THE OXFORD
CLASSICAL DICTIONARY

THE OXFORD CLASSICAL DICTIONARY

Edited by

M. CARY   A. D. NOCK

J. D. DENNISTON   W. D. ROSS

J. WIGHT DUFF   H. H. SCULLARD

With the assistance of

H. J. ROSE   H. P. HARVEY   A. SOUTER

OXFORD

AT THE CLARENDON PRESS

Oxford University Press, Ely House, London W.1

GLASGOW NEW YORK TORONTO MELBOURNE WELLINGTON
CAPE TOWN SALISBURY IBADAN NAIROBI LUSAKA ADDIS ABABA
BOMBAY CALCUTTA MADRAS KARACHI LAHORE DACCA
KUALA LUMPUR HONG KONG

FIRST PUBLISHED MARCH 1949
REPRINTED 1950, 1953, 1957, 1961, 1964, 1966

PREFACE

THE idea of the present work, the publication of which has been inevitably delayed by the war, was first conceived in 1933. It is designed to cover the same ground, though on a different scale, as the well-known dictionaries by Sir William Smith on Greek and Roman antiquities and on Greek and Roman biography, mythology, and geography. The eighth edition (1914) of Lübker's *Reallexikon* was taken as a general model, but with certain modifications in principle and with certain differences in emphasis. The present work is intended to be less purely factual than Lübker. It devotes more space to biography and literature, less to geography and to bibliographical information, aiming in this latter respect at no more than referring the reader to the best work, in English and foreign languages, on the various subjects. A special feature is the inclusion of longer articles designed to give a comprehensive survey of the main subjects and to place minor characters, places, and events, the choice of which has been necessarily selective, against their appropriate literary or historical background. The *terminus ad quem* is, generally speaking, the death of Constantine (337), and proportionately less space has been allotted to persons who lived later than the second century A.D.; but a few prominent figures of later ages, such as Augustine, Eustathius, Photius, Psellus, Thomas Magister, Triclinius, and Tzetzes, who are important for the student of classical antiquity, have been included. Christian writers, as such, have been excluded.

The editors of the dictionary at its inception were Mr. J. D. Denniston, for Greek literature; Professor J. Wight Duff, for Latin literature; Mr. (now Professor) H. M. Last, for Greek and Roman history and geography; Professor A. D. Nock, for Greek and Roman religion; the then Provost of Oriel, Dr. W. D. (now Sir David) Ross, for Greek and Roman philosophy, mathematics, and science. Professor R. G. Collingwood advised on matters concerned with art and archaeology until his death in 1943. In 1937 Professor Last found himself unable to continue his editorship, and his place was taken by Professor M. Cary and Dr. H. H. Scullard, who are alone responsible for the selection and form of articles on history, geography, law, archaeology, and art. In 1944 Professor Wight Duff died, and Professor A. Souter agreed to see the articles on Latin literature through the press; and in 1945 Professor H. J. Rose took over from Professor Nock the final stages of the editorship of articles connected with religion. In the autumn of 1939 Sir Paul Harvey undertook the complicated and laborious task of securing uniformity in such matters as spelling, transliteration, and abbreviations, and of adding the requisite cross-references. He had all but completed this work when in June 1948 illness compelled him to relinquish it. Professor Paul Maas has placed his many-sided learning at the Delegates' disposal in the final stages, and contributed the short bibliographical articles at the end of the book. Valuable help and advice have also been received from Mr. R. Syme and Professor A. Momigliano.

A list of contributors will be found on p. vii. At the end of the book three short bibliographical articles have been included as appendixes, listing the principal works of reference in the field of classical scholarship generally, the history of Greek and Latin literature, and Greek grammar.

Every effort has been made by the editors to incorporate the results of recent scholarship and to bring the work as much up to date as possible, but a task which involved communication with so many widely scattered contributors has been made much harder by the interruptions of war and the difficulties of present production. For any omissions therefore, particularly in the bibliographies, the reader's indulgence is sought.

June 1948

INDEX TO INITIALS OF CONTRIBUTORS

J. W. H. **A.**	John William Hey Atkins
R. G. **A.**	Roland Gregory Austin
W. B. **A.**	William Blair Anderson
A. **B.**	Adolf Berger
A. **O.**	André Oltramare
A. R. **B.**	Andrew Robert Burn
C. **B.**	Cyril Bailey
C. M. **B.**	Cecil Maurice Bowra
E. A. **B.**	Eric Arthur Barber
E. P. **B.**	E. Phillips Barker
G. L. **B.**	Godfrey Louis Barber
H. **B.**	Herbert Bloch
H. E. **B.**	Harold Edgeworth Butler
T. A. **B.**	Thomas Allan Brady
J. P. **B.**	John Percy Vyvian Dacre Balsdon
K. O. **B.**	Karl Oscar Brink
O. **B.**	Olwen Phillis Frances Brogan
R. H. **B.**	Reginald Haynes Barrow
R. J. **B.**	Robert Johnson Bonner
T. R. S. **B.**	Thomas Robert Shannon Broughton
W. **B.**	William Beare
A. H. **C.**	Allan Hartley Coxon
A. W. **P.-C.**	Arthur Wallace Pickard-Cambridge
D. J. **C.**	Donald John Campbell
F. S. **C.**	F. S. Cawley
G. E. F. **C.**	Guy Edward Farquhar Chilver
G. H. **C.**	George Henry Chase
H. **C.**	Harry Caplan
H. J. **C.**	Henry Joel Cadbury
J. M. **C.**	James Macdonald Cobban
M. **C.**	Max Cary
M. P. **C.**	Martin Percival Charlesworth
R. C. **C.**	Roger Clifford Carrington
R. P. **C.**	Robert Pierce Casey
S. **C.**	Stanley Casson
W. M. **C.**	William Moir Calder
A. M. **D.**	Arnold Mackay Duff
E. R. **D.**	Erik Robertson Dodds
J. D. **D.**	John Dewar Denniston
J. F. **D.**	John Frederic Dobson
J. W. **D.**	John Wight Duff
L. **D.**	Ludwig Deubner
M. S. **D.**	Margaret Stephana Drower
O. **D.**	Oliver Davies
S. **D.**	Sterling Dow
T. J. **D.**	Thomas James Dunbabin
C. F. **E.**	Charles Farwell Edson, Jr.
L. **E.**	Ludwig Edelstein
P. J. **E.**	Petrus Johannes Enk
S. **E.**	Sam Eitrem
V. **E.**	Victor Ehrenberg
W. M. **E.**	Walter Manoel Edwards
B. **F.**	Benjamin Farrington
C. **F.**	Charles Favez
C. J. **F.**	Christian James Fordyce
E. S. **F.**	Edward Seymour Forster
G. B. A. **F.**	Geoffrey Bernard Abbott Fletcher
G. C. **F.**	Guy Cromwell Field
J. E. **F.**	Joseph Eddy Fontenrose
K. von **F.**	Kurt von Fritz
P. B. R. **F.**	Peter Barr Reid Forbes
T. **F.**	Theodore Fyfe

A. W. G.	Arnold Wycombe Gomme
G. T. G.	Guy Thompson Griffith
H. T. W.-G.	Henry Theodore Wade-Gery
R. J. G.	Robert John Getty
S. G.	Stephen Gaselee
W. C. G.	William Chase Greene
W. K. C. G.	William Keith Chambers Guthrie
F. M. **H.**	Friedrich M. Heichelheim
G. **H.**	Gilbert Arthur Highet
G. M. A. **H.**	George M. A. Hanfmann
J. **H.**	J. Hammer
M. **H.**	Michael Holroyd
M. Hammond	Mason Hammond
N. G. L. **H.**	Nicholas Geoffrey Lemprière Hammond
R. **H.**	Reginald Hackforth
R. M. **H.**	Robert Mitchell Henry
T. **H.**	Thomas Little Heath
T. J. **H.**	Theodore Johannes Haarhoff
R. **W.-I.**	Reginald Pepys Winnington-Ingram
A. H. M. **J.**	Arnold Hugh Martin Jones
R. L. **J.**	Robert Leoline James
F. G. **K.**	Frederic George Kenyon
W. F. J. **K.**	William Francis Jackson Knight
J. A. O. **L.**	Jakob Aall Ottesen Larsen
J. F. **L.**	John Francis Lockwood
R. G. C. **L.**	Robert Graham Cochrane Levens
W. A. **L.**	William Allison Laidlaw
A. **M.**	Arnaldo Momigliano
E. C. **M.**	Edgar Cardew Marchant
E. H. **M.**	Ellis Hovell Minns
H. **M.**	Harold Mattingly
J. A. **M.**	James Alan Montgomery
J. F. **M.**	James Frederick Mountford
J. G. **M.**	Joseph Grafton Milne
J. L. **M.**	John Linton Myres
J. L. Matthews	John Lumley Matthews
P. **M.**	Paul Maas
R. **M.**	R. Mandra
R. Meiggs	Russell Meiggs
R. A. B. **M.**	Roger Aubrey Baskerville Mynors
W. S. **M.**	William Stuart Maguinness
A. H. McD.	Alexander Hugh McDonald
D. R.-MacI.	David Randall-MacIver
M. P. N.	Nils Martin Persson Nilsson
P. S. N.	Peter Scott Noble
S. G. O.	Sidney George Owen
A. J. D. **P.**	Alexander James Dow Porteous
A. L. **P.**	Arthur Leslie Peck
A. S. **P.**	Arthur Stanley Pease
F. N. **P.**	Frederick Norman Pryce
H. M. D. **P.**	Henry Michael Denne Parker
H. W. **P.**	Herbert William Parke
J. W. **P.**	John William Pirie
L. R. **P.**	Leonard Robert Palmer
M. **P.**	Maurice Platnauer
R. A. **P.**	Roger Ambrose Pack

C. H. R.	Colin Henderson Roberts	P. T.	Piero Treves
F. N. R.	Fred Norris Robinson	W. T.	William Telfer
G. C. R.	George Chatterton Richards	W. W. T.	William Woodthorpe Tarn
G. W. R.	Geoffrey Walter Richardson		
H. J. R.	Herbert Jennings Rose	P. N. U.	Percy Neville Ure
H. W. R.	H. W. Richmond		
I. A. R.	Ian Archibald Richmond		
J. C. R.	John Carew Rolfe		
R. R.	Richard George Frederick Robinson	A. W. van B.	Albert William van Buren
R. M. R.	Robert Mantle Rattenbury	J. J. van N.	John James van Nostrand
W. D. R.	William David Ross		
A. S.	Alexander Souter	A. H.-W.	Alun Hudson-Williams
C. S.	Charles Joseph Singer	A. J. B. W.	Alan John Bayard Wace
C. E. S.	Courtenay Edward Stevens	A. M. W.	Arthur Maurice Woodward
C. G. S.	Chester G. Starr	A. N. S.-W.	Adrian Nicholas Sherwin-White
C. H. V. S.	Carol Humphrey Vivian Sutherland	D. E. W. W.	Donald Ernest Wilson Wormell
E. T. S.	Edward Togo Salmon	E. H. W.	Eric Herbert Warmington
F. A. W. S.	Franz A. W. Schehl	E. J. W.	Edward James Wood
G. H. S.	George Hope Stevenson	F. A. W.	Frederick Adam Wright
H. H. S.	Howard Hayes Scullard	F. R. W.	Francis Redding Walton
O. S.	Otto Skutsch	F. W. W.	Frank William Walbank
R. S.	Ronald Syme	G. C. W.	George Clement Whittick
T. A. S.	Thomas Alan Sinclair	H. D. W.	Henry Dickinson Westlake
W. H. S.	Walter Hayward Shewring	J. W.	Joshua Whatmough
		T. B. L. W.	Thomas Bertram Lonsdale Webster
		T. E. W.	Thomas Erskine Wright
J. T.	Jonathan Tate	W. G. W.	William Gillan Waddell
L. R. T.	Lily Ross Taylor	W. N. W.	William Nassau Weech
M. N. T.	Marcus Niebuhr Tod	W. S. W.	William Smith Watt

SIGNS

ABBREVIATIONS USED IN THE PRESENT WORK

A. GENERAL

ad fin.	ad finem	l.c. or loc. cit.	loco citato
ad loc.	ad locum	lit.	literally
ad init.	ad initium	mod.	modern
al.	alias, aliter, etc.	n.	note
ap.	apud	n.d.	no date
arg.	argument	no.	number
art.	article	n. plur.	neuter plural
b.	born	N.S.	New Series
c, cc.	century, centuries	OE	Old English
c.	circa	OIr	Old Irish
comm.	commentary	ON	Old Norse
d.	died	O.T.	Old Testament
E.T.	see Engl. Transl.	op. cit.	opus citatum
ed.	editor, edition, edidit, or edited by	pl., pls.	plate, plates
Engl. Transl. or E.T.	English Translation	Ps.-	Pseudo-
esp.	especially	qu.	query
f., ff.	and following	q.v., qq.v.	quod vide, quae vide
fl.	floruit	rp.	reprint
Fr.	French	str.	strophe
fr., frs.	fragment, fragments	s.v.	sub voce
ib., ibid.	ibidem	Suppl.	Supplement
id.	idem	temp.	tempore, in the time of
inf.	infra	tr. or transl.	translation or translated by
Ir.	Irish	v., vv.	verse, verses
l., ll.	line, lines		

B. AUTHORS AND BOOKS

AJArch.	American Journal of Archaeology, 1897–	Aeschin.	Aeschines
		In Ctes.	*Against Ctesiphon*
AJPhil.	American Journal of Philology, 1880–	*In Tim.*	*Against Timarchus*
ARW	Archiv für Religionswissenschaft, 1898–	Aët.	Aëtius
		Alc.	Alcaeus
A.V.	see Beazley	Alcidamas, *Soph.*	Alcidamas, Περὶ σοφιστῶν
Abh. followed by name of Academy or Society	Abhandlungen	Alcm.	Alcman
		Alex. Polyh.	Alexander Polyhistor
Abh. sächs. Ges. Wiss.	Abhandlungen der sächsischen Gesellschaft der Wissenschaften	Altheim, *Hist. Rom. Rel.*	F. Altheim, *Römische Religionsgeschichte*, tr. H. Mattingly (1938)
Abh. zu Gesch. d. Math.	Abhandlungen zur Geschichte der mathematischen Wissenschaften, 1877–	Am. Ac. Rome	*Memoirs of the American Academy at Rome*, 1915–
Abh. zu Gesch. d. Med.	Abhandlungen zur Geschichte der Naturwissenschaften und d. Medizin, 1922–	Amm. Marc.	Ammianus Marcellinus
		Ammon.	Ammonius grammaticus
		Diff.	Περὶ ὁμοίων καὶ διαφόρων λέξεων
Acad. index Herc.	Academicorum philosophorum index Herculanensis editus a F. Buechelero (1869)	Anac.	Anacreon
		Andoc.	Andocides
Ael.	Aelianus	Anecd. Bach.	*Anecdota Graeca*, ed. L. Bachmann (1828–9)
NA	*De natura animalium*	„ Bekk.	*Anecdota Graeca*, ed. I. Bekker (3 vols. 1814–21)
VH	*Varia Historia*		
Aen.	Aeneid	„ Ox.	*Anecdota Graeca* e codd. MSS. Bibl. Oxon., ed. J. A. Cramer (4 vols., 1835–7)
Aesch.	Aeschylus		
Ag.	*Agamemnon*	„ Par.	*Anecdota Graeca* e codd. MSS. Bibl. Reg. Parisiensis, ed. J. A. Cramer (4 vols., 1839–41)
Cho.	*Choephori*		
Eum.	*Eumenides*	Ann. Épigr.	*L'Année Épigraphique* (published in *Revue Archéologique* and separately, 1888–)
Pers.	*Persae*		
PV	*Prometheus Vinctus*		
Sept.	*Septem contra Thebas*		
Supp.	*Supplices*		

Ann. Ist.	Annali del Istituto di Corrispondenza Archaeologica, 1829–
Anon. De Com. or Περὶ κωμ.	Anonymus De Comoedia
Ant. Class.	L'Antiquité classique, 1932–
Ant. Kunstpr.	see Norden
Ant. Lib.	Antoninus Liberalis
Met.	Metamorphoses
Anth. Lat.	Anthologia Latina, ed. A. Riese, F. Buecheler, and E. Lommatzsch (1869–1926)
Anth. Lyr. Graec.	see Diehl
Anth. Pal.	Anthologia Palatina
Anth. Plan.	Anthologia Planudea
Antig. Car.	Antigonus Carystius
Antip. Sid.	Antipater Sidonius
Anz. followed by name of Academy or Society	Anzeiger or Anzeigen
Ap. Rhod.	Apollonius Rhodius
Argon.	Argonautica
Apollod.	Apollodorus mythographus
Bibl.	Bibliotheca
Epit.	Epitome
Apollonius	Apollonius paradoxographus
Mir.	Mirabilia
Apollonius Dyscolus	
Pron.	De pronominibus
App.	Appian
BCiv.	Bella Civilia
Hann.	Ἀννιβαϊκή
Hisp.	Ἰβηρική
Ill.	Ἰλλυρική
Mac.	Μακεδονική
Mith.	Μιθριδάτειος
Pun.	Λιβυκή
Sam.	Σαυνιτική
Syr.	Συριακή
App. Verg.	Appendix Vergiliana
Apsines, Rhet.	Apsines, Ars Rhetorica
Apul.	Apuleius
Apol.	Apologia
Asclep.	Asclepius
De deo Soc.	De deo Socratico
De dog. Plat.	De dogmate Platonis
Flor.	Florida
Met.	Metamorphoses
Ar.	Aristophanes
Ach.	Acharnenses
Av.	Aves
Eccl.	Ecclesiazusae
Eq.	Equites
Lys.	Lysistrata
Nub.	Nubes
Plut.	Plutus
Ran.	Ranae
Thesm.	Thesmophoriazusae
Vesp.	Vespae
Ar. Byz.	Aristophanes Byzantinus
Aratus Phaen.	Aratus, Phaenomena
Prognost.	Prognostica
Arch. Ael.	Archaeologia Aeliana (Newcastle-upon-Tyne), 1815–
Arch. Anz.	Archäologischer Anzeiger in Jahrbuch des [kaiserlichen] deutschen archäologischen Instituts (JDAI)
Ἀρχ. Δελτ.	Ἀρχαιολογικὸν Δελτίον, 1915–
Ἀρχ. Ἐφ.	Ἀρχαιολογικὴ Ἐφημερίς, 1910–
Arch.-Epigr. Mitt. Österr.	Archäologisch-epigraphische Mittheilungen aus Österreich-Ungarn, 1877–97
Arch. Ert.	Archeologiai Értesítő, 1881–
Arch. Journ.	Archaeological Journal, 1845–
Arch. latein. Lexikogr.	Archiv für latein. Lexikographie u. Grammatik, ed. E. Wölfflin, 1884–1909
Arch. Pap.	Archiv für Papyrusforschung, 1900–
Archil.	Archilochus
Arist.	Aristotle
An. (Post.)	Analytica Posteriora
An. (Pr.)	Analytica Priora
Ath. Pol.	Ἀθηναίων Πολιτεία
Cael.	De Caelo

Arist. (cont.)	
Cat.	Categoriae
[Col.]	De Coloribus
De An.	De Anima
Div. Somn.	De Divinatione per Somnia
Eth. Eud.	Ethica Eudemia
Eth. Nic.	Ethica Nicomachea
Fr.	Fragmenta
Gen. An.	De Generatione Animalium
Gen. Corr.	De Generatione et Corruptione
HA or Hist. An.	Historia Animalium
Int.	De Interpretatione
[Lin. Ins.]	De Lineis Insecabilibus
[Mag. Mor.]	Magna Moralia
[Mech.]	Mechanica
Mem.	De Memoria
Metaph.	Metaphysica
Mete.	Meteorologica
[Mir. Ausc.]	see Mir. Ausc. under M
[Mund.]	De Mundo
[Oec.]	Oeconomica
Part. An.	De Partibus Animalium
Ph.	Physica
[Phgn.]	Physiognomonica
Poet.	Poetica
Pol.	Politica
[Pr.]	Problemata
Resp.	De Respiratione
Rh.	Rhetorica
[Rh. Al.]	Rhetorica ad Alexandrum
Sens.	De Sensu
Soph. El.	Sophistici Elenchi
Top.	Topica
[Xen.]	De Xenophane
Aristid. Quint.	Aristides Quintilianus
Aristox. Fr. Hist.	Aristoxenus, Fragmenta Historica
Harm.	Harmonica
Rhythm.	Rhythmica
Arn.	Arnobius
Adv. Nat. or Adv. Gent.	Adversus Nationes
Arnim (von)	see SVF
Arr.	Arrian
Anab.	Anabasis
Epict. Diss.	Epicteti Dissertationes
Peripl. M. Eux.	Periplus Maris Euxini
Tact.	Tactica
Art Bull.	Art Bulletin (New York), 1913–
Artem.	Artemidorus Daldianus
Asc.	Asconius
Corn.	Commentary on Cicero, Pro Cornelio de maiestate
Mil.	Commentary on Cicero, Pro Milone
Pis.	Commentary on Cicero, In Pisonem
Verr.	Commentary on Cicero, In Verrem
Ath.	Athenaeus
Ath. Mitt.	Mitteilungen des deutschen archäologischen Instituts, Athenische Abteilung, 1876–
Athenaeum	Athenaeum (Pavia), Nuova Serie, 1923–
Athenagoras, Leg. pro Christ.	Athenagoras, Legatio pro Christianis = Πρεσβεία περὶ Χριστιανῶν
Auct. ad Her.	Auctor ad Herennium
August.	Augustine
Ad Rom.	Expositio of Epist. ad Romanos
De civ. D.	De civitate Dei
In Evang. Iohan.	Tractatus in Evangelium Iohannis
Ep.	Epistulae
Retract.	Retractationes
Aul. Gell.	see Gell.
Aur. Vict., Caes.	Aurelius Victor, Caesares
[Aur. Vict.], De Vir. Ill.	[Aurelius Victor], De Viris Illustribus
Auson.	Ausonius
Cent. Nupt.	Cento Nuptialis
Grat. Act.	Gratiarum Actio
Mos.	Mosella
Ordo Nob. Urb.	Ordo Nobilium Urbium
Prof. Burd.	Commemoratio Professorum Burdigalensium
Technop.	Technopaegnion

BAct.	Bellum Actiacum: see *BAegypt.*	*Byz. und Neugr. Jahrb.*	*Byzantinisch-neugriechische Jahrbücher* (1920–)
BAegypt.	*Carmen de Bello Aegyptiaco sive Actiaco* (papyrus fragment)	*Byz. Zeitschr.*	*Byzantinische Zeitschrift,* 1892–
BAfr.	*Bellum Africum*		
BAlex.	*Bellum Alexandrinum*		
BCH	*Bulletin de Correspondance Hellénique,* 1877–	*CAF*	T. Kock, *Comicorum Atticorum Fragmenta* (1880–8)
BGU	*Berliner Griechische Urkunden (Ägyptische Urkunden aus den Kgl. Museen zu Berlin),* 1895–	*CAH*	The *Cambridge Ancient History* (1923–39)
BKT	*Berliner Klassikertexte, herausgegeben von der Generalverwaltung der Kgl. Museen zu Berlin,* 1904–	*CGF*	G. Kaibel, *Comicorum Graecorum Fragmenta* (1899)
		CHJ	*Cambridge Historical Journal,* 1924–
B.M.	British Museum	*CIA*	*Corpus Inscriptionum Atticarum* (1825–)
B.M. Coins, Rom. Emp.	*British Museum Catalogue of Coins of the Roman Empire,* 1923–	*CIE*	*Corpus Inscriptionum Etruscarum* (1893–)
BMQ	*British Museum Quarterly,* 1926–	*CIL*	*Corpus Inscriptionum Latinarum* (1863–)
B. phil. Woch.	*Berliner philologische Wochenschrift,* 1881–1920	*CISem.*	*Corpus Inscriptionum Semiticarum* (1881–)
BSA	*Annual of the British School at Athens,* 1895–	*CJ*	*Classical Journal,* 1905–
BSR	*Papers of the British School at Rome,* 1902–	*CMG*	*Corpus Medicorum Graecorum* (1908–)
		CML	*Corpus Medicorum Latinorum* (1915–)
Bacchyl.	Bacchylides	*CPhil.*	*Classical Philology,* 1906–
Baehr.	E. Baehrens	*CPL*	*Corpus Poetarum Latinorum* (1894–1920)
FPR	*Fragmenta Poetarum Romanorum,* 1886	*CQ*	*Classical Quarterly,* 1907–
PLM	see *PLM*	*CR*	*Classical Review,* 1887–
Basil. De Virg.	Basilius, *De Virginitate*	*CRAcad. Inscr.*	*Comptes rendus de l'Académie des Inscriptions et Belles-lettres,* 1857–
Beazley, A.V.	J. D. Beazley, *Attische Vasenmaler* (1925)	*CRF*	see Ribbeck
Beibl.	*Beiblatt*	*CSEL*	*Corpus Scriptorum Ecclesiasticorum Latinorum* (1866 ff.)
Beitr.	*Beitrag, Beiträge*		
Beloch	K. J. Beloch	Caes.	Caesar
Gr. Gesch.	*Griechische Geschichte*² (1912–27)	*BCiv.*	*Bellum Civile*
Röm. Gesch.	*Römische Geschichte bis zum Beginn der punischen Kriege* (1926)	*BGall.*	*Bellum Gallicum*
Bérard, Bibliogr. topogr.	J. Bérard, *Bibliographie topographique des principales cités grecques de l'Italie méridionale et de la Sicile dans l'antiquité* (1941).	Callim.	Callimachus
		Aet.	*Aetia*
		Ap.	*Hymnus in Apollinem*
		Cer.	„ „ *Cererem*
		Del.	„ „ *Delum*
		Dian.	„ „ *Dianam*
Ber. Sächs. Ges. Wiss.	*Berichte über die Verhandlungen der [Kgl.] sächsischen Gesellschaft der Wissenschaften zu Leipzig,* 1848	*Epigr.*	*Epigrammata*
		Jov.	*Hymnus in Jovem*
		Lav. Pall.	*Lavacrum Palladis*
Berger, Gesch. d. wiss. Erdkunde d. Gr.	H. Berger, *Geschichte d. wissenschaftlichen Erdkunde d. Griechen*² (1903)	*Calp.*	Calpurnius Siculus
		Carm. Arv.	*Carmen Arvale*
Berl. Abh.	*Abhandlungen der preuß. Akademie d. Wissenschaften zu Berlin,* 1786–1907; 1908–	*Carm. Epigr.*	*Carmina Epigraphica* ('pars posterior' of *Anthologia Latina*)
		Carm. Pop.	*Carmina Popularia* in Diehl's *Anth. Lyr. Graec.* ii, pp. 192–208
Berl. Klass. Text.	*Berliner Klassikertexte,* 1904–	*Carm. Sal.*	*Carmen Saliare*
Berve, *Alexanderreich*	H. Berve, *Das Alexanderreich aus prosopographischer Grundlage* (1927)	Cary-Warmington, *Explorers*	M. Cary and E. H. Warmington, *The Ancient Explorers* (1929)
Bibl. Éc. Franc.	*Bibliothèque des Écoles françaises d'Athènes et de Rome,* 1877–	Cass. Dio	Cassius Dio
Bidez–Cumont	J. Bidez and F. Cumont, *Les Mages hellénisés* (2 vols., 1938)	Cassiod.	Cassiodorus
		Var.	*Variae*
Blass, *Att. Ber.*	F. Blass, *Die Attische Beredsamkeit,* 2nd ed. 1887–98	*Cat. Cod. Astr.*	*Catalogus Codicum Astrologorum* (ed. F. Cumont et alii, 1898–)
Boll. Fil. Class.	*Bollettino di filologia classica,* 1894–1929; N.S. 1930–	*Cat. Lit. Pap.*	H. J. M. Milne, *Catalogue of the Literary Papyri in the British Museum* (1927)
Bonner Jahrb.	*Bonner Jahrbücher,* 1895–	Cato, *Agr.* or *Rust.*	Cato, *De Agricultura* or *De Re Rustica*
Bresl. phil. Abh.	*Breslauer philologische Abhandlungen*	*Orig.*	*Origines*
Bruns, *Font.*	C. G. Bruns, *Fontes iuris Romani antiqui*⁷ (1919)	*Catull.*	Catullus
		Celsus, *Med.*	Celsus, *De Medicina*
Budé	Collection des Univ. de France, publiée sous le patronage de l'Assoc. Guillaume Budé	Censorinus, *D.N.*	Censorinus, *De die natali*
		Chalcid. *in Tim.*	Chalcidius, *in Platonis Timaeum*
		Charisius, *Gramm.*	Charisius, *Ars Grammatica*
Buecheler, *Carm. Epigr.*	F. Buecheler, *Carmina Latina Epigraphica* (2 vols. with Supplem. by E. Lommatzsch, 1895–1926)	Christ–Schmid–Stählin	W. von Christ, *Geschichte d. griechischen Litteratur,* revised by W. Schmid and O. Stählin, II. i⁶ 1920, II. ii⁶ 1924. *See also* Schmid–Stählin.
Bull. Com. Arch.	*Bullettino della Commissione archeologica comunale in Roma,* 1872–		
Bull. Corr. Hell.	see *BCH*	*Chron. Marcell.*	Marcellinus, *Chronicon*
Bull. Ist. Dir. Rom.	*Bullettino del Istituto di diritto romano,* 1888–	*Chron. Min.*	*Chronica Minora*
		Chron. Pasch.	*Chronicon Paschale*
Burnet, *EGP*	J. Burnet, *Early Greek Philosophy*⁴ (1930)	Cic.	Cicero (Marcus Tullius)
Bursian	C. Bursian, *Geographie von Griechenland,* vol. ii (1872)	*Acad.*	*Academicae Quaestiones*
		Acad. Post.	*Academica Posteriora* (=Plasberg, Bk. IV)
Jahresb.	Bursian's *Jahresberichte über die Fortschritte der Altertumswissenschaft,* 1873–	*Acad. Pr.*	*Academica Priora* (= Plasberg, Bk. I)

Cic. (*cont.*)	
ad Brut.	*Epistulae ad Brutum*
Amic.	*De Amicitia*
Arch.	*Pro Archia*
Att.	*Epistulae ad Atticum*
Balb.	*Pro Balbo*
Brut.	*Brutus* or *De Claris Oratoribus*
Caecin.	*Pro Caecina*
Cael.	*Pro Caelio*
Cat.	*In Catilinam*
Clu.	*Pro Cluentio*
Corn.	*Pro Cornelio de maiestate* (fragmentary)
Deiot.	*Pro rege Deiotaro*
De Imp. Cn. Pomp.	see *Leg. Man.*
De Or.	*De Oratore*
Div.	*De Divinatione*
Div. Caec.	*Divinatio in Caecilium*
Dom.	*De Domo sua*
Fam.	*Epistulae ad Familiares*
Fat.	*De Fato*
Fin.	*De Finibus*
Flac.	*Pro Flacco*
Font.	*Pro Fonteio*
Har. Resp.	*De Haruspicum Responso*
Inv. Rhet.	*De Inventione Rhetorica*
Leg. Agr.	*De Lege Agraria*
Leg.	*De Legibus*
Leg. Man.	*Pro Lege Manilia* or *De Imperio Cn. Pompeii*
Lig.	*Pro Ligario*
Luc.	*Lucullus* or *Academica Posteriora*
Marcell.	*Pro Marcello*
Mil.	*Pro Milone*
Mur.	*Pro Murena*
Nat. D.	*De Natura Deorum*
Off.	*De Officiis*
Orat.	*Orator ad M. Brutum*
Phil.	*Orationes Philippicae*
Pis.	*In Pisonem*
Planc.	*Pro Plancio*
Prov. Cons.	*De Provinciis Consularibus*
QFr.	*Epistulae ad Quintum Fratrem*
Quinct.	*Pro Quinctio*
QRosc.	*Pro Roscio Comoedo*
Rab. Post.	*Pro Rabirio Postumo*
Red. Pop.	*Post reditum ad Populum*
Red. Sen.	*Post reditum in Senatu*
Rep.	*De Republica*
Scaur.	*Pro Scauro*
Sen.	*De Senectute*
Sest.	*Pro Sestio*
Sull.	*Pro Sulla*
Tog. Cand.	*Oratio in Senatu in toga candida* (fragmentary)
Top.	*Topica*
Tusc.	*Tusculanae Disputationes*
Verr.	*In Verrem*
Cicero, *Comment. Pet.*	Cicero (Quintus), *Commentariolum Petitionis*
Cichorius, *Röm. Stud.*	C. Cichorius, *Römische Studien*, 1922 (cited by chapter and section)
Claud., *Cons. Hon.*	Claudianus, *De consulatu Honorii*
Cons. Stil.	*De consulatu Stilichonis*
Clem. Al.	Clemens Alexandrinus
Protr.	*Protrepticus*
Strom.	*Stromateis*
Cod.	Codex
Cod. Iust.	*Codex Iustinianus*
Cod. Theod.	*Codex Theodosianus*
Codd. Lat. Ant. (Lowe)	E. A. Lowe, *Codices Latini Antiquiores* (1934–)
Coll. Alex.	see Powell
Collingwood–Myres, *Roman Britain*	R. G. Collingwood and J. N. L. Myres, *Roman Britain and the English Settlements*[2] (1937)
Comm. in Arist. Graeca	*Commentaria in Aristotelem Graeca*
Comp. Gr. Stud.	The *Cambridge Companion to Greek Studies*[4] (1931)
Comp. Lat. Stud.	The *Cambridge Companion to Latin Studies*[3] (1935)
Conon, *Narr.*	Conon Mythographus, Διηγήσεις
Const.	*Constitutio*
Conway, *Ital. Dial.*	R. S. Conway, *Italic Dialects* (1897)
Cook, *Zeus*	A. B. Cook, *Zeus: a Study in Ancient Religion* (vol. i, 1914; vol. ii, 1925; vol. iii, 1940)
Cornutus, *Theol. Graec.*	Cornutus (L. Annaeus), Ἐπιδρομὴ τῶν κατὰ τὴν Ἑλληνικὴν Θεολογίαν παραδεδομένων
Corp. poes. ep. Graec. lud.	*Corpusculum poesis epicae Graecae ludibundae*, vol. 1, *Parodia et Archestratus*, P. Brandt, 1888; vol. 2, *Syllographi Graeci*, C. Wachsmuth, 1885
Cos., Cos. suff.	Consul, Consul suffectus
Cramer, *Anecd. Par.*	see *Anecd. Par.*
Croiset, *Hist. Lit. Gr.*	Croiset (A. and M.), *Histoire de la littérature grecque*, i[4] 1928, ii[3] 1914, iii[3] 1913, iv[2] 1900, v 1928
Cul.	*Culex*
Cumont, *Rel. or.*	F. Cumont, *Les Religions orientales dans le paganisme romain*[4] (1929)
Cyril, *Adv. Iul.*	Cyrillus, *Adversus Iulianum*
DCB	*Dictionary of Christian Biography and Literature*, ed. H. Wace and W. C. Piercy, 1911.
D.H.	see Dion. Hal.
D.L.	see Diog. Laert.
Dam. *Isid.*	Damascius, *Vita Isidori*
Dar.–Sag.	Ch. Daremberg and E. Saglio, *Dictionnaire des antiquités grecques et romaines d'après les textes et les monuments* (1877–1919)
De Com.	see Anon. *De Com.*
De Sanctis, *Stor. Rom.*	G. De Sanctis, *Storia dei Romani* (1907–)
De Vir. Ill.	*De Viris Illustribus* (auctor ignotus)
Déchelette, *Manuel*	J. Déchelette, *Manuel d'archéologie préhistorique, celtique et gallo-romaine* (1908–14)
Dem.	Demosthenes
De Cor.	*De Corona*
Lept.	*Against Leptines*
Meid.	*Against Meidias*
Demetr. *Eloc.*	Demetrius [Phalereus], *De Elocutione* = Π. ἑρμηνείας
Demiańczuk, *Supp. Com.*	J. Demiańczuk, *Supplementum Comicum* (1912)
Democr.	Democritus
Dessau, *ILS*	H. Dessau, *Inscriptiones Latinae Selectae* (1892–1916)
Did. Iul.	Didius Julianus, see S.H.A.
Diehl, *Anth. Lyr. Graec.*	E. Diehl, *Anthologia Lyrica Graeca* (1925, 2nd ed. 1942)
Poet. Rom. vet.	*Poetarum Romanorum veterum reliquiae* (1911)
Diels, *Dox. Graec.*	H. Diels, *Doxographi Graeci* (1879)
Vorsokr.	*Fragmente der Vorsokratiker*[3] (1934)
Dig.	*Digesta*
Dio Cass.	Dio Cassius
Dio Chrys.	Dio Chrysostomus
Or.	*Orationes*
Diocl. Magn.	Diocles of Magnesia
Diod. or Diod. Sic.	Diodorus Siculus
Diog. Laert. or D.L.	Diogenes Laertius
Diogenian.	Diogenianus Paroemiographus
Diom.	Diomedes Grammaticus
Dion. Calliphon.	Dionysius Calliphontis filius
Dion. Hal. or D.H.	Dionysius Halicarnassensis
Ant. Rom.	*Antiquitates Romanae*
Comp.	*De Compositione Verborum*
De Imit.	*De Imitatione*
Dem.	*De Demosthene*
Isoc.	*De Isocrate*
Lys.	*De Lysia*
Pomp.	*Epistula ad Pompeium*
Rhet.	*Ars Rhetorica*
Thuc.	*De Thucydide*
Vett. Cens.	*De Veterum Censura*
Dion. Thrax	Dionysius Thrax
Dionys. Per.	Dionysius Periegeta
Diss.	Dissertation
Diss. Pan.	*Dissertationes Pannonicae* 1932–
Dittenberg. *SIG*	W. Dittenberger, *Sylloge Inscriptionum Graecarum*[3] (1915–24)

Diz. Epigr.	see Ruggiero
Donat.	Aelius Donatus
Dox. Graec.	see Diels
EGF	G. Kinkel, *Epicorum Graecorum Fragmenta* (1877)
EGP	see Burnet
EM	see *Etym. Magn.*
ERE	see Hastings
Enc. Brit.	*Encyclopaedia Britannica*
Ennius, *Ann.*	Ennius, *Annales*
Eph. Epigr.	*Ephemeris Epigraphica, Corporis Inscriptionum Latinarum Supplementum*, Berlin 1872–
Epicurus, *Ep.*	Epicurus, *Epistulae*
Epigr. Gr.	G. Kaibel, *Epigrammata Graeca ex lapidibus conlecta* (1878)
Epiph. *Adv. Haeres.*	Epiphanius, *Adversus Haereses*
Epit.	*Epitome*
Epit. Oxyrh.	*Epitome Oxyrhynchica* of Livy
Eratosth.	Eratosthenes
[*Cat.*]	[Κατασтερισμοί]
Ét. d'arch. rom.	Vol. I of *Annales de l'École des Hautes Études de Gand* (1937)
Etym. Gud.	*Etymologicum Gudianum*
Etym. Magn.	*Etymologicum Magnum*
Euc.	Euclid
Eudem.	Eudemus
Eunap.	Eunapius
VS	*Vitae Sophistarum*
Eup.	Eupolis
Eur.	Euripides
Alc.	*Alcestis*
Andr.	*Andromache*
Bacch.	*Bacchae*
Beller.	*Bellerophon*
Cyc.	*Cyclops*
El.	*Electra*
HF	*Hercules Furens*
Hec.	*Hecuba*
Hel.	*Helena*
Heracl.	*Heraclidae*
Hipp.	*Hippolytus*
Hyps.	*Hypsipyle*
IA	*Iphigenia Aulidensis*
IT	*Iphigenia Taurica*
Med.	*Medea*
Or.	*Orestes*
Phoen.	*Phoenissae*
Rhes.	*Rhesus*
Sthen.	*Stheneboea*
Supp.	*Supplices*
Tro.	*Troades*
Eus. or Euseb.	Eusebius
Chron.	*Chronica*
Hist. Eccl.	*Historia Ecclesiastica*
Praep. Evang.	*Praeparatio Evangelica*
Eust., *Il.*	Eustathius, *ad Iliadem*
Eutocius, *In Arch. circ. dim.*	Eutocius, *In Archimedis circuli dimensionem*
FCG	see Meineke
FGrH	F. Jacoby, *Fragmente der griechischen Historiker* (1923–)
FHG	C. Müller, *Fragmenta Historicorum Graecorum* (1841–70)
FPG	F. W. A. Mullach, *Fragmenta Philosophorum Graecorum* (1860–81)
FPL	see Morel
FPR	see Baehr. (Baehrens)
Farnell, *Cults*	L. R. Farnell, *The Cults of the Greek States* (1896–1909)
Hero-Cults	L. R. Farnell, *Greek Hero-Cults and Ideas of Immortality* (1921)
Festus, *Gloss. Lat.*	W. M. Lindsay's second ed. of Festus in his *Glossaria Latina*, vol. iv
Firm. Mat.	Firmicus Maternus
Err. prof. rel.	*De errore profanarum religionum*
Fleck. J. Suppl.	*Fleckeisens Jahrbücher für klassische Philologie*, Suppl. xxiv, 1898 = *Neue Jahrbücher f. d. klassische Altertum*
Frank, *Econ. Surv.*	*An Economic Survey of Ancient Rome*, Ed. T. Frank (5 vols., U.S.A. 1933–40)

Frazer, *GB*	J. G. Frazer, *The Golden Bough: a Study in Magic and Religion*[3] (13 vols., 1911–15)
Friedländer, *Rom. Life*	L. Friedländer, *Darstellungen aus der Sittengeschichte Roms*[9–10] (1921–23, revised by G. Wissowa); *Roman Life and Manners under the Early Empire* (Engl. Transl. from ed. 7, 1908–13)
Frontin.	Frontinus
Aq.	*De Aquae Ductu Urbis Romae*
Str.	*Strategemata*
Fronto, *Ep.*	Fronto, *Epistulae*
Fulg.	Fulgentius
Myth.	*Mitologiae tres libri*
Funaioli, *Gramm. Rom. Frag.*	H. Funaioli, *Grammaticae Romanae fragmenta* (1907, vol. i alone published)
GB	see Frazer
GDI	H. Collitz et alii, *Sammlung der griechischen Dialektinschriften* (1884–1915)
GGM	C. Müller, *Geographici Graeci Minores* (1855–61)
Gai. Inst.	Gaius, *Institutiones*
Gal.	Galen
Libr. Propr.	Περὶ τῶν ἰδίων βιβλίων
Nat. Fac.	Περὶ φυσικῶν δυνάμεων
Gell.	Aulus Gellius
NA	*Noctes Atticae*
Gercke–Norden	A. Gercke u. E. Norden, *Einleitung in die Altertumswissenschaft* (1927–)
German.	Germanicus
Arat.	*Aratea*
Gesch.	*Geschichte*
Gesch. der griech. Lit.	see Christ–Schmid–Stählin and Schmid–Stählin
Gesch. gr. Lit. Alex.	see Susemihl
Gesch. röm. Lit.	see Schanz and Teuffel
Gloss. Lat.	see Lindsay
Glotz, *Hist. grecque*	G. Glotz, R. Cohen, and P. Roussel, *Histoire grecque*, i–iv. 1 (1925–38)
Gnomon	*Gnomon, Kritische Zeitschrift für d. gesamte klassische Altertumswiss.*, 1925–
Gomperz	T. Gomperz, *Griechische Denker* (1896). Engl. Transl. ('Greek Thinkers'), vol. i, 1901; vol. ii, 1902; vol. iii, 1905; vol. iv, 1912.
Herk. Stud.	*Herkulanische Studien* (1866)
Gorg.	Gorgias
Hel.	*Helena*
Pal.	*Palamedes*
Gött. Anz.	*Göttingischer gelehrte Anzeigen*, 1739–
Gött. Nachr.	*Nachrichten von der Gesellschaft der Wissenschaften zu Göttingen*, 1845–
Gr. Gesch.	see Beloch
Gramm. Lat.	see Keil
Gramm. Rom. Frag.	see Funaioli
Greenidge–Clay, *Sources*	A. H. J. Greenidge and A. M. Clay, *Sources for Roman History*, 133–70 B.C. (1903)
Grenier, *Manuel*	A. Grenier, *Manuel d'archéologie gallo-romaine* (1931–4; = vol. v of Déchelette's *Manuel d'archéologie préhistorique*)
HR Rel.	see under Peter
Halm, *Rhet. Lat. Min.*	K. Halm, *Rhetores Latini Minores* (1863)
Harp.	Harpocration
Harrison, *Prolegomena*	J. E. Harrison, *Prolegomena to the Study of Greek Religion* (1903, 3rd ed. 1922)
Themis	*Themis: a Study of the Social Origins of Greek Religion* (2nd ed. 1927)
Harv. Stud.	*Harvard Studies in Classical Philology*, 1890–
Harv. Theol. Rev.	*Harvard Theological Review*, 1908–

Hastings, *ERE*	J. Hastings, *Encyclopaedia of Religion and Ethics* (12 vols., 1908–21; Index vol. 1926)
Hdn.	Herodianus
Hdt.	Herodotus
Head, *Hist. Num.*	B. V. Head, *Historia Numorum* (ed. 2, 1911)
Hell. Oxy.	*Hellenica Oxyrhynchia*
Heph.	Hephaestion
Heraclid. Pont.	Heraclides Ponticus
Hermes	*Hermes, Zeitschrift für klassische Philologie*, 1866–
Hermog.	Hermogenes
Id.	Περὶ ἰδεῶν
Inv.	Περὶ εὑρέσεως
Prog.	Προγυμνάσματα
Herod.	Herodas
Hes.	Hesiod
Op.	*Opera et Dies*
Sc. or *Scut.*	*Scutum*
Th. or *Theog.*	*Theogonia*
Hesp.	*Hesperia: Journal of the American School of Classical Studies at Athens*, 1932–
Hieron.	Hieronymus (Jerome)
ab Abr.	*ab Abraham*, the chronological reckoning from the first year of Abraham followed in Jerome's translation and enlargement of Eusebius' Chronicle
Adv. Iovinian.	*Adversus Iovinianum*
Chron.	*Chronica = ab Abr.*
De script. eccles. proleg.	*De scriptoribus ecclesiasticis prolegomena*
De Vir. Ill.	*De Viris Illustribus*
Ep.	*Epistulae*
Himer. *Ex. Nap.*	Himerius, *Excerpta Napolitana*
Hippoc.	Hippocrates
[*Ep.*]	*Epistulae*
Hippol.	Hippolytus
Haer.	*Refutatio omnium Haeresium*
Hist. Aug.	*Historia Augusta* (see S.H.A.)
Hist. Rom. Rel.	see Altheim
Hom.	Homer
Il.	*Iliad*
Od.	*Odyssey*
Homil. Clement.	*Clementine Homilies*
Hor.	Horace
Ars P.	*Ars Poetica*
Carm.	*Carmina* or *Odes*
Carm. Saec.	*Carmen Saeculare*
Epist.	*Epistulae*
Epod.	*Epodi*
Sat.	*Satirae* or *Sermones*
How and Wells	W. W. How and J. Wells, *A Commentary on Herodotus* (1912)
Hyg.	Hyginus
Fab.	*Fabulae*
Poet. Astr.	*Poetica Astronomica*
Hymn. Hom. Ap.	*Hymnus Homericus ad Apollinem*
Bacch.	„ „ „ *Bacchum*
Cer.	„ „ „ *Cererem*
Mart.	„ „ „ *Martem*
Merc.	„ „ „ *Mercurium*
Pan.	„ „ „ *Panem*
Ven.	„ „ „ *Venerem*
Hymn. Mag.	*Hymni Magici*
Hymn. Orph.	*Hymni Orphici*
hyp.	hypothesis
IG	*Inscriptiones Graecae* (1873–)
IG Rom.	*Inscriptiones Graecae ad res Romanas pertinentes* (1906–)
ILS	see Dessau
IPE	*Inscriptiones orae septentrionalis Ponti Euxini*, (1885)
Iambl.	Iamblichus
Myst.	*De Mysteriis*
Ibyc.	Ibycus
Il.	*Iliad*
Indo-Germ. Forsch.	*Indogermanische Forschungen*, 1891–
Inst. Iust.	*Institutiones Iustiniani*
Isae.	Isaeus

Isid.	Isidorus
Etym. or *Orig.*	*Etymologiae* or *Origines*
Isoc.	Isocrates
Bus.	*Busiris*
Paneg.	*Panegyricus*
It. Alex.	*Itinerarium Alexandri*
It. Ant.	*Itineraria Antonini Augusti*
JDAI	*Jahrbuch des [kaiserlich] deutschen archäologischen Instituts*, 1886– (contains *Archäologischer Anzeiger*)
JEg.Arch.	*Journal of Egyptian Archaeology*, 1914–
JHS	*Journal of Hellenic Studies*, 1880–
JÖAI	*Jahreshefte des Österreichischen Archäolog. Instituts in Wien*, 1898–
JRS	*Journal of Roman Studies*, 1911–
JTS	*Journal of Theological Studies*, 1899–
Jacobsthal–Neuffer	P. Jacobsthal and E. Neuffer, *Gallia Graeca* (1933)
Jahrb.	see [Neue] *Jahrb.*
Jahrb. f. cl. Phil. Suppl.	*Jahrbücher für classische Philologie, Supplementband*
Jahresb.	see Bursian
Jerome	see Hieron.
Jones, *Eastern Cities*	A. H. M. Jones, *The Cities of the Eastern Roman Provinces* (1937)
Joseph.	Josephus
AJ	*Antiquitates Judaicae*
Ap.	*Contra Apionem*
BJ	*Bellum Judaicum*
Vit.	*Vita*
Journ. Bib. Lit.	*Journal of Biblical Literature*, 1890–
Journ. Phil.	*Journal of Philology*, 1868–1920; Index, 1923
Journ. Sav.	*Journal des savants*, N.S. 1903–
Julian.	Julianus Imperator
Apophth.	*Apophthegmata*
Ep.	*Epistulae*
Mis.	*Misopogon*
Or.	*Orationes*
Just. *Epit.*	Justinus, *Epitome* (of Trogus)
κ.	κατά
KB	see Winter
KS	A. Kiessling and R. Schöll, ed. of Asconius
KZ	Kuhn's *Zeitschrift für vergleichende Sprachforschung*, 1851–
Kaibel	see *CGF* and *Epigr. Gr.*
Keil, *Gramm. Lat.*	H. Keil, *Grammatici Latini* (8 vols., 1855–1923)
Kern, *Inschr. von M.*	O. Kern, *Die Inschriften von Magnesia am Maeander* (1900–)
Orph. frag.	*Orphica Fragmenta* (1922)
Rel. d. Griech.	*Die Religion der Griechen* (1926)
Kl. Schr.	*Kleine Schriften* (of various authors)
Klass. Phil. Stud.	*Klassische Philologische Studien* herausg. von E. Bickel u. C. Jensen
Klio	*Klio, Beiträge zur alten Geschichte*, 1901–
Körte, *Men. Rel.*	A. Körte, *Menandri Reliquiae*
Kroll, *Rhet.*	W. Kroll, *Rhetorik* (1937; written as article for *PW*, but published separately)
Kühn	K. G. Kühn, *Medicorum Graecorum Opera*
LXX	*Septuagint*
L & S	Liddell & Scott, *Greek-English Lexicon*, 9th ed., revised by H. Stuart Jones (1925–40)
Lactant.	Lactantius
Div. Inst.	*Divinae Institutiones*
Laur.	Laurentian Library
Leipz. Stud.	*Leipziger Studien zur klassischen Philosophie*, 1878–95
Lex.	*Lexicon*
Lex. Mess.	*Lexicon Messanense*
Lib. Colon.	*Libri coloniarum*

Lind. Temp. Chron.	Chr. Blinkenberg, *Die Lindische Tempelchronik*, 1915
Lindsay, *Gloss. Lat.*	W. M. Lindsay, *Glossaria Latina* (Paris, 1930)
Lit. Gesch.	see Christ–Schmid–Stählin, Schmid–Stählin, Schanz, and Susemihl
Livy, *Epit.*	Livy, *Epitomae*
Per.	*Periochae*
Lobeck, *Aglaoph.*	C. A. Lobeck, *Aglaophamus* (1829)
Loeb	Loeb Classical Library
[Longinus], *Subl.*	[Longinus], Περὶ ὕψους
Luc.	Lucan
Lucian	
Alex.	*Alexander*
Anach.	*Anacharsis*
Catapl.	*Cataplus*
Demon.	*Demonax*
Dial. Meret.	*Dialogi Meretricii*
Dial. Mort.	*Dialogi Mortuorum*
Hermot.	*Hermotimus*
Hist. conscr.	*Quomodo Historia conscribenda sit*
Ind.	*Adversus Indoctum*
Iupp. Trag.	*Iuppiter Tragoedus*
Macr.	*Macrobii*
Nigr.	*Nigrinus*
Salt.	*De Saltatione*
Symp.	*Symposium*
Syr. D.	*De Syria Dea*
Trag.	*Tragoedopodagra*
Ver. Hist.	*Verae Historiae* 1, 2
Vit. Auct.	*Vitarum Auctio*
Lucil.	Lucilius
Lucr.	Lucretius
Lycoph.	Lycophron
Alex.	*Alexandra*
Lycurg.	Lycurgus
Leoc.	*Against Leocrates*
Lydus, *Mens.*	Lydus, *De Mensibus*
Mag.	*De Magistratibus*
Lys.	Lysias
MGH	*Monumenta Germaniae Historica*, 1826–
Macrob.	Macrobius
Sat.	*Saturnalia*
Malcovati, *ORF*	H. Malcovati, *Oratorum Romanorum Fragmenta* (Turin, 1930)
Manitius	M. Manitius, *Gesch. der lat. Lit. des Mittelalters* (1911–12)
Marcellin.	Marcellinus
Marm. Par.	*Marmor Parium* (*IG* 12(5), 444)
Marquardt	J. Marquardt
Privatleben	*Privatleben der Römer*, 2ᵉ Auflage, besorgt von A. Mau. 2 vols., 1886. These together make up vol. vii of *Handbuch der römischen Altertümer*, von Joachim Marquardt und Theodor Mommsen
Staatsverw.	*Römische Staatsverwaltung*² (1881–5)
Mart.	Martial
Spect.	*Spectacula*
Marx	F. Marx, *C. Lucilii Carminum Reliquiae* (1904–5)
Med. Nederl. Akad.	*Mededeelingen der Koninklijke Akademie van Wetenschappen*, 1896–
Med. Nederl. Hist. Inst. Rom.	*Mededeelingen van het Nederlandsch histor. Instituut te Rom*, 1921–
Meineke, *FCG*	A. Meineke, *Fragmenta Comicorum Graecorum* (1839–57)
Mélanges d'arch.	*Mélanges d'archéologie et d'histoire de l'École française de Rome*, 1881–
Mél. Masp.	*Mélanges Maspéro* (1934–7)
Men. Rel.	see Körte
Men.	Menander
Epit.	Ἐπιτρέποντες
Her.	Ἥρως
Pk.	Περικειρομένη
Sam.	Σαμία
Metr. Mus. Studies	Metropolitan Museum of Art, New York, *Studies*, 1928–
Meyer, *Forschungen*	Ed. Meyer, *Forschungen zur alten Geschichte* (1892–9)

Migne, *PG*	Migne, *Patrologiae Cursus, series Graeca*
PL	*Patrologiae Cursus, series Latina*
Min. Fel.	Minucius Felix
Oct.	*Octavius*
Mir. Ausc.	*De Mirabilibus Auscultationibus* (auctor ignotus)
Mnemos.	*Mnemosyne*, 1852–
Mommsen	Th. Mommsen
Ges. Schr.	*Gesammelte Schriften* (8 vols., 1905–13)
Röm. Forsch.	*Römische Forschungen* (2 vols. (1 in 2nd ed.), 1864–79)
Röm. Staatsr.	*Das Römisches Staatsrecht*, i, ii (ed. 3, 1887), iii (1888)
Röm. Strafr.	*Das Römisches Strafrecht* (1899)
Mommsen–Marquardt, *Manuel*	*Manuel des antiquités romaines* (1887–1907), a French transl. of Mommsen's *Römisches Staatsrecht*
Mon. Anc.	*Monumentum Ancyranum*
Mon. Ant.	*Monumenti Antichi pubblicati per cura della Reale Accademia dei Lincei*, 1890–
Mon. Piot	*Monuments Piot*, 1894–
Morel, *FPL*	*Fragmenta Poetarum Latinorum epicorum et lyricorum . . . post E. Baehrens*, ed. W. Morel (1927)
Münzer, *Röm. Adelsparteien*	F. Münzer, *Römische Adelsparteien u. Adelsfamilien* (1920)
Mus. Belge	*Musée Belge*, 1897–
Myth. Vat.	*Mythographi Vaticani*, ed. Bode (1834)
Nachr. Ges. d. Wiss. Gött.	see *Gött. Nachr.*
Naevius, *fr. com.*	Naevius, *fragmenta comoediarum*
Nauck	see *TGF*
Nemes.	Nemesianus
Cyn.	*Cynegetica*
Ecl.	*Eclogae*
Nep.	Nepos
Att.	*Atticus*
Epam.	*Epaminondas*
[Neue] *Jahrb.*	(1) *[Neue] Jahrbücher für Philologie und Pädagogik*, 1826–97 (2) *Neue Jahrbücher für d. klassische Altertum*, 1898–1925 (3) *Neue Jahrbücher für Wissenschaft und Jugendbildung*, 1925–36 ((1), (2), and (3) form a continuous series)
Nic.	Nicander
Alex.	*Alexipharmaca*
Ther.	*Theriaca*
Nic. Dam.	Nicolaus Damascenus
Nilsson, *Feste*	M. P. Nilsson, *Griechische Feste v. religiöser Bedeutung m. Ausschluss d. attischen* (1906)
Non.	Nonius
Nonnus, *Dion.*	Nonnus, *Dionysiaca*
Norden, *Ant. Kunstpr.*	E. Norden, *Die Antike Kunstprosa, vom 6. Jahrh. v. Chr. bis in d. Zeit d. Renaissance* (1898, rp. with supplements 1909)
Not. Dign. [*occ.*] [*or.*]	*Notitia dignitatum in partibus Occidentis Orientis*
Not. Scav.	*Notizie degli scavi di antichità*, 1876–
Nov.	*Novellae*
Nov. Com. Fragm.	see Schroeder
Num. Chron.	*Numismatic Chronicle*, 1861–
Numen.	Numenius
O.C.T.	Oxford Classical Texts
OGI	*Orientis Graeci Inscriptiones Selectae* (1903–05)
ORF	see Malcovati
Od.	*Odyssey*
Or.	*Oratio*
Origen, *c. Cels.*	Origen, *Contra Celsum*
Oros.	Orosius
Orph. *Lith.*	Orphica, *Lithica*
Ov.	Ovid

Ov. *(cont.)*	
Am.	*Amores*
Ars Am.	*Ars Amatoria*
Fast.	*Fasti*
Hal.	*Halieuticon Liber*
Her.	*Heroides*
Ib.	*Ibis*
Medic.	*Medicamina faciei*
Met.	*Metamorphoses*
Pont.	*Epistulae ex Ponto*
Rem. Am.	*Remedia Amoris*
Tr.	*Tristia*
Overbeck	J. Overbeck, *Die antiken Schrift-quellen zur Geschichte d. bilden-den Künste bei den Griechen* (1868)
π.	περί
PG	see Migne
PGM	*Papyri Graecae Magicae*, ed. by Karl Preisendanz, 2 vols., 1928–31
PIR	*Prosopographia Imperii Romani Sae-culi I, II, III* (1st ed. by E. Klebs and H. Dessau, 1897–8; 2nd ed. by E. Groag and A. Stein, 1933–)
PL	see Migne
PLG	T. Bergk, *Poetae Lyrici Graeci* (1882, rp. 1914–15)
PLM	*Poetae Latini Minores* (ed. E. Baeh-rens, 5 vols., 1879–83; rev. by F. Vollmer, only vols. i, ii, and v completed 1911–35)
PMG	see *PGM*
PPF	H. Diels, *Poetarum Philosophorum Graecorum Fragmenta* (1901)
PSAS	*Proceedings Soc. Antiq. Scotland,* 1866–
PSI	*Papiri Greci e Latini (Pubblicazioni della Società italiana per la ricer-ca dei Papyri greci e Latini in Egitto,* 1912–)
PW	A. Pauly, G. Wissowa, and W. Kroll, *Real-Encyclopädie d. klassischen Altertumswissenschaft* (1893–)
PAmh.	*Amherst Papyri,* 1900–
PAntin.	The *Antinoe Papyrus* of Theocritus
PBerol.	*Berlin Papyri*
PEleph.	*Elephantine Papyri* (1907)
PFouad	P. Jouguet and others, *Les Papyrus Fouad I* (1939)
PGiess.	*Griechische Papyri im Museum des ober-hessischen Geschichtsvereins zu Giessen*
PHib.	*Hibeh Papyri* (1906)
PIand.	*Papyri Iandanae* (1912–)
PLips.	*Griechische Urkunden der Papyrus-sammlung zu Leipzig*
PLondon	*Greek Papyri in the British Museum,* ed. F. G. Kenyon and H. I. Bell
PLund	*Papyri Lundenses*
PMilan.	*Papiri Milanesi*
POsl.	*Papyri Osloenses*
POxy.	*Oxyrhynchus Papyri,* ed. B. P. Grenfell and A. S. Hunt (1898–)
PRyl.	*Catalogue of the Greek papyri in the John Rylands Library at Manchester* (1911–)
PTeb.	*Tebtunis Papyri* (1902–38)
PVat. II	*Il Papiro Vaticano Greco II,* ed. M. Norsa and G. Vitelli (1931)
Parker, *Roman World*	H. M. D. Parker, *A History of the Roman World from A.D. 138 to 337* (1935)
Parod. Epic. Gr. Rel.	*Parodorum Epicorum Graecorum reli-quiae* (vol. i of *Corpusculum Poesis Epicae Graecae Ludibundae,* P. Brandt and C. Wachsmuth, 1888)
Parth.	Parthenius
Amat. Narr.	*Narrationum Amatoriarum libellus* (Ἐρωτικὰ παθήματα)
Paulus, *Sent.*	Julius Paulus, *Sententiae*
Paus.	Pausanias

Peripl. M. Rubr.	*Periplus Maris Rubri*
Pers.	Persius
Peter, *HR Rel.*	H. Peter, *Historicorum Romanorum Reliquiae* (vol. i², 1914)
Petron.	Petronius
Sat.	*Satura*
Pf.	R. Pfeiffer
Pfuhl	E. Pfuhl, *Malerei u. Zeichnung d. Griechen* (3 vols., 1923)
Pherec. or Pherecyd.	Pherecydes
Phil. Unters.	*Philologische Untersuchungen,* 1880–
Phil. Wochenschr.	*Philologische Wochenschrift,* 1921–
Philo	Philo Judaeus
CW	Edition of Philo Judaeus by L. Cohn and P. Wendland (Berlin, 1896–1916)
In Flacc.	*In Flaccum*
Leg.	*Legatio ad Gaium*
Philol.	*Philologus,* 1846–
Philol. Suppl.	*Philologus,* Supplement, 1860–
Philostr.	Philostratus
Imag.	*Imagines*
VA	*Vita Apollonii*
VS	*Vitae Sophistarum*
Phld.	Philodemus
Phlegon, *Mir.*	Phlegon, *Miracula*
Phot.	Photius
Bibl.	*Bibliotheca*
Pind.	Pindar
Isthm.	*Isthmian Odes*
Nem.	*Nemean* „
Ol.	*Olympian* „
Pyth.	*Pythian* „
Pl.	Plato
Alc.	*Alcibiades*
Ap.	*Apologia*
Chrm.	*Charmides*
Cra.	*Cratylus*
Cri.	*Crito*
Criti.	*Critias*
Epin.	*Epinomis*
Euthphr.	*Euthyphro*
Grg.	*Gorgias*
Hipparch.	*Hipparchus*
Hp. Mi.	*Hippias Minor*
La. or *Lach.*	*Laches*
Leg.	*Leges*
Menex.	*Menexenus*
Phd.	*Phaedo*
Phdr.	*Phaedrus*
Phlb.	*Philebus*
Prm.	*Parmenides*
Prt.	*Protagoras*
Resp.	*Respublica*
Symp.	*Symposium*
Soph.	*Sophista*
Tht.	*Theaetetus*
Ti.	*Timaeus*
Platner–Ashby, *Topog.*	S. B. Platner and T. Ashby, *A Topo-graphical Dictionary of Ancient Rome* (1929)
Dict.	
Plato Com.	Plato Comicus
Platon.	Platonius
Diff. Com.	*De Differentia Comoediarum*
Plaut.	Plautus
Amph.	*Amphitruo*
Asin.	*Asinaria*
Bacch.	*Bacchides*
Capt.	*Captivi*
Cas.	*Casina*
Cist.	*Cistellaria*
Curc.	*Curculio*
Men.	*Menaechmi*
Merc.	*Mercator*
Mostell.	*Mostellaria*
Stich.	*Stichus*
Plin.	Pliny (the Elder)
HN	*Naturalis Historia*
Plin.	Pliny (the Younger)
Ep.	*Epistulae*
Pan.	*Panegyricus*
Tra.	*Epistulae ad Traianum*
Plotinus, *Enn.*	Plotinus, *Enneades*
Plut.	Plutarch

Plut. (*cont.*)

Mor.	*Moralia*
Amat.	*Amatorius*
An seni	*An seni respublica gerenda sit*
Comp. Ar. et Men.	*Comparatio Aristophanis et Menandri*
Conv. sept. sap.	*Convivium septem sapientium*
De Alex. fort.	*De fortuna Alexandri*
De def. or.	*De defectu oraculorum*
De exil.	*De exilio*
De fac.	*De facie in orbe lunae*
De frat. amor.	*De fraterno amore*
De garr.	*De garrulitate*
De gen.	*De genio Socratis*
De glor. Ath.	*De gloria Atheniensium*
De Is. et Os.	*De Iside et Osiride*
De lat. viv.	*De latenter vivendo*
De mul. vir.	*De mulierum virtutibus*
De mus.	*De musica*
De prof. virt.	*De profectu in virtute*
De Pyth. or.	*De Pythiae oraculis*
De sera	*De sera numinis vindicta*
De superst.	*De superstitione*
De tranq. anim.	*De tranquillitate animi*
Quaest. conv.	*Quaestiones convivales*
Quaest. Graec.	„ *Graecae*
Quaest. Plat.	„ *Platonicae*
Quaest. Rom.	„ *Romanae*
Quomodo adul.	*Quomodo adulescens poetas audire debeat*
Vit.	*Vitae Parallelae*
Aem.	*Aemilius Paulus*
Ages.	*Agesilaus*
Alc.	*Alcibiades*
Alex.	*Alexander*
Ant.	*Antonius*
Arat.	*Aratus*
C. Gracch.	*Gaius Gracchus*
Caes.	*Caesar*
Cam.	*Camillus*
Cat. Mai., Min.	*Cato Maior, Minor*
Cic.	*Cicero*
Cim.	*Cimon*
Cleom.	*Cleomenes*
Crass.	*Crassus*
Dem.	*Demosthenes*
Demetr.	*Demetrius*
Flam.	*Flamininus*
Luc.	*Lucullus*
Lyc.	*Lycurgus*
Lys.	*Lysander*
Mar.	*Marius*
Marc.	*Marcellus*
Num.	*Numa*
Pel.	*Pelopidas*
Per.	*Pericles*
Phil.	*Philopoemen*
Pomp.	*Pompeius*
Pyrrh.	*Pyrrhus*
Rom.	*Romulus*
Sert.	*Sertorius*
Sol.	*Solon*
Sull.	*Sulla*
Them.	*Themistocles*
Thes.	*Theseus*
Ti. Gracch.	*Tiberius Gracchus*
Tim.	*Timoleon*
[Plut.], *Cons. ad Apoll.*	[Plutarch], *Consolatio ad Apollonium*
Vit. Hom.	*Vita Homeri*
X orat.	*Vitae decem oratorum*
Poet. Rom. Vet.	see Diehl
Poll.	Pollux
Onom.	*Onomasticon*
Polyaenus, *Strat.*	Polyaenus, *Strategemata*
Polyb.	Polybius
Pompon.	Pomponius
Porph.	Porphyry
Abst.	*De Abstinentia*
De Antr. Nymph.	*De Antro Nympharum*
Plot.	*Vita Plotini*
Powell, *Coll. Alex.*	J. U. Powell, *Collectanea Alexandrina* (1925)

Powell and Barber, *New Chapters*	J. U. Powell and E. A. Barber, *New Chapters in the History of Greek Literature* (1921); Second Series (1929); Third Series (J. U. Powell alone, 1933)
praef.	*praefatio*
Preisendanz	see *PGM*
Preller–Robert	L. Preller, *Griechische Mythologie*⁴, bearbeitet von C. Robert (1894)
Prisc. *Inst.*	Priscian, *Institutio de arte grammatica*
Procl.	Proclus
In Ti.	*In Platonis Timaeum commentarii*
Procop.	Procopius
Goth.	*De Bello Gothico*
Vand.	*De Bello Vandalico*
Progr.	*Programm*
Prop.	Propertius
Prosop. Att.	J. Kirchner, *Prosopographia Attica* (1901–3)
Prosop. Rom.	= *PIR*
Prudent.	Prudentius
c. Symm.	*contra Symmachum*
Perist.	*Peristephanon*
Ptol.	Ptolemaeus mathematicus
Alm.	*Almagest*
Geog.	*Geographia*
Harm.	*Harmonica*
Quint.	Quintilian
Ep. ad Tryph.	*Epistula ad Tryphonem* (introductory to the following)
Inst.	*Institutio oratoria*
Quint. Smyrn.	Quintus Smyrnaeus
RGVV	*Religionsgeschichtliche Versuche und Vorarbeiten*, ed. A. Dieterich, R. Wünsch, L. Malten, O. Weinreich, L. Deubner (1903–)
RK	see Wissowa
RLÖ	*Der römische Limes in Oesterreich* (1900–)
Rav. Cosm.	*Cosmographia Anonymi Ravennatis*
Reiff.	Reifferscheid (ed. Suetonius)
Rend. Ist. Lomb.	*Rendiconti d. R. istituto Lombardo di scienze e lettere*, 1864–
Rend. Linc.	*Rendiconti della reale accademia dei Lincei*, 6th Ser. 1892–1924; 7th Ser. 1925–
Rend. Pont.	*Rendiconti della pontificia accademia romana di archeologia*, 1921–
Rer. nat. scr. Graec. min.	O. Keller, *Rerum naturalium scriptores Graeci minores* (1877)
Rev. Arch.	*Revue archéologique*, 1844–
Rev. Bibl.	*Revue biblique*, 1892–
Rev. Ét. Anc.	*Revue des études anciennes*, 1899–
Rev. Ét. Grec.	*Revue des études grecques*, 1888–
Rev. Ét. Lat.	*Revue des études latines*, 1923–
Rev. Hist.	*Revue historique*, 1876–
Rev. Hist. Rel.	*Revue de l'histoire des religions*, 1880–
Rev. Phil.	*Revue de philologie*, Nouv. Sér. 1877–
Rh. Mus.	*Rheinisches Museum für Philologie*, 1827–, Neue Folge, 1842–
Rhet.	see Spengel
Rhet. Her.	*Rhetorica ad Herennium*
Rhet. Lat. Min.	see Halm
Ribbeck, *CRF*	O. Ribbeck, *Comicorum Romanorum Fragmenta*
TRF	O. Ribbeck, *Tragicorum Romanorum Fragmenta* [both in *Scaenicae Romanorum Poesis Fragmenta*³ (1897–8)]
Ritter and Preller	H. Ritter and L. Preller, *Historia Philosophiae Graecae*¹⁰ (1934)
Riv. d. Arch. Crist.	*Rivista di archeologia cristiana*, 1924–
Riv. Fil.	*Rivista di filologia*, 1873–
Riv. ital. per le sc. giur.	*Rivista italiana per le scienze giuridiche*, 1886–
Robert, *Bild und Lied*	Carl Robert, *Bild und Lied* (1881)
Robin	L. Robin, *La Pensée grecque et l'origine de l'esprit scientifique*² (1932); Engl. Transl. *Greek Thought*

Rohde, *D. gr. Roman*	E. Rohde, *Der griechische Roman u. s. Vorläufer*[3] (1914)
Röm.	*Römisch*
Röm. Forsch.	see Mommsen
Röm. Gesch.	see Beloch
Röm. Mitt.	*Mitteilungen des Deutschen Archäolog. Instituts, Römische Abteilung,* 1886–
Röm. Staatsr.	see Mommsen
Röm. Strafr.	„ „
Röm. Stud.	see Cichorius
Roscher, *Lex.*	W. H. Roscher, *Ausführliches Lexikon d. griechischen u. römischen Mythologie,* 1884–
Rose, *Handb. Gk. Myth.*	H. J. Rose, *Handbook of Greek Mythology*[3] (1945)
Rossbach, *Röm. Ehe*	A. Rossbach, *Untersuchungen über die römischen Ehe* (1853)
Rostovtzeff	M. Rostovtzeff
Roman Empire	*The Social and Economic History of the Roman Empire* (1926)
Hellenistic World	*The Social and Economic History of the Hellenistic World* (3 vols., 1941)
Ruggiero, *Diz. Epigr.*	E. de Ruggiero, *Dizionario epigrafico di antichità romana* (1886–)
Rut. Namat.	Rutilius Namatianus, *De Reditu*

SC	*Senatus consultum*
SEG	*Supplementum epigraphicum Graecum* (1923–)
S.H.A.	Scriptores Historiae Augustae
Alex. Sev.	*Alexander Severus*
Aurel.	*Aurelian*
Comm.	*Commodus*
Did. Iul.	*Didius Iulianus*
Hadr.	*Hadrian*
M. Ant.	*Marcus Antoninus*
Max.	*Maximinus*
Sev.	*Severus*
Spart.	*Spartianus*
Tyr. Trig.	*Tyranni Triginta*
Marc.	*Marcus*
SIG	see Dittenberg. *SIG*
SMSR	*Studi e materiali di storia delle religioni,* 1925–
SPCK	Society for Promoting Christian Knowledge
SVF	H. von Arnim, *Stoicorum Veterum Fragmenta* (1903–)
Sall.	Sallust
Cat.	*Bellum Catilinae* or *De Catilinae coniuratione*
H.	*Historiae*
Iug.	*Bellum Iugurthinum*
Satyr.	Satyrus Historicus
Vit. Eur.	*Vita Euripidis*
Sav. Zeitschr.	*Zeitschrift der Savigny-Stiftung für Rechtsgeschichte, romanistische Abteilung* (1862–)
Schanz, Schanz–Hosius	M. Schanz, *Geschichte d. römischen Literatur,* revised I[4] 1927 and II[4] 1935 by C. Hosius; III[3] 1922, Hosius and Krüger; IV. i[2] 1914 and IV. ii. 1920, Schanz, Hosius, and Krüger
Schmid–Stählin	W. Schmid and O. Stählin, *Geschichte d. griechischen Literatur,* I. i 1929, I. ii 1934. See also Christ–Schmid–Stählin
schol.	scholiast or scholia
Schol. Bern.	*Scholia Bernensia ad Vergilii bucolica et georgica,* ed. Hagen (1867)
Schol. Bob.	*Scholia Bobiensia*
Schol. Cruq.	*Scholia Cruquiana*
Schol. Dan. Aen.	*Scholia Danielis* (Pierre Daniel, first publisher in 1600 of Supplements to Servius' Commentary on Virgil)
Schol. Flor. Callim.	*Scholia Florentina in Callimachum*
Schroeder, *Nov. Com. Fragm.*	O. Schroeder, *Novae Comoediae fragmenta in papyris reperta exceptis Menandreis* (1915)

Scol. Anon.	*Scolia Anonyma* in Diehl's *Anth. Lyr. Graec.* II, pp. 181–92
Scol. Att.	*Scolia Attica* in Diehl's *Anth. Lyr. Graec.* II, pp. 181–9
Scymn.	Scymnus
sel.	selected
Semon.	Semonides
Sen.	Seneca (The Elder)
Con. Ex.	*Controversiarum Excerpta*
Controv.	*Controversiae*
Suas.	*Suasoriae*
Sen.	Seneca (The Younger)
Apocol.	*Apocolocyntosis*
Ben.	*De beneficiis*
Clem.	*De clementia*
Constant.	*De constantia sapientis*
Dial.	*Dialogi*
Ep.	*Epistulae*
Epigr.	*Epigrammata super exilio*
Helv.	*Ad Helviam*
Prov.	*De Providentia*
QNat.	*Quaestiones Naturales*
Tranq.	*De tranquillitate animi*
Serv.	Servius
Praef.	*Praefatio*
Serv. Dan.	see *Schol. Dan. Aen.*
Sext. Emp.	Sextus Empiricus
Math.	*adversus Mathematicos*
Pyr.	Πυρρώνειοι ὑποτυπώσεις
Sid. Apoll.	Sidonius Apollinaris
Carm.	*Carmina*
Sil.	Silius Italicus
Pun.	*Punica*
Simon.	Simonides
Simpl.	Simplicius
in Cael.	*in Aristotelis de Caelo Commentarii*
in Phys.	*in Aristotelis de Physica Commentarii*
Sitz. followed by name of Academy or Society	*Sitzungsberichte*
Sitz. Wien	*Sitzungsberichte der Akad. der Wissenschaften in Wien,* 1848–
Socrates, *Hist. Eccl.*	Socrates, *Historia Ecclesiastica*
Solin.	Solinus
Soph.	Sophocles
Aj.	*Ajax*
Ant.	*Antigone*
El.	*Electra*
Fr.	Fragments, *TGF* or A. C. Pearson (1917)
OC	*Oedipus Coloneus*
OT	*Oedipus Tyrannus*
Phil.	*Philoctetes*
Trach.	*Trachiniae*
Sozom.	Sozomen
Hist. Eccl.	*Historia Ecclesiastica*
Spengel, *Rhet.*	L. Spengel, *Rhetores Graeci* (1853–6 vol. I pars. ii. iterum ed. C. Hammer, 1894)
Stat.	Statius
Achil.	*Achilleis*
Silv.	*Silvae*
Theb.	*Thebais*
Steph. Byz.	Stephanus Byzantius or Byzantinus
Stith Thompson	Stith Thompson, *Motif-Index of Folk-Literature* (6 vols. in Indiana University Studies, 96–7, 100–1, 105–6, 108, 110–12; also published as FF Communication 106–9, 116–17, 1932–6)
Stob.	Stobaeus
Ecl.	Ἐκλογαί
Flor.	Ἀνθολόγιον
Stor. Rom.	see De Sanctis
Strab.	Strabo
Stud. Gesch. Kult. Alt.	*Studien zur Geschichte und Kultur des Altertums,* 1907–
Stud. Ital.	*Studi italiani di filologia classica,* 1893–
Studi stor.	*Studi storici per l'antichità classica* (1908–15)

Suet.	Suetonius
Aug.	*Divus Augustus*
Calig.	*Gaius Caligula*
Claud.	*Divus Claudius*
Dom.	*Domitianus*
Gram.	*De Grammaticis*
Iul.	*Divus Iulius*
Ner.	*Nero*
Poet.	*De Poetis*
Rel. Reiff.	*Reliquiae,* ed. Reifferscheid
Rhet.	*De Rhetoribus*
Tib.	*Tiberus*
Tit.	*Divus Titus*
Vit.	*Vitellius*
Vita Luc.	*Vita Lucani*
Suid.	Suidas
Supp. Aesch.	H. J. Mette, *Supplementum Aeschyleum* (1939)
Supp. Com.	see Demiańczuk
Supp. Epigr.	see *SEG*
Susemihl, *Gesch. gr. Lit. Alex.*	F. Susemihl, *Geschichte d. griechischen Litteratur in d. Alexandriner-Zeit* (1891–2)
Syll. Graec.	see *Corp. poes. ep. Graec. lud.*
Symb.	*Symbolum*
Symb. Philol. Danielsson	*Symbolae Philologicae O. A. Danielsson octogenario dicatae,* Upsala (1932)
Symmachus, *Relat.*	Symmachus, *Relationes*
T.	see Teubner
TAPA	see *Trans. Am. Phil. Ass.*
TGF	A. Nauck, *Tragicorum Graecorum Fragmenta*[2] (1889)
TRF	see Ribbeck
Tab. Agn.	*Tabula Agnoniensis*
Tac.	Tacitus
Agr.	*Agricola*
Ann.	*Annales*
Dial.	*Dialogus de Oratoribus*
Germ.	*Germania*
Hist.	*Historiae*
Tatianus, *Ad Gr.*	Tatianus, *Oratio ad Graecos*
Ter.	Terence
Ad.	*Adelphoe*
An.	*Andria*
Eun.	*Eunuchus*
Haut.	*H(e)autontimorumenos*
Phorm.	*Phormio*
Tert.	Tertullian
Ad Nat.	*Ad Nationes*
Adv. Valent.	*Adversus Valentinianos*
Apol.	*Apologeticus*
De Anim.	*De Testimonio Animae*
De Bapt.	*De Baptismo*
De Monog.	*De Monogamia*
De praescr. haeret.	*De praescriptione haereticorum*
De Spect.	*De Spectaculis*
Teubner or T.	Bibliotheca Scriptorum Graecorum et Romanorum Teubneriana (1849–)
Teuffel, Teuffel–Kroll	W. S. Teuffel, *Geschichte d. römischen Literatur*[6], vol. ii[7] by W. Kroll and F. Skutsch (3 vols., 1913–20). Engl. Transl. by G. C. Warr from L. Schwabe's revision of the 5th German ed. (2 vols., 1900)
Theoc.	Theocritus
Epigr.	*Epigrammata*
Id.	*Idylls*
Theog.	Theognis
Theoph. *ad Autol.*	Theophilus, *ad Autolycum*
Theophr.	Theophrastus
Caus. Pl.	*De Causis Plantarum*
Char.	*Characteres*
Hist. Pl.	*Historia Plantarum*
Theopomp.	Theopompus Historicus
Thuc.	Thucydides
Tib.	Tibullus
Timoth.	Timotheus
Pers.	*Persae*
Tod	M. N. Tod, *Greek Historical Inscriptions* (1933–48)

Trag. Adesp.	*Tragica Adespota* in Nauck's *Tragicorum Graecorum Fragmenta,* pp. 837–958
Trans. Am. Phil. Ass. or *TAPA*	*Transactions of the American Philological Association,* 1870–
trib.	*tribunus*
trib. pot.	*tribunicia potestas*
Tzetz.	Tzetzes
Chil.	*Historiarum variarum Chiliades*
UPZ	U. Wilcken, *Urkunden der Ptolemäerzeit* (1922–)
Ueberweg–Praechter, *Grundriss*	F. Ueberweg, *Grundriss d. Geschichte d. Philosophie,* Pt. i, *Das Altertum;* 12th ed. by K. Praechter (1926)
Ulp.	Ulpian
VCH	*Victoria County History*
Val. Max.	Valerius Maximus
Varro, *Ling.*	Varro, *De Lingua Latina*
Rust.	*De Re Rustica*
Sat. Men.	*Saturae Menippeae*
Vatin.	Vatinius
Vell. Pat.	Velleius Paterculus
Verg.	Virgil
Aen.	*Aeneid*
Catal.	*Catalepton*
Ecl.	*Eclogues*
G.	*Georgics*
Vit. Aesch.	*Vita Aeschyli* (O.C.T. of Aeschylus)
Vitr.	Vitruvius
De Arch.	*De Architectura*
Vopiscus, *Cyn.*	Vopiscus, *Cynegetica*
Vorsokr.	see Diels
Walz	C. Walz, *Rhetores Graeci* (9 vols., 1832–6)
Warde Fowler, *Rel. Exper.*	W. Warde Fowler, *The Religious Experience of the Roman People* (1911)
Warmington, *Indian Commerce*	E. H. Warmington, *The Commerce between the Roman Empire and India* (1928)
Westd. Zeit.	*Westdeutsche Zeitschrift für Geschichte und Kunst,* 1882–1909
Wien. Stud.	*Wiener Studien,* 1879–
Wilamowitz	U. von Wilamowitz-Moellendorff
Interpret.	*Aischylos Interpretationen* (1914)
Textg. d. gr. Lyr.	*Textgeschichte der griechischen Lyriker* (1900)
Wilhelm, *Urkunden*	A. Wilhelm, *Urkunden dramatischer Aufführungen in Athen* (1905)
Winter, *KB*	F. Winter, *Kunstgeschichte in Bildern* (1935 ff.)
Wissowa, *RK*	G. Wissowa, *Religion und Kultus d. Römer*[2] (1912)
Ges. Abh.	*Gesammelte Abhandlungen zur römischen Religions- und Stadtgeschichte.*
Xen.	Xenophon
Ages.	*Agesilaus*
An.	*Anabasis*
Ap.	*Apologia Socratis*
Cyn.	*Cynegeticus*
Cyr.	*Cyropaedia*
Hell.	*Hellenica*
Mem.	*Memorabilia*
Oec.	*Oeconomicus*
Symp.	*Symposium*
Vect.	*De Vectigalibus*
Z. für die öst. Gym.	*Zeitschrift für die österreichischen Gymnasien,* 1850–
Zeller, *Phil. d. Gr.*	E. Zeller, *Die Philosophie d. Griechen*
Gesch. d. gr. Phil.	*Grundriss d. Geschichte d. Griechischen Philosophie*[13] (1928)
Plato, etc.	*Plato and the Older Academy* (Engl. Transl. 1888)
Zonar.	Zonaras

NOTE TO THE READER

ROMANS have normally been listed under their *cognomina* rather than *nomina*. Bearers of the same name have usually been arranged in their chronological order, subject to a priority given to emperors and kings. But it has not been possible to do this in the case of the bearers of the names Dionysius, Julius, and Ptolemaeus; and for these a rough alphabetical order of their places of origin, or of their *cognomina*, has been adopted. Numerous cross-references have been given for the reader's assistance. Quantities of vowels have been indicated where readers might be in doubt, e.g. ANȲTUS, EURĪPIDES. In the bibliographies place of publication is not mentioned, except in the case of books in English published outside the United Kingdom. The abbreviations employed (a list of which is given on pp. ix–xix) are somewhat fuller than those in Liddell and Scott, *Greek–English Lexicon*, and in Lewis and Short, *Latin Dictionary*. In the spelling of Greek and Latin words the rules for transliteration adopted in the *Journal of Hellenic Studies* have been in general followed; but no attempt has been made to achieve a pedantic uniformity. Where there is an accepted English form of an ancient name, such as Hecuba, Clytemnestra, Phidias, Pisistratus, that form has been used. Similarly, such established forms of common nouns as *choregus, didascaliae, palaestra, scolia, strategus* have been thus spelt, while the Greek spelling has been retained for less familiar words such as *ephetai, hektemoroi, nauarchos*. For the names of Greek cities ending in -εια, -*eia* has normally been adopted; but -*ea* or -*ia* has been preferred in the case of some cities, e.g. Chaeronea, Mantinea, Alexandria, which are usually so spelt in English. The Greek final -ων in proper names has normally been transliterated -*on*, but not in such famous names as Plato and Zeno. The whole subject is one on which scholars differ, and it has been found necessary to impose a measure of uniformity in face of some disagreement. In the cases of I and J, U and V the following rules have been followed in principle; but many exceptions have been made where it seemed convenient. In headings J is normally used as initial letter for proper names, e.g. Janiculum, Jason, Josephus, Julius, Juvenal (but it would be eccentric to spell Iacchus, Iapetus, &c., where metre often demands the I, with a J): I for all other words, e.g. *iaculum, iudex, ius, iuvenes*. In the body of the articles J is used for names isolated in an English context, also for abbreviations: I for names in a Latin title, phrase, or quotation, and for things. Thus: Jugurtha *passim* in article on Marius, Juv. for Juvenal, but *Bellum Iugurthinum, ius civile, Lex Iulia, De vita Iulii Agricolae*. Consonantal U is used in Latin quotations (as opposed to phrases) alone: V everywhere else, including all headings.

THE OXFORD
CLASSICAL DICTIONARY

ABACUS, a counting-board, the usual aid to reckoning in antiquity. The Egyptians, Greeks, and Romans alike used a board with vertical columns, on which (working from right to left) units, tens, hundreds, or (where money was in question) e.g. ⅛ obols, ¼ obols, ½ obols, obols, *drachmae*, sums of 10, 100, 1,000 *drachmae*, and talents were inscribed. When an addition sum was done, the totals of the columns were carried to the left, as in our ordinary addition. The numbers might be marked in writing or by pebbles, counters, or pegs.   W. D. R.

ABARIS, a legendary servant of Apollo, similar to Aristeas (q.v.), and believed to be a Hyperborean (q.v.). He lived without food, and travelled everywhere bearing the golden arrow, the symbol of the god (Hdt. 4. 36). Pindar assigned him to the time of Croesus (fr. 283 Bowra). Later authorities tell of his presence in Athens (Suidas, s.v.) and of his helping the Spartans by directing the performance of sacrifices which prevented all plagues thereafter (Apollonius, *Mir.* 4).   W. K. C. G.

ABDERA, a Greek city in Thrace, near the mouth of the river Nestus. It owed its prosperity to its good wheat-lands and to a gap in the coastal mountains which facilitated trade with the Thracian interior; but it was exposed to attack through this gap. The original Greek settlement, founded by Clazomenae *c.* 650 B.C., was soon destroyed by the Thracians. A new colony from Teos established itself *c.* 500, and in the fifth century became one of the richest Aegean cities, paying 12–15 talents of tribute to the Delian League. In 376 it was rescued by Chabrias from Thracian marauders and joined the Second Athenian Confederacy. From 352 to 198 it was mostly under Macedonian rule; thenceforward it was a 'free city' under Roman rule. Though its inhabitants had a reputation for stupidity, they included the philosophers Protagoras and Democritus.   M. C.

ABORIGINES. Livy and Dionysius have preserved a puzzling tradition: that the neighbourhood of Rome was occupied originally by Siculi (*see* SICELS), who were expelled by *Aborigines* before the Romans themselves came. That Siculi were there is probable enough, but these Siculi themselves were what we should call 'aboriginal', for palaeolithic man hardly counts. The explanation may lie in the fact that Rome was occupied by Villanovans (q.v.) two or three centuries before the traditional date of its founding. Although actually their kindred, the Romans may have regarded these earlier forerunners as aborigines.   D. R.-MacI.

ABRAXAS, *see* AMULETS.

ABYDOS, Milesian colony on the Asiatic side of the Hellespont, at its narrowest point, opposite Sestos (*see* HERO AND LEANDER). In 411 B.C. the Spartan fleet was defeated by the Athenians near Abydos. In 200 the town, until then a free city, fought heroically against Philip V of Macedon, but was forced to surrender. Three years later Antiochus III made Abydos one of his chief bases of support. Later it probably belonged to Pergamum, but as an autonomous State.   V. E.

ACADEMY, (1) a park and gymnasium in the outskirts of Athens sacred to the hero Academus (or Hecademus); (2) the school or college established there by Plato, probably about 385 B.C. This was organized as a corporate body with a continuous life of its own and survived down to its final dissolution by Justinian in A.D. 529.

There can be little doubt that Plato's chief object in the foundation was to train men for the service of the State, and there is evidence that a number of his pupils played a considerable part in the political life of their cities. But his method of training consisted of a thorough education in science and philosophy, and the school is better known for its contributions to these subjects. Under Plato and his immediate successors a great deal of important work was done in mathematics and astronomy. But later more purely philosophical interests became paramount. In the third and second centuries B.C., under Arcesilaus and Carneades, the Academy became known as the chief sceptical school, though there is some doubt as to the exact length to which their scepticism went. In the following century this tendency was abandoned. After that we know practically nothing of the institution for several centuries, though occasional indications justify us in believing in its continued existence. It does not emerge into the light again until the fifth century A.D., when it appears as a centre of Neoplatonism, particularly under the leadership of Proclus. It was also active in the production of commentaries on Plato and Aristotle, some of which still survive and preserve information of great value.

Histories of Ancient Philosophy: Zeller; Gomperz; Robin. J. Burnet, *From Thales to Plato* (1914), ch. 12; G. C. Field, *Plato and His Contemporaries* (1930), ch. 3; W. Jaeger, *Aristotle*, ch. 1 (Engl. Transl. 1934); R. E. Witt, *Albinus and the History of Middle Platonism* (1937); T. Whittaker, *The Neo-Platonists* (1918), ch. 9.   G. C. F.

ACAMAS, in mythology, son of Theseus, brother of Demophon (qq.v.); eponym of the tribe Acamantis. When Diomedes went to Troy to ask for the return of Helen, Acamas accompanied him; Laodice, daughter of Priam, fell in love with him and had by him a son, Munitus (Parthenius, *Amat. Narr.* 16). After the Trojan War, according to one account, it was he, not Demophon, who came to Thrace and met and deserted Phyllis. While in Cyprus he opened a mysterious box she had given him, and, frightened by what he saw in it, galloped wildly away, fell, and was killed by his own sword (schol. Lycophron 495).   H. J. R.

ACARNAN, eponym of Acarnania; in mythology, son, with Amphoterus, of Alcmaeon (q.v.) and Callirhoë. When Alcmaeon was murdered, Callirhoë prayed Zeus, who was her lover, to make her sons grow up immediately; he granted her prayer, and they avenged his death on Phegeus and his sons (Apollod. 3. 91–3).   H. J. R.

ACARNANIA, a district of north-west Greece, bounded by the Ionian Sea, the Gulf of Ambracia, and the river Acheloüs. It contained a fertile plain along the lower Acheloüs, but was ringed off on other sides by mountains. Its inhabitants long remained semi-barbarous: in Thucydides' day they still went about wearing armour (1. 5). In the seventh century the seaboard was occupied by settlers from Corinth. With Athenian help the Acarnanians beat off later attacks by the Corinthian colonists (*c.* 437 B.C.) and by the Spartans (429–426 B.C.);

but they were subdued by Agesilaus in 390 and remained under Spartan rule until 375. They again allied with Athens, to resist Philip of Macedon (344), but subsequently became dependants of Macedonia. In 314, at the instance of Cassander, they replaced their early cantonal league by a federation of newly founded cities (their largest town being Stratus). Frequent frontier disputes with the Aetolians led to the partition of Acarnania between Aetolia and Epirus c. 255; but after the fall of the Epirote monarchy in 230 the Acarnanians recovered their independence and acquired from Epirus the island of Leucas. Though they sided with Philip V of Macedon against the Romans (200), they were allowed by the latter to retain their league until 30 B.C.

Hirschfeld, in *PW*, s.v. 'Akarnania'. M. C.

ACASTUS, in mythology, son of Pelias (*see* NELEUS); he took part in the Argonautic expedition and the Calydonian boar-hunt. When Peleus (q.v.) took refuge with him, Acastus' wife (variously named) loved him, and being repulsed, accused him to her husband of improper advances. Acastus, therefore, contrived to steal Peleus' wonderful sword and leave him alone on Mt. Pelion, where he was rescued by Chiron (*see* CENTAURS). Afterwards Peleus took Iolcus, putting to death Acastus' wife and, by some accounts, Acastus himself (Apollod. 3. 164–7, 173; schol. Ap. Rhod. 1. 224; cf. Paus. 3. 18. 16). H. J. R.

ACCA LĀRENTIA (less correctly **Larentina**), an obscure Roman goddess, whose festival (Larentalia or Larentinalia) was on 23 Dec. A story current in Sulla's time (Valerius Antias ap. Gell. 7. 7. 5–7) makes her a prostitute, contemporary with Romulus (or Ancus Martius, Macrob. *Sat.* 1. 10. 12), who became rich by the favour of Hercules and left her property to the Roman people; another, perhaps invented by Licinius Macer, says she was wife of Faustulus (q.v.), mother of the original Arval brothers (*see* FRATRES ARVALES) and adopted mother of Romulus (Macrob. ibid. 17). That she had another festival in April (Plut. *Quaest. Rom.* 35) is probably a mis-statement, but see E. Tabeling, *Mater Larum* (1932), 57.

The principal work on the subject is Mommsen, 'Die echte und die falsche Acca Larentia', in *Römische Forschungen*. H. J. R.

ACCENSI, *see* APPARITORES.

ACCENT, *see* GRAMMAR, PRONUNCIATION.

ACCIUS (in older books often **ATTIUS**), LUCIUS (170–c. 85 B.C.), Latin tragic poet, born at Pisaurum, of freedman parents, Roman in origin. He came to Rome, becoming famous as a tragic writer by 140. He was a friend of Brutus Gallaecus, and of the tragic poet Pacuvius. In 135 he visited Asia. He seems to have been a man of 'pushing' but not quarrelsome character, and posterity came to regard him as the central figure of Roman tragedy. *See* DRAMA, ROMAN, para. 6.

FRAGMENTS: (i) 660 lines from tragedies on Greek models—*Achilles, Aegisthus, Agamemnonidae, Alcestis, Alcmeo, Alphesiboea, Amphitryo, Andromeda, Antenoridae, Antigona* (not from Sophocles' play), *Armorum Iudicium, Astyanax, Athamas, Atreus, Bacchae* (following Euripides' extant play, but with original lyrics and *cantica*), *Chrysippus, Clytaemnestra, Deiphobus, Diomedes, Epigoni, Epinausimache, Erigona* (from Sophocles?), *Eriphyla, Eurysaces, Hecuba* (from Euripides' extant play?), *Hellenes, Io, Medea* (not from Euripides), *Melanippus, Meleager* (from Euripides?), *Minos, Myrmidones, Neoptolemus, Nyctegresia, Oenomaus* (from Sophocles), *Pelopidae, Philocteta* (not from Sophocles), *Phinidae, Phoenissae* (free adaptation from Euripides' extant play), *Prometheus, Stasiastae, Telephus, Tereus, Thebais, Troades.* (ii) 44 lines from unknown tragedies. (iii) 16 lines from the *praetexta* entitled *Aeneadae* or *Decius*

on the self-sacrifice of Decius Mus in battle at Sentinum, 295 B.C.; and 23 almost continuous and a few other lines from the *praetexta* entitled *Brutus* on the Tarquins' downfall. (iv) 22 unpoetical sotadic lines from *Didascalica* (9 or more books) on Greek sources of plays, stage-technique and equipment, and Roman stage-history. (v) 2 lines from *Pragmatica* (on stage-diction?). (vi) 9 hexameters from *Annales*, on festivals. (vii) 2 doubtful lines from *Parerga.* Accius also wrote *Praxidica* (agricultural?), saturnians for Gallaecus, and amatory poems, and made new rules for spelling (e.g. for long vowels *a, e, u,* put *aa, ee, uu;* for *i, ei;* for sound *ng,* put *gg,* etc.).

Fragments: E. H. Warmington, *Remains of Old Latin* ii (with transl.—Loeb 1936); O. Ribbeck, *TRF*³ (Teubner, 1897). Plays only: L. Mueller, *C. Lucili Saturarum Reliquiae; accedunt Acci (praeter scenica) carminum reliquiae* (1872). E. H. W.

ACCLAMATIO was public applause in Rome at marriages, funerals, and especially performances and triumphs. The emperor and his family were greeted in the circus, theatre, and Senate by fixed words in a fixed rhythm. Nero trained his Augustiani (the corps of young noblemen which he established) in Oriental forms of salutations. The *acclamatio* might be accompanied by shaking of handkerchiefs and throwing of flowers. In the Senate it replaced the *sententia* of the *senatus consultum* and was recorded in the *acta* from the time of Trajan. The popular *acclamatio* of magistrates after election by the Senate sanctioned the choice.

Mommsen, *Röm. Staatsr.* iii. 349, 951; Dar.–Sag. i. 18; L. Friedländer, *Rom. Life,* ii. 3–4; M. P. Charlesworth, *JRS* 1943, 4 ff. A. M.

ACESTES (Αἰγέστης, Αἴγεστος), in mythology, son of a Trojan woman of noble rank, exiled for some reason by Laomedon (various accounts in Dion. Hal. *Ant. Rom.* 1. 52. 1 ff.; Serv. on *Aen.* 1. 550; schol. Lycophron 953 ff.), and a non-Trojan father, usually said to be the Sicilian river-god Cri(m)nisus. He founded Egesta (Segesta) in Sicily, and hospitably received Aeneas (*Aen.* 1. 550). H. J. R.

ACHAEA (Ἀχαία) is a name derived from Ἀχαιοί, the common designation for Greeks in Hittite and Egyptian texts of 1400–1200 B.C. and in Homer, where it refers particularly to Achilles' men and Agamemnon's followers. In historical times it was restricted to south-east Thessaly (Ἀχαία Φθιῶτις), and the north coast of Peloponnesus, between Elis and Sicyon. Here a narrow territory, with good soil in the plains and on the hill-terraces, extends between the almost harbourless Corinthian Gulf and a steep range of mountains. Twelve small towns, forming a federal league, divided this territory; they met at the sanctuary of Poseidon Heliconius until Helice fell into the sea (after an earthquake in 373 B.C.), later generally at Aegium.

The Achaeans sent colonists to Sybaris, Croton, Metapontum, Caulonia in south Italy; otherwise they had an unimportant early history, remaining neutral in the Persian Wars and most of the wars between Greeks. In the third and second centuries the Achaean League (q.v.) became the chief power in Greece, eventually including nearly all the Peloponnesus and part of central Greece. After 27 B.C. this area became the senatorial province of Achaea (for its boundaries see Larsen, op. cit. inf., 437 ff.; J. Keil, *CAH* xi. 556 ff.).

E. Curtius, *Peloponnesos* i (1851), 403 ff.; Frank, *Econ. Surv.* iv, 259 ff.; E. Groag, *Die röm. Reichsbeamten von Achaia* (1939). T. J. D.

ACHAEA PHTHIOTIS, *see* PHTHIOTIS.

ACHAEAN LEAGUE. An early Achaean League, organized at an unknown date, lasted through the fourth century. The later and more famous Achaean League was founded in 280 B.C. by the union of four cities, to which the remaining Achaean cities soon were added. It acquired importance through the incorporation of non-Achaeans, who were admitted on terms of equality, so that Dorians and Arcadians could become Achaean statesmen. When Sicyon was admitted after the expulsion of its tyrant in 251, Aratus (q.v. 2) of Sicyon soon became the leading Achaean statesman and adopted a definitely anti-Macedonian policy. The later admission of Megalopolis and other Arcadian cities led to hostility with Sparta and paved the way for reconciliation with Macedonia. During the Cleomenic War (*see* CLEOMENES III) Aratus himself asked for Macedonian help and permitted the Achaeans to join the Hellenic League of Antigonus Doson (224). This alinement lasted till Achaea went over to Rome in 198. The new alliance led to the incorporation of almost the entire Peloponnesus, but also led to frequent clashes with the Roman authorities. After the Achaean War of 146 the League was dissolved, but a smaller Achaean League soon was organized and continued under the Empire.

At the head of the League were two generals until a single general was substituted in 255. Immediate re-election was forbidden, and prominent leaders commonly served every second year. Alongside of the general stood a board of ten *demiurgoi*, who shared in the administration and presided over the assemblies. A primary assembly, the *synkletos*, was summoned at irregular intervals to deal with questions of war and peace, and later also written communications from the Roman Senate. Any meeting could consider only the one subject announced beforehand; voting was by cities, and each city probably was given a number of votes in proportion to its size. Other business was brought before the *synodos*, which met several times a year. This is mentioned frequently, but its composition never clearly described. Consequently agreement has not yet been reached on the question whether it was a primary assembly, a representative assembly, or a combination of a *boule* and a primary assembly. *See also* FEDERAL STATES.

Polybius; Livy, bks. 31–45. G. Niccolini, *La confederazione achea* (1914); F. W. Walbank, *Aratos of Sicyon* (1933); A. Aymard, *Les Assemblées de la confédération achaienne* (1938) and *Les Premiers rapports de Rome et de la confédération achaienne* (1938). *See also under* FEDERAL STATES. J. A. O. L.

ACHAEMENIDS, descendants of Achaemenes (Hakhamanish), the eponymous founder of the Persian royal house. According to Herodotus (7. 11) and the Behistun inscription, he was the father of Teispes, ancestor of Cyrus and Darius. At first kings only of Parsumash, a vassal State of the Median Empire, the Achaemenids extended their sovereignty over Anshan and Parsa; Cyrus II (q.v.) challenged and conquered Astyages, and the Median Empire passed to the Persians (550 B.C.). Campaigns in the north and east, the conquest of Lydia and the defeat of Nabonidus of Babylonia, brought the whole of western Asia into one vast empire, to which Cambyses added Egypt. A collateral branch of the family assumed the succession with Darius (q.v.), the greatest of the Achaemenids. His reign marks the climax of Persian rule. Subsequent reverses, e.g. the failure of Xerxes' Greek expedition, and harem intrigues weakened the dynasty, until with the defeat of Darius III Codomannus by Alexander in 330 B.C. the line perished.

Classical sources for Achaemenid Persia: Herodotus; Ctesias, *Persica*; Xenophon, *Cyropaedia, Anabasis*, etc.; Strabo, bks. 11–17. Cuneiform: F. H. Weissbach, *Keilinschriften der Achämeniden* (1911). Archaeological: E. Herzfeld, *Archäologische Mitteilungen aus Iran* (1929–). Modern works: G. C. Cameron, *History of Early Iran* (U.S.A. 1936); C. Clemen, *Fontes historiae religionis persicae* (1920); A. Christensen, 'Die Iranier', *Handbuch der Altertumswissenschaft* iii. 1, 3; A. Godard, *L'Art de la Perse Ancienne* (1930); E. Meyer, *Geschichte des Altertums* iii (1937); P. M. Sykes, *History of Persia* i (1930); *CAH* iv, chs. 1, 9, 10; vi, ch. 12; *PW*, arts. on individual kings. M. S. D.

ACHAEUS (1), eponym of the Achaeans; in mythology, son of Poseidon (Dion. Hal. *Ant. Rom.* 1. 17. 3), Zeus (Serv. on *Aen.* 1. 242), Xuthus (Apollod. 1. 50), or Haemon (schol. *Il.* 2. 681).

ACHAEUS (2) of Eretria (b. 484–481 B.C.), Athenian tragic poet, wrote 44 (or 30 or 24) plays, the first produced about 447 B.C. (Suidas, s.v.). Of nineteen known titles more than half are probably satyric; the philosopher Menedemus thought his satyric plays second only to those of Aeschylus (Diog. Laert. 2. 133). The Alexandrians placed him in the *Canon* (*see* ARISTOPHANES 2) and Didymus wrote a commentary on him. Euripides is said to have adapted one line from him (Ath. 6. 270b) and he is twice quoted by Aristophanes (*Vesp.* 1081, *Ran.* 184). Athenaeus (10. 451c) describes him as lucid in style, but liable to become obscure and enigmatical.

TGF, 746–59. A. W. P.-C.

ACHAEUS (3) (d. 214 B.C.), grandson of Antiochus I, and general of Antiochus III. In 223 he recovered most of Seleucid Asia Minor from Pergamum; but he was encouraged by Antiochus' difficulties in the East to proclaim himself independent (220). His soldiers refused to follow him against Antiochus, but he maintained himself in Asia Minor until the king was at liberty to deal with him. After a two years' siege in Sardes he was betrayed to Antiochus and barbarously executed.

Polybius, bks. 5–6. G. T. G.

ACHARNAE, the largest Attic deme (the figure 3,000 hoplites in Thuc. 2. 20. 4 is too high), lay in a corner of the Attic plain, near the pass from the Thriasian plain. It had good corn and olive land and vineyards, but its special resource lay in the charcoal-burning on Mt. Parnes. Near Acharnae (at Menidi) is a beehive-tomb which received offerings continuously from the fourteenth to the fifth century.

Thuc. 2. 19–23; Aristophanes, *Acharnians*; A. Milchhöfer, *Karten von Attika* ii. 42 ff. T. J. D.

ACHATES, in mythology, faithful companion of Aeneas (*Aen.* 1. 312 and often); he killed Protesilaus (schol. *Il.* 2. 701).

ACHELOÜS, the longest of Greek rivers, rising in central Epirus and debouching after a course of 150 miles (mostly through mountain gorges) at the entrance to the Corinthian Gulf. Its lower reaches constituted the frontier between Acarnania and Aetolia. It had no value as a line of communications.

ACHERON, a river of Thesprotia in southern Epirus. In its upper course it ran through gloomy gorges, and it disappeared underground at several points. It was, therefore, reputed to lead to Hades, and an oracle of the dead was situated upon it (Hdt. 5. 92. 7).

ACHILLES (Ἀχιλλεύς), in mythology, son of Peleus and Thetis (qq.v.); usually said to be their only child, but cf. Lycophron 178 and schol. there. The etymology of his name is unknown, though a connexion with the river-name Acheloüs is possible. All the evidence goes to show that he was a man, real or imaginary, and not a 'faded' god, and that his widespread cult (Leuke in the Black Sea, Olbia, and elsewhere in that region; sporadically in Asia Minor; Epirus; doubtfully in Thessaly; Elis; Croton in Italy) is the result chiefly or solely of the *Iliad* (see Farnell, *Hero-Cults*, 285 ff.). His portrait was drawn once for all by Homer, and later writers merely added details from their own imagination, or possibly from obscure local legends of which we know nothing.

2. In the *Iliad* he appears as a magnificent barbarian, somewhat outside the circle of Achaean civilization, though highly respected for his prowess. He, alone among Homeric figures, keeps up the old practice of making elaborate and costly offerings, including human victims, at a funeral (*Il.* 23. 171 ff., condemned as 'evil deeds', 176); contrast the sceptical attitude of Andromache (22. 512–14). His treatment of the body of Hector is of a piece with this (22. 395, again stigmatized as 'unseemly deeds', and 24. 15 ff.). So also is his furious

and ungovernable anger, on which the whole plot of the *Iliad* turns; in 24. 560 ff. he is himself conscious of this weakness and afraid that it may overcome his chivalrous pity for Priam. When not roused by anger or grief, he is often merciful (21. 100 ff.), but in his fury he spares no one and has no respect even for a visible god (22. 15-20). Besides his valour in battle, he is a pathetic figure, being conscious of the fated shortness of his life (9. 410 ff., cf. 19. 408 ff.). He is capable of the most generous sentiments, witness his devoted friendship for Patroclus throughout the poem and his strong detestation of lying (9. 312), an unusual thing in a Homeric Greek.

3. He comes to Troy, apparently, of his own free will, not as in any sense a subject of Agamemnon, at the head of a contingent of fifty ships (*Il.* 2. 685), and there distinguishes himself in a series of engagements during which he takes twelve towns along the coast and eleven inland (9. 328–9), including Lyrnessos, where he captures Briseis (2. 690). Agamemnon, on being compelled to return his own captive, Chryseis, to her father (1. 134 ff.), takes Briseis from Achilles by way of compensating himself (ibid. 320 ff.). At this insult, Achilles refuses further service and begs his mother Thetis to move Zeus on his behalf (352 ff.). She succeeds in inducing the god to punish Agamemnon and his army; a false dream encourages the king to go out against the Trojans, who, hearing that Achilles is no longer fighting, profit by their strategic superiority (their reinforcements are close at hand, Agamemnon can get none from nearer than Greece) to offer battle, instead of merely standing on the defensive (9. 352 ff.). The result is a series of engagements in which Agamemnon loses far more men than he can afford (*Il.* 2–8). Now Agamemnon offers a full and handsome honour-price to Achilles, who puts himself in the wrong by refusing it (9 passim), but is later induced to let Patroclus go at the head of his followers, the Myrmidones (16. 1 ff.), to keep the Trojans from actually burning the Greek camp. Patroclus, however, is killed fighting (16. 786 ff.), and Achilles, on hearing the news, is frenzied with grief (18. 15 ff.), hastily reconciles himself to Agamemnon, goes out the next day, routs the Trojans, and kills Hector (19–22). He is wearing armour specially made for him by Hephaestus (18. 468 ff.), as his own had been worn by Patroclus and fallen into the hands of Hector. He then gives Patroclus a magnificent funeral (23) and, warned by his mother (24. 137), lets old Priam ransom Hector's body.

4. His death is foretold in the *Iliad* (22. 359–60); he is to be slain by Paris and Apollo. The *Odyssey* (24. 35 ff., a doubtfully authentic passage) describes the fight over his body, his funeral, and the mourning of Thetis and the other sea-nymphs over him. Later authors add the following details, among others.

5. He had his education from Chiron (see e.g. Pind. *Nem.* 3. 43 ff., developing *Il.* 11. 832). When the contingents were gathering for the Trojan War, Peleus, or Thetis, knowing that he would die at Troy, hid him in Scyros, dressed as a girl. Here he met Deidameia, daughter of Lycomedes, king of the island, who bore him Neoptolemus (q.v. 1). Calchas having told the Greeks that Troy could not be taken without him, Odysseus with other envoys found him and discovered his sex; after which he went willingly with them (so unnamed and rather doubtful cyclic poets in schol. *Il.* 19. 326, and many later writers). On the way to Troy, the Greeks landed in Mysia, and there Achilles wounded Telephus (q.v. 1) in battle, afterwards healing him (so the *Cypria*, which also makes Achilles marry Deidameia after the affair in Mysia). Still according to the same poem, the army then reassembled in Aulis, where the affair of Iphigenia (q.v.) occurred, went on to Tenedos, where Achilles and Agamemnon had a quarrel, and finally reached Troy, where a number of exploits of Achilles are recorded (killing of Cycnus and Troilus, checking of

a plan to abandon the enterprise, etc.). After the events in the *Iliad*, Troy was reinforced successively by the Amazon Penthesilea and by Memnon (qq.v.), who were both slain by Achilles. Immediately afterwards he was killed by Apollo (or Paris, or Apollo in the shape of Paris). So far the *Aethiopis*.

6. Further details are mostly erotic. Achilles and Patroclus were lovers (e.g. Aesch. fr. 135 Nauck); other loves were Troilus (Serv. on *Aen.* 1. 474), Polyxena daughter of Priam (Hyg. *Fab.* 110), Helen (Lycophron 171 f., where he merely dreams of her; Paus. 3. 19. 13, where he is united to her in Leuce), and, oddest and earliest, Medea (Ibycus and Simonides ap. schol. Ap. Rhod. 4. 814; Lycoph. 174; in the Elysian Fields). The story that he was made invulnerable by Thetis (save for the heel in which he traditionally got his death-wound, originally no doubt from a poisoned arrow) by being plunged into Styx is not found earlier than Statius (*Achil.* 1. 134, whereon see schol. 269). It is a common folk-tale.

A useful collection of references will be found in the art. 'Achilleus', in Roscher's *Lexikon*. H. J. R.

ACHILLES TATIUS (1) of Alexandria, author of the *Leucippe and Clitophon* (τὰ κατὰ Λευκίππην καὶ Κλειτοφῶντα) and probably the last of the extant Greek novelists, wrote not later than *c.* A.D. 300. His identification by Suidas with a writer of more serious works, including a treatise on the sphere (see next article and cf. Firmicus Maternus, *c.* A.D. 350), is difficult to credit, and the statement that he ultimately became a Christian bishop may be rejected as a reflection of the tradition about Heliodorus (q.v.). A. T. presents his story as a narrative heard from the hero's lips; but the setting, which is not plausible, is soon forgotten, though Clitophon continues to recount his experiences in the first person. The adventures, amorous and other, are according to pattern, but they are less heroically conceived and more sensationally treated. A. T., with Heliodorus in mind, seems to have attempted to substitute realism for idealism, but by stripping off the heroic glamour he only exposes the incredibility of the material. Perhaps he had little interest in his plot, which he is always ready to abandon in favour of some irrelevant or barely relevant digression. Though the rhetoric is at once more ambitious and more ridiculous than in the other novels, A. T. has a certain liveliness of style and power of description. He was popular in later times and much esteemed by Byzantine critics; Photius placed him second to Heliodorus only on moral grounds and wrote an epigram in praise of his novel (*Anth. Pal.* 9. 203).

Text and translation: S. Gaselee (Loeb). Commentary: F. Jacobs (1821). Style and diction: L. Castiglioni, *Riv. Fil.* 1906 and *Byz. und Neugr. Jahrb.* 1923; F. Garin, *Riv. Fil.* 1919; H. Dörrie, *de Longi Achillis Tatii Heliod. memoria* (1935). Life and work: S. Gaselee (Loeb); D. B. Durham, *CPhil.* 1938. *See also* NOVEL, GREEK. R. M. R.

ACHILLES TATIUS (2) (probably 3rd c. A.D.), author of a Greek commentary on Aratus, the only surviving part of his work Περὶ σφαίρας.

Ed. E. Maass, *Commentariorum in Aratum Reliquiae* (1898), 25; PW i. 247.

ACHILLEUS, rebel in Egypt, A.D. 296–7, not the Domitius Domitianus of the coins, but his chief assistant. Domitianus revolted in summer 296 and was conquered by Diocletian in person early in 297. His revolt was probably not related to that of Coptos and Busiris, but was due to economic distress connected with Diocletian's reform of the coinage.

Seston, *Mélanges d'arch.* (1938), 184 ff. H. M.

ACILIUS, GAIUS, Roman senator and historian, who interpreted for Carneades, Diogenes, and Critolaus in the Senate in 155 B.C., wrote a history of Rome, in Greek, from early Italian times to his own age, certainly to 184 B.C. (Dion. Hal. 3. 67. 5); it appeared *c.* 142 (Livy,

Per. 53: reading *C. Acilius*). His senatorial tradition is seen in the anecdote of Scipio and Hannibal (Livy 35. 14. 5). His work was reproduced in Latin by a Claudius, probably Claudius (q.v.) Quadrigarius, who would then have incorporated it in his annalistic form.

H. Peter, *HRRel.* i² (1914), pp. cxxi, 49; M. Gelzer, *Hermes* 1934, 48.   A. H. McD

ACILIUS, *see also* ATTIANUS, GLABRIO.

ACOUSTICS, *see* PHYSICS, para. 7.

ACRAGAS (Lat. *Agrigentum*), a Doric colony founded by Gela (582 B.C.) on fertile Sicanian territory in south-west Sicily, the birthplace of Empedocles and Philinus and powerful rival of Syracuse. Its tyrant Theron, Acragas' earliest personality apart from the half-mythical Phalaris (*c.* 565), helped Gelon of Syracuse to crush Carthage at Himera (480). After expelling Theron's son Thrasydaeus (471), Acragas became a wealthy, pugnacious democracy, possessing temples as amazing to modern visitors to Agrigento. It was, however, sacked by Carthage (405) and, although somewhat revived by Timoleon (338) and Phintias (286–280), its Punic Wars misfortunes prevented it from regaining real prosperity until it became a *civitas decumana* subject to Rome. By Verres' time it was quite wealthy and *c.* 43 B.C. obtained Roman citizenship. Although not mentioned in imperial history Acragas has always remained a large city, productive of grain, wine, olives, cheese, salt, sulphur, and textiles.

Strabo 6. 272. Diod. bks. 11–23. Thuc. 6. 4; bk. 7. Polyb. 1. 17 f.; 9. 27 (excellent description). Livy 24. 35; 25. 40 f.; 26. 40. Cic. *Verr. passim.* P. Marconi, *Agrigento* (1929). V. Bérard, *Bibliogr. topogr.* (1941), 40.   E. T. S.

ACRISIUS, in mythology, son of Abas, king of Argos, and his wife Aglaïa, father of Danaë and brother of Proetus (q.v.). After Abas' death the two brothers quarrelled; in their warfare they invented the shield. Proetus, defeated, left the country, returned with troops furnished by his father-in-law Iobates, and agreed to leave Argos to Acrisius, himself taking Tiryns; both were fortified by the Cyclopes. See schol. Eur. *Or.* 965. Cf. PERSEUS (1).   H. J. R.

ACROAMA, *see* ANAGNOSTES.

ACRON, HELENIUS (2nd c. A.D.), wrote commentaries (now lost) on Terence (*Adelphi* and *Eunuchus* at least) and Horace; but evidence for a commentary by him on Persius is slender. The extant pseudo-Acron scholia on Horace (ed. O. Keller, 2 vols., 1902–4) appear in three recensions of which the earliest dates from the fifth century. Alongside of excerpts from Porphyrion (q.v.), these scholia may contain genuine Acron material; but their attribution to him (not made in any MS. before the 15th c.) is probably due to a humanist. *See* SCHOLARSHIP, LATIN, and cf. Teuffel, § 365 a; Schanz–Hosius, § 601.   J. F. M.

ACROPOLIS, a detached hill-site containing a town or temples, but pre-eminently the *Athenian Acropolis*, a rocky eminence to the south of the Greek town, precipitous to north and east, sloping steeply to south but more accessible from west. As fortified in the sixth century B.C. it was roughly an oval about 1,000 × 480 ft., with main axis east and west and with approach steps thrust forward from west salient; it was a sanctuary site from very early times, associated later particularly with Athena. There are evidences of pre-Greek walls, but Cimon (q.v.) built great retaining walls on south and east early in fifth century B.C., when the principal buildings were the old Athena Temple or Hecatompedon (*c.* 550 B.C., enlarged *c.* 530), and the old Parthenon (*c.* 490), of which, as of other sixth-century temples in stone, important sculptural remains exist.

Under Pericles, after the destruction of Persian wars, the Acropolis was made glorious by the rebuilt Propylaea (q.v.), the little temple of Athena Niké beside it, and the rebuilt Parthenon (q.v.), the Erechtheum (q.v.) being added slightly later. The colossal statue of Athena Promachos, the precinct of Artemis Brauronia, and an adjacent hall (*Chalkotheke*, completed before 400 B.C.), were between Propylaea and Parthenon. There are foundations of other fifth-century buildings against the north wall. Though placing of buildings was influenced by structural and religious requirements, recent research (Stevens, op. cit. below) has shown that the approach to the Parthenon from the Propylaea was an ordered though asymmetrical scheme. On south slope outside the wall were, from east, the Theatre of Dionysus (6th c. B.C. and later), the Stoa of Eumenes (*c.* 260 B.C.), and the Odeon of Herodes Atticus (*c.* A.D. 167).

M. L. D'Ooge, *The Acropolis of Athens* (1908); G. P. Stevens, *The Periclean Entrance Court of the Acropolis of Athens* (New York, 1936). *See also* ATHENS (topography).   T. F.

ACROSTIC. Acrostics were perhaps composed in Latin earlier than in Greek. They were used by Ennius and the composers of Sibylline oracles (Cic. *Div.* 2. 110–12). Phlegon (q.v.) cites two examples from oracles (*Mir.* 10, pp. 76 ff., Keller). Cf. also *Anth. Pal.* 14. 148 (to Julian the Apostate), *GGM* 1. 238–9 (where the acrostic determines the authorship of a work), Dionysius Periegeta (*GGM* 2. 102 ff., 109 ff., 513 ff.), the acrostic prologues (of uncertain date) to Plautus' plays, and the beginning and end of the *Homerus Latinus*, giving (Silius) Italicus as the author. A comedy-prologue of the third century B.C. has a series of lines beginning with *a*, *β*, etc. (O. Schroeder, *Nov. Com. Fragm.* (1915), 65).

H. Diels, *Sibyllinische Blätter* (1890).   J. D. D.

ACTA. Under the Roman Republic magistrates took an oath, on entering office, to respect the laws of the State. With the fall of the Republic and the increasing scope and importance of the emperor's enactments (loosely called *Acta*), it was desirable that these should acquire a permanence comparable with that of the laws. Magistrates, therefore, emperors included (Dio Cass. 60. 10), took the oath to observe the *Acta* of previous emperors, except those whose *Acta*, directly after their death, were explicitly rescinded (*rescissio actorum*) or at least excluded from the oath. Thus no oath was taken to observe the *Acta* of Tiberius, Gaius, Galba, Otho, Vitellius, Domitian, or Caracalla; though it is clear, from the evidence of Gaius, *Inst.* 1. 33 (citing an edict of Nero) and *Digest* 48. 3. 2 (citing an edict of Domitian), that the wise enactments of even bad emperors might survive their death. The exact definition of *Acta* was not easy. The term was eventually held to cover the 'Constitutiones Principum' (i.e. *edicta*, *decreta*, and *rescripta*); but the difficulties arising from a loose definition of it were apparent when Julius Caesar's *Acta* were ratified by the Senate after his murder (Cic. *Phil.* 1. 16 ff.). A second difficulty concerned the relation of the *Acta* of the living emperor to those of his predecessors. The first recorded case of an oath to observe such *Acta* was that taken by all the magistrates to observe the *Acta* of Julius Caesar in 45 B.C. (Appian, *BCiv.* 2. 106). Similar oaths were taken to observe the *Acta* of Augustus in 29 and in 24 B.C. (Dio Cass. 51. 20; 53. 28). The more moderate emperors, as Tiberius and Claudius, sought to restrict the oath to the *Acta* of Divus Augustus, excluding their own *Acta* (Suet. *Tib.* 67; Tac. *Ann.* 1. 72; Dio Cass. 60. 10), but, with the increase of autocracy, the oath came to include the *Acta* of reigning emperors.

The *Acta Senatus* (or *Commentarii Senatus*) constituted the official record of proceedings in the Senate under the Roman Empire, the senator responsible for the record being, since the reign of Tiberius, selected by the emperor (Tac. *Ann.* 5. 4). The *Acta Diurna* were a gazette, whose daily publication dates from 59 B.C. (Suet. *Iul.* 20); it recorded important social and political news, and was read not only at Rome but also in the provinces (Tac. *Ann.* 16. 22). The *Acta Senatus* were preserved and could be consulted by senators. Tacitus used, or depended on authorities who used, both these (e.g. *Ann.* 15. 74) and the *Acta Diurna* (*Ann.* 3. 3).

J. P. B.

ACTAEON, in mythology, son of Aristaeus (q.v. 1) and Autonoë, daughter of Cadmus (q.v.). A keen hunter, he one day came upon Artemis bathing; offended at being thus seen naked by a man, she turned him into a stag and he was chased and killed by his own hounds; so first in Stesichorus ap. Paus. 9. 2. 3 (see Vürtheim, *Stesichoros' Fragmente und Biographie* (1919), 29); most famously in Ovid, *Met.* 3. 138 ff. Other versions of his offence were that he was Zeus' rival with Semele (Acusilaus, fr. 33 Jacoby = Apollod. 3. 30) or that he boasted that he was a better hunter than Artemis (Eur. *Bacch.* 339–40), and that he wished to marry Artemis (Diod. Sic. 4. 81. 4). But to see any deity uninvited brings destruction (Callim. *Lav. Pall.* 101–2). For representations in art of his death, cf. P. Jacobsthal, *Marburger Jahrbuch f. Kunstwissenschaft* v.   H. J. R.

ACTE, CLAUDIA, Nero's favourite freedwoman, came from Asia Minor; hence her alleged descent from the Attalidae. Nero's passion for her was encouraged by Seneca in Agrippina's despite. She became very wealthy. Replaced by Poppaea, she apparently remained at court, since she deposited Nero's remains in the tomb of the Domitii.

A. Stein, *PW* iii. 288; *PIR*[2], C 1067.   A. M.

ACTIO, *see* LAW AND PROCEDURE, ROMAN, II, para. 6.

ACTIUM, a flat sandy promontory on the Acarnanian coast, south of the entrance to the Ambracian Gulf, forming part of the territory of Anactorium. There was a temple of Apollo there at least as early as the fifth century B.C. Actium was the site of Antony's camp in 31 B.C., and gave its name to the naval battle fought just outside the gulf, in which he was defeated by Octavian.

Strabo 7. 324–5. For the campaign and battle: Horace, *Epod.* 9; Velleius 2. 84–5; Plutarch, *Antony*, 61–8; Dio Cassius 50. 9–35. Modern literature: J. Kromayer, *Hermes* 1899 and 1933; T. Rice Holmes, *Architect of the Roman Empire* i (1928); W. W. Tarn and G. W. Richardson, *JRS* xxi and xxvii (1931 and 1937).   G. W. R.

ACTORIONE, *see* MOLIONES.

ACUSILAUS, of Argos, lived 'before the Persian Wars' (Joseph. *Ap.* 1–13) and compiled Γενεαλογίαι, translating and correcting Hesiod, with ingenious conjectures but no literary merit.

FHG i. 100; *FGrH* i. 2.

ADAERATIO, a technical term in use during the Late Roman period for payment in money for official duties, especially taxes which had been originally payable in kind. The new institution developed as a consequence of an improvement in money economy throughout the Roman Empire after the reforms of Diocletian and Constantine. The expression was much later than the habit to which it gave the name. '*Adaeratio*' seems not to have been used before A.D. 409 and '*adaerare*' not before 383, the Greek equivalents ἀπαργυρισμός and ἐξαργυρισμός not before Justinian. Tax-debts in kind, and (somewhat later) part of the dues connected with the *annona* (q.v.), and even military obligations, could be discharged in money. Officials sold legally and illegally their remunerations in kind to tax-collectors against money allowances reckoned in genuine or (more often) fictitious market prices, until government decrees regulated such exchange rates for private and for official use.

Humbert, in Dar.-Sag. s.v.; O. Seeck, in *PW* s.v.   F. M. H.

ADAM-KLISSI, a mound in the plain of the Dobrudja (S. Rumania), containing two Roman monuments: (1) an altar inscribed with the names of at least 3,000 Roman soldiers, which commemorates the defeat of Cornelius Fuscus or (more probably) of Oppius Sabinus in the Dacian War of Domitian (A.D. 85); (2) a trophy, dedicated by Trajan to Mars Ultor in 109, to signalize his final victory over the Dacians. Below the mound Trajan founded a small town, Tropaeum Traiani.

B. W. Henderson, *Five Roman Emperors* (1927), 162–3, 302–7.

M. C.

ADEIA, permission given by the Athenian Ecclesia to make proposals or give information under special circumstances: e.g. proposals (1) to revoke sentences of *atimia* (q.v.), or to remit State debts; (2) to rescind a special clause forbidding the alteration of certain laws or decrees (Thuc. 2. 24. 1; 8. 15. 1); (3) to impose an *eisphora* (q.v.), or to borrow from the treasury of Athena. For a grant of *adeia*, at least in case (1) above, a quorum of 6,000 votes was necessary. *Adeia* was also necessary, for non-citizens, to make supplication to the assembly or lay information about crimes of which it took cognizance (*see* ECCLESIA). A similar procedure was observed in many other Greek States.   A. W. G.

ADHERBAL, *see* NUMIDIA.

ADIABENE (*Hadiab*), district of the two Zâb rivers in north Mesopotamia. A Seleucid eparchy, it became a vassal kingdom, later a satrapy, of Parthia, and was constantly involved in her internal disputes and in her wars with Rome. One of the dynasties of Adiabene embraced Judaism (Joseph. *AJ* 20. 17–37). After Trajan's conquest it became the Roman province Assyria (q.v.); the two names were thenceforward interchangeable.

M. S. D.

ADLECTIO. Under the Roman Republic a man could enter the Senate (*see* SENATUS) either by holding a magistracy or by having his name placed on the senatorial roll by the censors. Admission by this second means (which Sulla temporarily suppressed) was known technically as *adlectio* under the Principate. *Adlectio* was also employed to accelerate the magisterial careers of senators; an ex-quaestor, for instance, who was *adlectus inter praetorios*, like Germanicus in A.D. 9 (Dio Cass. 56. 17), could proceed directly to the consulship. Princes of the Imperial house might be adlected by the Senate—e.g. Germanicus and Drusus, son of Tiberius, in A.D. 9 (Dio Cass. 56. 17), following the precedent set for Octavian in 43 B.C. (Augustus, *Res Gest.* 1). Though the right of adlection had been largely employed by Julius Caesar, it was exercised cautiously by the first emperors, and only in connexion with the holding of an official *lectio senatus* or the tenure of the censorship: by Augustus probably, and certainly by Claudius (*ILS* 968) and by Vespasian and Titus (*ILS* 1024). After Domitian the right of *adlectio* was exercised as a normal power of the emperor. Men were adlected *inter quaestorios* (i.e. to the rank of ex-quaestors in the *cursus honorum*), *inter aedilicios*, *inter tribunicios*, *inter praetorios*. *Adlectio inter consulares* was an innovation of Macrinus and met with opposition (Dio Cass. 78. 13); under the constitution of Diocletian and Constantine it became common.

J. P. B.

ADMETUS, *see* ALCESTIS.

ADONIS (Ἄδωνις), in mythology, the son of Cinyras (q.v.), king of Cyprus, by an incestuous union with his daughter Myrrha or Smyrna, according to the usual myth (Ov. *Met.* 10. 298–559, 708–39). The beautiful youth was beloved by Aphrodite. While hunting he was killed by a boar, or, in some accounts, by the jealous Hephaestus, or by Ares disguised as a boar. Panyasis (in Apollod. *Bibl.* 3. 183) calls A. the son of Theias and Smyrna.

Aphrodite concealed the infant in a box and entrusted it to Persephone, who was unwilling to restore him till Zeus decreed that A. should spend part of each year on earth with Aphrodite, part in the underworld with Persephone. A. was a divinity of vegetation and fertility, whose disappearance marks the harvesting of the crops (cf. Euseb. *Praep. Evang.* 3. 11. 12). He is akin to the Babylonian Tammuz; the name Adonis may be simply the Semitic title 'Adon', 'Lord', by which he was known in Phoenicia. Byblus was especially sacred to A., and his death, which annually stained the river Adonis with his blood, was localized at the near-by Aphaca (Lucian *Syr. D.* 6–9). He was worshipped at Amathus in Cyprus, and it was probably from Cyprus that his cult was carried, by the fifth century, to Athens, where he was, at least partially, identified with Eros. His cult existed only in conjunction with that of Aphrodite (q.v., para. 3), to whom swine seem to have been sacrificed only where she was associated with A.

THE ADONIA. At Byblus there was a period of mourning for the dead A., followed by the day of his resurrection. At Alexandria the rites consisted of a magnificent pageant of the wedding of A. and Aphrodite; the next day women carried A.'s image to the sea-shore amid lamentations (Theoc. *Id.* 15). The mourning of the women and the setting out of the ephemeral 'Gardens of A.' on the house-tops marked the festival at Athens. There was perhaps considerable variation in the content as in the date of the festival, and much of the original intent of the rites appears to have been forgotten. In fifth-century Athens they were held in April, in Ptolemaic Egypt perhaps in September, while under the Empire the accepted date was 19 July. The cult was especially popular with women.

W. W. Baudissin, *Adonis und Esmun* (1911); J. G. Frazer, *Adonis Attis Osiris* i. Separate studies on the *Adonia*: M. P. Nilsson, *Griechische Feste* (1906), 384–7; F. Cumont, *Syria* 1927 and 1935; A. S. F. Gow, *JHS* 1938 (detailed commentary on Theoc. 15); F. R. Walton, *Harv. Theol. Rev.* 1938. F. R. W.

ADOPTIO, a legal act by which a Roman citizen—*sui* or *alieni iuris*—enters another family and comes under the *patria potestas* (q.v.) of its chief. When the adopted person is *sui iuris* the act is called *adrogatio*. The original development of *adrogatio* is an independent development; but it has some characteristics in common with *adoptio* in the strict sense (i.e. of a person *alieni iuris*), such as the artificial creation of a *patria potestas*, the *capitis deminutio* (*mutatio familiae*) of the adopted person, and the same effects with regard to the rights of succession and property.

2. *Adrogatio* effects the fusion of two families, for together with the *adrogatus* all the persons under his power (*potestas, manus*) and all his property pass into the family of the *adrogator*. In early times a public act was necessary for the validity of *adrogatio*: the vote of the *comitia curiata* preceded by an investigation by the pontiffs; by the time of Cicero the *comitia* were replaced by thirty lictors, who gave their assent as the representatives of the *curiae*. These forms of *adrogatio*, which were valid only for Rome, were inaccessible to the provincials, who, therefore, applied directly to the emperor: this was the origin of *adrogatio per rescriptum principis* which became obligatory after Diocletian. After Antoninus Pius *impuberes* could be adrogated, in post-classical times women too.

3. The *adoptio* of a *filius familias* had a more private character. It was executed according to a rule of the XII Tables (*see* PATRIA POTESTAS) by a complicated mechanism of three *mancipationes* effected by the natural father with two intervening manumissions made by the future adoptive father and a final collusive *vindicatio filii*. This procedure by which the father lost his *potestas* over the son and the adopter acquired it is described in

Gai. 1. 132, 134. These troublesome and antiquated formalities were finally abolished by Justinian; henceforth a *datio in adoptionem* (a declaration of the natural father in presence of the adopter and the child before the magistrate) was sufficient.

4. Adoption, since it was a method of acquiring *patria potestas*, could originally be by men only, and its object was that, in the absence of natural children, the family and its *sacra* should be carried on by the *heres*, who would also succeed to the family property. Adoption by women, allowed in post-classical times as a *solacium liberorum amissorum*, shows a change in conception. Other innovations were brought about by adopting the principle that *adoptio imitatur naturam*, of which one result was the rule introduced by Justinian that the adopter must be at least eighteen years older than the person adopted. Under him complete severance of the adopted person from his original family was no longer necessary.

5. The classical form of adoption gave to the adopted the position of a *filius familias* in the new family with all its duties and rights, especially in regard to inheritance. The new member of the family was bound to it by the agnatic and gentile tie. He received his adoptive father's name and rank: a plebeian adopted by a patrician became patrician and vice versa. For the defence of the adopted against the disadvantages of a premature *emancipatio* his right to the succession in the new family was preserved by a law of Antoninus Pius. By a further development the adopted person kept his right of succession in his former family and did not come under the *patria potestas* of the adoptive father (this is the *adoptio-minus plena* in Justinian's law; its roots lie in the popular law, cf. *PLips.* 28 and *POxy.* 9. 1206). Only in special cases, as in that of adoption by a natural ascendant, did the full effects of the ancient *adoptio plena* remain unaltered.

G. Desserteaux, *Effets de l'adrogation* (1892); W. W. Buckland, *A Text-book of Roman Law* (1921), ch. 3; R. Monier, *Studi Albertoni* i (1933); G. Castelli, *Scritti giuridici* i (1923), 165–97. A. B.

ADRASTUS, the name of several mythological persons, the only one of importance being the son of Talaus, king of Argos. His name, if it means 'the unescapable', is very appropriate to a warrior-prince and gives no grounds for supposing he was originally a god. In historical times he had a cult at Sicyon and Megara (see Farnell, *Hero-Cults*, 334 ff.). Probably much of the tradition concerning him is derived from the lost cyclic *Thebais*; whether it has any historical content is doubtful.

When a young man he was driven out of Argos by dynastic rivalries and took refuge in Sicyon with his mother's father Polybus (q.v.). He married Polybus' daughter and succeeded him as king (*Il.* 2. 572 and scholiast there; Pind. *Nem.* 9. 9 ff., with schol.); afterwards he returned to Argos, making terms with Amphiaraus (q.v.). While reigning there he received in his house Tydeus and Polynices (qq.v.), both exiles, and recognized in them the lion and boar to whom he had been bidden marry his daughters, Argeia (to Polynices) and Deipyle (to Tydeus) (see, e.g., Apollod. 3. 58–9). He then undertook to restore them, and began by attempting to set Polynices on the throne of Thebes. The army was led by himself, his two sons-in-law, and Parthenopaeus (originally Adrastus' brother, in later accounts son of Atalanta, q.v.), Amphiaraus, Capaneus, and Hippomedon—the famous Seven against Thebes; in some lists the exiles are omitted and Mecisteus and Eteoclus substituted (see Wilamowitz-Moellendorff, *Aischylos Interpretationen*, 97 ff.). On the way to Thebes the army halted at Nemea, and there were shown the way to water by Hypsipyle (q.v.). While she was thus engaged her charge, the baby Archemorus, was killed by a serpent; Amphiaraus secured her pardon and the Nemean Games were founded in memory of the infant (see especially Eur. *Hypsipyle*). The attack on Thebes was a complete failure, only Adrastus escaping home, thanks to his marvellous horse, Arion. Our chief authorities here are Aeschylus, *Septem* and some odes of Pindar, notably *Ol.* 6. 12 and *Pyth.* 8. Ten years later Adrastus led the sons of the Seven, the Epigoni, against Thebes with better success; the city fell, but Adrastus' son Aegialeus was killed in the fighting. According to the earlier story (Paus. 1. 43. 1) the aged Adrastus died of grief on the way home; a sensational and late account (Hyg. *Fab.* 242. 5) makes father and son burn themselves alive *ex responso Apollinis*.   H. J. R.

ADRIA, a Greek colony at the Po estuary, probably dating back to the sixth century, but of uncertain origin. It prospered by its trade with the Etruscan rulers of north Italy, but fell into decay in the fourth century, after the occupation of north Italy by the Gauls and the recession of the Adriatic Sea. The historian Philistus took refuge at Adria from Dionysius I of Syracuse and wrote his Σικελικά there.   M. C.

ADRIANUS of Tyre (*c.* A.D. 113–93), sophist, pupil and successor of Atticus Herodes at Athens. He subsequently taught rhetoric at Rome and his works included μελέται, epideictic speeches, and treatises on ἰδέαι and στάσεις.

ADRIATIC SEA (ὁ Ἀδρίας; *mare Adriaticum* or *superum*). This term was used indifferently with that of 'Ionian Sea' to denote the gulf between Italy and the Balkan Peninsula. Its southward limit was extended by some authors to include the sea east of Sicily. In prehistoric times it was a route by which Baltic amber (q.v.) and perhaps also Bohemian tin (q.v.) reached Italy and Greece. Greek exploration of the Adriatic was mainly the work of the Phocaeans, who penetrated to its upper end by 600 B.C. (Hdt. 1. 163); but Greek colonization was relatively late and sporadic. The southeast coast was settled from Corinth and Corcyra in the late seventh and the sixth centuries, their chief foundations being Apollonia and Epidamnus (qq.v.). Emigrants from Cnidos occupied Black Corcyra (*Curzola*), and Syracusans (probably refugees from Dionysius I) took possession of Issa (*Lissa*). But the north Dalmatian coast was not colonized. Temporary settlements were made by Rhodes in south Apulia (Strabo 14. 654; probably in the sixth century). In central Italy Ancona was a solitary Greek foundation. Adria and Spina (qq.v.) at the Po estuary throve temporarily on trade with the Etruscans, and finds of coins in the Po valley indicate Tarentine trade up the Adriatic in the fourth century.

Adriatic commerce and colonization were impeded by the brigandage of the Illyrians on the south Dalmatian coast, where deep recesses and off-shore islands provided ideal pirate bases. This nuisance was eventually suppressed by the Romans, who swept the Adriatic with a war-fleet after the First Punic War (229 and 219 B.C.), and from the time of Augustus patrolled it with a regular police flotilla. But Greek trade in the Adriatic fell away after 300 B.C., and the Romans made little use of this sea except on the crossings from Brundisium and Ancona (qq.v.).

R. L. Beaumont, *JHS* 1936, 159–204.   M. C.

ADROGATIO, *see* ADOPTIO.

ADULIS or **ADULE,** on west coast of the Red Sea (in Annesley Bay near Massowa), was used by Ptolemies II and III for elephant-hunts, and became an important export-mart for African and re-exported Indian wares, a caravan-route leading thence inland. Greeks and Indians frequented it. When the Axumite kingdom rose (1st c. A.D.; *see* AXUMIS) Adulis became their main port and base (for voyages to E. Africa and India), surpassing all

others in the third century A.D. Two famous inscriptions (combined in *OGI* 54) are among its monuments.

Periplus M. Rubr. 4; Ptol. *Geog.* 4. 7. 8; 8. 16. 11.   E. H. W.

ADULTERY. I. In GREEK STATES the punishment of adultery (μοιχεία) ordinarily took the form of private self-help. A law of Draco allowed a man to kill anyone caught in the act with his wife, mother, sister, or daughter; according to a law of Solon the offended husband could deal with the adulterer as he liked. The adulterer could, however, buy himself off by paying a money penalty. It was also open, alike to interested persons and to others in the first instance, to enter a legal prosecution against him. Penalties were very severe and differed in the individual States. The husband of a woman convicted of adultery was compelled to repudiate her, otherwise he became liable to *atimia* (q.v.) by a law of Solon. In the Greco-Egyptian papyri some marriage contracts (so the oldest one, *PEleph.* 1) prescribe a pecuniary penalty for adultery.

II. ROMAN LAW. The punishment of adultery (sexual intercourse of a married woman with a man other than her husband) was first regulated by Augustus in the *Lex Iulia de adulteriis coercendis* (*ante* 18 B.C.). The mention of a legendary law of Romulus (Dion. Hal. 2. 25), punishing the adulteress with death, is doubtless an anticipation of an old rule adopted in judgements of family councils or of the usage of killing the adulterous woman and her partner caught *in flagranti* (cf. Gell. 10. 23; Val. Max. 6. 1. 23). In the Republican period the repression of adultery became less rigorous; but a reaction against the decay of ancient custom was brought by the above-mentioned *Lex Iulia*, which introduced severe penalties. By this law the father was allowed to kill his adulterous daughter and her paramour, when caught in the act in his or her husband's house; a husband could in certain cases kill the adulterer, but not his wife. The normal penalty for adultery was the banishment (in the form of *relegatio*, q.v.) of both guilty partners—but *in diversas insulas*—confiscation of parts of their property, and for the woman the loss of half of her dowry. The husband was obliged to divorce immediately, otherwise he was punished as a *leno* (procurer). The accusation of adultery had to be made by the husband or the wife's father within sixty days after the divorce; after this time it could be made within four months by anyone, on the ground that the adultery was an offence against morality. A special criminal court (*quaestio*) was instituted for cases of adultery; it was presided over by a praetor, and had much work to do: Dio Cassius (76. 16) relates that in his first consulship there were about 2,000 suits for adultery pending. The procedure shows an interesting peculiarity: slaves could exceptionally be examined (under torture) against their *dominus*. Adultery committed by a *concubina* was treated as that of a married woman.

The penalties of the *Lex Iulia*, to which a special title is dedicated in Justinian's Digest (48. 5), were made more severe by the Christian emperors. Constantine introduced the death-penalty; Justinian confirmed it (*Nov.* 134. 10), and restored the husband's right to slay his adulterous wife, but he restricted the right of making a charge against the guilty persons to the relatives.

GREEK LAW: J. H. Lipsius, *Das attische Recht* i (1905), 429 f.; A. Berger, *Strafklauseln in d. Papyrusurkunden* (1911), 218.
ROMAN LAW: Mommsen, *Röm. Strafr.* (1899), 627 f., 688 f.; Ph. Lotmar, *Mélanges Girard* ii (1912), 143 f.; E. Volterra, 'Storia dell' accusatio adulterii', *Studi econ.-giur. dell' Univ. Cagliari* 1928; B. Biondi, 'Poena Adulterii', *Studi Sassaresi* xvi (1938).   A. B.

ADVOCATUS. The parties to a trial, under Roman procedure, could be assisted in both its stages, *in iure* and *apud iudicem*, by legal advisers, *patroni, oratores,* or *advocati.* (For the difference in this terminology, not very essential, see pseudo-Asc. in Cic. *Div.* 4, whose words imply that the advocate's part was a modest one: 'aut ius suggerit aut praesentiam suam accommodat amico'.) Being experienced in law and procedure, they helped the party with technical advice; but they were also expected to be versed in oratory, as their task often included the delivery of a speech on behalf of the client. The activity of advocates was supposed from the earliest times to be gratuitous; but it is certain that they did not refuse gifts or money for their services. The *Lex Cincia* (204 B.C.), and again Augustus, forbade this practice, but legislation remained fruitless, so that later emperors could not do other than recognize that the advocates—now defined as 'qui causis agendis quoquo studio operantur' (Ulp. *Dig.* 50. 13. 1. 11)—might receive a *honorarium* (or *palmarium*, if payment was conditional on the case being won). The intervention of an *advocatus* was considered in classical times so necessary that the praetor promised in his edict to assign one to those who were without legal assistance. Under the later Empire the standing of the advocates improved considerably, as the professional jurists became increasingly rare. They formed a special corporation and were attached to individual courts, where they could defend the interests of their clients, acting generally as their legal representatives (which they were not in earlier times). Diocletian in his *Edictum de pretiis* fixed the maximum fees for the different functions performed by advocates; Justinian limited the *honorarium* to 100 *aurei*. The majority of his collaborators at the composition of the Digest were advocates.

Mommsen, *Röm. Strafr.* 674 ff., 705 ff.; A. Checchini, *Studi di ordinamento proces.* i (1925), 110 ff.; L. Wenger, *Procedura civ. rom.* (transl. R. Orestano, 1938), 80, 320 f.   A. B.

AEACUS, in mythology, son of Zeus and Aegina (daughter of the river-god Asopus), ancestor of the Aeacidae, the (post-Homeric) genealogy being:

Aeacus=Endeis (daughter of Sciron of Megara)

Thetis=Peleus   Hesione=Telamon=Eriboea

Achilles=Deidameia   Teucer   Aias=Tecmessa

Neoptolemus   Eurysaces

Some accounts give Aeacus a third, illegitimate son, Phocus, who was killed by his brothers; they consequently left the island of Aegina (so named from their grandmother). Aeacus was celebrated for his piety. In response to his prayers a drought came to an end (Isoc. 9. 14–15 and later authors). Because the population of the island was scanty, or had died of a plague sent by Hera, he besought Zeus to help him, and the god turned a swarm of ants into men, who were, therefore, called Myrmidones (Hes. fr. 76 Rzach; Ov. *Met.* 7. 517 ff.). He judged between the gods (Pind. *Isthm.* 8. 25); built part of the walls of Troy (Pind. *Ol.* 8. 31; no other authority). After his death he became a judge of the dead (Isoc. loc. cit.; Plato, *Ap.* 41 a, *Grg.* 523 e).   H. J. R.

AEDESIUS (d. *c.* A.D. 355) of Cappadocia, Neoplatonist, pupil of Iamblichus and teacher of Maximus, Chrysanthius, Priscus, and Eusebius Myndius. He set up a school of philosophy in Pergamum. No writings remain; biography by Eunapius.

PW i. 941.

AEDILES. The aediles originated as two subordinate officials of the *plebs*, created to assist the tribunes, whose sacrosanctity they partly shared, either for the maintenance of the prison, or, as is more likely, to superintend the common temple (*aedes*) and cult of the *plebs*, that of Ceres (q.v.). Soon their functions began to extend to the administration of public buildings in general, particularly to the oversight of the archives, both *plebiscita* and *senatus consulta*. With the addition in 367 B.C. of two *aediles curules*, elected from the patricians, the aedileship became a magistracy of the whole people. After the admission of plebeians the curule magistracy was held alternately by either order, but in the Empire was omitted by patricians. The office was elective— either in the *concilium plebis*, or, for the *curules*, in the *comitia tributa*—and annual, being held after 367 for the consular, not the tribunician, year (*see* CALENDARS, para. 6). *Curules* ranked below praetors, *plebeii* at first below tribunes but eventually with the *curules*. The office was non-essential in the *cursus honorum*, but its connexion with the games rendered it useful to men with political ambitions, and it was the first office to confer full senatorial dignity and the *ius imaginis*. The competence of either branch was the same. Their duties were the *cura urbis*, *cura annonae*, and *cura ludorum sollemnium*. *Cura urbis* meant care for the streets of Rome, traffic regulations, public order in religious matters and cult practices, care for the water-supply and the market, especially the supervision of weights and measures. Consequently they had powers of minor jurisdiction. Fines exacted went to separate chests for *plebeii* and *curules*. Out of the *cura urbis* developed the *cura annonae*, the maintenance and distribution of the corn-supply (*see* ANNONA), a heavy charge until Julius Caesar created special *aediles Ceriales* for this duty, which passed under Augustus to the *praefectus annonae* and other officials. Care for the public games, which grew out of their urban administration, increased in importance with the growth of wealth and political rivalry in the later Republic, till the greater part of the expense was borne by the aediles as a means of gaining popularity and votes. Augustus, however, transferred the games to the praetors. The *ludi Romani* and the *Megalesia* fell to the *curules*, the *ludi Ceriales* and *plebeii* to the plebeians. Aediles are also found as the normal minor administrative officials of all Roman municipalities (*see* MUNICIPIUM), and in corporate bodies such as *vici* (*see* VICUS) or *collegia* (*see* CLUBS, ROMAN). *See also* AERARIUM.

Livy; Dion. Hal.; Cicero, *Verrines*, 2 and 5. 14. G. De Sanctis on origins, *Riv. Fil.* 1932; Kubitschek, 'Aedilis' in *PW*; E. Kornemann, *Klio* 1915; Mommsen, *Röm. Staatsr.* ii³. 470 f.   A. N. S.-W.

AEDITUUS (older **Aeditumus**), properly the keeper or sacristan of a consecrated building, *aedes sacra*. In practice two kinds of official were so named, (*a*) a man of rank and standing, who was responsible for the upkeep of the building, (*b*) a servant, often a slave, who did the actual work of cleaning, etc.

See Marquardt–Wissowa, *Röm. Staatsverw.* iii³. 214 ff.   H. J. R.

AËDON (Ἀηδών), in mythology, daughter of Pandareos, the son of Hermes and Merope. She married Zethus (q.v.) and had two children, Itylus and Neïs. Envying Niobe (q.v.), Amphion's wife, for her many children, she planned to kill them, or one of them, at night; but Itylus was sleeping in the same room as they and she mistook the bed and so killed him. In her grief, she prayed to be changed from human form, and became a nightingale (ἀηδών).

See schol. *Od.* 19. 518, and cf. Rose, *Handb. Gk. Myth.* 340.   H. J. R.

AEDUI, a Gallic tribe which occupied most of modern Burgundy. They appealed to Rome against the Arverni and Allobroges (121 B.C.) and received the title of *fratres consanguineique*. During the Gallic War they gave valuable though not whole-hearted support to Caesar, and when they finally joined Vercingetorix in 52 their support was lukewarm. Under the Empire they became a *civitas foederata*, and were the first tribe to furnish Roman senators. *Duoviri* replaced the *Vergobretus* as magistrates, and the hill-fort Bibracte was abandoned for Augustodunum (*c.* 12 B.C.). They took part unsuccessfully in the rebellions of Sacrovir (A.D. 21) and

Vindex (68). In the third century the region suffered heavily from civil war and barbarian invasion; the panegyrist Eumenius celebrates the relief measures of Constantius and Constantine.

CIL xiii. 400; O. Hirschfeld, *Kleine Schriften*, 186–200; C. Jullian, *Hist. de la Gaule* iii. 535–40; vi. 423–30. C. E. S.

AEGAE (modern *Vodena*), early capital of Macedon, commanding the route from the Macedonian plain to upper western Macedonia. Formerly called Edessa, it formed a base for the Macedonian conquest of the coastal plain *c.* 640 B.C., was renamed Aegae, and remained the cult-centre of the royal house even after Archelaus moved the court to Pella (q.v.). Its strong position is illustrated in S. Casson, *Macedonia, Thrace, and Illyria* (1926), fig. 69. N. G. L. H.

AEGEAN SEA, between Greece and Asia Minor. To it the modern name Archipelago was originally applied, but the ancient Greeks derived the name Aegean variously from Theseus' father Aegeus (q.v.), who drowned himself in it; from Aegea, Amazonian queen, who was drowned in it; from Aegae city. They subdivided it into *Thracian*, along Thrace and Macedonia to the north coast of Euboea; *Myrtoan*, south of Euboea, Attica, Argolis, west of the Cyclades; *Icarian*, along (Asiatic) coasts of Caria and Ionia; *Cretic*, north of Crete. Some, like Strabo, treated the last three as separate, ending the Aegean at Sunium in Attica. The whole Aegean contains many islands in three groups: along the Asiatic coast, including Lesbos, Chios, Samos, Rhodes; a small group off Thessaly; Euboea and the Cyclades, a continuation or reappearance of the mountains of the Greek mainland. E. H. W.

AEGEUS (*Αἰγεύς*), almost certainly a humanization of Poseidon of Aegae; hence Theseus (q.v.) is sometimes called his son, sometimes Poseidon's. In legend, however, he is a king of Athens, son (usually) of Pandion and Pylia, daughter of Pylas, king of Megara. Born in Megara, he afterwards conquered Attica. Probably Athenian claims to the Megarid in historical times have much to do with this and similar legends. Having no children, he consulted Delphi, and was told in riddling phraseology to be continent till he reached home (Eur. *Med.* 679, and schol.), but did not understand, and begat Theseus on Aethra, daughter of Pittheus, king of Troezen, who understood the oracle and purposely brought it to pass that the divinely ordained child should be his grandson. Later, he gave Medea a refuge on her flight from Corinth (*see* MEDEA), and married her; their son was Medus (Hyg. *Fab.* 26. 1, from some Alexandrian source). On her trying to poison Theseus when he arrived in Athens, Aegeus drove her out (different account in Hyginus, ibid. 2). Theseus freed him from the attacks of Pallas and his fifty sons, who were trying to overthrow him, and afterwards left for Crete to meet the Minotaur (*see* MINOS). On returning, however, he forgot to change the black sails of his ship, and Aegeus, seeing them and thinking his son dead, killed himself by leaping off the Acropolis or into the sea, hence, in this account (but see preceding article), called the Aegean (*Αἰγαῖον πέλαγος*) after him. See, for connected accounts, Plutarch, *Theseus*, and Apollod. 3. 206 ff. H. J. R.

AEGIMIUS, a legendary king, son (or father, schol. Pind. *Pyth.* 1. 121) of Dorus, eponym of the Dorians. Being attacked by the Centaurs, he asked Heracles to help him, and in gratitude for his aid adopted Hyllus (q.v.) and made him joint heir with his own sons—obvious Dorian propaganda.

AEGINA, an island in the Saronic Gulf, inhabited from late neolithic times and in contact with Minoan Crete and Mycenae. It was conquered *c.* 1000 B.C. by the Dorians under Deiphontes (q.v.), son-in-law of Temenus

of Argos. Early in the seventh century (probably) it fell to the Argive tyrant Pheidon and struck the first coins of Greece proper, the long-lived silver 'tortoises'. Throughout the archaic period it was a naval power, often in rivalry with Samos (war with King Amphicrates; voyages of Sostratus of Aegina and Colaeus of Samos; establishments at Naucratis (q.v.); attack *c.* 520 on Samians settled in Crete).

In 506 began the long struggle with Athens. The Athenian fleet that won Salamis was raised ostensibly against the Aeginetans who had 'medized' in 491; but at Artemisium, Salamis, and Plataea they fought on the Greek side, winning the prize for valour and much besides. To this period belongs the temple of Aphaea (q.v.) with its splendid sculptures now in Munich.

When Athens and Sparta became estranged, Aegina, the 'eyesore of the Piraeus', sided with the Peloponnesians. A decisive naval defeat in 459 led to its capture by Athens and incorporation in the Delian League (458), to which it paid 30 talents yearly. The Aeginetans helped to foment the Peloponnesian War, and on its outbreak were expelled from their island, which was occupied by Athenian cleruchs, among them the families of Aristophanes and Plato. Restored by Lysander in 405 they received a Spartan harmost, and till its bequest to Rome by Attalus of Pergamum the island played a minor, mainly passive, rôle. Its supreme glory is to have inspired some of Pindar's greatest poetry, including the eighth Pythian.

Herodotus; Thucydides; Xenophon, *Hellenica*; *Oxyrhynchus Papyri* v. 842, cols. 1, 2, 3; Pindar; *IG* i². 191 f.; A. Furtwängler and others, *Heiligtum der Aphaia* (1906); G. Welter, *Aegina* (1938, with good bibliography). P. N. U.

AEGIS, attribute of Zeus and Athena, usually represented as a goatskin. When Zeus shakes the aegis (*Il.* 17. 593 ff.) a thunder-storm ensues and he puts fear into the hearts of Achaeans. Athena and Apollo use the aegis to disperse enemies and to protect friends (*Il.* 15. 229, 307; 21. 400).

The aegis made by Hephaestus (*Il.* 15. 307 ff.) for Zeus is indestructible, resisting even lightning (*Il.* 21. 400). That of Athena (*Il.* 5. 738) is surrounded by Fear, Fight, Force, and Pursuit, and has a Gorgon-head in the centre. In art the aegis appears as an attribute of Athena from mid-sixth century on (A. Rumpf, *Chalkidische Vasen*, 143). It is shown as a short cloak worn over the shoulders or, like a shield, over the left arm; it is bordered with snakes and has often the head of Gorgo in the centre. It is assumed that originally the aegis was conceived as a storm-cloud (Aesch. *Cho.* 585) and came to be regarded as a goatskin because of the similarity of words αἴξ goat and καταιγίς hurricane.

Dar.-Sag. s.v.; N. Prins, *De Oorspronkelijke Beteekenis van de Aegis* (1931). G. M. A. H.

AEGISTHUS, in mythology, surviving son of Thyestes (*see* ATREUS; so Aesch. *Ag.* 1605); but a version apparently Sophoclean (see Dio Chrys. 66. 6; cf. Apollod. *Epit.* 2. 14; Hyg. *Fab.* 87 and 88. 3–4) makes him the incestuous offspring of Thyestes and his daughter Pelopia after the murder of the elder sons. His name suggesting the word αἴξ, a story is told, in connexion with that mentioned above, that he was exposed and fed by a she-goat (Hyg. ibid. and 252). When adult, he returned to Argos to avenge his father. All this is post-Homeric; the *Odyssey* (3. 517 ff.) evidently thinks of him as a baron having an estate near the domains of Agamemnon, and gives no reason for the quarrel except Aegisthus' intrigue with Clytemnestra (q.v.; cf. 1. 35 ff.). For his murder of Agamemnon and the revenge taken by Orestes, see the appropriate articles. H. J. R.

AEGRITUDO PERDIC(C)AE, an anonymous Latin epyllion narrating the calamitous love of Perdicas for his mother, Castalia. The ascription of the poem to Dracontius (q.v.) is unwarrantable, though it almost certainly belongs to his period.

Texts: Vollmer, *PLM* v². 238; *Anth. Lat.* no. 808.

A. H.-W.

AEGYPTUS, see DANAUS, EGYPT.

AELIA CAPITOLINA, see JERUSALEM.

AELIANUS (1), CLAUDIUS (c. A.D. 170–235), generally known as 'Aelian', of Praeneste, where he was pontifex. He taught rhetoric in Rome, but later confined himself to writing. Extant works: Π. ζῴων ἰδιότητος (*De Natura Animalium*), a collection of excerpts and anecdotes of a moralizing character, concerned chiefly with the animal world; Ποικίλη ἱστορία (*Varia Historia*), a similar collection dealing with human life and history; Ἐπιστολαὶ ἀγροικικαί, short stylistic exercises in letter form. Fragments exist, chiefly in Suidas, of Π. προνοίας and Π. θείων ἐναργειῶν, collections designed to illustrate the workings of providence and divine justice.

Aelian's philosophical ideas, notably that of universal reason as manifested in the animal creation, derive from Stoicism; he is especially bitter against the Epicureans. His excerpts, largely derived from intermediate sources (Sostratus, Alexander of Myndos, Pamphilus, etc.), often supplement our knowledge of earlier writers. He enjoyed a reputation for Attic purity of diction (Suidas, Philostratus); he affects simplicity (ἀφέλεια) and lack of arrangement. His works enjoyed great subsequent popularity. He is probably to be distinguished from the author of a *Tactica* (see article below).

Suidas; Philostr. *VS* 2. 31. Editions: R. Hercher 1858 (preface); id. (Teubner) 1864. Criticism: W. Schmid, *Atticismus* (1889) iii. 1 f. (language); M. Wellmann, *Hermes* xxvi (1891), xxvii (1892), xxxi (1896), li (1916) (sources of Π. ζ. ἱ.); F. Rudolph, *Leipz. Stud.* vii (1884) (sources of Π. ἱ.). W. M. E.

AELIANUS (2), author of a *Tactica* (in Greek), probably in Trajan's reign, on the long-dead Macedonian phalanx, mostly taken from Asclepiodotus (q.v.). Its value is slight.

Text: H. Köchly and W. Rustow, *Griechische Kriegsschriftsteller*, 1855.

AELIUS (1) **PAETUS CATUS,** SEXTUS (*cos.* 198 B.C.), a Roman jurist, was the author of the renowned work *Tripertita* which contained the law of the XII Tables, an account of its development by legal interpretation, and the forms of the *legis actiones*. The work was later known under the name *Ius Aelianum*; Pomponius says of it: 'ueluti cunabula iuris continet'. A. B.

AELIUS (2) **TUBERO,** LUCIUS, friend of M. Cicero and legatus to Q. Cicero in Asia, engaged in writing history; but of publication we have no proof. It possibly descended as material to his son, Q. Aelius (q.v. 3) Tubero, who shared his father's interest both in history and in the Pompeian cause. J. W. D.

AELIUS (3) **TUBERO,** QUINTUS, jurist and annalist, who fought on Pompey's side but became reconciled with Caesar, left politics after an unsuccessful prosecution of the Republican Q. Ligarius in 46 B.C., and wrote on jurisprudence and history (Pompon. *Dig.* 1. 2. 2. 46). He was reputed to be an expert in public and private law; he published several legal works which, however, did not enjoy a great popularity because of his *sermo antiquus*. In at least fourteen books, he treated Roman history from the origins to his own times; these fragments, however, may be from a monograph addressed to Oppius (Gell. 6. 9. 11). Livy cites him with Macer (4. 23. 1; 10. 9. 10), whom he may have taken as model. Pliny cites a Q. Tubero for astronomical data (*HN* 18. 235).

H. Peter, *HRRel.* i² (1914), pp. ccclxvi and 308; W. Soltau, *Livius' Geschichtswerk* (1897); cf. K. J. Beloch, *Röm. Gesch.* 106. A. H. McD.

AELIUS (4), LUCIUS (L. Ceionius Commodus, son of L. Ceionius Commodus), praetor in 130, *cos.* I in 136, and adopted (as 'L. Aelius Caesar') later in the same year (*CIL* vi. 10242) as Hadrian's successor; *trib. pot.*, Dec. 136–7; *cos.* II, 137. Elegant, luxurious, and consumptive, he nevertheless governed the two Pannonias well (136–7). He died on 1 Jan. 138, honoured but not deified. (*See also under* VERUS, L.)

S.H.A., *Had.* and *Ael.*; Dio Cassius 69; *PIR²*, C 605; H. Mattingly, *B.M. Coins, Rom. Emp.* iii (1936). C. H. V. S.

AELIUS (5) **PROMOTUS,** physician from Alexandria, probably belonging to the period between Hadrian and Pertinax (A.D. 138–93). He wrote a book on curative methods called Δυναμερόν, sections of which remain.

PW i. 528.

AELIUS, see also s.v. ARISTIDES, DONATUS, GALLUS, HADRIAN, HERODIAN, MARCIANUS, SEJANUS, STILO, THEON(3).

AELLO, see HARPYIAE.

AEMILIANUS, MARCUS AEMILIUS, emperor A.D. 253. While governor of Moesia he repelled a Gothic invasion and was saluted emperor by his troops (252). Next spring he invaded Italy and was accepted as successor to Gallus (*see* TREBONIANUS). His reign lasted only three months. When news reached Rome that Valerian had been proclaimed emperor, Aemilianus, who deserved a better fate, was assassinated by his own soldiers.

H. Mattingly, *JRS* xxv. 55–8. H. M. D. P.

AEMILIANUS, see also FABIUS (7), SCIPIO (11).

AEMILIUS, see AEMILIANUS, ASPER, LEPIDUS, PAPINIANUS, PAULLUS, REGILLUS, SCAURUS.

AENARIA (or **Inarime**—a fanciful derivation from *Il.* 2. 783): the largest island near Naples; nowadays Ischia. The activity of its now extinct volcano Epopeus ('Typhoeus' grave according to some; *Aen.* 9. 716) rendered sojourn difficult for its successive Euboean, Syracusan, Neapolitan, and Roman settlers (Strabo 5. 248 f.; Livy 8. 22). Aenaria was famous for its warm springs and potter's clay (whence its Greek name *Pithecusae*: Pliny, *HN* 3. 82).

V. Bérard, *Bibliogr. topogr.* (1941), 78. E. T. S.

AENEAS (1) (Αἰνείας or Αἰνέας), son of Anchises and the goddess Aphrodite, a famous Trojan leader in Homer's *Iliad* and the hero of Virgil's *Aeneid*. In the *Iliad* he is said to have been respected equally with Hector (5. 467), and honoured like a god (11. 58). He fought against Diomede (bk. 5), Idomeneus (bk. 13), and Achilles himself (bk. 20). His actions are not strikingly heroic, and more than once he is protected or rescued by one of the gods, to whom he exhibits marked piety (20. 298, 347). Aeneas was descended from the younger branch of the Trojan royal house (20. 230 ff.), and had a grudge against Priam, who came of the elder branch, for not giving him his due (13. 460). But he himself hoped to succeed to the kingship (20. 180), and Poseidon prophesies that he and his descendants will rule over the Trojans (20. 307). Aeneas is thus the one Trojan hero who has a definite future before him.

From this hint tradition developed the legend of his flight from Troy with his father Anchises (q.v.), his son Ascanius (q.v.), and his ancestral gods (*see* PENATES) (Xen. *Cyn.* 1. 15), and the legend of his subsequent wanderings. Arctinus represents him as retiring to Mt. Ida, and afterwards he was thought to have visited or founded many places on the mainland of Greece and elsewhere, which either had names resembling his own, like Ainos in Thrace and Aineia in Chalcidice, or possessed temples of Aphrodite, often with the cult-title Αἰνειάς, such as those in Leucas, at Actium, and at

Elymus in Sicily. This story of his wanderings was developed with the addition of other places, such as Delos and Crete, by later writers, especially by Hellanicus, Timaeus, and Dionysius of Halicarnassus. The association with Sicily acted as a stepping-stone both to Rome and to Carthage. Stesichorus may have asserted that Aeneas reached 'Hesperia', but the story that he came to Latium appears first in Hellanicus. It became popular after the wars with Greece, when patriotism urged the Romans to seek a founder within the cycle of Greek legend, but among the enemies of Greece. Among Roman writers this development is found in Naevius and Ennius, in Q. Fabius Pictor and later historians, including Livy. Considerations of chronology later made Aeneas the founder, not of Rome itself, but of Lavinium, the head of the Latin League. The connexion of Aeneas with Carthage was known to Varro, and there is a possible earlier reference to the meeting of Aeneas and Dido in a fragment of Naevius.

Virgil thus inherited a flat and disconnected story of Aeneas' wanderings, a legend of his association with the foundation of Rome, and a hero with no definite characteristics, except a scrupulous piety. Out of this material he constructed the epic of the *Aeneid*. The legends of the wanderings he wisely telescoped into the third book, while the association with Rome is developed into the great national theme of the poem. Virgil's portrait of Aeneas is based on the piety ascribed to him by Homer, but this is amplified in the full sense of the Roman *pietas* into a devotion to his father, to his mother and the gods in general, and to the great destiny of Rome. If to modern readers he still seems colourless, and his 'piety' monotonous, the key to the understanding of Virgil's Aeneas lies in the gradual strengthening of his character and purpose, which follows on his realization of his destiny as the founder of the Roman State.

The *Aeneid* ends with the slaying of Turnus by Aeneas, but other writers tell of his meeting with Dido's sister, Anna, on the banks of the Numicius (Ov. *Fasti* 3. 601 ff.) and of his purification in the river and his assumption to heaven with the title of Indiges (Ov. *Met.* 14. 581 ff.).   C. B.

AENEAS (2), commonly called *Tacticus*, probably the Aeneas of Stymphalus who was general of the Arcadian League in 367 B.C., wrote several military treatises (epitomized later for Pyrrhus), of which the one on the defence of fortified positions, probably written soon after 357, has survived. As advice to the defenders of a besieged town it is rather elementary, though it contains interesting details; but its real value is the light it throws on social and political conditions in early fourth-century Greece, for it is assumed throughout that the chief danger to the defence is not so much the enemy without the wall as the opposing faction within, who will betray the city if they can. Philologically, the work, as an early non-Attic document, has some interest for the study of the growth of the Hellenistic *Koine*.

E. Schwartz, 'Aineias (3)' in *PW*; Illinois Greek Club, *Aeneas Tacticus* (Loeb, 1923); L. W. Hunter, *Aineiou Poliorketika* (1927). W. W. T.

AENESIDEMUS of Cnossos, Sceptic, probably of the Ciceronian period. Philo seems to have borrowed from him an account of the τρόποι τῆς ἐποχῆς (grounds of suspense of judgement). Works: Πυρρώνειοι λόγοι, Ὑποτύπωσις εἰς τὰ Πυρρώνεια, Κατὰ σοφίας, Περὶ ζητήσεως, Πρώτη εἰσαγωγή. His aim was to restore the sceptical character which the teaching of the Academy had under Antiochus' influence lost. Diogenes Laertius (in the life of Pyrrhon) and Sextus Empiricus give many details of his teaching, which was substantially followed by Sextus himself. The τρόποι τῆς ἐποχῆς were directed against the reliability of the senses.

PW i. 1023.   W. D. R.

AENUS, a Greek colony in Thrace at the mouth of the river Hebrus, founded by Mytilene and Cyme. It stood at the head of a trade route up the Hebrus valley and across the Thracian isthmus to the Black Sea. Its prosperity in the fifth and fourth centuries (temporarily interrupted by the rise of the Thracian kingdom of Sitalces, q.v.) is attested by the high tribute which it paid in the Delian League and by its copious emission of coinage. Between 341 and 185 B.C. it passed through the hands of the Macedonian, Egyptian, and Pergamene kings; in 185 it was declared a free city by the Romans.

S. Casson, *Macedonia, Thrace, and Illyria* (1926), 255–9.   M. C.

AEOLIAE INSULAE (nowadays *Lipari Islands*), seven volcanic islands off north-eastern Sicily, named after their fancied connexion with Homer's island of Aeolus (*Od.* 10. 1, etc.). The largest, Lipara, contained a Cnidian-Rhodian colony (*c.* 579 B.C.) which practised piracy in the fourth century (Livy 5. 28). The islands became a Carthaginian naval station, which Rome captured in 252 B.C. and later assigned to the Sicilian province. Under the Republic Lipara was a *civitas decumana* (i.e. subject to tithe) but possessed Roman citizenship under the Empire. Volcanic eruptions were frequent on the islands, especially on Hiera (*Vulcano*), which was traditionally Vulcan's abode; to-day Strongyle (*Stromboli*) is the most active. Principal products: obsidian, sulphur, alum, pumice, coral.

Strabo 6. 275 f. (confused); Pliny, *HN* 3. 92 f.; Diod. 5. 7 f.; 23. 20; Thuc. 3. 88; Polyb. 1. 21. 39; Cic. *Verr.* 3. 84. L. Zagami, *Isole Eolie* (1939); V. Bérard, *Bibliogr. topogr.* (1941), 61. E. T. S.

AEOLIC, *see* DIALECTS, GREEK.

AEOLIS, the territory of the northernmost group of Greek immigrants to the western coast of Asia Minor, extending from the entrance of the Hellespont to the mouth of the Hermus—a linguistic and ethnological, not a geographical, unit. Near the end of the second millennium B.C. the Aeolians, deriving from Boeotia and Thessaly, planted their first settlements in Lesbos, and thence expanded northwards to Tenedos, and along the mainland coast to the east and south. The Troad was occupied much later (perhaps in the seventh century B.C.) by secondary colonization, principally from Lesbos. There must have been considerable racial fusion with the local barbarian inhabitants. Most of the Aeolian cities derived such prosperity as they enjoyed primarily from agriculture, commerce being of minor importance in Lesbos. The Aeolian settlements in the south were grouped together in a league, whose origin was probably religious. Its members were Aegae, Aegirusa, Cilla, Cyme, Gryneum (where the temple of Apollo was perhaps the central sanctuary of the league), Larissa, Myrina, Neonteichos, Pitane, Smyrna (later resettled by Ionians), and Temnos. The most important cities in the north were: Antandros, Assos, Cebren, Gargara, Ilium, Neandria, and Scepsis.

G. Hirschfeld, *PW*, s.v. 'Aiolis (3)'.   D. E. W. W.

AEOLUS, (1) the ruler of the winds; in *Od.* 10. 2 ff. a mortal, son of Hippotes; he lives in Aeolia, a floating island, with his six sons and six daughters, who have married one another; he can tie up the winds in a sack to prevent them blowing. In *Aen.* 1. 51 ff. he is a minor god and keeps the winds in a cave on Aeolia. Sometimes confused with (2) a son of Hellen (q.v.), eponym of the Aeolians and the Aeolidae:

Aeolus⊤Enarete

Cretheus	Sisyphus	Athamas	Salmoneus	Deïon	Magnes
Perieres	Macar(eus)	Canace	Alcyone	Peisidice	Calyce
	Perimede	(Arne	Tanagra	Melanippe)	

Canace killed herself, or was killed by her father, because of incest with Macareus (Ov. *Her.* 11). Arne, or Melanippe, became by Poseidon mother of (3), another ancestor of the Aeolians; see Hyg. *Fab.* 186 and Rose ad loc.; Euripides, frags. of Μελανίππη ἡ δεσμῶτις and *M. ἡ σοφή.*   H. J. R.

AEON, *see* AION.

AEPYTUS, in mythology, son of Cresphontes, king of Messenia, also called Cresphontes (see *TGF* 497) and Telephontes (Hyg. *Fab.* 137. 3). Escaping, as a child, when his father was killed by Polyphontes, he returned with false news of his own murder and, after narrowly escaping death from his mother Merope, killed Polyphontes, thus becoming king.   H. J. R.

AEQUI, primitive (Oscan-speaking?) mountaineers, inhabiting the valleys of the upper Anio, Tolenus, and Himella in central Italy (Strabo 5. 228, 231, 237; *Aen.* 7. 746). Expanding thence towards Latium, by 500 B.C. they held the mountains behind Tibur and Praeneste. During seventy years Hernici, Latins, and Romans found them, despite their small numbers (Livy 6. 12), even tougher enemies than their Volscian confederates (H. Last, *CAH* vii. 500). They established themselves on the Alban Hills and were not expelled until 431 (*see* ALGIDUS). Thereafter, however, Aequi are only casually mentioned until 304, when they apparently occupied their original central Italian area. Rome now almost exterminated them; she established Latin colonies at Carsioli and Alba Fucens, gave the surviving Aequi *civitas sine suffragio* and rapidly romanized them (Livy 9. 45; 10. 1. 9). The Aequian nation thus disappeared, although a *municipium Aequiculorum sive Aequiculanorum* is still recorded after 90 B.C. (Pliny, *HN* 3. 106); its name survives in the district Cicolano north of the Fucine Lake. Their name (*aequi*) gave rise to the tale that the Aequi invented the *ius fetiale* (Livy 1. 32).

R. S. Conway, *Italic Dialects* i (1897), 300 f.   E. T. S.

AEQUITAS, *see* PERSONIFICATIONS.

AERARIUM, derived from *aes*, denotes 'treasury'. The main *aerarium* of Rome was the *aerarium Saturni*, so called from the temple below the Capitol, in which it was placed. Here was kept the State treasure, originally mainly of bronze, *aes* (hence the name), but including also ingots of gold and silver and other valuables. With it was associated a public record office, the *tabularium* (q.v.).

The *aerarium* was controlled by the quaestors under the general supervision of the Senate, with a subordinate staff of *scribae, viatores,* etc. The *tribuni aerarii* (q.v.), men of a property-class a little below the *knights*, were probably concerned with making payments from the tribes into the treasury. The Roman mint was associated with the temple of Juno Moneta, but it is possible that the coinage of *aes*, as opposed to gold and silver, was, at first at any rate, associated with the *aerarium*. The *aerarium sanctius* was a special reserve, fed by the 5 per cent. tax on emancipations. Treasure was withdrawn from it in 209 B.C. and on other occasions. Caesar in 49 B.C. insisted on seizing the reserve for his own uses.

Caesar placed two aediles in charge of the *aerarium*, Augustus two *praefecti* (28 B.C.) and then two praetors (23). Claudius (A.D. 44) placed it again under the quaestors, Nero, finally, in A.D. 58, under two *praefecti*. The *aerarium* of the Empire at first dealt with important revenues, but stood, effectively, at the disposal of the emperor. It steadily lost ground to the *fiscus* (q.v.) and sank to be a mere city-chest of Rome. *See also* FINANCE, ROMAN.

The *aerarium militare*, founded by Augustus in A.D. 6 to provide for the pensioning of discharged soldiers, was fed by special grants and by the *vicesima hereditatum*, an estate-duty affecting only Roman citizens. It was administered by three praetors, at first drawn by lot, later nominated by the emperor.

O. Hirschfeld, *Die Kaiserlichen Verwaltungsbeamten* (1905), 8 ff., 18 ff.; *PW*, s.v.   H. M.

AERARIUS, at Rome, the citizen who, having no land-property, was not registered in any Servian tribe. He was exempted from voting and military service, but had to pay a poll-tax in proportion to his means. The half-citizens (*Caerites*, q.v.) who were not landowners, from 353 B.C. onwards; the Latins, even if they possessed estates; and the citizens of Capua after their rebellion (211), were also counted as *aerarii*. The class was suppressed (c. 312) by Appius Claudius and restored in 304 by Fabius Rullianus, who retained, however, the distribution of the *aerarii* among the four urban tribes. People punished with removal from their tribe for moral or military misbehaviour were also called *aerarii*.

W. Kubitschek, *PW*, s.v.; Mommsen, *Röm. Staatsr.* ii³. 392 ff.; strongly opposed by A. H. J. Greenidge, *Infamia* (1894), 106 ff., who attributes the origins and meaning of the word *aerarius* 'not to the tribes but to the centuries', and by P. Fraccaro, *Athenaeum* 1933.   P.T.

AES, bronze, i.e. copper, as generally used with alloy of tin, etc.

Aes, by itself, can denote (1) a document recorded in bronze, e.g. the ground-plan of a colony, (2) 'stipendium', 'military pay', and from that 'military service', (3) the bronze list of recipients of free corn (*aere incisi*). *Aes*, with explanatory adjectives, has a wide range of uses: thus *aes alienum* (or *circumforaneum*) = 'debt', *aes multaticium* = 'money raised by fines', *aes equestre* = the grant to the knight to buy his horses, *aes hordearium* = the allowance for the keep of the horses. *Aes et libra* represented the old method of purchase, by touching the scales with a piece of bronze.

All these uses depend on the fact that bronze was the first metal employed by the Romans to measure values (*see* COINAGE, ROMAN). Most important is the reckoning with cardinal numbers and the genitive *aeris*, representing originally pounds of bronze, but, subsequently, perhaps, smaller amounts, as the *aes* fell from the full pound to two ounces, one ounce, a half, and even a quarter. The characteristic meaning, however, seems to be the original, 'pounds', so that, even in later days, when the silver *sestertius* was the unit of reckoning, it was equated to the old pound of bronze. When Gaius gives the limit fixed by the *Lex Voconia* as 100,000 *aeris*, he does not mean anything different from the 100,000 *sestertii* recorded by Dio Cassius.

PW, s.v.; H. Mattingly, 'Aes and Pecunia', *Num. Chron.* 1943, 21 ff.   H. M.

AESCHINES (1) (c. 390–after 330 B.C.), the orator, son of Atrometus, an Athenian who, exiled by the Thirty, fled to Corinth. Returning to Athens some years later, he kept a school. Of A.'s early life we know little beyond what is recorded by the malice of Demosthenes, from which the only truth which emerges is that he was brought up in comparatively humble circumstances and had to earn his living at an early age. The fact that A. himself frequently boasts of his good education perhaps indicates an inferiority complex in this matter. He was first a clerk to some minor officials, and later an actor. He served as a hoplite at Mantinea and Tamynae, obtained political employment under Eubulus, c. 357 B.C., and was subsequently clerk to the Ecclesia. In 348 he was a member of the embassy sent to Megalopolis, when, having gone out as an opponent of Philip's designs, he came back with changed views, having recognized, as he says himself, that resistance was impracticable. Two years later he went with Demosthenes and others on the embassies which resulted in the peace of Philocrates. Demosthenes prepared to prosecute A. for taking bribes from Philip, and enlisted Timocrates as his fellow-prosecutor. A., however, prosecuted the latter as being a person of notorious evil character and therefore debarred from speaking in public. He appears to have proved his case. In 343 B.C. Demosthenes brought the action in which he and A. delivered the speeches entitled *De Falsa Legatione*, and A. was acquitted by a narrow majority. In 339 he delivered before the Amphictionic Council a provocative speech which led to the outbreak of the Sacred War. In 337, when Ctesiphon proposed to confer a crown on Demosthenes, A. impeached Ctesiphon for illegality; the case was not heard till 300, when A., having failed to obtain a fifth of the votes, was fined 1,000 *drachmae*. He retired to Asia Minor, where he lived, according to Plutarch, as a professional sophist.

2. Aeschines had no consistent policy: he was admittedly an opportunist. Demosthenes definitely accused him of changing front in consequence of bribes offered by Philip. A. admits having changed his views, but only when he found that the policy which he first advocated was impossible. He is further accused of having given false reports of Philip's intentions, with a view to misleading the public. It is more probable that he was himself misled: a self-made man, vain of his success, may well have been imposed on by the subtle flattery of the adroit diplomatist who was able to convince even Isocrates of the purity of his intentions. But he cannot be acquitted of bad taste and lack of serious judgement: his speech to the Amphictions, which led to a riot and caused a war, was due, as he admits, to momentary exasperation, and, disregarding the serious consequences, he glories in the effect of his oratory on the audience.

3. SPEECHES. *Against Timarchus*—who is accused of (a) private immorality, (b) prodigality, (c) corruption in public life.

On the Embassy: The charge of treason brought by Demosthenes really referred to the second embassy, though he implied that A. was corrupt both before and after. A. diverts attention by laying stress on the conduct of the first embassy, about which no specific charge had been laid. After an appeal for impartiality there follows an amusing narrative of the embassy. The main line of defence is that A. was himself deceived by Philip. He succeeds in thoroughly obscuring the issues, and the speech is a fine piece of advocacy.

Against Ctesiphon: A. proposes to prove that Ctesiphon's proposal was illegal, his statements about Demosthenes untrue, and the result of his action harmful. (a) As Demosthenes was subject to εὔθυνα (see EUTHYNA), it was illegal to propose to confer a crown on him; (b) it was illegal to make the proclamation in the theatre; (c) the assertion that Demosthenes had acted for the best interests of Athens was false. The first two charges are dealt with by legal argument, the third by a lengthy discussion of Demosthenes' public policy.

4. A man of dignified presence and fine voice, A. deprecated the use of extravagant gestures by an orator, preferring a statuesque pose. Proud of his education, he displays it by frequent quotation of poetry. In the use of historical argument he cannot compare with Demosthenes, but in a battle of wits he more than holds his own. His vocabulary is simple but effective, though occasional obscurities may be found in his sentences. Ancient critics ranked him lower than he deserves; the fact is that he was not aiming at literary perfection; his object was to produce a powerful effect on his audiences, and he was justified by the result. With no initial advantage of birth, education, or even principle, he raised himself by the force of his eloquence to a position of authority and importance.

For general bibliography, *see* ATTIC ORATORS; passages in Demosthenes, *de Corona*. Text: Blass (Teubner, 1908). Text and translation: Adams (Loeb); Martin and Budé (Budé). Commentaries: *In Ctes.*, Gwatkin and Shuckburgh; *Sur l'ambassade*, Jullien and Pérèra (1912). Index: S. Preuss (1896).   J. F. D.

AESCHINES (2) **SOCRATICUS** (4th c. B.C.), of the Athenian deme Sphettus, one of Socrates' most devoted adherents, was present at his master's condemnation and death. He founded no school of philosophy, but is said to have had Xenocrates as a pupil. He also wrote speeches for the law-courts, and taught oratory. He fell into great poverty, but found a refuge at the court of Syracuse; whether in the time of Dionysius I or in that of Dionysius II (i.e. after 368) is not known; he returned to Athens after the expulsion of Dionysius II in 356. He is best known as the author of Socratic dialogues which were highly esteemed for their style and their faithfulness to Socrates' character and way of speaking. Those which were pretty certainly genuine are Μιλτιάδης, Καλλίας, Ἀξίοχος, Ἀσπασία, Ἀλκιβιάδης, Τηλαύγης, Ῥίνων; seven others passed under his name, but were judged by antiquity not to have the genuine Socratic character.

Ed. H. Dittmar (1912); *PW* i. 1048.   W. D. R.

AESCHYLUS. (*See also* TRAGEDY.)

I. LIFE (525/4-456 B.C.)

1. Aeschylus, son of Euphorion of Eleusis, a member of a Eupatrid family, was born 525/4 B.C. (*Marm. Par.*) and witnessed the end of tyranny at Athens in his youth, and the growth of democracy throughout his life; he fought at Marathon (*Marm. Par.*), where his brother Cynegirus met a noble death, and probably at Salamis (schol. Aesch. *Pers.* 429; Pausanias (114. 5) adds Artemisium, and the *Life* Plataea, but these reports are much less certain). On the strength of Ar. *Ran.* 885–7 many have believed that he was initiated into the Mysteries. It is not clear what inference should be drawn from Aristotle's statement (*Eth. Nic.* 3. 1) that when accused of revealing the Mysteries, he replied that he did not know that what he said was something which might not be uttered. (Clement of Alexandria (*Strom.* 2. 461) says that he obtained acquittal by proving that he was not initiated; there is no agreement as to the plays in which the supposed revelation was made.) But his temperament was profoundly religious and intensely patriotic, and the effect upon it of the great events of his youth and manhood was seen in his assertion of the supremacy of Justice and his conception of Divine Government.

2. His first appearance in tragedy must have been very early in the fifth century (Suidas, s.v. 'Pratinas') and his first victory was in 484 (*Marm. Par.*). Of his extant plays, the earliest, the *Supplices*, cannot be certainly dated, the *Persae* was produced in 472, the *Septem contra Thebas* in 467, and the *Oresteia* (*Agamemnon*, *Choephoroe*, and *Eumenides* with the lost satyric *Proteus*) in 458; the *Prometheus* trilogy was probably one of his latest plays (see G. Thomson's edition). He paid probably two visits to the court of Hieron in Sicily, the first not many years after the foundation by Hieron in 476 of the new city of Aetna, the second after the production of the *Oresteia*. On the first visit he wrote a play (*Aetnae* or *Aetnaeae*) in honour of the new city, and gave a performance of the *Persae* at Hieron's request; the second ended with his death at Gela in 456. No better reason for these visits need be sought than the attraction of such a centre of literary men as Hieron's court; the causes imagined by old writers—his defeat by Sophocles in 468, or by Simonides in the composition of an epitaph on the heroes of Marathon, or the collapse of the wooden theatre during one of his plays, or the unpopularity caused by the terrifying effect of the *Eumenides*—may be dismissed. The epitaph on his monument at Gela, in which his fighting at Marathon is mentioned, but not his poetry, may (as Paus. 1. 14. 5 asserts) or may not have been composed by himself. After his death the Athenians decreed that anyone desiring to produce the works of Aeschylus should be granted a chorus by the archon

(*Vit. Aesch.*). In view of this, not too much must be made of Aristophanes' allusion (*Ran.* 807) to disagreements between Aeschylus and the Athenians; but, unless Aristophanes' picture of him is wholly wrong, we can believe that he was by temperament somewhat aloof and warm-tempered as well as high-souled. The figures in the *Life* and in Suidas giving the number of his plays and victories are uncertain or corrupt. The catalogue of his plays in the Medicean MS. includes 72 titles, but omits 10 plays ascribed to him elsewhere, most of them probably correctly. The statement in the *Life* that his plays gained many victories after his death may well be true.

II. Works

3. The trilogies or tetralogies of plays connected in subject which are certainly recorded are (1) the *Laius, Oedipus, Septem contra Thebas,* and the satyric *Sphinx.* (2) the *Prometheus Δεσμώτης, Pr. Λυόμενος,* and *Pr. Πυρφόρος;* (3) the *Oresteia* (see above); (4) the *Λυκούργεια,* including the *Edoni, Bassarides* or *Bassarai, Νεανίσκοι,* and satyric *Lycurgus.* No connexion of subject can be traced between the plays produced in 472—the *Phineus, Persae, Glaucus Potnieus,* and satyric *Prometheus;* but it is practically certain that there was a Danaid trilogy including the extant *Supplices,* the *Aegyptii, Danaides,* and probably the satyric *Amymone,* and a number of titles have been grouped together with considerable likelihood:

Myrmidones, Nereides, Phryges or *῞Εκτορος Λύτρα,* with choruses attendant upon Achilles, Thetis, and Priam (see Wilamowitz, *Interpret.* p. 245). A papyrus fragment of the first play has been recovered (*Supp. Aesch.* p. 31).

῞Οπλων Κρίσις, Threissae, Salaminii, the first turning upon the contest for the arms of Achilles, the second on the death of Ajax, the third perhaps on the misfortunes of Teucer.

Argivi, Eleusinii, Epigoni (or *Nemea, Argivi, Eleusinii*: see Wilamowitz, loc. cit. p. 68), dealing with the hostilities of Argos and Thebes; the *Eleusinii* corresponded in subject to Euripides' *Supplices.*

Lemnii, Hypsipyle, Argo, Cabiri, on the Argonautic story. (The *Nemea* may also have belonged to this group, and if so, one of the other plays must go. The statement in Ath. 10. 428 f. that Aeschylus brought drunkards on the stage for the first time in the *Cabiri* suggests a satyric play.)

Bacchae, Xantriae, Pentheus (order uncertain).

Δικτυουλκοί, Polydectes, and *Phorcides* (satyric, *IG* ii¹. 973), on the story of Perseus and connected legends. A papyrus fragment of the first-named has been published (*Supp. Aesch.* p. 71; D. L. Page, *Greek Literary Papyri,* 8 ff. (Loeb, 1940))

Besides these, the *Telephus* and *Mysi* probably belong to one group, the *Memnon* and *Ψυχοστασία* to another, and the *Ixion* and *Perrhaebides* to a third.

The titles not enumerated above include the *Athamas, Aetnae* or *Aetnaeae, Alcmene, Atalantae, Heliades, Heraclidae, Thalamopoioi* (possibly an alternative title for one of the plays of the Danaid trilogy), *῾Ιερεῖαι, Callisto, Cares* or *Europa* (of which a papyrus fragment exists), *Cressae, Niobe* (for a considerable fragment, see *Greek Poetry and Life,* 106 ff.; D. L. Page, op. cit. 2 ff.), *Palamedes, Penelope, Propompoi, Semele* or *Hydrophoroe, Toxotides* (on the death of Actaeon), *Philoctetes* (see Dio Chrys. 52), *Orithyia;* and the satyric plays, *Διονύσου Τροφοί, Θεωροὶ ἢ ᾽Ισθμιασταί, Cercyon, Κήρυκες, Circe, Leon, ᾽Οστολόγοι, Sisyphus* (possibly two plays, *Σ. δραπέτης* and *Σ. πετροκυλιστής), Ψυχαγωγοί.*

III. Character of his Work

4. It was Aeschylus who in all probability organized the external presentation of the drama on the lines which were to become traditional—the rich costumes, the decorative (though probably not in his time thick-soled) cothurni, the solemn dances. He seems to have had a special liking for gorgeous or impressive spectacular effects, such as were presented in the *Supplices* and *Eumenides* and, indeed, in nearly all his plays, though in a certain fondness for the barbaric (cf. Ar. *Ran.* 928 ff., 962 f.) and in some experiments in mechanical devices which may have bordered on the grotesque his successors did not follow him. The Egyptian and Oriental dresses in the *Supplices* and *Persae* are of a piece with his enjoyment of the geography of strange lands. The Persian Wars affected him as they affected Herodotus. His love of long and magnificent descriptions—the battle of Salamis in the *Persae,* the armour of the heroes in the *Septem,* the fall of Troy in the *Agamemnon*—is characteristic, and in a trilogy there was room for it. In other respects, too, he was a master of impressiveness—the long silences of some of his characters, the recurrent refrains (ἐφύμνια) of many choral odes, the solemn grandeur of Darius in the *Persae,* the litany of invocation in the *Choephoroe,* are sufficient illustrations. It must also have been he who created the tragic dialogue in the forms which became regular, though in him they sometimes show (especially in stichomythia, as compared e.g. with Sophocles) a certain stiffness, and there is not much adaptation of style to speaker. His characters are 'typical', in the sense that in most there is not much minute drawing of the details of character—Danaus is the cautious father, Pelasgus the constitutionally-minded king, Atossa the royal mother, Eteocles the champion and defender of his city, Prometheus the victim and the unyielding opponent of tyranny, and so on—and that most are the embodiment each of some great passion or principle which determines all their words and acts.

5. The characters share the greatness of the issues which are worked out in their destiny. A man's destiny depends on the interaction of two factors, his own will and the higher powers that rule the world; each of the great personages of Aeschylus possesses a will that can rise to the conflict; but the Clytemnestra of the *Agamemnon* stands above them all as one in whom the imagination of a poet is added to a commanding and relentless personality. Not that Aeschylus is incapable of pathos; but even in Cassandra there is no lack of strength.

6. His choruses are all very distinctly characterized, though still 'typical'; the foreboding solemnity of the old men of the *Agamemnon,* tremulous, not what they were, but not prepared to endure an Aegisthus, contrasts sharply with the fussy, noisy terror of the women in the *Septem;* and the tender sympathy of the Oceanids with the savage joy of the Erinyes in their horrible office. The chorus in most plays serves as a foil to set off in relief the character of the leading personage. Now and then, as in the Watchman in the *Agamemnon* and the Nurse in the *Choephoroe,* there is a thoroughly homely character with little human touches.

7. In the *Frogs* of Aristophanes Aeschylus is made to defend the 'high-flown' language with which he is taunted on the ground that great thoughts and minds need great words for their expression, in other words, that the grandeur of his style is of a piece with that of his characters and conceptions. The defence was a just one in a poet who had fought at Marathon; the critics belonged to an age when grandeur did not come naturally and was not taken seriously. He is not afraid of compound words of which each embodies a whole picture; of epithets strung together in a mass, passing rapidly from one metaphor to another, rather than giving for comparison (as Sophocles does) a single picture clearly and beautifully drawn; of phrases suggesting the outline of some great imaginative idea, not so minutely analysed as to be expressible in simple language. He lives in a world of metaphor, and his metaphors are

drawn from a wide range of sources in human life and the natural world, and if sometimes strange, often give pictures of incomparable beauty. He is fond of lines consisting of but three resounding words, and does not mind an occasional repetition or a neglect of the caesura.

8. The plot of an Aeschylean play is usually of the kind which Aristotle calls simple or straightforward (ἁπλῆ), i.e. uncomplicated by περιπέτεια or by recognition scenes of the kind which often compose the crisis in his successors' plays; events move relentlessly forward, as the divine plan works itself out. The connected trilogy was a form specially fitted for the presentation of the divine operation in its slow but certain working, and the forms of surprise, which were very telling and almost necessary when the action was confined to a single play and a single day, were less natural to Aeschylus. For what Aeschylus taught was the lesson of the ultimate justice of Providence, in whose designs the rival claims, whether of men or of supernatural powers, were at last reconciled and contending wills brought to work together within the universal scheme of ordered government and goodwill towards men, which is what the name of Zeus signifies to him, and in which there is room for both Apollo and the Eumenides. That at least was the moral of the *Oresteia* and the Prometheus trilogy, and probably of the Danaid trilogy also, as is strongly suggested in the choruses of the extant play. Everything that is of the nature of ὕβρις, unless it has become incurable, must be pruned of its selfishness and its excess—the Danaids' rejection of Aphrodite, the irreconcilability of Prometheus, the savagery of the age of the Titans and the Furies. Zeus himself (this is perhaps the boldest of Aeschylus' imaginations) has had to grow in wisdom and learn the spirit of good government. The current ideas of inherited evil, of the curse upon a house and the fatality of great prosperity, Aeschylus takes over but purifies. The curse will not fall on a man unless he calls it out by his own wrongdoing and so gives the demon in the house his chance, nor will wealth, perilous though it be, harm its possessor if he keeps himself free from ὕβρις; the stroke of Justice, however long delayed, will never fail to fall where it is deserved, but there may be at last, by the grace of God, an escape from the fatal chain of evil, and the cruellest suffering, like that of Io, may be seen in the end to have been only a step in a great and beneficent design of the Divine Will.

9. In the history of his own time, no less than in legend as he interpreted or refashioned it, Aeschylus read the same lessons. We cannot fully explain the echoes of the history of contemporary Argos in the *Supplices*, but the antithesis of tyranny and freedom was in the air the poet breathed, and it is not far below the surface in any play. The failure of Persia was unmistakably the downfall of ὕβρις, and as for Athens, the salvation of the State lay in freedom and righteousness and in the reconciliation, through moderation on either side, of rival claims—that is the moral of Athena's speeches in the *Eumenides*, a play which ends in a great festival of reconciliation, recalling at every point the Panathenaea, the festival of united Athens (see W. Headlam, *JHS* 1906).

BIBLIOGRAPHY

LIFE AND WORKS. M. Croiset, *Eschyle* (1928); H. W. Smyth, *Aeschylean Tragedy* (U.S.A. 1924); W. Porzig, *Aischylos* (1926); B. Snell, *Aischylos und das Handeln im Drama* (1928). A. E. Haigh, *Tragic Drama of the Greeks* (1896); M. Pohlenz, *Die griechische Tragödie* (1930); W. L. Kranz, *Stasimon* (1933); A. Lesky, *Die griechische Tragödie* (1938); G. Murray, *Æschylus* (1940).

TEXT. U. von Wilamowitz (1914); A. Sidgwick (O.C.T. 1902 incl. Fragments); G. Murray (O.C.T. 1937). *TGF*, pp. 3–128; H. J. Mette, *Supplementum Aeschyleum* (1939); P. Mazon (Budé, with French translation).

COMMENTARIES. A. Sidgwick (each play separately); Supplices, T. G. Tucker (1889); J. von Vürtheim (1928); Septem, T. G. Tucker (1908); Prometheus, G. Thomson (1932); Agamemnon, A. W. Verrall (2nd ed. 1904); W. Headlam (1910); Choephori, A. W. Verrall (1893); U. von Wilamowitz, *Das Opfer am Grabe* (1890); Tucker (1901); Eumenides, Verrall (1908); Oresteia, G. Thomson (1938). Also Wilamowitz, *Aischylos Interpretationen* (1914), *Lexicon Aeschyleum*, W. Dindorf (1876).

TRANSLATIONS. Prose: W. and C. E. S. Headlam. Verse: G. Murray (each play separately). A. W. P.-C.

AESCULAPIUS, latinized form of *Asclepius* (q.v.). A. was brought to Rome from Epidaurus at the instance of the Sibylline Books, perhaps seconded by Delphi, after a plague in 293 B.C. Legend told how the sacred snake, incarnating the god, itself chose the Insula Tiberina for its abode, and there on 1 January 291 a temple was dedicated to A. (Livy 10. 47; *epit.* 11; Ov. *Met.* 15. 622–745; *Fasti* 1. 289–94). The cult was patterned directly on that of Epidaurus, but of the minor deities there only Hygieia was received, to whom, from about 180 B.C. (Livy 40. 37) the name of the Italic goddess Salus was sometimes applied. They received a joint cult from the military in various parts of the Empire, but the relative strength of A. in Dacia and Spain may be due to Greek or Oriental elements there. The A. worshipped with Caelestis in and about Carthage is a Semitic god of the Eshmun type.

W. A. Jayne, *The Healing Gods of Ancient Civilizations* (U.S.A. 1925), ch. 7; J. Toutain, *Les Cultes Païens dans l'Empire Romain* i (1907), 330–8; E. J. and L. Edelstein, *Asclepius* (1945). F. R. W.

AESEPUS, god of the Mysian river of that name, Hesiod, *Theog.* 342.

AESERNINUS, grandson of Asinius Pollio (q.v.), an orator under Tiberius.

AESON, see JASON (1).

AESOP, see FABLE.

AESOPUS (1st c. B.C.), tragic actor, 'gravis' (Hor. *Epist.* 2. 1. 82), contemporary of Roscius (Quint. *Inst.* 11. 3. 111 'Roscius citatior, Aesopus gravior'), gave the young Cicero lessons in elocution. *Auct. ad Her.* (3. 21. 34) suggests that he was greatly his senior: as an optimate, he supported Cicero's recall from exile (*Sest.* 120–3), and returned to the stage for Pompey's *ludi*, 55 B.C., without much success (*Fam.* 7. 1. 2). See *Div.* 1. 80; *Tusc.* 4. 55; *QFr.* 1. 2. 14. His son, M. Clodius Aesopus, was rich enough to be a wastrel (Hor. *Sat.* 2. 3. 239; Pliny, *HN* 9. 122). G. C. R.

AETERNITAS, see PERSONIFICATIONS.

AETHER, see AITHER.

AETHERIAE PEREGRINATIO, see PEREGRINATIO AD LOCA SANCTA.

AETHIOPIS, see EPIC CYCLE.

AETHRA, in mythology, daughter of Pittheus, king of Troezen, and mother of Theseus by Aegeus (qq.v.). Since Theseus was often called son of Poseidon, various explanations grew up. Aethra was sent by Athena (hence called Apaturia, the Deceitful) to the island of Hiera or Sphairia, where Poseidon met her (Paus. 2. 33. 1); Poseidon visited her the same night as Aegeus (Apollod. 3. 208, Hyg. *Fab.* 37. 1); it was a tale invented by Pittheus to save her credit (Plut. *Thes.* 6). Her appearance as waiting-maid to Helen (*Il.* 3. 144) also needed explanation; a story, apparently as old as the Cycle (*Iliu Persis*, fr. 3 Allen, cf. Apollod. 3. 128), says the Dioscuri carried her off while Theseus was in Hades, as reprisal for his kidnapping of Helen, and her grandsons, Demophon and Acamas (qq.v.), fetched her home when Troy fell. H. J. R.

AËTION, painter (and sculptor?), dated by Pliny 352 B.C. In his most famous picture, the 'Marriage of Alexander and Roxane' (not before 327), Roxane was seated in the marriage chamber, Alexander standing before her, Hephaestion leaning on Hymen; Erotes fluttered round the chief actors and played with Alexander's arms in the background. A. was probably not the sculptor mentioned by Theocritus (*Epigr.* 8) and Callimachus (*Epigr.* 24).					T. B. L. W.

AËTIUS, Eclectic of the first or second century A.D., summarized in his Συναγωγὴ περὶ ἀρεσκόντων the opinions of the Greek philosophers on natural philosophy. These *Placita* are reproduced in the ps.-Plutarchean *Epitome* and in Stobaeus' *Eclogae*, and have been edited by H. Diels in *Doxographi Graeci* (1879), 273-444. They form one of our most important sources for the opinions of the philosophers whose works have for the most part perished.

PW i. 703:					W. D. R.

AETNA, (1) Europe's highest active volcano (10,758 feet), lying between Tauromenium and Catana in Sicily. Its fertile lower slopes produce excellent grapes; forests cover the middle slopes; the upper slopes are bare. Its eruptions, which reputedly drove the Sicani into western Sicily, greatly impressed the ancients, who commonly attributed them to a giant, either Typhon or Enceladus, buried beneath. Roman ruins near the summit prove that Aetna was frequently climbed (by Hadrian amongst others). Empedocles is said to have committed suicide there.

[Lucilius], *Aetna*; Strabo 6. 273 f.; Pind. *Pyth.* i. 20 f.; Aesch. *PV* 351 f.; Lucr. 6. 640 f.; Verg. *Aen.* 3. 570 f.; Gell. 17. 10. C. S. du Riche Preller, *Italian Mountain Geology* (1923).

(2) A town lay at the southern foot of the volcano near *Paterno*. Originally a Sicel settlement named Inessa, it was renamed Aetna in 461 B.C., when Hieron's Doric colonists, fleeing from Catana (q.v.), came there. Aetna was a Syracusan stronghold which Dionysius garrisoned with Campanians whom Timoleon ultimately ejected. Under the Romans it was a *civitas decumana* which Verres plundered unconscionably. Its subsequent history is unknown.

Strabo 6. 268; Thuc. 3. 103; Diod. bks. 11-16; Cic. *Verr.* 3. 23. 44; 4. 51.					E. T. S.

AETNA, Latin didactic poem in 646 hexameters, was placed among Virgil's minor works in early manuscripts. This ascription was doubted in Donatus' day, and very few accept it now. Style, metre, and language point on the whole to the early Silver Age; since the poem mentions the volcanic activity of Campania as extinct, it cannot be placed later than the earthquake of A.D. 63. Seneca, *Ep.* 79. 5, prompted the ascription to Cornelius Severus, Ovid's friend (an ascription supported by some later manuscripts), or to Lucilius Junior, Seneca's correspondent; but Seneca's words suggest a description of Aetna inside a larger work, not a separate poem on Aetna.

Rejecting mythological explanations, the unknown author argues that the controlling force behind eruptions is wind operating at high pressure in narrow subterranean channels, and that the volcanic fire, produced by friction, gets a nutritive material especially in the lava-stone (*lapis molaris*). The poem is embellished by digressions. One passage (224-73) extols physical science; another (604-46) narrates the devotion of two brothers who rescued their parents during an eruption. *Aetna* makes difficult reading, partly because of its corrupt text, partly because of the author's style. He strains after brevity, overloads words and phrases, indulges freely in metaphor and personification; in his terse mythological allusions, details are taken for granted as well known. Nevertheless, the work does not lack polish or animation; and one respects the author's earnest enthusiasm for the study of nature (*see* METEOROLOGY). Posidonius is probably the chief scientific source of *Aetna* (Sudhaus ed. 59-81); similarities of expression in Seneca's *Naturales*

Quaestiones seem to indicate, not a debt to Seneca, but a common source behind both works. Among poets, Lucretius and Virgil are the principal models.

Texts: H. A. J. Munro, 1867; E. Baehrens, *PLM* ii (1880), revised F. Vollmer, *PLM* i (1927); M. L. de Gubernatis (1911). With trans. (German) S. Sudhaus (1898); (French) J. Vessereau (1905); (English) R. Ellis (1901); J. W. and A. M. Duff, *Minor Latin Poets* (Loeb, 1934).					A. M. D.

AETOLIA, a country bordered on the west by the lower and middle valley of the river Acheloüs, and on the east by Mt. Oxya, the watershed between Aetolia and Malis. It contains the southern continuation of the Pindus mountain range. While the mountains of north Aetolia run north and south, the main range of southern Aetolia runs east and west, cutting off the rich plains of central Aetolia by Lake Conope and Lake Trichonis from the coast of the Corinthian Gulf. The coast between the mouths of the Acheloüs and the Euenus contains shallow lagoons but no good harbour. While five coastal towns, especially Pleuron and Calydon, were known to Homer, the religious centre of classical Aetolia lay inland at Thermum near Lake Trichonis, and its history was entirely that of a land power. Seclusion from the sea left Aetolia undeveloped in the fifth century B.C. (Thuc. 1. 5), little urbanized, and organized in tribes who formed a common front against Demosthenes' invasion (426 B.C.). The natural avenues of expansion lay into Acarnania and northwards to Amphilochia and Malis; but Aetolia did not develop successfully along those lines until the third century B.C.

W. J. Woodhouse, *Aetolia* (1897).					N. G. L. H.

AETOLIAN CULTS AND MYTHS. The chief divinities of Aetolia were Artemis, Apollo, and Athena (dedication of statues of all three by Aetolians at Delphi, Paus. 10. 15. 2; of Artemis and Apollo only, id. 10. 16. 6). The cult centre of Artemis Laphria was Calydon (later Patrae, id. 7. 18. 8-13); Apollo was worshipped at Calydon, but principally at Thermum; Athena is associated with Pleuron (Stat. *Theb.* 2. 726-31; Dion. Calliphon. 57-9 = *GGM* i. 240). At Phistyon the Syrian Aphrodite (*see* ATARGATIS), to whom the epithet Phistyis was here applied, shared a temple, from at least 213/12 B.C., with the Mother of the Gods and the Virgin (Parthenos), possibly local deities in origin; the cult is known only from inscriptions. The cults of Dionysus (cf. Paus. 7. 21. 1-5), Heracles, Zeus Soter, and some others are also known.

Prominent in myth are Aetolus, the reputed founder, and the family of Oeneus, Althaea, Meleager, and Deianira (qq.v.). For the Calydonian boar-hunt *see* MELEAGER.

J. de Keitz, *De Aetolorum et Acarnanum sacris* (Diss. Halle, 1911); W. J. Woodhouse, *Aetolia* (1897); for the inscriptions see *IG*² ix. 1 and G. Klaffenbach, *Sitz. Berl.* 1936; for the myths, C. Robert in L. Preller, *Griechische Mythologie* ii. 1 (1920), 85-100.					F. R. W.

AETOLIAN LEAGUE. The looser tribal organization of the Aetolians gave way during the fourth century B.C. to a federal State (*sympoliteia*, q.v.), which acquired considerable power already in the latter part of that century and retained it even during the first period of the Roman intervention. In the third century the Aetolians exercised a protectorate over Delphi and through their expansion secured a controlling interest in the Amphictionic League (*see* AMPHICTIONIES). Since they normally were hostile to Macedonia, they naturally became Rome's first active allies within Greece proper. Their later hostility to Rome and co-operation with Antiochus III proved their downfall. Their conquests and outside influence were lost, and in 189 B.C. the Aetolians were forced to accept a treaty as subject allies of Rome. The League was not dissolved, but all its importance and influence were gone.

At the head of the League was a general elected annually. The primary assembly had two regular meetings a year and could be summoned for special sessions. The *boule* or *synedrion*, in which the cities were represented in proportion to population, contained some thousand members. Hence, particularly in time of war, much of the leadership fell to a smaller body, the *apokletoi*, itself containing over thirty members, probably a committee of the *boule*. At no time did the leadership of the League pass out of the hands of the Aetolians proper. This was in part because more distant States were not made regular members but merely bound to the League by *isopoliteia* (q.v.), which involved civil rights, protection, and potential citizenship but no participation in federal affairs unless residence was established in a community possessing active citizenship. Grants of *asylia* (q.v.) by the Aetolians were not infrequent and were highly prized on account of their extensive use of piracy and the right of reprisal. *See also* FEDERAL STATES.

G. Klaffenbach, introduction to *IG*[1] ix. 1; R. Flacelière, *Les Aitoliens à Delphes* (1937). J. A. O. L.

AETOLUS (Αἰτωλός), eponym of the Aetolians. His legend seems to be founded on traditions of the relation between certain Greek peoples. Endymion, king of Elis, had three sons, Paeon, Epeios, and Aetolus; he set them to race at Olympia, promising the kingship to the winner. Epeios won, hence the ancient name *Epeioi* for the people of the district; Paeon left the country and gave his name to the district of Paeonia; Aetolus had later to leave because of a blood-feud, and went to Aetolia, which is called after him (Paus. 5. 1. 3–8). H. J. R.

AFER, GNAEUS DOMITIUS (d. A.D. 59), considered by Quintilian the best orator of his age. After his first spectacular success (the condemnation of Claudia Pulchra, cousin of the elder Agrippina, in A.D. 26), he enjoyed a distinguished, but sinister, reputation. Prosecuted by the Emperor Gaius in 39, he saved himself by flattery and was made consul (Sept. 39). J. P. B.

AFRANIUS (1), LUCIUS (b. *c.* 150 B.C.), Latin poet, was the most prolific composer of *comoediae togatae*, whose representation of domestic life in Italian towns he made more artistic and involved, with wider and coarser appeal. His plays were performed even in Imperial times, the most renowned being *Divortium*, *Epistula*, *Fratriae*, *Privignus*, *Vopiscus*. He admired Terence, from whom he confessedly borrowed, and was compared by Horace (*Epist.* 2. 1. 57) with Menander. He portrayed chiefly family life and the 'middle classes'. *See* DRAMA, ROMAN, para. 5.

Fragments: O. Ribbeck, *CRF*[2] 164 (3rd ed. Teubner, 1897). E. H. W.

AFRANIUS (2), LUCIUS (*cos.* 60 B.C.), of Picene birth (*ILS* 878), served under Pompey in Spain and against Mithridates, and was rewarded with the consulate of 60 B.C., being elected by flagrant bribery and proving most disagreeable to Cicero; 'quam ignauus et sine animo miles'. He became proconsul of one of the Gauls, probably Cisalpina, and perhaps gained a triumph. From *c.* 53 he governed Hispania Citerior as Pompey's legate with three legions, and in 49 commanded at Ilerda. Pardoned by Caesar, he returned to Pompey, though charged with treachery by other Pompeians. He escaped from Pharsalus, but was captured and executed after Thapsus. G. E. F. C.

AFRANIUS, *see also* BURRUS.

AFRICA, *see* LIBYA.

AFRICA, ROMAN. The Punic Wars (q.v.) made Rome heir to the Carthaginian Empire. In 146 B.C. Rome left most of the continental territory in the hands of Massinissa's descendants and annexed merely some of the fertile lands round Carthage. This new province (roughly equivalent to modern Tunisia) covered *c.* 5,000 square miles within a frontier from Thabraca to Hadrumetum; it was governed by a praetor from Utica (q.v.). Except for the new capital and six other favoured cities, most of the land became *ager publicus* (q.v.). Though the attempt of Gaius Gracchus to colonize Carthage failed, Roman and Italian merchants settled in Africa in large numbers. After the battle of Thapsus (46 B.C.) Caesar added to the province the Numidian territories of Juba I, and planned to restore Carthage as a Roman colony.

2. Augustus promoted urbanization by founding six colonies, fifteen *municipia*, and thirty *oppida libera* in Africa. He placed the province under a proconsul at Carthage with command of the Third Augustan legion. After the rising of Tacfarinas (q.v.), Gaius made the proconsul a purely civilian official, and handed the legion and Numidia over to the legate. The westward expansion was carried on by Claudius, who organized the two provinces of Mauretania. The frontier was pushed southward slowly as the result of successful wars (e.g. against Tacfarinas) and the Saharan campaigns under Septimius. Roman Africa reached its greatest extent under Caracalla. The frontier ran from the Cyrenaic border at Ara Philaenorum through Cydamus (mod. *Gadhamès*), Nefta, and Vescera (mod. *Biskra*) and then north-west through Auzia (mod. *Aumâle*) to reach the Atlantic south of Volubilis (q.v.) at Sala (mod. *Salé*).

3. This huge territory, on which the provincial organization of the Empire was imposed, was populated mainly by men of Berber stock, whose language survives to-day. Their chief tribal divisions were Garamantes in the Fezzan, Massyli and Masaesyli in the east and centre of the high plateaux, Moors in the west of the Atlas Mountains (q.v.), and Gaetulians in the Sahara. Phoenician colonies covered the coast from Leptis, through Hadrumetum, Carthage, and Caesarea, to Tingis on the Straits of Gibraltar, down the Atlantic seaboard to Lixus (mod. *Larache*). Inland other Phoenician communities had settled, and intermarriage had produced the so-called Libyphoenician race; they inhabited the numerous towns and practised an agriculture which made their country the granary of Rome. Phoenician divinities were worshipped side by side with primitive Libyan or Berber gods. Both the Punic and Berber languages persisted, though the official speech was Latin. Roman law was enforced in the lands near the network of Roman roads; but in the gaps native customs and even some form of native rule persisted. The proconsular province of Africa was the most completely romanized, and was always richer than Numidia and the Mauretanias.

4. The most fertile corn districts were the hinterland of Oea and Leptis, the Bagradas valley, and the country round Cirta; productivity depended on the magnificent water-system established by Rome. Other exports were oil, precious woods, marble, minerals, purple dyes, amphitheatre beasts, slaves, minerals, gold dust, and ostrich eggs. African wine was not highly esteemed. The great estates were run on slave labour, and the country was a paradise for sportsmen, as is shown by the mosaics, in which the Africans reached a high degree of skill. Surviving remains testify to great building activity, which lasted from the first century to the middle of the fourth. Till the Moslem invasion Roman Africa seems to have maintained a higher degree of continuous prosperity than any other part of the Empire.

5. A force of about 30,000 men sufficed to protect the four provinces, till Moorish and Gaetulian tribesmen raided successfully in the fourth century. The victory of the Vandals (q.v.) was due largely to religious dissensions. The Africans embraced Christianity with enthusiasm, and the work of Tertullian, Cyprian, and Augustine did much to mould the thought and organization of Western Christendom. But this same enthusiasm produced the Donatist and Circumcellion heresies. Yet Byzantine Africa was still vigorous enough to send Heraclius eastward to restore the power of Constantinople in the seventh century. His name ends the long list of emperors which Africa gave to the throne, a list beginning with Titus and Domitian, whose mother was born in Sabratha, and continuing through Clodius Albinus, the Severi, and Macrinus. The tie with the Eastern Empire lasted till the end of the seventh century, when the Berbers were defeated at Thysdrus (q.v.) and Carthage surrendered to Hassan.

Inscriptions: *CIL* viii and Supplements. *Inscriptions latines de l'Algérie* i (1922), ii (1938), by S. Gsell; *Inscriptions latines de l'Afrique* (1923), by R. Cagnat and J. Toutain; *Inscriptions latines de la Tunisie* (1944) by A. Merlin.
Atlas archéologique de la Tunisie (1st series by E. Babelon, etc., 1892–1913; 2nd series by R. Cagnat and A. Merlin, from 1914); *Atlas archéologique de l'Algérie* by S. Gsell (1902–11). A. N. Sherwin-White, 'Geographical Factors in Roman Algeria', *JRS* 1944, 1 f.
S. Gsell, *Histoire ancienne de l'Afrique du Nord* i–viii (1914–29); E. Albertini, *L'Afrique romaine*[4] (1937); S. Gsell, *Les Monuments antiques de l'Algérie* (2 vols. 1901); J. Toutain, *Les Cités romaines de la Tunisie* (1895); T. R. S. Broughton, *The Romanization of Africa Proconsularis* (U.S.A. 1929); E. Albertini, in *CAH* xi, ch. 12; R. M. Haywood in T. Frank, *Econ. Surv.* iv (1938); Rostovtzeff, *Roman Empire*, ch. 7; Pallu de Lessert, *Fastes des provinces d'Afrique* (2 vols. 1896–1901); R. Cagnat, *L'Armée romaine d'Afrique*[2] (1912); E. S. Bouchier, *Life and Letters in Roman Africa* (1913); H. Leclercq, *Afrique chrétienne* (1904); S. Gagé, 'Nouveaux aspects de l'Afrique chrétienne', in *Annales de l'École des Hautes Études de Gand*, i (1937); Essays in *Africa Romana* (1935). On the African *limes* see bibliography in A. Piganiol, *Histoire de Rome* (1939), 415.
W. N. W.

AFRICANUS, see CAECILIUS (6), JULIUS (1) *and* (2), *and* SCIPIO (5) *and* (11).

AFTER-LIFE. In Greek and Roman thought, bound by no generally received dogma or revelation, numerous and often contradictory concepts of the after-life existed side by side. These peoples were concerned primarily with this life, but, certain philosophers apart, a belief in some sort of survival after death was almost universal. That the dead live on in the tomb was perhaps the most primitive, and most enduring, concept of all. There they still feel human wants, which are satisfied both by the household objects buried or burned with the body and by the continued tendance regularly paid to the dead by their families. Already in Mycenaean times this tendance seems to have given rise, in the case of individuals especially powerful both in life and death, to the continuing cult of heroes by persons not related to them and eventually by the whole community. By a different line of development arose festivals such as the Attic Anthesteria in which the dead in general received attention.

2. The belief that the dead dwell together in a common, subterranean abode, the realm of Hades and Persephone, dark and gloomy like the grave, found its classic expression in Homer (especially *Od.* 11), and so became fixed as the popular eschatology of all antiquity. Thither all mortals must repair, there good and evil alike lead a shadowy and cheerless existence. The dead need nothing and are not to be feared, for Homer's aristocratic society, separated from the ancestral tombs, has forgotten or ignores the older ideas (which, however, reappear in the post-Homeric age), and the elaborate funeral rites are in the main but meaningless survivals.

3. A totally different conception, that of Elysium or the Isles of the Blest, situated at the ends of the earth, appears in Homer (*Od.* 4. 561–9) and Hesiod (*Op.* 167–73) as the place to which certain favoured heroes, exempted from death, are translated by the gods. Elysium appears to be a survival from Minoan religion; when a later age concerned itself with the fate of the blessed *dead*, Elysium was transferred to the nether regions, in conformity with Greek ideas and the Homeric picture.

4. By the sixth century the Eleusinian Mysteries, an old, probably pre-Greek, agrarian cult, through an associa-

tion of its chthonic divinities and the powers of the underworld, had begun to promise to its initiates a happier lot in the after-life (*Hymn. Hom. Cer.* 480–2; Ar. *Ran.* 154–8, 455–9); apparently, there as in this world they will continue to celebrate the Mysteries. A more clearly ethical note was struck in some mystic speculation, notably that reflected in Pind. *Ol.* 2 and frs. 131 and 133 Bergk. The divine origin of the soul was affirmed; popular ideas of punishment after death were combined with a doctrine of metempsychosis, and assurances of blessedness were held out to those who, throughout a series of existences in this and the other world, should lead pure lives. These or similar ideas were entertained by Pythagoreans and by Orphics, and had wide currency, but it is doubtful that there was any consistent doctrine of 'Orphism'.

5. Hitherto the hope of immortality had been at most based on intuition or religious teaching. Plato, whose eschatology was profoundly influenced by 'Orphism', however much he scorned its baser manifestations, first supplied this hope with a philosophic foundation, by arguments based on anamnesis, the Theory of Ideas, and ethical considerations. The precise nature of immortality he never defines, but his intense conviction that to the good man nothing but good can come and that the highest part of man's nature is allied to God has had far-reaching consequences.

6. Aristotle denied the power of survival to all but the intellectual part of man's tripartite soul, and even this is deprived of all sensibility. The Hellenistic age was, in general, little inclined to speculate on the after-life. The Academy adopted a thoroughly sceptical attitude. Epicurus and his followers attacked the fear of death with the claim that the soul, like the body, was composed of material atoms, and was dissipated at death. While some Stoics admitted a limited survival, at least of the souls of the wise, until the next cosmic conflagration, Panaetius denied even this. Posidonius, however, reverted to Platonic language and imagery, and the first century B.C. witnessed a considerable revival of interest in the after-life.

7. The Thraco-Phrygian cults of Dionysus and Sabazius and the hellenized mysteries of Attis and of Isis offered to many adepts the assurance of a blessed after-life—whether the dead was thought of as inhabiting the old underworld, or whether his continued existence was transferred to the celestial spheres. This belief in a celestial immortality, which was in no sense limited to the mystery religions, derived its popularity from the new concept of the universe as a series of concentric spheres around the earth and from philosophic speculations on the soul, whether in the Platonic sense of something from the world of Being which had descended into the world of Becoming, or the Stoic sense of something essentially Fire. Such ideas found easy acceptance in the cult of Mithras (q.v.), who was identified with the Sun, and in that more general solar piety which played so large a part in the later religious life of antiquity.

8. A final word on the specifically Italic concepts of the after-life: the ghosts of the dead join the undifferentiated mass of *Manes* or *Lemures* in the underworld (*Inferi*), and can return only at certain specified times, as at the feast of the Lemuria in May; no idea of divine retribution is discernible. On this primitive core of belief was superimposed the whole range of Hellenic conceptions, at first through Magna Graecia and through Etruria, which had combined Greek ideas with an elaborate demonology, and later by direct contact with Greece and the East. From the latter years of the Republic on, the Graeco-Roman world was essentially one in its development of religious and philosophic ideas of the after-life.

A. Brelich, *Aspetti della morte nelle iscrizioni sepolcrali dell' impero Romano* (Diss. Pannonicae 1, 7, 1937); F. Cumont, *After Life in*

Roman Paganism (U.S.A. 1922); *Recherches sur le Symbolisme funéraire des Romains* (1942); A. Dieterich, *Nekyia²* (1913); L. R. Farnell, *Greek Hero-Cults and Ideas of Immortality* (1921); W. K. C. Guthrie, *Orpheus and Greek Religion* (1935), ch. 5; C. H. Moore, *Ancient Beliefs in the Immortality of the Soul* (1931); M. P. Nilsson, *Minoan-Mycenaean Religion* (Lund, 1927), ch. 17; 'Early Orphism', *Harv. Theol. Rev.* 1935; A. D. Nock, *Harv. Theol. Rev.* 1932, 1940; E. Rohde, *Psyche* (Engl. Transl. of 8th ed., 1925); Mrs. A. Strong, *Apotheosis and After Life* (1915); I. M. Linforth, *The Arts of Orpheus* (U.S.A. 1941). *See* PSYCHE, SOUL, TRANSMIGRATION.

F. R. W.

AGAMEMNON, in mythology, son of Atreus and brother of Menelaus (qq.v.); king of Mycenae, or Argos; probably an historical person who, if not overlord of some or all of the princes of the Mycenaean era, was the most important of them.

In Homer, A. is commander-in-chief of the Greek expedition against Troy. In the *Iliad* he is a man of personal valour, but lacking resolution and easily discouraged. His quarrel with Achilles (q.v.) supplies the mainspring of the poem's action. The *Odyssey* (1. 35 ff.; 4. 512 ff.; 11. 405 ff.; 24. 96–7) tells how, on his return, he was carried by the wind outside his own territory to the barony of Aegisthus (q.v.), the lover of his wife Clytemnestra, sister of Helen, who treacherously set upon him and his men at a banquet and killed them all, Clytemnestra also killing Cassandra, daughter of Priam, whom A. had brought back with him. This story later authors retell with elaborations and small changes, e.g. the scene is generally (as in Aesch. *Ag.*) transferred to Argos.

The *Cypria* is the earliest evidence for the sacrifice of A.'s daughter Iphigenia (q.v.). The cause of it was the offence given to Artemis by A., who after a successful hunt boasted that he was a better hunter than she. Calchas, when the fleet was wind-bound at Aulis, explained that the goddess was the cause and the sacrifice must be made to appease her. Iphigenia was therefore sent for to Aulis on the pretext that she was to be married to Achilles. For sundry variants, see Rose, *Handbook of Greek Mythology²*, 119 and notes.

In other stories A. appears as a subsidiary figure, or is handled with more or less disregard of tradition, as in the fantastic perversion of the legend in Hyginus, *Fab.* 88.

In historical times A. had cults at several places (see Farnell, *Hero-Cults*, 321–2 and note 55). The remarkable statement (Lycophron 335 and 1369, with schol.) that A. was called Zeus at Sparta has never been satisfactorily explained. In any case, there is no earlier evidence for it, and it seems to be a development of the Hellenistic period.

Agamemnon's children in all accounts include Orestes (q.v.). A quite unsupported story (Hyg. *Fab.* 121), gives him an illegitimate son, Chryses, by his slave-concubine Chryseis (*Il.* 1. 111, etc.). His daughters are Chrysothemis, Laodice, and Iphianassa in *Il.* 9. 145; Iphigenia, whom Homer does not mention, seems to be a later substitution for Iphianassa.

H. J. R.

AGANIPPE, in mythology, daughter of the river-god Permessus (Paus. 9. 29. 5: spelling 'Ter-'), nymph of the spring of that name on Helicon (Callim. *fr.* 100ᵉ 4 Schneider), sacred to the Muses.

AGAPENOR (Ἀγαπήνωρ), in mythology, leader of the Arcadian contingent against Troy (*Il.* 2. 609); son of Ancaeus (q.v.). On the way back from Troy he arrived at Cyprus (Lycoph. 479 ff.), where he founded Paphos and a temple of Aphrodite and settled (Paus. 8. 5. 2).

AGASIAS, (1) sculptor, son of Dositheus, of Ephesus. He signed the Borghese warrior in the Louvre (Winter, *KB*, 382. 3), a nude figure striding forward to parry an attack from above, showing remarkable knowledge of anatomy and probably deriving from an earlier group. The signature and another from Thessaly are dated late second to early first century B.C.

(2) sculptor, son of Menophilus, of Ephesus, known from signatures in Delos, of about 100 B.C. One base may belong to the wounded warrior of Delos, part of a group (Winter, *KB*, 350. 1; C. Picard, *BCH* 1932, 491).

T. B. L. W.

AGATHARCHIDES, Greek grammarian and Peripatetic of Cnidos, became guardian to a young Ptolemy (? Soter II) of Egypt, *c.* 116 B.C.

WORKS: (i) Τὰ κατὰ τὴν Ἀσίαν, on the Diadochi; (ii) Τ.κ.τ. Εὐρώπην, on history ?323 B.C. to fall of Macedon; (iii) Περὶ τῆς Ἐρυθρᾶς θαλάσσης; [(iv) epitome of (iii), not A.'s? (v) on Troglodytes (q.v.)—same as (iii)?]; (vi) epitome of writers on (?) wonders; (vii) historical Ἐκλογαὶ ἱστοριῶν; (viii) Intercourse of Friends.

Extracts survive from (iii), in Photius and Diodorus bk. 3, dealing with elephant-hunts; name of 'Red' Sea, etc.; Ethiopians; gold-mining on Egypto-Ethiopian frontier; races and animals west of Red Sea; Arabians, especially Sabaeans.

FHG iii (historical fragments); *GGM* i. liv-lxxiii, 111-95 (Red Sea); E. H. Bunbury, *Hist. of Anc. Geog.* (1879) ii. 50 ff. E. H. W.

AGATHARCHUS (5th c. B.C.), painter, of Samos. He made scenery for Aeschylus (between 468 B.C. and 456 B.C., since Aristotle ascribes the introduction of scene-painting to Sophocles), and was compelled by Alcibiades (*c.* 430 B.C.?) to paint his house (with perspective scenes?). He wrote a book on scene-painting, which inspired Anaxagoras and Democritus to write on perspective. He was the first painter to use perspective on a large scale (isolated instances occur on vases from the late sixth century B.C.).

Overbeck, 1118–25; Pfuhl, 723; P. M. Schuhl, *Platon et l'art de son temps* (1933). T. B. L. W.

AGATHIAS (A.D. 536–82), surnamed *Scholasticus*, 'the advocate', was born in Aeolis, studied law in Alexandria and Byzantium, and practised it in Byzantium until his death. He is best known for his work as compiler of a *Circle* of epigrams on which the existing Anthology (q.v.) is based—see his preface (*Anth. Pal.* 4. 3). The Anthology contains about a hundred epigrams by him, mostly elegant but lifeless adaptations of Alexandrian themes and language. His history, *The Reign of Justinian*, a sequel to Procopius covering the years A.D. 552–8, is romantic and highly poetical in style.

W. S. Teuffel, *Studien und Charakteristiken* (1889), 296. G. H.

AGATHINUS, CLAUDIUS (*c.* A.D. 50–100), pupil of the Stoic L. Annaeus Cornutus and of Athenaeus of Attaleia (q.v. 3), the founder of the pneumatic school of medicine. He was the teacher of Archigenes (q.v.). Adopting some of the tenets of the empirical and methodical schools of medicine, he founded an eclectic school. Works: Περὶ ἐλλεβόρου; Περὶ ἡμιτριταίων (on tertian fevers); Περὶ σφυγμῶν (on the pulse).

PW i. 746. W. D. R.

AGATHOCLES (361–289 B.C.), tyrant of Syracuse. He became an officer and democratic leader in the Civil Wars after 325. Making himself tyrant (317), he endeavoured to conciliate the poor, and to reinforce army and fleet. In an attempt to extend his power, he brought on long wars with the Sicilian Greeks and Carthage. After great successes he was beaten by the Carthaginians and blockaded in Syracuse (311). He now resolved to attack Carthage in Africa. Having luckily escaped and effected his landing, he seriously threatened Carthage. Meanwhile, the Carthaginian attacks on Syracuse failed. Agathocles increased his power by incorporating the troops of Ophellas (q.v.). Feeling secure in Africa, he shortly returned to Sicily, where he fought hard against Acragas (308/7). But matters in Africa took a bad turn, and A., unable to improve them, left his army in the lurch (307/6). Carthage, however, was too weak to resume attack. After some concluding campaigns, A. reigned peacefully over east Sicily, assuming the title of king in 304. He subsequently was engaged in various operations in Italy. The last years of this adventurous and cruel man were spoilt by dreadful discord within his family. Renouncing the dynastic succession, he restored liberty to Syracuse by his last will. But the city could not bear liberty any more. Agathocles, the only Hellenistic king among western Greeks, and their last leader, left a heap of ruins.

Sources (deriving mostly from his enemy, Timaeus): Diodorus, bks. 19–21; Justin, bks. 22–3; Polyaenus, bk. 5. Modern Literature: H. J. W. Tillyard, *Agathocles* (1908); M. Cary, *CAH* viii, ch. 19; Glotz, *Hist. grecque* iv. 375 ff. V. E.

AGATHON, tragic poet, son of Tisamenus of Athens, and remarkable for his personal beauty, won his first victory at the Lenaea in 416 B.C., when he was probably under thirty years of age (Pl. *Symp.* 198 a). The *Symposium* of Plato represents a feast in honour of his victory. In 411 he heard and approved of Antiphon's speech in his own defence (Arist. *Eth. Eud.* 3. 5)—this may mean that his sentiments were not on the democratic side—and in the same year he was caricatured in Aristophanes' *Thesmophoriazusae*, but about 407 he went to the court of Archelaus in Macedonia (Ar. *Ran.* 83–5; Ael. *VH* 13. 4; *Anecd. Ox.* iv. 269), and died there, probably about 401. He came under the influence of the sophists, Gorgias and Prodicus (Pl. *Prt.* 305 d). His speech in Plato's *Symposium* is in the manner of Gorgias, and some quotations from his tragedies are in a pointed, epigrammatic style, probably due to sophistic influence. His originality was shown by the composition of a tragedy (*Antheus*, not Ἄνθος) in which characters and plot were his own invention, not taken from legend (Arist. *Poet.* 9), by making choral odes, for the first time, mere interludes (ἐμβόλιμα) without reference to the plot (ibid. 13), and by the free use in tragedy of the chromatic scale and various florid musical figures (Plut. *Quaest. conv.* 3. 1. 1). Aristophanes (*Thesm.* 101 ff.) parodies his lyrics and hints that they are voluptuous and effeminate. Aristotle also criticizes him (*Poet.* 8) for including too lengthy a story, such as the whole sack of Troy, within a single plot. He was evidently a 'modernizer' in tragedy, who sat loose to tradition but was not without genius, though less than forty lines of his work survive. (*TGF* 763–9.) A. W. P.-C.

AGATHOS DAIMON, see DAEMON.

AGDISTIS, a form of the Phrygian mother-goddess; at Pessinus Cybele (q.v.) was called A. (Strabo 469, 567). According to the myth (*see* ATTIS), she was originally androgynous. Her cult spread to various parts of Anatolia, to Egypt (by 250 B.C.), to Attica (with that of Attis in Piraeus 4th–3rd, cc., *IG* ii². 4671; at Rhamnus, 83/2 B.C.), Lesbos, and Panticapeum. At Lydian Philadelphia her private shrine (1st c. B.C.) enforced a strict moral code (*SIG* 985; O. Weinreich, *Sitz. Heid.* 1919). There and elsewhere A. appears with *theoi soteres*. *See* ANATOLIAN DEITIES.

H. Hepding, *Attis* (1903); Hiller v. Gaertringen, *ARW* 1926. Rhamnus inscription: K. A. Rhomaios, Ἑλληνικά 1928; P. Roussel, *Rev. Ét. Anc.* 1930. F. R. W.

AGELADAS, Greek sculptor of the Argive school. The earliest work associated with his name is a statue of an Olympic victor, Anochos, whose victory was in 520 B.C. He was also the reputed teacher of Myron, Polycletus, and Phidias (qq.v.). This would bring his activities down to about 470 and harmonizes with the general character of his work, so far as it is known. He was, like most of the leading sculptors of the fifth century, mainly a worker in bronze. His most famous work was the statue of Zeus at Ithome, said by Pausanias to have been made for the Messenians settled in Naupactus. It appears on silver coins of Messenia of the fourth century.

Both the style and the attitude of the Zeus, who strides forward hurling a thunderbolt, with an eagle perched on his left hand, indicate a date c. 470–460. He also made a statue at Aegium of 'Zeus as a Boy', representations of which appear on the Roman coins of that town; its attitude is similar to that of the Zeus of Ithome. The bronze statue of a god found recently in the sea off Artemisium is attributed by some to Ageladas. S. C.

AGENOR (Ἀγήνωρ), name of several mythological persons, the most important being the king of Tyre (or Sidon), father of Europa (q.v.). On the disappearance of his daughter, he sent out his sons to look for her, bidding them not come back without her; hence Phoenix, Cilix, and Cadmus founded respectively the Phoenician and Cilician peoples and Thebes in Boeotia. His genealogy, which varies somewhat (see Stoll in Roscher's *Lexikon*, s.v. 'Agenor'), links various Eastern peoples together. H. J. R.

AGENTES IN REBUS, under the Roman Empire, a corps of imperial agents, organized in *scholae* on military lines, under the control of the *magister officiorum* (q.v.). First heard of in A.D. 319, they replaced the *frumentarii* (imperial secret service agents) of the earlier Empire. Their employments were various. They might carry dispatches or supervise the imperial post. But what made them feared and hated, despite their humble birth and rank, was the fact that they travelled through the provinces as spies, collecting evidence of evasion of taxes and of treasonable conduct of every description.

O. Seeck, *PW*, s.v. H. M.

AGER CAMPANUS, *see* CAPUA.

AGER FALERNUS, *see* FALERNUS.

AGER PUBLICUS. I. IN ITALY. During her conquest of Italy Rome penalized such communities as offered a stubborn resistance or subsequently rebelled, by confiscating a part (usually a third) of their territories. The use to which the public land should be put was from an early date—according to tradition as far back as 486 B.C.—disputed between the patricians, who preferred to maintain public ownership, under which they could occupy it as *possessores* (see POSSESSIO), and the plebs, who wished it to be distributed among themselves. As the *ager publicus* grew by conquest, the patricians became more liberal. Some land was distributed to individuals (*viritim assignatus*); part of the territory taken from Veii was so treated in 393. More was allocated to colonies of Roman citizens; this practice, according to tradition, dates back to the early fifth century. Larger areas were devoted to the Latin colonies which Rome planted after the dissolution of the Latin League in 338. By the Licinio-Sextian laws of 367 (see STOLO) no citizen might occupy more than 500 *iugera* of this land.

The defections of the allied communities during the Second Punic War were punished by extensive confiscation of land, and the conquest of Cisalpine Gaul added large areas to the *ager publicus*. Most of the Gallic land was devoted to colonies, and the remainder was distributed in small holdings (173 B.C.). Elsewhere few colonies were planted, and vast tracts, especially in the south, remained in the hands of the State. The best of this land was leased by the censors and brought in a good rent to the State, but large tracts were occupied by *possessores*, being mostly used for ranching. The *possessores* were supposed to pay dues, and the size of their tenures was legally limited by the Licinio-Sextian laws. But the laws were regularly evaded or ignored, and the collection of dues was lax.

Under the agrarian law of Ti. Gracchus (133) a commission was set up to resume for the State public lands occupied in excess of the Licinio-Sextian limit (increased in favour of *possessores* who had sons) and to distribute them in small holdings, which were to remain public and pay a *vectigal*. Much land was distributed under this scheme, which was revived by C. Gracchus in 123–122 B.C., until in 119 the land commission was suppressed. C. Gracchus also planned several colonies, one of which at least was planted. By the agrarian law of 111 the Gracchan small holdings, whose *vectigal* had been abolished in 122, and the holdings of *possessores* within the Gracchan limit were declared private land, the *vectigal* which had been reimposed in 119 on the latter being abolished. After this law the following categories of land remained public: (*a*) open spaces at Rome; (*b*) roads; (*c*) lands leased by the censors, notably the *ager Campanus*; (*d*) lands assigned to Roman and Latin colonies and *municipia* corporately; (*e*) holdings allotted on condition of maintaining the roads; (*f*) lands granted to State creditors (*in trientabulis*); (*g*) pastures on which contiguous owners had exclusive rights (*compascua*); (*h*) all other public lands, which were henceforth to be common pasture. Sulla confiscated the territories of many cities which opposed him for the benefit of his veterans. Caesar in 59 distributed the *ager Campanus* to Pompey's veterans. Octavian in 30 expropriated cities which had favoured Antony to find land for his veterans, but compensated the owners in money or provincial land.

II. In the provinces. According to Gaius the *dominium* in all provincial soil was vested in the Roman people or the emperor; but this theory, which probably did not arise till the first century A.D., had no practical import. The public land acquired under the Republic comprised (*a*) the estates of prominent opponents, in so far as these were not immediately sold or given away; (*b*) the territories of cities which were, like Carthage and Corinth, destroyed or were merely, as were a few Sicilian and Pamphylian communities, punished by the loss of their lands; (*c*) the royal lands of kings who were deposed or bequeathed their kingdoms to Rome. These comprised some Macedonian estates, Attalid lands in the Chersonese, and an extensive tract of desert in Cyrenaica; the Bithynian and Pontic royal lands seem to have been assigned by Pompey to the cities of the new province. Most of the provincial public lands (except in Cyrenaica) seem to have been alienated by the beginning of the Principate, some, such as Carthage and Corinth, being devoted to Roman colonies. Under the early Principate more royal lands were added to the *ager publicus*, notably the γῆ βασιλική of Egypt and extensive domains in Cappadocia.

The *ager publicus*, both in Italy and the provinces, was swelled by *bona vacantia*, *caduca*, and *damnatorum*. These sources, negligible under the Republic, became important under the Principate owing to the severe *leges caducariae* passed by Augustus and to the frequent condemnations of wealthy men. All public lands gradually passed under the administration of the emperor, and most seem eventually to have been assimilated to the imperial estates; *see* DOMAINS (*b*, *Imperial*).

M. Weber, *Römische Agrargeschichte* (1891); E. G. Hardy, *Six Roman Laws* (1901), 35 ff.; J. Vančura, *PW* xii. 1150–85; Tenney Frank, *JRS* 1927, 141–61; L. Zancan, *Ager publicus* (1935); A. H. M. Jones, *JRS* 1941, 26–31. A. H. M. J.

AGESILAUS (444–360 B.C.), Spartan king, son of Archidamus and half-brother of Agis II, secured the succession in 399, largely through Lysander's influence, in preference to Leotychidas, whose legitimacy was suspect. Lysander had hoped to use Agesilaus for his own ends, but was quickly brought to heel. As commander in Asia Minor from 396, Agesilaus overran Phrygia and routed Tissaphernes, but failed to check the growing Persian naval menace. Recalled with his army in 394, he took the overland route and reached Coronea almost unopposed. The ensuing battle with the Boeotian and allied forces was a Pyrrhic victory, and Agesilaus had to evacuate the country. He won minor successes, however, in the vicinity of Corinth and in Acarnania

(391–388). He condoned, on grounds of expediency, Spartan intervention against Mantinea, Phlius, and Olynthus (in violation of the principle of autonomy enjoined by the peace of Antalcidas), and the still more flagrant occupation of the Cadmea by Phoebidas (382), and attempt on the Piraeus by Sphodrias (378). The alliance between Thebes and Athens resultant on this policy was unshaken by Agesilaus' invasions of Boeotia in 378 and 377. His refusal in 371 to admit Epaminondas' claim to represent all Boeotia at the peace congress in Sparta precipitated the Battle of Leuctra. In the years of Sparta's humiliation he organized the defence of the city (370 and 362) and sought to augment the State revenues by foreign service (in Asia Minor with Ariobarzanes 364, and in Egypt with Nectanebo 361). He died on the homeward voyage from Egypt (360).

Despite his poor physique and a strain of romanticism, Agesilaus was typically Spartan in his qualities and limitations. He was an efficient soldier, but a better tactician than strategist, and he failed to understand the importance of sea-power. The narrowness of his loyalties dissipated those moral assets by virtue of which alone Sparta could maintain her hegemony.

Ancient sources: Xenophon, *Agesilaus* (the encomiastic tribute of a personal friend), *Hellenica*; *Hellenica Oxyrhynchia*; Nepos, *Agesilaus*; Plutarch, *Agesilaus*. Modern literature: H. Lins, *Kritische Betrachtung der Feldzüge des Agesilaos in Kleinasien* (1914). D. E. W. W.

AGGENIUS URBICUS (perhaps 5th c. A.D.), *gromaticus*, author of a commentary on Frontinus' treatise *De controversiis agrorum*.

AGIADS (Ἀγιάδαι) was the name of the senior royal house at Sparta. The Agiad dynasty enjoyed a ceremonial precedence over the other (Eurypontid) house, but possessed no constitutional privileges. The most notable Agiad kings were Cleomenes I and III, Leonidas, and Pausanias (qq.v.).

AGIS II, son of Archidamus, king of Sparta *c.* 427–*c.* 399. Though active in the Archidamian War, he first gained distinction in the campaign of 418 against the Argives and other enemies of Sparta. After failing to utilize what appeared to be a strategic advantage, he subsequently outmanœuvred his opponents near Mantinea and won a decisive victory, which re-established Spartan prestige. In 413, adopting the suggestion of Alcibiades, he fortified Decelea as a permanent base for plundering Attica. Remaining here, he attempted to exert an autocratic control over Spartan policy, but his influence waned when the centre of war moved to Asia. He collaborated with Lysander in the blockade of Athens in 405–404, and in his last years reduced Elis by a successful invasion. Agis was a fine soldier whose qualities are underrated by Thucydides, but, like so many Spartan kings, he seems to have lacked constructive statesmanship.

Thucydides, bks. 5 and 8. H. D. W.

AGIS III, king of Sparta (338–331 B.C.), Eurypontid, organized the resistance of the Greeks against Macedonia during Alexander's Asiatic campaign. Assisted by the Persian admirals' gifts of ships and money, he assembled an army, consisting mostly of 8,000 Greek mercenaries, fugitives after Issus. He was successful in Crete and then in Peloponnesus, where some States revolted from Macedonia (331). Athens, however, stood aloof (in spite of Ps.-Dem. 17), and so did Megalopolis, Messene, and Argos. While besieging Megalopolis, Agis was forced to meet Antipater and an army almost twice as numerous as his own. After a hard struggle, he was beaten and died heroically. His death put an end to all Greek revolts against Alexander.

Arrian, Diodorus, Curtius. Berve, ii, no. 15; Tarn, *CAH* vi. 433 f.; Glotz, *Hist. grecque* iv. 194 f. V. E.

AGIS IV (*c.* 262–241 B.C.), son of Eudamidas, ascended the Eurypontid throne at Sparta in 244. Heavy mortgages, large estates in single hands, and a depleted citizen-body were evils he resolved to cure by a return to 'Lycurgus' constitution'. In 243, as ephor, his supporter Lysander introduced relevant bills; in 242 A. deposed new, reactionary ephors, and Leonidas, the Agiad king, whom he had already impeached, fled to Tegea. Supported by his rich uncle Agesilaus, A. now burnt the mortgages; this done, Agesilaus turned against him, and while A. was absent assisting his Achaean allies against Aetolia, Leonidas returned and seized power. Arriving back, A. took sanctuary: but the ephors decoyed him out and executed him.

High-minded but unrealistic, he fell before cleverer men: his death became the legend around which a new generation rallied.

Plut. *Agis.* K. J. Beloch, *Gr. Gesch.* iv (1928); W. H. Porter, *Hermathena* 1935. F. W. W.

AGNATIO, *see* PATRIA POTESTAS.

AGON, in Greek Comedy, *see* COMEDY (ORIGINS OF), para. 2; COMEDY (OLD), para. 8.

AGON HOMERI ET HESIODI, a Greek account of a competition in hexameter poetry between Homer and Hesiod, preceded and followed by other information about the origin, life, and death of each poet. The competition takes place at Chalcis (or Aulis), on the occasion of the games at Amphidamas' funeral, and his brother, Panedes, is one of the judges. Hesiod asks Homer questions, which he answers successfully, and then recites verses, apparently nonsense, to each of which Homer replies with another verse which makes sense of the verse propounded. Then Panedes orders each poet to recite his finest passage, and afterwards, though the audience favours Homer, crowns Hesiod and awards the prize, a tripod, to him, on the ground that he encouraged peaceful activities, whereas Homer described fighting. Hesiod dedicates the tripod, with an inscription, to the Muses of Helicon. The story in its present form is not earlier than Hadrian, who is mentioned in it, but much of the material is older. All the writers cited are early. The central part of the competition itself is almost certainly derived from the *Μουσεῖον* of Alcidamas, fifth century B.C., which is cited for an incident connected with the death of Hesiod, and to which Stobaeus (120. 3) attributes two verses of the *Agon* (78–9). Aristophanes quotes from it (*Pax* 1282–3 = *Agon* 119–20), and Plutarch (*Conv. sept. sap.* 10. 153 c–154 a) attributes to Lesches (q.v.) the initial verses of the central part of the *Agon* (96–101), but in a rather different version. The verses in the central part do not occur in our texts of Homer and Hesiod, but all appear old, fifth century or earlier. The origin of the story is probably Hesiod's claim (*Op.* 650–8) to have won a tripod in a competition at the funeral games of Amphidamas and to have dedicated it to the Muses. The competition in the *Agon* may well have formed part of a life of Homer, earlier than Archilochus, and possibly by Lesches himself.

Text: O.C.T., *Homeri Opera* v. 218–38. Criticism: A. Busse, *Rh. Mus.* lxiv (1909), 108–19; T. W. Allen, *Homer: the Origins and Transmissions* (1924), 20–7. W. F. J. K.

AGONES, public festivals at which competitors contended for a prize, were a distinctive feature of Greek life. Religious in origin, most of the games were under the patronage of a god or hero, the smaller gatherings depending on local support, the larger drawing spectators from all parts of the Greek world. The best-known were the Olympian, Pythian, Nemean, and Isthmian games, together with the Dionysia and Panathenaea at Athens (qq.v.). In most cases chariot-races, foot-races, and field events were the chief attractions, but at Athens the first place was given to the dramatic competitions in honour of Dionysus. *See also* ATHLETICS. Introduced at Rome in 186 B.C., contests in the Greek manner became fairly common towards the close of the Republic. A regular quinquennial festival (Neronia) was established by Nero, a quadrennial *Agon Capitolinus* by Domitian in A.D. 86, and an *Agon Solis* by Aurelian in 274.

Friedländer, ii. 117–30. F. A. W.

AGONIUM, name given to 9 Jan., 17 March, 21 May, and 11 Dec. in the Roman calendar. It does not denote a festival of any particular god, and the ancients were in doubt of its meaning, witness the etymologies (Festus, p. 9 Lindsay, and note in his larger ed. *Gloss. Lat.* iv. 104). Possibly it is a latinization of ἀγών, in its old sense of 'assembly'. The January entry may have displaced the name of the festival of Janus, presumably **Ianuar.*

H. J. R.

AGONOTHETES, *see* CHOREGIA.

AGORACRITUS, Greek sculptor, a native of Paros and pupil of Phidias. Pliny (36. 17) records that he was defeated in a competition for a statue of Aphrodite and sold his statue to the people of Rhamnus in Attica, where it served as a figure of Nemesis. Pausanias, however, attributes the statue of Nemesis at Rhamnus to Phidias, who made it from a block of marble brought by the Persians to make a trophy at Marathon. Pausanias gives a most detailed description of the statue and its base, which was adorned with high reliefs. Excavations at Rhamnus have revealed part of a colossal female head, now in the British Museum, which corresponds closely to the description of Pausanias. Antigonus of Carystus (quoted by Pliny) mentions that the statue at Rhamnus bore a tablet with the name of Agoracritus. Clearly antiquity was in doubt as to its authorship, but the attribution to Agoracritus is generally accepted to-day. Fragments of the reliefs on the bases have also been found. A Roman relief at Stockholm preserves versions of four of the figures on the base, clearly copied directly from the base itself. S. C.

AGORANOMOI (ἀγορανόμοι), overseers of the market, an office known in more than 120 Greek States. In classical times they were usually elected by lot. In Athens there were ten, five for the city and five for the Piraeus. They kept order in the market, saw to the quality and correct weight of goods, and collected market dues. They had power to punish small infractions of their rules with fines, from the proceeds of which they maintained and extended the market buildings; for graver offences they initiated prosecutions before the dicasteries and presided at the trials. *See also* METRONOMOI, SITOPHYLAKES, ASTYNOMOI. A. W. G.

AGRICOLA (1), GNAEUS JULIUS (A.D. 40–93), of Forum Julii (*Fréjus*), was son of Julius Graecinus, senator, and Julia Procilla; he married Domitia Decidiana, and had one son (died an infant) and one daughter. He was educated at the University of Massilia. He was *tribunus militum* to Suetonius Paulinus in Britain (A.D. 61); quaestor of Asia (64); *tribunus plebis* (66); praetor (68); commissioner for the recovery of temple property (68); recruiting officer for Mucianus (69); legate of the Twentieth Legion, in Britain (71–3); legate of Aquitania (74–7); consul (77); legate of Britain (from 77 or 78).

His career, in particular the British governorship, is described in his *Life* by Tacitus, his son-in-law. Previous experience in Britain, shrewd intelligence, provincial sympathies, and an exceptional eye for country, enabled Agricola both to pacify civilians and to advance far into Scotland, where his permanent outposts at Inchtuthil (*JRS* 1919, 111 ff.), Fendoch (*PSAS* lxxiii. 110–54) and Dealgin Ross (*JRS*, loc. cit.), with others yet undiscovered, blockaded the Highlands. The advance was by stages. North Wales was conquered (Tac. *Agr.* 18); the west coast ('silvas ac aestuaria', *Agr.* 20) was annexed. Then came a preliminary advance to the Tay (*Agr.* 22), gripping the Tweed crossing at Newstead and followed by a temporary consolidation between Forth and Clyde (*Agr.* 23) with forts at Mumrills and Cadder and signal-posts at Bar Hill and Croy Hill (Macdonald, *Roman Wall in Scotland*[2]). The fifth campaign was probably in the south-west (*Agr.* 24), where Agricolan penetration of Ayrshire is now proved (*Antiquity* xiii. 288). The sixth marked annexation beyond the Forth (*Agr.* 25) and campaigning up to the Highlands. In the seventh the Highlands were spurred to defeat at 'mons Graupius' (*Agr.* 29–38) on the fringe of Caledonia (q.v.). Agricola was then recalled after a rather specialized experience which did not fit him for service elsewhere. Roman historians were most struck by his circumnavigation of Britain *Agr.* 38; Dio Cass. 39. 50. 4; 66. 20. 1–2); kindred explorations were also made (Plut. *De def. or.* 18; cf. Dessau, *Hermes* xlvi. 156).

I. A. Richmond, *JRS* 1944, 34–45.   I. A. R.

AGRICOLA (2), SEXTUS CALPURNIUS, waged war as governor of Britain for Marcus and Verus (A.D. 163); was legate in the German phase of the Marcomannic War and governor of *Tres Daciae* in 167–8. British inscriptions attest his military building at Corbridge and Chesterholm in Tynedale and at Ribchester on the Ribble; also a change of garrison at Carvoran on Hadrian's Wall.

        I. A. R.

AGRICULTURE (Greek and Roman). The general technique of Greek and Roman agriculture, its utilization of most of the plants, animals, and tools employed until modern times, may have originated in the mesolithic and neolithic periods; but the beginning of the Iron Age, i.e. the dawn of history in Greece and Italy, witnessed a revolutionary change. The iron plough and other tools, now made of the new metal, increased agricultural production as never before. Most of the villagers of the Minoan and Mycenaean regions seem to have been serfs of their kings, but the periods of Homer, Hesiod, and Solon preferred small and economically independent agricultural units, and revolted successfully against the rule of big landlords. Small estates of knights and peasants were now the rule. A few slaves, together with their owner's family, did all normal work. Free labourers were employed during harvest and for tasks for which the farmers and their servants lacked sufficient time. Small irrigation works and canals were necessary almost everywhere. After a year of cultivation the land was left fallow for one, and in some regions, for two years and was ploughed in autumn, in spring, and in summer (in some regions only twice in the year). The production of corn, flax, and vegetables was supplemented by arboriculture, olive-culture, viticulture, and especially pasturage, which were the most lucrative forms of land work.

2. The period of classical Greece witnessed a rational differentiation of the various agricultural plants and their habits, of the different kinds of soil, and of the appropriate manures, and production was stimulated by the growing demand for corn and vegetables in the towns. The time had come for threefold rotation of crops (*IG* ii[2]. 2493 and Xen. *Oec.* 16. 12–15). The agricultural production of Greece must have increased very greatly when the soil could be continuously cultivated without being exhausted. No wonder that the first capitalistic slave estates were established at this time, and that capitalists investing in land began to lease to tenants tracts which were too large for their own or their stewards' management. Small estates remained nevertheless the rule in the Greek motherland, and were common also in Sicily and on the Black Sea coast.

3. From Alexander to Augustus Mediterranean agriculture was improved by many inventions (especially machines for hoisting water). Suitable varieties of plants

and animals were transferred from one part of the civilized world to another, and new crops developed in many countries. Attica seems to have produced 1,100,000–1,250,000 bushels of corn in Alexander's time, of which amount only c. 15–20 per cent. appears to have been wheat. The production of the Hellenistic East increased considerably. The two-crop system originating in the ancient East was improved under Greek management, and independent Greek cultivators were settled throughout the Seleucid Empire.

4. Ptolemaic Egypt introduced a remarkable controlled economy into its agriculture. Oil-seeds, corn, and textile plants had to be cultivated in each region of the Nile country according to an official schedule, which was revised each year. The seed, iron tools, and cattle for agriculture were commonly lent to the cultivators by the government. Almost the whole of the crop had to be paid (for taxes in kind, rent) or sold to the government, which built up a granary system for wheat export throughout the Nile country. Only a few large estates of distinguished owners were partly exempted. Handbooks on agriculture (the sources of Cato, Columella, the *Geoponica*, Mago, Varro) were used in this new cultivation system as well as by the more educated owners of large slave estates, which now superseded many of the peasant homesteads in all Mediterranean countries. Another characteristic of the same period was the surprising extent of division of labour and specialization in Greek and Roman agriculture, and very often the almost capitalistic calculation of expenses, revenues, and profits.

5. The highest standard of ancient cultivation was reached in the Italian agriculture of the later Republic and early Principate. Big slave estates prevailed here, so long as prisoners of war were cheap. The varieties of plants, the rotation of crops, and the other methods of cultivation, amelioration, irrigation, and manuring, bookkeeping, the organization and division of labour, the buildings, tools, and machines were carefully selected from the technical as well as from the economic point of view, and similar methods spread to the provinces.

6. The Roman *villa* (q.v.) of this period underwent decisive changes, as soon as slave economy ceased to pay. Estate management of the highest type had to be confined to comparatively small tracts, so far as cheap labour for it was available. Most of the land had to be given to small tenants who were gradually bound to the soil (*see* COLONUS). This development did not mean the collapse of Graeco-Roman agriculture, but its final preservation. The agricultural methods of small peasants had not been much improved during the prevalence of slave estates; but the landlords of necessity now saw to it that their tenants should learn as much of the results of scientific agriculture as was suitable for their small economic units.

7. The unification of Mediterranean agriculture as seen to-day was completed from the second century A.D. onwards by the popularizing of plants, animals, tools, machines, and methods of estate agriculture under the peasantry of the Empire. Germanic and Oriental prisoners of war, who were settled throughout the Empire, were similarly taught, and transferred such knowledge to their home countries. Agriculture did not break down in Europe after the conquest of the Western Roman Empire. On the contrary, the agriculture of middle and northern Europe was modelled on Late Roman lines; it was a fundamental heritage of the Ancient World. *See also* ARBORICULTURE, BEE-KEEPING, LATIFUNDIA, OLIVE CULTURE, PASTURAGE, VITICULTURE.

PW, s.v. 'Ackerbau'; Kornemann, ibid., s.v. 'Bauernstand' (Suppl. iv), 'Domänen' (Suppl. iv); Orth, ibid., s.v. 'Landwirtschaft'; Heichelheim, ibid., s.v. 'Sitos' (Suppl. vi). E. Bréhaut, *Cato the Censor on Farming* (1933). T. Frank, *CAH* viii, ch. 11; F. Örtel, ibid. x, ch. 13; xii, ch. 7; *Econ. Surv.* i–iv. H. Gummerus, 'Der römische Gutsbetrieb als wirtschaftlicher Organismus' (*Klio*, Suppl. 5, 1905). J. Hasebroek, *Griechische Wirtschafts- und*

Gesellschaftsgeschichte bis zur Perserzeit (1931). V. Hehn, *Kulturpflanzen und Haustiere in ihrem Uebergang aus Asien nach Griechenland und Italien, sowie in das übrige Europa* (1911). F. M. Heichelheim, *Wirtschaftsgeschichte des Altertums* (1938); Index s.vv. 'Dreifelderwirtschaft', 'Gutsbetrieb als Wirtschaftsorganismus', 'Landwirtschaft', 'Zweierntenwirtschaft'. W. E. Heitland, *Agricola* (1921). A. Jardé, *Les Céréales dans l'antiquité grecque* i (1925). G. Mickwitz, *Engl. Hist. Rev.* lii (1937), 577 f. Cl. Préaux, *L'Économie royale des Lagides* (1939). Rostovtzeff, *Roman Empire; Hellenistic World; A Large Estate in the Third Century B.C.* (U.S.A., 1922). E. Savoy, *L'Agriculture à travers les âges* i, ii (1935–6). M. Schnebel, *Die Landwirtschaft im hellenistischen Aegypten* (1924).   F. M. H.

AGRI DECUMATES, a territory including the Black Forest, the basin of the Neckar, and the Swabian Alb, annexed by the Flavian emperors between A.D. 74 and 98 to shorten communications between the Rhine and Danube armies, and lost to Rome *c.* A.D. 263. It had been occupied by the Helvetii and later by Suebi, but after the migration led by Maroboduus (*c.* 6 B.C.) there was no compact tribal community left, and a number of homeless Gauls settled there. The meaning of *Decumates* has been much disputed, but it is now widely held that the term was derived from the Celtic word for ten, the *Agri Decumates* thus consisting of ten units, possibly cantons (cf. the *Decempagi* of the Mediomatrici).

E. Hesselmeyer, *Klio* xxiv (1931), 1–37; E. Norden, *Alt-Germanien* (1934), 137–90; Tacitus, *Germania*, ed. Anderson (1938), 148–9. The only classical reference to the *Agri Decumates* is Tac. *Germania*, 29.   O. B.

AGRIGENTUM, see ACRAGAS.

AGRIMENSORES, see GROMATICI.

AGRIPPA (1) I (b. 10 B.C., 'Herod Agrippa'), son of Aristobulus (*see* HEROD THE GREAT), spent his youth at the Imperial court, whence, having dissipated his patrimony, he fled to Syria. He returned to Rome on borrowed funds in 36, but was imprisoned by Tiberius for treason. He had, however, ingratiated himself with Gaius, who in 37 appointed him king of Philip's tetrarchy and later of Antipas' also. He courageously withstood Gaius' attempt to desecrate the temple, and was appointed by Claudius, whose accession he assisted, king of Judaea (41), with the object of soothing the outraged feelings of the Jews. This he did, being a very popular ruler; but his gross extravagance and his ambitious foreign policy disquieted Claudius, who on his death in 44 annexed his kingdom. Though he is called 'Herod Agrippa' in the Acts of the Apostles (xii), he never bore the name of Herod.   A. H. M. J.

AGRIPPA (2) II (b. A.D. 17), son of Agrippa I, was appointed in 50 king of Chalcis, which in 53 he exchanged for Philip's tetrarchy and Abilene and Arcene; Nero added four toparchies of Galilee and Peraea. From 48 he appointed the high priests and managed the temple funds. He supported the prosecution of Cumanus by the Jews but upheld the Roman government, and in 66 endeavoured by suasion and later by military action to nip the rebellion in the bud. He supported Cestius Gallus, Vespasian, and Titus with troops and with advice, and was rewarded with an accession of territory. He is stated to have died in 100, but had ceased to reign before 93. He is referred to in the Acts of the Apostles (xxv and xxvi).   A. H. M. J.

AGRIPPA (3), M. VIPSANIUS (b. *c.* 63 B.C.), accompanied Octavian to Rome from Apollonia after the murder of Caesar, played a prominent part in the Perusine War, and was praetor in 40. Subsequently as governor of Gaul he suppressed a rebellion of the Aquitani and led a punitive expedition across the Rhine. During his consulship in 37 he superintended the training of Octavian's fleet, constructing a new harbour for the purpose near Baiae (Portus Julius). His naval victory at Mylae was of decisive importance in the war against

Sextus Pompeius, and at Naulochus his improved grapnel is said to have been highly effective. He took part in the Illyrian War of 35–33, and his vigorous naval operations in the campaign of Actium were the primary cause of Octavian's victory over Antony. Agrippa held a second consulship in 28 and a third in 27, assisting Augustus in carrying out a census and *lectio senatus*. When, on the occasion of a serious illness (23), Augustus handed him his signet-ring, he probably meant to indicate him as his most suitable successor. Agrippa's subsequent departure for the East, where he made Mytilene his head-quarters, is almost certainly to be explained as an administrative (possibly also a diplomatic) mission, though friction with C. Marcellus (q.v. 7) may have made his temporary absence advisable. He was recalled in 21 to represent Augustus in Rome and proceeded to Gaul and Spain, where he put an end to trouble with the Cantabri (19). In 18 he was associated with Augustus by the conferment of the *proconsulare imperium* and the *tribunicia potestas* for five years, these powers being renewed for the same term in 13. (In 13, if not in 18, he received an *imperium maius* like that of Augustus.) As one of the *XVviri sacris faciundis* he assisted in the celebration of the *ludi saeculares* in 17. His second mission to the East (16–13) is notable for the establishment of Polemo of Pontus in the Bosporan kingdom, the settlement of veteran colonies at Berytus and Heliopolis, and Agrippa's friendship with Herod and benevolent treatment of the Jews. He was sent to Pannonia, where there was danger of revolt, in 13, and died shortly after his return to Italy in the following year. He left his property to Augustus, and was buried in the imperial mausoleum.

Agrippa ably seconded Augustus in his restoration and improvement of the city of Rome. Among the public works erected at his expense were two new aqueducts (Julia and Virgo), public baths (Thermae Agrippae), and the Pantheon, and as aedile in 33 he reconditioned the sewers of Rome. He wrote an autobiography (now lost) and a geographical commentary (also lost, but used by Strabo and Pliny) from which a map of the Empire was constructed.

Agrippa was married three times: (1) to Pomponia (daughter of Atticus), who bore him a daughter, Vipsania; (2) to Marcella, niece of Augustus, whom he divorced in 21 to marry (3) the emperor's daughter Julia. By Julia he had three sons (Gaius Caesar, Lucius Caesar, and Agrippa Postumus) and two daughters (Agrippina and Julia).

Velleius, bk. 2; Josephus, *AJ* 12. 3 and 16. 2; Suetonius, *Augustus*; Appian, *BCiv.* bk. 5; Dio Cassius bks. 48–54. T. Rice Holmes, *Architect of the Roman Empire* (1928 and 1931); W. W. Tarn and M. P. Charlesworth, *CAH* x, chs. 2–3; M. Reinhold, *Marcus Agrippa* (U.S.A. 1933); R. Daniel, *M. Vipsanius Agrippa* (Breslau, 1933).   G. W. R.

AGRIPPA (4), POSTUMUS (12 B.C.–A.D. 14), third son of Agrippa and Julia, was born after his father's death in 12 B.C. and adopted by Augustus in A.D. 4. He was a youth of fine physique, but his depraved and contumacious character ultimately exasperated Augustus into disinheriting him. He was first sent to Surrentum, then condemned by the Senate to perpetual exile on Planasia (A.D. 7), where he was put to death immediately after the death of Augustus.

Velleius 2. 112; Tac. *Ann.* 1. 3–6. On the alleged visit of Augustus to Planasia, M. P. Charlesworth, *AJPhil.* xliv (1923), 145 ff.   G. W. R.

AGRIPPA (5), Sceptic, later than Aenesidemus (q.v.; date otherwise unknown). Diog. Laert. 9. 88 ff. ascribes to him five τρόποι τῆς ἐποχῆς (grounds of doubt), which are distinguished by Sext. Emp. *Pyr.* 1. 164 from those previously recognized by the Sceptics.

PW i. 897.   W. D. R.

AGRIPPINA. (1) VIPSANIA AGRIPPINA (d. A.D. 20) was daughter of M. Agrippa and granddaughter of Pomponius Atticus. Married to Tiberius, she bore him a son, Drusus, but he was forced by Augustus, against his will, to divorce her and marry Julia in 12 B.C. She then married Asinius Gallus (q.v. 5) and bore him at least five sons.

(2) AGRIPPINA MAJOR (c. 14 B.C.–A.D. 33), Vipsania Agrippina, the daughter of M. Agrippa and of Julia (daughter of Augustus). She married Germanicus (probably in A.D. 5), to whom she bore nine children. She was with Germanicus on the Rhine from 14 to 16 and in the East from 18 until his death in the following year. From 19 to 29 she lived in Rome, the rallying point of a party of senators who opposed the growing power of Sejanus. With Tiberius, whom she suspected (without evidence) of causing her husband's death, her relations were consistently bad, and he refused her request in 26 for leave to marry again. She was arrested in 29 on the instruction of Tiberius and banished by the Senate to Pandateria, where she starved to death in 33. She was survived by one son, Gaius (q.v. 1), and three daughters, Agrippina II, Drusilla, and Livilla.

(3) AGRIPPINA MINOR (A.D. 15–59), Julia Agrippina, the eldest daughter of Germanicus and Agrippina, was born on 6 Nov. A.D. 15 at Ara Ubiorum. In 28 she was betrothed to Cn. Domitius Ahenobarbus, to whom she bore one son, the later Emperor Nero, in 37. During the principate of her brother Gaius (37–41) her name, like those of her sisters, was coupled with the emperor's in vows and oaths; but when she was discovered at Moguntiacum late in 39 to be involved in the conspiracy of Gaetulicus, she was sent into banishment. She was recalled by her uncle Claudius, who married her in 49. Aided by Pallas, Seneca, and Burrus, she quickly achieved her ambitious purpose. Receiving for herself the title Augusta, she persuaded Claudius to adopt Nero as guardian of his own son Britannicus. She was generally believed to have poisoned Claudius, to make room for Nero (54). In the first years of Nero's rule she was almost co-regent with him but, after Pallas had fallen in 55 and Burrus and Seneca turned against her, she lost her power. In March 59 she was murdered at Baiae by a freedman, Anicetus, acting on Nero's instructions. She wrote an autobiography.   J. P. B.

AGROECIUS, fifth-century bishop of Sens, wrote a treatise *De Orthographia* (ed. Keil, *Gramm. Lat.* vii. 113–25) as a supplement to Flavius Caper (q.v.).

Cf. Teuffel, § 457, 11; Schanz–Hosius, § 1100.

AGYIEUS, god of roads, title of Apollo (q.v.).

AGYRRHIUS (c. 400 B.C.), Athenian democratic politician, restored the 'Theorika' (q.v.), and introduced payment for attendance at the Assembly, first one, later three obols.

Prosop. Att. 179.

AHALA, *see* SERVILIUS.

AHENOBARBUS, *see* DOMITIUS.

AIAS (*Αἴας*, Lat. *Ajax*). (1) Son of Telamon, king of Salamis, hence A. Telamonius (*see* AEACUS, TELAMON), but nowhere called an Aeacid till after Homer. In the *Iliad* he leads the Salaminian contingent (2. 557); he is of enormous (πελώριος) size, head and shoulders above the rest (3. 226–9). He is a blunt, stolid man, slow of speech, of unshakable courage, who repeatedly leads the Greek attack or covers the retreat. His stock epithet is 'bulwark (ἕρκος) of the Achaeans' and his characteristic weapon a huge shield, evidently of Mycenaean pattern. Fighting Hector in a duel, he has rather the better of it (7. 206 ff.); he draws a wrestling-match with Odysseus, strength against cunning (23. 708 ff.). He is one of the

three ambassadors who treat with Achilles (q.v.; 9. 169 ff.). In the *Odyssey* (11. 543 ff.) mention is made of his death in consequence of the arms of Achilles having been adjudged to Odysseus and not to him after the death of their owner. The story is probably that found in later authors, e.g. Sophocles (*Ajax*), that he went mad with anger and disappointment and finally killed himself; it was told in the *Little Iliad*.

In the *Great Ehoiai* (Hesiod, fr. 140 Rzach) and thence in Pindar (*Isthm.* 6. 34 ff.), Heracles visits Telamon and, standing on his lion-skin, prays that his new-born child shall be as stout (ἄρρηκτος) as the skin; Zeus, in answer, sends an eagle, αἰετός, and hence the baby is named Aias. From this develops (Lycophron 455 ff.) the tale that Aias was invulnerable save at one point, where the skin had not touched him when (in this version) he was wrapped in it. In the *Aethiopis* Aias carries off the body of Achilles, while Odysseus keeps off the Trojans (cf. *Od.* 5. 309). Of his death various stories were told; he died of an arrow-wound received from Paris, or, being invulnerable, was buried alive by the Trojans throwing clay on him (argument to Soph. *Aj.* ad fin.). When he killed himself his blood flowed on the ground and there sprang up the iris (ὑάκινθος), which also commemorates the death of Hyacinthus (q.v.); hence the markings on its petals recall the hero's name (*Αἴας—αἰαῖ*, see Ov. *Met.* 13. 394 ff.).

Aias had a cult in Salamis, Attica, Megara (?), the Troad, and Byzantium (Farnell, *Hero-Cults*, 307 ff. and note 58). That he was not originally a man at all, but a gigantic and supernatural being, is an ingenious theory (see, for instance, P. von der Mühll, *Der grosse Aias*, 1930) but based on slight evidence. Certainly from Homer on he was conceived as a very tall and powerful man, nothing more.

(2) Son of Oïleus or Ileus, the Locrian chieftain. Of his historical existence there is some proof in the Locrian custom of sending every year two virgins of their noblest families to serve in the temple of Athena of Ilium, if they were not killed on the way by the townspeople. From early in the third century B.C. the Aianteioi, the hero's own clan, undertook to furnish these girls (inscription published by A. Wilhelm, *JÖAI.* xiv (1911), 168 f.; for the custom in general, see Lycophron 1141 ff. and schol. there; Polybius 12, fr. 5, 6 Büttner–Wobst); it ended not very long before A.D. 100 or so (Plutarch, *De sera* 557 d), having lasted 1,000 years). It seems inconceivable that this should be the result of an imaginary person's fabulous crime, and therefore the classical explanation, that it is a penance for Aias carrying off the Palladium or raping Cassandra at the altar of Athena, during the sack of Troy, is by far the most plausible. See further Farnell, op. cit. 294 ff., and ibid. 293–4, for Aias' cult; A. Momigliano in *CQ* 39, 49.

In Homer Aias is leader of the Locrian contingent (*Il.* 2. 527 ff.); he is 'much lesser' than the son of Telamon (hence often called Aias the Lesser), quick-footed, and often paired with his greater namesake as a brave fighter. He is, however, of hateful character and on occasion grossly rude (as 23. 473 ff.). Athena hates him (ibid. 774; *Od.* 4. 502); in the latter passage he is drowned by Poseidon for blasphemy against the gods while scrambling ashore after shipwreck. In the *Iliu Persis* Aias drags Cassandra away from the altar of Athena, pulling the Palladium with her (cf. above). That he committed any further assault on her is not said by any author earlier than Callimachus (*fr.* 13 d Schneider); whether he invented this detail or had it from an older writer is not known.

That two heroes so unlike should have the same name is curious, and at the same time an argument against supposing that they were originally one.   H. J. R.

AIDOS (αἰδώς), *see* PERSONIFICATIONS.

AINOI (αἶνοι), see ARCHILOCHUS.

AION (Αἰών), a personification of (1) period of time, (2) passage of time, indefinitely long time (hardly eternity, except in thought deriving from Plato, *Tim.* 37 d). See PERSONIFICATIONS. In cult, (1) is represented by the festival at Alexandria (late and Greek but not unconnected with Egyptian ideas, see E. Norden, *Geburt des Kindes*, 28, and refs. there), at which an image was brought out of the inner sanctuary of the Κορεῖον, with the announcement that 'the Maiden (Κόρη) has brought forth Aion'. This is apparently the year; cf., for an allegedly Phoenician mythological figure of the same kind, Philon of Byblus ap. Euseb. *Praep. Evang.* 1. 10. 7. (2) perhaps in Eur., *Heracl.* 900, but cf. Wilamowitz–Moellendorff on *HF* 669; cf. Heraclitus, fr. 79 Bywater. In cult he is late, probably Orphic (Kern, *Relig. der Griechen* iii. 243), possibly Mithraic also (Cumont, *Textes et Monuments* i. 76; *Rel. or.* (4. 140 and note 46), cf. the Iranian Zervan Akarana. Mythologically, Aion is an important character in Nonnus, *Dionysiaca*. His connexion with a number of figures showing a lion-headed deity is problematical, cf. Cumont, *Textes*, loc. cit., Wernicke in *PW* ii. 1043, 33. An inscription to him, of 74–73 B.C., from Eleusis, *SIG*, 1125. Cf. Nock, *Harv. Theol. Rev.* xxvii (1934), 53 ff. on the complexity of ideas attaching to this term (and on the publicist or patriotic sense of *Aeternitas* at Rome); C. Bonner, *Hesperia* xii (1944), 30 ff. H. J. R.

AIORA, see ICARIUS.

AISA, see FATE.

AISYMNETES, according to Aristotle (*Pol.* 1285ᵃ), a supreme ruler appointed by some early city-states in times of internal crisis, for life, for a prescribed period, or till the completion of his task, e.g. Pittacus (q.v.). Aristotle defines the office as an elective tyranny, Dionysius (5. 73) compares the Roman dictator. These *aisymnetai* have affinities with the early lawgivers (Solon, Zaleucus, Demonax, etc.), the difference being one of local nomenclature. Inscriptions (*SIG* 38, 57, 272, 642, 955) show regular magistrates so called in Teos, Miletus, Naxos, Megara, Selinus, and Chalcedon. The word first occurs in *Od.* 8. 258, meaning a referee. P. N. U.

AITHER (Αἰθήρ), personification (q.v.) of the purer upper stratum of air (approximately the stratosphere), next to or identical with the sky; son of Erebus and Night (Hesiod, *Theog.* 124–5); of Chaos and Darkness (Hyginus, *Fab. praef.* 1); husband of Day and of Earth (ibid. 2–3). H. J. R.

AIUS LOCUTIUS, the unknown divine 'sayer and speaker' who, a little before the battle of the Allia in 390 B.C., bade one M. Caedicius tell the magistrates that the Gauls were coming. After their departure a precinct (*templum*) and shrine (*sacellum*) were dedicated near Vesta's shrine, on the Nova Via, where the voice was heard.

See Livy 5. 32. 6; 50. 5; Platner–Ashby, 4. H. J. R.

AJAX, see AIAS.

AKONTION (ἀκόντιον) see ARMS AND ARMOUR, GREEK.

ALABANDA, a city in northern Caria, on the Marsyas, a tributary of the Maeander, at the point where the road from Tralles branches to Halicarnassus and to the coast opposite Rhodes. Its site (now *Arabhisar*) between two hills is likened by Strabo to a pack-saddle. In the province Asia it was a *civitas libera* and the centre of a *conventus*. It was proverbial for opulence and comfort. W. M. C.

ALAE, a term originally denoting the two contingents of *socii* normally posted on the legion's flanks; after

90 B.C., it bore the more restricted sense of cavalry. When Augustus organized the *auxilia* the cavalry contingents commanded by equestrian *praefecti* were called *alae* and numbered either 1,000 or 500, subdivided into 24 and 16 *turmae* respectively. They commonly bore titles indicating the country from which they had been recruited (e.g. *Hispanorum*) or the emperor or general who had raised them (*Aelia, Siliana*) or as a mark of honour *Augusta, pia, fidelis*). See AUXILIA.

G. L. Cheesman, *The Auxilia of the Roman Army* (1914). H. M. D. P.

ALAMANNI (ALEMANNI), a Suebic people, descended from the Semnones, who late in the second century A.D. migrated from their home in Brandenburg. Early in the third century they broke through the *limes*, and Caracalla campaigned against them (213). Their attacks became serious in the thirties, and they made incursions into Upper Germany, Gaul, Raetia, and Italy. Gallienus defeated a horde near Milan, but had to abandon the *limes* territory of Upper Germany and Raetia, which the Alamanni then occupied. They did not cease to devastate Roman territory, and frequent Alamannic wars are recorded, notably those of Aurelian, Probus, and Julian. In the fifth century some of the Alamanni occupied Alsace, the Palatinate, and part of Switzerland; others had meanwhile spread over Raetia, and the modern Swabians are largely their descendants.

L. Schmidt, *Geschichte der deutschen Stämme* ii² (1915), 236–324. O. B.

ALANS, a nomadic tribe which entered Europe in the wake of the Sarmatians (q.v.) and was established in south-east Russia in the first three centuries A.D. The Alans repeatedly attempted to cross the Caucasus, and in 75 they raided Armenia and Parthia. But the Roman emperors from Nero and Vespasian onward fortified the western exits of the mountains against them, and Arrian, when governor of Cappadocia, beat off an attack by them. In the fourth century the Alans were swept across eastern and central Europe by the Huns. They found new homes in Spain (*c.* 410), but were soon absorbed here by their fellow-invaders, the Visigoths. Greek writers sometimes confused the Alans with the Albanians of the southern Caucasus.

M. Rostovtzeff, *CAH* xi. 94–7. M. C.

ALASTOR, in mythology, son of Neleus and brother of Nestor, q.v. Like all his brothers save Nestor himself, he was killed by Heracles (*Il.* 11. 693; Apollod. 1. 93). He married Harpalyce, daughter of Clymenus of Argos, but on the way home he was overtaken by Clymenus and robbed of his bride, for whom her father had an incestuous passion. To revenge herself, she killed her younger brother, cooked his flesh, and served it to her father at a feast. She then prayed to be taken from the world of men, and became a χαλκίς, here a night-bird of some kind (Parthenius 13, from Euphorion).

ἀλάστωρ, subst. or adj., in the latter case often with δαίμων added: an avenging power, as Aesch. *Ag.* 1501, where it is the supernatural agent who, according to Clytemnestra, exacts vengeance on Atreus' descendants for his crime (*see* ATREUS, AGAMEMNON). Hence the criminal himself, presumably as giving occasion for such punishment, e.g. Aesch. *Eum.* 236, where Orestes uses it of himself; hence occasionally a mere vague term of abuse, 'wretch', 'scoundrel', as Dem. 19. 305. H. J. R.

ALAUDAE ('the Larks'), a legion raised by Caesar in Gallia Narbonensis from non-citizens, and the earliest of its kind. In 47 B.C., when its soldiers were enfranchised, it received a number—V. It was probably destroyed in the disaster of Cornelius Fuscus in Dacia in A.D. 87.

Ritterling, *PW*, s.v. 'Legio'. H. M. D. P.

ALBA FUCENS, an ancient town just north of the Fucine Lake in central Italy, first mentioned as a Latin colony planted *in Aequis*, but near the Marsi, 303 B.C. (Livy 10. 1); perhaps the Via Tiburtina was now extended thus far east (see VIA VALERIA). Alba usually supported the Roman government, e.g. against Hannibal, the *socii* (90 B.C.), Caesar, and Antony; its recusant attitude in 209 was exceptional (App. *Hann.* 39; Livy 27. 9; 29. 15; *Epit.* 72; Caes. *BCiv.* 1. 15; Cic. *Phil.* 3. 6). Roman State prisoners were often kept here (Livy 30. 17; 45. 42; *Epit.* 61). Although not mentioned in Imperial times, imposing ruins at *Albe* and inscriptions attest its importance. E. T. S.

ALBA LONGA, nowadays *Castel Gandolfo* in the Alban Hills twelve miles SE. of Rome (T. Ashby, *Journ. Phil.* xxvii (1901), 37): a very ancient city traditionally founded by Ascanius *c.* 1152 B.C. (*Aen.* 3. 390 f.). Its necropolis contains tombs of *c.* 1100. Alba founded some, certainly not all, Latin cities (reject Livy 1. 52, *Aen.* 6. 773; and see I. G. Scott, *Am. Ac. Rome* 1929, 25). Apparently it once headed a league (of Prisci Latini? see Festus, p. 253 L.), the nature and members of which cannot be exactly determined: lists in Diodorus (7. 5), Dionysius (4. 92; 5.61), and Pliny (*HN* 3. 69), like surviving lists of Alban kings, are untrustworthy. The Romans destroyed Alba (*c.* 600 B.C.) and transported some of its inhabitants to Rome, where they became prominent (Julii, Tullii, etc.: Livy 1. 29 f.; Tac. *Ann.* 11. 24). Alba was never rebuilt, the untransported Albans remaining in neighbouring Bovillae, where their descendants, *Albani Longani Bovillenses*, preserved Alban cults and memorials until late times (*ILS* 6188 f.). The name Alba is preserved to-day by Albano. Latin *Albanum* means 'a villa on Alban territory': i.e. Domitian's, which Septimius Severus transformed into a legionary camp and which became the nucleus for the modern town. Alban wine and building stone (peperino) were famous.

G. Lugli, *Bull. Com. Arch.* 1917–20; *Ausonia* 1919–21; *Nuova Antologia* 1929; A. Doboşi, *Ephemeris Dacoromana* vi (1935), 240. E. T. S.

ALBANIA (Caucasian), the land (mod. *Shirvan*) adjacent to the eastern Caucasus and the western Caspian, separated from Armenia by the river Cyrus (*Kur*). Its Caspian flat-lands were fertile, but the Albanian people remained a rude and warlike folk of herdsmen, hunters, and fishers, who traded by barter. Under a common king they had twelve local chiefs and spoke twenty-six different dialects; their chief worship was an orgiastic cult of the moon-goddess. Albania was explored by Pompey in 65 B.C. and was occasionally attached to the Roman Empire as a client State.

Strabo 11. 491 ff.; Pliny, *HN* 6. 15, 29, 39; Ptol. *Geog.* 5. 12. E. H. W.

ALBANUS LACUS (mod. *Lago Albano*), a crater lake in the Alban Hills near Rome. Its wooded banks in Imperial times were studded with villas, e.g. Domitian's. Lacking natural outlets, its waters reach the Rivus Albanus, and thence the Tiber, via a tunnel through the crater rim built *c.* 397 B.C. The Romans reputedly excavated this *emissarium* to ensure the fall of Veii which, an oracle prophesied, awaited the overflowing of the lake (Livy 5. 15–19). Actually their motive was to carry off the waters rapidly for irrigation purposes (Cic. *Div.* 2. 69); otherwise seepage through the porous subsoil would waterlog the districts below. E. T. S.

ALBANUS MONS, the Alban Hills and more specifically their dominating peak (*Monte Cavo*, 3,115 feet), thirteen miles south-east of Rome. Until *c.* 1150 B.C. the Albanus Mons was an active volcano, preventing human habitation in Latium; the volcano, however, has been inactive in historical times. On the summit stood the

Latin federal sanctuary of Jupiter Latiaris where Roman consuls celebrated the *Feriae Latinae* (Dion. Hal. 4. 49; the antiquity of the festival probably is underestimated). Remains exist, not indeed of the temple, but of the Via Triumphalis leading to it; here at least five Roman generals celebrated ovations after being refused regular triumphs in Rome (e.g. Marcellus in 211 B.C.: Livy 26. 21). E. T. S.

ALBINOVANUS, CELSUS, *see* CELSUS (1).

ALBINOVANUS PĔDO, a poet-friend addressed by Ovid in *Pont.* 4. 10, author of a *Theseid*, is mentioned by Martial (1 *praef.*; cf. 5. 5. 6) as one of his models in epigram. The *Consolatio ad Liviam* (q.v.) and *Elegiae in Maecenatem* (q.v.), which Joseph Scaliger ascribed to him, are no longer considered his work. Under Tiberius he wrote a poem on Germanicus' North Sea expedition from which Seneca (*Suas.* 1. 15; cf. Baehr. *FPR*, p. 351) quotes over twenty hexameters as a typical Latin description of the ocean. Its rather turgid rhetoric does not exhibit the qualities in him which appealed to Martial; but the younger Seneca (*Ep.* 122. 15–16) calls him a 'fabulator elegantissimus' and gives his vividly amusing story about a noisy neighbour who turned night into day. J. W. D.

ALBINUS (1), pupil of Gaius and teacher of Galen (in A.D. 151–2), wrote a Prologue to Plato, in which the nature, classification, and order of the dialogues are discussed, and a text-book of Plato's philosophy (the latter ascribed wrongly in the MSS. to an otherwise unknown philosopher Alcinous). Both works contain an amalgam of Platonism with Peripatetic and Stoic elements; specifically Neoplatonic doctrines are merely hinted at.

Ed. C. F. Hermann in his *Plato*, 6. 147, 152 (1892); P. Louis (Paris) 1945. *PW* i. 1314. W. D. R.

ALBINUS (2) (4th c. A.D.), writer on metre and music. His works are lost.

Cf. Teuffel, § 405, 2 and § 407, 5; Schanz–Hosius, § 825.

ALBINUS, *see also* CLODIUS (4), POSTUMIUS (3, 4, and 5).

ALBION, ancient (Celtic or pre-Celtic) name of Great Britain (but not Ireland), first recorded *c.* 525 B.C. by a Massiliote seaman (quoted by Avienus, q.v.) who spoke of Ireland, two days' sail from Brittany, 'alongside the island of the Albiones'. The name 'Albion' was used by the author of *De Mundo* (who said that it and Ireland were bigger than the Mediterranean islands, but smaller than Ceylon), but it was soon ousted by the Celtic 'Britannia'. The Romans, connecting 'Albion' with *albus*, white, referred the name to the cliffs of Dover. E. H. W.

ALBOGALERUS, *see* APEX.

ALBUCIUS (1), TITUS (2nd c. B.C.), orator and Epicurean, of whose Hellenomania Lucilius makes fun (Marx, 88: cf. 84, where it is probably his style that is likened to a wriggly mosaic pavement).

ALBUCIUS (2) **SILUS**, GAIUS, Augustan orator and teacher of rhetoric, from Novaria. Though over-conscientious and not sure enough of himself, he could command a grand simplicity, and Seneca places him in the first rank (*Controv.* 7 *praef.* 1–9; Suet. *Rhet.* 6). C. J. F.

ALBUM, a whitened *tabula*, was used for publishing, in black writing, priestly notices, *fasti*, notices of *comitia* and Senate, *proscriptiones* and edicts (e.g. *album praetoris* with *formulae actionum*), also member rolls (e.g. *album senatorum, decurionum, iudicum, collegii*), and lists of recipients of corn. A. H. McD.

ALBUNEA, nymph of the *albulae aquae*, a sulphurous spring and brook rising at Tibur, where it forms the well-known waterfall, and flowing into the Anio. Near the fall was a dream-oracle (*Aen.* 7. 81 ff., needlessly doubted by Heinze and Wissowa, *RK* 211 note 4). Albunea herself was called a Sibyl (Varro ap. Lactant. *Div. Inst.* 1. 6. 12); Servius on *Aen.* 7. 84 equates her with Leucothea (q.v.) and says the god [*sic*] Mefitis is her subordinate. H. J. R.

ALCAEUS (1) (b. *c.* 620 B.C.), lyric poet, of Mytilene in Lesbos (Strabo 617), was still a boy when his brothers, Antimenidas and Cicis, overthrew the tyrant Melanchros (fr. 53, 7–8 Lobel = fr. 48 Diehl, Diog. Laert. 1. 74). Melanchros was succeeded by Myrsilus, who was helped by Deinomenes and Pittacus. Alcaeus' early years seem to have been spent in combating all three. At first he lost and went into exile at Pyrrha (schol. ad fr. 57 = 37), where he wrote fr. 55 = 35, and possibly frs. 87 = 30 and 6 = 119, in which political conditions are described in seafaring language. A fight followed, and to A.'s delight Myrsilus was killed (fr. 93 = 124). He was succeeded by Pittacus, with whom A. seems at first to have been friendly, since both fought against Athens at Sigeum (Diog. Laert. 1. 74) *c.* 600 B.C. Here A. lost his shield and celebrated the fact (fr. 193 = 49). On the conclusion of peace Pittacus became all-powerful, and was attacked by A., who regarded his election to power as an act of madness (fr. 109 = 87), and reviled him for his physical defects (Diog. Laert. 1. 81), his ambitious marriage (fr. 48 = 43), his riotous behaviour (fr. 50 = 45), and his craftiness (fr. 47 = 42). The result of the struggle was that soon after 600 B.C. A. went to Egypt (Strabo 37) and his brother Antimenidas became a mercenary of the king of Babylon (fr. 112 = 50). Alcaeus seems also to have been in Thrace (fr. 29 = 77) and to have had negotiations with the Lydians (fr. 47 = 42). Before Pittacus resigned his powers in 580 B.C. he forgave A. (Diog. Laert. 1. 75), who must have returned home. The rest of his life and the date of his death are unknown.

His works survive only in fragments. Edited by Aristophanes and Aristarchus in at least ten books (Heph. p. 74, 12 ff.), they seem to have been arranged according to subject, since Ὕμνοι (schol. Heph. p. 169, 28 ff.) and Στασιωτικά (Strabo 617) are mentioned, but the papyrus fragments give no indication of systematic arrangement. The remains indicate that A. wrote lyrical songs, usually monodies; many dealt with contemporary politics, while others are drinking-songs (frs. 96 = 91, 99 = 90, 108 = 94, 107 = 96, 128 = 66), sometimes with a meditative tinge (fr. 22 = 73), love-songs (fr. 49 = 44; cf. Theoc. 29–30, Hor. *Carm.* 1. 32. 11), hymns to Apollo (fr. 72 = 1), Hermes (fr. 73 = 2), and the Dioscuri (fr. 17 = 78). Sometimes he seems to write variations on themes of folk-song (fr. 10 = 123) or describes a festive scene (fr. 58 = 106). He writes in vernacular Aeolic, with occasional Homerisms. He uses two- or four-lined stanzas with a wide variety of metres, including the Greater and Lesser Asclepiads, the Sapphic and Alcaic stanzas, and other stanzas of his own invention. He occasionally employs an elaborate allegory (frs. 63 = 117 and 87 = 22), but normally he writes directly and easily, and is at his best in describing simple sights or emotions.

Texts: E. Lobel (1927); E. Diehl, *Anth. Lyr. Graec.* i. 4, pp. 86–159. Criticism: C. M. Bowra, *Greek Lyric Poetry* (1936), 141–85. C. M. B.

ALCAEUS (2) (4th c. B.C.), called by Suidas κωμικὸς τῆς ἀρχαίας κωμῳδίας, but from the titles of his plays clearly a Middle Comedy writer. His Πασιφάη took the fifth (last) prize in 388 B.C. (hyp. 4 Ar. *Plut.*). Fragments of eight plays survive, mostly mythological burlesques.

FCG i. 244–9; *CAF* i. 756 ff.; Demiańczuk, *Supp. Com.* 7. M. P.

ALCAEUS (3) of Messene (*fl.* 200 B.C.) has about twenty epigrams in the Greek Anthology, including several very interesting political lampoons on Philip V of Macedonia (see F. W. Walbank, *CQ* 1942–3). Plutarch (*Flam.* 9) says that one of them was sung throughout Greece; the king's fierce retort is also in the Anthology (*Anth. Plan.* 26 b). These are the earliest invective epigrams in the style taken up by Catullus and cultivated by so many lampoonists after him. A.'s iambics, which must have been pasquinades too, are lost. G. H.

ALCAMENES (*c.* 460–400 B.C.), Greek sculptor. He was probably an Athenian and may have been a pupil of Phidias, though he is sometimes described as his rival. His latest known work being a relief carved for Thrasybulus at Athens in 404–403, Pausanias attributed to him the carving of the west pediment of the temple of Zeus at Olympia. This attribution, however, cannot be accepted, though Alcamenes may have had some part in the completion or repair of the pediment. The only surviving work which can be attributed to him is a statue, now in the Acropolis Museum (no. 1358), of a woman and a small boy. This appears to be identical with a statue of Procne and Itys which, according to Pausanias, was dedicated by an Alcamenes on the Acropolis. Some scholars think that the dedicator and the sculptor are not identical, but the attribution is almost certainly correct. Perhaps Alcamenes contributed to the sculpture of the Erechtheum, and the similarity between the Procne and Itys and the Caryatids in style is noteworthy. S. C.

ALCATHOUS (Ἀλκάθοος or Ἀλκάθους), in mythology, son of Pelops and Hippodameia, to whom games (Alkathoia) were celebrated at Megara (Pind. *Isthm.* 8. 74 and schol. on *Nem.* 5. 46). A folk-tale (theme H 105, Stith Thompson) told by Dieuchidas (ap. schol. Ap. Rhod. 1. 517) says that, exiled for his share in the murder of his brother Chrysippus, he killed a lion (it haunted Cithaeron and had killed Euhippus, son of Megareus, king of Megara, who promised his daughter's hand and the succession to his throne to whoever slew it, Paus. 1. 41. 3), cut out its tongue, and when false claimants arose, used it to refute them. He then built temples to Apollo Agraios and Artemis Agrotera (Paus. ibid.) and walls for Megara; Apollo helped him, and rested his lyre on a stone still shown in Pausanias' time (ibid. 42. 2). His eldest son, Ischepolis, was killed on the Calydonian boar-hunt; one Callipolis brought the news and scattered the wood of a fire on which Alcathous was offering, whereat Alcathous killed him with one of the billets (ibid. 42. 6). H. J. R.

ALCESTIS (Ἄλκηστις), in mythology, a daughter of Pelias (*see* NELEUS) and wife of Admetus, king of Pherae in Thessaly. For some unknown reason she is the central figure of two interesting legends, one of them also moving and famous in literature, but both characteristic folk-tales.

(1) When she was of age to marry, many suitors appeared, but her father would not give her to any who could not fulfil the prescribed condition of driving wild beasts yoked to a chariot. This is of course one of the innumerable stories told of extraordinary tasks set wooers (see Stith Thompson, H 335). In this instance it does not appear that Pelias apprehended any danger from Alcestis' marriage, or had any special reason for wanting her at home. Admetus succeeded, thanks to a divine helper. Apollo had shortly before killed the Cyclopes who made Zeus' thunderbolts (cf. Eur. *Alc.* 1 ff.), because he did not dare to avenge the death of his son Asclepius (q.v.) on Zeus himself. In consequence, he was banished from heaven for a time (the common punishment of a human manslayer is here transferred to a god), and made to serve a mortal. Admetus was renowned for his piety and treated his divine serf with every consideration, employing him (appropriately, as

he is a god of flocks and herds, *see* APOLLO) to tend his horses or cattle. The god, in return for this, in a later form of the legend, because Admetus was very handsome and he loved him (first in Callimachus, *Ap.* 49, who does not mention the affair of the banishment) brought him a lion and a boar yoked, and he drove away with Alcestis behind this team (Hyg. *Fab.* 50. 51; source unknown; 50. 1 suggests another form of the story in which the successful candidate was allowed to choose whichever of Pelias' daughters he preferred).

(2) At the bridal feast, Admetus forgot to sacrifice to Artemis (Apollod. 1. 105, who also had the story of the lion and boar), and on opening the bridal chamber found it full of serpents. The snake being a chthonian creature for the most part, this was an omen of imminent death, and Apollo again intervened. By the primitive method of making the Fates drunk (Aesch. *Eum.* 728) he persuaded them to promise that if anyone else would die on Admetus' behalf, he might continue to live. But no one would consent to die, except Alcestis (Eur., ibid. 15 ff. He makes no mention of the portent, which indeed, if he had heard of it, would not fit his version of the story; his Alcestis has been married long enough to have two children past infancy). That there was any baseness in accepting her offer did not occur to tellers of the legend before Euripides; elsewhere Admetus is a wholly admirable character. So far, the tale embodies popular moralizing (a man's truest friend is a good wife). On the appointed day Alcestis accordingly died, i.e. the rest of her life was transferred to her husband, a piece of magic which Jason suggests to Medea (Ov. *Met.* 7. 168), but she declares it quite impossible, 'nec sinat hoc Hecate' (174). When gods were the agents, such difficulties did not exist. Now comes a form of the widespread tale (Tammuz and Ishtar is the oldest known form) of the recovery from the lower world of one of a pair of lovers. It is sometimes said (Apollod., ibid. 106) that Persephone sent Alcestis back of her own accord; but the usual version is that Heracles (q.v.) intervened. Admetus, with his usual piety, had received him hospitably in the midst of his own grief; by way of return for this, he set out to harrow Hell, and fought successfully either with Hades himself (Apollod., ibid.) or with the death-spirit, Thanatos, compelling him to give Alcestis back.

Some extraordinarily foolish theories have been evolved concerning this legend, mostly starting from the name of Admetus ('Unconquerable, Unsubduable'). He has been declared to be a sun-god, or, more absurd still, a death-god. The standard treatise is now that of A. Lesky, 'Alkestis, der Mythus und das Drama', in *Sitz. Wien,* 1925, which gives some account of these aberrations and puts forward a substantially correct explanation. It should have been obvious that to give the story point the characters must be human, or near enough to human to be capable of dying; even if originally husband and wife had been gods, the legend would not have been told of them till that fact was forgotten.

Apart from these tales, neither of the pair has much mythology. Admetus took part in the Argonautic adventure, (Hyg. *Fab.* 14. 2 and elsewhere); the Calydonian boar-hunt (Apollod. 1. 67); the funeral games over Pelias (chest of Cypselus in Paus. 5. 17. 9, where he drives a chariot; perhaps in imitation of this, Statius (*Theb.* 6. 310 ff.) makes him compete at the first Nemean games with a team of mares.

One account (Phanodemus ap. schol. Ar. *Vesp.* 1239) says that in his old age Admetus was driven into exile with Alcestis and their youngest child, Hippasus (the elder son, Eumelus, took part in the Trojan War, *Il.* 2. 713–14; he was a skilled charioteer, 23. 288–9, but had ill success in the chariot-race at Patroclus' funeral, ibid. 391 ff.; the daughter, Perimele, married Argos, son of

Phrixus, Ant. Liberalis 23). The cause of the exile is not known, and the story is plainly connected with the famous skolion (quoted by Ar. *Vesp.* 1238), Ἀδμήτου λόγον ὦταῖρε μαθὼν τοὺς ἀγαθοὺς φίλει, said by Phanodemus to refer to Admetus' kind reception by Theseus.

There appears to have been no hero-cult of either Alcestis or her husband.   H. J. R.

ALCHEMY is a body of doctrine characterized by

(*a*) Interest in the change of base matter into silver and gold.

(*b*) A belief that all matter is made up of the four elements, and of a fifth entity, the directed action of which can change the character of the whole.

(*c*) A belief that material events have a spiritual basis or even that matter and spirit are one. In the background lies a confused hylozoism. These are the main sources of a notorious obscurity.

(*d*) A delight in syncretism.

2. The word 'alchemy' is medieval and is an Arabic combination of the article with Greek *chemia* = Egypt (Plutarch), hence 'the Egyptian art'. This derives perhaps from an Egyptian word meaning black, and especially the black soil, which is Egypt as distinguished from the sandy desert. The Greek alchemical texts never used the word *chemia*, though one is ascribed to 'Chymes'. This name betrays a constantly recurring confusion between *chemia* and *chymeia* (= melting, fusion). The texts refer to their subject as 'The Work', 'The divine and sacred Art', etc. It is not yet possible to indicate the sources of Greek alchemy. The texts bear names of Greek, Egyptian, Hebrew, and Persian authors. The intense religious element in them recalls that of the Hermetic writings and suggests an Alexandrian atmosphere.

3. There is no early Latin alchemy. The technical sections of Pliny's *Historia naturalis* have no trace of the alchemical spirit.

4. Early Greek alchemical texts are almost all pseudonymous and commonly quoted under the names of their spurious authors. They fall into various schools which gradually pass out of the Classical period.

(*a*) *The School of Democritus* worked only by superficial colouring and by preparing alloys by fusion. The considerable *Physica et mystica* of 'Democritus' has no Christian or Jewish allusion and may be as early as the first century B.C. The mythology of the text of 'Isis' is early Gnostic. It may be about A.D. 100. Later is the text of 'Moses' which opens with Exodus xxxi. 2–5. A second- or third-century text was of 'Ostanes', the traditional name of the Persian teacher of the real Democritus.

(*b*) *The School of Mary the Jewess* employs complex apparatus for distillation and sublimation. Works in her name were not later than the first century A.D. They survive in numerous quotations. She is commemorated in the modern chemist's 'bain marie'. The text of 'Cleopatra' contains the earliest drawings of alchemical apparatus. Other texts are of 'Agathodaemon', 'Hermes', and 'Comarius'.

(*c*) *The School of Zosimus* of the third and fourth centuries, at least partly of Christian origin, has a commentatory character but also records experiments. Zosimus adhered specially to the ideas of Mary and Cleopatra. This early feminist collaborated with his 'sister' Theosebeia in an alchemical work of which there are substantial remains. Of one member of the school, Olympiodorus of Thebes in Egypt, we gain a clear picture since he wrote in A.D. 425 a history of his times of which an abridgement survives. With the numerous later schools we are not here concerned.

5. The Greek alchemists had at their disposal numerous substances, of which about forty can be identified as moderately pure. Nevertheless they had no criterion

of chemical purity, and it met their needs if substances looked like and, to a certain extent, behaved like those they sought, which were, above all, gold and silver. This could become fraudulent but was, in itself, an approach which necessarily followed from their doctrines.

6. The extreme difficulties of interpreting the descriptions and drawings of apparatus have, in some cases, been surmounted, notably for the complex *kerotakis* used for sublimation. The 'bain marie' itself has been in use for nearly 2,000 years.

M. Berthelot, *Collection des anciens alchimistes grecs* (4 vols. 1887–8); E. O. von Lippmann, *Entstehung und Ausbreitung der Alchemie* (1919); F. Sherwood Taylor, 'A Survey of Greek Alchemy' in *JHS* l (1930), 109; A. J. Hopkins, *Alchemy, Child of Greek Philosophy* (New York, 1934); *Catalogue des manuscrits alchimiques grecs* in course of publication by the Union Académique Internationale; *PW* i. 1338; A. J. Festugière, *La Révélation d' Hermès Trismégiste* i (1944). C. S.

ALCIBIADES (*c.* 450–404 B.C.), son of Cleinias, Athenian general and statesman. Brought up in the household of his guardian Pericles, he became the pupil and intimate friend of Socrates. His brilliance enabled him in 420 to assume the leadership of the extreme democrats, and his ambitious imperialism drew Athens into a coalition with Argos and other enemies of Sparta. This policy, half-heartedly supported by the Athenians, had to be abandoned after the Spartan victory at Mantinea (418). Though Alcibiades temporarily allied with Nicias to avoid ostracism, the two were normally at variance, and when the former sponsored the plan for a Sicilian expedition, Nicias vainly opposed it. Both were appointed, together with Lamachus, to command this armament, and received extraordinary powers (415). Alcibiades was suspected of complicity in the mutilation of the Hermae (q.v.) and other profanations at Athens, and soon after the fleet reached Sicily he was recalled for trial. He escaped, however, to Sparta, where he gave the valuable advice that a Spartan general should be sent to Syracuse and that a permanent Spartan post at Decelea in Attica should be occupied.

In 412 his mission to Ionia caused many allies of Athens to revolt, but he soon lost the confidence of the Spartans and fled to Tissaphernes. He tried to secure reinstatement at Athens by winning the support of Persia and fomenting an oligarchic revolution, but he could not induce Tissaphernes to desert the Spartan cause. The Athenian fleet at Samos appointed him general, and for several years he skilfully directed operations in Ionia and the Hellespont, winning a brilliant victory at Cyzicus in 410. He returned to Athens in 407 and was entrusted with an extraordinary command. Against the powerful combination of Lysander and Cyrus he could effect little, and when in his absence a subordinate suffered defeat at Notium (406), his enemies roused popular suspicion against him. He then withdrew, and in 404 through the influence of the Thirty Tyrants (q.v.) and Lysander he was murdered in Phrygia, where he sought refuge with Pharnabazus.

Alcibiades was an egoist whose career proved disastrous to Athens, but Thucydides justifiably censures the conduct of his countrymen, who twice discarded him when his genius might have been a decisive factor.

Thuc., bks. 5–8; Xen. *Hell.* bk. 1; Plato, *Alc.* 1 and *Symp.*; Plut. *Alc.* K. J. Beloch, *Gr. Gesch.*² ii, pt. 1, chs. 11–12; W. S. Ferguson, *CAH* v, chs. 9–12; Glotz, *Hist. grecque* ii, chs. 20–1; J. Hatzfeld, *Alcibiade* (1940); F. Taeger, *Alcibiades* (1943). H. D. W.

ALCIDAMAS (4th c. B.C.), rhetorician and sophist, was born at Elaea in Aeolis. He studied under Gorgias, and led the orthodox branch of Gorgias' followers, while Isocrates led the innovators; the difference consisted largely in the fact that Alcidamas emphasized the importance of a power of improvisation resting on wide knowledge, while Isocrates excelled in dialectical skill and delicacy of language. The works extant under Alcidamas' name are (1) Περὶ τῶν τοὺς γραπτοὺς λόγους

γραφόντων ἢ περὶ σοφιστῶν, (2) (spurious) 'Οδυσσεὺς κατὰ Παλαμήδους προδοσίας. The most important of the lost works seems to have been that called Μουσεῖον.

Ed. F. Blass, in his *Antipho* (1892), 183. *PW* i. 1533. W. D. R.

ALCIDES = HERACLES (q.v.).

ALCINOUS ('Αλκίνοος), in mythology, son of Nausithous (*Od.* 7. 63), husband of Arētē, his first cousin (ibid. 66), king of the Phaeacians in Scheria (ibid. 6. 12, etc.), father of Nausicaa (q.v.). He received Odysseus hospitably (*see* ODYSSEUS) and sent him to Ithaca on one of the magic ships of his people (13. 70 ff.), though he had had warning of the danger of such services to all and sundry (13. 172 ff.). In the Argonautic legend (see especially Ap. Rhod. 4. 993 ff.) the Argonauts visit Scheria (here called Drepane) on their return from Colchis; the Colchians pursue them there and demand Medea. Alcinous decides that if she is virgin she must return, but if not, her husband Jason shall keep her. Warned by Arētē, she and Jason consummate their marriage. H. J. R.

ALCIPHRON (2nd c. A.D.), Athenian sophist, whose letters, in imitation of Lucian, supposedly written by Athenians of the fourth century B.C., embody reminiscences of Menander, are written in familiar style, and vividly reflect the ordinary life of that time.

Text, M. A. Schepers (Teubner, 1905). Translation, F. A. Wright (1923). J. W. H. A.

ALCITHOE, see MINYAS.

ALCM(A)EON (1) ('Αλκμέων, 'Αλκμαίων), in mythology, son of Amphiaraus (q.v.). After the expedition of the Seven against Thebes, he avenged his father's death on his mother Eriphyle, and afterwards became, by command of Apollo, leader of the expedition of the Epigoni, which took Thebes (or the expedition came first, the matricide afterwards, contrast Asclepiades in schol. *Od.* 11. 326, with Apollod. 3. 86). Being maddened by the Erinyes, he left Argos and went to Psophis, where King Phegeus purified him and gave him his daughter Arsinoë or Alphesiboea, but as a famine visited the land he left, settled in the new land formed by the Achelous at its mouth, and therefore not seen by the sun when Eriphyle was killed, and married Achelous' daughter Callirhoë (*see* ACARNAN). But the brothers of Arsinoë waylaid and killed him, afterwards shutting their sister up in a chest and selling her as a slave. In Euripides' *Alcmeon at Corinth* he met Manto on his wanderings and had two children by her. H. J. R.

ALCMAEON (2) of Croton (*c.* 500 B.C.), pupil of Pythagoras, physician and scientist, wrote a book Περὶ φύσεως. Fundamentally a Pythagorean, he was also influenced by Heraclitus. He is best known for his list of contrary principles (Arist. *Metaph.* 986ᵃ27), and for his study of the human sense-organs. He is said to have been the first Greek to operate on the eye; his view that the eye is connected with the brain by pores was adopted by Empedocles and the Atomists (*see* ANATOMY, para. 1).

Testimonia and fragments in Diels, *Vorsokr.*⁵ i. 210–16. *PW* i. 1556. W. D. R.

ALCMAEONIDAE, a noble Athenian family which played a leading part in Attic politics in the seventh, sixth, and fifth centuries B.C. Its most prominent member was Cleisthenes (q.v., 2). Pericles was the son of an Alcmaeonid mother. *See also* CYLON. M. C.

ALCMAN (*fl.* 654–611 B.C., Jerome–Eusebius; 631–628 B.C., Suidas), lyric poet, who lived in Sparta in the second half of the seventh century B.C. While some (ap. Suid. s.v. 'Αλκμάν) said that he was a Laconian from Messoa, others (Crates ap. Suid.) said that he came from Sardes in Lydia, and support for this has been found in fr. 13, where the poet may be addressing himself. In the latter case he would be an Asiatic Greek. He is also said to have been a slave who was granted his liberty because of his skill (Heraclid. Pont. fr. 2). His fragments show no direct reference to contemporary history, though fr. 100 may refer to the end of a war, and fr. 44 may be a tribute to Spartan methods of government. His work seems to belong to the period of peace which followed the Second Messenian War, and is mainly concerned with Spartan feasts and festivals. He wrote lyrical poems which were later collected in six books (Suid. loc. cit.). These seem to have been mainly choral and to have often been sung by choirs of maidens. From one more than half survives (fr. 1). Beginning with a myth which illustrates the punishment of pride, it goes on to give personal remarks about the girls who sing and is very hard to interpret. It has been variously ascribed to festivals of Artemis, the Dioscuri, Dionysus, and Helen, seems to have been sung at night in some kind of competition against another choir, and has been thought to have its parts divided between different members of the choir, an unusual, though not impossible, occurrence in Greek poetry. Other fragments come from hymns to the Dioscuri (frs. 2–6), Hera (fr. 24), Athena (frs. 25–8), Apollo (frs. 29–34), and Aphrodite (fr. 35), while one seems to describe a nocturnal festival of Dionysus (fr. 37). He also wrote in hexameters what may have been Preludes to recitations of Homer. In these he sometimes varies a Homeric theme (fr. 73) or speaks about himself (fr. 94). He uses a literary language which includes Dorian and Aeolic elements and shows echoes from Homer. References to the Issedones, the Rhipean mountains, and King Kolaxais of Scythia may perhaps be taken from the work of Aristeas of Proconnesus. He writes with unaffected charm about simple matters such as birds (frs. 92–4), horses (fr. 1, ll. 45–9, 58–9), food (frs. 49, 55, 56), and with magic about night and sleep (fr. 58). Suidas says that he was the inventor of love-poems, but his fragments give no evidence on this beyond the tender emotions which he describes between the different members of a choir. His metres are varied and usually simple, though in fr. 58 he shows an advanced technique. It is not clear that he used a triadic structure in his verse.

Text: E. Diehl, *Anth. Lyr. Graec.* ii. 7–38. Criticism: H. Diels, *Hermes* 1896, 340–74; C. M. Bowra, *Greek Lyric Poetry* (1936), 16–76; J. A. Davidson, *Hermes* 1938, 440–58. C. M. B.

ALCMENE, in mythology, daughter of Electryon. When her husband Amphitryon (q.v.) killed her father by mischance, she left Argos for Thebes with him, but refused to allow him conjugal rights till he had avenged the death of her brothers on the Taphians and Teleboans. He gathered an army and set out; but during his absence his wife was visited by Zeus (*see* HERACLES). She thus bore Heracles to Zeus and Iphicles to Amphitryon ([Hesiod], *Shield* 1 ff.). The birth was delayed by Hera (*Il.* 19. 114 ff., much elaborated in Ov. *Met.* 9. 290 ff., Ant. Lib. 29, from Nicander). After the death of Heracles, she and her children were persecuted by Eurystheus; according to Euripides (*Heracl.*) they took refuge in Attica. Eurystheus attacked but was defeated and captured, the victory being bought by the sacrifice of Heracles' daughter Macaria to Persephone, in accordance with an oracle; Alcmene insisted on the death of Eurystheus. At her own death Alcmene was taken to the Islands of the Blessed and a stone substituted in her coffin (Pherecydes ap. Ant. Lib. 33. 3). She had a cult at Thebes and elsewhere (Farnell, *Hero-Cults*, 409). H. J. R.

ALCYONEUS, *see* GIANTS.

ALEMANNI, *see* ALAMANNI.

ALESIA, a town of the Mandubii, a client-state of the Aedui, modern *Alise-Ste Reine,* a hill-fort built by La Tène Celts. Excavation has revealed a Gallic town with *murus Gallicus.* In 52 B.C. Caesar besieged Vercingetorix here, and after beating off a large relieving army received his surrender. Siege-works corresponding to Caesar's minute description were discovered in 1860–5. A Gallo-Roman town on the hill, with important buildings, is in course of excavation. It suffered damage in A.D. 69 and c. 166, and in the third century, eventually falling into decay.

Caesar, *BGall.* 7. 68–89 (siege). Grenier, *Manuel* i. 206–25; ii. 702–12; J. Toutain, *Alésia gallo-romaine et chrétienne* (1933). C. E. S.

ALETES (Ἀλήτης), in mythology, (1) son of Hippotas. Asking at Dodona how he might become king of Corinth, he was told he should do so 'when one gave him a clod of earth on a day of many garlands'. He went there on a festival as a beggar, and was given earth by one of whom he asked bread; subsequently he became king through an intrigue (schol. Pind. *Nem.* 7. 155). (2) Son of Aegisthus, *see* ERIGONE (2). H. J. R.

ALEUADAE, the leading aristocratic family of Thessaly, who dominated the neighbourhood of Larissa. The military and political organization of the Thessalian national State was ascribed to Aleuas the Red. The earliest *tagus* (q.v.) who was certainly an Aleuad was Thorax; his intrigues with Persia caused a temporary eclipse of Aleuad influence after the invasion of Xerxes. The Aleuadae vigorously opposed the tyrants of Pherae and several times invited Macedonian intervention. Simus, at first a creature of Philip, later defied him, and the suppression of this movement against Macedonian domination finally broke the power of the Aleuadae. H. D. W.

ALEUROMANCY, *see* DIVINATION, para. 6.

ALEXANDER (Ἀλέξανδρος) (mythological), *see* PARIS.

ALEXANDER THE GREAT, *see* ALEXANDER (3).

ALEXANDER (1) **I,** king of Macedon c. 495–450 B.C. He submitted to Persia (492) and served with the Persian forces under Xerxes. Nevertheless he succeeded in helping the Greeks without arousing Persian suspicion; he advised the Greeks to abandon Tempe and is said to have given information to the Athenians before Plataea. For his services he was admitted as a Hellene to the games at Olympia, where he won a victory, and became proxenus at Athens. He endeavoured to hellenize his court, to which he invited Pindar. After the Persian retreat he annexed territory as far as the Strymon valley, capturing silver-mines in the Krusha Balkan, whence he issued the first Macedonian coinage on the standard used by Abdera. His further expansion was checked by the Delian Confederacy and Athens' reduction of Thasos. He was the first king of Macedon to enter Greek politics, to establish claim to Greek descent, and to introduce Greek ways into Macedonia.

F. Geyer, *Historische Zeitschrift,* Beiheft 19 (1930). N. G. L. H.

ALEXANDER (2) **II,** eldest son of Amyntas and king of Macedon 369–368 B.C. Invoked by the Aleuadae (q.v.) against Alexander of Pherae, he garrisoned Larissa and Crannon before a rebellion in Macedonia compelled him to return. Pelopidas ejected the Macedonian garrisons, arbitrated in Macedonia, and made alliance with Alexander. Shortly afterwards Alexander was murdered. He probably instituted the *pezetaeri* (*see* HETAIROI *and* ARMIES, GREEK AND HELLENISTIC, para. 4). N. G. L. H.

ALEXANDER (3) **III** of Macedonia ('the Great'), 356–323 B.C., son of Philip II and Olympias of Epirus. Aristotle became his tutor, and he early showed his powers of intellect and command. Despite serious quarrels with Philip, occasioned by palace intrigues and uncertainty as to the succession, Alexander did succeed without difficulty (336), and immediately devoted himself to the plan of invading Asia which was part of his inheritance. To invade the Persian Empire with limited objectives was not difficult, experience having shown that a Greek army could penetrate to Mesopotamia and, with good cavalry, might defeat any Persian army. Distances were great and communications sometimes difficult; but an army could usually live on the land, and had nothing to fear, west of Iran, from a national resistance of hostile populations.

2. Having secured Macedonia, Greece, and his northern frontiers, Alexander crossed the Hellespont (334) with an army of about 40,000 men, of whom fewer than half were Macedonians, and fewer than a quarter were Greek contingents from city-members of the Corinthian League. His immediate object was certainly to liberate the Greek cities in Asia. This was quickly achieved, after the battle of the Granicus (near the Hellespont) had reduced the Persian advance forces to defending a few strong places. He now disbanded his fleet and proceeded to 'defeat the Persian fleet on land', by conquering its remaining bases in Phoenicia and Egypt. Having completed the conquest of western and southern Asia Minor, he was brought to action by the Persian 'Grand Army'. The battle of Issus (near Alexandretta) was fought on ground unfavourable to the Persian cavalry; it was won by the steadiness of the Macedonian infantry and Alexander's brilliant cavalry leadership. Shortly after, he refused peace on favourable terms—the first certain sign that, exceeding the more restricted aims of the Greeks and probably of Philip, he intended to conquer the whole Persian Empire. But though the way to Babylon and the East lay open, he adhered to his original plan and spent the next year in occupying Phoenicia, Palestine, and Egypt. The capture of Tyre represents his greatest military achievement, and with it Persia ceased to be a Mediterranean Power.

3. In 331 Alexander left Egypt for Babylonia, where Darius had collected another 'Grand Army'. At the battle of Gaugamela (in the plain of Mesopotamia), he outmanœuvred and defeated the Persians on their own terrain; Darius escaped, but now became a mere fugitive. Alexander proceeded to occupy the Persian capitals (Babylon, Susa, Persepolis, Ecbatana), where the vast treasures of the Empire were stored. The sack of Persepolis, if not promoted by impulse, was probably intended to mark the end of the Persian monarchy; and the death of Darius after a stern pursuit left Alexander free to assume the title of *Basileus* (Great King) and to treat further resistance as rebellion (330). In a great sweep from the Caspian to the south-east slopes of Hindu Kush he found little opposition (330–329), but the conquest of Bactria and Sogdiana (Russian Turkestan) cost him nearly three years of hard fighting. Here was a national resistance broken only by time, a strategy adapted to new conditions, and a final gesture of reconciliation, Alexander's marriage with the Sogdian Roxane.

4. The Indian Expedition (327–325) extended the eastern frontiers of the Empire to the Hyphasis (Beas) and lower Indus. The nations of north-western India, unable to combine, presented to Alexander an opportunity like that which the disunion of Greece had given to Philip. The only formidable opponent was Porus (king of the Paurava), and the only great battle (the 'Hydaspes battle') was another triumph for Alexander's versatility. Having overrun the Punjab, he turned back because the army refused to follow him farther. The return journey to Persia became a voyage of discovery. With half of the army, part marching and part in ships newly built, he reached the Indus delta, whence the fleet was to make the unknown voyage to the Persian Gulf, while he took an equally dangerous land route to prepare its bases. This return march through Gedrosia has been called

Alexander's 1812; exaggerated though its horrors may have been, it was certainly the nearest that he ever came to a great disaster. The fleet suffered too, but arrived safe (325–324).

5. The last year of Alexander's life reveals how great would have been his difficulties had he survived. Misgovernment and disloyalty among his subordinates, a mutiny of his Macedonians, a rising of Greek soldier settlers in Bactria, imminent war in Greece—these were the fruits of his policy, which may conveniently be summarized under two heads, (*a*) Alexander's conception of conquest; (*b*) his conception of himself.

(*a*) In the government of the Empire he made only one important innovation, the separation of fiscal from military authority in the Western provinces, with a centralized financial administration. To peoples used to being ruled, the change of rulers meant little; with the former rulers themselves, the Iranian nobility, the case was different. With striking originality, Alexander adopted the style and ceremonial of a Persian king; he drafted Iranian cavalry into his army, and had 30,000 boys trained to fight in the phalanx. He married into the Iranian nobility and eventually made his highest officers do likewise, and encouraged mixed marriages by the soldiers. This bold policy was not wholly successful *vis-à-vis* the Iranians themselves: most of his Asiatic governors turned out badly. To many of his Macedonian officers it was odious from the first, and finally his plans for a new 'mixed' army occasioned the great mutiny of 324, when even the Macedonian soldiers, devoted hitherto, stated their grievances. To the Macedonians the situation was simple: they were the conquerors, the barbarians were the conquered. To Alexander it appeared that some at least of the barbarians should be partners in the Empire. It is even possible that Alexander was the first to conceive the idea of the essential unity of all mankind.

(*b*) It is practically certain that in 324 Alexander officially requested the Greek cities to treat him as a god (Aelian, *VH* 2. 19; Hyperides 5, col. 31; Arrian, *Anab.* 7. 23. 2): this act perhaps contains the clue to his inner personality and aims. It is usually interpreted as a political manœuvre, a means of evading his obligations to the Greek city-members of the Corinthian League (to all except Greeks the act was without meaning); but, if so, it was a very clumsy manœuvre, and failed of its purpose. Greek religion certainly allowed for the possibility of a man, a great benefactor, becoming a god; but there was no religious consciousness in Greece which could override the highly developed political consciousness, and there was no question of Alexander's deification appearing to any Greek as a 'revelation', or compensating for the loss of his political birthright, complete autonomy. Alexander himself, however, may have believed strongly in his own divinity: if Greeks in general could hail a benefactor as a god, who more likely to believe in his divinity than the benefactor himself? In 332–331 Alexander had gratuitously undertaken a long and dangerous march to the desert oracle of Ammon (oasis of Siwah), and his own propaganda later announced that he had been recognized as son of Ammon (Zeus) (Callisthenes ap. Strabo 17. 1. 43, and see AMMON). This may well have been a customary local formula addressed to a new pharaoh; but, equally, its effect can have been incalculable on one whose whole career reveals his extraordinary preoccupation with the gods of all nations and, perhaps, his emulation of the Greek gods Heracles and Dionysus in particular.

6. It remains a debated question whether Alexander aimed at a universal monarchy. The chief evidence supporting this view is probably not authentic (Diodorus 18. 4. 3 ff.); in fact, there is no sign that he intended in the immediate future anything more than exploration, and perhaps conquest, on his southern and northern frontiers (Arabia and the Caspian). His desire in India to conquer still farther was natural if, as is certain, he thought the eastern Ocean comparatively near. If he believed in his own divinity, that does not make him intent on conquering the West as well as the East, since no Greek god (except perhaps Zeus) was ever supposed to hold a universal rule. What is certain is that he would never have remained idle.

7. Alexander was undoubtedly the greatest general of his race and probably of antiquity. He profited by the splendid army of Philip, and by technical improvements in siegecraft; but this does not explain his achievement, which was due to a profound, if unconsidered, insight into the essentials of strategy, and a wonderful versatility. By temperament an inspired leader of cavalry and a 'monster of celerity', he could nevertheless be patient (siege of Tyre), and could fight a defensive battle until the moment came to strike (Gaugamela). No doubt he exposed himself too readily, and in leading a charge he lost control of the battle; yet to this personal courage and his powers of endurance he partly owed his continued ascendancy over officers and men, despite their accumulating grievances. As a ruler, he must be judged by his plans for the Empire (above), which were grand and original, but perhaps impossible of execution, even by himself. His foundations of new cities show a superb appreciation of strategic needs and economic possibilities. He was always eager to find some new thing, whether a new land or a new piece of knowledge. His favourite book was the *Iliad*, his favourite sport hunting, and his only relaxation the symposium. His character was 'heroic' rather than amiable: extravagantly brave and generous by nature, he was extravagantly passionate and revengeful when thwarted, and his few vices led him to great crimes. In him, the soul wore out the breast, and he died, in his thirty-third year, of a fever which might well have spared him had he ever known how to spare himself.   G. T. G.

BIBLIOGRAPHY

ANCIENT SOURCES. *Alexander-historians* (see under the separate names). There are supposed to be three main lines of tradition. (1) The 'good' tradition includes Alexander's official *Journal* (*see* EPHEMERIDES) written by Eumenes of Cardia, and such letters of his as are genuine; the geographical work of his bematists Baeton and Diognetus; the histories of Ptolemy I and Aristobulus, Nearchus' book, and some valuable information in Eratosthenes. (2) The anti-Alexander tradition of the Greek opposition, crystallized by the Peripatetic and Stoic schools: Alexander was a tyrant, and (to the Peripatetics) owed his success to Fortune. (3) The so-called vulgate tradition is no real tradition, but only a name used to embrace Cleitarchus and some lesser writers, as Onesicritus and Chares; roughly, it signifies popular beliefs as distinct from genuine history. Callisthenes, and the informative 'mercenaries' source' used by Diodorus and Curtius, come under no label. Many writers are known, from the fourth century B.C. to the fourth A.D., of whom nothing survives but the name or a few fragments; among them may be mentioned Anaximenes the rhetorician, Ephippus the gossip-monger, Androsthenes and Polycleitus the geographers, Nymphis and Marsyas of Pella, historians, Anticleides the antiquarian, Hegesias, rhetorician and untrustworthy historiographer. (For lists see Müller and Jacoby, below.)

Of extant writers, the most important, Arrian, is noticed under his name. Plutarch's *Life* of Alexander is compiled from every kind of source, good and bad; the first part of his *De Alexandri fortuna* is a young man's passionate protest against the slanders of Stoics and Peripatetics. Diodorus 17 is largely based on Aristobulus, overlaid with Cleitarchus and other matter. Curtius gives the full-length Peripatetic portrait, and some invaluable information mixed with much rubbish. Justin is almost worthless. Several extant works—the Metz *Epitome*, *Itinerarium Alexandri*, *P. Oxyrhynchus* 1798, *Codex Sabbaiticus* 29—illustrate the transition to the Romance. The problem of the modern historian is how far to use Diodorus and Curtius. C. Müller, *Scriptores rerum Alexandri Magni*, 1846; F. Jacoby, *FGrH* ii nos. 117–53, and the notes; H. Berve, *Das Alexanderreich* ii under the separate names (contemporaries only). For Ptolemy: H. Strasburger, *Ptolemaios und Alexander*, 1934; E. Kornemann, *Die Alexandergeschichte des Königs Ptolemaios I*, 1935. For others: articles 'Nearchos' (W. Capelle), 'Aristoboulos', 'Curtius' 31, 'Diodoros' 38 (E. Schwartz), 'Kleitarchos' (F. Jacoby), in *PW*. Full bibliographies in *CAH* vi. 592 ff. and in Glotz, *Hist. grecque* iv. i (1938), pp. 33 ff.; *see also* W. W Tarn, *Alexander the Great* ii (1948).   W. W. T.

MODERN LITERATURE. (*a*) *General histories.* K. J. Beloch, *Griechische Geschichte*[2] iii, pt. 1, ch. 16 (1922); J. G. Droysen, *Gesch. Alexanders des Grossen* (reprint 1917); Glotz, *Hist. grecque* iv, pt. 1, bk. 1 (1938); W. W. Tarn, *CAH* vi, chs. 12 and 13 (1927): *Alexander the Great*, 2 vols. (1948); G. Radet, *Alexandre le Grand* (1931); U. Wilcken, *Alexander der Grosse* (Engl. Transl. 1932).

(*b*) *Alexander's army.* H. Berve, *Alexanderreich*, pt. 1, 103; J. Kromayer and G. Veith, *Antike Schlachtfelder*, iv, pt. 3 (1924).

(*c*) *Administration and political ideals.* Berve, op. cit. 221; Ed. Meyer, *Kleine Schriften*[2] i (1920); W. W. Tarn, 'Alexander's Ὑπομνήματα' (*JHS* 1921, p. 1); Tarn, *Alexander the Great and the Unity of Mankind* (1933); U. Wilcken, 'Alexanders Zug in die Oase Siwa' (*Sitz. Berl.* 1928, p. 576); Wilcken, 'Alexander der Grosse und die hellenistische Wirtschaft' (*Schmollers Jahrbuch* 1921, p. 349).

(*d*) *Prosopography.* Berve, op. cit., pt. ii.

(*e*) *Review of recent literature.* Th. Lenschau, *Bursian* cxliv (1934), 78.   G. T. G.

ALEXANDER (4) IV of Macedonia (323–?310 B.C.), posthumous son of Alexander the Great and Roxane, succeeded to the Empire jointly with Philip Arrhidaeus, but never lived to rule, though the possession of his person was important to the 'legitimist' generals in the wars of the *Diadochi* (q.v.), and later (316) to Cassander (q.v.), the greatest enemy of Alexander's house. Prisoner though he then became, his name and cause were still useful to Antigonus in his efforts to re-unite the Empire under his own rule; and, correspondingly, his continued existence embarrassed Cassander, who finally put him to death.   G. T. G.

ALEXANDER (5) OF PHERAE, tyrant 369–358 B.C., nephew of Jason (q.v., 2). Throughout his tyranny he was opposed by Larissa and other cities, which refused to recognize him as *tagus* (q.v.). His enemies received occasional support from Thebes and became increasingly formidable, especially after Pelopidas had organized a Thessalian League modelled upon that of Boeotia. Pelopidas, who three times visited Thessaly, defeated him at Cynoscephalae in 364, and Pherae was subsequently compelled to join the Boeotian League. Alexander was at first an ally but later an enemy of Athens. In 358 he was murdered by the sons of Jason.

The cruelties attributed to Alexander by a tradition which glorified Pelopidas may well be exaggerated. He possessed great energy but little judgement, and, unlike Jason, attempted to crush the Thessalian cities rather than win them by diplomacy.

Diodorus, bk. 15; Plutarch, *Pelopidas*, 26–35. H. D. Westlake, *Thessaly in the Fourth Century B.C.* (1935), ch. 7.   H. D. W.

ALEXANDER (6) I, king of Molossia in Epirus, 342–330 B.C. Philip II of Macedon, his brother-in-law, placed him on the throne, expelling Arybbas and subjugating Cassopia; as king of the Molossi he united Epirus in the form of a symmachy with himself as *hegemon*. Invoked by Tarentum *c.* 333, he conquered most of south Italy, allied with Rome, and was defeated and killed at Pandosia; he had made Epirus an important power, coining gold and silver, and united to Macedon by his marriage with Cleopatra, sister of Alexander the Great.

G. N. Cross, *Epirus* (1932).   N. G. L. H.

ALEXANDER (7) II, king of Epirus 272–*c.* 240 B.C. During the Chremonidean War (see CHREMONIDES) he invaded Macedonia, was routed and deposed by the generals of Antigonus, who set up a republic (*c.* 263 B.C.). Restored with Aetolian help, he conquered Acarnania and divided it with Aetolia. He died shortly afterwards.

G. N. Cross, *Epirus* (1932).   N. G. L. H.

ALEXANDER (8) (b. *c.* 315 B.C.), of Pleuron in Aetolia (hence called *Aetolus*), made his name as a tragic poet and was included in the *Pleiad* at Alexandria. *Circa* 285–283 he was entrusted by Ptolemy Philadelphus with the *diorthosis* (preliminary sorting-out) of the tragedies collected for the Library. Later, *c.* 276, he appears at the court of Antigonus Gonatas in Macedonia.

WORKS. The only trace of A.'s tragedies is one title, Ἀστραγαλισταί (*Dice-players*), *TGF* 817. Two elegies are known, the *Apollo* and the *Muses*. The first was a collection of love-stories with unhappy endings, framed as a series of prophecies uttered by Apollo himself. Thirty-four lines (fr. 3) survive from the story of Antheus and Cleoboea; the language is learned and the style extremely dry. The *Muses* contained literary history. A striking appreciation of Euripides in anapaestic tetrameters (fr. 7) must come from a similar work. From two epyllia, *Halieus* (*Fisherman*) and *Circa* or *Crica*, only a fragment apiece survives. Other works mentioned are *Phaenomena* (A. met Aratus in Macedonia), *Epigrams*, and *Ionic Poems* (without music) in imitation of Sotades.

Texts: J. U. Powell, *Collectanea Alexandrina* (1925), 121–30. Modern literature: G. Knaack, 'Alexandros (84)' in *PW* i. 1447–8; W. von Christ, *Gesch. griech. Lit.* ii. 1⁶ (1920), 173–4.   E. A. B.

ALEXANDER (9) (*c.* 290–*c.* 245 B.C.), son of Craterus (q.v. 2), and his successor as viceroy of Corinth and Euboea, declared himself independent in 250–249 (not 252, as commonly held) at Ptolemy's instigation, and allied himself with the Achaean League. A short war with Athens and Argos ended in 249, Gonatas acquiescing in his usurpation. The Aetolian victory of Chaeronea (245) split his realm in two, and about this time he died (poisoned, an unlikely rumour claimed, by Gonatas), leaving his throne to Nicaea, his widow.

W. H. Porter, ed. Plutarch's *Aratus*, Introd. (1937).   F. W. W.

ALEXANDER (10) **BALAS** (d. 145 B.C.), pretended son of Antiochus IV, became king of Syria after the defeat and death of Demetrius I (q.v.). He was a pawn of Pergamum and Egypt and had support from the Roman Senate, which feared (unnecessarily) a revival of Seleucid power; as a king, he was incompetent. His reign (150–145) was ended by his expulsion and death; it is important mainly as marking the beginning of a period of civil wars which hastened the disintegration of the Seleucid Empire.   G. T. G.

ALEXANDER (11) 'Polyhistor', born *c.* 105 B.C. at Miletus or in Caria, came as prisoner of war to Rome; freed by Sulla (*c.* 80 B.C.), he took the name L. Cornelius Alexander; he was pedagogue to Cornelius Lentulus, and later taught C. Julius Hyginus. He was accidentally burnt to death at Laurentum. His vast literary output (*FHG* iii. 206–44) included works on various lands, Delphi, Rome, the Jews, wonder-stories, and literary criticism. A. followed Crates' school; industrious and honest, he lacked taste and originality.   F. W. W.

ALEXANDER (12) (2nd c. A.D.), son of Numenius, wrote a τέχνη in which the rival theories of Apollodorus and Theodorus were discussed; also Π. σχημάτων (based on Caecilius), which influenced later writers. *See also* ANONYMUS SEGUERIANUS.

Spengel, *Rhet.* i. 427–60, iii. 1–6, 9–40.   J. W. H. A.

ALEXANDER (13) **OF ABONUTEICHOS** (Ἀβώνου τεῖχος) in Paphlagonia, a contemporary of Lucian (q.v.), whose bitterly hostile account of him, Ἀλέξανδρος ἢ ψευδόμαντις (see M. Caster, *Études sur Alexandre ou le faux prophète*, 1938) is our chief source of information. He claimed to have a new manifestation of Asclepius (q.v.) in the form of a serpent called Glycon. With this divine aid, he gave oracles and conducted mysteries, from which he carefully excluded all unbelievers, especially Epicureans, and all Christians. He got a considerable following, a prominent member being a Roman of some standing, named Rutilianus. He was personally handsome and apparently popular with women especially; to what extent, if any, he believed his own doctrine can hardly be determined in the absence of any description of him other than Lucian's, which represents him as a thorough impostor, applying to him all the stock abuse of rhetorical controversial writings. The cult survived its author.

Cf. A. D. Nock in *CQ* xxii (1928), 160 ff.   H. J. R.

ALEXANDER (14) **OF APHRODISIAS** (fl. early 3rd c. A.D.), Peripatetic philosopher. He began lecturing at Athens in A.D. 198 or soon after, and dedicated his book Περὶ εἱμαρμένης to Septimius Severus and Caracalla. His teachers had been Aristocles of Messana, Herminus, and Sosigenes. He was the ablest of the Greek commentators on Aristotle, and is treated with great respect by his successors among these, who preserve many fragments of his lost works. He is singularly free from the mystical tendencies of his time. He assumes the indissoluble unity of the mental faculties and denies the immortality of the soul and the reality of time, but apart from a few such individual doctrines confines himself to the attempt to explain Aristotle's views without innovation or criticism. The extant commentaries are on *An. Pr.* 1 (ed. M. Wallies, 1883), *Top.* (ed. M. Wallies, 1891), *Mete.* (ed. M. Hayduck, 1899), *Sens.* (ed. P. Wendland, 1901), *Metaph.* (ed. M. Hayduck, 1891; only bks. 1–5 are by Alexander). There are also extant under his name a work of his own Περὶ ψυχῆς (ed. I. Bruns, 1887), Ἀπορίαι καὶ λύσεις, Ἠθικὰ προβλήματα, Περὶ εἱμαρμένης, Περὶ κράσεως καὶ αὐξήσεως (all ed. by I. Bruns, 1892). Of these Περὶ ψυχῆς 1, Περὶ εἱμαρμένης (tr. A. Fitzgerald, 1931), and Περὶ κράσεως καὶ αὐξήσεως are probably genuine. Ἰατρικὰ ἀπορήματα καὶ φυσικὰ προβλήματα and Περὶ πυρετῶν (ed. J. L. Ideler, *Physici et Medici Graeci Minores* (1841), 3, 81), and Προβλήματα ἀνέκδοτα (ed. U. C. Bussemaker, *Aristotelis Opera* (1857) iv. 291), are spurious.

PW i. 1453.   W. D. R.

ALEXANDER, *see also* SEVERUS (2), TIBERIUS (3).

ALEXANDRA, *see* CASSANDRA.

ALEXANDRIA was founded by Alexander the Great immediately after his conquest of Egypt; communication with Europe by sea was important, and none of the existing harbours on the Delta coast could accommodate a large fleet. Whether he designed to make it the capital of the country is unknown; it was not till after Ptolemy had established himself in possession of Egypt that the seat of government was transferred from Memphis to Alexandria. But it grew rapidly, and was made a centre of learning as well as of commerce and industry by the second and third Ptolemies. Under the Romans it was the one city that counted in the province; and, despite disasters in the third century, it did not begin to decline till the Arab conquest shifted the connexions of Egypt from Europe to Asia.

The plan of ancient Alexandria is difficult to reconstruct, as nearly all buildings have been destroyed and debris has covered the old levels. It lay on a neck between the sea and Lake Mareotis, and the island of Pharos was linked with the mainland by a mole, seven stades (*c.* ¾ mile) long, so as to provide a double harbour. The chief edifices were by the eastern harbour—the Emporium fronting the sea, the Palace on the east, the Caesareum and Theatre, probably also the Museum and Library, behind; a wide street intersected the city from east to west, by which was the Gymnasium. The only one of these of which the site is certain is the Caesareum. The Temple of Sarapis stood in the western quarter. Under the Ptolemies the city may have had a Senate, but there is no record of any action by it. Augustus definitely refused to grant any self-government, though the Alexandrian citizenship was allowed to continue and carried with it certain privileges—e.g. it was the avenue to Roman citizenship for an Egyptian. In 200 Alexandria was given a Senate by Severus, simultaneously with other Egyptian towns: it is not known to have done anything. Probably the control of the city was kept strictly in the hands of the Prefect: the only special local official mentioned is the head of the police. The Jews, who were numerous and inhabited a special quarter, had their own ethnarch and council under the Ptolemies, and Augustus confirmed these privileges.

E. Breccia, *Alexandrea ad Aegyptum* (1922); H. I. Bell, *JEg.Arch.* 1927, 171.   J. G. M.

ALEXANDRIA 'ad Issum', near Iskenderun (*Alexandretta*) on the Gulf of Issus, was probably Myriandrus re-founded by Alexander (333 B.C.). It lay six miles south-west of the Cilician Gates (hence the alternative name 'Alexandria of Cilicia'), and was also the key of the Syrian Gates (*Beilan Pass*).

ALEXANDRIA 'Arachosion' (of the Arachosii) or Alexandropolis, at or near Kandahar in Afghanistan, was founded or re-founded by Alexander, 329 B.C. It lay on an important trade-route between Merv (or else Meshed) and India through the Bolan and Mula Passes, Kabul, and Las Bela. It soon ceased to be a Greek town.

ALEXANDRIA 'Areion' (of the Arii), Herat in Khorassan, founded or re-founded by Alexander, was the chief town in Ariana. It lay on an important trade-route from Merv or else Meshed) through Kandahar to India.

ALEXANDRIA 'Eschate', or 'the Farthest' (*Khodjend?*), hurriedly founded by Alexander on the Jaxartes as a fortress held by Macedonians, Greek mercenaries, and local Asiatics, against savage peoples beyond. It was re-founded by Antiochus I as an 'Antiocheia'.

Arrian, *Anab.* 4. 1. 3; Curtius 7. 6.

ALEXANDRIA 'among the Paropamisadae' was a short-lived colony of Alexander, north of Kabul, at the junction of routes from Aria, Bactria, and India.

Arrian, *Anab.* 3. 28. 4 ff.; 4. 22. 5; Strabo 12. 514.   E. H. W.

ALEXANDRIAN POETRY. This term commonly denotes the Greek poetry, other than the New Comedy of Athens, composed between *c.* 300 and *c.* 30 B.C., and is justified by the fact that till 145 (expulsion of the scholars by Ptolemy Physcon) Alexandria, thanks to its library and museum, was the literary capital of the Greek world. The distribution of this poetry over the period indicated is very uneven. Two decades of fairly intense activity form a prelude to Alexandria's Golden Age, which itself only lasts from *c.* 280 to *c.* 240. The writers who follow are all Epigoni, and the second century B.C. is the least productive in the history of Greek poetry. But the beginning of the first century witnesses a St. Martin's Summer of Alexandrian poetry thanks to Meleager and his contemporaries. Meleager's *Garland* becomes known at Rome, and soon Parthenius and others introduce their pupils to Alexandrian poetry as a whole, which is thus enabled to play an important part in shaping the course of Roman poetry.

2. The struggles of the *Diadochi* discouraged the production of any poetry except Comedy and the Epigram, but *c.* 300 a revival becomes visible in the southeastern corner of the Aegean, both on the mainland (Zenodotus and Menecrates of Ephesus, Hermesianax and Phoenix of Colophon) and in the neighbouring islands, where the chief representatives were Philetas of Cos, Simias of Rhodes, and Asclepiades of Samos. The last-named, together with his associates Posidippus and Hedylus, was mainly important as an epigrammatist, but the other two exerted a wider influence. Both were scholars as well as poets and reviving the tradition of another scholar-poet, Antimachus of Colophon, set an example of a learned poetry, appreciable only by the cultivated few, which their successors followed almost as a matter of course. Though very little of their work survives, it seems that Philetas, Simias, and their contemporaries experimented in most of the poetical forms which the next generation commonly favoured, i.e. Narrative Elegy, Epyllion or Short Epic, Catalogue-poem, Hymn, Iambus, Didactic Poem, Epigram, and Paignion. After 280 the leading figures are Aratus of Soli, chiefly but by no means solely a didactic poet; Theocritus of Syracuse, best known for his pastorals but active in many other fields; Callimachus of Cyrene, the most representative Alexandrian poet, thanks to the clarity with which he formulated his poetic creed and the consistency with which he practised it; and finally Callimachus' opponent, Apollonius of Rhodes, who dared to question his former master's ruling and to compose an Epic in the grand manner. Contemporary with these poets was, it seems, Herodas of Cos, whose *Mimiambi* reflect the spirit of the age no less by the archaism of their form than by the modernity of their content. Of Alexandrian tragedy (though its seven most famous writers were known as the Tragic Pleiad) and Satyr-play little can now be established. The *Alexandra*, attributed to Lycophron, one of the Pleiad, probably belongs to the early second century.

3. In the quarrel between Callimachus and Apollonius the victory went to the former, but the question remained unsettled. Thus after the Golden Age, while Euphorion and Eratosthenes cultivate the Epyllion, Rhianus and others revert to the longer Epic. Moschus and Bion continue the Pastoral down to *c.* 100, and the didactic poems of Nicander of Colophon are best dated about the middle of the second century. But at Alexandria the savant had displaced the scholar-poet. For the poets referred to above see under their names.

4. The chief characteristics of Alexandrian poetry may be summarized thus:

Matter. Preferably this should be new, i.e. not invented by the poet, but not hitherto treated in verse. Hence the attractiveness for the Alexandrians of the so-called Local Legends, which they unearthed from prose-chroniclers. Hence also one justification for Didactic. But the less familiar types of earlier poetry, e.g. the Epic Cycle apart from Homer, the Hesiodic poetry, the Homeric Hymns, Stesichorus, and Pindar were other possible sources for material. Again the poet's own emotions find increased expression, not merely in intimate verse like the Epigram, but in the Iambus, Hymn, and Narrative Elegy. But Love, though a favourite theme of Alexandrian narrative poetry, finds little subjective expression outside the Epigram and some forms of Lyric.

Form. Few forms of earlier Greek poetry escaped imitation by the Alexandrians, but this imitation by no means precluded originality, which lay, as these poets thought, in a nice adjustment of their exemplars to the conditions of their own day and in subtle touches calculated to introduce novelty and variety. Thus the traditional forms are used for new purposes or the traditional dialect of a form is changed or the traditional vocabulary is given a fresh meaning. Some metres were refined, others were simplified. By conscious art the Alexandrians did all they could to rise above the limitations of their age.

G. Knaack, 'Alexandrinische Litteratur' in *PW* i. 1399–1407; W. von Christ, *Gesch. griech. Lit.* ii. 1⁶ (1920); F. Susemihl, *Geschichte der griechischen Litteratur in der Alexandrinerzeit* (1891–2); F. A. Wright, *A History of Later Greek Literature* (1932); E. A. Barber, *CAH* vii (1928), chap. 8; A. Couat, *La Poésie Alexandrine* (1882, Engl. Transl. by J. Loeb, 1931); Ph.-E. Legrand, *La Poésie Alexandrine* (1924); A. Körte, *Die Hellenistische Dichtung* (1925, Engl. Transl. by J. Hammer and M. Hadas, 1929); U. von Wilamowitz-Moellendorff, *Hellenistische Dichtung in der Zeit des Kallimachos* (1924); E. Rohde, *Der Griechische Roman und seine Vorläufer³* (1914).   E. A. B.

ALEXANDRIANISM, LATIN. The work of the 'Alexandrian' poets of the first century B.C. is distinguished from the earlier hellenizing movement, represented in epic and drama, by a difference of models and a corresponding difference of purpose. Their main interest was turned from the classical Greek writers to the poets of the third and second centuries, and their chief aim was not to graft on to Latin the best of Greek literature but to promote the ideals of technical perfection cultivated by the Alexandrians. Alexandrianism was primarily a movement of scholarship, and it found a natural home in Italy when the period of creative activity which had come with the Punic Wars and the first contacts of Rome with Hellenism had been succeeded by an age of criticism of which the beginnings are seen in Lucilius and Accius; and the social and political unrest in Italy which set in with the Gracchi may well have encouraged an ideal which turned men of letters away from the world upon themselves and on art for art's sake.

Four of the outstanding characteristics of the Greek Alexandrians reappear in their Latin followers: (1) the development of new *genres*, especially epyllion, elegy, and epigram, all miniature forms displacing the large-scale epic and drama; (2) a regard for form, for concinnity and symmetry in language and metre, which left a lasting impression on Latin literature; (3) the cult of erudition, seen in the vogue of didactic verse, mythological allusion, and novelty in story-telling; (4) the emergence of a subjective and personal way of writing—in elegiac and lyric a new individualism, in narrative a sentimental handling and a psychological interest. Two differences probably tempered the excesses of Alexandrian mannerism in transplanting: while in Greece Alexandrian literature was a literature of exhaustion, in Italy it was one of experiment and revolt, and most of the Italian Alexandrians, for all their *ars* and *doctrina*, were not confined, as were their masters, to the sheltered life of the study.

The movement begins with the work of poets writing near the beginning of the first century B.C. and bridging the gap between the old style and the new—the epigrams of Porcius Licinus, Pompilius, and Lutatius Catulus, the bizarre erotic poems of Laevius, and the didactic verse of Varro Atacinus. These pioneers were succeeded by a school of poets especially associated with Cisalpine Gaul, of which Catullus is the only surviving representative, but which also included Valerius Cato, Furius Bibaculus, Cinna, Calvus, Cornelius Nepos, and Ticidas. Thus established, Alexandrianism exercised its influence throughout the century. The mock-heroic *Culex* and the romantic *Ciris* of the *Appendix Vergiliana* are Alexandrian in technique, as were the lost elegies of Gallus; Virgil's *Eclogues*, and in a less degree the *Georgics*, show the influence of Alexandrian models, though in his maturer work Virgil learned to turn their lessons to his own purposes and to reconcile Alexandrian ideals with the tradition of Latin epic. The combination of learning with intense individualism in Propertius reflects his avowed allegiance to the masters of Alexandrian elegy, and Ovid's elegies owe much to the same sources, while the *Metamorphoses* and the *Fasti* are akin to the narrative verse of Callimachus, though in Ovid the influence of Alexandrianism is fused with that of the rhetoric of the schools. Cf. NEOTERICI. C. J. F.

ALEXIS (*c.* 372–270 B.C.), Middle Comedy poet, born at Thurii but naturalized at Athens, where he lived the greater part of his long life. His work (245 plays, Suidas) belongs partly to the New Comedy; of the 130 titles, many reveal (1) the love-motive (Παμφίλη, Ἐπίκληρος, Λευκαδία, Ὀρχηστρίς), (2) study of character-types (Κιθαρῳδός)—two features of the New Comedy. A. wrote only about twelve mythological burlesques, and seldom imitated tragedy. His fragments show sometimes real reflection and beauty of language: fr. 70, carnal love a blasphemy against true Love; fr. 219, life as a carnival;

fr. 228, old age as life's evening. An unusual type of play is Γραφή (fr. 40): a man fell in love with a 'picture', which possibly 'came to life', like Hermione's statue in the *Winter's Tale*. In Ὕπνος (fr. 240) Sleep is described in a riddle more elegant than the usual Middle Comedy riddles. In Λίνος (fr. 135) Linus, teacher of Heracles, has a library at his disposal. Fr. 36, Aristippus; fr. 94, legislation against philosophers, 307 B.C.; fr. 98, beauty-culture; fr. 108, part of a postponed prologue (of the New Comedy type); fr. 149, eulogy of cookery; fr. 257, a gate-crasher.

A lively scene (26 vv.), preserved on a Berlin papyrus of third century B.C. (*PBerol.* 11771; see M. Platnauer in Powell, *New Chapters in Greek Literature*, 3rd Ser., 166 f., and G. Norwood, *Greek Comedy*, 56 ff.) shows someone taking refuge at an altar before the temple of Demeter; here the Chorus, in addition to singing a lyric interlude denoted in a second fragment by XO]POY, as in Ar. *Eccles.* (see ARISTOPHANES), participates in the action of the play.

It was doubtless popular success that stimulated Alexis to write so many plays; and in Roman times also his fame was great (echoes in Plautus; as also in Caecilius and Turpilius; Gell. 2. 23. 1).

FCG iii. 382 ff.; *CAF* ii. 297 ff. D. L. Page, *Greek Literary Papyri*, i. 232–7 (Loeb). W. G. W.

ALFENUS VARUS, P.? (*consul suffectus* 39 B.C.; *praenomen* inferred from designation of P. Alfenus Varus, *cos.* A.D. 2, presumably his son, as P. f.) was according to the scholiast on Hor. *Sat.* 1. 3. 130 a shoemaker of Cremona who studied under Servius Sulpicius Rufus at Rome, attained some fame as a jurisconsult, became consul, and was accorded a public funeral (cf. Pomponius, *Dig.* 1. 2. 2. 44; Gell. 7 (6). 5. 1; Amm. Marc. 30. 4. 12). He and his son apparently were the only Cisalpines to reach the consulate under Augustus. Perhaps an early supporter of Octavian, Alfenus proved a severe land-commissioner in Cisalpine Gaul, though possibly he helped to restore Virgil's farm (Servius, on *Ecl.* 9. 10, erroneously names Alfenus as Pollio's successor as governor of Cisalpine Gaul, which in fact had become autonomous). Probably he was the Varus named in *Ecl.* 9; it is less certain whether *Ecl.* 6 was dedicated to him or to Quinctilius Varus. He provided Horace (l.c.) with the point of a joke and has been identified with the versifier whom Catullus called Suffenus (T. Frank, *CQ* xiv (1920), 160 ff.). H. H. S.

ALFIUS (ALPHIUS) AVITUS, a 'neoteric' (q.v.) of Hadrian's time, used iambic dimeters in poems on historical events.

Baehr. *FPR*; Morel, *FPL*.

ALGIDUS, the eastern section of the outer crater rim of the Alban Hills, famous for its temples of Diana and Fortune and its fashionable villas (Hor. *Carm. Saec.* 69; Livy 21. 62; Sil. 12. 536). The rim of the Alban Hills is here pierced by a narrow pass which the Aequi seized in the fifth century B.C. (Diod. 11. 40; implies the date 484). This pass, which the Via Latina (q.v.) later used, dominated the route to the Hernici; consequently Cincinnatus and other Roman generals strenuously tried to dislodge the Aequi, Postumius Tubertus finally succeeding in 431. E. T. S.

ALIENUS, see CAECINA (2).

ALIMENTA. The purpose of the *alimenta* in the Roman Empire was to give an allowance for sustenance to poor children, and this was achieved by the investment of capital in mortgage on land, the mortgage interest being paid to, and administered by, municipalities or State officials. The system originated in private philanthropy, the earliest known benefactor in this field being T. Helvius Basila in the late Julio-Claudian period (*ILS* 977).

A later philanthropist, the younger Pliny, who made a similar gift to Comum, has recorded his reasons for his endowment (*Ep.* 7. 18). Nerva (Aurelius Victor, *Epit.* 12) and Trajan were the earliest emperors to give money for this purpose. According to two Trajanic inscriptions (*ILS* 6675 ; 6509) from Veleia, near Parma, and from the Ligures Baebiani, near Beneventum, landowners who received sums of money from the emperor's gift gave security in land, to the value of as much as twenty times the sum received; on this sum they paid annual interest at the rate of 5 per cent. The total received annually in interest at Veleia was 52,200 sesterces, which was distributed among 245 boys, 34 girls, and 2 illegitimate children. The boys received 16 sesterces a month, the girls 12, and the illegitimate children 12 and 10 respectively. The system was widely advertised by Trajan, on one of the bas-reliefs of the arch at Beneventum and on coins with the legend ALIM[ENTA] ITAL[IAE] Its primary object was to increase the birth-rate among the poorer classes, partly, as Pliny suggests (*Panegyricus* 26), with a view to the recruiting of the Roman legions. Perhaps the system had a secondary object of assisting farmers—in as far as the emperors promoted the scheme by investing capital in land, instead of making an annual allowance for the purpose. As the system spread during the second century (in the provinces, as well as in Italy), a civil service was created for its administration, with a senatorial *praefectus alimentorum* at its head and subordinate equestrian *procuratores ad alimenta*. The *curatores* of the great roads of Italy also took part in this work.

PW, s.v.; *CAH* xi. 210 ff. (bibliography on p. 887); and (far the best account in English) B. W. Henderson, *Five Roman Emperors* (1927), 214–24. Coins, H. Mattingly and E. A. Sydenham, *The Roman Imperial Coinage* (1926) ii. 240. Illustrations of the bas-reliefs, Rostovtzeff, *Roman Empire*, 308, 314.   J. P. B.

ALISO, a fort on or near the Lippe established during the wars of Drusus, possibly the one mentioned by Dio (54. 33. 4) as set up in 11 B.C. 'at the point where the Lupia and the Elison unite'. The garrison resisted the advancing Germans after the defeat of Varus in A.D. 9 and regained the Rhine (Vell. Pat. 2. 120). Germanicus, in 15, refortified all the posts between Aliso and the Rhine and restored the road (Tac. *Ann.* 2. 7). Its site is uncertain; its identification with an important Roman fort excavated at Haltern, on the Lippe, thirty miles from the Rhine, is not widely accepted.   O. B.

ALLECTUS, probably *rationalis* (finance minister) of Carausius (whom he assassinated(A.D. 293)). After three years' rule he was overthrown by Constantius I, whose praetorian prefect, Asclepiodotus, defeated and slew him, probably somewhere in Hampshire.

P. H. Webb in *Num. Chron.*, 4th series, xxii. 127–71; and in Mattingly–Sydenham, *Roman Imperial Coinage* v, ii, 427–60, 558–70; E. Stein, *Geschichte des spätrömischen Reiches* (1928), i. 116.
                                                    C. E. S.

ALLEGORY, GREEK. As philosophy developed, many who valued its various doctrines were led by their admiration for the wisdom and inspiration of Homer and Hesiod to find similar views symbolically expressed in the early poetry. (The tendency survives, as in a modern scholar who depicts Homer as a pacifist because Zeus dislikes Ares in the *Iliad*.) Even the early philosophic critics of Homer's world-view accepted this standpoint, and competed with the poet by expressing their theories in 'poetic' style, whether by remoulding the myths to suit newer cosmogonies, or at least by using puns, personifications, and 'enigmas', either in verse (Parmenides, Empedocles) or in prose (Anaximander, Heraclitus). Hence the belief that Homer too 'philosophized in verse', and that allegorical treatment could make his teaching fully explicit. This belief was not altogether baseless, for Homer and Hesiod contain some

traces of speculative thought and some genuinely allegorical passages. Allegorical interpretation could not develop fully until philosophy had more or less attained an independent life and an abstract (non-mythical) language of its own. Its most flourishing period was the late fifth century B.C., when Metrodorus of Lampsacus, the most thoroughgoing of all allegorists, studied Homer's 'physical' doctrines, and other adherents of Anaxagoras as well as Heracliteans and Sophists specialized (as Plato shows) in the 'hidden meanings' (ὑπόνοιαι: ἀλληγορία is a later word) of the poets. Once this method had been initiated by the philosophers for its *positive* results, it began to be exploited by 'grammarians' (first, apparently by Theagenes of Rhegium (q.v.), who explained some allegories in Homer's Theomachy) for the *negative* purpose of defending morally offensive passages of Homer. But the leading allegorists were philosophers, who applied their treatment to offensive and inoffensive passages alike. The handmaid of this pseudo-science (never, be it noted, popular among the Greeks) was 'etymology' (q.v.), which dealt in the 'true' meanings, as revealed by assonances, of mythical words and names.

2. Plato attacked *positive* (philosophical) allegorism, chiefly on the ground that the authority of the poets (even if their teaching were ascertainable) cannot do duty for reasoned argument. *Negative* or defensive ('grammatical') allegorism he regarded as unimportant.

3. After Plato, among philosophers allegorism (mainly etymological) was practised by the Stoics (especially Chrysippus) for the illustration and corroboration of their own doctrines. This school, however, from Zeno (following Antisthenes, who was not an allegorist) onwards, admitted the presence of irrational 'opinion' (δόξα) in the poets, from which deeper meanings cannot be extracted. The Middle-Stoics laid still more stress on this element; hence Cicero's Balbus (unlike the grammarians) refuses to interpret the Theomachy; and the Platonizing Stoic, Ariston of Chios, rejected allegorism entirely. In the first century A.D. the Stoic Seneca regarded it as an aberration of the grammarians; but his contemporary, the Stoic Cornutus (in his *De Natura Deorum* = *Theologiae Graecae Compendium*, Teubner), tried to recall Stoicism to something like the position of Chrysippus. Plutarch was Platonic enough to reject allegorism, but the Neoplatonists (except Plotinus) revived it in a distorted and exaggerated form (see e.g. Porphyry, *De Antr. Nymph.*).

4. As for the grammarians, Alexandrian scholarship (Aristarchus, etc.) rejected the allegorical interpretations of Homer. But Crates and his school, under Stoic influence, adopted the practice for the defence of Homer's good fame. It is ultimately from these grammarians that the bulk of the allegories found in the Homeric scholiasts and in the collection (first century A.D.) known as Heraclitus' *Quaestiones Homericae* (a veritable curiosity of literature) is derived. Their view is that Homer either erred or allegorized (cf. [Longinus] Π. ὕψους 9. 7), but (unlike Longinus) they are sure that he did not err: if Zeus binds Hera (for example), this means that aether is the boundary of air, and the two 'anvils' are the other two elements. Such is the standpoint also of Strabo (a Stoic of sorts, who regarded myth as the treacle disguising the pill of historical and philosophical truth), [Plutarch] (*Vit. Hom.*), Maximus of Tyre (for whom poetry is elementary philosophy), Dio Chrysostom, and others. Some, but not all, of these used allegorical interpretation to vindicate Homer's omniscience against Plato.

5. Deliberately written allegories are rare in Greek and never extensive. Examples are Prodicus' *Choice of Heracles* (Xen. *Mem.* 2. 21) and Plato's parable of the Cave (*Resp.* 514 a).

J. Tate in *CR* xli. 214; *CQ* xxiii. 41, 142, xxiv. 1, xxviii. 105 and literature there cited; L. Radermacher, *Mythos und Sage bei den Griechen* (1938), especially p. 293, n. 10.   J. T.

ALLEGORY, LATIN. The main line of succession in allegorism leads from Stoicism not to Rome but to Alexandria; Origen, for example, had read Cornutus. Some Romans (Ennius, Varro), however, adopted Greek methods with the Roman gods, and the Stoic in Cicero's *De Natura Deorum* (2. 62–9) supplies examples of 'etymological' allegorism on these lines, deriving e.g. 'Neptunus' from 'nare'. But Horace, who knew Stoicism well, is more typically Roman in ignoring 'physical' and 'etymological' speculations, and merely contending for the moral meanings of the *Odyssey* (*Epist.* 1. 2) and of the tales of Orpheus and Amphion (*Ars. P.* 391 ff.). And though the word ἀλληγορία first appears in a Roman author (Cicero), it has only a very restricted use, as a term of rhetoric.

Unlike medieval allegorism, which led both before and after the Renaissance to the creation of allegories on a large scale (Dante, Spenser), these theories did not result in any such sustained parallelism as marks *The Pilgrim's Progress* or *The Tale of a Tub*. They merely encouraged certain poetic conceits (like calling the sea 'Neptune'), and numerous personifications, which range from Lucretius' Venus to the Philologia of Martianus Capella. These personifications are sometimes developed in poetry in a way which, as Propertius (2. 12) on the figure of Amor suggests, may indicate the influence of symbolic painting; this manner is most clearly seen in Ovid's picturesque Palace of the Sun, Home of Sleep, etc. (*Met.* 2. 1 ff.; 11. 592 ff.).

A few allegories come directly from Greek: Horace takes over Alcaeus' ship of State; Silius adapts the Choice of Heracles. Some rare examples are original and unsophisticated like Tarquin's message to his son or Menenius Agrippa on the belly and the other members (Livy 1. 54; 2. 32). The most novel tendency was the allegorical representation of contemporary persons and events: the shepherds of Virgil (and of his imitators) correspond (to a degree still disputed) with real persons. To some modern scholars Aeneas has seemed a similar disguise for Augustus. Actual allusions in the *Aeneid* to contemporary events may excuse such a view; just as Virgil's profundity and deliberate ambiguities may excuse the older interpretation of the *Aeneid* which, from the time of Donatus onwards, found there an allegory of ideas rather than of facts (see D. Comparetti, *Vergil in the Middle Ages* (tr. of 1st ed., 1895). i, ch. 8; D. L. Drew, *The Allegory of the Aeneid*, 1927.)   J. T.

ALLIA, nowadays probably the *Fosso Bettina* (T. Ashby, *Roman Campagna*, 71), a stream flowing into the Tiber eleven miles north of Rome, where the Gauls overwhelmed the Romans (390 B.C.). Despite Diodorus (5. 114) the battle probably occurred on the left bank of the Tiber (Livy 5. 37; Plut. *Cam.* 18). *See also* AIUS LOCUTIUS.
E. T. S.

ALLITERATION, *see* ASSONANCE.

ALLOBROGES, a tribe of Gallia Narbonensis, occupying modern Dauphiné and Savoy. The name seems to mean 'foreigners'. They were annexed to Rome in 121 B.C. by Cn. Domitius Ahenobarbus and Q. Fabius (q.v.) Maximus *Allobrogicus*. An attempted revolt was crushed by C. Pomptinus (61). On the other hand, they resisted the invitations of Catiline (63) and Vercingetorix (52). Under the Empire the name gives place to Viennenses (from the capital Vienna), surviving only as the protecting god, Allobrox.

C. Jullian, *Hist. de la Gaule* (1908), ii. 515; vi. 330–5.   C. E. S.

ALLOBROGICUS, *see* FABIUS (8).

ALOADAE, in mythology, Otus and Ephialtes, sons of Iphimedeia, wife of Alōeus, and Poseidon. They grew till they were nine fathoms tall and nine cubits broad when nine years old (*Od.* 11. 310–11). They imprisoned

Ares in a bronze vessel for thirteen months (*Il.* 5. 385 ff.); they meant to climb to heaven by piling mountains on each other, but were killed by Apollo before they grew up (*Od.* 11. 315 ff.). A later variant (Hyg. *Fab.* 28) says they tried to violate Artemis; Apollo sent a hind between them, and in shooting at it they killed each other. They were punished in Tartarus (Hyg. ibid. and Rose ad loc.). In their cult (see Schultz in Roscher's *Lexikon* i. 254) they have no such unholy characteristics.   H. J. R.

ALPHABET, GREEK. The various forms of local alphabet current in early Greece were all eventually derived from a Phoenician (Semitic) script which must have reached the Aegean in the course of trade certainly by the eighth century B.C. and probably much earlier. The most striking feature in the Greek adaptation of the Phoenician model is that by altering the original significance of *A E I O Y* Greek, unlike Phoenician, has achieved an independent representation of vowel-sounds.

An early form of Greek alphabet is represented by the oldest inscriptions of Thera, Melos, and Crete. In it, as in many other 'epichoric' or local alphabets, we find ϝ (= ɰ), Ϙ (= k before o and u), M (San, occurring frequently instead of Σ), and H = h. It lacks, however, Φ and X, using Π (or ΠΗ) and K (or KH) instead. Ψ and Ω are also absent. At a more developed stage the alphabets fall into two groups. Both groups have Φ and also X, but they differ in their use of the latter symbol. (1) The eastern alphabets used X = kh and some of them, notably those of the Greek cities of Asia Minor and of Argos, Corinth, and Megara, had Ψ = ps and Ξ = ks. Other places, e.g. Athens, used ΦΣ and ΧΣ for Ψ and Ξ. (2) The western alphabets current in Euboea and on the mainland outside the districts which followed the eastern system had X = ks and Ψ = (↓) = kh. They had no Ξ and expressed ps by ΦΣ.

One variety of the eastern alphabets, namely the East Ionic, eventually became predominant. In the Ionic dialect (as in many others) short e had a close quality (ẹ), but there were two forms of long e, one open and the other close (ẹ̄, ẹ̄). Through the loss of the h-sound in Ionic, the symbol H became superfluous. The East Ionic alphabet then employed it to represent ẹ̄, and invented a new form of O, namely Ω, to represent ọ̄. ẹ̄ and ọ̄ continued for a time to be denoted by E and O like the short vowels, but before 400 B.C. the development of the original diphthongs ei and ou into simple long vowels of close quality made it possible to use EI and OY not only for the original diphthongs but also for the ẹ̄ and ọ̄ that had never been diphthongal (e.g. εἰμὶ κοῦρος, older ΕΜΙ ΚΟΡΟΣ).

The Ionic alphabet was officially accepted at Athens in the archonship of Eucleides (403–402 B.C.) and thereafter gradually extended. Non-Ionic elements like ϝ lingered locally for some time, and local differences, especially in vowel-pronunciation, produced variations in spelling. As H could no longer express the rough breathing, a modification of it (Ⱶ) was used for this purpose in some areas and has given rise to the sign ʽ; another modification (⊣) has produced the sign for the smooth breathing.

A. Kirchhoff, *Studien zur Geschichte des griech. Alphabets* (1887) E. S. Roberts, *Introduction to Greek Epigraphy* i (1887); C. D. Buck, *Comparative Grammar of Greek and Latin*, pp. 68–73 (U.S.A. 1932); E. Schwyzer, *Griech. Grammatik* i (1934), 137–48.   J. W. P.

ALPHABET, LATIN. It has generally been held that the original Latin alphabet of twenty-one letters (A B C D E F Z H I K L M N O P Q R S T V X) was borrowed directly from the Greek alphabet of Cumae in Campania. This city, a colony of Chalcis in Euboea, was regarded as the most likely source, because the ancient forms of certain Latin letters strongly resemble the Cumaean equivalents. Modern opinion, however, favours the view that Latin, like Oscan and Umbrian, owes its alphabet only indirectly to the Greeks, but directly to the Etruscans. For Latin the immediate source is said to be an early form of Etruscan script, derived itself not from Campania but from a type of Greek alphabet current on the mainland of Greece north of the Corinthian Gulf. Be this as it may, the ultimate source is a western alphabet which contained the signs X = ks and H = h.

In the Latin adaptation of this alphabet the following points are noteworthy:

(1) C (⟨), i.e. Γ (Gamma), was at first used for k as well as for g. This peculiarity is usually ascribed to the influence of Etruscan, which made no distinction between voiceless and voiced stops (see PRONUNCIATION, GREEK, B. 1). Of the three signs thus available for the voiceless guttural, K was used originally before a, C before e and i, Ϙ (Greek Koppa) before o and u (as in Greek) and also before u. Eventually C was generalized for all positions except before u, where Ϙ continued. Relics of the old spelling are Kalendae and Kaeso. In the third century B.C. the introduction of G, a modification of C, gave the voiced guttural a separate symbol. C., Cn. = Gaius, Gnaeus are survivals.

(2) Z originally represented the voiced s (z), but was dropped when this sound became r in the fourth century B.C. Afterwards it was reintroduced to express ζ in words borrowed from Greek, and found its place then at the end of the alphabet, its original position having been occupied by G.

(3) For Latin f the nearest equivalent in Greek was the voiceless Digamma (FH) which occurred in some dialects, and which must have approximated in pronunciation to Scottish wh, i.e. hw. F is a simplified form of FH. This use of F (in Greek = u) made it necessary to express u as well as u by V. Y (another form of V) was added late in the Republican period to denote v (by then = ü) in words borrowed from Greek. I had to do duty for both i and j. The use of u and i for the vowels and v and j for the semivowels is a device of medieval times and not of the Latin period.

(4) An attempt to distinguish long vowels from short by writing the former double is attributed to the poet Accius (q.v.). Later the 'Apex' (a mark like an acute accent) was sometimes employed for the same purpose. ei for ī is common from about 150 B.C. after the diphthong ei had become ī in pronunciation. The occasional use of 'I longa' (e.g. FELICI) starts in Sulla's time.

(5) For double consonants a single letter originally sufficed. The reform in this respect belongs to the second century B.C. and is ascribed to Ennius.

W. M. Lindsay, *The Latin Language* (1894), 1–12; F. Sommer, *Handbuch der lateinischen Laut- und Formenlehre* (1914), 23–31; Stolz–Schmalz, *Lateinische Grammatik*⁵ (1926, revised, M. Leumann and J. B. Hofmann), 44–50. J. W. P.

ALPHESIBOEA, in mythology, daughter of Phegeus of Psophis and wife of Alcmaeon (q.v.). According to Propertius 1. 15. 15, she and not Callirhoë's children avenged him; perhaps a mere blunder, perhaps an unknown variant.

ALPHEUS (Ἀλφειός), the largest river of Peloponnesus, rises in south Arcadia near Asea and flows past Olympia to the Ionian Sea. Its waters were fabled to pass unmixed through the sea and to rise in the fountain of Arethusa at Syracuse (Pind. *Nem.* 1. 1; Ibycus, fr. 23 Bergk). T. J. D.

ALPS. Although the passes of the Alps were used for trans-European commerce since prehistoric times, the early Greeks had no knowledge of these mountains, though a vague notion of them may lurk in their speculations about the Hercynia Silva and the Rhipaean Mts. (qq.vv.); in Herodotus (4. 49) 'Alpis' is a tributary of the Danube. By the fourth century Greek travellers in north Italy and Provence brought information about a 'pillar'

or 'buttress' of the north (Ephorus ap. Scymn. 188); but Apollonius Rhodius (4. 627 f.) could still believe that the Rhône and Po were interconnected. The Roman conquest of Cisalpine Gaul and Hannibal's invasion of Italy (Polyb. 3. 50–6; Livy 21. 32–7; the pass remains unidentified) brought more detailed knowledge, and Polybius gave a good description of the western Alps, though he thought that they extended uniformly in a west–east direction. The campaigns of Caesar in Gaul, and of Tiberius in Switzerland and Austria, opened up the Alps thoroughly, and in the first two centuries A.D. at least five paved roads (Little and Great St. Bernard, Splügen, Maloja, and Brenner passes) were built across them. Strabo defined the curve of the Alps with substantial correctness, and graphically described their vegetation and the predatory habits of the valley populations.

The Romans distinguished the following chains: Alpes Maritimae, Cottiae (from Mte. Viso), Graiae (the St. Bernard section), Poeninae (Mt. Blanc–Mte. Rosa), Raeticae (Grisons), Noricae (Tyrol), Carnicae, and Venetae. They also gave the name of 'Alps' to the Austrian and Dalmatian mountains.

Cary–Warmington, *Explorers*, 120 ff. E. H. W.

ALTAR. The ancients distinguished between βωμός, *altare*, the altar of a supreme god, ἐσχάρα, *ara*, that of a hero or demi-god, and ἑστία, *focus*, a domestic altar, though these distinctions were not always observed. An altar for the indispensable sacrifice was a necessary adjunct of a cult (save in the case of infernal deities, to whom offerings were made in pits, βόθροι, *scrobes*); and the primitive heaps of stones or turf had been replaced as early as Minoan times by more regular forms. The open-air altars for burnt offerings at Greek temples often attained enormous size; the great altar of Pergamum was 40 feet high, while others at Syracuse and Parium are credited with a length of one stadium. Within the temples smaller altars served for incense or bloodless offerings. In Hellenistic times circular altars are common, while the Romans preferred the quadrangular form, and their cinerary urns were frequently in the form of altars. Altars were places of refuge, the suppliants being under the protection of the deity to whom the altar belonged.

E. Saglio, Dar.–Sag., s.v. 'Ara'; E. Pernice, *Die Hellenistische Kunst in Pompeji*, vol. v (1932); W. Altmann, *Römische Grabaltäre der Kaiserzeit* (1905). F. N. P.

ALTHAEA, see MELEAGER, OENEUS.

ALTHAEMENES, in mythology, son of Catreus, king of Crete. Warned by an oracle that he would kill his father, he left Crete for Rhodes. Long after, his father came to seek him; Althaemenes took him for a pirate and killed him (Diod. Sic. 5. 59; Apollod. 3. 12–16).

ALYATTES, fourth Lydian king (c. 610–560 B.C.), of the house of Gyges, finally drove out the Cimmerians, extended his dominion to the Halys, and made a war on Cyaxares the Mede (585), during which occurred an eclipse (perhaps the one foretold by Thales). After the conclusion of peace through Labynetus (Nebuchadrezzar) of Babylon he continued the Lydian campaigns against Ionia, conquered Smyrna, but was foiled by Clazomenae and Miletus. He built temples to Athene near Miletus and made offerings to Delphi. The vast round-barrow tomb of Alyattes described by Herodotus and Strabo is still visible.

Herodotus bk. 1; Strabo 13. 627. G. Radet, *La Lydie* (1893), 193–206. P. N. U.

ALYPIUS (3rd or 4th c. A.D.), the author of an extant Εἰσαγωγὴ μουσική, the fullest source of our knowledge of Greek musical scales.

Ed. C. Jan, *Musici Scriptores Graeci* (1895), 357–406. PW i. 1710.

AMAFINIUS, Gaius, older contemporary of Cicero, popularized the philosophy of Epicurus in Latin. Cicero refers to him disparagingly (*Acad. Post.* 1. 5; *Tusc.* 1. 6; 2. 7; 4. 6, 7).

PW i. 1714.

AMALTHEA (Ἀμάλθεια), in mythology, a nurse of Zeus, variously described as a nymph or a she-goat (details in Stoll, in Roscher's *Lexikon* 1. 262). Possibly she was originally a theriomorphic goddess (cf. Nilsson, *Minoan-Mycenaean Religion*, 466). Two principal legends, neither early, concern her. She was transformed into the star Capella (Aratus, *Phaen.* 162–4 and many later authors). Her horns were wonderful, flowing with nectar and ambrosia (schol. Callim. *Jov.* 1. 49). One of them broke off, and was filled with fruits and given to Zeus (Ov. *Fasti* 5. 121 ff.). This was the origin (the story is variously told) of the proverbial Ἀμαλθείας κέρας, *cornu Copiae*, first mentioned by Antiphanes ap. Ath. 503 b. It is very likely to be older than its connexion with Amalthea, for it is a widespread folk-motif, the magical object whose possessor can get anything he likes (or all he wants of some specific thing) out of it (see Stith Thompson, D 1470. 2. 3). Ovid has another version: when Achelous' horn was broken off in wrestling with Heracles (q.v.), the Naiads picked it up, filled it with flowers and fruit, and gave it to Bona Copia (*Met.* 9. 88–9); this is Latin, for there is no Greek goddess corresponding to Copia. H. J. R.

AMANUS, the name applied to the mountain horseshoe of Elma Dagh above Alexandretta, together with Giaour Dagh which trends north-eastwards. It is separated from Taurus by the deep gorge of the Jihun. It is crossed by great passes, the Amanid Gates (*Baghche Pass* from the Cilician plain to Zeugma), and the Syrian Gates (*Beilan Pass*) carrying a Roman road from Tarsus into Syria. The part of Mt. Amanus which Cicero reduced to order (*Att.* 5. 20. 3) must be the heights that end in Ras-el-Khanzir. E. H. W.

AMARANTUS of Alexandria (1st–2nd c. A.D.), an older contemporary of Galen (Gal. 14. 208, Ath. 8. 343 f), was the author of a commentary on Theocritus (*Etym. Magn.* 156. 30, 273. 41), perhaps based on Theon's notes, and of a work Περὶ σκηνῆς, which probably gave historical and biographical accounts of stage performances and performers (Ath. l.c. and 10. 414 e). J. F. L.

AMASEIA, the capital of the early kings of Pontus, with a magnificent fortress commanding the middle valley of the Iris and the chief Pontic roads. Pompey gave it municipal status and made it the administrative centre of a large territory. Under the Empire it became the metropolis of Galatic Pontus, and increased in importance with the development of the roads leading to the eastern frontier.

Strabo 12. 561; F. Cumont, *Studia Pontica* ii (1906), 138–82, iii (1910), 109–87; Jones, *Eastern Cities* (Index). T. R. S. B.

AMASIS (1) became pharaoh *c.* 569 B.C. as champion of the native Egyptians against Apries (q.v.), but later 'becoming philhellene' granted the Greeks Naucratis (q.v.), maintained a Greek bodyguard, allied himself with Lydia, Samos, Cyrene, and perhaps Sparta, and made gifts to Greek shrines. These foreign alliances were dictated by the Persian peril, which overthrew Egypt in 525, shortly after Amasis' death. His long reign was remembered as a time of peace and prosperity attested by numerous great buildings, and Amasis himself as a great but unconventional and sometimes deliberately undignified figure.

Herodotus 1. 77 and bks. 2 and 3; G. Maspéro, *Popular Stories of Egypt*, 281 ff. P. N. U.

AMASIS (2) (6th c. B.C.), potter, in Athens; probably father of the potter Cleophrades; known from eight signatures. The Amasis painter, who worked for him 555–525 B.C., painted black-figure *amphorae*, *oenochoae*, *lecythi*, cups. A formal but individual artist; note particularly his Apollo and Heracles (Boston), and Dionysus and Maenads (Paris).

J. D. Beazley, *JHS* 1931, 256; W. Kraiker, *Ath. Mitt.* 1934, 19. T. B. L. W.

AMAZONS (Ἀμαζόνες), in mythology, a people of female warriors, always situated on the borders of the known world (Themiscyra on the Thermodon, Aesch. *PV* 723–5, but they have been driven from there, Strabo, 11. 5. 4; on the Tanais, Pliny, *HN* 6. 19; the Caspian Gates, Strabo, ibid., citing Cleitarchus), and in all probability nothing more than the common travellers' tale of the distant foreigners who do everything the wrong way about, cf. Hdt. 2. 35. 2 (Egyptians). Attempts to find a sociological significance in the legend (Bachofen, *Mutterrecht*², 1897, 88 and elsewhere) or other explanation postulating a foundation of fact are mistaken. Why this particular tale caught Greek fancy and was elaborated we do not know.

2. *Amazon customs*. Generally it is stated that they provide for offspring by meeting at certain seasons with men of another race, afterwards keeping their female children but getting rid of or disabling the boys (Justin 2. 4. 9–10, Diod. Sic. 2. 45. 3); they destroy the girls' right breasts to prevent them getting in the way in battle, ibid.; hence their name, fancifully derived from ἀ+μαζός. Their deities are Ares (e.g. Ap. Rhod. 2. 385 ff.) and Artemis (see below). Their occupations are hunting and fighting, their weapons being especially the bow and the 'Amazonian' crescent-shaped shield, but also axe and spear, all used on horseback.

3. *Amazon legends*. In the *Iliad* they are warred upon by Bellerophon (q.v.; *Il.* 6. 186) and by Priam (3. 189). After Homer Arctinus (*Amazonis*) and others represent them as coming to the help of Priam after Hector's death under their queen Penthesilea (q.v.), daughter of Ares. Achilles kills her, but is accused of being in love with her by Thersites, whom he kills in anger (cf. Quint. Smyrn. 1. 538–810). With these stories are connected the numerous legends that this or that place in Ionia was founded by Amazons (especially Ephesus, Strabo 12. 3. 21 and 1, 4; Pind. fr. 157 Bowra; Tac. *Ann.* 3. 61. 2; cf. schol. *Il.* 6. 186). They are often connected also with the following legends.

4. Heracles (q.v.) and his campaign against the Amazons to get their queen's girdle produced an echo in the legend of Theseus (q.v.), modelled as usual on that of the greater hero. Either because he had been with Heracles or on account of an expedition he undertook on his own behalf (Plut. *Thes.* 26 gives several versions), the Amazons attacked him in force, reached Attica, and besieged him in Athens itself. A great battle took place on the date of the later festival Boedromia (Boedromion, unknown day), and a chthonian ceremony in Pyanopsion (?) was interpreted as a sacrifice to the dead Amazons. In general, there was a strong tendency, perhaps especially among antiquarians, to explain nameless monuments and festivals whose original meaning had been forgotten by relating them to this event (examples in Plut. ibid. 27). The result was that the Amazons were defeated, or at all events so stoutly resisted that they agreed to retire from Attica. For the further history of the Amazon Hippolyta (or Antiope), who had become Theseus' prisoner, see HIPPOLYTUS.

5. Of Hellenistic date, on the other hand, is the legend, or rather cycle, which represents Dionysus (q.v.) as meeting the Amazons and conquering them. It is part of his conquest of the East; references to it are found, e.g., in Tacitus, loc. cit. and Plut. *Quaest. Graec.* 56.

A Euhemerizing story in Diod. Sic. 3. 71. 4 represents them as his allies, and presumably goes back to some legend to that effect.

6. Representations of the Amazons in art are exceedingly common, the piquant contrast between their feminine beauty and their manly employments attracting artists of all periods of antiquity later than the archaic. Attica was especially rich in these monuments.

Besides the articles 'Amazonen' in Roscher's *Lexikon* and *PW* see especially W. R. Halliday in *The Greek Questions of Plutarch* (1928), 209–11. H. J. R.

AMBARVALIA (*Ambarvale sacrum, Lustratio agri*), (1) a private rite, described by Cato, *Agr.* 141; Verg. *G.* 1. 338 ff., cf. *Ecl.* 3. 77; 5. 75 and Servius ad locc.; Tib. 2. 1; see LUSTRATION. (2) A State rite, in which, since even the earliest *ager Romanus* had too large a circumference to be easily got about in one day, sacrifice was offered at particular points (Strabo 5. 3. 2). That this was identical with the sacrifice to the Dea Dia performed by the Arval Brothers has been repeatedly suggested (Wissowa, *RK* 562), but is rightly denied by A. Kilgour, *Mnemos.* 1938, 225 ff. H. J. R.

AMBER, a fossilized resin, occurring in Tertiary strata and particularly common along the Baltic. From the earliest periods it was highly valued, the bright colour suggesting sunlight. A treasure of 4,000 pieces found in Denmark is actually neolithic, but in the next periods export reduced the quantity available at home. In return for amber Denmark received bronzes from the Mediterranean; this lively commerce explains her early culture. Amber appears freely at Mycenae and sparsely in the Terremare (q.v.); in classical Greece it had little vogue. The trade with Germany, central Europe, and Italy lasted with some fluctuations for two thousand years. Till the late Iron Age the only source was the Baltic ('succinite'). J. M. de Navarro, partly inspired by O. Montelius, has deduced three main routes by plotting all finds on the map of Europe. The central route (early Bronze Age) ran from Jutland up the Elbe to the Saale, where it divided. One half went up the Moldau to the Danube at Passau, the other up the Saale and thence to Passau. From Passau this road crossed the Brenner. The western (middle Bronze Age) diverged from the central route in Thüringen and went to the Main, the Rhine, and the Neckar. The eastern (Iron Age) route, which began at Danzig, by destroying the monopoly of Jutland almost ruined Denmark. It led to the head of the Adriatic, and supplied the east coast of Italy with a particular abundance. Amber is seldom mentioned in classical writers, though its power of attraction interested observers as early as Thales. Pliny (*HN* 37. 45) emphasizes its extraordinary popularity in the Roman Empire. As late as the sixth century A.D. an embassy from the Baltic brought a large gift of amber to Theodoric.

Ebert's *Reallexikon der Vorgeschichte*, s.v. 'Bernstein'; J. M. de Navarro, *Geographical Journal*, Dec. 1925. D. R.-MacI.

AMBITUS, a 'going round' (cf. *ambire*), or canvassing for public office. Personal contact with the electors in Rome was naturally allowed, but propaganda throughout Italy or among provincial citizens, although legal, was generally open to criticism. The State soon intervened against bribery and intrigue. The alleged law *de ambitu* of 432 B.C. is probably either a forgery or an anticipation of the *Lex Poetelia* (358), which forbade propaganda outside Rome but was soon disregarded, or of a law passed in 314 against the *coitiones*, i.e. societies of illegal canvassers. The scandalous increase of electoral corruption in the early second century required an elaborated legislation. From the *Lex Cornelia Baebia* (181) down to the laws enacted by Cicero (*L. Tullia*, 63), Pompey (*L. Pompeia*, 52), and Caesar (*L. Iulia*, 49), attempts were made to stop bribery by threatening heavy penalties (death, exile for ten years or life, etc.). Municipal

authorities accordingly took steps to keep order in local elections. But the works of Cicero and the *Commentariolum petitionis consulatus* (64 B.C.) of his brother Quintus expose the uselessness of such precautions. In the Imperial age *ambitus* came to indicate an appointment illegally secured, and was punished with confiscation and deportation.

L. M. Hartmann, *PW*, s.v.; Mommsen, *Röm. Strafr.* (1899), 865 ff.; W. Kroll, *Die Kultur d. ciceronischen Zeit* (1933), i. 50 ff. P. T.

AMBIVIUS TURPIO, LUCIUS, actor and theatre-director in Terence's day. His experience as a player contributed much to the success of Caecilius Statius and Terence (q.v.). All Terence's plays were, the *didascaliae* record, produced by him.

AMBRACIA, a Greek city, situated north of the Bay of Actium, in the fertile valley of the lower Arachthus. It was founded as a Corinthian colony by Gorgos, son of the tyrant Cypselus. Its attempts to control the whole coastland of the Bay of Actium brought it into conflict with the Acarnanians and Amphilochians, who with Athenian aid inflicted a severe defeat upon the Ambracians in 426 B.C. Ambracia allied with Athens against Philip of Macedon, who subdued and garrisoned it. In 294 it was ceded by Cassander's son to Pyrrhus of Epirus, who made it his capital and spent lavishly on its adornment. In 229 it passed into the Aetolian League, from which it was wrested by the Romans after a siege (189). It then became a free city. M. C.

AMBROSIA and NECTAR, the food and drink respectively (but the reverse occasionally, see Ath. 39 a) of the gods. Their effect is to make those who take them immortal (Pind. *Ol.* 1. 60 ff., cf. *Il.* 5. 341–2). They will keep a corpse from decay (e.g. *Il.* 19. 38–9). The smell of ambrosia is extraordinarily sweet and will overpower bad odours (*Od.* 4. 445–6). Various things connected with the gods are 'ambrosial' (the fodder of Ares' horses, *Il.* 5. 369; the 'beauty', κάλλος, apparently a sort of magical wash, with which Athena treats Penelope, *Od.* 18. 192–3); mortals of high rank wear 'nectarean' garments (*Il.* 3. 385; 18. 25), perhaps 'sweet-smelling'. That nectar is originally some kind of honey-drink (mead?), ambrosia idealized honey, is probable (see Roscher in his *Lexikon* i. 282). H. J. R.

AMBRŎSIUS (St. Ambrose) (c. A.D. 337–4 Apr. 397), son of a *praefectus praetorio* in Gaul, and born there. After his father's death he received in Rome the best education, and entered on an official career. While still young he was appointed *consularis* of Aemilia and Liguria, with head-quarters in Milan. He was so esteemed that on Auxentius' death (374) the people chose him against his will as bishop of Milan, though a layman who had held none of the lower offices. He devoted himself ardently to the varied duties of his office. Already a great orator, he became a great preacher. He fought heresy. After Gratian's death (383) he became again important politically. He successfully opposed the Empress Justina (385, 386), who was an Arian. With equal force and tact he resisted the civil power in the interests of the Church. The Emperor Theodosius was forced by him to repent publicly for murders for which he was responsible.

His writings are not so voluminous as those of Jerome (see HIERONYMUS) or Augustine (q.v.), but are nevertheless considerable in bulk and quality. They are exegetical, ethical, dogmatic, oratorical, and epistolary. (Two contemporary works are falsely attributed to him: a commentary on St. Paul's Epistles, often now called 'Ambrosiaster', and the *Lex Dei sive Mosaicarum et Romanarum legum collatio*). The following illustrate his range: (1) *Hexaemeron* (6 books) on the Creation narratives in Genesis, *De Helia et Ieiunio* (important for history of morals), *De Nabuthe* (Naboth), *De Tobia, Enarrationes in XII psalmos Davidicos, Expositio in psalmum 118* (our 119), *Expositio Evangelii sec. Lucam* (10 books). These were all based on sermons. (2) *De Officiis Ministrorum*, based largely on Cicero *De Officiis*. (3) *De Fide, De Mysteriis, De Sacramentis*. (4) *De excessu fratris Satyri* (2 books), and 91 letters, where his greatness as bishop especially appears.

Works: Migne, *PL* xiii-xvii, *CSEL* (incomplete, 6 vols.); F. Homes Dudden, *The Life and Times of St. Ambrose* (1935). A. S.

AMBURBIUM, a rite of lustration (q.v.) for the city, corresponding to the Ambarvalia (q.v.), for the fields. It is probable that it was annual, though if so it must have been one of the *feriae conceptivae*, or movable festivals, for it appears in no calendar. Beyond this we have no certain knowledge, for the conjecture of H. Usener (*Weihnachtsfest²*, 310 ff.), that it was on 2 Feb. and ultimately christianized into Candlemas is too hazardous to accept even in the modified form proposed by Wissowa (*RK*, p. 142, n. 12), that it was held about then (see L. Delatte in *Ant. Class.* vi (1937), 114 ff.). Lucan (1. 592 ff.) describes an *amburbium* of some kind, but it was clearly an extraordinary ceremony. H. J. R.

AMBUSTUS, see FABIUS (1) and (2).

AMEIPSIAS, Athenian comic writer, contemporary with Aristophanes. The Κόννος (423 B.C.), attributed to him, was placed second to Cratinus' Πυτίνη and above Aristophanes' *Clouds* (hyp. 5 Ar. *Nub.*). Κόννος was Socrates' music-master, and the play probably ran on much the same lines as the *Clouds*. Socrates himself was a character (fr. 9) and the chorus consisted of Φροντισταί (Diog. Laert. 2. 27)—i.e. Sophists (cf. the Φροντιστήριον in the *Clouds*). Protagoras was not included (Ath. 5. 218 c). The Κωμασταί ('The Revellers'), likewise attributed to A., defeated Aristophanes' *Birds* and Phrynichus' Μονότροπος in 414 (hyp. 1 Ar. *Av.*; *IG* ii², 2325). But the Κόννος and Κωμασταί were perhaps by Phrynichus (q.v. 2). According to Aristophanes, a defeated rival, Ameipsias was a vulgar writer (φορτικός, *Nub.* 524) and his jokes banal (*Ran.* 15). Suidas, doubtless echoing Aristophanes, calls him ὑπόψυχρος.

FCG i. 199 ff.; *CAF* i. 670 ff. M. P.

AMELESAGORAS, author of a series of Greek miracle stories: cf. Ov. *Fasti* 6. 749 (see Frazer ad loc.), perhaps derived from A. Probably a priest of Eleusis. A fourth-century B.C. *Atthis* is doubtfully ascribed to him.

FHG ii. 21.

AMELIUS or **AMERIUS GENTILIANUS** (3rd c. A.D.), born in Etruria, was Plotinus' pupil A.D. 246–70. His literary work was devoted mainly to the exposition and defence of Plotinus' philosophy, of which, however, he had little true understanding.

PW i. 1822.

AMICUS AUGUSTI, a term used unofficially to indicate senators and equites who were admitted to the Roman Imperial court. The *amici* were graded (by a practice which, in private families, dated from C. Gracchus and Livius Drusus: Sen. *Ben.* 6. 34) as *primae, secundae*, or *tertiae admissionis*. The term was also used in a narrower sense to indicate those who were chosen from this larger body as the emperor's advisers (*consiliarii*) and travelling-companions (*comites*): cf. Suet. *Tit.* 7. 2; Pliny, *Pan.* 88. J. P. B.

AMISUS, a sixth-century colony of Phocaea or Miletus, situated at the head of the one easy road from the Euxine coast into the interior of Pontus. Pericles settled cleruchs in Amisus and renamed it Piraeus. It belonged to the Pontic kings by 250 B.C. Lucullus gave it freedom and additional territory, gifts that Pompey confirmed when he shaped its municipal constitution. It became a free and allied city under Augustus, and remained attached to the province of Bithynia and Pontus until Diocletian. Its territory included the fertile coastal plain of Themiscyra and was eventually extended westwards to the mouth of the Halys river. Its commercial prosperity is attested by its abundant coinage and the wide dispersal of its citizens.

Strabo 12. 547; F. Cumont, *Studia Pontica* ii (1906), 111 ff., iii (1910), 1 ff.; Jones, *Eastern Cities* (Index). T. R. S. B.

AMMIANUS MARCELLINUS (b. *c.* A.D. 330), last of the great Roman historians, was born into a good family at Antioch. After a creditable military career he wrote in Latin a work dealing with the years 96 to 378, which was thus a continuation of Tacitus. The first thirteen books have perished. Books 14 to 31 contain a very valuable narrative of the events of 353 to 378. Ammianus served under Ursicinus in the East, accompanied him to Italy and Gaul, and took part in operations against the Persians. He visited Egypt and Sparta, and in later life lived in Rome and wrote his history there, finishing it probably a few years after 390. He had a keen eye for human character, and, as Gibbon observed, was 'without the prejudices and passions which usually affect the mind of a contemporary'. He was a polytheist with a ready religious toleration. Latin was an acquired language for him, but he was very well read in several Latin authors. He often makes use of phrases from them, and he is fond of showing his learning in digressions. His style is far from homogeneous and is often overloaded with metaphor and ornament; his syntax also is peculiar, but he can write vivid narrative and strike out a splendid phrase.

Best edition, C. U. Clark's (Berlin, 1910–15). The following are valuable in themselves and for bibliographical references: W. Ensslin, 'Zur Geschichtsschreibung und Weltanschauung des Ammianus Marcellinus', *Klio*, Beiheft xvi (1923); H. Hagendahl, 'Studia Ammianea', *Uppsala Universitets Årsskrift* 1921; G. B. Pighi, *Studia Ammianea* (1935); id. *Nuovi Studi Ammianei* (1936); id. *I Discorsi nelle Storie d'Ammiano Marcellino* (1936); P. de Jonge, *Sprachlicher und historischer Kommentar zu Ammianus Marcellinus XIV* (1935–9); E. A. Thompson, *The Historical Work of A.M.* (1947). G. B. A. F.

AMMON (or **AMO[U]N**), originally the god of the city of Thebes in Egypt. During the age of the Egyptian Empire Ammon became an imperial deity whose worship struck roots in Nubia, Syria, and Libya. Ammon appears in Greek literature chiefly by reason of his cult at the oasis of Siwa, which became known to Greeks after the colonization of Cyrene in the seventh century. In the temple at Siwa there was an oracle of A. whose fame in the Greek world came to rival that of Delphi and Dodona. In Greece A. was usually portrayed on coins and elsewhere with a head of Zeus to which the curling ram's horns of A. were added. Pindar and Herodotus testify to the authority of the oracle of A., and we are told that it was consulted by Cimon, Lysander, and others. In the fourth century Athens had a theoric vessel named the Ammonis, and public sacrifices to A. were conducted by the magistrates. The oracle was probably at the height of its influence when it was visited by Alexander the Great. Alexander's question and the answer he received from the god are unknown to us, but some modern writers have asserted that Alexander went to the oracle to be deified. Actually the priests there did but employ a conventional form in greeting Alexander as the son of Zeus. The cult of A. seems to have been popular with some members of the Ptolemaic dynasty, but it certainly was not widespread in the Mediterranean world during the Hellenistic and Roman periods. We know of *thiasotai* of A. in Attica, and A. was connected in some way with the cult of Amphiaraus at Oropus (*IG* ii². 1282). Occasionally A. is included among the Egyptian deities, though there are only two such instances at Delos. Ammon is represented in sculpture chiefly by busts, masks, and relief medallions, most of which portray him in the conventional manner.

A. B. Cook, *Zeus* i (1914), 346 ff.; A. Erman, *Die Religion der Ägypter* (1934); E. Meyer, art. 'Ammon' in Roscher's *Lexikon*; A. Wiedemann, *Herodots Zweites Buch* (1890); U. Wilcken, *Alexander the Great* (1932). T. A. B.

AMMONIUS (1) (2nd c. B.C.), pupil and successor of Aristarchus (schol. *Il.* 10. 397; Suid. s.v.), wrote, besides a commentary on Homer (*POxy.* ii. 121), other works on the Homeric poems, e.g. a treatise on Plato's borrowings from Homer ([Longinus], *Subl.* 13. 3), and essays in defence of Aristarchus' recension of the Homeric text (schol. *Il.* 10. 397); these formed a valuable source for Didymus. For his commentary on Pindar (schol. *Ol.* I. 122 c) he used Aristarchus' work, but made independent additions (schol. *Nem.* 3. 16 b). The work on Aristophanes (schol. *Vesp.* 947), sometimes entitled Κωμωδούμενοι (ibid. 1239), probably discussed the individuals attacked in Old Attic Comedy. J. F. L.

AMMONIUS (2) **SACCAS** (3rd c. A.D.), of Alexandria, was born a Christian but reverted to the ancient religion of Greece. Among his pupils were Origen the Neoplatonist, Origen the Christian Father, Longinus, Herennius, and Plotinus (the latter from 232 to 242). He wrote nothing, and preferred that his philosophy should be kept secret, but Origen the Neoplatonist, Herennius, and Plotinus published portions of it. It was mystical in character, whence his nickname Θεοδίδακτος. In view of his influence on Plotinus he ranks among the founders of Neoplatonism, but his teaching was soon completely overshadowed by that of his pupil. *PW* i. 1863. W. D. R.

AMNESTY. There are few certain records of public amnesties in Greek States, the earliest one being the law of Solon (Plut. *Sol.* 19), who restored citizen rights to every man who had lost them, unless he was disfranchised for murder or tyranny. Another act of general reconciliation was the decree of the Athenian Assembly after the restitution of democracy (403 B.C.), which excluded only the Thirty Tyrants (q.v.) and some of their most important assistants. Aristotle (*Ath. Pol.* 39. 6) quotes its chief regulation: μηδενὶ πρὸς μηδένα μνησικακεῖν. The word *amnestia* is not used for this act before Plutarch; its first known use is in a Milesian inscription of the second century B.C. (*SIG* 633, l. 36). V. E.

AMOEBEAN VERSE, a device found mainly in bucolic poetry, consists of couplets or 'stanzas' assigned alternately to two characters (e.g. Theoc. 5 and 8; Verg. *Ecl.* 3 and 7; cf. Hor. *Carm.* 3. 9). Such passages are generally singing matches (sometimes preceded by mutual abuse) in which each theme introduced by one character is closely 'capped' by the other. J. F. M.

AMPELIUS, LUCIUS (2nd or possibly 3rd c. A.D.), published a *liber memorialis*, a handbook of knowledge, dedicated to a Macrinus, not necessarily the emperor of A.D. 217–18. It gives a summary of cosmography, geography with *miracula mundi*, mythology (Euhemeristic in tendency), and history (Oriental, Greek, and of the Roman Republic, with constitutional interests); incidental references to Trajan occur. Compendious in style, it was based, probably indirectly, on Nigidius Figulus and Varro, Alexandrian works, Euhemeristic genealogies of the gods, and, in the historical part, Cornelius Nepos, Trogus, the epitomized Livian tradition, and the tradition of the *De Viris Illustribus*.

Editions: E. Wölfflin (1854); E. Assmann (1935). Cf. E. Wölfflin, *De L. Ampelii libro memoriali* (1854). A. H. McD.

AMPHIARAI EXELASIS, *see* EPIC CYCLE, para. 5.

AMPHIARAUS(Ἀμφιάραος,Ἀμφιάρεως), in mythology, son of Oecles (or Apollo, Hyg. *Fab.* 70, a not unexampled genealogy for diviners). On the return of Adrastus (q.v.) from Sicyon, Amphiaraus made peace with him and married his sister Eriphyle (Apollod. 1. 103). Foreknowing the result of the expedition of the Seven against Thebes, he would not take part in it till Eriphyle, bribed by Polynices with the necklace of Harmonia, compelled him (for the necklace, see Rose, *Handb. of Gr. Myth.*[2], 185, 190, 194), it having been agreed between Amphiaraus and Adrastus that in case of differences between them she should decide. Before setting out, he commanded his children to avenge his death on Eriphyle and to make an expedition against Thebes (cf. ALCMAEON 1). He attacked Thebes at the Homoloian Gate (Aesch. *Sept.* 570), was driven off, and, as he fled, was swallowed up in a cleft in the ground made by Zeus' thunderbolt (rhetorical description, Stat. *Theb.* 7. 771 ff.; for continuous account, see Apollod. 3. 60–77). Thus originated the very famous oracular shrine of Amphiaraus (Farnell, *Hero-Cults*, 58–62; *see also under* OROPUS and AMMON).

Whether he was originally a man or a god is disputed; his name ('very sacred') points to the former, as ἱερός is not used of a god in classical Greek (though Hesiod, *Theog.* 21, uses it of the 'race of immortals'). H. J. R.

AMPHICTIONIES (from ἀμφικτίονες, 'dwellers round about') is the name for leagues connected with temples and the maintenance of their cults. Most important was the Amphictionic League organized around the temple of Demeter at Anthela near Thermopylae and later associated also with that of Apollo at Delphi (*see* DELPHIC ORACLE, para. 6). In the earliest form known the League consisted of the following twelve tribes: Thessalians, Boeotians, Dorians, Ionians, Perrhaebians, Dolopians, Magnetes, Locrians, Aenianes, Phthiotic Achaeans, Malians, and Phocians. Thus it was possible to control the League by reducing the small tribes of central and northern Greece, as was done by Thessaly in the sixth and Aetolia in the third century B.C. The League, in co-operation with Delphi, administered the temple of Apollo and its property and conducted the Pythian Games. In the *synedrion*, which met twice a year, each tribe had two votes cast by two *hieromnemones* (q.v.), alongside of whom stood a number of *pylagorai*, later replaced by *agoratroi*. The ecclesia was less important and is seldom mentioned. During the fourth century B.C. a board of *naopoioi* and later of *tamiai* supervised the rebuilding of the temple and the administration of its funds. The latter even issued Amphictionic coins.

The League was not without political importance. An old Amphictionic oath forbade destroying cities within the League or cutting off their water-supply. Later efforts at Panhellenic legislation included decrees concerning Dionysiac guilds and currency. Violators of Amphictionic laws were tried by the *hieromnemones*, who could even proclaim sacred war against offenders. Strong States, however, disregarded Amphictionic judgements, and the League was important politically chiefly as a tool of powerful States. Votes frequently were transferred from one State to another: Delphi acquired two, those of Phocis were transferred to Philip II, and the Aetolians assigned votes to their friends. They themselves probably were not admitted to the League, but by their conquests acquired direct control of the votes of others, the maximum recorded being fifteen. Under Augustus six votes were added for Nicopolis and the total for the first time increased (from 24 to 30). Under Hadrian there was a readjustment to secure a more just representation, but the details are unknown.

Ancient Sources: a selection of documents in *SIG*[3]. Modern Literature: G. Busolt, *Griechische Staatskunde* ii (1926), 1280 ff.; U. Kahrstedt, *Griechisches Staatsrecht* (1922), 383 ff.; R. Flacelière, *Les Aitoliens à Delphes* (1937); G. Daux, *Delphes au II*[e] *et au I*[er] *siècle* (1936). J. A. O. L.

AMPHILOCHUS, in mythology, brother of Alcmaeon (q.v. 1), and, in some accounts (as Apollod. 3. 82 and 86), his comrade in the expedition of the Epigoni and helper in slaying Eriphyle. After Homer he takes part in the Trojan War (e.g. Quint. Smyrn. 14. 366), and is celebrated as a diviner. He and Calchas left Troy together by land and came to Claros (Strabo 14. 1. 27). A number of local tales (or constructions of Greek historians) connect Amphilochus with the origins of places and peoples in Asia Minor, as Poseideion on the borders of Syria and Cilicia (Hdt. 3. 91. 1), the Pamphylian nation (ibid. 7. 91. 3), but above all the famous mantic shrine in Mallus (Strabo 14. 5. 16). Apollo killed him in Soli (Hesiod quoted ibid. 17).   H. J. R.

AMPHĪON (Ἀμφίων) and **ZETHUS** (Ζῆθος), in mythology, the sons of Antiope (q.v.) and Zeus. Left behind by their mother at birth, they were found and reared by a shepherd. Amphion was given a lyre by Hermes and became a wonderful musician; Zethus was a herdsman. When, after long captivity, their mother escaped, they were full grown, and recognizing her, they took her under their protection, killing or at least dethroning Lycus and putting to death his wife Dirce by tying her to the horns of a bull, as she had intended to do to Antiope. Dirce was turned into, or her bones were burned and thrown into, the spring which bore her name. Amphion and Zethus now proceeded to wall the city later known as Thebes (from Zethus' wife Thebe, Apollod. 3. 45; Thebe is a local nymph or minor goddess), Amphion drawing the stones after him by the magical music of his lyre. Amphion married Niobe (q.v.). See Euripides, fr. 179–227 Nauck, and later finds, Pickard-Cambridge in Powell, *New Chapters* iii. 105 ff.; Apollod. 3. 43 ff.; Hyg. *Fab.* 7–9.

It is doubtful whether the brothers (called also τὼ λευκοπώλω, the White Horses, or Horsemen) were originally gods or heroes; see for this and their cult in historical times Farnell, *Hero-Cults*, 212 ff.   H. J. R.

AMPHIPOLIS, the chief Greek city on the north Aegean coast. Situated on the river Strymon, at the point of its emergence from Lake Cercinitis, it was a centre of communications (as was implied by its original name, Ἐννέα Ὁδοί), and it controlled the western approach to the mines and timber standings of Mt. Pangaeus (q.v.). After an ineffectual attempt by Aristagoras of Miletus (497 B.C.), and by an Athenian force in 465, to wrest it from the Thracians, it was colonized by Athens in 437. In 424 the Spartan general Brasidas carried it by surprise, and two years later he decisively defeated the Athenian Cleon under its gates. Though nominally ceded back to Athens by the Peace of Nicias, it maintained its independence, beating off attempts at recovery by the Athenians in 416 and in 368–365. In 357 it was captured by Philip of Macedon, who had promised to restore it to Athens but kept it for himself. It remained under the Macedonian kings until 168, when it became for twenty years the capital of Macedonia Prima. With the decline of the Pangaeus mines Amphipolis lost its former importance.

S. Casson, *Macedonia, Thrace, and Illyria* (1926), *passim*. M. C.

AMPHIS, Middle Comedy poet, not anterior to Plato (fr. 6). His twenty-eight titles come chiefly from mythology and daily life, but Γυναικοκρατία, *Government by Women*, sounds like an Aristophanic theme, and Διθύραμβος (perhaps also Ἰάλεμος and Σαπφώ) dealt with musical innovations of the time. Fr. 30, on slovenly pronunciation ('κτὼ 'βολῶν for ὀκτὼ ὀβολῶν).

FCG iii. 301 ff.; *CAF* ii. 236 ff.   W. G. W.

AMPHISSA, in western (Ozolian) Locris, commands the route leading west of Mt. Parnassus from Doris to the Gulf of Crisa. Its traditional policy being enmity

with Phocis and alliance with Thebes, Amphissa played a leading part in the Third Sacred War (q.v.), and was reduced to dependence by Onomarchus in 353 B.C. Independent again after the collapse of Phocis, it proposed, probably in the interest of Thebes, that Athens be fined by the Delphic Amphictiony, but Aeschines countered by accusing Amphissa of sacrilege in cultivating the Sacred Plain of Crisa (340); from this sprang the Amphissaean War, in which Philip II of Macedon captured Amphissa and destroyed its walls (338).

N. G. L H.

AMPHISSUS, *see* DRYOPE.

AMPHITHALES, *see* CHILDREN.

AMPHITHEATRES. The earliest known Roman amphitheatre is that of the Sullan colony (*c.* 80 B.C.) at Pompeii, called by its builders *spectacula* (*CIL* x. 852). Pliny (*HN* 36. 117–20) ascribes the introduction of amphitheatres at Rome to Curio (q.v. 2), the first permanent building being erected by Statilius Taurus in 29 B.C., at a time when such buildings were being constructed far and wide throughout the Empire. Architecturally, such examples as those of Emerita (8 B.C.; *Arch. Journ.* lxxxvii. 113, pl. viii) with segmental arches, and of Nemausus (Nîmes), with heavy lintel construction, exhibit affinity to wooden prototypes, which continued to exist (Tac. *Ann.* 4. 62). The Pompeian amphitheatre, dug deep into the earth and retained by a low façade with external staircases, demonstrates also the connexion with the natural arena or earth mound, of which provincial examples abound. Imperial architects, however, rapidly evolved very large self-contained buildings, in which problems of access and circulation were solved by remarkably ingenious use of balanced vaulting systems. The most famous is the Colosseum (q.v.). The arena was honeycombed with underground passages for stage effects, comparable with those of Julius Caesar's *Forum Romanum* (*JRS* 1922, 8–9). The amphitheatre should be distinguished from the *ludus*, or gladiators' training-school, which has much less seating and a proportionately larger arena (Lundström, *Undersökningar i Roms topografi*, 22–5).

Ashby–Anderson–Spiers, *Architecture of Ancient Rome* See also bibliography s.v. COLOSSEUM. Methods of laying out the non-elliptical arena are discussed by J. A. Wright, *Archaeologia* lxxviii. 215.   I. A. R.

AMPHITRYON, in mythology, son of Alcaeus.

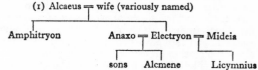

(1) Alcaeus ⚭ wife (variously named)

Amphitryon   Anaxo ⚭ Electryon ⚭ Mideia

sons   Alcmene   Licymnius

(2) Mestor (brother of Alcaeus) ⚭ Lysidice (dr. of Pelops)

Hippothoe ⚭ Poseidon

Taphius

Pterelaus

Comaetho

Taphius and the sons of Pterelaus quarrelled with Electryon and reaved his cattle. In recovering them, Amphitryon accidentally killed Electryon, and so had to leave his native Mycenae (or Argos), taking Alcmene and Licymnius with him. At her urging (*see* ALCMENE) he got together an army, partly by help of Creon I, king of Thebes, who made it a condition that Amphitryon should rid him of the uncatchable Cadmeian vixen, which was ravaging the country. Amphitryon obtained the help of Cephalus (q.v.) and his hound Laelaps, which never lost its quarry, and the impasse between the beast which could not be caught and the beast which must catch was settled by Zeus turning both to stone. Amphitryon proceeded against Pterelaus and his people the Teleboans, but could not take their city while Pterelaus lived, nor could the latter die till a golden hair which Poseidon had planted in his head was removed. Comaetho, being in love with Amphitryon, finally betrayed Pterelaus, and their city, Taphos, was taken. *See further* ALCMENE, HERACLES.

Apollodorus 2. 50 ff.; a somewhat different account in Arguments 4 and 5 to [Hesiod], *Shield*. H. J. R.

AMPLIATIO, a peculiarity of Roman criminal procedure in the time of the Republic, exceptionally admitted by some laws on criminal matters. We meet this institution particularly in trials for *repetundae*. When the jury was unable to come by majority to a decision, the evidence of guilt of the accused having been not quite sufficient either for condemnation or for discharge, they settled by the vote *non liquet* that the case was not quite cleared up and demanded by pronouncing the word *amplius* the reiteration of the evidence. The effect was not a simple adjournment, but a repetition of all proofs with the object of elucidating the case thoroughly. Normally *ampliatio* took place only once; but it lent itself to abuse before an unscrupulous jury: it is told, for instance, that in the trial of L. Aurelius Cotta on a charge of *repetundae* proceedings were repeated seven times. Such incidents perhaps caused the institution to fall into disuse in the early Principate. *See* LAW AND PROCEDURE, ROMAN, III.

J. P. Balsdon, *BSR* 1938, 109 ff. A. B.

AMULETS (Lat. *amuletum*), charms, objects worn for magical use, to protect the wearer against witchcraft, the evil eye, sickness, accidents, etc. (cf. modern mascots). Houses, walls, towns, etc., were protected in the same way. Any kind of material might be used, stones and metals as well as animals and plants, because every sort of material was supposed eventually to possess supernatural or magical virtue. Even parts of the body (hand, *fascinum, vulva*) had peculiar efficacy; thus the snout of a wolf, fixed upon the door, guarded against evil influences (Plin. *HN* 28. 157), etc. The efficacy of the amulet might be enhanced by engraved figures, e.g. deities or symbols, especially on stones and metals (cf. the so-called 'Abraxas gems' and the Solomon gems in Byzantine times). Inscriptions (magical formulas, unknown magic words, the 'great name', alphabets, anagrams) are here often added, but such inscriptions were also thought effective by themselves. A number of apotropaic charms written on papyrus have been found in Egypt, the classical home of every sort of magic (cf. also the illustrations in *POsl.* 1). The magical potency was secured and strengthened by a consecration of the amulet (cf. the procedure described in Orph. *Lith.* 366 ff.). The forms of amulets are innumerable (270 kinds are examined by Flinders Petrie, *Amulets*); notable are rings, nails, keys, knots, etc. Special importance derives from the place at which or the circumstances (fitting times, stellar influences) in which the amulet was found or made. A crossway and a burial-place are considered to endue anything there found (plants, bones, skulls) with magic powers. Remains of men whose death had been a violent one (shipwrecked men, etc.) were eagerly sought. 'Individual amulets' depend only on chance observation and vague ideas of connexion.

Belief in amulets remained active in Greece, as in Italy, in all classes of the populations through the whole of antiquity and still survives to-day.

Words for amulets: φυλακτήριον, περίαμμα, περίαπτον; *amuletum* (for etymology see Walde–Hofmann, *Lat. etym. Wörterbuch* i. 42), *bulla, crepundia, fascinum, alligatura* (later), etc.

Otto Jahn, 'Über den Aberglauben des bösen Blicks' (*Ber. Sächs. Ges. Wiss.* 1855, 28 ff.); Kropatscheck, *De amuletorum apud antiquos usu* (1907); Freire–Marreco, etc., art. 'Charms' in Hastings, *ERE*; E. Labatut, 'Amuletum' in *Dar.-Sag.*; E. Riess, 'Amulett', in *PW*; cf. Flinders Petrie, *Amulets* (1914). S. E.

AMULIUS, *see* ROMULUS AND REMUS.

AMYCLAE, an early town on the right bank of the Eurotas *c.* 3 miles south of Sparta, mentioned in the Homeric *Catalogue* as in the domain of Menelaus. According to tradition it was an Achaean stronghold which long resisted the Dorian invaders; after its conquest, which opened the way for their southward advance, it was incorporated in Spartan territory. But it retained its own magistrates, including three ἔφοροι (*IG* v. 1. 26, 2nd or 1st c. B.C.). Remains of the famous sanctuary and throne of Apollo Amyclaeus have been excavated on the hill of H. Kyriake (probably north of the ancient town).

Paus. 3. 18. 7–19. 6. For the sanctuary and throne: Frazer, *Paus.*, ad loc. A. Furtwängler, *Meisterwerke*, 693 ff.; *JDAI* xxxiii. (1918); *Ath. Mitt.* lii (1927). A. M. W.

AMYCUS, in mythology, king of the Bebryces, a savage people of Bithynia. He was of gigantic strength and compelled all comers to the land to box with him, the loser to be at the absolute disposal of the winner. When the Argonauts arrived in his country, Polydeuces accepted his challenge, and being a skilled boxer, overcame Amycus' brute force. In the fight Amycus was killed (Apollonius), or knocked out (Theocritus), and made to swear to wrong no more strangers, or, having lost the fight, was bound by Polydeuces (Epicharmus and Pisandrus ap. schol. Ap. Rhod. 2. 98). See Ap. Rhod. 2. 1 ff.; Theoc. 22. 27 ff. H. J. R.

AMYMONE (Ἀμυμώνη), in mythology, daughter of Danaus. While at Argos (*see* DANAUS) she went for water, was rescued from a satyr and seduced by Poseidon, who created the spring Amymone in commemoration (Apollod. 2. 14; Hyg. *Fab.* 169, 169 a).

AMYNTAS, king of Galatia 39–25 B.C. Originally a secretary of Deiotarus (q.v.), he commanded the Galatian auxiliaries of Brutus and Cassius at Philippi. He deserted after the first battle of Philippi, and after Deiotarus' death received from Antony a kingdom which eventually comprised Galatia and parts of Lycia, Pamphylia, and Pisidia. He accompanied Antony to Actium, but by a second timely desertion (before the battle of Actium) he won Octavian's favour and retained all his possessions. He died on a campaign against the unruly mountain tribes on the southern borders of his realm. M. C.

AMYNTOR (Ἀμύντωρ), in mythology, father of Phoenix (q.v.), son of Ormenus, king of Hellas (in the epic sense), (*Il.* 9. 447; see the whole passage), or of Eleon (ibid. 10. 266). Being jealous of Phoenix' attentions to his concubine, he cursed him (blinded him, according to Euripides, Ar. *Ach.* 421, cf. Ov. *Ibis*, 259), driving him from home. H. J. R.

ANABOLE, strictly used of the striking-up of a musical instrument, especially of a lyre, by a bard when he began to sing (*Od.* 1. 155, 8. 266: ἀνεβάλλετο, Pind. *Pyth.* 1. 14), but used in a special sense of a lyric solo introduced into a dithyramb (Ar. *Av.* 1385; Arist. *Rh.* 3. 9. 1) by Melanippides, Cinesias, and Timotheus. C. M. B.

ANACHARSIS (*c.* 600 B.C.), a hellenized Scythian sage. He travelled through Asia Minor and Greece imbibing Greek customs and showing great wisdom. When he tried to introduce the orgiastic worship of the 'Mother of the Gods' from Cyzicus to his country he was killed by the king (Hdt. 4. 76 f.). In the fourth century B.C. and later A. is described as one of the so-called Seven Sages, uttering the voice of unspoiled nature and criticizing the over-civilization of Greece (cf. Ephorus, *FGrH* 70: frs. 42; 158; 182 Jacoby; in this they were perhaps influenced by a work of the Cynic school). Maxims ascribed to him occur from Aristotle onwards. Writings falsely ascribed to him, as the so-called letters of A. (R. Hercher,

Epistologr. Graeci, 102 f.), and works like the biography by Diogenes Laertius (1. 101 f.) or Lucian's *A.*, display him with clearly Cynic characteristics. But certain important features of this later A. may well be old.

F. E. Bohren, *De septem sapientibus* (1867); R. Heinze, *Philol.* 1891; Von der Mühll, *Festschrift für H. Blümner* (1914); *PW* i. 2017.   K. O. B.

ANACREON (b. *c.* 570 B.C.), lyric poet, son of Scythinus, born at Teos (Suid. s.v. Ἀνακρέων), but left home *c.* 545 B.C. when it was threatened by the Persians (Strabo 644); to this he may refer in frs. 67 and 90. With other Teans he founded the colony of Abdera in Thrace (Suid., Strabo, l.c.). References to fighting here against Thracians may be seen in fr. 100, a commemorative epigram for a dead fighter, and in fr. 101. Here too he may have written fr. 88 to a Thracian girl. He was summoned to Samos by Polycrates, who wished him to instruct his son in music (Himer. *Ex. Nap.* in *Hermes* xlvi. 422), and he was with the tyrant when the fatal messenger came summoning the latter to his death (Hdt. 3. 121). He is said to have made many references to Polycrates in his poems (Strabo 14. 638), but none survive. To his Samian period must belong fr. 25 with its reference to civil strife, fr. 1 for the Magnesians on the Maeander, and many of his love-poems, which seem to have been to the taste of Polycrates. After the fall of Polycrates Hipparchus fetched him to Athens ([Pl.] *Hipparch.* 228 b); thence *c.* 514 B.C. he went to Thessaly, where two epigrams, fr. 107, a dedication by King Echecratidas, and fr. 108, a dedication by Queen Dyseris, show him consorting with royalty. He returned to Athens, where his memory was honoured later by Critias (fr. 8) and by a statue on the Acropolis (Paus. 1. 25. 1). Some of his poems seem to show traces of Attic language, and may belong to this period (frs. 44, 52, 96, 110). His death, at an advanced age, was said to be due to a grape-pip sticking in his throat (Val. Max. 9. 8). His works were edited by Aristarchus in six books of μέλη, ἴαμβοι, and ἐλεγεῖα (Heph. p. 68. 22; 74. 11 ff.). The first class contains his lyric poems, mostly monodic, such as hymns to Artemis (fr. 1), Eros (fr. 2), and Dionysus (fr. 3), love-songs to Cleobulus (frs. 3–4), and other convivial or sympotic poems (frs. 5, 11, 32, 37, 43). Of his iambic poems the most complete example is his cruel poem on Artemon (fr. 54). His elegiacs contain commemorative poems, dedications, and epitaphs. He writes in an Ionic vernacular with very few traces of Homeric or Aeolic language. His metres are usually simple. He favoured a stanza made of Glyconics with Pherecrateans for *clausulae*, and often used a minor Ionic verse with anaclasis, called Anacreontic after him. He is remarkable for his combination of fancy and wit, which prevents him from taking himself or others too seriously. His poetry is concerned mostly with pleasure, but this may well be due to the circumstances of its performance, and it is unwise to deduce too much about his character from it. *See also* IAMBIC POETRY, GREEK, *and* LYRIC POETRY, GREEK.

Text: H. Diehl, *Anth. Lyr. Graec.* i. 4, pp. 160–92.
Criticism: U. von Wilamowitz-Moellendorff, *Sappho und Simonides* (1913), 102–36; L. Weber, *Anacreontea* (1895); C. M. Bowra, *Greek Lyric Poetry* (1936), 284–316.   C. M. B.

ANACREONTIC, *see* METRE, GREEK, III (13).

ANAGNIA, chief town of the Hernici (q.v.), in a fertile area of Italy (*Aen.* 7. 684); nowadays *Anagni* with well-preserved walls. In 306 B.C. Anagnia became a *civitas sine suffragio* (*see* MUNICIPIUM) which Pyrrhus and Hannibal later ravaged (Livy 9. 42 f.; 26. 9; App. *Sam.* 10). In the second century it acquired full citizenship (Festus 155 L.) and remained a *municipium* under the Empire (reject *Lib. Colon.* p. 230). Vitellius' general Valens and Commodus' concubine Marcia were born here (Tac.

Hist. 3. 62; *ILS* 406). The numerous temples near Anagnia were still celebrated in Marcus Aurelius' time (Fronto, *Ep.* 4. 4).

S. Sibilia, *La Città dei Papi* (1939).   E. T. S.

ANAGNORISMOS, *see* TRAGEDY, para. 16.

ANAGNOSTES, a reader, often an educated slave, whose duty in Roman houses was to entertain his master and guests at table by an *acroama* in Greek and Latin. Cicero (*Att.* 1. 12) mentions his distress at the death of his young reader Sosthenes. He had one, however, who ran away (Vatin. ap. Cic. *Fam.* 5. 9. 2). Atticus kept very good readers whom he thought indispensable at dinner parties (Nep. *Att.* 13 and 14). Gellius (3. 19) records similar entertainment at dinner with the philosopher Favorinus. The word is used of a scholar giving a *recitatio* in a theatre (Gell. 18. 5). The *anagnostes* also took part in grammatical instruction.   J. W. D.

ANAGNOSTICI, *see* TRAGEDY, para. 21.

ANAHITA (*Anaitis*, Ἀναῖτις), Persian goddess of the fertilizing waters (*Zend-Avesta*, Yašt 5). Artaxerxes Ochus (358–338 B.C.) introduced the use of cult-images (Berossus ap. Clem. Alex. *Protr.* 5. 65. 3), and the cult spread to Armenia, Cappadocia, Pontus, and especially to Lydia. In Armenia sacred prostitution (q.v.) was practised (Strabo 532–3), and in Pontus A. possessed many *hierodouloi* (q.v.). In Lydia she was assimilated to Cybele and to Artemis Ephesia, and hence called Meter A. or Artemis A., but Iranian cult traditions also persisted (Paus. 5. 27. 5–6). She was often called the Persian Artemis. Bulls were sacred to her, and the *taurobolium* (*see* CYBELE, para. 3) perhaps originated in her cult. *See* ANATOLIAN DEITIES.

F. Cumont, *PW*, s.v. 'Anaitis'; *ERE*, s.v. 'Anahita'; *Rev. Arch.* 1905, i. 24–31; *CRAcad. Inscr.* 1915, 270–6 for exorcism by her priestess. In Roscher, *Lex.*, E. Meyer, s.v. 'Anaitis', Höfer, s.v. 'Persike'.   F. R. W.

ANAKES (Ἄνακες), old by-form of ἄνακτες, hence 'kings', 'lords'. A title especially of the Dioscuri (q.v., and see L & S⁹ s.v.), but also of the Tritopatores (?, q.v.), (Cic. *Nat. D.* 3. 53), and perhaps certain deities at Amphissa (Paus. 10. 38. 7, where MSS. have Ἄνακτες).

ANALOGIA, DE, Caesar's lost treatise inspired by the teaching of Antonius Gnipho (q.v.), written on a journey across the Alps (55 or 54 B.C.) and dedicated to Cicero. It defended the principle of Analogy (q.v.) and a reformed *elegantia* founded on the *sermo cotidianus*. Gellius (1. 10. 4) quotes from its first book the famous advice 'ut tamquam scopulum sic fugias inauditum atque insolens uerbum' (see Dahlmann, *Rh. Mus.* lxxxiv. 3).   J. W. D.

ANALOGY and **ANOMALY** were the watchwords of two opposing schools of thought about linguistic phenomena. In particular, the analogists held that nouns and verbs were capable of classification into orderly declensions and conjugations on the basis of similarity of form (ἀναλογία), whereas the anomalists were impressed by the many manifestations of irregularity (ἀνωμαλία) which actual usage sanctioned. Neither party viewed language in a true perspective or effected any appreciable change in living speech; but the discussion was not entirely barren in so far as it stimulated grammatical studies. The analogist at least had a standard he could apply in cases of genuine doubt; the strength of the anomalist's position lay in his readiness to accept language as he found it. Underlying the controversy was the question (already discussed in Plato's *Cratylus*; cf. Lucr. 5. 1028–90) whether language was a natural growth or an arbitrary convention; and though matters of style did not at first enter into the argument, the analogists tended to be allied with purists in their condemnation of barbarisms and solecisms, and anomalists with those who claimed a place for new coinages and modes of expression. Amongst the Greeks, the quarrel was most keenly pursued on the side of analogy by the grammarians of Alexandria (e.g. Aristophanes of Byzantium, Aristarchus, Dionysius Thrax), and on the side of anomaly by the Stoics (e.g. Chrysippus, who wrote four books Περὶ ἀνωμαλίας) and the scholars of Pergamum (e.g. Crates of Mallos). At Rome the Scipionic circle in their pursuit of *Latinitas* and *purus sermo* inclined to favour the analogical view (cf. Lucil. 964). Varro (*Ling.* bks. 8-10) gives both sides of the controversy but leans towards the analogists, as did Caesar (in his *De Analogia*, where he condemns the 'inauditum atque insolens uerbum'; cf. Gell. I. 10. 4) and 'Atticists' like Calvus. Cicero (e.g. *Orat.* 155-62), Horace (*Ars P.* 70-2), and Quintilian (I. 6) give greater weight to the claims of *consuetudo*.

E. Norden, *Ant. Kunst.* i. 184-94; J. E. Sandys, *Hist. of Class. Scholarship* i (*passim*); G. L. Hendrickson, *CPhil.* 1906, 97; F. H. Colson, *CQ* 1919, 24.   J. F. M.

ANATOLIAN DEITIES. The outstanding characteristic of Anatolian religion is the worship of a mother goddess and her youthful male consort, embodiments of the fertility principle, who reappear constantly under a diversity of local, differentiating names, epithets, and forms. There is some evidence (J. Keil, *JÖAI.* xviii. 1915) for a divine triad of mother, father, son, but this is a less constant feature. The apparent diversity which masks the basic similarity of the great pair is due in part to the strength of localism and to local differentiation and development, in part to the complex racial background of Asia Minor, and in part to identification with various Hellenic divinities, each of whom might fitly be thought to represent one facet of the native god's complex personality. Thus the male god, as supreme, might be called Zeus; as giver of oracles, Apollo; and as healer, Asclepius. Generally the goddess predominated in Asiatic cities, while in Hellenic foundations the god was accorded higher rank. The native names, such as Cybele (q.v.), Attis (q.v.), Ma, Wanax, seldom or never appear in Asia Minor on Greek inscriptions (though local epithets do), and are known chiefly from Neo-Phrygian documents or from outside Anatolia. According to Calder (*CR* xli (1927), 161-3) this shows that while speakers of the native languages used the old names, speakers of Greek did not, except in the Mysteries (cf. the mystic formula in Dem. *De Cor.* 260). Of the Mysteries themselves we know little, and that chiefly from non-Asiatic sources. *See* AGDISTIS; ANAHITA; ATTIS; CYBELE; EUNUCHS, RELIGIOUS; HIERODULOI; METRAGYRTES; PROSTITUTION, SACRED; SABAZIUS.

The inscriptions are our chief source of material: see especially the series *Monumenta Asiae Minoris Antiqua* (1928-), and numerous articles in *Anatolian Studies presented to Sir Wm. Ramsay* (1923), *Anatolian Studies presented to W. H. Buckler* (1939), and L. Robert, *Études anatoliennes* (1937). A valuable synthesis in F. Cumont, *Les Religions orientales dans le paganisme romain* (1929), ch. 3.
                                                                  F. R. W.

ANATOMY AND PHYSIOLOGY. The earliest records of true anatomical observations are in fragments of Alcmaeon (q.v. 2; *c.* 500 B.C.) of Croton. There can be no doubt that he actually dissected animals, discerning the optic nerves and the tubes between the nose and ear cavities now known as 'Eustachian'. He even extended his researches to embryology, describing the head of the foetus as the first part to develop—a justifiable interpretation of the appearances. His followers investigated especially the blood-vessels.

2. The theory of Empedocles (q.v.; *c.* 480 B.C.) of Acragas of four elements in opposites was to control medical thought for two millennia, but more immediately influential was his view taken from folk-belief that the blood is the seat of the innate heat (θερμὸν ἔμφυτον)— 'the blood is the life'. This led to the consideration of the heart as centre of the vascular system and chief

organ of the *pneuma* which was distributed by the blood-vessels. *Pneuma* was identified, in accord with certain philosophical tendencies, with both air and breath. These views of Empedocles were rejected by the important Coan Medical School, then becoming prominent, but were widely accepted elsewhere. Notably Diogenes of Apollonia, a contemporary of Hippocrates of Cos, was led to investigate the blood-vessels, and his account of the vascular system is the earliest that is intelligible.

3. Early members of the so-called 'Hippocratic Collection' (q.v.) are the treatises *On the sacred disease* of about 400 B.C. and *On the nature of man* which is but little later. The author of the former opened the skulls of goats and found the brain to resemble that of man in being cleft into symmetrical halves by a vertical membrane. The large veins of the neck are intelligibly described. The arteries are said to contain air, an idea gained from their emptiness in dead animals. *On the nature of man*, ascribed by Aristotle to Polybus, son-in-law of Hippocrates, contains the doctrine of the four humours. These—Blood, Phlegm (*pituita*), Black Bile (*melancholia*), and Yellow Bile (*cholē*)—make up the living body as the four elements make up non-living matter. This doctrine persisted till quite modern times and has left definite traces in the anatomical and pathological nomenclature of our own day.

4. An interesting Athenian practitioner of the middle and late fourth century B.C. was Diocles (q.v.) of Carystus. He drew his opinions from many sources, adopting the humours of Polybus and the innate heat of Empedocles, regarding with Aristotle the heart as seat of the intelligence but accepting also Sicilian pneumatism. His observations on the early human foetus are the first recorded. His work *On anatomy*, based to some extent on human material, has disappeared and we have no general early treatise on the subject. Our best representative of the anatomy of the fourth century is the tract in the Hippocratic Collection *On the heart*, of about 340 B.C. We cannot be sure that it is based on human dissection, but it discusses the anatomical similarities of man to animals. It places the innate heat in the heart. Air enters direct into the left ventricle, where takes place some subtle change of blood into spirit, and where too the intellect resides. The heart valves are described and experiments are suggested for testing their competence. There is the startlingly false statement—with a claim that it is verified by experiment—that, in drinking, some of the fluid passes to the lungs. This might be ascribed to textual confusion were not the same view expressed in Plato's *Timaeus* and other early writings. The *Timaeus* itself had little effect on medical teaching.

5. The direct contributions of Aristotle to human anatomy and physiology are unimportant and he did *not* dissect the human body. The text of his account of the heart is corrupt and incomprehensible, but it was in any event very inadequate, nor did he make any proper distinction between arteries and veins, though he gave fair descriptions of several of these vessels. On the other hand, he gave excellent accounts of certain organs from the standpoint of comparative anatomy. Some were illustrated by drawings, the first anatomical figures recorded. We can confidently restore certain of them, for example, that of the organs of generation. His nomenclature of the uterine organs is still partially retained.

6. Among the noteworthy errors of Aristotle is his refusal to attach importance to the brain. Intelligence he placed in the heart. This was contrary to the views of Diocles and other of his medical contemporaries, contrary to the popular view, and contrary to the doctrine of the *Timaeus*. Aristotle must have known all these, and it is conjectured that, having found the brain to be devoid of sensation, he concluded that it could not be associated with it. The function of the brain was to prevent the heart from over-heating the blood. This was effected by the cold Phlegm (*pituita*) secreted in the nose, supposedly by the brain, an idea preserved in our anatomical term 'pituitary body'.

7. After Aristotle's time Alexandria became the chief medical centre. Herophilus (q.v.; *c.* 300 B.C.) of Chalcedon was of the earliest Alexandrian scientific generation, was the first to dissect the body publicly, wrote a work *On anatomy*, and made numerous discoveries. He recognized the brain as the central organ of the nervous system and the seat of intelligence; distinguished the cerebrum from the cerebellum; described the fourth ventricle of the brain and even its 'calamus scriptorius', which he named (ἀνάγλυφος κάλαμος); and described the meninges and the 'wine-press' (torcular, ληνός), a confluence of veins which modern anatomists, following Galen, still name after him. He was the first to grasp the nature of nerves other than those of the special senses, and he distinguished motor from sensory nerves. The modern anatomical terms 'prostate' (ἀδενοειδεῖς προστάται) and 'duodenum'(δωδεκαδάκτυλον) are derived, through Galen, from him. We owe to him also the first description of the lacteals and the first clear differentiation of arteries from veins. Pulsation was for him an active arterial process. He wrote an anatomy for midwives and is the first medical teacher recorded—perhaps apocryphally—to have had a woman pupil.

8. Erasistratus (q.v.) of Chios, a younger Alexandrian contemporary of Herophilus, was the first to set forth a complete physiological scheme. Accepting the atomism of Democritus and its consequent 'materialism' he described the body as a mechanism, combining this with a pneumatic theory. Observing that every organ is equipped with a threefold system of branching vessels—veins, arteries, and nerves—he concluded that the minute divisions of these, plaited together, compose the tissues. Blood and two kinds of pneuma are the sources of nourishment and movement. Blood is carried by the veins, which take it to the heart. Air is taken in by the lungs and passing thence to the heart becomes changed into the first pneuma, the *vital spirit* (πνεῦμα ζωτικόν) which is sent to the parts of the body by the arteries. Carried by these to the brain it is there changed to the second pneuma, the *animal spirit* (πνεῦμα ψυχικόν), and distributed to the parts through the nerves, which are hollow.

9. The view of Erasistratus that the heart is the centre and source not only of the arterial system but also of the venous system was ahead of all opinion until Harvey (1628). Perceiving that arteries though empty in dead bodies, yet when incised in the living contain blood, he sought to explain the presence of the blood in them as due to the escape of pneuma through the wound leading to a vacuum by which blood was sucked into the arteries from the veins through fine intercommunications between artery and vein. The view that arteries contain air was experimentally disproved by Galen 450 years later, but Erasistratus, having realized that the two systems communicate at their periphery, was not very far from the conception of a circulation.

10. Erasistratus advanced on Herophilus' knowledge of the nervous system, giving detailed descriptions of the cerebral ventricles, which he regarded as filled with animal spirit. He observed the cerebral convolutions, noting their greater elaboration in man than in animals, associated, as he thought, with man's higher intelligence. He made experiments on the brain and meninges, traced the cranial nerves into the brain itself, and distinguished cranial sensory from cranial motor nerves. He also attained a clear view of the action of muscles in producing movement, regarding their shortening as due to distension by animal spirit.

11. After Erasistratus anatomy and physiology declined at Alexandria. The schools that arose at Pergamum, Smyrna, Corinth, and elsewhere were poor substitutes. The human body ceased to be dissected and when Galen began his studies about A.D. 145 it was difficult to find even a skeleton in these schools. Nevertheless, two Ephesians of the first Christian century produced noteworthy anatomical works. Of these Rufus gave to many parts of the eye the names by which they are still known, and in his book on the pulse claimed that the heart strikes the chest-wall during contraction. Had this critical observation been known to Galen it should have led him to modify his physiological scheme, perhaps in the direction of a circulation. Soranus of Ephesus wrote a book on pregnancy with figures of the uterus. Indirect medieval copies of these are the first surviving anatomical drawings exhibiting details ascertainable only by human dissection.

12. Anatomical and physiological science in antiquity reached both its climax and its end with Galen (q.v.; A.D. 129–99), who spent his early years gleaning in many schools the traditions of his predecessors. His active professional life was passed at Rome, where he gave public demonstrations. He never dissected a human body, but made numerous accurate anatomical and physiological studies on a variety of animals, among them the Barbary ape, the structure of which is not very different from that of man. He also experimented on dogs, bears, cattle, and pigs, being struck with the resemblance of the latter to human beings.

13. Galen elaborated a complete physiological scheme which was generally accepted until modern times. It involves three kinds of pneuma or spirit in addition to air. The basic principle of life was drawn from the world-pneuma of air by breathing. Entering the body through the windpipe it passes to the lung and thence to the left ventricle, where it encounters the blood. His view as to the changes that then take place in the blood was most ingenious, and the errors that it involved remained current till the seventeenth century.

14. Galen believed that chyle, brought from the digestive system by the portal vessel, reaches the liver, and that that organ has the power of enduing it with a pneuma, innate in all living substance, which came to be called the *natural spirit* (πνεῦμα φυσικόν). It then became venous blood. This is distributed by the liver through the venous system, ebbing and flowing in the veins.

15. One great branch of the venous system, a mere extension of a great trunk direct from the liver, was the cavity that we now call the right ventricle. The venous blood that entered this had two possible fates. Most of it, remaining awhile in the ventricle, left it to ebb back into the liver, having parted with its fumes or impurities, which were carried off to the lung and thence exhaled—hence the poisonous character of re-breathed air. A small fraction of the blood in the right ventricle, however, trickling through minute channels in the heart-substance, dripped slowly into the left ventricle. There, encountering the air brought through the lung, these drops of dark blood, charged with natural spirit, are elaborated into the higher *vital spirit*, which is the active principle of the bright arterial blood.

16. The arterial blood charged with vital spirits is distributed through the arteries to all parts of the body. Some passes to the so-called 'rete mirabile' (πλέγμα μέγιστον θαῦμα) at the base of the brain, and becomes charged with yet a third pneuma, the *animal spirit* derived from the brain. This is distributed by the nerves. The 'rete mirabile', absent in man, is well developed in cattle. It was from experiments and observations on them that this remarkable system was derived.

17. Of Galen's positive anatomical knowledge the best presentation is his great work *On anatomical procedure* in sixteen books, of which nine survive in Greek while the remainder have been recovered in modern times in Arabic translation. His treatise *On the uses of the parts*

of the body of man was the most popular of his general anatomical works. *On anatomical operations* is a superb experimental study. *On the anatomy of muscles* is an accurate and remarkable pioneer survey. *On bones, for beginners* is his only work based on human material and has influenced modern nomenclature. Among his terms current in modern anatomy are apophysis, epiphysis, trochanter, diarthrosis, and synarthrosis.

18. In pure anatomy Galen's best work was on the muscles, and his writings contain frequent references to the form and function of muscles of various animals. Thus the dissection of the muscles of the orbit and larynx was performed on the ox, while those of the tongue are described from the ape. Occasionally he indicates that he is aware of the difference between the muscles he is describing and those of man. His famous and intensely teleological description of the structure and functions of the hand was derived from that of the Barbary ape. There is perhaps in all literature no passage that is more confident as to the exact details of the divine intentions.

19. Galen's anatomical and physiological writings are both voluminous and detailed. They are, however, ill arranged, and, since he has no adequate technical nomenclature and is very argumentative, his meaning is often obscure. Though his account of the brain and of its related nerves is difficult, yet his classification and description of the cranial nerves remained in vogue until quite modern times, and part of his nomenclature of them survives even in current anatomy.

20. Perhaps Galen's most remarkable achievement was his experimental investigation of the spinal cord, the continuity of which at different levels was, he showed, necessary for the maintenance of certain functions. Injury between the first and second vertebrae caused instantaneous death. Section between the third and fourth produced arrest of respiration. Below the sixth it gave rise to paralysis of thoracic muscles, respiration being carried on only by the diaphragm. If the lesion were yet lower the paralysis was confined to the lower limbs, bladder, and intestines. Galen's knowledge of the functions of the spinal cord was not developed and indeed was not adequately appreciated until well into the nineteenth century.

21. Galen's scientific works are among the most influential of all time. Nevertheless he established no school and he had neither disciples nor followers. On his death in 199 the prosecution of anatomical and physiological inquiry ceased abruptly. Silence descends like a curtain; the classical period of the subject is over and the Dark Ages have begun.

BIBLIOGRAPHY

Remains of fifth-century anatomists in Diels, *Vorsokr.*[5] (1934). E. Krause, *Diogenes von Apollonia* (1908–9). M. Wellmann, *Die Fragmente der Sikelischen Aerzte, Akron, Philistion und des Diokles von Karystos* (1901). W. Jaeger, *Diokles v. Karystos* (1938). Aristotle's anatomy mostly in *Historia animalium*, trans. by D'Arcy W. Thompson (1910). The fragments of Herophilus and Erasistratus collected and translated by J. F. Dobson, *Proc. of Roy. Soc. of Med., Historical Section*, xviii (1924) and xx (1927). J. Ilberg, *Die Ueberlieferung der Gynäkologie des Soranos von Ephesos* (1910). Ch. Daremberg, *Œuvres anatomiques physiologiques et médicales de Galien* (2 vols. 1854). Max Simon, *Sieben Bücher Anatomie des Galen* (2 vols. 1906). J. S. Prendergast on Galen in *Proc. of Roy. Soc. of Med., Historical Section* xix (1926) and xxi (1928). Very little of Galen is translated into English; there is, however A. J. Brock, *Galen on the Natural Faculties* (Loeb, 1916) and a very good anonymous rendering of the famous passage *On the hand* by T. Bellott (1840). G. Senn, *Die Entwicklung der biologischen Forschungsmethode in der Antike* (1933). Survey by Charles Singer and C. Rabin, *A Prelude to Science* (1946).   **C. S.**

ANAXAGORAS (*c.* 500–*c.* 428 B.C.; Apollodorus ap. Diog. Laert. 2. 7), son of Hegesibulus, a native of Clazomenae, the first philosopher to reside in Athens. He came in 480, probably with Xerxes' army, and 'began to philosophize at Athens in the archonship of Callias (Calliades) at the age of 20, where he is said to have remained 30 years' (Demetrius of Phalerum ap. D.L.

ibid.). The teacher and friend of Pericles, he was indicted by the latter's enemies on charges of impiety and medism; but with Pericles' aid he escaped to Lampsacus, where he founded a school and died in general honour and esteem. Accounts of the trial vary: the probable date is 450, not 432 (as Ephorus ap. Diod. 12. 38 f. and Plut. *Vit. Per.* 32 state). A.'s astronomical views, the main ground of the charge, were influenced by the fall of the meteorite at Aegospotami in 468–467. Only one work is ascribed to him: from bk. 1 a score of fragments is preserved by Simplicius.

2. Conflicting testimonies make modern reconstructions of A.'s system problematic. He accepts, like Empedocles, the Eleatic denial of 'becoming' and void, but advocates a radical pluralism and an indefinitely complex matter. His Sphere is a 'mixture' containing 'seeds' (σπέρματα) of every qualitatively distinct natural substance, organic and inorganic: these (flesh, blood, bone, gold, etc.) are infinitely divisible into parts like each other and the whole—hence Aristotle's name for them, 'homoeomeries' (ὁμοιομερῆ)—and are A.'s 'elements'; Empedocles' are mixtures of seeds of all sorts (πανσπερμίαι). A. thus rejects contemporary atomism and, implicitly, Empedocles' less drastic pluralism. Seeds take their quality from their prevailing component (fr. 12); but actually, at every stage of division, imperceptible portions of *every* other 'qualitied' thing remain, for (fr. 11) 'in everything there is a portion of everything except mind (νοῦς)'. This last A. introduces as initiator of cosmic motion and animating principle of plants and animals. Mind, because itself separate and unmixed, can move other things.

3. Anaxagoras thus explains growth and nutrition without assuming qualitative change (cf. fr. 10): the characters which 'emerge' must have been present, imperceptibly, in the germ or food, and rendered apparent by regrouping. But much is obscure: modern controversy centres round the place of the contrary 'opposites' (the hot, the cold, etc.) in A.'s scheme. Tannery's view that these are the ingredients of the seeds has been modified by Burnet and Cornford. Cornford, identifying them with the 'things' of which there is something in everything, uses this dictum to explain the qualitative differences in the seeds only, not also, as do Aristotle and Burnet, biological changes. Bailey adopts the usual and literal (but uneconomical) interpretation, which was that of Aristotle and subsequent ancient authorities, that every seed contains a portion of every other; and apparently avoids a vicious infinite regress by assuming two forms of mixture: (1) complete fusion (σύμμιξις) in the All, from which seeds of different sorts are broken off; (2) compounding of these by juxtaposition (σύγκρισις) —a distinction scarcely justified by the texts.

4. Anaxagoras' cosmology is a closely knit part of the theory. *Nous* starts a rotatory motion (περιχώρησις) which gradually spreads. Thus seeds are separated out, the dense, moist, cold, and dark (ἀήρ) going to the centre, their opposites (αἰθήρ) to the circumference. The heavenly bodies are stones, torn from the earth, which motion renders red-hot (cf. ASTRONOMY). A. follows the Ionian tradition of a flat earth, but knows the cause of eclipses. He assumes only *one* world. (Cornford's arguments against Burnet in *CQ* xxviii (1934) are convincing.) Sense-perception depends on the contrast of unlikes.

5. Anaxagoras' great reputation in antiquity is endorsed on the whole by Aristotle. He solves the problem raised by Parmenides more subtly, if less simply, than the Atomists. His failure to use mind as a teleological principle, which Plato and Aristotle deplore, was fortunate for science.

BIBLIOGRAPHY

1. Ancient sources and text of fragments: Diels, *Vorsokr.*[5] (Kranz, 1934–7); Ritter and Preller[10] (1934). **2.** Modern literature: (i) General. Zeller–Nestle, *Philosophie der Griechen* i. 2[7] (1922) (E. T.

1881); Th. Gomperz, *Greek Thinkers*, i (1901); J. Burnet, *Early Greek Philosophy*[4] (1930; translates frs.) and *Greek Philosophy*, Part i: *Thales to Plato* (1914); L. Robin, *La Pensée grecque*[2] (1932); H. Cherniss, *Aristotle's Criticism of Pre-Socratic Philosophy* (U.S.A. 1935). (ii) Special. A. E. Taylor, *CQ* xi (1917), 81–7 (a convincing discussion of A.'s chronology); C. Bailey, *The Greek Atomists and Epicurus*, Appendix i (1928); F. M. Cornford, *CQ* xxiv (1930; two valuable articles); A. L. Peck, *CQ* xx (1926), xxv (1931) (three articles critical of usual views); *PW* i. 2076. A. J. D. P.

ANAXANDRIDES (4th c. B.C.), Middle Comedy poet who came to Athens from Rhodes or Colophon. His plays are dated by inscriptions from 382 to 349 B.C. (first victory, 376 B.C.); with 65 comedies he won 10 victories. Forty-two titles have survived, 15 denoting mythological burlesques. Aristotle, who often mentions him, says (*Rhet.* 3. 12) that Philemon (q.v. 5; not the famous comic poet) acted in Anaxandrides' plays.

Fr. 6, parody of style of Timotheus; fr. 39, an Athenian contrasts Egyptian and Athenian ideas and customs; fr. 41, wedding-feast of Cotys' daughter with Iphicrates; fr. 49, the quack doctor; fr. 52, cynical view of marriage.

FCG iii. 161 ff.; *CAF* ii. 135 ff. W. G. W.

ANAXARCHUS (4th c. B.C.) of Abdera, a follower of Democritus, with Sceptical tendencies, was the teacher of Pyrrhon the Sceptic. His nickname Εὐδαιμονικός implies that he treated happiness as the *summum bonum*. He accompanied Alexander the Great on his Asiatic campaigns and was much esteemed by him. He is usually represented in antiquity as a flatterer of Alexander, but this may be due to Peripatetic prejudice. He was cruelly put to death by the Cypriot prince Nicocreon.

Testimonia and fragments in Diels, *Vorsokr.*[5] ii. 235–40. *PW* i. 2080. W. D. R.

ANAXICRATES, admiral of Alexander the Great, *see* ARABIA.

ANAXILAS (1), tyrant of Rhegium, 494–476 B.C. He tried to take Zancle from Hippocrates (q.v. 1) by offering it to Samian refugees, but the Samians came to an agreement with Hippocrates. Later he succeeded in expelling them and settling other Greeks, especially Messenians (c. 490), from whom the town was renamed Messana. In 480, through antagonism to Gelon, he was on the Carthaginian side; afterwards he became dependent on Syracuse. In 477 he threatened Locri, but Hieron (q.v. 1) intervened; next year he died. The story in Paus. 4. 23 which connects him with Aristomenes (q.v.) is a mere invention.

Hackforth, *CAH* iv, ch. 11; Kroymann, *Sparta und Messenien* (1937), ch. 2. V. E.

ANAXILAS (2) (4th c. B.C.), Middle Comedy poet, whose name bespeaks a Dorian origin, and whose date is indicated by his burlesques (frs. 14 and 26) of Plato (who died in 347 B.C.) and his composition of a comedy Νεοττίς (cf. EUBULUS (2) and ANTIPHANES), named after the courtesan (31 vv. attempt to describe the type, fr. 22). His plays are mythological burlesques (Κίρκη, Ὧραι), or deal with daily life (Ἄγροικος, Αὐλητής). Ὑάκινθος πορνοβοσκός appears to combine both types; Βοτρυλίων is perhaps a vine-growing peasant; Μονότροπος, a study of a Timon-like character, is influenced by Phrynichus. Fr. 27 is on the 'new music' of the time: ἡ μουσικὴ δ' ὥσπερ Λιβύη πρὸς τῶν θεῶν | ἀεί τι καινὸν κατ' ἐνιαυτὸν θηρίον | τίκτει.

FCG iii. 341 ff.; *CAF* ii. 264 ff. W. G. W.

ANAXIMANDER (Ἀναξίμανδρος) (born 610 B.C.) of Miletus wrote the first Greek treatise in prose c. 546 B.C. He held that the origin (ἀρχή) of all things was the Infinite (τὸ ἄπειρον), which he regarded as the Divine, describing it as 'immortal and deathless' and as 'surrounding and governing' the innumerable worlds. Each world he envisaged as a community of conflicting opposites 'separated' out of the Infinite by the world-rotation and liable to inevitable 'punishment' for their mutual 'in-

justice'. He thereby first conceived the entire universe as subject to a single law. A. revolutionized astronomy by regarding our world no longer as hemispherical but as spherical; in the centre is the unsupported Earth, shaped like a truncated column, around which circle at even distances and in an inclined plane stars, moon, and sun. Hence he is credited, perhaps rightly, with discovering the obliquity of the ecliptic. He introduced into Greece the gnomon, which he used to determine the equinoxes, and drew the first map of the earth. *See also* ASTRONOMY.

Diels, *Vorsokr.*[5] i. 81–90; Burnet, *Early Greek Philosophy*[4], 50–71; W. Jaeger, *Paideia* (Engl. Transl[2]. 1945), 154–61; *PW* i. 2085. A. H. C.

ANAXIMENES (1) of Miletus (fl. c. 546 B.C.), junior and perhaps pupil to Anaximander (q.v.), maintained in simple Ionic prose that all things arise from air (ἀήρ), which when rarefied becomes fire, when condensed, progressively wind, cloud, water, earth, stone; all other things are formed from these. The Earth is thin and flat, floating on air; sun, moon, and stars are leaves of fire exhaled from the Earth and carried by air around it, setting behind high ground in the distant north. A.'s astronomy is retrograde from Anaximander's; but in his theory of condensation and rarefaction he is the first to conceive the cosmos as governed according not to a moral but to a physical law.

Diels, *Vorsokr.*[5] i. 90–6; Burnet, *Early Greek Philosophy*[4], 72–9; *PW* i. 2086. Zeller-Mondolfo, *La filosofia dei Greci* i[2] (1938), 206–38. A. H. C.

ANAXIMENES (2) of Lampsacus (c. 380–320 B.C.), historian and rhetorician, a pupil of Zoilus and instructor of Alexander. Fragments of his historical works—Ἑλληνικά, Φιλιππικά, and a *History of Alexander*—reveal rhetorical influences seen yet more clearly in his speeches, writings on Homer, and παίγνια. More significant is his *Rhetorica ad Alexandrum*, formerly attributed to Aristotle, the fourth-century origin of which is confirmed by the Hibeh Papyrus (1906), no. 26. As the sole surviving manual of early Sophistic rhetoric, it throws light on the teaching from Corax to Isocrates.

Spengel, *Rhet.* i. 169–242. J. W. H. A.

ANAXIPPUS, New Comedy poet, 'in the time of Antigonus and Demetrius Poliorcetes' (Suidas). Four comedies are plainly attributed to A.; and one fragment (49 vv.) of another is assigned to 'Anthippus'—probably a mistake for Anaxippus—the verbose but humorous speech of a cook who elevates the gastronomic art.

FCG iv. 459 ff.; *CAF* iii. 296 ff. W. G. W.

ANCAEUS (Ἀγκαῖος), in mythology, (1) son or grandson of Lycurgus of Arcadia (Hyg. *Fab.* 14. 14), an Argonaut (Ap. Rhod. 1. 164), the strongest next to Heracles, with whom he is paired (ibid. 426, 531, etc.), killed in the Calydonian boar-hunt (Ov. *Met.* 8. 315, 391 ff.). (2) son of Poseidon (Ap. Rhod. 1. 187) and king of the Leleges of Samos; often confused with (1) (as Apollod. 1. 112 and 126). A skilled navigator, he steered the *Argo* after Tiphys died (Ap. Rhod. 2. 894). He planted a vineyard and was told by his servant that he should not live to drink its wine. On the grapes ripening, he pressed some of the juice into a cup, but the man remarked πολλὰ μεταξὺ πέλει κύλικος καὶ χείλεος ἄκρου, and Ancaeus was killed by a boar before he could drink (schol. Ap. Rhod. 1. 188). H. J. R.

ANCHISES, in mythology, son of Capys and grandson of Assaracus, belonged to the younger branch of the Trojan royal house. Spoken of with respect in the *Iliad*, he is chiefly famed for his marriage with Aphrodite while pasturing herds on the slopes of Ida, from which union Aeneas was born. Forbidden to reveal the name of his son's mother, he is said to have boasted of it among his friends, and for this was blinded or lamed by lightning.

At the fall of Troy he was rescued by Aeneas, who carried him on his shoulders from the city, and subsequently shared his son's wanderings. Tradition gives many accounts of his death; Virgil places it at Drepanum in Sicily, and later describes him in the Elysian fields.

R. A. B. M.

ANCHISTEIS (ἀγχιστεῖς), the kinship-group, extending to second cousins, which was the basis of family law at Athens; also called συγγενεῖς. In cases of homicide, the nearest male relative within this limit had to prosecute; in cases of intestacy, the nearest male relative within this limit could claim the property. Relatives on the father's side had precedence, but the mother's relatives were included.

A. W. G.

ANCONA (Ἀγκών, so called from the shape of its harbour, which resembles an elbow-socket), a town of Italy in the territory of the Piceni, with the only good natural harbour on the central west coast, but with a poorly developed hinterland. It is first mentioned as a colony of refugees from Dionysius I of Syracuse. It was used by Cornelius Cinna as the mustering point of his expeditionary force against Sulla (84 B.C.), and it subsequently served as a port of embarkation to Dalmatia. Trajan rebuilt the harbour and erected a commemorative arch on a mound above it.

M. C.

ANCYRA (Ἄγκυρα, modern *Angora*), a city in that part of Phrygia settled by the Galatians, one of whose three tribes, the Tectosages, made it their capital. It lies in a strong position, around the steep fortified crag which formed its acropolis, at an important road junction, and rose to prominence as the capital of the province Galatia, as again to-day as the capital of Turkey. On the walls of the temple of Rome and Augustus, the ruins of which still stand, was inscribed the bilingual record of the reign of Augustus known as the *Monumentum Ancyranum*.

W. M. C.

ANDOCIDES (1) (c. 440–c. 390 B.C.), a member of an aristocratic family which, as he claimed, had been distinguished for three generations. In 415, shortly before the starting of the Athenian expedition to Sicily, Athenian feeling was shocked by two acts of sacrilege, the mutilation of the Hermae and the parody of the Mysteries of Eleusis by Alcibiades. A. was accused of participation in both these acts. He cleared himself in the case of the Mysteries, but admitted some knowledge of the Hermae incident. He was imprisoned, and in order, as he says, to save his father and others, decided to tell all that he knew. A sentence of *atimia* was passed on him, and he went abroad. In his speech *De Reditu*, some years later, he affirms that he knew of the plot and opposed it, that at the time when the sacrilege was committed he was incapacitated by an accident, and that he was induced by threats to say nothing about it. For some years he was engaged in commerce in various parts of the world. In 411 he provided oars for the Athenian fleet at Samos, and returned to Athens to plead for a remission of his sentence. The Four Hundred, who had now come into power, rejected his plea. In 410 he made another unsuccessful attempt, delivering the speech *De Reditu*; he was finally reinstated under the terms of the amnesty of Thrasybulus (403).

He took an active part in public life, speaking in the Assembly as a warm supporter of democratic ideals. In 399 he was accused of impiety on two counts, the more serious being that he had taken part in the Mysteries when he was legally disqualified from doing so. He defended himself successfully in the *De Mysteriis*. In 391 he was one of the envoys appointed to negotiate peace with Sparta. The attempt was unsuccessful. The Ps.-Plutarch states that he went into exile a second time, and we know nothing of his subsequent adventures.

SPEECHES

1. *De Reditu*, 410 B.C. In 415 A. made certain disclosures under a guarantee of immunity from punishment, but the decree of Isotimides excluded from the Agora and the temples all who had committed impiety and confessed it. The enemies of A. maintained that this decree applied to him. A. pleads his subsequent services to the State, particularly to the army at Samos, as a reason for his reinstatement.

2. *De Mysteriis*, 399 B.C. A. had returned to Athens under the general amnesty of 403, and four years later was charged with having transgressed the decree of Isotimides by taking part in the Mysteries and entering the temple of Eleusis. His adversaries (see [Lysias], *Against Andocides*) maintained that the amnesty was only political and did not extend to religious matters. A. here maintains that he was guiltless with regard both to the Mysteries and to the Hermae incident, and therefore the decree does not touch him. The speech is of great importance in relation to the history of the year 415.

3. *De Pace*, 390 B.C. A. argues unsuccessfully in favour of peace with Sparta on terms practically the same as those obtained three years later by the peace of Antalcidas.

4. *Against Alcibiades* is a rhetorical forgery of late date (Jebb, *Attic Orators* i. 134–6).

Four lost speeches were entitled Πρὸς ἑταίρους, Συμβουλευτικός, Περὶ τῆς ἐνδείξεως, and Ἀπολογία πρὸς Φαίακα.

Greek and Roman critics discovered in A. faults which, according to their canons, were serious; and admittedly the faults are there. He sometimes carries the use of parenthesis to absurd extremes; he cannot keep to one point at a time; his style is so loose that the argument is hard to follow. On the other hand, this inconsequential method of expression is at times effective, giving the impression of an eagerness which outruns premeditated art. He possessed a natural gift of expression, a fine flow of words, and a good narrative style. He was not a professional rhetorician, and if he neglected scholastic rules, it can at least be claimed for him that he was successful on his own unconventional lines.

For general bibliography *see* ATTIC ORATORS. Text: Blass–Fuhr (Teubner, 1913). Commentary, *De Mysteriis* and *De Reditu*, E. C. Marchant (1889). Index (to A., Lycurgus, and Dinarchus), L. L. Forman (U.S.A. 1897).

J. F. D.

ANDOCIDES (2) (fl. last quarter of 6th c. B.C.), a potter in Athens, known from six signatures. Two important artists worked for him: 1. Andocides painter. Painted amphorae and cups in black- and red-figure (the black-figure parts perhaps by another), red-figure, and white-figure technique. Successor of Execias (q.v.). 2. Menon painter (probably called Psiax; worked also for the potter Menon). Painted amphorae, hydriae, and small vases in black-figure, black- and red-figure, and red-figure technique.

J. D. Beazley, *Attic Black-figure* (1928), 25; *Attische Vasenmaler* (1923), 7, 9; G. M. A. Richter, *AJArch.* 1934, 547; H. R. W. Smith, *New Aspects of the Menon Painter* (1929). T. B. L. W.

ANDREAS (d. 217 B.C.), physician of Ptolemy IV (Philopator). Works: Νάρθηξ (a pharmacopoeia, with descriptions of plants and roots); Περὶ δακέτων (on snakebites); Περὶ τῶν ψευδῶς πεπιστευμένων (against superstitious beliefs); Περὶ στεφάνων (all lost except for fragments).

PW i. 2136.

ANDRISCUS, an Adramyttian adventurer, claiming to be Philip, the son of Perseus and Laodice, appeared as pretender to the Macedonian throne. On approaching Demetrius I of Syria, Laodice's brother, he was handed over to Rome, but escaped and with Thracian help invaded Macedonia, where by two victories and repressive measures he established control in 149 B.C.

Rejecting negotiations with Scipio Nasica, he defeated Juventius Thalna, but was crushed in 148 by Q. Caecilius Metellus.

Livy, *Per.* 48-50; Polyb. 36. 9-10 and 17; Zonar. 9. 28. G. Colin, *Rome et la Grèce* (1905), 608. A. H. McD.

ANDROGEUS (Ἀνδρόγεως), in mythology, (1) son of Minos (q.v.) and Pasiphaë, was treacherously killed by his defeated rivals after a victory in the Panathenaic games, or (in another version) was sent by Aegeus king of Athens against the Marathonian bull and destroyed by it. To avenge him Minos besieged Athens, and was only appeased by an annual tribute of seven youths and seven maidens to be thrown to the Minotaur. Later he was honoured in Phalerum as κατὰ πρύμναν ἥρως. (2) Greek leader killed at Troy (Verg. *Aen.* 2. 370-3).
R. A. B. M.

ANDROMACHE, in mythology, daughter of Eëtion king of Thebe and wife of Hector (q.v.; *Il.* 6. 395 ff.). Her father and brothers were killed by Achilles, her mother taken prisoner but ransomed (ibid. 414 ff.). After the fall of Troy her son Astyanax was put to death by the Greeks (*Little Iliad*, fr. 19 Allen; *Iliu Persis*) and she herself became Neoptolemus' slave (ibid.). She bore him a son, Molossus, eponym of the Molossians. According to Euripides (*Andromache*) she narrowly escaped death at the hands of Neoptolemus' wife Hermione (q.v.) during the visit to Delphi in which he was killed (*see* NEOPTOLEMUS). After his death (Euripides) or before his marriage (*Aen.* 3. 327-9) she was handed over to Helenus, with whom she lived the rest of her life in Epirus. H. J. R.

ANDROMEDA, in mythology, daughter of Cepheus king of the Ethiopians and his wife Cassiepeia or Cassiope (Κασσιέπεια, Κασσιόπη). A principal source of our information about her is apparently the *Andromeda* of Euripides (Nauck², pp. 392 ff.). Cassiepeia boasted that she was more beautiful than the Nereids; they complained to Poseidon, who flooded the land and sent a sea-monster to ravage it. On consulting Ammon, Cepheus learned that the only cure was to expose Andromeda to the monster, and she was accordingly fastened to a rock on the sea-shore. At this point Perseus (q.v.) came by on his way from taking the head of Medusa. He fell in love with Andromeda at sight, and got her and her father's consent to marry her if he could kill the sea-beast. This he did; but Andromeda's uncle Phineus, who had been betrothed to her, attacked him by open force (Ov. *Met.* 5. 1 ff.) or otherwise (ἐπιβουλεύοντος, Apollod. 2. 44). Perseus showed him and his followers the head of Medusa, turning them all into stone. He and Andromeda stayed for a time with Cepheus, and left their eldest son, Perses, with him; from Perses the Persian kings were descended. They then went on to Seriphus and thence to Argos and Tiryns, *see* PERSEUS. Their other children were Alcaeus, Sthenelus, Heleius, Mestor, Electryon, and a daughter Gorgophone (Apollod. 2. 43-9; other authorities in Nauck, loc. cit.). The story is of a type widely distributed (Stith Thompson R111. 1. 3) and may well have had a share in forming the legend of St. George and the dragon (Politis in Λαογραφία 4, 1913, p. 220 f.).

That Andromeda, Perseus, Cepheus, Cassiepeia, and the monster were all turned into the constellations bearing their names (the monster is Cetus) was asserted by Euripides, according to [Eratosthenes], *Catast.* 17, by the natural interpretation of his words; he may, however, merely mean that Euripides tells the story of her rescue. If the first interpretation is right, it is one of the very few Greek star-myths which can be traced back to an earlier date than the Alexandrian period.

See Manilius 5. 22 ff., 540 ff.; [Eratosthenes] 15-17; Hyginus, *Poet. Astr.* 2. 9-12; schol. German. *Arat.* pp. 77 ff., 137 ff., Breysig.
H. J. R.

ANDRON of Halicarnassus, author concerned with the genealogies of Greek cities and families (Συγγενικά or Συγγένειαι), a popular subject in the fourth century B.C. The ascription of an *Atthis* to him is improbable.

FGrH i. 10; *FHG* ii. 349.

ANDRONICUS, LIVIUS, *see* LIVIUS ANDRONICUS.

ANDRONICUS RHODIUS (1st c. B.C.), Peripatetic philosopher, who recalled the attention of the school to the works of Aristotle and Theophrastus, which had sunk into neglect. He arranged the works of both in the order in which those of Aristotle and in part those of Theophrastus have survived; on his arrangement of Aristotle's works is based the list preserved by Ptolemy. He wrote a treatise in at least five books on the order of Aristotle's works, with discussion of their contents and authenticity, an account of his life, and a transcript of his will. In his work he had the assistance of the grammarian Tyrannio. Andronicus' editorial work is probably to be dated about 40 B.C., and his assumption of the headship of the Peripatetic school at Athens shortly thereafter. The work *De Passionibus* which passes under his name (bk. 1, ed. X. Kreuttner, 1885; bk. 2, ed. K. Schuchhardt, 1883) is spurious.

PW i. 2164. W. D. R.

ANDROS, the most northerly of the Cyclades (q.v.). In the eighth century B.C. the island was dependent on Eretria. It submitted to Persia in 490, thus angering Athens, and later Pericles planted Athenian colonists there. About 410 it revolted from Athens; as a free State it entered the second Athenian confederacy (378-377). After the battle of Chaeronea the island came under Macedonian control, which remained more or less continuous until the occupation by Pergamene and Roman forces in 200. After 133 Andros was associated with the Roman province of Asia.

IG xii. 5; Bursian ii. 441 ff.; T. Sauciuc, *Andros* (1914).
W. A. L.

ANDROSTHENES, of Thasos, sailed with Nearchus (q.v. 3) and wrote an account of the voyage and of his subsequent exploration of the inner Persian Gulf and Bahrein. *See* ALEXANDER (3), Bibliography, Ancient Sources.

ANDROTION (4th c. B.C.), entered Athenian public life *c.* 386 and was engaged in military or diplomatic matters for the next forty years. Pupil of Isocrates. Accused by Demosthenes (*Or.* 22) in 354-353 of making an illegal proposal (παράνομα). His *Atthis* (q.v.), probably in ten books, was next in importance to that of Philochorus, being one of Aristotle's sources for the *Athenian Constitution*. It reached 346.

FHG i. 371. G. L. B.

ANGELS (ἄγγελοι), 'messengers'. Hermes was considered the messenger of the Olympians, and named Angelos (once Euangelos). The same function was attributed to Iris (in the *Iliad* and *Homeric Hymns*), and in Plato (*Cra.* 407 e, 408 b) the two are the divine *angeloi*. Hecate-Artemis is also designated as *angelos* (Sophron in schol. Theoc. 2. 12), which signifies her intercourse with the nether world and the dead. Hermes is once named the 'messenger of Persephone'. Thera has yielded interesting sepulchral inscriptions (Christian), in which the 'angelos' of the defunct is mentioned, *IG* xii. 3. 933 ff. (Index, p. 257; in no. 1238 the protective genius of the grave, cf. Hermes in Thessaly). The role of the angels became important in Gnostic and Neoplatonic systems (in the following order: gods, archangels, angels, demons, heroes); they were connected with the planets (under Jewish-Chaldaean influence), dominated metals and plants, and their names had magic virtues (see *PGM*, Index). Their cult flourished in Egypt and Asia Minor especially in the second and third centuries A.D. and gained new life with the Christians (Michael replacing Hermes, but also Apollo, etc.).

Th. Hopfner, *Griechisch-ägyptischer Offenbarungszauber* (vol. xxi and xxiii of Wessely's *Studien zur Paläographie und Papyruskunde* 1922, 1924) i, §§ 135 ff.; H. Leclercq, art. 'Anges' in Cabrol–Leclercq, *Dictionnaire d'archéologie chrétienne* i. 2, col. 2080–161. S. E.

ANGERONA, DIVA, a Roman goddess, worshipped on 21 Dec. (Divalia or Angeronalia), in the Curia Acculeia (Varro, *Ling.* 6. 23), or the *sacellum Volupiae*, where there stood on the altar a statue of Angerona with her mouth bound up and sealed (Macrob. *Sat.* 1. 10. 8; *CIL* i², p. 337). The ancients connected her name with *angina* (Festus, p. 16, 12 Lindsay) or *angor* (Masurius ap. Macrob. ibid.); Mommsen with *angerere*, 'to raise up', sc. the sun after the solstice.

See Wissowa, *RK* 241. H. J. R.

ANGITIA, or the **ANGITIAE**, Marsian goddess(es), principally worshipped on the Lacus Fucinus at Lucus Angitiae (now *Luco*), also at Sulmo, where the plural of the name is found (see, for the former, *Aen.* 7. 759). Her native name was Anagtia and she seems to have been a goddess of healing and very popular; see Conway, *Ital. Dialects*, 182, 289 f.; Wissowa, *RK* 49; Schirmer in Roscher's *Lexikon*, s.v. H. J. R.

ANICETUS, prefect of the fleet at Misenum, was freedman and tutor of Nero, who used him to murder Agrippina. Subsequently induced to confess himself Octavia's paramour, he was exiled to Sardinia (A.D. 62). *PIR*², A 589.

ANIMALS, DOMESTIC, see PETS.

ANIMALS, SACRED. Neither Greece nor Italy regarded any beast as an incarnate god in classical times (unlike Egypt, with the practices of which land they became familiar), but various animals were sacred in one sense or another. (1) A number of beasts and birds are connected with individual gods; thus, the eagle is associated with Zeus, the cow and the peacock with Hera, the owl with Athena, the bull with Dionysus, and so forth; in Italy, the wolf and the woodpecker are creatures of Mars (e.g. Plut. *Rom.* 4). For the Greek associations of animals and plants with deities, see Eustathius *in Il.*, p. 86, 36 ff., discussed by C. Reinhardt, *De Graecorum theologia* (1910), p. 90 ff. It is a tenable theory that some at least of these deities were originally theriomorphic. (2) Besides the consecrating of victims to gods and the dedication of a live creature to some deity (as the horses dedicated by Julius Caesar, Suet. *Divus Iulius* 81; such animals were unworked and called ἄφετοι in Greek, e.g. Pl. *Critias* 119 d) we occasionally hear of an animal living in a shrine, as serpents (q.v.) very commonly in chthonian cults (Erechtheus, on the Acropolis, Hdt. 8. 41. 2; Asclepius, Ar. *Plut.* 733); geese sacred to Juno (Moneta) (Livy 5. 47. 4). (3) Sporadically, we hear of some creature locally sacred and inviolable; e.g. tortoises on Mt. Parthenion (Paus. 8. 54. 7); these were regarded as sacred to Pan. Such phenomena have often been explained as survivals of totemism, but there is no evidence that this ever existed in Greece, see Rose, *Primitive Culture in Greece*, 47–51. Perhaps no one explanation can fit them all. *See also* BIRDS (SACRED). H. J. R.

ANIO (modern *Aniene*), a river of Italy rising in the Sabine country and separating it from Latium (Pliny, *HN* 3. 54). After flowing seventy-five miles west-south-west it joins the Tiber at the site of Antemnae just north of Rome. Landslides in A.D. 105 and later have changed but not destroyed its spectacular cascades at Tibur (Hor. *Carm.* 1. 7. 13; Pliny, *Ep.* 8. 17). It supplied two aqueducts, Anio Vetus (272 B.C.) and Anio Novus (A.D. 52),

and below Tibur was navigable (Strabo 5. 238). Recently found Neanderthal skulls indicate very ancient habitation of its valley.

G. Colasanti, *L'Aniene* (1906); T. Ashby, *Aqueducts of Ancient Rome* (1935), 54, 252. E. T. S.

ANIUS, in mythology, king of Delos and priest of Apollo. His mother Rhoeo being with child by Apollo, her father Staphylus son of Dionysus set her afloat in a chest, which stranded on Delos. A., when he grew up, married Dorippa and had three daughters, the Oenotropoe, Oeno, Spermo, and Elais, who could produce respectively wine, seeds, and oil, by grace of Dionysus. They thus supplied Agamemnon's army before Troy. A. received Aeneas (*Aen.* 3. 80). See Lycophron 170, and scholiast there. H. J. R.

ANNA, see DIDO.

ANNA PERENNA, a Roman goddess, whose festival was on 15 March, i.e. the first full moon of the year by the old reckoning (1 March being New Year's Day). It was popular and merry (see Ov. *Fasti* 3. 523 ff., with Frazer's commentary). She is usually explained as being a year-goddess, and her name thought of as created from the prayer 'ut annare perennareque commode liceat', 'for leave to live in and through the year to our liking' (Macrob. *Sat.* 1. 12. 6). See, however, Altheim, *Terra Mater* (1931), pp. 91 ff., who makes her 'Mother Perna', a form of Ceres with Etruscan connexions. She has no mythology, but Ovid (ibid.) tells two stories (? of his own invention), one identifying her with Anna the sister of Dido (545–656), the other with an old woman of Bovillae named Anna ('Granny'), who fed the plebeians during the secession to the Mons Sacer (663–74. On what follows, 675 ff., cf. Rose, *Handbook of Greek Mythology*, 324). H. J. R.

ANNAEUS, see CORNUTUS, FLORUS, LUCAN, SENECA.

ANNALS, ANNALISTS. From the beginning of Roman history to 400 B.C. only scanty records were preserved, but the main lines of tradition are authentic in the fourth century, and from c. 300 B.C. the *tabulae pontificum* (q.v.) gave regular records of magistrates and events of cult importance. These tables were the first annals, from which Ennius took the title of his historical epic; but their character was still purely sacral in Cato's day (*Origines*, bk. 4, fr. 77 Peter), and the variance in the foundation-dates of Rome indicates that the pontifical records were not in full chronicle form in the middle of the second century.

The senatorial historians, Fabius Pictor, Cincius Alimentus, Postumius Albinus, and C. Acilius (qq.v.), now appear, on M. Gelzer's reinterpretation of Cicero (*De Or.* 2. 51–2; *Leg.* 1. 5) and his study of the Fabian tradition, to have been not annalistic writers, but discursive historians, following the Hellenistic κτίσεις and episodic histories; Cato's *Origines* merely continued their work in Latin. If this view is accepted, the evidence of both pontifical records and historiography sets the first annalistic history in the latter part of the second century B.C.

Under Cato's influence the 'old' annalists, Cassius (q.v.) Hemina and Calpurnius Piso (q.v. 1), began the systematic reconstruction of Roman history. Then the publication of the *annales maximi* in eighty books, *ab initio rerum Romanarum usque ad P. Mucium pontificem maximum*, presumably by P. Mucius Scaevola himself (Pontifex Maximus from 131–130 to between 123 and 114 B.C.), set out in formal arrangement year by year the official events of the State, viz. elections and commands, civic, provincial, and cult business. The composition involved for the regal period legendary and antiquarian speculation, for the early Republic systematic reconstruction from the nucleus of records, and added to the framework of the *tabulae pontificum* from the fuller records in the archives.

The publication was definitive, and the new material and its formal arrangement determined the character of 'late' annalistic history from Cn. Gellius to the Sullan annalists and Livy. The influence of Isocratean historiographical theory allowed, probably Gellius, certainly Valerius Antias and Claudius Quadrigarius (qq.v.) to elaborate the ceremonial form and expand the records in the light of senatorial constitutionalism, legalistic antiquarianism, and family interests, with conventional rhetorical composition; this led, particularly with Antias, to inaccuracy, invention, and tendentious falsification.

The annalistic form was thus established as an historiographical γένος. Licinius Macer (q.v. 1) and Aelius Tubero (q.v. 2) in following it appear to have checked their material, but Livy accepted both material and arrangement in its Sullan form, and his work enshrines the annalistic tradition. The form was adapted to the narration of contemporary history, and was used by the Imperial annalists, imposing its conventions even on Tacitus.

H. Peter, *HRRel.* i² (1914), ii (1906). K. W. Nitzsch, *Die röm. Annalistik* (1873); L. Cantarelli, *Riv. Fil.* 1898, 209; E. Kornemann, *Die Priestercodex in der Regia* (1912); F. Leo, *Gesch. röm. Lit.* i (1913), 259; De Sanctis, *Stor. Rom.* i. 16; K. J. Beloch, *Röm. Gesch.* 86; M. Gelzer, *Hermes* 1933, 129; ibid. 1934, 46; ibid. 1936, 275 (for a criticism of these views see F. W. Walbank, *CQ* 1945, 15); J. E. A. Crake, *CPhil.* 1940. *See also* TABULA PONTIFICUM.
A. H. McD.

ANNIANUS, a 'neoteric' (q.v.) of Hadrian's time, composed *carmina Falisca* on country themes.

Baehr. *FPR*; Morel, *FPL.*

ANNICERIS, of Cyrene, philosopher of the Cyrenaic school, probably lived under Ptolemy I, who died 283 B.C. He, Hegesias, and Theodorus 'the godless' became leaders of three divergent branches of the school, his own originality consisting, so far as we know, in stressing the importance of sympathetic pleasure.

PW i. 2259.
W. D. R.

ANNIUS (and **ANNIA**), *see* FAUSTINA, FLORIANUS, GALLUS, LUCILLA, MILO, VINICIANUS.

ANNONA. This word, literally 'harvest', is almost always used in the sense of corn-supply. From the earliest times the Romans regarded it as a duty of the State to secure that the population of the city was adequately supplied with corn at a reasonable price; speculation in grain was punishable by law. Under the Republic the *cura annonae* devolved upon the aediles (q.v.), whose duties were considerably increased by the introduction of *frumentationes* (doles of cheap or free corn) by C. Gracchus. In 57 B.C. a special *cura annonae* was conferred upon Pompey. Two new aediles (*aediles Ceriales*) were created by Caesar. The corn-supply was made into an imperial department by Augustus, who delegated it to a *praefectus annonae*, an equestrian official of high rank. The *praefectus* held office for an indefinite period, and had subordinates in the Italian ports and in the provinces, where barns were erected for storage at the cost of the government. Officials connected with the *annona* (*aediles, praefecti, curatores*) are also found in the municipal towns, which followed the example of Rome in making public provision for essential foodstuffs. In the later Empire the word *annona* was used of a tax in kind, which was imposed by a special imperial order (*indictio*, q.v.; *see also* DIOCLETIAN, para. 7).

D. van Berchen, *Les Distributions de blé et d'argent à la plèbe romaine sous l'empire* (1939).
G. H. S.

ANONYMUS Ἀνταττικιστής, a contemporary opponent of Phrynichus the Atticist (q.v.), who cites from good, but not always Attic, writers many words condemned by Phrynichus. *See* LEXICA SEGUERIANA.

ANONYMUS περὶ ὕψους. *See* LONGINUS.

ANONYMUS SEGUERIANUS (3rd c. A.D.) wrote a τέχνη τοῦ πολιτικοῦ λόγου, including references to the work of Alexander (q.v. 12), son of Numenius, which throw light on first-century rhetorical teaching.

Spengel, *Rhet.* i. 427–60.

ANSER (1st c. B.C.), a salacious erotic poet. Nothing remains of his poems. The only unequivocal reference to him is in Ovid (*Tr.* 2. 435).

Cf. R. Unger, *De Ansere Poeta* (1858).

ANTAEUS (Ἀνταῖος), in mythology, a giant, son of Poseidon and Earth, living in Libya; he compelled all comers to wrestle with him and killed them when overcome (Pind. *Isthm.* 4. 56 ff. and schol. Plato, *Tht.* 169 b). He was defeated and killed by Heracles (q.v.). That he was made stronger when thrown, by contact with his mother the Earth (Apollod. 2. 115), seems a later addition to the story.
H. J. R.

ANTAGORAS OF RHODES (3rd c. B.C.), author of a *Thebais*, epigrams, and a *Hymn to Love*.

ANTALCIDAS (more correctly *Antialcidas*) (fl. 4th c. B.C.), Spartan agent and general, converted first Tiribazus (392 B.C.) and later Artaxerxes II (388) to the view that Persia had greater identity of interest with Sparta than with Athens. Having negotiated a Sparto-Persian alliance, he blockaded the Hellespont and forced Athens, and her allies, to agree to the peace which bears his name (386). Its terms abandoned the Greek cities of Asia Minor to Persia (Xen. *Hell.* 5. 1. 32–6). He undertook further diplomatic missions to Persia in 372 and 367, the second of which was a disastrous failure and may have occasioned his death by suicide.
D. E. W. W.

ANTEIA, *see* BELLEROPHON.

ANTENOR (1), in mythology, an elderly and upright counsellor in Troy during the siege, who advised the return of Helen to the Greeks, and in return for this (or, according to much later accounts, for betraying the city) was spared by the victors. Pindar says his descendants held Cyrene; but in the story current in Roman times he took with him the Eneti from Paphlagonia (who had lost their king at Troy) and, settling in Venetia at the head of the Adriatic, founded Padua.
R. A. B. M.

ANTENOR (2) (c. 540–500 B.C.), Athenian sculptor, famous as the sculptor of the first group of the Tyrannicides, Harmodius and Aristogiton (*see* CRITIUS). This group stood in the Agora at Athens, but was taken to Persia by Xerxes in 480. It was later restored to its place by Seleucus or Alexander. Two signed bases of this artist were found on the Acropolis at Athens. One of them belongs to a fine marble *kore* now in the Acropolis Museum (No. 681). The doubts which have been expressed as to the association of the base with the statue (see H. Payne, *Archaic Marble Sculpture from the Acropolis*, 31) may be dismissed. It is held by many that he was the sculptor of the archaic pedimental figures of the temple of Apollo at Delphi.
S. C.

ANTHESTERIA, the festival of the flowers, celebrated in the spring, in Athens on the 12th Anthesterion and (as the frequent occurrence of the month name Anthesterion shows) in many other Ionian towns. The day before had its name, Pithoegia, from the opening of the wine-jars. The festival had two aspects, on the one hand that of merriment and rejoicing and, on the other, that of gloom. On the chief day, the 12th, the new wine was ceremonially blessed before Dionysus; everyone carried in wine and drank of his own jug; hence this day was called Χόες, the Jugs. Small children were admitted to the festival and given little jugs; it was a school holiday. On the same day Dionysus was brought in on a ship set on wheels and married the wife of the (Archon-) Basileus, and in the evening, which according to religious reckoning belonged to the 13th, called the Χύτροι, pots with cooked fruits were brought to the dead. The derivation of the word from ἀναθέσσασθαι, 'to raise by prayer', i.e. the dead (J. E. Harrison, *Prol. to the Study of Greek Religion*, 48), must be rejected. The *carrus navalis* and the blessing of the wine are represented on vase-pictures, which by some scholars are referred to the Great Dionysia and the Lenaea respectively (*see* LENAEA).

M. P. Nilsson, *Studia de Dionysiis atticis* (1900), 115; *Gesch. d. griech. Religion* (1940) i. 550. L. Deubner, *Attische Feste*, 93 ff.
M. P. N.

ANTHOLOGIA LATINA as a title properly belongs to a collection of poems made by a certain Octavianus in 532–4 A.D. at Carthage. This work delighted the Middle Ages. Of its extant MSS. by far the best is the seventh-century Parisinus 10318, called also Salmasianus (from its owner Claude de Saumaise, 1588–1653). The first five books are missing. But from the *Praefatio* to Octavianus' own poems we may gather that they contained selections from poets that preceded the sixth century A.D. Other MSS., such as Thuaneus (Parisinus 8071) and Vossianus L.Q. 86, both of the ninth century, help to remedy their loss. The surviving books include Virgilian Centos, Serpentine Verses, Poems on Roses, Dido's Letter, Poems of the Vandals, The Vigil of Venus, and a host of other pieces dealing with a large variety of subjects.

From the sixteenth century onwards many collections of Latin poems have been arranged and published, notably those of Joseph Scaliger (1573), P. Burmann Secundus (1759–73), J. C. Wernsdorf (1780–99), E. Baehrens (1879–83), A. Riese and F. Buecheler (1894), and J. W. and A. M. Duff (Selections: *Min. Lat. Poets*, Loeb 1934, with excellent English translation). Such collections show the vast output of the minor Latin poets that usually are not easily accessible.

See C. Schubart, *Quaestionum de Anthol. Cod. Salmasiani Pars I* (1875); and the Prefaces of those scholars mentioned above.
R. M.

ANTHOLOGY, ἀνθολογία, 'bouquet', was first used of a collection of poems in the Byzantine period. The greatest classical anthology is the Palatine Anthology (quoted as *Anth. Pal.*) of Greek poetical epigrams—so called because the only manuscript was found in the Count Palatine's library at Heidelberg.

2. From the fourth century B.C. onwards many collections of epigrams by individual poets or on single subjects were made. The first really large critical anthology was the *Garland* of MELEAGER (q.v. 2), *c.* 90 B.C.), which contained epigrams attributed to about fifty poets from Archilochus down to Meleager himself. Most of them were elegiac; a few were in other metres; all were short, averaging eight lines. They were probably arranged in groups, the original epigram on any one theme being followed by imitations and variations; but there are traces of an alphabetical arrangement, by the first letter of each poem.

3. About A.D. 40 PHILIPPUS (q.v. 3) of Thessalonica collected a less abundant *Garland* of Greek epigrammatists since Meleager. He was more conservative—all his poets wrote in elegiacs, and conformed to certain easily defined patterns, erotic, epideictic, etc.

4. Large sections from both *Garlands* were included in the *Circle* of epigrams compiled about A.D. 570 by the Byzantine AGATHIAS (q.v.), who added many contemporary epigrams, and arranged them all by subject: his metrical contents-page (*Anth. Pal.* 4. 3) survives to give the scheme he followed.

5. Under the learned Emperor Constantine VII (912–59), CEPHALAS (q.v.) made the existing Anthology by rearranging those of Meleager, Philippus, and Agathias, and adding others such as Straton's homosexual poems. His arrangement is: (i) Christian epigrams, mainly on Byzantine churches; (ii) a description of statues in a Byzantine gymnasium (*c.* A.D. 500); (iii) inscriptions on statues in Attalus' temple to filial love (*c.* 183 B.C.); (iv) the prefaces of Meleager, Philippus, and Agathias; (v) love-poems; (vi) dedications; (vii) epitaphs; (viii) religious epigrams by St. Gregory (*c.* A.D. 350); (ix) epideictic epigrams—displays of wit and imagination on odd facts, famous people, great works of art; (x) comments on life and morality; (xi) convivial and satirical epigrams; (xii) poems on homosexual love; (xiii) epigrams in peculiar metres; (xiv) riddles; (xv) miscellaneous epigrams, including poems shaped like an egg and an axe.

6. The Anthology of Cephalas was re-edited in 1301 by the monk PLANUDES, who expelled many fine poems. His revision was the only known collection of Greek epigrams until the solitary manuscript of Cephalas was found (1606) and—after many vicissitudes—printed. The current text ends with the Planudean Appendix, a collection of nearly 400 epigrams, chiefly on works of art: they come from Planudes' edition, and ultimately from a lost book of Cephalas, but are not in the Palatine MS.

7. The Anthology is a mine of jewels choked with masses of lumber. Books i, ii, iii, viii, xiv are worthless; iv, xii, xiii, xv are curious, often (e.g. Meleager's preface) fascinating; the remaining books contain some tedious imitations, some trivialities, and some of the finest poetry in the world. *See* EPIGRAM.

BIBLIOGRAPHY
TEXTS: Jacobs (antiquated but complete); Stadtmüller (Teubner: books i–vii, part of ix); Waltz (Budé, i–vii). Sternbach *Anth. Plan. Appendix*.
TRANSLATIONS: W. R. Paton (Loeb); P. Waltz (Budé i–vii, good notes).
SELECTIONS: J. W. Mackail, *Epigrams from the Gk. Anth.* (1906, charming introduction); J. A. Pott, *Gk. love-songs* (1913); H. Macnaughten, *Masterpieces from the Anth.* (1924); H. Wolfe, *Others Abide* (1927).
STUDIES OF SPECIAL ASPECTS: R. Weisshäupl, *Die Grabepigramme der griech. Anthologie* (1889); J. A. Symonds, *Studies of the Gk. Poets* ii. 22 (3rd ed. 1893); N. Douglas, *Birds and Beasts of the Gk. Anth.* (1928); A. Wifstrand, *Studien zur griech. Anth.* (1926); X. Guglielmino, *Epigrammate satiriche nell' xi libro dell' Antologia* (1933). See bibliography to EPIGRAM.
G. H.

ANTIAS, *see* FURIUS (1), VALERIUS (10).

ANTICĀTO or **ANTICĂTONES** (Schanz–Hosius[4] viii. 1, § 118), two (?) lost books by Caesar (A. Dyroff, *Rh. Mus.* (N.F.) l. 481 ff., thinks one by Hirtius) answering eulogies on Cato, whose death at Utica occasioned laudatory discourses on republican heroes by Cicero, Brutus, and Fadius Gallus.
J. W. D.

ANTICLEA (Ἀντίκλεια), in mythology, daughter of Autolycus (q.v.), wife of Laertes, and mother of Odysseus (*Od.* 11. 84–5). Later (as Sophocles, *Phil.* 417 and schol.) Odysseus' real father is Sisyphus (q.v.).

ANTICYRA, Phocian town at the head of the gulf east of Cirrha. An excellent port and outlet for Phocian export, it shared the history of Phocis, being destroyed in 346 B.C. and captured by Roman generals. It gained a reputation from the medicinal plant hellebore (supposed to cure madness), which grew in its neighbourhood.
N. G. L. H.

ANTIDORUS (*c.* 300 B.C.) of Cyme was the first to abandon the name κριτικός and to call himself γραμματικός (Clem. Al. *Strom.* 1. 16. 79). He wrote a work on Homer and Hesiod, of which the form and content are unknown, and a treatise on λέξις, which was either a lexical study, perhaps of Homeric expressions, or a work on style (schol. Dion. Thrax, pp. 3, 7, 448 H.; schol. *Il.* 23. 638–9).
J. F. L.

ANTIDOSIS. An Athenian who had been put to a liturgy (q.v.) had a right to refuse it, by asking, at an officially fixed date, another wealthy citizen either to perform it in his stead or to agree to an exchange of properties. If the other citizen rejected this offer, a court decided which of them should perform the liturgy. Both parties had to divulge their whole estate on oath, three days after they had formally laid claim to their opponents' possessions before the magistrates. Only shares in the mines of Laurium had not to be declared, because they were free from liturgy obligations.

A. M. Andreades, *History of Greek Public Finance* (U.S.A. 1933), 283 f.; H. Francotte, *L'Antidosis en droit athénien* (1895).
F. M. H.

ANTIGENES (5th c. B.C.), Attic dithyrambic poet, who wrote a dedicatory poem for tripods won at the Dionysian competition by the Acamantis tribe. The poem, preserved at *Anth. Pal.* 13. 28, is written in couplets, the first line of which is a dactylic tetrameter followed by a trochaic dipody, the second an iambic tripody followed by an alcaic decasyllable. Nothing else is known of him or his work.

Text: E. Diehl, *Anth. Lyr. Graec.* ii. 119. Criticism: U. von Wilamowitz-Moellendorff, *Sappho und Simonides* (1913), 218–23.
C. M. B.

ANTIGONE (1). In the versions of the legend of Oedipus (q.v.) best known to us, he and Iocasta have four children, Eteocles, Polynices, Antigone, and Ismene, though Homer (*Od.* 11. 271 ff.) and the Cyclic epic *Oedipodia* (see Paus. 9. 5. 11) know nothing of offspring of the incest and the latter makes Euryganeia daughter of Hyperphas the mother of his children. Of these four, the two sons are part of the story from the cyclic *Thebais* onwards; the daughters seem to be a later addition, or at least are unimportant until the fifth century B.C. The earliest certain mention of either appears to be Mimnermus fr. 21 Bergk, from which, combined with Phocylides ap. schol. Eur. *Phoen.* 53 it appears that Ismene was 'in converse with Theoclymenus' (unknown in such a context, perhaps a mistake for Periclymenus, one of the Theban heroes) and was killed by Tydeus (q.v.) at the instance of Athena by the spring which bears her name, i.e. the source of the river Ismenus. Ion of Chios (fr. 12 Bergk; both this and the passage of Mimnermus are from Salustius' argument to the *Antigone*) said that both sisters were burned in the temple of Hera by Laodamas son of Eteocles, an otherwise unknown tale. Also, in the older stories neither the affair of the burial of Polynices nor the banishment of Oedipus is told. We have then a legend apparently of fifth-century Attic growth, whether pure invention or founded on some local tradition.

2. Omitting the spurious termination of the *Septem* of Aeschylus (latest discussion by P. Groeneboom, *Aeschylus' Zeven tegen Thebe* (1938), p. 245 ff.), our materials are the *OT*, *OC*, and *Antigone* of Sophocles and the fragments of Euripides, *Antigone*, with their derivatives. Taking the Sophoclean plays in the order of events in the story, not of their composition, in *OT* 1480 ff. Oedipus takes farewell of his children and commends them to the fatherly care of Creon; they are mute figures. In *OC* he is a wandering beggar, faithfully tended by Antigone. Ismene, here as elsewhere the less resolute character, remains at Thebes, but comes to Colonus (324 ff.) to bring them news of happenings there. Creon, whose character has deteriorated in this play, kidnaps both sisters in an attempt to force Oedipus to return, but is himself taken by Theseus and the girls rescued (818–1096). Antigone advises Oedipus to grant Polynices an interview (1181 ff.), and vainly begs her brother to abandon the attempt on Thebes (1414 ff.); they address each other in terms of deep affection. In the *Antigone* Creon has forbidden Polynices to be buried

after his and Eteocles' death at each other's hands (23 ff.); Antigone resolves to bury him despite this. Ismene is horrified, and will not do more than keep her secret (85). Antigone contemptuously casts her off and later (536 ff.) will have none of her attempts to confess herself a confederate. The attempt to give Polynices at least the formal minimum of burial succeeds (245 ff.), but later (407 ff.) Antigone is arrested while coming to pour libation and replace the dust which had been swept from the body. Creon now sentences her to be placed alive in a vault, despite the protestations of his son Haemon who is betrothed to her (635 ff.). In this he is doubly wrong, for it is impious to put a living person into the underground realm of Hades, and it is Antigone's betrothed husband who should deal with her (P. Roussel in *Rev. ét. grecques* (1922), 63 ff.; Rose in *CQ* 1925, 147 ff.). Tiresias warns him (988 ff.) that he is offending the gods by leaving dead bodies unburied; he sets out (1095 ff.) to bury Polynices and rescue Antigone, but finds her already dead by her own hand; Haemon kills himself over her body and Creon's queen Eurydice stabs herself from grief (1183 ff.).

3. Euripides, possibly using some tradition of the existence of descendants of Antigone, modified Sophocles' story; his play being lost, we have to reconstruct the plot chiefly from Hyginus (*Fab.* 72, which is not an accurate synopsis, see C. Robert, *Oidipus*, 381 ff.; Rose, *Modern Methods in Class. Myth.*, 40 ff.; J. Mesk in *Wien. Stud.* xlix. 1 ff.). Creon, acting more correctly than in Sophocles, handed over Antigone, when taken, to Haemon to be put to death. He, instead of doing so, hid her among shepherds, and had a son by her. The child lived, grew, and came to Thebes on the occasion of certain games. Since he naturally competed naked, Greek fashion, Creon recognized him as one of his own race, the Sparti, because he had on his body the peculiar birthmark like a spear-head which all that family bore (Hyg. *Fab.* 72. 3; Arist. *Poet.* 1454^b22, very likely from this play). He denounced the young man as a bastard (fr. 168 Nauck) and ordered the deaths, apparently, of Haemon and Antigone. Hereupon, according to Hyginus (72. 3) Heracles vainly interceded; fr. 177 is an apostrophe to Dionysus, and Aristophanes' argument to Sophocles' *Antigone* says that Antigone was 'given in marriage' to Haemon, from which, together with general probability, it seems likely that Dionysus was the intercessor (if indeed the quotation is not from the *Antiope*) and the play ended with a reconciliation and formal union of the lovers.

4. The story in Hyginus is itself evidence that some development took place in the legend after Euripides, possibly at the hands of the fourth-century tragedians (so Mesk). One additional detail, of unknown date of origin, is the appearance of Argia, wife of Polynices, to help Antigone bury him (Hyginus 72. 1; Statius, *Theb.* 12. 177 ff.); she meets Antigone by moonlight; they put Polynices' body on Eteocles' still burning pyre, the flames of which divide (cf. ETEOCLES); they are taken and sentenced to death by Creon, but rescued by the arrival of the Attic army under Theseus.

Although the above stories are not of Theban origin, they had been adopted in Thebes by Imperial times. Pausanias was shown (9. 25. 2) a place outside the walls called σύρμα Ἀντιγόνης, 'Antigone's drag', said to be the spot where she dragged the body of Polynices, as it was too heavy for her to lift, to lay it on the pyre of Eteocles (see above; this suggests that the legend was popularized there in a rather late form). It was one of several alleged monuments of the mythical past of the city, doubtless rather a by-product of the tourist trade than the result of a real tradition.

See material collected briefly in Jebb's introduction to his edition of Sophocles, *Antigone*; more in Stoll's arts. 'Antigone' and 'Ismene' in Roscher's *Lexikon*.
H. J. R.

ANTIGONE (2), in mythology, daughter of Eurytion son of Actor, king of Phthia. Peleus (q.v.) was purified by her father after the murder of Phocus (*see* AEACUS) and married her, with a third of the country for her dowry. Later he accidentally killed Eurytion at the Calydonian boar-hunt and fled to Iolcus (Apollod. 3. 163). H. J. R.

ANTIGONE (3), in mythology, daughter of Laomedon, king of Troy. Because she vied in beauty with Hera, the latter turned her hair into snakes; afterwards she, or the other gods, turned her into a stork, which therefore preys on snakes (Ovid, *Met.* 6. 93–5; Servius on *Aen.* 1. 27; *Myth. Vat.* 1. 179.) H. J. R.

ANTIGONUS (1) I (probably 382–301 B.C.), son of Philip, a Macedonian noble, first appears holding a command in Alexander's army (334). He was left as satrap of Phrygia (333). In Alexander's lifetime he did useful work in Asia Minor, but he gave no indication of his future greatness. His opportunity came when his friend Antipater (q.v. 1) gave him command over the royal army in Asia (321). His successful campaigns against the 'rebels' Alcetas (320) and Eumenes (320 and 318–316), and the death of Antipater (319), gave A., alone of the generals, a prospect of reuniting all Alexander's empire under himself, and this became his unceasing aim. The result was a coalition of the 'separatist' generals against him (Cassander in Macedonia, Ptolemy in Egypt, and Lysimachus in Thrace), but the war (315–311) left him as strong as before, though the occupation of Babylon and the Eastern satrapies by Seleucus (312) greatly reduced the area he controlled. The peace of 311 lasted only a year, and his separate attempts to crush Seleucus (310–309), Ptolemy (306–305), and Cassander (304–302) finally convinced them all (with Lysimachus) that A. must be crushed. In the decisive battle of Ipsus (in Phrygia) he was defeated and killed. Of his kingdom little is known. He is said to have governed well, and he certainly showed statesmanship in his policy towards the Greeks. His reputation rests on his greatness as a general, but in an age of peace he would probably have been a great ruler, and certainly could never have been a bad one.

Diodorus bks. 18–20; Plutarch, *Eumenes* and *Demetrius*. W. W. Tarn. *CAH* vi, ch. 15. G. T. G.

ANTIGONUS (2) II (*c.* 320–239 B.C.), surnamed *Gonatas* (Euseb. 1. 238; meaning unknown), son of Demetrius I and Phila, was in charge of Demetrius' Greek possessions after 287. In 285, having lost much of Thessaly to Pyrrhus, he made peace; on Demetrius' death (284–283) he took the title of king. In 280 he marched on Macedon, but was repelled; Sparta meanwhile stirred up revolts in Greece. After a naval campaign he made a lasting peace with Syria (278); and having defeated 20,000 Gauls near Lysimacheia, he seized Macedonia. For ten months Cassandreia resisted, but by 276, when he married Antiochus' sister, Phila, he was acknowledged king of Macedon. When in 274 Pyrrhus, back from Italy, attacked Macedon, many Macedonians deserted; Antigonus suffered defeats (274–273) and lost Thessaly and upper Macedonia. In 272, however, Pyrrhus invaded Peloponnesus, and A. joined with Sparta to destroy him. He now re-established his power as far as Corinth. Shortly afterwards, subsidized by Egypt, Athens and Sparta began the Chremonidean War against him (267–263/2), which ended with the fall of Athens. After a short-lived truce (261), he defeated Ptolemy at sea off Cos (258), thus securing the Aegean, and peace followed in 255. In 250–249, instigated by Egypt, Alexander, his governor of Corinth, revolted, and held Corinth with Chalcis until his death. But after defeating Ptolemy at sea off Andros (246), Antigonus tricked Alexander's widow, Nicaea, out of Acrocorinth (245). This fortress, however, Aratus seized in 243, and Antigonus' subsequent

Aetolian alliance proved fruitless; to this period belongs his patronage of Peloponnesian tyrants. In 241–240 he made peace with Achaea, and died in spring 239.

Blunt, honest, and tenacious, A. won not only Macedon, but also its people. Himself a philosopher, he gathered about him poets, philosophers, and historians; and his long reign, despite vicissitudes, re-established Macedon as a nation.

Ancient sources: Plut. *Demetr.*, *Pyrrh.*, *Arat.*; Justin. bks. 16 ff. For the early years the tradition echoes Hieronymus of Cardia, for the later the pro-Spartan Phylarchus. Inscriptions important. Modern literature: W. W. Tarn, *Antigonos Gonatas* (1913); *CAH* vii; W. Fellmann, *Antigonos Gonatas . . . und die griechischen Staaten* (1930). F. W. W.

ANTIGONUS (3) III (*c.* 263–221 B.C.), surnamed *Doson*, son of Demetrius the Fair (who was half-brother of Antigonus II), became guardian to Philip V on Demetrius II's death (229) and married Philip's mother Phthia (Chryseis). After expelling a Dardanian inroad he recovered most of Thessaly from invading Aetolians, but made an agreement leaving them Phthiotic Achaea, and renounced the re-establishment of Macedonian influence beyond Thermopylae. Early in 227, as sequel to a threatened mutiny by the army assembly, he took the title of king. An expedition to Caria in 227 was probably directed against Ptolemy: it brought acquisitions in the Aegean, alliances in Crete, and temporary gains in Caria; but the islands generally remained independent, and Macedonian sea-power now rapidly decayed. Meanwhile the Achaean League was crumbling before Cleomenes; in 227–226 A. received Achaean envoys favourably, and in 224, on Aratus' promise of Acrocorinth, he led his troops to the Isthmus. In two campaigns he recovered Arcadia, and in winter 224 set up a Confederacy of Leagues, with himself as president. In 222 he crushed Cleomenes at Sellasia and occupied Sparta. But immediately he was summoned to expel the Illyrians from Macedon; having burst a blood-vessel in battle, he died in summer 221, after providing for Philip's succession.

The Achaean alliance and the Confederacy stamp A. as a statesman of generous vision. His policy mainly followed traditional lines; but his rehabilitation of Macedon gave it new life and a strong material background for Philip's wilder policies.

Ancient sources: Polyb. 2; Plut. *Cleom.*, *Arat.*; Justin. bk. 28. Modern literature: W. W. Tarn, *CAH* vii; 'Phthia-Chryseis', *Athenian Studies presented to W. S. Ferguson* (U.S.A. 1940), 483 ff.; P. Treves, *Athenaeum*, 1934–5; S. Dow and C. F. Edson, *Harv. Stud.* 1937; J. V. A. Fine, *AJPhil.* 1940. F. W. W.

ANTIGONUS (4) of Carystus (fl. 240 B.C.), bronze-worker and writer, lived at Athens in touch with the Academy; worked under Attalus I at Pergamum.

WORKS. An inferior anecdotal collection survives, the (1) Ἱστοριῶν παραδόξων συναγωγή (O. Keller, *Rer. Nat. scr. Graec. Min.* i. 8 f.); Diog. Laert. and Athenaeus contain fragments from (2) *Lives of Philosophers*, personal character-sketches of contemporaries; (3) various works of art-history; (4) Περὶ λέξεως (Ath. 3. 88 a; 7. 297 a; probably this A.).

A reliable biographer with a flowing, periodic style, A. achieved considerable popularity. He helped to make the statues which celebrated Attalus' Gallic victory.

U. von Wilamowitz-Moellendorff, *A. v. Karystos* (1881). F. W. W.

ANTILOCHUS, in mythology, son of Nestor (q.v. 1), mentioned several times in the *Iliad* as a brave warrior and a fine runner (e.g. 15. 569–70). He brings Achilles the news of Patroclus' death (18. 2 ff.), drives cleverly in the chariot-race (23. 402 ff.), and courteously cedes the second prize to Menelaus (596). His death is mentioned (*Od.* 3. 111); it took place (*Aethiopis*, whence Pindar, *Pyth.* 6. 28 ff.) while he was defending his father against Memnon, when Paris had killed one of Nestor's horses and he called Antilochus to his help. H. J. R.

ANTIMACHUS (1) (probably b. *c.* 444), of Colophon, poet and scholar. It is possible that he competed in a poetic contest at the Lysandreia in Samos before Lysander (died 395), cf. Plut. *Lys.* 18. 8. Further, the evidence of Hermesianax, fr. 7, 41–6 and [Plutarch], *Cons. ad Apoll.* 9. 106 b may be accepted that he loved one Lyde (probably his mistress, not his wife), and wrote his narrative elegy with that title, a collection of 'heroic misfortunes', to console himself for her loss. Finally Heraclides Ponticus (fr. 91 Voss) records that Plato sent Heraclides to Colophon to collect A.'s poems. It is, therefore, probable that A. died fairly early in the fourth century B.C.

WORKS. Our sources mention five poems: *Thebais, Lyde, Deltoi, Artemis, Iachine* (?). The *Thebais* was an epic narrating the first expedition against Thebes. For his material A. probably drew not only on the Epic Cycle but also on lyric and tragic versions of the story of Thebes. The *Lyde* comprised at least two books, probably considerably more in view of A.'s reputation for prolixity, which the fragments detailing the voyage of the *Argo* seem to justify. Other legends mentioned included those of Demeter's wanderings, Bellerophon, and Oedipus. It is clear that except for the metre there was very little that was elegiac about the *Lyde*. Though it is possible that the poem contained a preface in which A. explained the circumstances that had produced it, there is no evidence that once embarked he turned aside from his narration of 'heroic misfortunes' to bewail his own. The laments which according to Hermesianax filled the poem must have been those of the heroes and heroines. Though others, e.g. Mimnermus, had inserted references to myth into their elegies, A. was the real founder of Narrative Elegy and found many imitators. The *Deltoi* (? *Tablets*) was perhaps a collection of short poems (? in elegiacs). The *Artemis*, if the first part of *PMilan.* 17 contains excerpts from this poem, was written in hexameters and its careful recording of the goddess's titles and cults recalls the *Hymn to Artemis* of Callimachus.

Later writers praised A. for his sobriety and virility, qualities which perhaps explain Plato's liking for his verse. But Callimachus (fr. 74 b) found him stodgy and involved. What little survives seems to justify the more unfavourable verdict. But A.'s real importance is that as a scholar (he edited Homer) no less than poet he anticipated by some 100 years the scholar-poets of Alexandria. Unlike his post-Cyclic predecessors, Pisander and Panyassis, he not only borrowed without change from early Epic, but also practised all the arts of 'interpretation', variation, and contamination which were to become so popular with the Hellenistic poets, and not least with Callimachus. In language, too, A. anticipates the Alexandrians. The scanty fragments contain many 'glosses', neologisms, and obscure periphrases.

Text: B. Wyss, *Antimachi Colophonii Reliquiae* (1936); for *PMilan.* 17 see also A. Vogliano, *Papiri della R. Università di Milano* i (1937), 41–65. G. Wentzel, 'Antimachos (24)', in *PW* i. 2433–6.　　　　　　　　　　　　　　　　　　　　　E. A. B.

ANTIMACHUS (2) of Teos, see EPIC CYCLE. *EGF*, p. 247.

ANTINOÖPOLIS (*Sheikh Abâdeh*), in Middle Egypt, founded in A.D. 130 by Hadrian in memory of Antinous, stood east of the Nile at the head of a new road to the Red Sea. Its constitution was Greek, modelled on that of Naucratis, with special privileges; hellenized inhabitants were brought, e.g., from Ptolemais; it was also the metropolis of an Egyptian nome. After Diocletian it was the administrative centre of the Thebaid. Considerable remains of public buildings existed in 1800, but have been destroyed. The cemeteries were excavated by Gayet, the mounds explored for papyri by Johnson.

E. Jomard, *Description de l'Égypte, Antiquités*, ch. 15, pls. 53–61; E. Kühn, *Antinoopolis* (1913); J. Johnson, 'Antinoë and its papyri' (*JEg.Arch.* 1914); H. I. Bell, *JRS* 1940, 133–47.　　　J. G. M.

ANTINOUS (1), in mythology, chief of Penelope's suitors, son of Eupeithes (*Od.* 1. 383); killed by Odysseus (22. 8 ff.).

ANTINOUS (2) (b. *c.* A.D. 110–12), Greek-born at Bithynium (= Claudiopolis) Bithyniae. His beauty and grace made him Hadrian's favourite; accompanying Hadrian up the Nile in 130, he was drowned, to Hadrian's bitter grief. His royal friendship and tragic death (some said he gave his life for Hadrian) aroused almost legendary fame. Deified, he was commemorated by the Egyptian city Antinoöpolis (q.v.), and by cults, festivals, and statues in many lands.

B. W. Henderson, *Life and Principate of the Emperor Hadrian* (1923), 130 ff.; see also *PIR²*, A 737.　　　　　C. H. V. S.

ANTIOCH (Ἀντιόχεια) (1), capital of Seleucid Syria, on the left bank of the Orontes, some 15 miles from the sea, was founded in 300 B.C. by Seleucus I, who transferred thither the 5,300 Athenian and Macedonian settlers whom Antigonus had planted at Antigoneia nearby in 307. These settlers occupied the first quarter of the city; the second was filled with the native inhabitants; a third and fourth were added by Seleucus II and Antiochus IV, no doubt for fresh settlers; Antiochus III after 189 B.C. enrolled exiled Aetolians and Euboeans in the city. Antioch also contained a large Jewish community, whose privileges were said to go back to Seleucus I. From the reign of Antiochus IV, who built a new council chamber, the city issued a municipal coinage, and from 149 to 147 autonomous coins as one of the Brother Peoples. Since it was the royal capital, its people played a large part in the dynastic revolutions of the later Seleucid era. After an interlude of Armenian rule (83–66) it was annexed by Pompey (64) and became the capital of the province of Syria; it was freed by Caesar (47). Having sided with Pescennius Niger it was in A.D. 194 degraded by Septimius Severus to a village of Laodicea, but was in 201 restored to its former rank, to which Caracalla added the title of colony. Antioch had a council numbering 1,200 and its people were divided into eighteen tribes: it ruled a very extensive territory. It was one of the greatest cities of the East, disputing the primacy with Alexandria. Its wealth must have been derived from its administrative position and from commerce: no industries are recorded save the Imperial mint. The scanty ruins are being excavated (*Antioch on the Orontes* i (1934), ed. G. W. Elderkin; ii (1938), ed. R. Stillwell).

K. O. Müller, *Antiquitates Antiochenae* (1839); E. S. Bouchier, *A Short History of Antioch* (1921).　　　　　A. H. M. J.

ANTIOCH (2) (Pisidian: Ἀντιόχεια Πισιδίας or more correctly πρὸς Πισιδίαν 'towards Pisidia'), a city in Phrygia (so Strabo, confirmed by inscriptions), lying near the Pisidian border, called 'the Pisidian' to distinguish it from the other Phrygian Antioch on the Maeander, and hence wrongly assigned to Pisidia by Pliny and others. It was a Seleucid foundation, settled by colonists from Magnesia-on-the-Maeander, occupying a plateau above the river Anthios (mentioned on its coins) close to the modern Yalovac. It was declared free by the Romans after the defeat of Antiochus the Great, but passed under Roman control as part of the kingdom of Amyntas (see GALATIA) in 25 B.C., and about the same time was made a Roman colony with the name Caesarea Antiochia. The colony was linked by military roads with the other colonies subsequently founded by Augustus to control Pisidia. Near it was a wealthy *hieron* of Mên Askaênos with wide estates and numerous temple-serfs (*hieroduloi*, q.v.), the site of which has recently been excavated. In the provincial reorganization of Diocletian Antioch was assigned to Pisidia.

Jones, *Eastern Cities* (see Index).　　　　　　　　　W. M. C.

ANTIOCH (3) (*Margiana*, modern *Merv*) was founded apparently by Alexander, destroyed by Asiatics, and refounded by Antiochus I. Here in a mountain-girt fertile plain a land-route from Seleuceia branched, forming silk-routes, (i) through Samarkand, (ii) through Balkh, to central Asia; a third went south through Herat and the Bolan Pass to India. E. H. W.

ANTIOCH-IN-PERSIS (4), the *Ionaca polis* ('Greek-town') of Ptolemy 6. 4. 2, probably stood on the Gulf of Bushire, whence a road must have run up to Persepolis, as now to Shiraz. It was founded by Seleucus I and re-colonized and enlarged by Magnesia-on-the-Maeander for Antiochus I (*OGI* 233). It was a Greek city, with Council, Assembly, and Prytanies, i.e. division into tribes; it worshipped the gods of Magnesia, and was the local centre for the official cult of the Seleucid dynasty. W. W. T.

ANTIOCHUS (1) **I** (Soter) (324–262 or 261 B.C.), son of Seleucus I (q.v.) and the Bactrian Apama. He ruled the eastern Seleucid territories from 293/2, and took over Seleucus' young wife Stratonice (whether for romantic or political reasons). On his accession (280) he renounced his father's ambitions in the West, and his treaty (279) with Antigonus (q.v. 2) Gonatas formed the basis of peace and friendship with Macedonia throughout the century. Northern Asia Minor, and later much of its southern and western coast, slipped from his grasp, the latter being lost mainly to Egypt ('First Syrian War', 276–272, and war of 266–261). His chief exploit was his defeat of the Gallic invaders of Asia Minor (276—'the Elephant Victory'), which earned him his cult-name 'Soter'. Of his personal character and internal policy little is known, except that he was the greatest founder of cities after Alexander (*see* COLONIZATION, HELLENISTIC). His elder son Seleucus became co-regent in the East (280), but proved a failure, and may even have been executed for treason. G. T. G.

ANTIOCHUS (2) **II** (Theos) (*c*. 287–247 B.C.), second son of Antiochus I and Stratonice. His reign (com-mencing 262 or 261) comprises the most obscure period of Seleucid history. Most of the known facts bear on his relations with Egypt, and show that, by the 'Second Syrian War' (260–255), in alliance with Macedonia, he recovered most of what Antiochus I had lost, namely the coast of Asia Minor (except Pergamum, Caria, and Lycia) and places in Coele Syria. His Egyptian marriage, however (to Berenice, daughter of Ptolemy II, 252), and repudiation of Laodice with her children, created a 'succession question' which became acute on his death. G. T. G.

ANTIOCHUS (3) **III** ('the Great') (241–187 B.C.), second son of Seleucus II (q.v.), succeeded (223) to a kingdom already reduced by separatist movements (Bac-tria and Parthia), which threatened to spread to Media, Persis, and Babylonia and to Asia Minor (*see* ACHAEUS 3). His aim from the first was to restore and expand. His first attempt to conquer Ptolemaic Syria and Palestine was foiled by a Ptolemaic victory at Raphia ('Fourth Syrian War' 219–216). But by his 'Anabasis' in the East (212–206) he acquired Armenia, and regained Parthia and Bactria, as vassal kingdoms; and his demonstrations in 'India' (Cabul valley) and 'Arabia' (across the Persian Gulf) earned him, like Alexander, the title of 'Great'.

But Antiochus' expansion policy was ruined by his failure to recognize the advent of a new Power in the eastern Mediterranean, Rome. His notorious secret treaty with Philip V of Macedonia to partition the over-seas possessions of Egypt (202) was not directed against Rome; but the Senate, already suspicious of Philip, took alarm when Antiochus, after conquering Ptolemaic Syria and Palestine (202–198), invaded Europe to recover Thrace (196). In the protracted diplomatic exchange of 196–193 he and the Senate were at cross purposes, and finally he lost patience and invaded Greece. He was defeated by the Romans in two land battles, at Thermo-pylae and Magnesia (ad Sipylum), and also lost a naval campaign to them. By the peace of Apamea (188) the Seleucid Empire ceased to be a Mediterranean Power, though it remained a great continental Power in Asia. Despite these errors of judgement in dealing with Rome, the triumphs of his youth, his unfailing energy, and his high conception of the Seleucid task in Asia suggest that Antiochus really was a great man.

Ancient sources: the most important is Polybius, directly in bks. 2–21 (ed. Büttner-Wobst), and indirectly in Livy bks. 30–8. Modern literature: M. Holleaux, *Rome, la Grèce, et les monarchies hellénistiques* (1921), and in *CAH* viii, chs. 6, 7; W. W. Tarn, ibid. vii. 723 ff. G. T. G.

ANTIOCHUS (4) **IV** (Epiphanes) (*c*. 215–163 B.C.), third son of Antiochus III, became king in 175. The tradition about him is unfavourable, mainly because of his policy towards the Jews. He controlled Judaea firmly (if tact-lessly), because it was strategically important as a frontier province; and he wished to hellenize the Jews, because he believed in hellenization in general. But the result, apparent only after his death, was to stimulate and revive Jewish nationalism. Despite his reputation for eccentricity, Antiochus was probably a sound states-man: his policy of urbanization, especially in the East, represents a notable achievement at this date. His Egyptian war (169–168), 'preventive' in motive, could certainly have achieved the annexation of Egypt, had Rome not intervened. Finally, the Eastern expedition, on which he met his death, shows that he was alive to the nascent danger from Parthia. G. T. G.

ANTIOCHUS (5) **V** (Eupator) (*c*. 173–162 B.C.), son of Antiochus IV, reigned less than two years through the regent Lysias, and was put to death in Antioch when Demetrius I (q.v. 8) arrived from Rome to claim his throne. G. T. G.

ANTIOCHUS (6) **VI** (Epiphanes Dionysus) (*c*. 148–138 B.C.), son of Alexander (q.v. 10) Balas and Cleopatra Thea (daughter of Ptolemy VI). In the revolt at Antioch against Demetrius II (q.v. 4) he was put forward by the general Diodotus (later called Tryphon) as heir to the throne formerly usurped by his father. Tryphon soon deposed (142) and later killed him (138). G. T. G.

ANTIOCHUS (7) **VII** (Sidetes) (*c*. 159–129 B.C.), second son of Demetrius I (q.v. 3) of Syria, succeeded his brother Demetrius II, who had become a prisoner in Parthia (139). Able and energetic, he quickly defeated and killed the pretender Tryphon in Antioch (138), reconquered Palestine (135–134), and temporarily re-covered Babylonia from Parthia (130). But his eventual defeat and death in battle against the Parthians brought about the final loss of the Seleucid provinces in the East. G. T. G.

ANTIOCHUS (8) (Hierax) (*c*. 263–226 B.C.), second son of Antiochus II and Laodice, became independent ruler of Seleucid Asia Minor when his brother Seleucus II was occupied with the 'Third Syrian War' (246–241). He defeated Seleucus' attempt to recover Asia Minor ('War of the Brothers', *c*. 239–236), allying himself with traditional enemies of the Seleucid House, Pontus, Bithynia, and Galatians. This last alliance, however, embroiled him with the rising power of Attalus I of Pergamum, who drove him from Asia Minor (236–228). After an unsuccessful attempt to raise Syria and the East against Seleucus, he became an exile (227), and died by violence in Thrace. G. T. G.

ANTIOCHUS (9) of Syracuse, Greek logographer of the fifth century B.C., author of a history of Sicily in Ionic, reaching from Cocalus to 424 B.C., and of Italy. His style, according to Strabo (p. 254), was simple and old-fashioned. *See* HISTORIOGRAPHY, GREEK, para. 2.

FHG i. 181-4. J. D. D.

ANTIOCHUS (10) of Ascalon (b. *c.* 130–120 B.C.), founder of the 'fifth Academy', became the pupil, at Athens, of Philo (q.v.) of Larissa and of the Stoic Mnesarchus. In 88 he accompanied Philo to Rome, and made the acquaintance of L. Lucullus. He had probably already reacted against the teaching of Philo, and he soon abandoned the Scepticism of the Middle and New Academy and reverted to the teaching of the Old Academy. He was head of the Academy at Athens in 79–78, when Cicero attended his lectures. He joined Lucullus again at the time of the Second Mithridatic War (73), and died about 68. His doctrine was an eclectic one in which he maintained the essential agreement of the Academic, Peripatetic, and Stoic philosophies; in spite of lack of originality he had much influence. Cicero quotes him frequently.

PW i. 2493. H. M. Strache, *D. Eklektizismus v. Antiochos v. Askalon* (1921). W. D. R.

ANTIOCHUS (11) of Athens (not later than A.D. 300), author of a popular compilation of astrological lore.

Ed. A. Olivieri, *Cat. Cod. Astr.* i. 108, and F. Boll, ib. vii. 128. PW i. 2494 and Suppl. 4. 32.

ANTIOPE (Ἀντιόπη), in mythology, daughter of the river Asopus (*Od.* 11. 260) or Nycteus, king of Boeotia (tragedians, especially Euripides, see schol. ad loc.). Her story has come down chiefly through Euripides' tragedy *Antiope*, now lost (*see* AMPHION). Zeus loved her and approached her in the form of a satyr (Ov. *Met.* 6. 110; Nonnus, *Dion.* 16. 243). She then fled from her father to Sicyon, where she married Epopeus; Nycteus, dying by his own hand, bade his brother Lycus punish her. He attacked Sicyon, killed Epopeus, and carried Antiope off. Either then (Apollod. 3. 43) at Eleutherae, or before meeting Epopeus (Hyg. *Fab.* 8. 2) she bore her twin sons. Lycus and his wife Dirce put her in a dungeon and tormented her till at length she escaped; *see further* AMPHION. H. J. R.

ANTIPATER (1) (Ἀντίπατρος) (397–319 B.C.), Macedonian general. He was one of Philip II's right-hand men in war and in diplomacy; in 347–346 he helped to negotiate the peace between Philip and Athens. After Philip's death he aided Alexander in the struggle for the succession, and during Alexander's absence in the East he was governor of Macedonia and 'general of Europe' (334–323). He made himself disliked in Greece by giving support to oligarchs and to tyrants, but he obtained the assistance of the Greek League founded by Philip, when Agis III (q.v.) of Sparta organized rebellion against Macedon, and defeated him decisively at Megalopolis (330).

After the death of Alexander, Antipater was caught by surprise when the Athenians, Aetolians, and Thessalians rose in revolt, and had to sustain a siege in Lamia; but after the arrival of Macedonian reinforcements and a victory at Crannon he broke up the rebel league (323–322). He now imposed a more oligarchic form of government upon Athens and drove Demosthenes, whose surrender he demanded, to commit suicide. In 321 he joined a coalition of Macedonian generals against the regent Perdiccas, and after Perdiccas' death he obtained the regency from a conference of generals at Triparadisus in Syria. He remained a loyal servant of the Macedonian dynasty, and his death in 319 precipitated the break-up of Alexander's empire.

Diodorus, bks. 17–18, *passim*. J. Kaerst, in *PW*, s.v. 'Antipatros'; Berve, *Alexanderreich* ii, no. 94. M. C.

ANTIPATER (2) of Tarsus (2nd c. B.C.), Stoic, successor of Diogenes (q.v. 3) of Babylon as head of the school at Athens and teacher of Panaetius. He defended himself in many writings against the criticisms of Carneades, and committed suicide at a great age. His views differed little from those of Chrysippus. Named works: Περὶ θεῶν, Περὶ μαντικῆς. His definition of the end of life (Stob. *Ecl.* 2, p. 76, 11, ed. Wachsmuth) has some importance in the history of ethics.

Testimonia and fragments: in H. von Arnim, *SVF* iii. 244-58. PW i. 2515. W. D. R.

ANTIPATER (3) of Sidon (fl. 130 B.C.), Greek epigrammatist, knew and influenced Q. Lutatius Catulus and other Republican poets (Cic. *De Or.* 3. 194). The Greek Anthology contains about seventy-five of his epigrams—mostly artificial epitaphs and epideictic pieces. With his passion for rhetorical effect, he occasionally strikes out a fine phrase, but he is usually trivial or strained. For his life and character, see Meleager (*Anth. Pal.* 7. 428).

P. Waltz, *de A. Sidonio* (1906). G. H.

ANTIPATER (4) of Tyre (1st c. B.C.), who introduced Cato of Utica to the Stoic philosophy, died shortly before 44 B.C. Works: Περὶ καθήκοντος, Περὶ κόσμου, Περὶ οὐσίας, Περὶ ψυχῆς, Περὶ γάμου, Περὶ γυναικὸς συμβιώσεως.

PW i. 2516.

ANTIPATER (5) of Thessalonica (1st c. B.C.–1st c. A.D.), Greek epigrammatist, became in about 11 B.C. a client of L. Calpurnius Piso Frugi, the cultured statesman for whose sons Horace wrote the *Ars Poetica*. His latest datable poem belongs to the years A.D. 12–15. In the Greek Anthology there are about eighty of his epigrams—graceful, witty, and unimportant; his attitude to life and art closely resembles Ovid's.

C. Cichorius, *Römische Studien* (1922), viii. 6. G. H.

ANTIPHANES (c. 388–c. 311 B.C. (Capps, *AJPhil.* xxi (1900), 54 ff.)), Middle Comedy poet (two poets, some think), of foreign birth, was granted Athenian citizenship by Demosthenes (Anon. *De Com.*); wrote many plays (?260, ? 365), some to be read, others to be produced elsewhere than at Athens: about 120 titles are known, including Ἀνθρωπογονία (*POxy.* iii. 427). Many titles denote mythological burlesques (Ἄδωνις, Ἀφροδίτης γοναί), some are from occupations (Ἰατρός, Κιθαρῳδός, even Τριταγωνιστής) or characters (Ἄγροικος, Φιλοπάτωρ), others are proper names (Νεοττίς, Χρυσίς), and a few are of unusual type—Ποίησις (fr. 191, comparison of Tragedy and Comedy), Παροιμίαι (introducing a character like Sam Weller, whose speech is lavish in proverbs), Πρόβλημα and Σαπφώ (both dealing in riddles, spoken in hexameters). Over 300 fragments survive, of varied content (fr. 1, parody of Sophocles; fr. 18, parody of Euripidean prologue; frs. 52, 182, ridicule of dithyrambic bombast; fr. 55, lesson in cottabos-playing; fr. 85, contempt for old-fashioned poetry; fr. 122, on the Lyceum; frs. 124, 169, references to Philip of Macedon and Demosthenes; fr. 221, cynical humour at the expense of matrimony; fr. 304, speech frozen in winter, thawed out in summer).

FCG iii. 3 ff.; *CAF* ii. 12 ff. W. G. W.

ANTIPHATES, in mythology, king of the gigantic Laestrygonians in the *Odyssey* (10. 106). On Odysseus sending three of his crew to inquire who the people are, he kills one for his dinner, the others escaping. His people then destroy all Odysseus' fleet save his own ship. H. J. R.

ANTIPHILUS of Byzantium (1st c. B.C.–1st c. A.D.), Greek epigrammatist, can be dated by his poem on Tiberius' retirement to Rhodes (5 B.C.–A.D. 2) in *Anth. Pal.* 9. 178. He has about fifty poems in the Greek

Anthology, more than half of which are rhetorical paradoxes, or descriptions of queer accidents in which the hunter is caught or the biter bit. But three or four (e.g. 9. 71, 546) are vivid and forcible. In his love of point and surprise, he was a direct predecessor of Martial.

K. Prinz, *Martial u. das griech. Epig.* (1911): K. Müller, *Die Epig. des Antiphilos v. Byzanz* (1935). G. H.

ANTIPHON (1)(*c.* 480–411 B.C.), the Attic orator. A man of strong aristocratic prejudices, he never, or very seldom, appeared in court or spoke in public, but gained a great reputation by speeches composed for others. He suddenly came to the front in 411 B.C. as the brain of the oligarchic conspiracy, and was the leader of the extremists against the moderate counsels of Theramenes. He went with Phrynichus and eight others to negotiate peace with Sparta in the hope of obtaining support for the oligarchs. The mission failed, and the murder of Phrynichus was followed shortly by the fall of the Four Hundred and the flight of the leaders to Decelea. Antiphon and Archeptolemus remained, and were tried, condemned, and executed. A. delivered, in his own defence, the finest speech of the kind which had ever been heard (Thuc. 8. 68). When congratulated by Agathon on its brilliance, he replied that he would rather have satisfied one man of good taste than any number of common people (Arist. *Eth. Eud.* 1232b7).

2. WORKS. The *tetralogies* are oratorical exercises designed to show in outline how speeches should be composed both for attack and defence. Each set contains (*a*) the prosecutor's opening speech, (*b*) the first speech for the defence, (*c*) the prosecutor's reply, and (*d*) the defendant's conclusion. *First Tetralogy:* a murder case tried before the Areopagus. *Second Tetralogy:* a boy has been accidentally killed by a javelin in the gymnasium, and the boy who killed him is charged with murder. *Third Tetralogy:* an old man, assaulted by a young man, has died of his wounds. *The Murder of Herodes* deals with a real case. Herodes and the accused were on a voyage together; one night H. went ashore and disappeared; later, his companion was accused of murder. It is possible that the charge was trumped up to injure the defendant's father, who was unpopular in Mytilene on political grounds (§§74–80). *On the Choreutes* (*c.* 412 B.C.), defence of a *choregus* who has accidentally caused the death of a boy singer by giving him a drug to improve his voice. *Against a Stepmother:* a young man accuses his stepmother of having employed a slave-woman to poison his father. This may be a rhetorical exercise. A few fragments of other speeches survive; some of these may be the work of Antiphon (2), the sophist.

3. When Antiphon began to write there was no tradition of prose style in the Attic dialect. His contemporary Gorgias wrote in Attic, but his influence cannot have been much felt before 427 B.C., when he first visited Athens. A., then, was free to make experiments. The result was a style which, though crude at times, is always vigorous and precise. He was the first of extant writers to pay careful attention to 'periodic' expression, as opposed to the 'running' style, which is more suitable to narrative than to argument. He indulges freely in antithesis both of word and of thought, and is able to join together clauses so neatly balanced that they correspond even in the number of syllables. In vocabulary, he avoids colloquialisms, and has some partiality for poetical words. Some of the peculiarities of Thucydides may be traced to his influence.

4. He established a standard form of structure—an introduction, describing the circumstances of the case; a narration of the facts; arguments and proofs, sometimes interspersed with evidence; lastly, a peroration.

5. His manner is as dignified as his style; he frequently appeals to divine law, which punishes the guilty even though he may escape human justice; he avoids persona-

lities, though in the *Herodes* the speaker exhibits a righteous indignation against his persecutors. He relies on *a priori* probabilities (arguments from character, etc.) at least as much as on the evidence of witnesses.

For general bibliography see ATTIC ORATORS. Text: Blass–Thalheim (Teubner, 1914). Text and Translation: Gernet (Budé). Index: F. L. van Cleef (U.S.A. 1895). J. F. D.

ANTIPHON (2) of Athens (5th c. B.C.), contemporary with Antiphon the orator and often confused with him, sophist and interpreter of dreams, mentioned by Xenophon and Aristotle as an opponent of Socrates. Works: Ἀλήθεια, Περὶ ὁμονοίας, Πολιτικός, Περὶ κρίσεως ὀνείρων.

Testimonia and frs. in Diels, *Vorsokr.*⁵ ii. 334–70. PW i. 2529. W. D. R.

ANTIPHON (3), tragic poet at the court of the Elder Dionysius of Syracuse, by whom he was put to death (Plut. *Quomodo adul.* 27; Philostr. *VS* i. 15. 3). *TGF* 792.

ANTISTHENES (1) (*c.* 455–*c.* 360 B.C. (Diod. 15. 76)), son of Antisthenes of Athens and of a Thracian woman (Diog. Laert. 6. 1; Seneca, *Constant.* 18. 5), one of the most devoted followers of Socrates (Xen. *Symp.* 8. 4; *Mem.* 3. 11. 17). He was considered founder of the Cynic sect (Diog. Laert. 1. 15; 6. 13) and probably influenced the philosophy of Diogenes of Sinope, from whose nickname ὁ κύων the name of that sect is derived. He also influenced the doctrine of the Stoics.

The main principles of his philosophy were the following. Happiness (εὐδαιμονία) is based on virtue (ἀρετή). Virtue is based on knowledge and therefore can be taught. This is done through investigation into the meaning of words (ὀνομάτων ἐπίσκεψις). For he who knows the meaning of a word knows also the thing which it denotes. Whoever knows what virtue is cannot but act virtuously. Whoever has attained this knowledge can never lose it. Most pleasures (ἡδοναί) are treacherous and do not contribute to happiness. Only the pleasure which is the result of exertion (πόνος) is lasting and unobjectionable. The best government is that of the wise man.

He revered Heracles because he led a life of virtue and exertion, and considered Cyrus the model of a wise monarch. He preferred Odysseus to Ajax because he considered wisdom superior to brutal strength. He wrote dialogues (*Heracles, Aspasia, Cyrus, Protrepticus,* and others), interpretations of Homer, and fictitious orations (*Ajax, Odysseus*).

Antisthenis fragmenta coll. A. W. Winckelmann (1842); Diogenes Laertius 6. 1–19; F. Dümmler, *Antisthenica* (1882); K. v. Fritz, *Hermes* lxii. 453–84; *Rh. Mus.* N.F. lxxxiv (1935), 19–45; R. Dudley, *A History of Cynicism* (1937), 1–16; F. Sayre, *Diogenes of Sinope* (1938), 48–70; *PW* i. 2538. K. von F.

ANTISTHENES (2) of Rhodes (fl. early 2nd c. B.C.), wrote Διαδοχαὶ φιλοσόφων; also a history, perhaps of Rhodes, down to his own time (used by Polybius via Zeno).

FHG ii. 174–83.

ANTISTIUS (1) VETUS, GAIUS (1st c. B.C.), under whose father Caesar had served in Spain, became Caesar's quaestor (date uncertain). In 45 B.C. in Syria he opposed Caecilius Bassus, but in 44 he joined the Liberators. He was legate of Octavian against the Salassi (*c.* 34), *cos. suff.* (30), and legate in Spain, perhaps as governor of Hispania Citerior (26–24).

*PIR*², A 770; R. Syme, *The Roman Revolution* (1939), see index. A. M.

ANTISTIUS (2) LABEO, MARCUS (d. before A.D. 22), one of the most prominent Roman jurists, lived in the time of Augustus. Of plebeian extraction, he was by political conviction a republican; his official career ended with the praetorship, for he refused the consulate offered to him by Augustus. In his legal work he showed great independence of mind and was a bold innovator ('plurima innouare instituit'). His learning was enormous: besides mastering his special branch of knowledge, to which he was introduced by his father (who was also a jurist), and by other teachers, including Trebatius Testa and some of the disciples of Servius Sulpicius (qq.v.), he was expert in dialectics, in the history of Latin language and grammar, and in philosophy. Gellius (13. 10. 1) emphasizes his knowledge of ancient Roman literature. Labeo was a voluminous writer: it was his practice to spend six months in every year with his pupils in Rome, and to devote the remainder of the year to writing in the country. He is said to have written about 400 volumes (Pompon. *Dig.* 1. 2. 2. 47). We know from the citations by other jurists the titles of the following works of L.: *Pithana* (collection of decisions on individual cases, very instructive); *Responsa*; *Epistulae*; a large treatise *De Iure Pontificio* (15 books); a commentary to the Praetor's Edict. After his death his posthumous works, *Posteriora* (at least 40 vols.) were published. These are known only by quotations in other jurists, and by a large Epitome made by Javolenus (q.v.) and freely excerpted by the compilers of the *Digest*.

He was a contemporary of Ateius Capito (q.v.), and if Pomponius' account is true, it was the political and personal antagonism between them which originated the schools of jurists named later *Sabiniani* and *Proculiani*. Labeo enjoyed a high reputation not only with his contemporaries but also with the best jurists of the classical epoch. It is notable that a leader of the Sabinians published an edition of his posthumous works, though he was a precursor of the opposite school.

A. Pernice, *M. Antistius Labeo* i (1873). O. Karlowa, *Röm. Rechtsgeschichte* i. 677 ff. (1882). P. Krüger, *Gesch. der Quellen des röm. Rechts²* (1912), 154 ff. A. B. & J. W. D.

ANTISTIUS (3) **VETUS**, LUCIUS (d. A.D. 65), consul with Nero in A.D. 55, was legate of Germania Superior (55–6) and planned to connect the Rhine with the Rhône. In 62 he vainly urged his son-in-law Rubellius Plautus to take up arms against Nero. Proconsul of Asia (c. 64), he anticipated condemnation by suicide (65). He is perhaps the writer who was source for Pliny, *HN* 3–6.

PIR², A 776; Ritterling, *Fasti des röm. Deutschland*, 16; Schanz–Hosius, *Röm. Litteratur* ii (1935), 653. A. M.

ANTIUM (modern *Anzio*), roadstead of Latium. Legends envelop its origin, but apparently it was Latin in the sixth century B.C. (Dion. Hal. 1. 72; Polyb. 3. 22). Shortly thereafter Volsci captured it, and for 200 years Antium was apparently the principal Volscian city. Most fifth-century records concerning it, including the record of the Latin colony in 467, are untrustworthy: the notorious annalist Valerius Antias hailed from here. But in the fourth century it was the centre of Volscian resistance to Rome, that ended only when Maenius (q.v.) captured the Antiate fleet and made possible the establishment of a citizen colony, 338 (Livy bks. 2–8; Dion. Hal. bks. 4–10). Antiate pirates, however, continued active even after 338 (Strabo 5. 232). After being sacked by Marius, Antium became a fashionable resort with celebrated temples (App. *BCiv.* 1. 69; 5. 26; Hor. *Carm.* 1. 35). Caligula and Nero were born here and, like later emperors, patronized the town (Suet. *Calig.* 8; *Ner.* 6). Antium nevertheless gradually declined. A pre-Julian calendar, ruined villas, and famous *objets d'art* like the Apollo Belvedere have been found here.

K. Lehmann-Hartleben, *Antiken Hafenanlagen des Mittelmeeres* (1923), 190. E. T. S.

ANTONIA (1) (b. between 54 and 49 B.C.), daughter of the triumvir M. Antonius and Antonia. She was promised to the son of the triumvir Lepidus, but in 34

married the rich Pythodorus of Tralles. Her daughter Pythodoris married Polemo I, king of Pontus.

Mommsen, *Eph. Epigr.* i. 270; ii. 263. Drumann–Groebe, *Gesch. Roms* i². 380. A. M.

ANTONIA (2) **MAJOR** (b. 39 B.C.), eldest daughter of M. Antonius and Octavia, was the wife of L. Domitius Ahenobarbus. Her son, Cn. Domitius, was Nero's father. Tacitus (*Ann.* 4. 44; 12. 64) calls her Antonia Minor.

PIR², A 884. A. M.

ANTONIA (3) **MINOR** (36 B.C.–A.D. 37), younger daughter of M. Antonius and Octavia, married the elder Drusus (c. 16 B.C.), and refused to marry again after his early death. She gave information to Tiberius leading to the discovery of the conspiracy of Sejanus. Gaius (Caligula) at first conferred numerous honours upon her, but later appears to have resented her interference (though the charge that he drove her to suicide is at least doubtful). Her children were Germanicus, Livilla, and Claudius (later emperor).

Josephus, *AJ* 18. 6; Plutarch, *Antony* 87; Dio Cassius 51, 58–60, and 66. G. W. R.

ANTONIA (4), daughter of Claudius and Aelia Paetina, married in A.D. 41 Cn. Pompeius Magnus and afterwards Faustus Cornelius Sulla. Her first husband was put to death by Claudius, the second by Nero. She was killed some months after the Pisonian conspiracy, in which her complicity is doubtful. That her refusal to marry Nero after Poppaea's death caused her condemnation is improbable.

PIR², A 886. A. M.

ANTONINIANUS (coin), *see* AURELIUS (2), COINAGE, ROMAN, para. 15.

ANTONINUS LIBERALIS, mythographer, probably of Antonine times, published a Μεταμορφώσεων συναγωγή, based on Hellenistic sources, e.g. Nicander.

Text. E. Martini, *Mythographi graeci* ii. 1, p. 61: E. Oder, *De Antonino Liberali* (1886).

ANTONINUS PIUS (*Titus Aurelius Fulvus Boionius Antoninus*) (A.D. 86–161), born at Lanuvium, was son of Aurelius Fulvius (of consular stock settled originally at Nemausus) and Arria Fadilla (also of provincial but consular descent). He adopted a senatorial career, serving as quaestor and praetor and (in 120) as consul; already he had married Faustina (q.v. 1). Appointed *IVvir consularis*, he administered this legal office in Etruria and Umbria, where he owned much property. Proconsul of Asia between 133 and 136, he gained fame for his integrity, and afterwards joined Hadrian's *consilium*. Scrupulous, loyal, and gentle, he thus earned the respect of Hadrian, who, on the death of L. Aelius (q.v.), proposed him as successor. Antoninus was adopted by Hadrian (138), himself adopting both M. Annius Verus (= M. Aurelius, q.v.), Faustina's nephew, and L. Ceionius Commodus (= L. Verus, q.v.), son of Aelius. During Hadrian's last months, Antoninus, now holder of proconsular and tribunician power, was virtual ruler: his authority and modest arguments equally secured Hadrian's consecration. The succession (10 July 138) was smooth: the Senate conferred on him the title 'Pius' (devout), and that of 'Augusta' on Faustina. The title 'Pater Patriae', refused at first, he accepted in 139, with the consulship (afterwards held in 140 and 145).

2. His policy was unsensational, but beneficent and mildly progressive. Accession-gifts were remitted entirely for Italy, and as to one-half for the provinces. Italy (with its opportunities for a country gentleman's life) claimed, with Rome, his chief attention, and returned to senatorial control with the removal of the *IVviri consulares* (S.H.A. *M. Ant.* 11. 6). Completely deferential to the Senate (of which no member was put to death), he nevertheless conceded it no new powers, and used his advisory *consilium* on all matters. General administration was increasingly centralized: rotation of office became slower, good officials (at home and abroad) remaining unchanged for years; and permanent home-officials were *consiliarii*. Imperial control of jurisdiction continued, with experts to assist.

3. Antoninus dispensed nine 'liberalities' (to a total of 800 *denarii* a head); founded the 'Puellae Faustinianae' to commemorate Faustina (died 140–1); lightened the provincial burden of Imperial Posts; helped many communities financially; and carried out much public building. But he cut down unnecessary public expenditure, and at his death left 675 million *denarii* in the Treasury (Dio Cass. 74. 8. 3). Modest and plain-living himself, he disciplined both freedmen and imperial procurators. Confiscation was rare, judicial clemency frequent.

4. Foreign affairs, though Antoninus' influence encouraged peaceful settlement, were uneasy. About 140–1 the British frontier was advanced (*see* WALL OF ANTONINUS); but the Brigantes were later to revolt. A restive Germany was further insulated by settling Britons in the Neckar lands. Revolt in Numidia and Mauretania (*c.* 145–50) was followed by Jewish and Egyptian risings. Dacian trouble (*c.* 158) caused the tripartition of the province under procurators (159). Kings were assigned to the Colchian Lazi; to the Quadi; and to the Armenians, whom Parthia was warned to leave untouched, though hostilities occurred later (*ILS* 1076); and Abgar of Edessa was admonished for aggressive conduct.

5. With the succession assured, and himself—another Numa—high in respect, Antoninus quietly developed the centralization of government, relying chiefly on a friendly Senate. Rome and Italy (which he perhaps never quitted as emperor) were the focus of his *pietas*; and his medallions (struck 140–4) advertising the coming 900th anniversary of Rome (147) show his conception of Rome's spiritual ascendancy. He died at Lorium on 7 March 161, entrusting the State to M. Aurelius. Deified by universal accord, he received all the usual honours.

BIBLIOGRAPHY

I. ANCIENT SOURCES. (*a*) *Literary authorities*: The account of Antoninus in *Historia Augusta* is uncritical. Minor references in Aurelius Victor and Eutropius; and fragments of Dio Cassius bk. 70. The *Meditations* of M. Aurelius and Fronto's *Letters* contain frequent allusions to Antoninus.
(*b*) *Inscriptions*: W. Hüttl, *Antoninus Pius* ii (1933); *PIR*², A 1513.
(*c*) *Coins*: H. Mattingly and E. A. Sydenham, *The Roman Imperial Coinage* iii (1930); H. Mattingly, *B.M. Coins, Rom. Emp.* iv (1940); P. L. Strack, *Untersuchungen zur römischen Reichsprägung des zweiten Jahrhunderts* iii (1937); J. Toynbee in *CR* 1925, 170.
II. MODERN LITERATURE. E. E. Bryant, *The Reign of Antoninus Pius* (1895); G. Lacour-Gayet, *Antonin le Pieux et son temps* (1888); W. Hüttl, op. cit. i (1936); H. M. D. Parker, *Roman World* (1935), part i; W. Weber in *CAH* xi (1936), ch. 9; C. H. Dodd, *Num. Chron.* 1911, 6–41; P. von Rohden, *PW*, s.v. 'Aurelius (138)'.

C. H. V. S.

ANTONIUS (1), MARCUS (143–87 B.C.), was praetor in 102, consul in 99, and censor in 97. In 102 he made a preliminary drive against the pirates off the south coast of Asia Minor and established the province of Cilicia (q.v.). At Rome he gave support to the *Optimates* and opposed the party of Saturninus; he perished in the Marian massacres. Antonius was also a distinguished orator. Eschewing Greek refinements and appeals to emotion, he carried his point by sharp reasoning and skilful marshalling of his argument. None of his speeches has been preserved.

Cicero, *Brutus*, 139–42. M. C.

ANTONIUS (2) 'CRETICUS', MARCUS (d. *c.* 72 B.C.), son of (1) and father of the triumvir. He shared his son's amiable disposition and spendthrift habits. As praetor in 74 B.C. he was invested with a general commission (*imperium infinitum*) on sea against the Mediterranean pirates, but showed none of the organizing ability which his task required. After some heavy requisitioning in Sicily he operated off the coasts of Liguria and Spain, where he perhaps assisted Pompey by cutting Sertorius' sea communications (74–73). Leaving the west Mediterranean still exposed to pirate raids, he made further severe requisitions in the Aegean area, only to sustain an ignominious defeat in a pitched battle against the pirates of Crete (72). He died of illness shortly afterwards.

P. Foucart, *Journal des Savants* 1906, 569 ff. M. C.

ANTONIUS (3) HYBRIDA, GAIUS, son of M. Antonius (1), a notorious spendthrift. Expelled from the Senate in 70 B.C., he stood for the consulship of 63 in association with Catiline. He was elected with Cicero, who won over his colleague from Catiline by surrendering to him the province of Macedonia. After Catiline's flight to north Italy, A. took over the troops in Etruria, but was not present at the final battle near Pistoria.

Antonius' inglorious record in Macedonia led to his trial for misgovernment (59). Despite Cicero's defence he was condemned. Recalled from exile by Caesar, he was censor in 42. J. M. C.

ANTONIUS (4), MARCUS (*c.* 82–30 B.C.), 'Mark Antony' the triumvir, eldest son of Antonius (2) Creticus, was born probably in 82 B.C. After a dissipated youth he distinguished himself as a cavalry commander under Gabinius in Palestine and Egypt (57–55), and subsequently joined Caesar's staff in Gaul, where he served his quaestorship in 51. As tribune in 49 he defended Caesar's interests in the Senate, joining him at Ravenna before the outbreak of the Civil War and taking part in the campaigns in Italy and Greece. He had been left in charge of Italy in 49, and was sent back as Caesar's representative after Pharsalus, being appointed *magister equitum*. Probably because of a temporary estrangement, he took no part in the Dictator's last campaigns, but in 44 he was his colleague in the consulship. After the Ides of March he at first adopted a conciliatory attitude towards the Liberators, but he made an unscrupulous use of Caesar's papers, and his recruiting of armed supporters, followed by the irregular enactment of a law which gave him Cisalpine Gaul and Gallia Comata for five years (June), caused general apprehension. Decimus Brutus was supported in his refusal to surrender Cisalpine Gaul by the Senate and Octavian (with whom Antony had quarrelled), and Antony was compelled by reverses at Forum Gallorum and Mutina (April 43) to retreat to Gallia Narbonensis. He was joined there, however, by the governors of the Western provinces (Lepidus, Pollio, and Plancus), and subsequently reconciled with Octavian.

2. By the *Lex Titia* (November 43) Antony, Lepidus, and Octavian were appointed *Triumviri Rei Publicae Constituendae* for five years. The proscription of their political and personal enemies in Rome was followed by the defeat of Brutus and Cassius at Philippi (42), where Antony established his reputation as a general. He then proceeded to Asia Minor (41), met Cleopatra at Tarsus, and spent the following winter in Egypt. His brother's defeat in the Perusine War compelled him to return to Italy in 40, but a new agreement was reached at Brundisium, by which he received the Eastern provinces (east of Illyricum) and married Octavian's sister Octavia. He left for the East after the treaty of Misenum (39), but met Octavian again at Tarentum in 37, when they agreed to renew the Triumvirate for another five years. In 36 Antony's expedition against the Parthians ended in a disastrous retreat. At the end of 37 he had again met Cleopatra, and in 35 he offended Octavian by forbidding

Octavia to visit him. In 34 he annexed Armenia on the pretext of the king's desertion in 36, and celebrated a triumph at Alexandria. His conduct there and his donations of territory to Cleopatra and her children had alienated many of his supporters, and in 32 Octavian induced the Senate to deprive him of his authority and declare war on Cleopatra. Decisively defeated at Actium (31), Antony attempted to defend Egypt, but the general defection of his governors in the Eastern provinces made his cause hopeless. He committed suicide before Octavian's entry into Alexandria (30).

3. Of fine physique, and with a constitution which excesses and hardships alike failed to ruin, Antony was a natural soldier, and his courage, affability, and generosity made him a great soldiers' leader. As a politician, though by no means unskilful, he was sometimes led into serious errors by his irascible temper and self-will.

4. Antony was married four times: (1) to Fadia, (2) to Antonia, (3) to Fulvia (c. 46), and (4) to Octavia (40). He left three daughters and two sons (Antyllus and Iullus Antonius). If he contracted a formal marriage with Cleopatra it was not valid in Roman law. She bore him three children: Alexander, Ptolemy, and Cleopatra.

Cicero, *Letters* and *Philippics*; Caesar, *BGall.* bks. 7 and 8, *BCiv.* bks. 1 and 3; Velleius, bk. 2; Josephus, *AJ* bks. 14 and 15; Plutarch, *Antony*; Appian, *BCiv.* bks. 2–5; Dio Cassius, bks. 41–53. Modern literature: V. Gardthausen, *Augustus und seine Zeit* (1891); Drumann–Groebe, *Gesch. Roms* i; T. Rice Holmes, *Architect of the Roman Empire* i (1928); F. E. Adcock, M. P. Charlesworth, and W. W. Tarn, *CAH* ix and x; J. Kromayer, *Hermes* xxix, xxxi, xxxiii, xxxiv (1894 ff.). G. W. R.

ANTONIUS (5), Gaius, second son of Antonius (2) Creticus and brother of the triumvir. As Caesar's *legatus* in 49 B.C. he was blockaded by a Pompeian fleet on the island of Curicta and taken prisoner. After his praetorship in 44 he set out for Macedonia, but was besieged and captured in Apollonia by M. Brutus (March 43). He tried to incite the troops of Brutus to mutiny and was executed by his order early in 42.

Cicero, *Letters* and *Philippics*; Caesar, *BCiv.* 3. 10 and 67; Plutarch, *Brutus*, 26 and 28; Appian, *BCiv.* bks. 2 and 3; Dio Cassius, bks. 41–7. Modern literature: Drumann–Groebe, *Gesch. Roms* i; Ganter, *Jahrb. f. Philologie* (1894). G. W. R.

ANTONIUS (6), Lucius, third son of Antonius (2) Creticus. He served his quaestorship in Asia in 50 B.C., and as tribune in 44 carried a law giving Caesar special powers in the appointment of magistrates, and an agrarian law under which he himself served as one of the commissioners. In the war of Mutina he was *legatus* to his brother Marcus. As consul in 41 he asserted the rights of his office against Octavian, and championed the Italians dispossessed by the latter's settlements of veterans. The ensuing civil war ended in the surrender of Lucius at Perusia (40). He was then sent as Octavian's legatus to Spain, where he appears to have died soon afterwards.

Cicero, *Letters* and *Philippics*; Josephus, *AJ* 14. 10; Appian, *BCiv.* bk. 5; Dio Cassius, bks. 45–8. Modern literature: V. Gardthausen, *Augustus und seine Zeit* i (1891); Drumann–Groebe, *Gesch. Roms* i; T. Rice Holmes, *Architect of the Roman Empire* i (1928). G. W. R.

ANTONIUS (7), Marcus, 'Antyllus', the name given by the Greeks to Marcus Antonius, elder son of the triumvir and Fulvia. In 37 B.C. (at Tarentum) he was betrothed to Octavian's daughter Julia. He assumed the *toga virilis* after Actium and was put to death by Octavian after the capture of Alexandria. G. W. R.

ANTONIUS (8), Iullus, second son of the triumvir and Fulvia, was praetor in 13 B.C., consul in 10, and probably proconsul of Asia. In 2 B.C. he was convicted of adultery with Julia, daughter of Augustus, and committed suicide. He married Marcella, niece of Augustus (21 B.C.), and had a son Lucius. G. W. R.

ANTONIUS (9) **CASTOR**, perhaps a freedman of M. Antonius, was one of the Elder Pliny's sources for botany (*HN* 25. 9).

M. Wellmann, *Hermes* lix (1924); *PW* i. 2615.

ANTONIUS (10) **MUSA**, physician of Augustus, whom in 23 B.C. he cured of a serious illness. Apparently he was the first to introduce hydropathy at Rome. He wrote a work in several books on the properties of drugs. The extant works that pass under his name—*De herba botanica* and *De tuenda valetudine ad Maecenatem*—are spurious and later.

Ed. E. Howald and H. E. Sigerist, *CML* iv (1927); *PW* i. 2633. W. D. R.

ANTONIUS (11) **DIOGENES** (c. A.D. 100), author of a fantasy in twenty-four books called *The wonderful things beyond Thule* (Τὰ ὑπὲρ Θούλην ἄπιστα), of which Photius' abstract is extant. The story, which in spite of a love interest is less a romance than an aretalogy, had little or no influence on the development of the Greek Novel.

Text: R. Hercher, *Erotici Scriptores Graeci* i (Teubner). *See also* NOVEL, GREEK. R. M. R.

ANTONIUS, *see also* FELIX, GNIPHO, GORDIAN, PALLAS, PRIMUS, SATURNINUS.

ANTYLLUS (2nd c. A.D.), physician, belonged to the pneumatic school; his chief contributions to medicine were in the sphere of dietetics, general therapeutics, and especially surgery. Works: Περὶ βοηθημάτων (on medicine); Χειρουργούμενα (on surgery); Περὶ ὑδροκεφάλων: all lost except for frs. *See* SURGERY, para. 6.

PW i. 2644. W. D. R.

ANTYLLUS, *see also* ANTONIUS (7).

ANUBIS, originally one of several local gods of the dead in Egypt, is represented on the monuments as a jackal. In Hellenistic times his cult is both celestial and infernal and he is sometimes identified with Hermes under the name Hermanubis. He is an important member of the cult of the Egyptian deities only at Delos, though we know of a *thiasos* which worshipped him at Smyrna. In the Roman period he is represented at times as a soldier in armour. T. A. B.

ANYTE (fl. 290 B.C.), Arcadian poetess, is known from twenty charming Doric epigrams in the Anthology. Twelve are dainty mock-epitaphs on pet animals (a fancy which she invented); most of the others are little nature-lyrics filled with the quiet, pure emotion which characterizes the Peloponnesian school of epigrammatists. *See* EPIGRAM.

R. Reitzenstein, *Epigramm und Skolion* 123 (1893). G. H.

ANYTUS (5th–4th c. B.C.), a wealthy Athenian and a democratic leader. General in 409 B.C., he failed to prevent the loss of Pylus, and is said to have escaped condemnation only by bribery. After the war, he was one of the restorers of democracy with Thrasybulus, proving himself an honest and moderate politician. Plato (*Meno* 90 f.) introduces him as a well-bred man, but a passionate enemy of the sophists. He probably did not belong to the circle of Socrates, as some sources hint. He became Socrates' chief accuser, less for private reasons than from an honest belief that he was doing the best for Athens. Accounts about his banishment and murder may be later inventions.

Prosop. Att. 1324. V. E.

AORNOS, the mountain stronghold between the Swat and Indus rivers captured by Alexander (327–326 B.C.), has been identified by Sir Aurel Stein with Pir-sar, north of Buner. Two great ridges, Pir-sar and Una-sar, converge at right angles; the 'rock' is Bar-sar on Pir-sar, cut off from the Una ridge (along which Alexander attacked) by the Būrimār ravine (across which he constructed his ramp). The operations can only be understood from a map, which shows what a great feat of arms it was. 'Aornos' may represent Una (Unra).

Sir A. Stein, *On Alexander's Track to the Indus* (1929), chs. 17–22, with maps. W. W. T.

APAMEA, a city on the Orontes which replaced the Macedonian military colony of Pella. It was founded by Seleucus I, or perhaps Antiochus I. It was the capital of a satrapy and the military head-quarters of the Seleucid kingdom. A natural fortress, it was seized by Caecilius Bassus in 46 B.C. and endured a long siege. During the Principate it made only one issue of coins (under Claudius), but ruled a large territory; its citizen population numbered 117,000 under Augustus. Its ruins are being excavated (reports in *L'Antiquité classique* 1932, 1935–6). Apamea was the place where the Romans concluded a peace with Antiochus III (q.v.) in 188 B.C.
A. H. M. J.

APARCHE, votive gift to a god. The custom which is expressed by the Latin word *votum* (q.v.), that a gift is promised and given if a certain condition is fulfilled by the god, was common in Greece too (cf. *Il.* 6. 305 ff.); it is expressed by the word εὐχή. The words ἀπαρχή, ἀκροθίνια express the idea that a part of something gained is given to the god. Generally these gifts were understood as a χαριστήριον, thank-offering. Cf. *IG* i². 625 εὐχωλὴν τελέσας σοι χάριν ἀντιδιδούς.

H. Beer, Ἀπαρχή *und verwandte Ausdrücke in griechischen Weihinschriften* (Diss. München, 1914). M. P. N.

APATURIA, a festival characteristic of the Ionians (among the Dorians the Apellai (q.v.) corresponds to it). It is chiefly known from Athens, where it was celebrated by the phratries in the month of Pyanopsion (Oct.–Nov.). Its three days were called (1) δορπία (from a late meal), (2) ἀνάρρυσις (from the sacrifice of an animal), (3) κουρεῶτις. On this last day the children and young adult men and newly married wives were enrolled in the phratry. Three sacrifices are mentioned in connexion with this enrolling: the μεῖον (the lesser one) was probably brought on behalf of a child introduced into the phratry; the κούρειον (cf. κουρεῶτις) has its name from the shearing of the hair of the ephebes; the γαμήλια from the introduction of the newly married young women. *See also under* AETHRA.

L. Deubner, *Attische Feste*, 232 ff. Note above all the inscription of the phratry of the Demotionidae, *IG* ii². 1237 = *SIG*³ 921. M. P. N.

APELLA (ἀπέλλα; probably related to Ἀπόλλων), the Spartan Assembly, which retained many features of the Homeric Ἀγορά. Instituted, or at least defined, by the *Rhetra* of Lycurgus, it met once every month, and all Spartiatai (perhaps only on attaining the age of thirty) could attend. Summoned originally by the kings, it was later (? 6th c.) convoked and presided over by the ephors. It could merely consider proposals put before it by the ephors or the Gerousia. It expressed its opinion by acclamation, and if this seemed indecisive, by formal division

Its functions were to decide disputed royal successions; to appoint military commanders; to elect ephors and other magistrates and members of the Gerousia; to decide on peace or war and the conclusion of treaties; and to approve the emancipation of helots. Any proposed change in the laws required its approval. Its authority was diminished—perhaps only temporarily—by the addition to the *Rhetra* ascribed to the time of Polydorus and Theopompus, empowering the kings and the Gerousia to set aside misguided decisions.

We hear also of a μικρὰ ἐκκλησία (Xen. *Hell.* 3. 3. 8) apparently convoked on urgent occasions, but its composition is uncertain.

Arist. *Pol.* 2. 11. 6 (comparison with Carthage); Plut. *Lyc.* 6. 7. 25. G. Busolt, *Griechische Staatskunde* (1926), 691 ff.; U. Kahrstedt, *Griechisches Staatsrecht* i. 255 ff. A. M. W.

APELLAI. Ἀπέλλα is a Dorian word signifying assembly-place, assembly (*see preceding article*). In the plural it signifies a festival corresponding to the Athenian Apaturia (q.v.) at which the new members of the *gens* were introduced. The name of the month Apellaios proves that it was widely spread among the Dorians; otherwise it is only known through the inscription of the Labyadai at Delphi (*SIG*² 438).

M. P. Nilsson, *Gesch. d. griech. Religion* i. 524. M. P. N.

APELLES (4th c. B.C.), painter, of Colophon, later of Ephesus (sometimes called Coan because of the Coan Aphrodite). Pliny dates him 332 B.C. (by Alexander). He was taught first by Ephorus of Ephesus, then by Pamphilus (q.v.) of Sicyon. When in the Sicyonian school, he helped Melanthius to paint the victorious chariot of the tyrant Aristratus. He painted portraits of Philip, Alexander, and their circle, and a self-portrait. Anecdotes connect him with Alexander, Ptolemy, and Protogenes. He died in Cos while copying his Aphrodite, probably early in the third century.

SELECTED WORKS: 1. Aphrodite Anadyomene, in Cos, later in Rome. Aphrodite rising from the sea, wringing out her hair. 2. Alexander with the thunderbolt, in Ephesus. Alexander darker than nature so that the thunderbolt stood out. 3. Calumny, preceded by Envy, Intrigue, and Deception, and followed by Repentance and Truth, dragging her victim before a man with large ears, attended by Ignorance and Superstition. 4. Sacrifice, in Cos. Described by Herodas (4. 59). The tone of his pictures was due to a secret varnish. He wrote a book on painting; he claimed to know when to take his hand from a picture (contrast Protogenes), and that his works had charm, χάρις (contrast Melanthius).

Overbeck, 591, 1067, 1073, 1090, 1446–8, 1481, 1687, 1726, 1745, 1748–9, 1751, 1759, 1766, 1772, 1774, 1827–1906, 1921; Pfuhl, 801. T. B. L. W

APENNINES, Italy's mountain backbone, branch off from the Alps near Genoa. At first they are of moderate height (3,000–4,000 ft.) and run eastwards forming the southern boundary of Cisalpine Gaul (Northern Apennines); then, near Ariminum, they turn south-east, follow the line of the Adriatic coast and attain great altitudes—9,560 feet at the Gran Sasso (Central Apennines); approaching Lucania they become lower again, swing south and occupy virtually all south-west Italy (Southern Apennines: the granite Sila mountains of the Bruttian Peninsula, although geologically distinct, are generally reckoned a prolongation of the limestone Apennines. Italy's volcanic mountains, however—Albanus, Vesuvius, Vultur—are independent of the Apennine system). The 800-mile Apennine chain is not continuous and unbroken, but consists of tangled mountain masses of varying width, interspersed with numerous upland passes and fertile valleys suitable for agriculture or summer pasturage. Offshoots are numerous, e.g. Apuan Alps (Liguria), Volscian Mountains (Latium); some are completely separated from the main range, e.g. Mons Garganus (Apulia). The Apennines feed most Italian rivers except the Po and some of its tributaries, but, not being perennially snow-capped, supply inadequate amounts of water in summer, when consequently the rivers become mere rills or torrent-beds. The Apennines contain numerous mineral springs but little mineral wealth. In antiquity their cheeses, wolves, bears, goats, extensive forests, and brigands were famous.

Polybius 2. 16; 3. 110 includes Maritime Alps in the Apennines; Strabo 2. 128; 5. 211; Lucan 2. 396–438; Varro, *Rust.* 2. 1. 5, 16; Pliny, *HN* 11. 240; 16. 197. C. S. du Riche Preller, *Italian Mountain Geology* (1923). E. T. S.

APER, MARCUS, an advocate of Gallic origin who attained the praetorship. He apparently visited Britain, perhaps as *tribunus laticlavius*. Tacitus studied his rhetorical methods, and in the *Dialogus* introduces him as a utilitarian defending lucrative court-oratory in the modern style as against poetry and the older fashions (Tac. *Dial.* 2; 5–10; 16. 5–23). G. C. W.

APEX, a sort of mitre worn by Roman *flamines* and some other priests, or more properly the top of it (Suetonius ap. Servius on *Aen.* 2. 683, 'apex proprie dicitur in summo flaminis pilleo uirga lanata, hoc est in cuius extremitate modica lana est'. The *virga* was a twig or spike of olivewood (Festus p. 9. 30 Lindsay); the *lana* was a woollen thread, *apiculum*, with which apparently the spike was tied on (ibid. 21. 10). The lower part of the head-dress was the *galerus*; that of the *flamen Dialis* was called *albogalerus*, being made of the skins of white victims sacrificed to Jupiter (ibid. 9. 29; Varro ap. Gel. 10. 15. 32). This was a close-fitting conical cap (Varro, *Ling.* 7. 44).

See K. A. Esdaile, *JRS* i. 213 ff.; Wissowa, *RK* 499. H. J. R.

APHAEA (Ἀφαία), a goddess worshipped in Aegina, where the ruins of her temple (famous for its pedimental sculptures, now in Munich) are still extant. She was identified with Britomartis (q.v.; Paus. 2. 30. 3); i.e. she was of similar character to Artemis (q.v.). H. J. R.

APHRODISIUS, SCRIBONIUS, a slave instructed by Horace's teacher, Orbilius, took up the subject of Latin orthography and passed strong criticisms on the work of Verrius Flaccus (q.v.). Scribonia, Augustus' first wife, freed him (Suet. *Gram.* 19).

APHRODITE, Greek goddess of love, beauty, and fertility. The meaning of the name is uncertain, though the Greeks, from Hesiod on (*Theog.* 188–206), derived it from ἀφρός, 'foam', and told of the birth of A. from the sea. She was worshipped throughout almost all of the Greek world; the sanctuaries at Paphos and Amathus in Cyprus, at Cythera, and at Corinth were especially renowned. To Homer she is 'the Cyprian', and it was probably from the meeting of Greek and Semite in Cyprus that A., who is certainly akin to Astarte and Ishtar, entered Greece, though the Hellenic goddess doubtless owes something to earlier Aegean divinities, such as Ariadne, whose cults she absorbed. Greek tradition consistently pointed to an Eastern origin for A. (cf. Hdt. 1. 105; Paus. 1. 14. 7), and it was from Cyprus that Adonis, the consort of Astarte-Aphrodite, was later to come to Athens. But the process of hellenization has already gone far in Homer, who makes A. the daughter of Zeus and Dione, and the wife of Hephaestus; Ares, in later myth her husband, appears in the lay of Demodocus (*Od.* 8. 266–366) as her paramour. Aeneas is her son by the Trojan Anchises (*Il.* passim; *Hymn. Hom. Ven.* 5), and she is ever the partisan of the Trojans (another hint of her non-Hellenic origin) but no warrior, and when she is wounded by Diomedes, Zeus reminds her that her sphere is not war but love (*Il.* 5. 428–9).

2. Primarily, she is a goddess of generation and fertility, and in poetry often seems little more than a personification of the sexual instinct and the power of love. Occasionally she presides over marriage, and the bearded A. of Cyprus seems to be an androgynous type arising from the marriage ritual (*see* HERMAPHRODITUS), but marriage was a domain largely pre-empted by Hera. Prostitutes, however, considered A. their patron (cf. Aphrodite Πόρνη, Ἑταίρα, Ath. 13. 572 e–573 a), and there was sacred prostitution (q.v.) in her cult at Corinth, but in general the public cult, at least, was staid and even austere.

3. The goddess of vegetation appears most clearly in Cyprus and wherever else Adonis (q.v.) was worshipped with A. Here too belong the cult names A. ἐν Κήποις, A. Ἄνθεια, and her associations with the Charites, the Horae, and Eros (qq.v.) (cf. the sanctuary of Eros and A. ἐν Κήποις on the north slope of the Acropolis, O. Broneer, *Hesp.* 1932, 1935). The powers of fertility are generally chthonian (A. Μελαινίς, Paus. 2. 2. 4; 8. 6. 5; 9. 27. 5; A. Ἐπιτυμβία at Delphi, Plut. *Quaest. Rom.* 269 b), and to this trait may be due her frequent association in cult with Hermes (q.v.).

4. Aphrodite was widely worshipped as a goddess of the sea and seafaring (A. Ποντία, Εὔπλοια). The armed A. (ὡπλισμένη) or goddess of war (A. Ἀρεία, Στρατεία) was worshipped in Sparta, Cyprus, Cythera, and elsewhere; this warlike character is probably a direct survival from her Oriental prototypes, and may also explain her associations, chiefly in myth, with Ares (q.v.).

5. Two very common titles are Οὐρανία and Πάνδημος, but the philosophical interpretation of these as representing intellectual and common love (Pl. *Symp.* 180 d–181; Xen. *Symp.* 8. 9–10) is unjustified. The title Urania, in fact, seems frequently a mark of the Oriental goddess, and was a cult name at Cyprus, Cythera, and Corinth. It was also applied to various foreign goddesses (e.g. the Scythian Argimpasa, Hdt. 4. 59; the Arabian Allat, Hdt. 3. 8; Venus Caelestis = Astarte at Carthage). Pandemus, on the other hand, the 'goddess of the whole people', represents the highest political idea to which A. attained, notably at Athens, but also at Erythrae, Thebes, Cos, and Megalopolis.

6. Apart from Hermes, A. has no strong associations in cult with the major Hellenic gods. Nor are her festivals, except in Cyprus, of great importance, though that at Delos, where A. has replaced Ariadne, was very ancient (Plut. *Thes.* 21; Callim. *Del.* 306–13), and several States had a month named for A. The myrtle and the dove are sacred to A. (cf. dove used for lustration of temple of Pandemus, *IG* ii². 659); the sacrifice of swine seems to mark the fertility cult and the presence of Adonis.

7. In the Hellenistic period the name 'Syrian A.' (on Delos A. Ἁγνή) designates Atargatis (q.v.).

8. The poets, as in the fragment of Aeschylus' *Danaides* and the magnificent exordium of Lucretius, exalt A. as the cosmic generative force pervading all nature.

L. R. Farnell, *Cults of the Greek States* ii (1896), chs. 21–3; M. P. Nilsson, *Griechische Feste* (1906), 362–87; L. Preller–C. Robert, *Griechische Mythologie*⁴ (1894) i, 345–85. *See* VENUS. F. R. W.

APHRODITE IN ART. Greek art took several hundred years to achieve a truly individual vision of Aphrodite. Archaic art represents A. either in the Oriental type of a nude goddess or as a standing or seated figure distinguished only by attributes from other goddesses.

Classical art of the fifth century endows A. with majestic beauty and grave charm. The famous images by Phidias, Alcamenes, and Agoracritus (A. W. Lawrence, *Class. Sculpt.* 1929) are lost, but we can admire in originals the poetic charm of Aphrodite rising from the sea (Ludovisi Throne), the quiet dignity of Aphrodite on the swan (painted cup, London), the harmony of Aphrodite and Eros in the Parthenon frieze. An A. on a tortoise and an A. leaning on a pillar reflect monumental images of Periclean times (Schrader, *Phidias*, 1924).

'The finest statue not only of Praxiteles but of the whole world is the Aphrodite for the sight of which many had sailed to Cnidos', says Pliny. Carved about the middle of the fourth century and known through Roman copies, this statue showed the goddess laying her garment on a hydria before taking a bath. The first convincing representation of the beautiful female nude, distinguished by an evasive charm, the Cnidian A. became a model for the numerous A.s of Hellenistic and Roman times. Of these the best known are A. of Cyrene, the popular Venus de Milo, the crouching A. by the Bithynian Doidalsas, the armed A. of Acrocorinthus, and the various types described as 'Venus Genetrix'.

Blinkenberg, *Knidia* (1933); A. W. Lawrence, *Later Greek Sculpture* (1927); O. Broneer, *The Armed Aphrodite* (1930); M. Bieber, *Röm. Mitt.* 1933. G. M. A. H.

APHTHONIUS, AELIUS FESTUS (3rd c. A.D.), wrote four books *De Metris*, which now form the bulk of the *Ars Grammatica* of Marius Victorinus (ed. Keil, *Gramm. Lat.* 6. 31–173). This incorporation (not due to Victorinus himself) was effected before A.D. 400.

Cf. Teuffel, § 395; Schanz–Hosius, § 829. J. F. M.

APICIUS, a proverbial gourmet under Augustus and Tiberius (Plin. *HN* 10. 13, Tac. *Ann.* 4. 1), committed his experience in *cuisine* to writing (Sen. *Helv.* 10. 8: schol. Juv. 4. 23). The *De Re Coquinaria* under his name was compiled some centuries later (C. T. Shuch, 1867; Giarratano and Vollmer, 1922). J. W. D.

APICULUM, *see* APEX.

APION, son of Posidonius, a Greek (or Graeco-Egyptian) of Alexandria, pupil of Didymus, and successor to Theon as head of the Alexandrian school. He was later at Rome, under Tiberius and Claudius. He was nicknamed Πλειστονίκης (by himself), *cymbalum mundi* and *propriae famae tympanum* (by Tiberius and Pliny, Plin. *HN* Pref.), and, for his industry, Μόχθος. He wrote on Egypt (cf. Josephus, *Ap.*; and Gell. 5. 14. 10–30); he called up (so he said) Homer's spirit to ascertain the poet's parentage and birthplace, but published no account of the proceedings, and compiled, *inter alia*, an alphabetically arranged Homeric glossary, based, as was usual, on Aristarchus, and preserved only in fragments and in the derivative work of Apollonius Sophistes.

Fragments: *FHG* iii. 506–16. A. Ludwich, *Philol.* lxxiv (1917), 205; lxxv (1919), 90. P. B. R. F.

APIS, the sacred bull worshipped in Memphis. His cult attained national prominence and under Ptolemaic and Roman rulers official recognition was given to it and to the feast-days connected with it. When the sacred animal died, a successor was chosen and the dead beast was mummified and entombed during a period of sorrow and fasting which lasted for seventy days. Apis is mentioned a few times in Greek inscriptions as one of the gods included among the Egyptian deities, but his chief importance for Graeco-Roman religion lies in the fact that the cult of Sarapis (q.v.) originated in the worship of the Osirified (*see* OSIRIS) Apis bulls entombed in the temple at Memphis. T. A. B.

APODEKTAI, a board of ten officials at Athens, who received all the moneys from the revenue-collecting departments and paid them over to the spending departments, under the supervision of the Boule. They were instituted by Cleisthenes; from the time of Pericles they were appointed by lot.

APOLLINARIS, *see* SIDONIUS, SULPICIUS (4).

APOLLO (Ἀπόλλων, Epic also Ἀππόλλων or Ἀπόλλων, as *Il.* 1. 14), the most Greek of all gods, in art the ideal type of young, but not immature manly beauty. His functions are especially music, archery, prophecy, medicine, and the care of flocks and herds; with agriculture he has much less to do. He is often associated with the higher developments of civilization, approving codes of law (as Hdt. 1. 65. 6), inculcating high moral and religious principles (as id. 6. 86. 15; Aelian, *VH* 3. 44), and favouring philosophy (e.g. he was said to be the real father of Plato). In matters of ritual, especially of purification, his oracles are commonly regarded as the supreme authority. Politically, he is especially prominent in suggesting or approving schemes of colonization (Apollo Archegetes, q.v.). His cult was panhellenic and he is regularly spoken of with profound respect, some of the war-time plays of Euripides being an exception.

2. His name is of uncertain etymology, perhaps not Greek. Of his origin there are two principal theories.

(1) He comes from somewhere north of Greece. In support of this it is urged that his seats of worship are numerous and ancient in the north; the legendary Apolline people, the Hyperboreans (q.v.), are always thought of as northerners and are real enough to send yearly offerings to Delos which follow a route from the north (Hdt. 4. 33; cf. Farnell op. cit. infra, 99–100); and the ritual of the Stepteria points north also. (2) He is Asianic, for his title Λύκειος and the name of his mother Leto suggest Lycia and the Lycian *Lada*; he has numerous connexions with that country and with the Oriental sacred number seven (e.g. his birthday is the seventh of the month, Hesiod, *Op.* 771); he is especially worshipped at Troy and warmly supports the Trojans in Homer. For a short selection of the literature on this question, which is yet undecided, see Rose, *Handb. of Gk. Myth.*, 158 n. 2; add Bethe, 'Apollon der Hellene', in Ἀντίδωρον (Göttingen, 1924).

3. It was conjectured as early as the fifth century B.C. (Euripides, fr. 781, 11–13 Nauck; Aesch. ap. [Eratosth], *Catast.* 24 is uncertain) that Apollo was the Sun, and this theory prevailed in Hellenistic and Imperial times and was for a while revived by modern scholars. It lacks, however, any real evidence (see Farnell, 136 ff.). It is more likely that the god's origins are to be sought in his titles of Nomios and Lykeios. If he was a god of herdsmen in wild country, it is highly probable that his interests would include archery, music, and medicine, and that he should be somehow connected with their worst enemy, the wolf, is equally reasonable; he can both send and stay that and other plagues. How and where he became a prophetic god is not known, but he is so from our earliest records.

4. Of his oracular shrines, Delphi was the chief, though others were important, notably Branchidae and Claros in Ionia, whereof the latter was particularly prominent in Hellenistic times. The method of divination was by possession, the medium (commonly female, as at Delphi) being filled with the god, or his inspiration (see further Farnell, 179 ff. and DELPHIC ORACLE). Of his ritual perhaps the most remarkable was the Delphic Stepteria, held every eight years. In this, a boy, apparently personating the god, was led to a hut near the temple, called the palace of Python (see below); this was set on fire; the boy went away into supposed banishment; and finally all concerned were purified at Tempe and came back by the traditional sacred route known as the Pythian Way (see Farnell, 293). The ancients regarded the ritual as a sort of play commemorating the killing of Python (see below). Delphi, through the enterprise of its clergy, became the nearest approach to a Vatican which Greece possessed, though it had no formal authority to enforce its advice. Delphic propaganda may be traced in the tendency to introduce Apollo as adviser, inspirer, etc., into any and every myth which contains a prophet or a prediction. Delphi claimed to be the centre of the world, the famous stone called the *omphalos* (navel) marking the very spot. In art, Apollo is often represented as sitting on this, but the actual seat of his medium, the Pythia, was a tripod, hence continually associated with Apollo and his oracles.

5. Apollo's earliest adventure (for his birth at Delos, *see* LETO) was the killing of Python, a formidable dragon which guarded Delphi (in the earliest version, the Homeric Hymn to the Pythian Apollo, 300 [122], it is a female and unnamed). He also killed Tityos, a giant who offered violence to Leto, *Od.* 11. 580. For other divine vengeances, *see* ALOADAE, NIOBE.

6. Of his many loves, the most famous was that for Coronis, mother of Asclepius (q.v.). For the adventures to which Asclepius' death led, *see* ALCESTIS. Very interesting is the tale of his unsuccessful rivalry with Idas (q.v.) for Marpessa. Another object of his affections was Cassandra (Alexandra), daughter of Priam. To win

her he gave her the gift of prophecy, but having received it she would not grant him her love. He could not recall his gift, but made it futile by causing her always to be disbelieved(Aesch. *Ag.* 1202 ff.). Somewhat similar, probably modelled upon this, is the story of the Cumaean Sibyl, as told by Ovid (*Met.* 14. 132 ff.). He bade her choose whatever she wished, and she asked to live as many years as she held grains of sand. But she forgot to ask for permanent youth, and, having denied him, received no more favours from him; hence she grew so old that she finally hung in a vessel, saying, when asked what she wanted, that she wished to die (Petronius, *Sat.* 48. 8; see Campbell Bonner in *Quantulacunque, Studies presented to Kirsopp Lake . . .* (U.S.A., 1937), 1 ff.). By Cyrene, granddaughter of the river Peneus, he became father of Aristaeus (q.v.); he was first attracted to her by observing her courage and prowess in hunting on Mt. Pelion, where she was fighting a lion bare-handed, and carried her off to that part of Africa which was afterwards named after her (Pind. *Pyth.* 9. 17 ff.; it was a foundation-legend of the colony of Cyrene, see L. Vitali, *Religione Cyrenaica* (1932), 107 ff.).

7. Apollo was usually impartial in politics, though he shows Troy great favour in the *Iliad*. His principal departures from this attitude were during the Persian Wars, when he was partial to the Persians, and the Peloponnesian War, when he was whole-heartedly of the Spartan faction, hence Euripides' attitude, see above.

8. In Italy, Apollo was introduced early, partly through Etruria (cf. the famous statue of him from Veii), partly direct from Greek settlements. Although now and then equated with native gods (as the deity of Soracte, *Aen.* 11. 785), he never had a generally accepted identification. At Rome his Republican cult seems to have been primarily that of a god of healing (the Vestals addressed him as *Apollo medice, Apollo Paean*, Macrob. *Sat.* 1. 17. 15) and of prophecy (cf. SIBYLLA, QUINDECIMVIRI). He had a shrine, *Apollinar*, outside the Porta Carmentalis, and a temple was erected in consequence of the plague of 433 B.C. Augustus, who had a special devotion to him, partly owing to the nearness of the battle of Actium to one of his temples, erected a magnificent temple on the Palatine (thus receiving him *intra pomerium*), to which the celebrated library was attached. Thenceforward, under the Empire, Apollo Palatinus was in some sort the equal of Jupiter Optimus Maximus. See Wissowa, *RK* 293 ff. *See also* DELPHIC ORACLE, OMPHALOS; STONES, SACRED.

9. Besides the appropriate sections and articles of the handbooks and dictionaries of mythology, see, for the cult, etc., of Apollo, L. R. Farnell, *Cults of the Greek States* iv (1907), 98 ff., cited above as 'Farnell'; *see also* ARISTEAS (1). H. J. R.

APOLLODOREANS (*Apollodorei*), followers of Apollodorus (q.v. 5) from Pergamum. He belonged to the older and stricter Attic school, and taught Octavian rhetoric (Suet. *Aug.* 89; Tac. *Dial.* 19). His followers are mentioned by Quintilian, *Inst.* 2. 11. 2; 3. 1. 18. They insisted on rigidly observing rhetorical rules and on retaining in order four indispensable parts of a legal speech, *prooemium, narratio, argumentatio, peroratio*, whereas their opponents, the Theodoreans (q.v.), keen on political oratory, claimed that rules depended on circumstances and that *argumentatio* was essential. The Apollodorean method emphasized explanatory *narratio* (q.v.) in speeches (Sen. *Controv.* 2. 1. 36) and contrasted with that of the *Theodorei*, who did not think clearness and brevity always advisable (Quint. *Inst.* 4. 2. 32).

See M. Schanz, 'Die Apollodoreer und die Theodoreer', *Hermes* xxv (1890). J. W. D.

APOLLODORUS (1) (5th c. B.C.), painter, of Athens. Pliny dates him 408 B.C., but he must have been painting by 430, if Zeuxis (q.v.) 'entered the door opened by

Apollodorus'. He was the first to represent appearance (*species*) and was known as σκιαγράφος. Σκιαγραφία, common in Plato for illusionistic painting, means primarily plastic shading by gradation of colour; on vases shading is not used for human figures until 425–400. Although only two of his pictures are mentioned, his importance was fully recognized in antiquity.

Overbeck, 1641–7; Pfuhl, 734; R. G. Steven, *CQ* 1933, 150; A. Rumpf, *JDAI* 1934, 10. T. B. L. W.

APOLLODORUS (2) of Gela. New Comedy poet, contemporary of Menander according to Suidas. He has been identified with Apollodorus (q.v. 3) of Carystus, but Pollux 10. 138 and inscriptional evidence (see E. Capps, *AJPhil.* xxi. 45) prove his separate existence.

FCG iv. 438 ff.; *CAF* iii. 278 ff. W. G. W.

APOLLODORUS (3) of Carystus, New Comedy poet, more famous than Apollodorus (q.v. 2) of Gela, and sometimes referred to simply as Apollodorus. Apollodorus 'the Athenian comic poet' composed forty-seven dramas and won five victories (Suidas); probably Apollodorus of Carystus obtained Athenian citizenship. A contemporary of Posidippus, he produced his first play *c.* 285 B.C. Ἑκύρα was the original of Terence's *Hecyra*: Ἐπιδικαζόμενος, of Terence's *Phormio*. Terence frequently translated the Greek *verbatim* (Donatus)— evidence of his high opinion of the Greek poet. Fr. 5, the folly of war; fr. 7, whimsical humour.

FCG iv. 440 ff.; *CAF* iii. 280 ff. See E. F. Krause, *De Apollodoris Comicis* (1903); M. Schuster, *De Apollodoris Poetis Comicis* (1907). W. G. W.

APOLLODORUS (4) of Alexandria, physician and scientist of the beginning of the third century B.C. His chief work, Περὶ θηρίων or Λόγος θηριακός (on poisonous creatures), was the primary source for all the later pharmacologists of antiquity (e.g. Numenius, Nicander, Heraclides of Tarentum, Sostratus, Aelian, Sextius Niger, Pliny, Dioscorides, Archigenes, Aemilius Macer). He seems also to have written a work Περὶ θανασίμων (or δηλητηρίων) φαρμάκων.

Frs. in O. Schneider, *Nicandrea*, 181 ff. *PW* i. 2895. W. D. R.

APOLLODORUS (5) of Pergamum (*c.* 104–22 B.C.), rhetor who taught Octavianus and others at Rome. His Τέχνη, dedicated to C. Matius, was translated into Latin by C. Valgius Rufus; but his real influence was due to his oral teaching, which was challenged by Theodorus (q.v. 3) of Gadara. Both followed Hermagoras; but whereas to Apollodorus rhetoric was a science (ἐπιστήμη) with fixed rules, to Theodorus it was an art (τέχνη) with freer methods. This clash of theories, influenced by the opposition of Analogy and Anomaly in grammar, was keenly debated during the first century A.D. (*see* RHETORIC, LATIN, para. 3). J. W. H. A.

APOLLODORUS (6) of Athens (b. *c.* 180 B.C.), pupil of Aristarchus, left Alexandria (*c.* 146 B.C.), perhaps for Pergamum, and later moved to Athens, where he remained until his death. He was a scholar of great learning and varied interests.

WORKS. 1. Chronological: Χρονικά or Χρονικὴ σύνταξις, dedicated to Attalus II of Pergamum, was written in comic trimeters and dealt in considerable detail with successive periods of history, important incidents, philosophical schools, the life and work of individuals from the fall of Troy (1184 B.C.) to 144 B.C.; later it was continued, not certainly by A. himself, down to 119 B.C. 2. Mythological: *Bibliotheca* (Βιβλιοθήκη), a study of Greek heroic mythology. The extant work of this name, which presents an uncritical summary of the traditional Greek mythology, belongs to the first or second century A.D. 3. Theological: Περὶ θεῶν, a rationalistic account of Greek religion, much used by later writers. 4. Geographical: a commentary on the Homeric Catalogue of

Ships, an important work of scholarship based on Eratosthenes and Demetrius of Scepsis, and containing many quotations from poets and historians and many criticisms of earlier writers; Strabo found it a valuable source for books 8 to 10 of his *Geography*. The Γῆς περίοδος or Περὶ γῆς, a geographical guide-book in comic trimeters, was probably a later forgery. 5. Critical and exegetical: commentaries on Epicharmus and Sophron; these probably included a critical recension of the text. 6. Etymological: Ἐτυμολογίαι or Ἐτυμολογούμενα or Γλῶσσαι.

F. Jacoby, *FGrH* ii. B. 244 and *Apollodors Chronik* (1902); [*Bibliotheca*], R. Wagner in *Mythographi Graeci*, i (1894), J. G. Frazer, with translation (Loeb, 1921); C. Robert, *De Apollodori bibliotheca* (1873); R. Münzel, *De Apollodori περὶ θεῶν libris* (1883). J. F. L.

APOLLODORUS (7) of Damascus, a Greek townplanner and architect who worked at Rome in the first century A.D. He planned the Forum of Trajan and designed, or supervised, the Basilica and Column of Trajan, and other adjacent architecture. When the temple of Venus and Rome was built by Hadrian, he advised that it should be raised on an artificial platform. He was banished by Hadrian in A.D. 129, and later put to death. For his surviving work on *Engines of War* see C. Wescher, *La Poliorcétique des Grecs* (1867), 137 ff. H. W. R.

APOLLODORUS (8) of Seleuceia on the Tigris, Stoic philosopher, the author of an *Ethics* and a *Physics* cited by Diog. Laert. 7. 102, 129; 125, 135. He also wrote logical works. Testimonia in H. von Arnim, *SVF* iii. 259–61.

PW i. 2894.

APOLLONIA was the name of several Greek towns. The chief of these was in Illyria, near the mouths of the rivers Aoüs and Apsus, with relatively easy communications across Mt. Pindus to Thessaly and Macedonia respectively. It was founded as a Corinthian colony by Periander (possibly with an admixture of Corcyraean settlers—Wade-Gery, *CAH* iii. 553 n.). It is rarely mentioned before the Hellenistic period, when it was acquired in turn by Cassander and by Pyrrhus as an outlet on the Adriatic. Its main importance was as a base for Roman expeditionary forces in the Balkans. First occupied by the Romans during the Illyrian War of 229 B.C., it was the starting-point of their Greek and Macedonian campaigns in the second century. After 146 it was one of the terminal points of the Via Egnatia (q.v.), and it was Caesar's head-quarters in the campaign of Dyrrhachium (48). In 45–44 Caesar gathered an army at Apollonia for his Eastern campaigns, and at his death his grand-nephew Octavius was stationed there as a cadet. M. C.

APOLLONIUS (1) **RHODIUS** (3rd c. B.C.) of Alexandria or less probably Naucratis, but generally called the Rhodian owing to his retirement to Rhodes. Born *c.* 295 B.C., A. was a pupil of Callimachus (*Vitae*, Suidas). According to *Vita* i (Mooney, p. 1) he turned late to writing poetry. This conflicts with the following statement of the same authority that A. gave a recitation of the *Argonautica* while still a stripling (ἔτι ἔφηβον ὄντα), was badly received, and retired to Rhodes, where he revised the poem, which then became famous. Unless ἔφηβον is here an error for νεανίσκον, a term used by Tzetzes (Kaibel, *CGF* 31. 13) to describe Callimachus' official position at the court, it is best to regard the story as a tendentious invention. At any rate, *POxy*. 1241, a list of Alexandrian librarians, establishes that A. held that post after Zenodotus and before Eratosthenes. *Vita* ii represents A. as being appointed librarian after his return from Rhodes, but this dating and Suidas' statement that A. succeeded Eratosthenes as librarian probably originate in a confusion with Apollonius the Eidograph, who is now known (from *POxy*. 1241) to

have followed Eratosthenes in this office. On the whole it is likely that A. succeeded Zenodotus as librarian *c.* 260, held the post till the accession of Euergetes in 247, and then retired to Rhodes, where he remained till his death. A.'s famous quarrel with Callimachus may have been caused not only by their differing about the type of Epic suitable to the age, but also by friction at the library, where Callimachus, who was never librarian, was presumably A.'s subordinate.

WORKS. *Verse*. In the fashion of the day A. wrote poems, from which a few hexameters survive, on the Foundation (κτίσις) of Alexandria, Naucratis, Caunus, Cnidos, Rhodes, possibly Lesbos. A poem called *Canobus* was in choliambics. Of his *Epigrams* only *Anth. Pal.* 11. 275, an attack on Callimachus, is extant. A.'s *magnum opus* was the *Argonautica*, narrating the *Argo*'s voyage to Colchis by the Propontis and Black Sea (bks. 1–2), the winning with Medea's aid of the Golden Fleece (bk. 3), and the return by the Danube, Po, Rhône, Mediterranean, and northern Africa (bk. 4). At six places in bk. 1 the scholia cite the version of the *proekdosis* (= the first edition), but the differences from the present text are not important.

Apollonius' vocabulary is mainly taken from Homer, but in the Alexandrian manner he is continually varying and 'interpreting' the Homeric words and phrases. Indeed his greatest achievement as a stylist lies in this subtle adaptation of Homer's language to describe a new world of romantic sentiment. For the subject-matter it is evident that A. consulted a great number of authorities, and the excellent scholia record many of his sources. They include prose-chroniclers as well as poets. It is in fact this passion for completeness which ruins the artistic effect of all but the third book. There, however, in recounting the birth and progress of Medea's love for Jason, A. shakes off the trammels of his erudition and in his subtle and moving analysis of a young girl's first love, attended by many doubts and difficulties, rises to heights which none of his contemporaries, even Theocritus, ever equalled. For the rest A.'s *forte* lies in his similes, his descriptive powers, and on occasion his gift for suggesting atmosphere. His characterization is weak, Jason in particular being a colourless figure, and the poem lacks all unity except that inherent in the theme itself. Metrically A.'s hexameter follows Homer rather than Callimachus.

Prose. A. had some repute as a scholar. A tract of his *Against Zenodotus* is mentioned, also works on Archilochus, Antimachus, and Hesiod.

TEXTS: R. C. Seaton (1929); R. Merkel (1854); C. Wendel, *Scholia Vetera* (1935); Fragments: J. U. Powell, *Collectanea Alexandrina* (1925), 4–8. Text and translation: R. C. Seaton (Loeb, 1912).
COMMENTARIES: G. W. Mooney (1912); M. M. Gillies (*Bk. 3*, 1928).
GENERAL: G. Knaack, 'Apollonios (71)', in *PW* ii. 126–34; Christ-Schmid-Stählin ii. 1⁶ (1920), 140–6. E. A. B.

APOLLONIUS (2) of Perga (*c.* 262–190 B.C.), called the 'great geometer' (Geminus ap. Eutocius), was born at Perga in Pamphylia. He spent a long time in Alexandria studying with the successors of Euclid during the reign of Ptolemy Euergetes (247–222). He visited Ephesus and Pergamum, where he stayed with Eudemus of Pergamum, to whom he dedicated the first three books of his *Conics* in a second and improved edition; the first edition in eight books he had presented, as he says, prematurely, to Naucrates, a geometer at whose instance he had taken up the subject. The fourth and remaining books were dedicated, after Eudemus' death, to King Attalus I (241–197 B.C.).

Of the *Conics* four books survive in Greek, and three more in Arabic; the eighth is lost. Serenus and (according to Suidas) Hypatia wrote commentaries on it; Pappus added a number of lemmas. Eutocius' commentary on the first four books is included in the definitive edition of the Greek text by J. L. Heiberg (Teubner, 1891–3). The first important edition was the Latin translation of the first four books by Commandinus (Bologna, 1566) which included the lemmas of Pappus and Eutocius' commentary. The *editio princeps* of the Greek text is that of Edmund Halley (1710), which includes also a Latin translation of books 5–7 from the Arabic version by Thâbit b. Qurra (826–901). [A fragment of book 5 (up to Prop. 7) was edited by L. Nix (Leipzig, 1889).]

Previous writers on conic sections had generated them from separate right circular cones, 'right-angled', 'acute-', and 'obtuse-angled' respectively. Apollonius was the first to produce all three from the most general cone, right or oblique; he expressed their fundamental properties in terms of the traditional 'application of areas'; hence the names *parabola* (παραβολή), ellipse (ἔλλειψις), and *hyperbola* (ὑπερβολή) first given to the curves by Apollonius. Books 1–4 he describes as an elementary introduction; books 5–7 are specialized investigations; book 5 (on normals) is the most difficult and advanced, including propositions which lead immediately to the determination of the *evolute* of any conic.

Pappus (bk. 7) describes shortly the contents of six other treatises by Apollonius, each in two books. (1) *Λόγου ἀποτομή*, *Cutting-off of a ratio*: this alone survives, in Arabic (Latin translation by Halley, 1706): (2) *Χωρίου ἀποτομή*, *Cutting-off of an area*: (3) *Διωρισμένη τομή*, *Determinate section*: (4) *'Επαφαί*, *Tangencies*, (5) *Τόποι ἐπίπεδοι*, *Plane Loci*, (6) *Νεύσεις*, *Inclinationes* or *Vergings*. There have been many attempted restorations, e.g. of (5) by Fermat, van Schooten, and Robert Simson, of (6) by Marino Ghetaldi, Alex. Anderson, and Samuel Horsley (1770). The great problem of (4)—the drawing of a circle to touch three given circles—has attracted the most distinguished mathematicians; Vieta (1540–1603), van Roomen (1561–1615), and Newton (in *Arithmetica universalis*) gave solutions of it. Apollonius also wrote a *Comparison of the dodecahedron with the icosahedron* (v. Hypsicles, pref. to 'Eucl. bk. 14'), a *General Treatise*, *Καθόλου πραγματεία* (v. Marinus on Euclid's *Data*), and works on the *Cylindrical Helix* (Κοχλίας), on the *Burning-Mirror* (Περὶ τοῦ πυρίου), and on *Unordered Irrationals* (v. schol. on Eucl. 10. 1). An arithmetical work, *'Ωκυτόκιον* ('quick delivery'), calculated limits closer than those of Archimedes to the value of π. Apollonius invented a system (of 'tetrads') for expressing large numbers as the sum of units and successive powers of the myriad (10,000), *see* PAPPUS; he showed how to work with a system in which (practically) 10,000 is substituted for 10 as the base of the scale of notation.

In astronomy Apollonius was an exponent, if not the inventor, of the hypotheses of eccentric circles and epicycles respectively.

Editions of the *Conics*, other than those above mentioned, include: a German translation by A. Czwalina (1926), T. L. Heath, *Apollonius of Perga*, *Treatise on Conic Sections*, in modern notation (1896), H. G. Zeuthen, *Die Lehre von den Kegelschnitten im Altertum* (1886), Paul ver Eecke, *Les Coniques d'Apollonius de Perge, œuvres traduites pour la première fois du grec en français avec une introduction et des notes*.   T. H.

APOLLONIUS (3) (3rd c. B.C.), the finance minister of Egypt for about twenty years from 262 B.C., held an estate of some three square miles at Philadelphia in the Fayûm; it was reclaimed land, tenable at the king's will. His development of the estate can be traced from the correspondence of Zenon, his right-hand man; he was specially interested in the improvement of live-stock, horticulture, and viticulture. He had extensive business operations in Egypt and the Levant and owned a merchant fleet, as is shown by the same correspondence; there is also mention in it of properties in Alexandria and at Memphis which he seems to have possessed. Zenon, a Carian from Caunus, entered his service soon after his appointment to office, and settled at Philadelphia probably in 256; thereafter he managed Apollonius' estates, and acquired businesses of his own, which he carried on for some years after Apollonius disappears as a landholder at Philadelphia (c. 242). Of his associates the most important was Cleon, an engineer employed in the reclamation of the Fayûm, whose works are recorded in other papyri besides those of Zenon.

M. Rostovtzeff, *A Large Estate in Egypt* (1922); *Social and Economic History of the Hellenistic World* (1941); C. C. Edgar, *Zenon Papyri in the University of Michigan Collection* (1931).
                                                                        J. G. M.

APOLLONIUS (4) (2nd c. B.C.) of Alabanda, ὁ μαλακός, a pupil of Menecles of Alabanda. He founded a school of rhetoric at Rhodes, visited by Scaevola (121 B.C.) and M. Antonius (98 B.C.).

APOLLONIUS (5) perhaps of the 2nd c. B.C., author of *'Ιστορίαι θαυμάσιαι*, a compilation from Aristotle, Theophrastus, Aristoxenus, etc.

Ed. O. Keller, *Rerum Naturalium Scriptores* i. 43–56. *PW* Suppl. iv. 45.

APOLLONIUS (6) (1st c. B.C.), sculptor, son of Archias, of Athens. Known from signature in Athens and on bronze herm of Polyclitus' Doryphorus (Winter, *KB* 393. 3); three other herms from the same villa in Herculaneum are probably also his.

APOLLONIUS (7), sculptor, son of Artemidorus, brother of Tauriscus (q.v. 2).

APOLLONIUS (8), sculptor, son of Nestor, of Athens. Works: 1. Belvedere torso in the Vatican (Winter, *KB* 394. 2), perhaps the Amycus on Roman coins of Sparta. 2. Bronze boxer in the Terme (Winter, *KB* 339. 1). Both are new creations, combining Hellenistic realism with classical reminiscence. The signatures are dated about 50 B.C. Apollonius may also have made the cult statue of Jupiter Capitolinus, dedicated 69 B.C., which is reflected in small bronzes.   T. B. L. W.

APOLLONIUS (9), sculptor, son of Tauriscus (q.v.); late first century B.C.

APOLLONIUS (10) of Citium, an Alexandrian physician of about 50 B.C. Works: (extant) commentary on Hippocrates *Περὶ ἄρθρων*; (lost) *Πρὸς τὰ τοῦ Ταραντίνου* (against Heraclides); *Πρὸς Βακχεῖον*; *Curationes*.

Ed. H. Schöne, 1896. *PW* ii. 149.

APOLLONIUS (11) **MOLON** (1st c. B.C.), rhetor, a native of Alabanda and pupil of Menecles. He lectured at Rhodes, visited Rome (87 and 81 B.C.), taught Cicero and other Romans, and won success as a pleader. He wrote on rhetoric and attacked both philosophers (*K. φιλοσόφων*) and Jews (*K. 'Ιουδαίων*).   J. W. H. A.

APOLLONIUS (12) **MYS**, member of the Herophilean school of medicine, worked for many years in Alexandria, towards the end of the first century B.C. He wrote *Περὶ τῆς 'Ηροφίλου αἱρέσεως*, *Περὶ εὐπορίστων φαρμάκων*, and *Περὶ μύρων*.

PW ii. 149.

APOLLONIUS (13) **SOPHISTA** (c. A.D. 100) compiled a *Lexicon Homericum* which is extant in an abridged form (ed. I. Bekker, 1833). A fragment of the unabridged work survives in a Bodleian papyrus. He used especially the commentaries of Aristarchus, on whose critical method he throws valuable light, and the glossary of Apion.   J. F. L.

APOLLONIUS (14) of Tyana (*'Απολλώνιος ὁ Τυανεύς*), a Neopythagorean sage. According to our only full account, Philostratus' *Τὰ ἐς τὸν Τυανέα 'Απολλώνιον* (time of Septimius Severus, see Rose, *Handb. of Gk. Lit.*

403, W. Nestle, *Griechische Religiosität*, iii. 123 ff.), he was born at Tyana in Cappadocia, apparently about the beginning of the Christian era, and survived into the Principate of Nerva (for other datings, and the few known facts about him, see J. Miller in *PW* ii. 146 ff.). He led the life of an ascetic wandering teacher, possessed miraculous powers, visited distant lands, including India, was in danger of his life under Nero and again under Domitian, and saw by clairvoyance the latter's death (Philostr. 8. 25–6, cf. Cassius Dio 67. 18). Philostratus is highly untrustworthy (cf. W. R. Halliday, *Folklore Studies* (1924), last essay), and references elsewhere scanty; but Apollonius' existence and Pythagoreanism need not be doubted. An anti-Christian writer, Hierocles of Nicomedia, paralleled Apollonius with Christ, which provoked a reply (extant) from Eusebius. Of his writings (see Suidas, s.v., p. 623 Bernhardy) there survive some doubtfully authentic letters and a fragment of his treatise *On Sacrifices* (Τελεταὶ ἢ περὶ θυσιῶν).   H. J. R.

APOLLONIUS (15), son of Mnesitheus, named *Dyscolus*, of Alexandria (2nd c. A.D.). Of his life little is known, except from his works: these are distinguished, even among grammarians, for obscurity of style and asperity of manner; but his method is genuinely critical, and his zeal for correcting errors extends to his own (cf. *Syntax*, p. 231. 15 Bekk.). For the history of grammar from Dionysius Thrax to his own day he is our chief source of information.

Of his twenty-nine works, mostly on syntax, named in Suidas, four survive—on the *Pronoun, Conjunction, Adverb*, and *Syntax*. A conspectus of his doctrines is given in the *Syntax*, which deals mainly with Article, Pronoun, Verb, Preposition, and Adverb, successively. He approaches syntax from the parts of speech, not the sentence, beginning with the establishment of the 'correct' order of these, assuming that there must be a proper order for them as there is, in his view, for the alphabet; and he has much argument disproving such current opinions as that the function of the article is to distinguish genders, and that ὦ is its vocative. As a result, although he correctly settles many details, acutely arguing from function, not form, he nevertheless achieves no comprehensive, organic, system of syntax. His work is marked by a constant quest for principle. 'We must investigate what *produces* solecisms, and not merely adduce examples.' '*Why* do some verbs take the genitive, not the accusative?' In discussing forms and constructions he makes much use of alleged ἀναλογία (*see* CRATES OF MALLOS), e.g. insisting on ἵμι, not εἶμι, by 'analogy' from the plural and dual; also τεθείκωμαι (pf. pass. subj.). He also makes use of what he recognizes to be false analogy (συνεκδρομή), as when he explains that the usage γράφει τὰ παιδία (nominative) is permitted because it sounds the same as when παιδία is accusative, in which case the syntax is normal.

His own syntax shows both extreme carelessness, e.g. in bad order, pleonasm, ellipse, and anacoluthon, and also the idioms of his day, e.g. ἐὰν c. indic., εἰ c. subjunct., increased confusion of negatives (ἐπεὶ μή constantly), and odd uses of conjunctions and prepositions. He had a wide knowledge of literature and was familiar with Latin. Inevitably, perhaps, he falls short of the comparative and historical methods available, if not always adopted, to-day. But it would be hard to overestimate his influence on later Greek and Latin grammarians, notably Priscian, or to quarrel with Priscian's tribute, 'maximus auctor artis grammaticae'.

Edition, by Uhlig and Schneider in Teubner's *Grammatici Graeci*. E. Egger, *Apollonius Dyscole: Essai sur l'hist. d. théories gramm. dans l'antiquité* (1854).   P. B. R. F.

APOLLONIUS (16) of Tyre, the hero of an anonymous romance widely known in the Middle Ages. The oldest extant version (5th–6th c. A.D.) is in Latin, *Historia*

Apollonii regis Tyri; but matter and style suggest that there was a Greek original of the second to third century A.D.

Text and Prolegomena: ed. Riese (Teubner). *See also* NOVEL, LATIN.   R. M. R.

APOLLOPHANES, according to Suidas an Athenian comic writer. Once victorious, c. 400 B.C. (*IG* ii². 2325). In the Κρῆτες a character is introduced apparently speaking Doric.

FCG i. 266–7; *CAF* i. 797 ff.; Demiańczuk, *Supp. Com.* 9.

APOPHRADES, unlucky, forbidden days, characterized by gloomy rites (Plato, *Leg.* 800 d), e.g. the Plynteria (Plut. *Alc.* 34), on which no assembly or court was held. Such were also the last two days of the Anthesteria, on which the dead visited their old houses and people chewed buckthorn and smeared the doors with pitch to protect themselves. They were properly called μιαραὶ ἡμέραι as opposed to καθαραί.

E. Rohde, *Psyche* i. 237, n. 3.   M. P. N.

APOTHEOSIS, *see* RULER-CULT.

APPARITORES, public servants who attended Roman magistrates (cf. *apparere*). The most important classes were *scribae, lictores, viatores* (qq.v.), *accensi*, and *praecones*. They were generally freedmen or sons of freedmen. They received an annual salary from the State. Although their appointment was technically annual, they were soon permitted to retain their posts indefinitely. They formed corporations which were legally recognized by the State. It is uncertain whether the *apparitores* wore any characteristic uniform.

Mommsen, *Röm. Staatsr.* i³. 332 ff.; P. Habel, *PW*, s.v.   P. T.

APPELLATIO. As an institution of the Roman civil procedure *appellatio* was introduced (according to the prevalent opinion) only in the latest form of classical proceedings, the *cognitio extra ordinem*. The judgement of the private *iudex* in Republican times was not subject to appeal. The oldest not unquestionable records of civil appeal date from the times of the first emperors. *Appellatio* is the act by which a litigant disputes a judgement, and its effect is that the controversy is brought before a higher magistrate, normally before the one who appointed the magistrate of the lower instance. *Appellatio* in its developed phase had to be effected either orally (the pronouncing of the word *appello* sufficed) or in writing (*libelli appellatorii*) at the court of the magistrate whose decision was impugned; he was then obliged to transmit all the documents in the case to the competent higher magistrate with a written report (*litterae dimissoriae, apostoli*). Judgement was given after a new trial in which fresh evidence was admitted. The appellate judge could confirm or reverse the judgement of the lower court, or alter it as he thought fit, even in favour of the respondent. A frivolous appellant had to pay to his adversary four times the costs of the appeal proceedings. Constantine punished him by relegation *in insulam* and confiscation of half of his property. Justinian reverted to mere pecuniary sanctions. His legislation reformed the institution thoroughly (many of its norms have passed into modern legislation); and his *Nov.* 82 settled the rule that all judgements except those of the praetorian prefect are appealable.

In the widest sense *appellatio* is any recourse to a higher magistrate for the alteration or abolition of a decree of a lower one. In this sense the term is used with respect to ordinary administrative decisions of magistrates and judgements delivered in criminal cases. In the language of the later classical jurisprudence (since Scaevola) the term *appellatio* is used indiscriminately with *provocatio* (cf. *Dig.* 49. 1 and *Cod. Iust.* 7. 62), the proper field of which in former times was criminal jurisdiction. Thus imperial constitutions speak of *appellatio* or *provocatio* against a nomination as *decurio* or *scriba* (*Cod. Just.* 7. 62. 4. 7).

E. Perrot, *L'Appel dans la procédure de l'ordo iudiciorum privatorum* (1907); C. Sanfilippo, *Contributi esegetici alla storia dell'appellazione* i (1934); H. F. Jolowicz, *Histor. Introduction to the Study of Roman Law* (1932), 406, 459. For criminal procedure: Mommsen, *Röm. Strafr.* (1899), 275 ff., 468 ff.; J. L. Strachan-Davidson, *Problems of the Roman Criminal Law* (1912), ii. 176 ff. A. B.

APPENDIX VERGILIANA According to Suetonius (ed. Reifferscheid, p. 58) Virgil wrote in his youth *Catalepton, Priapea, Epigrammata, Dirae, Ciris, Culex,* and *Aetna*. Servius (A.D. 400) adds the *Copa*. A ninth-century library catalogue mentions a Virgilian MS. containing also the *Moretum* and the post-Virgilian *Elegiae in Maecenatem*. Evidently the *Epigrammata* belong to the *Catalepton*.

1. The *Catalepton* (κατὰ λεπτόν, (?) 'trifles') contains fourteen short, for the greater part charming little poems, differing in metre and contents; an epilogue, possibly by the publisher, is sometimes added as a fifteenth. There are those who take all the poems to be Virgil's; others again consider them spurious. It is generally admitted that numbers 9, 13, 14 (in Vollmer's edition) were not composed by Virgil. There is reasonable certainty that numbers 1, 3, 5, 7, 8 are Virgilian and the rest are perhaps his.

2. *Priapea* (3), to which Pliny (*Ep.* 5. 3. 2) may allude, when he ascribes 'uersiculos seueros parum' also to Virgil.

3. *Dirae* ('maledictions'), called down by an unknown poet upon an estate from which he was expelled by a veteran when the arable land was distributed.

4. *Lydia*, an elegy (in the MSS. united with the preceding poem) in which the poet (most probably the same as the author of the *Dirae*) mourns the absence of his beloved.

5. *Ciris*, a Hellenistic epyllion, relating how Scylla, daughter of King Nisus of Megara, became the cause of her father's death, because she had conceived love for Minos, her country's enemy. The gods changed her into a sea-bird called Ciris. The *Ciris* is probably neither the work of Cornelius Gallus nor a youthful poem of Virgil's (see Bibliography, below). It contains elements drawn from Lucretius and Catullus and lavishly uses Virgilian verses and phrases. Though on the whole rather clumsy, it contains some fine psychological pictures.

6. *Culex*. A shepherd kills a gnat that has stung him to warn him against a snake. Later on, the insect's ghost blames him for his ingratitude and explains the torments and the blessings of the nether world. Lucan (Suet. *Vita Luc.* p. 50 Reiff.), Statius (*Silv.* 1. praef.) and Martial (8. 56. 20) mention a Virgilian *Culex*. Following Donatus, who tells us that Virgil wrote the *Culex* when sixteen, some assume that our poem is an immature work of the poet's youth which he published later with a dedication to Octavius before June 44 B.C.; for after that date Octavius was named Octavianus. The verse-structure, however, which points to a later period of Augustan poetry, the stilted, obscure language, some vulgar forms, and the indubitable imitation of Virgilian phrases (cf. *Cul.* 275 and *Aen.* 6. 431; *Cul.* 292 and *Ecl.* 8. 48) prove the *Culex* to be a spurious poem that shortly after Ovid's time was attributed to Virgil.

7. *Copa*, 'the Hostess'. An elegy bubbling over with the joy of life, too cheerful, however, to allow ascription to Virgil.

8. *Moretum*, 'Salad', relates the way in which a farmer prepares his breakfast on a dark winter morning. The poem charms by its unadorned realism. Poet unknown.

9. *Aetna*: see article AETNA.

BIBLIOGRAPHY
TEXTS: O.C.T. (Ellis), Teubner (*PLM* i, Vollmer).
COMMENTARIES: Catalepton, Th. Birt, *Jugendverse und Heimatpoesie Vergils* (1910); E. Galletier, *Epigrammata et Priapea* (1920); Dirae, Lydia, A. F. Naeke, *Carm. Valerii Catonis* (1847); Ciris, M. Lenchantin de Gubernatis (1930); R. Helm (1937); Culex, F. Leo (1891); Ch. Plésent (1910).
TRANSLATION: H. R. Fairclough, with text, Loeb (*Virgil* ii).
STUDIES OF THE APPENDIX: A. Rostagni, *Virgilio Minore* (1933). Dirae, P. J. Enk, *Mnemos.* 1919, 382; Ciris, F. Skutsch, *Aus Vergils Frühzeit* (1901, by Gallus); R. Helm, *Hermes* 1937, 78, (post-Virgilian); Culex, Ch. Plésent, *Le Culex: Étude sur l'alexandrinisme latin* (1910, spurious); E. S. Jackson, *CQ* 1911, 163 (Virgil's); W. Holtschmidt, *De Culicis sermone et tempore* (1913, spurious). P. J. E.

APPIAN (*Appianos*) of Alexandria, born at latest under Trajan, experienced the Jewish rising of A.D. 116, held office in Alexandria, and after gaining Roman citizenship moved to Rome, becoming a knight, probably *advocatus fisci*, and, through the influence of Fronto, *procurator Augusti*; an old man under Antoninus Pius, he then wrote his 'Ρωμαϊκά. Ethnographic in arrangement, this work treated in turn the Roman conquests: Bk. i Βασιλική, ii 'Ιταλική, iii Σαυνιτική, iv Κελτική, v Σικελικὴ καὶ Νησιωτική, vi 'Ιβηρική, vii 'Αννιβαϊκή, viii Λιβυκή (Καρχηδονιακή, Νομαδική), ix Μακεδονικὴ καὶ 'Ιλλυρική, x 'Ελληνικὴ καὶ 'Ιωνική, xi Συριακή, xii Μιθριδάτειος; xiii–xvii 'Εμφυλίων (the Civil Wars, bks. 1–5); xviii–xxi Αἰγυπτιακῶν (the conquest of Egypt); xxii 'Εκατονταετία, xxiii Δακική, xxiv 'Αράβιος (the Empire to Trajan and the Dacian and Arabian campaigns). The final Παρθικὴ γραφή was not written. Bks. vi–ix, xi–xvii are complete, except for Νομαδική (viii) and Μακεδονική (ix), which with i–v are fragmentary; x, xviii–xxiv are lost.

The extant tradition goes back ultimately, in its successive parts, to an early annalist (perhaps Cassius Hemina), Polybius, Posidonius, Fannius (possibly), Sallust, Asinius Pollio, Livy, the memoirs of Augustus and Messalla, possibly Nicolaus of Damascus; but it came immediately from the tendentious, constitutionalistic, literary composition of an imperial annalist, writing under Augustus or Tiberius, whom Appian adapted to his ethnographic form. Loyal and honest, an admirer of Roman imperialism, he wrote in the plain κοινή, and though interested solely in wars and ignorant of Republican institutions and conditions, preserves much valuable material, most notably in bk. 1 of the *Civil Wars*.

Texts: L. Mendelssohn (1879–81); P. Viereck, *Bell. Civ.* (1905); H. E. White (1912–13, Loeb). E. Schwartz, *PW* ii. 217; J. Carcopino, *Autour des Gracques* (1928), ch. 1; A. Klotz, *Appians Darstellung des zweiten Punischen Krieges* (1936). A. H. McD.

APPIUS, see CLAUDIUS.

APPULEIUS, see SATURNINUS.

APRIES (*Hophra*), fourth pharaoh (589–570 B.C.) of the Saite XXVIth dynasty, relied like his predecessors on Ionian and Carian mercenaries. He made unsuccessful attempts to conquer Phoenicia and Cyrene, and was overthrown by a rising against his mercenaries which set Amasis on the throne.
Herodotus 2. 161 f., 4. 159. P. N. U.

APSINES of Gadara (c. A.D. 190–250), Athenian rhetor and rival of a certain Fronto of Emesa, author of Π. σχημάτων, Ζητήματα, and Μελέται. His Τέχνη (Spengel, *Rhet.* i. 331–414), which has come down with many interpolations, owed much to Hermogenes and is the latest complete τέχνη to survive. J. W. H. A.

APULEIUS, born (c. A.D. 123) of wealthy parents at Madauros in Africa (August. *De Civ. D.* 8. 14), was educated first at Carthage (*Flor.* 18), later at Athens (*Apol.* 72). After much travel (*Apol.* 23) he apparently visited Rome (*Met.* 11), whence he returned to Africa. Later setting forth on a journey to Egypt he fell sick at Oea (*Tripoli*) c. A.D. 155, where he was visited by an old friend, Sicinius Pontianus; the latter was anxious about his widowed mother Pudentilla, now betrothed to her brother-in-law, Sicinius Clarus. Pontianus, being on bad terms with his uncle, proposed to A. that he should marry Pudentilla; after some hesitation, A., finding the widow wealthy and attractive, took her to wife. Sicinius Aemilianus (brother of Sicinius Clarus) accused A. of having won her love by magic. The case was tried at Sabrata before the proconsul, Claudius Maximus. A. defended himself with vigour (*Apologia*) and was acquitted, but left Oea for more congenial surroundings. He is next heard of at Carthage, enjoying renown as poet, philosopher, and rhetorician (c. A.D. 161). He was appointed chief priest of the province (*Flor.* 16), and delivered many florid declamations after the manner of the rhetoricians of the 'second Sophistic'. Statues were erected in his honour at Carthage and at Madauros (the base of the latter has been discovered). He may have had a son named Faustinus. The date of his death is uncertain.

WORKS. (1) *Apologia* (or *Pro se de Magia*) is one of the most interesting and certainly the oddest of all Latin speeches. At times an almost childish display of wild rhetoric and shallow sciolism, at times a vigorous and skilful defence, it gives a unique description of provincial life and throws a curious light on superstitions of the age. For its theme see above.

(2) The *Metamorphoses* (better known as 'The Golden Ass') is the sole Latin novel that survives entire. A delightful work, imaginative, humorous, and exciting, it tells the adventures of one Lucius who, being too curious concerning the black art, is accidentally turned into an ass, and thus disguised, endures, sees, and hears many strange things. He is at last restored to human shape by the goddess Isis. At the outset a Greek (1. 1), at the close he is identified with A. himself (11. 27), and the story of his initiations into the mysteries of Isis and Osiris is probably autobiographical. Many stories are embedded in the novel, the most famous being the exquisite tale of Cupid and Psyche (4. 28–6. 24). A briefer version of the novel, falsely attributed to Lucian, also exists (Λούκιος ἢ ὄνος). Both works probably derive from the same original, the lost *Metamorphoses* of Lucius of Patras (Photius 96 b, 12 Bekker). The story of Cupid and Psyche may be an adaptation of the Greek of 'Aristofontes Atheneus' (Fulg. *Myth.* 3. 6). The date is uncertain (an early work according to Purser, late (c. A.D. 180) according to Helm).

(3) The *Florida* are excerpts from declamations on varied themes, mainly trivial and showing an extravagance typical of the author. They contain much that is curious and amusing, while the description of the death of the comic poet Philemon has real beauty. They were largely composed between A.D. 160 and 170.

(4) The *De Dogmate Platonis*, an exposition of the philosophy of Plato, showing neither knowledge nor understanding. Bk. 1 deals with P.'s life and physical doctrine; bk. 2 (dedicated to 'my son Faustinus') sets forth his ethics. Bk. 3, in which he promised to deal with his dialectic, is missing; some have held that the Περὶ ἑρμηνείας, a treatise on formal logic, is the third book, but it is regarded by others as spurious.

(5) The *De Deo Socratis* is a flamboyant declamation on the δαιμόνιον of Socrates, probably based on a Greek original.

(6) The *De Mundo* is a translation of the Περὶ κόσμου falsely attributed to Aristotle; it too is dedicated to Faustinus.

(7) *A Latin translation* of a passage from Menander's Ἀνεχόμενος: Baehrens, *PLM* iv. 104.

(8) *Lost Works:* Poems (*Apol.* 6, 9; *Flor.* 9, 17, 18, 20); Speeches (*Apol.* 24, 55; *Flor.* 16; August. *Ep.* 138. 19); *Quaestiones Naturales*, *De Piscibus* (*Apol.* 36, 38, 40), *De Re Rustica*, *De Arboribus*, *Astronomica*, *Arithmetica*;

De Republica, *De Proverbiis*; *Epitome Historiarum*; *Eroticus*; *Quaestiones Conviviales*; a translation of Plato's *Phaedo*; a novel entitled *Hermagoras* (Priscian, *Gramm. Lat.* 2. p. 85).

(9) *Spuria: Asclepius, Herbarius, De Remediis Salutaribus, Physiognomonia*.

The style of A. is a development of Asianism (*see* RHETORIC), which finds its nearest parallel in Pliny (*HN* 9. 102; 10. 3; 10. 81). There is no justification for calling it African Latin. It is florid and extravagant, richly coloured with poetry, full of strange words, Graecisms, archaisms (*see* ARCHAISM), and idioms drawn from colloquial Latin; its fullest and most perfect development is seen in the *Metamorphoses*, where it finds appropriate scope and at times rises to great heights of beauty (e.g. *Met.* 11. 1). The works of A. are tinged throughout by his personality—a rhetorician posing as philosopher, peacock-proud and full of an immense store of undigested and superficial learning. But his novel won him deserved renown. Indeed St. Augustine was not certain that he had not actually been turned into an ass, and warns the faithful against those who extol him as a thaumaturge whose powers surpassed those of Christ himself (*Ep.* 136. 1; 138).

TEXTS: Met., R. Helm (1907, 1912, 1931); Apol., R. Helm (1905); Flor., R. Helm (1910). De Deo Soc., Asclep., De Dog. Plat., De Mundo, Περὶ ἑρμηνείας, P. Thomas (1908). Herbarius, E. Howald and H. E. Sigerist, *CML* iv (1927).
COMMENTARIES: complete, F. Oudendorp (1764 (1823)), G. F. Hildebrand (1842). Apol., H. E. Butler and A. S. Owen (1914); C. Marchesi (1914). Cupid and Psyche, L. C. Purser (1910).
TRANSLATIONS: Apol. and Flor., H. E. Butler (1909); P. Vallette (1924). Met., W. Adlington (1566 and (revised by S. Gaselee) 1915); H. E. Butler (1910).
STYLE: *Die antike Kunstprosa*, E. Norden (1898); M. Bernhard, *Der Stil des A.* (1927); *Index Apuleianus*, W. Oldfather, etc. (U.S.A. 1934).   H. E. B.

APULIA, a rather unhealthy region of south-eastern Italy (cf. Varro, *Rust.* 1. 6), extending from Mons Garganus to Calabria; nowadays *Puglia*. Its arid soil is fertile, especially in the coastal and northern plains; southern Apulia contains numerous hills, including Mons Vultur. Apulian wool was famous, summer migration of flocks having been practised there continuously since early times (Varro, *Rust.* 2. 1; Pliny, *HN* 8. 190). Its inhabitants were indiscriminately called Apuli; they included Messapic-speaking Peucetii and Daunii as well as Apuli proper who dwelt about Mons Garganus and spoke Oscan (Strabo 6. 283 f.). Although lacking Greek colonies, Apulia was much hellenized by 300 B.C. Between 326 and 317 it became subject to Rome, largely voluntarily, and remained loyal against Pyrrhus (Livy 8. 25, 37; 9. 12. 9 f., 20; Zonar. 8. 5). In the Hannibalic and Social Wars, however, many Apulians revolted (Livy 22. 61; Appian, *BCiv.* 1. 39); the consequent devastation ruined Apulia. Chief towns: Teanum, Sipontum, Luceria, Arpi, Herdonia, Venusia, Canusium, Barium.

R. S. Conway, *Italic Dialects* i (1897), 22.   E. T. S.

AQUAE ET IGNIS INTERDICTIO, *see* EXSILIUM.

AQUAE SULIS (modern *Bath*) attained importance since the first century A.D. from its hot springs. The water was led to a partly underground oblong building containing a great bath (73 ft. by 29 ft.) and three other swimming-baths. Hot air baths, stoked by coal-fires, were later added at either end. To the north were at least two porticoed courtyards, one containing the temple of Sul Minerva; Corinthian pilasters and fragments of the pediment (25 ft. wide) are extant, the latter containing the famous Gorgon sculpture. Though a small place (25 acres), Bath was visited even by continentals. It was completely destroyed by the Saxons, and the bath establishment was choked up and forgotten.

F. J. Haverfield in *VCH* (*Somerset*) i. 219–88; W. H. Knowles, *Archaeologia* lxxv. 1–18.   C. E. S.

AQUEDUCTS are justly regarded as one of Rome's most distinctive contributions to architecture and hygiene. Rome's first aqueducts, Aquae Appia (312 B.C.) and Anio Vetus (272 B.C.), were tunnelled, no doubt owing much to inherited experience drawn from making the far older drainage-channels (*cuniculi*) and emissaries cut in the soft tufaceous Latian valley-floor. Possibly this experience weighed with the builders even more than military considerations, which favoured the hidden underground channel. Such tunnels, like early railway tunnels, were cut in short lengths reached by vertical shafts, which later served for inspection and cleaning. To cross ravines and narrow valleys or to reach elevated points a conduit carried on arches was required, short bridges occurring sparingly on the Anio Vetus, as at Ponte Taulella, long arched sectors for the first time upon Aqua Marcia (144 B.C.). An alternative method of conveyance, employed for the Anio Vetus at Ponte Lupo, was the inverted siphon (Vitr. 8. 7; *ILS* 5348). All these principles were strikingly developed in the wide Imperial world, the Pont du Gard near Nemausus (*Nîmes*) and the aqueduct of Segovia furnishing the most famous examples of storied bridges, the Aquae Marcia (144 B.C.), Claudia, and Anio Novus (A.D. 38–52) of Rome itself offering the most remarkable series of arched substructions, the four aqueducts of Lyons the finest series of inverted siphons, made of lead pipes in series bedded upon concrete. The cost and upkeep of these works was high. Aqua Marcia cost 180,000,000 sesterces, and Pliny (*Ep.* 10. 37) quotes 3,329,000 sesterces for the aqueduct of Nicomedia in Bithynia. The quality of work varied very much also (cf. Frontin. *Aq.* 120–2; *ILS* 5795). Smaller towns thus contented themselves with simpler underground systems, which were also much in vogue in military forts and fortresses, where wooden pipe-lines were often used. The channels and their course remained public property, often demarcated by *cippi*, and the water, on arrival, was distributed from *castella*, as at Nîmes and Thuburbo Maius, to public fountains, baths, and private consumers, the latter relying much upon overflow (*aqua caduca*). Supplies were regulated by gauge-pipes of standard bore (*calices*) or by time-limits (*CIL* vi. 1261, viii. 448). Development of water-power, as on the Aqua Traiana (A.D. 109; s.v. JANICULUM), was rare. Rents were not designed to cover running costs or capital charges, and the works were usually a liability to the community rather than a source of income.

Frontinus, *De Aquis Urbis Romae*. T. Ashby, *Aqueducts of Ancient Rome* (1935); E. B. Van Deman, *The Building of the Roman Aqueducts* (U.S.A. 1934); G. de Montauzan, *Les Aqueducs antiques de Lyon* (1909); E. Samesreuther, *Bericht der Röm.-Germ. Kommission* xxvi (1936), 24–157.   I. A. R.

AQUILA ROMANUS (3rd c. A.D.), rhetorician, whose treatise *De figuris sententiarum et elocutionis* (ed. Halm, *Rhet. Lat. Min.* 22–37) was partly based on the Greek of Alexander Numenius, but contains illustrations from Cicero's works (often misquoted from memory).

Cf. Teuffel, § 388, 1; Schanz–Hosius, § 837.   J. F. M.

AQUILA, see also PONTIUS (3) *and* SIGNA MILITARIA.

AQUILEIA, a city seven miles from the head of the Adriatic. In 186 B.C. Transalpine Gauls occupied this fertile site, which controls roads across the Julian Alps. Rome ejected them and founded a Latin colony (181 B.C.) to forestall similar intrusions and to exploit neighbouring gold-mines (Livy 39. 22, 54; 40. 34; H. Mattingly–E. S. G. Robinson, *Date of Roman Denarius* (1933), 22). Aquileia became a great military, commercial, and industrial stronghold; its amber trade was especially important (Strabo 4. 207 f.; 5. 214). In Imperial times it was a *colonia*, sometimes dubbed *Roma secunda*, the capital of *Venetia et Istria*, one of the world's largest cities, until razed by Attila in 452 (Auson. *Ordo Nob. Urb.* 65 f.; Amm. Marc. 21. 11 f.; Procop. *Vand.* 1. 330).

Its inhabitants fled to the neighbouring lagoons of Venice. Aquileia became a malaria-stricken village, but was still an important patriarchate in the fifteenth century. Ancient remains are numerous.

A. Calderini, *Aquileia Romana* (1930); A. Degrassi, *Riv. Fil.* 1938, 132 ff.   E. T. S.

AQUILIUS (1) (fl. c. 174–154 B.C.), supposed Latin author of *Boeotia* (*Boeotis*?), a *comoedia palliata* which Varro attributed to Plautus. *See* DRAMA, para. 4.

O. Ribbeck, *CRF*² 33 (3rd ed. Teubner, 1897).   E. H. W.

AQUILIUS (2), MANIUS, consul in 129 B.C., completed the war against Aristonicus, succeeding Perperna, and settled the province of Asia. He was accused *de repetundis*, but acquitted. The Senate, however, took away Phrygia from the king of Pontus, to whom it had been assigned by Aquilius.

C. Gracchus, apud Gellium 11. 10.   M. H.

AQUILIUS (3), MANIUS, a legate of Marius in the Cimbric campaigns, was consul with Marius in 101 B.C., and proceeded to crush the slave revolt in Sicily, the rebel leader Athenion being killed. Through the influence of Marius and the oratory of M. Antonius, Aquilius was acquitted on a charge of maladministration in Sicily. Sent to Asia, he successfully ejected Mithridates' forces from Cappadocia and Bithynia, and blackmailed Nicomedes whom he restored to Bithynia; but in 88 he was driven from Bithynia by Mithridates and captured. Mithridates poured molten gold down his throat to rebuke Roman avarice.   M. H.

AQUILIUS (4) **GALLUS**, GAIUS, a Roman jurist in the last century of the Republic, disciple of the celebrated Q. Mucius Scaevola (q.v.), and a teacher of law in his turn. He was praetor in 66, contemporarily with Cicero; and he died between 55 and 44 B.C. 'Vir magnae auctoritatis et scientia iuris excellens' (Val. Max.). He is the creator of the *stipulatio Aquiliana*, which served for transferring all kinds of debts into one general *stipulatio*, so that they could be discharged by the convenient means of *acceptilatio* (*Dig.* 46. 4. 18. 1), and of the *iudicium de dolo* (Cic. *Nat.D.* 3. 30. 74; *Off.* 3. 14. 60).
                                                 A. B.

AQUILIUS, *see also* REGULUS (2).

AQUINCUM, on the Danube at Buda-Pest, originally an Illyrian-Celtic settlement, was later the capital of Pannonia Inferior and an important Roman base against the Quadi and Sarmatae-Iazyges. *Auxilia* were quartered there probably from the time of Tiberius. Later, apparently from A.D. 114, Legio II Adiutrix was garrisoned at Aquincum, but it may have been there under Domitian and then only detached for the Dacian wars. Perhaps Legio X Gemina was at Aquincum between 103 and 107, and a short stay of Legio IV Flavia is probable between 161 and 211. The *canabae* (q.v.) near the camp had their own administration (cf. 'dec(urio) canab(arum)' in an unpublished inscription quoted by Kuszinsky, op. cit. infra, p. 186, no. 499). Aquincum became a *municipium* (*Aelium*) under Hadrian, and a *colonia* (*Septimia*) under Septimius Severus. When the Romans gradually relinquished Pannonia (c. 400), Aquincum (last mentioned in Sid. Apoll. 5. 107) was also given up.

W. Tomaschek, *PW*, s.v.; K. Kuszinsky, *Aquincum* (1934); J. Szilágyi in *Laureae Aquincenses* (1938), 287–311.   F. A. W. S.

AQUITANIA, a name originally applied to the area of modern Gascony, occupied apparently by mixed Ligurian and Iberian population with a slight Celtic tinge. It consisted of a number of small and obscure tribes, which were conquered by Caesar's lieutenant, P. Licinius Crassus, and finally subdued by Augustus after campaigns in 38 and 27 B.C. In Augustus' provincial organization Aquitania was extended to include the tribes of the Loire, a measure which, as Strabo (4. 1. 1) complains, made ethnographical nonsense of the name; but by the third century the original Aquitanian tribes, which had coalesced to nine (*novem populi*), secured their administrative independence. Of these, Ausci and Convenae enjoyed Latin rights, while Lugdunum Convenarum and Elusa are called *coloniae* at various dates. Nevertheless, the level of romanization was nowhere high.

O. Hirschfeld, *Kleine Schriften* (1913), 209; C. Jullian, *Hist. de la Gaule* (1908), ii. 449. C. E. S.

ARA PACIS, a monument dedicated by the Senate, as Augustus records in his Testament, to commemorate his safe return from Gaul and Spain. It stood on the Campus Martius under the modern Palazzo Fiano. The altar, which was adorned with reliefs representing the *suovetaurilia* or sacrifice at the ceremony of dedication 30 Jan. 9 B.C.), stood in a walled precinct (11·6 × 10·6 metres) with doors on the east and west. The wall was sculptured with reliefs in two tiers: internally, festoons and ox-heads above, panelling below; externally, the lower frieze was filled with foliage, the upper contained on east and west mythological panels, on north and south a representation of the consecration procession (4 July 13 B.C.) with portraits of the imperial family and court. These reliefs rank among the most important products of Augustan art.

Several sculptured slabs were brought to light about 1568; others were found in 1859 and 1903. They were identified as parts of the Ara Pacis by F. von Duhn in 1879. In 1937–8 the site was thoroughly explored and the monument re-erected as far as possible on the bank of the Tiber.

G. Moretti, *L'Ara Pacis Augustae* (1938). F. N. P.

ARABIA. Greeks of the Classical period knew little about Arabia. The Babylonian king Nabonidus had resided at Teima; Darius I, astride the 'incense route' in the north-west, had drawn a tribute of spices from the south, like Sargon and Sennacherib before him. But knowledge really began with Alexander. In preparation for his intended circumnavigation his admiral Hieron sailed down the Persian Gulf to Ras Mussendam, and Anaxicrates down the Red Sea through Bab-el-Mandeb to the south coast; the south-east (Oman) long remained unknown. The Seleucids planted some settlements along the coast between the Euphrates and Gerrha, and had a trade arrangement with Gerrha, which supplied Seleuceia with spices. Ariston explored down to Bab-el-Mandeb for Ptolemy II, and that king, to chastise the hostile Nabataeans of Petra, tapped the 'incense route' south of them by a trade arrangement with the Lihyanites of Dedan (Al-'Ula); Miletus settled for him a colony, Ampelone, as a sea-port for Dedan. The fourth–third-century kingdoms in the south were Minaea on the Red Sea, Katabania at the Straits, and Sabaea, the Hadramaut, and Mahra along the south coast; by the second century Minaea had vanished, and a Sabaean-Homerite confederacy (Himyarites) dominated Yemen. In the first century Petra grew great, and the Nabataeans finally extended from Damascus to Dedan. The interior was always unknown. Arabia exported frankincense and myrrh, gold and gems, and re-exported Indian spices and other products. The principal routes were the 'incense route' from Sabaea through Medina, Dedan, and Petra to Syria, and routes from Dhofar to Gerrha, from Gerrha across to Petra, and from Egypt to Babylonia via Jauf. Till Augustus' time the southern Arabs were jealous intermediaries of the sea-trade between India and Egypt; Roman Egypt, with direct voyages to south Arabia and India, broke their monopoly, and also diminished the importance of the 'incense route'. Augustus sent an expedition to conquer Sabaea, which

failed; the story that he ruled Aden cannot be true. Subsequently the south was let alone, Rome being content with her sea trade; but Trajan made Nabataea a Roman province, with its capital at Bostra, and constructed a great road through it from the Red Sea to Damascus.

M. Cary and E. H. Warmington, *Ancient Explorers*, ch. 4; J. G. C. Anderson, *CAH* x. 247 ff.; W. W. Tarn, *JEg.Arch.* 1929, p. 9. W. W. T.

ARACHNE (i.e. 'Spider'), in Ovid, *Met.* 6. 5 ff., a Lydian woman, daughter of Idmon of Colophon, so skilled in weaving as to rival Athena, whom she challenged to a competition when the goddess visited her to warn her. On Athena destroying her web, she hanged herself and Athena changed her to a spider. This seems to be originally a folk-tale (Stith Thompson A 2091. 1, 2231. 5). H. J. R.

ARADUS, an ancient Phoenician town on an island off the Syrian coast, whose kings ruled a large area on the mainland. Confirmed by Alexander, the dynasty was suppressed in 259 B.C. and its dominions dismembered. The Aradian republic extorted from Seleucus II during his war with Antiochus Hierax the rights of coinage and of harbouring exiles (*c.* 239) and gradually became independent. In the early first century B.C. it reconquered most of its old mainland territory, but having resisted Antony in 38 B.C. was deprived of it. A. H. M. J.

ARAE FLAVIAE, modern *Rottweil* on the Neckar. In A.D. 74 the Roman Rhine–Danube frontier was shortened by carrying a road south-eastwards from Strasbourg to the Danube. A fort was built at the point where another road coming up from Windisch (Vindonissa) joined the first, and the town Arae Flaviae was founded there. Some fine houses of this period, probably belonging to officials, have been excavated. Domitian advanced the frontier farther and removed the garrison, and after A.D. 100 Rottweil lost its importance, being afterwards no more than a station on the road from Switzerland. O. B.

ARAROS (Ἀραρώς), son of Aristophanes, who according to Ar. *Plut.* hyp. 4 wrote Araros' first two productions, Κώκαλος (? victorious 387 B.C.) and Αἰολοσίκων, 'συστῆσαι Ἀραρότα τοῖς θεαταῖς βουλόμενος'. The series of A.'s own plays began, according to Suidas, about 375 B.C.

FCG i. 343–6; *CAF* ii. 215–19. M. P.

ARATEA, Latin poems translated from the Φαινόμενα and Προγνώσεις of Aratus (q.v.) (1) by Cicero, partly extant, a portion being in about 480 hexameters besides detached fragments of *Phaenomena* and *Prognostica* (Baehr. *PLM* i. 1–28; Cicero, ed. C. F. W. Müller, p. 4 v. 3, 360–94; W. W. Ewbank, *The Poems of Cicero*, 1933), sometimes inaccurate and monotonous; (2) by Germanicus, *Phaen.*, 725 hexameters, and fragments amounting to over 200 verses of *Progn.* (Baehr. *PLM* i. 142ff.; A. Breysig, Teubner² 1899), a more poetic and more independent adaptation than Cicero's, in which the imperial author corrects some astronomical errors in the original; (3) by Avienus (q.v.) in the fourth century, *Phaen.* in 1325, *Progn.* in 553 hexameters (Breysig, 1889), considerably expanded from the Greek. Cf. G. Sieg, *De Cic., German., Avieno Arati interpretibus* (1886).
J. W. D.

ARATUS (1), of Soli in Cilicia (*c.* 315–240/239 B.C.), was first taught by Menecrates of Ephesus, perhaps in that town. Later he went to Athens, where he imbibed Stoicism from Zeno and was introduced to Antigonus (q.v. 2) Gonatas. Antigonus *c.* 276 invited A. to the Macedonian court, where he celebrated the king's marriage to Phila, half-sister of Antiochus I, in a *Hymn to Pan*. Later A. went to Syria and joined Antiochus' court. There he completed his edition of the *Odyssey*, but eventually returned to Macedonia, where his death preceded that of Antigonus in 240/239.

WORKS. Aratus' best-known work, still extant, is an astronomical poem, entitled *Phaenomena*. This, undertaken at the request of Antigonus, versifies a prose treatise or treatises of Eudoxus of Cnidos (*c.* 390–337). After a proem to Zeus (1–18), and a brief reference to the poles, A. describes the northern and southern fixed stars (26–453), the circles of the celestial sphere (462–558), and the risings and settings of stars (559–732). The remainder of the poem (733–1154) deals with weather signs, in spite of a separate title (Προγνώσεις διὰ σημείων) an integral part of the poem. The *Phaenomena* achieved immediate fame (cf. *Anth. Pal.* 9. 25 (Leonidas of Tarentum); Callimachus, *Epigr.* 27) and found many commentators (the names of 27 are known); but the astronomical mistakes, which some commentators tried to remove by altering the text, were widely criticized, especially by Hipparchus (*c.* 190–120 B.C.), whose commentary survives. Nevertheless the poem enjoyed a great reputation among both Greeks and Romans (cf. Cic. *De Or.* 1. 69) till the end of antiquity. Latin translations of it were made by Varro of Atax, Cicero, Germanicus, Avienus (*see* ARATEA). A.'s style is sober, being modelled on Hesiod, and the language, drawn mostly from Homer, is relatively simple (there are few 'glosses'), but the poem is not easy reading owing to the nature of the subject-matter. There are some bad errors in the formation of Epic words, and some neologisms. The metre is fairly correct, but the refinements introduced by Callimachus are lacking. The Stoic creed pervades the whole poem, while poetic colour is provided by digressions, the longest being the descriptions of the Golden Age (98–136) and of storms at sea (408–35).

Aratus wrote many other poems, now lost, e.g. *Epikedeia*, *Epigrams* (cf. *Anth. Pal.* 12. 129), *Elegies* (Macrob. 5. 20. 8), *Hymns*, *Paegnia*, and a collection of short poems with the title Τὰ κατὰ λεπτόν (the meaning is uncertain), from which the *Catalepton* attributed to Virgil takes its name. Other lost works have astronomical or medical titles.

TEXTS: E. Maass, *Arati Phaenomena* (1893); *Commentariorum in Aratum reliquiae* (1898).
GENERAL LITERATURE: G. Knaack, 'Aratos (6)' in *PW* ii. 391–9; E. Maass, *Aratea* (1892); G. R. Mair, *Callimachus, Lycophron, Aratus* (Loeb, 1921), 359–473; W. W. Tarn, *Antigonos Gonatas* (1913), 223–56; Christ–Schmid–Stählin ii. 1⁶ (1920), 163–7.
                                                              E. A. B.

ARATUS (2) (271–213 B.C.), a Sicyonian statesman, educated at Argos, his refuge after his father's murder (264). He recovered Sicyon in 251, united it to the Achaean League for defence against Macedon, and solved its economic difficulties by subsidies from Ptolemy Philadelphus, whom he visited personally. As General of the League, normally each alternate year from 245, he seized Acrocorinth in 243 and defeated Gonatas' Aetolian allies at Pellene (241). In alliance with Aetolia (239–229) he frequently attacked Athens and Argos; additions to the League included Megalopolis (235) and Argos (229), and on Demetrius II's death (229) Aratus helped to liberate Athens. However, Spartan aggression cancelled these advances. Defeated at Mt. Lycaeus and Ladoceia (227) by Cleomenes III, he realistically opened negotiations with Macedon, and Doson's arrival in 224 preserved the League from disruption. In the crisis he held special powers, judicial and administrative. On Philip V's accession he called in Doson's Confederacy against Aetolian aggression (220); in the subsequent war he successfully exposed the treachery of the court cabal under Apelles, and after the peace of Naupactus (217) vigorously resisted Philip's anti-Roman policy and proposed seizure of Ithome. His death (213), probably from consumption, was attributed popularly to Philip.

His *Memoirs* (Ὑπομνηματισμοί: Polyb. 2. 40) were pro-Achaean and apologetic in tone, and less reliable than Polybius claims (2. 40. 4).

Though not without personal rancour (e.g. against Lydiades or Aristomachus of Argos), Aratus' actions usually revealed a sound statesmanlike basis. His failure to organize a strong army was serious; but his major decisions were almost invariably correct, and both as a diplomatist and guerrilla leader he carried adaptability to the height of greatness.

Polyb. 2. 37–71; bks. 4–5; Plut. *Agis, Cleomenes, Aratus*. F. W. Walbank, *Aratos of Sicyon* (1933); W. H. Porter, ed. Plutarch's *Aratus*, introd. (1937).   F. W. W.

ARAUSIO, a town in Gallia Narbonensis, modern *Orange*; the scene of a great Roman defeat in 105 B.C. A probably posthumous Caesarian colony was founded here under the title *Colonia firma Iulia Secundanorum Arausio*. The theatre, the gymnasium (?), a temple, probably of the Imperial house, and a triumphal arch, all of Caesarian or Augustan date, still survive. The last, re-dedicated to Tiberius in A.D. 28, may have fronted the north gate of the town wall, much of which is elsewhere preserved. The *territorium* was laid out in centuriated plots; fragments of the allotment plan are extant.

L. Chatelain, *Monuments romains d'Orange* (1909); J. Formigé, *Le prétendu Cirque d'Orange* (1927); I. A. Richmond, *JRS* xxiii. 151.
                                                              C. E. S.

ARAXES, properly the Armenian river now called Aras, Ras, or Yerash, rising in Bin Geul Dagh, then flowing eastwards across Erzerum and the Mogan Steppe. Until A.D. 1897 it joined the Kur (ancient Cyrus), but now flows separately into the Caspian. Swift and turbulent now, in Graeco-Roman times it marked a trade-route from the Caspian and the Cyrus to Artaxata and Asia Minor. Herodotus confuses the Aras with the Iaxartes or the Oxus. Xenophon calls it Phasis, his Araxes being probably the Khabur. The 'Araxes in Persis' is probably the Bendamir or Kum Firuz.   E. H. W.

ARBITER, *see* IUDEX.

ARBITRATION, GREEK. The submission of a dispute to a neutral person or body, whose verdict the disputants engage themselves in advance to accept, was recognized among the Greeks from a very early period, and legend and history alike attest its frequent application. There is evidence for the existence of public arbitrators in numerous States, e.g. Sparta, Gortyn, Ephesus, and Lampsacus, but we have detailed knowledge only about Athens. There private διαιτηταί, not necessarily citizens, were frequently employed to settle claims on an equitable rather than on a legal basis (Arist. *Rhet.* 1. 13), while public arbitrators, appointed from citizens in their sixtieth year, were used, especially in the fourth century, for the settlement, under the auspices of the 'Forty', of private claims exceeding 10 drachmas in value, so as to lighten the work of the public courts (Arist. *Ath. Pol.* 53). Once accepted by both parties, the arbitral award became legally binding, but inasmuch as either party had the right of appeal to the law-court, these public διαιτηταί must be regarded as mediators rather than as arbitrators in the strict sense. Another important application of the same principle was the practice, especially frequent in the Hellenistic age, whereby a State invited a friendly neighbour-State to send a tribunal (δικασταὶ μετάπεμπτοι, ξενικὸν δικαστήριον) to deal with civil, and sometimes also with criminal, cases affecting its citizens; the visiting judges sought first to settle disputes 'out of court', but where the method of conciliation (σύλλυσις) failed, they had the right to pronounce legal judgements.

2. But it was in the field of inter-State relations that arbitration attained its greatest influence. Whether the Greeks originated this device for substituting equity for force is uncertain, but it was assuredly they who made it a recognized and frequent means of averting wars. The earliest recorded cases, such as the Spartan arbitration between Athens and Megara regarding the possession of Salamis, are known only from semi-legendary traditions; but the original text survives of an award of about 450 B.C. (*SIG* 56), by which Argos sought to compose existing differences between her two Cretan colonies Cnossos and Tylissus and to prevent their future recurrence. From 450 peace-treaties normally contained a clause binding the contracting parties to submit to arbitration all eventual disputes (e.g. Thuc. 1. 78. 4, 140. 2, 144. 2, 145; 4. 118. 8; 5. 18. 4, 79. 4); and we may assume that this course was frequently followed, though circumstances sometimes arose in which the exacerbation of public feeling and the difficulty of finding a suitable arbitrator led to the neglect of this provision. Athens seems to have claimed the right to act as arbitrator in disputes among the members of her Empire (Plut. *Per.* 25), and later the Greek Leagues sought by similar means to secure internal harmony.

3. It is upon inscriptions that we depend for our detailed knowledge of the operation of the arbitral machinery, the size, composition, and appointment of the tribunals, their procedure, the nature of the evidence laid before them, the formulation and publication of their awards, the penalties attaching to their infraction, and the character of the boundary-delimitations carried out by frontier commissions. Among the fullest and most interesting accounts of this kind are those relating to the arbitrations of King Lysimachus and, later, the Rhodians between Samos and Priene (*OGI* 13, *SIG* 599, 688), of the Megarians between Corinth and Epidaurus (*SIG* 471), of the Calydonians between Perea and Melitea in Thessaly (ib. 546 B), of the Senate between Melite and Narthacium (ib. 674), of the Mylasians between Magnesia and Priene (ib. 679), of the Milesians between Sparta and Messene (ib. 683), of the Magnesians between Itanus and Hierapytna (ib. 635), and of the Cnossians between Lato and Olus (ib. 712; *Inscriptions de Délos*, 1513).

For the Athenian διαιτηταί see M. H. E. Meier, *Die Privatschiedsrichter u. d. öffentlichen Diäteten Athens* (1846); B. Hubert, *De arbitris atticis et privatis et publicis* (1885); A. Pischinger, *De arbitris Atheniensium publicis* (1893); T. Thalheim in *PW* v. 313 ff.; G. Busolt, *Griech. Staatskunde* (1920–6), 485 ff., 1111 ff.; R. J. Bonner, *CPhil.* ii. 407 ff., xi. 191 ff.; J. H. Lipsius, *Das attische Recht u. Rechtsverfahren* (1905), i. 220 ff.; H. C. Harrell, *Public Arbitration in Athenian Law* (1936). For the ξενικὰ δικαστήρια see E. Sonne, *De arbitris externis quos Graeci adhibuerunt* (1888); Thalheim in *PW* v. 573 f.; Busolt, op. cit. 557 f. For inter-State arbitration see Sonne, op. cit.; H. F. Hitzig, 'Altgriech. Staatsverträge über Rechtshilfe', in *Festschrift F. Regelsberger* (1907); C. Phillipson, *International Law and Custom of Ancient Greece and Rome* (1911), ii. 127 ff.; A. Raeder, *L'Arbitrage international chez les Hellènes* (1912); M. N. Tod, *International Arbitration amongst the Greeks* (1913), *Sidelights on Greek History* (1932), 37 ff.; Busolt, op. cit. 1257 ff.
M. N. T.

ARBITRATION, ROMAN. The history of Roman arbitration begins with the interference of Rome as a great power in the politics of the Hellenistic world. Rome took the place of the kings who had often acted as international arbitrators between the free cities and leagues of the Greeks. Such disputes were referred to the Senate, which decided the general issue, but sometimes left particular points to a third party with local knowledge for settlement. Rome did not, in the earliest period, enforce the acceptance of her arbitral awards. While not abusing her influence, Rome tended to accept the state of affairs at the time when the appellants first came under her influence as the standard of reference. This practice tended, as her authority increased, to merge into the defence of the privileges of her allies. With the formation of provinces and the consolidation of the Empire, arbitration lost its international character, since, except by special permission, which was sometimes allowed, notably in Sicily, the subject peoples could not turn elsewhere. But senatorial adjudication of disputes between provincial States of all categories continued to be frequent till the third century of the Empire. Such arbitration tended to merge with the general provincial administration, and was gradually replaced by the activity of special commissioners such as the *curatores* and *correctores civitatum*. Its existence illustrates the lively political self-consciousness of the cities of the Roman Empire.

Ancient sources: Polybius, Livy bks. 30–45. Documents in Abbott and Johnson, *Municipal Administration in the Roman Empire* (1927). Modern literature: ibid. ch. 11; and E. De Ruggiero, *L'arbitrato pubblico presso i Romani* (1893). A. N. S.-W.

ARBORICULTURE. Neolithic Europe knew apple, and perhaps pear-, cherry-, and plum-trees; the ancient Oriental regions also knew fig-trees and date-palms, pistachio-, carob-, walnut-, peach-, lemon-, pomegranate-, and almond-trees. Greece after the Persian Wars and especially in the Hellenistic age, as well as Italy after 200 B.C., imported and cultivated all these fruit-trees, so far as climate permitted. Under the Roman emperors many of them reached the Rhine, the Danube, and the Atlantic coast, and spread into Germanic and Slavic Europe, and from Iran even to China. Fig- and date-trees had great economic importance for the Asiatic and African parts of the Mediterranean world and for southern Greece from Minoan times. The scientific experience of Greece and Rome was used for arboriculture with remarkable results. Orchards flourished everywhere, the methods of their cultivation being well known to us from papyri and contemporaneous authors. Cultivation of trees useful for their wood is found in the Ptolemaic Empire. State plantations of them were established, private plantations encouraged and even commandeered to lessen the scarcity of wood in Egypt. *See* AGRICULTURE.
F. M. H.

ARCADIA, a mountainous area in central Peloponnesus, approaching the sea only in the south-west, near Phigalia. Its small valleys have a hard climate but are not infertile. Most of it is drained by the Alpheus and its tributaries, but large parts have no overground outlet for their waters, which disappear through swallow-holes; hence the north and east valleys either held lakes (Pheneus, Stymphalus) or became flooded. The most prosperous parts were the eastern plains, with Orchomenus, Mantinea, Tegea, lying at about 2,000 feet, and the Alpheus valley, where lay Heraea, the first Arcadian place to coin and one of the religious centres of Arcadia (C. Seltman, *Greek Coins*, 97). The rest of Arcadia, particularly the mountain valleys, was a land of villages. Arcadia therefore carried little weight in the politics of Greece; its chief strength was man-power, and from the early fifth century we hear of Arcadian mercenaries. From the mid-sixth century it came under Spartan hegemony, but was often ready to revolt. Under Epaminondas' direction an Arcadian League was formed as a counterweight to Sparta, but was weakened by particularism. For Arcadian participation in the Achaean League see MEGALOPOLIS.

The dialect, related to Cypriot, was a survival of the pre-Dorian speech of Peloponnesus. The pastoral character of Arcadian life was shown in their myths and cults, many of them rude and savage, and the charming small bronze figurines of shepherds, etc.

Paus. bk. 8 and Frazer's Commentary; W. Lamb, *BSA* 27. 133 ff.; C. Callmer, *Studien zur Geschichte Arkadiens* (1943). T. J. D.

ARCADIAN CULTS AND MYTHS. All the usual gods were worshipped in Arcadia; the most remarkable features of the cult were (1) Zeus on Mt. Lycaeon had a holy place, to enter which was death (by stoning, if it was deliberate; mysteriously within a year, if otherwise). It was reported as early as the time of Plato that human sacrifice was practised there, and that he who tasted the flesh of the human victim became a wolf. (2) Poseidon's shrine at Mantinea stood open but might not be entered;

one Aepytus who disregarded this was blinded by a mysterious wave. (3) Hermes by most reports was born on Mt. Cyllene; there is little doubt that his cult originated in that region. (4) Demeter at Lycosura was associated with a goddess Despoina, said to be her daughter by Poseidon; at Phigalia she was shown horse-headed and bore the surname of Black; at Thelpusa, that of Erinys. In other words, she was a local goddess identified with the normal Demeter, but of more formidable character. (5) Pan is universally said to be an Arcadian god, as was natural enough, considering that the country was largely pastoral. (6) Before a festival at Aliphera sacrifice was made to a godling called Myiagros, 'fly-catcher', and it was believed that after this flies would not trouble the worshippers. Of myths, the most important was the claim of the Arcadians that Zeus was born in their country, and the source of the river Neda had sprung up for Rhea to wash herself and her infant. It was a kind of proverb or standing joke that the Arcadians had lived there since before the moon was created. *See also* ARES.

W. Immerwahr, *Die Kulte und Mythen Arkadiens* (1891).
                                                        H. J. R.

ARCADIUS of Antiocheia, a grammarian, of the later Empire, who wrote a (lost) Ὀνοματικόν (table of noun inflexions). To him is falsely ascribed an extant epitome from Herodian, probably made by Theodosius (end of 4th c. A.D.), and interpolated in the sixteenth century.

Edition (Hdn. Epitome): E. H. Barker (1820).   P. B. R. F.

ARCADO-CYPRIAN, *see* DIALECTS, GREEK.

ARCAS, eponym of Arcadia, son of Zeus and Callisto (q.v.). Being left without a mother, he was reared by Maia. His grandfather Lycaon, to test the omniscience of Zeus, killed him and served up his flesh. The god overthrew the table, destroyed the house with a thunderbolt, turned Lycaon into a wolf, and restored Arcas to life. Later, meeting Callisto in bear-shape, Arcas pursued her into the precinct of Zeus on Mt. Lycaon. Both thus incurred the death-penalty (cf. ARCADIAN CULTS; Ovid, *Met.* 2. 496, says nothing of the shrine but only that he did not know her and was about to kill her), when Zeus turned them respectively into the Great Bear and Arctophylax.

Hyginus, *Poet. Astr.* 2. 1 and 4.   H. J. R.

ARCESILAS I, II, III, IV, second, fourth, sixth, and eighth kings of the house of Battus, which ruled Cyrene (q.v.) from its foundation (630 B.C.) till after 460 B.C. Arcesilas I (*c.* 590–574) inherited the original settlement of colonists from Thera. Arcesilas II (the Cruel) succeeded *c.* 560 to a city which Battus II had reinforced with settlers from Peloponnesus, Crete, and other islands; he quarrelled with his brothers, who seceded and founded Barca with Libyan support, and was defeated and murdered by them. He is probably the Arcesilas figured in the famous cup in Paris (*CAH*, Plates i. 378) seated on board ship watching the stowage of bales of merchandise (silphium?, wool?). Arcesilas III succeeded Battus III on a throne diminished by the democratic reforms of Demonax, a lawgiver called in from Mantinea; helped by Polycrates of Samos and Cambyses of Persia, whose vassal he became, he regained personal power, but leaving Cyrene to be governed by his mother Pheretime retired to Barca, where he was murdered *c.* 510. The last Arcesilas is immortalized in Pindar's fourth Pythian (462), which pleads the cause of a political exile from Cyrene. A few years later Arcesilas himself was exiled and the dynasty ended.

Herodotus 4. 154–67, 200–5.   P. N. U.

ARCESILAUS (1) (*Arcesilas* in Cicero, Ἀρκεσίλαος; *c.* 315–241/40 B.C., Diog. Laert. 4. 44, 61), founder of the sceptical or middle (and new) Academy (D.L. 4. 28;

etc.). He was the son of Seuthes, or Skythes, of Pitane in Aeolia (Hermipp. ap. D.L. 4. 28). On the death of his father his elder brother intended to make him a rhetor. Instead he went to Athens and became a pupil of Theophrastus; finally he was won over by Crantor to the Academy (D.L. 4. 29. 43; Numen. ap. Euseb. 14. 6. 2). An intimate friendship connected him with his new teacher as well as with Polemon and Crates, successively presidents of the Academy (D.L. 4. 22; etc.). Upon the death of Crates (probably 268–265), general recognition of his superiority caused a rival to resign, and he became president of the School (D.L. 4. 32). His teaching opened a new and flourishing period of Academic philosophy. He left no writings (D.L. 4. 32; Plut. *De Alex. Fort.* 4, p. 328).

His chief polemic was directed against the dogmatic theory of knowledge brought forward by the Stoics (Cic. *Acad.* 1. 44) for merely ethical purposes. The Stoics maintained that there was a criterion of truth which they found in a specific kind of sense-perception, called the 'irresistible' or 'convincing perceptions' (καταληπτικαὶ φαντασίαι). A. replied that wrong perceptions under certain circumstances were as convincing as right ones (Cic. *Luc.* 27; Sext. Emp. *Math.* 1. 154; cf. the other arguments, 150 f.).

After disproving the Stoic theory of apprehension A. goes on to deny the possibility of any knowledge: 'if apprehension does not exist, all things will be non-apprehensible' (Sext. ib. 155). This denial became a watchword of Academic scepticism (Sext. *Pyr.* 1. 3). Consequently he not only adopted the attitude Socrates assumes in Plato's early dialogues but even the agnosticism of the Sceptic Pyrrhon (Sext. *Math.* 1. 155, cf. *Pyr.* 1. 233, etc.). But Pyrrhon's crude criticism started from an ethical basis and aimed at an ethical goal, imperturbability of mind. A. on the other hand founded a sceptical theory of knowledge based on certain parts of Socratic and Platonic teaching and on his own refutation of the then established dogmatic philosophy, the Stoic.

Study of A.'s ethics makes this difference still clearer. To him moral philosophy was of secondary importance. He withdrew it from the main line of his criticism by holding that in practical life it was enough to find the most sensible reasons for an action. As the criterion for a practical question he only offers the 'reasonable' (εὔλογον) which is, without philosophic doctrine, sufficient to secure achievement in life (Sext. *Math.* 1. 158).

It is not easy to see how the Platonist A. was able to deal with the dogmatic elements of Plato's own philosophy. But at least it can be said that, in a time given to dogmatic overstatement, he upheld, if somewhat rigidly, the Socratic power of clear thinking. A. originated the school of logical scepticism which played an important role in the development of the philosophical mind.

H. von Arnim in *PW* ii. 1164; see also the bibliography under SCEPTICS.   K. O. B.

ARCESILAUS (2) (1st c. B.C.), sculptor, friend of L. Lucullus, working in Rome. Works: 1. Statue of Venus Genetrix for temple dedicated by Julius Caesar in 46 B.C. For reduced reproduction see M. Bieber, *Röm. Mitt.* 1933, 261. 2. Statue of Felicitas for Lucullus. 3. Centaurs carrying nymphs, for Asinius Pollio. 4. Lioness with Cupids for Varro. 5. Plaster model for crater with reliefs. His models, *proplasmata*, were sold at a high price. Probably a versatile adapter rather than an original artist.   T. B. L. W.

ARCHAEOLOGY, CLASSICAL. Classical Archaeology may be defined as the study which is concerned with the reconstruction of the ancient life of Greece and Rome by means of the discovery, classification, and interpretation of its material remains. In so far as such a study produces papyri or inscriptions, it is allied to the literary studies of the ancient world. In so far as it recovers works of art it is allied to the more general study of the History of Art. Its contributions to the study of ancient history are direct and obvious.

2. The founder of Classical Archaeology was Cyriac de' Pizzicolli (usually known as Cyriac of Ancona), who travelled in Greece between 1412 and 1447, and searched for works of art and inscriptions. His note-books, which have never been adequately published, contain a mass of important epigraphical material.

3. After his day little further was done except by agents who set out to purchase antiquities for the great collectors of the seventeenth and early eighteenth centuries. This was helpful to the study of ancient art, but not based on sound knowledge. The first serious contribution to an organized study of antiquity in Greece was the work of the Society of Dilettanti (founded in England in 1732), who sent out in the late eighteenth century well-organized expeditions to study the antiquities of Athens and Asia Minor. The work of Stuart and Revett, two of their best representatives, is of prime importance.

4. In 1835, shortly after the Declaration of Independence in Greece, much good work was done in the clearing of the Acropolis at Athens. One of the earliest journals of Classical Archaeology was the Ἀρχαιολογικὴ Ἐφημερίς, which began to be published at this time.

5. Excavation in Italy commenced with the uncovering of Herculaneum and Pompeii at the end of the eighteenth century. The opening of Etruscan tombs in the early nineteenth century, while largely a matter of looting and organized commercial excavation, did nevertheless add enormously to our knowledge of Greek vase-painting, as well as of Etruscan archaeology. Unfortunately the Greek vases in Etruscan tombs were for a long time classified as Etruscan.

6. The foundation of the German Institute of Archaeology in 1829 followed upon the activities of Lessing and others, and in Germany the organized study of Classical Archaeology grew up more rapidly than elsewhere. But it was not until c. 1870 that any large-scale organized excavations were undertaken, when H. Schliemann began work on the Homeric sites of Mycenae and Troy. Twenty years later Schliemann's operations at Troy were resumed in a more scientific fashion by W. Dörpfeld, and in 1901 Sir Arthur Evans brought to light the palace of Minos at Cnossos. The Acropolis at Athens, Delphi, and Olympia were subjected to close excavation by Greek, French, and German scholars respectively (c. 1880); minor sites elsewhere were also extensively studied, and material was thus accumulated for the intensive study of Greek art and epigraphy. Schools and institutes were founded by many countries in Athens and in Rome, and on their work and activities most of the modern organization of the study of Classical Archaeology is based. The exploration and identification of classical sites has also been carried on in more systematic fashion since the nineteenth century. The work of Col. Leake in Greece, of Sir W. M. Ramsay and others in Asia Minor, and of T. Ashby in the environs of Rome, has been of special value in finding suitable spots for excavation.

7. Classical Archaeology is concerned with all aspects of the history, social and artistic, of Greece and Rome from the time when those two lands achieved a distinct character and coherent existence. Any period prior to the Bronze Age does not strictly come under consideration. Classical Archaeology can justly interest itself in the Early Iron Age in Greece and Italy, or in Asia Minor and Cyprus, but earlier periods are concerned only in so far as anything in Classical Greece or Italy is derivative from the Bronze Age.

8. Classical Archaeology falls into the following sections:

(i) The study of art as such, including the study of sculpture (from small bronzes and terra-cottas to colossal figures in marble and bronze), of vase-painting, painting in general, and decorative or ornamental art. The study of vase-painting (as apart from the study of pottery) has, owing to the enormous mass of material available, become a subsidiary study in itself with its own methods and organization.

(ii) The study of architecture. This covers all forms of building from the largest temples to the smallest houses and shrines.

(iii) The study of epigraphy, a highly expert branch of work. All inscriptions, whether incised on stone and metal, or painted on vases or on any other medium, constitute the material of this study. The archaeologist is the producer of the material, the epigraphist its interpreter.

(iv) Numismatics. This, though a vast and important branch, is still an essential part of Classical Archaeology as a whole.

(v) The study and classification of ancient pottery. Since pottery is one of the principal clues to the chronology of ancient sites, its organization as a special study is essential. The pottery at any given site is the first and main study of the excavators; its importance cannot be over-estimated. Vase-painting, considered as art, is a subject that properly belongs to (i) above.

9. Contacts of Greek and Roman civilization with outside lands and other modes of culture make it essential that the Classical Archaeologist should make himself acquainted with the art and archaeology of other lands. Of these, Persia, Egypt, and Assyria, with perhaps the later Hittite world, are most important. S. C.

ARCHAISM in Latin. The efforts of Ennius to hellenize Latin literature diverted the literary language of Rome away from the popular dialect, and literary Latin became in a sense a dead language. Writers wishing to invigorate their style would introduce from everyday speech words which came in time to appear archaic. We still find in Ennius the original quantity of terminations (e.g. *ponebāt*), nominatives in *-ōr* and *-ā* and elision of *-s* before consonants. The first declension genitive is always in *-āī* or *-ās*, the old genitive plural, e.g. *deum*, is common, and obsolete pronouns e.g. *mis, olli, sas*, and verbs like *morīmur, fūimus*. Many of these forms were metrically convenient for later writers, but, apart from such considerations, the success and prestige of the *Annales* stamped such archaisms firmly upon the literary language. Forms thus reintroduced are frequently of popular origin, and it is difficult to disentangle the archaic and the popular elements. Modernizing scribes have removed much of the archaic from Cato, but he still shows archaisms such as *praefamino* (imperative) and *prohibessis*. In Caesar and Cicero Latin prose reached its zenith of classical purity, but in Sallust we come to one who deliberately imitates the ancients. He is full of old words, e.g. *prosapia, obsequela, dextumus*, and recalls early comedy in his fondness for frequentatives. In inflexion he uses e.g. *fide* (dat.), *vis* (acc. pl.), *nave* (adv.), *senati, nequitur*. Lucretius too is given to archaism, chiefly to show his admiration for Ennius. He uses forms like *im, endo, alid, rabies* (genit.), *vapōs* (nomin.), *scatit, confluxet, recesse*, infinitives in *-ier, escit, siet, fuat* and elision of pre-consonantal *-s*. Archaisms are naturally not frequent in the impassioned poetry of Catullus, but some of the above are convenient and he shows *alis, alid, deposivit, componier, tetulit, recepso*. Horace's *Epistles* and *Satires* have many colloquialisms and a few archaisms, e.g. *erepsemus, surrexe*. Virgil, though a keen antiquarian, keeps archaism within bounds, retaining just enough to give to his work a grateful flavour of antiquity, e.g. *aulāī, olli, iusso, admittier*. The Latinity of Propertius is quite peculiar. He shows many archaisms both in vocabulary and inflexion, e.g. *tergit, lenibunt,* *nullo, toto, uno* (= *nulli*, etc.). The not infrequent archaisms in Livy occur mostly in legal formulae and hardly affect the general tone of his work, for by his time the struggle between the graecizing and archaizing schools had ended in victory for the former. Persius (1. 76–8) mocks Neronian archaizers, and this recurrent phenomenon reappears in Hadrian's time, when it became fashionable to prefer Ennius to Virgil. In Fronto and Apuleius we see a deliberate return to the obsolete diction of Ennius and Cato; and even Gellius, whose language is much purer, is full of archaisms like *edulcare, recentari, aeruscator*. In Christian writers, who wrote for the people at large, archaic words which had never died out of the spoken language again came into their own.

A. Ernout, *Recueil de textes latins archaïques* (1938), and texts of authors mentioned in the article.   P. S. N.

ARCHEBULEAN, *see* METRE, GREEK, III (15).

ARCHEDEMUS of Tarsus, Stoic philosopher, probably a pupil of Diogenes (q.v. 3) of Babylon.

Testimonia in von Arnim, *SVF* iii. 262–4. *PW* ii. 439.

ARCHEDICUS, New Comedy poet, who foully slandered Demochares, nephew of Demosthenes (Polyb. 12. 13), in order to gain favour with Antipater.

FCG iv. 435 ff.; *CAF* iii. 276 ff.

ARCHEGETES (Ἀρχηγέτης), i.e. 'leader', 'guide', a title of Apollo (q.v.) in several places, e.g. Naxos in Sicily (Thuc. 6. 3. 1); of Heracles at Sparta (Xen. *Hell.* 6. 3. 6); of Asclepius near Tithorea (Paus. 10. 32. 12). It signified that the god either personally shared in, or had shown approval of, the foundation of the colony or other institution in question and would protect it. *Archegetis* (ἀρχηγέτις) is used in like manner of goddesses.   H. J. R.

ARCHELAUS (1), philosopher (fl. 5th c. B.C.), probably of Athenian birth, was a pupil of Anaxagoras (q.v.) and followed him in the main, but in some details adhered to the view of the older Ionian school. He held that the warm and the cold were produced out of the original Mixture by rarefaction and condensation, and agreed with Diogenes of Apollonia in assigning great importance to the part played by air. He is said to have taught Socrates, but it is improbable that he anticipated Socrates by engaging in ethical speculation.

Testimonia and frs. in Diels, *Vorsokr.*⁵ ii. 44–9. *PW* ii. 454.   W. D. R.

ARCHELAUS (2), king of Macedon *c.* 413–399 B.C. He organized the military strength of Macedonia by training infantry and building forts and roads (Thuc. 2. 100), and sought to foster hellenization by bringing Greek artists, especially Euripides, to his court, and by celebrating games at Dium. Moving his court from Aegae to Pella near the coast and adopting the Persian coin standard, he developed Macedonian trade. He maintained friendly relations with Athens, averted the revolt of Elimiotis by a marriage alliance, and captured Pydna (410); *c.* 400 he put the philo-Macedonian party into power at Larissa, probably annexing Perrhaebia.

F. Geyer, *Historische Zeitschrift*, Beiheft 19 (1930).   N. G. L. H.

ARCHELAUS (3) (fl. 1st c. B.C.), Greek general of Mithridates VI, perhaps from Sinope or Amisus. After overrunning Bithynia and most of central Greece ('First Mithridatic War', 88–85 B.C.), he was twice defeated by Sulla, and commissioned by Mithridates to negotiate a peace. Falling under suspicion of treasonable dealings with Sulla, on the renewal of war (83) he deserted to Rome, and he assisted Lucullus early in the third war (74). His only defeats were by Rome's best general with an army better, and not much smaller, than his own.

Appian, *Mithridatica* 18 ff.; Plutarch, *Sulla* 11 ff. For army figures, see esp. Memnon (frs. 31–2, in *FHG* iii. 535 ff.). G. T. G.

ARCHELAUS, *see also* LAELIUS (3), CAPPADOCIA.

ARCHEMORUS see HYPSIPYLE, ADRASTUS.

ARCHERS (Greek and Hellenistic). In Homer the chieftains, except Teucer, Pandareus, and Paris, did not use the bow in war, but the rank and file did. In classical times the Persians were dreaded for their attacks with arrows, but Greek citizens were not organized into regular bodies of archers. Archery, which had gone out of normal use, was kept up only in Crete and the backward parts of Greece, such as Acarnania. Cretan archers, who were specially renowned, were frequently employed at all periods to supplement the ordinary citizen-soldier. Athens also in the fifth century imported Scythian mercenaries who acted both as police and as soldiers, and were reinforced by additional recruits from the poorer citizens up to a total of 1,600 (Thuc. 2. 13. 8). Mounted archers were few in the classical period. In the Hellenistic armies under Oriental influence the use of archers, whether mounted or on foot, was somewhat more frequent, but only the Parthians made them the main arm of their offensive.

H. Hommel, *PW* s.v. τοξόται; R. Cagnat, Dar.-Sag. s.v. 'Sagittarii'; W. W. Tarn, *Hellenistic Military and Naval Development* (1930), 87 ff.   H. W. P.

ARCHERS (Roman), *see* MERCENARIES, ROMAN.

ARCHESTRATUS of Gela, a contemporary of Aristotle, styled ὁ τῶν ὀψοφάγων Ἡσίοδος ἢ Θέογνις (Ath. 6. 310 a). Wrote a Ἡδυπάθεια, a sort of gastronomical Baedeker, the source of Ennius' *Hedyphagetica*.

P. Brandt, *Corpusc. poes. ep. graec. ludibundae* (1888), i. 114–93.   J. D. D.

ARCHIAS, AULUS LICINIUS (2nd–1st c. B.C.), a Greek poet of Antioch, arrived in Rome before the end of the second century B.C. He celebrated Marius' Cimbric victory, and the Mithridatic victories of L. Licinius Lucullus, who obtained for him the citizenship of Heraclea in Lucania (93 B.C.). Under the Lex Plautia Papiria he acquired Roman citizenship. This was contested by Gratius (62), and defended successfully by Cicero (*Pro Archia*). Cicero hoped for a laudatory poem from him, but (*Att.* 1. 16. 15) in vain, as he was engaged by the Metelli. He improvised in verse (Quint. *Inst.* 10. 7. 19). His epigram on the infant Roscius discovered asleep with a serpent coiled round him is mentioned by Cicero (*Div.* 1. 79): it may be inferred he was alive in 45. Haupt and Th. Reinach have attributed to him some of the forty-one epigrams in the Greek Anthology headed 'Archias'. Mackail doubts Reitzenstein's opinion that he is the elder Archias, implied by the title Ἀρχίας νεώτερος (*Anth. Pal.* 9. 91).

F. Susemihl, *Gesch. gr. Lit. Alex.* i. 900.   G. C. R.

ARCHIDAMUS, the name of several Spartan kings. The most notable were:

ARCHIDAMUS II, who reigned from 469 (?) B.C. (476, Diodorus) to 427–426; grandson of Leotychidas (q.v.). He distinguished himself on the occasion of the Spartan earthquake in 464, and in operations against the rebel Messenians, after which we hear nothing of him for thirty years. Having failed to dissuade Sparta from going to war with Athens, he led the Peloponnesian forces to invade Attica in 431, 430, and 428; and to attack Plataea in 429. He left two sons, Agis II and Agesilaus II (qq.v.).

Thuc. bks. 1 and 2, passim; Diod. 11. 63–4.

ARCHIDAMUS III, who reigned from 360–359 to 338, son of Agesilaus II. He brought back the Spartan army after Leuctra (371), in which Diodorus wrongly states that he took part, and fought against the Arcadians (367, 364). He distinguished himself in the defence of Sparta against Epaminondas (362), and supported the Phocians in the Sacred War, but returned in disgust at the duplicity of their commander Phalaecus (347–346). Invited to help Tarentum against the Lucanians, he landed with a force in Italy but soon fell in battle at Manduria (338). Isocrates' *Archidamus* purports to be the appeal of the king to a congress at Sparta (366–365) to refuse the Theban demand for the recognition of the independence of Messene. Pausanias mentions a statue of him at Olympia.

Xen. *Hell.* bks. 5–7; Diod. bks. 15 and 16; Plut. *Ages.* 19, 33–4, 40; Paus. 3. 10. 3–5; 6. 4. 9. Niese, *PW*, s.v. 'Archidamos'; E. Meyer, *Forschungen* ii. 505–6. A. M. W.

ARCHIGENES of Apamea in Syria, pupil of Agathinus (q.v.); well-known physician at Rome in the time of Trajan (A.D. 98–117). He belonged to the eclectic school, but was chiefly influenced by the doctrines of the pneumatic school. The leading principle of his therapeutics was to combat the eight δυσκρασίαι (bad temperaments). Galen's theory of the pulse was borrowed from that of Archigenes, while at other points Galen reacts against his teaching. Works: Περὶ τῶν κατὰ γένος φαρμάκων; Περὶ τόπων πεπονθότων; Περὶ καστορίου χρήσεως; eleven bks. of letters of medical advice; and many others: all lost except for frs.

PW ii. 484. W. D. R.

ARCHILOCHEAN, *see* METRE, GREEK (14).

ARCHILOCHUS, iambic and elegiac poet, of Paros, son of Telesicles (Ael. fr. 80) and a slave-woman. His date is disputed. The ancient authorities vary from the time of Romulus, 753–716 B.C. (Cic. *Tusc.* 1. 1. 3), to that of Gyges, who died *c.* 652 B.C. (Hdt. 1. 12). The eclipse of the sun mentioned in fr. 74 is usually taken to be that of 6 April, 648 B.C., but may be that of 14 March, 711 B.C. Since Archilochus took part in the colonization of Thasos (Euseb. *Praep. Evang.* 6. 8), and this is dated *c.* 708 B.C. (Clem. Al. *Strom.* 1. 333 b), the earlier date is more probable. If so, Archilochus mentions contemporary events in the Lelantine War (fr. 3) and the destruction of Magnesia (fr. 19). Little is known of his life except of warfare in Thasos, and his quarrels with Lycambes in his attempts to marry Neobule (Hor. *Epist.* 1. 19. 23 ff.). Fr. 18 does not prove that he went to Magna Graecia. He was killed in battle (Plut. *De sera* 7). Considerable remains of his work survive: (1) elegiac epigrams, probably songs sung to the flute over the wine, often about himself, sometimes influenced by epic language, but remarkable for their strongly personal note, whether about war (frs. 3, 6, 7) or wine (fr. 4); (2) iambic trimeters, also about himself, though in fr. 22 another character is represented as speaking. In them he seems to have assailed Lycambes (fr. 24), and fr. 25 has been referred to Neobule; (3) trochaic tetrameters catalectic, including lines on the colonization of Thasos (frs. 52–4), the approach of war (fr. 56), his own misfortunes (frs. 58, 67), the eclipse of the sun (fr. 74), and his own skill in poetry (frs. 76–7); (4) epodes, or stanzas of mixed metres, of which there are different types: (*a*) frs. 81–7 iambic trimeter followed by hemiepes, (*b*) frs. 88–97 iambic trimeters followed by iambic dimeters, and (*c*) fr. 104 dactylic hexameters followed by iambic dimeters. In this class he composed αἶνοι, fables of traditional character about the fox and the monkey, the fox and the eagle, the fox and the hedgehog, probably with personal references to himself and his circumstances; (5) tetrameters of mixed rhythms, (*a*) frs. 107–11, paroemiacs and ithyphallics, (*b*) frs. 112–17, dactylic tetrameters and ithyphallics; (6) Pindar (*Ol.* 9. 1) attributes to him the song of victory used by victors at Olympia. He was regarded as a great innovator (Plut. *De mus.* 28) in metre, language, and subjects, and the fragments support this reputation. They are less violent and abusive than we might expect (cf. Pind. *Pyth.* **2.** 99). His language is mostly colloquial Ionic, though

in his elegiacs he admits epic forms. *See also* IAMBIC POETRY, GREEK.

TEXT: E. Diehl, *Anth. Lyr. Graec.* i. 3, pp. 3–49.
CRITICISM: A. Hauvette, *Archiloque, sa Vie et ses Œuvres* (1905); A. A. Blakeway, 'The Date of Archilochus' in *Greek Poetry and Life* (1936), 34–55; F. Jacoby, 'The Date of Archilochus', *CQ* xxxv (1941), 97–109. C. M. B.

ARCHIMEDES (*c.* 287–212 B.C.), the greatest mathematician of antiquity, born at Syracuse, killed at the sack of the city by Marcellus, was the son of Phidias, an astronomer, and was on intimate terms with King Hieron II. He studied for some time in Alexandria, where he met Conon of Samos and Eratosthenes, and then returned to Syracuse. History knows him (1) as the inventor of a water-screw (κοχλίας) and of clever machines used against the Roman besiegers, (2) for his boast of being able to move a great weight by a very small force ('give me a place to stand on and I will move the earth', πᾷ βῶ καὶ κινῶ τὰν γᾶν, Simplicius *in Phys.* 1110. 5 d), (3) for his determination of the proportions of gold and silver in a crown made for Hieron (εὕρηκα, εὕρηκα), (4) for his planetarium ('sphere') which was taken to Rome, where it was seen by Cicero (*Rep.* 1. 21. 22, etc.) and probably by Ovid (*Fasti* 6. 277). His tomb, by his wish, showed a cylinder circumscribing a sphere with the ratio 3/2 which he discovered between them (Cic. *Tusc.* 5. 64 f.).

Archimedes' works extant in Greek are: *On the Sphere and Cylinder* bks. 1 and 2, *Measurement of a Circle*, *On Conoids and Spheroids*, *On Spirals*, *Plane Equilibriums* (Ἐπίπεδοι ἰσορροπίαι) bks. 1 and 2, *Sand-reckoner* (Ψαμμίτης, *Arenarius*), *Quadrature of a Parabola*, *On Floating Bodies* (Περὶ ὀχουμένων) bks. 1 and 2, and the *Method* (Ἐφόδιον)—the Greek text of the last two only discovered in 1906, by Heiberg. Lost works named by various writers include: Περὶ ζυγῶν, on balances or levers (Pappus 8), Κεντροβαρικά (Simplicius on *De Caelo* 543. 24 Heib.), Κατοπτρικά, Theory of mirrors (Theon on Ptol. *Alm.* 1, p. 29 ff.), and on thirteen semi-regular solids (Pappus 5. 352–8). A book of lemmas coming from the Arabic includes interesting propositions on the *salinon* (? 'salt-cellar') and ἄρβηλος ('shoemaker's knife'), and a method of trisecting any angle; Arabic tradition refers to yet other works and has preserved some, notably the inscribing of a regular heptagon in a sphere (see T. L. Heath, *Manual of Greek Mathematics*, 340–2).

In geometry, building upon the 'method of exhaustion' invented by Eudoxus, and extending it, Archimedes performs operations equivalent to the use, with us, of the integral calculus; thus he finds the area of a parabola and of a spiral, the surface and volume of a sphere and any segment thereof, the volumes of any segments of the conicoids of revolution. The newly discovered *Method* is of special interest, since it explains a 'mechanical' method (weighing pairs of infinitesimal parts of two different figures separately against one another) by which he discovered many of his results. In the *Measurement of a circle* Archimedes uses regular polygons of 96 sides inscribed and circumscribed respectively to a circle, and finds by pure arithmetic upper and lower limits ($3\frac{1}{7}$ and $3\frac{10}{71}$) to the value of π; he starts from approximate values of $\sqrt{3}$, and gives approximations to the square roots of many large numbers. An arithmetical *tour de force* is the *Sand-reckoner*, in which he describes an original system for expressing in language very large numbers; it amounts to a scale of notation in which 100,000,000 is substituted for 10 as the base; by this means Archimedes works out at 10^{63} the number of grains of sand which, on certain assumptions, the universe would contain. A *cattle-problem* contained in an epigram addressed to Eratosthenes (edited by Lessing in 1773) is a problem in indeterminate analysis (seven equations between eight unknowns, with other conditions) leading to prodigious figures.

In *mechanics* Archimedes establishes the theory of the lever and finds the centre of gravity of triangles and quadrilaterals, any segment of a parabola, a semicircle, a hemisphere, a segment of a sphere, etc. Lastly, in Περὶ ὀχουμένων he invented the whole science of hydrostatics, dealing with the behaviour of different bodies when floating in a fluid, according to their shape and to what we call their specific gravity. *See also* PHYSICS, paras. 3, 4, and 6.

The *editio princeps* is that of Gechauff, Basel 1544. A Latin translation of five treatises by Commandinus followed in 1588 (Venice). J. Torelli's edition in Greek and Latin (Oxford 1792) was the standard edition until the appearance of Heiberg's definitive Greek text with Latin translation (2nd edition 1910–15, Teubner). See also: German translation by E. Nizze (1824); French translations by F. Peyrard (2nd ed. 1808) and (recent) by Paul ver Eecke; T. L. Heath, *The Works of Archimedes* (in modern notation) (1897); PW ii. 507. T. H.

ARCHIPPUS, Athenian comic dramatist, victorious 415–412 B.C. (Suidas: several fragments point to a similar *floruit*). In his best-known play, Ἰχθύες (probably shortly after 403 B.C.), the fishes declare war on man, and a treaty is made for an exchange of prisoners, the gourmets most obnoxious to the fishes being handed over to them. The Ῥίνων no doubt satirized the statesman of that name and so is after 403 B.C. (Isoc. 18. 6). A. seems to have been an imitative writer. His Ἰχθύες probably owes something to Ar. *Av.*, his Ἡρακλῆς γαμῶν to Epicharmus' Ἥβης γάμος, and possibly his Πλοῦτος (probably after Ar.'s first *Plutus*, 408 B.C.) to Aristophanes'. His contemporaries derided his frigid puns (schol. Ar. *Vesp.* 481), some of which survive in the fragments.

FCG i. 205 ff.; CAF i. 679 ff. M. P.

ARCHITECTURE. I. GREEK. Greek architecture began about the middle of the seventh century B.C.; approximately at that time the first temples which can be called Greek were built, the earliest known example being the Dorian Temple of Hera (Heraeum) at Olympia. There were two main streams of development, Dorian and Ionian, the former being firmly planted in the West till the second century B.C., with centres in Greece proper, south Italy (Magna Graecia), and Sicily; a parallel Ionian development prevailed from *c.* 600 B.C. in west and south-west coast lands (Ionia, Lycia, and Caria) and adjoining islands of Asia Minor. Both streams preserved separate architectural character throughout; in Greece (at Athens and Delphi) during the sixth and fifth centuries B.C., and at Locri in Magna Graecia (an Ionian colony) we find Ionian buildings in Dorian lands.

2. Though the temple (q.v.) is the supreme architectural type, there are others, mostly civic, well worth study. The Hall of Mysteries (Telesterion) at Eleusis (6th and 5th c.), the Thersilion at Megalopolis (a unique pillared hall—*c.* 370 B.C.), and the Arsenal at the Piraeus (*c.* 347 B.C.) may be mentioned. From *c.* 350 till *c.* 100 B.C.—or, broadly speaking, in the period called 'Hellenistic', there are remains of buildings showing interesting plan and structure (e.g. the 'Hypostyle Hall' at Delos and the Heroön at Calydon), large monumental quality (e.g. the Mausoleum (q.v.) at Halicarnassus), and small monumental quality (e.g. the Choragic Monument of Lysicrates and the 'Tower of the Winds' at Athens); in addition there is a wealth of evidence about domestic buildings in the fifth to second centuries, notably from Olynthus, Priene, and Delos (see TOWNS). Theatres (q.v.) and halls of assembly (Miletus and Priene) also gave opportunity for architectural treatment.

3. All Greek architecture was strictly governed by the expressions of post and beam (trabeated) construction known as the Doric, Ionic, and (to a slight extent) Corinthian Orders; the arch, though known by 200 B.C., was practically never used. It is essential to realize,

firstly, that the beam, or entablature, and the base, or stylobate, combine with the column (q.v.) to form an Order, the two former being even more important, as they were used in wall treatments as well as in columnar treatments, securing the emphasis of the horizontal element which is the hall-mark of all classical architecture; secondly, that Greek architectural forms outlasted Greece, politically, completely saturating Roman decorative expression, which, in the Near East even as late as the second century A.D., maintained essentially Greek qualities. The term 'Graeco-Roman', vaguely understood in an architectural sense, can be used with certainty for Order treatments in most of the structures that are Roman in date up to the end of the first century B.C., and often much later.

4. The Orders had their origin in wooden originals: in Doric this can be seen particularly in entablatures, while the Doric column capital shows the influences of Minoan and Mycenaean prototypes; in Ionic the capital developed from Near Asian (Aeolic) and from further eastern forms. Before the end of the sixth century B.C. both Doric and Ionic temples had become perfect stone and marble expressions, construction being flawless and without the use of mortar; utmost refinement was the ideal, stone, where used, being finished with thin stucco, and both stone and marble coloured with admirable taste. The Corinthian Order, also fully coloured, was first used in the latter part of the fifth century; some rudimentary examples (one, at Epidaurus, remarkably fine) are known from Greek and Hellenistic times, but this Order was really a Graeco-Roman achievement.

II. ROMAN. The Romans were skilful users of the artistic genius of the Greeks in regard to pure architecture, and even Roman works of civic development were an extension of ideas already evolved in Greek lands. The Roman Forum took the place of the Greek Market (*Agora*), and there was nothing new in the underlying principles of Roman temples, theatres (q.v.), palaces (q.v.), domestic buildings, or even basilicas (q.v.), though baths (q.v.) and amphitheatres (q.v.) were new types; but the Romans became constructors of first-rate ability by a mastery in the use of the semicircular arch, borrowed from the Etruscans and from native Syrian masons. The trabeated principle was never abandoned, but was associated with arched forms externally (e.g. in the Colosseum (q.v.) at Rome, and with vaulted and domical forms internally (e.g. in baths). By a gradual process of transition the expressions of the Greek Orders were changed into forms which have become the accepted modern ones through their exploitation in the Italian Renaissance. For columnar treatments of exceptional strength (e.g. in Triumphal Arches) a fourth Order, the 'Composite', was used; the capital being a fusion of Ionic and Corinthian which had its origin in the fourth century B.C. The profusely carved and dentilled cornice of the Corinthian and Composite Orders, enriched with modillions, was the most important architectural feature bequeathed by the Romans to posterity.

2. Roman arched forms supported and sometimes reinforced the concrete used for their vaults and domes (*see* BUILDING MATERIALS). Though the fully developed pendentive dome on a square plan was used by the Romans at Gerasa (Syria) at the end of the second century, it was not adopted in the West, but the large rotunda known as the Pantheon (q.v.), the so-called 'Temple of Minerva Medica' (3rd or 4th c.), and other circular or polygonal structures from the time of Hadrian to that of Constantine, had an important influence on Early Christian and Byzantine churches of centralized type. *See also* AQUEDUCTS, BRIDGES.

3. The outstanding contribution of Greek architecture to posterity was its perfecting of the Orders, and of Roman architecture the constructive ability and sheer magnitude of its greatest buildings; but the Orders are

of paramount importance—their survival value has been unique in the history of architectural development. Apart from their Orders, the Parthenon (q.v.) and the tiny Monument of Lysicrates at Athens would lose all their expression; and structures such as these are immortal.

D. S. Robertson, *Greek and Roman Architecture*[2] (1943); W. J. Anderson, R. P. Spiers, and W. B. Dinsmoor, *The Architecture of Ancient Greece*[3] (1927); W. J. Anderson, R. P. Spiers, and J. Ashby, *The Architecture of Ancient Rome*,[3] (1927).   T. F.

ARCHITHEORIA, *see* LITURGY.

ARCHIVES. I. GREEK (ἀρχεῖα: this name originally applied to all offices of magistrates; it did not acquire its special sense until the Hellenistic period). The predecessors of Greek archives were the officials called *mnemones*, 'remembrancers'. They were gradually displaced through the necessity of having public records in writing and under the custody of the State. Even Sparta possessed an archive (which included the Delphic oracles). But generally the institution of public archives started in the fifth or fourth century B.C.; in Athens a centralized record-office was perhaps not instituted before 403. The name of the record-offices varied, temples often being used, as the Metroön in Athens. All records kept in archives were written on white wooden tablets or papyrus. They constituted the originals (αὐτόγραφα), while all inscriptions in public places were copies (ἀντίγραφα). There were, of course, all kinds of records in the archives; most of them contained a register of landed property. Registration of public records became increasingly general; in most Hellenistic States it seems to have been made optional for everybody to deliver private records to the archive, and it became compulsory to lodge certain legal documents there. The registration of landed property and generally the preservation of records was nowhere more elaborate than in Ptolemaic and Roman Egypt.

E. Weiss, *Griech. Privatrecht* i (1923), 356 ff., 391 ff. Busolt-Swoboda, *Griech. Staatskunde* i. 484 ff., ii. 1036 ff. Kahrstedt, *Klio* 1938, 25 ff.

II. ROMAN (*tabularia*, from *tabulae*, the usual word for records). The chief archive was the *aerarium populi Romani*. This was at first housed in the temple of Saturn in the Forum, after 78 B.C. in the so-called *tabularium* on the south-east side of the Capitol. Originally the treasury, it contained from early times all documents relating to financial administration, and later on almost all official records were deposited there, including laws, *plebiscita*, *senatus consulta*, Imperial constitutions and decrees. Various officials, chiefly the *quaestores urbani*, were concerned with the administration of the *aerarium*. Among the other archives the most important were the temple of Ceres (where copies of plebiscites and, in early times, of *senatus consulta* were lodged), and the *tabularium Caesaris*, where all documents relating to landed property were kept in Imperial times. Documents concerning foreign affairs, e.g. treaties, were stored in bronze copies on the Capitol. All provinces and *municipia* had their own archives. Private records were generally not admitted, until Marcus Aurelius ordered that the birth of every Roman child was to be registered at the *aerarium* of the provincial *tabularium*.

Mommsen, *Röm. Staatsr.* passim, esp. ii. 1. 545 ff.; Sachers, *PW*, s.v. 'Archive'.   V. E. and A. H. McD.

ARCHONTES, the general term for all holders of office in a State. But the word was frequently used of a particular office, originally at least the highest office of the State. *Archontes* are found in most States of central Greece, including Athens, and in States dependent on or influenced by Athens.

2. In Athens there were at first three archons, the *basileus*, the polemarch, and the archon (*eponymos*), this being probably the order in which they were first instituted. The royal house of Medontidae (*see* CODRUS) continued to hold a hereditary life-office (probably as *basileis*, not as *archontes eponymi*, as Aristotle says) after the institution of polemarch and archon, the two latter being presumably elective. Later (*c.* 750 B.C.?) the three archons were made ten-yearly, and in 683 yearly magistrates; all rights of the Medontidae had disappeared. Shortly after this the number of archons was increased to nine by the addition of six *thesmothetai* (q.v.). They were elected by the people and were the chief magistrates of the State. The *archon eponymos* was the most important because he had the widest range of duties. Political struggles in the seventh and sixth centuries centred round the elections to this office till the tyranny of the Pisistratids, who arranged that one of themselves or their adherents should hold it. In 487 the lot (first from an elected body of 500, later without pre-election) was introduced as the mode of their appointment, and therewith their political importance ended. No influential politician held the office afterwards; before 487 Solon, Hippias, Themistocles, and Aristides had been archons.

3. The nine archons and the secretary to the *thesmothetai* were each chosen from one of the ten *phylae*. Solon's arrangement was preserved, by which the archonship was open only to men of the highest or two highest census-classes (*see* SOLON); it was opened to the *zeugitai* in 457, never formally to the *thetes*, though questions were not asked if one of the latter was chosen.

4. All ex-archons after their *euthyna* (q.v.) entered the Areopagus, and remained life-members of that council. This added considerable importance to their office in early times; after the introduction of the lot as the method of election, the Areopagus too lost its political importance.

5. Like most public offices in Greece, the archonship involved wide judicial as well as executive duties. In early times the nine archons tried cases entirely themselves (except those involving life or citizen rights, where there was trial by the Areopagus or appeal to the citizenbody). The relationship between the archons and the Heliaea (q.v.) in the sixth century is obscure. In the developed democracy the archons (and other magistrates) were only required to examine a case to decide if it could be brought at all, and if so in what court, to collect the evidence, and to preside at the trial (*see* DICASTERIES).

6. The *archon eponymos* was so called because he gave his name to the year: the list of eponymous archons was kept continuously from 683 B.C., but the term *eponymos* was not officially used before Roman Imperial times. He was chief magistrate until 487 and always remained the nominal head of the State. His archonship was a civil office, and was concerned especially with the protection of property; on entry into office he took an oath that at the end of his year everyone should hold what he held at the beginning: that is, he guaranteed the citizens against disorder and arbitrary executive action. Since property involved inheritance, the archon had to protect the family (and in particular orphans and heiresses), and in his judicial capacity had charge of all cases involving family and inheritance rights. He regulated certain religious festivals, particularly the City Dionysia, and had the charge of lawsuits arising from them.

7. The *Basileus* had certain religious duties and presided over the Areopagus. He had charge of the Lenaea and the Mysteries (q.v.), and in general of all the religious duties of the former kings. He introduced lawsuits arising from these, and also those between claimants for a priesthood. His jurisdiction included all charges of impiety, and all homicide cases (because a man guilty of shedding blood must be kept away from sacred places till purified). *See also* POLEMARCHUS, THESMOTHETAI.

Aristotle, *Ath. Pol.* chs. 3, 8, 13, 55–9.   A. W. G.

ARCHYTAS of Tarentum flourished in the first half of the fourth century B.C. He was visited by Plato, and had a great reputation in antiquity. He is said to have been the founder of mechanics; he distinguished harmonic progressions from arithmetical and geometrical; he solved the problem of doubling the cube, by means of two half-cylinders. He worked out the ratios which underlie the relations of successive notes in the enharmonic, the chromatic, and the diatonic scales. In philosophy he belonged to the Pythagorean school. Frs. of his mathematical works remain, but the other frs. cited as from him are late fabrications.

Testimonia and frs. in Diels, *Vorsokr.*⁵ i. 421–39. *PW* ii. 600.
W. D. R.

ARCISIUS (Ἀρκείσιος), in mythology, father of Laertes and grandfather of Odysseus (q.v.); his own parentage is variously given. In one story, his mother was a she-bear (Ἀρκείσιος—ἄρκτος), Aristotle in *Etym. Magn.* 144. 25.

ARCTINUS of Miletus (? 8th c. B.C.), epic poet; author of the *Aethiopis* and *Iliu Persis.* and probably of the *Titanomachia. See* EPIC CYCLE.

EGF, pp. 3, 6–8, 33–6, 49–52.

ARDEA, a city of the Rutuli, a Latin people. Although three miles distant from the sea it served as a port for Latium. Archaeological remains (ditch and wall defences, acropolis, and temples that long served as federal sanctuaries for the Latin League) confirm the tradition that Ardea was once an important city, worthy of signing a separate treaty with Rome (444 B.C.). In 442 a Latin colony strengthened Ardea against the Volsci and in 390 Camillus, it was said, set out from here to repel the Gauls. Apparently, too, Ardea remained loyal in the Latin War (Livy 8. 12). Ardea began its decline *c.* 300 and malaria accelerated the process. However, the erection of numerous villas and possibly the dispatch of a Hadrianic colony prevented the village from entirely disappearing. In Republican times Ardea served as a State prison; later its fields supported the Imperial elephants.

Verg. *Aen.* bks. 7–12; Dion. Hal. 1. 72; Livy 4. 7; 5. 43 f.; 39. 19; Cato fr. 58 P.; Strabo 5. 232; Diod. 12. 34; *Lib. Colon.* p. 231. B. Tilly, *Vergil's Latium* (1947), 31 ff.
E. T. S.

AREITHOUS (Ἀρηΐθοος), a mythological character, surnamed Κορυνήτης, i.e. Club-man, because he fought with a club of iron; his armour had been given him by Ares. Lycurgus the Arcadian caught him in a narrow road where he had no room to swing his club, ran him through with a spear, and took his armour (*Il.* 7. 138 ff.).
H. J. R.

ARELATE, a town in Gallia Narbonensis, modern *Arles-sur-Rhône.* The *periplus* of Avienus (679) mentions a Greek town Theline which preceded 'Arelatus', and the 'Rhodanusia' of Ps.-Scymnus (206) was presumably in the vicinity; but archaeological vestiges are slight (cf. Jacobsthal–Neuffer, *Préhistoire* ii. 51). Arelate came into importance with the construction of the 'Fossae Marianae', and was used as a naval base by Caesar against Massilia (49 B.C.). A colony of veterans of the sixth legion was founded here in 46 ('colonia Iulia Paterna Arelate sextanorum'), but the town was much enlarged, as appears, by Augustus, to whom the earliest surviving town-wall, and probably the still visible east gate, are due. The *territorium* was created mainly at the expense of Massilia. Early buildings still partially surviving are the forum, amphitheatre (136 m. × 107 m. externally), and the theatre. The principal importance of Arelate was due to its position as a port of trans-shipment for sea-going vessels which were under the control of the five corporations of *navicularii Arelatenses.* In the Later Empire it acquired importance as the occasional residence of emperors, in the fourth century a mint was set up, and in the

fifth it became the seat of the praetorian prefecture. Extensive baths (*La Trouille*) date from this period, and though the area within the walls was reduced, Ausonius (19. 73–80) and the Emperor Honorius (Haenel, *Corpus legum*, 238) attest its prosperity. After various vicissitudes it was annexed by the Visigoths in A.D. 476.

L. A. Constans, *Arles antique* (1921); Grenier, *Manuel* i. 289–95; ii. 493–9.
C. E. S.

ARELLIUS FUSCUS, Augustan rhetor, perhaps a Greek. His style was brilliant but affected and undisciplined (Sen. *Controv.* 2 praef. 1). Ovid was one of his many pupils (ib. 2. 2. 8–9).

AREOPAGUS (officially ἡ Βουλὴ ἡ ἐξ Ἀρείου πάγου), the oldest Council at Athens, originating in the king's advisory body of chief men. It had also from earliest times a special jurisdiction in cases of homicide (including wounding with intent and arson); in this capacity it met on the hill known as the Areopagus (*see* ATHENS (TOPOGRAPHY)), as a Council in the Stoa Basileios. The Basileus (*see* ARCHONTES, para. 7) presided at its meetings; from the time of the three archons, or more probably from that of the nine, it received into its ranks all ex-archons who had passed a *dokimasia* (q.v.) before it.

Since the archons (until 456 B.C.) were chosen exclusively from the nobles or the rich, the Areopagus would naturally become a powerful oligarchic body, like the Senate at Rome, and as its members were appointed for life would be far stronger than the yearly archons. According to Aristotle it not only controlled the magistrates before Solon but had the administration of affairs practically in its hands; and Solon made it particularly the guardian of the new constitution. It had specific powers to punish offenders (presumably offending magistrates, for the archons had jurisdiction in ordinary civil and criminal cases). Yet in fact there was no tradition of its ever playing an important part in the history of Athens during the seventh and sixth centuries: the archonship is the chief office and the centre of party struggles. After 487, when the lot was introduced for the archonship, the political power of the archons, and therefore ultimately of the Areopagus, declined. We are told indeed that after 480, owing to its unshaken courage before and after Salamis, it recovered much of its influence; there is probably some truth in this— Themistocles and Aristides were both members, and they may have been greatly helped by the Council's action; but there is no reason to believe that it almost ruled Athens for a number of years, putting a brake on the democratic advance. On the contrary Salamis gave a great impulse to the growth of the democratic sailor-class. In 462–461 the democrats, led by Ephialtes, carried a series of laws taking from the Areopagus its power of 'overseeing' the constitution and its control over the magistrates; this marks the end of its influence, but that had been effectively undermined by the reform of 487.

For the rest of the fifth and in succeeding centuries it remained a highly venerated court for the trial of homicide (and a few minor cases arising from certain religious cults): much talked about by sentimentalists who wanted 'the old constitution' back, ignored by all in practical politics. There was some revival of its activities after 338; it seems to have taken some part in hunting down traitors and cowards, and it was given the commission of examining the affair of Harpalus (q.v.) in 325–324 and reporting to the dicasteries. But even then, and in later oligarchic attempts to restore it, it never gained any real political power.

Aristotle, *Ath. Pol.*, passim.
A. W. G.

ARES (Ἄρης, Aeolic Ἄρευς; etymology unknown, but good Greek formation), the Greek war-god, not in the sense of a warlike deity who leads his people into battle.

but rather a deification of warlike spirit. F. Schwenn, *ARW* xxii (1923–4), 224 ff., finds difficulty in supposing this possible for early times and suggests that Ares was originally a deity of vegetation, who became a war-god secondarily by some unknown process. There is, however, no reason to assume that Ares was worshipped by the earliest Greeks. He is unpopular, is an important god only in Thebes and perhaps Athens (contrast Mars, q.v.), belongs especially to the northern and western communities (Aetolia, Thessaly, etc.), and has been considered by some to be of Thracian origin (Farnell, op. cit. infra, 399 ff.). It is conceivable that he was 'projected' from some widespread rite of war-magic, earlier than civilization in any Greek people. He never develops into a god with any moral functions, like Zeus or Apollo, and in mythology he appears either as instigator to violence or as a tempestuous lover, a divine *miles gloriosus*. He frequently has Aphrodite (q.v. para. 4) as his partner (e.g. at Thebes they are the parents of Harmonia, *see* CADMUS); he is associated with her, Athena, and Enyo in his temple at Athens (Paus. 1. 8. 4). It must be noted that Aphrodite (q.v.), like many mother-goddesses, has warlike qualities. Hence, as she is also thought of as wife of Hephaestus, the story that Ares is her paramour (*Od.* 8. 266 ff. and often later). In his ritual perhaps the most remarkable feature is that at Tegea he was worshipped by women under the title of Γυναικοθοίνας (Paus. 8. 48. 4); it should be remembered that women are often active in war-magic. Dogs were sacrificed to him (under his common title of Enyalios) at Sparta (Plut. *Quaest. Rom.* 290 d; Paus. 3. 14. 9), a procedure associated with purifications and deities of an uncanny sort, such as Hecate.

In mythology, although son of Zeus and Hera, he is commonly the helper of foreign peoples, such as the Trojans, or unusually warlike ones, as the Amazons (q.v.). He is the father, by various mothers, of numerous children, mostly sons and commonly of warlike, often violent and outrageous character, as Ascalaphus (*Il.* 13. 518; 15. 113 for Ares' fury at his death); Diomedes the Thracian (*see* HERACLES); Cycnus the brigand (*see* ibid.); Meleager in some versions of the story (Hyg. *Fab.* 14. 16); Phlegyas, eponym of a whole people of impious raiders and ferocious fighters (Paus. 9. 36. 2). Such genealogies seem to waver between the complimentary (a brave warrior is a 'shoot from Ares' stock', ὄζος Ἄρηος, in Homer) and the uncomplimentary, the god's own character being ferocious and unlovely. That he is the father of Eros (Simonides, fr. 24 Diehl) is a by-product of the original lack of any association between Eros and Aphrodite. Of his daughters, Harmonia has already been mentioned; by Agraulus daughter of Cecrops (*see* ATTIC CULTS AND MYTHS) he became the father of Alcippe, who was violated by Halirrhothius son of Poseidon. Killing him, he was tried by the Areopagus and acquitted (Apollod. 3. 180) or sent into a year's serfdom (Panyassis ap. Clem. Alex. *Protr.* p. 26, 22 Stählin). As early as Hesiod (*Th.* 934) Aphrodite bears him his Homeric attendants Deimos and Phobos (Fear and Rout). Cicero (*Nat.D.* 3. 60) adds Anteros to the family from some late author.

In Rome he was identified with Mars (q.v.).

Much material collected in Roscher's *Lexikon*, s.v. 'Ares' (Stoll-Furtwängler). Brief account in Rose, *Handbook of Gk. Myth.*², 157–8. For his cult, see especially Farnell, *Cults of the Greek States* v. 396–414. H. J. R.

ARETAEUS of Cappadocia, medical author, a contemporary of Galen (*c.* 150–200), wrote in Ionic in imitation of Hippocrates. Works (extant but incomplete): Περὶ αἰτιῶν καὶ σημείων ὀξέων καὶ χρονίων παθῶν; Περὶ θεραπείας ὀξέων καὶ χρονίων παθῶν; (lost) Περὶ πυρετῶν; Περὶ γυναικείων; Περὶ φυλακτικῶν; Χειρουργίαι. His main merit is that he builds on the solid foundations of Archigenes (q.v.).

Ed. K. Hude, *CMG* ii (1923). *PW* ii. 669. W. D. R.

AREUS (*c.* 312–265 B.C.), son of Acrotatus, succeeded his grandfather, Cleomenes II, on the Spartan throne (309–308). In 280 he invaded Aetolia, after organizing a Peloponnesian coalition against Macedon; on his repulse this collapsed. In 272 he returned hurriedly from helping Gortyn in Crete, to drive Pyrrhus back from Sparta, and assisted in his destruction at Argos. During the Chremonidean War he failed to force Craterus' Isthmus lines to relieve Athens; in 256 he fell outside Corinth. He was the first Spartan king to hold an elaborate court and to issue silver coins.

K. J. Beloch, *Griech. Gesch.* iv (1928). F. W. W.

ARGAS, citharode and poet of the first half of the fourth century B.C., renowned for his badness (Plut. *Dem.* 4, schol. Aeschin. 2. 99). Hence his name was used as a term of abuse of Demosthenes by Aeschines (2. 99).

ARGEADAE, *see* MACEDONIA, para. 2.

ARGEI. On 16 and 17 March a procession went *ad Argeos* (Ov. *Fasti* 3. 791–2), i.e. to the twenty-seven *Argeorum sacraria* (Varro, *Ling.* 5. 45) scattered about Rome. On 14 May (15, Dion. Hal. *Ant. Rom.* 1. 38. 3), the Vestals, pontiffs, and others threw from the Pons Sublicius into the Tiber twenty-seven effigies of men in old-fashioned clothing (Ov. op. cit. 5. 621 ff.; Dion. Hal. loc. cit.; Varro, op. cit. 7. 44 and Ennius quoted there; see further Frazer on Ovid, loc. cit.). The ancients commonly explained this as a surrogate for human sacrifice (Ov. ibid., and other passages). Of moderns, Wissowa holds a similar view (art. 'Argei' in *PW*, = *Gesammelte Abhandlungen*, 211 ff.), and dates it from the third century B.C., the age of the document quoted in Varro, *Ling.* 5. 47 ff. This is generally rejected. That it is a vegetation-rite, with the well-known drowning or bathing of a sort of Jack-in-the-Green, is unlikely, if only from the number of the figures (why more than one?) (L. Deubner in *ARW* xxiii (1925), 299 f.); it remains most likely that, as Frazer suggests (*Fasti of Ovid*, iv. 91 and references there), the puppets are 'offerings to the river-god to pacify him' and induce him to spare the real persons using the bridge or otherwise approaching the stream. H. J. R.

ARGEIA, *see* ADRASTUS.

ARGENTARIUS (1), MARCUS (fl. 1 B.C.), is the liveliest of the Graeco-Roman epigrammatists whose works crowd the Greek Anthology. A heavy drinker (see his address to a bottle, *Anth. Pal.* 6. 248), he was poor and unsuccessful; but his vein of coarse humour never deserted him, though his sense of propriety often did. He is probably the Latin-speaking Greek rhetor cited by the elder Seneca (*Suas.* 5. 6, *Controv.* 2. 6. 11). G. H.

ARGENTARIUS (2), Augustan rhetor, a Greek; a slavish follower of Cestius (Sen. *Controv.* 9. 3. 12–13). He may be identical with the epigrammatist of the Greek Anthology.

ARGENTORATE, modern *Strasbourg*. The Celtic name (silver fort) hints at a pre-Roman settlement, of which traces have been found. Perhaps first occupied as one of Drusus' *castella* by 'Ala Petriana Treverorum'. It was garrisoned *c.* A.D. 12–43 by Legio II Augusta, then by legionary detachments including one of XXI Rapax, who constructed the first basalt wall. *Circa* A.D. 80 Legio VIII was transferred here. Its fortress (606 × 300 m.) was defended by an earth bank with 90 cm. thick revetment wall of small blocks and brick borders. From the third century Argentorate was exposed to barbarian attacks (an incident of which was Julian's victory, A.D. 357), and for increased protection the wall was fronted by another, 2 m. 50 cm. thick, of re-used masonry with bastions *c.* 25 m. apart. In this period the *canabae* (q.v.), previously important, were given up and the civil population crowded into the fortress.

R. Forrer, *Strasbourg-Argentorate* (1927).   C. E. S.

ARGONAUTS ('Αργοναῦται), one of the oldest Greek sagas, based originally on a perhaps real exploit of the semi-historical Minyae, known as early as Homer (*Od.* 12. 70), probably elaborated into something like its present form at Miletus (Colchis as goal of the voyage; Miletus had an extensive Black Sea trade). The chief surviving accounts are Pindar, *Pyth.* 4; Apollonius Rhodius, *Argonautica* (both of these, especially the latter, have very helpful scholia); Valerius Flaccus, *Argonautica* and the 'Orphic' *Argonautica*; Apollodorus, 1. 107 ff.; Hyginus, *Fab.* 12 ff. The later authors all draw more or less on Apollonius, but not exclusively. Many of the episodes were represented in art.

2. Aeson son of Cretheus (*see* AEOLUS) was deprived of the kingship of Iolcus in Thessaly by his half-brother Pelias. His young son Jason (q.v.), on reaching manhood, came to reclaim the throne. Pelias was afraid to refuse openly, so induced him (how, accounts vary) first to go and fetch the Golden Fleece (*see* ATHAMAS) from Colchis. With the help of Hera, who favoured him and had been insulted by Pelias, he got together a band of the noblest heroes in Greece (lists differ widely, owing no doubt to ambitious families, many not Minyan, claiming an ancestor in the *Argo*; but all include Argos (q.v. 3*b*), Tiphys the helmsman, Lynceus, whose sight was preternaturally keen, and a few more, among them Heracles and Orpheus, both manifest intruders; cf. also Rose, *Handb. of Gk. Myth.²*, 295). Argos built him a ship, the *Argo*, by help of Athena; she was the first longship ever made. They set sail for Colchis and had several adventures by the way. At Lemnos (*see* HYPSIPYLE) they stayed a year with the women of the island; at Cyzicus they were hospitably received by the eponym of the island and Heracles rid him of the Gegeneis who infested the hills. Driven back by a storm, they killed Cyzicus in a scuffle at night, and mourned for him. At Cios, Heracles' page Hylas was carried off by water-nymphs and he, staying to look for him, was left behind. After visiting the Bebryces (*see* AMYCUS) they touched at Salmydessus and learned from Phineus (q.v.) that to get to the Euxine they must pass the Clashing Rocks (Symplegades), which he advised them to test by seeing if a dove could fly between them before they met. The dove did so, and the *Argo* likewise passed; in some accounts the rocks became stationary (at the present Dardanelles). Arrived finally at Colchis, they were confronted with a task set by King Aeetes; they must yoke a pair of fire-breathing bulls, plough a field, sow it with teeth from Cadmus' dragon (*see* CADMUS), and overcome the warriors who should spring up. This Jason succeeded in doing with the help of Medea (q.v.), and, still by her advice, he took the Fleece that same night and fled, accompanied by her.

3. The story now divides into several main variants, conditioned partly by the geographical ideas of different periods, partly by the desire to bring the Argonauts into connexion with places traditionally Minyan. (1) They returned the way they came. (2) Because they did not want to face the Symplegades again or for some other reason, they ascended the river Phasis, got to the stream of Ocean, and so sailed around till they reached the Mediterranean again. (3) They went up the Ister (Danube), thence got into the Eridanus (fabulous, but in part the Po), down it to some part of the Mediterranean, and so home. (4) From the Ister they got (via the Rhine?) into the North Sea, and so down to the Straits of Gibraltar and through them. The subsidiary adventures vary accordingly; some of the commonest are, that they reached Africa and there met a Triton who showed them the way through the shallows near Cyrene and foretold the founding of the colony by one of their descendants (Pind. ibid. 19 ff.); they passed the Sirens (*see* ODYSSEUS) and were protected against their song by Orpheus' still more lovely playing (Ap. Rhod. 4. 891 ff.); they came to Crete, and there encountered Talos, q.v., who guarded the island. Medea charmed him into a magic sleep, and he was killed by destroying the fastening that closed his one vein, thus letting out his blood, or whatever corresponded to it in him (Ap. Rhod. 4. 1638 ff., Apollod. 140–1; details vary, however). For their meeting with Alcinous, *see* s.v.

4. Not only is the story diversified with details which are pure *Märchen* (a feature of many sagas, since one good story attracts another; cf. Rose in *Folklore* (1935), 16 f.) but the motive of the voyage is of the same sort, together with two principal episodes at least. To send a hero on a dangerous journey to get rid of him, to confront a dangerous visitor with tasks, to be helped in those tasks by the daughter of a tyrant, wizard, or other formidable person, are all well-known themes (Stith Thompson, nos. H 1211, H 900, G 530. 2), and the Golden Fleece itself seems a sort of magical treasure, the kind of thing which fairy heroes go to look for. If a real voyage underlies the tale, it is deeply buried.

Good collection of material in Roscher's *Lexikon*, arts. 'Argo', 'Argonautai' (Seeliger). Interesting discussion in J. R. Bacon, *Voyage of the Argonauts* (1925).   H. J. R.

ARGOS (1), a city in the southern part of the Argive plain, three miles from the sea, at the foot of the Mycenaean and classical acropolis called Larissa. A lower hill, the Aspis, was enclosed in the walls. Both were occupied from the Early Bronze Age; most of the classical city lay in the plain.

In the *Iliad* Argos was the kingdom of Diomed, who owned Agamemnon's leadership; also, in a wider sense, Agamemnon's empire. In the Dorian invasion Argos fell to Temenus, the eldest of the Heraclids. It probably was the base from which the Dorians occupied northeast Peloponnesus, and retained the overlordship until the eighth or seventh century, when its ascendancy was challenged by Sparta. Early in the seventh century a strong king, Pheidon (q.v.), defeated the Spartans, coined the first Greek money in Aegina, presided in person over the Olympic Games, and made Argos the first power in Greece. But his power died with him, checked perhaps by the rise of Corinth. Henceforth Argos maintained a suspicious neutrality, fighting once a generation with Sparta. Her heaviest defeat was *c.* 494 B.C., when Cleomenes was barely repelled from the walls by the women of Argos, rallied by the poetess Telesilla. In 480–479 the Argives observed a benevolent neutrality towards Persia. Shortly afterwards they set up a democracy. They were repeatedly allied with Athens against Sparta (461, 420, 395), but remained an ineffective power. Argos sided with Philip II of Macedon and was one of the last cities to join the Achaean League, after a period of rule by tyrants. The territory of Argos in classical times included Mycenae, Tiryns, Nauplia, Asine, and other strongholds in the Argive plain, but not the cities of the Acte east of Argos, nor Phlius and Cleonae in the northern hills. The great Argive goddess was Hera, worshipped at the Heraeum six miles north of Argos. The minor arts were important in the earliest period, but from the seventh century they shared in the general decline. Argive sculptors of the early classical period were pre-eminent; the greatest was Polycletus (q.v.).

H. T. Wade-Gery, *CAH* iii. 527 ff.; A. Boethius, 'Zur Topographie des dorischen Argos', in *Strena Philologica Upsaliensis* (1922), 248 ff. Excavations: C. W. Vollgraff, *BCH* 1904, 1906, 1907, 1920; *Mededeelingen der Koninklijke Akademie van Wetenschappen*, Afdeeling Letterkunde, Deel 66, 87 ff.; 71 ff. (summaries in French); C. Waldstein and others, *The Argive Heraeum* (1902–5); C. W. Blegen, *Prosymna* (1937); Ἀρχ. Ἐφ. 1937, 377 ff.; *AJA* 1939, 410 ff.   T. J. D.

ARGOS (2), the chief place of the Amphilochians at the head of the Bay of Actium. Captured by the Ambracians *c.* 437 B.C., it was set free by the Athenians and assisted Athenian operations in north-west Greece in the early stages of the Peloponnesian War.

ARGOS (3), in mythology, (*a*) a monster, of variously stated parentage, who had a third eye in the back of his neck, or four eyes, two before and two behind (Pherecydes and the anonymous epic *Aegimius* ap. schol. Eur. *Phoen.* 1116), or many eyes (Aesch. *PV* 678 and most authors). He was of huge strength and size, and killed a bull and a satyr which were troubling Arcadia; he also took vengeance on the killers of Apis the son of Phoroneus (Apollod. 2. 4). When Io (q.v.) was turned into a heifer, Hera set Argos to watch her (Aesch. loc. cit.), but by command of Zeus, Hermes killed him (Apollod. ibid. 7 and many authors). He turned into a peacock (Moschus, 2. 58 ff., schol. Ar. *Av.* 102), or Hera took his eyes to deck its tail (Ov. *Met.* 1. 722–3). (*b*) An Argonaut, builder of the *Argo*, see ARGONAUTS. His parentage and nationality are variously given. (*c*) Eponym of the city Argos, Apollod. 2. 2–3. H. J. R.

ARGOS, CULTS AND MYTHS OF. The most famous cult of the Argolid was that of Hera, whose great temple, however, was not in Argos itself but some distance away (*see* HERA). In the city itself, on the lower acropolis (the Aspis), stood a very ancient temple of Athena (*see* Vollgraff in *Mnemos.* lvi, 319). Of great importance in historical times was Apollo Lykeios, whose temple stood in the Agora (Soph. *El.* 6 f.; Paus. 2. 19. 3); its foundation was ascribed to Danaus (q.v.). Myths connected with the city and district are innumerable, nearly every important legend touching them at some point; more local are the lists of Argive kings, of which the oldest is in a βουστροφηδόν inscription from the Aspis (Vollgraff, *Mnemos.* lix. 369 ff.): Potamos (?Inachus), Sthenelas son of Echedamidas, Hippomedon, Charon (otherwise unknown as a hero), Adrastus (q.v.), Orthagoras, Cteatus, Aristomachus, and Ichonidas. See, for later lists, Apollod. 2. 1 ff., Hyg. *Fab.* 124. H. J. R.

ARGUMENTUM, an explanation of the circumstances in which the action of a play is supposed to open, addressed direct to the audience by the speaker of the prologue (which may be deferred, cf. Plaut. *Cist.* 155). The *argumentum* forms part of all the prologues of Plautus except in the *Asinaria* and *Trinummus* (where we are informed that it is unnecessary); no doubt it was often translated from the Greek original (cf. the exposition uttered by Agnoia in Menander's *Perikeiromene*); it may vary from a brief statement (as in the *Truculentus*) to a detailed account (e.g. *Amph.* 97–150). Frequently it anticipates the plot to some extent. Terence abandoned the *argumentum* altogether. Cf. HYPOTHESIS.

G. Michaut, *Plaute* (1920), i. 101–8. W. B.

ARIADNE, in mythology, daughter of Minos (q.v.) and Pasiphaë. When Theseus (q.v.) came to Crete, she fell in love with him and gave him a clue of thread by which he found his way out of the Labyrinth after killing the Minotaur. He then fled, taking her with him, but (magically?) forgot and left her on Naxos (Dia). It is generally said that Dionysus found her there and married her; but Plutarch (*Thes.* 20, from Paeon of Amathus) preserves a curious local legend and custom. Theseus left her there pregnant, and she died in childbed. In commemoration of this, every year at Amathus a young man imitated a woman in childbed in honour of Ariadne Aphrodite (*see* APHRODITE, para. 1). It is probable that Ariadne was originally a goddess.

Rose. *Handb. of Gk. Myth.* 184, 265, and notes. H. J. R.

ARICIA, nowadays *Ariccia*, a city at the foot of the Albanus Mons, sixteen miles south-east of Rome, on the edge of a remarkably fertile volcanic depression (*vallis Aricina*; the impressive, beggar-infested viaduct, which carried the Via Appia across this (Juv. 4. 117), survives). Founded in mythical times, Aricia was a powerful city in early Latium: under Turnus Herdonius it organized resistance to Tarquinius Superbus, helped Aristodemus of Cumae to crush the Etruscans (*c.* 505 B.C.), supplied the Latin League with a meeting-place (*caput aquae Ferentinae*), and was prominent in the Regillus battle and the following treaty, *foedus Cassianum* (499–493). In 446 Aricia quarrelled with Ardea over boundaries. After participating in the Latin War it received Roman citizenship (Festus, p. 155 L. represents this, probably inaccurately, as partial citizenship), and became a prosperous *municipium* (Cic. *Phil.* 3. 15). Such it remained, despite its sack by Marius (Livy, *Epit.* 80; *Lib. Colon.*, p. 230), until barbarian invasions ruined it. Aricia was the birthplace of Augustus' mother Atia, and is celebrated for its wealthy Temple of Diana Nemorensis, whose ruins still exist nearby in the woods surrounding Lake Nemi; its presiding priest was a runaway slave who had murdered his predecessor.

Strabo 5. 239; Verg. *Aen.* 7. 761 f.; Livy 1. 50 f.; etc. G. Florescu, *Ephemeris Dacoromana* iii (1925) (documented). A. E. Gordon, *Cults of Aricia* (U.S.A., 1934). E. T. S.

ARIES, *see* SIEGECRAFT, ROMAN.

ARIMASPEANS. A legendary people of the far North, between the Issedones and the Hyperboreans. They were one-eyed, and fought with griffins who guarded a hoard of gold. Aristeas was said to have written an epic about them (Hdt. 3. 116, 4. 13 and 27; Aesch. *PV* 803 ff.). W. K. C. G.

ARIMINUM, nowadays *Rimini* with imposing Augustan monuments, an Umbrian and later Gallic town on the Adriatic which became a Latin colony, 268 B.C. (Vell. Pat. 1. 14; K. J. Beloch, *Röm. Gesch.*, 490, for magistrates; A. Sambon, *Monnaies ant. de l'Italie* (1903), 88, for coins; E. T. Salmon, *JRS* 1936, 58, for the *Ius Arimini*). An important harbour and road-centre, Ariminum was the key to Cisalpine Gaul, controlling the bottle-neck between Apennines and Adriatic (Polyb. 3. 61, etc.; Livy 24. 44, etc.; Strabo 5. 217). It remained loyal to Rome against Hannibal (Livy 27. 10) and obtained Roman citizenship *c.* 89 B.C. (Pliny, *HN* 3. 115). Surviving sack by Sulla, occupation by Caesar, confiscation and colonization by the Triumvirs, attacks by Flavians (A.D. 69) and Goths (538), it became a member of the *pentapolis maritima* subject to the Ravenna exarchs (App. *BCiv.* 1. 67; 4. 3; Plut. *Caes.* 32; Tac. *Hist.* 3. 41; Procop. 2. 10).

G. A. Mansuelli, *Ariminum* (1941). E. T. S.

ARION (Ἀρίων) (fl. 628–625 B.C.), son of Cycleus, of Methymna in Lesbos (Suidas, s.v.), spent most of his life at the court of Periander, paid a profitable visit to Italy and Sicily, returned to Corinth after being thrown overboard and carried to land, it was said, by a dolphin (Hdt. 1. 23). He was an important figure in the history of the dithyramb, which he composed himself and taught Corinthian choirs to perform. He seems to have made it formal and stationary and to have given his poems names, i.e. definite subjects. Suidas connects him with the birth of tragedy, but this probably means no more than that his type of dithyramb helped eventually to produce tragedy. Nothing survives of his work, and a piece attributed to him by Aelian (*NA* 12. 45) is certainly spurious, being probably work of the fifth century B.C.

Text. Diehl, *Anth. Lyr. Graec.* ii. 5–6. A. W. Pickard-Cambridge *Dithyramb, Tragedy and Comedy* (1927), 20–22. C. M. B.

ARION (Ἀρείων), in mythology, the wonderful horse of Adrastus (q.v.); at Thelpusa in Arcadia (Paus. 8. 25. 5) he was said to be the offspring of Poseidon and Demeter in horse-shape. He could speak (Propertius 2. 34. 37). He belonged successively to Poseidon himself, Copreus, Heracles (see CYCNUS), and Adrastus (schol. *Il.* 23. 346).
                                                                    H. J. R.

ARIOVISTUS, king of the Suebi, invaded Gaul *c.* 71 B.C. at the invitation of the Sequani, and defeated the Aedui, then the pre-eminent Gallic tribe. He invited more Germans and defeated at Magetobriga (site unknown) a combined Gallic attempt to eject him. The Senate ratified his conquests by the title of 'friend'. In 58, however, Caesar, influenced by the petitions of Gallic chiefs, picked a quarrel with him, and after a difficult campaign routed him in the plain of Alsace. His death is mentioned incidentally in *BGall.* 5. 29.

Caesar, *BGall.* 1. 31–53; Cicero, *Att.* 1. 19. 2; Rice Holmes, *Ancient Gaul*, 37–67, 553–5, 636–57.   C. E. S.

ARISBE, name of two cities: (1) in the Troad, from Arisbe daughter of Merops, wife of Priam, or Paris, afterwards of Hyrtacus, or daughter of Teucer of Crete and wife of Dardanus; (2) in Lesbos, from Arisbe daughter of Macar. Stephanus Byzantinus, s.v.

ARISTAEUS (1), son of Apollo and Cyrene (daughter of Hypseus, king of the Lapithae), a god or hero, protector of cattle and fruit-trees, whose cult originated in Thessaly, but is found also in Cyrene, Ceos, Boeotia, and elsewhere. Pindar in *Pyth.* 9 tells how Apollo, enamoured of Cyrene in Thessaly, carried her off to Libya, where Aristaeus was born. Virgil in *G.* 4. 315–558 narrates an otherwise unknown story of Aristaeus, which he is said by Servius on doubtful authority to have substituted for a eulogy of Gallus after his disgrace. Aristaeus had offended the nymphs by pursuing Eurydice, wife of Orpheus, who in her flight was bitten by a serpent and died. The nymphs in revenge destroyed his bees. On his mother's advice he takes counsel of Proteus, who explains the cause of his misfortune. Cyrene urges him to sacrifice cattle to the nymphs. Returning after nine days Aristaeus finds bees swarming in the carcasses.
                                                                    C. B.

ARISTAEUS (2), of Croton, son-in-law and first successor of Pythagoras, is said to have written works on mathematics. In an extant fr. of a work Περὶ ἁρμονίας ascribed to him, the eternity of the world is inferred from that of God.

PW ii. 859.

ARISTAEUS, *see also* ICARIUS (1).

ARISTAGORAS (1) (fl. *c.* 500 B.C.), son-in-law of Histiaeus (q.v.), in whose absence he ruled Miletus. In 499 B.C. he persuaded the Persians to undertake an expedition against Naxos. On the failure of this enterprise he profited by the widespread discontent of the Ionians to raise them in revolt. He restored freedom to Miletus, and combated the other tyrants, who all had Persian support. In winter 499–498 he went to Greece to obtain help. Refused by Cleomenes of Sparta, he was successful in Athens and Eretria, but their small and temporary help was ineffective. Before the final failure of the revolt Aristagoras, who was a mere adventurer, emigrated to Myrcinus in Thrace, there to perish with his companions in a fight against the Thracians.

Hdt. bk. 5. M. Cary, *CAH* iv. 216 ff.; De Sanctis, *Riv. Fil.* lix (1931).   V. E.

ARISTAGORAS (2), comic writer of uncertain date. His Μαμμάκυθος ('The Simpleton') was possibly a *réchauffé* of Metagenes' Αὖραι (Ath. 13. 571 b).

FCG i. 218; *CAF* i. 710.

ARISTARCHUS (1) of Samos (*c.* 310–230 B.C.), mathematician and astronomer, was a pupil of the Peripatetic Straton of Lampsacus. He is famous as the author of the heliocentric hypothesis in astronomy, that 'the fixed stars and the sun remain unmoved, and that the earth revolves about the sun in the circumference of a circle, the sun lying in the middle of the orbit' (Archimedes, *Sand-reckoner*); he combined with this the rotation of the earth about its own axis (Plutarch, *De fac. in orbe lunae*, ch. 6). His only extant treatise, *On the sizes and distances of the sun and moon*, is, however, on the geocentric basis. Starting with six 'hypotheses', the treatise has eighteen propositions combining clever geometry with facility in arithmetical calculation. The ratios of sizes and distances which have to be calculated are really equivalent to trigonometrical ratios, and Aristarchus finds upper and lower limits to their values on the basis of assumptions equivalent to well-known theorems in trigonometry. Aristarchus is said to have invented an improved sun-dial, the σκάφη (Vitruv. 9. 8), and to have added $\frac{1}{1623}$ of a day to Callippus' estimate of 365¼ days as the length of the year.

The Greek text of Περὶ μεγεθῶν καὶ ἀποστημάτων ἡλίου καὶ σελήνης was edited by John Wallis (1688, see *Opera Mathematica* 1693–8), Fortia d'Urban (1810), E. Nizze (1856), T. L. Heath, *Aristarchus of Samos* (1913); *see also* Pappus 6. 554 f. (Hultsch); Latin translation by Commandinus (1572); German translation by A. Nokk (1854).   T. H.

ARISTARCHUS (2) of Samothrace (*c.* 217-215 to 145-143 B.C.) belonged to the school of Aristophanes of Byzantium at Alexandria and was tutor of Eupator, son of Ptolemy Philometor. He succeeded Apollonius ὁ εἰδογράφος as head of the Alexandrian Library (*c.* 153 B.C.). On the accession of Ptolemy Euergetes II (145 B.C.) he left Alexandria for Cyprus, where he died. With him scientific scholarship really began, and his work covered the wide range of grammatical, etymological, orthographical, literary, and textual criticism. He was styled ὁ γραμματικώτατος (Ath. 15. 671 f.), and for his gift of critical divination was nicknamed μάντις by Panaetius (Ath. 14. 634 c). His name has often been used to typify the complete critic (e.g. Cic. *Att.* 1. 14. 3, Hor. *Ars P.* 450). The school which he founded at Alexandria and which lasted into the Roman Imperial period had many distinguished pupils, e.g. Apollodorus and Dionysius Thrax. His writings fall into three main groups:

1. Critical recensions (διορθώσεις) of the text of Homer, Hesiod, Archilochus, Alcaeus, Anacreon, Pindar. For these, particularly for his double recension of the *Iliad* and *Odyssey*, he used symbols to indicate his suspicions of the genuineness of verses, wrongful repetition, confused orders of verses, etc. (see SCHOLARSHIP, GREEK). In his treatment of textual problems in Homer he was more cautious than his Alexandrine predecessors and sought to remove corruption, conjecture, and interpolation by scrupulous regard for the best manuscript tradition, by careful study of the Homeric language and metre, by his fine literary sense, by emphasis on the requirements of consistency and appropriateness of ethos, and by his practice of interpreting a poet by the poet's own usage. But his work seems to have had comparatively little influence on the traditional text of Homer.

2. Commentaries (ὑπομνήματα) on Homer, Hesiod, Archilochus, Pindar, Aeschylus, Sophocles, Ion, Aristophanes, Herodotus.

3. Critical treatises (συγγράμματα) on particular matters relating to the *Iliad* and *Odyssey*, e.g. the naval camp of the Greeks; and polemics against other writers and scholars, e.g. against Philetas and the *Chorizontes* (see HOMER, para. 6), especially Xenon.

K. Lehrs, *de Aristarchi studiis Homericis*³ (1882); A. Ludwich, *Aristarchs homerische Textkritik* (1884–5); D. B. Monro, *Homer's Odyssey*, Appendix (1901); B. P. Grenfell and A. S. Hunt, *Amherst Papyri* (1901), ii. 12; P. Cauer, *Grundfragen der Homerkritik*³ (1923); A. Römer, *Die Homerexegese Aristarchs* (ed. E. Belzner 1924).   J. F. L.

ARISTARCHUS (3) of Tegea, a contemporary of Euripides, dated by Eusebius (*Chron.* 2. 105) 455–454 B.C.; said by Suidas (s.v.) to have written seventy tragedies and won two victories. His plays included *Tantalus*, *Achilles* (adapted by Ennius), *Asclepius* (a thank-offering for recovery from illness, Suid, s.v.). No precise meaning can be attached to Suidas' statement that Aristarchus πρῶτος εἰς τὸ νῦν μῆκος τὰ δράματα κατέστησεν.

A. W. P.-C.

ARISTEAS. (1) of Proconnesus, a legendary servant of Apollo (cf. ABARIS), and reputed author of a poem on the Arimaspeans (q.v.). His story has three features of especial interest for Apolline religion (Hdt. 4. 13): (*a*) Ecstasis, literal separation of soul from body. A. produces the semblance of death and appears at the same time elsewhere. (*b*) The taking of non-human shape. A. accompanies Apollo in the form of a raven. (*c*) Missionary spirit. The object of A.'s miraculous disappearance from Cyzicus and reappearance at Metapontum is to spread the cult of the god.

(2) For the 'letter of Aristeas', *see* SEPTUAGINT.

W. K. C. G.

ARISTIAS (5th c. B.C.), son of Pratinas (q.v.) of Phlius, contended against Aeschylus in 467, when Aeschylus produced his Theban tetralogy and Aristias the *Perseus*, *Tantalus*, *Antaeus* (?), and his father's Παλαισταὶ Σάτυροι (Arg. Aesch. *Sept.*). He achieved some fame as a composer of satyric plays (Paus. 2. 13. 5). His name is doubtfully restored, two places below that of Sophocles, in the list of Dionysiac victors in *IG* ii¹. 977 a.   A. W. P.-C.

ARISTIDES (Ἀριστείδης) (1) (b. 520 B.C. or earlier), Athenian statesman and soldier. He was strategus in the Marathon campaign (490–489), and archon eponymus in 489–488; he belonged therefore to the richest class (*see* ARCHONTES). He was ostracized in 483–482, and recalled in the general amnesty two years later. He led the Athenian hoplites who landed on the islet of Psyttaleia in the battle of Salamis, and in 479 he held supreme command over the Athenian army at Plataea. Immediately after he worked with Themistocles to secure the rebuilding of the walls of Athens against the wishes of Sparta. In 478 he commanded the Athenian contingent of the Greek naval forces, and was chiefly responsible for the secession of the Asiatic and island Greeks from the Spartan Pausanias (q.v.). These now followed the lead of Athens; the Confederacy of Delos was formed (spring 477), and A. fixed the quota of each contributory State. Aristotle (*Ath. Pol.* 24) says that he also initiated the policy of democratic 'state-socialism'; but this is doubtful. Otherwise nothing is recorded of him after 477.

He died (perhaps 468 B.C.) a poor man, if the story is true that the State had to support his children. His reputation for honesty went back to his contemporaries, and later became proverbial. The later conventional biography made him in all ways the opposite and opponent of Themistocles, honest, conservative, and hoplite against the deceitful, radical, sailor. He may have opposed Themistocles' naval policy in 483–482, but they worked together, not only in 480 and 479, but in the formation of the maritime league.

Plutarch, *Aristides*.   A. W. G.

ARISTIDES (2), painter, of Thebes, pupil of Euxinidas (late 5th c. B.C.), and teacher of Euphranor (q.v.). His use of encaustic was further developed by Praxiteles (q.v.). Probably father and teacher of Nicomachus, whose son and pupil (see below) has been confused with the elder Aristides by Pliny. The statement that he was the *first* to represent the soul, the affections, and the emotions, though his colour was rather hard, is more credible of early than late fourth-century painting. He

probably painted the Baby creeping to its dying mother's breast (before 335) and the Suppliant whose prayers could almost be heard.

ARISTIDES (3), painter, son of Nicomachus. Of Pliny's list the 'Battle of Greeks and Persians' (for Mnason of Elatea) probably, and the portrait of Leontion, pupil of Epicurus (after 306), certainly, were by the younger Aristides.

Overbeck, 1762, 1772, 1778–85; Pfuhl, 789, 814; H. Fuhrmann, *Philoxenes von Eretria* (1931), 72.   T. B. L. W.

ARISTIDES (4) of Miletus (*c.* 100 B.C.), author or compiler of the lost Μιλησιακά, is credited, probably falsely, with several other works, including Ἰταλικά, pseudo-historical anecdotes with a novelistic tendency (*FHG* iv. 320 ff.). Ancient references indicate that the Μιλησιακά were erotic, often obscene, stories (Ov. *Tr.* 2. 413–14; Plut. *Crass.* 32; [Lucian], *Amores* 1). The genre, exemplified perhaps by Lucian's *Asinus*, had little influence on the Greek Novel; but the Μιλησιακά, translated into Latin by Cornelius Sisenna (Ov. *Tr.* 2. 443–4; fragments in Buecheler–Heraeus, *Petronii Saturae*), were notorious at Rome, where *Milesiae* (*fabulae*) became a generic title for erotic tales. Specimens are extant in Petronius (e.g. *The Widow of Ephesus*, 111–12) and Apuleius, who calls his *Metamorphoses* a Milesian composition. *See also* NOVEL, GREEK.   R. M. R.

ARISTIDES (5), AELIUS (A.D. 117– or 129–89), famous sophist, educated at Pergamum and Athens, who travelled through Egypt, lectured in Asia Minor and Rome (A.D. 156), and endured a long illness at Smyrna. Unskilled as a teacher, he contributed little to rhetorical study. The [Aristides] τέχναι (Spengel, *Rhet.* ii. 459 ff.), falsely ascribed to him in Byzantine times, consist of two treatises (Π. πολιτικοῦ καὶ ἀφελοῦς λόγου) by different second-century writers, which possibly influenced Hermogenes in writing his Π. ἰδεῶν. His main achievement consisted of ceremonial speeches (55 survive), including μελέται, sacred discourses (ἱεροὶ λόγοι), eulogies of Athens (Παναθηναϊκός), Rome, and Smyrna, an attack on philosophy (Π. ῥητορικῆς), and compliments to the emperor. All are written in Attic style; and with their glowing periods, rhetorical devices, and refined feeling, they represent the fine flower of sophistic eloquence. To later ages his work represented a genuine part of the legacy of Greece.

Text, W. Schmid (Teubner, 1926). Commentary, W. Dindorf (1829). Criticism, A. Boulanger, *Aelius Aristide et la sophistique dans la province d'Asie* (1923); C. A. de Leeuw, *Aelius Aristeides als Bron voor de Kennis van zijn Tijd* (1939).   J. W. H. A.

ARISTIDES (6) QUINTILIANUS (probably 3rd or 4th c. A.D.), author of an extant work Περὶ μουσικῆς, a compilation based partly on Aristoxenus (q.v.), partly on older authorities such as Damon. The metaphysical background savours of the teaching of Porphyry and Iamblichus, and A. may be reckoned as a Neoplatonist.

Ed. A. Jahn (1882). *PW* ii. 894.   W. D. R.

ARISTIPPUS, (1) a citizen of Cyrene and a companion of Socrates. His date is uncertain, but he was probably somewhat older than Plato. He appears, from the earliest evidence, to have been a professional teacher of rhetoric, a man of luxurious habits and, for a time, a courtier of Dionysius I. But his close friendship with Socrates, which is undoubted, suggests that there must have been something more in him than appears from this. He has sometimes been described as the founder of the so-called Cyrenaic school (*see* CYRENAICS), but this is almost certainly a mistake for

(2) a grandson of above through his daughter Arete. He appears to have been the first to teach the characteristic doctrine of this school, that immediate pleasure was the only end of action. This was combined with

a sensationalist theory of knowledge and the belief that the present moment is the only reality. But it is uncertain how much of these developments should be ascribed to Aristippus himself.

Zeller, ii. 1⁴. 336–40, 361–9; T. Gomperz, *Greek Thinkers* (E.T. 1905) ii. 209–45; Robin (E.T.), 169–73; G. B. L. Colosio, *Aristippo di Cirene* (1925). (1) *PW* ii. 902; (2) *PW* ii. 906. G. C. F.

ARISTOBULUS (1) of Cassandreia, Alexander-historian, was one of the Greek technicians with the army. He wrote before Ptolemy I; his history was used by Arrian to supplement Ptolemy, was Strabo's basis for Alexander in India, and was largely the basis of Diodorus Bk. 17, though overlaid with Clitarchus and other material. He was better on geography and natural history than on military matters; but he knew much that was really important about Alexander himself, and must have had his confidence. *See* ALEXANDER (3), Bibliography, Ancient Sources. W. W. T.

ARISTOBULUS (2), an Alexandrian Jew, probably of the second half of the second century B.C., author of a commentary on the Pentateuch which is known only through quotations by Clement, Anatolius, and Eusebius. This has been thought by some scholars to be a much later work (of the 3rd c. A.D.) falsely ascribed to Aristobulus; but the character of the quotations does not necessitate this conclusion. If the earlier date be accepted, the book is the earliest evidence of contact between Alexandrian Jewry and Greek philosophy. Its object was twofold, to interpret the Pentateuch in an allegorical fashion and to show that Homer and Hesiod, the Orphic writings, Pythagoras, Plato, and Aristotle had borrowed freely from a supposed early translation of the O.T. into Greek. Though A. toned down the anthropomorphism of the O.T., his thought remained Jewish and theistic; it did not accept the pantheism of the Stoics nor anticipate the Logos-doctrine of Philo.

PW ii. 918; Zeller, *Phil. d. Gr.* iii. 2⁴. 277–85. W. D. R.

ARISTOBULUS (3), *see* JEWS, para. 2.

ARISTOCLES (1) of Pergamum (2nd c. A.D.), Peripatetic, studied under Herodes Atticus at Rome (c. A.D. 130–40) and practised as a sophist and teacher of rhetoric at Pergamum, and as a travelling lecturer in Ionia and Italy, and became consul. Works: Τέχνη ῥητορική; letters; Μελέται; an address to the Emperor Ἐπὶ τῇ διανεμήσει τοῦ χρυσίου.

PW ii. 937. W. D. R.

ARISTOCLES (2) of Messana in Sicily (2nd c. A.D.), Peripatetic, teacher of Alexander (q.v. 14) of Aphrodisias. Works: Περὶ φιλοσοφίας; Πότερον σπουδαιότερος Ὅμηρος ἢ Πλάτων; Τέχναι ῥητορικαί; Περὶ Σαράπιδος; Ἠθικὰ βιβλία. His history of philosophy was probably superior to that of Diogenes Laertius in insight, his chief interest being in tracing the development of doctrine and in philosophical criticism.

Testimonia and frs. in Mullach, *FPG* iii. 206–21. *PW* ii. 934. H. Heiland, *Aristoclis Messanii Reliquiae* (1925). W. D. R.

ARISTOCRACY, the 'rule of the best', was originally the rule of the nobility. In Homeric times the king's authority and, in an equal measure, the importance of the assembly of the people, had become limited by the chiefs of the noble families. The nobles, pretending to share descent from the gods with the king, were the ruling class of the city-state (*see* POLIS). They were the landowners, and owners of live-stock, mostly living in town, prominent by birth, wealth, and personal prowess. They formed a class of knights (ἱππεῖς), connected by their unwritten laws of nobility, and by the old social and religious communities of tribe, brotherhood, and family

(*see* PHYLAE, PHRATRIAI, GENOS). The nobles governed the State by means of the council of the *Gerontes*, whose authority long remained unquestioned. After the eighth century B.C., however, military tactics changed, and rows of heavy-armed foot-soldiers (hoplites) displaced knights fighting in single combat. By subsequent economic evolution, new sources of wealth (mines, trade, industry) arose, and were utilized by nobles as well as by other people. In these circumstances aristocracy changed its character, and non-aristocrats rose to the same level as the nobles. Either the smaller communities, especially the phratries, were opened to the non-nobles, or else new ones with analogous rights were founded. Aristocracy became oligarchy (q.v.). Later on, especially among philosophers, aristocracy was a political and moral ideal, the rule of the best and wisest men. V. E.

ARISTODEMUS (1), *see* HERACLIDAE.

ARISTODEMUS (2), the traditional hero of the First Messenian War. When the Messenians had withdrawn to their stronghold of Ithome in the fifth year of the war, he offered his daughter for sacrifice to the gods below, in response to a Delphic oracle. Eight years later he was elected king, and after carrying on guerrilla warfare for five years, signally defeated the Spartans. But in the following year he slew himself in despair on his daughter's grave.

Paus. 4. 9–13. For the value of his traditions, *see* ARISTOMENES (1) *and* MESSENIA. A. M. W.

ARISTODEMUS (3) of Cumae repulsed Etruscans and others who were attacking the city (524 B.C.) and became Cumae's tyrant by exploiting his consequent popularity. By defeating the Etruscans again at Aricia in 505 or earlier A. helped to break their power in Latium. After the Regillus battle he harboured Tarquinius Superbus, and died c. 492. Our principal accounts are vague and exaggerated; nevertheless Aristodemus is an historical figure, the earliest such at Cumae.

Dion. Hal. 7. 2 f.; Plut. *De Mul. Vir.* 26. G. De Sanctis, *Stor. d. Rom.* i. 450 f. E. T. S.

ARISTODEMUS (4), of unknown date (? 4th c. A.D.), compiled a history of Greece which included at least the period 480–431 B.C., perhaps as a handbook for students of rhetoric. The fragments suggest that its historical value was negligible.

FGrH ii A 493; ii C 319. G. F. Hill, *Sources for Greek History*, see Index. H. H. S.

ARISTOGITON (Ἀριστογείτων) (6th c. B.C.), Athenian tyrannicide. He and Harmodius, both of noble family, planned to kill the tyrant Hippias and his younger brother Hipparchus, in consequence of a private quarrel (514 B.C.). The plot miscarried: only Hipparchus was killed. Harmodius was at once cut down by Hippias' guards, Aristogiton arrested and executed (after torture, it is said). As the tyranny was overthrown three years later, the two were popularly supposed to have made this possible, and were ever after called the Liberators. Simonides wrote a poem in their honour, statues of them were set up in the agora (and new ones erected when these were carried off by Xerxes in 480), and their descendants for all time honoured with the right to meals in the Prytaneum (*see also* CRITIUS). A. W. G.

ARISTOMENES (1), the traditional hero of the Second Messenian War. Secretly enlisting support from Argos and Arcadia, he led a revolt against Sparta, and soon won a striking victory at Stenyclarus. Defeated in the battle of 'The Great Trench' owing to the treacherous desertion of Aristocrates the Arcadian, he rallied the survivors and held out for eleven years, twice escaping after capture. After the fall of his stronghold, Eira, he lived in exile at Rhodes.

Paus. 4. 14–24, following Rhianus, a Cretan poet of the fourth century B.C., whose works are lost. The story of Aristomenes and of Aristodemus (q.v.) was much embellished by legend, probably after the founding of Messene in 369.
Modern discussions: E. Schwartz, *Philol.* 1937, 19 ff. J. Kroymann, *Neue Philologische Untersuchungen* xi (1937).   A. M. W.

ARISTOMENES (2) (5th–4th c. B.C.), Athenian comic writer, contemporary of Aristophanes (Suid.). He produced Ὑλοφόροι (or Κολεοφόροι, 'The Sheath-bearers': so *IG* xiv. 1097) in 424 B.C. (Ar. *Eq.* arg. 2) and Ἄδμητος in 388 (Ar. *Plut.* arg. 4). A.'s dramatic activity probably lasted from c. 439 to 388 B.C. (*IG.* ii². 2325). In Διόνυσος ἀσκητής the effeminate Dionysus turns athlete (Poll. 3. 150).

FCG i. 210 ff.; *CAF* i. 690 ff.   M. P.

ARISTON (1) of Chios, pupil of Zeno of Citium, founded an independent branch of the Stoic school and was, about 250 B.C., the most influential philosopher at Athens, with the exception of Arcesilaus. He apparently left behind him no writings except letters. He represented a return towards the views of the Cynics, taking no interest in logic or physics, and rejecting Zeno's recognition of a distinction between the προηγμένα and the ἀποπροηγμένα (preferable and non-preferable) among things indifferent, and holding that the end of life is ἀδιαφορία, complete indifference to them all.

Testimonia in H. von Arnim, *SVF* i. 75–90. *PW* ii. 957.
W. D. R.

ARISTON (2) of Ceos, Peripatetic, may have succeeded Lycon (who died 226 or 225 B.C.) as head of the Lyceum. He was a writer of some accomplishment, but not a philosopher of importance. Diog. Laert. seems to have derived from him the wills of the first four heads of the school—Aristotle, Theophrastus, Straton, Lycon—with biographies of them and lists of their chief works. Works: Ἐρωτικὰ ὅμοια (a collection of anecdotes); a supplement to Theophrastus' Περὶ ὑδάτων; a work on education; Τιθωνὸς ἢ περὶ γήρως; Λύκων. He continued the Theophrastean tradition of the writing of Χαρακτῆρες, and was influenced in his writing of them by the lively style of Bion (q.v. 1) of Borysthenes.

PW ii. 953.   W. D. R.

ARISTON (3) of Alexandria, a Peripatetic associated with Antiochus of Ascalon at Alexandria in 87 B.C. He is quoted by Simplicius as an authority on Aristotle's *Categories*.

PW ii. 956.

ARISTON (4) explorer, *see* ARABIA.

ARISTONICUS (1) (d. 128 B.C.), an illegitimate son of Eumenes II of Pergamum. He led a formidable popular rising after the death of Attalus III and the bequest of his kingdom to Rome (133–130). His motives may have been mainly nationalistic and anti-Roman, but his appeal was to the depressed classes, especially slaves and non-Greeks: the name *Heliopolis* ('City of the Sun') in connexion with his projected State, and the presence of Blossius (formerly tutor of the Gracchi), suggest a 'Utopian' programme of social revolution. After some early successes in the field he was captured by Roman forces and put to death.   G. T. G.

ARISTONICUS (2), son of Ptolemaeus, an Alexandrian grammarian of the Augustan age. He was an opponent of Crates of Mallos. Much of his chief work—on the Aristarchan recensions of Homer—is preserved in our scholia (cf. Nicanor). He also wrote Περὶ ἀσυντάκτων ὀνομάτων and commentaries on Hesiod and Pindar.   P. B. R. F.

ARISTONOUS (3rd c. B.C.), son of Nicosthenes, a Corinthian citharode. On a *stele* found at Delphi (*BCH* xvii (1894), 563 ff.) the Delphians give to him and his descendants certain privileges because of his hymns to the gods. The date has been fixed at 222 B.C. by Pomtow (*Klio* 1914, 305). Then follows a Paean to Apollo of forty-eight lines written in regular eight-lined stanzas of glyconics and pherecrateans.

E. Diehl, *Anth. Lyr. Graec.* ii. 297–300; J. U. Powell, *Collectanea Alexandrina*, 162–4; Powell and Barber, *New Chapters* 1. 45.
C. M. B.

ARISTONYMUS, comic writer, contemporary of Aristophanes (schol. Pl. *Ap.* 19 c), whom he attacks in his Ἥλιος ῥιγῶν.

FCG i. 196–7; *CAF* i. 668–9.

ARISTOPHANES (1) (c. 450–c. 385(?) B.C.), the only writer of Old Comedy of whose plays some (eleven) have survived entire, an Athenian of the tribe of Pandion, son of Philippus (schol. Pl. *Ap.* 19 c; Anon. Περὶ κωμ. 11). He seems to have lived, or owned property, in Aegina (*Ach.* 654)—a fact which gave rise to accusations from his rivals of foreign birth. The date of his death is uncertain. His last play, *Plutus*, was staged in 388, but he subsequently wrote Κώκαλος and Αἰολοσίκων for his son Araros to produce (*Plut.* hyp. 4). He died therefore probably c. 385.

2. OLD COMEDIES. Taking the plays in chronological order, as far as possible, we get:

427. Δαιταλῆς, which gained second prize (schol. *Nub.* 529). The play represented the officially selected twelve 'banqueters' at the feast of Heracles (Ath. 6. 235 c), who, with their twelve 'sons', formed the chorus (G. Norwood, *Gk. Comedy*, 280), and contained an ἀγών between two brothers, ὁ σώφρων τε χὠ καταπύγων (*Nub.* 529).

426. Βαβυλώνιοι; a 'political' play which attacked τάς τε κληρωτὰς καὶ χειροτονητὰς ἀρχὰς καὶ Κλέωνα (schol. *Ach.* 377). The chorus consisted of Athenian allies represented as the slaves of the Athenian Δῆμος (Suid. s.v. Σαμίων ὁ δῆμος). If this view is correct, the 'Babylonians' must have formed a παραχορήγημα (see COMEDY, OLD, para. 9). This attack on himself and the public criticism of Athens' treatment of her allies brought upon the poet an impeachment by Cleon (*Ach.* 377–82).

(?) 426. Δράματα ἢ Κένταυρος, introducing Heracles.

425. Ἀχαρνῆς (*Acharnians*): produced (like Βαβυλώνιοι) διὰ Καλλιστράτου; won first prize.

424. Ἱππῆς (*Knights*): the first of Aristophanes' plays, so far as we know, produced ἰδίῳ ὀνόματι; won first prize.

(?) 424. Γεωργοί: a 'peace' play, probably on the lines of *Acharnians*.

423. Νεφέλαι (*Clouds*). Aristophanes was much disappointed at only gaining third prize and is said (hyp. 5 and 6) to have produced a second edition (διασκευή). That at least the *parabasis* of the play as we possess it belonged to this διασκευή is clear from its reference (553) to Eupolis' *Maricas* (421 B.C.). It is probable that this διασκευή was never staged and that what we possess is an amalgam of the two editions.

(?) 423. Ὁλκάδες ('The Merchantmen'): another 'peace' play.

422. Σφῆκες (*Wasps*): produced διὰ Φιλωνίδου; gained second prize. It is probable that the play that won first prize on this occasion, the Προαγών (or Πρόαγων) 'of Philonides', was really the work of A. We know (schol. *Vesp.* 61) that A. wrote a Προαγών in which he brought on the stage and ridiculed Euripides.

421. Εἰρήνη (*Peace*): gained second prize.

Three plays may probably be dated shortly after 421: Δαίδαλος, a mythological parody introducing Zeus' deception of Leda by means of Daedalus' devices; Δαναΐδες, also a mythological parody; Δράματα ἢ Νίοβος, possibly a second edition of Δράματα ἢ Κένταυρος.

(?) 420. Εἰρήνη δευτέρα, probably a διασκευή of the extant play.

(?) 420. Γῆρας: the chorus seems to have consisted of rejuvenated old men (Ath. 3. 109 f). Possibly the play depicted the new age of peace expected after the Peace of Nicias. We may assign the Ὧραι to about this time if, as seems probable, it contained some parody of Euripides' Erechtheus (produced 422). The play seems to have contained an ἀγών between the older and the more recently introduced gods (e.g. Sabazius, fr. 566) leading to the expulsion of the latter from Athens (Cic. Leg. 2. 15).

419–412. Ἀνάγυρος: seems to have travestied the tragic story of the revenge taken by the eponymous god of the Attic deme Ἀναγυροῦς on a farmer who had damaged the trees of his sacred enclosure. Πολύιδος satirized soothsayers and the like, and may possibly refer to the revulsion against that class felt and expressed by Athens after the Sicilian expedition (Thuc. 8. 1. 1).

415–404. Ταγηνισταί (lit. 'The Broilers'; possibly ' The Roisterers', cf. Eup. fr. 351) seems to have attacked the jeunesse dorée and possibly Alcibiades among them.

414. Ὄρνιθες (Birds): produced διὰ Καλλιστράτου; gained second prize.

414. Ἀμφιάρεως: produced διὰ Φιλωνίδου (Αν. hyp. 3); a sickly and superstitious old man, accompanied by his wife, goes to the shrine of the hero Amphiaraus at Oropus and returns cured. The play probably contained an 'incubation' scene like that in the Plutus.

(?) 413. Ἥρωες: seems to have dealt with the Athenian neglect of hero-worship; the chorus was composed of 'heroes'.

(?) 412. Λήμνιαι (title taken from the Lemnian women who entertained the Argonauts): seems to have satirized the immorality of Athenian women.

411. Λυσιστράτη (Lysistrata): produced διὰ Καλλιστράτου.

411. Θεσμοφοριάζουσαι (Thesmophoriazusae): the date is calculable from various scholia.

(?) 410. Τριφάλης: almost certainly an attack on Alcibiades under the title Τριφάλης (deriv. φαλλός; cf. τριγέρων, τρίδουλος, etc.). The Φοίνισσαι (after 409) seems to have been a parody of Euripides' play.

408. Γηρυτάδης (from γηρύειν, cf. Χαιρητάδης from χαίρειν) probably dealt with the badness of contemporary poets and an attempt to recall some of the older and better ones from Hades (frs. 149, 150). (For another view see Norwood, op. cit. 290–2.)

(?) 408 (schol. Plut. 173) Πλοῦτος πρότερος.

(?) 407. Θεσμοφοριάζουσαι δεύτεραι.

405. Βάτραχοι (Frogs): produced διὰ Φιλωνίδου and awarded first prize.

405–400 (certainly before 399) Τελεμησσῆς: the Telmessians were a Carian tribe and much given to the practice of divination (Cic. Div. 1. 94). This play, like the Πολύιδος, was evidently directed against soothsayers.

391. Ἐκκλησιάζουσαι (Ecclesiazusae). The communism depicted in this play is so like that of the fifth book of Plato's Republic that there is probably some connexion between the two, though which came first is not certain. Probably the Eccl. followed and to some extent parodied the Republic. Still, communism was a regular topic in the philosophical schools, and A. may have been travestying that of Antisthenes.

Though it is a mistake to postulate any sharply defined chronological division between Old and Middle Comedy, it is not unreasonable to assign the death of the Old to the period which separates the Frogs from the Eccl. The latter, with its restricted and non-lyrical chorus and its lack of all personal-political colouring, may definitely be regarded as a Middle Comedy.

3. MIDDLE COMEDIES. After 399 Πελαργοί ('The Storks'): the stork was renowned for its pietas (Αν.

1354–7; Aesop. 76); it is possible that this play tells the story of an ungrateful son brought in some way to respect and love his parents.

388. Πλοῦτος δεύτερος: whatever may have been the plot and general character of the first Plutus (see above), there is no doubt that the Plutus we possess (the second) is a Middle Comedy. Its subject-matter is domestic, not political, and the chorus is reduced to a minimum. Indeed, the various indications ΧΟΡΟΥ (two such occur even in Eccl. 729 and 876) suggest not so much a chorus properly speaking as a series of musical interludes entirely unconnected with the play.

387. Αἰολοσίκων, written by A., but given by him for production to his son Araros (q.v.). The title derives from (a) Aeolus, the incestuous marriage of whose children Euripides had taken as the plot of his Aeolus, and (b) Σίκων, a famous chef (Sosipater, fr. 1, line 14 (CAF iii. 315)). The play—a Middle Comedy with no chorus (Platon. Diff. Com. 5)—presumably contained a travesty of the myth, an attack on Eur., and satiric criticism of the luxury and debauchery of the Athenians.

387. Κώκαλος: another play written by A. for Araros (Plut. hyp. 4). It was obviously a mythological burlesque of the story of Minos' violent death at the hands of Cocalus, king of Camicus in Sicily. Sophocles treated the same theme in his Καμικοί (cf. Soph. fr. 323–7). According to the first Vita (no. 11 of Dübner's Prolegomena to the Scholia) the play contained a seduction (φθορά) and a recognition scene (ἀναγνώρισις) καὶ τἆλλα πάντα ἃ ἐζήλωσε Μένανδρος. It was, in fact, New Comedy. Of the four disputed plays (Dübner, l.c.) the attribution of Ναυαγός to A. is very uncertain. The Νῆσοι is better attested; we may reasonably suppose that it was a 'peace' play with a chorus of islands belonging to the Athenian Empire on the lines of the Βαβυλώνιοι.

4. From the first the reputation of A. has stood high. With four first prizes, three second, and one third his success surpassed that of any other writer of comedy, so far as literary or epigraphic sources allow us to judge. It is clear from the speech which Plato puts into his mouth (Symp. 189 c ff.) that the Athenian philosopher appreciated him, and we are told in the first Vita that he introduced his plays to Dionysius, king of Syracuse. The Alexandrian critics ranked him with Cratinus and Eupolis (e.g. Platon. Diff. Com.—probably derived from Dionysiades' Χαρακτῆρες), though from Plutarch's Σύγκρισις Ἀρ. καὶ Μενάνδρου it is clear that the taste of a later generation, to whom the politics of fifth-century Athens meant little or nothing, preferred the New Comedy writer. An epigram (Anth. Pal. 9. 186) of Antipater of Thessalonica speaks of his poetry as 'steeped in Dionysus' and praises his outlook on life. Horace (Sat. 1.4.1) and Quintilian (10.1.66) mention him, Cratinus, and Eupolis as the main writers of Old Comedy; Cicero (Orat. 29) and the younger Pliny (Ep. 1.20.19) quote him. It is difficult briefly to estimate the merits of so many-sided a genius as Aristophanes. As a poet his choruses put him at once in the front rank. Though metrically less complicated than those of tragedy, they have a freshness and charm only equalled in some of the simpler lyrics of Sophocles and Euripides. As a dramatist he is all but unrivalled in the invention of comic situations, in parody, in satire, in wit, and in downright farce. Of humour he has little or none, for humour is of the emotions, and A. was rather a man of intellect and imagination. His weaknesses as a playwright are plot-construction (a matter in which he was no doubt hampered by tradition) and character-drawing; for, though he is a brilliant depicter of types, he never created a character like, say, Falstaff.

Except in a few instances, notably those of Cleon and Euripides, his attacks, violent as they generally are, are good-tempered. His strong political bias towards aristocracy never made him really anti-democratic. He was, as Kaibel has well said, μισοδημάγωγος, not μισόδημος. Aristophanes was always 'in opposition'; but his objections to the Government were not so much those of an oligarch as of a pacifist in the best sense of the term, of one, that is, who desired an honourable peace with Sparta. And not only in politics was A. a natural conservative. He had a strong mistrust of, and dislike for, social, religious, literary, and musical innovations, and he had no hesitation in hotly attacking the authors of such. Nor are his the attacks of a fogy or a Philistine. Stripped of their 'comic' exaggeration they are the criticisms of a man who realized that much of what is called progress often ends in a cul-de-sac.

See also COMEDY, OLD; COMEDY, MIDDLE; LITERARY CRITICISM, GREEK, para. I.

The individual plays have been constantly re-edited, and it is impossible to do more than mention a few outstanding modern editions such as Starkie's *Acharnians* (1909), *Clouds* (1911), and *Wasps* (1897), Neil's *Knights* (1909), Herwerden's *Peace* (1897), Sharpley's *Peace* (1905), Radermacher's *Frogs* (1922), Tucker's *Frogs* (1906). Of complete exegetical editions the best is that of van Leeuwen (in Latin; 1893–1906): also good is Rogers (1902–16) with a brilliant verse translation (text and translation only re-edited in Loeb ed.). Scholia: Dübner (1883), Rutherford (1896–1905).
Concordance: H. Dunbar (1883). Index: O. J. Todd (U.S.A. 1932). General: A. Couat, *Aristophane et l'ancienne comédie antique* (1902); M. Croiset, *Aristophane et les partis à Athènes* (1906; Engl. Transl. Loeb, 1909); J. van Leeuwen, *Prolegomena ad Aristophanem* (1909); T. Zieliński, *Gliederung der altatt. Komödie* (1885); P. Mazon, *Essai sur la composition des comédies d'Aristophane* (1904); G. Murray, *Aristophanes* (1933); Kaibel, 'Aristophanes' in *PW*; G. Norwood, *Greek Comedy* (1931), 202–312; V. Ehrenberg, *The People of Aristophanes*² (1951). M. P.

ARISTOPHANES (2) of Byzantium (c. 257–180 B.C.), pupil at Alexandria of Zenodotus, Callimachus, and Eratosthenes, succeeded Eratosthenes as head of the Alexandrian Library (c. 194 B.C.). He was a scholar of wide learning, famous for his linguistic, literary, textual, and scientific researches, and for his systematic study of punctuation and accentuation.

2. His edition of the *Iliad* and *Odyssey* made a distinct advance on the work of Zenodotus and Rhianus. Despite some capriciousness and boldness of treatment, due to a subjective method of criticism, his work showed much critical acumen; e.g. he was the first to put the end of the *Odyssey* at 23. 296. In his textual criticism he used symbols to show his doubts of the genuineness or satisfactoriness of verses (see SCHOLARSHIP, GREEK).

3. Besides editions of Hesiod's *Theogony*, Alcaeus, and Anacreon, he produced the first collected edition of Pindar, whose works he arranged in seventeen books; in his texts of the lyric poets A. used signs to mark the ends of metrical *cola*. He probably compiled a complete and standard edition of Euripides, each volume of which perhaps contained eight plays (*CIA* ii. 992), and also the first critical edition of the comedies of Aristophanes; but to a later date belong the metrical ὑποθέσεις, traditionally ascribed to him, on seven of these comedies (see HYPOTHESIS). He was responsible for the somewhat unsatisfactory grouping of fifteen dialogues of Plato in trilogies.

4. His select lists of the best classical poets seem, along with those of Aristarchus, to have provided the basis for the classification of writers in the Alexandrian canon. He corrected and supplemented the biographical and literary information contained in the *Pinakes* of Callimachus. Introductions to some plays of Aeschylus, Sophocles, and Euripides, based on the *Didascaliae* of Aristotle and on Peripatetic research, are extant in an abbreviated form (see HYPOTHESIS). In the Π. προσώπων he treated the character-types in Greek Comedy. His interest in Menander led him to compile the treatise Παράλληλοι Μενάνδρου τε καὶ ἀφ' ὧν ἔκλεψεν ἐκλογαί.

5. Of his lexicographical works the most important was the Λέξεις (or Γλῶσσαι), which perhaps consisted of a series of special studies classified according to dialect or to subject. He produced two books of proverbs in

verse (schol. Soph. *Aj.* 746) and four in prose (schol. Ar. *Av.* 1292). See PAROEMIOGRAPHERS.

6. The grammatical treatise Περὶ ἀναλογίας, in which he attempted to define the rules of Greek declension, was probably directed against Chrysippus' Περὶ ἀνωμαλίας and began the long controversy between Analogists and Anomalists (see ANALOGY).

7. The work Περὶ ζῴων appears to have been based on the studies of Aristotle, Theophrastus, and the Paradoxographers (q.v.).

A. Nauck, *Aristophanis Byzantini grammatici Alexandrini fragmenta* (1848); K. Lehrs, *de Aristarchi studiis Homericis*³ (1882); U. von Wilamowitz-Moellendorff, *Textgeschichte der griechischen Lyriker* (1900); B. P. Grenfell and A. S. Hunt, *Oxyrhynchus Papyri* (1899), ii. 121, 122, *Amherst Papyri* (1901), ii. 17; I. Wagner, *Die metrische Hypotheseis zu Aristophanes* (1908). J. F. L.

ARISTOTLE (Ἀριστοτέλης) (384–322 B.C.), son of Nicomachus, of the medical guild of the Asclepiadae, was born at Stagirus (later Stagira) in Chalcidice. Nicomachus was the physician and friend of Amyntas II of Macedonia, and A. may have spent part of his boyhood at the court of Pella; he probably acquired in his father's surgery his interest in physical science. At the age of 17 he entered Plato's school at Athens, and here he remained to the death of Plato in 348–347, first as a pupil, later as a 'research student' working in comparative independence. It seems likely that in the study of zoology, even at this early date, he struck out a fresh line of research. When Plato was succeeded by Speusippus, who represented a tendency of Platonism repugnant to A., its tendency to 'turn philosophy into mathematics', he left the Academy, along with Xenocrates. They accepted an invitation from a former fellow-student in the Academy, Hermeias, the ruler of Atarneus and Assos in Mysia, who had gathered round him a small Platonic circle; at Assos they stayed till the fall and death of Hermeias in 345, and A. married Hermeias' niece Pythias. From Assos he went to Mitylene, in the neighbouring island of Lesbos; his choice of a residence may have been due to Theophrastus, a native of the island. To his stay at Assos, and especially at Mitylene, belong many of his zoological inquiries; the island lagoon of Pyrrha is often mentioned in the *Historia Animalium*. In 343–342 Philip of Macedon invited him to come to Pella to act as tutor to Alexander. His teaching of Alexander was probably mainly in Homer and the dramatists, but he also composed for him a work on *Colonists* and one on *Monarchy*, and his instruction of Alexander in politics may have sown the seeds of his own interest in the subject. Any close intimacy with Alexander seems to have ended with the latter's appointment as regent for his father in 340; A. probably then settled in Stagira.

2. In 335, soon after the death of Philip, A. returned to Athens. Outside the city to the north-east, probably between Mt. Lycabettus and the Ilissus, lay a grove sacred to Apollo Lyceius and the Muses; here A. rented some buildings and founded a school; the buildings included a covered court (περίπατος) from which the school took its name. Here he collected manuscripts—the prototype of all the great libraries of antiquity—maps, and probably a museum of objects to illustrate his lectures, especially those on zoology. Alexander is said to have given him 800 talents to form the collection, and to have ordered the hunters, fowlers, and fishermen of the Empire to report to A. any matters of scientific interest; and the story probably has some foundation in fact. A. laid down rules for his community, and established common meals, and a symposium once a month. Above all he organized research on a grand scale, of which the account of the constitutions of 158 Greek States was a good example. Under his leadership Theophrastus carried on studies in botany, Eudemus in the history of philosophy, and Aristoxenus in music.

3. At some time during his second residence in Athens Pythias died, and A. lived afterwards with Herpyllis, by whom he had a son Nicomachus. On the death of Alexander in 323, Athens became the scene of an outbreak of anti-Macedonian feeling. A charge of impiety was brought against A., and rather than let the Athenians 'sin twice against philosophy' he left the school in Theophrastus' hands and retired to Chalcis, where he died in 322 of a disease of the digestive organs. Diogenes Laertius has preserved his will, in which he makes careful provision for his relations, secures his slaves from being sold, and arranges for the freeing of some of them; his will affords clear evidence of a grateful and affectionate nature.

4. An ancient tradition describes him as bald, thin-legged, with small eyes and a lisp in his speech, and as being noticeably well dressed. We are told further that he had a mocking disposition which showed itself in his expression. A number of extant statues, e.g. one in the Vienna Museum, probably represent him.

5. The works connected with his name may be divided into three classes: (A) early popular works published by himself, mostly in dialogue form, and now lost; (B) memoranda and collections of materials for scientific treatises, also now lost; (C) philosophical and scientific works, still extant. Apart from the *Athenaion Politeia*, the whole extant Aristotelian corpus, so far as it is authentic, belongs to the third class; of the other two our knowledge rests on frs., and on three lists which have come down from antiquity. (A) The dialogue *On Rhetoric*, or *Grylus*, modelled on the *Gorgias*, was probably written not long after the death of Grylus in 362–361. Somewhat later, probably, was the *Eudemus*, or *On the Soul*, named after Eudemus of Cyprus, who died in 354–353. This was modelled on the *Phaedo* and accepted the doctrines of pre-existence, transmigration, and recollection. To the same period belongs the *Protrepticus* (probably not a dialogue), an exhortation to the philosophic life which was very popular in antiquity and furnished Iamblichus with materials for his *Protrepticus*, and Cicero with a model for his *Hortensius*. The dialogue *On Philosophy*, which gave an account of the progress of mankind largely Platonic in character but asserting the eternal pre-existence of the world and opposing the doctrine of Ideas and of Idea-numbers, belongs to about, or just after, the date of the earliest parts of the *Metaphysics*, i.e. to A.'s Assos period. To the period of his tutorship of Alexander belong *Alexander*, or *About Colonists*, and *On Monarchy*. Less is known of the other dialogues—*Politicus*, *Sophistes*, *Menexenus*, *Symposium* (all probably modelled on Platonic dialogues of the same names), *On Justice*, *On the Poets*, *Nerinthus*, *Eroticus*, *On Wealth*, *On Prayer*, *On Good Birth*, *On Pleasure*, *On Education*.

(B) We know, from ancient accounts, of very large collections of historical and scientific facts which were made by Aristotle, sometimes in co-operation with others. The majority of these have been lost, and exist only in fragments. They must be dated during his headship of the Lyceum. *Pythionicai*, a list of the victors at the Pythian games, was compiled *c.* 335–334; *Nomima*, a collection of barbaric customs, and *Dicaiomata Poleon*, Pleas of the Cities, after 330. Of the *Politeiai*, accounts of the constitutions of Greek States, the *Athenaion Politeia* (written *c.* 329–328) was recovered from the sands of Egypt in 1890. Other collections of materials now lost were *Didascaliai* (records of the dramatic performances at Athens), *Aporemata Homerica* (Homeric problems), *Olympionicai* (records of victories at Olympia). A. also made great collections of materials on physical problems which were added to by successors, and worked up into the extant *Problems*.

(C) The works in the extant corpus may be classified as follows:

(*a*) Genuine: *Prior Analytics, Posterior Analytics, Topics, Sophistici Elenchi* (= *Top.* 9); *Physics, De Caelo, De Generatione et Corruptione, Meteorologica* (bk. 4 perhaps by Straton); *De Anima* and the following works known collectively as *Parva Naturalia: De Sensu et Sensibilibus, De Memoria et Reminiscentia, De Somno, De Somniis, De Divinatione per Somnum, De Longitudine et Brevitate Vitae, De Vita et Morte, De Respiratione; Historia Animalium* (bk. 10 and perhaps bks. 7, 8, 21–30, 9 are spurious, ? 3rd c. B.C.), *De Partibus Animalium, De Incessu Animalium, De Generatione Animalium; Metaphysics* (the earliest parts, bks. *A, Δ, K* (first part), *Λ, N* belong to the Assos period); *Nicomachean Ethics; Politics; Rhetoric; Poetics* (a fragment).

(*b*) Probably genuine: *De Interpretatione, De Motu Animalium, Eudemian Ethics* (probably earlier than *Eth. Nic.*).

(*c*) Of doubtful genuineness: *Categories, Magna Moralia.*

(*d*) Spurious: *De Mundo* (probably written between 50 B.C. and A.D. 100), *De Spiritu* (? *c.* 250 B.C.), *De Coloribus* (? by Theophrastus or Straton), *De audibilibus* (? by Straton), *Physiognomonica* (? 3rd c. B.C.), *De Plantis* (the original perhaps by Nicolaus of Damascus), *De Mirabilibus Auscultationibus* (compiled at dates ranging perhaps from the 2nd to the 6th c.), *Mechanica* (? by Straton), *Problems* (compiled perhaps as late as the 5th or 6th c.), *De Lineis Insecabilibus* (? by Theophrastus or Straton), *Ventorum Situs* (perhaps an extract from a work by Theophrastus), *De Xenophane, Zenone, Gorgia* (more properly *De Melisso, Xenophane, Gorgia*) (1st c. A.D.), *De Virtutibus et Vitiis* (*c.* 100 B.C.–A.D. 100), *Oeconomica* (of different periods, from 300 B.C. to A.D. 400), *Rhetorica ad Alexandrum* (? beginning of 3rd c. B.C.).

6. Strabo tells us (13. 54; cf. Plutarch, *Sull.* 26. 1) that Theophrastus left A.'s MSS. to Neleus of Scepsis in the Troad, whose successors kept them in a cellar to protect them from the book-collecting kings of Pergamum. They were sold (*c.* 100 B.C.) to Apellicon, who edited them badly. In 84 B.C. Sulla took them to Rome, where they were edited first by Tyrannion and then by Andronicus of Rhodes, towards the end of the first century B.C. Andronicus' edition is the basis of our present corpus. Until these editions were produced, the now extant works of A. were unknown to the world, and he was known only through the works which are now lost. But when once the existing works came to be known, they were commented on by a series of commentators, mostly Neoplatonists, beginning with Aspasius (fl. *c.* A.D. 110) and ending with Sophonias (*c.* 1300).

7. The extant works were not prepared for publication, but they are for the most part too full and elaborate to be mere notes for lecture purposes. They rather suggest memoranda meant to be shown to students who had missed the lectures, and to preserve a more accurate record than memory or the notes of students could provide. The indications of date are slight; there are references which indicate that some of the works were begun early, and several which show that they were finished late in A.'s life. Many references imply an Athenian audience. The writings would probably reflect a progressive withdrawal from Plato's influence. Using this and other indications of date, we may say that A. began by writing dialogues on the Platonic model, but that in the latest of these his protest against Plato's 'separation' of the Forms began to be felt. To the period of his stay in the Troad, in Lesbos, and in Macedonia belongs the earliest form of the extant works largely Platonic in character—the *Organon*, *Physics*, *De Caelo*, *De Generatione et Corruptione*, *De Anima* 3, *Eudemian Ethics*, the oldest parts of the *Metaphysics* and the *Politics*, and the earliest parts of the *Historia Animalium*. To the second Athenian period belong the rest of his works of research—*Meteorologica*, the works on psychology and biology, the *Constitutions*, and the other historical researches, the *Nicomachean Ethics*, the *Poetics*, the *Rhetoric*, and the completion of the works begun in the middle period.

8. It is impossible in a few pages to offer any useful summary of A.'s philosophy; for a philosopher's conclusions are worth little without his reasons for them, and A.'s reasons cannot be stated briefly. It may be more useful to offer a more general characterization. The main lines of his thought were to a large extent determined by his association with Plato and the Academy; and if we may distinguish his philosophical from his scientific works (though the distinction is only one of degree), it may be said that there is hardly a page of them which does not betray Plato's influence. The dialogues written before Plato's death seem to have shown little originality, and even in *Metaph. A*, written in the Assos period, Aristotle thinks of himself as still a member of the Platonic school. But by that time important differences begin to be apparent. A. was an Ionian, with all the Ionian interest in observation and in the world of change. He felt unable to follow Plato in asserting the 'separate' existence of the Ideas, and unable to accept unchanging Ideas (as he mistakenly assumes that Plato did) as sufficient explanation of the facts of change and motion. The later development of Plato's thought, in which numbers took the place of Ideas as the explanation of the universe, he thought at least equally unsatisfactory. He is sometimes described as 'no mathematician', but this is an exaggeration. He was probably abreast of the mathematics of his time; he was interested in the astronomical theories of Eudoxus and Callippus (*Metaph. Λ.* 8) and his discussion of the problems of infinity and continuity is masterly. But he did not realize to anything like the same extent as Plato the importance of mathematics as the foundation of physical science. It is true that 'God always geometrizes'; in physical science mathematical precision is all-important, and from his failure to realize this he was led, in his physical works, to adopt and reason from assumptions which to common sense, in the absence of exact measurement, were highly plausible, but were mistaken; so that his influence on dynamics and on astronomy was a retarding one. The science in which he was most at home was biology, in which, in its early stages, exact measurement is less important. Here his combination of close observation with acute reasoning made him *facile princeps* among the ancients. 'Linnaeus and Cuvier have been my two gods,' Darwin wrote, 'but they were mere schoolboys to old Aristotle.' It is possible that Plato stimulated him to this study; for at least one other member of the school, Speusippus, tried his hand at biology. But in the main A. was here reverting to the Ionian, pre-Socratic tradition of curiosity about all sorts of natural phenomena.

9. The same passion for research was shown in his vast collections of materials about the constitutions of Greek States, the history of the drama, the history of the Pythian games; apparently nothing was too great or too small to rouse his curiosity. One may even say that his political thought was to some extent modelled on his biological researches. He took over his original classification of constitutions from Plato's *Politicus*, with a difference. But in one passage (*Pol.* 1290^{b}21–1291^{b}13) he envisages a classification which takes account of the various forms assumed in various States by the organs of the body politic, as biological classification takes account of the forms assumed by the bodily organs; and we can see in *Pol.* 4 and 6 an attempt to achieve for States such a precise description of their types as he gives for animals in the *Historia Animalium*.

10. His mind has two well-marked characteristics. One is a sort of inspired common sense which makes him avoid extremes in any direction. In theory of knowledge he is neither a rationalist nor an empiricist; he recognizes the parts played both by the senses and by the intellect. In metaphysics he is neither a spiritualist nor a materialist; he admits the claims both of mind and of body, and regards the two as inseparable elements in the living being. In ethics he is neither a hedonist nor an ascetic; he recognizes in pleasure an element, though a secondary and consequential one, in the good life. In politics he is neither an aristocrat nor a democrat; he advocates the rule of the middle class, which he regards as the steadiest element in the State. He often writes what will not bear very close scrutiny; for many distinctions have become clear through later philosophical discussion that were not clear in his day. But by virtue of his strong common sense he rarely writes what anyone would regard as obviously untrue.

11. The other leading characteristic of his mind is its tidiness and love of order; and by this philosophy has greatly benefited. For one thing, we owe to him, in the main, the classification of the sciences with which we habitually work. He divides them into the theoretical, which aim simply at knowledge, the practical, which aim at improving conduct, and the productive, which aim at the production of things useful or beautiful; and among the theoretical he distinguishes mathematics, which studies things that are eternal and unchangeable but not substantial, physics, which studies things substantial but subject to change, and 'first philosophy' or theology, which studies what is both eternal and substantial (*Metaph. E.* 1). And what is more important, he practises what he preaches. In a dialogue of Plato we are apt to find metaphysics and ethics, psychology and politics, all present together; the variety is part of the charm, but sometimes leaves the reader perplexed as to what Plato is mainly driving at. To logic, to physical science, to zoology, to psychology, to metaphysics, to ethics, to politics, to rhetoric—to each A. devotes one or more works in which, though with many false starts, he sticks to one great subject with a wonderful feeling for relevance; the continuity he achieves is the more remarkable because none of the extant works was revised for publication, and several if not all of them consisted originally of separate essays which he never brought formally into a whole. So it is that, while there have always been philosophers who derived more inspiration from Plato, the working programme of the philosophical sciences has owed more to A.

12. His orderliness of mind shows itself also in the development of a terminology which has been of great service to philosophy. When we talk or write philosophy, we use a vocabulary which derives more from him than from anyone else; and much of it has entered into the speech of all educated men. Universal and particular, premise and conclusion, subject and attribute, form and matter, potentiality and actuality—these are a few of the many antitheses which he first introduced by name. They have their danger, and much harm has been done by the glib repetition of them when the danger has not been recognized; but they have provided philosophy with a framework that has been of great service.

13. His love of classification is another result of his orderliness of mind. The leading categories—substance, quality, and relation—received their names from Plato; but the idea of a complete classification of the *summa genera* of nameable entities seems to be A.'s own; for Plato never attempts a classification of categories in this sense, and the 'greatest kinds' of the *Sophistes* correspond rather to the *transcendentalia* which characterize all existing things. Again, A. has a much more elaborate classification of the faculties of the soul than Plato. But it may be noted that he is singularly free from the dangers of faculty psychology. He thinks it important to mark off mental activities into their kinds, but he does not think he has explained activities by referring to the faculties of which they are the manifestation; and his distinction of the faculties is accompanied by an awareness of the links between them. Sensation, for him, is of particulars, and knowledge of universals; but sensation is of particulars as characterized by universals, and knowledge is of universals as exemplified in particulars. Again, he has a most elaborate classification of animal kinds; but these form a *scala naturae* in which the transition from one kind to another is never very wide, and the lower kinds present analogues of what is found in the higher.

14. A.'s work has till recently been treated as a closed system of doctrine all held by him simultaneously, and much ink has been wasted in the attempt to reconcile the irreconcilable. This tendency requires correction in two ways. First, while some of his works (most notably the account of the syllogism in the *Prior Analytics*) proceed with assured mastery from point to point, others (e.g. *De An.* 3, the *Metaphysics*, and the *Politics*) are little more than a series of ἀπορίαι to which only tentative answers are given. Secondly, Mr. Case and, on a much larger scale, Prof. Jaeger have shown that there is a great deal more development in his doctrine than has hitherto been recognized. As Prof. Jaeger has shown, the general tendency is from Platonic otherworldliness to a growing interest in the phenomena of the world around us. Yet A., while he became more of a scientist, probably did not become less of a philosopher. The last book of the *Physics* and Λ of the *Metaphysics*, which cannot be dated early (since they presuppose the highly original treatment of the infinite and the continuous, to which apparently nothing in the Academy showed the way), show him still seeking for a super-sensuous explanation of change in the sensible world.

For Aristotle's views on ANATOMY AND PHYSIOLOGY, ASTRONOMY, AFTER-LIFE, see under those titles. *See also* DIALOGUE, GREEK, para. 4; LITERARY CRITICISM (Greek), para. 3; METEOROLOGY; MUSIC, § 2; PAROEMIOGRAPHERS; PHYSICS, para. 2.

BIBLIOGRAPHY

LIFE, WORKS, AND DOCTRINE. Diog. Laert. 5. 1. R. Eucken, *Die Methode d. Aristotelischen Forschung*, 1854. V. Rose, *De A. Librorum Ordine et Auctoritate*, 1854; *A. Pseudepigraphus*, 1863. A. Gercke in *PW* ii. 1012. T. Gomperz in *Griechische Denker* 3, 1902 (Engl. Transl. 4, 1912). T. Case in *Enc. Brit.*[11], 1910. F. Brentano, *A. u. seine Weltanschauung*, 1911. A. E. Taylor, *Aristotle*[3], 1919. O. Hamelin, *Le Système d'A.*, 1920. E. Zeller, *Ph. d. Gr.* ii. 2[4], 1921 (Engl. Transl. 1897). W. Jaeger, *Aristoteles*, 1922 (E.T. 1934). J. L. Stocks, *Aristotelianism*, U.S.A. 1925. G. R. G. Mure, *Aristotle*, 1932. W. D. Ross, *Aristotle*[3], 1937. M. Schwab, *Bibliographie d'A.* 1896.

TEXTS. I. Bekker, 1831 (with invaluable *Index Aristotelicus* by H. Bonitz, 1870). Teubner texts of all the works except *Cat., Int., An. Pr.* and *Post., Mete., Mund., Gen. An.; Fr.*, ed. V. Rose. *Rh. Al.* is in Spengel-Hammer's *Rhetores Graeci* (Teubner). O.C.T., *Cael.* (D. J. Allan), *Eth. Nic.* (I. Bywater), *Poet.* (id.), *Ath. Pol.* (F. G. Kenyon). *Mete.*, F. H. Fobes, Cambridge, U.S.A. *Mund.*, W. L. Lorimer, Paris, 1933. *Xen.*, H. Diels, 1900.

COMMENTARIES. *Comm. in A. Graeca*, Berlin, 1882–1909, with *Supplementum Aristotelicum*, 1882–1903. *Organon*, J. Pacius, 1597; T. Waitz, 1844–6. *An. Post.*, J. Zabarella, 1578. *Soph. El.*, E. Poste, 1866. *Ph.*, W. D. Ross, 1936; bk. 2, O. Hamelin, 1907. *Cael., Gen. Corr., Mund., Parva Naturalia*, J. Pacius, 1601. *Gen. Corr.* and *Mete.*, J. Zabarella, 1600. *Gen. Corr.*, H. H. Joachim, 1922. *Mete.*, J. L. Ideler, 1834–6. *De An.*, G. Rodier, 1900; R. D. Hicks, 1907. *Sens.* and *Mem.*, G. R. T. Ross, 1906. *De Vita et Morte* and *Resp.*, W. Ogle, 1897. *Hist. An.*, H. Aubert and F. Wimmer, 1868. *Part. An.*, W. Ogle, 1882. *Gen. An.*, H. Aubert and F. Wimmer, 1860. *Metaph.*, H. Bonitz, 1848–9; W. D. Ross, 1924. *Eth. Nic.*, J. A. Stewart, 1892; J. Burnet, 1900; bk. 5, H. Jackson, 1879; bk. 6, L. H. G. Greenwood, 1909; bk. 10, G. Rodier, 1897. *Eth. Eud.* A. T. H. Fritzsche, 1851. *Pol.*, F. Susemihl, 1879; W. L. Newman, 1887–1902; F. Susemihl and R. D. Hicks (Bks. 1–5), 1894. *Ath. Pol.*, J. E. Sandys[2], 1912. *Rh.*, L. Spengel, 1867; E. M. Cope and J. E. Sandys, 1877. *Poet.*, S. H. Butcher[3], 1902; I. Bywater, 1909; D. S. Margoliouth, 1911; A. Rostagni, 1927. *Fr.*, R. Walzer, 1934. *Col.*, C. Prantl, 1849. *Mech.*, J. P. van Cappelle, 1812. *Musical Problems*, F. A. Gevaert and J. C. Vollgraff, 1899–1902. *Lin. Ins.*, O. Apelt in *Beiträge zur Gesch. d. Gr. Philosophie*, 1891. *Oec.* 1, B. A. van Groningen, 1933.

TRANSLATIONS. Oxford Transl., ed. J. A. Smith and W. D. Ross, 1908–31. With text, Loeb series (all except *An. Post., Top., Soph. El., Mete., Mund., Hist. An., Gen. An., Fr.*).

STYLE AND DICTION. H. Bonitz, *Aristotelische Studien*, 1862

(syntax). R. Eucken, *De A. Dicendi Ratione*, Diss., Gött., 1866 (particles); *Ueber d. Sprachgebrauch d. A.*, 1868 (prepositions).

STUDIES OF PARTICULAR WORKS. J. Zabarella, *Opera Logica*, 1578. H. Bonitz, *Ueber d. Categorien d. A.*, 1853. F. A. Trendelenburg, *Elementa Logices Aristoteleae*[9], 1892. O. Apelt, *Kategorienlehre d. A.* in *Beiträge zur Gesch. d. Gr. Philosophie*, 1891. H. Maier, *Syllogistik d. A.*, 1896–1900. G. Calogero, *I Fondamenti della Logica aristotelica*, 1927. H. v. Arnim, *Das Ethische in A. Topik*, 1927. F. Solmsen, *Entwicklung d. aristotelischen Logik u. Rhetorik*, 1929. J. W. Miller, *The Structure of Aristotelian Logic*, 1938. J. Zabarella, *De Rebus Naturalibus*, 1590. H. Bergson, *Quid A. de loco senserit*, 1889. O. Gilbert in *Die Meteorologischen Theorien d. gr. Altertums*, 1907. P. Duhem, in *Le Système du Monde* i, 1913. A. Mansion, *Introd. à la physique aristotélicienne*, 1913. G. Sorof, *De A. Geographia*, 1886. P. Bolchert, 'A. Erdkunde v. Asien u. Libyen', in *Quellen u. Forsch. zur alten Gesch. u. Geog.*, 1908. A. E. Chaignet, *Essai sur la Psych. d'A.*, 1883. F. Brentano, *A. Lehre vom Ursprung d. menschlichen Geistes*, 1911. J. B. Meyer, *A. Thierkunde*, 1855. L. Robin, *Théorie Platonicienne des Idées et des Nombres d'après A.*, 1908. W. W. Jaeger, *Studien zur Entstehungsgesch. d. Metaph. d. A.*, 1912. F. Ravaisson, *Essai sur la Métaph. d'A.*[2], 1913. J. Chevalier, *Notion du Nécessaire chez A. et ses prédécesseurs*, 1914. J. Stenzel, *Zahl u. Gestalt in Plato u. A.*, 1924. H. v. Arnim, *Die Entstehung der Gotteslehre d. A.*, 1931; *Die drei aristotelischen Ethiken*, 1924; *Eudemische Ethik u. Metaphysik*, 1929; *Nochmals die aristotelischen Ethiken*, 1929. R. Walzer, *Mag. Mor. u. aristotelische Ethik*, 1929. K. O. Brink, *Stil u. Form d. pseudaristotelischen Mag. Mor.*, 1933. W. Oncken, *Die Staatslehre d. A.*, 1870. E. Barker, *The Political Thought of Plato and A.*, 1906. H. v. Arnim, *Die Politischen Theorien d. Altertums*, 1910. M. Pohlenz, *Staatsgedanke u. Staatslehre d. Griechen*, 1923. H. v. Arnim, *Zur Entstehungsgesch. d. aristotelischen Politik*, 1924. E. M. Cope, *Introd. to A.'s Rhetoric*, 1867. O. Kraus, *Neue Studien zur aristotelischen Rhetorik*, 1907. L. Cooper, *The Poet. of A., its Meaning and Influence*, New York, 1924. J. Bernays, *Zwei Abhandlungen über d. aristotelische Theorie d. Drama*, 1880; *Die Dialoge d. A.*, 1863. E. Kaibel, *Stil u. Text der 'Αθ. πολ.*, 1893. U. v. Wilamowitz-Moellendorff, *Aristoteles u. Athen*, 1893 (on *Ath. Pol.*). W. L. Lorimer, *The Text Tradition of Ps.-A. De Mundo*, 1924; *Some Notes on the Text of Ps.-A. De Mundo*, 1925. C. Stumpf, *Ps.-aristotelischen Probleme über Musik*, 1897.   W. D. R.

ARISTOXENUS, born at Tarentum between 375 and 360 B.C., philosopher and musical theorist. He received a musical training from his father Spintharus and from Lamprus of Erythrae (not the Lamprus mentioned by Plato, *Menex.* 236 a). For some time he lived at Mantinea; and during a sojourn at Corinth (after 343) he became familiar with the exiled Dionysius the Younger (fr. 9). At Athens he became the pupil of the Pythagorean Xenophilus and finally of Aristotle. His reputation amongst his fellow-pupils at the Lyceum was such that he expected to succeed to the headship of the school; but the master passed him over in favour of Theophrastus. A. is said by Suidas to have assailed Aristotle's memory; but though he retailed scandalous stories about Socrates (fr. 25–30) and alleged that most of Plato's *Republic* was plagiarized from Protagoras (fr. 33), the one extant reference he makes to Aristotle by name (*Harm.*, p. 31) is laudatory. Whether he ever returned to Italy is unknown; nor is there any evidence about the date of his death. Suidas gives the number of his books as 453.

2. WORKS (a) *Principles and Elements of Harmonics*, of which three books are in part preserved. The first deals with the scope of the subject, movements of the voice, pitch, notes, intervals, and scales; ii covers the chief topics of i, but includes keys (τόνοι), modulation, and the construction of melody (μελοποιΐα) also, and is more polemical in tone; iii contains twenty-seven theorems on the legitimate combinations of intervals and tetrachords in scales. These three books do not give a complete theory of music; nor are they from a single work. The most probable view is that we have the remains of two treatises, the *Principles* ('Αρχαί = i) and the *Elements* (Στοιχεῖα = ii and iii), both of which have suffered partly by curtailment and partly by the insertion of passages from other treatises. Further details of A.'s musical theory are found in later writers such as Plutarch (*De mus.*), Cleonides, Aristides Quintilianus; and a short fragment on Harmonics printed in *POxy.* iv. 667 is probably from some work of A.

(b) *Elements of Rhythm* ('Ρυθμικὰ Στοιχεῖα), of

which part of the second book is extant. It deals with the nature of rhythm (defined as a τάξις ἀφωρισμένη χρόνων), the primary unit of rhythm (ὁ πρῶτος χρόνος), feet, their distribution between arsis and thesis, and their differences. Since A. refers to his earlier writings on musical theory (p. 282), this work is possibly later than the *Harmonics*. Porphyry on Ptol. *Harm*. (p. 78 Düring) quotes from a work entitled Περὶ τοῦ πρώτου χρόνου; and passages based on A.'s theory of rhythm are found in later authors, especially the Byzantine Michael Psellus (11th c.). An important fragment (*POxy*. i. 9), on the rhythmization of cretic sequences, is attributed to a treatise by A. on rhythmical composition (see Powell and Barber, *New Chapters in Gk. Lit*. ii. 178).

(*c*) Other musical works were: *On Music* (Περὶ μουσικῆς, at least four books; cf. Ath. 14. 619 d), *On Melody* (Π. μελοποιίας, at least four books; cf. Porph. p. 125), *On Listening to Music* (Π. μουσικῆς ἀκροάσεως), *On Keys* (Π. τόνων), *On Auloi and Musical Instruments* (Π. αὐλῶν καὶ ὀργάνων), *On the Boring of Auloi* (Π. αὐλῶν τρήσεως), *On Aulos-Players* (Π. αὐλητῶν), *On Tragic Poets* (Π. τραγῳδοποιῶν), *On Dancing in Tragedy* (Π. τραγικῆς ὀρχήσεως); and the obscurely entitled Πραξιδαμάντεια seems to have contained musical material.

(*d*) Works of a biographical, historical, and miscellaneous character were: the *Lives* (Βίοι ἀνδρῶν, including biographies of Pythagoras, Archytas, Socrates, and Plato), *Pythagorean Maxims* (Πυθαγορικαὶ ἀποφάσεις), *Comparisons* (Συγκρίσεις), *Educational Laws* (Νόμοι παιδευτικοί), *Political Laws* (Νόμοι πολιτικοί, at least eight books; cf. Ath. 14. 648 d), *Historical Notes* ('Ιστορικὰ ὑπομνήματα), *Short Notes* (Τὰ κατὰ βραχὺ ὑπομν.), *Miscellaneous Notes* (Σύμμικτα ὑπομν., at least sixteen books; cf. Photius *Bibl*., p. 176), *Scattered Notes* (Τὰ σποράδην), and *Table Talk* (Σύμμικτα συμποτικά).

3. Aristoxenus' presentation of the science of Harmonics differed in many important particulars from that of his predecessors and exercised a potent influence for many centuries (*see* MUSIC). His pride in his own achievements, his combativeness, his tedious proofs of the obvious, and his parade of logic are sometimes irritating; but he shows himself a worthy pupil of Aristotle in his method of expounding by definition and subdivision into categories, and his system of musical theory is distinctly superior to the empirical and half-mystical investigations of the Pythagoreans. He also had a deep interest in the ethical and educational value of music and showed a strong preference for the older styles of composition. The fundamental importance of his work on rhythm has also long been recognized. Like other Peripatetics, A. did not restrict his inquiries to a single subject; but most of what has been preserved from his other works is quoted for its value as gossip. For his philosophical views we have only the evidence of Cicero (*Tusc*. 1. 19) that A. regarded the soul as a 'tuning' (*intentio*, ἁρμονία) of the body. This opinion, which would be attractive to a musician, may have been taken from the later Pythagoreans; for a somewhat similar view is expounded by Simmias the Theban, disciple of Philolaus, in *Phaedo* 86 b; but it is quite inconsistent with the earlier Pythagorean doctrine of transmigration and could not have been countenanced by Aristotle.

BIBLIOGRAPHY

LIFE AND WORKS. Suidas; and cf. C. von Jan in *PW* ii. 1057.
TEXTS. Harm.: Meursius (Leyden, 1616), Meibomius (Amsterdam, 1652), P. Marquard (1868), R. Westphal (in *Aristoxenos* ii, 1893), H. Macran (1902); and add *POxy*. iv. 667. Rhythm: Morelli (with *Aristidis oratio*, etc., Venice, 1785), R. Westphal (in *Lehrsätze der gr. Rhythmiker*, 1861 and in *Aristox*. ii, 1893), P. Marquard (1868); and add *POxy*. i. 9. Fragments: C. Müller, *FHG* ii. 269–92; F. Wehrli, *Aristoxenos* (1945).
COMMENTARIES. R. Westphal, *Lehrsätze* (1861), *System der ant. Rhythmik* (1865), *Theorie der mus. Künste der Hellenen* (1885–89), *Aristoxenos* (1883–93); H. Macran, *Aristoxenus* (1902); L. Laloy,

Aristoxène de Tarente (1904, with a useful lexicon); C. A. Williams, *Aristoxenian Theory of Musical Rhythm* (1911).
TRANSLATIONS (of *Harm*.). Latin: Gogavinus (Venice, 1542: reprinted in Westphal, *Aristox*. ii); Meibomius (1652). German: P. Marquard (1868). French: C. E. Ruelle (1871). English: H. Macran (1902). Müller gives a Latin version of the fragments.
J. F. M.

ARIUS DIDYMUS (1st c. B.C.) of Alexandria, philosophical teacher of Augustus. Works: a *Consolatio* addressed to Livia on the death of Drusus: a doxographical work of which Stobaeus preserves two long frs. on the Stoic and Peripatetic ethics. He is described as a Stoic, but seems to have shown an eclecticism similar to that of Antiochus of Ascalon, by whom he was influenced.

Ed. Diels in *Doxographi Graeci*, 447–72. *PW* ii. 626. W. D. R.

ARMENIA, a mountainous country of Asia. Strabo (11. 520 ff.) describes it as bounded on the east by Media Atropatene, on the north by Iberia, Albania, and Colchis, and on the west and south by the Euphrates, Cappadocia, and Commagene. The country was variously divided at different periods; some districts, e.g. Sophene, Gordyene, were often independent principalities. The Romans distinguished between Armenia Major, the whole plateau east of the Euphrates, and Armenia Minor, a small kingdom to the west of it.

Once the seat of the independent kingdom of Urartu, Armenia was incorporated into the Persian Empire, in which it formed a satrapy. Xenophon (*An*. 4. 2 and 3) describes the country as he saw it. Under Seleucid rule the Armenian cantons were administered by local governors, but after Magnesia (189 B.C.) the natives declared their independence, and one king, Artaxias, became sovereign over all Armenia Major, though nominally subject to Rome. The imperialistic ambitions of Tigranes the Great (q.v.) led the Republic to tighten its hold; after the campaigns of Lucullus and Pompey Armenia became a Roman protectorate. Thenceforward it was the subject of a continual tug-of-war between the two world-powers, Rome and Persia, each seeking to maintain control. A dynasty of Arsacid princes founded by Tiridates (q.v. 1) generally managed to maintain a balance, remaining Parthian in sympathy while professing friendship to Rome. Trajan temporarily reversed Roman policy by annexing the country.

Armenia was the first kingdom officially to adopt Christianity, and the new religion and its persecution by the Sassanids fostered a nationalistic spirit. In A.D. 387 the country was divided between Persia and Byzantium. The Arabs conquered it *c*. A.D. 653.

SOURCES. (1) Classical: for the relations between Rome and Armenia see especially Strabo, bk. 11; Plutarch (*Lucullus, Pompey, Antony*); Tacitus (*Ann*. 12–15); Dio Cassius, bk. 68; Ammianus Marcellinus. (2) Oriental (unreliable): V. Langlois, *Collection des historiens de l'Arménie* (1877). (3) Numismatic: E. Babelon, *Les Rois de Syrie, d'Arménie et de la Commagène* (1890). No coins were minted in the Arsacid period.
MODERN WORKS: P. Asdourian, *Die politischen Beziehungen zwischen Rom und Armenien* (1911); A. Christensen, *L'Iran sous les Sassanides* (1936); K. Güterbock, *Römisch-Armenien und die römischen Satrapien* (1900); C. F. Lehmann-Haupt, *Armenien einst und jetzt* (1910–31); J. Sandalgian, *Histoire documentaire de l'Arménie* (1917); E. Stein, *Gesch. des spätrömischen Reiches* (1929); F. Tournebize, *Histoire politique et religieuse de l'Arménie* (1900); *PW*, s.v. 'Armenia' (Baumgartner), 'Persarmenia' (Sturm), and individual kings. M. S. D.

ARMIES, GREEK AND HELLENISTIC. The composition of the Homeric army is never clearly stated in the epic, and was no doubt never exactly defined. Generally there is a distinction drawn between the champions (πρόμαχοι) and the general mass of soldiers (πληθύς). Probably only the chieftains were fully armed and armoured; the common soldiers equipped themselves as best they could.

2. There is no direct continuity between the Homeric army and the classical. In the latter (for which the Athenian can be taken as typical) the organization was based on the tribal system and property-qualification. The citizen of any age between eighteen and sixty, if not disabled, might be required at need to serve the State in a military capacity, as horseman, hoplite, or light-armed soldier, according to his assessment. In practice the hoplite was the chief unit. Cavalry were scarce in Greece, apart from Thessaly and Macedon, neither of which was a great military power between 550 and 375 B.C. The usual proportion of hoplites to cavalry in an army was ten to one. Light-armed citizen troops had no fixed equipment: they were only called out *en masse*, when an army marched πανδημεί into a neighbouring State or to resist such an invasion. Their numbers might be large, but their military efficiency was slight. The Athenian hoplites were organized into ten tribal regiments; the cavalry were grouped into two divisions of five tribes each and were led by two hipparchs. Total numbers on the Athenian army-list (κατάλογος) are never clearly stated; the most important summary is in Thuc. 2. 13. 6 ff., which admits of various interpretations. Ordinarily young men from eighteen to twenty and older men from fifty upwards were retained for garrison duty only. The age-classes required were called up by reference to their year-archons (ἐπώνυμοι) or in the fourth century soldiers were alternatively summoned by the detachment (ἐν τοῖς μέρεσιν). The only standing army in fifth-century Athens were the τοξόται, archers mostly employed for police duties. They numbered 1,600 and were mainly hired from abroad.

3. Every Greek army had its local peculiarities, but the State with the most individual system was Sparta, where all the full citizens were equals, and therefore none was less than hoplite in status. Their cavalry were few and unsatisfactory. In the Persian wars the Spartans sent to Plataea a force of 5,000 citizens as hoplites, supported by 5,000 *perioeci*. At that period they were divided into five territorial regiments, but at the battle of Mantinea (418 B.C.) the regiments were seven in number, subdivided into πεντηκοστύες and ἐνωμοτίαι, and in addition there was an eighth, separate, Scirite λόχος of 600. Thucydides reckoned the main hoplite force at Mantinea as 4,298 men, excluding the Scirites, and described them as five-sixths of the Spartan army. The number of cavalry at this period had been raised to 700 (Thuc. 4. 55. 2). The early fourth century saw a further reorganization into five *morae*, subdivided into λόχοι, πεντηκοστύες, and ἐνωμοτίαι. The extent to which the army at Mantinea or later was composed of a blend of Spartans and *perioeci* is uncertain, but the best theory is that Spartans and *perioeci* were incorporated in the same organization, and that the changes of system correspond to increasing proportions of *perioeci* and declining numbers of Spartiates. During the Peloponnesian War the Spartans were also compelled more and more to use Helots for foreign expeditions and garrison duty abroad. They were sent out under the command of one Spartiate with perhaps another Spartan or two as his lieutenants. In the fourth century Sparta like other Greek States was forced to employ mercenaries (q.v.).

4. The Macedonian army is best known as it was organized under Alexander the Great, but no doubt his system was taken over directly from Philip II, and its general lines may be much older. At that time the infantry consisted of the πεζέταιροι, about 3,000 strong, who formed the phalanx (q.v.), and the ὑπασπισταί, probably about twice as many, who were more lightly armed. The *corps d'élite* of the Macedonian cavalry were the ἑταῖροι, grouped in eight ἶλαι; but Alexander also had at his command large forces of Thessalian cavalry as well as Thracians, and special light-armed levies, such as the Agrianes. In addition he led into Asia the forces of his Greek allies and a certain number of mercenaries.

5. The armies of the *Diadochi* were in practice little else than mercenary bands, but with the founding of the Hellenistic kingdoms new national armies were established. (1) The army of the Ptolemies is best known from Polybius' account (5. 65) of the battle of Raphia (217 B.C.), and from many casual references in inscriptions and papyri. The main divisions were (a) native Egyptians, (b) Macedonians, and (c) mercenaries. Of these the Macedonians were the most important, drawn from settlers with an obligation to provide military service, but the standing army mostly consisted of mercenaries who supplied the palace guard. (2) The army of the Seleucids was remarkable for the great variety of nationalities from which it drew its soldiers. Its phalanx was armed in the Macedonian style, but was no doubt of very mixed blood, and was raised from the military settlers (κάτοικοι). (3) The Macedonian army was still in theory based on its former system of citizen levies, but actually the man-power of Macedon had been seriously exhausted, and in later periods barbarian mercenaries from the north had to be hired in large numbers. (4) In the Hellenistic period the Achaean and Aetolian Leagues were the chief military powers among the Greek States. Their forces were composed in varying proportions of citizens and mercenaries. They copied the royal armies in having more varied types of troops, and tended more and more to depend on professional soldiers.

See also ARCHERS, ARMS AND ARMOUR, ARTILLERY, HOPLITES, MERCENARIES (GREEK), WAR (ART OF).

J. Kromayer and G. Veith, *Heerwesen und Kriegführung der Griechen und Römer* (1928); P. Monceaux, Dar.-Sag., s.v. 'Exercitus'. On the Spartan army, G. Dickins, *JHS* xxxii (1912), 1 ff.; and on Hellenistic armies, G. T. Griffith, *The Mercenaries of the Hellenistic World* (1935).   H. W. P.

ARMIES, ROMAN.

Traditional accounts of the early Roman army are tendentious and may often reflect later conditions. It seems, however, probable that from the first military service was regarded as an essential feature of citizenship, but as the poor could not provide suits of armour, in practice service devolved upon the rich. This inequality was lessened by two reforms. (a) Citizens were grouped for service in accordance with their means (traditionally since Servius Tullius). Thus the richest provided the cavalry and the poorest the light-armed troops. (b) As the need for longer campaigns grew, entailing a maximum liability of sixteen years' service, pay was introduced to compensate the cost of armour (traditionally *c.* 400 B.C.). Thus gradually the State assumed responsibility for the maintenance of its soldiers.

2. By the time of the Punic Wars the Roman army consisted of a citizen militia levied according to seasonal requirements from citizens possessing a certain property qualification (although in a crisis even slaves might be enrolled), and organized in legions under consuls and military tribunes. The *Socii* were obliged by treaty to provide contingents, of equal numbers (theoretically) with those of Rome. These were called *alae*, and gradually superseded the legionary cavalry and light-armed troops. They were commanded by *praefecti*, half of whom were Roman officials under the supreme control of the consuls.

3. This system of military service was radically altered by the Marian army reforms and the enfranchisement of Italy. By the former service in the legions was opened to all Roman citizens, and a professional army voluntarily enlisted replaced the conscript militia. By the latter Italians became eligible for legionary service. Consequently the separate contingents of *Socii* disappeared, and the Roman army now consisted of legions, and of *auxilia* raised outside Italy. During the last century of the Republic long-period commands (sometimes of five or even ten years) became increasingly common. The military executive thus became divorced from the civil government, and the Republican army disintegrated into a series of professional armies owing loyalty each to its own general.

4. Out of the armies of the triumvirs Augustus established a permanent standing army, composed of legions recruited from Roman citizens and *auxilia* from provincials, who were enfranchised after their service. The former were commanded by senatorial *legati*, the latter by equestrian officers, both under the supreme control of the *princeps*. In addition Augustus constituted the Praetorian Guard (*see* PRAETORIANI).

5. During the next two centuries no substantial alterations were made, apart from the gradual elimination of differences between legions and *auxilia*. With Septimius Severus, who widened the areas of praetorian recruitment, began a policy of democratization, which culminated in Gallienus' removal of senators from military commands. At the same time with the influx of barbarians the army lost its national character, and the Roman stock became increasingly effete.

6. In the reorganization consummated by Constantine the Imperial forces were divided into a mobile field army and stationary frontier garrisons. The former comprised the flower of the troops, the latter soon degenerated into local militias. The praetorians were disbanded, and in place of their prefects *magistri militum* assumed the highest command under the emperors.

See further ARMS AND ARMOUR, ARTILLERY, AUXILIA, COMITATENSES, FABRI, LEGATI, LEGION, LIMITANEI, MAGISTER MILITUM, MERCENARIES (ROMAN), PALATINI, PRAEFECTUS, PRAETORIANI, WAR (ART OF).

Kromayer–Veith, *Heerwesen und Kriegführung der Griechen und Römer* (1928); *PW* s.v. 'Exercitus'; H. M. D. Parker, *The Roman Legions* (1928). H. M. D. P.

ARMILUSTRIUM, *see* AVENTINE, MARS.

ARMINIUS (*c.* 18 B.C.–A.D. 17), chief of the Cherusci. He had Roman citizenship, served in the Roman auxiliary forces, and attained the rank of *eques*. In A.D. 9 he secretly organized the struggle against the Romans. By the report of a rising he attracted three Roman legions, commanded by P. Quinctilius Varus, to the Teutoburgian Forest and cut them to pieces. In 15 he fought against Segestes, whose daughter Thusnelda he had married. Segestes was helped by Germanicus (q.v.), and Thusnelda fell into the hands of the Romans. In 16, though beaten by Germanicus and wounded, Arminius again thwarted the Roman conquest of Germany. In 17, with the help of the Semnones and Langobardi, he entered into war with Maroboduus, but was treacherously killed. He was a prudent tactician and a master of surprise attack; his greatness was recognized by Tacitus: 'liberator haud dubie Germaniae.' Only the Roman, not the German tradition, preserved his memory. The identification of Arminius with the Siegfried of German legend is wrong.

Sources: Velleius 2. 118; Tacitus, *Ann.* 1–2; Strabo 7. 291; Frontin. *Str.* 2. 9. 4; Florus 2. 30 (4. 12); Cass. Dio 56. 19. General literature: *PIR²*, A 1063; R. Syme, *CAH* x. 373; L. Schmidt, *Geschichte d. deutschen Stämme* i² (1938), 100; E. Hohl, 'Neues von Arminius', *Antike (Alte Sprachen und deutsche Bildung)* 1943, 49–60. A. M.

ARMS AND ARMOUR, GREEK. Homeric equipment is a special subject. No single description applies to all the passages, but a large number are best interpreted in connexion with Minoan and Mycenaean armaments, which are known from such representations as those on the Shaft-grave daggers. Their characteristic armour is a figure-of-eight-shaped shield made of one ox-hide and swung from the neck by a strap. The only protection used with it was a helmet. The chief weapon was a long rapier-like sword. Towards the end of the Bronze Age this style was displaced by the use of a much smaller round shield carried on the arm. This change involved the addition of a breastplate and greaves, while the sword became shorter and was used for cut as well as thrust. In the Homeric poems the champions begin by throwing spears at each other, and when these are gone they proceed to close combat with swords.

The standing type of the archaic and classical soldier is the hoplite (q.v.). This was ultimately derived from the soldier of the transition to the Iron Age. The trend was towards heavier armour and fighting based on weight of man-power. Shields were made of bronze, and spears and swords of iron. In addition hoplites wore breastplates, greaves, and helmets as defensive armour. The spear as used by hoplites and cavalry had become a pike for thrusting, not throwing, and was usually some nine feet in length. Only light-armed troops and some light cavalry used instead the throwing spear (ἀκόντιον). Along with the use of the spear as a pike, the sword (at least of the Athenian hoplite) had developed a short, straight-edged blade; it could only be used for very close fighting.

The fourth century saw the evolution of a more flexible type of equipment than the hoplites. Experiments were first made with the peltast (q.v.), but the final change was the establishment of the Macedonian type as employed in the phalanx (q.v.). The spear (σάρισα) was increased still more in length to a maximum of 17 feet, and the shield reduced to a small target carried on the arm. The different ranks of the phalanx used different lengths of spear. The equipment for light-armed infantry and light- and heavy-armed cavalry was also specialized at this period.

J. Kromayer and G. Veith, *Heerwesen und Kriegführung der Griechen und Römer* (1928). Homeric: W. Reichel, *Homerische Waffen* (1901). Hoplite: M. P. Nilsson, 'Die Hoplitentechnik und das Staatswesen', *Klio* xxii (1929), 240 ff. Hellenistic: W. W. Tarn, *Hellenistic Military and Naval Developments* (1930). H. W. P.

ARMS AND ARMOUR, ROMAN. In the regal and early Republican period the Roman infantry fought as a phalanx and was equipped on the Greek model (possibly under Etruscan influence). The *hasta* or thrusting spear was the chief offensive weapon, and the defensive armour varied with the individual's means. The richest soldiers had corselets and light round shields (*clipei*), and, in common with the less opulent, greaves and helmets.

2. By the time of Polybius, however, the *pilum* or throwing spear had replaced the *hasta* as the Roman national weapon, and was carried by the first two lines (*hastati* and *principes*). For close fighting the two-edged cut-and-thrust Spanish sword had been introduced. The *clipeus* was superseded by an oval *scutum*, while for the Greek corselet was substituted a Celtic coat of mail. By contrast with the heavy-armed legionary the *velites* were equipped with only a small round buckler (*parma*) and a light spear (*iaculum*). The legionary cavalry wore a helmet and cuirass, and carried a *clipeus* and a two-pointed spear (*hasta, tragula*), but no sword. The *Socii* were probably armed like their corresponding Roman contingents.

3. During the last century of the Republic the *pilum* became universal in the legion, and its construction was improved so as to increase its penetrative powers. The oval was replaced by a rectangular cylindrical shield, and greaves were abolished. In short, Greek equipment was gradually supplanted by types of armour partly indigenous and partly adopted from Gaul and Spain.

4. Under the Principate the arms of the legionary and the auxiliary were differentiated. Among the former there were few important changes, apart from modifications made in the cuirass. Of special interest is the *lorica segmentata* represented on Trajan's column, which consisted of breast and back plates strengthened by iron hoops round the body and arms. By contrast with the legionary *pilum* and *gladius*, the auxiliary infantry and cavalry carried a *hasta* and *spatha* or long sword; the former had oblong and the latter oval-shaped shields instead of the *scutum*. In addition there was a number of specialist contingents, whose names indicate their equipment (*funditores, sagittarii*).

5. The Roman army eventually lost its national character. *Pilum* and *gladius* were replaced by *spiculum* and *spatha*, and in the *Notitia Dignitatum* many units bore titles indicating their methods of fighting, e.g. *clibanarii* and *catafractarii*, the iron-clad horsemen of Persian pattern.

P. Couissin, *Les Armes romaines* (1926); Kromayer–Veith, *Heerwesen und Kriegführung der Griechen und Römer* (1928).
H. M. D. P.

ARNŎBIUS wrote about A.D. 305 in Numidia seven books *Adversus Nationes*. They make a detailed attack on ancient paganism in which much curious learning, derived partly from Varro, is preserved. The style is not unpleasant, its most unexpected feature being the constant reminiscences of Lucretius, which make it clear that the author knew the *De Rerum Natura* by heart. His Christianity is especially to be inferred from his hostility to paganism. He is the first dated Latin writer to use the word *deitas*.

C. Marchesi, *Adversus Nationes*, (1934); E. Löfstedt, *Arnobiana* (1917); F. Gabarrou, *Le Latin d'Arnobe* (1921); H. Hagendahl, *La Prose métrique d'Arnobe* (1937). A. S.

ARPINUM, a Volscian hill-town in the Liris valley; nowadays *Arpino*, with interesting polygonal walls. Rome captured Arpinum from its Samnite conquerors and gave it *civitas sine suffragio*, 305–303 B.C. (Diod. 20. 90; Livy 9. 44; 10. 1). After 188 it enjoyed full citizenship, being administered as a *praefectura* and, after 90, as a *municipium* (Livy 38. 36; Festus 262 L.; Cic. *Planc.* 20). Subsequently Arpinum is seldom mentioned. It is famed as the birthplace of Marius and Cicero (Juv. 8. 237 f.); remains, possibly of Cicero's villa, still exist nearby.

L. Ippoliti, *Il luogo di nascita di Marco Tullio Cicerone* (1936) —with bibliography. E. T. S.

ARRETIUM, modern *Arezzo*. Strabo, who mentions Arretium as important in late days, describes it as the most inland of Etruscan cities. Evidently it was later than most. Its early history is barely revealed by occasional gleams; we do not even know when Arretium became Roman. In 301 B.C. its ruling family were the Cilnii. A hundred years later its wealth is revealed by the supplies furnished to Scipio's fleet (Livy 28. 45). That its commercial magnates were lovers of art is shown by two bronze masterpieces now in the Florence Museum. The Minerva is a copy of some Greek original of the fifth century; but the Chimaera is a work of striking originality. In the first century B.C. Arretium became famous for its red pottery, whose moulded figures are in the finest late Hellenistic style (*see* TERRA SIGILLATA). D. R.-MacI.

ARRHA SPONSALICIA, see MARRIAGE, LAW OF.

ARRIA (1) **MAJOR,** the wife of Caecina Paetus, professed Stoicism. When her husband was condemned by Claudius for his part in the conspiracy of Camillus Scribonianus (A.D. 42), she stabbed herself and gave Paetus the dagger saying, 'Paete, non dolet' (Plin. *Ep.* 3. 16; Martial 1. 13). A. M.

ARRIA (2) **MINOR,** daughter of Arria (1), was wife of P. Clodius Thrasea (q.v.) Paetus, mother of Fannia (who became wife of Helvidius Priscus), and relative of Persius. She wished to die beside her condemned husband (A.D. 66), but was forbidden. Banished by Domitian, she returned to Rome under Nerva, and was a friend of Pliny the Younger. A. M.

ARRIAN (FLAVIUS ARRIANUS, 2nd c. A.D.) of Bithynia governed Cappadocia under Hadrian and defeated the great Alan invasion of 134. He was a pupil of Epictetus, whose teaching reinforced his natural sense and honesty; if he claimed to imitate Xenophon, it was his only affectation. He preserved the valuable *Discourses* of Epictetus; and beside military treatises and his lost

History of Parthia he wrote a history of Alexander's successors, based on Hieronymus of Cardia (large fragments alone survive); the *Indike*, an account of India from Megasthenes and Nearchus, with a reproduction of Nearchus' account of his voyage; and his chief book, the *Anabasis*, his history of Alexander. He calls Ptolemy I and Aristobulus his sources, but his main source was Ptolemy, Aristobulus being used to supplement him; the vulgate and stories he quotes as λεγόμενα, 'so they say'. His sober narrative is the basis of Alexander's history, a welcome contrast to the romanticism, the slander, the absurd stories, so often met elsewhere. Purists condemn Arrian's style; it is more important that he wrote plainly and eschewed rhetoric. He is not a compiler, but a real historian who tried to go to the best sources; he illustrates Polybius' dictum that only men of action could write history, and but for this practical soldier we should know little enough about Alexander.

See ALEXANDER (3), Bibliography, Ancient Sources.
W. W. T.

ARRIUS ANTONINUS, grandfather of the Emperor Antoninus Pius, wrote Greek poems which recalled Callimachus and Herodas according to Pliny (*Ep.* 4. 3. 3–4).

ARRIUS, *see also* VARUS (4).

ARRUNTIUS (1), LUCIUS, was proscribed in 43 B.C., but escaped to Sextus Pompeius. He returned to Italy after the treaty of Misenum and commanded a division of Octavian's fleet at Actium. He was consul in 22, and as *XVvir sacris faciundis* took part in the *Ludi Saeculares* in 17. In spite of his wealth Arruntius was noted for the simplicity and severity of his life. He wrote a history of the (First?) Punic War.

Velleius 2. 77, 85 and 86; Seneca, *Ep.* 114. 17–19; Tacitus, *Ann.* 11. 6 and 7. G. W. R.

ARRUNTIUS (2) **STELLA,** LUCIUS (*cos.* A.D. 101), poet-patron of Martial and Statius, gave games to celebrate Domitian's Sarmatian victory: wrote love-poems on Violentilla, whom he afterwards married (Mart. 1. 7; 4. 6; 5. 11. 2; 7. 14. 5; Stat. *Silv.* 1. 2).

ARRUNTIUS (3) **CELSUS** (2nd c. A.D.), miscellanist, whose (lost) works included a grammar and (possibly) commentaries on Terence and Virgil.

Teuffel, § 365 a, 3; Schanz–Hosius, § 606, 5.

ARRUNTIUS, *see also* SCRIBONIANUS (1).

ARS, a treatise. This meaning of the word, based on the opposition (common in literary criticism) between *ars* (τέχνη) and *natura* (*ingenium*, φύσις), is first found in the *Ad Herennium*. The term is used mainly for technical works (*ars grammatica, ars arithmetica*); but *Ars Amatoria* was certainly Ovid's own title (cf. 2. 162). Horace's *Ars Poetica* is first so named by Quintilian (8. 3. 60). J. F. M.

ARSACIDS, the royal dynasty of Parthia (q.v.) *c.* 250 B.C.–A.D. 230. Arsaces, rebelling against the Bactrian satrap of Antiochus II Theos, became the first king of Parthia, and his descendants (some 38 in number) bore his name as an official title. The Arsacids rapidly made Parthia a world-power second only to Rome: on the west they drove the Seleucids from Mesopotamia and more than once invaded Syria; in the east they reached India and extended their influence over the Indo-Scythian kingdoms. Their relations with Rome were generally hostile, yet they performed a great service to the western world in halting the constant menace of nomadic invasion from the north-west. Politically, the Arsacids were the heirs of the Achaemenids, from whom they claimed descent. They too made Media the centre of their empire and Ecbatana their capital; Ctesiphon (q.v.) was their winter residence. Although not themselves Persians, they adopted Persian religion and customs, and organization into satrapies.

SOURCES. Classical: Plutarch (esp. *Crassus* and *Antony*); Josephus (E. Täubler, *Die Parthernachrichten bei Josephus*, 1904); Tacitus (*Ann.* 13-15); Dio Cassius (passim).

Babylonian cuneiform texts (valuable for chronology): A. T. Olmstead, *CPhil.* 1937; J. N. Strassmaier, *Zeitschr. f. Assyriologie* iii (1888).

Chinese texts: F. Hirth, *China and the Roman Orient* (1885); J. J. M. de Groot, *Chinesische Urkunden zur Geschichte Asiens* (1921-6).

Coins (important): W. Wroth, *Parthia* (B.M. Cat.), 1903); R. H. Macdowell, *Coins from Seleucia* (1936).

GENERAL HISTORIES. G. Rawlinson, *The Sixth Oriental Monarchy* (1873); A. von Gutschmid, *Geschichte Irans* (1888); N. C. Debevoise, *Political History of Parthia* (1938). *PW*, arts. on individual kings.

Rome and Parthia: A. Günther, *Beiträge zur Geschichte der Kriege zwischen Römer und Parthern* (1922); R. P. Longden in *JRS* 1931; *CAH* ix, x, xi. M. S. D.

ARSINOE, in mythology, *see* ALCMAEON (1).

ARSINOE I (b. *c.* 300 B.C.), daughter of Lysimachus (q.v.) and of his first wife Nicaea. She married Ptolemy II when crown prince (*c.* 289-288), and had by him at least three children, Ptolemy III, Berenice Syra, and a Lysimachus. She was accused of plotting to kill her husband and was banished to Coptus (279-274). Her motive was perhaps jealousy, as Arsinoë II had returned to Egypt a short time before. F. M. H.

ARSINOË II (*Philadelphus*) (*c.* 316-270 B.C.), daughter of Ptolemy I and Berenice I. She married (*c.* 299-298) Lysimachus (q.v.), who was strongly under her influence and gave her the towns of Heraclea, Tius, Amastris, and Cassandreia as special domains. After Lysimachus' defeat and death and a short marriage to her step-brother Ptolemy Ceraunus, Arsinoë fled to Egypt. She married her brother Ptolemy II in 276-275 or perhaps a year earlier. Her influence as queen was decisive in the policy of Egypt. The Fayûm, colonized at this time, was called Arsinoites after her. F. M. H.

ARSINOË III (*Philopator*) (b. *c.* 235 B.C.), daughter of Ptolemy III and Berenice II. She married her brother Ptolemy IV in 217, but fell into disfavour during his last years and was burnt to death in a deliberately started palace fire in 206-205 or 204-203, shortly before or after her husband's death.

See PTOLEMY. F. M. H.

ARSINOË (*Crocodilopolis*) was developed by Ptolemy Philadelphus as the metropolis of the district which he reclaimed in the Fayûm; its Egyptian predecessor was unimportant. The ruins are extensive, but have not been systematically excavated; they were the first source of papyri exploited in the Fayûm, and have produced large numbers of Roman and Byzantine documents. J. G. M.

ARSINOË (*Cleopatris*), now *Ardscherud* near Suez, at the northern end of the gulf, founded by Ptolemy II, was the capital of the Heroöpolite nome, and the terminal point of a canal from the Pelusiac arm of the Nile. It became one of the chief Egyptian ports, despite shoals and south winds, carrying Red Sea trade, but much less than Myos Hormos and Berenice (qq.v.). Near it Trajan established a garrison at Clysma, at the end of a new canal (from *Baboul*), cleared periodically through several centuries.

Warmington, *Indian Commerce*. E. H. W.

ART, *see* ARCHITECTURE, ART (GREEK RELIGIOUS), GEMS, MOSAIC, PAINTING, PORTRAITURE, POTTERY, SCULPTURE, VASE-PAINTING.

Bibliography: Springer, Michaelis, Wolters, *Die Kunst des Altertums* (1923); F. Winter, *Kunstgeschichte in Bildern*, i, *Das Altertum* (1912-); A. Rumpf, *Griechische und römische Kunst*[4] (1931); H. Brunn, *Griechische Kunstgeschichte* i-ii (1893-7); H. B. Walters, *The Art of the Romans* (1911); E. Strong, *Art in Ancient Rome* (2 vols, 1929). See also the chapters on Art in *CAH*.

ART, GREEK RELIGIOUS. Greek art, at least until the time of Alexander the Great, was essentially a civic and religious art, devoted primarily to the adornment of the city and the glorification of the gods who protected it.

2. For the four centuries between 1100 and 700 B.C. our information is scanty. A formal, geometric style of decoration took the place of the naturalistic curvilinear schemes of the Bronze Age, as is shown especially by the painted vases and crudely modelled figurines in bronze and terra-cotta. Some of these served religious purposes: large vases painted with scenes of death and burial sometimes marked the graves of the dead, and smaller vessels were placed in the graves and dedicated as offerings at shrines; and the bronze and terra-cotta figurines were also used as offerings. The shrines were for the most part, however, simple structures of wood and crude brick which have left few traces. Greek writers frequently mention wooden statues of divinities which were regarded as very early works and some of these, no doubt, were products of the 'Geometric Period'. The most famous of such images was the ancient Athena in the Erechtheum. Although the forms of the great Olympian divinities were well established at this time, as appears clearly in the Homeric poems, the artist apparently was unable to represent them.

3. It was only in the seventh century, and largely as a result of contact with the Orient, that an advance was made. On vases and bronzes of this time the gods and heroes gradually appeared, often in forms that suggest the influence of the East, like the winged nature goddess with animals, who was most commonly equated with Artemis and sometimes given her characteristic bow and quiver. Even when, towards the end of the seventh century, larger sculpture in stone was attempted, it was only by means of attributes that gods and goddesses were distinguished, the same types being used for divinities and human beings.

4. The Archaic Period (600-480 B.C.) was characterized by rapid progress in all the arts. Temples of stone, generally Ionic in Asia Minor and Doric on the mainland and in the West, replaced the earlier simple shrines. Each of these contained in the principal chamber a statue of the divinity to whom it was dedicated; pediments with scenes from mythology, at first in painted relief, later with painted statues in the round, and the metopes and friezes offered other space for decoration. The pedimental sculptures from the temple of Aphaea at Aegina, now in Munich, with the stiff central figure of Athena and the freely posed but still archaic figures of fighting Greeks and Trojans, show the progress that had been made just before 480 B.C. Throughout the Archaic Period statues in stone and statuettes in bronze and terra-cotta were dedicated as offerings at the sanctuaries of the gods and so have some religious character; excellent examples are found in the great series of female figures from the Acropolis at Athens, each holding an offering in the extended hand. Not infrequently, however, such figures were characterized as divinities by their attributes, and the figurines in clay and bronze placed in the tombs exhibit similar types.

5. The period from the Persian Wars to the end of the fifth century marks the first great flowering of the Greek genius in all fields, when many works were created which later generations looked upon as masterpieces. It was a period of high idealism when the types for many of the gods were fixed for all later time. The great Apollo from the west pediment of the temple of Zeus at Olympia, which was dedicated about 456 B.C., though still slightly archaic, is a marvellous embodiment of the Homeric ideal of 'blessed gods who live forever'. More famous were other statues which we know only in inadequate copies: the gold and ivory Zeus made by Phidias for the temple at Olympia, which according to Quintilian 'seems to have added something to the established religion'; the gold and ivory Athena in the Parthenon at Athens by the same sculptor; the Hera made by Polycletus for a new temple of the goddess at her shrine near Argos. In the fifth century even purely human figures were idealized; the men and women who appear in the great Panathenaic procession on the frieze of the Parthenon do not differ greatly from the gods who await them. The painted vases of the mid-fifth century exhibit similar qualities and are generally believed to reflect the style of Polygnotus and other painters of the time who decorated the walls of temples and public buildings with elaborate compositions, mostly mythological in subject, such as the Greeks at the sack of Troy and the Slaying of the Suitors.

6. This high level was not long maintained. The fourth century witnessed many changes, especially in the direction of a more human conception of the gods and a greater individuality, both in the artist and in his product. The famous Hermes of Praxiteles found at Olympia, in spite of the skilful execution, lacks the grandeur of the fifth-century Apollo from the same site; and his most famous statue, the nude Aphrodite of Cnidos, was a more human goddess than the creations of the fifth century, such as the Aphrodite on the so-called Ludovisi Throne in Rome and the companion relief in Boston. No doubt we should feel the same about the famous Aphrodite Rising from the Sea by the contemporary painter Apelles, if that work were preserved. It is characteristic of the fourth century, also, that the lesser divinities of the Greek pantheon were more frequently represented than in earlier periods. In the list of Praxiteles' works are found Eros, Peitho, Pan, Satyrs, and Nymphs. Another innovation appeared in statues and groups that represent abstractions, such as Peace Carrying Wealth by Cephisodotus (an altar to Peace is said to have been set up for the first time in Athens in 374 B.C.), Fortune and Wealth by Xenophon.

7. The spread of Greek culture to many lands, which resulted from the conquests of Alexander the Great, brought many changes. In the new cities which were founded by Alexander and his successors temples were erected to Greek divinities as well as to local gods, and the worship of Oriental divinities, such as Sarapis, Isis, and Harpocrates, spread to Greece itself. The sculptors of the Hellenistic Age (dated usually from the death of Alexander in 323 B.C.) based their creations upon the types established in earlier times, but modified them to embody contemporary ideas, which were in the direction of more slender forms, more theatrical poses, and greater realism in detail. The Aphrodite of Melos is less stocky than the fourth- and fifth-century models by which it was inspired; the Apollo Belvedere (a Roman copy of a Hellenistic original) shows well the theatrical quality; the Demeter and the Artemis from the great group by Damophon of Messene suggest individual character much more than the highly idealized forms of earlier days. The Tyche of Antioch, created early in the third century by Eutychides and worked out as an elaborate allegory of the town itself, was the ancestress of many similar representations of a goddess who became immensely popular, the Fortune of the individual city. The erudite character of much Hellenistic sculpture is well illustrated by the Battle of the Gods and Giants which decorated the great Altar of Zeus and Athena at Pergamum. In the high relief of this elaborate composition are found Aether and other divinities who can have had little real significance even to the Greeks themselves, and in the treatment of the figures with their contorted poses and bulging muscles gods and giants alike are hardly to be distinguished from contemporary athletic types. The gods have descended from Olympus and become much more like ordinary mortals. The diffuse and varied character of Hellenistic art accurately reflects the disintegration of Greek civilization in its last phase.

E. Buschor, *Greek Vase Painting* (translated by G. C. Richards, 1921); Winifred Lamb, *Greek and Roman Bronzes* (1929); A. W. Lawrence, *Classical Sculpture* (1929), *Later Greek Sculpture* (1927); Gisela M. A. Richter, *The Sculpture and Sculptors of the Greeks* (U.S.A., 1929); D. S. Robertson, *Handbook of Greek and Roman Architecture* (1929). *See also* RELIGION, MINOAN-MYCENAEAN.

G. H. C.

ARTABAZUS (*c.* 387–*c.* 325 B.C.), son of Pharnabazus (q.v.) and Apame. His consistent loyalty to Artaxerxes II (q.v.) was rewarded by his appointment as satrap of Dascyleum, a position which was hereditary in his family. Under Artaxerxes III he revolted, and, aided successively by Chares and Pammenes, held out until 352, when he was forced to seek refuge in Macedonia. His return to Persia was arranged by Mentor, his brother-in-law, in 345. After Gaugamela he fled with Darius III, but deserted from Bessus to Alexander, who made him satrap of Bactria, a command which he resigned in 328.

D. E. W. W.

ARTAVASDES I of Armenia succeeded his father Tigranes before 52 B.C., and was Rome's ally when Crassus invaded Mesopotamia; but Orodes' simultaneous invasion of Armenia brought him over to Parthia's side, and he married his sister to Orodes' son Pacorus. The story of the performance of the *Bacchae* at the wedding feast in the Armenian capital has led to a suggestion that Artavasdes, who is said to have written Greek 'histories', was the unknown historian whom Plutarch followed in the Parthian part of his *Life* of Crassus; but the unknown was certainly an eastern Greek. Artavasdes remained Parthia's ally till Antony's invasion in 36, when Canidius defeated him and he became (in name) an ally of Antony; he deserted in the critical battle, and in 34 Antony punished him by conquering Armenia and leading him in triumph at Alexandria. Contrary to Roman custom, Antony spared his life; later he was put to death by Cleopatra.

W. W. Tarn, *CAH* ix, ch. 14, x, ch. 3; *The Greeks in Bactria and India* (1938), 51 ff.   W. W. T.

ARTAXATA, the capital city of Armenia, on the river Araxes, in the district of Ararat, *c.* 20 miles south-west of Erivan. It was founded by Artaxias I, traditionally with the advice and assistance of Hannibal (Strabo 11. 528; Plut. *Luc.* 31). It was several times captured by the Romans during their invasions of Armenia; Corbulo burnt it in A.D. 58 (Tac. *Ann.* 13. 41); it was rebuilt by Tiridates brother of Vologeses (q.v.) and renamed Neronia (Dio Cass. 63. 7), but reverted to its old name. It was finally destroyed by Statius Priscus (A.D. 163). M. S. D.

ARTAXERXES (1) **I** (*Macrocheir*), king of Persia, son of Xerxes and Amestris, began his forty years' reign on his father's assassination in 464 B.C. He overcame disaffection in the court, in Bactria, and in Egypt, which, through Athenian support, resisted until 454. The peace of Callias (449) regulating relations with Athens was, on balance, a Persian diplomatic success. He was dominated by his mother; but his generous treatment of Themistocles, and of the Jewish and Egyptian minorities, suggests political sense rather than weakness.   D. E. W. W.

ARTAXERXES (2) **II** (*Mnemon*) (*c.* 436–358 B.C.), son of Darius II and Parysatis, ascended the Persian throne in 404. After crushing Cyrus' rebellion and repelling Spartan intervention in Asia Minor (peace of Antalcidas 386), he twice failed in the attempt to recover Egypt (385–383 and 374). He succeeded in suppressing the Satraps' Revolt (366–358), largely through mutual distrust among his enemies. His incapacity and subservience to the will of his mother and of his wife, Statira, caused a progressive decline and disintegration of the Empire.

D. E. W. W

ARTAXERXES (3) **III** (*Ochus*) succeeded his father, Artaxerxes II, in 358 B.C. He secured his position by the wholesale execution of his brothers, and by crushing Orontes and Artabazus. In 343 (after a previous failure in 351) he reconquered Egypt with the aid of Mentor, who later recovered western Asia Minor. He was poisoned by his minister Bagoas in 338. Though he misjudged the strength of Macedonia, his achievement in restoring the power and prestige of the central government indicates high qualities of statecraft and leadership.

W. Judeich, *PW*, s.v. 'Artaxerxes (3)'.   D. E. W. W.

ARTAXERXES (4) (*Ardashir*), the name of several Sassanid kings, the greatest being Artaxerxes I (A.D. 211–12 to 241), founder of the New Persian empire of the Sassanids. Taking advantage of the confusion in the eastern part of the Roman Empire to assume the king-ship of Istakhr, and then to conquer the neighbouring principalities one by one, he finally defeated Artabanus V of Parthia in battle and entered Ctesiphon in 224. After further campaigns his empire included Iran, Afghanistan, and Baluchistan to the Oxus, Babylonia, Mesopotamia, and Armenia. He was responsible for the political and religious organization of the Sassanian Empire, and he founded many cities. He maintained friendly relations with Rome and with the neighbouring Arab principalities.

M. S. D.

ARTEMIDORUS (1) of Tarsus (2nd and 1st cc. B.C.), grammarian. For his edition of the Bucolic Poets he wrote *Anth. Pal.* 9. 205. *See also* GLOSSA (Greek).

ARTEMIDORUS (2) (*fl.* 104–101 B.C.), a Greek of Ephesus, voyaged along Mediterranean shores, outer Spain (and Gaul?), and in Alexandria wrote eleven geographical books (Περίπλους, Τὰ γεωγραφούμενα, Γεω-γραφίας βιβλία), often quoted. His records, especially of distances in western regions, including (misapplied) use of Roman measurements, were fair, with errors and confusions. For eastern waters and Ethiopia A. relied on Agatharchides (q.v.), adding distances and details as far as C. Guardafui; for India, on Alexander's writers and Megasthenes (q.v.). He made two calculations of the inhabited world's length and two of its breadth, without determining positions by latitude and longitude.

Berger, *Gesch. d. wiss. Erdkunde d. Gr.* iv, 38 ff.; E. H. Bunbury, *Hist. of Anc. Geog.* ii (1879), 61 ff.   E. H. W.

ARTEMIDORUS (3) (late 2nd c. A.D.), born at Ephesus, lived at Daldis in Lydia, travelled extensively to collect dreams, and wrote an extant treatise (’Ονειροκριτικά) on their interpretation, a topic which had attracted the attention of serious men, as well as anecdote-mongers, since the Alexandrian age; also Οἰωνοσκοπικά and Χειρο-σκοπικά (palmistry). A. is important for the study of ancient folklore.

Text, R. Hercher (1864). W. Reichardt, *De Artemidoro Daldiano* (1894); R. Dietrich, *Beiträge zu A.* (1910).   J. D. D.

ARTEMIS (Ἄρτεμις, occasionally Ἄρταμις), a goddess universally worshipped in historical Greece, but in all likelihood pre-Hellenic. The name yields no Greek etymology, Ἄρταμις being probably a popular assimila-tion of it to ἄρταμος (slaughterer, butcher; see O. Kern, *Relig. der Griechen* i. 102). For features indicating a specifically Minoan origin, see Nilsson, *Minoan-Myce-naean Religion*, 432 ff. She is often confused with Hecate and Selene (qq.v.), with the former owing to resemblance of character and functions, with the latter through learned speculation. Her proper sphere is the earth, and specifically the uncultivated parts, forests and hills, where wild beasts are plentiful; it is true that she

is often a city-goddess, but this is a secondary develop-ment of her importance, especially among women; cf. Wilamowitz-Moellendorff, *Glaube der Hellenen* ii. 148, for a good sketch of her. Her place among the deities was not won immediately, for she plays a feeble and even ridiculous part in the *Iliad* (21. 470 ff.); but she is already a daughter of Zeus, 'lady of wild things' (πότνια θηρῶν), sister of Apollo, a huntress and a 'lion unto women' (483), because their sudden and painless deaths are ascribed to her. Her functions as a birth-goddess and a bringer of fertility to man and beast, together with health to their offspring when born (she is often κουρο-τρόφος), are still obscure, at all events in the aristocratic circles for which Homer wrote; we may believe that even then she was made more of among the common people. Of mythology she has not much; for the story of her birth as Apollo's twin, *see* LETO; it is certain that she had originally nothing to do with him. The principal adventure which she never shares with her brother is the slaying of Orion (q.v.). But it is highly probable that many of the stories of women or nymphs who bear children were originally myths of Artemis (or some similar goddess), for being a giver of fertility she can hardly have been other than a mother-deity herself (see Farnell, op. cit. infra, p. 442 ff.); the strongest instance is perhaps Callisto, whose name is suspiciously like Artemis' title καλλίστη. However, for historical Greeks she was a virgin goddess, though a friend and helper of women in childbirth.

Concerning her cult, it is characteristic that she seldom has the larger cattle sacrificed to her. Goats are a com-mon offering, and at Patrae Artemis Laphria was annually given a holocaust of wild beasts and birds, presided over by a priestess in a chariot drawn by stags like Artemis' own (Callimachus, *Dian.* 98 ff.; see Paus. 7. 18. 12, J. Herbillon, *Cultes de Patras*, 55 ff.). It is not, however, certain that this was as primitive a rite as it seems. Else-where her votaries simulate beast-shape, suggesting a theriomorphic form of Artemis herself. At Brauron in Attica, little girls in saffron dresses (to imitate the tawny hide of the bear?) danced before her; they were said ἀρκτεύειν, to play the bear, and were themselves called ἄρκτοι (Ar. *Lys.* 645 and schol.; Deubner, *Attische Feste*, 207). The existence of the word νεβεύειν, to play the fawn, suggests a similar rite in Larissa and Demetrias (Liddell–Scott⁹ s.v., in add. et corr.; P. Clement, *Ant. Class.* iii (1934), 401 ff.). At Halae a pretence of human sacrifice was made, a few drops of blood being drawn from a man's throat with a sword (Eur. *IT* 1450 ff.); actual human sacrifice at Phocaea is alleged (Pythocles ap. Clem. Alex. *Protr.* p. 32, 7 Stählin; doubtfully authentic). These are some of her most characteristic and unusual rites; in many places there probably was little to distinguish her cult from that of any other important deity. That she develops into a city-goddess has already been said; occasionally she shows a connexion with agriculture (Farnell, p. 455 ff.).

Artemis is very often identified with foreign goddesses of a more or less similar kind. Mythologically, the most important of these identifications is with the goddess of a barbarous people in the Tauric Chersonese (*Crimea*), whose cult was said to have been imported by Orestes to Halae (see above). Historically, that having the widest-reaching results was probably with the great goddess of Ephesus, which was in many ways essentially right, though the two cults had quite independent origins. From Ephesus the worship of this 'Artemis' was carried to Massilia by the Phocaeans, and thence again it made its way to Rome, where the Aventine temple of Diana (q.v.) had a statue modelled on the Ephesian type (Strabo 4. 1. 5).

Identifications with other goddesses in Greece itself, besides Hecate and Selene, were not uncommon. A clear example is the so-called Artemis Orthia of Sparta, where it is archaeologically certain that Orthia came thither with the Dorians, and therefore cannot have been originally the same as a pre-Hellenic deity; see *Artemis Orthia* (Hellenic Society, supp. paper No. 5, 1929), 399 ff. No doubt many identifications were so complete that they now escape our notice.

Several recent treatises are mentioned above. The best collection of material is still Farnell, *Cults of the Greek States* ii. 425 ff., though some of his conclusions on minor points must now be given up.   H. J. R.

ARTEMISIA I, princess of Caria, ruled under Persian suzerainty over Halicarnassus, Cos, Nisyrus, and Calyndus. She accompanied Xerxes' expedition with five ships, perhaps as commander of the Asiatic Dorians. According to Herodotus, whose account (probably based on a Halicarnassian source) is strongly biased in her favour, she vainly urged Xerxes not to attack at Salamis (probably a prophecy *ex eventu*); she fought prominently in the battle and escaped pursuit by sinking an intervening Calyndian vessel. Afterwards she urged Xerxes to immediate retreat and transported part of his family to Ephesus.
                                                   P. T.

ARTEMISIA II succeeded her brother and husband Mausolus (q.v.) of Caria in 353–352 B.C. In his memory she completed the Mausoleum (q.v.), and promoted a literary competition attended by the most famous rhetoricians (Isocrates, Theodectes, etc.); Theopompus won the prize. In 350 an attack on Rhodes by democratic exiles, relying on the support of Athens which Demosthenes (*Or.* 15) vainly tried to secure, gave Artemisia a pretext to subdue Rhodes and the adjacent islands. She died soon afterwards.

U. Kahrstedt, *Forschungen* (1910), 22 f., 114 f.; A. Momigliano *Riv. Fil.* 1936, 54 ff.; K. J. Beloch, *Griech. Geschichte*² (1923), pt. 2, 142 ff.   P. T.

ARTEMISIUM, a promontory on the north-west coast of Euboea, so called from a temple of Artemis Proseoa on this site. The place is perhaps to be identified with the village of *Potaki* near the Bay of Penki. For the battle of Artemisium, *see* PERSIAN WARS.

G. B. Grundy, *The Great Persian War* (1901), 321 ff.   P. T.

ARTEMON (1) (probably not later than 2nd c. B.C.), sometimes identified with A. (2) of Cassandreia or A. (3) of Pergamum, edited the letters of Aristotle with notes on the art of letter-writing (Demetr. *Eloc.* 223, David on Arist. *Cat.* 24ª28 Brandis).

ARTEMON (2) of Cassandreia (perhaps 2nd or 1st c. B.C.) wrote two bibliographical treatises, sometimes regarded as parts of a single work: (1) *On the Collection of Books*, (2) *On the Use of Books*, in the second book of which he discussed the three types of scolion.

FHG iv. 342 f.

ARTEMON (3) Ὁ ἀπὸ Περγάμου, also styled ὁ ἱστορικός, perhaps identical with A. (2) of Cassandreia, Cassandreia being his birthplace, Pergamum the scene of his literary activity (similar discrepancies in appellation often occur). He is several times mentioned in the scholia to Pindar for explanations based on history (ἀφ' ἱστορίας), and probably wrote a commentary on some of the *Odes*.

PW ii. 1446–7.   J. D. D.

ARTEMON (4) of Miletus wrote, during Nero's reign, a book on dreams which come true, with special reference to cures by Sarapis, cited by Artemidorus.

FHG iv. 340; *PW* ii. 1448.

ARTEMON (5) of Magnesia, date uncertain. Author of *Famous Exploits of Women* (Τῶν κατ' ἀρετὴν γυναιξὶ πεπραγματευμένων διηγήματα), from which Sopater made excerpts.

PW ii. 1447.

ARTILLERY. Greek artillery represents an early stage in the logical improvement of man's primitive weapons, the bow and the sling, against which men had learned to protect themselves with body-armour, shields, or city-walls. The catapult (*katapeltes*) was originally a strengthened bow built on a stand, and fired arrows only. With the materials then available, the increase of power thus obtained was limited, but necessity produced a new invention, the torsion catapult; here the power was produced by many tightly twisted strands of an elastic material (often women's hair), which could be tightened still more with a windlass and then released suddenly. Its first certain use is by Alexander against Tyre (332 B.C.); he may have learned it from the Phoenicians, just as Dionysius I may have borrowed from Carthage when he introduced the earliest form of catapult into Greek warfare (*c.* 400 B.C.).

The perfected weapon assumed two forms: it shot either arrows (καταπέλτης or ὀξυβελής), or large stones (πετροβόλος—fire-baskets could be substituted), and each was effective up to 200 yards. Though Dionysius had used catapults from land against ships, and Alexander to cover his crossing of a great river, their natural function was as siege-weapons (*see* SIEGECRAFT), equally necessary to besiegers and defenders alike, as is illustrated by Demetrius' siege of Rhodes (306). In the field, the slingers and archers held their ground, because of their greater mobility and rapidity of 'fire'. Nor could naval warfare profit by artillery, because the ships could not bear the extra weight without a fatal loss of speed.

After 300 there were no important technical improvements, though scientific research produced, besides treatises, an occasional interesting freak. Artillery never became a deciding factor in ancient warfare, except perhaps when it was still, comparatively, a novelty. In sieges it was the superior will, rather than the better material, which most often prevailed, as the Romans showed at Syracuse and Carthage and elsewhere. Rome added to the Greek technique nothing except the Roman will to succeed.

W. W. Tarn, *Hellenistic Military and Naval Developments* (1930), 101 ff.: E. Schramm, in *Heerwesen und Kriegführung der Griechen und Römer* (J. Kromayer and G. Veith, 1928), 209 ff., with bibliography and illustrations.   G. T. G

ARULENUS RUSTICUS, JUNIUS, tribune of the plebs A.D. 66, praetor 69, possibly *cos. suff.* 92, Stoic philosopher and friend of Thrasea (q.v.) Paetus. Thrasea prevented him from vetoing the *senatus consultum* by which he was condemned to death. He fought for Vitellius against Vespasian and was put to death by Domitian because of a panegyric upon Thrasea and Helvidius Priscus (about 93).   A. M.

ARUSIANUS MESSIUS (late 4th c. A.D.), grammarian, compiled an alphabetical list (*exempla elocutionum*) of nouns, adjectives, verbs, and prepositions which have more than one construction (ed. Keil, *Gramm. Lat.* 7. 449–514). His citations from Sallust's *Historiae* are particularly valuable.

Teuffel, § 427, 4; Schanz-Hosius, § 839.   J. F. M.

ARVAL BRETHREN, *see* FRATRES ARVALES.

ARVERNI, a Gallic tribe, occupying modern Auvergne. Craniometry and archaeology agree in assuming a considerable pre-Celtic survival among the population. The Arverni are reported as having long contested the primacy of Gaul with the Aedui (Caesar, *BGall.* 1. 31. 3). In 207 B.C. they treated with Hasdrubal (Livy 27. 39. 6), and in the next century, under Luernius and his son Bituitus, their empire, according to Strabo (4. 2. 3), stretched as far as the Pyrenees, the Ocean, and the Rhône. Bituitus was, however, defeated near the Rhône by Cn. Domitius Ahenobarbus and Q. Fabius Maximus

(121), and subsequently arrested at the peace conference, the Arvernian Empire being reduced to suzerainty over some neighbouring tribes. In 52 Vercingetorix (q.v.), son of a former Arvernian king, led the Gallic revolt against Caesar, and defeated an attempt upon the hill-fort capital, Gergovia. Under Augustus the capital was moved to Augustonemetum (*Clermont-Ferrand*), and the tribe lost its powers of suzerainty; but it seemingly obtained the position of *civitas libera*. Its principal temple—of Mercury Dumias—on the Puy-de-Dôme was famous for a statue erected by the Greek Zenodorus at the cost of forty million sesterces (Pliny, *HN* 34. 45). The region was devastated in the third century by the Alamanni, and after a heroic struggle was ceded to the Visigoths in A.D. 475.

C. Jullian, *Hist. de la Gaule* ii. 546–52, iii. 1–19; O. Hirschfeld, *Kleine Schriften* (1913), 200–1.   C. E. S.

ARX, *see* CAPITOL.

ASCALABUS, in mythology, son of Misme, an Attic woman. His mother gave Demeter (q.v.), who was looking for Persephone, a vessel of water, meal, and pennyroyal; he laughed at her for drinking it greedily, and she threw what was left of it over him, whereat he became a spotted lizard.

Anton. Lib. 24, citing Nicander; Ov. *Met.* 5. 446 ff.   H. J. R.

ASCALAPHUS, in mythology, (1) son of Ares (q.v.); (2) son of Orphne (Ov. *Met.* 5. 539), a nymph of the river Acheron, or Gorgyra (Apollod. 1. 33), and Acheron. When Persephone was carried off by Pluto (*see* HADES), Demeter obtained from Zeus a promise that she should return if she had eaten nothing in the lower world. Ascalaphus had seen her eat a few pomegranate-seeds and betrayed her; Persephone turned him into an owl (Ovid) or Demeter put him under a great stone (Apollod.).
                                        H. J. R.

ASCANIUS, the son of Aeneas (q.v.). According to Virgil, his mother was the Trojan Creusa, and he accompanied his father to Italy after the fall of Troy (*Aen.* 2). Livy (1. 3) mentions an alternative version, that he was born from Aeneas' marriage to Lavinia after the foundation of Lavinium; and tells how he became king on Aeneas' death, but later left Lavinium and founded Alba Longa on the Alban Mount. Latin authors also call him Iulus, and the *gens Iulia* claimed descent from him.
                                        W. S. W.

ASCLEPIAD, *see* METRE, GREEK, III (11).

ASCLEPIADES (1) of Tragilus (4th c. B.C.), pupil of Isocrates, wrote a work, Τραγῳδούμενα, on the myths of Greek tragedy and their treatment (*FGrH* i. 12), which probably became an important source for Mythographi.

ASCLEPIADES (2), whose pen-name was *Sicelidas* (fl. 270 B.C.), the most brilliant of the Alexandrian epigrammatists, has some forty poems in the Anthology, mainly on love. Exquisitely tender and imaginative, but clear and economical in expression, they distil the quintessence of the love-elegy and drinking-song into the inscriptional form of the epigram. A. was probably the first to introduce into love-poetry many of the erotic themes and symbols (e.g. Love the archer) which have become part of world-poetry. He was a close friend of Hedylus and Posidippus (q.v. 2); Callimachus was deeply influenced by him.

R. Reitzenstein, *Epigram und Skolion* (1893), 96 ff.   G. H.

ASCLEPIADES (3) of Prusa in Bithynia practised medicine in Rome, where he died at an advanced age (about 40 B.C.). A sensualist and materialist, influenced by Epicurus and Heraclides Ponticus, he accepted the atomic theory, rejecting all teleology and stressing the importance of phenomenal appearances. Opposed to the theory of humours and of the healing power of nature, he explained health as the unhindered movement of the bodily corpuscles, disease as their inhibited movement. His therapy, consisting in diet rather than in drugs, was based on the principle *tuto, celeriter, iucunde*, and made him equally well liked by high and low. Owing to its consistency and originality, his system influenced contemporary and later physicians and philosophers.

TEXT: Fragmenta, Ch. G. Gumpert (1749), not complete. List of writings: Susemihl, *Gesch. gr. Lit. Alex.* ii. 439.
LITERATURE: Summary, F. Überweg–K. Praechter, *Die Philosophie d. Altertums* (1926), 138 f., besides W. A. Heidel, *Harv. Stud.* 1911; T. C. Allbutt, *Greek Medicine in Rome* (1921); M. Wellmann, *PW* ii. 1632, still important, though antiquated in general characterization.   L. E.

ASCLEPIADES (4) of Myrleia in Bithynia (1st. c. B.C.) worked in Spain, and wrote on the history of Bithynia, and of scholarship; on Homer and Theocritus; and, as Atticist analogist, Περὶ ὀρθογραφίας. He insisted that grammar was a τέχνη: cf. Sext. Emp. *Math.* 1. 60–72.
                                     P. B. R. F.

ASCLEPIODOTUS (1st c. B.C.), probably Posidonius' pupil, wrote on Greek and Macedonian military tactics. His book, the earliest extant specimen of a school treatise on a virtually dead branch of the military art, is a pedantic drill-book, in which the phalanx too often becomes a mathematical scheme. Probably it largely reproduces a lost work of Posidonius; but some things may go back through Posidonius to Polybius, and occasionally it gives an item of real value, as e.g. that the famous Thessalian cavalry fought in a rhomboid formation.

K. K. Müller, 'Asklepiodotos' in *PW*; Illinois Greek Club, *Asclepiodotus* (Loeb, 1923).   W. W. T.

ASCLEPIUS (Ἀσκληπιός, basic non-Ionic form Ἀσκλαπιός), hero and god of healing. In the *Iliad* he is a mortal, the 'blameless physician', taught his art by Chiron. To Hesiod and Pindar (*Pyth.* 3) he was the son of Apollo and Coronis, daughter of Phlegyas. Coronis proved faithless and with her lover Ischys was slain by Artemis, but Apollo (or Hermes, Paus. 2. 26. 6) snatched the unborn A. from the pyre, and entrusted him to Chiron. For daring to restore Hippolytus to life, he was slain by a thunderbolt of Zeus. There were conflicting versions (cf. Paus. 2. 26. 3–7): Epidaurus (supported by Delphi) claimed to be his birthplace, and told how he was exposed by Coronis-Aigle and nurtured by a goat; in Messenia, Apollo and the Leucippid Arsinoë were considered his parents, in southern Arcadia, Arsippus and Arsinoë. His wife is generally called Epione, and his children include Machaon and Podalirius, the physicians of the *Iliad*, and the personifications Hygieia, Panaceia, Iaso, and (an Athenian addition) Aceso.

2. While many writers have classed A. with the chthonian deities, Farnell has adduced strong evidence to show that he was in origin a hero, later elevated to full divinity; as a god, despite a few chthonian traits (e.g. the snake and possibly the rite of incubation), his associations are with the celestial divinities. His primary function, healing, is no criterion of his nature, for that art might be practised by gods, whether celestial or chthonian, or by heroes (cf. ἥρως ἰατρός at Athens). Unlike Trophonius, with whom he has been erroneously identified, he was not, except in a limited sphere, a giver of oracles, and even though, as Σωτήρ, he was on rare occasions invoked to protect from shipwreck and other ills, healing remained his chief concern.

3. The cult possibly originated at Tricca in Thessaly (Strabo 437; home of Machaon, *Il.* 4. 202), though the birth story is localized in eastern Thessaly. Thence he was carried, perhaps by the 'Phlegyans', into Phocis, where he was called Ἀ. Ἀρχαγέτας (Paus. 10. 32. 12), and Boeotia, and now probably originated his fateful alliance with Apollo. In the Peloponnesus, the cult at Titane

contained certain archaic features (Paus. 2. 11. 6–8), and Hygieia may be native here. The cult at Gerenia in Messenia derived from Tricca, and even Epidaurus, despite its pretensions, never entirely forgot the Thessalian origin of A. At Epidaurus the hero, through his association with Apollo Maleatas, first attained real prominence, and Epidaurus became the metropolis from which many of the later shrines were founded: at Athens in 420 B.C. (with some non-Epidaurian influence), Pergamum (apparently 4th c.), Rome in 293–291 B.C. (*see* AESCULAPIUS), Balagrae of Cyrene (Paus. 2. 26. 9), and, in some degree at least, Lebene in Crete. At Cos local tradition (Herod. 2. 97) insisted on a Triccan origin. In instituting new shrines, a sacred snake, representing the god, was fetched from the mother temple; the famous story (Lucian, *Alex.*) of the charlatan Alexander's quackery at Abonuteichos is illuminating. Of the Hellenistic temples the greatest were at Epidaurus and Cos (cf. Herodas 4); under the Empire Pergamum ranked highest, and thence in Pausanias' time the cult was carried to Smyrna (Paus. 2. 26. 9).

4. The cult appealed strongly to the rising individualism of the fourth and ensuing centuries, since it provided a close personal relationship with the divine and could evoke a fervid personal devotion (as with Aelius Aristides) seldom found in the formal State religion. The number and magnificence of the temples and the quantities of ex-votos attest its popularity. The central feature of the cures was the ritual of incubation, amply described by Aristophanes (*Plut.* 653–747). Many of the recorded cures are sheer miracles, and while much was accomplished by auto-suggestion and the workings of faith, use was also made of pragmatic therapeutic methods: dietetic regimens, baths (at Pergamum in radio-active springs), and exercise. In a sense the great sanctuaries were sanatoria, equipped with theatres, gymnasia, and baths, but how far the secular physicians, sometimes designated as Asclepiadae, derived their science from the priestly craft remains an open question, though the foundation of the temple at Cos (mid-4th c.) was perhaps due largely to disciples of Hippocrates. The chronic invalid Aelius Aristides is a valuable witness for the methods employed in his time in the cult. *See* MEDICINE, II.

5. Usually associated with A. were his children, especially Hygieia, personified Health; Telesphorus is a late Pergamene addition to the cult. The sacred snake regularly assists in the cures, sometimes also dogs, to which, at Piraeus, sacrifices were even ordained (*IG* ii². 4962). The organization of the cult followed normal lines; likewise the festivals for A., the Asclepieia, consisted of the usual hymns, processions, and sacrifices. Of the various paeans to A. one, especially famous, continued in use at Athens for 500 years and more, and copies have been found also at Erythrae, in Macedonia, and in Egypt; late antiquity ascribed it to Sophocles, probably because of his famed 'reception' of A. at Athens and consequent heroization as Δεξίων. Of epithets of A. may be mentioned Σωτήρ, common on inscriptions, and Παιάν; Zeus A. is late, as is σωτὴρ τῶν ὅλων and the title μύστης.

6. In art A. generally appears as a mature, bearded man, similar to Zeus, but with a kindlier, milder expression; Calamis and Scopas portrayed him as beardless, and Boethus as a child. His most constant attributes are the staff (cf. rite of τῆς ῥάβδου ἀνάληψις at Cos, Hippocr. *Ep.* 11, p. 778 Kühn), and the snake, often coiled about the staff. Generally the god is standing, as in the fifth-century original from Emporion in Spain (R. Carpenter, *The Greeks in Spain* (U.S.A. 1925), 104 ff.); in the famous chryselephantine statue by Thrasymedes at Epidaurus, described by Pausanias (2. 27. 2) and figured on coins, A. is seated, the staff in his left hand, his right extended above the head of a serpent, and beside the

throne lies a dog. The scroll or tablet which he sometimes bears probably represents medical learning.

L. R. Farnell, *Greek Hero Cults* (1921), ch. 10; E. J. and L. Edelstein, *Asclepius* (2 vols., U.S.A. 1945); W. H. D. Rouse, *Greek Votive Offerings* (1902), ch. 5; A. Walton, *The Cult of Asklepios* (U.S.A. 1894); U. v. Wilamowitz-Moellendorff, *Isyllos von Epidauros* (1886). Special topics: R. Herzog, *Wunderheilungen von Epidauros* (1931); on paeans, J. H. Oliver, *Hesp.* 1936; F. Kutsch, *Attische Heilgötter und Heilheroen* (1913); on A. and Sophocles, F. R. Walton, *Harv. Stud.* 1935; W. S. Ferguson, *Harv. Theol. Rev.* 1944, 86; P. Schazmann and R. Herzog, *Kos*, vol. i, *Asklepieion* (1932); O. Deubner, *Das Asklepieion von Pergamon* (1938). F. R. W.

ASCONIUS PEDIANUS, QUINTUS (9 B.C.–A.D. 76; Hieron. *Chron.* on 76, the year he became blind being 64; see Clark), of Padua ('Livius noster', Asc. 68 [on Cic. *Corn.*]; Sil. *Pun.* 12. 212), a 'historicus clarus'. Quintilian (1.7.24) makes probable an early relationship with Livy. Servius on *Ecl.* 4. 11 implies that he knew Asinius Gallus (d. A.D. 33); Suid. s.v. Ἀπίκιος connects him with Iunius Blaesus, *cos.* A.D. 10, not the consul of 28 (E. Klebs, *PW*). Lost writings are (1) *Vita Sallustii*, [Acron] on Hor. *Sat.* 1. 2. 41. (2) *Symposion*, imitating Plato, on physical exercises as promoting health and longevity (Suid., and Plin. *HN.* 7. 159). (3) *Contra obtrectatores Vergilii* (Donat. ap. Suet.). We possess only a fragment of his commentary on Cicero's orations (*Pis.*, *Scaur.*, *Mil.*, *Corn.*, *Tog. Cand.*), written between A.D. 54 and 57. It elucidates their history and chronology, on the basis of Cicero's published (and unpublished) works, except the letters to Atticus. Poggio found a ninth-century MS. at St. Gall: his copy is in Madrid (P. Matritensis). It was also copied by Sozomenus of Pistoja (S. Pistoriensis), and by Bartolomeo di Montepulciano (Laur. 54, 15). Included in *Sangallensis* was a fifth-century commentary on *Div. Caec.*, *Verr.* 1 and 2 to § 35. This is of grammatical character, and is quoted as Pseudo-Asconius.

A. C. Clark, *Q. Asconii Pediani Commentarii* (O.C.T. 1907); *Scholiastae Ciceronis Orationum recensuit Th. Stangl* ii (1912). G. C. R.

ASCULUM PICENUM, the capital of Picenum, strongly placed amid imposing mountains near the Adriatic on the R. Truentus (Strabo 5. 241); nowadays *Ascoli Piceno*, with numerous ancient remains. Rome captured Asculum in 268 B.C. and continued the Via Salaria to it (Florus 1. 14). The Social War broke out here, but the Romans recovered the town after a two-year siege and grimly punished it (App. *BCiv.* 1. 38, 47, 48). In imperial times it was a *colonia* (Pliny, *HN* 3. 111). Asculum Picenum should be distinguished from Asculum (better Ausculum) in Apulia (nowadays *Ascoli Satriano*), where Pyrrhus defeated the Romans in 279 B.C. E. T. S.

ASELLIO, SEMPRONIUS, historian, military tribune at Numantia in 134–133 B.C., wrote a history (*res gestae*) of his own times, not in annalistic form (*annales*), but, presumably under the influence of Polybius, with pragmatic treatment. Perhaps beginning at the destruction of Carthage, it included the year 137 B.C. in bk. 4, Ti. Gracchus' death in bk. 5, and Livius Drusus' death (91 B.C.) in bk. 14. In a celebrated fragment on the function of history (Gellius 5. 18. 8), he distinguishes between pragmatic *historia* and formal *annales*.

H. Peter, *HRRel.*² (1914), pp. ccxlii and 179; W. Stelkens, *Der röm. Geschichtsschreiber Sempr. Asellio* (1867); W. Eggert, *Sempr. Asellio* (1869); M. Gelzer, *Hermes* 1934, 46. A. H. McD.

ASIA (continent). The name was probably derived from 'Assiuva', the Hittite designation of north-west Asia Minor; in Homer (*Il.* 2. 461) it denoted the hinterland of Ionia. Between 800 and 500 B.C. Greek explorers realized the existence of great land-masses beyond Europe and included all of these under 'Asia'. After 500 they separated Africa from Asia and fixed the boundaries of Asia at Suez and (usually) at the R. Don.

Herodotus knew that a route led up the Don and into the Asian steppe; he had a fairly accurate conception of the Persian Empire as far as Babylonia, and sporadic information about Arabia, Iran, and north-west India; like most Greeks before Alexander, he gave Asia Minor a narrow neck at its eastern base. Greek knowledge of Asia progressed little until Alexander opened up the continent as far as the Syr Daria, the Himalayas, and the Jhelum, and the sea route between India and the Persian Gulf. The Hellenistic Greeks obtained some knowledge of the Ganges valley (*see* MEGASTHENES), and met Chinese travellers advancing across the Tarim basin (*see* SERES). But inner Arabia remained a secret to them, and their knowledge of the Caspian basin was inferior to that of Herodotus (*see* CASPIAN SEA, PATROCLES). The irruptions of the Parthians (250 B.C.) and of the Tochari and Sacae (150) into Iran virtually cut off the Greeks from central Asia.

In the second century A.D. the Roman emperors secured greater freedom of travel through the Parthian dominions, and Greek traders, advancing to Daraut Kurghan, renewed contact with Chinese merchants and gained knowledge of the Pamirs, Tianshan, and Altai. In the first two centuries A.D. Greek traders also opened up the Indian coast as far as C. Comorin, and occasionally visited the Bay of Bengal and the Gulf of Tongking.

Cary–Warmington, *Explorers*, 56 ff., 130 ff. *See also* ARABIA, BACTRIA, HIPPALUS, INDIA, TAPROBANE.   E. H. W.

ASIA (Roman province). Attalus III of Pergamum bequeathed his kingdom to the Romans, and at his death in 133 B.C. it was constituted as *provincia Asia* by M' Aquilius (*see* AQUILIUS 2). Originally the province consisted of Mysia, Lydia, Ionia, and almost certainly Caria; Phrygia was given to Mithridates Eupator of Pontus, and was not incorporated in the province till 116. Between 80 and 49 the *conventus* of Laodicea, Apamea, and Synnada, which lay along the route by which the governor of Cilicia travelled to his province, were for convenience assigned to Cilicia. From 49 B.C. till A.D. 297 Asia included all the territory from Tyriaion to the sea, with the adjacent islands; it was bounded on the north by Bithynia, on the south by Lycia, and on the east (after 25 B.C.) by Galatia.

The province Asia was rich in natural resources and in the products of agriculture and industry (its dyed wool fabrics were famous), and its harbours were entrepôts for the trade which crossed it by the Hermus and Maeander valley routes from the interior of Asia Minor and countries farther east. On this wealthy land the Roman Republican governors and capitalists descended like vultures, and its hatred of Rome had grown to white heat when it joined Mithridates in 88–84 B.C. and massacred 80,000 Italian residents in one day. In 84 Sulla reorganized Asia and brought order into its system of taxation; this year was used as the beginning of the provincial era in the eastern part of the province till the end of the Imperial period. Asia continued to suffer from arbitrary exactions during the civil wars; order and prosperity returned to it with the foundation of the Principate. At the partition of provinces between Augustus and the Senate Asia became Senatorial, with a governor of consular rank who governed as proconsul. The governor landed and resided at Ephesus, and was assisted by three legates and a quaestor.

Asia was a conglomeration of city territories; several of these cities had been autonomous in the Attalid period, and a few of those retained a titular freedom under the Romans. The cities, under the authority of the governor, continued to be administered by their own councils and magistrates, often with the assistance of a *logistes* appointed by the emperor, who controlled finance and expenditure. For purposes of jurisdiction the province was divided into *conventus*, according to

Pliny nine in number; later others were added. Provincial unity was expressed in the *commune Asiae* (κοινὸν Ἀσίας), a General Assembly of all the cities in the province, which met annually in this or that city, provided for the official worship of Rome and Augustus, organized games and festivals, and made representations to the emperor, sometimes with good effect, on matters concerning the administration of the province. In the first two centuries of the Empire Asia enjoyed great prosperity, of which memorials survive in splendid ruins and handsome monuments all over the country, as well as in the works of Dio Chrysostom and Aelius Aristides. The province shared in the universal sufferings of the third century, and in the fourth century, when the Anatolian roads led no longer westwards to Greece and Rome, but northwards to Constantinople, it lost its age-long position as an entrepôt of inter-continental trade. Meantime Diocletian, about A.D. 297, had divided Asia into seven provinces: *see*, e.g., LYDIA, PHRYGIA.

V. Chapot, *La Province romaine d'Asie* (1904); T. R. S. Broughton, in Frank, *Econ. Surv.* iv, pt. 4; Jones, *Eastern Cities*, ch. 2.
                                                                    W. M. C.

ASIANISM, *see* RHETORIC, GREEK, para. 6.

ASIATICUS, *see* SCIPIO (7), VALERIUS (18).

ASINIUS, *see* GALLUS (5), POLLIO.

ASIUS of Samos (? 7th or 6th c. B.C.), poet (Ath. 3. 125 b ποιητὴν παλαιόν); author of genealogies, satirical poetry in hexameters (on the luxury of the Samians), and elegiacs.

EGF 202–5.

ASKOLIASMOS (ἀσκωλιασμός), a country sport in Attica. The players tried to keep their balance while jumping on an inflated and greasy wineskin (ἀσκός). The occasion seems to have been the Rural Dionysia (*see* DIONYSIA; Cornutus, *Theol. Graec.* p. 60, 23 Lang; Suidas, s.v.; Verg. *G.* 2. 384). That it was a religious or magical ceremony and that it belonged to any other festival seem to be mis-statements; see L. Deubner, *Attische Feste* (1932), 117, 135.   H. J. R.

ASMONIUS (5th c. A.D.), author of works on grammar and metre (now lost) which Priscian used.

Teuffel, § 445, 8; Schanz–Hosius, § 825.

ASPASIA, a Milesian woman who came to Athens as a courtesan and became attached to Pericles, who divorced his wife (between 450 and 443 B.C.), and lived with her thereafter, as his mistress. Naturally the political enemies of Pericles took the opportunity of attacking her; but these charges are not more trustworthy than other scandals of the law-courts and comedy. Aristophanes parodies them admirably in his story of the origin of the Peloponnesian War (*Ach.* 515–39). Aspasia's intellectual attainments, on the other hand, are attested directly by the Socratics (especially Aeschines), and indirectly by comedy: she was Hera to the Olympian Pericles, Deianira to his Heracles, and so forth. About the beginning of the Peloponnesian War, perhaps when Pericles' own position was weakened in consequence of the pestilence, she was prosecuted for 'impiety', but acquitted, Pericles pleading for her. She had a son by him, Pericles the younger, who was specially legitimated after the death of Pericles' two sons by his first wife. After Pericles' death in 429 she apparently became the mistress of Lysicles, a popular leader, who was killed in 428. She lived on in Athens and was buried there.   A. W. G.

ASPASIUS (c. A.D. 100–150), Peripatetic. His commentaries on Aristotle's *Cat.*, *Int.*, *Metaph.*, *Ph.*, and *Cael.*, and his *Libellus de naturalibus passionibus* are lost; his commentary on the *Eth. Nic.* survives in part (ed. G. Heylbut, 1889).

PW ii. 1722.

ASPENDUS, a Greek colony in Pamphylia, claiming descent from Argos. Though assessed as a member of the Delian League (*IG*[2] i. 64), it preferred Persian rule, even resisting Alexander. Occupied by Ptolemy I, it was later subject to the Seleucids till 189 B.C., when C. Manlius admitted it to the alliance of the Roman people; though no longer free it still vaunted this title on its Imperial coins. It was an important harbour and its wealth is attested by its ruins.

K. Lanckoroński, *Städte Pamphyliens* (1890) i. 85–124.
A. H. M. J.

ASPER, AEMILIUS (late 2nd c. A.D.), wrote commentaries (now lost) on Terence, Sallust (*Historiae* and *Cat.*), and Virgil, which dealt with subject-matter and diction and included parallels from Greek and Latin authors. Aelius Donatus (q.v.) probably borrowed freely from him. The *ars* extant under his name (ed. Keil, *Gramm. Lat.* 5. 547–54) is apocryphal.

Teuffel, § 374, 1; Schanz–Hosius, § 598.
J. F. M.

ASPRENAS, the name of two Augustan rhetoricians, Lucius and Publius, whose declamations are mentioned in Seneca's *Controversiae* and *Suasoriae*.

Teuffel, § 267, 2.

ASSONANCE, GREEK. Assonance is the recurrence of a sound in words which strikes the ear. The definition is, of necessity, subjective; and the Greek ear seems not to have noticed recurrences which strike our ear harshly; e.g. Eur. *Alc.* 160 ἐλούσατ', ἐκ δ' ἐλοῦσα; *IT* 1339, *Phoen.* 1174, *Or.* 238, Soph. *Phil.* 372. The Greeks tolerated such homoeoteleuta as Thuc. 2. 43. ὁ μετὰ ῥώμης καὶ κοινῆς ἐλπίδος ἅμα γιγνόμενος ἀναίσθητος θάνατος (cf. [Andoc.] 4. 39, Pl. *Leg.* 949 c, Dem. 18. 238). Euripides, however, was taunted, perhaps unfairly, with putting in too many sigmas (Plato Com. fr. 30, Eubulus fr. 26–7).

(1) ALLITERATION. There are a few apparently intentional examples in Homer (e.g. Φ 181 χύντο χαμαὶ χολάδες, more in Aeschylus, not so many in Sophocles and Euripides. Alliterations in π are the most numerous. (The commonness of π as an initial letter does not wholly account for this.) Next come α and κ. The most famous example is Soph. *OT* 371 τυφλὸς τά τ' ὦτα τόν τε νοῦν τά τ' ὄμματ' εἶ. Cf. also Aesch. *Ag.* 819–20, *Cho.* 89, 566, Soph. *El.* 210, Eur. *Hipp.* 1201–2, *Phoen.* 488–9. In the prose of the pre-Socratics alliteration undoubtedly plays a part (cf. Heraclit. fr. 25, Democr. frs. 164, 193, 215, 258, Gorg. fr. 11. 4, 8), also perhaps in Thucydides (1. 69. 1, 81. 5–6; 6. 9. 1; 7. 68. 1), and Plato (*Ap.* 39 a, *Resp.* 609 a, *Leg.* 634 e, 666 e, 688 e, 730 c, 923 a), while it is virtually absent from Herodotus, Xenophon, and the orators. Plato's use of assonance is perhaps a legacy from earlier philosophers. At Pl. *Symp.* 197 d Agathon) ἐν πόνῳ, ἐν φόβῳ, ἐν πόθῳ, ἐν λόγῳ κυβερνήτης the medial assonance is no doubt intentional.

(2) RHYME. Theognis (in marked contrast to Tyrtaeus) has leonine rhyme in one pentameter out of seven (cf. 173–83, 390–6), which can hardly be accidental. There is little evidence for intentional rhyme in epic, or in tragedy, but we can perhaps, as Herrmanowski suggests, detect a tendency to employ it in proverbs (e.g. Soph. *OT* 110–11) and in *loci communes* at the end of a scene (e.g. Eur. *Med.* 408–9). There are more examples in comedy (e.g. Ar. *Ach.* 30–4, 1087–92, *Pax* 341–4; Alexis fr. 141. 9–13). Rhyme is clearly present in some of the late *Anacreontea* (e.g. 38). In prose, Demosthenes does not seek rhyming clauses, perhaps actually avoids them, while in Gorgias, Isocrates, and writers of the Isocratean school they are an important part of the stock-in-trade, and double rhyme is often employed (e.g. Isoc. 4. 18 καινῶς διελθεῖν ... ἀρχαίως εἰπεῖν).

(3) PUNNING ASSONANCE, extending over the greater part of the two words, including Cicero's 'immutatione litterae quasi quaesitae venustates' (*Orat.* 84). With us the pun is usually humorous, though Mussolini was not joking when he said that the Mediterranean is a *via* for other nations, *vita* for the Italians. With the Greeks it was often serious (Aesch. *PV* 693 ψύχειν ψυχάν), sometimes the means for enforcing a philosophical lesson. Thus Aesch. *Ag.* 177 πάθει μάθος, Heraclit. fr. 114, Democr. fr. 57, Pl. *Grg.* 493 a (σῶμα–σῆμα, πίθος–πιθανός). But in Plato the pun, including puns on proper names, is often humorous or semi-humorous (*Leg.* 803 a τροπιδεῖα–τρόποις, 834 d Κρὴς οὐκ ἄχρηστος, 956 e κληρώσεις–πληρώσεις, *Epin.* 982 e πορείαν–χορείαν), sometimes with a hit at the sophists (*Symp.* 185 c Παυσανίου παυσαμένου, *Grg.* 492 b λόγον καὶ ψόγον, in Callicles' mouth, *Prt.* 345 b χρόνου–πόνου, a backhanded compliment to Protagoras). Gorgias' λαβοῦσα–λαθοῦσα (fr. 11. 4) is a typical sophistic instance, and φήμη–μνήμη, ῥώμη–γνώμη are common form in this style. Xenophon sometimes indulges in naïve puns (e.g. *An.* 2. 2. 1 Μένων–ἔμενε). For punning on proper names, see ETYMOLOGY, para. 1.

O. Dingeldein, *Der Reim b. d. Griechen und Römern* (1892); C. Riedel, *Alliteration b. d. griech. Tragikern* (1900); P. Herrmanowski, *De homoeoteleutis quibusdam tragicorum* (1881); K. Polheim, *Die lateinische Reimprosa* (1925), pp. 133–57 (rhyme in Greek prose).
J. D. D.

ASSONANCE, LATIN. In Latin, *alliterative* assonance regularly marks both popular and literary usage; its artistic employment helped to bring beauty and sonority to the language. In popular speech it occurs in proverbs ('fortes fortuna iuuat', 'mense Maio malae nubunt'—see Otto, *Sprichwörter*, p. xxxii), in various formulae (e.g. *manu mancipio*), and in prayers ('pastores pecuaque salua seruassis', Cato, *Agr.* 141). In the literary tradition, it forms an important structural principle of Saturnians (cf. Anglo-Saxon verse); Ennius and the dramatists commonly use it, sometimes crudely ('nec cum capta capi nec cum combusta cremari', Ennius, *Ann.* 359 Vahlen[3]), sometimes with a proverb-like jingle ('ex malis multis malum quod minumum est, id minume est malum', Plautus, *Stich.* 120), often showing fine imagination ('lassitudinemque minuam manuum mollitudine', Pacuvius 246 Rib.[2]; cf. Ennius passim); finally in Virgil it becomes a supremely subtle servant of emotion (e.g. *Aen.* 4. 651 ff.). Prose shows analogous development, but in later ages Apuleius and Fronto recall the more obtrusive methods of the early poets.

Another form of assonance, inherent in Latin grammatical structure and often combined with alliteration, is *homoeoteleuton*. Perhaps because final syllables were so slightly stressed, the Romans tolerated such juxtapositions as 'cum studium audientium tum iudicium mire probaui' (Pliny, *Ep.* 3. 18. 8), 'pleniore ore laudamus' (Cicero, *Off.* 1. 61); yet extremes were not approved—see Quintilian 9. 4. 41, on Cicero's phrase 'res mihi inuisae uisae sunt', and Juvenal 10. 122, on Cicero's notorious verses (cf. Servius on *Aen.* 3.183). But homoeoteleuton is often used with deliberate effect: see Virgil, *Aen.* 6. 314, 'tendebantque manus ripae ulterioris amore'; Cicero, *Cael.* 77, 'ciuem bonarum artium, bonarum partium, bonorum uirorum', and 63, 'in balneis deliteuerunt: testes egregios! dein temere prosiluerunt: homines temperantes!' (cf. *Scaur.* 45).

The parallel structure of Latin rhetorical prose, combined with homoeoteleuton, often produces a species of *rhyme*. This already appears in magic formulae ('terra pestem teneto, salus hic maneto', Varro, *Rust.* 1. 2. 27). It is noticeable in Cicero (cf. *Cael.* 63 above), and later becomes exaggerated in Apuleius (e.g. *Met.* 11. 25, 'spirant flamina, nutriunt nubila, germinant semina, crescunt germina'), Tertullian, and St. Augustine. In poetry, Plautus, Terence, the tragedians, Ennius, Cicero show similar tendencies; Virgil uses rhetorical rhyme often, with much charm. When the Christian hymn-form began to supersede quantitative verse, conscious poetic rhyme developed. Sedulius and Venantius Fortunatus (5th and 6th centuries) first used it extensively, but its full development came only in the eleventh century, together with that of the 'leonine' hexameter with disyllabic rhyme (found occasionally in Virgil and other classical poets).

E. Wölfflin, in *Ausgewählte Schriften* (1933); E. Norden, *Antike Kunstprosa* (1915); J. Marouzeau, *Traité de stylistique appliquée au Latin* (1935); W. J. Evans, *Allitteratio Latina* (1921); F. J. E. Raby, *Christian Latin Poetry* (1927), with useful bibliography; F. Brittain, *The Medieval Latin and Romance Lyric* (1937). R. G. A.

ASSOS, an impregnable site on the Gulf of Adramyttium, facing south towards Lesbos (it was originally colonized from Methymna) and controlling the coast road. The harbour is artificial. The public buildings rose in terraces on the steep hill-side in a unified architectural scheme; impressive fortifications are still extant. Except in the fourth century B.C. the history of Assos is inseparable from the general history of the Troad. Ariobarzanes was besieged here in 365. Subsequently Hermeias made Assos the centre for a school of Platonists, amongst whom Aristotle was numbered. It was the birthplace of the Stoic philosopher Cleanthes.

D. E. W. W.

ASSYRIA (Greek and Roman), the name applied by Herodotus (1. 178, 185, etc.), Xenophon (*Cyr.* 2. 5) and later writers (e.g. Pliny) to the whole country between the Armenian and Iranian mountains and the Syro-Arabian desert. More properly, Assyria denoted the ancient kingdom on the Upper Tigris, bounded on the north and east by the Masius range and the Kurdish hills—the centre of the great Assyrian Empire (*c.* 1000–612 B.C.). In the Parthian period the kingdom of Adiabene (q.v.) comprised most of the old territory of Assyria; in A.D. 115 Trajan formed the province of Assyria, but this was abandoned by Hadrian. Assyria was a satrapy of the Sassanid Empire. Part of the Parthian city of Asshur, the ancient capital, can be reconstructed from excavations on the site.

W. Andrae, *Das wiedererstandene Assur*, 1938. M. S. D.

ASTARTE, *see* APHRODITE, paras. 1 and 5.

ASTERIA, in mythology, sister of Leto (q.v.), mother, by Perses, of Hecate (q.v.). Being pursued by Zeus (Callimachus, *Del.* 38; Hyginus, *Fab.* 53, and several other authors; Nonnus, *Dion.* 2. 125, says it was Poseidon), who was in love with her, she turned into a quail, leaped into the sea (or was thrown into it), and then became Ortygia, i.e. Quail Island, afterwards Delos; the time and occasion of her turning into a quail are variously told. As her name means Starry, it appears as if the story were put together from disparate elements, perhaps an idea that the island was originally a falling star, i.e. meteorite, and also a desire to explain its alleged old name. See for more material Schirmer in Roscher's *Lexikon*, s.v. H. J. R.

ASTEROPE, *see* STEROPE.

ASTRAGALUS. Knucklebones (ἀστράγαλοι) were used especially by Greek women, in various simple games such as children now play with stones, and were also employed as dice. The four long faces of the knucklebones were of different shapes, one flat, one irregular, one concave, and one convex, and in dicing these had the value respectively of 1, 6, 3, 4. F. A. W.

ASTROLOGY. Ancient astronomy sought to reduce to mathematical order the apparent motions of the heavenly bodies. Astrology was concerned with the supposed effects of these heavenly bodies on human destinies. Its fundamental faith was that a universal 'sympathy' binds heaven to earth. And, as astronomy by prolonged observation had learned to predict the recurrence of heavenly phenomena, astrology professed to be a science which could forecast the earthly happenings which depend on the heavenly. This view of things, with its blend of religious and scientific elements, was first elaborated in the temples of Mesopotamia, and spread thence to Egypt. It had no great influence on Greek life until after the death of Alexander, when Greeks and Orientals mingled in the kingdoms of the Seleucids and Ptolemies. From this time on it became an increasingly important factor in the civilization of Greece and Rome, reaching its apogee in Imperial times, and affecting every level of society. It is only the underworld of astrology that is represented by the casters of horoscopes, the *Chaldaei* and *mathematici*, assailed by Roman magistrates and satirists. At its highest it commanded the ardent allegiance of the best minds of the ancient world. Hardly a branch of ancient culture remained unaffected by it. The Stoic philosophers, trained in Greek thought, partially secularized this ancient temple wisdom, but gave it fresh currency. The astronomers Hipparchus and Ptolemy believed in it. It affected medicine profoundly. It found poetical expression in the *Astronomica* of Manilius and architectural embodiment in the Pantheon. It supplemented the *Ius Civile* by the concept of Natural Law. *See also* FATE, para. 7.

A brilliant short account will be found in F. Cumont, *Les Religions orientales dans le paganisme romain*[4] (1929), ch. 7, where full bibliographical information is supplied. The same writer's *L'Égypte des astrologues* (1937) gives striking demonstration of the fresh light thrown on the ancient world by the progress of this branch of study. B. F.

ASTRONOMY. The Ionian Greeks obtained their first astronomical knowledge from Egypt and Babylon. Thales (*c.* 624–547 B.C.) probably learnt from Egypt the division of the solar year into 365 days and the inequality of the astronomical seasons; he wrote on the solstices and equinoxes. He advised mariners to sail by the Little Bear rather than the Great Bear. He learnt from the Babylonians the period of 223 lunations after which eclipses recur; this enabled him to prophesy the solar eclipse of 28 May 585 B.C. The Doxographers (q.v.) attribute to him many other things which it is not likely that he knew. Anaximander (q.v., *c.* 611–546 B.C.) put forward a remarkable theory of the evolution from a vortex of our universe and of an infinite number of worlds; for him the heavenly bodies consisted of opaque circular rings with fire shining through at one opening; the earth is poised aloft supported by nothing; it is like a tambourine in shape. Anaximander brought from Babylon the *polos* and the *gnomon* or sun-dial (Hdt. 2. 109). He was the first to speculate on the sizes and distances of the sun and moon; he was the first who ventured to draw a map of the inhabited earth. Pythagoras and Parmenides declared that the earth is spherical; Pythagoras held that there were antipodes (Diog. Laert. 8. 26); he recognized that the sun, moon, and planets revolve in circles of their own in a sense contrary to that of the daily rotation (Theon of Smyrna, p. 150). Later the Pythagoreans made the earth also to be a planet revolving, like the others, about the 'central fire' (Arist. *De Caelo*, Simplicius, Aëtius 2. 7. 7, etc.); the 'harmony of the spheres' was their doctrine (Arist. *Metaph.* 986ᵃ1, etc.). Anaxagoras (q.v.) held that the heavenly bodies were thrown off from a central revolving mass by centrifugal force (Aët. 2. 13); that the sun is a red-hot stone and the moon earth (Hippol. *Haer.* 1. 8); that the moon receives its light from the sun (Plato, *Cratylus*, 409 a). In 433–432 B.C. Meton put forward the '19-year cycle' consisting of 235 months, making the year $365\frac{5}{19}$ days. Callippus (q.v. 2) in 330–329 substituted a 76-year cycle giving 940 months, containing 27,759 days and making the year $365\frac{1}{4}$ days

(Geminus, *Isagoge* 8. 57–60). Plato's astronomy in the main followed that of Pythagoras (*Resp.* 10. 616–17, *Timaeus* 37 d–e, 38 c–d, 40 b–d), but he is said in later years to have repented of placing the earth in the centre (Plut. *Quaest. Plat.* 8. 1, *Numa* 11). Plato realized the apparent irregularities in the movements of the planets (*Tim.* 40 b–d). Eudoxus explained the movements of the planets by an elegant system of simultaneously revolving concentric spheres (Arist. *Metaph.* 1073^{b}17–1074^{a}15, Simpl. on *De Caelo* 496–7 Heib.). Callippus modified the system by adding further spheres. Aristotle himself tried to turn the theoretical into a mechanical system (ibid.). Heraclides of Pontus (q.v. 5, *c.* 388–315 B.C.) declared that the sun and the fixed stars are stationary, but that the earth revolves about its axis in about 24 hours (Simpl. on *De Caelo* 444. 31–445. 5 Heib.). He also held that Mercury and Venus revolve about the sun like satellites (Chalcidius on *Timaeus*, ch. 110). Aristarchus (q.v. 1) was the first to put forward a heliocentric hypothesis with the earth also revolving round the sun (Archimedes, *Sand-reckoner*); his treatise *On the sizes and distances of the sun and moon* assumes the geocentric standpoint. Seleucus of Seleuceia supported Aristarchus' heliocentric hypothesis (Plut. *Quaest. Plat.* 8. 1). Apollonius (q.v. 2) of Perga discussed the hypotheses of eccentric circles and epicycles respectively for explaining the phenomena (Ptol. *Syntaxis* 12. 1). Autolycus (q.v. 2) of Pitane is the author of the earliest extant mathematical text-book in Greek, *On the moving sphere*, which is closely akin to the *Phaenomena* of Euclid, and of another treatise *On risings and settings*. Eudoxus (q.v. 1) wrote two astronomical works, the *Mirror* (Ἔνοπτρον) and *Phaenomena*, to which Aratus was indebted for many of the data in his poem the *Phaenomena* (see Hipparchus *In Arati et Eudoxi phaenomena* 1. 2. 2). Hipparchus (q.v. 3), the greatest of the Greek astronomers, born at Nicaea in Bithynia, belongs to the second century B.C. Apart from his *Commentary on the Phaenomena of Eudoxus and Aratus*, his astronomy is known to us through Ptolemy's *Syntaxis*. He worked upon the hypotheses of eccentric circles and epicycles, on a geocentric system. He was the first to make systematic use of trigonometry; he compiled a Table of Chords in a Circle. He made great improvements in the instruments used for observations; he compiled a catalogue of 850 stars; he discovered the Precession of the Equinoxes. Finally Ptolemy (q.v. 3, *c.* A.D. 150) wrote his great *Syntaxis* (originally called Μαθηματικὴ σύνταξις), giving definitive form to Hipparchus' astronomy, dealing very fully with the eccentric and epicycle hypotheses and including a definite theory of the motions of the five planets.   T. H.

ASTURES, a tribe of north-western Spain, holding the northern coastline between the Callaeci and the Cantabri, and reaching south across the mountains to the Durius (*Douro*). Before their conquest by Augustus they were known as rude and predatory highlanders. The Augustan census estimated 240,000 free men divided between the Transmontani of the north and the Augustani of the south. Pacified by Roman legions (26–19 B.C.), the Astures furnished gold, chrysocolla, minium, horses, and auxiliary troops. Asturia was but slowly and partially romanized. Pliny mentions only one municipality, Asturica Augusta (*Astorga*) 'urbs magnifica'. An intricate road system, to aid transport of minerals, was constructed by the emperors from Augustus to Gratian.

A. Schulten, *Los Cantabros y Astures* (1943).   J. J. V. N.

ASTYANAX or *Scamandrius* (*Il.* 6. 402), in mythology, young son of Hector and Andromache (qq.v.). At the capture of Troy he was flung from the walls by Neoptolemus (q.v.; *Little Iliad*, fr. 19 Allen) or killed by Odysseus (*Iliu Persis*).

ASTYDAMAS, the name of two poets of the fourth century B.C., father and son. The father was the son of Morsimus the son of Philocles (nephew of Aeschylus) (Suidas, s.v.). It is uncertain to which some of the records about 'Astydamas' refer. One of the two was a pupil of Isocrates (436–338 B.C.) in rhetoric before he became a poet. The elder produced his first play in 398 B.C., and one of the two (probably the son) won his first victory in 372 (*Marm. Par.* 71). The elder is said to have lived to the age of sixty (Diog. Laert. 2. 43; Diod. Sic. 14. 43. 5), and if this is true the inscriptional records (*IG*² ii. 2320) which note Dionysiac victories in 341 with the *Achilles*, *Athamas*, and *Antigone*, and in 340 with the *Parthenopaeus* and *Lycaon* must refer to the son, and the ascription by Suidas and Photius of the *Parthenopaeus* to the father must be a mistake. The Athenians were so delighted with this play that they erected a statue to the poet in the theatre, and a fragment of the base of this survives, but he was not allowed to inscribe on it the conceited verses which made his name a byword for vanity (Suidas, s.v. σαυτὴν ἐπαινεῖς). The son was evidently famous in his day. Aristotle notes (*Poet.* 14) that in his *Alcmaeon* he made the hero kill his mother unwittingly instead of deliberately as in the original legend, and Plutarch (*De Glor. Ath.* 7) speaks with very high praise of the *Hector*. Of the two poets less than twenty lines in all are preserved.

TGF 777–80. See Wilamowitz, *Aischylos Interpretationen* 238–9.
                                                 A. W. P.-C.

ASTYDAMEIA, see PELEUS.

ASTYNOMOI, an office found mostly in the Ionian States. In Athens there were five for the city and five for the Piraeus, elected by lot for one year. Their principal duties were to keep the streets clean and free of obstruction. They also had duties in relation to festivals; and in particular (at least *c.* 326) they enforced certain sumptuary laws. They could inflict small fines and introduce to the law courts more important cases within their jurisdiction. They had slaves as assistants. In many States they also had harbour and market duties (*see* AGORANOMOI).   A. W. G.

ASTYOCHE, in mythology, sister of Priam and daughter of Laomedon (qq.v.; Apollod. 3. 146). She married Telephus (q.v.; Quint. Smyrn. 6. 135) and bore Eurypylus, who came to the Trojan War and was killed by Neoptolemus with many of his people, γυναίων εἵνεκα δώρων (*Od.* 11. 521). This the commentators explained either of the gift of a wife (Hermione) by Menelaus to Neoptolemus, or of the gift by Priam to Astyoche of the golden vine which was given Tros by Zeus as compensation for the loss of Ganymedes (*Little Iliad*, fr. 6 Allen), etc. See Eustathius *in Odyss.*, p. 1697, 30 ff.   H. J. R.

ASYLIA means a guarantee against seizure of property by citizens of another State exercising the right of reprisal. Whenever there were no arrangements for the settlement of disputes between States the party wronged claimed the right to use self-help and to seize the property (e.g. a ship or its cargo), not only of the offending party, but of other citizens and metics of his State. Such seizure was designated by the verb συλᾶν and related words. Rights of reprisal were often proclaimed by one State against another. When *asylia* was granted to individuals it meant that whatever claims there were against his State his personal property was safe from seizure at the hands of citizens and residents of the State bestowing *asylia*. This form of *asylia* could be given to entire States. Another form, connected with a locality and not applying to the property of its citizens abroad, was the recognition by other States of the inviolability of a sanctuary or a sanctuary and the city in which it was located. Such sanctuaries were used as places of refuge; hence the later meaning of 'asylum'.

E. Schlesinger, *Die griechische Asylie* (1933), assembles the evidence and cites earlier literature. J. A. O. L.

ATACINUS, *see* VARRO (3).

ATALANTA ('Ἀταλάντη), in mythology, daughter of Iasus, son of Lycurgus of Arcadia, and Clymene, daughter of Minyas (Apollod. 3. 105), or of Schoeneus, son of Athamas (Hesiod, fr. 20 Rzach). Boeotian and Arcadian legends often show connexion, but there is no need to suppose two heroines of the same name here, for she is in all probability a by-form of Artemis (q.v.). She was a huntress, averse to marriage, loved by (1) Meleager (q.v.); Parthenopaeus was her son by him (Hyg. *Fab.* 99. 1, a late story, see Rose ad loc.); (2) Melanion (Milanion, i.e. Μειλανίων, Prop. 1. 1. 9), her first cousin (Apollod., ibid.), or Hippomenes. She would marry no one who could not beat her in a foot-race (in Hyg. *Fab.* 185. 2, she follows the suitor and spears him if she can catch him; perhaps a reminiscence of a religious rite, see Rose ad loc.). Melanion, or Hippomenes, got three golden apples from Aphrodite and delayed her by throwing them, thus winning. Their son was Parthenopaeus in most accounts. But (by the anger of Aphrodite, to whom he forgot to pay his vow, Ov. *Met.* 10. 681 ff.) he lay with her in a holy place (Apollod. 108, Hyg., ibid. 6, Ov., ibid. 686); for this impiety they were turned into lions. In some versions (as Prop. 1. 1. 9) there is no race, but Melanion wins Atalanta's affection when hunting with her. H. J. R.

ATARGATIS (Aramaic 'Atar-'Ata, according to Ronzevalle 'the divine 'Ātā': cf. the epithet ἀγνή applied to her at Delos) or *Derceto*, the goddess of Hieropolis-Bambyce in Syria. Her temple, rebuilt *c.* 300 B.C. by Stratonice, wife of Seleucus I, was plundered by Antiochus IV and by Crassus, but was still in Lucian's day one of the greatest and holiest in Syria. Her consort was Hadad; his throne was flanked by bulls, that of A. by lions. At Ascalon, A. was represented as half woman, half fish. Fish and doves were sacred to her; the myth records that, having fallen into a lake, A. was saved by the fish ([Eratosth.] *Cat.* 38), or, in another version, that A. was changed into a fish, and her daughter Semiramis into a dove (Diod. Sic. 2. 4. 2–6; 2. 20. 1–2; Ov. *Met.* 4. 44–8). Late in the third century B.C. her cult appears in Egypt, Macedon, and, with civic status, at Phistyon in Aetolia and (early 2nd c.) at Thuria in Messenia. Natives of Hieropolis founded a shrine on Delos in 128–127, of which Athens soon took control. A. was worshipped also in a number of other Hellenic cities, whereas in the West (apart from Rome, where Nero favoured her for a while) only a few dedications, from Italy, the Danubian provinces, and England, have been found. Since A. was primarily a fertility goddess, the Greeks often recognized in her a form of Aphrodite, but generally she was simply the 'Syrian Goddess'. Astrologers identified her with the constellation Virgo, and a third-century 'creed' found in England (*CIL* vii. 759) accepts the *dea Syria* as one of several names or manifestations of the universal goddess. At Thuria her cult included mysteries. Lucian, *De Dea Syria*, describes the cult in Syria; Apuleius, *Met.* 8–9, the life of her wandering Galli. *See* EUNUCHS, RELIGIOUS; FISH, SACRED; METRAGYRTES.

C. Clemen, *Lukians Schrift über die syrische Göttin* (1938); F. Cumont, *PW*, s.v. 'Atargatis', 'Dea Syria', Dar.-Sag. s.v. 'Syria Dea'; S. Ronzevalle, *Mélanges de l'Université Saint Joseph* (Beyrouth), 1940; P. Roussel, *Délos Colonie Athénienne* (1916), 252–70; F. R. Walton, *Reallexikon f. Antike u. Christentum*, s.v. 'Atargatis' F. R. W.

ATE, the personification of infatuation or moral blindness, in which right and wrong, advantageous and ruinous conduct cannot be distinguished. She is the subject of an elaborate allegory in *Il.* 19. 90 ff., the earliest in Greek, where she is daughter of Zeus (an early instance of the problem of the moral responsibility of Deity). She is daughter of Strife and sister of Lawlessness (Hes. *Theog.* 230). H. J. R.

ATEIUS PRAETEXTATUS PHILOLOGUS, LUCIUS, one of the chief scholars of the Ciceronian age. Born at Athens, he became a captive of war in 86 B.C., was brought to Rome and manumitted. He claimed to have written 800 books on all kinds of subjects (*miscellanea*, ὕλη) and took the name Philologus as an indication of his interests. According to Suetonius (*Gram.* 10) he helped Sallust by compiling a *Breviarium Rerum Romanarum* and Asinius Pollio by advising about the style of his history. Festus mentions his *Liber Glossematorum* and Charisius a work entitled *An amaverit Didun Aeneas*.

G. Funaioli, *Gramm. Rom. Frag.*, 137–41; Teuffel, § 211, 1; Schanz-Hosius, § 195, 6. J. F. M.

ATEIUS, *see also* CAPITO.

ATELLANA sc. FABULA, the Roman 'Punch-and-Judy', an improvised, masked performance; its stock characters were Maccus, 'Clown', Pappus, 'Gaffer', Bucco, 'Fatcheeks', Dossennus, 'Hunchback' (?) (? identical with Manducus, 'Champ-jaws'). Perhaps developed from the Doric farce of Magna Graecia (cf. burlesque element) in the Oscan towns of Campania, especially Atella. It achieved early popularity in Rome, where its performance came to be monopolized by amateurs (?). It became literary in the hands of Pomponius and Novius (qq.v.; temp. Sulla); surviving fragments illustrate its coarseness. Later performed by professionals as occasional interlude.

Schanz-Hosius i. 245–53; A. Nicoll, *Masks, Mimes and Miracles* (1931; popular account, illustrated). W. B.

ATESTE, the modern *Este* in Venetia, twenty-five miles from Padua. Until the sixth century A.D. the Adige, which is now nine miles to the south, flowed through Este. This aided a commerce, which was partly seaborne, with all the head of the Adriatic. From 800 to 200 B.C. the Atestines formed a very important trading community, rivalling the Bolognese, with whom they had culturally and racially very much in common. Ateste and Bononia became equally renowned for their metal-work. They were the Birmingham and Sheffield of Iron-Age Italy. The trade of Ateste was especially transalpine; its products can be traced from Carniola to the Brenner. A noticeable efflorescence of style under Etruscan influence *c.* 500 B.C. died down when the north Etruscan colonies were destroyed by the Gauls a century later. Ateste, never conquered by Gauls or Romans, retained its independence till 184 B.C., when it was peaceably annexed. D. R.-MACI.

ATHAMAS, in mythology, son of Aeolus (q.v. 2) and a character in a variously told story of a stepmother's cruelty (Stith Thompson, S31). He married first Nephele (a cloud-goddess), then Ino daughter of Cadmus (q.v.; the order is reversed in Philostephanus ap. schol. *Il.* 7. 86; Hyg. *Fab.* 4, professedly from Euripides, introduces a third wife, Themisto, but omits Nephele). Nephele bore him Phrixus and Helle, and Ino in her turn Learchus and Melicertes. Ino was jealous of her stepchildren, and therefore caused the seed-corn to be roasted; when it consequently failed to grow, and Delphi was consulted, she induced the messengers on their return to say that the sacrifice of Phrixus and Helle, or Phrixus alone, was demanded. Nephele saved them, or him, by means of a golden-fleeced ram given by Hermes; the ram brought Phrixus to Colchis, where he married Chalciope, daughter of Aeetes. Helle fell into the strait thenceforth named Hellespont (q.v.) after her. *See further* ARGONAUTS. In Hyginus, loc. cit., Themisto tries to murder the stepchildren and fails in the same manner as Aëdon (q.v.); cf. Stith Thompson, K1611. See Hyg. *Fab.* 1–5; Apollod. 1. 80 ff.; Ov. *Fasti* 3. 851 ff.; [Eratosthenes] 19; Hyg. *Poet. Astr.* 2. 20; schol. German. *Arat.*, pp. 79, 142 Breysig. Several of these say that the ram became the constellation Aries. Cf. Pickard-Cambridge in Powell, *New Chapters* iii. 97. The rest of Athamas' story is less folk-tale and more myth. Because Ino had nursed Dionysus, Hera drove Athamas and her mad; Athamas killed Learchus, Ino ran from him carrying Melicertes, leaped into the sea, and she and her son were transformed into deities, Leucothea and Palaemon (Apollodorus and Hyginus, supra; Ov. *Met.* 4. 416 ff.; Rose, *Handbk. Gk. Myth.* 150 and authorities there cited).

At Halos in the Thessalian Achaia, the senior member of the clan claiming descent from Athamas was sacrificed to Zeus Laphystios if he entered the city hall. This was explained as retribution for Athamas' joining Ino in plotting against Phrixus (Hdt. 7. 197. 1).   H. J. R.

ATHEISM. 'Denial of the gods' (τὸ μὴ νομίζειν θεοὺς [εἶναι], J. Tate in *CR* l. 3 and li. 3) might mean atheism in the modern sense or a distaste for pagan mythology compatible with deep religious faith. The earliest motive for it was the moral inadequacy of the gods as depicted by Homer and Hesiod. Thus Xenophanes (q.v.) adduced the crimes imputed to them, and added that men everywhere created gods in their own image. Yet he upheld the existence of the divine, and taught a kind of pantheism. However, in the fifth century Ionian speculation and the Sophistic movement did make possible the doubt or denial of any form of deity. ἄθεος later became the term for this philosophical atheism (but see below). Of famous thinkers prosecuted for ἀσέβεια in this century, though political motives usually played a part in such prosecutions, Anaxagoras (q.v.) was a rationalist who sought to explain everything by natural causes and doubtless (though positive evidence is lacking) an atheist in the modern sense. Protagoras' (q.v.) position was strictly agnostic. Socrates (q.v.) is a more complex case. Perhaps the gods of his personal belief were not those of the State, but he conformed to official cults and was a man of deep religious feelings, sure of divine guidance. Often quoted for positive atheism is the fragment of the *Sisyphus* of Critias (q.v., fr. 23 Diels), which describes the gods as human inventions in the interests of law. Among the poets, Pindar defends the tradition by gently purging the myths of their crudities, Euripides exclaims against the folly of believing in such gods. Atheism was attributed to other contemporary philosophers, and Plato's attack in *Laws* 10 suggests that it was widespread in the next century. Aristotle's intellectual conception of divinity left no room for the traditional personal gods (*Metaph.* Λ 8 *fin.*), and the theological argument started in the Socratic schools led naturally to scepticism, and in one case at least—Theodorus the Cyrenaic—to actual atheism.

Besides 'unbelieving', ἄθεος meant 'abandoned by the gods', wicked, godless. (See lexica and K. Latte in *ARW* xx. 264.) The question of belief had not in general the importance which it has to-day (cf. A. D. Nock, *Conversion* (1933), p. 10 f.), and the word tended to be a term of abuse rather than a reasoned description, e.g. as applied to the Christians (Nock, *Sallustius* (1926), p. lxxxviii). Yet cf. also Theophrastus in Porph. *Abst.* 2. 7 and Plutarch *De Superst.*, where ἀθεότης is discussed and defined as a 'lack of sensitiveness to the divine'; also evidence in F. Cumont, *L'Égypte des astrologues* (1937), p. 135.

In general, see A. B. Drachmann, *Atheism in Pagan Antiquity*, London and Copenhagen, 1922.   W. K. C. G.

ATHENA (Ἀθάνα, Ἀθήνη, Ἀθηναίη(-α), Ἀθηνᾶ). The patron goddess of Athens in Attica and Athens in Boeotia, also extensively worshipped in many other places in Greece proper and the colonies and islands. There is no reasonable doubt that she is originally pre-Hellenic. Her name shows the non-Greek suffix -*na* found also, e.g., in Μυκῆναι; her most famous cult, that at Athens on the Acropolis, is on the site of a Mycenaean palace, the 'house of Erechtheus' of *Odyssey* 7. 81, cf. *Iliad* 2. 549; hence her constant association with other heroes, as Tydeus, Diomedes, and Odysseus. In Minoan fashion, she takes on occasion the form of a bird, as *Od.* 3. 371–2 (the owl, though regularly associated with her in classical times, is not the only bird with which she is connected in cult). Her peculiar cult-statues, female yet fully armed, resemble the Mycenaean shielded goddess (*Ath. Mitt.* xxxvii (1912), p. 129 ff. and plate viii, often reproduced elsewhere). The conclusion is hardly avoidable (Nilsson, *Die Anfänge der Göttin Athene* (1921); *Minoan-Mycenaean Religion*, 417 ff.) that she is the tutelary goddess of Cretan and Mycenaean princes, especially the latter, retained in popular cult when the ancient citadels came to be reserved for the gods and not for rulers. Presumably she had been fervently worshipped by the subjects of those princes; at all events, she continued to hold a very high rank and to develop in several directions.

2. Besides her connexion with citadels, and consequently with cities (e.g. Verg. *Ecl.* 2. 61–2; *see* ZEUS), she has a rather decided association with water, hence her epithet *Tritogeneia*, whereof the first two syllables have something to do with water, though their exact meaning is unknown (cf. Farnell, op. cit. infra, 265 ff.). This, however, did not result in her becoming a deity of the sea, even by way of Athens' naval power; the hold of Poseidon was probably too strong.

3. She is regularly regarded as virgin.* That she is interested in fertility, both animal and vegetable, is not remarkable; she is a goddess of the State and on such increase its continued existence depends.

4. Her most conspicuous functions are perhaps those connected with war. She has a certain tendency to become a war-goddess in general, a kind of female Ares, as in *Iliad* 17. 398, where she is coupled with him as an expert in battles and liable to violent wrath; neither of them could have 'found fault with' the fury of the contest over the body of Patroclus. Normally, however, she is warlike in the sense that she fights for, or leads to battle, her chosen people, or hero (as Diomedes, *Il.* 5. 856, where she guides his spear into Ares' flank; Eur. *Heracl.* 349–50, where, though Hera leads the Argives, Athena leads Athens to fight against them). Or she protects them, as a strong warrior might a weaker one (Solon, fr. 3. 3–4 Diehl), though this does not refer only to war but to shielding Athens against all dangers. Hence also she is the inventor of sundry warlike implements, as the war-chariot (*Hymn. Hom. Ven.* 13) and the trumpet (she was called Σάλπιγξ in Argos, Paus. 2. 21. 3).

5. But, being female and goddess of that city which was perhaps nearer than any other in Greece to being industrialized, she is also a patroness of arts and crafts. Among these, spinning and weaving take a prominent place, as might be expected, and in general she is the goddess of women's work (*Hymn. Hom. Ven.* 14–15). But her influence extends much further than this, for all manner of handicraftsmen worship her, or regard her as their teacher, as potters (Ps.-Hdt. *Vit. Hom.* 32; the scene is Samos, indicating that such worship of Athena is in no way purely Attic), goldsmiths (*Od.* 6.

---

* Her Elean title of Μήτηρ need mean no more than that mothers worshipped her, cf. the strange titles 'Maid', 'Wife', and 'Widow' applied to Hera (q.v.), and see Farnell, 302 ff., yet cf. E. Fehrle, *Kultische Keuschheit* (1910), 183 ff.

233, again wholly unconnected with Athens). In Athens the Chalceia (literally the festival of smiths, χαλκῆς) was held in her honour, though Hephaestus seems to have had some share in it (Deubner, p. 35 f.). It is in such connexions as this that her title Ergane, 'the work-woman', is especially appropriate, and here also that her functions overlap to some extent those of Hephaestus, thus explaining their mythical connexion; see below. She is on occasion goddess of medicine also, since that is a highly skilled occupation, but this seems to be a development rather of Minerva (q.v.; see Ov. *Fasti* 3. 827).

6. Identifications between Athena and foreign goddesses are fairly numerous, e.g. Neith in Egypt (Plato, *Tim.* 21 e), a Libyan goddess whose name is unknown (Hdt. 4. 180. 2), and, most familiar, the Italian Minerva. It is not always possible to tell what caused the identification. Of Greek goddesses subordinate to her, the best known is Nike, whose temple on the Acropolis is one of the best preserved; she also had some connexion with Hygieia, whose name she bore as a title (Paus. 1. 23. 4).

7. That she became ultimately allegorized into a personification of wisdom is a not unnatural development of her patronage of skill; she passes from one sense of σοφία to another. The process has already begun in Hesiod (*Theog.* 886 ff.), where Metis, i.e. Good Counsel, is her mother (cf. Rose, *Folklore* (1935), 27 f.).

8. The principal myth concerning her is her birth, without mother (but cf. Hesiod, above), from the head of Zeus. It was fully developed by the time of Pindar (*Ol.* 7. 35; cf. scholiast there); Zeus' head was split with an axe by Hephaestus (or some other deity, the details varying in different accounts), and the goddess sprang out, fully armed and uttering her war-cry. Helios, adds Pindar, let his sons in Rhodes know of this, so that they might be the first to sacrifice to the new power. They did so, but in such haste that they forgot to take fire with them, and so offered the victims unburned, whence, as Athena was pleased with their devotion, the custom continued at her shrine among them. This is the goddess of Lindus, probably not originally Athena at all, who is not worshipped in this fashion, not being a chthonian goddess.

9. The above is no doubt a Rhodian myth; the following is Athenian. Hephaestus desired to marry her, and Zeus consented, but gave her leave to repulse his attentions. They struggled together, and his seed fell on the earth, which thus became fertile and in due season produced a boy. Athena took charge of the infant (possibly she was originally his actual mother, see above), hid him in a chest guarded by serpents and gave it to the daughters of Cecrops to keep, with instructions not to open it. They disobeyed, and at the sight of the serpents (or whatever the chest contained; chests are very common receptacles of sacred objects which must not be looked at at all, or only after some rite of initiation) they were so terrified that they leaped off the Acropolis and so perished. The child was called Erichthonius and remained a favourite of Athena (Rose, *Handb. Gk. Myth.*² 110 and references). In Attica also she strove with Poseidon for ownership of the land; she produced the olive-tree, thus outdoing the miracles which he performed, and won the contest; see POSEIDON.

10. That she was originally thought of as theriomorphic is not proved but suggested by her stock epithet γλαυκῶπις ('bright-eyed' or 'owl-faced'?).

Useful collections of facts and references, Farnell, *Cults of the Greek States*, i. 258 ff., and the larger classical dictionaries. Attic cults, L. Deubner, *Attische Feste* (1932), 9 ff.; non-Attic, M. P. Nilsson, *Griechische Feste* (1906) 84 ff. H. J. R.

ATHENAEUM, Hadrian's famous institute for lectures and recitations by rhetors and other literary men. Aurelius Victor (*Caes.* 14) calls it 'ludum ingenuarum artium'.

ATHENAEUS (1) (fl. *c.* A.D. 200), of Naucratis in Egypt. His only extant work, Δειπνοσοφισταί ('The Learned Banquet'), was probably completed after the death of Commodus in A.D. 192 (ib. 537 f); other chronological inferences are uncertain. It belongs to the polyhistoric variety of the symposium form (*see* SYMPOSIUM LITERATURE), practised earlier by Aristoxenus and Didymus. It is now in fifteen books (originally perhaps 30); there is also an Epitome, which covers existing gaps. At the 'banquet', which extends over several days, philosophy, literature, law, medicine, and other interests are represented by a large number of guests, who in some cases bear historical names (e.g. Galen and Ulpian of Tyre); a Cynic philosopher is introduced as a foil. The symposiac framework, if not devoid of occasional humour, is artistically far below the Platonic standard, though recalling certain passages of Plato; it is subordinate in interest to the collections of excerpts which are introduced into it. These relate to all the materials and accompaniments of convivial occasions; they are drawn from a vast number of authors, especially of the Middle and New Comedy, who are otherwise unrepresented; they are valuable both as literature and as illustrating earlier Greek manners. The order of these extracts sometimes suggests the use of lexica (Didymus, Pamphilus) or of διδασκαλίαι (*see* DIDASCALIA); but A. has collected much independently from the great writers; it is often difficult to judge which method he has pursued.

Ancient source: Suidas. Text: G. Kaibel (Teubner, 1887–90). Text and translation: C. B. Gulick (Loeb, 1927–41), 7 vols. Commentary: J. Schweighäuser (1801–7). Criticism: R. Hirzel, *Dialog* (1895) ii. 352. F. Rudolph, *Philol. Suppl.* vi (1891) (sources); K. Mengis, *Stud. Gesch. Kult. Alt.* x (1920) (composition); C. A. Bapp, *Leipz. Stud.* viii (1885) (music and lyric); K. Zepernick, *Philol.* lxxvii (1921) (trustworthiness). W. M. E.

ATHENAEUS (2), author of an extant work on siege-engines (Περὶ μηχανημάτων) may probably be dated in the second century B.C.

Ed. R. Schneider, *Abh. d. Gesellsch. d. Wissensch. zu Göttingen* (Ph.-hist. Kl.) N.F. 12 (1912).

ATHENAEUS (3) of Attaleia practised medicine in Rome under Claudius (A.D. 41–54). Like many other physicians of that time he founded a new school, that of the Pneumatists. Imbued with Stoic ideas, but well trained in philosophy in general, Athenaeus assumed as basic elements the four qualities, together with the *pneuma* as the fifth. Health and disease he explained through their *eukrasia* (good temperament) and *dyskrasia* (bad temperament). His physiology was dependent on Aristotle. Details of his pathology are unknown. His system apparently was important in its speculative formulation rather than in its practical consequences. Athenaeus, who considered medical knowledge as part of general education, devised most elaborate dietetic rules, in which he included pedagogical as well as medical precepts, differentiated according to the different stages of life. The ideas of Athenaeus were highly estimated by Galen.

Text: Fragments from Oribasius, *Veterum et Clarorum Medicorum Graecorum Opuscula*; Ch. F. Matthaei, *Mosque* (1808), not complete. Literature: M. Wellmann, 'Die pneumatische Schule', *Phil. Unters.* 1895, *PW* ii. 2034; no clear distinction between Athenaeus and the teaching of his followers, whose importance seems exaggerated; cf. also T. C. Allbutt, *Greek Medicine in Rome* (1921); for the early history of Pneumatic theories, E. Neustadt, *Hermes* 1909; W. Jaeger, *Hermes* 1913; Allbutt, loc. cit. 224. L. E.

ATHENS (Ἀθῆναι) (HISTORICAL OUTLINE). The Athenian claim to 'autochthony' had at least this much truth, that Attica was comparatively little disturbed at the time of the Dorian and Boeotian migrations. The tradition that it was ruled by kings till *c.* 1000–900 B.C. is also trustworthy. We may believe as well that Attica was originally divided into several 'kingdoms', with the king in Athens exercising a vague suzerainty; but whether the union into one State (the *synoecism*) was achieved by 'Theseus' (i.e. in the thirteenth century) is very doubtful. As elsewhere in Greece the monarchy was succeeded by an aristocracy, when the archonship became the principal magistracy (*see* ARCHONTES). Though the archonship became an annual office in 683–682, and the Thesmothetai (q.v.) were instituted, the aristocracy retained and increased their control of affairs until Solon's legislation (594); for they not only monopolized political office, but had acquired most of the land, the peasants being reduced to serfdom and sometimes slavery. An attempt by Cylon (c. 632) to overthrow them had failed; and Draco's code (c. 624–621) left their powers untouched. In the ninth and eighth centuries Athens produced magnificent 'geometric' pottery, in the seventh the crude but vigorous 'Early Attic'. Sculpture was comparatively little developed. Writing was in use from at least 700.

2. Solon laid the foundations of democracy by establishing economic freedom, by making the Ecclesia independent of the archons, by instituting the Heliaea and making the magistracies responsible to the people. He did not, however, secure internal peace; and after many years of struggle the popular leader Pisistratus made himself tyrant (first in 561–560 and finally c. 545). The tyranny lasted till 511, when his son Hippias was driven out. The sixth century saw a remarkable development of Athens. Her pottery, by its technical and artistic excellence, practically drove its rivals from all foreign fields; sculpture flourished; Solon was himself the earliest Attic poet, and the tyrants attracted poets from elsewhere—Athens was becoming a cultural centre. Material prosperity greatly increased, in agriculture, manufacture, and trade; many foreigners settled in Athens, and by 500 the population was already large.

3. The attempt of the aristocrats to gain control after the expulsion of Hippias failed, and the reforms of Cleisthenes established a true democracy (*see* ECCLESIA, BOULE, AREOPAGUS). An active foreign policy was at first checked by an unsuccessful intervention in the Ionian Revolt (499); but the immense military and moral effort of Athens in two Persian wars (490 and 480–479) established her position as the most energetic and enterprising State in Greece; a fact, however, which soon drew her into rivalry with Sparta, the accepted leader. Sparta's refusal to champion the Greek States which had revolted from Persia after 479 gave Athens her chance; in 477 the Confederacy of Delos was founded, comprising most of the Aegean islands and the Greek cities of the Asiatic and Thracian coasts. The war with Persia was successfully continued till Cimon's victory at the Eurymedon (c. 467). Athens had a severe check when she supported an Egyptian revolt (459–454); but by the peace of 449 Persia practically recognized the Athenian Empire, agreeing not to send her fleet west of Phaselis and of the Bosporus, nor her army nearer than three days' march of the Ionian cities. Before this, war had broken out with the Peloponnesians, in which Athens lost the battle of Tanagra (457), but won the campaign, conquering Boeotia and winning over Phocis, and gaining victories over Corinth and Aegina. Meanwhile she had reduced to submission a few seceding States in the League; she now strengthened her position by improving her fleet, by cleruchies (q.v.) and garrisons, by a better organization of the tribute, and by supporting democracies against oligarchies, by encouraging the States to look upon herself as their capital, and later by introducing her own coinage in the subject cities. The League had become an Athenian Empire. In 447 Boeotia and Phocis recovered their independence; but by the Thirty Years' Peace (445) the Peloponnesians recognized the Empire.

4. By the development of tragedy and later of comedy, history, and oratory, Athens had become indisputably the literary centre of Greece. During the ascendancy of Pericles, painting and sculpture flourished there as never

before; between 447 and 431 the Parthenon, the Propylaea, and many other buildings were completed. Most Greeks eminent in art, letters, and science visited Athens, and many settled there. Socrates, himself an Athenian, laid the foundations of mental and moral science in an enduring manner, and assured to Athens the primacy in philosophical studies. Trade prospered, for Athens preserved the peace of the seas. But peace did not last long. Sparta was jealous, the rest of Greece nervous; in 431 the Peloponnesian League and the Boeotians declared war, 'to free Greece from the tyrant city'. The war lasted, with an interval of uneasy peace, for twenty-seven years. By 404 the whole political structure of Cimon's and Pericles' generations was in ruins: Athens was a dependant of Sparta under the heel of the Thirty Tyrants (q.v.), her Long Walls (q.v.) destroyed, her fleet reduced to a dozen ships, her population barely half its former total.

5. Yet Athens made an astonishingly quick recovery. By 403 she had regained her democracy and her autonomy; ten years later she had a fleet, had rebuilt the Long Walls, and had successfully revolted with other cities against Spartan imperialism. In 377 a new maritime league was formed; in 376 Chabrias won back for Athens supremacy at sea. Athens supported Thebes in her struggle against Sparta till after Leuctra (371), and later assisted Sparta against Thebes, striving for a balance of power. But when Philip of Macedon began his policy of expansion (359), Athens could not decide definitely between war and peace, and became involved in halfhearted wars. The maritime league lost its most powerful members in the Social War (356–355); but Athens was still strong at sea and controlled the Hellespont, indispensable for her food supplies. Inspired by Demosthenes, Athens resisted Philip successfully in the Bosporus region in 340; but after the defeat at Chaeronea (338) she was glad to secure peace with Philip with the loss of the Hellespont. Overawed by Alexander in 335, Athens reorganized her forces during his absence in the East; but in the war of 323–322 she was defeated on land and sea. She now had to admit a Macedonian garrison in Munychia, and to modify her constitution. It was the end of Athens as a considerable military power.

6. The fourth century was a time of material prosperity, and trade and manufacture had quickly revived; the arts and letters (especially oratory, at its greatest in Demosthenes) were as vigorous as before. Though an Athenian dicastery had condemned Socrates to death in 399 (on grounds that were largely political—*see* SOCRATES), philosophy and science still flourished and under the leadership of Plato and Aristotle were at their height. But after 322, though comedy, philosophy, and physical and historical science continued active in Athens, the decline in creative thought began; after 300 Zeno and Epicurus were her greatest figures, and, recognized by all as the cultural centre of the Greek world, she began to live on her past. Politically the story of the century after Alexander was one of frequent struggles to rid herself of Macedonian domination, often temporarily successful, but always with the help of one or other of the *Diadochi*, who, if successful, abused his power; they all wanted her as an ally and a military station; she was finally crushed between them in the war against Antigonus Gonatas (q.v., 266–262), and her independence forfeited. She was free again in 228; and as a small State had comparative peace, while Rome was establishing her power in Greece. Her last independent action was when she sided with Mithridates against Rome. Reduced by Sulla after a siege (87–86), she pleaded her glorious past; but he retorted that he was there to punish rebels, not to learn ancient history. Thereafter Athens was a cultured university town to which men came from all parts of the Roman Empire, but with no history, and no creative

thought. *See also* PERSIAN WARS, PELOPONNESIAN WAR, and the articles on individual Athenians and particular political institutions.

Ancient sources: the Ἀτθίδες (q.v.) or special histories of Athens (written in the fourth and third centuries) have all been lost except Aristotle's *Constitution of Athens*. Modern works: besides the general histories of Greece, see G. de Sanctis, *Storia della repubblica ateniese*[2] (1912); M. L. W. Laistner, *History of the Greek World from 479 to 323 B.C.* (1936); P. Cloché, *La Politique étrangère d'Athènes de 404 à 338 av. J.-C.* (1934); W. S. Ferguson, *Hellenistic Athens* (1911); P. Graindor, *Athènes de Tibère à Trajan* (1931), *Athènes sous Hadrien* (1934); J. Day, *An Economic History of Athens under Roman Domination* (U.S.A. 1942). A. W. G.

ATHENS (TOPOGRAPHY). There are three great building periods in Athens: Pisistratus, Pericles, Hadrian. Few remains of the first are visible, but many fifth-century buildings had sixth-century predecessors.

2. The centre of Athens was the Acropolis, a long rocky hill, one of many in the Attic plain, easy of access only at the west. A Mycenaean fortress and palace (Ἐρεχθῆος πυκινὸς δόμος) occupied it. There was much sixth-century building, which was destroyed by the Persians; fragments of buildings and sculpture were used to extend the level surface when the Acropolis was walled by Themistocles and extended by Cimon. (For the extant buildings dating from 450–400 B.C. *see* ACROPOLIS, ERECHTHEUM, PARTHENON, PROPYLAEA). The only considerable post-classical work on the Acropolis is the tower of Agrippa outside the Propylaea.

3. Below the Acropolis to the south lies the Roman Odeum of Herodes Atticus (the no longer extant Odeum of Pericles lay east of the theatre); the theatre of Dionysus, the oldest Greek theatre, with a temple of Dionysus Eleuthereus; and many monuments for choregic victories, including those of Thrasyllus, above the theatre on the Acropolis wall, and Lysicrates, to the east. West of the Acropolis is the prominent monument of Philopappus (1st c. A.D.), the *Pnyx* (q.v.), and many house-walls and foundations cut in native rock. On the eastern and northern slopes, various small sanctuaries in the rock; north-west the Areopagus, with rock-cut seats; under the north side of the Acropolis lay the Agora, recently being excavated (for identification of Bouleuterion, Tholos, Metroön, and other excavated buildings see H. A. Thompson, *Hesperia* vi, 1 ff.). The buildings adjoining the Roman Agora, to the east, are well preserved (the Stoa of Attalus, Library of Hadrian, and Tower of the Winds, where Byron lodged). Above the Agora to the west is the Hephaesteum (so-called Theseum), a nearly complete Doric temple of mid-fifth century; farther on, the *Dipylon* (q.v.). The chief cemetery lay here; other graves have been found outside the walls on the north, and in the Agora; until the sixth century family burying-places within the inhabited area were in use. The walls are visible at the Dipylon and behind the Pnyx; fragments have been found north of Stadion Street.

4. Hadrian added a new quarter towards the Ilissus, marked by an arch standing near the Olympieum (q.v.). There are many Roman remains in the Royal gardens. Beyond the Ilissus the modern stadium is on the site of the Panathenaic stadium.

General topography: Paus. bk. 1, and Frazer's commentary; J. E. Harrison and M. de G. Verrall, *Mythology and Monuments of Ancient Athens* (1890); Harrison, *Primitive Athens as described by Thucydides* (1906); E. A. Gardner, *Ancient Athens* (1902); W. Judeich, *Topographie von Athen*[2] (1931). Acropolis: M. Schede, *The Acropolis of Athens* (Engl. Transl. 1924); M. P. Balanos, *Les Monuments de l'Acropole* (1938); O. Walter, *Athen, Akropolis* (1929) (short guide). Early buildings: T. Wiegand, *Die archaische Poros-architektur der Akropolis* (1904). Buildings: F. C. Penrose, *The Principles of Athenian Architecture*[2] (1888); J. H. Middleton, *Plans and Drawings of Athenian Buildings* (1900). Building accounts: W. B. Dinsmoor, *AJArch.* 1913, 1921. Agora: *Hesperia* passim. Theatre: E. Fichter and R. Herbig, *Das Dionysos-Theater in Athen* (1935–6). Olympieum: G. Welter, *Ath. Mitt.* 1922, 61 ff.; 1923, 182 ff. Walls: F. Noack, 'Die Mauern Athens', *Ath. Mitt.* 1907, 123 ff., 437 ff. T. J. D.

ATHLETICS. The two main branches of athletics as practised by the Greeks were: (i) Athletics proper, where the essential feature is the competition (ἆθλος) with its concomitant the prize (ἆθλον), although this latter is often of no intrinsic value, the real prize being the honour of victory. (ii) Gymnastics, the training of the body by a system of exercises in which the naked limbs are allowed full play, part of that physical education which the Greeks closely connected with their art, music, and medicine. The Romans never took either of these seriously: they thought that training for athletics took too much time, and as for gymnastics they considered that nakedness in public was disgraceful, 'flagiti principium'.

2. The gymnastic exercises which the athlete practised fall into three classes, depending respectively on strength of body, of leg, and of arm. To the first class belong boxing and wrestling, to the second running and jumping, to the third throwing the discus and javelin. The last five of these, boxing being excluded, formed the Greek *Pentathlon*, a combined competition in five events, arranged to suit the all-round athlete, and calling not only for strength but also for grace, agility, and skill. The foot-race was taken first and then the jump, the javelin, and the discus; and probably only those who gained a certain number of marks in these first four competitions were allowed to enter for the wrestling.

3. There are many varieties of foot-races; long, short, for men, for boys, for men in armour. In the *Pentathlon* the race may have been the *diaulos*, a quarter-mile, but there is no certainty. Nor can we judge the standard of performances: it is probable that the Greeks were better at long distances than at sprints, but the pictures of runners on the vases show that as far as style goes they were not inferior to the moderns. Jumping was comparatively simple, for the Greeks had neither high jumping, pole-jumping, nor hurdle-races: long jumping was the only form, standing and running, and this was done from a take-off into a pit with the help of jumping-weights. In throwing the javelin and the discus their regular training in body poise and muscular development gave the Greeks a great advantage over our athletes. The javelin was a thin pole about 5 feet long, with a thong fastened near its centre. The movements in throwing, the short steps of the run, and the final turn of the body, are plainly shown in the vase-paintings. For throwing the discus we have Myron's statue, the Discobolus. The athlete has swung the discus backwards, turning head and body to the right, and the force of the throw depends largely on the swing of the whole body. *See also* BOXING, DISCUS, GYMNASIUM, PANKRATION, WRESTLING.

E. N. Gardiner, *Athletics of the Ancient World* (1930). F. A Wright, *Greek Athletics* (1925); C. Alexander, *Greek Athletics* (1925); C. A. Forbes, *Greek Physical Education* (1929); B. Schröder, *Der Sport im Altertum* (1927). F. A. W.

ATHOS, a headland on the easternmost of the Chalcidian promontories, with a conspicuous pyramid-shaped peak rising to 6,350 feet. In 492 B.C. a Persian fleet was destroyed near it by a storm. To avoid the passage round Mt. Athos, Xerxes dug a canal through the neck of the promontory (483–481). This had a length of 1½ miles, a breadth of 65–100 feet, and a depth of 6–10 feet. The upcast earth was piled up to a height of 50 feet. Despite the doubts expressed by ancient and modern writers, the canal was undoubtedly completed.

Hdt. 7. 22–4; Strabo 7. 331. A. Struck, *Neue Jahrb.* 1907, 115–30. M. C.

ATIA MAJOR (daughter of M. Atius Balbus and of Julia, Caesar's sister) was the wife of C. Octavius and the mother of C. Octavius (the future Augustus) and of Octavia minor. After her husband's death in 59 B.C. she married L. Marcius Philippus. She tried to dissuade her son from accepting the inheritance of Caesar. She died in 43. The legend that she had given birth to Augustus by Apollo had some circulation. A. M.

ATIA MINOR, younger daughter of M. Atius Balbus and aunt of Augustus. She married a Marcius Philippus (probably L. Marcius Philippus, son of the step-father of Augustus and consul in 38 B.C.) and had a daughter Marcia.

J. G. Frazer, *Fasti of Ovid* iv. 350–3. G. W. R.

ATILIUS (1) **CALATINUS,** Aulus (*cos.* I, 258 B.C.), fought successfully in Sicily, and as consul II (254) stormed Panormus. He was the first dictator to lead an army outside Italy—to Sicily in 249. He was censor (247). He was buried near the Porta Capena (epitaph, Cic. *Sen.* 61), and was reckoned by Cicero among the most famous men of old. H. H. S.

ATILIUS (2) **SERRANUS,** Aulus, praetor in 192 B.C., commanded the Roman fleet against Nabis and Antiochus (192–191). Praetor again (173), he renewed the treaty relations with Syria on Antiochus Epiphanes' accession. Envoy to Perseus in 172 with Q. Marcius Philippus, he was consul in 170, in Liguria.

Livy 35–6; 42. 6, and 37 ff. De Sanctis, *Stor. Rom.* iv. 1, pp. 135, 173, 275. A. H. McD.

ATILIUS (3), Marcus, contemporary with Caecilius, composed *comoediae palliatae* of which very few fragments remain (*see* DRAMA, para. 4). He had a reputation for harshness, and could stir the emotions deeply. Licinius, in Cic. *Fin.* 1. 5, applies the term 'ferreus scriptor' to an Atilius who translated Sophocles' *Electra.*

Fragments: O. Ribbeck, *CRF*[2], 32 (3rd ed. Teubner, 1897). E. H. W.

ATILIUS (4) **FORTUNATIANUS** (4th c. A.D.), metrician. The first part of his *Ars* (*metrica*) deals with general principles, the second with Horatian metres (ed. Keil, *Gramm. Lat.* 6. 278–304). The work depends largely on earlier writers, especially Caesius Bassus (q.v.).

Cf. Teuffel, § 405, 3; Schanz–Hosius, § 827. J. F. M.

ATILIUS, *see also* REGULUS.

ATIMIA, the loss of all or some civic rights in a Greek city. It originally implied outlawry, but later, especially in Athens, involved the loss of active rights only (or of some only of these). Deprivation might be temporary: a state-debtor's *atimia* ended automatically when the debt was paid. Permanent deprivation of all active rights was the punishment for treason, bribery (of a magistrate), cowardice in face of the enemy, perjury in a law-court (after three convictions), and some offences against the citizenship laws. Permanent deprivation of some rights only was applied (1) if a man brought a *graphe* (q.v.) and (*a*) dropped it, or (*b*) failed to get one-fifth of the votes at the trial; (2) if a man had been convicted three times in a γραφὴ παρανόμων; (3) for certain moral offences. A. W. G.

ATIUS, *see* BALBUS (1).

ATLANTIS, i.e. '(the island) of Atlas', 'the island lying in the Atlantic'. A very large island off the Straits of Gibraltar, which, according to myth, once ruled south-west Europe and north-west Africa, till, in an expedition to conquer the rest, its kings were defeated by the prehistoric Athenians (Plato, *Tim.* 24 e ff.). Its constitution is the chief subject of the unfinished *Critias.* Wholly fictitious, though vague accounts of real islands in the Atlantic may have given Plato the hint, it is interesting as the oldest surviving philosophical wonderland in

Greek, a predecessor of Euhemerus' Panchaia (*see* EUHEMERUS), and of Iambulus (Diod. Sic. 2. 55–60).

Cf. W. A. Heidel, *Proc. American Acad. of Arts and Sciences* 1933, 189 ff.; J. Bidez, *Bull. acad. roy. Belgique* 1934, 101 ff. H. J. R.

ATLAS ("Ατλας), probably 'very enduring', ἀ intensive +root of τλᾶν; in mythology a Titan, son of Iapetus and Clymene (Hesiod, *Theog.* 509). He is guardian of the pillars of heaven (*Od.* 1. 53); but later (as Hesiod, ibid. 517, Aesch. *PV* 347 ff.), he himself holds the sky up. Both are well-known popular explanations of why the sky does not fall (see Stith Thompson, A665. 2, A842). A. became identified with the Atlas range in north-west Africa, or a peak of it (first in Herodotus 4. 184. 5–6); sky-supporting mountains are also popular (Stith Thompson A665. 3), and found elsewhere in Greek (Ap. Rhod. 3. 161, on which see Gillies ad. loc.); a later tale explaining that Perseus had turned him into stone with the Gorgon's head is in Ovid, *Met.* 4. 655 ff. He was variously rationalized into a king (Plato, *Critias* 113 a), a shepherd (Polyidus ap. schol. Lycophron, 879), and an astronomer (Diod. Sic. 3. 60. 2). From his position in the far west, he is naturally brought into conjunction with the Hesperides (q.v.), as in Ovid, loc. cit.; he is their father in Diod. Sic. 4. 27. 2. In Homer (*Od.* loc. cit.), he is father of Calypso, but usually his daughters are the Pleiades (favourite subjects of popular speculation, Stith Thompson A773), Alcyone, Celaeno, Electra, Maia, Merope, Sterope, and Taygete, whose names and local connexions (Maia with Arcadia, Electra with Troy, etc.) show that the African localization of their father is no part of their story. Besides his connexion with Perseus (see above) he encountered Heracles (q.v.), when the latter was seeking the apples of the Hesperides. Atlas offered to fetch them if Heracles would uphold the sky meanwhile; he then refused to take back the burden, until forced or cheated into doing so by the hero (e.g., Pherecydes ap. schol. Ap. Rhod. 4. 1396). Atlas upholding the sky was represented in art from early times, is a favourite subject in Hellenistic art, and develops into an ornamental support. H. J. R.

ATLAS MOUNTAINS, the great range which formed the backbone of Roman Africa. Its highest peaks are in the Great Atlas to the west, and Greek legend converted them into the bowed shoulders of the god who held up the heavens (see preceding article). The chain slopes eastward through Middle and Little Atlas to the Aurès and Medjerda ranges. On the north the Atlas buttresses the Tell or fertile coastal plain. Southward the mountains slope down to the Saharan desert, which runs eastward to touch Lesser Syrtis (q.v.). Between Tell and Sahara are the High Plateaux with much good grazing land; in the centre and the east lie the shotts or salt lakes. Suetonius Paulinus crossed Mt. Atlas in A.D. 42 (Pliny, *HN* 5. 14–15).

A. N. Sherwin-White, *JRS* 1944, 1 ff. W. N. W.

ATREUS, in mythology, son of Pelops (*see* TANTALUS) and husband of Aërope. From late epic on (*Alcmaeonis* ap. schol. Eur. *Or.* 995) he and his brother Thyestes are at variance. Hermes was wroth with the whole house for the death of his son Myrtilus (*see* PELOPS) and gave them a golden ram, the possession of which carried the kingship with it; Thyestes got this from Aërope, whose paramour he was; Atreus banished him, but later pretended a reconciliation. At the banquet held to consummate this, Atreus served up to Thyestes the flesh of the latter's own children, at which the sun turned back on its course in horror. *See further* AEGISTHUS. In another version (Apollod. *Epit.* 2. 12) Atreus by advice of Hermes offers to let Thyestes, who has seized the throne, keep it till the sun turns back; Thyestes agrees, and Zeus immediately turns the sun backwards, the rest of the story following much as above. There are numerous other variants; the story was much elaborated by the tragedians, see for instance Eur. *El.* 699 ff.; *Or.* 995 ff.; Seneca, *Thyestes*, passim. Continuous narratives, Apollod., loc. cit.; Hyg., *Fab.* 86–8; more in Roscher's *Lexikon*, art. 'Atreus' (Furtwängler). H. J. R.

ATRIUM, see HOUSES (ITALIAN).

ATRIUM VESTAE, an ancient precinct, east of the *Forum Romanum*, comprising the *aedes* and *lucus Vestae, Regia, domus publica,* and *domus Vestalium.* Republican remains of the last two underlie the existing *domus Vestalium,* built after Nero's fire of A.D. 64. The western ritual-kitchen is Flavian, while the eastern *exedra,* once fronting a closed garden behind Nero's small peristyle, is Hadrianic. The Antonines, uniting the rooms grouped about the Neronian courtyard, added second and third stories. The enlarged peristyle now visible is Severan. Later additions are of minor significance.

E. Van Deman, *Atrium Vestae* (U.S.A. 1909). I. A. R.

ATROPOS, see FATE.

ATTA, TITUS QUINCTIUS (d. 77 B.C.), Latin poet, composed *comoediae togatae,* elegiac epigrams, and perhaps *satura.* Fragments, and titles of eleven plays, survive. He excelled in character-drawing, especially feminine. See DRAMA, para. 5.

Fragments: O. Ribbeck, *CRF²,* 160 (3rd ed. Teubner, 1897).

ATTALEIA, a city of Pamphylia, founded by Attalus II, perhaps with Athenian settlers; on its Imperial coins the city boasts kinship with Athens. In 79 B.C. it was mulcted of its territory by Servilius Isauricus for its complicity with the pirate king Zenicetes. These lands were probably utilized by Augustus for settling veterans, but Attaleia was not made a colony, a status which it achieved only in the late third century. There are some classical ruins.

K. Lanckoroński, *Städte Pamphyliens* (1890),i. 7–32. A. H. M. J.

ATTALUS I (SOTER) of Pergamum, 269–197 B.C., son of Attalus and nephew of Eumenes I, whom he succeeded (241). He was the first to refuse 'tribute' to the Galatians, and his great victory over them (before 230) was commemorated by his cult-name *Soter,* by the triumphal monument at Pergamum famous for its 'dying Gaul', and probably by the title of King (which Eumenes had never taken). His counter-attack on Antiochus Hierax, who had co-operated with the Galatians, gained him all Seleucid Asia Minor except Cilicia (229–228); but Achaeus (223–220), and later Antiochus III (216–214), deprived him of most of his conquests.

Attalus also inaugurated a 'western' policy which was to give a new turn to the history of Pergamum. The dangerous ambitions of Philip V of Macedonia prompted him to support Philip's enemies the Aetolians, first with subsidies (220–217), and later with troops and a fleet (209–207). After the peace of Phoenice (205), Attalus replied to Philip's acts of aggression near the Hellespont by renewing the war in alliance with Rhodes (201), and securing Roman intervention against Macedon in common with the Rhodians. During the 'Second Macedonian War' he co-operated with the Romans by sea. He died shortly before the final victory.

An excellent general and diplomatist, Attalus raised Pergamum almost to the rank of a Great Power. Between Philip and Antiochus, he chose to live dangerously, and his approach to Rome, though brilliantly successful in its immediate rewards (*see also* EUMENES II), ultimately made Pergamum a pawn of Roman policy, besides precipitating the collapse of the Hellenistic political system. Apart from politics, Attalus was a notable patron of literature, philosophy, and the arts, and enjoyed a conspicuous domestic happiness with his wife Apollonis of Cyzicus and their four sons. G. T. G.

ATTALUS II (PHILADELPHUS), 220–138 B.C., second son of Attalus I, and brother of Eumenes II, whom he succeeded (160–159). Before 160 he showed himself a skilful soldier and diplomatist, and was conspicuously loyal to Eumenes, whom he could probably have supplanted, with Roman support, at any time after 168 (*see* EUMENES II). As king, he fulfilled the (by now) traditional Pergamene part of watch-dog for Rome in the East. He equipped and supported the pretender Alexander Balas to win the Seleucid throne from Demetrius I (153–150); and in return Rome supported him in his two wars with Bithynia. Like all the Attalids, he was genuinely interested in letters and the arts. G. T. G.

ATTALUS III (PHILOMETOR EUERGETES), *c.* 170–133 B.C., son of Eumenes II and successor of Attalus II (138). His short reign was famous only for its dénouement, the 'Testament of Attalus' bequeathing the kingdom of Pergamum to Rome (*OGI* 338). Its motive has never been perfectly explained, especially as Attalus was comparatively young and presumably did not expect a premature death. But the revolution after his death (*see* ARISTONICUS I) suggests that he may have made and published this testament partly as an insurance against social revolution while he survived.

For bibliography, *see under* PERGAMUM. G. T. G.

ATTHIS ('Aτθίς), a type of literature dealing specifically with the history of Attica which became popular *c.* 350–200 B.C. under the influence of the Sophists and Peripatetics and the general conception fostered by Isocrates and the Orators of a return to the past glory of Athens. Hellanicus' history of Attica (Thuc. 1. 97), one of a series dealing with various States, was not strictly an *Atthis.* Cleidemus was the first atthidographer, followed by Androtion, Demon, Philochorus, Phanodemus, Melanthius, Amelesagoras, Ister. The last produced a final authoritative version. Characteristics of the *Atthides* are their chronological arrangement and emphasis on mythology and origins of cults. Most atthidographers held priestly or political offices and produced other works on religious antiquities. Scholia to Aristophanes and the *Marmor Parium* show their accepted value for dates. Often used by commentators on the Orators for constitutional and topographical details.

See Wilamowitz, *Aristoteles und Athen* i. 8. *See also* HISTORIOGRAPHY, GREEK, para. 5. G. L. B.

ATTIANUS, PUBLIUS ACILIUS (*Röm. Mitt.* xviii (1903), 63 ff.), an equestrian of Italica, guardian and adviser of the young Hadrian (q.v.), was almost certainly *praefectus praetorio* when Trajan died, helping Plotina to secure Hadrian's succession. Replaced by Q. Marcius Turbo (q.v.) in 119 (perhaps after exaggerating the rumoured plotting of the four 'consulars'), he was made a senator, of consular rank, as a mark of honour.

S.H.A. *Hadr.*; Dio Cassius 69; *PIR²,* A 45; R. H. Lacey, *The Equestrian Officials of Trajan and Hadrian, &c.* (Diss. Princeton, 1917), p. 16, no. 37. C. H. V. S.

ATTIC, see DIALECTS, GREEK.

ATTIC CULTS AND MYTHS. The chief goddess was of course Athena, her festivals being Arrhetophoria (Pyanopsion and Scirophorion; for the month-names, *see* CALENDARS), Procharisteria (early spring; both the above are agricultural), Callynteria and Plynteria (Thargelion; ceremonial cleansing of temple and statue), Panathenaea (q.v., Hecatombaeon 28, Great Panathenaea every four years), and Chalceia (last day of Pyanopsion). Other gods and goddesses were celebrated at the following festivals: Demeter and Core—Scira (*see* SCIROPHORIA, Scirophorion 12), Thesmophoria (q.v., Pyanopsion 10 at Halimus, 11–13 at Athens), Haloa (Poseideon), Chloia (early spring, to Demeter Chloë and Core, at Eleusis), Lesser Mysteries at Agrae (Anthesterion),

Greater Mysteries beginning at Athens and ending at Eleusis (Boedromion 15–22: see MYSTERIES). Dionysus—Anthesteria (q.v., Anthesterion 11–13; apparently a blend of his worship with an All Souls feast), Lenaea (q.v., Gamelion ?12), Rural Dionysia (see DIONYSIA, Poseideon), Great or City Dionysia (Elaphebolion 9–13 or 14, see J. T. Allen in *Univ. of Calif. Publns.* xii, pp. 35–42; this and the Lenaea were the great dramatic festivals), Oschophoria (Pyanopsion ?8). Kronos—Kronia (Hecatombaeon 12). Zeus—Diasia (Anthesterion 23, to Zeus Meilichios, see ZEUS), Dipolieia (Scirophorion 14), Diisoteria (Scirophorion, at Piraeus), and some minor feasts. Apollo—Thargelia (q.v., Thargelion 7), Pyanopsia (Pyanopsion 7). Artemis—Munichia (Munichion 16); Brauronia (at Brauron, unknown date, see ARTEMIS), Tauropolia (Halae, unknown date), Elaphebolia (unknown, gave its name to the month Elaphebolion). There were also festivals, of which not much is known, to Poseidon, Hephaestus, Prometheus, the Eumenides, and some minor deities.

The best-known myths have to do with Athena and Poseidon (qq.v.). Heroic and aetiological tales centre around the vague and contradictory line of kings, dealing mainly with Cecrops (see CULTURE-BRINGERS), Erichthonius, Erechtheus (q.v.), and above all Theseus (q.v.). There is besides the story of Cephalus (q.v.) and Procris, and a few others little known. *See also* BENDIS, ERIGONE, NEMESIS.

L. Deubner, *Attische Feste* (1932). H. J. R.

ATTIC ORATORS. Caecilius of Calacte in the Augustan age wrote 'On the style of the ten orators', namely Antiphon, Andocides, Lysias, Isocrates, Isaeus, Lycurgus, Aeschines, Demosthenes, Hyperides, Dinarchus. This 'canon', though ignored by Dionysius, was recognized by the Ps.-Plutarch, Quintilian, and later writers. Its origin is unknown, but the arbitrary inclusion of a definite number of names in such a class is characteristic of Alexandrian scholarship.

Ancient sources: Pseudo-Plutarch, *Lives of the Ten Orators*; Dionysius of Halicarnassus, *De Verborum Compositione* and *Letters to Ammaeus*; Demetrius, *De Elocutione*; Hermogenes Περὶ ἰδεῶν; [Longinus], *On the Sublime*. Modern works: F. Blass, *Die attische Beredsamkeit*[2] (1887–98); R. C. Jebb, *The Attic Orators from Antiphon to Isaeus*[2] (1893); J. F. Dobson, *The Greek Orators* (1919); Grote, *History of Greece*; *CAH* vii; Croiset, *Histoire de la litt. grecque* v. Texts: *Oratores Attici*, I. Bekker (1828); do. G. S. Dobson (1828); Text and translation of *Minor Attic Orators*, K. J. Maidment (2 vols. Loeb). *Selections from the Attic Orators* (text and commentary), R. C. Jebb (2nd ed. 1888). Indexes: T. Mitchell, *Index in Oratores Atticos*. C. Rehdantz, *Indices zu Demosthenes neun philippischen Reden*, 4th ed. (1886) revised by Blass. See also under the names of the various orators.

J. F. D.

ATTICA, a triangular promontory of about 1,000 sq. m., the easternmost part of central Greece, separated from Boeotia by Mt. Parnes. Most of it consists of small interconnected plains; the Thriasian plain (where Demeter gave corn to man), the Attic plain, larger but stonier, and the Mesogeia, an undulating and fertile land of vine and olive, in a cup of low hills with easy access south and east to the sea. Pentelicum and Hymettus, with their marble quarries, and other smaller hills, stand out of these plains. The south-east, with the silver mines of Laurium and temples of Sunium, is a mass of hills; the north is hill-country, well wooded, with patches of good land, the largest round Aphidna and Marathon. The soil, though light, is as good as in most of Greece; but its natural riches lay in mines, marble, and excellent potter's clay.

In early times Attica contained several independent settlements; the tradition of twelve townships fused by Theseus into a single Athenian State is borne out by rich Mycenaean cemeteries at Eleusis, Marathon, and in the Mesogeia. The synoecism was probably gradual, and went on until the seventh century (see ELEUSIS). Cults from the country-side were brought to Athens (e.g. Artemis Brauronia, the Eleusinian goddesses); this continued after the synoecism (e.g. Dionysus from Eleutherae). Later acquisitions, Salamis, Eleutherae, Plataea, Oropus, did not become part of Attica. Attica was less affected than most of Greece by the great migrations, and continuity from Mycenaean to Hellenic times is well demonstrated in its remains.

Down to the sixth century the country districts had a vigorous and largely independent life, as is shown by finds of rich sanctuaries and cemeteries, particularly in the Mesogeia. During the fifth century, with the adoption of an aggressive foreign policy depending on sea-power and sea-borne trade, Attica became an appendage to Athens which might be disregarded in emergency (as in the Peloponnesian War), but Aristophanes shows the survival of an Attic, as distinct from Athens–Piraeus, patriotism. *See also* ACHARNAE.

General literature: W. Wrede, *Attika* (1934); *Attische Mauern* (1933); E. A. Gardner and M. Cary, *CAH* iii. 571 ff.; A. Milchhöfer and W. Judeich, *PW*, s.v. 'Attika'. Topography: E. Curtius and A. Milchhöfer, text to *Karten von Attika* (1881–1900). Special subjects: R. Lepsius, *Geologie von Attika*; S. C. Atchley, *Wild Flowers of Attica* (1938). History; S. Solders, *Die Ausserstädtischen Kulte und die Einigung Attikas* (1931). *See also* ATHENS. Maps: Greek Staff, 1 : 20,000; British Staff, 1 : 100,000; Curtius–Kaupert, *Karten von Attika* 1 : 25,000; of remains visible in 1881–1900, some have disappeared, some are not ancient. T. J. D.

ATTICUS (1), TITUS POMPONIUS (109–32 B.C.), a Roman *eques*, was an intimate friend and correspondent of Cicero. He derived his surname from long residence at Athens (88–65), whereby he escaped Sulla's proscription. His sympathies were with the *Optimates*, but even after his return to Rome he took no active part in politics, and lived on good terms with conservatives and Caesarians alike. His vast wealth was founded on his estates in Epirus and increased by his manifold business activities, which ranged from banking to publishing; he also inherited a large fortune from his miserly uncle Q. Caecilius. Though frugal, he was a discriminating patron of the arts, with a real appreciation of Greek culture, and his house on the Quirinal was a well-known literary centre. He survived the Civil Wars by consistently showing himself a friend to all and an ally to none (see esp. Nepos, *Att.* 8), and he enjoyed the favour of Octavian until his death.

Atticus' calculating policy of neutrality is hard to justify even when covered by the cloak of Epicureanism, but he had many attractive qualities. His urbanity, discretion, and ready sympathy made him an ideal confidant for Cicero. Atticus himself published the full, though one-sided, correspondence between the two.

Cicero's *Letters to Atticus* (in sixteen books) illuminate the character of both; a letter to him from Brutus also survives (*ad Brut.* 17). His own letters have perished with his other literary works. Cornelius Nepos' *Life* is detailed, but fulsome and uncritical.

G. Boissier, *Cicero and His Friends* (Engl. Transl. 1897); H. Ziegler, *Titus Pomponius Atticus als Politiker* (U.S.A. 1936).

J. M. C.

ATTICUS (2), JULIUS, like Graecinus (q.v.), a Latin writer on vines in Tiberius' time, who was a source for Columella (3. 17. 4).

ATTICUS (3) (c. A.D. 150–200), Platonist, opposed the infiltration of Peripatetic elements into Platonism, but himself introduced into it certain doctrines proper to Stoicism.

PW ii. 2241.

ATTIS, in mythology, the youthful consort of Cybele (q.v.) and prototype of her eunuch devotees. The myth exists in two main forms, with many variants. According to the Phrygian tale (Paus. 7. 17. 10–12; cf. Arn. *Adv. Nat.* 5. 5–7), the gods castrated the androgynous Agdistis (q.v.); from the severed male parts an almond tree sprang and by its fruit Nana conceived A. Later Agdistis fell in love with him, and to prevent his marriage to another caused him to castrate himself. Agdistis is clearly a doublet of Cybele, though Arnobius brings them both into his account. Ovid (*Fasti* 4. 221–44) and others change many details, but keep the essential aetiological feature, the self-castration. In a probably Lydian version A., like Adonis, is killed by a boar. The story of Atys, son of Croesus, who was killed by the Phrygian Adrastus in a boar-hunt (Hdt. 1. 34–45) is an adaptation of this, and attests its antiquity, though the Phrygian is probably the older version.

In Asia Minor A. bears his native name only in the Neo-Phrygian inscriptions, though the high priest and, under the Empire, all members of the priestly college at Pessinus had the title Attis. A. is sometimes called Papas or Zeus Papas. He appears only rarely in Greece, but at Rome attained official status under Claudius. Like Adonis, he was fundamentally a vegetation god and the equinoctial spring festival centred about his death and resurrection. Under the Empire he was invested with celestial attributes, and became a solar deity, supreme, all-powerful, and sometimes it seems a surety of immortality to his initiates. In art he is generally represented as an effeminate youth, with the distinctive Phrygian cap and trousers. See ANATOLIAN DEITIES; CYBELE; EUNUCHS, RELIGIOUS.

J. Carcopino, *Mél. d'Arch. et d'Hist.* xl (1923), 135–59, 237–324; F. Cumont, *Les Religions orientales dans le paganisme romain* (1929); H. Hepding, *Attis* (1903); H. Graillot, *Le Culte de Cybèle* (1912).   F. R. W.

ATTIUS, see VARUS (1).

AUCTOR AD HERENNIUM, see RHETORICA AD H.

AUCTORITAS PATRUM, see PATRUM AUCTORITAS.

AUDAX (probably 6th c. A.D.), grammarian, whose *De Scauri et Palladii Libris excerpta* is extant (ed. Keil, *Gramm. Lat.* 7. 320–62).

Cf. Teuffel, § 408, 4 and § 482, 4; Schanz–Hosius, § 1105.

AUFIDIUS (1) **BASSUS** (fl. 1st c. A.D.), the Imperial historian, an Epicurean and subject to ill health, which prevented a public career, wrote on the German Wars (*Bellum Germanicum*), probably under Tiberius and glorifying his achievements. He also wrote a history of his times, probably under Claudius, which may have begun with Caesar's death, certainly included Cicero's death (Sen. *Suas.* 6. 18; 23), and was continued by the Elder Pliny under the title *a fine Aufidii Bassi*. This indicates an inconspicuous closing point, which may fall in A.D. 31, but is, on the evidence of Tacitus' use of Pliny, better set in A.D. 50. Cassiodorus followed him for the consul lists of 9 B.C.–A.D. 31. In authority he ranks among the great historians of the early Empire (Quint. 10. 1. 103).

H. Peter, *HRRel* ii (1906), pp. cxxxv, 96; Ph. Fabia, *Les Sources de Tacite* (1893), 185, 355; cf. F. Münzer, *Rh. Mus.* 1907, 161. F. A. Marx, *Klio* 1933, 323.   A. H. McD.

AUFIDIUS (2), GNAEUS, in Cicero's boyhood wrote a 'Graeca historia', possibly of Rome (*Tusc.* 5. 112).

AUFIDIUS (3), MODESTUS, commentator on Virgil and Horace, in the first century A.D.

AUGE, see TELEPHUS.

AUGURES, official Roman diviners, forming a *collegium* which consisted originally of three but was gradually increased to sixteen members (Livy 10. 6. 7–8 and *periocha* 89; Dio Cassius 42. 51. 4), one of the *quattuor amplissima collegia*. Etymology uncertain; the traditional derivation from *aui*+*ger(o)* would give **auger*, not *augur*; that from the root *aug(eo)*, see E. Flinck in

Ann. Acad. Scient. Fennicae xi (1921), 3 ff., suggests rites of fertility rather than divination, but the transition is not impossible, cf. AUGURIUM CANARIUM. Their business was not to foretell the future, but to discover by observation of signs, *auguria*, either casually met with, *oblativa*, or watched for, *impetrativa*, whether the gods did or did not approve a proposed action. The most characteristic signs were given by birds (hence the traditional etymology). These might be chickens, which were carried by armies in the field for the purpose; food was given to them, and if they ate it so as to drop some from their beaks, that was an excellent sign ('tripudium solistimum', Cicero, *Div.* 2. 72, where see Pease). If wild birds were observed, the augur marked out a *templum* (cf. DIVINATION), i.e. he designated boundaries by word of mouth (see e.g. Varro, *Ling.* 7. 7–8, which gives the formula) within which he would look for signs, and divided this space into *sinistra*, *dextra*, *antica*, and *postica* (*pars*); the significance of the flight or cry of the bird varied according to the part in which it was heard or seen. The officiant faced south or east (Rose in *JRS* xiii (1923), 82–90). Such observations prefaced every important action public or (at least in early times) private, but to accept or reject augural advice was the responsibility of the magistrate or other person performing the action. For *augurium salutis*, see SALUS, and for augury in general see DIVINATION; ETRUSCANS, para. 4.

Bouché–Leclercq, *Histoire de la Divination* iv. 209 ff.; Wissowa, *RK²* 523 ff.   H. J. R.

AUGURINUS, SENTIUS (? *Serius*), a young friend praised by Pliny (*Ep.* 4. 27; 9. 8) for writing 'Poems in Little' (*poematia*) marked by charm and tenderness, but sometimes by satire. Pliny quotes eight hendeca-syllabics by him in the manner of Catullus and Calvus.

Baehr. *FPR*; Morel *FPL*.   J. W. D.

AUGURIUM CANARIUM. Ateius Capito in Festus, p. 358, 27 Lindsay, says that reddish (*rutilae*) bitches were sacrificed *canario sacrificio pro frugibus*, to 'deprecate' the fierceness of the Dog-star. Cf. Fest. (Paulus), p. 39, 13, from which it would appear that the place was near the Porta Catularia and the time fairly late summer, since the crops were yellowing (*flauescentes*). This seems to be the *sacrum canarium* of Daniel's Servius on *G.* 4. 424. The ritual name, however, was *augurium canarium*, as is shown by Pliny, *HN* 18. 14, who quotes from the *commentarii pontificum* (q.v.) the direction that the days (*dies*; it is not clear whether the rite lasted more than one day or the various days for different years are meant) for it should be fixed 'priusquam frumenta uaginis exeant nec (et *codd.*, *corr.* Ulrichs) antequam in uaginas perueniant', that is to say some time in spring (see L. Delatte in *Ant. Class.* vi (1937), 93 ff.). The name probably means '*augurium* of the dog-days'. It is most unlikely that it was a sacrifice to the Dog-star; it may have been an augury in the sense that omens for the result of the harvest were taken from the victims, but if the second etymology given under 'AUGURES' is right, it is tempting to make it mean 'ceremony of increase for the dog-days'. There is no evidence, though some probability, that the augurs took part and no reason to suppose it performed in honour of any god.   H. J. R.

AUGUSTA, title of Imperial ladies, see AUGUSTUS, AUGUSTA.

AUGUSTA (1) **EMERITA** (now *Mérida*), a colony in south-western Spain founded by Augustus (25 B.C.) chiefly with veterans of legions V and X. Connected with Baetica by a 64-arch bridge over the Anas (*Guadiana*), it was the terminus of many roads leading to the north and west. It became the capital of the province of Lusitania (q.v.). The city was indebted to

Agrippa for its theatre (restored by Hadrian), to Otho for economic favours, to Trajan for its bridge. Many of its Roman monuments have been preserved.

J. R. Mélida, *Mérida* (1929). J. J. V. N.

AUGUSTA (2) **PRAETORIA** (now *Aosta*), a colony founded with 3,000 Praetorians on the Duria Major in Cisalpine Gaul by Augustus (24 B.C.); it was here that Terentius Varro had encamped the previous year when subjugating the Salassi (Strabo 4. 206; Cass. Dio 53. 25). Standing at the Italian end of the Great and Little St. Bernard Passes over Pennine and Graian Alps respectively, Augusta became and still remains the capital of this whole region (*Val d'Aosta*).

For inscriptions see P. Barocelli, *Inscriptiones Italiae* i, fasc. 1 (1932); for Roman monuments, F. Haverfield, *Ancient Town Planning* (1913). F. Eyssenhardt, *Aosta und seine Alterthümer* (1896). P. Toesca, *Aosta* (1911). E. T. S.

AUGUSTA (3) **TAURINORUM** (now *Torino, Turin*), an important Augustan *colonia* in Cisalpine Gaul, situated at the foot of the Mont Genèvre Pass over the Cottian Alps and at the confluence of the Duria Minor and the Po, which here became navigable (Pliny, *HN* 3. 123). Originally the capital of the Taurini, who were probably celticized Ligurians, it is apparently identical with the Taurasia captured by Hannibal, 218 B.C. (App. *Hann.* 5). Tacitus (*Hist.* 2. 66) records its burning in A.D. 69. Ancient authors seldom mention it. The modern city preserves the ancient street plan.

F. Haverfield, *Ancient Town Planning* (1913), 87; G. Bendinelli, *Torino Romana* (1928). E. T. S.

AUGUSTA (4) **TREVERORUM** (now *Trier* or *Trèves*) was founded by Augustus. It rapidly became the chief city of north-east Gaul, and an important trade-centre between Gaul and the Rhineland; its colonial status, if not already conferred by Augustus, may date from Claudius. It was the seat of the *procurator provinciae Belgicae et duarum Germaniarum*; Postumus made it his capital, a precedent followed by Maximian and Constantius Chlorus, and it remained the capital of the Prefecture of Gaul from 297 until early in the fifth century, when it was abandoned to the Franks. Its bishop enjoyed a corresponding importance.

Trèves grew far beyond the original settlement, to cover 700 acres. Notable ruins, mostly of the period when the city was frequently the Imperial residence, were standing till recently—the 'Porta Nigra' (a late Roman gateway), remains of public halls incorporated in the cathedral and another church, baths, and the first-century amphitheatre; the modern bridge rests on Roman piers. Excavation has revealed an extensive temple quarter (already used in pre-Roman times) outside the town, comprising about seventy shrines, a theatre, and priests' dwellings. Pottery (including Samian ware) and cloth manufactured in Trèves were widely exported; the city had an Imperial mint from at least 296 and was also a centre of the Moselle wine trade.

Rau, s.v. 'Treveri' in *PW* viA 2320 ff. K. Schumacher, *Siedelungs- und Kulturgeschichte der Rheinlande*, Bd. ii (1923). O. B.

AUGUSTA (5) **VINDELICORUM** (now *Augsburg*) probably dates from *c.* A.D. 6–9, when the legion stationed at Oberhausen nearby was sent away. It lay at the centre of a network of important roads and was from the first the administrative and trading centre of Raetia (cf. Tac. *Germ.* 41). Hadrian raised it to municipal status (122–3), and after the reorganization under Diocletian it remained the civil capital of Raetia Secunda. It became the seat of a bishop. Nothing of Roman Augsburg remains above ground, but numerous sculptures and smaller objects have been found. O. B.

AUGUSTALES, *see* RULER-CULT.

AUGUSTINUS, AURELIUS (St. Augustine, A.D. 354–430), was born at Tagaste in Numidia, 13 November A.D. 354, of a father Patricius, a heathen town-councillor in straitened circumstances, and a Christian mother, Monnica. Educated at Tagaste, Madauros, and Carthage, he was highly distinguished in his studies, more so in Latin than in Greek. His view of life was greatly influenced by Cicero's lost dialogue *Hortensius*, and he belonged to the Manichean sect for several years. He left Carthage to reside in Rome (383) and obtained a chair of rhetoric in Milan, 384. There the preaching and private influence of Ambrose (q.v.) helped towards his conversion, 386. Nor must the great influence of Neoplatonism on his mental make-up be ignored. In 387 after baptism he left Milan, and after a period in Rome reached his native country towards the end of 388. He received priest's orders, 391, at Hippo Regius, where he became co-bishop, 395, and subsequently sole bishop. Except for many short journeys in the interests of the Faith he remained there till his death, 28 Aug. 430.

With a loving and sympathetic nature, an excellent education, tireless industry, and an unwearied devotion to the Christian faith, when once he had surrendered to it, it is not surprising that Augustine has exercised on subsequent Christian thought a greater influence than any other Father. He fulfilled all the duties of a bishop, preaching and writing in a manner never surpassed.

His surviving works are in bulk about six times those of Cicero. In his *Retractationes* he reviewed his writings down to 427 and pointed out what he then regarded as errors in them. Here there is space to allude merely to the most important: *De Doctrina Christiana* (4 books); *Confessiones* (c. 400) in thirteen books, of which the first ten are autobiographical and the others concerned with the earlier chapters of Genesis; *De Catechizandis Rudibus*, a manual of Christian education; *De Trinitate* (completed 416), his greatest dogmatic work; *De Consensu Evangelistarum*, on the 'synoptic problem'; *De Civitate Dei* (22 books, 413–26), the most carefully written, the most learned, and the greatest of his works, in which ancient paganism may be said to have received its death-blow (*see* PHILON 4); *Enarrationes in Psalmos*, his longest work and his finest piece of exposition; *Tractatus in Evangelium Iohannis*, 125 sermons on the Fourth Gospel; *Contra Iulianum* and *Opus Imperfectum contra Iulianum*, a refutation of the most learned of the Pelagians; some 500 sermons, interesting also from the semi-colloquial latinity in which they abound; about 300 epistles, mostly of dogmatic import. It should be mentioned that Augustine was also a careful reviser of certain portions of the Latin Biblical text, such as the *Psalms* and the *Epistles of St. Paul*, in this respect quite worthy to be named beside Jerome, though his inferior in purely linguistic knowledge.

Works: Migne, *PL* 32–47; new sermons by G. Morin, *Miscellanea Agostiniana* i (1930); many works in *CSEL*; *Confessiones*, F. Skutella (Teubner, 1934), annotated, Gibb and Montgomery (1927); *De Civitate Dei*, Dombart and Kalb (Teubner), C. Weyman (Munich); *De Catech. Rud.*, J. P. Christopher (U.S.A. 1926); cf. É. Gilson, *Introduction à l'Étude de Saint Augustin* (1931). A. S.

AUGUSTODUNUM (modern *Autun*), a town in Gallia Belgica, founded *c.* 12 B.C. in the plain of the Arroux to replace the hill-town Bibracte. It was laid out on a large scale (area *c.* 490 acres), and important buildings (including two town gates) survive. It was celebrated as a centre of learning both in the first and in the fourth centuries A.D. It suffered for its fidelity to Claudius II (A.D. 269), and was ruined after a seven-month siege. Its restoration under Constantius I is celebrated by Eugenius, master of the local 'Scholae Maenianae'. But the reduced perimeter of the town wall shows its depopulation.

H. de Fontenay, *Autun et ses Monuments* (1889); F. J. Haverfield, *Ancient Town Planning* (1913), 121–3; Grenier, *Manuel* i. 337–45. C. E. S.

AUGUSTUS (63 B.C.–A.D. 14). C. Octavius, born on 23 Sept. 63 B.C., was brought up by his mother Atia (q.v.), Caesar's niece, as his father C. Octavius (q.v.) died in 59. His teachers gave him a taste for literature and philosophy, but Caesar himself introduced him to Roman life. Aged twelve, he pronounced the *laudatio* of his grandmother Julia; he was appointed pontifex; in 46 B.C. he accompanied his great-uncle in his triumph. Despite delicate health, he joined Caesar in Spain in 45. At Apollonia, where he had been sent with his friends, M. Agrippa and Salvidienus Rufus, to complete his studies, he learnt of Caesar's sudden death. The opening of Caesar's will revealed that Octavius had been adopted and made his chief heir by the dictator. He decided to return to Italy and to avenge Caesar. The unexpected situation imposed new duties and stimulated new ambitions. Caesar had lived long enough to afford an inspiring example, but had died soon enough not to destroy the Roman traditionalism of his heir. Octavius was cautious and superstitious, but exceptionally mature, clever, and decided. In Italy he gained Cicero's sympathy and Antony's distrust. He celebrated the *ludi Victoriae Caesaris* and, while linking himself with the moderate Republicans, did not overlook Caesar's veterans. During the conflict between Antony and Dec. Brutus (q.v. 6) he obtained from the Senate the rank of senator and propraetor, and emerged victorious from the war of Mutina (43 B.C.). But when the Senate refused their champion due honours, his legionaries forced his appointment as consul. He was recognized as Caesar's adopted son under the name of Gaius Julius Caesar Octavianus. He soon reached a compromise with Antony and M. Lepidus (q.v. 3). By the *Lex Titia* (27 Nov. 43) they secured official acknowledgment of themselves as triumvirs *rei publicae constituendae* for five years. Octavian obtained Africa, Sicily, and Sardinia as his provinces. When on 1 Jan. 42 Caesar was recognized as a god, Octavian became *divi filius*. In the triumviral proscriptions (q.v.) he was as ruthless as his colleagues: ambition and a touch of puritanical fanaticism made him cruel. During the campaign of Philippi he suffered from ill health. Thereafter he received Spain, Sardinia, and for a short time Africa, and supervised the distribution of land to the veterans. This task and the suppression of the rebellion of L. Antonius (q.v. 6), in which Salvidienus Rufus, M. Agrippa, and C. Maecenas became his close collaborators, strengthened his hold on Italy and Gaul (40 B.C.). In a transitory attempt to conciliate Sextus Pompeius, who held Sicily and Sardinia, Octavian married his relative Scribonia (q.v.). In Oct. 40 the pact of Brundisium sealed a new reconciliation with Antony, who married Octavian's sister, Octavia; Virgil's fourth Eclogue records the contemporary enthusiasm. Octavian divorced Scribonia and married Livia (q.v.), who shared his traditionalism and simplicity and thus became a permanent force in his life. Salvidienus Rufus was now condemned to death, since he was suspected of meditating revolt. In 38, when war with Pompeius broke out, Octavian probably assumed the *praenomen* of *imperator* (q.v.), which was ratified in 29 by the Senate. In 37 at Tarentum Antony and Octavian confirmed their agreement and had their triumviral powers extended for another five years (until Dec. 33?). With the defeat of Pompeius and the downfall of Lepidus (36) the West was in the hands of the *divi filius*.

2. Octavian was already winning over public opinion in Italy. He put himself under the protection of Apollo. He was perhaps granted *sacrosanctitas* or some other form of tribunician privilege. He disbanded legions and founded colonies. He saw definitely that his task was to establish peace and restore Italy. The opposition to Antony and Cleopatra reinforced his position at a moment in which the consciousness of a united Italy was just formed. Between 35 and 33 B.C. his campaigns

in Illyricum and Dalmatia, although not entirely successful, strengthened the eastern borders of Italy. Great attention was given to the adornment of Rome, especially under the aedileship of Agrippa (33 B.C.). Octavian's party had originally won more support from the Italian municipalities, but now a considerable part of the Roman aristocracy joined. Antony's callousness towards Octavia added a family justification to the rivalry. The triumvirate was not renewed, but Octavian, like Antony, did not abandon power and prepared for war against his partner. In Oct. 32 Italy and the western provinces swore allegiance to Octavian. They became his clients—an important step towards the Principate and a substitute for his triumviral powers. War was declared only against Cleopatra. In 31 Octavian's position became more regular when he assumed the consulship, which he held every year until 23 B.C.

3. Octavian overthrew Antony in the campaign of Actium (Sept. 31), founded Nicopolis (q.v.), and ascribed his success to Apollo. In August 30 he became master of Egypt and its treasure. His arrangements in the East mainly preserved the dispositions of Antony. In 30 libations for his *genius* were granted by the Senate; his tribunician competence was perhaps extended; he was authorized to create patricians. In 29 he celebrated his triumph and the temple of Janus was closed. Many legions were disbanded; new distributions of land were granted. In 28 Octavian held the census with Agrippa, reduced the Senate to some 800 members (later to 600), was appointed *princeps senatus*, revived ancient religious ceremonies, and dedicated a temple of Apollo on the Palatine. His policy was increasingly founded upon his prestige as victor, peace-bringer, and defender of Roman tradition. He was teaching the Italian people that Roman traditions were their traditions and old Roman virtue the eternal foundation of the Roman State. Poets, historians, and artists were at his side. The Republic had to be solemnly restored, because the Republic was deeply rooted in tradition. Yet the restoration had to be reconciled with the obvious fact that Octavian never seriously thought of laying down his power. He effectively controlled the State through his money and his soldiers (*see* ARMIES, ROMAN, 4).

4. On 13 Jan. 27 B.C., Octavian transferred the State to the free disposal of the Senate and People, but he received Spain, Gaul, and Syria (in addition to Egypt) for ten years as his province with the greater part of the army, while preserving his consulate (*see* IMPERIUM). On 16 Jan. he received among many honours the title Augustus (see following article), which proclaimed his superior position in the State. The month Sextilis was called Augustus. A golden shield was set up in the Senate-house with an inscription commemorating his valour, clemency, justice, and piety. Possibly he was granted other powers. The Republic was restored, because his powers depended on the Senate and were formally to last only for ten years. Yet the forces in his hands were overwhelming and supported a moral authority even greater. Half the Empire had already sworn allegiance to him. The oath was extended to the other provinces, and probably the soldiers took a special oath of allegiance to him. In the East the cult of Augustus was associated with the existing cult of Roma. In the West many forms of worship, especially of his *genius*, were wide-spread.

5. Expansion of the frontiers and reinforcement of the Roman penetration in semi-conquered territories were equally considered. The frontiers between Egypt and Ethiopia were secured by the campaigns of Cornelius Gallus (29 B.C.) and C. Petronius (25). Augustus himself directed the main phase of the final submission of Spain and the urbanization and organization of Spain and Gaul (27–25). In 25 Terentius Varro (q.v. 4) Murena crushed the Salassi in Val d'Aosta, but Aelius Gallus failed to conquer Arabia Felix (25–24). Galatia was annexed (25) and Juba appointed king of Mauretania. These were difficult years: Augustus was critically ill in 25 and 23 B.C. In 26 Cornelius Gallus (q.v. 3) was condemned. In 23 the conspiracy of Terentius Varro Murena was discovered and young Marcellus (q.v. 7), who had married Augustus' daughter Julia in 25, died. As Augustus had no son, the problem of a successor was urgent. Constitutional reforms seemed necessary. In 24 Augustus had been granted dispensation from certain laws. In July 23 he resigned the consulship, but obtained an *imperium proconsulare maius* in the senatorial provinces and the *tribunicia potestas* for life; this included the absolute right of veto and involved complete control of the State —the very end of the Roman Republic. Agrippa was honoured with an eastern command (23) and the hand of Julia (21); their sons Gaius and Lucius were eventually regarded as the future heirs. In 22 Augustus refused the dictatorship, but accepted the *cura annonae*; Gallia Narbonensis (in 22) and Hispania Baetica were transferred to senatorial administration. Augustus' travels in Sicily, Greece, and Asia (22–19) were probably of great importance for the civil organization; the most apparent result was the reconciliation with Parthia, which recognized the Roman protectorate in Armenia. An expedition against the Garamantes in Africa was successful (19). Possibly some consular privileges were granted to Augustus by the Senate in 19. Moral and religious reforms marked the years 18 and 17 B.C. The *lex Iulia de adulteriis* made adultery a public crime; the *lex Iulia de maritandis ordinibus* made marriage nearly compulsory and offered privileges to married people. A *lex sumptuaria* tried to reduce luxury. Members of senatorial families were forbidden to marry into families of freedmen. In 17 the *ludi saeculares* were celebrated. In 18 the powers of Augustus were extended for five years, while a co-regency was conferred upon Agrippa, and a new *lectio senatus* was held. In 17 Augustus adopted Gaius and Lucius, and in 14 he gave the Bosporan kingdom to Polemo of Pontus—an unsuccessful settlement. Three years of residence by Augustus in Gaul (15–13) marked the importance of the organization of Gaul and its frontiers. T. Statilius Taurus was left in Rome as *praefectus urbi*. In 16–15 Raetia and Noricum were annexed as Imperial provinces. About 15–14 the Imperial mint of Lugdunum was founded, and the Senate was reduced to controlling the copper coinage. At latest from 12 B.C. (when a new *lectio senatus* was made), the organization of the senatorial and equestrian orders and the *iuvenes* (qq.v.) was complete. In 13 the powers of Augustus and Agrippa were extended for five years. Agrippa's death in 12 was a blow. The death of Lepidus left the post of Pontifex Maximus open: Augustus, the head of the Roman Empire, became also the head of the Roman religion (12).

6. The substitution of Tiberius' and Drusus' influence for that of Agrippa was marked by new military activity. In several campaigns the frontier of Illyricum was advanced to the Danube (13–9 B.C.) and later Moesia was made a province. Meanwhile Drusus attempted to advance the Rhine frontier to the Elbe. In 9 the Ara Pacis (q.v.) was dedicated and (in 7?) the *collegia* (see CLUBS, ROMAN) were revised. In 8 the powers of Augustus were extended for ten years. Some time between 12 B.C. and A.D. 1 the Homonadeis in southern Galatia were defeated and in 6 Paphlagonia was added to Galatia. In 6 Tiberius received *tribunicia potestas*, but shortly afterwards retired to Rhodes through jealousy of Gaius Caesar, who in 5 was proclaimed *princeps iuventutis*.

7. The great creative period of the life of Augustus was over. His best collaborators were dead, including the poets, Virgil and Horace. Livy was left to witness his decline, Ovid to experience the severity of his moral code. Augustus politically favoured the upper classes, but he was careful to appeal in some measure to every class. The division of Rome into fourteen *regiones* in 7 B.C. gave the opportunity for associating the cult of the *genius* of the Emperor with the popular cult of the Lares Compitales. By the *leges Fufia Caninia* (2 B.C.) and *Aelia Sentia* (A.D. 4) manumission was limited and certain classes of slaves were excluded from the possibility of Roman citizenship. Augustus was also conservative in bestowing citizenship on provincials. In 2 B.C. he was saluted as *pater patriae*; he also banished Julia (q.v. 2). The deaths of Lucius Caesar (A.D. 2) and Gaius Caesar (A.D. 4) thwarted Augustus' plans for the succession, and he was compelled to adopt Tiberius, who again received *tribunicia potestas* for ten years. In A.D. 3 Augustus' own powers were extended for ten years. In A.D. 6 a new system was introduced to pay discharged soldiers from an *aerarium militare* (see AERARIUM); this superseded the necessity of founding military colonies, the last revolutionary survival. The privileged position of Italy in taxation was reduced by the imposition of two new taxes on legacies and sales. A body of seven *cohortes* of *vigiles* (q.v.) was established. In foreign affairs the year A.D. 6 was marked by the annexation of Judaea as a province and by the Pannonian rebellion which suddenly revealed the weakness of the Roman army, which had been reduced to twenty-eight legions (apart from the *auxilia*) and had been posted on the borders without a central reserve. Tiberius took three years to crush the rebellion (6–9), while the loss of three legions under Varus (q.v. 2) in Germany in 9 confirmed the insufficiency of the military organization. Augustus was shocked and decided to abandon Germany and to retain only twenty-five legions: conquest would involve increasing the army. The year A.D. 9 saw the last social law (*lex Papia Poppaea*), which mitigated the *lex Iulia de maritandis ordinibus* and offered further inducements to having children. In A.D. 13 Tiberius received *tribunicia potestas* and *imperium proconsulare* for another ten years. Augustus himself was granted ten more years of power. In April A.D. 13 he deposited his will in the house of the Vestals. It included a *breviarium totius imperii* (a summary of the military and financial resources) and the so-called *Monumentum Ancyranum* (q.v.). His mausoleum had been ready for many years. He died on 19 Aug. A.D. 14 at Nola, and on 17 Sept. the Senate decreed that he should be accepted among the gods of the State.

8. He had preserved the calm beauty of his person until his old age. He had never forgotten his studies, but no philosophic influence is demonstrable in his government. He wrote a pamphlet against Brutus about Cato Uticensis, an exhortation to philosophy, an autobiography dealing with the period before about 25 B.C., a biography of Drusus, a short poem about Sicily, a book of epigrams—all lost—and planned a tragedy on Ajax. His style was clear and simple, but, if necessary, majestic as his mind. When he entered political life, republican liberty was already dead. He tried to establish a government in which an accurate balance of classes and of countries gave the predominance to Roman tradition and Italian men without offending the provinces and without diminishing the Greek culture. He gave peace, as long as it was consistent with the interests of the Empire and with the myth of his glory. But he intended especially that the peace was to be the internal peace of the State. He assured freedom of trade and wealth to the upper classes. He did his enormous work in a simple way, living a simple life, faithful to his faithful friends. His superstition did not affect the strength of his will. Yet, as he never thought of real liberty, so he never attained to the profound humanity of the men who promote free life.

SOURCES: *Monumentum Ancyranum* (q.v.); Suetonius, *Life* (ed. Adams, 1939); Appian, *BCiv.* (only until 35 B.C.); Dio Cassius 45 ff.; Velleius Paterculus, etc. The contemporary poets and monuments are invaluable. For the coins see *British Museum Catalogue* i (1923). The minor fragments of Augustus' works are collected in H. Malcovati, *Caesaris Augusti . . . fragmenta*² (1928).

GENERAL LITERATURE: *CAH* x (1934) is the best reference-work, but cf. Mommsen, *Röm. Staatsr.*, especially vol. ii³ (1887) and M. Hammond, *The Augustan Principate* (U.S.A. 1933). Later works: A. v. Premerstein, *Vom Werden und Wesen des Prinzipats* (1937); *Augustus, Studi in occasione del Bimillenario Augusteo* (1938); R. Syme, *The Roman Revolution* (1939); J. Buchan, *Augustus Caesar* (1937); H. Andersen, *Cassius Dio und die Begründung des Prinzipates* (1938). G. Rodenwaldt, *Kunst um Augustus* (1942); M. Hammond 'Hellenistic influences in the structure of the Augustan principate', *Am. Ac. Rome* 1940, 1; P. de Francisci, 'Genesi e struttura del principato Augusteo', *Mem. Accad. Italia* 1941; W. Kolbe, *Klio* 1943, 26; M. Grant, *From Imperium to Auctoritas* (1946). For the portraits see O. Brendel, *Ikonographie des Kaisers Augustus* (1931) and *Augustus*, p. 374. See also K. Hönn, *Augustus im Wandel zweier Jahrtausende* (1938).   A. M.

AUGUSTUS, AUGUSTA (Gk. Σεβαστός, Σεβαστή). On 16 Jan. 27 B.C. Octavian received the title 'Augustus' from the Senate, wisely preferring this to the alternative offer of 'Romulus'. The word *augustus* had been used in Republican times at Rome only in a religious context— 'sancta uocant augusta patres', Ovid wrote (*Fast.* 1. 609) —and was readily contrasted with *humanus*. Though Augustus apparently intended that the title should be carried by his successor (Suet. *Tib.* 26), Tiberius at first hesitated to accept it (Dio Cass. 57. 2. 1; 8. 1. Compare the similar conduct of Vitellius in A.D. 69, Tac. *Hist.* 2. 62; 80.). It was held by all Roman emperors except Vitellius, and never by any other member of the Imperial family. The title 'Augusta' was bequeathed by Augustus to his wife Livia, granted by Gaius to his grandmother Antonia, by Claudius to his wife Agrippina, and by Nero to Poppaea. From Domitian's time it was normally conferred, on the initiative of the Senate, upon the wife of the reigning emperor.   J. P. B.

AULE, see HOUSES, GREEK.

AULIS, where the Greek fleet collected before sailing to Troy, is a small hill on the Euripus with a little land-locked harbour north and a deep bay south. The emigrants to Aeolis also claimed to have sailed thence (Strabo 9. 401), and Hesiod names it as a port (*Op.* 651); but it had no important later history.   T. J. D.

AULOS, see MUSIC, § 9.

AURELIA, Caesar's mother, of the house of Cotta, detected P. Clodius (q.v. 1) at the celebration of the Bona Dea. She died in 54 B.C.

AURELIANUS, LUCIUS DOMITIUS (c. A.D. 215–75), played a prominent part in the military plot that destroyed Gallienus (q.v., early A.D. 268). Appointed by Claudius II to the chief command of the cavalry, he served with distinction against the Goths, and, after the death of Claudius, was raised to the throne by the army in place of Quintillus (c. Mar. 270).

2. Barbarian invasions claimed his first attention. He defeated the Vandals in Pannonia and then repulsed a dangerous attack on Italy by the Juthungi, after a serious defeat at Placentia. A victory over the same people on the Danube, usually placed earlier, may belong to this same campaign. He then visited Rome, punished disaffected senators, quelled a serious rising of the 'monetarii', and surrounded Rome with walls, to prevent a surprise attack by the barbarians (*see* WALL OF AURELIAN). He also disposed of three rivals in the provinces—Septimus, Urbanus, and Domitianus.

3. Zenobia (q.v.), ruling Palmyra for her young son, Vaballathus, had occupied Egypt and Asia Minor up to Bithynia. Coins were struck for Vaballathus at Alexandria and Antioch as colleague of Aurelian. But the Emperor refused the compromise. He marched eastward, stopping on the way to repulse the Goths on the Danube

and withdraw the Romans from old Dacia to new Dacia on the right bank, and was only delayed for a short time by the siege of Tyana. The main Palmyrene army under Zabdas met him north of Antioch on the Orontes. Aurelian won a complete victory, occupied Antioch, stormed a post at Daphne, and advanced to Emesa. Here he again triumphed with some difficulty over the Palmyrene heavy cavalry. The provincials were won over by Aurelian's leniency, and Zenobia now withdrew to Palmyra. Aurelian followed and began the siege. Hampered at first by the desert tribes, Aurelian soon broke down resistance. Zenobia was captured on her way to seek aid from Persia, and Palmyra surrendered. At Emesa Aurelian held a trial and condemned Zenobia's chief adviser, Longinus, to death (summer 272).

4. Marching back westward, Aurelian defeated the Carpi on the Danube, but was recalled by the revolt of Palmyra. Striking without delay, Aurelian deposed the new king, Antiochus, and reduced Palmyra to a village. A wealthy merchant of Alexandria, Firmus, who tried with the aid of the Blemmyes to save Zenobia's cause, was soon crushed.

5. Aurelian now turned west and ended the Gallic Empire at Châlons, assisted by the desertion of the Emperor Tetricus himself (early 274). Tetricus, led with Zenobia in Aurelian's triumph, was then appointed 'corrector Lucaniae'.

6. Early in 275 Aurelian set out against Persia, but was murdered at Caenophrurium, near Byzantium, in a military plot, fostered by his secretary Eros (Mnestheus?). Some six months passed before Tacitus was appointed to succeed him—the army offering the choice to the Senate, the Senate shirking the dangerous responsibility.

7. Aurelian was an able but stern administrator. He suppressed informers and peculators, cancelled arrears of debts, issued bread in place of corn to the poor of Rome, and distributed free oil, pork, and salt. He seems to have given public organization to the guilds of bakers and shippers. He reformed the coinage, issuing new money for the old. In 274 he instituted the State cult of *Sol dominus imperii Romani*, with *pontifices* of senatorial rank. To the Senate he was a severe *paedagogus*. Towards the Christians he was at first not unfriendly and decided the strife between Paul of Samosata and Domnus for the see of Antioch in favour of the latter. But at the time of his death he was planning to renew the persecutions. Excessive severity marred a career of notable public service.

H. Mattingly, *CAH* xii. 297 ff.; Parker, *Roman World*, 194 ff.; L. Homo, *Essai sur le règne de l'empereur Aurélien* (1904); E. Groag, *PW*, s.v. 'Domitius (36)'.   H. M.

AURELIUS (1), **MARCUS** (*M. Annius Verus*) (A.D. 121–80), was son of Annius Verus (of consular Spanish stock, and brother of Faustina the Elder, q.v.) and Domitia Lucilla. He early gained the favour of Hadrian, who justly nicknamed him 'Verissimus', made him a Salian priest when only eight, betrothed him in 136 to the daughter of L. Aelius (q.v. 4), and supervised his education, the best teachers of rhetoric, grammar, philosophy, and law being employed to form his frank, serene, and sensitive character. With Aelius' son Lucius (=L. Verus, q.v.), he was adopted (as 'M. Aelius Aurelius Verus Caesar') by Antoninus Pius (q.v.) in 138. Quaestor in 139, and consul I with Pius 140, he was betrothed to Pius' daughter (his own cousin Faustina the Younger, q.v.), whom he married in 145, as *cos.* II; a daughter's birth (146) brought him also tribunician and proconsular power. Now aged twenty-five, a son-in-law of Pius, himself a father, and enjoying limited co-government with Pius, Marcus held a position clearly excelling that of Lucius (not *cos.* I until 154). This student, frail and yet austerely athletic, continued to live with Pius in close friendship and trust, ever loyal and deferential.

About 146–7 he deserted rhetoric, taught by his faithful Cornelius Fronto, for Stoic philosophy, which inspired all his future life.

2. Succeeding, as M. Aurelius Antoninus, on 7 Mar. 161, Marcus immediately petitioned the Senate that L. Verus, his fellow-consul, should receive (as L. Aurelius Verus) tribunician and proconsular power, and the title 'Augustus', in joint authority with himself; for the first time the Principate was collegiate, and the tie was emphasized by Verus' betrothal to Marcus' daughter Lucilla (q.v.), commemorated by a fresh alimentary institution. Revolt in Britain and Chattan aggression were settled; but in the East the Parthians, seizing Armenia, defeated two Roman armies and, in March 162, Marcus sent Verus thither with a strong force. Indulgent and dilatory, Verus did not arrive until 163; but Statius Priscus soon recovered Armenia (163–4), and Avidius (q.v.) Cassius invaded Mesopotamia and made it a Roman protectorate (166). Returning, Verus' troops brought a pestilence which swept the world. German tribes poured across the upper and lower Danube about 166, attacking even north Italy. Two new legions were hastily recruited; able generals and Marcus' insistence on a strong Dacia, now made a 'consular' province with two legions, saved a critical situation. Marcus and Verus reached Aquileia in 168; the invaders sought terms, and Italy was freed. Returning to Rome with Marcus in early 169, Verus died of apoplexy, relieving Marcus of an embarrassing partner.

3. Marcus now contemplated the permanent subjection of central and south-eastern Europe north of the Danube. After auctioning Imperial treasures to replenish the treasury, and marrying Lucilla to Ti. Claudius (q.v. 15) Pompeianus, he left Rome (169). From 170 to 174 he fought the Marcomanni and Quadi; and he successfully attacked the Sarmatian Iazyges (175). 'Marcomannia' and 'Sarmatia' came near provincialization. But plans were shelved when Avidius (q.v.) Cassius revolted; and Marcus merely defined a neutral zone north of the Danube, and settled, in depopulated areas south of the river, semi-romanized tribesmen under obligation to defend the frontiers—the first step in the de-romanization of the frontier-provinces. Cassius, proclaimed emperor (175) in Syria and Egypt, was soon murdered. But Marcus set out in alarm for Syria. In 176 he visited Egypt (uneasy since a Delta revolt in 172), and returned, via Syria, to Rome, to celebrate a great triumph. In 177 German tribes again vexed Pannonia, and Marcus, leaving Commodus (now 'Augustus', consul, holder of tribunician and proconsular power, and married to Crispina) in Rome, went north, defeating the Marcomanni (178). Now he could have possessed their territory, with that of the Quadi and Iazyges; but he died, swiftly and peacefully, on 17 Mar. 180. Consecrated by acclamation, he was sincerely mourned; the famous sculptured column was set up to commemorate his exploits.

4. Ironically, war thus dominated the philosopher's reign. To this is due much of the intensity of his 'Meditations'—devotional reflections, compiled in solitude during his campaigns, and breathing high Stoic principles. But Stoicism endangered Empire: 'self-sufficiency' did not encourage wide administrative experience based on personal contact: hence Marcus' faulty judgement in choosing Commodus as successor, and hence, too, increased bureaucracy. Circuit judges (iuridici) were revived for Italy (see HADRIAN); alimenta, fiscus, annona, and even the care of minors, were controlled by permanent officials; registration of free-born children was compulsory; the various grades of officialdom received distinguishing titles. Marcus' obvious duties were faithfully discharged: jurisdiction claimed his full care; and Senate and Knights were honourably treated. But generally he was an improver rather than an innovator: foresight and imagination were lacking. Long wars and many largesses (seven—a total of 850 denarii per head) emptied a treasury which auctions could not relieve; even the silver coin in currency dropped sharply in volume. The plague further depressed a weakening economy; local towns (their finances tottering) had commissioners imposed; and municipal initiative declined.

BIBLIOGRAPHY

ANCIENT SOURCES. (a) *Literary authorities*. The substantive but uncritical life of Marcus in the *Historia Augusta* is confused by interpolation. Copious excerpts from bks. 71–2 of Dio Cassius furnish useful material. The lives of L. Verus, Avidius Cassius, and Commodus in the *Historia Augusta* bear on that of Marcus. Minor references in Aurelius Victor and Eutropius. The *Meditations* of Marcus and Fronto's *Letters* are valuable evidence for Marcus' personal character. See A. S. L. Farquharson, *The Meditations of the Emperor Marcus Antoninus*, 2 vols. (1945).
(b) *Inscriptions*. PIR², A 697.
(c) *Coins*. H. Mattingly and E. A. Sydenham, *The Roman Imperial Coinage* iii (1930); H. Mattingly, *B.M. Coins, Rom. Emp.* iv (1940).
MODERN LITERATURE. H. D. Sedgwick, *Marcus Aurelius, a Biography*, &c. (1921); U. von Wilamowitz-Moellendorff, *Kaiser Marcus* (1931); A. von Premerstein, 'Untersuchungen zur Geschichte des Kaisers Marcus' in *Klio* xi–xiii (1911, 1912, 1913); H. M. D. Parker, *Roman World* (1935), part i; W. Weber in *CAH*. xi (1936), ch. 9; C. H. Dodd (Eastern and Danubian campaigns in the light of the coinage) in *Num. Chron.* 1911, 209 ff., 1913, 162 ff.; P. von Rohden, *PW*, s.v. 'Annius (94)'. See also bibliography in *CAH* xi (1936), 894 f.　　　　　C. H. V. S.

AURELIUS (2) ANTONINUS, MARCUS (A.D. 188–217), commonly called CARACALLA, became emperor in A.D. 211 (for early career *see* SEPTIMIUS SEVERUS, PLAUTIANUS).

After Septimius' death he made peace with the Caledonians and returned to Rome, where he assassinated his brother Geta, and became sole emperor in defiance of his father's wishes (212) (*see* GETA 1). To secure his position he bought the support of the Praetorians and the Legio II Parthica, and persecuted his brother's partisans.

In 213 Caracalla set out for Germany. Realizing that the army was his mainstay, he sought by indulgences to his soldiers to win for himself a popularity which his cruel and cowardly nature did not spontaneously arouse. Yet he was not devoid of strategical ability. The stone wall from Hienheim to Lorch was completed, and the Pfahlgraben in Upper Germany received its final form. In September the Alamanni were defeated and the Cenni (? Chatti) bought off by a subsidy.

Caracalla's next objective was the East, where in his assumed role of a second Alexander he hoped to realize his Utopia of a Romano-Iranian Empire. The year 214 was spent on the Danube fighting the Carpi and mobilizing an army, which included a phalanx of 16,000 equipped on the Macedonian model. Reaching Antioch in 215 the Emperor delayed his declaration of war against Parthia till the next year owing to disturbances in Alexandria. In 216 he invaded Media and spent the winter at Edessa preparing for a more intensive campaign, but was assassinated near Carrhae in April 217 (*see* OPELLIUS MACRINUS).

Caracalla's chief reform was his edict granting citizenship to all communities inside the Roman Empire except the *dediticii* (q.v. *and see* CITIZENSHIP, ROMAN). To pay for his extravagances (e.g. Baths at Rome) he increased by 5 per cent. the taxes on inheritances and manumissions, and resorted to a policy of monetary inflation by the issue of a new coin called the *Antoninianus*.

Herodian 4. 1–13; Dio Cassius 77–8; S.H.A.; W. Reusch, *Der Historische Wert der Caracalla-vita*; A. H. M. Jones, *JRS* xxvi. 223–35; Parker, *Roman World*, 89–101, 115–28; M. Besnier, *Histoire romaine* iv. 56–76; *CAH* xii, ch. 1, § 5.
　　　　　H. M. D. P.

AURELIUS (3) VICTOR, SEXTUS, an African, governor of Pannonia Secunda, A.D. 361, and *praefectus urbi*, 389, published *Caesares*, probably in 360, from Augustus to Constantius (360). Based on Suetonius, this Imperial history treated biographical material after a moralizing fashion, in the tradition of Sallust and Tacitus; the writer is heathen, interested in prodigies. The *Origo Gentis*

Romanae and *De Viris Illustribus* (Republican biography) associated with the *Caesares* in a *historia tripertita* are not by his hand; nor is the *Epitome de Caesaribus* (to Theodosius I, A.D. 395), which at the beginning follows the *Caesares*.

Ed. F. Pichlmayr (1911). A. H. McD.

AURELIUS, *see also* ANTONINUS, CARINUS, CARUS, COMMODUS, COTTA, MAXENTIUS, NUMERIANUS, PROBUS, SEVERUS.

AUREOLUS (proclaimed emperor A.D. 268), commander of the new cavalry corps based on Milan, helped Gallienus (q.v.) to overthrow Ingenuus in Pannonia (A.D. 258–9) and then, in 261, through his lieutenant Domitianus, crushed the Macriani, advancing westwards, on the borders of Thrace. Serving with Gallienus in Gaul in 263, by slackening his pursuit he allowed Postumus (q.v.) to escape. In 268, while Gallienus was fighting the Goths, Aureolus revolted in Raetia. Gallienus, returning, defeated him and besieged him in Milan. Coins of that mint, struck in the name of Postumus, prove Aureolus' alliance with the Gallic emperor. When Gallienus was assassinated, Aureolus surrendered to Claudius, but he had been proclaimed emperor during the siege, and his own soldiers killed him.

CAH xii. 173, 185–6, 189 ff.; Parker, *Roman World*, 168 ff., 181 ff. H. M.

AURUM CORONARIUM, a contribution in gold exacted by generals of the Roman Republic for the provision of crowns at their triumph. This gold seems to have been provided partly by the conquered people and partly by the province which the *triumphator* had governed. A law of Caesar (59 B.C.) enacted that it should not be demanded until a triumph had been formally decreed. Augustus prided himself on refusing *aurum coronarium* from the cities of Italy (*Mon. Anc.* 21). Later emperors accepted it fairly freely from the provinces (Spain and Gaul provided crowns to celebrate the conquest of Britain), but seldom from Italy. In the fourth century the burden of providing it fell upon the *decuriones* (q.v.). G. H. S.

AUSONES, *see* CAMPANIA.

AUSŎNIUS, DECIMUS MAGNUS (d. *c.* A.D. 395), was born at Bordeaux about the beginning of the fourth century. His studies were pursued at Bordeaux and Toulouse. For thirty years he taught in his native town, first as *grammaticus*, then as *rhetor*. Distinguished enough to attract the attention of the court, he was called by Valentinian to Trèves to be tutor to Gratian. He was on the staff of father and son in the campaigns against the Alamanni (368–9). After holding minor positions he became governor of Gaul, and later of other provinces. Finally, in 379, he was made consul. After the murder of Gratian (383) he returned to his early home, and added to the number of his poems, enjoying epistolary intercourse with various eminent men.

His numerous poems, written in various metres (hexameter, elegiac, hendecasyllabic, etc.), do not come so near the classical standard as those of Claudian, but are nevertheless of considerable interest, both in subject-matter and style. There are over a hundred epigrams, some of which are in Greek and others translated from Greek. There are twenty-five letters. His correspondence with Paulinus (q.v.) of Nola is the most notable part of these. The *Ephemeris* includes many poems in various metres, dealing with daily life. The *Parentalia* is a collection of short poems in memory of deceased relatives of the poet. The *Commemoratio Professorum Burdigalensium* is of great interest for the history of education. The *Ordo Nobilium Urbium* describes twenty notable cities of the Roman world. This account by no means exhausts the list of the minor poems, throughout which the author's minute knowledge of Virgil is apparent and his Christian faith is not obtruded. *See also* CENTO (LATIN).

His most important poem is the *Mosella*, still a charming guide-book to that river. It is in 483 hexameters, and describes in considerable detail the various fish to be found in it as well as some of the fine buildings on the banks and other features, not forgetting the vines, to be expected in such a laudatory poem.

Ed. R. Peiper (Teubner, 1886); H. G. Evelyn White, 2 vols. (Loeb, 1919–21); *Mosella*, C. Hosius (3rd ed., 1926). A. S.

AUSPICIUM, a term used by the Romans for certain types of divination, particularly from birds (*avis, specio*), designed to ascertain the pleasure or displeasure of the gods towards matters in hand. Despite ancient and modern attempts at definition, *auspicia* are hardly to be differentiated from *auguria*, and are not limited to signs derived from the number, position, flight, cries, and feeding of birds—particularly the sacred chickens, for which see AUGURES—but extend to other animals (Paul. ex Fest. p. 244 M. s.v. *pedestria auspicia*) or to inanimate phenomena. Festus and Paulus, pp. 261–262 M., record five types: *ex caelo, ex avibus, ex tripudiis, ex quadripedibus, ex diris*. Private auspices were early largely abandoned, save for weddings (Cic. *Div.* 1. 28), but public ones, taken by magistrates possessing the *ius auspiciorum* (or *spectio*) were important in civil and military life, and were retained by Cicero in *Leg.* 3. 10. They appear at elections, inauguration into office, entrance into a province, etc., and in the conduct of wars the phrase *ductu auspicioque* frequently recurs (*Thes. Ling. Lat.* v. 2171, 8–27). Since ex-officials, however, and, later, imperial legates lacked the *ius auspiciorum* (Cic. *Nat.D.* 2. 9, *Div.* 2. 76–7), even public auspices eventually fell into neglect, and at times pains were taken to avoid observing signs divinely vouchsafed (Cic. *Div.* 2. 77–8).

Observation was usually made from a *tabernaculum*, by a professional attendant of the magistrate (Cic. *Div.* 2. 71–2 preserves the ritual in the case of the sacred chickens), and *auspicia minora* (of the lesser magistrates) were sometimes superseded by *auspicia maiora* of consuls, praetors, or censors (Gell. 13. 15. 4). *Vitium*, a ritual defect or oversight, often nullified auspices, but *peremnia*, or rites at the crossing of streams (Cic. *Div.* 2. 77, Serv. *Aen.* 9. 24) provided against one type of *vitium*. Recrossing the *pomerium* (the bound between the civil and military spheres) required the taking of new auspices in order to avoid *vitium*, a famous instance being narrated by Cic. *Div.* 1. 33. For the military *auspicia ex acuminibus* see especially Cic. *Div.* 2. 77 and Pease ad loc.

For the subject in general and for bibliography, *see* DIVINATION. A. S. P.

AUTOCRATES, called an Athenian writer of Old Comedy by Suidas, who adds (no doubt wrongly) ἔγραψε καὶ τραγῳδίας. We know of only one play, Τυμπανισταί ('The Drummers').

FCG i. 270; *CAF* i. 806. H. J. R.

AUTOLYCUS (1), in mythology, maternal grandfather of Odysseus. He 'surpassed all men in thievery and (ambiguous) swearing', by favour of Hermes (whose son he is in later accounts), *Od.* 19. 394 ff.; one of his thefts, *Il.* 10. 267; later stories in von Sybel in Roscher's *Lexikon, s.v.* H. J. R.

AUTOLYCUS (2) of Pitane (fl. *c.* 310 B.C.), astronomer and author of the earliest Greek mathematical text-book that has come down to us entire, *On the Moving Sphere* (Περὶ κινουμένης σφαίρας), a geometrical work treating of the poles and the principal circles of the sphere; many of its propositions are used by Euclid in his *Phaenomena*. Another work of Autolycus, in two books, is Περὶ ἀνατολῶν καὶ δύσεων, *On risings and settings* ('true' and 'apparent').

Both works are edited by F. Hultsch (Teubner, 1885); see also Pappus (bk. 6) on the 'Little Astronomy' (Μικρὸς ἀστρονομούμενος). Autolycus, in a controversy with Aristotherus, criticized Eudoxus' hypothesis of concentric spheres on the ground that it did not account for the planets being at different distances from the earth at different times (Simpl. on *De Caelo* 504–5 Heib.).

PW ii. 2602.   T. H.

AUTOMEDON, in mythology, Achilles' charioteer, son of Diores (*Il.* 17. 429 and often); hence by metonymy, any charioteer, as Juvenal 1. 61.

AUTONOMY, one of the leading ideas of the Greek *polis* (q.v.), meant to the *polis* not merely the right of self-government, but the right and the possibility of using its own laws and constitution. Therefore in the Peloponnesian War Sparta pretended to be fighting for the autonomy of the Greek States, which in the Athenian Empire had been forced to establish democratic governments. Autonomy was mostly connected with, but not clearly distinguished from, the idea of freedom (*eleutheria*). Though mainly concerning the interior life of the *polis*, autonomy was, since the fourth century B.C., an instrument of inter-Hellenic policy, and the chief reason of the failure of all attempts to create a Greek empire. As Persian and Macedonian supremacy over Greek towns was mainly based on local tyrants or oligarchies, autonomy thereafter implied a free democratic constitution. Under the Hellenistic kings, however, the autonomy of the Greek States was often very precarious, and sometimes it did not exclude even a royal garrison, compulsory taxation, or actual supervision by a king's official.

V. Ehrenberg, *Der Griechische Staat* (Gercke–Norden, *Einleitung in d. Altertumswissenschaft*[3] iii (part 3), 43 f., 82 ff.); A. Heuss, *Stadt und Herrscher des Hellenismus*, 240 ff.   V. E.

AUTRONIUS PAETUS, PUBLIUS, was consul designate with P. Cornelius Sulla in 66 B.C., but their election was declared void because of bribery. He joined Catiline in the two unsuccessful conspiracies. He escaped arrest in 63, but was condemned in 62. He went into exile at Epirus, where he still was during Cicero's banishment.
                                                         A. M.

AUXESIA and DAMIA, obscure goddesses of fertility (Hdt. 5. 82. 2 ff.), worshipped at Epidaurus and Aegina, with ritual abuse (ibid. 83. 4); at Troezen, with ritual stone-throwing (Λιθοβόλια, Paus. 2. 32. 2), where the local legend made them Cretan virgins stoned in a disturbance. *See* BONA DEA.   H. J. R.

AUXILIA. During the last two centuries of the Republic Rome made good her deficiency in cavalry and light-armed troops with contingents raised outside Italy. These *auxilia* greatly increased in number during the civil wars and formed the nucleus of the permanent auxiliary army established by Augustus (*see* MERCENARIES). This force was recruited from provincials who had not yet received the franchise. Thus in the Julio-Claudian period Gallia Comata and Hispania Tarraconensis provided a large quota of *auxilia*, while Narbonensis and Baetica, two romanized provinces, were areas for legionary recruiting. Service was sometimes, as with the Batavi, accepted in lieu of tribute. At first the different units were normally stationed near their homes, but after the revolts in Pannonia (A.D. 6–9) and of Civilis (A.D. 69) this policy was gradually abandoned. Spanish auxiliaries are found in Illyricum as early as the Principate of Tiberius, and after A.D. 70 many German and Gallic units were sent to Britain. As their numbers were kept up by local recruiting, the *auxilia* gradually lost their native character, and the titles borne by the units ceased to indicate the origin of their soldiers. Exception must be made of the Oriental cohorts of archers, which were maintained at strength by drafts from their home countries.

2. The auxiliary units bore titles which were normally geographical (*Asturum, Lusitanorum, Gallica*), but sometimes honorific (*Augusta, Pia, Fidelis*), or indicative of the general or *princeps* who raised them (*Siliana, Aelia*). They were numbered, but not consecutively, a fresh series starting when new regiments were enlisted some time after the original levy. This inconvenient system renders difficult any assessment of the total strength of the *auxilia*. Probably it ranged from 130,000 under Augustus to approximately 225,000 in the second century.

3. The *auxilia* comprised both cavalry and infantry, the former organized in *alae*, the latter in *cohortes*, either 1,000 or 500 strong, while there were some mixed units (*cohortes equitatae*). They were commanded by *praefecti*, who at first were commonly tribal chiefs or ex-centurions and later young equestrians. Under them were centurions and decurions.

4. After twenty-five years' service, which in the second century coincided with his discharge, an auxiliary soldier received the franchise for himself and his descendants. After A.D. 140 these privileges were restricted to personal citizenship and legalization of future but not existing offspring.

5. During the second century the *auxilia* became assimilated to the legions and after Caracalla's edict their distinctive character was largely lost. In the barbarian invasions of the third century many units were destroyed, and in the Constantinian reorganization *alae* and *cohortes* are relegated to the *Limitanei*. *See* ALAE, COHORS, DIPLOMA, PRAEFECTUS.

G. L. Cheesman, *The Auxilia of the Imperial Roman Army* (1914); W. Wagner, *Die Dislokation der römischen Auxiliarformationen in den Provinzen Noricum, Pannonien, Moesien und Dakien* (1938).
                                                  H. M. D. P.

AUXUME, *see* AXUMIS.

AVENTINE, an abrupt plateau overlooking the Tiber and separated from the other hills of Rome by the Murcia valley. It formed *regio* XIII of Rome, while an eastward lobe (*regio* XII, *Piscina publica*) was known as *Aventinus* to Dionysius, Varro, and Festus, and later as *Aventinus minor*, though perhaps not originally so called (Cic. *Div.* 1. 107, quoting Ennius). The hill was *ager publicus* (q.v.), given to the *plebs* for settlement in 456 B.C. It already held two pre-Republican temples, to Diana, patroness of a Latin league, and to Luna; also the Loretum, reputed a regal tomb, and the *armilustrium* (where arms were ritually purified). These connexions are with Latium rather than Rome, and the hill lay until A.D. 49 outside the *pomerium* (q.v.). Other early temples were those of Juno Regina (396–392 B.C.) and Jupiter Libertas (238 B.C.), the latter housing Varro's library presented by Asinius Pollio. Here also dwelt Ennius (q.v.), in the plebeian quarter whose early and thriving prosperity is represented by the *clivus Publicius*, a street development of 238 B.C.   I. A. R.

AVERNUS, a deep lake near Puteoli. Its unusual name (fancifully derived from ἀ-όρνις), its reputed immense depth, and its situation amid gloomy-looking woods and mephitic exhalations inspired the belief that it led to the underworld (Strabo 5. 244; Verg. *Aen.* 6. 237 f.; Lucr. 6. 740 f.; Livy 24. 12). Agrippa temporarily remedied its lack of a natural outlet.   E. T. S.

AVERRUNCUS, minor Roman deity who averts (*averruncat*) evil, Varro, *Ling.* 7. 102.

AVIANUS (fl. *c.* A.D. 400), Roman fabulist; he dedicated his forty-two fables in elegiac metre to Macrobius (q.v.) Theodosius, author of the *Saturnalia*. Nothing more is known of his life. His chief source is the Greek fabulist, Babrius. With few exceptions, his fables are expanded paraphrases of their Babrian prototypes; and the exceptions are probably based on lost fables of Babrius. A.'s style is picturesque; he expands his models by elaborating the descriptive element; but his effort to introduce Virgilian and Ovidian phrases produces a strained and sometimes mock-heroic effect. Mingled with classical echoes, there are frequent instances of a degenerate Latin (R. Ellis ed. xxxvi ff.). The metre is correctly Ovidian except for a few lapses showing the decline of metrical strictness in A.'s age. Paraphrases, scholia, and quotations show that A. was popular in medieval schools. Stronger evidence is afforded by the *promythia* and *epimythia* attached to some of the fables to point a moral. Most of these were composed in medieval times; but some *epimythia* may come from A. himself.

Texts: E. Baehrens, *PLM* v (1883); R. Ellis (1887); (with translation) J. W. and A. M. Duff, *Minor Latin Poets* (Loeb, 1934). A. M. D.

AVIDIUS (1) NIGRINUS, Gaius, probably son of Avidius Nigrinus, plebeian tribune in A.D. 105, governed Achaea (perhaps temporarily an imperial province) with special powers (*SIG*³ 827; cf. *CIL* iii. 107). Possibly he was also governor of Upper Moesia. Rich, influential, and well connected (he was father-in-law of L. Aelius, q.v. 4), he was thought to be Hadrian's selected successor; but he became involved in the conspiracy of the four 'consulars' against Hadrian (q.v.) in 118, and was killed by senatorial order, with his complicity unproved or at least unpublished.

S.H.A. *Had.*; Dio Cassius, bk. 69; *PIR*², A 1408; cf. *CAH* xi (1936), 220. C. H. V. S.

AVIDIUS (2) CASSIUS, Gaius (d. A.D. 175), son of the equestrian C. Avidius Heliodorus (a rhetorician of Cyrrhus in Syria, and an official under Hadrian and Antoninus Pius), was consul early in the reign of M. Aurelius (q.v. 1) and afterwards governor of Syria. He sternly drilled the Syrian legions into efficiency, thrust east against Parthia, subdued Mesopotamia and captured Seleuceia and Ctesiphon (A.D. 165–6). Subsequently given supreme command over all the East (with Egypt, where he quelled a revolt in 172), he proclaimed himself emperor in 175, with the support of Egypt and of all the East save Cappadocia and Bithynia; false reports of M. Aurelius' death helped him, and even Faustina the Younger (q.v.) was said to be in collusion. Three months later he was assassinated. Avidius issued no coinage.

S.H.A. *Avidius Cassius*; Dio Cassius 72; *PIR*², A 1402; P. Lambrechts, *La Composition du Sénat romain . . . (117–192)* (1936), p. 117, no. 694. See also under AURELIUS (1). C. H. V. S.

AVIENUS, Festus Ruf(i)us (4th c. A.D.), Latin writer to whom are ascribed: (i) *Descriptio Orbis Terrae* (title varies), 1,394 extant hexameters (material based, sometimes closely, but with omissions, additions, and amplifications, on Dionysius Periegetes, q.v. 10) describing noteworthy things in physical and political geography, and reproducing in vigorous style much ancient ignorance which learned contemporaries could have corrected; (ii) *Ora Maritima*, 703 extant iambics (from a much larger work?) mostly about the coast from Massilia to Gades, with little order and much irrelevance, full of ancient nomenclature and ignorance, but giving interesting material from early records of Greek and Carthaginian voyages in the Atlantic c. 500 B.C.; (iii) *Aratea Phaenomena* (1,325 extant hexameters) and *Aratea Prognostica* (552 hexameters) based on Aratus, sometimes closely,

often expanding, attractive in style; (iv) three short works (two personal, one on the Sirens and Ulysses). Avienus, born at Vulsinii, held high office. See DIDACTIC POETRY, LATIN.

Texts: A. Holder (1887); *Ora Maritima*, A. Schulten and P. Bosch-Gimpera (1922); A. Berthelot (1934). E. H. W.

AVILLIUS FLACCUS, Aulus, a friend of Tiberius and prefect of Egypt (A.D. 32–8). He was friendly to the Greek elements in Egypt and therefore his policy was anti-Jewish. Philo (q.v. 1) directed Εἰς Φλάκκον against him. In 38 he was unexpectedly arrested, condemned at Rome, perhaps on a charge of plotting with Ti. Gemellus and Macro, banished to Andros, and later put to death.

H. I. Bell, *CAH* x. 309; H. Box, *Philonis Alexandrini in Flaccum* (1939); A. v. Premerstein, *Alexandrinische Geronten vor Kaiser Gaius* (1939). A. M.

AVĪTUS, Alcimus Ecdicius, Bishop of Vienne (c. A.D. 490–518), a vigorous opponent of Arianism, author of sermons, letters, a biblical epic in five books, and a short poem on chastity.

Edition: Peiper, *MGH* (1883).

AXAMENTA (n. pl.), hymns in Saturnian verse sung by the Salii, apparently not addressed to individual gods (Paul. ex Fest. p. 3, 12 tr.).

AXE, DOUBLE, in Minoan religion, *see* RELIGION (MINOAN-MYCENAEAN), para. 1.

AXINOMANCY, *see* DIVINATION, para. 6.

AXIONICUS, Middle Comedy poet, perhaps late in the period (fr. 2 mentions Gryllis, a parasite of one of Alexander's generals). In Φιλευριπίδης, 'Lover of Euripides', fr. 4 is modelled on a tragic monody.

FCG iii. 530 ff.; *CAF* ii. 411 ff.

AXONES, the white wooden tablets of laws, in the Prytaneum at Athens, revolving on an axis. Draco's and Solon's laws were written on them, and they were quoted by the number of the *axon*; the highest known number is sixteen (Plut. *Sol.* 23. 4). Copies of Solon's laws were published on similar pillars of stone, the so-called κύρβεις. They were used elsewhere, too, as a fragment found at Chios shows.

Swoboda, *PW*, s.v. V. E.

AXUMIS or **AUXUME** (mod. *Axum*), a city in the Tigré province of Abyssinia. In the first century A.D. it became the royal seat of the Habashat or Axumites, who, through their port Adulis, traded busily with Arabians, Greeks, Romans, and Indians, eclipsing Meroë. In the second century A.D. the Axumites were powerful in Somaliland and possibly in Arabia also, controlling much of the traffic to India from that time until far in the Byzantine era. Fragments of their history are known from inscriptions and classical references. Some of the kings were Christians, and important relations were maintained with the West. The summit of Axumite influence was reached in the fourth and fifth centuries A.D.

See A. Wylde, *Modern Abyssinia* (1901) (for antiquities); Warmington, *Indian Commerce*, index, 'Axumites' (for commerce); J. Bent, *The Sacred City of the Ethiopians* (1893), appendix by D. Müller (inscriptions); Pietschmann, *PW*, s.v. E. H. W.

B

BABRIUS, VALERIUS (?), probably a hellenized Roman, who composed not later than the second century A.D. (*POxy.* 10, n. 1249) μυθίαμβοι Αἰσώπειοι, being versions in choliambic metre of existing fables, together with some original additions. The work was originally in ten books (Suidas); in the existing MS. tradition it consists of two, of which the second is incomplete. The metre and the language, which is that of everyday life, are well adapted to the subject-matter. The collection enjoyed great popularity.

Sources: Suidas; Avianus (*prooem.*). Editions: W. G. Rutherford (comment., 1883); O. Crusius (Teubner, pref., 1897). Criticism: O. Crusius, 'De B. aetate', *Leipz. Stud.* ii (1879).   W. M. E.

BABYLON (1) (mod. *Bâbil*), ancient capital of the south Semitic kingdom of Mesopotamia (*see* BABYLONIA) on the river Euphrates. It was one of the greatest cities in the ancient world. Herodotus, who claimed to have visited it, gives a somewhat inaccurate description of its wonders (1. 178–87). It attained its highest prosperity under the Chaldean kings of the New Babylonian Empire. Its history thenceforward is one of gradual decline. The Persians, who conquered it in 538 B.C., made it the chief city of the Babylonian satrapy; it was the winter residence of the Great King. Alexander, like Cyrus, entered Babylon without resistance; his project of rebuilding it and making it the capital city of his empire was frustrated by his death there in 323.

In Hellenistic times Babylon was still a prosperous city with a considerable Greek population. A frequent bone of contention among Alexander's successors and twice the centre of revolt against the Seleucids, it was more than once sacked. It suffered still more from the foundation of Seleuceia (q.v. 1) as the new commercial centre of Babylonia (Pliny, *HN* 6. 122). In the Parthian period Babylon again became the chief city of a satrapy, but it declined rapidly; Trajan in A.D. 115 found little but ruins. Many of the public buildings, temples, palaces, etc., and the city walls have been excavated.

R. Koldewey, *Das wiedererstehende Babylon* (Engl. Transl. 1915). E. Unger, *Babylon* (1931).

(2) Fortified town at the head of the Delta of Egypt; the head-quarters of a Roman legion under the Early Empire.   M. S. D.

BABYLONIA, the more southerly of the two ancient kingdoms of Mesopotamia. Its geographical limits were not clearly defined. Ptolemy (5. 20) says that it was bounded by Mesopotamia, Arabian desert, the Persian Gulf, and the river Tigris. It was sometimes included in the wider designation Assyria (q.v.).

In 538 B.C. the New Babylonian Empire fell before the Persians, and the country became an Achaemenid satrapy. Conquered by Alexander and intended as the centre of his empire, it was disputed among the *Diadochi*; Seleucus I Nicator founded Seleuceia (q.v.) to replace Babylon as the capital city. When the eastern portion of the Seleucid Empire passed to the Parthians, Babylonia became an important commercial and administrative centre; Ctesiphon, the Parthian residence, became the capital of the Sassanids.

Through all vicissitudes, until the Sassanian epoch, Babylonia retained its ancient civilization, the religion, cuneiform writing, and economic organization which it had inherited from Sumer. An attempt of Antiochus Epiphanes to hellenize it failed. In the Greek cities the native element was at first segregated, but most of the numerous Greek residents became orientalized, as the numerous business documents from Babylon and Orchoi (*Uruk*) testify. The country played an important part, politically and commercially, as the bridge between East and West. It was far more extensively cultivated than to-day, and was proverbially fertile (Hdt. 1. 193; Strabo 16. 742).

K. Holzhey, *Assur und Babel in der Kentniss der griechisch-römischen Welt* (1921); J. Jordan, *Uruk-Warka* (1928); E. Meissner, *Babylonien und Assyrien* (1920); P. Schnabel, *Berossos und die babylonisch-hellenistische Literatur* (1923); M. Rostovtzeff, *Seleucid Babylonia* (U.S.A. 1932), *CAH* vii, ch. 5. *See also* SELEUCEIA. Cuneiform Texts: A. T. Clay, *Legal Documents from Erech* (1913); M. Rutten, *Contrats de l'époque séleucide* (1935); S. Smith, *Babylonian Historical Texts* (1924).   M. S. D.

BACCHAE, *see* MAENADS.

BACCHANALIA, the Latin name of the Dionysiac *orgia*. They are especially known because of the harsh measures taken by the Roman Senate to repress them. The decree of 186 B.C. is preserved (*CIL* i. 196; *ILS* 18), and Livy (39. 8–18) has a long account. They were widespread in southern Italy. The first trace is an inscription of the fifth century B.C. from Cumae forbidding those who were not initiated in the Bacchic mysteries to be buried in a certain place (figured in Cumont, op. cit. infra, p. 197). Evidently they came from Campania to Rome, bringing much disorder under the cover of religion. It has been suggested that there is a connexion between the decree mentioned and a regulation of the Bacchic mysteries in Egypt by Ptolemy IV at the end of the third century B.C. (C. Cichorius, *Römische Studien*, 1922, p. 21). In the first centuries A.D. the Dionysiac mysteries were very popular, as is proved e.g. by the many sarcophagi with Dionysiac motifs and the paintings in the Villa Item at Pompeii (their interpretation is highly controversial). Very important is the large inscription of Agrippinilla from the beginning of the second century A.D. enumerating the officials of a Bacchic *thiasus*. Cumont is of the opinion that Oriental elements were dominant, but it seems that these mysteries were fundamentally Greek.

F. Cumont, *Les Religions orientales dans le paganisme romain*⁴, 195 ff.; T. Frank, *CQ* xxi (1927), 128 ff. The inscription in the Metropolitan Museum is edited by A. Vogliano and F. Cumont, *AJArch.* xxxvii (1933), 215 ff. M. P. Nilsson in *Studi e materiali della storia di religioni*, x (1934), 1 ff. The paintings of the Villa Item, A. Maiuri, *La villa dei misteri*; *JDAI* xliii, pls. 5–9; *JRS* iii (1913), pls. 8–13.   M. P. N.

BACCHIADAE, *see* CORINTH (para. 2), CYPSELUS.

BACCHEIUS (Βακχεῖος) **GERON,** author of an Εἰσαγωγὴ τέχνης μουσικῆς, lived in the time of Constantine (A.D. 274–337). The work is in the form of question and answer; while following in the main the tenets of Aristoxenus, it borrows freely from other schools of musical theory.

Ed. C. Jan, *Musici Scriptores Graeci* (1895), 283–316. *PW* ii. 2790.   W. D. R.

BACCHUS, *see* DIONYSUS, para. 3.

BACCHYLIDES (fl. 5th c. B.C.), lyric poet, of Iulis in Ceos, son of Midylus (*EM* 582, 20) and nephew of Simonides (Strabo 486, Suid. s.v. Βακχυλίδης). He may have been born about 524–521 (*Chron. Pasch.* 304. 6), though Eusebius–Jerome gives his *floruit* both in 467 B.C. and in 431 B.C. Remains of fourteen epinician odes and six dithyrambs found in 1896 at Al-Kussiyah may be arranged tentatively in a chronological order. He seems to have followed the fortunes of his uncle Simonides and to have been employed by the same patrons, a fact which sometimes brought him into competition with

Pindar, who was almost his contemporary. His first activities may have been in Thessaly (fr. 15, Ode 14) and Macedonia, where he wrote his Encomium for Alexander son of Amyntas (fr. 20 B). About 487 B.C. he wrote Ode 13 for Pytheas of Aegina, and Ode 12 may belong to the same period. Again like his uncle, he wrote dithyrambs for the competitions at Athens, notably Ode 19, and Ode 18, which is unique in being a dialogue between the leader of the chorus, who takes the part of Aegeus, and the remainder, who represent his followers. It is not clear whether this is a survival of an older form of dithyramb or has been influenced by the technique of Attic drama. Ode 17, which may belong to the early years of the Delian League, is really a paean sung by a Cean choir at Delos. The date of Ode 10, written for an Athenian victor in the Isthmian Games, is not known. About 476 B.C. Bacchylides accompanied Simonides to Sicily as the guest of Hieron (Ael. *VH* 4. 15) after writing Ode 5 for Hieron's victory in the horse-race at Olympia, an event celebrated by Pindar in *Ol.* 1. In Sicily he seems to have incurred the dislike of Pindar, who is thought to make disparaging references to him in *Ol.* 2. 86–8, *Pyth.* 2. 72–3, *Nem.* 3. 80–2. It is not known how long he stayed in Sicily, but his connexion with it was maintained with Ode 4 for Hieron's victory in the Pythian horse-race of 470 B.C., for which Pindar wrote *Pyth.* 1, and Ode 3 for the Olympian chariot-victory of 468 B.C., when Pindar may have written *Pyth.* 2. To his later years belong Odes 6 and 7 for Lachon of Ceos in 452. He is said to have been exiled to the Peloponnese (Plut. *De exil.* 14), and in this period he may have written Ode 9 for Automedes of Phlius, and the dithyramb *Idas* for the Lacedaemonians (20). The date of his death is not known.

Bacchylides also wrote hymns (frs. 1–2), paeans, of which fr. 4 contains a fine eulogy of peace, processional songs (frs. 11–13), maiden-songs (Plut. *De mus.* 17), hyporchemata (frs. 14–16), encomia, like that to Alexander (fr. 20 B) and to Hieron (fr. 20 C). His reputation has suffered by the comparisons with Pindar, which are at least as old as 'Longinus' (*De Subl.* 33). His gifts are of a different kind: a brilliant clarity and sense of narrative, a real love for the games which he describes, an absence of didactic fervour, a choice command of epithets, and occasional moments of magical beauty.

Text: B. Snell (Teubner, 1934). Commentaries: R. C. Jebb (1905); H. Jurenka (1898); A. Taccone (1907). Criticism: A. Severyns, *Bacchylide* (1933): W. K. Prentice, *De Bacchylide Pindari artis socio et imitatore* (Diss. Halle, 1900). C. M. B.

BACIS. Although used by Herodotus (8. 20) as if a proper name, later references make it clear that B. was the generic title of a class of inspired prophets, characteristic of the growth of ecstatic religion in the seventh and sixth centuries B.C.

E. Rohde, *Psyche* (Engl. Transl. 1925), 292 ff.

BACTRIA with southern Sogdiana (northern Afghanistan and part of Russian Turkestan) was the country of the middle Oxus, a fertile irrigated land known to Greeks as the Jewel of Iran. Traditionally the home of Zoroaster and the Zend Avesta, it formed a Persian satrapy which also included part of the Jaxartes basin (northern Sogdiana) and was often governed by an Achaemenid prince. It fought desperately against Alexander, and the Seleucids had Sogdian blood through Seleucus' wife Apama. In Persian times it was middleman for the Siberian gold supply, but the route was cut before the Greek period. As an independent kingdom under Euthydemus and his son Demetrius (qq.v.) the country attained great prosperity and included, besides Sogdiana, Merv, part of Khorasan, and Ferghana (Kwarizm its kings never ruled). Bactria had no gold and little silver, and Euthydemus' attempt to restore the gold route failed; its strength, which enabled it to hold off the nomads and annex

northern India, was due to its fertility, good government, and extensive trade; it was middleman for the overland trade between India and the West, and was beginning to reach out to Mongolia and China. The Seleucid eparchies (subdivisions of satrapies) were turned into satrapies, i.e. primary units of administration, an example followed throughout Asia. The capital, Alexandria-Bactra (*Balkh*), was probably only semi-Greek, and few Greek cities are recorded, but there was a large Greek settlement, which implies many military colonies; the essential matter, however, was that the Euthydemids made a united country, both securing the co-operation of the Iranian barons, who furnished its famous cavalry, and transforming the open peasant villages into quasi-autonomous communities within walls. After Demetrius' death Eucratides' line ruled till about 130 B.C., when Bactria was conquered by the nomad Yueh-chi (Kushans). As Tocharistan, they governed it for centuries; the country became a centre of Buddhism, and (after 106) Bactra was the clearing-house for the overland Chinese trade.

W. W. Tarn, *The Greeks in Bactria and India* (1938), passim. W. W. T.

BAEBIUS TAMPHILUS, MARCUS, praetor in 192 B.C., with an advance guard covered the Roman landing in Greece against Antiochus. Consul in 181, he transported 40,000 mountain Ligurians to Samnium (*Ligures Corneliani et Baebiani*, *ILS* 6509). To him are attributed the Baebian measure on the number of praetorships (Livy 40. 44. 2) and the *Lex Baebia de ambitu* (Livy 40. 19. 11).

Livy 35. 20–4; 36; 40. 38. F. Münzer, *Röm. Adelsparteien und Adelsfamilien* (1920), 195. A. H. McD.

BAETICA, the heart of the province originally (197 B.C.) called Farther Spain. As the territory occupied by the Romans increased, a clear-cut line between Hither and Farther Spain was formed beginning at the Mediterranean south of Carthago Nova (*Cartagena*) and running west-north-west to the Anas (*Guadiana*) at Lacimurga (*Villavieja*); thence northward to the Pyrenees. Augustus separated the prosperous and pacified area from the less settled west (Lusitania, q.v.) by a line roughly parallel to the Anas from Lacimurga to the Atlantic, and assigned the new province, Baetica, to the Senate. Four *conventus* (Gades, Corduba, Astigi, Hispalis) made convenient judicial circuits for the 175 towns of the province (Pliny, *HN* 3. 7). Most important was the rich Baetis (*Guadalquivir*) valley from which wine, oil, wheat, honey, sheep, fish, copper, lead, cinnabar, and silver were exported to Rome. The wealth of the country attracted pirate-bandits from Africa (A.D. 178), while the Vandals tarried there long enough to attach their name to the country (*Andalusia*). The cultural contribution of Spain to Rome was made by the predominantly Baetic Spanish school of letters of the first century A.D.

R. Thouvenot, *Essai sur la province romaine de Bétique* (1940). J. J. VAN N.

BAGAUDAE, Gallic peasants of the later Empire who took to brigandage. A rebellion of Bagaudae was crushed by Maximian in A.D. 285, but they are mentioned in the fifth century as still active against the State.

Jullian, *Hist. de la Gaule* vii. 51–6; viii. 174–6; *MGH* ix. 660; Salvian, *de Gubernatione Dei* v. 24.

BAIAE, a town on an inlet of the Bay of Naples, reputedly named after Baios, Odysseus' companion (Strabo 5. 245). Baiae never became a *municipium*; originally perhaps the port of Cumae, it remained Cumaean territory. Its sulphur-springs (whence its earlier name *Aquae Cumanae*: Livy 41. 16), mild climate, and beautiful surroundings made it a fashionable, even licentious, resort (Mart. 11. 80). Imposing villas were erected here by

Julius Caesar, Caligula, Nero, Alexander Severus, and others. Baiae declined owing to malaria, already present in Republican times (Cic. *Fam.* 9. 12), and earthquakes.

E. T. S.

BALBINUS, Decius Caelius Calvinus and **PUPIE-NUS MAXIMUS,** Marcus Clodius, members of a board of twenty appointed for the defence of Italy against Maximinus, were after the deaths of Gordian I and II chosen joint emperors by the Senate (A.D. 238). The former belonged to a noble family, the latter was an experienced officer. Constitutionally, on the model of the consulate, they had equal powers, each being Pontifex Maximus; but Balbinus was entrusted with the civil administration and Pupienus with the command of the army. To placate the soldiers, Gordian III was given the status of Caesar.

At the news of Maximinus' murder Pupienus proceeded to Aquileia and sent back the former's legions to their provinces, and with his German bodyguard returned to Rome to share a triumph with Balbinus and Gordian. For a few days the joint government worked smoothly, but soon the Emperors became jealous. The issue was, however, decided by the Praetorians, who resented the Senate's action and disliked the presence of a German bodyguard in Rome. The two Emperors were dragged from their palace and murdered after ruling for three months (*see* GORDIAN I and III).

For bibliography *see* MAXIMINUS (1). H. M. D. P.

BALBUS (1), Marcus Atius, born at Aricia, was husband of Caesar's sister Julia, and father of Atia, Augustus' mother. Praetor before 59 B.C., he was commissioner for the *Lex Iulia agraria* (59).

M. Grant, *From Imperium to Auctoritas* (1946), 150 ff.

BALBUS (2), Lucius Cornelius (*Maior*), of Gades, acquired Roman *civitas* for service against Sertorius, taking his *nomen* probably from the consul of 72 B.C. (cf. Cic. *Balb.* 19). He removed to Rome, where his political sense and the wealth derived from his adoption (*c.* 59) by Theophanes of Mytilene gave him enormous influence. Chief architect of the coalition of 60 B.C., he gradually shifted his allegiance from Pompey to Caesar, serving the latter as *praefectus fabrum* in Spain and Gaul, and later managing his interests in Rome. In 56 he was prosecuted for illegal usurpation of the *civitas*, and successfully defended by Cicero in the extant speech. In the Civil War he was outwardly neutral, and persistently tried to persuade Cicero and Lentulus (q.v. 7) Crus to join him. Actually he favoured Caesar, and after Pharsalus became, with Oppius, Caesar's chief agent in public affairs. In 44 he supported Octavian, though cautiously, and in 40 became Rome's first foreign-born consul. Author of a published diary (now lost), and recipient and editor of Hirtius' commentaries, he had wide literary interests over which he constantly corresponded with Cicero. He bequeathed 25 *denarii* to every citizen of Rome.

On the difficult constitutional questions connected with Balbus see F. Münzer, *PW*, s.v. 'Cornelius (69) Balbus', 1261 ff. See also R. Syme, *The Roman Revolution* (see Index), and M. Grant, *From Imperium to Auctoritas* (1946), 6. G. E. F. C.

BALBUS (3), Lucius Cornelius (*Minor*), nephew of Balbus (2), joined Caesar in the Civil War, and in 44–43 B.C. was quaestor to Asinius Pollio, who complained of his tyrannical conduct at Gades and of his absconding with the pay-chest. He was honoured by Augustus with a pontificate and consular rank, was proconsul of Africa, and triumphed over the Garamantes (19 B.C.). Balbus built a 'new town' and docks at Gades and a theatre in Rome.

Cicero, *Fam.* 10. 32; Strabo 3. 169; Velleius 2. 51; Dio Cassius 54. 25. Modern literature: Drumann–Groebe, *Gesch. Roms* ii. 523–5. G. W. R.

BALEARES INSULAE. The name *Gymnesiae* (Γυμνήσιαι), used by early Greek voyagers, was replaced by *Baliares* or *Baliarides* from an Iberian original. The spelling was changed to *Baleares* in the Augustan period. Roman names of each island were *Maiorca* (formerly *Columba*), *Minorca* (formerly *Nura*), *Capraria, Menaria, Tiquadra*, and *Cunicularia* (formerly *Hannibalis*). Urban units included Iberian *Tuci*, Phoenician *Bocchori* and *Guiuntum*, and Roman *Palma* and *Pollentia* on Maiorca. Minorca had Iberian *Sanisera* as well as Phoenician *Mago* and *Iamo*. The characteristics of the natives most frequently mentioned by classical writers were their cave-homes, the absence of gold and silver, inhumation, polyandry, and their exceptional skill in the use of the sling. Although Roman title to the islands was recognized by the treaty of 202 B.C., they were only pacified in 121 by Q. Caecilius Metellus (Balearicus). Copper coins were minted under Tiberius by some of the towns, all of which received the Latin Right (*see* IUS LATII) from Vespasian. For administrative purposes the islands were attached to the *conventus Carthaginiensis* of Hither Spain. Diocletian made them an independent province. Escape from the severity of barbarian invasions may be inferred from the late reference (*Not. Dign.* 11. 71, ed. Seeck) to the Balearic dye-works, *bafii*. J. J. Van N.

BALL GAMES. We know from Homer that ball games were played in early Greece, for it was a lost ball that roused Odysseus from his sleep in the bush and led to his discovery by Nausicaa. At Athens in the fifth century they were overshadowed by gymnastic exercises, but they were popular with youths, as recent archaeological evidence shows. A sculptured relief built into the Themistoclean ring-wall at Athens, and rediscovered in 1922, shows the details of a 'hockey match'. The ball is on the ground in the middle; two youths with sticks are engaged in a 'bully' for it; on either side of them stand two other pairs of youths with sticks.

Another relief represents a throw-in from the touch-line: one youth is preparing to throw, the rest are waiting either to seize the ball in the air or to tackle the next possessor. This game, *Phaeninda*, was played with a small, hard ball and bore some resemblance to our Rugby, except that the ball was thrown and never kicked. Another game, more akin to our lacrosse, was played with a lighter ball, the Greek *sphaira*, Latin *follis*. Here tackling was not allowed, and the ball was thrown from hand to hand while the players were running at full speed. In a third type of game (*trigon*), the players were three in number and stood at the corners of a triangle, throwing balls quickly one to the other; both hands were used and caddies supplied the players with missiles.

Galen, *On the small ball* (*Scripta Minora* i, p. 93). F. A. W.

BALLISTA (or *Callistus*), praetorian prefect of Valerian, rallied the Romans at Samosata after his capture and dealt severe blows to the Persians on the Cilician coast. In A.D. 260, he joined Macrianus in setting up the younger Macrianus and Quietus as rivals to Gallienus. When the Macriani marched west, Ballista stayed with Quietus in Emesa, but, after their defeat, fell a victim to Odenathus.

H. M.

BALLISTA, *see* SIEGECRAFT, ROMAN.

BANKS. Loans and deposits were known to the Indo-European and Semito-Hamitic tribes, as their languages prove. The Ancient Oriental cultures had even an encashment business and exchange bills. But banking as a trade could not develop until the invention of coins allowed specialized bankers sufficient opportunities for a living. Institutions which may be called private banks are found in Mesopotamia from the seventh century B.C.; but banking business was here not separated from the administration of large estates. In early Greece the temples (e.g. the Artemisium at Ephesus) had almost regional monopolies of banking. But in the classical period the τραπεζῖται, who originated in the sixth century as money-changers and set up their 'tables' at festivals and markets, took over the business of the temples. By the fourth century they provided most of the loans and held most of the deposits, and individual bankers of note appeared (*see* PASION). Whether endorsements could be performed in classical Greece and in contemporaneous Mesopotamia is not certain; various new types of loans appear in our sources at this time (*see* BOTTOMRY LOANS, USURY). On the other hand, banking remained a risky trade. A banker's death meant loss of valuable customers and connexions, if not bankruptcy. The firms were small and banking terminology and bookkeeping remained simple. Many bankers combined banking with commerce or manufacture.

2. In the city-states of the Hellenistic age the more important temples, private firms, and the cities themselves carried on the banking business without much change. But the Ptolemaic Empire created a public banking system which represents for us the most highly developed banking organism of antiquity. A network of royal banks was spread over the whole of Egypt with a central bank in Alexandria, provincial banks in all district capitals, branch establishments in smaller localities, and institutes of minor importance, which were let out to private bankers under the State bank's control. Thousands of employees found occupation in this vast institution, which had a monopoly for the banking business of Egypt, collected revenues, and paid out the charges of the monarchy. Endorsements (*PTeb.* 890) and even primitive exchange bills occur here. Lending was not monopolized by this State bank; the owners of large estates and the temples lent large sums to peasants and business people.

3. The Roman banks of the second and first centuries B.C. were comparatively small firms. The main business was done by *equites* and other men of wealth and not by specialized bankers. Their methods, however, were progressive. The so-called *permutatio*, a method of clearing between banks in and outside Rome, allowed payments to provincial residents and vice versa without actual transfer of money.

4. Augustus divided the Egyptian State bank into small and independent local institutions. The banking structure of Republican Rome (with local variations) spread over the whole Empire. Slowly the banks of the Principate lost most of their paying business (money exchange and lending) to local owners of large estates, a primitive state of affairs which became common throughout the rural districts of the Byzantine Empire. The few banks which survived the breakdown of Roman coinage during the third century A.D. were indispensable for financial State transactions, and were therefore compulsorily enrolled in the *corpus collectariorum*, which was controlled by the government. Most of the earlier banking procedure was codified by Justinian and preserved by Europeans and Arabs throughout the Middle Ages.

A. Calderini, *Aegyptus* xviii (1938), 244 ff.; J. Corver, *De Terminologie van het Crediet-Wezen in het Grieksch* (1934); T. Frank, *Economic Survey of Ancient Rome* i–iv (U.S.A. 1933–8); A. Früchtl, *Das Geldgeschäft bei Cicero* (1912); J. Hasebroek, *Hermes* lv (1920), 113 ff.; F. M. Heichelheim, *Wirtschaftsgeschichte des Altertums* (1938), Index s.v. 'Bankmässige Geschäfte und Berufe'; R. Herzog, *Tesserae Nummulariae* (Abhandlungen der Giessener Hochschulgesellschaft i, 1919); E. Kiessling, s.v. 'Giroverkehr' in *PW* Suppl. iv; B. Laum, s.v. 'Banken' in *PW* Suppl. iv; F. Oertel in R. von Pöhlmann, *Geschichte der sozialen Frage und des Sozialismus in der antiken Welt*, ii³ (1925), 529 f.; Cl. Préaux, *L'Économie royale des Lagides* (1939), 280 f.; W. L. Westermann, *Journ. of Economic and Business History* iii (1931), 30 ff. F. M. H.

BANTIA, an Apulian or possibly Lucanian town near Venusia (Pliny, *HN* 3. 98; Hor. *Carm.* 3. 4. 15), nowadays *Santa Maria di Banzi.* The great Marcellus fell near here in 208 B.C. (Livy 27. 25). Its (originally Messapic?) inhabitants spoke Oscan in Republican times, as a surviving copy of its municipal regulations demonstrates (the famous *Tabula Bantina* of *c.* 120 B.C.: R. S. Conway, *Italic Dialects* i. 22 f.). Under the Empire Bantia was a *municipium.* E. T. S.

BARBATUS, *see* SCIPIO (1).

BARCINO (nowadays *Barcelona*), *Colonia Faventia Iulia Augusta Pia*, a native foundation with traditions of origin both Greek and Phoenician. Granted colonial immunity by Caesar, Barcino received full colonial status from Augustus. It was far less important to the Romans than Tarraco, but gradually took the lead in the third century. Inscriptions record the gifts of wealthy citizens and the service of many Imperial-cult officials. These, like the literary references, are chiefly of late date.
J. J. VAN N.

BARYGAZA (*Broach*), near the mouth of the Nerbudda, on the Gulf of Cambay. After discovery by Hippalus (q.v.) of the use of monsoon winds, Greek ships sailed thither direct from Aden; conducted by royal pilots from the Kathiawar coast and towed to the town, they brought merchandise, presents, and Roman coins. To Barygaza were brought Indian and Chinese products from the north through Modura (*Muttra*) and Ozene (*Ujjain*), and from eastern and central India chiefly through Tagara (*Thair?*) and Paethana (*Paithan*). Barygaza sent Indian ships to the Persian Gulf, Somaliland, and Arabia. It was the chief port for Greek and Persian trade in north India.

Peripl. Mar. Rubr. passim; Ptol. *Geog.* 7. 1–6. Warmington, *Indian Commerce*, index (for commerce). E. H. W.

BASILICA, a Roman form of building consisting of a rectangular roofed hall, with or without exedras, which served as a social or commercial meeting-place, associated with a forum. The earliest known was at Rome, built by Cato (184 B.C.). More important, because still preserved, is that at Pompeii, *c.* early first century B.C., a hall about 185 feet × 71 feet (exclusive of porch at east and tribunes at west end), containing inner hall about 148 feet × 40 feet surrounded by columns; in effect the Greek peripteral temple turned outside in, and possibly influenced by Greek or Hellenistic pillared halls. An advance was made with the Basilica Iulia (central area 260 feet × 60 feet) and Basilica Aemilia, in the Roman Forum, both *c.* 50 B.C. and later, which had double surrounding aisles with arcades (open on one side to the Forum) and galleries, above which the central area was lit by a clerestory. This type of building—of which Trajan's Basilica had the important addition of two semicircular halls—influenced Christian basilican churches in fourth and later centuries, but more important structurally was the Basilica Nova of Maxentius, near the Roman Forum, finished by Constantine, *c.* A.D. 313, and doubtless derived from the central halls of the Thermae (*see* BATHS). This was in essence a vast vaulted hall, 265 feet × 195 feet, with only four internal supports linked by arches to piers projecting from side walls, and providing a buttressed superstructure to the central clerestoried compartment roofed with a groined vault in three bays; each compartment of the aisles being barrel-vaulted at a lower level. The clear span of the central vault was 76 feet; the height from floor to crown of vault 114 feet.

See ARCHITECTURE, and R. Schultze, *Basilika* (1928) T. F.

BASSAE, in south-west Arcadia, near Phigaleia, the site of one of the best-preserved Greek temples. This was dedicated to Apollo, and built by Ictinus, the architect of the Parthenon. The orientation, determined seemingly by that of an earlier building, was towards the north instead of east, and the early sunlight, instead of entering through the main doorway, was admitted to the *adytum* through an opening of unique kind in the eastern side-wall. Unique too were the ten engaged Ionic columns which decorated the side-walls of the *cella* internally, and the single central Corinthian column—one of the earliest of its kind, and one of the most beautiful—between the *cella* and the *adytum*. The sculptured frieze (now in the British Museum) shows that it belonged to the late fifth century. *See* ICTINUS.

Paus. 8. 41. 7 ff.; C. R. Cockerell, *The Temples . . . at Aegina and . . . Bassae* (1860); W. B. Dinsmoor, 'The Temple of Apollo at Bassae', *Metr. Mus. Studies* iv. 204 ff.; *AJArch.* 1939, 27 ff.
T. J. D. and H. W. R.

BASSARIDES, *see* MAENADS.

BASSULUS, *see* POMPONIUS (5).

BASSUS (1), CAESIUS (1st c. A.D.), a friend of the satirist Persius and editor of his work. He himself was a lyric poet, and Quintilian (10.1.96) mentions him as the only one whose name might appear with that of Horace in a canon of Roman lyric poets. He is possibly the author of a metrical work to which later writers refer and part of which is preserved in a corrupted form under the name of Atilius Fortunatianus (ed. Keil, *Gramm. Lat.* vi. 255–72). The treatise *De Metris* printed in Keil, *Gramm. Lat.* vi. 305–12, is spurious.

Cf. Teuffel, § 304, 1–2; Schanz–Hosius, § 385.   J. F. M.

BASSUS (2), SALEIUS, an epic writer of poetic genius who died young (Quint. *Inst.* 10. 1. 90, Juv. 7. 80). Vespasian assisted him financially (Tac. *Dial.* 5. 2; 9. 8).

BASSUS, *see also* AUFIDIUS, GAVIUS, LOLLIUS (3).

BASTARNAE, a roving tribe which first appeared on the lower Danube *c.* 200 B.C. They were enlisted by Philip V and Perseus of Macedon against their enemies in the northern Balkans, and by Mithridates against the Romans. They defeated C. Antonius *c.* 62 B.C., but were subdued by M. Crassus (29–28), and henceforth they generally appear as subject-allies of Rome. They were transplanted to the southern bank of the Danube by Probus. Earlier writers were uncertain as to the nationality of the Bastarnae, but it may be inferred from Strabo (7. 306), Pliny (*HN* 4. 100), and Tacitus (*Germ.* 46. 1) that they were Germans.
M. C.

BATAVI, a German tribe on the Rhine delta. They were an offshoot of the Chatti (Tac. *Germ.* 29). They probably became allies of Rome between 16 B.C. and 13 B.C.; and about 8 B.C., owing to the importance of their territory as a naval base, they were brought into the Empire as a *gens foederata*, supplying men for the Roman army but paying no taxes. Their contingents were organized into auxiliary regiments under their own chiefs (Tac. *Hist.* 1. 59; 4. 12); Batavi also served in the Imperial bodyguard (Suet. *Calig.* 43). After the revolt of their chieftain Civilis (q.v.) in A.D. 69–70, the Batavian regiments were disbanded, and the new *cohortes Batavorum* of second-century inscriptions were sent to serve away from their homeland. The Batavi disappear after 300, on the arrival of Salian Franks in their country, but their name is preserved in the district of Betuwe. *See also* NOVIOMAGUS.   O. B.

BATHS, the most important buildings of the Romans, probably the earliest to arrange halls and rooms in association symmetrically. Evidences exist in most provincial towns, but the great Baths (*Thermae*) in Rome itself overshadowed all others in size and magnificence. The earliest, the Baths of Agrippa (*c.* 20 B.C.), led the way; those built by Caracalla and Diocletian are the best preserved; all conformed, with variations, to a general type of community centre, cultural as well as physical, and on a vast scale.

The Baths of Caracalla had a main building, approximately a rectangle of 750 feet × 380 feet, placed in an enclosed and nearly square space about 33 acres in extent, raised 20 feet above surrounding ground level with vaulted storerooms underneath. A vaulted Central Hall (*not* a *tepidarium*) 183 feet × 79 feet was the kernel of the building: it gave access at its ends through spacious vestibules to enclosed courts (*palaestrae*, with separate baths for athletes), on its south side to the *tepidarium* and thence to the domed *calidarium*—a circular chamber about 115 feet in diameter, flanked by rooms for poets and philosophers—and on its north side to a large swimming-pool (*frigidarium*), perhaps partly unroofed, flanked by halls for spectators and dressing-rooms (*apodyteria*); a nobly conceived plan and an impressive treatment, as the immense vaulted roof of the central hall—with clerestory windows—rose high above the adjacent roofs.

The surrounding enclosures of the great *Thermae* were treated with equal care, partly garden (*xystus*)—either colonnaded or laid out with formal trees—and partly open-air gymnasium, with, on east and west and (partially) north or south sides, various promenade rooms; on the south side the central space contained a theatre and a stadium. The main buildings were heated by underground furnaces and floor ducts (hypocausts), which conveyed warmed air to flues behind the walls of the various compartments. Architectural accessories were sumptuous, marble mosaic being used for the floors; marble for the columns, the casing of the superstructure, seats, etc.; and painted decoration for the stuccoed upper walls and vaults.

Anderson, Spiers, and Ashby, *The Architecture of Ancient Rome*[3] (1927), ch. 6; G. T. Rivoira, *Roman Architecture* (1925).   T. F.

BATO (1), the Dalmatian, chieftain of the Daesitiates, raised rebellion in Illyricum in A.D. 6, raided the Dalmatian coast, fought against the Romans in the valley of the Save, and, after the capitulation of his Pannonian allies in A.D. 8, retreated southwards. After vainly defending several forts against the Romans, he surrendered and was interned at Ravenna (A.D. 9).   R. S.

BATO (2), the Pannonian, like his Dalmatian namesake, revolted, tried to capture Sirmium (A.D. 6), and shared in the subsequent fighting, but surrendered in A.D. 8 at the river Bathinus. Soon after, however, the Dalmatian chieftain captured and killed him.   R. S.

BATON (Βάτων), New Comedy poet in the first half of the third century B.C.; an anecdote links him with Cleanthes (d. 251) and Arcesilaus (d. 240). The fragments mainly deride the inconsistency of philosophers, but praise Epicurus.

FCG iv. 499 ff.; *CAF* iii. 326 ff.   W. G. W.

BAUBO (*Babo*), a female daemon of primitive and obscene character, doubtless originally a personification of the *cunnus*. She appears in the Orphic version of the Rape of Kore (Kern, *Orph. Frs.* 49 ff.), and on inscriptions from Paros and Asia Minor, and is mentioned by Asclepiades of Tragilus (Harpocration s.v. Δυσαύλης) as mother of the Anatolian Mise. She has been thought to have a part in the Eleusinian Mysteries (Ch. Picard in *Rev. Hist. Rel.* xcv (1927)), but see L. Deubner, *Attische Feste* (1932), 83, n. 3. She survives in modern folklore (R. M. Dawkins in *JHS* xxvi (1906)). Other references in Picard, l.c. and W. K. C. Guthrie, *Orpheus and Gk. Rel.* (1935), 136.   W. K. C. G.

BAUCIS, *see* PHILEMON (1).

BAVIUS (1st c. B.C.), a poetaster, rescued from oblivion by Virgil's contempt (*Ecl.* 3. 90).

BEE-KEEPING had the same importance for non-tropical antiquity from palaeolithic times onwards as sugar production has now. The culture of bees seems to have begun as early as the Mesolithic period. Solon introduced a law which regulated bee-keeping. Greek towns (Teos, Theangela) and the Ptolemaic Empire introduced special taxes on bee-keeping and carefully organized enterprises for honey-production. Different methods of bee-keeping and breeds of bees were developed, the most important progress being made during the centuries between Alexander and Augustus. One bee-hive would produce 1–2½ and occasionally 3 *chous* (*c.* 6–18 pints) of honey at one harvesting. The best honey came from Attica (Hymettic region), Theangela, Chalybon, Cos, Calymna, Rhodes, Lycia, Coracesium, Thasos, Cyprus, several districts of Syria, Sicily (especially the Hyblaean region near Syracuse), Liguria, Noricum, and the south of Spain, the main honey-exporting countries of the Ancient World. The practical experience of many generations of Greek and Roman bee-masters was finally codified by a number of Greek and Latin authors, the most distinguished being Aristotle, Virgil, Varro, and Columella.

P. D'Héronville, *Mus. Belge* xxx (1926), 161 f.; J. Klek, *PW*, s.v. 'Bienenzucht' (Suppl. iv); J. Klek and L. Armbruster, *Archiv für Bienenkunde* i. 6; ii. 17; iii. 8; vii (1919–26); Olck, *PW*, s.v. 'Biene', 'Bienenzucht'; L. Robert, *Ant. Class.* iv (1935), 170 f.   F. M. H.

BELGAE. According to Caesar, a population-group of this name occupied lands to north of Seine and Marne. They were the fiercest inhabitants of Gaul and boasted of their German blood (cf. Strabo 4. 196). Certain tribes, he says, had settled in Britain, and Belgae are actually located there by later geographers. The Gallic Belgae were subdued by Caesar in 57 B.C., but continued to give trouble for thirty years more.

Among the Gallic Belgae, archaeology distinguishes two cultural provinces separated by the Ardennes. The northern part is a backward region with Hallstatt characteristics; to the south, traditions of the Marne culture, notably the pedestal-urn, persist. Both experienced German penetration, cremation (a German practice) being normal. The northern group was reinforced under the Empire by new settlers and rose suddenly to great prosperity under the stimulus of the Rhine market.

An exodus from the southern (pedestal-urn) group into Britain occurred *c.* 75 B.C., which developed into the kingdom of Cassivellaunus, whose descendants extended their rule over all the south-west. About the time of Caesar's conquest, or perhaps after, a further exodus settled in Hampshire and Berkshire, spread over west (but not east) Sussex, and influenced the culture of the neighbouring Durotriges. Their rulers were the house of Commius (q.v.) and their culture was characterized by Bead-rim pottery.

Characteristics of the Belgae were their preference for woodland sites both for towns and for agricultural development, and their fondness for things Roman, which, however, made them no less hostile to Roman invasion; it appears, indeed, that it was Belgic areas which led opposition to the Roman conquerors.

C. F. C. Hawkes and G. C. Dunning in *Arch. Journ.* lxxvii. 150–335. The 'Second Belgic Invasion' has been attacked by Mrs. Cunnington (*Antiquaries Journal* xii. 27–34) and R. E. M. Wheeler (ib. xv. 275; *JRS* xxix. 88); but Hawkes has defended himself (*Proc. Hampshire Field Club* xiii. 160–3).   C. E. S.

BELISARIUS, see JUSTINIAN.

BELLEROPHON (Βελλεροφῶν, Βελλεροφόντης). In *Il.* 6. 155 ff., Glaucus the Lycian gives the following account of his ancestor Bellerophontes; the genealogy is Sisyphus—Glaucus I—Bellerophontes—Isandros, Hippolochus and Laodameia, Sarpedon being the son of Laodameia, and Glaucus II of Hippolochus. He was a man of remarkable beauty and valour, a native of Ephyre

(generally identified with Corinth). Proetus, king of the Argives,* had a wife Anteia (Stheneboea in later accounts) who tried to tempt Bellerophon, and when he refused, told Proetus that he had tried to seduce her (cf. ACASTUS; Stith Thompson, K 2111). Proetus then sent Bellerophon to Lycia (in later accounts the king of Lycia, Iobates, was Proetus' father-in-law) with a letter to the king asking for his execution (cf. Stith Thompson, K 978). On reading this, the king set him first to fight the Chimaera (q.v.), then the Solymi, then the Amazons, and finally laid an ambush for him. Bellerophon survived all these trials, and the king made peace with him and married him to his own daughter. Afterwards, Bellerophon became 'hated of all the gods' and wandered along on the πεδίον Ἀλήϊον (to Homer at least the 'plain of wandering'). Later, he accomplishes his tasks with the help of the winged horse Pegasus, which Athena helped him to catch (Pind. *Ol.* 13. 63 ff.); he used him to take vengeance on Stheneboea (Euripides, *Sthen.*) and offended by trying to fly on him to heaven (Eur. *Beller.*). See further Rose, *Handb. Gk. Myth.* 270 f.   H. J. R.

* In Homer there is no hint that Ephyre was not in his domains; later, e.g. schol. *Il.* 6. 155, the geography is modernized, and Bellerophon has to leave Corinth because of a blood-feud and take refuge at Argos.

BELLO AEGYPTIACO (*sive* **ACTIACO** *sive* **ALEXANDRINO**), **CARMEN DE**, fragments of a papyrus from Herculaneum, possibly part of Rabirius' poem on Antony's defeat (E. Bickel, *Gesch. d. röm. Lit.* (1937), 441).

Baehrens, *PLM* i. 218; *see* PAPYROLOGY, LATIN.

BELLONA, the Roman war-goddess, older *Duellona*, rarely *Bellola*. Whether independent in origin or an offshoot of Mars, she is early, her name occurring in the formula of *devotio* (Livy 8. 9. 6). She had, however, no *flamen* and no festival, and her temple was vowed in 296 B.C. and built somewhat later (Livy 10. 19. 17). It was in the Campus Martius, near the altar of Mars, and often used for meetings of the Senate when held *extra pomerium* (Platner–Ashby, 82). Before it stood the *columna bellica*, used in formal declarations of war, cf. FETIALES. She was occasionally identified with Nerio, the ancient cult-partner of Mars (Augustine, *De civ. D.* 6. 10), commonly with the Greek war-goddess Enyo, and in Imperial times at latest with the Cappadocian goddess Mâ.

Wissowa, *RK* 151, 348; Nock, *CAH* xii. 425.   H. J. R.

BELLUM AFRICUM, a record of Caesar's war in Africa (winter 47–46 B.C.). Its ninety-eight chapters are monotonous to the layman, but as military history it is painstaking and straightforward. Both style and matter suggest that the author was a trained soldier, tribune or centurion, who took part in the campaign, though not a man in Caesar's confidence; however, the claims of Hirtius (q.v.) to editorship are still upheld.

O. Seel, 'Hirtius', *Klio*, Beiheft 1935; cf. T. Rice-Holmes, *The Roman Republic* iii (1923), 274.   G. E. F. C.

BELLUM ALEXANDRINUM, a work continuing Caesar's commentary on the Civil War. Thirty-three chapters describe the war at Alexandria from the point at which Caesar left off; then follow the campaign of Calvinus (q.v. 2) against Pharnaces (chs. 34–41), the war in Illyricum (chs. 42–7), and the disturbances during Q. Cassius' tenure of Spain (chs. 48–64), both in the winter 48–47, and finally Caesar's campaign against Pharnaces (chs. 65–78) ending in the victory of Zela (2 Aug. 47). The style is cultured and the writer was well informed; he may well have been Hirtius (q.v.), who, however, took no part in the Alexandrian war.

For bibliography, *see* HIRTIUS, with T. Rice-Holmes, *The Roman Republic* iii (1923), 483–4.   G. E. F. C.

BELLUM CIVILE. (1) Caesar's books on the war begun in 49 B.C. (2) The poem of 295 hexameters introduced into Petronius' *Satyricon* (119–24) to illustrate Eumolpus' implied criticism on the management of the same subject by Lucan, who is not named. J. W. D.

BELLUM HISPANIENSE, an account of the campaign which ended at Munda (45 B.C.), written by an eyewitness, probably from Caesar's army. The text is deplorable; but many meaningless passages are caused by the author's illiteracy and his incapacity to understand anything difficult. The work is interesting mainly as a study in half-educated Latin, which combines colloquialism with quotations from Ennius and schoolboy rhetoric.

Cf. O. Seel, 'Hirtius', *Klio*, Beiheft 1935; T. Rice-Holmes, *The Roman Republic* iii (1923), 298. G. E. F. C.

BELLUM HISTRICUM, a lost epic on the Istrian War of 125 B.C. by Hostius, probably grandfather of Propertius' 'Cynthia', i.e. Hostia (4.20.8).

See Morel, *FPL* 33.

BELLUM SEQUANICUM, historical epic (lost) by Varro Atacinus (q.v.) written in Caesar's time on his war with Ariovistus.

Morel, *FPL* 99.

BELUS (*Βῆλος*), hellenization of Ba'al, Bel, sometimes recognized as a divine title (Zeus Belus, Hdt. 1. 181. 2; Marduk?), oftener taken as the name of an ancient oriental king (of Assyria, Serv. on *Aen.* 1. 642); father of Dido (ibid.); ancestor of the founder of the dynasty of the Heraclidae in Lydia (Hdt. 1. 7. 3); father of Danaus (q.v.); founder of the rulers of Persia (Ov. *Met.* 4. 213). It thus forms a stopgap name for foreign genealogies, as Creon for Greek. H. J. R.

BENDIS (*Βένδις, Βενδῖς*), a Thracian goddess, worshipped with orgiastic rites in Thrace (Strabo, 10. 3. 16, p. 470); at the Piraeus, where her cult was introduced during Socrates' lifetime (Plato, *Resp.* 327 a, 354 a), presumably by resident Thracians (cf. W. S. Ferguson, *Hellenistic Athens* (1911), 216), she had processions, a torch-race on horseback, and a vigil. The date was Thargelion 19 (Deubner, *Att. Feste*, 219). She was apparently represented as carrying two (hunting?) spears (Hesych., s.v. δίλογχον). Cf. now Ferguson, *Harv. Theol. Rev.* 1944. H. J. R.

BENEVENTUM, on the river Calor in southern Italy. Originally a stronghold of the Hirpini Samnites named Malventum, it fell some time after 300 B.C. to the Romans, who made it a Latin colony, changing its ill-sounding name to Beneventum, 268 B.C. (Vell. Pat. 1. 14; Festus p. 25 L.). Thereafter its *territorium* expanded and Beneventum flourished. Under the Republic it was a military base, later an opulent *municipium*; under the Empire a *colonia* and important road-centre (Viae Appia, Traiana); under the Lombards a duchy. The ancient remains include Trajan's arch. (Polyb. 3. 90; Livy 27. 10, etc.; Strabo 5. 250.)

Beloch, *Röm. Gesch.* 489, for magistrates; A. Sambon, *Monnaies antiques de l'Italie* i (1903), 114, for coins. E. T. S.

BERENICE. (1) BERENICE I, daughter of Lagus (father of Ptolemy I) and Antigone, was born c. 340 B.C., and died between 281 and 271. She married a Macedonian Philippus. The issue of this marriage were Magas, king of Cyrene, Antigone (m. Pyrrhus of Epirus), and other daughters. Berenice, already a widow, came to Egypt with her aunt Eurydice, who married Ptolemy I. The step-sister of the king, she presently (c. 317) became his mistress and succeeded Eurydice as his wife. Their children were Arsinoë II and Ptolemy II Philadelphus.

(2) BERENICE SYRA, daughter of Ptolemy II and Arsinoë I, was born c. 280 B.C. She married the Seleucid king Antiochus II after the Second Syrian War (252). Laodice, the king's divorced first wife, murdered Berenice and her son by Antiochus after his death in 246, before Ptolemy III could bring help.

(3) BERENICE II, daughter of King Magas of Cyrene and of Apama, daughter of Antiochus I, was born c. 273 B.C. She was betrothed to Ptolemy III, but after Magas' death Demetrius, a Macedonian prince, was called in by her mother to marry her. Berenice led a rebellion against them both, and Demetrius was killed by her orders. She married Ptolemy III in 247, who called a star 'Berenice's curls' after her, as Callimachus and Catullus tell us. After her husband's death she became joint ruler with her eldest son Ptolemy IV, but was murdered by him in 221. He nevertheless appointed a special Alexandrian priestess in his mother's honour in 211–210, the ἀθλοφόρος Βερενίκης Εὐεργετίδος. *See* PTOLEMY. F. M. H.

BERENICE (4) (b. A.D. 18), daughter of Agrippa I (q.v.), was married first to Marcus, brother of Ti. Julius Alexander, then to her uncle Herod of Chalcis. On his death (48) she lived for long with her brother Agrippa II, in incest, it was said. To quiet scandal she induced Polemon II, then king of Olba in Cilicia, to marry her c. 65, but soon parted from him and returned to her brother. Titus fell in love with her when he was in Judaea (67–70), and when she visited Rome in 75 lived openly with her. He was, however, dissuaded from marrying her, and when she revisited Rome in 79 repulsed her advances. A. H. M. J.

BERENICE, the name of several Hellenistic towns. Chief among them were: (i) a foundation of Ptolemy II on the Egyptian coast of the Red Sea below *Ras Benas*, connected with Coptus on the Nile by a desert camel-track supplied with cisterns and stations. It became the chief Egyptian port for Arabia, east Africa, and India in the first and second centuries A.D. (Warmington, *Indian Commerce*, 6 ff., 51 ff., 73 ff.); (ii) *Berenice Panchrysos*, on the African coast of the Red Sea near the gold-mines of *Jebel Allaki*; (iii) *Berenice Epideiris* on the same coast at the Straits of Bab-el-Mandeb. E. H. W.

BEROSUS or **BEROSSUS** (*Βηρωσός*) (fl. c. 290 B.C.), priest of Bel, author of history of Babylon (*Βαβυλωνιακά*) in three books dedicated to Antiochus I. Book 1 dealt with origins to the Flood, bk. 2 reached Nabonassar (747 B.C.), and bk. 3 the death of Alexander. Value lay in transmission of Babylonian history and astronomy to the Greek world.

FHG ii. 495. E. A. B.

BERYTUS (mod. *Beirut*), a Phoenician city. It issued a municipal coinage, inscribed both in Greek and in Phoenician, from the reign of Antiochus IV, at first as Laodicea in Phoenice, later under its old name. In 80 B.C. it became a free city, and in c. 15 B.C. a Roman colony, with *ius Italicum*, two legions being settled in it by Agrippa. It received at this time a large accession of territory, including Heliopolis, which it lost under Septimius Severus. A great trading town, it was also famed for its wine and linen, and from the third century for its school of Roman law. A. H. M. J.

BESTIA, LUCIUS CALPURNIUS, an Optimate politician. As tribune in 120 B.C. he recalled Popillius Laenas from exile. As consul (111) he was sent to Numidia, against Jugurtha (with Scaurus as legate); having wisely admitted Jugurtha to terms, he was condemned in 110 under the Mamilian commission (*see* MAMILIUS 3). He later returned from exile, but left Rome again in 90, to escape trial under the Varian law (*see* LEX, LEGES). M. H.

BETROTHAL. In Greece a formal betrothal (ἐγγύησις) was a necessary preliminary to a wedding. At Rome this ceremony (*sponsalia*) did not inevitably lead to a marriage, and was merely a preliminary business arrangement. The intending bridegroom, or his father, approached the girl's father and opened negotiations, which were concerned chiefly with the amount of her dowry. If the bride's father gave his consent, the affair was settled, nor was the lady consulted. It was usual to celebrate the occasion with a family party where the future bride and bridegroom exchanged gifts, which were forfeited if either party later broke the contract. This, however, was the only penalty in Roman law, which did not allow breach-of-promise actions.   F. A. W.

BIBACULUS, MARCUS FURIUS, born at Cremona 103 B.C. (Jerome), is coupled with Catullus as a lampooner by Quintilian and Tacitus, by the latter expressly as attacking 'the Caesars', and has been conjecturally attached to Catullus' circle. A few phalaecians preserved by Suetonius (*Gram.* 11) suggest humour and felicity of phrase. Horace (*Sat.* 2. 5. 40) twits him with tripe-inspired epic bathos, and Acron (ad loc.) credits him with an epic on Caesar's Gallic Wars, to which some lines quoted from a Furius by Macrobius (*Sat.* 6. 1) not improbably belong. He is also assigned an *Aethiopis*.

Certain difficulties (notably age-discrepancy as regards Catullus; anti-Caesarianism and Caesarian epic) commend the suggestion that Bibaculus is divisible into: (1) Jerome's M. Furius Bibaculus, the epic poet, (2) a younger Bibaculus, the lampooner, born about 82 B.C.

Morel, *FPL* 80–3.   E. P. B.

BIBRACTE (modern *Mont-Beuvray*), a hill-fort, the original capital of the Aedui. Here in 52 B.C. the supreme command was conferred by a pan-Gallic council upon Vercingetorix. Its inhabitants were transferred c. 12 B.C. to a new town in the plain, Augustodunum (*Autun*), but inscriptions—*deae Bibracti*—at Autun kept the old name alive, and a cult survived on the site itself. Excavations have revealed numerous houses of the Gallic town, all rectangular and of dry stone, some with *atria* and even hypocausts. An important metal-workers' and enamellers' quarter was also revealed.

Bulliot, *Fouilles du Mont Beuvray* (1899); Déchelette, *Fouilles du Mont Beuvray de 1897 à 1901* (1904); id. *Manuel* ii. 946–57.
                                                        C. E. S.

BIBULUS (1) MARCUS CALPURNIUS, Caesar's colleague in aedileship and praetorship, and finally in the consulate of 59 B.C., when after being forcibly prevented from vetoing the agrarian law he attempted from his house to invalidate legislation by 'watching the heavens'. His only departure from strict Republicanism was to propose Pompey's consulate in 52. In 51 he governed Syria, and resisted the Parthians tenaciously. In the winter 49–48 he wore himself to death, trying to prevent Caesar's crossing to Epirus. He married Porcia, daughter of Cato and future wife of Brutus.   G. E. F. C.

BIBULUS (2) LUCIUS CALPURNIUS, son of (1) and Porcia, joined his stepfather Brutus and was proscribed; but after Philippi he passed over to Antony, and became his *praefectus classis* and finally governor of Syria, where he died in 32 B.C. He frequently attempted mediation with Octavian. His book on Brutus was an (indirect?) source of Plutarch (*Brutus* 13; 23).

PW iii. 1367; H. Peter, *HRRel.* ii, p. lxvii; R. Syme, *The Roman Revolution* (1939), see index.   A. M.

BIDENTAL. By Etruscan use, when lightning had struck any place, the supposed fragments of the bolt were collected, buried while a formula was pronounced (Lucan 1. 606–7), and the place walled in (ibid. 8. 864) and inscribed *fulgur conditum* or the like; it was tabu (ibid. 1. 608, 'dat . . . numen'), and anyone touching it was *incestus* (Hor. *Ars P.* 471). This was called a *bidental*.

See C. O. Thulin, *Etruskische Disciplin* (1909), i. 92 ff. H. J. R.

BIOGRAPHY, GREEK. The impulse to celebrate the individual finds early expression in the dirge and funeral oration; but not until the fifth century, with its conscious recognition of the individual in various arts, do the first traces of biographical literature appear in Greece. Many of THUCYDIDES' sketches approximate to this *genre*; and ION OF CHIOS and STESIMBROTUS described important contemporary figures. In the fourth century appeared ISOCRATES' *Evagoras* and XENOPHON's *Memorabilia* and *Agesilaus*, all forerunners of biography proper; though Isocrates' claim that the *Evagoras* was the first prose encomium of a living person is exaggerated. Meanwhile the Platonic corpus was developing the figure of Socrates.

2. ARISTOTLE gave biography a new impetus. Under his influence interest in ethical and cultural problems encouraged the writing of βίοι, 'ways of life' of peoples and individual types (e.g. CLEARCHUS; DICAEARCHUS); simultaneously the history of rhetoric and the chronology of refinements in that art were recorded in compilations, and Aristotle himself gave such researches a literary form. Directly associated with THEOPHRASTUS was ARISTOXENUS, who stamped the so-called peripatetic biography with its most typical characteristics—combinations of legendary material, scandal, polemics, an interest in literary innovations, and a popular literary form in which character was revealed through a man's actions. DURIS was more directly interested in personality, a trend carried further by PHAENEAS, IDOMENEUS, and NEANTHES, who treated not only literary figures but also, occasionally, men of action. CHAMAELEON set a popular fashion by deducing wild stories from the works of those for whom reliable biographical data were scanty, a precedent followed by HERMIPPUS OF SMYRNA, SATYRUS, who ignored the distinction between men of letters and men of action, and SOTION, who instituted the διαδοχή—a semi-biographical account of successive teachers and pupils in various fields.

3. About 240 B.C. ANTIGONUS OF CARYSTUS displayed a new accuracy in describing contemporaries from personal knowledge; and in the scholarly atmosphere of Alexandria there grew up a biographical form, which revalued the findings of the Peripatetics and re-established their chronological data. Commentaries and epitomes called for biographical introductions, which generally shed their narrative character: between the particulars of a writer's birth and death short notes gave specific details of his mode of life, friends, students, works, etc. Typical of this school is Posidonius' pupil, JASON; and HERACLIDES LEMBUS took still further a literary form which led ultimately to SUETONIUS.

4. Meanwhile, historians too, after Alexander, stressed the individual personality; POLYBIUS, in his *Histories* (e.g. 10. 2) and *Life of Philopoemen*, and after him PANAETIUS, are associated with a development to which such memoir-writers as ARATUS had contributed. There is, however, no proof that peripatetic biography continued, treating political and military figures (as Leo claims). Two hundred years later PLUTARCH's *Lives* mark a new achievement, without continuous links with either previous biographers or Hellenistic historians. Like the Peripatetics Plutarch is discursive, and in contrast to the Alexandrians normally lets his hero's character be deduced from his actions; though his scheme is flexible, each *Life* forms a whole, generally with a strong moral bias. The *Comparisons* reveal his keen interest in psychology.

5. Later PHILOSTRATUS rhetoricized and EUNAPIUS broke up the Alexandrian form; Alexandrian too in

origin, though more learned, were the Neoplatonist biographies of PORPHYRY and MARINUS. Of the abridging and synthesizing of the materials of the literary biography an example survives in DIOGENES LAERTIUS. Much of Greek biography has perished. It seems clear, however, that the Peripatetic form, for all its weaknesses, constituted an artistic unity, though it failed to portray the development of character; whereas the Alexandrian studies, which had most influence at Rome, remained an accumulation of material lacking internal cohesion.

F. Leo, *Die griech.-röm. Biographie nach ihrer litt. Form* (1901); W. Uxkull-Gyllenband, *Plutarch u. die griech. Biographie* (1927); D. R. Stuart, *Epochs of Gk. and Roman Biography* (U.S.A. 1928); N. I. Barbu, *Les Procédés de la peinture des caractères . . . dans les biographies de Plutarque* (1934). F. W. W.

BIOGRAPHY, ROMAN (including AUTOBIOGRAPHY and MEMOIRS). The Romans from early times had customs which laid foundations for biography without Greek influence: songs at banquets praising illustrious men (Cic. *Tusc.* 4. 3); and dirges (*neniae*) at their funerals; eulogies at the obsequies of eminent citizens (*laudationes funebres*). Dionysius (*Ant. Rom.* 5. 17) records the oration on Brutus by Valerius Publicola; he does not know whether this was a new custom, but he is positive that it was of Roman origin. These were early committed to writing (Cic. *Sen.* 12) and preserved as family records in a wing of the *atrium*, where were also exhibited masks of distinguished ancestors, arranged so as to form a family-tree. Finally, a Roman's career was recorded in his funerary inscription, which was highly prized and looked forward to during life. These condensed biographies, especially the *laudationes*, were gradually elaborated by such details as justification of a person's conduct, domestic affairs, including regularly his property, and sometimes intimate private matters, as in the *laudatio Murdiae* (*CIL* vi. 2. 10230). Leo (op. cit. infra, 226), denies the derivation of Roman biography from the *laudationes*, but the opposite view is convincingly upheld by Stuart (op. cit. infra, chs. 7 and 8). On autobiography as original with the Romans, though not under that name, which is modern, see West, *Roman Autobiography*.

2. Direct information on the subject is scanty, because of the small number of surviving works, an inconsiderable part of those which once existed. Jerome (Migne, *PL* xxiii. 821, *prolog. ad Dextrum in librum de illustribus*; cf. Suet. *Reliquiae* ed. Reifferscheid (1860), p. 3), besides Suetonius Tranquillus, from whose lost preface to the *De Viris Illustribus* the saint derived his information, names as his predecessors Varro, Santra, Nepos, and Hyginus. The omission of Tacitus is noteworthy; the *Agricola* is certainly a biography, but might naturally be regarded by Suetonius as history. Varro's place in the list suggests him as the founder of the genre, and doubtless Suetonius so regarded him; nothing of Varro's in that line has survived, for the *Imagines* is not biography. Of Santra we know little; he approved the work of Curtius Nicias on Lucilius (Suet. *Gram.* 14), and expressed an opinion as to the authorship of Terence's plays (id. *Poet.* 4). On Nepos as biographer, see under his name. Of Julius Hyginus' works Gellius (1. 14. 1) cites book 6 of *De Vita Rebusque Illustrium Virorum*, and (6. (7). 1. 2) a *Life of Scipio Africanus* (cf. 3. 4. 1); Asconius (*Pis.* 12) cites his *De Viris Claris*. On Suetonius and Valerius Probus, *see* SUETONIUS (2).

3. The impulse to justify or to exalt an individual led to the writing of memoirs, autobiographical and biographical. Of the former we know of those of C. Gracchus (Cic. *Div.* 1. 36); of M. Aurelius Scaurus in 3 books (Cic. *Brut.* 112); of P. Rutilius Rufus in 5 books (Charisius, *Gramm.* 1. 139. 18 Keil; Suet. *Rel.*, p. 105 Reiff.); of Q. Lutatius Catulus (Cic. *Brut.* 132); of Sulla (bk. 22 was finished by Cornelius Epicadus, Suet. *Gram.* 12; *Rel.*, p. 110 Reiff.); of Varro (Charisius, *Gramm.* 1. 89. 28

Keil); Cicero wrote a prose account of his own consulship in Greek (whether the Latin version was made is uncertain) and a poem on the same subject (*Att.* 1. 19. 10); of Augustus in 13 books, extending to the Cantabrian War (Suet. *Aug.* 85); of Agrippa (*Schol. Bern.* on Verg. *G.* 2. 162); of Tiberius (Suet. *Tib.* 61); of Claudius (id. *Claud.* 41.3); of Agrippina the younger (Tac. *Ann.* 4. 53); of Hadrian (S.H.A. *Hadr.* 16); of Severus (S.H.A. *Sev.* 18). The only surviving autobiography, the *Confessions* of Augustine, differs from the others in showing the development of a human soul. Memoirs written by others are very numerous: on Pompey and on Pompey's father by L. Voltacilius Plotus (Suet. *Rhet.* 3; *Rel.*, p. 214 Reiff.); on Caesar by Oppius (id. *Iul.* 53, cf. 52. 2); on Cicero by Tiro in 4 books (Asc. *Mil.* 43); on Cato Uticensis by Cicero (*Att.* 12. 40. 1); by Fadius Gallus (Cic. *Fam.* 7. 24. 2); by Brutus (Cic. *Att.* 12. 21); and by Munatius Rufus (Plut. *Cat. Min.* 37); on Drusus by Augustus (Suet. *Claud.* 1. 5); on Pomponius Secundus by the elder Pliny (Plin. *Ep.* 3. 5. 3); on Thrasea Paetus by Arulenus Rusticus and on Helvidius Priscus by Herennius Senecio (Tac. *Agr.* 2); on Ambrosius by his secretary Paulinus. The custom of eulogizing the emperor on receiving the consulship was common, as in some of the twelve surviving *Panegyrici Latini* (q.v.).

F. Leo, *Griech.-Röm. Biogr.* (1901); D. R. Stuart, *Epochs of Greek and Roman Biogr.* (U.S.A. 1928); W. H. D. Suringar, *De Romanis Autobiographis* (with fragments, 1846); A. F. West, *Roman Autobiography* (U.S.A. 1901); G. Misch, *Geschichte der Autobiographie*, Bd. I, *Das Altertum*, ed. 2 (1931). J. C. R.

BION (1) (*c.* 325–*c.* 255 B.C.), frequently referred to as *Bion the Borysthenite*, son of a freedman and of a former hetaera of Borysthenes (= Olbia). Because of a fraud committed by his father the family was sold into slavery. But as slave of a rhetorician Bion received a good education, was later set free, and inherited the fortune of his master. He went to Athens and studied in the Peripatos (under Theophrastus) and the Academy (probably under Xenocrates). But he was more strongly influenced by Crates the Cynic and by Theodorus the atheist and hedonist. Diogenes Laertius includes him among the adherents of the Academy. But he did not follow any particular philosophical creed. He imitated the caustic humour, the criticism of conventions, and the shamelessness of the Cynics, and preached the Cyrenaic doctrine that happiness is achieved by adapting oneself to circumstances. He wandered from town to town lecturing for money. In his writings, which later influenced Roman satire, he used a highly eclectic style.

Sillographi Graeci, ed. C. Wachsmuth, 73–7; Diogenes Laertius 4. 46–58. R. Heinze, *De Horatio Bionis imitatore* (1889); R. Dudley, *A History of Cynicism* (1937), 62–9; *PW* ii. 483. K. VON F.

BION (2) (fl. probably *c.* 100 B.C.), of Phlossa near Smyrna. Seventeen fragments have been preserved from his *Bucolica*. Some pieces seem complete, others to be excerpted from longer poems (? a *Hyacinthus*, a *Galatea*). The bucolic element is very slight. The theme of several pieces is playfully erotic, but in others B. is sententious and in one fragment, where he dwells on the vanity of human effort, seems to strike a more personal note. B.'s style is easy and the language simple. Since the Renaissance B. has also been credited with the *Lament for Adonis*, a highly coloured composition in ninety-eight hexameters, which some MSS. wrongly assign to Theocritus. While this has the same theme as Theocritus 15 and in certain features (e.g. the refrain) recalls Theocritus 1, the lyrical treatment is more akin to that found in certain hymns of Callimachus, though B. goes far beyond the latter in emotionalism. The chief argument for B.'s authorship of the *Lament for Adonis* is drawn from the references to the poem in the *Lament for Bion*, a work of some disciple of B., not, as some MSS. assert, of Theocritus or Moschus. According to the *Lament for Bion* B. spent most of his life in Sicily. The fragmentary *Epithalamius of Achilles and Deidameia*, an epyllion introduced by two bucolic interlocutors, has also been assigned by some to B., but without real justification.

Texts: U. von Wilamowitz-Moellendorff, *Bucolici Graeci*[2] (1910), 122, 130, 140; Ph. Legrand, *Bucoliques grecs* ii (1927), 185–218. General literature: G. Knaack, 'Bion (6)', in *PW* iii. 481–2. E. A. B.

BIOTTUS (2nd c. B.C.), Greek comic poet, mentioned only in didascalic lists. His Ποιητής was produced in 168–167 B.C., followed later by his Ἀγνοῶν (*IG* ii². 2323, 212 and 238). No fragments remain.

CAF iii. 366.

BIRDS, SACRED, see ANIMALS, SACRED; some further particulars are given here. One of the most noteworthy associations of a bird with a deity is that of the swan with Apollo (for material, see Sir D'A. W. Thompson, *Glossary of Greek Birds*[2], 180–4, q.v. in general for legends concerning birds). It was a fixed ancient belief that it could sing, at least when dying, an idea perhaps founded on the cry of the Whooper Swan; certainly no other species makes any but a harsh noise. It was also the form taken by Zeus to approach Leda (refs. ibid. 183), and there are several stories of metamorphoses into swan-form; when Horace hopes to become one, *Carm.* 2. 20. 9 ff., he means that he is to be recognized as a true poet, Apollo's singer. The connexion of the sparrow (στρουθός) with Aphrodite, as Sappho, fr. 1. 10, is not unreasonably to be explained by its fertility and lustfulness; the dove (περιστερά) is associated with her most probably because of her Oriental connexions, it being the sacred bird of more than one Asianic mother-goddess (Atargatis, Lucian, *Syr. D.* 14; Ishtar and others). In the case of deities with pre-Hellenic connexions, the occasional bird-form which they assume (cf. ATHENA, para. 1) may plausibly be associated with the epiphanies of Minoan divinities in that shape (see Nilsson, *Minoan-Mycenaean Religion*, 285 ff.); but some birds, e.g. Hermes' cock and Hera's peacock, are much later than their owners, being comparatively recent introductions into Greece. H. J. R.

BIRTHDAY (γενέθλιος ἡμέρα, *natalis*, sc. *dies*). The classical Greeks seem to have paid but little attention to the anniversary of their births. A child's birth was the occasion of congratulatory visits from friends and relations, and presents might be made to the child (Aesch. *Eum.* 7–8); but this was not confined to the actual day of the birth, but was carried out when the child was first seen by the giver, hence the name ὀπτήρια for such a present (Callim. *Dian.* 74, there given to an infant three years old); the word also means a sacrifice made by the father on first seeing the child (Eur. *Ion* 1127). Another word was γενέθλια, also used both of the sacrifice (ibid. 653, 805) and of the gift (Hesych., s.v.). But there is no definite proof of the yearly recurrence of this or of the family festival which accompanied it (Plato, *Symp.* 203 b) earlier than the date (conjecturally late 4th c.) of the Greek original of Plautus, *Pseudolus*, in which much stress is laid on it being Ballio's birthday (165 ff.). The nearest approach is the fact that the days of the month associated with gods are interpreted as being their birthdays as early as Hesiod, *Op.* 771 (a passage doubtfully part of the original poem) and *Hymn. Hom. Merc.* 19; it may therefore have been the custom to have some kind of remembrance, monthly rather than yearly, of the birthdays of human beings.

2. In Hellenistic times birthdays were more observed, particularly in the case of kings and other great persons. One of the most familiar instances of this is found on the Rosetta stone (*OGI* 90. 46), where the Egyptian clergy decree solemnities for 'the day on which the birthday feast of the King is held'. This may of course have been connected in other cases, as it certainly was in this one, with the divine or quasi-divine honours given them; we may compare the celebration after their deaths of the birthdays of distinguished men in and just before that period, as Aratus at Sicyon (Plut. *Arat.* 53) and the founders of various philosophical schools. These had in some cases been regularly heroized and in others received from their followers and successors in the schools something like heroic honours, analogous to those paid to the founder of a city or colony. But some royal personages themselves kept their own birthdays as feasts, analogous to but more splendid than those of ordinary individuals in Rome or a modern country; Cleopatra VII is an example, Plut. *Ant.* 73, where it is expressly noted that on a special occasion she refrained from making any display on her birthday. It is quite possible that the growing belief in the personal *daimon* has something to do with the increased importance of the birthday in the case of private individuals (e.g. *Anth. Pal.* 6. 227; the epigrammatist Crinagoras sends a friend a piece of plate for a birthday present); to celebrate the birthday was to celebrate the anniversary of the deity's first manifestation of his care. See, for the belief, Th. Hopfner, *Griechisch-ägyptischer Offenbarungszauber* i, par. 117 ff.

3. In Rome certainly a like belief had a direct connexion with birthday ceremonies, which are testified to from Plautus onwards (supposing that not all his references are taken over from Greek models) and even for quite humble persons, as Verg. *Ecl.* 3. 76, where a slave is speaking. This was the universal cult of the Genius (q.v.), attested for birthdays by Tibullus (2. 2. 5); at a birthday sacrifice 'ipse suos Genius adsit uisurus honores'. It was to him, then, that the ceremonial of the day was directed. Since in classical times he was precisely equivalent to the Greek personal *daimon*, it may be that Greek influence played a part; but certainly the Romans celebrated not only private birthdays and those of emperors but also the *natales* of cities and all manner of institutions, since every one of them had its genius. The *natalis* of a temple, however, is presumably an annual honour done its god.

W. Schmidt, *Geburtstag im Altertum* (1908), and in *PW* vii. 1135 ff. H. J. R.

BIRTHDAY POEMS, see GENETHLIACON.

BITHYNIA, a territory in north-west Asia Minor, originally confined to the peninsula of Chalcedon, but gradually extended eastward to Heraclea and Paphlagonia, southward to the Mysian Olympus, and westward to Mysia and the Propontis. Although much of the land is mountainous, the Sangarius river and the valleys that run back from the Propontis form fertile plains and provide relatively easy communications. It was a well-watered region producing good timber, excellent pasturage, and all manner of fruits and grains (except olives), possessing fine quarries of marble, and good harbours, and crossed by the chief roads to the Anatolian plateau and to Pontus.

2. The Bithynians were of Thracian origin, and long kept their tribal identity among the peoples about them. They warred constantly with the Greek colonies on the coast, preserved a measure of autonomy under the Persian régime, and in 297 B.C. founded a dynasty of Thracian stock, beginning with King Zipoetes. By a combination of aggressive policies and judicious alliances (especially with the Galatians, whom they invited into Asia in 279), the Bithynian kings protected themselves against the Seleucids and their rival Heraclea and extended their power to Inner Paphlagonia, to the valleys of Nicaea and Prusa, and finally to the cities of the coast. They were active founders of cities, especially Nicomedes I and II and Prusias I, fostered commerce, to which the tribesmen had previously been inhospitable, and showed an interest in Greek culture. Wars with Pergamum in the second century lost Prusias I and II some territory, but otherwise there were slight changes until in 74 Nicomedes IV bequeathed his kingdom to Rome (*see* NICOMEDES I–IV).

3. In organizing the province of Bithynia-and-Pontus Pompey apparently divided all the land among the cities for convenience in maintaining order and collecting taxes. Nicaea, for instance, extended in later times as far as Dorylaeum. In the early Empire Bithynia-and-Pontus was at first a senatorial province, but the importance of the great highway to the eastern frontier and of maritime connexions with the Euxine coasts led imperial procurators to assume more than their regular authority. Special legates were sent under Trajan and Hadrian (Pliny and Julius Severus), and finally Marcus Aurelius made it Imperial. In the time of Pliny and Dio Chrysostom peculation by magistrates, unwise and extravagant building, bitter rivalries between cities, and social discontent within individual cities (for the native Bithynians, long an inferior class, were pressing for equal privileges) created a bad situation, which they did their best to remedy.

E. Meyer and G. Brandis, *PW*, s.v.; Th. Reinach, *Trois royaumes de l'Asie Mineure* (1888); M. I. Rostovtzeff, *BSA* xxii (1918), 1 ff.; Jones, *Eastern Cities*, 148 ff. T. R. S. B.

BITON (*Βίτων*) (3rd or 2nd c. B.C.), the author of a small extant work on siege-engines (*Κατασκευαὶ πολεμικῶν ὀργάνων καὶ καταπαλτικῶν*) and of a lost work on optics.

Ed. A. Rehm and E. Schramm, *Abh. d. Bayer. Akad. d. Wissench.*, Ph.-hist. Abt., N.F. ii, 1929. *PW* iii. 545.

BITON, *see also* CLEOBIS.

BLAESUS of Capreae (? 2nd or 1st c. B.C.), author of *σπουδογέλοια* (perhaps akin to Menippus' satires).

Kaibel, *CGF* 191.

BLANDUS, RUBELLIUS, from Tibur, as the first *eques* to teach rhetoric, marked the rise in professional status (Sen. *Controv.* 2, *praef.* 5). He trained Papirius Fabianus who in turn taught the younger Seneca. He is perhaps the historian cited by Servius on Verg. *G.* 1. 103.

BLITHO, SULPICIUS, *see* SULPICIUS.

BOADICEA, *see* BOUDICCA.

BOCCHUS, king of Mauretania at the time of the Jugurthine War. Bestia (q.v.) in 111 B.C. rejected Bocchus' offer of alliance. He took the part of his son-in-law, Jugurtha, in the later stages of the war, though at the price of the cession of all western Numidia. With Jugurtha, he nearly defeated Marius at Cirta; but was finally induced by Sulla's daring diplomacy to surrender Jugurtha. He retained western Numidia. Bocchus II ruled with his brother Bogud (q.v.), *c.* 50–38 B.C., and alone until *c.* 33.

BOEOTIA, a district of central Greece, bordering on Attica, and of similar extent. Its heart consisted of the plains of Orchomenus and Thebes, which were good wheat-land and bred horses (for the flooding of the northern plain, *see* ORCHOMENUS, COPAIS). The south is rough and mountainous, with good harbours on the Corinthian Gulf, but not easy of access; the north is hill country with a narrow seaboard; the east rolling country watered by the Asopus. The south-east frontier is formed by Cithaeron and Parnes, the north-west, with Phocis and Locris, is not clearly marked.

The Boeotians came from Thessaly before the Dorian invasion. Their dialect is most closely related to Thessalian and Aeolic, but has west Greek (Dorian?) elements, and, in the south-east, traces akin to Arcadian. Orchomenus and the Oropus district were relatively late additions to the Boeotian territory. Twenty-nine small Boeotian towns are named in the Homeric Catalogue.

Some disappeared, others were absorbed by more powerful neighbours; in classical times the independent cities numbered about a dozen. The importance of Boeotia in Greek history varied with the degree of Theban control (*see* THEBES 1), though some of her rivals, Thespiae and Plataea, had more attractive histories. The Boeotians were, on the whole, a self-contained agricultural people who did not share in the overseas expansion of Greece. The proverb *Βοιωτίαν ὖν* referred to their riches, and the slowness with which the Athenians taunted them. It is preserved by Pindar, the greatest of a number of Boeotian poets from Hesiod downwards who give it the lie. The Boeotian contribution to ancient music was also important. Artistically Boeotia was always backward.

Paus. bk. 9 and Frazer's commentary; Strabo 9. 400 ff. A. W. Gomme, 'The Topography of Boeotia', *BSA* xviii. 189 ff.; W. A. Heurtley, 'Notes on the Harbours of S. Boeotia', ib. xxvi. 38 ff.; W. R. Roberts, *The Ancient Boeotians* (1895); M. Feyel, *Polybe et l'histoire de Béotie* (1942). T. J. D.

BOEOTIA, CULTS AND LEGENDS. Stories of the earliest population are scanty and poor (see Paus. 9. 1. 1 and 2; cf. Cauer in *PW* iii. 640–2). We may instance the shadowy figure of Aon, eponym of the Aones (Steph. Byz., s.v.; schol. Stat. *Theb.* 1. 33), son of Poseidon. Most of the tradition concerning Orchomenus is lost (cf. MINYAS) and the bulk of the surviving tales are Theban (*see* ADRASTUS, AMPHIARAUS, AMPHION, ANTIGONE, CADMUS, ETEOCLES, OEDIPUS). Much of what we know is owing to Pausanias. Cf. HERACLES.

Of cults, several are remarkable. Plataea had the Daedala, apparently a sacred marriage (*see* MARRIAGE, SACRED), combined with a remarkable fire-ceremony (Paus. 9. 3. 3 ff., cf. Plutarch, vol. vii, pp. 43–50 Bernardakis). At Orchomenus existed the ancient cult of the Charites (Pind. *Ol.* 14. 4; Paus. 9. 38. 1, cf. Farnell, *Cults* v. 428). On Helicon was the shrine of the Muses, said to have been founded by Otus and Ephialtes (Paus. 29. 1 ff., Farnell, ibid. 435). Thespiae had the cult of Eros (Paus. 27. 1), and a virgin priestess of Heracles (ibid. 6); Lebadea the oracle of Trophonius (q.v.). At Chaeronea a stick said to be the sceptre of Agamemnon was the chief deity (Paus. 40. 11, see de Visser, *Die nicht menschengestaltigen Götter* (1903), 112). At Thebes itself may be mentioned the cult of Apollo *Σπόδιος*, the very ancient worship of Aphrodite, the so-called tomb of Amphion and Zethus and the fertility-magic attaching, Athena's title of Onca and the imported cult of Hector (Paus. 11. 1 and 2; 16. 3; 17. 4; 18. 5), also the remarkable sanctuary of the Cabiri (q.v.) (ibid. 25. 5; see Kern in *PW* x. 1437 ff.). For a list of Boeotian cults, see Nilsson, *Griechische Feste*, topographical index under 'Böotien'.

For contacts with Arcadian myths and cults, see V. Bérard, *Les Cultes arcadiens* (1894), index under 'Béotie'. H. J. R.

BOEOTIAN, *see* DIALECTS, GREEK.

BOETHIUS, ANICIUS MANLIUS SEVERINUS (*c.* A.D. 480–524), son of the consul for 487, was *cos.* in 510. He was high in the confidence of Theodoric at Ravenna since early manhood, but, becoming involved in a charge of high treason brought against his friend Albinus, he was thrown into prison and executed. He wrote in prison the *De Consolatione Philosophiae*, a dialogue between himself and a figure representing philosophy, interspersed after the fashion of the Menippean Satire with verses in various metres, in which, though a Christian, he employs arguments of pagan philosophy. He was a prolific writer and exercised a wide influence in the Middle Ages by his works on arithmetic and music, and his translations and commentaries (see ENCYCLOPAEDIC LEARNING): he wrote on Aristotle's *Categories*, on his *Περὶ ἑρμηνείας*, on Porphyrius' *εἰσαγωγή* to Aristotle's *Categories*, and on Cicero's *Topica*. He had projected translations (with commentaries) of the whole of Aristotle and Plato, but the plan was only partly carried out. He wrote also theological treatises on the Trinity and in opposition to Eutyches and Nestorius.

T. Hodgkin, *Italy and her Invaders* (1892–9), iii. 466 ff.; H. F. Stewart, *Boethius, a Study* (1891); *Cons. Phil.* ed. Weinberger (1934).
R. M. H.

BOETHUS (1) (2nd c. B.C.), sculptor and metal-worker, son of Athenaion, of Calchedon. Works (dated): (*a*) signature of dedication made by Boethus to Athena of Lindus about 180 B.C. in gratitude for the office of proxenus; (*b*) signature of statue of Antiochus IV (175–164 B.C.) in Delos (undated); (*c*) boy strangling a goose, bronze; marble copies in Munich, etc. (Winter, *KB* 370. 1–2). Herodas (4. 31) mentions an earlier marble group of the same subject (perhaps Winter, *KB* 370. 3); (*d*) statue of Asclepius as a boy; (*e*) signed bronze archaizing herm, found in the sea near Mahdia, probably support for winged boy also found there (Winter, *KB* 310. 1); (*f*) hydria, an heirloom stolen by Verres from Pamphilus of Lilybaeum; (*g*) a particular kind of couch, 'lectus Boethiacus', may have been invented by Boethus.

Overbeck, 1597–9, 2167, 2184; G. M. A. Richter, *Sculpture and Sculptors* (1930), 297; F. Studniczka, *Artemis und Iphigenie* (1926), 69; R. Herzog, *JÖAI* 1903, 215. T. B. L. W.

BOETHUS (2) (2nd c. B.C.), sculptor, son of Apollodorus, of Carthage. Known from signature in Ephesus and Pausanias' description of gilded boy in Heraeum at Olympia (Overbeck, 1596).

BOETHUS (3) of Sidon (fl. 2nd c. B.C.), pupil of Diogenes of Babylon, was an unorthodox member of the Stoic school. In distinction from Chrysippus' monistic psychology he propounded a dualistic one, in which the rational faculties νοῦς and ἐπιστήμη were opposed to the irrational, ὄρεξις and αἴσθησις. A similar dualism appears in his derivation of soul from air and fire, of which the latter was probably regarded as the basis of reason. Similarly he rejected Pantheism and divided the universe into a part which was divine—the sphere of the fixed stars—and a part which was not. His divergences from orthodox Stoicism seem to be due to Aristotelian influence. He devoted himself specially to the study of astronomy and meteorology. Works: a commentary on Aratus' *Phaenomena*, Περὶ φύσεως, Περὶ εἱμαρμένης.

Testimonia in von Arnim, *SVF* iii. 265–7; *PW* iii. 601.
W. D. R.

BOETHUS (4) of Sidon, Peripatetic philosopher of the time of Augustus, a pupil of Andronicus of Rhodes and probably also of Xenarchus. After Andronicus' death he seems to have been head of the school at Athens. His commentaries on Aristotle are referred to by later Greek commentators, but none of them has survived.

PW iii. 603. W. D. R.

BOGUD (*Bogudes*, Βόγος, Βογόνας), king of Mauretania Tingitana, became Caesar's ally in 49 B.C.; in 48 he helped Q. Cassius in Spain; in 45 in the battle of Munda his cavalry played a decisive part. He declared for Antony, and after an unhappy attack on Spain, lost his kingdom. He fell at Methone in the Peloponnese fighting against Agrippa (31). A. M.

BOII, Gauls who entered Italy c. 400 B.C. (reputedly via the Great St. Bernard) and established themselves between the Po and the Apennines, ousting Etruscans and Umbrians. Their chief city was Bononia. Their Iron Age civilization was not altogether primitive. Defeated by Rome c. 282 B.C., they signed a 45-year truce. They were conquered again at Telamon (225) and submitted until Hannibal's arrival encouraged them anew; with Ligurian and other allies they continued fighting Rome until they were subjugated, massacred, and mulcted of

half their territory in 191. Military roads and colonies (Bononia, Parma, Mutina) consolidated the Roman victory and the Boii disappeared from Italy either through expulsion or assimilation (Livy 5. 35; 21–35; Polyb. 2. 17 f.; 3). Boii are also recorded in Gaul, where they supported the Helvetii, were defeated at Bibracte (58 B.C.), and settled on Aeduan territory (Caes. *BGall.* 1. 5. 28; 7. 9). Bohemia, which preserves their name, likewise contained Boii from early times until their extermination by Burebistas the Dacian c. 50 B.C.

The relationship of these various Boii is commonly but somewhat unconvincingly explained as follows (Strabo 5. 213): large numbers left the parent Gallic stock, entered Italy, were expelled thence after 191 and settled in Bohemia.

For bibliography see CISALPINE GAUL. E. T. S.

BOIO, an ancient Delphic priestess, to whom was attributed an 'Ορνιθογονία (description of transformations into birds) of unknown date.

J. U. Powell, *Collectanea Alexandrina*, 23–4.

BOLANUS, see VETTIUS (4).

BOLUS of Mendes in Egypt, writer of the third or second century B.C. He is mentioned in Suidas (s.v. Βῶλος Δημοκρίτειος and Β. Μενδήσιος Πυθαγόρειος, who is the same person) as writer of *mirabilia* and magical books. Some of these were fastened on Democritus' name, especially the medicine-book 'On sympathies and antipathies'. Later B.'s own name may have been used for similar pseudo-Democritean literature.

See PARADOXOGRAPHERS.

Susemihl, *Gesch. gr. Lit. Alex.* i. 482, 901; ii. 674; E. Oder, *Rh. Mus.* 1890, 70 f.; *PW* iii. 676. K. O. B.

BONA DEA, a Roman goddess worshipped exclusively by women. Her proper name was allegedly Fauna, daughter (Varro ap. Macrob. *Sat. i. 12. 27*) or wife (Sex. Clodius ap. Arn. *Adv. Nat.* 5, p. 190, 2 Reifferscheid, cf. Plut. *Quaest. Rom.* 20) of Faunus (q.v.). Her official nocturnal ceremonial was held yearly at the house of the chief magistrate, under the leadership of his wife and with the assistance of the Vestals (Cic. *Har. Resp.* 37; Plut. *Caes.* 9). The room was decorated with vine-branches and other plants and flowers, myrtle, however, being excluded. Wine was brought in, but called milk and the covered jar containing it a honey-pot (Macrob. ibid. 25, and the other passages cited). It is not known how much of this was native and how much due to the superimposed ritual of Damia (cf. AUXESIA; Festus, p. 60, 1 ff. Lindsay). The sacrifice to Bona Dea was a sow (Macrob. ibid. 23), and her temple on the Aventine below the *saxum*, hence her title Subsaxana (Platner–Ashby, 85).

See Wissowa *RK* 216 ff. H. J. R.

BONONIA (1) (mod. *Bologna*), in Cisalpine Gaul, has always been a place of consequence. Villanovan settlements occupied the site from c. 1050 until 500 B.C. when Etruscans founded Felsina there. Felsina became the chief Etruscan city north of the Apennines (Pliny, *HN* 3. 115), but fell first to the Boii then to Rome (196 B.C.), and acquired the name Bononia (Livy 33. 37). Subsequently as Latin colony, *municipium*, Imperial *colonia*, or part of the Ravenna exarchate, Bononia was always important (Livy 37. 57; Festus p. 155 L.; Tac. *Ann.* 12. 58; Procop. *Goth.* 3. 11). Antony, Octavian, and Lepidus met near here to establish the Second Triumvirate (*CAH* x. 19). As a centre of the north Italian road system Strabo 5. 216 f.), Bononia flourished and was able to survive a conflagration in A.D. 53 and Alaric's attack in 410 (Tac. loc. cit.; Zosim. 6. 10). (2), see GESORIACUM.

For BONONIA (1) see the bibliography under CISALPINE GAUL, and A. Grenier, *Bologne, Villanovienne et Étrusque* (1912); A. Ducati, *Storia di Bologna* (1928). E. T. S.

BONOSUS (3rd c. A.D.), son of a Gallic mother, but of British descent, was commander of the Roman fleet at Colonia Agrippinensis on the Rhine. Losing a squadron through carelessness to the Germans and fearing punishment, Bonosus revolted. He found some support in Gaul and among the barbarians, but was crushed by Probus after a bitter struggle (A.D. 280). H. M.

BONUS EVENTUS, personified 'good result', originally good harvest (Varro, *Rust.* 1. 1. 6), then success in general. He had a temple on the Campus Martius (Amm. Marc. 29. 6. 19), and was a popular deity, to judge by the many inscriptional dedications to him.

See Wissowa, *RK* 267. H. J. R.

BOOKS, GREEK AND LATIN. I. GREEK.

1. Although there is now ample evidence of the use of writing in the Near East (Egypt, Palestine, Syria, Mesopotamia, Crete) long before the earliest Greek literature, and a consequent presumption of its use in Greece, there is nothing to show what writing-material was used for the Homeric and Hesiodic works. Presumably it was either leather or papyrus. Herodotus (5. 58) records a tradition that the Ionians had once, when papyrus was scarce, made use of skins, as certain barbarous peoples did in his day. The word for 'book' among the Ionians was διφθέρα, which seems to imply a primitive use of leather as writing-material, at any rate in Asia Minor; but the form in which Herodotus states the fact proves that, so far back as Greek memory went in his day, papyrus was the normal material. It may therefore be taken as certain that, at least from the beginning of the period of the lyric poets, books were normally written on papyrus; and this continued to be the case throughout the classical and Hellenistic periods.

2. From the classical period no specimens survive. Papyrus is a perishable material, and it is practically only from the exceptionally dry soil of Egypt that Greek MSS. on papyrus have been recovered. These all date after the introduction of Greek settlers by Ptolemy I. The first discovery of papyri was made in 1778 (with partial publication, 1788), but it is only since 1877, and especially since 1891, that they have been discovered in considerable quantities, so that now we possess several hundreds of literary MSS. (generally in fragments only) from the last quarter of the fourth century B.C. to the first half of the seventh century A.D. How fully their evidence applies to the earlier period can only be matter for conjecture.

3. Papyrus, as a writing-material, was made from the pith of a water-plant (*Cyperus papyrus*), which then grew plentifully in the Nile (Plin. *HN* 13. 68 ff.). The pith was cut into thin strips, which were laid down in two layers, in one of which the fibres were laid horizontally, and in the other vertically. The two layers were fastened together by water, glue, and pressure, and the surface polished to perfect smoothness. The size of the sheets was governed by the length to which the strips could be cut without weakness, the widest being the best. Specimens are known as broad as 15 in., but normal measurements from Greek times range from about 9 in. downwards. In height a roll might be as much as 12 or 13 in. (one Egyptian papyrus reaches 19 in.); but 8 or 9 in. is a more normal size for literary rolls, ranging down to 5 in. for a book of poetry, or even 2 in. for a booklet of epigrams. In the Roman market names were given to various qualities according to their size; but these categories cannot be identified in the extant specimens.

4. The sheets thus formed (κολλήματα) could be used singly (as for letters) or glued together side by side to form a roll. Pliny states that a roll (*scapus*) never consisted of more than twenty sheets (i.e. about 15 ft.); but this can only apply to the unit of sale. For practical use the *scapus* could be cut up if less were needed, or leng-

thened by attachment to another. Egyptian rolls are known which exceed 100 ft.; but for Greek rolls the evidence shows that 30–35 ft. was about the maximum. This, with a normal writing, would suffice for one book of Thucydides; a book of Plato's *Republic* would require not much more than half of this.

5. The writing was arranged in columns (σελίδες), which do not correspond with the κολλήματα. For poetry the width of a column was dictated by the length of the verse; in a sumptuous Homer it may reach 9¾ in., but 5 in. would be more normal. For prose, 4 in. (including margin) is exceptionally wide, 2 to 3 in. normal. The number of lines varies with the height of the column and the size of the writing; but numbers less than 25 or more than 45 are exceptional. The number of letters in a line varies. There were fixed rules governing the division of words at the end of a line, and to meet these the outer (right-hand) edge of the column was uneven. About 18 to 25 letters to a line is normal; less than 16 is almost unknown. Conjectures based on the number of lines in a column or of letters in a line are therefore precarious.

6. The writing on papyrus was normally on the side on which the fibres lay horizontally (*recto*); but frequently the other side (*verso*) of a document or literary text was subsequently utilized. Such copies were, however, for private use, or, possibly, represent a form of cheap production for the market. Very rarely the text on the *recto* is continued on the *verso*; such rolls are known as *opisthograph*, and references to them occur in ancient authors, as marks either of the poverty of the writer or the excess of his matter (Lucian, *Vit. Auct.* 9; Ezek. 2. 10; Pliny, *Ep.* 3. 5. 17; Juv. 1. 6). Since the writing on the *recto* almost invariably precedes that on the *verso* (there are a few exceptions in the 3rd c. B.C.), valuable evidence for dating may sometimes be obtained from this fact.

7. Margins between columns are generally small, but those at the top and bottom of a roll (especially the finer specimens) may extend to 1½ or 2 in., or even more. Here lines or words accidentally omitted are sometimes written, generally with an arrow to indicate the place where they should be inserted. Marginal annotations are rare in extant papyri.

8. Helps to the reader are strikingly rare. Words are not separated; enlarged initials are not used. Accents are very rare, the chief exceptions being in lyric poems, such as the papyri of Alcman and Bacchylides; and even here their occurrence is only sporadic. A rough breathing is occasionally inserted where misunderstanding might arise. Punctuation is uncertain and arbitrary; it takes the form either of a single point, generally about level with the top of the letter (there is no systematic use of high, medial, and low points), or of leaving a short space at the end of a clause. A short stroke (παράγραφος) is sometimes placed below the beginning of a line in which a break occurs; and the same symbol is used in dramatic pieces to indicate a change of speaker. Titles are placed at the end (*see* SUBSCRIPTIONES); but in the Herodas MS. titles of individual poems have been prefixed by the original scribe, and in the Bacchylides MS. they have been added in the margin by another hand. The normal means of identifying the content of a roll was a label (σίλλυβος) of papyrus or vellum, which projected from it as it lay on a shelf or in a box (*see* LIBRARIES).

9. The papyrus roll continued to be the main vehicle of literature down to the end of the third century A.D.; but it is now evident, from recent discoveries in Egypt, that at least from the beginning of the second century papyrus books were sometimes produced in *Codex* form, i.e. the modern form with leaves arranged in quires. Whether this was actually an invention of the Christian community in Egypt, with the object of being able to include more than a single Gospel or Epistle in one book, is unknown, but it was certainly predominantly used by them; for while all pagan MSS. in the second century and 95 per cent. of them in the third century are rolls, the majority of Christian MSS. are codices.

10. A papyrus Codex was formed by taking a sheet twice the width of the page desired, and folding it once vertically, thus producing a quire of two leaves. By similarly treating a number of sheets simultaneously, a quire could be made of any desired size. Specimens exist from quires of 2 leaves (Chester Beatty Gospels and Acts) to quires of 118 leaves (Chester Beatty Ezekiel, Daniel, and Esther); but these seem to have been early experiments, and eventually it was found convenient to form quires of 10 or 12 leaves. All the later codices are of this type. Since usually sheets which were to form a quire were laid, before folding, with the *recto* uppermost, after folding *verso* pages preceded *recto* in the first half of each quire, and *recto* preceded *verso* in the second half. If it was desired, for the sake of uniform appearance, to have *recto* pages facing *recto*, and *verso verso*, at each opening of the Codex, this result could be obtained by laying the sheets, before folding, with *recto* and *verso* alternately uppermost; and examples of this exist.

11. Most extant papyrus codices have only one column to a page, but there are some examples with two, e.g. the Chester Beatty Numbers and Deuteronomy. A few early codices are exceptionally tall and narrow; e.g. the Chester Beatty Ezekiel (14 × 5 in.), *PAmh.* 460 (11 × 4½ in.), but most range between about 12 × 8 and 8 × 7 in.

12. Besides the change from papyrus roll to codex, which barely affects non-Christian literature before the fourth century, the beginnings of the use of vellum have to be observed. Vellum or parchment (there is no regularly observed distinction between the terms) is a development of the use of leather, being a material produced by the preparation of the skins of cattle, sheep, and goats. The skins are washed, scraped to remove the hair, smoothed with pumice, and dressed with chalk. There is a slight difference between the hair-side and the flesh-side, the former tending to be darker, but to retain the ink better.

13. According to Varro (Plin. *HN* 13. 70) vellum was invented at Pergamum when Ptolemy (Epiphanes, 205–182 B.C.) placed an embargo on the export of papyrus, in order to hamper the growth of the library of his rival bibliophile, Eumenes II of Pergamum (197–159 B.C.). Vellum cannot in fact have been then first used as a writing-material, since documents on vellum have recently been found so far away from Pergamum as Dura on the Euphrates, with dates equivalent to 196 and 190 B.C.; but it may well be that Eumenes was the first to use it as a vehicle for literature, and this is somewhat confirmed by its Greek name, περγαμηνή. Its use at this early date was, however, local, and probably temporary; for it is certain that papyrus remained in use as the principal book-material until a much later date. The evidence from Egypt shows that in that country at least vellum made no headway before the end of the third century. Two fragments may be as early as the end of the first century, but the total number earlier than the fourth century is negligible. It is likely that the use of vellum was greater in other countries, but all present evidence goes to show that the main change-over from papyrus to vellum took place in the first half of the fourth century. Constantine, on his acceptance of Christianity as the State religion, ordered 50 copies of the Scriptures for the churches of Constantinople, and these were to be written on vellum; and at about the same time Jerome records that the papyrus MSS. in the library of Caesarea, having become worn by use, were replaced by vellum copies. Even from Egypt there is a marked increase in the number of vellum fragments discovered, while the quality of the papyrus MSS. deteriorates. From this period also come the first and finest vellum codices now extant, the Vatican and Sinaitic codices of the Greek Bible; and

the earliest Latin codices (Virgil, Cicero, Terence, Livy, N.T.) are assigned to the fourth or early fifth century. But this is to pass from the classical period to the history of the transmission of texts of classical authors through the Middle Ages down to the invention of printing.

II. LATIN.

1. Latin literature depends almost wholly on Greek, and it is practically certain that Latin books in the Classical period followed the Greek model. The Romans themselves had little knowledge of any earlier stage. Livy quotes no authority earlier than the second century B.C. for the existence of archives written on linen (*libri lintei*) of the time of the kings; and the word *liber* itself seems to imply a time when writings were inscribed on bark. But no literature survives (if it was ever written down) from these earlier periods, and for all practical purposes it may be taken as certain that the main vehicle of Latin literature as we know it was the papyrus roll (*charta, volumen*).

2. For the exterior form of Latin books we have more evidence from contemporary descriptions and allusions than we have for Greek, but much less in the way of extant specimens. Egypt has produced far fewer Latin fragments than Greek, and these add practically nothing to our knowledge of the form of papyrus books. What has been said of Greek books must be taken as applying to Latin. Allusions in Catullus, Propertius, Tibullus, and especially Martial add details of their external appearance. A good example is the description in Catullus' poem on Suffenus, 22. 4–8. The better class of rolls were furnished with rollers (no specimens of these have been found in Egypt), the projecting knobs of which (*cornua, umbilici*) might be made ornamental in colour or material. The roll when not in use might be enclosed in a vellum cover (*membrana, paenula*), which could be coloured and fastened with coloured strings. The papyrus itself might be soaked in cedar oil (Hor. *ArsP.* 332), and the title attached to it (*titulus, index*) might be coloured. When not in use, rolls were stored in boxes or buckets (*capsa, capsula, scrinium*), or laid on shelves or in pigeon-holes (*nidi*). The booksellers' shops in Rome were to be found mainly in the Argiletum, with advertisements of their wares suspended on the columns of the porticos in their front (Cic. *Att.* 12. 32; Mart. 1. 117. 9 ff.).

3. The Latin authors also contain many references to another form of writing-material, namely the tablets (*tabellae, pugillares*) which were used as note-books. These were normally of wood, which could either be whitened to receive ink, or covered with wax, on which writing was inscribed with a *stilus*. Two tablets fastened together with string (which could be secured with a seal, if desired) could form a closed letter which the recipient, after smoothing over the wax, could return with his answer (Ovid, *Am.* i. 12. 1; August. *Ad Rom.*: Migne, *PL* xxxiii. 80). Or they could contain a legal contract, the substance of which, for greater convenience and security, was repeated on the outside. Or again several tablets could be fastened together with thongs, forming a sort of wooden codex.

4. It is indeed probable that the tablet with several leaves gave the original idea of the Codex as a book form, and that vellum first came into use for note-books, and was treated in the same way. *Membrana*, the Latin word for vellum, also means note-book (Hor. *Sat.* 2. 3. 2); the μεμβράναι mentioned in St. Paul (2 Tim. iv. 13) were probably his note-books. Evidence of the early use of vellum for books is provided by Martial, who in his descriptions of gifts at the Saturnalia includes a number of books (14. 183–95). Some of these are specifically said to be *in membranis*, implying that the others were of the more ordinary material, papyrus; but their exact nature is a puzzle. All are of large works, totally out of scale for a Christmas present, and a point is made that a great work is comprised in a small compass; the *Iliad* and *Odyssey* in *pugillares membranae*, all Virgil in a *breuis membrana*, all Livy even *pellibus exiguis*. Evidently some form of extract or epitome is meant, and all the evidence is against the use of vellum as a serious competitor with papyrus until the fourth century, from which time fine vellum codices are extant, and vellum became the principal vehicle of Latin literature. *See also* LIBRARIES.

W. Schubart, *Das Buch bei den Griechen und Römern²*, (1921); F. G. Kenyon, *Books and Readers in Ancient Greece and Rome* (1932). Earlier works, still useful, but lacking the information derived from the most recent discoveries of papyri in Egypt, are: Th. Birt, *Das antike Buchwesen* (1882); V. Gardthausen, *Griechische Palaeographie, I. Das Buchwesen im Altertum* (1911); E. Maunde Thompson, *Introduction to Greek and Latin Palaeography* (1912).
F. G. K.

BOOKSELLERS, *see* SOSII.

BOREAS, the North wind. Cult of or magic practices directed towards winds are fairly common in Greece (*see* WIND-GODS and Farnell, *Cults* v. 448–9; more in Fiedler, *Antiker Wetterzauber* (1931)). The most famous worship of Boreas was in Attica (Hdt. 7. 189, for his help against the Persians at Artemisium). Mythologically, he was 'son-in-law' of the Athenians, having carried off his bride, Oreithyia, daughter of King Erechtheus, from the Areios Pagos or the banks of the Ilissus (Plato, *Phdr.* 229 c–d). By her he had two sons, Zetes and Calais (*see* CALAIS AND ZETES).

Apart from this, hardly anything is told of him which does not arise from his physical characteristics. He is, for instance, son of Eos and Astraeus (Hes. *Theog.* 378–80), along with Zephyrus and Notus; in other words, winds come down out of the sky, where the stars and dawn are an idea which competes with the conception of them as underground beings (as a kind of ghosts, cf. HARPYIAE, or because they come from below the horizon?), to whom black victims are sacrificed (e.g. Ar. *Ran.* 847). Even his begetting of horses (as *Il.* 20. 223) is a simple mythologizing of the speed of wind, or perhaps of some such belief as that in Verg. *G.* 3. 275, that mares can be impregnated by wind.
H. J. R.

BORYSTHENES, a river of Scythia (modern *Dnieper*). According to Herodotus (4. 53) it was the largest river after the Nile and the Ister (*Danube*), being navigable for forty days from the sea. This statement, and his failure to mention the falls at Dnieprostroi, show that Herodotus was unacquainted with the upper course of the Borysthenes. But the glowing terms in which he described its fisheries and meadows were not ill founded. The Borysthenes was the chief Greek trade route into Scythia, but this trade (as the record of finds shows) did not extend beyond the region of Kiev.
M. C.

BOSCOREALE, a village on the slopes of Vesuvius near Pompeii. Several *villae rusticae*, buried in the eruption of A.D. 79, have been found in its vicinity. One, excavated in 1893–4, is famous for the discovery of a treasure of silver plate, but the rustic character of the villa suggests that the treasure was brought from elsewhere at the time of the catastrophe. The villa was mainly agricultural, and the arrangement of the rooms can be determined with certainty. A second villa, discovered four years later, was residential in type and remarkable for a beautiful series of wall-paintings of the first century B.C.
R. C. C.

BOSPORUS, a narrow strait joining the Black Sea with the Mediterranean and dividing Asia and Europe. Its direction is NE.–SW. and it is 17 miles long, and from 600 yards at the narrowest to 3,300 at the broadest in width. The current runs swiftly from the Black Sea into the Mediterranean, breaking against Serai Point, the

shores of ancient Byzantium. The strait has been worn away in a fairly recent geological past as the exit for the water of the Black Sea, which was originally a lake. The Bosporus is noted for its wealth of fish, and many ancient Greek coastal towns bore fish as the device on their coins. The name records the legend of the crossing of Io (q.v.). In antiquity it was called the Thracian Bosporus to distinguish it from the Cimmerian Bosporus connecting the Sea of Azov and the Black Sea.
S. C.

BOSTRA, a commercial town in the north of the Nabataean kingdom. In A.D. 105 it was refounded by Trajan as the capital of the province of Arabia. From *c.* 125 it was the camp of Legio III Cyrenaica and was made a colony by Severus Alexander. The ruins are considerable.

R. E. Brünnow and A. von Domaszewski, *Die Provincia Arabia* iii (1909), 1–84.
A. H. M. J.

BOTANY. Among the Greeks, as among other peoples, knowledge of herbs was linked with medicine. It was somewhat esoteric and, from an early date, certain drugs were imported from overseas, notably from Egypt, Mesopotamia, and even India. Plant-lore was the special preserve of the rhizotomists (ῥιζοτομικοί), who were differentiated from the physicians and doubtless represent an earlier cultural stratum. They were sometimes of evil reputation; Sophocles speaks of them almost as poison-mongers. In gathering plants they practised complex rituals of which fragments are preserved by Theophrastus and Pliny.

2. The Hippocratic Collection mentions some three hundred herbal drugs but tells almost nothing of the plants themselves. Nevertheless, in the first half of the fourth century botany was emerging as a separate discipline and attention was paid to it at the Academy even before it was taken up at the Lyceum. Perhaps under the influence of the former, but chiefly inspired by Sicilian pneumatic views (*see* ANATOMY AND PHYSIOLOGY), is the Hippocratic work *On the nature of the embryo* of about 360 B.C. It discusses germination of seeds and growth of plants and contains the first attempt at a vegetable physiology.

3. Aristotle treated plants as a lower order of beings than animals, linked with them through the 'zoophytes', continued downward into non-living matter, and possessing only the lowest of the three faculties of soul. Of his work *On Plants* only a corrupt abstract survives. We have, however, several treatises on plants by his pupil Theophrastus (372–287 B.C.), and among them are the only ancient botanic works worthy of the name of science.

4. Theophrastus felt the need of a technical terminology and began to develop it. Like his master he was deeply interested in generation and, having examined the germination of seeds, with extraordinary acuteness made the distinction between monocotyledons and dicotyledons. In this and in many other matters he showed himself fully capable of following morphological homologies. Though ignorant of the nature of sex in flowers he had an approximately correct notion of the relation of flower and fruit, distinguished hypogynous, perigynous, and epigynous types, and regarded the relation of flowers to fruit as the essential floral element. He had a clear view of plant distribution as dependent on soil and climate and, benefiting by the knowledge available from Alexander's expeditions, came near to a statement of geographical plant regions. He has numerous good descriptions of the forms, habits, habitats, fructification, cultivation, and uses of plants, of which he discusses more than 400 kinds.

5. The Alexandrian school produced no botanical works of significance. Important, however, was the work of the rhizotomist Crateuas (q.v., *c.* 100 B.C.), who served Mithridates VI of Pontus. He wrote a herbal in which

each plant was represented by a figure. Of this there survives a substantial fragment, copied from a very ancient and perhaps almost contemporary original. Since Crateuas plant representation has been an important department of botany.

6. The *Natural History* of Pliny (A.D. 23–79) records many current views on the nature, origin, and uses of plants. Being quite uncritical it is more interesting for folk-lore than for botany. On a higher plane is the *Materia Medica* of Dioscorides (*c.* A.D. 60), which consists of a series of short accounts of plants arranged without system but accompanied with terse descriptions which sometimes include habits and habitats. It is the most widely read botanical work ever penned. Early MSS. of versions and translations of it are to be numbered by the hundred. Many of its plant names have passed into modern terminology. After Dioscorides there was no extension of botanical knowledge in antiquity.

7. Difficulties in identifying the plants of Dioscorides led very early, perhaps during his lifetime, to the preparation of copies of his herbals provided with pictures of the plants. A magnificent representative of this practice in uncial letters is the Juliana Anicia MS. of 515 at Vienna, the earliest surviving complete Greek herbal. Illustrated Latin versions, abridgements, and modifications of Dioscorides were prepared in the time of Cassiodorus (A.D. 490–585), and a Latin work based on one of these versions but bearing the name of Apuleius is the commonest early medical text. A splendid half-uncial MS. of this *Herbarius Apuleii* at Leyden is almost contemporary with Cassiodorus himself and is our earliest complete Latin document of this type.

8. The question of the identification of plants mentioned by classical writers frequently arises and can be answered for certain distinctive or economically important species. The question, however, ignores the semantics of plant-names. A modern plant-name—even a 'popular' one—presupposes a conception of species and of their constancy and limitations and an idea of classification that was absent in antiquity. Greek and Latin writers, like modern unlettered peasants, constantly called the same plant by different names and different plants by the same name. The question as to what a particular writer meant by a particular plant-name is therefore, with the exceptions mentioned above, normally unanswerable.

J. Berendes, *Des Pedanios Dioskurides aus Anazarbos Arzneimittellehre* (1902); H. Bretzl, *Botanische Forschungen des Alexanderzuges* (1903); A. de Premenstein, *De codicis Dioskuridei Aniciae Julianae historia etc.* (1906); E. L. Greene, *Landmarks of Botanical History* (U.S.A. (Smithsonian Institute), 1909); E. Howald and H. E. Sigerist, *Antonii Musae De herba vettonica Liber, Pseudo-Apulei Herbarius*, etc. (1927); Charles Singer, 'The Herbal in Antiquity', *JHS* xlvii (1927); G. Senn, *Die Pflanzenkunde des Theophrast im Eresos* (1933); R. Strömberg, *Theophrastea, Studien zur botanischen Begriffsbildung* (1937); R. M. Dawkins, 'Semantics of Greek Plant Names', *JHS* lviii (1938). C. S.

BOTTOMRY LOANS (ναυτικόν, ναυτικὸς τόκος; *fenus nauticum* or *pecunia traiecticia*), are known from the fourth century B.C. They took the place of modern shipping-insurance, because they were repayable only if the ship or the cargo which had been pledged for them (especially in Greek law), safely reached its place of destination (ἑτερόπλουν) or returned to the original port (ἀμφοτερόπλουν), according to the terms of a written contract. The debt was not forfeited if ship or cargo was lost by the debtor's fault. Creditors and debtors could be groups of persons in partnership.

The biggest loan we know of amounts to 70 *minae*. During the fourth century the rate charged for a voyage from Athens to the Pontus and back was 30 per cent. on the amount of the loan, from Sestus to Athens 12½ per cent., and from Byzantium to Athens 10–12 per cent. Roman law from Justinian onwards allowed a rate (*usurae maritimae*) up to 12½ per cent. on *fenus nauticum*.

The creditor had the right to send a supercargo (ἐπίπλους), often a freedman or slave, with the ship to control loading, unloading, and repayment. Attic as well as Roman law made elaborate regulations for this institution, which represented an important form of capital investment.

Klingmüller, *PW*, s.v. 'fenus'; Berger, ibid., s.v. 'iactus'; Schwahn, ibid., s.v. ναυτικὸς τόκος; U. E. Paoli, *Studi di diritto attico* (Pubblicazioni dell' Università di Firenze, v.s. ix (1930), pt. I). F. M. H.

BOUDICCA (name uncertain, but 'Boadicea' has neither authority nor meaning), wife of Prasutagus, who was established as client-king of the Iceni (East Anglia) by the Romans. On his death (A.D. 61) he had left the Emperor coheir with his daughters, but imperial agents maltreated his family. Under Boudicca the Iceni, assisted by the Trinovantes, rose in rebellion while the governor, Suetonius Paulinus, was occupied in the west. Colchester, London, and Verulamium were successively sacked. Venturing a battle, however, with Paulinus' main force, Boudicca's troops were easily routed, and she herself took poison.

Tacitus, *Ann.* 14. 31–7; *Agr.* 16. 1–2; Dio 62. 1–12. Collingwood-Myres, *Roman Britain*, 99–104. C. E. S.

BOULE in Greek States, originally the council of nobles which the king summoned to advise him; later a specially appointed council to undertake, on behalf of the citizen-body, the day-to-day affairs of State. Its range of competence was equal to that of the citizen Assembly. In an oligarchy it might be in some respects independent of the Assembly—e.g. it might have the right of summoning the Assembly only when it wished; in a democracy it was its servant, acting as a general purposes committee. In the former, members might be elected by vote (perhaps from a restricted number of citizens) or sit by hereditary right, for a term of years, or for life; in a democracy, members were generally chosen by lot, and served for a year only. Every 'constitutional' State (hereditary monarchy, oligarchy, or democracy) had a Boule of one kind or another.

2. In Athens, Solon (q.v.) established a Boule of 400, 100 from each *phyle* (q.v.), perhaps elected by vote, its members not confined to the rich, and serving for a year only; its especial duty was to prepare business for the Ecclesia, which was thus freed from the control of the Areopagus. This Boule survived the tyranny; Cleisthenes enlarged it to 500, 50 from each of the new *phylae*, so many from each deme in proportion to its population (*see* DEMOI), elected by lot to serve for a year. All citizens over thirty were eligible, but no one could serve more than twice, and not in successive years. Its members were paid, 5 obols a day in Aristotle's time. It met daily except on festival days; and its functions were to carry on all the business of the State in conjunction with the magistrates, and to prepare business for the Ecclesia: nothing that it had not considered could come before the Ecclesia (q.v.); all magistrates therefore had to bring proposals before it first. Its presidents, who prepared its business, were from its own members; and it also provided the presidents of the Ecclesia; both Boule and Ecclesia were thus free of control by the magistrates. Its meetings were normally open to the public; but it could sit in secret if it so decided. *See also* PRYTANIS, GRAMMATEIS, PROEDROI.

3. It had a very wide competence. It conducted many forms of *dokimasia* (q.v.). It received all foreign envoys. It had special duties in relation to the navy—the care of the ships and of the docks, the provision of new ships each year. Its financial duties were also important, the letting of State property and receiving of rents, the borrowing from temple treasuries, the handing over of funds from each annual group of treasurers to their successors, the receiving of the allies' tribute in the fifth century—all was done in its presence; and it supervised the magistrates' accounts of public money (*see* EUTHYNA, LOGISTAI). It had the care of public buildings, and of certain State cults and sacrifices (with ten *hieropoioi* from its own members). It was responsible for the preservation of all State archives (*see* GRAMMATEIS).

4. It had certain judicial powers in matters which would come before the Ecclesia (by *eisangelia*, q.v.), such as treason, conspiracy against the constitution, or public riot: it could arrest citizens pending trial, and could itself fine up to a limit of 500 drachmas.

5. The Boule was the keystone of the democratic constitution; but it never dominated the State, as one might expect a body with its wide powers to have done. This was due to its constantly changing membership, which precluded the growth of an exclusive corporate feeling. Since a large proportion of the citizen-body (not less than one-third in the fifth century, and one-half in the fourth) passed through its ranks, it accurately reflected popular sentiment.

Aristotle, *Ath. Pol.*, passim. A. W. G.

BOUPHONIA, *see* SACRIFICE.

BOVIANUM UNDECIMANORUM, capital of the Pentri Samnites: modern *Bojano*. Conquered by Rome *c.* 311 B.C., it remained loyal during the Hannibalic War. In the Social War, after temporarily serving as a capital for the Italians, it was reduced to a village by Sulla. Under Vespasian veterans from Legio Undecima Claudia colonized it: hence its name.

Strabo 5. 250; Livy 9. 28. 31; 25. 13; App. *BCiv.* 1. 51; Pliny, *HN* 3. 107. E. T. S.

BOVIANUM VETUS, capital of the Caraceni Samnites and, in Imperial times, a colony of veterans: modern *Pietrabbondante*, with well-preserved remains of a theatre and temple. Rome first captured it in 298 B.C.

Livy 10. 12; Pliny *HN* 3. 107; Mommsen, *CIL* ix. 257. E. T. S.

BOXING. There were three stages in the history of ancient boxing, depending largely upon the methods of protecting or reinforcing the fist. Until 400 B.C. it was customary to wind soft strips of leather—μειλίχαι—round the hands and arms, which served like our light gloves to protect the knuckles and so increased the power of attack, but did not in themselves add to the severity of the blow. Early in the fourth century the μειλίχαι were superseded by gloves—σφαῖραι—made of hard pieces of leather with protecting and cutting edges, like our knuckle-dusters. From these the Roman *caestus* was developed, where the glove was weighted with pieces of iron and metal spikes placed in position over the knuckles.

In Greek boxing there was no ring and therefore little close fighting; there were no rounds and therefore the pace was slow; there was no classification by weight, and therefore the heavier the man the greater his chance of success. As thongs or gloves were always used on the hands, wrestling was impossible and the defence was all-important. Body-hitting was not practised to any extent, and in the later periods a fight was usually decided by a knock-out blow on the jaw. But in the earlier times the Greek boxer used both hands freely, was active on his feet, and had a considerable variety of attack.

Theocritus, 22. 87–111. K. T. Frost, *JHS* 1906, 213 ff. F. A. W.

BRANCHIDAE, *see* DIDYMA.

BRASIDAS (d. 422 B.C.), Spartan general. Though prominent from 431, he held only subordinate commands until 424, when he was sent with a small force of Helots and Peloponnesians to damage Athenian interests in Thrace. After saving Megara from an Athenian attack, he hurried northwards and rapidly won several important cities, including Amphipolis and Torone. He continued operations in Thrace after the conclusion of the armistice between Athens and Sparta in 423, by supporting the revolt of Scione and Mende, though he was unable to protect them adequately. In 422 he heavily defeated and killed Cleon in a surprise attack at Amphipolis, but was himself mortally wounded.

Brasidas' resourcefulness and his talent for winning confidence wherever he went gained the admiration of Thucydides and permanently injured the Athenian cause in a vital area.

Thucydides, bks. 4–5. H. D. W.

BRAURONIA, *see* ARTEMIS.

BRENNUS (1), the Gallic king who traditionally captured Rome (in 390 B.C. or, according to Polybius' chronology, 387), and made the famous utterance: 'Vae victis.' Since neither Polybius nor Diodorus mentions him, it has been suggested that Brennus is a title which was mistaken for a name, or that historians transferred to him the name of the Gallic chieftain who invaded Greece in 279 B.C. But the former hypothesis is disproved on philological grounds, and the Greek accounts of Brennus, which can be traced back to fourth-century authors, are anterior to the coming of the Celts. P. T.

BRENNUS (2), leader of the Galatian invasion in 279 B.C. Following on the heels of another body of Gauls under Bolgius, Brennus overran Macedonia and invaded Greece in autumn. Checked by a Greek coalition at Thermopylae, he detached a column into Aetolia, turned Thermopylae by the pass into Doris, and attacked Delphi. The detachment in Aetolia and the main column under Acichorius were harassed by guerrilla tactics, while Brennus was wounded at Delphi. During the general retreat northwards the Gauls were attacked by the Thessalians; Brennus committed suicide, and few escaped. N. G. L. H.

BREVIARIUM, *see* EPITOME (LATIN), PERIOCHAE.

BREVIS BREVIANS, Latin phonetical tendency between fourth and first centuries B.C., a 'short' syllable 'shortening' a following long one which is preceded or followed by an accent. Hence *calĕfacio* (from *cālēfácio*), but *ferŭefacio*. A comprehensive study setting out the conditions under which shortening becomes permanent (*benĕ* and *malĕ*, but cf. e.g. *probĕ*) is wanted. Poetry in general accepts the shortened forms only when they have become stabilized, but early drama shows *breuis breuians* in active operation in scansions like *bonĭs, quid ĕst, pessim(e) ŏrnatus.* Cf. PLAUTUS, para. 5 (Prosody). O. S.

BRIAREŌS, *see* HECATONCHEIRES.

BRIDGES. Remains of pre-Roman bridges in the Hellenic world are few and their dating rests upon no sound basis. Culverts near Mycenae are indistinguishable from remains assigned to the fifth century near Epidaurus, while bridges in the neighbourhood of Athens are even less securely dated. The Bosporus bridge of Darius was built by Mandrocles of Samos (Hdt. 4. 83, 87–8). The Etruscan 'bridges', as at Veii and Vulci, are tunnelled spurs of natural rock, the built structures in stone being in fact Roman. For, while the wooden bridge (*pons sublicius*) is associated with the very existence of Rome, the stone bridge is a relatively late development, the earliest dated example being *pons Aemilius* (Livy 40. 51. 4) of 179 B.C., given an arched superstructure in 142 B.C., and followed by *pons Mulvius* (q.v.) in 109 B.C. and *pons Fabricius* in 62 B.C. Typical of the state of affairs outside Rome is Strabo's description (4. 1. 12 of the Narbonese *via Domitia* or the statement of Augustus (*Mon. Anc.* 4. 19): 'refeci uiam Flaminiam ... [. . . et pontes in ea] omnes praeter Muluium et Minucium.' Nearly all monumental bridges thus belong to the Imperial age. In Italy the most complete are those of Augustus at Ariminum and of Hadrian at Rome, the most imposing those of Augustus at Narnia and at Ausculum, the most curious the bold foot-bridge of Val de Cogne (*JRS* 1939, 149). But they are far outclassed in length by the Augustan bridge at Emerita and in height by the famous bridge which several Spanish communities combined to erect over the Tagus gorge at Alcántara (A.D. 106). The tradition of wooden bridge-building, however, continued in the hands of military engineers (*BSR* xiii. 34). Caesar's description of his temporary wooden bridge on the Rhine (*BGall.* 4. 17) is famous (cf. *CR* 1908, 144). Vegetius (1. 10) describes pontoon bridges of boats, while many bridges of timber more durably constructed than these must have carried even the most important trunk roads. Bridges spanning powerful rivers, however, were usually built with stone piers and wooden superstructure, as the Flavian Rhine bridge at Moguntiacum or Trajan's Danube bridge, the latter some 1,120 metres long, with stone piers and segmental arches of timber. British examples are the Thames bridge at London, the Tyne bridges at Corbridge and Newcastle upon Tyne (*pons Aelius*), where stone piers of the same kind are known to have been used. At Arelate (*Arles*) there was a famous permanent bridge of boats (Auson. *Ordo Nob. Urb.* 77. *Not. Scav.* 1914, 286).

R. Delbrück, *Hellenistische Bauten in Latium* i (1907); Ashby-Anderson–Spiers, *Architecture of Ancient Rome*; I. A. Richmond, *BSR* xiii. 7, 28. I. A. R.

BRIGANTES, the most populous tribe in Britain (Tac. *Agr.* 17), whose territory, spanning the island (Ptol. *Geog.* 2. 3. 16), included the legionary fortress of Eburacum (*York*), a capital at Isurium (*Aldborough*), forts at Olicana (*Ilkley*), Cataractonium (*Catterick*), and Vinovium (*Binchester*), and native *oppida* at Camulodunum (*Almondbury*), *Stanwick*, and Rigodunum (perhaps *Ingleborough*). Native coinage is confined to Yorkshire. Early relations with Rome were friendly; later strife in the royal household compelled annexation by Cerialis and Agricola in A.D. 71–9 (Tac. *Agr.* 17, 20). The Pennines and the forests of Lancashire and Durham were intersected by garrisoned roads (Tac. *Agr.* 20) and lead-mining began by A.D. 81 (*CIL* vii. 1207). In the Ouse basin civil life gave rise to a town at Isurium and widespread villas, as at Well, Castledykes, Gargrave, or Dalton Parlours. Systematic pacification of the uplands was a commonplace under Hadrian (Juv. 14. 196), but under Pius the tribe apparently lost much territory following unlawful raiding (Paus. 8. 43). The eponymous goddess *Brigantia* won local fame (*CIL* vii. 200, 203, 875, 1062; *Eph. Epigr.* vii. 920; ix. 1120, 1141). I. A. R.

BRIGANTIA (mod. *La Coruña*?), one of the mystery towns of Roman Spain. The name, obviously Celtic, is found in Dio, Orosius, and two itineraries (*Bricantia* in *Rav. Cosm.*). The evidence from the itineraries and Ptolemy would place it in or near modern Betanzos. But the lighthouse ascribed to it by Dio and Orosius is apparently that of La Coruña (*CIL* ii. 2559, 5639). Ptolemy's name, *Flavium Brigantium*, marks it as a recipient of Vespasian's grant of the Latin Right (*see* IUS LATII). J. J. Van N.

BRIMO, name or title of a goddess, often identified with Persephone (q.v.; as *Etym. Magn.* 213, 49), Hecate (q.v.; as ibid.; Ap. Rhod. 3. 861), or Demeter (q.v.; as Clem. Alex. *Protr.* p. 13, 4 Stählin). At Eleusis it was proclaimed that she had borne 'a holy child Brimos' (Hippolytus, *Haer.* 5. 8. 40, p. 96 Wendland, where both names are said to mean 'strong'). H. J. R.

BRISEIS, in mythology, daughter of Briseus of Lyrnessus and widow of Mynes; Achilles' slave-concubine, taken from him by Agamemnon and afterwards restored (*Il.* 1. 392; 19. 60, 296 and contexts).

BRITANNIA (the form Πρετανικαὶ νῆσοι, used apparently by the earliest Hellenic visitor, Pytheas (c. 300 B.C.) should be cognate with Irish (q-Celt) *cruithin* (= Picts)). At the beginning of the Christian era the culture of Britain was divided fairly sharply by a line from Tyne to Exe, corresponding to a geological contrast of the Palaeozoic 'Highland' and the Caenozoic 'Lowland' zone. In the 'Highland zone', Bronze Age conditions prevailed among peoples of neolithic ancestry; in the 'Lowland' waves of Celts had imposed Iron Age cultures, the latest of whom, the Belgae (q.v.), overran the south-east (first arrival c. 75 B.C.). Caesar's invasions (55 and 54 B.C.), at least, retarded the formation of a Belgic 'imperium', which was, however, realized by Cunobelinus (d. c. A.D. 41); but disturbances in his old age invited intervention. A grotesque demonstration by Caligula (A.D. 40) indicated the trend of Roman policy, which was resumed by Claudius, who invaded Britain after Cunobelinus' death (A.D. 43). The army (four legions with accompanying *auxilia*) quickly overran the 'Lowland Zone' (A.D. 43–48), and a revolt under Boudicca (q.v.; A.D. 61) was crushed; but where Celtic civilization was combined with 'Highland Zone' conditions, as in east Wales (Silures) and Yorkshire (Brigantes), little was effected until the campaigns of an able succession of Flavian governors. The last of these, Agricola (probably A.D. 78–85), advanced far into Scotland, but after his recall the army was reduced to a garrison footing of three legions (making with the *auxilia* a strength of c. 50,000). After a period of optimism, the destruction of a legion (IX) compelled a decision, and c. A.D. 122 a definite frontier-line was drawn (Hadrian's Wall). Rome had lost the initiative in Britain, a fact which anticipates the high-water mark of progress soon reached in the Empire itself. Britain, indeed, is, in every respect of romanization, last in advance, first in retreat. This is its historical significance.

2. Britain was a typical imperial province, and its local government imitated the Gallic cantonal system. A late author (Gildas, 3) mentions twenty-eight *civitates*, which included, eventually, four *coloniae* (Colchester, Lincoln, Gloucester, York). New towns were created in Roman style, where even artisans wrote Latin. The negative aspect of romanization, however, was the virtual extinction of an attractive native art, based on the La Tène style. Moreover, the social organization was hardly advanced enough to respond to rapid urbanization and certain excavated towns show immediate and accelerating decay (Uriconium, Verulamium).

3. Rural life follows closely the lines of pre-history. Areas of easy settlement, heavily populated since the Bronze Age, continue so, and the normal unit of habitation, the village of rough huts, persists, as it does in little romanized 'Highland zone'. Elsewhere the farm isolated, though often in local groups, is the norm. Less romanized (and far less literate) than the towns, the villas and even the villages show increased prosperity, so that a system of rural exchange, based on barter and a mainly fiduciary coinage, attained by the fourth century a surprisingly high level of stability. Moreover, the mineral wealth (mainly in argentiferous lead mines worked as early as A.D. 49) increased the value of the province to Rome.

4. After Hadrian, political history was fairly uneventful. The northern tribes continued troublesome, and c. A.D. 142 Antoninus Pius decided to push the frontier up to the Forth–Clyde isthmus (Antonine Wall). But the new line was never very satisfactory, and by the end of the century (exact date still controversial) was abandoned.

5. The usurpation of Albinus (A.D. 193–6) illustrates an evil from which the province was later to suffer, the removal of its garrison for overseas adventures; an incursion from the north ensued. The campaigns of Severus, however (A.D. 208–11), re-established the *status quo* behind Hadrian's Wall, which he had restored. Meanwhile a policy of entrusting responsibilities of defence to semi-independent *gentes* with military support behind had been tried out in Wales, perhaps as early as Hadrian, and was eventually employed in the north. It coped well enough with attacks from Ireland and Scotland; but the growing strength of Saxon piracy made necessary the erection of signal-stations and forts along the eastern and southern coasts (begun *c.* A.D. 280).

6. Britain, however, held firm, and the attempt of a Menapian seaman, Carausius, to blackmail Diocletian, by seizing it, into recognizing him as colleague caused little internal disturbance. Carausius, in fact, was assassinated in A.D. 294, and in A.D. 297 the Imperial authority was re-established by Constantius Chlorus. From now Britain, already divided into two by Severus, was administered as four provinces. Christianity began to reach it, but old ways were still strong, and pagan temples were actually built *de novo*.

7. Continuous attacks, however, were undermining its powers of resistance and recovery; and a general assault in A.D. 367 was accompanied by a revolt of the frontier garrison. Order was restored with difficulty, but a vast capital destruction had been suffered. Adventurers, Maximus (A.D. 385) and Constantine (A.D. 409), withdrew the garrison, and it is doubtful whether after A.D. 409 there was ever a Roman army there again. Left to itself, Britain resisted its invaders; but it was the leaders of the Celtic *gentes* of the west who came to the front, and Roman ways gave place to the underlying Celtic. To compensate for the vanished garrison, Saxons from overseas were enrolled as *foederati*; they soon revolted and invited their Teutonic fellows. In the struggle of Celt and Teuton, Roman Britain disappeared almost completely (the precise extent of survival is very controversial), even Christianity vanishing from the Lowland zone. But, in truth, the Roman element was already in retreat, and in the Highland zone, though men spoke of 'Romania' and wrote Latin on the tombstones, the spirit was Celtic and the old Celtic art broke forth, though hesitatingly, once more.

Chief sources: Caesar, *BGall.* 4. 20–36; 5. 8–23. Tacitus, *Ann.* 12. 31–40; 14. 29–39; *Agricola.* Dio Cassius 60. 19–23; 76. 11–13. Chief modern works: T. Rice Holmes, *Ancient Britain and the Invasions of Julius Caesar* (1907); F. Haverfield and G. Macdonald, *Roman Occupation of Britain* (1924); R. G. Collingwood, *Archaeology of Roman Britain* (1930); R. G. Collingwood and J. N. L. Myres, *Roman Britain and the English Settlements²* (1937: fundamental, with full bibliography); C. H. V. Sutherland, *Coinage and Currency in Roman Britain* (1937); T. D. Kendrick, *Anglo-Saxon Art* (1938). C. E. S.

BRITANNICUS (TIBERIUS CLAUDIUS CAESAR) (A.D. 41–55), son of Claudius and Messalina. His stepmother Agrippina induced Claudius to adopt her son L. Domitius (Nero), and contrived to remove the tutors and officers of the guard who were loyal to Britannicus, thus ensuring her son's succession on the Emperor's sudden death in 54. The death of Britannicus in 55 was no doubt due to foul play. According to the general belief he was poisoned by Nero's order.

Tacitus, *Ann.* bks. 11–13; Dio Cassius, bks. 60–1. B. W. Henderson, *Life and Principate of the Emperor Nero* (1903). G. W. R.

BRITOMARTIS (the name means 'sweet maid' in Cretan, Solinus 11. 8), a Cretan goddess, identified with Artemis (Solinus loc. cit. and Hesychius s.v.). She had a temple near Cydonia (Strabo 10. 4. 13). Minos loved her; she avoided him for nine months and finally, to escape him, leaped over a cliff into the sea, was caught in fishermen's nets (hence called Dictynna from δίκτυον),

got away to Aegina, escaped from him again into a grove of Artemis, and was thenceforth worshipped there as Aphaea (q.v.).

See Callimachus, *Dian.* 189 ff.; Pausanias 2. 30. 3; Antoninus Liberalis 40 (no author quoted); [Verg.] *Ciris* 286 ff.; Rose, *Handb. of Gk. Myth.* 117f. H. J. R.

BRIZO, a goddess worshipped by women at Delos, especially as protectress of sailing (Semus of Delos ap. Athen. 8. 335 a–b = *FHG* iv. 493). Her name is derived from βρίζειν 'to sleep', and she was credited with sending prophetic dreams. Bowls of all sorts of food, except fish (cf. FISH, SACRED), were offered to her in sacrifice. F. R. W.

BRONZE. The ancients used the words χαλκός, *aes*, indiscriminately for copper and for the harder and more fusible bronze, the compound of copper and tin. Implements of bronze are found in Egypt and Mesopotamia before 3000 B.C., and by 2000 B.C. (the Middle Minoan period of Crete) the general use of bronze and the normal composition of the mixture (one part of tin to nine of copper) were established. Until the introduction of iron bronze remained the sole metal for utilitarian purposes, and afterwards it continued in general use to the end of antiquity for sculpture and many domestic objects. Brass (ὀρείχαλκος, *orichalcum*, a mixture of copper and zinc) is not found before Roman Imperial times, when a white metal formed by the addition of lead to bronze is also in use.

Copper is widely found in classical lands, where the principal sources of supply are, for Greece, Chalcis in Euboea and Cyprus, and, for Italy, Bruttium, Etruria, and Elba, while under Roman rule Spain produced largely. Tin (q.v.) is much rarer, though a little is still worked in Asia Minor; but Herodotus speaks of the metal as coming from the extremities of Europe (3. 115), and Spain, Brittany, and Cornwall seem to have been the main sources.

Several varieties of bronze were distinguished in antiquity—Corinthian, Delian, Aeginetan, Syracusan, Campanian—but these cannot be identified. The technical processes employed were: hammering into plates which were riveted together (σφυρήλατον), used in the making of utensils and, during the archaic period, of statues; and casting with wax, either solid (usually in the case of small statuettes) or hollow over a core of clay or plaster (πρόπλασμα, argilla) to produce large-scale sculpture. Relief decoration was produced in repoussé work (ἐμπαιστική); incised ornament is also common, especially on mirrors. Tin and copper solders were used in addition to riveting for joins. The dull patina of bronzes in museums is the result of time; ancient bronzes were kept bright, and the surface was often coated with gold or silver, or variegated with damascening and inlay, while enamelling on bronze was a Celtic practice.

Pliny, *HN* bk. 34. H. Blümner, *Technologie und Terminologie der Gewerbe und Künste bei Griechen und Römern* iv; Kluge and Lehmann-Hartleben, *Die Antiken Grossbronzen*; W. Lamb, *Greek and Roman Bronzes* (1929); see also the introductions to the *Catalogues of Bronzes* of the British Museum (by H. B. Walters, 1893) and of the Metropolitan Museum, New York (by G. M. A. Richter), 1915). F. N. P.

BRUCTERI, a powerful German tribe which in the time of Augustus dwelt north of the Lippe, separated by the Teutoburger Wald from the Cherusci, whom they joined in the wars of A.D. 9–17. Within their territory lay the important sanctuary of Tamfana. After 58 they spread southwards into lands vacated by the Usipi, and encouraged by their prophetess Veleda they played an important part in the war of Civilis (69–70). They resumed hostilities *c.* 75–8, but were defeated, and Veleda was captured; about 97 they were disastrously defeated by the Chamavi and Angrivarii. They later probably joined the Frankish confederation. O. B.

BRUNDISIUM (Βρεντέσιον), the best harbour on the east coast of Italy, consisting of two sea-arms which penetrate deeply into the land, and the nearest Italian town to the east Adriatic coast. It was believed to have been occupied by Cretan colonists in prehistoric times, and to have subsequently received settlers from Tarentum; but it usually figures as a native Messapian town until 246 B.C., when the Romans constituted it a Latin colony. It became the terminal point of the extended Via Appia (q.v.), and since the Illyrian War (229) it was the regular port of embarkation for Roman armies crossing to Greece or Epirus. In 49 Caesar vainly attempted to cut off Pompey's retreat from Italy by capturing it. In 40 it was put under siege by Antony when Octavian sought to prevent his return to Italy, and was the scene of the subsequent negotiations between the triumvirs. In Roman times it was also of continuous importance as the starting-point of passenger traffic to Greece.

For the sieges, see Caesar, *BCiv.* 1. 24–8; Dio Cass. 48. 27–30.
M. C.

BRUTTEDIUS (BRUTTIDIUS) NIGER, aedile A.D. 22; prosecuted Silanus for *maiestas* (Tac. *Ann.* 3. 66). He was a pupil of Apollodorus (Sen. *Controv.* 2. 1. 35–6). He was tempted to woo imperial favour by delation, and is probably the Bruttidius of Juv. 10. 83. His account of Cicero's death (Sen. *Suas.* 6. 20 f.) comes from an historical work by him.

Peter, *HRRel.* 2. 90–1.
J. W. D.

BRUTTII inhabited the rugged south-west peninsula of Italy (modern Calabria; the name Bruttium lacks ancient authority). Earlier inhabitants were Morgetes and Oenotri (= Sicels?) and Chones (= Illyrians). Sabellian Lucani appeared near Laus *c.* 390 B.C., defeated the Thurians (Polyaenus 2. 10), and imposed their Oscan language on the peninsula. In 356 the oscanized inhabitants, asserting their independence from the Lucani, became known as Bruttii—probably a pre-Sabellian name which the Lucani adopted as their word for 'runaways' (Diod. 16. 15; Strabo 6. 253 f.; Justin. 23. 1) The Bruttii conquered several Greek colonies on the fertile coastlands, became themselves partly hellenized (Festus, p. 31 L.), and reached their apogee in the third century. Rome, however, subjugated them for supporting Pyrrhus and seized half the Sila Forest (Zonar. 8. 6; Dion. Hal. 20. 15). When they revolted to Hannibal, Rome confiscated additional territory, ringed them round with colonies (Buxentum, Tempsa, Vibo, Croton, Thurii), and practically enslaved them (App. *Hann.* 61). Consequently the separate nation of Bruttii disappeared. In 71 B.C. Spartacus, following Hannibal's example, based his operations on Bruttian territory. Once famous for its ships' timber and pitch, Hannibalic depredations started its decline (but see Cassiod. *Var.* 8. 31). Chief towns: Consentia, Clampetia, and Greek coastal colonies.

R. S. Conway, *Italic Dialects* i (1897), p. 3; H. Kanter, *Kalabrien* (1930); J. Whatmough, *Foundations of Roman Italy* (1937), 335; G. Slaughter, *Calabria, the First Italy* (U.S.A. 1939).
E. T. S.

BRUTUS (1), LUCIUS JUNIUS, the founder of the Roman Republic, is probably an historical figure; there is no reason to suppose that he was a god, or that his exploits were retrojections of achievements by later members of the *gens Iunia*. His consulship in 509 B.C., and his alleged attempt to humanize some primitive cults, may be later embellishments. The story of the capital punishment which he inflicted on his sons, and of his victory over the Etruscans at Silva Arsia, where he was killed, form part of an early popular legend.

W. Schur, *PW*, Suppl. v. 356 ff.
P. T

BRUTUS (2) **CALLAICUS**, DECIMUS JUNIUS (*cos.* 138 B.C.), subjugated Lusitania and Callaecia, 'triumph-

ing' in 136. He accompanied C. Sempronius Tuditanus against the Iapudes (129) and opposed C. Gracchus (121). He was a patron of poets, especially of Accius.

F. Münzer, *PW* x. 1021.

BRUTUS (3) **DAMASIPPUS**, LUCIUS JUNIUS, a leading Marian and praetor in 82 B.C. During Sulla's campaign in Italy Brutus, at Rome, received a message of despair from the younger Marius, then besieged at Praeneste; and, as a result, he assassinated many leading citizens, including P. Antistius, C. Carbo, L. Domitius, and Scaevola, the Pontifex Maximus. He was soon afterwards defeated and killed by Sulla.
M. H.

BRUTUS (4), MARCUS JUNIUS, tribune of the plebs 83 B.C., proposed that Capua should be made a colony. In 77 as Lepidus' partner he commanded the forces in Cisalpine Gaul. He surrendered to Pompey, but was slain.

F. Münzer, *PW* x. 972.

BRUTUS (5), MARCUS JUNIUS (QUINTUS CAEPIO) (probably 85–42 B.C.), the tyrannicide, son of Marcus Junius Brutus (tribune 83 B.C.) and adopted by his uncle Q. Servilius Caepio. In 58 he accompanied Cato to Cyprus, and in 53 was quaestor to Appius Claudius in Cilicia. He joined Pompey in the Civil War, but was pardoned by Caesar after Pharsalus. In 46 he was governor of Cisalpine Gaul, and in 44 *praetor urbanus*. After the conspiracy against Caesar, in which he played a leading part, Brutus found it impossible to remain in Rome; he was given a corn commissionership, but in August (probably), after a quarrel with Antony, left Italy for Greece. With the support of Q. Hortensius, governor of Macedonia, he raised an army, won over the troops of Vatinius in Illyricum, and captured Gaius Antonius in Apollonia (March 43). The Senate gave him command of the forces in the Balkan peninsula and (after Mutina) an *imperium maius* in the eastern provinces (co-ordinate with that of Cassius). After a campaign against the Bessi in Thrace he crossed to Asia Minor, subjugated the Lycians, and returned with Cassius to Thrace to encounter Antony and Octavian (42). He committed suicide after his defeat in the second battle of Philippi.

Brutus impressed his contemporaries by his moral earnestness and independence, but he was naturally a student rather than a man of action. He had a considerable reputation as an orator, and was the author of political and philosophical works (*see also under* DIALOGUE, LATIN).

In 46 Brutus divorced his first wife, Claudia, to marry Cato's daughter Porcia, who died shortly before him.

Cicero, *Letters* and *Philippics*; Plutarch, *Brutus*; Appian, *BCiv*, bks. 2–4; Dio Cassius, bks. 44–7. Modern literature: G. Boissier, *Cicéron et ses amis* (1865); Tyrrell and Purser, *Correspondence of Cicero* vi³, pp. cix–cxxiv; Drumann–Groebe, *Gesch. Roms* iv (but cf. Gelzer in *PW* x. 973–1020 for a more sympathetic appreciation); M. Radin, *Marcus Brutus* (1939).
G. W. R.

BRUTUS (6) **ALBINUS**, DECIMUS JUNIUS, son of Decimus Brutus (consul 77 B.C.) and adopted by a Postumius Albinus. As a young man he served under Caesar in Gaul and distinguished himself by his naval victory over the Veneti (56). He successfully commanded a Caesarian fleet at Massilia in 49, and was appointed governor of Transalpine Gaul, where he suppressed a rebellion of the Bellovaci (46). Decimus Brutus took part in the conspiracy against Caesar in spite of the marked favour shown him by the dictator (he was consul designate for 42). In December 44 he refused to surrender Cisalpine Gaul to Antony, was besieged in Mutina, and released by the victory of Hirtius and Octavian. He was then given chief command of the senatorial forces and crossed the Alps to encounter Antony in Gallia Narbonensis. Deserted by Plancus (governor of Gallia Comata), he planned to join Marcus Brutus in Macedonia, but was abandoned by his army, captured by a Gallic chief, and put to death by Antony's order.

Cicero, *Letters* and *Philippics*; Caesar, *BGall.* bks. 3 and 7, *BCiv.* bks. 1 and 2; Velleius 2. 56–87; Appian, *BCiv.* bks. 2 and 3; Dio Cassius bks. 44–6. Modern literature: B. C. Bondurant, *Decimus Junius Brutus Albinus* (Chicago, 1907); Drumann–Groebe, *Gesch. Roms.* iv; Tyrrell and Purser, *Correspondence of Cicero* vi², pp. lxxxiv–lxxxix. G. W. R.

BRYGUS, potter, in Athens, late sixth to early fifth century B.C. Known from nine signatures. His best artist, the Brygus painter, decorated red-figure cups, plastic vases, etc. Note particularly Komos (Würzburg), Sack of Troy (Paris).

BRYSON of Heraclea on the Pontus, sophist, was probably a pupil of Eucleides of Megara and a teacher of Pyrrhon (qq.v.). He is best known as the author of an inconclusive attempt to square the circle (Arist. *An. Post.* 75ᵇ4; *Soph. El.* 171ᵇ16, 172ᵃ3).

PW iii. 927.

BUBASTIS, a local cat-headed goddess of the city of Bubastis. Early identified with Isis, she was also identified by the Greeks with Artemis. A temple of Bubastis existed at Memphis, one of the many temples in the great complex of sacred structures there. Bubastis appears with the Egyptian deities, or with some of them, at Delos, Ostia, Nemi, and Rome. T. A. B.

BUCEPHALUS (or **BUCEPHALAS**), favourite horse of Alexander the Great, died after the battle on the Hydaspes (326 B.C.). In its memory, Alexander founded the town of Bucephala on the site. *See also* HORSES.

BUCOLICA, *see* PASTORAL POETRY.

BUILDING MATERIALS. I. GREEK. The regions surrounding the Aegean and Adriatic are rich in limestones, and it was by these, and particularly by certain marbles, that the character of classic Greek architecture was largely determined. The white marbles, including that from Mt. Penfelicus, which was used on the Parthenon (q.v.), were generally preferred, and when possible were used for almost every visible architectural part, even roof-tiles and ceilings of small span. In some cases (e.g. the Erechtheum—q.v.) even ceilings of comparatively large span were worked in marble; but wood was more usual, cedar being preferred. Construction of entire buildings in marble was, however, only possible in a few places. Elsewhere the less important parts were usually in one of the coarser limestones, loosely included in the term *poros*. In such cases a marble-like appearance was often obtained by applying a skin of fine marble stucco. Temple cells of plastered sun-dried brick were not unknown. The finest masonry was usually entirely or mainly mortarless, the blocks being worked to a very fine joint and bonded by concealed cramps of bronze. Externally bronze was used for the openwork grilles of temples and for many decorative purposes.

II. ROMAN. The Romans also made great use of limestones, though in their outlying lands they used whatever material was at hand. For Vitruvius, as for his Greek masters, marble was the preferred material. Rome herself, in addition to the Greek marbles and Egyptian granites which she imported under the Empire, was well supplied locally. The hard, strong, honey-coloured limestone, travertine (sometimes classed as a marble), from Tibur (*Tivoli*), was excellent for most structural purposes, and as a facing hardly inferior to marble; while the soft, light, easily worked volcanic *tufa*, abounding in the immediate vicinity, was useful for general purposes, and particularly as a filling for the cores of walls, vaults, substructures, etc. and as an aggregate and surface-key for plaster in concrete work.

III. The volcanic dust, *pozzolana*, deserves mention for the peculiar strength which it lent to Roman mortar and concrete. Concrete, little used before the Hellenistic period, became under the Empire a material of major importance. Replacing the puddled clay rubble, it soon grew, because of its superior strength, to be the chief weight-bearing agent—the facings being often reduced to mere protective or decorative skins. The through-stones and bonding courses necessary in the older technique were, however, often retained as safeguards, and in the great vaults and domes of the emperors, whose construction was greatly facilitated by the use of concrete, light arches and groins of brick were used to direct the stresses conveniently. The loads were sometimes reduced by the insertion of hollow pots or light fillings of tufa or pumice. Baked brick came into general use with concrete, and was much used in combination with it, as well as by itself and in combination with sun-dried brick. Bronze was used for decorative purposes, and occasionally for the framework of roofs. Windows of glass or mica were fairly common in Rome in the first century A.D., and large transparent conservatories for fruit were known to Martial.

IV. GENERAL. The Homeric poems, with their admiration for cedar and ivory, and for polished stone and burnished metal-work, always had an effect on the choice of materials and finishes. For work of the less permanent kinds sun-dried brick, usually raised on a stone footing, often plastered internally and externally, and at times combined with timber reinforcements or framing, was an almost universal walling material. So too was unwrought stone, dry-jointed or mortared with clay. Thatch of grass or reeds seems to have been fairly common in pre-classic times, and continued in use in certain districts, for humble classes of work. Tiles of terra-cotta were widely used, and in some regions the old tradition of terra-cotta roof-ornaments continued unbroken. Plaster finishes were generally very good, and when polished were hardly distinguishable from marble.

Vitruvius, *De Architectura*; *see also* bibliography s.v. ARCHITECTURE. H. W. R.

BUPHONIA, *see* SACRIFICE.

BURDIGALA, a town in Gallia Aquitanica, modern *Bordeaux*. An important port, trading even with Britain, it had many strangers in the population. A praetor is mentioned as executive magistrate. Of remains, the amphitheatre (Palais-Gallien, perhaps as early as second century) and the important temple of Tutela (destroyed by Louis XIV) are notable. In the late Empire a reduced enceinte, c. 700×450 m., rectangular with bastions, was built. It was the birthplace (c. A.D. 320) of Ausonius, who celebrated its university. It fell under Visigothic rule from c. A.D. 413.

C. Jullian, *Inscriptions romaines de Bordeaux* (1887–90); Grenier, *Manuel* i. 410. C. E. S.

BUREBISTAS, king of the Dacians, built up an extensive but impermanent empire in the Danubian lands (c. 60–44 B.C.). With the aid of a priest called Decaeneos he carried out a religious and moral reform in Dacia, pulling up all the vines (Strabo, 303 f.). In Pannonia he defeated and annihilated the Boii and other Celts; he harried the Greek cities on the coast of the Pontus; and he spread his power southwards over the Danube into Thrace. Pompey negotiated with him for assistance in 48 B.C. (cf. *SIG*³ 762: decree in honour of the ambassador Acornion of Dionysopolis). Caesar was intending to march against him in 44. But Burebistas himself was assassinated about this time and his empire broke up into four or five separate kingdoms. R. S.

BURIAL, see DEAD, DISPOSAL OF.

BURRUS, SEXTUS AFRANIUS, procurator of Livia, Tiberius, and Claudius, came from Gallia Narbonensis (Dessau, *ILS* 1321). As Agrippina's favourite, he was appointed sole *praefectus praetorio* by Claudius in A.D. 51 and retained his post under Nero. He was Nero's tutor and adviser for many years and with Seneca responsible for the first period of Nero's government (see NERO). Unaffected in 55 by an unfounded accusation of conspiracy, he played an uncertain part in Agrippina's murder, but opposed Nero's designs against Octavia. He died in 62, probably not by poison.

P. v. Rohden, *PW* i. 712; *PIR*², A 441. A. M.

BUSIRIS, according to Greek mythology, an Egyptian king, son of Poseidon, who slaughtered on the altar of Zeus all foreigners who entered Egypt. Heracles is said to have come to Egypt and killed the wicked king with all his followers. Among classical writers, Herodotus, Euripides, Isocrates, Diodorus, Virgil, Arrian, and others, it was a popular myth. T. A. B.

BUTEO, see FABIUS (4).

BUTES, name of several figures of Attic legend: (1) son of Teleon, an Argonaut who, charmed by the Sirens' song, plunged into the sea, but was rescued and taken to Lilybaeum by Aphrodite, by whom he became the father of Eryx. (2) Son of Poseidon Erechtheus (or of King Pandion), legendary ancestor of the family of the Eteobutadae, hereditary priests of that god in the Erechtheum. (3) Son of Boreas, driven mad by Dionysus for the rape of the nymph Coronis. R. A. B. M.

BYBLIS, see NYMPHS.

BYRSA, see CARTHAGE (TOPOGRAPHY).

BYSSUS (βύσσος). The exact nature of this substance is uncertain. It was probably a variety of flax rather than cotton, and of Egyptian origin. Mummies in Egypt were wrapped in white byssus, and the Persians wore belts of the same stuff (Hdt. 2. 86; 7. 181). But there was also a byssus, golden in colour and almost worth its weight in gold, which was grown in Greece at Elis, and was woven at Patrae into a very light tissue, like our crêpe de chine, suitable for women's garments.

Tertullian, *De cultu feminarum*, 13. F. A. W.

BYZANTIUM was reputed to have been founded by Megarian colonists in 667 B.C. on a pre-existing settlement called Lygos. It was situated at the apex of a promontory bounded on the south by the Propontis, on the north by the Golden Horn, and projecting eastwards into the Bosporus. The area occupied corresponded roughly with the present area of the Old Serai, extending westwards to a point near the Column of Constantine. Finds of early Hellenic pottery and inscriptions near this point establish the limits of the city. A secondary colonization from Megara followed in 628. The wealth of the city was almost certainly founded on the fisheries of the Bosporus. Byzantium was seized by the Persians in the reign of Darius, but later joined in the Ionian revolt. After the battle of Plataea Pausanias freed it from the Persians. In 440 the Byzantines revolted from the Athenian rule, and again in 411, but were subdued in 408 by Alcibiades. Byzantium was captured by Lysander in 403 after the battle of Aegospotami. When the Ten Thousand arrived at its gates, they were inhospitably treated and, in retaliation, occupied the city. It was besieged by Philip of Macedon in 340, and subsequently assaulted continuously by Gallic tribes resident in Thrace. The divine intervention of Hecate in 340 was commemorated on coins of the city by the symbol of the Crescent and Star, which thus reached Islam from a Greek source. Other Bosporan cities also used this symbol, which was later inherited by the Turks. It was besieged and captured by Septimius Severus in A.D. 196 and then for the first time was organized on Roman lines. Septimius constructed the Hippodrome and other buildings in the neighbourhood. On 11 May 330, it was officially re-founded by Constantine and renamed New Rome. This name, however, soon gave way to that of Constantinopolis. S. C.

C

CABIRI, non-Hellenic deities, probably Phrygian (earlier theories of Phoenician origin are not borne out by recent researches, Kern, *Rel. d. Griech.* i. 235 ff.), who promoted fertility and (at least from the fifth century) protected sailors. Their numbers varied, but one tradition gave four names, Axierus, Axiocersa, Axiocersus, Cadmilus (schol. Ap. Rhod. 1. 917). The Greeks also gave them the common title of Μεγάλοι θεοί, and connected their worship in different places with more familiar cults, those of Demeter (material in Farnell, *Cults* iii. 367, n. 256), Hermes (ib. v. 11 and 16) and Dionysus. With the first and last they had certainly an initial kinship, if the assumption of Phrygian origin is correct. (This would also facilitate the identification with the Corybantes and Curetes which took place in the Hellenistic period.) Their chthonian nature is confirmed by phallic rites and the presence of sacrificial pits at Samothrace and Thebes (Kern, l.c.). The historic centre of their worship was Samothrace, where mysteries were celebrated (Hdt. 2. 51; Ar. *Pax* 276), but it existed on other islands, notably Lemnos, and in Asia Minor (see MYSTERIES). On the mainland, the cult is found from the sixth century at Anthedon on the Boeotian coast and near Thebes. Pausanias' statement (4. 1. 7) that the Theban cult was founded from Athens was denied by Wilamowitz, but may be true. Probably under Orphic influence (W. K. C. Guthrie, *Orpheus and Gk. Rel.* 123 ff.), it acknowledged an elder Cabirus and a child, and identified the former with Dionysus. The ἄνακτες παῖδες worshipped at Amphissa were thought by some to be the C. (Paus. 10. 38. 7: cf. s.v. ANAKES). After Alexander the cult spread rapidly over the Greek world. At Samothrace it was patronized by the Ptolemies, and later by the Romans (*BCH* xlix (1925), 245 ff., 258; Kern, op. cit. iii. 118; K. Lehmann-Hartleben, *AJArch.* xliii (1939), xliv; J. H. Oliver, ib. xliii. 464 ff.). In this period the C. were often confused with the Dioscuri (q.v.), who shared their character as seamen's gods. In art we have representations of a pair of C., a younger and an older, the older, bearded figure usually reclining while the younger stands, (best exemplified by the Κάβιρος and Παῖς at Thebes, but there are traces of the same pair in Samothrace), and later they became a pair of youths indistinguishable from the Dioscuri; so on coins, where also a hammer-wielding C. appears.

For a summary of the Cabiri n art, see O. Kern in *PW* x. 1477 ff. W. K. C. G.

CACUS and CACA (etymology uncertain; connexion with Caeculus founder of Praeneste, of whom a miracle involving fire is related, Servius on *Aen.* 7. 678, has often been suggested but remains unproved). The former is represented in *Aen.* 8. 190 ff. (cf. Dion. Hal. *Ant. Rom.* 1. 39. 2 ff., Prop. 4. 9) as a savage fire-breathing monster, son of Volcanus (q.v.), who lived on the Palatine (Aventine, Virgil, but the Scalae Caci on the Palatine, see Platner–Ashby, 465, go far to prove him wrong) and terrified the country-side with his brigandage till he stole some of the cattle of Geryon from Heracles (q.v.), and was overcome and killed by the latter. Servius on *Aen.* 8. 190 says that he was betrayed by his sister Caca, and by way of reward she was given a shrine 'in quo ei pervigili igne sicut Vestae sacrificabatur' (so the best MS., F; 'in quo ei per virgines Vestae sacrificabatur' the rest). This makes it tolerably plain that originally Cacus and Caca were a divine pair, the fire-god and fire-goddess of the Palatine settlement. H. J. R.

CADMEA (Καδμεία), see CADMUS and LEONTIADES.

CADMUS, in mythology, son of Agenor, king of Tyre. When his sister Europa (q.v.) disappeared, Agenor sent Cadmus with his brothers Cilix and Phoenix (the eponyms of Cilicia and Phoenicia), to seek her, with instructions not to return without her. Cadmus arrived at Delphi and was advised to settle where a cow, which he should find on leaving the temple, lay down. She led him to the site of Thebes, where he built the Cadmea, the citadel of the later town. To get water he killed a dragon, the offspring of Ares, and had to undergo a term of servitude. By advice of Athena, he sowed the dragon's teeth, and there came up a harvest of armed men, whom he killed by setting them to fight one another. Five survived and became the ancestors of the nobility of Thebes, the Spartoi (traditionally 'sown men'). He married Harmonia, daughter of Ares and Aphrodite, to whom he gave a robe and a necklace made by Hephaestus; the latter especially played a part in later events, *see* AMPHIARAUS. Their children were Ino, Semele, Autonoë, and Agaue (*see* ACTAEON, ATHAMAS, DIONYSUS, PENTHEUS). Cadmus introduced writing into Greece (i.e., the 'Phoenician', or North Semitic alphabet). In their old age he and Harmonia went away to Illyria and finally were turned into serpents. *See* ALPHABET.

O. Crusius in Roscher's *Lexikon*, s.v. H. J. R.

CADMUS OF MILETUS, *see* LOGOGRAPHERS.

CAECILIA (1) **METELLA,** daughter of L. Metellus Delmaticus, wife of M. Aemilius Scaurus (*cos.* 115 B.C.), and afterwards fourth wife of Sulla. She bore him twins, Faustus (quaestor in 54) and Fausta (later wife of Milo). In 86 she escaped to Greece. In 81 Sulla divorced her, when she was dying, to avoid contaminating his triumph.

CAECILIA (2) **METELLA,** daughter of Q. Caecilius Metellus Creticus, wife of a certain M. Crassus, probably the triumvir's son. Her tomb is preserved almost intact on the Via Appia (Dessau, *ILS* 881).

CAECILIA (3) **ATTICA** (b. 51 B.C.), daughter of Atticus. She was married to Agrippa through the good offices of Antony (37 B.C.?). Subsequently suspicion of misconduct led to the removal of her tutor, a freedman of Atticus. She was the mother of Vipsania Agrippina (q.v.).

Cornelius Nepos, *Atticus* 12.

CAECILIUS (1) **STATIUS** (d. 168 B.C.), an Insubrian Gaul, came to Rome as a slave and was subsequently manumitted. After initial failure he was enabled by the support of Ambivius (q.v.) Turpio to succeed Plautus as Rome's chief comic dramatist. He is said to have died one year after his friend Ennius. We possess about forty titles (mostly Greek) and nearly 300 lines of his comedies. Volcacius ranks him above all other writers of *palliatae*; elsewhere he is praised for plot (presumably he followed well-chosen originals unusually closely), *gravitas*, and emotional power. Gellius cites three passages (about 30 lines in all) from his *Plocium*, together with the original Greek, to show how he has sacrificed subtlety and natural grace for cheap effects. The passages quoted, while certainly coarser than the Menander, are perhaps more vivid as well as more farcical. Emotional power is shown in the angry father's outburst (quoted by Cicero):

egone quid dicam? egone quid uelim? quae tu omnia tuis foedis factis facis ut nequiquam uelim . . .

His *gravitas* appears in such familiar maxims as

saepe est etiam sub palliolo sordido sapientia,

or the reference to the tree-planter, who

serit arbores quae saeclo prosint alteri.

There is some suggestion of satirical power in the references to an *un*mercenary courtesan and a lover who finds his father embarrassingly—openhanded! Cicero calls Caecilius a bad Latinist; Velleius attributes to him 'dulces Latini leporis facetiae'.

Text: (with trans.) E. H. Warmington, *Remains of Old Latin* (Loeb, 1935) i. W. B.

CAECILIUS (2) of Novum Comum, one of Catullus' friends, composed a poem on Cybele (Catull. 35).

CAECILIUS (3) **EPIROTA**, QUINTUS, a man of letters of the Augustan age. He was the freedman of Atticus and the friend of Cornelius Gallus, after whose death (26 B.C.) he opened a school where he taught small groups of pupils. According to Suetonius (*Gram.* 16), he was the first to give public lectures on Virgil and other contemporary poets.

Cf. Teuffel, § 263, 1; Schanz–Hosius, § 352. J. F. M.

CAECILIUS (4) of Calacte, a freedman of Jewish stock (originally Archagathus), taught rhetoric at Rome under Augustus. Of his writings only fragments remain (ed. by E. Ofenloch, 1907). Two works dealt with history; and a τέχνη, a lexicon (Attic), and an important treatise *On figures* (Kroll, *Rhet.* § 33) represented his technical writings. More significant were his critical works, two of which, including K. φρυγῶν, were attacks on Asianism; while his treatise Π. τοῦ χαρακτῆρος τῶν δέκα ῥητόρων, embodying the first mention of the earlier canon, was notable for its biographical sketches and aesthetic appreciations. Other studies included an inquiry into the authenticity of Demosthenes' orations, a criticism of Lysias, comparisons of Demosthenes with Aeschines and Cicero, and a treatise (Π. ὕψους), which drew from 'Longinus' his famous work. Together with Dionysius of Halicarnassus he helped to disengage literary criticism from technical instruction and to establish Attic standards in oratory and prose style. J. W. H. A.

CAECILIUS (5) **JUCUNDUS**, LUCIUS (1st c. A.D.), a Pompeian auctioneer, known from a pair of 'herms' found in his atrium, which bore realistic busts of the owner, and from a series of 127 waxed tablets, mostly receipts recording the proceeds of auction sales that Jucundus conducted, and dating with two exceptions from A.D. 52 to 62.

CIL iv. 3340. R. C. C.

CAECILIUS (6) **AFRICANUS**, Sextus (c. A.D. 150), a Roman jurist, disciple of Salvius (q.v.) Julianus. He attended the courses of his teacher even in his riper years, and published the precious and instructive material collected during his discussions with him. His only known work, *Quaestiones* (9 books), contains for the most part the views (*responsa* and *quaestiones*) of his master, edited without any systematic arrangement, and introduced with a simple '*ait*', '*inquit*', or '*respondit*', without the name of his author (Julian). He is not a fluent writer, indeed his texts are sometimes hardly intelligible. A reconstruction of this work has been edited by D. Lenel, *Sav. Zeitschr.* li (1931). Another work, *Epistulae*, is known only by its title.   A. B.

CAECILIUS, *see also* METELLUS.

CAECINA (1) **SEVERUS**, Aulus (*cos. suff.* 1 B.C.), a *novus homo* and an experienced soldier. Attested as legate of Moesia in A.D. 6, when he rescued Sirmium from the Pannonian insurgents, but had to protect his province from Dacian and Sarmatian raiders. In 7, commanding with M. Plautius Silvanus an army of five Roman legions, he won a great battle north-west of Sirmium and marched to join Tiberius at Siscia. In 14 he was legate of Germania Inferior and had trouble with a mutiny. In the following year he nearly suffered a serious disaster when crossing the 'pontes longi' on his return from the Ems to the Rhine. In 21 he proposed without success that wives should not be permitted to accompany their husbands on provincial commands.
         R. S.

CAECINA (2) **ALIENUS**, Aulus (*cos. suff.* A.D. 69), born at Vicetia, was quaestor of Baetica in 68 and active for Galba. He is described as 'decorus iuventa, corpore ingens, animi immodicus, scito sermone' (Tac. *Hist.* 1. 53). Legate of a legion in Germania Superior, he was largely instrumental in the elevation of Vitellius, one of whose army-columns he led across the Great St. Bernard to Italy and to victory at Bedriacum. Honoured and enriched by Vitellius, and dispatched northwards to arrest the Flavian invasion, he negotiated with the enemy and was deposed from command by his own troops. Rescued after the fall of Cremona, Caecina acquired the favour of Vespasian, but conspiring, so it is alleged, with Eprius (q.v.) Marcellus c. 78–9, he was summarily executed.
         R. S.

CAECUS, *see* CLAUDIUS.

CAELIUS RUFUS, Marcus, of equestrian birth, associate of Catiline (63 B.C.), and protégé of Cicero and Crassus, supplanted Catullus as lover of Clodia (q.v.); but by the year 57 the affair was over, and litigation began against the Atratini, backed by Clodia, culminating in 56 when Caelius, defended by Cicero in the existing speech, was acquitted of *vis* (including poisoning). Tribune and opponent of Pompey in 52, in August 50 Caelius, now aedile, declared for Caesar; but in 48 Caesar's reluctance to cancel debts shook his enthusiasm, and as *praetor peregrinus* he opposed the official policy of Trebonius, *praetor urbanus*. The *senatus consultum ultimum* (q.v.) being passed, Caelius fled, joining Milo to start insurrection in Italy. He was captured and executed at Thurii (48).

Seventeen letters to Cicero (*Fam.* 8) show brilliant political insight, with agreeable attacks on the more pompous personalities; fourteen are written to Cilicia on Roman affairs. His wit made him a master of invective, of which Quintilian (4. 2. 123) quotes a superb example from his prosecution of C. Antonius (59 B.C.). He is addressed in Catullus 77 and almost certainly in 79.
         G. E. F. C.

CAELIUS, *see also* BALBINUS.

CAENEUS ($K\alpha\iota\nu\epsilon\acute{\upsilon}s$), a Lapith (*see* CENTAURS), of whom three principal stories are told. (1) He was invulnerable, and therefore the Centaurs disposed of him by hammering him into the ground (Pind. fr. 150 Bowra, cf. Hyg. *Fab.* 14. 4 and Rose ad loc.). (2) He set up his spear to be worshipped (schol. in Ap. Rhod. 1. 57, in *Il.* 1. 264). (3) He was originally a girl, Caenis, loved by Poseidon, who gave her (invulnerability and) a change of sex (*Aen.* 6. 448 and Servius there, and scholiasts as above). He was son of Elatus of Gyrtone (*Il.* 2. 746 and schol. 1. 264, Ap. Rhod. 1. 57).   H. J. R.

CAEPIO (1), Quintus Servilius (*cos.* 106 B.C.), leader of the Optimate party during the rise of Marius. He triumphed in 108 B.C. for achievements as propraetor in Lusitania. Elected consul for 106 about the time of Metellus' triumph, Caepio struck at Marius' partisans the *Equites* by his law (*Lex Servilia Caepionis*) which probably transferred the jury-courts to the Senate. In Gaul he took and plundered Tolosa, and in 105, as proconsul, refused to co-operate with the consul Cn. Mallius, a *novus homo*, against the Cimbri; both their armies were heavily defeated at Arausio. Caepio was deprived of his *imperium* by popular vote, was accused by the tribune Norbanus, and was condemned in 103. There had previously been a *quaestio extraordinaria* about the *aurum Tolosanum* which had been largely lost in transit. Caepio retired to Smyrna.

J. Lengle, *Hermes* 1931, 302 ff.   M. H.

CAEPIO (2), Quintus Servilius, son of Caepio (1), was quaestor in 100 B.C.; he opposed Saturninus and in return (in 99) was unsuccessfully charged with *maiestas*. In 92–1 he supported the *Equites* against the Senate and his own brother-in-law Drusus, and vainly accused M. Aemilius Scaurus, who counter-attacked with a charge of *ambitus*. He fell in the Social War in 90.

Münzer, *Röm. Adelsparteien*, 292–4, 298–302.   H. H. S.

CAEPIO (3), Fannius, headed a conspiracy against Augustus in 22 B.C. When prosecuted by Tiberius before the *quaestio maiestatis* he attempted to escape but was betrayed and executed.

Velleius 2. 91 and 93; Macrobius, *Sat.* 1. 11. 21.

CAERE (modern *Cervetri*) was one of the wealthiest Etruscan cities, situated 6 miles from the coast and 30 miles north of Rome. Dionysius and others state that an important town preceded the Etruscan; this is confirmed by Villanovan graves. Caere always maintained good relations with Rome; indeed Roman youths were sent there for education. It was granted *hospitium* in 390 and *civitas sine suffragio* later (*see* CAERITES). Of the city and its port Agylla little trace remains, but there are extensive cemeteries which include many monumental tumuli. The graves are laid out in streets like a town; the passages and chambers which pierce the great tumuli are often replicas of the living-rooms in an Etruscan house. These are cut in the tufa; and the tumulus above them, sometimes 40 or 50 yards in diameter, is finished with masonry and earth. The earliest tumuli are of c. 700 B.C.; they continued in use down to the fourth century B.C. The most famous is the Regolini-Galassi. Its contents (now in the Vatican Museum), together with the princely tombs of Praeneste and Vetulonia, form our most valuable source of information for the best orientalizing period of art and commerce. Results of recent excavations are in the Villa Giulia Museum at Rome.

G. Dennis, *Cities and Cemeteries of Etruria*[3] (1883); O. Montelius, *La Civilisation primitive en Italie* i, ii (1895–1910); G. Pinza, *Mat. per etnogr. toscano-laziale* (1915); Ebert's *Real-Lexikon* (1925); D. Randall-MacIver, *Villanovans and Early Etruscans* (1924); R. Mengarelli, *Studi Etruschi* i (1927), 145; xi (1937), 77.   D. R.-MacI.

CAERITES. The ancient accounts of the so-called Caerite franchise are contradictory. They confuse together the earliest and the final stages of development of *civitas sine suffragio*. Caere received this status (*see* MUNICIPIUM) either as a reward for protecting the Vestal Virgins during the Gallic invasion of 390 B.C. (Gellius' and Strabo's view), or as a punishment for an otherwise unspecified revolt during the third century, which was possibly Livy's view. The latter is more probable, because the connexion with the Gallic invasion is unknown to Livy, and the common belief that the status of Caere was *ignominiosum* fits only the later date. The notion that Caere was the first *municipium* is a deduction from the improbable connexion of its franchise with the events of 390 B.C.

Mommsen, *Rom. Staatsr.* iii. 1. 572, n. 3; A. N. Sherwin-White, *The Roman Citizenship* (1939), 50 ff.; and *see under* MUNICIPIUM.
A. N. S.-W.

CAESAR (1), GAIUS JULIUS, b. 102 B.C. (Mommsen's date; traditionally 100; 101, according to Carcopino, *Mélanges Bidez* i. 36), was nephew of Marius' wife; Sulla, in sparing his life, said he could see many Marii in him. The significance of his early actions is doubtful: he served in Asia and Cilicia (81–78) and in 77 prosecuted Dolabella (*cos.* 81); as quaestor in 68 he extolled the *gens Iulia* in a funeral oration over his aunt, Marius' widow, and on his return from his province, Spain, intrigued with the Transpadani. Certainly by his aedileship in 65 he was Crassus' (q.v.) ally, and was accused of complicity in a plot to murder the consuls (the 'First Catilinarian conspiracy') and in designs on Egypt. In 63 he engineered the trial of C. Rabirius (q.v.), and again upheld the 'popular' view of the *senatus consultum ultimum*, when he opposed the execution of the Catilinarians, proposing instead confinement in the municipalities. In the same year, after heavy bribery, he was elected Pontifex Maximus. His praetorship (62) was temporarily suspended when he supported Metellus Nepos (q.v.), and in the Bona Dea trial (May 61) he refused to depose against Clodius (q.v.), though he divorced his wife Pompeia, for 'Caesar's wife must be above suspicion'. His praetorian province was Hispania Ulterior, whence he returned in 60, asking that while he waited outside Rome for a triumph he might stand for the consulate. The Senate under Cato's influence refused, whereupon Caesar surrendered the triumph and by forming an alliance with Pompey and Crassus (the 'First Triumvirate') secured the consulate of 59. From the outset he raised troops and disregarded the veto of his colleague Bibulus (q.v.): wags spoke of 'the year of Julius and Caesar'. The *publicani* received remission on the Asiatic tax contracts for 61; two *leges agrariae*, the second distributing Campanian land, provided land for Pompey's veterans, and Pompey's Eastern *acta* were confirmed; Caesar colonized Novum Comum, passed a useful *Lex de repetundis*, compelled publication of the Senate's transactions, and transferred Clodius to the plebeians. But the chief measure of the year was a *Lex Vatinia*, which revoked the Senate's allocation to Caesar of an insignificant province, and conferred on him Cisalpine Gaul and Illyricum for five years, incidentally legalizing his possession of an army. The Senate added Transalpine Gaul, and Caesar left early in 58, to be engaged for the next nine years on the Gallic Wars (q.v.). Starting as a dangerous *popularis*, he returned as the resolute destroyer of the Republic. At first Piso, his father-in-law (*cos.* 58), and Clodius (q.v.) protected his interests; but by April 56 the attacks of Domitius (q.v. 3) looked dangerous, and Caesar met Pompey and Crassus at Luca. Pompey and Crassus became consuls for 55, and renewed Caesar's command for five years more, themselves receiving equivalent terms of *imperium* under a *Lex Trebonia*. Caesar was temporarily safe; thereafter he received from the Senate *supplicationes* of

unprecedented length for his Gallic successes, and bribed nobles in Rome, and cities and kings abroad, to foster his designs. But in 54 his daughter Julia (q.v. 1) died, and in 53 Crassus was killed. Caesar approved of Pompey's measures in 52 (*BGall.* 7. 6), and gained on balance from Pompey's *Lex de Iure Magistratuum*, for his tribunes could now veto attempts to recall him before he could stand for the consulate, which a law of this year enabled him to do *in absentia*. But the crux was whether Pompey, who now had a fresh *imperium*, would support these attempts at recall. Although he opposed in 51 the motion of M. Marcellus (q.v. 4), after much hesitation he threw in his lot with Caesar's opponents. The final compromise of Caesar's tribune Curio (q.v. 2) failed, and on 1 January 49 the Senate voted that Caesar lay down his command. On 10 January Caesar crossed the Rubicon.

2. Caesar rapidly overran Italy, but failed to prevent Pompey's crossing to Greece. He therefore turned to Spain, where he forced Pompey's lieutenants Afranius and Petreius to surrender after some brilliant manœuvring near the town of Ilerda. In 48 he effected a crossing to Epirus, Antony later bringing the bulk of his army. Shortage of troops frustrated his blockade of Pompey at Dyrrhachium, and a sortie by Pompey inflicted considerable loss. But reinforced by Domitius Calvinus in Thessaly, Caesar fought a set battle agains (Pompey's force (still far superior numerically) at Pharsalus, where the courage of his veterans in withstanding cavalry brought complete victory (9 August 48). He pursued Pompey to Egypt, and was involved through the winter in a difficult war against Ptolemy XIII and the Alexandrians, which ended in the establishment of Cleopatra, now his mistress, as queen. He proceeded to Asia Minor and defeated Pharnaces (q.v. 2) of Bosporus at Zela, the battle which occasioned his famous boast, 'Veni, vidi, vici'. He returned to Rome, but in January 46 landed in Africa, where after four months he overcame the Pompeian forces under Scipio at Thapsus. The wars seemed over, and he celebrated four triumphs, Gallic, Alexandrian, Pontic, and African; but in 45 he was called to Spain to fight Pompey's sons and Labienus, and his victory at Munda was his hardest battle.

3. On his return from Ilerda Caesar was made dictator to hold elections, in October 48 he was again appointed, in 46 he became dictator for ten years, and in 44 for life. He secured his consulate for 48, and in 46 and 45 held nine months' consulates, the last without a colleague. In 44 he received tribunician *sacrosanctitas*, in 46 a *praefectura morum*. Other powers and honours, including a full *tribunicia potestas*, he refused, but received extraordinary emblems of royalty, statues, a purple robe, and a temple to his Clementia, and a *flamen* (M. Antonius); and his head appeared on coins of 45–44. But full deification was given only after his death. The reforms of his period of power were necessarily sporadic and incomplete: he reduced the number of recipients of corn dole and abolished *collegia* (q.v.), but settled veterans in Italy and outside, founding numerous colonies, many for commercial reasons, especially Corinth and Carthage; he curtailed indiscriminate emigration and ordained that at least one-third of Italian herdsmen be freemen; he carried out public works in Italy, prepared standard regulations for Italian municipal constitutions, carried sumptuary laws, introduced the Julian calendar (beginning 1 Jan. 45 = 709 A.U.C.), and abolished tax farming in Asia and perhaps in other provinces. His revision of debts was moderate, and offended extremists like Caelius (q.v.). He was lavish in granting citizenship (Cisalpine Gaul received it from a *Lex Roscia* in 49), and went outside Italy in recruiting the Senate, which he enlarged to 900. At the time of his death he was preparing wars against Parthia and Dacia. His famous 'clemency', which reached its climax with the recall of M. Marcellus (q.v.), did much to conciliate the aristocracy. But his powers and honours, and especially

perhaps his control of offices, even though he refused the title *Rex* in 44, were intolerable even to men who had been of his party, and on the Ides of March 44 he fell to a conspiracy led by M. Brutus and C. Cassius, and died at the foot of Pompey's statue. To every citizen he left 300 sesterces, repeating a previous gift; his largesse to his soldiers had also been considerable, though their loyalty to him, the chief factor in his power, was in the main spontaneous. He married Cornelia, daughter of Cinna, who died in 68, then Pompeia (above), and in 59 Calpurnia (q.v.); among his numerous mistresses the most famous after Cleopatra was Servilia, half-sister of Cato, and mother of Brutus.

4. WRITINGS: seven books *De Bello Gallico*, each covering a year from 58 to 52 (completed to 50 by Hirtius, q.v.) and three *De Bello Civili* (text—R. du Pontet, O.C.T., 1900). Both works show Caesar as the simple, efficient patriot, fighting necessary wars; but the propaganda (cf. *BCiv.* 1. 1-11; 3. 31-3, 82-3) never breaks unduly the masterly descriptions of warfare, studied in all later ages. The Commentaries were a new literary genre; their style (cf. Cicero, *Brutus*, 262; Hirtius' preface to bk. 8) is lucid and compressed, entirely free from rhetoric, and the diction is simple but brilliantly chosen. Caesar was an atticizer, and there exists a verse epigram to Terence, the 'puri sermonis amator' (*FPL*, 91); his *Analogia* and *Anticato* (*see* CATO 5) have not survived. As an orator he was second only to Cicero.

5. Caesar's style mirrors the clear vision which was his outstanding quality. His generalship, unsurpassed in antiquity, rested chiefly on his sense of the moment to strike. As a statesman he had abandoned the palliatives of earlier reformers, and the urban populace was no longer first in his mind: the inchoate programme of his dictatorship finds coherence in the promotion of good government, economic development, and greater social equality in Italy and in the Empire as a whole. Yet his radicalism, however far-seeing, went too far for the Italy of his day; and though the stories of trousered Gauls in the Senate or of an intended transference of the capital to the East are fabrications, they point the direction in which Caesar was moving. But he legislated almost in spite of himself: the man who by 46 could say 'satis diu uel naturae uixi uel gloriae' (Cic. *Pro Marcello* 32) had personal position rather than reform as his ambition, and the Civil War (see Caes. *BCiv.* 1. 9. 2) was fought to save his *dignitas*. He was not, like Augustus, economical in the powers he held, nor did he understand the indirect exercise of *auctoritas*; again, the exaggerations of our sources about his honours, royal and divine, reveal something which even contemporaries thought about him. But his impatience was characteristic of his zest for life; his continued accessibility moved the reluctant Cicero, and his culture is another proof of his astonishing versatility, which makes him one of the most impressive characters of antiquity.

BIBLIOGRAPHY

ANCIENT SOURCES (*a*) Documents: Bruns, *Fontes Iuris Romani*[7], 15-18, 28. (*b*) Literary: Caesar's own writings (above), with the *Bella* (*Alexandrinum, Africum, Hispaniense*, qq.v.); Cicero, Correspondence (ed. Tyrrell and Purser, esp. vol. vii, Index), and Speeches (esp. *De Provinciis Consularibus, Pro Marcello, Pro Ligario, Pro Rege Deiotaro, Philippics* 1 and 2); Sallust, *Bellum Catilinae* (a moderate Caesarian's propagandist attempt to show Caesar's dissociation from extremism), *In Caesarem senem* 1 (contemporary, if not Sallustian; and cf. H. Last, *CQ* 1923-4). Of later writers Suetonius (*Divus Iulius*) is the most valuable, based on a collation of varied contemporary sources, not always used with judgement; Plutarch, *Caesar* (and cf. *Pompey, Cicero, Cato Minor, Brutus, Antony*) perhaps draws on Nepos; Dio, bks. 36-44, probably drawing on Livy, an important source for Caesar's honours, but often anachronistic and apt to record proposals as facts; Appian, *BCiv.* 2, has not the merits of bk. 1; Lucan, *De Bello Civili*, is a source for the Civil War.

MODERN LITERATURE (*a*) General: Mommsen, *History of Rome* iv-v, trans. W. P. Dickson (1895); T. Rice Holmes, *The Roman Republic* (1923); M. Cary and F. E. Adcock in *CAH* ix (1932); J. Carcopino, *César* (*Histoire générale*, ed. G. Glotz, *Histoire*

romaine ii, 1936); E. Meyer, *Caesars Monarchie und das Principat des Pompejus*[2] (1919); R. Syme, *The Roman Revolution* (1939), pp. 1-96. M. Gelzer, *Caesar der Politiker und Staatsmann* (1941). (*b*) Military: T. Rice Holmes, *Caesar's Conquest of Gaul*[2] (1911); J. Kromayer, *Antike Schlachtfelder* (1904-31). (*c*) The issue between Caesar and the Senate: Mommsen, 'Die Rechtsfrage', *Ges. Schr.* iv. 92; C. G. Stone, *CQ* 1928-9; C. E. Stevens, *AJPhil.* 1938; F. E. Adcock, *CQ* 1932; J. P. V. D. Balsdon, *JRS* 1939 (the present writer follows mainly the last two); G. R. Elton, *JRS* 1946. Full bibliography in *CAH* ix. 954. (*d*) Miscellaneous: E. G. Hardy, *Some Problems in Roman History* (1924); R. Syme, 'Caesar, the Senate and Italy', *BSR* 1938; J. Carcopino, *Points de vue sur l'impérialisme romain* (1934), 89; L. R. Taylor, *The Divinity of the Roman Emperor* (1931); M. Cary, 'Notes on the Legislation of Julius Caesar', *JRS* 1929. G. E. F. C.

CAESAR (2), LUCIUS JULIUS (*cos.* 90 B.C.), an Optimate politician, in spite of his democratic connexions. As consul in the Social War, Caesar passed the *Lex Iulia* admitting loyal allied communities to citizenship; he registered them in eight old or ten new tribes as censor, with P. Crassus, in 89. He commanded in Campania in 90, with some success, and was continued in command in 89. He was murdered in 87 by Fimbria. M. H.

CAESAR (3), LUCIUS JULIUS (*cos.* 64 B.C.), son of Caesar (2) and uncle of M. Antonius. He was *duumvir perduellionis* with Caesar (63) and voted for the death of the Catilinarians. He was legate of Caesar in Gaul (52-49) and prefect of the city (47). After Caesar's death he became a Republican and was proscribed, but was saved through the appeals of his sister Julia. He wrote a book *De Auspiciis*.

F. Münzer, *PW* x. 468. A. M.

CAESAR (4), SEXTUS JULIUS, fought in Spain against Pompey (49 B.C.); in 47 he was quaestor and afterwards governor of Syria, where he was killed (46).

F. Münzer, *PW* x. 477.

CAESAR (5), LUCIUS JULIUS, son of Caesar (3), as Pompey's follower and Caesar's relative played an important part in the negotiations of 49 B.C. between Caesar and Pompey. He repaired to Africa and in 46 was with Cato in Utica. Though pardoned, he was afterwards killed.

F. Münzer, *PW* x. 471. M. H.

CAESAR (6), GAIUS, eldest son of Agrippa and Julia, born in 20 B.C. and adopted by Augustus in 17. In 5 B.C., when he assumed the *toga virilis*, he was designated consul for A.D. 1, admitted to the Senate, and saluted by the *equites* as *Princeps Iuventutis*. In 1 B.C. he was sent to the East, where he had a conference with the Armenian king and installed a Roman nominee on the Armenian throne. He was, however, seriously wounded in the siege of Artagira, and died in Lycia on his way back to Italy (A.D. 4).

Monumentum Ancyranum 3. 1 and 5. 29; Velleius 2. 101-2; Dio Cassius, bks. 54 and 55. G. W. R.

CAESAR (7), LUCIUS, second son of Agrippa and Julia, born in 17 B.C. and adopted by Augustus. In 2 B.C., when he assumed the *toga virilis*, he received the honours previously conferred on his brother Gaius. He died at Massilia, on his way to Spain, in A.D. 2.

Monumentum Ancyranum 3. 1; Velleius 2. 102; Dio Cassius 54. 18; 55. 9-12. G. W. R.

CAESAR (8) **STRABO**, GAIUS JULIUS VOPISCUS, orator, curule aedile 90 B.C., killed by the Marians with his elder brother Lucius in 87, was responsible for a novel and stagey kind of pleading, presumably influenced by his own tragedies.

Cic. *Brut.* 177; *De Or.* 3. 30; Malcovati, *ORF* ii (1930), 193 ff.

CAESAREA (1) **OF CAPPADOCIA** (formerly Mazaca), was created by the Cappadocian kings to be their capital. Ariarathes V gave it a Greek constitution (the laws of Charondas, q.v.) under the name of *Eusebeia under the Argaeus*, which was changed to *Caesarea* by Archelaus in 12-9 B.C. From A.D. 17 it was the capital of the province of Cappadocia and an Imperial mint. A. H. M. J.

CAESAREA (2) **OF PALESTINE** (previously Strato's Tower) was captured by Alexander Jannaeus (a Jewish king of the Maccabaean dynasty) in 104 B.C., restored by Pompey in 63, and granted in 30 by Octavian to Herod, who from 22 to 10 rebuilt it on a grandiose scale and provided it with a huge artificial port, renaming it *Caesarea*, and the harbour *Portus Augusti*. The population was mainly Syrian, but there were many Jews, who under Nero unsuccessfully claimed the citizenship; they were massacred in A.D. 66. Vespasian made Caesarea a colony, immune from *tributum* (q.v.) *capitis*; Titus added immunity from *tributum soli*. It was the capital of Judaea under both the procurators and the legates. An important commercial town, it also had a purple dyeing industry.

A. H. M. J.

CAESAREA (3) (modern *Cherchel*), a seaport in Mauretania. The old Carthaginian trading-station of *Iol* became Caesarea when Juba II (q.v.) and Cleopatra Selene made it the capital of their Mauretanian kingdom and a centre of Greek art. Under Claudius it received a colony of veterans and became the residence of the procurator of Mauretania Caesariensis. With a population of 100,000, Caesarea became the third most important African port; it traded with the Mediterranean and Atlantic, and was a naval base. Its best-known citizen was Macrinus (q.v.). Sacked by Moors and Vandals, it was refortified by Belisarius.

P. M. Duval, *Cherchel et Tipasa* (1946). W. N. W.

CAESARION was the nickname conferred by the Alexandrians upon Ptolemy Caesar (47-30 B.C.), a son of Cleopatra VII. He was titular joint ruler of Egypt with his mother from 42, and was destined to be her successor. The paternity of Caesarion is under dispute. Cleopatra and Antony proclaimed him a son of Caesar, and this was the prevalent, albeit not the universal, belief of ancient writers. (For the opposite view, see J. Carcopino, *Annales de l'école des hautes études de Gand* 1937, 37 ff.) Octavian, who saw in him a possible rival, put him to death. M. C.

CAESELLIUS VINDEX, LUCIUS (early 2nd c. A.D.), wrote a miscellany (now lost) entitled *Stromateus* or *Lectiones antiquae*.

Cf. Teuffel, § 352, 1; Schanz-Hosius, § 593.

CAESENNIUS, *see* PAETUS.

CAESTUS, *see* BOXING.

CAESURA, *see* METRE, GREEK, II; METRE, LATIN, II.

CAKES. The ancients, especially the Greeks, had an enormous variety of cakes and bread (lists in Pollux 6. 72 ff., Athenaeus 643 e ff., cf. the lexicographers under the names of the different kinds). Of these, many were used in sacrifices (material collected in Lobeck, *Aglaophamus*, 1060 ff.; see also Eitrem, *Opferritus*, index under 'Kuchen'). Examples are the ἀμφιφῶν, stuck with lights and sacrificed to Artemis Munichia (Ath. 645 a; the βασυνία, of wheat-flour and honey, sacrificed to Iris (ib. 645 b); many kinds were in shapes of animals, etc. (ib. 646 e, 647 a; schol. Thuc. 1. 126. 6, and often). Cakes are the poor man's offering (Porphyry, *Abst.* 2. 16), and often prelude a greater sacrifice (as Ar. *Plut.* 660 and schol.). The usual Latin name for a sacrificial cake is *libum* (as Ov. *Fasti* 1. 127-8). H. J. R.

CALABRIA, in antiquity the flat and arid but fertile south-eastern promontory or 'heel' of Italy, inhabited by Messapii (q.v.). Its prehistoric monuments resemble those of Sardinia. The Lombards seized Calabria c. A.D. 700, whereupon the Byzantines transferred its name to the south-western promontory or 'toe' of Italy—the Calabria of to-day.

Strabo 6. 277-83; Pliny, *HN* 3. 99-103. E. T. S.

CALAIS and **ZETES,** in mythology, sons of Boreas (q.v.), hence often called together the Boreadae. They took part in the expedition of the Argonauts (q.v.), and, being winged, freed Phineus from the Harpies (q.v.). They persuaded the others to leave Heracles behind at Cios (*see* HYLAS), for which he afterwards killed them, setting over their grave two stones, of which one moves when the north wind blows (Ap. Rhod. 1. 211, 1298; 2. 240 ff.). H. J. R.

CALAMIS (c. 480-450 B.C.), Greek sculptor. No works survive that can be attributed to him. But he was the author of what was probably one of the first colossal-scale bronze statues ever made, the Apollo at Apollonia Pontica, which was 30 cubits in height and cost 500 talents to make. The silver coins of this city preserve a version of the statue as a design. He was distinguished for his grace and refinement and for his skill at making figures of horses, but almost nothing is really known about his style. Neither the school nor the place of origin of Calamis is known. S. C.

CALCEUS, *see* DRESS, para. 4.

CALCHAS, in mythology, son of Thestor; a diviner who accompanied the Greek army to Troy (*Il.* 1. 69 ff.). He reveals the reason for the plague on the camp (ibid.) and foretells the length of the war (2. 300 ff.). After Homer he is introduced into several episodes, as the sacrifice of Iphigenia (q.v.; Aesch. *Ag.* 201 ff., from the *Cypria* directly or otherwise); the building of the Wooden Horse (Verg. *Aen.* 2. 185, cf. Quint. Smyrn. 12. 3 ff.), and generally the actions fated to capture Troy. After the war he went to Claros, and there met Mopsus (q.v.). It had been foretold that Calchas would die when he met a better diviner than himself; Mopsus answered a question which he could not answer (the number of figs on a tree), and Calchas died of mortification (Strabo 14. 1. 27). Another story of his death is that he died laughing at a prophecy that he would not live to drink the wine of his vineyard (Servius on Verg. *Ecl.* 6. 72); cf. ANCAEUS.

H. J. R.

CALEDONIA, the name used by Tacitus and Dio Cassius for the Scottish Highlands, beyond the *ciuitates trans Bodotriam sitas* (*Agr.* 25). Others use the adjective, sometimes of inland Britain (Florus 1. 45. 18; Stat. *Silv.* 5. 2. 142), mostly of north Britain, referring to its seas (Lucan 6. 37), its north cape and monument with Greek letters (Solinus 22; Mommsen, *Addit.* 234), its frosts (Claudian *IV Cons. Hon.* 26), fauna (id. *I Cons. Stil.* 2. 247), pearls (Auson. *Mos.* 68), and people (Mart. 10. 44. 1; Claudian, *Laus Serenae* 45; Sid. Apoll. *Carm.* 7. 89). Its wooded hills (*saltus*) were early famous (Florus 1. 17. 3, 1. 45. 18; Plin. *HN* 4. 102) but vaguely located (op. cit.) until Ptolemy (*Geog.* 2. 3. 8) placed δρυμὸς Καληδόνιος south-west of Beauly Firth. The name survives (Watson, *Celtic Place-names of Scotland*, 21) in Dunkeld, Rohallion, and Schiehallion. It occurs as a personal (*Eph. Epigr.* vi. 1077) and tribal (*ILS* 4576) name.

Agricola (q.v.) defeated the *Caledonii* without conquering them. In A.D. 197 they broke a treaty with Rome (Dio Cass. 75. 5), were reduced by Severus in 209, but broke faith again in 210-11 (id. 76. 15). Dio (76. 12) divides non-Roman Britain into *Caledonii* and *Maeatae*; his description does not reflect Iron Age conditions and may go back much earlier (cf. Hübner, *PW*, s.v.). Ammianus (27. 8. 5) distinguishes *Dicalydones* (cf. Ptol. *Geog.* 2. 3. 1, ὠκεανὸς Δουηκαληδόνιος) and *Verturiones*, the latter of Fortrenn (Watson, op. cit. 68-9). I. A. R.

CALENDARS. Almost every ancient community had a calendar of its own, differing from others in names of months and date of New Year. All were, at least originally, lunar or soli-lunar (see TIME-RECKONING). The months were either simply numbered (Protos was the first month in Phocis, September the originally seventh month in Rome) or named after festivals held or deities specially worshipped in them (Dios and Apellaios, the first two Macedonian months, from Zeus and Apollo; Anthesterion at Athens, from the Anthesteria; Martius in Rome and several other Italian communities, from Mars). Some of the Greek month-names are at least as old as Hesiod (Lenaeon, *Op.* 504; 8th c.?); both they and the Italian names are usually adjectival, the word for 'month' being expressed or understood.

2. Greek months were divided into thirds, at least where we have any information as to a division. The first ten days were the 'rising' month, μὴν ἱστάμενος, and numbered forwards, as with us: Βοηδρομιῶνος ἱσταμένου πέμπτη, on Boedromion 5; the next ten also numbered forwards, and most commonly in the style Βοηδρομιῶνος πέμπτῃ ἐπὶ δέκα, Boedromion 15; the last ten or nine, the 'waning' (φθίνων) month, were numbered backwards, or forwards from the twentieth, εἰκάδες. The last day of the month was commonly called τριακάς, or thirtieth, in Athens ἔνη καὶ νέα, 'old and new'. In Italy, at all events in Rome, days were numbered backwards from the three fixed points, the *kalendae* (new moon), *idus* (full moon) and *nonae* (the ninth day, counting inclusively, before the Ides). Thus *ante diem octavum kalendas Apriles* is 25 March; *pridie nonas Iunias* is 4 June.

3. Of Greek calendars, the least imperfectly known is the Athenian. It began as near as might be to the summer solstice (longest day), and its months were Hecatombaeon, Metageitnion, Boedromion, Pyanopsion, Maemacterion, Poseideon, Gamelion, Anthesterion, Elaphebolion, Munichion, Thargelion, and Scirophorion. All are named after festivals, some very obscure to us and probably to fifth- and fourth-century Athenians, which occur in them. The intercalary month (see TIME-RECKONING) was obtained by inserting a Second (δεύτερος) or Later (ὕστερος) Poseideon. Every month was either 'full' (πλήρης) or 'hollow' (κοῖλος), i.e. respectively thirty and twenty-nine days long; normal total 29½ × 12 = 354 days.

4. The original Roman calendar consisted of ten months only, the later March–December, and must therefore have had an uncounted gap in the winter, between years (see especially Ov. *Fasti* 1. 27 ff., with Frazer's note; cf. Nilsson, *Time-Reckoning*, 223). The Republican calendar, represented for us by the fragmentary *Fasti Antiates* (see Mancini in *Not. Scav.* 1921, 140 for first publication) and literary descriptions (notably Censorinus 20. 4 ff., Macrob. *Sat.* 1. 13. 1 ff.; their chief ultimate sources are no doubt Varro and Verrius Flaccus), was introduced from Etruria by Tarquinius Priscus (so Junius Gracchus ap. Censorinum, ibid.), as is shown among other things by the month-name *Iunius*, pure Latin *Iunonius*, clearly connected with the Etruscan form of Juno's name, *Uni*. It is earlier, however, than the Capitoline temple (traditionally not dedicated till after the expulsion of the kings), for of the feast-days which it marks in large capitals none is connected with that cult. January, as containing the festival (*Ianuar*, presumably the *Agonium* of later calendars, 9 Jan.) of the god of gates who was on his way to be a god of all beginnings, must have been intended to be the first month, but the revolution which expelled the Etruscan dynasty put a stop to this and March remained the first of the year till 601/153. March, May, Quintilis (July), and October had 31 days each (Ides on 15th, Nones on 7th), February 28 and the rest 29 (Ides on 13th); total, 355.

5. To intercalate, a 'month' of 22 or 23 days, called *Mercedonius* or *Intercalaris*, was placed between the 23rd and 24th of February. This intercalating was so clumsily done that by the time of Julius Caesar the civic year was about three months ahead of the solar. In his capacity of *Pontifex Maximus*, he intercalated sufficient days to bring

the year 708/46 to a total of 445 days (Censorinus, ibid. 8), which was thus the 'last year of the muddled reckoning', 'ultimus annus confusionis' (Macrob. ibid. 14. 3). From the next year onwards the Egyptian solar calendar (see TIME-RECKONING) was adapted to Roman use, by inserting enough days in the shorter months to bring the total up to 365 and arranging for the insertion of a day, not a month, between 23 and 24 February in leap year (hence called bissextile year, since the date *a. d. vi. kal. Mart.* occurs twice in it; the non-existent date '29 February' is a modern absurdity). No substantial change was made thereafter till the reforms of Gregory XIII (promulgated by Bull, 24 Feb. 1582), whose calendar is now in general use.

6. The official year of the consuls (and of most other Roman magistrates) was appointed in 153 B.C. to begin on 1 Jan. That of the *tribuni plebis* began on 10 Dec.

W. Kubitschek (see TIME-RECKONING); M. P. Nilsson, *Primitive Time-Reckoning* (Lund, 1920); 'Entstehung und religiöse Bedeutung des griechischen Kalendars', in *Lunds Universitets Arsskrift*, N.F., Avd. 1, Bd. 14, Nr. 21; 'Zur Frage von dem Alter des vorcäsarischen Kalenders', in *Strena philologica Upsaliensis* (1922); G. Thomson, 'The Greek Calendar' (*JHS* 1943, 52 ff.); F. Altheim, *History of Roman Religion* (1938), p. 104 ff. H. J. R.

CALES, an Auruncan or Sidicinan town on the borders of Campania, nowadays *Calvi* (Strabo 5. 237; Polyb. 3. 91; Verg. *Aen.* 7. 728; Beloch, *Röm. Gesch.* 388). In 334 B.C. the Via Latina was probably extended to Cales, which became a Latin colony and the centre of Roman supremacy in Campania (Livy 8. 16; 10. 20). A *quaestor navalis* was stationed there (Tac. *Ann.* 4. 27; text uncertain). Cales was an important base in the Hannibalic War but, sustaining heavy losses, refused Rome further aid in 209 (Livy 27. 9). Rome reinforced it in 184 B.C. (Dessau, *ILS* 45). In Ciceronian and Imperial times Cales was a *municipium* (q.v.), and the birthplace of Vinicius, Velleius Paterculus' patron (Cic. *Leg. Agr.* 2. 86; Tac. *Ann.* 6. 15). The fertile Ager Calenus was famous for its pottery. Numerous monuments survive.

A. Sambon, *Monnaies antiques de l'Italie* i (1903), 353; C. L. Woolley, *JRS* 1910, 199; K. J. Beloch, *Röm. Gesch.* 489. E. T. S.

CALIDARIUM, see BATHS.

CALIDIUS, MARCUS, praetor 57 B.C., a leading Atticist pupil of Apollodorus in oratory (q.v.; cf. RHETORIC, LATIN). His gifts in speaking are handsomely praised by Cicero (*Brut.* 274 ff.).

Fragments: H. Malcovati, *ORF* iii.

CALIGA, see DRESS, para. 4.

CALIGULA, see GAIUS (1).

CALLEVA ATREBATUM, modern *Silchester*, on the Hampshire–Berkshire border. Recent excavations have not revealed pre-Roman occupation, so that the significance of CALLEV on coins of Epillus, son of Commius, is obscure. A Roman town was enclosed by a polygonal earthwork, perhaps after Boudicca's revolt (A.D. 61), and c. 100 was laid out in *insulae*. A flint wall erected c. 200 reduced the enclosed area to c. 100 acres. The land within it was completely excavated 1890–1909. Shops, a dyeing industry, and some 60 houses were exposed, and of public buildings a *forum* with *basilica*, baths, a presumed *hospitium*, five small temples, and a small Christian church. The population was perhaps c. 2,000. The town was eventually deserted after a period of slumdom.

Recent excavations (Mrs. Cotton) unpublished; those of 1890–1909, *Archaeologia* lii–lxii; earlier work (important) ib. xl. 403–16; xlvi. 329–65; l. 263–80. Partial summaries in *VCH* (*Hants*) i. 271–84, 350–72. Pottery: T. May, *Catalogue* (1916). C. E. S.

CALLIAS (1) (5th c. B.C.), son of Hipponicus, of one of the richest families in Athens. He was cousin to Aristides (q.v.), and married Elpinice, sister to Cimon (q.v.). He is said to have distinguished himself at the battle of Marathon; he won the chariot-race at Olympia three times. He is chiefly known as the head of the embassy which went to conclude peace with Persia in 449, a peace which recognized each party's sphere of influence —Persia agreeing not to send a fleet west of Phaselis in south Asia Minor and of the Bosporus, nor to send troops within three days' march of the west coast, Athens leaving to Persia all to the east of that line, as well as Cyprus and Egypt. The reality of this treaty was impugned by Theopompus, and has been doubted by modern scholars (see Grote, pt. ii, ch. 45; *CAH* v. 469-71). He is also said to have been one of the negotiators of the Thirty Years' Peace with Sparta (446-445). A. W. G.

CALLIAS (2), Athenian comic writer, victorious in 446 B.C. (*IG* ii². 2318, 2325), and said to have been a rival of Cratinus (Schol. Ar. *Eq.* 527). He was perhaps still active, as a litigant or a dramatist, after 403. His Πεδῆται mentions Socrates as a teacher of Euripides (fr. 11) and Aspasia of Pericles (fr. 15) and so is attributable to *c.* 431. (The Callias who wrote a γραμματικὴ τραγῳδία (Ath. 7. 276 a; 10. 448 b, 453 c) was a different person, an elder contemporary of Strattis).

FCG i. 213 f.; CAF i. 693 ff.; Demiańczuk, *Supp. Com.* 27 f.; Capps in *CPhil.* i. 219. M. P.

CALLIAS (3) (*c.* 450-370 B.C.), an Athenian nobleman, notorious for his wealth and his extravagance. He was ridiculed by comic poets, and attacked by Andocides, whom he accused of sacrilege. More sympathetic pictures of his house and life are given by Xenophon (*Symposium*) and Plato (*Protagoras*). He was general in 391-390, and took part in the famous victory of Iphicrates (q.v.) over Spartan hoplites. As an old man, he was a member of the embassy sent to Sparta in 371-370.

Swoboda, *PW*, s.v. 'Kallias (3)'. V. E.

CALLIAS (4) of Syracuse, lived at the court of Agathocles, tyrant of Syracuse (316-289 B.C.), and wrote a history of his reign in twenty-two books, variously described as Τὰ περὶ Ἀγαθοκλέα, Περὶ Ἀγαθοκλέα ἱστορίαι, etc. It so favoured Agathocles that Callias was suspected of accepting bribes; so Diod. Sic. (21. 17. 4) who, however, probably only knew Callias through the medium of Agathocles' enemy, Timaeus. The history had little influence on the tradition, which remained unfavourable to the tyrant, although, apart from the account written by Agathocles' brother, Antandrus, it was the first important work on this subject.

FHG. ii. 382 and iv. 657. G. L. B.

CALLICRATES (1), a Greek architect of the fifth century B.C. He was associated with Ictinus and the sculptor Phidias in the building of the Parthenon (q.v.).

CALLICRATES (2) (d. 149-148 B.C.) of Leontium, the Achaean pro-Roman statesman, in opposition to Lycortas after the death of Philopoemen, announced in Rome in 181-180 B.C. his policy of subservience to Rome. General in 180-79, he repatriated Spartan and Messenian exiles, and restored Spartan local rights. In 168 he prevented assistance to Egypt. After the Third Macedonian War, with the detention of the leading independent Achaean politicians in Italy, he maintained his ascendancy with Roman support, despite his unpopularity with the masses, until his death.

Polyb. 24. 8-10; 29. 23-5; 30. 13, 29, 32. G. Colin, *Rome et la Grèce* (1905), 233. De Sanctis, *Stor. Rom.* iv. 1, pp. 247, 347. A. H. McD.

CALLICRATIDAS, Spartan admiral, who succeeded Lysander (q.v.) in 406 B.C. Though hampered by partisans of Lysander and rebuffed by Cyrus, he increased the Peloponnesian fleet, defeated a squadron under Conon at Mytilene, and blockaded it there. Leaving 50 ships to maintain the blockade, he proceeded with 120 to attack

an Athenian relief fleet of 150. In a battle off the Arginusae Islands he suffered a heavy defeat and was drowned. He displayed energy, spirit, and sincerity, but his qualities are perhaps overrated by authorities hostile to Lysander.

Xenophon, *Hellenica* 1. 6. 1-33; Diodorus 13. 76-9, 97-9; Plutarch, *Lysander* 5-7. H. D. W.

CALLIMACHUS (1), Athenian polemarch and commander-in-chief in the campaign of Marathon (490 B.C.). He accepted Miltiades' plan to meet the Persians in the field. His part in the actual battle, in the last stage of which he was killed, has been obliterated by the personality and achievements of Miltiades, but his share in the victory was fully recognized in the wall-paintings on the Stoa Poikile (*c.* 460 B.C.), where he was portrayed among the Athenian gods and heroes, and in two surviving epigrams (Tod, *Greek Historical Inscriptions*, 13).

H. Berve, *Miltiades* (1937), 78 ff.; C. Robert, *Die Marathonschlacht in der Poikile* (1895), 19 ff. P. T.

CALLIMACHUS (2), Greek sculptor, perhaps an Athenian. He was reputed to have been the inventor of the Corinthian capital in architecture. This may well be true, since the Corinthian capital first occurs (at Bassae) in the third quarter of the fifth century, the period when Callimachus seems to have been active. He was noted as the first artist to employ the running-drill as a major instrument in carving. It is first so used about 440 B.C. He was known to artists as κατατηξίτεχνος—the man who spoiled his art by over-elaboration. This may well have been the consequence of his peculiar use of the drill.

S. C.

CALLIMACHUS (3) (*c.* 305-*c.* 240; Aul. Gell. 17. 21, 40 puts his *floruit* shortly after 264), of Cyrene, son of Battus (hence Battiades in *Epigr.* 35; Catull. 65. 16; Ov. *Am.* 1. 15. 13, etc.). He is described as pupil of Hermocrates of Iasos. Early in life C. migrated to Alexandria and became a schoolmaster in its suburb Eleusis. Soon he was recommended to Ptolemy Philadelphus and given employment at the library, apparently with the title νεανίσκος τῆς αὐλῆς (Tzetzes in Kaibel, *CGF* 31. 13). Employed as cataloguer of the library, he produced a *catalogue raisonné* in 120 volumes with the title Πίνακες τῶν ἐν πάσῃ παιδείᾳ διαλαμψάντων καὶ ὧν συνέγραψαν, the first scientific literary history. He was on intimate terms with the courts of Philadelphia and Euergetes and their consorts. Nevertheless his literary critics were numerous and persistent, including such well-known names as Asclepiades and Posidippus. It is possible that the dispute originated, early in C.'s career, over the merits of Antimachus' poetry (cf. *Anth. Pal.* 9. 63 (Asclepiades); 12. 168 (Posidippus); Callim. fr. 74 b). Soon the controversy turned on C.'s own poetic abilities, his opponents declaring that he was incapable of composing 'one continuous poem in many thousands of verses', i.e. an Epic in the traditional manner. C. met them by the assertion that such compositions were out of date, and confined himself to the production of short poems complete in themselves or loosely connected in a larger work (*see* EPYLLION). In C.'s later years the *Argonautica* of Apollonius Rhodius marked a rebellion in principle against C., Apollonius' former teacher, and provoked the famous quarrel. *Hymn Ap.* 105-13 and the *Retort to Critics* (*POxy.* 2079) are concerned with this later phase, Pontus in the former being perhaps Apollonius, and the Telchines, Pontus' offspring in myth, his supporters. C. was victorious and Apollonius retired to Rhodes. Soon afterwards, in 246-245, C. wrote the *Lock of Berenice*. His death may be dated *c.* 240.

WORKS

Verse: C.'s longest and most famous work was the *Aetia* (Αἴτια, *Causes*), produced probably *c.* 270, but reissued with a new preface, the *Retort to Critics*, towards the close of his life. It was a narrative elegy in four books and contained 3,000–4,000 lines. In the prologue (cf. *Anth. Pal.* 7. 42) C. described himself as transported in a dream from Libya to Helicon and there interrogating the Muses about myth, history, and ritual. It is uncertain how far in the poem this framework was maintained, as also what continuity existed between the various *Aetia* or elegies. The new *Diegeseis* (*Expositions*) of C.'s poems (*PMilan*. 18), which include bk. 4 and the end of bk. 3, testify to a certain degree of grouping by subject-matter. The longest fragments all come from papyri, *Acontius and Cydippe* (fr. 9 Pf.), *Pollis' Banquet* (fr. 8 Pf.), *Sacrifice of Zancle* (*POxy*. 2080). While the *Aetia* secured for C. his supremacy in Elegy (Quintilian, *Inst.* 10. 1. 58 calls him 'princeps elegiae'), he also wrote numerous elegies of the occasion. The best known is the *Lock of Berenice* (Catullus 66, cf. Barber in *Greek Poetry and Life*, 343–63). Others were a *Victory Ode for Sosibius* (fr. 60 Pf.) and an *Epithalamius for Arsinoë* (fr. 196). The *Iambi* were a collection of thirteen or fourteen shortish pieces. In 1–3, 5, and 14 C. satirizes contemporary morals; in 4 and 13 he deals with his literary critics; 6 describes Phidias' statue of Zeus at Olympia for an intending tourist; 7–11 are more on the lines of the *Aetia*; 12 celebrates the birth of a daughter to a friend Leon. The favourite metres are the scazon and iambic trimeter, but some pieces are in epodic form and there are other experiments. A veritable *lanx satura*, the *Iambi* must have influenced Roman Satire. Of C.'s Lyrics (Μέλη) very little survives, but enough to prove his skilful use of a variety of metres, some of them his own invention. His galliambics probably served as a model to Catullus and Varro. The longest fragments (Fr. 1 Pf.) come from the *Funeral Ode for Arsinoë* (d. 270), in archebuleans. Epic on the grand scale was avoided by C. on principle. Instead he composed epyllia (*see* EPYLLION), the most famous being his *Hecale*, a poem of perhaps 1,000 lines, narrating Theseus' encounter with the Bull of Marathon, but working in an account of the hero's earlier life and devoting most space to the old dame Hecale, at whose hut he spent the night previous to the encounter, and concluding with her death and the honours paid to her by Theseus. The poem also contained a remarkable digression in which the speakers are birds; the connexion of this with the main narrative remains obscure. Another branch of epic is represented by the *Hymns*, of which I–IV and VI are in hexameters, V in elegiacs. Up to a point C.'s model is the *Homeric Hymns*. C.'s *Hymns*, however, were not intended to be recited at a public festival, still less to accompany religious ritual. They are literary pieces, meant for reading or recitation to a select audience. I, II, and IV contain political propaganda. The style varies. I (Zeus) reads at times like a humorous report of a learned controversy. III (Artemis) approximates to an epyllion. IV (Delos), which competes with the Homeric Hymn to the Delian Apollo, comes nearest to the traditional manner. II (Apollo), V (Bath of Pallas), and VI (Demeter) represent C.'s greatest originality in this department. By a combination of dramatic mime and lyric the poet brings to life the spectacle itself and the emotions of the spectators. In V and VI a 'Holy Story', pathetic in V, grotesquely gruesome in VI, contributes an epic element. I–IV are in the epic dialect, V–VI in Doric. Of C.'s *Epigrams* some sixty survive. More interesting than the dedications and epitaphs, though some of the latter are excellent, are the occasional pieces, prompted by C.'s own experiences and emotions, especially during his early manhood. Of C.'s tragedies, comedies, and satyr-plays mentioned by Suidas nothing now survives. Almost as shadowy are a riddle poem on Athena and the *Grapheium*, which contained literary criticism. The *Ibis*, a wilfully obscure poem in mockery of Apollonius, gave Ovid the idea for his poem with the same title, but cannot be reconstructed from the latter. The *Diegeseis*, for example,

show that Ovid's *Ibis* incorporates several stories from the *Aetia*.

Prose. Besides the *Pinakes* C. wrote many other works in prose, e.g. a *Chronological Register of the Athenian Dramatic Poets*, a study of Democritus' writings and language, numerous encyclopaedias (*About Nymphs, Birds, Games, Winds, Rivers,* etc.), collections of Paradoxa, and Glosses.

The time is not yet ripe for a just appreciation of C. The publication of further new fragments is imminent, and still more material is known to exist. Already, however, it is clear that C. was a poet of far greater originality and wider compass than was commonly allowed. His amazing productivity (Suidas credits him with more than 800 volumes) was accompanied, as regards his poetry, by a boldness in experiment and a versatility of style which offended the conservatives of his generation, but justify the great reputation he enjoyed in later ages.

TEXTS: U. von Wilamowitz-Moellendorff, *Callimachi Hymni et Epigrammata*[4] (1925); O. Schneider, *Callimachea* (1870, 1873); R. Pfeiffer, *Callimachi Fragmenta Nuper Reperta* (ed. maior 1923); *Oxyrhynchus Papyri* xvii (1927), 45–72; A. Vogliano, *Papiri della R. Università di Milano* i (1937), 66–173. For further references to the new texts see H. Herter, Bursian's *Jahresbericht* lv (1937), 82–217, and E. Cahen in A. Couat, *La Poésie alexandrine sous les trois premiers Ptolémées* (1882, Engl. Transl. by J. Loeb, 1931), 548 ff. A. W. Mair, *Callimachus, Lycophron, Aratus* (Loeb, 1921), and E. Cahen, *Callimaque* (1922) give the hymns, epigrams, and a selection of the fragments, new and old.
GENERAL: H. Herter, 'Kallimachos (6)', in *PW*, Supplement-band v. 386–452; E. Cahen, *Callimaque et son œuvre poétique* (1929); id. *Les Hymnes de Callimaque* (1930). E. A. B.

CALLINUS, elegiac poet, of Ephesus, lived in the first half of the seventh century B.C., when Cimmerians and Trerians were attacking Phrygia, Lydia, and Ionia (Strabo 627, 647). He refers to them in frs. 3 and 4. He also refers to the destruction of Magnesia by the Ephesians (Ath. 525 c.). His one long fragment (fr. 1) summons men lying at a feast to take up arms and defend their country, and attributes the rank of demi-god to the brave fighter. It is written in epic language, but with certain originalities of phrasing.

Text: E. Diehl, *Anth. Lyr. Graec.* i. 1, pp. 3–5. Commentary: T. Hudson-Williams, *Early Greek Elegy* (1926), 71–81. Criticism: C. M. Bowra, *Early Greek Elegists* (1938), 13–16. C. M. B.

CALLIPHON, philosopher of uncertain date (probably not before Ariston of Chios and Hieronymus of Rhodes, who flourished *c.* 250 B.C.). Cicero says he held that the supreme good consists in the union of pleasure and virtue.

PW x. 1656.

CALLIPPUS (1), an Athenian, of Lamptrae, one of the early pupils of Isocrates, mentioned by him with others of his disciples to whom golden crowns were awarded for their public services (Isoc. 15. 93). We are not justified in identifying him with the man against whom Demosthenes wrote a 'private' speech for Apollodorus (*see* Dem. *c. Callippum*). Another Callippus, of Paeania, was prosecuted by Hegesippus for proposing an illegal decree ([Dem.] 7. 43). J. F. D.

CALLIPPUS (2) of Cyzicus (*c.* 370–300 B.C.), perhaps the greatest Greek astronomer of his time, went with Polemarchus to Athens, where he stayed with Aristotle. He corrected and added to Eudoxus' theory of concentric spheres designed to account for the movements of the sun, moon, and planets (Simpl. *in Cael.* 493, 5–8 Heib.); Callippus added two more spheres in each case for the sun and moon, and one more for each of the planets (as to these changes see Arist. *Metaph.* 1073[b] 32–8, Simpl. l.c. 497, 17–24). Callippus proposed the '76-year cycle' containing 27,759 days and consisting of 940 months—28 intercalary—as an alternative to Meton's cycle of 19 years (Geminus, *Isagoge* 8. 57–60); the first 76-year cycle began in 330–329 B.C. T. H.

CALLIRHOË (1), in mythology, daughter of the river Achelous; for her story, see ACARNAN, ALCMAEON; (2) a virgin of Calydon, vainly loved by Coresus, priest of Dionysus there, in a romantic and obviously late legend (Paus. 7. 21. 1–5).

CALLISTHENES of Olynthus, Aristotle's nephew, already known for works on Greek history, but not a wise man, accompanied Alexander's expedition as its historian. In his history he wrote up Alexander as champion of Panhellenism, partly propaganda against the Greek opposition; but he also made him son of Zeus, a far-reaching extravagance. He quarrelled with Alexander in 327 by opposing the introduction of *proskynesis* (his reasons remain doubtful), and was executed for alleged complicity in the Pages' conspiracy, which made the Peripatetic school Alexander's enemies for ever. *See* ALEXANDER (3), Bibliography, Ancient Sources.   W.W.T.

CALLISTO, probably in origin a by-form of Artemis Καλλίστη; in mythology, daughter of Lycaon. She was loved by Zeus and bore him Arcas (q.v.). Either Artemis, angered at her unchastity, or Hera then turned her into a she-bear; or she was shot by Artemis. In her transformed shape, either Artemis mistook her for a real bear and killed her, or her own son pursued her (as a quarry, or because she was trespassing on the precinct of Zeus Lycaeus), when Zeus took pity on them and transformed him into the constellation Arctophylax, her into the Great Bear.

See Apollodorus 3. 100–1; Ps.-Eratosthenes 1 and 8; Ov. *Met.* 2. 405 ff., *Fasti* 2. 155 ff.   H. J. R.

CALLISTRATUS (1), a διδάσκαλος of Old Comedy, possibly himself a comic poet, but better known as the man under whose name Aristophanes produced his three earliest plays.

CALLISTRATUS (2) of Aphidna, nephew of Agyrrhius (q.v.), was a talented orator and financier, who influenced Athenian policy from 377 to 361 B.C. Having prosecuted the ambassadors who proposed peace with Sparta in 391, he was elected strategus in 378 when the Second Athenian Confederacy was founded. He is known to have organized the finances of the confederacy and is believed to have inspired its liberal constitution. With Iphicrates he prosecuted Timotheus for misconduct in 373 and acted as strategus in 372, when Spartan naval power was broken. Realizing that Thebes was becoming more dangerous than Sparta, he negotiated the peace of 371 with Sparta (Xen. *Hell.* 6. 3. 10 f.). Endeavouring to maintain the balance of power between Thebes and Sparta, he proposed the dispatch of Iphicrates to aid Sparta in 369. Since his policy failed to check Thebes, he was impeached and only saved by his oratory (366). When Timotheus' policy of imperialism failed, Callistratus perhaps regained popular favour by negotiating alliance with Arcadia, but in 361 he was impeached, and was condemned to death *in absentia*. After reorganizing the finances of Macedonia for Perdiccas II, he landed in Attica and was put to death. A realist and constructive statesman, he was thwarted by the rise of Thebes.

P. Cloché, *La Politique étrangère d'Athènes 404–338 B.C.* (1934).   N. G. L. H.

CALLISTRATUS (3), pupil of Aristophanes of Byzantium, edited Homer and other authors, and wrote Σύμμικτα, quoted by Athenaeus. He attacked his fellow-pupil Aristarchus for departing from his master's doctrines.

CALLISTRATUS (4), a Roman jurist of the later Classical period (first half of the 3rd c. A.D.). He was of Greek origin, his Latin is full of Greek reminiscences, and his interest lay in the legal life of the Hellenistic provinces and the Imperial rescripts directed to them.

Works: *Quaestiones*, four books *De Iure Fisci, Institutiones,* an exposition of the edictal law (with a title of which the meaning is not quite clear: *Ad Edictum Monitorium*), and of the procedure *extra ordinem* (*De Cognitionibus*). A. B.

CALLISTRATUS (5) (3rd or 4th c. A.D.), a sophist who wrote Ἐκφράσεις (descriptions) of fourteen statues, in imitation of the Εἰκόνες of Philostratus of Lemnos.

Text, C. Schenkl and E. Reisch (Teubner, 1902). Translation, A. Fairbanks (Loeb, with Philostratus, 1931).

CALLISTUS, GAIUS JULIUS, a freedman of the Emperor Gaius, who took part in the conspiracy leading to Gaius' murder in A.D. 41. Under Claudius he acquired great wealth and power in the post of *a libellis*. (On the question whether he was appointed later than A.D. 43, see A. Momigliano, *Claudius*, 103.) He prudently refused help to Narcissus in accomplishing Messalina's downfall, but later was unsuccessful in championing the claims of Lollia Paulina to be Claudius' (fourth) wife. Agrippina, no doubt, secured his dismissal after Claudius' death, for nothing more is heard of him (see CLAUDIUS 1).   J. P. B.

CALLISTUS, *see also* BALLISTA.

CALLIXENUS (fl. *c.* 155 B.C.), a Rhodian Greek, wrote Περὶ Ἀλεξανδρείας. Athenaeus (5. 196 a; 203 e) quotes C. on ships built by Ptolemy Philopator and on a πομπή of Philadelphus.

PW x. 1751–4.

CALPURNIA (1), daughter of L. Piso Caesoninus (*cos.* 58 B.C.), married Caesar in 59, cementing an alliance between her husband and father. Though Caesar would have divorced her to marry Pompeia in 52, her affection for him was great, and she attempted to keep him from the Senate on the Ides of March (Plut. *Caes.* 63). After Caesar's murder she handed his papers and 4,000 talents to Antony.   G. E. F. C.

CALPURNIA (2), second wife of Pliny the Younger, whom she accompanied to Bithynia.

CALPURNIUS (1) **SICULUS,** TITUS (fl. A.D. 50–60), was the author of seven pastorals associated until 1854 with four others which Haupt proved to be by Nemesianus (q.v.). C.'s Neronian date is clear from allusions to the comet of A.D. 54 (1. 77–83), to the amphitheatre of 57 (7. 23–24), to Nero's speech for the people of Ilion (1. 45), and to the handsome young and divine ruler welcomed as the restorer of a Golden Age in 1, 4, and 7. These are his three courtly poems, placed at the beginning, middle, and end of the collection, while 2, 3, 5, and 6 are more strictly rural. In 2 Crocale's praises are sung alternately by a shepherd and a gardener (an innovation in pastorals); in 3 (possibly the earliest) Lycidas has thrashed his faithless sweetheart but swears repentance in a pretty love-song; 5 is an old herdsman's advice to his foster-son on managing goats and sheep, while 6 is a singing-match broken off by the ill temper of the competitors. Of the court-pieces, 1 represents two shepherds finding a poem by Faunus cut into the bark of a tree to prophesy a new Golden Age—they hope that their poetry will reach the Emperor through their patron Meliboeus; and 4, the longest eclogue (169 lines), hints that they have had some success; 7 gives Corydon's impressions of the amphitheatre built by Nero at Rome.

The problems concerning C. have produced many theories. His name may imply that he was son of a freedman of C. Calpurnius Piso, who conspired against Nero in 65: the epithet 'Siculus' may mean literally 'Sicilian' or symbolize the poet's debt to Theocritus. 'Meliboeus' in 1 and 4, described as learned and a new Maecenas, has been questionably identified with Seneca, with Piso, and others. An additional question touches the authorship of the contemporary Einsiedeln eclogues (q.v.), which some have unconvincingly ascribed to C. It has further been debated whether he could have written the *Laus Pisonis* (q.v.).

The situations, names, and phraseology in C.'s poems are often reminiscent of Virgil, to whom he does notable homage in 4. 64–72. There are signs of the influence of Ovid, Propertius, and Tibullus. C. can take a cue from Theocritus and follow it up with some independence. He shows skill in coherent dialogue when he employs amoebean verse in eclogues 2, 4, and 6. *See also* PASTORAL POETRY, LATIN, para. 5.

LIFE AND WORKS. Clementina Chiavola, *Della vita e dell' opera di Calpurnio Siculo* (1921).
TEXT: E. Baehrens, *PLM* iii; H. Schenkl, *Calp. et Nemes. bucolica* (1885) and in Postgate, *CPL*; C. Giarratano, *Calp. et Nemes. bucolica* (1924).
COMMENTARY: C. H. Keene, *Eclogues of Calp. and Nem.* (1887).
TRANSLATIONS: E. J. L. Scott (octosyllabic verse; 1890); J. W. and A. M. Duff (prose; Loeb, 1934).
SPECIAL STUDIES: M. Haupt, *De carminibus bucol. Calp. et Nemes.* (1854) ('Meliboeus' = Calp. Piso); F. Chytil, *Der Eclogendichter Calp. u. seine Vorbilder* (1894) ('Meliboeus' = Columella); F. Skutsch, 'Calp. Sic.' in *PW*; J. Hubaux, *Les Thèmes bucoliques dans la poésie latine* (1930); E. Cesareo, *La poesia di Calpurnio Siculo* (1931).   J. W. D.

CALPURNIUS (2) **FLACCUS** (2nd c. A.D.), author of declamations (*see* DECLAMATIO, para. 1) from fifty-three of which excerpts survive (Schanz–Hosius–Krüger, *Röm. Lit. Gesch.* 1922, 153).

G. Lehnert, *Calp. Flacc. Declamationes* (1903).

CALPURNIUS, *see also* AGRICOLA, BESTIA, BIBULUS, CRASSUS, PISO.

CALVINUS (1), GAIUS SEXTIUS (*cos.* 124 B.C.), in 123, following Flaccus' war in south Gaul, defeated the Salluvii, and founded a small settlement of Roman veterans at Aquae Sextiae (*Aix-en-Provence*).

CALVINUS (2), GNAEUS DOMITIUS, with C. Memmius, his fellow-candidate for the consulate in 54 B.C., made an infamous compact with the then consuls (Cic. *Att.* 4. 17. 2); this Memmius disclosed, but despite the disturbances which followed Calvinus was elected consul in July 53 for the rest of that year. In the war he fought for Caesar, against Scipio in Thessaly, against Pharnaces who defeated him at Nicopolis, and in Africa. In 42, while bringing reinforcements to the triumvirs, he was trapped on the Adriatic by Ahenobarbus, and lost his whole force. But he was made consul again in 40, and afterwards governed Spain, with notorious severity to the troops; in 36 he triumphed, and from his spoils decorated the Regia (q.v.).   G. E. F. C.

CALVISIUS SABINUS, GAIUS, served under Caesar in the Civil War, and was appointed governor of Africa (45 B.C.). He was consul in 39, and commanded a fleet for Octavian in 38. In 28 he triumphed 'ex Hispania'.

Appian, *BCiv.* 5; Dio Cassius, bk. 48.

CALVUS, GAIUS LICINIUS MACER (82–47 B.C.), Roman orator and poet, son of the annalist C. Licinius Macer (d. 66 B.C.). He left twenty-one speeches; the names of five have been preserved, one of which was against Vatinius, defended on the occasion (54 B.C.) by Cicero. Calvus was an orator of the Attic school. His speeches were the product of careful research and painstaking polish and compression, but lacked ease, vigour, and freshness (Cic. *Brut.* 283–4; *Fam.* 15. 21. 4; Quint. 10. 1. 115; Tac. *Dial.* 18, 21, 25). His poetic output was somewhat similar to that of Catullus, whose friend he was and with whom he is grouped by Horace (*Sat.* 1. 10. 19), Propertius (2. 25. 4), and Ovid (*Am.* 3. 9. 62). He wrote light, sportive pieces, fierce lampoons, elegies (including a lament for his wife or mistress, Quintilia, Prop. 2. 34. 89–90; cf. Catull. 96), an epithalamium,

and an epyllion entitled *Io* (presumably presenting many Alexandrian features), from which Ovid probably borrowed. Fragments of his speeches and poetry are few and brief.

H. Malcovati, *ORF* iii (1930), 167 ff.; W. Morel, *FPL* (1927); F. Plessis, *Calvus* (fragments, commentary, *testimonia*, biographical and literary study, 1896).   A. M. D.

CALVUS, *see also* SCIPIO (3).

CALYPSO (Καλυψώ, 'she who conceals'), a nymph, daughter of Atlas (q.v.; *Od.* 1. 14 and 50 ff.). She lived on the island of Ogygie, 'where is the sea's navel', i.e. a great way from any known land, and there received Odysseus when shipwrecked on his way from Circe's island (cf. ODYSSEUS). Though she promised to make him immortal if he would stay and be her husband (5. 209), he desired to return home; therefore, at the command of Zeus, conveyed by Hermes (5. 105 ff.) she let him go in the eighth year (7. 259–61), providing him with materials and tools to construct a makeshift boat (σχεδίη, 5. 251; the description shows that it was not a 'raft'). After Homer, little is added to her story. In the *Odyssey* nothing is said of her having children by Odysseus; but in Hesiod, *Theog.* 1017–18 (an interpolation?) she has two sons, Nausithous and Nausinous. More commonly her son (by Odysseus or Atlas; in post-Homeric genealogies she is often daughter of Oceanus or Nereus) is Auson, eponym of Ausonia (S. Italy), also called son of Circe (see, e.g., schol. Ap. Rhod. 4. 553 and Eustathius on Dionysius Periegeta, 78).   H. J. R.

CAMARINA, a Dorian colony near mod. *Scoglitti* in southern Sicily, was founded (599 B.C.), then destroyed (553), by Syracuse. Hippocrates of Gela refounded (491), and Gelon of Syracuse again destroyed it (484). Founded a third time—again by Gela (461)—Camarina became prosperous but, itself comparatively weak, necessarily supported stronger States, e.g. Leontini (427) and then Athens (424) against Syracuse, Syracuse against Athens (413). The Camarinaeans, disobeying Delphi, drained a nearby marsh, thus exposing their city: hence the proverb μὴ κίνει Καμάριναν (= 'let sleeping dogs lie'). After 406 Camarina was subject to Carthage, was temporarily liberated by Timoleon (339), and was finally destroyed during the First Punic War (258).

Hdt. 7. 154 f.; Thuc. 4. 25; 6. 5, 75; Diod. 11. 76; 13; 14; 16; 19; 20; 23; Polyb. bk. 1. B. Pace, *Camarina* (1927); J. Bérard, *Bibliogr. topogr.* (1941), 44.   E. T. S.

CAMBYSES (*Kambuiya*), son of Cyrus the Great; king of Persia 529–521 B.C. The main achievement of his reign was the conquest of Egypt in 525 B.C. (Hdt. 3. 1–15). He planned further military expeditions against Carthage, Ethiopia, and Siwa Oasis, but the first proved impracticable, the second was a partial failure, and in the third the Persian force perished in the desert. These misfortunes may have changed him from a wise and tolerant ruler to the tyrannical madman of Herodotus' account. He died in Syria while returning to suppress the rebel Gaumata, the pseudo-Smerdis.

J. V. Prašek, 'Kambyses', *Alte Orient* xiv. 2 (1913); *PW*, s.v. 'Kambyses' (C. F. Lehmann-Haupt).   M. S. D.

CAMELS. The camel of the Graeco-Roman and Iranian worlds, including Bactria, was the one-humped Arabian species; the two-humped 'Bactrian' camel belonged to India, China, and central Asia; the 'Bactrian' camel sent to Xerxes with the Saca tribute is depicted at Persepolis as an Arabian with two humps. Camels were common draught animals in Ptolemaic and Roman Egypt; Alexander and Ptolemy I utilized swift dromedaries for messages across the desert; Antiochus III had a camel corps, as had Romans (*dromedarii*) and Parthians later. But the real use of camels in war was shown by Surenas (q.v.), though seemingly he had no imitators.
                                                      W. W. T.

CAMENAE, Roman goddesses, identified since Livius Andronicus (*Odissia*, fr. 1) with the Muses. They seem, however, to be water-deities, having a grove and spring outside the Porta Capena (Plut. *Numa* 13; Platner–Ashby, 89) whence the Vestals drew water daily, also a little shrine (*aedicula*, Servius on *Aen.* 1. 8, who says it was of bronze and dedicated by Numa; its dedication-day was 13 Aug., *fast. Antiates*). Libation was made to them with milk and water (Serv. Dan. on Verg. *Ecl.* 7. 21). Their shrine, being struck by lightning, was removed to the temple of Hercules Musarum (Servius, first citation above).

See Wissowa, *RK* 219. H. J. R.

CAMEOS, *see* GEMS.

CAMERINUS, *see* SULPICIUS (3).

CAMILLA, a legendary Volscian maiden, whose father, Metabus, in flight fastened her to a javelin, dedicated her to Diana, and threw her across the Amisenus river. After life as a huntress she joined the forces of Turnus, engaged in battle, and was killed by the Etruscan Arruns. Virgil alone (*Aen.* 7. 803; 11. 539–828) relates her story. *See* HARPALYCE. A. S. P.

CAMILLUS (1), MARCUS FURIUS, the saviour and second founder of Rome after the Gallic invasion (387 B.C.). The splendour of his career is emphasized by the continuous embellishments which the account of it underwent from the fourth century B.C. onwards. Political pamphleteers, especially from the time of Sulla, exploited the story of Camillus for propaganda purposes: so Livy (5. 51 ff.) puts into his mouth a programme foreshadowing the Roman traditionalism of Augustus' policy. Camillus' earliest and greatest victory was the capture of Etruscan Veii (c. 396 B.C.); soon afterwards he reduced Falerii. As a war memorial a golden basin was dedicated to Apollo in the treasury of the Massiliotes at Delphi. This fact need not be questioned, since contacts had already been established, through Etruria, between Rome and the Greek world, while Greek fourth-century historians (e.g. Aristotle) dealt with Camillus' career. Tradition alleged that Camillus, who had been exiled for appropriating some booty, retired to Ardea in exile, where he was appointed dictator when the Gauls attacked Rome: he levied an army, defeated the Gauls, and recovered the gold with which the Romans had bought off the invaders. Whether Camillus was ever actually exiled or not, the story was obviously invented to balance the defeat on the Allia and, despite traces of accounts drawn from the contemporary legends, the main elements in it were borrowed from the trial of the Scipios. If Camillus did nothing to prevent the catastrophe, nobody contributed more whole-heartedly to Rome's subsequent recovery. Although his home policy aimed at reasserting patrician influence, and he crushed the sedition of M. Manlius (q.v. 1) by force, his military reforms proved nevertheless favourable to the plebeians, since they gave recognition to individual merit and provided public pay, and he supported the plebeian claims to the supreme magistracies. Camillus' policy of appeasement at home enabled him successfully to lead the Romans against the Aequi and Volscians, although his subsequent victories were undoubtedly exaggerated by tradition.

For source-criticism: Mommsen, *Röm. Forsch.* ii. 321 ff.; O. Hirschfeld, *Kl. Schriften* (1913), 273 ff.; E. Täubler, *Klio* 1912; E. Burck, *Die Erzählungskunst des T. Livius* (1934), 109 ff.; F. Altheim, *Epochen d. röm. Gesch.* i (1934), 164 ff.; A. Momigliano, *CQ* 1942, 111 ff. P. T.

CAMILLUS (2), LUCIUS FURIUS, a son of Camillus (1). As consul in 349 B.C. he defeated the Gauls through the

efforts of Valerius (q.v. 3) Corvus. Probably this success, and not a fictitious Auruncan victory in 345, induced him to dedicate the temple of Juno Moneta.

Livy 7. 28. F. E. Adcock, *CAH* vii. 587. E. T. S.

CAMILLUS (3), LUCIUS FURIUS, a grandson of (1). In 338 B.C. he and his fellow-consul, C. Maenius, crushed the Latins and dissolved the Latin League—an exploit that earned them honorific statues in the Forum (Livy 8. 13). Camillus' second consulship (325) was undistinguished owing to illness (Livy 8. 29). E. T. S.

CAMILLUS, an acolyte in Roman cult, fem. *camilla*. They might be the children of the officiant, but must have both parents alive (*pueri patrimi et matrimi*), be below the age of puberty, and of course free-born.

See Marquardt–Wissowa, *Staatsverw.* iii. 2. 227.

CAMPANIA lies between the Apennines and the Tyrrhenian Sea in Italy, extending from Latium to the Surrentine promontory. This fertile, volcanic plain annually produced three, sometimes four, cereal and vegetable crops. Its roses, fruits, olives (from Venafrum), and wines (from the isolated mountains Vesuvius, Gaurus, Massicus, Callicula) were also famous. In the Bay of Naples it possessed an excellent harbour, and Puteoli (q.v.) became Italy's chief port. The mild climate and beautiful luxuriousness of Campania constantly attracted invaders and reputedly sapped the martial energies of its inhabitants (Polyb. 3. 91). After 750 B.C. Greeks began colonizing the coast, drove back the indigenous population (known traditionally as *Ausones*), and extended their influence even to Rome (*see* CUMAE). In the interior c. 600 an invading Etruscan minority established a league of twelve cities headed by Capua, but failed to capture Cumae (Polyb. 2. 17). The Greeks indeed badly defeated these Campanian Etruscans in 474. Invading Sabelli (q.v.), however, proved irresistible: they captured Capua c. 440, Cumae c. 425, and imposed their language on and merged with the indigenous population (Diod. 12. 31. 76; Livy 4. 37); henceforth the Campanians are called Osci (q.v.). This name, as its *-co-* suffix shows, is pre-Sabellian (for Sabellian tribal names had an *-no-* suffix, *-co-* like *-(a)ti-* being non-Sabellian. Cf. Ardeates, Ardeatini). These Osci, although more civilized than their Samnite or Roman neighbours and although skilled mercenary soldiers, were no match for fresh Sabellian invaders and consequently sought Roman protection c. 343 B.C. Thereafter, although the Oscan and Greek languages long survived here, Campanian history is linked with Roman (*see* CAPUA). Campania witnessed heavy fighting in the wars of the Republic and suffered disasters like the eruption of Vesuvius. Nevertheless it remained a prosperous area with an excellent road-system and numerous villas. After Augustus Campania included Latium; indeed the name was ultimately restricted to Latium, the *Campagna* of to-day.

Strabo 5. 242; Pliny, *HN* 3. 59 f.; Florus 1. 16. 3. K. J. Beloch, *Campanien²* (1890); R. S. Conway, *Italic Dialects* i (1897), 51; A. Sambon, *Monnaies antiques de l'Italie* i (1903), 137; R. M. Peterson, *Local Cults of Campania* (Rome, 1919); J. Day, *Yale Classical Studies* iii (1932), 167 (well documented); J. Whatmough, *Foundations of Roman Italy* (1937), 292; G. Spano, *La Campania felice nelle età più remote* (1941). E. T. S.

CAMPS. When the Roman camp (*castra*) was described by Polybius (6. 27–32) about 143 B.C., its stereotyped form was already taken for granted; indeed, no Roman historian troubles to describe it. It is associated with the earliest annals of Roman history (cf. Livy 10. 32. 9; 34. 46. 8; 40. 27. 1–7; 41. 2. 11), but its origins are doubtful. R. Lehmann-Hartleben assigns its introduction to the Etruscans and would connect it with Assyrian war-entrenchments (*Die Traianssäule* (1926), 10), while others would connect it with the *terremare* (q.v.) settlements of prehistoric Italy, too often assumed to be normally symmetrical (*Antiquity* xiii. 320). The augural principles associated with its planning certainly appear in the earliest Roman colonies of which we have archaeological knowledge, and its development is undoubtedly a Roman invention.

Polybius describes a camp for a consular army of two Roman legions with an equivalent number of Italian allies. It is square, and faces in the most convenient direction (contrast *Veget.* 1. 23). Its plan is based upon the general's tent (*praetorium*, q.v.) and the 100-foot street (*via principalis*), parallel therewith. The legions (each grouped as 1,200 *hastati*, 1,200 *principes*, 600 *triarii*, and 1,200 *velites*) and the bulk of the allies were encamped by *centuriae* (then of 60 men each) and *turmae* in parallel divisions along streets at right angles to the *via principalis*, and were divided at the position of the fifth cohort by a second large cross-street, hence called *via quintana*. The *praetorium* is flanked by six tribunes' tents disposed along the *via principalis*, with open spaces behind them serving respectively as *forum* and *quaestorium*. Then comes a third cross-street, behind which lay the *extraordinarii* (selected allied troops) with *auxilia* (foreign levies) on the flanks. The enclosing rampart (*vallum*) and ditch (*fossa*) were divided from the host by an *intervallum* 200 feet wide, serving for booty, and probably for the *velites*, about whose position there is ambiguity (Stolle, *Das Lager und Heer der Römer* (1912), 94–104). There are many points of resemblance between this Polybian plan and the camps of the second century B.C. excavated by A. Schulten at Numantia (q.v.), though the allotment of space differs considerably, maniples being grouped round a square rather than in long narrow *strigae*.

An imperial camp of the third century A.D. (*Rh. Mus.* xlviii. 243) is described in the anonymous treatise *De Munitionibus Castrorum*. While Polybius had tried to describe common practice, this imperial camp is treated as a mere exercise in castrametation, using factors unlikely to be found in conjunction. The differences are striking. The proportion of the whole work is not square but *tertiata*, one-third being called *praetentura* and two-thirds *retentura*. Auxiliaries and irregulars take the place of *extraordinarii* and occupy the whole *praetentura*. The *via quintana* has moved to behind the *praetorium*. The legionaries are quartered around the whole encampment, lying between the *intervallum* and a street called *via sagularis*. The unit for all regulars is no longer the maniple, but the *centuria* of 80 men. The *quaestorium* has moved to behind the *praetorium* and such institutions as the hospital (*valetudinarium*), of which Polybius makes no mention, have appeared. Archaeology does not supply examples of Imperial camps on so large and detailed a scale as the Republican camps at Numantia. For defences and outlines, the British groups of Northumberland and Scotland are unrivalled. At Masada, west of the Dead Sea, there is a remarkable series of small siege-camps, filled with temporary buildings in the manner of Numantia, while the manœuvre-camps of Cawthorn should also be noted.

H. Stuart Jones, *Companion to Roman History* (1912), 226 ff.; A. Schulten, *Numantia* i–iv (1914–31); Kromayer–Veith, *Heerwesen und Kriegsführung der Griechen und Römern* (1928); for Northumberland examples, I. A. Richmond, *Northumberland County History* xv. 116–29; for Scottish examples, W. Roy, *Military Antiquities of the Romans in North Britain* (1793); for Masada, *Antiquity* iii. 195 f. and *Zeitschrift des Deutschen Palästina-Vereins* lvi; *De Munitionibus Castrorum*, ed. Lang (1848), von Domaszewski (1887).   I. A. R.

CAMPUS MARTIUS, originally the Tiber flood-plain bounded by the Pincian, Quirinal, and Capitoline hills of Rome, was once pasture, though Tarquin grew corn there, and, being outside the *pomerium* (q.v.), was used for army musters and exercises, for the *comitia centuriata*, and for foreign cults, as of Pluto and Proserpine, Apollo (431 B.C.), and Bellona (296 B.C.). Republican public

works, the *Villa Publica* (435 B.C.), *Forum Holitorium*, *Circus Flaminius* (221 B.C.), *Porticus Octavia* (168 B.C.) and *Minucia* (110 B.C.), and many unidentified temples, as in the *Forum Boarium* and Piazza Argentina, soon overran its south end. The *Theatrum Pompei* (52 B.C.), with huge *porticus*, foreshadows the immense buildings of the Augustan *viri triumphales*, the temple of Neptune by Domitius Ahenobarbus (*c.* 32 B.C.), *amphitheatrum Tauri* (29 B.C.), the *Mausoleum*, gardens, and crematorium of Augustus (28 B.C.), *porticus Octaviae* (27 B.C.), the *Saepta Iulia* (q.v., 26 B.C.), Agrippa's Baths, water-garden, aqueduct (q.v.), Pantheon (q.v.) and *porticus Argonautarum* (25 B.C.), the theatres of Marcellus and Balbus (the latter with *Crypta*) of 13 B.C., a monumental sun-dial (10 B.C.) of which the gnomon was an obelisk of Psammetichus II, and the *Ara Pacis* (q.v., 9 B.C.). Imperial buildings came to fill the remaining space. Gaius projected an amphitheatre, and perhaps built the *Iseum et Serapeum* vowed by the triumvirs. Nero built *thermae* (A.D. 62–4). Domitian erected the *Templum Divorum* (*Vespasiani et Titi*), a *stadium* (now Piazza Navona), and *odeum*. Hadrian added the *basilicae* of Matidia and Marciana, with a temple to the former. Pius honoured Hadrian with a temple (A.D. 145), and is himself commemorated by a crematorium and *columna Divi Pii*, with famous panels on its base, while the *templum divi Marci* is associated with the more famous Column, with spiral reliefs of the Marcomannic wars.   I. A. R.

CAMULODUNUM, modern *Colchester* (Essex). A site to the west of the Roman (and modern) town, was occupied *c.* 10 B.C. by the Belgic conquerors of the Trinovantes and was the capital and mint of Cunobelinus (q.v.), as well as the principal trading port of Britain (cf. Fox, *Proc. Prehist. Soc. E. Anglia* vii. 159). Captured in Claudius' campaign of A.D. 43, it served as a base for the conquest of Britain, and in 50 a colony (*colonia Victricensis*) was founded close by, which was probably at first the provincial capital. This unwalled town was sacked by Boudicca in 61 and was subsequently rebuilt in regular *insulae* to cover an area of *c.* 108 acres. Its defences were a clay bank, to which, as appears, a stone wall was added *c.* A.D. 100. Important remains are the substructures of a temple (probably not that of Divus Claudius), an underground structure with drains (possibly a Mithraeum), and the monumental west (Balkerne) gate. Samian pottery was made here in the second century. Its subsequent history is virtually unknown: a *censitor civium Romanorum* is mentioned (*ILS* 2740, 2nd c.), and it was possibly the seat of a bishopric (*Eng. Hist. Rev.* lii. 196, n. 1).

Summaries in *CIL* vii. 33–6; *JRS* ix. 139–69; *Royal Commission on Historical Monuments* (NE. Essex), 20–32. Recent excavation (mainly on the pre-Roman site) summarized in *JRS* and *Trans. Essex Arch. Soc.* See also C. F. C. Hawkes and M. R. Hull, *Camulodunum* (1947). Pottery: T. May, *Catalogue* (1930).   C. E. S.

CANABAE, the name given to the civil settlements that grew up around the legionary fortresses, e.g. at Moguntiacum, Carnuntum, and Lambaesis. Their inhabitants were Roman citizens, many of whom were discharged soldiers returning to the scene of their military service. *Canabae* were *vici* (q.v.) and had magistrates with the titles of *magistri* or *curatores*, and probably a local council. During the second century A.D. many of them were given the status of *municipia* (q.v.).

Soldiers who give *castris* as their birthplace were born in the *canabae* of the camp where their fathers, who had contracted an illegal marriage, were stationed.

M. Rostovtzeff, *Social and Economic History of the Roman Empire* (1926), passim.   H. M. D. P.

CANALS. Although the science of irrigation was highly developed in Mesopotamia and Egypt, and was familiar to the Romans, whose irrigation works in the province of Africa enabled it to provide Rome with corn, few navigable canals were constructed in antiquity. Proposals to canalize rivers by diverting their course met with some religious opposition (Hdt. 1. 174; Tac. *Ann.* 1. 79). Xerxes' famous canal across Athos was seldom imitated. From very ancient times (Hdt. 2. 158) a canal, which was reopened by Trajan, connected the Nile with the Gulf of Suez. The idea of constructing a canal across the Isthmus of Corinth appealed to Caesar and Caligula, and work was begun on it under Nero (Suet. *Nero* 19; Plin. *HN* 4. 45), but not completed. Tacitus (*Ann.* 13. 53) mentions a scheme for connecting the Moselle to the Saône by a canal, to connect the North Sea and the Mediterranean. Pliny (*Tra.* 41–2, 61–2) asked Trajan for the services of an engineer (*librator*) to connect a lake in Bithynia with the sea by means of a canal; his letters show that the Romans were familiar with the use of the sluice (*cataracta*). Nero proposed the construction of a canal from the Bay of Naples to the Tiber (Tac. *Ann.* 15. 42; Suet. *Nero* 31). The most successful canals made by the Romans were near the mouths of rivers. Corbulo connected the Meuse with the Rhine (Tac. *Ann.* 11. 20), and Drusus linked the Rhine with the Zuyder Zee (ib. 2. 8). Marius facilitated the approach to the Rhône by the construction of the *Fossae Marianae*, through which seafaring ships were enabled to enter the east mouth of the river (Strabo 4. 183, Plut. *Mar.* 115).

M. L. de la Blanchère, Dar.-Sag., s.v. 'Fossa'. G. H. S.

CANDIDATUS, a candidate for a magistracy. Officially named *petitor* (his rivals were therefore styled *competitores*), he was called *candidatus* because he wore a white, or whitened, toga when greeting electors in the forum. He was then accompanied by a slave (*nomenclator*) who reminded him of the names of the electors, and by a crowd of partisans (*sectatores*), mostly freedmen, whose task was to secure votes by bargaining and bribing, either directly or through special agents. The *divisores* were charged with distributing money to the voting members of the tribes. To prevent or limit canvassing, legislation *de ambitu* (*see* AMBITUS) was enacted, but unsuccessfully. A radical change occurred when Tiberius 'recommended', that is in fact appointed, at least some of the candidates. From Vespasian onwards *all* candidates were recommended by the emperors, who conferred upon them the title of *candidati Caesaris* as a mark of favour.

Mommsen, *Röm. Staatsr.* i³. 477 ff.; ii³. 921 ff.; W. Kubitschek, *PW*, s.v. P. T.

CANIDIUS CRASSUS, PUBLIUS, was legatus to Lepidus in 43 B.C., and subsequently one of Antony's most trusted officers. He fought in the Perusine War and became *consul suffectus* after the peace of Brundisium. He was sent to Armenia in 37, subdued the Iberians and Albanians in the Caucasus, and subsequently joined Antony in the Parthian expedition. Canidius was left in command of Antony's army at Actium, escaped before its surrender, and rejoined Antony in Egypt, where he was put to death by Octavian after the occupation of Alexandria.

Velleius 2. 85–7; Plutarch, *Antony*; Appian, *BCiv.* 5. 50; Dio Cassius 49. 24. G. W. R.

CANINIUS (1) REBILUS, GAIUS, a *novus homo* and legate, who served Caesar well against Vercingetorix. In 49 B.C. he was sent by Caesar to Pompey to arrange a compromise. He fought in Africa and later in Spain. On the last day of 45, on the sudden death of a consul, Caesar appointed him consul for a few hours. A. M.

CANINIUS (2) RUFUS, of Comum, a neighbour of the younger Pliny, much occupied with his land estates, but possessing an epic bent which Pliny encouraged, as he did in the case of Octavius Rufus and others. His literary interests are discernible from Pliny's letters to him (1. 3; 2. 8; 3. 7; 6. 21; 7. 18; 8. 4; 9. 33). J. W. D.

CANIUS RUFUS, from Gades, a poet friend of Martial, who alludes to his versatility and merriment in epigram 3. 20 (cf. 1. 61. 9; 1. 69).

CANNAE, a village on the south bank of the Aufidus in Apulia, the site of Hannibal's great victory in 216 B.C. L. Aemilius Paullus and C. Terentius Varro (qq.v.) with perhaps 48,000 infantry and 6,000 cavalry (rather than the 90,000 which Polybius implies) faced Hannibal's 35,000 infantry and 10,000 cavalry. Hannibal's convex crescent-shaped formation gradually became concave under pressure of the Roman centre which, being thus encircled and finally surrounded by Hannibal's cavalry in the rear, failed to break through and was cut to pieces. The long-debated question whether the battlefield lay north or south of the river now appears to be settled in favour of the south by the reported discovery of a large military cemetery there.

Polybius 3. 107–18. Livy 22. 43–9. *See also* PUNIC WARS. For excavations, see *Arch. Anz.* 1938, 717. H. H. S.

CANTABRI, a sea-coast and mountain tribe of Spain situated east of the Astures (q.v.). Their poverty and primitive characteristics are described by Strabo (3. 3. 7–8, pp. 155–6), who ascribes to them a sort of gynaecocracy (3. 4. 18, p. 165). They were finally reduced by the Romans in campaigns from 26 to 19 B.C. which were led by Augustus (26–25) and Agrippa (19). Those who survived this Cantabrian War were either deported from their mountain homes or remained under the supervision of Roman troops. Juliobriga (nowadays *Reinosa*) is the only known Roman foundation. Pliny mentions *plumbum nigrum*, or lead, and magnetic iron, as natural resources.

On the wars see D. Magie, *CPhil.* 1920, and R. Syme, *AJPhil.* 1934. A. Schulten, *Los Cantabros y Astures* (1943). J. J. VAN N.

CANTHARUS, Athenian comic poet, victorious in 422 B.C. (*IG* ii². 2318). His Σνμμαχία seems to have dealt with the ostracism of Hyperbolus in 417.

FCG i. 251; *CAF* i. 764–6; Demiańczuk, *Supp. Com.* 28.

CANTICA, the lyric or musical portions of a Latin comedy (e.g. in Plautus) as contrasted with *diverbium*. Lyric *cantica* scarcely exist in Terence. *See* METRE. LATIN, I (B).

CANTORES EUPHORIONIS, *see* NEOTERICI.

CANULEIUS, GAIUS, tribune of the plebs in 445 B.C., is reputed to have enacted a *rogatio* or *Lex Canuleia* that allowed intermarriage between patricians and plebeians, probably by recognizing the legitimacy of children of plebeian mothers, and by admitting them to the patrician *gentes*. Livy's lively but historically almost worthless account contains difficulties (e.g. the carrying of the law in the tribal assembly, and its connexion with the first plebeian attempts to win admission to the consulate), but the fact and approximate date of the law are indisputable.

G. De Sanctis, *Stor. d. Rom.* ii. 55 ff. On the question of intermarriage between patricians and plebeians see now H. Last, *JRS* 1945, 31 ff. P. T.

CANUS, *see* JULIUS (3).

CANUSIUM (nowadays *Canosa*), on the river Aufidus, was an Apulian city, probably of Daunian origin (cf. Pliny, *HN* 3. 104), although late-Canosan pottery, necropolis finds, coins, and language indicate much hellenization by 300 B.C. (cf. Hor. *Sat.* 1. 10. 30). After submitting to Rome (318 B.C.), Canusium remained faithful until the Social War, which apparently caused it to decline somewhat (Strabo 6. 283; Livy 9. 20; App. *BCiv.* 1. 42, etc.). However, situated on the Via Traiana, it soon recovered to become a *municipium*, an Antonine *colonia*, and the chief Apulian city in the sixth century (Procop. 3. 18). For a list of its decurions (A.D. 223) see Dessau *ILS* 6121 (cf. 8703 *b*, 5188).

N. Jacobone, *Canusium* (1925). E. T. S.

CAPANEUS (Καπανεύς), in mythology, son of Hipponous and father of Sthenelus (*Il.* 4. 367; Hyg. *Fab.* 70. 1); one of the Seven against Thebes, cf. ADRASTUS. As he climbed on the walls, boasting that not even Zeus should stop him, he was destroyed by a thunderbolt (Aesch. *Sept.* 427; Eur. *Phoen.* 1172 ff. (from the cyclic *Thebais*?)).

H. J. R.

CAPELLA, MARTIANUS, *see* MARTIANUS CAPELLA.

CAPER, FLAVIUS (late 2nd c. A.D.), grammarian, whose lost treatises *De Latinitate* (containing citations from old Latin authors) and *De Dubiis Generibus* were freely used by later writers. The *Orthographia* and *De Verbis Dubiis* extant under his name (ed. Keil, *Gramm. Lat.* vii. 92–107; 107–12) are apocryphal.

Cf. Teuffel, § 374, 3; Schanz–Hosius, § 599. J. F. M.

CAPITE CENSI, *see* CENTURIA.

CAPITO (1), GAIUS ATEIUS, tribune of the plebs 55 B.C., opposed Pompey and Crassus. He announced adverse prodigies (which Crassus disregarded) and was consequently punished in 50 with a *nota censoria* (Cic. *Div.*1. 29).

CAPITO (2), GAIUS ATEIUS, a Roman jurist of the first decade of the Empire. He came of a modest family, but obtained the consulship (in A.D. 5), and was *curator aquarum* from A.D. 13 to 22, the year of his death. With his contemporaries 'maximae auctoritatis fuit' (Pompon. *Dig.* 1. 2. 2. 47). As a disciple of the jurist Ofilius, he was contemporary and rival of Antistius (q.v. 2) Labeo. Their political, scientific, and personal antagonism was the origin—if Pomponius' account is true—of the schools of jurists, the Sabinians (Sabinus was a disciple of Capito) and Proculians. Capito was conservative in his legal doctrines, whilst Labeo was an independent innovator. They were also political adversaries, but in an inverse sense: Capito approved of the new constitution, Labeo was an obstinate republican, even under the new régime. His activity as a writer was considerable: a comprehensive work *De Iure Pontificio*, a large collection entitled *Coniectanea* (there was a chapter *de iudiciis publicis*, another *de officio senatorio*); a monograph *De Iure Sacrificiorum*. He is rarely quoted by the jurists, but more plentifully by non-legal authors (Gellius, Plinius, Festus, Macrobius).

P. Jörs, *PW*, s.v. 'Ateius (8)'; B. Kübler, *Gesch. d. röm. Rechts* (1925), 259 ff. Collection of passages preserved in non-legal authors' works in Huschke–Seckel–Kübler, *Jurisprudentia anteiustiniana* i² (1908), 62–72. A. B.

CAPITO, *see also* SINNIUS.

CAPITOL, CAPITOLIUM, or MONS CAPITOLINUS, one of the hills of Rome: an isolated mass left by erosion, with two peaks, Capitolium proper and Arx. At all periods it constituted less a part of the inhabited area of the city than a citadel and sanctuary: it is mentioned chiefly in connexion with religious observances, especially triumphs, and with military operations. It was crowned by the Tarquins' temple, dedicated in 509 B.C. by a first consul of the Republic to Jupiter Optimus Maximus, Minerva, and Juno, who had been previously installed on the Quirinal (Varro, *Ling.* 5. 158). The original platform of the temple (55 m. by 60 m. in area), still exists; but the original temple, embellished in 296, 275, 193, 179, and 142, was burnt in 83 B.C. The new temple of Lutatius Catulus (69 B.C.), renovated and repaired by Augustus in 26 and 9 B.C., was burnt down in A.D. 69, while Vespasian's temple perished in the fire of A.D. 80. Domitian's building, dedicated two years later, cost 12,000 gold talents and lasted until A.D. 455, when Gaiseric the Vandal plundered it. The Tarpeian Rock (q.v.) lay close by, on the south-west shoulder of the hill. On the north summit of the hill, originally distinguished as the *arx*, lay the temple of Juno Moneta (344 B.C.), the *auguraculum* (an augur's observation post with primitive hut), and the temple of Concordia (216 B.C.). On the col between the hills lay the curious *aedes Veiovis* (Vitr. 4. 8. 4) and the *asylum inter duos lucos* associated with Romulus. The east face of the hill was occupied by the Tabularium (q.v.) and the approach-road (*clivus Capitolinus*), paved in 174 B.C.

Both hill and the temple of Jupiter were reproduced in many cities of Italy and the Roman West, and either hill or temple or both in Roman Byzantium; Jerusalem, as refounded by Hadrian, was styled *Aelia Capitolina*. The right to erect such *Capitolia* was at first probably reserved for Roman *coloniae*. A. W. V. B. and I. A. R.

CAPPADOCIA at one time designated the whole region between the Halys and the Euphrates, and from the Euxine Sea to Cilicia; but the northern part became 'Cappadocian Pontus' or simply 'Pontus' (q.v.), and the central and southern part Greater Cappadocia. This latter consists of a rolling plateau, almost treeless in its western portion, some broken volcanic areas in the centre and west (the cone of Mt. Argaeus reaches 12,000 ft.), and the ranges, for the most part well watered and well timbered, of the Taurus and Antitaurus. A rigorous winter climate limits production to hardy cereals and fruits. Grazing was always important; the Persian kings levied a tribute of 1,500 horses, 50,000 sheep, and 2,000 mules, and Roman emperors kept studs of race-horses there. Mines are mentioned of quartz, salt, Sinopic earth, and silver. Since the passes were frequently closed in winter the country was isolated, and consequently developed slowly.

The Medo-Persian conquest led to the formation of an Iranian nobility with feudal dominion over considerable districts. Besides these there existed large areas owned by temples and ruled by priests, such as the territories of Ma of Comana and Zeus of Venasa. Nobles and priests often rivalled the authority of the kings. The ordinary people lived in villages on the large estates or as serfs on the temple territories, supplying their masters with labour and revenues and the raw material for an active slave-trade.

The satrap Ariarathes refused to submit to Alexander; his descendants added Cataonia to their possessions, and were recognized as kings from *c.* 255 B.C. Ariarathes IV supported Antiochus III against Rome at Magnesia in 190, but he and his successors thereafter adopted a philo-Roman policy. Their efforts at hellenization and urbanization made slow progress, as Mazaca and Tyana remained almost the only cities. Devastated by Tigranes of Armenia in the Mithridatic Wars, Cappadocia was restored by Pompey, who gave the king large loans for reconstruction. Antony replaced this line, which had proved disloyal in the Parthian invasion, with the energetic Archelaus, who renamed Mazaca Caesarea and founded Archelais (Garsaura). He lost favour in Rome in his old age, and the military importance of Cappadocia led to its annexation in A.D. 17. A procuratorial province until Vespasian, it was joined with the Galatian complex under a consular legate until Trajan, after whom Pontus and Cappadocia remained united to the time of Diocletian. The eleven royal *strategiai* remained the basis of the provincial administration. Development of commerce from the West, the transfer of legions to the upper Euphrates, and the system of military roads aided the belated advancement of native communities to city rank, but at most they hardly occupied a third of the territory. Imperial estates, beginning with the royal properties, steadily increased through confiscations.

Th. Reinach, *Trois royaumes de l'Asie Mineure* (1888); *CAH* ix. 211 ff.; xi. 606 ff.; Jones, *Eastern Cities*, 175 ff.; W. E. Gwatkin, 'Cappadocia as a Roman Procuratorial Province', *Univ. of Missouri Studies* v (1930), no. 4. T. R. S. B.

CAPRARIA, see BALEARES INSULAE.

CAPREAE (nowadays *Capri*), a beautiful, mountainous island near Naples (Strabo 5. 248). Neolithic people once dwelt here, and, in prehistoric times, legendary Teleboae (*Mon. Ant.* 1924, 305; Verg. *Aen.* 7. 735). In historical times Capreae was Neapolitan territory until Augustus, who often stayed here, gave Neapolis Aenaria in exchange (Suet. *Aug.* 92). Tiberius spent his last ten years on Capreae, amid wild debaucheries according to incredible ancient records. Ruined villas afford tangible memorials of his sojourn; he is said to have built twelve, named after various deities (Tac. *Ann.* 4. 67). After Tiberius the Caesars avoided Capreae except as a place of banishment, e.g. for Commodus' wife and sister (Dio Cass. 72. 4). Although arid, Capreae was fertile, but in antiquity never experienced municipal organization. The Romans knew its famous Blue Grotto.

H. E. Trower, *Book of Capri* (1924); A. Maiuri, *Breviario di Capri* (1938). E. T. S.

CAPROTINA. a title of Juno (q.v.), derived from the Nonae Caprotinae (7 July), i.e. Nones of the Wild Fig (*caprificus*), under which maid-servants had a sham fight with stones, etc., and abused each other. It seems to be an old rite of fertility (fig-juice as equivalent to milk? cf. the Akikuyu rite in *Man* 1913, No. 3), grown unintelligible and relegated to slaves, though free-born women also sacrificed on that day (Macrob. *Sat.* 1. 11. 36); see further Wissowa, *RK* 184. H. J. R.

CAPSA, CAPSULA, see BOOKS, II. 2.

CAPUA, a city of Campania. Archaeological evidence indicates that Capua was founded *c.* 600 B.C., probably by Etruscans; it was certainly Etruscan in the sixth century (Vell. Pat. 1. 7; Livy 4. 37). Capua gave its name to the entire surrounding plain, *Ager Campanus* (i.e. *Capuanus*), later called Campania (q.v.). But it specifically dominated the immediately neighbouring territory (Falernus Ager, Casilinum, Calatia, Suessula, Acerrae, Atella). Other Campanian cities (Suessa, Teanum, Nola, Nuceria, Neapolis, Cumae) pursued independent policies. After 474 B.C. Etruscan power in Campania declined and *c.* 440 Sabelli (q.v.) seized Capua, indefensible owing to its position in the open plain, and oscanized it (Diod. 12. 31). Henceforth the Campani of Capua are frequently mentioned. Threatened by fresh Sabellian invaders *c.* 343, they sought Roman protection but immediately proved treacherous. Accordingly Rome confiscated the Falernus Ager, gave Roman citizenship to the *equites Campani* and *civitas sine suffragio* (see MUNICIPIUM) to the other Campani (Livy 7. 29–8. 14). Capua, however, retained its Oscan language and magistrates (*meddices*), the latter with somewhat curtailed powers after 318 when *praefecti Capuam Cumas* were appointed (Mommsen, *Röm. Staatsr.* ii³. 608). After 312 the Via Appia linked Capua still more closely to Rome. In the Samnite Wars Capua behaved equivocally and witnessed much fighting (Diod. 19. 76; Livy 9. 25); it continued, however, to prosper, becoming indeed proverbial for its luxuriousness and pride (Ath. 12. 36). By 218 it rivalled Carthage and Rome (Florus i. 16. 6). In 216 Capua revolted to Hannibal, but in 211 Rome recaptured and severely punished it, executing its prominent citizens, depriving the remainder of political rights, and confiscating its territory, which as Roman public domain was partly used for colonies (194) but mostly rented out at a substantial profit until distributed to 20,000 colonists by Julius Caesar (59) (Livy 23. 2 f.; 26. 14 f.; Cic. *Leg. Agr.* 1. 7; Vell. Pat. 2. 44). Capua itself remained a populous town, but without municipal privileges until after 90 B.C. (Cic. *Sest.* 10). It suffered in the wars of the late Republic but under the Empire was a prosperous *colonia*, Augustus particularly favouring

it (Dio Cass. 49. 14). It had declined somewhat, but was still a considerable city when Vandals sacked it (456). Saracens finally destroyed Capua (840), the church of Santa Maria alone escaping to give the town its modern name (*Santa Maria di Capua Vetere*). Its refugees settled at Casilinum, the Capua of to-day. Capuan perfumes and bronzes were famous (Cic. *Sest.* 19; Pliny *HN* 34. 95). Its large amphitheatre proves its fondness for gladiatorial shows; see also SPARTACUS.

J. Heurgon, *Capoue préromaine* (1942); R. S. Conway, *Italic Dialects* i (1897), 99; A. Sambon, *Monnaies antiques de l'Italie* i (1903), 387; *Not. Scav.* 1924, 353 (for the magnificent Mithraeum); also see bibliography under CAMPANIA. E. T. S.

CAPUT, see DEMINUTIO CAPITIS.

CAPYS (1), father of Anchises (*Il.* 20. 239); (2) companion of Aeneas (*Aen.* 10. 145) and founder of Capua; (3) king of Alba Longa (Livy 1. 3. 8).

CARACALLA, see AURELIUS (2).

CARATĂCUS (the form Caractacus is found only in an inferior manuscript), son of Cunobelinus. With his brother Togodumnus he led the south-eastern Britons in the early struggles against the Roman invaders, and after the capture of Camulodunum (A.D. 43) he escaped to the tribes of the West (Silures and Ordovices), where he renewed hostilities against the governor Ostorius Scapula, by whom, however, he was defeated somewhere in the hills of the Welsh border. He fled to Cartimandua, queen of the Yorkshire Brigantes, who surrendered him to the Romans (51). Tacitus puts into his mouth a rhetorical speech delivered at Rome to Claudius, who spared his life. A Welsh genealogy of some authority (*Y Cymmrodor* ix. 151) indicates that his great-grandson took a name Scaplaut (=Scapulatus) cognate with that of his conqueror, and the name Caratacus itself reappears (e.g. *Eph. Epigr.* ix. 982).

Tacitus, *Ann.* 12. 33–7; Collingwood-Myres, *Roman Britain*, 75–96. C. E. S.

CARAUSIUS, MARCUS AURELIUS MAUS(AEUS?) (cf. Dessau, *ILS* 8928), a Menapian of mean origin who was appointed *c.* A.D. 287 to a command in the English Channel. He aroused, however, the suspicions of Maximian and fled to Britain, where he proclaimed himself Emperor. An unsuccessful attempt to suppress him led to a settlement whereby he could represent himself as a colleague of the Emperors (*c.* 290) and extend his rule over north-eastern Gaul. His remarkable realm utilized the support of Franks and possibly Picts; and he may have instituted the fortification of the Saxon shore. The Caesar Constantius, however, ejected him from Boulogne (293), and he was assassinated by his *rationalis* Allectus. His name was perpetuated by post-Roman 'tyrants' (cf. *Num. Chron.*³ vii. 191–219; *Inscr. Christ. Brit.* 136) and in medieval fable.

P. H. Webb, *Reign and Coinage of Carausius* (1907) (reproducing sources); C. Jullian, *Hist. de la Gaule* vii. 75–84; E. Stein, *Gesch. des spätrömischen Reiches* (1923), 97, 116; Collingwood-Myres, *Roman Britain*, 276–7; C. H. V. Sutherland, *Coinage in Roman Britain* (1937), 62–71. C. E. S.

CARBO (1), GAIUS PAPIRIUS (d. 119 B.C.), a strong supporter of the Agrarian Law of Tiberius Gracchus, and a *IIIvir* for its execution from 129 B.C. As tribune, in 131, he furthered democratic legislation. His desertion of C. Gracchus at the end of 122 is perhaps a symptom of Gaius' alienation of moderate opinion. It won him the consulship for 120, when he defended Opimius; but when L. Crassus accused him, in 119, he committed suicide. Perhaps the story that Carbo had assassinated Scipio Aemilianus dates from this trial. Carbo's motives are usually taken to have been purely self-seeking, but Crassus' later regret for his part in Carbo's fall is a reason for doubt. Cicero praises his oratorical powers.

J. Carcopino, *Autour des Gracques* (1928). M. H.

CARBO (2), GNAEUS PAPIRIUS (d. 82 B.C.), Marian leader, chief helper of Cinna, and chief party-leader after his death, was consul in 85, 84, and 82 B.C. Little is known of his career, apart from the war against Sulla in Italy. Carbo then led the Marians in north Italy; honours were even when he met Sulla at Clusium, and Carbo never lost a battle except when he and Norbanus failed in an attack on Metellus Pius' camp near Faventia, losing 10,000 killed besides 6,000 by desertion. Carbo fled to Africa with an army after Sulla's victory in Italy; thence he went to Sicily, where he was captured. Pompey had him executed in 82.   M. H.

CARCERES, *see* CIRCUS.

CARCINUS (1), son of Xenotimus of Thoricus, a tragic poet mercilessly ridiculed, with his sons, by Aristophanes (*Pax* 781 ff., *Vesp.* 1497 ff.) and other comic poets. He is probably identical with the general mentioned by Thucydides (2. 23).

CARCINUS (2), son of Xenocles(1) and grandson of Carcinus (1), a tragic poet who is said to have written 160 plays (Suidas, s.v.) and won 11 victories (*IG*² ii. 2325, according to a probable restoration) in the fourth century. He passed much time at the court of the younger Dionysius of Syracuse (Diod. Sic. 5.5.1). He is referred to by Aristotle, *Poet.* 16 (the recognition scene in the *Thyestes*) and 17 (a mistake in theatrical management in the *Amphiaraus*), *Eth. Nic.* 7. 8 (the endurance of Cercyon in the *Alope*), *Rhet.* 2. 23 (an argument in the *Medea*—apparently she did not kill her children in this play) and 3. 16 (arguments of Iocasta in the *Oedipus*), and Plutarch (*De Glor. Athen.* 7) praises his *Aërope*. The phrase Καρκίνου ποιήματα is said to have been applied to obscure poems (Suidas s.v., etc.) but only on the strength of a single passage in the *Orestes*.
TGF 797–800.   A. W. P.-C.

CARCINUS (3) **OF NAUPACTUS** (? 7th–6th c. B.C.), epic poet, probable author of the *Naupactia*, a Catalogue of Famous Women. *See* EPIC CYCLE.
EGF 198–202.

CARIA, a region of south-western Asia Minor, extending northward in historical times to the river Maeander. Its interior is on the whole less rugged than that of southern Asia Minor in general, and in ancient times it was noted for its excellent figs; but it is cut off from the seaboard by coastal ranges. The Carians were probably a native people, akin to the Lydians; they dwelt in villages under cantonal dynasts. In the prehistoric age they settled in the Cyclades and perhaps also in Crete, and Greek authors attributed to them a short 'thalassocracy' in the eighth century. In historical times they often went abroad on mercenary service, but they lost their overseas possessions. Under Persian rule they constituted a separate satrapy; but they participated actively in the Ionian Revolt, and some of their communities joined the Delian League (till *c.* 440 B.C.). In the fourth century the dynasts Hecatomnus (397–377) and Mausolus (q.v.; 377–351) spread Greek culture in Caria, and its urbanization progressed under Hellenistic and Roman rule. It frequently changed hands in the Hellenistic period; in 129 B.C. it became part of the Roman province of Asia.
Strabo 651–64. Bürchner, *PW*, s.vv. 'Karer', 'Karia'.   M. C.

CARINUS, MARCUS AURELIUS, elder son of Carus (q.v.), left by him as Caesar in the West, when he marched against Persia (A.D. 282). Made Augustus before his father's death, Carinus succeeded him as colleague of Numerian and crushed the rebel 'corrector Venetiae', Julianus, in battle near Verona. Early in 285 Diocletian, appointed Emperor to succeed Numerian, ended a

difficult campaign at the battle of the Margus in Moesia. Carinus, victorious in the fight, was killed by an officer whose wife he had seduced. He bears an evil name for luxury and cruelty, but some allowance must be made for the enmity of the rival faction.
CAH xii. 321 ff. Parker, *Roman World*, 219 ff.   H. M.

CARISTIA, a Roman family feast, otherwise *cara cognatio*, celebrated on 22 Feb., immediately after the *dies parentales* (Feb. 13–21); Ovid (*Fasti* 2. 617 ff.), who says it was a reunion of the surviving members of the family after the rites to the departed; Valerius Maximus (2. 1. 8), adding that no outsiders were admitted and any family quarrels were then settled. It is mentioned under the date in the calendar of Philocalus and under February in the *Menologia Rustica*.   H. J. R.

CARMEN, a term having a range of extended applications to oracular responses, prophecies, incantations, *carmina triumphalia*, *neniae*, epitaphs (*Carmina Epigraphica*, Bücheler, 1895–7), or legal formulae even in prose (Livy 1. 26. 6, 'lex horrendi carminis'). Apart from its broad meaning of 'poetry' including epic, drama, lampoon, it remains the regular Latin word for either actual song or poetry of lyric type. It is in this sense that the term is applied to Horace's *Odes* or his *Carmen Saeculare*; and it is also in this sense that it is applied to the earliest remains of Latin in ritual hymns or heroic lays. Some of these may be mentioned here.

2. The *carmen arvale* and *carmen Saliare* represent the few surviving remains of the older native Latin literature in Saturnian metre. The name 'Saturnian' testifies to their antiquity, being attributed to the metre later in order to link it up with 'the age of Saturn'. The *carmen arvale* (q.v. for linguistic aspects), discovered at Rome in the latter part of the eighteenth century, is one such relic. It is a late (early 3rd c. A.D.) copy of an ancient litany of the *fratres arvales* (q.v.), an official group of twelve men whose business it was to perform the lustral ceremonies of the spring agricultural festivals by means of dances (*tripudium*) and sacrifices (*suovetaurilia*) and prayer. The actual inscription which we possess is an invocation to the Lares and to Mars, who seems to appear here as a god of vegetation. The brotherhood survived certainly till A.D. 240, under the third Gordian, as is proved by an inscription found at Rome in 1914 (Dessau, *ILS* 9522).

3. The *carmen Saliare* (q.v. for linguistic aspects) is represented by a few fragments surviving from verses (*axamenta*) chanted by the Salian priests (who also were priests of Mars) during the March processions when the sacred shields were carried. The text (E. Diehl, *Poet. Rom. Vet.* 1) is doubtful, and in later times was hardly understood even by those who recited or recorded it, if we may judge from what Horace and Quintilian tell us.

4. We have the evidence of Cicero (*Tusc.* 4. 3; *Brut.* 75; cf. Varro ap. Non. Marcell. 76), who quotes the authority of Cato's *Origines*, that among the earlier Romans it was the custom at banquets to sing the praises of famous men to the flute. This evidence led Niebuhr in the nineteenth century to put forward the theory that there originally existed a large body of popular epic poetry in Latin, which contained accounts of the glorious deeds of old, from which these banquet songs (*carmina convivalia*) and the legendary tales recounted by Livy drew their material. This theory was warmly welcomed at the time, but, in view of material evidence and the attacks made upon it by Taine, it has now been generally abandoned. Rostagni, however (*La Letteratura di Roma*, 1939, 45 ff.), holds that the epic germs in these primitive *carmina* were not entirely destroyed by Hellenism but influenced Roman poets.

5. Of a later composition, the *carmen Nelei* (q.v.), five fragments are preserved by Festus and Charisius. This

was in iambic senarii, perhaps a tragedy or a dramatic descriptive poem. Neleus' exposure was dealt with by Sophocles in his play *Tyro*, now lost, and the *carmen Nelei* may possibly derive from it. It is mentioned by Charisius in connexion with Livius' *Odissia*, and this together with its archaic vocabulary shows it to be of a similar date. It may mark the transition to the *fabulae praetextae* introduced by Naevius.

6. In the primitive Saturnian *carmina* lay the rudimentary beginnings of Latin lyric, but much development had to take place under the influence of Greek models before the literary *carmina* of the first century B.C. could be produced (*see* LYRIC POETRY, LATIN). Pliny (*Tra.* 96. 7) uses *carmen* in the traditional meaning of 'hymn' when he reports that the Christians 'carmen Christo quasi deo dicere secum inuicem'. A. L. P.

CARMEN ARVALE (*see* CARMEN, para. 2). The Arval ritual-hymn would be invaluable if we possessed a correct copy. Unfortunately what we have (text: E. Diehl, *Altlateinische Inschriften*, 118) is most corrupt and its interpretation therefore doubtful. *Lases* equals *Lares*, *enos* may be *nos*, and *Marmar*, *Marmor* may be reduplicated forms of *Mars*. If *semunis*, *advocapit* represent *sēmōnes*, *advocabit* then they show dialectal changes, the former $\delta > \bar{u}$, the latter (Faliscan?) $b > p$. It was already obscure before the time of Aelius Stilo (see Schanz-Hosius i, p. 18). E. Norden, *Aus altrömischen Priesterbüchern* (1939), thinks the hymn not a pure relic of Italian ritual but influenced by Greek. P. S. N.

CARMEN DE FIGURIS, anonymous Latin poem (*c.* A.D. 400), describing figures of speech in 186 hexameters. Three lines are devoted to each figure, explaining its name and giving one or two examples. Material largely taken from Rutilius (q.v. 2) Lupus. Prosody late, aphaeresis of final *s*, and ancient forms (*indupetravi*, *prosiet*) imitating pre-classical poetry. *See* DIDACTIC POETRY, LATIN.

Baehr. *PLM* iii. 272. O. S.

CARMEN DE PONDERIBUS ET MENSURIS, a Latin didactic piece of 208 hexameters, fourth to fifth century A.D., at one time erroneously ascribed to Priscian, but of uncertain authorship (see Teuffel or Schanz). It deals with weights and measures (giving Greek and Latin names), with the specific weight of different liquids, and with a test for an alloy of silver and gold. *See* DIDACTIC POETRY, LATIN.

Baehr. *PLM* v. J. W. D.

CARMEN NELEI. Of this dim work five fragments (19 words) survive, embedded in Charisius and Festus. Charisius ranks it for age with the *Odissia* of Livius. The metre and content of three fragments suggest, if anything, a drama.

Baehr. *FPR. See also* CARMEN.

CARMEN SALIARE. The fragments of the ritual-hymn of the Saliar priests (text: E. Diehl, *Poet. Rom. Vet.* 1) have come down in far too corrupt a state to allow us certainty of interpretation. It was already unintelligible in Republican times to the priests themselves. Interesting are the syncopated form *cante* (= *canite*), the termination of *tremonti* (cf. Dor. φέροντι), the diphthong, and -*s*- of *Leucesie* (= *Lucerie* 'god of light'), and the archaic superlative *dextumum*. The rest is quite uncertain and obscure.

Schanz-Hosius, i. 18. P. S. N.

CARMENTIS or **CARMENTA** (the latter form is found in Greek authors and very rarely in Latin, as Hyg. *Fab.* 277. 2), mythologically a prophetess, mother of Evander; she (Hyg. ibid.; Isid. *Etym.* 1. 4. 1 and 5. 39. 11) or more commonly he (as Tac. *Ann.* 11. 14. 4) taught the Aborigines to write. As she is also called a nymph

(as *Aen.* 8. 336), she may have been a water-goddess; certainly she was a goddess of birth, worshipped by matrons (Plut. *Rom.* 21, *Quaest. Rom.* 56). Hence there are sometimes two Carmentes, Prorsa and Postverta (Varro ap. Gell. 16. 16. 4); her, or their, relation to the triad Parca Nona Decima, or Nona Decuma Morta (ibid. 3. 16. 11) is obscure, as is also the question whether Carmentis or the Carmentes are the older.

See Wissowa, *RK* 220. H. J. R.

CARMINA MARCIANA, *see* MARCIUS (1, *vates*).

CARMINA TRIUMPHALIA, songs sung, in accordance with ancient custom, by soldiers at a *triumphus* (q.v.), either in praise of their victorious general or in a satiric ribaldry supposed to avert the evil eye from him.

Cf. Livy, 3. 29; 4. 53; 5. 49; 45. 38; Suet. *ul.* 49; 51; 80; Plin. *HN* 19. 144; Baehr. *FPR*, 330 f. J. W. D.

CARNEA (Κάρνεια), a Doric festival, whose frequent occurrence is proved by the name of the month Karneios (Aug./Sept.) which is common to most Doric calendars; this month was considered to be holy. Details are known from Sparta. A meal took place in bowers like tents in a military fashion and there was a race of youths called σταφυλοδρόμοι. A youth put *taeniae* on his head and ran away; if he was overtaken by the others, it was a good omen, if not, a bad one. The festival belonged to Apollo, but he has certainly ousted an old god Karnos or Karneios. The fact that κάρνος signifies 'ram' has given rise to various hypotheses; the interpretation of the festival is uncertain.

S. Wide, *Lakonische Kulte* (1893), 74 ff.; M. P. Nilsson, *Griech. Feste*, 118 ff.; *Gesch. d. griech. Rel.* i. 501 f. M. P. N.

CARNEADES (214/213–129/128 B.C. (Apollod. ap. Diog. Laert. 4. 65, etc.)), of Cyrene, son of Epicomus (Diog. Laert. 4. 62, etc.), founder of the so-called Third or New Academy (Sext. Emp. *Pyr.* 1. 220, etc.). He became president of the Academy after his teacher Hegesinus. Together with the Stoic Diogenes of Babylon and the Peripatetic Critolaus he was a member of the famous Athenian delegation of philosophers sent to Rome in 156–155. The lectures he delivered there became famous because of their dialectical and rhetorical power as well as their moral independence (Plut. *Cat. Mai.* 22; Cic. *Luc.* 137; Gell. 6. 14. 8, etc.). The school flourished under his presidency (Cic. *Luc.* 16; *De Or.* 1. 45; *Acad. Index Herc.* col. 23 f.; D.L. 4. 63), which he resigned in 137–136. His younger namesake C. succeeded him (Apollod. fr. 98 Jacoby; *Acad. Index* col. 29. 38; 30. 1; 24; 28). Shortly before his death he went blind (D.L. 4. 66). He was worshipped by his school (Suid. s.v.) and won great fame in Greece and Rome. He left no writings (Cic. *Luc.* 98; D.L. 4. 65).

2. Carneades gave a new systematic form to the criticism of dogmatic philosophies, and religious and moral opinions. His polemic against theological views, especially those of the Stoa, against their anthropocentric theory of providence against any sort of fatalism, and against divination, penetrated deeply into the mind of the later Greco-Roman world. The subject of his lectures in Rome was a *disputatio in utramque partem*, after the Academic manner, on the problem of justice. Cicero used them for the third book of the *De Re Publica*; so it is possible in this case to learn from a wider context the power and independence of his reasoning.

3. In a discussion of all aims of human endeavour, the later so-called *Carneadea divisio* (Cic. *Fin.* 5. 16 f.), he disputed the pros and cons of each. Such a discussion, which brought all philosophies down to the same argumentative level, is an important preparation for the forthcoming eclecticism.

4. There was a positive side to C.'s scepticism, his

theory of probability. Like Arcesilaus he denied all possibility of knowledge, and applied this especially to the Stoic criterion (Sext. Emp. *Math.* 7. 159–65). As in the case of his predecessor, this argument leads to the withholding of judgement (ἐποχή: Cic. *Luc.* 108; *Nat. D.* 1. 11; etc.). Nevertheless he admitted different stages of clearness in human perception. A perception which carries conviction C. called 'convincing or probable presentation' (πιθανὴ φαντασία; Sext. *Math.* 7. 184 f.).

5. Carneades might well be called the greatest systematic figure in ancient scepticism. He developed and systematized its polemic side, and by his theory of probability he devised a new philosophical method.

H. von Arnim in *PW* x. 1964, s.v. 'Karneades'; see also the bibliography under SCEPTICS. K. O. B.

CARNEISCUS, Epicurean of the third or second century B.C., author of Φιλίστας, a discussion of friendship in which Praxiphanes (q.v.) was criticized.

Ed. W. Crönert, *Kolotes u. Menedemos* 60 (1906). *PW* x. 1993.

CARNUNTUM, on the Danube between Petronell and Deutsch-Altenburg, was the most important Roman fortress on the Danube frontier. Near the ancient Celtic settlement an earth camp for one legion was erected, probably under Augustus; this was converted into a stone fortress in A.D. 73. First belonging to Noricum, Carnuntum was added to Pannonia, probably in A.D. 16 or later when legio XV Apollinaris was transferred there. This legion remained at Carnuntum (except A.D. 62–71) till it was relieved by legio XIV Gemina (114 or earlier). The civil town became a *municipium* (q.v.) under Hadrian, and a *colonia* (q.v.) (*Septimia*) under Septimius Severus, who was proclaimed Emperor there. It was often visited by emperors: thus M. Aurelius wrote there the second book of his *Meditations*; Diocletian, Galerius, and Maximian met there in 308; Valentinian stayed at Carnuntum in 375, and ordered the camp to be reconstructed. Carnuntum was flourishing in the second century before its destruction in the Marcomannic Wars, after which it was soon rebuilt. Under Septimius Severus the civil town increased largely, but later diminished. About 400 Carnuntum was burnt down. Temples, private houses, baths, two amphitheatres, military and civil burial-places have been excavated.

Kubitschek, *PW*, s.v. 'Carnuntum'. *RLÖ* i (1900)–xviii (1937), passim. W. Kubitschek–S. Frankfurter, *Führer durch Carnuntum²* (1923). R. Noll, etc., *Carnuntum 1885–1935* (Vienna, 1935). *Berichte des Vereines Carnuntum in Wien.* F. A. W. S.

CARPENTUM, see CARRIAGES.

CARRHAE (mod. *Charran*), in north Mesopotamia, was the site of the battle (53 B.C.) which ended Crassus' invasion of Parthia. Crassus, deficient in cavalry and with unacclimatized troops, reached the Belik river below Carrhae, where Surenas was awaiting him with his 10,000 horse-archers and his camel train, reinforced by 1,000 cataphracts (mailed knights). Though outnumbered thrice over, his horse-archers poured arrows into the Roman square with impunity till dark; in the night most of the survivors, abandoning their wounded, found temporary refuge in Carrhae. After a rest, Crassus tried to escape by night; but his army, completely demoralized, broke up, and when at daybreak Surenas overtook him, the troops refused to fight. He surrendered to Surenas, who meant to send him alive to Orodes, but a scuffle started in which he perished. Of his 44,000 men, 10,000 escaped; the rest were killed or captured.

W. W. Tarn, *CAH* ix. 606 ff. W. W. T.

CARRIAGES were in common use from the beginnings of Roman history (Livy 1. 34), and a great variety of types are mentioned. Driving in the streets of Rome, and probably of other towns, was forbidden except to high officials on great occasions, but the complaints of

Seneca and Juvenal about the noise of vehicles suggests that the rule was not strictly enforced (Sen. *Ep.* 56; Juv. 3. 237). For rapid journeys the carriage most frequently used was the two-wheeled *cisium* or *essedum*, which attained considerable speeds. A form of two-wheeled carriage used at festivals was the *carpentum*, which was also used for travelling. The usual vehicle to employ on long journeys was the four-wheeled *rheda*, which held several people and baggage (Juv. 3. 10). A similar type was the *carruca*, in which it was possible to sleep. Carriages were sometimes highly ornamented and plated with silver and gold (Mart. 3. 72). The horses or mules were harnessed to a yoke, and traces were used only when several animals were required. Change of horses was provided at the *mansiones* on the great roads, and thus Caesar was enabled to travel 100 miles a day (Suet. *Iul.* 57).

W. A. Becker, *Gallus* (Engl. Transl. 1898), 345 ff. G. H. S.

CARRUCA, see CARRIAGES.

CARTHAGE (*Kart-Hadasht*; Καρχηδών; *Carthago*). The traditional foundation of the great Tyrian colony at Carthage in north Africa about 814 B.C. has been immortalized by Virgil in his story of Queen Dido. But the vigorous Phoenician seamen, who founded 'the New City', do not appear to have instituted monarchy; it was under aristocratic rule that they soon outstripped Utica, Hadrumetum, and other older foundations. Carthage's situation opposite the western end of Sicily presented an opportunity of dominating the shores of the western Mediterranean, while the Bagradas valley supplied food in abundance. Her nobles seemed to have kept their blood pure; but the lower class intermarried with the native Berbers or Libyans, and this mixed Libyphoenician stock built up the wealth of Carthage as seamen and farmers.

2. That Carthage took the lead among the colonies, factories, and trading-stations along the African coast, after Tyre had been weakened by Assyria, was largely due to her oligarchical constitution. This made for stability and roused the admiration of Aristotle (*Pol.* 2. 8). Her chief magistrates were two shophets (Lat. *suffetes*), who were elected annually; they worked with the Council of Three Hundred and the Popular Assembly. But these two bodies gradually lost power to the Court of the Hundred and Four Judges and the Boards of Five. Only rarely could the Assembly assert its power against the nobles, as when Hannibal used it after Zama to attack the venality and corruption of the mercantile oligarchy. Warned by the attempt of Malchus and the fears inspired by Mago's family in the sixth century, the ruling class used the Court and the Boards successfully to guard against an ambitious shophet using the army to make himself dictator.

3. There was a party which favoured the acquisition of a land empire; Carthage occupied some territory in the Bagradas valley, and taught the Berbers agriculture in such places as Thugga (q.v.) and civic government by shophets. This expansion was made possible by a mercenary army, officered by Carthaginians. But the predominant party looked to the sea. Eastward Greek encroachments were checked at the Syrtes (q.v.), and the grudging allegiance of Leptis and Oea (qq.v.) was secured. The Phoenician colonies, which stretched westward to Tingi (q.v.) and Lixus (modern *Larache*), acknowledged Carthaginian leadership, though Utica remained aloof. From these ports Carthage drew a revenue which made her the richest city in the western Mediterranean by the third century B.C.

4. The northern shore of the Mediterranean and the great islands presented a different problem. From *c.* 600 B.C. it was clear that rival claims to control them must lead to war between Etruscans, Carthaginians, and

Greeks. The westward thrust of Phocaea and Massilia was crushed off Alalia in Corsica by the Etruscan and Carthaginian fleets (c. 535). The latter gradually established its influence in Corsica and Sardinia, as Etruscan power weakened, and revived the Tyrian hold on Gades, Malaca, and other parts of southern Spain. Earlier Malchus had won successes in Sicily, and the western end of the island was held for Carthage by Panormus, Lilybaeum, and Drepanum.

5. For three centuries Carthaginians and Greeks fought intermittently for Sicilian territory and the allegiance of Sicans, Sicels, and Elymians. In 480 B.C. a great Carthaginian army under the shophet Hamilcar was defeated at Himera by the tyrants Gelon and Theron. His grandson, Hannibal, avenged him by destroying Himera (409); but the ensuing wars with Dionysius of Syracuse ended with Carthaginian power confined to the west of the island. Agathocles carried the war into Africa, but was defeated near Tunis (307).

6. With Rome Carthage had concluded treaties in 508 and 348, in which she guarded jealously her monopoly of maritime trade, while abstaining from any interference in Italy. When Pyrrhus attacked (280), her fleet helped Rome to victory. But sixteen years later Sicilian politics brought the two Powers into conflict and precipitated the Punic Wars (q.v.), which ended with the destruction of the city (146).

7. Rome decreed that neither house nor crop should rise again. But Carthaginian blood survived. The grim pantheon, which had nerved the Phoenician warriors in battle and siege, still persisted, and Africa continued to worship Baal-Hammon, Taanit-pene-Baal, Eshmoun, and Melkart. Proof of the practice of human sacrifice is found in the bones dug up on Djebel Bou Kornein and Tiberius' decree of repression. Urban life and the rule of shophets continued in many Berber towns. Mercantile and maritime ability went on, though there were no more great long-distance voyages, such as that of Hanno in 550. Carthage never developed an art of her own, and was content to copy Greece and Egypt. She manufactured and exported carpets, rugs, purple dyes, jewellery, pottery, lamps, tapestry, timber, and hides. Her great carrying trade passed to Italians and Greeks. Her agricultural skill, which had made excellent use of the richly phosphated Tunisian plain, profited her Roman conquerors and her Berber subjects; Mago's thirty-two books on scientific farming were translated into Latin.

8. The site of Carthage was too attractive to remain unoccupied for long. The attempt of C. Gracchus (q.v.) to establish the colony of Junonia on the suburban land failed, but the city site was colonized by Caesar and Augustus. It received colonial rank (see COLONIZATION, ROMAN) and became the capital of proconsular Africa. Great buildings rose on Byrsa Hill, and by the second century A.D. Carthage had become one of the most flourishing cities of the Empire. A few urban troops and a cohort of the Third Augustan legion sufficed to keep order. But through his control of the African corn-trade, the proconsul was a potential danger to the emperor, as was shown by the rebellions of Clodius (q.v.) Macer and the Gordians (q.v.).

9. Carthage became an outstanding educational centre, especially famous for orators and lawyers. In the third century the genius of Tertullian and the devotion of Cyprian made her a focus of Christianity. Her bishop held himself the equal of the bishop of Rome, and she played a great part in establishing western Christianity on lines very different from the speculations of the Greek churches. As a great Catholic stronghold, she fought against the Donatist heresy. When the Vandals (q.v.) overran Africa, she became the capital of Gaiseric and his successors. After Belisarius' victory Catholicism was restored on stricter lines. Carthage remained loyal to

the East Roman Empire and beat off the earlier Moslem invasions, until captured in 697.

Carthaginian inscriptions in CISem. i (1881); L. Müller, Numismatique de l'Afrique ancienne (1860–74); S. Gsell, Histoire ancienne de l'Afrique du Nord (1914–28); G. De Sanctis, Stor. Rom. iii (1) (1916); O. Meltzer, Geschichte der Karthager, i–ii (1879–96), iii (by U. Kahrstedt, 1913); V. Ehrenberg, Karthago (1927); M. P. Charlesworth, CAH viii. 484 ff.   W. N. W.

CARTHAGE (Topography). Carthage was situated on part of a peninsula projecting seawards within the Gulf of Tunis. Topographical details are extremely controversial and the remains of Punic Carthage small. The earliest settlement (probably c. 800 B.C.; there is no archaeological evidence to support the late tradition cf a prior settlement in the 13th c.) perhaps lay near the coast east of the Byrsa Hill, to which it gradually spread (this view is supported by recent excavation—Comptes Rendus 1939, 294 ff.). Despite some modern doubts, the traditional identification of the Punic citadel (the Byrsa) with the Hill of St. Louis, and of the ancient harbours with the Salammbo lagoons, may be retained. The Byrsa walls, which probably measured 1,060 metres in length (Revue Africaine 1934, 336), were destroyed in 146 B.C. and refortified by Theodosius II (A.D. 424) and Belisarius (553). If the walls of Punic Carthage were twenty-one miles in circumference (Livy, Epit. 51), a large part of the area must have been sparsely populated. The main harbour (Cothon) was artificial; it comprised an inner circular naval port and an outer rectangular commercial basin. Many cemeteries have been found, the earliest burials being seventh century B.C. There are traces of Roman colonial delimitation of the land: plots of 125 acres for Junonia, of 1¼ acres for the settlement of Caesar and Augustus (C. Saumagne, Journ. d. Savants 1931, 56). Remains of cisterns, an aqueduct, amphitheatre, theatre, houses, and the proconsular palace survive from Roman Carthage. See especially Appian, Pun. 8. 95 ff., Strabo 17. 3. 4, Orosius 4. 22.

Besides the articles named above, see R. Oehler, PW, s.v. 'Karthago'; H. P. Hurd, The Topography of Punic Carthage (U.S.A. 1934); D. B. Harden, Greece and Rome ix. 1; P. Gauckler, Nécropoles puniques de Carthage (2 vols. 1915); R. Cagnat, Carthage, Timgad, Tebessa (1912); A. Audollent, Carthage romaine (1901). Cf. S. Gsell, Rev. Historique 1927, 225; L. Carton, Pour visiter Carthage (1924).   H. H. S.

CARTHAGO NOVA, a town in Hispania Citerior, to-day Cartagena. It lay on a peninsula within one of the best harbours of the Mediterranean. Originally named Mastia, it was refounded as New Carthage by Hasdrubal in 228 B.C. as a base for the Carthaginian conquest of Spain. It was captured by Scipio Africanus in 209, visited by Polybius in 133 (described in 10. 10), and made a colony (Col. Iulia Victrix N.C.) by Julius Caesar or more probably by Octavian after a prior grant of Latin rights by Julius (cf. M. Grant, From Imperium to Auctoritas (1946), 215 ff.). During the Empire it was overshadowed by Tarraco, though remaining an important city until its destruction by the Vandals (A.D. 425). It was famous for the neighbouring silver-mines, which brought the Roman treasury a daily revenue of 25,000 drachmae, for a fish sauce called garum, for mackerel, and for esparto grass (spartum) used for ropes, baskets, and sandals.

For the topography see H. H. Scullard, Scipio Africanus (1930), Appendix I, and the literature there cited.   H. H. S.

CARUS, MARCUS AURELIUS, praetorian prefect of Probus, rebelled in Raetia in A.D. 282, and, after Probus had been murdered by his troops, announced to the Senate his accession as Emperor. Leaving Carinus as Caesar in the West, Carus marched east against Persia with his younger son and Caesar, Numerian. On the way he defeated the Quadi and Sarmatae on the Danube. Carus invaded Persia and captured Ctesiphon, but, venturing on a further advance, was 'killed by a thunderbolt'—more probably by treachery on the part of Aper, the praetorian prefect. Suspect to the Senate as a nominee of the army, Carus yet ranks as 'medius', between good and bad emperors.

CAH xii. 321 ff.; Parker, Roman World, 219.　　H. M.

CARVILIUS (1) **MAXIMUS,** Spurius, twice consul with Papirius Cursor, in 293 B.C. when he conquered the Samnites at Cominium and dedicated a statue of Jupiter Capitolinus made from their armour (Livy 10. 43; Pliny, HN 34. 43); and in 272, when he closed the series of triumphs over the Samnites (Zonar. 8. 6). His censorship (Vell. Pat. 2. 128) probably belongs to 289.　　E. T. S.

CARVILIUS (2), freedman of Spurius Carvilius Maximus, one of the consuls of 235 B.C. 'The Romans were late in beginning to teach for payment, and the first of them to open an elementary school was Spurius Carvilius' (Plut. Quaest. Rom. 59). It is unlikely that Carvilius' school was the first to be opened at Rome, where literacy is attested c. 450 B.C. (Livy 3. 44). Cicero's statement, that boys in the early Republic were required to learn the XII Tables by heart, points to the probability of schools existing before 250. Plutarch's statement simply means that Carvilius was the first to open a school for pay, earlier teachers having depended on voluntary gifts from pupils.

According to Plutarch, Carvilius was the first to differentiate between the letters C and G (Quaest. Rom. 54). Some scholars have attributed the distinction to Appius Claudius.

A. Gwynn, Roman Education (1926), 29 ff.; H. Jordan, Kritische Beiträge zur Gesch. der lateinischen Sprache, 157; L. Havet, Rev. Phil. ii. 16.　　T. J. H.

CARYATIDES, a Greek term for columns or pilasters the shafts of which were carved in the form of draped females. The most famous caryatides are those of the Athenian Erechtheum, one of which is now in the British Museum. Others have been found at Delphi. The term seems to have been sometimes used for non-columnar statues.　　H. W. R.

CASCA LONGUS, Publius Servilius. Two Servilii Cascae were conspirators against Caesar. Publius was the first to strike. Tribune of the plebs (43 B.C.), he was compelled to flee and joined Brutus. The two brothers killed themselves after Philippi (Anth. Latina, no. 457).

F. Münzer, PW ii A. 1788.　　A. M.

CASPIAN SEA (also called 'Hyrcanian' from its SE. coast). This large and brackish inland water was correctly described by Herodotus as a lake. In spite of partial exploration by Greeks, all subsequent writers thought that the Oxus and Iaxartes flowed into it; many believed that it was joined to the Black Sea (by the river Phasis), or to the Sea of Azov; and the prevalent view was that a channel linked it with a not far distant Northern Ocean. The first of these opinions may have had apparent support from the remains of a prehistoric channel between the Caspian and the Aral Sea, and the last may have been prompted by a vague knowledge of the Volga. About 285 B.C. Patrocles (q.v.) sailed up both sides, but failing to reach the north end, gave currency to the belief that one could sail from the Caspian to India by the Northern Ocean. Renewed exploration after the reign of Tiberius led to the rediscovery of the Volga ('Rha' in Ptolemy), and Ptolemy restated the truth that the Caspian is a lake, though he got its shape wrong.

Cary-Warmington, Explorers, 136 ff.; A. Herrmann, PW, s.v. 'Kaspisches Meer'.　　E. H. W.

CASSANDER (c. 358-297 B.C.), son of Antipater (q.v.), joined Alexander in Asia (324). They seem to have disliked one another intensely, but the tradition which makes him Alexander's murderer is false. When the Empire began to split up, Cassander drove the regent Polyperchon from Macedonia and most of Greece (319-316); henceforth his aim was to keep what he held, which involved resisting the efforts of Antigonus to reunite the Empire under himself. These efforts he finally joined in defeating (with Ptolemy, Lysimachus, and Seleucus) by the decisive victory of Ipsus (301). His last four years were devoted mainly to consolidating his position at home.

Ruthlessly efficient though he was in politics, Cassander was no barbarian. He founded two great cities, Cassandreia and Thessalonica (Salonika), and he rebuilt Thebes. As befitted the slayer of Alexander's mother, son, and widow, he had friends among the Peripatetics, the literary group which did most to create a tradition hostile to Alexander.

Diodorus, bks. 18-20; W. W. Tarn, CAH vi, ch. 15, and vii, 75 ff.　　G. T. G.

CASSANDRA or **ALEXANDRA,** in mythology, daughter of Priam (q.v.). In Homer, nothing is said of her being a prophetess; she is mentioned (Il. 13. 365) as being the most beautiful of Priam's daughters, and (in 24. 699 ff.) she is the first to see the body of Hector being brought home. Nor is it clear that post-Homeric epic enlarged on the Homeric picture; its principal new episode, assuming that Homer did not already know of it, is her mishandling by Aias (q.v. 2) the Locrian. How old the tradition of her prophetic gifts is we do not know, but in surviving literature it appears first in Pindar, Pyth. 11. 33 (474 or 454 B.C.; if the latter, then later than Aeschylus, Agamemnon, with which it has points of contact; perhaps both draw on the Oresteia of Stesichorus). In Agam. 1203 ff., Apollo has given her the power of prophecy, to win her love; as she cheats him, he turns the blessing into a curse by causing her always to be disbelieved. Later authors follow this form of the story, which indeed Aeschylus seems to imply was already well known when he wrote. There is, however, another (schol. Il. 7. 44 and Eustathius p. 663, 40) which says that she and Helenus, when children, had their ears licked by serpents while asleep and so got their prophetic gift. She commonly appears, in Tragedy and elsewhere, as foretelling vainly the evil results of successive events, such as the birth of Paris, and finally warning the Trojans against the Wooden Horse (as Verg. Aen. 2. 246). On the basis of this, Lycophron (Alexandra) takes occasion to put into her mouth a forecast of mythological and historical adventures of both Trojans and Greeks from the war to his own day. For her story see AGAMEMNON, AIAS (2). For her cult, or that of a goddess confounded with her, see Farnell, Hero-Cults, 329 ff. H. J. R.

CASSIANI, see SABINUS (2).

CASSIODORUS (Flavius Magnus Aurelius Cass. Senator, c. A.D. 487-583), scion of a distinguished Bruttian family, was, except for Boethius, the most important writer of the sixth century A.D. After serving in public capacities (consul, magister officiorum, praetorian prefect) for forty years, he retired (c. 550) to the monastery of Vivarium, which he founded in Bruttium, and there devoted himself to collecting a library and writing theological and encyclopaedic works. During his official career he published: Orationes (fragments ed. by L. Traube in Mommsen's ed. of Variae, 465-84); Chronica, a universal history from Adam to A.D. 519 (ed. Mommsen, MGH, auct. ant. xi. 120-61); Historia Gothica in twelve books (known only from extracts made by Iordanes); and Variae, a collection in twelve books of correspondence and official documents for which he had been responsible (ed. Mommsen, MGH, auct. ant. xii. 10-385). After his retirement he published: Institutiones divinarum et saecularium litterarum (see ENCYCLOPAEDIC LEARNING), of which the second part, preserved in longer and shorter versions, was widely used in the Middle Ages (ed. R. A. B. Mynors, 1937); *De Orthographia* (ed. Keil, *Gramm. Lat.* vii. 143–210), and various biblical commentaries (in Migne *PL*, vols. lxviii (under name 'Primasius') to lxx). He also edited a translation made by his friends from Josephus; and to a certain Epiphanius he entrusted the compilation of a *Historia ecclesiastica tripartita* (in Migne, *PL*, vol. lxix). His importance lies not only in his writings but also in the example he gave to the monks of his own and other foundations not to neglect the literature and learning of pagan Rome.

Teuffel, § 483; Schanz–Hosius, § 1044; M. Manitius, *Geschichte der lat. Lit. des Mittelalters* i (1911), 36–52.　　　　J. F. M.

CASSIOPEIA (Cassiepeia or Cassiope), *see* ANDROMEDA.

CASSITERIDES ('Tin Islands'), a name applied
generically to all the north Atlantic tin lands, but especially to Cornwall and the Scillies (which may have served as depots for Cornish tin). They were probably first discovered by Phoenicians or Carthaginians from Gades; the latter eventually established an open-sea route from north-west Spain. A Greek named Midacritus (*c.* 600 B.C.?) is recorded to have imported tin from Cassiteris island (Plin. *HN* 7. 197), but it is doubtful whether he actually reached the Cassiterides. The Carthaginians kept their tin-routes secret, hence Herodotus (3. 115) doubted the existence of the Cassiterides. Pytheas (q.v.) visited the miners of Belerium (*Land's End*) and their tin depot at Ictis (q.v., *St. Michael's Mt.*); but it was left to a Roman, P. Crassus (probably a governor in Spain *c.* 95 B.C.), to make the tin-routes generally known. Strabo, who enumerates ten Cassiterides (the Scillies group contains 30 islands), describes the Cornish tin and lead mines and the black cloaks and long tunics of the natives. The importance of the Cornish mines declined in the first century A.D., after the discovery of tin deposits in Spain. *See also* TIN.

Strabo 3. 175–6; T. R. Holmes, *Ancient Britain* (1907), 483 ff.; F. J. Haverfield, *PW*, s.v. 'Kassiterides'.　　　　E. H. W.

CASSIUS (1) VECELLINUS, SPURIUS, consul in 493
B.C., yet bearing a plebeian name, mediated the treaty made then between Rome and the Latins. This established peace throughout Latium, providing for mutual military assistance on equal terms, and held good till *c.* 380. Dubious legends attached to the name of Spurius need cast no doubt upon the treaty. Its effect is discernible beneath the surface of Livy's narrative, which tends, through pride, to obscure the fact that Rome was only an equal partner.

For bibliography, *see under* LATINI. A. N. Sherwin-White, *The Roman Citizenship* (1939), 20 ff.　　　　A. N. S.-W.

CASSIUS (2) HEMINA, LUCIUS, the first Latin
annalist, treated Roman history from early Italian times (bk. 1) and the founding of Rome (bk. 2) to the Second Punic War (bk. 4), writing before the Third Punic War (cf. the title *Bellum Punicum posterior* of bk. 4); but fr. 39 (146 B.C.) indicates an extension. His interest in Italian origins, in etymological, religious, and social antiquities, and in synchronism (fr. 8), reflects the influence, especially, of Cato's *Origines*.

H. Peter, *HRRel.* i² (1914), pp. clxv and 98. T. Frank, *Life and Literature in the Roman Republic* (1930), 172.　　　　A. H. McD.

CASSIUS (3) DIONYSIUS of Utica, wrote (1) (88
B.C.) a Greek translation (with additions) of the work of the Carthaginian Mago on agriculture, which became the standard work on the subject, used by all its successors in antiquity; (2) Ῥιζοτομικά, a compilation much used by Pliny the Elder.

PW iii. 1722.　　　　W. D. R.

CASSIUS (4) LONGINUS, GAIUS, consul 73 B.C.
with M. Terentius Varro Lucullus, brought forward the *Lex Terentia Cassia*, which distributed five *modii* of corn a month to a limited number of recipients (40,000 people?) in Rome, not necessarily gratis. He was defeated by Spartacus near Mutina in 72. He testified against Verres (70), and supported the Manilian law (66, *see* MANILIUS 2).

F. Münzer, *PW* iii. 1727. For the *lex*: M. Rostovtzeff, *PW* vii. 174.　　　　A. M.

CASSIUS (5) LONGINUS, QUINTUS, was Pompey's
rapacious quaestor in Spain in 54 B.C. In 49, as one of the two tribunes who supported Caesar, he fled to his camp and later summoned the Senate. Sent to Spain, he was surprised by a rebellion of provincials and soldiers, while preparing an expedition against Juba (48). With the help of Bogud he resisted, but left his province on the arrival of his successor, and perished by shipwreck.

F. Münzer, *PW* iii. 1740.　　　　A. M.

CASSIUS (6) LONGINUS, GAIUS, the tyrannicide,
was quaestor to Crassus in 53 B.C., rallied the defeated army after Carrhae, and won a military reputation by his defence of Syria against Parthian attacks. He was tribune in 49. In the Civil War he commanded a Pompeian fleet, but was pardoned by Caesar after Pharsalus and may have taken part in the campaign against Pharnaces. *Praetor peregrinus* in 44, he played a leading part in the conspiracy against Caesar. Prevented by popular hostility from discharging his duties in Rome, he was given a corn commissionership, but left Italy in August (probably) for Syria, where Staius Murcus and Marcius Crispus put their armies at his disposal. The rebel Caecilius Bassus followed suit, a force on its way from Egypt to Dolabella was intercepted, and Dolabella's army captured in Laodicea (probably July 43). The Senate had given Brutus and Cassius supreme authority in the eastern provinces after Mutina, but after Octavian's *coup d'état* they were outlawed. In 42, having subdued the Rhodians, who refused their support, Cassius crossed with Brutus to Thrace and encountered Antony and Octavian at Philippi. In the first battle his camp was captured, and probably under the impression that the battle was entirely lost he committed suicide.

More keen-sighted and practical than Brutus, Cassius seems nevertheless to have been less respected and less influential. He was a man of violent temper and sarcastic tongue, a strict disciplinarian, and ruthless in his exactions. The charge of covetousness may have been well founded; but there is no convincing evidence that he was influenced by petty motives in the conspiracy against Caesar. Cassius married Junia Tertia (Tertulla), sister of Brutus.

Cicero, *Letters* and *Philippics*; Caesar, *BCiv.* 3. 5 and 101; Velleius, bk. 2; Josephus, *AJ*, bk. 14; Plutarch, *Crassus*, *Caesar*, and *Brutus*; Appian, *BCiv.* bks. 2–4; Dio Cassius bks. 40–7. Modern literature: Tyrrell and Purser, *Correspondence of Cicero*, vi², pp. cii–cviii; Drumann–Groebe, *Gesch. Roms.* ii.　　　　G. W. R.

CASSIUS (7) LONGINUS, GAIUS, a prominent
Roman jurist, *cos. suff.* A.D. 30, proconsul of Asia 40–1, *legatus* of Syria 45–9. Exiled by Nero in 65 to Sardinia, he was recalled by Vespasian and died soon after. His principal work was the *Libri iuris civilis*, known through a revised edition of Javolenus and citations in later jurists' works. Cassius was a disciple of Sabinus and enjoyed high authority as a teacher and respondent, so that after the death of Sabinus he became the leader of the Sabinian school; hence its name *schola Cassiana* (*Cassiani*). *See* SABINUS (2).　　　　A. B.

CASSIUS LONGINUS, *see also* LONGINUS.

CASSIUS (8) **PARMENSIS** (i.e. of Parma) was, like Cassius (6) Longinus, among Caesar's murderers. Horace (*Epist.* 1. 4. 3) thinks of Albius (Tibullus) as writing poetry to surpass that of this Cassius (confused by the scholiasts with an inferior poet Cassius Etruscus, Hor. *Sat.* 1. 10. 61). J. W. D.

CASSIUS (9) **SEVERUS**, Augustan orator whose speeches were brilliant but bitter (Sen. *Controv.* 3 *praef.*; Quint. *Inst.* 10. 1. 116; 12. 10. 11; Tac. *Dial.* 19 and 26). Like T. Labienus (q.v.), he had his works publicly burned (Tac. *Ann.* 1. 72; 4. 21; Suet. *Calig.* 16). He died in the 25th year of his exile about A.D. 34 (Euseb. *Chron.*) J. W. D.

CASSIUS (10) **CHAEREA**, a centurion in Lower Germany in A.D. 14. In 41, as a tribune in the Praetorian Guard, he was mocked by Gaius for his supposed effeminacy. He played a leading part in the latter's murder (41). On Claudius' accession he was executed. J. P. B.

CASSIUS (11), a Roman physician of the time of Augustus and Tiberius (31 B.C.–A.D. 37). His specific for the relief of colic was famous in antiquity. *PW* iii. 1678.

CASSIUS (12), Ἰατροσοφιστής, the author of Ἰατρικαὶ ἀπορίαι καὶ προβλήματα φυσικά, not earlier than the 3rd century A.D. The author must have been a rather eclectic member of the pneumatic school of medicine.
Ed. J. L. Ideler, *Physici et Medici Graeci Minores* (1841) i. 144. *PW* iii. 1679. W. D. R.

CASSIUS DIO, see DIO CASSIUS.

CASSIUS, see also AVIDIUS (2).

CASSIVELLAUNUS, king presumably of the Catuvellauni (Herts.), appointed supreme commander of the south-eastern Britons on the occasion of Caesar's second invasion (54 B.C.). After an initial defeat in Kent, he endeavoured to avoid battle and hamper his enemies' foragers—strategy which much embarrassed Caesar, who was able, however, to capture his capital (probably Wheathampstead, cf. R. E. M. Wheeler, *Verulamium*, 20). A peace was arranged through Caesar's agent Commius, by which Cassivellaunus agreed to pay a tribute and allow the independence of the Trinovantes (Essex). His coinage is believed to be represented by the uninscribed 'Whaddon Chase' type (Brooke, *Antiquity* vii. 278).
Caesar, *BGall.* 5. 11. 8; 18–22. Collingwood–Myres, *Roman Britain*, 46–51. C. E. S.

CASTOR AND POLLUX. The cult of the Dioscuri (q.v.) was introduced into Rome at an early date, traditionally (Livy 2. 20. 12; 42. 5) in 484 B.C., in consequence of a vow made by A. Postumius at the battle of Lake Regillus. In this connexion the famous legend (of Greek origin) arose, that they actually took part in the battle and brought word of it to Rome (Dion. Hal. *Ant. Rom.* 6. 13. 1–2). Their temple was in the Forum (cf. Platner-Ashby, 102), and was commonly called *aedes Castoris*, the two brothers being not infrequently referred to as *Castores*. Several indications point to the introduction of the cult from Tusculum (Wissowa, op. cit. infra, 269 f.); there is no evidence that it was under the control of the *quindecimviri* (q.v.), like normal Greek or other foreign worships. The most outstanding feature of the ritual was the close connexion of the brethren with the *equites*, whose ceremonial parade (*transvectio equitum*) took place on 15 July, the traditional date of the battle (Dion. Hal., ibid. 4). For the age of this, see S. Weinstock in *SMSR* xii (1937), pp. 10 ff. A controversial point is the connexion of the Castores with Juturna, whose *lacus* in the Forum is near their temple. F. Altheim, 'Griechische Götter im alten Rom' (*RGVV*

xxii, 1 (1930), pp. 4 ff.), argues that her name has an Etruscan suffix (θur), means 'daughter of Jupiter' or the like, and indicates close association between her and them. This is controverted by several scholars, who would hold the nearness of the places of worship to be merely fortuitous.
G. Wissowa, *RK* 268–71 for convenient assemblage of references. H. J. R.

CASTOR OF RHODES, rhetorician, possibly to be identified with the son-in-law of Deiotarus, the Galatian Tetrarch, published Χρονικά, synchronistic tables of Oriental, Greek, and Roman history, from the Assyrian Belus and Ninus and the Sicyonian Aegialeus to Pompey (61–60 B.C.), adding the mythical period of Greek kings to the tables of Eratosthenes and Apollodorus; the work was used by Varro, Julius Africanus, and Eusebius.
FGrH ii B, 1130; BD, 814. A. H. McD.

CASTULO, a city of the Oretani situated near the upper Baetis (*Guadalquivir*) in the Saltus Castulonensis (*Sierra de Segura*). Its importance, indicated by the title *urbs valida ac nobilis*, derived from the lead and silver mines nearby, and from its situation on an old route from Valentia to Corduba. Hannibal chose a wife from Castulo. The Cornelii in its inscriptions are apparently descendants of natives enfranchised by the Scipios who campaigned in the district during the Hannibalic War.
M. Acedo, *Castulo* (1902). J. J. Van N.

CATACOMBS, a term derived from κατὰ κύμβας, a locality close to the church of St. Sebastian on the Via Appia, three miles south of Rome. The name may refer to the natural hollows across which the road passes or to an inn-sign, but was in use in the fourth and fifth centuries A.D. for the Christian cemetery associated with St. Sebastian's in the form *ad catacumbas* or *catacumbae*. This famous cemetery was a series of narrow underground galleries and tomb-chambers, cut in the rock. Their walls were lined with tiers (up to seven are known) of coffin-like recesses for inhumation, holding from one to four bodies apiece and sealed with a stone slab or with tiles. The affinity to *columbaria* (q.v.) is evident, but the type itself seems to have been immediately derived from Jewish catacombs (H. W. Beyer and H. Lietzmann, *Die Katakombe Torlonia* (1930)), where Jews, like Christians, remained a household of the faithful, united in death as in life. Catacombs were not confined to Rome: examples are known at Albano, Alexandria, Hadrumetum, Kertsch, Naples, Malta, and Syracuse. All are associated with soft rocks, where tunnelling was easy.

The catacombs at Rome, however, are much the most extensive, stretching at least 350 miles. Their distribution, along the main roads outside the city, is explained by their growth out of, or side by side with, pagan cemeteries lying beyond the city boundary in conformity with the law. That of St. Priscilla, on the Via Salaria, grew out of the burial-ground of the Acilii Glabriones (q.v.), persecuted under Domitian. Domitilla's contemporary catacomb, on the Via Ardeatina, developed from the vestibule of the Flavii. St. Paul's catacomb, on the Via Ostiensis, contains dated epitaphs of A.D. 107, 111, and 217. Other important groups include those of St. Sebastian, where the bodies of SS. Peter and Paul rested; St. Callixtus, containing the bodies of fifteen popes, and St. Praetextatus, all on the Via Appia.

The tomb-chambers (*cubicula*), containing table-tombs and arched recesses (*arcosolia*) for the bodies of saints, martyrs, and popes, are important for the development of later Christian crypts and depositories of relics; while the catacombs also saw the first development of Christian art, with frequent reference to acceptable Jewish legend and to Christian miracles, and with less obvious reference to Christ as Orpheus or the Kriophoros. The catacomb of St. Pontianus contained a baptistery. Heretical Gnostic beliefs are represented in the *hypogaeum* of Trebius Justus, on the Via Latina. Minor furniture included lamps, portrait medallions of glass, and *ampullae*, whose contents may well have varied between perfumes, consecrated wine, and martyrs' blood.

The presence of these large cemeteries is explained partly by the size of the Christian community in Rome and partly by the long periods of toleration. By about a century after the official recognition of the Church, the catacombs passed into desuetude, becoming centres of pilgrimage.

M. Besnier, *Les Catacombes de Rome* (1909); O. Beyer, *Die Katakombenwelt* (1927); O. Marucchi, *Le Catacombe romane* (1933); P. Styger, *Die römische Katakombe* (1935); G. Wilpert, *Le pitture delle catacombe* (1903). On the Jewish catacombs at Rome cf. G. B. Frey, *Rend. Pont.* xii. See also G. B. De Rossi, *Roma sotterranea* (1864–77; new series started in 1909 by O. Marucchi); *Notizie degli Scavi*, passim; *Atti dell' Accademia pontificia*, passim; *Nuovo bolletino di archeologia cristiana*, passim; *Rivista di archeologia cristiana*, passim. I. A. R.

CATAFRACTARII, *see* ARMS AND ARMOUR, ROMAN.

CATALEPTON, *see* APPENDIX VERGILIANA.

CATALEXIS, *see* METRE, GREEK, I (3).

CATANA (Κατάνη, modern *Catania*), a Greek colony, was founded by Naxos in 729 B.C. on Sicel territory in eastern Sicily. Like other Chalcidian States it used the legislation of its semi-mythical lawgiver Charondas (q.v.), and incurred Syracusan enmity: Hieron actually drove the Catanaeans to Leontini, replacing them with Dorian colonists (476). These latter, however, were soon ejected: they went to Inessa–Aetna (*see* AETNA), Catana's Chalcidian inhabitants returned (461), and the city prospered. During the Syracusan expedition (415) Catana was the Athenian base of operations (Thuc. bk. 6). Subsequently it was subject successively to Dionysius' Campanian mercenaries, Carthage, Callippus, Mamercus, Timoleon, Agathocles, Carthage again, Pyrrhus, Rome. A *civitas decumana* under the last, Catana was a flourishing grain port (and, appropriately, an ancient centre of Ceres-worship). Servile wars, earthquakes, and eruptions from nearby Aetna, during one of which Catana's celebrated *Pii Fratres* rescued their parents after the manner of Aeneas, merely interrupted its prosperity. Catana became a *colonia* under Augustus (Pliny, *HN* 3. 89) and has always remained a large city.

Strabo 6. 268 f.; [Lucilius], *Aetna*, 602 f.; Paus. 10. 28. 4; Diod. bks. 11, 13, 14, 16, 19, 22; Cic. *Verr.* passim; Auson. *Ordo Nob. Urb.* 11. A. Holm, *Catania antica* (1925). J. Bérard, *Bibliogr. topogr.* (1941), 45. E. T. S.

CATAPULT, *see* ARTILLERY, SIEGECRAFT.

CATILINE (LUCIUS SERGIUS CATILINA) was an active lieutenant of Sulla, both in the Civil War and in the proscriptions. After governing Africa as propraetor for two years, he returned to Rome in 66 B.C. to find that an impending prosecution for misgovernment prevented him from standing for the consulate (Asconius 79 f.). The candidates elected, Autronius and P. Sulla, had been unseated for bribery; with them he concerted a wild scheme to murder the new consuls at the beginning of 65 (Cic. *Cat.* 1. 15). The plot was exposed, but a senatorial inquiry was soon abandoned.

After trial and acquittal in 65 Catiline stood for the consulship of 63 with C. Antonius. His defeat by Cicero embittered him, and in 63 he came forward again with a programme for the abolition of debts, calculated to appeal to all the discontented classes (Cic. *Cat.* 2. 18 ff.). After a second defeat he abandoned constitutional methods and organized a far-reaching conspiracy. Cicero was well informed of Catiline's plan and, supported by the 'last decree' of the Senate (21 Oct. 63: Asconius 5),

took active steps to foil the projected rising. On 8 Nov., after being openly attacked by Cicero in the Senate, Catiline himself withdrew from Rome to the forces his lieutenant Manlius had collected in Etruria. By the help of some Gaulish informers Cicero was able to expose and execute Lentulus (q.v. 4) and the other ring-leaders in Rome. Catiline's army was outnumbered and ill equipped; unable to break through to Gaul, he turned to face the army of Antonius near Pistoria (Jan. 62) and fell fighting bravely.

Of great physical strength, reckless, ambitious, and unscrupulous, Catiline yet had a certain plausible charm which blinded many to his true nature (Cic. *Att.* 1. 2; *Sull.* 81; *Cael.* 12 ff.). It seems, however, clear that neither Caesar nor Crassus, who had supported his candidature in 64, was implicated in the second plot.

ANCIENT SOURCES: Cicero's letters and speeches (esp. *In Catilinam*, 1–4, and *Pro Sulla*) and Asconius' *Commentarii* are of the first importance. Sallust's *Bellum Catilinae* must be regarded as a political pamphlet, exonerating Caesar. Dio Cassius (bks. 36 and 37), Appian (*BCiv.* bk. 2), Suetonius (*Iul.*), and Plutarch's *Lives* are also helpful.

MODERN AUTHORITIES: C. John, *Die Entstehungsgeschichte der catilinarischen Verschwörung* (1876); G. Boissier, *La Conjuration de Catilina* (1905); E. G. Hardy, *The Catilinarian Conspiracy* (1924); M. Cary, *CAH* ix, ch. 11 (1932); J. Vogt, *Cicero und Sallust über die catilinarische Verschwörung* (1938). J. M. C.

CATIUS, TITUS, an Insubrian, mentioned by Cicero (*Fam.* 15. 16) as a recently deceased writer on Epicureanism.

CATO (1) 'CENSORIUS', MARCUS PORCIUS (234–149 B.C.), was born of peasant stock in Tusculum. He fought as a youth in the Second Punic War and was at Metaurus (207). His proof of legal ability and stern traditional morality impressed L. Valerius Flaccus, with whom he began his political career. Quaestor in 204, he was in Sicily, and on his return via Sardinia brought Ennius to Rome (203–202). Plebeian aedile in 199, he became praetor in Sardinia in 198, expelling usurers; *Leges Porciae de sumptu provinciali* and *de provocatione* are probably to be dated here. Consul in 195 with L. Valerius Flaccus, he opposed the repeal of the *Lex Oppia* and took the province of Spain; here, after extensive operations, he settled the administration and initiated the development of Roman rule.

2. After distinguished service under Manius Acilius Glabrio at Thermopylae (191), he prosecuted Q. Minucius Thermus (190), and, himself a candidate, supported charges of peculation against Glabrio in the censor elections for 189. He instigated and openly helped the attacks on L. Scipio, aiming to destroy the predominance and Hellenistic influence of Scipio Africanus. His success led to his censorship in 184 with L. Valerius Flaccus, at a time when social deterioration among nobles and people gave his doctrines full scope. He taxed luxury, strictly revised the senatorial and equestrian rolls, and checked the publicani; he also spent heavily on building, e.g. 1,000 talents on the sewerage system. He represented a policy of reconstruction, moral, social, and economic. The character of colonization at this time does not necessarily prove a predominantly agrarian policy on his part; he treated senators, *equites*, people, Latins, and provincials with equal regard to their traditional place in the State. This conservatism was associated with hatred of things Greek entering into Roman life, and he disguised his wide knowledge by a rustic pose in the cultivated senatorial society, which added ill manners to his natural robustness. He supported the *Lex Baebia* in 181, and opposed its modification and the repeal of the *Lex Orchia*; he attacked M. Fulvius Nobilior after the latter's censorship (179–178). In 171 he was patron in the Spanish appeal against extortion, prosecuting P. Furius Philus. He supported the *Lex Voconia* (169), favoured the independence of Macedonia, and rejected war against

Rhodes (167), and attacked Sulpicius Galba for his opposition to Aemilius Paullus' triumph. In 155 he spoke against the Athenian embassy of philosophers, and in 154 upheld the case of Ptolemy Philometor in the Egyptian question.

3. His embassy to Carthage (157 or 153), when he saw the new prosperity of the old enemy, brought into his policy the demand for the destruction of Carthage. The reason probably lies less in any commercial consideration than in distrust of Carthaginian resurgence and moral indignation at its character. In 151 he supported the return of the Achaean hostages, favoured Attalus II in a dispute with Prusias II, and approved of the prohibition of re-election to the consulship. In 150, despite the opposition of Scipio Nasica, he saw war declared on Carthage. In 149 he attacked Sulpicius Galba on behalf of the Lusitanians. He died in 149 aged eighty-five years, leaving two sons, Cato Licinianus by his first wife, Cato Salonianus by a second marriage; the latter was grandfather of Cato Uticensis.

4. Cato's whole policy appears based on a conception of traditional government and life, with the single aim of establishing social solidarity again in Rome and Italy, administrative control in the West, but no more than security, with justice, in the East. His thought found expression also through his strong natural literary talent. He published his speeches: Cicero knew more than 150, and we have fragments of 80. He wrote an encyclopaedia for his first son, including agriculture, rhetoric, and medicine, and separate treatises on medicine, jurisprudence, and military science. We know of letters to his son, apophthegmata, and the *Carmen De Moribus*, a gnomic book of morality; the *Catonis Disticha* date from Imperial times.

5. The *De Agri Cultura*, written *c.* 160 B.C., dealt with the development of vine, olive, and fruit-growing and grazing for profit in Latium and Campania; for all its lack of form, its details of old custom and superstition, and its archaic tone, it was an up-to-date work directed from his own knowledge and experience to the new capitalistic farming. The *Origines* in seven books, written from *c.* 168 to 149, following the Hellenistic κτίσεις histories and the senatorial historiography, included Aeneas, the founding of Rome (751 B.C.), the kings in bk. 1, the foundation traditions of the Italian cities in bks. 2 and 3, the Punic Wars to Cannae in bk. 4, the Rhodian debate of 167 B.C. in bk. 5, the prosecution of Sulpicius Galba (149) in bk. 7. He used Fabius Pictor, Hellenistic legends, local traditions, inscriptions, later inserting his own speeches; his treatment was discursive (*capitulatim*) and pragmatic, and, unlike the senatorial historiography, omitted the names of generals. The work, the first of its kind in Latin, inspired historical study and founded prose style; for to the principle of 'rem tene, uerba sequentur' he joined plain rhetorical device, including imitation from Greek, and a sense of effect in sentence structure and vocabulary. The style is the man, and if his talent moved narrowly in the expanding field of imperial politics, it touched greatness in his literary stimulus to the Roman tradition.

Livy 29. 25; 32. 27; bks. 34, 36, 38-9; 43. 2; 45. 25; Cicero, *De Senectute*; Nepos, *Cato*; Plutarch, *Cato Maior* (see R. E. Smith, *CQ* 1940); H. Malcovati, *ORF* i (1930), pp. 17, 153. G. Cortese, *De M. Porcii Catonis vita, operibus et lingua* (1885); O. Jaeger, *M. Porcius Cato* (1892); P. Fraccaro, *Atti di Mantova* (1910), 104; *Studi stor.* 1910, 129; ibid. 1911, p. 1; W. Drumann-P. Groebe, *Geschichte Roms* v. 102 (1912); De Sanctis, *Stor. d. Rom.* iii. 2, pp. 507, 517; iv. 1, pp. 163, 438, 447, 579; T. Frank, *CAH* viii, 639; B. Janzer, *Hist. Unters. zu den Redenfragmenten des M. Porcius Cato* (1937); A. H. McDonald, *JRS* 1938, 161, and *CHJ* 1939, 137. Texts: *De Agri Cultura*, H. Keil (1882-94); index by R. Krumbiegel (1897); G. Goetz (1922); E. Bréhaut, *Cato the Censor on Farming* (1933); W. D. Hooper-H. B. Ash (Loeb, 2nd imp. 1934); H. Jordan, *M. Catonis praeter librum de re rustica quae exstant* (1860); H. Peter, *HRRel.* i, pp. cxxvii, 55; H. Malcovati, loc. cit. E. Norden, *Antike Kunstprosa*² (1909), 164; J. Hörle, *Catos Hausbücher* (1929); R. Till, 'Die Sprache Catos', *Philol.* Suppl. xxviii (1936). A. H. McD.

CATO (2), GAIUS PORCIUS (*cos.* 114 B.C.), grandson of Cato (1). Once a follower of Tiberius Gracchus, he changed sides—presumably before or during C. Gracchus' agitation. He was condemned *de repetundis* after his defeat, as consul in 114 B.C., by the Scordisci in Macedonia, was exiled in 110 by the Mamilian Commission for his dealings with Jugurtha and died at Tarraco. M. H.

CATO (3), LUCIUS PORCIUS (*cos.* 89 B.C.), as tribune in 100 B.C. opposed Saturninus. In the Social War he defeated the Etruscans in 90, and as consul (89) defeated the Marsi, but was killed in a subsequent skirmish.

CATO (4), GAIUS PORCIUS (*trib.* 56 B.C.), 'adulescens nullius consili, sed tamen ciuis Romanus et Cato' (Cic. *QFr.* 1. 2. 15), in 59 B.C. openly called Pompey 'priuatus dictator' when prevented from prosecuting Gabinius. In 56 as tribune, it was supposed in Crassus' pay, he attacked Pompey again over the Egyptian business and tried to deprive Lentulus Spinther of his Cilician command. But after Luca he postponed the consular elections in the interests of Pompey and Crassus. Milo made him ridiculous by buying his gladiators and auctioning the 'familia Catoniana'. In 54 he was accused of violating the *Leges Fufia* and *Iunia Licinia* (*see* LEX, LEGES), and though apparently acquitted he is not heard of again. G. E. F. C.

CATO (5) UTICENSIS, MARCUS PORCIUS (95-46 B.C.), great-grandson of Cato (1), nephew of Livius Drusus, and brought up in the Livian household with the children of his mother's marriage to Cn. Servilius Caepio. His reputation for rectitude was already formed when in 63 he became tribune-designate to check Metellus Nepos (*see* METELLUS 10), supported Murena's (q.v.) prosecution, and intervened powerfully in the Senate to secure the execution of the Catilinarians. As tribune he conciliated the mob by increasing the doles of cheap corn, but in all else remained uncompromising; Cicero (*Att.* 1. 18. 7; 2. 1. 8) deplores the impracticability by which he prevented revision of the Asian tax-contracts (61 B.C.) and frustrated every overture of Pompey (q.v.) until the 'Triumvirate' was formed. In 59 he opposed Caesar obstinately and was temporarily imprisoned, but next year Clodius removed him by compelling him to undertake the annexation of Cyprus, over which, though King Ptolemy killed himself and Cato's accounts were lost on the voyage home, his reputation for fairness remained unimpaired. After Luca he persuaded his brother-in-law Domitius (q.v. 3) not to despair of the consulate, but the two were driven from the field; and Vatinius by bribery defeated Cato for the praetorship, which he subsequently obtained in 54. In 52, forsaking his principles, he supported Pompey's consulate; he himself stood for 51, but failed. In the war he strove to avert bloodshed of citizens but resolutely followed Pompey: he served in Sicily, whence Curio expelled him, then in Asia, and during the campaign of Pharsalus held Dyrrhachium. After Pompey's defeat he joined the Pompeians in Africa, composed their quarrels, and had Scipio made general. During the war he governed Utica with great moderation, and was honoured by the inhabitants when after Thapsus he compassed his famous death.

His character was unamiable: his first wife Antistia proving unfaithful he lent the second, Marcia, daughter of Philippus (*cos.* 56), to Hortensius. But his constitutionalism, a mixture of Stoicism and old Roman principles, was genuine. After death he was more dangerous than ever to Caesar, who in his *Anticato*, a reply to Cicero's pamphlet *Cato*, pitched the hostile case too high, and left the fame of Cato's life and death to give respectability to the losing side, and to inspire 'Republicans' a century later: 'uictrix causa deis placuit, sed uicta Catoni' (Lucan i. 128).

Sources: Plutarch's *Cato Minor* is wholly laudatory but rich in anecdote. See also the sources cited s.v. CAESAR (1). G. E. F. C.

CATO, see also VALERIUS (12).

CATREUS (Κατρεύς), in mythology, son of Minos and Pasiphaë, father of Althaemenes, Aërope, Clymene, and Apemosyne. In consequence of the prophecy that one of them should kill him (see ALTHAEMENES) he sold Aërope and Clymene, who, however, married respectively Pleisthenes, who here replaces Atreus as father of Agamemnon and Menelaus, and Nauplius, her sons being Palamedes and Oeax. Apemosyne was killed by Althaemenes, who did not believe her when she told him that she had been violated by Hermes, and supposed her unchaste. See Apollod. 3. 12 ff.   H. J. R.

CATTIGARA (τὰ Καττίγαρα), important city-port of the Sinae (Southern Chinese) near the mouth of river Cottiaris. *Circa* A.D. 100, one Alexander discovered it by sea from India, on a gulf inhabited by fish-eaters. Cattigara may be *Hanoi* or *Kian-chi* in the Gulf of *Tongking*, or possibly *Canton*. After the Gulf of Siam Ptolemy makes the Chinese coast face west, so that by mere calculation with his figures Cattigara would fall in Borneo.

Ptol. *Geog.* 1. 14. 4–10, etc.; 7. 3. 3; 8. 27. 14. G. E. Gerini, *Journ. Royal Asiatic Soc.* 1897, 551 ff.; Warmington, *Indian Commerce*, 109, 125–6, 129, 177; A. Herrmann, *PW*, s.v. 'Kattigara'.
                                                                          E. H. W.

CATULLUS (1), GAIUS VALERIUS (c. 84–c. 54 B.C.), Roman lyric, erotic, and epigrammatic poet, was born at Verona. Jerome (*Chron. Euseb.*) says he was born in 87 B.C. and died aged thirty; but he was alive in 55 when Caesar first invaded Britain and Pompey obtained his second consulship (Catull. 11; 29; 45; 113). Most probably he lived from 84 to 54. His father was notable enough to entertain Julius Caesar, doubtless in Cisalpine Gaul (Suet. *Iul.* 73) on his assize circuit. Catullus himself was wealthy (4; 31; 44; 68. 35) in spite of temporary embarrassments (10; 13). He came to Rome about 62 and quickly made friends in literary and fashionable society. His infatuation for the 'Lesbia' of his poems began this year. She was, it is now generally held, Clodia (q.v.), sister of Cicero's enemy P. Clodius (q.v. 1) Pulcher and wife of Q. Caecilius Metellus (q.v. 3) Celer, governor of Cisalpine Gaul in 62 and consul in 60. About ten years his senior, a woman of many lovers, she but played with the youth's affections. It seems she at one time encouraged him to hope for marriage (70), but before Metellus' death in 59 Catullus knew her inconstancy. The same year his brother died in the Troad. In deepest sorrow Catullus went home to Verona for a while; returning to Rome, he found established in Clodia's affections M. Caelius (q.v.) Rufus, Cicero's friend and correspondent. Agonized pleadings and reproaches had no effect and he tried to steel his mind against love (76). In 55 he composed a bitter and final farewell to Lesbia (11). Meanwhile, in 57, he had gone to Bithynia on the staff of the propraetor C. Memmius (q.v. 2). After visiting his brother's tomb near Troy (101), he returned by yacht to Italy in 56 (46; 31; 4) with the poet Cn. Helvius Cinna (q.v. 4). At the end of this journey he wrote his rapturous salutation to the promontory of Sirmio on Lake Garda. His last years were spent in or near Rome in literary composition and social pleasures. Besides Cinna, his literary friends were C. Licinius Calvus, Q. Cornificius, Furius Bibaculus, Q. Hortensius, Cornelius Nepos, and others. He was anti-Caesarian personally, if not politically; some of his bitterest satire is directed against Caesar and his *praefectus fabrum* Mamurra (29; 54; 57; 93). But finally Catullus was reconciled with Caesar (Suet. *Iul.* 73).

2. One hundred and sixteen poems are extant; but three (18–20) are spurious and omitted in modern editions. Arranged neither by chronology nor by subject, they nevertheless fall into three main groups: (*a*) 1–60,

short poems on various topics in lyric, sportive, erotic, abusive, or satiric vein; the metres are varied, but phalaecians (hendecasyllabics) and, to a lesser degree, scazons prevail; (*b*) 61–4, longer pieces; two wedding hymns (61 and 62); the *Attis* (63), a story in tempestuous galliambics of a youth who became a eunuch-acolyte of Cybele; the *Marriage of Peleus and Thetis* (64), an epyllion (q.v.) in 408 hexameters; (*c*) 65–116, all in elegiac metre. Of these 65–8 and 76 may be called elegies. The rest are short poems of epigram type, as miscellaneous in spirit and content as 1–60. Poems on Lesbia occur in both (*a*) and (*c*).

3. Though Catullus' sources are mainly his own experience, observation, and genius, he owes much to earlier models. Laevius set the example of fitting Greek lyric metres to the Latin language; part of 64 contains imitations of his contemporary Lucretius; otherwise his debt to Roman literature is slight. But he draws for metre, technique, and sometimes for content on Greek poets, especially Sappho (notably 51), Pindar, Archilochus, Hipponax, and the Alexandrians. For many Catullan motifs, prototypes exist in the Greek Anthology (O. Hezel, *C. und das griechische Epigramm* (1932); A. L. Wheeler, see bibliography infra). But Catullus freely alters his models according to personal experience; his poems therefore bear a highly individual stamp.

4. Alexandrian influence was strong in his circle. The epithet *doctus* applied to him later (Ovid, *Am.* 3. 9. 62; Tib. 3. 6. 41; Mart. 1. 61. 1) practically means Alexandrian. Catullus' Alexandrianism (q.v.) is shown in his avoidance of drama and epic, his translation of Callimachus' *Lock of Berenice* (66), his experiment in epyllion (64), his adoption of Hellenistic motifs, his mythological and geographical allusions (especially in 11; 55; 64–6; 68), his use of balanced antithesis and various poetical artifices such as anaphora in manifold forms (J. van Gelder, *Woordherhaling bij C.*, 1933), and a partly symmetrical scheme (O. Friess, *Darstellungskunst Catulls*, 1929). He avoids, however, the worst Alexandrian faults: obscurity, over-cleverness, excess of erudition and allusiveness. *See also* ARCHAISM.

5. His great virtue is sincerity. Strong and simple utterance is given to deep feeling, whether love or hate for Lesbia, sorrow for his brother, or rapture over a friend's home-coming; he ranks with Sappho and Shelley among the greatest lyric poets of all time. His tenderness can appear even when he is not portraying his own concerns, as in the picture of babe and parents in 61. 209–13. His satire is sharp, lucid, and direct, whether aimed at miser, kleptomaniac, or dull writer, at ugliness, peculation, or immorality. Equally sincere is his feeling for nature. His raptures over Sirmio come straight from the heart. His similes are often drawn from Alpine scenery or from plants and flowers (e.g. 11. 22; 61 passim; 62. 39; 68. 57). He can construct word-pictures of extraordinary vividness, and here his fondness for colour is often apparent.

6. Catullus' diction, prevailingly clear, direct, and simple (perhaps influenced by Italian folk-songs), presents some noticeable features. His lighter poems have a colloquial ring. He makes sudden changes in the person, animal, or thing addressed (3; 27; 28; 46). For himself he uses the first person or *Catullus* or *tuus Catullus* or apostrophizes himself in the vocative, often changing his practice within a single poem (6; 7; 8; 11; 13; 14; 38; 44; 56; 58; 72; 76; 79). Diminutives are frequent (Ellis, *Comm.* xxx), many doubtless of his own creation. Sometimes they have real diminutive force, but more often express tenderness or contempt.

7. In his hexametric poems (62 and 64) he is much more polished and less prosaic than Lucretius. He only once (64. 141) ends a word at the end of the second foot without a strong caesura in that foot. Elision is comparatively rare. He has an Alexandrian tendency towards spondaic fifth feet. His frequent closing of the sense at the end of lines with the corresponding rarity of enjambement makes for monotony. In elegiacs Catullus is uncouth compared with later elegists. The pentameter is marred by elisions at its caesura and in its later feet; it often ends in a word of three, four, or five syllables.

8. Catullus' influence was insufficiently recognized in antiquity. His adoption of Greek lyric metres and refinement of the hexameter pointed the path to Horace and Virgil respectively. To his epigrams Martial is indebted; and, as Catullus played a part in developing elegy out of epigram, he may be called the precursor of the Roman elegists. In the fourteenth century much is owed to him by Petrarch and other Italian humanists.

See also ALEXANDRIANISM, ELEGIAC POETRY (LATIN), EPYLLION, LYRIC POETRY (LATIN), para. 4.

Editions: K. Lachmann (1829, 1861, 1874); E. Baehrens, Commentary (1885); R. Ellis, Commentary² (1889), Text (O.C.T. 1904); W. Kroll (1929). Translations: J. Cranstoun (1867); T. Martin (1875); F. W .Cornish (Loeb, 1913); Sir W. Marris (1924); F. A. Wright (1926). Other literature: L. Schwabe, *Quaestiones Catullianae* (1862); A. Couat, *Étude sur C.* (1875); G. Lafaye, *C. et ses modèles* (1894); T. Frank, *C. and Horace* (1928); A. L. Wheeler, *C. and the Traditions of Ancient Poetry* (U.S.A. 1934); E. A. Havelock, *Lyric Genius of C.* (1939).   A. M. D.

CATULLUS (2), a well-known Neronian mime-writer (Juv. 8. 185 ff., 13. 111; Mart. 5. 30. 3), whose lost works include a noisy piece *Phasma* (The Ghost) and a realistic one, *Laureolus*, in which the crucifixion of a notorious bandit was staged (Mart. *Spect.* 7. 4; Suet. *Calig.* 57; Joseph. *AJ* 19. 1. 13).   J. W. D.

CATULUS (1), GAIUS LUTATIUS, was consul in 242 B.C. when Rome determined to renew naval warfare against Carthage. His great service was his decision to attack when a Carthaginian fleet appeared off Aegates Insulae (W. Sicily); there he terminated the First Punic War by a naval victory, 10 March 241. He negotiated peace terms with Hamilcar.   H. H. S.

CATULUS (2) QUINTUS LUTATIUS (*cos.* 102 B.C.), an Optimate leader and the first of his family to reach the consulship for over a century, became one of the chief men of the State. He was, however, defeated three times in his candidature for the consulship, during the coalition of *Equites* and Democrats: his successful rivals were C. Atilius Serranus, 106 B.C.; Cn. Mallius, 105; C. Flavius Fimbria, 104. As Marius' colleague in the consulship in 102 Catulus failed to prevent the entry of the Cimbri into Italy: he had awaited them near Verona, and was forced back into the plains, but avoided a decisive battle. In 101, with Marius, he destroyed the Cimbri at Vercellae: according to surviving accounts, Catulus' army bore the brunt of the fighting. Catulus was active against Saturninus in 100. He served in the Social War. Having been proscribed by the Marians in 87, he committed suicide.

An aristocrat of the highest education and culture, Catulus had close connexions with the Scipionic circle, and succeeded Laelius Sapiens as a centre of culture (Cic. *Tusc.* 5. 56). He thus became a link between that circle in its latest phase and its most brilliant intellectual descendant, Cicero. Like Scipio Aemilianus, he combined military, political, and literary prestige, though the group of figures around him, such as Antipater of Sidon and Archias, Furius of Antium, Q. Roscius, and Valerius Aedituus, were rather representative of literature. His learned freedman Lutatius Daphnis, originally bought for 700,000 sesterces, was, Suetonius tells us (*Gram.* 3), jokingly called 'Pan's darling' by the Laevius Melissus whom some identify with Laevius (q.v.), author of an *Erotopaegnia*, and others consider non-existent (F. Lammert, *Hermes* lxii (1927), 251–3). Büttner's contention that Porcius Licinus (q.v.) belonged to the Scipionic

circle in Catulus' time is unlikely in view of Porcius' biased verses on Terence's relation to his patrons (D'Alton, *Roman Literary Theory and Criticism* (1931), 64). As a philosopher, Catulus was according to one source (Cic. *Acad. Pr.* 2. 148) an Academic-Sceptic of the school of Carneades, according to another (*De Or.* 3. 182) a Peripatetic. He composed speeches, among them a funeral oration on his mother Popillia—the first instance of a Roman woman so honoured. The charm and purity of his style are often praised by Cicero, who introduced him as a character in the *De Oratore*. Cicero eulogizes his fine pronunciation of Latin, while his command of Greek won the admiration of the Greeks themselves. He wrote a memoir on his own consulship in a charming Xenophontean style, which has probably coloured our accounts of the period. A work *communis* (*-es*) *historia* (*-ae*) is attributed to him, apparently a popular treatment of myths and local legends similar to Timaeus' κοιναὶ ἱστορίαι. We know further of two erotic epigrams. In one, imitating a theme of Callimachus, the author declares his desire to recapture his lost soul that his beloved Theotimus possesses, but fears that if he does so he may lose his body too. The other epigram addresses the actor Roscius.

Cf. Malcovati, *ORF* ii, 66 f., 154 f.; W. Morel, *FPL* 43; R. Büttner, *P. Licinus u. der litterarische Kreis des Q. Lutatius Catulus* (1893).   M. H. and L. R. P.

CATULUS (3), QUINTUS LUTATIUS (*cos.* 78 B.C.), opposed the subversive intrigues of his colleague Lepidus (q.v. 2) and finally defeated him outside the walls of Rome. In 70 Catulus acted as *iudex* at the trial of Verres, and shortly afterwards he became *princeps senatus* in all but name and title. As the recognized leader of the conservative party he opposed the proposals of Gabinius (q.v. 2; 67) and Manilius (q.v. 2; 66). In 65 he held the censorship with Crassus (q.v. 4), but the divergence between their aims led to stalemate (Plut. *Crass.* 13). His defeat by Caesar in the pontifical election of 63 was a bitter blow to him. He died in 61 or 60.

Catulus was a 'conservative' who was not blind to the faults of the Senate (Cic. *Verr.* 1. 15. 44). He was neither a brilliant general nor an outstanding orator; but his steadiness and his integrity were universally acknowledged (Cic. *Leg. Man.* 17. 51; *Sest.* 47. 101).

Sources: scattered references in Cicero; Plutarch's *Lives* of Pompey, Crassus, Caesar, and Cato; Appian, *BCiv.* bk. 1 and (after 68 B.C.) Dio, bks. 37–8.   J. M. C.

CAUCASUS. For long the Greeks knew only the name and great size of this range. Herodotus describes it as a vast high mountain with many primitive peoples, skirting the west side of the Caspian, and he knew of the Derbent pass. Others believed that it contained many lakes and large rivers. Alexander mistook the Hindu-Kush for part of the Caucasus, thus causing some confusion in Greek literature. Not much more was learnt until Pompey subdued the Iberi (*see* IBERIA). Strabo could give details of the Caucasus—a well-wooded barrier between the two seas and connected with the Armenian heights and Mt. Taurus; he described the customs of the natives and their use of snow-shoes and hides which served as toboggans. No accounts survive of subsequent discoveries.

Strabo 11, esp. pp. 499–506; Ptol. *Geog.* 5. 9. 14, 15. E. H. W.

CAUDEX, see CLAUDIUS (5).

CAUDINE FORKS, the narrow defile where a Roman army was trapped by, and surrendered to, Gavius Pontius (q.v.), 321 B.C. (Livy 9. 2–6). It lay in the territory of the Caudini Samnites, somewhere between Capua and Beneventum, but cannot be certainly identified. The Arienzo–Arpaia valley, the traditional site, contains the significantly named hamlet Forchia, but seems too small;

an objection that applies also to the valley between S. Agata de' Goti and Moiano. The plain between Arpaia and Montesarchio, although large enough, does not fit Livy's description.

See E. T. Salmon, *JRS* 1929, 12 and the literature there cited.
E. T. S.

CAUPONES, *see* COMMERCE, para. 7.

CAVALRY, *see* ARMIES, AUXILIA.

CAVES, SACRED. It would appear that Greek cave-sanctuaries mostly belong either to pre-Hellenic cults or to Oriental importations: an exception is perhaps the cave-shrines of the Nymphs, common from Homer (*Od.* 13.347 ff.) on. The most famous is that of Zeus on Mt. Dicte in Crete (cave of Psychro, Nilsson, *Minoan-Mycenaean Religion*, 393). This was vaguely remembered as his birthplace and belongs to the cult of the Cretan god identified with him. Hardly less celebrated was the cave of Trophonius at Lebadea (Farnell, *Hero-Cults*, 21; description, Paus. 9. 39. 5 ff.). Here the date of the cult is unknown. In Italy, one of the most celebrated holy caves was the Lupercal on the Palatine, where the Luperci met for their ritual (see Platner–Ashby, 321). This is undoubtedly old, but we have no reason to suppose the ceremony pre-Italic. Of imported cults in both countries, that most closely connected with caves, or artificial underground vaults, was Mithraism (*see* MITHRAS).

For Cybele and caves, cf. L. Robert, *Mélanges Bidez* (1934), 795 ff.; A. J. Festugière, *Rev. Bibl.* xliv (1935), 382 f. H. J. R.

CEBES of Thebes, pupil of Philolaus the Pythagorean, and later of Socrates, plays an important part in the discussions in the *Phaedo*, and in the *Crito* is represented as one of those who were prepared to spend money in helping Socrates to escape from prison. The extant dialogue (probably belonging to the 1st c. A.D.) called Κέβητος Θηβαίου Πίναξ makes no pretence to be by Socrates' friend, and has been ascribed to him by a mere error. It presents an eclectic doctrine which in spite of its Pythagorean setting owes more to Plato, Aristotle, and the Stoics than to the Pythagoreans.

Ed. K. Praechter (1893). *PW* xi. 102. W. D. R.

CECROPS (Κέκροψ), mythical first king of Athens (though Actaeus is sometimes called first king), was a child of the Attic soil, though some late writers said that he was of Egyptian or Cretan origin. Sometimes it is said that his father was Hephaestus. As an indication of his autochthonous origin Cecrops is often represented as of serpent shape below the waist. By Aglauros or Agraulos, daughter of Actaeus, he had three daughters, Pandrosos, Herse, and Aglauros II. He was succeeded upon the throne by Cranaus. According to some writers there were two Cecropes who had ruled in Athens, the second being a son of Erechtheus.

Among late writers Cecrops had the reputation of having been a great benefactor of mankind. The story that he had instituted monogamy among men had its origin in a rationalistic interpretation of his double nature. He was also credited with the institution of burial of the dead and with the invention of writing. During his reign the contest of Athena and Poseidon for possession of Athens took place, and in some accounts he was judge of the contest. In a small structure on the Acropolis at the south-west corner of the Erechtheum the Athenians saw the tomb of Cecrops.

Ancient sources: Eur. *Ion* 1163 f.; Apollod. 3. 177 ff.; Paus. 1. 5. 3; schol. Ar. *Plut.* 773. Modern literature: C. Robert, *Griechische Heldensage* (1920), 137–9; H. J. Rose, *Handbook of Greek Mythology* (1928), 261 f. J. E. F.

CEIONIUS, *see* VERUS.

CELAENO, *see* HARPYIAE.

CELER, *see* METELLUS (9).

CELSUS (1) ALBINOVANUS, a friend of Horace (*Epist.* 1. 3. 15–20; 8. 1) and author of poems in which he showed himself too free a borrower.

CELSUS (2), AULUS CORNELIUS, under Tiberius (A.D. 14–37), wrote an encyclopaedia comprising agriculture, medicine, military science, rhetoric, and probably philosophy and jurisprudence (*see* ENCYCLOPAEDIC LEARNING). Apart from a few fragments of the other sections only the medical books are preserved. The work, dealing with the whole of medicine, is most important for the reconstruction of Hellenistic doctrines. The introduction outlines briefly but admirably the history of medicine up to the author's time. Celsus, a layman, writing for his own instruction and that of other laymen, selected with sound judgement his material from different sources (*see* SURGERY, para. 7). In philosophy he was a follower of the Sextii; in medicine he was influenced most strongly by Themison. The Latin of Celsus, the 'Cicero medicorum', became the model of Renaissance writing when his book, almost unnoticed in antiquity and in the Middle Ages, was rediscovered and printed at a very early date.

BIBLIOGRAPHY

TEXT: F. Marx, *CML* i (1915); text criticism, H. Lyngby, *Textkritiska studier till Celsus' Medicina* (Göteberg, 1931).
TRANSLATION: with text, Loeb; James Greive (1756).
LITERATURE: Celsus' book not based on one Greek original, O. Temkin, *Bull. of the Inst. of the Hist. of Med.* 1935; opposite theories summarized, Marx, l.c. lxxiv; M. Wellmann, *Arch. f. Gesch. d. Med.* 1925; Celsus as philosopher, A. Dyroff, *Rh. Mus.* 1939. General: J. Ilberg, *Neue Jahrb.* 1907; Wellmann, *PW* iv. 1273. L. E.

CELSUS (3), PUBLIUS JUVENTIUS, a distinguished Roman jurist, was born before A.D. 77, praetor 106 or 107, *legatus* of Thrace, twice consul (the second time 129), member of Hadrian's *consilium*. He was chief of the school of Proculians and successor to his father, Juventius C., in this position. Probably his disciple, he surpassed the father considerably. Author of *Epistulae*, *Commentarii*, *Quaestiones*, and of excellent, chiefly casuistic *Digesta* (in 39 books)—a later work, written probably after the new redaction of the Edict under Hadrian. Celsus had a profound knowledge of the earlier literature, which he often cites, but he is not seldom a severe and even rude critic of other jurists' views, being himself an independent -spirited thinker. His constructions are original; his language is clear and as independent as his mind: no jurist's vocabulary is so rich in cutting expressions as his.

F. Stella Maranca, *Intorno ai frammenti di Celso* (1915). A. B.

CELSUS (4), author of the first comprehensive philosophical polemic against Christianity, the Ἀληθὴς λόγος, written *c.* A.D. 178–80, of which the greater part is quoted in Origen's *Contra Celsum*; and of a book of advice to converts from Christianity. Celsus wrote from the standpoint of a Greek and a Platonist, but put certain objections to Christianity in the mouth of Jews in Egypt familiar with the Logos-theory. The Ἀληθὴς λόγος is important evidence for the knowledge of, and attitude towards, the Christianity of the Greek world; it shows knowledge of Gnostic sects as well as of the 'Great Church'. Celsus' criticism became part of the material for the Neoplatonic polemic against Christianity.

PW iii. 1884; O. Glöckner, *Celsi Ἀληθῆς λόγος* (1926). W. D. R.

CELSUS, *see also* ARRUNTIUS (3).

CELTIBERIANS, a powerful people of north central Spain. The name should be interpreted as proof of an intrusion of Iberians into territory once held by Celts (Schulten, op. cit. infra). A mingling of blood and of cultures resulted, but the combination was dominantly

Iberian. The poverty of the country dictated a simple life. Possibly the most valuable and certainly the most valued possession was the military equipment of the individual. The Hispanic (Iberian) sword, which became standard equipment for the Roman legionary, attained its best form and quality in Celtiberian workshops. The most dramatic events of their long struggle with Rome (intermittently from 195 to 133 B.C.: first Celtiberian War 181–179, second 153–151, third or Numantine 143–133) are concerned with Numantia (q.v.), the most important town of Celtiberia. Even after the Celtiberi were conquered their influence persisted. The comb and mantilla of nineteenth-century Spain have been traced to Celtiberian originals.

A. Schulten, *Numantia*, 4 vols. (Munich, 1914–31): a completely documented introduction (i. 1–160) describes the land and people of Celtiberia. For a different view of Celtiberian origins, see P. Bosch Gimpera, *Etnología de la Península Ibérica* (1932). J. J. Van N.

CELTS, a name applied by ancient writers to a population group occupying mainly lands north of the Mediterranean region from Galicia and Ireland in the West to Galatia in the East. Their unity is recognizable by common speech and common artistic tradition. (1) Dialects of Celtic are still spoken (Ireland, Scotland, Wales, Brittany), or are attested by inscriptions, quotations, and place-names in this area. The language seems closely akin to the Italian group, showing like it a division between 'q' and 'p' renderings of the velar guttural. The significance of this division is still obscure. (2) The artistic unity is expressed in the La Tène style (called from the Swiss type-site), which appears c. 500 B.C. It derived principally from living Italo-Greek styles, but archaic Hellenic motives which had survived in a Villanovan backwater are also noticeable, as well as eastern influences conveyed by way of Scythia. Out of these chronologically and regionally different borrowings the Celts evolved a very idiosyncratic art of swinging, swelling lines, at its best alive and yet reposeful.

2. This Celtic culture obviously flowed over earlier cultural regions, and the origin of the Celts is still uncertain, not least because the La Tène style appears somewhat catastrophically, and its relations to the preceding Hallstatt artistic phase are difficult to determine. It is generally supposed that a Celtic diffusion from southern Germany was part of the general migrations induced by worsening climatic conditions in the later Bronze Age. Bosch Gimpera sees the earliest Celtic movement in an invasion of Catalonia (c. 900 B.C.); subsequent movements overflowed France and north-west Spain. Celts may have reached the British islands in the later Bronze Age (c. 900), and the Hallstatt invasions of the sixth century and later were fairly certainly Celtic. Southward the Celts penetrated Italy, sacking Rome in 390; eastward they penetrated into Bohemia (Boii), descended the Danube, and raided Delphi (279). Another band crossed the Hellespont (278), and founded a State (Galatia), where Celtic was still spoken in the fifth century A.D.

3. The ancients knew the Celts as fierce fighters and superb horsemen, and noticed the savagery of their religious rites conducted by the priesthood, the Druids, who derived their doctrine from Britain. But Celtic political sense was weak, and they were crushed between the migratory Germans and the power of Rome, to be ejected (e.g. from Bohemia and south Germany), or more or less assimilated (as Belgae, q.v.) by the former, and conquered outright by the latter. Only in the far West did a vital Celtic culture persist, to borrow again from the Mediterranean, and to flower in works of art such as the Book of Kells, and of the spirit, as in the achievement of the Celtic saints, Columbanus, Gallus, and Aidan.

BIBLIOGRAPHY

Regional prehistoric studies (often very important) are enumerated in de Navarro's *Survey of Research on an Early Phase of Celtic Culture* (1937).

SOURCES: J. Dinan, *Monumenta Historica Celtica* (1911); J. Zuriker, *Fontes Religionis Celticae* (1934–6).

LANGUAGE: G. Dottin, *Langue gauloise* (1920, with *corpus* of Celtic inscriptions); A. Holder, *Altkeltischer Sprachschatz* (1891–6); H. Pedersen, *Vergleichende Grammatik der keltischen Sprachen* (1909–13); R. Thurneysen, *Handbuch des Altirischen* (1909); L. Weisgerber, *Sprache der Festlandkelten* in xx. *Bericht Röm.-Germ. Kommission* (1931), 147–226.

GENERAL: J. Déchelette, *Manuel d'Archéologie préhistorique* (1910–14); J. M. de Navarro, *CAH* vii (1928), 41–74; T. Rice Holmes, *Caesar's Conquest of Gaul*[2] (1911); H. Hubert, *Rise of the Celts* (1934); C. Jullian, *Histoire de la Gaule*, i–iii (1908); R. E. M. Wheeler, in Eyre's *European Civilization* ii (1935), 159–279.

C. E. S.

CENOMANI, Gauls, reputed to be Aulerci, who established themselves in Cisalpine Gaul c. 400 B.C. (Polyb. 2. 17; Strabo 5. 216). Their territory lay around Lake Garda. Chief towns: Brixia and probably Verona and Bergomum (Livy 5. 35). The Cenomani usually supported Rome, e.g. in 225 B.C. against Boii and Insubres and in 218 against Hannibal (Polyb. 2. 23, 24, 32; Livy 21. 55). In 200, however, they joined Hamilcar, but were quickly subjugated and romanized, disappearing from history (Livy 31. 10; 32. 30). In 49 B.C. Gallia Transpadana, including the Cenomani district, obtained Roman citizenship. For bibliography *see* CISALPINE GAUL.

E. T. S.

CENSOR (cf. *censere*, to estimate) was the title of a Roman magistrate who, although lacking *imperium* and the right to an escort of lictors, nevertheless possessed great authority, since he controlled public morals and supervised the leasing of public areas and buildings. The censorship was probably instituted c. 443 B.C. as a patrician and civil magistracy, in order to make up and maintain the official list of citizens, or *census* (q.v.). If a citizen was found guilty of suppressing or delaying information about his status and property, the censors (who always numbered two, in obedience to the principle of collegiality) were empowered to take judicial proceedings against him. The enrolment of the population, which generally took place in spring (probably in May), ended in a religious ceremony called *lustrum* ('cleansing', *see* LUSTRATION). Originally this ceremony was held *quinto quoque anno*, i.e. every four years, but from 209 B.C. onwards the formula was taken to mean every five years, and the interval between two celebrations was called a *lustrum*. The censors entered their office in early spring and the tenure lasted for eighteen months, the revised roll being issued twelve or fifteen months after their appointment. This registration took place in a special building in the Campus Martius. The *equitum census*, i.e. the making up of the list of those liable to cavalry service, was held in the Forum. The censors had the right of striking off the names of those who had given false statements, or who no longer merited the privilege of fighting as knights, owing to unbecoming behaviour at home or on military service, for bad administration of provinces, public property, and the like.

The censorship became accessible to the plebeians at the latest in 351 B.C., and one of the *Leges Publiliae* of 339 declared that at least one censor must be a plebeian, although two collegiate plebeian censors were not elected until 131. The power of the censors reached its zenith in the third and second centuries, largely owing to the *Lex Ovinia* (c. 312 B.C.), which empowered the censors to keep the senatorial rolls and revise them periodically, a function previously fulfilled by the consuls: they were to strike off such senators as had not observed the *ordo magistratuum* or had acted against law and public morality. The authority of the censorship was greatly reduced by Sulla and, although down till the Augustan age several distinguished citizens still filled the office, yet the censorship was doomed, and was rendered a dead letter when Domitian appointed himself censor for life. Thereafter other officials were entrusted with the censorial functions.

Mommsen, *Röm. Staatsr.* ii². 1, 334 ff.; J. W. Kubitschek, *PW,* s.v.; H. F. Jolowicz, *Hist. Introduction to the Study of Roman Law* (1939), 36 f., 50 ff.; A. Klotz, *Rh. Mus.* 1939; R. V. Cram, *Harv. Stud.* 1940 (fasti). **P. T.**

CENSORINUS (3rd c. A.D.), a Roman grammarian, (Prisc. 1. 4. 17) wrote *De Accentibus* (lost), and a 'De Die Natali uolumen illustre' (Sid. Apoll. *Carm.* 14 (*Epist.* § 3)), which is preserved. It is dedicated to Q. Caerellius on his forty-ninth birthday in A.D. 238. The parade of erudition is affected. The first part deals with human life from birth to death, and the influence of the planets; the second with time and its divisions, apparently an abstract of Varro, *Antiquitates rerum humanarum,* bks. 14–19. In the archetype MS. the last pages were lost as well as the beginning of an encyclopaedic work which was copied along with it, and has been quoted (since L. Carrion's edition, Paris, 1583) as *fragmentum Censorini.*

Editions: O. Jahn (1845); F. Hultsch (1867); J. Cholodniak (1889). On sources (Suetonius, etc.), Schanz–Hosius–Krüger, *Gesch. röm. Lit.* iii (1922). **G. C. R.**

CENSUS, a national register which was prepared at Rome from the time of the kings for taxation and military service. The holding of a census was at first the duty of the king, then of the consuls, and from 443 B.C. of the censors (q.v.). A census was normally held at intervals of five years. The citizens were registered in tribes and distributed into five classes according to their wealth: each class was subdivided into *seniores* and *iuniores.* They were required to state their full name and age and the amount of their property (*Lex Iulia Municipalis,* 145). The names of women and children were not included in the census, but parents gave information about their families (Dion. Hal. *Ant. Rom.* 4. 15). Under the later Republic the census was taken very irregularly, but it was revived by Augustus, who held it three times (*Mon. Anc.* 8). The last regular census was held in Italy by Vespasian and Titus: it had come to be unnecessary here, as Italians had become exempt from direct taxation and normally from compulsory military service. The taking of a census was concluded with a religious purification (*see* LUSTRATION). In the *Lex Iulia Municipalis* the chief magistrates of Italian towns are ordered to take a census simultaneously with the holding of one in Rome, and this must have been done earlier in communities possessing Roman citizenship (see Livy 29. 15).

In some provinces, e.g. Sicily (Cic. *Verr.* 2. 131), a local census was held even in Republican times, but it was not till the reign of Augustus that the census was organized by the Imperial Government. Information could be easily acquired in the municipalized senatorial provinces. Augustus was well informed by 7 B.C. about the wealth of the people of Cyrene (*SEG* ix. 1. 8). But new machinery had to be set up in the more backward provinces, where organized city life did not exist. A census was held in Gaul in 27 B.C., A.D. 14 and 61, and the census held in Judaea after its annexation in the governorship of Quirinius is famous. Most of the inscriptions referring to officials of the census come from imperial provinces. The governor was normally responsible and records the fact in his inscriptions, but many other men of senatorial and later of equestrian rank were concerned with the matter (*ILS* iii, Index, p. 351), and unimportant officials were entrusted with the duty in particular districts, e.g. Q. Aemilius Secundus, who when prefect of a cohort conducted the census of Apamea under Quirinius (*ILS* 2683). The census-return included full details of the character and extent of cultivated land and the number of slaves owned (*Dig.* 4. 15. 4), and of other forms of property. This information was necessary to those responsible for levying the *tributum soli* and

tributum capitis. It was probably the duty of governors to keep the register up to date, but no regular census-period seems to have been prescribed.

A. H. J. Greenidge, *Roman Public Life* (1901), 221 ff., 429 ff. **G. H. S.**

CENTAURS, a tribe of wild, beast-like monsters usually thought of as having the upper part of a human being and the lower part of a horse. Centaurs live in woods or mountains of Elis, Arcadia, and Thessaly. In the *Iliad* they are described as 'beasts' (φῆρες; and cf. *Od.* 21. 303). Possibly the conception of horse-shaped centaurs originated with the horse-breeders of Thessaly. Myths of Centaurs must be very old, since they occur in Homer, in late Mycenaean, and in early orientalizing art. For the Greeks Centaurs are representative of wild life, animal desires, and barbarism. They are lustful and over-fond of wine. Their fight against the Lapiths, whose king Peirithous invited Centaurs to his marriage (*Il.* 1. 262; 2. 742; *Od.* 21. 295 ff.; [Hes.] *Sc.* 178 ff.) is famous. Either one (Eurytion) or several Centaurs attempted to rape the Lapith women. In the ensuing fray the Centaurs were routed, although they killed the invulnerable Caeneus. Heracles had a clash with Centaurs when he visited the Centaur Pholus. Attracted by the smell of wine, Centaurs assailed Heracles with rocks and stones, but were beaten back with fire-brands and arrows and fled to Cape Malea.

Individual Centaurs have myths of their own. Nessus offered to carry Deianira across the river Euenus and then attempted to rape her (Archilochus in Dio Chrys. 60). Heracles killed him with his sword or with arrows. This scene is a great favourite with archaic vase-painters. Before Nessus died he gave to Deianira the garment which later caused the death of Heracles (Soph. *Trach.*). Chiron was the wise and kind old medicine-man among the Centaurs. He is of divine origin, son of Kronos and Philyra (Apollod. 1. 9; Pherecyd. in schol. Ap. Rhod. 1. 554), well versed in medicine (*Il.* 4. 219) and other arts, and educates divine children and heroes, Achilles, Asclepius, and Jason. He also helps Peleus to woo Thetis (*Cypria* fr. 2; Apollod. 3. 170). Chiron had a cult in Thessaly.

The Centaurs are sometimes children of Ixion (q.v.), but in Pindar the offspring of Centaurus, son of Ixion and Nephele, who mated with mares near Mt. Pelion (Pind. *Pyth.* 1. 36).

In art, the earliest Centaurs brandish boughs or hunt. The Nessus episode appears in the seventh century B.C. (J. M. Cook, *BSA* 1934–5, 191). The fight with the Lapiths occurs on the famous François vase and in sculpture on the pediment of the temple of Zeus in Olympia. Later, Centaurs join the Dionysiac *thiasus* and are so shown on Roman funeral reliefs. (Cf. Nonnus, *Dion.* 14. 49, 143, 193.)

P. V. C. Baur, *Centaurs in Ancient Art* (1912); J. E. Harrison, *Prol. to the Study of Greek Religion* (1922), 380; P. Kretschmer, *Glotta* 1919; H. Payne, *Necrocorinthia* (1932). **G. M. A. H.**

CENTO. I. GREEK. A patchwork (*cento,* a patchwork cloak) of existing verses, sometimes humorous in intention, sometimes not. Trygaeus' improvisation at Ar. *Pax* 1090–4 is an early example, and in the *Frogs* (1264 ff., 1285 ff., and 1309 ff.) the cento is pressed into the service of literary criticism. Lucian (*Symp.* 17) mentions a 'very funny song', made of a medley of Hesiod, Anacreon, and Pindar. Cf. also *Anth. Pal.* ix. 381–2. Ὁμηροκέντρωνες were composed in Byzantine times, e.g. by the Empress Eudocia in the fifth century A.D. Many parodies, e.g. the one of Homer quoted by Dio Chrysostom in *Or.* 32 (see Brandt, *Corpusc. poes. ep. graec. ludib.,* pp. 100 ff.) are virtually centos.

G. Kaibel, *Epigrammata Graeca e lapidibus conlecta* (1878), 1009; E. Stemplinger, *Das Plagiat in der griech. Lit.* (1912), 193–5. **J. D. D.**

[180]

II. LATIN. In Latin, cento-making originated when an age fertile in perversity began to look for amusement in Virgil. Lines from his poems, learned by heart in school, were strung together to form a new whole, 'de inconexis continuum, de diuersis unum, de seriis ludicrum' (Ausonius, *Cent. Nupt.*, *praef.*). Such works were the *Medea* of Hosidius Geta, a contemporary of Tertullian, the anonymous *De Alea*, and Ausonius' *Cento Nuptialis*, written at Valentinian's request *c.* A.D. 368, an unpleasantly clever poem whose preface clearly explains the author's method and purpose.

Parody gave way to demonstrations of Virgil's 'anima naturaliter Christiana'. In the fourth century, the poetess Proba wrote biblical history in cento form; Pomponius modelled his *Tityrus* on the first Eclogue. Other centos are the *De Incarnatione Verbi* (formerly attributed to Sedulius) and the *De Ecclesia*, in which the author (probably Mavortius, author also of a *Iudicium Paridis*) deprecates the title 'Maro Iunior'. In 494 Pope Gelasius decreed 'centimetrum de Christo, Vergilianis compaginatum uersibus, apocryphum'.

References in Isidore show continued interest in cento; it reappears in Columban (6th c.), Waldram (9th c.), and in the tenth-century *Ecbasis Captivi*, although other authors besides Virgil are now drawn upon.

Baehrens, *PLM* iv. 191 ff.; O. Delepierre, *Tableau de la littérature du centon* (London, 1874–5); D. Comparetti, *Virgilio nel Medio Evo*, 1872; revised ed. vol. i, 1937 (tr. E. F. M. Benecke, 1895; rp. 1929), 53 f.; F. J. E. Raby, *Christian Latin Poetry* (1927), *Secular Latin Poetry* (1934); Schanz, *Gesch. d. röm. Lit.* iv. 1, ed. 2 (1914), pp. 31, 219 ff.; Manitius, *Gesch. d. lat. Lit. des Mittelalters* i. 185, 597, 618.   R. G. A.

CENTUMVIRI, a special court of justice in Rome, created not before 240 B.C. and probably about 150 B.C., for more important civil lawsuits, particularly for all kinds of *vindicationes* and for *causae hereditariae* (*hereditatis petitio, querella inofficiosi testamenti*). The *centumviri* functioned only in the second stage of civil proceedings in place of the private *unus iudex*; the procedure *in iure* in these cases was reserved for the magistrate as in normal proceedings. For each particular case allotted to the *centumvirale iudicium* a special tribunal was selected, presided over firstly by a magistrate, later by a member of the Decemviral College (*see* VIGINTISEXVIRI), and composed of an unknown and rather numerous group of judges taken from the centumviral panel. It is noticeable that the whole college did not number a hundred persons, but 105 (three from each *tribus*), and later even 180. We do not know precisely for what reasons a matter was brought before the *centumviri*; it may be that the special importance of the case (for instance the high value of an inheritance) was decisive for this purpose, perhaps also a consideration of a procedural character, such as an agreement or a common petition of both the parties. The question whether the stage *apud iudicem* should come before the *centumviri* had to be settled in the preliminary proceedings *in iure*, because in such cases procedure by *legis actio sacramento* was prescribed even in later times, when the formulary procedure was otherwise obligatory. The practice of the centumviral courts had a great influence on the development of the Roman law of succession.   A. B.

CENTURIA was the smallest unit of the Roman legion. Each legion contained 60 centuries (*see* LEGION, para. 1; MANIPULUS).

According to tradition, Servius Tullius founded a new political assembly based on the centuries. The real date of this reform is doubtful, and many scholars prefer the middle or the end of the fifth century B.C. The assembly consisted of 18 centuries of horsemen, 6 of which were called *sex suffragia*, and 170 centuries of foot-soldiers. The foot-soldiers were divided into five *classes* (q.v.) according to their census. The first class fell into 40 centuries of *iuniores* (between 17 and 45 years) and 40 of

seniores (between 46 and 60); the second, the third, and the fourth into 10 centuries of *seniores* and *iuniores* apiece, and the fifth into 15 of each category. Five centuries of non-combatants, including one of *capite censi* (*proletarii*), were attached; two of these centuries (of *fabri*) were apparently ranked with the first class. The age limit of sixty for the *seniores* disappeared in the centuries of the comitia.

Between 241 and 218 B.C. the distribution of the centuries underwent a reform about which Livy (1. 53. 12) and Cicero (*Rep.* 2. 22. 39) leave us uncertain, except to show that its object was to correlate the centuries and the local tribes, and that the first class was reduced to 70 centuries. Some scholars hold that each class was now equally divided into 35 centuries of seniors and 35 of juniors; but others hold that the number of the centuries remained fixed at 193.

The name *centuria* was also used for the block of 100 *heredia* (little allotments, theoretically each of 2 *iugera*), which was the unit for the delimitation of the *ager publicus*.

See COMITIA.

Domaszewski and Kubitschek, *PW* iii. 1952. For the Servian classification, G. W. Botsford, *The Roman Assemblies* (1909), 66; A. Rosenberg, *Untersuchungen zur römischen Zenturienverfassung* (1911); P. Fraccaro, 'La storia dell' antichissimo esercito romano e l'età dell' ordinamento centuriato', *Atti II Congresso Studi Romani* (1931) (fundamental); id. *Athenaeum* 1934, 57; G. De Sanctis, *Riv. Fil.* 1933, 289; A. Momigliano, *Studia et documenta historiae et iuris* ii (1938), 509; H. H. Scullard, *A History of the Roman World* (1935), 448; H. Last, *JRS* 1945, 31. For the reform of the third century, Rosenberg and Momigliano opp. cit., G. De Sanctis, *Stor. Rom.* iii. 1 (1916), 376; P. Fraccaro, *Studi in onore di P. Bonfante* (1929), 105.   A. M.

CENTURIO. The centurions were the principal professional officers in the Roman army. There were sixty in each legion. In the post-Marian army each of the ten cohorts had six centurions: *pilus primus, pilus posterior, princeps prior, princeps posterior, hastatus prior*, and *hastatus posterior*. Apart, however, from those of the first cohort there was little difference in rank among the six centurions of each cohort. Consequently a centurion was promoted from cohort to cohort, not infrequently with a change of legion, until he reached the first cohort. He had now entered the *primi ordines*, and inside this group a strict seniority was observed, with the post of *primus pilus* as the final honour.

During the Republic centurions were selected from the common soldiers; under the Principate some of them were *ex equite Romano*, i.e. men who had started and then resigned an equestrian career, or ex-praetorians (*evocati*). They were attracted by high pay (five times that of the praetorian soldier), and good prospects on retirement. *See also* PRIMIPILUS.

In the pre-Marian army the maniple (*see* MANIPULUS) was commanded in battle by the centurion of the right-hand century; when the cohort (*see* COHORS) superseded the maniple each was probably commanded by its *pilus prior* centurion.

Centurions are also found in the *Auxilia* and the Praetorians (qq.v.), but without the distinguishing titles of their legionary counterparts.

H. Wegeleben, *Die Rangordnung der römischen Centurionen*; A. von Domaszewski, *Die Rangordnung des römischen Heeres* (1908); H. M. D. Parker, *The Roman Legions* (1928).   H. M. D. P.

CEPHALAS, CONSTANTINUS, a Byzantine Greek of the tenth century, compiled the great Palatine Anthology (q.v.) of Greek epigrams. Little is known of his personality: he was one of the many industrious collectors, like 'Suidas', who were set to work to preserve relics of classical antiquity by the learned emperor Constantine VII Porphyrogennetos (912–59).   G. H.

CEPHALUS, a hero, apparently Attic. He is eponym of the Attic *genos* Κεφαλίδαι (Hesych. s.v.), marries Procris (q.v.), and lives at Thoricus (Pherecydes, infra).

He has, however, connexions outside Attica, for he takes part with his hound in the hunt for the Teumessian vixen (see AMPHITRYON), in the Cyclic *Epigoni* (fr. 2 Allen); he marries Clymene daughter of Minyas (*Nostoi*, fr. 4 Allen). His principal adventures are: (1) his affair with Eos (q.v.), first in Hesiod (*Theog.* 986), where their son is Phaëthon the attendant of Aphrodite. Generally (e.g. Ov. *Met.* 7. 704, supported by much earlier evidence from art, see Roscher's *Lex.* s.v.), she carries him off. (2) His jealousy of Procris. To test her, he stayed away for eight years, came back in disguise, and succeeded in obtaining her favours (schol. V on *Od.* 11. 321, citing Pherecydes). (3) Her jealousy of him, because he spent so much time hunting (Pherecydes, ibid., cf. Ovid, ibid. 796 ff.). Learning that he was accustomed to call for a cloud, νεφέλη (Pherec.), or a breeze, *aura* (Ovid), to cool him, she supposed this the name of a mistress, followed him in hiding, and was killed by his throwing-spear, which he flung at her supposing her to be a beast (the spear never missed, Ov., ibid. 683; further fanciful details of the legend, Hyg. *Fab.* 189). That Cephalus was eponym of Cephallenia (Arist. in *Etym. Magn.* 144. 26), is hardly more than a pun. His father is regularly Deïon or Deïoneus. H. J. R.

CEPHEUS (Κηφεύς), name of four or five mythological persons, the best-known being the father of Andromeda (q.v.). Though generally called an Ethiopian from Euripides on, he and consequently the whole legend are very variously located; for particulars cf. Tümpel, in Roscher's *Lexikon* ii. 1109-13. H. J. R.

CEPHISODORUS (1) (fl. *c.* 400 B.C.), writer of Old Comedy (*IG* ii². 2325; Lys. 21. 4 Κηφισοδότῳ codd.). The Ἀντιλαΐς satirized the ἑταίρα Laïs.

FCG i. 267-9; CAF i. 800-2.

CEPHISODORUS (2) of Thebes, pupil of Isocrates, wrote a history of the Sacred War and a treatise directed against Aristotle.

FHG ii. 85-6.

CEPHISODOTUS (1), sculptor, Athenian, probably father of Praxiteles (q.v.), and a brother-in-law of Phocion. Pliny dates 372, probably by the Irene group. Selected works: 1. Irene and the infant Plutus, on the Areopagus (the Irene cult was introduced 375); marble copies at Munich, etc. (Winter, *KB* 293. 3). 2. Hermes with the infant Dionysus; *attributed* from likeness to Irene. 3. Dionysus; marble copies in the British Museum, etc. (Winter, *KB* 293. 4). 4. Hygieia; original head in Athens, copies in Melchett collection, etc. Cephisodotus develops Phidian tradition, forerunner of Praxiteles.

Overbeck, 878, 1137-43; B. Ashmole, *BSR* x. 1. T. B. L. W.

CEPHISODOTUS (2), sculptor, Athenian, son of Praxiteles. Pliny dates 296 B.C. (inscription of 344-343, published as signature of Cephisodotus, probably refers to dedicator). Selected works: 1 (with his brother Timarchus). Lycurgus and his sons, probably after Lycurgus' death 323. 2 (with Timarchus). Menander, in the theatre at Athens, probably after Menander's death, 291; copies of head at Boston, etc. (Winter, *KB* 320. 4). 3 (with Timarchus). Statues on the altar of the Asclepieum at Cos (Herod. 4. 1-26); fragments have been discovered. 4 (with Euthycrates, son of Lysippus). Anyte (fl. 284). 5. Symplegma (erotic group) in Pergamum. 6. Leto, later on the Palatine; reproduced on the Sorrento base. He continued the Praxitelean tradition into the third century.

Overbeck, 1331-41; M. Bieber, *JDAI* 1923-4, 242. T. B. L. W.

CEPHISSUS (Κηφισός), the name of several rivers, the best known being the Attic and the Boeotian Cephissus. The Attic Cephissus was the main river of the Plain of Athens, gathering all sources of the mountains around, and emptying itself into the bay of Phalerum; its water, divided into many trenches, irrigates the plain west of Athens (cf. Soph. *OC* 685). The Boeotian Cephissus springs from the northern Parnassus, near Lilaea, and waters the plains of Phocis and northern Boeotia, debouching into the lake Copaïs.

Bölte, *PW*, s.v. 'Kephissos'. V. E.

CERBERUS, monstrous dog guarding the entrance to the lower world. According to Hesiod (*Theog.* 311) C. is the son of Typhon and Echidna, has fifty heads and a voice like bronze. He is often referred to simply as 'the dog of Hades'. The canonical type of C., established in late archaic and classical literature and art (Eur. *HF* 611), shows him with three heads and mane or tail of snakes. C. is most frequently mentioned in connexion with the descent of Heracles to Hades (*Il.* 8. 367; Apollod. 2. 5. 12). With the permission of Hades Heracles dragged C. out of the lower world, showed him to Eurystheus, and then returned him to Hades. This episode is depicted with much gusto on the Caeretan *hydriae* in the Louvre and the Museo Villa Giulia (E. Pfuhl, *Malerei und Zeichnung der Griechen*, pl. 36, fig. 154, and G. Q. Giglioli, *Arte etrusca*, 1934, pl. 128, 3). The same scene appeared on the Amyclaean throne (Paus. 3. 18. 9, Frazer).

S. Eitrem, *PW*, s.v. 'Kerberos'. G. M. A. H.

CERCIDAS (*c.* 290–*c.* 220 B.C.), of Megalopolis, was friendly with Aratus of Sicyon, who sent him *c.* 226 to Antigonus Doson to ask the latter's intervention on behalf of the Achaean League against Cleomenes (Polyb. 2. 48). In 222 before the battle of Sellasia C. is mentioned as the leader of 1,000 men from Megalopolis (Polyb. 2. 65). Other authorities refer to C.'s success as a lawgiver, alluding probably to the restoration of liberty at Megalopolis after the tyranny of Lydiadas (235). An alternative description of C. as a Cretan (Diog. Laert. 6. 76) may indicate his residence in the island during that tyranny. Outside politics, C. attained fame as a Cynic philosopher and poet.

WORKS. Literary sources have preserved only nine short fragments of C.'s verse. Of these one (fr. 14 Powell) is cited from the *Iambi*. It proves that the work was in the choliambic or scazon metre and may come from a diatribe against luxury. An attempt has been made (by A. D. Knox, *The First Greek Anthologist*, 1922) to claim C. as the editor of an anthology of moralizing verse preserved in several papyri, and possibly the author of some of the pieces written in scazons. But C.'s best-known work was his *Meliambi*, i.e. poems lyrical in form, but satiric in content. Substantial remains, preserved in *POxy.* 1082, show that C. was a skilful and original metrist and a keen critic of social conditions in his day. Though a member of the property-owning class, he makes himself in these poems the mouthpiece of the poor and oppressed, and attacking the cult of wealth and its attendant vices exhorts his fellows to mend their ways while there is yet time. In his use of verse to inculcate the Cynic view of life and in his mixture of the earnest and the jesting C. was clearly influenced by Crates of Thebes, whose example was followed about the same time by Menippus of Gadara (qq.v.); but his opinions seem to have been formed chiefly by the example of the sect's founder, Diogenes, to whom he pays a glowing tribute (fr. 1), and by the teaching of Bion (q.v.) the Borysthenite. The so-called 'Diatribe Style', of which Bion is the reputed founder, finds frequent illustration in C.'s verse, but he combines with it other features, such as new and lengthy compounds, which derive rather from the dithyramb, Old Comedy, and Timon of Phlius. His skilful use of citations from Homer, of whose poetry he is said to have been a warm admirer, and from Euripides is in the Cynic vein. The language of the *Meliambi* is a literary Doric which avoids local peculiarities and pedantic consistency. *See also* IAMBIC POETRY, GREEK.

Texts: J. U. Powell, *Collectanea Alexandrina* (1925), 201–19; A. D. Knox, *Herodes, Cercidas, and the Greek Choliambic Poets* (Loeb, 1929), 190–238; E. Diehl, *Anthologia Lyrica* iii (1923), 305–14. General literature: G. A. Gerhard, 'Kerkidas (2)', in *PW* ix. 294–308, also *Phoinix von Kolophon* (1909); J. U. Powell and E. A. Barber, *New Chapters in the History of Greek Literature* (1921), 1–12. E. A. B.

CERCOPS OF MILETUS (? 6th c. B.C.), epic poet, to whom (or to Hesiod) is ascribed the *Aegimius* (on the Dorian hero Aegimius who fought against the Lapithae). *EGF* 82–5.

CEREALIS, *see* JULIUS (4).

CERES, an ancient Italian corn-goddess, commonly identified in antiquity with Demeter (q.v.). Her name (Oscan *Kerri-*, see the 'Curse of Vibia', Conway 130, 1) suggests that of Cerus ('in carmine Saliari Cerus manus intellegitur creator bonus', Festus, p. 109, 7 Lindsay), but in cult she is found associated not with him but with Tellus Mater (q.v.). This is shown by the juxtaposition of their festivals (Fordicidia, to Tellus, 15 April; Cerialia, 19 April) and the fact that the *feriae sementiuae* are celebrated in January in honour of both (Ov. *Fast.* 1. 657 ff., on which cf. Frazer). The occurrence of the Cerialia on the calendars and the existence of a *flamen Cerialis* testify to the antiquity of Ceres' cult at Rome, but her whole early history is extremely obscure, particularly her relations, if any, with non-Italian (Greek) deities; see, for some ingenious conjectures, Altheim, *Terra Mater* (1931), 108 ff. One of the many difficulties is to determine whether the rite of swinging attested by 'Probus' on Verg. *G.* 1. 385–9 as used at the *feriae sementiuae* is really, as he says, borrowed from the Attic αἰώρα (*see* ERIGONE) or an independent development. Another is the question whether the long list of minor deities invoked by the officiant on the same occasion (Servius on *G.* 1. 21) arises out of genuinely early ideas or is a relatively late priestly elaboration (see Rose in *JRS* iii (1913), 233 ff.).

There is, however, no doubt that Ceres' most famous cult, that on the Aventine (introduced 493 B.C.), is largely under Greek influence. She is there worshipped with Liber and Libera, the triad apparently representing the Eleusinian group of Demeter, Kore, and Iacchus (but see Altheim, op. cit. 15 ff.). The temple became a centre of plebeian activities, was supervised by the plebeian *aediles Cereris*, and was connected with the *ludi Ceriales* which became a prominent feature of the Cerialia. To this Greek cult belongs also, no doubt, the annual festival conducted by the women in August, called Greek and an initiation by Cicero (*Leg.* 2. 21); also probably Ceres' occasional association with the underworld (as in the 'Curse of Vibia', above), the purely Roman goddess in this connexion being Tellus (as Livy 8. 6. 10). *See also* MUNDUS.

Wissowa, *RK* 191 ff., 297 ff.; F. Altheim, *A History of Roman Religion*, passim. H. J. R.

CERIALIS CAESIUS RUFUS, QUINTUS PETILLIUS (*cos. suff.* A.D. 70, *cos.* II *suff.* 74), a relative of Vespasian. Legate of Legio IX Hispana in Britain, he suffered a serious defeat in the revolt of Boudicca (61). With the Flavian forces at the capture of Rome, he was sent to restore order in Gaul and the Rhineland. He won a battle at Rigodulum, captured the city of the Treveri, and then proceeded to deal with Civilis and Classicus: after confused fighting the latter capitulated (towards the end of 70). Cerialis was next appointed legate of Britain (71–4), in which command he shattered the power of the Brigantes and made extensive conquests in northern England (cf. Tac. *Agr.* 17). Nothing more is heard of him after his second consulship. R. S.

CERSOBLEPTES, a king of the Odrysae in south-east Thrace from 360 to 342 B.C. In the early part of his reign he was a rival of Athens for the possession of the Thracian Chersonese. Hampered by the presence of two pretenders to his throne, he ceded to the Athenians the whole peninsula except the town of Cardia (358–357). He subsequently drew closer to Athens, under the threat of Macedonian aggression, but he did not obtain an alliance, and was excluded from the peace of 346. In the same year he capitulated to Philip of Macedon, and after a rebellion in 342 he was deposed. M. C.

CERVIDIUS, *see* SCAEVOLA (5).

CESTIUS (1) (EPULO), GAIUS, tribune and praetor of the Augustan age; among his heirs was M. Agrippa. A pyramid was erected on the Via Ostiensis as his tomb (*ILS* 917).
PIR², C 686.

CESTIUS (2) PIUS, LUCIUS, Augustan rhetor, a Greek from Smyrna; a popular teacher distinguished for his conceit, his outspoken wit, and his dislike of Cicero, to several of whose speeches he wrote answers (Sen. *Controv.* 7 *praef.* 8–9).

CESTIUS (3) GALLUS, GAIUS (*cos. suff.* A.D. 42), was legate of Syria from 63 (or 65) to 67. In 66 he marched into Palestine to restore calm, but failed to occupy Jerusalem and on his withdrawal was defeated at Beth-horon. He died in 67.
PIR², C 691.

CETHEGUS, GAIUS CORNELIUS, a Roman senator who conspired with Catiline. He was left in Rome with P. Lentulus Sura to murder the leading senators. He was condemned to death (63 B.C.).

CETO, *see* GORGO.

CEYX, in mythology, (1) king of Trachis, friend of Heracles, and father-in-law of Cycnus son of Ares ([Hesiod], *Sc.* 354 ff.). (2) Son of the Morning Star; husband of Alcyone daughter of Aeolus (1) or (2). He and his wife were turned into the birds which bear their names (see Sir D'A. W. Thompson, *Glossary²*, s.vv.) as punishment for calling themselves Zeus and Hera (Apollod. 1. 52); or, he was drowned and she, finding his body, leaped into the sea and both were changed by the pity of the gods (Ov. *Met.* 11. 410 ff.). H. J. R.

CHABRIAS (d. 357 B.C.), a professional soldier who after 390 B.C. fought successfully for Athens and for the rebellious kings of Cyprus and Egypt. He invented a useful method of defence against hoplites. After the naval victory over Sparta near Naxos (376) he gained many allies for the Athenian Confederacy, together with Timotheus (q.v.), whom he subsequently impeached. He was elected general several times. Finally accused of treachery, but acquitted (after 366), he once more supported an Egyptian king, Tachus, against Persia, together with old Agesilaus (q.v.; 360). In 357 he fell at Chios, fighting gallantly.

Nepos, *Chabrias*; Xen. *Hell.* 5. 1 ff.; Diod. 15. 29 ff. Cf. *Prosop. Att.* 15086. H. W. Parke, *Greek Mercenary Soldiers* (1933). V. E.

CHAEREA, *see* CASSIUS (10).

CHAEREMON (1), tragic poet of about the middle of the fourth century B.C., wrote a *Centaur* which Aristotle (*Poet.* 1) calls 'a rhapsody in which all metres were mixed'. The term 'rhapsody' may imply some affinity to epic poetry; his plays were better adapted for reading than for performance (Arist. *Rh.* 3. 12) and indulged in far-fetched and artificial metaphors, some of which might almost be parodies of the style of Aeschylus, though others are picturesque. Athenaeus' description of him (13, p. 608 d) as 'especially fond of flowers' is supported by several fragments in which they are mentioned, and a passage from the *Oeneus* shows some descriptive power and feeling for beauty of colour. A few epigrammatic and even cynical lines also survive.

TGF 781–92. A. W. P.-C.

CHAEREMON (2), a Stoic, teacher of Nero, wrote, *inter alia*, on astronomy, history, and grammar (Σύνδεσμοι παραπληρωματικοί). Not extant.

CHAEREPHON, of Sphettus in Attica, an enthusiastic disciple of Socrates. He was banished by the Thirty Tyrants and returned with Thrasybulus in 403, but died before the trial of Socrates in 399. He is best known as having drawn from the Delphic oracle the saying that Socrates was the wisest of men; the story is related both by Plato and by Xenophon, and there is no reason to doubt its truth. Suidas refers to works of Chaerephon, but these were early lost.

PW iii. 2028. W. D. R.

CHAERIS, a pupil of Aristarchus, whose text of Homer he defended, wrote also a commentary on Pindar and Aristophanes, and a Τέχνη γραμματική, all lost.

CHAERONEA (Χαιρώνεια), in the Cephissus valley, was the northernmost town of Boeotia. It was subject to Orchomenus in the fifth century. It owes its fame to its position on the through route from northern Greece, and to the defeat of the Athenians and Thebans by Philip in 338 B.C., which is commemorated by a colossal stone lion. In 86 Sulla won a decisive victory there over Mithridates' armies. Plutarch was born and lived at Chaeronea, and kept alive its customs.

N. G. L. Hammond, 'The two battles of Chaeronea', *Klio* xxxi (1938), 136 ff.; G. Soteriades, *Ath. Mitt.* xxviii (1903), 301 ff.; xxx (1905), 113 ff. T. J. D.

CHALCEDON, a Megarian colony, situated across the Bosporus at seven stadias distance from Byzantium, and now occupied by the suburb of *Kadiköy*. It was reputed to have been founded seventeen years before Byzantium, and Herodotus relates how the Persian general Megabazus called it the 'city of the blind' because its founders had failed to perceive the superior advantages of the site of Byzantium. S. C.

CHALCIDICE, the southern projection of Macedonia, ending in the three promontories of Pallene, Sithonia, and Acte. Its population consisted of two tribes, the Chalcidians and the Bottiaei, who were closely related to the Greeks, and of settlers from Greece proper (mostly from Chalcis and Eretria), who colonized the promontories in the seventh and sixth centuries. The principal Greek cities were Olynthus and Potidaea (qq.v.) on the isthmus of Pallene; Scione and Mende on its sheltered south-west face; and Torone on the south-west face of Sithonia. Chalcidice in general supplied timber to Greece, and Mende exported wine.

For protection against Macedonian expansion after the Persian Wars the Chalcidian Greeks joined the Confederacy of Delos, but in 424 B.C. Olynthus and several other towns were freed from Athenian control by Brasidas, and the remainder became independent in 404. Under the leadership of Olynthus the Chalcidian cities now formed a league which was extended to comprise the Macedonian town of Pella (c. 385). The league was disbanded after a siege of Olynthus by the Spartans (383–381), but was promptly re-formed. It joined the Second Athenian Confederacy, but soon broke away, and so became an easy prey to Philip of Macedon, who transplanted many of its inhabitants and repeopled Chalcidice with Macedonian veterans.

E. Harrison, *CQ* 1912, 93, 165; A. B. West, *History of the Chalcidian League* (Madison, 1919). *See also* OLYNTHUS. M. C.

CHALCIS, the chief city of Euboea (q.v.), commanding the narrowest part of the Euripus channel. In the eighth century B.C. Chalcis planted colonies in Sicily, and in the seventh on the north Aegean shores. It was a great manufacturing and trading city, famous for its pottery and metal-work, and was a successful rival with its neighbour Eretria for control of the Lelantine plain; but in 506 it was compelled to cede part of the plain to Athenian cleruchs. The city made common cause, however, with Athens during the invasion of Xerxes. She led a revolt of Euboea against Athens (446), but was defeated and became a tributary ally until 411. A member of the second Athenian Confederacy, from 350 she was a focus of Macedonian intrigues until 338, when, by imposing a Macedonian garrison, Philip II created here one of the three 'fetters' or 'keys' of Greece. The city was a great trade centre of Hellenistic Greece, but was involved in the Macedonian and Syrian wars against Rome. For its participation in the Achaean League's struggle against Rome, Chalcis was partly destroyed (146); sixty years later it served as a base for the Pontic general Archelaus.

Strabo 10. 445–8. W. A. L.

CHALDAEI, *see* ASTROLOGY.

CHALKOTHEKE, *see* ACROPOLIS.

CHALYBES, a people of the south-east coast of the Euxine, famed in Greek legend as the first workers of iron, which from early times they sent southward across Asia Minor and westward to the Aegean. Geographical sources locate them at various points from Paphlagonia to Colchis. Xenophon and Strabo appear to place them among the mountain tribes south of Trapezus, but both also mention other Chalybes near Cerasus who worked iron mines. The traveller W. J. Hamilton saw ancient iron workings near this spot. T. R. S. B.

CHAMAELEON of Heraclea Pontica, Peripatetic writer, perhaps Theophrastus' contemporary; no biographical details exist. C. wrote works on satyric drama and comedy, and studies of a number of early poets, probably including Sophocles and Euripides, deducing biographical data from their works and references to them in comedy. These works, which were anecdotal and uncritical, are often cited by Athenaeus. His philosophical writings (Προτρεπτικός, Περὶ μέθης, Περὶ ἡδονῆς (this last attributed to Theophrastus), Περὶ θεῶν) closely followed the Aristotelian tradition.

Fragments in E. Köpke, *De Cham. Heracleota* (1856); additions listed by Wendling, *PW*, s.v. F. W. W.

CHAONES, *see* EPIRUS.

CHAOS. 'The very first of all Chaos came into being', says Hesiod (*Theog.* 116); it is noteworthy that he implies by the verb (γένετο, not ἦν) that it did not exist from everlasting. What it was like he does not say; the name clearly means 'gaping void'. Later, presumably influenced by the ὁμοῦ πάντα of Anaxagoras (q.v.), it is described (Ov. *Met.* 1. 5 ff.) as a mixture of the 'seeds' (*semina*) or potentialities of all kinds of matter. H. J. R.

CHARAX of Pergamum, living probably late in the period between Nero and the 6th c. A.D., published a World History in forty books, the Ἑλληνικά including at least ten books on Greek saga in Euhemeristic and allegorical fashion; Roman history began in bk. 12, with a second *syntaxis* for the Empire. He also wrote Χρονικά.

FGrH ii. A, 482; C, 312. A. H. McD.

CHARES (1), Athenian general and *condottiere* who after 366 B.C. was engaged in various successful wars for Athens. In 357, after obtaining the surrender of the Chersonesus from Cersobleptes (q.v.), he became commander in the Social War in succession to Chabrias, but went off to join the rebellious satrap Artabazus (q.v.). After the peace (355) he accused his colleagues, and became one of the military leaders against Philip, fighting at Olynthus, in Thrace, at Byzantium, at Chaeronea. His surrender being demanded by Alexander (335), he escaped to Sigeum, and in 332 he commanded in Mytilene on the Persian side. He died soon after, probably in Sigeum.

Prosop. Att. 15292. H. W. Parke, *Greek Mercenary Soldiers* (1933). V. E.

CHARES (2), of Mytilene, Alexander's chamberlain, wrote a history of him such as a chamberlain would write, full of court ceremonial and personal gossip; but he probably witnessed the attempt to introduce *proskynesis* (prostration as a sign of obeisance), which he described. *See* ALEXANDER (3), Bibliography, Ancient Sources. W. W. T.

CHARES (3), a writer of Γνῶμαι, from which over fifty lines are preserved, in a mutilated state, in a papyrus of the early third century B.C.

Powell and Barber, *New Chapters* i. 18.

CHARIDEMUS (4th c. B.C.), Euboean mercenary leader. He fought alternately for the Athenians, whose citizenship he gained, and for their enemy, the Thracian king Cotys (*c.* 360 B.C.). Having joined the satraps' revolt (362), he again went to Cotys, and after his murder he supported Cotys' young son Cersobleptes, whose sister he married. He was, however, highly honoured by Athens for helping to restore the Chersonesus to Chares. Expelled from Thrace by Philip of Macedon, he was Athenian general again, but met with little success. After Chaeronea, he was to be surrendered to Alexander (335), but escaped and entered Persian service. He is said to have been executed by Darius for his outspokenness (333).

Prosop. Att. 15380. H. W. Parke, *Greek Mercenary Soldiers* (1933). V. E.

CHARISIUS, FLAVIUS SOSIPATER (late 4th c. A.D.), African grammarian. His *Ars grammatica* is a compilation and alongside of elementary material contains sections copied from learned sources which he names (e.g. Remmius Palaemon, Julius Romanus) and from which he took citations of Ennius, Lucilius, Cato, etc. It is to these borrowings that his work owes its value. Of the original five books, the first lacks its introduction, the fourth (dealing with style and metre) has gaps, and the fifth has to be pieced together from various sources. H. Keil's edition (*Gramm. Lat.* i. 1–296; 534–65) is now superseded by that of K. Barwick (1925).

Cf. Teuffel, § 419, 1–2; Schanz–Hosius, § 833. J. F. M.

CHARITES, goddesses personifying charm, grace, and beauty. Like the Nymphs and the Horae, the C. are originally indefinite in number and stand for the joy and beauty produced by the blessings of fertile nature and by other things that evoke spontaneous emotion of pleasure. They make roses grow (Anacr. 44. 1 Bergk), they have myrtles and roses as attributes, and the flowers of Spring belong to them (*Cypria* ap. Ath. 15. 682 e). Their varying names bespeak their qualities: *Thaleia*, the Flowering; *Auxo*, the Grower; *Kale*, the Beautiful; *Euphrosyne*, Joy; *Aglaia*, the Radiant, etc. In their further development C. reflect the development of the truly Greek notion of *charis*. As representatives of beauty and grace they are naturally connected in mythology with Aphrodite (Paus. 6. 24. 7), but they are also present at all divine and human celebrations where Olympian joy prevails. They bestow their qualities of beauty and charm, on the one hand physical beauty (*Anth. Pal.* 7. 60), on the other intellectual, artistic, and moral 'wisdom, beauty, and glory' (Pind. *Ol.* 14. 6). In the Hellenistic poet Hermesianax, Peitho (q.v.), Persuasion, becomes one of the Charites. C. are fond of

poetry, singing, and dance (Hes. *Th.* 64; Theog. 15) and perform at the wedding of Peleus and Thetis. χάρις is, however, not only grace but also favour and gratitude for favour. In Athens, statues of benefactors and decrees in their honour were placed in the precinct of Demos and Charites (W. S. Ferguson, *Hellenistic Athens*, 212, 238), and Aristotle says that 'the sanctuary of the C. is placed in a prominent position' so that those seeing it may be reminded to requite one another's benefits (ἀνταπόδοσις, sc. χάριτος, *Eth. Nic.* 5. 1133ᵃ3).

Charites are always daughters of Zeus, but their mothers vary. From Hesiod on (*Th.* 907) their usual number is three. They play secondary parts in many myths and are connected with many divinities. Their most important cults were in Orchomenus, Paphos, Athens, and Sparta (Paus. 9. 35). Statues of C., shown as draped female figures, were seen in many archaic and classical sanctuaries. The type of three nude C., known through countless Roman copies, may go back to a famous Hellenistic painting. The Charites were Latinized as *Gratiae*.

S. Gsell, in Dar.–Sag., s.v. 'Gratiae'. G. Rodenwaldt, *JRS* 1938, 60. G. M. A. H.

CHARITON, author of a Greek novel called *Chaereas and Callirhoe* (Τὰ περὶ Χαιρέαν καὶ Καλλιρόην), describes himself as a native of Aphrodisias and secretary to the orator Athenagoras. The names of the author, his birthplace, and his employer are so closely relevant to his story that all have been suspected; there is, however, inscriptional evidence for the names Chariton and Athenagoras at Aphrodisias in Caria. Papyrus fragments date C. not later than the second century A.D., and the introduction of a genuine historical character (Hermocrates) confirms his position as the earliest extant Greek novelist.

Chaereas and Callirhoe, in the novel, are married at Syracuse; but soon after, in a fit of jealousy, Chaereas strikes his wife so severely that she is taken for dead and duly buried. Tomb-robbers find her alive, take her to Miletus, and sell her as a slave. For the sake of Chaereas' child she consents to marry her master, Dionysius. Chaereas, in the course of his search, is himself captured and enslaved. His master competes with Dionysius for the affections of Callirhoe, and the Persian king, asked to arbitrate, joins the competition. News of the revolt of Egypt separates the suitors. Chaereas escapes and joins the Egyptians, whose fleet he leads to victory. He captures the women of the Persian court, including Callirhoe, with whom, in spite of the defeat of the Egyptian army, he sails back to Syracuse and lives happily ever after.

Chariton's style, though rhetorical, is simpler than that of most of the novelists. He introduces a number of Homeric tags and quotes or reflects New Comedy on occasion; but he tells a complicated story with commendable clarity and does not indulge in irrelevant discussions.

Text: W. E. Blake (1938). Commentary: J. P. D'Orville (1750). Translation: W. E. Blake (1939). Style and diction: St. Heibges, *De clausulis Charitoneis* (1911) (full bibliography in Blake's edition). Life and work: A. Calderini, *Le avventure di Cherea e Calliroe* (1913); B. E. Perry, *AJPhil.* 1930. See also under NOVEL, GREEK. R. M. R.

CHARMADAS (fl. *c.* 107 B.C.), member of the New Academy and pupil of Carneades. Sextus Empiricus describes him as having founded, with Philon of Larissa, the Fourth Academy. We learn from Cicero that he attacked the ordinary schools of rhetoric as Plato had done in the *Phaedrus*.

PW iii. 2172. W. D. R.

CHARMIDES (d. 403 B.C.), an Athenian of noble family, nephew and ward of Critias, uncle of Plato, and member of the Socratic circle. He is mentioned in Pl. *Symp.* 222 b, *Prt.* 315 a, Xen. *Mem.* 3. 6. 1, 7. 1–9, and plays a large part in the Platonic dialogue that bears his name. According to Xen. (*Mem.* 3. 7) he was encouraged by Socrates to take up political life. He assisted Critias in the oligarchic revolution of 404 and fell with him in battle in 403, when the democrats returned under Thrasybulus.

PW iii. 2174. W. D. R.

CHARMS, *see* AMULETS.

CHARON (1), in Greek mythology, the aged ferryman in Hades who for an obolus conveyed the shades of the dead across the rivers of the lower world. As a fee for C. the Greeks used to put a coin into the mouth of the dead. He is first mentioned in the *Minyad* and by Aeschylus (*Sept.* 842) and introduced by Aristophanes in the *Ranae* (183). In art he is first seen on a terra-cotta of the sixth century B.C. He was painted by Polygnotus in Delphi (Paus. 10. 28. 1) and is often shown on white-ground *lecythi.* The Etruscans knew a demon *Charun* who is perhaps a hellenized native hammer-god. Virgil's famous description of C. (*Aen.* 6. 298–315) embodies some Etruscan features.

O. Waser, *Charon, Charun, Charos* (1898); F. De Ruyt, *Charun* (1934). G. M. A. H.

CHARON (2), son of Pythocles, of Lampsacus, reputed born under Darius, and alive 'in the Persian War' (Suidas) is quoted for Themistocles' arrival in Persia (465–464 B.C.), and as an earlier contemporary of Herodotus, and (like Hellanicus) as his model. But neither Herodotus nor Thucydides seems to use him. Plutarch, criticizing Herodotus, treats C. as independent and trustworthy. He wrote Περσικά, Ἑλληνικά, and other descriptions of peoples and cities, including his birthplace (Ὧροι Λαμψακηνῶν); on a *Journey beyond the Pillars of Heracles*; and on *Magistrates of Lacedaemon*, perhaps chronological. Fragments illustrate his concise descriptions and narratives, his interest in romances, local legends, and folk-lore. He thus stands between the 'older historians'(Dion. Hal. *Thuc.* 5) and the rationalized history of Herodotus. Unlike Dionysius of Miletus, he attempted Ἑλληνικά as well as Περσικά; unlike Hellanicus, a general history of the Greeks. He stands to Sparta and Crete as Hellanicus to Athens and Argos. But he wrote neither chronology and literary history like Damastes, nor technology like Hippias (q.v. 2).

FHG i. 32–5, ii. 627–8; Jacoby, *Stud. Ital.* N.S. xv (1898), 207; L. Pearson, *Early Ionian Historians* (1939), ch. iv. J. L. M.

CHARONDAS, the lawgiver of his native town Catana, and other Chalcidic colonies, especially Rhegium. He is often associated with Zaleucus (q.v.), but he lived later, probably in the sixth century B.C. Aristotle emphasizes the precision of his laws, but he may have included later measures under the name of Charondas. His laws were plainly much concerned with family right, but they seem to have embraced almost all departments of life. We do not know whether he established a new constitution, but he certainly was an aristocrat.

Aristotle, *Politics*, passim; Diodorus, 12. 11–19. Adcock, *CHJ* ii (1927), 95 ff.; Mühl, *Klio* xxii (1929) 105 ff., 432 ff. V. E.

CHARYBDIS, a sort of whirlpool or maelstrom in a narrow channel of the sea (later identified with the Straits of Messina, where there is nothing of the kind), opposite Scylla (q.v.; *Od.* 12. 101 ff.); it sucks in and casts out the water three times a day and no ship can possibly live in it. Odysseus, carried towards it by a current when shipwrecked, escapes by clinging to a tree which grows above it and dropping into the water when it is cast out (432 ff.).

Hence proverbially, a serious danger, as Horace, *Carm.* 1. 27. 19; Augustine, *In Evang. Iohan.* 36. 9. H. J. R.

CHATTI, a powerful German tribe who inhabited the wooded, hilly country of the upper Weser basin, into which they moved *c.* 100 B.C. from lands on the Ruhr.

On the migration eastwards of the Suebi they expanded into the Main valley and across the Taunus. They joined with the Cherusci in the rising against Varus, and Germanicus in revenge destroyed their chief town, Mattium (probably the Altenburg, by Metze-Niedenstein). After the recall of Germanicus they fell out with the Cherusci and were mainly responsible for their permanent eclipse. A sub-tribe, the Mattiaci, which had established itself around Wiesbaden, made terms with Rome, but the Chatti themselves were a constant menace. Domitian drove them from the Taunus (A.D. 83 and 89) and created the Roman *limes* to guard it. The Chatti again made raids in 162 and 170, and fought Caracalla in 213. The Alamanni drove them out of the Main basin and thereafter they are not mentioned, but it is possible that they joined the Franks in their wars with the Empire. It is generally held that the Hassi (Hessi) mentioned by St. Boniface and Einhard are their descendants.

L. Schmidt, *Geschichte der deutschen Stämme* ii² (1915), 347–66. O. B.

CHAUCI. The Chauci (Maiores and Minores), one of the chief West German tribes at the time of the Augusto-Tiberian wars, occupied the coastlands between Ems and Elbe, and a wide stretch of territory inland. The coast-dwellers inhabited artificial hillocks in the marshes (Plin. *HN* 16. 2 f.). The Chauci became clients of Rome in A.D. 5, but by 41 they had regained their independence, and in 41 and 47 they made raids on the Gallic coast; in 69–70 they helped Civilis (q.v.). It is thought that at a later date they became merged with the Saxons. O. B.

CHERSONESUS. (*a*) The *Thracian Chersonesus* or Gallipoli peninsula. This territory had a double importance in Greek history, as a wheat-growing district which produced a surplus for export, and more especially because it lay on a main passage between Europe and Asia. It was occupied in the eighth and seventh centuries by settlers from Miletus and other Ionian towns, the chief colonies being Cardia (near the Bulair isthmus) and Sestos (q.v.), at the principal crossing-point of the Dardanelles. It passed into the hands of the elder Miltiades, probably by arrangement between Pisistratus and the native Thracian population, for whose protection he fortified the Bulair isthmus (*c.* 560 B.C.). It remained in the possession of his family until 493, when the younger Miltiades (q.v.), who had held the peninsula as a vassal of King Darius, abandoned it to the Persians. After the Persian Wars it was at once brought into the Delian League by the Athenians, who established colonies at Sestos, Callipolis, and elsewhere (*c.* 450). After a period of Spartan domination (404–386) the Athenians recovered control, but had some difficulty in keeping out the Thracian dynasts, and in 338 they ceded the peninsula to Philip of Macedon. After passing through the hands of various Hellenistic rulers, most of the Chersonese became a domain of the Pergamene kings (189). In 133 a large part of it was converted into Roman *ager publicus*, and under Augustus into an imperial estate.

(*b*) The *Tauric Chersonesus* or Crimea. The main attractions of the Crimea to the Greeks were the fisheries of the Cimmerian Bosporus (Straits of Kertch), the corn-lands of the interior, and the partial protection which its peninsular situation gave against the mainland peoples of Russia. It was colonized by Milesians and other Ionians in the seventh century. The principal settlement was Panticapaeum on the Bosporus. In 438 most of the Chersonese came under the rule of a dynasty of Thracian stock but of Hellenic culture, under whom it attained great prosperity as a granary of Greece (*see* SPARTOCIDS).

(*c*) The *city of Chersonesus*, situated on the Crimean Riviera near Sevastopol, in a vine-growing district. This Milesian colony was refounded at some later date by Dorians from Heraclea Pontica. After a long period of independence it sought protection from Mithridates VI against Scythian inroads (c. 115 B.C.), and from his death in 63 B.C. until the third century it remained in the hands of his descendants, who held it as vassals of Rome. Nero provided it with a Roman garrison, and Hadrian gave it further protection by means of a wall across the Crimea. It remained an outpost of Greek civilization until the thirteenth century.

E. H. Minns, *Scythians and Greeks* (1913), 493–553. S. Casson, *Macedonia, Thrace and Illyria* (1926), 210–28. M. C.

CHERUSCI, a German tribe on the middle Weser. In A.D. 4 Tiberius incorporated them in the Empire as *foederati*; troops were recruited from them, and members of their ruling house, including Arminius, were made Roman citizens. The Cherusci headed the rising of A.D. 9 and after the destruction of Varus' army they maintained their ascendancy. Arminius was able to meet Germanicus in open battle and inflict heavy loss upon him, and to defeat King Maroboduus (q.v.). The Romans, however, fomented the jealousies in the Cheruscan royal house, and Arminius gradually lost power. The Cherusci were also weakened by internal strife and protracted wars with the Chatti, and the Chauci seized much of their land. Rome furnished them with a king in 47; another of their kings, Chariomerus, driven out by the Chatti because of his pro-Roman policy, was befriended by Domitian. The Cherusci then disappear from history. O. B.

CHILDREN. The role of children in the religious life of antiquity was not inconsiderable, no doubt partly because of their sexual purity (see E. Fehrle, *Die kultische Keuschheit* (1908–10), 112). Hence also in magic the prescription of child-mediums (*PGM* 5. 1; S.H.A. *Did. Iul.* 7. 10; in black magic, child victims, Hor. *Epod.* 5. 12 ff.; Lucan 6. 710). In family cult, an unmarried daughter would on occasion sing or lead off the hymn at the beginning of a symposium, when the third libation was poured (Aesch. *Ag.* 243 ff.). In like manner, after a Roman family dinner, one of the children would announce that the portion of food offered to the household gods was acceptable ('deos propitios', Servius on *Aen.* 1. 730; more in W. Warde Fowler in Hastings, *ERE* iii. 545). This was readily extended to public cult. Apart from the common occurrence of choirs of boys, girls, or both (Fehrle, loc. cit.), a striking instance is the ceremonial of the Arrhephoroi at Athens, wherein little girls, after long preparation, were entrusted with the carrying of very sacred objects from the Acropolis to the temple of Aphrodite in the Gardens (Paus. 1. 27. 3, cf. L. Deubner, *Attische Feste*, 9 ff.). Cf. also the ritual at Brauron (*see* ARTEMIS). That the vestals (q.v.) develop out of the services of young daughters in domestic hearth-cult is practically certain. Generally speaking, the presence of a παῖς ἀμφιθαλής, *puer patrimus et matrimus*, was necessary for all manner of rites, public and private, as diverse as a Roman marriage and the cutting of the olive-garlands at Olympia. H. J. R.

CHILDREN'S SONGS, GREEK. Pollux (9. 123) gives a list of eighteen παιδιαί, children's songs often accompanied with some sort of action, and adds details about χαλκῆ μυῖα, a kind of Blind Man's Buff, χελιχελώνη a kind of Prisoner's Base, and (9. 113) χυτρίνδα, a kind of Catch. Another such game was ἄνθεμα (Ath. 629 c).

Diehl, *Anth. Lyr. Graec.* ii. 202–4; J. M. Edmonds, *Lyra Graeca* iii. 536–43. C. M. B.

CHILDREN'S SONGS, LATIN. Children's singing-games and nursery songs, such as those of English origin published by Cecil Sharp and Alice Gomme in recent years, must have been known to children throughout the ages, and there can be no doubt that songs were sung to children, and by children, in Latin as in any other language, but they have suffered the fate of other childish things at the hands of grown-up *littérateurs*. Our informa-

tion about Latin songs is very meagre. From a scholium on Persius (3. 16) it appears that nurses used to sing *lalla, lalla* as a lullaby to squalling children who refused to go to sleep, and references elsewhere to the way in which nurses talk to babies tell us no more than we should have known without them. The ditty (*puerorum nenia*) used by children playing King-of-the-castle is quoted by Horace (*Epist.* 1. 1. 59–63) and the scholium gives a fuller version of the words: 'rex erit qui recte faciet; qui non faciet, non erit.' Another quotation ('habeat scabiem quisquis ad me uenerit nouissimus') apropos of a tag in the *Ars poetica* (417) seems to have a similar origin. The 'ancient lays' sung at banquets by *pueri modesti* (Varro ap. Non. 76) are obviously not to be classed as children's songs. A. L. P.

CHILON (Χίλων), Spartan ephor (556/5 B.C.), was the first to yoke the ephors alongside the kings (Diog. Laert. 1. 68). The statement that he aided King Anaxandridas to overthrow the tyrannies at Sicyon and Athens (*PRyl.* 18) seems impossible on chronological grounds. He is credited by modern scholars with a stricter enforcement of the Spartan training and a change in Sparta's foreign policy. Universally accepted as one of the 'Seven Sages' (Plato, *Prt.* 343 a), he was worshipped as a hero at Sparta, but mainly for his political services (Paus. 3. 16. 4).

G. Dickins, *JHS* 1912, 17 ff.; J. Wells, *Studies in Herodotus* (1923), 44–54; V. Ehrenberg, *Neugründer des Staates* (1925), 7–54. A. M. W.

CHIMAERA, properly 'she-goat'; a triple-bodied monster, 'lion before, serpent behind, she-goat in the middle' (*Il.* 6. 181), of divine race (Hesiod, *Theog.* 319 ff., explains that it was the offspring of Typhon and Echidna) and fire-breathing, slain by Bellerophon (q.v.). In art, the goat is represented by the head and neck of one protruding from the creature's back, as in the famous bronze Chimaera at Florence (*CAH*, vol. i of plates, pp. 336–7). This is so oddly inorganic as to suggest an early misunderstanding of some kind, and there is much to be said for the theory of Anne Roes (*JHS* liv. (1934), 21 ff.) that originally (in Oriental art) it had wings ending in a goat-like head, a type known to exist (ibid. 23 and illustrations there). H. J. R.

CHIONIDES, called by Suidas πρωταγωνιστὴς τῆς ἀρχαίας κωμῳδίας and dated by him eight years before the Persian War, i.e. 487–486 B.C., when he probably gained the prize at the first official competition in 486. When Aristotle says (*Poet.* 3. 1448[a]33) that Chionides and Magnes came some time *after* Epicharmus (fl. 487), he probably means no more than that Epicharmus was an older contemporary of theirs. Three fragments of his Ἥρωες survive (Poll., Suid.). The genuineness of his Πτωχοί was doubted even in antiquity (Ath. 4. 137 e, 14. 638 d). Suidas mentions also a Πέρσαι ἢ Ἀσσύριοι. Wilamowitz (*Hermes* ix. 335 ff.) believed that all three plays were the work of later writers. See COMEDY, OLD, paras. 2 and 3.

FCG i. 27 ff.; *CAF* i. 4–7. M. P.

CHIOS, a large island lying off the Erythraean peninsula, roughly oblong in shape, but narrowing towards the centre through the broad indentation on the lengthy western side. The mountains of the north give way to fertile plains in the south. Chios was renowned in antiquity for its wine, corn, figs, and gum-mastic. The city of Chios, the focus of political, economic, and cultural life, was founded at the finest harbour of the eastern seaboard, and became highly prosperous. From the time of Homer (whose birthplace it claimed to be) Chios had a distinguished literary tradition, and schools of artists working in stone and metal flourished on the island.

After its occupation by Ionian settlers Chios was a consistent ally of Miletus against Phocaea, Erythrae, and

Samos. Incorporated in the Persian Empire under Cyrus, it fought heroically in the Ionian Revolt, and was devastated after Lade. As a member of the Delian Confederacy, Chios remained loyal until 413; Athenian efforts to retake the city proved ineffective. It was pro-Athenian during the fourth century B.C. until the Social War (357–355), which resulted in a temporary Carian domination. Its relations with Rome were cordial; in 86 it was sacked by Zenobius, Mithridates' general, the inhabitants being transported to Pontus. Sulla restored them to their homes, and Chios enjoyed the privileges of a free city under the Empire, until these were suspended by Vespasian.

L. Bürchner, *PW*, s.v. 'Chios'. D. E. W. W.

CHIRON (X[ε]ίρων), *see* CENTAURS, para. 2.

CHITON (χιτών), *see* DRESS, para. 2.

CHLAMYS, *see* DRESS, para. 2, and EPHEBI.

CHLOË, i.e. 'green', title of Demeter as goddess of the young green crops. She had a shrine near the Acropolis at Athens (Paus. 1. 22. 3) and a festival, the Chloia, perhaps on Thargelion 6 (Deubner, *Attische Feste*, 67).

CHOERILUS (1), an Athenian tragic poet, according to Suidas (s.v.) wrote plays from 523 B.C. onwards, competed against Aeschylus and Pratinas, and, as some said, made innovations in the tragic mask and costume. Only one of his plays, the *Alope*, is known by name. One or two bold metaphors are quoted from him (*TGF* 719–20). He is probably not the Choerilus described in a line of an unknown writer (quoted by Plotius *de metris*) as 'King among the Satyrs'. A. W. P.-C.

CHOERILUS (2) **OF SAMOS,** epic poet; admirer and friend of Herodotus; employed by Lysander to celebrate his exploits; ended his days in Macedon, at the court of Archelaus; author of a *Persica*, on the Athenian victory over Xerxes, which was decreed at Athens to be recited with Homer's poetry, and of a *Samiaca*; several times cited by Aristotle. *See* EPIC CYCLE.

EGF 265–72. Criticism: A. F. Näke, *Choerili Samii quae supersunt . . .* (1817). W. F. J. K.

CHOERILUS (3) **OF IASUS,** epic poet; travelled with Alexander the Great; paid to celebrate him; a bad poet (Hor. *Epist.* 2. 1. 232–4; id. *ArsP.* 357–8; Porphyrion ad loc.).

EGF 308–11

CHOËS (Xóες), *see* ANTHESTERIA.

CHOLIAMBUS = scazon; *see* METRE, GREEK, II (3).

CHOREGIA. The main part of the expense of the production of dithyramb, tragedy, and comedy at the Dionysiac festivals at Athens was laid upon individual citizens of sufficient wealth. For dithyramb these *choregi* were chosen by the ten tribes (Arg. ii to Dem. *Meid.*, cf. Ar. *Av.* 1403–4); for tragedy and comedy by the *Archon Eponymus* (Arist. *Ath. Pol.* 56); about the middle of the fourth century B.C. the appointment for comedy was transferred to the tribes (ibid.). No one could be obliged to serve as *choregus* until a year had elapsed after his last period of office (Dem. *Lept.* 8), but any citizen might volunteer to serve (Lys. 21. 1–6; Aeschin. *In Tim.* 11–12; Harp. s.v. ὅτι νόμος). No one under forty years of age might be *choregus* to a dithyrambic chorus of boys. The smaller expenses of dithyrambs performed at the Thargelia, Panathenaea, and Hephaestea were also laid upon individual *choregi* (Antiphon 6. 11, Lys. 21. 2) and the same system was applied to some other entertainments, such as the exhibition of pyrrhic dancers (Isae. 5. 36). *Choregia* for the men's dithyramb, which involved a

chorus of fifty members and the most highly skilled flute-players, was much more expensive than for tragedy; the boys' dithyramb and comedy might cost less than either (Lys. 14. 29, 42; 21. 1–5).

Choregia at the Great Dionysia probably began shortly before 500 B.C. for dithyramb and tragedy, and about 486 for comedy. The dates for the Lenaea are unknown. For a few years from 405 onwards, when there may have been a lack of rich men, *choregia* at the Great Dionysia was shared between two *choregi* (Schol. Ar. *Ran.* 404); this arrangement probably terminated in the city about 394. (Such *synchoregia* at certain Rural Dionysia is attested by several inscriptions of later dates in the fourth century). About 318 a State-appointed *agonothetes* was instituted to manage the festivals and share the expense with the State, which is frequently named in inscriptions as *choregus* (ὁ δῆμος ἐχορήγει), but *choregi* reappear, with or without an *agonothetes*, in inscriptions of the first century A.D. (See Haigh, op. cit. inf., 54, 55.)

Dithyrambic poets were assigned to the several *choregi* by lot, and the *choregi* then drew lots for the order of choice of a flute-player—a matter of great importance (Dem. *Meid.* 13–14; Antiphon 6. 11). It is probable that tragic and comic poets were also assigned by lot, but there is no record. *Choregi* had nothing to do with the selection, payment, or dresses of actors (see Haigh, op. cit., pp. 57 ff.), but they selected the members of the chorus, with the help of an agent (χορολέκτης, Arist. *Pol.* 3. 3), provided a room for their practices, and paid the expense of their costumes and training (Arg. i to Dem. *Meid.*; Pseudo-Xen. *Ath. Pol.* 1. 13, etc.). As it was a misfortune for a *choregus* to be assigned to a bad poet, so it was important for a poet to have a liberal *choregus*, since it depended upon him whether a play was well or badly presented in respect of costumes, mute characters (attendants, etc.) and other additions to the setting (παραχορηγήματα). An ambitious or public-spirited *choregus*, like Nicias, might provide a magnificent spectacle and so win the victory; a mean one, hiring cheap costumes, could ruin a play (Antiphanes fr. 204; Dem. *Meid.* 16, 61; Arist. *Eth. Nic.* 4. 6; Pollux 7. 78), though a negligent *choregus* might be brought to book by the archon (Xen. *Hieron* 9. 4).

The prize won by a successful *choregus* for dithyramb was a tripod, which he subsequently dedicated, often as a part of a more elaborate monument—the extant monuments of Lysicrates and Thrasyllus are instances—and the locality where most of the Dionysiac tripods were collected was named 'the Tripods'. Those gained at the Thargelia were erected in the precinct of Apollo Pythius (Paus. 1. 20. 1, etc.). The *choregus* for comedy did not receive the tripod, nor, almost certainly, did the *choregi* for tragedy; they erected tablets commemorating their victory, and some of these survive. There remain also some laudatory inscriptions erected by fellow-tribesmen or citizens in honour of public-spirited *choregi*. The choregic system was in use in many cities besides Athens, and a large number of inscriptions testify to its continuance in these to the end of the second century B.C., and in some much later. *See also* LITURGY.

A. Brunck, *Inscriptiones Graecae ad Choregiam pertinentes* (Diss. Philol. Halenses vii (1886)); E. Reisch, *De musicis Graecorum certaminibus* (1885) and art. Χορηγία in *PW* iii. 2 (1899); E. Capps, *Introduction of Comedy into the City Dionysia* (1903); A. Wilhelm, *Urkunden dramatischer Aufführungen in Athen* (1906); A. E. Haigh, *Attic Theatre*[3] (1907), Ch. 2 and App. B; K. J. Maidment in *CQ* xxix (1935), 1 ff.; A. W. Pickard-Cambridge, *Dithyramb, Tragedy and Comedy* (1937). A. W. P.-C.

CHORUS, *see* TRAGEDY, COMEDY, DRAMA (ROMAN).

CHREIA, a collection of witty or clever sayings, so called because designed for utility (χρησίμου τινὸς ἕνεκα Hermog. *Prog.* c. 3); one of the varieties of *progymnasmata* (q.v.). Such collections were already being made in the fourth century B.C., e.g. by Theocritus of Chios and Demetrius of Phalerum. Some biographies of philosophers, e.g. that of Diogenes by Diogenes Laertius, consist largely of *Chreiai*. The greatest extant collection is the *Gnomologium Vaticanum*, published in *Wien. Stud.* ix–xi (1887–9). The *Chreia* of Machon (q.v.) is a collection of scurrilities. J. D. D.

CHREMONIDES (fl. 270–240 B.C.), Athenian nationalist statesman, pupil of Zeno. In 267–266 he carried a decree by which Athens joined the Peloponnesian anti-Macedonian coalition, supported by Ptolemy (*IG* ii². 1. 686 and 687). The subsequent war, named after him (Ath. 6. 250 f.), ended with the surrender of Athens in 263–262. He found refuge with Ptolemy, and as Egyptian admiral was defeated off Ephesus by Agathostratus of Rhodes (258); he was still admiral c. 240.

K. J. Beloch, *Griech. Gesch.* iv (1928); W. W. Tarn, *JHS* 1934. F. W. W.

CHRISTUS PATIENS, a play in 2,610 verses describing the Passion of Our Lord, bearing the name of Gregory the Nazianzene, but probably written by a Byzantine of the eleventh or twelfth century. It contains a very great number of lines from Euripides, and some from Aeschylus and Lycophron. It is of doubtful use for the textual criticism of Euripides (see Murray's Euripides, O.C.T. vol. i, p. viii), but portions of the lost end of the *Bacchae* have been recovered from it (O.C.T. vol. iii).

Text: J. G. Brambs (Teubner, 1885). J. D. D.

CHRYSEIS (Χρυσηΐς), in mythology, daughter of Chryses, priest of Apollo at Chryse. She was taken prisoner and given to Agamemnon as his gift of honour (γέρας). On her refusal to let her father ransom her, Apollo, at Chryses' prayer, sent a plague on the Greek camp, which was not stayed till she was returned to him. Agamemnon compensated himself by taking Briseis (q.v.) from Achilles, thus starting the quarrel between them (*Il.* 1. 11 ff.). In a late legend (Hyg. *Fab.* 121) she has a son by Agamemnon. H. J. R.

CHRYSIPPUS (c. 280–207 B.C.), son of Apollonius of Soli (Cilicia), successor of Cleanthes as head of the Stoa. He came to Athens about 260 and there first attended the lectures of Arcesilaus, then head of the Academy. From him he got the training in logic and dialectic which he later used to great advantage in fighting the scepticism of Arcesilaus and the Middle Academy. He was converted to Stoicism by Cleanthes, whom he succeeded in 232. He devoted his life to elaborating the Stoic system in almost innumerable works and to defending it against the attacks of the Academy. He was so successful that his philosophy became identified with Stoic orthodoxy, and obscured that of his predecessors, from whom he differed in many points, especially in his logic and theory of knowledge. The catalogue of his works given by Diog. Laert. 7. 189–202 is not completely preserved.

Fragments: von Arnim, *SVF* ii. 1–348; iii. 3–205; Diogenes Laertius 7. 179–202; M. Pohlenz, 'Zenon und Chrysipp', *Nachricht. Götting. Gesellsch. Fachgruppe* i, N.F. ii, no. 9. *PW* ii. 2502. K. von F.

CHRYSOGONUS, LUCIUS CORNELIUS, Sulla's favourite freedman, placed the name of the murdered Sex. Roscius on the list of the proscriptions in order to purchase his confiscated property and afterwards accused Roscius' son of parricide (*see* ROSCIUS 1).

F. Münzer, *PW* iv. 1281.

CHRYSOTHEMIS, see AGAMEMNON.

CHYTROI (Χύτροι), see ANTHESTERIA.

CICERO (1), MARCUS TULLIUS, third successive bearer of the name, was born at Arpinum, 3 Jan. 106 B.C., and put to death in the proscriptions, 7 Dec. 43. His family was connected with the Marii. His mother, Helvia, was a careful housewife (*Fam.* 16. 26). His father who, being delicate, was devoted to literature rather than agriculture, took a house in the Carinae at Rome, to give his sons Marcus and Quintus (b. 102) a good education. Plutarch says C. distinguished himself at school. In these early days he began his lifelong friendship with Atticus, three years his senior, and he met Caesar (probably, J. Carcopino, *Mélanges Bidez*, 35–69) five years his junior (*Prov. Cons.* 17. 40). Though Atticus took him to the lectures of the Epicurean Phaedrus (*Fam.* 13. 1), he preferred those of the Academic Philon of Larissa (*Brut.* 306). But the residence in his father's house of Diodotus, the blind Stoic, from 87, made him familiar with Stoic tenets (*Tusc.* 5. 113, *Att.* 2. 20. 6). In 91 he assumed the *toga virilis*, and in 89 during the Social War had brief military experience on the staff of Pompeius Strabo, when doubtless he met Pompey, his junior by half a year. In Rome he attended the receptions of Scaevola the augur, and after his death those of Scaevola the Pontifex Maximus. His preparation for public life was prolonged by the troublous times. As a boy he had listened to the great orators, M. Antonius and L. Crassus; at nineteen he heard Apollonius Molon lecture in Rome. His first appearance in the senatorial courts was in a civil case, *Pro Quinctio*, in 81. His real début was a successful defence of Sex. Roscius of Ameria on a charge of parricide in 80, in which his bold invective against Chrysogonus (q.v.), Sulla's favourite, was covered by skilful flattery of Sulla. He also maintained the right of a lady of Arretium to sue and be sued, although Sulla had disfranchised her native town. In 79 he went abroad for two years (for his health, *Brut.* 314, not for fear of Sulla, as in Plut. *Cic.* 3), attended the lectures of Antiochus, Philon's successor, at Athens, and received instruction in rhetoric from Demetrius there, and at Rhodes from Molon, who cured him of a tendency to the redundant ornament of the Asiatic school. At Rhodes he must have sat under Posidonius.

2. Returning to Rome established in health, he spoke for Roscius the actor (some think it was ten years later) and pleaded other *causas nobiles* (*Brut.* 318). About this time he married Terentia; their daughter Tullia was probably born in 76, when his public career began with the quaestorship. He was an Italian *eques* and the *Equites* were then estranged from the *Optimates*. In 75 he was sent to Lilybaeum under the good governor Sex. Peducaeus. A later governor was the infamous Verres, who systematically robbed the Sicilians, relying on bribery of his future judges and the support of the Metelli. The scandal created by his behaviour, and the energy of C. in securing evidence and obtaining a conviction nine days after the opening of the trial (70), led to the passing of the *Lex Aurelia* which left to senators only a third of the membership of the courts. In this case C. established his equality with Hortensius as leader of the Roman Bar. Of the Verrine orations he delivered only his claim to be prosecutor (*Div. Caec.*) and in substance the first pleading, but he also published his second pleading in five parts, as a damning indictment of senatorial misgovernment. Prosecution was unusual for him, and soon afterwards he defended Fonteius on a charge of misgoverning Narbonensis. In 69 he held the office of curule aedile, the expense of which he says (*Off.* 2. 59) was not great; Plutarch says the grateful Sicilians financed him. In 68 he acquired his villa at Tusculum, which, though he offered it for sale in 57, he retained till his death. In 66 he was praetor, and presided at the trial and condemnation of the historian Macer (*Att.* 1. 4. 2). He successfully defended Cluentius, charged with poisoning.

3. In his first *contio* he supported the Manilian Law to supersede Lucullus by Pompey for the Mithridatic War. He hoped to be Pompey's nominee for the consulship, and took the popular side in defending Cornelius on a charge of *maiestas*. He summoned Atticus from

Athens to assist his canvass, and to conciliate Atticus' 'noble' friends (*Att.* 1. 2. 3). But he would hardly have been elected for 63, had not his chief opponent been Catiline who, formerly a Sullan, was now dangerous from the senatorial point of view as an open advocate of *novae tabulae*. C. on the other hand, as a representative *eques*, was a safe man.

4. Once elected, he was obliged to oppose the various moves of the *populares* under the leadership of Caesar and of Crassus, who was obsessed by dislike of Pompey. C. succeeded in defeating the agrarian measures of the tribune Rullus, but was unable to prevent the condemnation of the aged senator Rabirius for the murder of Saturninus, thirty-seven years before. When Catiline was again rejected at the polls for 62 (Sept. ?), C., who knew that an armed insurrection was about to break out in Etruria, denounced Catiline to his face in the Senate on 8 Nov., and caused him to leave Rome, explaining to the people next day what had happened. By good luck, he secured from the Allobrogian envoys, then in Rome, evidence of the guilt of the chief remaining conspirators, including the praetor Lentulus, and five were arrested. C. described the conspiracy to Senate and People; on 5 Dec. the Senate met to consider their fate. Silanus, consul-elect, proposed the death penalty, Caesar confiscation of property and life imprisonment, thereby admitting that the Senate had to take action. C. (in a speech not extant) said he would execute either penalty, but Cato turned the scale in favour of death. Their execution, however, was dangerous to C., since after the condemnation of Rabirius no *popularis* would admit that C. was really authorized to execute them.

5. On 5 Jan. 62 Catiline and the rebels in the field were annihilated; but before that Metellus Nepos arrived straight from Pompey's camp and was elected tribune. He showed his hand by forbidding C. to address the people on laying down office, and in the early months of 62 continued to attack C. with Caesar's support, proposing to summon Pompey from the East. The Senate suspended both praetor and tribune; so Caesar went off to Spain and Nepos returned to Pompey. That there had been an anarchic conspiracy can hardly be doubted, for Sallust paints Catiline as black as C. does, and C. claims to have crushed it by reconciling *Equites* and Senate in a *concordia ordinum*, which, however, soon began to break up. Pompey returned and disbanded his troops before he had secured lands for them. Having, in spite of C.'s support, failed to get this by the *Lex Flavia*, he formed a secret alliance with Caesar, consul-elect for 59, and Crassus; C. was invited to join this coalition and did not finally refuse until Dec. 60 (*Att.* 2. 3. 3). This involved his retirement from public life in 59, and as he still declined appointments which would have implied submission to the Triumvirs and ensured his personal safety, his banishment by the law of the tribune Clodius followed early in 58. C. bitterly resented the apathy of the senatorial leaders and ascribed this to jealousy (*Att.* 3. 15. 2; 4. 5. 1). Soon Pompey found Clodius intolerable, and C. was recalled by law and compensated in 57.

6. He then resumed his practice at the Bar (*For Sestius, For Caelius, Against Vatinius*) and Pompey made Quintus his legate in Sardinia. But when C. gave notice of a motion in the Senate to reconsider Caesar's agrarian legislation, Caesar acted with his usual celerity. After seeing Crassus at Ravenna, he met Pompey at Luca, and the Triumvirate was patched up. C. was notified both through his brother and directly that he must submit or suffer, and in his speech *On the Consular Provinces* came to heel, eulogizing Caesar, but gratifying his animosity against Piso and Gabinius, the consuls of 58 who had helped to exile him, by proposing their recall from Macedonia and Syria. From then till the outbreak of the Civil War he was on friendly terms with Caesar, who appointed Quintus his legate, and with Pompey. But when, after the deaths of Crassus and Julia, the two became estranged, C. leant more and more to Pompey, who was driven into the arms of the *Optimates*. During these years he had to defend personal enemies, Vatinius who was acquitted and later showed gratitude, and Gabinius who was condemned; but he also had an extensive private practice. He could not save Milo from condemnation *de vi* (the speech we have is worked up for publication), but the death of Clodius relieved him of personal fears. From 52 to 46 his voice was hardly heard in the courts or Senate. In 51 very unwillingly he went as proconsul to Cilicia, where, though he had not to face a Parthian invasion, he superintended military operations on Mt. Amanus.

7. By the time of his return civil war was inevitable. After long hesitation he went to Pompey's camp, but after Pharsalus submitted to the conqueror, before whom he pleaded *For Marcellus* and *For Ligarius* in 46, *For King Deiotarus* of Galatia in 45. He had nothing to do with Caesar's murder, though, when once convinced that Caesar would not rule constitutionally but establish a despotism, he applauded the deed. After Caesar's death he became violently opposed to Caesar's pinchbeck imitator, the consul Antony, with whom, however, he was anxious not to break as late as 21 June 44 (*Fam.* 16. 23. 2). Before the end of 47 he had divorced Terentia; he does not seem to have been on good terms with her since 57, thinking her dishonest in money matters. In 46 he married his young ward Publilia, but after Tullia's death (Feb. 45) he sent her away, and refused to take her back. He then solaced himself with writing, in which he was immersed at the time of Caesar's murder.

8. On 17 July 44 he set out for Athens to visit his son, but, hearing of a meeting of the Senate called for 1 Sept., determined to return, and reached Rome on 31 Aug. Antony having attacked him in his absence on 1 Sept., he delivered the *First Philippic* as his ultimatum in Antony's absence on 2 Sept. Antony renounced his friendship, retired to Tibur to compose an invective, and delivered it on 19 Sept. The *Second Philippic*, an elaborate answer, was not delivered, but (probably) made public after Antony finally left Rome on 25 Nov. C. returned to Rome on 9 Dec. and led the Senate in opposition to Antony, delivering many speeches of which we possess twelve, until Octavian marched on Rome and assumed the consulship, 19 Aug. 43. Of the last miserable months of C.'s life we know little. On 7 Dec. 43 he bravely faced death, having been sacrificed by Octavian to the animosity of Antony.

WORKS

1. **Verse, original and translation.** *Prose translation.* An heroic poem on Marius; an early effort, for Scaevola praised it (*Leg.* 1. 1); but the fifteen lines we possess seem mature in style. We hear from Plutarch (*Cic.* 2) of a *Pontius Glaucus* in trochaic tetrameters. Of his translation of Aratus' *Phaenomena* 500 lines remain, and of his *Prognostica*, mentioned in 60 (*Att.* 2. 1. 11) and perhaps a youthful work revised, twenty-seven (see DIDACTIC POETRY, LATIN). His much derided poem on his consulship was written in 60, and that on his exile (*De Temporibus Suis*) after 57. Besides, we have numerous passages from Homer and the tragedians, metrically rendered, in his philosophical works. His frequent quotations from Ennius, Terence, and other early poets show his familiarity with the national poetry.

He tells his son (*Off.* 2. 24. 87) that at nineteen he translated Xenophon's *Oeconomicus*; he also translated Plato's *Protagoras*, and the speeches of Demosthenes for, and of Aeschines against, Ctesiphon; but the short preface to them mentions the trial of Milo and was not written before 52.

2. **Orations** (58, some incomplete, survive: about 48

are lost). *Pro Quinctio* (81). *Pro Sex. Roscio Amerino* (80), *Pro Roscio Comoedo* (77?), *In Caecilium Divinatio*, *In Verrem Act.* I, *Act.* II. i–v (70). *Pro Tullio, Pro Fonteio, Pro Caecina* (69), *Pro Lege Manilia, Pro Cluentio* (66), *Contra Rullum* I–III, *Pro C. Rabirio perduellionis reo, In Catilinam* I–IV, *Pro Murena* (63). *Pro Sulla, Pro Archia* (62). *Pro Flacco* (59), *Post reditum ad Quirites, Post reditum in Senatu, De Domo sua* (57). *De Haruspicum responso, Pro Sestio, In Vatinium, Pro Caelio, De Prov. Cons., Pro Balbo* (56). *In Pisonem* (55). *Pro Plancio, Pro Rabirio Postumo* (54). *Pro Milone* (52). *Pro Marcello, Pro Ligario*, (46). *Pro Rege Deiotaro* (45). *Philippicae* I–XIV (44–43).

3. Rhetorica. *De Inventione* (84), the first instalment of an unfinished work (he uses *Auctor ad Herennium*). *De Oratore*, three books dedicated to Quintus (55). *Oratoriae Partitiones*, a dialogue with his son (c. 54). Fragment, *De Optimo Genere Oratorum* (52). *Brutus* or *De Claris Oratoribus* (surveying the past century of oratory) and *Orator*, mainly autobiographical, both dedicated to Brutus (46). *Topica* adapted from Aristotle, and written in seven days (44).

4. Philosophica (in dialogue (q.v.) form, most fully developed in *De Leg.*). *De Republica*, six books imperfectly preserved, published in 51 (*Att.* 5. 12. 2; *Fam.* 8. 1. 5); here he seems to have used Plato, Panaetius, and Polybius. The sublime 'Dream of Scipio', with which the work ends, following the heroic soul into a future life, was alone known, till in 1820 Cardinal Mai discovered almost a third of the treatise in a fourth- or fifth-century Vatican palimpsest.

De Legibus. Three books are preserved, but Macrobius quotes from a fifth. It was probably begun in 52 (*Leg.* 2. 17. 42), but as it is not given in the list in *Div.* 2. 1, was probably not published till after his death. In 48 Matius (*Fam.* 11. 27. 5) urged him to write on philosophy. He did not begin till Feb. 45, after Tullia's death, with the lost *De Consolatione*. After Munda (17 March) he wrote *Hortensius*, adapted from Aristotle, the exhortation to the study of philosophy which so powerfully influenced St. Augustine. Then came the first draft of the *Academica* in two books. In the first (lost) Catulus expounded the position of Carneades. In the second Lucullus attacked it and C. defended suspense of judgement. Later he recast the work in four books, dedicated to Varro, of which we possess part of the first (*Academica Posteriora*) and *Lucullus* (*Academica Priora*). He must have largely followed the *Sosus* of Antiochus (*Acad.* 2. 11). The work gave him much trouble (*Att.* 13. 16; 13. 25. 3). By 29 May he had begun *De Finibus Bonorum et Malorum*, five books on views of the chief Good and chief Evil. He refuted the positions of both Epicureans and Stoics, probably using Antiochus as his authority. The work was dedicated to Brutus. *Tusculanarum Quaestionum libri quinque* grew out of discussions with Hirtius, Pansa, and Dolabella at Tusculum in 46. It is not certain what author he followed. He quotes Crantor verbatim 3. 12 and criticizes Antiochus 5. 22. Bk. I 'On fear of death'; II 'Is pain an evil?'; III and IV 'On distress and its alleviation, pain and its remedies'; V 'Virtue is sufficient for happiness'. Concurrently with these he wrote three books *De Natura Deorum*, expounding Epicurean, Stoic, and Academic theologies, following Zeno, Posidonius, and Clitomachus respectively. The Academic spokesman is careful to reconcile his philosophic scepticism with maintenance of the traditional Roman religion. To this *De Divinatione* in two books, and *De Fato*, dedicated to Hirtius, are appendixes: superstition is differentiated from religion, and determinism from fatalism. *Cato Maior*, or *De Senectute*, and *Laelius*, or *De Amicitia*, both dedicated to Atticus, were reliefs to his mind after the Ides of March. When he wrote *Paradoxa Stoicorum* is uncertain; probably parts are of different dates. *De Officiis* in three

books, in the first two of which he follows Panaetius, but not slavishly (2. 17. 60) and in the third writes independently, was dedicated to his son and completed by 5 Nov. 44. To the list the lost *Cato*, which provoked replies from Caesar and Hirtius, and the lost *De Gloria* must be added. The total output between Feb. 45 and Nov. 44 and the high quality of the work so rapidly done are astonishing.

5. Letters (931 in Tyrrell and Purser). Sixteen books *Ad Familiares*, arranged and successively published by Tiro, his freedman and literary executor. Sixteen books *Ad Atticum* covering (with gaps) the years 68 to 44. Nepos saw them, and says they almost gave a connected history of the period. But Asconius (A.D. 54) did not know them, and they are first quoted by Seneca, *c.* A.D. 62–5. What led to their publication about 60 we do not know. Petrarch in 1345 rediscovered them with the three books to Quintus, and two books of correspondence with Brutus, a mere fragment of the nine books that once existed (Nonius). The authenticity of the extant letters to Brutus (with one possible exception) has been vindicated by Purser and Sjögren; but the epistle to Octavian is spurious.

6. Cicero's verse, though derided by Juvenal (10. 122–6), is interesting for the development of the Latin hexameter. It can be claimed that he transmitted to Lucretius and Catullus the older type of Latin versification, but he was not in sympathy with contemporary Alexandrianism, the νεώτεροι (*Att.* 7. 2. 1) or *cantores Euphorionis* (*Tusc.* 3. 19. 45). Jerome (*Chron.* ad ann. Abr. 1922) says he 'emended' Lucretius' poem, about which he and his brother corresponded soon after the poet's death in 54 (*QFr.* 2. 9. 3 is unfortunately corrupt). As an orator he was supreme in the courts for years. His *copia uerborum* is sometimes excessive ('no word can be added to Cicero', Quint. *Inst.* 10. 1. 106), but his vocabulary is rich and impeccable. In passionate passages of the *Catilinarians* and *Philippics* he equals Demosthenes. When (*Phil.* 2. 119) he quotes *Cat.* 4. 2, 3, and repeats his twenty-year-old assurance that death cannot come untimely to a senator, this is surely unique in history. He himself thought the Attic style of Calvus, Caesar, and Brutus frigid and jejune, while he equally disliked the other extreme, the Asianism of Hortensius. In philosophy he only claims to be a translator (*Att.* 12. 52. 3) 'ἀπόγραφα sunt; uerba tantum adfero quibus abundo'), but more truly he is an adapter of Greek thought and often an independent critic, as of Epicurus in *Fin.* 2. From the Academy's suspense of judgement, and reliance on probability as a sufficient guarantee of truth and guide of life, he never departed. He was the first important prose author to introduce Greek philosophy to Roman readers, and he created a Latin philosophical vocabulary.

7. Of his letters nine-tenths were written unaffectedly to relations and intimate friends, without thought of publication; occasionally, when this is not so, we see the difference in the rhythmical structure (*Att.* 4. 1; *Fam.* 1. 9; letters to Appius Claudius in *Fam.* 3). He did not contemplate publication till 9 July 44 (*Att.* 16. 5. 5), and the intention was not carried out. *See* LETTERS (LATIN), paras. 2 and 3.

Cicero moulded the Latin language into an incomparably clear and effective vehicle of thought, so that, in spite of brief reactions, his style affected centuries, and his rhythms were stereotyped in the Papal Chancery (*see* RHETORIC, LATIN, para. 2). Finally Erasmus had to write his *Ciceronianus* to claim liberty to add to his vocabulary and not to use pagan terms for Christian subjects. C. constantly maintained the necessity for an orator to have a basis of literary culture (*Orator* 12) and thus strengthened his power of writing (*see* LITERARY CRITICISM, LATIN, para. 2). He was, for a Roman, unusually witty and skilled in repartee (for a specimen of *altercatio* see *Att.* 1. 16. 10), and he made enemies (Clodius and Octavian) by his smart utterances. He did not cast himself for the statesman's part, though the consulship was to him, as to all upper-class Romans, the goal of ambition, but twice in his life he had to face emergencies. He was obliged subsequently to praise his action in 63 (it was a mistake to speak of his *res gestae* to Pompey) just because it was attacked as illegal and unnecessary (*Quint. Inst.* 11. 1. 18); in rhetorical and philosophical writings he is uniformly modest, cf. *Tusc.* 4. 52. In the second crisis he staked and lost his life. Because we know so much from himself of his preliminary vacillations we are apt to forget how he acted. Quintilian quotes him as saying: 'I am not timid in facing dangers, but in attempting to guard against them.' As to his alleged 'conceit', it is only fair to quote *Planc.* 64–5 or *Att.* 4. 5. 1. Any public man whose private letters were published would be exposed as much as Cicero to the charge of insincerity. In political life he was not, *pace* Mommsen, a trimmer, but a moderate man who was loyal to the Constitution. He was not far-sighted or politically wise enough to initiate reforms himself, but he was resolute in opposing reform by violence or revolution. Nepos (*Att.* 16. 4) says of him: 'he not only foretold what happened in his lifetime, but even predicted what is taking place to-day.'

BIBLIOGRAPHY

LIFE AND WORKS: *CAH* ix (1932), chs. 11–12 (M. Cary), 15–17 (F. E. Adcock), 18 (E. E. Sikes), 19 (J. Wight Duff); x (1934), ch. 1 (M. P. Charlesworth); G. Boissier, *C. et ses amis* (1865, ed. 10, 1895, Engl. Transl. 1897); J. L. Strachan-Davidson, *C. and the Fall of the Roman Republic* (1894); E. G. Sihler, *C. of Arpinum* (U.S.A. 1914); J. C. Rolfe, *C. and His Influence* (1923); Th. Zieliński, *C. im Wandel der Jahrhunderte*⁴ (1929); G. C. Richards, *C., a Study* (1935). See also *PW* viA (1937), 827–1274, s.v. 'M. Tullius (29) Cicero' (by various authors).

TEXTS: J. G. Baiter and C. L. Kayser, *Op. Omnia*, 11 vols. (1860–9), re-ed. C. F. W. Müller, and for rhet. works G. Friedrich; also later Teubner series by new editors, with improved orthography.

Orations, O.C.T. (A. C. Clark and W. Peterson); *Asconii orationum quinque Cic. enarratio* (A. C. Clark), 1907. *Rhetorica*, O.C.T. (A. S. Wilkins). *Philosophica*, C. F. W. Müller (1898).

Letters, O.C.T. (L. C. Purser); H. Sjögren *Ad Brut.* 1910, *Ad Q.* 1911, *Ad Att.* (incomplete), 1916, Uppsala; *Ad Fam.* 1925, Teubner.

COMMENTARIES: (1) Orations, C. Halm, revised by Laubmann and Sternkopf (1886–93). G. Landgraf, *Rosc. Am.* (1914); E. Thomas, *Div. Caec.*, *Verr.* (Paris, 1894); W. Peterson, *Verr.* 1907), *Clu.* (1899); H. A. Holden, ²*Planc.* (1881), *Sest.* (1883); J. S. Reid, *Arch.* (1879), *Balb.* (1878), *Sull.* (1882), *Mil.* (1897); W. E. Heitland, *Mur.* (1875); J. C. Vollgraff, *Cael.* (1887); R. G. Austin, *Cael.* (1933); H. E. Butler and M. Cary, *Prov. Cons.* (1924); T. B. L. Webster, *Flacc.* (1931); J. E. B. Mayor, *Phil. II* (1865); J. D. Denniston, *Phil. I, II* (1926). A. C. Clark, *Mil.* (1895). (2) Rhetorica, A. S. Wilkins, *De Or.* (1881–92); J. E. Sandys, *Orator* (1885). (3) Philosophica, J. S. Reid, *Acad.* (1885); *De Fin. I, II* (1925); J. B. Mayor, *Nat. D.* (1885); J. N. Madvig, *De Fin.* (1876); W. M. L. Hutchinson, *De Fin.* (1909); T. W. Dougan and R. M. Henry, *Tusc.* 1905–34; H. A. Holden, *De Off.* 1891. (4) Letters, R. Y. Tyrrell and L. C. Purser, *The Correspondence of C.*, 6 vols.+index (1885–1933); A. Watson, *Select Letters* (1870; new ed., W. W. How and A. C. Clark, 1925–6).

TRANSLATIONS of various orations in Oxford Translation and Loeb series; *Philosophical works* (Loeb); H. Rackham, *Fin.*, *Acad.*, *Nat. Deor.*; J. S. Reid (*Fin.*, *Acad.*); J. E. King, *Tusc. Disp.*; C. W. Keyes, *Rep.*, *Leg.*; W. Miller, *De Off.*; *Letters*, E. S. Shuckburgh, 4 vols. (1903); E. O. Winstedt, *Att.* (Loeb), W. Glynn Williams, *Fam.*, *QFr.* (Loeb), G. E. Jeans, *Watson's Selection* (1880).

STYLE AND DICTION: J. Lebreton, *Études sur la langue et la grammaire de C.* (1901); Th. Zieliński, *Das Clauselgesetz in C.'s Reden* (1904), *Der constructive Rhythmus in C.'s Reden* (1920); H. D. Broadhead, *Latin Prose Rhythm* (1928).

SPECIAL STUDIES: Orelli and Baiter, *Onomasticon Tullianum* (1838); A. H. J. Greenidge, *The Legal Procedure of C.'s Time* (1901); C. F. Lehmann, *De Cic. epist. ad Att. recensendis et emendandis* (1892); H. Sjögren, *Commentationes Tullianae* (1910); W. Kroll, *Die Kultur der Cic. Zeit* (1933); O. E. Schmidt, *Der Briefwechsel des C.* (1893), *Ciceros Villen* (1899); R. Hirzel, *Der Dialog* (1895); J. Galbiati(us), *De fontibus Ciceronis librorum ... de rep. et de legibus quaestiones* (1916); B. Farrington, *Primum Graius homo* (1927); W. W. Ewbank, *The Poems of Cicero* (1933); M. Pohlenz, *Antikes Führertum* (1934); L. Labowsky, *Die Ethik des Panaitios* (1934); M. van der Bruwaene, *La Théologie de Cicéron* (1937; bibliography on C.'s sources). G. C. R.

CICERO (2), QUINTUS TULLIUS (102–43 B.C.), shared the education of his elder brother Marcus (1), but though he accompanied him to Athens in 79 did not take to oratory or philosophy. He had, however, a library of Greek and Latin books (*QFr.* 3. 4. 5) and some literary taste: thus he relieved the tedium of winter-quarters in Gaul by writing tragedies (*QFr.* 3. 6. 7). Marcus did Quintus a bad turn by bringing about his marriage with the masterful Pomponia, Atticus' sister, in 69 (Nepos, *Att.* 5), but the ill-assorted union (*Att.* 5. 1. 3–4) lasted till 44. Pilia, Atticus' wife, took the husband's side (*Att.* 5. 11. 7).

2. Quintus' career followed his brother's. He was plebeian aedile in 65 and praetor in 62. He probably wrote the *Commentariolum Petitionis* to assist Marcus' election to the consulship. In 61 he went as proconsul to Asia; *QFr.* 1. 1 and 2 are long letters of advice for his third year of office. The brothers did not meet till M.'s return from exile, which Q. did his best to promote. Pompey then made Q. his legate in Sardinia, and through him M. was warned to submit to the Triumvirs (56). Early in 54 M. procured Q.'s appointment as legate to Caesar in Gaul. In winter 54–53 he held out against the Nervii till relieved (*BGall.* 5. 52), but in 53, when in charge of Aduatuca, he disobeyed orders and nearly caused a disaster (ib. 6. 36 ff.). He was in Gaul winter 52–51 (ib. 7. 90); but was available in the middle of 51 to go as M.'s legate to Cilicia, where he conducted military operations.

3. Like his brother, Q. joined Pompey, but after Pharsalus he and his son tried to ingratiate themselves with Caesar by blaming M. (*Att.* 11. 9 and 10). That the brothers were subsequently reconciled is shown by Q.'s introduction as an interlocutor in *De Div.* and *De Leg.*, though there are no letters, the correspondence to Q. only covering 60–54 B.C. They were together at Tusculum when they heard they were proscribed, and started to flee, but soon parted. Q. and his son, being betrayed by slaves—while M.'s did all they could to save their master—were put to death (Dec. 43).

4. Quintus had wit and power of self-expression, but his lack of self-control and tendency to exaggeration (*Fam.* 16. 26 and 27) stood in his light. Though a competent soldier, he had no political capacity; he owed to his brother's aid his praetorship and province, and acquitted himself fairly well in both offices.

See W. Wiemer, *Q. Tullius Cicero* (Diss. Jena, 1930). G. C. R.

CICERO (3), QUINTUS TULLIUS junior (67–43 B.C.), son of (2) and nephew of the orator (1), was educated under his uncle's supervision during his father's absences from Rome in Sardinia and Gaul. He told his uncle about 'the squabbles of our womenfolk' (*QFr.* 2. 5. 2). In Cilicia his uncle found him deceitful and difficult to manage. He gave him the *toga virilis* at Laodicea, 17 Mar. 50; the youth had then managed to reconcile his parents (*Att.* 6. 7. 1). After Pharsalus he showed base ingratitude in abusing his uncle to Caesar and the Caesarians; but Hirtius snubbed him, and Dolabella and Pollio both wrote to warn Cicero. After acting as aedile at Arpinum in 46, he went to Spain, then turned to Antony (*Att.* 14. 17. 3) and afterwards to Brutus (*Att.* 15. 19. 2; 21. 1). He shared his father's fate in Dec. 43.

G. C. R.

CICERO (4), MARCUS TULLIUS (b. 65 B.C., *Att.* 1. 2), only son of the orator (1) and Terentia, was educated under his father's supervision, but needed the spur (*Att.* 6. 1. 12). Along with his cousin he was taken to Cilicia and visited King Deiotarus (*Att.* 5. 17. 3). In March 49 he received the *toga virilis* at Arpinum (*Att.* 9. 6. 1), and then commanded a cavalry squadron in Greece (*Off.* 2. 13. 45). After serving as aedile at Arpinum in 46 he wanted to go to Spain (*Att.* 12. 7. 1), but consented instead to attend

Cratippus' lectures at Athens. He was idle and extra-vagant, but wrote to Tiro promising amendment (*Fam.* 16. 21). He then served under Brutus, who praised him (*Brut.* 2. 3. 6), and a legion of C. Antonius surrendered to him (*Phil.* 10. 6. 13). After Philippi he joined Sextus Pompeius, but took advantage of the amnesty of 39 B.C. As colleague of Octavian in the consulship (from 13 Sept. 30) he overthrew the statues of Antony and executed the *damnatio memoriae*. He was afterwards proconsul of Asia (in 29–28 according to M. Grant, *From Imperium to Auctoritas* (1946), 385) and (perhaps or) legate of Syria. Seneca remarks (*Ben.* 4. 30) that he owed his consulship to his father, and he was chiefly remembered as a toper (Plin. *HN* 14. 147). G. C. R.

CILICIA, a region of south Asia Minor, of varying extension. The name was sometimes applied to the entire mountain zone of south Asia Minor, and to Cappadocia; but it usually referred to two districts of widely different character, (1) Cilicia Tracheia ('Rough Cilicia'), a deeply fissured limestone plateau of the central Taurus range, and (2) Cilicia Pedias, the plain between Mts. Taurus and Amanus.

Cilicia Tracheia was of little consequence, except as a haunt of pirates, who established their bases here from prehistoric to Roman times, and as a source of ship-timber for the navies of Egypt. Cilicia Pedias was important both by reason of its abundant crops (especially of flax and grapes) and as a land of passage between Asia Minor and Syria (by way of the 'Cilician Gates' in Mt. Taurus and the 'Syrian Gates' in Mt. Amanus). It received immigrants from Greece in prehistoric times, in the early first millennium, and in the Hellenistic age, the chief settlements being at Soli, Mallus, and (later) Alexandria-ad-Issum. Under their influence the natives became partly hellenized and founded cities of their own, e.g. at Tarsus (q.v.). After a period of vassalage under Assyrian monarchs Cilicia Pedias passed into Persian hands, but retained its own dynasts. In the Hellenistic age it was a bone of contention between Seleucids and Ptolemies; from 246 to 197 it was mostly under Ptolemaic rule.

The Romans first constituted a province of Cilicia in 102; but this was merely a chain of coastguard stations along the mountain rim of south Asia Minor. After the pirate drive of Pompey (67) the province was extended to include the mountainous interior and Cilicia Pedias. Under Augustus it probably disappeared altogether, the mountain zone being transferred to Galatia, and Cilicia Pedias to Syria. Under Vespasian Cilicia Pedias and Tracheia were re-combined into a separate province.

Strabo, 533–51, 667–76; Jones, *Eastern Cities*, ch. 8. M. C.

CIMBRI, a German tribe from north Jutland, where the district of Himmerland preserves their name. To-wards the end of the second century B.C. over-population and encroachments by the sea drove them to migrate, in company with the Teutoni (q.v.) and Ambrones. From the Elbe they arrived, by a roundabout route, in Noricum, where they defeated a Roman consular army (113 B.C.). They then turned west and entered the Helvetian terri-tory between the Main and Switzerland, where a few of them settled; vestiges of a Cimbric element in the popu-lation are perhaps implied by inscriptions to Mercurius Cimbrianus at Miltenberg and Heidelberg (*ILS* 4595, 4596, cf. 9377). About 110 they entered the Rhône valley, defeating M. Junius Silanus and then turning into the centre of Gaul. In 105 they were again in the south, where they won the great victory of Arausio (*Orange*), and then entered Spain, whence the Celtiberians drove them out. They now moved towards Italy. Marius defeated the Teutoni and Ambrones, who took the western route, at Aquae Sextiae (*Aix-en-Provence*) in 102, and in 101 destroyed the Cimbri, who had travelled

round the Alps and entered Italy by the north-east, near Vercellae, in the Po valley. A few of the Germans had remained in northern Gaul; the later Aduatuci were their descendants. A remnant of the Cimbri was found in Jutland by the naval expedition sent by Tiberius in A.D. 5 (*Mon. Anc.* 26).

L. Schmidt, *Geschichte der deutschen Stämme. Die Westgermanen*² (1938), i. 3 ff.; Tacitus, *Germania*, ed. Anderson (1938), 171 ff. O. B.

CIMMERIANS (Κιμμέριοι), to Homer a fabulous people 'on whom the sun never looks'. They emerged into history when from south Russia they entered Asia Minor over the Caucasus (there may have been a subsidiary invasion by the north-west) towards the end of the eighth century B.C. They settled round Lake Van and fought the Assyrians until, under Essarhadon (681–668 B.C.), they moved westwards into Asia Minor on a destructive plundering expedition resembling that of Timur in A.D. 1402. They broke the power of Phrygia, overran Lydia (Sardes was captured about 657), and attacked the Greek cities on the west coast, with varying success. The effect of the Cimmerian invasion was to weaken Lydian pressure on the Greek cities and to leave Phrygia devastated and an easy prey to Lydia. W. M. C.

CIMON (*c.* 512–449 B.C.). Athenian statesman and soldier, son of Miltiades (q.v.). On his father's death in 489 he paid the fine of fifty talents which had been im-posed upon him. *Circa* 480 he married Isodice, grand-niece of Cleisthenes, thus connecting himself with the Alcmaeonidae. Elected *strategus* in 478–477, he helped Aristides to form the Delian League. He was again *strategus* when he drove Pausanias (q.v.) out of Byzantium and later captured Eion, the last Persian stronghold in Thrace (perhaps both in 476). Soon after he captured Scyrus, and brought from there 'the bones of Theseus' in triumph to Athens. He is not said to have taken part in the war against Naxos (469 or 468), though the anec-dote of his giving judgement for Sophocles against Aeschylus at the Dionysia represented him as *strategus* in 469–468. His greatest military achievement soon followed (in 468 or 467)—the Eurymedon campaign, in which the Persian fleet was totally destroyed, and several Greek cities, as far east as Phaselis, joined the League. He reduced Thasos, which had seceded from the League, after a two years' siege (465–463). He was prosecuted on his *euthyna* (q.v.) by the democrats when he returned in 463, but was acquitted. He persuaded the Athenians to assist Sparta against the insurgent helots, and himself led out a large force of hoplites (462). He was, however, soon sent home by the Spartans (who suspected Athenian intrigues with the helots), and with this ignominy Cimon's great influence at Athens ended. The democrats, led by Ephialtes and Pericles, stripped the Areopagus (q.v.) of most of its powers either during his absence or after his failure, and he was ostracized in 461. Four years later Cimon asked to be allowed to fight against the Spartans at Tanagra to prove his loyalty; this was refused, but he was recalled soon after. He took little part in politics, however, till 451 or 450, when he arranged a Five-Year Truce with Sparta. He led a last expedition against Persia in 449, to recapture Cyprus. On this campaign he died, and peace with Persia followed (see CALLIAS I).

In the later biography, represented by Plutarch, Cimon figured as a large-hearted, expansive, genial conserva-tive; his policy one of goodwill towards the allies, friend-ship with Sparta, and war against the national enemy—the opposite in all things of Pericles. There is some truth in this, but the Egyptian war took place during his exile, and he was as active as Pericles in opposing by force secession from the League; attacks were made on his character, some of them by Stesimbrotus, who came from Thasos.

Plutarch, *Cimon.* A. W. G.

CINAEDIC POETRY, verses recited by κιναιδολόγοι, such as Sotades and Timon of Phlius. Originally accompanied by oriental instruments (Demetr. *Eloc.* 37; Polyb. 5. 37. 10), they were later recited (Plin. *Ep.* 9. 17. 1; Strabo 648). They were of a satirical and scurrilous character (Petron. *Sat.* 23. 2) and said to be of Ionian origin (Ath. 620 e; cf. Plaut. *Stich.* 769). C. M. B.

CINAETHON OF LACEDAEMON, epic poet, of uncertain date; supposed author of a *Telegonia* (? *Theogonia*), an *Oedipodea*, the *Ilias parva*, a *Heraclea*, and perhaps genealogies; to be distinguished from Cynaethus (q.v.). *See* EPIC CYCLE.

EGF 4, 8, 38, 196–8, 212.

CINCINNATUS, LUCIUS QUINCTIUS, an historical figure, although details of his career probably were derived from popular poetry. In 458 B.C., according to tradition, when Minucius was besieged by the Aequi on Mt. Algidus, Cincinnatus was appointed dictator and dispatched to his rescue. He defeated the Aequi, freed Minucius, resigned his dictatorship after sixteen days, and returned to his farm beyond the Tiber. The story later underwent embellishments (e.g. the *Prata Quinctia* may have suggested the name of the hero, and various features may have been borrowed from the account of the rescue of C. Minucius in 217 B.C.), but undoubtedly it is based on more than the misinterpretation of some monument, a false etymology, or reduplication. But the story of Cincinnatus' second dictatorship in 439 has no foundation. P. T.

CINCIUS ALIMENTUS, LUCIUS, Roman senator and historian, was praetor in Sicily in 210–209 B.C., and was captured by Hannibal (Livy 21. 38. 3). His history of Rome, written in Greek, set the foundation of the city in 729–728 B.C. and reached his own times. With the work of Fabius Pictor, it formed the basis of the senatorial historical tradition, especially of the Second Punic War. The constitutional antiquarian of the same name wrote towards Augustan times.

H. Peter, *HRRel.* i² (1914), pp. ci, 40; M. Gelzer, *Hermes* 1934, 48. A. H. McD.

CINEAS, a skilful Thessalian diplomat, famous for his observations that Rome's Senate was an assembly of kings and war with Rome a battle with a hydra. King Pyrrhus (q.v.) sent him at least once and possibly twice to Rome to negotiate peace. His terms, however, proved unacceptable.

Livy, *Epit.* 13; Plut. *Pyrrh.* 11 ff.; Appian, *Sam.* 10 f. E. T. S.

CINESIAS (c. 450–c. 390 B.C.), dithyrambic poet, of Athens, connected with the abolition of the Chorus from Attic comedy (Schol. Ar. *Ran.* 404), twice engaged in legal proceedings with Lysias, who disapproved of him (Lys. 21. 20; fr. 73). No fragments of interest survive from his work, but Aristophanes refers to him at *Av.* 1377; *Lys.* 860; *Eccl.* 330; *Ran.* 1437; fr. 198, and Plutarch (*De mus.* 30) regarded him as a corrupter of Attic music. *See* MUSIC § 10. C. M. B.

CINNA (1), LUCIUS CORNELIUS (*cos.* 87, 86, 85, 84 B.C.), patrician leader of the democratic party and father of Cornelia, first wife of Julius Caesar. As consul for 87, he impeached Sulla, whom he had sworn to support. On Sulla's departure for the East he proposed the recall from exile of Marius and his partisans. His colleague Cn. Octavius defeated this proposal, and the Senate deposed Cinna from the consulship; whereupon he raised a force of Italians, and with Sertorius' help blockaded Rome. Their entry with Marius into the city was followed by a massacre of Sulla's supporters.

Cinna's successive consulships with democratic colleagues—Marius, and then L. Flaccus, in 86; Cn. Carbo, in 85 and 84—amounted to a 'dictatorship'. We know little (and that only from hostile sources) of the measures then taken, apart from Flaccus' law remitting three-fourths of debts and the restoration of Sulpicius' distribution of the Italian voters throughout the tribes—carried out by censors of 86, or at any rate completed by 84. Cinna's government, however, must be credited, most probably, with the return to the issue of pure silver coinage, after a period of debased *denarii* (see MARIUS 3).

Cinna made great preparations to resist the return of Sulla after his campaigns in Greece, but was killed in a mutiny at Brundisium. M. H.

CINNA (2), LUCIUS CORNELIUS, son of (1) above, took part in the revolt of Lepidus, joined Sertorius in Spain, and returned under the *Lex Plotia de reditu Lepidanorum*. Praetor in 44, he expressed approval of the murder of Caesar, was attacked on his way to attend the Senate (17 Mar.), and rescued by Lepidus. He procured the recall of the exiled tribunes Flavus and Marullus. His wife was the daughter of Pompey.

Plutarch, *Brutus*, 18 and 20; Appian, *BCiv.* 2. 121 and 126. Drumann-Groebe, *Gesch. Roms* ii. 508 f. G. W. R.

CINNA (3), GNAEUS CORNELIUS, son of (2) above and Pompeia, daughter of Pompey. He plotted against Augustus during his absence in Gaul (possibly 16–13 B.C.), but was pardoned at the instance of Livia and was consul in A.D. 5.

Seneca, *Clem.* 1. 9; Dio Cassius, 55. 14 and 21 f. G. W. R.

CINNA (4), GAIUS HELVIUS, tribune 44 B.C., carried a law deposing his colleagues Flavus and Marullus, who had offended Caesar. After Caesar's funeral he was mistaken for L. Cornelius Cinna and lynched by the mob. He is usually identified with a friend of Catullus', of whose works only fragments survive. *See* ZMYRNA.

G. W. R.

CINXIA, see JUNO.

CINYRAS, mythical king of Cyprus and ancestor of the Cinyrades, the priests of Aphrodite–Astarte at Paphos (Tac. *Hist.* 2. 3). C. represents the Phoenician culture in Cyprus, and so is called king of Byblos (Strabo 755) or son of Sandocus, a Syrian immigrant to Cilicia (Apollod. *Bibl.* 3. 14. 3). Founder of the cult of Aphrodite in Cyprus, C. introduced sacred prostitution (q.v.) there. He was the father of Adonis (q.v.) through unwitting incest with his daughter, Myrrha or Smyrna (Ov. *Met.* 10. 298 ff.); this story was sometimes told of Theias, who is also given as the father of C. As musician and seer, C. is the son and favourite of Apollo. His name became proverbial for riches and beauty.

Cf. Roscher, *Lex.* and *PW*, s.v. 'Kinyras'; J. G. Frazer, *Adonis Attis Osiris* i, ch. 3. F. R. W.

CIRCE, in Homer (*Od.* 10. 210 ff.) a goddess living on the fabulous island of Aeaea (ib. 135), later identified, in Italy, with the promontory of Circeii in Latium. She is very powerful in magic; her house is surrounded by wild beasts who fawn on new arrivals (later, as *Aen.* 7. 19–20, they are men changed by her spells) and she turns Odysseus' men into swine. He is helped by Hermes to resist her spells by means of the herb moly, forces her to restore his men, and lives with her for a year, after which she gives him directions for his journey home, *see* ODYSSEUS. She is sister of Aeetes and daughter of Helios and Perse (*Od.* 137–8). In Hesiod (*Theog.* 1011 ff., spurious?) she bears Odysseus two sons, Agrios and Latinus (*see further* ODYSSEUS). She touches the Argonautic legend, receiving Jason and Medea, and purifying both from the murder of Absyrtus (Ap. Rhod. 4. 557 ff.). H. J. R.

CIRCUS, an enclosure for chariot-racing, planned with parallel sides and semicircular end, all fitted with seats, and with an axial rib (*spina*) marked at each end by turning-posts (*metae*) dividing the area into two runs. The seating was arranged in storied groups. At the open end were the curved stables (*carceres*) for twelve teams of horses, who competed four, six, eight, or even twelve at a time under the colours of the different factions. These were red and white at first (Tertull. *De Spect.* 5 and 9) and presently green (Suet. *Gaius* 55) and blue (Suet. *Vit.* 7), Domitian's purple and gold (Suet. *Dom.* 7) being temporary. There were seven laps to each race, measured by movable eggs and dolphins, the emblems of the Heavenly Twins and Neptune, the horse gods (Dio Cass. 49. 43. 2).

The earliest example of a *circus* at Rome is the *Circus Maximus*, in the Murcia valley between the Palatine and Aventine hills, reputed to be of kingly origin, adorned during the Republic (Livy 8. 20. 1; 33. 27. 4; 39. 7. 8; 40. 2. 1; 41. 27. 6), and rebuilt by Caesar (Pliny, *HN* 36. 102). The second was the *Circus Flaminius* of 221 B.C., in the Campus Martius. The third was the *Circus Gai et Neronis* (Pliny, *HN* 36. 74) or *Vaticanus* (ib. 16. 201), the site of Christian martyrdoms, close to the later St. Peter's basilica. Best preserved of all is the Circus of Maxentius on Via Appia, outside the city, dedicated in A.D. 309 (*ILS* 673).

In Italy, the *circus* is not infrequent, examples being known at Bovillae, Asisium (*CIL* xi. 5390), and Aquileia. The hippodromes of Constantinople, Alexandria, and Antioch were famous throughout the East. In the West, examples are known in Gaul at Lugdunum (*CIL* xiii. 1919), and Vienne; at Emerita, Toletum, Tarraco, Balsa, Zafra, and Urso in Spain, which was famous for its racing-stables (Plin. *HN* 8. 166). I. A. R.

CIRIS (κεῖρις), *see* APPENDIX VERGILIANA.

CIRRHA, the port of Delphi in the Crisaean Gulf in classical times, identified with the modern *Maghoula*. The name is the same as Crisa (q.v.), so that the two places are sometimes confused. The settlement was destroyed *c.* 600 B.C. by the Amphictionic League, because its inhabitants had molested the pilgrims to Delphi. It possessed prehistoric tin-works. O. D.

CIRTA (modern *Constantine* in Algeria), a strong rock-fortress, commanding the gorges of the Ampsaga (*Rummel*), was the capital of Syphax and then of Masinissa, who encouraged the settlement of Italian merchants, and linked Cirta to the ports of Rusicade (*Philippeville*) and Chullu (*Collo*). Micipsa strengthened its fortifications, and introduced Greeks from Cyrene. Jugurtha captured it from Adherbal (112 B.C.) and massacred the Italian inhabitants. For help in overthrowing Juba I, Sittius (q.v.) was granted Cirta and the surrounding country by Caesar (46 B.C.). His veterans settled there, and the new colony remained the capital of a rich agricultural district. Among communities associated politically and economically with Cirta were Rusicade, Chullu, Cuicul (*Djemila*), Milev (*Milah*), and Thibilis (*Announa*). Cirta's great prosperity in the second and third centuries A.D. depended on its crops, marbles, and copper-mines. Its best-known citizen was Fronto (q.v.). Cirta became a centre of the Donatist heresy and was weakened by religious quarrels. But, rebuilt by Constantine, it retained its importance under Byzantine rule.

L. Leschi, *Rev. Africaine* 1937. W. N. W.

CISALPINE GAUL, the fertile, populous region between Apennines and Alps in north Italy. The migration of Gauls into Italy via the Brenner (*c.* 400 B.C.) was one phase of the great Celtic expansion (Livy 5. 33 f. mistakenly makes the Gauls arrive via the Western Alps *c.* 600). These Gauls, although successfully resisted by the Veneti, gradually ousted the Etruscans, pushed back the Umbrians and Ligurians, and made the Cisalpine area their own. Their gift for poetry, their art and material culture imply a certain degree of civilization; their iron implements, e.g. badly tempered swords, have been recovered from their inhumation burials. But in many ways they were savages: they practised head-hunting and human sacrifice and were addicted to drunken brawling. Occasionally they built excellent fortifications, but many Gallic settlements were mere collections of primitive huts. The Gauls were not very cohesive; they tended to form in groups around individual and often mutually hostile chieftains. Expert horsemen, they were savage fighters, ever ready to live either by plunder or by serving as mercenaries. In the fourth century B.C. their marauding bands, one of which captured Rome (390), terrorized Italy. After 330, however, with an adaptability perhaps not surprising in so unstable a nation, these restless adventurers settled down about the Po and became skilful agriculturalists. However, they retained their fighting qualities, as their annihilation of a Roman army at Arretium (284) proves. Subsequently they waged long and ultimately unsuccessful wars against Rome: *see* BOII, CENOMANI, INSUBRES, SENONES. Since any *tumultus Gallicus* threatened her national existence Rome pursued a policy of denationalization and even extermination; by 150 B.C. few Gauls remained in the Cisalpine plain (Polyb. 2. 35; Sall. *Iug.* 114; Cic. *Phil.* 8. 3). South Italians, including many Romans, replaced them and Cisalpine Gaul became known as Gallia Togata. Cimbri, who threatened it in 101, were repulsed by Marius. In 89 the Transpadane region received *Ius Latii*, the Cispadane apparently Roman citizenship. Probably it was Sulla who organized the Cisalpine province with the Rubicon as its southern boundary (but see O. Cuntz, *Polybius u. s. Werk* (1902), 32). Roman citizenship was extended to the Transpadane region in 49, and in 42 the province was incorporated into Italy. Under Augustus the tribes inhabiting the Alpine foothills were conquered; thus the Alps became the frontier of Italy (Pliny, *HN* 3. 138). Its remarkable productivity and flourishing woollen trade enriched Cisalpine Gaul. 'Est enim ille flos Italiae, illud firmamentum imperi populi Romani, illud ornamentum dignitatis' (Cic. *Phil.* 3. 13). In Strabo's time (5. 217 f.), as in ours, it contained more large wealthy towns than any other part of Italy.

ANCIENT SOURCES: Strabo (5. 212 ff.) gives a valuable general account of Cisalpine Gaul, marred by anachronisms. Polybius' historical and geographical outline of Cisalpine Gaul down to the Hannibalic War, despite certain inaccuracies, is sober and scientific (books 2 and 3). For events after 202 the chief source is Livy 30–36, a confused account vitiated by rhetorical elaborations. Justin, Diodorus, Appian, and Dio Cassius are the principal subsidiary sources.

MODERN LITERATURE. A. Bertrand and S. Reinach, *Les Celtes dans les vallées du Pô et du Danube* (1894); C. Jullian, *Histoire de la Gaule* i (1908); F. von Duhn in *Reallexikon der Vorgeschichte* (1924) s.v. 'Kelten'; *CAH* vii, ch. 2 (J. M. de Navarro); ch. 17 (L. Homo); ch. 25; viii, ch. 11 (T. Frank); H. Hubert, *Les Celtes* (2 vols., 1932; with good bibliography); J. Whatmough, *Prae-Italic Dialects* ii (1933), 166; *Foundations of Roman Italy* (1937); G. E. F. Chilver, *Cisalpine Gaul, Social and Economic History from 49 B.C. to the Death of Trajan* (1941).

SPECIAL SUBJECTS. For the extension of Latin rights and Roman citizenship see Asconius p. 3 Cl.; Dio Cassius 41. 36; Bruns, *Fontes*[7] 16, 17 (= *Lex Rubria*: see E. G. Hardy, *Some Problems in Roman History* (1924), 43, 207); J. Marquardt, *Römische Staatsverwaltung* i[2] (1881), 61 f. E. T. S.

CISIUM, *see* CARRIAGES.

CITHARA, *see* MUSIC, § 9.

CITIZENSHIP, GREEK (πολιτεία, a word which also denotes (i) the citizen body, (ii) the constitution). In Greek city-states citizenship was originally not an individual right; it meant membership of a political and social community (*see* POLIS). Descent from full citizen parents always conferred citizen status, and also membership of the smaller communities of family, *genos*, and *phratria* (qq.v.). This was an inheritance from the aristocratic *Polis*. In oligarchies, however, it was more important to own landed property or to be wealthy than to be well born, and in democracies the rule of descent from citizen parents (ἐξ ἀμφοῖν ἀστοῖν) was not strictly enforced until democracy became well established. Besides, the State could grant and withdraw citizenship. Such grants were seldom made in earlier times, except occasionally by tyrants or other leaders bent on increasing the number of their adherents; but they became frequent after the fourth century B.C. Inscriptions recording grants of citizenship were very numerous in all cities. Finally citizenship became an empty honour which might be obtainable by purchase, and in many cases people obtained two or more citizenships. Citizenship was lost either by *atimia* (q.v.) or banishment. The rights of full citizens were equal in substance, and so were the duties (taxes, military service, etc.). The general duties of a citizen, e.g. submission to law, defence of the State and its Constitution, worship of the State gods, were often confirmed by oath. In most cases citizenship granted to a stranger carried all the rights of a born citizen. In the Hellenistic Leagues every citizen of a member-state acquired a second citizenship, that of the League.

E. Szanto, *Griechisches Bürgerrecht* (1892); V. Ehrenberg, in Gercke–Norden, *Einleitung in die Altertumswissenschaft*[3] (1932) iii. 3; U. Kahrstedt, *Staatsgebiet und Staatsangehörige in Athen* (1934).
V. E.

CITIZENSHIP, ROMAN. Roman citizenship depended either upon birth—descent from Roman parents on both sides, though one parent might be a *peregrinus* possessing *conubium*—or upon a grant made by the People. It implied rights, privileges, and duties, *iura*, *honores*, *munera*. All citizens, after the union of the Orders, possessed *conubium* etc., and, under the Republic, voting rights (*suffragium*) in the various assemblies, unless specifically disfranchised (*aerarii*). The system of wealth classification limited the value of the *suffragium* and determined eligibility for magistracies (*honores*) and liability to *munera* (q.v.), especially military service. *Honores* were thus supplementary; there was no *ius honorum*. Rome gradually extended her citizenship to her allies and subjects, in whose incorporation *civitas sine suffragio* (s.v. MUNICIPIUM) or *ius Latii* (q.v.; also LATINI) formed an intermediary stage. Citizenship brought the new Romans within the orbit of *iura*, *munera*, and *honores*, and entailed the surrender to Rome of the sovereignty of the community concerned. Thus Roman citizenship was incompatible with that of another State. Incorporated communities retained, however, some rights of local self-government (*see* MUNICIPIUM). These principles, worked out in the incorporation between 380 and 250 B.C. of those places which formed the Roman territory down to 90 B.C., were revived by the incorporation of all Italy after the Social War (*see* SOCII, MUNICIPIUM, COMMERCIUM, LATINI). The consequent increase in the number of *municipia* inaugurated a change in the theory of Roman citizenship. Rome ceased to be a city-state and became the *communis patria* of all Italy. Municipal affairs began to supplant the Forum as the centre of interest for the mass of citizens. Next came the extension of the citizenship to provinces. In the Second Triumvirate colonies and municipalities were regularly established overseas, provincial peoples were granted Latin rights and citizenship. Throughout the Principate these processes continued, accelerated by the regular grant of citizenship to legionary recruits and discharged auxiliaries of provincial extraction, until the western provinces became Roman both in civilization and social rights (*see* COMMERCIUM). Finally the *constitutio Antoniniana* conferred citizenship upon all free inhabitants of the Empire (A.D. 212), without, however, affecting the status of their communities. (Cf. MUNICIPIUM, COLONIZATION, IUS ITALICUM.) The citizenship gradually lost its political importance, apart from the value of *ius provoca-*

tionis (*see* APPELLATIO): the *munus militare* disappeared with the disuse of compulsory recruiting; the abolition of *comitia* made the *ius suffragi* illusory; senatorial *honores* fell to only the most distinguished of provincial citizens, though the municipal aristocracy commonly aspired to equestrian rank. But the social content remained unchanged, despite some assimilation of the rights of *peregrini* to those of citizens (cf. s.v.). By the age of the Antonines, however, citizenship was mainly valued as a symbol of imperial unity, for the doctrine of the incompatibility of two citizenships had broken down with the frequent extension of the franchise to individual members of non-Roman communities (*see* PEREGRINI), and the political ambitions of ordinary men were fully satisfied by the service not of Rome but of their local municipalities. Consequently the spread of *civitas Romana* led to the elaboration of the theory that Rome was the *communis patria* of the whole civilized world.

For bibliography, *see* COLONIZATION, LATINI, MUNICIPIUM.
Ancient sources: add *CIL* xvi; *Digest* passim; *ILS* 212; *PGiess.* 40; Aelius Aristides, Εἰς Ῥώμην; Tertullian, *Apol.*, etc. Modern views: H. M. Last in *CAH* xi; A. N. Sherwin-White, *The Roman Citizenship* (1939); J. Vogt, *Ciceros Glaube an Rom* (1935).
Particular studies: J. G. C. Anderson, *JRS* 1927 (the Cyrenean Edicts). E. Kornemann, 'Conventus' in *PW*. P. Lambrechts, *La Composition du Sénat Romain* (Antwerp, 1936). A. Stein, *Der Römische Ritterstand*. B. Stech 'Senatores Romani', *Klio*, Beiheft X. Cf. C. S. Walton, *JRS* 1929; R. Syme, *BSR* xiv. On *Const. Antonin.* A. H. M. Jones, *JRS* 1936. Also s.v. CLAUDIUS (1).
A. N. S.-W.

CITY-FOUNDERS (κτίσται, οἰκισταί, *conditores*) played an important part in the city-state. In the Greek homelands, where the true origin of cities was no longer known, a god or legendary hero was looked upon as founder. But the founder is of greatest significance in the period of Greek colonization. No city sent out a band of colonists without appointing a founder, who had complete power over the colony until the new city's foundation was accomplished. If a band of exiles founded a city they selected one of their number to be founder. When a colony founded a colony in its turn, it always summoned a founder from the mother-city. The founders received heroic honours (*see* HERO-CULT) after death; there was probably no *polis* without a founder's cult. Sometimes a city changed its founder, thus symbolizing some important change in its constitution or fortunes, as when Amphipolis ousted Hagnon for Brasidas. Hadrian through his benefactions received the name of founder from many cities.
J. E. F.

CIVILIS, GAIUS JULIUS (1st c. A.D.), a noble Batavian and commander of a Batavian cohort, had personal grievances against the Roman government. When Antonius Primus wrote to him in A.D. 69, inciting him to create a diversion and so prevent Vitellian reinforcements from going to Italy, Civilis fomented a war of liberation under pretext of supporting Vespasian. With help from Germans beyond the Rhine he attacked the legionary camp of Vetera, but was beaten off. The revolt, however, spread widely, finding support in the winter of A.D. 69–70 among Gallic tribes like the Treveri and Lingones. Roman troops at Novaesium took an oath of allegiance to the 'imperium Galliarum' and Vetera fell at last. But meanwhile the Flavian generals were approaching. Cerialis (q.v.) won a battle near Trier and the Gallic movement collapsed. After mixed fighting along the Rhine towards the Batavian territory, Civilis finally capitulated. His fate is not known.

E. Stein, *PW*, s.v. 'Julius (186)'.
R. S.

CIVITAS (territorial), like the Greek πόλις, from meaning originally any autonomous State, came to be applied under the Empire to any self-governing municipal unit, irrespective of its civic category. But technically it denoted the least privileged grade of provincial communities possessing local autonomy, however circumscribed (*see*

PEREGRINI). Their form of government was republican, with magistrates, council, and a constitution fixed according to local custom. The development of *civitates* out of an unorganized village or tribal system was the first step in the municipal development of backward areas, notably in Spain and Africa. The *civitates*, which might later be given Roman municipal status (*see* MUNICIPIUM), were the basis of the provincial administration. The governors and procurators worked through them, leaving to the local authorities the actual performance of e.g. the census surveys and collection of taxes (*see* DECURIONES, MUNUS, MUNICIPIUM).

For bibliography *see* MUNICIPIUM, SOCII.   A. N. S.-W.

CLAROS, seat of a cult and oracle of Apollo near Colophon. It was a very ancient sanctuary, undoubtedly of pre-Hellenic origin, but it seems unlikely that the oracle was anything like so old. The cult-myth connects the oracular establishment with Delphi and the prophet Calchas. But Herodotus never mentions it, and the earliest evidence belongs to the fourth century B.C. Only in the Roman Imperial period does it appear to have attained great renown.

The god's vehicle was a male prophet, who heard only the names and number of the consultants, then retired into a grotto, drank the waters of a sacred spring, and uttered his responses in verse. He was assisted by a priest and a thespiode.

Ancient sources: Strabo 642 f.; Tacitus, *Ann.* 2. 54; Iamblichus, *Myst.* 3. 11. Modern literature: K. Buresch, *Klaros* (1889); Ch. Picard, *Ephèse et Claros* (1922). Such excavation as has been done is reported by Th. Macridy-Bey and Ch. Picard in *BCH* xxxix (1915), 33–52.   J. E. F.

CLASSICIANUS, GAIUS JULIUS ALPINUS, perhaps originated from the Treveri. As procurator of Britain (A.D. 61) he favoured a policy of conciliation, and begged Nero to recall the harsher Suetonius (q.v.) Paulinus. His tombstone was found in London.

F. Cottrill, *Antiquaries Journal,* 1936, p. 1; E. Birley, ib. 207; R. G. Collingwood, *Roman Britain*[2] (1937), 103.   A. M.

CLASSICUS, JULIUS, of royal stock among the Treveri (related presumably to C. Julius Classicianus, q.v.), and commanding as *praefectus* a cavalry regiment of his own tribe, joined Julius Civilis (q.v.) when his revolt spread into Gaul at the beginning of 70. Julius Tutor and the Lingonian Julius Sabinus were his close associates in the founding of the 'imperium Galliarum'. Classicus displayed great dash and vigour, shared in most of the fighting against the remnants of the Rhine legions and the generals of Vespasian, and remained loyal to Civilis, apparently to the end. His ultimate fate is unknown.
                      R. S.

CLASSIS was at first the whole Roman army; later it was a division of the army in the reform attributed to Servius Tullius. Connected with the ancient meaning is also *classis* as 'navy'. In the Servian constitution the property owners were divided into five *classes* (apart from 18 centuries of *equites* and 4 centuries of *fabri, cornicines,* and the like). The first three *classes* were infantry of the line, the last two light-armed troops.

The property ratings of the *classes* were perhaps at first expressed in terms of land or agrarian produce, and subsequently in terms of money. The monetary scales were variously given by ancient writers; probably they underwent several alterations (Livy 1. 43; Dion. Hal. 4. 16; Polyb. 6. 23. 15; 6. 19. 2; Gellius 6. 13; Gaius 2. 274; ps.-Asc. *Verr.* 2. 1. 41; Dio Cassius 56. 10; Cic. *Rep.* 2. 22.). See CENTURIA.

A. H. J. Greenidge, *Roman Public Life* (1901), 68; G. De Sanctis, *Stor. Rom.* ii. 198, iii. 1, p. 353; H. Stuart Jones, *CAH* vii. 432; T. Frank, *Econ. Survey* i. 19; A. Piganiol, *Annales d'histoire économique et sociale* v (1933), 113; E. Cavaignac, *Rev. Phil.* 1934, 72; H. Mattingly, *JRS,* 1937, 99; E. F. D'Arms, *AJPhil.* 1943, 424.
                      A. M.

CLAUDIAN (CLAUDIUS CLAUDIANUS) lived in Rome and in Milan, A.D. 395–404. Born probably in Alexandria (his first writings were in Greek), he eulogized in Latin the consuls of 395, and became poet-laureate of Stilicho and the Emperor Honorius. Claudian's panegyrics, invectives, and short poems are important historical documents: after 404, when he married a protégée of Serena, niece and adopted daughter of Theodosius, he disappears completely. His statue in bronze, erected by the Emperor 'poscente senatu' (25. 9), bore an honorific inscription (*CIL* vi. 1710), now in Naples Museum.

WORKS. (1) *Panegyric on Probinus and Olybrius,* 395. (2) *Against Rufinus* (2 books), attacking the praetorian prefect, whose murder and dissection are exultantly rehearsed. (3) *War against Gildo* (526 vv., incomplete). (4) *Fescennine Verses.* (5) *Epithalamium of Honorius and Maria* (Stilicho's daughter), 398. (6) *Against Eutropius* (2 books), attacking the eunuch chamberlain, consul 399. (7) *Panegyrics* on consulships of Honorius (396, 398, 404), Manlius (399), Stilicho (400). (8) *Gothic War,* on Stilicho's victory over Alaric, 402. (9) *Shorter Poems: The Old Man of Verona* (idyll, 22 vv.), eulogy of Serena, epithalamium of Palladius and Celerina, *Gigantomachia* (unfinished). (10) *Rape of Proserpine* (unfinished and undated, 3 books), mythological epic, showing skill in picturesque description.

With amazing command of Latin, Claudian, even in official poems, can attain the standard of Silver Age poets (*see* EPIC POETRY, LATIN, para. 3). He is a master of allegory, mythological allusion, elaborate similes; his bold imagination and splendour of diction give power and elevation to many passages. His poems show occasional grace and charm, but much epigram, terse and vigorous, and conceits such as 'nusquam totiensque sepultus' (5. 453); in the political panegyrics and invectives eulogy and savage satire are unrestrained. He writes enthusiastically of Rome the Mother (24. 150 ff.).

BIBLIOGRAPHY

LIFE AND WORKS. P. Fargues, *Claudien: Études sur sa Poésie et son Temps* (1933). T. Hodgkin, *Claudian* (1875). J. H. E. Crees, *Claudian as an Historical Authority* (1908).

TEXTS. Birt, *MGH* x (1892). Koch (Teubner, 1893). *In Eutrop.* (comment.), P. Fargues (1933). *In Ruf.,* H. L. Levy (1935).

COMMENTARIES. Heinsius (1650, 1665). Gesner (1759).

TRANSLATIONS. M. Platnauer (prose, with text, Loeb, 1922). R. M. Pope, *Rape of Proserpine* (verse, 1934).   W. G. W.

CLAUDIUS (1) (TIBERIUS CLAUDIUS NERO GERMANICUS, 10 B.C.–A.D. 54), the Emperor, was born at Lyons on 1 Aug. 10 B.C. and was the youngest son of the elder Drusus (q.v. 3) and of Antonia minor. Overshadowed by the strong personality of his elder brother Germanicus, and hampered by a weak constitution and continual illness (he suffered from some sort of paralysis: see T. de C. Ruth, *The Problem of Claudius,* Baltimore, 1924), he received no public distinction from Augustus beyond the augurate and held no magistracy under Tiberius, who considered his 'imminuta mens' an obstacle to high preferment (Tac. *Ann.* 6. 46). He first held office when on 1 July A.D. 37 he became suffect consul with his young nephew, the Emperor Gaius; for the rest, he received little from Gaius but insults. His proclamation as emperor in 41 was largely accidental. After Gaius' murder he was discovered in the palace by a soldier, hiding behind a curtain in fear of murder; he was dragged to the Praetorian Camp and saluted by the Praetorian Guard while the Senate was still discussing the possibility of restoring the Republic. The Senate did not easily forgive him, and many senators supported the fruitless revolt of Scribonianus in Dalmatia in the following year. Chosen by the Guard, Claudius emphasized his interest in the army—a policy all the more necessary because of his own lack of military distinction. Claudius took a personal part in the invasion of Britain (43) and was present at the capture of Camulodunum. By the end of his principate he had received twenty-seven imperial *salutationes*.

2. Though he was consul four times during his principate (in 42, 43, 47, and 51) and censor in 47–8, in policy he reverted from the pretentious absolutism of Gaius (who was, however, spared an official *damnatio memoriae*) to a less autocratic form of principate. He went farther than his predecessors in extending the *civitas* (see e.g. the Volubilis inscription) and in the foundation of new colonies (e.g. Camulodunum in Britain). This liberal aspect of his policy is well revealed in his speech advocating that the chiefs of Gallia Comata should be granted the *ius honorum* (Dessau, *ILS* 212). With the Senate he was unpopular, not because he curtailed its powers, but from the circumstances of his accession and because of the insistence with which he urged its members to take their responsibilities seriously (see e.g. *BGU* 611). Other causes of his unpopularity were his intense interest in jurisdiction, especially the hearing of cases *intra cubiculum principis*, and the political power of his wives and freedmen. Claudius' principate is marked by the emergence of rich and powerful freedmen, especially Narcissus, his *ab epistulis*, and Pallas, his *a rationibus*. These private secretaries exercised ministerial functions and were, no doubt, heavily bribed by candidates for preferment. Claudius was incurably uxorious. His first wife bore him two children who died in infancy. Aelia Paetina, his second wife, bore him a daughter (Claudia Antonia, A.D. 27–66). He was married at the time of his accession to Valeria Messalina, and had by her a daughter Octavia (born before 41, and later married to Nero) and a son, Britannicus (q.v.), born in 41 or 42. Messalina succumbed in 48 to the intrigues of Narcissus, and Claudius then married his niece Agrippina, who could count on the support of Pallas. She persuaded Claudius in 50 to adopt her son Nero as guardian of his own son Britannicus (four years Nero's junior). Four years later Claudius died: it was generally believed that Agrippina handed him a poisoned dish of mushrooms (13 Oct. A.D. 54). He was, nevertheless, consecrated and was the first emperor after Augustus to receive this distinction. The *Apocolocyntosis*, probably by Seneca, is a satire on his consecration.

3. Claudius had in his youth acquired from Livy a thorough knowledge of Roman history and great respect for Roman religion and tradition. He celebrated the *Ludi Saeculares* in A.D. 47, founded a College of Haruspices, expelled Jews from Rome (though in Judaea and in Alexandria he did his best to still the disturbances resulting from the anti-Semite policy of Gaius), and in Gaul he suppressed Druidism. He wrote books on Etruscan and Carthaginian history, on dicing and on the history of Augustus' principate ('a pace ciuili'—i.e. from 27 B.C.). He also wrote an autobiography. None of these works has survived.

4. Claudius added a number of provinces to the Roman Empire: Britain (whose invasion had, perhaps, been contemplated by Gaius), the two provinces of Mauretania (whose last king, Ptolemy, had been deposed and executed by Gaius), and Thrace (in A.D. 46).

5. Ancient writers ascribed the responsibility for Claudius' administration, both on its good and its bad side, to his freedmen and wives. This view is now untenable for the early part of his principate, thanks to the fortunate chance that Claudius thought and wrote in a style as inimitable as it is grotesque. A large number of imperial enactments are preserved in inscriptions and on papyri, covering a great variety of administrative problems. Unquestionably they were dictated by Claudius himself and they show, all of them, however grotesque their thought and language, profound administrative common sense. In the last four years of his principate,

however, his powers were failing and Agrippina and Pallas exercised strong influence on his policy.

ANCIENT SOURCES: Tacitus, *Annals* bks. 11–12 cover the period A.D. 47–54, but we do not possess Tacitus' account of the first six —unquestionably the best and most important—years of Claudius' principate. For the rest, we depend chiefly on Dio Cassius bk. 60 and on Suetonius, *Divus Claudius*. For other sources, see *CAH* x. 973 f. The most important inscriptions and papyri (all of which are published by M. P. Charlesworth in *Documents illustrating the reigns of Claudius and Nero* (1939)) are the letter to the Alexandrians (see H. I. Bell, *Jews and Christians in Egypt*), the Volubilis inscriptions (*Ann. Épig.* 1916, 42; 1924, 66), the Anauni edict (*ILS* 206), the speech on the *ius honorum* of the Gauls (*ILS* 212; see on this, Ph. Fabia, *La Table Claudienne de Lyon*), and *BGU* 611.
MODERN LITERATURE: A. Momigliano, *Claudius* (1934); M. P. Charlesworth, *CAH* x. 667–701 and full bibliography ibid. 975–7; V. M. Scramuzza, *The Emperor Claudius* (U.S.A. 1940). J. P. B.

CLAUDIUS (2) **II (GOTHICUS)**, MARCUS AURELIUS (VALERIUS), one of the chief officers of Gallienus, chosen, after his assassination, to succeed him as emperor (early A.D. 268). Whether privy to the murder or not, he soon established friendly relations with the Senate, which had hated Gallienus. He calmed the troops by a donative, and interfered in Rome to check the massacre of Gallienus' friends.

His first act was to dispose of Aureolus, who surrendered in Milan, but was put to death by his own men. His second was to defeat the invading Alamanni near Lake Benacus, after an initial cavalry defeat. Aurelian was appointed to command the horse.

In the west, the Gallic Empire, under Postumus and his successors, Marius and Victorinus, continued to hold aloof. But Spain returned to its allegiance, and a corps was placed at Grenoble, under Placidianus, to protect Narbonensis. When Augustodunum (Autun) revolted, however, Claudius sent no aid, and the city had to surrender to Victorinus.

The main achievement of Claudius was the decisive defeat of the Goths, who, even after Gallienus' great victory, were plundering the Balkans. Claudius won two great battles, at Doberus and Naissus, and finally broke up their great host, absorbing many as soldiers or *coloni*. At the same time he took energetic steps against the pirate squadrons in the Aegean.

In the east, the Palmyrene government had begun by recognizing Claudius, but before the end of his reign had occupied Egypt and had pushed northward to Bithynia.

Claudius died of plague at Sirmium early in 270. He had ruled in harmony with the Senate and was acclaimed as the great patriot, who had 'devoted' his own life to the State and had earned the title of 'Gothic conqueror'.

CAH xii. 189 ff., 225, 231; Parker, *Roman World*, 185 ff.; P. Damarau, *Kaiser Claudius II Goticus* (1934). H. M.

CLAUDIUS (3), APPIUS (decemvir, 451 B.C.), despite his patrician descent, supported the plebeian claims for a written code of laws and became the leader of the decemvirs. While his policy and high birth attracted the patricians, he pleased the plebeians by sharing power with their representatives at least in his second year of office. He thus hoped that the plebeians would compromise, and consent to abolish the tribunate in return for admission to the highest magistracies. His success as a lawgiver is attested by the survival of the decemviral code despite the violent opposition which his policy aroused. His ultimate failure (that he was murdered or escaped assassination by suicide is probable but not certain) together with the gloomy recollections of the civil struggle in which his dictatorship ended (*see* VERGINIA), gave rise to the legend of Appius' tyranny, which, embellished with details taken perhaps from the deeds of the later Claudii, ultimately overshadowed his work and memory.

Mommsen, *Röm. Forsch.* i. 295 ff. P. T.

CLAUDIUS (4) **CAECUS**, APPIUS (*cos.* 307 and 296 B.C.), stands out as the first clear-cut personality in Roman history. He has rightly been compared with the aristocratic founders of Athenian democracy for, although a patrician, Appius used his censorship (*c.* 312 B.C.) to increase the part taken by the lower classes in managing public affairs. He made citizens of low birth and even sons of freedmen senators. Their support, and also heavier taxation, enabled him to build during the eighteen months of his censorship the first aqueduct (*Aqua Appia*) and the Via Appia (q.v.) on which he founded a market (*Forum Appi*). Whether he distributed the landless citizens of Rome throughout all the existing tribes, independently of their income, in order to establish a balance of power between the urban and the agrarian population, which alone had hitherto enjoyed full political rights, is a matter of dispute, although the step accords with his policy. He transferred the cult of Hercules from private to public superintendence, and perhaps helped Cn. Flavius (q.v.) to publish a book of forms of legal procedure. Despite his reforms Appius could still rely on senatorial support, as his subsequent career shows. As consul in 307 and 296 (when he dedicated a temple to Bellona) and praetor in 295, he took an active part in the wars against the Etruscans, Sabines, and Samnites. Despite his old age and blindness, Appius was still one of the most authoritative statesmen when he persuaded the Senate to reject Pyrrhus' peace proposals (*c.* 280). The speech he delivered on that occasion soon became famous, was poetically elaborated by Ennius, and still circulated in the age of Cicero. Appius was the first Roman prose-writer and author of moral apophthegms (e.g. 'faber est suae quisque fortunae'), which probably owed much to Graeco-Pythagorean sources.

Mommsen, *Röm. Forsch.* i. 301 ff.; P. Lejay, *Rev. Phil.* 1920; K. J. Beloch, *Röm. Gesch.* 481 ff.　　　　　　　P. T.

CLAUDIUS (5) **CAUDEX**, APPIUS (*cos.* 264 B.C.), formally commenced the First Punic War by crossing to Sicily with two legions. He relieved Messana by successive attacks on the camps of Hieron and Hanno (Polyb. I. 11–12, 15). Philinus, however, described these Roman engagements as unsuccessful.　　　　　　　H. H. S.

CLAUDIUS (6) **PULCHER**, PUBLIUS, held the Sicilian command as consul in 249 B.C. To intensify the naval blockade of Lilybaeum he attacked the Carthaginian fleet at Drepana. The Carthaginian admiral, however, fell on the flank of the Roman line as its head entered Drepana harbour. Claudius lost 93 of his 123 ships in this the only serious Roman naval defeat in the First Punic War. The pious attributed his defeat to his disregard of religious form before the battle: when told that the sacred chickens would not eat, he drowned them: 'let them drink'. He was court-martialled and fined, and died soon afterwards.

Polybius, I. 49–52.　　　　　　　H. H. S.

CLAUDIUS (7), QUINTUS, *tribunus plebis* in 218 B.C., was author of a law which forbade senators and their sons to own sea-going vessels capable of carrying over 300 *amphorae* (*c.* 225 bushels). Small vessels would suffice to transport their agricultural produce. Perhaps he is to be identified with the praetor of 208.

Livy 21. 63.　　　　　　　H. H. S.

CLAUDIUS (8) **PULCHER**, GAIUS, augur (195 B.C.), praetor (180), was consul in 177, when, after repatriating Latins in Rome, he closed the Istrian War and crushed a Ligurian rising, recapturing Mutina in 176. He was military tribune in Greece in 171. Censor in 169 with Ti. Sempronius Gracchus, he intervened in the levies for Greece; his severity against the *Equites* brought a prosecution in which he was nearly convicted. On the commission for settling Macedonia he died in 167. Strong-willed and conservative, he represented the traditional authority of the Senate in Roman and Italian affairs.

Livy 40. 37; 41. 9–18; 43. 14–16; 45. 15. De Sanctis, *Stor. Rom.* iv. 1, p. 611.　　　　　　　A. H. McD.

CLAUDIUS (9) **PULCHER**, APPIUS, as consul (143 B.C.) defeated the Salassi in Transpadane Gaul and was censor, probably in 136, with Q. Fulvius Nobilior. As *Princeps Senatus*, he gave powerful support to the programme of his son-in-law, Tiberius Gracchus, serving with him and Gaius on the first board of *IIIviri* under the *Lex Agraria* of 133. He died perhaps in 130.

J. Carcopino, *Autour des Gracques* (1928), 200.　　　　M. H.

CLAUDIUS (10) **PULCHER**, APPIUS, was praetor in 89 B.C. His soldiers in Campania deserted to Cinna (87). He was expelled from the Senate (86). He was consul (79) with P. Servilius, and proconsul in Macedonia, where he won some victories against the neighbouring tribes; he died in 76.

Münzer, *PW* iii. 2848.　　　　　　　A. M.

CLAUDIUS (11) **QUADRIGARIUS**, QUINTUS, the Sullan annalist, wrote a history of Rome in at least twenty-three books, from the Gallic sack to his own times. Bk. 3 included the Pyrrhic War, bk. 5 the battle of Cannae, bk. 6 the year 213 B.C., bk. 9 (probably) Ti. Gracchus at Numantia, bk. 13 the year 99 B.C., bk. 19 the year 87 B.C.; the latest date preserved is 82 B.C., the latest book 23. If he is the Claudius who translated Acilius (Livy 25. 39. 12; 35. 14. 5), he presumably adapted the senatorial historian's material to his own annalistic form; the ἔλεγχος χρόνων of Κλώδιος (Plut. *Numa* 1) is scarcely his. The choice of opening point shows his care in handling tradition, although in composition he may have used the Hellenistic, especially the Isocratean, methods of narrative elaboration. This, however, was probably not exaggerated, as by Valerius Antias. His style, as the fragments show, was simple, his vocabulary plain, with an archaic grace (Gellius 9. 13; 15. 1; 13. 29 (28)). He ranks with Valerius Antias as the leading annalist before Livy, and Livy followed him throughout his work.

H. Peter, *HRRel.* i² (1914), pp. cclxxxv, 205. W. Soltau, *Livius' Geschichtswerk* (1897); B. Sypniewska, *De Cl. Quad. fragmentis* (1922); M. Gelzer, *Hermes* 1935, 269; M. Zimmerer, *Der Annalist Q. Claudius Quadrigarius* (1937).　　　　A. H. McD.

CLAUDIUS (12) **PULCHER**, APPIUS, son of no. 10, accompanied his brother-in-law Lucullus to Asia. He was praetor (57 B.C.), then governor in Sardinia. As consul (54) with L. Domitius Ahenobarbus, he made a notorious compact to secure their successors' election for money. He was proconsul in Cilicia (53–51) and after two prosecutions censor (50). He followed Pompey in 49 and died before Pharsalus. He wrote a work on augural discipline, the first book of which he dedicated to Cicero. He appears in the *De Re Rustica* of Varro and was a correspondent of Cicero's.

F. Münzer, *PW* iii. 2849.　　　　　　　A. M.

CLAUDIUS (13), TIBERIUS, a freedman from Smyrna, served the emperors from Tiberius to Domitian. Secretary *a rationibus* of Nero, he was given equestrian rank by Vespasian, banished by Domitian, but recalled on the intercession of his son Claudius Etruscus (Statius, *Silv.* 3. 3).

Stein, *PW* iii. 2670; *PIR*², C 763.　　　　　　A. M.

CLAUDIUS (14) **ETRUSCUS**, the wealthy son of (13) above and (Tettia?) Etrusca, patron of Statius and Martial, was probably knighted by Vespasian. He obtained from Domitian the recall of his exiled father. Statius' *Silvae* 3. 3 is dedicated to him.

Stein, *PW* iii. 2719; *PIR*², C 860.　　　　　　A. M.

CLAUDIUS (15) **POMPEIANUS**, TIBERIUS, son of an equestrian of Antioch, rose to senatorial rank and pursued a brilliant career: *c.* A.D. 167 he was governor of Lower Pannonia, where he stemmed the German invasions. Subsequently *cos.* I, he married Lucilla (q.v.), widow of L. Verus (q.v.), in 169, holding a second consulship in 173. He was now the trusted friend of M. Aurelius (q.v. 1), and his commander in all major campaigns. Under Commodus (q.v.) he retired into private life, thus escaping the repercussions of Lucilla's plot, but, though aged and infirm, emerged again under Pertinax, who, like Didius Julianus after him, vainly pressed him to a share of the imperial administration.

PIR², C 973; P. Lambrechts, La Composition du sénat romain . . . (117–192) (1936), p. 120, no. 705. C. H. V. S.

CLAUDIUS (16) **MAMERTINUS** is the author of a speech delivered on 1 Jan. A.D. 362 in Constantinople, in which he thanked the Emperor Julian for the gift of the consulship. The kernel of the speech is an exaggerated eulogy of Julian. Involved in an embezzlement charge, he fell into disgrace in 368. See PANEGYRIC, LATIN. A. S.

CLAUDIUS, see also BRITANNICUS, DRUSUS, MARCELLUS, NAMATIANUS, NERO, TACITUS.

CLAUSULA, see PROSE RHYTHM.

CLAVUS ANGUSTUS, LATUS. The angustus clavus was a narrow, the latus clavus a broad, purple stripe (possibly two stripes) stitched to the border of the Roman toga. The former indicated equestrian, the latter senatorial, rank. Under the Roman Empire the latus clavus was worn before admission to the Senate, on the assumption of the toga virilis, by sons of senators as a right (though, perhaps, the formal consent of the emperor was required; cf. Suet. Aug. 38. 2); by others who aimed at a senatorial career (e.g. Ovid and his brother, Trist. 4. 10. 28 f.; Dio Cass. 59. 9. 5), with the emperor's special permission. Military tribunes in the legions were distinguished as tribuni angusticlavii or tribuni laticlavii according as they were pursuing the equestrian or the senatorial cursus honorum. J. P. B.

CLEANTHES (331–232 B.C.), son of Phanias of Assos, disciple of Zeno of Citium and his successor as head of the Stoic School from 263 to 232. With him the sober philosophy of Zeno became pervaded by religious fervour. He considered the universe a living being, God as the soul of the universe, the sun as its heart. In ethics he stressed disinterestedness, saying that doing good to others with a view to one's own advantage was comparable to feeding cattle in order to eat them. He contended that evil thoughts were worse than evil deeds, just as a tumour that breaks open is less dangerous than one which does not. Most famous among his works is his hymn to Zeus.

A. C. Pearson, The Fragments of Zenon and Cleanthes (1891); H. von Arnim, SVF i. 103–39; Poetical Fragments, J. U. Powell, Coll. Alex. (1925), 227–31; Diog. Laert. 7. 168–76; PW xi. 558. K. von F.

CLEARCHUS (1) (c. 450–401 B.C.), a Spartan officer and a stern disciplinarian, held commands in the Hellespontine region from 409 onwards. He refused to withdraw from Byzantium in 403, was ejected by Spartan troops, and sought refuge with Cyrus II, who commissioned him to recruit, and later to command, the Greek mercenaries forming the core of his army. At Cunaxa his refusal to expose his right flank made possible the decisive Persian cavalry charge. He held his troops together after the battle, but, with the other officers, was treacherously arrested at a conference with Tissaphernes and executed. D. E. W. W.

CLEARCHUS (2), Middle Comedy poet, late in that period, his name standing among the victors four places before Timocles (IG ii.² 2325. 154). Fr. 3 (The Corinthians) says no one would carouse if the headache came before the debauch!

FCG iv. 562 ff.; CAF ii. 408 ff. W. G. W.

CLEARCHUS (3) of Soli, in Cyprus (fl. c. 250 B.C.), a polymath, wrote βίοι (of people and individuals), paradoxes, an encomium on Plato, and zoological and mystical works. These are learned but sensational; attacks on luxury reveal a Peripatetic background (FHG ii. 302).

O. Stein, Philol. 1931, 258–9. F. W. W.

CLEDONIUS (5th c. A.D.), grammarian who taught in Constantinople and wrote an Ars (ed. Keil, Gramm. Lat. v. 9–79) which is explanatory of the Ars of Donatus. The treatise is preserved only in a sixth-century Berne codex which is our oldest MS. of a grammatical work.

Cf. Teuffel, § 472. 1; Schanz–Hosius, § 1101. J. F. M.

CLEDONOMANCY, see DIVINATION, para. 5.

CLEIDEMUS or **CLEITODEMUS** (fl. c. 350 B.C.), the oldest atthidographer, if we except Hellanicus. The Atthis, in more than four books, was his chief work. The first two books dealt with the monarchic period, and are most often cited, his main interest being presumably in the earlier history. These two books are also referred to under the title Πρωτογονία. The fragments show a tendency to rationalize myths and an interest in etymology.

FHG i. 359. G. L. B.

CLEISTHENES (1) (6th c. B.C.), Athenian statesman, son of Megacles (q.v.) and Agariste (see CLEISTHENES 2). He was of the family of Alcmaeonidae (q.v.), which had quarrelled with Pisistratus; though it is possible that he returned from exile and became archon c. 525–524 B.C. If so, the Alcmaeonidae were exiled again, perhaps after the murder of Hipparchus in 514. An attempt by them to overthrow the tyranny failed at Leipsydrium (date uncertain; perhaps before 514). While in exile the Alcmaeonidae had gained influence at Delphi, and induced the oracle to urge Sparta (then engaged in driving out tyrants and setting up oligarchies in many States and thereby extending the Peloponnesian League) to overthrow the tyranny at Athens. With Spartan help Hippias was expelled; but the noble families at Athens soon quarrelled, and Cleisthenes joined or formed a democratic party to oust his rival Isagoras. The latter was elected archon in 508–507, and called in Sparta again (perhaps the Spartan troops had helped to secure his election). Cleisthenes withdrew, but was soon recalled, and his democratic constitution finally established. According to a doubtful story in Herodotus, he attempted to get help from the Persian satrap at Sardes for the probable war with Sparta; but the terms, complete submission to Persia, were too high. Nothing further is known of him; the complete darkness which veils his last years is one of the curiosities of history.

For his constitutional reforms see ARCHONTES, BOULE, ECCLESIA, DEMOI, PHYLAE, STRATEGI. A. W. G.

CLEISTHENES (2) of Sicyon, the greatest tyrant of the house of Orthagoras, which ruled for the record period of a century (c. 665–565 B.C.). His reign (c. 600–570) was marked by a strong movement against the Argive Dorian culture and ascendancy: the three traditional Dorian tribes were renamed Piggites, Swinites, Assites, while the non-Dorian was called Archelaoi (Rulers); Argive rhapsodes were suppressed and the ancient Argive hero Adrastus persuaded to find a tomb elsewhere. His daughter Agariste (mother of the Athenian Cleisthenes) married the Alcmaeonid Megacles, after her suitors had spent a year in the tyrant's palace like successors of the suitors of Penelope. In the First Sacred War (q.v.) Cleisthenes took a leading part; he destroyed Crisa and for a while appears to have controlled the sea approach to Delphi.

Herodotus 5. 67–9; 6. 126–31. P. N. Ure, Origin of Tyranny (1922), 258–64, footnotes. P. N. U.

CLEITARCHUS of Alexandria, Alexander-historian, was a secondary writer who was never in Asia and wrote under Ptolemy II, some time after 280 B.C. Little certainty can be obtained about his history, but the belief that Diodorus bk. 17 substantially represents it is baseless; probably it was a bad historical novel, unfavourable to Alexander and making him an imitative character with a taste for massacres. His sources were probably largely popular beliefs, though he sometimes used and embellished Aristobulus and may have drawn on the poets who accompanied Alexander. Diodorus and Curtius did use him, but as secondary material only. No critic of antiquity has a good word for him; but he was much read under the early Roman Empire, and influenced the Romance. *See* ALEXANDER (3), Bibliography, Ancient Sources. W. W. T.

CLEITODEMUS, *see* CLEIDEMUS.

CLEITUS (1) ('the Black') (*c.* 380–328 or 327 B.C.), a Macedonian of noble birth and some distinction as a commander of cavalry. His fame, however, rests on two events: he saved Alexander's life at the battle of the Granicus; and he was himself killed by Alexander nearly seven years later, in a drunken quarrel, though the underlying grounds of difference were political questions of the first importance (Arrian, *Anab.* 4. 8. 1 ff.; Plutarch, *Alex.* 51, and—more hostile to Alexander—Curtius Rufus 8. 1. 19 ff.).

Berve, *Alexanderreich*, no. 427. G. T. G.

CLEITUS (2) (d. 318 B.C.), a Macedonian noble, served under Alexander in Asia without distinction. Sent home with Craterus and the 'veterans' (324), he played an important part in the Lamian War as admiral of the Macedonian fleet which closed the Dardanelles to the Greeks after two victories (322). For his continued loyalty to Antipater he was rewarded with the satrapy of Lydia (321), from which Antigonus expelled him (319). He became Polyperchon's admiral with the task of preventing Antigonus from invading Europe, but was defeated by Nicanor near the Bosporus and killed in Thrace soon afterwards. G. T. G.

CLEMENS, FLAVIUS (*cos.* A.D. 95), son of Flavius Sabinus and husband of Flavia Domitilla (the niece of Domitian), a person of inoffensive habits ('contemptissimae inertiae'), who was put to death, along with his wife, for *maiestas* soon after he laid down the consulate. They are said to have been guilty of ἀθεότης, or following Jewish practices (Dio 67. 14), and may have been Christians, as later tradition alleges. Domitian intended the succession to go to the two small sons of Clemens; they are not heard of after 96. R. S.

CLEMENT OF ALEXANDRIA (TITUS FLAVIUS CLEMENS) was born *c.* A.D. 150, probably at Athens, of pagan parents. He was converted to Christianity and travelled extensively seeking instruction from Christian teachers and finally from Pantaenus, head of the Catechetical School of Alexandria, at that time an unofficial institution giving tuition to converts. Clement had a wide acquaintance with Greek literature; his writings abound in quotations from the Platonic and Stoic philosophers; also from Homer, Hesiod, and the dramatists (frequently drawn, it is thought, from anthologies and other secondary sources). His *Protrepticus* shows familiarity with the Greek Mysteries. After ordination he succeeded Pantaenus as head of the school, some time before 200, and held the office till *c.* 202, when, on the outbreak of the persecution under Septimius Severus, he left Alexandria and took refuge, perhaps with his former pupil Alexander, then bishop of Cappadocia and later of Jerusalem. Clement died between 211 and 216. Much of his writings is lost, but the following im-

portant works survive nearly complete. These are: (1) The Προτρεπτικὸς πρὸς Ἕλληνας or 'Hortatory Address to the Greeks' (*c.* 190), designed to prove the superiority of Christianity to the pagan religions and philosophies. (2) The Παιδαγωγός or 'Tutor' (*c.* 190–5), an exposition of the moral teaching of Christ, not only in its general method, but also in detailed application to special points of conduct, such as eating and drinking, dress, and the use of wealth. (3) The Στρωματεῖς or 'Miscellanies' (probably *c.* 200–2), in eight books, the first seven dealing in the main with the subordination and inferiority of Greek to Christian philosophy. The eighth book is a fragment on Logic. In one of the MSS. two further pieces follow, generally known as *Excerpta ex Theodoto* and *Eclogae propheticae*.

The *Quis dives salvetur?* (Τίς ὁ σωζόμενος πλούσιος;) is an extant homily urging detachment from worldly goods. The Ὑποτυπώσεις or 'Sketches' (of which only fragments survive) was probably an exegetical work consisting of notes on passages of the Scriptures.

Clement's conception of Christianity has been criticized as tinged with Hellenism and humanism and as doctrinally imperfect. His name is often found in Christian calendars on 4 Dec., but in 1748 Benedict XIV expressly excluded him from the Roman martyrology. His writings, however, have much charm and are characterized by serenity and hopefulness.

TEXTS: J. Potter (2 vols., 1715); R. Klotz (1831–4); W. Dindorf (Oxford, 1869); Migne, *PG* viii and ix; O. Stählin (4 vols., 1905–36, in *Die griechischen christlichen Schriftsteller*); *Exc. ex Theod.*, R. P. Casey (1934).
GENERAL LITERATURE: Eusebius, *Hist. Eccl.*; B. F. Westcott in *DCB*, s.v.; C. Bigg, *The Christian Platonists of Alexandria* (Bampton Lectures of 1886); O. Bardenhewer, *Geschichte der altkirchlichen Literatur* (ii², 1914), 40–95; B. J. Kidd, *A History of the Church to A.D. 461* (1922), i, ch. 15.

CLEOBIS and BITON, the two Argive brothers mentioned by Solon to Croesus, in Herodotus' story (1. 31), as among the happiest of mortals. Their mother, presumably as Cicero says (*Tusc.* 1. 47) a priestess of Hera, found that her oxen were not brought in time for a festival, and they drew her car the 45 stades to the temple. She prayed to the goddess to grant them the greatest boon possible for mortals, and Hera caused them to die while they slept in the temple. The Argives honoured them with statues at Delphi, which have been discovered, their identity being ensured by an inscription.

SIG 5 *Supp. Epigr.* 3. 395. Cf. Ch. Picard, *Rev. Hist. Rel.* xcvi (1927), 365 ff. W. K. C. G.

CLEOMEDES (probably *c.* A.D. 150–200), astronomer, author of a popular work Κυκλικὴ θεωρία μετεώρων (*De Motu Circulari Corporum Caelestium*), largely founded on Posidonius, but with a certain number of optical discoveries which appear to be original.

Ed. H. Ziegler (1891). *PW* xi. 679. W. D. R.

CLEOMENES (1) **I** (reigned *c.* 519–487 B.C.), a Spartan king, the son of Anaxandridas by his second wife, and half-brother to Dorieus, Leonidas, and Cleombrotus, whom Anaxandridas' first wife bore him later. He pursued an adventurous and at times unscrupulous policy in Greece. He sought to embroil Athens with Thebes by referring the request of the Plataeans for help against Thebes to Athens (probably early in his reign, as Thuc. 3. 68 implies). He launched an unsuccessful attack upon the Athenian tyrant Hippias in 511, but taking the field in person expelled him in 510. Three years later he interfered unsuccessfully on behalf of Isagoras against Cleisthenes, and in 506, when he mobilized the full Peloponnesian levy to restore Hippias, he was frustrated by the defection of the Corinthians and the obstruction of his colleague Demaratus (q.v.).

Disliking distant commitments, he refused to interfere in the affairs of Samos (*c.* 515), and to support the

Ionian Revolt. His ruthless destruction of the Argive army near Tiryns (probably in 494) was a wanton attack on an unoffending neighbour. His attempt to punish Aegina for submitting to Darius was thwarted by Demaratus, but with support from a Delphic oracle he secured Demaratus' deposition on a charge of illegitimacy. When this was proved to be baseless, he fled and stirred up revolt among the Arcadians. Recalled to Sparta, he soon met a violent end. According to Herodotus he killed himself in a fit of insanity.

Herodotus (5. 39 ff.) underrates Cleomenes; J. Wells, *Studies in Herodotus* (1923), 74 ff., is too lenient. A. M. W.

CLEOMENES (2) **III** (c. 260–219 B.C.), son of Leonidas, king of Sparta, imbibed ideals of social revolution from his wife Agiatis, Agis IV's widow. Becoming king in 235, he first moved in 229, when he annexed Tegea, Mantinea, Orchomenus, and Caphyae from Aetolia. Having provoked Achaea into war (228), he secured victories at Mt. Lycaeus and Ladoceia (227); he now seized despotic power at home (winter 227–226) and set up a 'Lycurgan' régime, cancelling debts, dividing up land, and restocking the citizen body from *perioeci* and metics. After his capture of Mantinea and victory at Hecatombaeum, a peace conference was called, but postponed owing to his illness; but meanwhile Aratus had opened negotiations with Antigonus III and war recommenced. By seizing Argos (225) and besieging Corinth (224) Cleomenes threatened to shatter the Achaean League; but Antigonus reached the Isthmus, Argos revolted, and Cleomenes was reduced to the defensive. In winter 223 he took Megalopolis; but after a decisive defeat at Sellasia (July 222) he fled to his patron Euergetes in Egypt. Imprisoned by Euergetes' successor, he broke out, tried in vain to stir up revolution in Alexandria, and committed suicide (winter 220–219).

An idealist and a nationalist, Cleomenes used social revolution as the tool of Spartan expansion. He was able to inspire allegiance, and his ideals lived on after him; but he devised no means of securing his gains.

Polyb. 2. 45–70; Plut. *Cleomenes, Aratus*. F. W. Walbank, *Aratos of Sicyon* (1933); W. H. Porter, ed. Plutarch's *Aratus*, introd. (1937). F. W. W.

CLEOMENES (3) of Naucratis was appointed financial manager of Egypt and administrative chief of the eastern Delta district by Alexander in 332–331 B.C. He was entrusted with the completion of Alexandria, and became a citizen of it. He made himself satrap of the whole of Egypt after a few years without the consent of Alexander, but was afterwards recognized and pardoned by him. Cleomenes became *hyparchus* of Egypt, with Ptolemy I as satrap, in 322–321; but the future king of Egypt brought serious charges against him, and executed him afterwards. The tricks with which Cleomenes exploited Egypt's wealth and collected 8,000 talents are described in Ps.-Aristotle's *Economics*.

A. M. Andreades, *Bull. Corr. Hell.* liii (1929), 1 f.; F. M. Heichelheim, s.v. 'Sitos' in *PW*, Suppl. vi. 863 f.; G. Mickwitz, *Vierteljahrschrift für Soz.- und Wirtschaftsgesch.* xxxii (1939), 11 f.; F .Stähelin, s.v. 'Kleomenes' in *PW*. F. M. H.

CLEON (d. 422 B.C.), Athenian politician, the son of a rich tanner. His first known action in politics was to attack Pericles in 431 and 430; he succeeded him as 'leader of the people'. He proposed the decree to execute all the men of Mytilene after its revolt in 427 (rescinded next day). In 426 he attacked the *Babylonians* of Aristophanes as a libel on the State. Next year, after the Athenian victory at Pylos, he frustrated the Spartan peace proposals, and later accused the generals in charge of the siege of Sphacteria of incompetence. Nicias offered to resign the command to him, and he was compelled to take it; he was completely successful, forcing the Spartans to surrender. In 425 he carried a measure doubling or trebling the tribute paid by the allied States,

and increased the dicasts' pay from two to three obols. In 423 he proposed the decree for the destruction of Scione and the execution of all its citizens. In 422–421 he was strategus and set out to recover Amphipolis for Athens, but miserably failed, being defeated by Brasidas and killed.

We have a vivid picture of Cleon in Thucydides and Aristophanes. Both were clearly prejudiced against him, but the portrait must be in essentials true: a very forcible speaker, as ready to tell the people their faults as to flatter them, vulgar in manner, vain (his one success at Sphacteria carried him away), above all, narrow-minded and short-sighted. He wore the mantle of Pericles, but was as inferior to him in ability as he was different in manner. By the fourth-century orators he is spoken of with respect; in the later history he is the conventional vulgar demagogue. A. W. G.

CLEONIDES (beginning of 2nd c. A.D.), author of an Εἰσαγωγὴ ἁρμονική, one of the best sources for the harmonic theory of Aristoxenus (q.v.) of Tarentum.

Ed. C. Jan, *Musici Scriptores Graeci* (1895), 167–207, and H. Menge, *Euclidis Opera* 8 (1916), 186. *PW* xi. 729. W. D. R.

CLEONYMUS (fl. 305–270 B.C.), younger son of Cleomenes II, guardian to his nephew Areus, who ascended the Spartan throne in 309–308. In 303–302, answering a Tarentine appeal with 5,000 mercenaries, he forced the Lucanians to make peace, annexed Metapontum, and seized Corcyra. When Tarentum revolted he returned to Italy, but was defeated, and soon lost Corcyra. In 293 he helped Boeotia ineffectively against Demetrius; in 279 he seized Troezen, and attacked Messene and Megalopolis. Banished from Sparta c. 275 (Plut. *Pyrrh.* 26), he last appears accompanying Pyrrhus' Laconian invasion (272). Violent, and soured by missing the throne, he was a constant foe of the Antigonids.

K. J. Beloch, *Griech. Gesch.* iv (1928). F. W. W.

CLEOPATRA I (c. 215–176 B.C.), daughter of Antiochus III and Laodice. She married Ptolemy V in 193 and ruled after her husband's death in 180 as regent for her young son, Ptolemy VI, but died four years later. Her foreign policy was pro-Seleucid, as was natural, and she was therefore called Syra by her subjects. Her official name was θεὰ ἐπιφανής and μήτηρ. F. M. H.

CLEOPATRA II, daughter of Ptolemy V and Cleopatra I, was born between 185 and 180 B.C. She married her brother, Ptolemy VI, c. 175–174. Later she was co-regent with Ptolemy VI and his brother Ptolemy VIII from 170 until Ptolemy VI was restored as sole ruler. After his death in 146 Cleopatra's further life was a continuous struggle for power against her brother Ptolemy VIII by open war (short regency for Ptolemy VII in 146, rebellion 132–124) or diplomacy (marriage to Ptolemy VIII in 144, conciliation in 124). She survived her second husband, but died in 116 or 115. F. M. H.

CLEOPATRA III, daughter of Ptolemy VI and Cleopatra II. Ptolemy VIII seduced and married her in 142 B.C., and made her his co-regent, as a counterweight against her mother's influence. After his death in 116 her eldest son, Ptolemy IX, was made co-regent against her will. She incited unsuccessful rebellions in 110 and 108, but succeeded in 107 in giving her second son, Ptolemy X, his brother's throne. Her last years were filled with quarrels with this second son, who was accused by many of matricide. *See* PTOLEMY. F. M. H.

CLEOPATRA VII was second daughter of Ptolemy (q.v.) Auletes. Her traditional portrait is partly a product of Roman hatred. A Macedonian princess, with no Egyptian blood, she was attractive rather than beautiful, highly educated, a good organizer, fearless, and amazingly alive. Brought up at a corrupt court, she was always her own law. Some Alexandrians apart, she was popular in Egypt; alone of Macedonian monarchs she spoke her people's language, and if her interest in their religion was as much political as personal, she did feel herself daughter of Re (the sun-god) more seriously than Alexander had felt himself son of Ammon. Almost certainly she never loved any man. Her two love affairs were to gain power, for the keynote of her character was intense ambition; that, and her fire, her mysticism, and her legend, bring her nearer to Alexander than any other of his successors. An exile of 22 when Caesar reached Egypt, she became his mistress to recover her throne, bore him a son, and followed him to Rome in the hope of something greater. After his death she returned to Egypt, until in 41 Antony summoned her to Tarsus. She became his mistress, and he visited her at Alexandria, where he treated her, not as a Roman client-queen, but as an independent monarch; but in 40 he quitted Alexandria, and she did not see him again for four years. Then, late in 37, convinced that further co-operation with Octavian was impossible, he again came eastward, and this time married her; she was the stronger of the two, but was loyal to him to the end. Next year she persuaded him that war with Octavian was inevitable and that he must make one supreme effort for victory. Any Macedonian had much to avenge upon Rome, but few more audacious schemes have ever been conceived than her design of conquering Rome by means of Romans. At Antony's triumph over Armenia in 34 she publicly appeared in the guise of Isis; and at the following 'Donations of Alexandria' he expressly made her overlord of the East as Queen of Kings; the real meaning, not expressed, was that he was Roman Emperor and she Roman Empress. An unknown Greek prophesied that after overthrowing Rome she would reconcile Europe and Asia and inaugurate the reign of Justice and Love; whether she had any such thoughts cannot be said. In any case, Antony's dual position as Roman magistrate and Cleopatra's husband steadily became impossible, and at Actium the refusal of his fleet (i.e. his legions) to fight ended her dream. Egypt offered to rise for her, but she forbade the useless sacrifice; she hoped Octavian would crown one of her sons in her stead. Octavian played her till he had secured her person and treasure and then disillusioned her and gave her an opportunity for suicide. She used an asp, because it was Re's minister; her death meant that she went home to her father the Sun-god. Whatever her faults, the Roman conquerors raised an unwilling monument to her greatness: they had feared her, a woman, as they had feared none other but Hannibal.

W. W. Tarn, *JRS* 1932, 135 (the Cleopatra prophecy); *CAH* x, chs. 2 and 3.
W. W. T.

CLEOPHON (1) became the democratic leader at Athens after the restoration of democratic rule in 410 B.C. He introduced the διωβελία, a dole of two obols a day, the allotment of which is unknown. He apparently managed Athenian finances between 410 and 406; he was honest and died poor, and seems to have been efficient. But he was as violent in his manner as Cleon. He attacked both Critias and Alcibiades; and prevented the peace terms offered by Sparta after Cyzicus in 410 from being accepted, and again after Aegospotami in 405. He was prosecuted and condemned to death in 404.
A. W. G.

CLEOPHON (2), Athenian tragic poet of whose plays some titles (Suidas, s.v.) but no fragments survive. Aristotle mentions his lack of idealism (*Poet.* 2), his prosaic style (ibid. 22; *Rh.* 3. 7), and illustrates from him a method of evading a question (*Soph. El.* 15).
A. W. P.-C.

CLEOSTRATUS of Tenedos, *see* CONSTELLATIONS, para. 3.

CLEPSYDRA, *see* CLOCKS.

CLEROMANCY, *see* DIVINATION, para. 6.

CLERUCHY (κληρουχία), a special type of Greek colony, in which the settlers retained their original citizenship and did not form an autonomous community. It was almost confined to Athens in the time of the Empire. Every settler was allotted a parcel of land (κλῆρος), normally sufficient to maintain him as *zeugites* (q.v.) and so as a hoplite; they were chosen from the poorest citizens. The cleruchy thus served a double purpose: it helped the poor of Athens and provided a garrison, to prevent either disaffection or attack from without. The most important cleruchies were in Salamis (*c.* 509 B.C., but perhaps earlier), Chalcis (506–490), Lemnos and Imbros (perhaps before 480), Scyros (*c.* 475), Hestiaea in Euboea (445), Naxos, Andros, and the Chersonese (*c.* 450), Aegina (431), Lesbos (427). All these, except Salamis, were abolished in the last stages of the Peloponnesian War. Early in the fourth century Lemnos, Imbros, and Scyros were resettled, and remained Athenian till Roman times; Samos was colonized in 360–350, but lost in 322.

Though the settlers retained their Athenian citizenship, their military duties kept them in their new homes, where they formed communities with self-government in local affairs: they had a boule, ecclesia, *phylae*, magistrates on the Athenian pattern. In the fourth century at least they were supervised by yearly *epimeletae* and *strategi* from Athens. An archon was sent from Athens to Salamis; but the settlers there could exercise political rights in Athens. The cleruchs had the military duties of citizens, and often served abroad; they participated in Athenian festivals.

The size of the cleruchies varied from 1,000 settlers or more (Lemnos, Imbros, the Chersonese) to 200 (Andros). The cleruchs may have numbered 10,000 all told by 430.
A. W. G.

CLIBANARII, *see* ARMS AND ARMOUR, ROMAN.

CLIENS. In Ancient Rome a client was a free man who entrusted himself to another and received protection in return. In the late Republic and early Empire, clientship was essentially a social hereditary status consecrated by usage and reflected in the law. The rules of the law were far more binding for the special case of the freedman, who was *ipso facto* 'cliens' of his former owner (*see* FREEDMEN). The ordinary client might receive daily food, often converted into money (*sportula*), or assistance in the courts. In return he helped his patron in his political and private life, and showed him respect, especially by greeting him in the morning. Client and patron could not bear witness against one another, or at least the evidence could not be enforced. Dionysius (*Ant. Rom.* 2. 9–10) records other rules, many of which were out of use or are mere conjectures, for instance that the client must try to ransom his patron.

The Twelve Tables recognized the tie of clientship: 'patronus si clienti fraudem fecerit sacer esto'.

In Imperial times the client was practically confused with the parasite. Martial describes himself as a client. Clients were called *salutatores* because of their duty of daily salutation and *togati* because custom compelled them to wear the toga, by that time obsolescent.

In the provinces (especially in Gaul) the Roman clientship superimposed itself on pre-existing local forms of social ties.

Mommsen, *Röm. Forsch.* i (1864), 354; id. *Röm. Staatsr.* iii. 54; A. v. Premerstein, *PW* iv. 23; L. Friedländer, *Darstellungen aus d. Sittengeschichte Roms* i⁹ (1919), 223; ii. 230; J. Carcopino, *Daily Life in Ancient Rome* (1941), 171. *See also* PATRONUS.
A. M.

CLIPEUS, see ARMS AND ARMOUR, ROMAN.

CLITOMACHUS (Κλειτόμαχος), (187/6–110/9 B.C.), Academic (*Acad. index Herc.* col. 25. 15). He was a Carthaginian, originally called Hasdrubal (l.c., col. 25. 1 f.; Diog. Laert. 4. 67; etc.). After having studied Greek for four years, at the age of twenty-eight he became a pupil of Carneades. In 140–139 he opened a school of his own in the Palladium, and in 127–126 he was elected president of the Academy (*Acad. index*). During a serious illness he committed suicide (Stob. *Flor.* 7. 55).

Clitomachus, a rigid sceptic, was the literary exponent of Carneades, who had left no writings. He is said to have composed about 400 books (D.L. 4. 67), often, however, only notes of Carneades' lectures (cf. Cic. *Tusc.* 3. 54). Well-known writings of his were four books *About the withholding of assent* (Περὶ ἐποχῆς, cf. Cic. *Luc.* 98); *On the sects* (Π. αἱρέσεων, D.L. 2. 92); a work dedicated to the Roman poet Lucilius, another to L. Censorinus, on the principles of the theory of knowledge (Cic. *Luc.* 102). Moreover, it is likely that the greater part of the account of the New Academy in Cicero, Plutarch, and Sextus Empiricus is based on C.

PW xi. 656. K. O. B.

CLITUMNUS, a river near Trebiae in Umbria, famous for the white sacrificial kine on its banks (Verg. *G.* 2. 146). It flowed into the Tinia, and subsequently into the Tiber. Shrines of the personified Clitumnus and other deities adorned its source (called *Sacraria* in the Itineraries), attracting numerous tourists (Pliny, *Ep.* 8. 8; Suet. *Cal.* 43). E. T. S.

CLIVUS PUBLICIUS, see AVENTINE.

CLOACA MAXIMA, a canalized stream draining north-east Rome from the Argiletum to the Tiber by way of the Forum Romanum and Velabrum. Tradition ascribed its regulation to Tarquinius Superbus, and branch drains of the fifth century B.C. do exist. Much of the existing sewer, nowhere older than the third century B.C., is due to M. Vipsanius Agrippa in 33 B.C. I. A. R.

CLOATIUS VERUS, Augustan grammarian, who besides other works (e.g. Macrob. *Sat.* 3. 6. 2) wrote three books on derivations (some sound, some unsound) of Latin words from Greek (Gell. 16. 12): probably the 'Cloatius' cited six times by Verrius.

Teuffel, § 263.

CLOCKS. The hours (ὧραι, *horae,* not in the modern sense till Aristotle; δυώδεκα μέρεα τῆς ἡμέρης, Hdt. 2. 109. 3, but see J. E. Powell in *CR* liv. 69 f.) were told in antiquity (1) by the sundial, ὡρολόγιον or -εῖον, *solarium,* consisting of a pointer, γνώμων, casting its shadow (hence the instrument is sometimes called σκιοθήρας) upon a convex surface, σκάφη (also πόλος, as being a sort of model of the sky) or (less commonly) a flat one. The inventor was Anaximandros (Favorinus ap. Diog. Laert. 2. 1; Pliny, *HN* 2. 187 says Anaximenes), and the idea itself Babylonian (Hdt. loc. cit.). (2) By the water-clock, κλεψύδρα, *clepsydra,* ὑδροσκοπεῖον, consisting of (*a*) a vessel from which water flowed through a small orifice, (*b*) a graduated container into which the water flowed. But if the water-level in (*a*) was allowed to grow lower, the rate of flow would decrease; hence it was necessary either to keep the level in (*a*) constant or in some other way to compensate for the decrease. See Heron of Alexandria, vol. 1, p. 506. 23 Schmidt (Teubner, 1899), and the elaborate clock of Ctesibius (Vitruvius, *De arch.* 9. 8. 2 ff.). Ordinary clocks were, however, anything but accurate (Seneca, *Apocol.* 2. 2).

Convenient assemblage of facts in A. Rehm, *PW,* s.v. 'Horologium'. Cf. W. Kubitschek, *Grundriss der antiken Zeitrechnung* (1928), 188 ff. H. J. R.

CLODIA, sister of Clodius (q.v. 1) and wife of Q. Metellus Celer; already before her husband's death (59 B.C.) the most profligate woman of the aristocracy, possessing also considerable political power. Catullus (q.v.) made her into his Lesbia; by 58 Caelius (q.v.) was her lover, but later branded her as a 'quadrantaria Clytaemnestra'. Cicero's *Pro Caelio* is the most vivid picture of her; in his *Letters* she is βοῶπις (Juno), accused of incest with her brother (cf. Catull. 79).

L. Schwabe, *Quaestiones Catullianae* (1862), 54 ff.; T. Frank, *Catullus and Horace²* (1928), 81; Teuffel-Schwabe, *History of Roman Literature* (1900), i. 392. G. E. F. C.

CLODIANUS, see LENTULUS (3).

CLODIUS (1) PUBLIUS, brother of App. Claudius Pulcher (*cos.* 54), preached mutiny to Lucullus' troops in 68 B.C., and appeared as collusive prosecutor of Catiline in 64. In December 62 he caused a political crisis by appearing in woman's clothes at the festival of Bona Dea, held in the house of Caesar (*Pontifex Maximus*), whose wife Pompeia was his mistress. Though Clodius was finally acquitted of sacrilege by bribed jurors, Cicero had given evidence destroying his alibi; and to be revenged Clodius eventually obtained through Caesar in 59 a *traductio in plebem,* and was elected tribune for 58. He bribed the people with free corn and restoration of *collegia*; then, after repealing the *Leges Aelia* and *Fufia* (see LEX, LEGES), he passed a law outlawing anyone who had put citizens to death without trial. Cicero went into exile; Clodius removed Cato (q.v. 5) to Cyprus, and rewarded for their acquiescence the consuls, Gabinius and Piso, with the provinces of Syria and Macedonia. Clodius then turned against Pompey, allowing the escape of Tigranes, son of the Armenian king, threatening Pompey's life, and perhaps suggesting repeal of the *Lex Iulia Agraria.* He continued these attacks after Cicero's recall, over the questions of the corn supply and Egypt; but after Luca he lost Caesar's backing, and the rest of his life was spent in brawls against the rival gangs of Milo (q.v.), whom Pompey originally set against him. On 18 January 52 Milo murdered Clodius, then candidate for the praetorship, and the people, regarding Clodius as their champion, burned the Senate house as his pyre.

Sources: Cicero, esp. *De Domo, Pro Sestio,* and Correspondence (ed. Tyrrell and Purser, vols. i and ii); Asconius, esp. pp. 6–10, 26–49, KS.; and the texts and general modern works cited s.v. CAESAR (1) in the present work. On Clodius as Caesar's agent in 58–56 see L. G. Pocock, *CQ* 1924–5. G. E. F. C.

CLODIUS (2) MACER, LUCIUS, *legatus* in Africa in A.D. 68, revolted to Galba and cut off the corn-supply of Rome. He acted as a champion of the Senate, called himself propraetor, and raised a new legion I Macriana liberatrix. Galba had him executed.

E. Groag, *PW* iv. 79; *PIR²,* C 1170; H. Mattingly, *B.M. Coins of R.E.* i. 285. A. M.

CLODIUS (3) QUIRINALIS, PUBLIUS, from Arelate in Gaul, taught rhetoric in the Neronian age.

CLODIUS (4) ALBINUS, DECIMUS, a native of Hadrumetum in Africa, belonged to a noble family. After distinguished military service he was at the time of Commodus' death governor of Britain. As a potential candidate for the principate he was at first placated by the title of Caesar, but after Niger's death was proclaimed by Septimius a public enemy on the score of alleged treasonable correspondence with the Senate. In reply Albinus was saluted Augustus by his army, and in A.D. 196 he crossed to Gaul in the vain hope of securing the support of the German legions before marching on Rome. He was killed in a battle near Lugdunum in 197.

Herodian 2. 15, 3. 7–8; Dio Cassius, bk. 73; O. Hirschfeld, *Kleine Schriften* (1905), 411 ff. *See also* SEVERUS, SEPTIMIUS. H. M. D. P.

CLODIUS, *see also* PUPIENUS S.V. BALBINUS, TURRINUS.

CLOELIA, a Roman girl given as hostage to Porsenna (q.v.). She escaped to Rome by swimming the Tiber, but was handed back to Porsenna who, admiring her bravery, freed her and other hostages. An equestrian statue on the Via Sacra celebrated her exploit, in which modern hypercriticism sees an aetiological myth woven round an image of Venus Equestris.   H. H. S.

CLOTHO, *see* FATE.

CLUBS, GREEK. The clubs here discussed may be defined as voluntary associations of persons more or less permanently organized for the pursuit of a common end, and so distinguishable both from the State and its component elements on the one hand, and on the other from temporary unions for transitory purposes. Despite the large number and great popularity of clubs in the Greek world, both in the Hellenistic and in the Greco-Roman period, literature makes surprisingly few references to them, and the available evidence consists almost entirely of inscriptions and, in the case of Egypt, papyri. These provide a picture which, if incomplete, is at least vivid and detailed.

2. Greek clubs, sacred and secular, are attested as early as the time of Solon, one of whose laws, quoted by Gaius (*Dig.* 47. 22. 4), gave legal validity to their regulations, unless contrary to the laws of the State; and we hear of political clubs (ἑταιρίαι) at Athens in the fifth century B.C. (Thuc. 3. 82; 8. 54; 65). In the classical period the societies known to us are mostly religious, carrying on the cult of some hero or god not yet recognized by the State, such as the votaries (ὀργεῶνες) of Amynus, Asclepius, and Dexion, the heroized Sophocles. With the close of Greek freedom, clubs become much more frequent and varied, and though many of them have religious names and exercise primarily religious functions, their social and economic aspects become increasingly prominent and some of them are purely secular. They are found throughout the Graeco-Roman world, but are specially common in the cosmopolitan trade-centres such as Piraeus, Delos, Rhodes, in Egypt, and in the flourishing cities of Asia Minor, and they appear to have played a valuable role in uniting in a common religious and social activity diverse elements of the population—men and women, slaves and free, citizens and aliens, Greeks and 'barbarians'. On the titles and aims of these guilds, their cults and festivals, their social and economic aspects, their membership and officials, their organization and finance, much light has been thrown by inscriptions, fully discussed by Poland (see below).

3. From the multifarious societies so revealed, incapable of a wholly satisfactory classification, three groups may be singled out for mention.

(a) Among the religious guilds a leading place is taken by those of the Dionysiac artistes (οἱ περὶ τὸν Διόνυσον τεχνῖται), which devoted themselves to the promotion of music and the drama. The earliest and most prominent of these was the Attic σύνοδος, founded probably in the early third century B.C. (though some scholars assign it to the late fifth) and traceable down to the close of the Roman Republic. Slightly later and less influential was the Isthmian and Nemean κοινόν, a federation of several local σύνοδοι with its centre at Thebes and branches at Argos, Chalcis, and elsewhere. To the third century belongs a similar κοινόν in Asia Minor, οἱ ἐπ' Ἰωνίας καὶ Ἑλλησπόντου, with Teos as its original centre, favoured by the Attalid kings, while in Egypt and Cyprus a guild of τεχνῖται flourished under the patronage of the Ptolemies. Under the Empire further titles and privileges were showered, especially by Hadrian, on the σύνοδος, a federal reorganization of the Dionysiac guilds, οἱ ἀπὸ τῆς οἰκουμένης περὶ τὸν Διόνυσον τεχνῖται, the existence of which is last attested in A.D. 291.

(b) In various cities wholesale merchants (ἔμποροι) formed associations of their own (Poland, 107 ff.), and in Athens they combined, for some purposes at least, with the shippers (ναύκληροι). In the second century B.C. two vigorous and wealthy societies, in which these two elements unite with the warehousemen (ἐγδοχεῖς), meet us on the island of Delos, the *Heracleïstae* of Tyre and the *Poseidoniastae* of Berytus (W. A. Laidlaw, *History of Delos* (1933), 212 ff.); the large and well-appointed clubhouse of the latter, which apparently served religious, social, and commercial ends, has been completely excavated (*Explor. archéol. de Délos*, vi).

(c) Numerous guilds, some of which probably date from the classical period, are composed of fellow-workers in the same craft, industry, or trade, such as doctors, bankers, architects, producers of woollen or linen goods, dyers, fullers, launderers, tanners, cobblers, workers in metal, stone, and clay, builders, carpenters, farmers, gardeners, fishers, bakers, pastry-cooks, barbers, embalmers, transport workers. Their main function was religious and social rather than economic; and though we hear of troubles at Ephesus in which the guilds play a leading part (Acts xix. 24 ff.; *Anatolian Studies presented to W. M. Ramsay*, 27 ff.), their chief object was not to modify conditions of labour or to champion the interests of the workers against their employers, but to offer their members opportunities of pleasurable intercourse in leisure hours.

4. Religious feeling and observance entered deeply into every department of Greek life, and among a people with so developed a social sense religion naturally tended to be an affair of the group rather than of the individual. Hence arose one of the main incentives to the formation of associations, and such glimpses as we gain of their activities suggest that religious rites played a prominent, though rarely (except at the earliest stage) the sole role therein. Deities not recognized by the State were thus worshipped by their devotees, groups of compatriots settled in some foreign city, e.g. the Phoenicians and the Egyptians resident in Delos or Piraeus, maintained their native cults, most of the club-gatherings probably opened with some religious ceremony, and we have numerous references (e.g. *IG* ii². 1275) to the participation of the guild in the funeral rites of its members, the provision or protection of their tombs, or the perpetuation of their cult as 'heroes'. Significant also is the large proportion of guild-names (Poland, *Geschichte*, 33 ff.; 57 ff.) which indicate religious activities (συνθύται, θεραπευταί, θρησκευταί, μύσται, etc.) or are derived from divinities (Ἀθηναϊσταί, Ἀφροδισιασταί, Ἡρακλεϊσταί, etc.), while their officials frequently bear titles of an unmistakably religious character. 'No point', remarks Poland, 'is more important for the historical evolution of the whole phenomenon than its relation to the deity. This is far more prominent than in the case of the Roman *collegia*; indeed, for many associations these religious aspects are the only thing which we learn about them.' A picture of unsurpassed vividness and detail is presented by an inscription (*SIG* 1109, translated in Tod, op. cit. inf. 86 ff.) of the second half of the second century A.D., which records the proceedings, punctuated by the interjections of enthusiastic members, of a general meeting of the Athenian society of Iobacchi, followed by a verbatim text of the new statutes of the society unanimously adopted thereat. These deal with the admission and subscriptions of members, the dates of periodical meetings, the maintenance of order and the penalties imposed for any disorderly behaviour, the religious ceremonies (including a sermon and a dramatic performance by officers and members of the society) which marked the principal meetings, the celebration of any auspicious event in the life of any member, the duties and privileges of the treasurer, and the attendance of members at the funeral of any of their number. There we see the por-

trayal of typical club-life, the social activities of which are founded upon and suffused by a common religious interest and loyalty.

In general see E. Ziebarth, *Das griech. Vereinswesen* (1896); J. Oehler, *Zum griech. Vereinswesen* (1905); F. Poland, *Geschichte d. griech. Vereinswesens* (1909); M. N. Tod, *Sidelights on Greek History* (1932), 69 ff. For specific aspects or regions: M. San Nicolò, *Aegyptisches Vereinswesen zur Zeit der Ptolemäer u. Römer* (1913–15); J. P. Waltzing, *Les corporations professionnelles* (1895); P. Foucart, *Des associations religieuses chez les Grecs* (1873); F. Poland, s.v. 'Technitae' in *PW* VA. 2473 ff.; M. Radin, *Legislation of the Greeks and Romans on Corporations*. The decrees and laws of the Attic societies are collected in *IG* ii.² 1249–369; those of the Delian corporations in *Inscriptions de Délos*, 1519–23; for a selection of inscriptions relating to clubs *SIG*³ 1095–120, Michel, 961–1018; for Egyptian religious associations A. D. Nock, etc., *Harv. Theol. Rev.* xxix. 39 ff.   M. N. T.

CLUBS, ROMAN. The Latin words corresponding most closely to the English 'club' are *collegium* and *sodalicium* (*sodalitas*). The former was the official title of the four great priestly colleges, *pontifices*, *VIIviri epulonum*, *XVviri sacris faciundis*, and *augures*, and the word had religious associations even when the object of the club was not primarily for worship. Few, if any, *collegia* were completely secular. Some took their name from a deity or deities, e.g. Diana et Antinous (*ILS* 7212), Aesculapius et Hygia (ib. 7213), Hercules (ib. 7315, etc.), Silvanus (ib. 7317), and their members were styled *cultores*. Even when their name was not associated with a god *collegia* often held their meetings in temples, and their clubhouse (*schola*) might bear the name of a divinity (*ILS* 7218: *Schola deae Minervae Aug.*). The *collegia* illustrate the rule that all ancient societies from the family upwards had a religious basis.

2. Plutarch (*Numa* 17) attributes to Numa the foundation of certain *collegia*, but it is doubtful whether many existed before the Second Punic War. Complete freedom of association seems to have prevailed down to the last century of the Republic, though the action taken by the Senate against the *Bacchanales* in 186 B.C. shows that the government might intervene against an objectionable club. In the Ciceronian age the *collegia* became involved in political action; many were suppressed in 64 B.C. and again by Caesar, after a temporary revival by Clodius. By a *Lex Iulia* (probably A.D. 7, *ILS* 4966) Augustus enacted that every club must be sanctioned by the Senate or Emperor. This sanction is sometimes recorded on club inscriptions, and it undoubtedly was freely given, though the policy of different emperors varied ('Trajan absolutely forbade the formation of clubs in Bithynia: Plin. *Tra.* 34). An extant *senatus consultum* (*ILS* 7212) shows that general permission was given for burial clubs (*collegia funeraticia* or *tenuiorum*), provided that the members met only once a month for the payment of contributions. In practice these clubs engaged in social activities and dined together on certain occasions, e.g. the birthdays of benefactors. After A.D. 100 the government seems to have viewed the clubs with little suspicion.

3. Many *collegia* were composed of men practising the same craft or trade, e.g. smiths, clothworkers, carpenters, sailors; but there is no evidence that their object was to maintain or improve their economic conditions. In most cases they were probably in name burial clubs, while their real purpose was to foster friendliness and social life among their members. Many clubs of *iuvenes* existed mainly for sport, and associations were formed among ex-service men (*veterani*). Several lists of members survive (e.g. *ILS* 6174–6; 7225–7). These are headed by the names of the *patroni* (*ILS* 7216 f.), wealthy men, sometimes of senatorial rank, who often had made gifts to the clubs. The members bore titles recalling those borne by municipal officials. The presidents were *magistri* or *curatores* or *quinquennales* (who kept the roll of members). Below these came the *decuriones*, and then the ordinary members (*plebs*). The funds were sometimes

managed by *quaestores*. In these clubs the humbler population found some compensation for their exclusion from municipal honours. The fact that at the distributions of money or food a larger share was given to the officials or even to the *patroni* implies that the object of the clubs was not primarily philanthropic, though they no doubt fostered goodwill and generosity among their members. *See also* INDUSTRY, paras. 2, 5, and 7.

4. The evidence is almost entirely epigraphic, though Cicero often refers to the political activity of *collegia*. See *ILS* ii. 2, ch. 15 and iii. 2, pp. 710–25. Modern works: J. P. Waltzing, *Étude historique sur les corporations professionnelles chez les Romains* (1895 ff.); E. Kornemann, s.v. 'Collegium' in *PW*; S. Dill, *Roman Society from Nero to Marcus Aurelius* (1905), 251 ff.; E. G. Hardy, *Studies in Roman History* i (1906), 129–50 (Christianity and the *Collegia*).   G. H. S.

5. As stated above, there existed in Rome (and elsewhere in the Roman world) many private *collegia* (*sodalicia*, *sodalitates*, etc.: for a list of the names in use, see A. De-Marchi, *Il culto privato di Roma antica*, pt. ii (1903), p. 75, the standard work on the subject), all theoretically dedicated to the cult of some deity or deities. The general objection to *sodalicia* which existed under the Empire did not extend to societies of this kind, provided they conformed to the rigid regulations laid down in a *senatus consultum* preserved for us at least in part in the records of the *cultores Dianae et Antinoi* of Lanuvium (*CIL* 14. 2112, and cf. *Dig.* 47. 22. 1). The two classes of *collegia* which were allowed or tolerated seem to have been (*a*) those consisting wholly of poor persons who made small contributions to a common end (frequently the burial of deceased members; this was the purpose of the Lanuvian association already mentioned and of many others which are known). Such societies might meet once a month, presumably for business purposes, for our inscriptional evidence (see De-Marchi, loc. cit. 90) testifies to more frequent meetings which were purely social or purely religious. (*b*) Societies wholly and genuinely religious in their character, provided of course that the *religiones* in question were not in themselves objected to, as in the classical instance of the Bacchanalian conspiracy (Livy 39. 8 ff., and the *S.C. de Bacanalibus*, Bruns, *Fontes* 7, no. 36). Such an attitude seems implicit in the words (*Dig.*, ibid. 1), 'religionis causa coire non prohibentur'. It would seem that one handle against the Christians was that they formed illicit associations (Pliny, *Tra.* 96 (97). 7), and some slight evidence that they associated themselves on occasion under some such inconspicuous title as *cultores Verbi* (De-Marchi, op. cit. 162, note 4). Very often, however, the *collegium* was religious in little more than the adoption of a patron deity. One of the commonest forms of association was a trade-guild or a local group of fellow-craftsmen. Thus, we hear of a group of *cultores Liberi patris caupones* (*CIL* 8. 9409), where the worship of the wine-god by tavern-keepers is obviously appropriate. In other cases the divine patron might be unconnected with the trade but generally or locally prominent, as in the *collegium fabrum Veneris* of *CIL* 3. 1981. Other *sodalicia* would appear to have been merely clubs meeting for some kind of common entertainment. Political associations were frowned upon by the emperors (Pliny, loc. cit. and ibid. 34 (43). 1).   H. J. R.

CLUENTIUS HABITUS, AULUS, of Larinum, was the central figure in two remarkable criminal cases. In 74 B.C. he charged his stepfather Oppianicus with attempting to poison him. Each side practised wholesale bribery, and finally Oppianicus was condemned by seventeen votes to fifteen. In the hands of the tribune Quinctius, who had conducted the defence, the trial assumed political importance. Oppianicus died in 72; in 66 his son charged Cluentius with his murder. The brilliant advocacy of Cicero probably secured his acquittal. See Cicero, *Pro Cluentio*, and, for the political implications of both trials, W. Peterson's edition (1899).   J. M. C.

CLUSIUM, the modern *Chiusi*, situated in central Italy near Lake Trasimene, was conquered later than the coastal towns by the Etruscans. Seldom mentioned in history after the episode of Lars Porsenna (q.v.), it is very important archaeologically. Originally the Umbrian *Chamars*, it retained much of its pre-Etruscan indivi-duality, notably in burial customs. Cremation was never replaced by inhumation. The consequent use of anthro-pomorphic urns led to the remarkable development of a sensitive plastic talent. Seen first in 'canopics' it develops in figures and bas-reliefs. Examples in Chiusi, Florence, and (totally neglected) Palermo museums. Round Chiusi are fine painted tombs.

R. Bianchi-Bandinelli, *Clusium* (1925); D. Levi, *Il Museo civico di Chiusi* (1935).   D. R.-MacI.

CLUVIUS, *see* RUFUS (7).

CLYMENE, name of a dozen different heroines (for one *see* CATREUS), the best known being the mother of Phae-thon (q.v.), wife of Merops, king of Ethiopia. Meaning simply 'famous', it is a stopgap name, like Creusa, Leucippus, etc., used where there was no genealogical or other tradition.   H. J. R.

CLYMENUS, (1) euphemistic title of Hades, especially at Hermione (Paus. 2. 35. 9, cf. Lasos ap. Athen. 624 e). (2) The fabulous founder of the temple there, an Argive (Paus. ibid.). (3) Name of several other mythological persons, the best known being the father of Harpalyce, *see* ALASTOR. Variants to the story given there are that his daughter's transformation (to an owl, in this account) took place while she was fleeing from him (*Paradoxo-graphi*, p. 222 Westermann), where she is called Nycti-mene, apparently by confusion with a like story of Epopeus, king of Lesbos (Hyg. *Fab.* 204), and that he killed her (ibid. 206) and himself (ibid. 242. 4, Parthenius 13).   H. J. R.

CLYTEMNESTRA(*Clytaem(n)estra, Κλυταιμ(ν)ήστρα*; the shorter form is better attested; *Clutaemestra*, Livius Andronicus, trag. 11, by iambic shortening), daughter of Tyndareos, sister of Helen and the Dioscuri and wife of Agamemnon (qq.v.). For her murder of her husband, *see* AGAMEMNON.

Her legend was a favourite one among post-Homeric authors, and the central interest being her infidelity and murder, all manner of motives are discovered; for in Homer she is a weakly good woman (*Od.* 3. 266), over-persuaded by the energetic scoundrel Aegisthus, and 'hateful' (ibid. 310) or 'accursed' (11. 410) only in retrospect. Her sole active cruelty is to kill Cassandra (11. 422). Stesichorus (fr. 17 Diehl) blames Aphrodite, who made Tyndareos' daughters unfaithful because he had neglected her. Aeschylus (*Ag.* passim) and others after him (but the motive may be earlier, see Pindar, *Pyth.* 11. 22 ff., cf. CASSANDRA) give her a double in-centive, the sacrifice of Iphigenia (q.v.), and anger at Agamemnon's infidelities, the latter a non-Homeric reason. He also makes her a strong character, the leader in the whole affair, while Aegisthus is a blustering weakling (cf. *Od.* 3. 310, ἀνάλκιδος Αἰγίσθοιο). Sopho-cles and Euripides in their *Electras* still make her the more prominent figure, but tend to increase the re-lative importance of Aegisthus again; Euripides (*El.* 1105–6) makes her somewhat sorry for all that has happened. In Aeschylus, again, she tries to resist Orestes (*Cho.* 889 ff.) and threatens him with the Erinyes (924), whom her ghost afterwards stirs up against him (*Eum.* 94 ff.); in the other tragedians she merely pleads for life.

Her part in other legends is small; she brings Iphigenia to Aulis (Eur. *IA* 607 ff.), and Telephus (q.v.) gets a hearing from the Greeks by acting on her advice (Hyg. *Fab.* 101. 2; ? Euripidean). Her name occasionally occurs as a common noun meaning 'adulteress' (as Quintilian, *Inst.* 8. 6. 53), or 'murderess' (see Horace, *Sat.* 1. 1. 100, where 'fortissima Tyndaridarum' stands for Clytaemnestra). *See further* ELECTRA.

Abundant ancient and modern references in Höfer in Roscher's *Lexikon* ii. 1230 ff.   H. J. R.

CNIDOS, a Greek colony (probably from Argos), situated at the south-west tip of Asia Minor. It produced a famous vintage, and by the sixth century it had trade connexions with Egypt (Naucratis) and southern Italy (Tarentum). But its chief titles to renown were its medical school, its statue of Aphrodite (by Praxiteles), and the observatory of its chief citizen, the astronomer Eudoxus (q.v.).

After a vain attempt to isolate itself by perforating the isthmus on which it stood, Cnidos fell under Persian rule (*c.* 540 B.C.). In the fifth century it formed part of the Delian League, but little is known of its political connexions after 400. It repeatedly changed rulers in Hellenistic times, and in 129 became a *civitas libera* in the Roman province of Asia. Remains of two temples and of the town walls are still visible.

C. T. Newton, *Travels and Discoveries in the Levant* (1865) ii, ch. 44.   M. C.

CNOSSOS (*Κνωσσός, Κνωσός*) covers a low hill in the Kairatos valley three miles from the sea in the centre of the north coast of Crete. Its history begins with the earliest known habitation of Crete in the Neolithic Age. A deep deposit shows the gradual progress of human culture over a long period of time and that Cnossos even then was an important and populous place. In the late Neolithic Age small huts with two rooms were in use. With the begin-ning of the Early Bronze Age (*c.* 3000 B.C.) and contacts with Egypt and Asia Minor which lasted throughout till the final destruction of the Palace, the standard of life improved and houses with two stories arose. Though finds of pottery prove that Cnossos was continuously inhabited, architectural remains are few, since the levelling and terracing of the hill for the building operations which began early in the Middle Bronze Age swept away earlier structures. In this Middle Bronze Age (2200–1600) the hill-top became a large central court with independent blocks of buildings grouped round it. Beyond these to the north and west lay other courts, and approaches from the north–south road across the island were made to Cnossos as an official centre. The Palace grew as the period progressed. The isolated blocks were linked together, the west court enlarged, magazines built on the west and north-west, the north, south, and west entrances were made, the drainage system laid out, and the later Domestic Quarter was begun.

2. At the end of the second phase of the period (*c.* 1700) the Palace suffered disaster, perhaps the first of a series of earthquakes, and the third phase marks the rise of the Palace as it appears to-day. New architectural features occur in the construction of floors, of columns, and of ashlar masonry. The Grand Staircase with its five flights and the Domestic Quarter in its main lines were built. The north and south entrances were remade, and in the magazines and shrines treasure cists were provided. The theatral area or north court was extended. This Palace, richly decorated with frescoes, suffered from another earthquake just before the close of the period (*c.* 1600) and this involved more remodelling. The west porch was built, the west court extended, the central court paved, and the south porch received its final form and generally, except for the Throne Room, the Palace took the form which has survived. The Royal Tomb,

half tomb and half shrine, was built at this time. Some large private houses adjoining the Palace began to encroach upon it and a flourishing and populous town had now grown up all round it. The first and second phases of the Late Bronze Age (*c.* 1600–1400) added little except the Throne Room system and much fresco work applied to walls repaired and replastered. The built tombs at Isopata nearby belong to this age. About 1400 the Palace was destroyed by fire either caused by yet another earthquake or by an enemy attack. In the last phase of the Bronze Age the Palace was partially reoccupied, and to this stage belong the shrine of Double Axes and a large cemetery. The site lay deserted from the opening of the Early Iron Age and a Greek temple was later built over the ruins. Cnossos, however, continued as a town through the Early Iron Age and the Greek settlement of the island. Tombs of this and the succeeding orientalizing and archaic periods show that it passed through the same stages of cultural evolution as other Greek cities. Through the classical and Hellenistic periods it was one of the leading Cretan States and the rival of Gortyn, to which its leadership passed after the Roman conquest. Cnossos was a powerful and rich city, made foreign alliances, struck coins, and survived till about the fourth century A.D. Its ruins have yet to be explored. *See also* MINOS.

A. J. Evans, *Palace of Minos at Knossos* (1921–36); J. D. S. Pendlebury, *Archaeology of Crete* (1939). A. J. B. W.

COCCEIUS, *see* NERVA.

CODEX, *see* BOOKS, I. 9.

CODEX (legal). The earliest collections of Imperial constitutions, made for the use of practitioners and scholars, were the *Codex Gregorianus* (published *c.* A.D. 291) and *Hermogenianus*, a supplementary collection to the first, with constitutions of Diocletian and his co-regents of 293 and 294 (published 295). Some constitutions of the subsequent years were inserted later. Whilst these collections were private compilations (of unknown authors; written presumably in Beyrout), the *Codex Theodosianus*, a creation of Theodosius II (published 438), was an official code. It contains in sixteen books constitutions from the time of Constantine.

Following the example of Theodosius, Justinian ordered in 528 (only half a year after his accession to the throne) the compilation of Imperial constitutions, but this publication (edited on 7 April 529) at once became obsolete because of the very copious legislation of 530 and the concurrent composition of the *Digesta* (q.v.) by an editorial commission presided over by Tribonianus (q.v.). A new edition was therefore an urgent necessity: it appeared as *Codex repetitae praelectionis* (534), a year after the *Digest*. Tribonianus was again the head of the editorial commission, the members of which were former collaborators in the composition of the *Digest*. The collection comprehends in twelve books constitutions of various types from Hadrian to Justinian (the latest is of 4 November 534). The three codes mentioned above were used in its preparation; the greatest part of the collection is occupied by constitutions of Diocletian. Earlier constitutions are not rarely interpolated in a similar manner as the jurists' works in the *Digest* but not so freely.

Justinian's constitutions issued after the publication of the second Code (written mostly in Greek) are called *Novellae Constitutiones*; but a collection of them was not published by the Emperor, though he intended to do so. Three unofficial collections are known; the largest one was published under Tiberius II.

The best edition of Justinian's Codex is that of P. Krueger, *Corpus iuris civilis* ii[10] (1929). The 3rd vol. of the *Corpus Iuris Civilis*, edited by R. Schöll and W. Kroll (4th ed., 1912) contains the *Novellae*. Important works of reference: C. Longo, 'Vocabolario delle Costituzioni di Giustiniano' (*Bull. Ist. Dir. Rom.* x);

R. v. Mayr, M. San Nicolò, *Vocabularium Codicis Iustiniani* i (1920), ii (1923). Fr. Schulz, in *Studi Bonfante* i, *Acta Congressus Iuridici Internationalis* i (1935); P. Noailles, *Les Collections de Novelles* i, ii (1912, 1914). A. B.

CODRUS, an early king of Athens. According to the story current in the fifth century his father Melanthus, of the Neleid family in Pylos, came as a refugee to Attica, championed Athens against Boeotia in single combat, and became king. When Attica was invaded by the Dorian Heraclids, who had heard from Delphi that they would be victorious if Codrus' life were spared, a friendly Delphian informed the Athenians of this oracle. Codrus thereupon went forth in woodcutter's garb, invited death by starting a quarrel with Dorian warriors, and so saved his country (see Lycurg. *Leoc.* 84–7). For this deed he was worshipped as a hero; he was succeeded by his son Medon (by another version, the kingship ended with Codrus). Other sons led the Attic colonization of Ionia.

No family of Codridae or Melanthidae is known in Athens. On this ground the historical character of Codrus has been denied. But the Medontidae were a leading family—Solon, Pisistratus, and Plato belonged to it; there was a (presumably ancient) shrine of Neleus, Basile, and Codrus at Athens (*IG* i². 94); and Codridae are known in Ionia. J. E. F. and A. W. G.

COELE SYRIA, *see* SYRIA, para. 1.

COELIUS (1) **ANTIPATER,** LUCIUS, jurist, rhetorician, and historian, the teacher of L. Crassus, writing after 121 B.C., introduced to Rome, from Hellenistic models, the form of the historical monograph. He wrote in seven books on the Second Punic War, Cannae appearing in bk. 1, Scipio's landing in Africa in bk. 6, the capture of Syphax in bk. 7; the work was dedicated to L. Aelius Stilo, the grammarian. Coelius used not only Roman sources, including family archives (Livy 27. 27. 13), but Silenus' Carthaginian account (Cic. *Div.* 1. 24. 49); his relation to Polybius is uncertain. Some antiquarian fragments indicate perhaps another work, certainly digressions. His style was Asianic, with rhythm, echoes of Ennius, striking word-order, and vivid presentation; he composed speeches within the narrative. The work was epoch-making, and its authority was recognized by Cicero, Brutus, Livy, who used him, and Hadrian.

H. Peter, *HRRel.* i² (1914), pp. ccxi, 158; O. Meltzer, *De L. Coelio Ant.* (1867); E. Norden, *Antike Kunstprosa* i (1923), 176; De Sanctis, *Stor. Rom.* iii. 2. 176. A. H. McD.

COELIUS (2) **CALDUS,** GAIUS, a *homo novus*, was tribune in 107 B.C.; he obtained the extension of written voting to trials for *perduellio* (*Lex tabellaria*). He was praetor (99) and consul (94).

COEMPTIO, *see* MANUS.

COERCITIO, the right, held by every higher magistrate, of compelling reluctant citizens to obey his orders and enactments, by inflicting punishment. Against this compulsion, which magistrates exercised not as judges but as the holders of executive authority, no appeal was admitted. The law of *provocatio*, however, made it illegal to issue a capital sentence as a purely coercive measure. *Coercitio* was, therefore, applied in historical times in the case of minor offences only, and took the form of imprisonment, exactment of pledges, fine, relegation, and possibly flogging. But in military law magisterial compulsion always retained much of its primitive severity. *See also* LAW AND PROCEDURE, III. 10.

Mommsen, *Röm. Staatsr.* i³. 163 ff.; *Röm. Strafr.* (1899), 35 ff.; J. L. Strachan-Davidson, *Problems of the Roman Criminal Law* (1912) i. 97 ff.; K. J. Neumann, *PW*, s.v. P. T.

COGNATIO, *see* PATRIA POTESTAS.

COGNITIO, see LAW AND PROCEDURE, II. 5 and III. 3.

COHORS. In the early Roman Republic the infantry provided by the *socii* was organized in separate *cohortes* of varying strength under Roman and native *praefecti.* In the legions the cohort was first used as a tactical unit by P. Scipio in Spain, and after the Marian reforms permanently superseded the maniple. There were ten cohorts in a legion, and for administrative purposes each was subdivided into three maniples and six centuries (*see* MANIPULUS).

In the *Auxilia* the infantry units numbering either 500 or 1,000, and bearing territorial or honorific surnames (e.g. *Gallica, fidelis*), were called cohorts; they were commanded by *praefecti* or *tribuni.*

The Praetorians, perhaps on the model of the *cohors praetoria* or Republican general's bodyguard, the urban troops, and the *vigiles*, were organized in cohorts 1,000 strong under tribunes. Troops specially levied were also grouped in cohorts, e.g. *cohortes voluntariorum, cohortes levis armaturae.* (*See* ALAE, AUXILIA.)

Kromayer–Veith, *Heerwesen und Kriegführung der Griechen und Römer* (1928). H. M. D. P.

COINAGE, GREEK. Greek coinage began in the metal trade: merchants dealing in the precious metals made up their goods in lumps of a handy size and stamped these with their marks as a guarantee of quality. The earliest examples come from western Asia Minor, and may be of the ninth century B.C.; the metal used is the natural alloy of gold and silver now called electrum. The coins were marketed as bullion, so that standardization of weight was unnecessary, though local standards can be traced in some groups; the marks all seem to be of private persons, and the only legend known, 'I am the mark of Phanes', supports this idea. Such private ventures would have no value as specie. The first series of coins struck closely to standard comes from Lydia, and was probably issued by the Mermnadae (*see* LYDIA), who could require their subjects to accept them at forced values. Their lead was followed by the Greek cities of the coast, whose badges begin to appear on coins probably before 700; and the Aeginetans, the partners of those cities in the trade with Egypt, took up the idea and struck coins of silver, the metal of which they had the best supply.

2. In Greece the measure of values, at this time, was a conventional one expressed in a handful of iron spits, the drachma; to this the first Aeginetan coins seem to have had no fixed relation, but were regarded as staters, i.e. units of bullion, and fractions of staters. But about 650 Pheidon of Argos reformed the currency within his sphere of influence, by giving the Aeginetan unit the value of two drachmas, and so replacing the iron tokens by silver ones. This created the Aeginetan standard for coinage, in which an ingot of about 90 grains of silver represented a drachma. When the fact that an artificial value could thus be set on a lump of metal was realized, other States which controlled supplies of silver started coinages on their own standards, Corinth soon after 650 and Chalcis in Euboea about 625. These both got their metal from the Paeonian mines in the Balkans, not, as did Aegina, from the islands, and adopted lighter standards, Corinth one of about 45 grains of silver to the drachma and Chalcis about 65, with a common stater.

3. Till about 600 most of the currency of Greece was probably struck at these three centres, either with their own badges or with those of their commercial clients, in the form of their units of coinage, didrachms at Aegina and Chalcis and tridrachms at Corinth. But in the sixth century the use of coins for local business became more general, and many cities began to issue smaller denominations for retail trade; Boeotia provides a good instance of this practice. The greatest development was at Athens, where Solon made the Euboean drachma into a commercial weight, and Pisistratus adopted the tetradrachm as his unit and initiated a coinage in which the exact amount of silver in a stater could be known without any test; he derived his metal from the mines of Laurium, and so could dictate the price, as the city could later when the mines passed into its possession.

4. The great commercial coinages usually adhered steadily to the same types: the earliest issues bore a type on one face only, first the signet of the merchant and then the badge of the city. In the sixth century types began to appear on the reverse face as well, to distinguish denominations; the first instance in Greece was probably at Corinth, where experiments in modifying the obverse type for the same purpose had previously been tried. Another use of the second field for types is found in Boeotia, where the leading cities put the shield, the badge of the Boeotian League, on the obverse and their own badges on the reverse. But till the end of the century the types in Greece were practically limited to badges or to local deities. There was more freedom of choice in Sicily, where not only artistic but advertising elements affected the types: the cock of Himera and the parsley of Selinus may be badges, but the dolphin of Zancle seems to call attention to the advantages of the harbour; the racing-chariots, which became very popular in the next century, were probably in the first case personal types, for which rural parallels are found among the Thracian tribes. The only fifth-century coinage in Greece which shows such an attempt at medallic appeal was that of the Eleians, struck for the Olympic festivals and of remarkable artistic merit. The commemorative intent is clear in the *Dāmareteion* of Syracuse, issued after the victory at Himera in 480, which is of exceptional size and virtually a war-medal; a similar issue was made once at Acragas and several times at Syracuse in later years, but a single issue at Athens is the only instance outside Sicily till Hellenistic times.

5. Till the fifth century the only metal used for coinage in Greece was silver; the cities of the Asiatic coast continued to strike electrum, and Croesus and the Persian kings made gold their standard. Towards the end of the fifth century a few Greek gold coinages began to appear, the earliest probably at Thasos, and these became more numerous in the fourth; but the issues were small, judged by the rarity of specimens now known, except in the case of the staters of Lampsacus, which began about 390 and with Persian darics supplied the bulk of the gold in the Greek markets till Philip II of Macedon flooded them with his coins. Bronze was first struck in Sicily by the Greek cities early in the fifth century, to suit the wants of the Sicels and Elymians, who, like the Italian tribes, were accustomed to measure their values in bronze. It was not used for coinage in Greece till after 400, if emergency issues are left out of account; but the advantages of small change were quickly realized, and by the end of the fourth century most important Greek cities had their regular bronze currency. The old iron spits probably continued in use at Sparta till the end of the fourth century, and a few iron coins of Argos exist; but in this case, as in that of other base metal coins, it is difficult to decide whether they were official issues or fraudulent copies.

6. Plated coins were produced in Greece as early as the sixth century, the first recorded by ancient authors being the electrum staters of Polycrates of Samos; and the frequent occurrence, in hoards, of coins chopped to test their goodness, especially in the Near East, is evidence that the practice of plating was a recognized danger to the merchant. Gold and silver were seldom debased in official issues of the earlier periods, the most notable instance being the base silver of Lesbos; but in the fourth century debased gold was issued in Sicily, and Carthage followed suit. Under the Roman Empire the depreciation of Greek currencies continued, till the last survivors,

the staters of the kings of Bosporus, which had originally been gold, ended in the fourth century A.D. as bronze. A similar deterioration is found in the silver coinages of the eastern provinces, beginning under the Hellenistic kings, and in Egypt and Syria recourse to lead occurs. This decay, however, was really in sympathy with the collapse in Roman credit, and belongs to Roman economic history.

7. There was a notable change in the Greek coinages after Alexander the Great had made an attempt, probably suggested by the action of the Athenians in the time of their empire in the fifth century, to develop a world currency on a single standard. In addition to the three Greek standards, local standards had grown up, especially in Thrace, Asia Minor, and Phoenicia, to suit the local values of silver, and there were wide differences between bullion and specie prices. The system of Alexander, which was based on the Attic standard, with gold in a fixed relation to silver, and bronze subsidiary, could last only as long as the Empire held together and its rulers dictated currency values; as soon as it broke up, the local conditions governed the markets as before. The Successors generally tried to keep to the Alexandrian standard for their regal issues; but by the second century in the East they had to resort to dual coinages. The kings of Pergamum struck royal Attic tetradrachms and commercial Asiatic ones, the Seleucids had a supplementary series of Phoenician standard, and the Ptolemies were driven on to a copper standard. Cities which obtained sufficient autonomy generally returned to the old local standard; Alexandrian types and weights lingered on for some time, in Asia Minor till the middle of the second century, but as a rule the Attic standard was followed in Greece, the Phoenician in the Syrian region, and the Asiatic between them. The issue of large silver pieces tended to concentrate in a few important trade centres; but there was a great extension in the production of bronze in the smaller towns for local use.

8. The general character of the types placed on the city coinages had begun to show some change in the fifth century, and this process went further in the fourth: the old badges on the obverses were replaced by heads or figures of deities, and the reverse types were often associated in idea with the deities so portrayed. After Alexander the custom grew up of putting on the obverse the head of the ruler who issued the coin. Alexander's likeness never appeared on his own coins, but Lysimachus and Ptolemy Soter first put the head of Alexander, the one as the son of Ammon, the other as the founder of Alexandria, on their coins; then Ptolemy substituted his own portrait, an example followed by the Seleucids and lesser houses.

9. The end of Greek coinage was gradually effected by the growth of Roman influences. The first to disappear were naturally the issues of Italy and Sicily, which, so far as silver was concerned, were killed by the change of the Roman unit from bronze to silver in or about 217 B.C.; bronze lingered on in diminishing quantity for a time, the last 'Greek' issues in Italy being at Paestum under Tiberius. In Greece itself silver continued to be struck on the old basis at Athens till Augustus, and a fair number of cities issued bronze. These issues, however, became restricted to occasions such as festivals or imperial visits, even at commercial centres like Corinth and Patrae; an exceptional output of small bronze coins in the Peloponnesus under Severus and Caracalla may have had military connexions. In Asia Minor the Greek standard lasted longer. Asiatic staters were struck at several cities till Hadrian, and there was a steady issue of silver at Caesarea in Cappadocia till the middle of the third century; many cities had quasi-autonomous bronze coinages, which are evidence of the local demand. The bulk of the bronze, however, was of the commemorative

class: even small towns occasionally struck showy coins, and the 'Imperial Greek' of Asia is a series remarkable not only for the number of places at which it was issued, but for the artistic merit and interest of many of the types.

10. All the issues came to an end in the troubles of the reign of Gallienus, except at a few cities in the south-west, where coins of Claudius Gothicus, Aurelian, and Tacitus were struck. Syria and Phoenicia were still more independent of Rome for their coinage: till the Empire they continued to follow their old standard, and, after Augustus had opened an Imperial mint at Antioch which seems to have posed as an eastern partner of Rome, the values were based on the drachma. There were large issues on the Antiochene model at other cities, particularly at Tyre, whose autonomous series did not end till Vespasian, and under the Severan house the number of subsidiary mints for tetradrachms was increased. Other cities, as in Asia Minor, struck commemorative bronze freely till the middle of the third century. Egypt stood absolutely apart, and the Alexandrian series inherited from the Ptolemies lasted on, though much depreciated, till the reform of Diocletian in 296. The coinages of Africa and the western provinces, sometimes called Greek, need not be considered here; after the Roman organization of the countries, they had nothing in the way of coinage that was not essentially Roman.

BIBLIOGRAPHY

INTRODUCTORY. G. F. Hill in CAH iv, ch. 5; K. Regling, Münzkunde (Gercke–Norden² (1931) ii, pt. 2); J. G. Milne, Greek Coinage (1931). For general reference, G. F. Hill, Handbook of Greek and Roman Coins (1899); F. von Schrötter, Wörterbuch der Münzkunde (1930).

ADVANCED. The only complete history of Greek coinage is B. V. Head, Historia Numorum² (1911); for pure numismatics it is indispensable. The second part ('Description historique') of E. Babelon, Traité des monnaies grecques et romaines (1901–) had got as far as Alexander, except for Italy and Sicily, at the author's death; the introduction in part i gives a valuable survey. P. Gardner's History of Greek Coinage goes down to 300 B.C. only, but is particularly useful in its treatment of the economic side. For illustrations of the coins, the handiest plates are in the British Museum Guide to the Principal Coins of the Greeks (1932), designed as a companion to Head's Historia; some additional material may be found in C. T. Seltman's Greek Coins (1933); the plates of the Sylloge Nummorum Graecorum, published for the British Academy, are excellent, especially in vol. ii, the Lloyd Collection of Italian and Sicilian issues (1933).

ART AND TYPES. K. Regling, Die Antike Münze als Kunstwerk (1924), is the most comprehensive study of the whole history of Greek numismatic art. For the general classification of the types, P. Gardner, Types of Greek Coins (1883), gives the best account; for their origin and meaning, G. Macdonald, Coin Types (1905).

METROLOGY. The problems of Greek coin-standards are still controversial. There is much material for study in E. Pernice, Griechische Gewichte (1894), O. Viedebantt, Antike Gewichtsnormen und Münzfüsse (1923), and A. Segrè, Metrologia e circolazione monetaria degli antichi (1928). Certain points have been discussed recently in W. Giesecke, Antikes Geldwesen (1938).

BIBLIOGRAPHY. There is a full bibliography up to 1911 in Head's Historia, but no adequate supplement to his has been produced, except with regard to hoards in S. P. Noe, Bibliography of Greek Coin-hoards² (1937). The volumes of the British Museum Catalogue of Greek Coins published since 1911 contain information up to the dates of their issues; otherwise the only way of discovering all that has been written on a particular series is by searching indexes.
                                                                          J. G. M.

COINAGE, ROMAN. All mentions of coinage under the kings and the early Republic are quite unhistorical. Rome reckoned values in terms of oxen and sheep (hence pecunia from pecus) down to c. 450 B.C., in uncoined bronze (aes rude) until after 300 B.C.

2. Until recent years the origin of Roman coinage was placed in Campania (c. 340). While Capua struck silver didrachms, the bronze as and its parts were cast for Rome and Latium. But it is now becoming clear that the whole development is to be placed somewhat later.

3. In 289 B.C. triumvirs of the mint were appointed, and their first task was to cast aes in bars weighing about six pounds each and bearing types on both sides. These

bars, usually known as *aes signatum*, bear no marks of value, and, while certainly currency, were not certainly coin. Other bars, of more primitive style, with simple patterns as types, are perhaps a little earlier, but not specifically Roman in origin.

4. In 269 B.C. Rome struck her first silver: didrachms, marked ROMANO, in Greek style, with token bronze attached. There were four series, each with its distinctive types, probably struck at Rome and at three Italian mints for three of the Italian *quaesturae*. At the same time, the bronze *as* was cast, at the weight of a pound, with multiples and subdivisions. Each denomination had its characteristic types and mark of value, but no ethnic. In the main the bronze runs parallel to the silver. The system was bimetallic: silver for the cities, heavy bronze for the old-fashioned country-side. In two of the silver series the standard was Neapolitan (didrachm of *c.* 113·0 grains), in one Alexandrian (*c.* 109·5 gr.), in one reduced Tarentine (?) (*c.* 102·5 gr.). The standards of the *as* were 240 scruples in two mints, 288 in one, and 300 in one. Of the mints, one was certainly Rome, two others possibly Beneventum and Tarentum; the exact site of the fourth is uncertain, but it served the north and north-east.

5. The First Punic War seems not to have affected the coinage in any notable way. But soon after (perhaps in 235 B.C.) a change was made. While the same four mints continued to issue, the types were varied or changed, the legend ROMA replaced ROMANO, and the standards were regularized: everywhere the didrachm of 6 scruples (102·5 gr.) and the *as* of 240. The change probably did not take place at the same time in all mints. The date given above (235 B.C.) seems to be true of Rome, and possibly of two other mints: the fourth struck the old ROMANO issue as late as *c.* 220 B.C. The new types of the Roman mint were 'Young Janus'–Jupiter and Victory in car for the *quadrigatus*, Janus–Prow for the *as*. The victoriate, a drachm, with types Jupiter–Victory and trophy, seems to have originated outside Rome, but to have come later to represent the half *quadrigatus*.

6. The impact of the Hannibalic War on Roman institutions was violent. Of the four mints, only Rome struck throughout the war. The monetary unit, the *as*, was reduced from 240 scruples to 144 in 217 B.C., further to 72 about 209 B.C. The silver, we are told, was also debased. If, as is probable, the didrachm of pure silver was equal to 6 *asses* of 240 scruples each, it would equal 10 of 144 and 20 of 72 scruples.

7. After the war it seems probable that Rome went back for a short time to the libral standard of the *as* (240 scruples). One, but probably only one, of the Italian mints resumed issue. Not that all coinage proceeded from Rome itself, but the mints were now auxiliaries of Rome, using her types. About 187 B.C. a new silver piece, the *denarius*, began to be struck in Bruttium. It grew in favour and range; reduced a little from its original weight, it settled down to rank as the equivalent of the Attic drachm, and, *c.* 170 B.C., definitely replaced the *quadrigatus* as the standard silver coin of Rome. The *denarius* was marked X, its half and quarter, the *quinarius* and *sestertius*, V and IIS; the *as*, the unit, was now struck (not cast) at a weight of something over 2 oz., with the types Janus–Prow. The *quinarius* and *sestertius* soon disappeared, but the victoriate continued, for a time, to be struck beside the *denarius*: it bore no mark of value and was probably struck, as bullion, for foreign trade.

8. Gold had been struck, probably *c.* 217 and 209 B.C., with *obv.* 'Young Janus' and *rev.* Two warriors striking a treaty, in a style very close to the *quadrigati*. At a date near 170 a new series, with *obv.* Mars and *rev.* Eagle, appeared, with marks of value, LX, XXXX, and XX (*asses*): gold is valued very low in terms of silver,

probably owing to a purely temporary cause, a 'gold-rush' near Aquileia.

9. From *c.* 200 B.C. foreign coinage is reported as pouring into Rome, in volume hitherto unknown: the 'argentum Oscense' from Spain, the gold Philippus of Macedon, and the two tetradrachms, Attic and cistophoric, from the East.

10. The *as* gradually fell to about an ounce in weight and, in the age of the Gracchi, was retariffed at sixteen to the *denarius*. Under the stress of the Social War, the *as* was reduced to half an ounce and soon afterwards ceased to be struck. Then, or perhaps earlier, the *denarius* suffered serious debasement, but seems to have recovered its fineness under Sulla. Plated coins, however, continued to be issued, mainly at any rate, by forgers. The victoriate was reintroduced, before 100 B.C., as the half of the *denarius*, and the *sestertius* too was again struck. Gold was issued sporadically from Sulla onwards, to become regular under Caesar.

11. The mint of Rome was in the temple of Juno Moneta. It was assisted by subsidiary mints in Italy, and by mints in the western provinces. From Sulla onwards provincial mints became increasingly numerous and important, in East as in West. Roman coins rarely give the rank of the moneyer, but, apart from the regular *IIIviri aere argento auro flando feriundo*, quaestors, aediles, and other magistrates struck.

12. The original types of the *denarius*—head of Bellona on obverse, Dioscuri charging on reverse—were slow to change. But, by the end of the Republic, a great variety of types was in use, often referring more directly to the family history of the moneyers than to the fortunes of the State.

13. The Empire brought with it serious changes. The Senate soon ceased to issue gold and silver from its mint at Rome, and the Emperor took over this coinage, though he chose at first to strike, as *imperator*, at provincial centres, notably Lugdunum. *Aes* was struck in collaboration by Senate and Emperor, as holder of the tribunician power: it regularly bore the mark S C, 'Senatus Consulto'. Provincial and civic issues completed the scheme. They were mainly in bronze and, after the reign of Gaius, were almost restricted to the East. Triumvirs of the mint continued to be appointed and presumably had a hand in the *aes* coinage. The gold and silver was struck by imperial slaves and freedmen.

14. The coinage comprised *aureus* and half-piece in gold, *denarius* and half-piece in silver, *sestertius*, *dupondius*, and *semis* in orichalcum (brass), *as* and *quadrans* in copper. Twenty-five *denarii* went to the *aureus*, sixteen *asses* to the *denarius*. It was a bimetallic system, with both gold and silver struck exceedingly fine.

15. Nero reduced the *aureus* from $\frac{1}{42}$ to $\frac{1}{45}$ of a pound, the *denarius* from $\frac{1}{84}$ to $\frac{1}{96}$, and mixed 10 per cent. of alloy with the silver. As the debasement of the silver, once begun, increased till it reached nearly 40 per cent. under Septimius Severus, the coinage came to rest more and more on an essential gold basis. Caracalla, in A.D. 215, issued a double *denarius* (the *Antoninianus*) at something below its proper weight. Abandoned by Severus Alexander the coin was restored by Balbinus and Pupienus and, by the reign of Philip, had practically ousted the *denarius*. The *aureus*, reduced by Caracalla to $\frac{1}{50}$ of a pound, gradually fell in weight; by the reign of Gallienus gold was struck on no single apparent standard. The debasement of the silver continued, and, in A.D. 259, the *Antoninianus* sank to be a mere copper piece, coated with silver. Under Trajan Decius it had fallen to the value of a *denarius*: now it fluctuated at low and irregular values in the market. The *aes* coinage ran an even course down to Gallienus: Trajan Decius struck the *quadrans* after long intermission and introduced a double *sestertius*. But, when the silver piece collapsed, this coinage was suspended.

16. In A.D. 274 Aurelian called in the old money and issued new. He struck no regular *aureus*, and no good silver piece, but a slightly improved piece of bronze coated with silver. The mark XX.1 (20 = 1?) defined its value—perhaps '1 unit (*sestertius*) equals 20 *asses* or 2 *denarii*'. This reform, though never fully accepted in the West, carried the Empire over the immediate crisis.

17. The main mint of the early Empire was Rome for all metals: imperial and senatorial mints probably worked in close harmony. Provincial mints of imperial coin—Antioch, Milan, Siscia—then gradually arose to supply the needs of the armies. Local coinage gradually declined: the only mint to survive till Diocletian was Alexandria. The imperial coinage centred round the person of the emperor and discoursed, with discreet eloquence, on his achievements and aspirations.

18. Diocletian, after standardizing his *aureus* at 70, and then at 60, to the pound, carried through a complete reform of the coinage in A.D. 296. He struck an *aureus* of 60 to the pound, a silver piece of 96 to the pound, a large piece of silver-coated bronze, and a smaller piece with radiate head. It appears probable that the *aureus* was valued at 25 silver pieces, 100 larger and 200 smaller pieces of silvered bronze; the smaller piece was really the piece of Aurelian, reduced to half its original value. Constantine, *c.* A.D. 312, introduced the lighter *aureus* of 72 to the pound, the famous *solidus*. Silver was hardly struck between A.D. 305 and 330. Then the $\frac{1}{96}$ of the pound reappears, succeeded, *c.* 350, by the *siliqua* ($\frac{1}{120}$ pound) and the *miliarense* ($\frac{1}{60}$). The subsidiary coinage of silvered bronze went through a series of changes and reductions, only partially intelligible to us. One reform fell under Constantius II (A.D. 348), another under Julian (363). *Pecunia maiorina* and *centenionalis* were names of coins, not yet certainly identified. In the main, the *solidus* stood apart, in a privileged position, commanding a premium on its nominal value. Its issue was long regarded as the special prerogative of the Roman emperor and the barbarian successor-states were slow to usurp the right.

19. All coinage after A.D. 296 was issued from imperial mints, carefully distributed to cover imperial needs—at Rome, Treveri, Lugdunum, Arelate, Siscia, Sirmium, Thessalonica, Nicomedia, Heraclea, Antioch, Alexandria and the rest. The types of the coins became more formal and referred rather to permanent aspects of the State than to specific events. Each denomination tended to have its special reverse type. The mints were under *rationales*, dependent on the *comes sacrarum largitionum*. False moneying was rife and was savagely repressed by edict.

20. The gradual development of independent money-systems among the barbarians of the West and the great reform of Anastasius in the East belong to another story.

BIBLIOGRAPHY

(a) GENERAL. H. Mattingly, *Roman Coins* (1928); G. F. Hill, *Historical Roman Coins* (1909); K. Regling in *PW* s.v. 'Münzwesen' and in Gercke–Norden, *Einleitung in die Altertumswissenschaft*, 'Münzkunde'.

(b) EARLY ITALY AND THE ROMAN REPUBLIC. E. J. Haeberlin, *Aes Grave* (1910); E. A. Sydenham, *Aes Grave* (1926); H. Mattingly and E. S. G. Robinson, 'The Date of the Roman Denarius' (*Proc. Brit. Academy*, 1933); H. Mattingly, 'The First Age of Roman Coinage', *JRS* 1945; for a somewhat different view, J. G. Milne, *JRS* 1946; H. A. Grueber, *British Museum Catalogue of Republican Coins*, 3 vols. (1909); E. Babelon, *Description historique et chronologique des monnaies de la République romaine* (1885, 1886; *Nachträge* by Max von Bahrfeldt, 1897, 1900); M. von Bahrfeldt, *Die römische Goldmünzenprägung während der Republik und unter Augustus* (1923).

(c) THE ROMAN EMPIRE. M. Grant, *From Imperium to Auctoritas*, *A Historical Study of Aes Coinage in the Roman Empire 49 B.C.–A.D. 14* (1946); H. Mattingly, *British Museum Catalogue of Coins of the Roman Empire* (4 vols., Augustus to Commodus, 1923–40); H. Mattingly, E. A. Sydenham, and C. H. V. Sutherland, *The Roman Imperial Coinage* (vols. I–IV, ii, Augustus to Pupienus; vol. V, i and ii, Valerian to Diocletian, 1923–38); H. Cohen, *Description historique des monnaies frappées sous l'Empire romain* (8 vols., 2nd ed.,

1884–92); M. Bernhart, *Handbuch zur Münzkunde der römischen Kaiserzeit* (1926); P. L. Strack, *Untersuchungen zur römischen Reichsprägung des zweiten Jahrhunderts* (vols. i–iii, Trajan–Antoninus Pius, 1931–7). On coins as a source for imperial history cf. H. Mattingly, *CAH* xii. 713–20.   H. M.

COITIONES, *see* AMBITUS.

COLACRETAE, *see* KOLAKRETAI.

COLCHIS, the region at the east end of the Euxine Sea, just south of the Caucasus mountains; the legendary home of Medea and the goal of Jason's expedition. The land was rich in timber, flax, hemp, wax, and pitch, and Phasis was the terminus of a northern trade route to central Asia. Its people consisted of many tribes; seventy languages, it is said, could be heard in the markets of Dioscurias. Greeks established trading posts on the coast. Colchis was conquered by Mithridates; it appears later in the kingdom of Polemon. Under Hadrian there were Roman forts along the coast and the tribal chiefs were nominated by Rome.

Strabo, 11. 496–9; Arrian, *Peripl. M. Eux.*   T. R. S. B.

COLLATINUS, *see* TARQUINIUS (3).

COLLATIO LUSTRALIS, under the Roman Empire, the contribution, levied every five years (*lustrum*), on earnings in trades and professions, normally paid in gold and silver by weight, only the lowest charges being paid in silver or copper coin. Landowners were supposed to be exempt; otherwise, exemptions (e.g. to the clergy) were only grudgingly allowed. This *collatio*, which was largely directed towards paying donations to the troops. was felt as an intolerable burden. Its five-year period coincided with the period of the imperial vows. But vows could be for more than one emperor or be celebrated in advance of their time, and the occasions of levy were continually being multiplied. Introduced by Constantine I, the tax was abolished by Anastasius.   H. M.

COLLEGIA, *see* CLUBS, ROMAN.

COLLEGIUM

(1) Any private association of fixed membership and constitution (*see* CLUBS, ROMAN).

(2) A board of officials (or strictly speaking, of more than two officials).

The principle of collegiality was so common a feature of all Republican magistracies at Rome that its origins were embodied in the mythical figures of Remus and Titus Tatius (q.v.). To prevent the rise of a new monarchy disguised under the names of consulship or dictatorship, it was ordained that every magistracy should be filled by at least two officials, and in any case by an even number. They were to possess equal and co-ordinate authority, but subject to mutual control. Thus a decision taken by one consul was legal only if it did not incur the veto (*intercessio*) of the other. This principle led to alternation in the exercise of power, depending on age (*collega maior*), or, under the Empire, on domestic circumstances, the married being preferred to the single. Alternation gradually became a purely honorary distinction.

Mommsen, *Röm. Staatsr.* i³. 27 ff.   P. T.

(3) The name *Collegium* was also applied to the two great priesthoods of the *Pontifices* (q.v.) and the *Augures* (q.v.) and to the *duoviri* (later *decemviri* (q.v.) and *quindecimviri*) *sacris faciundis*, who had charge of the Sibylline oracles and of the *Graecus ritus* in general. Minor religious 'Colleges' were the *Collegia Compitalicia*, concerned with the worship of the *Lares* (q.v.) at the *compita*, the *Collegium Capitolinorum*, responsible for the *Ludi Capitolini*, and the *Collegium Mercatorum*, who presided over the worship at the temple of Mercurius. The lesser priesthoods were known as *Sodalitates* (*see* SODALES).

Wissowa, *RK*², pp. 404, 483–5.   C. B.

COLLUTHUS, *see* EPIC POETRY, GREEK, para. 9.

COLOMETRY, *see* STICHOMETRY ad fin.

COLON, *see* METRE, GREEK, I.

COLONI, *see* COLONUS.

COLONIA, *see* COLONIZATION, ROMAN.

COLONIA AGRIPPINENSIS (*Colonia Claudia Ara Augusta Agrippinensium*), modern *Cologne*.

In 38 B.C. Agrippa transferred the friendly tribe of the Ubii (q.v.) from the right to the left bank of the Rhine, and *c.* 9 B.C. an altar for the Imperial cult (Tac. *Ann.* i. 57) was consecrated at their tribal capital. About the same time two legions were stationed close by. These were transferred to Neuss and Bonn *c.* A.D. 35, and in 50 Claudius founded a colony in honour of Agrippina his wife (Tac. *Ann.* 12. 27) which was laid out in regular form, perhaps within the former cantonments. A fine naval harbour, the head-quarters of the Rhine fleet, was built a little upstream and a large mercantile port developed between the colony and the river. The colonists and the Ubii merged rapidly, and the latter only adhered unwillingly to Civilis in 69–70. Cologne suffered in the wars of the third century, and its fortifications were strengthened, partly by Gallienus. The city was taken by the Franks in 355, but Julian drove them out the following year. They retook it in 463.

From the first century Cologne was the chief commercial city of the Rhineland and the capital of *Germania Inferior*; it became a bishopric not later than the third century. Various manufactures are attested, and its glass was exported all over western and northern Europe. Part of the walls of Roman Cologne still stand (A.D. 1939), and large portions remain of the bridge-head fortifications at Deutz.

K. Schumacher, *Siedelungs- und Kulturgeschichte der Rheinlande* ii (1923); A. Grenier, *Archéologie gallo-romaine* (1931), 345 ff.
O. B.

COLONIZATION, GREEK (750–500 B.C.).

The character of early Greek colonization was primarily agrarian (Thuc. 1. 15; Hdt. 4. 150 ff., on Cyrene; Strabo 257, on Rhegium; Strabo 380, Archilochus in Athenaeus 4. 167, on Syracuse; the corn ear on coins of Metapontum). There was, however, considerable trade between Greece and neighbouring lands, even before 800 B.C. (Blakeway, *BSA* xxxiii). The seamen who carried Geometric pottery to Sicily and to Cumae no doubt helped to direct the peasant colonists; and some very early colonies, far afield, seem to have been primarily trading posts, e.g. the first settlements at Sinope and at Cumae (Burn, *World of Hesiod* (1936), 179 ff.).

2. Sicily and south Italy formed the most important colonial area. Chalcis (with recruits from other States) planted Rhegium, Zancle (later Messene), Naxos, Catana, Leontini; Corinth founded Syracuse and the half-way house of Corcyra; Megara settled Sicilian Megara. In Italy Sybaris, Croton, Metapontum were colonized by Achaeans, Tarentum by Spartans, Locri by Locrians. There are traces of Eretrians around Cumae and at Corcyra before the Corinthians (Thuc. 6. 3–5; Strabo, bks. 5 and 6; etc.). All these foundations were of the late eighth century save Cumae, which was older. A generation later came eastern Greeks—Rhodians and Cretans to Lindii on the 'Cold Stream' of Gela (Thuc. 6. 4), and Colophonians to Siris (Justin 20. 2).

3. After two further generations there was apparently a concerted thrust farther west, when Selinus was founded by the western Megara and Himera by Zancle (*c.* 630). Phocaea opened up the Adriatic and the farther west, Massilia being the greatest of numerous colonies in Liguria and Spain (*c.* 600). Gela founded Agrigentum *c.* 585; but a Rhodo-Cnidian settlement of Lilybaeum, *c.* 580, was foiled by the natives, and soon after this

Carthage first intervened in Sicily (Justin 18. 7). Thereafter the Greeks made little progress and even lost some outposts (e.g. Maenace near Malaga and Alalia in Corsica, both Phocaean) in face of the opposition of Carthage and Etruria (Hdt. 1. 163–7; 5. 43–7; Strabo 156).

4. In Africa, Carthage and Egypt stopped Greek expansion, save round Cyrene, and at the unique treaty-port of Naucratis (Hdt. 4. 150–60; 2. 178). In the Levant Sennacherib claimed to have 'drawn the Ionians like fish from the sea, and given peace to Cilicia and Tyre'; Phoenicians maintained their foothold in Cyprus, though even during the Persian Wars Greek traders had at least a 'factory' at Ras Shamra in Phoenicia; Cymaean Side and Samian Nagidus and Celenderis remained small and half barbarous; in Lycia, Rhodian Phaselis alone became important.

5. In Thrace the natives imposed a barrier; but Thasos, colonized from Paros, prospered exceedingly, and Maronea (Chian), Aenos (Lesbian), and Abdera (Teian) ultimately grew rich on wine and the slave-trade. The peninsulas of Chalcidice offered sheltered sites, but restricted territory; here Andros, Chalcis, and Eretria founded many cities (Thuc. 4. 84; 103; 123); but Olynthus and Amphipolis were not Greek till the fifth century.

6. In Propontis, Mytilene (at Sestos), Teos (Cardia), Phocaea (Lampsacus), Colophon (Myrlea), Paros and Erythrae (Parion), were among the early colonizers; then Miletus, with Abydos, Cyzicus, etc., almost monopolized the passage. But Megara, evidently friendly with Miletus, occupied Chalcedon (675 B.C.), Selymbria (a first venture into Thrace), and finally Byzantium (657).

7. After this, Pontic colonization began in earnest. Of Miletus' numerous colonies, the greatest were Panticapaeum; Olbia (*c.* 645) tapping the 'Black Earth Belt'; Sinope; Trapezus. Megarian Heraclea in Bithynia became a considerable land-power, and founded Heraclea in Crimea, Callatis, Mesembria, etc. Phocaean Amisus (566) was probably, like Samian Perinthus (599), the result of armed monopoly-breaking (cf. Plut. *Quaest. Graec.* 57). The economic importance of the Pontus was immense; its contribution to Greek culture negligible—physical conditions were too different. Hellenism flourished essentially between the isotherms 40° for January and 80° for July. Outside these limits, roughly, are found some Greek settlements, but little Greek art or thought. There was, however, something to broaden the mind of old Greece in the spectacle of a land 'where an earthquake is considered a portent, and where they grow corn for export' (Hdt. 4. 17; 28), no less than in the strange peoples of Africa and Asia.

8. Late and exceptional was the 'Corinthian Empire' in north-west Greece. Epidamnus (*c.* 625), Apollonia, Ambracia, Anactorium, Leucas, with Potidaea in Chalcidice (594), were all Cypselid foundations, representing a coherent, personal plan. Here alone Greeks, with 'tyrannical' ruthlessness, colonized among Greeks; and here alone, before the Athenian cleruchies (q.v.), Greek colonies remained politically dependent on the mother city. The attempt to keep Corcyra similarly dependent, however, probably led to the 'earliest Greek naval battle' (Thuc. 1. 13), and provoked a feud. Cf. the Corcyraean claim that 'colonists are not sent out to be subjects, but to be equals'; and the Corinthian reply that they only expected 'to be acknowledged leaders and receive the customary respect' (ib. 34; 38).

9. The customary honours included preferential treatment at temples, games, etc.; but Corinth's 'over-magistrates' at Potidaea (ἐπιδημίουργοι, Thuc. 1. 56) remained exceptional. Political independence, however, was compatible with filial feelings. Rich, spectacular Syracuse sought help from compact, stable Corinth against Athens or Carthage; Tarentum from Sparta;

Perinthus from Samos. If a colony colonized, she asked for a Founder from the *metropolis* (e.g. Thuc. 1. 24). If two cities colonized jointly, one was the official metropolis, the other might give the colony its name (e.g. Cumae, Naxos, Gela—officially Lindii). Amphipolis, in revolt from Athens, made Brasidas its 'Founder' instead of Hagnon the Athenian (Thuc. 5. 11). Filial friendship was often reinforced by a thriving trade, which comprised not only metal and valuables, as before, but colonial food and metropolitan objects of industry. With the growth of a trading class and specialist manufactures, aristocracies became outworn and 'tyrants' arose as leaders of the unenfranchised. Thus, through colonization, the whole politics and economy of Greece were revolutionized; and thus in turn the need for large-scale colonization was brought to an end. See also articles on various cities.

J. L. Myres, *CAH* iii, ch. 25; A. Gwynn, *JHS* 1918, 88 ff.; A. R. Burn, *JHS* 1935, 130 (chronology).   A. R. B.

COLONIZATION, GREEK (5th and 4th cc.), *see* CLERUCHY.

COLONIZATION, HELLENISTIC.
The diffusion of Greek settlers through Asia and Egypt in the century after Alexander's conquests was as far-reaching in every sense as the earlier colonial movements. Greece in the fourth century had suffered cruelly from unemployment, but now the Macedonian rulers of the new lands needed Greek soldiers for their armies, and a Greek population attached to themselves (as their native subjects were not), to occupy places strategically or economically important. Alexander himself gave the lead. His greatest colony, Alexandria in Egypt, was the type of the new city, founded with an eye to trade and to creating a splendid Greek centre of administration. His military settlements in Sogdiana were likewise imitated by his successors wherever they had turbulent subjects to restrain or a dangerous frontier to hold.

In Egypt, apart from Alexandria itself (q.v.), the colonizing process was mainly for military purposes. Land (*kleros*) was assigned to soldiers individually, with a military obligation which passed to each occupant in successive generations. The 'cleruchs' did not form political communities, a lack which probably explains the failure, in time, of the Ptolemaic system to fulfil its original military object.

In Asia, the military *kleros* carried the same obligations; but the wide, open spaces allowed, and even demanded, communal groups of settlers. Most of the new Greek 'cities' began as military colonies. The possibilities of colonization on these lines were realized by Antigonus I and probably by the Ptolemies in their Asiatic provinces; but the greatest work was done by the first two Seleucids. Clusters of colonies in Bactria-Sogdiana to guard the northern frontier, in Media to preserve vital communications and overawe hill-tribes, in Asia Minor and Syria to facilitate quick mobilizations in war-time, formed the backbone of the Seleucid military system, and ultimately of Greek civilization in Asia. Naturally they did not remain mere military centres. Greek civilians went to live there, and many foreigners; and in time they became self-governing cities (*poleis*) with the normal Greek institutions and the minimum of political interference from the king. Their citizen-body probably consisted always of Greeks (or Macedonians, Thracians, etc.) only, and Greek was always the official language, even in cities with large native populations. Only in northern India, in the 'Greek' empire of Demetrius and Menander in the second century B.C., are there signs of a more liberal policy towards the conquered, dictated partly by the fewness of the Greek immigrants, but partly, too, by the political genius of Demetrius. In India the bold experiment did not survive to leave a permanent impression; but in the Near and Middle East the new cities, with all their limitations, remained for centuries the great representatives of civilization under Roman, and even under Parthian, rule.

V. S. Tscherikower, *Die hellenistischen Städtegründungen von Alexander dem Grossen bis auf die Römerzeit* (1927); W. W. Tarn, *The Greeks in Bactria and India* (1938), especially ch. 1 ('The Seleucid Settlement'), 118 ff. (Bactria); 243 ff. (India); E. Bikerman, *Institutions des Séleucides* (1938), 74 ff. and 157 ff.; Rostovtzeff, *Hellenistic World* (1941).   G. T. G.

COLONIZATION, ROMAN.
The earliest colonies of Roman citizens were small groups of 300 families sent to garrison the Roman coastline at Ostia, Antium (338 B.C.), and Tarracina (329 B.C.). Others were added as the Roman territory expanded, through reluctance to maintain a permanent fleet. In 218 there were twelve such *coloniae maritimae*. After 200 B.C. citizen colonies were used to guard the coasts of Italy in general. *Coloni* retained their Roman citizenship because the early colonies were within Roman territory, and were too small to form an independent *res publica*; colonies might be a mere enclave within an existing community. Thus citizen colonies are distinct from Latin colonies which, though largely manned by Romans, were autonomous States established outside Roman territory (*see* LATINI, IUS LATII). *Coloni maritimi* were normally exempt from legionary service, though the exemption was revocable, and were bound not to absent themelves by night from their colonies in time of war. *C.* 177 B.C. the system of citizen colonies was reorganized. They were assimilated to Latin colonies, and the use of the latter abandoned. Henceforth citizen colonies are large—from two to five thousand men—and are employed for the same purposes as Latin colonies formerly. Generous allotments of land were given and their internal organization was changed also. They remained citizen colonies but received extensive powers of local government with annual magistrates—*duoviri*, *praetores*, or *duoviri praetores*—a council, *consilium*, and priestly officials. Not many of the new style were founded till the Gracchan age, when a further change took place in their employment. Henceforth colonies were founded not for strategic but for political reasons, either as an emigration scheme for the proletariat or to provide for veteran soldiers. But under the Principate strategic centres were usually chosen for such colonies.

2. The first foundation outside Italy was the Gracchan Junonia at Carthage. Its charter was revoked, but the *coloni* retained their allotments. In 118 B.C. Narbo Martius was successfully founded in Provence despite senatorial objections to overseas colonies. Marius settled veterans in Africa and Corsica, but not in regular colonies. Caesar and the Second Triumvirate established the practice of transmarine foundations. Some colonists were still drawn from the civilian population, notably at the refounding of Carthage and Corinth, also at Urso in Spain. Such colonies were known as *coloniae civicae*, being exceptional. Colonies sent to places where native communities already existed encouraged the romanization of the latter, which eventually received citizenship and municipal rights and coalesced with the colony. Augustus established numerous colonies not only in Narbonensis, the Spanish provinces, Africa, and Mauretania, but also in the East, notably the group in Asia Minor, surrounding the rebellious Homonadenses. Claudius began the regular colonization of the Balkan provinces and the northern frontier. These processes continued till Hadrian. Thenceforth no new colonies were founded. The increasing tendency to local recruitment of legionaries rendered veteran colonies unnecessary. Instead, the title of colony and *ius coloniae* became a privilege increasingly sought out by *municipia* as the highest grade of civic dignity. This process began when

Claudius conferred the title upon the capital cities of certain Gallic communes, but only became considerable in the second century (see MUNICIPIUM, IUS ITALICUM). Colonies usually adopted the names of their founders and subsequent benefactors, sometimes to an extravagant degree.

3. The arrangements for local government in Caesarean and Imperial colonies were a more complex development of the earlier system. Colonial magistracies were always more uniform than municipal magistracies, and soon came to resemble a standardized, small-scale replica of the Roman Constitution. Hence the later popularity of the *ius coloniae*. *Duoviri iure dicundo* replaced consuls and praetors; then came aediles and sometimes quaestors. *Pontifices* and augurs looked after cults and religion. The census was taken by *duoviri quinquennales*, replaced in some Italian colonies by *censores*. Ex-magistrates passed into the council of *decuriones* (q.v.), sometimes called *conscripti*.

4. Colonization was sometimes unofficial. In the later Republic casual immigrants established *pagi* and *conventus* (qq.v.) *civium Romanorum* in native communities, thus spreading Roman civilization and forming the basis of future *municipia*. See also AGER PUBLICUS.

ANCIENT SOURCES. (1) Republic: Scattered references in Livy, Cicero (esp. *Leg. Agr.* bk. 2), etc. Inscriptions, esp. Dessau, *ILS* 6687. (2) Empire: Strabo and Pliny, etc. Inscriptions, *CIL* passim.
MODERN LITERATURE. (1) Republic: K. J. Beloch, *Röm. Gesch.*; E. Kornemann, 'Colonia' in *PW* (lists); H. Rudolph, *Stadt und Staat im römischen Italien* (1935); F. Wilson in *BSR* xiii (on Ostia); A. N. Sherwin-White, *The Roman Citizenship* (1939). (2) Empire. Above, and Abbott and Johnson, *Municipal Administration in the Roman Empire* (1926); T. S. R. Broughton, *The Romanization of Africa Proconsularis* (1929); E. Kornemann, 'Conventus' in *PW*; Premerstein, 'Ius Italicum' in *PW*; Rostovtzeff, *Roman Empire*; M. Grant, *From Imperium to Auctoritas* (1946). A. N. S.-W.

COLONUS. (a) A member of a *colonia* (see COLONIZATION, ROMAN). (b) A tenant farmer. *Ager publicus* (q.v.) and municipal domains were normally let to *coloni*, as were the estates of private landlords when slave gangs were abandoned in the first century B.C., and also imperial estates. Private and imperial estates were usually managed by bailiffs (*vilici*), often slaves or freedmen of the owner, or farmers-general (*conductores, mancipes*), who cultivated a home farm and let the other farms to *coloni* and collected their rents. The rent was at first usually a fixed sum of money, later generally a share of the crops; on African estates the *coloni* also owed a few days' labour in the year on the home farm. On some municipal estates the tenure was perpetual, so long as a fixed rent charge (*vectigal*, q.v.) was paid. Nominally leases were for five years, but tenure tended to become hereditary. Perpetual tenure by emphyteutic leases (see EMPHYTEUSIS) was granted to *coloni* who reclaimed waste land. In the fourth century *coloni* were forbidden to abandon their farms, and their children were obliged to succeed them.

R. Clausing, *The Roman Colonate* (1925); M. Rostovtzeff, 'Studien zur Geschichte des römischen Kolonates' (*Arch. Pap.*, Beiheft i, 1910). A. H. M. J.

COLONUS (Κολωνὸς ἵππιος, as distinguished from Κολωνὸς ἀγοραῖος, on which the so-called Theseum stands), Sophocles' birthplace, is a hill a mile north of Athens, where Oedipus found refuge and was buried. The assembly which set up the Four Hundred in 411 B.C. was held in the sanctuary of Poseidon Hippios. There stood the bronze threshold of Hades, by which Theseus and Pirithous descended. The olives and nightingales have given place to a water-tower. T. J. D.

COLOR in rhetoric is often applied to embellished diction, but also specially to a plausible excuse or palliation of an offence debated in a *Controversia*. In this sense it enters into the title of the elder Seneca's collection. As a conjecture of motive or explanation for some

act, it is contrasted with a *quaestio* which can be supported by arguments (*Controv.* 1. 5. 9). The danger was that a *color* might be too far-fetched (1. 6. 9 'longe arcessito colore') or supremely silly (9. 4. 22 'colorem stultissimum induxit'). Seneca quotes many examples for approval or disapproval. About the Vestal who survived being thrown from the Tarpeian rock, he cites Junius Otho's *color* 'Perhaps she prepared for her punishment and practised falling from the time when she began her offence'! (1. 3. 11), an intolerable fatuity from the author of four books on *colores*! (2. 1. 33). J. W. D.

COLOSSEUM, the medieval name of Amphitheatrum Flavium, near the Colossus Neronis, built by Vespasian over Nero's 'stagnum domus aureae'. The axes measure 188 metres and 156 metres, the height 48·50 metres. Vespasian dedicated in A.D. 79 two stories faced in travertine and treated in Doric and simplified Ionic arcades respectively. Titus added a third, Corinthian, arcade carrying a fourth tier of blind arcading broken by windows set alternately in its *podium* and panels, the former windows being surmounted by bronze *clipei*. Next came mast-corbels for the awning, worked by sailors. The seating was in three tiers, two in Vespasian's building, the third, with standing-room above it, in the addition by Titus. The arena was cut off by a fence and high platform carrying marble chairs for guilds and officials, and, on the short axes, imperial or magisterial boxes. The arena was floored in timber, covering dens for beasts, mechanical elevators, and drains. Audiences, estimated at 45,000, were regulated outside the building in a plot bordered by bollards, and held tickets corresponding to the numbered arcades, whence an elaborate system of staircases commodiously served all parts of the auditorium.

The amphitheatre was restored by Nerva and Trajan (*CIL* vi. 32254-5), Pius (S.H.A., *Pius* 8), between 217 and 238 (Dio Cass. 78. 25; S.H.A. *Elagabalus* 17, *Alex. Sev.* 24, *Max. et Balb.* 1. 14), in 250 (Hieron. *ab Abr.* 2268), after 442 (*CIL* vi. 32086-9) and 470 (*CIL* vi. 32091-2, 32188-9), about 508 (*CIL* vi. 32094) and in 523 (Cassiod. *Var.* 5. 42).

G. L. Taylor and E. Cresy, *Architectural Antiquities of Rome* (1874), 114-29; C. Hülsen, *Röm. Mitt.* 1897; H. M. R. Leopold, *Med. Nederl. Hist. Inst. Rom.* iv. 39-76; A. von Gerkan, *Röm. Mitt.* 1925; G. Cozzo, *Architettura ed Arti decorative* ii. 273-91. I. A. R.

COLOTES (1), Greek sculptor and pupil of Phidias, native of Paros. He was the assistant of Phidias at Elis when Phidias was constructing the famous chryselephantine statue of Zeus. Colotes himself made an ivory statue of Asclepius at Cyllene. No work of his survives. S. C.

COLOTES (2) of Lampsacus (4th-3rd c. B.C.), pupil and fanatical admirer of Epicurus. Works: Against Plato's *Lysis*; Against the *Euthydemus* (both ed. by W. Crönert in *Kolotes u. Menedemus*, 1906); Against the *Gorgias*; Against the *Republic*; "Ὅτι κατὰ τὰ τῶν ἄλλων φιλοσόφων δόγματα οὐδὲ ζῆν ἔστιν. From Plutarch *Adv. Coloten* we learn that the last-named work tried, in a superficial and ill-informed way, to show that any theory of knowledge other than the empiricism of Epicurus affords no secure basis for practical life.

PW xi. 1120. W. D. R.

COLOURS, SACRED. Three colours are especially important for sacral purposes in antiquity; they are white, black, and red, the last being understood in the widest possible sense, to include purple, crimson, even violet (cf. E. Wunderlich, 'Die Bedeutung der roten Farbe im Kultus der Griechen und Römer', 1925 (*RGVV* xx. 1) 1 ff.).

White is in general a festal colour, associated with things of good omen, such as sacrifices to the celestial gods (white victims are regular for this purpose in both Greece and Rome). See for instance *Il.* 3. 103, where a white lamb is brought for sacrifice to Helios (q.v.); the scholiast rightly says that as the Sun is bright and male, a white male lamb is brought for him, while Earth, being dark and female, gets a black ewe-lamb (cf. Verg. *G.* 2. 146 for the white bulls pastured along Clitumnus for sacrificial purposes). It is the colour of the clothing generally worn on joyous occasions (e.g. Eur. *Alc.* 923, Martial 4. 2, whereon see Friedlaender); of horses used on great festivals such as (probably) that of Demeter and Persephone at Syracuse (Pind. *Ol.* 6. 95, cf. J. Rumpel, *Lex. Pindaricum*, 1883, s.v. λεύκιππος, and cf. LEUCIP-PUS). In Rome, white horses drew the chariot of a *triumphator* (Marquardt, *Staatsverw.* ii.² 586).

Black on the contrary is associated with the chthonian gods and mourning (Homer and Euripides, ll.cc.), and with the dead (hence the Erinyes wear sombre clothing, φαιοχίτωνες, Aesch. *Cho.* 1049, as infernal powers). There are, however, exceptions. At Argos, white was the mourning-colour (Socrates of Argos in Plut. *Quaest. Rom.* 26); Plutarch's assertion that white was the colour of Roman mourning will hardly pass muster, see Rose, *Rom. Quest. of Plut.* (1924), 180. Hence to wear it at a festival was both ill-mannered and unlucky (Martial, l.c., cf. Ov. *Ib.* 102 and the scholiast there). The above facts easily explain why 'white' and 'black' respectively mean 'lucky' and 'unlucky' when used of a day, etc. The natural association of white with light and black with darkness is explanation enough, but it may be added that white garments are conspicuously clean (cf. *Od.* 4. 750 for clean clothes at prayer), black ones suggest the unwashen condition of a mourner; cf. DEAD, DISPOSAL OF. See further G. Radke, *Die Bedeutung der weissen und der schwarzen Farben* (Diss., Berlin, 1936).

Red has more complicated associations, for which see Wunderlich, op. cit. It would seem to suggest blood, and therefore death and the underworld (hence, e.g., the use of red flags in cursing, Lysias 6. 51), but also blood as the source or container of life, wherefore a red bandage or wrapping of some kind is common in ancient, especially popular medicine, and also the ruddy colour of healthy flesh and various organs of the body, wherefore it is associated with rites of fertility on occasion (e.g. statues of Priapus, Hor. *Sat.* 1. 8. 5). Perhaps because red, or purple, is the colour of light, red is on occasion protective, e.g. the *praetexta* of Roman magistrates and children. But it is also associated with the burning heat of summer, cf. AUGURIUM CANARIUM.

Other colours are of little or no sacral importance, but it may be noted that the veil (*flammeum*) of a Roman bride, often stated to be red, is distinctly called yellow (*luteum*) by Lucan (*Phars.* 2. 361) and Pliny (*HN* 21. 46).

H. J. R.

COLUMBARIUM. (1) A Roman dove-cot. These were sometimes small and fixed in gables (*columina*), sometimes very large tower-like structures (*turres*), fitted with nesting niches in rows, perches, and running water.

(2) *Columbarium* was also applied to the sepulchral chambers of large households or of *collegia* (Mommsen, *De collegiis*, 93), where ash-chests and urns were stored in pigeon-holes (*loci, loculi*). These appear originally in Etruria (G. Dennis, *Cities and Cemeteries of Etruria* i². 10, 26), but are a feature of large Roman slave and freedmen groups attached to given households. The most striking are those of the Empress Livia, containing some 3,000 urns, the well-preserved *columbarium* of Pomponius Hylas, between Viae Appia and Latina, and the three *columbaria* of Vigna Codini (*CIL* vi. 4418-880, 4881-5178, 5179-538), all within the later city wall of Rome.

G. Lugli, *The Classical Monuments of Rome* i (1929), 400 ff.
I. A. R.

COLUMELLA, LUCIUS JUNIUS MODERATUS, contemporary and fellow-countryman of Seneca, was a Spaniard of Gades with a hereditary interest in agriculture. He served as tribune in the Legio VI Ferrata in Syria and Cilicia, *c.* A.D. 36 (*CIL* ix. 235). He afterwards acquired an estate near Ardea in Latium.

WORKS. The subjects of the *De Re Rustica* (*c.* A.D. 60) are: bk. 1, general precepts; bk. 2, land and crops; bks. 3 and 4, vines; bk. 5, land dimensions, trees; bks. 6 and 7, domestic animals; bk. 8, poultry, fish-ponds; bk. 9, wild cattle, bees; bk. 10 (in verse, supplementing Virgil's *Georgics*), gardening; bk. 11, bailiff's duties, calendar; bk. 12, duties of bailiff's wife. Columella's *De arboribus* also survives, an earlier and briefer treatment of the subject of *De R. R.* bks. 3-5. His *Adversus Astrologos* and *De Lustrationibus etc.* are lost.

Columella writes as a practical and scientific farmer, desirous of reviving Roman agriculture; he deplores the importation of foreign corn, the multiplication of country-seats and the absenteeism of landowners; he advocates hard work and personal supervision. He quotes Mago, the Carthaginian, as well as Greek and Latin agricultural writers, his sources including Cato, Varro, Hyginus, Virgil, Tremellius Scrofa, Celsus, Graecinus, Julius Atticus. His prose style, which in the prefaces is almost Ciceronian, is always lucid and appropriate, and, though sensitive to landscape and colour, he avoids the temptation of fine writing. In bk. 10, though his Muse sometimes soars on wings borrowed from Virgil, he reproduces the language rather than the spirit of his master.

BIBLIOGRAPHY

LIFE AND WORKS. Schanz-Hosius, § 496; Teuffel, § 293. Wight Duff, *Lit. Hist. Rome, Silver Age*, 160 ff.; Summers, *Silver Age of Lat. Lit.* 283 ff.; Heitland, *Agricola*, 250 ff.; V. Barbaret, *De C. vita et scriptis* (1887); W. Becher, (same title) (1897).
TEXTS. V. Lundström (1897, etc.); Bk. 10, Postgate (*Corp. Poet. Lat.* ii); H. B. Ash (see below).
COMMENTARIES. Gesner (1772-4); Schneider (1794); Ress (1795).
TRANSLATION. Anon. (London, 1745); H. B. Ash (i-iv, 1941, Loeb).
STYLE AND DICTION. Kottmann, *De elocutione C.* (1903); F. Prix, *Sprachl. Unters. zu C.* (1883); M. Ahle, *Sprachl. Unters. zu C.* (1915); W. Schröter, *De C. Vergilii imitatore* (1882); E. Stettner, (same title) (1894); V. Lundström, *Eranos*, xiv-xvii; H. B. Ash, *CJ* xviii. 328 ff.
E. S. F.

COLUMNA BELLICA, *see* BELLONA, FETIALES.

COLUMNS, detached supporting members in Greek and Roman architecture which are circular in section, or similar partly detached members called 'engaged' columns. The earliest forms were of wood. Neither columns nor engaged columns should be confused with 'pillars', i.e. supporting members which are rectangular in section, though an engaged column may form part of a larger supporting member known as a 'pier'. From the earliest times important Greek stone or marble columns were, or were intended to be, fluted, i.e. decorated with parallel concave channels for the whole height of the column shaft, though convex ridges having a similar decorative function are sometimes found in early work. The columns of the sixth-century Temple of Artemis at Ephesus had 44 flutes, but 20 flutes for Doric (exceptionally 16 and 24) and 24 for Ionic and Corinthian, became standardized; both Ionic and Corinthian columns having deep channels (nearly or quite semicircular in section) divided by fillets, in place of the shallow channels of Doric columns which meet on a fine edge. Roman columns of polished granite or marble were sometimes unfluted; or, when fluted, the flutes were partly filled in for one-third of the height from the base.

Greek Doric columns had a shaft and a capital. Greek Ionic and Corinthian columns and nearly all Roman columns had a base in addition. Practically all classical column shafts had 'diminution', i.e. a diminishing diameter from the base upwards, and most of them had *entasis*, i.e. a slight swelling of the shaft to correct any impression of hollowness. Occasionally, Graeco-Roman Corinthian columns had 'counter-diminution', i.e. a re-entering curve, producing the greatest diameter at about one-third of the shaft height above the base.

Sir Banister Fletcher, *A History of Architecture on the Comparative Method*[10] (1938), 86, 99, 122. T. F.

COMEDY (GREEK), ORIGINS OF.
Aristotle (*Poet.* 3–5) could find no recorded evidence about the early stages of Greek Comedy before the second decade of the fifth century B.C. He says that it developed (and the context shows that he is thinking mainly of the actor's share) from the share taken by the leaders of phallic processions like those which continued in vogue in many parts of Greece in his own day, and the statement (which may be a conjecture) is doubtless intended to account for the presence of an actor in phallic costume in the Old Comedy; but it happens that none of the phallic processions of which accounts are preserved shows any near affinity to early comedy, and the phallic actor has possibly a different origin. He further records a claim of the Dorians of Megara to have originated both Sicilian and Attic Comedy—the former because Epicharmus was a Dorian of Megara Hyblaea in Sicily, the latter as having arisen out of a form of Comedy which developed during the democratic period in the history of Megara in Greece; and passing references in other authors suggest that the Athenians of the fifth century knew something of a Megarian Comedy of an unrefined kind. The one thing about which Aristotle seems to be certain is that Comedy originated in some kind of κῶμος, in the performance of a band of revellers.

2. Of the two types of Comedy which are found in the fifth century—the non-choral Sicilian Comedy of Epicharmus, and the Old Comedy of Athens, with a chorus as important as the actors—the former had no distinguished composer after Epicharmus and fell away into (or was supplanted by) the mime and by the performances of actors called φλύακες, of which many pictures survive on South Italian vases; the latter received the recognition of the State at Athens in 486 B.C., and are mainly known to us through the surviving plays of Aristophanes. Both appear to have derived important elements from Dorian and Peloponnesian sources, in particular the phallic actor and (at Athens) his costume, and the burlesque of a variety of stock characters, human and superhuman. These seem to have figured in little plays without a chorus—like the later mimes—sometimes (as at Sparta) presenting such characters as a quack doctor, or a food-stealer or orchard-robber, or a grotesque old man or old woman. The two latter are often found in Comedy, as is a Peloponnesian dance, the *Kordax*, commonly associated with the old woman; and the quack doctor may have been one of the many types of pretentious humbug whose discomfiture is part of the stock-in-trade of the Old Comedy. These performances in Sparta and elsewhere seem to have been mainly associated with the worship of Artemis in some of her more primitive forms; but early Corinthian vases give us pictures of demonic (and perhaps also of human) figures, which are apparently Dionysiac, and which wear practically the same costume—grotesque padding under a tight-fitting garment, with or without the phallus—as was worn by comic actors on the Attic stage; and since the Dionysiac demons of Attica were not of this type, it is a probable inference that Attic Comedy derived this costume from the Peloponnese. Megara may have served as a half-way house between the Peloponnese and Athens. It is not known when or how these Dorian and non-choral elements came to be combined with those derived from the Athenian κῶμος, and no recorded form of κῶμος corresponds exactly with what is required to explain the

typical forms of Attic Comedy, though some come near to it, and probably comic poets borrowed freely from any source, and also invented freely for themselves. In Aristophanes the general lines of Comedy, particularly in the early scenes, are fairly constant. A ludicrous person appears with a brilliant and extravagant idea for setting the world to rights or getting out of some difficulty; a chorus bursts in either in furious opposition or in enthusiastic support; there is a scene of violent argumentation or horse-play, calming down into a set debate (*agōn*); and when the conclusion of this is reached, the chorus turn to the audience—in a κῶμος it would be to the bystanders watching the revel—and deliver addresses to them which alternate with brief chants to the gods. These addresses and chants may contain a good deal of personal satire, like the exchanges of raillery between other Greek processions and the bystanders. The literary form of these elements in Comedy is singularly constant—the symmetrical structure and the use of long metres (anapaestic, iambic, trochaic, and others) almost throughout; and it does not seem extravagant to suppose that there must have been some form of κῶμος following the same sequence, viz. *parodos* (entrance etc. of chorus), *proagōn* leading to *agon* or debate, *parabasis* (addresses to audience separated by brief chants), and that into this performance there came to be introduced the phallic actor of Dorian mime (unless indeed the leading person in the κῶμος was sometimes phallic already) and the play of character-types.

3. The other main group of scenes which, with those just described, goes to compose Attic Comedy is mainly in iambic trimeters. In these scenes the play of character-types predominates, though the chief personage in the earlier group of scenes usually takes a leading part, often confronting and discomfiting a series of other characters in rapid succession. Aristophanes shows an increasing skill in combining these two main elements in Comedy—doubtless originally separate—into a unity.

4. The κῶμος was often entirely non-dramatic; the revellers pretended to be no one but themselves, whereas the primitive Dorian performers were entirely dramatic. But one particular semi-dramatic form of κῶμος was certainly Attic and contributed to Comedy, viz. the masquerade of revellers disguised as animals, of which various early forms are known (partly from vase-paintings), and which probably suggested the choruses of Birds, Frogs, Wasps, Goats, Storks, Fishes, Riders on horseback, etc., which the Attic poets employed.

5. If an 'origin' is required for the normal ending of a Comedy in a feast, it is enough to suggest that a κῶμος would naturally have ended so. The fact that Comedy at Athens was at first particularly associated with the Lenaea suggests that a κῶμος of the type required to explain it may have formed part of that Dionysiac festival, but the various elements (whether Dorian or Attic) composing Comedy probably go back to times before the introduction of the Dionysiac worship into which they were later absorbed, and belong to that stock of primitive customs and amusements which seem to be common to humanity everywhere. A. W. P.-C.

COMEDY (GREEK), OLD.
Old Greek Comedy falls into two main divisions: (1) Sicilian Comedy and (2) Attic Comedy. Of (1) we know very little, except that it was written in Doric, that it had no chorus, and that it dealt with subjects of general interest, contained a plot, and was free from personal and political satire. Some of its 'stock' characters (e.g. the parasite) foreshadow New Comedy. Except for the shadowy Phormis the only exponent of whom we know anything is Epicharmus (*c.* 530–440 B.C.), who wrote (to judge from the fragments) mythological burlesques, comedies (or farces) of manners, and scenes of everyday life—perhaps not unlike the

mimes of, e.g., Herodas. Sicilian Comedy seems to have died out early, giving place to the Old Attic Comedy.

2. This was at first acted by amateurs (ἐθελονταί: Arist. *Poet.* 1449ᵇ2) and obtained official recognition later than Tragedy. It is likely that in early times Tragedy was acted at the Great Dionysia (March) and Comedy at the Lenaea (January), though later both forms of drama were exhibited at both festivals. In spite of this 'the archon gave a chorus' to Comedy (i.e. Athens officially recognized and subsidized it) at the Dionysia earlier than at the Lenaea. Suidas (s.v. Χιωνίδης) assigns the first comic ἀγών to 486 B.C. This date is more or less confirmed by epigraphic evidence, for we know from the dramatic *fasti* (*IG* ii². 2318) that Magnes won a Dionysiac victory in 472, while in the Victors' list (*IG* ii². 2325) his name stands sixth, which fact sets the start of the comic ἀγών some years earlier than 472. The date of the first comic ἀγών at the Lenaea is put with much probability by Capps (*AJPhil.* xxviii. 179 ff.) as 441–440 B.C.

3. Little is known of the earliest writers of Attic Comedy. Epicharmus (q.v.) is said by Aristotle (*Poet.* 1448ᵃ33) to have lived πολλῷ πρότερος Χιωνίδου καὶ Μάγνητος; but Aristotle himself admits that he knows little of the early history of Comedy διὰ τὸ μὴ σπουδάζεσθαι ⟨αὐτήν⟩ (*Poet.* 1449ᵃ38), and it is more likely that Epicharmus was an older contemporary of the other two. Suidas gives Chionides' first (?) victory as 486. Still more shadowy are the names of Euetes, Euxenides, and Myllus whom Suidas (s.v. 'Epicharmus') gives as active in Athens *c.* 484. Of Euxenides nothing further is known. Euetes occurs in the list of *tragic* victors. Myllus (= the Squinter) may have been no more than a stock character of farce (cf. Latin *Dossenus*, etc.). He is, however, mentioned by Diomedes (together with Susarion and Magnes) and by the paroemiographers. Magnes (q.v.) is the first comic writer who is more than a name.

4. The normal number of competing comedies was five—so Arist. *Ath. Pol.* 56. 3, a figure confirmed for the years 440–431 by a Roman inscription (*IG* xiv. 1097), for 388 B.C. by Ar. *Plut.* arg. 4, and for the end of the fourth century by didascalic inscriptions (Wilhelm, op. cit. inf. 43 ff.). The number was reduced to three during the Peloponnesian War, doubtless from motives of economy (args. to Ar. *Ach.*, *Eq.*, *Vesp.*, *Ran.*). The production of each play was financed by the *choregus* (see CHOREGIA); the chorus was trained either by the poet himself as διδάσκαλος or by a friend acting as such. For leave to produce at the Dionysia the poet applied (χορὸν αἰτεῖν) to the Archon (Arist. *Ath. Pol.* 56. 5), at the Lenaea to the *Archon basileus* (ib. 57. 1). It seems probable that at least in the fifth century not more than one play could be produced by any one διδάσκαλος at the same festival. According to arg. Ar. *Vesp.* Aristophanes gained first prize with his *Wasps* produced διὰ Φιλωνίδου, while Philonides won second prize as his own διδάσκαλος; but it is likely that the words διὰ Φιλωνίδου should be excised. In the fourth and third centuries, however, there are undoubted cases of two plays produced by one διδάσκαλος. It is clear from schol. Ar. *Eccl.* 102 and *Ran.* 367 that the *poet* received the pecuniary prize; and in the Victors' list it is the *poet's* name that appears. In the *fasti*, however (i.e. in the *official* list), the name of the διδάσκαλος is inscribed.

5. At the Athenian festivals new plays were regularly produced, and it was very rarely that an old one was restaged. Not until 339 B.C. do we get the regular reproduction of an old play unaltered—the reacting of the *Frogs* (arg. 1, Ar. *Ran.*) was exceptional. On the other hand, a poet could *rewrite* and reproduce a play, as Aristophanes rewrote the *Clouds* and Teleclides the Στερροί (*IG* xiv. 1098ᵃ). Old plays were also frequently reproduced at various *country* Dionysia (cf. Aeschin. 1. 157, and see Körte in *Gnomon* xi. 631 ff.).

6. The question whether the State could, or ever did,

interfere with a poet's παρρησία is a vexed one. Schol. Ar. *Ach.* 67 mentions a law περὶ τοῦ μὴ ⟨ὀνομαστὶ⟩ κωμῳδεῖν as in force from 439 to 437 B.C., and schol. Ar. *Av.* 1297 attributes another such law to Syracosius in 415 B.C. (Antimachus' Ψήφισμα mentioned in Schol. Ar. *Ach.* 1150 is a palpable misinterpretation of the passage). It is more probable, however (so Körte, art. in *PW*), that no such 'law' ever existed, though politicians could and did bring private actions against libellous poets, as did Cleon against Aristophanes after the production of the *Babylonians* (schol. Ar. *Ach.* 378) and possibly Alcibiades against Eupolis after that of the *Baptae*, though tradition (Platon. *Diff. Com.* § 4; Cic. *Att.* 6. 1. 18) attributes to Alcibiades more violent methods.

7. The subject-matter *par excellence* of Old Comedy is personal invective, mainly against political characters and individuals otherwise notorious. The politicians attacked were, as a rule, those of the popular party, such as Pericles, Cleon, Hyperbolus; though the poets are not to be supposed to be themselves necessarily of oligarchic sympathies. Besides politicians, poets, philosophers, and musicians came frequently under the poet's lash; e.g. Euripides, Socrates, and Connus (Socrates' music master, attacked by Ameipsias in a comedy bearing his name). Another (and later—*see* CRATES 1) class of Comedy, not to be sharply differentiated from the comedy of invective, is what may be called the comedy of fantasy, typified by Aristophanes' *Birds*. A third type is mythological burlesque; a type perhaps commoner in Middle Comedy but well established in Old Comedy, as the titles of Aristophanes' plays (if nothing else) would suggest. Mythological burlesque is traceable from Epicharmus down, and Platonius (*Diff. Com.* § 7) is wrong in saying that such plays had neither chorus nor parabasis. Cratinus' Ὀδυσσῆς had both (frs. 144–6). Another type again is the comedy of everyday life. Out of this developed New Comedy. Comedies of this class are rare in the fifth century, though we find a certain number, mostly with the names of ἑταῖραι as titles. Broadly speaking, the comic poets did not specialize individually in particular genres.

8. Old Comedy, to judge from what remains of it, was written on a fixed plan. First came (A) the 'Attic' part (see above) lasting until the *parabasis*. This comprised (1) the *prologue*—not the ῥῆσις *prologue* of, e.g., Euripides, but a scene descriptive to the audience of the subject matter of the play. The slaves' dialogue in Ar. *Eq.* is a good example. Next (2) the *parodos* or entrance of the chorus. Then the development of the plot, which generally contained (3) an ἀγών, the set contest or dispute that figures in nearly all Aristophanes' plays. (There is none in *Ach.* or *Thesm.*; in *Eq.* and *Nub.* there are two.) Part (A) is written partly in iambic trimeters, partly in other measures. The *parabasis* (B) is the address of the poet made through the chorus and *coryphaeus* to the audience. It is generally (*Av.* and *Thesm.* are exceptions) unconnected with the action of the play and concerned with personal and political questions of the time. The third main division of Old Comedy is (C) the 'Dorian' or episodic part. This is a series of scenes of a more or less farcical character in which the main personage of the play puts to flight various unwelcome visitors. These scenes are always written in iambic trimeters and are interpunctuated by short choric songs. Occasionally, as in Ar. *Ran.*, they are broken by the ἀγών, which in this case, exceptionally, comes after the *parabasis*. The episodes are brought to an end by the *exodus*, a κῶμος consisting usually of the main character and the chorus. This κῶμος is lacking in Ar. *Nub.* and *Thesm.*

9. As in fully developed Tragedy, the number of actors was limited to three—first, according to Tzetzes (Kaibel, *CGF* 18) by Cratinus. Aristotle (*Poet.* 1449ᵇ3) says 'no one knows who fixed the number of comic actors'. These actors were grotesquely padded before

and behind and furnished with leather phalli and masks. The chorus probably numbered twenty-four (Poll. 4. 109; scholl. Ar. *Av.* 297; *Ach.* 211) and was divided into two semi-choruses. It was dressed in appropriate costume (e.g. as birds in Ar. *Av.*), part of which it removed in order to dance (Ar. *Ach.* 627, ἀποδύντες; schol. *Pax* 729). Sometimes a play had a secondary chorus (παραχο-ρήγημα); cf. Ar. *Ran.*, in which the μύσται form the chorus, the Frogs the παραχορήγημα. The leader of the chorus was the *coryphaeus*. It seems likely that where the chorus sang in two semi-choruses the coryphaeus would lead semi-chorus A, a secondary coryphaeus leading semi-chorus B.

BIBLIOGRAPHY

Fragmenta Comicorum Graecorum, A. Meineke (5 vols., 1839–57) containing valuable introduction; *Comicorum Atticorum fragmenta*, T. Kock (3 vols., 1880–8); *Comicorum Graecorum Fragmenta*, G. Kaibel (1899)—Doric Comedy only: all published; A. Wilhelm, *Urkunden dramatischer Aufführungen in Athen* (1906)—deals with the important 'dramatic' inscriptions; E. Capps, *Introduction of Comedy into the City Dionysia* (1903); P. Geissler, *Chronologie der altattischen Komödie* (1925); J. Denis, *La Comédie grecque* (2 vols., 1886); A. W. Pickard-Cambridge, *Dithyramb, Tragedy, and Comedy* (1927); G. Norwood, *Greek Comedy* (1931); T. Zieliński, *Die Gliederung der altattischen Komödie* (1885); A. Körte, art. 'Komödie' in *PW* (1921).   M. P.

COMEDY (GREEK), MIDDLE.

From Old Comedy there was continuous development through the Middle period (*c.* 400–*c.* 320 B.C.) into the New: Middle merged into New, yet separate names are convenient. (Earlier Greek criticism recognized ἀρχαία and καινή (or νέα) only, e.g. Arist. *Eth. Nic.* 1128ᵃ22; μέση was added later. *See* PLATONIUS.) Development was accompanied by decrease in variety of interest, the New Comedy being almost entirely devoted to the dramatization of love-plots.

2. The downfall of Athens, 404 B.C., vitally affected the comic stage: other themes replaced those which had evoked the brilliant wit and extravagant fancy of Aristophanes and his contemporaries, and Comedy was led to adapt its structure to the conduct of a play of intrigue by greatly diminishing the role of the chorus and developing the importance of the ἐπεισόδια. In Aristophanes' *Plutus* (388 B.C.) the transition to Middle Comedy is already visible: χοροῦ (MSS.) indicates an interpolated lyric (ἐμβόλιμον), loosely connected with the comedy. Lyric measures are found in Middle Comedy fragments (e.g. Eubulus frs. 104, 105, *CAF* ii. 199), some in monodies (Axionicus fr. 4, *CAF* ii. 413, parodying Euripides). Evidence for chorus in Middle Comedy: Alexis fr. 237 and papyrus fragment, Timocles fr. 25 (*CAF* ii. 462); Heniochus fr. 5 (ibid. 433). But the chorus is no longer the poet's mouthpiece.

3. Aristotle (*Eth. Nic.* 4. 1128ᵃ20) attests that the Comedy of his time (the developed Middle Comedy) had renounced (with the phallus and the paunch) the αἰσχρο-λογία of Old Comedy, replacing it by ὑπόνοια; and the extant remains of Middle and New Comedy, with negligible exceptions, bear this out. Personal invective (κωμῳδεῖν ὀνομαστί) against contemporaries was not discarded so quickly or completely as obscenity (Pl. *Leg.* 11. 935 e; Isoc. *On Peace* 14; Aeschin. 1. 157): indeed, a greater proportion of titles are proper names in Middle Comedy than in Old. Political attacks are found early in the period (and one comparatively late—Mnesimachus' *Philippus*; and *see* TIMOCLES). Courtesans and philosophers (Aristophon's Πλάτων, and passages on Plato and the Academy, Pythagoreans, the Lyceum, Cynics, and Cyrenaics) were prominent subjects. Parasites, gluttons, fishmongers, and cooks played a large part; eating and drinking were endlessly discussed. (The above-mentioned characters, with others, e.g. old men, young men, and slaves, appeared regularly as stock 'characters', and were further elaborated in the New Comedy.) Burlesque of mythology (well established in Old Comedy, q.v., para. 7) became common in Middle Comedy—in two types,

(1) directly from the myth, (2) from the treatment of the myth by some tragedians, especially Euripides, but also Sophocles, and less frequently Aeschylus. This παρα-τραγῳδεῖν influenced the diction, representation, and structure of Comedy.

4. Before long, the realistic depiction of daily life (not unknown in Old Comedy, q.v., para. 7) became the chief aim in Comedy (cf. the titles of Antiphanes and other Middle Comedy poets). Ordinary, commonplace life is no easy subject to treat interestingly on the stage; and Antiphanes (fr. 191, Ποίησις) contrasts the comic poet's more difficult lot with the tragedian's, whose plot is already familiar, and the *deus ex machina* at hand—the comic writer has no such resources.

5. By study, or parody, of Tragedy, especially of Euripides (as well as by observation of life), comic poets learned to employ certain motives—the love-motive, and the exposure of children with their subsequent recognition. Such titles as Ἀντερῶσα (Antiphanes, Nicostratus) and the many names of foreign women (Ὀλυνθία, Μιλησία) show that love is an important element in certain plays; cf. the Greek Middle Comedy original of Plautus' *Persa*. Again, the tragic motive of flight to the altar (used in Aristophanes, *Thesm.* 689 ff.) appears in the Alexis papyrus.

6. Numerous fragments show that the most striking characteristic of Middle Comedy is observation of contemporary types and manners (ὁ ζωγράφος, ὁ μεμψίμοι-ρος). Yet not a single comedy can be reconstructed with any degree of certainty, since the extant passages were quoted to illustrate food and drink, moral principles, or lexicography—not dramatic technique nor comic force. (Contrast New Comedy, which papyrus discoveries have revealed in some detail.)

7. In Middle Comedy diction and metre are much less elaborate than in the Old. Beside iambic trimeter and trochaic tetrameter, there is occasional use of iambic tetrameter; more frequently, anapaestic systems and dactylic hexameters (one elegiac distich, Antiphanes fr. 149). For the few lyric measures see supra, para. 2, and EUBULUS.

8. To 57 poets Athenaeus assigns more than 800 plays: we know the names of about 50 poets (many of them non-Athenians), Antiphanes, Anaxandrides, Eubulus, Alexis, Timocles (qq.v.) being the most prominent.   W. G. W.

COMEDY (GREEK), NEW.

New Comedy continues the development begun by Middle Comedy away from the imaginative and fantastic. The chorus is almost altogether divorced from the action: a band of revellers (Alexis fr. 107, Menander, *Epit.* 242: cf. the κῶμος of Old Comedy) are, on their first appearance, announced as invading the stage, and they give an *entr'acte* performance of singing and dancing. Later, their entrances are unannounced. So little connexion has the chorus with the play that among the *dramatis personae* of Menander's Ἥρως, the chorus is not noted. But exceptions occur, e.g. the chorus of fishermen in the original (by Diphilus) of Plautus' *Rudens*. In any performance the stage need not be continuously occupied.

2. The stock characters are shown by numerous masks (Pollux 4. 143–54, cf. C. Robert, *Die Masken der neueren Komödie* (1911)—9 types of old men (e.g. the πάππος, lenient or severe; the πρεσβύτης, choleric or phlegmatic), 11 types of young men (e.g. town-bred or country-bred, sanguine or despairing lover), 7 slaves, 3 old women, and 14 young women of three different classes; also, different types of parasite, soldier, cook, and others—mostly recognizable in the fragments as well as in the masks.

3. Personal ridicule (one means of providing comic relief in plots which became increasingly serious) is directed against parasites, gluttons, and the like; and there are isolated attacks upon philosophers (Philemon, Φιλόσοφοι) and others, e.g. by Philippides and Arche-

dicus (qq.v.). Plays are occasionally named after contemporaries, e.g. *Amastris* (Diphilus), after the niece of Darius and founder of the town in Pontus; *Arsinoe* (Posidippus), after the wife of Ptolemy Philadelphus.

4. A few mythological plays were written, but titles are deceptive: thus Menander, *Ἥρως*, deals with ordinary life, the god Heros being the speaker of the prologue. Comedies are named after occupations (*Γεωργός*, *Ἁλιεῖς*), relationships (*Ἀδελφοί*, *Δίδυμαι*), origin (*Καρχηδόνιος*, *Ἀνδρία*), character (*Κόλαξ*, *Δεισιδαίμων*), prominent objects in the plot (*Δακτύλιος*, *Θησαυρός*), personal names (Thaïs, Thrasyleon); sometimes a present participle summarizes the plot or one episode (*Ἐπιτρέποντες*, from its arbitration scene). From the time of Alexis (apparently a pioneer in love-plots), love became the mainspring of the play (with few exceptions, e.g. the originals of Plautus' *Captivi* and *Trinummus*), yet within the limits of this theme there is infinite variety of detail.

5. To the influence of Old Comedy may be assigned the breach of illusion by direct appeal to the spectators (Men. *Epit.* 567, *Sam.* 54, 114, 338, and in a prologue *Pk.* 51), and the use of 'asides'.

6. The preponderating influence of Euripides (already marked in Middle Comedy) is seen in the dramatic treatment of modern problems, in the profusion of moral maxims, in the use of the monologue, the recognition-scene, the isolated prologue, and the prologue-god (which in Comedy may be a mere abstraction: in Menander, *Ἄγνοια* (*Pk.*), *Ἥρως θεός* (*Her.*), *Τύχη*, *Ἔλεγχος*; in Philemon, *Ἀήρ*; Anon., *Φόβος*, *Διόνυσος*). The plot of Menander's *Epit.* owes a debt to Euripides' *Auge* and *Alope* (see Körte, *Men. Rel.* i, p. xx).

7. The New Comedy is predominatingly serious in tone, with elements of pathos and grave reflection; its cosmopolitan character is due partly to the number of non-Athenian poets, partly to the universal interest of its plot of sentiment.

8. Metres are even fewer and less elaborate than in Middle Comedy, but the trochaic tetrameter is still used for whole scenes. Diphilus has a series of dactylic hexameters (fr. 126), and, exceptionally, an archilochian (fr. 12). Menander uses anapaests in *Leucadia*, frs. 312, 313. Diction has developed towards the *Κοινή*; hence the criticisms of the Atticist purists, Phrynichus and Pollux, in the second century A.D., who condemned neologisms; but in plays of daily life the living speech of contemporary Athens must be followed.

9. About 70 names of New Comedy writers are known to us, the three most eminent being Menander, Philemon, and Diphilus (qq.v.).

Meineke, Kock, Denis, Norwood, Körte (as under OLD COMEDY). P. E. Legrand, *Daos*, 1910 (Engl. Transl. J. Loeb, *The New Greek Comedy*, 1917). K. J. Maidment, 'The Later Comic Chorus', *CQ* xxix (1935), 1–24. Other works s.v. MENANDER.   W. G. W.

COMEDY (LATIN), *see* DRAMA, ROMAN.

COMINIANUS, (early 4th c. A.D.), grammarian. His *Ars*, compiled for school use, is not extant, but is referred to respectfully by Charisius and was probably the basis of Dositheus (q.v.).

Cf. Teuffel, § 405. 1; Schanz–Hosius, § 825.

COMITATENSES, i.e. units forming the emperor's *comitatus*, were one of the two divisions in the Roman field army as reorganized by Constantine. They comprised both cavalry (*vexillationes*) and infantry (*legiones*) and were under the command of the *magistri militum*. *See* PALATINI.

R. Grosse, *Römische Militärgeschichte*, 88–93. Parker, *Roman World*, 273–5.   H. M. D. P.

COMITES. Under the Principate *comes Augusti* meant first a legal and after A.D. 161 a military adviser who accompanied the *princeps* on his journeys abroad. In the

Constantinian reorganization *comes* was an honorary title conferred upon the leading military and civil functionaries. The *magistri militum* and sometimes the *duces* were so honoured, and all members of the *sacrum consistorium* were graded as *comites* in one of three classes.

Comites was also the title of mobile cavalry units which first appear in the time of Diocletian.

O Seeck, *PW*, s.v. 'Comites'.   H. M. D. P.

COMITIA. In Rome *comitium* was the place of assembling; *comitia* meant an assembly of the Roman People summoned in groups by a magistrate with *ius agendi cum populo*. The convocation had to be on a proper day (*comitialis*), after the *auspicia* had been taken, on an inaugurated site. When only a part of the People was summoned, the assembly was strictly a *concilium* (Gell. 15. 27). When the whole People were summoned, but not by groups, the assembly was a *contio* (q.v.). In the *comitia* the majority in each group determined the vote of the group. The *comitia* voted only on business presented to them by magistrates, and they could not amend proposals. As the three main divisions of the Roman People were *curiae*, *centuriae*, *tribus* (qq.v.), the three types of *comitia* were *curiata*, *centuriata*, *tributa*. A special form of the *comitia curiata* and *centuriata* was the *comitia calata* (probably always summoned by the *pontifices*). The resolutions of the *comitia* (and probably of the *concilia plebis*) depended for their validity on a formal ratification by the patrician senators (*see* PATRUM AUCTORITAS).

2. (*a*) *Comitia curiata.* The most ancient *comitia* were the *curiata* (see CURIA 1), dating from the age of the kings. Their competence was progressively limited by the *comitia centuriata*. In historical times they formally confirmed the appointment of magistrates by a *lex curiata de imperio* (q.v.), and witnessed the installation of priests, adoptions, and the making of wills, when the *pontifex maximus* presided at these ceremonies. The monthly announcement by the *pontifices* of the day on which the *nonae* would fall was probably made before the *curiae*. In Cicero's time the 30 *curiae* were represented in the *comitia* only by 30 lictors (Cic. *Leg. Agr.* 2. 12. 31).

(*b*) *Comitia centuriata.* The *comitia centuriata*, on a timocratic basis (*see* CENTURIA), were traditionally instituted by Servius Tullius. Many modern scholars prefer a later date (after 450 B.C.). The enacting of laws, the election of the magistrates *cum imperio* and of the censors, the declaration of war and peace, and the infliction of the death penalty (subject to *provocatio*, q.v.), were concerns of *comitia centuriata*. An interval (*trinundinum*—probably of twenty-four days) was observed after the notification of a meeting, during which preliminary discussions (*contiones*) of the proposals (*rogationes*) were held. In the judicial *comitia* a preliminary investigation before a *contio* had to be held, lasting for three days; after a *trinundinum* and perhaps a further *contio* the vote was taken. The *comitia centuriata* met 'extra pomerium' (q.v.), usually in the Campus Martius, in military order. But in the last period of the Republic the voting centuries were no longer identical with the tactical field-units. The *Lex Caecilia Didia* (98 B.C.) forbade the presenting in the same bill of proposals dealing with unrelated subjects. The formula by which the magistrate proposed the law was: 'uelitis iubeatis Quirites rogo'. Approbation was expressed by the formula 'uti rogas'; rejection by 'antiquo'. The method of voting is described s.v. VOTING (2). The voting groups were unequal, and the wealthier citizens consequently exercised a preponderating influence. In the third century B.C. this disparity was lessened; but the *comitia centuriata* never became democratic.

(*c*) *Comitia plebis tributa.* The assemblies of the plebs were not strictly *comitia* but a *concilium*. But when *plebiscita* were given equal validity with the laws (287 B.C.), the *concilium plebis* was as a rule called *comitia*. It was divided in conformity with the territorial tribes (*see* TRIBUS). In them the tribunes of the plebs and the plebeian aediles were elected, trials were held for non-capital offences, and nearly every form of business was enacted. The procedure was quicker than in the *comitia centuriata*.

(*d*) The *comitia populi tributa* were founded in imitation of the *comitia plebis tributa*, at an uncertain date. They differed from the former in that they were convoked by consuls or praetors, and patricians were admitted. They elected quaestors, *aediles curules*, *tribuni militum a populo*, enacted laws, and held minor trials.

3. From *c.* 250 B.C. the Pontifex Maximus and from 104 B.C. (except during the period from Sulla to 63 B.C.) *pontifices*, *augures*, and *decemviri sacrorum* were elected by special *comitia* of seventeen tribes.

4. The *comitia* in Rome decayed with the extension of the Roman territory, which made it impossible for individuals to attend, and with the growing oligarchic spirit of the leading class, which avoided any reform of them. An attempt of Augustus to give to the *decuriones* of the colonies a chance to vote without coming to Rome was too late (Suet. *Aug.* 46). The election of magistrates was transferred to the Senate by Tiberius; only the declaration of the result (*renuntiatio*) was still performed before the People. The judicial functions also lapsed; and the last law known to us is an agrarian law of A.D. 98. The *comitia* continued a formal existence at least until the third century A.D.

5. The *municipia* and *coloniae* had *comitia*, at which (in Republican times and at least in the first century of the Empire) magistrates were elected. In Republican times they had also some legislative powers.

See also CURIA (1), CENTURIA, CLASSIS, LEX CURIATA, TRIBUS.

Mommsen, *Röm. Staatsr.* iii (1887); G. W. Botsford, *The Roman Assemblies* (U.S.A. 1909). Cf. W. Liebenam, *PW* iv. 679; A. H. J. Greenidge, *Roman Public Life* (1901); G. Rotondi, *Leges publicae populi Romani* (1912). Recent discussions: H. Siber, *Sav. Zeitschr.* 1937, 233; G. Beseler, ibid. 356; C. H. Brecht, ibid. 1939, 261; U. Kahrstedt, *Rh. Mus.* 1917, 258; H. Last, *JRS* 1945, 31; F. Cornelius, *Unters. zur frühen röm. Geschichte* (1940); A. G. Roos, *Med. Nederl. Akad.* 1940, n. 3.   A. M.

COMITIUM, the open place of assembly of Rome (Varro, *Ling.* 5. 155; Livy 5. 55), situated in the Forum and ritually orientated by the cardinal points. To north lay the *curia* (q.v. 2), to south the *rostra* (q.v.), to west the *carcer* and *basilica Porcia*. The area was finally restricted by Caesar (*see* SAEPTA IULIA) to a small space containing the successive Republican *rostra* respectively associated with all but the first and last of five levels ranging from the sixth century B.C. to 52 B.C. The numerous monuments and statues which filled it have perished, excepting the ancient group consisting of a *sacellum*, a tufa cone, and an archaic *cippus* of ritual law (*ILS* 4913), all sealed in damaged condition below a black marble pavement (*lapis niger*) itself at least once altered in position.

Mommsen, *Ann. Ist.* 1845, 288–318; Van Deman, *JRS* 1922, 6–11; E. Gjerstad, *Opusc. Archeol.* ii (1941), 97–159.   I. A. R.

COMMAGENE, in north Syria, became an independent kingdom in 162 B.C. when its governor, Ptolemy, revolted against the Seleucids. Its king Antiochus I submitted to Pompey in 64 B.C. and was rewarded with a piece of Mesopotamia; he was deposed by Antony in 38 B.C. for abetting the Parthian invasion. Tiberius annexed the kingdom in A.D. 17, but it was restored by Gaius in A.D. 38 to King Antiochus IV, who, after being deposed by Gaius, was reinstated by Claudius in 41 and reigned till 72, when Vespasian, on account of his alleged Parthian sympathies, finally annexed the kingdom and

incorporated it in Syria. The royal house claimed descent, through the satrapal dynasty of Armenia, from Darius, and, by a marriage alliance with the Seleucids, from Alexander; its genealogy and its religion, a superficially hellenized Zoroastrianism, are illustrated by the pretentious funeral monument of Antiochus I. On the annexation the country was divided into four city territories, Samosata (the royal capital, founded by King Samos *c.* 150 B.C.), Caesarea Germanicia (founded by Antiochus IV in A.D. 38), Perrhe, and Doliche. Commagene remained a separate κοινόν within the province of Syria.

E. Honigmann, *PW*, Suppl. iv (1924), 978–90.   A. H. M. J.

COMMENDATIO. Under the Roman Republic distinguished consulars influenced the elections of magistrates by open canvassing (*suffragatio*) on behalf of their friends. This practice, when employed by an emperor, was known as *commendatio*, and the recommended candidates (*candidati Caesaris*) were elected without opposition. Augustus at first canvassed in person (Suet. *Aug.* 56), but after A.D. 8 (Dio Cass. 55. 34) announced the names of his candidates in writing. *Commendatio* was first employed for magistracies between the quaestorship and the praetorship (for which the Princeps recommended four candidates; Tac. *Ann.* 1. 15), but by the end of Nero's principate it was employed for the consulship also (Tac. *Hist.* 1. 77). The *Lex de imperio Vespasiani* (Dessau, *ILS* 244) granted to the emperor the right of *commendatio*, apparently for all magistracies without limitation of number. Henceforth the consuls appear to have been the emperor's nominees (cf. Pliny, *Pan.* 77, 'praestare consulibus ipsum qui consules facit').   J. P. B.

COMMENTARII (ὑπομνήματα) were memoranda, originally of a private character, e.g. *tabulae accepti et expensi*, note-books for speeches, legal notes, etc. Their public use (excluding the false *commentarii regum*) developed in the priestly colleges (e.g. *commentarii pontificum*, *augurum*), and in the magistracies (e.g. *commentarii consulares*, *censorii*, *aedilium*), and with the provincial governors. Under the Empire, the *commentarii principis*, like the Hellenistic ἐφημερίδες, represented a court journal, and the system spread in the Imperial administration, under the influence of the ὑπομνηματισμοί of the *praefectus Aegypti*. The emperors' *commentarii* of campaigns and audiences, constitutions, rescripts, epistles, and edicts, had official authority.

From the business *commentarii* arose the literary form, autobiographical in character, written in plain style as a basis of full history, yet directed to the reading public, e.g. Sulla's ὑπομνήματα and, above all, Caesar's *commentarii*.

A. von Premerstein, *PW* iv. 726; A. Rosenberg, *Einleitung und Quellenkunde zur röm. Geschichte* (1921), p. 2; cf. J. B. Bury, *Ancient Greek Historians* (1909), 232.   A. H. McD.

COMMENTARII or LIBRI PONTIFICUM, general name for the records kept by the *Collegium Pontificum* in Rome. They included *commentarii sacrorum*, of which an idea may be formed from the existing *acta Arvalium* and *acta ludorum saecularium*, save that these are records of ritual actually performed, the pontifical *commentarii* rather directions for the performance of ritual when necessary. They probably contained not only this, but also the text of prayers, sacred laws, and other relevant matter. The details are often extremely obscure, since neither the *commentarii* themselves nor any sufficient number of what may be safely regarded as verbatim quotations have come down to us. How old any kind of written liturgy, etc., was in Rome we do not know.

G. Rohde, 'Die Kultsatzungen der römischen Pontifices' (*RGVV* xxv (1936)).   H. J. R.

COMMERCE, GREEK AND ROMAN. A certain amount of trade with valuable raw materials and products of craftsmanship can be proved for neolithic Greece and Italy from finds and excavations, and in an increasing degree for the same regions during the Bronze and Iron Ages. Many early traders seem to have been warriors, sailors, pirates, and craftsmen simultaneously. Those of the Minoan and Mycenaean town cultures were, perhaps, employees and serfs of their rulers after the model of the Ancient Oriental cultures. They had connexions with and brought their products to all Mediterranean coasts and even to middle Europe. We have no evidence of barter in cheap products in these early communities, but its existence is self-evident.

2. The development of Greek trade after the migrations of the earliest Iron Age is closely connected with the invention of coins, and especially those of small denominations, during the eighth and seventh centuries B.C. The sale of cheap goods like corn, oil, pottery, small hardware, etc., became easier and paid better than exchange by barter. The Phoenician traders in valuable products of foreign countries lost their earlier importance for Greece and Italy, and gave way to native trade centres (e.g. Corinth, Athens, Aegina; the ports of Asia Minor, the Black Sea, and Magna Graecia). Three Greek commercial crafts developed during the seventh and sixth centuries B.C., all free and independent, but without much working capital, those of the *naukleros* (a sea-merchant with his own ships), the *emporos* (a sea-merchant using the ships of others), and the *kapelos* (a petty trader in small districts).

3. The Classical Greek Age carried Hellenic trade habits to neighbouring countries. Greek imports and exports of cheap goods, corn, oil, wine, cattle, Corinthian, Attic, and other pottery, metal products, etc., as well as inter-regional commerce, grew in such a degree that the markets of Athens and of other towns became surprisingly efficient, and their *kapeloi* were able to specialize in single products and crafts like those of middlemen for imported products. The sea-merchants began to specialize as well, e.g. as foreign agents and as exclusive transport merchants. Some of the *emporoi* became land merchants. *Deigmata* (mercantile exchanges) were built in great ports. 'Corners' of merchant associations tried occasionally to increase prices. The foreign population of Athens grew enormously. Greek imports of valuable foreign products were also more intensive than in earlier centuries, Greece being wealthier than before the Persian Wars. Greek export trade with valuable merchandise reached the Atlantic coasts and India.

4. Rome became, during the same period, a modest river port and centre of communications for the middle Italian trade, and had a certain importance for the salt trade of its neighbours. It introduced market days and festivals (*nundinae, ludi Apollinares, ludi Romani, ludi plebeii*), and created the *Forum Boarium* for foreign merchants. The beginnings of the Roman law of sales were of future importance.

5. The campaigns of Alexander, the *Diadochi*, and the Roman generals from the Punic Wars to Augustus unified the immense region between the Atlantic Ocean and India, the Sahara, Rhine, Danube, and the Ukraine. The Greek economic structure was imitated everywhere, but not without being modified and adapted to new conditions. The towns of the Greek mother country, and many of the *poleis* and hellenized Phoenician towns in the East, preserved much of the economic structure of the pre-Alexandrian days. Main centres of such an economic type were Syracuse, Tarentum, Naples, Carthage, Massilia, and Cyrene in the West; Alexandria in Egypt, Corinth, Athens, Ephesus, Miletus, Apamea, Delos, and Rhodes in the old country; Olbia, Tanaïs, Byzantium, Thessalonica, and Sinope in the North, Antioch on the Orontes, Seleuceia in Pieria, Sidon, Tyre, Seleuceia on the Tigris, and Alexandria Charax in the East. The main trade was in cheap goods, the commercial crafts and their trading methods were not materially altered, but trade associations became more common and some of the *emporoi* were more specialized than during the classical period.

6. On the other hand, compulsory State planning was the most characteristic trade condition for the Egyptian country-side, for Hellenistic India, and to a lesser degree the more barbaric regions of the Seleucid, the Pergamenian, the southern Arabian, and the Parthian Empires, which slowly developed a separate Semitic-Iranian Hellenism. In Ptolemaic Egypt, for example, the trade in oil, soda, salt, perfumes, beer, mining products, textile, leather, and metal products, and (perhaps) papyrus was monopolized, so that the government was able to control the price and quality of such merchandise and to claim special fees for the right to buy and to sell, very few enterprises being privileged. Prices and trade conditions of corn, cattle, fish, game, wood, wine, slaves, and the whole of the import and export trade were more or less government-controlled.

7. Roman civilization followed the Greek example, but modified it. Italy's essential imports of cheap products could not be paid for in full by her trading exports. Therefore the supply of Rome with corn and raw materials for military purposes was largely dependent on tribute. The exports of Italy, especially those in pottery, hardware, wine, and oil, spread over the whole of the Mediterranean during the last two centuries B.C., but by political as well as economic methods. The foreign trade in valuable products was much more important in the Latin than in the Greek part of the Ancient World. Rome was the economic centre. Its main ports were Puteoli and later Ostia; its main provincial import and export harbours Narbo and Arelate in Gaul; Utica, Cyrene, and Cirta in Africa; Athens, Delos, Pergamum, Ephesus, Apamea, Antioch, and Alexandria in the East. The Roman commercial crafts (*navicularii* (= *naukleroi*), *mercatores* (= *emporoi*), *caupones* (= *kapeloi*)) of the second century B.C. and their trade conditions were similar to the Greek ones, but not so specialized; but from the first century B.C. onwards *caupo* (and later *kapelos* as well) meant an innkeeper, *mercator* a *kapelos* or a small *emporos*. The great capitalists, already known from Alexander's time in the East, became a special craft, that of the *negotiatores*, who were at the same time merchants, bankers, and owners of workshops and large estates. They almost superseded the Greek type of great *emporoi* and absorbed the main business in all Roman provinces up to the time of Caesar.

8. A large area of the Old World remained outside the Greek, Latin, and not very different Semitic-Iranian regions of Hellenism, which were in close commercial intercourse. Britain, Germany, southern Russia, western Siberia, and India were visited by Mediterranean merchants; but their trade habits had to be assimilated to alien conditions. Valuable products of the Hellenistic world even reached China and central Africa, as finds and Chinese reports prove.

9. The time of the Roman Principate began with an absolute commercial supremacy of Rome and Italy, and free Empire trade (wherever advisable). It ended with a far-reaching economic autarky of the Roman provinces and State control over commerce. Britain and Dacia only were added to the central zone of ancient commerce during that period. The foreign trade of the Roman Empire was considerable, as finds and many Latin and Greek words in Irish, German, Pahlavi, Semitic, Iranian, and even a few in Indian and Mongolian languages prove. A few Roman merchants reached China, and Chinese merchants seem to have come to Iran and the most eastern parts of the Empire.

10. The internal changes were more revolutionary. The imports and exports of most of the earlier centres for cheap products gradually lost importance for private buyers, because such merchandise could be and, as a rule was, produced locally or in a consumer's own province. In such circumstances only the inter-provincial import and export of valuable goods remained lucrative from about the third century A.D. A considerable amount of local trade was done by large estates and State institutions which did not require real merchants for this purpose. During the first century A.D. the *negotiatores* had spread as *pragmateutai* to the Hellenistic East, and the merchants and traders had been able to specialize in the Hellenistic way throughout the Latin provinces of the Empire, and in regions and provinces like Egypt which had not known free trade during the Hellenistic period; but from about the time of Hadrian all important commercial crafts had to be saved from complete collapse by the Roman government. The *collegia* (*see* CLUBS) of merchants—originally private organizations—were bound, regulated, and privileged by the State, first those of the transport merchants, then those of the other crafts. The Hellenistic trade control had not been completely dissolved by the Roman government in many provincial regions. Now a new compulsory system with characteristic legal regulations arose wherever State necessities were concerned. The end of free trade for many centuries had come. Prices and trade conditions were controlled by magistrates whenever difficulties arose.

11. The commerce of the Late Roman Empire up to the Islamic conquest has often been underestimated. This was no period of 'house-economy'. The trade in valuable products was equal to that of earlier centuries. Jewels, perfumes, valuable textiles, and glasses of the Mediterranean world were well known in northern Europe, Abyssinia, India, central and even eastern Asia. Trade in cheap products had suffered owing to Diocletian's system of taxation in kind, the decrease of the Roman and Greek town population during the third century A.D., and the autarky of many large feudal and church estates; but it was doubtless on the average superior to that of classical Greece (with the exception, perhaps, of Athens). The markets of Rome, Alexandria, Antioch, Constantinople, and many other towns were in normal years as full as ever of all that the population required. On the other hand, the strict and well-organized government control of the conditions of sale, and the codification of Roman commercial law, were novelties. Foreign trade was, if possible, restricted to certain frontier places, so that arms for prospective enemies as well as raw materials and victuals, which happened to be scarce in the Empire, could not be exported. Profitable imports, e.g. Chinese silk, became State monopolies. Government officials controlled the quality and prices of all merchandise in their districts as well as the quantities allowed to a merchant. The variety of products is well known from Diocletian's Price Edict and the Church Fathers. On the other hand, the purchasing of the Empire population had much decreased, and only in big towns and very wealthy country districts could the earlier specialization of commercial crafts be maintained to any extent. Not much difference existed, as a rule, between *negotiator* and *mercator*, between *emporos* and *kapelos*. Traders were very often craftsmen at the same time, and comparatively few big merchant firms remained; but on the whole the standard of Late Roman commerce was sufficient for the needs of the period, and we may justly consider its controlled organization as indispensable for the future world-wide progress of commerce during the Islamic and the later European Middle Ages.

See AMBER; BANKS' BOTTOMRY LOANS; INTEREST (RATE OF); MONEY; MONOPOLIES; USURY.

BIBLIOGRAPHY
J. L. Myres in *CAH* iii, ch. 25; M. N. Tod, ibid. v, ch. 1; T. Frank, ibid. viii, ch. 11; M. Rostovtzeff, ibid. viii, chs. 18, 20; xi, ch. 3; W. W. Tarn, ibid. ix, ch. 14; F. Örtel, ibid. x, ch. 13; xii, ch. 7. G. Calhoun, *The Business Life of Ancient Athens* (U.S.A. 1926). M. P. Charlesworth, *Trade Routes and Commerce of the Roman Empire*[2] (1926). V. Ehrenberg, *The People of Aristophanes* (1943). M. Finkelstein, *CPhil.* xxx (1935), 320 f. T. Frank, *An Economic History of Rome*[2] (U.S.A., 1927). T. Frank, *Economic Survey of Ancient Rome* i–iv (U.S.A., 1933–41). G. Glotz, *Le Travail dans la Grèce ancienne* (1920). J. Hasebroek, *Trade and Politics in Ancient Greece* (1933). F. M. Heichelheim, *Wirtschaftsgeschichte des Altertums* (1938), Index s.v. 'Fernhandel', 'Güterumlauf', 'Kaufmannsberuf', 'Nahhandel'. G. Jennison, *Animals for Show and Pleasure in Ancient Rome* (1937). H. Michell, *The Economics of Ancient Greece* (1940). G. Mickwitz, *Vierteljahrsschr. für Soz. und Wirtschaftsgesch.* 32 (1939), 3 ff.; *Geld und Wirtschaft im römischen Reiche des 4. Jahrh. n. Chr.* (1932). Cl. Préaux, *L'Économie royale des Lagides* (1939). Rostovtzeff, *Roman Empire*; *Hellenistic World*. E. H. Warmington, *The Commerce between the Roman Empire and India* (1928).   F. M. H.

COMMERCIUM was the right of any *Latinus* (*see* LATINI) to enter into contracts with a Roman according to the forms of Roman law and enforceable in the Roman courts without recourse to the *ius gentium* (and vice versa). Without it a foreigner could only secure his rights by the help of the *praetor peregrinus*. *Conubium* similarly was the right to contract a legal marriage with a member of another State without either party forfeiting inheritance or paternity rights. Without *conubium* a Roman's children by a foreigner took the citizenship of the foreigner. These complementary rights formed an essential part of *ius Latii* (q.v.). Their development, unparalleled in the Ancient World until the later stages of some Greek cities, belongs to the period before the growth of large States in Latium, and was encouraged by the continental environment of the numerous small *populi* of the plain-dwellers, *Latini* (q.v.). In 338 B.C. Rome temporarily suspended these rights between certain Latin peoples, and again between certain Hernici in 308. This was only a temporary expedient in punishment for their revolts. The Latin colonies, including the so-called 'Last Twelve' founded between 268 and 181 B.C., all shared these rights not only with Rome but with one another, for, being often contiguous and also adjacent to Roman colonies, they could not flourish without such connexions. These *iura* also formed the chief practical benefit of *civitas sine suffragio* (*see* MUNICIPIUM), and could be granted to other *socii Italici* by special dispensation. By the Social War they were perhaps common throughout Italy. Under the Empire *conubium* was sometimes withheld from *ius Latii*, but the spread of Roman citizenship inside Latin communities rendered this rare. The grant of either to *peregrini*, however, remained exceptional. *Conubium cum peregrinis mulieribus* was thus given as a reward upon discharge to the praetorian troops, when required, and also along with the citizenship to the auxiliary troops drawn from the provinces.

These conceptions could also be applied to the relations between any communities of *peregrini*. Thus in 168 B.C. Macedonia was split up into four districts which were forbidden *commercium* or *conubium*, as an exceptional expedient to avoid the creation of a new province.

For bibliography, *see* LATINI, IUS LATII.   A. N. S.-W.

COMMIUS, appointed king of the Atrebates by Caesar 57 B.C., acted as cavalry leader and general diplomatic agent, especially in Britain. He joined the revolt of 52, however, and evaded attempts at capture and assassination. He finally retired to Britain, where he founded a dynasty (British Atrebates; apparently not at Calleva).

C. Hawkes and G. C. Dunning, *Arch. Journ.* lxxxvii. 291–4.
          C. E. S.

COMMODIANUS, probably of Arles and of the fifth century A.D. Two works of his survive: *Instructiones*, two books of short poems on numerous topics of importance to humble Christians, and *Carmen Apologe-*

ticum (1,060 verses), a metrical defence of Christianity against the still powerful paganism. Much of his work is accented verse.

Ed. B. Dombart (*CSEL* xv (1887)); A. F. van Katwijk, *Lexicon Commodianeum* (1934); H. Brewer, *Kommodian von Gaza* (Paderborn, 1906). A. S.

COMMODUS, Lucius Aelius Aurelius, sole emperor A.D. 180–92, elder son of Marcus Aurelius, was born in A.D. 161. During his father's principate he was gradually advanced to the status of joint-ruler which he attained in A.D. 177 (Caesar in 166, *imperator* in 176, consul, *tribunicia potestas*, and Augustus in 177). In 177, after his marriage to Crispina, he accompanied his father to the second German-Sarmatian War.

2. After his father's death (partly as a measure of economy, but more essentially from a desire to return to the enjoyments of life in Rome) Commodus concluded peace, imposing restrictions upon inter-tribal intercourse in return for a subsidy and the evacuation of conquered territories. On reaching the capital he celebrated a triumph, and changed his name to Marcus Commodus Antoninus.

3. At first Commodus retained some of his father's ministers, e.g. Tarrutenius Paternus as praetorian prefect. But soon he resorted to government by means of favourites and open hostility to the Senate, which was exacerbated by an abortive conspiracy promoted by Lucilla and Ummidius Quadratus (182). For the next six years Rome was virtually governed by the praetorian prefects Perennis (182–5) and Cleander (186–9), and continuous war was waged against the Senate.

4. Commodus finally came under the influence of his concubine Marcia, his chamberlain Eclectus, and Laetus, who became praetorian prefect in 191. The intoxication of power seems to have deranged his mind. Senatorial persecutions were redoubled, Rome was rebaptized *Colonia Commodiana*, and the Emperor regarded himself as the incarnation of Hercules (title of *Hercules Romanus*). To perfect the impersonation he determined to appear in public on 1 January 193 as both consul and gladiator, and this so outraged the feelings of his advisers that they suborned an athlete called Narcissus to strangle him.

5. During this period the Empire was untroubled by foreign wars. The only serious unrest was in Britain, where the Antonine Wall was breached and south Scotland overrun. Order was restored by Ulpius Marcellus, and a subsequent mutiny of the legions put down by the future Emperor Pertinax.

Herodian, bk. 1; Dio Cassius, bk. 72; S.H.A.; J. M. Heer, *Der historische Wert der Vita Commodi*; W. Weber, *CAH* xi, ch. 9, §§ 7, 8; Parker, *Roman World*, 26–51. H. M. D. P.

COMMUNES LOCI, the 'commonplaces' or 'general arguments' of Latin rhetoric (as in Cic. *Orat.* 47; 126; *De Or.* 3. 106; Quint. *Inst.* 2. 1. 9) (cf. κοινοὶ τόποι in Arist. *Rhet.* 1. 2 ad fin.; 2. 18–19; 23–4). They included a wide range of topics of universal character capable of being introduced by a speaker into appropriate parts of his oration (*see* PROOEMIUM). Being part of the rhetorical training (e.g. studies of character, good or bad, serviceable for eulogy or invective, or of general themes like envy, avarice, honour, fickleness of fortune), they were often recollected and employed in declamation or in forensic pleadings. They influenced also poets of the Silver Age like Persius and Lucan, who aimed at giving condensed and fresh expression to a 'commonplace'. J. W. D.

COMMUNIO, common ownership by two or more persons of a *res communis* or of an undivided group of objects (inheritance), originating in a contract by the will of the parties (*societas*, *see* CONTRACT), or, independently of their intention, in a common inheritance or legacy. A joint owner might freely dispose only of his share by legal transaction (alienation, pledging, giving in usufruct);

dispositions of the whole *res communis* depended on the consent of all owners (*domini*). Manumission of a common slave was subject to special rules. Material alterations in the common object (constructions, plantations), intended or initiated by one joint owner, could be vetoed by any other. Controversies between joint owners were adjusted by an action for division of property (*actio communi dividundo*; *actio familiae erciscundae*, for division of inheritance was of earlier date). The judge divided the common object among the co-owners in proportion to their shares, or, if the object was indivisible, made an award for equalizing payments. The judge's *adiudicatio* vested the property. Profits, expenses, and damages, incurred by individual joint owners, were also apportioned by the judge, who distributed them among all owners according to their shares.

A. Berger, *Zur Entwicklungsgeschichte der Teilungsklagen* (1912); S. Riccobono, *Essays in Legal History*, Intern. Congress of Historical Studies 1913; J. Gaudemet, *Régime juridique de l'indivision* (1934). A. B.

COMPARATIVE PHILOLOGY, *see* PHILOLOGY, COMPARATIVE.

COMPASCUA, *see* AGER PUBLICUS.

COMPERENDINATIO, *see* GLAUCIA.

COMPITALIA, *see* LARES.

COMPRECATIONES. Aulus Gellius (13. 23. 1–2), quotes from the *libri sacerdotum populi Romani*, that is to say the *commentarii pontificum* (q.v.), the following forms of address, which he calls *comprecationes deum immortalium* (since they are in the accusative, it would appear that some verb meaning 'to invoke' is to be supplied): *Luam Saturni, Salaciam Neptuni, Horam Quirini, Virites Quirini, Maiam Volcani, Heriem Iunonis, Moles Martis Nerienemque Martis*. It is clear that each pair consists of a well-known deity associated with an obscure one, or in two cases, a plurality of such. Since family relationships among Roman deities are unknown, and Gellius distinctly says that these prayers 'ritu Romano fiunt', no such word as *uxor* or *filia* can be supplied (contrast, e.g., *Terentia Ciceronis, Tullia Ciceronis*). It therefore remains to suppose that the genitives mean that the lesser deity is somehow active in the sphere presided over by the greater one. Cf. K. Kerényi in *SMSR* ix (1933), 17 ff. H. J. R.

COMUM, the modern *Como*, was the birthplace of the elder and the younger Pliny; the latter had two famous villas on the lake. The civilization of all this district emerges as a distinct entity as early as the tenth century B.C. It was not creative, only receptive; so that the best of the antiquities housed in the museum of Como are imports. Weapons are numerous, including fine swords of Hungarian types. A lively trade with Picenum on the Adriatic is proved rather by finds near Lago Maggiore than by the scanty discoveries at Como. The Golaseccans of Lake Maggiore were kinsmen of the Comacines. Both practised cremation, like the Villanovans, from whom, however, they can be distinguished. After 500 B.C. the whole lake region was strongly affected by Etruscan commerce, which spread from the newly founded Etruscan colonies north of the Apennines. During the Roman Republic the district was predominantly Celtic. In 89 Pompeius Strabo placed settlers at Comum and in 59 Caesar established a Roman colony (Novum Comum) of which the legality was questioned (cf. Rice Holmes, *Roman Republic*, ii. 317 ff.). For later history cf. G. E. F. Chilver, *Cisalpine Gaul* (1941), Index, s.v. D. R.-MacI.

CONCILIABULUM, a type of large village which down to the Social War formed political centres for the Roman country-folk. They replaced the *tribus rusticae*, whose structure as civic units was shattered by the territorial expansion of Rome in the third century. Beginning 'beyond the tenth milestone' they covered the Roman territory except where other *oppida* existed. Official announcements were published in them, but as in other villages, their powers of self-government were slight, since they possessed neither municipal territory nor jurisdiction (*see* VICUS) until during the Ciceronian age they were assimilated to *municipia* (q.v.).　A. N. S.-W.

CONCILIUM was a general name for any Assembly; it was often used to denote the Popular Assemblies at Rome, especially the Plebeian Assembly (*Concilium Plebis*, *see* COMITIA).

The *Concilia Provinciarum* were provincial parliaments, consisting of delegates from the constituent cities or tribes of a province or of several associated provinces. They developed out of the κοινά or cult-assemblies which sprang up in the province of Asia (29 B.C.) and elsewhere in the Greek East for the worship of Augustus. They were introduced into the Western provinces by Augustus himself, who deputed his stepson Drusus to inaugurate a *concilium* of the four Gallic provinces at Lugdunum (12 B.C.), and they eventually received an official organization which covered the whole of the Roman Empire except Egypt.

The *concilia* or κοινά (as they were called in the Eastern provinces) ordinarily met once a year at a central point of their district (e.g. Carthage in Africa, Ephesus, Pergamum, or Smyrna in Asia). Their primary function was the worship of 'Roma et Augustus', and their president was also chief priest of this cult. Games and festivals were often associated with the religious ceremonies. But the *concilia* also served as channels of communication between the provinces and the emperors, and in the first century A.D. they often rendered good service in reporting on bad governors and facilitating their condemnation in the Roman courts. But they never acquired powers of legislation or taxation; they lost all significance in the troubled times of the third century; and an attempt by Constantine to reanimate them (without emperor-worship) proved ineffectual.

G. W. Botsford, *The Roman Assemblies* (U.S.A. 1909), ch. 6; E. G. Hardy, *Studies in Roman History* i (1906), ch. 13; P. Guiraud, *Les Assemblées provinciales dans l'empire romain* (1887); E. Kornemann, *PW*, s.v. κοινόν (Suppl. iv) and 'Concilium'.　M. C.

CONCORDIA, personification of agreement between members of the Roman State or of some body or bodies within it (*Concordia provinciarum, militum* or *exercituum, imperi*, etc., on coins; occasionally inscriptions are dedicated to the *Concordia* of a town, guild, or the like). Her oldest and principal temple, near the Forum (Platner–Ashby, pp. 138 ff.), was allegedly dedicated by Camillus in 367 B.C. (end of disturbances over the Licinian Rogations), restored by L. Opimius in 121 B.C. (death of C. Gracchus) and re-dedicated by Tiberius in A.D. 10 as Concordia Augusta, which from then on became a frequent title, apparently with reference to agreement between members of the Imperial family. She had also a shrine near the above temple, dedicated in 304 B.C. (Livy 9. 46. 6), and another on the Arx, (Livy 22. 33. 7; 23. 21. 7). The former was a political gesture, the latter commemorated the end of a mutiny. See Wissowa, *RK*[2] 328 f. *See* HOMONOIA.　H. J. R.

CONCUBINATUS, *see* MARRIAGE, LAW OF.

CONDITORES, *see* CITY-FOUNDERS.

CONDUCTOR signified any kind of contractor, but more particularly a person who rented from the Roman government the right of collecting certain sources of revenue. In the course of the second century A.D. individual *conductores* (with whom *socii* might be associ-

ated) took the place of the companies of *publicani* (q.v.) as collectors of the *vectigalia* (q.v.). Inscriptions (*ILS* 1461 ff., 1851 ff.) prove that *conductores* were responsible for *portoria* (q.v.), mines, fishing-rights, etc. In the mining village of Vipasca (*ILS* 6891) the word is used not only of those who worked the mines but of dyers, shoe-makers, hairdressers, etc., who had been granted a monopoly. Much information about *conductores* can be derived from the complaints addressed to Commodus by the tenants of the Imperial *saltus* in Africa (*ILS* 6870). They were evidently wealthy men who acted as intermediaries between the government and its tenants, and were able to secure the collusion of the *procuratores* (q.v.), to whose supervision they were subject, in opposing the *coloni*.

H. Pelham, *Essays* (1911), 284 ff.; M. Rostovtzeff, 'Geschichte der Staatspacht', *Philol. Suppl.* ix.　G. H. S.

CONFARREATIO, the oldest and most solemn form of Roman marriage, confined to patricians and in classical times obligatory for the three *flamines maiores* and the *rex sacrorum*, who must also have been born of such marriages (Gaius 1. 112). The ceremony is imperfectly known, but outstanding features were that bride and bridegroom sat with veiled heads on joined seats, which were covered with the hide of a sheep (Servius on *Aen.* 4. 374); a cake of *far* (spelt) was used in some way (perhaps eaten by the parties), and the whole rite was in honour of Jupiter Farreus (Gaius, ibid.). The *flamen Dialis* and the Pontifex Maximus were present (Servius on Verg. *G.* 1. 31) and there must be ten witnesses (five, a sacred number, for each of the two *gentes* concerned?) (Gaius, ibid.). The marriage was indissoluble save by an elaborate ceremony, *diffarreatio* (Festus, p. 65. 17 Lindsay, cf. Plutarch, *Quaest. Rom.* 50; see Rose ad loc.; he speaks of 'horrible, extraordinary, and dismal rites'). *See* MARRIAGE CEREMONIES, para. 3, and MANUS.

Rossbach, *Die römische Ehe* (1853), 95 ff.; P. E. Corbett, *The Roman Law of Marriage* (1930), 71.　H. J. R.

CONGIARIUM. Under the Republic this term designated gifts of wine or oil made by magistrates, candidates for office, or generals. Later these distributions consisted, at first mainly, and then exclusively, of money. From the time of Augustus *congiaria* were given by emperors only or under their authority, and were associated with such events as the accession of a new emperor, imperial birthdays, victories, or the erection of buildings. The recipients were probably identical with the *plebs frumentaria* who received doles of corn. Instead of money they often received *tesserae nummariae* exchangeable for cash, of which a great number have survived.　G. H. S.

CONGUS, *see* JUNIUS (1).

CONON (1) (*c.* 444–392 B.C.), an Athenian of noble birth. He was admiral of the squadron based on Naupactus in 414, and from 407 to 405 commanded the fleets operating in the Aegean and Hellespont. At Aegospotami he alone of the Athenian generals was on the alert, and slipped away to find refuge with Euagoras. He inspired the programme of reviving Persian sea-power, and his efforts were crowned with success when he annihilated the Spartan fleet at Cnidos (394). He crossed in triumph to Athens, completed the rebuilding of the Long Walls, and even dreamed of a new Athenian empire. The visit of Antalcidas to Tiribazus in 392 converted the satrap to a pro-Spartan policy. Conon, who was in Sardis on a diplomatic mission, was arrested, and although he succeeded in escaping, died shortly afterwards.

H. Swoboda, *PW*, s.v. 'Konon (3)'.　D. E. W. W.

CONON (2) of Samos (3rd c. B.C.), astronomer and mathematician. After travelling in the western part of the Greek world in search of astronomical and meteorological observations, he settled in Alexandria. He is best known for his discovery (c. 245 B.C.) of the new constellation Βερενίκης Πλόκαμος between Leo, Virgo, and Boötes, recounted in Catullus' imitation (c. 66 B.C.) of Callimachus' elegy on the Coma Berenices. He wrote an astronomical work De Astrologia of which nothing remains, and was well known for his researches into solar eclipses. In mathematics, he wrote a work Πρὸς Θρασυδαῖον on the mutual sections and contacts of conic sections. He was a close friend of Archimedes, who always praises highly his mathematical work, and regrets his early death.

PW xi. 1338. W. D. R.

CONON (3), mythographer, who dedicated his work to Archelaus Philopator (Philopatris) of Cappadocia (36 B.C.–A.D. 17), published διηγήσεις, fifty tales from Greek saga, Atticist in style, based on a Hellenistic handbook, and preserved in Photius.

FGrH i. 190, 499.

CONSCRIPTI. This obscure term may refer either to an official list or album of senators, the patres 'on the list'; or to an early union of two different kinds of senators—i.e. patres ⟨et⟩ conscripti—either patricians and plebeians, though the struggle of the Orders renders this unlikely, or the patres of different communities incorporated in Rome. A. N. S.-W.

CONSECRATIO, the process of making anything into a res sacra. We are best informed of the ceremonial in the case of a temple (aedes sacra) and the ground on which it stood. The latter must be the property of the Roman people; e.g. Trajan saw no objection to the moving from its place of an old temple at Nicomedia, because it could not have been dedicated in Roman form (Plin. Tra. 49, 50; cf. Mommsen, Staatsr. iii. 734). Furthermore, dedication must be authorized by the State (Cic. Dom. 136). Usually the Senate, the People, or in later times the emperor appointed some person, or persons (duumviri, Livy 23. 21. 7 and often), with a natural tendency, if the temple had been vowed by a magistrate in office, to appoint him or some relative. It remained for the gods to accept the gift through their earthly agents, the pontifices (e.g. Justinian, Inst. 2. 1. 8). It was proper for the whole college to be present (Cic., ibid. 117); the minimum requisite was for one of them to be there. He held one of the postes of the entrance door and pronounced the necessary formula (ibid. 119, 121). Like all ceremonies, this must be gone through without interruption, hesitation, or stumbling (e.g. ibid. 134, 141; Pliny, HN 11. 174). The dedicator also held a doorpost (Livy 2. 8. 7), and went through a form of prayer (ibid. 8), dictated to him by the pontiff (Cic., ibid. 138, 'quid praeiri . . . ius fuerit' and Livy, infra), containing a clause to the effect that he gave the building (or other object) to the god (Servius on Verg. G. 3. 16). The ceremony was necessary also if a new building was put up on ground already consecrated (Livy 9. 46. 6).

Of the other consecrations less is known; the goods of a condemned man were on occasion consecrated by a magistrate, who covered his head, employed a fluteplayer to drown ill-omened sounds, and had by him a small portable altar (foculus) for incense (Cic. ibid. 123–4).

A title-deed (lex dedicationis) seems regularly to have been drawn up, at all events for important dedications. To judge by the provincial specimens which alone have been preserved (Bruns, Fontes, nos. 90, 92) it was recited by the dedicator under the direction of the pontiff and contained a precise statement of the size of the ground on which the object stood, the conditions under which it was to be used, etc. See DEDICATIO.

Convenient assemblage of material (requiring some revision) in Marquardt-Wissowa, Staatsverw. iii.² 269 ff. H. J. R.

CONSENTES DI, the Roman version of the Athenian Twelve Gods. Their gilt statues stood in the Forum (Varro, Rust. 1. 1. 4), later apparently in the Porticus Deorum Consentium (see Platner–Ashby, p. 421); as there were six male and six female, they may well have been the twelve worshipped at the lectisternium (q.v.) of 217 B.C. (Livy, 22. 10. 9), Jupiter and Juno, Neptune and Minerva, Mars and Venus, Apollo and Diana, Volcanus and Vesta, Mercury and Ceres (Wissowa RK 61). H. J. R.

CONSENTIUS (5th c. A.D.), grammarian. His extant treatises De nomine et verbo and De barbarismis et metaplasmis (ed. Keil, Gramm. Lat. v. 338–85, 386–404) are excerpts from a complete grammar. His illustrations drawn from the speech of his own times make him valuable for the study of vulgar Latin.

Cf. Teuffel, § 472. 3; Schanz–Hosius, § 1103. J. F. M.

CONSILIUM PRINCIPIS. A Roman magistrate was always at liberty to summon advisers in deliberation or on the bench. Under the Roman Empire a body of advisers summoned by the emperor acquired the character of a Privy Council. At first it was unofficial, and no more than an indeterminate collection of 'amici Caesaris' who had been summoned by the Princeps to act as assessors in a judicial inquiry (Tac. Ann. 3. 10; 14. 62) or as advisers in problems of administration. Hadrian went farther and, in judicial inquiries, summoned 'amici', 'comites', and jurisconsults, 'quos tamen senatus omnes probasset' (Vita 18). Severus Alexander established a regular consilium of seventy members, who assisted him in the framing of constitutiones; twenty of them were jurisconsults, the rest the Emperor's nominees, chiefly, no doubt, senators (Vita 16). Its members were known as consiliarii Augusti, some of them—perhaps only the equites—receiving salaries. The body was reorganized under Diocletian, membership being made permanent, and its name was changed to sacrum consistorium (q.v.). This consilium is to be distinguished from the regular consilium established by Augustus, and known as the consilium semestre, consisting of the two consuls, one member of each of the other colleges of magistrates, and fifteen senators chosen by lot, who retained their membership for six months (Dio Cass. 53. 21. 4 ff.; Suet. Aug. 35. 3). This body prepared business for the Senate in collaboration with the Princeps (see, for example, the senatus consultum conveyed in the fifth of the Augustan edicts from Cyrene, JRS 1927, p. 36). Its character was altered slightly in A.D. 13 and again after Tiberius' accession, but the institution came to an end after Tiberius retired from Rome in A.D. 26. J. P. B.

CONSISTORIUM, SACRUM (θεῖον συνέδριον), the Imperial Council from the fourth century onwards (see CONSTANTINE, para. 6), so called because it was necessary to stand (consistere) in the presence of the emperor. The consilium (q.v.) of the early Empire had important advisory functions, and Hadrian had given it added authority and prestige. But both its composition and its business depended entirely on the will of the emperor. The heads of bureaux were not expressly excluded, but were certainly not regularly called.

The consistorium of the fourth century resembled the consilium in its entire dependence on the emperor. It differed from it both in the increased formalism of its proceedings and in its usual composition; for the emperor, though still free to choose at pleasure, actually made a practice of summoning to the consistorium all heads of departments—the quaestor sacri palatii, the comes sacrarum largitionum, and the other comites and magistri. The business was prepared by the magister officiorum and included all matters reserved for the emperor's personal decision. The emperor himself held the presidency and his judgements could not be set aside, but the advice of so many experts on subjects falling within their competence—foreign policy, internal legislation, finance, etc.—must have carried very serious weight.

O. Seeck, *PW*, s.v. H. M.

CONSIVA, *see* OPS.

CONSOLATIO. Outlined by Democritus, raised to the dignity of a *genre* by Crantor, and influenced from Bion's time by the Diatribe (q.v.), of which it became one of the characteristic forms, the 'Consolation' was introduced at Rome by Cicero. The Latin *consolationes* which have come down to us concern chiefly death, sometimes exile, rarely other misfortunes. Simple letters or philosophic treatises, they differ according to the author's style and personality, the circumstances which dictated them, and the character of the recipient. Yet they all wear a fundamental likeness. Eclectic, they draw upon the same arsenal of arguments (*solacia*) carefully catalogued, arguments which the *epicedium* (q.v.) in part borrows from them.

Of these *solacia*, one group is applicable to the afflicted person, the other to the cause of the affliction. Among the former the commonest thoughts are: Fortune is all-powerful—one should foresee her strokes (*praemeditatio*). Has a loved one died?—remember that all men are mortal; the essential thing is to have lived not long but virtuously; time heals all ills; yet a wise man would seek healing not from time but from reason, by himself putting an end to his grief; the lost one was only 'lent'—be grateful for having possessed him. As to death, the cause of the affliction, it is the end of all ills: the one who is lamented does not suffer; the gods have sheltered him from the trials of this world. To these *loci communes* consolers sometimes add eulogy of the dead, and almost always examples of men courageous in bearing misfortune.

Their exaggerated intellectualism distrusts feeling— reason is the supreme consoler. One of them, however— Seneca—views family affections as precious sources of comfort. Christian consolers (Ambrose, Jerome, Paulinus of Nola), while resorting to pagan arguments, were enabled to renew the *genre* by the stress laid upon feeling and by the character of their inspiration, which was at once biblical, ethical, and mystic.

In the following list of the chief Latin *consolationes*, their subjects, if other than death, are indicated in brackets: Cic. *Fam.* 5. 16, 18 (exile); 6. 1 (exile, war); *Brut.* 1. 9; fragments of Cicero's *Consolatio* written on Tullia's death; *Tusc.* 1 and 3; Sulpicius ap. Cic. *Fam.* 4. 5; Sen. *Dial.* 6 (*ad Marciam*), 11 (*ad Polybium*), 12 (*ad Helviam matrem*; exile); *Ep.* 63, 81 (ingratitude), 93, 99, 107 (runaway slaves).

A. Gercke, *De Consolationibus* (*Tirocinium philologum* Berl.) 1883; K. Buresch, 'Consolationum . . . historia critica' (*Leipz. Stud.* ix. 1), 1886; E. Boyer, *Les Consolations chez les Grecs et les Romains*, 1887; C. Martha, *Études morales sur l'antiquité*[3] (1896), 135–89; J. D. Duff, *Sen. Dial.* 10, 11, 12 (two last being *Consolationes*), 1915; Ch. Favez, Introductions to his edns. of Sen. *Ad Helviam* (1918) and *Ad Marciam* (1928); *La Consolation latine chrétienne* (1937).
C. F., transl. J. W. D.

CONSOLATIO AD LIVIAM, an elegiac poem of condolence, of 474 lines, addressed to the Empress Livia on the death of her son Drusus, campaigning in Germany 9 B.C., whose body was brought to Rome for burial. It is assigned to Ovid in the fifteenth-century manuscripts and the *editio princeps* Romana (1471), but is obviously not his work. If he had written it, he would not have passed over without mention this loyal effusion among his appeals for mercy. Its verbosity conflicts with his delicate touch; the frequent elisions and certain expressions are not in his manner. It was attributed to Albinovanus Pedo by J. J. Scaliger, and by Haupt to some humanist on insufficient grounds (*Opusc.* 1. 315). The author, a Roman *eques* (202 'adsumus omnis eques'), professes to have attended Drusus' funeral. The poem may have been written then. But its excessively rhetorical structure, hackneyed commonplaces, and reminiscences of Seneca's *Consolations* suggest rather that it is a fictitious exercise composed considerably later in imitation of Ovid, from whom the author borrows continually, even whole lines. He also plagiarizes from Lucretius (359, 369), Tibullus (281, 415), and Propertius (330, 466).

Texts: Teubner *PLM* ii. 2 (Vollmer); Paravia (Lenz), full introd. and apparatus. Commentary: A. Witlox (Maestricht, 1934). Translation: J. H. Mozley, *Ovid: Art of Love* etc. (Loeb, 1929). S. G. O.

CONSTANTINE, known to history as 'the Great', FLAVIUS VALERIUS CONSTANTINUS (*c.* A.D. 274–337), was born at Naïssus, the son of Constantius Chlorus and his wife or concubine, Helena. Although Constantius (q.v.) had to put away Helena, Constantine could not but attract attention by his ability and energy. He was with Diocletian at Alexandria in 296, served with Galerius against Persia, and was at his court in 305, when the old Augustus abdicated. The new ruler, Galerius, with both Caesars—Severus and Maximin Daia—devoted to him, was superior in all but name to his fellow-Augustus, Constantius, and Constantine was virtually a hostage for his father's good behaviour. In 306 Constantius requested Galerius to release Constantine for service in Britain; Galerius reluctantly consented. Constantine, fearing interruption by Severus, hastened to Britain and assisted his father in Scotland. When Constantius died at York (25 June), Constantine was proclaimed Augustus by the troops, urged on by the Alamannic king, Crocus; he seemed better qualified than his half-brothers, sons of Theodora, to carry the family fortunes. Galerius, smothering his resentment, granted Constantine the rank of Caesar; the rank of Augustus of the West was given to Severus.

2. The rise of Maxentius in Rome and the wars that ensued with Severus and Galerius reacted on the fortunes of Constantine. The old Emperor Maximian, returning to power to help Maxentius, visited Constantine in Gaul, gave him in marriage his daughter Fausta (once already betrothed to him in 293) and the title of Augustus. Constantine made no move, while Galerius invaded Italy and then retreated in disorder, but he sheltered Maximian when driven from Rome after a vain attempt to depose his son. At the Conference of Carnuntum in 308 Constantine was called on to resign the title of Augustus and become Caesar again, under Licinius as second Emperor. Both he and Maximin Daia resented the slight. They refused to be satisfied with the makeshift title of 'Filii Augustorum' and claimed and held the full rank of Augustus. In Gaul, meanwhile, Constantine had kept himself and his army in training against Franks, Alamanni, and Bructeri. He was absent on one of these expeditions in 310 when Maximian, restless and discontented, seized Massilia. Constantine turned and forced the old man to surrender and commit suicide. Deprived by this tragic incident of the moral support of the Herculian dynasty, Constantine claimed a new dynasty of his own, the Solar, derived from his ancestor Claudius (q.v. 2) Gothicus.

3. In 311 Galerius died and a new grouping of powers began. Constantine and Maxentius prepared for a fight to the death and sought support in Licinius and Maximin Daia respectively. Early in 312 Constantine invaded Italy, broke up a stubborn resistance in the north by great victories near Turin and Verona, and then marched on Rome. Maxentius gave battle and found defeat and death at the Mulvian Bridge. Welcomed as deliverer by the Senate, Constantine replaced Daia as senior Augustus. In 313 Licinius visited Milan, married Constantia, sister of Constantine, and with him issued certain regulations in favour of the Christians, known as the

'Edict of Milan'. Licinius then struck down his eastern rival, Maximin, and the two kinsmen emperors were left to rule East and West in harmony. The concord was unstable. A first war, fought in 314–15, was decided in favour of Constantine by victories at Cibalae and in the Mardian plain. The occasion was Constantine's attempt to make a third emperor, Bassianus, in Illyricum; the result was the cession to Constantine of territory as far as Thrace. Valens, appointed colleague by Licinius, was sacrificed. In 317 Crispus and Constantine II, sons of Constantine, and Licinius II, son of Licinius, were appointed Caesars. But trouble soon arose again. Licinius, jealous and suspicious, began to persecute the Eastern Christians. In 323 Constantine, in beating back a Gothic invasion, violated the territory of Licinius; war followed. Victorious in great battles by land and sea— Adrianople, Chrysopolis, and the Hellespont—Constantine forced the abdication of Licinius, who soon afterwards was executed.

4. Constantine now held the whole Empire, reunited under his own hand. Abroad his prestige stood unshaken. In 332 he repulsed Goths on the Danube and settled 300,000 Sarmatians within the Empire for its defence. A Persian war that was gathering did not break until after his death. Between 325 and 330 he built the new Christian capital of the East, new Rome, Constantinopolis (see CONSTANTINOPLE). A third son, Constantius II, became Caesar in 323 and a fourth, Constans, in 333. But in 326 Crispus, the eldest son, was accused by Fausta of an attack on her virtue and put to death. Fausta herself, charged with false accusation, was the next victim. The true facts are lost, but this imperial tragedy was a grave scandal to the Christian Church, to which Constantine now lent his full support. At the Council of Nicaea (A.D. 325) and in subsequent negotiations he succeeded in abating the strife of Athanasians and Arians that had threatened to split the Church.

5. Constantine planned to leave his Empire to his three sons, Constantine II, Constantius II, and Constans, and to the sons of his half-brother Delmatius, the younger Delmatius and Hannibalianus. Delmatius, who had put down a rebel, Calocoerus, in Cyprus, in 335, was to rule in Illyricum, while Hannibalianus was to have a kingdom to the south of the Black Sea. After Constantine had died, in full communion with the Church, in 337, the army massacred the side-branches of the family and secured the succession for the sons.

6. It is with full justice that Constantine bears the title of 'the Great'. He was a general of outstanding ability, an administrator and legislator of great talent and energy, a ruler of integrity, though too fond in his later years of unworthy friends and flatterers. With Diocletian he ranks as the re-founder of the Empire. It is impossible to decide in detail what parts belong to each, but to Constantine may be safely attributed the full development of the new status of the *praefecti praetorii*, the new imperial *consistorium* (q.v.) with its high officers and *comites*, and the new army, with its standing corps and frontier militia contrasted—not to mention a new money-system, with the famous gold *solidus* as its chief piece. But it is in the field of religion—as the instrument of the Christian Revolution—that Constantine rises to his full historical stature. Inheriting from his father, Constantius, a gentle and tolerant attitude to religion, Constantine was deeply impressed by the heroism of the Church under persecution. The audacity of his attack on Maxentius seems to imply that he felt assured of the spiritual support of the Christian God against the magic arts of his enemy. Victor, he showed marked favour to the Church, relieved it of all disabilities, and legislated in its interests. Within the Church, he fought hard for unity. A united Empire needed a united Church to support it. That was the reason why Constantine strove so hard, though without success, to bring the Donatists

of Africa back to their obedience, and why, throughout the Arian controversy, he used his whole influence to find a formula in which all could unite. He felt himself to be a 'servant of God' in a special sense, a 'bishop of those that are without'—the pagans and the aliens.

7. Constantine was baptized only on his death-bed, but his whole attitude shows that, long before that, he had passed from a vague monotheism to a definite belief in the power (*virtus*) of the God of the Christians. Statesman he certainly was and able to bend to his will a Church weak after persecution and unable to bear success. But he was no intellectual or sceptic. It was not without strong emotions and ardent faith that Rome's restorers could bring her through her great crisis. Constantine saw where the strength of the Empire lay and that recognition gave him the key to the new age that was waiting to be unsealed.

N. H. Baynes, 'Constantine the Great and the Christian Church' (*Proceedings of the British Academy* 1929) with full bibliography; Jakob Burckhardt, *Die Zeit Konstantins des Grossen*³ (1898); Ed. Schwartz, *Kaiser Konstantin und die christliche Kirche*² (1936); O. Seeck, *Untergang der antiken Welt*, Bd. i–iii; Parker, *Roman World*, 240 ff.; *CAH* xii. 342 ff., 678 ff.; A. Alföldi, *The Conversion of Constantine* (1948). H. M.

CONSTANTINOPLE. Byzantium (q.v.) in virtue of its unrivalled natural position, had always enjoyed great commercial prosperity and had occasionally played its part in history, under the Athenian Empire, with Lysimachus, in the war between Septimius Severus and Pescennius Niger. It was near Byzantium that Crispus in A.D. 324 won a decisive sea-victory for his father over Licinius. It was not without reason, then, that Constantine, seeking a site for a new Christian capital of the East, chose Byzantium.

2. The building of the new city—New Rome, or, more commonly, Constantinopolis—began in 324, but was only concluded in May 330. It was splendidly equipped with new buildings, and the grand natural harbours were developed. A new Senate, to match the Roman, was created and Roman noble families were induced by various offers to migrate. The poor too, like the poor of Rome, received their corn-dole. Paganism, even if not entirely excluded, as the statues of Cybele and of Constantine himself as Helios prove, had little place in a city destined to be the Christian metropolis. Constantinople became the centre of administration in the East. Its mint was one of the most active, and its 'Tyche Anthousa', is often represented beside that of Rome on Imperial coins. Special issues, from all mints, of Constantinopolis, with Victory on prow on reverse, and of Urbs Roma, with she-wolf and twins, celebrated the capitals, new and old, side by side.

3. As the Western Empire declined and fell, Constantinople rose steadily in oecumenical fame and standing. It became the firm rock, on which the Christian Empire of the East could rest, while the storms of attack, from Persian and Arab, from Bulgarian and Slav, broke against it in vain. Even the last and deadliest enemy, the Turk, was checked for centuries by its walls, even if the restored empire of the Palaeologi could only retain a very restricted independence. At the same time, the old commercial supremacy of the city was slowly sapped by Venetians and Genoese.

4. Constantinople was a Christian city and bore the symbols of the faith on its imperial coins. The Patriarch, under the shadow of the Emperor, could never attain the independence of the Pope of Rome; but he ranked as second in the hierarchy, and, after the final break between the Churches in 800, as supreme in the Greek Orthodox Church.

5. Constantinople had its seven hills and fourteen regions. It was extended by Theodosius II and Heraclius, and had a strong double wall. It was famous for its harbours—the Golden Horn, Sycae, etc.—its great

streets (such as Ἡ Μέσος), its palaces, squares, and aqueducts. The Hippodrome was often a centre of political demonstrations as well as of chariot races. Famous among its churches were Ἡ Ἁγία Σοφία, built by Justinian I in 532, Οἱ Ἅγιοι Ἀπόστολοι, and Ἡ Ἁγία Θεοτόκος τῶν Βλαχερνῶν. The population, never as large as that of Rome in its prime, may have been over half a million, with the Greek element predominating from about the eighth century.

Oberhummer, *PW* s.v.; C. Diehl, *Constantinople* (1924). For the history of the Byzantine Empire see bibliography s.v. ROME.
H. M.

CONSTANTIUS CHLORUS, FLAVIUS VALERIUS, of Dardanian stock, served with distinction as officer and governor, and was called by Diocletian in A.D. 293 to become Caesar of the West. To marry Theodora, daughter of Maximian, he had to put away Helena, his wife or concubine, the mother of Constantine.

The first task allotted to Constantius was the recovery of rebel Britain. In 293 he stormed Boulogne, after cutting it off by a dam from the sea; but Allectus, who murdered Carausius, was left in peace for three years. In 296 Maximian came up to guard the Rhine, and Constantius and his praetorian prefect, Asclepiodotus, put to sea. Asclepiodotus, landing in fog near Clausentum (*Bitterne*), routed and killed Allectus in Hampshire. Constantius, separated from him, came up the Thames and reached London in time to cut to pieces the marauding surv'vors of the beaten army. Constantius showed mercy to the island and restored its defences. In 298 he gained a spectacular victory over the Alamanni at Langres.

The abdication of Diocletian in A.D. 305 left Constantius in the West as senior Augustus, but hampered by his Caesar, Severus, a creature of Galerius. Constantine remained with Galerius, virtually as a hostage. In 306 Constantius asked that his son might be restored to him. Constantine, travelling with desperate speed, reached Britain just in time to help his father in a last victory, over the Picts, and to succeed him when he died at York.

Constantius was an able general and a generous and merciful ruler. Though not a Christian himself, he was as lenient to the Christians under persecution as his loyalty to Diocletian would allow. The stories of his descent from Claudius (q.v. 2) Gothicus are of doubtful value.

CAH xii. 328 ff., 342 ff.; Parker, *Roman World*, 227 ff., 238, 240 f., 292 f.
H. M.

CONSTELLATIONS. The first evidence of knowledge of the constellations possessed by the Greeks appears in the poems of Homer and Hesiod. Homer speaks of the Pleiades, the Hyades, Orion, the Great Bear ('also called by the name of the Wain, which turns round on the same spot and watches Orion; it alone is without lot in Oceanus' bath', *Od.* 5. 271 f.), Sirius ('called Orion's dog', 'rises in late summer', 'a baleful sign, for it brings to suffering mortals much fiery heat'), the 'late-setting' Boötes. Hesiod mentions the same stars, his name for Boötes being, however, Arcturus. The inference is that, at first, the observations of the sky were all directed to practical utility, the needs of persons following various callings, the navigator, the farmer, etc. The stars served as signs to guide the sailor, or as indications of the weather, times, and seasons. Calypso tells Odysseus to sail in such a way as always to keep the Great Bear on his left. Hesiod marks the time for sowing at the beginning of winter by the setting of the Pleiades in the early twilight, or the early setting of the Hyades or Orion, the time for harvest by the early rising of the Pleiades, threshing-time by the early rising of Orion, vintage-time by the early rising of Arcturus, and so on; for Hesiod, spring begins with the late rising of Arcturus. Then,

later, legends came to be attached to the various constellations, often owing to supposed resemblances in shape, and poetic fancy played its part.

2. (1) Orion, Ὠρίων (Ὠαρίων, Hesiod), was perhaps the constellation to which a Greek legend was earliest attached. A Boeotian legend made him a mighty hunter, ultimately killed by Artemis, or, according to a later version, by a scorpion sent by her. In art he is represented with a club in his right hand, a sword dependent from his belt (ξιφήρης Ὠρίων, Eur. *Ion* 1153) and a lion's skin on his left arm. In Pseudo-Eratosthenes *ad Arat.* an alternative name Ἀλεκτροπόδιον ('cock's foot') appears. The three stars of the belt were in Latin *Iugulae*, and in Greek astrological texts Χάριτες ('graces').

(2) *The Great Bear*, ἡ Ἄρκτος = the Wain, ἡ Ἄμαξα, which is no doubt the earlier name. To the former name attaches the story that Callisto, beloved of Zeus, was turned into a bear by Hera and thereon placed by Zeus in the heavens. Another story is that the two bears were placed in the heavens as constellations, and that they were two bears which had hidden and nourished Zeus, when a youth, in Crete for a year (Arat. 30–5). With the 'Wain' is connected the name of the star called Βοώτης ('oxen-driver') by Homer; when the Wain becomes the Bear, Boötes is naturally called Arcturus (Ἀρκτοῦρος, 'Bear-guard', Hesiod; Ἀρκτοφύλαξ, Eudoxus and Arat. 92). Another name for the Great Bear was ἑλίκη (Arat. 3; Apoll. Rhod. 3. 1105) implying convolutions; one interpretation is 'snail's-house', from a supposed resemblance in shape; the other rests on the revolution of the Bear round the pole. The Romans called it *Septentriones*, 'seven threshing-oxen' (*trio* = 'threshing-ox' in Varro and Gellius) going round and round. Βοώτης would be the suitable attendant for such a team, and perhaps there was an earlier Greek name corresponding to *Septentriones* which dropped out of use.

(3) *The Little Bear*. The Greeks, we are told, sailed by the Great Bear, the Phoenicians by the Little Bear (Arat. 39). Thales advised the Greeks to follow the Phoenician lead, the reason being that the Little Bear is the better guide to the position of the north pole. The Little Bear was commonly called *Cynosura* (κυνόσουρα, 'dog's tail', Arat. 36); another name was 'Callisto's dog' (schol. in Arat. 27).

(4) *Boötes* (Βοώτης), *Arcturus* (Ἀρκτοῦρος, Ἀρκτοφύλαξ) see *Great Bear*.

(5) *Hyades*, Ὑάδες, a group consisting of one star of the first and four of the third magnitude, the morning setting of which marked for Hesiod the time for ploughing. The name is derived from ὗς, 'swine', and it was regarded as representing a sow with four young; this is a more likely derivation than the alternative one from ὕειν, 'to rain', because it corresponds to the Latin *suculae* (Cic. *Nat. D.* 2. 111).

(6) *Pleiades*, a group of seven stars of fifth magnitude near the Hyades. Hesiod calls them the seven daughters of Atlas by Pleione; their names were Halcyone, Merope, Celaeno, Electra, Sterope, Taÿgete, Maia (Arat. 262 f.). The name Pleiades may be derived from πλεῖν, 'to sail', since their early rising in spring marks for Hesiod the beginning of the sailing season. The spelling of the word as Πελειάδες is, however, supposed to justify the early Greek view of them as a flight of doves. Another significant name for them is βότρυς, cluster or bunch of grapes (schol. on *Il.* 18. 486). The Latin name is *Vergiliae* (Plaut. *Amph.* 275), perhaps derived from *virga*, a twig.

3. *The Zodiac*. It seems now to be established that the Greeks obtained their knowledge of the twelve signs of the zodiac and the constellations in them from the Babylonians, to whom the Egyptians were similarly indebted. It was probably Cleostratus of Tenedos who imported this knowledge into Greece in the second half of the sixth century B.C. (see Pliny *HN* 2. 3; Hyginus, *Poet. Astr.* 2. 13). The pictorial representations of the

constellations, or most of them, passed over to Greece, as has been inferred from a number of boundary stones (see G. Thiele, *Antike Himmelsbilder* (1898), 10 f.; F. J. Boll, *Sphaera* (1903), 201 f.).

(7) The *Ram* (Κριός). According to Pliny this name was first used by Cleostratus, but it may be Babylonian. It marked for Hipparchus the spring time. The story is that it was the ram with the golden fleece which bore Phrixus and Helle over the sea (whence 'Hellespont'). It was sacrificed to Zeus, who placed it among the stars; the fleece was the object of the Argonauts' quest.

(8) The *Bull*, Ταῦρος, perhaps also a Babylonian name, is in the Greek legend the bull of the Europa-story.

(9) The *Twins*, Δίδυμοι, *Gemini*. They were variously identified as Castor and Pollux, Amphion and Zethus, Theseus and Heracles, Apollo and Heracles, Triptolemus and Iasion. The notion of them as Apollo and Heracles seems to go back to the time when the Greeks first became acquainted with the signs of the zodiac, and is supported by Ptolemy; they appear, however, in Babylonian texts as representations of the god Nirgal, the flaming summer-heat (Boll, 125).

(10) The *Crab*, Κάρκινος, *Cancer*, the fourth sign of the zodiac, was easy, from its appearance, to picture as a crab. An earlier name for it was ὄνων φάτνη, 'Asses' Crib' (see Arat. 898 f.), representing a crib and two asses.

(11) The *Lion*, Λέων, *Leo*, the fifth sign, was associated with the hot harvest-season. Kugler identified it with the Babylonian Urguta (literally 'Big Dog'). Greek legend made it the Nemean lion killed by Heracles.

(12) The *Virgin*, Παρθένος, *Virgo*, the sixth sign, is represented with wings and holding an ear of corn (στάχυς, *spica*). Aratus tells the story that she was the daughter of Zeus and Themis and dispensed justice on the earth, but, when men became vicious, she was translated to heaven; hence the alternative name for the constellation, Δίκη, Justice. She became, later, associated with the succeeding sign, the *Scales*, Ζυγός, *Libra*; hence the treatment of *Spica* by Aratus as a separate constellation. Other names attached to the constellation from time to time were: Demeter (because of her holding the ear of corn), Athena, Isis, Atargatis, Tyche (= Τύχη Ps.-Eratosth. *Cat.* 9), and Erigone, daughter of Icarius or Icarus (Manilius 5. 251).

(13) The *Scales*, Ζυγός, *Libra*. The original Greek name was χηλαί, Claws (of the Scorpion). The idea of the *Balance* came later; it was suggested by the equality of night and day at the equinox. The *Scales* were at first represented as held in the claws of the Scorpion; later, separated from the Scorpion, they were pictured either alone or as held by a female or male figure.

(14) The *Scorpion*, Σκορπίος, seems to be of Babylonian origin. The Greek story is that it was sent by Artemis to kill Orion.

(15) The *Archer*, Τοξότης, *Sagittarius*, was represented sometimes as a Centaur, sometimes as a creature with two feet, standing upright. Ps.-Eratosth. (*Cat.* 28) says of him: 'Most men call him a Centaur. Others dispute this, because he does not appear to have four legs, but stands upright and shoots with his bow. But none of the Centaurs used a bow. This (figure), though a man, has horse's feet, and, like Satyrs, a tail.'

(16) The *Sea-Goat* or *Horned Goat*, Αἰγοκέρως, *Capricornus*, the tenth sign of the zodiac, is of Babylonian origin. It is a Goat-Fish, with the head of a goat and a fish-tail. Epimenides identified it with the Cretan goat which brought up Zeus; others make it Pan under the name *Aegipan*. Theogenes caused it to be adopted as part of the Arms of Augustus, and it was put on the banners of the Augustan legions (Thiele, 69).

(17) *Aquarius*, Ὑδροχόος, *water-pourer*. 'The man that holds the watering-pot' of the rhyme is represented as pouring out water from an urn variously described as ὑδρία, κάλπις, or κάλπη, *urna*. Legends identify it

sometimes with Deucalion, sometimes with Ganymede.

(18) The *Fishes*, Ἰχθύες, *Pisces*, twelfth sign of the zodiac, are two stars of the third magnitude, one north and one south, tied together by δεσμά or σύνδεσμός (Arat. 243, 245). The northern one was also called 'swallow-fish' by the Chaldaeans = χελιδονία ἰχθῦς, the other ὁ νότειος (schol. in Arat. 242, Boll 196). The idea of this constellation came perhaps from the *Water* (ὕδωρ) of which Aratus made a separate constellation (Thiele 13).

4. After the time of the Ionian philosophers and the recognition in Greece of the signs of the zodiac comes a period in the fifth century when the constellations (their observed positions, risings, and settings) were used by Meton, Euctemon, and Democritus for the purposes of the calendar (παραπήγματα) and weather-indications (ἐπισημάσιαι). By the time of Eudoxus (first half of 4th c.) the following constellations were known and described in literature, with various legends attached. We take first those in the northern hemisphere.

(19) *Lyra*, Λύρα, containing the bright star Vega, is mentioned in connexion with the Twins. Apollo being one of the Twins, the association is appropriate, as legend has it that Apollo presented the lyre to Orpheus. The Lyre was used by Democritus and Euctemon for calendar-making (Diels, *Vorsokr.*⁵ ii. 143); it was also of significance in the calendar of Caesar (Plut. *Caesar*, 50).

(20) The *Swan* (Ὄρνις, 'Bird', *Olor*, *Cygnus*), belonging, like the *Eagle*, to the Milky Way, touches the northern tropic circle. Aratus (279) says that its right wing stretches out to the right hand of Cepheus. Legend connects it with the story of Leda and the Swan.

(21) The *Eagle*, Ἀετός, *Aquila*, was used by Democritus (Diels, loc. cit.). According to the legend, Zeus used the Eagle to carry Ganymede to Olympus.

(22) The *Dolphin*, Δελφίς, *Delphinus*, known to Democritus (Diels, *Vorsokr.*⁵ ii. 144), and used for the calendar by Euctemon and Eudoxus, was supposed to have been placed in the heaven by Poseidon for having helped him towards his marriage to Amphitrite.

(23) The *Horse*, Ἵππος, *Equus*, a constellation on the equator with back southwards; according to Aratus (283) his head is touched by the hand of the Ὑδροχόος, 'water-pourer', in the *Catasterismi* and later he became Pegasus.

(24) The *Crown* (northern), Στέφανος, *Corona*, is mentioned by Aratus (71), next after the *Kneeler* (Heracles), as placed in the heaven to commemorate Ariadne; also used for the calendar by Euctemon. Its principal star, Gemma, is of the second magnitude.

(25) The *Charioteer*, Ἡνίοχος, *Auriga*, a constellation between the Twins, the Bull, and the north pole, was first conceived as a man holding reins and driving a horsed chariot (Thiele 4. 28; Boll 111); he was then combined by astronomers with a still older constellation, the goat, Αἴξ, *Capella*, with two kids (Ἔριφοι), so that he carries the former on his shoulder and the latter on his left hand. Legend associates him with Bellerophon.

(26) The *Kneeler* (ὁ ἐν γόνασιν) is described by Aratus as 'like to a toiling man resting' on one knee with both arms raised, and the tip of his right foot on the head of the Dragon. He is represented as Heracles, with a club in his right hand and the lion's skin on his left arm, in his fight with the Dragon which watched the Garden of the Hesperides. Others identified him with Theseus, Ixion, Prometheus, etc.

(27) The *Serpent-holder* (Ὀφιοῦχος, *serpentarius*) holds a serpent in his hands. His head is near and opposite to the Kneeler; he is above the Scorpion. Identified by Ps.-Eratosth. *Cat.* 20 with Asclepius, and so with Ὑγίεια.

(28) The *Dragon*, Δράκων, *Draco*, passes in and out enclosing the Bears in coils turned opposite ways. Its tail at first marked the north pole; its head is under the

foot of the Kneeler (Heracles). It was variously identified with the dragon killed by Cadmus, the dragon which watched over the Garden of the Hesperides, or the Python killed by Apollo.

(29) *Cassiopeia* (earlier spelling *Cassiepeia*), a group of stars represented (*a*) by Aratus (192–3) as in the form of a key, (*b*) as a queen sitting on a throne with arms uplifted as if in agony about her daughter Andromeda. In another picture she is shown chained to two trees.

(30) *Andromeda* is represented by Aratus (203) as having her hands bound, agreeably to the story (cf. Eur. fr. 124 N.).

(31) *Perseus* is pictured running, unclothed save for a chlamys, with a sword in his right hand, wings on his feet, and Medusa's head in his left hand. Aratus (249–50) does not mention the Gorgon's head. The constellation includes Algol (of the second magnitude).

(32) *Cepheus*, husband of Cassiopeia and father of Andromeda. His position in the heavens is described by Eudoxus (ap. Hipparch. *in Arat.* 1. 2. 11) and Aratus (179 f.). His upraised right hand touches the Swan's right wing; his feet are just below the tail of the Little Bear.

(33) The *Arrow* ('Οϊστός, *Sagitta*) is under the Eagle. It is supposed to represent the arrow with which Heracles killed the Eagle gnawing the liver of Prometheus.

(34) The *Triangle* (called Δελτωτόν, Arat. 233) is below Andromeda, between her and the Ram (Eudoxus ap. Hipparch. *in Arat.* 1. 2. 13).

The southern constellations are the following:

(35) *Cetus* (Κῆτος, the *Sea-Monster* or *Whale*), represented as the Sea-Monster sent to kill Andromeda, is some distance south of her and Perseus. Its head is on the equator, near to the feet of the Ram (cf. Arat. 354). It is said to occupy more space in the heavens than any other constellation.

(36) The *Eridanus* (or Ποταμός, *River*), alternatively called Oceanus and by some identified with the Nile. Eudoxus described it as Ποταμός, starting from the left foot of Orion and lying below the Cetus (Hipparch. *in Arat.* 1. 8. 6). The legend connects it with Phaëthon who fell into it when struck by Zeus with a thunderbolt. Later combined with ὕδωρ from Aquarius (Boll, 136–8).

(37) The *Hare* (Λαγωός, *Lepus*), a constellation described as under the feet of Orion and pursued by the Great Dog (Sirius) behind it (Arat. 338).

(38) The *Great Dog*, Κύων, *Canis Major*. Its feet lie, like the bend of the river Eridanus, on the southern tropic (Eudoxus ap. Hipparch. *in Arat.* 1. 10. 37). The bright star of the constellation, *Sirius*, was known to the Egyptians, who began their year from the day after the early morning rising of Sirius, which also marked the rising of the Nile.

(39) *Procyon*, Προκύων, *Antecanis*, the *Little Dog*, was called Procyon because its morning rising is just before that of Sirius, its position being a little more to the north (schol. *in Arat.* 450. It is just under the Twins. Cf. Hipparch. *in Arat.* 2. 2. 13. etc.)

(40) *Argo*, Ἀργώ, is described by Aratus (349–50) as being marked by stars only in the half of the ship from the mast to the stern. Hipparchus objects to this part of the description. Argo's position is near the hind legs and the tail of the Great Dog.

(41) The *Southern Fish* ('Ιχθῦς Νότιος, *Piscis Australis*) is described by Aratus (386–8) as being under the Sea-Goat (Αἰγοκερώς) and turned towards the Cetus. It receives the water poured out by Aquarius. It is alternatively called the *Great Fish* (schol. in Arat.).

(42) The *Water-Snake* ("Υδρα Arat. 444, 519; "Υδρας Hipparch. *in Arat.* 1. 11. 9). Its head reaches the middle of the Crab, its coils are below the Lion and its tail above the Centaur. On its coils respectively are the *Bowl* (Κρατήρ) and the *Raven* (Κόραξ). It was identified with the Hydra killed by Heracles (schol. in Arat. 443). The scholium also has the story that the Raven is a servant

of Apollo who was sent to fetch a cup of pure water for a sacrifice; the servant found a fig-tree on the way and waited for the figs to ripen; ultimately he carried back to Apollo a snake and the cup, saying that the snake had prevented him from drawing the water from the spring.

(43) The *Centaur* (Κένταυρος) contains one star of the first and five of the second magnitude. According to Eudoxus (ap. Hipparch. *in Arat.* 1. 2. 20) and Aratus (501–3) its back is along the winter tropic, like the Argo and the middle of the Scorpion; Aratus says (437–8) that the part like a man is under the Scorpion and the hinder (equine) part under the *Claws*. Hipparch. *in Arat.* 1. 8. 19–23, correcting this, says that it is almost wholly under Virgo except for the right shoulder, right hand, and forelegs, which are partly under the Claws. In his left hand he is supposed to hold a thyrsus, and a hare dependent; on his right lies an animal (Θηρίον) which has been differently understood as a dog or a wolf or a panther (Boll, 143–8).

(44) The *Altar* (Θυτήριον, *Ara*) is in front of the fore-feet of the Archer (between them and the fore-feet of the Centaur). Aratus uses the name θυτήριον (403), Eudoxus and Hipparchus θυμιατήριον (Hipparch. *in Arat.* 1. 8. 14; 11. 9, etc.); so Ptolemy.

(45) The *Southern Crown*, Στέφανος νότιος, is under the feet of the Archer. It is probably identical with the nameless stars δινωτοὶ κύκλῳ in Aratus (400). The name Στέφανος is later than Hipparchus but is used by Geminus and Ptolemy. Alternative names, according to schol. *in Arat.* are Οὐρανίσκος, Prometheus, wheel of Ixion ('Ιξίονος τροχός). Others again call it πλοῖον (Boll, 150).

5. We may assume that Eudoxus gives in his works on observational astronomy, entitled *Phaenomena* and the *Mirror* ("Ενοπτρον) respectively, a description of all the constellations known in his time. According to Hipparchus (*In Arati et Eudoxi phaenomena* 1. 2. 2) the books were separate works, though they agreed in all but a few particulars. Hipparchus quotes freely from both. The *Mirror* may have been the earlier work and the *Phaenomena* an improved edition of it. The poem of Aratus, *Phaenomena*, was a popular version of Eudoxus so far at least as lines 19–732 are concerned. The commentary of Hipparchus gives three names which do not appear in Aratus: Πρόπους (= η of the Twins). In a text from Teucros a variant Τρίπους occurs (as to this see Boll, 126 f.); Προτρυγητήρ, *Vindemiatrix*, herald of the vintage = ε of *Virgo*; *Canopus*, omitted in Aratus, according to schol., because not visible in Greece, = α of Argo: on this see Hipparch. *in Arat.* 1. 11. 7. Called the 'pilot of Menelaus'.

6. Geminus (Εἰσαγωγὴ εἰς τὰ φαινόμενα, c. 3) gives a list of the constellations, which he divides into three classes, those in the zodiac and those to the north and south of it respectively. The list does not differ substantially from that given above, but Geminus mentions separately the following stars:

The *Crib* (Φάτνη); two *Asses* ("Ονοι): as to these see under *Crab* (10) above: Καρδία λέοντος (the Heart of the Lion, *Cor Leonis*, which Hipparchus calls ὁ ἐν τῇ καρδίᾳ τοῦ λέοντος), with the alternative name Βασιλίσκος, *Regulus*; Λίνοι, *Bands*, between the two fishes in the constellation of that name, and Συνδεσμός, *Knot* (see *Fishes* (18) above); "Οφις, the *Snake* held by Ophiuchus; Προτομὴ "Ιππου καθ' "Ιππαρχον = *Equuleus*, *Little Horse* (apparently Hipparchus has not the name, but Ptolemy has); Θυρσόλογχος, *Thyrsus-staff*, which according to Hipparchus 'the Centaur wields'; "Υδωρ, the *water* from Aquarius (see *Eridanus* (36) above); Κηρύκιον καθ' "Ιππαρχον, 'Herald's staff', according to Hipparchus' (= *Caduceus*), mentioned by Valens as held in Orion's left hand (not Greek but Egyptian in origin, Boll, 134, 167 f.); Γοργόνιον, the *Gorgon's Head*, 'at the end of Perseus' right hand'; 'the small stars close together at the end of

Perseus' right hand are made into the Ἅρπη (Sickle)'; Βερενίκης πλόκαμος, *Coma Berenices*, so called by the courtier-astronomer Conon in honour of Berenice and celebrated in the poem of Callimachus: Ptolemy (*Alm.* 2. 56) calls this last constellation Πλόκαμος simply.

7. The *Milky Way*, Γαλαξίας κύκλος, is described by Aratus (400) as 'that wheel with glaring eyes all round which they call Milk'. Democritus was the first to recognize that it consisted of stars packed very closely together. The name arose out of the legend of Hera's milk which was spilt when she refused the breast to the infant Heracles. Popularly and poetically it was variously regarded as the way to the Home of the Gods, the one-time orbit of the sun, Phaëthon's course, the souls' meeting-place, etc.

8. Hipparchus made a catalogue of 850 stars or more. Ptolemy (*Alm.* bks. 7-8) has one of 1,022 stars grouped under 48 constellations. It may be noted that Ptolemy retains the old name Χηλαί, *Claws*, for the *Scales*. He includes some stars which have not hitherto been mentioned: (*a*) *Antares* in the *Scorpion*, (*b*) *Antinous*, a group of six stars classified under the *Eagle*. On the other hand, Ptolemy does not mention the Χάριτες (*Graces*)— see under *Orion* (1) above.

9. The positions of the various constellations and stars in the heavens were shown on globes or 'spheres' (cf. the Σφαιροποιΐα of Archimedes). Even Thales and Anaximander are credited by the Doxographi with the construction of such globes. Eudoxus is certain to have had one; so had Hipparchus; and Ptolemy must have had access to some copy of it (see *Alm.* bk. 8 c. 1 ad fin., Thiele, op. cit. ch. 2). The globe on the shoulders of the Atlas Farnese in the Naples Museum represents such a globe, and is attributed to a date not later than A.D. 150. It shows the constellations with the principal great circles on the heavenly sphere, but not individual stars; the positions of the constellations show that the artist avoided the mistakes of Aratus pointed out by Hipparchus; he was aware, and made use, of Hipparchus' corrections. A fragment of a similar globe of blue marble is preserved in the Berlin Museum (No. 1050 A); this has separate stars shown in yellow colour within the contour of the figures representing the constellations.

10. After the time of Alexander the Great an astrological point of view becomes more and more dominant in astronomical works, and there is more admixture of Egyptian and Babylonian with Greek elements. Distinctive names *Sphaera graecanica* and *Sphaera barbarica* appear for the first time in Latin works by P. Nigidius (q.v.) Figulus bearing these titles, a few fragments of which are preserved; the *Sphaera barbarica* gave the Egyptian accounts of the fixed stars and legends connected with them, perhaps also the Babylonian. But Nigidius drew from Greek sources. One of these may be Asclepiades of Myrleia (1st c. B.C.); Teucros 'the Babylonian' (1st c. A.D.) and Antiochus (perhaps 3rd c. A.D.) were acquainted with the *Sphaera barbarica* (see Boll, *Sphaera* 413). Berosus (q.v., 3rd c. B.C.) and Nechepso-Petosiris (q.v., about 160 B.C.) may also have been intermediaries for Babylon and Egypt respectively. Astrology among the Romans was represented by Manilius and Firmicus Maternus (qq.v.); the latter follows Manilius closely, but cites as his authorities a certain Abraham and Achilles.

11. In Teucros and Antiochus Egyptian influence is very marked; they have alternative Egyptian names for various constellations, such as the following: Τυφῶν, *Typhon* = the Great Bear, *Osiris* = Orion, *Anubis* (in connexion with the Osiris-Orion group), *Isis*, a seated figure holding or feeding her son Horus, Κυνοκέφαλος (perhaps two constellations were so called, one of them being a dog-headed *Ape*, see Boll, 218 f., etc.), Ταυρο-κέφαλος Βοώτης, 'Bull-headed Boötes', with a plough (Boll, ch. 10).   T. H.

CONSTITUTIONES, the generic name for legislative enactments by Roman emperors, which were made in different forms. In the first place the emperors possessed the *ius edicendi* like all higher magistrates (see EDICTUM); imperial *edicta* were issued for enactments of a general character (cf. Augustus' edicts from Cyrene, Caracalla's edict on citizenship), to a less extent for law reforms. This purpose was better served by *decreta* (decisions in civil or criminal trials passed by the emperor) and *rescripta* (imperial decisions upon special points of law, in answer both to petitions, *libelli*, addressed to him by a litigant, and to the inquiry of a judicial official in complicated cases, *relationes*). The *rescripta* were also called *epistulae*, when directed in the form of a letter to the inquiring official or *subscriptiones* when written on the *libellus* itself and signed by the emperor. These forms of constitutions gave occasion to legislative innovations, for their statements of law exceeded often the sphere of mere interpretation of existing law and laid down new legal rules which, though issued in particular cases, became authoritative and binding for all, as coming from the emperor himself. Another type of *constitutiones* was the imperial instructions given to officials, especially to provincial governors, *mandata*, which were more concerned with administrative matters. Exceptionally they touched civil law, e.g. in dealing with legal relations marriage, wills) of military persons. An excerpt of a *liber mandatorum* is preserved on a papyrus (*BGU* v. 1) known as *Gnomon of the Idios Logos* (a high official of the financial administration in Egypt).

The constitutional basis of the emperor's legislative power was at the beginning of the Principate not quite clear, apart from *edicta* as expressions of his magisterial *imperium* (*proconsulare*). The first emperors used therefore to give effect to their legislative intentions by means of the Senate, before whom they pronounced personally (*oratio*) or by a *quaestor* their motion for approval by the senators. The resolution of the Senate became later a mere formality, so that an imperial *oratio* was simply a kind of publication of an imperial law. And generally the constitutions were soon recognized as having the force of law (*legis uicem* [*uigorem*] *optinent*). The innumerable quotations of imperial rescripts in the works of the classical jurists excerpted for the *Digest* show how productive was this activity of the emperors in the times of the Antonines and their successors. Some titles of the *Digest*, especially those which deal with criminal law and procedure, abound in mentions of imperial constitutions. From the time of Diocletian and Constantine the legislative power of the emperors was unlimited: they issued directly general enactments (*leges generales*), laying down new legal rules with unrestricted validity. For collections of constitutions, *see* CODEX.

For bibliography see under LAW AND PROCEDURE, ROMAN, § 1 (textbooks on the Sources of Roman Law).   A. B.

CONSUL, the supreme civil and military magistrate of Rome under the Republic. The etymology of the word *consul* is uncertain: it has variously been derived from *cum-esse* (Niebuhr), from *cum-salire* (Mommsen), and from *consulere* (De Sanctis). In any case it was not the original designation of the chief magistrates. It is proved by Livy (3. 15. 12), and by the Greek translation of their title (στρατηγός or στρατηγὸς ὕπατος), that they were in the first instance called 'praetores'. This name (from *prae-ire*, to march ahead) and its Greek equivalent emphasize the military character of the magistracy. The name of 'consul' came into use before 366 B.C., for by this date the title *praetor* was reserved for another magistrate, the *praetor urbanus* (see PRAETOR).

According to the traditional account, which has the support of the *fasti* (q.v.), the head magistrates were two in number from the beginning. An alternative theory (propounded by De Sanctis, *Storia dei Romani* i. 403 ff.)

maintains that the original board consisted of three *praetores* (probably the military commanders of the three original tribes), of whom two took special charge of military functions, while the third praetor discharged civilian duties; by 366 the board had been split into two separate offices, that of the 'consuls' (as the military commanders came to be called), and that of the *praetor urbanus* (who retained the older title with the distinctive epithet *urbanus*). In 367 B.C. the Licinian law opened the consulship to the plebeians. The law, often violated by the patricians, was confirmed by a plebiscite in 312 B.C., by which representatives of the two orders shared the consulship until 172, when for the first time two plebeian consuls were elected.

Throughout the Republic candidates for the consulship were elected by the people in the *comitia centuriata*, but, as they were proposed by the senators from their own ranks, liberty of voting was greatly restricted. It disappeared under the Empire when the *comitia centuriata* was suppressed and the emperors either recommended the candidates or themselves assumed the consulship. Under the Republic the consuls entered office on 15 March (after 153 B.C. on 1 January) and retained it for a whole year; under the Empire they retained it from two to four months only. Consequently, while Republican consuls, except *suffecti* (that is, appointed in case of the death, illness, or resignation of a consul), both gave their names to the year, despite differences of rank arising from their age (*collega maior*) or the polling (*collega prior*), Imperial consuls did so only if they entered office on 1 January (*consules ordinarii*, to be distinguished from their successors *consules suffecti*). A further distinction depended on whether Imperial consuls were single or married, and the number of their children. Moreover, the emperors often appointed themselves or their relatives and protégés consuls, entirely disregarding the legal age limits, which had been carefully fixed in 180 B.C. by the *Lex Villia Annalis*. In the age of Cicero no one under forty could be elected consul; under the Empire children were invested with the office, which was conferred upon Honorius at birth. But the consulship survived in the Western Roman Empire until A.D. 534.

Mommsen, *Röm. Staatsr.*, ii². 1. 74 ff.; G. De Sanctis, *Stor. d. Rom.* i. 403 ff. (cf. *Riv. Fil.* 1929, 1 ff.); B. Kübler, *PW* s.v.; M. Holleaux, Στρατηγὸς ὕπατος (1918). **P. T.**

CONSUS, a Roman god whose festivals (Consualia) were on 19 Aug. and 15 Dec., possibly in connexion with the ending respectively of the harvest and the autumn sowing. He seems connected with Ops (q.v.), by the dates of his festivals. The most reasonable explanation of his name is that it is connected with *condere* and he is the god of the store-bin or other receptacle for the garnered grain. This, as corn was often stored underground, may account for his subterranean altar in the Circus Maximus, uncovered only on his festival days (Varro *Ling.* 6. 20; Dion. Hal. *Ant. Rom.* 2. 31. 2); for its alleged inscription (Tert. *De Spect.* 5) see v. Blumenthal and Rose in *ARW* xxxiii. 384; xxxiv. 111. The ancients commonly supposed his name to have something to do with *consilium* (Dion. Hal., ibid. 3) or, because his altar lay in the Circus, identified him with Poseidon Hippios (Livy 1. 9. 6). He had also a temple on the Aventine, probably vowed or dedicated by L. Papirius Cursor about 272 B.C. (see Platner–Ashby, 141). His characteristic offering was first-fruits (Dion. Hal. ibid.). Horses and asses were garlanded and rested on his festival (Plut. *Quaest. Rom.* 48, whereon see Rose). Whether he was originally honoured with circus games is doubtful. **H. J. R.**

CONTAMINATIO, 'spoiling'. Terence's enemies accused him of 'contaminating' his originals; he replies that he would rather imitate the 'carelessness' of Naevius, Plautus, and Ennius than the 'dull laboriousness' of his rivals. The only liberty to which he confesses is that he has sometimes borrowed from a second Greek original. Modern scholars consequently assume that *contaminatio* could mean 'blending of originals', and that this is the procedure which Terence attributes to Naevius and others. Of the countless attempts to discover traces of 'blending' in Plautus only three are recognized as successful by P. Enk (*Rev. Phil.* 1938, iv; cf. G. Michaut, *Plaute* ii. 239 ff.). But I. Waltz (*Rev. Ét. Lat.* 1938, ii) argues that even in Terence's prologues *contaminare* means simply 'spoil'. The charge against Terence would, then, be that his translations were not faithful; and this charge, as he says, could be brought against earlier dramatists also. He glosses over the fact that his alterations differed from those made by earlier dramatists in being deliberate; but surely in speaking of their 'carelessness' he absolves them from any suspicion of so delicate a procedure as the blending of originals.

W. Beare, 'Contamination in Plautus and Terence', *Rev. Phil.* xiv (1940). **W. B.**

CONTIO (*conventio*) was a public gathering which even non-citizens, though illegally, used to attend. It was summoned by a magistrate or priest, either as a preliminary to legislation, in which case the measures to be passed were announced, or as a political assembly, called to discuss questions of public moment or the programmes of the political leaders. A magistrate could cancel a meeting summoned by an inferior (*contionem avocare*), and a tribune could veto or adjourn it (*intercessio* and *obnuntiatio*). The right of addressing the audience (*contionem dare*) depended on the will of the president who addressed the assembly from the platform (*ex superiore loco*), while the debaters spoke *ex inferiore loco*. The meetings generally took place near the rostra, in daytime, on *dies fasti*. As the kings had done, so the emperors alone summoned the meetings to address the people in solemn circumstances.

Mommsen, *Röm. Staatsr.* i². 191 ff.; W. Liebenam, *PW* iv. 1149 ff.; G. W. Botsford, *The Roman Assemblies* (1909), 139 ff.; A. H. J. Greenidge, *Roman Public Life* (1911), 158 ff. **P. T.**

CONTRACT, ROMAN LAW OF. For the earliest forms of binding by agreement, *see* NEXUM, STIPULATIO. The developed Roman law embraced a whole system of obligations arising from a free agreement (*conventio*, *obligatio*; *contractus*, which did not become common as a technical term until the 2nd c. A.D., signified agreements recognized by *ius civile* as actionable). The extension and consolidation of *actiones* for protecting contractual obligations were supported in a large measure by the praetorian law of the late Republic. The classical Roman law did not elaborate any general conception of contract as a binding agreement; it recognized only some typical circumstances which, by agreement of the parties, produced one-sided or reciprocal obligations. According to a classification of Gaius (3. 89), repeated by Justinian (*Inst.* 3. 13. 2), four groups of contracts were distinguished according to the specific instrument employed for creating an obligation: (*a*) *res*, an actual handing over of a thing to the future debtor; (*b*) *verba*, a solemn declaration (*stipulatio*, q.v., *dotis dictio*, see MARRIAGE); (*c*) *litterae*, written entries in the account books of the creditor; (*d*) *consensus*, where a mere consent sufficed for a valid agreement. The informal real contracts (*a*) were: (1) *mutuum*, a loan of money or natural products (e.g. corn), obligating the debtor to return the sum loaned or an equivalent in quantity, kind, and quality of the products received for consumption. The payment of interest (with a maximum of 12 per cent., reduced by Justinian to 4 per cent.) required a special agreement; (2) *commodatum*, a gratuitous loan of an object for use, to be returned by the borrower after the agreed time; (3) *depositum*, gratuitous custody of another's property without any right of use or other profit for the depositee, who was obliged to return the object to the depositor on demand; (4) *fiducia*, a pledge (*see* SECURITY). Under the group of consensual contracts (*d*) were included: (1) *emptio–venditio*, sale. This contract is effected when the parties have agreed on the object of sale and its price (estimated in money): henceforth the risk of the depreciation or destruction of the object sold passes to the buyer, and damage caused by accident falls upon him; on the other hand, he has the benefit of any increase in its value. The vendor was obliged to surrender to the buyer exclusive possession of the object sold, and to guarantee him against a third person's claims; he was also responsible for latent defects in the object. Special rules for the sale of slaves and beasts were introduced by the aediles' edict. (2) Hire (*locatio–conductio*), of a movable or immovable object, of services (*operae*), except certain liberal arts, or an undertaking to perform a piece of work (*opus*). (3) *Mandatum*, an undertaking to perform a gratuitous service for another (*mandator*) on his request. (4) *Societas*, when two or more persons contribute capital or labour, or even an entire property (as when an undivided inheritance was enjoyed in common by the coheirs, *consortium*), to be exploited for a common purpose. Profits and losses were divided between all partners (*socii*) according to their shares in the union. The consensual and real contracts created rights and obligations which were mostly of reciprocal character, and would vary more particularly in regard to the liability of the debtor for failure to safeguard the object entrusted to him (responsibility for *custodia, dolus, culpa*). The bilateral character of contractual obligations (apart from *mutuum* and the verbal contracts, which affected unilateral duties) gave occasion to a whole system of *actiones*, called generally by the name of the contract itself (*actio depositi, commodati, empti, venditi, locati, conducti, mandati, pro socio*). Sometimes special actions were introduced for a particular liability (as for secret defects in the sale). The action against a debtor in a case of *mutuum* was *condictio*. For agreements which did not fall within the above-mentioned types of recognized contracts the magistrate could grant an exceptional protection by an action called *in factum*. Later post-classical constructions extended the sphere of uch reciprocal agreements not falling within the named contracts (and called therefore by the modern theory 'innominate'), and endowed them with legal protection (*actio praescriptis verbis*), if one party had performed his duties according to the agreement.

See the text-books mentioned under LAW AND PROCEDURE, ROMAN, § 1. P. De Francisci, *Synallagma* i (1913), ii (1916). P. Bonfante, *Scritti giuridici* ii. S. Riccobono, *Studi Bonfante* ii (1930); *Corso di diritto romano: Stipulationes, contractus, pacta* (1935). V. Arangio-Ruiz, *Responsabilità contrattuale*² (1933). P. Collinet, *Law Quarterly Review* 1932. A. B.

CONTROVERSIA, the more advanced form of *declamatio* (q.v.), is best illustrated in the collection by the elder Seneca (q.v.), who recorded the treatment of debatable themes by the chief speakers of his day. He mentions *controversiae* as a recent term for Cicero's *causae* (*Controv.* 1 praef. 12). The debate was on some disputable point of law, usually fictitious and unreal, though as an exercise it was designed to equip for practice in law courts. The figures include pirate chiefs with or without a susceptible daughter, tyrants, mutilators of exposed children, poisoners, fathers implacably disinheriting sons. Unlikelihood of theme favoured imagination and ingenuity of argument, but served to make the exercise too scholastic to be serviceably forensic. Many *controversiae* look like novels in brief, and might be fitted with such titles as 'The young man with a kind heart who was twice disinherited', 'The Vestal Virgin who wrote love-poetry', 'The strange case of a son and stepson indistinguishable in looks'. Neat *sententiae* for and against are freely introduced; the skeleton statement of legal points involved comes in the *divisio*; and *colores*

(q.v.), or arguments professing to illumine motives, are quoted by Seneca from contemporary rhetors. It is surprising how much can be said to defend or condemn persons arraigned under the imaginary laws which are cited. The value of Seneca's collection lies partly in its illustration of the cleverly pointed *sententiae* which entered so inextricably into Silver Latin literature, and partly in its picture of the manner of argument adopted by contemporary speakers. Their straining after rhetorical effect and their use of far-fetched arguments or foolish *colores* are not spared by Seneca (e.g. *Controv.* 7. 5. 10; 9. 2. 27; 10 praef. 10). *See* EDUCATION, III. 3. J. W. D.

CONTUBERNIUM (from *taberna*), (1) the common life of soldiers occupying the same quarters; (2) any companionship; (3) the living together of slaves as husband and wife. Slaves could not contract *iustae nuptiae* (*see* MARRIAGE, LAW OF), but from early times a slave was allowed to marry a slave woman of the *familia*, and family life was increasingly recognized in practice and in law (*Dig.* 33. 7. 12. 7 rules that a testator could not will the separation of parents and children); literature, inscriptions, and law-books use *maritus, uxor, coniunx* instead of *contubernalis*, and show that an unbroken family life could generally be counted on.

For bibliography, *see* SLAVES. R. H. B.

CONUBIUM, *see* COMMERCIUM.

CONVENTUS, a word used in two main senses: (1) administrative divisions of a province, in the leading city of each of which justice was administered (*conventus iuridicus*, in the eastern provinces *dioecesis*). These areas were determined by the *Lex Provinciae*, and often cut across pre-existing divisions. They developed some independence, and in the Principate sometimes had their own priests of the imperial cult (*ILS* 6931–2). (2) Associations of Roman citizens resident in provincial centres (*conventus civium Romanorum*). In the Republic (notably at Delos) they included non-enfranchised Italians as well as citizens proper. They are found only in places where citizenship was rare, and thus disappear early in the Principate from the romanized Western provinces; they are unknown in *coloniae* and *municipia*. At this period in such provinces as Raetia, Aquitania, and Lugdunensis, their members were drawn from all over the province. Their organization resembled that of *collegia* (*see* CLUBS, ROMAN). Under the Republic they elected *magistri*, who were often associated with a religious cult. In the Principate their president was normally a *curator civium Romanorum*, probably chosen by themselves. The *conventus* took part in the worship of the emperors, and priests of particular emperors are found among their members (*ILS* iii. 1. 587). G. H. S.

CONVERSION, abandonment, more or less sudden, of one way of living in favour of another, a genuine phenomenon and occasionally testified to in antiquity. The most famous case is that of the young rake Polemon, who strayed into Xenocrates' lecture-room and was so impressed by his discourse on temperance that he turned philosopher (Diog. Laert. 4. 16). Horace professes (*Carm.* 1. 34) to have been converted from materialism by thunder from a clear sky, which at least shows that such a thing was supposed possible. But religious conversion, i.e. the abandonment of one religion for another, did not take place under polytheism; a believer in certain gods would not cease to believe in them because he was attracted to and became a devotee of another. A mystery-cult might attract a man to a religious life as a monastic order does to-day, but that again is not abandonment of former beliefs. Only Judaism and Christianity produced conversions in this sense.

A. D. Nock, *Conversion* (1933), and in *Pisciculi Franz Joseph Dölger dargeboten* (1939), 165 ff., also forthcoming art. 'Conversio' in *Reallex. f. Ant. u. Christ.* H. J. R.

COPA, see APPENDIX VERGILIANA.

COPAÏS, a lake, now drained, which in early days covered most of the west plain of Boeotia. It took its name from Copae on its north side. The swallow-holes on its east side were cleared and enlarged, and canals dug north and south to lead the Cephissus and other streams to them round the edge of the plain. Shafts for uncompleted tunnels were also bored on the low hills in the north-east corner and between Copaïs and Lake Hylice on the east. The drainage works were usually ascribed to the Minyans of Orchomenus; to the Mycenaean period belongs the fortress of Gla, on what afterwards became an island in the lake. The outlets were said to have been blocked by the Theban hero Heracles: perhaps the Thebans stopped them during their wars against Orchomenus. In classical times, in spite of attempts to drain it, the lake was always swampy, and famous for eels (Ar. *Ach.* 880 ff.).

E. J. A. Kenny, *Annals of Archaeology and Anthropology* 1935, 189 ff.; U. Kahrstedt, *Arch. Anz.* 1937, 1 ff.   T. J. D.

COPTUS (mod. *Keft*), on the right bank of the Nile, was a station on a well-equipped camel-track through the desert to Berenice on the Red Sea. This route became the principal link between the Mediterranean and Eastern waters. It was developed by Augustus; in the third century it temporarily fell into the hands of the native Blemmyes and was almost destroyed by Diocletian (A.D. 292), but recovered and maintained itself in the Byzantine Age. Part of a customs tariff survives on a papyrus from Coptus.

Warmington, *Indian Commerce*, 6 ff., 14-16, 50-1, 104-5; Kees, *PW* s.v. 'Koptos'.   E. H. W.

CORAX of Syracuse (5th c. B.C.) wrote the first manual on rhetoric, based on legal practices in Sicily after the Fall of the Tyrants (Arist. *Rhet.* 2. 24; Cic. *Brut.* 46). It dealt with forensic oratory, defined rhetoric as an art of persuasion, advocated the use of probable (εἰκός) arguments, and prescribed three sections (προοίμιον, ἀγῶνες, ἐπίλογος) for every speech.   J. W. H. A.

CORBILO (mod. *Corsep?, Coron?*), a town of the Veneti on the Loire, to which British tin was shipped for conveyance across Gaul to the Mediterranean coast. The transit across Gaul was made in thirty days. Scipio Aemilianus (c. 135 B.C.) met traders from Corbilo at Massilia or Narbo, but failed to extract information about Britain from them.

Strabo 4. 190; Diod. 5. 22; Cary, *JHS* 1924, 172 ff   E. H. W.

CORBULO, GNAEUS DOMITIUS, son of the *consul suff.* of A.D. 39, was *consul suff.* (year unknown). In 47 as legate of Germania Inferior he successfully fought against the Chauci led by Gannascus, but was not allowed by Claudius to go farther. A strict disciplinarian, he made his troops dig a canal between the Meuse and Rhine. Proconsul of Asia under Claudius, he was entrusted as a *legatus* of Cappadocia and Galatia with the command against Parthia in the war about the control of Armenia, which broke out after Nero's accession, but which started in earnest only in 58, when Corbulo had reorganized the Roman army in the East. He captured Artaxata and Tigranocerta, installed Tigranes as king of Armenia, and received the governorship of Syria. But Tigranes was driven out of Armenia, the war was renewed in 61, and at Corbulo's request a separate general, Caesennius Paetus (q.v.), was sent to Armenia. After Paetus' defeat, Corbulo obtained in 63 a *maius imperium*, restored Roman prestige, and concluded a durable agreement with Parthia: Tiridates, the Parthian nominee to the throne of Armenia, admitted a Roman protectorate. Corbulo probably did not abuse his popularity, but his son-in-law Vinicianus (q.v.) conspired. In 67 Nero invited Corbulo to Greece and compelled him to commit suicide. His daughter Domitia Longina became wife of Domitian in 70. It was the homage of the new dynasty to the name and influence of the greatest general of his time. The account of his achievements in Tacitus (*Ann.* bks. 12–15) and Dio Cassius (bks. 60–3) derives ultimately to a great extent from Corbulo's own memoirs.

Stein, *PW*, Suppl. iii. 394; M. Hammond, *Harv. Stud.* 1934, 81; J. G. C. Anderson, *CAH* x. 758, 880. Portrait: F. Poulsen, *Rev. Arch.* 1932, 48.   A. M.

CORCYRA (Κέρκυρα), modern *Corfu*, the northernmost and most important of the Ionian islands. It owed its prosperity in part to its fertile soil, but especially to its situation at the starting-point of two main Greek trade-routes, along the coast of Illyria, and across the Adriatic to Italy and Sicily. It was popularly identified with the Phaeacia of the *Odyssey*. Its first Greek settlers came from Eretria (Plut. *Quaest. Graec.* 11; c. 700 B.C.?); but these were supplanted, perhaps after the first Greek naval battle, traditionally dated 664 B.C. (Thuc. 1. 13), by the Corinthians. It shared with Corinth the foundation of Epidamnus (q.v.), and perhaps of other colonies in Illyria; but it resented the dominion of the tyrant Periander, and after his death it became a competitor of Corinth in Adriatic waters. Pursuing a policy of isolation, it stood out of the Persian Wars; but in 435 it was drawn into open hostility against Corinth, in consequence of a scramble for the control of Epidamnus, and to escape defeat it sought an alliance with Athens (433), which it renewed several times. It received protection from the Athenian fleet in 433, and again in 427 and 425, when Corinthian fleets attempted to co-operate with disaffected elements on the island; in 427 and 425 the Corcyrean democracy disgraced its victory by wholesale massacre of the oligarchs. In 410 Corcyra shook off the Athenian connexion, but in 375 it joined the Second Athenian Confederacy, and so drew upon itself a Spartan expeditionary force, which it beat off after a prolonged siege (373). By 360 it had again detached itself, but c. 340 it rejoined Athens in a vain attempt to prevent the intrusion of Macedonia into Adriatic waters. After the death of Alexander it became an object of dispute between various mainland dynasts, Cassander, Demetrius, and Pyrrhus, and was occupied for a time by the Syracusan tyrant Agathocles. In 229 it was captured by the Illyrians, but was speedily delivered by a Roman fleet and remained a Roman naval station until at least 189. At this period it was governed by a prefect (presumably nominated by the consuls), but in 148 it was attached to the province of Macedonia.

Thuc. 1. 24–55, 3. 70–85, 4. 46–8; Xen. *Hell.* 6. 2; J. Partsch, *Die Insel Korfu* (1887).   M. C.

CORDUBA (nowadays *Cordova*), a pre-Roman city on the middle Baetis (*Guadalquivir*), first mentioned as a foundation of M. Claudius Marcellus, 152 B.C. It was granted colonial status, as *colonia Patricia*, by Pompey or his sons (during the Pompeian occupation of 46–45 B.C. according to M. Grant, *From Imperium to Auctoritas* (1946), 4). Pompeian in sympathy, Corduba was taken by Caesar in 45 B.C. Under the emperors it became the religious, and possibly also the administrative, centre of Baetica. Inscriptions reflect an active business life in which men of diverse origins shared. Local mines (*Mons Marianus*) and pasture-lands for sheep increased Corduba's wealth. It was the birthplace of Lucan and the two Senecas.   J. J. Van N.

CORFINIUM, near the modern *Pentima*, controlled a strategic bridgehead of the river Aternus in Italy. It occupied a strong site on the Via Valeria near the Adriatic (Strabo 5. 241). As capital of the Paeligni, whose name the neighbouring church of San Pelino preserves, Corfinium must always have been important; but it is first mentioned during the Social War when the Italians made it their seat of government and renamed it Italia, intending it to become the permanent capital of Italy (90 B.C.). They were quickly obliged, however, to transfer their seat of government to Aesernia, and the ultimate fate of Corfinium in the Social War is unknown: presumably the Romans captured it and made it a municipium (Diod. fr. 37; Vell. Pat. 2. 16). In 49 B.C., garrisoned by Domitius Ahenobarbus, it offered temporary resistance to Julius Caesar (Caesar, *BCiv.* 1. 15 f.; App. *BCiv.* 2. 38; Suet. *Iul.* 33 f.; Lucan, 2. 478 f.). Subsequently Corfinium received colonists on several occasions, but apparently was never styled *colonia* (*Lib. Colon.* 228, 255). Inscriptions indicate that it was a flourishing *municipium* in Imperial times, but its later history is unknown. Presumably it was destroyed in medieval times. E. T. S.

CORINNA, lyric poetess, of Tanagra (fr. 2; Paus. 9. 22. 3), elder contemporary of Pindar, with whom various legends, none very trustworthy, connect her (Suidas s.v. Κόριννα; Plut. *de Glor. Ath.* 4; Ael. *VH* 13. 25; schol. Ar. *Ach.* 720). She wrote narrative lyrical poems on Boeotian subjects for a circle of women (fr. 2), with titles such as *Boeotus, Seven against Thebes, Euonymie, Iolaus, Return of Orion.* A papyrus at Berlin contains substantial remains of two poems. In the first (fr. 4) she describes a contest in song between the mountain gods Cithaeron and Helicon. Since Helicon is defeated, the contest may stand for the competition between her own kind of art and that of the Hesiodic school. In the second the seer Acraephen foretells the high destiny of the daughters of Asopus, who are married to gods. The material used may go back to Eumelus of Corinth, and is based on legends of colonization. Both are written in regular stanzas of fixed length in which a metre is repeated and the stanza closed with a *clausula.* She uses simple verse-forms, such as minor ionics and choriambic dimeters. She also wrote lyric nomes, and fr. 5 B, called *Orestes,* seems to be a choral hymn for a spring festival. Her text is in the reformed Boeotian spelling of the fourth century and must have been transliterated from what she wrote. She normally keeps to her own dialect, but sometimes admits Aeolic and Homeric forms.

Text: E. Diehl, *Anth. Lyr. Graec.* i. 4, 193–206. W. Crönert, in *Rh. Mus.* lxiii. 166–89. Commentary, etc.: U. von Wilamowitz-Moellendorff, in *Berl. Klass. Text.* v (2), 19–55. C. M. Bowra, in Powell and Barber, *New Chapters in Greek Literature* iii. 21–30, and 'The Daughters of Asopus' in *Hermes* lxxiii (1938), 213–21. C. M. B.

CORINTH, the isthmus city controlling communications between north Greece and Peloponnesus and the eastern and western seas. The city lay north of the citadel (Acrocorinth), two to three miles from the sea, with ports, Lechaeum and Cenchreae, on both gulfs. Finds of geometric, Mycenaean, and pre-Mycenaean pottery from Korakou near Lechaeum show that a city existed in prehistoric and Homeric times, though in the epic it takes a subordinate place (*Il.* bks. 2 and 13, and, under the name *Ephyre*, bk. 6).

2. At the Dorian conquest Corinth probably fell to Temenus the conqueror of Argos. Later the kingship gave place to the Dorian oligarchy of the Bacchiadae, under whom Corinth founded Corcyra and Syracuse (both traditionally 734 B.C.), led the way in shipbuilding (Ameinocles of Corinth built ships for Samos in 704) and naval warfare (battle with Corcyra, 664), and developed a great pottery industry. In its latest phase the Bacchiad government may have fallen under the ascendancy of Pheidon of Argos. C. 657 it was overthrown by the tyrant Cypselus, under whose house Corinth reached its greatest prosperity and power (commemorated by dedications at Olympia and Delphi), while the discontented Bacchiad Demaratus emigrated to Tarquinii, an event epoch-making in the history of Rome (Blakeway, *JRS* 1935, 129–49).

3. Archaeological evidence invalidates the attempts of some moderns to postdate the Corinthian tyranny, and supports the dating of fourth-century historians, according to which Periander died in 585, and his nephew and successor Psammetichus (Cypselus II) was overthrown soon after.

4. The tyranny was replaced by a constitutional government, based apparently on an inner cabinet of eight and a council of eighty (Nic. Dam. 60). Trade still flourished and craftsmen still enjoyed special consideration. The city fostered friendly relations with the rising powers of Athens and Sparta; mediated between Athens and Thebes over Plataea (519), between Athens and Cleomenes of Sparta (507), Gela and Syracuse (491); supported Sparta against the medizing Polycrates of Samos, and Athens against Aegina; and fought well against Persia at Salamis, Plataea, and Mycale.

5. With the growth of Athenian imperialism Corinth's relations to Athens deteriorated, though even at the revolt of Samos from Athens in 440 she opposed Peloponnesian intervention; but Athenian interference at Megara and in the Corinthian Gulf had already led to fighting between Athens and Corinth in 459, and disputes between Athens and Corinth over Corcyra and Potidaea led to the outbreak in 431 of the Peloponnesian War. Corinth suffered severely, losing ships, trade, and colonies, and after the temporary peace of 421 was for a while estranged from Sparta, but at Mantinea in 418 was again fighting on the Spartan side. The Sicilian expedition of 415 increased her hostility to Athens: Corinthians under Gylippus took a leading part in the struggle at Syracuse and till the fall of Athens in 404 continued among Athens' most implacable foes. But shortly afterwards Corinth combined with Athens, Argos, and Boeotia to make war against the tyrannical rule of Sparta. During this 'Corinthian War' (395–386) a democratic government was established c. 392 with Argive help, but after the war it was replaced by an oligarchy. In the troubled times of Epaminondas and Philip II Corinth aimed at a neutral policy in Greece proper, but when Sicilian Greeks sought help against local tyrants and Carthage she sent out Timoleon in 344 and helped to repeople Syracuse, whose coins now showed the Corinthian *pegasus*. After the battle of Chaeronea (338) Corinth was made the gathering place of the new Hellenic League; here Philip, its author, and Alexander proclaimed their crusade against Persia.

6. In the Hellenistic period Corinth became a centre of industry, commerce, and commercialized pleasure, and also a key fortress that frequently changed hands in the dynastic struggles of the period. In 243 it joined the Achaean League; in 224 it sided against Aratus and Macedon with Cleomenes III of Sparta, and on the latter's overthrow passed again under Macedon till Flamininus' victory over Macedon in 198–6, when it was declared free like all other Greek cities and became the chief city of the Achaean League. As such it suffered heavily when Rome sought to curtail the League's power, and in 146 it was completely destroyed by Mummius.

7. Refounded in 44 B.C., it became the capital of the province of Achaea and was visited by apostles, emperors (including Nero, who made a vain attempt to cut a canal through the Isthmus), philosophers, Gothic hordes, and earthquakes. Its destruction by one of these last in A.D. 521 is cited by Procopius as evidence that God was abandoning the Roman Empire.

The evidence of ancient sources on Corinth is highly scattered among such authors as Herodotus, Thucydides, Xenophon, Strabo, Diodorus, Plutarch, Tacitus, Pausanias, Himerius, Libanius, Zosimus, Malalas. Chief modern literature: J. G. O'Neill, *Ancient Corinth* (1930); H. G. Payne, *Necrocorinthia* (1931). Excavation reports in *JHS, AJArch., Hesperia.* P. N. U.

CORIOLANUS, GNAEUS MARCIUS, was probably the eponymous hero or god of the Volscian town Corioli, from the capture of which he was reputed to have won his *cognomen*. He is said to have withdrawn from Rome when charged with tyrannical conduct and opposing the distribution of corn to the starving plebs; he then led a Volscian army against Rome, from which he was only turned back by the entreaties of his mother Veturia and his wife Volumnia (491 B.C.); he was then put to death by the Volscians. The sources of Dionysius 8. 62 and other evidence show that the story did not arise from the misinterpretation of any monument (especially the temple of the *Fortuna Muliebris*, reputedly built where Coriolanus' womenfolk had met him). Nor was it a fiction invented either to glorify some patrician family, or in imitation of some incidents in Greek history (although some details may have been added from the stories of Achilles or Themistocles), or, finally, to provide an example of some legal customs and institutions. Rather, the legend reflects the period when Rome suffered severely from famine and Volscian pressure.

Mommsen, *Röm. Forsch.* ii. 113 ff.; W. Schur, *PW*, Suppl. v. 653 ff.; E. T. Salmon, *CQ* 1930.   P. T.

CORIPPUS, FLAVIUS CRESCONIUS, *see* EPIC POETRY, LATIN, para. 3.

CORNELIA (1), mother of the Gracchi, the second daughter of Scipio Africanus, married Ti. Sempronius Gracchus after her father's death, and had twelve children, alternately boys and girls, until Sempronius' death in 154 B.C. She did not remarry, even refusing the hand of Ptolemy VII (Euergetes II, Physcon), but devoted herself to the education, in Greek culture, of her three surviving children, Tiberius, Gaius, and Sempronia, who married Scipio Aemilianus. Hostile tradition held that she supported her sons' revolutionary policy, but in fact she appears to have restrained them, e.g. checking Gaius' attack on Octavius (q.v. 2). The fragments of two letters attempting to dissuade Gaius from his political career, preserved in MSS. of Nepos, are, however, of doubtful authenticity, although Cicero knew letters by her (*Brut.* 58. 211). She outlived her sons, residing in Misenum, still prominent in State circles, her home a centre of culture. Tradition made her the model of Roman matronhood.

Plutarch, *Tiberius* and *Gaius Gracchus*. J. Carcopino, *Autour des Gracques* (1928), 47, 107; on the letters, H. Malcovati, *Athenaeum* 1920, 77; E. von Stern, *Hermes* 1921, 273 n. 1; J. H. Theil, *Mnemos.* 1929, 347.   A. H. McD.

CORNELIA (2), a cultured lady, daughter of Metellus (*cos.* 52 B.C.), in 55 married P. Crassus, the triumvir's son, who died with his father, and in 52 Cn. Pompeius, whom she accompanied after Pharsalus to Egypt, where she saw him murdered. She returned to Italy.

CORNELIUS (1), GAIUS, tribune in 67 B.C., in association with Gabinius introduced several popular reforms, the most important of which laid down that the praetors should abide by their own edicts. A proposal to introduce drastic measures against bribery at elections was considerably watered down by the Senate; Cornelius was also compelled to agree to a compromise when he attacked the right of the Senate to grant private dispensations. In 66 he was charged with *maiestas*, and the case came to court in 65. Cornelius, who was defended by Cicero, was acquitted by a large majority.

See Asconius, *In Cornelianam*. W. McDonald, 'Tribunate of Cornelius', *CQ* xxiii (1929).   J. M. C.

CORNELIUS (2) **NEPOS** (*c.* 99–*c.* 24 B.C.), born in Cisalpine Gaul, moved to Rome, but took no part in politics; he was intimate with Cicero, with whom he exchanged letters, and with Pomponius Atticus after 65.

Catullus dedicated his book to N. in eulogistic verses. Fronto tells us that N. was also a transcriber of books.

WORKS: 1. *De Viris Illustribus*, in at least sixteen books (Charisius, *Gramm.* 1. 141. 13 Keil), comparing Greeks and Romans. The categories of generals, historians, kings, poets, and probably orators, are certain. It was published before the death of Atticus, apparently in 34; before 27 a second edition appeared, including non-Greeks and expanding the *Atticus*. Of this we have *De Excellentibus Ducibus Exterarum Gentium* (see Loeb *Nep.* 357 ff.), and two Lives from *De Historicis Latinis*, besides fragments.

2. *Lost Works*: *Love Poems* (Plin. *Ep.* 5. 3. 1 ff.); *Chronica*, a universal history in three books (Catull. 1); *Exempla*, anecdotes in at least five books (Gell. 6. (7). 18. 11); *Life of Cato* (Nep. *Cato* 3. 5); *Life of Cicero* (Gell. 15. 28. 2); a work on Geography (Plin. *HN* 5. 4).

Nepos was the writer of the first surviving biography under its author's name, and the first biographer to compare Romans with foreigners, probably prompted by Varro's *Imagines*. His defects are hasty and careless composition (perhaps less marked in his first edition) and lack of control of his material. He is mainly eulogistic, with an ethical aim, but also gives information about his hero's environment. As historian his value is slight; he names many sources, but rarely used them at first hand. He follows mainly the 'plain' style (Gell. 6 (7). 14), but with colloquial features and many archaisms, not used for artistic effect, but from indifference. His rhetorical training appears in attempts at adornment, neither uniform nor discriminating.

BIBLIOGRAPHY

LIFE AND WORKS: Introduction to Commentaries and Translations; Leo, *Griech.-Röm. Biogr.* (1901), ch. 10; D. R. Stuart, *Epochs of Greek and Roman Biogr.* (U.S.A. 1928), 121, 193, 216, 238, 251.
TEXTS: O.C.T. (Winstedt); Teubner (Halm, Fleckeisen); O. Wagner (Leipzig, 1922).
COMMENTARIES: Staveren (ed. Bardili² 1820); K. Nipperdey (Berlin, 1849: Nipp.-Witte¹¹, 1913); Browning-Inge (1887).
TRANSLATIONS: with text, J. C. Rolfe (Loeb, 1929); A. M. Guillemin (Budé, 1923).
STYLE AND DICTION: B. Lupus, *Sprachgebrauch des Corn. Nep.* 1876; Introdd. to Nipp.-Witte, and to Translations.   J. C. R.

CORNELIUS (3) **SEVERUS,** Augustan poet. Of his hexameter poem on the Sicilian War of 38–36 B.C., perhaps part of a longer *Res Romanae*, Quintilian says (10. 1. 89) that if he had maintained the level of the first book he would have been second only to Virgil; Seneca (*Suas.* 6. 26) quotes a passage of twenty-five hexameters on Cicero's death. The nature of the 'carmen regale' ascribed to him by his friend Ovid (*Pont.* 4. 16. 9) is unknown. *Cf.* AETNA.   C. J. F.

CORNELIUS (4) **LABEO** (? second half of 3rd c. A.D.) wrote a (lost) history of Romano-Etruscan religion.

CORNELIUS, *see also* BALBUS, CETHEGUS, CHRYSOGONUS, CINNA, COSSUS, DOLABELLA, FUSCUS, GALLUS, LENTULUS, MERULA, PALMA, SCIPIO, SISENNA, SULLA.

CORNIFICIUS (1), QUINTUS, orator and poet, friend of Catullus (38. 1; cf. Ov. *Tr.* 2. 436; Cic. *Fam.* 12. 17–30), wrote a lost epyllion *Glaucus* (Morel, *FPL*). He played a creditable part in defending Illyricum against the Pompeians in 48 B.C., was sent to the East (as governor of Cilicia?) in 46, and appointed governor of Africa Vetus in 44. In the War of Mutina he sided with the Senate, was attacked by T. Sextius (governor of Africa Nova), and defeated and killed near Utica (42 or 41).

Bell. Alex. 42–7; Cicero, *Letters*; Plutarch, *Caesar*, 43 and 51; Appian, *BCiv.* 3. 85, 4. 36, and 53–6; Dio Cassius 48. 17 and 21. Modern literature: F. L. Ganter, *Philol.* liii (1894), 132–46; Drumann-Groebe, *Gesch. Roms* ii. 531–5.   J. W. D. and G. W. R.

CORNIFICIUS (2), LUCIUS, a friend of Octavian, in 43 B.C. accused Brutus of Caesar's murder. In the war against Sex. Pompeius he was admiral; he was surrounded with three legions near Tauromenium, but escaped and joined Agrippa at Tyndaris (36). He was consul in 35, and proconsul of Africa; he celebrated a triumph in 32 and used to ride on an elephant at Rome in commemoration of his successes.

*PIR*², C 1503.   A. M.

CORNIFICIUS, by some regarded as the author of *Rhetorica* (q.v.) *ad Herennium*, cannot be certainly identified among several Cornificii.

CORNU COPIAE, *see* AMALTHEA.

CORNUA, *see* BOOKS, II. 2.

CORNUTUS, LUCIUS ANNAEUS, born *c.* A.D. 20 at or near Leptis, as a freedman of Seneca, or of one of his relatives, assumed the name Annaeus, and became a teacher of philosophy and rhetoric at Rome, *c.* A.D. 50, including Lucan and Persius among his pupils. Persius dedicated to Cornutus his fifth satire, and in 62 bequeathed him a sum of money, which he refused to accept, and his library. In collaboration with Caesius Bassus, Cornutus edited the posthumous poems of his disciple, omitting any passage which might appear to contain allusions to Nero. Probably involved in the conspiracy of Piso, Cornutus was exiled in 66; whether he later returned to Rome and resumed his literary activity is a matter of dispute. Cornutus was equally versed in Greek and Latin literature and wrote on Aristotle's logic (in Greek), and on rhetoric, the poetry of Virgil, etc. (in Latin). His one extant work is the ἐπιδρομὴ τῶν κατὰ τὴν Ἑλληνικὴν θεολογίαν παραδεδομένων, or Summary of the traditions concerning Greek mythology; in this he expounds, mainly following Chrysippus, the principles of Stoic criticism of myths, which he explains allegorically. In the Middle Ages scholia on Persius and Juvenal were wrongly attributed to him: cf. Teuffel, § 299. 2; Schanz–Hosius, § 451.

TEXTS: C. Lang (Teubner). The fragments of Cornutus' minor works collected by R. Reppe, *De L. Annaeo Cornuto* (1906). Modern literature: P. Decharme, *La Critique des traditions religieuses chez les grecs anciens* (1905); *PW* i. 2225.   P. T.

CORONIS, in mythology, daughter of Phlegyas, and mother of Asclepius (qq.v.). While with child by Apollo, she had an intrigue with (or married) Ischys son of Elatus, an Arcadian. Apollo learned this from a crow which brought word to Delphi (Pindar emends the story; he knew it by his own omniscience), and sent Artemis to kill Coronis. But when she was on the funeral pyre, he took the unborn child from her womb and gave him to Chiron to bring up (so Hesiod, fr. 123 Rzach; Pindar, *Pyth.* 3. 24 ff.). The local legend of Epidaurus omits the affair of Ischys and the killing, and says Coronis was also called Aegla (Isyllus, 46 ff.). Apollo turned the crow black for bringing the bad news (Ov. *Met.* 2. 632).

H. J. R.

CORPUS TIBULLIANUM, *see* TIBULLUS.

CORRECTOR, a type of official first mentioned under Trajan, who sent Sex. Quinctilius Maximus to Asia 'ad ordinandum statum liberarum ciuitatum' (Pliny, *Ep.* 8. 24). Pliny's own position in Bithynia was similar, though he was styled 'legatus pro praetore', and replaced the ordinary governor. As a rule the activities of *correctores* (λογισταί, ἐπανορθωταί, διορθωταί) were confined to the supervision of the *liberae civitates*, which in strict law stood outside the jurisdiction of the governor. They were commonest in Achaea, where free cities were numerous; but they are found in other senatorial provinces such as Sicily and Asia, and do not seem to have superseded the

governors. They were generally of praetorian rank, though *consulares* are found among them after A.D. 200. From *c.* 250 the name appears in Italy, foreshadowing its inclusion in the provincial system by Diocletian. In the later Empire it is used of the governors of certain districts of Italy (*CAH* xii. 392 ff.).

A. V. Premerstein, s.v. 'Corrector' in *PW*; J. Marquardt, *Staatsverw.* i² (1881), 227 ff.   G. H. S.

CORSICA (Κύρνος), a rugged island in the Mediterranean off western Italy, consisting mostly of mountains that rise 9,000 feet and fall sheer into the sea on the west. The eastern coast, however, has good harbours. The tradition that Corsica's earliest inhabitants were Iberians mixed with Ligurians is credible but unprovable. About 535 B.C. Carthaginians, helped by Etruscans, expelled the colony which Phocaeans had established at Alalia thirty years earlier. By sending expeditions in 259 and 231, Rome ousted the Carthaginians and organized Corsica with Sardinia as one province (subsequently in Imperial times, exactly when is unknown, Corsica became a separate province). Rome colonized Mariana and Aleria on the east coast but exercised only nominal authority over the wild interior. Corsica produced ship-building timber, bitter-tasting honey, granite, cattle; the Romans did not work its mines. Vandals, Goths, Ravenna Exarchs, and Saracens successively followed the Romans as masters of the island.

Strabo 5. 223 f.; Pliny, *HN* 3. 80 (number of Corsican towns exaggerated); Hdt. 1. 165 f.; Diodorus 5. 13 f.; Theophr. *Hist. Pl.* 5. 8. 1; Seneca's picture of Corsica as inhospitable and unhealthy (*Dial.* 12. 7 f.; *Epigr.* 1 f.) is untrustworthy: Corsica was his place of exile. In general ancient authors seldom mention Corsica. E. Michon, *Mélanges de l'École française de Rome* xi (1891), 106; F. von Duhn, *Italische Gräberkunde* (1924) i. 112; E. Pais, *Storia della Sardegna e della Corsica* (1923).   E. T. S.

CORSTOPITUM, a Roman military post near Corbridge, Northumberland. The name, possibly corrupt, is of uncertain etymology (Corstopitum, *It. Ant.* 464. 3; Corielopocarium, *Rav. Cosm.* 432. 6). Here the road from York to Scotland bridged the Tyne, branching to Carlisle and Tweedmouth. The place began as a Flavian bridge-head fort, with timber buildings and turf rampart (*Arch. Ael.* ser. 4, xv. 255) garrisoned by the *ala Petriana milliaria* (*Eph. Epigr.* vii. 995). It lay empty when Hadrian's Wall was built, but important buildings were erected in A.D. 139 (*Arch. Ael.* ser. 4, xiii. 274) and 140 (*Eph. Epigr.* ix. 1146) under Lollius Urbicus (q.v.) and in 163 (*Eph. Epigr.* ix. 1381–2) under Calpurnius Agricola (q.v.), presumably connected with the re-occupation of Scotland. Severus and his sons built granaries *c.* 205 (*Eph. Epigr.* ix. 1144, 1156), a large unfinished courtyard-building (probably a storehouse), and also legionary forges, all restored or altered under Constantius I (*c.* 297) and Valentinian I (369). Late fourth-century silver plate, gold rings (*CIL* vii. 1300), and a gold coin-hoard attest prolonged use as an administrative centre.

Arch. Ael. ser. 3, iii–xi; ser. 4, xv, xvii.   I. A. R.

CORUNCANIUS (1), TIBERIUS, from Tusculum, consul in 280 B.C., triumphed over the Etruscans and guarded Rome against Pyrrhus' advance. He was the first plebeian Pontifex Maximus (253) and an early jurist: 'primus profiteri coepit' (Pompon. *Dig.* 1. 2. 2. 38), i.e. admitted the public, or at any rate students, to his consultations. Thus jurisprudence became professional instead of a mystery.

H. H. S.

CORUNCANIUS (2), GAIUS and LUCIUS, formed the Roman embassy to Teuta, the Illyrian queen, in 230 B.C., demanding satisfaction for the murder of Italian merchants by Illyrian pirates; this was refused, and they were themselves attacked, L. Coruncanius being killed. This outrage precipitated the First Illyrian War.

Polyb. 2. 8. M. Holleaux, *CAH* vii. 831.   A. H. McD.

CORVINUS, see VALERIUS (15).

CORVUS, see VALERIUS (3).

CORYNETES (Κορυνήτης), see PERIPHETES.

CORYPHAEUS, see COMEDY (GREEK), OLD, para. 9.

CORYTHUS, the name of several obscure mythological persons, including (1) son of Zeus and husband of Electra (q.v.) daughter of Atlas; his sons were Dardanus and Iasius (Iasion), see DARDANUS; Servius on *Aen.* 3. 167. (2) Son of Paris and Oenone (qq.v.). His story is variously told; the least unfamiliar account is in Parthenius, 34, from Hellanicus and Cephalon of Gergis. He came to Troy as an ally; Helen fell in love with him and Paris killed him. Nicander, quoted ibid., calls him son of Paris and Helen. H. J. R.

CŌS, one of the Sporades islands, probably colonized from Epidaurus. In the Peloponnesian War it suffered from both Spartans and Athenians. In 366, after internal strife, the townships (*demoi*) were merged in one capital city, on the north-east coast. The island revolted successfully from Athens in 354, but came under the control of Alexander of Macedon. It subsequently oscillated between Macedon, Syria, and Egypt, to find its greatest glory as a literary centre under the protection of the Ptolemies and as the home of Philetas and Theocritus. In the second century Cos was loyal to the Romans, even before it became a *libera civitas* in the province of Asia. The Emperor Claudius, influenced by his Coan physician Xenophon, conferred *immunitas* on the island. Here in the fifth century B.C. Hippocrates laid the foundations of medical science.

Strabo 14. 657–8. W. R. Paton–E. L. Hicks, *Inscriptions of Cos* (1891); R. Herzog, *Koische Forschungen und Funde* (1899); A. Maiuri, *Nuova Silloge epigrafica di Rodi e Cos* (1925); Herzog, etc., *Kos: I. Asklepieion* (1932); A. N. Modona, *L'Isola di Coo nell' Antichità classica* (1933), with bibliography. W. A. L.

COSCINOMANCY, see DIVINATION, para. 6.

COSCONIUS, QUINTUS (1st c. A.D.), a scholar who wrote on grammar and law. His works are lost.

Cf. Teuffel, § 159. 7; Schanz–Hosius, § 196. 2.

COSSUS, AULUS CORNELIUS, the hero of two alleged wars with Fidenae (437–435 and 428–425 B.C.) of which only the second is probably historical. He won the *spolia opima* (q.v.) by killing Lars Tolumnius of Veii, whose inscribed breastplate he dedicated to Jupiter Feretrius. This inscription was read by the Emperor Augustus, who stated that Cossus performed the feat as consul in 428 (Livy 4. 20). This fact need not be interpreted as an invention of Augustus' designed to block the claim of M. Crassus (q.v. 6) to a triumph. According to other traditions Cossus was military tribune in 437 and *magister equitum* in 426. H. H. S.

COTTA (1), GAIUS AURELIUS, as consul in 75 B.C., carried a law to rescind the measure of Sulla, by which tribunes of the plebs were debarred from proceeding to higher magistracies. His speeches were noted for their neat style and sharp reasoning, but have not survived. He modelled his speaking on M. Antonius (q.v. 1) of the previous generation (Cic. *Brut.* 201–3). It was at his house that Cicero's dialogue *De Natura Deorum* was represented as taking place; and in bk. 3 Cotta is the champion of the Academic philosophy (cf. *De Or.* 3. 145). (The oration imputed to him in Sallust *H.* 2. 47 (Maurenbrecher) is Sallust's own invention.) M. C. and J. W. D.

COTTA (2), MARCUS AURELIUS, brother of (1) above, as consul in 74 B.C. was sent to defend the new province of Bithynia from invasion by Mithridates VI of Pontus. With a small army and improvised fleet he rashly engaged

the king's main forces near Chalcedon, sustaining a severe defeat, and the loss of his fleet in a counter-attack. In 73–70 he helped Lucullus to conquer Pontus, reducing several of the coast towns. His rapacity in plundering the city of Heraclea led to his subsequent conviction for embezzlement (67).

Memnon, chs. 30–59 (*FHG* iii. 541–57). M. C.

COTTA (3), LUCIUS AURELIUS, brother of (1) and (2) above, as praetor in 70 B.C. proposed a law that the juries should be composed of equal numbers of senators, *equites*, and *tribuni aerarii*. In 66 he accused the consuls designate of corruption and became consul for 65 and censor in 64. He supported the proposal for Cicero's return from exile. On the eve of Caesar's murder it was rumoured that he would propose the proclamation of Caesar as king. Caesar's mother, Aurelia, was his kinswoman.

Münzer, *PW* ii. 2485; *CAH* ix. 338, 737. A. M.

COTTIUS, MARCUS JULIUS, son of a native king named Donnus, offered no opposition to Augustus' pacification of the Alpine regions and was recognized as ruler over a number of native tribes with the title of *praefectus civitatium* (*ILS* 94, cf. Pliny, *HN* 3. 138). He erected an arch in honour of Augustus at Segusio (*Susa*) in 7–6 B.C. (*ILS* 94), and improved the road over the Mt. Genèvre (Ammianus 15. 10. 2). The territory, annexed by Nero after the death of his son, was commonly known as the *Alpes Cottiae*. R. S.

COTTUS, see HECATONCHEIRES.

COTYS, COTYT(T)O (Κότυς, Κοτυ(τ)τώ), a Thracian goddess worshipped with orgiastic rites (Aesch. fr. 57 Nauck). Her cult was privately practised in Athens in Eupolis' time, and included some rite of washing or dipping, see the fragments of his *Baptae* in *CAF* i. 273 ff. For her cult in other Greek communities see Schwenn, *PW* xi. 1551. H. J. R.

COVELLA, see JUNO.

CRAGUS, a Lycian god identified with Zeus (Lycophron 542 and schol.), humanized into a son of Tremiles (eponym of the Tremileis or Lycians), after whom Mt. Cragus was named (Steph. Byz. s.v.).

CRANNŌN, a city of Thessaly, commanding a small level area among the low hills which separate the eastern and western plains. The Scopadae, the leading local family, were rivals of the Aleuadae (q.v.), but *c.* 515 B.C. they were involved in a mysterious disaster and lost much of their influence. The smallness of its plain and the proximity of Larissa checked its development. A Pheraean named Deinias became tyrant of Crannon, probably in the fourth century, and with support from the tyrants of Pherae. In the Lamian War Antipater defeated the Greek confederates near Crannon (322). H. D. W.

CRANTOR of Soli in Cilicia (*c.* 335–*c.* 275 B.C.), philosopher of the Old Academy. After he had won fame in his native town he became a pupil of Xenocrates (Diog. Laert. 4. 24). He lived in intimate friendship with Polemon, Crates, and his great pupil Arcesilaus, to whom he left his belongings (D.L. 4. 22; 24; 29).

With his commentary on Plato's *Timaeus* C. opened the long line of commentaries on Plato. His work *On grief* (Περὶ πένθους) was famous as the best ancient *Consolatio*, renowned for its religious and philosophic depth as well as for its style.

F. Kayser, *De C. Academico* (1841, the fragments); Mullach, *FPG* iii. 131–52. E. Zeller, *Plato*, etc., Engl. Transl. (1888), 619 f.; K. Buresch, *Leipz. Stud.* 1887; F. Susemihl, *Gesch. d. gr. Lit. Alex.* i. 118 f.; *PW* xi. 1585. K. O. B.

CRASSUS (1) **MUCIANUS**, PUBLIUS LICINIUS (*cos.* 131 B.C.), married Clodia, sister of App. Claudius, Ti. Gracchus' father-in-law, and was father of Licinia, wife of C. Gracchus. A jurist and Greek scholar, he was a strong supporter of Tiberius Gracchus' land-law, and his successor as *IIIvir*. Though Pontifex Maximus, he insisted on leaving Italy in 131 to command in Asia against Aristonicus, but was killed after an initial setback in the campaign (130). M. H.

CRASSUS (2) **DIVES**, PUBLIUS LICINIUS (*cos.* 97 B.C.), commanded in Spain after his consulship and triumphed (Lusitania) in 93. He served under L. Caesar in the Social War, and was his colleague as censor in 89. Proscribed by the Marians in 87, Crassus committed suicide. M. H.

CRASSUS (3), LUCIUS LICINIUS (*cos.* 95 B.C.), statesman and orator, was the husband of Mucia (daughter of Q. Scaevola 'Augur') and the father of Licinia, who married the younger Marius. In 119 B.C. when only twenty-one, he made his mark by accusing Carbo, the renegade Gracchan, and further advertised his support of the Gracchan party by the foundation of Narbo Martius (*Narbonne*). But his democratic ardour soon cooled; in 113 the Vestal Licinia, his first cousin, was condemned in spite of Crassus' speech in her defence, and in 106 he supported the consul Caepio's judiciary law. In 95 as consul, with his colleague Scaevola 'Pontifex', he carried a law for expelling the Latins from Rome; the motive may have been to prevent the illegal extension of the franchise, but one result was certainly to intensify the agitation which led to the Social War. He also defended the younger Caepio. In 92 he was censor, and quarrelled with his colleague Ahenobarbus. He strongly supported the reforms of the younger Drusus, and died suddenly after making a powerful speech in Drusus' favour. In many respects his career foreshadows that of Cicero, who admired him greatly; and it is probably right to consider Crassus as a moderate, and above all a constitutionalist. As an orator, his only contemporary rival was Antonius. M. H.

CRASSUS (4) **DIVES**, MARCUS LICINIUS, the triumvir (b. *c.* 112 B.C.) and the younger son of Crassus (2), was, as commander of the successful right wing, largely responsible for Sulla's victory at the Colline Gate. His astute speculation in real estate rapidly marked him out as the leader of the business interests in Rome. In 72 B.C., as praetor, he was appointed to take over from the discredited consuls the command against Spartacus (q.v.), whom he defeated just before Pompey arrived from Spain to share his laurels. The two rivals suspended their hostility and joined forces. Together they were elected consuls for 70, when they did much to undo what was left of Sulla's constitution.

Crassus remained bitterly jealous of Pompey, and his aim from 67 onwards was to strengthen his position at Rome against Pompey's return from the East (Sallust, *Cat.* 17. 7). He persuaded the Senate to hush up the First Catilinarian Conspiracy, hoping to use the conspirators for his own purposes. In 65 he instigated an unsuccessful proposal for the annexation of Egypt, and as censor he tried, despite the opposition of his colleague Catulus, to gain fresh support by enfranchising the Transpadane Gauls. He bought over Julius Caesar, who was heavily in debt, and in 63 they sponsored the far-reaching agrarian law of Rullus (q.v.). He supported Catiline at the consular elections of 64, but he cautiously kept aloof from the conspiracy of 63.

Pompey returned late in 62, and through Caesar's agency the two rivals were in 60 brought into alliance as members of the 'First Triumvirate' (Dio 37. 56). During the next four years Crassus kept in the background, but he was to a large extent the moving spirit behind the activities of Clodius; in 56 he was again intriguing for a commission in Egypt. Meanwhile his relations with Pompey became increasingly strained, but at the Conference of Luca Caesar prevented the impending break-up of the Triumvirate. Re-elected consul with Pompey (55), Crassus shared his colleague's credit for a series of constitutional reforms. More important for himself was the big military command for which he had longed; the *Lex Trebonia* awarded him the province of Syria for five years with extraordinary powers.

Crassus raised troops with some difficulty, and left Rome late in 55 for a Parthian campaign. After a preliminary invasion of western Mesopotamia in 54, he crossed the Euphrates again in 53 and headed east across the desert. He was hemmed in near Carrhae by the Parthians, whose elusive bowmen broke the morale of his forces. Retreat became a rout and Crassus met his death through treachery.

Such was the ignominious end of a strangely ineffectual career. Crassus' aim was power. His money bought him influence, his general affability gave him friends (Plut. *Crass.* 3). Yet when the opportunity came he achieved little, because he had no clear-cut programme and no political ideals.

Sources: Fragments of Sallust's *Histories* (ed. B. Maurenbrecher, 1891-3); Plutarch's *Life of Crassus* (based, for the earlier years, on Sallust); Dio Cassius, bks. 37-40; Appian, *BCiv.* bk. 1; scattered references in Cicero's letters and speeches. C. Deknatel, *De Vita M. Crassi* (1901); A. Garzetti, *Athenaeum* 1941-5. For Parthian expedition see: P. Groebe, *Hermes* 1907; K. Regling, *Klio* 1907; W. W. Tarn, *CAH* ix, ch. 14. J. M. C.

CRASSUS (5), PUBLIUS LICINIUS (*c.* 85-53 B.C.), younger son of the triumvir. He accompanied Caesar to Gaul, first as *praefectus equitum* (58), then as *legatus* (57). In the victory over Ariovistus his resolute handling of the reserve was decisive. In 57 he subdued the coastal Gallic tribes and perhaps explored the Cassiterides (Strabo 3. 175-6). In 56 he defeated the Aquitanians. He returned to Rome in 55 and married Cornelia, daughter of Metellus Scipio. He commanded a body of Gallic horse under his father in the Parthian war of 53. His vigorous leadership involved them in heavy losses which he refused to survive.

Münzer, *PW* s.v. 'Licinius (63)'. C. E. S.

CRASSUS (6), MARCUS LICINIUS (*cos.* 30 B.C.), grandson of M. Crassus (4), was at first a partisan of Sex. Pompeius, then an Antonian. The precise date of his desertion to Octavian has not been recorded; the consulate was probably his reward. Appointed proconsul of Macedonia, he conducted highly successful campaigns in 29 and 28 (Dio Cass. 51. 23 ff.). Having killed a king of the Bastarnae with his own hands, he claimed the *spolia opima*, to the annoyance of Octavian, himself jealously monopolizing military glory. The claim was rebutted on the grounds that Crassus had not been fighting under his own auspices; Octavian may have used as an argument the linen corslet in the temple of Jupiter Feretrius, which purported to show that Cornelius Cossus (q.v.) was consul (not merely military tribune) when he earned the *spolia opima*. The incident may have accelerated the regulation of Octavian's constitutional position (as E. Groag argues, *PW* xiii. 283 ff.). Crassus was permitted to hold a triumph (27), after which nothing more is heard of this ambitious (and perhaps dangerous) *nobilis*.

E. Groag, *PW* s.v. 'Licinius (58)'; R. Syme, *Roman Revolution* (1939), see Index. R. S.

CRASSUS (7) **FRUGI LICINIANUS**, GAIUS CALPURNIUS, of a long and illustrious line, was suffect consul under Domitian. Conspiring against Nerva, he was exiled to Tarentum. His plotting against Trajan caused his removal to an island, where, becoming suspect in Hadrian's reign, he was slain by a procurator (perhaps unbidden) while trying to escape.

S.H.A. *Hadr.*; Dio Cassius, bk. 68; *PIR*², C 259. C. H. V. S.

CRASSUS, see also CANIDIUS, NINNIUS, OTACILIUS.

CRATERUS (1) (c. 370?-321 B.C.), Macedonian officer of Alexander the Great. Beginning as commander of a *taxis* (brigade) of Macedonian infantry (at the Granicus), he advanced to be senior *taxiarch* (at Issus and Gaugamela), and, after Parmenion's death, virtually Alexander's second-in-command. When the army was divided he frequently held separate commands, and distinguished himself particularly in Bactria and Sogdiana (329-328), and in India at the Hydaspes battle. In 324 he was delegated to lead home the discharged Macedonian veterans, and to replace Antipater as regent of Macedonia and overseer of Greece, a distinction which illustrates Alexander's confidence in him. He was generally recognized as the best soldier on Alexander's staff, and he would certainly have played a commanding part among the 'Successors', had he not been killed in the very first battle, against Eumenes of Cardia, near the Hellespont.

Berve, *Alexanderreich*, no. 446. G. T. G.

CRATERUS (2) (321–c. 255 B.C.), son of Craterus (1) and Phila, Antipater's daughter, was appointed governor of Corinth and Peloponnesus (c. 285), and later viceroy of Attica and Euboea, by his half-brother, Antigonus II, whom he served loyally. In 271 he tried to assist Aristotimus, the Elean tyrant (Plut. *Mor.* 253 a), and in 266 checked Areus of Sparta at the Isthmus (Paus. 3. 6. 4-6).

The ψηφισμάτων συναγωγή, a collection of Athenian decrees with a scholarly commentary, was probably the work of this Craterus.

F. Jacoby, *PW* s.v. 'Krateros (1)'; W. W. Tarn, *Antigonos Gonatas* (1913); *CAH* vii. F. W. W.

CRATES (1), Athenian comic poet. Aristotle (*Poet.* 5. 1449b5) says he was the first to drop the comedy of personal invective and invent plots of a general character. This would seem to date C. earlier than Cratinus. But that C. was the later is clear from the fact that he appears later on the victors' list (*IG* ii². 2325), that Anon. Περὶ κωμ. deals with Cratinus first, and that Aristophanes (*Eq.* 526 ff.) clearly mentions C. as the younger poet. Eusebius puts his *floruit* as 450 B.C. Suidas and Anon. Περὶ κωμ. attribute seven plays to him, and the former gives six titles: Γείτονες, Ἥρωες, Θηρία, Λάμια (*The Vampire*), Πεδῆται (*The Prisoners*—an odd title; perhaps a mistake for Παιδιαί, *Games*; Poll. 9. 114), Σάμιοι. In the Γείτονες drunkards were first introduced on the comic stage (Ath. 10. 429a). The Θηρία depicted a Golden Age, in which no one ate meat, and slaves were unnecessary, since everything a man needed came to him of its own volition. It had a chorus of animals, and contained an ἀγών between an upholder of the simple life and a lover of luxury. The Σάμιοι was probably political in tone. Too little remains for an estimate of C., but Aristophanes (*Eq.* 537-40) represents him as a neat and finished poet whose literary resources were meagre.

FCG i. 58 ff.; *CAF* i. 130 ff.; Demiańczuk, *Suppl. Com.* 29, 30. M. P.

CRATES (2) (c. 365-285 B.C.), son of Ascondas of Thebes, Cynic philosopher. Having come to Athens as a young man he first attended the lectures of Bryson of the Megaric School, but was soon converted to Cynicism by Diogenes of Sinope and decided to live henceforth in Cynic poverty. He married Hipparchia, sister of Metrocles of Maronea, having converted both brother and sister to Cynicism. In her company he led a wandering life, preaching the gospel of voluntary poverty and independence, consoling people in distress, and reconciling enemies. He became so universally beloved that people wrote on their doors 'welcome to Crates, the good spirit' (Julian, *Or.* 6. 201 b). He wrote a great many poems, mostly by revising the poems of famous poets so

as to give them a Cynic content. His letters were praised for their style, but those which have come down to us are spurious. He is said by Diogenes Laertius (6. 98) to have written tragedies of a very lofty character in which his philosophy was displayed. One fragment expresses cosmopolitan sentiments.

H. Diels, *PPF* 216 ff.; *TGF* 809-10; Diogenes Laertius 6. 85-93; E. Schwartz, *Charakterköpfe* ii. 1-26; D. R. Dudley, *A History of Cynicism* (1938), 42-53; *PW* xi. 1625. K. von F. and A. W. P.-C.

CRATES (3) of Mallos, son of Timocrates, was a contemporary of Demetrius of Scepsis (Strabo 14. 676) and Aristarchus. He visited Rome, probably in 168 B.C., when his lectures, during his recovery after breaking his leg in the Cloaca Maxima, greatly stimulated Roman interest in scholarship (Suet. *Gram.* 2). He was the first head of the library at Pergamum, and wrote, *inter alia*, on Homer, Hesiod, Euripides, Aristophanes, and Aratus, usually with a philosophic and antiquarian bias; on Attic; and on 'anomaly'. See also *Anth. Pal.* 11. 218.

The Pergamenes and the Alexandrians were divided on the rival principles of 'analogy' and 'anomaly' in language. Aristophanes and Aristarchus, of Alexandria, in editing Homer sought the correct form (or meaning) of a word by collecting and comparing its occurrences in the text, a procedure more novel in their age than in ours. Further, they tried to classify words by their types of form (cf. our declensions), in order by reference to the type to decide what was correct in any doubtful or disputed instance. Thus in Homer Aristarchus accented Κάρησος after Κάνωβος, πέφνων after τέμνων, οἰῶν after αἰγῶν; and similarly as to inflexions (see APOLLONIUS (15) DYSCOLUS). Crates, on the contrary, borrowed his linguistic principles from the Stoics. Not only words (see ETYMOLOGY) but literature likewise they thought a μίμησις θείων καὶ ἀνθρωπείων (Diog. Laert. 7. 60), an accurate reflection of truth, and on this basis they carried to ludicrous extremes the allegorical method of interpretation, in order to secure the support of Homer for Stoic doctrines. In such features as inflexion they saw only confusion wrought upon nature's original products by man's irregular innovations and perversions. Cleanthes had named this unruly principle of language ἀνωμαλία, illustrating it without much difficulty from the Greek declensions. This term and doctrine, and the allegorical method, were adopted by Crates and his school, to whom, consequently, the Alexandrian classification of forms (Crates seems to have written chiefly on noun anomalies) seemed futile in practice and wrong in principle.

The Alexandrians did valuable work; yet they had inevitable difficulty in deducing their types and rules from the facts: in such discrepancies, and when they proceeded by 'analogy' to adapt the facts to their rules, as even Aristarchus sometimes did, Pergamene criticism was, so far, justified. But neither did the Stoics (and Pergamenes) themselves follow usage *simpliciter*, but only usage controlled by their theory: cf. Diog. Laert. 7. 59.

The controversy gained importance with the growth of purism (see GLOSSA), and its extension from Greek to Latin. An Alexandrian compromise appears in Aristarchus' pupil, Ptolemy Pindarion, which is later derided by the extreme anomalist Sext. Emp. *Math.* 1. 201: and see Lucian, *Pseudologista*. Reconciliations were attempted by Varro, Caesar, Cicero, and the Elder Pliny, but the problem remained unsettled. 'Quare mihi non inuenuste dici uidetur, aliud esse Latine, aliud grammatice loqui' Quint. *Inst.* 1. 6. P. B. R. F.

CRATEUAS, pharmacologist, at the court of Mithridates the Great (111-64 B.C.), after whom he called a plant 'Mithridatia' (Plin. *HN* 25. 62). C. is the author of a comprehensive and scientific work on pharmacology ('Ριζοτομικόν, schol. Nic. *Ther.* 681) in at least three books ([Gal.] *De virtute centaurea*, 2). Of a more popular character was another book which contained coloured pictures of plants with notes underneath indicating their medical use (Plin. *HN* 25. 8). C.'s works are much used in Sextius Niger and Dioscorides. They exercised a strong influence on all later medicine and pharmacology.

Dioscurides ed. M. Wellmann (1906–14) iii. 139 f. (fragments); M. Wellmann, 'Krateuas', *Abh. Gött. Ges.* 1897; *PW* xi. 1644.
K. O. B.

CRATINUS, always regarded, with Aristophanes and Eupolis, as one of the greatest of Athenian comic poets (Hor. *Sat.* 1. 4. 1; Quint. 10. 1. 66; Platon. *Diff. Com.* 1). His dates are uncertain: born probably c. 484 B.C.; died probably c. 419 (if we may assume that the reference to his death in Ar. *Pax* 700 ff. is a joke). Definitely datable plays are: Χειμαζόμενοι (425; arg. Ar. *Ach.*); Σάτυροι (424; arg. 2 Ar. *Eq.*); and Πυτίνη (423; arg. 5 Ar. *Nub.*). C.'s comedies fall into two not sharply differentiated classes: (A) personal or political satires; (B) mythological burlesques. Of (A) may be cited the Ἀρχίλοχοι (? 448). This play contained a dispute between Archilochus and some cyclic poets (frs. 2 and 6). The Πανόπται ridiculed the Sophists. In the Πυτίνη (written as a practical answer to Aristophanes' imputations (*Eq.* 531–6) of senility) C. satirizes himself as a drunkard. A chorus of friends try to prevent C.'s desertion of his true wife Κωμῳδία in favour of Μέθη and other such mistresses (fr. 183). To effect this they break all C.'s wine-jars (fr. 187), leaving him with but one empty one (fr. 190). C. makes a speech in his own defence (frs. 185–6). Of class (B) we may mention the Ὀδυσσῆς, a burlesque (διασυρμός) of the Odyssey. The chorus consisted perhaps half of Odysseus' companions and half of Cyclopes. The play seems to have contained a novelty (νεοχμὸν ἄθυρμα; fr. 145), viz. the arrival in the orchestra of Odysseus and his company in a ship (cf. Lohengrin's swan). The Πλοῦτοι was a skit on the Golden Age. The Θρᾷσσαι (prob. 443, as it contains a reference (fr. 71) to Pericles' escape from ostracism (444)) was an attack on the Thracian goddess Bendis, whose orgiastic rites had been introduced into Athens. The Σερίφιοι burlesqued the Perseus myth. The Νέμεσις contained both elements, for, though a burlesque on the story of the egg which produced Helen—Nemesis, not Leda, is said to have laid it (fr. 108)—yet it seems that Pericles was satirized under the character of Zeus (fr. 111) and Aspasia under that of Helen. Thanks to a comparatively recently found papyrus (*POxy.* iv. 69 ff. (no. 663)), which gives us the hypothesis of the play, we know more about the Διονυσαλέξανδρος (430). It had a chorus of Satyrs. Dionysus (not Paris) gives the golden apple to Aphrodite, who, as a reward, enables him to elope with Helen to Troy. On the arrival of the Greek fleet Dionysus hides Helen and changes himself into a ram (fr. 43). Paris discovers them, keeps Helen for himself, and hands over Dionysus to the Greeks. In this play, as the hypothesis says, Pericles is satirized in the guise of one of the characters (obviously Dionysus) for having brought war on the Athenians.

C.'s style is vigorous and direct. Aristophanes (*Eq.* 526–30) likens him to an impetuous torrent that sweeps all before it. The Anon. Περὶ κωμ. (6) detects an Aeschylean quality in him, and Platonius (*Diff. Com.* 2. 14) compares him to Archilochus and calls him αὐστηρὸς ταῖς λοιδορίαις, but criticizes his faulty construction (οὐκ ἀκολούθως πληροῖ τὰ δράματα). The Alexandrian scholar Callistratus edited Cratinus with notes (at any rate the Θρᾷτται (Ath. 11. 495a)); Galen (*Libr. Propr.* 17) wrote two books on C.'s πολιτικὰ ὀνόματα, and Symmachus also seems to have produced an edition of the poet (Hdn. 2. 495; cf. schol. Ar. *Vesp.* 151).

FCG i. 43 ff.; *CAF* i. 11 ff.; Demiańczuk, *Suppl. Com.* 30 ff.
M. P.

CRATIPPUS OF ATHENS, author of a continuation of Thucydides' history to Conon's restoration of Athenian naval power, at least to 394 B.C., was, according to Dionysius of Halicarnassus (*Thuc.* 16), contemporary with Thucydides, but appears rather to be a late Hellenistic historian, claiming antiquity for the sake of authority.

FGrH ii A, p. 13; c, p. 2; E. Schwartz, *Hermes* 1909, 496.
A. H. McD.

CRATYLUS, a younger contemporary of Socrates. He pressed the doctrine of Heraclitus to an extreme point, denying to things even the slightest fixity of nature. According to Aristotle he was Plato's first master in philosophy, and Plato drew the conclusion that since fixity does not exist in the sensible world there must be a non-sensible world to account for the possibility of knowledge. Plato in his *Cratylus* makes Cratylus maintain that falsehood is impossible and that all words in all languages are naturally appropriate to the meanings in which they are used, and exhibits him as a glib and unscientific etymologist.

Testimonia in Diels, *Vorsokr.*⁵ ii. 69–70; *PW* xi. 1660. W. D. R.

CREMATION, see DEAD, DISPOSAL OF.

CREMONA, a Latin colony, founded in 218 B.C. as a bulwark against Insubres and Boii on the north bank of the Po in north Italy (Polyb. 3. 40; Tac. *Hist.* 3. 34). Cremona staunchly supported Rome against Hannibal, although thereby it suffered so severely that in 190 it required additional colonists (Livy 21. 56; 27. 10; 37. 46). Its territory was confiscated for a colony of veterans c. 41 B.C. (Verg. *Ecl.* 9. 28). However, it continued prosperous until its destruction by Vespasian's troops in A.D. 69 (Tac. *Hist.* 3. 33 f.). Thereafter, although an important road centre, Cremona did not really revive until the ninth century. E. T. S.

CREMUTIUS CORDUS, AULUS, the historian, writing under Augustus (Suet. *Tib.* 61. 3) and Tiberius, treated the period from the Civil Wars to at least 18 B.C. (Suet. *Aug.* 35. 2). He refused to glorify Augustus, and celebrated Cicero, Brutus, and Cassius, 'the last Roman'. Prosecuted for treason at the instigation of Sejanus (Tac. *Ann.* 4. 34–5), he committed suicide (A.D. 25). His work was burnt, but copies, preserved by his daughter, were republished under Gaius (Dio 57. 24. 4). The Elder Pliny and Seneca used his work.

H. Peter, *HRRel.* ii (1906), pp. cxiii and 87; G. M. Columba, 'Il processo di Crem. Cordo', *Atene e Roma* 1901. A. H. McD.

CREON (Κρέων), a stopgap name ('prince', 'ruler') given to several subsidiary figures, as (1) a king of Corinth. Medea and Jason (qq.v.) visited him, and Medea killed him by magic and fled, leaving her children behind (Creophylus ap. schol. Eur. *Med.* 264); the children were killed by the Corinthians. Euripides himself makes her kill Creon's daughter, Jason's betrothed, with a poisoned costume which catches fire when worn, Creon being killed in trying to save her (*Med.* 1136 ff.), and murder her own children (ibid. 1273 ff.). (2) An early king of Thebes, sometimes confused with (3). He purified Amphitryon (q.v.) from blood-guilt on his arrival in Thebes, helped him in his campaign against the Teleboans, and afterwards married his daughter Megara to Heracles (Apollod. 2. 57. 70). (3) Brother of Iocasta, see OEDIPUS. He offered her hand and the kingdom to anyone who would rid Thebes of the Sphinx (Eur. *Phoen.* 45 ff.). After Oedipus' fall and again after the death of Eteocles he became king, or regent, of Thebes, see ANTIGONE (1). During the attack by the Seven he lost his son Menoeceus (q.v.). According to the Attic account, Theseus was persuaded to intervene and compel him to grant burial to the bodies of the Seven (Eur. *Supp.*, passim). In Statius (*Theb.* 12. 773 ff.) Theseus kills Creon in the resulting battle. (4) The oldest occurrence of the name is *Il.* 9. 84, where he is father of Lycomedes, commander of part of the Greek outpost; otherwise unknown.

H. J. R.

CREPIDATA, see FABULA.

CRESCONIUS CORIPPUS, FLAVIUS, see EPIC POETRY, LATIN, para. 3.

CRESILAS (later 5th c.), Greek sculptor, famous for a statue of Pericles, of which the head survives in poor Roman copies in the British Museum and the Vatican gallery. It is uncertain whether the portrait of Pericles was a complete statue or only a herm. Three bases of statues by him, bearing his signature, were found on the Acropolis at Athens, and one at Hermione. One of the bases on the Acropolis states that it is a statue of Hermolycus son of Diitrephes. A second is the base of the portrait of Pericles. He is also recorded to have made a statue of a wounded Amazon. A Roman copy of a wounded Amazon in the Capitoline Museum at Rome is thought to be a version of this work. It may also be identical with the statue of an Amazon which Cresilas contributed in a competition, in which Phidias took the first place and Cresilas the third.

S. C.

CRESPHONTES, see HERACLIDAE.

CRETE. I. PREHISTORIC. The earliest population yet known in Crete is that of the Neolithic Age, which seems to have lasted long. This people probably reached Crete from south-west Asia Minor. They dwelt first in caves and some distance from the coast, and spread thinly about east and central Crete. By the end of the age (3100–2800 B.C.) they had begun to live in small two-roomed huts grouped in villages. With the Early Bronze Age the population had increased, reinforced perhaps by a fresh wave from Asia Minor. Towns were built, especially on the east coast, houses were larger, and metals were used—gold, silver, copper, lead. Burial took place in large ossuaries. Settlement in central Crete extended slightly westward, but not till the last phase of the Late Bronze Age (1400–1150) does there seem to have been any habitation in West Crete. In south Crete a strong Egyptian influence suggests that at the end of the Second Dynasty refugees fled across the sea to Crete. North Crete was in touch with the Archipelago. In the Middle Bronze Age (*c.* 2200–1600) population increased in the centre and south, but declined in the east. Towns developed and the first palaces arose. Building improved and ashlar work began. Copper developed into bronze, the potter's wheel was introduced, and writing evolved from a pictographic to a linear script. Cretan culture in this age is more uniform, and the island was prosperous. Manufactures and arts flourished, and by 1600 carving and fresco painting were freely practised. There was overseas trade with the Archipelago, Egypt, and the Levant. This prosperity continued through the first two phases of the Late Bronze age (1600–1400). Palaces and houses grew larger, were better equipped and even luxurious. Metal-work improved, and carving, writing, and fresco painting were commonly practised. Overseas commerce was now extended to the mainland of Greece. The road system and the tablets and store chambers of the palaces suggest a well-organized administration. About 1400 the palaces were destroyed and the power of Crete collapsed. The large centres of population suffered and small towns took their place, but there was no break in civilization, and inhabitation began in west Crete. The end of the old system may have been due to an earthquake, or to some political upheaval perhaps caused

by Greek raids from the mainland. *See also* CNOSSOS; MINOS; PHAESTUS.

J. D. S. Pendlebury, *The Archaeology of Crete* (1939).

A. J. B. W.

II. GREEK AND ROMAN. In historical times Crete was predominantly Dorian, having been colonized by Dorians probably from Peloponnesus. These divided themselves into city-states: Homer speaks of a hundred cities. The names of over forty are known, of which the most powerful were the rivals Cnossos and Gortyn, and Cydonia (colonized from Aegina). Apart from the absence of kings, the Cretan type of constitution and society resembled the Spartan, which may have been derivative. The chief magistrates were called *kosmoi*. The history of Crete is largely that of the independent cities. Disputes between them, especially about territory, led so often to war that a contract for arbitration (κοινοδίκιον) was framed for the cities of the Cretan league (κοινὸν τῶν Κρηταιέων) and supplemented by arbitration treaties (σύμβολα).

Crete was geographically important as a station on the trade-routes from the Sporades and Cyprus to Egypt. But the island lay outside the main currents of Greek history; she refused to aid the defence against Persia in the fifth century. Cretan mercenaries, however, often took part in the wars of Hellas. From the middle of the third century her foreign relations centred on the new and unstable league and the intrigues of Macedon. In 216 the cities accepted Philip V as protector, but strife soon returned. At the end of this century Crete was reputed a home of pirates second only to Cilicia. These activities were encouraged by Philip, who realized his hope of thereby injuring Rhodes (155). The pirates supported Mithridates VI of Pontus against Rome, and when M. Antonius intervened to chastise them he was beaten off Cydonia (74); but Q. Metellus with three legions crushed the islanders and destroyed Cnossos (68/7). Crete became a Roman province, and was united with Cyrene at least from the time of Augustus. The old league was adapted as a *concilium provinciae*. In the early Empire Roman traders were numerous at Gortyn, where an imperial mint was established. *See also* ARCHERS.

Hom. *Od.* 19. 172 ff.; Strabo 10. 474–84; Arist. *Pol.* 2. 10; Polyb. 6. 45–7. Bursian ii. 529 ff. Mijnsbrugge, *The Cretan Koinon* (New York, 1931); Karo and Bürchner, *PW* s.v. 'Kreta'.

W. A. L.

CREUSA (Κρέουσα), feminine of Creon (q.v.). The best-known 'princesses' who bear this quasi-name are: (1) daughter of Erechtheus king of Athens. She was violated by Apollo and bore a son whom she exposed; Hermes brought him to Delphi, and thence after growing to young manhood he was brought back to Athens by Creusa's husband Xuthus, who supposed him his own son and called him Ion (q.v. 1). He became the ancestor of the Ionians (Eur. *Ion*). (2) Wife of Aeneas and mother of Ascanius; she died in trying to escape from Troy and her ghost warned Aeneas of his future adventures (*Aen.* 2. 651 ff.).

H. J. R.

CRETIC SEA, see AEGEAN SEA.

CRINAGORAS (b. *c.* 70 B.C.), elegiac poet, of Mytilene, son of Callippus, took part in embassy to Caesar at Rome in 45 B.C., and to Augustus in 26–25 B.C. In Rome he was the friend of Octavia, and there wrote his epigrams nos. 29, 11, and 41. No. 29 is concerned with the marriage of Octavia's stepdaughter to Juba, no. 19 with Tiberius, no. 31 with Drusus. Ep. 24 has been connected with the disaster of Varus. He is more interesting for his connexions with others than for his own sake, since his work is usually rhetorical and undistinguished.

Text: M. Rubensohn, *Crinagorae Mytilenaei Epigrammata* (1888). Criticism: J. S. Phillimore, *Dublin Review* 1906; E. Norden, 'Das Germanenepigramm des Krinagoras', in *Sitz. Berl. Akad.* 1917, 668–79; C. Cichorius, *Röm. Stud.* viii (1922), 4ff. C. M. B.

CRISA, the name applied to a site on a spur close to the modern Chryso, on the road from the coast to Delphi. The place was occupied as a refuge-settlement after the destruction of Cirrha (q.v.) in the First Sacred War (*see* SACRED WARS).

CRISPUS, *see* VIBIUS (3).

CRITIAS (*c.* 460–403 B.C.), one of the Thirty Tyrants at Athens, of an aristocratic family, to which Plato's mother (his first cousin) also belonged. He was an early associate of Socrates, and of the sophists, and was himself active as a writer (*see below*). He was implicated in the mutilation of the Hermae, but released on the evidence of Andocides. He seems to have played but a small part in the Revolution of the Four Hundred (q.v.), perhaps from hostility to Phrynichus. After their overthrow he proposed the recall of Alcibiades and the denunciation of the dead Phrynichus as a traitor; on the restoration of the full democracy he was exiled. He retired to Thessaly, where (according to Xenophon) he intrigued with the *penestae* (the serfs) against their masters. On the surrender of Athens in 404 he returned and was made one of the Thirty (q.v.). He soon proved himself the most unscrupulous and violent and vicious of them all, at least according to the democrats and rival oligarchs; he caused the death of his colleague Theramenes. He was killed fighting against Thrasybulus (q.v.), spring 403. His reputation did not recover after his death; but Plato, much as he disliked the excesses of the Thirty, honoured his memory in his Dialogues.

Critias wrote elegiac poems and tragedies. In later days it was uncertain whether certain plays were the work of Euripides or of Critias (*Vit. Eur.*). A long fragment of the *Sisyphus* gives a rationalistic account of the belief in the gods, and the *Pirithous*, which is described by Ioannes Diaconus *In Hermogenem*, and of which some fragments are known from papyri, is probably his work (*TGF* 770–5, Powell and Barber, *New Chapters in Gk. Lit.* iii. 148 ff.). A. W. G. and A. W. P.-C.

CRITICISM, LITERARY, IN ANTIQUITY, *see* LITERARY CRITICISM.

CRITIUS (fl. *c.* 480–470 B.C.), Greek sculptor who invariably worked together with another named Nesiotes. Five statue bases bearing their combined signatures have been found on the Acropolis at Athens. They are most famous for their group of the Tyrannicides, to replace that by Antenor which had been taken by Xerxes to Persia. It stood in the Agora at Athens, and a part of its base with inscription has recently been found there. Our knowledge of that group is derived from a Roman copy, now in Naples, and from copies of the head of Harmodius in New York, and of Aristogiton in the Vatican and at Madrid. Critius was probably an Athenian; his style is strong and clear-cut, deeply influenced by a Peloponnesian tradition. An original of his period in the Acropolis Museum is attributed by some to him. S. C.

CRITO (Κρίτων) (1), a contemporary and devoted friend of Socrates, referred to in Plato's *Apology, Phaedo,* and *Euthydemus*. In the *Crito* he plans for Socrates to escape from prison. Seventeen (lost) dialogues ascribed to him by Diogenes Laertius are of doubtful authenticity.

PW xi. 1932.

CRITO (Κρίτων) (2), one of the latest poets of the New Comedy; he won second prize with Ἐφέσιοι in 183 B.C. and with Αἰτωλός in 167. From Φιλοπράγμων, *The Busybody*, eight lines are preserved, in which Criton calls the Delians παράσιτοι τοῦ θεοῦ.

FCG iv. 537 ff.; CAF iii. 354 f.

CRITO (Κρίτων) (3), a Neo-Pythagorean, probably of the first century B.C. or the first century A.D., who produced a work claiming to be a product of the early

Pythagorean school—Κρίτωνος ἤτοι Δαμίππου Πυθαγορείου περὶ φρονήσεως καὶ εὐτυχίας. Three frs. are quoted by Stobaeus.

PW xi. 1933.

CRITO (Κρίτων) (4), physician at Trajan's court *c.* A.D. 100 (his full name was T. Statilius Crito). We have (in Galen) considerable frs. of his works Κοσμητικά and Περὶ τῆς τῶν φαρμάκων συνθέσεως.

PW xi. 1935.

CRITOLAUS (early 2nd c. B.C.) of Phaselis in Lycia (Plut. *De exil.* 14. 605 b), Peripatetic. As president of the school he perhaps succeeded Ariston of Ceos (see Zeller 479, n. 1). He was a member of the famous embassy of philosophers to Rome in 156–155, and lectured there (Gell. 6. 14. 10). He died in his eighty-third year (Lucian, *Macr.* 20).

The activities of the post-Aristotelian school had been scholarly rather than philosophical. Critolaus reintroduced into the Peripatos metaphysical speculation. Thus he brought the school into closer contact with important doctrines of Aristotle (Antiochus ap. Cic. *Fin.* 5. 14). He defended the Aristotelian theory of the world's eternity ably against the Stoa (Philo, *De aetern. mundi* 11 f.). Cicero quotes a fine passage on the value of the soul (*Tusc.* 5. 51). His ethics, as well as his psychology, is probably not free from Stoic influence. He carried on a controversy against popular rhetoric.

Susemihl, *Gesch. gr. Lit. Alex.* i. 153; Zeller, *Aristotle,* etc., Engl. Transl., ii. 479; R. Harder, *Ocellus Lucanus* (1925), 151 f.; W. Theiler, *Gnomon* 1925, 151 f.; 1926, 150 f.; 590 f.; *PW* xi. 1930. K. O. B.

CROESUS, last king of Lydia (*c.* 560–546 B.C.), son of Alyattes. He secured the throne after a struggle with a half-Greek half-brother, and completed the subjugation of the Greek cities on the Asia Minor coast. His subsequent relations with the Greeks were not unfriendly; he contributed to the rebuilding of the Artemisium at Ephesus and made offerings to Greek shrines, especially Delphi; anecdotes attest his friendliness to Greek visitors and his proverbial wealth (cf. the famous Κροίσειοι στατῆρες). The rise of Persia turned Croesus to seek support in Greece and Egypt, but Cyrus anticipated him: Sardis was captured and Croesus overthrown. His subsequent fate soon became the theme of legend: he is cast or casts himself on a pyre, but is miraculously saved by Apollo and translated to the land of the Hyperboreans or becomes the friend and counsellor of Cyrus.

Herodotus, bk. 1; Nic. Dam. frs. 65, 68; Pindar, *Pyth.* 1. 94; Bacchylides 3. *British Museum Cat. Sculpture* (1928) I. i. 38; Louvre, *Vases antiques gr.* 197; G. Radet, *La Lydie* (1893), 206–59. P. N. U.

CROMMYON (Κρομμυών), **SOW OF,** *see* PHAEA.

CRONUS, *see* KRONOS.

CROTON (Κρότων), nowadays *Cotrone*. Originally a Messapic settlement (J. Whatmough, *Prae-Italic Dialects* ii. 258), Croton became an Achaean colony *c.* 710 B.C. Its situation, near the celebrated temple of Hera Lacinia in the 'toe' of Italy on an indifferent but important harbour, was bracing (Strabo 6. 261 f.; Polyb. 10. 1). Croton became a flourishing city twelve miles in circumference; it founded some colonies (Terina, Caulonia) and dominated others (Lametium, Scylletium). Famous for its doctors, athletes (including Milon, q.v.), Heracles cult, and especially for its Pythagorean brotherhood (between *c.* 530 and 455), Croton reached its apogee after destroying Sybaris (510). It even sent a ship to the battle of Salamis (Hdt. 8. 47). Shortly thereafter, however, its defeat by Locri and Rhegium presaged its decline. Although still populous when captured by Dionysius (379), internal, Lucanian, Bruttian, Pyrrhic, and Hannibalic wars ultimately ruined Croton. A Roman colony (194

B.C.) failed to revive it (Diod. 14. 103 f.; 19. 3, etc.; Livy 24. 3; 34. 45).

See the bibliography s.v. MAGNA GRAECIA and add D. Randall-MacIver, *Greek Cities of Italy and Sicily* (1931); P. Larizza, *Crotone nella Magna Grecia* (1934); J. Bérard, *Bibliogr. topogr.* (1941), 48.
                   E. T. S.

CRUS, *see* LENTULUS (7).

CRYPTEIA, *see* KRYPTEIA.

CTEATUS, *see* MOLIONES.

CTESIAS (late 5th c. B.C.) of Cnidos, Greek doctor at the Persian court who assisted Artaxerxes at the battle of Cunaxa, and was sent as envoy to Evagoras and Conon, 398 B.C. Author of a history of Persia (Περσικά) in twenty-three books, written in Ionic; also of the first separate work on India ('Ινδικά). See J. Gilmore, *Fragments of the Persika of Ctesias* (1888).   G. L. B.

CTESIPHON, on the river Tigris, *c.* sixty miles above Babylon. Founded as a Parthian military camp opposite the Hellenistic Seleuceia (q.v.), it became the winter residence of the Arsacids. After the destruction of Seleuceia (A.D. 165) it was the chief city in Babylonia. Artaxerxes made it the capital of the new Sassanian Empire, and his successors built palaces and added new suburbs. In 636 the 'seven cities' of Ctesiphon were taken by the Arabs. Part of the fortifications still stand, and the impressive ruins of a Sassanid palace.

M. Streck, 'Seleucia und Ktesiphon', *Alte Orient* xvi. 3/4 (1917); O. Reuther, *Antiquity* 1929, 434 ff.   M. S. D.

CUICUL (modern *Djemila*), a mountain-town lying between Cirta and Sitifis. Originally a *castellum*, dependent on Cirta, it became a colony under Nerva. In the second century A.D. it received an influx of romanized Berbers; agricultural prosperity developed and many public buildings were erected by generous citizens. Under the Severi Cuicul doubled its size; its best-known citizen was Claudius Proculus, who became governor of Numidia. Its extensive ruins include a Christian basilica, baths, theatre, baptistery, Caracalla's arch, and the temple of the *gens Septimia*.

A. Ballu, 'Ruines de Djemila', *Rev. Africaine*, 1921; Y. Allias, *Djemila* (1938).   W. N. W.

CULLEO, QUINTUS TERENTIUS, a senator, captured by the Carthaginians and released by Scipio in 201 B.C.; to show his gratitude he marched in Scipio's triumphal procession in a freedman's cap. As *tribunus plebis* (189) he carried a measure to enrol sons of freedmen in the rustic tribes. As praetor (187) he examined the evidence of unlawful registration by Latins on the citizen roll. The statement (Antias, apud Livy) that he was chairman of a special *quaestio* set up to try L. Scipio belongs to a false account of the procedure then adopted. H. H. S.

CULT, DOMESTIC, *see* WORSHIP (HOUSEHOLD).

CULTS, ARCADIAN, MACEDONIAN, etc., *see* ARCADIAN, MACEDONIAN, etc.

CULTURE-BRINGERS. All folk-lore (see Stith Thompson, A 500 ff.) contains stories of persons, divine or human, who introduced mankind in primitive days to the arts, religious observances, etc. Greek tradition is no exception. Prometheus (q.v.) is the great culture-hero of Attic belief (Aesch. *PV* 442 ff.); Cadmus (q.v.) introduces letters; Triptolemus, by direction of Demeter (q.v.), teaches men to plant corn. Similar Latin stories are late and artificial; for examples, *see* JANUS, SATURNUS. Gods figure occasionally in this capacity (Athena invents horsemanship, Dionysus introduces the vine, etc.). Lists of such inventors are late, but common, see Kremmer, *De catalogis heurematum* (Diss. Leipzig, 1890). H. J. R.

CUMAE, Italy's earliest Greek colony, founded on the coast near Naples by Chalcis, traditionally in 1050, actually *c.* 750 B.C., in fertile territory inhabited in pre-Hellenic times but now deserted. After its foundation Greek civilization spread farther in Italy (A. Blakeway, *JRS* 1935, 135). Cumae soon acquired wealth and power. From 700 to 500 it exercised wide dominion and colonized Neapolis, Dicaearchia (= Puteoli), Abella, distant Zancle (= Messana), and possibly Nola. Cumae is inseparably associated with the Sibyl whose oracular cavern still exists (*Aen.* 6); but its first real personality is Aristodemus (q.v. 3), who repulsed the Etruscans. In 474 Cumae with Syracusan aid crushed Etruscan power in Campania, but was itself conquered by Sabelli (q.v.) *c.* 425 and became an Oscan city (Diod. 11. 51; 12. 76). Subsequently coming under Roman control it obtained *civitas sine suffragio* in 338 and *praefecti Capuam Cumas* in 318. It staunchly supported Rome in the Hannibalic and Social Wars, discarded Oscan for Latin in 180, and ultimately obtained full citizenship. But, as Puteoli rose, Cumae, despite repeated colonizations and the erection of villas nearby, declined. However, its inaccessible citadel was still strategically important in Belisarius' time.

R. S. Conway, *Italic Dialects* i (1897), 85; A. Sambon, *Monnaies antiques de l'Italie* i (1903), 139, 283; E. Gabrici, *Monumenti Antichi* xxii (1913–14); D. Randall-MacIver, *Greek Cities of Italy and Sicily* (1931), 1; J. Van Ooteghem, *Étud. Classiques* 1936, 606; A. Maiuri, *Altertümer der phlegräischen Felder* (1938); J. Bérard, *Bibliogr. topogr.* (1941), 50. See too the bibliography s.v. MAGNA GRAECIA.   E. T. S.

CUNAXA, northward from Babylon, was the scene of the battle between Cyrus (q.v. 2) the younger and Artaxerxes II (401 B.C.). Artaxerxes' scratch army—he had only two satraps with him besides Tissaphernes—consisted of perhaps 30,000 infantry (Xenophon's estimate of 900,000 is ridiculous), but at least 6,000 horse. Cyrus, who had brought only 2,600 horse, had failed before he started. Tissaphernes, with Artaxerxes, was in the centre with a strong cavalry force; Cyrus put his 10,400 Greek hoplites under Clearchus on his right instead of opposite Tissaphernes, and took the centre himself with only 600 horse; Ariaeus with Cyrus' Asiatic troops was on the left. Clearchus routed the infantry of Artaxerxes' left, but neglected to turn against his centre; while he uselessly pursued the beaten infantry, Tissaphernes threw in his cavalry, killed Cyrus, outflanked Ariaeus who fled, and gained a decisive victory.

W. W. Tarn, *CAH* vi, p. 7.   W. W. T.

CUNICULARIA, *see* BALEARES INSULAE.

CUNOBELLINUS, son of Tasciovanus, king of the Catuvellauni at Verulamium. He may have conquered the Trinovantes of Essex before his father's death, and succeeded (*post* 12 B.C.) to a kingdom which ultimately embraced south-east Britain, so that he was styled 'rex Britanniarum' (Suetonius, *Calig.* 44. 2). His capital and mint at Camulodunum (Lexden Heath, near the later colony) became a notable centre of Roman imports, and his coins bear Latin inscriptions and emblems of mythology. His relations with Rome were friendly, but *c.* A.D. 40 a quarrel with his son Amminius, who fled to Rome, prompted Caligula's abortive demonstration. He died before 43; and a mound at Lexden Heath may be his grave (*Archaeologia* lxxvi. 241–54). He was prominent in medieval fable, whence Shakespeare derived the material for 'Cymbeline'.

Sir J. Evans, *Coins of the Ancient Britons*, 284–348; T. Rice Holmes, *Ancient Britain*, 361–70; C. Hawkes and G. C. Dunning, *Archaeological Journal* lxxxvii. 257–62, 311–14; Brooke, *Antiquity* vii. 285–8.   C. E. S.

CUPID AND PSYCHE, *see* APULEIUS.

CUPIDO AMANS, a short anonymous Latin poem, 3rd c. A.D., in 16 hexameters.

Anth. Lat. (Riese) 240. J. W. and A. M. Duff, *Minor Latin Poets* (Loeb, 1934).

CURA, CURATOR, *see* GUARDIANSHIP.

CURATOR, a term applied to a great variety of persons, other than magistrates, to whom specific duties were allotted. Under the Republic *curatores viarum* are frequently mentioned (*ILS* 5800, 5892; Cic. *Att.* 1. 1. 2); and in the Principate the disappearance of the censorship as an ordinary magistracy led to the creation of various *curae*, of which the most important were the *cura viarum* (*see* ROADS), the *cura aquarum*, the *cura aedium sacrarum locorumque publicorum*, and the *cura riparum et alvei Tiberis*. These were entrusted to boards of senators holding office for indefinite periods. The term was also applied in municipal towns to men performing special duties, e.g. *curator kalendarii*, *curator muneris gladiatorii*, and sometimes to officers of *collegia* (*see* CLUBS, ROMAN).

A special use of the term was to designate the imperial officials who were appointed from the time of Nerva and Trajan to supervise the finances of towns in Italy and the provinces. Their appearance marks the beginning of the interference of the central government in the affairs of municipalities, which was later to deprive them of all independence. The *curatores* (*logistae*) of particular cities were distinct from the *correctores* (q.v.), who controlled larger areas. In the first instance they were merely advisers whose consent was required for any unusual expenditure, and there is no evidence that their services were unwelcome (*ILS* 5918a). By the third century they practically superseded the ordinary magistrates, and the *curator* became a permanent mayor. *Curatores* might belong to the senatorial or to the equestrian order. The great majority exercised their authority in the cities of Italy, but they are found in provincial cities before the end of the second century A.D.

ILS iii. 1. 358; iii. 2. 685; E. Kornemann, s.v. 'Curator' in *PW*; W. Liebenam, *Philol.* lvi. 290 ff.; J. Marquardt, *Staatsverw.* i² (1881), 162 ff.; F. F. Abbott and A. C. Johnson, *Municipal Administration* (1926), 90 ff.; C. Lucas, 'Notes on the Curatores Rei-Publicae of Roman Africa', *JRS* 1940.   G. H. S.

CURETES, (1) a people hostile to the Calydonians (*Il.* 9. 529). (2) Semi-divine beings (Hesiod. fr. 198 Rzach, calls them θεοί) inhabiting Crete, who protected the infant Zeus by dancing about him and clattering their weapons so that his cries were not heard (Callim. *Jov.* 52 ff., and many authors). The origin of the legend is plausibly derived from the Cretan rite (see J. Harrison, *Themis²* 1 ff.; Nilsson, *Minoan-Mycenaean Religion*, 475 ff.) of a ceremonial (not provably a dance) in honour of Zeus Kouros. They are often confused with the Corybantes attendant on Rhea (see Rose, *Handbook of Greek Mythology*, 171). See further H. Jeanmaire, *Couroi et Courètes* (1939), and for the religious confraternity bearing this name at Ephesus in and after the time of Strabo, Ch. Picard, *Éphèse et Claros* (1922), 279 ff., etc.   H. J. R.

CURIA (1) was the most ancient division of the Roman People, already existing under the Kings. The *curiae* were thirty in number (ten for each Romulean tribe). Some bore local names (Foriensis, Veliensis), others personal ones (Titia). They were probably composed of families, who were, originally at least, neighbours. Probably both patricians and plebeians were always included (Dionysius 4. 12. 20). The head of the *curia* was the *curio*; the head of the college of the *curiones* was a *curio maximus*, who until 210 B.C. was always a patrician. The *curiae* were probably the basis of the oldest military organization and certainly the elements of the oldest Roman assembly (*see* COMITIA). Each *curia* had its own place of worship called after the *curia*.

Curia was also the name given to the assembly-places of many other corporations, and especially of the Senate-house (see below). As a voting section of the citizens the *curia* is attested in Latium (Lanuvium) and in many Italian and provincial *municipia* and *coloniae*, both of Latin and Roman status. It was especially common in Africa. During the Empire *curia* was also the usual name for the municipal Senates, to which the elections of the magistrates were transferred from the people. It was largely constituted from ex-magistrates chosen for life (at least in the West) and in the Late Empire turned into a hereditary caste, called the *curiales*, whose lives and property were under the control of the State as security for the collection of taxes. *See also* CURIALIS, DECURIONES.

G. Humbert, Dar.-Sag. i. 2. 1627; Kübler, *PW* iv. 1819; Mommsen, *Röm. Staatsr.* iii. 99; F. Altheim, *Epochen d. röm. Geschichte* i (1934), 70; W. Warde Fowler, *The Roman Festivals* (1899), 71, 306. For the *curiae* in *municipia* W. Liebenam, *Städteverwaltung im römischen Kaiserreiche* (1900), 214; Mommsen, *Juristische Schriften* i. 303.   A. M.

CURIA (2), the Senate-house of Rome, situated on the north side of the Comitium (q.v.) in the Forum and ascribed to Hostilius. It was restored by Sulla in 80 B.C., burnt after the death of Clodius in 52, and rebuilt by Faustus Sulla. Julius Caesar began a new building in 44, forsaking the old orientation by cardinal points, which was restored by Domitian, and later by Diocletian after the fire of Carinus. The Caesarian plan, always retained, was a sumptuous oblong hall (25·20 × 17·61 m.), with central door facing a magistrates' dais and lateral marble benches. The hall was separated from the record-office (*secretarium senatus*) by an *atrium* or *chalcidicum*, dedicated by Domitian to Minerva. Diocletian's building, of tile-faced concrete coated with imitation stucco block-work, still exists to full height.   I. A. R.

CURIALIS (earlier *Decurio*, q.v.), the member of a *curia* or senate of a *municipium*. In the early Empire the position, though burdensome, was coveted, as a mark of rank and wealth, and as the door to municipal office. But after the reforms of Diocletian and Constantine, the position of the *curiae* rapidly deteriorated. The honour was not entirely lost, but the burdens and responsibilities increased out of all proportion. Not only were the *curiales* responsible for all local offices and their expenses, but also for the collection of taxes; in case of deficit they were often called upon to make good. The result was a double movement—of the *curiales* to escape from their rank, of the government to bind them to it or to assign fresh members to the office, by way of punishment.
                                                H. M.

CURIATIUS MATERNUS, senator, poet, and dramatist, at whose house the scene of Tacitus' *Dialogus* is laid. A lover of *nemora et luci secretum*, he speaks there as champion of poetry. His (lost) *praetextae*, *Domitius* and *Cato*, belong to Vespasian's time.

CURIO (1), GAIUS SCRIBONIUS (*cos.* 76 B.C.), son of a famous orator, opposed Saturninus in 100 B.C. and was tribune in 90. He besieged Athens with Sulla. As consul he opposed the restoration of the tribunician power. Proconsul in Macedonia (75–73), he defeated the Dardanians. He spoke for P. Clodius at his trial, but afterwards became Cicero's friend and Caesar's enemy. In 55 he published a dialogue against Caesar.
    F. Münzer, *PW* ii A 862; Schanz–Hosius i. 351.   A. M.

CURIO (2), GAIUS SCRIBONIUS, son of (1), was, as a young man, implicated in the mysterious conspiracy of Vettius (q.v. 3). On his election as tribune for 50 he was, in spite of his aristocratic connexions, bought over for Caesar by his agent Balbus. He consistently opposed the attempts of the Senate to recall Caesar (Cic. *Fam.* 8. 11. 3), proposing instead that both Pompey and Caesar should give up their armies (Plut. *Pomp.* 58). It was he who bore Caesar's ultimatum to the consuls in late December; early in January he fled from Rome to Ravenna with Antony.

In the Civil War Curio won Sicily for Caesar (April 49)

and thence crossed to Africa. After initial successes he besieged the Pompeian commander Varus in Utica; but an attempt to surprise a relief force sent by King Juba led to a crushing Roman defeat. Curio himself died fighting; he was a reckless but loyal lieutenant who served Caesar well.

Caesar, *BCiv.*; Appian, *BCiv.* bk. 2; Dio, bks. 40 and 41; Cicero, *Epp. ad Fam.* 2. 1–7 are addressed to him.　　　　J. M. C.

CURIUS, *see* DENTATUS.

CURSES. A curse is in general a wish, expressed in words and with magical effect, that evil may befall a person or persons or, eventually, the curser himself.

I. The Greek word ἀρά reflects a prehistoric stage of Greek religion, signifying the address to supernatural forces, prayer as well as curse (personified as Ἀρά, secondarily combined with Erinys, goddess of revenge; cf. ἀρητήρ in the *Iliad*). Originally the curse (just as its opposite, the blessing) worked by its own inherent quality (*mana*), the power of its magic formula; this may be spoken or written or both; it may also be accompanied or symbolized by action (cf. the modern Greek φασκέλωμα and the Italian *il fico*, etc.), the gesture and the intonation intensifying the emotional character of the curse. The curse was always a powerful weapon in the hands of the weak and the poor, as also against unseen or unknown foes. So we often meet with such imprecations (*dirae*) in funeral inscriptions against those who violate graves (especially in Asia Minor). Numerous leaden tablets (magic nails, amulets, etc., cf. the magic papyri), inscribed with imprecatory formulas or words or signs, testify to the popularity of cursing (ἀναθεματίζειν), resorted to in all centuries by all sorts of people on any provocation (in the 4th c. B.C. even by well-to-do Athenians). When the tablets are buried in tombs, not only the spirits of the dead are invoked, but also the infernal deities, Persephone, Hades, Erinyes (cf. *Il.* 9. 453 ff.); elsewhere Hermes, Gaia, Demeter (at Cnidos), Hecate, and all sorts of demons are favourites (cf. the Roman *devotio*: see s.v.). Especially to be noted are the 'hereditary curse', infectious through generations (cf. Aeschylus' *Oresteia*), and the curse, uttered in vain, that returns to the curser, destroying him and his family (cf. *SIG*³ 41. 14). The ἀραί, *dirae*, developed into a special literary genus (cf. Sophron, Ovid's *Ibis*, Horace *Epod.* 10; Tib. 1. 5. 49 ff.). Later Christians might use ancient curses in inscriptions, simply prefixing a cross.

II. In the development of human society and ethics the curse plays an important role, just as does the oath (the two being often combined, cf. *Il.* 3. 279). The curse, expressed by the community through its representatives (magistrates, priests), had an enormous effect (cf. the blessing or curse uttered by parents or dying people). The culprit ('infecting' his countrymen, as Plato puts it, *Leg.* 9. 881 e 5) was thus in the position of a man guilty of sacrilege, and so the legal powers could enforce their rights even in cases where only the gods could help. Enemies and traitors were cursed, just as those who removed landmarks or maltreated guests and suppliants. The curses of the Bouzygai (*see* SACRIFICE) at Athens may illustrate how ethical principles might be enforced by cursing the offenders, and 'public curses' were as terrifying to the Greeks (cf. the *dirae Teiae*, *SIG* 37–8) as to the Romans (cf. Crassus on his departure for the Orient, Plut. *Crass.* 16). The weakening of the fear of the old gods already recognizable in official use in the third century B.C. reduced the importance of the curse, but we can still see its effect in ecclesiastical ritual.

Kurt Latte, *Heiliges Recht* (1920), 61 ff.; E. Ziebarth, *Hermes* xxx. 56 ff. Cf. W. W. Fowler, *Roman Essays and Interpretations*, 15 ff.; N. G. Politis, *Laographia* iv. 601 ff.; Westermarck, *Origin and Development of the Moral Ideas* (Index s.v. 'Curse' in vol.i i); A. E. Crawley, Hastings, *ERE* iv. 367 ff.; *IG* iii. 3; A. Audollent, *Defixionum Tabellae* (1904); R. Wünsch, *Antike Fluchtafeln*² (1912).
　　　　S. E.

CURSOR, *see* PAPIRIUS.

CURTIUS, the hero of an aetiological myth invented to explain the name of *Lacus Curtius*, a pit or pond in the Roman Forum, which by the time of Augustus had already dried up. Three Curtii are mentioned in this connexion: (1) a Sabine Mettius Curtius who fell off his horse while fighting against Romulus; (2) the consul of 454 B.C. who consecrated a site struck by lightning; (3) most important, the brave young knight M'. Curtius who, in obedience to an oracle, to save his country, leaped armed and on horseback into the chasm which suddenly opened in the Forum.

Platner–Ashby, *Topogr. Dict.* 310 f.　　　　P. T.

CURTIUS MONTANUS was prosecuted under Nero for his satiric poems, and excluded from holding any public office (Tac. *Ann.* 16. 28; 29; 33). He became, however, one of Domitian's advisers (Juv. 4. 107).

CURTIUS, *see also* RUFUS.

CYBELE (Κυβέλη; Lydian form Κυβήβη, Hdt. 5. 102), the great mother-goddess of Anatolia, worshipped with her youthful lover Attis (q.v.), god of vegetation. Pessinus in Phrygia was her chief sanctuary, and the cult appears at an early date in Lydia. The queen or mistress of her people, C. was responsible for their well-being in all respects; primarily she is a goddess of fertility, but also cures (and sends) disease, gives oracles, and, as her mural crown indicates, protects her people in war. The goddess of mountains (so Μήτηρ ὀρεία; Meter Dindymene), she is also mistress of wild nature, symbolized by her attendant lions. Ecstatic states inducing prophetic rapture and insensibility to pain were characteristic of her worship (cf. especially Catull. 63).

2. By the fifth century C. was known in Greece, and was early associated with Demeter (H. Thompson, *Hesperia* vi (1937), 206) and perhaps with a native Μήτηρ θεῶν, but except possibly for such places as Dyme, Patrae (Paus. 7. 17. 9; 20. 3), and private cult associations at Piraeus, where Attis also was worshipped, it is likely that the cult was thoroughly hellenized. C. was officially brought to Rome from Asia Minor in 205–204 (for the conflicting legends see Graillot, op. cit. inf., ch. 1), but under the Republic, save for the public games, the Megalesia, and processions (Lucr. 2. 624 f.), she was limited to her Palatine temple and served only by Oriental priests (Dion. Hal. *Ant. Rom.* 2. 19. 3–5). After Claudius admitted Attis to public status, the priesthood was opened to citizens, and was henceforth controlled by the *XVviri sacris faciundis* (see QUINDECIMVIRI). The cycle of the spring festival, while not fully attested till later, perhaps took form then. The rites began on 15 March with a procession of the Reed-bearers (*cannophori*), and a sacrifice for the crops. After a week of fastings and purifications, the festival proper opened on the 22nd with the bringing of the pine-tree, symbol of Attis, to the temple. The 24th was the Day of Blood, commemorating the castration and probably the death of Attis. The 25th was a day of joy and banqueting, the Hilaria, and after a day's rest the festival closed with the ritual bath (*Lavatio*) of Cybele's image in the Almo. The rubric for the 28th (*Initium Caiani*) may refer to initiations in the Vatican Phrygianum. Of these initiations we know little. The formulae preserved (Firm. Mat. *Err. prof. rel.* 18; Clem. Al. *Protr.* 2. 15) mention a ritual meal; the carrying of the κέρνος, a vessel used in the *taurobolium* to receive the genitals of the bull; and a descent into the παστός, probably an underground chamber where certain rites were enacted.

3. The ritual of the *taurobolium* originated in Asia Minor, and first appears in the West in the cult of Venus

Caelesta (i.e. -is) at Puteoli in A.D. 134 (*ILS* 4271, but cf. 4099 of 108 A.D.). From the Antonine period, numerous dedications to C. and Attis record its performance in this cult 'ex vaticinatione archigalli' (i.e. with official sanction), on behalf of the emperor and the Empire. From Rome the rite spread throughout the West, notably in Gaul. It was performed also on behalf of individuals, and was especially popular during the pagan revival, A.D. 370–90. In the rite, the recipient descended into a ditch and was bathed in the blood of a bull, or ram (*criobolium*), which was slain above him (Prudent. *Perist.* 10. 1011–50). It was sometimes repeated after twenty years; one late text (*ILS* 4152) has 'taurobolio criobolioq. in aeternum renatus' (a concept possibly borrowed from Christianity), but in general the act was considered rather a 'thing done' for its own value than as a source of individual benefits.

4. A belief in immortality was part of the cult from early times, perhaps under Thracian influence. In Anatolia, C. and Attis were the guardians of the grave, and the after-life may at first have been thought of as a reunion with Mother Earth. Later, Attis became a solar god, and he and C. were regarded as astral and cosmic powers; there is some evidence that the soul was then thought to return after death to its celestial source.

5. Thanks to its official status and early naturalization at Rome, the cult spread rapidly through the provinces, especially in Gaul and Africa, and was readily accepted as a municipal cult. Its agrarian character made it more popular with the fixed populations than with the soldiery, and it was especially favoured by women.

6. Cybele is generally represented enthroned in a *naiskos*, wearing either the mural crown or the *calathos*, carrying a patera and tympanum, and either flanked by lions or bearing one in her lap.

See also AGDISTIS, ANAHITA, ANATOLIAN DEITIES, ATTIS, EUNUCHS, METRAGYRTES.

J. Carcopino, *Mél. d'Arch. et d'Hist.* xl (1923); F. Cumont, *Religions Orientales*⁴ (1929); L. R. Farnell, *Cults of the Greek States* iii (1907); J. G. Frazer, *GB*³ iv (1914) (= *Adonis Attis Osiris*²); H. Graillot, *Le Culte de Cybèle* (1912); H. Hepding, *Attis* (1903); M.-J. Lagrange, *Rev. Bibl.* 1919; Schwenn, s.v. 'Kybele' and Oppermann, s.v. 'Taurobolia', in *PW*; in Roscher, *Lex.*, Drexler and Höfer, s.v. 'Meter', Rapp, s.v. 'Kybele'. F. R. W.

CYCLADES, the islands regarded as circling round the sacred isle of Delos. According to ancient tradition the Carians once inhabited them, and were driven out by Minos, king of Crete. There is archaeological proof that the culture of the Cyclades in the second millennium resembled that of Crete. About 1000 B.C. Ionic-speaking settlers from continental Greece occupied these islands. In the eighth century Eretria exercised control over some of them, as did the tyrants Pisistratus (Athens), Polycrates (Samos), and Lygdamis (Naxos) in the sixth; but no Power could protect the islanders from the invading Persian fleet in 490. After the Persian Wars the islanders entered an Athenian Confederacy centred at Delos (478–477), and Athens soon became mistress of the Cyclades. They were also enrolled in the second Athenian Confederacy (378–377), but the triumph of Philip of Macedon ended Athenian hegemony. Antigonus of Macedon founded a League of Islanders with head-quarters at Delos. In the prolonged struggle between Macedon and Egypt in the third century the Cyclades often changed masters; late in the century they suffered from Cretan piracy and the rivalries of Pergamum, Rhodes, and Syria. In the Mithridatic War the islands were reduced by Archelaus (88), nor was tranquillity restored until the triumph of Augustus.

Bursian, ii. 438 ff.; *IG* xii. 5 (1909), vii–xxxvii. Prehistory: O. Montelius, *La Grèce préclassique* i (1924), 93–111. Cf. *Ath. Mitt.* ix. 156 ff.; xi. 15 ff. Pottery: C. Dugas, *Les Céramiques des Cyclades* (1925). W. A. L.

CYCLIC POETS, *see* EPIC CYCLE.

CYCLOPES (Κύκλωπες), gigantic one-eyed beings of whom at least two separate traditions exist. In Homer they are savage and pastoral; they live in a distant country, having no government or laws. Here Odysseus (q.v.) visits them in his wanderings and enters the cave of one of them, Polyphemus, who imprisons him and his men and eats two of them morning and evening, until they escape by blinding him, while in a drunken sleep, and getting out among the sheep and goats when he opens the cave in the morning (*Od.* 9. 106 ff.). Polyphemus is son of Poseidon, and the god, in answer to his prayer for vengeance, opposes the home-coming of Odysseus in every possible way, bringing literally to pass the curse that he may return alone and find trouble when he arrives (ibid. 532–5). Out of this, or by conflation of it with some local legend, grows the story of the amorous Polyphemus (Theocr. 11 and elsewhere). He lives in Sicily (one of many identifications of Homeric with later known western places) and woos Galatea (q.v.).

But in Hesiod (*Theog.* 149) the Cyclopes are three, Brontes, Steropes, and Arges (Thunderer, Lightener, Bright), who make thunderbolts and in general are excellent craftsmen; they are like the gods except that they have but one eye each, and are sons of Earth and Heaven. They often appear (as Callim. *Dian.* 46 ff.) as Hephaestus' workmen, and often again are credited with making ancient fortifications, as those of Tiryns, and other cities of the Argolid (schol. Eur. *Or.* 965). There they are called ἐγχειρογάστορες, simply 'workmen' (Wilamowitz-Moellendorff, *Glaube der Hellenen* i. 277). Schol. Hesiod, *Theog.* 139, makes these builders a third kind of Cyclopes.

See Roscher in his *Lexikon*, s.v. 'Kyklopen', and S. Eitrem in *PW*, s.v. H. J. R.

CYCNUS, (1) a son of Ares, a brigand, waylaying and robbing those who brought tithes to Delphi (Arguments 2 and 3 to [Hesiod], *Sc.*). According to that poem, Heracles and Iolaus met him in company with Ares himself in the precinct of Apollo (58). Clad in his armour, the gift of the gods, and drawn by Arion (q.v.; 120), Heracles asked Cycnus to let him pass, then, as he would not, engaged with him, encouraged by Athena (325 ff.), killed him, and then, when Ares attacked him, wounded the god in the thigh. Pindar (*Ol.* 10. 15) says Heracles fled before Cycnus, which the scholiast explains, quoting Stesichorus, as meaning that he at first fled before Ares. He also says that Cycnus' object was to build a temple of skulls to Apollo. (2) Son of Poseidon. He was killed by Achilles before Troy, according to several authors from the *Cypria* on. Ovid (*Met.* 12. 83 ff.) adds that he was invulnerable and Achilles choked him to death; Poseidon then turned him into a swan (κύκνος). (3) King of Liguria, kinsman of Phaethon (q.v.); mourning for his death, he also became a swan (Hyg. *Fab.* 154. 5). (4) Son of Apollo, a handsome boy. Because a much-tried lover left him, he drowned himself in a lake, ever after frequented by swans, into which he and his mother, who also drowned herself, were turned (Antoninus Liberalis 12). H. J. R.

CYCNUS, *see* TENES.

CYLON, an Athenian nobleman; winner of the *stadion* and *diaulos* at Olympia, perhaps 640 B.C. He married the daughter of Theagenes, tyrant of Megara, and with his help and a few friends seized the Acropolis at Athens with a view to a tyranny (632 or 628). The masses, however, did not follow him, and he was besieged. He himself escaped; his friends surrendered and, though suppliants at an altar, were killed. Hence arose the ἄγος, or taint, which attached to those said to be responsible, especially to Megacles the archon and his family, the Alcmaeonidae. A. W. G.

CYME, the most important and powerful of the Aeolian cities on the seaboard of Asia Minor, occupying a site of natural strength midway between the mouths of the Caicus and the Hermus, and facing north-west towards Lesbos. Its history is a record of external domination, by Persians (though Cyme participated in the Ionian Revolt, and belonged to the Delian League and the second Athenian Confederacy), Seleucids, Attalids, and Romans. A severe earthquake devastated the city in A.D. 17. Hesiod's father came from Cyme to Boeotia. Its most distinguished son was Ephorus. The inhabitants were famous for their easy-going temperament.

D. E. W. W.

CYNAETHUS of Chios, rhapsode; interpolated Homer; supposed author of the *Homeric Hymn to Apollo*; said to have been the first to recite Homer at Syracuse in 504 B.C. (? 704: T. W. Allen, *Homer, the Origins and Transmission* (1924), 65–66). *See* RHAPSODES.

CYNAXA, *see* CUNAXA.

CYNEGEIRUS, brother of Aeschylus, fought and fell at Marathon (490 B.C.) in a bold attempt to seize a Persian ship by the stern. This exploit was immortalized in the Painted Portico (*c.* 460), and was variously elaborated by historians (e.g. the source of Justin 2. 9. 16 ff.) and rhetoricians (e.g. Polemon). P. T.

CYNEGETICA, books on management of dogs for hunting; *see* GRATTIUS, NEMESIANUS, OPPIAN, XENOPHON (1).

CYNICS (κυνικοί), followers of the principles of Diogenes of Sinope, who had received the nickname of κύων (dog) because he rejected all conventions, tried to live on nothing, and advocated and practised shamelessness (ἀναίδεια). Since Antisthenes had probably influenced the philosophy of Diogenes, many considered and still consider him the real founder of the sect.

The Cynics were never organized in a school like the Stoics, Epicureans, Peripatetics, etc., and had no elaborate philosophical system. Since therefore everybody was at liberty to adopt those of Diogenes' principles which appealed to him and to neglect the rest, there has been and still is much argument as to who was a true Cynic and who was not. The variety was greatest during the century following the death of Diogenes. His most faithful disciple Crates of Thebes preached the gospel of simplicity and independence, and comforted many in those troubled times by demonstrating that he who needs next to nothing, renounces all possessions, and keeps aloof from social entanglements, can live happily in the midst of war and disorder. Onesicritus adapted Cynic philosophy to the life of a soldier or sailor, and compared Diogenes' principles with those of the Indian ascetics. Bion of Borysthenes and Menippus imitated Diogenes' caustic wit in their satirical writings. They were the first to mingle Cynicism with Hedonism. Cercidas derived theories of social reform from Cynic doctrines. Crates and Teles originated the type of Cynic who wandered all over Greece with stick and knapsack, teaching and preaching.

After having flourished in the third century B.C., Cynicism gradually faded out in the second and first centuries B.C., retaining only some literary influence (Meleager of Gadara). It was revived in the first century after Christ. The beginnings of this revival are unknown; but under the reign of Vespasian and his successors the Orient and Rome swarmed with Cynic beggar philosophers (Dio Chrys. 32. 10). Educated men like Dio himself, however, also adhered to Cynic principles; and the contrast between the true Cynic and the depraved Cynicism of the beggar philosophers became a commonplace in the literature of the Empire (Dio, Lucian,

Julian). While the aristocratic opposition to the emperors was connected with Stoicism, middle-class criticism was sometimes voiced by Cynics who contrasted their ideal of the philosopher king with the actual conduct of the emperors. They therefore were frequently banished from the capital.

Outstanding among the Cynics of the first and second century after Christ were Demetrius, Dio, Demonax, Peregrinus Proteus, Oenomaus of Gadara, Sostratus, and Theagenes. Only very few Cynics of the following centuries acquired any renown. The last one mentioned by name is Sallustius, who lived at the end of the fifth century (Suidas s.v.; Dam. *Isid.* 342ᵃ 27 ff.). But the Cynic beggar philosophers are frequently alluded to in literature up to the sixth century.

D. R. Dudley, *A History of Cynicism* (1938). K. von F.

CYNTHIA, the name under which Hostia was celebrated in the love-poetry of Propertius (q.v.).

CYPARISSUS (Κυπάρισσος), i.e. Cypress, in mythology son of Telephus (q.v.), a Cean (Ov. *Met.* 10. 106 ff.), who grieved so much at accidentally killing a pet stag that the gods turned him into the mournful tree; or a Cretan, who was so metamorphosed while fleeing from the attentions of Apollo, or Zephyrus (Servius on *Aen.* 3. 680). H. J. R.

CYPRIA *see* EPIC CYCLE.

CYPRIAN (*Caecilius Cyprianus qui et Thascius*) lived from about A.D. 200 to 258, when he was martyred. After the best rhetorical training that Carthage could provide, he entered on an ecclesiastical career which culminated in the bishopric of Carthage. He regarded Tertullian as his 'magister', but writes a much better style than he, a style formed before his conversion in the same school of rhetoric as that of Apuleius. It is evident that Cyprian had read Cicero, Virgil, and Seneca. His writings have all to do with Christian topics. The [*Testimonia*] *Ad Quirinum* and the *Ad Fortunatum* consist almost entirely of exact citations from the Latin Bible used by him, and are invaluable, as both localized and dated. Among his other works are his letters, his *Ad Donatum, De (Catholicae) Ecclesiae Unitate*, and *De Lapsis* (backsliders in the Decian persecution).

Ed. W. von Hartel (*CSEL* iii, 1868–71); E. W. Benson, *Cyprian, His Life and Times* (1897); H. v. Soden, *Das Lateinische Neue Testament in Afrika* (1909); E. W. Watson, 'The Style and Language of St. Cyprian' (*Studia Biblica* iv (1896)); H. Koch, *Cyprianische Untersuchungen* (1926). A. S.

CYPRUS, an island in the Levant immediately south of Cilicia. Its extreme measurement is 140 × 60 miles, and it is shaped like the skin of an animal, with the neck pointing towards Syria. Recent excavations have revealed the existence of a neolithic culture of high quality lasting from *c.* 4000 to 3000 B.C. It was followed by a native Bronze Age which was a period of increasing prosperity and culture. In the fifteenth century B.C. direct contact on an extensive scale was made with Mycenaean Greece, perhaps through the medium of Rhodes. Contacts with Asia Minor and Syria began earlier and were continuous. The Mycenaean contacts brought about a widespread change in the island which from 1400 onwards developed urban life and culture on Mycenaean lines. All the main elements of Mycenaean life are found except architecture, Mycenaean tomb-types, and Mycenaean road-systems. It is probable that the copper mines of the island first began to be worked in the fourteenth century. Salamis seems to have been the chief Mycenaean city, and its connexions with Syria have been illustrated by recent finds at Ras Shamra (*Ugarit*). Among the Mycenaean imported elements of culture was a mode of writing, a variant of the Minoan script, which reached Cyprus through the Mycenaean colonists. The name of

Cyprus at this time seems to have been Alashia, as in Hittite and Egyptian texts. The Cypriot script of the Bronze Age survived into the Classical period and was used as a vehicle for Greek down to about 400; but inscriptions also prove the survival of a non-Greek tongue in the Classical age. Egyptian connexions were constant, and in 1450 Cyprus came under Egyptian domination.

2. Cyprus was only slightly affected by the Dorian invasion and no Dorian settlement was made on the island, although its neighbour Rhodes was completely dorianized. The Greek stock of the island, which probably took root at the time of the Mycenaean immigration, must therefore be Achaean. The survival of Achaean dialect forms (mostly as Arcadian) in the Cypriot Greek of the Classical age indicates the continuity of this original Mycenaean-Achaean stock. The survival of the Bronze Age script also testifies to the absence of any catastrophic change in the island at the Iron Age. But Cyprus shared in the general changes of the time, and Iron Age peoples from Syria seem to have moved into the island c. 1000 B.C. Cypriot art was altered and deeply modified. Perhaps c. 800 Phoenicians entered the island and settled in the cities. But their influence was never profound. Cyprus was known to Homer, but not intimately. In 709 and again in 670 it fell under Assyrian rule. In the sixth century it was virtually annexed by Egypt and from 569 to 525 it was ruled by Euelthon of Salamis, as governor for the Egyptians. At the same time each Cypriot city retained a semi-autonomous kingship. Such kingdoms of Cyprus went back to the Bronze Age and continued down to Ptolemaic times.

3. The City-State never gained a foothold in Cyprus, whose traditions of kingship probably derived from the Achaeans. In 525 Cyprus fell to the Persians under Cambyses. In 498 an abortive attempt was made by Cypriots to join the Ionian Revolt. After the Persian Wars Cyprus was finally liberated by Cimon. But the island did not regain its freedom from the Phoenicians until one of the greatest Cypriots, Evagoras of Salamis, organized in 411 a wider movement of phil-Hellenism. At the peace of Antalcidas in 387 Persia gained control again. In 350 the Cypriot kings revolted and the island was free. In 333 the island declared for Alexander, and at his death passed to Antigonus. Later it fell to Ptolemy and remained under the Egyptian dynasty for nearly two and a half centuries. It became a Roman province in 58 B.C. At its annexation the island was systematically drained of its wealth, which was poured into Roman coffers. It became a district of the province of Cilicia.

J. L. Myres, *Handbook to the Cesnola Collection* (1914); R. Gunnis, *Historic Cyprus* (1936); S. Casson, *Ancient Cyprus* (1937); Sir G. F. Hill, *A History of Cyprus* (1940). S. C.

CYPSELUS, tyrant of Corinth c. 655–625 B.C., son of Eetion, who traced descent from the pre-Dorian Lapithi, and Labda, a lady of the ruling Dorian clan of the Bacchiadae. Oracles foretold his destiny, and he escaped destruction by the Bacchiads only through being hidden as a babe in a jar (*cypsele*). After reaching manhood Cypselus, again with oracular support from Delphi, overthrew the Bacchiads and made himself tyrant. Herodotus calls him blood-thirsty, but later writers contrast his mild rule with that of his son Periander. He had no bodyguard; probably his severity was confined to the nobility while the masses supported him. The fine local pottery (late Protocorinthian and early Corinthian) was exported (especially to the West) in immense quantities throughout his reign. On the route to Italy and Sicily he founded the colonies of Leucas, Ambracia, and Anactorium. The earliest Corinthian coins may go back to him, as may also some of the dedications made by his house at Olympia and Delphi.

Herodotus 5. 92; Nic. Dam. fr. 58. P. N. Ure, *Origin of Tyranny* (1922), ch. 7, footnotes. P. N. U.

CYPSELUS, CHEST OF, a chest of cedar wood, exhibited at Olympia in the temple of Hera, and reputed to be the one in which the infant Cypselus (q.v.) was hidden. Either Cypselus himself or his son Periander dedicated the chest as a thank-offering. The very detailed description by Pausanias of the chest and its decoration suggests that it was a work of Corinthian art in the period of the tyrants. The decoration was executed in ivory, in gold, and in the cedar wood of the chest itself; apparently it was a form of inlay work rather than of relief. No specimen of work of this kind survives. The decoration and composition conform to our knowledge of Proto-Corinthian and Corinthian painting, and may be compared with that of the François vase.

J. G. Frazer, *Notes to Pausanias*, 5. 17. 5; H. Stuart Jones, *JHS* 1894, 30 ff. S. C.

CYRANIDES (Βίβλοι κυρανίδες or κοιρανίδες), a Greek work, in four books, on the magical curative properties of stones, plants, and animals. The name is of uncertain origin. If κυρανίδες is its original form, this may mean 'inscribed on columns' (from a Coptic word) —that being the account the work itself gives of its history; if κοιρανίδες, it means 'queens among kings'. The compilation may be ascribed to the first or second century A.D., though part of it may go back to the Hellenistic age. It describes itself as the work partly of Cyranus king of Persia and partly of Harpocration (the medical and astrological writer).

Ed. C. E. Ruelle in F. de Mély, *Les Lapidaires de l'antiquité et du moyen âge*, ii (1898–9). *PW* xii. 127. W. D. R.

CYRENAICS, the 'minor Socratic' school founded at Cyrene by Aristippus (q.v.; fl. c. 400–365), which became the pioneer of Epicureanism. The chief other members were Theodorus, Hegesias, and Anniceris. The main tenet of the school was the treatment of the pleasures of the senses as the end of life. The school seems to have come to an end c. 275 B.C.

Zeller, *Ph. d. Gr.* ii. 1⁴. 336–88. W. D. R.

CYRENE, a port lying north of Great Syrtis (q.v.). The Delphic oracle encouraged Theraeans and Cretans to found Cyrene c. 630 B.C.; these early settlers intermarried with the Berbers. Fresh colonists came from Peloponnese and the islands (570). Barca, Euhesperides (*Bengazi*), and other cities were founded, and the Cyrenaic pentapolis formed a prosperous centre of Hellenic civilization between the Phoenician tripolis to the west and the Egyptians to the east. The limestone plateau of Cyrene was rich in corn, silphium, wool, and dates.

The original founder became king of Cyrene, assumed the name Battus (Libyan for 'king'), and established a dynasty (*see* ARCESILAS). Under Battus III Cyrene received a liberal constitution from Demonax of Mantinea; but this was abolished by Arcesilas III. Attacked unsuccessfully by Apries of Egypt, the city came to terms with Amasis. Battus IV reduced Barca and its neighbours to subjection. Cyrenaica maintained contact with mainland Greece; it built a treasury at Olympia, and Pindar celebrated the sporting triumphs of Arcesilas IV (*Pyth.* 4). Cyrene submitted to Cambyses, and formed part of Darius' empire. On recovering its independence it sheltered the Athenian survivors from the Egyptian expedition (c. 455). In the fourth century it was famous for its mathematicians and philosophers, and was prosperous enough to supply the mother-country with corn in the great famine of 330 B.C.

Alexander made Cyrene an ally, and Ptolemy joined it to his Egyptian kingdom. In spite of occasional separations the connexion was maintained till Ptolemy Apion bequeathed Cyrene to Rome (96 B.C.). After twenty-two years of chaos, during which the royal lands fell into private hands, it became a province, to which Crete was added in 67. Augustus allotted it to the Senate; but his edicts (see following article) show that the emperor intervened on occasion. Its tranquil existence was shattered by violent Jewish outbreaks under Trajan; though Hadrian imported colonists into the devastated province, its prosperity declined. Cyrene was reunited with Egypt under the Later Empire. Its recently excavated ruins have revealed outstanding examples of Greek art and architecture.

U. von Wilamowitz-Moellendorff, *Kyrene* (1928); L. Malten, *Kyrene* (1911); R. Paribeni in *Diz. Epig.* s.v. 'Cyrenae'; *CAH* iii. 666 ff., iv. 109 ff. (bibliog., pp. 628-9), xi, ch. 16 (bibliography of excavation reports, p. 928); E. S. G. Robinson, *British Museum Catalogue of the Greek Coins of Cyrenaica* (1929); Jones, *Eastern Cities*, ch. 12; P. Romanelli, *La Cirenaica romana* (1943). W. N. W.

CYRENE, EDICTS OF, five edicts of Augustus, discovered in an inscription of Cyrene, published in 1927. The first four belong to 7-6 B.C. and apply to the senatorial province of Cyrenaica and Crete alone; the fifth (which introduces a *senatus consultum*) belongs to 4 B.C. and applies to the whole Empire. The documents definitively prove that Augustus received an *imperium maius* over the senatorial provinces and demonstrate the emperor's ably balanced policy towards the provincials.

In the first edict Augustus establishes the procedure that criminal cases involving a capital charge against a Greek should be tried by mixed Graeco-Roman juries of a certain census, unless the accused prefers to have an entirely Roman jury. The system is modelled on the *quaestiones perpetuae* of Rome. Roman citizens except Greeks who had received Roman citizenship are not allowed to be accusers in cases involving murders of Greeks. The second edict approves the conduct of the governor towards some Roman citizens. The third establishes that the provincials who have obtained Roman citizenship should continue to share the burdens of their original Greek community unless they had special privileges. Under the fourth, all legal actions between Greeks, other than capital ones, were to have Greek judges, unless the defendant preferred Roman judges. The fifth edict communicates a *SC* which establishes that charges of extortion can be examined by five senatorial judges, after a preliminary examination by the whole Senate. This marks a beginning of the judicial function of the Senate.

Text in *SEG* ix. 1, 1938 v. 8. Short English commentary: J. G. C. Anderson, *JRS* 1927, 33; 1929, 219. Standard works: A. v. Premerstein, *Sav. Zeitschr.* 1928, 419; 1931, 431; J. Stroux–L. Wenger, *Abh. d. Bayer. Akad.* xxxiv (1928), 2 Abt.; F. De Visscher, *Les Édits d'Auguste découverts à Cyrène* (1940). Cf. H. M. Last, *JRS* 1945, 93. A. M.

CYRUS (1) (*Kurash*), son of Teispes, the founder of the Achaemenid Persian Empire (559-529 B.C.). According to a legend of his birth and upbringing (Hdt. 1. 107-30), he was related to Astyages, king of Media (denied by Ctesias, *Persica* exc. 2). Heir only to the throne of Anshan, he soon challenged his Median overlord. Capturing Astyages, he entered Ecbatana in 549 B.C. Thenceforward the Persians became the ruling race, though their kinsmen the Medes still held privileged positions in the State. Cyrus' defeat of Croesus of Lydia (Hdt. 1. 71 ff.) gave him Asia Minor, that of Nabonidus, Babylonia, Assyria, Syria, and Palestine. Campaigns in the north and east extended his boundaries over almost all the Iranian plateau. The extent of his conquests is known from the lists of peoples subject to Darius. This vast empire he administered with wisdom and tolerance. In the conquered territories he was welcomed as a liberator; he respected their customs and religion, honouring Marduk at Babylon and freeing the captive Jews to build their temple in Jerusalem. To the Greeks he became a model of the upright ruler.

There are conflicting legends of his death (Xen. *Cyr.* 8. 7. 2 ff.; Hdt. 1. 204 ff.); it is probable that he died in battle. His grave is at Pasargadae (Strabo 15. 730; Arrian, *Anab.* 6. 29. 8).

The best sources for Cyrus' reign are the official cuneiform records: F. H. Weissbach, *Keilinschriften der Achämeniden* (1911). Classical sources: Hdt. bk. 1; Ctesias, *Persica* bks. 7-9; Xen. *Cyropaedia* (a fanciful biography). Modern works: J. V. Prašek, 'Kyros der Grosse', *Alte Orient* xiii. 3 (1912); F. H. Weissbach, *PW* Suppl. iv (1924) s.v. 'Kyros (6)'. *See also under* ACHAEMENIDS. M. S. D.

CYRUS (2) **II,** younger son of Darius II and Parysatis, and his mother's favourite. He was given an overriding command in Asia Minor in 408 B.C. when he had barely come of age. In Sardes he met Lysander; their friendly co-operation meant victory for Sparta in the Peloponnesian War. Cyrus was summoned to the court in 405 on his father's fatal illness, but Arsaces, the elder brother, succeeded as Artaxerxes II, and only Parysatis' influence saved Cyrus when accused of treason by Tissaphernes. On his return to Asia Minor he began to gather mercenaries (amongst whom Xenophon enlisted), ostensibly for an expedition against Pisidia. In the spring of 401 he set out with some 20,000 men; his true destination was not revealed until the army struck the Euphrates at Thapsacus. At Cunaxa (q.v.), some forty-five miles from Babylon, Artaxerxes made his stand. Cyrus' deficiency in cavalry proved fatal, and he lost his life in a desperate attack on his brother's bodyguard. He had youthful faults of impetuosity and superficiality, but his personal charm, his energy, and his gift of leadership, were the qualities of a potentially great ruler.

Xenophon, *Anabasis* and *Hellenica*; Ctesias, *Persica*. F. H. Weissbach, *PW* Suppl. iv (1924) s.v. 'Kyros (7)'. D. E. W. W.

CYTHERA, an island off the south-east promontory of Peloponnesus, formerly called 'the purple island' (Πορφυροῦσα) from its rich *murex* deposits. It passed from Argive into Spartan possession (*c.* 600 B.C.) and received a Spartan garrison and governor (Κυθηροδίκης); its inhabitants were *perioikoi*. Herodotus relates that King Demaratus, in advising Xerxes to occupy it, quoted Chilon's saying that it would have been better sunk beneath the sea. Captured by Nicias (424 B.C.), it became a base for Athenian raids into Laconia; and it was again held by Athens from 393 to 386.

R. Leonhardt, 'Die Insel Kythera', *Petermann's Mitteilungen*, Ergänzungsheft 128 (1899); O. Maull in *PW* s.v. A. M. W.

CYZICUS, a Milesian colony traditionally founded in 756 and refounded in 675, on the island of Arctonnesus, among a Myso-Phrygian population. The site rivalled Byzantium in defensibility and commercial importance. The island could be joined to or cut off from the mainland at will; it sheltered two harbours, and practically all the shipping of the Propontis came to Cyzicus to avoid the inhospitable northern shore. Its coinage of electrum staters, called Cyzicenes, became famous everywhere.

Cyzicus was a member of the Delian League, to which it gave the largest annual contribution from the Hellespontine region, nine talents. It was the scene of Alcibiades' naval victory over the Spartans in 410. It preserved much of its commercial importance in the fourth century, and continued to do so in the Hellenistic age, when it cultivated especially good relations with the Attalid kings. Under Rome it remained a free city and was rewarded with an increase of its already large territory for its courageous resistance in 74 to Mithridates. Loss of freedom for a time and some diminution of territory followed the killing of Roman citizens, probably trade rivals, in 20 B.C. Further outbreaks caused definitive loss of the privilege in A.D. 25. Hadrian built a huge temple at Cyzicus, probably giving the city at the same time the titles of *metropolis* and *neocorus*. Later emperors gave aid after earthquakes. An earthquake in the reign of Justinian gave him a chance to use the marbles of Cyzicus in Saint Sophia.

F. W. Hasluck, *Cyzicus* (1910); Jones, *Eastern Cities*. T. R. S. B.

D

DACIA was the country situated in the loop of the lower Danube, consisting mainly of the plateau of Transylvania, but extending in a wider sense to the Seret and the Vistula. The Dacians were an agricultural people. Under the influence of Celtic invaders in the fourth century they partly absorbed Celtic culture and developed the gold, silver, and iron mines of the Carpathians. From *c.* 300 B.C. they traded with the Greeks by way of the Danube; from the second century they also had relations with the Greek towns of Illyria and with Italian traders. Their chief import was wine.

The separate Dacian tribes were united *c.* 60 B.C. by a chieftain named Burebistas (q.v.), who extended his rule to south-west Russia, Hungary, and the Balkan peninsula as far as the Roman border. After his death his empire broke up, and for 100 years the Dacians merely made sporadic raids across the Danube. But the threat from Burebistas to Roman territory was not easily forgotten. In 44 Caesar was preparing to sweep up the Dacians south of the Danube; Antony and Octavian sought alliance with Dacian tribal kings. When a chieftain named Decebalus reunited Dacia, Domitian made a preventive attack upon him A.D. 86–9. This invasion remained indecisive, but Trajan made two further attacks (101–2 and 105–6) which resulted in the death of Decebalus and the capture of his chief stronghold, Sarmizegethusa. *See* DECEBALUS. The two Dacian wars of Trajan were commemorated by the sculptured reliefs on Trajan's column (*see* FORUM TRAIANI).

Dacia was now constituted into a Roman province, but its territory was restricted to the Aluta in the east, and to a line short of the Carpathians and the river Theiss in the north and west. New settlers were introduced from Dalmatia and the eastern provinces, and the mines were exploited more intensively. Colonies and *municipia* of Italian type were established, the most important being Sarmizegethusa and Apulum. After the Gothic invasions of A.D. 250–70 Dacia was abandoned by the Romans.

Dio Cass. 68. 6–14 (Trajan's campaigns). V. Pârvan, *Dacia* (1928: Dacian culture); Brandis in *PW* s.v.   M. C.

DACTYLS, IDAEAN, *see* IDAEAN DACTYLS.

DAEDALA, *see* MARRIAGE (SACRED) *and* BOEOTIA (CULTS).

DAEDALUS, a legendary artist, craftsman, and inventor of archaic times. He has a significant name, for artful works were called δαίδαλα. His father (Paus. 9. 3. 2) Eupalamus or 'Skillhand' was descended from Erechtheus (Pherecydes, *FGrH* i. 146). D. was born in Athens, but had to leave the city because he killed his nephew Perdix who surpassed him in skill (Suidas s.v. Πέρδικος ἱερόν). He went to Crete, where he made the cow for Pasiphaë, the labyrinth for the Minotaur, a dancing ground (χορός), a small wooden statue of Aphrodite, and the famous thread for Ariadne. Enraged by the aid that D. had rendered to Pasiphaë, King Minos imprisoned him and his son Icarus, but D. constructed two pairs of artificial wings and flew away. He crossed safely to Sicily; Icarus, however, approached the sun too closely so that the wax of his wings melted and he drowned in the Aegean Sea.

In Sicily D. was protected by the Sicanian king, Cocalus; Minos, who arrived in pursuit of D., was suffocated in a steam bath (constructed by D.?) by the daughters of Cocalus (A. C. Pearson, *Fragments of Sophocles* ii, p. 3). D. had constructed in Sicily a reservoir for the river Alabon, a steam-bath at Selinus, a fortress near Agrigentum, and a terrace for the temple of Aphrodite on Mt. Eryx (Diod. 4. 78 after Antiochus).

Daedalus was also considered the inventor of carpentry and of such things as the saw, the axe, the plumb-line, the auger, and glue. He also invented the mast and the yards of boats (Pliny, *HN* 7. 198). As tangible evidence of his skill a folding chair was shown in the temple of Athena Polias on the Acropolis (Paus. 1. 27. 1). His skill in metal-work was attested by the golden honeycomb in the temple of Aphrodite on Eryx. A multitude of archaic temples and archaic statues, especially wooden ones in Greece and Italy, were believed to be by his hand (Overbeck, *Antike Schriftquellen* (1868), 119). He first made figures which had open eyes, walked, and moved their arms from their sides, whereas earlier works had their feet closed and their arms fixed to their sides (Suid. Δαιδάλου ποιήματα). Several later archaic artists were considered pupils of Daedalus, and a demos of the *phyle* Cecropis in Attica was named the Daedalids.

The legend of Daedalus unites many heterogeneous elements. Certain features seem to go back to Cretan and Dorian tales, others betray an Attic origin. The propensity of the Greeks to recognize their own gods and legends in foreign countries enabled them to recognize works of Daedalus in architecture and sculpture of the natives in Sicily, Sardinia, and even in the pyramids of Egypt (Diod. 4. 30; 1. 97; Paus. 9. 17. 3). Since the name of Daedalus had come to stand for art of extremely archaic character, any very archaic statue was easily ascribed to Daedalus. The notion of uncanny superhuman skill inherent in the character of Daedalus accounts for such folkloristic traits as the legend of living statues (Eur. *Hec.* 836). The chronology of the Daedalids being faulty (Robert, *Archäologische Märchen* (1886)), it is not possible to determine the lifetime of D. from ancient authors. It is also controversial whether a historical artist D. gave the impetus to the formation of the legends, or is a purely mythological figure representative of accomplished craftsmanship.

Daedalus is represented on vases, gems, and in sculpture in Greece (J. D. Beazley, *JHS* 1927, 222) and Etruria (G. M. A. Hanfmann, *AJArch.* 1935, 189 ff.), and in Roman wall-painting and sculpture usually with Icarus or Pasiphaë.

C. Picard, *Manuel arch. grecque* i (1935), 77; W. Miller, *Daedalus and Thespis* (1931), ii. 1; B. Schweitzer, *Xenokrates von Athen* (1932), 20.   G. M. A. H.

DAIMACHUS of Plataea (first half of 4th c. B.C.), is Ephorus' source for early Boeotian history, and is important if Jacoby rightly assigns to him the *Hellenica* from Oxyrhynchus (q.v.; *Nachrichten Gesellsch. d. Wissensch. zu Göttingen* 1924, i). A younger Daimachus wrote ʾΙνδικά a century later.

FGrH ii. 65 and 66. *FHG* ii. 440.   G. L. B.

DAIMON (δαίμων). In Homer this word may be applied to one of the great gods, but its use has peculiar features. It has no feminine form and no plural (this is frequent in later literature). It has been observed that, whilst the Homeric poet in his own narrative constantly refers to the anthropomorphic gods, in the words which he puts in the mouth of his personages the cause of events is ascribed not to these but to a *daimon*, or a general phrase, θεός τις, θεοί, Ζεύς, is used. *Daimon* appears to correspond to the supernatural power, the mana, not as a general conception but in its special manifestations. δαιμόνιος is 'strange', 'incomprehensible'. As *daimon* refers to the lot of a man, the word comes sometimes near the significance of 'fate', σὺν δαίμονι, πάρος τοι δαίμονα δώσω. An expression occurring in tragedy, ὁ παρὼν δαίμων, proves that the old reference to a special manifestation was not forgotten, although a general sense is frequent in later writers, e.g. in the compounds ὀλβιοδαίμων, εὐδαίμων, κακοδαίμων. Heraclitus says: ἦθος ἀνθρώπῳ δαίμων 'a man's character is his fate', but 'fate' is not quite a correct translation. Finally people spoke of a good and an evil *daimon* of a man, which follows him through his life. The application of the word to cult gods is extremely rare, but it was appropriate to less well-defined gods. Hesiod calls the deceased of the Golden Age *daimones*, and Aeschylus in the same sentence calls the ghost of Darius δαίμων and θεός. Thus the word seemed to be appropriate to lesser gods. Since Plato *daimones* were conceived of as beings intermediate between gods and men, and Xenokrates allowed that they were of a mixed nature, and that ἡμέραι ἀποφράδες (*see* APOPHRADES) and festivals involving mourning, fasting, or improper language belonged to beings of this nature—an idea developed by Plutarch (R. Heinze, *Xenokrates*, 167 f.). Finally, Christianity which made the pagan gods evil beings impressed upon the word the significance which 'demon' now has in common language.

M. P. Nilsson, *ARW* xxii (1924), 363 ff.; *Gesch. d. griech. Religion* i. 201 ff.; H. J. Rose, *Harv. Theol. Rev.* xxviii (1935), 243; E. Hedén, *Homerische Götterstudien* (1912); K. Lehrs, *Populäre Aufsätze²* (1875), 243 ff. M. P. N.

DALMATIA, a land on the east coast of the Adriatic, north of Epirus, was inhabited by the warlike Dalmatians of the Illyrian group, but to some degree celticized. The Dalmatians once formed part of the Illyrian kingdom of Scodra (*see* ILLYRICUM), but revolted from Genthius and therefore preserved their independence after his defeat by the Romans in 168 B.C. As the Dalmatians continuously threatened their neighbours, the Romans intervened and forced them to acknowledge Roman supremacy (156–155 B.C.). There was further fighting in 119 and a revolt in 78–77; in 51 the Dalmatians defeated the troops which Caesar sent against them. In the Civil War the Dalmatians sided with Pompey and beat Caesar's lieutenants, Q. Cornificius and A. Gabinius, but agreed to pay taxes in 46. But fighting was renewed in 45; after the campaigns of Asinius Pollio (39) the Dalmatians were finally subdued by Octavian (*see* ILLYRICUM). After two revolts in 16 and 11–10 their great fight for independence in the Illyrian-Pannonian revolt of A.D. 6–9 (or *bellum Delmaticum*: *ILS* 3320) failed, and Tiberius established the *pax Romana*, which was only once disturbed by the unsuccessful revolt of Camillus Scribonianus (q.v.), the governor of Dalmatia in A.D. 42. After its subjugation by the Romans Dalmatia formed part of Illyricum. After the creation of a separate province of Pannonia (q.v.) Dalmatia was occasionally called *superior provincia Illyricum*, and later, probably under the Flavians, received the official name 'Dalmatia'. It was then an imperial province under a *legatus Augusti pro praetore*, who resided at Salonae. In the third century it was put under equestrian administration, apparently in consequence of the reform of Gallienus. Under Diocletian Dalmatia was divided into *Dalmatia* with Salonae as capital, and *Praevalitana* or *Praevalis* with Scodra as capital, the former belonging to the *dioecesis Pannoniarum*, the latter to the *dioecesis Moesiarum*.

C. Patsch, *PW* s.v.; *Sitz. Wien* 214 i (1932), 215 iii (1933); *Archaeologisch-epigraphische Untersuchungen zur Geschichte der röm. Provinz Dalmatien* i–viii (Wissenschaftl. Mitteilungen aus Bosnien und der Herzegovina iv (1896)–xii (1912)). Ruggiero, *Diz. Epigr.* iv/1 (1924) 20 ff.; this includes a list of governors, to which must be added [Pollenius] Auspex (Dessau, *ILS* 8841) and C. Iulius [Ale]xianus (*JÖAI* xix/xx, 1919, Bbl. 293 ff.). C. Daicoviciu, 'Gli Italici nella provincia Dalmatia' in *Ephemeris Dacoromana* v (1932), 57–122. A. Betz, *Untersuchungen zur Militärgeschichte der römischen Provinz Dalmatien* (1939). F. A. W. S.

DAMASCUS was the capital of Demetrius III and Antiochus XII, under whom it issued municipal coins (some under the name of Demetrias, which the city received during Demetrius' reign). Menaced by the Ituraeans, it invited Aretas III to protect it in 85 B.C., but was independent in 69. Annexed by Pompey in 64, it was granted by Antony to Cleopatra, reannexed by Octavian, granted by Gaius to the Nabataean kingdom, and finally annexed *c.* 62. It was made a colony by the Emperor Philippus. It derived its wealth from the caravan trade, from its woollen industry, and from the multifarious products of its territory, which included not only its own fertile oasis but from 24 B.C. a large (formerly Ituraean) area up to Mt. Hermon. The only surviving monument is the *peribolos* wall of the temple of Zeus.

G. Watzinger and K. Wulzinger, *Damaskus* (1922). A. H. M. J.

DAMASTES (mythological), *see* PROCRUSTES.

DAMASTES of Sigeum, a contemporary of Herodotus and pupil of Hellanicus, wrote on *Events in Greece* (he mentioned a Persian visit of Diotimus, a *strategus* of 433–432 B.C.); on *Poets and Sophists*; on *Peoples and Cities*; on the *Ancestors of those who fought at Troy*: his *Periplus* was based on Hecataeus. Strabo (1. 3. 1) criticized Eratosthenes for trusting him.

FHG ii. 65; *FGrH* i. 5. J. L. M.

DAMIA, *see* AUXESIA.

DAMNATIO IN METALLA, *see* LAW AND PROCEDURE, iii. 11.

DAMNATIO MEMORIAE. This formed part of the penalty of *maiestas* in the graver form of *perduellio* (qq.v.). It implied that the *praenomen* of the condemned man might not be perpetuated in his family, that images of him must be destroyed and his name erased from inscriptions. Bad emperors were not exempt from such a fate. Nero (Suet. *Nero* 49) and Didius Julianus (Dio Cass. 73. 17) were declared *hostes* and condemned to death by the Senate in their lifetime. In other cases the Senate voted a posthumous *damnatio memoriae* (which included *rescissio actorum*). Claudius prevented the Senate from condemning the memory of Gaius (Dio Cass. 60. 4. 5); but formal decrees were passed after the deaths of Domitian (Suet. *Domit.* 23), Commodus (*Vita* 20), and Elagabalus (*Vita* 17).

F. Vittinghoff, *Der Staatsfeind in der röm. Kaiserzeit* (1936). J. P. B.

DAMNUM. Some cases of unlawful damage to property were dealt with in the XII Tables, e.g. damage committed by quadrupeds or in violation of agricultural interests (illicit cutting of trees or crops, grazing on another's pasture, and the like). But these were only special provisions; general rules on this matter were first laid down by a statute of unknown date (probably of the 3rd c. B.C.), *Lex Aquilia*, which introduced civil liability of the wrongdoer for wrongful killing or injuring another man's slave or beast (belonging to a herd), and for damage done to other kinds of property by burning, breaking, or destroying. The interpretation of jurists and the praetorian edict considerably extended the narrow provisions of the law to other kinds of damage, enlarged the circle of persons qualified to bring into operation the *actio legis Aquiliae* or the corresponding praetorian *actio in factum* —originally only the proprietor of the damaged object could require indemnity—and reformed the manner of appraising the value of the damage. The title IX. 2 of the *Digest* demonstrates how fertile was the contribution of the classical jurisprudence in the evolution of these doctrines.

H. F. Jolowicz, *Law Quarterly Review* 1922; D. Daube, ibid. 1936. A. B.

DAMOCLES, courtier of Dionysius I. When he excessively praised the tyrant's happiness, the latter symbolically feasted him with a sword hung by a hair over his head (Cic. *Tusc.* 5. 61, and passim).

DAMON (1), Pythagorean from Syracuse, famous for his friendship with Phintias (not Pythias). An oft-told story: Phintias, sentenced to death by Dionysius (I or II), and reprieved, comes back at the last moment to save Damon who had gone bail for him.

DAMON (2), Athenian musician, teacher of Pericles, later ostracized for his influence on him. Also called Damonides.

Prosop. Att. 3143.

DAMON (3), Athenian, one of the earliest and most important Greek writers on music, a pupil of Prodicus, much esteemed by Socrates and Plato. Plato ascribes to him (*Resp.* 400 a–c) views about the ethical effects of various rhythms, and Plato's own views about the ethical effects of different scales can probably also be traced to Damon (*Resp.* 424 c). Much in Aristides Quintilianus is probably due to him. He is said to have invented the 'relaxed Lydian' mode (ἡ ἐπανειμένη Λυδιστί).

Testimonia and frs. in Diels, *Vorsokr.*⁵ i. 381–4. *PW* iv. 2072.
W. D. R.

DAMONIDES, *see* DAMON (2).

DAMOPHILUS, a celebrated painter and modeller of doubtful date. Pliny says that he and a certain Gorgasus 'united both arts in the decoration of the temple of Ceres at Rome near the Circus Maximus' (*HN* 35. 154). He may perhaps be identified with the painter Demophilus of Himera (ibid. 61) and with Demophilus the author of a treatise on proportion (Vitruvius, bk. 7 praef.). H. W. R.

DAMOPHON (2nd c. B.C.), sculptor, of Messene, repaired Phidias' Zeus at Olympia. Made statues of gods and goddesses for Messene, Aigion in Achaea, and Megalopolis, and large groups for Messene, Megalopolis, and Lycosura in Arcadia. The last comprised Demeter and Despoina enthroned, Artemis, and a Titan Anytus. The heads of Demeter, Artemis, and Anytus and part of Despoina's veil have been discovered (Winter, *KB* 373. 1–4). The style is academic in its reminiscences of the fifth and fourth centuries. The veil accurately copies contemporary textiles. Other works have been attributed to Damophon on grounds of style.

Overbeck, 745; 1557–64; B. Ashmole in *Greek Sculpture and Painting* (1932), 91; the veil, A. J. B. Wace, *AJArch.* 1934, 107; other works, A. W. Lawrence, *Later Greek Sculpture* (1927), 121.
T. B. L. W.

DAMOXENUS, New Comedy poet, foreign to Athens, as his name signifies; he mentions Epicurus, and Adaeus of Macedon who perished at Cypsela, 353 B.C. Fr. 2, a cook philosophizes; fr. 3, a handsome youth plays ball.

FCG iv. 529 ff.; *CAF* iii. 348 ff.

DANAË, *see* ACRISIUS, PERSEUS.

DANAUS. The following genealogy, artificial but not very late (it is due to Pherecydes, fr. 21 Jacoby), shows the relationships of Danaus.

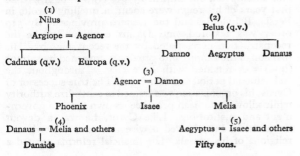

Since the names Aegyptus, Danaus, and Phoenix are simple eponyms of the Egyptians, Danai, and Phoenicians, the artificial nature of the whole is clear; but it may be taken as representing the historical theory of the day. Danaus' direct ancestry is:

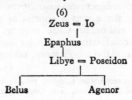

This adds the eponym of North Africa to the complex; this detail is as old as Aeschylus, *Supp.* 313 ff.

Of Danaus' daughters, only two are named in any old source (the lists in Apollod. 2. 16–20 and Hyg. *Fab.* 170 are late and artificial). These are Amymone (q.v.), and Hypermestra. Of Aegyptus' sons, only Lynceus has a real name; the rest are given names in the above lists. The two fathers quarrelled; to settle the dispute Aegyptus was desirous that his sons should marry Danaus' daughters, while Danaus and his offspring were strongly opposed. (This has no sociological significance, see Rose in *Folk-Lore* xxvii. 226 ff.) As the weaker party, Danaus and his family fled to Argos, where they claimed help and shelter from their kin; the story, with numerous subsidiary details, is in Apollodorus (2. 12 ff.), Pausanias (2. 16. 1 ff.; 19. 3–7; 25. 4; 37. 1–2); Hyginus (*Fab.* 168 ff.). The oldest parts of it doubtless go back to the *Danais* (Rose, *Handbook of Greek Lit.* 69) and much is due to the Aeschylean trilogy of which the *Suppliants* is the surviving part. Aegyptus' sons pursued them, and Danaus consented to the marriage, secretly instructing his daughters to kill their husbands on the wedding night. Except Hypermestra, who spared her husband Lynceus and helped him to escape, they obeyed him. Danaus imprisoned Hypermestra, but finally, perhaps through the intervention of Aphrodite (Aeschylus, fr. 44 Nauck), released her.

So far the story is fairly consistent in its main outlines, though many details differ in different authors. It now divides into three main accounts. (*a*) Lynceus returned, killed Danaus and his daughters except Hypermestra, and became king and ancestor of the royal Argive line (schol. Eur. *Hec.* 886). (*b*) The daughters were purified by Athena and Hermes (Apollod. 22) after burying the heads of their husbands in Lerna, their bodies outside the city, a strange detail never satisfactorily explained. Danaus married them off by offering them as prizes in a foot-race (Pind. *Pyth.* 9. 112 ff.). (*c*) They were punished in Hades by being set to fill a leaky jar with water ([Plato], *Axiochus,* 371 e, and often later, as Hor. *Carm.* 1. 11. 22 ff.). Here again, no generally accepted explanation exists.

Campbell Bonner in *Harv. Stud.* xiii. 129 ff. H. J. R.

DANCING. Ancient dancing bore little resemblance to that of the modern ball-room. It had some affinity with the ballet, but its scope was wider and it depended far less on musical accompaniment. Like the ballet it was an art of movement, a form of mental expression with the body as its medium.

At first the dance was a ritual ceremony. Such gods as Athene and Apollo were approached in the solemn measures of the *Hyporchema*, while Artemis and Dionysus were worshipped in the wild ecstasy of the Maenads' dance. From the temple it passed to the theatre, and the tragic dance came long before the tragic drama. There was the round dance of the dithyramb, *Turbasia*; the square dance of tragedy, *Emmeleia*; the single dance of comedy, *Kordax*; and the combined dance of the satyric chorus, *Sikinnis*. Every dance had two elements, movement and gesture, the movements—*phorai*—being taught in the gymnasia, the gestures—*schemata*—reserved for professional dancers.

Under the Roman Empire the dance assumed a new form in the hands of the 'pantomimes', Pylades and Bathyllus. The subject was usually taken from Greek mythology, and there was a chorus of singers with an orchestra and elaborate stage setting. The interest centred in the chief dancer, who by gestures and conventional signs told the whole story, taking each character in turn.

Athenaeus, *Deipnosophistae* 1. 25–7, 37–40; 14. 25–30. Lucian, Περὶ ὀρχήσεως. M. Emmanuel, *The Greek Dance* (Engl. Transl. 1916). F. A. W.

DANUVIUS, the Roman name for the Danube. Originally it referred to the upper course of the Danube only, the part below the Iron Gates being known as Ister (q.v.). The upper course of the Danube remained unknown to the Greeks. Herodotus (2. 33) said that its source was in Pyrene (the Pyrenees?), Ephorus in the 'Pillar of the North' (the Alps?), Timaeus in the Hercynian Forest (q.v.), Timosthenes in a Celtic lake, Apollonius Rhodius in the Rhipaean Mts. (q.v.). The identity of the Danuvius and the Ister was first asserted by Sallust(fr. 3. 79 M.), probably as a result of Octavian's Illyrian expedition in 35 B.C. In 16 B.C. Tiberius discovered the real sources, and in 13–12 the bend of the middle course (Strabo 7. 289). Strabo described the Danube with considerable accuracy and Ptolemy knew its windings (*Geog.* 3. 8. 3; 8. 7. 2). E. H. W.

DAPHNE ('laurel'), in mythology, daughter of a river-god (Ladon, generally; Peneus, Ov. *Met.* 1. 452; but Phylarchus and Diodorus of Elaea made her daughter of Amyclas, eponym of the town Amyclae, Parthenius 15). Apollo loved her, and, as she would have none of him, pursued her; fleeing from him, she prayed for help and was turned into the tree bearing her name.

H. J. R.

DAPHNE, a park near Antioch, dedicated by Seleucus I to the royal gods, especially Apollo. It contained their temples, which were served by priests appointed by the Crown, and a theatre, stadium, etc., where the kings celebrated games in their honour. Daphne was famed for its natural beauties and was a favourite and not very reputable pleasure resort of the Antiochenes. Pompey enlarged its area, and it appears under the Principate to have been the property of the emperors, who had a palace there in the fourth century and protected its famous cypresses. The Antiochenes, however, celebrated their Olympia in its precincts. A theatre has been excavated.

Antioch on the Orontes ii (1938), ed. R. Stillwell. A. H. M. J.

DAPHNIS, in mythology, a Sicilian shepherd. According to Stesichorus (ap. Aelian, *VH* 10. 18) and Timaeus (ap. Parth. 29) he was son or favourite of Hermes, and loved by a nymph, Echenaïs, who required of him that he should be faithful to her. This he was, till a princess made him drunk and so won him to lie with her. Thereupon the nymph blinded him; he consoled himself by making pastoral music, of which he was the inventor, or it was first invented by the other shepherds, who sang of his misfortunes; the language of our sources is ambiguous. But Theocritus 1. 66 ff. tells allusively a different story. In this, apparently, Daphnis will love no one, and Aphrodite to punish him inspires him with a desperate passion. Sooner than yield to it he dies of unsatisfied longing, taunting and defying her to the end, mourned by all the inhabitants of the country, mortal and immortal, and regretted by the goddess herself.

H. J. R.

DARDANI, a warlike Illyrian tribe, which was in its eastern parts intermingled with Thracians, in the south of Moesia Superior. The Dardani first appear as a united nation under a king in 284 B.C. Their frequent raids harassed the kingdom of Macedonia as well as the later Roman province. Thus they were fought by Sulla (85 B.C.), Appius Claudius Pulcher (78–76), C. Scribonius Curio (75–73); after unsuccessful campaigns under Antonius Hybrida (62) and L. Calpurnius Piso (57) the troops of M. Antonius engaged the Dardani (39); finally they were subdued by M. Licinius Crassus apparently without fighting (29 or 28). *Alae* and *cohortes Dardanorum* are known (see indexes of *CIL* xvi and Dessau, *ILS*).

Patsch, *PW*, s.v.; id. *Sitz. Wien*, 214. 1 (1932). F. A. W. S.

DARDANUS. In *Iliad* 20. 215 ff. we have the genealogy Zeus–Dardanus–Erichthonius–Tros, and thereafter

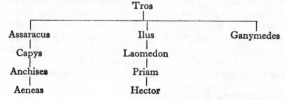

But as Priam is regularly called Δαρδανίδης, which by Homeric usage is either son or grandson of Dardanus, this passage is probably an interpolation. Later authors give two accounts of Dardanus. (*a*) He was a Samothracian, son of Zeus and Electra and brother of Iasion; either because he was driven out by Deucalion's flood (Lycophron 72–3 and schol.) or because Iasion was killed by the thunderbolt for assaulting Demeter (Apollod. 3. 138, a later form of the old ritual myth in *Od.* 5. 125 ff.), Dardanus left Samothrace and came to the mainland; for another account, see Diodorus Siculus 5. 48–9. (*b*) He and Iasius (Iasion) lived originally in Italy, their real or reputed father being Corythus (1) (q.v.); either the brothers separate, Iasius going to Samothrace and Dardanus to the Troad, or Dardanus kills Iasius. Servius on *Aen.* 3. 167 mentions three other accounts, that he was an Arcadian, a Cretan, and a native of the Troad. The constants are that he was Electra's son and founded Dardania. H. J. R.

DARES OF PHRYGIA, priest of Hephaestus at Troy (*Iliad* 5. 9) and reputed author of a lost pre-Homeric account of the Trojan War (Aelian, *VH* 11. 2). A supposed Latin prose translation survives, *Daretis Phrygii de Excidio Trojae Historia* (5th c. ?), with an alleged dedication by Sallust to Cornelius Nepos. It has little merit, but was widely used by medieval writers on the Trojan War. *See* DICTYS CRETENSIS.

Text: F. Meister (Teubner), 1873. G. C. W.

DARIUS I (*Dariavaush*), Achaemenid king of Persia, 521–486 B.C. He came to the throne after overthrowing a usurper, Gaumata the Magian, who was impersonating Bardiya (Smerdis), the dead brother of Cambyses (King and Thompson, op. cit. inf. 13–61; Hdt. 3. 68 ff.). The first years of his reign were spent in quelling revolts in Persia, Babylonia, and the Eastern provinces. By 519 order was restored, and Darius could undertake the reconstruction necessitated by the recent anarchy. His division of the Empire into provinces governed by satraps (q.v.) was retained with little change throughout the Achaemenid period and even later. The true successor of Cyrus, his organization was framed to centralize authority while allowing to each province its own form of government and institutions. Like Cyrus, he was a devout Zoroastrian, but showed a wise tolerance towards the religions of his vassals. His financial reforms created a new national economy based on a yearly fixed tax. His campaigns were designed to consolidate the frontiers of the Empire; he developed commerce, building a network of roads, exploring the Indus valley and the Mediterranean, and connecting the Nile with the Red Sea by canal.

In 512 Darius penetrated into Europe on a punitive expedition against the Scythians. A revolt of the Greek cities in Ionia was suppressed; he then prepared to punish the Greeks for their interference. Storms off Mt. Athos checked this expedition, and a third, undertaken after further preparation, ended in a Greek victory at Marathon (490 B.C.). Darius died soon after.

G. B. Grundy, *The Great Persian War* (1901); L. King and R. Campbell Thompson, *The Sculptures and Inscriptions of Darius the Great at Behistun* (1907); J. V. Prašek, 'Dareios I', *Alte Orient* xiv. 4 (1914). M. S. D.

DARIUS II, son of Artaxerxes I, ruled over Persia 424–405 B.C. On his father's death he emerged triumphant from a dynastic struggle. His subsequent misgovernment, due in part to the influence of his consort and half-sister Parysatis, who proved much the stronger character, gave rise to a succession of abortive revolts, in Syria, in Lydia (before 413), and in Media (410). More serious was the loss of Egypt in 410. These set-backs were partially balanced by the successful intervention of Persian diplomacy, directed by Tissaphernes, Pharnabazus, and Cyrus, in the Peloponnesian War.

D. E. W. W.

DARIUS III (*c.* 380–330 B.C.), a collateral of the Achaemenid house, was raised to the throne in 336 by the vizier Bagoas, who met the same death at Darius' hands as he had himself inflicted on Artaxerxes III and Arses. In Alexander's invasion Darius was outgeneralled and outfought at Issus and Gaugamela, his defeats being aggravated by his personal cowardice. He attempted to rally the Eastern provinces, but was hunted down in 330, and his own followers, who had previously deposed him in favour of Bessus, stabbed him to death on Alexander's approach.

H. Swoboda, *PW*, s.v. 'Dareios'. D. E. W. W.

DEA DIA, a corn-goddess worshipped by the Fratres Arvales; chief festival in May.

Henzen, *Acta fratrum Arualium* (1874), pp. 3 ff.

DEA SYRIA, see ATARGATIS.

DEAD, DISPOSAL OF. Cremation and inhumation were the only native methods in the classical cultures, others being known (e.g. Hdt. 2. 86–8; Ap. Rhod. 3. 202–7 and Nymphodorus ap. scholiast, ibid.), but not normally practised. It does not appear that these two methods corresponded to different eschatological beliefs. In some cases they arose from racial difference (the Terremare people in Italy cremated, the Villanovans inhumed), but even this is not invariable (Homer's people always cremate, but seem to be descended from the inhuming Mycenaeans). In the Roman Empire considerations of economy or convenience had a good deal to do with the choice (see A. D. Nock in *Harv. Theol. Rev.* xxv (1932), 357), and this may well have been true elsewhere. The essential thing was apparently to cover the body, burned or not, with earth (three handfuls will do for a ceremonial burial, Hor. *Carm.* 1. 28. 35, which is wholly Greek in tone; Antigone scatters a thin coating of dust over Polyneices, Soph. *Ant.* 255–6); the Roman definition of a buried body was one of which no bone showed above ground (Q. Mucius Scaevola ap. Cic. *Leg.* 2. 57, see the whole passage), or in a vault of some kind, such as a natural or artificial cave. Such constructions often held a number of bodies, e.g. the *columbaria* used in Imperial Rome and many earlier erections; pits

in the earth, when used, varied considerably in size, pattern, and the number of corpses they contained.

2. This covering cut off the dead from the sight of the celestial gods, with whom they had no more to do (see Soph. *Aj.* 589, and its imitation in Verg. *Aen.* 11. 51), thus avoiding pollution or offence of them and their altars (cf. Soph. *Ant.* 1016 ff.). It was also a kindness to the departed, who were generally held to need burial in order to admit them to the lower world (e.g. *Il.* 23. 71 ff.; *Aen.* 6. 325—*Od.* 24. 1 ff. is abnormal and such passages as *Aen.* 2. 646, Lucan 7. 819 are philosophical, not popular). Hence it was a universal act of piety to bury, or at least allow the burial of, any dead person, friend or foe; to be left unburied was the lot of certain criminals after execution (at Athens, Plat. *Resp.* 4. 439 e, with Adam's note; traitors were so used, e.g. Soph. *Ant.* 26 ff., imitated by Aesch. *Sept.* 1013 ff. (a spurious passage); Soph. *Aj.* 1047 ff.; Roman law regularly allowed the burial of executed criminals, *Dig.* 48. 24, with occasional exceptions, Tac. *Ann.* 6. 29. 2). Suicides were sometimes given abnormal burial, or even none (Athens, see Aeschines 3. 244, hand of corpse buried separately; Rome, 'cautum fuerat in pontificalibus libris ut qui laqueo uitam finisset, insepultus abiceretur', Servius on *Aen.* 12. 603; but this certainly was not regularly observed).

3. A regular funeral (ταφή, *funus*) was carried out as follows, omitting local, national, and chronological differences (see below). After the body had been bathed (e.g. *Il.* 7. 425; *Aen.* 6. 219), dressed (in clothes such as might have been worn in life, not in a shroud), and laid on a couch, it was lamented by the relatives and others present (excess in this respect was forbidden in classical times, e.g., by the XII Tables 10. 4 Bruns) and then carried to the place of burning or inhumation (ἐκφορά, *exsequiae*), attended by a more or less large crowd. The pyre, if the body was burned (πυρά, *rogus*), was often, in archaic Greece and under the Empire in Rome, an elaborate structure, and the amount of grave-gifts burned with the body or placed in the tomb might be very large, though customs varied enormously, the classical tendency being towards moderation in this respect also (see, e.g., Plutarch, *Solon* 21, XII Tables 10. 2 Bruns). The ashes, in a case of cremation, were placed in a vessel, the shape, material, and size of which varied in different times and places; for an unburned body a coffin (σωρός or λάρναξ, *capulus*) would normally be used, while later the stone sarcophagus, often elaborately carved, became very popular with those who could afford it. In either case, body and container would be put in one of the receptacles already described. If the body could not be found, a funeral would still be held, a dummy of one kind or another being sometimes used (example in *JHS* lvi (1936), 140). The tomb, then and at intervals afterwards, became the centre of family ritual directed towards the dead.

4. Of the differences in funeral practice above referred to, the following are the most interesting and important. In the Heroic Age of Greece, as described by Homer (especially *Il.* 23, funeral of Patroclus), the whole ceremony was most elaborate. This may be due, as regards some details, to the fact that Achilles (q.v.) retains some of the manners of an earlier time. Achilles himself, as chief mourner, is fasting and unwashed (43 ff.) till the rites are completed. The body lies in state and is formally bewailed by the women (19. 282 ff.; cf. 24. 664 and 710 ff., the mourning for Hector). In a hot climate the ceremony probably did not last long; in the *Iliad* both Patroclus and Hector are miraculously kept from decay (19. 29 ff.; 23. 184 ff.), and the lying-in-state continues for several days. When the pyre is complete, the body is brought to it by a procession of warriors in full armour, and is covered with hair shorn from the mourners' heads; Achilles, as chief mourner, holds the head of the corpse during the procession, and he and

some others keep watch over the pyre till morning. Then beasts are slaughtered and their fat laid about the body, together with other food-offerings and sacrifices of horses, dogs, and human beings, presumably to attend the dead in the next world (127 ff.). After the pyre has burned, the ashes are quenched with wine and the bones collected and put in an urn (237 ff.). A barrow of earth is then heaped above them (245 ff.), which was often marked by a post or other such object (331). Both the barrow and the post were called σῆμα, the former also τύμβος.

5. Of the funerals of the Minoan and Mycenaean ages we know nothing, but the tombs varied very much in size, elaboration, and number and value of offerings buried with the dead (see e.g. M. P. Nilsson, *Minoan-Mycenaean Religion*, 257; H. Schliemann, *Mycenae and Tiryns*, 41 ff., 88 ff.). Nor is it known whether it was the custom then to have the elaborate games after the funeral proper which are described in Homer (*Il.* 23. 259 ff.). Every contestant receives a prize of some sort, and some of them were the property of the dead; this possibly represents a compromise between burying all his goods with him and allowing them to be inherited.

6. In the classical Greek period some remnant of the ancient magnificence was still to be seen in public funerals, especially those given at Athens to citizens killed in war (Thuc. 2. 34), on which occasion a speech in their honour was made by one of the leading men (ἐπιτάφιος λόγος).

7. In Rome the funeral of a prominent man of good family, whose ancestors had held public office, was a remarkable ceremony. After the wailing (*conclamatio*) the corpse was laid out, fully dressed (in official robes, if he himself was or had been a magistrate), on a bed in the *atrium*, feet to the door. The household was *funesta*, i.e. in a state of taboo, not to be approached by, e.g., a pontiff, and to mark it as such, cypress or pitch-pine was hung outside the door. This condition lasted till a certain time after the funeral, when the heir formally swept out the pollution of death from the house with a special sort of broom (Festus, p. 68. 8 ff. Lindsay). The corpse was escorted to the place of inhumation or cremation, not only by living relatives and the general public, who were formally invited to attend, but by his dead kin, represented by actors or other suitable persons wearing their *imagines* (q.v.) and official robes. There were also professional mourning women, *praeficae*, who sang a dirge, *nenia* (q.v.), and musicians, often so noisy as to make the din almost proverbial (Hor. *Sat.* 1. 6. 43). The origin of all this was probably Etruscan; for details and references, see S. Marquardt, *Privatleben*, pp. 2, 346 ff. In the case of a son, the funeral might be conducted at night with very little ritual, in which case the household did not become *funesta* (Rose in *CQ* 17 (1923), 191 ff.). For Roman funerals, see further LAUDATIO FUNEBRIS, GLADIATORS.

8. Both Jews and Christians objected to cremation, which thus became ultimately extinct, and the latter in early times to elaborate sepulchres, hence the simple *loculi* or niches characteristic of the catacombs. Later they, when able to afford it, fell in with the common use of sarcophagi. See above, para. 3.

LITERATURE. No modern book deals exclusively and professedly with the subject as a whole; all the handbooks and encyclopaedias of classical antiquities contain sections and articles devoted to it.

H. J. R.

DEAE MATRES, a group of divinities whose worship is found chiefly in the Celtic and German provinces of the Roman Empire. There is no clear reference to them in the ancient writers, but more than seven hundred monuments of their cult (mostly inscribed) have been found. They are numerous in Cisalpine Gaul, Gallia Narbonensis, Gaul proper, lower Germany, and Britain, and rare in Rome and Spain. Those in Britain and Rome,

perhaps also in Spain, seem due to the army. The divinities are called *Matres, Matrae* (? inferred doubtfully from *Matris* and *Matrabus*), or *Matronae*, the last being perhaps their real Celtic name, though it is also common in Germanic territory. Ματρεβο (at Nîmes) is also generally recognized as a Celtic form.

The monuments range in date from the time of Caligula to that of Gordianus. The earliest are on Celtic territory, and the flourishing period of the cult among the Germans appears to have been between A.D. 100 and 250. From these facts it has been usually inferred that the worship was taken over by the Germans from the Celts; but a number of scholars have recently argued that the Germans had such female divinities long before their contact with Celtic influence. In the lack of positive evidence it must be left undecided whether the Germans borrowed the cult from the Celts, or both peoples inherited it independently from Indo-European or took it over from some previous population in Europe.

The *Matres* are usually represented in triads, three draped figures sitting under a canopy and often holding baskets of fruit. There are variations in dress and posture, and on a very few monuments all three figures are standing. In the case of other groups of five or two, or even of single figures, the identification with *Matres* is doubtful. The single figure of the so-called 'equestrian Matrona' is now held to be Epona (q.v.).

The functions of the goddesses are hard to determine precisely, and they doubtless belong to a stage of religion in which 'departmental gods' were not clearly distinguished. The baskets of fruits and similar symbols suggest divinities of wealth and fertility. Most of the epithets on the inscriptions are local or tribal, but others (*Gabiae, Ollogabiae, Alagabiae*) indicate again the giving of bounty. The association, on various monuments, with *Parcae, Iunones, Campestres,* and *Suleviae* points to a number of other functions. Perhaps the *Matres* were primarily protecting divinities of persons or family groups, whose powers were freely extended till they covered on the one hand the interests of women (*Iunones*) and on the other military affairs (*Campestres*). The cult apparently always belonged chiefly to the humbler classes in the provinces, though the dedicants in many cases must have possessed considerable means.

In addition to the general treatises cited under RELIGION, CELTIC, note M. Ihm, in *Bonner Jahrbücher* 1887; the same author in Roscher ii. 2464 ff., s.v. 'Matres'; Heichelheim in *PW* xiv. 2213 ff., s.v. 'Matres'; J. De Vries, 'De Nederrijnsche Matronenvereering', in *Tidjschr. v. Nederl. Taal- en Letterkunde* l. 87 ff. Monuments discovered later have been reported in successive volumes of the *Revue Archéologique* and the *Bonner Jahrbücher*. Some of the most interesting discoveries of recent years have been shrines or temples of the *Matres*. See especially *Bonner Jahrb.* cxix. 307 ff., cxxxiii. 213 ff.

F. N. R.

DEATH, *see* THANATOS.

DECAPROTI (δεκάπρωτοι) first appear in A.D. 66 and become common throughout the Eastern provinces of the Roman Empire in the second and early third centuries; the office was abolished in Egypt and probably elsewhere in A.D. 307–8. *Decaproti* were probably in origin a finance committee of the city council, concerned with civic revenues and endowments. By the second century they were collecting imperial taxes and levies, and in the third this was their chief function; in Egypt they were responsible for the imperial land revenue. They were liable to make good deficits from their own property. Normally ten in number, the board had a varying membership, sometimes increasing to twenty. They were elected, and probably held office for five years.

E. G. Turner, *JEg.Arch.* 1936, 7–19. A. H. M. J.

DECARCHIES, (1) the committees, usually of ten oligarchic and pro-Spartan citizens, installed by Lysander after the Peloponnesian War in cities detached from the

Athenian Empire. Possessing full executive powers, and sometimes supported by a garrison under a Spartan commander, they collected their cities' share of the Spartan war-tax levied by Sparta (Arist. *Ath. Pol.* 39. 2). The Thirty Tyrants (q.v.) and the Ten at the Piraeus are the best-known examples. Many decarchies, especially in the Asiatic cities, were abolished in the reaction against Lysander (403–402 B.C.); the rest fell after the Spartan defeat at Cnidos (394) or by the King's Peace (386). (2) The same name was given to the governments instituted by Philip II of Macedon in the Thessalian cities in 344. A. M. W.

DECEBALUS, king of the Dacians, acquired prominence through his war against Domitian (A.D. 85–9) and organized his realm. Though defeated by Roman armies, he was able to secure a favourable peace from Domitian when the revolt of the German and Sarmatian allies beyond the Danube imperilled the whole frontier, namely recognition, a subsidy, and the loan of skilled artisans. The growth of his power seemed dangerous to Trajan, who made war upon him and, after two campaigns (101–2), imposed fairly stringent terms of peace. Decebalus, it is said, did not abide by them: war began again in 105 with a serious Dacian incursion into Moesia. Trajan now resolved to make an end and convert Dacia into a Roman province. The land was invaded, Sarmizegethusa, the capital, was taken. Decebalus, hunted down, evaded capture by suicide (106). R. S.

DECELEA (Δεκέλεια), on the foothills of Mt. Parnes overlooking the Attic plain as far as the Piraeus, was occupied by the Spartans from 413 to 404 B.C. as a permanent post on Attic soil. The slight remains of fortification belong probably to the early fourth century.
Thuc. 7. 19. 27–8. A. Milchhöfer, *Karten von Attika* vii–viii. 2 ff.
T. J. D.

DECEMPRIMI, the ten senior members of the local council of a Latin or Roman municipality, formed with the yearly magistrates a group which in times of crisis represented the community in dealings with the central government. They are mentioned in the Republican period only, but in the fully developed Empire a similar group of *decaproti* (q.v.) emerges as specially liable to Rome for the collection of the imperial taxes. The connexion between the two groups is obscure. *See* DECURIONES. A. N. S.-W.

DECEMVIRI was the name given to several Roman magistracies held by ten men:
(1) *Decemviri stlitibus iudicandis* judged suits to decide whether a man was free or a slave. It is doubtful whether they are to be identified with those *iudices* whose *sacrosanctitas* was declared together with that of the tribunes (Livy 3. 55). They are first definitely attested in a document *c.* 139 B.C. By Augustus they were probably made sectional presidents of the centumviral tribunal. *See* CENTUMVIRI, VIGINTISEXVIRI.
(2) *Decemviri sacris faciundis* kept the Sibylline books. Originally *duoviri*, they were increased to *decemviri* in 367 B.C. to include plebeians, and in Sulla's time to *quindecimviri*.
(3) *Decemviri legibus scribundis*. Tradition records that in 451 B.C. the Roman constitution was suspended and complete power was entrusted to ten patricians to prepare a code of laws. They prepared ten tables of law, and a new college of *decemviri* was appointed for 450 to complete the work. Although the new board included plebeians, it composed two additional tables which were unfavourable to the plebeians (e.g. codifying the prohibition of intermarriage between the Orders). It was dominated by Ap. Claudius (q.v. 3) and retained office until the murder of Verginia (q.v.) led to its resignation.

The ancient constitution was restored and the consuls of 449 published the Twelve Tables. The substantial authenticity of the tradition (apart from the single episodes) depends on the reliability of the *Fasti*, which is now acknowledged. Further, since tradition pictures the second decemvirate as hostile to the plebeians, it would have hardly invented the plebeian *decemviri*. Thus both colleges may be accepted. The Twelve Tables (q.v. for the content) represent a compromise between patricians and plebeians. It is doubtful whether the decemvirate was contemplated as a provisional magistracy or as one designed to replace permanently the consulate and tribunate. The majority of patricians and plebeians, however, were probably unfavourable to the second *decemviri*, fearing their tyrannical tendencies.
Diod. 12. 24–6; Livy 3. 31; Dionysius 10. 54; Cic. *Rep.* 2. 36. E. Täubler, *Untersuchungen zur Geschichte des Decemvirats* (1921); cf. G. De Sanctis, *Riv. Fil.* 1924, 266; W. Soltau, *Sav. Zeitschr.* 1917, 1; J. Elmore, *CPhil.* 1922, 128. *See also* TWELVE TABLES.
A. M.

DECIDIUS SAXA, LUCIUS, described by Cicero as 'ex ultima Celtiberia' but deriving from Italian and probably Samnite stock (compare the proscribed Cn. Decidius defended by Caesar), was admitted to the senatorial career by Caesar, becoming tribune of the plebs in 44 B.C. He had previously been a centurion or an equestrian officer. An Antonian partisan, Saxa commanded along with C. Norbanus the advance-guard of the Caesarians in the campaign of Philippi. Later governing Syria for Antony, he was defeated and killed in the Parthian invasion (40).
R. Syme, *JRS* 1937, 127 ff. R. S.

DECIUS, the Emperor, *see* DECIUS (4).

DECIUS (1) MUS, PUBLIUS, performed heroic but probably legendary feats as military tribune in the perhaps apocryphal First Samnite War (343 B.C.; Livy 7. 34 f.). During his consulship (340) a battle with the Latins, somewhere in Campania (E. Pais, *Storia di Roma* iv. 196), made him famous. Actually Decius may not have been present (K. J. Beloch, *Röm. Gesch.* 374); he was popularly believed, however, to have ensured Rome's victory by solemnly 'devoting' himself and the enemy to the gods below and then charging into the enemy ranks to his death (Livy 8. 9)—an exploit more probably to be attributed to his son. For the possibility of his Capuan origin see J. Heurgon, *Capoue préromaine* (1942), 260 ff. E. T. S.

DECIUS (2) MUS, PUBLIUS, son of (1) above, consul in 312, 308, 297, 295 B.C.; censor in 304. Duris, a contemporary, mentions his death at the battle of Sentinum (295) (*FHG* ii. 479, fr. 40). Later tradition (Livy 10. 28) insisted that this was another case of *devotio* (see preceding article); in fact, if any *devotio* is historical, it is probably his (but see K. J. Beloch, *Röm. Gesch.* 440). Even so, the real hero of Sentinum probably was his colleague, Fabius (q.v. 3) Rullianus. E. T. S.

DECIUS (3) MUS, PUBLIUS, son of (2) above, consul 279 B.C. Pyrrhus defeated him at Ausculum. The story that he, like his father and grandfather, 'devoted' himself in the battle is unknown to most ancient authorities and should probably be rejected (Plut. *Pyrrh.* 21; Dion. Hal. 20. 1). E. T. S.

DECIUS (4), GAIUS MESSIUS QUINTUS, emperor A.D. 249–51, a native of Pannonia, but connected on his mother's side with an old Italian family, was city prefect before being appointed by Philip to the Danubian command (*see* PHILIPPUS 1). After Philip's death he was accepted by the Senate and assumed the surname of

Trajan. The first year of his reign was peaceful, and extensive road-making was undertaken. A special financial office, somewhat reminiscent of the censorship, was created and given to the future Emperor Valerian. In an attempt to revive the State religion the Church was vigorously persecuted as a disintegrating element in the Empire, and Christians were obliged to make a declaration of conformity before specially constituted commissions.

In 250–1 Moesia was invaded by two armies of Goths. Decius succeeded in relieving Nicopolis, but was too late to save Philippopolis. He next attempted to cut off the Goths' retreat, but after an initial success at Abrittus near Adamklissi was trapped through the treachery of his lieutenant, Trebonianus (q.v.) Gallus, and cut down by the enemy.

Zosimus 1. 22–3; Zonaras 12. 20; Wittig, *PW*, s.v. 'Messius'; Parker, *Roman World*, 157–61; *CAH* xii, ch. 6, §§ 1, 5.

H. M. D. P.

DECLAMATIO (perh. originally a translation of κατή-χησις, 'dinning into the ears', F. H. Colson, *CR* 1922, 116–17) long retained a nuance of excessively loud and over-vehement oratory (Cic. *Planc.* 19. 47; Tac. *Dial.* 35. 6), though late in Cicero's lifetime it had come to mean an oratorical exercise on an invented theme. Such themes were not unknown to Greek *rhetores* about the time of Demetrius of Phaleron (Quint. *Inst.* 2. 4. 41). Philostratus (*VS* § 507, ed. Kayser) regards Aeschines as the founder of 'the second Sophistic', which brought in stock characters of the type found in declamations—the tyrant, the rich man, the poor man. The old abstract subjects were replaced by subjects which reproduced in a fictitious manner a public debate or a judiciary case, on the ground that this sort of practice would qualify for politics or the law court. The inclusion of such exercises in education at Rome may have been due to Molon of Rhodes about 84 B.C. In any case, declamation grew to be the culminating practical exercise which most effectively applied the principles taught by professors of rhetoric; and its manner, its inventiveness, its quest after striking *sententiae* are of vital importance for its influence on the Latin style of the Silver Age. From the elder Seneca's collection, commonly known as *Controversiae* and *Suasoriae*, and from the pseudo-Quintilianean *Declamationes* we can best understand the nature of the declamatory oration. The variety and ingenuity of the arguments therein adduced for or against a thesis show declaimers at work and are typical of the rhetoric of several centuries. The stock subjects are also represented by the brief excerpts from over fifty declamations of Calpurnius Flaccus (1st or 2nd c. A.D.; ed. G. Lehnert, 1903); and the similarities pervading declaimers' themes are indicated by T. S. Simonds, *Themes treated by the Elder Seneca* (U.S.A. 1896).

2. There were two main sorts: (1) *suasoria* (q.v.), in which some eminent character is imagined to deliberate with himself or to have advice tendered to him at a political or strategic crisis, e.g. 'Should Sulla abdicate?' (Juv. 1. 16) or 'Should Cato commit suicide?' (Pers. 3. 45). Here the basis is chiefly historical. Hannibal can be told that his daring push across the Alps leads but to the glory of furnishing a rhetorical theme ('ut pueris placeas et declamatio fias', Juv. 10. 107). (2) *controversia* (q.v.), handling a fictitious case in imitation of actual pleadings in court. Here we meet condensed stories, sometimes of romantic flavour, and move in a realm of far-fetched laws affecting such figures as the daughter and captive of a pirate-chief, a condemned Vestal, a disinherited son.

3. The handling of imaginary problems as if before a court ('cum sit declamatio forensium actionum meditatio', Quint. 4. 2. 29) aimed at producing readiness and assur-

ance in a speaker. In this lay a danger. Quintilian (10. 7. 21) comments on the vanity of showy *declamatores* ready to speak glibly on any theme the moment it was propounded. This emphasizes the unreality of undisciplined rhetoric. Much earlier the orator Crassus had feared lest the passion for applause might turn rhetorical academies into 'ludos impudentiae', and his reasons for closing by censorial edict the establishments of the *rhetores Latini* are given in Cicero, *De Or.* 3. 24. 93–5 (cf. Quint. 2. 2. 12). The qualities of a good declaimer are recognized in Seneca, *Controv.* 3 *praef.* 7–8, but in the same preface (12–18) strictures are cited from Severus Cassius on the remoteness of declamations from the real arena of Senate or forum. Caustic remarks are made about 'toiling in dreamland' ('cum declamo . . . uideor mihi in somniis laborare'), about the absurdity of training a sea-pilot on a fishpond, and about the declamatory standard by which great public speakers like Asinius Pollio and Messalla Corvinus were foolishly ranked as inferior to professors of rhetoric such as Cestius or Latro. There are many passages which allude to the pernicious influence of the proud parent keen on hearing his son declaim show-pieces (Pers. 3. 45–7; Quint. 2. 7. 1; 10. 5. 21; Stat. *Silv.* 5. 3. 215–17; Juv. 7. 160–6). Similar views had justified Pollio in contrasting the genuine *orator forensis* with the *orator scholasticus*, and in remarking that success in the one capacity did not guarantee success in the other (Sen. *Controv.* 2. 3. 13; 3 *praef.*). Quintilian has salutary improvements to suggest in declamations (2. 10), and the bad effects of unreal themes are condemned by Tacitus, *Dial.* 35.

4. Yet, with all its faults, declamation laid a powerful hold on Romans under the Empire. In an age of restricted free speech, the hall for the declaimer and his often highly critical audience provided an artificial forum. Alongside of the fashionable literary readings (*recitationes*), increasingly rife from Pollio's day, declamations formed an occupation or intellectual sport for the leisured and cultivated Roman. He did not necessarily forswear the exercise when he left the rhetorical school. Cicero claims that no one kept declamation up longer than he, *Tusc.* 1. 4. 7. Juvenal, a medieval *Vita* says, 'ad mediam fere aetatem declamauit animi magis causa quam quod scholae se aut foro praepararet', and the effect on his style is obvious. The habit spread from Rome to Gaul, Spain, Africa, and other parts of the Empire, so that the traditional declamatory spirit is bequeathed to Christian Latin apologetics. Pagan themes continued to be set in schools, which explains why the works of Ennodius, bishop of Pavia late in the fifth century A.D., contain declamations similar to those in Seneca. Effective declamations kept their vogue as patterns long after their authors' times; e.g. those of Junius Gallio, Seneca's friend, were still studied in Jerome's day along with Cicero and Quintilian.

See CONTROVERSIA, DECLAMATIONES PS.-QUINT., QUINTILIANUS, RHETORIC (LATIN), and SUASORIA.

E. Norden, *Die antike Kunstprosa* (1898), i. 248 ff.; H. Bornecque, *Les Déclamations et les déclamateurs d'après Sénèque le père* (1902); G. Boissier, 'Declamatio' in Dar.–Sag.; W. Kroll, 'Rhetorik' in *PW*; J. de Decker, *Juvenalis Declamans* (1913; bibliogr.); J. W. Duff, 'Education, Roman' in *ERE*, and *Lit. Hist. of Rome in Silver Age*, ch. 2. For legacy of declamation to later Latin lit., F. J. E. Raby, *Hist. of Secular Latin Poetry in Mid. Ages* (1934).

J. W. D.

DECLAMATIONES PSEUDO-QUINTILIANEAE, a title given to two sets of rhetorical pieces ascribed, very questionably, by manuscripts to Quintilian. The one set consists of 19 longer and more elaborate declamations, the other of 145 shorter pieces (the latter part of a collection once numbering 388). Ritter edited the shorter ones, and, unlike most modern critics, accepted them as by Q., but believed that the longer declamations fall into four groups, differing in date and authorship, though one group might, he thought, come from the school of Q. In the fourth century Jerome and Servius quote from the longer ones as by Q. They may have been collected in the period of Gellius and Apuleius. It seems impossible to identify, as Ritter does, the shorter declamations with one of the two works mentioned by Q. (1 *proem.* 7) as having been published from notes by enthusiastic pupils; and a survey of the more fantastic, far-fetched, sensational themes of both sets indicates a difference in spirit from Q., who reminds us (2. 10. 5) that we shall look in vain among cases of contract and interdict for 'wizards', 'pestilence', 'oracles', 'stepmothers crueller than those in tragedy', and other features still more romantic (*fabulosa*). The shorter declamations contain a *sermo* (sometimes more than one *sermo*) sketching useful lines of argument for pupils' guidance, and the rhetorical handling is exemplified in *declamatio*.

Texts: in P. Burman's ed. of Quintilian (Leiden, 1720, still very serviceable); C. Ritter, *M. Fab. Q⁴. declamationes quae supersunt cxlv* (1884); G. Lehnert, *Declamationes xix maiores* (1905, not satisfying). Special Studies: C. Ritter, *Die Quintilianischen Deklamationen* (1881); R. Reitzenstein, *Studien zu Q.'s grösseren Dekl.* (1909, suspects even more varied authorship than Ritter does); G. Golz, *Der rhythmische Satzschluss in d. grösseren pseudo-Quint. Dekl.* (1913, infers considerable variety of authorship from examination of *clausulae*); Y. Englund, *Ad Q⁴. qui feruntur declamationes maiores adnotationes* (1934). On authenticity and nature of the themata see literary histories of Teuffel–Kroll–Skutsch, Schanz–Hosius, and Wight Duff.   J. W. D.

DECRETUM, *see* CONSTITUTIONES.

DECUMA.
Tithes on agricultural produce were paid by tenants on the *ager publicus* (q.v.) of Italy (Appian, *BCiv.* 1. 7), and by the landowners in the provinces of Sicily and Asia under the Roman Republic, which maintained the taxes previously levied by the native kings. Owing to the variability of the yield it suited the government to let out to *publicani* (q.v.) the right of collection. In Sicily this was done in Syracuse, so that local companies could compete. The *decumae* of Asia, which lasted from the time of C. Gracchus till the dictatorship of Caesar, were let in Rome to Italian companies. The *decumani* were regarded as the leading members of the *societates publicanorum* (Cic. *Verr.* 2. 175). The government had a right of pre-emption (at a fair price) on another tenth of the harvest (*alterae decumae*).   G. H. S.

DECUMATES, *see* AGRI DECUMATES.

DECURIONES,
the local councillors of the fully developed Roman municipal system, both in colonies and municipalities, whether Latin or Roman. They were recruited from the ex-magistrates and by censorial appointment at the quinquennial census, holding office for life. The qualifications were those required for the magistracies and included criteria of wealth, age, status, and reputation. The minimum age-limit of twenty-five was frequently neglected, minors of influential families being elected *honoris causa*. The *decuriones*, whose number varied with the size of the municipality, formed the *consilium* of the magistrates, and in practice controlled the public life of the community. Local administration and finance, the sending of deputations and petitions to Rome or to the provincial governors, the voting of honorary decrees and statues, fell to them, since the popular assemblies played little part except at the magisterial elections. The *decuriones* were also responsible for collecting the imperial taxes due by their municipality, and personally liable in case of default, a liability which became an intolerable burden in the later Empire and led to the breakdown of the municipal system. The decurionate became an hereditary inescapable *munus* of the wealthy, who degenerated from a ruling class to a tax-collecting caste, known as *curiales* (q.v.). For bibliography *see* MUNICIPIUM.   A. N. S.-W.

DEDICATIO,
the other side of *consecratio* (q.v.). Strictly speaking, only one who is himself in touch with *res sacrae*, in other words a priest expert in the ways of the gods, can consecrate anything; hence we do not hear, for instance, that M. Horatius Pulvillus consecrated the Capitoline temple, but that he dedicated it. But the owner (State or individual) of a *res profana* can if he chooses give it to a god, as he might to another human being or another State. This giving to a god, or removing from the secular (*noa, profanus*) sphere into the sacred (*tabu, sacer*) being accomplished in due form, the object, which a moment before anyone might handle, because it was a common thing, now becomes charged with *numen*, and to have anything to do with it requires more or less precaution and observance of proper ritual. Thus, a block of carved stone is in itself unremarkable, but if it has been dedicated to a god for use as an altar, it is impiety to touch it save in the performance of an act of worship, usually sacrifice (Hor. *Carm.* 3. 23. 17).

Though only objects dedicated and consecrated by permission or direction of the State could in Roman law be really *res sacrae* (*see* CONSECRATIO), in practice anyone might privately dedicate, e.g., a chapel on his own property to such gods as he chose to worship, though occasionally a non-Roman cult was prohibited by decree of the Senate or other competent authority.   H. J. R.

DEDICATIONS.
I. GREEK. In the early period of Greek literature dedication, in the modern sense, of literary works did not exist. When Hesiod, Theognis, and Empedocles addressed poems to Perses, Cyrnus, and Pausanias, their intention was not that of a modern dedicator, to gratify the dedicatee or obtain a *cachet* from his name. The person addressed was no more than a target for the arrows of instruction or exhortation. Nor, obviously, do the *Epinicians* of Pindar come into account here. The first Greek to dedicate a book seems to have been Dionysius Chalcus, who in the middle of the fifth century B.C. dedicated his poems to a friend (Ath. 15. 669 d–e). In the fourth century Isocrates (*To Nicocles*) and perhaps Theophrastus (Ath. 4. 144 e) adopted the practice, which became extremely common in the Hellenistic age. Thus Archimedes addressed his *Psammites* to Gelon, Apollonius of Perga the first three books of his *Conica* to Eudemus, the last five to Attalus I. Diogenes Laertius actually finds it 'arrogant' in Chrysippus to 'write so many books and dedicate none of them to a king' (7. 185), and mentions (4. 38) the only king to whom Arcesilaus did *not* dedicate anything. In the Roman period of Greek literature the practice remains frequent. Notable examples are the literary treatises of Dionysius of Halicarnassus (some in the form of letters) and the anthologies of Meleager and Philippus (*Anth. Pal.* 4. 1–2).

II. LATIN. The dedication of a literary work is not a difficult technical problem in the case of a collection of small poems. Thus Horace simply prefaces the first book of his *Odes* with a poem addressed to Maecenas (cf. *Epod.* 1. 4; *Sat.* 1. 1). Many of the *Epistulae* in bk. 1 address friends (e.g. Tibullus 1. 4. 1, 'Maecenas docte' 1. 19. 1), and such addressing verges on dedication; but Horace intentionally places *Epist.* 2. 1 before 2. 2 (written earlier) as an introduction addressed to Augustus. Propertius scatters mentions of his friends throughout his work, linking them to his predominant love-theme. Lucretius happily combines the dedication to Memmius with the invocation of Venus. Virgil is less successful. In *Eclogue* 3 a herdsman mentions the name of Pollio; the sixth begins with lines addressed to Varus having nothing to do with the poem; while the unity of the eighth is broken by the lines on Pollio's Illyrian expeditions. The *Georgics* (1. 2) are appropriately addressed to Maecenas (cf. 4. 2).

Formal dedications, like Spenser's letter to Raleigh explanatory of *The Faërie Queene* with his dedication to

Queen Elizabeth, or like the elaborate addresses introducing eighteenth-century writings, were not the usage in Latin classics—many were subconsciously directed to posterity rather than to contemporaries. Apart from the technique of a dedication, formal or informal, there is its value for light thrown on an author's circle or the date of a work. Thus Persius addresses friends like Macrinus or Caesius Bassus in different satires; Valerius Flaccus invokes Vespasian early in his *Argonautica* and by allusions to Titus and Domitian shows that he began his poem after A.D. 70; Martial, like Statius, prefixes to some of his books a prose letter: e.g. he dedicates bk. 8 to Domitian and bk. 12 to a friend Priscus excusing himself for three years' indolence in Spain.

Regarding prose writings, one may instance the *De Natura Deorum* as one of five philosophical treatises dedicated by Cicero to Brutus, and the second edition of the *Academica*, dedicated to Varro, of whose learning Cicero stood in some trepidation. Velleius Paterculus dedicated his work to M. Vinicius, and Valerius Maximus his to Tiberius. Seneca's *Consolationes* may be taken as dedicated to their addressees: his three books *De Ira* were dedicated to his brother Novatus; his seven *De Beneficiis* to Aebutius Liberalis. Quintilian addressed his *Institutes* to Vi(c)torius Marcellus as the real begetter of his undertaking.

R. Graefenhain, *De more libros dedicandi ap. scr. Graec. et Rom. obvio* (1892); F. Stephan, *Quomodo poetae Graecorum Romanorumque carmina dedicaverint* (1910); J. Ruppert, *Quaestiones ad hist. dedicationis librorum pertinentes* (1911). J. D. D.
L. R. P.
J. W. D.

DEDITICII were individuals, communities, or nations which made a formal, unconditional surrender of themselves, their property, territory, and towns to the Roman State. *Deditio* was usually performed by defeated enemies who preferred to throw themselves on Rome's mercy— *deditio in fidem*—rather than suffer total sack and destruction—*expugnatio*. But any community which wished to place itself under the total protection of Rome could surrender by *deditio*. *Dediticii* were regarded as suppliants and usually treated with generosity. They had no political rights and were *cives nullius certae civitatis*, until Rome settled their future status, either by restoring to them the right of self-government, *leges et iura*, and recognizing them as ordinary *peregrini* (q.v.), or even by granting them the status of a *civitas libera* (see SOCII) or, on occasion, full treaty rights (see FOEDUS). *Deditio* is not itself a form of treaty-alliance, nor is it normally a permanent status, although the *Lex Aelia Sentia* (A.D. 4) placed slaves of ill repute who were given their liberty in the category of *dediticii* instead of granting them Roman citizenship.

Ancient sources: Livy, passim, esp. bks. 1–10; Caesar, *BGall.*, passim. Modern views: A. Heuss, *Klio*, Beiheft xxxi; E. Täubler, *Imperium Romanum.* Cf. A. H. M. Jones, *JRS* 1936, 223 ff.
A. N. S.-W.

DEFIXIO, *see* MAGIC, para. 8.

DEIANIRA (Δηάνειρα), in mythology, daughter of Oeneus (q.v.) and wife of Heracles. He first heard of her from Meleager's ghost in Hades, according to Bacchylides 5. 170. He won her in combat from Achelous (cf. AMALTHEA), and on the way home he entrusted her to the centaur Nessus to carry across a river; Nessus tried to assault her and Heracles killed him with one of his poisoned arrows. Dying, he gave Deianira some of his blood, assuring her it was a potent love-charm. Years later, when she had borne Heracles several children, he brought Iole home from Oechalia; Deianira, to regain his affection, smeared the blood on a garment and sent it him. The poison caused his death, whereat she killed herself. See Sophocles, *Trachiniae.* H. J. R.

DEÏDAMEIA (Δηιδάμεια), *see* ACHILLES, para. 5.

DEIOTARUS, tetrarch of the Tolistobogii (in W. Galatia), and subsequently king of all Galatia. In the third Mithridatic War he consistently supported the Romans. He was rewarded by Pompey with part of east Pontus (64 B.C.), and in 52 or 51 he received from the Senate Lesser Armenia and most of Galatia, together with the title of king. For his adherence to Pompey in the Civil War he was temporarily deprived of his new acquisitions by Caesar. Accused before Caesar at Rome (45 B.C.) of various acts of insubordination, he was defended by Cicero, whose son he had befriended during Cicero's governorship of Cilicia. After Caesar's death Deiotarus resumed his lost territories and bought recognition from Antony. He supported Brutus and Cassius at Philippi, but by his timely desertion to Antony he retained his kingdom, and by the murder of a rival tetrarch (c. 42) he acquired all Galatia. He died in 40. Deiotarus trained his infantry in Roman fashion; one of his corps subsequently became the Legio XXII Deiotariana.

B. Niese, *PW* s.v.; F. E. Adcock, *JRS* 1937, 12–17. M. C.

DEIPHOBUS (Δηΐφοβος), in mythology, son of Priam; he plays a fairly prominent part in the fighting in the *Iliad*, and in the *Odyssey* is associated with Helen (5. 276), and the hardest fighting at the capture of Troy is about his house (8. 517–20). All later authors say he was married to Helen after Paris' death. H. J. R.

DEIPHONTES (Δηϊφόντης), in mythology, a descendant in the fifth generation of Heracles. He married Hyrnetho, daughter of Temenus king of Argos, and was favoured by him above his own sons, who therefore murdered their father and strove with Deiphontes, with results variously described by different authors (collected by Stoll in Roscher's *Lexikon* s.v.). H. J. R.

DEIPYLE, *see* ADRASTUS.

DELIA, the name under which Plania was celebrated in the love-poetry of Tibullus (q.v.).

DELIAN LEAGUE, THE, is the modern name applied to the confederacy organized in 478–477 B.C. to continue the naval war against Persia. As a *symmachia* (q.v.) it resembled the Peloponnesian League in leaving the determination of its policy to an assembly, and in entrusting the leadership in war to one State, Athens. Yet it was organized without a break between Athens and Sparta, and was meant to be neither a counterblast against the Peloponnesian League nor an instrument of Athenian power. Its membership eventually rose to c. 200 States. The Assembly met at Delos, and Athens theoretically had no predominant influence in it, but, like other States, cast one vote only. An advance over the older league was the existence of a treasury, which was kept at Delos till 454, when it was transferred to Athens. Members supplied either ships or money, and the money was used by Athens for the maintenance of the fleet. The original assessment of Aristides is said to have called for 460 talents a year, but details concerning collections are available only for the period beginning 454. Actually the position of Athens was stronger than indicated by the constitution. The smaller States followed her lead in the Assembly and the larger States that opposed her were outvoted. Furthermore, the League had been organized as a permanent offensive and defensive alliance, so that secession could be treated as rebellion. Revolting States, when subdued, were by treaties made into subject allies. Gradually most members lost their independence, meetings of the Assembly were discontinued, the treasury was transferred to Athens, and the League was transformed into an empire.

ANCIENT SOURCES: G. F. Hill, *Sources for Greek History*[2] (1907), ch. 1: add Thucydides 3. 10–11 (representation in assembly).

MODERN LITERATURE: Accounts in histories of Greece and handbooks of constitutional antiquities; especially J. B. Bury, *History of Greece*[2] (1913), 328 ff. The constitution and purpose of the League are discussed by Larsen in *Harv. Stud.* 1940. On the finances of the League see B. D. Meritt, H. T. Wade-Gery, and M. F. McGregor, *The Attic Tribute Lists*, vol. i (U.S.A. 1939). J. A. O. L.

DELICTUM, *see* LAW AND PROCEDURE, III. 4.

DELOS, a small island regarded as the centre of the Cyclades. According to legend the birthplace of Apollo and Artemis, it was from earliest historical times sacred to Apollo, who was honoured by song, dance, and games in a festival (*panegyris*), to which came men and women from the islands and coasts of the Aegean as early as the eighth century (cf. *Homeric Hymn to Apollo*). The island had once been occupied, according to Thucydides, by Carian sea-rovers, who were driven out by Minos of Crete. The pre-Hellenic inhabitants, of whose occupation stone huts on Mt. Cynthus afford evidence, were displaced by colonists from continental Greece before 1000 B.C., and the island was already famous in the *Odyssey*. Its history proper begins in the sixth century, when Pisistratus, to further his control of the Cyclades, purified Delos, and the Samian tyrant Polycrates extended his patronage.

2. When the invading Persian fleet arrived in 490 Datis respected the sanctuary. In 478–477, when a maritime league was formed to ensure Greek independence, Delos was naturally chosen as seat of the common treasury (*see* DELIAN LEAGUE). On the removal of the treasury to Athens Delos came under more direct Athenian control, but did not pay tribute. In 426 Athens again purified the island, and Nicias inaugurated a quinquennial festival in a *theoria* of great pomp. After the Peloponnesian War Athenian control of Delos was interrupted until the formation of Athens' second maritime confederacy (378/7), when the administration of the Delian temples was reorganized under Athenian officials called Amphictiones (cf. 'Sandwich Marble', *IG* ii. 1635). When Athens lost her sea power, her administration of Delos ended (314).

3. Henceforth for a century and a half the sanctuary was administered by local officials known as *hieropoioi*, while Egypt and Macedon contended for hegemony of the Aegean. During this period Delos enjoyed the usual institutions of a city-state. For the supervision of the temple of Apollo, and all edifices within his *temenos*, the Ecclesia entrusted its powers to the *hieropoioi*, who ranked next to the Archon, the head of the State. The first political relationship of the free Delians was with the League of Islanders (i.e. Cyclades), the formation and protection of which are attributed by some to the Ptolemaic kings. The federal treasury—perhaps the seat of the League—was at Delos, where federal festivals were from time to time instituted in honour of the Hellenistic princes who happened to be paramount in the mid-Aegean. Delian monuments of this period reveal the pretensions not only of the Egyptian and Macedonian but also of the Pergamene and Syrian kings. Early in the third century Delos was a centre of the corn-trade of the Aegean; buyers came from Macedonia and other northern places. A colony of foreigners was growing up, foreign banking-firms flourished; the occurrence of Italian names indicates commercial bonds with south Italy. Delos enjoyed a kind of neutrality; but at last she presumed to support Perseus of Macedon against Rome, and after his defeat at Pydna Rome handed over the island to her ally Athens, who removed the old inhabitants and sent her cleruchs to replace them (166). To damage Rhodian trade, Delos was made a free port.

4. In the third great period of Delian history the chief annual magistrate of the Athenian colony bore the title *Epimeletes*. After a servile outbreak (*c.* 130) there was a wider organization of the Athenians and foreign traders.

Already there existed guilds (κοινά) of Italian residents (*Hermaistai*, or *magistreis Mirquiri*, and others), also powerful Oriental guilds (e.g. *Poseidoniastai* of Berytus). Traders' vessels filled the Sacred Harbour and the Merchant Harbour, and slaves constituted one of the chief commodities of exchange. Decline, however, set in after Archelaus, general of Mithridates of Pontus, sacked the island in 88; and in 69 the pirates, allies of Mithridates, attacked Delos, now a Roman naval centre, and enslaved the inhabitants. After Pompey suppressed the pirates some measure of prosperity returned; but before the end of the century the trade-routes had changed, and Delos was soon abandoned.

5. The archaeological exploration of Delos, carried on by the French School (Athens) from 1873, has revealed the remains of public buildings—temples, porticoes, theatre, gymnasium, etc., also of warehouses and private houses; these, with a wealth of inscriptions, make a notable addition to the knowledge of Greek civilization.

F. Durrbach, *Choix d'Inscriptions de Délos* (1921–2); P. Roussel, *Délos colonie athénienne* (1916); *Délos* (1925); W. A. Laidlaw, *A History of Delos* (1933); M. Rostovtzeff, *CAH* viii, ch. 20, § 3 (with full bibliography); id. *Social and Economic History of the Hellenistic World* (1941). W. A. L.

DELPHI is situated on the lower southern slopes of Parnassus, some 2,000 feet above the Gulf of Corinth. It was the most ancient and sacred sanctuary in Greece. It attained importance as early as 1600 B.C., for a Minoan fountain spout of that date was found near the temple, and it was also occupied in the Mycenaean period.

For the history of the oracle, see the following article. The sanctuary consisted of a *temenos* enclosed by a wall. Inside it were the monuments dedicated by the States of Greece to commemorate victories and public events, together with some twenty 'treasuries' (q.v.), a small theatre, and the main temple of Apollo (q.v., para. 4) to which the Sacred Way wound up from the road below. The original temple, a primitive and small building, was destroyed by fire in 548. Objects of value saved from it at this time have recently (1939) been found buried under a stone of the Sacred Way. The second temple was completed in 510, largely with the help of donations from the Athenian family of Alcmaeonidae (q.v.), then living at Delphi in exile. This new temple (partly described in the *Ion* of Euripides) was destroyed by an earthquake in 373. A new temple was built by subscription, its pedimental sculptures being made by two Athenians, Praxias and Androsthenes. This building survived until Roman times and was repaired by Domitian. The *adyton* or Holy of Holies, where the priestess gave the oracles, was below the south-west corner of the temple. A stone known as the *omphalos* (q.v.), the reputed centre of the earth, was found here; it bore the inscription ΓΑΣ (the 'Stone of Earth', the original deity of the oracle), and is dated *c.* 600 B.C. A marble omphalos of Roman period has also been found.

The sanctuary was attacked by the Persians in 480 and by the Gauls in 279, but suffered little damage. Nero despoiled it of 500 statues. Julian attempted a revival of the sanctuary, but the oracle announced to him its own decline, and in A.D. 390 it was finally closed by Theodosius in the name of Christianity. Excavations were begun by French archaeologists in 1880, when the village of Kastri was removed from the site to its present position.

F. Poulsen, *Delphi* (1920); E. Bourguet, *Les Ruines de Delphes* (1914); P. de la Cost-Messelière, *Au Musée de Delphes* (1936). S. C.

DELPHIC ORACLE, in classical times the supreme oracle of Greece, presided over by Apollo. Its site was supposed to be the centre of the earth, marked by the sacred navel-stone (*omphalos*, q.v.). It had been a holy place from remote antiquity (remains of pre-Greek sacrifices have been found), and the presiding genius was originally an earth-spirit. Apollo was recognized by the Greeks themselves as a late-comer (Aesch. *Eum.* 1 ff., etc.). Aeschylus' account emphasizes the peaceful nature of the transfer to Apollo, but the legend of his killing a chthonian monster (*Hymn. Hom. Ap.*, Eur. *IT* 1244 ff.) suggests a different and more plausible tradition; the ecstasies and sex of the Pythia may be due to the original chthonian nature of the cult (but cf. K. Latte, *Harv. Theol. Rev.* xxxiii (1940), 9 ff.).

2. Responses were given by the Pythia, a young woman (in later times elderly, Parke, op. cit. infra, 257), in a state of frenzy induced by means not now ascertainable with certainty. Faith in the power of the god to take possession was complete, and the consequent emotional suggestion would doubtless add powerfully to the effect of such practices as chewing bay-leaves (Apollo's plant) or drinking holy water. Excavation has rendered improbable the post-classical theory of a chasm with mephitic vapours. The riddle of the prophecies is not entirely soluble. Efficient accumulation and use of information can account for much, but there remain exceptions, such as the response about the wisdom of Socrates, whose explanation will always be a mystery. After purification and sacrifice, inquirers approached the oracle in an order determined partly by lot. Right of precedence might be granted as a privilege (προμαντεία, Farnell, *Cults* iv. 214 n.). A male prophet put their question and interpreted the Pythia's answer, commonly in verse. Advice was sought both by private individuals (e.g. concerning marriage, childlessness, commercial enterprises) and States. Slaves were manumitted by dedication to the Delphic god.

3. In religion Delphi gave answers on all questions of cult, fostering the worship of Olympian and local deities impartially and adopting a generally conservative attitude on religious questions. The best way to worship was 'according to ancestral custom' or 'the City's custom' (Parke, 326, n. 2). It seems, however, to have welcomed Dionysus—with whose ecstatic worship Delphic prophecy has been thought to have much in common—and assisted in the propagation of his cult. At Delphi itself Dionysus was received into partnership, his grave was shown in the inner sanctuary, and for three winter months Apollo was believed to hand over the shrine to Dionysus and retire to the far north. The trieteric festivals of Dionysus at Delphi were orgiastic, and women were officially sent from the Greek States (including Athens) to take part in them. An authority on all cult-practices, Apollo was above all the god of *katharsis*, especially purification after homicide, from which the primitive conception of automatic *miasma* never entirely disappeared.

4. Politically, Delphi came to the fore in the great period of colonization, its advice being regularly sought on the choice of site and patron deity. Tradition assigned many laws of Greek cities also to the god, e.g. the constitution of Lycurgus at Sparta. Other political prophecies, with a few striking exceptions difficult to explain, suggest extensive knowledge of the situation and a leaning to conservatism which did not exclude attempts (not always successful) at a politic adaptation to changing conditions. Thus in spite of aristocratic sympathies, Delphi is said to have foretold the power of most of the tyrants (Pisistratus is an exception), it favoured Croesus until his fall, discouraged Greek resistance to Persia, was pro-Spartan in the Peloponnesian War, supported Philip of Macedon.

5. Questions of individual morality, which were left untouched by the city-states, deeply interested the oracle, and it seems to have shown great firmness on moral issues. It sponsored the notion that purity was a matter, not only of ritual, but also, and primarily, of the spirit, and that the intention might be more important than the

deed. (Cf. esp. the story of Glaucus, Hdt. 6. 86, and other examples in Parke, 386 ff.) In this it reached the high-water mark of religious ethic in pagan antiquity. The famous exhortations carved on the temple, though not especially exalted in tone, were also moral precepts—'Know thyself' and 'Nothing too much'.

6. The importance of Delphi is above all that it provided a meeting-place for the otherwise isolated city-states of Greece. The unique position and universal prestige which it enjoyed, and which were necessary if it was to discharge this function, cannot now be completely accounted for, but besides the impressiveness of its prophetic method (as contrasted with 'sane' procedures like the inspection of victims or the flight of birds), one may mention the attraction of its famous Panhellenic Pythian games (founded after the First Sacred War about 590 B.C.) and its connexion with a powerful religious league of Northern States, the Delphic Amphictiony (*see* AMPHICTIONIES). The early history of the Amphictiony is obscure, but it seems certain that its original centre was farther north, and Delphi was probably not included until the middle of the seventh century. In the fifth century, with the recognition of Delphi as a common centre of worship, the Amphictionic Council became representative of the Greek States as a whole (Parke, 193). Macedon was admitted to membership after the assistance given by Philip against the Phocians in the Third Sacred War (355–346 B.C.).

7. In Hellenistic times the influence of Delphi and of the League rapidly declined, though the new kings thought it due to their royalty to flatter the oracle, which was still a centre of information for the Greek world. Delphi was seized by the Aetolian League about 300 B.C. and suffered later from barbarian invasions. Its treasure was unscrupulously used by Sulla. Under the Roman Empire it enjoyed a somewhat artificial revival in Hadrian's time, but astrology provided an alternative source of prophecy and there were rival oracles. The decline of Delphi was already almost complete when Christianity became the official religion under Constantine.

On the general subject of oracular prophecy, *see* ORACLES, DIVINATION.

For a full account of the Delphic oracle and bibliography, see H. W. Parke, *A History of the Delphic Oracle* (1939); also K. Latte, *PW* xviii. 839 ff. W. K. C. G.

DEMADES (fl. 350–319 B.C.), Athenian politician. A brilliant orator and diplomat, who recognized that Athens must come to terms with Macedon and did not scruple to stand in Macedonian pay, he rendered good service after the battle of Chaeronea, when he checked the intransigence of the Athenian people, rebuked Philip's insolence, and secured honourable terms of submission for Athens. After Philip's death he survived an impeachment by Hyperides, and when Alexander marched into Greece he again mediated between Athens and Macedon (335). During Alexander's absence in the East he remained in power, together with Phocion; he prevented Athens from supporting King Agis III (q.v.) against Macedon, and he procured the deification of Alexander. Accused of receiving a bribe from Harpalus (q.v.), he offered no defence and was fined; and after Alexander's death he was disfranchised. Reinstated in 322 to avert Antipater's attack on Athens, he used his influence to procure the death of Demosthenes and Hyperides. In 319 he was detected by Cassander in an intrigue with Antigonus, and was summarily executed by him while on an embassy to Macedonia. Nothing survives of his speeches (which were not committed to writing) except some picturesque phrases, e.g. 'Macedon without Alexander would be like the Cyclops without his eye'. A fragment ὑπὲρ τῆς δωδεκετείας, included in the oratorical Corpus, is certainly not by Demades.

P. Treves, in *Athenaeum*, 1933. N. G. L. H.

DEMARATUS, a Spartan king, *c.* 510–491 B.C. He obstructed his colleague Cleomenes I (q.v.) on the invasion of Attica (506), and again when he prevented the arrest of the medizing party at Aegina (491). Dethroned on a false charge of illegitimacy by Cleomenes, he fled to King Darius. He accompanied Xerxes in 480, possibly in hopes of recovering his throne from the victorious Persians, and repeatedly warned him (according to Herodotus) that Sparta would infallibly resist him. Rewarded for his (unspecified) services with four cities in Asia Minor, he resided there until his death, many years later. A. M. W.

DEMETER (Δημήτηρ), the Greek corn-goddess, identified in Italy with Ceres (q.v.). It seems certain that the last two syllables of her name mean 'mother', but the first is more difficult. The ancient explanation, that δη- is a by-form of γη- and she is the 'earth-mother', breaks down owing to the absence of evidence of any such by-form of that or any other word beginning with γ. More likely, especially in view of Nilsson's demonstration (see below) that her most famous cult turns wholly on the processes connected with corn, is the suggestion of Mannhardt (see Farnell, op. cit. infra, 29 f.) that it is to be connected with ζειά, spelt, although this also is dubious, seeing that the form δηαί is attested (by Hesychius, s.v.) only as the Cretan for 'barley', and Demeter is not particularly connected with Crete, and the Dorian and other dialects call her Δαμάτηρ, indicating an *a*, not an *e* in the original form of her name.

2. Of her functions, however, there is no doubt. She is the goddess who governs the fruits of the earth, especially, though not quite exclusively, bread-corn. She would appear to have thrown off very early a younger double of herself, the 'Virgin' (Κόρη), who is regularly (not quite invariably) worshipped with her, and seems to be essentially the power which is in the corn itself and appears and disappears with it. Being thus connected with very important happenings at the surface of the earth, it is in accordance with a common tendency of Greek and other religions that she should become associated also with the depths of the earth; so Demeter becomes in mythology the mother-in-law, Kore (Persephone) the wife, of the death-god. It may reasonably be conjectured that originally the latter was the consort, not of Hades, but of Pluton, god of the wealth (especially the wealth of corn) which the earth produces. The story, first found in the Homeric Hymn to Demeter, is that Hades carried off Kore; Demeter, after vainly searching for her daughter, wandered to Eleusis and there was received, in disguise as an old woman, into the house of Celeus the king, to nurse his son. She put the child in the fire every night to burn his mortal nature away, but was interrupted by Metanira, Celeus' wife, and so hindered from making him immortal as she had planned. She then revealed herself to the Eleusinians, who built her a temple. Meanwhile Zeus, to persuade her to come back to Olympus and to let the earth bring forth, had Kore returned to her; but Kore, as she had eaten some pomegranate-seeds in the other world, could not return entirely, but spends some part of every year underground. As Nilsson (*ARW* xxxii. 79 ff.) points out, the myth agrees well with the historical celebration of the Eleusinian Mysteries (see MYSTERIES) and with Greek climatic conditions. The Great Mysteries are in Boedromion, 16–17 and 19–22, and connected with the return of Kore; the time is early autumn, when the fields are growing green again after the drought of summer. The Lesser Mysteries of Agrae are in Anthesterion; it is spring, and they lead up to the summer harvest and the following period of dryness, during which Kore, the young corn or seed-corn, is indeed under the earth, stored away in the great grain-jars. That the ritual of the Mysteries (which at Eleusis, are even older than Demeter, being

pre-Hellenic) had to do with the death and rebirth of the corn and that in time hopes of human immortality came to be read into this ritual is fairly clear, but the details remain extremely obscure (see bibliography below). Eleusis claimed to be the centre from which knowledge of agriculture sprung, Demeter having sent Triptolemus the Eleusinian to teach the rest of mankind (Callimachus, *Cer.* 20–2; Ov. *Met.* 5. 645; and many authors and representations in art).

3. Of other festivals of Demeter, one of the most famous and widely spread was the Thesmophoria (q.v., to Demeter Thesmophoros, 'bringer of treasures'). In Athens it was held on Pyanopsion 11–13, and consisted of a series of rites, largely magical, performed by women for the fertility of the soil; connected with it was the ritual of the Scirophoria (q.v.), on Scirophorion 12.

4. In Arcadia Demeter appears as the consort of Poseidon (probably in his capacity of 'earth-holder' or husband of Earth, γαιήοχος, see POSEIDON). The Black Demeter of Phigalia and the Demeter Erinys of Thelpusa were both said to have been mated with by Poseidon in horse-shape, and the former was shown horse-headed (Paus. 8. 25. 4 ff., 42. 1 ff.), while it was doubtful if the child she bore was a foal or the local goddess Despoina. That a darker side of her nature was stressed here is clear from her titles. However, even the normal Demeter could be very formidable, since being a giver of plenty she could also bring famine. When Erysichthon (q.v.) offended her it was insatiable hunger that was his punishment. Another trace of her tendency to become a goddess of the depths of the earth and not simply of the corn is shown in the Athenian use of Δημήτρειοι, 'Demeter's people', as a euphemism for the dead (Plut. *De fac.* 943b).

5. Since she is a mother-goddess, the question who her husband is was never consistently answered. In Arcadia (see above) he was Poseidon; according to Hesiod (*Theog.* 912–13) Zeus was Persephone's father; a story, probably a very old ritual myth, in the *Odyssey* (5. 125 ff.) says that she lay with Iasion (cf. DARDANUS) in a ploughed field, and that when Zeus heard of it he killed Iasion with the thunderbolt. To be the consort of a mother-goddess is very dangerous, cf. ANCHISES. Hesiod adds (ibid. 969 ff.) that their child was Plutus (q.v.). This is characteristic for all such goddesses; the important thing is that they should be fertile, not that they should be wives.

Of literature on the subject, only a small selection can be given. Farnell, *Cults* iii. 29 ff. is the best collection of facts concerning her cult; add Deubner, *Attische Feste*, 40 ff., for her Attic, Nilsson, *Griechische Feste*, 311 ff., for her non-Attic festivals. H. J. R.

DEMETRIAS, a city of Magnesia on the Gulf of Pagasae. Formerly located below Mt. Pelion, it is now proved to have adjoined Pagasae on the western shore of the inner bay. Demetrius Poliorcetes founded it *c.* 293 B.C. by a 'synoecism' of many small Magnesian towns; he built massive fortifications and made the best use of an admirable site, so that it became important as a military and commercial centre. Though occupied by a Macedonian garrison as one of the 'fetters of Greece', it enjoyed some measure of self-government. Liberated from Philip V by Rome, Demetrias supported the Aetolians and Antiochus in 192–191 and was accordingly restored to Macedonia, under whose control it remained until the overthrow of Perseus. After a second liberation it gradually declined.

The adjacent sites of Demetrias and Pagasae have been more thoroughly investigated by archaeologists than any in the interior of Thessaly.

F. Stählin and E. Meyer, *Pagasai und Demetrias* (1934). H. D. W.

DEMETRIUS (1), writer of Old Comedy (Diog. Laert. 5. 85). His Σικελία may be assigned to *c.* 400 B.C.

CFG i. 264–6; *CAF* i. 795–6.

DEMETRIUS (2) of Phalerum (b. *c.* 350 B.C.), son of Phanostratus, Athenian writer and statesman, escaped death as a pro-Macedonian in 318, and was made absolute governor at Athens by Cassander. During his ten years' *strategia* he limited military and other service, passed sumptuary laws, and established νομοφύλακες. When Poliorcetes took Athens (307), D. fled to Boeotia, and was later librarian at Alexandria (297). He died in disgrace under Philadelphus.

WORKS: moral treatises, popular tales, declamations, histories, literary criticism, rhetoric, and collections of letters, fables, and proverbs. Though an outstanding orator, D. produced mainly a superficial amalgam of philosophy and rhetoric. He assisted his fellow Peripatetics, and under him Athens enjoyed peace.

FGrH ii B 228. W. S. Ferguson, *Hellenistic Athens* (1911).
F. W. W.

DEMETRIUS (3) I of Macedonia, *Poliorcetes* (336–283 B.C.), son of Antigonus I, married (321) Antipater's daughter Phila. His first important campaign was against Eumenes (317–316); his first independent command, against Ptolemy, ended in disaster at Gaza (312). Nevertheless he became henceforth the brilliant instrument of his father's policy of reuniting Alexander's empire. His best performances were in Cyprus (306), which he won from Ptolemy by the naval victory of Salamis, and in Greece (307 and 304–302), where his enthusiasm (perhaps genuine) for Greek autonomy and his revived 'League of Corinth' achieved more than many victories. His famous siege of Rhodes (305) was a failure, and would have been unimportant politically had it succeeded; it repays study as a military *tour de force* and an apt expression of 'the Besieger's' personality.

The defeat of Ipsus and the death of Antigonus (301), for which Demetrius, by his impetuosity, was partly to blame, destroyed Antigonus' empire in Asia, and reduced Demetrius' power to a precarious thalassocracy. But he kept a foothold in Greece, and after Cassander's death (297) and the murder of two kings and the queen-mother, he had (through Phila) the best claim to the throne of Macedonia, and he was accepted as king by the army (294).

He was always a conqueror rather than a ruler, and age taught him no wisdom. While he established his control over Greece (293–289), he planned to regain his father's empire in Asia. He possessed the finest man-power and the greatest fleet; but the Macedonians, who wanted peace not war, deserted to Lysimachus and Pyrrhus when they simultaneously invaded Macedon; and Demetrius had lost his kingdom (288). He led into Asia no 'Grand Army', but a small force of mercenaries (287). He was trapped in Cilicia and surrendered to Seleucus (285), who hospitably encouraged him to drink himself to death (283). 'Bonis initiis malos euentus habuit.'

Diodorus, bks. 19, 20; Plutarch, *Demetrius*. W. W. Tarn *CAH* vi, ch. 18; vii, ch. 3.
G. T. G.

DEMETRIUS (4) 'the Fair' (ὁ καλός), son of Demetrius (3) Poliorcetes, and half-brother of Antigonus Gonatas. He was sent by Antigonus to take Cyrene from Ptolemy II (*c.* 255 B.C.). He gained Cyrene without opposition, but was murdered soon after at the instance of Berenice II (q.v.).
M. C.

DEMETRIUS (5) II of Macedonia (*c.* 276–229 B.C.), son of Antigonus II and Phila, defeated Alexander of Epirus and dethroned him in 264 (Justin. 26. 2. 11). On succeeding Gonatas (*see* ANTIGONUS 2) in 239 he divorced Stratonice, Antiochus I's daughter, who had no male issue, and married an Epirote princess, Phthia, also called Chryseis. (His marriage to Nicaea, Alexander of Corinth's widow, was probably unconsummated: Plut. *Arat.* 17.) The Aetolian League, which sought to annex Epirote Acarnania, now united with Achaea against Macedon

('Demetrian War'). Active at first in the west, Demetrius saved Acarnania, but lost Atintania; he assisted Argos against Achaea, and detached Boeotia, part of Phocis, and Opuntian Locris from Aetolia; in 233 his general Bithys defeated Aratus. About this time, however, the Epirote monarchy was overthrown and the new republic joined the Leagues; Demetrius allied himself with Agron of Illyria to protect Acarnania, but was called north by a Dardanian inroad. Defeated, he died in 229, leaving one son, Philip, by his wife Phthia.

A shadowy figure, Demetrius by his lack of vigour brought the Macedonian monarchy to a low ebb.

Plut. *Aratus*; Justin. bk. 28. V. Costanzi in *Saggi di Storia antica offerti a G. Beloch* (1910); K. J. Beloch, *Griech. Gesch.* iv (1928); P. Treves, *Rendiconti Accademia Lincei* 1932.
F. W. W.

DEMETRIUS (6) of Pharos (d. 214 B.C.) betrayed Corcyra to Rome (229) and became a dynast in north-west Illyria. He helped Antigonus at Sellasia (222). In 220, breaking the treaty with Rome, he sailed past Lissus, to ravage the Aegean islands. Pursued by the Rhodians, he sold his assistance against Aetolia to Macedon. When expelled by the Romans (219), he fled to Philip V, whose anti-Roman policy he mainly inspired. In 215 he urged Philip to seize Ithome, and later perished in a rash expedition against Messene. Polybius (3.19.9) characterizes him as foolhardy, and wholly without judgement.

Polybius (the only reliable account). M. Holleaux, *Rome et la Grèce* (1921).
F. W.

DEMETRIUS (7) of Bactria (d. 167 B.C.), eldest son of Euthydemus (q.v. 2) and his half-Seleucid queen (*see* DIODOTUS I), succeeded to the Bactrian throne about 190 B.C. He annexed the Seleucid provinces east of the Persian desert, and soon after 184 invaded northern India to restore the native Mauryan Empire under his own rule. Making skilful use of the political position, which threw the Buddhist world on to his side, he almost succeeded; his general Menander captured the capital Pātaliputra (*Patna*), while Apollodotus occupied Kathiawar, Barygaza (*Broach*), and probably Ujjain; and he began to rebuild Taxila as his Indian capital. He was consciously imitating Alexander, and intended, following his ideas, to make of his empire a kind of partnership of Greek and Indian, typified by his bilingual coinage. Many names of the Greek satrapies in India have been recovered; he founded three name-cities, Demetrias in Arachosia, in Sind (*Patala*), and on the Oxus (*Termedh*). But many Bactrian Greeks disliked his Indianizing policy; in 168 Eucratides, cousin of Antiochus IV, invaded Bactria and raised a revolt; next year Demetrius was killed, and Bactria with its Iranian provinces fell to Eucratides.

Cambridge History of India i, chs. 17, 22; W. W. Tarn, *The Greeks in Bactria and India* (1938), passim.
W. W. T.

DEMETRIUS (8) I SOTER of Syria (187–150 B.C.), second son of Seleucus IV. As a hostage in Rome he saw the kingdom pass first to his uncle (Antiochus IV) and then to his cousin (Antiochus V). In 162 he escaped and won the throne for himself. He crushed the rebel general Timarchus in the East and reconquered the insurgent Jews in Palestine (161). His ability made him feared by neighbouring Powers and suspect to Rome (though the Senate had recognized his title in 160). He died in battle against a pretender, Alexander Balas, whom the kings of Pergamum and Egypt had suborned against him.
G. T. G.

DEMETRIUS (9) II NICATOR of Syria (*c.* 161–126 B.C.), eldest son of Demetrius I, reigned 145–141 and 129–126. In 141 he made war upon Parthia, but was captured, and did not obtain his release until 129. His reign well illustrates the difficulties of the later Seleucids. He won his kingdom from one pretender, lost part of it almost immediately to a second, and was finally murdered after losing the remainder to a third.
G. T. G.

DEMETRIUS (10) of Scepsis in the Troad (b. *c.* 214 B.C.), grammarian, archaeologist, and polymath, wrote 60 books on the 60-line Trojan catalogue (*Il.* 2).

DEMETRIUS (11) **IXION** (2nd c. B.C.), a grammarian, contemporary with Aristarchus, who seceded from Alexandria to Pergamum and disputed Aristarchan textual principles. He also compiled an Atticist Lexicon.

DEMETRIUS (12) **LACON** (2nd c. B.C.), Epicurean, pupil of Protarchus of Bargylia and younger contemporary of Zeno of Sidon. He criticized Carneades' attack on the possibility of proof, and expounded Epicurus' doctrine of time. Ed. W. Crönert, in *Kolotes u. Menedemos* (1906), p. 100, and V. De Falco (1923).

PW iv. 2842. W. D. R.

DEMETRIUS (13) (probably 2nd or 1st c. B.C.) compiled in Greek a short guide to letter-writing which enumerates twenty-one types of letter, with one or two examples of each type (ed. V. Weichert, 1910).

DEMETRIUS (14) of Magnesia (fl. 50 B.C.), friend of Atticus, wrote in Greek on concord (Περὶ ὁμονοίας), and on homonymous towns and writers; much of his biographical detail was transmitted to Diog. Laert.

FHG iv. 382.

DEMETRIUS (15), the unknown author of a Greek treatise *On Style* (Π. ἑρμηνείας: *De Elocutione*), of uncertain date. That he was not Demetrius Phalereus (2 above), the traditional author, would seem certain: and as its date is probably best assigned to the first century A.D. (Roberts, ed. 49 ff.: see, however, Kroll, *Rhet.*, § 20), the attempt to identify him with Demetrius (q.v. 16) of Tarsus (Roberts, ed. Loeb, 272–9) is worthy of note. The work, which is of considerable value, embodies Peripatetic teaching, discusses diction and its arrangement, four types of style and the epistolary art, and probably forms part of the first-century movement for establishing classical standards in literary art.

Editions: L. Radermacher, 1901; W. Rhys Roberts, 1902; W. Rhys Roberts (Loeb), 1927. E. Orth, *Demetrios vom Stil*, 1923 (German translation, with bibliography). J. W. H. A.

DEMETRIUS (16) of Tarsus (late 1st c. B.C.), a grammarian, one of the characters in Plutarch's *De defect. orac.*, where he is said (c. 2) to be on his way home from Britain to Tarsus. Perhaps identical with a D. who dedicated two tablets with Greek inscriptions, now in the York Museum; and possibly also Demetrius (15). See W. Rhys Roberts, in Loeb *Demetrius*, pp. 272–9.

DEMETRIUS (17) the Cynic lived in Rome under Gaius, Nero, and Vespasian, and belonged to the strongly anti-monarchical branch of the Cynic school. He was exiled to Greece under Nero (A.D. 66) but returned in the time of Vespasian.

PW iv. 2843.

DEMETRIUS (18) of Troezen (probably 1st c. A.D.), wrote works on literary history (Ath. 1. 29a). The only known title is that of his work on philosophers, Κατὰ σοφιστῶν (Diog. Laert. 8. 74).

DEMETRIUS (19), Jewish historian, *see* JEWISH GREEK LITERATURE.

DEMETRIUS, *see also* TRICLINIUS.

DEMINUTIO CAPITIS. The civil capacity in Roman law depends on three elements: freedom (*libertas*), Roman citizenship (*civitas*), and membership in a Roman family (*familia*). The loss of one of these three *status* effects the loss of the *caput*, the civil capacity (*capitis deminutio*). *Caput* signified originally the individual person by which a group of persons, *populus* or *familia*, has been diminished and not directly the civil capacity (cf. *Inst. Iust.* 1. 16. 9) as in the classical meaning of the term. Classical Roman law distinguished three degrees of *deminutio capitis*. (*a*) *Maxima*, when the individual lost his freedom (by enslavement). This involved the further loss of his *civitas* and family, for only a free man could be *civis* and member of a family. (*b*) *Media* (or *minor*), when a person has lost the citizenship with the consequent dissolution of family ties (this happened in the case of *aquae et ignis interdictio*, and later with *deportatio*, or when a Roman citizen became *peregrinus* or Latin); the *libertas*, however, remained untouched. (*c*) *Minima*, when somebody has lost the membership of his family (*mutatio familiae*). In this case it is indifferent whether he enters at the same time another family or becomes a head of a family himself. The *deminutio capitis minima* occurs with *adoptio* (q.v.), *adrogatio, emancipatio, in manum conventio, datio in mancipium*. The origin of *deminutio capitis* is obscure. The rigid organization of the ancient Roman family explains the fact that in ancient times *deminutio capitis minima* was treated on a par with the two other forms, in spite of essential differences which distinguished the legal institutions from which the various degrees of *deminutio capitis* originated. In later development the effects of *deminutio capitis maxima* and *media* remained unaltered, except in so far as the principles of the *ius gentium* moderated the effects of *deminutio capitis media*. But the consequences of *deminutio capitis minima* (dissolution of agnatic ties and therewith the suppression of the rights of inheritance and guardianship, extinction of debts, of personal servitudes and partnership, failure of will, and so on) were considerably diminished already in the Classical period, together with the weakening of the institution of the Roman family. These reforms were due to the praetorian law, in which the emphasis on cognatic relationship was one of the chief features. In Justinian's law *deminutio capitis minima* lost its actuality for the most part.

Ancient sources: Gaius 1. 162–4; Ulp. *Epit.* 2. 13; *Inst. Iust.* 1. 16; *Dig.* 4. 5. F. Desserteaux, *Études sur la formation historique de la capitis deminutio* i (1909), ii (1919–26), iii (1928). W. W. Buckland, *A Text-Book of Roman Law*² (1932), ch. 3. U. Coli, *Capitis Deminutio* (1922). P. Bonfante, *Corso di diritto romano* i (1925), 123 ff. A. B.

DEMIURGOI (δημιουργοί), 'public workers', are in Homer such independent craftsmen as metal-workers, potters, and masons, and also seers, doctors, bards, and heralds (though not beggars! *Od.* 13. 383). Plato and Xenophon use the word thus. But in pre-Solonian Athens they comprised all who gained their livelihood other than from the soil, perhaps including wage-earners. They enjoyed a short-lived right of supplying two of the archons (580 B.C.) (Arist. *Ath. Pol.* 13. 2); they do not subsequently appear as a separately organized class. As the highest, often eponymous officers, *demiurgoi* appear in several States; though perhaps of greatest antiquity in Elis and Achaea, they are most often mentioned in Dorian records. Their exact function varied from State to State. In the Achaean League they formed a council of ten, who assisted the general; the Arcadian League imitated this organization, based originally on local representation, as also in Elis, where the *demiurgoi* formed a special caste. *Demiurgoi* appear in the Argolid, Megarid, Messenia, Thessaly, Delphi, Locris, Phocis, Crete, and several Aegean islands; examples from Cilicia, Pamphylia, and Pisidia date from Roman times.

Evidence mainly epigraphical. V. v. Schoeffer, *PW* s.v. 'Demiurgoi'; M. Guarducci, *Riv. Fil.* 1930.

DEMOCEDES of Croton (6th c. B.C.), one of the most famous physicians of his time, practised first in Aegina and Athens, then at the court of Polycrates of Samos. After the murder of Polycrates in 522 B.C. he won much favour at the court of Darius, but later returned to Croton; on the defeat of the aristocrats by the democrats under Theages he fled to Plataea. He married a daughter of the wrestler Milon.

Testimonia in Diels, *Vorsokr.*⁵ i. 110–12. *PW* v. 132. W. D. R.

DEMOCHARES (*c.* 360–275 B.C.), Athenian orator and democratic statesman, who rose to power after the expulsion of Cassander's agents in 307. During the 'Four Years' War' against Cassander (307–304) he fortified Athens and made an alliance with Boeotia. Exiled *c.* 291 (not earlier, as Plut. *Demetr.* 24 suggests), he returned in Diocles' archonship (288–287), and recovered Eleusis from Macedon. He secured financial aid from Lysimachus, Antipater, and Ptolemy; and in 280–279 (archon: Gorgias) had a decree passed honouring Demosthenes, his uncle. Sincere and patriotic, he was handicapped by doctrinaire political views.

His written works consisted of Speeches, and a History, mainly of Athens, in over twenty-one books, rhetorical and lacking in objectivity.

F. Jacoby, *FGrH* ii. 79; *Lives of X Orators*, p. 851 (decree passed by Demochares' son Laches, 271–270); W. S. Ferguson, *Hellenistic Athens* (1911); K. J. Beloch, *Griech. Gesch.* iv. 2 (1928), 445.
F. W. W.

DEMOCRACY (δημοκρατία, the 'rule of the people'). This term becomes common with Thucydides and Aristophanes, but is known to Herodotus (6. 43), and is presumed by Aeschylus (*Supp.* 604). The germs of Greek democracy grew from the fact that the *polis* (q.v.) derived from the old assembly of the armed people, and always preserved some traces of that origin. Beginning with Thersites (*Il.* 2. 212), there were always movements against the rule of the noble and the rich, as the lower ranks of free people tried to win full citizenship. The development to democracy may be first perceived in Hesiod and Solon. The suppressed and exhausted demos found leaders in tyrants or lawgivers, and during the sixth and fifth centuries B.C. most of the city-states achieved a more or less democratic constitution. The ideas of law, freedom, and equality began to predominate. (The expression for equality, *isonomia*, is sometimes used for democracy itself.) Athens became the most perfect and by its power the most influential democracy. Its ideal form is proclaimed by the Periclean Funeral Speech (Thuc. 2. 35 ff.).

The sovereign authority in democracy was the Assembly, which decided by majority. The principal task of the council (*see* BOULE) and the magistracies (q.v.) was to prepare measures and to carry them into effect. In the Assembly and popular courts almost the whole people participated, and as council and magistracies were continuously changing their personnel, the people became the actual ruler. Every citizen had full liberty of speech (παρρησία), but even the most extreme democracy could not dispense with leadership. In the fifth century one or more of the *strategi* (q.v.) ruled in fact, in the fourth century government was controlled by unofficial and irresponsible leaders ('demagogues'). That was one of the reasons for the decline of democracy. Other reasons were: the ease with which the Assembly could make and unmake laws, the strong individualism arising from the very ideals of freedom and equality, and the general mistrust of any person who grew powerful. Political philosophers always regarded democracy, and especially its 'deviation', ochlocracy, as a bad constitution.

Schoeffer, *PW*, Suppl. i. 346 ff.; T. R. Glover, *Democracy in the Ancient World* (1927); G. Glotz, *The Greek City* (1929). V. E.

DEMOCRITUS, *c.* 460 (Apollodorus, ap. Diog. Laert. 9. 41; Thrasylus, ibid., gives 470) to *c.* 370 B.C., 'a young man in the old age of Anaxagoras, 40 years his junior' (D.L. l.c.), son of Hegesistratus (al. Athenocritus or Damasippus), a wealthy citizen of Abdera in Thrace, adopted the Atomic theory of his master Leucippus (q.v.), with whom his name is constantly conjoined. Accounts of his life, spent mainly in study, teaching, and writing as head of the school at Abdera, are legendary. In childhood magi left behind by Xerxes with his father taught him Oriental lore, and, as a young man he is said to have spent his patrimony in extensive travel in Egypt and the East. Contemporary tradition (Glaucon of Rhegium, ap. D.L. 9. 38) mentions a Pythagorean teacher, and association with Philolaus (Apollod. ap. D.L. ibid.) and Anaxagoras, as well as Leucippus (D.L. l.c. 34), is asserted on weak evidence. Demetrius of Phalerum (ap. D.L. l.c. 37) denies the story of his visit to Athens, where he saw Socrates but was unrecognized (fr. 116). Nicknamed 'Wisdom' (Σοφία) in his lifetime for his encyclopaedic learning, and, in later antiquity, 'the laughing philosopher' (Γελασῖνος: cf. Hor. *Epist.* 2. 1. 194; Juv. 10. 33), he lived to a great age (90, Diod. 12. 11; 100–9, ap. D.L. l.c. 39, 43). Plato never mentions him, but Aristotle pays great attention to his views. Cicero praises his style for its ornateness, rapidity of motion, and clarity.

2. WORKS: Of an edition by Thrasylus (1st c. A.D.) in tetralogies only the list of 70 titles (ap. Diels, A 33) and 200–300 fragments, mostly ethical, some spurious, survived from antiquity. D.'s writings covered almost every field: Ethics (Tetrs. 1, 2); Physics, with Psychology and Logic (3–6); Mathematics and Astronomy (7–9); Music and Poetics (10, 11); Technical (12, 13); 'causes' (9 bks.); miscellaneous (9 bks.). The following are noteworthy philosophically: *On Cheerfulness* (Περὶ εὐθυμίης 2. 3), defining the moral ideal; the *Greater* and the *Lesser World Systems* (Μέγας and Μικρὸς διάκοσμος, 3. 1, 2), the former ascribed to Leucippus; *On Mind* (Περὶ νοῦ, 4. 3) by Leucippus, and *On the Senses* (Περὶ αἰσθησίων 4. 4), both psychological; *Guarantees* (Κρατυντήρια, 6. 1) and *On Logic or The Canon* (Περὶ λογικῶν ἢ κανών, 6. 3) which contained his theory of knowledge.

3. Ancient writers after Theophrastus failed to distinguish the respective contributions of Leucippus and D. to Atomist doctrine: D. probably supplied its refinements and elaborate theory of knowledge. The ultimate principles are atoms and void: the former—real or body —innumerable tiny particles, homogeneous in substance, infinitely various in shape and (D. adds) size, indivisible (ἀδιαίρετα, ἄτομα), solid, compact, and unmodifiable; the latter, infinite empty space (τὸ κενόν)—unreal, but existent. D. contrasts the Nothing (οὐδέν) with the Something (δέν) —where these invisible reals move in all directions, colliding and interweaving and forming things by aggregation. That D. held Epicurus' theory of an original perpendicular fall of the atoms due to their weight is, despite conflicting testimony (see Bailey, op. cit. inf., 130–2), unlikely. Burnet argues (*EGP*⁴ 341 f.) that Leucippus and D. considered weight a derivative property, a function of size within the 'Whirl'. Aristotle's complaint (*Metaph.* 985ᵇ19) that they omitted to assign any cause for atomic motion is unfair. They took it as ultimate and eternal, referring it to 'necessity' (ἀνάγκη: Arist. *Gen. An.* 789ᵇ2; D.L. 9. 45), or 'natural law'.

4. Differences in the shape, arrangement, and position of the atoms in compound bodies, by variously affecting the senses, generate the 'secondary qualities' of colour, sound, etc., which exist only by convention (νόμῳ, fr. 125). Soul (identified with mind) is material, composed of fine, round, fiery atoms distributed over the body. 'True-born' knowledge (γνώμη γνησίη) of atoms (and void) comes from direct contact with soul atoms, 'bastard' (σκοτίη), via the senses. Both depend on

'idols' (εἴδωλα, δείκελα) which objects shed. In vision an idol stamps an impression on the intervening air, which then appears, distorted, as an image in the pupil (ἔμφασις).

5. Aristotle's thrice-repeated remark (*De An.* 404ᵃ27; *Metaph.* 1009ᵇ12 f.; *Gen. Corr.* 315ᵇ9) that D. 'found truth in sense-appearance' because he identified mind with soul (*De An.*), or thought with sense (*Metaph.*), must be understood from his own standpoint of belief in intelligibles (νοητά), not as implying a narrow sensationalism and ignoring D.'s account of true cognition of (physical) realities. D.'s own fragments (ap. Diels B 6–11; cf. 117), quoted by Sextus, show that he refused to take sense at its face value, and looked deeper for truth. His attack on the relativism of his fellow-townsman Protagoras (Sextus ap. Diels A 114; Plut. ibid. B 156) proves him to be no sceptic.

6. Democritus shared Leucippus' theory of the generation of innumerable 'Worlds' by action of a 'whirl' which originates spontaneously (ἀπὸ ταὐτομάτου) or by chance (ἀπὸ τύχης); this does not imply contingency, as Aristotle's criticism (*Ph.* 196ᵃ24–ᵇ8) might suggest, but rather the operation of undesigned and inscrutable mechanical causes (cf. Bailey, op. cit. inf. 139–43). His astronomy is reactionary, with its Milesian notion of a flat, disk-shaped earth.

7. Democritus' ethical fragments hardly afford evidence for a systematic theory of conduct. His ideal of inner contentment is lofty but self-centred, and his acute reflections on human life lack the moral depth of Socrates and Plato.

8. Aristotle thought highly of D., who approaches Aristotle himself in the volume of his writings and the breadth of his learning. The loss of his works is serious. Epicurean physics and modern materialism derive largely from him.

1. Ancient sources: Diels, *Vorsokr.*⁵ (Kranz, 1934–7); Ritter and Preller¹⁰ (1934). 2. Modern literature. (i) General: Zeller–Nestle, *Philosophie der Griechen* i. 2⁷ (1922) (Engl. transl. 1881); Th. Gomperz, *Greek Thinkers* i (1901); J. Burnet, *Greek Philosophy, Part* i: *Thales to Plato* (1914); L. Robin, *La Pensée grecque*² (1932); H. Cherniss, *Aristotle's Criticism of Pre-Socratic Philosophy* (U.S.A. 1935). (ii) Special: P. Natorp, *Die Ethika des Demokritos* (1893); A. Dyroff, *Demokritstudien* (1899); C. Bailey, *The Greek Atomists and Epicurus* (1928); A. Brieger, *Die Urbewegung der Atome und die Weltentstehung bei Leucipp und Demokrit* (1884); H. C. Liepmann, *Die Mechanik der Leucipp-Democritischen Atome* (1885); O. Hamelin, *La Pesanteur de l'atome dans le système de Démocrite* (1888); L. Mabilleau, *Histoire de la Philosophie atomistique*; A. Goedeckemeyer, *Epikurs Verhältnis zu Demokrit* (1897); H. Weiss *CQ* xxxii (1938; D.'s theory of cognition); *PW* v. 135. A. J. D. P.

DEMODOCUS, the minstrel of Alcinous (q.v.), blind but very gifted (*Od.* 8. 44–5; 62–4). He sings of the loves of Ares and Aphrodite (ibid. 266 ff., if genuine), is sent an honourable portion of meat by Odysseus at Alcinous' feast (474 ff.), and makes him weep with his songs of the Trojan War (521 ff.). H. J. R.

DEMOI (δῆμοι), in general, villages, like κῶμαι; of political importance at Athens since the legislation of Cleisthenes. He took the natural groups which formed townships in Attica, and gave them a part in both local and State administration. As local corporations they were responsible for certain police duties (such as were performed by the *astynomoi*, q.v., in the city); they could hold land and had their own cults and officials (a treasurer, priests, etc.); measures were passed at meetings of all the members (*demotai*), presided over by the *demarchos*. Each deme registered its own members, youths being entered at a deme-meeting on the completion of their eighteenth year, and on these registers every citizen depended for recognition of his citizen-rights, though a rejected applicant might appeal to a dicastery. From each deme were chosen the *bouleutai*, in numbers proportionate to the membership of the deme; and the demes carried out financial duties on behalf of the State,

such as keeping a register of property held within the deme for the purposes of *eisphora* and *liturgies* (qq.v.). Metics (q.v.) also were registered in their demes of residence. In this way a census of the adult male citizen and metic population, of wealth, and of the production of cereals was kept.

As the demes were originally natural townships, they varied greatly in size. There were at least 150 in the fifth century (over 170 later); they averaged about 3 members each in the Boule, but Acharnae had 22 members (in the 4th c. at least), some from 10 to 15, many only one or two. Athens contained seven or eight demes within the walls and many others in the environs. After their first institution the demes ceased to be purely territorial, for a man belonged to his father's deme wherever he resided; with the drift of the country population to Athens and Piraeus they tended to develop from territorial units to kinship groups.

Demes are also found in other States, as Cos and Rhodes (after 408–407), and in many under the influence of Athens.

A. W. Gomme, *The Population of Athens in the Fifth and Fourth Centuries B.C.* (1933), ch. ii. A. W. G.

DEMON (*c.* 300 B.C.), wrote an *Atthis* and a large collection of proverbs (Περὶ παροιμιῶν). The latter was widely quoted by writers of *Paradoxa*, but its explanations are generally false and popular.
FHG i. 378.

DEMON, antiquarian, *see* PAROEMIOGRAPHERS.

DEMONAX of Cyprus (2nd c. A.D.), Cynic philosopher, known only by the life of him ascribed to Lucian. He was of good family but elected to live in poverty; his teachers were Epictetus, Timocrates of Heraclea, Agathobulus, Demetrius. He avoided the grossest excesses of the Cynic school; he admired Socrates and Aristippus as well as Diogenes. He cannot be credited with any independent philosophical views. He starved himself to death when nearly 100 years old.
PW v. 143. W. D. R.

DEMOPHANES and **ECDELUS** (not Megalophanes and Ecdemus, as Plut. *Phil.* 1; cf. Ziegler, *Rh. Mus.* 1934, 228 f.) (3rd c. B.C.), two Megalopolitans, followers in exile of Arcesilaus of the Athenian Academy, and renowned for their services to the republican cause, in 251 B.C. helped Aratus to liberate Sicyon, and about the same time had the tyrant Aristodemus murdered, thus freeing their own city. After the assassination of Demetrius the Fair (q.v. 4) they were called in to establish a federal constitution in Cyrene (*c.* 250). They were later famous as Philopoemen's teachers. F. W. W.

DEMOPHON (Δημοφῶν), in mythology, son of Theseus and brother of Acamas (q.v.). He and his brother, being shadowy figures, are often confused, both being lovers of Laodice and Phyllis. His part in the Trojan War is the doublet of his brother's. While returning he stayed in Thrace and there met Phyllis, a princess who fell in love with him. He left her, promising to return when he had settled affairs at Athens, but she, weary with waiting, hanged herself and was turned into an almond-tree, which put forth leaves when Demophon came at last and embraced it (Servius on Verg. *Ecl.* 5. 10; Hyg. *Fab.* 59; Ov. *Her.* 2). The Athenians claimed to possess the Palladium (q.v.), which came somehow into Demophon's hands (Suidas s.v. ἐπὶ Παλλαδίῳ; Clem. Al. *Protr.* p. 36, 15 ff. Stählin). H. J. R.

DEMOSTHENES (1) (d. 413 B.C.), son of Alcisthenes, Athenian general. After an unsuccessful invasion of Aetolia in 426 he won two brilliant victories against a Peloponnesian and Ambraciot army invading Acarnania.

In 425 his occupation of Pylos led to a most valuable success, the capture of a body of Spartan hoplites on the adjacent island of Sphacteria. He surprised Nisaea in 424, but failed to take Megara, and in a triple attack on Boeotia, for which he was perhaps responsible, he was unable to land troops at Siphae, since the enemy was forewarned. In 413 he commanded the armament sent to reinforce Nicias at Syracuse. After failing to regain Epipolae by a night attack, he urged the abandonment of the siege, but evacuation was delayed until the Athenians lost control of the sea and were driven to attempt escape by land. The rearguard, led by Demosthenes, surrendered on the sixth day, and he was subsequently executed.

Though never a politician, Demosthenes favoured the war-party and collaborated with Cleon. His strategy tended to be over-elaborate, but he was a skilful tactician, and his gallant leadership in difficult situations merited a better fate.

Thucydides, bks. 3, 4, 7. B. W. Henderson, *The Great War between Athens and Sparta* (1927), chs. 4-6 and 9. H. D. W.

DEMOSTHENES (2) (384-322 B.C.), the orator, son of Demosthenes of the deme Paeania in Attica. When D. was seven years old his father died, leaving the management of his estate to his brothers, Aphobus and Demophon, and a friend, Therippides. The trustees mismanaged the business, and D. at the age of eighteen found himself almost without resources. He claimed his patrimony from his guardians, who spent three years in attempts to compromise. In the meantime, D. was studying rhetoric and legal procedure under Isaeus; at twenty-one he brought a successful action against his guardians, but two more years elapsed before he received the remnants of the property. He was now engaged in the profession of *logographos*, and was also giving lessons in rhetoric. The latter profession he followed certainly till 345, when public affairs began to engross his attention.

2. He is said to have tried as a young man to speak in the Ecclesia, but to have failed, because his voice was weak and his delivery imperfect. We may set aside the legends of his declaiming with pebbles in his mouth and reciting on the sea-shore amid the thunder of the waves, but doubtless he submitted himself to a rigorous training which partially overcame his disabilities, though, if we may believe Aeschines, he was not successful at extempore speaking. Internal evidence justifies the tradition that he carefully studied the works of Thucydides, Plato, and Isocrates. As a *logographos* he did not specialize in any one class of cases; his extant speeches show a very wide range of subject and a remarkable grasp of legal technicalities.

3. The reputation gained in private causes led to his being employed as an assistant to official prosecutors in public trials, and the speeches against Androtion, Timocrates, and Aristocrates (355-352 B.C.) bear witness to his ability on this higher level. His first appearance in the courts was at the trial of Leptines (354); in the same year he spoke in the Ecclesia (*On the Symmories*) and again in 353 (*For the people of Megalopolis*). In 351 he started on his political career with the first of the famous series of *Philippics*. All the great political speeches fall within the period 351-340, when D. was in opposition. During this time a great change was coming over Greek politics. Philip, who had come to the throne of Macedon in 359, had in eight years united the seemingly incompatible elements in his kingdom, created a national spirit out of tribal feuds, and established a national army, gradually throwing over the mercenaries on whom he at first relied. The Athenians had not hitherto realized the significance of the rise of this new power; D., with keener insight, foresaw the danger not only to Athens but to Greek liberty in general, and henceforward

devoted his life to the task of averting it. The splendid series of *Philippic*, *Olynthiac*, and other speeches ends with the *Third Philippic*, the finest of them all.

4. By the end of this period the anti-peace party, led by Hyperides and Lycurgus, had gained strength. A vigorous policy was pursued, and one of D.'s greatest triumphs was that he persuaded Athens to offer alliance to Thebes, her ancient enemy. After the battle of Chaeronea, 338 B.C., D. was engaged for a time in internal affairs, e.g. the repair of fortifications. In 336 the death of Philip revived the hopes of the city-states, but the prompt action of Alexander shattered them. Alexander demanded that D., with other orators, should be surrendered to him, but they were saved by the intervention of Demades.

5. In 344 D. had impeached Aeschines (*De Falsa Legatione*) for his conduct in connexion with an embassy to Philip. Aeschines is accused of having, from corrupt motives, led the people into concluding a dishonourable peace; there was a strong presumption of Aeschines' guilt, but little proof, and he was acquitted. The enmity between the two orators smouldered on for many years, and finally burst out in the famous trial *De Corona* (330). Aeschines had accused Ctesiphon of illegality on three counts in proposing that a gold crown should be awarded to D. (see *Aeschines*). This was a mere pretext, and the real issue was a review of the political life of the two opponents. Aeschines in his speech *Against Ctesiphon* had discussed in detail the public actions of D. from 357 to 330; D. defended himself and made a vigorous counter-attack. The verdict was against Aeschines, and modern opinion is inclined to accept it as just.

6. The last phase of D.'s life begins with the mysterious case of Harpalus; this man, who was governor of Babylon, accepting (in 324) a false rumour of Alexander's death, made off with the king's treasure and sailed to Athens with 6,000 followers. On the motion of D., he was refused admittance, but on dismissing his army he was allowed to enter. Alexander demanded his surrender, but D. temporized by proposing that he should be kept as a prisoner and the treasure stored in the Parthenon. Harpalus subsequently escaped, and the treasure remaining was found to be short by 370 talents of the sum which he had declared. On the motion of D. himself the Areopagus made an investigation, and declared that D. had received 20 talents for helping Harpalus to escape. He was brought to trial and condemned to pay a fine of 50 talents; being unable to do so, he went into exile at Troezen. The extant speeches for the prosecution by Hyperides and Dinarchus are not explicit, and the question to what extent D. was guilty or innocent must remain undecided.

7. On the death of Alexander (323) D. made a tour of the Peloponnese to organize a joint effort against Macedon. He was recalled from exile, and his fine paid from the public funds. After the victory of Antipater at Crannon, Athens received a Macedonian garrison, and Demades carried a decree for the execution of D. and Hyperides. D. took sanctuary in the temple of Poseidon at Calauria, but being pursued there he sucked poison concealed in the end of his pen, and so died (322).

8. WORKS

(a) *Private law-court speeches* (δίκαι). The series of private speeches begins with those against Aphobus and Onetor (363-362), in which D. claimed recovery of his property from his guardians, and continues throughout his life (*Against Dionysodorus*, 323-322). Several private speeches attributed (perhaps wrongly) to D. were delivered on behalf of the Apollodorus who was D.'s opponent in the *For Phormio*. The speech *For Phormio* (350) and the first *Against Stephanus* (349; the second *Stephanus* is undoubtedly spurious) raise a question of professional morality. Pasion, the banker, appointed his chief clerk Phormio trustee for his sons; the elder son, Apollodorus, subsequently claimed a sum of money allegedly due to him, but Phormio proved that the claim had been settled some years previously. Apollodorus then prosecuted Stephanus, one of Phormio's witnesses, for perjury. If, as Plutarch states, D. wrote *Stephanus* A as well as *For Phormio*, he was guilty of a serious breach of faith, for while the earlier speech extols Phormio's character, the later one contains insinuations against him. The evidence for the authenticity of *Stephanus* A is, however, inconclusive (Paley and Sandys II, xxxix–l; Pickard-Cambridge, *Demosthenes*, 220–4). Aeschines asserts that D. showed to Apollodorus a speech composed for Phormio, but this may be a misrepresentation of some attempt by D. to act as mediator.

The subjects of the private speeches include guardianship, inheritance, claims for payment, bottomry-loans, mining rights, forgery, trespass, assault, etc. In the *Callicles* (which has flashes of humour, seldom found in D.) the plaintiff alleges that the defendant has flooded his land by blocking a watercourse; in the *Conon*, a brilliant piece of writing, combining Lysianic grace and Demosthenic force, some dissolute young rowdies and their father are summoned for assault. The *Polycles* gives a vivid picture of the trierarchic system.

(b) *Political law-court speeches* (γραφαί). *Against Androtion* (355), written for Diodorus, who prosecuted Androtion for an illegal proposal. *Against Leptines* (354), delivered by D. in person. Leptines proposed the abolition of the hereditary immunity from taxation granted to public benefactors. *Against Timocrates* (353), written for Diodorus. Timocrates proposed that Androtion and others, guilty of embezzlement, should be given an extension of time for repayment. *Against Aristocrates* (352), written for Euthycles, is important as an authority for the law of homicide. *Against Midias*, 347 B.C. Midias, a personal and political enemy of D., had slapped the latter's face at the Greater Dionysia when D. was providing a chorus. D. maintains that Midias has committed sacrilege in assaulting a public official engaged on sacred duties. This powerful speech was greatly admired by Lord Brougham. It has flashes of effective irony (cf. § 174), and supplied [Longinus] (*Subl.* 20) with a fine example of the effect produced by repetition combined with asyndeton. *On the Embassy*, 344 B.C. D. accuses Aeschines of having been bribed by Philip to conclude a dishonourable peace. *On the Crown* (330; see above), the most famous of D.'s speeches, is long and lacking in systematic arrangement. It purports to be a defence of Ctesiphon, but the main theme is the contrast between the speaker's public life and that of Aeschines, the prosecutor. The private life of Aeschines also comes in for severe treatment. *Against Aristogiton*, i and ii (325–324), an attempt to crush a sycophant. Weil considers the second spurious. *Against Neaera* and *Against Theocrines* (both *c.* 340) are probably not by D. but by unknown contemporary writers.

(c) *Political speeches* (λόγοι συμβουλευτικοί). The earliest of these is the *Symmories* (354), in which, while discrediting a rumour that Persia is planning to invade Greece, D. urges the necessity of preparation and introduces a scheme of naval reform. In the *Megalopolitans* (353) D. supports the people's request for help against Sparta; in the *Liberty of the Rhodians* (351) he supports the Rhodians' request for help against Artemisia, widow of Mausolus of Caria. In the *First Philippic* (351) and the three *Olynthiacs* (349) D. emphasizes the rapid growth of Philip's power, and the need to meet it with equal resolution. He hints in the *First Olynthiac*, and says openly in the *Third*, that the Theoric Fund must be used for military purposes, to aid Olynthus. In the *Peace* (346), while disapproving of the peace of Philocrates, D. urges that, once made, it should be kept. In the *Second Philippic* (344) he exposes Philip's duplicity, and

contrasts his singleness of purpose with Athenian vacillation. In the *Chersonese* (341) he defends Diopeithes, an Athenian admiral, charged by Philip with plundering some of his subjects, and argues that Athenian admirals are compelled to shift for themselves if the State votes them no supplies. The *Third Philippic* (341), the finest of D.'s deliberative speeches, is characterized by its broader view of the political situation. It is no longer a question merely of Athenian interests; the liberty of Greece as a whole is threatened. The speech is extant in two forms, and it is generally believed that Demosthenes was responsible for both; but it is uncertain which is the final form. The *Fourth Philippic* suggests that Persia might be asked to help against Philip. The speech is a compilation, about one-third being taken from the *Chersonese*, while other passages may have been borrowed from speeches now lost. *On the Halonnese* (342), *see* HEGESIPPUS (1). *On the Treaty with Alexander* is generally assigned to an unknown contemporary of D. The six *Letters* are doubtful, the *Epitaphios* and *Eroticus* almost certainly spurious. The collection of 56 *prooemia* may be genuine (*see* PROOEMIUM).

9. D. had many rivals in his lifetime; but later critics considered him the greatest of the orators. His claim to greatness rests on his singleness of purpose, his obvious sincerity, and his lucid and convincing exposition of his argument. In many instances he produces a great effect by the use of a few ordinary words. In his most solemn moments his style is at its plainest and his language most moderate. A master of metaphor, he uses it sparingly, and hardly at all in his most impressive passages. His style varies infinitely according to circumstances; sometimes as simple as Lysias, now polished like Isocrates, again almost as involved as Thucydides, he follows no scholastic rule; long and short periods follow each other, or are mingled with passages in the running style not according to any regular system. Thus his carefully prepared utterances give an impression of spontaneity. Such was his control of language that he was generally able to avoid hiatus (q.v.) without any dislocation of the order of words. He had an instinctive aversion to a succession of short syllables, and even tribrachs are of comparatively rare occurrence.

10. In his public orations no personal enmity is allowed to interfere with his judgement; his political opponents are not abused or even mentioned by name; it is the policy, not its supporters, that he attacks. In the forensic speeches the case is different: not content with argument, the speaker calls up all his forces of irony, sarcasm, and invective. Ridiculous stories, probably false or at least much exaggerated, about the ancestry and private life of Aeschines served to raise a laugh at the time, but do not increase the orator's reputation.

BIBLIOGRAPHY

ANCIENT SOURCES: the speeches of Aeschines; Lucian's *Demosthenis Encomium*; Plutarch's *Life of D.*

TEXTS: Teubner, ed. *maior*, Fuhr–Sykutris, 3 vols. (1914–27), ed. *minor* Blass–Fuhr, vols. i–ii (1928–33); Blass, vol. iii (1923); O.C.T., Butcher–Rennie, 3 vols. Text with translation, J. H. Vince, *Forensic and Political Speeches* (3 vols. Loeb); M. Croiset, *Harangues de D.* (Budé); A. T. Murray, *Private Orations* (5 vols., in progress, Loeb).

COMMENTARIES: H. Weil, *Plaidoyers politiques de D.*, 2 vols. (1883–6); *Harangues de D.*, 1 vol. (2nd ed. by Dalmeyda); Paley and Sandys, *Select Private Orations*, 2 vols.; *Androtion and Timocrates*, W. Wayte; *Midias*, W. W. Goodwin; *Leptines*, J. E. Sandys; *the Crown*, W. W. Goodwin; *Philippics, Olynthiacs, Peace, Chersonese*, 2 vols., J. E. Sandys.

TRANSLATIONS: *Orations*, C. R. Kennedy, 5 vols. (Bohn); A. W. Pickard-Cambridge, *Public Orations of D.*, 2 vols.; Lord Brougham, *On the Crown*.

CRITICISM: (i) General: S. H. Butcher, *Demosthenes*; A. W. Pickard-Cambridge, *D. and the Last Days of Greek Freedom*; A. Schaefer, *D. und seine Zeit*. (ii) Special: P. Treves, 'Apocrifi Demostenici' (in *Athenaeum* of Pavia, 1936); J. Sykutris, *D.'s Epitaphios*; C. D. Adams, 'The Fourth Philippic' (in *CPhil.* 1938); R. Rühling, 'Against Spudias' (in *Hermes* 1936). Index: S. Preuss, 1892. In addition, for general bibliography, *see* ATTIC ORATORS.

J. F. D.

DEMOSTHENES (3) of Bithynia (? 2nd c. B.C.), epic poet, author of *Bithyniaca*.

FHG iv. 384-6.

DENTATUS (1), LUCIUS SICINIUS (or SICCIUS), called by ancient writers 'the Roman Achilles', was a legendary embodiment of the civic and military virtues of the plebeians in their struggles against both patricians and external enemies. Since the chronology of his largely fictitious career was unknown, Siccius was later connected with the Decemvirs, by whose leader, Appius Claudius, he is said to have been treacherously murdered.

P. T.

DENTATUS (2), MANIUS CURIUS, Roman plebeian hero, consul in 290, 284 (*suffectus*), 275, 274 B.C.; censor in 272. After ending the Samnite War (290), he conquered Sabines (q.v.) (290), Senones (284), Pyrrhus (275), Lucani (274). He triumphed in 290 (the sources incredibly say twice) and 275. About 289 Curius partly drained Lake Velinus and in 272 commenced Rome's second aqueduct (*Anio Vetus*). He died in 270. The rhetorical accounts of his humble birth, incorruptibility, and frugality resemble the tales told of C. Fabricius (q.v.) Luscinus, and derive largely from Cato who idealized him.

Polyb. 2. 19; Livy, *Epit.* 11 and 14; Florus 1. 13; Val. Max. 4. 3. 5; 6. 3. 4; Cic. *Att.* 4. 15. 5. E. T. S.

DENTISTRY in antiquity was part of general medicine; diseases of the teeth were explained and treated in accordance with the theories on other diseases. The operative technique was excellent (the Hippocratic treatment of the fracture of the mandible is famous); extractions were performed at an early date. The methods of preserving the teeth, however, consisted mainly of medicinal and dietetic means; fillings for that purpose were unknown. Loose teeth were fastened with gold wire (Hippocrates, *Π. ἄρθρων* 32; *The XII Tables* 10. 8). Toothache being considered a chronic disease and one of the greatest torments (Celsus 6. 9), hygienic prescriptions were extensively advocated. Cleansing of the teeth with tooth-powder, the tooth-pick (*dentiscalpium*), chewing (σχινίζειν τοὺς ὀδόντας) were recommended in addition to innumerable remedies against bad breath, a favourite topic of Latin epigrammatists. False teeth were set, but only by technicians, the artificial teeth being carved from ivory or other animal teeth. Such protheses, used by the Etruscans and Romans, served primarily to hide physical defects and to correct deficiencies of speech, but had probably to be removed before meals. Physicians and dentists refrained from making protheses, either on account of their technical insufficiency, or because their importance for the process of digestion was not appreciated.

V. Guerini, *A History of Dentistry* (U.S.A. 1909), surveys the Etruscan excavations and other archaeological findings. K. Sudhoff, *Gesch. d. Zahnheilkunde²* (1926), dissertations on ancient authors enumerated, pp. 75, 97, 102. W. Artelt, 'Gesch. d. Anatomie d. Kiefer u. d. Zähne', *Janus* 1929. Instruments, J. S. Milne, *Surgical Instruments in Greek and Roman Times* (1907). L. E.

DEPORTATIO, *see* EXSILIUM, RELEGATIO.

DERCETO, *see* ATARGATIS.

DETERMINISM, *see* FATE.

DETESTATIO SACRORUM. A patrician, if *sui iuris*, had certain rites belonging to his *gens* (*sacra gentilicia*) to perform. If, therefore, he wished to become legally the son of a member of another *gens* (*arrogatio*) or cease to be a patrician (*transitio ad plebem*), he must, after investigation by the pontifices to make sure that the rites of his own *gens* did not become extinct, attest before

them and the *comitia calata* that he renounced them. This was called *detestatio sacrorum*. See Gellius 5. 19. 5-10; 15. 27. 3, cf. 7. 12. 1; Cicero, *Dom.* 34 ff., *Orat.* 144; Servius on *Aen.* 2. 156; Mommsen, *Röm. Staatsr.* ii³. 37; iii. 38 f., 136 ff. H. J. R.

DEUCALION (Δευκαλίων), name of several mythological persons, the only important one being Prometheus' son, the Greek Noah. When Zeus flooded the earth in wrath at the sins of the Bronze Age, or of Lycaon (q.v. 2), he and his wife Pyrrha, daughter of Epimetheus, by Prometheus' advice built an ark (λάρναξ, Apollod. 1. 47) and floated in it till the waters subsided. When their ark grounded, they were advised by Themis, or Hermes, to throw their mother's bones over their shoulders. Realizing that this meant the stones of the earth, they did so, and those thrown by Deucalion became men, those thrown by Pyrrha, women (Ov. *Met.* 1. 318 ff.; Apollod. 1. 46 ff.). They became the parents of Hellen (q.v.; ibid. 49). H. J. R.

DEVA, the river *Dee*, whence the name was applied to the legionary fortress at its mouth, modern Chester. The earliest discovered occupation is *c.* A.D. 70, and the permanent fortress with stone buildings was probably constructed by Agricola in 79 (*ILS* 3704a), perhaps for Legio II Adiutrix and XX Valeria victrix. A reconstruction soon after may denote reorganization when II Adiutrix left (*c.* 86). Another rebuilding after 150, following extensive destruction, may be connected with the evacuation of the garrison for Albinus' campaigns (196). Portions of the fortress wall of block-work with internal towers (enclosing *c.* 56 acres), the *praetorium*, two other colonnaded buildings (*scholae*?), and typical 'legionary' barrack blocks are known; there was an extramural amphitheatre, and extensive civil settlements and cemeteries.

F. Haverfield, *Catalogue of Inscribed Stones* (1900); R. G. Collingwood, *Archaeology of Roman Britain* (1930), 19-23; P. H. Lawson, *Chester Archaeological Journal* xxvii. 163-9; C. E. Stevens, ib. xxxv. 49-52. For recent work, R. Newstead ib. xxix. 1-40 (amphitheatre); xxxiii. 5-117; xxxiv. 5-46; *Liverpool Annals* xxii. 19-30; xxiii. 3-50. C. E. S.

DEVERRA, *see* PILUMNUS.

DEVOTIO. It was open to a Roman general, if the battle was going against him, to vow (*deuouere*) himself and the enemy's army with him to Tellus and the Manes (Livy 8. 9. 4 ff.). He wore his ceremonial costume (*toga praetexta*), with his head covered (*uelato capite*) and his feet on a weapon (*telum*, probably a spear or javelin; perhaps to bring himself into direct contact with Mars, cf. Mars Hasta). One hand touched his chin (? cf. the dedicator holding the door-post of the temple he dedicates, see CONSECRATIO). He then recited after a pontifex a formula of prayer asking for victory and the destruction of the enemy. At the end of this, he said: *legiones auxiliaque hostium mecum deis manibus Tellurique deuoueo.* Then, girt with the *cinctus Gabinus* (see GABII), he sought death among the enemy. He might, however, substitute for himself any soldier from a legion (ibid. 10. 11), presumably with a corresponding change of formula. If he or his substitute was killed, the gods had clearly accepted the vow and must therefore accept the rest of it. If the substitute was not killed, but the victory won, an image at least 7 feet high must be buried in his place; if the general was not killed, he could never again offer sacrifice acceptably. The enemy must not get the weapon on which he had stood. H. J. R.

DEXIPPUS, PUBLIUS HERENNIUS (fl. *c.* A.D. 253-76), Athenian Sophist and statesman, published a Χρονικὴ ἱστορία to A.D. 269-270 in twelve books, a history of the *Diadochi* in four books, and Σκυθικά, a work on the

Gothic Wars from A.D. 238 to Aurelian, preserved largely in Zosimus. In rhetorical composition and in style he follows Thucydides.

FGrH ii A, p. 452; C, p. 304; E. Schwartz, PW v. 288.
A. H. McD.

DI CONSENTES, see CONSENTES DI.

DI PATRII, see THEOI PATROOI.

DI PENATES, see PENATES.

DIADEM (διάδημα), a blue band with white spots which was fastened round the Persian king's upright head-dress, the tiara. When Alexander conquered Darius he adopted this band as an emblem of royal power, and his example was followed by his successors. Refused by Julius Caesar in 44 B.C., the symbol of Oriental monarchy was adopted by Constantine in A.D. 325 and became part of the insignia of the Roman emperors.
F. A. W.

DIADOCHI (Διάδοχοι, 'Successors'). This term was applied in a special sense to the more important of Alexander the Great's officers who ultimately partitioned his empire, viz. Antigonus I, Antipater, Cassander, Lysimachus, Ptolemy I, Seleucus I (qq.v.). The 'age of the *Diadochi*' represents a period extending from Alexander's death (323 B.C.) at least to the battle of Ipsus (301), which ended the efforts of Antigonus I (q.v.) to reassemble the whole empire under his own rule, and perhaps to the battle of Corupedium (281), which fixed the main political boundaries of the Hellenistic world for the next century.
G. T. G.

DIAERESIS, see METRE, GREEK, II (1).

DIAGORAS, lyric poet, of Melos. Though Eusebius–Jerome gives his *floruit* as 466 B.C., he seems to have been active in the last quarter of the fifth century (Ar. *Av.* 1071 ff., *Nub.* 828 ff.). Renowned for his atheism (Cic. *Nat. D.* 1. 2, 63), he disparaged the Mysteries (schol. Ar. *Av.* 1071; *Lys.* 6. 17), was condemned to death, and fled (Diod. Sic. 13. 6). Fragments, perhaps from *Encomia*, show no trace of atheism, and the story was that he lost his faith because the gods did not punish a man who broke his oath (Sext. Emp. *Pyr.* 9. 53).

Text: E. Diehl, *Anth. Lyr. Graec.* ii. 126–7. Criticism: U. von Wilamowitz-Moellendorff, *Textg. d. griech. Lyr.* (1900), 80–4.
C. M. B.

DIALECTIC. If Aristotle really said that Zeno discovered dialectic (Diog. Laert. 9. 25), he was inaccurate. Zeno set the example of exploring the consequences of an hypothesis, and Socrates set the example of seeking truth by question and answer alone; but the creator of the notion of dialectic was Plato (*Resp.* 531–9, and Adam's commentary, esp. ii. 168–79). He regards it as the highest of human arts, by which men attain the greatest insight into the best things. It deals solely with the unseen, not even using the visible as an aid. Its only medium is speech, the responsible use of question and answer in the pursuit of truth. He represents it sometimes as the synopsis of the one in the many and the many in the one, by which we define realities and discern which fall under which; sometimes as the exploration of the consequences of an hypothesis, by which we render our opinions more systematic. Once he suggests that dialectic can ultimately overcome its hypothetical character and reach the 'unhypothesized beginning' (*Resp.* 511 b). For Aristotle (see *Top.* 1. 1–2 and *Soph. El.* 34), its hypothetical character makes it inferior to deduction from premisses known to be true. Nevertheless, it has its uses: (1) ultimate premisses, which cannot themselves be deduced, can sometimes be made evident by exploring the consequences of their denial, and that is hypothetical

thinking; (2) dialectic provides good training; (3) even winning the argument is worth something, and Aristotle's handbook of dialectic, the *Topics*, gives disproportionate attention thereto. See R. Robinson, *Plato's Earlier Dialectic* (1941), 65–96.
R. R.

DIALECTS, GREEK. From the inscriptional evidence it appears that each of the Greek city-states possessed and used in its public documents its own individual dialect. This multitude of dialects falls into three distinct groups: (1) Attic-Ionic, spoken in Attica, the Ionic colonies on the southern seaboard of Asia Minor, and certain islands; (2) Achaean, comprising (a) Aeolic in Lesbos and the neighbouring mainland and, with an admixture of West Greek elements, in Thessaly and Boeotia; (b) Arcado-Cyprian, which is not employed in extant literature; (3) West Greek comprising (a) North-West Greek in Phocis, Locris, Elis, and Aetolia, and (b) Doric in the Peloponnese and the Doric colonies in various islands and Magna Graecia.

2. The dialects of the literary texts are not identical with those that appear in the inscriptions. This is not due merely to manuscript corruption but to the strict literary formalism that forced a Greek writer to use the traditional language of the genre he was practising in preference to his native dialect. The dialect was, in fact, regarded as an integral part of the particular art form. Thus the epic dialect, arising from a fusion of Aeolic and Ionic elements, was utilized by all writers of Greek epic down to Byzantine times. The elegy was a creation of the Ionians. Yet because the hexameter was traditionally wedded to the epic dialect, it is this dialect (in an ionicized form) that appears in elegy whether by Ionians like Archilochus and Callinus, the Laconian Tyrtaeus, the Athenian Solon, or the Megarian Theognis. Similarly the choric ode was developed among the Dorians; consequently Pindar, a Boeotian, Bacchylides, an Ionian, and the Attic dramatists must give their language at least a Doric flavour. It was because of this traditionalism in language that only few of the Greek local dialects achieved literary rank, and even these few discard much that would have seemed narrow and provincial. In this respect, too, Greek art idealized: the language itself represents a compromise between individual and local peculiarities.

3. The EPIC DIALECT is basically Ionic, the most characteristic features of which are the change of ā>η, the ν *ephelkustikon*, the pronouns ἡμεῖς, ἡμᾶς, ὑμεῖς, ὑμᾶς, the particle ἄν and the infinitive in -ναι, and verbal forms in -σαν (ἔδοσαν, ἔθεσαν, etc.). It contains, further, numerous Aeolic elements such as ἄμμε, ὔμμε, etc., datives in -εσσι, genitives in -οιο, infinitives in -μεν(αι), and the particle κε. The dialect exhibits, further, features from different chronological stages of the language, and there can be little doubt that so composite and artificial a language is a product of a long poetical tradition which passed from an Aeolic to an Ionic sphere.

4. The language of Hesiod is practically identical with that of Homer. He has a few Aeolisms absent from Homer which may come from his native Boeotian—αἴνημι, τριηκόντων, etc. We find, further, Dorisms derived possibly from Locris, where he settled: τέτορα, ἦν 'they were', acc. plur. -ᾰς, and participles like δήσᾰς. The epic dialect exercised a strong influence on all subsequent poetry, which constantly exhibits such features as -οιο, -εσσι, the omitted augment, and the inconsistent treatment of ϝ.

5. MELIC POETRY. The intensely personal character of this genre precluded any rigid formalism of language. The poems of Sappho and Alcaeus are written in their native Lesbian dialect. Characteristic are the ο in στρότος, βροχέως, etc., the diphthongs in αὔως, ναύοις, χεύατο, etc., the diphthong which appears after the loss of ν before ς (παῖσα, Μοῖσα, λίποισα, and the acc. plur.

ἀπάλαις, στεφάνοις, etc.), the double consonants in ἔμμι, ὔμμε, σελάννα, φαεννός, etc., datives in -εσσι, infinitives in -μεναι, and the -μι conjugation of contracted verbs (κάλημι, etc.). It would be absurd to attribute hyper-Aeolisms to native speakers. It follows that φαῖμι, Κρονίδαις, and the like are later corruptions.

6. Anacreon of Teos used his native Ionic with but few Aeolisms or epicisms (πτερύγεσσι, ὀχάνοιο, δακρυόεσσα, etc.).

7. Corinna of Tanagra wrote in Boeotian. Characteristic are εο>ιο (ἐκόσμιον), preservation of ϝ (ϝάδομη), verbal forms in -νθι and -νθη, ἴων for ἐγώ, τύ, τίν, τεοῦς, τεῖν for σύ etc., and βανά = γυνή. The text in our version appears with the later orthography (αι>η, η>ει, ει>ι, οι>υ). The usual epic features are present.

8. For the CHORIC ODE the traditional dialect was Doric, the chief characteristics of which are the retention of ā and ϝ, the preservation of the group τι (δίδωτι, ϝίκατι, etc.), aorists in -ξα (ἐδίκαξα), the article τοί, ταί, 1st pers. plur. in -μες (φέρομες), futures in -σεω, and the particle κα. Alcman, though he writes in the language of Sparta, nevertheless avoids certain local peculiarities such as the change of intervocalic -σ- to -h- (Ποhοιδάν). In view of the influence of Lesbian Melic poetry on the choric ode it is not surprising that Apollonius (*Pron.* 107. 13) describes Alcman as συνεχῶς Αἰολίζων. Aeolic features are ἔμματα, κλεννά, ἔχοισα, etc. Epic influence is apparent in ἔδμεναι, παίδεσσι, the free augment, etc. As with Corinna, the orthography of our text has been modernized: σιός (θεός) embodies a change of θ>s first attested in the fourth century B.C.

9. The language of the other poets of this genre (Stesichorus, Ibycus, Simonides, Bacchylides, Pindar) has no such close connexion with a local dialect. It is an artificial creation, a mixture, varying with the individual author, of Aeolic, Ionic, and epic elements with the basic Doric, which is progressively reduced to a few representative elements such as ā, genitives like Κρονίδᾱ, Μουσᾶν, and verbal forms like πτάσσουτι.

10. IAMBIC AND TROCHAIC poetry were written in Ionic. Hipponax, in particular, and his imitator Herodas, used an especially popular variety containing many non-Hellenic words. Solon, however, apart from quotations and reminiscences of epic and Ionic poetry, used his native Attic dialect. This dialect appears, further, in the trimeters and tetrameters of Attic drama. It has been suggested that the few Doric elements present indicate a possible Doric origin of this particular art form.

11. COMEDY. Both Epicharmus and Sophron employed the popular dialect of Syracuse, where the common Doric was infused with local peculiarities such as ψίν (σφίν), κίκραμι (κέραννυμι), κάρρων (κρέσσων). Even so popular a genre, however, did not wholly escape the influence of epic and tragedy.

12. PASTORAL POETRY. The dialects affected by Theocritus (epic in *Id.* 12, 22, and 25, Lesbian in 28–30, and 'choral' Doric in 16–18 and 24) have that combination of the learned and the artificial that we expect from an Alexandrian poet. Even the fuller Doric, in which the majority of the idylls are written, has been designated a 'salon-Doric'. For while it contains the common Doric features enumerated above, its artificiality is revealed by hyper-Doric forms like φιλάσω. The dialect contains a few more locally restricted Dorisms such as the acc. plur. in -ος, ἐντί = εἰσί, infinitives in -εν, and the 2nd pers. sing. in -ες (συρίσδες), which may derive from the Doric of Sicily or Cos. The usual epic elements are present (see above). Aeolic colouring is given by the predominance of participial forms in -οισα, but γελάοισα is hyper-Aeolic for γέλαισα.

13. EPIGRAM. The earliest inscriptional epigrams were written in the local dialects, so that even the Ionian Simonides composed the epigrams he wrote for Doric cities in a conventional Doric. The local peculiarities of the epigrams have often been obscured in the tradition: thus the manuscript version of the epitaph on the Corinthians who fell at Salamis contains the words ποτ' ἐναίομεν, whereas the stone itself presents the Doric ποκ' ἐναίομες. The poets of this genre drew largely on Homeric material in composing their hexameters, but the oldest epigrams exhibit fewest traces of this influence. It is noteworthy that even such borrowings assume a native guise: thus Ποσειδάωνι ἄνακτι appears in a Corinthian epigram as Ποτειδάϝωνι ϝάνακτι.

14. PROSE. A prose literature was first developed in Ionia, and Ionic became the language of historical and scientific prose: representative names are Hecataeus of Miletus, Antiochus of Syracuse, Hellanicus of Lesbos, and Hippocrates from Cos; even the Athenian Thucydides gave his history an Ionic flavour by avoiding local Attic peculiarities such as ττ and ρρ. The early λογογράφοι wrote in a simple unadorned Ionic. Herodotus, however, was a more self-conscious artist and dignified his native Ionic with archaic speech forms—uncontracted verbs, iterative imperfects (ποιέσκε), and the numerous epic expressions which earned him the epithet Ὁμηρικώτατος.

15. Our estimate of the Homeric elements in the dialect of Herodotus must be linked with an examination of the textual tradition, for our manuscripts present a picture of his dialect which can hardly be authentic. We find hyper-Ionic forms like Κροίσεω, and suspicion is cast on the genuineness of the uncontracted verb forms by impossibilities such as κέεται, which is a false resolution of κεῖται. Moreover, the fact that another hyper-form νοῦσος is identical with the Homeric form, where it is metrically conditioned, whereas the derived verb, which does not occur in Homer, has the normal form νοσέω suggests that the text of Herodotus was corrupted at an early date by editors ignorant of the Ionic dialect who 'ionicized' his language while regarding the Homeric epics as a source of early Ionic. Thus they took the omission of the augment to be an Ionic trait. This led to curious misunderstandings. The augmented imperfect of ὁράω, for instance, was *ἠϝοραον, which in Ionic would appear as ἑώρων. The editors ionicized this by omitting the first vowel, so that the manuscripts present the impossible ὤρων, the true unaugmented form being ὅρων. Ionic, further, was distinguished from Attic by the crasis of o+a>ω: thus ἑωυτῷ contrasts with Attic ἑαυτῷ. It is perhaps to a false generalization of this equivalence of ωυ and αυ in the respective dialects that we owe the Herodotean θῶυμα. At any rate this form never appears in the inscriptions, which present, on the contrary, examples of θαύμων, θαύμασις. Similarly the extension of the form αὐτέων to the masculine and neuter rests on a misunderstanding of the relationship of the true Ionic feminine form αὐτέων to the contracted Attic αὐτῶν. Both rest on an early αὐτάων, which in primitive Ionic would appear as αὐτήων.

16. THE Κοινή. The liquidation of the independent city-states and the political unification of Greece encompassed the destruction of the ancient dialects and their absorption into a new common language. Xenophon, who passed his life among Greeks of different origin and dialect, epitomizes this process and may be regarded as the first writer of the κοινή. It was in this common language that the Septuagint and the Greek New Testament were written. In the first century the archaist revival we know as Atticism strove to approximate the language of prose literature to that of classical Attic. In spite of numerous revolts this archaistic literary language has maintained itself against the increasingly divergent popular language, so that the modern Greek must learn the καθαρεύουσα which he writes in addition to the δημοτική which he speaks.

A. Thumb, *Handbuch der griechischen Dialekte* (1909; 2nd ed. Pt. 1, 1932); C. D. Buck, *The Greek Dialects* (1928); A. Meillet, *Aperçu d'une histoire de la langue grecque* (1930). L. R. P

DIALECTS, ITALIC. Latin together with Oscan and Umbrian as well as the dialects of various mountain tribes of central Italy, Marsi, Marrucini, Hernici, Vestini, etc., forms the Italic branch of the Indo-European family of languages. This excludes, in the north, Celtic, Ligurian (now generally considered Indo-European, cf. Kretschmer, Kuhn's *Zeitschr. f. vgl. Sprachforschung*, 38. 108), and Venetic (of Illyrian origin); in central Italy, Etruscan (q.v.); and, in the south, Messapian (probably Illyrian in descent). But the term Italic Dialects is more commonly confined to Oscan and Umbrian, the two chief non-Latin dialects of the group. Oscan inscriptions have been found in Samnium, Campania, Apulia, Lucania, Bruttium, but Pompeii, and more recently Capua, have furnished most. The earliest are coin-legends of *c.* 450–350 B.C., while the latest are graffiti from the walls of Pompeii after the first earthquake in A.D. 63. Most are written in the Oscan alphabet, which is derived through Etruscan from Chalcidic Greek. But a few, including the longest, the Tabula (q.v.) Bantina, are in the Latin alphabet, while others from south Italy are in Greek. Oscan was more than a mere *patois*. While Latin was still confined to Rome and Latium, Oscan was the chief language of central Italy. Our knowledge of Umbrian is derived almost entirely from the Tabulae (q.v.) Iguvinae, a more extensive document than any representing any other dialect save Latin. Some of the tablets are written in the Umbrian alphabet, also derived through Etruscan from Greek, the rest in the Latin alphabet. The following are some of the main features which distinguish Osco-Umbrian from Latin.

(a) PHONOLOGY

(i) q^u g^u appear as *p, b* (Latin *qu, u*): O. *pis*, U. *pisi* (= quis). O. *bivus* (= vivi).

(ii) Syncope of short medial vowels: O. *actud* (= agito).

(iii) *nd > nn*: O. *upsannam* (= operandam).

(iv) *s* retained before nasals: O. *fisnam* (= fanum), U. *sesna* (= cena).

(v) *bh, dh > f*: O. *tfei*, U. *tefe* (= tibi).

(vi) *kt > ht, pt > ft*: O. *Uhtavis* (= Octavius), O. *scriftas*, U. *screhto* (= scriptae).

(vii) *ks > ss, s*: O. *destrst* (= dextra est).

(b) MORPHOLOGY

(i) First decl. genit. sing. ends in -*ās* (cf. paterfamilias), also nomin. plur.

(ii) Second decl. genit. sing. ends in -*eis*; dat. sing. in *oi*; nomin. plur. both nouns and pronouns in -*ōs*; genit. plur. only in -*ōm*.

(iii) Third decl. genit. sing. in -*eis* (from *i* stems); accus. sing. of consonantal stems in -*om* (from *o* stems); in the nomin. plur. consonantal and vocalic stems are kept distinct, the former ending in -*ēs* with syncope of the *e*, the latter in -*ēs* as in Latin: O. *humuns* (= homines) but *trís* (= tres).

(iv) In the verb, moods, tenses, voices are like Latin, but

(a) Present infin. active ends in -*om*: O. *ezum*, U. *erom* (= esse).

(b) Future indic. has -*s*- (it is a short vowel *s*- aorist subjunctive): O. *deiuast* (= iurabit) U. *ferest* (= feret).

(c) Future perfect has -*us*-: O. *dicust* (= dixerit), U. *benust* (= venerit).

(d) Characteristic of the perfect is an -*f*- type: O. *aikdafed* (= decrevit). Oscan has also a -*tt*- perfect, and Umbrian an -*l*- and -*nki*- perfect, but the -*vi*- and -*s*-types of Latin are lacking.

(e) A peculiar third sing. passive is e.g. O. *sakrafir*, U. *ferar* (= feratur).

(c) SYNTAX

The syntax is very similar to the Latin with some differences in case-usage. Thus

(i) the locative is quite common: O. *eisei terei* (= in eo territorio).

(ii) Genitive of time: O. *zicolom XXX nessimum* (= in diebus XXX proximis).

(iii) The genitive of respect is much less restricted than in Latin.

(d) VOCABULARY

There is a considerable number of words in Osco-Umbrian which do not appear at all or in the same form in Latin, though they can be paralleled in other Indo-European languages:
e.g. *her-* (= velle): O. *herest*, U. *heri*. Cf. χαίρω.

touta- (= civitas): O. *toutad praesentid* (= populo praesente).

medes- (= ius): O. *meddiss*, U. *mersto* (= iustum). Cf. *modus*.

hontro- (= inferus): O. *huntruis* (= inferis), U. *hondra* (= infra).

ner- (= vir): O. *nerum* (genit. plur.), U. *nerf* (accus. plur.). Cf. *Nero*.

pur- (= ignis): U. *pure-to* (= ab igne). Cf. πῦρ.

ais- (= sacer): O. *aisusis* (= sacrificiis). Cf. Etrus. *aisar* (= dei), L. *aestimo*.

Peculiar to Oscan are, e.g.:

deiua- (= iurare) connected with *deiuo (= deus).

egmo- (= res). O. *egmazum* (genit. plur.).

eituam (= pecuniae). Also in Marrucinian.

feihúss (= muros). Cf. τεῖχος: same root as L. *fingo, figura*.

puklum (= filium). Also Paelignian *puclois* (= pueris).

tanginom (= sententiam). Cf. L. *tongere* and Engl. 'think'.

Peculiar to Umbrian are, e.g.

anouihimu (= induitor). Same root as L. *induo, exuo*.

gomia (= gravidas). Cf. L. *gemo* and γέμω.

nertru (= sinistro). Cf. νέρτερος.

uend- (= vertere): U. *ahauendu* (= avertito). Cf. Engl. 'wind'.

Many words are used in a sense either unknown in Latin or passing out of use. Thus

O. *kasit* (= caret) means *decet, oportet*.

O. *castrous* (= castrum), U. *castruo* means *fundus*.

O. *carneis* (= caro), U. *karu* means 'portion', cf. κείρω. But Umbrian also has the meaning 'piece of flesh'.

U. *emantur* (= accipiantur) shows the original meaning of Latin *emo*, 'take', found in compounds *adimo, demo*.

O. *urust* (oro) is used in the technical sense 'plead, argue': cf. Festus 'orare antiquos dixisse pro agere'.

BIBLIOGRAPHY

R. S. Conway, *The Italic Dialects* (with grammar and glossary, 2 vols. 1897; exhaustive collection of material containing inscriptions, glosses, lists of proper names, and place-names). C. D. Buck, *A Grammar of Oscan and Umbrian*² (1928; excellent account of both). R. von Planta, *Grammatik der oskisch-umbrischen Dialekte* (1892–7).
P. S. N.

DIALEXEIS, see DISSOI LOGOI.

DIALOGUE, GREEK. Diogenes Laertius (3. 48) defines a dialogue as 'a discourse consisting of question and answer on some philosophical or political subject, with due regard to the characters of the persons introduced and the choice of diction'. It is essentially a μίμησις, an artistic reproduction of 'good talk' or informal discussion in which, while a single theme is pursued, some digression and inconsequence is permissible and proper; the theme must be of more than topical interest, though it usually arises out of the experiences of particular persons at a particular time.

2. The most important source of dialogue was the actual conversation of Socrates with all and sundry; yet the Σωκρατικὸς λόγος is foreshadowed in the incorporation of quasi-philosophical conversations in the narrative of Herodotus and Thucydides, notably that between Solon and Croesus (Hdt. 1. 30–2) and the Melian Dialogue (Thuc. 5. 85–113). The influence of Attic Drama is also plain, and the affinity to dialogue of the Mimes of Sophron is recognized by Aristotle.

3. The earliest Socratic dialogues may have been simply notes taken by those who talked with or listened to Socrates (cf. Pl. *Tht.* 142–3); later these developed into freer μιμήσεις in the hands of Plato, Xenophon, Aeschines (of whom considerable fragments survive), and other disciples. Plato's dialogues differ widely in literary merit: some show supreme dramatic power and artistry; in others the dialogue form becomes almost a convention, the chief speaker (sometimes an unnamed 'stranger') a mouthpiece for Plato's own teaching, and the interlocutors otiose. Of the earlier works Jaeger's saying is true, that 'his desire was to show the philosopher in the dramatic instant of seeking and finding, and to make the doubt and conflict visible'; for such an aim dialogue was wholly suitable.

4. Aristotle's dialogues, extant only in fragments, won him high literary fame in antiquity. Most were written before the death of Plato. Although some fragments show Aristotle still retaining the Socratic technique of question and answer, his usual method was probably that of long expository speeches, like those in Cicero's dialogues, with the leader (sometimes Aristotle himself) summing up.

5. After a long and almost total eclipse, dialogue reappears with Plutarch and Lucian. Some fourteen genuine dialogues of Plutarch survive, philosophical or semi-philosophical in character. His best work lacks Plato's depth and dramatic power, yet has a quiet charm and illuminates for us the interests of contemporary cultured society. In Lucian the influences of Socratic dialogue, the New Comedy, and Menippus combined to stimulate a genius unique amongst ancient writers. Though he employed many other forms, his fame rests principally on his satiric dialogues, brilliant exposures of every sort of dogma, prejudice, and humbug. In the twilight of classical antiquity dialogue is still represented in the work of Julian and Synesius.

Aeschines Socraticus, ed. H. Krauss (Teubner, 1911); Aristotle, Fragments, ed. Valentin Rose (Teubner, 1886); A. and M. Croiset, *Histoire de la litt. grecque* (1910–14) iii (Plato, Xenophon, etc.), v (Plutarch and Lucian); M. Croiset, *Essai sur la vie et les œuvres de Lucien* (1882); H. W. and F. G. Fowler, *Lucian* (Engl. Transl. with introduction, 1905); R. Hirzel, *Der Dialog* (1895); id. 'Plutarch' (*Das Erbe der Alten* iv, 1912); W. Jaeger, *Aristoteles* (1923); Engl. Transl. by R. Robinson).
R. H.

DIALOGUE, LATIN. The art of dramatic dialogue early attained a high proficiency in Rome, especially in the comedies of Plautus and Terence, the Roman public being quite keen to appraise the quick give and take of conversation, as is shown by the popularity of the *altercationes* in forensic rhetoric (Cic. *Brut.* 164). Dialogue played a considerable part in the *Satura* from the time of Ennius, one of whose *saturae* seems to have been a dialogue between *Mors* and *Vita*; and many satires of Lucilius, Horace, and Persius are largely dialogue, though it plays a smaller part in Juvenal. Prose dialogue at Rome began with M. Junius Brutus, who composed his three books *De Iure Civili* in the form of dialogues with his son (Cic. *De Or.* 2. 224). These, like Cicero's, and the Roman dialogue generally, followed the Aristotelian rather than the Platonic model: the principal part in each dialogue was played by one interlocutor (sometimes the author himself) who expounded his view dogmatically in long speeches, the part of the other characters being reduced to a minimum. Each dialogue was preceded by a *mise en scène* giving the place and the occasion of, with

the names of the participants in, the conversation. Cicero's long series begins with the political dialogues, *De Republica* and *De Legibus*, proceeds to the rhetorical dialogues (*De Oratore, Orator,* and *Brutus*), and ends with the philosophical and theological *Academica, De Finibus, Tusculanae Disputationes, De Divinatione, De Natura Deorum,* etc. While Cicero's dialogues reproduced the conversation and manners of high society, a less polished, though not more Roman, stratum was represented in Varro's dialogue *De Re Rustica.* Seneca's *dialogi* are dialogues only in name. The prose dialogue is taken up into the novel in Petronius' *Satyricon* and to a less extent in Apuleius' *Metamorphoses.* Tacitus' *Dialogus* resumes the Ciceronian tradition in its discussion of the decline of oratory; but the art is almost lost by the time of Boethius' *De Consolatione.* Minucius Felix used the dialogue form in his *Octavius* in the interest of Christian polemic, a use which persisted till the time of St. Augustine.

R. Hirzel, *Der Dialog* (2 vols. 1895); R. E. Jones in *AJPhil.* lx. 3 (1939), 307 ff.
R. M. H.

DIANA (root DI, cf. Zeus, Iup-piter; probably 'bright one', which says nothing for or against ancient and modern theories of her identity with the moon), an Italian goddess anciently identified with Artemis (q.v.). Altheim (*Griechische Götter,* 93 ff.) supposes her cult actually derived from that of Artemis Orthia, through Etruria, but see A. E. Gordon in *Trans. Am. Phil. Ass.* lxiii (1932), 177 ff.; *California Pubs. in Class. Arch.* ii (1934), 11. Her cult was widespread; see Birt in Roscher's *Lexikon* i. 1003–4 for details. One of her most famous shrines was on Mt. Tifata near Capua (Vell. 2. 25. 4 and elsewhere in literature, supported by much inscriptional evidence); the name Tifata means 'holm-oak-grove' (Festus, 503. 14 Lindsay), which suits Diana's character as a wood-goddess (see below) excellently. Most famous of all was her ancient cult near Aricia (on the shore of the volcanic lake known as *Speculum Dianae,* below the modern Nemi, i.e. *nemus*). Her temple stood in a grove, and the cult is said to have been founded by Egerius Baebius (?) of Tusculum, *dictator Latinus* (Cato, *Orig.* 2, fr. 21 Jordan). It was therefore an old religious centre of the Latin League and it is probable, though direct proof is lacking, that the foundation of her temple on the Aventine, traditionally by Servius Tullius (Livy 1. 45. 2 ff.), was an attempt to transfer the headquarters of this cult to Rome, along with, what Livy mentions (ibid. 3), the headship of the League. See further REX NEMO-RENSIS, and for the Massiliote and Ephesian connexions of the Aventine temple, see ARTEMIS.

That she was largely a goddess of women is shown by the processions of women in her honour at Aricia (Prop. 2. 32. 9–10; Ov. *Fasti* 3. 268–9), also by the character of many of the votive offerings there, which have clear reference to children and childbirth; see further Frazer on Ovid, ibid. 267, Wissowa *RK* 248. That she is a moon-goddess (see Preller–Jordan, *Römische Mythologie*[3] i. 312) is an idea resting on no real evidence (cf. JANUS). Warde Fowler (*Religious Experience,* 235) plausibly calls her a 'wood-spirit', for certainly she is commonly worshipped in wooded places. The central idea of her functions would seem to have been fertility, especially human, though probably not confined to that; for the development of such a deity into one of political importance, cf. Juno and Hera.

At Aricia she was associated with Egeria (q.v.), and Virbius, an obscure male deity (Ov. *Met.* 15. 544; Servius on *Aen.* 7. 84 and 761; see HIPPOLYTUS). Identifications with foreign deities are common all over the West.
H. J. R.

DIATRIBE. For examples of the διατριβή in Greek, characteristic of the Cynic and Stoic schools, *see* EPICTE-TUS, TELES. A large number of Roman writers, even when not professed philosophers, imitated the Greek διατριβή. Cato in his speeches resorts to the polemic methods of the popular moralists of Greece. In Lucilius the employment of diatribist writings is above all literary. On the other hand, Varro's satires are so much akin to Menippus' works that they can be in their general features reconstituted thanks to comparison with the dialogues of Lucian, another successor of Bion's disciple. Even Cicero in the *Tusculans* and *Cato Maior* presents long passages inspired by the opponents of systematic philosophy—by Ariston of Chios in particular. From this epoch of soul-stirring moral crisis, the popular preachers in their harangues to Roman crowds had recourse to the arsenal of themes belonging to the diatribe. Horace mocks them, but he willingly admits that his own satires are *Bionei sermones*; and his independence of thought does not debar him from using the same weapons. Among his contemporaries one must segregate the disciples of Q. Sextius (q.v. 2), founder of a sect which was rather original in spite of the eclectic character of its doctrine. Its ascetic vegetarianism is based, not on Pythagorean metaphysical conceptions, but on reasons of empirical ethics and hygiene which rest diatribic themes on the exercise of the will. Fabianus, an important 'Sextian', had an enormous influence upon the schools of rhetoric.

The elegiac poets and the prose-writers (especially Livy) who urge a return to the simplicity of ancient times found, like the fabulist Phaedrus, in this tradition, rejuvenated in accordance with the Roman spirit, those moralizing *loci communes* which appeared suitable to the needs of their period.

Seneca's works mark the point of departure for a fresh evolution, a neo-Stoicism in which, thanks to him, the diatribe makes its formal re-entry into philosophy. Notwithstanding manifold inconsistencies, Seneca towards the end of his life becomes more and more faithful to the moral principles which he had borrowed from Bion and Ariston. If Lucan and Persius return to orthodox Stoicism, Juvenal, the last of the great Roman satirists, is especially influenced by *rhetores* whose diatribist themes he develops at length.

Among Christian writers Tertullian shows what profit the advocates of the new religion could draw from this pagan tradition.

One sees that the role played by this movement of ideas was considerable in Roman literature. Its predominantly pragmatic and empiric character suited the practical spirit of the Latin people and agreed with their moralizing purposes.

R. Heinze, *De Horatio Bionis imitatore* (1889); H. Weber, *De Senecae genere dicendi Bioneo* (1895); R. Schütze, *Iuvenalis ethicus* (1905); P. Wendland, *Die hellenistisch-römische Kultur* (1907); C. Favez, *Senecae ad Helviam matrem de consolatione* (1918); A. Oltramare, *Les Origines de la diatribe romaine* (1926); Th. Brandt, *Tertullians Ethik* (1928). A. O. (transl. J. W. D.)

DICAEARCHUS, a Greek from Messana, who lived most of his life in the Peloponnese, especially at Sparta; pupil of Aristotle and contemporary of Theophrastus. Fragments only survive of his works:

I. POLITICAL. (i) Βίος Ἑλλάδος, the first attempt at a universal history of culture, from the Golden Age to D.'s time. (ii) Πολιτεῖαι (*Constitutions*) of Pellene, Corinth, Athens, and Sparta. (iii) Τριπολιτικός, perhaps a delineation of a 'mixed' constitution, containing elements of monarchy, aristocracy, and democracy. Probably this and others of D.'s works were in dialogue form. (iv) Ὀλυμπιακός and Παναθηναϊκός, both probably in form political orations. (v) Περὶ τῆς ἐν Ἰλίῳ θυσίας, on Alexander's sacrifice before the battle at the Granicus.

II. BIOGRAPHY AND LITERARY HISTORY. (i) Βίοι, on the lives and writings of Plato and other philosophers. (ii) Π. Ἀλκαίου, probably a biography and an exegetical commentary. (iii) Works on Homer, titles unknown.

(iv) Ὑποθέσεις τῶν Σοφοκλέους καὶ Εὐριπίδου μύθων (*see* HYPOTHESIS).(v) Π. μουσικῶν ἀγώνων,on competitions in music and poetry. The last three works were important sources for later scholars, containing much information about Homer and the Dramatists.

III. PHILOSOPHICAL. (i) Π. ψυχῆς, a dialogue on the corporeal nature and mortality of the soul, apparently consisting of two parts, Λεσβιακός and Κορινθιακός. (ii) Π. φθορᾶς ἀνθρώπων, maintaining that man is destroyed more by man than by natural disasters. (iii) A work on future things, title unknown, but apparently not identical with (iv) Π. μαντικῆς. (v) Ἡ εἰς Τροφωνίου κατάβασις, 'Descent into the Trophonian Cave', including immoralities of priests therein. (vi) Letter (? philosophical) to Aristoxenus.

IV. GEOGRAPHICAL. Περίοδος γῆς, cartography (and description?) of the known world, establishing for geographers a main parallel from the Straits of Gibraltar to the Himalayas; it included perhaps 'Measurements of Mountains in Greece', whose heights D. over-estimated.

Dicaearchus was a learned, fertile, and remarkably versatile author, of an original and genuinely scientific turn of mind. He influenced many subsequent writers, including Eratosthenes, Cicero, Josephus, and Plutarch. Cicero, who admired him greatly (*Att.* 2. 2. 6; 13. 31; *Tusc.* 1. 77), took him as the exemplar of the βίος πρακτικός, Theophrastus as that of the βίος θεωρητικός.

FGrH ii. 225 ff.; GGM i. 97-110, 238-43. PW xxv. 546-63.
E. H. W.

DICAEOGENES, a tragic poet, probably of the latter half of the fifth century B.C., wrote a *Medea* and a *Cyprians* (Aristotle, *Poet.* 16, mentions the recognition scene).

TGF 775-6.

DICASTERIES. At the institution of Athenian democracy in the time of Cleisthenes, the Heliaea (q.v.) ceased to be a court of appeal and became a court of first resort. The date was probably *c.* 487-486 B.C., when the importance of the archons was diminished by the substitution of sortition for election in their appointment. But whatever the occasion of the change, it was only natural that the growing democracy should seek more judicial power, for as Aristotle (*Ath. Pol.* 9) observes, κύριος ὢν ὁ δῆμος τῆς ψήφου (judicial ballot), κύριος γίγνεται τῆς πολιτείας.

2. It was obviously impossible for the entire Heliaea to sit on every case. Accordingly 6,000 were annually selected to serve in panels called dicasteries. This number was chosen because in the case of νόμοι ἐπ' ἀνδρί and ostracism a quorum of 6,000 was required. Thus the 6,000 dicasts represented the Athenian people. The whole group was sworn annually. The designation of the oath as ἡλιαστικός indicates that it belongs to the time of Solon. The oath was as follows:

I shall vote according to the laws and the decrees of the Athenian people and the Council of the Five Hundred, but concerning things about which there are no laws, I shall decide to the best of my judgement, neither with favour nor enmity. I shall judge concerning those things which are at issue and shall listen impartially to both the accusation and the defence.

Though the oath was annual, the dicasts were constantly reminded of it by litigants.

3. At first the dicasts served without pay. Remuneration was first suggested by Aristides, but was carried out by Pericles as a political manœuvre (*c.* 450 B.C.). By a convenient legal fiction the representative character of the total number of dicasts was extended to each section. Thus each court was independent, and no one could call it to account. But the dicasts represented current public opinion, because they were apportioned among the demes in each tribe according to their number and population. At first each section, numbering 500(Bonner and Smith, *Administration of Justice* i (1930), 235 ff.), not 600 as is commonly believed, was assigned to a court

for a whole year. For important cases several dicasteries could be combined. An even vote was an acquittal, like the Scottish verdict 'not proven'.

4. At the end of the fifth century there was a change in the method of manning the courts. The number of jurors was still nominally 6,000. All eligible citizens who offered for service were accepted and divided into ten sections. The first ten letters designated the sections, the next ten marked the courts. On days when court sessions were to be held all jurors were summoned. By a system of lot each court could be filled. Odd numbers —201 or 401 or 501—were used with the assurance that the trial would start with the full number.

5. A third system of recruiting dicasteries is described by Aristotle (*Ath. Pol.* 60 ff.; cf. H. Hommel, op. cit. inf.). The date of its introduction is uncertain, but in all likelihood it coincides with the introduction of written evidence in 378–377. Under this system it seems certain that the same men remained in the same section year after year. The annual allotments were confined to new applicants. It is difficult to interpret the intricate details of the assignments of dicasts to the court in which they would sit; its effect was to render impossible the bribery of dicasts, which was not unknown in the fifth century.

6. Each litigant appeared before the dicastery and was expected to speak in his own behalf, but he could always recite a speech written for him by a professional *logographos*. A litigant who was obviously incapable of speaking in his own behalf could obtain a substitute by permission of the court. Advocates (συνήγοροι) were always permitted to speak for a defendant. Until 378 evidence was presented orally as in modern courts; afterwards all evidence was reduced to writing and read by the clerk of the court when called for by the speaker. The verdict of a court was final, though on rare occasions the Ecclesia annulled or quashed a verdict or granted a pardon to a condemned defendant. In certain classes of cases a successful suit for perjury against a witness enabled a litigant to reopen the case.

7. The dicasts were judges of both law and fact. The presiding magistrate's task was to see that the case came to court in proper fashion; he did not issue an instruction to the jury after the hearing of the case. The dicasts reached a verdict without the charge of an expert jurist or an opportunity of discussing a case in private such as modern juries enjoy. Their verdict, reached by a majority or equal vote, was a mere affirmation or negation. As each court was independent, there were no legal precedents. But when a speaker cited parallel cases, they unquestionably had some effect on the dicasts. It is difficult to believe that 500 or more amateurs could try a case fairly. But the Athenians had some advantages: they could neither be browbeaten nor bribed, their numbers gave them confidence, and the system of selecting them made bribery impossible.

R. J. Bonner, *Lawyers and Litigants in Ancient Athens* (U.S.A. 1927); R. J. Bonner and G. Smith, *The Administration of Justice from Homer to Aristotle* (2 vols.; U.S.A. 1930–8), esp. i. 226 ff., 367 ff.; J. H. Lipsius, *Das attische Recht und Rechtsverfahren* (1905–15); Busolt–Swoboda, *Griechische Staatskunde* ii (1926), 1151 ff.; H. Hommel, *Heliaea* (Philol. Suppl.-Band xix, Heft ii, 1927); S. Dow, *Hesperia* 1937, Suppl. i. 198 ff.; id. *Harv. Stud.* l. 1 ff.
R. J. B.

DICING. Gambling with dice, the American crap game, was a popular amusement in Greece; in Rome, although nominally illegal except during the Saturnalia, it became a national vice. There were two kinds of dice, the four-sided astragalus (Lat. *talus*) and the six-sided cubus (Lat. *tessera*); and two, three, or four dice could be used. Sometimes the best throw was when all the dice showed different numbers, but usually the highest score was four sixes, *Venus*, the lowest four aces, *Canis*. The dice were thrown from a box; loaded dice were not unknown.
F. A. W.

DICTA CATONIS ('Dionysius', sometimes added to Cato's name, remains a puzzle), the title given to a versified handbook of morality, partly pagan, partly Christian, which, dating in its original form probably from the third century A.D., was widely studied in the Middle Ages and translated into many European languages. The title 'Cato' was perhaps an unknown author's recognition of Cato the Elder as the first moralist of Rome.

The collection consists of (*a*) its most important part, four books of hexameter *Disticha* (288 lines); (*b*) preceding them, 57 *breves sententiae* in prose; (*c*) four short *praefationes*, that to bk. 1 being in prose, the rest in hexameters; (*d*) 16 additional lines from the Zürich and Verona MSS. of 'Cato'; (*e*) 78 single lines (*Monosticha*), besides a considerable number of lines of Catonian origin (Baehrens thought 52) in a *carmen monostichon* constituting rules for life, *Praecepta Vivendi*. Baehrens accepted the ascription of the *Praecepta* to Columbanus, but its affiliation is rather with a poem ascribed by Dümmler to Alcuin (205 lines published by Dümmler, *MGH, Poet. lat. aevi Carolini* i. 275, 1880). This ascription Boas supports with proofs in *Alcuin und Cato* (1937), reprinting Dümmler's text with marginal notes to indicate borrowings from *Disticha* and *Monosticha*. Alcuin, he believes, used, not the medieval vulgate of 'Cato', but a manuscript of the same family as the Veronese fragment.

The collection has bequeathed many debatable questions, e.g. which are the oldest parts, the prose or the verse? whether or not there once existed a larger *Corpus Catonianum*? how much is pre-Christian? what alterations were made by a Carolingian recension?

The maxims, not without worldly cunning and selfishness, inculcate on the whole a homely morality: they represent, as proverbs do, the experience of the past, traceable sometimes to Greece, though occasionally the influence of Horace or Ovid appears. The final couplet of the *Disticha* (4. 49) emphasizes the terseness aimed at.

Text: Baehrens, *PLM* iii. 214–42 (1881); G. Némethy; with translation, J. W. and A. M. Duff, *Min. Latin Poets* (Loeb, 1934). For language, metre, and survival among European peoples, F. Skutsch, *PW* v (1905), 358 ff. A series of articles by M. Boas deal with the MSS. and relevant questions: e.g. *Rh. Mus.* lxvii (1912); *Mnemos.* xliii (1915), xliv (1916); *Rh. Mus.* lxxii (1917); *Philol.* lxxiv N.F. xxviii (1917), lxxv N.F. xxix (1918), lxxxiii N.F. xxxvii (1926); *Die Epistola Catonis* (Akad. Amsterd., 1934); *Alcuin und Cato* (1937).
J. W. D.

DICTATOR. The dictatorship, which is found as a permanent office in other Latin States, was added to the Roman constitution soon after the expulsion of the kings to provide a temporary, extraordinary magistracy in military—and later domestic—crises, *rei gerundae causa*. Any connexion with Etruscan or Oscan magistracies is obscure (*see* MEDDIX). Originally a major colleague of the consuls, known as *praetor maximus*, the dictator soon became completely independent, holding undivided authority of military character, not subject to veto or appeal, both abroad and at Rome. Twenty-four lictors indicated his quasi-regal power, which, however, was rather a concentration of the consular authority than a limited revival of the kingship. The dictator was not elected by the people, but nominated by a consul on the Senate's proposal. A *lex curiata* confirmed the nomination. After 361 B.C. *consulares* were normally selected, earlier the 'best man' was chosen. The dictator (who was also known as *magister populi*, master of the infantry) immediately appointed a *magister equitum* (q.v.) as his subordinate. Other magistrates remained in office but were subject to the dictator, who held his post for six months at most, but usually retired earlier, as soon as his particular task was done. This time limit rendered the dictatorship comparatively useless outside Italy, and its importance declined in the third century. Dictators were increasingly employed for minor purposes—holding elections or celebrating festivals or fixing the 'sacred nail', etc.—and popular agitation, long unsuccessful, was able by 300 B.C. to subject the dictatorship to *provocatio* (q.v.). Despite a revival during the invasion of Hannibal it was never again employed for its original purpose after 216 B.C., perhaps because of senatorial jealousy of independent authorities. After 202 B.C. even the dictators with limited competence were no more appointed. Later dictatorships (*see* SULLA, CAESAR) differed widely from the original in scope and purpose.

Ancient sources: Livy bks. 1–25 and Dion. Hal. passim; Polybius etc. Modern views: Liebenam, 'Dictator' in *PW* v, with Westermeyer, 'Magister Equitum', ibid. suppl. (lists); Mommsen, *Röm. Staatsr.* ii. 141 ff.; K. J. Beloch, *Röm. Gesch.* 75 ff.; A. Rosenberg, *Staat der alten Italiker* (1913), 89 ff.; E. Meyer, *Kleine Schriften* (1924), ii. 272. A. N. S.-W.

DICTIO DOTIS, *see* MARRIAGE, LAW OF, para. 8.

DICTYNNA, *see* BRITOMARTIS.

DICTYS CRETENSIS, a Cretan of Cnossos, companion of Idomeneus at Troy, and reputed author of a Trojan War diary, actually composed perhaps in the second or third century A.D. (*PTeb.* ii. 268). This work, supposedly discovered during Nero's reign, was translated into Latin prose by L. Septimius (fourth c.?) and with Dares (q.v.) formed the chief source drawn upon by medieval writers on the Troy-saga.

Text: F. Meister (Teubner, 1872) G. C. W.

DIDACTIC POETRY, GREEK, includes under one name many works which have little in common, except that their subject-matter is not love or war but science, philosophy, or some art or craft. The Greeks themselves hardly regarded it as a separate genre, but classed it under the general head of ἔπη. In the earliest times we can perhaps discern two main roots from which it sprang. On the one hand, there is an interest in myth and genealogy, and here we see its relation to hymn and epic; on the other, a natural desire to accumulate and hand on a store of recorded experience, whether in the practical or moral sphere, enriched with proverb and fable, and in this way akin to the utterance of oracles and seers. That such subjects should be expressed in hexameter verse is natural to an age in which literature is to be handed down in the memory and published by recitation. Both these strains can be traced in our earliest surviving poems, which come not from Ionia but from mainland Greece, and are grouped round the name of Hesiod. We can distinguish somewhat sharply between the guide to right conduct both with heart and hand, called *Works and Days*, and the *Theogony* with other works now lost (such as the *Ehoiai*, a catalogue of the heroines from whom noble families claimed their descent) —the former a moving personal appeal aiming at right action, which has been compared not unprofitably with Horace's *Epistles* and the prophecies of the Old Testament; the latter mere versified cosmogony and mythology, aiming at right information, and much more obviously influenced by Homer. Later work of the same school, now lost, included the proverbial philosophy of the *Sententiae Chironis*, and poems on astronomy—an easy extension from the agriculture of the *Works*—and perhaps geography. In the seventh and sixth centuries the purely moral element in Hesiod is continued in the work of Phocylides of Miletus; but henceforward it was to be expressed rather in the elegiac and iambic poets, whom we do not regard as didactic in the strict sense of the word, and later in the prose diatribe. The religious movements of the time found utterance in the oracles and *Theogony* of Epimenides, and in the early verse-literature of Orphism. But the most remarkable flowering of didactic poetry is to be seen in the work of the great philosophers of the Ionian school. It might be thought

that the growth of speculation would have led merely to the development of a simple prose style adequate to express its results with lucidity, for science is concerned with thoughts, poetry with feelings; but the passionate personal conviction of the early thinkers raised their subject to a level apt for poetical expression, and both in their interest in cosmogony and in their desire to make converts to right thinking they are the direct heirs of Hesiod. Add to this that the first philosophical poet, Xenophanes of Colophon, was already a poet in other metres, and we see why no effort was made before about 500 B.C. (Heraclitus) to exploit the latent resources of prose. But for his example, it is hard to think that his younger contemporary, Parmenides of Elea, would have chosen to write in verse, for his style is crabbed and his ear faulty. In Empedocles of Acragas, on the other hand, great intellectual force is allied with burning conviction, command of language, and an imagination both powerful and lively; and though Aristotle denies him the name of poet, the fragments of his works *On Nature* (Περὶ φύσεως) and *Purifications* (Καθαρμοί) incline us to regard him as one of the outstanding figures in Greek literature. Didactic poetry was never to achieve such heights again.

In fifth-century Athens the writing of didactic, as of epic, poetry was not in fashion; but in Alexandrian times, when systematization of knowledge was in vogue and increased attention was paid to the works of Hesiod, there arose a most flourishing school. The Greeks had always regarded edification as a poet's legitimate aim; and they attached great importance to literary form, even in subjects so unpromising as veterinary science. In this period they derived a pleasure which we cannot always share from the perusal of works in which mere technical details were expounded in flowing Homeric verse— pleasure seemingly enhanced if the author, a mere 'metaphrast', had no personal knowledge of his theme, but was known to be simply versifying an accepted prose treatise on the subject. We may leave on one side poems on local history and antiquities, for they partake to a certain extent of the nature of epic or hymn and are not always written in hexameters, and may concentrate on didactic poets in the narrow sense. Of these the first, at the end of the fourth century, is Menecrates of Ephesus, who wrote a poem now lost on husbandry (Ἔργα), inspired no doubt by the *Works and Days*. It was his pupil, Aratus of Soli in Cilicia, whose *Phaenomena*, a transposition into hexameters of the prose treatise of Eudoxus on the constellations, achieved a popularity truly phenomenal, and with its free adaptation of epic language set the fashion for all succeeding work of the same kind. His follower, Nicander of Colophon, shows the style at its most unreadable to our taste, for in his poems on snakes (Θηριακά) and antidotes for snakebite (Ἀλεξιφάρμακα)—others on agriculture and beekeeping are lost—outlandish subjects are allied with a love of rare and uncouth words. But the fashion had come to stay. The favourite themes were medicine (including the magical properties of precious stones), astronomy, and geography. Thus we hear of the *Phaenomena* and *Chorography* of Alexander of Ephesus in the Ciceronian age; of the *Sights of Italy* (Ἰταλικὰ θεάματα) and the Ἀπολυτικά (possibly on methods of painless suicide) of Heliodorus of Athens in the first century B.C. or A.D.; the antidote described by Andromachus of Crete, Nero's physician, in 174 elegiac verses; the Ἰατρικά in 42 books of Marcellus of Sidē under Marcus Aurelius; and very many more, which are mere names to us. Only four surviving works are of any importance. The Ἀποτελέσματα ascribed to Manetho, which were given their present form perhaps in the fourth century A.D. but incorporate earlier material, are of some value to the student of ancient astrology. The long geographical poem (Οἰκουμένης περιήγησις) of Dionysius Periegetes in the reign of Hadrian (he also wrote a *Λιθικά*, on precious stones) is enlivened with descriptions, though its aim is the purely practical one of imparting instruction; and it enjoyed very great popularity down to Byzantine times. The five books on fishing (*Ἁλιευτικά*) and four on hunting (*Κυνηγητικά*) under Oppian's name, written by two different poets living under Marcus Aurelius and Caracalla, are the most readable productions of this later school, for in them the technical theme is diversified with epic colouring, with similes, moral reflections, and picturesque detail, and the intent is purely to give pleasure. These are the last real fruit of the didactic tradition in Greek poetry, for henceforward the practical intention already noticed in Dionysius holds the field, and if information is expressed in verse, it is to make it more easily got by heart at school. R. A. B. M.

DIDACTIC POETRY, LATIN,

as was to be expected, is strongly influenced by Greek, and most of the Roman writers are translating or adapting Greek models. But at Rome the tradition produces poetry which is often of higher quality, and sometimes in the very first rank, partly because the authors usually convey more of a personal interest in their subject, partly because they are better poets. In the early period of Latin literature it is doubtful how far one can speak of didactic poetry. The *Hedyphagetica* of Ennius, a rendering of Archestratus' Greek work on gastronomy, seems from the surviving fragment more akin to satire; and of a remarkable series of poems in various metres on criticism and literary history —Accius' *Didascalica*, and the work of Porcius Licinus and Volcacius Sedigitus—we know too little to speak with certainty. The same is true of Q. Valerius Soranus, the friend of Cicero; and even the latest of these poems on literary themes, Horace's *Ars Poetica*, has more the character of an epistle or *sermo* than of didactic poetry properly so called. It is in the Ciceronian age that the Greek tradition begins to bear full fruit at Rome. There is first the example of Empedocles. The translation of his work by a certain Sallustius is known only from an unfavourable judgement in one of Cicero's letters and the contemporary *De Rerum Natura* of Egnatius from two brief fragments. But it was Empedocles who inspired Lucretius to express his passionate conviction of the truth of Epicurean philosophy in a long hexameter poem, as he acknowledges in one of the noblest tributes ever paid by one great poet to another; and the genius, the power, and originality of the result enabled Latin didactic poetry in the next generation to achieve a masterpiece which the Alexandrian school by itself would have been powerless to beget. For the other great influence in the last century of the Republic is that of Aratus and his followers. Aratus' *Phaenomena* enjoyed in Roman literary circles the same inexplicable popularity as among the Greeks, and Cicero's *Prognostica*, an adaptation of it made by him in early youth, is the first of a series of similar enterprises spread over four and a half centuries; also the most important, for it had considerable influence on both Lucretius and Virgil. The *Chorography* of P. Varro (q.v. 3) Atacinus, perhaps based on Alexander of Ephesus, and the *Theriaca* and *Ornithogonia* of Aemilius Macer (q.v. 2), who no doubt followed Nicander, seem to have been little more than attempts to naturalize the Alexandrian didactic poem in Roman dress. It is far otherwise with Virgil's *Georgics*. It is fashionable to regard these as a didactic poem on husbandry, and indeed the title—already used by Nicander—and the author's claim to be the Roman Hesiod, lend colour to this view. But their didactic element is in a sense accidental; they are something absolutely new in the beauty and splendour of their language and the masterly variety of their construction, and their real subject is not farming, but Rome and Italy and nature and the life of man.

The subsequent popularity of didactic poetry on many trifling subjects we know from Ovid's reference in *Tristia* 2. 471–92. His own position is peculiar. The *Halieutica* (if it be his) is on traditional lines, and so was perhaps his lost *Phaenomena*; but the *Medicamina faciei femineae* and the *Ars Amatoria*, with its palinode the *Remedia Amoris*, are rather parodies of the genre, brilliantly adapted as befits the theme to elegiac verse. His contemporary Grattius (q.v.) in the *Cynegetica*, presumably adapted from a Greek source but enlivened by a genuine feeling for the subject, shows that under the inspiration of the *Georgics* even a writer not of the first rank could produce work that can be read with pleasure; and we should feel the same of the remarkable *Astronomica* of Manilius, were it not for the obscurity of his distasteful theme. The undying popularity of Aratus appears from the new rendering of the *Phaenomena* by Germanicus Caesar, under Tiberius; its success, from the body of scholia that was later to gather round it. But didactic poetry was never again to be written by men of real poetic talent; and though under the Julio-Claudian Principate an unknown author was provoked by the example of Lucretius to write a crabbed poem on Mt. Aetna, later ascribed to Virgil, though Columella, the writer on agriculture, accepting the challenge thrown out in the *Georgics*, clothed his tenth book (on gardening) in competent hexameters, the old tradition was played out. Nemesian's (q.v.) fragmentary poem on hunting, written late in the third century, is its last manifestation. Already, towards the end of the second, a new type shows itself, in which the desire to impart information is everything, the poetry nothing: the voluminous works on grammar and metres of the skilful versifier Terentianus Maurus and the jejune collection of medical prescriptions by Q. Serenus seem—like the anonymous *Carmen de figuris* and *Carmen de ponderibus et mensuris* (qq.v.) of two centuries later—almost to announce the onset of the Middle Ages. The same love of instruction causes one more lengthy adaptation of Aratus in the second half of the fourth century by Avienus (q.v.), whose *Ora maritima* (written in iambics) is not without its value; and Dionysius Periegetes is translated by the same Avienus, and in the sixth century by Priscian, no doubt for use in schools. The Latin didactic poem serves henceforth for schoolbooks, or for Christian polemic and edification. R. A. B. M.

DIDASCALIA.

The word means primarily the 'teaching' of a play or dithyramb to the chorus which was to perform it by a poet or the professional trainer employed, and then, more generally, the production of the play or dithyramb. (In Plutarch and other late writers the term may also be applied to the group of plays performed.) In the plural *Διδασκαλίαι* refers to the records of performances, including the names of victorious tribes, *choregi*, poets, actors, and flute-players for each year, and of the plays performed at the Dionysiac festivals; Aristotle's lost works included one book entitled *Διδασκαλίαι* and one book of *Νῖκαι Διονυσιακαὶ ἀστικαὶ καὶ Ληναϊκαί*. These must have been completed from the official records; it is not known whether these were engraved on stone from the first or not; but it is generally agreed that the inscriptions, of which large fragments remain (*IG* ii². 2318–25, with some other scraps), and which were probably engraved in the third century or late fourth century B.C., were based on the work of Aristotle so far as this went, and brought up to date afterwards; and that Aristotle was also the source from which Alexandrian and other scholars (including the authors of the Arguments to the plays in our manuscripts) must have drawn; it is not known how far his researches went beyond the official records, nor in what year his record began. The inscription numbered *IG* ii². 2318 probably carried the record back to 502 B.C. or a few years earlier,

and is generally thought to correspond to Aristotle's
Νῖκαι; the other inscriptions are likely to have drawn
upon his Διδασκαλίαι.

See E. Reisch in *PW* v. 1 (1903), s.v. 'Didaskaliai'; A. Wilhelm,
Urkunden dramatischen Aufführungen in Athen (1906); E. Capps,
Introduction of Comedy into the City Dionysia (1903), and arts. in
AJPhil. xx and xxi, *AJArch.* for 1900, and *Hesperia* xii. 1 (1943);
A. E. Haigh, *Attic Theatre³*, ch. 2 and Appendix B (1907); G.
Jachmann, *De Aristotelis didascaliis* (1909).　　　　A. W. P.-C.

DIDASCALIAE at Rome. Plautus' *Stichus* and *Pseudolus* (in A), Terence's plays and Donatus' commentary
thereon are prefaced by brief remarks concerning first
performance, games at which performed, presiding
magistrates, producer, composer and type of music,
Greek original, order of play in author's works, consuls
of the year, etc. They were often incomplete; varying
in different manuscripts; source unknown; nevertheless
of fundamental importance.

See Schanz–Hosius, *Gesch. röm. Lit.* i⁴ (1927), 105.　　W. B.

DIDIUS (1), TITUS, an Optimate and the first member of his family to reach the consulship (98 B.C.). As
tribunus plebis (103) he was driven from the tribunal by
his colleague Norbanus, during the trial of Q. Caepio
(q.v. 1). He was praetor (101) and defeated the Scordisci
in 100 in Macedonia. Later, as proconsul in Spain, he
cut to pieces nearly 20,000 of the Vaccaei, was saluted
Imperator, and triumphed (in 93). As consul, with Q.
Metellus Nepos, he passed the famous *Lex Caecilia Didia*,
forbidding 'tacking' and imposing an interval of three
nundinae between the promulgation of a law and voting
on it. He fell in the Social War (89).

For his tribunate, see J. Lengle, *Hermes* 1931.　　M. H.

DIDIUS (2) **JULIANUS**, MARCUS, a rich senator, was
chosen by the praetorians after a mock auction of the
Empire to succeed Pertinax, in preference to the latter's
father-in-law Flavius Sulpicianus. His election was no
less unpopular with the populace (*see* PESCENNIUS NIGER)
than with the army, and at Carnuntum the legions proclaimed Septimius Severus emperor. Julianus attempted
negotiations, but his fate was sealed when Severus bought
the support of the praetorians. Upon their direction the
Senate deposed Julianus, who was murdered in his
deserted palace on 1 June A.D. 193.

Herodian 2. 6–13; Dio Cassius bk. 73; S.H.A.; Parker, *Roman
World*, 56–60.　　H. M. D. P.

DIDIUS, *see also* GALLUS (6).

DIDO, legendary daughter of a king of Tyre, known by
Virgil as Belus; she is said to have had the name of
Elissa at Tyre, and to have been called Dido (? 'The
Wanderer') at Carthage. Her husband, called Sychaeus
by Virgil, was murdered by her brother Pygmalion, now
king of Tyre, and Dido, escaping with some followers
to Libya, there founded Carthage. At this point legends
diverge. The older story, narrated by Timaeus, was that
in order to escape marriage with the king of Libya
(Iarbas in Virgil) Dido built a pyre as though for an
offering and leapt into the flames. The Roman form of
the story, which gained currency at the time of the Punic
Wars and was probably followed by Naevius and Ennius,
brought Aeneas to Carthage, but Varro, who adopts it,
makes Dido's sister Anna, not Dido herself, perish for
love of Aeneas. The story contained in the first and
fourth books of the *Aeneid* may have been invented by
Virgil himself. Aeneas, shipwrecked on the coast of
Libya, is brought by Venus to the palace and entertained
by Dido, who falls in love with him. After a while
Aeneas departs, warned by Mercurius to leave Carthage
and pursue his destiny, and Dido throws herself on the
pyre. Ovid in *Heroides* 7 presents Dido's lamentation

in a rhetorical form. Modern sentiment has reviled
Aeneas' treatment of Dido, but his desertion of her in
obedience to divine command is an essential element in
his 'piety' (*see* AENEAS 1).

For the sources see A. S. Pease, Vergil, *Aen.* 4. 14 ff.　　C. B.

DIDYMA, also called **Branchidae,** seat of an oracle of
Apollo, eleven miles from Miletus. Before the Persian
wars Didyma was governed by the hieratic family of the
Branchidae, who traced their descent from the hero
Branchus. The Persians burned the temple in 494.
After Alexander's conquest of Miletus in 334 the cult
was reorganized. The Milesians built for it the largest
temple of the Greek world. The cult was thenceforth
administered directly by the city; the prophet was elected
annually and assisted by two treasurers (ταμίαι) and an
executive board (κόσμοι). A prophetess, as at Delphi,
was the mouthpiece of the god. An annual agonistic
festival, the Didymeia, was made pan-Hellenic early in
the second century B.C.

Ancient sources: (*a*) Milesian inscriptions relating to Didyma
are scattered through many publications; see especially B. Haussoullier, *Rev. Phil.* from 1895 to 1926; Th. Wiegand, *Milet: Ergebnisse der Ausgrabungen* (1899–); a number of the more important
are included in Dittenberger, *SIG* and *OGI*. (*b*) Valuable literary
sources are Hdt. 1. 157 f.; 5. 19; Conon, *Narr.* 33, 44; Iambl. *De
Myst.* 3. 11; Pausanias and Strabo, passim. Modern literature:
H. Gelzer, *De Branchidis* (1869); B. Haussoullier, *Milet et le Didymeion* (1902); H. Knackfuss, *Didyma: Die Baubeschreibung* (1939).
J. E. F.

DIDYMUS (1) (*c.* 80–10 B.C.) belonged to the school
founded at Alexandria by Aristarchus (q.v. 2) and himself
taught there. A scholar of immense learning and industry
(cf. his nicknames Χαλκέντερος and Βιβλιολάθας, the
latter because of occasional self-contradictions due to his
having forgotten what he had said in earlier books), he
is said to have written 3,500 or 4,000 works. His importance for literary history consists primarily in his
careful compilations of the critical and exegetical work
of earlier scholars. He was not an original researcher,
but rather a discriminating variorum editor and a
scrupulous transmitter of learning that might otherwise
have been lost.

WORKS: 1. He sought to reconstitute lost recensions
by Aristarchus of the Homeric text by the comparison of
copies and by the examination of A.'s commentaries and
special treatises. His results were much used by the
scholiasts. 2. Commentaries, with abundant mythological, geographical, historical, and biographical information,
on Homer, Hesiod, Pindar, Bacchylides, Choerilus,
Aeschylus, Sophocles, Ion, Euripides, Achaeus, Cratinus,
Aristophanes, Phrynichus, Eupolis, Menander, Thucydides, Antiphon, Isaeus, Isocrates, Aeschines, Demosthenes, Hyperides, Dinarchus. Much of the oldest
scholia to Pindar, Sophocles, Euripides, and Aristophanes
is ultimately derived from D. A papyrus fragment of
his commentary on Demosthenes' *Philippics* illustrates
well his compilatory method. 3. Lexicography: Λέξεις
τραγικαί and Λέξεις κωμικαί. These collections formed
a valuable source for scholiasts and lexicographers, e.g.
Hesychius. *On Corrupt Expressions, On Expressions of
Doubtful Meaning, Metaphorical Expressions, On Proverbs,*
a chief source of the extant works of the *Paroemiographi*
(q.v.). 4. Grammar: *On Orthography, On Analogy among
the Romans, On Inflexions.* 5. Literature and antiquities:
On Lyric Poets, Ξένη ἱστορία (on myths and legends),
Miscellany (Σύμμικτα συμποσιακά), *On the Axones of
Solon,* works on the death of Aeneas, the birthplace of
Homer, etc., and a polemic against Cic. *Rep.,* which was
answered by Suetonius.

M. Schmidt, *Didymi Chalcenteri grammatici Alexandrini fragmenta*
(1854); A. Ludwich, *Aristarchs homerische Textkritik* (1884–5);
H. Diels u. W. Schubart, *D. Kommentar zu Demosthenes* (1904);
A. Körte, *Rh. Mus.* 1905; P. Foucart, *Mémoires de l'Institut
National de France* 1909.　　J. F. L.

DIDYMUS (2), CLAUDIUS, the Younger (1st c. A.D.), an Atticist lexicographer, wrote on the incorrect diction of Thucydides (Περὶ τῶν ἡμαρτημένων παρὰ τὴν ἀναλογίαν Θουκυδίδῃ), abridged the *Attic lexicon* of Heracleon of Ephesus, and wrote a monograph comparing Latin with Greek. P. B. R. F.

DIEKPLUS (διέκπλους), a naval manœuvre which the Greeks apparently borrowed from the Phoenicians in the Persian Wars. The ships of one line, feinting to ram the galleys of the opposing line, swept between them (διεκπλεύσαντες), damaging their oars or rudder-oar, and circled about to strike the helpless craft in the rear. To prevent this, a fleet was drawn up in two lines, either in file, as at Artemisium (U. Wilcken, *Hermes* 1906, pp. 103 ff.), or in staggered formation, as at Arginusae (Xen. *Hell.* 1. 6. 29). With the heavier ships of Hellenistic times, the insertion of *lembi* in the lines (Polyb. 16. 4. 8 ff.), and the Roman reliance on boarding (ibid. 1. 22–3, 51), the *diekplus* lost importance. C. G. S.

DIES FASTI, NEFASTI. On the Roman calendar (*see* CALENDARS) certain days were marked *F*, meaning *fas* or *fastus*, literally 'days of speaking', when the formal words necessary to transact legal business might be spoken, i.e. the courts were open and the day was not a festival. Others were *N(efasti)*, when for one reason or another legal business might not be done (properly speaking, it was not impossible, but to do it was a *uitium* and must be expiated by a sacrifice). See Varro, *Ling.* 6. 29 ff. for other classes of days: *C(omitialis)*, when public assemblies might be held; *EN(dotercisus)* or *intercisus*, lawful during the pause in the middle of the sacrificial ritual; *Q(uando) ST(ercus) D(elatum) F(as)*, 15 June, when the shrine of Vesta (q.v.) was cleansed; *Q(uando) R(ex) C(omitiauit) F(as)*, 24 March, 24 May, when the *rex* (q.v.) *sacrorum* had certain formal duties. On existing calendars, the sign NP, probably *nefas, feriae publicae*, is used somewhat erratically for many of the *dies nefasti*. *Dies religiosi* are any days, whether *nefasti* or not, supposed to be unlucky, e.g. the anniversary of Cannae. H. J. R.

DIESPITER, by-form of *Iuppiter* (see JUPITER), e.g. Horace, *Carm.* 3. 2. 29.

DIETETICS was originally the regulation of life for those who were training for the games, and this type of dietetics was practised as long as games were held. In the fifth century Herodicus of Selymbria, Plato says (*Resp.* 406 a), tried to heal the sick by prescribing a certain regimen; from then on dietetics became an established means of treating patients, like surgery or pharmacology.

Still more important than dietetics for athletes and the sick was that for the healthy as advocated by Greek physicians. If diseases due to a disturbance of the bodily balance can be healed by diet, it must be likewise possible to prevent diseases by a diet which preserves this balance undisturbed. Such prevention is the more necessary since the bodily balance is constantly changed by whatever a person does, eats, or drinks, by exercises and the seasons; it must be constantly restored so as to avoid the danger of falling into disease at almost any moment. The healthy no less than the sick, it was therefore claimed, should fall under the permanent supervision of the physician.

For their dietetic rules the physicians determined with minute accuracy the quality of all factors influencing the body from without or within. They regulated with great care every detail of life according to the necessities of health alone, and without paying any attention to the demands of business activities, politics, or normal life. They admitted that the poor had to content themselves

with what was possible for them, but wanted the rich, who alone had the means of living a healthy life, to do so, even if it meant giving up everything else. Strange as it seems, people accepted this medical philosophy, believing as they did that health is the greatest blessing in this life of uncertainty and change. Such ideas became the more plausible, at least for the upper classes who were not restrained by any considerations of occupation, especially since political independence was gradually destroyed in the city-states. Yet even among the poor dietetic measures in as far as they could be applied were very common.

There can be no doubt that the demand of physicians on the healthy was responsible for much nervousness. People became too conscious of their bodies; besides, they were unable to endure sudden and unforeseen changes, and in addition tended to remain aloof from all useful activity, a consequence deplored by philosophers and statesmen. Yet it was not until Greek medicine was transmitted to the Romans that a certain change took place. The Romans insisted that the healthy man could do whatever he pleased, for otherwise he could not fulfil his duties as a citizen; dietetics they thought only good for weaklings and scholars. In the Roman Empire, however, even this opposition was overcome. With the rise of autocratic government and the beginning of the archaistic movement the Greek conception won the day and its reign was uncontested until the heathen ideal of bodily health vanished before the new God.

ANCIENT SOURCES: Hippocrates, Περὶ διαίτης ὑγιεινῆς; Περὶ διαίτης bks. 1–4; Galen, Ὑγιεινόν, bks. 1–6; Philostratus, Περὶ γυμναστικῆς.
MODERN LITERATURE: general, L. Edelstein, *Die Antike* (1931). Relation to gymnastics, L. Englert, *Studien z. Gesch. d. Med.* (1929). Medical content, J. Marcuse, *Diätetik im Alterthum* (1899). L. E.

DIEUCHIDAS of Megara (4th c. B.C.) wrote annals of Megara (Μεγαρικά), and ascribed the recension of Homer to Solon.
FHG iv. 388.

DIFFARREATIO, see MARRIAGE, LAW OF, para. 9.

DIFFERENTIAE, distinctions between words of similar form (*ora, hora*) or meaning (*metus, timor, pavor*) formulated by rhetoricians and grammarians as an aid to correct diction. The earliest Latin examples are in the *Ad Herennium* and Varro's *De Ling. Lat.* Many *differentiae* were discussed by miscellanists (Suetonius in his *Prata*, Aulus Gellius), by lexicographers (Verrius Flaccus, Nonius especially in bk. 5), and by grammarians. Anonymous lists compiled from various sources were sometimes attributed to great names (*Diff. Catonis*, etc.) and many items were incorporated in glossaries. Many *differentiae*, however, do not correspond with the actual usage of Latin authors.

G. Goetz, art. 'Differentiae' in *PW*; Schanz-Hosius, § 1121. J. F. M.

DIGAMMA, see ALPHABET.

DIGESTA, a title applied by the classical jurisprudence to systematic, comprehensive treatises on the law as a whole, and by Justinian to the main part of his codification, published after the first Codex and *Institutiones*. An alternative name for this part of Justinian's work was *Pandectae*, a counterpart of Greek origin to the Latin name formed from *digerere*. By the constitution of 15 December 530, beginning with the words 'Deo auctore', the Emperor initiated the work by giving instructions to his minister of justice Tribonianus (q.v.) for its composition by the collection of passages from the works of classical jurists. Precisely three years later the collection was published by the Constitution 'Tanta', which contains precious indications on the origin and formation of the work, but nothing on the method by which the editorial commission (five professors and eleven advocates under the presidency of Tribonian) accomplished their task. The *Digesta* came into force on 30 December 533. They contain excerpts from works of jurists of more than three centuries; the earliest are C. Mucius Scaevola and Labeo, the latest Modestinus, Hermogenianus, and Charisius. Justinian records that two thousand books with three millions of lines were read by the compilers for this purpose, but only a twentieth, 150,000 lines, were selected. A not quite accurate list of authors and works excerpted (Index Florentinus) is annexed to the best manuscript of the *Digest*, preserved at Florence. The collection is divided into fifty books, the books into titles with headings taken chiefly from the praetorian edict. Each fragment has an *inscriptio* indicating its author and the work from which it is taken. The order of books and titles follows generally that of the commentaries on the edict.

It was certainly a strange idea of the Emperor or his counsellors to construct a code of existing law by compiling passages written three to five centuries before, and presenting them as his own opinion (const. 'Omnem' 6: 'omnia nostra facimus'). The compilers, moreover, did not restrict themselves to collecting legal rules and formulations of a general character: they copied passages with historical reminiscences, etymological observations, quotations taken from Homer, polemics and divergent opinions, precious of course from a historical point of view, but superfluous and embarrassing in a work which according to a strict order of Justinian should have been a codification, since the jurists' opinions were to be considered as substantive and valid law. The task of the compilers was very difficult; the mosaic compilation of more than 9,000 fragments could not produce a perfect result; repetitions and contradictions were unavoidable (though strictly forbidden by Justinian) in such an enormous work, completed in less than three years. Another reason for the insufficiency of the work was the order of the Emperor that the compilers might alter and reform everything that seemed to them 'superuacuum, imperfectum uel minus idoneum' (const. 'Tanta' 10). Such alterations, accomplished in the classical texts by omissions, additions, or substitutions in a very large measure, are called 'interpolations' ('emblemata Triboniani'). They concern partly institutions of civil law or procedure obsolete in Justinian's times, as abolished by law or custom (e.g. *mancipatio, in iure cessio, res mancipi, dotis dictio, fiducia, cognitor, vindex, vadimonium*, and some more). Mention of all these antiquated matters was suppressed and replaced by modern expressions. The tendency to restrict the classical texts had the effect that several passages were often fused into one fragment, longer argumentations were omitted or shortened so as to produce not infrequently an unintelligible or chaotic text. On the other hand, superfluous additions were made in explanation of a word or a rule. But a great number of interpolations were far from being merely formal alterations, as when the classical decision was restricted to special matters of fact or changed into an opposite one in conformity with the new law of imperial constitutions of post-classical times, and with reforms of Justinian himself, or under the influence of new legal doctrines and ideas. It is clear that such a method of adapting old classical texts to new tendencies, rules, or necessities sometimes brought a confusion into the precise constructions and opinions of the classical jurists, the more so as the Byzantine compilers wrote different Latin from the jurisprudence of the first three centuries of the Empire. In the modern science of Roman law the discovery of interpolations (already known as such in the 16th c.) has engaged most attention, and justly so, for the distinction of the classical law from that of Justinian depends on the recognition of the original classical text. The real value of the detection of an interpolation (which

must mostly remain hypothetical) does not, however, lie in the mere purification of a text from alterations or additions, but in the right appreciation of the alteration itself, of its reforming character and its position in the development of a legal institution or idea. It remains to be observed that the manuscripts excerpted by Justinian's compilers contained corruptions, mistakes of copyists, additions (glosses) and marginal notes of the earlier users of them. Many of these alterations subsequently passed into the official manuscript of the *Digest*, partly by inadvertence of the Byzantine copyists, partly by intention, on the order of the compilers, to whom such notes seemed a useful extension of the classical original. Therefore not everything which seems to come from another hand than that of classical jurists is an intentional, substantial interpolation, i.e. a legal reform. The modern literature of Roman law has made enormous progress in distinguishing the classical law from Justinian's and his collaborators' innovations, but very often an exaggerated tendency to find new interpolations has produced erroneous opinions. Interpolations are assumed without sufficient justification (especially on the basis of the fallacious linguistic criterion), and errors are committed in the historical evaluation of suspected texts.

Modern editions: Mommsen, *Digesta Iustiniani* (2 vols. 1866, 1870); Mommsen, P. Krueger, *Corpus iuris civilis* i (14th stereotyped ed. 1922, with indication of interpolations). A pocket edition by Bonfante, Fadda, Ferrini, Riccobono, Scialoja contains some useful suggestions (vol. i, 1908; vol. ii, 1931). Important works of reference: A. Guarneri-Citati, *Indice delle parole e frasi ritenute interpolate*[2] (1927); Supplem. in *Studi Riccobono* i and *Festschrift für P. Koschaker* i (1939). *Index Interpolationum quae in Iustiniani Digestis inesse dicuntur* (initiated by L. Mitteis and edited under the direction of E. Levy and E. Rabel; 3 vols. and 1 Suppl., 1929–35). *Vocabularium iurisprudentiae Romanae*, in 5 volumes (not yet finished, edited by B. Kübler). See also the bibliographies under LAW AND PROCEDURE, ROMAN, § 1, and JURISPRUDENCE (text-books on the sources of Roman Law). A. B.

DIKE (*Δίκη*), personification, mostly literary, of Justice. One of the Horae (Hesiod, *Theog.* 902), she reports to Zeus the wrong-doings of men (*Op.* 256 ff.), and similar ideas occur in later authors. In Aratus (*Phaen.* 96 ff.), she is the constellation Virgo, who finally left the earth when the Bronze Age began; some (as Ov. *Met.* 1. 149–50) call her Astraea in this connexion. In art she is sometimes shown punishing Injustice (see Paus. 5. 18. 2; cf. von Sybel in Roscher's *Lexikon* i. 1019). She catches an evil-doer (Eur. *Heracl.* 941); will not suffer a murderer to live (*Acts* xxviii. 4), perhaps from popular (pagan) belief. Cf. Schrenk in G. Kittel, *Theologisches Wörterbuch zum Neuen Testament* ii. 180 ff. H. J. R.

DIKE (*δίκη*) in Athenian practice might mean any lawsuit, but technically it was a private suit in which the plaintiff appeared in his own behalf, as distinguished from *γραφαί* or other processes, in which any one might be plaintiff. Normally *δίκαι* correspond to modern civil actions. Marked exceptions are prosecutions for homicide and perjury: the former could be instituted only by a relative of the deceased, the latter by the person injured by the illegal evidence.

Δίκαι were either *πρός τινα* (*ex contractu*) to settle a claim, or *κατά τινος* (*ex delicto*) to determine damages. Where the court assessed the damages, a second trial was held to decide between the damages asked by the plaintiff and those suggested by the defeated defendant. Such *δίκαι* were called *τιμηταί*, others *ἀτίμητοί* because damages were fixed by law. R. J. B.

DINARCHUS (*Δείναρχος*) (b. *c.* 360 B.C.), the last of the 'ten orators'. A Corinthian by birth, he lived at Athens, and studied under Theophrastus. Being a *metoikos*, and therefore debarred from public speaking, he composed a large number of speeches for others. The first of these was written *c.* 336, but he did not come into prominence till *c.* 324, when he wrote a speech against Demosthenes in the Harpalus affair (*see* DEMOS-THENES). He prospered particularly after the death of Alexander, when, as his biographer Dionysius of Halicarnassus remarks, the other orators having been executed or banished, there was nobody left worth mentioning. Under the oligarchy established by Cassander, 322–307 B.C., he was active and prosperous, but on the restoration of democracy in 307 he retired to Chalcis in Euboea, where he lived till 292. Returning to Athens, through the intercession of Theophrastus, he was robbed of a large sum of money by his host Proxenos, and brought the latter to justice. Nothing is known of his life after this, nor the date of his death.

WORKS. Of sixty speeches which Dionysius considered genuine we possess only three—*Against Demosthenes*, *Against Aristogiton*, and *Against Philocles*, which are all connected with the affair of Harpalus. The authenticity of the first of these was doubted by Demetrius, but it is very similar to the others in style and matter. Three other speeches, *Against Boeotus II*, *Against Theocrines*, and *Against Mantitheus*, which appear in the Demosthenic Corpus, have sometimes been ascribed to D.

Dinarchus marks the beginning of the decline in Attic oratory. He had little originality, except some skill in the use of new metaphors; he imitated his predecessors, especially Demosthenes (Hermogenes, *Id.* 2. 11 calls him κριθινὸς Δημοσθένης, 'a small-beer Demosthenes'), but developed no characteristic style of his own. He knew the technique of prose composition and had command of all the tricks of the orator's trade. He was competent up to a point, but his work is careless and lacking in taste. Thus, the arrangement of his speeches is incoherent; his sentences are long and formless, certain figures of speech, e.g. epanalepsis and asyndeton, are ridden to death, and his invective is so exaggerated as to become meaningless. Numerous examples of minor plagiarisms are collected by Blass (*Att. Ber.*² iii. 2. 318–21); in particular, a passage about Thebes in *Demos.* 24 is based on Aeschines 1. 133, and *Aristog.* 24 is suggested by Demosthenes 9. 41.

For general bibliography, *see* ATTIC ORATORS. Text, Blass (Teubner, 1888). Index, *see* ANDOCIDES.　　　　　　　　J. F. D.

DINON (Δίνων rather than Δείνων) of Colophon, father of Cleitarchus (q.v.), wrote a history of Persia in at least three *syntaxeis* (perhaps Assyria, Media, Persia), certainly down to Artaxerxes Ochus. Following Ctesias' Περσικά, it represents the trend towards the romantic Alexander-histories. Widely read, it is used in Plutarch's *Artaxerxes*.

FHG ii. 88.　　　　　　　　A. H. McD.

DIO (1) COCCEIANUS, later called **Chrysostomus** ('the golden-mouthed') (*c.* A.D. 40–after 112), Greek orator and philosopher. He was born in Prusa (now *Brussa*) in Bithynia of a family of high social standing in their city (*Or.* 44. 3; 46. 2). He gained renown as an orator and sophist, and was able to play a political role. In 82 he became involved in a political intrigue in Rome (*Or.* 13. 1) and was banished from Italy and his native province by decree of Domitian. He then wandered about for years in the Balkans and Asia, earning his livelihood by occasional humble work (Philostr. *VS* 7. 29). This sudden and complete change of life created an entire change of mind. He turned to philosophy, and based his life on the Cynic doctrine. Convinced of his divine mission (e.g. *Or.* 32. 12) as a doctor of the soul, he went about healing mankind by his example and his orations. Under Nerva he was allowed to end his exile. Henceforth he combined a new political career at home and a rhetorical one throughout the Empire with his work as a preacher and philosopher. His influence was at its height under Trajan, to whom he delivered the speeches 'On the duty of a prince'. He was a champion of Greek

patriotism within the Roman Empire, and, like Plutarch, a representative figure of Greek culture in the late first century of Imperial Rome. *See* LITERARY CRITICISM IN ANTIQUITY, 1. 6.

As a philosopher D. with his eclecticism of Stoic and Cynic ideas is not in the least original. What makes his orations worth reading is the fact that he understands philosophy deeply enough to take it as a basis of active life, and propounds it with a considerable power of style. A corpus of eighty speeches (with a few *falsa*) is preserved.

Texts: H. v. Arnim (1893–6); G. de Budé (Teubner, 1915–19); Loeb (with transl., in progress). Studies: H. v. Arnim, *Leben u. Werke des Dio von Prusa* (1898, important); C. Martha, *Les Moralistes sous l'empire Romain*⁷ (1900); *PW* v. 848; Ueberweg-Praechter, *Grundriss*¹² 506. Style: W. Schmid, *Der Attizismus* in Norden, *Kunstprosa*² ii.　　　　　　　　K. O. B.

DIO (2) CASSIUS (*Cassius Dio Cocceianus*) of Nicaea (Bithynia), son of Cassius Apronianus, governor of Cilicia and of Dalmatia, entering the Senate under Commodus, became praetor (A.D. 193), *consul suffectus* (before 211), and consul for the second time with Alexander Severus in 229. Besides a biography of Arrian and a work on the dreams and portents of Septimius Severus, he wrote a Roman history from the beginnings to A.D. 229, of which bks. 36–54 (68–10 B.C.) are fully preserved, 55–60 (9 B.C.–A.D. 46) in abbreviation, 17, 79–80 in part. Xiphilinus (11th c.) epitomized from bk. 36 (missing Antoninus Pius and M. Aurelius' first years); Zonaras (12th c.) gives the tradition of bks. 1–21, 44–80 in bks. 7–11 of his Ἐπιτομὴ Ἱστοριῶν, following Xiphilinus from Trajan.

The narrative, which took ten years to prepare and twelve years to write, appears to be based on an early annalistic tradition, Polybius with annalistic 'contamination', Livy (from 68 to 30 B.C.), Imperial annalistic tradition (common to Tacitus, if Tacitus himself is not used), memoirs, and possibly Arrian's Παρθικά, and for contemporary events his own high authority. Ignorant of Republican institutions and conditions, from Caesar he used his Imperial constitutional experience, at first colouring events with his ideas of Imperial absolutism (cf. Maecenas' speech in 52. 14–40), but later handling his material with full knowledge. Annalistic in arrangement, although modified to meet requirements of subject-matter, his narration concentrated on political aspects, avoiding details and technicality, and giving a rhetorical narrative in Thucydidean style.

Texts: J. Melber (1890–1928 Teubner); U. P. Boissevain (1895–1931); E. W. Cary (1914–27, Loeb); cf. E. Schwartz, *PW* iii. 1684.　　　　　　　　A. H. McD.

DIOCLES (1) (d. after 412 B.C.), democratic lawgiver in Syracuse, and opponent of Hermocrates (q.v.). Some scholars distinguish two Diocles, an elder one, a lawgiver who received worship as a hero, and the politician of 412. But this remains a mere hypothesis.

Diodorus, bk. 13. W. Hüttl, *Verfassungsgeschichte von Syrakus* (1929), 85 ff.　　　　　　　　V. E.

DIOCLES (2) (fl. *c.* 410 B.C., Suidas), comic poet, born at (?) Athens. Several of the titles (Βάκχαι, Θυέστης, Κύκλωπες) suggest mythological burlesque. Μέλιτται presumably portrayed a republic of industrious bees. He may be the Diocles who is said to have invented a sort of harmonica, consisting of saucers struck with a wooden hammer (fr. 15).

FCG i. 251 ff.; *CAF* i. 766 ff.　　　　　　　　M. P.

DIOCLES (3) of Carystus, according to Pliny the second physician after Hippocrates in time and fame, a contemporary of Aristotle (384–322 B.C.), lived at Athens. He was the first physician to write in Attic, avoiding hiatus. His books dealt with animal anatomy, physiology, aetiology, symptomatology, prognostics, dietetics, botany. The fragments show the influence of the Sicilian school of which his father, Archidamus, was also an adherent, and of Empedocles (four humours, importance of the heart, the pneuma), of Hippocrates (the body considered as organism), of Aristotle (methodological concepts and terminology). Diocles' originality, it seems, consists in uniting these different trends. That in the details of scientific research he was independent is certain.

Text: fragments, M. Wellmann, *Die Fragmente d. sikelischen Ärzte* (1901); M. Fränkel, *D. Carystii fr. quae supersunt*, Diss. Berl. (1840). Literature: general discussion, Wellmann, l.c., and *PW* v. 802. W. Jaeger, *D. v. Karystos* (1938), points to Aristotelian influence and argues for a later date of Diocles than had formerly been assigned; the date 340–260 B.C. (Jaeger, *Sitz. Berl.* 1938) seems too late; cf. review of Jaeger's book by L. Edelstein, *AJPhil.* 1940.

L. E.

DIOCLES (4) (probably 1st c. B.C.), mathematician. He wrote a work Περὶ πυρείων (on burning-glasses). He invented the 'cissoid' curve as a means of doubling the cube, and may have been the inventor of the parabolic burning-glass.

PW v. 813.

DIOCLES (5) of Magnesia (it is not known which Magnesia), a younger friend of the Cynic Meleager of Gadara, therefore probably born *c.* 75 B.C. He must have lived part of his life in Cos. He is mentioned only by Diogenes Laertius, who describes him as the author of an Ἐπιδρομή (compendium) τῶν φιλοσόφων. Diogenes makes large use of this work, but Nietzsche went much too far in describing Diogenes' work as simply an epitome of that of Diocles.

PW v. 798.

W. D. R.

DIOCLES (6), Greek rhetor of the Augustan age, whose declamations betrayed moderate Asianist tendencies.

Sen. *Controv.* 7. 1. 26.

DIOCLETIAN (GAIUS AURELIUS VALERIUS DIOCLETIANUS), originally named Diocles, a Dalmatian of low birth, who rose to be commander of the Emperor Numerian's bodyguard. Chosen by the army near Nicomedia in November A.D. 284 to avenge his master's death, he at once struck down the praetorian prefect, Aper. Marching westward to meet Carinus, he ended an arduous campaign at the battle of Margus (early 285) and, by showing mercy to the hostile faction, assured a lasting peace. He at once chose Maximian, an old comrade, to be his Caesar and sent him to Gaul to suppress the revolt of the Bagaudae. Quickly victorious, Maximian was raised to the rank of Augustus early in 286.

2. The two emperors had wars to fight on Danube and Rhine, against Sarmatians, Franks, and Alamanni. In 289 they joined forces in Raetia against the Chaibones, and in the winter of 289–90 met in state at Milan. In the East Diocletian set up a Roman nominee, Tiridates III, as king of Armenia and asserted Roman supremacy in Mesopotamia. In 291 (?) he suppressed the revolt of Coptos and Busiris in Egypt. But, in the West, Carausius, admiral of the Channel fleet, revolted in 286 to escape condemnation for neglect of duty, seized Britain and a part of northern Gaul, and frustrated all attempts to reduce him. The emperors found it politic to grant him peace and recognition in 289.

3. To increase the stability of his government Diocletian in 293 established his famous 'tetrarchy'. Himself Augustus of the East he took Galerius to be his Caesar, while to Maximian, Augustus of the West, was assigned Constantius Chlorus. The two Caesars put away their wives to marry the daughters of their Augusti. The main military problems of the reign now came up for settlement. Constantius blockaded Bononia (*Boulogne*) by a dam and wrested it from Carausius, who was soon afterwards murdered by his assistant, Allectus. A great expedition in 296 under Constantius and his praetorian prefect, Asclepiodotus, destroyed Allectus and recovered Britain, which now entered on a new age of prosperity. In 298 Constantius gained a spectacular victory over the Alamanni at Langres. Maximian in 297 crossed to Africa and defeated the troublesome confederacy of the Quinquegentanei. In Egypt a fresh revolt broke out under Domitius Domitianus and Achilleus in 296, but was suppressed by Diocletian in person at Alexandria in 297.

4. Galerius had at first been engaged in defending the frontiers and reclaiming waste land in Illyricum. In 297 he settled the Carpi in Pannonia. But a determined attack on the Empire by Narses of Persia now called him to the assistance of his Augustus. Defeated in the first campaign near Carrhae, Galerius was permitted to bring up reinforcements and correct his error. Invading Armenia, he gained a complete victory over the king and destroyed his will to fight by capturing among the booty the royal concubines. Diocletian moderated the zeal of Galerius and granted peace on reasonable terms, annexing only some minor provinces and establishing Nisibis as trade-depot between the two empires.

5. In 303 Diocletian visited Rome for the first time, to celebrate his *Vicennalia*. A collapse in health the following year almost cost him his life, and on 1 May 305 he abdicated with Maximian, leaving Constantius and Galerius Augusti in West and East respectively, with Severus and Maximinus Daia as their Caesars. His years of honoured retirement were spent at Salonae, broken only by a return to public life, in 308, to help Galerius to re-establish order in the government at the Conference of Carnuntum. Diocletian died in 313, saddened by the civil wars, the collapse of his system, and the persecution of his kindred by Maximinus Daia and Licinius.

6. Diocletian deservedly ranks as the refounder of the Empire, completing and systematizing the changes demanded by the anarchy of the third century. The Imperial office, as we have seen, was divided. Two Augusti, with two Caesars as adjutants and destined successors, administered different sections of the Empire. Diocletian, as chief, ensured unity of purpose. The provinces were greatly increased in numbers by subdivision, and were grouped in twelve dioceses (*see* DIOECESIS), each under a *vicarius* of the *praefecti praetorio*. Each Augustus and Caesar had his own prefect, and these prefects began to rank as financial and administrative, rather than as military, officers. The civil and military commands were permanently separated. Asia and Africa were still governed by proconsuls, all other provinces by senators or equestrian *praesides*. Each of the four rulers had his staff (*comitatus*), and new capitals, Nicomedia, Treviri, and Sirmium, rose by the side of Rome.

7. In finance, too, Diocletian introduced extensive reforms. The new system of taxation was based on the *iugum*, the unit of land, and the *caput*, the human unit, and was liable to revision every fifteen years (*indictio*). Besides money payments the *annona*, payment in kind, was regularly levied. In the coinage Diocletian at first contented himself with stabilizing the gold piece at 70, and later at 60, to the pound. But in A.D. 296 he carried through a complete reform. Beside the gold piece of 60 to the pound was struck a piece of good silver, at 96 to the pound, with subordinate issues of silvered bronze and plain bronze. Alexandria, the last surviving Greek mint, was closed, and all coinage was now Imperial, issued from a number of centres. The masses of silvered bronze already in circulation were probably reduced in value. This led to distrust of the coinage, desperate spending, and an abrupt rise in prices, which Diocletian strove, without much success, to combat by his *Edictum de maximis pretiis* of A.D. 301. Italy lost her ancient privilege and paid taxes with the provinces. Despite the general excellence of the financial administration, the expenses of four courts and the lavish expenditure on new buildings put a heavy strain on the taxpayer.

8. In the army discipline was restored and efficiency enhanced. The legions were reduced in size, but greatly increased in numbers. The *élite* of the army was now concentrated in the standing army, the *palatini*, and *comitatenses*; the frontier troops were militia of inferior quality. The chief command was assigned to *magistri peditum* and *equitum*.

9. To raise the dignity of the Imperial office Diocletian assumed the forms and trappings of royalty, and required obeisance (*adoratio*) from his subjects. His own dynasty, the Jovian, stood under the protection of Jupiter, the Herculian of Maximian under that of Hercules. A stern love of old Roman discipline and tradition gradually led Diocletian to attack the Christian Church. Beginning with a purge of the army and civil service, Diocletian was led on by Galerius to direct persecution in 303. The burning of the palace of Nicomedia embittered feeling, and the persecution became increasingly severe, passing from attack on buildings and sacred books to actual bloodshed. Carried on with varying intensity over the whole Empire, it had apparently triumphed by the time that Diocletian abdicated. The persecution was the one grave mistake in a career of enlightened public service.

H. Mattingly *CAH* xii, ch. 9, 323; Parker, *Roman World*, 220 ff., 262 ff.; G. Costa in *Diz. Epig.* ii. 1793 ff.; K. Stade, *Der Politiker Diokletian und die letzte große Christenverfolgung* (1926); W. Ensslin, *Zur Östpolitik des Kaisers Diokletian* (1942); W. Seston, *Dioclétien et la tétrarchie* i (1946). 　　　　　　　　　 H. M.

DIODORUS (1) of Sinope (fl. *c.* 350 B.C.), Middle (or New?) Comedy poet, brother of Diphilus (q.v.): a family monument included both brothers as Athenian citizens (Wilhelm, *Urkunden*, p. 60). Two of his plays (Μαινό-μενος, Νεκρός) are dated 353 B.C. Fr. 2, the ways of the parasite.

FCG iii. 543 ff.; *CAF* ii. 420 ff. 　　　　　　　　　 W. G. W.

DIODORUS (2) **CRONUS** of Iasos (fl. *c.* 300 B.C.), one of the masters of Megarian dialectic. Among his pupils were Zeno of Citium and Arcesilaus, both of whom owed much to him. He repeated the arguments of Zeno of Elea against the possibility of motion; his most famous argument, the κυριεύων, was directed against the possibility of that which is not actual, and played a considerable part in controversies over freewill.

PW v. 705. 　　　　　　　　　 W. D. R.

DIODORUS (3) **SICULUS** of Agyrium, flourished under Caesar and Augustus (to at least 21 B.C.), wrote (*c.* 60–30 B.C.) a World History, his Βιβλιοθήκη, in forty books from the earliest times to Caesar's Gallic War (54 B.C.). He began with an ἀρχαιολογία: bk. 1 Egypt, bk. 2 Mesopotamia, India, Scythia, Arabia, bk. 3 North Africa, bks. 4–6 Greece and Europe (1–5 fully preserved, 6 fragmentary); bks. 7–17 covered from the Trojan War to Alexander the Great, bks. 18–40 from the *Diadochi* to Caesar (11–20 fully preserved, 21–40 fragmentary). The narrative reproduces in its successive parts the tradition of Hecataeus, Ctesias, Megasthenes, Dionysius Scytobrachion, Ephorus, Theopompus, an historian of Alexander who is perhaps Cleitarchus, Hieronymus (perhaps through Agatharchides), Duris, Diyllus, Philinus, Timaeus, an early Roman annalist not necessarily Fabius Pictor, Polybius, Artemidorus, Posidonius. This material was added to the framework of a chronographical work, dependent on Apollodorus, like that of Castor of Rhodes. Despite his universal conception of history and his aim of writing for the Graeco-Roman world, his work is undistinguished, with confusion arising from the different traditions and chronologies, a compilation only as valuable as its authorities.

Texts: I. Bekker (1853–4); L. Dindorf (1866–8); F. Vogel–C. T. Fischer (1888–1906); C. H. Oldfather (1933–, Loeb). Cf. E. Schwartz, *PW* v. 663; A. Momigliano, *Enciclop. ital.* xii. 924; N. G. L. Hammond, *CQ* 1937, 79; ibid. 1938, 137; A. Klotz, *Rh. Mus.* 1937, 206. 　　　　　　　　　 A. H. McD.

DIODOTUS (1), satrap of Bactria-Sogdiana under Antiochus I and II. Under the latter he began to act independently, and struck coins with Antiochus' name and types but with the monogram DIO, which *may* represent Diodotus. In 246 Seleucus II, in his struggle with Ptolemy III, gave a sister to Diodotus to ensure his support; their daughter married Euthydemus (q.v. 2). Probably Diodotus took the royal title, for in the state-cult of the Euthydemid kings he bore the cult-name Soter; the earlier coins with the legend 'Of king Diodotus' have recently been ascribed to him instead of his son Diodotus II. 　　　　　　　　　 W. W. T.

DIODOTUS (2), Stoic, teacher of Cicero *c.* 85 B.C., lived later in Cicero's house. He died *c.* 60 and made Cicero his heir.

PW v. 715.

DIOECESIS. To facilitate the control of the provincial governors by the central bureaucracy Diocletian divided the Empire (including Italy) into twelve dioceses, each administered by a *vicarius*. These *vicarii* were representatives of the praetorian prefects, and being equestrians were of lower rank than the senatorial governors, all of whom, except the proconsuls of Asia, Africa, and Achaea, were subject to vicarial authority. The dioceses corresponded to the spheres of the *vicarii*, except the diocese of Italy, which extended to the Upper Danube. The provinces north of the Apennines were under the *vicarius Italiae* at Milan; the rest of the mainland, with Sicily, Corsica, and Sardinia, was controlled by a special *vicarius in urbe Roma*. The jurisdiction of the *vicarii* was concurrent with that of the praetorian prefects, and appeals from their decisions went directly to the emperor.

Parker, *Roman World*, 263–5. 　　　　　　　　　 H. M. D. P.

DIOGENES (1) of Apollonia (prob. Phrygian, not Cretan Apollonia), son of Apollothemis and younger (?) contemporary of Anaxagoras (cf. Diog. Laert. 9. 57; fl. *c.* 440 or 430 B.C.), was an eclectic philosopher, carrying on the Ionian tradition with additions from Anaxagoras and Leucippus. Little is known of his life. He almost certainly visited Athens, where his views aroused prejudice and were parodied by Aristophanes in the *Clouds* (423 B.C.).

WORKS: *On Nature* (Περὶ φύσεως), from which Simplicius quotes extensive fragments. Others cited, *Against the Sophists* (i.e. Cosmologists), a *Meteorology*, and *The Nature of Man*, are mere titles.

Diogenes revives the teaching of Anaximenes, whom he could scarcely have 'heard' (D. L. ibid.), that the primary substance is Air, endowing it with mind or intelligence, divinity and all-disposing power. Its infinite transformations are effected by rarefaction and condensation. D. argues that if things in the world, including Empedocles' elements, are to be affected by one another, they must be differentiations of the same underlying substance (fr. 2). Air is also the principle of soul and intelligence in living creatures, and essentially alike in all; it differs, however, in degrees of warmth for different species and individuals. D.'s physiological theories of generation, respiration, and the blood are important in the history of medicine, and Aristotle has preserved his account of the veins (*Hist. An.* 511^{b}30 f.). His cosmology follows traditional lines, with its flat round earth, but bears some resemblance to that of Anaxagoras. The heavenly bodies are pumice stones filled with fire. But he is no mere reactionary: like the Hippocratic writers he displays the scientific interest in details typical of his age. *See also* ANATOMY AND PHYSIOLOGY, para. 2.

Ancient sources and text of fragments: Diels, *Vorsokrat.*[5] (Kranz, 1934–7); Ritter and Preller[10] (1934). Modern literature: Zeller–Nestle, *Philosophie der Griechen* i. 2[7] (1922) (Engl. Transl. 1881); Zeller–Mondolfo ii (1938); J. Burnet, *Early Greek Philosophy*[4] (1930, translates frs.); *PW* v. 764. 　　　　　　　　　 A. J. D. P.

DIOGENES (2) (c. 400–c. 325 B.C.), son of Hicesias of Sinope, ὁ κύων, founder of the Cynic sect. According to some authors (Diog. Laert. 6. 20–1) he came to Athens as an exile after he and his father, who had been in charge of the mint in Sinope after 362 (*Recueil général des monnaies grecques de l'Asie Mineure*, 193), had been accused of παραχαράττειν τὸ νόμισμα. At Athens he lived in extreme poverty and continued παραχαράττων τὸ νόμισμα in a metaphorical sense, by rejecting all conventions. Whether he was a personal disciple of Antisthenes (D.L. 6. 21 and passim) is doubtful on chronological grounds. But he seems to have been influenced by his philosophy, since there are many similarities in outlook, and since the originality of Diogenes apparently consisted more in the way in which he applied his philosophy in everyday life than in his theories as such.

2. His main principles were the following: Happiness is attained by satisfying only one's natural needs and by satisfying them in the cheapest and easiest way. What is natural cannot be dishonourable or indecent and therefore can and should be done in public. Conventions which are contrary to these principles are unnatural and should not be observed.

3. From this there results in practical life self-sufficiency (αὐτάρκεια), supported by ἄσκησις (training of the body so as to have as few needs as possible), and shamelessness (ἀναίδεια). Mainly on account of the latter quality Diogenes was called κύων (dog), from which appellation the name of the Cynics is derived.

4. He illustrated his simple principles by pointed utterances and drastic actions. He probably wrote dialogues and tragedies, the latter in order to show that the tragic heroes could have avoided misfortune by following his principles. But many of the works attributed to him by later authors were spurious.

5. Although Theophrastus described his way of living and his disciple Metrocles collected anecdotes about him, the tradition about his life is obscured by the fact that soon after his death he became a legendary figure and the hero of pedagogic novels (Eubulus, Cleomenes) and satirical dialogues (Menippus, Bion). The tradition on his philosophy was obscured by the tendency of the Stoics to attribute their own theories to him because they wanted to derive their philosophy from Socrates through the succession Antisthenes, Diogenes, Crates, Zeno.

6. It is uncertain whether Diogenes lived in Corinth for many years (so *D.L.* 6. 71; Dio Chrys. 8. 4; Julian, *Or.* 7. 212), and how, when, and where he died, since the tradition is conflicting.

7. His disciple Crates spread his philosophy. D. had great influence on later literature through his caustic wit. He is stated (*D.L.* 6. 73, 80) to have written tragedies in which his doctrines were expounded, but the plays named as his were also ascribed to others. They were probably never acted.

Diogenes Laertius 6. 20–81; tragic fr. in Nauck, *TGF* 807–9. E. Schwartz, *Charakterköpfe* ii. 1–26; K. von Fritz, *Philol.* Suppl.-Bd. xviii. 2; *Studi di Filologia Class.* N.S. v. 133–49: D. R. Dudley, *A History of Cynicism* (1937), 17 ff.; F. Sayre, *Diogenes of Sinope* (1938); *PW* v. 765.   K. von F.

DIOGENES (3) of Seleuceia on the Tigris, commonly called Diogenes of Babylon (c. 240–152 B.C.), pupil of Chrysippus, succeeded Zeno of Tarsus as head of the Stoic school. He visited Rome in 156–155 and greatly stimulated interest there in the Stoic creed. His most famous pupil was Panaetius, and his main influence was on the grammatical doctrine developed by the school. Works: Περὶ φωνῆς τέχνη; Διαλεκτικὴ τέχνη; Περὶ τῆς Ἀθηνᾶς; Περὶ μαντικῆς; Περὶ τοῦ τῆς ψυχῆς ἡγεμονικοῦ; Περὶ εὐγενείας (all lost).

Testimonia and frs. in von Arnim, *SVF* iii. 210–43. *PW* v. 773. W. D. R.

DIOGENES (4) of Tarsus, Epicurean of uncertain date, but probably identical with the author of a book on ποιητικὰ ζητήματα (who fl. c. 150–100 B.C.).

PW v. 776.

DIOGENES (5) of Oenoanda in Lycia, Epicurean of about the second century A.D. Faced with the approach of death he decided to proclaim to the widest possible audience the main principles of the Epicurean gospel; so he ordered the erection of a big Epicurean inscription in an open place. The work is a collection of single treatises, mainly about problems of Ethics and Physics. We find also the correspondence of a mother and a son, probably Epicurus himself.

The inscription is interesting more as a human document of a faithful Epicurean mind than as a philosophical work. But the account D. gives of the doctrines of his master is clear and shows some understanding of the questions involved. The main part of the inscription was discovered in 1884.

Text: J. Williams, Leipzig 1907 (with comm.). Studies: Ueberweg–Praechter, *Grundriss*¹² 578 f.; *PW* Suppl. v. 153.   K. O. B.

DIOGENES (6) **LAERTIUS**, author of a preserved compendium of ancient philosophy, of about the first half of the third century A.D. His name is probably modelled on the Homeric Διογένης Λαερτιάδης.

His work is a mixture of biography and doxography, as its title proves: 'History of philosophy, or on the lives, opinions, and apophthegms of famous philosophers'. It was never brought up to the standard of a literary or scientific book, but remained a collection of more or less classified quotations and excerpts. Nevertheless, to us the work is of the greatest importance, as most of our biographical knowledge of ancient philosophers is derived from it.

The book is arranged in so-called 'successions' (*see* PHILOSOPHY, HISTORY OF). In the early stages of its use it was mutilated, as a sketch of the original plan shows (ed. Rose, *Hermes* 1866).

TEXTS: H. G. Huebner (1828); C. G. Cobet (1850, with Lat. transl.); Loeb (with Engl. transl.); in critical editions: book 3, edd. Breitenbach, Buddenhagen, etc. (1907); book 5, life of Aristotle, *see* ARISTOTLE; book 8, ed. A. Delatte (1922); book 10, *see* EPICURUS. STUDIES: U. von Wilamowitz, *Phil. Unters.* iii. 1880, *Epistula ad Maassium*; E. Schwartz in *PW* v. 738 (standard work); E. Howald, *Philol.* 1917; *Hermes* 1920; A. Delatte, *La Vie de Pythagore de Diogène Laerce* (1922); R. Hope, *The Book of D. L.* (1930, an account of modern research).   K. O. B.

DIOGENIANUS (1), Epicurean. Eusebius quotes many passages from his polemic against Chrysippus' doctrine of fate. His date is unknown, but he probably belongs to the second century A.D., when the polemic of the New Academy against Chrysippus was at its height.

Ed. A. Gercke, *Jahrbücher für klassische Philologie*, Suppl. 14. 748. *PW* v. 777.   W. D. R.

DIOGENIANUS (2), of Heraclea, of the age of Hadrian. Besides geographical indexes, a collection of proverbs, and other works, he compiled in five books an alphabetically arranged epitome of the Lexicon of Pamphilus as abridged by Vestinus. This epitome was used by Hesychius, who refers to it under the title of Περιεργοπένητες.

Edition, E. L. von Leutsch and F. G. Schneidewin, *Paroemiographi* i. 177, ii. 1. Norden, *Hermes* xxviii (1892), 625.   P. B. R. F.

DIOMEDES (Διομήδης), in mythology (1) a Thracian, son of Ares and Cyrene, king of the Bistonians (Apollod. 2. 96). To capture his man-eating horses was the eighth labour of Heracles (q.v.).

(2) Son of Tydeus (q.v.), and Deipyle, daughter of Adrastus (q.v.; Hyg. *Fab.* 69. 5 and often). He took a

prominent part in the Trojan War, wounding Aphrodite and Ares by help of Athena, and overcoming a number of the foremost Trojans (*Il.* 5. 1 ff.), but behaving chivalrously to his hereditary guest-friend Glaucus the Lydian (q.v.; ib. 6. 119 ff.). He and Odysseus raid the Trojan camp, killing Rhesus (q.v.; 10. 219 ff.). Throughout the poem, and especially in the second half, he is the author of wise and bold counsels. His part in the expedition of the Epigoni against Thebes (cf. ADRASTUS) is mentioned in the *Il.*; (4. 406, cf. Apollod. 3. 82 ff.). In the post-Homeric Trojan cycle he is conspicuous. He shared with Odysseus in the murder of Palamedes (q.v.; Paus. 10. 31. 2, quoting the *Cypria*). He and Odysseus brought Philoctetes from Lemnos (Hyg. *Fab.* 102. 3; cf. PHILOCTETES). The same pair stole the Palladium from Troy (Hesychius and Suidas s.v. Διομήδειος ἀνάγκη, from the *Little Iliad*). Two other cycles of his adventures are: (*a*) In Calydon; his grandfather Oeneus having been robbed in old age of his kingship by the sons of Agrius, Diomedes killed them all but two, gave the throne to Oeneus' son-in-law Andraemon, and brought Oeneus to the Peloponnesus (Apollod. 1. 78). (*b*) After the return from Troy he found his wife Aegialeia unfaithful, came to Italy, where his companions were turned into birds (Stith Thompson, *Index*[2] 88), and finally received heroic or divine honours after his death or disappearance (Farnell, *Hero-Cults*, 289 ff.). H. J. R.

DIOMEDES (3) (late 4th c. A.D.), grammarian, who wrote an *Ars grammatica* in three books (ed. Keil, *Gramm. Lat.* i. 299–529). His work is of value because, though he rarely mentions his sources, he clearly relied upon earlier grammarians who discussed and illustrated the usages of Republican authors. Parallels between his work and that of Charisius (q.v.) seem to indicate that he borrowed from his contemporary.

Cf. Teuffel, § 419. 3; Schanz-Hosius, § 834. J. F. M.

DION (c. 408–354 B.C.) was a relative and minister of Dionysius I; but falling under the spell of Plato, he became opposed to tyranny. He tried to exert a liberalizing influence upon the young Dionysius II, but like Plato himself he failed, and had to leave Syracuse (366). For many years he stayed in Greece, closely attached to the Academy. But the hostility of Dionysius grew, and Dion decided to attack him. With only a small force he succeeded in winning Syracuse, and other cities joined him. But he had internal enemies, being a haughty aristocrat and not a popular leader like his former friend Heraclides, who outstripped him by gaining a great naval victory over Dionysius' admiral Philistus. The intrigues against Dion increased, and he and his soldiers were expelled, only to be recalled soon after, when Syracuse was again attacked by Dionysius. Once more the city was liberated, but Heraclides' intrigues continued, and finally Dion had to allow his assassination. After his rather ideological attempt at a constitution according to Platonic ideas, he became 'a tyrant in spite of himself'. In 354 he was murdered by order of Callippus, a supposed friend and Platonist.

Plato's letters (esp. 7 and 8); Plutarch, *Dion*; Diodorus, bk. 16. R. Hackforth, *CAH* vi. 272 ff.; R. v. Scheliha, *Dion* (1934) (idealizing). V. E.

DIONE (Διώνη), consort of Zeus at Dodona, Farnell, *Cults* i. 39, who conjectures that she is the local form of the Earth-Mother; but her name is simply a feminine of Zeus (cf. Cook, *Zeus*, ii. 350 and note 6), which suggests rather a sky-goddess. Nothing definite is known of her cult; if the original consort of Zeus, she was ousted by Hera (q.v.), and from Homer (*Il.* 5. 370) on she is one of his mistresses or secondary wives, mother of Aphrodite, or even Aphrodite herself. H. J. R.

DIONYSIA. Many festivals of Dionysus had special names, e.g. the Anthesteria (q.v.), the Lenaea (q.v.), etc.; the latter are, however, in inscriptions styled Διονύσια τὰ ἐπὶ Ληναίῳ or ἐπιλήναια Δ. (Aristotle, *Ath. Pol.* 57; *IG* ii[2]. 1496 A, *b* 105, 1672, 182) and the term Dionysia was given to such festivals at which dramatic performances took place. With the great and ever increasing popularity of the drama, Dionysia were instituted almost everywhere; their origin is found in Athens. Athens had (*a*) τὰ κατ' ἀγρούς, (*b*) τὰ ἐν ἄστει or τὰ μεγάλα Δ. The old opinion that the Lenaea were part of the Anthesteria and the urban equivalent of the rustic Dionysia (revived by W. Dörpfeld–E. Reisch, *Das griechische Theater*, 1896, pp. 9 ff.; contra, M. P. Nilsson, *Studia de Dionysiis atticis* (1900)) is clearly wrong, for the festivals cannot be separated from the months named from them; the month of Gamelion in which the Lenaea were celebrated was in other Ionian towns called Lenaion. The rustic Dionysia were celebrated in Poseideon and the city Dionysia in Elaphebolion.

(*a*) Rustic Dionysia are known from many Attic demes through inscriptions, but only because of the dramatic performances which took place at them, and these are obviously borrowed from the city Dionysia. Fortunately Aristophanes gives a vivid description of the procession at the merry rustic festival (*Ach.* 247 ff.). First comes the daughter of Dicaeopolis as *kanephoros*, then two slaves carrying the phallos, and last Dicaeopolis himself singing an obscene lay in honour of Phales. Plutarch, *Non posse suav. vivi sec. Epic.* 1098b, mentions the cries and the riot at the rustic Dionysia. A special feature was the ἀσκωλιασμός, youths balancing on a full goat-skin; see ASKOLIASMOS.

(*b*) The City Dionysia were celebrated in honour of Dionysus Eleuthereus. This god was introduced into Athens by Pisistratus from the village of Eleutherae in the borderland between Attica and Boeotia. A temple was built to him on the southern slope of the Acropolis, and a second temple was erected close at hand, probably in the last years of the fifth century B.C. The orchestra where the dramatic performances took place was adjacent; the stone theatre was built by Lycurgus about 330 B.C. The fact that tragedy has its origin in this cult militates against the commonly accepted opinion of Aristotle that tragedy and satyric drama alike arose from the dithyramb. At Eleutherae Dionysus was called μελαναιγίς, 'he who is clad in a black goat-skin', and a myth tells of a duel between Xanthus and Melanthus in which Dionysus appeared. It has been supposed that the origin of tragedy is to be found in the mourning for the slain god (M. P. Nilsson, *Neue Jahrb.* xxvii (1911), 673 ff.).

The City Dionysia was a great festival to which people flocked from all parts. The statue of Dionysus was brought to a temple in the Academy and, coming hence, the god made his epiphany with much pomp; phalli were carried in the procession, which went to the temple on the southern slope of the Acropolis where sacrifices were performed. Inscriptions give the information that, after the sacrifice, the ephebes carried Dionysus into the theatre by torchlight in order that he might be present at the dramatic performances (M. P. Nilsson, *JDAI* xxxi (1916), 336 ff.; P. Stengel, ib. 340 ff.). When the theatre was filled with people the surplus of the State revenues was carried through the orchestra and the sons of men who had fallen in war were given panoplies.

The performances at the City Dionysia comprised lyric choruses sung by men and boys as well as tragedies and comedies. The Marmor Parium, ep. 43, gives the information that Thespis performed the first drama ἐν ἄστει at a date which is mutilated, but must fall between 542 and 520 B.C.; Suidas says 535. Comedy was introduced later, a few years before the Persian Wars (see COMEDY, OLD). For the very important but badly mutilated inscriptions which enumerate the victories see A. Wilhelm, *Urkunden dramatischer Aufführungen (Sonderschriften des österreichischen archäologischen Instituts* vi) (1906).

L. Deubner, *Attische Feste* (1932), 134 ff.; A. E. Haigh, *The Attic Theatre*[3], revised by Pickard-Cambridge (1907); A. W. Pickard-Cambridge, *The Theatre of Dionysus in Athens* (1946).   M. P. N.

DIONYSIUS (1) I (*c.* 430–367 B.C.), tyrant of Syracuse, was a former adherent of Hermocrates (q.v.). After the failure of the Syracusans to relieve Agrigentum in 406, Dionysius, supported by Philistus, the historian, caused the assembly to elect new generals, among whom he was one. Later he supplanted his colleagues, obtained a bodyguard, and was regularly re-elected *strategos autokrator*—a constitutional tyrant. Defeated by the Carthaginians, he lost the support of the wealthy class, who attempted an unsuccessful revolution. To consolidate his power he signed a very unfavourable treaty with Carthage, and converted Ortygia into a fortified residence. His adversaries' property was distributed among aliens and freed slaves. Aided by mercenaries, he began a process of military expansion. He destroyed Naxos, settled mercenaries in Catana, and transplanted the citizens of Leontini to Syracuse. At Syracuse he fortified Epipolae and built a castle at Euryalus. He constructed a great fleet and remarkable war-machines. His aim was clearly to expel the Carthaginians from Sicily (398). He took Motya, but the tables were turned by the arrival of Himilco (397), who drove him out, defeated his fleet, and besieged Syracuse until driven off by plague and Spartan intervention. A secret agreement between Himilco and Dionysius is improbable. Dionysius' authority was now established over Greek and Sicel towns. A new Carthaginian attack was repelled in 392, and he styled himself 'archon of Sicily'. An extensive movement of population assured his domination.

His ambitions extended to southern Italy, where in alliance with Locri (he married a Locrian, Doris) and Lucanian tribes he established his authority after a victory near the Elleporus (388) and the destruction of Rhegium (386). He concluded an alliance with the Molossian Alcetas and probably with Taras. He may have established colonies at Issa, Ancona, and Hadria to control the Adriatic (but the evidence is doubtful). He helped Sparta against Athenian naval predominance and against Thebes, checked Etruscan piracy, and probably entered into relations with Rome. His State was the first great political construction of the Greeks in the West. But Dionysius had checked the Carthaginians only at the expense of the Greek cities against which he launched barbarian populations. His mercenaries exhausted his financial resources. His oppression had to be concealed by external splendour. He sought popularity in Greece: in Athens for political convenience his tragedy *The Ransom of Hector* was awarded the first prize in 367. Plato, who visited him, was sent away in disgrace.

A new outbreak of hostilities with Carthage *c.* 383 involved the cities of south Italy. Heavily defeated at Cronium (382?; 375?), Dionysius had to abandon Selinus and Thermae. His fresh attack in 368 was stopped before the impregnable Lilybaeum. He died in 367.

Dionysius composed tragedies, which he exhibited at Athens and Olympia, as well as in Sicily; but though, as noted above, he won the first prize at the Lenaea with the Ἕκτορος Λύτρα in 367, his plays are generally represented as very poor work (Cramer, *Anecd. Par.* i. 303; Diod. Sic. 15. 6, 74, etc.) and are ridiculed by poets of the Middle Comedy (e.g. in Ephippus fr. 16 and in Eubulus' *Dionysius*). His use of the desk of Aeschylus and his purchase of the pen, writing-tablets, and harp of Euripides (Lucian, *Ind.* 15) failed to kindle any inspiration which could justify his vanity in regard to his work. Gram-

marians give instances of his misuse of words in accordance with fanciful etymologies.

Principal source: Diodorus, bks. 13–15 (partly from Timaeus, partly perhaps from Theopompus). K. J. Beloch, *Griechische Geschichte*, iii[2]. 1–2 (1922–3); J. B. Bury, *CAH* vi (1927), 108; M. L. W. Laistner, *A History of the Greek World from 479 to 323 B.C.* (1936), 268; G. Glotz–R. Cohen, *Histoire grecque* iii (1936); R. L. Beaumont, *JHS* 1936, 202–3. *See also* SICILY, SYRACUSE. For Dionysius' tragedies see *TGF* 793–6.   A. M. and A. W. P.-C.

DIONYSIUS (2) II, eldest son of Dionysius I, succeeded his father in 367–366 B.C., when about thirty. He stopped the war with the Carthaginians, but he continued the Spartan alliance and retained some hold in south Italy, founding two colonies in Iapygia. Weak, inexperienced, and probably dissolute, he was also cultured, the author of poems and philosophic dissertations, and the host of philosophers (Plato, Aeschines, Aristippus, Xenocrates, Speusippus). An historian, Philistus, was his minister. Dion (q.v.), backed by Plato, tried to transform him into a model monarch of a philosophic State, but both were eventually dismissed by him (366). His power rested on mercenaries and his court was disunited. Dionysius, wishing to preserve the friendship of Plato, induced him to return (361), but the result was a complete breach. In Dionysius' absence (357) Dion seized Syracuse, although Ortygia resisted till 355. Dionysius held Rhegium till *c.* 351 and Locri till 347–346, when he again seized Syracuse by treachery. In 345 he was blockaded in Ortygia by some Syracusans and Carthaginians and also by Timoleon (q.v.) whom a rival party had summoned to help. He surrendered to Timoleon and obtained a safe conduct to Corinth, where he lived many years.

Sources: Plato, *Epist.* 3, 7, 8 (see G. Pasquali, *Le lettere di Platone*, 1938); Diodorus, bks. 15–16; Plutarch and Nepos, *Lives of Dion and Timoleon*. B. Niese, *PW* v. 904; R. Hackforth, *CAH* vi; R. v. Scheliha, *Dion, die platonische Staatsgründung in Sizilien* (1934). *Also see* PLATO, SICILY, SYRACUSE.   A. M.

DIONYSIUS (3), AELIUS, an important Atticist lexicographer, of the age of Hadrian. He compiled ten books of Ἀττικαὶ λέξεις. See PAUSANIAS (4).

DIONYSIUS (4) **THE AREOPAGITE,** an Athenian mentioned in Acts xvii. 34 as converted at Rome by St. Paul's preaching. Of the works ascribed to him, (1) Περὶ τῆς οὐρανίας ἱεραρχίας, (2) Περὶ τῆς ἐκκλησιαστικῆς ἱεραρχίας, (3) Περὶ θείων ὀνομάτων, (4) Περὶ μυστικῆς θεολογίας, (5) 11 letters, (6) a Liturgy, the four first-named are a daring fusion of Christianity with Neoplatonism, and had an enormous influence throughout the Middle Ages. They are certainly not by St. Paul's Dionysius; they may be as early as A.D. 350 or as late as 500. It has been conjectured that the ascription of them to the Areopagite is due to confusion between him and another Dionysius (? Dionysius of Rhinocolura, *c.* 370), but it is more likely that the author deliberately tried to pass them off as the work of a contemporary of St. Paul.

PW v. 996. Ed. Migne, *PG*, vols. 3, 4.   W. D. R.

DIONYSIUS (5) of Byzantium (fl. *c.* A.D. 175), a Greek. Of his Ἀνάπλους τοῦ Βοσπόρου, 'Voyage up the (Thracian) Bosporus', part of a Latin translation survives (Pierre Gilles, *de Bosp. Thrac., Libri III*).

GGM II. i ff.; Gk., C. Wescher, 1874.

DIONYSIUS (6) **CHALCUS** (5th c. B.C.), poet, so called after his introduction of bronze currency into Athens; he took part in the colonization of Thurii (Plut. *Nic.* 5), wrote sympotic elegies, some of which began with a pentameter (Ath. 602c), of a somewhat riddling character, with notable metaphors.

Text: E. Diehl, *Anth. Lyr. Graec.* i. 1, pp. 88–90. Criticism. R. Reitzenstein, *Epigramm und Skolion* (1893), 51; U. von Wilamowitz-Moellendorff, *Hellenistische Dichtung* (1924) i. 97.   C. M. B.

DIONYSIUS (7) of Halicarnassus, rhetor and historian, taught at Rome (30–8 B.C.), where he was the leading spirit of an influential literary circle. Of his critical writings (30–8 B.C.), the most original was *On the Arrangement of Words* (Π. συνθέσεως ὀνομάτων: *De comp. verb.*, an illuminating inquiry into an artistic word-order. Important, too, was the work *On the Ancient Orators*, which traced the development of Attic oratory on biographical and aesthetic lines. Its first section (Lysias, Isocrates, Isaeus) remains; and part of the second section possibly survives in the fine appreciation of Demosthenes in Π. τῆς Δημ. λέξεως. Representative also was Π. μιμήσεως (fragments only), which dealt with imitation, authors to be imitated, and methods of imitating. The rest of his writings, occasional in kind, included Π. τοῦ Θουκυδίδου χαρακτῆρος, in which the matter and style of Thucydides were discussed, *On Dinarchus*, investigating the authenticity of Dinarchus' speeches, the *First Letter to Ammaeus*, confuting Demosthenes' alleged indebtedness to Aristotle, a *Second Letter to Ammaeus*, supplementing his previous remarks on Thucydides, and a *Letter to G. Pompeius*, in which Plato's inferiority as a stylist was reaffirmed. The τέχνη (Ps.-Dion.), falsely ascribed to him and consisting of precepts on epideictic oratory, was probably a later compilation. As a critic D. stands high, though in places his work is conventional and uninspired. At his best he is a masterly exponent of the subtleties of style, a keen aesthetic critic, and a pioneer in critical methods (biographical, historical, and comparative) who recalled to his age the literary standards of classical Greece (*see* LITERARY CRITICISM IN ANTIQUITY, I. 5).

His historical work, *Antiquitates Romanae* ('Ρωμαϊκὴ ἀρχαιολογία), which in twenty books covered from the κτίσις of Rome to the First Punic War, represents the application of his historical theories to the annalistic tradition. Careful study of the sources loses in effect through critical inability and ignorance of early Roman conditions; much of value is obscured, much of a misleading character is added, in his elaborate rhetorical composition.

Texts, etc.: *Dionysii Hal. Opuscula* ed. Usener and Radermacher (1899–1929); *On Lit. Comp.* ed. Roberts (1910); *Three Lit. Letters*, ed. Roberts (1901); *Ant. Rom.* C. Jacoby (1885–1925); Cary (Loeb, in progress, 1937–); *Vett. Cens.* (Hudson ii. 122–7) = Περὶ μιμήσεως B (Usener-Radermacher ii. 202. 18–214. 2). Criticism: E. Schwartz, *PW* v. 934.   J. W. H. A.

DIONYSIUS (8) of Heraclea on the Pontus (*c.* 328–248 B.C.) studied under Heraclides Ponticus, Menedemus, and Zeno, and became one of the most voluminous writers of the Stoic school. He also wrote poetry (including a tragedy, Παρθενοπαῖος) and was an admirer and imitator of Aratus. An attack of illness in old age led him to abandon the Stoic creed that pain is not an evil and to adopt the view that pleasure is the end of life (hence his nickname ὁ μεταθέμενος). He starved himself to death.

Testimonia in von Arnim, *SVF* i. 93–6. *PW* v. 973. W. D. R.

DIONYSIUS (9) of Miletus, *see* LOGOGRAPHERS.

DIONYSIUS (10) 'PERIEGETES', Greek author, *c.* A.D. 300, of Περιήγησις τῆς οἰκουμένης in 1,185 hexameters (for schoolboys?), describing pleasantly the known world chiefly after Eratosthenes, taking little account of subsequent discoveries: land, elliptic (east–west), three continents; ocean, with inlets; Mediterranean; Libya; Europe; islands; Asia. Lost works attributed to D.: Βασσαρικά = Διονυσιακά; Λιθικά (on gems); 'Ορνιθιακά; Γιγαντιάς.

GGM II. xv ff., 103 ff. E. H. Bunbury, *Hist. Anc. Geog.* (1879) ii. 480 ff.; *PW* v. 915–25.   E. H. W.

DIONYSIUS (11) of Philadelphia, reputed author of an extant poem, 'Ορνιθιακά, which may, however, be by Dionysius Periegetes.

Ed. F. S. Lehrs, *Poetae Bucolici et Didactici* (1851). *PW* v. 925.

DIONYSIUS (12) of Samos, Hellenistic 'cyclographer', published a κύκλος ἱστορικός in seven books, a mythographical romance or, perhaps more probably, a mythological handbook.

FGrH i 178, 491. E. Schwartz, *PW* v. 932.

DIONYSIUS (13) SCYTOBRACHION, an Alexandrian grammarian of the second or first century B.C., who appears to be cited also as Dionysius of Mytilene (or Miletus), wrote a mythological romance, Euhemeristic in tone and claiming authority by false reference to old writers. He treated of the Argonauts, followed here by Diodorus (bks. 3–4), the Trojan War, Dionysus and Athena, and the Amazons, and wrote Μυθικὰ πρὸς Παρμένωντα.

FGrH i. 228, 509. E. Schwartz, *De Dionysio Scytobrachione* (1880) and in *PW* v. 929.   A. H. McD.

DIONYSIUS (14) of Sinope, Middle (?) Comedy poet. The learned cook provides humour in one piece (fr. 2).

FCG iii. 547 ff.; *CAF* ii 423 ff.

DIONYSIUS (15) of Thebes, poet, teacher of Epaminondas (Nep. *Epam.* 2), regarded by Aristoxenus (ap. Plut. *De mus.* 31) as a practiser of the old style of music.

DIONYSIUS (16) surnamed THRAX, son of Teres, of Alexandria, was a pupil of Aristarchus and later a teacher of grammar and literature at Rhodes, where his pupils provided him with the silver for a model to illustrate his lectures on Nestor's cup (Athenaeus 489, 492, 501). His most enduring work was the extant Τέχνη γραμματική, an epitome of pure grammar as developed by the Stoics and Alexandrians (*see* GRAMMAR). The work is essentially Alexandrian, but there are traces of Stoic influence. It defines grammar as an ἐμπειρία, but includes ἀναλογία (*see* CRATES (3) OF MALLOS) among its parts; classifies accents, stops, letters, and syllables; defines the parts of speech, with lists of their qualifications (cases, moods, etc.), and subdivisions, if any, giving examples; and concludes with some paradigms of inflection. To the four Stoic cases the vocative (κλητική) is subjoined; the adjective (ἐπίθετον) is still one of many classes of noun; the ἄρθρον includes both ὁ ἡ τό (with vocative ὤ) and ὅς, our relative pronoun. There is no treatment of syntax in the work. It had, however, an immediate vogue which lasted until the Renaissance, and its authority was continued in the catechisms derived from it which then took its place. Latin grammar early fell under its influence (see, e.g., Remmius Palaemon), and through Latin most of the modern grammars of Europe are indebted to it.

Edition: Uhlig, in Teubner's *Grammat. Gr.* Scholia: Hilgard, same series.   P. B. R. F.

DIONYSIUS (17) (? 2nd c. A.D.), a Greek, son of Calliphron, author of 'Αναγραφὴ τῆς 'Ελλάδος (for schoolboys?); 150 feeble iambics survive: preface (acrostics); Ambracia–Peloponnesus; [gap]; Cretan cities; Cyclades and Sporades Islands.

GGM I. lxxx, 238–43.

DIONYSUS, the god much more of an emotional religion than of wine (q.v.). He is rarely mentioned in Homer, for, like Demeter, he was a popular god who did not appeal to the Homeric knights, but the myth that Lycurgus persecuted him and his nurses is told (*Il.* 6. 130 ff.). From Hesiod (*Theog.* 940 ff.) on, his parents are Zeus and Semele (q.v.).

2. The general opinion, shared both by ancient and modern authors, that he came from Thrace is well founded. His cult was widely spread in Thrace (*see* RELIGION, THRACIAN), and the Thracian and Macedonian women were especially devoted to his orgia. The myths of invasions of Boeotia and Attica by Thracians are not to be wholly disregarded. They may be ascribed to the

very beginning of the last millennium B.C., and the Thracians may have brought the cult to Greece. Boeotia and Attica were its chief seats; in the Peloponnese it is less common. Myths, e.g. of Pentheus and the daughters of Minyas, prove that it swept over Greece like wildfire and that the cause was its ecstatic character which seized chiefly on the women. They abandoned their houses and work, roamed about in the mountains, whirling in the dance, swinging thyrsi and torches; at the pitch of their ecstasy (*see* ECSTASY) they seized upon an animal or even a child, according to the myths, tore it apart and devoured the bleeding pieces (Farnell, op. cit. infra, 302 ff.). This so-called omophagy is a sacramental meal; in devouring the parts of the animal the maenads incorporated the god and his power within themselves. Dionysus was sometimes believed to appear in animal form; he is called 'bull', 'bull-horned', etc. He himself and his maenads are clad in fawn-skins. Sometimes it is told that the maenads wore masks. The mask was characteristic of his cult; his image sometimes consisted of a mask and a garment hung on a pole, but these masks are human. This feature reminds us of primitive customs and is important with regard to the fact that the drama has its origin in the cult of Dionysus. The descriptions of his orgia referred to, in which the votaries are depicted as capable of all kinds of miracles, possessed by the god, enjoying communion with wild life, vegetable and animal, and able to overcome any human resistance (e.g. Eur. *Bacch.* 680 ff.), are mythical and literary, but votaries did in fact bear the god's name, *bakchoi* (Pl. *Phaed.* 69c). Orgia of a milder kind were celebrated in historical times on Mt. Parnassus by official cult associations of women, and there is a trace of the omophagy in a State cult. The frenzy of the orgia was tamed by Apollo, who admitted Dionysus at his side at Delphi and brought his cult into the gentler forms of State religion.

3. Ancient authors say, however, that Dionysus also came from Phrygia. The Phrygians, who were a Thracian tribe, believed that Dionysus (cf. Phrygian Diounsis: W. M. Calder, *CR* xli (1927), 160 ff.) was bound or slept in the winter and was free or awake in the summer. They knew also of a child-god. This Dionysus is apparently a god of vegetation. His other name, Bacchus, is a Lydian word. It is remarkable that the Dionysiac festivals of the Lenaea (q.v.) and the Anthesteria (q.v.), the spring festival in which Dionysus made his epiphany coming from the sea, are common to all Ionians, whilst other festivals of Dionysus are isolated. At Delphi Dionysus was venerated as a child in a winnowing fan and awakened by certain rites. It seems that Dionysus in a somewhat changed form came from Asia Minor across the sea. This Dionysus was a god of the vegetation, not of the crops but of the fruit of the trees including the vine. Moreover, he seems to have a certain connexion with Minoan religion. The phallus which was carried in the Dionysiac processions belongs to him as a god of fertility; he is never represented as phallic himself, but the Sileni and Satyrs who surround him are; they are daemons of fertility. This Dionysus was the god of wine, but wine has no great place in his cult in the early age, especially not in the orgia. The festivals of viticulture are few and rarely attributed to him, and we find him connected with a variety of plants—corn (Diod. Sic. 4. 4. 2), trees (Farnell, pp. 96, 118 ff.), figs (Ath. 3. 78c; Hesychius s.v. συκάτης, ivy (Eur. *Bacch.* 106 etc.). On Attic vases he is, however, constantly represented with a drinking-horn, or a cantharus, and vine branches. As time went on, he was more and more thought of as the god of wine, and we hear of wine-miracles in certain festivals.

4. A point of view particularly emphasized by some scholars is that he was the Lord of souls. The opinion of Rohde that the belief in immortality was introduced into Greece by Dionysus is now abandoned. While others, e.g. Miss Harrison, refer to the fact that the

Anthesteria was devoted to the dead, these rites have nothing to do with Dionysus; the connexion had no intrinsic reason. Other similar festivals are too little known. But among the mystics Dionysus was associated with the Nether World, an idea which perhaps originated among the Orphics, in whose doctrines Dionysus had a great place. Thus Dionysus was introduced into mysteries other than the old orgia, but no one of them can be proved to be of old origin. Such mysteries became very popular in the Hellenistic and even more in the Roman age. In spite of the opinion of Cumont, these late mysteries of Dionysus seem to owe more to Greek than to Oriental tradition. That the idea of a happier life in the other world prevailed in them is proved by the fact that sarcophagi are often decorated with Dionysiac myths. Until the early part of the fifth century B.C. Dionysus is represented as a full-grown, bearded man, later as a delicate, playful youth. His myths are numerous. Not to speak of his early adventures in escaping from Hera's jealousy (*see* ATHAMAS), his campaigns in the East are known to Euripides: their extension to India is modelled after those of Alexander the Great; they were celebrated in a voluminous epic by Nonnus at the end of antiquity.

E. Rohde, *Psyche*; Farnell, *Cults of the Greek States* v. 85 ff.; J. E. Harrison, *Proleg. to the Study of Greek Religion*, 364 ff.; M. P. Nilsson, *Gesch. d. griech. Religion* i. 532 and, for the Minoan connexions, *Minoan-Mycenaean Religion*, 492 ff.; W. F. Otto, *Dionysos* (1933), is highly speculative. The festivals: Nilsson, *Studia de Dionysiis atticis* (Lund 1900); *Griech. Feste*, 258 ff.; L. Deubner, *Attische Feste*, 93 ff. The late mysteries: F. Cumont, *Les Religions orientales dans le paganisme romain*[1], 195; *AJArch.* N.S. xxxvii (1933), 232 ff.; Nilsson, *Studi e materiali di storia delle religioni* x (1934), 1 ff.; H. J. Rose, *Handbook of Greek Mythology*[2], 149 ff.
M. P. N. and H. J. R.

DIOPHANTUS of Alexandria (fl. *c.* A.D. 250) was the first Greek to make any approach to an algebraical notation. He wrote Ἀριθμητικά in thirteen books, six of which survive, and a tract on Polygonal Numbers. A third work, Πορίσματα, is lost, but some propositions in the theory of numbers are quoted from it in the *Arithmetica*. Diophantus works with numbers purely arithmetically and not geometrically as did the Pythagoreans. In the preface to the *Arithmetica* he defines 'species' of numbers, which are, besides units (denoted by M^O for μονάδες), the various powers up to the sixth of the unknown quantity, for which he appropriates the word ἀριθμός denoted by the symbol ς. Its powers he denotes by $Δ^Y$ (for δύναμις, square), K^Y (for κύβος, cube), etc. He has a symbol ⋀ for *minus*, denoting λεῖψις, a 'wanting', contrasted with ὕπαρξις, 'forthcoming' or *plus*. Minus, he explains, multiplied by a plus gives minus, minus by minus, a plus. Expressions containing more than one 'species' he arranges according to powers, first the positive terms, then the negative terms all together. He shows how to solve simple and quadratic equations; he does not recognize negative roots of equations or negative numbers standing by themselves. His problems are mostly indeterminate or semi-determinate equations (single or simultaneous) of the second degree, and his methods are extraordinarily varied and ingenious; his object is always to find a solution in positive numbers (not necessarily integral as generally required in modern indeterminate analysis). The typical sort of problem solved is this: to find three numbers such that the product of any two of them *plus* their sum, or *plus* any given number, is a square. It was Diophantus' work which led Fermat to take up the theory of numbers, in which he made his world-famous discoveries. The *editio princeps* of the Greek text is that of C. G. Bachet, 1621; second edition, with Fermat's notes, 1670. The standard text is now that of Paul Tannery (Teubner). Other editions are: German, by Wertheim (1890); English (in modern notation) by T. L. Heath (1910); French translation by Paul ver Eecke (Bruges and Paris).   T. H.

DIOS wrote a history of Phoenicia cited by Josephus (*AJ* 8. 147–9; *Ap.* 1. 113–15).

DIOSCORIDES (1) (fl. 230 B.C.), last of the great Alexandrian poets, has some forty epigrams in the Greek Anthology. The majority are erudite and skilful conceits on remote subjects—artificial epitaphs on historical figures (e.g. 'inventors' like Atys and Thespis) or paradoxical anecdotes. The rest—save one hate-poem, *Anth. Pal.* 11. 363—are lively, ironical, realistic love-poems in the sharpest epigrammatic style.   G. H.

DIOSCORIDES (2) **PEDANIUS** (1st c. A.D.) of Anazarbus, army physician, was well versed in pharmacological literature and had studied the subject of his interest from early youth in extensive travels before composing his book; he was ambitious as expert rather than as writer. All this he tells us himself. He lived under Claudius and Nero (41–68); Erotianus mentions him.

WORKS: 1. Π. ὕλης ἰατρικῆς, bks. 1–5, almost 600 plants, nearly 1,000 drugs. 2. Π. ἁπλῶν φαρμάκων, or Εὐπόριστα, bks. 1–2.

The *Materia medica* is a conscious attempt to give a system, not an alphabetical list of drugs. Remedies from the vegetable, animal, and mineral kingdoms are described in careful subdivisions. The observation is minute, the judgement sober and free from superstition. Dioscorides' book superseded all earlier literature and became the standard work of later centuries, in the East no less than in the West. *See* BOTANY, para. 6; MEDICINE, 1 j.

BIBLIOGRAPHY

TEXT. *Materia medica*, M. Wellmann, i–iii (1907–14), contains both works; Wellmann's proof of genuineness of the second work (*Die Schrift d. D. Π. ἁπλῶν φαρμάκων*, 1914) not wholly convincing. Certainly spurious, Π. δηλητηρίων φαρμάκων; Π. ἰοβόλων, K. Sprengel, in C. G. Kühn, *Medici Graeci* xxvi (1830); *De herbis femininis*, H. F. Kästner, *Hermes* 1896; list of plant synonyms, Wellmann, *Hermes* 1898.
TRANSLATIONS. Latin, H. Stadler, *Romanische Forschungen* (1896 seq.); H. Mihǎescu, *Iași* (1938). English, R. T. Gunther, *The Greek Herbal of Dioscorides* (1934).
LITERATURE. Survey, M. Wellmann, *PW* v. 1131, here Π. ἁπλῶν φαρμάκων spurious. Ch. Singer, *Studies in the History and Method of Science* ii (1921), also for illustrations (Codex Julia Anicia). T. C. Allbutt, *Greek Medicine in Rome* (1921). Arabic tradition, M. Meyerhof, *Quellen u. Studien z. Gesch. d. Naturw. u. d. Med.* (1933), 103.   L. E.

DIOSCORIDES, see also DIOSCURIDES.

DIOSCURI (Διόσκουροι, Attic -κοροι), the Sons of Zeus, a title (*Hymn. Hom.* 33. 1, of uncertain date; Hdt. 2. 43. 2; and often in Attic authors; not in any early passage) of the Tyndaridae (cf. TYNDAREUS), Castor and Polydeuces (latinized Pollux). They are the brothers of Helen, *Il.* 3. 237 ff., where it is apparently stated that they are dead, but cf. *Od.* 11. 300 ff., where they are 'alive' although 'the corn-bearing earth holds them', and the author explains that they are honoured by Zeus and live on alternate days, 'having honour equal to gods'. Here and in Hesiod they are sons of Tyndareus and Leda; later, as in Pindar (*Nem.* 10. 80), Polydeuces is son of Zeus, his twin Castor of Tyndareus, and at Polydeuces' request they share his immortality between them, living half their time below the earth, the other half in Olympus. The Homeric hymn (supra) makes them both sons of Zeus, and an account of which there is no certain mention earlier than Horace (*Sat.* 2. 1. 26) makes them both born from an egg, like their sister (*see* HELEN). They had a cult in Lacedaemon, where they were symbolized by the *dokana*, two upright pieces of wood connected by two cross-beams (Plut. *De frat. amor.* 478 a–b), and in many other States, chiefly but not exclusively Dorian (Argos, Athens, Dorian colonies in Sicily, etc.). *See* ANAKES.

2. The chief events in their mythology are three. When Theseus kidnapped Helen they made an expedition to Attica, recovered her and carried off Aethra (q.v. for references). They took part in the Argonautic expedition, and on it Polydeuces distinguished himself in the fight against Amycus (q.v.). Their final exploit on earth was the carrying off of the two daughters of Leucippus, the Leucippides, Phoebe and Hilaeira. Thereupon the nephews of Leucippus, Idas and Lynceus, pursued them (Pind. op. cit. 60 ff., who makes it a cattle-raid; Theoc. 22. 137 ff.). In the resulting fight Castor and both the pursuers were killed; the sequel of the shared immortality has already been mentioned, but some ingenuity seems to have been spent in determining whether they have since been always together or always separate, one being in Hades while the other is in Olympus (Rose, *Handbook of Greek Myth.* ²249, note 4). They are often identified with the constellation Gemini (as Ps.-Eratosthenes 10), and are connected with stars as early as Euripides (*Hel.* 140). Of the miracles attending their cult, the most famous is that connected with the battle of the Sagra, which gave rise to the Roman story of their appearance at Lake Regillus (Cic. *Nat. D.* 2. 6). The Locrians, being at war with the Crotonians, appealed for help to Sparta and were told that they might have the Dioscuri, whom they accepted. In the battle, which resulted in a complete victory for them, two gigantic youths in strange dress were seen fighting on their side (Justin 20. 3. 8; Suidas s.v. ἀληθέστερα τῶν ἐπὶ Σάγρα).

3. It is a still unsettled controversy whether they are in origin heroes of more than usual celebrity and popularity (they received divine honours here and there) or heroized ('faded') gods. In favour of the former view it may be urged that the earliest evidence (Homer, Hesiod fr. 94. 13, 27, and 31 Rzach) knows nothing of their being anything more than important human beings, honoured after death as several others of their kind were; that they do not become more than heroes till relatively late and even in late traditions and theologizings retain much of their human origin, becoming stock examples of the possibility of transcendent human virtue attaining superhuman rank (as Horace, *Carm.* 3. 3. 9). For such a career a close parallel can be found in that of Heracles (q.v.). On the other side, however, can be cited a not inconsiderable list of divine twins, the most celebrated being the Sanskrit Açvins. These are often connected with horses; the Dioscuri are on occasion λευκόπωλοι, 'riders on white steeds', and Castor especially is a notable horseman. They not uncommonly have astral connexions, such as we have seen the Dioscuri have, though not very early and possibly only through one of their most picturesque functions, that of saviours of those in peril from storms at sea. In this capacity they appear as twin lights of St. Elmo's fire, which it would not be a hard thing to confuse mythologically with stars; see, for instance, Pliny, *HN* 2. 101. Certainly they are not infrequently seen in art with stars over the curious round caps which they wear. Moreover, possible traces of other twin gods have been discovered elsewhere in Greece, as for instance the Theban pair, Amphion and Zethus (*see* AMPHION), who are also sons of Zeus. But it cannot be said that these arguments are cogent as against the earlier date of the Homeric and Hesiodic passages; the original divine nature of the twins is no more than a possibility.

4. There is but one important identification of the Dioscuri with other figures; they tend to be confused with the Cabiri (q.v.). See, for some very interesting monuments connected with this and similar cults, F. Chapouthier, *Les Dioscures au service d'une déesse* (1935); in these, they (or deities identified with them) are grouped on either side of Helen. The connecting link is the common function of rescuing mariners.

Farnell, *Hero-Cults*, 175 ff., for their cult and the controversy as to their origin. Fuller references to their legends and art-monuments in the appropriate articles of the larger classical dictionaries, as Roscher's *Lexikon*.   H. J. R.

DIOSCURIDES or **DIOSCORIDES** (1st c. B.C. or A.D.) is reputed to have written *On Customs in Homer*, in which he is said to have interpolated the Homeric text, *On the Life of Homer's Heroes, Recollections* of sayings of famous men, *The Spartan Constitution, On Institutions.* But these may not all be the work of one D.

FHG ii. 192 ff.   J. F. L.

DIOTIMA, legendary priestess at Mantinea and teacher of Socrates; Plato in *Symp.* 201d puts in her mouth his metaphysic of love. It is impossible to say whether Plato's fiction had any basis in fact, since we have no independent testimony.

PW v. 1147.

DIOTIMUS of Thrace (fl. 250 B.C.), who was a poor schoolmaster in Gargara, is the author of ten epigrams in the Greek Anthology: several of them (e.g. 7. 173, 261) are full of the deep, pure pathos which is characteristic of the 'Peloponnesian school' of epigrammatists.

Wilamowitz-Moellendorff, *Hellenistische Dichtung* (1924), i. 143.
                                                              G. H.

DIPHILUS of Sinope, brother of Diodorus (q.v. 1) of Sinope, New Comedy poet, born probably before 340 B.C.; he outlived Menander (Philemon in his *Φάσμα*, later than 289 B.C., mentioned Diphilus as living—Plaut. *Mostell.* 1145). Wrote about 100 plays, winning three Dionysiac victories (1st Lenaean victory, *c.* 316 B.C.). About sixty titles are known—many of them common to other poets, and nine being mythological (e.g. *Heracles, Theseus*). His admiration for 'golden' Euripides, fr. 60 (a parasite's behaviour), was shared by other poets of New Comedy. Many interesting fragments of this 'live' poet—e.g. fr. 38, unfilial conduct of Ctesippus, son of Chabrias; fr. 43, a master-cook selects his employers with care; frs. 69, 70, Archilochus and Hipponax as Sappho's lovers; fr. 91, a vigorous description of an ugly woman.

A play of Diphilus was the original of Plautus' *Rudens*; the *Κληρούμενοι*, of Plautus' *Casina*; the *Συναποθνήσκοντες*, of the lost play of Plautus, *Commorientes* (Terence, *Ad. prol.* 6, used a scene omitted by Plautus); and possibly *Σχεδία*, of Plautus' *Vidularia*. The influence of Diphilus upon the Roman stage attests his popularity and power as a comic poet.

FCG iv. 375 ff.; *CAF* ii. 541 ff. See Coppola, *Atene e Roma* (1924), 185–204.   W. G. W.

DIPLOMA, a small bronze tablet recording the privileges granted to a soldier on the completion of his service or, as regularly after the first century A.D., on his discharge. These *diplomata*, of which some 160 are extant, were given to auxiliaries, *classiarii*, and members of the praetorian and urban cohorts. Down to the principate of Antoninus Pius the auxiliary and marine received personal citizenship, the legalization of his past or future marriage, and civic rights for his descendants. After A.D. 140, by which time Roman citizens also were enlisted in the *auxilia*, the form was brought into line with the *diplomata* granted to the praetorians. Citizenship was given to those requiring it, but *conubium* was now only prospective.

The legionary did not normally receive a *diploma*. The only exceptions to this rule are the two Adiutrices legions recruited from *classiarii* in A.D. 68–9, and some soldiers of X Fretensis who were non-citizens enlisted in the same crisis.

CIL xvi (texts of diplomata; ed. H. Nesselhauf). G. L. Cheesman, *The Auxilia of the Roman Army* (1914); J. Lesquier, *L'Armée romaine d'Égypte* (1918).   H. M. D. P.

DIPYLON, the gate by which the Sacred Road to Eleusis left Athens, and much of the traffic from Piraeus passed. Outside lay the outer Ceramicus (the inner Ceramicus being by the Agora). This was a burying-place from the early Bronze Age, and from late Mycenaean times was Athens' chief cemetery. Magnificent monuments lined the roads, among those identified being those of Alcibiades' family and of the Spartans killed at Piraeus in 403. The Athenians who fell in battle were buried here, and here Pericles' Funeral Speech was spoken.

W. Judeich, *Topographie von Athen*[2] (1931), 135 ff., 400 ff (modified by the results of recent excavations); progress reports in *Ath. Mitt.* and *Arch. Anz.*   T. J. D.

DIRCE, *see* AMPHION.

DIRGE in Greek literature. The ancient critics seem to have distinguished between two kinds of dirge, the *ἐπικήδειον* sung actually over the dead body (Procl. ap. Phot. *Bibl.* 321a30), and the *θρῆνος*, a song sung in memory of the dead (Ammon. *Diff.* p. 54). The difference does not seem to have been observed by the Alexandrian editors of the lyric poets, and the Dirges of Simonides (frs. 7–12) and of Pindar (frs. 114–23) may well have included both kinds. The earliest evidence for such dirges is in *Il.* 18. 50–1, 314–16, 24. 472–4. In these a company laments, but the leader has a special part as *ἔξαρχος*. Cf. E. Reiner, *Die rituelle Totenklage der Griechen* (1938).

For the dirge in Latin literature see EPICEDIUM, NENIA.
                                                              C. M. B.

DISCORDIA, *see* PERSONIFICATIONS.

DISCUS (*δίσκος*), a flat circular piece of stone or metal, somewhat thicker in the centre. The old stone discus was heavier than the metal, sometimes weighing rather more than the 15 pounds which is the normal weight of the shot in our putting. The metal discus, usually of bronze, which became general during the fifth century B.C., was lighter and smaller, extant specimens varying in diameter from 6 to 9 inches, in weight from 3 to 9 pounds. It was thrown from a space defined by lines in front and either side. For the method of throwing, *see* ATHLETICS.   F. A. W.

DISSOI LOGOI (labelled by H. Stephanus *Διαλέξεις*), a short surviving sophistic work written in Doric about 400 B.C., perhaps in Cyprus, perhaps at Cyrene. The contents have no originality; they are reminiscent now of Protagoras, now of Hippias, now of Gorgias, and confirm Plato's account of the ethical relativism characteristic of the Sophists.

Ed. Diels, *Vorsokr.*[5] ii. 405–16.   W. D. R.

DITHYRAMB. The origin of the word *διθύραμβος* is not known, though it is almost certainly not of Hellenic origin. It first appears in Archilochus (fr. 77), who calls it the song of Dionysus and says that he, under the influence of wine, leads others in singing it. It was, then, from the beginning a choral song to Dionysus, though it need not yet have had any very definite form. It was reduced to order by Arion at Corinth *c.* 600 B.C., when it was sung by a regular choir and made to treat of a definite subject. From Corinth it was brought to Athens by Lasos of Hermione (Suidas s.v. *Λᾶσος*), and it soon became a subject for competition at the fes vals of Dionysus. The first victor is said to have been Hypodicus of Chalcis in 509–508 B.C. (*Marm. Par.* 46). Hence till about 470 B.C. it attracted poets of great eminence such as Simonides, who won fifty-six prizes (fr. 79), Lasos, Pindar (frs. 60–77, not all for Athens), and Bacchylides (Odes 15–21). At this period it was composed like other choral odes, with regular strophe and antistrophe. The surviving fragments do not suggest any close connexion of their subjects with Dionysus or any special Dionysiac spirit, though the large element of narrative in them may be due to Arion's example. But about 470 B.C. its character began to change. The change, associated with the names of Melanippides, Cinesias, Philoxenus, and Timotheus, was largely musical, and since no note of their music survives, it is hard to estimate what happened. In the main the music seems to have become more important than the words and to have led to a degeneration of the text. A protest against this movement is to be seen in some lines of Pratinas (fr. 1). Other elements in the change were the abolition of the correspondence of strophe and antistrophe, the introduction of solo-songs, and the development of a pompous, affected language. The movement continued into the fourth century in the hands of Polyidus and Telestes. After the fourth century the dithyramb seems to have lost its importance, even at Athens, though before 300 B.C. the State took charge of the expenses of production. Inscriptions from Delos, from 286 to 172 B.C., show that at the Delian Dionysia and Apollonia competitions were still held, as they were at Miletus in the third century and at Teos and Samos in the second. Polybius (4. 20) notes that the Arcadians commonly sang dithyrambs in his time. The habit lasted in Athens into the Imperial age, though no fragments of importance survive.

A. W. Pickard-Cambridge, *Dithyramb, Tragedy, and Comedy* (1927), 5–82.   C. M. B.

DIVERBIUM, dialogue in a comedy as distinct from *cantica* (q.v.).

DIVINATIO. Divination (q.v.), when professionally exercised, was regarded at Rome from the time of Tiberius as a crime and punished with confiscation of property and *relegatio* (q.v.). In spite of this and similar later prohibitions of all forms of *divinatio* (*vaticinatio*) and especially of the art of *astrologi* (called *mathematici*), all these 'improbandae artes contra quietem publicam' did not pass out of fashion, especially as some emperors tolerated this profession, which was practised mostly by foreigners from the Orient (*Chaldaei*). Under the late Empire the prohibition was repeatedly renewed. Diocletian strictly forbade the *ars mathematica*; Constantius (A.D. 357) made divination into a capital offence: 'sileat omnibus perpetuo diuinandi curiositas'; his constitution was included in Justinian's Code (9. 18. 5). It was equally a punishable offence to consult soothsayers.

Divinatio had another meaning in criminal procedure. When several persons came forward as prosecutors of the same criminal act, the magistrate determined in a special intermediate *iudicium*, attended by a *consilium* of jurors, who should be the accuser. *See* QUAESTIO.   A. B.

DIVINATION. Prediction by supernatural means of future events and interpretation of past occurrences is found throughout Greek and Roman civilization, showing contacts at various points, such as necromancy, prophecy, extispicy, or astrology, with Oriental cultures. The present account sketches Greek and Roman uses together, and for the sake of brevity neglects much of their chronological development.

2. Our most important ancient source, Cicero's *De Divinatione*, in 1. 11 and 2. 26 (possibly after Posidonius), divides the art into natural (or intuitive) and artificial (or inductive) types, though the two may at times overlap in practice, as with dreams. The former of these is immediate in its application, the latter supplements observation by *coniectura*.

3. Of Natural Divination no form seems more primitive than dreams, often mentioned from Homer onward. These might either be understood by the dreamer or require professional interpreters, whose lore, based partly on empiricism but chiefly on supposed resemblances (Arist. *Div. Somn.* 2. 464ᵇ7), was preserved in practical dream-books, such as the *Onirocritica* of Arte-

midorus and Astrampsychus, or discussed in theoretical works, like Aristotle (op. cit.), Synesius, *De Insomniis*, and Macrobius, *Comm. in Somnium Scipionis*. A specialized form is incubation (q.v.; ἐγκοίμησις), practised at health-shrines, like those of Asclepius, by persons desirous of cures, and hence called iatromancy. Necromancy, or evocation of spirits of the dead, is already well developed in *Od.* 11, but though long employed, especially at certain localities (*psychomantia*), it was less respectable than most other methods. Related to it are lecanomancy, elaeomancy, hydromancy, and catoptromancy, in which forms of the dead or of gods or demons appear on the surface of liquids or on mirrors.

4. Very important is prophecy (*vaticinatio*), in which the *vates* acts as the medium or mouthpiece (προφήτης) of a divine or demonic power possessing him, the process being related to poetic inspiration, and known as ἐνθουσιασμός; cf. [Arist.] *Probl.* 30. 1. 954ᵃ34–8. Lists of such seers are given by Hopfner in *PW* xiv (1928), 1267–8. Like telepathy and clairvoyance and like the ventriloquists (ἐγγαστρίμυθοι), the freer forms of prophecy, such as those of the shadowy Bacis (q.v.) and Musaeus (q.v. 1), seem hardly to have become institutionalized, but with the Sibyls (q.v.) and the oracles (q.v.), e.g. Delphi (q.v.), Dodona (q.v.), Lebadea, Oropus, and Ammon (q.v.), prophetic power became resident at fixed sites, where a succession of media regularly answered consultants. See, however, PROPHECIES.

5. Artificial Divination may be roughly divided into prognostications from animate beings or from plants, and those from lifeless objects. Its oldest type is perhaps augury (*see* AUGURES) or the observation and interpretation of the number, species, flight, cries, eating, and other symbolic acts of birds. Cicero (*Div.* 1. 92) mentions Phrygians, Pisidians, Cilicians, Arabs, and Umbrians as specialists in this art, but it was common in Greece from the time of Tiresias, Melampus (Porphyry, *Abst.* 3. 3), and Calchas (*Il.* 2. 308–32), and at Rome was entrusted to the college of augurs (*see* AUSPICIUM). Auguries might be deliberately sought (*inpetratiua*) or offered to men unsought (*oblatiua*; cf. Serv. *Aen.* 6. 190), a variety of the former type more convenient for military use being the Roman observation of the sacred chickens (alectryonomancy). Similar features might be noted in the case of other animals, especially from their chance appearances during a journey (ἐνόδια; cf. A. S. Pease on Cic. *Div.* 1. 26). Still more important were indications derived from human beings, e.g. from their involuntary motions or twitchings (παλμός, salisatio), from sneezing, and from the large class of omens (or cledonomancy), i.e. utterances prophetically significant, like tragic irony, in a way not realized by the speaker, who is here, as in motions and sneezings, merely the tool of a temporarily possessing, superhuman, power (e.g. *Od.* 18. 112–17). Other types depend upon the morphology rather than the actions of animate beings, and include teratological births, palmistry or chiromancy (Poll. 2. 152), and the interpretations of physiognomists. But most important, during a long period and over a wide geographic range, is extispicy (or haruspicy), based on observation of the entrails—especially the liver (hepatoscopy) of sacrificial animals, for which *see* HARUSPICES. Predictions were also derived from miraculous growths and actions of plants, e.g. of 'birth-trees' (see Donat. *Vit. Verg.* p. 2 Brummer), the residence of an 'external soul'.

6. Divination from lifeless objects has varied forms. The classification by Varro (ap. schol. Dan. *Aen.* 3. 359; Isid. *Etym.* 8. 9. 13) into four elemental groups (*geomantis, aëromantis, pyromantis, hydromantis*) is suggestive but unduly formal. There may here be mentioned, however, empyromancy, or the behaviour, when placed on a sacrificial fire, of such objects as incense (libanomancy), flour (aleuromancy), or eggs (oöscopy). In omoplatoscopy (or scapulomancy) the shoulder-blade of

the victim was observed when heated over the coals. Other objects, such as axes (axinomancy), spindles (sphondulomancy; Poll. 7. 188, where numerous other detailed types of divination are named), and sieves (coscinomancy) also appear, but rhabdomancy, or the use of the rod for prognostication, seems to belong primarily to neighbouring cultures. Numerous are the uses of lots (cleromancy), in which a divine power guides the fall of dice or knuckle-bones (astragalomancy) or the drawing (often by the hand of an innocent child) of inscribed *sortes* from some receptacle. This practice was often localized at particular sites, such as Claros, Praeneste, Antium, the fountain of Clitumnus, and Patavium. The inscribed lot is naturally later in origin than the introduction of writing, and from it was perhaps derived bibliomancy, or the random consultation of books to discover prophetic advice. The great poets were often so used (rhapsodomancy), perhaps as being themselves divinely inspired. Thus we find the *sortes Homericae*, the *sortes Vergilianae*—eight cases in the *Augustan History* alone—and, with the Christians, the *sortes Biblicae*.

7. The interpretation of weather-signs (as in Aratus 733) approaches more nearly to empirical science, yet many unusual meteorological phenomena (storms, meteorites, aurora borealis, etc.) and many arising from the earth (earthquakes, faulting, etc.), as well as teratological births of men and beasts (see above), were called *ostenta*, *portenta*, *monstra*, *prodigia* (q.v.) (Cic. *Div.* 1. 93), and considered precursors of social, political, or dynastic changes. Such were recorded in priestly records (especially at Rome) and used as sources by various historians (e.g. Livy, from whom Julius Obsequens, by a reverse process, compiled his *Prodigiorum liber*). For the vast field of astrology in its various forms, increasing with the Oriental influences following the conquests of Alexander, *see* ASTROLOGY.

8. Popular belief at most periods commonly accepted older, socially or politically established, forms of divination, though many looked askance upon others as charlatanry. Some philosophers also accepted the art with little question, but Xenophanes, the Epicureans, Carneades, and others rejected it, and Panaetius expressed doubts of its reality. Some Peripatetics admitted intuitive but disallowed inductive divination (Cic. *Div.* 1. 5, 113; 2. 100), but most Stoics (notably Posidonius) vigorously defended both types, basing their justification upon the powers of gods, fate, and nature (Cic. *Div.* 1. 125), or upon the doctrine of συμπάθεια. Mystics in the second century of our era, and later, attempted to revive interest in the Delphic oracle, which was in Cicero's time (*Div.* 1. 37–8; cf. Plut. *De Pyth. or.*; *De Def. or.*) already in neglect, and various collections of oracles, with infiltration of Christian elements, date from this period. Yet after a fitful respite, during which apologists like Origen attacked pagan divination as the work of malign demons, Theodosius, in the fourth century, by a series of edicts forbade various mantic rites, and though these sometimes survived under Christianized guise the prestige of the pagan divination was at an end.

BIBLIOGRAPHY

GENERAL. A. Bouché-Leclercq, *Histoire de la Divination dans l'antiquité* (4 vols. 1879–82; the most comprehensive work). Id. in Dar.-Sag. ii. 292–319. W. R. Halliday, *Greek Divination* (1913). T. Hopfner in *PW* xiv. 1258–88.

NATURAL DIVINATION. Dreams: B. Büchsenschütz, *Traum u. Traumdeutung im Alterthum* (1868); J. Fischer, *Ad Artis Veterum onirocriticae Historiam Symbola* (1899); S. Luria, 'Stud. z. Gesch. d. ant. Traumdeutung' (*Bull. de l'Acad. d. Sc. de l'U.R.S.S.* 1927, 441–66 and 1041–72). Necromancy: L. Fahz, *De Poetarum Romanorum Doctrina magica* (1904); E. Rohde, *Psyche* i⁸ (1921), 213. Lecanomancy: W. R. Halliday, op. cit. 145–62. Catoptromancy: J. Delatte, *La Catoptromancie grecque et ses dérivés* (1932). Clairvoyance: E. R. Dodds, 'Telepathy and Clairvoyance in Classical Antiquity', in *Greek Poetry and Life* (1936), 364–85. Prophecy: E. von Lasaulx, *Über d. prophetische Kraft d. menschlichen Seele* (1858); E. Rohde, *Psyche*, ii⁸. 38–69. Oracles: see s.v.

ARTIFICIAL DIVINATION. Augury, etc.: on Roman augury I. M. J. Valeton in *Mnemos.* xvii (1889); xviii (1890); xix (1891); xx (1892); xxi (1893); xxiii (1895); xxv (1897); xxvi (1898); G. Wissowa in *PW* ii. 2313–44; E. Flinck, 'Auguralia u. Verwandtes' in *Ann. Acad. Sci. Fennicae*, Ser. B, xi (1921). For augural *fasti* A. Bouché-Leclercq, op. cit. iv (1882), 363–72; V. Spinazzola in E. de Ruggiero, *Diz. epigr.* i. 790–5, 804–10; G. Howe, *Fasti Sacerdotum . . . Aetatis imperatoriae* (1904), 27–32. On the augural books: P. Regell, *De Augurum publicorum Libris* (1878); id., *Fragmenta auguralia* (1882); id., *Comment. in Libr. aug. Frag.* (1893). On other animal omens: L. Hopf, *Thierorakel u. Orakelthiere* (1888). Birthtrees: W. Mannhardt, *Ant. Wald- u. Feldkulte* i² (1904), 44–51; ii (1905), 23–31; J. G. Frazer, *GB* xi³ (1914), 159–68. Involuntary Motions: H. Diels, 'Beitr. z. Zuckungslit. d. Okzidents u. Orients' (in *Abh. Berlin* 1907, iv. 1–42; 1908, iv. 1–130, with text of Melampus, Περὶ παλμῶν). Sneezing: A. S. Pease on Cic. *Div.* 2. 84 (with bibliography); 'P. Saintyves' (= E. Nourry), *L'Éternuement et le bâillement* (1921). Extispicy: on Chaldaean origins, M. Jastrow Jr., in *Proc. Amer. Philos. Soc.* xlix (1908), 646–76; id., in *Stud. in Honor of C. H. Toy* (1912), 143–68. For Etruscan and Roman practice: G. Blecher, *De Extispicio* (1905); C. O. Thulin, *Die etruskische Disciplin*, 3 vols. (1905–9); id. in *PW* vii. 2431–68. For fasti of the haruspices: A. Bouché-Leclercq, op. cit. iv. 376–7; C. O. Thulin in E. de Ruggiero, *Diz. Epigr.* iii. 644–8. Empyromancy: A. Bouché-Leclercq, op. cit. i. 178–82. Libanomancy: R. Ganschinietz in *PW* xii. 2551–2. Omoplatoscopy: R. Hercher in *Philol.* viii (1853), 166–8, editing Psellus, Περὶ ὠμοπλατοσκοπίας καὶ οἰωνοσκοπίας. Coscinomancy: R. Ganschinietz in *PW* xi. 1481–3. Rhabdomancy: W. Gundel in the same, i A 13–18; F. J. M. De Waele, *The Magic Staff or Rod in Greco-Roman Antiquity* (1927). But cf. W. R. Halliday, op. cit. 226–8. Lots: G. Glotz and H. Lécrivain in Dar.-Sag. iv. 1401–18; F. Heinevetter, *Würfel- u. Buchstabenorakel in Griechenland u. Kleinasien* (1912). Prodigies: L. Wülker, *Die geschichtl. Entwicklung d. Prodigienwesens bei d. Römern* (1903); F. Luterbacher, *Prodigienglaube u. Prodigienstil d. Römer* (1904); P. Stein, *Τέρας* (1909); O. Weinreich in *Tübing. Beitr. z. Altertumsw.* v (1929), 200–464 (on miraculous openings of doors). VIEWS OF PHILOSOPHERS. General: G. Wolff's ed. of Porphyry, *De Philos. ex Orac. haur.* (1860), 54–65; F. Jaeger, *De Oraculis quid veteres Philosophi iudicaverint* (1910). On particular schools: C. Wachsmuth, *Die Ansichten d. Stoiker ü. Mantik u. Daemonen* (1860); H. von Arnim, 'Plutarch ü. Dämonen u. Mantik' (in *Verh. d. k. Akad. v. Wetensch. te Amsterdam*, N.S., xxii. ii (1921)); K. Reinhardt, *Kosmos u. Sympathie* (1926), 214–75.   A. S. P.

DIVISIO, used in Cicero and Quintilian of logical and rhetorical division, occurs in the title of Seneca's collection of specimen debates. Part of each *controversia* is devoted to a dissection of the strict legal questions involved (e.g. *Controv.* 9. 5. 6; 10. 2. 8–9): it is a skeleton line of argument showing the structure of a speech (*Controv.* 1. 4. 6). The *divisio* had to avoid overelaboration; for Seneca (*Controv.* 7 *praef.* 1), criticizing Albucius' handling of *controversiae*, says it was too sketchy for a declamation but too full for a *divisio*.

See H. Bornecque, ed. of Sen. *Controv. et Suas.*², Introd. p. ix.   J. W. D.

DIVISORES, *see* CANDIDATUS.

DIVITIACUS (1) (1st c. B.C.), an Aeduan Druid, leader of the philo-Roman party. After the defeat of his tribe by Ariovistus (c. 61 B.C.) he appealed unsuccessfully for help at Rome. He regained influence against his brother Dumnorix by supporting Caesar (58), whom he urged in the name of the Gallic tribes to expel Ariovistus. In 57 he assisted Caesar by attacking the Bellovaci and secured favourable terms for them.

Caesar, *BGall.* 1. 16–20; 31–2; 2. 5–15; Cicero, *Div.* 1. 41. 90.

DIVITIACUS (2), king of the Suessiones c. 100 B.C. and overlord of other tribes both in Gaul and Britain.

Caesar, *BGall.* 2. 4. 7.   C. E. S.

DIVORTIUM, *see* MARRIAGE, LAW OF, para. 9.

DIYLLUS of Athens, author of a universal history (Ἱστορίαι) in twenty-six books including that of Sicily for the period 357–297 B.C. The first part (σύνταξις) began with the Sacred War and overlapped Ephorus' narrative down to 341, and the second and third parts continued with increasing detail until the death of Cassander, 297. D. was one of the major sources of Diodorus and was considered a satisfactory authority by Plutarch.

FGrH ii. 73; *FHG* ii. 360.   G. L. B.

DOCHMIUS, see METRE (Greek) III (7).

DODONA (Δωδώνη), seat of a very ancient oracle of Zeus in the mountains of Epirus. Zeus, with the epithet Naios, had Dione as his consort. According to the cult-myth a pigeon (πελειάς) flying from Egyptian Thebes had lighted on an oak tree at Dodona, and with human voice had directed the founding of an oracle. This oak was the centre of Zeus' cult; in the rustling of its leaves the god's will was divined. Perhaps other signs were interpreted too: the flight and cooing of the sacred pigeons, the murmurs of the sacred spring, the resounding echoes of a bronze gong. The consultants wrote their questions upon lead tablets; the tablets preserved reveal that the questions were frequently of a trivial nature. Both men and women served Zeus and Dione and interpreted their will. The priests were called Selli (Σελλοί) 'of unwashed feet, who couch upon the ground' (*Il.* 16. 235). Our sources call the women not only prophetesses (προφήτιδες, προμάντεις) and priestesses (ἱέρειαι), but also 'old women' (γραῖαι) and 'pigeons', whence the pigeon of the cult-myth.

ANCIENT SOURCES. (*a*) Inscriptions: a number of the lead-tablet inscriptions of consultants' questions are published in Collitz, *Dialekt-Inschriften*, 1557–98, and in *SIG*³, 1160–6. (*b*) Literature: Hom. *Il.* 16. 233–5, *Od.* 14. 327 f. — 19. 296 f.; Hdt. 2. 55–7; Strabo 327–9 and bk. 7, frs. 1–3 (Jones).
MODERN LITERATURE: P. Gardner, *New Chapters in Greek History* (1892), 403–12; L. R. Farnell, *Cults of the Greek States* i (1896), 38–40; A. B. Cook, *JHS* xxii (1902), 5–28; M. P. Nilsson, *Gesch. griech. Rel.* i (1941), 396–400; A. H. Krappe, *Rev. Arch.* 5 sér. xxxvi (1932), 77–93; J. Friederich, *Dodonaica* (1935). The nineteenth-century excavations are reported in C. Carapanos, *Dodone et ses ruines* (1878); more recent excavations are reported by D. Evangelides in Πρακτικὰ τῆς ἐν Ἀθήναις Ἀρχαιολογικῆς Ἑταιρείας (1930–2). J. E. F.

DOGS. From early times in Greece and Italy the dog was the companion and the friend of man, although he had not then lost some of the qualities which in his wild state he shared with the wolf and jackal. In Greek towns, even in the fifth century B.C., dogs often roamed in bands feeding upon the garbage of the streets, and Thucydides (2. 50) in his account of the plague at Athens notes that the dogs refused to eat the corpses left un-buried. In Homer, however, we see the dog in his gentler aspect, when on the return of Odysseus the old hound Argus wags his tail and pricks up his ears in recognition of his master (*Od.* 17. 290 ff.).

The ancients knew of many varieties of dogs. The best-known was the huge Molossian, whose open jaws, strong teeth, and loud bark are described by Lucretius (5. 1063). From Greece also came the Laconian and the Arcadian hounds, the latter fierce animals supposed to have a strain of the lion in them. In Italy the chief breeds were the Umbrian and Salentine, equally useful as sheep-dogs or hunters; and from our island in the third century A.D. the Romans imported the bulldog and the terrier. A white Laconian was considered best as a sheep-dog, a black Molossian as a guardian of the house; and all alike were used in hunting. For pet dogs see PETS.

Oppian, *Cynegetica*; Grattius, *Cynegeticus*; Nemesianus, *Cynegeticus.* F. A. W.

DOKANA, see DIOSCURI, para 1.

DOKIMASIA, the examination of candidates for office at Athens, before the *thesmothetai* (except candidates for the Boule, who were examined by the outgoing Boule). Men already chosen, whether by lot or by vote, but primarily the former, were formally interrogated to as-certain whether they were eligible: e.g. whether they were thirty years old; whether (in the case of certain offices at certain periods, e.g. the archonship: see ARCHONTES) they belonged to a particular census-class; and whether they were not precluded from one office, because they had held it before, or were holding another, or through being under some form of *atimia* (q.v.). A. W. G.

DOLABELLA (1), GNAEUS CORNELIUS, consul 81 B.C. and afterwards governor of Macedonia, was rewarded with a triumph for his victory against the Thracians. Accused in 77 *de repetundis* by Caesar in a famous speech now lost, he was acquitted.

Münzer, *PW* iv. 1297–8. A. M.

DOLABELLA (2), GNAEUS CORNELIUS, praetor 81 B.C., plundered Cilicia (80–79) aided by his legate Verres; impeached by M. Aemilius Scaurus and betrayed by Verres, he was banished.

DOLABELLA (3), PUBLIUS CORNELIUS, commanded a Caesarian fleet in the Adriatic (49 B.C.) and fought in the campaigns of Pharsalus, Thapsus, and Munda. As tribune in 47, he provoked serious riots in attempting to carry a law for the cancellation of debts. After the murder of Caesar he at first associated himself with the conspirators, but Antony won his support by allowing him to assume the consulship which Caesar had intended for him. At the same time his drastic intervention against worshippers of Caesar (April 44) was enthusias-tically approved by the Republicans. Towards the end of the year he left for Syria, which had been assigned to him by the Assembly for five years, captured Smyrna by surprise, and put to death Trebonius, governor of Asia. The Senate declared him a public enemy (February 43), he was besieged by Cassius in Laodicea, and committed suicide to avoid capture (probably July 43). Dolabella was notorious for his dissipation, and was invariably in debt. His second wife was Cicero's daughter Tullia.

Cicero, *Letters* and *Philippics*; Plutarch, *Antony* 9–11; Appian, *BCiv.* bks. 2–4; Dio Cassius, bks. 41–7. Drumann–Groebe, *Gesch. Roms* ii. 486–97. G. W. R.

DOLABELLA (4), PUBLIUS CORNELIUS (*cos.* A.D. 10), was legate in Dalmatia (14–*c.* 20), where he kept the legions quiet and used them in a big programme of road construction. In 23–4, as proconsul of Africa, he ended the war against Tacfarinas (q.v.).

*PIR*², C 1348. A. M.

DOMAINS. (*a*) CIVIC. Most cities owned land cor-porately. Some was acquired by conquest, some by escheat, some by confiscation. When cities came under Roman rule, conquest was ruled out, and escheated and confiscated estates normally went to the Roman People. The cities, however, continued to acquire territory, chiefly by gifts and bequests; though they could not inherit under Roman law, they probably could do so under peregrine law (till A.D. 212), and legacies were legalized by Nerva; moreover, *fideicommissa* were doubt-less always valid. The domains owned by a city did not necessarily lie within its territory; Arpinum owned land in Cisalpine Gaul and Cos estates in Cyprus. The rent from domains was often an important part of the civic revenues.

(*b*) IMPERIAL. The nucleus of the imperial domains was formed by the estates of successive emperors, which normally passed to their successors. They were enlarged by a vast flow of bequests not only from friends, depen-dents, and freedmen, but from strangers: some em-perors refused to accept bequests from persons unknown to them, but others were so grasping as to quash wills under which they did not benefit. Furthermore, the estates of persons condemned for *maiestas* were some-times bestowed on the emperor; by the second century this was probably the regular practice. In Egypt the imperial domains were, from the Flavian period, managed by a special department (λόγος οὐσιακός) separately from the public lands. In other imperial provinces, where there were only scattered public domains, they and the imperial estates were probably administered by the same staff. In the public provinces the emperor's procurators, who at first managed only his estates, later, perhaps under the Flavians, assumed control of public lands; at this date the domains in Africa were grouped in *regiones* and *tractus*. Public and imperial domains were thus assimilated (except in Egypt) and were both included in the *patrimonium*.

(*c*) ROYAL. Alexander and the Successors claimed to own the land of their kingdoms, excluding the Greek cities. This theory was most vigorously exploited by the Ptolemies in Egypt. They granted lands, it is true, to the gods in perpetuity, to their friends for life, and to their soldiers at first on a life and later on a hereditary tenure, and they even granted private possession in perpetuity of some land. But they seem to have maintained their title to the land which was granted (γῆ ἐν ἀφέσει), and the rest, the royal land (γῆ βασιλική), they exploited directly by rack-renting it to the peasants. In Cyrenaica also the Ptolemies seem to have claimed ownership of all the land save the territories of the Greek cities. The Seleucids also made grants of land to their friends and soldiers, but they did not generally disturb tenures, but merely levied the customary dues from the natives. They gradually alienated the χώρα βασιλική by gifts and sales to cities, or to individuals with permission to incorporate the land in cities; by founding new cities; and by recognizing native communities as cities. When the Attalids succeeded to Seleucid Asia Minor, they probably found little royal land. The Bithynian and Cappadocian kings owned extensive royal lands. The Macedonian and other European kings, on the other hand, possessed little— probably only family estates and the territories of communities which had been conquered and destroyed.

(*d*) SACRED. Many gods owned land; especially in Egypt and Asia Minor. These were probably acquired in the main by gifts and bequests; partly perhaps by the foreclosure of mortgages, for the gods, controlling large reserves of cash, engaged extensively in money-lending. In Egypt the sacred lands were administered by the Crown under the Ptolemies, and the Roman government maintained the system. In Asia Minor the sacred lands were often managed by the high priests of the god, some of whom were independent dynasts or subject only to the suzerainty of the Crown. In cities the sacred lands were generally administered by public magistrates, and with the spread of cities the independent temples of Asia Minor mostly passed under municipal control.

O. Hirschfeld, *Kleine Schriften*, pp. 516–75, 1902 (for (*b*)). M. Rostovtzeff, *Studien zur Geschichte des römischen Kolonates* (*Arch. Pap.* Beiheft i, 1910); id. *Social and Economic History of the Hellenistic World* (1941; for (*c*) and (*d*)). E. Kornemann, *PW*, Suppl. iv. 227–68.   A. H. M. J.

DOMINIUM. In ancient Roman law ownership of things was closely connected with the power over persons: the rights of a *pater familias* over wife and children were similar to those over slaves and cattle; they all derived from his sovereign position as head of the *familia* (a term which included both persons and objects in the household, see PATRIA POTESTAS). The more developed law differentiated between rights over persons and rights over things, as also between the transactions for their transfer, for all of which *mancipatio* had previously been sufficient. The classical jurisprudence conceived ownership (*dominium, proprietas*), without precise definition, as an unrestricted right of control over physical objects. It was absolute, exclusive, and complete. Consequently, when several persons owned a thing in common, neither did each of them hold *dominium* of the whole, nor did each of them hold *dominium* of a determined part (e.g. a single floor of a building). They owned ideal, abstract parts, expressed in fractions (see COMMUNIO). Restrictions of *dominium* were at first imposed for religious reasons only, or for avoiding a nuisance to neighbours; they were gradually extended in later times in order to protect public interests.

The ancient law knew only *dominium ex iure Quiritium*, which, being an institution of the old *ius civile*, was open to Roman citizens only. The quiritary owner (the only one who could assert 'res mea est') could transfer the ownership of *res mancipi* by transactions of the *ius civile*, viz. *mancipatio* (q.v.) and *in iure cessio* (a kind of collusive process in which the transferrer, as defendant in the trial, did not contradict the plaintiff's claim to own the transferred object). By a later development, however, the praetors introduced means of protecting ownership not acquired by these methods, or ownership of *res nec mancipi*. In this way a praetorian type of ownership (*in bonis habere*) arose, which was defended by special praetorian remedies, even against the quiritary owner. A 'praetorian' owner became a 'civil' one by uninterrupted possession of an object for one year (if movable) or two years (if immovable). This method of acquiring quiritary property was called *usucapio*. The contrast between quiritary and praetorian ownership disappeared in Justinian's law (see POSSESSIO).

Ch. Appleton, *Histoire de la propriété prétorienne*, i, ii (1889–90); V. Scialoja, *Teoria della proprietà*, i, ii (1928–31); P. Bonfante, *Corso di diritto romano* ii. 1 (1926).   A. B.

DOMITIAN (TITUS FLAVIUS DOMITIANUS), son of the Emperor Vespasian, was born on 25 October A.D. 51. His youth was spent in obscurity until 69, when his father's rebellion against Vitellius suddenly brought him into prominence. After a narrow escape from death Domitian found himself, on the murder of Vitellius, temporarily at the head of affairs in Rome. This brief taste of power, which abruptly ended with Vespasian's arrival in 70, coloured Domitian's whole outlook. He had dreamed of heading a Germanic invasion and of rivalling his brother's exploits; instead, he found himself condemned to a position of inferiority. Vespasian intended him to succeed the childless Titus, and he held two ordinary consulships (73 and 80) and five suffect consulships; yet neither under Vespasian nor under Titus did he exercise any real power.

2. The effect which this long suppression had on Domitian's naturally proud and ambitious character was unfortunate. When he finally succeeded Titus in 81 he was an embittered and jealous man, determined to exert his powers to the full. His reign falls into two halves. Down to the rebellion of L. Antonius Saturninus (q.v. 3) in 88 Domitian avoided bloodshed and ruled firmly but equitably; afterwards he became more and more ruthless, until his reign culminated in a Terror (93 to 96).

3. Domitian accentuated the absolutist tendencies of Vespasian. He was consul ten times during his principate, using the office merely for the purpose of giving his name to the year. He wore the dress of a *triumphator* even in the Senate and was accompanied by twenty-four lictors. He habitually exercised the right of *adlectio*, using it to draft distinguished *equites* and provincials into the Senate, while in 84 or 85 he became *censor perpetuus*. This was a serious blow to the Senate, whose composition he now completely controlled. He only consulted it perfunctorily, relying for advice on the *consilium principis*, in which senators and *equites* served equally. In fact Domitian broke the spirit of the Senate, compelling it to vote as he willed, and, after 88, bringing back all the horrors of *maiestas* and *delatio*. This was partly caused by financial embarrassment, though, as his major expenses occurred before 93, it may be argued that revenge was at least as important a motive. The increase of legionary pay from 300 to 400 *denarii* annually, military campaigns, extensive public works and buildings, such as the temple to Jupiter on the Capitol, the temple to Jupiter Custos on the Quirinal, and his magnificent Alban villa, in addition to *congiaria* amounting in all to 225 *denarii* a head, all helped to swell expenditure.

4. In foreign policy Domitian aimed at strengthening existing frontiers, and his much-maligned campaign against the Chatti in 83 was really a successful attempt to annex Mt. Taunus and complete the line of defence from Main to Neckar. In 85 the Dacian king Decebalus inflicted a heavy defeat on Oppius Sabinus, legate of Moesia. Another defeat followed in 86, and the Roman general Sabinus was slain and an eagle captured. In 87 the Roman forces won a great victory at Tapae; but under pressure from a defeat of the Pannonic army, which he was leading in person, at the hands of the Marcomanni and Quadi, Domitian made an honourable peace with Decebalus and returned to Rome to triumph in 89. The Sarmatians inflicted some further defeats on the Romans, and in 92 Domitian, taking the field in person, won some success. The only other serious fighting was that of Agricola (q.v.) in Britain; Agricola was recalled in 84, possibly because Domitian was jealous of his success.

5. In general administration of the Empire Domitian showed himself careful and efficient, choosing good governors and punishing bad ones. Procurators and freedmen were strictly controlled, and exaction of taxes was severe but fair. Domitian also made serious attempts to raise the general standard of morality, and, as censor, strictly enforced the laws against immorality, suppressed castration, and checked theatrical licence. In 83 he executed three Vestal Virgins for immorality. In 90 the Chief Vestal, Cornelia, was condemned to be buried alive.

6. Domitian's strictness on the question of public morality accorded ill with the sensuality of his private life, and this was one of the many causes of the opposition with which he met from the aristocracy and philosophers. Other causes were his attempt to impose Greek refinement on the Romans, his virtual suppression of the Senate, and the Oriental flattery of himself which amounted, at least unofficially, to an assumption of semi-divine honours. Earlier Domitian had treated this opposition with comparative indifference, but in his later years, feeling that he could trust nobody, he turned to persecution. The philosophers, whom he twice banished from Italy (89 and 95), were not so serious a menace: their chief danger was that they supplied theoretical arguments to justify the aristocratic opposition. Many plots were made, though our authorities give the most flimsy reasons for Domitian's executions. The fact that the Emperor was childless increased both his own suspicion and the hopes of the plotters; until he executed him in 95, Domitian had destined the two sons of Flavius Clemens as his heirs; what he intended to do afterwards we do not know.

7. A vicious circle was thus set up; every unsuccessful plot caused more executions, which in their turn led to another plot. In 96 the Emperor's own wife, Domitia, feeling herself insecure, joined with the two praetorian prefects and some of the court officials in a plot which succeeded, and Domitian was murdered. The real significance of his reign lies in the fact that a rapid and permanent advance was made towards absolute monarchy.

Principal ancient sources: Suet. *Dom.*; Dio Cass. bk. 67; Statius, *Silvae*; Plin. *Pan.* Modern literature: *PIR*, F 176; Weynand, in *PW*, s.v. 'Flavius (77)'; S. Gsell, *Essai sur le règne de l'empereur Domitien* (1894); R. Syme, *JRS* 1930, and C. H. V. Sutherland, *JRS* 1935 (on Domitian's finances). *See also under* VESPASIAN.

R. L. J.

DOMITIANUS, TITUS FLAVIUS, son of Flavius Clemens and Flavia Domitilla; he and his brother were adopted by Domitian and received respectively the names of Domitian and Vespasian. Their tutor was Quintilian.

Stein, *PW* vi. 2596.

DOMITILLA, FLAVIA, Domitian's niece, was accused with her husband, the consul Flavius Clemens, in A.D. 95 of atheism, probably because she favoured Christian (rather than Jewish) rites. She was exiled. The early-Christian Coemeterium Domitillae on the Via Ardeatina is somehow connected with her. Eusebius 3. 18, which refers to Domitilla as a niece of Clemens, is probably a simple mistake, not evidence for another person.

Stein, *PW* vi. 2732; H. Leclercq, *Dict. d'arch. chrétienne* iv. 1401; P. Styger, *Die röm. Katakomben* (1933), 63. A. M.

DOMITIUS (1) **AHENOBARBUS**, GNAEUS, plebeian aedile (196 B.C.), praetor (194), and consul in 192, in Gaul. In the absence of Scipio Africanus he was in effective command at Magnesia. He may have been in Greece in 169–168 and 167, but this Domitius may be his son, consul in 162.

Livy 35. 22 and 40; 37. 39; 44. 18; 45. 17; Appian, *Syr.* 30. De Sanctis, *Stor. Rom.* iv. 198. A. H. McD.

DOMITIUS (2) **AHENOBARBUS**, GNAEUS (*cos.* 122 B.C.), won great glory as proconsul in 121 by his conquest of the Allobroges in south Gaul, whither the king of the Salluvii had fled after Calvinus' victories. He used elephants with great effect at the battle of Vindalium near Avignon. The annexation of Narbonese Gaul followed, after Domitius had treacherously seized Bituitus, king of the Arverni, at a conference. The Via Domitia, from Provence to the Pyrenees, was founded by him; and he started the practice of erecting monuments (like that at St. Rémy) in the form of towers on the site of a victory. He was censor with Metellus Delmaticus (115). M. H.

DOMITIUS (3) **AHENOBARBUS**, LUCIUS (*cos.* 54 B.C.), husband of Cato's sister Porcia, supported Verres (Cicero then calls him 'princeps iuuentutis'—*Verr.* 2. 1. 139) and resisted Manilius (q.v. 2) in 66 B.C. Relentlessly hostile to the 'Triumvirate', in 58 (as praetor) and in 56 he specifically threatened Caesar's position in Gaul, the scene of his own grandfather's victories; he thus precipitated the conference of Luca, which postponed his consulate to 54. In 49 the Senate granted him Gaul, but his march northwards, unsupported by Pompey, ended in capitulation at Corfinium, though by Caesar's clemency he survived to defend Massilia and to fall at Pharsalus. Domitius could mobilize clients from the Marsi and Paeligni and tenants from the great estates which Sullan bounty had given him. But his pretensions sometimes made him ridiculous (cf. Caelius in Cic. *Fam.* 8. 14), his stupidity was proverbial, and he shared the brutality of his *gens* (Suet. *Nero* 2). G. E. F. C.

DOMITIUS (4) **AHENOBARBUS**, GNAEUS (*cos.* 32 B.C. and son of (3) above), fought on the Pompeian side in the Civil War and accompanied Brutus to Macedonia in 44. In 43 he was condemned (perhaps unjustly) for participation in the murder of Caesar, and proscribed. From 42 to 40 he commanded a fleet in the Adriatic against the Triumvirs, but he joined Antony before the treaty of Brundisium, was appointed governor of Bithynia, and took part in the Parthian expedition (36) and the operations against Sextus Pompeius in Asia Minor (35). Domitius was consul in 32, but left Rome for Ephesus when civil war threatened. He opposed the personal participation of Cleopatra in the war and went over to Octavian before Actium, already suffering from a fever which proved fatal.

Appian, *BCiv.* bks. 4 and 5; Dio Cassius, bks. 47–50. Drumann-Groebe, *Gesch. Roms.* iii. 24–8. G. W. R.

DOMITIUS (5) **AHENOBARBUS**, LUCIUS (*cos.* 16 B.C.), the husband of Antonia, the elder daughter of M. Antonius and Octavia, the Princeps' sister. Alleged to have been proud, blood-thirsty, and addicted to chariot-racing, he was aedile in 22, when he behaved arrogantly

to the censor Plancus; proconsul of Africa (12); legate of
Illyricum between 7 and 2, when he marched from the
Danube to the Elbe, setting up an altar to Augustus on
the farther bank of the latter river. The direction of his
march is uncertain. Next, in command of the army of
Germany, he constructed the causeway across the
marshes between the Rhine and the Ems known as the
pontes longi, after which nothing more is heard of him.

R. Syme, *Roman Revolution* (1939), see Index. R. S.

DOMITIUS (6) **MARSUS**, Augustan poet, acknowledged by Martial as one of his models (1 *praef.*; 2. 77;
5. 5. 6; 8. 56. 24). To light poetry he added an epic
Amazonis (4. 29. 8). An epigram by him is attached to
the *Vita* of Tibullus, but his remains are too slight for a
literary estimate.

Baehr. *FPR*; Morel, *FPL*. J. W. D.

DOMITIUS, *see also* AFER, AURELIANUS, CALVINUS,
CORBULO, NERO, ULPIAN.

DOMUS AUREA (Golden House) was the palace of
Nero, built after the great fire of Rome in A.D. 64,
covering the south slope of the Oppian Hill and surveying the ornamental lake later covered by the Colosseum
(q.v.) and the temple of Claudius on the Caelian. As
befitted its situation in a royal park, the main wing of
the palace (now covered by the courtyard and reservoirs
of the baths of Trajan) followed Hellenistic landscape
architecture, with frontal colonnade and angular planning, permitting different vistas to be enjoyed. The
treatment, however, is domestic when compared with
the Flavian palace on the Palatine. Only the vestibule
to the palace, on the site of Hadrian's temple of Venus
and Roma, attained monumental proportions and was
approached by the great colonnades of the new Sacra
Via (q.v.).

T. Ashby, *Topographical Dictionary of Ancient Rome*, s.v.; G.
Lugli, *Roma antica* (1946), 348 ff.; Van Deman, *AJArch.* 1923,
383–424, and *Am. Ac. Rome*, v. 115–26; A. Boethius, *Eranos* xliv
(1946), 442. I. A. R.

DONATIVUM, a supplement to the annual pay of a
soldier in the legions and the praetorian and urban
cohorts. Originally a share in booty, donatives were paid
in money by emperors to commemorate a joyful event
(e.g. the fall of Sejanus), or left in their wills. After
Claudius each new accession was the occasion for a
donative. The amount granted to each praetorian was
at first, like his pay, three times that of the legionary,
but gradually, because of the political importance of the
Guard, the difference became disproportionately greater.
When Hadrian adopted L. Aelius Caesar the legionary
got 225, the praetorian 5,000 *denarii*.

H. M. D. Parker, *The Roman Legions* (1928); M. Durry, *Les
Cohortes prétoriennes* (1938). H. M. D. P.

DONATUS (1), AELIUS, the most famous grammarian
of the fourth century A.D., who numbered amongst his
pupils the future St. Jerome. He wrote two *artes* and
commentaries on Terence and Virgil. (i) The *Ars minor*
(ed. Keil, *Gramm. Lat.* iv. 355–66), intended for beginners, deals, in the form of question and answer, with the
eight parts of speech. (ii) The *Ars maior*, or *secunda*
(ed. Keil, ibid. 367–402), is more comprehensive and
includes the *vitia et virtutes orationis*. These works
became favourite school-books in the Middle Ages.
(iii) The extant Terence commentary (which omits the
Heautontimorumenos) is not in its original form but is
apparently a (6th c.) compilation made from two copies
found in the margins of Terence MSS. P. Wessner (ed.
2 vols., 1902–5) prints the commentary as found in our
manuscripts; H. T. Karsten (ed. 2 vols., 1911–12)
attempts to restore the original form. In this work
Donatus owed much to Aemilius Asper (q.v.). (iv) Of
the Virgil commentary only the preface (ed. Wölfflin,

Philol. xxiv. 154) and the life of Virgil with an introduction to the *Eclogues* (ed. J. Brummer, *Vit. Verg.* 1912)
are extant. But the commentary of Servius (q.v.) contains much material derived from it, and the so-called
Servius Danielis is claimed to be virtually Donatus (cf.
E. K. Rand, *CQ* 1916, 158–64). Some of the more
learned notes in glossaries (e.g. the *Liber Glossarum*) may
also come ultimately from Donatus' commentary. *See
also* SCHOLARSHIP, LATIN, IN ANTIQUITY, and cf. Teuffel,
§ 409; Schanz–Hosius, § 832. J. F. M.

DONATUS (2), TIBERIUS CLAUDIUS (late 4th c. A.D.),
wrote a continuous (but tedious) commentary (*Interpreta-
tiones Vergilianae*) in twelve books on the *Aeneid* (ed.
H. Georgii, 2 vols., 1905–6), in which he deals with the
poet's thought, style, rhetoric, and learning. It has no
clear affiliation with earlier or contemporary commentators and is mentioned by no later writer.

Cf. Teuffel, § 431. 5; Schanz–Hosius, § 248. 3. J. F. M.

DORIANS, the last of the northern invaders into Greece
(*c.* 1100–1000 B.C.), who settled especially in Elis,
Laconia, Argos, Corinth, Sicyon, Epidaurus, Megara,
and Aegina, and crossed the seas to occupy Crete, Melos,
and Thera, and the south coast of Asia Minor. Greek
tradition associated the invasion with the return of the
Heraclidae and traced the route of invasion from Doris
(q.v.) via Delphi (where the priesthood came of Dorian
families) to Naupactus, whence the invaders crossed by
sea into Peloponnesus. As they spoke a dialect of Greek,
it is probable that they were of related stock to the earlier
invaders and had previously inhabited the fringes of the
Mycenaean world. Of the tribes commonly found in
Dorian communities, the Hylleis, Dymanes, and Pamphyli, the first probably represented the eastern stream
of invasion via Delphi, the second the western stream via
Elis (the ethnic -*anes* being north-west Greek), and the
third the general ruck of less important tribes. The area
whence the invaders came was probably Epirus and
south-west Macedonia.

Culturally the Dorian invaders were inferior to the
Mycenaeans; bringing little with them except the iron
slashing sword and the spectacle fibula, they ended
Mycenaean civilization and plunged Greece into the
Dark Ages, in which Geometric pottery—regarded by
some as Dorian, by others as degenerate Mycenaean
art—developed and reached its acme at Athens. In the
Orientalizing and Archaic periods the Dorian element
contributed largely to the development of Greek art
in architecture, pottery, sculpture, and choral lyric.
They possessed a restraint and architectonic power which
blended with Ionic Greece in Athens to produce the
acme of Greek art. Politically the Dorians split into two
main channels; at Sicyon, Corinth, Argos, and Aegina the
Dorian conquerors gradually lost their monopoly of
franchise and became merged in the subject people; but
Sparta and Crete retained a peculiar political form, in
which the subject-peoples were serfs and dependents,
while the franchised Dorians constituted a ruling military class, with a special organization of men's clubs.

K. O. Müller, *History and Antiquities of the Dorian Race* (Engl.
Transl. 1830); J. L. Myres, *Who were the Greeks?* (1930); W. A.
Heurtley, *BSA* xxviii. 159 f.; N. G. L. Hammond, *BSA* xxxii. 131 f.;
T. C. Skeat, *The Dorians in Archaeology* (1934). N. G. L. H.

DORIC, *see* DIALECTS, GREEK.

DORIEUS, a younger half-brother of the Spartan king
Cleomenes I (q.v.). Jealousy and discontent drove him,
probably with Cleomenes' approval, to lead a colonizing
expedition to Cinyps on the north African coast (near
mod. *Tripoli*), whence the Carthaginians expelled him
after three years. Returning to Sparta he next founded
a settlement in west Sicily near Heraclea Minoa, where,
before long, he and most of his followers were killed

by the joint forces of Segesta and the Phoenicians. According to a doubtful tradition Dorieus had previously taken part with Croton in the destruction of Sybaris (510 B.C.). A. M. W.

DORIS, a small area in central Greece enclosing the headwaters of the Cephissus. Its small plain, containing the Tetrapolis of Pindus, Erineus, Boeum, and Cytinium, is traversed by the route from Malis to Phocis which turns the defences of Thermopylae and was used by the Persians and Galatians. The Dorians of Peloponnesus, and the Spartans particularly, claimed Doris as their metropolis (Tyrtaeus, fr. 2); possibly during the invasion period a section of Dorian invaders halted there. Represented on the Amphictionic Council, Doris was championed by Sparta (Thuc. 1. 107). In the fourth century it fell into the power of Onomarchus and later of Philip. Fourth-century walls are extant at Cytinium.

N. G. L. H.

DOROTHEUS of Sidon (1st or beginning of 2nd c. A.D.), an astrological poet who had great vogue with the Arabian astrologers.

Ed. (along with Manetho) H. Koechly (1858). *PW* v. 1572.

DOS, see MARRIAGE, LAW OF, paras. 7–8.

DOSIADAS, author of a poem called Βωμός because of its shape, preserved in *Anth. Pal.* 15. 26 and manuscripts of Theocritus, written in mixed metres and purporting to be a dedication by Jason, in extremely obscure, allusive language. The poem is a παίγνιον like the *Syrinx* of Theocritus and seems to come from the same circle and age.

Text: J. U. Powell, *Collectanea Alexandrina*, 175–6 with notes; U. von Wilamowitz-Moellendorff, *Bucolici Graeci*, 152–3.
Criticism: Wilamowitz, *De Lycophronis Alexandra* (1884), 12 ff. C. M. B.

DOSITHEUS (1) of Pelusium (fl. *c.* 230 B.C.), pupil of the astronomer Conon. He continued a connexion between the Alexandrian astronomers and Archimedes which had begun with the latter's studies in Alexandria; Archimedes dedicated several of his books to D. Observations by him on the times of appearance of the fixed stars (some of them made at places farther north than Alexandria) and on weather-signs are recorded in the *Parapegma* of Geminus and elsewhere. He wrote a work Πρὸς Διόδωρον in which he discussed Aratus' *Phaenomena* and Eudoxus' researches, and a work on the calendar, Περὶ τῆς Εὐδόξου ὀκταετηρίδος.
PW v. 1607. W. D. R.

DOSITHEUS (2), surnamed *Magister* (possibly late 4th c. A.D.), grammarian, whose bilingual *Ars grammatica* (ed. Keil, *Gramm. Lat.* vii. 376–436; J. Tolkiehn, 1913) was intended for Greeks who wished to learn Latin. The Latin part was probably based on the *Ars* of Cominianus, and the Greek (now interspersed with the Latin) was originally interlinear. Under D.'s name there are also preserved in various forms the remains of a bilingual school-book now known as the *Pseudo-Dositheana Hermeneumata* (ed. G. Goetz, *Corp. Gloss. Lat.* iii). Originally it contained twelve sections: vocabularies, *Hadriani sententiae, fabulae Aesopiae, de manumissionibus, narratio de bello Troiano*, etc. The contents are of various dates (some possibly 3rd c. A.D.) and have value for the light they throw on social life.

Cf. Teuffel, § 431. 7–8; Schanz–Hosius, § 836. J. F. M.

DOSON, surname of Antigonus III (q.v.).

DOSSĒN(N)US (Hor. *Epist.* 2. 1. 173) probably identical with Manducus, the guzzler in *Atellana* (q.v.).

DOUGGA, see THUGGA.

DOXOGRAPHERS, designation of those ancient authors who wrote on the doctrines of philosophers.

This type of literature was inaugurated by Aristotle, who used to discuss the views of his predecessors in the introductory chapters of his systematic works. His disciple Theophrastus was the first to write a special work on the subject. He collected the doctrines of the Pre-Socratics in sixteen books (φυσικῶν δόξαι) and arranged them according to topics, the first book dealing with the first principles (περὶ ἀρχῶν), the last (most of which is preserved) with the theory of sense-perception. The works of the Hellenistic authors who wrote on the lives (περὶ βίων) and of those who wrote on the succession of the philosophers (περὶ διαδοχῶν) contained doxographic elements. This is especially true of the history of philosophy ('Επιδρομὴ τῶν φιλοσόφων) of Diocles of Magnesia. Some of this material has found its way into the work of Diogenes Laertius.

Arius Didymus, the teacher of Augustus, wrote a summary (ἐπιτομή) of the doctrines of the Stoics. A complete doxography of the philosophy of the pre-Christian era was composed by Aëtius (1st or 2nd c. after Christ). A great part of his work is preserved in the Pseudo-Plutarchean *Placita* and in the *Eclogae* of Stobaeus. It was also used by Galen in his history of philosophy and by Theodoret.

Doxographi Graeci ed. H. Diels (1879); J. Burnet, *Early Greek Philosophy*[4], 33–7. K. von F.

DRACO (Δράκων), an Athenian lawgiver, who drew up a code of laws with prescribed rules of procedure and fixed penalties (621 B.C.). He made no changes in the constitution (Arist. *Pol.* 1274[b]15; the constitution attributed to him by Arist. *Ath. Pol.* 4 is no longer regarded as genuine). The purpose of the code was to allay the discontent of the masses. In a measure this object was achieved. No longer could the aristocratic magistrates apply and modify the law in the interests of the nobility.

The governing class was doubtless further influenced in appointing a lawgiver by the fact that a murderer had come to be regarded as polluted. Owing to the danger of pollution and the possibility of serious blood-feuds, homicide could no longer be dealt with by the families concerned. The State provided courts to try all homicides who did not take refuge in exile (*CAH* iv. 28).

The view that Draco used the judicial decisions of the magistrates as recorded by the *thesmothetai* has been challenged. But there is evidence in the extant part of his code dealing with unpremeditated homicide that he reduced to writing the customary law of his day, particularly in practice and procedure (Tod, *Greek Historical Inscriptions*, 87). For example, there is no formula for the interdict against an alleged or unknown slayer. Some loose form of the interdict must long have been in use.

Solon (q.v.) revised or repealed all of Draco's laws except those dealing with homicide, because the penalties were too severe. When Draco was asked why he made penalties so severe, he replied that small offences deserve death and for greater crimes he knew of no more severe penalty. The orator Demades said that Draco's laws were written in blood, and Aristotle (*Pol.* 1274[b]13) says there was nothing noteworthy about them except the severity of the punishments. R. J. B.

DRACON of Stratonicea, in Caria, predecessor or contemporary of Dionysius Thrax; author of a number of works on grammar, metric, and particular lyric poets (Sappho, Alcaeus, and Pindar), cited by Suidas. The extant Π. μέτρων ποιητικῶν ascribed to him (text, G. Hermann, 1812) has been shown to be a sixteenth-century forgery.

PW v 1662–3. J. D. D.

DRACONTIUS, Blossius Aemilius, a Christian Latin poet who flourished as an advocate at Carthage towards the end of the fifth century A.D. For eulogizing in verse a foreign prince he was imprisoned by Gunthamund, the Vandal king, but subsequently released. His secular works, of small poetic value, marked by free treatment of legend and unrestrained rhetoric, consist of a collection of short hexameter poems entitled *Romulea*, including rhetorical exercises, epithalamia, and mythological epyllia (*Hylas, De Raptu Helenae, Medea*); the anonymous *Orestis Tragoedia*, now proved Dracontian, probably belongs to this collection. The Christian poems, written in prison, comprise (*a*) a short elegiac poem of repentance addressed to the king (*Satisfactio*), (*b*) *De Laudibus Dei* in three books of hexameters; this, his chief work, shows considerable poetic imagination, appeals by its warm personal interest, but is marred by digressions, repetitions, and lack of unity. D. displays an impressive knowledge both of Scripture and of classical Roman literature. Though he is well versed in the poetic diction, exhibiting numerous echoes of the classical poets, his language is often harsh and obscure, the syntax audacious, and the prosody faulty. That the anonymous *Aegritudo Perdicae* is Dracontian cannot be proved.

Editions: F. Vollmer, *MGH* (1905), *PLM* v² (1914). Cf. *PW* v. 1635 ff.; Teuffel–Kroll iii⁶. 466 ff.; Schanz iv. 2. 58 ff.; F. J. E. Raby, *Christian Latin Poetry*, 1927. A. H.-W.

DRAMA, GREEK, see COMEDY, TRAGEDY.

DRAMA, ROMAN. The Romans enjoyed rhetoric and spectacle; they had also a keen appreciation of satire and repartee. The germ of their drama is perhaps to be found in the rude exchange of banter at harvest-home festivals (*see* FESCENNINI). In 364–363 B.C. Etruscan dancers took part in an expiatory ceremony at Rome; the foreign, professional dance was then grafted on to the native mime, and the result was the *satura* (q.v.), a medley of dialogue, song, and dance, performed to music by professionals (*ludii, histriones*). The decisive advance to a continuous plot was made by the Tarentine Greek, Livius Andronicus, who in 240 B.C. produced at the Ludi Romani a Greek tragedy and comedy (?) in translation. Eight titles and forty lines of his tragedies are preserved; his *Aiax Mastigophorus* seems to have been a clumsy version of the *Ajax* of Sophocles. The three comic titles—The Blade, i.e. the Swashbuckler (?), the Maid (?), the Dancer (?)—with the fragments, point to New Comedy as their source. The metres include the iambic senarius, the trochaic septenarius, and the cretic; the three forms of dramatic delivery (speech, recitative, and song) therefore go back to Livius. He acted in his own plays; we are told that after his voice had become overstrained he employed a boy to sing the *cantica* while he himself accompanied the words in dumb-show (Mirmont, *Ét. sur l'ancienne poés. Lat.* 75 ff.). Little as subsequent generations thought of Livius, he seems to have given Roman tragedy and comedy their abiding form.

2. With Naevius (7 titles of tragedies, 2 *praetextae*, together nearly 70 lines; 34 comedies, some of uncertain title, over 100 lines), apparently a Campanian, we are conscious of a more national spirit: 'libera lingua loquemur ludis Liberalibus!' His achievements were (1) to develop the *palliata* (adaptation of New Comedy); (2) to create the *praetexta* (Roman historical drama); (3) to make drama topical; (4) to give it style. Though tragedy was not his chief interest, he gave it a Roman note:

laetus sum laudari me abs te, pater, a laudato uiro.

The very titles of the comedies are full of life—the Nighthawks (*Agrypnuntes*), Derby Day (*Agitatoria*), Solomon Levi (?) (*Apella*), the Girl of Tarentum (a notable flirt:

alii adnutat, alii adnictat, alium amat, alium tenet . . .);

When we read in the *Soothsayer* of how to entertain guests from Praeneste or Lanuvium, we feel that we are not far from native comedy (*togata*). His interest in Roman history manifested itself in two original plays, the *Romulus* and the *Clastidium* (the latter of which dealt with the victory of Marcellus in 222). Irrepressible boldness of utterance, a gift of epigram, and a taste for scandal brought Naevius into ill-favour with the Scipios and the Metelli; the lesson of his downfall was not lost on his contemporary Plautus (q.v.), whose *palliatae* are free from all but the most innocuous political allusions.

3. Ennius (239–169), a failure in comedy, has left us 20 titles of tragedies, with some 400 lines. A new power over language is manifest in the oath of Achilles:

per ego deum sublimas subices
umidas, unde oritur imber sonitu saeuo et spiritu.

The lyrical dialogue in his *Iphigenia* conveys a sense of night's grandeur and mystery not unworthy of the original by Euripides (*IA* 1 ff.):

quid noctis uidetur in altisono
caeli clupeo?
superat temo
stellas cogens etiam atque etiam
noctis sublime iter.

With Ennius' interest in Euripides (from whom he also translated the *Hecuba*, the *Medea*, and many other plays) went a rationalizing and humanitarian spirit:

ego deum genus esse semper dixi et dicam caelitum;
sed eos non curare opinor quid agat humanum genus;
nam si curent, bene bonis sit, male malis, quod nunc abest.

The famous words of Medea must have sounded strangely in Roman ears:

nam ter sub armis malim uitam cernere
quam semel modo parere.

Effective Roman rhetoric is found in Agamemnon's reply to Menelaus in the *Iphigenia*:

egone plectar, tu delinquas: tu pecces, ego arguar?

where a comparison with Eur. *IA* 385 supports Cicero's remark that the great Roman tragedians translated 'non uerba sed uim'. Effective use of metre is found in the change from recitative to song in Cassandra's ravings:

adest, adest fax obuoluta sanguine atque incendio!
multos annos latuit: ciues, ferte opem et restinguite!
iamque mari magno classis cita
texitur: exitium examen rapit . . .

The melodramatic tendency of Roman tragedy is illustrated by the repeated choice of the banquet of Thyestes as a dramatic subject; madness, too, is a frequent theme. Another passage in Ennius' *Iphigenia*, quoted by Gellius as part of a chorus:

otio qui nescit uti, plus negoti habet . : :

illustrates (1) the retention of the chorus in Roman tragedy (?), (2) the independence of Ennius, who appears to have substituted soldiers for the maidens of Euripides, (3) the recurrent note of pedantry in Roman drama. One or two lines are left of the *Sabinae* and the *Ambracia*, which may have been *praetextae*. Later generations, while recognizing Ennius' greatness as a poet, never seem to have ranked him as a dramatist with Pacuvius or Accius (qq.v.).

4. Meanwhile comedy was represented by Caecilius and Terence (qq.v.). The other writers of *palliatae* are hard to date; Trabea (q.v.) has left us a vigorous picture of a lover's eagerness, Atilius (q.v. 3) the title *Misogynus* ('Woman-hater'), Aquilius (q.v. 1) a parasite's diatribe against sun-dials, which Varro assigned to Plautus on grounds of style (in fact there was much confusion as to authorship, and much misuse of Plautus' name); Luscius (q.v.) Lanuvinus, Terence's arch-enemy, achieved some success by his faithful versions of Menander; Licinius (q.v. 2) Imbrex has left us two lines which seem to have been borrowed from Plautus. Turpilius (q.v.; died

103 B.C.) has left 13 titles and over 200 lines; the titles are Greek (like all our other titles of post-Caecilian *palliatae*), but the variety of metres and the somewhat rough style remind us of the earlier period. Turpilius had enough independence to change the opening monologue of Menander's Ἐπίκληρος into a dialogue; his *Demiurgus* was still performed in Cicero's time, and his *Leucadia* (from Menander), the story of the hideous boatman endowed by Venus with the magical power to win the love of all women, suggests that New Comedy was not yet exhausted as a source of promising themes. But the *palliata* seems for some time to have been fighting a losing battle against cruder forms of entertainment, and with the death of Turpilius it came to an end.

5. *Fabula Togata.* As the *palliata* grew more Greek in tone a natural reaction led to the creation of the 'comedy in native dress', also, apparently, called the *fabula tabernaria* or 'private-house comedy'. Three writers are mentioned: perhaps the earliest and most typical is Titinius (q.v. 1; date unknown), of whom we have 15 titles and about 180 lines. The *Fullonia* shows us the fullers, those stock butts, engaged in a dispute with the weavers. In the *Barbatus* an embroiderer remarks that he has given up his employment. In the *Setina* or 'Girl of Setia' (a town in the Pontine marshes) a timid suitor for the heiress is encouraged by a friend. There is a contemptuous reference in the *Quintus* to speakers of Oscan and Volscian, who know no Latin. We are in a respectable, workaday Italian world, where betrothal, marriage, and family relationships play a larger part than mercenary gallantries, and where the 'cunning slave' of the *palliata* is conspicuous by his absence. T. Quinctius Atta (q.v.; died 77 B.C.) has left 11 titles and 20 lines; such titles as 'The Aedile's Games', 'The Megalensian Games' indicate that he found material in the public festivals. The *Aquae Caldae* depicted life at a 'fast' watering-place, where the 'ladies of the town' infuriated respectable women by dressing like them. Titles such as 'The Aunt', 'The Mother-in-law', remind us that the author was renowned for his portrayal of female character. The title *Satura* recalls the pre-Livian drama—perhaps not unlike the *tabernaria*. Atta still held the stage in Horace's day. L. Afranius (q.v. 1; 44 titles, 300 lines) was a greater figure; he admired and imitated Terence, Menander, and others, as he confesses without shame. He employed the prologue, both explanatory (like Menander) and polemical (like Terence); his plots may have resembled those of New Comedy. His *Simulans*, in which a father-in-law by skilful strategy outwits and brings to repentance an errant son-in-law, was still very much alive in the time of Cicero; his *Incendium*, in which a fire was shown on the stage, was revived, characteristically, by Nero. But for a writer of 'native comedy' to have to draw on Greek sources (including peculiarly Greek immorality) was a confession that the days of the *togata* were numbered. The title *Bucco Adoptatus*, if genuine, suggests that Afranius even borrowed from the Campanian farce; if so, he pointed the way which popular drama was to take after his death (*see* ATELLANA *and* MIMUS).

6. In tragedy Pacuvius was succeeded by Rome's favourite tragedian, L. Accius (q.v. ?170–c. 86), whose activity, self-confidence, and fiery temperament are partly revealed in the surviving fragments (40–50 titles of tragedies, 2 of *praetextae*—the *Brutus* and *Decius*—and about 700 lines). The main qualities of his work—violent emotion, flamboyant character-drawing, powerful rhetoric, especially in repartee—are all exemplified in the famous reply of the tyrant Atreus—'oderint dum metuant'. The titles cover the whole tragic field—Trojan, Theban, Aetolian, the legends concerning Bacchus, Hercules, the Argonauts, the Pelopidae, etc. Modern statements as to Accius' treatment of his Greek originals are mostly derived from Ribbeck's guesswork; it seems

clear, however, that a fragment of the *Phoenissae* is a translation of Euripides' opening lines:

> sol qui micantem candido curru atque equis
> flammam citatis feruido ardore explicas ...

Another fragment of the same play,

> egredere, exi, ecfer te, elimina urbe!

when compared with Euripides (593, 614, 636) shows equally clearly the heightening of rhetorical effect which we may believe to have been characteristic of Accius. That his work, in spite of its acknowledged harshness, was appreciated by the Romans is shown by Cicero's expressed admiration and frequent quotations, by Virgil's imitations, and above all by the popularity of his plays and splendid leading roles down to the end of the Republic. Some may find a more poetic quality in such occasional passages as:

> excita saxis suauisona echo
> crepitu clangente cachinnat,

but it is difficult, when reading the last great dramatist of the Republic, to forget that drama itself is soon to give place to rhetoric.

7. *Theatre, production, etc.* There are frequent references in Plautus' plays to a seated audience; in 194 special places were assigned to the senators. The 'best' seats were placed close to the stage, which was of wood, low, long, and deep; on it appeared all the performers. Behind rose the green-room, the front wall of which, with its conventional three doors, served as a permanent back-cloth; at each end of the stage were the side-entrances: that to the right of the spectators was supposed to lead to the Forum or 'near distance', that to the left to more remote parts. There was at first no curtain; scenic decoration was of the simplest; changes of scene within the course of a play were unknown. The use of masks as early as the time of Naevius seems indicated by two of his titles—*Personata* (? 'The Masked Lady'), *Quadrigemini* ('The Twins twinned'); with doubling of parts a troupe of five actors could perform practically any play of Plautus. Choral singing was at first unknown; crowds were represented by one actor and some mutes. The flute-player was present throughout the course of a play to accompany the recitative and song and occasionally to while away an empty-stage interval.

8. *Decline of drama.* After Accius the writing of tragedy seems to have become an amusement for noble dilettanti like C. Julius Caesar Strabo (curule aedile in 90 B.C.). We do not know that his works were produced; the supply of new plays for the stage seems to have almost ceased. Yet the Ciceronian period was in a sense the Golden Age of the theatre; the tragedies and comedies of earlier writers were frequently produced and highly popular. It was an age of great actors: Aesopus 'starred' in such parts as the title-role of Accius' *Atreus*; Roscius was famed for his playing of Ballio in Plautus' *Pseudolus*. The crowd seems to have known its 'classics' well; public interest was heightened by the search for topical allusions, as when in 57 the mention of the banished Telamon (in Accius' *Eurysaces*) caused a demonstration in favour of the banished Cicero. We can understand why the authorities in 44 B.C. banned the performance of Accius' *praetexta*, the *Brutus*. The theatres had now become vast and splendid, the performances gorgeous; the use of such devices as the drop-curtain (mentioned by Cicero) made possible elaborate scenic effects. In 55 B.C. Pompey gave Rome its first stone theatre, seating 9,000 persons (Huelsen's estimate—Pliny says 40,000); the spectators were treated to a performance of Accius' *Clutemestra* in which 600 mules were led across the stage as part of Agamemnon's booty. Such barbaric display was itself a mark of decadence; soon the crowd were to find all that they wanted in spectacle, music, and farce, while the writing of plays became a mere literary exercise; thus Quintus Cicero wrote four in sixteen days.

9. *The Empire.* We possess scarcely a line of the two outstanding tragedies, the *Thyestes* of Varius (said to have been produced at the games in celebration of Actium) and the *Medea* of Ovid (who denies that he had written for the theatre, *Tr.* 5. 7. 27); for Asinius Pollio see Hor. *Carm.* 2. 1. 9–10. After the coming of pantomime in 22 B.C. tragedy seems to have survived chiefly in the form of excerpts sung on the stage (cf. Suet. *Ner.* 21), e.g. perhaps the *carmina* of the tragedian Pomponius Secundus which exasperated the spectators in A.D. 47 (Tac. *Ann.* 11. 13). The nine tragedies attributed to Seneca, with our solitary *praetexta*, the *Octavia*, do not read as though meant for production, but their influence on Renaissance drama was destined to be great. Of comedy, threatened by mimes and Atellanae, we hear even less. Melissus invented the *trabeata* (*see* FABULA); *togatae* were written for recitation (Juv. 1. 3); Fundanius composed *palliatae.* *Togatae* were sometimes performed (cf. *togatarium*, Suet. *Aug.* 45), but perhaps these were old classics (see para. 5 supra on Afranius). In the fourth century we find Arnobius (*Adv. Gent.* 7. 33) apparently referring to a production of Plautus' *Amphitruo.*

O. Ribbeck, *Scaen. Rom. Poes. Frag.*; W. Merry, *Fragments of Roman Poetry*; Ribbeck's *Römische Tragödie*; the literary histories of J. Wight Duff and Lamarre; E. Fiechter, *Baugeschichtliche Entwicklung des antiken Theaters*, 78 ff.; Friedländer ii. 95–100 (Engl. Transl.); M. Bieber, *The History of the Greek and Roman Theater* (1939). W. B.

DREAMS, *see* DIVINATION, para. 3.

DRESS. There are three striking points of difference between ancient and modern dress. Firstly, both in Greece and Rome women's dress in outward appearance was very similar to men's, and a Greek wife could, and often did, wear her husband's cloak out of doors. Secondly, there was very little fashionable alteration in the garments worn by both sexes, and none of our present-day bewildering changes in the body contour. Thirdly, wearing apparel was usually home-made and the same piece of home-spun cloth could serve as a garment, a blanket, or a shroud.

2. The two garments worn in Greece by men and women alike were the tunic (χιτών) and the cloak (ἱμάτιον). These were rectangular pieces of stuff, woollen or linen, and were draped according to individual taste. The tunic had two main varieties, the Ionian made of linen, the Dorian made of wool, this latter being the earlier kind of women's dress. In length it was rather more than the wearer's height, in breadth about twice the span of her arms. Before wearing it was first folded along the upper edge so that the overlap reached to the waist, and then doubled lengthways. The open ends were usually sewn up, but the Spartan women pinned them together. The tunic hung from the shoulders, arm-holes being provided on each side. It was secured at the waist with a girdle. The Ionian tunic was of much lighter stuff, and was bunched up round the waist with one or two girdles, the lower part hanging straight; while for outdoor wear a heavier garment was usually thrown over it. In early times when women at Athens were wearing the Dorian tunic, the men wore the Ionian; but *c.* 450 B.C. the women changed to the Ionian dress and the men adopted for active exercise a much shorter woollen garment reaching to the knee and drawn by fastenings to the left shoulder so as to leave the right arm bare. Their ordinary dress, however, was the cloak (ἱμάτιον), which was sometimes arranged in elaborate folds covering the whole body, but usually was drawn away from the right shoulder. For riding a short flowing cape (χλαμύς) was worn (*see also* EPHEBI).

3. A Roman lady had three sorts of garments, a *tunica*, a *stola*, and a *palla*. The *tunica interior* was sleeveless, a brassière—*strophium*—often being worn with it: over this for ordinary occasions was drawn a much longer tunic with sleeves, the *stola*, which had a broad flounce sewn on at the bottom, half covering the feet when the *stola* was girded up into folds under the breast. Third came the *palla*, a rectangular piece of stuff like the Greek ἱμάτιον, worn only out of doors and draped according to the wearer's taste. The men of Rome wore a *tunica* resembling the Greek χιτών and an outer garment, the *toga* (q.v.), which they probably adopted from the Etruscans.

4. At first the toga was worn alone next to the skin, but later one or more tunics underneath became usual—Augustus in cold weather wore four—and at all times the tunic was the usual indoor dress. Senators had a broad purple stripe in front, *latus clavus* (q.v.), knights two narrow stripes, *angustus clavus* (q.v.). There were, however, other garments worn on special occasions. The *synthesis* was a light brightly coloured robe especially suited for banquets; the *lacerna* an open mantle, fastened by a brooch on the shoulder, used in cold weather; the *paenula*, a sleeveless cloak, with a hole for the neck and a hood attached, used especially by travellers.

5. The Greeks had a broad-brimmed hat (*petasos*) for men and a round one for women, but seldom wore them: when their heads needed covering they drew up their cloaks. They had a simple form of sandal with a heavy sole for outdoor wear; at home they went barefoot. The Romans followed the Greeks as regards headwear, but besides sandals they had two special kinds of boot, the *caliga*, a heavy marching boot for soldiers, laced on the instep and secured by thongs, and the *calceus*, made in the case of senators of red leather with an ivory crescent and with thongs wound round the legs and tied twice in front.

Lady Evans, *Chapters on Greek Dress* (1893); E. B. Abrahams, *Greek Dress* (1908); A. J. B. Wace and Lady Evans in *Comp. Gr. Stud.*; L. M. Wilson, *The Clothing of the Ancient Romans* (1938). F. A. W.

DROMEDARII, *see* CAMELS.

DRUIDS, *see* RELIGION, CELTIC.

DRUSILLA, JULIA (probably A.D. 16–38), the second daughter of Germanicus and Agrippina. She was married to L. Cassius Longinus (*cos.* A.D. 30) and afterwards to her cousin M. Aemilius Lepidus. Her name, like her sisters', was compulsorily included in vows and oaths after the accession of her brother Gaius. She was his favourite sister, and it was rumoured that their relations were incestuous. She was named as Gaius' heir during his illness (late 37), but died in 38. Public mourning was enforced throughout the Empire and, though there was no precedent in Roman history for the consecration of a woman, she was consecrated as Panthea, probably on the anniversary of Augustus' birthday. J. P. B.

DRUSUS (1), MARCUS LIVIUS (*cos.* 112 B.C.), as tribune in 122 B.C. vetoed the proposals of C. Gracchus in his second tribunate, which he outbid by a scheme for twelve Roman colonies—never established—coupled with the exemption of Latins from corporal punishment. His continued popularity is hard to explain, if his proposals were merely dishonest. As consul in 112 he retrieved the recent failure of C. Cato in the Balkans, pursuing the Scordisci beyond the Danube. He died, probably in 109, while censor with Scaurus. M. H.

DRUSUS (2), MARCUS LIVIUS, son of (1) above, husband of Servilia (daughter of Q. Caepio, q.v. 1), brother of Livia (wife of the younger Caepio, praetor 91), and probably adoptive father of Livius Drusus Claudianus, whose daughter Livia married Augustus. Drusus was a senatorial leader who tried to combine Senate and *Equites*, while championing the Italians' claim to Roman citizenship. Proud and severe, he lavished his wealth in gaining political influence. The supporters of his proposals for reform from the side of the Senate included many leaders, such as Scaurus, Bestia, and L. Crassus; but while gaining adherents from all ranks, Drusus antagonized the selfish majority in each party. As tribune in 91 B.C. he revived his father's colonial schemes; proposed to give back the jury courts to the Senate, which, however, was to be doubled by the inclusion of 300 *Equites*; and offered the franchise to all Italians. This legislation was carried *en bloc*, contrary to the *Lex Caecilia Didia* (see DIDIUS 1) of 98; and force was used. Caepio, who had quarrelled with him and divorced Livia some years before, started an active opposition which was headed by the consul Marcius Philippus; and after a period of violent agitation, and various threats of large-scale Italian movements to support Drusus, the Senate declared all Drusus' legislation invalid. Drusus himself died by violence; his supporters were attacked in the law courts; and the Italians openly rebelled (Social War). Cicero's chief aims, the *Concordia Ordinum* and *Consensus Italiae*, were largely based on Drusus' ideas.

E. G. Hardy, *CR* 1913, 261 ff.; P. A. Seymour, *Engl. Hist. Rev.* 1914, 417 ff.; C. Lanzani, *Riv. Fil.* 1912, 272 ff. M. H.

DRUSUS (3), NERO CLAUDIUS (38–9, B.C.), son of Ti. Claudius Nero and Livia Drusilla, was born in 38 B.C., about the time when his mother was divorced by Nero and married Octavian. After his father's death he was educated by Octavian. He married Antonia minor, daughter of M. Antonius, and had three children: Germanicus, Livilla, and Claudius. Already in 18 B.C. he was quaestor by privilege; in 15 with his brother Tiberius he subdued the Raetians and Vindelicians. In 13 he was appointed legate of the Three Gauls and organized the census of 12, when he dedicated an altar to Rome and Augustus at Lugdunum. Augustus considered him his best general, as he entrusted him with the invasion of Germany (12). The main difficulty being the transport of supplies, Drusus built a canal to connect the Rhine with the Ocean (*fossa Drusiana*), which apparently proved of little value. He used as his chief base Vetera (q.v.) and later Mogontiacum. In 12 B.C. he subdued the Frisii and routed the Sugambri, Bructeri, and Chauci, but his fleet was damaged on its return. In 11 he subdued the Usipetes and reached the Weser. He built fortifications of uncertain position. Augustus refused him a triumph; he had to be satisfied with an *ovatio*. In 10 he fought the Chatti. In 9 as consul he fought the Suebi, Marcomanni, and Cherusci and reached the Elbe; the Roman fortifications in Germany were improved. He died unexpectedly in summer camp. His work as an explorer had been extremely audacious; his military successes were more apparent than real. He was popular and was considered to hold Republican sentiments. He was buried in the mausoleum of Augustus. The Senate attributed to him and his descendants the surname of Germanicus. A cenotaph was built at Mogontiacum. An unknown poet wrote for his mother the *Consolatio ad Liviam* (q.v.).

*PIR*², C 857; Stein, *PW* iii. 2703; R. Syme, *CAH* x. 349; L. Schmidt, *Geschichte d. deutschen Stämme* i² (1938), 93. For the birth-date J. Carcopino, *Rev. Hist.* clxi (1929), 225. Portraits: L. Curtius, *Röm. Mitt.* 1935, 260. A. M.

DRUSUS (4) JULIUS CAESAR (c. 13 B.C.–A.D. 23), the son of Tiberius (later Emperor) and Vipsania. He married Claudia Livia (Livilla), sister of Germanicus. He was successful in suppressing the mutiny of the Pannonian legions after Augustus' death, was consul in A.D. 15, and commanded in Illyricum A.D. 17–20, celebrating a triumph on his return to Rome. He was consul again in 21, was given the *tribunicia potestas*—and therefore indicated as Tiberius' prospective successor—in 22,

but died in the next year, poisoned—it was later suspected—by his wife, who had been seduced by Sejanus. He was popular, though dissolute and cruel, and his relations with Germanicus (q.v.) were friendly, in spite of mischief-makers. His son Tiberius Gemellus was put to death by the Emperor Gaius; his last-known male descendant (through his daughter Julia) was Rubellius Plautus, who was murdered by Nero's orders in 62.

R. S. Rogers, *Studies in the reign of Tiberius* (1943). J. P. B.

DRUSUS (5) JULIUS CAESAR (A.D. 7–33), as second of the surviving sons of Germanicus and Agrippina, was regarded, after the deaths of his father in 19 and of Drusus, son of Tiberius, in 23, as a likely successor to Tiberius after his elder brother Nero. Sejanus secured his arrest in 30 (a year after Agrippina and Nero were arrested), and he died, imprisoned in the palace, in 33.
J. P. B.

DRYOPE, in mythology, daughter of Dryops (q.v.). Apollo possessed her by a trick and she had by him a son, Amphissus, who became king of the city so called. Her mortal husband was Andraemon, son of Oxylus. The nymphs, who had long been her playfellows, finally carried her off and made a spring and a poplar appear where she had been; she became the nymph of the spring, and her son built a sanctuary for the nymphs. So far Nicander in Ant. Lib. 32. Ovid, *Met.* 9. 330 ff., says that while suckling Amphissus she wanted flowers for him to play with and by mishap plucked lotus-flowers, which were the nymph Lotis transformed. The plant trembled and bled, and when Dryope tried to run away she turned into a lotus-tree. H. J. R.

DRYOPS, eponym of the Dryopes; his parentage is variously given, and the history of his people, allegedly Pelasgian, i.e. pre-Hellenic, obscure, but they are stated to have emigrated widely (from the Spercheius valley to Parnassus, the Argolid, Arcadia, etc.); hence perhaps the differing stories which make him the son of gods or men belonging to several of these regions.

Weizsäcker in Roscher's *Lexikon*, s.v. Cf. DRYOPE. H. J. R.

DUCETIUS, native Sicel leader who after the fall of the Syracusan tyrants (460 B.C.), inspired by his knowledge of Greek political life, sought to accomplish a federation of the Sicels and to subdue the Sicilian Greeks. He seems to have formed a great power with its centre in the new town of Palici. First allied to Syracuse, he then became hostile to the Greeks, and was beaten by Syracusans and Acragantines (450). Deserted by his own friends, he appeared in Syracuse as a suppliant, was pardoned and sent to Corinth. Some years later, however, during a war between Syracuse and Acragas he returned and founded a colony of Sicels and Greeks at Cale Acte. While preparing to re-establish his leadership he suddenly died (c. 440), and the Sicels soon after abandoned all resistance.

Diod. 11. 78, 88 ff.; 12. 8. 29; Hackforth, *CAH* v. 155 ff. V. E.

DUILIUS, GAIUS, consul (260 B.C.), censor (258), and *dictator com. hab. caus.* (231). As commander of Rome's newly created fleet Duilius liberated Segesta and defeated the Carthaginian fleet off Mylae in Sicily, thanks largely to the adoption of the *corvus* (260). He celebrated the first naval triumph. In the Forum a column (*columna rostrata*) was erected, ornamented with the bronze beaks (*rostra*) of the captured vessels with a laudatory inscription, of which a copy (or restoration) of Imperial times exists (Dessau, *ILS* i. 65. Cf. a briefer elogium, ibid. 55). Duilius was escorted through Rome by night with torches and music, a Greek rather than Roman honour. From the booty of Mylae he built a temple to Janus in the Forum Holitorium. H. H. S.

DUMNORIX, brother of Divitiacus (q.v. 1) and leader of the anti-Roman party among the Aedui. He conspired in 61 B.C. with Orgetorix, the Helvetian. He acted against Caesar, who only spared him at Divitiacus' request. Ordered in 54 to accompany Caesar to Britain, he refused but was cut down in attempting to escape.

Caesar, *BGal*. 1. 3. 9; 18-20; 5. 6-7.　　　C. E. S.

DUOVIRI NAVALES. First chosen by the Roman people in 311 B.C., after the annexation of Campania (Livy 9. 30. 4), the *duoviri navales* 'for repairing and equipping the fleet' were thereafter elected or appointed, apparently at irregular intervals as need arose, until *c.* 150 B.C. This post was created for the defence of the Italian coasts; it played no part in Rome's great wars, for the ordinary squadron of a *duovir navalis* comprised only ten warships (Livy 40. 18. 7-8).　　　C. G. S.

DUOVIRI PRAETORES, IURE DICUNDO, QUINQUENNALES, see COLONIZATION, ROMAN, paras. 1 and 3.

DURA, see EUROPUS.

DURIS (1), potter and vase painter in Athens, working 510-465 B.C. Known from one potter's and thirty-two painter's signatures. Painted red-figure cups, etc., including ὅπλων κρίσις (Vienne), Eos and Memnon (Paris). A fine but slightly mannered artist, who continues into the early classical period.

Beazley, *A.V.* 199; id. *Attic White Lekythoi* (1938), 12.　T. B. L. W.

DURIS (2) (*c.* 340-*c.* 260 B.C.), son of Scaeus (Paus. 6. 13. 5), tyrant of Samos, historian and critic, a pupil of Theophrastus.

WORKS: (1) Various writings on literature, music, and painting, anecdotal in character. (2) *Samian Chronicle*, 2 books mentioned. (3) *Histories* ('Ἱστορίαι or Μακεδονικά (Ath.); 'Ελληνικά (Diog. Laert.)): at least 23 books, becoming increasingly fuller, and covering from 370 to *c.* 280. (4) *History of Agathocles*: four books cited (excerpts, Diod. Sic. bks. 19-21). D.'s historical influence was small: he aimed at sensationalism in style and matter.

FGrH ii A 76.　　　F. W. W.

DUX, a title sometimes given during the third century A.D. to an officer performing duties above his rank (e.g. *primipili* as *duces legionum*). After the separation of civil and military authority by Diocletian, the command of the provincial armies was given to equestrian *duces*. In the Constantinian army they continued to serve as generals of the frontier armies with the titles of *dux provinciae* or *dux limitis*. Sometimes they received the honorary rank of *Comes* (*Not. Dign. Or.* xxxi-xlii).

R. Grosse, *Römische Militärgeschichte*, 8-11; 152-80. H. M. D. P.

DYEING. Of the fabric arts dyeing was the most commercialized and Tyre remained through the whole period of classical history the chief centre of the dyeing industry. The dyestuffs were derived either from vegetable substances such as orchilla, saffron, reseda, madder-root, and gall nuts, or from small living creatures. Scarlet, for example, came from the *coccus*, a grub found on the bark of the ilex tree; purple from the shell-fish *purpura*, *murex* (*see* PURPLE). In Greece and early Rome dyeing was comparatively simple, but under the Roman Empire it became one of the great luxury trades, and enormous sums were squandered on red, purple, and violet dyes.

H. Blümner, *Technologie der Griechen und Römer²* i. 225 ff.　　　F. A. W.

DYMANES, see DORIANS.

DYRRHACHIUM (modern *Durazzo*), originally the name of the headland under which the city of Epidamnus was situated, became the name of the town itself *c.* 300 B.C. (it first appears on coins of the 5th c.). The city passed successively through the hands of Cassander and Pyrrhus. In 229 it was besieged by the Illyrians, but was delivered and occupied by a Roman force. It served, together with Apollonia (q.v.), as a base for the Roman armies in Greece and the Balkan lands, and in 148 became the terminal point of the northern fork of the Via Egnatia (q.v.). In 48 Pompey made Dyrrhachium into his main base on the Adriatic, and he beat off an attack by Caesar on his entrenched camp nearby. After the battle of Actium Octavian drafted evicted partisans of Antony from Italy to Dyrrhachium.

Caesar, *BCiv.* 3. 41-72.　　　M. C.

E

EBURACUM ('Εβόρακον, Ptol. *Geogr.* 2. 3. 10; 8. 3. 7; Eboraci, *Cod. Iustinian.* 3. 32. 1; S.H.A. *Severus* 19, etc.; *JRS* xi. 102; *CIL* vii. 248; Eburacum, *It. Ant.* 466. 1, etc.; *Eboracen(sis)*, *JRS* xi. 102; *Ebur(acenses)*, *Eph. Epigr.* iii, p. 123), modern *York* on the Ouse. Here, on the east river-bank, lay the fortress of Legio IX Hispana, founded during the campaigns of Cerialis in A.D. 71-4, and rebuilt by Agricola *c.* 79 and under Trajan in 108 (*CIL* vii. 241). In 122 Legio VI Victrix replaced the Ninth. The fortress was rebuilt after destruction by the Maeatae (a tribe from Scotland) in 197 and again after Pictish invasions a century later. It was the seat of the northern command and capital of Lower Britain (*CIL* xiii. 3162); Severus and Constantius I died there. The *canabae*, west of the Ouse, became a *colonia* by the third century, with trade connexions extending to Bordeaux (*CIL* vii. 248; *Eph. Epigr.* iii, p. 123; *JRS* xi. 102), and a bishopric before A.D. 314.

S. N. Miller, *JRS* xv. 176; xviii. 61; S. Wellbeloved, *Eburacum* (1842).　　　I. A. R.

ECBATANA (*Agbatana*, mod. *Hamadan*) in northern Media, on the Iranian plateau. Traditionally founded by Deioces (Hdt. 1. 98) as the capital city of the Median

Empire, it became the summer capital of the Achaemenid Empire, and like Susa and Babylon a royal residence (Strabo 11. 522-4; Xen. *Cyr.* 8. 6. 22). Alexander captured Ecbatana in 330 B.C. and plundered a vast sum from the treasury (Strabo 15. 731). It remained a royal residence in Parthian times. The site has not yet been systematically excavated; the palace and fortifications are described by Herodotus (1. 98), by Polybius (10. 27. 6 ff.), and others.　　　M. S. D.

ECCLESIA (ἐκκλησία, in some States ἁλιαία, ἀγορά, ἀπέλλα), the meeting of citizens summoned as of right (ἔκκλητοι); the ultimate sovereign power in constitutional States, whether monarchy, oligarchy, or democracy. In a democracy all adult males who were citizens by birth were members; in an oligarchy membership might be restricted to those possessed of a certain standard of wealth or of a particular birth qualification. In a democracy the Ecclesia not only elected and dismissed the magistrates (such as were not chosen by lot) but controlled their activities, and those of the council; it dealt with all political matters, administrative (as the conduct of wars), legislative (*see* NOMOTHETAI), financial, and, in certain State cases, judicial (*see* EISANGELIA). In an oligarchy or a monarchy the Ecclesia was more restricted: it decided alliances, war and peace, and (generally) questions affecting the life or status of a fellow-citizen, and elected magistrates; but the magistrates or the council had a greater sphere of activity unimpeded by the Ecclesia, and in practice they were better able to control its proceedings.

2. At Athens the summoning of the Ecclesia and the preparation of its agenda was the duty of the Boule (q.v.); but the Boule was by law compelled to summon it four times in each prytany (see PRYTANIS), and could summon it at other times if it thought fit or if the *strategi* demanded it. The Ecclesia could discuss nothing without previous consideration by the Boule; but it could order the Boule to bring a matter before it at its next meeting, and any amendment to a proposal by the Boule could be discussed. The agenda were fixed beforehand; and in times of war proposals by the *strategi* had a certain precedence. The president of the Ecclesia was a particular *bouleutes* for the day (see PRYTANIS, PROEDROI) —no one ever presided more than once in his life; the *prytaneis* or *proedroi* were responsible for the orderly conduct of the meeting. Any citizen might speak in debate and initiate amendments or administrative motions—magistrates had no privilege. Ambassadors and heralds of foreign States were given permission to address the Ecclesia directly. Voting was normally by show of hands, sometimes it was secret (e.g. in ostracism, q.v.); a simple majority decided the issue, but when the rights of an individual citizen were affected, a quorum of 6,000 votes was necessary (see ADEIA).

3. What proportion of the citizens on the average attended the Ecclesia we do not know: 6,000 was perhaps one-seventh of the total in 431, about one-quarter a hundred years later; but it was a traditional number, fixed when the population was lower. The oligarchs in 411 asserted that there were never as many as 5,000 at a meeting (Thuc. 8. 72. 1), but that was a party statement, and the circumstances were abnormal. After the war, when the masses were impoverished, payment to induce attendance was introduced, at first one obol, but by 327 it had risen to six obols, and nine for one meeting each prytany.

The Agora was the meeting-place in many cities, (hence ἀγορεύειν = to speak in the Ecclesia); at Athens it was changed to the larger area of the Pnyx hill; from the fourth century meetings were held in the theatre of Dionysus, and sometimes also in Piraeus.

Aristotle, *Ath. Pol.*, passim. A. W. G.

ECDELUS, see DEMOPHANES.

ECHECRATES of Phlius (fl. *c.*'367 B.C.), pupil of Archytas and Eurytus, was one of the last members of the Pythagorean school, and survived to the time of Aristoxenus. In Plato's *Phaedo*, Phaedo recites to Echecrates, apparently in the Pythagorean συνέδριον at Phlius, the account of Socrates' last discourses and death. Plato is said to have visited Echecrates at Locri.

Testimonia in Diels, *Vorsokr.*⁵ i. 443. PW v. 1910. W. D. R.

ECHECRATIDAE, see PHARSALUS.

ECHIDNA, i.e. 'Snake' in mythology, a monster, child either of Phorcys and Ceto or of Chrysaor and Callirhoë daughter of Oceanus (Hesiod, *Theog.* 295 ff., where it is not clear which parents are meant). She was half-woman, half-serpent, mated with Typhon (q.v.), and bore Orthus (Geryon's hound), Cerberus, and the Hydra (see HERACLES), the Chimaera (q.v.), and, by Orthus, the Sphinx and the Nemean lion. H. J. R.

ECHION, ('Εχίων, 'snake-man'), (1) one of the surviving Sparti, see CADMUS; he married Agave and begat

Pentheus (q.v.). (2) Son of Hermes and Antianeira, daughter of Menetus. He and his twin brother Erytus joined the Argonauts (q.v.; Ap. Rhod. 1. 51 ff.). Their home was Pangaeon (Pind. *Pyth.* 4. 180) or Alope (Apollonius). They joined the Calydonian boar-hunt (Ov. *Met.* 8. 311). H. J. R.

ECHO ('Ηχώ). There are two mythological explanations of echoes, neither very early. (*a*) Echo was a nymph vainly loved by Pan, who finally sent the shepherds mad and they tore her in pieces; but Earth hid the fragments, which still can sing and imitate other sounds (Longus 3. 23). (*b*) See NARCISSUS (1). H. J. R.

ECLECTICISM denotes the attitude of selecting doctrines from different systems of philosophy. It began in the second century B.C., when the struggle between the great philosophical schools had lost its importance in favour of principles common to them all. Eclecticism was anticipated to some extent by the scepticism of Carneades, who criticized all systems on the same level. Two generations later the Academic Antiochus of Ascalon maintained that there was no real difference between the old doctrines of the Academy, the Peripatos, and the Stoa. Panaetius and Posidonius erected systems on the Stoic basis, which were meant to incorporate valuable parts of Platonic and Aristotelian teaching and to unite them in a new entity. The greatest example of systematized eclecticism in this sense is Neoplatonism, which contains and amalgamates in itself essential parts of the earlier systems.

In a different sense the term Eclectic might be applied to Roman philosophers like Cicero or Seneca who selected ideas from different Greek schools and tried to apply them to Roman needs.

The term has often been used in modern histories of ancient philosophy, especially by Zeller, *A History of Eclecticism in Greek Philosophy* (Engl. Transl. 1883). K. O. B.

ECLOGA (ἐκλογή), originally a selection, and so sometimes a fine passage from a work (Varro ap. Charisium p. 120. 28 K.: cf. Cicero's *eclogarii*, *Att.* 16. 2. 6; equivalent to his ἄνθη, ibid. 11. 1). *Eclogae* is common in the wide sense of *brevia poemata* (schol. Cruq. Hor. *Sat.* 2. 1). Suetonius (*Vit. Hor.*) calls Hor. *Epist.* 2. 1 an *ecloga*, and grammarians gave the name to the *Epodes*. Pliny, *Ep.* 4. 14. 9, thinks it suitable for his own sportive hendecasyllabics; Statius (*Silv.* prefaces to bks. 3 and 4) calls some of his *Silvae* by the term, and Ausonius his poem *Cupido cruci adfixus*. Its most famous application is to Virgil's *Bucolics*. It may not be Virgil's own title, though it has some MS. authority, and Suetonius seems to know it when recording certain *Antibucolica* (*Vit. Verg.*). Applied to the pastorals of Calpurnius and Nemesianus (see PASTORAL POETRY, LATIN), it was perpetuated in Carolingian and Renaissance usage.

See G. Knaack, *PW* v (1905), s.v. J. W. D.

ECONOMIC LIFE, see AGRICULTURE; ARBORICULTURE; BANKS; BEE-KEEPING; COINAGE; COLONUS; COMMERCE; DOMAINS; FINANCE; INDUSTRY; INTEREST, RATE OF; LATIFUNDIA; MONEY; MONOPOLIES; OLIVE CULTURE; PASTURAGE; VITICULTURE, etc.

ECPHANTIDES, the oldest of the comic poets (so Arist. *Eth. Nic.* 1122ᵇ20). Yet he cannot have been much older than Cratinus, for both poets mention the demagogue Androcles (Schol. Ar. *Vesp.* 1187) murdered in 411 (Thuc. 8. 65. 2). His first victory fell about 457 B.C. (*IG* ii². 2325). Two titles (? Πεῖραι, *IG* ii². 3091; Σάτυροι, Ath. 3. 96c) and five fragments survive. His obscurity or dullness won him the sobriquet Καπνίας (schol. Ar. *Vesp.* 151). M. P.

ECSTASY (ἔκστασις). In classical and good Hellenistic Greek this word and the corresponding parts of ἐξίστημι describe either a pathological condition, madness or unconsciousness, or, colloquially, the state of being 'beside one's self' with anger, etc. (Liddell–Scott[9], s.vv.); Aristotle, *Mem.* 451[a]9, is a very dubious contrary instance. Later they signify a trance-state in which the soul, quitting the body, sees visions, as Acts x. 10; xxii. 17 (SS. Peter and Paul respectively have symbolic revelations). A state of this sort is clearly meant to be induced by the ritual of *PGM* iv. 475 ff.; cf. Dieterich, *Mithrasliturgie*[2], pp. 2 ff. (the magician mounts up to heaven). The loftiest application of the word is to the Neoplatonic union with deity, Plotinus, *Enn.* 6. 9. 11. Contrast ἐνθουσιασμός, in which the subject's body is possessed by a god. See further Hopfner, *Offenbarungszauber* ii, pars. 79 ff.; 102, and Fr. Pfister, *Pisciculi Franz Joseph Dölger dargebracht* (1939), 178 ff.; the word is characteristic of transcendental sects and philosophies.
                                                                            H. J. R.

ECUS (EQUUS) OCTOBER, see MARS.

EDESSA (mod. *Urfa*), capital of Osroene, favourably situated in a fertile plain, though the river Skirtos (*Kara–Kuyur*) which flowed through the city occasionally caused disastrous floods. It was founded as a colony by Seleucus I, and named after the Macedonian Edessa (Aegae). When Osroene claimed independence, traditionally in 132 B.C., it became the royal residence, and played an important part in the Romano-Parthian wars. Its sympathies were often with the Arsacids when prudence dictated compliance with Rome. Captured and sacked by L. Verus, it finally became a Roman colony (Dio Cass. 77. 12), and thereafter issued a copious coinage. Christianity reached Edessa early, and the town became the most important bishopric in Syria. It was several times besieged and once captured by the Sassanid Persians; Heraclius recovered it, but in A.D. 639 it fell to the Arabs.

A. R. Bellinger and C. B. Welles, in *Yale Class. Stud.* v (1935), 95 ff.; R. Duval, *Histoire politique, religieuse et littéraire d'Edesse* (1892); L. Hallier, *Untersuchungen über die Edessa Chronik* (1892); Jones, *Eastern Cities*, ch. 9.   M. S. D.

EDICTUM. The higher Roman magistrates (*praetores, aediles, quaestores, censores*; in the provinces the governors) had the right to proclaim by edicts legal provisions which they intended to observe in the discharge of their office (*ius edicendi*). These communications, originally oral (hence 'edicta'), were later published in the Forum; their validity was restricted to the period of the issuing magistrate's office. Legally they ceased to be binding when the magistrate left his post (normally after a year), but customarily they were reconfirmed by his successors, so that for the most part the rules laid down in the edict remained continuously valid. Among the magisterial edicts those of the *praetor urbanus* were of special importance for the development of the civil law. Apart from models of *formulae*, they granted new actions and jurisdictional and executive remedies, thus creating indirectly a mass of new rules (*ius praetorium*) to be observed by the people in order to obtain judicial protection. On the order of Hadrian the jurist Salvius (q.v.) Julianus composed a new and thoroughly revised edition of the praetorian edicts called *Edictum perpetuum* (*c.* A.D. 130). Confirmed by a *senatus consultum*, it acquired a permanent form. It was a codification of praetorian law only, and not of the whole civil law. The edict of the *aediles curules* concerning the trade in animals and slaves was perhaps annexed to it. From that time the right of the praetors to initiate new edicts was abolished. An ingenious reconstruction of Hadrian's Edict has been made by O. Lenel, *Edictum perpetuum*[3] (1927).   A. B.

EDICTUM DE MAXIMIS PRETIIS, see DIOCLETIAN, para. 7.

EDUCATION. I. In a survey of Greek and Roman education the following types may be distinguished:

1. The 'Heroic' Age (13th c. B.C.), as pictured by Homer, trained a man to be a good speaker and an effective member of the State. 'Peleus sent me forth', says Phoenix to Achilles, 'to teach you all this' (military science and political institutions) 'to be a speaker of words and a doer of deeds' (*Il.* 9. 443).

2. The education of certain Dorian States, like Crete and Sparta, emphasized rigid discipline and war-training, with a strong tendency, as in Sparta after Lycurgus, to neglect art and science.

3. Ionian education, more elastic and humane, with a lively interest in art, science, and philosophy, aimed, in its best days, at the education of the whole man. This type of training is found first in Ionic Asia Minor and then, from the sixth century B.C., at Athens. Here the Sophists developed the rhetorical tradition, imported from Sicily in the fifth century, and introduced professional studies.

4. The Hellenistic schools (Alexandria, followed by Pergamum, Antioch, Rhodes, etc.), which emphasized the intellectual side of education, continued the tendency to specialization, particularly in rhetoric, and inaugurated an age of universal scientific learning (mainly 3rd–1st cc. B.C.).

5. Meantime Rome practised her own home-made system of education from the seventh century to the middle of the third, emphasizing personal and political behaviour in accordance with ancestral practice.

6. With the advent of Greek letters came intellectual interests. The Ciceronian ideal of *humanitas* envisaged the man who combines abstract learning with sound character and avoids undue specialization. The educated Roman was now bilingual. Visiting lecturers, like Crates of Mallos, repeated the work of the Sophists at Athens.

7. The Ciceronian ideal passed into the Imperial period and influenced Quintilian, though Rhetoric now showed signs of artificiality due to specialization on form and style as opposed to content. This tendency appeared, too, in the Greek world, where Rhetoric became fashionable. But Plutarch strongly emphasized the moral aspect of education.

8. From A.D. 300 two significant changes took place: the gradual disappearance of Greek from the West, which ended the bilingual tradition of Roman schools, and the rise of Christian education, which largely took over the framework and, to some extent, the substance of the pagan system. Quintilian reappeared in the precepts of Jerome.

9. Graeco–Roman education passed into the Middle Ages and beyond. The Seven Liberal Arts of Martianus Capella (5th or, according to some, 3rd c. A.D.), resting ultimately on Varro's lost *Disciplinae*, formed the two parts of the medieval curriculum: the *Trivium* (grammar, which, as the Art of Letters, might include literature, rhetoric, and dialectic, the last ranging from bare logic to the combination of pagan and Christian philosophy that led to Scholasticism), and the *Quadrivium* (geometry, including some geography, arithmetic, astronomy, and music). As late as the seventeenth century the exercises contained in the *Rhetores Graeci* were used in the schools of Europe.

II. THE STATE AND EDUCATION.

1. In early society the child was trained to conform to the pattern of the group: only so could there be safety against hostile strangers or jealous gods. In early Rome and in Sparta laws and conventions played a large part in education. Even in Cicero's time children learned the Twelve Tables by heart. In Sparta the boy was rigorously trained to be hard and military and, if need be, cunning;

in Rome more stress was laid on moral character. In Dorian Crete we hear of common meals and troops led by a group-leader (*paidonomos*), which seems to indicate State control such as we find in Sparta after 550 B.C. But in early Rome the control lay with the *paterfamilias*: the child was educated 'in gremio matris', and the first school was not opened until the third century B.C. (*see* CARVILIUS (2)). At Athens a doubtful tradition ascribes school regulations to Solon (594 B.C.), and in the next century Herodotus mentions a school in Chios, Thucydides a school at Mycalessus in Boeotia, and Anaxagoras a school at Clazomenae.

2. The first recorded State contribution was made in 480, when the Trezenians undertook to educate refugee Athenian children at the public cost. Athenian schools up to the fourth century B.C. seem to have depended on private enterprise alone. According to the inscriptions, the first school to receive regular endowment was one in Miletus in the third century B.C., salaries at first being equivalent to sailors' pay under Pericles. Endowments eventually became widespread, and although the status of ordinary teachers was low, distinguished lecturers received relatively large sums. Hippias received about £80 from an insignificant town; on the other hand, he frequently lectured to the Spartans without wringing a single obol from them. Liberal presents sometimes replaced regular pay: Dionysius gave Plato 80 talents. At Athens the State trained youths from 18 to 20 (*see* EPHEBI), and an inscription of *c.* 350 B.C. (*SIG* 956) commends a *strategus* for attending to the education of children. In Hellenistic times the inscriptions, especially in Asia Minor, show many instances of State schools.

3. At Rome the State took more interest in education as time went on. Julius Caesar enfranchised teachers of the liberal arts; Vespasian appointed Greek and Latin professors of rhetoric (at a salary of about £850) to State-supported chairs. Trajan provided for the education of 5,000 children, and the younger Pliny endowed a school at Novum Comum. Marcus Aurelius established the first Imperial chairs at Athens. By the third century A.D. the emperors had, for the most part, assumed control of the schools. Antoninus Pius made provincial towns responsible for the upkeep of schools and gave them the right to appoint teachers under Imperial supervision. Diocletian fixed by edict the fees of all teachers. The *Codex Theodosianus* shows how completely both students and teachers came to be controlled by the emperor. Justinian dealt the death-blow to the pagan schools by expelling non-Christian teachers and forbidding pagan philosophy (A.D. 529). But academic freedom had declined ever since the control of the universities by the Ptolemies in alliance with the capitalist *bourgeoisie* in the third century B.C., an alliance that was continued by the later Roman emperors.

III. CONTENT AND METHODS

1. At Athens, as at Rome, religious and ethical ideas had a large place in elementary education. The child was initiated into State ceremonials and taught how to behave to men and gods. Plato says that parents charged the master to pay far more attention to their childrens' good behaviour than to their letters and harp-playing (*Prt.* 325d). In this respect the poet was the great teacher in the ancient world. When the boys have learned their letters 'they are furnished with works of good poets to read . . . and are made to learn them by heart' (ibid.). Hence the marked predominance of poetry in the curricula of Greek and Roman schools. Even music is to be studied for moral profit, so that children may become 'more gentle and harmonious and rhythmical'. Modesty of demeanour and self-restraint (σωφροσύνη, *continentia*) are greatly emphasized. The person of the boy was guarded by a slave (*paedagogus*), who escorted him to school and supervised his conduct.

2. In intellectual matters Athens received the torch from Ionia—the Dorian States had little to contribute—and fostered an enthusiasm for thought and knowledge. From 6 to 14 the boy attended the elementary school; from 14 to 18 the high school; and then for two years he trained as an *ephebus*. His elementary studies consisted of reading, simple arithmetic, and music—the whole being called μουσική (a word indicating connexion with the Muses or the arts inspired by them; cf. MUSEUM). For physical training, γυμναστική, he went to a *Paidotribes* with whom boys of 8 to 12 exercised in the *palaestra*, which was usually private, as distinct from the public *gymnasion* for adults. The Romans did not include these gymnastic exercises in the school curriculum; instead, they indulged in various sports on the Campus Martius. The secondary school at Athens, attended only by the richer class, concerned itself with mathematics, rhetoric, and literary studies. Grammar and metre are mentioned, and sometimes art. University or college education was supplied by the wandering Sophists and by the schools of philosophy like Plato's Academy. Plato favoured the seminar type of instruction; Isocrates the formal lecture; while Aristotle combined the two. The Sophists were objective, practical, fee-charging, versatile, vocational. Deeper search for fundamental principles was left to the philosophers, who regarded study as coextensive with life. Aristotle was Plato's student for twenty years. 'We must learn', says Seneca, who inherited this tradition of scholarship, 'as long as we lack knowledge: and that means, as long as we live.' For the State university of Alexandria *see* MUSEUM.

3. When Greek studies affected Rome (*c.* 240 B.C.) the school of the elementary teacher (*litterator*) appeared. The three R's were taught, and Horace comments on the prominence given to arithmetic by the practical Roman. After the Second Punic War came the secondary school of the *grammaticus*, whose pupils read texts aloud with careful attention to pronunciation and enunciation, and learned passages by heart. The master added a commentary (*enarratio*) on literary or philosophical points. The *Progymnasmata* of Aphthonius (4th c. A.D.) are specimens of studies preparatory to the school of the *rhetor*, which dates at Rome from the first century B.C. Here the students' tasks consisted of speeches on a given theme advocating a course of action (*suasoriae*) such as the retirement of Sulla from public life, or else debates (*controversiae*). These speeches were often marred by artificiality, a tendency that was increased by the cult of the epigram (γνώμη, *sententia*), which had always been part of rhetoric but became particularly prominent under the Empire. Works like Quintilian's *Institutio Oratoria* show how largely rhetoric bulked in education and how wide was its field.

4. The Romans were bilingual in their schools from Livius (q.v.) Andronicus until the fourth century A.D.; the Greeks were conscious monoglots. According to Petronius, Quintilian, and the younger Pliny, Greek took precedence in the Roman schools. Greek slaves were also used to escort the pupils and to talk Greek with them (hence the derivative meaning of *paedagogus*: teacher). Latin rhetors were forbidden to teach at Rome in 92 B.C. The reasons for this may have been political, but there was also the idea, based on the prestige of Greek letters, that the main object of education was to learn Greek. Greek tutors in Roman homes played an important part from the second century B.C, and many a Greek library found its way to Rome. Bilingualism undoubtedly helped to train the political imagination of the Roman and to give him an understanding of other races. This ultimately had a bearing on Roman imperialism.

5. At their best, the educators of Greece and Rome aimed at 'wholeness' and held that the educated man combined moral, intellectual, and physical excellence. At Athens an uneducated body was as much a disgrace

as an untrained mind. Plato opposed the narrowly vocational education of the lesser Sophists. Isocrates, Cicero,
and Quintilian stressed the importance of a wide education, of an attitude of mind that sees things in their
context and appreciates their relationships. They opposed the sterility into which rhetoric fell through undue
specialization. In two respects education covered too
narrow a field. (1) The education of girls was neglected
at Athens, though it received a larger place in Sparta
and in Rome. Yet women were admitted to Plato's
Academy, and there were women professors like Hypatia
at Alexandria. (2) Training in the technical arts was not
included among the *artes liberales*, i.e. those fit for a
liber or free man, as opposed to a slave. But the ideal of
humanitas remains a priceless, if neglected, legacy from
the ancient world.

K. Freeman, *Schools of Hellas* (1907); F. Winter, *Schulunterricht
auf griechischen Vasenbildern*; E. Ziebarth, *Aus dem griechischen Schulwesen*[2] (1909); H. v. Arnim, *Leben und Werke des Dion von Prusa*
(1898); U. v. Wilamowitz-Moellendorff, Appendix to *Antigonos von
Karystos* (*Philol. Untersuch.* iv (1880))—on the legal status of the
philosophic schools; P. Girard, *L'Éducation athénienne*[2] (1891);
L. Grasberger, *Erziehung und Unterricht im klassischen Altertum*
(1864–81); J. W. Walden, *The Universities of Ancient Greece* (1913).
A. Gwynn, *Roman Education* (1926); C. Barbagallo, *Lo stato e
l'istruzione pubblica nell' impero romano* (1911); C. Jullien, *Les
Professeurs de littérature à Rome* (1885); G. Rauschen, *Das griechisch-
römische Schulwesen* (1901); M. Roger, *L'Enseignement des lettres
classiques d'Ausone à Alcuin* (1905); T. J. Haarhoff, *Schools of Gaul*
(1920)—4th and 5th centuries A.D.; *The Stranger at the Gate* (1938)—
bilingualism. F. H. Cramer, 'Why did the Roman Universities
fail?' (*Harvard Educ. Rev.* ix. 2 (1939)).   T. J. H.

EETION ('Ηετίων), name of eight different mythological
persons (see Schultz in Roscher's *Lexikon*, s.v.). The
only well-known one is the father of Andromache (q.v.),
king of the Cilician city of Thebe. Achilles captured and
plundered the city, killing Eetion and his sons, but giving
him honourable burial (*Il.* 6. 414 ff.).   H. J. R.

EFFATUS (AGER, LOCUS). An augur (*see* AUGURES)
who marked out a *templum* on the ground was said
liberare effarique that space (see Servius on *Aen.* 1. 446),
that is to free it (from profane use, cf. Livy 5. 54. 7)
by the use of the proper words. But *effari* was used of
marking off land for other purposes; the ground on
which Rome (and presumably other cities regularly
founded) stood was *ager effatus* (Gellius 13. 14. 1). H. J. R.

EGERIA (etymology uncertain, whether from *egero*, cf.
infero: inferius; or connected with the gentile name
Egerius, and if the latter, whether the goddess or the
gens is prior), a goddess, probably of water, worshipped
in association with Diana (q.v.), at Aricia (Verg. *Aen.* 7.
762–3), and apparently with the Camenae (q.v.) outside
the Porta Capena (Juvenal 3. 17 and Mayor ad loc.).
Women with child sacrificed to Egeria for easy delivery
(Festus, p. 67. 25 Lindsay; Wissowa, *RK*, pp. 100, 219,
248 f.; cf. Altheim, *Griechische Götter*, 127; A. E. Gordon, *Univ. of California Publications in Classical Archaeology* ii (1934), 13 f.). She was said to have been Numa's
consort and adviser (Livy 1. 21. 3 and often); cf. NUMA.
                                                        H. J. R.

EGESTA, *see* SEGESTA.

EGG (*in ritual*). Eggs play no great part in ancient
ritual. They occur in chthonian offerings, Nilsson in
ARW xi. 530 ff. (as life-givers?); an egg is one of the
materials used for purifying the ship of Isis (Apuleius,
Met. 11. 16; not Greek ritual); but they were used for
Greek purifications also (Lucian, *Dial. Mort.* 1. 1;
Catapl. 7), including the so-called Hecate's suppers
(schol. Lucian, p. 125. 24 Rabe); probably in the Greek
instances simply as articles of food, either for the impurities to pass into so that they might be thrown away,
as food otherwise tainted might be, or as bribes to the
uncanny powers which they might eat instead of any-

thing more valuable. At meals, eggshells were smashed
or pierced to prevent sorcerers using them (Pliny, *HN*
28. 19). There was also a form of divination, ᾠοσκοπία,
by putting eggs on the fire and observing how they
sweated or burst; Orpheus was supposed to have written
on this (Kern, *Orphicorum fragmenta*, 333).   H. J. R.

EGNATIUS, GELLIUS, Samnite general who organized
the coalition of Samnites, Gauls, and Etruscans whose
defeat at Sentinum made Rome mistress of central Italy,
295 B.C. (Polyb. 2. 19; Livy 10. 21. 29). Egnatius, like
the Roman general Decius (q.v.) Mus, fell in the battle.
The suggestion that Egnatius is only a fictitious composite of two other Samnite generals, *Gellius* Statius
(captured 305) and Marius *Egnatius* (Social War hero),
is unconvincing.   E. T. S.

EGNATIUS, *see also* RUFUS.

EGYPT UNDER THE GREEKS AND ROMANS.
Egypt had been little affected by Greece before Alexander's conquest. Trade with Greece had mainly consisted
in bartering corn for silver at Naucratis, and foreign
manufactured articles rarely went up country. Greek
mercenaries were employed at times, but did not settle;
and travellers like Herodotus and Plato collected information but imparted none. Whether Alexander
formed any plans for hellenizing Egypt is unknown:
his one foundation there, Alexandria, was primarily a
seaport, and he does not seem even to have garrisoned
Memphis, the strategic centre of the lower Nile valley,
while the south was left to itself. He was formally
recognized as king at Memphis, and then passed out of
Egyptian history. If he had any scheme, it would doubtless be known to Ptolemy Soter, if to anyone; but how
far Ptolemy's organization of Egypt was his own and how
far inherited from Alexander can only be guessed.

2. The development of Alexandria as the home of a
new Graeco-Egyptian culture was begun by Soter: a
typical instance of the syncretism attempted is the conception of Sarapis built up by a committee of theologians. Ptolemais, founded to control Upper Egypt,
was more purely Greek in its organization; also reclaimed
lands in the Fayûm were given to veterans of the army,
providing a reservoir of troops and a guard for the desert
frontier. But Hellenism did not spread amongst the
natives for many decades; stray references, e.g. to
gymnasia in some provincial towns, are the only indications of Greek influence. Ptolemy Philadelphus, less
occupied with external policy than his father, could pay
more attention to the advancement of culture in Alexandria, and spent money freely in securing Greek writers
and artists; but he had to make concessions to Egyptian
ideas, e.g. by issuing a copper coinage on the local
standard to circulate alongside of the Greek silver.
Attempts to introduce Greek practices, e.g. that of Apollonius in farming, were short-lived; the recruiting of
Egyptians to be trained in a phalanx in 218 was more
significant of their recovery of position than of the growth
of Hellenism. The difference in tone between the decree
formulated by the synod of priests at Canopus in 237
and that similarly passed at Memphis in 196 shows the
revival of nationalism in religion.

3. The second century B.C. witnessed a gradual supersession of Greeks by Graeco–Egyptians in the Alexandrian official circles. In the reign of Epiphanes the last
Ptolemaic possessions outside Africa, except Cyprus,
were lost, isolating Egypt from the Greek political
world; and the Ethiopian rulers of Meroe had pushed
their frontier down to Philae. The latter probably
fostered risings in the Thebaid, and the constant dynastic
quarrels of the royal house, which started with the sons
of Epiphanes, disturbed the whole country. To these
in part the numerous concessions granted to the natives

may be ascribed, as bribes for their support; but the Egyptian element at court must also have counted for something in securing them. Polybius seemingly found no pure Greeks even at Alexandria: he described the population as Egyptians, mercenaries, and Alexandrians of mixed stock; and, as there was little to tempt fresh Greek settlers, the Graeco-Egyptians would tend to become more and more Egyptian.

4. Greek influence, in short, was never more than a veneer in the interior of Egypt under the Ptolemies. In Alexandria the Museum maintained a contact with Greek culture, particularly in philosophy, which absorbed some Egyptian elements, but it did not touch the natives; the Greek language was used officially, but the evidence of the study of Greek literature diminishes after the third century, and the native language persisted, to revive as Coptic; the Greek gods were only known in the country as synonyms for local deities, and in the artificial triad of Sarapis, Isis, and Harpocrates the latter two, who were mainly Egyptian in their attributes, were more generally worshipped than Sarapis. The royal house itself became egyptianized, in sympathies if not in blood: the monuments relating to it, especially in temples, are predominantly Egyptian; and the whole policy of government was changed accordingly in its orientation.

5. The Roman conquest of Egypt had disastrous results. Augustus did not add Egypt to the Empire of the Roman People, but treated it as a personal estate, which was exploited without any consideration for the welfare of the inhabitants. The wealth of the land had not been seriously depleted under the Ptolemies: there is little evidence of destitution, and, though the conditions of life outside the towns were primitive, they did not deteriorate. Roman rule was marked by decay for over three centuries: the revenues were spent abroad and capital was drained to Rome, land went out of cultivation, and many of the agriculturists were reduced to vagabondage. It was not till the Imperial authority grew weaker in the fourth century that there was any revival of prosperity in Egypt: then large estates of a feudal type were formed in some districts, in others monastic bodies acquired considerable properties—for both of which analogies can be found in Ptolemaic times —and contemporary documents suggest a distinct amelioration in the life of the natives. The changes in the administration of Egypt under the Roman emperors illustrate this point. Augustus probably intended to keep the existing scheme of organization in being when he conquered the country: certainly many of the Ptolemaic official titles were retained, and the functions of these officials were seemingly little altered; the chief novelty, the Prefect, might be described as a viceroy substituted for a king. But, as the machinery had to be gradually adapted to a new ideal of government, the Ptolemaic civil service lost such independence as it had possessed— for instance, the heads of the former finance department, the *dioecetes* and *idiologus*, became of executive instead of administrative rank, and the presence of an army of occupation deprived the *epistrategus* of his military powers. In the lower grades of officials, whose main duties were in the collection of revenues for the emperor, there was a steady trend towards compulsory service: many of the Ptolemaic taxes had been farmed freely, but under the Romans the posts became liturgies. The local magistrates, under various titles—gymnasiarch, *exegetes*, eutheniarch, *cosmetes*, *agoranomus*—had one common responsibility, that of making up the sum assessed upon their town, if they could not extract it from the collectors, or these from the taxpayers. Septimius Severus attempted to remedy matters by converting the bodies of magistrates into senates, presumably with the idea of increasing the local control; but as the burden on the community as a whole was not lightened, the measure did nothing to check the impoverishment of the country.

6. In Alexandria Roman rule completed the fusion of the Greek and Egyptian elements, which thereafter formed a nationalist opposition to the imperial officials; the gymnasiarchs were usually in the forefront of any popular movement. There was apparently some revival of Greek culture, as shown by the study of Greek literature, and Sarapis worship became more influential. Hadrian may have realized the possibility of improving the condition of the country, by encouraging this tendency, when he founded Antinoopolis on a Greek model; but though his foundation prospered, his experiment was not repeated, except by Septimius Severus in a summary and ill-considered fashion. Romanization was never attempted: veterans from the army settled sporadically in the country, but they were soon absorbed into the mass of the natives; Latin was hardly ever used, except in official or military documents, or studied; formal mention of the emperors was occasionally made in Egyptian style on temple walls, and Roman festivals were occasionally observed, but in neither case was there any real meaning. In Byzantine times a resident in Egypt might boast of Macedonian descent, or quote Homer; no one showed any knowledge of the existence of Rome. *See also* PTOLEMY.

BIBLIOGRAPHY

ANCIENT SOURCES. There is no connected account of any period in the history of Egypt under Greek or Roman rule, and very little first-hand evidence of value, except for passages in Polybius and the *De bello Alexandrino*. The scraps of information given by Roman writers are far from trustworthy. The important inscriptions can be found in *OGI* and *IGRom*. The papyri discovered and published during the last fifty years provide the chief material: their evidence is necessarily fragmentary, but they have revolutionized the old views on the social and economic conditions of the country.

MODERN LITERATURE. (a) General history: M. L. Strack, *Die Dynastie der Ptolemäer* (1897); A. Bouché-Leclercq, *Histoire des Lagides* (1903–7); E. R. Bevan, *History of Egypt under the Ptolemaic Dynasty* (1927); J. G. Milne, *History of Egypt under Roman Rule* (1924); W. Schubart, *Aegypten von Alexander dem Grossen bis auf Mohammed* (1922).

(b) Military: J. Lesquier, *Les Institutions militaires de l'Égypte sous les Lagides* (1911); id. *L'Armée romaine d'Égypte d'Auguste à Dioclétien* (1918).

(c) Organization: L. Mitteis und U. Wilcken, *Grundzüge und Chrestomathie der Papyruskunde* (1912); A. Stein, *Untersuchungen zur Geschichte und Verwaltung Aegyptens unter römischer Herrschaft* (1915); O. W. Reinmuth, *The Prefect of Egypt from Augustus to Diocletian* (Leipzig, 1935); V. Martin, *Les Épistratèges* (1911); E. Biedermann, *Der Βασιλικὸς γραμματεύς* (1913); P. Jouguet, *La Vie municipale dans l'Égypte romaine* (1911); B. A. van Groningen, *Le Gymnasiarque des métropoles de l'Égypte romaine* (1924); F. Oertel, *Die Liturgie* (1917).

(d) Taxation: U. Wilcken, *Ostraka aus Aegypten und Nubien* (1899); V. Martin, *La Fiscalité romaine en Égypte aux trois premiers siècles de l'Empire* (1926); S. L. Wallace, *Taxation in Egypt from Augustus to Diocletian* (1938).

(e) Social and Economic: Claire Préaux, *L'Économie royale des Lagides* (1939); M. Rostovtzeff, *Social and Economic History of the Roman Empire* (1926); id. *Social and Economic History of the Hellenistic World* (1941); A. C. Johnson, *Economic Survey of Ancient Rome—Roman Egypt* (1936); J. G. Winter, *Life and Letters in the Papyri* (1933).

(f) Religion: W. Otto, *Priester und Tempel im hellenistischen Aegypten* (1905–8).

References to numerous articles in periodicals will be found, classified, in the bibliographies to *CAH* vii, ch. 4; x, ch. 10; xi, ch. 16. The bibliography of Graeco-Roman Egypt published annually in the *Journal of Egyptian Archaeology* gives particulars of articles which have appeared since the preparation of these volumes.
                                                            J. G. M.

EGYPTIAN DEITIES. The chief deities of Egyptian origin worshipped in the Graeco-Roman world were Sarapis, Isis (qq.v.), and Harpocrates (*see* HORUS). Anubis (q.v.) appears with the group in some places and Ammon, Bubastis, and Osiris (qq.v.) at others. Temples of these deities such as the one at Delos, for instance, might contain among the 'associated gods', in addition to those mentioned, a dozen or more Egyptian, Greek, or syncretized deities. A minor deity of the group was sometimes Bes, an old, crude, comic god much beloved by the common people. The popularity of Bes, Harpocrates, and other minor members of the cult was enhanced by the influence of the pottery industry which sent out from Alexandria many statuettes, jars, jugs, and vases with representations of these deities. In the Hellenistic age most of the foundations of the cult of the Egyptian deities in the Aegean area seem to have become public cults very quickly, and most of their ceremonies and properties came under the regulation and direction of the magistrates of the city States. In connexion with many of these cults there were societies of *melanephoroi* and some system of periodic services was probably carried out. In the later period, especially in the West as, for instance, at Pompeii, the cult was probably served by a professional priesthood, and at many of the temples the old Egyptian mysteries of Osiris were celebrated. Something of the nature of these mysteries is disclosed to us by Apuleius in his *Metamorphoses* (bk. 11), and Plutarch (*Concerning Isis and Osiris*) shows how they could receive a philosophic interpretation. The cult of the Egyptian deities was one of the last great pagan worships to succumb to Christian pressure. The temple at Alexandria was destroyed about 391, but the cult lingered longer at Philae. The cult seems to have commanded strong interest among official classes in Rome during the fourth century.

A. Alföldi, *A Festival of Isis in Rome under the Christian Emperors of the Fourth Century* (Diss. Pann. ii. 7, Budapest, 1937); T. A. Brady, *The Reception of the Egyptian Cults by the Greeks* (Univ. of Missouri Studies x. 1935); F. Cumont, *Les Religions orientales dans le paganisme romain* (1929); S. Dow, 'The Egyptian Cults in Athens' (*Harv. Theol. Rev.* xxx, 1937); G. Lafaye, *Histoire du culte des divinités d'Alexandrie* (1884); J. G. Milne, 'Graeco-Egyptian Religion' (*ERE* vi, 374–84); A. D. Nock, *Conversion* (1933); P. Roussel, *Les Cultes égyptiens à Délos* (1916); J. Toutain, *Les Cultes païens dans l'empire romain* (1907–). *See also under* ISIS, SARAPIS.   Y. C. B.

EHOIAI or EOIAI, see EPIC POETRY, GREEK, para. 5, and HESIOD.

EIDYLLION, see PASTORAL POETRY, GREEK.

EILEITHYIA(E) (*Εἰλείθυια(ι)*), the goddess(es) of birth, identified by the Romans with (Juno) Lucina (q.v.). She has, or they have, no myth properly speaking, appearing simply as a subordinate figure in various stories of birth, see HERACLES, LETO. She is often identified with, or her name used as a title of, Hera, from whom she may have developed; she is identified also with Artemis (q.v.), owing to that goddess's functions in connexion with childbirth (see, for instance, Farnell, *Cults* i. 247, n. 28c; ii. 567–8, n. 41). She is also on occasion the daughter of Hera (as Pausanias 1. 18. 5 (Crete)), or the partner of Artemis (as Diod. Sic. 5. 72. 5, where she and Artemis are both daughters of Zeus). At Olympia, where she is associated in cult with Sosipolis (for whom see Farnell, *Cults* ii. 611; Nilsson, *Minoan–Mycenaean Religion*, 503, n. 2), she seems to be one of the nurse-goddesses not uncommon in Minoan cult. Her cult is widespread and she occasionally develops into a city-goddess.   H. J. R.

EINSIEDELN ECLOGUES, two incomplete Latin pastorals (87 hexameters together) first published in 1869 by Hagen from a 10th-century MS., early products of Nero's reign. In the first a competing shepherd belauds the minstrelsy (Nero's) which eclipsed that of Mantua (Virgil's); in the second the shepherd Mystes sings the return of the Golden Age. The authorship, sometimes credited to Calpurnius Siculus, remains unsolved. *See* PASTORAL POETRY, LATIN, para. 5.

Text: E. Baehrens, *PLM* iii; A. Riese, *Anthol. Lat.* nos. 725, 726; C. Giarratano (with Calp. and Nemes., 1924). Translation (with text): J. W. and A. M. Duff, *Minor Latin Poets* (Loeb, 1934). Special Study: S. Loesch, *Die Einsiedler Gedichte* (with text, facsimile, 1909) [supports Lucan's authorship, whose works present Stoic parallels to Apollo's praises, Ecl. 1. E. Groag, *PW* iii. 1379, maintains Calpurnius Piso's authorship.]   J. W. D.

EIRENAEUS (*Latine*, Minucius Pacatus), a grammarian of the Augustan age, pupil of Heliodorus the metrist, and cited by Erotian. *See also* GLOSSA (GREEK).

EIRENE, peace personified. Apart from her appearance as one of the *Horae* (Hesiod, *Theog.* 902), and a number of mentions in poetry (serious, Bacchylides, fr. 3 Jebb; Euripides, fr. 453 Nauck; semi-serious, Aristophanes, *Pax* 221 ff.), she has no mythology and little cult. The famous statue of her by Cephisodorus (see Roscher's *Lexikon* i. 1222 and the various handbooks of Greek art) is an embodiment in visible form of the poetical passages; the goddess holds on one arm the infant Plutus. At Athens, however, we hear of actual worship of her at a public festival; at the Synoikia (schol. Ar. *Pax* 1019), on Hecatombaeon 16, a sacrifice was offered to her, which the scholiast says was bloodless (perhaps a mere conclusion from the text of Aristophanes there, see Deubner, *Attische Feste*, 37 f.). It dates from the peace with Sparta in 374 (Isocrates 15. 109–11). Two or three times the name is found applied to a heroine or Bacchante (see Roscher, ibid.), but not for women till much later.   H. J. R.

EISANGELIA (*εἰσαγγελία*), in Athenian practice signified an information, but since it was largely used in cases that came before a political body, it is most conveniently rendered 'impeachment', that is to say a trial before a political body.

An impeachment could be brought before the Areopagus (in earlier times), the Boule, and the Ecclesia. The Boule might try a case at once and impose a fine within its competence, or send the case to court where a suitable penalty could be demanded. Again, the Boule might put the case on the calendar of the Ecclesia. In very unusual cases the Ecclesia might itself try the case. Otherwise it was turned over to a court.

In the so-called *εἰσαγγελτικὸς νόμος* (Hyperides 4. 7) which grew out of Solonian legislation (Arist. *Ath. Pol.* 8. 4) certain crimes are specified that had to be tried by *εἰσαγγελία*, viz. attempts to overthrow democracy, betrayal of military forces or possessions of the State, acceptance of bribes as an orator. The procedure was mandatory also against an arbitrator who had failed in his duty. The case came before the board of arbitrators. *Εἰσαγγελία* was commonly used in cases of wrongdoing that were novel and not mentioned in any criminal law. In later times the process was abused and trivial infractions of the law were thus tried.   R. J. B.

EISPHORA, the name of an extraordinary property tax in ancient Greece which is known from Aegina, Athens, Mende, Messene, Miletus, Mytilene, the Koinon of the Nesiotes, Orchomenus, Potidaea, Siphnus, Sparta, Syracuse, and the Ptolemaic Empire. It was a quantitative land tax in Mende and in Ptolemaic Egypt, a quantitative property tax in Messene, a distributable property tax in Potidaea and fourth-century Athens, and a property tax of some kind in fifth-century Athens and other States mentioned.

Pollux 8. 130—a much disputed passage which might nevertheless be trustworthy, at least in its dating—recalls a progressive *eisphora* system introduced by Solon. Thuc. 3. 19 (for 428–427 B.C.) and the (perhaps) earlier inscription *IG* i². 92 are the first certain sources for an *eisphora* in Athens.

The tax was remodelled at Athens in 378–377. The whole taxable capital in the State had to be valued (the amount of the first assessment being 5,750 talents). The taxpayers were divided into *symmoriae* which were financially nearly equal. A certain percentage of the whole assessment ($\frac{1}{100}$, $\frac{1}{50}$, $\frac{1}{12}$, etc.) had to be paid, as the necessity arose. Even fortunes exempt from liturgies (q.v.) had to be assessed for the *eisphora*. Some years after 378–377 the so-called *proeisphora* was introduced, according to which the 300 richest citizens had to pay the whole levy in advance and reimbursed themselves later on from the other taxpayers.

For bibliography see FINANCE (GREEK AND HELLENISTIC), SYMMORIA. B. A. van Groningen, *Mnemos.* lvi (1928), 395 f.; W. Schwahn, *Rh. Mus.* lxxxii (1933), 247 f.   F. M. H.

EKPHRASIS, the rhetorical description of a work of art, one of the types of *progymnasma* (rhetorical exercise, q.v.). Similar, but shorter, descriptions in verse are common in the *Anthology.* The efflorescence of the representational arts in the second century A.D. gave an impetus to this type of writing, of which Nicostratus of Macedonia (2nd c. A.D., author of an *Εἰκόνες*) is perhaps the first exponent. Lucian's *De Domo* (*Περὶ τοῦ οἴκου*) is on the same lines. In his *Imagines* (*Εἰκόνες*) the beautiful Pantheia is compared to famous works of art. The earliest extant collection is that of Philostratus (q.v. III), perhaps not descriptions of actual pictures. *See also* CALLISTRATUS (5) *and* PAULUS (2).

On the description of works of art in Greek literature, in general, see P. Friedländer, *Johannes von Gaza und Paulus Silentiarius* (1912), 1–103.   J. D. D.

ELAGABALUS (1), the Baal of Emesa in Syria. His young priest, on becoming emperor in A.D. 218 (see the following art.), carried to Rome the sacred black stone, or baetyl, of E., enshrined it on the Palatine with the Carthaginian Caelestis as its bride, and for a brief period made the 'deus invictus Sol E.' the chief deity of Rome.
F. R. W.

ELAGABALUS (2) (Roman emperor A.D. 218–22), whose real name was Bassianus, was a son of Julia Soaemias and grandson of Julia Maesa (*see* JULIA 5 and 6), and at his native Emesa was priest of the local Sun-god (Elagabalus). In his fifteenth year he was saluted Augustus under the title of M. Aurelius Antoninus (218; *see* MACRINUS). After the defeat of Macrinus he spent the winter at Nicomedia indulging with his mother in the fanatical excesses of his religion, and only reached Rome in 219. For three years the city witnessed unparalleled scenes of debauchery. Two magnificent temples were built for the Sun-god, whose midsummer festival was celebrated by his priest with a ceremonial no less ludicrous than obscene. Nor was Elagabalus merely a religious pervert; he was treacherous and extravagant without honour or responsibility. The command of the Praetorians was given to an ex-actor and the care of the food-supply to a hairdresser. Moral depravity was the passport to administrative preferment.

In alarm for her own position and the continuance of the Severan dynasty Maesa induced the Emperor to adopt his cousin Alexianus, and to entrust the secular administration to him (221). Jealousy and intrigue ensued till an opportune bribe by Mamaea, Alexianus' mother, induced the Praetorians to murder Elagabalus and his mother (222).

Herodian 5. 5–8; Dio Cassius, bk. 79; S.H.A. Parker, *Roman World,* 102–5; M. Besnier, *Histoire romaine* iv. 79–87; K. Hönn, *Quellenuntersuchungen zu den Viten des Heliogabalus und des Severus Alexander; CAH* xii, ch. 1, § 6.   H. M. D. P.

ELATEA (*Ἐλάτεια*), a Phocian town of strategic importance; commanding the routes from Phocis to Boeotia by the Cephissus valley, from Phocis to Opus on the Euboean Straits, and from Boeotia to Thermopylae over Mt. Callidromus. The most famous citizen of Elatea was Onomarchus (q.v.). Philip II of Macedon occupied it in September 339 B.C., threatening Boeotia a few miles south and Athens which lay three days' march distant; by fortifying the town he blocked all routes from Boeotia northwards. In 305 Cassander, while occupying the same position, was defeated by the Athenians under Olympiodorus (q.v.).   N. G. L. H.

ELATUS (*Ἔλατος*), 'Driver', the name of (1) a Trojan ally killed by Agamemnon (*Il.* 6. 33); (2) one of Penelope's wooers (*Od.* 22. 267); (3) the eponym of Elatea (Paus. 8. 4. 2–4); (4) a Centaur (Apollod. 2. 85); (5) a Lapith, father of Polyphemus the Argonaut (schol. Ap. Rhod. 1. 40); father of Taenarus eponym of Taenaron (ibid. 102).   H. J. R.

ELEATIC SCHOOL (*Ἐλεατικὸν ἔθνος,* Pl. *Soph.* 242d), a philosophical school founded about 540 B.C. at Elea in Lucania, by Xenophanes. The chief later members were Parmenides, Zeno, and Melissus (who fl. *c.* 440). The school seems not to have survived as a school after Melissus. Its common tenet was monism. In Xenophanes this was essentially the protest of a monotheist against polytheism. In Parmenides it was a materialistic monism, thinking of the universe as an undifferentiated sphere, denying the existence of plurality or change, and resting on reason as against the testimony of the senses. Zeno's contribution was a brilliant criticism of the paradoxes involved in a belief in plurality and change; Melissus attempted, but with much less success, to defend the theory against the rising tide of pluralism, as represented by Empedocles and Leucippus.   W. D. R.

ELECTRA (*Ἠλέκτρα,* Doric *Ἀλέκτρα*), in mythology, (1) daughter of Oceanus, wife of Thaumas, mother of Iris and the Harpyiae (q.v.; Hesiod, *Theog.* 265 ff.). (2) Daughter of Atlas, one of the Pleiads, born in Arcadia (Apollod. 3. 110), usually located on Samothrace (as Ap. Rhod. 1. 916 and schol. there); mother by Zeus of Dardanus (q.v.) and Iasion (Iasius) (schol., ibid.). (3) Daughter of Agamemnon and Clytemnestra (qq.v.). She does not appear in Epic, the first certain mention being in the *Oresteia* of Stesichorus (see Vürtheim, *Stesichoros' Fragmente und Biographie,* 46). Where Stesichorus, or his alleged predecessor Xanthus of Lydia (ibid.), found the name is quite unknown; one or the other made a bad pun on it in defiance of quantity, interpreting the Doric form as meaning 'unwedded', as from α privative+*λέκτρον.* In Tragedy she becomes one of the central figures of the story. Sophocles (*El.* 12) makes her rescue Orestes (q.v.), then a young child, from the murderers of his father. In the *Choephoroe* of Aeschylus she is unalterably hostile to her mother and Aegisthus (q.v.), welcoming her brother, joining with him in the invocation to Agamemnon's ghost, but not actively helping the killings. Her role in Sophocles is similar, but more developed. In Euripides (*El.*), she is almost a monomaniac from hate and brooding over her wrongs, helps to kill Clytemnestra, and at once goes half-mad with remorse. In his *Orestes* she appears as a desperately faithful nurse and helper to her mad brother, and shares his wild exploits throughout; ibid. 1658 and Hyg. *Fab.* 122. 4, she marries Pylades; in Hyginus (ibid. 1–3) she meets Orestes and Iphigenia at Delphi and nearly kills the latter, who she thinks has murdered him. The source of this story is unknown, see Rose ad loc. For her appearances in art, see Robert, *Bild und Lied,* 150 ff. It is fairly clear that the development of her story is due to the poets mentioned and their fellows, not to tradition.
H. J. R.

ELECTRICITY, *see* PHYSICS, para. 8.

ELECTRYON, *see* AMPHITRYON, LICYMNIUS (1).

ELEGIAC POETRY, GREEK. The Greek elegiac is a development of the epic hexameter in the direction of melic verse by adding to it a so-called 'pentameter', which consists of two 'hemiepes' verses combined into a single line in the form:

$$-\smile\smile-\smile\smile-|-\smile\smile-\smile\smile-$$

The pentameter is a single unity in so far as the final syllable of the first half must be long and hiatus is not allowed between it and the following syllable, but it reveals its construction from two separate parts by the break which is required at the end of the first half and does not allow a word to be carried from one half to the other. The word ἐλεγεῖον, first used by Critias (fr. 2. 3), is connected with ἔλεγος, and in antiquity there was a popular notion that the elegiac was in some sense a lament, the 'flebilis elegeia' of Ovid (*Am.* 3. 9. 3). This seems highly unlikely, since most early types of elegiac have no relation to laments. It is more likely that ἔλεγος is connected with some foreign word for 'flute', such as survives in Armenian *elegn-*, and that the elegiac was originally a flute-song. This is supported by the references to the flute in early elegists such as Archilochus (fr. 123 Bergk), Mimnermus (Strabo 14. 643), and Theognis (241, 533, 825, 943), and by the use of the flute for purposes for which the elegiac was used, such as military life and convivial occasions. The inventor of the elegiac is not known, and the ancients who ascribed it variously to Archilochus, Callinus, and Mimnermus may have known no more than we do. It makes its first appearance at the end of the eighth century and may have found most of its characteristic uses at an early date. It seems to have started in Ionia, but to have found its way quickly to the mainland of Greece. Its main uses may be classified. (1) Sympotic. Flute-songs were sung over the wine, and the elegiacs of Archilochus (frs. 1–13), though they belong mostly to camp-life, are of this kind. So, too, is Callinus fr. 1, as its opening words μέχρις τεῦ κατάκεισθε; show, though it is full of martial spirit. This type may be seen in all the known fragments of Mimnermus, in the collection ascribed to Theognis, in some short pieces of Anacreon (frs. 96, 100, 102), and in poets of the fifth century like Ion of Chios and Critias. To this class belong certain short poems sung in memory of dead men, like the Attic couplet on Cedon (*Scol. Att.* 23), which are sometimes mistaken for epitaphs. (2) Military. Long elegiac poems of an exhortatory kind were addressed to soldiers by Tyrtaeus, and it seems to have been his example which emboldened Solon to use the elegiac as a means for political discussion and propaganda. (3) Historical. Mimnermus told the history of Smyrna in his elegiac *Smyrneis*, Semonides that of Samos, Panyassis that of the Ionian colonization. This type may well have been a development of the first type, since Mimnermus certainly included historical pieces in his *Nanno*. (4) Different from these types was the use of the elegiac for inscribed dedications. The earliest known case comes from Perachora in the last quarter of the eighth century B.C., while examples are attributed, without certainty, to Archilochus (fr. 16) and Anacreon (frs. 107–8). It is not known why the elegiac was used for this purpose. (5) Epitaphs. The elegiac was also used in inscriptions to commemorate the dead, who were either made to speak in the first person or had something simple said about their name, home, etc. This seems to have become a popular use in the middle of the sixth century B.C., especially in Attica, and may perhaps have been derived from the commemorative elegiac. Both epitaphs and dedications were inscribed without the author's name, and though many are attributed to well-known poets, such as Simonides, the attributions are extremely uncertain. The elegiac epitaph survived for centuries and was still popular in the fourth century A.D. (6) Lament. This use seems to have existed and even to have been popular at an early date in the Peloponnese, since Echembrotus (*c.* 586 B.C.) was famous for his elegies sung to the flute and for their gloomy character (Paus. 10. 7. 4). No early examples of this kind survive, but perhaps traces of it may be seen in the epitaph on the Athenian dead of Coronea (*CQ* xxxii. 80–8), in the elegiacs of Euripides (*Andr.* 103–16), and in Plato's lines on Dion of Syracuse (fr. 6). These main types survived until the end of the fifth century, and probably till the

end of the fourth. After this the differences between them tended to be obliterated and the elegiac was put to new uses, largely because instead of being composed for a practical end it was often composed as a literary exercise. About 300 B.C. the changes were already apparent, and may perhaps be connected with the names of Anyte and Addaeus; in the next generation, that of Philetas and Asclepiades, there is no doubt about them. With these, and later, authors the elegiac is used in the following new ways: (1) Descriptive. Scenes are described, of country or town life, or even from mythology. This became more and more popular and lasted into the Byzantine age. (2) Love-poems. On the whole this type is very rare in the sixth and fifth centuries, though the second book of Theognis shows its existence. It was a department of the sympotic elegy. It was developed in intensity and intimacy by Plato, and became common at Alexandria. (3) Imitations of earlier forms, especially of dedications and epitaphs, which were often written just as literary pieces and betray themselves by their lack of exactness in giving names and their occasional confusion of real epitaphs with commemorative elegies. Along with these new forms the old forms survived and were still popular. After comparative inactivity in the fourth century the elegiac developed a new strength in the third, and was one of the forms of poetry most popular with the Alexandrians, who seem to have made its rules stricter and to have polished its technique. In the Roman period it continued its life and had a considerable flowering in the Augustan age, to which Antipater of Thessalonica, Bianor, and Euenus belong. The tradition was carried on in the first century A.D. by Antiphilus and Julius Polyaenus, and in the second by the distinguished figure of Lucian. After a century of comparative barrenness there was a considerable revival in the fourth century, when the Emperor Julian used the form and Palladas was the last distinguished pagan to express his feelings in it. Even in the sixth century, when classical Greek was a dead language, it was still used for the composition of elegiacs by such notable poets as Agathias Scholasticus, Paul the Silentiary, and Macedonius. After this outburst in the reign of Justinian it seems to have passed into disuse, though lines attributed to Cometas (*Anth. Pal.* 9. 586) may have been written as late as the reign of Constantine VII (A.D. 911–59).

Texts: E. Diehl, *Anth. Lyr. Graec.*; J. M. Edmonds, *Elegy and Iambus* (Loeb); T. Hudson Williams, *Early Greek Elegy* (1926).
Criticism: C. M. Bowra, *Early Greek Elegists* (1928).
C. M. B.

ELEGIAC POETRY, LATIN. While a few epigrams survive in the fragments of earlier writers (Ennius, Porcius Licinus, Q. Lutatius Catulus, Publilius), the first poet to use the metre with frequency is Catullus; he shows not only a great advance in poetic power and technique, but writes long elegies (66–8) as well as epigrams, while there is reason to believe that other poets of his circle (Calvus, Cinna, Cornificius) did the same. But the first Roman to write elegy on a large scale was Cornelius Gallus, in whose four books of *Amores*, of which but one line survives, the Latin love-elegy came to birth. Tibullus, Lygdamus, Propertius in his poems to Cynthia, and Ovid in his *Amores*, all follow in the footsteps of Gallus. The love-elegy finds no exact parallel in extant Greek poetry, nor is there any sure evidence for the existence of a prototype in any of the lost works of Greek elegists. It draws on many sources, Lyric, Epigram, Pastoral, and the New Comedy, is coloured throughout with illustrations drawn from Greek mythology, and (more especially in Propertius and Ovid) is strongly influenced by the schools of rhetoric. Love, however, is not the sole theme of elegy. Propertius hails Philitas and Callimachus as his masters in the learned mythological style. His aetiological poems in book 4 find their inspiration in the *Aitia* of Callimachus. The same is true of the *Fasti* of Ovid, whose *Ibis* also, the most Alexandrian of Roman elegies, has presumably some kinship with Callimachus' poem of the same name. But Ovid is also an innovator, giving a new rhetorical turn to elegy and inventing fresh types, such as the *Heroides*—brilliant rhetorical monologues, based on legendary themes, and cast in the form of letters—and as the *Ars Amatoria* and *Remedium Amoris*—cynical instructions to not too reputable lovers, shameless if witty travesties of didactic poetry, finding their germ in the New Comedy and the less respectable aspects of the love-elegy. Even his letters of exile (*Tristia* and *Epp. ex Ponto*) are in their way a novelty. Outside the ranks of the Augustan specialists in elegy stand other poets. Sulpicia's handful of elegies are genuine love-lyrics, akin rather to the epigrams of Catullus and the Greek Anthology. Virgil's elegies contained in the *Catalepton* are but slight and trivial, but his *Copa* (if it *be* his) is a gem, the most Greek of Latin elegies. To these must be added the *Nux*, the two *Elegiae in Maecenatem*, and the *Consolatio ad Liviam* (qq.v.). They have been attributed to Ovid, but their authorship is uncertain, and even their date is disputed. See, however, *Nux* in article on Ovid.

2. With Ovid's death the great age of Elegy comes to an end. The *Anthologia Latina* has preserved a number of elegies (mainly epigrams) attributed to Seneca and to Petronius. The former are of no great worth or interest, the latter are many of them charming. Martial a generation later makes free and skilful use of the epigram; he is often witty and entertaining, and occasionally has genuine charm. After him, though elegy survives, it is almost uniformly devoid of any real merit save for a very few fine poems by Claudian, occasional flashes of beauty in Ausonius, and the remarkable *Itinerarium* of Rutilius Namatianus, which, though uneven in quality and unduly rhetorical, has passages and couplets of real grandeur.

3. *The Metre.* The hexameter differs from the heroic hexameter in no respect save that it tends to be more dactylic than that of Virgil and his predecessors, and that the employment of long endings (4- or 5-syllable words) is rarer still. The pentameter in its earlier stages admits long endings (3-, 4-, or 5-syllable words) following Greek practice, though they are less common, and show a steady decrease, until in Ovid the disyllabic ending becomes the rule. Elision is rarer (after Catullus) both in the hexameter and the pentameter than in the hexameter when employed alone—and rarest of all in the last dactyl of the pentameter. Further, the couplet (unlike the Greek) is generally self-contained; and in cases where a sentence is continued through two or more couplets there is normally at least a comma at the end of the pentameter. The elegiac couplet is first found in full maturity in Tibullus. Catullus had not fully mastered the technique; it is not improbable that Cornelius Gallus largely contributed to its perfection.

PW, s.vv. 'Elegie' (Crusius), 'Epigramm' (Reitzenstein). K. F. Smith, *Tibullus* (1913), 13–29; H. E. Butler and E. A. Barber, *Propertius* (1933), xxxv–lxvi; A. L. Wheeler, *Catullus and the Traditions of Ancient Poetry* (1934) (also *CPhil.* v. 28–40; 440–50; vi. 56–77); A. A. Day, *The Origins of Latin Love-Elegy* (1938).　　H. E. B.

ELEGIAE IN MAECENATEM. Tradition ascribes to Virgil two such *Elegiae*, which in the MSS. have been wrongly made into one, but which Scaliger divided. As they were written after Maecenas' death (8 B.C.), Virgil (d. 19) cannot be the author. In the former elegy the unknown poet tells us that Lollius (either consul 21 B.C., cf. Horace, *Carm.* 4. 9. 33, or another Lollius) made him write this poem. This elegy defends Maecenas against the charge of weakness and love of ease.

The second elegy contains the farewell words of the dying Maecenas, who gives utterance to his gratitude towards his friend Augustus.

The question of their date is answered differently. By some they are dated shortly after Maecenas' death; on the strength of *El.* 1. 1–2 many ascribe to the same poet the anonymous *Consolatio ad Liviam*. Others rightly reject this on account of metre and diction, though it must be admitted that the Maecenas elegies follow the *Consolatio* in places. As both *Consolatio* and Maecenas elegies borrow from Ovid's *Metamorphoses*, *Tristia*, and *Ex Ponto* (I–III), it is probable that the Maecenas elegies were written not before A.D. 13.

BIBLIOGRAPHY

TEXTS: O.C.T. (*Appendix Vergil.* Ellis); Teubner (*Poet. Lat. min.* i, Vollmer).
COMMENTARY: J. Middendorf (diss. Marburg 1912).
TRANSLATION: J. W. and A. M. Duff (with text) *Min. Lat. Poets* (Loeb, 1934).
DATE: F. Skutsch, *PW* iv. 944 (1901, 8 B.C.); F. Lillge, *De Eleg. in Maec. quaest.* (1901, 8 B.C.); B. Axelson, *Eranos* (1930, p. 1, not before Statius); A. Witlox, *Consolatio ad Liviam*, p. xiv (1934, under Nero).
STYLE AND METRE: Th. A. A. M. Copray (diss. Nimeguen 1940, *Eleg. in M.* not by the poet of *Consol.*).　　P. J. E.

ELEMENTS. Hesiod conceived the Universe as a family of divine powers descended partly from the Void and partly from the Earth. The early Ionian cosmologists (Thales, Anaximander, Anaximenes, Heraclitus) saw it as not only originating from, but as consisting of and returning to, a single substance, which 'envelops and governs' it as the Divine. Parmenides regarded Nature as the product of the mixture in different proportions of two self-identical 'forms' (μορφαί), Light and Night, existing (like all Nature) only 'in convention', and transferred to a Daemon the world-government exercised by the Ionian ἀρχή. These 'forms' Empedocles converted into four real 'roots' (ῥιζώματα), viz. Earth, Air (αἰθήρ), Fire, Water, which are the ultimate, exclusive, and eternal constituents of the Universe. He thus founded the conception of physical elements.

For this conception Plato introduced the name στοιχεῖα, the 'letters' or 'ABC' of the book of nature (*Tht.* 201 e; *Soph.* 252b). He himself maintained that not the Empedoclean 'roots' but the geometric figures constituting them are alone genuine 'elements' (*Ti.* 48b; 54d). Aristotle (*Metaph. Δ* 3) defined and classified the usage of στοιχεῖον, embracing now, among other things, the elementary demonstrations inherent in all mathematical and logical proof (whence Euclid's '*Elements*'). The physical sense, however, prevailed, though the metaphor was forgotten; so that when St. Paul speaks of 'beggarly elements' (*Galatians* iv. 9) he refers to the natural phenomena worshipped by the superstitious. In Latin Lucretius, continuing the old image of letters for atoms, first translated στοιχεῖα by *elementa*; which term Cicero presently adopted to denote the Empedoclean 'roots'.

H. Diels, *Elementum* (1899).　　A. H. C.

ELEPHANTINE, on an island below the first cataract of the Nile, had been a military and business frontier station and a religious centre in Pharaonic times; but under the Ptolemies its religious importance was gradually transferred to the island of Philae above the cataract, and the Roman camp and customs station were at Syene, on the east bank of the river. The buildings seen by Jomard on Elephantine have nearly all been destroyed; the only interesting monument that remains is the Nilometer mentioned by Strabo. Many ostraca, chiefly customs receipts, have been found. The temples on Philae, mainly Ptolemaic and early Roman, are now submerged except at low Nile.

E. Jomard, *Description de l'Égypte, Antiquités*, ch. 3, pls. 30–7; H. G. Lyons, *Report on the Temples of Philae* (1908).　　J. G. M.

ELEPHANTS. War-elephants came to the Western world from India. Alexander's desperate battle with the 200 elephants of Porus proved their utility; and though he never used them in battle himself, they played a considerable part in the wars of his Successors. They could be deadly the *first* time, against untried infantry; but they soon lost their terrors, and the Macedonians used them primarily as a screen against cavalry, though at Raphia (217 B.C.) they led Antiochus' attack. When Indian elephants became a Seleucid monopoly, Ptolemy II and Carthage imported Indian trainers and broke in African elephants, the Ptolemies getting theirs from Ethiopia and the Red Sea hinterland, Carthage from Numidia and Mauretania. The oft-repeated story that the African was smaller and weaker than the Indian is a thoughtless literary *cliché*; the heavy weights recorded for Ptolemaic tusks are conclusive. Indians and Africans met at Raphia, and the Africans, heavily outnumbered, were defeated; but the African elephants of Carthage contributed greatly to the defeat of Regulus, and pulled Carthage through in her war with her mercenaries, even storming the mercenaries' camp (the only recorded success of elephants against a fortified position). The last important elephant battle was Magnesia in 189; they lingered among the Seleucids and in Numidia, and Juba I had some at Thapsus. The Romans first encountered elephants ('Lucanian oxen') in Pyrrhus' army, but seldom used them in battle. They frequently exhibited them in beast hunts.

S. Reinach, in Dar.-Sag., s.v. 'Elephas'; W. W. Tarn, *Hellenistic Military and Naval Developments* (1930), ch. 2. W. W. T.

ELEPHENOR, in mythology, leader of the Abantes of Euboea (*Iliad* 2. 540), killed by Agenor (4. 463–70). He is son of Chalcodon in both passages; Hyginus (*Fab.* 97. 10) says his mother was Imenarete, a dubious name. Lycophron 1034 and the schol. there make him survive the Trojan war, previous to which he had gone into exile from Euboea for accidentally killing his grandfather Abas. H. J. R.

ELEUSINIA, a word signifying games celebrated at Eleusis, never the Eleusinian Mysteries. The games were celebrated every fourth year (the second of the Olympiad) and on a lesser scale every second year. The prize was a certain quantity of grain from the Rarian field. We know also of a procession and certain sacrifices.

A. R. van der Loeff, *De ludis Eleusiniis* (1903); L. Deubner, *Attische Feste*, 91 ff. M. P. N.

ELEUSIS, the next town of Attica after Athens and Piraeus, on a land-locked bay with a rich plain, was an important prehistoric settlement, and its rich eighth- and seventh-century graves prove wide foreign contacts (J. D. P. Pendlebury, *Aegyptiaca* (1920), 79 ff.). It remained independent of Athens, with its own kings, until the seventh century (*Hymn. Hom. Cer.* 96–7; 473 ff.). The mysteries celebrated in honour of Demeter and Persephone attracted visitors from all Greece. Work of all periods is visible in their sanctuary; the small early apsidal temple was replaced under Pisistratus by the magnificent *telesterion*, a square hall with rock-cut seats like a theatre, which was rebuilt and enlarged by Ictinus. There was much building in Roman times, including the splendid Propylaea. The acropolis, held by the Thirty Tyrants in 403, was naturally strong; the walls and many houses are preserved. *See also* DEMETER, MYSTERIES.

K. Kourouniotes, *Eleusis* (Engl. Transl. 1936); F. Noack, *Eleusis* (1927). T. J. D.

ELIS, the plain of north-west Peloponnesus, famed for horse-breeding. It was occupied by a people akin in race and language to the Aetolians, coming in from the north. Their small neighbours of Pisa, Lepreum, and Triphylia long kept an uneasy independence. Their boundaries with the Arcadians of Heraea were established by treaty (Tod 5; early 6th c.?). The Eleans presided over the Olympic Games, traditionally set up in 776 B.C.; but they may not have had effective control until

two centuries later (*see* PISA). They lived a country life and had little concern with politics; a council of 90 life members formed a closed circle within the oligarchy (Arist. *Pol.* 1306ª12 ff.). They were early and loyal allies of Sparta, until in 420 Sparta championed the independence of Lepreum, whereupon Elis joined Athens and Argos; she was punished in 399 with the loss of Triphylia, which after 369 was united with Arcadia. Elis was now for a brief period a moderate democracy. In the third century the Eleians were allies of Aetolia and fought frequent wars with the Arcadians.

The town of Elis on the Peneus was built *c.* 471, and replaced Olympia as a political centre. It was an open and extensive town.

Philippson and Swoboda, *PW*, s.v. Excavations: *JÖAI* 1911, Beiblatt 97 ff.; 1913, Beibl. 145 ff.; 1915, Beibl. 61 ff. T. J. D.

ELIS, SCHOOL OF, was founded by Phaedo (q.v.; Diog. Laert. 1. 19; 2. 105; 126). Little is known of the members of the school other than its founder.

ELISSA, see DIDO.

ELOCUTIO NOVELLA, a phrase used by Fronto (q.v.) in writing to his pupil M. Aurelius expressing the modern style of Latin which he advocated. This fresh mode was a reaction against the outworn conventions of the Silver Age and an attempt to combine the virile elements of Early Latin authors with the vigorous current of contemporary speech. Gellius and Apuleius also represent the movement.

See J. Wight Duff, *Lit. Hist. Rome* (*Silver Age*), 651–2. J. W. D.

ELOGIUS, QUINTUS, Augustan writer of memoirs cited as a first-hand authority on the Vitellian family by Suetonius (*Vit.* 1).

ELYSIUM, see AFTER-LIFE.

EMANCIPATIO is the release of a *filius* or *filia familias* from family ties and the *patria potestas* by a voluntary renunciation of the *pater familias*. The *emancipatus* became hereby a person *sui iuris* and, if male, a *pater familias* even though he had not yet a family of his own. *Emancipatio* signified for him a *capitis deminutio minima* (see DEMINUTIO CAPITIS) with all its consequences. *Emancipatio* was accomplished in the classical period in the following manner: the father sold his child (subject to a *fiducia* or trust) three times by *mancipatio* to a reliable man, who then on his part released the *mancipatus* (being now with him *in mancipio*) by means of three manumissions (or, as a Latin document of *emancipatio* from the third century A.D. shows, by *remancipationes*). According to a rule of the Twelve Tables (see PATRIA POTESTAS) the father was deprived of his *potestas* over the son by the three sales. For the emancipation of a daughter and of a grandson one sale was sufficient. The post-classical period simplified the forms of *emancipatio*. The Emperor Anastasius introduced *emancipatio per rescriptum principis* when the son was absent; Justinian sanctioned this form as a general one and created moreover the form of *emancipatio* by simple declaration of the father before the magistrate.

Ancient sources: Gaius, *Inst.* 1. 132; *Inst. Iust.* 1. 12; *Dig.* 1. 7; *Cod.* 8. 48 (49). Modern literature: P. Moriaud, *La Simple famille paternelle* (1910); Cf. the republication of the Latin documents by P. M. Meyer, *Juristische Papyri* (1920) no. 9; P. Bonfante, *Corso di diritto romano* i (1925), 60 ff. A. B.

EMBATERION. The ἐμβατήριον was properly a marching-tune (Polyb. 4. 20. 12). Hence it was also a marching-song, such as the Spartans sang when under arms (Ath. 630 f.; schol. Dion. Thrax 450. 27), like the anapaests attributed to Tyrtaeus (*Carm. Pop.* 18–19; cf. Dio Chrys. 2. 59).

EMBLEMA, see MOSAIC.

EMBOLIMON, *see* AGATHON, TRAGEDY.

EMMELEIA, *see* DANCING.

EMPEDOCLES (c. 493–c. 433 B.C.; 444–441, his *floruit* ap. Diog. Laert. 8. 74, is too late), son of Meton and grandson of the Empedocles who won the horse-race at Olympia in 496, belonged to the aristocracy of Acragas in Sicily. Combining the rôles of philosopher, scientist, poet, orator, and statesman with those of mystagogue, miracle-worker, healer, and claimant to divine honours, he acquired legendary fame. Tradition associates him with Pythagoreans, and Theophrastus (ap. D.L. 8. 55) calls him a follower and imitator of Parmenides. He championed democracy at Acragas after 472, declined an offer of the kingship, was later exiled and fled to the Peloponnese, where he recited his *Purifications* at Olympia. He visited Thurii shortly after its foundation (Apollod. ap. D.L. 8. 52). The place and manner of his death, about which there are conflicting stories, are unknown. He died aged 60 (Aristotle ap. D.L. 8. 52; 74).

2. WORKS: two hexameter poems of considerable poetic merit (totalling 5,000 verses), (1) On Nature (Περὶ φύσεως), (2) Purifications (Καθαρμοί). About 350 verses of (1) and 100 of (2) are extant. Other writings are probably wrongly ascribed.

3. Empedocles' philosophy is the first pluralistic answer to Parmenides. Accepting the Eleatic contention that real being is permanent, he denies its unity and immobility. The All is a spherical *plenum*: within it four ultimate kinds or 'roots' (ῥιζώματα), fire, air, water, and earth—to which E. assigns divine names—mingle and separate under the contrary impulses of Love (Φιλία) and Strife (Νεῖκος), pictured as mobile fluids, to cause the arising and perishing of 'mortal things'. Generation and decay are nothing save the compounding (in fixed ratios) and dissolution of eternally unchanging 'elements'. E. imagines a World-cycle in which Love, the unifier of unlikes, and Strife, which divides and so joins like to like, alternately predominate. The four stages are: (i) Love controlling the Sphere, with the elements wholly mingled and Strife enveloping it on the outside; (ii) Strife passing in and Love going out; (iii) Strife victorious and the elements completely separated; (iv) Love returning and Strife withdrawing. Our world (cf. Aristotle, Gen. Corr. 334ᵃ6; Cael. 301ᵃ14) falls in period (ii): sexual generation has succeeded a phase of 'whole-natured forms' (fr. 62). A corresponding world occurs in (iv), where union in haphazard wise of limbs and organs, originating separately, produces monsters (frs. 57–61).

4. Empedocles' cosmology, described by the doxographers, begins with the separating off of the elements, first of all air and fire. His obscure astronomy mingles penetration with naivety. Two hemispheres, a bright and a dark, revolving round the spherical earth, produce day and night. The sun is the rays of the diurnal hemisphere focused back from the earth's surface. More significant are his biological theories of pores and 'effluences' and of vision, later adapted by Plato and Aristotle. He explains sense-perception on the principles of symmetry and 'like perceives like'. The blood round the heart is the organ of thought.

5. The *Purifications*, prima facie a complete contrast to the poem *On Nature*, shows E. in close relationship with the Orphic tradition in Acragas (cf. Pindar, *Ol.* 2) and raises the problem of reconciling its doctrine of transmigration with the physical teaching. But the theological and mystical flavour of the cosmological poem, and the remarkable parallels with the religious (exhibited by Cornford and Kranz), point to a possible vindication of the unity and consistency of his thought.

6. Empedocles' theory of matter is a step on the road to Atomism; and Aristotle, after criticism, incorporates

it in his own philosophy. E. was, through his disciple Gorgias, the parent of Sicilian rhetoric, and Galen calls him the founder of the Sicilian medical school. His importance in Greek thought is far-reaching.

ANCIENT SOURCES AND TEXT OF FRAGMENTS: Diels, *Vorsokr.*⁵ (Kranz, 1934–7); Ritter and Preller¹⁰ (1934).
MODERN LITERATURE. (1) General: Zeller–Nestle, *Philosophie der Griechen* i. 2⁷ (1922) (E.T. 1881); Th. Gomperz, *Greek Thinkers* i (1901); J. Burnet, *Early Greek Philosophy*⁴ (1930; translates frs.) and *Greek Philosophy Part i: Thales to Plato* (1914); L. Robin, *La Pensée grecque*² (1932); H. Cherniss, *Aristotle's Criticism of Pre-Socratic Philosophy* (U.S.A. 1935). (2) Special: J. Bidez, *La Biographie d'Empédocle* (1894); C. Millerd, *On the Interpretation of E.* (U.S.A. 1908); F. M. Cornford, *From Religion to Philosophy* (1912); E. Bignone, *Empedocle, Studio critico* (1916); W. Kranz, *Hermes* lxx (1935); PW v. 2507. A. J. D. P.

EMPHYTEUSIS. States and municipalities used to lease deserted land for cultivation at a small annual rent, *vectigal* (hence the land was called *ager vectigalis*), for a long period (hundred years) or in perpetuity. The legal position of the tenant was not much inferior to ownership: his rights were transferable by alienation or succession and enjoyed in a certain measure the same protection as ownership. An analogous practice based on similar conditions, but for much shorter terms and stronger accentuation of the owner's rights, was applied under the late Empire to imperial domains in the provinces and, later, to great private estates. From the fusion of the two institutions (the second of which was called *ius emphyteuticarium* from Greek ἐμφύτευσις) arose the *emphyteusis* invented and precisely defined by Justinian (*Cod.* 4. 66. 2–4). It was a peculiar contract, being neither a mere lease nor a purchase, which was also applied to ecclesiastical and private estates. When the holder was in arrears with the rent for three years the owner could revoke the *ius emphyteuticarium*, though the contract was valid in perpetuity. The land also returned to the owner if the holder allowed it to deteriorate or failed to pay his dues to the State.

L. Mitteis, *Zur Gesch. der Erbpacht im Altertum* (1901); G. Baviera, *Scritti giuridici* i (1909), 187 ff.; V. Arangio-Ruiz, *Istituzioni di dir. rom.*⁴ (1937), 253 ff.; F. Lanfranchi, *Studi sull' ager vectigalis* i (1938–9). A. B.

EMPORIAE (nowadays *Ampurias*), a colonial foundation of Massilia situated on the coast in north-eastern Catalonia (about 75 miles north-east of Barcelona). A tradition of unfriendly relations with the native Indigetes is related by Livy. Towards Rome Emporiae displayed an unwavering loyalty. It was the starting-point of Roman military operations in 218, in 210, in 197 B.C., and was Pompey's base against Sertorius. Caesar settled some veterans in Emporiae after the civil wars and apparently gave to the citizens Roman citizenship. Excavations (reported in *Anuari, Institut d'estudis Catalans*) have uncovered the remains of a Roman military camp, breakwater, wall, pagan temple, Christian chapel, and coins (pre-Roman to Augustus).

P. Bosch Gimpera, *Emporion* (1929). J. J. Van N.

EMPOROS, *see* COMMERCE, paras. 2 and 11.

EMPUSA, a Greek bogy-woman, appearing in fantastic forms (see Ar. *Ran.* 288 ff., the scholiast there, and the lexicographers s.v.). Later demonology took her more seriously: Philostratus (*VA* 2. 4) recommends abusing her if met, whereupon she will flee squeaking; she is an amorous fiend, like a Lamia, who will sooner or later eat her human lover (4. 25); Apollonius rescues a young man from her. H. J. R.

EMPYROMANCY, *see* DIVINATION, para. 6.

ENA, SEXTILIUS, a Spaniard from Corduba, who wrote narrative verse on events of the Augustan period (Sen. *Suas.* 6. 27).

See Baehrens, *FPR*; Morel, *FPL*.

ENCAUSTIC, the technique of painting on stone or wood with heated wax as a medium for applying colours (Plin. *HN* 35. 149). Encaustic decoration of architecture and ships preceded its use for pictures. Statues were coloured encaustically, which explains the statement that the technique was perfected by Praxiteles (q.v.); Praxiteles particularly liked those of his statues which were painted by Nicias (q.v. 2). The chief encaustic painters in Pliny's list are Polygnotus, Pamphilus, Pausias (qq.v.), Aristides (q.v. 2), and Nicias. The majority of the preserved mummy portraits (first to fourth century A.D.) are painted in encaustic on wood and show the combined use of brush and spatula for applying colours.

Overbeck, 1072, 1751, 1817; Pfuhl, 660, 796, 816, 821, 921.
T. B. L. W.

ENCOMIOLOGICUS, *see* METRE (GREEK) III (15).

ENCOMIUM (ἐγκώμιον, from κῶμος, 'revel'), originally applied by Pindar (q.v.) to the songs with which a victor was escorted home from an athletic contest; hence, any laudatory composition, whether in verse or prose. The prose form may be a serious study of a real person, e.g. the *Euagoras* of Isocrates, a sincere appreciation of the life and character of the king of Salamis; but the term more usually connotes a type of sophistical exercise in prose, often dealing with the virtues of some legendary character. We possess an *Encomium of Helen*, attributed to Gorgias, though its authenticity is very doubtful; and the lost works of Gorgias' pupil Alcidamas, 'The Praise of Death' and 'The Praise of Naïs', may be put in the same class. The best known *encomia* are those of Isocrates—the *Busiris* and the *Helen*; but these are frankly critical exercises, the former addressed to Polycrates, who had written on the same theme, the latter an answer to the *Helen* of Gorgias. Isocrates first points out the faults into which the author has fallen, and then shows how he himself would have treated the subjects. Polycrates had also written an *Encomium on Mice*; Isocrates speaks scornfully of those who write encomia of bumble-bees and salt. In a later age Lucian, in addition to a semi-serious essay, in dialogue form, on Demosthenes, let his fancy play with an *Encomium of the House-fly*. J. F. D.

ENCTESIS. Ἔγκτησις, ἔμπασις, and related words, commonly further defined by the addition of γῆς καὶ οἰκίας, are used to describe the right to own real property within a State. Since this right normally belonged only to citizens, it became the practice to make special grants of *enctesis* to foreigners, generally together with other rights and honours such as *proxenia* and even *isopoliteia*. Examples and formulas are given by W. Larfeld, *Handbuch der griechischen Epigraphik* (1902–7), i. 520 ff.; ii. 794 f. J. A. O. L.

ENCYCLIA, *see* FINANCE, GREEK, para. 6.

ENCYCLOPAEDIC LEARNING. In Greece the Sophists were the first who claimed to impart to pupils all the knowledge they might want in daily life. We are especially told of Hippias of Elis (Pl. *Hp. Mi.* 368b; Cic. *De Or.* 3. 127) that he mastered all the subjects of instruction (τέχναι), later on called by Aristotle (*Pol.* 1337ᵇ15) ἐλευθέριαι ἐπιστῆμαι, or the branches of knowledge requisite for a freeman. Among them were: astronomy, geometry, arithmetic, music, and grammar. When Quintilian (*Inst.* 1. 10. 1) speaks of 'orbis ille doctrinae quem Graeci ἐγκύκλιον παιδείαν uocant', he means the ordinary course of instruction for a pupil before taking up his special subject of study. Notwithstanding the value the Greeks attached to encyclopaedic knowledge, they never got so far as to compose an encyclopaedia.

2. It was reserved for the practical-minded Romans to lay down in a compilation the results attained by the scientific researches of the Greeks. Shortly after 184 B.C. M. Porcius Cato wrote a work for the benefit of his son on medical science, agriculture, and rhetoric, perhaps also on military science and jurisprudence.

3. Much more important was Varro's encyclopaedia, the *Disciplinae* in nine books on (i) *grammatica*, (ii) *dialectica*, (iii) *rhetorica*, (iv) *geometria*, (v) *arithmetica*, (vi) *astrologia*, (vii) *musica*, (viii) *medicina*, (ix) *architectura*. The first seven books formed the foundations for the so-called seven liberal arts, which as *trivium* (grammar, dialectic, rhetoric) and as *quadrivium* (geometry, arithmetic, astronomy, and music) were still practised in the Middle Ages.

4. During the reign of Tiberius, A. Cornelius Celsus (q.v. 2) composed an encyclopaedia named *Artes* probably containing the subjects agriculture, medicine, military science, rhetoric. Of these only the *libri medicinae* have come down to us. Pliny's *Naturalis Historia* (A.D. 77) is an encyclopaedia of nature and art. C. Suetonius Tranquillus' *Prata* was rather a collection of 'uaria et miscella et quasi confusanea doctrina' (Gellius, *Praef.* 5) than a real encyclopaedia.

5. In the fifth century the *artes liberales* were once more treated, by Martianus (q.v.) Capella between 410 and 439) in his bizarre work, *De Nuptiis Philologiae et Mercurii*. This encyclopaedia comprises, however, only the first seven *artes* dealt with by Varro. Neither is the book a strictly scientific manual, as Martianus dishes up his only half-understood learning borrowed from various sources in the shape of a Menippean satire, i.e. in prose alternated with poetry. The wedding of Mercury with Philology is the background that serves as a setting to the whole.

6. Anicius Manlius Severinus Boethius (q.v., *c.* 480–524) was so far interested in encyclopaedic learning that he made arithmetic, music, geometry, and astronomy the foundation of his purely philosophical works laid down in four text-books.

7. In the sixth century it was Flavius Magnus Aurelius Cassiodorus (q.v.) Senator who wanted to give the monks of his monastery 'Vivarium' a summary of the worldly sciences in his *Institutiones*. Therefore he laid down in seven chapters the seven liberal arts.

8. Finally mention must be made of the *Etymologiae* or *Origines* by Isidorus (q.v.) of Seville (*c.* 570–636), an encyclopaedia which, starting from etymology, treated everything briefly that seemed to him worth knowing. When at the end of the seventh century civilization on the Continent began to decline more and more, the monasteries of England offered a refuge for the study of the *artes* (Beda and Alcuin).

M. Guggenheim, *Die Stellung der liberalen Künste oder encyklischen Wissenschaften im Altertum* (1893); E. Norden, *Die antike Kunstprosa* ii (1909); 670; *PW* Suppl. vi. 1256. P. J. E.

ENDELECHIUS, Christian rhetorician and friend of Paulinus Nolensis (*c.* A.D. 395), probably identical with 'Severus Sanctus id est Endeleichus', in Pithoeus' heading (1596) of a pleasant idyll *De mortibus boum* in thirty-three lesser asclepiadean strophes (Riese's *Anthologia* no. 893). The poem, a dialogue between cowherds, recommends Christianity as an efficacious protection from cattle-plague. O. S.

ENDOWMENTS can be divided into two groups, those given to State institutions and public corporations, and the private ones. The first group was called *epidoseis* in Greece, if the givers were citizens, and was the only one permitted in Roman law. The *epidoseis*, known since the Peloponnesian War, and an important factor in town finances, were given in money or in kind (especially in corn). There was a difference between 'gifts' and *epidoseis* in Athens; the purpose of the *epidoseis* (cancellation of debts, war expenses, public buildings and roads, libraries, foundation of schools and offices, corn provision, public festivals, distribution of food, etc.) and the terms on which they were to be collected, had to be defined in a published decree.

The private endowments had very different purposes. We hear of donations to temples and synagogues, sacrifices, processions, the making of statues of gods, festivals for kings and Roman emperors, sacrifices for a dead person or care for his grave, donations and legacies to gymnasia, sports festivals, and clubs. The gifts were often in real estate (land, houses, and even villages). If the donation was intended to last for a long period or for ever, an administrative body had to be appointed and rules laid down how a given capital should be invested and how its interest should be applied.

Many precautionary measures against betrayal of trust were provided (oaths, witnesses, State control, fines and punishment, legal actions, curses, blessings, disavowal of the endowment or its transfer to another body, etc.). Several hundreds of such endowments are known to us, a symbol of the public generosity of the ancients. The economic crisis of the third century A.D. marked the approximate end of these general endowments, which were superseded by donations to the Christian Church. *See* FINANCE, GREEK AND HELLENISTIC.

O. Broneer, *Hesperia* viii (1939), 181 f.; B. Laum, *Stiftungen in der griechischen und römischen Antike* i, ii (1914); A. Kuenzi, *Epidosis* (1923). H. Volkmann, *Neue Jahrb. f. Antike* (1939), 3 f. F. M. H.

ENDYMION ('Ἐνδυμίων), in mythology, a remarkably beautiful young man, either king of Elis (Apollod. 1. 56 and others) or a Carian (Aristophanes ap. Hesych., s.v. 'Ἐνδυμίωνα); his grave was shown on Latmos (Hesych. ibid., Paus. 5. 1. 5), or at Elis (ibid.). Of several tales told of him (see v. Sybel in Roscher's *Lexikon*, s.v.) the most celebrated is that he was loved by the Moon. In the Elean version (Paus. ibid. 4) she bore him fifty daughters, evidently the fifty months of an Olympiad; usually (as Apollod., loc. cit.), he sleeps everlastingly, either because Zeus granted it to him as a boon or for some other reason.
H. J. R.

ENGYESIS, *see* MARRIAGE, LAW OF.

ENIPEUS ('Ἐνιπεύς), god of a river (in Thessaly, or Elis, schol. *Od.* 11. 238, cf. Strabo 8. 3. 32), loved by Tyro, daughter of Salmoneus (q.v.). As she wandered beside it, Poseidon took the form of the river-god and possessed her, making a wave curve over them to hide them. She bore Pelias and Neleus. H. J. R.

ENJAMBEMENT, *see* METRE, GREEK, 1.

ENNIANISTA, 'an enthusiast for Ennius', a title claimed by a reader (ἀναγνώστης) who gave public *recitationes* clamorously applauded in the theatre at Puteoli from Ennius' *Annales*. The incident, recorded by Gellius (18. 5), illustrates archaizing taste in the second century A.D. J. W. D.

ENNIUS, QUINTUS (239–169 B.C.), 'father of Roman poetry', was born at Rudiae in Calabria. Educated in Greek culture, he learned to speak Latin, Greek, and Oscan, became a centurion in the Roman army, served in Sardinia (204), and was brought by Cato (whom he taught Greek literature) to Rome, where he lived frugally on the Aventine, first by teaching Greek. Soon he was writing poetry, mostly dramatic, and became a friend of enlightened and influential Romans, especially Scipio Africanus and M. Fulvius Nobilior and his son Quintus. E. accompanied Marcus on his Aetolian campaign (189) and described it in the play *Ambracia*, being given Roman citizenship in 184 through Quintus. Acquaintance with the poets Livius, Naevius, and Plautus is not apparent, but he knew Caecilius Statius, while Pacuvius was his nephew. In 169, still poor, still producing plays, he

died of gout. E. was of a convivial nature, but his seventy years indicate no drunkard. Surviving fragments include: (i) about 550 lines from *Annals*—eighteen books of an epic which established the Greek hexameter in Latin, and described Roman history to 171 B.C. in often uncouth, often ruggedly magnificent, verse, following Homer in inspiration, verbal and descriptive details, and use of similes, but making full play with alliteration, assonance, and the resonance of Latin (*see* EPIC POETRY, LATIN). (ii) About 400 lines from at least twenty tragedies with Greek subjects and models (those asterisked being based on Euripides): *Achilles* from Aristarchus, *Ajax*, *Alcmeo*, *Alexander**, *Andromacha** (not from the extant 'Ἀνδρομάχη), *Athamas*, *Cresphontes*, *Erechtheus**, *Eumenides* based on Aeschylus' extant play, *Hectoris Lytra* (contaminated from an Aeschylean trilogy?), *Hecuba** (Euripides' extant play), *Iphigenia** (Euripides' extant 'I. ἐν Αὐλίδι), *Medea** (Euripides' extant play and his lost *M. ἐν Αἰγεῖ), *Melanippe** (ἡ σοφή), *Nemea*, *Phoenix*, *Telamo*, *Telephus**, *Thyestes*. E. freely translated, compressed, augmented, and adapted. (iii) Two *fabulae praetextatae*—*Ambracia* (see above), *Sabinae* (on the Rape of the Sabines). (iv) Lines from comedies. (v) Thirty-one lines from four or six books of *Satires* in various metres, including Greek fables and criticism of morals and politics. (vi) Hexameters and *septenarii* from *Scipio*, on Africanus' victory over Hannibal (202 B.C.). (vii) Some *Epigrams* (epitaphs). (viii) Lines (sotadics) from *Sotas*, translated apparently from the coarse poet Sotades (3rd c. B.C.). (ix) Three lines from *Protrepticum* (*Praecepta?*): Greek model. (x) Eleven lines of *Hedyphagetica* ('Delikatessen'), adapted from Archestratus, on edible sea-fish. (xi) Fourteen lines from a didactic poem *Epicharmus* on nature and the four elements. (xii) *Euhemerus* or *Sacra Historia* in septenarii (summarized by Lactantius in prose), rationalizing, after Euhemerus, old Greek mythology; chiefly about Jupiter. E. was revered by all literary Romans, as e.g. Cicero and Quintilian show. His epic influenced Lucilius and, still more, Virgil. *See* ARCHAISM; DIDACTIC POETRY, LATIN; DRAMA, para. 4.

Fragments: J. Vahlen, *Ennianae Poesis Reliquiae*[3] (1928); E. H. Warmington, *Remains of Old Latin* i (Loeb, with translation); Ethel M. Stuart, *The Annals of Q.E.* (1925); O. Ribbeck, *Scaenicae Romanorum Poesis Fragmenta*[2] (3rd ed. Teubner). Cf. Ribbeck, *Die römische Tragödie* (1875); E. Norden, *Ennius u. Vergilius*. E. H. W.

ENNODIUS, MAGNUS FELIX (A.D. 473/4–521), of Gaul, Bishop of Pavia, author of a biography of his predecessor Epiphanius, a panegyric of Theodoric (both works of historical importance), letters, model speeches, miscellaneous poems (sacred and secular), and other writings. Preoccupation with form dominates his work.

Editions: Hartel, *CSEL* (1882); Vogel, *MGH* (1885). A. H.-W.

ENOPLION, *see* METRE, GREEK, III (6).

ENYO, Greek war goddess, *see* BELLONA. Also one of the *Graiae* (q.v.).

EOIAI or **EHOIAI,** *see* EPIC POETRY, GREEK, para. 4, *and* HESIOD.

EOS ('Ἠώς, ῎Εως, *Aurora*), the dawn-goddess, a figure of mythology rather than cult. She is daughter of Hyperion and Thea (qq.v., Hesiod, *Theog.* 372); she drives over the sky in a chariot and pair (*Od.* 23. 246), the horses being Lampos and Phaethon, i.e. Shiner and Bright. In other words, she is an important luminary, but less so than the Sun with his four-horse car. Her stock epithets, especially in Homer, are ῥοδοδάκτυλος (rosy-fingered) and κροκόπεπλος (saffron-robed), with obvious reference to the colour of the sky at dawn.

For some unknown reason, she is imagined as very amorous; an aetiological myth (Apollod. 1. 27) attributes this to the jealousy of Aphrodite, because Eos had been Ares' mistress. Hence most of the stories about her consist of kidnappings of handsome men to live with her (? a euphemism for sudden and mysterious death, see E. Rohde, *Psyche*[4], index under 'Entrückung'). The oldest of these lovers, so far as our documents go, is Tithonus; she leaves his bed to shine (*Od.* 5. 1). In *Hymn. Hom. Ven.* 218 ff. she asks Zeus to make him immortal, but forgets to ask immortal youth for him; so at last he becomes helpless with old age although he talks perpetually, and she shuts him up in a bedchamber. An old, perhaps original form of the story (see J. Th. Kakridis in *Wien. Stud.* xlviii. 25–38), is that in Hellanicus (fr. 140 Jacoby), that he became a cicada, which chirps ceaselessly. Memnon (q.v. 1), was their son. A quite obscure lover is Clitus, a cousin of Amphiaraus (q.v., *Od.* 15. 250). Cephalus (q.v.) is much better known; in Ovid, *Met.* 7. 711 ff., Hyginus, *Fab.* 189. 2–3, it is Eos who suggests to him that he should try Procris' constancy. In Hyginus also (ibid. 5 ff.) Artemis gives Procris the means to be revenged on Cephalus. This opposition between the amorous and the virginal goddess might be suggested by *Od.* 5. 121 ff.; there Eos makes Orion (q.v.), her lover, and the jealousy of the gods finds expression in Artemis killing him with her arrows, an unusual detail, for she regularly kills women, not men.

In art, Eos is a common and picturesque figure, hence her occurrence in modern paintings also. H. J. R.

EPAMINONDAS (d. 362 B.C.; date of birth uncertain) was a pupil of Lysis the Pythagorean, but his early career is otherwise in doubt. Though he co-operated actively in the restoration of Theban power (379–371 B.C.), his individual part is not distinguishable till 371, when he was Boeotarch for the first time. While representing Thebes at the peace negotiations he refused to allow the Boeotian cities to be separately sworn, and consequently Agesilaus with the concurrence of Athens excluded Thebes from the treaty. Epaminondas was one of the commanders who met the invading Spartan army at Leuctra. Here he introduced the variant of a slanting attack by the left wing, which had been strengthened to the depth of fifty men (λοξὴ φάλαγξ). The crushing defeat of the Spartan army which followed made Epaminondas famous. More than a year later he invaded the Peloponnese (winter 370–369) to help the Arcadians to throw off Spartan control. When this was achieved without fighting, Epaminondas made the first recorded invasion of the Eurotas valley. He pressed home the moral advantage of this operation by establishing Messenian independence. His later invasions of the Peloponnese (369 and 367) had less effect. In 364 he decided to challenge the Athenian supremacy at sea, and led a fleet as far as Byzantium. But when war broke out again in Arcadia he commanded the Boeotians, and after a daring attempt to seize Sparta by surprise, he won an inconclusive victory at Mantinea, where he died of wounds.

The nobility of Epaminondas' character greatly impressed tradition. His political creations, independent Messenia and Arcadia, survived with somewhat different consequences than he had intended. His new strategy ended the military supremacy of Sparta and led to the innovations of Philip II and Alexander.

Plutarch's *Life* (as excerpted by Paus. **9. 13** ff.); H. Swoboda, *PW*, s.v. 'Epaminondas'. H. W. P.

EPAPHRODITUS (1), Nero's freedman and secretary, helped him to unmask the Pisonian conspiracy and accompanied him in his final flight. He was again secretary (*a libellis*) of Domitian, by whom he was killed (A.D. 95), apparently because he had helped Nero to commit suicide. Epictetus (q.v.) was his slave. He is probably not the man to whom Flavius Josephus dedicated his *contra Apionem* and *Jewish Antiquities*.

Stein, *PW* v. 2710; R. Laqueur, *Der jüdische Historiker Flavius Josephus* (1920), 23; L. A. Constans, *Mélanges d'arch.* 1914, 383. A. M.

EPAPHRODITUS (2) of Chaeronea (1st c. A.D.) in his youth was a slave of the Alexandrian scholar Archias, who became his teacher. After obtaining his freedom from the governor of Egypt, M. Mettius, he taught at Rome and acquired a large library. He died in the reign of Nerva at the age of seventy-five.

WORKS: Commentaries on Homer's *Iliad* and *Odyssey* (Steph. Byz. s.v. Λαπίθη, etc.; *EM* 165. 3, etc.), which dealt with etymology, grammar, and interpretation. Commentaries on Hesiod's *Scutum* (*Etym. Gud.* 36. 13) and Callimachus' *Aetia* (schol. Aesch. *Eum.* 2). Λέξεις, probably an etymological work (schol. Ar. *Vesp.* 352). Περὶ στοιχείων (schol. Theoc. 1. 117). J. F. L.

EPEISODIA, *see* TRAGEDY, para. **14.**

EPEIUS ('Επειός), in mythology, (1) son and successor (as king of Elis) of Endymion (q.v.; Paus. 5. 1. 4). (2) Maker, with the help of Athena, of the Wooden Horse (*Od.* 8. 493). He was son of Panopeus, a poor warrior but an excellent boxer (*Il.* 23. 664 ff.); casts the weight very badly (ibid. 839–40). In Stesichorus (*Iliu Persis*, fr. 1 Vürtheim; Athenaeus, 457a) he is water-carrier to Agamemnon and Menelaus, and Athena pities his hard toil and (presumably) inspires him. This may be local tradition or Stesichorus' invention. H. J. R.

EPHEBI (ἔφηβοι), meant in general youths who had reached the age of puberty. But in the legal and technical sense it had a different meaning. At Athens a youth who had reached the age of 18 was known as an *ephebus*. He now spent one year in military training and a further year doing garrison duty under the supervision of the State. By the third century B.C., as the number of *ephebi* fell, the period of training was reduced to one year. Six trainers were appointed by the State to conduct his physical and military and naval exercises, and his morals were supervised by a publicly appointed board. At the end of his training he was formally presented with a spear and a shield, and swore on oath that he would not bring shame on his weapons (Pollux 8. 10. 5).

His duties included attendance at public functions like feasts, processions, and the meetings of the Ecclesia, and sometimes intellectual studies. During his training he enjoyed immunity from taxes and could not be prosecuted. He wore his hair short and assumed a broad-brimmed hat (πέτασος) and short cloak (χλαμύς).

From the fourth century *ephebeia* spread through the Greek world, especially in Asia Minor; the inscriptions suggest that the length of service was generally one year, (e.g. *CIG* 3665—Cyzicus). During the Roman Empire *ephebeia* passed out of State control, though its functions continued to be of a public character. Its character became athletic, cultural, and religious rather than military, and admission depended on selection (ἔγκρισις) by the existing members.

When *ephebeia* was instituted in Athens is a vexed question. A clear use of the term in its legal sense is not found before the fourth century. Xenophon's use (*Cyr.* 1. 2. 4, etc.) is probably general and does not refer to Athens. Nevertheless many scholars believe that *ephebeia* was instituted at Athens at the beginning of the fifth century, if not earlier. T. J. H.

EPHEMERIDES (ἐφημερίδες), diaries, a term applied particularly to the Royal Journal of Alexander the Great, kept by Eumenes (q.v. 3) of Cardia and his assistant Diodotus of Erythrae. Its character has been deduced mainly from the internal evidence of a few surviving citations. It was candid, detailed, and catholic, recording, besides the personal affairs of Alexander, military and administrative memoranda. Though probably intended mainly for administrative purposes, it was almost certainly the ultimate basis of the so-called 'official tradition' concerning Alexander (q.v. 3, Bibliography, Ancient Sources), which survives in the work of Arrian (q.v.). The record began probably not later than 336 B.C.; it may even have been inherited from Philip. Its publication after Alexander's death is thought to have been in abridged form only; but this view is not supported by the citation (if genuine) of Philinus (Plut. *Mor.* 623e).

Fragments in *FGrH* ii B i, No. 117 (1927). J. Kärst, *PW*, s.v.; H. Endres, *Die offiziellen Grundlagen der Alexanderüberlieferung* (1913).   G. T. G.

EPHESIA GRAMMATA, formulae used in learned magic, see Eust. *Od.* 1864, 15. *Cf.* MAGIC, 6.

EPHESUS, a city at the mouth of the Caÿster on the west coast of Asia Minor, which rivalled and finally displaced Miletus, and owing to the silting up of both harbours has itself been displaced by Smyrna as the sea-port and emporium of the trade of the Maeander valley and of the great trade route which traverses it. Ephesus was founded by Ionian colonists under the leadership of Androclus, son of the Athenian king Codrus, a couple of miles from the holy place of the Anatolian goddess called Artemis by the Greeks, close to which was the old Anatolian township which was merged in the Greek city and gave it the character of a Graeco-Oriental community. Ephesus maintained itself against the Cimmerians and also against the Lydian kingdom until its capture by Croesus, who contributed to the construction of the first temple of Artemis and dedicated the columns fragments of which are preserved in the British Museum. Under the Persians Ephesus shared the fortunes of the other seaboard cities; it was a member of the Delian Confederacy, but revolted *c.* 415 B.C. and presently sided with Sparta. The temple was burned down on the night of the birth of Alexander the Great, under whose control the city passed in 334. The city was replanned by Lysimachus *c.* 286 and passed with the kingdom of Attalus III to the Romans in 133. It had meantime grown to a size and importance rivalled in the East only by Alexandria in Egypt and Antioch in Syria, and under the Roman Empire it was the real (though not the titular) capital of the province Asia, and the residence of the proconsul. At this time, as earlier, the Temple treasury acted as a bank, in which deposits were made by cities, kings, and private persons. Acts xix gives a vivid picture of conditions in Ephesus in the middle of the first century A.D. In the provincial reorganization of Diocletian, Ephesus became the metropolis of the reduced province of Asia. The temple and part of the city have been excavated.

Jones, *Eastern Cities* (see Index).   W. M. C.

EPHETAI (ἐφέται) were a commission of the Areopagus (q.v.), 51 in number, who were sent to sit in judgement on minor cases of homicide in the courts of the Palladium and the Delphinium, and at Phreatto. Before the State took cognizance of murder, a homicide either fled the country or took refuge in a sanctuary where he could in safety arrange to make compensation to the relatives of his victim. In later times homicides who felt that they had a reasonable excuse for their acts fled to the asylum of a temple, in whose precinct the trial was held. The common view is that regular dicasts were substituted for *ephetai* shortly after the revision of Draco's laws in 409–408 B.C. But a more attractive view is that the change was made by Pericles in the middle of the fifth century when he completed the reform of the Areopagus begun

by Ephialtes and himself. The name *ephetai* was retained long after they had become dicasts, even in such official documents as Draco's revised homicide code.

Gertrude Smith, 'Dicasts in Ephetic Courts', *CPhil.* 1924, 353 ff.; Bonner and Smith, *Administration of Justice* i (1930), 97 ff.   R. J. B.

EP(H)IALTES ('Εφιάλτης, 'Επ-), in mythology, (1) a giant; (2) one of the Aloadae (q.v.); also (3) a demon of nightmare. See Rose, *Handbook Gk. Myth.*[2] 57; 60 f.

EPHIALTES (4) (d. 462–461 B.C.), Athenian statesman. He took part apparently in the campaign of Eurymedon under Cimon (q.v.), 468 or 467 B.C. He was a fierce enemy of the nobles, personally incorruptible, and attacked many of them for their administration. He opposed the sending of help to Sparta in 462 during the helot revolt. With the help of Pericles, now beginning his political career, he carried measures stripping the Areopagus of most of its privileges, 462–1; but so great was the hatred that he had aroused that he was murdered later in the same year.   A. W. G.

EPHIALTES (5), of Trachis, is said to have shown to Xerxes the pass by which the Persians outflanked Leonidas at Thermopylae. The Delphic Amphictions set a price on his head (479 or 478), and the Spartans honoured as a hero another Trachinian who assassinated Ephialtes from personal motives (some ten years later, on his return from Thessaly, where he had taken refuge).   P. T.

EPHIPPUS (1), Middle Comedy poet, named in the Victors' List immediately before Antiphanes with one victory (*IG* ii[2]. 2325. 145). The twelve known titles include Βούσιρις: the character of the drunken Heracles attracted poets now, as in the days of Old Comedy. Ridicule is frequent (e.g. in Ναυαγός, of Plato and his school—a full-length portrait of an elegant Academician). Fr. 5 (how a fish bigger than Crete is prepared by whole States) has an obscure, but very early, reference to Celts or Gauls.

FCG iii. 322 ff.; *CAF* ii. 250 ff.   W. G. W.

EPHIPPUS (2), an Olynthian hostile to Macedonia, contemporary with Alexander, wrote a pamphlet of malicious gossip which started the legend of Alexander's excessive drinking. *See* ALEXANDER (3), Bibliography, Ancient Sources.

EPHORS ("Εφοροι, usually derived from ἐφορᾶν, but perhaps to be connected with οὖρος, 'a guardian'). Magistrates of this name existed in several Dorian States (Sparta, Thera, Heraclea Lucaniae). At Sparta they were five in number, presumably representing the five villages of the Spartan community, elected annually by the citizens, and the senior ephor gave his name to the year. Combining executive, judicial, and disciplinary powers, they profited by the scarcity of written laws, and by the fifth century B.C. they dominated the State (subject only to their rendering account to their successors). Their powers over the monarchy rested on the tradition that when the kings were at variance the ephors should decide, and on a monthly exchange of oaths with the kings, by which in return for the king's swearing to observe the laws, the ephors promised them their support. They had a general control over each king's life and conduct, could prosecute them before the Gerousia, and enforce their appearance before their own board at the third summons. Two ephors accompanied the king on campaign to watch his conduct. They negotiated with representatives of other States, and convoked and presided over the Gerousia and Apella. In the event of war they gave orders for mobilization and dispatch of the army.

Besides possessing general powers of civil jurisdiction they could depose and prosecute other magistrates. In trials before the Gerousia they both presided and executed the sentences. In disciplinary matters they enforced the Lycurgan κόσμος for the citizens, including supervision of the State education; they dealt more arbitrarily with the *perioeci*, and even more so with helots, through the *Krypteia* (q.v.). Abolished by Cleomenes III (*c.* 227 B.C.), they were revived later and survived until at least A.D. 200.

The origin of the ephorate is much disputed. Ancient writers variously ascribed it to Lycurgus, to King Theopompus (*c.* 750 B.C.), or even to a later founder. It may have been a primitive Dorian institution which was reorganized by Lycurgus (i.e. at the *synoecismus* of Sparta) and further strengthened under Theopompus.

A. M. W.

EPHORUS of Cyme (*c.* 405–330 B.C.), contemporary of Theopompus and a pupil of Isocrates. His various works included a history of Cyme (Ἐπιχώριος λόγος), a treatise on style (Περὶ λέξεως), and two books (Περὶ εὑρημάτων) which aimed at satisfying the demand for popular information on diverse topics characteristic of the period. E.'s importance rests on his universal history (Ἱστορίαι) in thirty books. Beginning with the Return of the Heracleidae on the theory that this was the first period of verifiable fact, it reached the siege of Perinthus, 341. Book 30 was added by his son Demophilus to complete the work with an account of the Sacred War. The arrangement was on a subject system (Diod. Sic. 5. 1. 4) merging later into an annalistic framework.

Our knowledge of E. largely depends on the fact that he was the chief source of Diodorus bks. 11–16, whose abridgement follows him very closely (see fr. 191). He consulted numerous authorities, correcting Herodotus by Ctesias, using a strongly biased Athenian source for the Pentecontaetia, perhaps Hellanicus or Androtion, and colouring Thucydides' account of the Peloponnesian War under the influence of fourth-century pamphleteers. He wisely preferred the Oxyrhynchus historian (q.v.) to Xenophon, and consulted Callisthenes and political pamphlets like those of Lysander and Pausanias. Although he failed in criticism of sources and was no military expert, he was, except for Xenophon, the most important historian of the fourth century. His influence lasted well into the Roman Empire. *See also* HISTORIOGRAPHY, GREEK, para. 4.

FGrH ii. 70; FHG i. 234. G. L. Barber, *The Historian Ephorus* (1935, with bibliography). G. L. B.

EPHYMNION, *see* METRE.

EPHYRE, *see* CORINTH.

EPIC, *see* DIALECTS, GREEK.

EPIC CYCLE, ἐπικὸς κύκλος, a collective name for certain epic poems, neither Homeric nor Hesiodic (cf. schol. Heph. 126. 20), composed by poets who are described as very ancient (Clem. Al. *Strom.* 1. 21. 132. 1), after the Homeric poems between *c.* 800 and *c.* 550 B.C., and later collected into a series.

2. A cycle, κύκλος, was a collected series either of documents, as the Orphic κύκλος, or of information, as the κύκλοι of Dionysius κυκλογράφος, who collected Homeric and other legends, and of Asclepiades of Tragilus, who compiled legends from tragedies only. The ἐπικὸς κύκλος was a series of epic poems, selected and arranged to make the story of Troy complete, from the union of Ouranos and Ge to the final settlement of the family of Odysseus after his death. The name is not found before the Christian era, and the collection of poems may or may not have been known to the Alexan-

drians. Aristarchus used the adverb κυκλικῶς, and Callimachus (*Epigr.* 29. 1) wrote ἐχθαίρω τὸ ποίημα τὸ κυκλικόν; but neither need refer to early 'cyclic' epic.

3. The Epic Cycle was extant in the second century A.D., as quotations show, but it was lost probably not long afterwards. Information about it is derived from notices, including inscriptions of Roman date (*EGF*, pp. 3–4) and quotations, and from an epitome of it in the *Chrestomathia* of Proclus (probably a writer of the second century A.D., not the fifth-century Neoplatonist), which is preserved in the *Bibliotheca* of Photius (O.C.T. *Homeri opera*, v. 95–109); Proclus may have depended on an earlier prose epitome, or, more probably, on the actual texts of the poems.

4. According to Proclus, the Epic Cycle included, before the *Iliad* begins, a *Theogonia*, a *Titanomachia*, and the *Cypria*; between the *Iliad* and *Odyssey*, the *Aethiopis*, the *Ilias Parva*, the *Iliu Persis*, and the *Nostoi*; and after the *Odyssey* the *Telegonia*. Also called cyclic are an early *Thebaid* and the later *Thebaid* of Antimachus of Colophon. Apparently, either the Trojan Epic Cycle included poems on the Theban legends, regarded as preliminary to the Trojan story, or there were strictly two cycles, a Theban and a Trojan. Many other epic poems existed, on subjects other than Thebes and Troy, and though they are not known to have been collected into cycles, they could be loosely included under the general conception of cyclic poetry.

5. The text of the Epic Cycle was to some extent fluid. According to available evidence, the *Ilias Parva* and the *Iliu Persis* overlapped and disagreed in details. There was an *Amphiarai Exelasis*, which may have been the same as the early *Thebais*, or a part of it, as the Τειχομαχία is part of the *Iliad* (bk. 12). The *Telegonia* was said to include a complete book by a different poet. Some of the earlier poems were at first attributed to Homer, but from the fifth century, as critical interest increased, they were attributed to other poets, with much difference of opinion, but sometimes on the evidence of local knowledge.

6. There was much in the cyclic epic which was alien from Homer's taste or from his time, especially superstitions and brutalities, probably survivals from a period before Homer, and also wider knowledge of the world, acquired subsequently to him. The poems were composed out of material such as Homer used, but without his freedom in the alteration and adaptation of it. They lacked the Homeric unity and dramatic movement (Arist. *Poet.* 23. 1459ᵃ; cf. eund. *Rh.* 3. 14. 4, 6, 1415ᵃ). But at first the earlier cyclic poems were highly valued and closely followed, as by Sophocles (Ath. 7. 277e) and Pindar (schol. Pind. *Ol.* 6. 15; *Nem.* 10. 114, etc.). In the fifth century epic was revived by Panyassis and others, partly in the cyclic tradition. Their work was admired, enthusiastically by some contemporaries, and also by later critics, but sometimes with more reserve (Suid. s.v. Πείσανδρος; Quint. *Inst.* 10. 1. 53–4; Dion. Hal. *Vett. Cens.* 2. 3; Cic. *Brut.* 51). From the fourth century, perhaps under the influence of Aristotle, the great superiority of Homer to other epic poets came to be better recognized, and eventually Cyclic Epic was read for ordered information rather than as poetry (Procl. *Epit.*). The word 'cyclic' acquired a disparaging connotation; but that is at least partly due to the banal qualities of prose compilations called κύκλοι, and of the learned poets who used them, and not wholly, if at all, to the cyclic epic. But there was certainly a tendency in these poems, shown especially in the *Telegonia*, to exploit exhausted material inartistically. Like the French poets after the great age of the *Chansons de Geste*, the Greek poets fell into a 'manie cyclique'. But the evidence is not sufficient to justify contradiction of the early Greek opinion that there was merit in some cyclic poems; and at any rate Greek epic continued to be composed, with little intermission and frequent infusion of new vitality, until the beginning of the Byzantine age.

7. The following is a list of the more important poems in hexameter verse, neither Homeric nor Hesiodic, down to the fifth century B.C.:

THE EPIC CYCLE, THE TROJAN WAR. *Theogonia*, beginning with the marriage of Ouranos and Ge with which the Epic Cycle is said to have started (Phot. *Bibl.* 319 a Bekker); there were probably several poems of this name. *Titanomachia*, by Arctinus or Eumelus (qq.v.), or anonymous (Ath. 7. 277d). *Cypria*, ? eighth century; wrongly attributed to Homer (Hdt. 2. 117); perhaps by Stasinus (q.v.); on the abduction of Helen. *Aethiopis*, eighth century; probably by Arctinus (q.v.); continuation of the *Iliad* to the quarrel for the arms of Achilles. *Ilias Parva*, ? seventh century; probably by Lesches (q.v.); continuing to the reception of the Wooden Horse into Troy. *Iliu Persis*, eighth century; probably by Arctinus (q.v.), continuing to the start of the Achaeans for home. *Nostoi*, ? seventh century; probably by Hegias or Agias of Troezen; on the homeward voyage, including the vengeance of Orestes. *Telegonia*, sixth century; by Eugammon (q.v.); continuation of the *Odyssey* to the death of Odysseus at the hands of Telegonus, and the union of Telegonus with Penelope and of Telemachus with Circe; said to have included the *Thesprotis* of Musaeus (Clem. Al. *Strom.* 6. 2. 25. 2), which may, however, have been an earlier version of the *Telegonia*.

POEMS ON THEBES WHICH MAY OR MAY NOT BELONG TO THE EPIC CYCLE. *Oedipodea*, ? eighth century; attributed to Cinaethon (q.v.); there may have been more than one poem so named. *Thebais*, eighth century; mentioned very early as by Homer (Callinus ap. Paus. 9. 9. 5); otherwise anonymous; much admired; called cyclic (Ath. 11. 465e); there were other poems so named, one by Antimachus (q.v.) of Colophon. *Amphiarai Exelasis*, attributed to Homer (Suid. s.v. Ὅμηρος); possibly identical with, or part of, the *Thebais*. *Epigoni*, ? seventh century; attributed to Homer (Hdt. 4. 32), and to Antimachus of Teos (schol. Ar. *Pax* 1270).

POEMS ON HERACLES. *Heraclea, Heracleis*; probably there were several poems so named, attributed to Cinaethon (q.v.) and others, especially Peisander (q.v.) of Cameirus. *Minyas*, on Heracles, Meleager, Thamyris, and others. *Oechaliae Halosis*, attributed to Homer and to Creophylus (Suid. s.v. Ὅμηρος; Strab. 14. 638).

POEMS ON THE ARGONAUTS. *Aegimius*, ? sixth century; attributed to Hesiod and to Cercops (Ath. 11. 503d). *Argonautica*, attributed to Epimenides (Diog. Laert. 1. 111). *Naupactia*, perhaps by Carcinus (q.v.). *Corinthiaca*, by Eumelus (q.v.).

OTHER EARLY EPIC POEMS. *Alcmaeonis, Atthis, Danais, Phocais, Phoronis, Theseis.*

POEMS OF THE EPIC REVIVAL. *Heraclea*, by Panyassis (q.v.). *Thebais*, by Antimachus of Colophon (q.v.). *Persica*, by Choerilus (q.v. 2) of Samos.

TEXTS: G. Kinkel, *Epicorum Graecorum Fragmenta*, 1877; O.C.T. *Homeri opera*, v. 93–151; F. Dübner, *Asii, Pisandri, Panyasidis, Choerili et Antimachi fragmenta* (1838).
CRITICISM: F. O. Welcker, *Der epische Cyclus oder die Homerischen Dichter*, i² (1865), ii (1849); D. B. Monro, *JHS* iv (1883), 305–34, v (1884), 1–41; U. von Wilamowitz-Moellendorff, *Homerische Untersuchungen* (1884), 328–80; R. Volkmann, *Über Homer als Dichter des epischen Kyklos* (1884); Andrew Lang, *The World of Homer* (1910), 197–221; John A. Scott, *The Unity of Homer* (U.S.A. 1921); E. Bethe, *Homer, Dichtung und Sage*, ii (1922), 371–83; T. W. Allen, *Homer, the Origins and Transmission* (1924), 51–77. *See also* EPIC POETRY.   W. F. J. K.

EPIC POETRY, GREEK. The Greek epic must originally have consisted of lays sung by bards in camp, at court, and in public gatherings. Homer depicts Achilles as singing κλέα ἀνδρῶν (*Il.* 9. 189), and his sketches of bards in the *Odyssey* show professional poets at work. These poets sing of the recent past and draw

their power from the Muse. This may mean that they improvise, and the probability is that the Greek epic, like other primitive epics, was originally improvised. The poet would learn the traditional formulae of his art and by means of these he would be able to provide the song for which he was asked and to suit its length to the conditions demanded by each occasion when he had to perform. Such lays would vary in length, though pre-Homeric poems must normally have been much shorter than the *Iliad*. For the *Iliad* shows the technique of short lays in the way in which its episodes can be detached from the whole and treated as complete unities in themselves. The bard would learn not merely formulae, but the traditional devices of his craft, such as similes, repeated lines and passages, conventional epithets, stock characters, and the like. Since he composed not to be read but to be heard, he had to concentrate on the essentials of narrative and omit irrelevant and unimportant details. In consequence epic narrative is more loosely knit than the modern novel and can more readily admit inconsistencies real and apparent.

2. Of pre-Homeric epic nothing survives. All that we have is the *Iliad* and the *Odyssey*. These presuppose a long line of predecessors in the stories which they assume their hearers to know, in the characters who are labelled with traditional epithets, in their occasionally inexact use of stock phrases. But Homer's originality may be guessed from the architectural unity which he gives to both his poems, from the life which he breathes into his characters, who are far more than tradition can ever have made them, in his moral sensibility, which is often at war with the more brutal standards of the heroic age which he describes, in the personal tastes and touches which he inserts into his similes. He seems to come at the end of a period of epic art and to sum up in himself all its characteristics. For this reason, no doubt, his works were preserved when his forerunners were forgotten, and for this reason he exerted an incalculable influence on later Greek poetry. Whether his poems were written down early or not does not affect the degree of his influence, which may be seen in all later Greek epic.

3. This influence must have appeared most obviously in the so-called Cyclic poets (*see* EPIC CYCLE). In the centuries after Homer other poets took up his stories and filled the gaps between the *Iliad* and *Odyssey* or before and after them. The *Cypria* provided a prelude to the *Iliad*, the *Aethiopis* told of the death of Achilles, the *Little Iliad* and the *Sack of Troy* of the events which ended the Trojan War, the *Returns* of the adventures of heroes other than Odysseus on their way home, and the *Telegonia* of the death of Odysseus. The scanty fragments suggest that their style belonged to the same tradition as Homer's, even if it was not directly influenced by him. Where they differed was in composition. Their authors lacked his capacity for building a single poem and fell into detached episodes. For this, and no doubt for their inferior poetic talent, they were forgotten when he was remembered.

4. Outside this Homeric cycle there were other epic cycles of which vague hints have survived. Boeotian legends were told in the *Oedipodea*, *Thebais*, and *Successors*; the *Titanomachia* told of Zeus' war against the Titans; the *Capture of Oechalia* of an episode in the life of Heracles. These poems were shorter than Homer's—the *Oedipodea* had 6,600 lines and the *Thebais* 7,000, and their chief interest is that they preserved ancient stories for later poets, lyric and tragic, to use. Of the same age but not quite of the same kind was the *Corinthiaca* of Eumelus of Corinth. Though this too dealt with the heroic age, it seems to have taken great liberties with tradition and to have falsified it in the interests of Corinthian national pride.

5. The *Theogony* and *Works and Days* of Hesiod are written in the epic metre and language and may possibly

have been influenced by Homer. The first is an attempt to clarify the confused traditions of Greek mythology, the second is a personal document about farming addressed to the poet's unsuccessful brother. Their differences from the Homeric epic are enormous, but they were written not for princes and soldiers but for farmers. They are the product of the mainland, where life was harder than in Ionia, and Hesiod has less belief in the heroic virtues than Homer had. Yet they are epic in their interest in the past, their language, their technique. Moreover, Boeotia seems to have had its own epic tradition, which was more concerned with old stories than these two poems were. For among the other poems attributed to Hesiod the collection known as the *Ehoiai* or *Catalogue of Women* seems to have told a large number of ancient tales. The only complete specimen is the *Shield of Heracles*, which is certainly later than Hesiod. It, and the other fragments, show that Hesiodic epic was more primitive than Homeric; its scope was smaller, its characterization less complete, its language less rich.

6. The Homeric text was preserved by the so-called Homeridae (q.v.) or sons of Homer, whose special task it was to recite it at festivals and public gatherings. Sometimes before beginning his recitation a bard would recite a composition of his own. Such poems, written in the epic manner, were called προοίμια or Preludes. They are known to have been composed by Terpander, who brought Homer's works to Sparta, and a collection of them survives in the book of *Homeric Hymns* (T. W. Allen, W. R. Halliday, and E. E. Sikes, 2nd ed., 1936). These poems differ considerably in date: the *Hymn to Demeter* is certainly early, the *Hymn to Pan* may be later than 500 B.C., but the collection shows how well the tradition of Homeric language was preserved and how carefully the poets modelled their own style on Homer's. These Ionian poets seem to have had a better gift for narrative than the Hesiodic school and to have concentrated less on the mere telling of a tale. They show an abundant fancy and a fine appreciation of the imaginative possibilities of their themes.

7. When the recitation of Homer became a fixed part of Athenian life in the sixth century, the composition of epic had almost ceased to be a reality in Greece. The society which produced it had ceased to exist, and its heroic standards had disappeared with the development of the city-state. But poets still attempted it. Some, like Epimenides and Onomacritus, used it as a vehicle for their new ideas about religion; others like Peisander, Panyassis, and Antimachus continued to tell the old stories. But their failure was known even to them; for Choerilus of Samos complained that the land of the Muses was now divided up and no new chariot was available to those who wished to enter the race (fr. 1). He indeed tried to find subjects for epic in more recent history and wrote about the Persian Wars, but it seems that he met with no great success. These poets realized that they could hardly use the language of Homer, and Antimachus seems to have tried to vary his style with archaic words and neologisms. But if we may judge by what the Alexandrians said of him, he succeeded merely in making himself absurd.

8. At Alexandria the epic revived, but in new conditions. It was now meant to be read, not heard; its poets aimed at precision and delicacy of language and avoided the traditional formulae; its construction was much affected by the contemporary taste for mythology, geography, picturesque scenes, and tender feelings. For their themes they went to the past, though not necessarily always to the heroic past. For while Rhianus wrote about local legends in Thessaly and Elis, his influential *Messeniaca* dealt with early Spartan history, or rather invented a whole new set of legends for it which were gravely accepted as fact by Pausanias. The only complete work of this time is the *Argonautica* of Apollonius Rhodius. Though he seems to have made use of Eumelus

and was accused of an attachment to outworn forms, he shows little of the true epic temper in his work, which is full of tender sentiment and elaborate descriptions, while his method of construction really owes more to Alexandrian Idylls than to Homer. In the third century Euphorion also wrote epic. Though he was much admired, he seems to have been a dry and dull writer, interesting more for his learning than for his powers of narrative. Epic was much disparaged by Callimachus, and popular taste seems to have turned against it. For in the later Alexandrian age and the first three centuries A.D. there is no Greek epic of interest known to us.

9. In the fourth and fifth centuries A.D. taste changed, and the epic revived. This movement, which may be regarded as a last manifestation of the pagan spirit in literature, is well known through the works of Quintus Smyrnaeus, Colluthus, and Tryphiodorus. These poets look beyond Alexandria to the early epic, especially to the Homeric cycle, on which they drew generously for their subjects. Quintus picked up the story of the *Iliad* where Homer left it and practically bridged the gap between it and the *Odyssey*. Colluthus wrote a short *Rape of Helen* in a simple style, and Tryphiodorus told again an old story in his *Capture of Troy*. Rather later than these poets are two others who pursue more original paths. Musaeus' *Hero and Leander* owes nothing to Homer either in theme or manner. It is a story of love, told with great force and feeling. The *Dionysiaca* of Nonnus is even more remarkable. In its enormous scope it tells every known adventure of Dionysus, and spares nothing to achieve an emphatic, rhetorical effect. Its language, copious and repetitive, seems to be its author's invention and to forecast a new age in literature.

Text: G. Kinkel, *Epicorum Graecorum Fragmenta* (1877), and see under the various authors mentioned.   C. M. B.

EPIC POETRY, LATIN. Of the earliest history of the Latin epic little is known. That the native Saturnian metre was adapted for narrative poetry is proved by its employment by Livius Andronicus and Cn. Naevius, but Cato's statement (fr. 118 Peter, *HRRel.*) that heroic lays were sung at Roman banquets 'apud maiores' does not prove the existence of epic poetry before the third century. L. Livius Andronicus (284–204) translated the *Odyssey* into Saturnian verse, and Cn. Naevius (c. 269–199) wrote his *Bellum Punicum* in the same metre. The scanty fragments of both display a rough vigour hampered by an unsuitable medium, and it was not until Q. Ennius (239–169), a Calabrian who obtained Roman citizenship in 184, adopted in his *Annales* the Greek hexameter as his metrical model that the history of the Latin epic really begins. The *Annales*, as the title implies, is a chronicle of the history of Rome in verse from the time of Romulus until the year 181, the first twelve books (down to 196) being published first and the remainder in probably two sections, bks. 13–15 (to 189), and bks. 16–18 just before the death of the author; the history of the First Punic War was treated cursorily as it had formed the main subject of Naevius' epic. Both poets, after the fashion of the Hellenistic epic, attempted to give to an historical record the form of an epic poem; but Ennius, adopting and naturalizing the Greek epic hexameter, with higher poetical gifts and a finer literary sense than his elder contemporary produced a work which, admired and imitated by Virgil, continued to be regarded as a virile and dignified monument of Roman literary achievement. The chronicle in verse retained until the Augustan age its position as the normal form of the Latin epic, though only scanty fragments survive: Hostius, who wrote a *Bellum Histricum*, A. Furius of Antium, M. Furius Bibaculus of Cremona who wrote a poem on Caesar's Gallic War, P. Terentius Varro of Atax (82–37), who, besides a free translation of the *Argonautica* of Apollonius Rhodius, composed a *Bellum Sequanicum*, are little more than names. Even Cicero attempted the epic. But no attempt seems to have been made until the Augustan age to produce an imaginative poem upon an historical subject which could be described as an epic as distinct from a mere narrative in verse. P. Vergilius Maro (70–19), after writing the *Eclogues* and the *Georgics* turned his attention to the composition of an historical epic, the *Aeneid*, upon which he spent the last ten years of his life, and which he left unfinished. By the choice of Aeneas as the hero of his poem Virgil avoided at once the annalistic form inseparable from the historical narrative and the combination of the panegyric and the epic hardly to be avoided in the treatment of contemporary events; he left his imagination free and he was able to give a form to his subject which would have satisfied Aristotle's definition of the epic. By abandoning the chronology followed by Ennius, which made Romulus the grandson of Aeneas, he found room for the line of Alban kings and was able to treat the whole history and antecedents of Rome as the distant prophecy of a destiny as yet remote and unrealized. A narrative that moved in the heroic age might fitly borrow from Homeric precedent; but Virgil's extensive borrowing from Homer, particularly in the later books of the poems, did not prevent him from drawing as well upon other Greek authors (esp. Apollonius Rhodius) and his Latin predecessors. He enriched the narrative of his hero's wanderings in search of Italy and of his final triumph there by the episode (inspired by the Alexandrian school and the *Argonautica* of Apollonius) of Dido's passion for him in the fourth book, and his *descensus Averni* in the sixth. He puts into his lips the story of the last days of Troy; and the episode of Nisus and Euryalus, the story of Camilla, the tragic figures of Mezentius and Lausus, and of Evander and Pallas, the description of the mustering of the Italian clans, are all proofs of the creative imagination which used a wide poetic heritage for its own purposes. The dramatic quality of his theme is emphasized by the careful insistence upon the reaction to the same circumstances of the contrasted characters of Aeneas and Turnus, and in the episode of Dido. The speeches are carefully (but unobtrusively) composed according to the dictates of rhetorical theory. Virgil succeeds in avoiding the monotony in his predecessors' handling of the hexameter; and by varying the pauses and by careful attention to the contrast and succession of vowel sounds, imparts a musical quality to his verse which no other Latin poet attained. The influence of the scholarship to which Varro had given such an impetus is reflected in Virgil's archaeological interests and particularly in his references to religious ceremonies and ancient customs; and all is put at the service of a lofty patriotism and a deep human sympathy and insight.

2. The latter part of the Augustan age saw a great production of epic poetry on mythological subjects (Ov. *Pont.* 4. 16): Cornelius Severus wrote a *Bellum Siculum* of some merit (Quint. *Inst.* 10. 1. 89), and Albinovanus Pedo wrote a *Theseis* and (apparently) a Roman epic (Sen. *Suas.* 1. 15). In Nero's reign M. Annaeus Lucanus (39–65) wrote his *De bello civili*, an epic in ten books on the civil war between Caesar and Pompey. In the choice of a Roman historical subject Lucan reverts to the pre-Virgilian tradition, but his treatment opens a new chapter in the Latin epic. He not merely abandoned the tradition of the Homeric and Hellenistic epic (followed by Ennius and Virgil) by dispensing with direct supernatural action in his story, but he changed the method of treatment of the human elements. The story was no longer treated objectively and allowed to enforce its own moral but was made the vehicle for the poet's own subjective attitude to the historical events recorded. Upon whatever sources now lost Lucan may have relied (R. Pichon, *Les Sources de Lucain*, 1912) he cannot be acquitted of carelessness and inaccuracy in geographical

and historical matters. In place of a consecutive narrative of events he selects episodes upon which he dwells with a singular force and brilliancy, often spoiled by exaggeration and lack of taste, throwing over the whole the rhetorical *color* to be expected from his Stoic republican sympathies. The divine intervention of the epic tradition is inadequately replaced by the idea of destiny (*fatum, fortuna*) which pervades the poem and by his morbid interest in necromancy. The numerous speeches are embellished by every device of the *controversia* and the *suasoria*, and the same 'pointed', artificial style is used also for the narrative and descriptive passages. Of this style Lucan was a master and used it with such striking effect that Roman classical poetry never after succeeded in shaking off his influence.

3. Under the Flavian dynasty the epic flourished; the Emperor Domitian himself attempted it in youth, as did also, not without success, Saleius Bassus (Quint. *Inst.* 10. 1. 90). The work of three epic poets has survived from this period, C. Valerius Flaccus Setinus Balbus (d. *c.* A.D. 90, Quint. loc. cit.), Silius Italicus (25–101), and P. Papinius Statius (*c.* 40–*c.* 96). Of the three Valerius Flaccus has the most genuine poetic gift. Reverting to the mythological epic of the Augustan age, he composed the *Argonautica*, of which eight books survive, following in the main the version of Apollonius Rhodius but with so many transpositions and variations as to make it virtually a different legend. The composition lacks the Virgilian firmness and precision: while Jason is the principal figure, it is not upon his person, but upon the quest of the Golden Fleece that the main interest is centred; and Valerius Flaccus never succeeds, as Virgil does in the case of Aeneas, in making him a genuine character of the heroic age. He is rather a figure of the Hellenistic period, just as his Medea lacks the simplicity and freedom from self-consciousness of the Greek legend. While Valerius keeps the traditional divine machinery, he is clearly influenced by the eschatological preoccupation of the mystery religions and imports it into his picture of the earlier time. He acknowledges by imitation on almost every page the influence of the *Aeneid*; but he cannot borrow either the Virgilian temper or the Virgilian style throughout, and his verse betrays too much the influence of the rhetoric of Lucan at a lower level. Statius, too, in his *Thebais* and his unfinished *Achilleis* chooses subjects from Greek mythology. He endeavours to import into his treatment of the heroic ages a new realism of detail. He is at times not unsuccessful in the attempt to combine descriptions of natural scenery and phenomena with his account of the actions and feelings of his characters and has a lively fancy for realistic details. But his style is so laborious and overloaded, under the combined influence of Alexandrian learning and Roman rhetoric, he is so fond of verbal and phraseological innovation, as to conceal his real poetical merits. While he tries to borrow felicitous phrases from Virgil, he lacks altogether the power to vary the cadence of his line and there are passages of unbearable metrical monotony. In contrast to Statius and Valerius Flaccus, Silius Italicus is in the annalistic tradition. His *Punica* is an attempt in seventeen books at a poetical narrative of the career of Hannibal up to the battle of Zama. His verse, while technically careful, is monotonous; and he tries to diversify his narrative of events, taken mainly from Livy, by imitating every epic device met with in his reading of previous poets. But he is capable of some competent descriptive passages and a few ingenious phrases. After the Flavian period the popularity of the epic seems to have declined until the time of Claudian. Most of the work of Claudius Claudianus (d. *post* 404) dealing with historical subjects is frankly panegyric or invective: his *De bello Gildonico* is a fragment; but in the *De raptu Proserpinae*, Claudian shows a perfect mastery of the epic style and metre. He has a vivid and colourful fancy, and many of his descriptions are of a smooth and finished polish hardly surpassed in Latin; but he falls short of the sober balance and *gravitas* of the best period. C. Sollius Modestus Apollinaris Sidonius (*c.* 430–79) continued the practice of the panegyric disguised as an epic poem; but Flavius Cresconius Corippus, who followed the same practice, added to it the composition of an epic, *Iohannis*, in eight books on the Byzantine campaign against the Mauretanians under Johannes the *magister militum* in Africa in not unpleasing verse.

Besides the general histories of Latin literature, Teuffel–Kroll, Schanz–Hosius, Wight Duff, and the relevant articles in *PW*, see L. Ziegler, *Das Hellenistische Epos* (1934); O. Ribbeck, *Gesch. der röm. Dichtung* 3 vv. (1887); W. Y. Sellar, *The Roman Poets of the Republic²* (1881); *The Roman Poets of the Augustan Age* i (1877); E. Norden, *Ennius u. Vergilius* (1915); E. Bellessort, *Virgile* (1920); R. Heinze, *Virgils epische Technik* (1915; ed. 3, 1928); E. E. Sikes, *Roman Poetry* (1923); W. C. Summers, *The Silver Age of Latin Literature* (1920). R. M. H.

EPICASTE (= *Iocasta*), see OEDIPUS.

EPICEDION DE MORTE DRUSI, a less authentic title for the *Consolatio ad Liviam* (q.v.).

EPICEDIUM (ἐπικήδειον sc. μέλος, *see* DIRGE), in Latin literature a poem in honour of a dead person. The term is not found in Latin before Statius; the thing itself is older, for the *nenia* and *laudatio funebris* (qq.v.) contained its essentials. But Greek influence was needed to weld these into a literary genre. Originally a song of mourning chanted over a corpse (*cadauere nondum sepulto*, in contrast with ἐπιτάφιον, Serv. ad Verg. *Ecl.* 5. 14), it came to mean simply a poem honouring a deceased person, scarcely distinguishable from a θρῆνος (*see* DIRGE). It was cultivated at Alexandria; it is not therefore surprising that the first Roman poets to attempt it were Calvus and Catullus. The *epicedium* sometimes fell also under the influence of the *Consolatio* (q.v.), without, however, losing its identity; its chief aim was to lament the dead, not to console survivors. Further, it is closely related to metrical epitaphs, several of which (Buecheler, *Carm. Epigr.* 1109; 1111; 1189; 1237) are really *epicedia*.

The constituent elements in the *epicedium* are lamentation and eulogy. Accompanying these (notably in the *Consolatio ad Liviam* or *Epicedion Drusi*, and in Statius) are consolatory reflections—irrevocability of fate, necessity of submission, faith in survival. Other customary features consist in frequent employment of mythology, apostrophes or invocations, indignation against destiny or the gods, thoughts on the vanity of birth or youth or merit, justification of lament, hope or assurance that the dead will be received in the other world by the *Manes*, finally (in Statius) description of last hours and of obsequies.

The metres are principally the hexameter and the elegiac distich. Length varies considerably: the shortest pieces are about 10 lines long; the longest (*Consol. ad Liv.*) is 474. Their literary worth is also very variable: contrast a masterpiece by Propertius with the poverties of the *Elegiae in Maecenatem*.

The chief *Epicedia* are: Catullus 101; Verg. *Ecl.* 5. 20–44; *Aen.* 6. 860–86; Hor. *Carm.* 1. 24; Propert. 3. 7; 18; 4. 11; Ov. *Am.* 3. 9; *Pont.* 1. 9; *Consol. ad Liviam* and *Elegiae in Maecenatem* (authors unknown); Mart. 5. 37; 6. 85; Stat. *Silv.* 2. 1; 6; 3. 3; 5. 1; 3; and 5; Auson. *Epiced. in patrem*; *Parentalia*.

Some *Epicedia* semi-parodically concern animals: Catull. 3; Ov. *Am.* 2. 6; Stat. *Silv.* 2. 4 and 5. Martial represents the pointed form where the dead animal is less the central theme than an occasion for a rhetorical subtlety.

O. Schantz, *De ... consolatione ad Liviam deque carminum consol. ... historia* (1889); A. Pais, 'Degli epicedii latini' (*Riv. di filol.* xviii, 1890). F. Vollmer, ed. of Stat. *Silv.* (1898), 316–17; O. Crusius in *PW*, s.v.; E. Galletier, *Étude sur la poésie funéraire romaine d'après les inscriptions* (1922), 200–10, 267–8; G. Herrlinger, *Totenklage um Tiere in der ant. Dichtung* (1930). C. F. transld. J. W. D.

EPICHARMUS (5th c. B.C.), Sicilian writer of comedy, born at Syracuse (Theoc. *Epigr.* 18), according to Arist. *Poet.* 1448ᵃ33 at Hyblaean Megara, or in Cos (Diog. Laert. 8. 3). Contemporary of Hieron, king of Syracuse (478–467 B.C.; *Marm. Par.* v. 71; Clem. Al. *Strom.* 1. 353 P.), whom Epicharmus mentions (fr. 98) as having stopped Anaxilaus of Rhegium from destroying Locri in 476 B.C. He lived to the age of 90 (Diog. Laert. 8. 78) or 97 (Lucian *Macr.* 25) and may be dated roughly 530–440 B.C. Said by Suidas to have started, with Phormis, Syracusan comedy, and by Aristotle (*Poet.* 1449ᵇ5) to have introduced 'plot' (μῦθος) into his plays. Wrote some 35 to 52 comedies. 35 titles survive. Of these 18 are mythological; some about Heracles, and many from the Homeric saga, e.g. Ὀδυσσεὺς αὐτόμολος (Odysseus, sent as a spy to Troy, hesitates to go, and wonders what excuse he can make to the Greeks (fr. 99)), Κύκλωψ, Τρῶες, Σειρῆνες. Many plays seem to burlesque the gods: e.g. the Τριακάδες (? referring to the month-end feast of Hecate), Ἥβης γάμος (fr. 54, Poseidon as fishmonger), Βούσειρις (fr. 21, the greed of Heracles). Some are controversial in type: e.g. Λόγος καὶ Λογίνα (? 'Male and Female Reason', whatever that may mean), Γᾶ καὶ Θάλασσα ('does Earth or Sea give greater blessings to men?'), Ἐλπὶς ἢ Πλοῦτος. Some suggest Middle Comedy subjects: e.g. Ἀγρωστῖνος (= Ἄγροικος, The Countryman); and even New Comedy is foreshadowed by such 'stock' characters as, e.g., the parasite. The Θεαροί depicts an embassy sightseeing at Delphi (fr. 79). The Πέρσαι may be a parody of Aeschylus. The Χύτραι perhaps depicts a potter's dream of wealth.

Epicharmus' plays seem to have been farces rather than comedies proper. There was apparently no chorus, for the plural titles (Θεαροί, Χορευταί, etc.) refer to *actors*. No lyric fragments are found, though some are in anapaestic metre and stage music is mentioned (frs. 127 and 210). Though farcical, the plays are written in literary (not vulgar) Doric and must have made their appeal to a cultured audience. They contain much philosophizing (e.g. frs. 170–3) and some parodies of Homeric style (fr. 99). Introduced into Athens probably for reading rather than performance, they doubtless influenced Attic comedy; cf. Archippus' Ἡρακλῆς γαμῶν, from Epicharmus' Ἥβης γάμος, and Aristophanes, according to the Scholiast, imitates Epicharmus at *Pax* 185 (E. fr. 125) and again (probably) in his *Telmesses* (Ar. fr. 530, cf. E. fr. 149). Among the well-known fragments may be cited fr. 246 αὗτα φύσις ἀνθρώπων ἀσκοὶ πεφυσαμένοι (cf. Petron. *Satyr.* 42 'heu, heu, utres inflati ambulamus'), and fr. 249 νοῦς ὅρη καὶ νοῦς ἀκούει· τἄλλα κωφὰ καὶ τυφλά. Tradition makes him a pupil of Pythagoras. The younger Dionysius of Syracuse wrote a book on him (Suidas, s.v. 'Dionysius') and the second-century-B.C. grammarian, Apollodorus, edited his works in ten volumes with notes (Porph. *Plot.* 24). Besides plays, Epicharmus is credited by Diog. Laert. (8. 78) with physical, medical, and ethical treatises.

Kaibel, *CGF* i. 88 ff.; A. O. F. Lorenz, *Leben und Schriften des Koers Epicharmos* (1864); A. W. Pickard-Cambridge, *Dithyramb, Tragedy, and Comedy* (1927), 353–415; A. Olivieri, *Frammenti della commedia greca* (1930). M. P.

EPICRATES, Middle Comedy poet, of Ambracia. In fr. 11 (before 347 B.C.) Epicrates cleverly describes scientific research in botany by Plato and his disciples.

FCG ii. 365 ff.; *CAF* ii. 282 ff.

EPICTETUS (1) (fl. 520–500 B.C.), potter and vase-painter in Athens, known from one potter's and thirty painter's signatures, chiefly on red-figure cups with dainty compositions. One vase signed by Epictetus is attributed to the Cleophrades painter, a successor of Euthymides (q.v.) and a forerunner of the strong style, who painted from 510 to 480; he should perhaps be known as Epictetus II.

Beazley, *A.V.* 24; *Der Kleophrades Maler* (1933); W. Kraiker, *JDAI* 1929, 141; G. M. A. Richter, *AJArch.* 1936, 100.
T. B. L. W.

EPICTETUS (2), (*c.* A.D. 55 to *c.* 135), of Hierapolis (Phrygia), Stoic philosopher. He grew up as a slave of Epaphroditus, a freedman, who held the important office *a libellis* under Nero and again under Domitian. His master allowed him to attend the lectures of Musonius Rufus and later set him free. He then began to teach philosophy in Rome. When in 89 Domitian banished the philosophers from Rome, he went to Nicopolis (Epirus), where he continued teaching to the end of his life. He acquired a large audience and many distinguished followers, among them Flavius Arrianus (*see* ARRIAN; *cos. c.* A.D. 130), who collected his lectures (διατριβαί), probably in eight books, four of which have come down to us, and later published a summary of his philosophy in the famous Manual (ἐγχειρίδιον). Through these posthumous publications he had great influence on the Emperor M. Aurelius.

Though Epictetus considered logic useful because it prevents us from being deceived by faulty arguments (Arrian 1. 17), he was but little interested in the purely theoretical side of philosophy, except theology. He taught that the universe is the work of God, and that Divine Providence manifests itself in its unity and order.

Contrary to the early Stoics he did not teach for the few and for the self-reliant, but for the many and the humble. He used to say that only he who had become aware of his weakness and his misery could profit from the teaching of the philosophers. He taught the common brotherhood of man. Wrongdoers, he thought, should not be punished as criminals, but pitied, because they are more unhappy than their victims.

Like the early Stoics he wanted to make man free and independent of the vicissitudes of fortune. We must not, he said, let our happiness depend on things which are not in our power. The only thing which is always in one's power is one's own self and one's will. This we must keep unblemished. We must be indifferent to death, pain, and illness, and even the loss of our dearest relatives must not touch us. For all this not only belongs to the external world, but also happens through Divine Providence, which is always good.

Epicteti Dissertationes ab Arriano digestae ed. H. Schenkl² (1916); A. Bonhöffer, *Epiktet und die Stoa* (1890); *Die Ethik des Stoikers Epiktet* (1894); Th. Colardeau, *Étude sur Épictète* (1903); D. S. Sharp, *Epictetus and the New Testament* (1914); *PW* vi. 126.
K. von F.

EPICURUS (Ἐπίκουρος), 17th Gamelion 342/1–271/70 B.C. (Apollod. ap. Diog. Laert. 10. 14 f.), famous Athenian philosopher. He was the son of the Athenian Neocles of the deme Gargettus and his wife Charaestrata. He belonged to a family of ancient nobility, the Philaedae (Metrod. ap. D.L. 10. 1). His own parents, however, are not likely to have been well-to-do, since they went out with many other colonists to Samos in 352/1 to make their fortune. There Neocles taught as a schoolmaster (Sotion and others ap. D.L. 10. 1; 4). E. was probably born in Samos. He went back to Athens in his eighteenth year (D.L. 10. 1) to pass the examination required of an *ephebus* (δοκιμασία). He used to say himself that he began to show philosophical interest at the age of fourteen (D.L. 10. 2). His first philosophical lessons he had with the Platonic Pamphilus, while still at Samos (Ariston ap. D.L. 10. 14). On his departure from Athens he joined his family again in Colophon, where they had gone after quitting Samos owing to the political situation (D.L. 10. 1). In Teos, not far from Colophon, he probably studied under the Democritean philosopher Nausiphanes (Ariston and Apollod. ap. D.L. 10. 13–14), of whom he used to speak very contemptuously in later

years (D.L. 10. 8; Sext. Emp. *Math.* 1. 3). E. may have been introduced by him to Democritus' philosophy (cf. Ariston ap. D.L. 10. 14). In 311/10 he opened a school of his own at Mytilene, and later one at Lampsacus. He soon was joined by devoted pupils, and after five years, in 306, he went to Athens to compete with the great philosophical schools. There he bought a house and the famous garden (κῆπος) as the domicile of his school, to which it gave its name. He was the first philosopher to admit female members to an organized school. He lived in Athens, except for a few journeys, for more than thirty-six years, leading a simple, remote, and hidden life with his pupils. In his will he left the garden and the school to Hermarchus of Mytilene (ap. D.L. 10. 17).

2. In his community (θίασος) the founder himself enjoyed a kind of worship even during his life. His birthday was a celebrated feast. This and similar customs he ordered in his will to be observed after his death (Epic. ap. D.L. 10. 18). The life he lived with his friends in the community was simple, contrary to the gossip of enemies of the sect (cf. D.L. 10. 4 f.; 11 f.).

3. WRITINGS. As the number of E.'s works Diogenes Laertius (10. 26) mentions the immense figure of three hundred rolls. All the main works are lost. The greatest loss is his writing *On nature* (Περὶ φύσεως) in thirty-seven books (D.L. 10. 27), of which we have only a few fragments in ancient writers and on papyrus. A most valuable source is the tenth book of Diogenes Laertius, which gives a *Vita*, the preserved works 1–4, and good doxographic material.

4. The preserved works are:

(1) The letter to Herodotus (like the recipients of 2 and 3 a pupil of E.), the only comprehensive review of E.'s natural philosophy which has been preserved. Its style is crabbed and difficult.

(2) The letter to Pythocles, probably only an abridgement of a work of E., giving an account of his meteorology.

(3) The letter to Menoeceus, the shortest and clearest of the three. Its subject is the ethical theory.

(4) Κύριαι δόξαι (*Principal Doctrines*), a kind of breviary which could be learnt by heart. It contains forty ethical aphorisms.

(5) *Sententiae Vaticanae*, a collection of eighty almost entirely ethical aphorisms, discovered in 1888 in a Vatican MS. by C. Wotke.

5. DOCTRINES. E. defines philosophy as the attempt to gain happiness by means of discussion and reasoning (Sext. Emp. *Math.* 11. 169). He divides it into three parts, Ethics, Physics, and the axiomatic part, called *Canonice* (κανονικόν), usually taken together with the Physics (D.L. 10. 30).

(1) *Canonice*. E. regards sense-perception (αἴσθησις) which is common to mankind as the one and only basis of knowledge (Sext. *Math.* 8. 9; cf. D.L. 10. 31). Fallacy may arise when we begin to reason, or to form opinions or judgements (δόξα, ὑπόληψις) out of the material with which the senses have been furnished. The only proof we can find lies again in perception. If there are sensations proving or, at least, not disproving them, opinions are right, otherwise wrong (D.L. 10. 31 f., etc.).

(2) *Physics*. For the needs of his new theory E. was brought back to the teaching of Democritus and the old atomism. Like Democritus he holds that sensation is due to 'effluences' leaving material things and entering our senses by means of the sense-organs. He assumes that things continuously throw off from their surfaces small 'images' or 'idols' (εἴδωλα, *imagines*) of unsurpassable fineness of texture, shaped like the solid bodies and flying with so incredible a speed that they cannot be seen moving. In this way our senses come, so to speak, in direct touch with the objects (Epicur. *Ep.* 1. 46 f.; Lucr. 4. 270 f.). This seemed to confirm the teaching of his Canonice.

The effluence of 'idols' is due, according to Democritus and E., to the motion of the atoms which constitute every concrete object. With Democritus E. believes that only the existence of two things can be finally proved: the atoms and the void. The atoms have to be accepted, because in all destruction there must be a last imperishable element. The void is necessary as the place through which bodies move (*Ep.* 1. 39 f.). E., however, differs considerably from his predecessor by granting a kind of arbitrary character to the movement of the atoms which causes them to swerve from their original straight movement (παρεγκλίνειν, *declinare*; Lucr. 2. 216 f.). This accounts for the first and all further collisions of atoms, and avoids the blind necessity of Democritus' mechanism.

Everything is due to the atoms and their movement: this perishable world as well as the infinite number of other worlds, including men and gods. At death the atoms of the soul are dispersed and sensation ceases immediately (*Ep.* 1. 63 f.; Lucr. 3. 328 f.; Usener p. 378 f.). The gods are anthropomorphic and made out of the finest atoms. In the distances between the worlds (*intermundia*) they live a blessed and perfect life, free from any concern with this or any other world (Lucr. 3. 18 ff.; 5. 146 f.; 1167 ff., etc.).

(3) *Ethics.* By his Physics E. wants to free mankind from the fear of death, of the gods, of the great metaphysical and physical powers which seem to surround him. He wants to remove every disturbance from without. So he advises man not to take part in public life (D.L. 10. 119), to avoid marriage and begetting of children (Clem. Al. *Strom.* 2. 23), to withdraw from the world and to live hidden (λάθε βιώσας: Plut. *De lat. viv.* 1128). As the natural human aim and the highest good E. recognizes 'pleasure' (ἡδονή: *Ep.* 3. 128 f.), led again by the evidence of our desires and feelings. But he firmly declines to identify this with the 'pleasure of the profligates' (*Ep.* 3. 131). Pleasure, as he understands it, is mainly negative, meaning freedom from pain and trouble, imperturbability (ἀταραξία), and an independent and peaceful state of body and mind (*Ep.* 3).

6. In Epicurus' time man had lost the old bonds of State and religion. His philosophy is a gospel intended to free humanity from old traditions and fears, and to give it a new belief instead. This was the gospel of the independent and untroubled human soul which has withdrawn from public life and found a new and reliable basis in the joy of its simple and pure existence.

BIBLIOGRAPHY

H. Usener, *Epicurea* (1887; standard work, containing the preserved writings 1–4 (see para. 4, supra) and the fragments, except the papyr. frs. of Περὶ φύσεως).
EDITIONS, TRANSL., AND COMM.: E. Bignone (1922; text, sel. frs., and notes); P. von der Muehll (1922; text); C. Bailey (1926; text, Engl. trans., sel. frs., comm.); Budé (Lucr. vol. i); Loeb (Diog. Laert. 10); for frs. of Περὶ φύσ., see list in Bailey p. 391 f., add esp. A. Vogliano, *Epicuri et Epicureorum scripta* i (Berlin, 1928).
MODERN LITERATURE (selection): E. Zeller, *Stoics, Epicureans, and Sceptics*, Engl. Transl.; J. Woltjer, *Lucreti philosophia cum fontibus comparata* (1877); C. Giussani, *Studi Lucreziani* (Lucr. vol. i, 1896); W. Crönert, *Kolotes u. Menedemos* (1906); Linde, *De Epicuri vocabulis ab optima Atthide alienis* (Thesis, Breslau, 1896); F. Merbach, *De Epicuri canonica* (1909); R. D. Hicks, *Stoic and Epicurean* (1911); Überweg-Praechter, *Grundr.*[11] §§ 60–2; C. Bailey, *The Greek Atomists and E.* (1928); C. Jensen, *Ein neuer Brief E.* (Abh. Ges. Göttingen, 1933); H. Widmann, *Beiträge zur Syntax E.* (1935); E. Bignone, *L'Aristotele perduto e la formaz. filos. di E.* (1936, traces for the first time the connexion with the works of the early Aristotle; important though often too fanciful); W. Schmid, *E.' Kritik der platon. Elementenlehre* (1936); B. Farrington, *Science and Politics in the Ancient World* (1939), 118 ff.; *PW* vi. 133.
K. O. B.

EPIDAMNUS, a joint colony of Corcyra and Corinth, founded *c.* 625 B.C. to exploit the Illyrian trade up the Genusus valley. This trade was at first constituted as a monopoly for the benefit of the ruling oligarchy, which further strengthened its ascendancy by restricting industrial pursuits to public slaves. By 435 the commons

had nevertheless gained control and expelled the oligarchs; when put under siege by the latter, they invoked the aid of Corcyra, and when this was refused they applied to Corinth. The Corinthians reinforced the democracy with new settlers, but shortly after the city was recaptured by the Corcyraeans. This scramble of Corinthians and Corcyraeans for Epidamnus was a contributory cause of the Peloponnesian War. For the later history of Epidamnus, *see* DYRRHACHIUM.

Thuc. 1. 24–9. M. C.

EPIDAURUS, one of the small States of the Argolic Acte, on a peninsula of the Saronic Gulf. It was originally Ionic, but dorized from Argos (Paus. 2. 26. 1); unlike Argos, it used a 'Western' alphabet. It owed religious dues to Argos (Thuc. 5. 53), but was politically independent, and at one time controlled Aegina (Hdt. 5. 82). Its fame lay in the sanctuary of Asclepius, situated in an inland valley. Entered by a propylaeum, the sanctuary contained a temple of Asclepius (early 4th c.), other small temples, porticoes, baths, a gymnasium and palaestra, inns and priests' houses. The chief extant buildings are the *tholos*, a round building of the mid-fourth century by Polyclitus the younger, with beautiful Corinthian columns, and one of the most perfect of Greek theatres, which well preserves its fourth-century plan. The building accounts of temple and *tholos* are preserved. Though there are earlier dedications, the buildings and the chief fame of Asclepius belong to the fourth and later centuries. The cult, originally perhaps Thessalian, was transferred from Epidaurus to other towns, notably to Athens and Rome (Paus. 2. 26. 8). The inscriptions recording cures, wrought by sleeping in a dormitory attached to the temple and following the prescriptions of the priests, are important for the history of ancient medicine.

P. Kavvadias, Τὸ ἱερὸν τοῦ Ἀσκληπίου ἐν Ἐπιδαύρῳ (1900); *Fouilles d'Épidaure* (vol. i only, Athens, 1893); Ἀρχ. Ἐφ. 1918, 115 ff. A. Defrasse, *Épidaure* (1895; architectural restorations); R. Herzog, *Die Wunderheilungen von Epidauros* (1931). T. J. D.

EPIDOSIS, *see* ENDOWMENTS.

EPIGENES (1) of Sicyon is said (Suidas s.vv. Θέσπις and Οὐδὲν πρὸς τὸν Διόνυσον) to have been the 'first tragic poet', and may have composed 'tragic choruses' of the type which Herodotus (5. 67) speaks of as produced at Sicyon in the sixth century B.C., having reference to the sufferings of heroes, but transferred by the tyrant Cleisthenes to the worship of Dionysus. A. W. P.-C.

EPIGENES (2), Middle Comedy poet, dated before 376 B.C. by his reference to Hecatomnus, king of Caria.
FCG iii. 537 ff.; *CAF* ii. 416 ff.

EPIGONI (Ἐπίγονοι), sons of the Seven against Thebes (*see* ADRASTUS). They were: Alcmaeon and Amphilochus, sons of Ampharaus; Aegialeus, of Adrastus; Diomedes, of Tydeus; Promachus, of Parthenopaeus; Sthenelus, of Capaneus; Thersander, of Polynices; Euryalus, of Mecisteus. (Apollodorus, 3. 82; a different list, Hyginus, *Fab.* 71.) H. J. R.

EPIGRAM

I. THE EPIGRAM: GREEK, GRAECO-ROMAN, AND BYZANTINE.

Epigram, ἐπίγραμμα, means 'inscription' and in practice a metrical inscription. Throughout 1,000 years of development the poetic epigram never wholly lost its original meaning. There are four stages in its history.

(1) *Archaic.* The first verse-epigrams appear about the seventh century B.C. on votive offerings, tombstones, and occasionally signposts (Plato, *Hipparch.* 228d). They are usually in one or more hexameter lines or elegiac couplets, sometimes even in iambics. Their style, enriched with Homeric decorations, is as ornate as is

compatible with their function. Throughout this period an epigram is essentially a graceful mnemonic. Thus a tombstone-verse contains the name, city, family, and age of the dead, and usually the manner of his death. Phrases of regret are not often added, though impersonal reflections sometimes are. This restraint and purpose made the epigram into an artistic form. Along with the elegiac couplet, the epigram was developed by the Ionians: from about 550 B.C. the Attic inscriptions become more and more graceful, and more and more Ionic. The first great poet to write inscriptions was Simonides, whose few authentic epigrams show a grave intensity of emotion which is actually increased by their brevity and impersonality. Throughout the fifth and fourth centuries, Greek verse-inscriptions show an increasing delicacy and pathos which is largely due to his example; other poetic influences, such as that of tragedy, further purified their style.

(2) *Hellenistic*. The Hellenistic age loved trifles, and it loved to change and expand the scope of literary forms. Therefore it made several fundamental changes in the meaning of the epigram—(i) by cultivating purely artificial epitaphs and votive inscriptions, called epideictic, 'for display', because they could not be carved on a real tomb or tablet, e.g. poems on long-dead historical personages, famous works of art, small perishable offerings, dead animals; (ii) by infusing the subjective emotion of the elegy and drinking-song into the brief memorable form of the poetic inscription. In this period two different schools have been postulated. The 'Peloponnesian' school wrote chiefly in Doric, often about country life and scenery: it was quiet, objective, straightforward. To it belonged the pastoral painter Anyte, Nossis servant of Aphrodite, Perses of Thebes, and the great Leonidas of Tarentum. The 'Ionian' school, centred in Samos and Alexandria, was more social and sophisticated; it wrote of love and wine, literature and art, in a far more complex style and vocabulary. Its leader was Asclepiades, with his friends Hedylus and Posidippus; he was followed by Callimachus and Dioscorides. Invective epigrams began in the third century B.C. with Alcaeus of Messene. The definition of epigram, thus enlarged, was made to include short poems by great poets of the past: the works of Archilochus, Sappho, Anacreon, and others were combed for 'epigrams', and forged epigrams were attributed to Aeschylus, Plato, and other notabilities. The metre of the epigram in this period was almost exclusively the elegiac couplet.

(3) *Graeco-Roman*. In 196 B.C. Alcaeus of Messene had extolled T. Flamininus, the 'liberator' of Greece. The Greek world now began to address, influence, and even praise Rome. Here, without sketching the history of epigram at Rome (for which *see* LATIN EPIGRAM below), it is appropriate to remark on some examples of Greek influence or departures from it. Ennius' fine epitaph on himself (the first extant Latin elegiac poem) is essentially Hellenistic in spirit, for it could not be carved on any tomb; but it is charged with a new Roman pride and solidity. Q. Lutatius Catulus, who was consul in 102 and knew the Greek epigrammatist Antipater of Sidon, joined two friends in writing rudimentary love-epigrams in the Alexandrian manner. By the time of Catullus and Calvus all forms of the Greek epigram were being successfully imitated in Rome—notably the invective epigram, which always suited Roman taste. Varro's picture-book *Imagines* had a descriptive epigram under each portrait. The fashion grew, until we hear of epigrams by almost everyone who pretended to culture (Cicero, Caesar, Augustus, Maecenas, Tiberius), anonymous collections by groups of friends (the *Priapea*), and venomous pasquinades against unpopular emperors. For humorous and spiteful epigrams the Romans used hendecasyllables and scazons as well as elegiacs. Meanwhile, Meleager (*c.* 90 B.C.) had given the Greek epigram a great impetus

by publishing his *Garland* of the greatest Greek literary epigrams; and in A.D. 40 Philippus compiled another to supplement it. Greek writers at this time tended to concentrate on complimentary and epideictic epigrams (Crinagoras, Antipater of Thessalonica, Antiphilus, and Erucius); but there was more real life in the convivial and amorous poetry of Philodemus and Argentarius. The genius of the Romans for satire appears in their preference for derisory epigrams: fools, knaves, and misfits are the targets of Roman epigrammatists in both languages. Nero patronized Martial's predecessor Lucillius (not the great satirist, Lucilius), whose Greek epigrams, all satirical and usually very funny, were closely imitated by the much less graceful Nicarchus. Martial's poems, more than half of them satirical in intention and pre-eminently perfecting the trick, comparatively rare in Greek, by which the epigram leads up to a surprise, were never improved upon by his Roman successors; and we find that the epigrams of Hadrian ('animula uagula blandula') and of Ausonius revert to a more Greek type. In Greek the strange gloomy figure of Palladas, a lonely disillusioned pagan (*c.* A.D. 400), closes this period, and marks the end of original poetry.

(4) *Byzantine*. The revival of Greek literature which began in the fifth century produced a number of Byzantine epigrammatists. Agathias made a large collection of epigrams called the *Circle*, including many contemporary poems, paraphrases of themes, and patterns invented by classical writers: their language and metre are correct, but to know their models is to despise them. He inserted numerous poems by himself and his friend Paulus Silentiarius. Agathias' collection, enlarged yet further by Constantine Cephalas in the tenth century, became our present *Anthology* (q.v.).

II. THE LATIN EPIGRAM

There is a difficulty in demarcating epigram from elegy (q.v.) most felt in their earlier stages. Their histories are intertwined and complementary, for elegy, though its origin lies in the sung lament, retains much in common with sepulchral epigram. But the widening content of epigram also widened the gap between them. Latin poets could note among Greek epigrammatists the extension of the form from a commemorative inscription on tomb, shrine, or work of art to lines on life or death, on ethical themes, on love or any striking event capable of giving the impulse towards terse summary or incisive mockery. It is significant that the liberation of a slave in Petronius' *Satyricon*, 55, is said to demand an 'inscriptio' or epigrammatic record, whereupon Trimalchio composes a few halting lines. Such occasional poetry may be as varied as human experience, so that in Martial, for instance, we find epigrams which could not be called elegies. The occasional epigram becomes an exercise-ground for wit and satire, different from the emotional tone of elegy; and the severance is emphasized by the choice, for the short poem, of various metres—hendecasyllabic, scazon, even hexameter (as Martial claims, 6. 65), besides the elegiac couplet. Martial indeed (12. 94) contrasts epigram as a separate literary genre with *epos*, tragedy, lyric, *saturae*, and *elegi*; while Pliny (*Ep.* 4. 14. 9) says his own hendecasyllabics may be equated indifferently with *epigrammata*, *idyllia*, *eclogae*, or *poematia*.

In studying Latin epigrams there are two further difficulties—the difficulty of dating many Greek epigrammatists preserved in the *Anthology*, so as to determine possible influence, and the difficulty caused by the disappearance of many collections of epigrams by Latin authors. What time has left offers only a meagre view of epigram-writing at Rome. Thus, we cannot estimate the literary worth of three authors, Marsus, Pedo, and Gaetulicus, acknowledged by Martial as his models besides Catullus, whose epigrammatic power we fortunately can judge.

The ancient tradition of the epitaph is exemplified in the three extant pieces by Ennius, and in one by Pompilius, while to Papinius belongs the satiric banter of two lovers ('Ridiculum est . . .'). From Varro's *Hebdomades* six pieces survive, mostly memorial verses of which the best known are on (? or by) Naevius, Plautus, and Pacuvius. Two love-poems by Valerius Aedituus have come down; unhappily, but for a line, the *Amores* of Cornelius Gallus are lost (for love-elegies see ELEGIAC POETRY, LATIN). We have remains, disappointingly insignificant, of compositions by Lutatius Catulus and his circle, and by the neoteric poets, Bibaculus, Calvus, Cinna, Ticidas, and others. Julius Caesar's lines on Terence represent literary compliment and contrast with the anonymous couplet reproaching Sallust for the theft of archaic words from Cato. Scraps have survived by Cicero, Ovid, and Manilius; more has been left of the *Catalepton* and *Priapea* (qq.v.).

Under the Empire, Asinius Gallus is one of those who continued the satiric epigram (the ex-boxer turned professor). Nero's reign yields the collections ascribed to Petronius and Seneca (see J. Wight Duff, *Lit. Hist. Rome, Silver Age*, 193–5, 246–7); Lucan has a distich of moral advice. From the Flavian age comes the memorial couplet written by Verginius Rufus for his tomb as his claim to have saved the imperial power 'non sibi sed patriae', and we know that Pliny was himself the author and the begetter in others of epigrams; but the pre-eminent figure of the day in this line, and the greatest name in the history of epigram, was his friend Martial (q.v.). Gellius (19. 9) heard a concert of 'charmingly sweet ἐλεγεῖα by recent poets'; and in the numerous *epigrammata* of Ausonius, mainly elegiac, we meet a wide variety of subjects where both Martial and Greek originals are models. Claudian's shorter poems include several in epigrammatic style—sepulchral, satiric, complimentary, descriptive. Roman sepulchral epigrams are usually miniature elegies, modelled on Augustan poets, but very seldom distinguished by originality. The luxurious Vandal State in Africa produced (c. 530) a brief crop of epigrammatists and anthologies like the *Codex Salmasianus*: metrically lax and aesthetically disgusting, they make us regret Martial. The persistence of epigram-writing during the Middle Ages and the Renaissance was largely due to the continued influence of Martial.

It is almost impossible to find a general definition which will sum up the history of the Greek and Latin epigram, and cover all known epigrams, literary and inscriptional; but certain fundamental characteristics are clear throughout. It is a short direct poem, usually in elegiacs, sometimes in hendecasyllables, rarely in hexameters; it expresses one single thought which is rather more intellectual and analytical than lyrical and passionate; the thought is usually voiced as a comment on a new and symbolic situation—the death of a friend, the breaking of a lover's vow, the dedication of an offering, the sudden realization of some incongruity or some beauty. The modern epigram bears the stamp of Martial and Catullus, and has become a brief, pointed, witty remark, instead of the vaguer but richer form which the Greeks filled with such manifold and delicate emotion.

BIBLIOGRAPHY

I. *The Epigram: Greek, Graeco-Roman, and Byzantine.*

TEXTS. G. Kaibel, *Epigrammata Graeca ex lapidibus conlecta* (1878); T. Preger, *Inscriptiones Graecae metricae e scriptoribus praeter Anthologiam collectae* (1891); E. Hoffmann, *Sylloge epigrammatum Graecorum* (1893); H. Stadtmüller, *Anthologia Palatina* (1894–); J. W. Mackail, *Select Epigrams from the Greek Anth.* (1906); W. R. Paton, *Greek Anthology* (Loeb, 1916); J. Geffcken, *Griechische Epigramme* (1916); F. Hiller von Gaertringen, *Historische griechische Epigramme* (1926); Walz i–viii.

GENERAL WORKS. J. A. Symonds, *Studies of the Greek Poets* ii. 22 (3rd ed. 1893); F. Plessis, *Épitaphes* (1905); J. Geffcken, 'Studien

zum griech. Epigramme', *Neue Jahrb.* 1917; R. Reitzenstein, 'Epigramm', in *PW* vi. 71. And see ANTHOLOGY.

SPECIAL STUDIES. (a) *Archaic period*: H. Gutscher, *Die attischen Grabschriften* (1890); U. v. Wilamowitz, *Sappho und Simonides* (1893).
(b) *Hellenistic period*: R. Reitzenstein, *Epigramm und Skolion* (1893); U. v. Wilamowitz-Moellendorff, *Hellenistische Dichtung* I. ii. 2 (1924); Herter in Bursian 1937.
(c) *Graeco-Roman period*: C. Cichorius, *Römische Studien* (1922) viii, 295–375; R. Keydell in Bursian, vol. ccxxx (1931), p. 141; X. Guglielmino, *Epigrammate satiriche nell' xi libro dell' Antologia*; F. Brecht, *Philol. Suppl.* xxii, 1930 (humorous epigrams).
(d) *Byzantine period*: B. Stumpo, *L'epigramme a Costantinopoli nel secolo vi* (1926).
And see individual epigrammatists.

II. *The Epigram: Latin.*

TEXTS. For surviving epigrams by many Latin poets or of unknown authorship see Baehrens, *FPR* and Morel, *FPL*; *Anthol. Lat.* Buecheler-Riese, *Cod. Salmas.*, etc. i. 1 and 2; *Carmina Epigraphica*, ii. 1 and 2; 3 (supplem. E. Lommatzsch, 1926); *Priapea* and *Catalepton*, Baehrens, *PLM* ii. 158–77; Vollmer, *Append. Verg.* (1927), 126–42. Petronius' poems: Baehrens, *PLM* iv. 87–101; Loeb ed. of *Satyricon*, 1913. Seneca's poems: Baehrens, *PLM* iv. 55–87.

Consult 'Epigramm' (Reitzenstein) in *PW* vi. 71–111; C. Cichorius, *Röm. Stud.* (1922), 295–375; E. Galletier, *Étude sur la poésie funéraire romaine* (1922); E. Lissberger, *Das Fortleben d. röm. Elegiker in d. Carmina Epigraphica* (1934); K. Prinz, *Martial u. das griech. Epigramm* (1911); O. Autore, *Marziale e l'epigramma greco* (1937).
G. H. and J. W. D.

EPIGRAPHY, GREEK, * is the study of inscriptions written on durable material, such as stone or metal, in Greek letters and expressed in the Greek languages. Coin-legends are regarded as falling within the province of the numismatist, painted mummy-labels and ink-written texts on ostraca (fragments of coarse pottery), specially numerous in and characteristic of Egypt, are claimed by the papyrologist, and painted inscriptions forming part of the original decoration of vases (97) are assigned primarily to ceramics, though texts subsequently incised on pottery and the stamps on Rhodian and other amphorae are usually deemed epigraphical materials. The study covers an area coextensive with the lands inhabited or visited by Greeks who left behind written memorials, and a period of well over a millennium, from the appearance of the earliest extant examples of Greek writing down to the close of the fourth century or even later, when Greek merges into Byzantine history. The materials are to a large extent scattered in the various places where they were found, though much has been done to collect and protect them in museums in Greece (especially the Epigraphical and Acropolis Museums at Athens and the local collections at Eleusis, Corinth (23), Sparta, Olympia (24), Thebes, Delphi (25), etc.), Asia Minor, Egypt (notably at Alexandria (46) and Cairo (47)), and elsewhere; there are important collections, e.g. in Berlin, Paris (45), the British Museum (44), and the Ashmolean Museum at Oxford.

2. Epigraphical studies have a very long history (2, 9, 10). Herodotus discusses, in the light of archaic dedications copied by him at Thebes, the Phoenician origin of the Greek alphabet and its later modification under Ionian influence (Hdt. 5. 53–61), and he frequently appeals to inscriptions as historical sources, as do also Thucydides and most of the Greek historians and orators. Philochorus edited a collection of Ἐπιγράμματα Ἀττικά early in the third century B.C., and about the same time Craterus published a Ψηφισμάτων συναγωγή with historical commentary, while a century later Polemo of Ilium received the nickname στηλοκόπας for his tireless attention to the inscribed records. The study revived in the fifteenth century with the activity of Ciriaco de' Pizzicolli (Cyriac of Ancona) in copying ancient inscriptions in the course of his travels, and the seventeenth and eighteenth centuries witnessed a dozen attempts to collect the available material in *corpora*. The modern period opens with the travels of Pouqueville, Leake, Gell, Osann, Letronne, and others, August Boeckh's acceptance

---
* In this article figures in brackets refer to the corresponding items in the appended Bibliography.

in 1815, under the auspices of the Berlin Academy, of the task of preparing a new and comprehensive *corpus* on a geographical basis (20), and the issue by J. Franz in 1840 of the first adequate general work on Greek epigraphy (6). Thus were laid the foundations on which scholars have built during the past century, aided by the enhanced opportunities of travel which followed the liberation of Greece, the systematic excavations carried out by Greek and foreign archaeologists on many Hellenic sites—the Acropolis, Corinth (23), Olympia (24), Delphi (25), Delos (21, 29), Gortyn, Priene (35), Miletus, Pergamum (36), Magnesia (34), Sardis (37), and others, of which the most recent and prolific is the Athenian Agora—and the improved technique of decipherment, restoration, and publication, in which the 'squeeze' and the photograph play a valuable part. The most ambitious and fruitful enterprise of this period is that of the Berlin Academy, which, shortly before the completion of Boeckh's great work, embarked on the publication of a series of *corpora*, united in 1903 under the single title of *Inscriptiones Graecae* (21), which should contain all the Greek inscriptions of Europe; the Vienna Academy undertook the preparation of a *corpus*, of which only the first-fruits have appeared (22), of Asia Minor; and Syrian (40) and Egyptian *corpora* are planned or already begun.

3. Greek epigraphy comprises two main provinces, palaeographical and historical, though there is a certain overlap between them in so far as palaeographical criteria are used for the determination of the provenance and the date of an inscription, and so for its assignment to its historical context.

I. Inscriptions afford by far the earliest extant examples of Greek writing, and are thus invaluable for the study of the origin and development of the Greek alphabet and script (8–12, 16, 17). The persistent tradition which spoke of the Phoenicians and their semi-mythical King Cadmus as those who taught the Hellenes to write is confirmed by the use of the word φοινικήϊα (Hdt. 5. 58; *SIG* 38. 37) to denote letters, by the 'retrograde' direction of the earliest Greek inscriptions, by the Greek letter-names, by the identical order of the alphabets of Phoenicia (as inferred from the cognate Hebrew) and of Greece (as indicated by many early *abecedaria*, by the numerical values given to the letters, and by the unbroken tradition of the Greek language), and by the striking resemblances between the letter-forms used in the most archaic inscriptions of the Greeks and their Phoenician counterparts, as found, e.g., in the inscription of Ahiram from Byblus and on the 'Moabite Stone'. The Phoenician alphabet of twenty-two consonants the Greeks rapidly and skilfully transformed into an instrument suited for the representation of their own language, either discarding or giving new phonetic values to letters they did not require, and making further additions, as utility or consistency demanded, at the close of the alphabet, which, as they first learned it, ended with T. In this process of development and adaptation each community or group of communities made its own experiments, and thus a large number of local variations arose (58), but the resultant alphabets fall into four main classes: (1) those of Crete, Thera, and early Melos, in which ΞΦΧΨ are lacking, (2) those of Attica and certain islands, in which ΦΧ represent the sounds φχ, but ΞΨ are wanting, (3) the 'Eastern Group', including also Corinth, Argos, and Sicyon, in which ΞΦΧΨ represent ξφχψ respectively, and (4) the 'Western Group' in which Ξ is not used and ΦΧΨ represent φξχ respectively. The original 'retrograde' direction of the script gave place to the 'boustrophedon' style, in which the lines run alternately from right to left and from left to right, and this was succeeded by the exclusive use of the left-to-right direction. Greek aesthetic sense, notably that of the Athenians, demanded greater simplicity, symmetry, and uniformity in the letter-forms and insisted

on their arrangement in straight horizontal lines. Indeed, in the sixth century B.C. the 'stoichedon' style appears, and enjoys, especially at Athens, a long vogue; in this there is an exact alinement of letters not only horizontal but also vertical (59). Down to the close of the fifth century Athens used an alphabet of only twenty-one letters,

ΑΒΛΔΕΙΗΘΙΚΙΜΝΟΓΡΣΤΥΦΧ,

in which Ε denotes ε, ει, η, Ο denotes ο, ου, ω, and Η retains its original value as an aspirate; but in 403 B.C. the Milesian alphabet of twenty-four letters was officially adopted in its place, and soon all Greece followed the Athenian lead and used the alphabet

ΑΒΓΔΕΙΗΘΙΚΑΜΝΞΟΓΡΣΤΥΦΧΨΩ.

Since that time the Greek alphabet has neither gained nor lost a letter, though various influences modified their forms. (1) The fourth century witnessed an excessive simplification, due perhaps in part to economic motives, leading to the frequent representation of Α or Δ by Λ, of Η or Ν by ΙΙ, etc.; but this hampered the reader and proved a passing phase, dying out in the third century. (2) Another temporary fashion was the substitution of rectilinear for curved forms, partly in the engraver's interest and partly because of the archaic appearance of some of the resultant forms. (3) Far more lasting and potent was the tendency towards elaboration of the script, due to a recoil from the old simplicity and a desire to display the designer's ingenuity; this led to the addition of serifs or of 'apices' to the letters, the substitution of Α for A, and the invention of various ornamented forms, and flourished in the two centuries before and after Christ, but died down c. A.D. 200. (4) Ultimately the influence of the cursive style triumphed, and the epigraphical script became a mere copy on stone of the forms convenient to papyrus or parchment, with its tendency to make the letters taller and narrower, to substitute curved for straight lines, and to reduce or eliminate the necessity of removing pen from paper. We thus reach an alphabet of the type

ΑΒΓΔΕΖΗΘΙΚΛΜΝΞΟΠΡΣΤΥΦΧΨΩ.

Numbers were either written out in words or indicated by numeral signs. The Greek numeral systems are of two classes, in the first of which there are many striking local divergences. (1) In the acrophonic system (60), illustrated by inscriptions from about 460 to 100 B.C. and used sporadically even later, the initial letters of πέντε, δέκα, ἑκατόν, etc., stand for the values indicated by those words; Ι represents the unit; and there are usually compound signs for 50, 500, 5,000, etc. Thus in Attica ΜΧΧΗΓΑΔΔΔΓΙ = 12186 and ΤΤΡΓΗΓΗΙΙC = 2 talents, 5607 drachmas, 2½ obols. (2) In the alphabetic system, traceable back to the fifth century, widespread in the Hellenistic period and completely dominant by 100 B.C., the letters in their alphabetical order (with the retention of Ϝ and Ϙ in their original places after ε and π and the addition of Ͻ after ω) indicate the nine units, nine tens and nine hundreds, so that ΤϘΗ = 398 and ΜΒΡΠΕ = 12186. Frequently these alphabetic numerals, which are used for ordinal as well as for cardinal numbers, are distinguished by a superposed horizontal line. Inscriptions also furnish abundant materials for the study of Greek punctuation, ligature, monogram, and abbreviation, which consists in the omission either of the end or of some part of the interior of a word; the latter method of contraction is especially frequent in, but by no means confined to, the *nomina sacra*, e.g. Θ(εό)s, Χ(ριστό)ν, Κ(ύρι)ε.

II. Even more important than the form of inscriptions is their content. They are historical documents as well as palaeographical specimens, and there is no aspect of Hellenic thought or speech, writing or action on which they do not throw valuable light. Apart from such outstanding documents as the Attic tribute quota-lists and assessments (82–3), the law-code of Gortyn (48), the the chronological table known as the 'Parian Marble' (49), the poems of Isyllus and Maiistas, the Delphic paeans, the cure-records from the Epidaurian Asclepieum, the official autobiography of Augustus in the bilingual *Monumentum Ancyranum* (50–1), Diocletian's Edict (52), and the philosophical confession of Diogenes of Oenoanda, inscriptions with their authentic, first-hand, contemporary records, characterized by extraordinary detail and objectivity, immeasurably enrich our knowledge of the ancient world (4, 5). They offer materials, often the sole materials available, for the study of all the Greek dialects (61–3); they provide uniquely valuable evidence of grammatical and orthographical usage and of phonetic changes (64); they give to the student of Greek literature thousands of dedicatory poems, metrical epitaphs, and other verse compositions (69–71), as well as countless examples of prose and extensive records of dramatic contests and victories (87); they preserve several hymns accompanied by the musical notes to which they were chanted. To the archaeologist they supply hundreds of signatures of sculptors (90), potters, and painters. In the sphere of religion we owe to them a wealth of detailed knowledge of cult titles and ritual laws (91), temple organization and finance, priestly appointment and tenure, religious festivals and societies, oracles, confessions and thanksgivings, prayers and curses (92), not to speak of the light they throw upon Jewish and Christian beliefs and practices (13–15, 65–8). In the political realm they preserve the *ipsissima verba* of laws, decrees (very many of which record the bestowal of citizenship, προξενία (76), and other privileges) (73), edicts and rescripts (75), treaties (74), arbitral awards (5, 77–9), legal judgements (80), economic and fiscal regulations, financial records (81), specifications and accounts relating to public buildings (88–9), boundaries of States or public domains, lists of eponymous or other magistrates, census-surveys, and other documents, confirming, correcting, or supplementing the data derived from literary sources. Finally, in the field of private and social life, where literature is least helpful, inscriptions aid us with their countless records of legal and commercial transactions—contracts, sales, leases, mortgages and guarantees, loans and deposits, wills and endowments (85), dowries and manumissions of various types, civil or religious—of clubs and societies (5, 98–9), schools and scholars, examinations and prizes (86), their thousands of stamped amphora-handles and mercantile inscriptions (84), and their myriads of epitaphs with varying formulae, often revealing interesting local peculiarities (93–6). Even where such inscriptions are of little or no value individually, they frequently serve, taken in large numbers, as the bases of inductions which are of real importance, linguistic or historical.

BIBLIOGRAPHY

The fullest epigraphical bibliography is (1) J. J. E. Hondius, *Saxa loquuntur* (1938), 55 ff. Here only a brief selection can be given.

History of the study: (2) S. Chabert, *Histoire sommaire des études d'épigraphie grecque* (1906).

Introductory: (3) C. T. Newton, *Essays on Art and Archaeology* (1880), 95 ff.; (4) M. Cary, *Documentary Sources of Gk. History* (1927); (5) M. N. Tod, *Sidelights on Gk. History* (1932).

General accounts: (6) J. Franz, *Elementa Epigraphices Graecae* (1840); (7) S. Reinach, *Traité d'épigraphie grecque* (1885); (8) E. S. Roberts–E. A. Gardner, *Introduction to Gk. Epigraphy*, i. *Archaic Inscriptions*, ii. *Attic Inscriptions* (1887–1905); (9) W. Larfeld, *Handbuch d. griech. Epigraphik* (1902–7); (10) id., *Griech. Epigraphik*[3] (I. von Müller's *Handbuch* i. 5; 1914); (11) F. Hiller von Gaertringen, *Griech. Epigraphik* (Gercke–Norden's *Einleitung* i. 9; 1924); (12) A. Rehm, *Die Schrift u. d. Schriftzeugnisse* (W. Otto's *Handbuch d. Archäologie* i (1937), 182 ff.).

Christian Epigraphy: (13) O. Marucchi, *Christian Epigraphy* (1912); (14) C. M. Kaufmann, *Handbuch d. altchristlichen Epigraphik* (1917); (15) J. Jalabert–R. Mouterde, *Inscriptions grecques chrét.* in *Dict. d'archéol. chrét.* vii (1926), 623 ff.

Facsimiles and photographs: (16) H. Roehl, *Inscriptiones Graecae antiquissimae* (1882); (17) id. *Imagines inscr. Graec. antiquiss.*[2] (1907); (18) O. Kern, *Inscriptiones Graecae* (1913); (19) J. Kirchner, *Imagines inscr. Atticarum* (1935).

Corpora, i.e. complete collections for given localities: (20) A. Boeckh, &c., *Corpus Inscriptionum Graecarum* (1825–77); (21) *Inscriptiones Graecae* (1873–) [includes Europe only: (i[2], ii/iii[2]) Attica; iv Argolis (iv[2]. 1 Epidaurus); v Laconia, Messenia, Arcadia; vi* Elis, Achaea; vii Megaris, Boeotia; viii* Delphi; ix Phocis, Locris, Aetolia, Acarnania, Ionian Islands, Thessaly (ix[2]. 1 Aetolia); x* Epirus, Macedonia, Thrace, Scythia; xi† Delos; xii† Aegean Islands except Delos; xiii* Crete; xiv Sicily, Italy and W. Europe]; (22) *Tituli Asiae Minoris* (1901–) [i, ii Lycia]; (23) B. D. Meritt, *Corinth* viii.1 (1931); (24) W. Dittenberger–K. Purgold, *Inschriften von Olympia* (1896); (25) *Fouilles de Delphes* iii (1909–); (26) M. G. Demitsas, 'Η Μακεδονία (1896); (27) E. Kalinka, *Antike Denkmäler in Bulgarien* (1906); (28) B. Latyschev, *Inscriptiones antiquae orae septentrionalis Ponti Euxini* i[2], ii, iv (1890–16); (29) *Inscriptions de Délos* (1926–); (30) W. R. Paton–E. L. Hicks, *Inscriptions of Cos* (1891); (31) A. Maiuri, *Nuova silloge epigrafica di Rodi e Cos* (1925); (32) M. Guarducci, *Inscriptiones Creticae* (1935–); (33) *Monumenta Asiae Minoris Antiqua* (1928–); (34) O. Kern, *Inschriften von Magnesia am Maeander* (1900); (35) F. Hiller von Gaertringen, *Inschriften von Priene* (1906); (36) M. Fränkel, *Inschriften von Pergamon* (1890–5); (37) W. H. Buckler–D. M. Robinson, *Sardis* vii.1 (1932); (38) W. M. Ramsay, *Cities and Bishoprics of Phrygia* (1895–7); (39) W. Judeich, *Altertümer von Hierapolis* (1898); (40) L. Jalabert–R. Mouterde *Inscr. grecques et latines de la Syrie* (1929–); (41) *Publications of the Princeton Univ. Archaeological Expeditions to Syria* iii (1907–22); (42) F. Preisigke–F. Bilabel, *Sammelbuch griech. Urkunden aus Ägypten* (1915–); (43) G. Oliverio, *Documenti antichi dell' Africa Italiana* i, ii (1932–6).

Collections: (44) *The Collection of Ancient Greek Inscriptions in the British Museum* (1874–1916); (45) L. Robert, *Collection Froehner* i: *Inscr. grecques* (1936); (46) E. Breccia, *Iscrizioni greche e latine* [Alexandria Museum] (1911); (47) J. G. Milne, *Gk. Inscriptions* [Cairo Museum] (1905).

Single inscriptions: (48) J. Kohler–E. Ziebarth, *Das Stadtrecht von Gortyn* (1912); (49) F. Jacoby, *Das Marmor Parium* (1904); (50) E. G. Hardy, *The Monumentum Ancyranum* (1923); (51) J. Gagé, *Res gestae Divi Augusti* (1935); (52) T. Mommsen–H. Blümner, *Der Maximaltarif des Diocletian* (1893).

Selections: (53) G. Dittenberger, *Sylloge Inscriptionum Graecarum*[3] (1915–24); (54) G. Dittenberger, *Orientis Graeci Inscriptiones Selectae* (1903–5); (55) C. Michel, *Recueil d'inscr. grecques* (1900–27); (56) E. L. Hicks–G. F. Hill, *Manual of Gk. Historical Inscriptions* (1901); (57) M. N. Tod, *Selection of Gk. Historical Inscriptions* i[2] (1946), ii (1948).

Script: (58) A. Kirchhoff, *Studien zur Geschichte d. griech. Alphabets*[4] (1887); (59) R. P. Austin, *The Stoichedon Style in Gk. Inscriptions* (1938); (60) M. N. Tod, 'The Gk. Numeral Notation' in *British School Annual* xviii. 98 ff.; xxviii. 141 ff.

Grammar and dialect: (61) H. Collitz, F. Bechtel, &c. *Sammlung d. griech. Dialekt-Inschriften* (1884–1915); (62) E. Schwyzer, *Dialectorum Graecarum exempla epigraphica*, (1923); (63) C. D. Buck, *Introduction to the Study of the Gk. Dialects*[2] (1927); (64) K. Meisterhans, *Grammatik d. attischen Inschriften* (3rd ed. by E. Schwyzer, 1900).

Special classes or topics: (65) H. Grégoire, *Recueil des inscr. grecques-chrétiennes d'Asie Mineure* (1922–); (66) G. Lefebvre, *Recueil des inscr. grecques-chrét.* d'Égypte (1907); (67) J. B. Frey, *Corpus Inscriptionum Iudaicarum* (1936–); (68) S. Klein, *Jüdisch-palästinisches Corpus Inscriptionum* (1920); (69) G. Kaibel, *Epigrammata Graeca ex lapidibus conlecta* (1878); (70) E. Hoffmann, *Sylloge epigrammatum Graecorum* (1893); (71) F. Hiller von Gaertringen, *Historische griech. Epigramme* (1926); (72) R. Cagnat–G. Lafaye, *Inscriptiones Graecae ad res Romanas pertinentes* i, ii, iv (1911–27); (73) H. Swoboda, *Die griech. Volksbeschlüsse* (1890); (74) R. von Scala, *Die Staatsverträge d. Altertums* (1898); (75) C. B. Welles, *Royal Correspondence in the Hellenistic Period* (1934); (76) P. Monceaux, *Les Proxénies grecques* (1886); (77) E. Sonne, *De arbitris externis* (1888); (78) A. Raeder, *L'arbitrage internationale chez les Hellènes* (1912); (79) M. N. Tod, *International Arbitration amongst the Greeks* (1913); (80) R. Dareste–B. Haussoullier–Th. Reinach, *Recueil des inscr. juridiques grecques* (1891–1904); (81) B. D. Meritt, *Athenian Financial Documents* (1932); (82) id.–A. B. West, *The Athenian Assessment of 425 B.C.* (1934); (83) id.–H. T. Wade-Gery–M. F. McGregor, *The Athenian Tribute Lists* (1939–); (84) R. Hackl, *Merkantile Inschriften auf attischen Vasen* (1909); (85) B. Laum, *Stiftungen in d. griech. u. röm. Antike* (1914); (86) E. Ziebarth, *Aus. d. griech. Schulwesen*[2] (1914); (87) A. Wilhelm, *Urkunden dramatischer Aufführungen in Athen* (1906); (88) A. Choisy, *Études épigr. sur l'architecture grecque* (1884); (89) H. Lattermann, *Griech. Bauinschriften* (1908); (90) E. Loewy, *Inschriften griech. Bildhauer* (1885); (91) I. de Prott–L. Ziehen, *Leges Graecorum Sacrae* (1896–1906); (92) A. Audollent, *Defixionum tabellae* (1904); (93) H. Gutscher, *Die attischen Grabschriften* (1889–90); (94) E. Loch, *De titulis Graecis sepulcralibus* (1890); (95) K. Strausberg, *De titulis Graecis sepulcralibus* (1937); (96) H. Stemler, *Die griech. Grabinschriften Kleinasiens* (1909); (97) D. M. Robinson–E. J. Fluck, *A Study of the Gk. Love-names* (1937); (98) E. Ziebarth, *Das griech. Vereinswesen* (1896); (99) F. Poland, *Geschichte d. griech. Vereinswesens* (1909).

* Not published by 1948.   † Partially published.

On almost every aspect of the study light is thrown by the works of M. Holleaux (esp. *Études d'épigraphie et d'histoire grecques*, 1938–), L. Robert, U. von Wilamowitz-Moellendorff (esp. *Kleine Schriften*, v. 1 (1937)), and A. Wilhelm (esp. *Beiträge zur griech. Inschriftenkunde* (1909)). Current discoveries and discussions are collected in J. J. E. Hondius, *Supplementum Epigraphicum Graecum* (1923–); biennial surveys of recent epigraphic books and articles are provided by M. N. Tod, in *JHS* and *JEg.Arch.*

M. N. T.

EPIGRAPHY, LATIN.

EPIGRAPHY, LATIN. Latin epigraphy is concerned with the remains of Latin inscribed on stone or metal (but not coins or gems), while palaeography deals with writings on parchment or papyrus. But epigraphy has regard not only to the form of the inscription (e.g. lettering, abbreviations) but also to the subject-matter, and so impinges in varying degree on philology, history, antiquities, law, and many other departments of classical study. Inscriptions range from casual scratchings on stone to important official documents incised on metal or stone. Most inscriptions belong to the early Empire, and throw a flood of light on numerous aspects of life about which the literature has little to say, e.g. the stations, promotions, movements, nationality of soldiers; the imperial civil service; the life of slaves and freedmen; trade; municipal government; religious cults; roads and boundaries; and indeed the general life of the provinces.

2. Inscriptions are usually classified somewhat as follows: (i) *tituli* (ἐπιγράμματα): inscriptions relating to individuals, usually connected with the object bearing the inscription, e.g. *tituli sepulchrales, sacri, honorarii,* or inscriptions on public works and portable objects as e.g. lamps, lead pipes; (ii) *acta* (γράμματα): public or private documents, e.g. *foedera, leges, plebiscita, senatus consulta, leges collegiorum, decreta* of magistrates or emperors, public documents of a sacred character, private documents. To illustrate the variety of topics covered by inscriptions it will be convenient to follow (in the main) the classification adopted by H. Dessau in his *Inscriptiones Latinae Selectae.*

3. Under *monumenta historica liberae reipublicae* fall such inscriptions as the *S.C. de Bacchanalibus* of 186 B.C. embodied in an official letter (Dessau, *ILS* 18), *lex agraria* of 111 B.C. (*CIL* i². 2. 585), inscriptions on boundary stones (*cippi*) set up by C. Gracchus, the 'Tables of Heraclea', containing an assortment of laws by Caesar (*ILS* 6085), *elogia*, i.e. inscriptions (often laudatory) appended to statues of famous men set up, e.g., in the *forum Augusti*, a few of which are contemporary (*ILS* 1–17, 43–68. *Inscriptiones Italiae* XIII, fasc. iii: *Elogia* (1937)). With this group may be mentioned also the *fasti consulares* and the *acta triumphorum* (*CIL* i². 1; *Inscript. Ital.* XIII, fasc. i (1947)).

4. Under the heading *tituli imperatorum domusque imperatoriae* (*ILS* 70–839) are grouped most valuable inscriptions which give information about the powers (e.g. *ILS* 244), offices, and titles held by the emperors (and on them we are often dependent for dates), events of their principates, their campaigns and travels, their rescripts and letters (e.g. *ILS* 423) and edicts (e.g. *ILS* 214), petitions sent to them and their replies, their public works, and their speeches. For the great record put up by Augustus, *see* MONUMENTUM ANCYRANUM.

5. Numerous inscriptions refer to *viri et mulieres ordinis senatorii* (*ILS* 862–1312) and to *viri dignitatis equestris* (*ILS* 1313–472), and illustrate, e.g., the official careers of the noble families and the lines of promotion; the distinction between senatorial and imperial provinces, their relative importance and the changes in their status; the rise of new families and the disappearance of old; the careers of the *equites* in the civil service. The study of the relative importance assigned to offices or of the provincial origin of officials may contribute largely to the understanding of the policy of an emperor, as e.g. of Vespasian and his new equestrian nobility of office.

6. Inscriptions relating to *ministri domus Augustae condicionis libertinae et servilis* (*ILS* 1473–876) and to *apparitores et servi publici* (*ILS* 1877–975) reveal the amazing variety of duties, many very responsible, which fell to the lower grades of the civil service in every quarter of the Empire. The names and origins of these humble officials often show something of the nationalities making up the population of a given place, while their functions and positions reveal in great detail the administrative system and illustrate the nature and function of slavery.

7. *Tituli militares* are indispensable for an understanding of the Roman army. Not only do they show the ranks and duties, lines of promotion, and terms of service within the army, but they also give information about the stations and movements of troops, about recruitment and the policy of using troops in their own area of recruitment or sending them elsewhere. The relationship between military service and citizenship, and thus the function performed by the army in civilizing the Roman world, can be appreciated from the inscriptions. Indeed *tituli militares* together with *tituli municipales* will show the process by which the camp and its *canabae* grew into a Roman township, often the origin of towns still flourishing to-day.

8. A few inscriptions refer directly to men well known as writers (e.g. the younger Pliny's career is given in *ILS* 2927), but more often men and women who are not much more than names in Latin literature are made real by chance information about them preserved in inscriptions.

9. *Tituli sacri et sacerdotum* (*ILS* 2957–5050) show the organization of religious cults, the spread of Roman cults into the provinces and of Oriental cults into the West. They are invaluable for the study of the growth of emperor worship. For our knowledge of the syncretism of religions, of the persistence of ancient cults and names and obscure deities of Gaul and Britain, of the nature and diffusion of Mithraism and kindred matters we are almost entirely indebted to inscriptions.

10. Inscriptions relating to *ludi* (*ILS* 5051–316) are common and range from lists of victorious horses and gladiators to the briefest prayer that a favourite 'colour' may win. Public works and buildings, roads, tunnels and aqueducts, the contracts and undertakings of building firms or emperors, technical details about sites and leases may be studied in other inscriptions (*ILS* 5317–6043).

11. *Tituli municipales* (*ILS* 6044–7210) form a large group and give abundant information about municipal life and government; from them we learn of the charters of townships, of their government and officials, of the gratitude and bequests of public men and private citizens, of the relations of the townships with the central government, of their origin, growth, wealth, financial instability, and decay. The charter of Malaca (*ILS* 6088) is an excellent example.

12. But inscriptions reveal also many aspects of humble life. Hence we can learn much of the *collegia* of the lower grades of society (*ILS* 7211–365); the numerous *tituli* relating to every kind of trade, craft, and occupation (*ILS* 7366–817) reveal the complex nature of life under the Empire and enable important deductions to be drawn about economic conditions. Of great human interest are the numerous epitaphs (*ILS* 7818–8560) put up by humble people, which record valuable details of family life and reveal clearly the feelings and affections of people whom the literature passes by; many are remarkably intimate and moving records of genuine emotion.

13. There are many other types of inscription of which mention must be omitted, and, though the information given by each inscription may be trivial, cumulatively it is of importance. For example, the stamps on wine-jars or lamps or medicine pots or tiles may yield, when gathered together, important conclusions of economic or military or geographical significance.

14. For the philologist inscriptions are of great value in furnishing evidence as to Italic dialects, the growth of the Latin language, changes in spelling and pronunciation. The kind of Latin spoken in the provinces can be studied and provincialisms of usage and pronunciation are easily accumulated.

15. The processes of cutting inscriptions need not be minutely described. The line along which the inscription was to run was marked with a stretched cord stained with colour and 'snapped' on to the stone; sometimes a faint line was cut. The letters were cut with a chisel (*scalprum*) and hammer; there is some evidence that they were painted first, and that the outline was sketched by means of a template. Sometimes the letters, when completed, were picked out with vermilion. Large bronze letters were occasionally fixed to the stone by pegs, and when the letters have been lost the inscription can be read by means of the holes. Inscriptions on bronze (prepared by an *aerarius*) were chased by a *caelator*, and the word *incidere* is used of cutting inscriptions on bronze as well as on stone; sometimes the letters were filled with white lead.

16. The kind of lettering used in inscriptions varies according to its date and purpose and the material on which it is made. The characters change very considerably from the time of the earliest known inscription (*c.* 600 B.C., the *fibula* of Praeneste *CIL* i², p. 320) till the *scriptura monumentalis* reached full development under Augustus and the early Empire: *litterae quadratae* (the *quadrator* squared the stones) became a recognized type familiar in the best inscriptions of, say, the time of Trajan; they are bold, rounded, and unornamented. The *scriptura actuaria* was derived from the flowing letters shaped naturally by a brush. The term *scriptura cursiva* is used to denote the letters of graffiti (writings on walls) which are akin to running handwriting. Individual letters vary much in the different *scripturae*. To save space letters were often run together or joined by 'ligatures'. From *c.* 90 B.C. to A.D. 250 an apex, shaped usually like an acute accent, was used (by no means always) to denote a long vowel. Sometimes dots above the foot of the line indicate the end of a word and less commonly small ivy leaves (*hederae distinguentes*) mark breaks.

17. Inscriptions are generally composed with extreme brevity to save space and lend dignity. But brevity is obtained also by drastic and elaborate abbreviation of words; this constitutes one of the main difficulties in beginning a study of inscriptions (handbooks usually contain a glossary of the main abbreviations). Certain words are more usually abbreviated than written in full, and the method of abbreviation on the whole follows defined rules. It is a convention in printing inscriptions that the letters necessary to complete an abbreviation are printed in round brackets ( ).

18. Inscriptions are dated (i) by subject-matter; for the assigning of a date most exact and detailed knowledge may be necessary, (ii) by the form of the letters or some peculiarity in phrase or order or spelling; on the other hand, badly cut letters occur in the best period. Forgeries have frequently been manufactured, chiefly in the Renaissance, to support a particular scholar's view or to glorify a family; but many of them contain imperfections or slips by which modern knowledge can prove their spuriousness.

19. A great many, perhaps most, inscriptions are imperfectly preserved; for the stones have often been damaged and used again for later building. But restoration of the whole inscription from a few surviving fragments can often be made with confidence by scholars who have knowledge of epigraphic usage and Roman history. Restorations are conventionally enclosed in square brackets [ ] in printing.

BIBLIOGRAPHY

About A.D. 800 a monk made a collection of Latin inscriptions, which was later found at Einsiedeln in Switzerland; thereafter many collections have been made, on which we rely for some inscriptions now lost, as also on manuscript notes made by Italian painters copying ancient buildings. The plan of a complete *Corpus Inscriptionum Latinarum* (*CIL*), conceived first in Copenhagen and encouraged in France, was carried out in Germany, chiefly on the initiative of Mommsen. The first volume appeared in 1863. The collection is arranged on a geographical basis: i *Inscr. Latinae antiquissimae* (down to 44 B.C.), Fasti and Calendars; ii Spain; iii Egypt, Asia, Greek provinces of Europe and Illyricum; iv *Inscr. Parietariae* of Pompeii, &c.; v Gallia Cisalpina; vi Rome; vii Britain; viii Africa; ix Calabria, Apulia, Samnium, Sabini, Picenum; x Bruttii, Lucania, Campania, Sicilia, Sardinia; xi Aemilia, Etruria, Umbria; xii Gallia Narbonensis; xiii Tres Galliae et duae Germaniae; xiv Latium vetus; xv Urbis Romae Instrumentum domesticum; xvi Diplomata militaria. Many volumes contain 'parts' or 'supplements' made necessary by new discoveries. Before incorporation in a supplement new inscriptions are published in *Ephemeris Epigraphica*. See also *Inscriptiones Italiae* (1931–). The best known selection is that of H. Dessau, *Inscriptiones Latinae Selectae* (Berlin, 1892–1916) with 9,522 inscriptions and Latin commentary.

The chief general treatments are: J. E. Sandys, *Latin Epigraphy*[2] (1927, revised by S. G. Campbell), with full bibliography, and R. Cagnat, *Cours d'épigraphie latine*[4] (1914). See also Lietzmann, *Kleine Texte* (which include 'Res gestae divi Augusti', 'Alt-lateinische Inschr.', 'Vulgär-lateinische Inschr.', 'Pompeianische Wandinschr.'); Bücheler, *Carmina Epigraphica* (Teubner, 1895–7); G. McN. Rushforth, *Latin Historical Inscriptions, illustrating the history of the Early Empire*[2] (1930); C. G. Bruns, *Fontes Iuris Romani antiqui*[7] (1909); R. H. Barrow, *A Selection of Latin Inscriptions* (1934). See also bibliographies under separate provinces (AFRICA, &c.), MONUMENTUM ANCYRANUM, MUNICIPIUM.   R. H. B.

EPILYCUS, cited by Athenaeus as a writer sometimes of Old (4. 140a) Comedy, sometimes of Middle (e.g. 1. 28e). The Κωραλίσκος has a Doric title, and was written partially in Doric.

FCG ii. 887 f.; *CAF* i. 803 f.; Demiańczuk, *Supp. Com.*, p. 40.

EPIMELETES. (a) In Greek cities this title was given either to regular magistrates who managed special departments, such as the water supply, the docks, or festivals, or to special commissioners elected for some temporary need, such as the erection of a public building. (b) In Ptolemaic Egypt the *epimeletes* was in the third century the chief financial official of the *nomos* (q.v. 1). In the second century he was subordinate to ὁ ἐπὶ τῶν προσόδων, and he was sometimes responsible for a part of a nome only. (c) In the Roman period *epimeletes* is often the translation of the Latin *curator*.   A. H. M. J.

EPIMENIDES, religious teacher and wonder-worker of Crete. According to Plato (*Leg.* 1. 642d) he was at Athens, performing religious rites and prophesying, about 500 B.C. Others said that he purified the city after the slaughter of Cylon's associates about 600 B.C. (Arist. *Ath. Pol.* 1, etc.; Diels, *Vorsokr.*[5] i. 29 f.). With the variations in date go the legends of his great age (157 or 299), and miraculous sleep of fifty-seven years (Diog. Laert.; Diels, ib. 28). The stories of wanderings out of the body (cf. Suidas; Diels, ib. 29) rank him with Aristeas, Hermotimus, etc., but his god was the Cretan Zeus, and Plutarch says that the men of the time called him Κούρης νέος (Diels, ib. 30). Tradition assigned to him a *Theogony* and a *Cretica*, also *Katharmoi* and other mystical writings.

Sources and fragments in Diels–Kranz, *Vorsokr.*[5] i. 27–37.
W. K. C. G.

EPINOMIA, see PASTURAGE.

EPIPHANY. In Homer the gods regularly appear visibly and have dealings with men—fighting, helping, loving (cf. RELIGION, MINOAN-MYCENEAN). Poetic or mythical epiphanies, regarded as belonging to the distant past, persist throughout Greek literature, and sometimes serve the ends of religion by giving the *aition* for a living cult, e.g. the Homeric Hymn to Demeter. Even the *märchenhaft* story of Baucis and Philemon suggests this by its ending. Dionysus especially appeared with manifestations of power to compel unbelievers, as in Euripides' *Bacchae*. In historical epiphanies the cult-motive is always prominent. In the famous story of Philippides, Pan demands worship at Athens in return for his help (Hdt. 6. 105). Two common types are (i) epiphanies to help or terrify in battle, frequent in Herodotus (8. 64; 8. 36 ff., etc.), and cf. in Roman saga the Dioscuri at Lake Regillus (Dion. Hal. *Ant. Rom.* 6. 13); (ii) healing epiphanies. Asclepius in effecting cures always *appeared* to the sufferer, usually in a dream (incubation) but sometimes waking (Isyllus-inscr. and *SIG* 803). Frequent Hellenistic inscriptions record epiphanies connected with the foundation of cults (e.g. the *Soteria* at Delphi; Dionysus 'in the tree' at Magnesia, Kern, *Inschr. von M.* 215 b). The genuineness of the belief cannot be doubted (cf. *Acts* xiv. 10–12), though cases of fraud were recognized (Pisistratus, Hdt. 1. 60). The term *epiphaneia* was used also to denote miracles in which the deity was not thought to be seen (Dion. Hal. *Ant. Rom.* 2. 68). Deified living rulers were hailed as θεοὶ ἐπιφανεῖς, because their power was felt. In general see F. Pfister in *PW* Suppl. iv. 277 ff.; A. D. Nock, *JHS* xlviii (1928), 38 ff.; cf. also the remarks of Nock in 'A Vision of Mandulis Aion', *Harv. Theol. Rev.* xxvii (1934), 53–104, esp. 67 ff.

W. K. C. G.

EPIROTA, *see* CAECILIUS (3).

EPIRUS ("Ηπειρος, 'Mainland'), north-west area of Greece, from Acroceraunian point to Nicopolis, with harbours at Buthrotum and Glycys Limen (at Acheron's mouth); bordered on south by Gulf of Ambracia, and on east by Pindus range with pass via Metsovo to Thessaly. Three limestone ranges parallel to the coast and the Pindus range enclose narrow valleys and plateaux with good pasture and extensive woods; alluvial plains were formed near Buthrotum, Glycys Limen, and Ambracia. Epirus had a humid climate and cold winters. In terrain and in history it resembled upper Macedonia. Known to Homer only for the oracle at Dodona, and to Herodotus as the home of Dorian invaders and for the oracle of the dead by Acheron, Epirus received Hellenic influence from Ambracia and Corcyra. Theopompus knew fourteen Epirote tribes, probably of Dorian and Illyrian stocks, of which the Chaones held the plain of Buthrotum, the Thesproti the plain of Acheron, and the Molossi the plain near Dodona, which forms the highland centre of Epirus with an outlet southwards to Ambracia. The unification of Epirus in a symmachy led by the Molossian king was finally achieved by Alexander (q.v. 6), brother-in-law of Philip II of Macedon. The invasions of Italy led by Alexander and Pyrrhus both ended in failure; a weakened Epirus was the victim of attack from Aetolia, Macedon, and Illyria, until in *c.* 232 B.C. the Molossian monarchy fell. The Epirote republic with a federal assembly at Phoenice (near Buthrotum) was involved in the wars between Rome and Macedonia, culminating in 167 B.C. with the sack of Epirus and deportation of 150,000 captives. Under the Roman Empire roads were built through Epirus, and Roman colonies founded at Buthrotum and Nicopolis. Ancient remains indicate that Epirus flourished in Hellenistic and declined in Roman times.

C. Klotzsch, *Epeirotische Gesch. bis zu 280 v. Chr.* (1911); G. N. Cross, *Epirus* (1930); M. P. Nilsson in *Lunds Universitets Årsskrift* 1909, no. 4; Carapanos, *Dodone et ses ruines* (1878); D. Evangelides in Ἠπειρωτικὰ Χρονικά, 1935; N. G. L. Hammond in *BSA* 1934; H. Treidler, *Epirus im Altertum* (1917); H. H. Scullard, *JRS* 1945, 58 ff. N. G. L. H.

EPISTATES. (*a*) At Athens the ἐπιστάτης τῶν πρυτάνεων, chosen daily by lot from the *prytaneis*, during his day of office held the State seal and keys, and in the fifth century B.C. presided in council and assembly. In the fourth century he selected the *proedri* by lot, and from them, also by lot, the ἐπιστάτης τῶν προέδρων who presided. Similar ἐπίσταται are found in other Greek cities; but sometimes the title is equivalent to the Athenian *prytaneis*. (*b*) In Ptolemaic Egypt the *epistates* was a royal official who administered justice in each *nomos* and sub-district. These officials were distinct from the ἐπιστάται τῶν φυλακιτῶν (*see* POLICE, GREEK). (*c*) In Ptolemaic Egypt the ἐπιστάτης ἱεροῦ was the superintendent, probably appointed by the Crown, of a native temple. (*d*) In all Hellenistic kingdoms the ἐπιστάτης was a high commissioner appointed by the king to control a subject city. He sometimes, perhaps generally, had a royal garrison to maintain public order. He frequently exercised an informal and in theory probably voluntary jurisdiction, settling suits out of court, preferably by arbitration. At Thessalonica and at Seleuceia in Pieria he is known to have possessed a constitutional power of veto over legislation.

On (*d*), M. Holleaux, *BCH* 1933, 25–31; A. Heuss, *Klio*, Beiheft xxxix (1937), 23 ff.; 58 ff. A. H. M. J.

EPISTOLOGRAPHY, *see* LETTERS.

EPISTULA AD PISONES, commonly known as *Ars Poetica*, see HORACE.

EPITADEUS, a Spartan ephor, who (probably soon after 400 B.C.) introduced a law authorizing the transfer of Spartan land-lots by gift or bequest, a method perhaps already much practised in secret. To this measure, and to the wealth accruing to Sparta after the Peloponnesian War, the concentration of the territory of Laconia and Messenia in a few hands (Arist. *Pol.* 2. 1270ᵃ) was mainly due. A. M. W.

EPITAPHIOS, a funeral speech, delivered, according to Athenian custom, by a citizen chosen on the grounds of his high moral and mental qualities (Thuc. 2. 34), at a public funeral of those who had fallen in battle.

The conventional form comprised a tribute to the virtues of the dead, a summary of their country's glorious achievements in the past, a consolation to their relatives, and an exhortation to the survivors to imitate their virtues. Thucydides professes to record in full the speech thus delivered by Pericles at the end of the first year of the Peloponnesian War. The speaker follows the usual form, except that, instead of enlarging on past history, he tells of the glories of Athens in her maturity.

As a contrast to the impersonal austerity of Pericles we have the speech of Hyperides on Leosthenes and others who died in the Lamian War (322 B.C.). Hyperides, who was an intimate friend of the dead general, shows deep personal feeling, and a unique feature of this speech is his reference to the hope of personal immortality. A passage in Lycurgus (*Leoc.* §§ 39–40) is in effect a condensed *Epitaphios* on the dead at Chaeronea.

In addition to these genuine speeches we possess a florid fragment by Gorgias and a speech, composed under Gorgian influence, attributed to Lysias, which, though it cannot be referred with certainty to any definite occasion, may well be genuine (see J. Walz, 'Der Lysianische Epitaphios' (*Philol.* Suppl. 29. 4)). A similar composition attributed to Demosthenes is almost certainly spurious. Finally Socrates in Plato's *Menexenus* recites a funeral speech which, he affirms, was composed by Aspasia to be delivered by Pericles. J. F. D.

EPITHALAMIUM, GREEK. The ἐπιθαλάμιον was strictly a song sung by young men and maidens before the bridal-chamber (Dion. Hal. *Rhet.* p. 247), like the contents of Sappho's Book 7, Theocritus 18, etc. It was distinguished from the γαμήλιος, which could be sung at any festival connected with a wedding (Eust. 1541. 49), and from the ὑμέναιος, the processional song which accompanied the newly wed couple to their home, and is described by Homer (*Il.* 18. 491–6) and Hesiod (*Sc.* 273–80).   C. M. B.

EPITHALAMIUM, LATIN. If Virgil's fourth eclogue is excluded, there are extant some seventeen Latin verse epithalamia. Epithalamia by Calvus, Ticidas, and Ovid are among those that have perished. The earliest and finest extant examples are the sixty-first and sixty-second poems of Catullus, who also in his sixty-fourth poem recounts the love and marriage of Peleus and Thetis. The influence of Sappho is discernible in Catullus, and her influence, direct or indirect, is sometimes suggested in the later rhetorical epithalamia of epic character. There are single examples by Statius, Ausonius (a cento), Paulinus of Nola, Ennodius, Venantius Fortunatus, and Luxorius (a cento). *Anthologia Latina* (Riese) 742 is an anonymous epithalamium. Claudian, Sidonius, and Dracontius have each left two epithalamia. A few verses by Gallienus are described as an epithalamium (S.H.A. *Gallieni Duo* 11. 8, and *Anthologia Latina* 711). The *Medea* of Seneca contains an epithalamium (56–115) which may well have owed something to one in Ovid's lost play with that title. The *De nuptiis Philologiae et Mercurii* by Martianus Capella is in mixed prose and verse, and a thing apart.

R. Reitzenstein, 'Die Hochzeit des Peleus und der Thetis', *Hermes* xxxv (1900), 73–105; A. L. Wheeler, 'Tradition in the Epithalamium', *AJPhil.* li (1930), 205–23; E. A. Mangelsdorff, *Das lyrische Hochzeitsgedicht bei den Griechen und Römern* (1913); J. Fries, *Ein Beitrag zur Ästhetik der römischen Hochzeitspoesie* (1910); C. Morelli, 'L'epitalamio nella tarda poesia latina', *Studi Italiani di Filologia Classica*, xviii (1910), 319–432.   G. B. A. F.

EPITHETS, DIVINE. In considering the very numerous surnames or epithets of gods it is necessary first to distinguish between those appearing only as literary (especially epic) ornaments and those known to have been used in cult. Thus we have no proof that Athena was ever addressed in ritual as γλαυκῶπις; it is her stock epithet in Homer, Zeus' pet-name for her (*Il.* 8. 373). It seems unlikely that Ares was prayed to as βροτολοιγός; he is so addressed by Athena (*Il.* 5. 31), which is a very different thing, and it is his stock epithet (as ibid. 846). In Latin such ornaments are abundant; thus in Virgil, Mars is *durus* (*Ecl.* 10. 44); *impius* (*G.* 1. 511); *indomitus* (*Aen.* 2. 440); *saeuus* (*Aen.* 11. 153). These are certainly not cult-epithets, and in some cases the name of the god hardly means more than 'war, strife'. The epithet is purely poetical in *Aen.* 9. 717, where he is called *armipotens*, and in 11. 8 where *bellipotens* is used instead of his name. But there are many border-line cases, hard to decide. We have no instance of Athena being called Pallas in cult, yet it is not easy to suppose that so familiar a name was never used for her by worshippers; Zeus' stock epithet, 'cloud-gatherer' appears in the voc., νεφεληγερέτα, in epic in many places where it is syntactically a nom., strongly suggesting that its form had become fixed by some ancient liturgical phrase, which, however, is quite lost to us. Now and then an epithet is used to avoid mentioning an ill-omened name; Hades in Sophocles, *OC* 1606, is Zeus χθόνιος, and in Aesch. *Supp.* 231 he is even Zeus ἄλλος.

2. But coming to those epithets which are guaranteed by their occurrence in liturgical formulae, dedications, and the official names of temples, we may distinguish the following classes. (1) Purely local, meaning that the deity in question is worshipped, or has a temple or altar, at such-and-such a place. Thus Apollo Δήλιος is simply Apollo who is worshipped in Delos, and differs from the Pythian, or any other similarly named Apollo, no other-

wise than as Our Lady of Lourdes does from Our Lady of Loretto. Dionysus Κυδαθηναεύς (Dittenberger, *SIG* 109. 16 and elsewhere) is nothing but the Dionysus who has a cult in the Attic deme Κυδαθήναιον. The Bona Dea (q.v.) Subsaxana gives rather the address of her temple than any characteristic of her own; cf. St. Mary's le Strand, St. Martin's in the Fields. Such titles are of no more than topographical interest. At most they may tell us something of the history of the cult, if the title does not fit the immediate locality; a Demeter Ἐλευσία worshipped at Pheneos in Arcadia (Paus. 8. 15. 1) manifestly has something to do with the famous cult at Eleusis, and the local legend said as much. In like manner, the vow of a temple to Venus Erucina, i.e. the Aphrodite of Eryx, in Rome (Livy 22. 9. 10) was made by advice of a Sibylline and therefore Greek oracle. (2) Titles indicating association with another god. These are often of some historical importance, and at times puzzling. Apollo Κάρνειος (*SIG* 736. 34 and 69) has behind him a history of identification, cf. CARNEIA; Athena Ἡφαιστία (ibid. 227. 20) need surprise no one, in view of the resemblance of some functions of the two deities; but it is less easy to see why she had a temple at Megara under the title Αἰαντίς (Paus. 1. 42. 4). In Latin these most characteristically take the form, not of an adjective applied to the god's name but of a genitive following it, as in the much-quoted *conprecationes* (q.v.) in Gellius 13. 23 (22). 2, *Luam Saturni, Salaciam Neptuni, Horam Quirini*, etc. Here in all cases the first of the pair is the less important, and the phrases mean 'Lua (etc.) who is associated with or belongs to the sphere of activity of Saturnus (etc.)', as is now pretty generally agreed. Adjectives are, however, used in the *Tabulae Iguvinae*, as I A 3, *Iuve Krapuvi* (*Ioui Grabouio*), 8, *Trebe Iuvie* (*Trebo Iouio*), though the meaning of the first adjective is not certain. (3) Undoubtedly the largest and most important class of epithets, however, have reference to the functions of the god or goddess, either in general or with reference to some particular occasion on which his or her power was manifest. Thus, Zeus has a great number of titles denoting his control of the weather and all that depends on it; he is Βροντῶν, Thunderer, Κεραύνιος, God of the Thunderbolt, Ὄμβριος, Sender of Rainstorms, Ὑέτιος, Rainer, and as a natural consequence Γεωργός, Farmer; also Οὔριος, God of Favourable Winds, and so forth. Examples may be had from Farnell, *Cults* (index under 'Zeus'), and references there; the corresponding entry in the index to A. B. Cook's treatise on Zeus would supply abundant instances of every kind of title mentioned in this article. Aphrodite has epithets denoting her power over the sexual life of mankind, as Ἀμβολογήρα, 'delayer of old age'; her connexion with love whether licit or illicit, for example Πάνδημος 'Goddess of the whole people', in her Athenian worship as a deity of marriage (Farnell, ii. 658), and on the other hand Ἑταίρα and even Πόρνη (ibid. 667). These last belong to an extremely curious sub-class in which the characteristics of the worshipper are transferred to the deity; both signify the goddess who is worshipped by harlots. Hera in like manner is called Παῖς, Τελεία, and Χήρα at her three shrines in Stymphalus, in other words Maid, Wife, and Widow (Paus. 8. 22. 2); she naturally received the worship of women of all ages and conditions. The local legend was somewhat at a loss to explain the third title, since Zeus cannot die, and invented a quarrel between the two leading to a separation; clearly the sense of such epithets was no longer remembered when Pausanias wrote.

3. Of epithets referring to a particular manifestation of a god's activity two Roman examples may be given. Mars Ultor (see Platner–Ashby, pp. 220, 329) owed his title to his supposed intervention on Augustus' behalf at Philippi and apparently in the recovery of the standards taken by the Parthians. Jupiter's titles

Custos and Conservator (Tacitus, *Hist.* 3. 74) refer *inter alia* to the thank-offerings made him by Domitian after his escape from the Vitellians when they took the Capitol.

4. Epithets having reference to the higher (moral or civic) qualities of a deity are not uncommon, though less so than those which are due to his natural functions. It is to be noted that there is a tendency in later ages to read such qualities into an old title; thus Athena Προναία at Delphi, so named from the fact that her shrine was in front of the temple of Apollo, had so decided an inclination to become Πρόνοια that some manuscripts of Herodotus 8. 37. 2 have been infected by it. As genuine examples may be instanced Apollo Ἀρχηγέτης (see APOLLO), Athena Βουλαία (of the Senate), Venus Verticordia.

5. Late hymns, for instance those of the Orphic collection, have a strong tendency to heap up epithets, including the most unheard-of and fanciful, e.g. no. 28 (Abel), to Hermes.

C. F. H. Bruchmann, *Epitheta deorum quae apud poetas Graecos leguntur* (Teubner, 1893); J. B. Carter, *De deorum Romanorum cognominibus* (Teubner, 1898) and *Epith. deor. q. a. p. Latinos leguntur* (Teubner, 1902) are useful, but there is room for a large and exhaustive work.   H. J. R.

EPITOME (ἐπιτομή). I. GREEK.

The production of summaries or abbreviated versions of longer works, especially scientific works, was much practised in the post-classical era. Thus Pamphilus' Glossary was reduced from 95 books to 30, and then to 5. Strabo was often epitomized (*GGM* 2. 529 ff.). Aristophanes of Byzantium epitomized Aristotle's *Historia animalium*, and the epitome was later epitomized by Sopatros. The first two books of Athenaeus and part of the third survive only in an epitome. But the most important of all Greek epitomes is Proclus' prose summary of the *Epic Cycle*, which has come down to us through Photius, and is a most important source for Greek mythology.   J. D. D.

II. LATIN. In Rome the mental lethargy of late Imperial times betrayed itself in a demand for potted-history books. Works of the dimensions of Livy's history dismayed the reading public and the demand was met in two ways: (1) by the *breviarium*, which aimed at giving a short and concise survey of history (*see* FLORUS, AURELIUS VICTOR, EUTROPIUS, RUFIUS FESTUS); (2) by the epitome, which offered condensed versions of, or extracts from, the works of others—an obvious danger to the survival of the originals. Among the latter is the so-called *Epitome Caesarum*, a hotch-potch account of Imperial history from Augustus to Theodosius which in the first eleven chapters betrays relationship with Aurelius Victor's *Caesares*. Another epitome is the work *De viris illustribus urbis Romae* which is preserved along with the *Caesares*. This gives a history of regal and republican times in the form of biographies. From the style, omissions, and obscurities it is evidently an epitome whose source is probably independent of, and antecedent to, Livy.

Apart from these we may regard as epitomizers L. Septimius, who contracted the last four books of his *Dictys* into one, and the so-called 'Hegesippus', who in his adaptation of Josephus' *Jewish War* compressed books 5, 6, and 7 of the original into one. We have, further, an epitomized version of Julius (q.v. 13) Valerius' translation of the Alexander Romance.

The *Epitome Juliani* is a sixth-century translation and an epitome of some 122 *Novellae* (Νεαραὶ διατάξεις) of Justinian.

Epitomes did not always prevent the preservation of originals. Vitruvius and his abbreviator Faventinus have both survived. Two abridgements did not destroy Valerius Maximus. Pliny's *Natural History* weathered epitomizing and excerpting. Half of Seneca's *Con-*

troversiae and about three and a half decades of Livy are extant despite summaries. But in some cases the abridgement triumphed: e.g. Justinus supplanted his foundation Trogus.

Cf. M. Galdi, *L'Epitome nella letteratura latina* (1922). *See* PERIOCHAE.   L. R. P. and J. W. D.

EPŎNA,

a goddess associated with horses and mules, worshipped by the Romans, and sometimes held to be an old Italic divinity. But the name is purely Celtic. (Cf. Gaulish *epo-redias*, 'equorum domitores'; Breton *ebeul*, colt; Ir. *ech*, horse.) Epona is mentioned by Juvenal (8. 157) and several other authors. Numerous monuments are preserved, chiefly in eastern Gaul, northern Italy, and the regions of the Rhine and the Danube, and the dedications are mostly by soldiers. In fact the cult was transported so far by the army that it has been called 'the most widespread of Gaulish myths'. The goddess is represented as riding a horse or mare, or sitting among horses and mules and feeding them. She sometimes has the same symbols as the *Deae Matres* (q.v.), and the plural form *Eponabus* (like *Matribus*, *Campestribus*) appears on one inscription. It is conjectured that a cult of the horse itself may have preceded the worship of the horse-goddess and been superseded by it.

For references in texts and inscriptions see A. Holder, *Altceltischer Sprachschatz*, s.v. 'Epona'. The principal study of the cult is by S. Reinach, in the *Rev. Arch.* 3rd ser. xxvi, xxxiii, xxxv, xl. For an attempt to explain the myth by Irish and Welsh stories see H. Hubert, in the *Mélanges Vendryes* (1925), 187 ff.   F. N. R.

EPONIA, see FINANCE, GREEK, para. 6.

EPONYMOI (ἐπώνυμοι)

are those who give their name to anybody or anything. They were of three kinds in antiquity. (1) Gods were the *eponymoi* of cities, as Apollo of Apollonia and Athena of Athens. (2) Heroes were the *eponymoi* of tribes, demes, and families. When Cleisthenes divided the Athenians into ten tribes, the Delphic oracle chose ten Attic heroes to be their *eponymoi*; forty-two other heroes became the *eponymoi* of the successive years of military service from 18 to 59. (3) In many cities the presiding magistrate was the eponym of the year, as the archon in Athens, the *stephanephoros* in Miletus, the consuls in Rome.   J. E. F.

EPOPEUS

(Ἐπωπεύς; corrupted to Epaphus by Hyginus, *Fab.* 7. 1; 8. 2–3), the king of Sicyon who protected Antiope (q.v.). He is post-Homeric, first in the *Cypria*, where a version of his story was told in an episode (Proclus ap. Phot.). Eumelus (in Paus. 2. 1. 1) said that he was son of Alōeus the son of Helios, and father of Marathon, the eponym of the Attic region of that name.
                                            H. J. R.

EPRIUS MARCELLUS, TITUS CLODIUS.

Born at Capua of humble parentage, he is first heard of as *praetor peregrinus* in A.D. 48. As *legatus Lyciae* he was guilty of extortion, but by bribery secured both his own acquittal and the exile of one of his accusers (57). In 66 he was *cos. suff.* I, and in the same year, with Cossutianus Capito, he accused the Stoic Thrasea (q.v.) Paetus. For this Nero rewarded him with five million sesterces (c. £50,000). He was subsequently on terms of bitter enmity with Helvidius (q.v.) Priscus, who attempted to prosecute him in 70. For attacks by Helvidius upon him see Tac. *Hist.* 4. 6–8; 43. From 70 to 73 he was *proconsul Asiae*, and on his return *cos. suff.* II (May 74). He continued to enjoy great influence with Vespasian until 79, when he conspired with Caecina Alienus and was forced to suicide. He was a biting and effective orator (Tac. *Dial.* 5. 7; 8. 1; *Ann.* 16. 22 and 29). He also held the offices of augur, *curio maximus*, and *sodalis Augustalis*.

PIR[2], C 915.   R. L. J.

EPULONES, the latest in date of the *quattuor amplissima collegia* of Roman priests. They were first instituted in 196 B.C. (Livy 33. 42. 1), and were then three in number (*tresviri epulones*), the bill for their creation being brought in by C. Licinius Lucullus, then tribune of the plebs, who was himself one of the first members. Their business was to organize and supervise the *epulum Iovis* and the similar public banquet which had by that time become a prominent feature of several festivals, as the *Ludi Romani* (cf. Cicero, *De Or.* 3. 73). They were later increased to seven and continued to be called *septemviri epulones*, although under Caesar their number became ten (Dio Cassius 43. 51. 9).

Wissowa, *RK* 423; 518; Marquardt–Wissowa, *Staatsverw.* iii². 347 ff. and references there.   H. J. R.

EPYLLION (ἐπύλλιον, diminutive of ἔπος), a literary type popular from Theocritus to Ovid, was a narrative poem of about 100 to 600 hexameters; the subject was usually taken from the life of a mythical hero or heroine, the love motif being prominent in later epyllia. Some dialogue and at least one speech generally appear. The distinctive feature is the digression; this occurs in all extant epyllia except Theocritus' *Hylas* and the majority of the legends in Ovid's *Metamorphoses*. Usually introduced as a speech, less commonly as a description of a work of art, the digression makes a contrast to the main plot in either subject or details. Owing something to catalogue poems and Homeric hymns, the epyllion was evolved in the Alexandrian age. Formal artistry, learned allusions, romantic and even morbid themes were in varying degree prominent. The epyllia of Theocritus (*Hylas*, *Heracliscus*, and—if his—*Heracles Leontophonos*) and of his school (Moschus's *Europa* and Bion's fragmentary *Achilleis*) are mainly successions of exquisite pictures; plot and character-drawing are comparatively slight. Callimachus in the fragmentary *Hecale* (published about the time when Theocritus died) developed a more complex plot. Dialogue was increased; the character of Hecale—possibly also of Theseus—was carefully constructed; the picturesque element, though not abandoned, was subordinated to the psychological. Euphorion (b. 276 B.C.), represented by some titles and fragments, wrote at least six epyllia. Allusive and obscure (Cic. *Div.* 2. 133), he probably dropped the picturesque element, popularized the criminal love-story, and concentrated interest on the heroine. None of the other Greek epyllia are known. Parthenius (1st c. B.C.) may have written epyllia; but his Περὶ ἐρωτικῶν παθημάτων (thirty-six prose love-stories, full of violence, treachery, and unfaithfulness, dedicated to Cornelius Gallus for use εἰς ἔπη καὶ ἐλεγείας) shows the morbid sensationalism preferred by Euphorion's successors.

Latin epyllia followed either the idyllic or the psychological type, either Theocritus or Euphorion. The idyllic group (to which may have belonged Cicero's *Alcyone*, Calvus' *Io*, and Cornificius' *Glaucus*) is represented by Catullus' *Peleus and Thetis*, the *Culex*, and Virgil's *Aristaeus* (in *G.* 4). Plot and character are indeed more developed in these than in the earliest epyllia; but their strength lies in graceful and vivid pictures. Catullus, however, while idyllic in main subject, develops Ariadne's character in the digression, thus introducing a novel point of contrast—an innovation followed by Virgil with the Orpheus and Eurydice digression in his *Aristaeus*. The *Aristaeus* shows the epyllion at its highest. Supremely natural, Virgil raises it out of the studied artificiality which hitherto encumbered it. He excels his predecessors in technique, pathos, vividness; single lines or words often form pictures. The psychological group is typified by the *Ciris*, which narrates the love-inspired treachery of Scylla. Frequently learned and obscure, it is perhaps by Gallus. Epyllia by Gallus (probably indicated in Verg. *Ecl.* 6. 31 ff.; cf.

F. Skutsch, *Aus Vergils Frühzeit*, 1901, c. 2) and Cinna's *Zmyrna* were almost certainly similar. This type is brought to its climax by the epyllia in Ovid's *Metamorphoses*. He makes some use of the picturesque method; like Virgil he can construct scenes out of a few words. But he excels in the psychological development of the heroine, especially through a set speech. Occasionally rhetoric betrays him into unnaturalness; but his diction has an easy flow, and his skill as a new teller of old stories is extraordinary. After Ovid, the epyllion was abandoned. The success of the *Aeneid* popularized epic, while the stock of epyllion subjects was almost exhausted. No one seemed original enough to develop historical or fictitious epyllia.

M. M. Crump, *Epyllion from Theocritus to Ovid* (1931). A. M. D.

EQUES, EQUESTER ORDO. *Eques* means firstly 'horseman', 'cavalryman', secondly 'knight', a member of that second rank of nobility in Rome from which horsemen were drawn. *Equester ordo* was the collective name for those knights. The *ordo* ranked as one of the permanent classes of the Roman population, but lacked a regular political organ.

2. The general lines of the history of the knights are as clear as the detail is obscure. The *equites* were originally the State cavalry, serving on horses provided by the State (*equo publico*). Their function in the army was certainly more important than later. They were only distinguished as a class in so far as a certain *census* was considered necessary to maintain the position. Later, the *equites equo publico* sometimes proved insufficient for the need, and during the siege of Veii (c. 400 B.C.) service for additional knights, *equo suo*, was added. Later still the Romans ceased to employ home cavalry to any extent and depended almost entirely on their allies. Small bodies of cavalry were still attached to the legions, but the *equites* came to serve mainly in posts as officers. Until the age of the Gracchi there was nothing to prevent a senator from serving as a knight. Service was from the age of 17 to 46, and the pay was three times that of the infantryman; 10,000 *sestertii* were allotted for the purchase, 2,000 for the keep of the horses. The knights were reviewed at each *lustrum* by the censors, who could, as a mark of censure, order the horse to be sold. A public parade, *transvectio*, instituted in 312 B.C., took place every four years.

3. Gaius Gracchus created a new order in the State, by excluding senators from service as knights, and by giving definite political functions to the class from which knights were drawn—certainly only completing a process that must have begun in the Second Punic War. He gave to the knights the seats on the juries, hitherto held by the Senate, and set them to collect the taxes of Asia; a regular equestrian census, usually assumed to have been 400,000 *sestertii*, was probably established. Henceforward, the knights were always rivals, often enemies of the Senate. Sulla was their enemy, Cinna their friend, Cicero the advocate of 'concordia ordinum'—friendly collaboration of knights and Senate. The jury-seats, restored to the Senate by Sulla, were divided between senators, knights, and *tribuni aerarii* in 70 B.C. In 67 B.C. special seats in the theatre were re-assigned to the knights by L. Roscius Otho. As tax-collectors, the knights fought to secure easy contracts and a free hand in the provinces. The knights suffered heavily under the proscriptions. On several occasions proposals were made to recruit new members of the Senate from their ranks.

4. In the *comitia centuriata*, under the 'Servian Constitution', there were eighteen centuries of knights, and from them the *centuria praerogativa* was chosen by lot. Twelve of these centuries certainly contained *equites equo publico*: the remaining six, known specially as the *sex suffragia*, may have included senators also. Later antiquarians traced the whole system back to the kings. Romulus appointed 300 *celeres* (*trossuli*); Tullus Hostilius, after incorporating Alba Longa, raised the number to 600; Tarquinius Priscus, hindered by an augur from increasing the centuries, doubled the numbers in each (6 × 200 = 1,000). Servius Tullius treated these as twelve centuries and added six more, or, according to another account, found six and added twelve. But there is a very wide historical gap between the kingly period and the eighteen centuries that certainly existed in the late Republic (for a possible reference to twelve, and not eighteen, see Livy 43. 16. 14).

5. Augustus revived the *recognitio*, and combined it with the *transvectio*, which now became annual. The corps of knights (τέλος) was organized in *turmae* under *seviri*. Princes often held the title of *princeps iuventutis* (q.v.). The number was no longer restricted to 1800. The emperor could assign the *equus publicus* at will to any man of free birth, blameless character, and the necessary census of 400,000 *sestertii*. Men over thirty-five were allowed to return the horse, if they chose. The *equester ordo*, in its looser sense, included as well as *equites equo publico*, ex-knights and the sons of senators before they assumed senatorial rank. The distinctive marks of the *ordo* were the *tunica* with narrow border (*angusticlavia*) and the golden ring.

6. From the knights the emperors drew officers for the army (tribunes and *praefecti*), jurymen, procurators, and other civil servants. The crowns of the equestrian career were the prefectures of the Praetorian guard and of Egypt. Hadrian extended their employment at the expense of freedmen and gave them such posts as *a rationibus* and *ab epistulis*. The knights steadily gained at the expense of the Senate, and, in the third century, displaced senators from many provincial posts and from the military commands. In the fourth century the knights survived as a social order, but with diminished political importance.

Kübler, *PW*, s.v.; A. Stein, *Der römische Ritterstand* (1927); C. W. Keyes, *The Rise of the Equites in the Third Century of the Roman Empire* (Princeton, 1915). H. M.

EQUIRRIA, see MARS.

EQUITES SINGULARES IMPERATORIS, probably created by the Flavians, were a mounted bodyguard of the emperor. Chiefly Germans and Pannonians, they numbered at first 500 and later 1,000. Legally their status was that of *Auxilia*, but in practice they formed part of the Praetorian guard. They had their own camp near the Lateran under the command of two Praetorian tribunes.

A. von Domaszewski, *Die Rangordnung im römischen Heere* (1908). H. M. D. P.

ERANOS. In Homer and later authors this word meant a meal to which each partner contributed his share; but from the fifth century B.C. it was mostly a loan, free of interest, given to an individual by a number of friends. Creditors could form a club under an ἀρχέρανος, ἐρανάρχης, or προστάτης ἐράνων, who paid out the loan and received it in repayment. Each partner's claim was transferable, and repayment of sums greater than the original loan could be agreed upon, so that an *eranos* could be profitable business. Papyri from Alexandria suggest that this type of loan was often used by Hellenistic Jews to evade the biblical prohibition of interest.

E. Leider, *Der Handel von Alexandria* (1933), 82 f.; E. Ziebarth, *PW*, s.v. F. M. H.

ERASISTRATUS of Ceos, physician, lived in Alexandria together with and after Herophilus (first half of the 3rd c. B.C.). His school still flourished in Galen's time; his books were read as late as the fourth century A.D. A scholar and philosopher rather than a practitioner, Erasistratus became more and more interested in scientific research, which included even quantitative experiment; working incessantly, he tried to complete his knowledge and did not shrink from admitting earlier mistakes. On the basis of the Democritean atomism and in connexion with Straton's system he apparently developed original ideas (e.g. that of a discontinuous vacuum); although relying on mechanistic principles of explanation, such as the *horror vacui*, he also believed that nature does nothing in vain. His anatomical studies led to the clear distinction of sensory and motor nerves; in post-mortem dissections he recognized the changes of the body due to disease; he was interested in comparative anatomy. In physiology he studied the growth of the body and the process of digestion; he theorized on the flow of the blood through the veins and that of the pneuma through the arteries. All diseases he explained by one cause, viz. plethora, repletion of the body through undigested nutrition; yet he did not neglect the local differences of illness nor the constitution of the patient. In therapy he emphasized the dietetic method and violently opposed phlebotomy and purgation.

BIBLIOGRAPHY

TEXT. R. Fuchs, *Erasistratea* (Diss. Berl. 1892); *Hermes* 1894, pp. 171–203. Erasistratus in the fourth century A.D., Themistius, Or. 20. List of writings, Susemihl, i. 810.
TRANSLATION AND COMMENTARY. J. F. Dobson, *Proceedings of the Royal Society of Med.*, Section Hist. of Med. (1927), indispensable translation and interpretation of more important fragments.
MODERN LITERATURE. Survey, M. Wellmann, *PW* vi. 333. Quantitative experiment, H. Diels, *Sitz. Berl.* 1893, pp. 101–27; W. Jaeger, *Hermes* 1913, pp. 58–65. Charles Singer, *Enc. Brit.*[14] s.v. 'Medicine, History of'. L. E.

ERATOSTHENES of Cyrene (*c.* 275–194 B.C.), pupil of Callimachus and Lysanias, after spending several years at Athens, where he came under the influence of Arcesilaus and Ariston, accepted the invitation of Ptolemy Euergetes to succeed Apollonius Rhodius as head of the Alexandrian Library. The most versatile scholar of his time, he was the first to call himself φιλόλογος. By the Alexandrian specialists he was styled βῆτα, 'second-rate', and πένταθλος, 'all-rounder'.
WORKS. 1. Literary criticism. Opposing the allegorical interpretation of Homer, he maintained that a poet wishes to charm, not to instruct. His most important work of scholarship was the treatise *On Ancient Comedy*, in at least twelve books; this was not a chronological study, but consisted of discussions of literary, lexical, historical, and antiquarian matters, and dealt with problems of the authorship and production of plays. He corrected Lycophron and Callimachus, and his work was much used by Aristophanes Byz. for his editions of the comic poets and by Didymus for his lexicon of comedy. His Καταστερισμοί treated the constellations and their mythology; the extant work of this name is probably not genuine. 2. Chronology. Χρονογραφίαι represented the first scientific attempt to fix the dates of political and literary history. He also compiled a list of Olympian victors. 3. Mathematics, astronomy, geography. Besides investigating arithmetical and geometrical problems (cf. his 'sieve' method of finding prime numbers), he dealt in *Platonicus* with mathematical definitions and with the principles of music, and he wrote geometrical works *On Means* and *Duplication of the Cube*. In his treatise *On the Measurement of the Earth* he treated mathematical geography, calculating with a high degree of accuracy the circumference of the earth and the magnitude and distance of the sun and moon. He was the first systematic geographer, and his *Geographica* (Γεωγραφικά), in which he sketched the history of the subject and dealt with physical, mathematical, and ethnographical geography, is often mentioned, sometimes disapprovingly, by later geographers, e.g. Strabo. 4. Philosophy. His essays had perhaps a mainly ethical interest. He wrote also a history of philosophy. 5. Poetry. His short epic *Hermes* described the

birth of the god, his youthful exploits, and his ascent to the planets. The short epic *Anterinys* or *Hesiod* dealt with the death of Hesiod and the punishment of his murderers. [Longinus] (*Subl.* 33. 5) praises the elegy *Erigone*, which told the myth of Erigonus and his daughter.

FGrH ii B 241 (1929–30); G. Bernhardy, *Eratosthenica* (1822); C. Strecker, *De Lycophrone Euphronio Eratosthene comicorum interpretibus* (1884); T. L. Heath, *A Manual of Greek Mathematics* (1931); E. Hiller, *E. carminum reliquiae* (1872); J. U. Powell, *Collectanea Alexandrina* (1925); [*Catasterismi*], A. Olivieri in *Mythographi Graeci* iii. 1 (1897); Sir E. H. Bunbury, *History of Ancient Geography* I. xvi (1879); H. Berger, *Geschichte der wissenschaftlichen Geographie der Griechen*[2] 406 ff.; 441 ff. (1903). J. F. L.

ERECHTHEUM, the third outstanding building on the Athenian Acropolis, begun in 421 B.C. and finished, after a lapse, in 407 B.C.; built of Pentelic marble, with friezes of black Eleusis stone to take applied white marble relief sculpture. Exact details of its construction are known from a contemporary inscription. It is tempting to accept W. Dörpfeld's restoration of the original design as a long rectangular building with projecting porches placed centrally on the sides, but there are no certain evidences of this. The main structure is divided into four compartments: the largest (east cella) has a prostyle-hexastyle Ionic portico; the west end is closed by a wall with engaged columns and corner piers. At this end is a unique and boldly projecting (though small) south feature—the 'porch of the maidens', with draped female figures (caryatids) serving as supports— and, nearly opposite on the north side, a still more boldly projecting porch with Ionic columns (partly reassembled in early twentieth century) standing on a lower level and having the tallest Order of the whole composition. Though the general form of the Erechtheum hardly conveys a homogeneous impression, the perfection of the design of its porches, and its beauty of detail—the capitals on north and east, the carved wall bands and the north door being unrivalled—make it the most notable Greek Ionic building in existence. *See* ALCAMENES. For the origin of the Erechtheum *see* ERECHTHEUS.

G. P. Stevens and J. M. Paton, *The Erechtheum* (U.S.A. 1927). T. F.

ERECHTHEUS (Ἐρεχθεύς), a fabulous king of Athens, often confused with Erichthonius (*see* ATHENA) and perhaps identical with him originally. Like him, Erechtheus was son of Earth and reared by Athena, *Iliad* 2. 547 ff., where his worship is mentioned (for which see Farnell, *Hero-Cults*, 11; *Cults* i. 393; iv. 47–52). Cf. *Od.* 7. 80 f., from a comparison of which with the other Homeric passage it would seem that Athena and Erechtheus were honoured together in a predecessor of the historical Erechtheum (the old royal palace?). The chief legend of Erechtheus concerns his daughters, of whom there were three (Eur. fr. 357 Nauck; *Ion* 10 adds a fourth, Creusa q.v. 1). They included Chthonia (Erechtheus' children vary greatly from one account to another, for obvious genealogical reasons); when Eumolpus (q.v.) the Thracian, son of Poseidon and Chione, invaded Attica, Erechtheus inquired of Delphi how he might win the victory. He was told that he should do so if he sacrificed one of his daughters. Chthonia, therefore, was sacrificed by consent of her mother Praxithea, probably by her own also, the story forming the plot of Euripides' *Erechtheus*, known by its frequent citations in later authors (to those quoted in Nauck, 464 ff. add Hyginus, *Fab.* 46 and 238. 2, and Rose ad locc.). The other daughters killed themselves; Erechtheus' own fate is variously told.

H. J. R.

ERETRIA, a city of Euboea, mentioned in the Homeric Catalogue. Eretria planted colonies on the north Aegean coasts, especially at Pallene. A great trading centre and rival of Chalcis, it was defeated in the struggle for control of the Lelantine plain, and declined in importance, though Aristagoras of Miletus sought its aid for the Ionic revolt against Persia. In the avenging expedition sent by Darius the city was besieged and burnt. *Circa* 445 B.C. Athens planted a colony, but in 411 Eretria revolted with the rest of Euboea. A member of the second Athenian Confederacy (378–377), it again revolted (349), and subsequently was the victim of Athenian and Macedonian intrigues. In the second Macedonian war Quinctius Flamininus sacked the city, which after the Roman victory was nominally free. Eretria took little part in the struggle of the Greek leagues against Rome, and in the time of Augustus still ranked as the second city of Euboea (q.v.). W. A. L.

ERETRIA, SCHOOL OF, founded by Menedemus (q.v.) as a continuation of the school of Elis, is mentioned by Diog. Laert. 1. 17–19; 2. 105; 126; Strabo 9. 393; Cic. *Acad.* 2. 129. Menedemus had a large following, but only one follower, Ctesibius, is known by name. The last trace of the school is in the title of a work of the Stoic Sphaerus against it. W. D. R.

ERICHTHONIUS, an Attic hero, usually son of Hephaestus; for the circumstances of his birth, *see* ATHENA. But Apollodorus (3. 187), says 'some' name Atthis daughter of Cranaus as his mother. Being born, he was taken care of by Athena, who put him into a chest and gave him into the charge of the daughters, or a daughter, of Cecrops (q.v.; Eur. *Ion* 21 ff.; 270 ff., and later authors, as Apollod. ibid. 189; Hyg. *Fab.* 166. 4–5); all agree that they opened the chest, which Athena had forbidden them to do, and then out of fright (because the child had wholly or partly serpent form or had a serpent with him) or driven mad by the anger of the goddess, leapt off the Acropolis and so were killed. Or the serpent killed them (Apollod. ibid.). This scene is not very common in art, but the birth is a fairly popular subject, see Furtwängler-Reichhold, *Gr. Vasenmalerei* iii. 95 and plate 137. Erichthonius became king of Athens, fostered the cult of Athena (Apollod. ibid.), received from Athena two drops of the blood of the Gorgon (q.v.), of which one poisoned and the other healed (Eur. *Ion* 999 ff.), and was the inventor or introducer of sundry things, as chariot-driving ([Eratosth.] *Catast.* 13; Hyg. *Poet. Astr.* 2. 13; hence he is sometimes identified with the constellation Auriga), silver (Hyg. *Fab.* 274. 4). He is often confused with Erechtheus (q.v.). H. J. R.

ERIDANUS (Ἠριδανός), mythical river, having Electrides (Amber-) Islands at its mouth. Named by Hesiod (*Theog.* 338) as a real river, the Eridanus was placed first in unknown northernmost Europe, or in western Europe, flowing into the Northern Ocean. Herodotus (3. 115) and Strabo (5. 215) doubted its existence. Aeschylus called it 'Spanish', meaning the Rhône (see Plin. *HN* 37. 32).

Greek authors from the time of Pherecydes agreed to identify the Eridanus with the Po, and Roman writers followed suit (since there are no islands at the mouth of the Po, some authors sought these in the east Adriatic). The description of the Eridanus as an amber-river may embody the memory of an early amber-route from Jutland up the Elbe and Rhine (Rhenus) and down the Rhône (Rhodanus) or across the Alps to north Italy (*see* AMBER). E. H. W.

ERIGONE (Ἠριγόνη), in mythology, (1) daughter of Icarius (q.v.), loved by Dionysus, who approached her disguised as a grape-cluster (Ov. *Met.* 6. 125). When she found her father's body she hanged herself, and the Athenian virgins began to do the same till her ghost was appeased by the αἰώρα and other honours (Hyginus, *Fab.*

130 and *Poet. Astr.* 2. 4; cf. Rose, *Greek Myth.*³ 154 f.).
(2) Daughter of Aegisthus (q.v.) by Clytaemnestra (q.v.).
She was rescued by Artemis from Orestes (q.v.), who
had killed her brother Aletes and wanted to kill her, and
made a priestess in Attica (Hyg. *Fab.* 122. 3). According,
however, to Cinaethon ap. Paus. 2. 18. 6, Orestes had
by her an illegitimate son Penthilus.   H. J. R.

ERINNA, poetess, of the Dorian island of Tēlos (Suid.
s.v. *Ἤριννα*), who probably lived at the end of the fourth
century B.C., not, as Suidas says, in the time of Sappho,
since her art shows affinities to that of Theocritus, and
Asclepiades seems to have edited her work (*Anth. Pal.*
7. 11). Writing in local Doric with a few Aeolisms, she
was famous for her *Distaff* (*Ἠλακάτη*), a poem in 300
hexameters in memory of her friend Baucis. Remains of
this on a papyrus have recently been added to the few
lines known from quotations, and show that in it Erinna
described experiences of girlhood shared with Baucis and
lamented her death. The title may refer to the time of
spinsterhood which it describes. She herself died at the
age of nineteen (*Anth. Pal.* 7. 11. 2). There also survive
three epigrams, one dedicatory (*Anth. Pal.* 6. 352) and
two inscriptions for Baucis' tomb (*Anth. Pal.* 7. 710 and
712). A line from what seems to have been a Propempticon (fr. 2) is of doubtful authenticity (Ath. 283d).

Text: E. Diehl, *Anth. Lyr. Graec.* i. 4, pp. 207–13; P. Maas, in
Hermes 69 (1934), 206–9. Criticism: C. M. Bowra, in *Greek Poetry
and Life* (1936), 325–42.   C. M. B.

ERINYES, spirits of punishment, avenging wrongs
done to kindred, especially murder within the family or
clan (cf. ORESTES, ALCMAEON), but also lesser offences
(see *Il.* 9. 454, 571; 15. 204), even against those who are
no kin but have a claim on our pity (beggars, *Od.* 17. 475,
though there it is rather hoped than stated that there are
such avengers for them if wronged). They once stop a
violation of the course of nature (*Il.* 19. 418), where they
silence the horse Xanthus, given human utterance
temporarily by Hera (407). Hence the dictum of Heraclitus (fr. 29 Bywater = 94 Diels–Kranz), that if the sun
left his course the Erinyes would find him. But these
passages go much beyond popular ideas, more in keeping
with which are their associations with oaths (*Il.* 19. 259;
Hesiod, *Op.* 803–4).

   This early connexion of the Erinyes with offences other
than manslaying makes against Rohde's theory (*Psyche*⁴ i.
270) that originally an Erinys is the ghost of the person
slain, though this will fit the other facts (close connexion
with blood guilt, greater importance of the Erinyes of an
elder brother or a parent, doubtful potency of those of a
beggar; see the Homeric passages above) very well. It is
on the whole more reasonable to suppose that they were
from the first curses, actual or conditional, personalized,
as Farnell argues (*Cults* v. 438–9), since a curse (cf.
CURSES) is not a mere form of words but the stirring up of
mysterious powers which work automatically when once
set going. They are early associated with Earth (Hesiod,
Theog. 185; cf. *Il.* 19. 259), which helps to explain
Demeter Erinys (cf. DEMETER), an earth-goddess, as
repository of powers of vengeance. As they regularly
work by disturbing the mind (*Od.* 15. 233–4), it is understandable that very similar deities are called *Maniai*
(Paus. 8. 34. 1). Being of the earth, they are often confused with kindlier powers who send fertility, Eumenides,
Σεμναί, etc.; their cult under their own name is extremely rare (see Farnell, ibid. 437 ff.).   H. J. R.

ERIPHUS, Middle Comedy poet, as the two mythological titles, *Αἴολος* and *Μελίβοια*, suggest.
   FCG iii. 556 ff.; *CAF* ii. 428 ff.

ERIS, personification of strife (discord, rivalry, competition; there are two kinds, one bad and one good, the
latter being emulation between fellow-workers, Hesiod,

Op. 11 ff.). Generally, however, she is definitely Strife.
Thus she accompanies Ares in Homeric battle-scenes, as
Il. 4. 440–1, where she is his sister and companion;
Theog. 225 ff., she is daughter of Night and mother of
Battles, Slaughters, Disputes, Lawlessness, etc.

   She emerges into fuller mythical personality in the
Cypria. Zeus, having decided on the Trojan War, to
relieve Earth of the burden of so many human beings
(fr. 1 Allen), lets Eris be present at the marriage of
Peleus and Thetis (qq.v.). There she stirs up a quarrel
between the goddesses as to which is the most beautiful,
this leading to the Judgement of Paris (see PARIS) and so to
the war. But the details are uncertain; we have no written
pre-Alexandrian authority for the 'apple of Discord'.
In Hyginus, *Fab.* 92. 1, from a Greek source perhaps
about contemporary with the Emperor Claudius (see
Rose, *Hygini Fabulae*, p. viii), Eris (Discordia) comes to
the door, throws in an apple, and says the most beautiful
may pick it up; other authorities (listed by v. Sybel in
Roscher's *Lexikon* i. 1338. 50 ff.) make her inscribe the
apple 'for the fairest'. This is obvious *Märchen* (see
FOLKTALES), but when it was added to this myth is
unknown.   H. J. R.

EROS, god of love in Greek mythology. Eros personified does not occur in Homer, but the Homeric passages
in which the word *eros* is used give a clear idea of the
original significance. It is the violent physical desire
that drives Paris to Helen, Zeus to Hera, and shakes the
limbs of the suitors of Penelope (*Il.* 3. 442; 14. 295; *Od.*
18. 212). A more refined conception of this E. who
affects mind and body appears in the lyric poets of the
sixth and seventh centuries B.C. Because his power
brings peril he is pictured as cunning, unmanageable,
cruel (Alcman 36 Diehl; Ibycus 6 Diehl; Sappho 137
Diehl; *Theog.* 1231); in Anacreon and in vase-paintings
he smites the lovestruck one with an axe or a whip
(*Deltion* (1927–8), 106). He comes suddenly like a wind
and shakes his victims (Sappho, Ibycus); Furtwängler
recognized a pictorial equivalent of this image in the E.
who carries off a girl on vases and gems. E. is playful,
but he plays with frenzies and confusion. On the other
hand, E. symbolizes all attractions which provoke love.
He is young and beautiful, he walks over flowers, and the
roses are 'a plant of E.' of which he makes his crown
(*Anacreontea* 53. 42). He is sweet and warms the heart
(Alcman 101 Diehl). Sappho sums up his essence, calling
him 'bitter-sweet'.

2. Already Hesiod connects E. with Aphrodite (q.v.
para. 3 and see *Theog.* 201), but many authorities hold
this connexion not to be original. With Himeros and
Pothos he is a constant companion of Aphrodite, although
he can appear with any god, whenever a love story is
involved, e.g. as *ἀμφιθαλής* at the marriage of Zeus and
Hera (A. D. Nock, *CR* 1924, 152).

3. Hesiod seems to have transformed the Homeric
conception of E. Although he describes E. in terms
almost identical with Homer as the god who 'loosens the
limbs and damages the mind', he also makes him together with Earth and Tartarus the oldest of gods, all-
powerful over gods and men. Building on this idea of
E. as a cosmic principle Parmenides found a place for
E. (Diels, *Vorsokr.*⁵ i. 243, fr. 13), perhaps as the power
which leads contrasts together? This philosophic conception contributed to the Euripidean picture of omnipotent
Eros (Ath. 13. 561), took abstruse mythological shape in
Orphic cosmogonies (Ar. *Av.* 693), and formed the background for the famous Platonic discussions of E. in
Symposium and *Phaedrus*.

4. Hellenistic poets continue the more playful conception of Anacreon and sing the tricks which E. plays
on mortals, the tribulations of those who try to resist
him, and the punishments which he receives for his
misdeeds. His bow and arrows, first mentioned by

Euripides (*IA* 548 f.), play a great part in these accounts. He becomes a humanized genre figure in Rococo style. Frequently a plurality of Erotes is introduced (Athen. 13. 562; *Anacreontea*; *Anth. Pal.*; Ap. Rh. 3. 114). The usage originated because the Greeks drew no sharp distinction between love passion and the god who symbolized it; both could multiply. For the relation of E. to Psyche *see* PSYCHE. E. had some old cults and enjoyed much individual worship. He was always the god of love directed towards female as well as male beauty. Hence his images in the gymnasia, his cult by the Sacred Band in Thebes (Ath. 13. 561; 602), and the altar in Athens erected by the lover of Hippias (Ath. 13. 602 d). As a god of fertility E. is celebrated in the very old cult in Thespiae, and in the joint cult with Aphrodite on the north slope of the Athenian Acropolis. In Thespiae E. was represented by an aniconic image; in Athens phallic symbols have been found in the sanctuary. In both cults festivals were celebrated; that in Thespiae was called Erotidia. The festival in Athens was celebrated in the spring month of Munichion (O. Broneer, *Hesperia* 1932, p. 31; 1935, p. 125). In Philadelphia the worshippers called themselves Erotes after the god. In Athens a procession of Erotes is represented on a relief performing the functions of worshippers. Another cult centre was Parion in Mysia.

5. In art Eros grows young. He begins as a fairly grown up boy in the archaic period, is a young boy in classical art, and becomes a playful putto in the Hellenistic age.

O. Waser in *PW*, s.v.; A. B. Cook, *Zeus* ii. 2 (1925), 1039; C. T. Seltman, *BSA* 1923–4, 87; P. Friedländer, *Studi e testi* (1939), 53. G. M. A. H.

EROS, STABERIUS, *see* STABERIUS.

EROTIAN, grammarian and doctor of the Neronian age, compiled an extant glossary to Hippocrates.

EROTOPAEGNIA, *see* LAEVIUS.

ERUCIUS (Ἐρύκιος), author of fourteen epigrams in the Anthology, came from Cyzicus, but bore a Roman name. His career and character are little known; but he attacks Parthenius (*Anth. Pal.* 7. 377) and he seems to imitate Virgil's *Arcades ambo* (*Ecl.* 7. 3 = *Anth. Pal.* 6. 96. 1), although it is very rare for a Greek to copy Roman poetry. Thus he was writing about the beginning of the Principate, 30 B.C. His poems are chiefly suave little dedications and anecdotes.

C. Cichorius, *Röm. Stud.* viii. 3 (1922). G. H.

ERYCIAS, ERYCIUS, *see* ERUCIUS.

ERYSICHTHON, in mythology, son of Triopas, of Dotion in Thessaly. Wanting timber, he was so misguided as to start cutting down a sacred grove of Demeter, though warned not to do so by the goddess herself in human form. He was thereupon plagued with insatiable hunger, to satisfy which he ruined himself and all his household. Thus far Callimachus (*Cer.* 23 ff.); the tale can be traced back no earlier than Hellanicus (Crusius in Roscher's *Lexikon* i. 1373. 56). Lycophron (1393, where see schol.; cf. Ov. *Met.* 8. 847 ff.) says he had a daughter Mestra, granted by her lover Poseidon power to change shape. She was sold in various beast-forms, escaped and came back to be resold, and he lived on the proceeds. See Zielinski in *Philol.* l. 138 ff. = *Iresione* ii. 1 ff. H. J. R.

ERYTHEIA, 'the red, or blushing, one', i.e. sunset-coloured. Name of (1) one of the Hesperides (Apollod. 2. 114). (2) The daughter of Geryon, and also his island (Steph. Byzant., s.v.; Paus. 10. 17. 5); for both (1) and (2) *see* HERACLES.

ERYTUS, see ECHION (2).

ERYX, an Elymian settlement and a mountain (*Monte San Giuliano*) above Drepana in west Sicily. Dependent on Segesta in the fifth century B.C., Eryx was occupied later by the Carthaginians, though temporarily seized by Pyrrhus (278 or 277). Phoenician masons' marks are found on the walls, and Punic legends appear on the coinage from the fourth century. The Elymian settlement, perhaps on a lower height than the famous temple of Astarte-Aphrodite-Venus (where is the modern town of S. Giuliano), was evacuated in 259, when the inhabitants were transferred to Drepana. L. Junius seized both heights and established a fort on the lower slopes to isolate Drepana (248). Hamilcar Barca captured the old town, but not the Temple and lower fort (244); thus he failed to relieve Drepana, although maintaining his position until 241. On recent somewhat disappointing excavations in the Temple area see *JHS* 1936, 218–20. H. H. S.

ESQUILINE. The name, in the form *Esquiliae* (from *ex-colo*, cf. *inquilinus*), denoted the eastern plateau formed in Rome by *montes Oppius* and *Cispius*, the *regio Esquilina* being the second of the Republican Four Regions (Varro, *Ling.* 5. 49–50). Under the Kings and much later it was used as a cemetery (von Duhn, *Italische Gräberkunde* i. 468), ultimately for paupers (Hor. *Sat.* 1. 8. 8–13). It was included by the Republican Wall and provided later sites for Nero's Golden House and Trajan's *Thermae*. Under Augustus the name was applied to Regio V, outside the Republican Wall, containing various gardens and the Sessorium, an imperial residence. The Arch of Gallienus (*CIL* vi. 1106) recalls the *porta Esquilina* of the Republican Wall. I. A. R.

ETEOBUTADES, *see* BUTES (2).

ETEOCLES, (1) an ancient king of Orchomenus, founder of the local cult of the Charites (Paus. 9. 34. 9 ff.). (2) In mythology, the elder son of Oedipus (q.v.). After the blinding and retirement of their father, he and his brother Polynices twice insulted him, once by setting before him certain vessels which had belonged to Laius and once by giving him a portion of meat less honourable than a king should have (Cyclic *Thebais*, frs. 2 and 3, Allen). He therefore cursed them (for conjectural details, see Rose, *Handbook of Greek Myth.*² 221, n. 28), and the curse was fulfilled thus. He and Polynices agreed to reign in alternate years, Eteocles taking the first year. Polynices left Thebes and married Argeia (*see* ADRASTUS). At the end of the year Eteocles would not give up his throne; Polynices returned with the Seven, and the two brothers met and killed each other. See references in Rose, loc. cit. H. J. R.

ETEOCLUS, son of Iphis, a somewhat obscure Argive hero. At a fairly early stage of the tradition he seems to have replaced Parthenopaeus (q.v.) as one of the Seven against Thebes, cf. ADRASTUS (see Paus. 10. 10. 3). Then Aeschylus (*Sept.* 458) or his authority included both him and Parthenopaeus, apparently so as to be able to leave Adrastus out of the actual assault; hence later writers (as Soph. *OC* 1316 and Eur. *Supp.* 872) use the same list.

See Wilamowitz-Moellendorff, *Aischylos Interpretationen* (1914), 100. H. J. R.

ETHIOPIA, the land of the Ethiopians or 'Burnt-Faced Men', was a name usually applied by the Greeks to any region in the far south (but north of the Equator). Under the influence perhaps of Homer (*Od.* 1. 22, etc.), who distinguished between Western and Eastern Ethiopians, Aeschylus (*Supp.* 284–6) made the Ethiopians extend to India, and Herodotus (esp. 3. 17–23; 7. 69–70) distinguished between the woolly-haired Ethiopians (negroes) and the straight-haired ones (primitive Indians). The tendency to confuse Ethiopians with Indians continued throughout ancient times (e.g. in Aesch. *Supp.* 284 ff.). But from Herodotus onward Ethiopia designated especially the lands south of Egypt—Nubia, Sennaar, Kordofan, and north Abyssinia. This country was visited since 665 B.C. by the Greeks, some of whom penetrated in the wake of Cambyses as far as Korosko, and various Ethiopian peoples became known in Greece by their tribal names. Under the Ptolemies the African coast was explored by sea as far as Somaliland and Cape Guardafui; the Blue and the White Nile and the Atbara were clearly distinguished (*see* NILE); and the Ethiopian city of Meroë (q.v.) received a veneer of Hellenic culture (Diod. 3. 38 ff.; Strabo 16. 773–4; 785–7). An Ethiopian raid into Egypt (25 B.C.) was repelled by the Romans, who established a frontier area from Assuan and Maharrakah. In the first century A.D. a powerful Ethiopian State arose in Abyssinia (*see* AXUMIS).

E. A. W. Budge, *The Egyptian Sudan* (1907); P. Paulitschke, *Geogr. Erforschung des afrikanischen Kontinents* (1884).   E. H. W.

ETRUSCANS, the most important of the numerous peoples which compose the mosaic of early Italy. 'The renown of their name filled the whole length of Italy from the Alps to the Sicilian Strait' (Livy 1. 2. 5). Servius, however, is mistaken when he infers (*ad Aen.* 10. 145) that they subjugated the whole peninsula. At the time of their widest power, 500 B.C., they had not penetrated south of Salerno, beyond which the way was barred by their commercial rivals and bitter enemies the Greeks. On the Adriatic side no trace of an Etruscan has been found from at least Ascoli to Otranto. Therefore they never politically dominated more than a third of Italy.

2. To their original territory (modern Tuscany) they soon added by conquest and settlement Umbria and Latium. A further extension into Campania was complete by *c.* 550. The trans-Apennine colonies from Milan to Bologna were founded just before 500 B.C. But at this moment the incipient empire began to crumble. Greeks and Romans struck the first blows. The war which followed the expulsion of the Tarquins from Latium was quickly followed by the campaign in which Aristodemus (q.v. 3) drove the Etruscans out of Campania. Hieron of Syracuse helped to destroy the common enemy in the naval battle of Cumae, 474 B.C. Twenty years later the Syracusans captured Corsica and Elba. Already in 480 B.C. had begun the bitter duel between Veii and Rome which ended only in 396 B.C. The Gauls destroyed the young colonies in the region of the Po about 390 B.C. Thus, early in the fourth century only the core of their original settlements remained in Etruscan hands, and these were lost piecemeal to Rome in the next two hundred years. This decline was due in part to the Etruscans' incapacity for united military or political action: their confederation of twelve cities was formed for religious purposes alone. So Rome was able to subdue all their great cities, Caere, Tarquinii, Vulci, one by one.

3. To a great extent this individualism may be traced to the circumstances of the original settlement. Modern opinion has rallied to the view almost universally held in antiquity that the Tyrseni or Tyrrheni were colonists from Asia Minor, if not perhaps actually from Lydia, as Herodotus (1. 94) so circumstantially narrates. The tradition was never questioned by any writer till Dionysius of Halicarnassus in the time of Augustus. It was explicitly endorsed by historians as early as Timaeus, and was accepted by the Etruscans themselves, who had their own chronology and must certainly have preserved their own family traditions. It seems, therefore, mere perversity on the part of Dionysius to question it. His garbled and doubtfully authentic copy of the Lydian

Xanthus was no trustworthy authority, and in any case did not contradict the story of Herodotus except by omission. There are, however, a few scholars who maintain by more modern reasoning that the Etruscans were autochthonous. Their views seem irreconcilable with the linguistic evidence. There can be no doubt that the migration was made by sea, and it had probably begun before 800 B.C. Archaeology has disproved Niebuhr's never well-grounded theory of an invasion by land over the Alps. The oldest cities, Tarquinii, Caere, Vulci, Vetulonia, Populonia, were all on the sea-coast, whereas inland towns such as Orvieto, Perugia, Arezzo were later offshoots. It is improbable that the first colonists came all at once. The analogy of the Northmen in Great Britain suggests rather that they arrived at intervals and in no great numbers. Each city was probably founded by an independent chief who owed no loyalty to his fellow-chiefs. These ruled as princes over an earlier population which eventually survived them.

4. The language was unique. If autochthonous, it could only be a survival from a general pre-Aryan stratum in the western Mediterranean, with which, however, it has no recognizable affinities. The philologists deny that it has anything in common with Indo-European languages and give a valuable independent support to the Herodotean tradition by tracing affinities with Eastern languages (*see* ETRUSCAN LANGUAGE). Only nine of the 8,500 known inscriptions, of which the majority are obviously funereal, contain more than 30 words. The material, therefore, though sufficient for morphological study, is too slight to allow any hope of decipherment. Except for a score of glosses given by classical writers the meaning of no single Etruscan word is known. It need not be assumed that there was no literature, but certainly none has survived. The wall-paintings in many tombs afford vivid glimpses of Etruscan life. These show them as a luxurious and light-hearted people, much given to horse-racing, dancing, and every kind of music. Some gloomy pictures of the underworld may be partly influenced by Greek Pythagoreanism. Of their own religion little is known, except that divining and augury formed an important accessory to it. The Roman augurs and haruspices learned their arts originally from the Etruscans, who, even in the late Roman Empire, were still famous for proficiency in these arts.

5. The Etruscan domination of Latium, culminating in the Tarquin dynasty, had deep and lasting effects on Roman life, as witness the schematization and equipment of the army, and many details of pomp and ceremonial. The rude peasantry from the Alban and Sabine hills was organized, disciplined, educated by Etruscan standards. Further, all Italy owed a great debt to these rivals and precursors of the Greeks. Etruscan excellence in the arts is still too little appreciated. The statues lately discovered or identified are of first-rate quality, and singularly original in character. They include the Apollo of Veii, the Chimaera of Arezzo, the Lateran wolf, the three warriors in New York, the woman's figure in Ny Carlsberg Glyptothek, and, at a later period, the Orator of Trasimene. In the minor arts the Etruscans were unsurpassed. Etruscan *situlae* and other bronzes were exported to the remotest parts of Europe. Art connoisseurs collected 'Etrusca sigilla'. The goldsmiths' work at Vetulonia equalled the finest in Ionia. Even an Athenian exquisite in the fifth century (see Athenaeus 1. 28) boasts of the gilded Etruscan vase that decorates the house.

BIBLIOGRAPHY

No works published earlier than 1900 can be recommended except some philological studies and the always valuable G. Dennis, *Cities and Cemeteries of Etruria*[3] (1883).

GENERAL WORKS: D. Randall-MacIver, *The Etruscans* (1927); R. A. L. Fell, *Etruria and Rome* (1924); M. A. Johnstone, *Etruria past and present* (1930); P. Ducati, *Le Problème étrusque* (1938);

B. Nogara, *Gli Etruschi e la loro civiltà* (1933); articles in *Enc. Brit.*, *Enciclop. Italiana*, and Ebert's *Real-Lexikon*.

ART: P. Ducati, *Storia dell' arte etrusca* (2 vols., 1927); G. Giglioli, *L'arte etrusca* (1936); F. Poulsen, *Etruscan tomb-paintings* (1922); F. Weege, *Etruskische Malerei* (1921); J. D. Beazley, *Etruscan Vase Painting* (1947).

DETAIL OF EXCAVATIONS: Randall-MacIver, *Villanovans and Early Etruscans* (1924); G. Pinza, *Museo Etrusco Gregoriano* (1915); annual periodical, *Studi Etruschi*.

LANGUAGE: *Corpus Inscriptionum Etruscarum*, i (Leipzig, 1893–1902); ii, fascicules i–iii (1907–36). D. R.-MacI.

ETRUSCAN LANGUAGE.

Of all the languages of ancient Italy the most difficult is Etruscan, about the origin of which little more can be stated with certainty than that it is not Indo-European. In spite of determined efforts to connect it with other better-known languages it is now generally agreed that we must rely for a solution of its problems upon the internal evidence of the records themselves. Besides a considerable number of Etruscan words preserved in Greek and Latin authors we possess some eight thousand inscriptions dating from the seventh century B.C. to the time of Augustus. They mostly contain little but proper names and are not very helpful, but two are longer, the Cippus Perusianus and the tablet of S. Maria di Capua. There is also a long liturgical text written on the wrappings of an Egyptian mummy now in the museum of Zagreb. The alphabet is a variety of the Greek with the omission of several characters which Etruscan did not need. The only added sign is 8, meaning *f*, which was common in Etruscan but unknown in Greek. Etruscan used only voiceless stops (*p*, *t*, *k*), which tended to become spirants; hence variations in pure Etruscan words, e.g. *sec* or *seχ*, and in borrowings from Greek, e.g. *sporta* (σπυρίδα), *triumpus* (θρίαμβος). It also had a strong initial stress-accent which caused weakening or loss of medial vowels, e.g. *Menle* (Menelaos), *Aχle* (Achilleus).

In Greek names masculine gender is shown by -*e* (*Hercle*), feminine by -*ai*, -*ei* (*Phersipnai*, *Elenei*), but in true Etruscan words the feminine is in -*i*, *larθ* : *larθi*. In vocalic stems the genitive is in -*s*, *seθre* : *seθres*, and in consonantal in -*us*, *velθur* : *velθurus*. Characteristic is the genitive in -*l* denoting filiation, e.g. *Pumpunial* (= son of Pumpuni, i.e. Pomponia). All that is certain about the verb is that the 3rd sing. perfect ends in -*ce*, e.g. *tece* (= has raised), *turce* (= has given). On dice we have the numerals from 1 to 6, *maχ*, *zal*, *θu*, *huθ*, *ci*, *śa*, but which is which has not been decided. Tens were formed by adding -*alχ*, thus *ci* : *cealχ*. The meaning of a considerable number of words is known, e.g. *ais* (= god; plur. *aisar*), *puia* (= wife), *clan* (= son), *usil* (= sun), *tiv* (= moon). Herodotean tradition connects Etruscan with Lydian, with which it has affinities; the ending -*ηνος* (*Τυρρηνοί*) is Asianic. The language of the Stele of Lemnos is also akin, and Caucasian affinity is possible.

PW, s.v. 'Etruskisch'; also numerous articles and references in *Glotta*; E. Fiesel, *Etruskisch* (1931). P. S. N.

ETRUSCAN RELIGION, see RELIGION (ETRUSCAN).

ETRUSCUS, see CLAUDIUS (14).

ETYMOLOGICA

(Greek). The earliest etymological studies are known only from (usually nameless) reproduction in the philosophers. The first known title is the Περὶ ἐτυμολογίας of Heraclides Ponticus, now lost, as also the Ἐτυμολογικά of Chrysippus. Under Atticist influence etymology flourished among the later Alexandrians and under the early Empire, e.g. in the lexica of Eirenaeus, Demetrius Ixion, and Caecilius of Calacte. These works were absorbed by Dionysius, Vestinus, Phrynichus, and others of the second century A.D. From them, and from later redactions and conflations, e.g. by Orus, Orion, and Helladius, the Byzantine *Etymologica* are mainly derived. *See* ETYMOLOGICUM MAGNUM.

R. Reitzenstein, *Geschichte d. gr. Etymologika*, 1897. P. B. R. F.

ETYMOLOGICUM MAGNUM,

an extant lexicon of uncertain date, but used by Eustathius, who became Archbishop of Thessalonica in A.D. 1175, and based mainly on the E. Gudianum (of *c.* A.D. 1100) and the E. Magnum Genuinum, the E. Gud. itself being a conflation of the E.M.G. and the E. Parvum, both of which were completed (the E.P. in A.D. 822) under the direction of Photius.

E. Magnum: T. Gaisford, 1841. P. B. R. F.

ETYMOLOGY

(in Greek and Roman times). Men have always seemed prone to toy with derivations and to see lessons in mere words. Thus in *Od.* 19. 562–7 the gates of *ivory* and *horn* by their very names—in Greek—proclaim the *frustration* and *fulfilment*, respectively, of the dreams that pass through them. Proper names have always been especial objects of such interest. L. Lersch (*Sprachphilosophie d. Alten*, pt. 3. 3–17) quotes some 70 examples—a selection only—mainly from Homer, Hesiod, Pindar, and Tragedy. Thus Aias is related by Sophocles to αἰάζειν, by Pindar to αἰετός; Euripides connects Zethus with ζητέω. (*See* ALLEGORY, GREEK.)

2. Unfortunately, Greek etymology did not remain the sport of amateurs, but was involved in sophistic and philosophical speculations on the origin of everything, including, inevitably, language. Was 'horse', or, it might be, some other—perhaps unrevealed—name, as much a natural property of the animal as its shape and constitution, or was a name only an artificial label by convention attached to this or that? Many of the Greek thinkers adopted the former view, with its consequences. Cratylus, pupil of Heraclitus, said that knowledge of Nature's names was required for real speech; without that utterance was mere noise. Indeed, in his old age, despairing of ascertaining Nature's names, he gave up utterance and used only gestures. Such a theory is paralleled in primitive (and later) practices, when, for example, healing virtues in things are deduced from their names, and the prescription swallowed with as much faith as the medicine: cf. E. S. McCartney, *AJPhil.* xlviii (1927), 326; Huc, *Travels in Tartary*, etc. i. 75.

3. If, then, words are not mere tokens of sensation and belief, to trace them to their ultimate origins would elucidate not the history of human opinion but Nature's own ἔτυμος λόγος. From this theory, constantly active though repeatedly challenged, arose a systematic practice of etymology, not only among its adherents. Early examples, with parodies of his own, figure largely in Plato's *Cratylus*, sometimes hitting the truth, if only by accident. Aristotle, who rejected the theory, has derivations: δίκαιον, δικαστής, from δίχα (*Eth. Nic.* 1132ᵃ 31), μακάριον from χαίρω (ibid. 1152ᵇ7), σωφροσύνη (after Pl. *Cra.* 411 e) from σῴζειν τὴν φρόνησιν, and (cf. Athenaeus 40b) μεθύειν from drinking μετὰ τὸ θύειν.

4. The Stoics, accepting the naturalistic theory, sought to relate the apparent chaos of current language to the rule of law hypothetically pervading Nature's works, by four principles stated in the Augustinian *Principia Dialecticae*. Nature forms words (i) κατὰ μίμησιν, by imitating things, e.g. *stridor*, *clangor*, or their impressions on the senses, as *crux* and *voluptas* are, respectively, unpleasant and pleasant in name (sound) as in fact; (ii) καθ' ὁμοιότητα, e.g. *crura*, which are 'longitudine atque duritia inter membra cetera ligno crucis similiora'; (iii) not from the thing but from something associated with it in one of various relations, viz. (*a*) *per efficentiam*, as 'foedus a foeditate porci'; (*b*) *per effecta*, as 'puteus quod eius effectum potatio est'; (*c*) *per id quod continetur*, as *urbs* from *orbis*; (*d*) *per id quod continet*, as *horreum* from *hordeum*; (*e*) by metonymy, as *mucro* for *gladius*; (iv) κατ' ἀντίφρασιν, as 'lucus, quod minime luceat', 'bellum, quod res bella non sit'. The operation of natural law was obscured, so they said, by human irregularity, ἀνωμαλία (*see* CRATES (3) OF MALLOS).

5. The Atticist movement (*see* GLOSSA, GREEK) furnished a new impulse for etymologists, and a new aim, viz. to test the admissibility of a word to 'correct use' by relating it to its στοιχεῖον, which in the derivative had probably suffered loss, accretion, metathesis, crasis, or other mutation. In this connexion a terminology for many such πάθη was evolved; cf. Pseudo-Trypho, Περὶ παθῶν. Atticism regarded not the usage of good writers but what was right for them to use (see Phrynichus; *contra*, Sext. Emp. *Math.* 1. 98). Etymology appears with analogy as a touchstone of diction in the Atticist Eirenaeus (of the Augustan age), and remained one of the criteria of fully developed purism, Greek and Latin. 'Latinitas est incorrupte loquendi obseruatio secundum Romanam linguam; constat autem, ut adserit Varro, his quattuor: natura (meaning *etymologia*), analogia, consuetudine, auctoritate' (Diom. 439). This new etymology appears in Philoxenus (1st c. B.C.) and is fully developed in Seleucus (under Tiberius), whose results resemble those of the *Cratylus*, from which he borrows.

6. At Rome (as elsewhere) aetiological etymologies were early popular: 'nomina haec numinum in indigitamentis inueniuntur, i.e. in libris pontificalibus, qui et nomina deorum et rationes nominum continent' (Serv. on Verg. *G.* 1. 21). There are also examples in the early poets. Under Greek influences the etymological fashion took firm hold of Latin literature and scholarship, with like results as in Greek: Paullus s.v. 'miles': 'militem Aelius (i.e. Stilo) a mollitia κατ' ἀντίφρασιν dictum putat: sic ludum (school) dicimus, in quo minime luditur' (cf. Quint. *Inst.* 1. 6); cf. Diom. and paragraph 4, supra.

7. It would be idle to analyse minutely a practice, popular and highly esteemed, often surprisingly correct and even acute (cf. Pl. *Cra.* 405c–d), which constantly produced such results as, ἕσπερος, ἀπὸ τοῦ ἔσω περᾶν πάντα τὰ ζῷα, and, γραμματική, διὰ τὸ τήκειν καὶ καθαίρειν τὰ γράμματα, and, ἔντερον, παρὰ τὸ ἐντὸς ῥέειν: so we are told that the (Greek) vowels number seven because there are seven planets. Neither Greeks nor Romans, early or late, came within reach of a scientific, historical method in etymology. Their rules are but statements of their arbitrary practices, with a multiplication of terminology that did nothing for the advancement of knowledge.

E. Schwyzer, *Griechische Grammatik* (1939), 29–45; F. Müller, *De veterum imprimis Romanorum studiis etymologicis* (1910); K. Woldt, *De analogiae disciplina apud grammaticos Latinos* (1911).—See also under GRAMMAR, GLOSSA (GREEK). P. B. R. F.

EUADNE, *see* EVADNE.

EUAGORAS, *see* EVAGORAS.

EUANGELUS appears to be a New Comedy poet. One fragment (10 trochaic tetrameters) is preserved of Ἀνακαλυπτομένη—a master discusses with a cook the preparations for a wedding-banquet.

FCG iv. 572; CAF iii. 376.

EUANTHIUS (4th c. A.D.), author of a commentary on Terence. The only parts remaining are certain sections of the treatise *De comoedia* which is now prefixed to the commentary of Aelius Donatus (q.v.).

Cf. Teuffel, § 405. 4; Schanz–Hosius, § 836. 1.

EUBOEA, also called Long Island (*Makris*), since it stretched from the Gulf of Pagasae to Andros. The chief cities from ancient times were Chalcis and Eretria (qq.v.). Other cities were Histiaea, Geraestus, and Carystus, famous for its marble. In the eighth century Chalcis and Eretria were powerful mercantile cities, rivals of Corinth, and, as pioneers, established colonies on the north-west shores of the Aegean and in Italy and Sicily. A rival with Chalcis for control of the Lelantine plain, Eretria was defeated, and her control of Andros, Tenos, and

Ceos passed to Athens, who later compelled Chalcis to cede part of the plain (506). In 490 the Persian general Datis attacked Euboea and captured Eretria and Carystus. Euboean contingents fought the Persians at Salamis and Plataea. Owing to Boeotian intrigues, the whole island revolted from Athens in 446, but it was reconquered by Pericles, who planted cleruchies in it. The cities remained tributary allies of the first Athenian Confederacy, but revolted in the Peloponnesian War (411). They were enrolled in the second Athenian Confederacy (378–377) and incorporated in a Euboean League (341). After much turmoil, while the Thebans and Philip II of Macedon intrigued against Athens, the whole island came under the control of the Macedonian monarchy, by whose fortunes it was affected for the rest of the third century. In 196 Flamininus, the liberator of Greece, revived the Euboean League. Euboea was temporarily occupied by Antiochus of Syria (192–191); for aid given to the Achaean League against Rome its League was dissolved (146). The island was attached to the province of Macedonia, and fell into decay in the Roman Imperial period.

Bursian ii. 395–438; *CAH* iii. 754 (bibliography); *IG* xii. 9. 143 ff. W. A. L.

EUBULEUS (Εὐβουλεύς), properly a euphemistic title of Hades, 'the good counsellor' (schol. Nic. *Alex.* 14 and elsewhere); one of a group of Orphic chthonian deities (Kern, *Orph. frag.* 32 c–e). He is humanized into a swineherd (fr. 51), son of Dysaules and brother of Triptolemus, who gave Demeter news of the rape of Persephone; or his swine were swallowed up with Persephone, which is why swine are thrown into chasms at the Thesmophoria (fr. 50). H. J. R.

EUBULIDES of Miletus, dialectician of the Megarian school, taught at Athens. He wrote a lampoon against Aristotle. He is said to have taught Demosthenes dialectic and rhetoric. He is best known for his eristic arguments, of which the most famous are the ψευδόμενος and the σωρίτης; but some of those ascribed to him by Diogenes Laertius are of older date.

PW vi. 870. W. D. R.

EUBULUS (1), (*c.* 405–330 B.C.), Athenian politician and rhetor. Some of his notable measures were the recall of Xenophon (q.v.), the peace after the Social War, and the peace of Philocrates. He was a realistic and pacifist politician, as we know from Demosthenes. Most remarkable was his financial policy, which directed Athenian administration from *c.* 354. He was able to increase (perhaps to treble) the public revenues, to expend more on the *theorika* (q.v.), and to introduce a public building policy without adding to regular taxation. He was an honest and thrifty statesman, but more cannot be said with certainty of his financial methods. It has been suggested, but never proved, that Xenophon's *De Vectigalibus* was influenced by or described his policy.

A. M. Andreades, *A History of Greek Public Finance* i (U.S.A. 1933), Index s.v. J. Kirchner, *PW* s.v. 'Eubulos'. F. M. H.

EUBULUS (2), Middle Comedy poet (described by Suidas as standing on the border-line between Old and Middle). He composed 104 plays (with which he won six Lenaean victories)—most of them (judging by over 50 extant titles) mythological burlesques or parodies of tragedy (e.g. Ἀγχίσης, Αὔγη), but some are character-types (Σκυτεύς), others, women's names (Νεοττίς, Πλαγγών). E. is outstanding for variety of metre: frs. 104 (dactylic tetrameters, with iambic clausula), 35, 78, 105, 139.

Many interesting passages: fr. 10, parody of Euripidean epilogue; fr. 12, in Boeotian dialect; fr. 25, the ways of a tyrant, Dionysius of Syracuse; fr. 90, the spoilt lap-dog;

frs. 116–17, the catalogues of good and bad women. In Σφιγγοκαρίων (named from a slave who talked like the Sphinx), fr. 107, the riddles beloved of Middle Comedy writers have a prominent place.

FCG iii. 203 ff.; *CAF* ii. 164 ff.; Demiańczuk, *Supp. Com.* 40 f.

W. G. W.

EUCLEIDES (1) of Megara (*c.* 450–380 B.C.), pupil of Socrates and founder of the Megarian school. He was a strict adherent of Eleatic monism, and tried unsuccessfully to combine it with Socrates' ethical teaching, treating the Good, God, reason, and the several virtues as merely names for the Eleatic One. It has been thought (by Schleiermacher and others) that he developed a theory of Ideas before Plato, but the evidence is rather that the Megarian school criticized the theory of Ideas, and that Plato retorts on them in the *Republic, Theaetetus, Parmenides,* and *Sophistes.*

PW vi. 1000. W. D. R.

EUCLEIDES (2), Athenian archon in 403–402 B.C., which, being the year of the re-establishment of democracy, is very often quoted. From that time Athenian inscriptions used the Ionian instead of the Attic alphabet, an important fact for epigraphical research. V. E.

EUCLEIDES (3), the mathematician, *see* EUCLID.

EUCLID (Εὐκλείδης) of Alexandria (fl. *c.* 300 B.C.) lived under Ptolemy I (306–283) and founded a school at Alexandria; his fame rests on his great text-book the *Elements,* στοιχεῖα, in thirteen books (Books 1–6 on plane geometry, 7–9 on the theory of numbers, 10 on irrationals, 11–13 on solid geometry). This work at once superseded those of earlier writers of Elements (Hippocrates of Chios, Leon, Eudoxus, Theudius). Euclid made full use of his predecessors' work but added much of his own, while altering the whole arrangement. Most of the MSS. contain the recension by Theon of Alexandria, but the Vatican MS. 190 containing an earlier edition was discovered and edited by F. Peyrard (1814–18), and forms the basis of the authoritative text by J. L. Heiberg (Teubner). Commentaries were written by Heron of Alexandria, Pappus, Simplicius. Fragments of these have come down to us, mostly through the Arabic (an-Nairīzī); but most valuable of all is the extant commentary of Proclus on Book I edited by Friedlein in 1877. The so-called 'Book 14' is by Hypsicles; 'Book 15' is an inferior compilation by a pupil of Isidorus (7th c. A.D.).

Of other works by Euclid some belong to elementary geometry: (1) the extant *Data*; (2) the lost *Pseudaria, Fallacies* (see Proclus, p. 70); (3) *On Divisions* (of figures), (Διαιρέσεων βιβλίον), discovered in the Arabic and edited by F. Wolpcke (1851; new edition by R. C. Archibald, Camb. 1913).

To higher geometry belong the following: (1) three books of *Porisms* (Πορίσματα), (2) *Surface-loci* (Τόποι πρὸς ἐπιφανείᾳ), (3) four books of *Conics* (Κωνικά). These works are lost, and all we know of them is contained in Pappus (7, on the 'Treasury of Analysis'). Important attempts to restore the *Porisms* were made by Robert Simson and Michel Chasles. Other extant works are: the *Phaenomena,* an astronomical text-book containing 16 or 18 propositions in sphaeric geometry, partly based on Autolycus' *On the Moving Sphere*; *Optics*; these are included, with *Catoptrica* (not genuine in its present form), in the Teubner edition by Heiberg and Menge. Euclid wrote also on 'The Elements of Music': two works are attributed to him, the *Sectio canonis* (Κατατομὴ κανόνος) and an *Introduction to Harmony,* the former only containing excerpts from the original work, the latter being by Cleonides, a pupil of Aristoxenus; both are included in the Heiberg–Menge edition. *See also* MATHEMATICS.

BIBLIOGRAPHY

The *Elements* were first translated (from the Arabic) by Athelhard of Bath (about A.D. 1120) and Johannes Campanus (13th c.); the first printed edition contained Campanus' translation (Erhart Ratdolt, Venice, 1482). 1505 saw the first translation from the Greek text, by Bartolomeo Zamberti. The *editio princeps* of the Greek text is that of Simon Grynaeus (Basel, 1533); the Latin translation by Commandinus is dated 1572; the first English translation was by Henry Billingsley, 1570. The Oxford edition of the Greek text by David Gregory (1703) contained the complete works of Euclid. The standard edition is *Euclidis opera omnia* by Heiberg and Menge (Teubner). Modern translations of the *Elements* are : T. L. Heath, *The Thirteen Books of Euclid's Elements*² (1910); F. Enriques, *Gli Elementi d'Euclide e la critica antica e moderna* (1925–36). T. H.

EUDEMUS of Rhodes (second half of the 4th c. B.C.), pupil of Aristotle. We do not possess any record of his life, although there was a biography by a certain Damas (Simpl. in Arist. *Phys.* p. 924. 13 Diels). In later years he appears to have opened his own school, probably in Rhodes (if one may combine E. ap. Simpl. *Phys.* p. 732. 32, taken from a lecture on Physics, with l.c. p. 923. 11 where he writes from outside Athens to Theophrastus about the same subject). That he stood closer to Theophrastus than to other Peripatetics is proved by the fact of their correspondence as well as the conservative character of their studies.

Eudemus' most important works concerned the history of science and civilization. He wrote a History of arithmetic and geometry, a History of astronomy, and a History of theology (Τῶν περὶ τὸ θεῖον ἱστορία). These books, with Theophrastus' historical works, are the basis of all later knowledge in these fields. He also compiled a paraphrase of Aristotle's *Physics* for which he inquired from Theophrastus about the reading of a sentence. He followed closely his master's text but noted and explained difficulties and gave the books a new grouping. Important features of the later Peripatetic commentaries can be traced back to E. and his generation. He also wrote on logic and rhetoric. On the *Eudemian Ethics* see ARISTOTLE.

L. Spengel, *Eudemi Rhodii Perip. fragm.* (1866 and 1870; not sufficient); Simpl. in Arist. *Phys.* ed. H. Diels, Index s.v.; U. Schoebe, *Quaestiones Eudemeae* (Thesis, Halle 1931; frs. of and comm. on the first book of the *Physics*). Studies: Brandis, *Handbuch d. griech.-röm. Philos.* iii. 1. 215 f.; 256 f.; Zeller, *Aristotle,* etc., Engl. Transl. ii. 417 f.; *PW* vi. 895. K. O. B.

EUDORUS (1), in mythology, a Myrmidon captain, son of Hermes and Polymele (*Il.* 16. 179 ff.).

EUDORUS (2) of Alexandria (fl. *c.* 25 B.C.), eclectic philosopher. Chief works (lost): Διαίρεσις τοῦ κατὰ φιλοσοφίαν λόγου; commentaries on *Timaeus, Categories, Metaphysics,* Aratus' *Phaenomena*; Περὶ τοῦ Νείλου. He is reckoned as a Platonist but owed much to Stoicism.

PW vi. 915.

EUDOXUS (1) of Cnidos (*c.* 408–355 B.C.), a brilliant mathematician and astronomer, was a pupil of Archytas in geometry and of Philistion in medicine. At 23 he went to Athens, attended lectures by Plato, and returned to Cnidos. From about 381–380 B.C. he stayed in Egypt studying astronomy and making observations. Thereafter he founded a school at Cyzicus; later, about 368 B.C., he transferred it to Athens. Finally, returning to Cnidos, he was elected to legislative office. In astronomy he wrote books entitled *The Mirror* ("Ἔνοπτρον) and *Phaenomena* (see Hipparchus, *In Eudoxi et Arati phaenomena* 1. 2. 2); but his greatest achievement was his hypothesis of concentric spheres by which he thought to explain geometrically the movements of the sun, moon, and planets; this made each planet describe, on the surface of a sphere, a curve like a figure-of-eight, which he described as a *horse-fetter* (ἱπποπέδη). In geometry he is famous as the creator (1) of the general theory of proportion, applicable alike to commensurable and incommensurable magnitudes, which is expounded in Euclid's

Books 5–6; (2) of the 'method of exhaustion', fundamental in Greek geometry, for measuring and comparing the areas and volumes of curvilinear plane and solid figures: this he applied to finding the volumes of a pyramid and a right circular cone, and to proving that circles are to one another as the squares, and spheres are to one another as the cubes, on their diameters respectively (see Euclid 12. 5–10, 1–2, 16–18). He also solved, by means of a special curve, the problem of doubling the cube. Other works were on *Geography* and on the *Octaëteris*, eight-year cycle (Diog. Laert. 8. 87; 90).

On the hypothesis of concentric spheres see Aristotle, *Metaph. Λ* 8. 1073ᵇ17–1074ᵃ14; Simpl. on *De Caelo* 488. 18–24; 493. 4—506. 18 Heib.; Schiaparelli, *Le sfere omocentriche di Eudosso, di Callippo e di Aristotele* (1875: German translation by W. Horn, *Abh. zur Gesch. d. Math.* (1877), 101–98); T. L. Heath, *Aristarchus of Samos*, 193–211.   T. H.

EUDOXUS (2) of Rhodes (fl. 225–200 B.C.?), historian, perhaps identical with the author of Περίπλοι (*GGM* i. 565), which may have formed a part of E.'s histories.

FHG iv. 407–8; *PW* vi. 1. 930.

EUDOXUS (3) of Cyzicus (2nd c. B.C.), Greek navigator. After 146 B.C. he was sent by Ptolemy Euergetes II of Egypt with a stranded Indian guide to find the sea-route to India; sent again later, he was on his return blown some way down east Africa, consorted with natives, returned to Alexandria with some wreckage there said to be part of a ship of Gades (*Cadiz*), decided that Africa could be circumnavigated, and determined to go round it to India, avoiding Ptolemaic exactions. Having collected cargoes at various ports, he set out from Gades, with music-girls, doctors, and carpenters on board, but was driven aground south of Morocco. Returning, he saw perhaps Madeira, failed to persuade Bocchus of Morocco to help him, cut across land to the Mediterranean, and, with much greater equipment, sailed again down west Africa, and disappeared.

Strabo 2. 98–102. J. Thiel, *Eudoxus van Cyzicus* (1939, in Dutch); Cary–Warmington, *Explorers*, 70–1, 98–103, with modern authorities.   E. H. W.

EUENUS of Paros (5th c. B.C.), poet and Sophist, of whom some twenty elegiac verses and two hexameters have come down. He gave metrical form to the rules of rhetoric and added to current terminology (Pl. *Phdr.* 267a).

EUETES, said by Suidas to have been an Athenian writer of comedy contemporaneous with Epicharmus, but it is likely that Suidas is really referring to the similarly named tragedian of about that date.

EUGAMMON of Cyrene (6th c. B.C.), epic poet, author of the cyclic *Telegonia* (see EPIC CYCLE).

EGF 57–9.

EUGEON of Samos, *see* LOGOGRAPHERS.

EUGRAPHIUS (early 6th c. A.D.), author of a commentary on Terence (ed. P. Wessner in *Donati Commentum*, iii. 1). His interest is chiefly in the rhetorical qualities and characterization of the plays and often he does little more than paraphrase the text of Terence. He probably knew the commentary of Donatus on Terence and that of Servius on Virgil. The work is found in two versions, one of which contains interpolations.

Cf. Teuffel, § 482. 3; Schanz–Hosius, § 1117.   J. F. M.

EUGUBINE TABLETS, *see* TABULAE IGUVINAE.

EUHEMERISM, *see* EUHEMERUS.

EUHEMERUS (*Euemerus*, Εὐήμερος) of Messene (cf. the best sources in *FGrH* 63 Jacoby), in the service of Cassander (q.v.) 311–298 B.C. E.'s fame is based on the anthropological theory of the gods which he put forward in a novel of travel, the *Sacred Scripture* ('Ιερὰ ἀναγραφή, Diod. 6. 1. 3; Athen. 14. 658e). In this book he gave an account of a fabulous journey which he claimed to have made to the island Panchaia in the Indian Sea. There he had seen in the temple of Zeus a large golden column on which were written the deeds (πράξεις) of Uranus, Kronos, and Zeus. From this he found that the gods of popular worship had originally been great kings and conquerors to whom mankind had shown their gratitude for astounding and helpful deeds by worshipping them as gods (Diod. 6. 1 f.; 5. 41 f.). E. systematized, perhaps not without the influence of Oriental, especially Egyptian, anthropomorphic theology, a deep-rooted Greek feeling which denied fixed boundaries between gods and great men. The rationalist tendency of his time as well as the tremendous deeds of Alexander had certainly prepared the way for his conception.

The theory seems to have made little impression on the Greeks, but Diodorus (q.v.) Siculus, apparently taking the romance for fact, embodied it (frs. of his sixth book). In Latin it had more success after the publication of the *Euhemerus* of Ennius (q.v.), and euhemerizing accounts of such mythological figures as Faunus exist. The Christian writers, especially Lactantius, liked to use it as an evidence of the real nature of the Greek gods. E.'s name survives in the modern term 'euhemeristic', applied to mythological interpretation which supposes certain gods (e.g. Asclepius) to be originally heroes.

G. Némethy, *Euhemeri reliquiae* (1889); Jacoby, *FGrH* 63; J. Vahlen, *Ennianae poes. reliquiae*², cxx f.; 223 f. Studies: R. von Pöhlmann, *Gesch. der sozialen Frage* (ed. 3, 1925), 293–305; P. van Gils, *Quaestiones Euemereae*, Thesis, Kerkrade–Heerlen 1902; *PW* vi. 952.   K. O. B. and H. J. R.

EUMELUS of Corinth (? 8th c. B.C. or later), epic poet; author of a *Corinthiaca* (of which a prose epitome was subsequently made), a Βουγονία (perhaps dealing with the story of Aristaeus), a processional ode (*Prosodion*), and other poems. *See* EPIC CYCLE.

EGF 185–95.   W. F. J. K.

EUMENES (1) I of Pergamum (d. 241 B.C.) was the son of a Eumenes of Tios and succeeded his uncle Philetaerus as ruler (never king) of Pergamum in 263, when he threw off Seleucid suzerainty with Egyptian assistance. After defeating Antiochus I near Sardes (262), he greatly extended his frontiers, and though he probably lost most of his gains to Antiochus II (c. 258), he maintained his independence till his death. He regularly bought immunity from the plundering bands of the Galatians.   G. T. G.

EUMENES (2) II (d. 160 or 159 B.C.) was the eldest son of Attalus I of Pergamum, whom he succeeded (197). He continued Attalus' policy of co-operation with Rome, and was perhaps mainly responsible for embroiling Rome with Antiochus (196–192), as Attalus had done with Philip V. In the war against Antiochus Eumenes assisted Rome with his fleet, and later stood a short siege in Pergamum; at Magnesia (189) he commanded the right wing with distinction. The peace of Apamea (188) gave him the Thracian Chersonese and most of Seleucid Asia Minor; and he secured these gains by cultivating the goodwill of Rome, which was further shown by the Senate's intervention in his favour, so as to end his wars with Bithynia (186–185) and Pontus (183–180). He was naturally the champion of the *status quo* in the East, and hence unpopular with all dissatisfied parties. The 'Third Macedonian War' (171–168), long regarded as 'inevitable', was hastened by his visit to Rome to accuse Perseus (172). Rome's failure to win the war quickly is said to have induced him to negotiate secretly with Perseus; but he cannot have seriously considered reversing a successful policy of thirty years.

Nevertheless, he certainly forfeited the Senate's confidence, though it was only transferred to his brother Attalus.

Eumenes was a worthy successor to Attalus I, and carried his policy to its logical conclusion, greatly to the advantage of Pergamum (taking the short view). His ability is unquestioned, and the unfavourable tradition is due partly to this very success, which made him many enemies. His best memorial was perhaps the city of Pergamum itself, which he adorned with a splendid sequence of buildings.

For bibliography, *see under* PERGAMUM.   G. T. G.

EUMENES (3) of Cardia (c. 362–316 B.C.), secretary to Philip of Macedon and to Alexander. He became (330?) principal secretary (ἀρχιγραμματεύς), and kept the Royal Journal (*see* EPHEMERIDES), which he perhaps published after Alexander's death. Some military experience, too, came his way, but it was in the wars of the 'Successors' (*see* DIADOCHI) that he proved himself a born general. He remained steadfastly loyal to the legitimate heirs and to the idea of a united Empire, and co-operated with the regents against the separatist generals. Driven from Asia Minor by Antigonus, he escaped to the Eastern satrapies, where he organized a fresh 'loyalist' front. After the indecisive battle of Paraetacene (317), Eumenes' fate was decided at Gabiene by the desertion of his picked Macedonian corps. He was executed by vote of the Macedonians of both armies. He was the Themistocles of the period, an able Greek among able Macedonians, their equal in warcraft, their superior in diplomacy, which included skilful management of his Macedonian colleagues by tact, and of his Macedonian soldiers with the aid of an Alexander-cult instituted by him.

Diodorus, bk. 18 passim; Plutarch, *Eumenes*. Berve, *Alexanderreich*, no. 317; A. Vezin, *Eumenes von Kardia* (1907).   G. T. G.

EUMENIUS (fl. 3rd–4th c. A.D.), of Greek origin, was, like his grandfather, a teacher of rhetoric. By oratorical skill he became *magister memoriae* at court. Constantius subsequently made him head of the school at Autun, a position less dignified, but much more highly paid. After the destruction of the school in war, Eumenius rebuilt it at his own expense, and delivered a carefully composed oration on the occasion of the reopening (A.D. 297) in which there is much flattery of the ruling powers. Perhaps some other speeches in the collection *Panegyrici* are also his work. *See* PANEGYRIC, LATIN.   A. S.

EUMOLPUS, mythical ancestor of the Eleusinian clan of the Eumolpidae, as his son Ceryx was of the Κήρυκες. According to Apollod. 3. 201 ff. he was son of Poseidon and Chione daughter of Boreas (q.v.). To conceal her shame, she threw him into the sea; Poseidon saved him, brought him to Ethiopia, and entrusted him to his daughter Benthesicyme. When adult, he married Benthesicyme's daughter, but also tried to rape her other daughter, for which he was banished. During his exile he visited Eleusis, where he founded the Mysteries (Lucian, *Demon.* 34), or at least became somehow connected with them (Plut. *De Exil.* 607b). Finally he succeeded Tegyrius, a Thracian king, but was sent for again by the Eleusinians to help them against Erechtheus (q.v.), in which campaign he was killed. Further details of his story are obscure and contradictory, see Engelmann in Roscher's *Lexikon* s.v.   H. J. R.

EUNEOS (Εὔνεως), and **THOAS** (Θόας), sons of Jason and Hypsipyle (q.v.). They came to Nemea while their mother was in captivity there, and were admitted to the house by her; later, they recognized her and took her away (Eur. *Hyps.* frs. 3 and 41 Hunt).

EUNUCHS, RELIGIOUS, generally self-castrated, were frequently associated with the cult of the Anatolian mother-goddess. The custom probably originated here,

rather than with the Semites, among whom it is found as a religious institution chiefly at Hierapolis–Bambyce, where many of the cultural ties were with Anatolia. Best known are the Galli of Cybele and Atargatis, who were temple attendants or wandering mendicants (cf. METRAGYRTES) rather than priests (Lucian, *Syr. D.* 43); they are seldom mentioned in inscriptions. Though the Archigalli in the West seem not to have been eunuchs, the heads of the cult at Pessinus, the Attis and Battakes, probably were, at least in earlier times. There were eunuchs in the service of Hecate at Lagina (*BCH* 1920, 79; 84), and Strabo (641) says that the Megabyzi, the chief priests of Artemis at Ephesus, were formerly eunuchs.

Many explanations of the practice have been offered, as that the act was intended to increase the fertility of the goddess or to assimilate the worshipper to her. These may have been contributory or secondary ideas, but the basic motive was probably the desire to make oneself permanently pure. Certain rites only the chaste could perform; the eunuch, at least in a negative sense, possesses the purity of a virgin or child (at Ephesus virgins were the colleagues of the Megabyzus). In other words, the importance lay not in the act but in its consequences.

The chief ancient sources are Lucian, *Syr. D.*, Catullus 63, *Anth. Pal.* 6. 217–20, and the texts collected in H. Hepding, *Attis* (1903) and F. Cumont, *L'Égypte des astrologues* (1937), 132–3. A *lex sacra* of Eresus forbidding Galli entrance to a sanctuary, *CR* 1902, 190; the Galli at Rome, J. Carcopino, *Mél. d'Arch. et d'Hist.* (1923). Origins of rite and comparative material: A. D. Nock, *ARW* 1925; L. H. Gray in *ERE*, s.v. 'Eunuch'.   F. R. W.

EUPATRIDAE, (1) a general term for nobles by birth; (2) a particular term in Athens for a well-defined class, a 'peerage', like the *patricii* (q.v.) in Rome. Presumably they were the descendants of the original royal counsellors, who claimed also an exclusive right to the archonship, or to the three major archonships (*see* ARCHONTES). In that case the Areopagus (q.v.) was exclusively Eupatrid. This right was abolished by Solon (q.v.), who established an aristocracy of wealth and deprived the magistracy and Areopagus of their sole right to interpret and administer the laws. The right to interpret certain religious 'laws' was retained under the democracy by a few Eupatrid families.

H. T. Wade-Gery, *CQ* 1931, 1 ff.   A. W. G.

EUPHANTUS of Olynthus, tutor of Antigonus Gonatas, to whom he dedicated a treatise Περὶ βασιλείας. He also wrote contemporary history ('Ιστορίαι) and several tragedies.

FGrH ii. 74; *FHG* iii. 19.

EUPHEMUS. A hero, son of Poseidon, connected with the foundation-legend of Cyrene. Sailing with the Argonauts, he was given a clod (symbol of sovranty) by Triton as they returned from Libya, and told (in Pindar's account) that if he dropped it into the sea near Taenarum his descendants in the fourth generation would rule in Libya. It fell, however, by Thasos, whence, in the seventeenth generation after E., Battus colonized Cyrene. (Pindar *Pyth.* 4. See EURYPYLUS (3), also Hdt. 4. 150 and Ap. Rhod. 4. 1730.)

In Homer (*Il.* 2. 846) a Euphemus is mentioned as leader of the Cicones, and in Plato (*Phdr.* 244a) one as father of the poet Stesichorus. According to Hesychius, E. was an epithet of Zeus in Lesbos.

EUPHORBUS, in mythology, a Dardanian, son of Panthoos, who wounded Patroclus (*Il.* 16. 806 ff.), and was afterwards killed by Menelaus (17. 45 ff.). Pythagoras claimed to have been Euphorbus in a former incarnation and to recognize his shield (Hor. *Carm.* 1. 28. 9 ff., and commentators there).

EUPHORION (1), son of Aeschylus, is said (Suidas, s.v.) to have exhibited plays written by his father but not produced in his lifetime, and to have won four victories with them. In 431 B.C. he defeated both Sophocles and Euripides (Arg. Eur. *Med.*). A. W. P.-C.

EUPHORION (2) (b. *c.* 276 B.C.), of Chalcis in Euboea, studied philosophy at Athens. In poetry he was a pupil of Archebulus of Thera. After enriching himself by a liaison with the elderly widow of Alexander, ruler of Euboea and Corinth, he was appointed librarian at Antioch in Syria by Antiochus the Great (223–187) and was buried there or at Apamea (Suidas).

WORKS. (1) *Verse.* Apart from epigrams (*Anth. Pal.* 6. 279; 7. 651) E. seems to have confined himself in the main to the composition of epyllia and composite epics, akin to catalogue-poems, on mythological subjects. Suidas mentions three works, *Hesiod, Mopsopia or Miscellanea* (Ἄτακτα), *Chiliades.* The second was a collection of Attic legends, Mopsopia being an old name for Attica. The third guaranteed the eventual punishment of persons who had defrauded E. of money by a recital of oracles fulfilled after the lapse of 1,000 years. Of the further titles cited in the fragments seven are proper names, perhaps those of the addressees. The content of these poems was apparently mythological, as was certainly that of seven others, among which the *Thrax* seems to have been a medley of myths. The *Curses or Goblet-thief* was directed against a man who had robbed E. of such an article and, if fr. 9 belongs to this poem, imprecated on the thief many unpleasant ends recorded in myth; cf. Ovid's *Ibis.* The *Replies* (Ἀντιγραφαί) to *Theodoridas* was also in verse, a poetic epistle. The attribution to E. of love-elegies in the Roman manner is based on a misunderstanding. (2) *Prose.* The following works are cited, *About the Isthmian Games, About the Aleuadae,* a lexicon to Hippocrates.

The scantiness of E.'s surviving fragments makes an estimate of his work difficult. In subject-matter he seems to have preferred the Trojan Cycle, local legends of a gruesome character, and topics of aetiology and geography. His narrative technique consisted in undue amplification of detail and vain repetition, leading up to very summary treatment of the climax (frs. 44, 51; Lucian, *Hist. conscr.* 57). His sentiment was mawkish (fr. 92) and he indulged in childish etymologies (frs. 57, 136). His proverbial obscurity is due partly to the many and difficult mythological references, partly to his language, of which 'glosses' (cf. *Anth. Pal.* 11. 218, an attack on E. by Crates of Mallus) and neologisms, including truncated words, formed an important part. His basic vocabulary was drawn from Homer, whom he termed 'untouchable' (fr. 118), but he was also indebted for this and for many themes to Hesiod and others. The papyrus fragments reveal him as a barefaced plagiarist of his immediate predecessors, Callimachus and Apollonius Rhodius. But [Lycophron] in the *Alexandra* is probably E.'s debtor. *See also* EPYLLION.

Euphorion exercised considerable influence on later poets. Among the Greeks, Nicander, Parthenius, Nonnus imitate his language or borrow his themes. At Rome his epyllia (*see* EPYLLION) were well known to the generation of Catullus and Gallus (hence *cantores Euphorionis,* Cic. *Tusc.* 3. 45). Virgil's debt to him for subject-matter is illustrated by Servius. Of extant Latin poems the *Ciris* perhaps reproduces E.'s technique most closely.

Texts: J. U. Powell, *Collectanea Alexandrina* (1925), 28–58. For the latest papyri see K. Latte, *Philol.* xliv (1935), 129–55. General literature: F. Skutsch, 'Euphorion (4)', in *PW* vi. 1174–90; A. Meineke, *Analecta Alexandrina* (1843), 3–168; F. Scheidweiler, *Euphorionis fragmenta* (1908). E. A. B.

EUPHRANOR, sculptor and painter, of the Isthmus; later settled in Athens. Pliny dates him 364 B.C. (by battle of Mantinea). Pupil of the elder Aristides

(q.v., 2). His sculptures, some of them colossal, included Paris, Alexander and Philip in chariots, and a Priestess of great beauty. No probable attributions have been made. His paintings included Cavalry battle before Mantinea, Theseus with Democracy and Demos, the Twelve Gods. He wrote on symmetry and colours. Critics remarked on his large heads and slim bodies, but he seemed to portray the dignity of heroes and himself called his Theseus 'beef fed', in contrast to the 'rose fed' Theseus of Parrhasius (q.v.). T. B. L. W.

EUPHRATES, the longest river of western Asia, and the more westerly of the Two Rivers of Mesopotamia. Rising in the Armenian mountains, it flows south-west to the Taurus, then south-east, receiving its three main tributaries the Murat Su, the Balikh, and the Khabur on the left bank. In the alluvial plain of Babylonia, which it inundates yearly, it was in antiquity connected with the Tigris (q.v.) by numerous navigation and irrigation canals. In classical times it was crossed by a number of bridges, e.g. at Zeugma (q.v.) and Babylon. It served as a political boundary between Armenia and Cappadocia, Sophene and Commagene, etc. (Strabo 16. 746–9; Pliny 5. 83; Ptol. 5. 12). Between 53 B.C. and A.D. 63, and again after the withdrawal of Trajan, it separated Rome from Parthia; the forts along its west bank guarded the *limes* of the Empire against the Sassanids.

F. R. Chesney, *Expedition for the Survey of the Rivers Euphrates and Tigris* i, ii (1850); V. Chapot, *La Frontière de l'Euphrate* (1907). M. S. D.

EUPHRON, New Comedy poet, dated *c.* 270 B.C. by his allusion to Nicomedes of Bithynia (fr. 11. 2). Of nine titles three (Θεῶν ἀγορά, Θεωροί, Μοῦσαι) show E.'s personal liking for burlesques.

FCG iv. 486 ff.; *CAF* iii. 317 ff. W. G. W.

EUPHRONIUS (late 6th–early 5th c. B.C.), potter and vase-painter in Athens, known from twelve signatures. He signed four red-figure vases as painter (510–500 B.C.), notably calyx crater with Heracles and Antaeus (Paris), and psycter with hetaerae (Leningrad). Experimented with new positions, character contrast, etc., within ripe archaic conventions. As potter he employed: (1) Panaetius, painter (500–480), who painted six cups for Euphronius, including Theseus and Amphitrite (Paris), Heracles and Eurystheus (London), and many other lively scenes. (2) Onesimus, cup painter; continues style of (1) in direction of grace and charm. (3) Pistoxenus, painter. Painted white ground cup (Berlin, about 475), also Heracles and Linus (Schwerin), and Aphrodite cup (British Museum). Has been identified with painter of Penthesilea cup (Munich). An early classical artist with much Polygnotan *ethos.*

Beazley, *A.V.* 58; 165; 172; 260; *Vases in Poland* (1928), 21 (Panaetius, painter); W. Technau, *Röm. Mitt.* 1931, 189 (Onesimus); H. Diepolder, *Penthesileamaler* (1936). T. B. L. W.

EUPOLEMUS (fl. *c.* 150 B.C.), a hellenized Jew, wrote Περὶ τῶν ἐν τῇ Ἰουδαίᾳ βασιλέων, a popular history of the Jews in a rhetorical style (*FHG* iii. 207–30).

EUPOLIDEAN, *see* METRE, GREEK, II (7).

EUPOLIS (fl. *c.* 430–410 B.C.), regarded in antiquity as one of the three greatest of Old Comedy writers (Platon. *Diff. Com.* 1; Quint. 10. 1. 66; Hor. *Sat.* 1. 4. 1). Born at Athens, probably in 445, as Suidas says he first exhibited in his seventeenth year; son of Sosipolis (Suid.). The old tradition which told how Alcibiades drowned him on his way to Sicily (Platon. *Diff. Com.* 4; Ov. *Ibis* 593 f.) in punishment for E.'s attack on him in the Βάπται was denied by Eratosthenes (Cic. *Att.* 6. 1. 18). Suidas attributed to E. seventeen plays and seven victories; anon. Περὶ κωμ. 2. 10 gives the number of plays as fourteen, the first 429 B.C. The Αἶγες (earlier than 423

B.C.) introduces a musical Sophist (fr. 11), and the plot may have resembled Ar. *Nub.* The *Βάπται* (? c. 416 B.C.) attacked Alcibiades (fr. 69) and his friends as worshippers of the Thracian goddess *Κοτυτώ*, whose rites contained lascivious dances (Juv. 2. 91 and schol.). The *Δῆμοι* may now with confidence be assigned to 412 B.C. (Körte, *Hermes* xlvii. 276 ff.). Papyrus finds have added much to our knowledge of its contents (Powell, *New Chapters in Greek Literature*, 3rd ser. 161–3). Its chorus consisted probably of *Μαραθωνομάχαι*. In the episodic part of the comedy various former *προστάται τοῦ δήμου* (Solon, Myronides, Aristides) are recalled from Hades to help Athens in her hour of need. Another scene depicts the expulsion of a *συκοφάντης* by a *δίκαιος ἀνήρ* (probably = Aristides). The *συκοφάντης* has tried to impeach a *ξένος* for violation of the Mysteries—a clear reference to the scandal of 415 in which Alcibiades was implicated. The *Κόλακες* (421 B.C.) contained an attack on Callias, son of Hipponicus (Ath. 5. 218b, c; schol. Ar. *Av.* 284), who is satirized as squandering his money on loose living and the parasites who presumably formed the chorus. The *Μαρικᾶς* (Hesych. *Μαρικᾶν· κίναιδον· οἱ δὲ ὑποκόρισμα παιδίου ἄρρενος βαρβαρικόν* (MSS. -*κοῦ*)) was produced in 421 (schol. Ar. *Nub.* 553). It attacked the demagogue Hyperbolus under the name M., as Ar. *Eq.* attacked Cleon under the name of the Paphlagonian; indeed, the two plays seem to have been so much alike that, while Aristophanes accused E. of plagiarism, E. retorted by claiming to have collaborated with Aristophanes (Ar. *Nub.* 553; E. fr. 78). The *Πόλεις* is probably to be assigned to 422 (*Hermes* xxx. 443 ff.). Cities of the Athenian Empire (e.g. Tenos (fr. 231), Chios (fr. 232), etc.) formed the chorus. The play probably had a political motive: that of persuading Athens to deal gently with her dependants. The *Ταξίαρχοι* (perhaps 427 B.C., and, if so, E.'s earliest datable play; see Wilamowitz, *Phil. Unters.* i. 64 ff.) shows the effeminate Dionysus learning the arts and rigours of the military life from the Athenian general Phormio.

Of the remaining plays the title of the *Ἀστράτευτοι ἢ Ἀνδρόγυνοι* (*The Shirkers*) explains itself. The *Αὐτόλυκος* attacked the favourite of Callias. The *Νουμηνίαι* may have been a mythological burlesque, like Epicharmus' *Τριακάδες*. The *Προσπάλτιοι* was perhaps a satire on litigiousness. The *Φίλοι* introduced the famous beauty, Demus, and may have been an attack on paederasty. The *Χρυσοῦν γένος* seems to have satirized Cleon. The fragments of E., though comparatively numerous, are too short to enable us to form any judgement on the poet's worth. Antiquity, as has been said, ranked him high, and we have, for what it is worth, the opinion of Platonius. He (*Diff. Com.* 2. 16) attributed to E. more *χάρις* than to Aristophanes and less *πικρότης* than to Cratinus. He further (ib. 2. 15) calls him *εὐφάνταστος* ('imaginative') *κατὰ τὰς ὑποθέσεις* and *εὔστοχος περὶ τὰ σκώμματα*.

FCG i. 104 ff.; ii. 426 ff.; *CAF* i. 258 ff.; Demiańczuk, *Suppl. Com.* 41 ff.   M. P.

EURÍPIDES. (*See also* TRAGEDY.)

I. LIFE (485?–406? B.C.).

1. Euripides was probably born in 485 B.C. (*Marm. Par.*). He was son of Mnesarchus or Mnesarchides, of the deme of Phlya, and Clito, who according to the comic poets were respectively a shopkeeper and a greengrocer, but according to Philochorus, a respectable historian, were people of good position. Possibly his father had an agricultural estate in Salamis, the poet's home from early life. The authorities for his life (Satyrus, Gellius 15. 20, the 'Life' in certain MSS., Suidas, etc.) retail much unreliable gossip; but it may well be true that he was a disciple of Anaxagoras, whose doctrines sometimes appear in the plays, and that he associated with Prodicus, Archelaus, Protagoras, and Socrates, and was influenced

in his thought by them. (Socrates is said to have been an enthusiastic admirer of his tragedies.) He is described as devoted to books, and passing much time in study and writing in a cave by the sea in Salamis. He held a local priesthood of Zeus at Phlya; he once went to Syracuse as member of an embassy (Arist. *Rh.* 2. 6 and schol.), and he probably served as a soldier like other citizens. Otherwise he seems to have lived mainly in retirement, and possibly on this account was credited with a morose and unsociable temperament. He had three sons, one of whom brought out some of his plays after his death. The malicious stories about his domestic life need not be believed, but it may be true that Cephisophon, a member of his household, helped him in composing the music for his plays (Ar. *Ran.* 944, and fr. 580 K. etc.).

2. His first appearance in a tragic contest was in 455, when he was placed third; his first victory was in 441. He won only five victories (one of them posthumously), covering 20 plays out of the 92 which he composed. Of the 78 (or 74) known to Alexandrian scholars only 7 or 8 were satyric. He produced new plays at the Piraeus and elsewhere, as well as at Athens. He composed also the elegy for the Athenian soldiers who fell in Sicily. He was constantly attacked by the comic poets, and his advanced views were probably ill received at first by Athenian audiences, though after his death he became, and remained for generations, the most popular of the three great tragedians. Not long before his death, i.e. in 408 or 407, he left Athens, some said on account of the ridicule of his fellow citizens, but no further explanation is given. After a stay in Magnesia (in Thessaly), where he was honourably received, he went to the court of Archelaus in Macedonia, where he composed a play in the king's honour, as well as the *Bacchae* and other plays. He died there, probably at the beginning of 406, and was buried at Arethusa; a cenotaph was erected to him at Athens.

II. WORKS

3. Of the 19 extant plays those which can be certainly dated are the *Alcestis*, 438 B.C. (produced in place of a satyric play with the *Cressae*, *Alcmaeon in Psophis*, and *Telephus*; the group won the 2nd prize); *Medea*, 431 (placed 3rd, with the *Philoctetes*, *Dictys*, and *Θερισταὶ Σατυροί*), *Hippolytus*, 428 (1st prize); *Troades*, 415 (placed second; the plays were *Alexander*, *Palamedes*, *Troades*, *Sisyphus*); *Electra*, 413; *Helena*, 412; *Orestes*, 408 (with the *Oenomaus* and *Chrysippus*). The *Bacchae* was probably composed in 407 (produced in or after 406, with the *Iphigenia in Aulis* and *Alcmaeon in Corinth*). The *Heraclidae* is probably to be dated about 430 or 429, the *Hecuba* about 425, the *Supplices* about 420, the *Andromache* (not performed at Athens) about 419, the *Hercules Furens* possibly about 416 (but the indications are very uncertain); the *Ion* and *Iphigenia in Tauris* seem to show the poet's later style (especially as regards versification) and may fall between 413 and 408, and the *Phoenissae* and *Hypsipyle* appeared shortly before Aristophanes' *Ranae* (produced in 405), i.e. probably 409 or 407. The satyric *Cyclops* cannot be dated. (For evidence, see editions, and Haigh, *Tragic Drama*, ch. iv.) Of the lost plays not mentioned above, the *Andromeda* appeared in 412 (Ar. *Thesm.* 1060), the *Erechtheus* and *Cresphontes* probably in or soon after 421, the *Stheneboea* before 422. The extant *Rhesus* is probably not that written by Euripides, but its date is keenly disputed.

4. From the Trojan Cycle and legends closely connected with it Euripides drew the stories of about twenty plays, but his subjects are more or less evenly spread over a wide range of mythology, and he has recourse to some purely local legends attached to places outside Attica (as in the *Cresphontes*, a Messenian story). His only Dionysiac play was apparently the *Bacchae*.

5. Much new light has been thrown on some of the lost plays by papyri published since Nauck's *Tragic Fragments*; see Powell and Barber, *New Chapters*, iii. 105–51 and D. L. Page, *Greek Literary Papyri* i. 54–135 (Loeb, 1942).

III. CHARACTER OF HIS WORK

6. Aeschylus and Sophocles were not out of harmony with the ordinary religious beliefs and conventions of their time. But to Euripides the traditional legends implied that the morality of the gods was lower than that of good men; and at the same time the advanced thought of the day, as expressed e.g. by Protagoras, declared itself baffled by all questions affecting the gods; scientific theories were accounting for natural phenomena by physical causes and dispensing with divine action, and, by the time when most of Euripides' extant plays were being written, the Peloponnesian War had generated, as Thucydides makes plain, widespread scepticism as to the existence of any divine government of the world. With these movements of thought Euripides was strongly in sympathy. At the same time he was intensely interested in the human mind and emotions as he saw them in living individuals, and he set himself to show what the effect on real minds and emotions must have been, if the events described in the legends had really taken place. In most of the earlier extant plays (and in some later) it is with the mind and feelings of women that he is occupied —first Alcestis (accompanied by a masterly portrait of unconscious selfishness suddenly becoming conscious in Admetus); then the long series of distraught or de-humanized victims of cruelty, divine or human— Phaedra (in the *Hippolytus*), Medea, Hecuba, Andromache, the women of the *Troades*, Electra, Creusa (in the *Ion*), all portrayed with a vividness and an understanding which both in its insight and in its painfulness was a new thing. In some lost plays also the central person was one afflicted with some horrible or morbid passion—Pasiphae, Canace, Stheneboea; or the victim of a god's lust, doomed to misery through no fault of her own—a Melanippe or an Antiope. Set against these were men either purely selfish (like Jason) or deadened to human feeling by supposed reasons of State, types of the political mind, masking cruelty with ingenuity of argument. (Aristotle, *Poet.* 15, feels that these characters may be sometimes needlessly bad—like Menelaus in the *Orestes*.) More rarely the victim of divine savagery is a man, Heracles, for instance, in the *Hercules Furens*. Besides such studies there are the incomparable pictures of maidens going willingly to death: Polyxena, Macaria, Iphigenia at Aulis, and doubtless the daughter of Praxithea in the lost *Erechtheus*; and there are good men—Theseus in the *Heracles*, Pylades, and others. The first interest of the poet in all these is in themselves, as human beings acted upon in different ways by experiences of a terrible or pitiful kind. But he also faces without evasion the moral to which their stories pointed as regards the government of the world. Sometimes his speakers may doubt or even roundly deny the existence of the gods, or speak very plainly as to their character; or they may declare their disbelief in the legends (*HF* 1346) or may rationalize them as Teiresias does in the *Bacchae*; or they may substitute the Laws of Nature or the Aether or Reason for what had been called God, or (especially in some later plays) may declare there is no power in the universe but Chance. Because the oracles were the official organs of the supposed will of the gods, they and the priests who administered them fall into the same condemnation, along with the purveyors of miracle-stories designed to bolster up the public worship by which priests and seers lived. But apart from such passages, the two main interests of the poet are reconciled by means of the normal structure of his plays. It is generally true that each play apart from the beginning

and end is a purely human drama, treated as if the agents were men and women who might have lived yesterday and who suffer as living men and women would suffer; only at the beginning and end, as a rule (the *Hercules Furens* is an exception), does it appear that all the misery is the work of the gods, and we are left to draw the moral. Not that Euripides is blind to the extraordinary beauty to be found in the religion of Greece; such a figure as Artemis in the *Hippolytus* and the amazing loveliness of the *Bacchae* are a sufficient refutation of this; but behind is always (and not least in the *Bacchae* itself) a sense of the falseness and cruelty of the gods, so that it is in human beings alone (and in the slave and the peasant no less than in those in high station) that the poet finds humanity.

7. In expressing these interests in drama Euripides often presents scenes such as have exposed him to criticism, not usually very intelligent, in ancient and modern times. Aristophanes and Plato thought that he lowered the dignity of Tragedy by his heroes in rags; others, disapproving of the minute analysis and display of abnormal passions and overwrought emotions, have been blinded to the poet's intense and truthful sympathy. But if there are some scenes so painful as to be almost intolerable, and if the poet seems at times to multiply distressing scenes almost wilfully, there is something much more profound than mere sensationalism in this; while in regard to some of the most pathetic and even agonizing scenes, it is well to remember that these presented the incidental consequences of war; and what these might be Euripides knew only too well. It was in the year before the production of the *Troades* that the Athenians had sacked Melos.

8. In his detestation of war Euripides never varies, and it appears in many plays; but his patriotism as a citizen of Athens is also strong. Perhaps it is for an idealized Athens, the upholder of the oppressed and of freedom, that he chiefly cares; the *Heraclidae* and the *Supplices* and the character of Theseus in more than one play illustrate this, and even the fine chorus of praise in the *Medea* is prompted by the part played by Aegeus as the friend in need. But he has also a hatred of Sparta which sometimes leads him—particularly in the *Andromache* and in the characters of Alcmene in the *Heraclidae* and of Menelaus generally—to say 'what the poet and not what the plot demands'. His attacks upon Apollo and the oracle of Delphi may be partly due to the pro-Spartan policy of the oracle in the war, though the fact that Delphi was the religious centre of Greece would be reason enough. Generally he is proud of his own free city, and even makes Theseus the author of its democracy (*Supp.* 353), but he has no mercy on demagogues, and in *Supp.* 244 ff. it is the μέσοι πολῖται, neither rich nor poor, that are spoken of as the saviours of the State, while in *Or.* 903–22 and in the portraiture of Electra's labourer husband he shows his respect for the honest working man. The debates on such subjects have been criticized as undramatic, but are perhaps less so in a drama in which the heroic story is treated as if it were a story of contemporary life.

9. The traditional stories had no special sacredness for Euripides, and he varies and invents freely. The plots of the *Helena* (with the virtuous Helen and the finely conceived Theonoe), the *Ion*, the *Iphigenia in Tauris*, and the *Orestes* are for the most part his own; so is Electra in her cottage with her peasant husband; and his treatment of the Theban story both in the *Phoenissae* and in the lost *Oedipus* and *Antigone* departed far from any existing versions (see C. Robert, *Oidipus*). Characters like the barbarian kings, Theoclymenus and Thoas, are a bold departure from convention. Now and then he presented plays in which there was almost as much of fairy-tale as of tragedy; the *Helena* and *Andromeda* (produced together in 412) and the *Phaethon* are examples, and perhaps some of the plays which he offered in place of the conventional satyric plays may have been of a semi-tragic type. It happens that a large proportion of the extant plays have a relatively happy ending; but we know from Aristotle (*Poet.* 13) that most of his plays ended unhappily, and it is precisely for this reason that he describes him as the 'most tragic of poets', 'in spite of his faulty management in other respects'.

10. In some plays Euripides is probably open to the criticism which Aristotle brings against 'episodic' plots and scenes which have no causal connexion with the plot or with the preceding scenes. The *Troades* is a series of pathetic scenes, without much structural necessity to connect them, but justified as illustrating one common theme. The *Phoenissae* is almost what Aristotle would call an ἐποποιϊκὸν σύστημα, the tragedy of Iocasta and that of Menoeceus being grafted on to that of the hostile brothers (which had been enough for one play of Aeschylus). The last part of the *Heraclidae* is very slightly connected with the rest and seems to be dictated by animosity against Sparta. In the *Supplices* the self-immolation of Evadne and the mourning of her father are criticized as a sensational 'extra'; and there are other instances. It is seldom difficult for a careful reader to see the motive of these scenes, and the same is true of the scenes which are semi-comic—the arming of Iolaus in the *Heraclidae* (where there is some pathos in the comedy); some parts of the *Helena*; the lament of the absurd Phrygian slave in the *Orestes*. But where Euripides wanted to construct an almost perfect plot he did so, for instance in the *Hippolytus*, the *Ion*, and the *Iphigenia in Tauris*; and if some of the recognition scenes, for which he was famous, are somewhat artificial, others are convincing as well as astonishing, and combine pathos and joy with consummate mastery.

11. The formal prologue, spoken sometimes by a god, sometimes by a human character, giving genealogies, stating the circumstances in which the action originates, even (in some plays) forecasting the issue, and the epilogue, spoken usually by a god *ex machina*, who issues orders and pronounces prophecies, are often criticized. In fact, they preserve the supernatural atmosphere which was demanded of Greek Tragedy, while leaving the poet free to construct in the rest of the play his purely human drama; and the prologue, by giving the bare facts at once (and incidentally making the audience aware of any new version of the story which the poet has designed), enables the whole interest to be thrown into the study of the characters and their feelings in reaction to each turn of the plot. The epilogue very rarely (if ever, in extant plays) provides by divine intervention a solution of an otherwise insoluble tangle, in the way suggested by Horace (*Ars P.* 191), but in addition to preserving the religious setting (though not always to the credit of the gods) it often connects the events of the play with the life of Athens, introducing the institution by the god of some hallowed custom or solemnity familiar to the Athenians—a proceeding perhaps undramatic, but humanly very intelligible. Some of the prologues spoken by human beings are very finely in character, and in no way external to the action, and in both prologue and epilogue the poet frequently shows his own view of the morality of the story, and at the same time, by the vision they afford of past and future, sets it against a larger background. It should be added that when the play is read, much more when it is acted, the impressiveness of these prologues and epilogues is their abundant justification.

12. Of the other non-choral elements, the speeches of the messengers in many plays are masterpieces of glowing description, rising in style somewhat above the simple beauty of the language of the dialogue, without being rhetorical in any bad sense. Rhetoric does at times carry the poet away elsewhere: in the elaborate debates on set themes and in the denunciations of classes of persons whom the poet dislikes he shows the less attractive side of the culture of his day in a way which is out of proportion to what the play requires, but it is fine vigorous work, both in thought and style. In a number of plays the chorus also appears to be less intimately connected with the plot than Aristotle (*Poet.* 18) would like, though it might be answered that the function of the chorus in Euripides is sometimes to afford relief from the plot by transferring the spectator to a larger and more spiritual atmosphere than the brutality of the story affords, that the choral odes which are really irrelevant to the general situation are few, and that a great number are actually prompted by the particular situation of the moment or have a special function at that point in the play. An ode which is really detached from the context (like the description of the shield of Achilles in *Electra* 432 ff.) is in fact exceptional, and careful study will usually discover what is in the poet's mind. The more frequent substitution of lyric dialogues between chorus and actor for set choral odes, while it may point to a certain disintegration of the choral form of tragedy, is certainly a testimony to the interest of the chorus in the action and the persons who act. It should be added that in many of the choral odes there are descriptive passages of indescribable beauty.

13. In so far as the chorus was really a difficulty, it was because Euripides, more than Aeschylus and Sophocles, developed intrigue as an element in drama, and it is difficult to conduct an intrigue smoothly in the presence of fifteen constant spectators of both parties; the binding over of the chorus by one party to keep the secret is sometimes unnatural and sometimes (as in the *Ion*) ends in its betrayal. In the *Alcestis* and the *Helena*, where there were good reasons for leaving the orchestra empty for a moment, this is effected quite naturally. The very great compression of the events supposed to have taken place during a choral ode in the *Supplices* and the lost *Stheneboea* was exceptional.

14. In the music which accompanied the choral odes, and in the lyric dialogues and monodies which Euripides introduced freely, he probably followed the new school of emotional music, which aimed at expressing by sound every change and degree of intensity in feeling without observance of any formal rule or symmetry. In the same way he frequently abandons the conventional anti-strophic form, particularly in the lyric expression of individual passion or grief. We can no longer trace the full effect of the lyric metres which he uses in rapid succession, and the music is lost. Critics like Aristophanes and Plato found the new style over-emotional and unwholesome, and Aristophanes laughed at Euripides' repetition of words and trilling of syllables so as to fit the music (a very familiar thing in modern opera); but it was a natural consequence of the poet's intense interest in real minds and feelings that he should refuse to be fettered by the old conventions.

15. As the creator of the love-drama Euripides was the forefather of the New Comedy, which took over some of the most effective parts of his technique, above all the many forms of intrigue and of recognition scene, and learned much from his style as well as from his psychological insight. If at first respectable Athens was shocked at him, he was destined to be the mainspring of future Greek literature for centuries, and the interests which he first introduced into drama have been and still are the life blood of romance both in verse and prose.

BIBLIOGRAPHY

LIFE AND WORKS. H. Frey, *Der Βίος Εὐριπίδου des Satyros* (Diss. 1920); A. E. Haigh, *Tragic Drama of the Greeks* (1896); M. Pohlenz, *Die griechische Tragödie* (1930); P. Decharme, *Euripide et l'esprit de son théâtre* (1893, Engl. Transl. by J. Loeb, 1905); G. Murray, *Euripides and his Age* (*Home University Library*, 1914); A. W. Verrall, *Euripides the Rationalist* (1895) and *Four Plays of*

Euripides (1905); W. Nestle, *Euripides, der Dichter der griechischen Aufklärung* (1901); P. Masqueray, *Euripide et ses idées* (1908); H. Steiger, *Euripides, seine Dichtung und seine Persönlichkeit* (1912).

TEXT. R. Prinz and N. Wecklein (1878–1902); G. Murray, O.C.T. (1901–9, 2nd vol. revised 1913); H. von Arnim, *Supplementum Euripideum* (1913, including Satyrus' *Bíos*); *TGF* 361–716.

COMMENTARIES. F. A. Paley (3 vols., 2nd ed., 1872–80); H. Weil, *Sept Tragédies d'Euripide* (3rd ed., 1905); **Alcestis,** C. S. Jerram (4th ed., 1895), W. S. Hadley (1896), L. Weber (1930); **Andromache,** A. R. F. Hyslop (1900), G. Norwood (1906); **Bacchae,** J. E. Sandys (4th ed., 1900), E. Bruhn (1891); E. R. Dodds (1944); cf. G. Norwood, *The Riddle of the Bacchae* (1908), A. W. Verrall, *The Bacchants of Euripides and other Essays* (1910); **Cyclops,** D. M. Simmonds and R. R. Timberlake (1927); **Electra,** J. D. Denniston (1939); **Hecuba,** W. S. Hadley (1894); **Helena,** A. C. Pearson (1903); **Heraclidae,** A. C. Pearson (1907); **Hercules Furens,** U. von Wilamowitz-Moellendorff (2nd ed., 1895), A. Gray and J. T. Hutchinson (2nd ed., 1886); **Hippolytus,** J. P. Mahaffy and J. E. Bury (1881), W. S. Hadley (1889), U. von Wilamowitz-Moellendorff (1891); **Ion,** U. von Wilamowitz-Moellendorff (1926), A. S. Owen (1939); **Iphigenia in Aulis,** C. E. S. Headlam (1889), E. B. England (1891); **Iphigenia in Tauris,** E. Bruhn (1894), M. Platnauer (1938); **Medea,** D. L. Page (1938); **Orestes,** N. Wedd (1895); **Phoenissae,** A. C. Pearson (1909); **Supplices,** T. Nicklin (1936); **Troades,** R. Y. Tyrrell (1897); **Rhesus,** W. H. Porter (1916). For lost plays (esp. papyrus fragments) see G. Italie (*Hypsipyle*, 1923), Pickard-Cambridge in Powell, *New Chapters* iii. 105–51 (1933), and D. L. Page, *Greek Literary Papyri* i. 54–135 (Loeb, 1942). Cf. also, on textual problems, U. von Wilamowitz-Moellendorff, *Analecta Euripidea* (1875).

TEXT AND TRANSLATION (French). L. Méridier, H. Grégoire, and L. Parmentier (Budé, 1923–5, 4 vols. published).

TRANSLATIONS. A. S. Way (Loeb); G. Murray (8 plays separately).

INDEX. B. W. Beatson (1830).

SCHOLIA. Ed. E. Schwartz (1887–91). A. W. P.-C.

EUROPA (Εὐρώπη), in mythology, daughter of Agenor king of Tyre (cf. CADMUS), or of Phoenix (Φοῖνιξ, 'the Phoenician', *Il.* 14. 321): i.e., her father, originally nameless, is later given an appropriate name 'the proud one', first in Herodotus (4. 147. 5). Zeus loved her, and so turned himself into, or sent, a beautiful bull, which swam to the sea-shore where she was playing and enticed her by its mildness to climb on its back. Once there, she was carried away to sea, and landed in Crete. There she bore Zeus two or three children, Minos, Rhadamanthys, and, in post-Homeric accounts, Sarpedon (in other words, the later forms of the legend reflect a belief, true or false, of a connexion between Crete and Lycia; Apollod. 3. 2 ff.). For their subsequent adventures, see under their names. She was then married to Asterius, king of Crete, who adopted her sons. Zeus gave her the bronze man Talōs (Ap. Rhod. 4. 1643; cf. ARGONAUTS, TALOS) to guard the island, a hound which never missed its quarry ([Eratosthenes] 33; cf. AMPHITRYON), and a javelin which never missed its mark (ibid., cf. Ov. *Met.* 7. 681 ff.). These passed afterwards to Minos, thence to Procris (q.v.) for curing a disease which afflicted him, and so to her husband Cephalus. After her death Europa was worshipped as a goddess, her festival being the Hellotia (Nilsson, *Griechische Feste*, 95), i.e. she was popularly identified with some Cretan goddess. For a Cretan myth resembling hers, see Nilsson, *Minoan-Mycenaean Religion*, 480 f. The bull became the constellation Taurus ([Eratosth.] 14). H. J. R.

EUROPE. The name Εὐρώπη originally stood for central Greece (*Hymn. Hom. Ap.* 250; 290). It was soon extended to the whole Greek mainland and by 500 B.C. to the entire land-mass behind it. The boundary between the European continent and Asia was usually fixed at the river Don. Homer vaguely knew dark regions of the west and north, but his range of information hardly extended north of Greece or west of Sicily.

The Mediterranean seaboard of Europe was chiefly opened up by the Greeks between 800 and 500 B.C. (*see* COLONIZATION, GREEK). The Atlantic coasts and 'Tin Islands' were discovered by the Phoenicians (*see* CASSITERIDES); Pytheas (q.v.) circumnavigated Britain and followed the mainland coast at least to Heligoland. The Baltic Sea was probably not entered by Greek or Roman

ships; Scandinavia was almost wholly unknown, and Thule (q.v.) remained a land of mystery.

The prehistoric amber (q.v.) routes across Europe from Jutland and the Baltic were unknown to later explorers. The Greeks penetrated by way of the Russian rivers as far as Kieff or perhaps Smolensk; central and north Russia remained to them a land of mythical peoples and of the fabulous Rhipaean Mts. (q.v.); north of the Balkans they located the equally mythical Hyperboreans (q.v.). Greek pioneers ascended the Danube to the Iron Gates, and the Rhône perhaps to Lake Leman. But Herodotus had only a hazy notion of central Europe, and the Hellenistic Greeks knew little more (*see* ALPS, HERCYNIAN FOREST).

The land exploration of Europe was chiefly accomplished by the Roman armies. These completed the Carthaginian discovery of Spain; under Caesar they made Gaul known; under Augustus' generals, M. Crassus, Tiberius, and Drusus, they opened up the Balkan lands, the Alpine massif, and the Danube basin (*see* DANUVIUS). Roman traders rediscovered the amber route from Vienna to the Baltic, and Trajan revealed the Carpathian lands by conquest (see DACIA). Tiberius and Drusus also overran west Germany to the Elbe, but central Germany remained outside known Europe.

Cary–Warmington, *Explorers*, 12 ff.; 108 ff.; 229 ff. E. H. W.

EUROPUS (*Dura*) on the middle Euphrates, founded as a Seleucid military colony *c.* 300 B.C. At first mainly Greek in character, it became gradually orientalized; the Arsacids refortified the city, and under Parthian rule it thrived by commerce and agriculture. Occupied by the Romans in A.D. 165, it became a strongly garrisoned fortress on the Euphrates *limes*, but its prosperity rapidly declined. It was besieged and destroyed by the Sassanids *c.* A.D. 257.

The importance of Europus is mainly archaeological. Excavation of the material remains has added considerably to our knowledge of life and culture in Mesopotamia under Hellenistic, Parthian, and Roman rule. The discoveries include well-preserved architectural remains, temples of Greek and Oriental gods, a Christian church and a synagogue, public and private secular buildings, and a Roman camp; frescoes and reliefs of great value for the history of art and religion; military equipment; inscriptions, parchments, and papyri including fragments of a Seleucid code, numerous Greek contracts, and important Roman military archives.

F. Cumont, *Les Fouilles de Doura-Europos 1922–3* (1926); J. Johnson, *Dura Studies* (U.S.A. 1932); M. Rostovtzeff and collaborators, *Excavations at Dura-Europos, Preliminary Reports* i–viii (U.S.A. 1929–39); M. Rostovtzeff, *Caravan Cities* (1932) (on which D. Schlumberger in *Gnomon* xi (1935), 82 ff.); id., *Dura-Europos and its Art* (1938). M. S. D.

EURYALE, see GORGO.

EURYBIADES, a Spartan nobleman, was the first recorded admiral of the Peloponnesian League (481–480 B.C.). Despite the smallness of Sparta's contingent (10 ships at Artemisium, 16 at Salamis), he held chief command over the allied Greek fleet against Xerxes. He gave general support to Themistocles (a ridiculous story alleges that he was bribed at Artemisium), but opposed his scheme to cut off Xerxes' retreat after Salamis by breaking the bridges over the Hellespont. A statue seems to have been erected in his honour at Sparta.

G. B. Grundy, *Great Persian War* (1901), 543 ff.; C. Guratzsch, *Klio* 1925, 62 ff. P. T.

EURYCLEIA, Odysseus' nurse, a woman of good family bought by Laertes (*Od.* 1. 429 ff.). She recognizes Odysseus (19. 392 ff.); keeps the maids in their quarters while the Wooers are killed (21. 380 ff.).

EURYCLES, GAIUS JULIUS, ruler of Sparta, was son of Lachares, who was executed by Antony. He fought at Actium on the side of Octavian, from whom he obtained

Roman citizenship. He exercised a sort of tyranny; his influence extended over the Eleutherolaconian towns and other parts of Greece. Cythera, which Augustus perhaps handed over to Sparta, was his personal possession. About 7 B.C. he was at the courts of Herod the Great and of Archelaus of Cappadocia, making mischief in the former. Repeatedly accused, he was exiled by Augustus (date uncertain), but he regained power, which he transmitted to his son Laco. He was probably dead before Tiberius' accession. The games known as Eurycleia were long maintained at Sparta.

E. Kjellberg, *Klio* xvii (1921), 44; E. Kornemann, *Abh. Schles. Gesell.* 1929; *CAH* xi. 561.   A. M.

EURYDICE (1) (*Εὐρυδίκη*, 'wide-judging', i.e. 'princess', a stopgap name like Creusa, q.v.), name of a dozen mythological characters, the best-known being Orpheus' wife (cf. ORPHEUS). Pursued by Aristaeus (q.v.), she was fatally bitten by a snake. Orpheus then descended to Hades and so charmed the infernal powers by his playing that he was permitted to bring her to the upper world again if he did not look back at her on the way. Breaking this taboo, he lost her. See especially Verg. *G.* 4. 454 ff., and for the distribution of the story, Stith Thompson, F 81. 1.   H. J. R.

EURYDICE (2), originally called *Adeia* (337–317 B.C.), daughter of Amyntas (nephew of Philip II of Macedon) and Cynane (illegitimate daughter of Philip II), was betrothed to the feeble-minded Philip Arrhidaeus before 323 when he succeeded to Alexander's throne (jointly with Alexander's infant son). Her royal blood endeared her to the Macedonian soldiers, whose protection enabled her to marry Philip Arrhidaeus (322), make trouble for the regent Antipater (321), depose his successor Polyperchon from the regency, and try to rule Macedonia, using Cassander as her minister, and excluding Alexander's son from the succession (317). Her undoing was Olympias, against whom the Macedonians would not fight. Philip and Eurydice became her prisoners, and after Philip's murder Eurydice obeyed an order to commit suicide. In an age of violence her blood, brains, and courage were not enough.

G. H. Macurdy, *Hellenistic Queens* (1932), 40 ff. and 48 ff.   G. T. G.

EURYPONTIDS (*Εὐρυπωντίδαι*) was the name of the junior royal house at Sparta. The most notable Eurypontid kings were Agesilaus, Agis II and IV, Archidamus II, and Leotychides (qq.v.). *See also* AGIADS.

EURYPYLUS, in mythology, (1) son of Euhaemon; leads a contingent to Troy (*Il.* 2. 736); takes part in several battle-scenes and is wounded; healed by Patroclus (11. 809 ff.). According to the local legend of Patrae (Paus. 7. 19. 6 ff.), after the war he looked into a chest which contained an image of Dionysus made by Hephaestus, and went mad. He was promised at Delphi a cure when he found a 'foreign sacrifice'. Coming to Patrae, he found human sacrifice practised there, which, according also to Delphi, was to stop when a foreign king brought a foreign god. Both oracles were thus fulfilled and the cult of Dionysus established there. Some, however, made this Eurypylus son of Dexamenus. (2) Son of Telephus (q.v.) and Astyoche sister of Priam (q.v.). (3) Son of Poseidon, a Triton, who meets the Argonauts and gives one of them, Euphemus, a lump of earth as pledge of possession of part of Africa (Cyrene) (Pind. *Pyth.* 4. 20 ff., Ap. Rhod. 4. 1551 ff.).   H. J. R.

EURYTION, in mythology, (1) Geryon's herdsman, *see* HERACLES. (2) A centaur (*Od.* 21. 295 ff.); getting drunk and misbehaving at Peirithous' wedding-feast, he began the quarrel between centaurs and men. (3) Brother of Pandarus (q.v.; Verg. *Aen.* 5. 495 ff.). (4) *See* PELEUS.

EURYTUS, *see* MOLIONES.

EUSEBIUS of Caesarea in Palestine, also surnamed *Pamphili*, after the Christian scholar who was his friend and patron in early life; his long life falls within the limits A.D. 260 and 340, covering the great crisis of the Christian Church. From early days Eusebius resided at Caesarea, where he worked in the school of biblical study established by Pamphilus and having as its kernel the library of Origen. In the great persecution, 303–10, Palestine suffered severely and Caesarea was the usual scene of the trials. The work of the school was interrupted, but the library seems to have escaped destruction. Pamphilus was beheaded in 310, but Eusebius himself got off with a short detention and was sometimes reproached later for his failure to 'witness'. In 311, after the edict of toleration, Eusebius succeeded Agapius as bishop of Caesarea. A little later he came into close personal contact with Constantine and remained in favour throughout his life. In the Arian controversy and at the Council of Nicaea Eusebius represented a moderate position, which, though unsatisfactory to Athanasius and the extremists, had the support of the Emperor. Eusebius cannot long have survived his patron.

Eusebius was the ablest and most fertile of the first generation of Christian men of letters in an Empire that was rapidly becoming Christian. Of his works, the *Chronica*, based largely on Julius Africanus, forms an important foundation of our knowledge of the chronology of Greek and Roman history. The *Church History* was written to satisfy the natural curiosity now felt in the rise of the Church to its new importance. The *Preparation of the Gospel*, similarly, was designed to show how pagan history had led up to the Christian revelation. In the *History* is included a special record of the martyrs of Palestine, invaluable as our one reliable witness to the detailed history of the persecution. A tract *Against Hierocles* confuted one of the bitterest of the enemies of the Church. Eusebius' *Life of Constantine* falls admittedly under the heading of panegyric, and sacrifices something of its historical value to the demands of its class. But Eusebius was writing of times he had lived in and of a man whom he had personally known and esteemed, and he is above suspicion of deliberate fraud. The historical importance of the *Life*, therefore, remains considerable and should not be too heavily discounted.

Most works in the Berlin Corpus, *Griech. Christl. Schriftsteller. Ecclesiastical History* translated by Kirsopp Lake and J. E. L. Oulton in Loeb Classics. *Praeparatio Evangelica* ed. E. H. Gifford (1903). E. Schwartz, *PW*, s.v.   H. M.

EUSTATHIUS (12th c. A.D.), born and educated at Constantinople, was deacon at St. Sophia and taught oratory until in 1174 he received the bishopric of Thessalonica. In 1175 he obtained the title of archbishop, in which position he continued till his death (*c.* 1194). His works of classical scholarship were written before 1175. Henceforward he devoted himself to the practical duties of his spiritual office and to combating the prevailing corruption of monastic life.

WORKS. (1) Classical. *Commentary on Pindar*, of which only the introduction survives; this gives information about lyric poetry (especially Pindar's) and Pindar's life, and shorter notes on the Olympian games and the pentathlon. The *Paraphrase of Dionysius Periegetes* has discursive scholia, valuable for citations from earlier geographers, historians, the complete Stephanus Byz., and the lost works of Arrian. The *Commentaries on Homer's Iliad and Odyssey* (Παρεκβολαὶ εἰς τὴν Ὁμήρου Ἰλιάδα [Ὀδύσσειαν]) are a vast compilation, in which the *Iliad* commentary is twice as long as that on the *Odyssey*. Prefaces deal with the differences between the poems and with the cultural importance of Homer. The notes discuss chiefly questions of language, mythology (interpreted allegorically), history, and geography. Their value consists particularly in the assemblage of material drawn from the old scholia and the lost writings of earlier scholars and lexicographers. His quotations from classical authors are taken mostly at second-hand.

(2) His other works include a history of the conquest of Thessalonica by the Normans; several polemics, e.g. the famous treatise *Inquiry into Monastic Life*; letters to the Emperor, church dignitaries, and others; speeches and addresses, homilies and tracts, some of which have historical value. E. was the outstanding scholar and orator of his time, enthusiastic for the traditional learning, for the preservation of books, for sound principles of education, and for the moral reawakening of monasticism.

Commentaria ad Iliadem et Odysseam, G. Stallbaum (1825–30); T. L. F. Tafel, *Eustathii Metropolitae Thessalonicensis opuscula* (1832); J. P. Migne, *Patrologia Graeca* cxxxv, cxxxvi (1864); A. B. Drachmann, *Scholia Vetera in Pindari Carmina* iii (1927).
                                                                J. F. L.

EUSTOCHIUS of Alexandria, physician, became a pupil of Plotinus in Plotinus' old age (Porph. *Plot.* 7) (prob. *c.* A.D. 265), and is said to have edited his master's works.

PW vi. 1489.

EUTERPE, *see* MUSES.

EUTHYCLES, writer of (?) Old Comedy (Ath. 3. 124 b). We possess but two titles, Ἄσωτοι ἢ Ἐπιστολή and Ἀταλάντη, the first of which looks more like Middle than Old Comedy.

FCG ii. 890; *CAF* i. 805.

EUTHYDEMUS (1) of Chios, Sophist, an older contemporary of Socrates. In the *Euthydemus* Plato presents him as a ridiculous figure. He has sometimes been thought to be unhistorical and merely a mask for Plato's criticism of Antisthenes. His historicity is proved by independent references by Aristotle; but Plato may have used him quite freely for the purpose of pillorying eristic views and arguments.

PW vi. 1504.   W. D. R.

EUTHYDEMUS (2) of Magnesia (3rd–2nd c. B.C.), probably a satrap of Diodotus II, removed him and became king of Bactria–Sogdiana. In 208 B.C. he was attacked by Antiochus III, who failed to subdue him and left him his crown. He made Bactria into a strong and quasi-national State, winning the support of the natives and shielding Iran from the northern nomads (*see* BACTRIA). After Antiochus' departure he took two satrapies from Parthia, conquered some part of Chinese Turkestan, and made an expedition northwards, probably to the Lake Issyk Kul country; Seleucid territory he never touched. He invented a new state-form, under which princes of the blood ruled groups of satrapies as sub-kings, with the right of coining. He died about 190. *See* DEMETRIUS (7).   W. W. T.

EUTHYMIDES (end of 6th c. B.C.), vase-painter in Athens, known from six signatures on large red-figure vases, including Arming of Hector (Munich). He breaks with archaic conventions; his heavy figures show new studies of movement.

Beazley, *A.V.* 63; *Greek Vases in Poland* (1928), 13; L. Talcott, *Hesperia* 1936, 59.   T. B. L. W.

EUTHYMUS. Temesa in south Italy was haunted by the ghost of Polites (q.v.), a companion of Odysseus, whom the inhabitants had killed for raping a girl. It could be kept quiet only by giving it the prettiest girl in Temesa every year. One year, when the sacrifice was to be made, Euthymus, a notable boxer, said to be son of the river Caecinus, arrived, pitied and then loved the girl, encountered the ghost, and drove it off for ever (Paus. 6. 6. 4–11).   H. J. R.

EUTHYNA, the examination of accounts which every officer of the State underwent on expiry of his office, at Athens and generally elsewhere. It was primarily an examination into the handling of public money, by ten *logistai* (q.v.) at Athens. If the *logistai* were not satisfied, or if some qualified citizen brought a charge against a magistrate, they must bring the matter before a dicastery and preside at the trial. Even after discharge the magistrate was not entirely free; for thirty days after, ten *euthynoi*, chosen by lot by the Boule from its own number, were prepared to examine any complaint, on a public or private matter, against an outgoing magistrate, and, if it was sound, brought it before a dicastery.

In democratic States the *euthyna*, though in the vast majority of cases a formality, was the most effective means for the control of the executive; and it put a powerful weapon into the hands of the sycophants (q.v.).

Aristotle, *Ath. Pol.* ch. 48.   A. W. G.

EUTROPIUS, the historian, who took part in Julian's Persian campaign (A.D. 363) and was *magister memoriae* of Valens, published a survey of Roman history (*Breviarium ab urbe condita*) in ten books. Beginning with Romulus, he reached the Sullan Civil War in bk. 5, Caesar's death in bk. 6, and covered the Empire to Jovian's death (A.D. 364) in bks. 7–10. The subject-matter for the Republic is based upon the Epitome of Livy, for the Empire upon the end of the Epitome, an expanded adaptation of Suetonius, and an 'Imperial history', closing with personal knowledge of events. The work is short, but well balanced, showing good judgement and impartiality. It was translated into Greek by Paeanius about 380, adapted into Greek by Capito of Lycia, and used by Hieronymus (Jerome), Orosius, Isidore, and Paulus Diaconus.

Editions: H. Droysen (ed. minor 1878; ed. maior 1879); C. Wagener (1884); F. Rühl (1887). W. Pirogoff, *De Eutropii breviarii A.U.C. indole ac fontibus* (1873); J. Sorn, *Sprachgebrauch des Eutropius* (1892); M. Galdi, *L'epitome nella lett. latina* (1922).
                                                                A. H. McD.

EUTYCHES (6th c. A.D.), author of an *Ars de verbo* in two books (ed. Keil, *Gramm. Lat.* v. 447–89) and of a treatise *De aspiratione* (now incorporated in the *De orthographia* of Cassiodorus; ed. Keil, *Gramm. Lat.* vii. 199–202).

Cf. Teuffel, § 482. 1; Schanz–Hosius, § 1116.

EUTYCHIDES (early 3rd c. B.C.), sculptor and painter of Sicyon, pupil of Lysippus. Works: (1) Statue of Timosthenes, a boy victor at Olympia. (2) Tyche of Antioch. Tyche seated, supported by the river god Orontes and crowned by Seleucus and Antiochus. Many copies of Tyche and Orontes have survived, the best probably the marble group in the Vatican (Winter, *KB* 340. 1). The bold composition is Lysippan; the drapery has a new realism. The original of a seated girl in the Conservatori (Winter, *KB* 371. 4) is ascribed to Eutychides because of its likeness in composition. (3) Eurotas. A copy has been recognized in a river-god in the Vatican (Winter, *KB* 340. 2). (4) Dionysus, belonging to Asinius Pollio.

Overbeck, 1516; 1530–6.   T. B. L. W.

EUTYCHIUS PROCULUS (2nd c. A.D.), author of (lost) grammatical works.

Cf. Teuffel, § 357. 4; Schanz–Hosius, § 606. 7.

EUXENIDES, mentioned by Suidas as an Athenian writer of comedy contemporaneous with Epicharmus.

EUXINE SEA was the Greek name for the Black Sea. (The origin of this name is uncertain; perhaps it was invented by the early Greek colonists 'ad captandum', like medieval 'Greenland'.) This sea apparently remained closed to traffic from the Aegean in prehistoric times, and the voyage of the Argonauts (*c.* 1250 B.C.?) was probably an adventure in unknown waters. The Euxine was opened up in the eighth and seventh centuries by Milesians and other Ionian Greeks; by 600 it had become ringed with Greek settlements (*see* COLONIZATION, GREEK), and it remained a Greek lake until the Middle Ages. The earliest surviving description of the Euxine Sea is by Herodotus, who had personal knowledge of its northern coasts and gave a fairly accurate account of it, though he greatly over-estimated its length. A more detailed description of the south coast is contained in the geographical work attributed to Scylax (*c.* 340 B.C.). An excellent survey of the whole coast was written by Arrian in the days of Hadrian; a later 'Periplus of the Euxine Sea' is an extract from this work and from other Greek geographies.

Herodotus, bk. 4, esp. chs. 85-6; Scylax, chs. 67-92; Arrian, *Periplus Maris Euxini*; Ps.-Arrian, with same title. The last three works in *GGM* i.   M. C.

EVADNE (*Εὐάδνη*), in mythology, (1) a daughter of Poseidon, who became by Apollo mother of Iamus, ancestor of the prophetic clan of the Iamidae in Olympia (Pind. *Ol.* 6. 29 ff.). (2) Daughter of Iphis and wife of Capaneus, one of the Seven against Thebes. She burned herself on his funeral pyre (Eur. *Supp.* 980 ff.).   H. J. R.

EVAGORAS (*Εὐαγόρας, c.* 435-374/3 B.C.), a member of the Teucrid house, the traditional rulers of Cyprian Salamis. Exiled during his youth, which fell in a period of Phoenician domination, he gathered some fifty followers at Soli in Cilicia, and with their aid established himself as ruler of Salamis in 411. His subsequent policy aimed at strengthening Hellenism in Cyprus by cooperation with Athens, and his court became a centre for Athenian *émigrés*, of whom Conon was the most distinguished. A clash with Persia was ultimately inevitable, but he postponed the issue by assisting in the revival of Persian sea-power culminating in the triumph of Cnidos. War finally came in 390 and dragged on for ten years. In alliance with Akoris of Egypt, Evagoras at first more than held his own. He not only extended his rule over the central cities of Cilicia, but also captured Tyre and dominated Phoenicia. In 382 Persia mobilized an overwhelming armament. Evagoras lost control of the sea at Citium in 381, and was forced to sue for peace, obtaining not unfavourable terms through dissensions among the Persian commanders. In 374 he was assassinated in a palace intrigue.

K. Spyridakis, *Evagoras I von Salamis* (1935).   D. E. W. W.

EVANDER (*Εὔανδρος*), in Greece a minor god or daemon, belonging to the circle of Pan and worshipped in Arcadia, especially at Palantion, where he had a temple; in Italy connected with the worship of Faunus (identified with Pan) and regarded as the first settler at Rome. According to tradition he was the son of Hermes and of a nymph, daughter of the river-god Ladon, known as Themis and identified in Italy with the prophetic goddess Carmenta (or Carmentis). Through Atlas, grandfather of Hermes, he was connected with the Trojan Dardanus (Verg. *Aen.* 8. 134-7). A more human genealogy made him the son of Echemos of Tegea, whose grandfather was Pallas (q.v. 2). As a boy he is said to have welcomed Priam and Anchises in Arcadia and conducted them to the city of Pheneos (*Aen.* 8. 165). He left Arcadia owing either to the hostility of Argos or to a famine, and reaching Italy landed on the left bank of the Tiber and made a settlement on the neighbouring hill, which he called after his native city (or his grandfather) Pallanteum (*Aen.* 8. 54), afterwards the Collis Palatinus. He instituted there the worship of Faunus (Pan Lycaeus) and established the Lupercalia (q.v.; Ov. *Fasti* 2. 279 ff.). According to Virgil, Hercules visited him and slew the monster Cacus, who had stolen

his cattle; Evander in memory established the cult of Hercules at the Ara Maxima (*Aen.* 8. 185-275; Livy 1. 7). Aeneas, on the outbreak of war against the Latins, made his way up the Tiber and appealed to Evander for aid. Evander welcomed him as a kinsman, conducted him over the site of the future Rome and sent back with him his own son Pallas, who was subsequently slain in battle by Turnus (*Aen.* 10). Evander was thus used by the Romans to supply a legendary connexion between Greece and Rome and an aetiological explanation of place-names and cults.   C. B.

EVOCATIO. Gods, being in a sense the highest class of citizens, are sometimes thought of as conquered when their city is taken (Verg. *Aen.* 1. 68 = 8. 11, 'uictos penatis', sc. of Troy), but more commonly (as Aesch. *Sept.* 218, on which see Groeneboom; Verg. *Aen.* 2. 351 f.) as leaving it. It was therefore not unnatural to hasten the fall of a city by inducing its gods to leave it, especially that god which particularly protected it. This the Romans did by promising the deity a cult in Rome at least as good as the one given by the city in question (Pliny, *HN* 28. 18); formula of evocation, Macrobius, *Sat.* 3. 9. 7-8. See Wissowa, *RK* 383 and note 7; W. Warde Fowler, *Rel. Exper.* 206.   H. J. R.

EXECIAS (*Ἐξηκίας*) (third quarter of 6th c. B.C.), potter and vase-painter in Athens, known from nine signatures (two vases are inscribed 'Execias painted and made'). Painted amphorae, calyx craters, cups, pinakes. Note particularly Achilles and Ajax dicing (Vatican), death of Ajax (Boulogne), both excellent compositions showing a psychological insight unique in black-figure.

W. Technau, *Exekias* (1936); O. Broneer, *AJArch.* 1938, 161.   T. B. L. W.

EXEGETES (*ἐξηγητής*), an interpreter or expounder, usually of sacred lore. Herodotus (1. 78. 2) gives this title to the college of diviners at the Telmessian oracle in Lycia. Best known are the *exegetai* of Athens, who, according to the most probable interpretation of the evidence, were of two kinds: those chosen by the Delphic oracle (*Πυθόχρηστοι*) and those elected by the people (*οἱ ὑπὸ τοῦ δήμου καθεσταμένοι* or *χειροτονητοί*). Probably there were three of each kind, chosen for life from the Eupatridae. The *Pythochrestoi* were selected by the Pythia from a list nominated by the Athenian people. Also we find at Eleusis the *exegetai* of (or from) the Eumolpidae, probably three in number. Their functions were confined to the Eleusinian cult, and they probably antedated the Athenian domination of Eleusis. *Exegetai* are attested in other cities too: e.g. the *Pythioi* of Sparta, who resemble the *Pythochrestoi*.

In general the *exegetai* were keepers of religious tradition. They gave advice on sacrifices, festivals, foundations of new cults, and especially rites of purification. They interpreted oracles and omens. It is reasonable to suppose that the *Pythochrestoi* were consulted on the interpretation of Delphic oracles and on all matters affecting Athenian relations with Delphi. Non-Delphic subjects were in the hands of the elective board.

Ancient sources: Suidas, Timaeus, Harpocration, **s.v.** Modern literature: P. Schoell, *Hermes* xxii (1887), 562-5; J. Toepffer, *Attische Genealogie* (1889), 68-76, 177; Ph. Ehrmann in *RGVV* iv (1908), 3; A. Persson, *Die Exegeten und Delphi* (1918).   J. E. F.

EXILIUM, *see* EXSILIUM.

EXODOS, *see* TRAGEDY, para. 14.

EXSILIUM. A Roman citizen or *peregrinus* being threatened by criminal proceedings on account of a capital crime could—even after their inception—leave Roman territory and escape to that of another State before a capital sentence was pronounced against him. This voluntary self-banishment, called *exsilium* (later the same term was used for indicating the banishment pronounced by a judgement in a criminal trial), was tolerated by the magistrates; in the last century of the Republic, however, it became a legal institution, when magistrates were strictly ordered to allow the condemned person time to escape before executing the capital sentence. Thus *exsilium* became a substitute for the death penalty. Its effect was to prohibit the return of the wrongdoer to Roman territory. After his escape a decree, more administrative than jurisdictional in character, pronounced by the *comitia* or a high magistrate, excluded him from all legal protection and threatened him with death in case of illicit return (*aquae et ignis interdictio*). In later times *exsilium* lost its strict technical meaning, being used not only by historians and orators, but even in some juridical texts (if they are not interpolated) indiscriminately for voluntary and involuntary emigration, for legally prescribed banishment, for escape before and after judgement, and generally for all categories of expulsion, from the mildest form of *relegatio* (q.v.) to the severest one of *deportatio*. Because of these different uses of the word we must consider in each case whether it refers to temporary or perpetual expulsion, whether or not it is followed by loss of citizenship, by confiscation (total or partial) of property, and so on. In its old technical sense *exsilium* was perpetual and general, without any gradation; it resulted in loss of citizenship and of all property. *See* RELEGATIO.   A. B.

EXSUPERANTIUS, *see* JULIUS (5) EXSUPERANTIUS.

EXTISPICY, *see* DIVINATION, para. 5, and HARUSPICES.

EYE, MEDICAL TREATMENT OF, *see* OPHTHALMOLOGY.

EZECHIEL, *see* JEWISH GREEK LITERATURE.

F

FABIANUS PAPIRIUS, a philosopher of the older school (Sen. *Dial.* 10. 10), pupil of the elder Sextius and of Blandus, taught the younger Seneca. His declamations are copiously illustrated in Sen. *Controv.* bk. 2: cf. *praef.* 4–5.

FABIUS (1) **AMBUSTUS,** QUINTUS, was *tribunus militum consulari potestate* in 391 B.C. Another tradition assigned his office to 390 and made him responsible for the Gallic attack on Rome, since as ambassador at Clusium he had treacherously murdered a Gallic chief. Thanks to the authority of his father or to his popularity among the plebeians, he had escaped an attempted patrician prosecution. This story was no doubt invented as an honourable explanation of the Roman defeat at the Allia. It may, however, be inferred from Livy (6. 1. 6–7) that the Roman military chiefs were actually prosecuted after the Celts had retired, although sudden death or suicide seems to have saved Fabius.

O. Hirschfeld, *Kl. Schr.* (1913), 269 ff.; Ed. Meyer, *Kl. Schr.* ii (1924), 312 ff.   P. T.

FABIUS (2) **AMBUSTUS,** MARCUS, *princeps senatus* and a patrician leader after the Gallic catastrophe, aimed at re-establishing patrician influence at home and at reasserting the power of Rome over her neighbours. Successful against the Hernici in 356 B.C. and in 354 against the Tiburtini, over whom he triumphed, he was defeated in the same year, being consul for the third time, by Tarquinii. Appointed dictator in 351, he failed to prevent the readmission of the plebs to the consulate. The attempts in the traditional account to conceal or ignore his defeat in 354 demonstrate his authority and that of his family.

K. J. Beloch, *Röm. Gesch.* 352, 361 ff.   P. T.

FABIUS (3) **MAXIMUS RULLIANUS,** QUINTUS, a hero of the Samnite Wars; consul 322, 310, 308, 297, 295 B.C., censor 304 (after 310 his colleague was always P. Decius Mus), dictator 315 (Diod. 19. 101 records a second, probably apocryphal, dictatorship in 313). He celebrated triumphs over Samnites, Etruscans, Gauls. Of the exploits attributed to Rullianus the following deserve mention: his Samnite victory (325), when the dictator Papirius Cursor apparently impeached him for fighting against orders; his defeat by Samnites at Lautulae (315); his Etruscan expedition, reputedly through the Ciminian Forest (310); his annihilation of the Samnite, Gallic, Etruscan coalition at Sentinum (295) (*see* EGNATIUS). The untrustworthy account of Rullianus in our principal source, Livy (bks. 8–11), whom details in Diodorus, Valerius Maximus, Frontinus, and others supplement, derives partly from Fabius Pictor but more from later annalists. It borrows incidents from the career of Rullianus' great-grandson, Fabius Cunctator; e.g. Rullianus–Papirius Cursor resemble Cunctator–Minucius; the censor Rullianus restricting the rabble to four city tribes suggests Cunctator confining freedmen to three tribes; Rullianus rescuing his son, the consul Fabius Gurges (292) (*see* PONTIUS 1), anticipates Cunctator serving under his own son (213 B.C.).

F. E. Adcock, *CAH* vii, ch. 18 (with bibliography).   E. T. S.

FABIUS (4) **BUTEO,** MARCUS (*cos.* 245 B.C.), censor 241 and *princeps senatus*. His naval victory off Aegimurus and subsequent shipwreck are improbable. Probably he, not Fabius Cunctator, delivered the Roman ultimatum at Carthage in 218. As dictator he filled up the Senate after Cannae (216).   H. H. S.

FABIUS (5) **MAXIMUS VERRUCOSUS, CUNCTATOR,** QUINTUS, consul I (233 B.C.), triumphed over the Ligurians; censor (230), consul II (228), dictator I (between 221 and 219, probably 221). He probably did not deliver the Roman ultimatum to Carthage (*see* FABIUS 4). After the disaster at Trasimene he was elected dictator II, but quarrelled with his *magister equitum*, M. Minucius (q.v.) Rufus. By religious observances he restored the people's morale and stated his policy of dogging Hannibal's heels and avoiding further pitched battles. He allowed Hannibal to ravage Campania unchecked and later at Callicula to cross the Apennines to Apulia, being duped by the Carthaginian advance at night behind a herd of oxen with burning faggots tied to their horns. Fabius' strategy of exhaustion, which was opposed by many Romans, was only justified as a temporary expedient, since there was yet no real reason to distrust the Roman legions. But when these were defeated at Cannae (216) Fabius' policy had to be continued and the abusive title Cunctator, the Delayer, now became an honour: 'unus homo nobis cunctando restituit rem' (Ennius, Vahlen, 12. 370). As consul III (215) in Campania Fabius covered the road to Rome, while Marcellus and Gracchus parried Hannibal's attacks; as consul IV (214) he helped to recover Casilinum. In 213 he served as legate to his inexperienced son, now consul. In 209 he was consul V and *princeps senatus*; he recovered Tarentum through internal treachery. He strenuously opposed Scipio's determination to invade Africa, and died in 203. He was pontifex for twelve years, augur for sixty-two. A typical example of the older Roman patrician, courageous, cautious, and unimaginative, Fabius inspired admiration rather than affection. Rightly called the Shield of Rome, he at length wore down Hannibal's strength: 'subsequendo coercuit' (*Elogium*). It was Scipio's bolder strategy which humbled Carthage—yet it was Fabius that had made its application possible. H. H. S.

FABIUS (6) PICTOR, QUINTUS, Roman senator and historian, who took part in the Second Punic War, consulting the Delphic oracle after Cannae, wrote a history of Rome in Greek, the first of the senatorial histories interpreting Roman institutions and policy to the Greek world. It treated the Greek association of Roman origins in Aeneas, set the foundation of the city in 747 B.C., and passed, probably in discursive fashion, to the Gallic and Punic Wars and his own times; his use of Diocles of Peparethus (Plut. *Rom.* 3; 8) is now disputed. Polybius, though criticizing his Roman bias (Polyb. 1. 14; 58; 3. 8–9), follows his authority. Dionysius and Livy cite him; Diodorus' use is uncertain. The Latin annals, if not a later adaptation, may belong to Ser. Fabius, the work *de iure pontificio* to Fabius Servilianus. Fabius' history, political in purpose, probably owed more to Hellenistic historiography than to the pontifical tradition, and it set the standard for senatorial history.

H. Peter, *HRRel.* i² (1914), pp. lxix, 5, 112; F. Leo, *Gesch. der röm. Lit.* i (1913), 85; K. J. Beloch, *Röm. Gesch.* 95; M. Gelzer, *Hermes* 1933, 129; 1934, 46. Cf. for detailed bibliography, Schanz-Hosius i (1927), 172. A. H. McD.

FABIUS (7) MAXIMUS AEMILIANUS, QUINTUS (*c.* 186–130 B.C.), born of L. Aemilius Paullus and Papiria and adopted by the Fabii Maximi, accompanied Paullus to Greece in 168. Praetor in Sicily (149); consul (145), he consolidated the position against Viriathus in Spain (145–144) and led an embassy to Crete (140). Legate at Numantia in 133, he died in 130. His career followed the rise of his brother, Scipio Aemilianus.

Livy 44. 35; 45; Plutarch, *Aemilius Paulus*; Appian, *Hisp.* 65. A. Schulten, *Numantia*, i (1914), 273, 353, 367. A. H. McD.

FABIUS (8) MAXIMUS ALLOBROGICUS, QUINTUS (*cos.* 121 B.C.), the son of Fabius (7). With Domitius (q.v. 2) he conquered the Allobroges and defeated the Arverni, then predominant in Gaul; the annexation of Gallia Narbonensis followed, as also the Roman alliance with the Aedui. 120,000 Gauls are said to have fallen in Fabius' victory at the confluence of the Rhône and Isère. From his spoils Fabius erected a triumphal arch at Rome. He was censor in 108. M. H.

FABIUS, *see also* FULGENTIUS, MAXIMUS, QUINTILIANUS, VALENS.

FABLE (αἶνος, μῦθος, λόγος, ἀπόλογος), a feature of the popular tradition of the Greek as of other races. It is typically an anecdote of animal life with a moralizing application; it may, however, be drawn from inanimate nature or directly from human experience. It is questionable whether Greek Fable is substantially indebted to that of any other race. Foreign and colonial sources are occasionally mentioned; e.g. Libya (Aesch. fr. 139), Egypt (Pl. *Phdr.* 275b), Lydia (Callim. *POxy.* 1011), Sybaris (Ar. *Vesp.* 1259). Instances of its employment occur throughout Greek literature; among the earliest are Hesiod *Op.* 202 and Archilochus frs. 86 and 89; it is not found in Homer. The earlier popular type upon which writers drew appears to have been in prose-form. By the end of the fifth century B.C. the body of native Fable was in general ascribed to Aesop, said to have been a slave in Samos in the sixth century (Hdt.

2. 134); his name is already familiar to Aristophanes and Plato. There is no extant Greek collection of fables as such before that of Babrius (q.v.). Demetrius of Phalerum composed Λόγων Αἰσωπείων συναγωγαί (Diog. Laert. 5. 80); these were presumably in prose. At a later period Fable was found useful in rhetorical training (Hermogenes Προγυμνάσματα ad init.), and further collections were made with this object, e.g. the δεκαμυθία of Nicostratus (Suid. Νικ.) in the second century A.D. The Fable so adapted reached its final form in the medieval collections, being regularly associated with the name of Aesop.

LATIN FABLE. As represented in Latin literature Fable is in general derivative from the Greek Aesopic form. It was well adapted for use in the *Satura*, especially in that of the Horatian type. Aulus Gellius (2. 29) cites part of an adaptation by Ennius of an Aesopic fable; Lucilius (988 Marx) uses another. Horace sometimes gives fables *in extenso* (*Sat.* 2. 6. 79 ff.; *Epist.* 1. 7. 29 ff.), sometimes merely alludes to them (*Sat.* 2. 3. 299; *Epist.* 1. 3. 19). The first extant Latin collection was in iambic verse, by Phaedrus (q.v.), a freedman of Augustus, who published his five books under Tiberius and Caligula. The MS. tradition is probably the result of selection; an Appendix of fables ascribed to Phaedrus is added. Phaedrus acknowledges his formal debt to Aesop, whilst seeking to improve upon him (4 *prol.* 11). The collection includes besides definitely Aesopic material much that is derived from the author's experience or imagination. He writes professedly (1 *prol.* 3) for entertainment and instruction; at the same time a desire for literary recognition is certainly a leading motive. He incurred the displeasure of Sejanus (3 *prol.* 41), no doubt on account of indiscreet allusions to contemporary events. He has been called a better story-teller than fabulist (Nisard); he is certainly at his best in anecdote, whilst his work lacks in general the peculiar genius of the best Greek Fable. His versification is adroit and finished; and in the terse and vigorous simplicity of his style he shows himself a not unworthy pupil of the preceding epoch. His diction is in general classical, but shows traces of contemporary tendencies. The Phaedrian collection was later paraphrased in prose under the title of *Romulus* (the 'Latin Aesop'). In the third century Titianus, of whose work nothing further is known, composed prose fables (Auson. *Ep.* 16 *praef.*); the extant collection of Avianus (4th or 5th c.), consisting of forty-two fables in elegiac verse, is of no particular literary merit. These later authors appear to have drawn principally on Babrius.

BIBLIOGRAPHY

A. Hausrath, *PW* vi (1909), xix (1938), (Phaedr.); Christ i⁶ (1912), ii (1920–4); W. G. Rutherford, ed. *Babrius* (introd.; 1883); E. Rohde, *Der gr. Roman²* (App.), 1914; Teuffel-Kroll⁶ i (1916), ii (1920) (Phaedr.), iii (1913) (Avian.); D. Nisard, *Poètes lat. d. l. décad.* i (1877) (Phaedr.); L. Hervieux, *Les Fables latines* (1893); O. Crusius, *PW* ii (1896) (Avian.); A. Hausrath, *Jahrb. f. cl. Phil. Suppl.* xxi (1894). Editions: (Gr. Aesop) K. Halm (Teubner 1889); (Babrius) W. G. Rutherford (1883); (Phaedr.) L. Müller (Teubner, 1903); J. P. Postgate (1919); (Avian.) C. Lachmann (1845); (*Romulus*) G. Thiele (1910). W. M. E.

FABRI. In the early Roman Army there were two separately organized centuries of *fabri*. These men were less sappers and gunners, whose work was done by the ordinary legionary, than smiths skilled in the repair of arms. They were commanded by *praefecti*.

By the time of Caesar, and probably much earlier, the *fabri* were absorbed into the ranks of the cohort, and the *praefectus fabrum* became a sort of A.D.C. to the general, his work bearing no relation to his title. H. M. D. P.

FABRICIUS LUSCINUS, GAIUS, hero of the war with Pyrrhus (q.v.), consul in 282, 278 B.C., censor in 275. He negotiated for Rome with Tarentum (284) and with Pyrrhus (280, 278). He rescued Thurii from Sabellian besiegers (282) and was twice awarded triumphs for his victories over Bruttii, Lucani, Samnites, and Tarentines. His personality lies concealed under the rhetorical stories of his poverty, austerity, and incorruptibility: he rejected alike bribes from Pyrrhus and the proffered aid of would-be poisoners of Pyrrhus. Similar tales are told of the other plebeian hero M'. Curius Dentatus (q.v.), whom Cicero (cf. *Paradoxa* 50) constantly cites with Fabricius as a typical specimen of Roman virtue.

Livy, *Epit.* 13 f.; Dion. Hal. bk. 19 f.; Val. Max. 1. 8. 6; Plut. *Pyrrhus*; App. *Sam.* 9; Gell. 3. 8. E. T. S.

FABULA (besides meaning 'story', 'talk', 'fable') was the general Latin term for 'play'; special types were *F. Atellana* (*see* ATELLANA); *crepidata*, possibly = *palliata* (*crepida* was a type of Greek shoe, worn with the *pallium*); *palliata*, adaptation of Greek New Comedy (*see* DRAMA; *pallium* = Greek cloak); *praetexta(ta)*, serious drama on Roman historical subjects (*see* DRAMA; *praetexta* was the magistrate's toga); *riciniata*, a mime (*see* MIMUS II; *ricinium*, properly a woman's mantle, which could be used to veil the head; possibly this made it useful in the mime); *saltica*, libretto for pantomime (*see* PANTOMIMUS); *stataria*, 'quiet' play, opposed to *motoria*, 'bustling' play (cf. Ter. *Haut.* 36-40); *tabernaria*, 'private-house comedy' (?), apparently identical with *togata*; *togata*, Roman comedy, nearly always concerned with lower life (*see* DRAMA); *trabeata*, a form of *togata* dealing with upper middle-class life, invented by Maecenas' freedman Melissus (the *trabea* was worn by the *equites*). W. B.

FADIUS GALLUS, MARCUS, friend of Cicero, who addresses to him *Fam.* 7. 23-7. In 45 B.C. he was among those who wrote anti-Caesarian eulogies of Cato. *See* ANTICATONES.

FALERNUS AGER, a section of Campania between the Mons Massicus and the Volturnus taken by Rome from Capua (338 B.C. or later) and distributed among Roman citizens (Livy 8. 11. 22; 9. 41). Its exact extent and the origin of its name are alike uncertain. Its celebrated wine was already deteriorating in Pliny's day (Hor. *Carm.* 1. 20, etc.; Athenaeus 1. 26c; Pliny, *HN* 14. 62). E. T. S.

FALISCI. The Faliscans were the inhabitants of the Ager Faliscus, around Mt. Soracte in south-east Etruria. Their principal city was Falerii (*Città Castellana*). They form a link between Etruscans and Latins, sharing their characteristics but not completely identifiable with either. Their language was a dialect of Latin, but Etruscan inscriptions occur. The mixture of burial rites also suggests the presence of two races, even apart from Sabine infiltration. Their culture was predominantly Etruscan from the eighth century onwards, but with a strongly individual note, especially in the painted pottery. Politically the fortunes of Falerii and its neighbours were inseparably bound up with Veii. Indeed Cato believed Capena to have been the mother city of Veii. Capena, Fidenae, and the Faliscans were the only allies of Veii against Rome, so that the capture of Veii by Camillus entailed the surrender of Falerii and Capena (*c.* 395 B.C.). On a pretext of disaffection the Romans totally destroyed Falerium Vetus (241) and moved its inhabitants to a neighbouring plateau, where the Roman walls are still preserved (*Falleri*).

Monumenti Antichi iv; F. von Duhn, *Italische Gräberkunde* (1924; summary and scanty bibliography); A. Della Seta, *Catalogue of Villa Giulia Museum at Rome* (1918; Faliscan tombs and temples). D. R.-MacI.

FALX MURALIS, *see* SIEGECRAFT, ROMAN.

FAMA, *see* PHEME.

FAMILIA, *see* PATRIA POTESTAS.

FANNIUS, GAIUS (*cos.* 122 B.C.), the Gracchan annalist, son-in-law of Laelius and pupil of Panaetius, served at Carthage (146 B.C.) and in Spain (141), and became tribune (142), praetor (between 133 and 131 ?), and consul (122), opposing C. Gracchus' Italian legislation in a celebrated speech (Cic. *Brut.* 26. 99-100). He wrote a history, perhaps from the origins of Rome, but probably of his own times (this depends on the date of the *Drepana* reference of fr. 3). He included speeches verbatim in his narrative, like Cato, and portrayed contemporary personalities. His work was authoritative, recognized by Cicero, Sallust, who praised its *veritas*, and Brutus.

H. Peter, *HRRel.* i² (1914), pp. cxciii, 139; E. Kornemann, *Klio* Beiheft 1 (1903), 21; P. Fraccaro, *Athenaeum* 1926, 153; T. Frank *Life and Literature in the Roman Republic* (1930), 175. A. H. McD.

FANNIUS, *see also* CAEPIO.

FASCES, probably of Etruscan origin (iron *fasces* have been found at Vetulonia), were rods (of elm wood, later of birch) tied by a red thong into a bundle from which an axe (*securis*) projected. They symbolized regal and later magisterial authority. They were carried on their left shoulders by the lictors, who never laid them aside, except as an act of mourning or homage (*fasces submittere* or *demittere*), or when magistrates addressed popular audiences in order to symbolize the subordination of executive authority to that of the law. The privilege of carrying *fasces* was granted also to religious officials (e.g. the *flamen Dialis* and the Vestal Virgins) and eventually to presidents of public games. When a magistrate was dismissed or punished his *fasces* were destroyed.

Mommsen, *Röm. Staatsr.* i³. 373 ff.; G. De Sanctis, *Riv. fil.* 1929; Samter, *PW*, s.v. P. T.

FASTI, the old calendar of *dies fasti* and *dies nefasti* for legal and public business, which received definite publication by Cn. Flavius in 304 B.C. (Livy 9. 46. 5), came to cover also lists of eponymous magistrates (*fasti consulares*), records of triumphs (*fasti triumphales*), and priestly lists (*fasti sacerdotales*). We know of the sacral calendars of Fulvius Nobilior (189 B.C.) and Verrius Flaccus (at Praeneste), and have fragments of the pre-Julian calendar of Antium (*c.* 70 B.C.) and twenty calendars from the close of the Republic to Claudius; also *fasti* of the Feriae Latinae and two rustic *menologia*, and in book form the calendar of A.D. 354, the *fasti Idaciani*, and the *Chronicon Paschale*. Of *fasti consulares* we have the exemplar of Antium (*c.* 70 B.C.) and the *fasti Capitolini*, which were set up on or near the new Regia (q.v.) of 36 B.C. and then continued to A.D. 13; the *ludi saeculares* were added, until A.D. 88. *Fasti triumphales* appear in the fragments of Tolentino and Urbisaglia, and also from the Regia, where a list from Romulus to 19 B.C. was added about 12 B.C., presumably by Augustus as Pontifex Maximus.

The authenticity of the *fasti* is now scarcely to be doubted, but they represent a systematic reconstruction, the opening of the *fasti triumphales* being based on the *annales maximi*, the *fasti Capitolini* owing something to a work like that of Verrius Flaccus or Atticus. The reconstruction was necessarily speculative, perhaps tendentious, for the fifth century B.C., based merely on a nucleus of records; but it was sound in its main lines for the fourth century, and from *c.* 300 B.C. appears consistently accurate, presumably using full regular records. This suggests that the inclusion of magistrates' names and cult notices (from which the triumph lists came) followed directly on the Flavian publication, and may be associated with the *tabulae pontificum* (q.v.).

Inscript. Italiae XIII, i (1947); C. Cichorius *De fastis cons. antiquissimis* (1886); De Sanctis, *Stor. Rom.* i. 1; G. Costa, *L'originale dei fasti consolari* (1910); *I fasti consolari* (1910); E. Pais, *Fasti triumphales pop. Rom.* (1920-3); *I fasti trionfali del popolo Romano* (1930); G. Moretti, *Not. Scav.* 1925, 114; K. J. Beloch, *Röm. Geschichte*, 1 ff.; F. Altheim *Epochen der röm. Geschichte* ii (1935), 298. A. H. McD.

FASTING (νηστεία), in the sense of abstinence from all food for a stated time, such as a day, is very rare in classical religions, both Greek and Roman. There is, for instance, no evidence whatever that anyone, priest or layman, was expected to come fasting to a sacral meal such as normally followed the killing of a victim. For Greece, however, we may cite two well-known instances. At the Thesmophoria the second day was called Nesteia, at all events at Athens (cf. ATTIC CULTS AND MYTHS), because, as it would appear, the women conducting the rite took no food then; there was a day at Taras (Tarentum) having the same name (cf. Aelian, VH 5. 20, who gives an aetiological story not to be taken too seriously); it probably was part of some rite of Demeter or a similar deity. In like manner, the *ieiunium Cereris* at Rome (Livy 36. 37. 4–5) was instituted by advice of the Sibylline Books, and therefore belongs to the Greek, not the native cult of that goddess. The other outstanding example of a ritual fast in Greece is, like the former, connected with the cult of Demeter. The Eleusinian formula in Clem. Al. *Protr.* 2. 21. 2 (p. 16. 18 Stählin) specifies that the initiate had fasted before drinking the *kykeōn*. Details are, however, lacking. Various statements to the effect that some person would not eat (e.g. Achilles after the death of Patroclus, *Il.* 19. 303 ff.; the beasts after the death of Daphnis, when they show human grief, Verg. *Ecl.* 5. 25–6) should not, therefore, without further proof, be taken to imply ritual fasting. The general prescription of light diet, that the body might hinder the soul as little as possible, for those engaged in divination, especially by dreams, extended to actual fasting in some cases, to judge from Tert. *De Anim.* 48.

The later mystery-cults, on the other hand, seem to have used ritual fasting quite commonly, e.g. that of Attis (Sallustius, *De dis et mundo* iv, p. 8. 22 Nock). It is to be remembered that they are not Greek but Oriental in origin. The many prescriptions of fasting in the use of magic (q.v.) are not all evidence for any prolonged abstinence; for example, the application of the remedy in Pliny, *HN* 26. 93 (the touch of a naked girl's hand). She should do it *ieiuna ieiuno*, but this condition is satisfied if the ceremony is carried out before operator or patient has breakfasted. However, some examples of real fasting, extending on occasion over more than one day, are to be found (see Ziehen, loc. cit. infra, 94. 43 ff.).

What might be called partial fasting, i.e. abstinence during a certain period or for the whole of life from some specified food or class of foods, is common enough. The best-known examples are the vegetarian diets of the Orphics (*see* ORPHISM) and Pythagoreans (*see* PYTHAGORAS; also J. Haussleiter, *Der Vegetarismus in der Antike*, 1935), but many others exist, as the food-taboos of the *flamen Dialis* at Rome (he might not, e.g., eat beans, Gellius 10. 15. 12) and the very curious restriction on the priestess of Athena Polias at Athens, who might not eat green cheese unless it was imported (Strabo 9. 1. 11).

L. Ziehen in *PW* xvii. 88–107. H. J. R.

FATE. In Homer we find many sombre reflections on various powers, such as *moira*, *aisa*, or the *daimon*, which seem sometimes to thwart the desires of man and again to leave him free to commit acts of folly. Unlike the poet himself, who usually prefers some more definite ascription, the Homeric hero, when quoted, regularly alludes to one of these rather vaguely conceived forces. Of special interest is *moira*, because in Homer and Hesiod alone there are references enough to suggest the probable evolution from a common noun to a personification, and thence to a divinity and finally a trio of goddesses. At first the word, like *aisa*, denotes the 'lot' or 'rightful portion' of the individual, but since man's inescapable lot is death, it becomes specialized in this sense, thus early acquiring a fatalistic connotation; and personifica-

tion begins as soon as *moira*, qualified as 'mighty', 'ill-omened', or 'baneful', is said to hurry a warrior to his appointed doom (e.g. *Il.* 5. 83; 12. 116). Since, however, Moira always remains distinct from Thanatos (cf. Hesiod, *Theog.* 211), she is never the actual agent of death, but often motivates it indirectly, as, for example, when she forces Hector to wait alone before the walls of Troy (*Il.* 22. 5; cf. 24. 132; another case, *Il.* 19. 87 ff.). An extended fatalism leads naturally to the belief that a man's death is determined at the time of his birth, a fact which explains the occasional association of Moira, in later times, with Eileithyia (e.g. Pindar, *Ol.* 6. 42; *Nem.* 7. 1). The notion of breaking the thread of life, beginning as a figure of speech, perhaps leads to that of spinning it. At first such spinning may be done by 'the gods' (*Od.* 20. 196; 1. 17; 8. 579; 11. 139) or 'the *daimon*' (*Od.* 16. 64) as well as by *aisa* (*Il.* 20. 128) or *moira* (24. 209), but since spinning is normally an occupation of women it is later restricted to the *Klothes* (*Od.* 7. 197) or 'Spinners', regarded as goddesses, and to the Moirai, who appear as a plural, however, only once in Homer (*Il.* 24. 49). Finally, when the course of life intermediate between birth and death comes also to be determined by fate, fate's task is trebled, and so the Moirai become definitely a trio. Their names are not found in Homer, but are first given by Hesiod (*Theog.* 901 ff.): Lachesis, who assigns the lot, Clotho, who spins the thread of life, and Atropos, who 'cannot be stayed', i.e. from severing it. Euripides (fr. 623 Nauck) pictures them as seated at the throne of Zeus, and Hesiod makes them daughters of Zeus and Themis (*Theog.* loc. cit.), though in Pindar (fr. 30 Schroeder) it is they who serve Themis as bridal attendants. Their relation to Zeus is not without difficulty, for at times they might seem to be independent of his will or even above it. Yet such phrases as '*moira* of the gods' (*Od.* 3. 269), 'divine *moira*' (Plato, *Ap.* 33c), and '*aisa* of Zeus' (*Il.* 17. 322; *Od.* 9. 52) show rather that it is he who determines fate and is bound by it only in somewhat the sense that a man is bound by his given word. Thus, in *Il.* 16. 433 ff., Zeus could save Sarpedon, though his time has run out, and would like well to do so, but declines when reminded by Hera that he would be virtually setting the laws of the universe at naught (cf. Pindar, *Paean* 6. 92 ff.).

2. The three fates of Latin poetry are the Parcae. Originally a Roman goddess of birth (cf. *parere*; Varro ap. Gell. 3. 16. 10), Parca was identified with the Moirai owing to a false etymology (cf. *pars*), and so trichotomized. As we have seen, the Moirai, too, were sometimes present at a birth. Plato makes Ananke, 'Necessity', their mother (*Resp.* 10. 617c), and places in her lap an adamantine spindle on which the world itself turns (ibid. 616c, ff.); Macrobius (*Sat.* 1. 19. 17) says that Ananke and Tyche (i.e. Fortuna) preside at one's birth along with Daimon and Eros; and Horace (*Carm.* 1. 35. 17) completes the circuit by associating Necessitas with Fortuna. The Latin Fata, or Tria Fata, like the Parcae, were assimilated to the Moirai of the Greeks; *fatum* signifies 'that which has been spoken' (cf. *fari*), i.e. 'decreed', as by some prophetic agency (cf. Isidore, *Orig.* 8. 11. 90).

3. Destiny, variously designated, played an important role in certain legends of the epic cycle which supplied the tragedians with situations rich in dramatic conflict. Perhaps freedom and predestination are most nicely balanced in Sophocles' *Oedipus Rex*, whose hero appears to struggle without avail against forces which drive him to patricide and incest. Yet, according to the *Poetics* of Aristotle, his downfall is really the result of some 'flaw' or 'error' of his own, the much-debated *hamartia*.

4. The philosophical doctrine of necessity begins its development in the writings of the Pre-Socratics, whose references to it are often phrased in poetic language because they could not entirely escape the influence of religious teachings. Subject to many minor qualifications, we may say that they believed in a sort of physical determinism. The defect which both Plato and Aristotle saw in their work was that they failed to recognize an external, final cause. Actually, a tentative approach to this can be discerned in some of the Pre-Socratics, notably Anaxagoras, who is said, however, to have disappointed the youthful Socrates because he did not definitely make his *nous* a final cause (Pl. *Phd.* 97c). This step was taken by Anaxagoras' disciple, Diogenes of Apollonia, the first teleologist.

5. Plato's dramatic methods of discussion left his ethical endorsement of responsibility imperfectly reconciled with the determinism of his theodicy. Aristotle enriched the speculation on the subject by criticizing in detail the work of his predecessors, distinguishing more carefully the various types of causation, and beginning a new attack from two different angles. First he showed that the notion of contingency or potentiality emerges from the fact that, of two mutually contradictory statements of particular, future content, either appears equally true. Then he constructed his ontological system, which culminated in his final cause, the prime mover; and this, once discovered, made it difficult in turn to retain contingency. His attempt to derive it from 'non-being' was a sort of compromise; the harsh alternative, chosen by such fatalists as the Megarians and Stoics, perhaps even Chrysippus (see below), was to reject it except as an illusion.

6. Of the atomists, Democritus had regarded necessity as strictly mechanical, identified with the endless motion of the atoms as an ultimate natural law; but he had neglected to extend this determinism to his ethics, where chance and free will reappear inexplicably. Epicurus, preferring to refashion physics in the interest of his moral teachings, devised the atomic 'swerve' as a somewhat naïve guarantor of freedom. The early Stoics clung to divination as revealing that all-powerful destiny which they saw in the pure reason of the supreme being. Confronted by the problem of evil, they asserted that it exists only at the human level, not the divine, and as the natural opposite of good. Chrysippus, who sought another, more adequate answer, strove to save at least the illusion of contingency, deliberation, and freedom of choice with his difficult theories of 'confatal acts' and 'assent'.

7. The pseudo-science of astrology acquired great importance in the early centuries of our era because it was thought to reveal the workings of a destiny so absolute as to render prayers and sacrifices entirely useless (cf., for example, Suet. *Tiberius* 69). The Ptolemaic system of astronomy appeared to give a rational basis for this belief. Those Oriental deities which promised, by virtue of their sovereignty over the stars, to release men from the rule of fate acquired thereby a special attraction for the superstitious. The Christian apologists also offered relief from the oppression of fate by insisting that man is free to create his own life of good or ill (e.g. Min. Fel. *Oct.* 36. 1).

General literature: St. G. Stock, 'Fate (Greek and Roman)', in Hastings, *ERE* v. 786–90; Gundel in *PW* vii .2622–45. Discussion of the many contexts of *moira*: Weizsäcker, in Roscher's *Lexikon* ii. 3084–102; Eitrem, *PW* xv. 2449–97, and *Symbolae Osloenses* xiii (1934), 47–64; Nilsson, *ARW* xxii (1923–4), 385–90. *Ananke, Parca,* and *fatum*: Wernicke, *PW* i. 2057–8; Otto, ibid. vi. 2047–51; Peter, in Roscher's *Lexikon* iii. 1569–70 and i. 1444–52. References to the latest literature on *hamartia*: Pack, *AJPhil.* lviii (1937), 418–36; lx (1939), 350–6. Fate and freedom in philosophy: Greene, *Harv. Stud.* xlvi (1935), 1–36; xlvii (1936), 85–129; English, *University of Toronto Studies* (Philology and Literature Series), no. xi (1938). P. Shorey, *The Unity of Plato's Thought,* University of Chicago Decennial Publications, 1st Series, vol. vi (1904), 129–214; J. Chevalier, *La Notion du nécessaire chez Aristote* (1915); C. Bailey, *The Greek Atomists and Epicurus* (1928); Gercke, *Jahrb. f. cl. Phil. Suppl.* xiv (1885), 691–781; Duprat, *Archiv. f. Gesch. d. Phil.* xxiii (1910), 490–511; Patch, *Speculum* iv (1929), 62–72. Fate in later religious thought: A. D. Nock, *Conversion* (1933), 101–2; *CAH* xii. 421, 468; *Sallustius,* lxx ff.; W. C. Greene, *Moira: Fate, Good and Evil, in Greek Thought* (Cambridge, Mass., 1944). R. A. P.

FATUUS, *see* FAUNUS.

FAUNUS (from root of *favere,* 'kindly one', euphemistic), a *numen* anciently identified with Pan, whose festival (5 Dec., Horace, *Carm.* 3. 18. 10) was kept in the *pagi* with dancing and merry-making. He was primarily of the forests, and especially connected with the mysterious sounds heard in them, hence his titles (or identification with) Fatuus and Fatuclus (Servius on *Aen.* 6. 775), both meaning 'the speaker'. As a god of herdsmen he was further identified with Inuus, whose name the ancients connected with *inire* and interpreted as the fertilizer of cattle (ibid.). He had female counterparts, Fauna (cf. BONA DEA) and Fatua (Cornelius Labeo in Macrob. *Sat.* 1. 12. 21). A more formidable side is shown by his identification (Servius, ibid.) with Incubo, a *numen* either of nightmare or (Petronius, *Sat.* 38. 8) of buried treasure. He was on occasion oracular (*Aen.* 7. 81 ff.; Dion. Hal. 5. 16. 2–3 and elsewhere). For his alleged connexion with the Lupercalia (q.v.), see Rose in *Mnemosyne* 60. 386 ff.

Cf. Wissowa, *RK* 208 ff. H. J. R.

FAUSTINA (1) the Elder (*Annia Galeria Faustina*), daughter of M. Annius Verus (*cos.* III in 126), and aunt of M. Aurelius, married the future Emperor Antoninus (q.v.) Pius *c.* A.D. 110 or later, bearing him two sons and two daughters (including Faustina (2) the Younger). She became 'Augusta' on his accession (138). Late tradition questioned her character; but the pair lived in harmony until her death (140/1), when Antoninus consecrated her and named his new charity (*Puellae Faustinianae*) after her.

PIR², A 715. C. H. V. S.

FAUSTINA (2) the Younger (*Annia Galeria Faustina*), younger daughter of Antoninus (q.v.) Pius, born *c.* A.D. 125–30, was betrothed by Hadrian's wish to L. Verus (q.v.). But in 139 Antoninus betrothed her anew to her cousin M. Aurelius (q.v.), whom she married in 145, becoming 'Augusta' after her first child's birth in 146. Ancient authority groundlessly interpreted her lively temperament as a sign of faithless and disloyal character, not above collusion with Avidius (q.v.) Cassius. She accompanied Marcus during his northern campaigns (170–4) and—now 'Mater Castrorum'—to the East in 175. There she died, consecrated by Marcus, who apparently loved her genuinely. A second charity of *Puellae Faustinianae* commemorated her.

See under AURELIUS (MARCUS); *also PIR²,* A 716. C. H. V. S.

FAUSTULUS, probably a by-form of Faunus (q.v.; if a deity *favet,* he is *faustus*), but humanized into a herdsman, husband of Acca (q.v.) Larentia, who found Romulus (q.v.) and Remus being suckled by the she-wolf. In a further rationalization his wife was the she-wolf herself (*lupa,* loose woman, prostitute). He reared the twins, and on Remus being brought before Numitor for an act of brigandage, told Romulus the whole story, whereupon the twins and their grandfather killed Amulius.

Livy 1. 4. 6 ff. H. J. R.

FAVENTINUS, MARCUS CETIUS, made an abridgement of Vitruvius (q.v.) which Palladius and Isidorus used.

FAVONIUS EULOGIUS, a rhetor from Carthage in Augustine's time, wrote a *Disputatio de somnio Scipionis* (ed. Holder, 1901).

FAVORINUS (Φαβωρῖνος) (*c.* A.D. 80–*c.* 150), famous rhetor and polyhistor. He was born in Arelate in Gaul, a hermaphrodite. His defect was obvious from his body and his voice (ἀνδρόθηλυς καὶ εὐνοῦχος, Philostr. *Vit. Soph.* 1. 8; Suid. s.v.; etc.). He learned Greek very early; later he preferred to use it in everyday talk and in his writings. His teacher was Dio Chrysostom. In later years he lived in Rome as a favourite of the Emperor Hadrian. For some time he was in disgrace with the Emperor and was exiled to Chios (Papyr. in *Studi e Testi*, 53 col. 14). His keen competitor as an orator was Polemon (Kavvadias, Δελτίον, 1892). But F. was renowned also as a scholar and philosopher. Among his friends was Plutarch, among his numerous pupils Herodes Atticus, Fronto, and Gellius.

Little has been preserved of his many writings; of the lost works the most important were a 'Miscellaneous history' (Παντοδαπὴ ἱστορία) in twenty-four books (Phot. *Bibl.* 103b), an encyclopaedic work whose scheme was akin to Aelian's Ποικίλη ἱστορία, and the 'Memoirs' (Ἀπομνημονεύματα). Notable among his philosophical works was 'Pyrrhonian modes' (Πυρρώνειοι τρόποι) in ten books (Philostr. *VS* 1. 8; Gell. 11. 5. 5; Diog. Laert. 9. 87) in which he discussed the 'modes' (τρόποι) of Aenesidemus (q.v.).

Two speeches under the name of Dio Chrysostom have been ascribed to F. with great probability (nos. 37 and 64). Lately a declamation 'On exile' (Περὶ φυγῆς) has been found on papyrus (*PVat.* 11).

J. L. Marres, *De F. Arel. vita, studiis, scriptis*, 1853 (not sufficient); Th. Colardeau, *De F. Arel. studiis et scriptis*, Thèse Grenoble, 1903; E. Zeller, *Philosophie der Griechen* iii. 2⁴. 76 f.; A. Goedeckemeyer, *Gesch. d. gr. Skeptizismus*, 1905, 248 f.; B. Häsle *Favorin Über die Verbannung*, Thesis Berlin, 1935; *PW* vi. 2078. K. O. B.

FEBRIS, the *numen* of fever (it is rash to assume that it was malaria, the early history of which is imperfectly known, see P. Fraccaro in *Studi etruschi*, ii. 3 ff.). She had three temples in Rome alone (Valerius Maximus 2. 5. 6), in which *remedia* (amulets?) which had proved efficacious were placed. Dedications to her have been found in various parts of the Roman Empire (see Wissowa, *RK* 246), some of which call her Tertiana and Quartana, clearly referring to malaria. H. J. R.

FEBRUUM, technical term of Roman ritual for anything used in a ceremony of purification.

See Ovid, *Fasti* 2. 19 ff.; Frazer, *Fasti of Ovid* ii. 277 f.

FEDERAL STATES first appear in Greece in the fifth century B.C., were most numerous and influential in the Hellenistic age, and continued under Rome as local governments in parts of Greece and Asia Minor. Though their influence on the course of events was considerable, they are particularly important as one of the two chief instruments used by the Greeks for creating unities larger than city-states, namely the *symmachia* (q.v.) and the federal State (*sympoliteia*, q.v.). Organizations of both types usually are called leagues. A distinguishing mark is that while the *symmachia* claimed to preserve the freedom of its members, the *sympoliteia* limited their freedom by the creation of a federal government. Hence the King's Peace led to the dissolution of the Boeotian and other federal leagues.

2. Federal States developed from tribal units (Boeotians, Arcadians, etc.), and so frequently, even in Roman Imperial times, a federal league was called an *ethnos* instead of a *koinon*, and c. 300 B.C. the States of Greece were classified as *ethne* (federal States and tribal States) and *poleis* (*IG*² iv. 1. 68). In some tribes cities developed early, but did not cause the dissolution of the tribe, and such conditions in time led to the growth of federal States. In other tribes, e.g. the Aetolians, a looser ethnic organization was long retained and later transformed into a *sympoliteia*. In either case, if a large league was to be developed, it was necessary to overstep the ethnic boundary and incorporate States outside the tribe. This policy was not employed extensively before the third

century B.C., when it was used most successfully by the Achaeans.

3. From the very beginning oligarchic States seem to have been more ready than democratic States to adopt representative government, though it must be noted that information is so scanty as to make generalizations dangerous. There is extant a description of the oligarchic Boeotian League as it was in the early fourth century. Citizenship depended on a property qualification, apparently the hoplite census, and the local governments were uniform with one-fourth of the active citizens serving as the *boule* and the rest as the *ecclesia*. For federal purposes the country was divided into eleven parts. Thebes, with subject communities, controlled four; Orchomenus and Thespiae, together with smaller communities grouped with them, controlled two each; Tanagra, one; the other two districts each included three towns. Each of the eleven parts furnished one Boeotarch, sixty federal *bouleutai* and an unknown number of judges supplied equal contributions to the federal treasury, and furnished 1,000 hoplites and 100 horsemen to the army. The other numbers are precise, those for the soldiers (obviously) approximate; undoubtedly all active citizens of military age could be called. The federal *boule* was the final authority and thus the federal government was representative. The League, founded about 447 B.C., was dissolved at the King's Peace. The later league of the time of Epaminondas was democratic; it had Boeotarchs, and a primary assembly meeting at Thebes and dominated by the Thebans. The Arcadian League organized in 370 had a form of government that suggests democracy with a *boule*, a primary assembly called the Ten Thousand, and a single general as its chief executive. An inscription which mentions the *boule* also lists fifty *damiorgoi* by cities showing an inequality of representation, thus suggesting, whatever was their relation to the *boule*, a system of representation in proportion to population also for this body.

4. Whatever the constitutional form, the government of a federal State, through relatively greater activity of magistrates and council and less full attendance at meetings of the primary assembly, in practice functioned more nearly like a representative government than that of a normal city-state. The Boeotian League and many of the later leagues took the step outright and dispensed with the primary assembly, which, however, was retained by the Aetolians and Achaeans. The Thessalian League, organized in 194 B.C., had as its chief organ of government a *synedrion* of over 300 members; each of the four Macedonian republics organized in 167 B.C. had a *synedrion* consisting of elected representatives; and the Lycian League flourishing in the same period is said by Strabo to have had a *synedrion* in which the cities, depending on their size, each had one, two, or three votes. The Lycian inscriptions from Imperial times at first surprise the reader by quoting decrees passed by an *ecclesia*, but closer study shows that this was itself a representative body.

5. Only a few of the better-known States have been mentioned. Notice also that, when dates have been given to a league, these apply only to the government described and do not exclude the existence of a league with a different form of government at other times.

ANCIENT SOURCES. Boeotian constitution: *Hell. Oxy.* 11. Arcadian *damiorgoi*: *SIG* 183 (date: M. Cary, *JHS* 1922, 188). Thessalian *synedrion*: *IG* ix. 2. 261. Lycian League: Strabo 14. 664; documents in *IGRom.* iii.

MODERN LITERATURE. General: E. A. Freeman, *History of Federal Government* (ed. Bury, 1893); G. Fougères in Dar.-Sag., s.v. 'Koinon'; H. Swoboda, *Staatsaltertümer* (1913) in Hermann's *Lehrbuch der griechischen Antiquitäten*⁶; G. Busolt, *Griechische Staatskunde* ii (1926), 1395–575; *CAH*, vols. vi–viii. Special: Federal coinage, M. O. B. Caspari, *JHS* 1917. Lycia: A. H. M. Jones, *The Cities of the Eastern Roman Provinces* (1937), ch. iii. Macedonian republics, Lycia, and Hellenistic representative assemblies: Larsen, *CPhil.* 1945. J. A. O. L.

FELICITAS, a goddess of good luck, not heard of till the middle of the second century B.C., when L. Licinius Lucullus dedicated her temple on the Velabrum (see Platner–Ashby, 207); another was planned by Julius Caesar and erected after his death by M. Aemilius Lepidus where the Curia Hostilia had stood (ibid.). She is associated with Venus Victrix, Honos, and Virtus at Pompey's theatre (*Fast. Amit.* on 12 Aug.); with the Genius Publicus and Venus Victrix on the Capitol (ibid., 9 Oct.); with the *numen Augusti* (*Fast. Praenest.* on 17 Jan.). Thereafter she is important in official cult under the emperors, appearing frequently on coins (*Felicitas saeculi* with figure of the goddess) and in addresses to the gods in dedications, etc., immediately after the Capitoline triad.

See Wissowa, *RK* 266–7.　　　　　　　　　　H. J. R.

FELIX, MARCUS ANTONIUS, freedman of Antonia, Claudius' mother, was brother of Pallas. Perhaps sent in A.D. 52 to Samaria with the rank of procurator during the trial of Ventidius Cumanus, he was soon appointed procurator of Judaea, where unrest increased during his administration. He was St. Paul's judge. Accused by the Jews of Caesarea, he was acquitted. He married (1) Drusilla, grand-daughter of Antony and Cleopatra, and (2) Drusilla, daughter of Agrippa I. He was succeeded by Festus *c.* 60.

PIR[2], A 828; E. Schürer, *Geschichte des jüdischen Volkes* i[4]. 571; A. Momigliano, *Annali Scuola Normale Pisa* iii (1934), 388. A. M.

FENESTELLA (52 B.C.–A.D. 19 or, possibly, 35 B.C.–A.D. 36), the antiquarian annalist, wrote a Roman history in at least twenty-two books, perhaps from the origins, certainly to 57 B.C.; the citations of Asconius reflect his special authority for the Ciceronian period. The fragments, which, however, may come also from works on constitutional and social antiquities, show his wide antiquarian interests and critical ability, in the Varronian tradition. The Elder Pliny used him, and an epitome was made. *See* SCHOLARSHIP, LATIN, IN ANTIQUITY.

H. Peter, *HRRel.* ii (1906), pp. cix, 79; L. Mercklin, *De Fenestella* (1844); J. Poeth, *De Fenestella* (1849).　　　　A. H. McD.

FENUS NAUTICUM, see BOTTOMRY LOANS.

FERALIA, Roman All Souls' Day, 21 Feb., last of the *dies parentales* (beginning at noon on 13 Feb.), during which each household made offerings at the graves of its dead (Ovid, *Fasti* 2. 533 ff.). It is marked N[p] in Imperial calendars (cf. DIES FASTI), but F in the Fasti Antiates; what public ritual, if any, was performed and whether any change in this respect took place under Augustus is unknown.　　　　　　　　　　　　　　　　　H. J. R.

FERIAE CONCEPTIVAE, see FESTIVALS, AMBURBIUM.

FERONIA (Fē-, Verg. *Aen.* 7. 800; Horace *Sat.* 1. 5. 24; and elsewhere), an Italian goddess, officially received in Rome before 217 B.C. (Livy 22. 1. 18), and given a temple in the Campus Martius (*Fast. Arval.* on 13 Nov.). Her principal place of worship was the *lucus Capenatis*, later Lucus Feroniae, near Mt. Soracte (Cato, *Orig.* 1, fr. 26 Jordan; Verg. *Aen.* 7. 697; Strabo 5. 2. 9; Pliny, *HN* 3. 51). Her cult, however, is shown by inscriptional and other evidence to have been widely spread in central Italy (see Wissowa, *RK* 285 f.). Of her functions and the etymology of her name, which may be Etruscan, nothing is known, and the ancients seem to have been equally uncertain, to judge by the variety of guesses recorded (Wissowa, ibid. 286). Strabo (loc. cit.) says that a ceremony of fire-walking was performed in her precinct, but this seems to be a confusion with the so-called Apollo of Soracte (see Verg. *Aen.* 11. 785 ff. and commentators there). Near Tarracina slaves were set free in her shrine (Servius on *Aen.* 8. 564).　　　　　　　　　　　　H. J. R.

FESCENNINI (VERSUS), ribald wedding-songs (Catull. 61. 126–55); cf. the licentious verses sung by soldiers at triumphs. Ancient etymologies were: Fescennium, a town in Etruria, and *fascinum* (= witchcraft, which the songs were supposed to avert). Similar verses were said to be exchanged at harvest-festivals between masked entertainers; such performances were thought, perhaps rightly, to have been the origin of drama (q.v.). For a possible parallel see Hor. *Sat.* 1. 5. 51–70; but see *PW*, s.v. 'Fescennini'.　　　　　　　　　W. B.

FESTIVALS. A festival is a sacred rite repeated yearly or with regular intervals of a certain number of years (every eight, four, two years; in this case there is often a lesser celebration in the intervening years, and except for the Dionysiac orgia, the enlargement consists of games); it is celebrated by an assembly at a certain time and after the introduction of the calendar on a certain day or certain days, often at full moon. The Roman custom of *feriae conceptiuae*, the day of which was fixed by the magistrate within certain limits, is not known in Greece. A remarkable circumstance is that most of the old festivals took place at full moon, generally on the twelfth day of the lunar month, except for those of Apollo which fell on his holy day, the seventh, and those of his sister Artemis which fell on the day before. It is apparent that many rites are pre-deistic, i.e. magical rites efficient without the interference of any personal god, and only subsequently attached to the cult of a god. Sometimes a great god took possession of a festival which belonged to a lesser god—as happened with Apollo and the Hyacinthia, in which a preliminary sacrifice was offered to the hero Hyacinthus, in fact a pre-Greek god.

Aristotle remarks that in early times festivals chiefly took place after the harvesting of crops and fruits, and in fact a survey of the Greek festivals of early origin proves that most of them are agrarian. This corresponds to the old mode of life in which the people subsisted on the products of their own land, and to the fact that agrarian customs are bound up with the seasons and in consequence easily conform to a calendrical regulation. Even at an early date people flocked together to a sanctuary at a given time. Their original purpose was to perform worship, but to this were added games, merry-making, and markets. Such festivals were called *panegyreis* and take place even in modern Greece in a manner very reminiscent of the old. The most famous of the ancient *panegyreis* are the great games, the Olympia, Pythia, etc. (qq.v.).

The state of things described above was already in an early time changed by town life. The cult was the concern of the State and its magistrates had charge of it. They performed the rites and arranged the festivals. Almost every god who was not too unimportant had his festival day on which the people went to his temple. Although old rites were carefully preserved, the procession and the sacrifice including the meal that followed became the most prominent parts of the festival, in which great pomp was displayed. The sixth century B.C., in which great temples were built, marked a great advance in this direction, especially due to the tyrants. The Athenian democracy developed this during its heyday; the lavish sacrifices were a means to humour the people. In early times the colonies sent embassies (θεωροί: see THEOROI) to the festivals of the mother town, and the cities to the national games. The Athenians enjoined on their colonies and allies to send sacrificial animals, etc., to the Panathenaea and the Great Dionysia, and on these occasions displayed their glory to them. In the Hellenistic age it became very common for the cities to send embassies to each others' festivals, especially to the games. New festivals were instituted, many in commemoration of political events, but these are uninteresting, comprising only processions, sacrifices, and games. The festivals were for a great part an expression of the political aspirations of the cities. The old rites are extremely important for the history of Greek religion and its gods.

M. P. Nilsson, *Griech. Feste mit Ausschluss der attischen* (1906); L. Deubner, *Attische Feste* (1932); P. Stengel, *Die griech. Kultus-altertümer*³, 190 ff. (including the games); Nilsson, *Gesch. d. griech. Religion* i. 778 (the *panegyreis*). M. P. N.

FESTUS (1), PORCIUS, succeeded Felix as a procurator of Judaea *c.* A.D. 60 (date very uncertain). He fought against the Sicarii and a pseudo-prophet and was involved in the controversy between the Jews and Agrippa II. He carried on the trial against St. Paul, whom he sent to Rome (Acts xxv–xxvi). He died after a short period of office. A. M.

FESTUS (2), SEXTUS POMPEIUS (late 2nd c. A.D.), scholar, epitomizer of the *De significatu verborum* of Verrius Flaccus (q.v.). Of his work (alphabetically arranged in twenty books) the first half is lost. Festus himself was epitomized in the eighth century by Paulus Diaconus. The standard edition (including Paulus) is that of W. M. Lindsay (1913) whose later edition in *Glossaria Latina* iv (93–467) incorporates Festus material gleaned from glossaries. *See* SCHOLARSHIP, LATIN, and cf. Teuffel, § 261. 4–7; Schanz–Hosius, § 341. J. F. M.

FESTUS, *see also* RUFIUS.

FETIALES, Roman priestly officials who conducted international relationships, as treaties and declarations of war. They were twenty (Varro ap. Non. 529), forming a *collegium* (Livy 36. 3. 7), variously said to have been founded by one or another of the kings; who its head was is not known, but it deliberated on questions affecting the state of war or peace (Varro, ibid.), though only in an advisory capacity, like all clerical *collegia*; the commonwealth decided what action should be taken.

Our chief informant as to their ritual is Livy. He states (1. 24. 4 ff.) that to make a treaty two *fetiales* were sent. One of these was the *uerbenarius* or *uerbenatus* (see Pliny, *HN* 22. 5; Varro ap. Non. 528), who carried herbs (*uerbenae, sagmina*) from the Arx; the other was the *pater patratus*, perhaps 'the father (full citizen, patrician) who accomplishes' (the ceremony; for this rare active use of *-tus*, see Krahe in *ARW* xxxiv (1937), 112). He, after the terms of the treaty had been read aloud in the presence of the other State's *fetiales*, pronounced a conditional curse on Rome if she were the first to break it, confirming this by killing a pig with a *lapis silex*, probably a neolithic implement, cf. JUPITER; STONES, SACRED. On occasion several pairs of *fetiales* might be sent (Livy 30. 43. 9).

If an injury were received from another State, the *pater patratus* crossed the border, first announcing, with his head veiled in a woollen garment (*filum*), who he was and what he came for, calling on Jupiter, *fas*, and the boundaries themselves to hear him and swearing to Jupiter that his errand was just. This formula was several times repeated at various stages of the journey. If within thirty-three days satisfaction was not given, he formally denounced the offending nation to all the gods and returned to Rome. The Senate would then be consulted by the chief magistrate, and, if it voted for seeking satisfaction *iusto pioque bello*, the *fetialis* went once more to the boundary, and there, after formally declaring a state of war in the presence of at least three adults, cast across it either an ordinary spear or a cornel stake sharpened and hardened in the fire (*hastam prae-ustam sanguineam*; to translate the last word by 'bloody' is a many times refuted blunder) (Livy 1. 32. 5 ff.). In case of war with a distant nation, the spear was cast upon a piece of land near the *columna bellica* (see BEL-

LONA), which by a legal fiction was considered hostile territory. This was first done in the war with Pyrrhus (Servius on *Aen.* 9. 53 (52)), and was still in use under Marcus Aurelius (Dio Cassius 71. 33. 3; see Frazer on Ov. *Fast.* 6. 206). Other functions of the *fetiales*, however, as the formal claim (*clarigatio*) for satisfaction, described above, seem to have gone comparatively early out of use. By a kind of pun, the origin of the *ius fetiale* was credited to the Aequicoli ('Plain-dwellers', misunderstood as 'cultivators of equity').

See Wissowa, *RK* 550 ff.; T. Frank, *Roman Imperialism*, ch. 1; *CPhil.* 1912; Mommsen–Marquardt, *Manuel* i. 280 ff., vii. 377; Samter, 'Fetiales' in *PW*. H. J. R.

FIBULA (περόνη, πόρπη). The primitive brooch or fibula, of violin-bow form resembling the modern safety-pin, is found in late Bronze Age times in Greece, northern Italy, and central Europe. A single centre of diffusion is highly probable, but it is uncertain whether that centre should be sought in the north or south. The case for the north has been weakened by recent lower dating of the central European examples, and it is now widely accepted that the fibula is an Aegean invention, developed *c.* 1300 B.C. out of a Minoan type of pin which had the end bent to prevent slipping. By further bending until the end, flattened into a catch, could engage the point, the fibula was produced, and the addition of a spiral coil at the angle to increase the tension is also of early date. Later improvements enlarge the bow so as to grip more cloth. Large fibulae from mainland Greece, of late Geometric times, extend the catchplate; the Cypriote type has a double-arched bow, the Asiatic a stilted one. The 'spectacle' type, in which the bow is replaced by spiral coils of wire, is considered of Danubian origin by some authorities. After 600 B.C. the fibula falls into comparative disuse in Greece, and no new types appear until Roman times. In Italy the development is unbroken and the types more varied: the bow looped, bent, threaded with disks, or thickened into the 'leech' or 'boat' form; the catchplate set transversely or fantastically prolonged. In the fifth century the simpler 'Certosa' type becomes universal and gives rise to the La Tène forms, in which the spiral spring is bilateral, and ultimately to the Roman in which, under the early Empire, a hinge replaces the spiral.

C. Blinkenberg, *Fibules grecques et orientales* (1926); J. L. Myres, *Who were the Greeks?* (University of California Press, 1930), 405–25; O. Montelius, *Civilisation primitive en Italie*, Pt. i (1895). F. N. P.

FIDEICOMMISSUM. A testator could leave individual objects to a person other than his heir by legacy (*legatum*) or *fideicommissum*. Several forms of *legata* were in use, the most commonly applied being: (1) *per vindicationem*, which transferred ownership to the legatee directly, so that he might claim the object by *vindicatio* (q.v.); (2) *per damnationem*, which imposed upon the heir the obligation to transfer the object to the beneficiary. Whereas a *legatum* had to be left in a prescribed form, and was chargeable only on a *heres* appointed by *testamentum*, a *fideicommissum* was a simple, informal request of the testator, addressed to any person who benefited from his inheritance (by will or on intestacy, by legacy or even by *fideicommissum*), to give one or more objects to a third person (*fideicommissarius*). The request was commonly made in the words 'fidei tuae committo' (hence the name *fideicommissum*). Originally not enforceable, *fideicommissum* from the time of Augustus became actionable in special courts, where the official, acting by *cognitio extra ordinem*, had a wide discretion in interpreting the testator's will. A *fideicommissum* was not necessarily a gift of single objects. It might be a gift of the inheritance, in whole or in part. In this case it meant a kind of universal succession, the *fideicommis-sarius* being *heredis loco*. To avoid refusal by the fiduciary successor, which would make void the *fideicommissum*, later legislation gave him the right of keeping a quarter of the property in trust, in conformity with a Republican statute which preserved for the heir a quarter of the inheritance free from legacies and other burdens. In Justinian's law the provisions concerning *legata* and *fideicommissa* were amalgamated, and the distinction between the two fell into abeyance.   A. B.

FIDEPROMISSIO, see STIPULATIO.

FIDES, the Roman personification of good faith. Although her temple (on the Capitol, near that of Jupiter, with whom she is closely connected) is no older than 254 B.C. (see Platner–Ashby, p. 209), her cult is very old, said to have been founded by Numa (Livy 1. 21. 4). Livy also gives details of her ritual; the *flamines* (q.v.), meaning probably the *flamines maiores*, drove to her shrine in a covered carriage drawn by two beasts, and the sacrificer must have his hand covered with a white cloth. A pair of covered hands is indeed her symbol, as often on coins commemorating the *fides* of the Augusti, the legions, etc., in Imperial times. Since giving the hand is a common gesture of solemn agreement, the symbolism is natural.

Wissowa, *RK* 133 f.   H. J. R.

FIMBRIA, GAIUS FLAVIUS (d. 85 B.C.), a violent supporter of the Marian party. At Marius' funeral in 86 Fimbria tried to assassinate Q. Scaevola 'Pontifex'. Sent as second-in-command of Flaccus' forces to the East, he fomented a mutiny, and murdered his chief (86); thereafter, he fought with success in Asia against Mithridates, whom he might have captured but for Lucullus' refusal to co-operate with him. On Sulla's arrival in Asia, he was deserted by his troops and committed suicide (85).   M. H.

FINANCE, GREEK AND HELLENISTIC. Conclusions on the revenue and expenditure of the Minoan and Mycenean kings are at present only guesswork based on excavations and doubtful figures in Minoan inscriptions believed to be accounts. Homeric finance was simple. The kings had comparatively high expenses for household, wars, and hospitality; their revenues came from the royal estate (*temenos*), from gifts (*dotinai*), personal services and customary contributions (*themistes*) of the people, from piracy, presents of foreign merchants and other foreigners, tributes and war-booty.

2. Sparta kept many Homeric characteristics up to the Classical period. No regular taxes existed, except a small contribution in kind to the kings. The helots paid nothing to the State, but gave a share of their crops to their Spartan landlords. The *perioikoi* may have paid a small tribute in kind to the kings, who also had a privileged share of the spoils. Irregular war revenue was derived from the enemy, from contributions of allies, or primitive collections within the community.

3. Exceptional expenses for court and bodyguards, public works, colonization, and wars were characteristic of the finances of the Greek tyrants, and it was, as a rule, impossible for them to pay all these out of the ordinary taxes. Confiscations, irregular levies, monopolies, the undemocratic poll-tax on free citizens, and even extortions had to be introduced to fill the always empty treasuries of such governments.

4. The financial system of the Greek cities, democratic and oligarchic, was more developed. Athens took the lead and was very often the model for smaller communities. The usual expenditure was concerned with police, army, navy, fortifications, ambassadors, palaestrae, gymnasia, education (a Hellenistic innovation), sacrifices, religious festivals, public works (those of Pericles were famous), distribution of money (*see* THEORIKA), corn, and other foodstuffs, salaries of State officials and of citizens entrusted with official duties (e.g. the Councillors,

Dicasts, and Ecclesia of Athens), honorary distinctions (e.g., entertainment in the Prytaneum at Athens), and the maintenance of orphans, invalids, and crippled soldiers.

5. The State revenues of Greek cities were varied. Most towns had a considerable income from State property, especially mines (e.g. the famous silver mines of Laurium in Attica), quarries, houses, and State domains. Court fees and fines at Athens and other towns were another important source of revenue. Direct taxes were, as a rule, only paid by foreigners, non-citizens, and despised professions (e.g. by *metoikoi*, freedmen, *hetairai*, certain craftsmen and traders). The indirect taxes brought a greater return. The custom dues of Attica at the beginning of the fourth century B.C. amounted to 2 per cent. on both exports and imports (during the fifth century, perhaps, only to 1 per cent.). Of like importance were the customs of the Bosporus and Black Sea ports during the Classical period, of Rhodes and the Egyptian ports during the Hellenistic. Treaties made by Athens and other towns, many of which are preserved, provided for delivery, under favourable conditions, of corn and materials for army and navy.

6. Excise duties existed, at least in the smaller cities of Greece. They may have been influenced, in some cases, by the practice of Hellenistic monarchies. The so-called *eponia* represented *ad valorem* gate tolls, auction taxes, and taxes on sales. They were in some places varied for real estate, slaves, cattle, bread, wheat, wine, etc. Another group of excise duties was called *enkyklia*, a Greek term which may be rendered as 'taxes on transport'. Belonging to this group of indirect taxes were harbour rights and dues, fishing rights in lakes and in the ocean, ferry taxes payable from shippers, pasturage taxes, duties for the use of public scales, and for the use of temple precincts for business purposes. In addition, there were a few land and cattle taxes during the Hellenistic period, and Classical as well as Hellenistic monopolies (q.v.). Certain liturgies (q.v.) had to be performed regularly too.

7. An important item of the Athenian Empire's budget in the fifth and fourth centuries, as well as of other hegemonic States, consisted in tribute and contributions from allies and subject States. The *phoros* of Aristides amounted to 460 talents, a sum which was subsequently increased. A certain amount of external revenue was derived from lands in the cleruchies (q.v.) of Athens and other powerful towns which belonged to the ruling State and were rented out as in the mother country. The regular revenues of Athens, the richest town of Classical Greece, were not always sufficient to meet expenditure. Irregular sources of income included *eisphora*, *epidoseis* and other endowments, sale of State property, public loans (often compulsory), selling of political rights and honours, tampering with the coinage, war booty, and financial expedients. The Athenian Empire and the temple States of Delphi and Olympia were able to collect large State treasures in times of peace.

8. Remarkable financial systems were developed in the Ptolemaic and Seleucid Empires, Syracuse, Hellenistic India, and other Hellenistic monarchies. The best-known of these, the Ptolemaic organization, may be described as an example. A planning economy regulated the Empire's budget. Attic and other city-state institutions were imitated. The expenditure was similar to that of the tyrants, but on a much larger scale. Monopolies (q.v.) were most important for the revenues. The whole country-side was farmed out as State land under rigorous State control of agriculture. The Greek poll-taxes, *eponia* and *enkyklia*, were used on a wider scale than in the *poleis*. The Ptolemaic control of agriculture, banking, commerce, and industry of Egypt's administrative units reminds us of the planning economies of the eighteenth and twentieth centuries A.D. As Greek *polis* economy

has influenced all later public financial organization in countries with free economy, so most later tendencies to planned economy from Byzantium and Hellenistic India to modern times seem to show a clear connexion with such Hellenistic systems. *See* EISPHORA; ENDOWMENTS; LITURGY; MONOPOLIES; SYMMORIA; THEORIKA.

A. M. Andreades, *A History of Greek Public Finance* i (Cambridge, Mass., 1933); G. Busolt–H. Swoboda, *Griechische Staatskunde* i, ii (1920–6); M. N. Tod, in *CAH* v. 1; M. Rostovtzeff, ibid. vii. 4, 5; viii. 19; F. M. Heichelheim, *Wirtschaftsgeschichte des Altertums* (1939), Index, s.v. 'Staatswirtschaft'; Rostovtzeff, *Hellenistic World*; F. M. Heichelheim, *Economic History* (1938), 1 f.; Cl. Préaux, *L'Économie royale des Lagides* (1939); H. Michell, *The Economics of Ancient Greece* (1940).   F. M. H.

FINANCE, ROMAN. At the basis of the finance of the Republic lay the authority of the Senate. In no department of State was its power more steadily exercised, in none were attacks on it more bitterly resented.

2. The general budgeting was in the hands of the censors, appointed every *lustrum* (four years) from 443 onwards. They revised the census classes, leased or sold public land, gave out public works on contract, and arranged for necessary buildings and repairs: the moneys allotted for the last purpose were termed *ultra tributa*. When the provincial taxes came to be sold to companies of knights it was the censors who held the auction. The decay of the censorship in the late Republic must have led to serious financial confusion. The details of administration fell to the quaestors—the urban, two in 467 B.C., later increased to four—and the Italian (*quaestores classici*), four instituted in 265. As provinces arose overseas, a quaestor was attached to the governor in each. The general abroad had a very free hand in the disposal of the booty (*see* MANUBIAE), and was seldom called to strict account, if his general policy was approved. The prosecution of the Scipios for their financial management in the war against Antiochus was exceptional. The aediles could levy fines and devote the money to works of public use.

3. Roman taxation was mainly indirect, consisting of customs-duties (*portoria*) and such special taxes as that on the manumission of slaves. The direct tax, *tributum*, was mainly levied for war, at a rate of 1 in 1,000 of the census: it could be treated as an advance, repayable at the State's convenience, as for example in 187 B.C. Provincial taxes were largely collected indirectly by *publicani*, who farmed them from the censors—an endless source of corruption and waste. Sicily paid a tithe (*decumana*). The State treasury was the *aerarium* (q.v.) *Saturni*, with a special reserve *aerarium sanctius*.

4. Augustus left the *aerarium* in the control of the Senate, but took an interest in its administration and the appointment of its chiefs. The censorship was not restored as a regular office. The emperors at once took over many of its functions, and occasionally held the office. Domitian became censor for life, and, though later emperors refused the title, they retained the powers. New treasuries arose—the imperial treasury (*fiscus*), the crown property (*patrimonium*), the *aerarium militare*. Septimius Severus added a new private chest, the *res privata* (qq.v.). Quaestors continued to function in Rome and the senatorial provinces: the quaestors of Italy were gradually abandoned. The emperor's own financial agents, in Rome and the provinces, were the procurators. The *a rationibus* was a chief Minister of Finance. Customs-duties were still levied for provinces or groups of provinces—the *IIII publica Africae* and the *XL Galliarum* are examples. The emperors gradually replaced the wasteful system of farming by direct collection. A *vicesima hereditatum* was levied on inheritances of Roman citizens, while other indirect taxes affected the sale of goods, the sale and emancipation of slaves, etc.

5. The third century brought a collapse of the coinage, disorganization of business, and catastrophic rises in prices. The *annona*, the levy in kind, largely replaced cash levies. Diocletian, in his new census, revised every fifteen years (*indictio*, q.v.), relied on two new units—the *iugum*, unit of land, and the *caput*, unit of human labour. The chief financial officer, *comes sacrarum largitionum*, controlled a large staff of *rationales* and assistants. Taxation became technically efficient, but terribly oppressive. The final collapse of the West was largely due to the financial exhaustion of the tax-payer.

J. Marquardt, *Staatsverw.* ii² (1884), 3 ff.   H. M.

FIRMICUS MATERNUS, JULIUS, of Syracuse, wrote (A.D. 334–7) an astrological treatise *Mathesis* in eight books (ed. Kroll–Skutsch–Ziegler, 1897–1913), the first containing an apologia for astrology. F. urges the highest moral integrity on the astrologer. The conflict between destiny and freedom of will he resolves on Stoic lines: the soul, being divine, can triumph over the stars. F. shows small technical knowledge; his merit, if any, is rhetorical and stylistic. Later, converted to Christianity, F. wrote a fanatical *De errore profanarum religionum* (ed. Ziegler, 1907) urging Constantius and Constans to eradicate paganism. Dom Morin's attribution of *Consultationes Zacchaei et Apollonii* (ed. 1935) to this author has not gained universal acceptance.   L. R. P.

FIRST FRUITS. The rite of bringing first fruits to the gods is not strongly characterized in ancient Greece. It is comprised under the rite known as *panspermia*, the bringing of a mixture of fruits at various festivals, sometimes cooked in a pot (at the Thargelia and the Pyanopsia). Θαλύσια are, according to the lexicographers, *aparchai* (q.v.) of the fruits and also the first loaf baked after the threshing. The opinion has been advanced that the offering of first fruits represents the breaking of the taboo imposed upon the unripe fruits; in the opinion of the Greeks themselves they were brought in order to ensure fertility; they were also called εὐετηρία, i.e. a Good Year. They survive in ecclesiastical usage to-day under the ancient name κόλλυβα.

M. P. Nilsson, *Gesch. d. griech. Rel.* i. 147.   M. P. N.

FISCUS, a basket or chest, hence a treasury—the distinctive name given, under the Roman Empire, to the main imperial treasury as against the *aerarium* (q.v.) *Saturni*.

The origin of the *fiscus* is obscure. It certainly existed under Claudius, whose powerful freedman Pallas, *a rationibus*, raised it to high importance. That some centre of imperial finance already existed under Augustus is proved by the accounts that he left at his death. Whether the *fiscus* yet existed as a chest, distinct from the provincial *fisci* and the *patrimonium*, is less certain.

The *fiscus* was under the *a rationibus*, usually a freedman down to Hadrian, afterwards a knight. His first assistant was perhaps the *procurator summarum rationum*. Disputes between the *fiscus* and the public were assigned by Claudius to the jurisdiction of his procurators. Nerva appointed a special praetor to try such cases in Rome. Hadrian instituted a new department of *advocati fisci*, to plead in the courts.

The *fiscus* dealt with the main revenues and charges of the emperor in his public capacity. For a survey of its business under Domitian, see Statius, *Silvae* 3. 3. 86 ff. The *fiscus* steadily grew at the expense of the *aerarium Saturni*, but as the emperor virtually controlled both, the distinction was largely illusory. It appears, however, that revenues from imperial provinces originally passed into the *aerarium*.

In strict theory, the *fiscus* was the property of the emperor, as the *manubiae* of the general. But he was under the strongest moral obligation to account for his use of it, and he could only leave it to his successor. There was much room for variation in practice, according to the greater or less degree of strictness with which the emperor interpreted his obligations. The *fiscus Asiaticus* received the dues of Asia, the *fiscus Iudaicus* the special tribute paid, from Vespasian onward, by Jews.

O. Hirschfeld, *Die kaiserlichen Verwaltungsbeamten*[2] (1905); H. Mattingly, *The Imperial Civil Service of Rome* (1910); Rostovtzeff in *PW*, s.v.; H. Last, *JRS* 1944, 51 ff.; C. H. V. Sutherland, *AJPhil.* 1945.   H. M.

FISH, SACRED. Fish were held sacred by various Oriental peoples. The Egyptian priests abstained from fish (Hdt. 2. 37) and there were local tabus on particular species. The Syrian reverence for fish early impressed the Greeks (Xen. *An.* 1. 4. 9); the temples of Atargatis (q.v.) regularly contained a pool for them, and a *lex sacra* from Smyrna (*SIG* 997) deals with their care. Atargatis punished with illness eaters of fish (Menand. fr. 544, Kock), and the tabu may have originated in the unwholesomeness of the local species. Her priests, however, ate them daily in a ritual meal (Mnaseas, *FHG* iii. 155), and they were a sacred food also in Thracian and Samothracian mystery cults, perhaps through Oriental influence; Julian (*Or.* 5. 176d) says they were sacrificed in certain mystic rites (*and see* VOLCANUS). The early Christian symbolism of Ἰχθύς may be in part connected with their sanctity in Syria, but its popularity was enhanced by its equation with the formula Ἰ(ησοῦς) Χ(ριστὸς) θ(εοῦ) υ(ἱὸς) σ(ωτήρ), which constituted a convenient confession of faith. *See* BRIZO.

F. Cumont, *PW*, s.v. 'Ichthys'; F. J. Dölger, Ἰχθυς, 1910–.
                                                          F. R. W.

FLACCUS, VERRIUS, a freedman, the most erudite of the Augustan scholars and teacher of the grandsons of Augustus. His works (now lost) included *Libri rerum memoria dignarum* (freely used by Pliny the Elder), *De obscuris Catonis*, *Libri rerum Etruscarum*, and *De orthographia*. The *Fasti Praenestini* (*CIL* i[2]) were also drawn up by him. But he is best known for his lost *Libri de significatu verborum* in which he quoted freely from the earlier Republican authors. His material he arranged in alphabetical order and devoted several books to each letter. From the epitome made by Festus (q.v.) we can gain some idea of the richness of learning contained in this work of Verrius Flaccus, which was a quarry for the scholars of the immediately succeeding generations.

Cf. Teuffel, § 261. 1–3; Schanz-Hosius, §§ 340–1a.   J. F. M.

FLACCUS, cognomen of Horace (q.v., Q. Horatius Flaccus).

FLACCUS, *see also* AVILLIUS, CALPURNIUS, FULVIUS, SICULUS, VALERIUS (6), (7), (8), (13), (19).

FLAMINES. The word *flamen* appears to mean 'priest' or 'sacrificer', cf. Old Islandic *blót*, 'sacrificial feast', etc. (Walde, *Lat. etym. Wört.*, s.v.). In Rome the *flamines* were a group of fifteen priests, three *maiores* and twelve *minores*, forming part of the *collegium pontificum*. Each was assigned to the cult of one god (though he might on occasion take part in the worship of some other; e.g. the flamen Quirinalis conducted the ritual of the Robigalia, Ov. *Fasti* 4. 910); Varro, *Ling.* 5. 84, Cicero, *Leg.* 2. 20. The three *maiores* were the flamen Dialis, of Jupiter; Martialis, of Mars; Quirinalis, of Quirinus (Gaius 1. 112). The first of these was obliged to observe an amazingly elaborate system of taboos, all designed to keep his extremely holy person from any pollution or bad magic (list, with authorities, Marquardt–Wissowa, *Staatsverw.*[2] iii. 328 ff.); it is probable that the observances of the other two were, at least originally, hardly less complicated. It is further highly likely that the Dialis represented an ancient king, see Rose, *Roman Questions of Plutarch*, 111. Of the twelve *minores* we know the following ten: Volturnalis, Palatualis, Furinalis, Floralis, Falacer, Pomonalis (these seem to have

been the last six, Festus, p. 144. 12 ff. Lindsay; all six in Ennius ap. Varr. op. cit. 7. 45); Volcanalis (Varr. op. cit. 5. 84), Cerialis (*CIL* xi. 5028), Carmentalis (Cicero, *Brut.* 56), Portunalis (Festus, p. 238. 9 Lindsay), but the order of precedence of these four is unknown. Their deities were respectively Volturnus, Pales, Furrina, Flora, Falacer, Pomona, Volcanus, Ceres, Carmentis, and Portunus.   H. J. R.

FLAMININUS (1), TITUS QUINCTIUS (*cos.* 198 B.C.), the victor of Cynoscephalae, was military tribune under Marcellus (208 B.C.), propraetor *extra ordinem* at Tarentum (205–204), and for his philhellenism and diplomatic address became consul in 198, not yet thirty, to win the support of Greece against Philip V in the Second Macedonian War. After Cynoscephalae (197) he confined Philip in Macedonia, rejected Aetolian claims in Thessaly, and in 196 at the Isthmian Games proclaimed the freedom of Greece; in 195 he forced Nabis to surrender Argos. In 194 he evacuated Greece, and the Greek cities honoured him as deliverer. In 194–193 he upheld against Antiochus' envoys the Roman guardianship of Greek autonomy in Asia Minor, and in 193–192 suppressed Nabis, but failed to check the pro-Syrian policy of Aetolia. After Thermopylae (191) he procured a truce in Greece. Censor in 189 with M. Marcellus, his liberal policy appears in the restoration of the Campanians' census rights. In 183 he demanded the surrender of Hannibal from Prusias. He died in 174; a son was consul in 150 and a grandson consul in 123. Ambitious and idealistic, he was in his philhellenism and policy a rival rather than a protégé of Scipio Africanus, and this, with his diplomacy and generalship, made him the Senate's best instrument in establishing a protectorate over an autonomous Greece.

Polyb. bks. 17–18; Livy, bks. 32–6; 38. 28 and 36; 39. 51; Plutarch, *Flamininus*. G. Colin, *Rome et la Grèce* (1905), 82; L. Homo, *Revue historique* cxxi (1916), 241; cxxii (1916), 1; F. Münzer, *Röm. Adelsparteien und Adelsfamilien* (1920), 117; De Sanctis, *Stor. Rom.* iv. 1. 76; M. Holleaux, *CAH* viii. 169; A. H. McDonald, *JRS* 1938, 155; A. Aymard, *Les Premiers rapports de Rome et de la confédération achaienne* (1938); F. W. Walbank, *Philip V of Macedon* (1940); F. M. Wood, *TAPA* 1939 and *AJPhil.* 1941.   A. H. McD.

FLAMININUS (2), LUCIUS QUINCTIUS (*cos.* 192 B.C.), curule aedile (201 B.C.), praetor (199), commanded the Roman fleet in Greece in 198 and 195 for his brother T. Flamininus. Consul in 192, he was guilty of oppression in Gaul, for which on moral grounds Cato expelled him from the Senate in 184.

Livy 33. 16 ff.; 34. 26 ff.; 35. 20–2; 39. 42–3. Plutarch, *Flamininus* 18–19.   A. H. McD.

FLAMINIUS, GAIUS (*cos.* I, 223 B.C.), the greatest democratic leader before the Gracchi to challenge the senatorial government. *Tribunus plebis* in 232 B.C., despite bitter senatorial opposition he carried a timely measure to distribute to the poor the *ager Gallicus et Picenus*, recently confiscated from the Senones. A doubtful aristocratic tradition (preserved by Polybius) alleges that this caused the beginning of 'the demoralization of the people' and by annoying the Gauls hastened the Gallic invasion of 225; further, it was alleged that his own father opposed Flaminius. As praetor in 227 he was the first to hold that office in Sicily. Consul I (223), he led the first Roman army across the Padus and defeated the Insubres: accounts which assign the victory to the legions' efficiency in spite of their general's rashness are suspect. He 'triumphed' at the People's wish despite senatorial objection. He was *magister equitum* to his enemy Q. Fabius Maximus (221). As censor (220) he built the Via Flaminia (q.v.) and the circus Flaminius. The reform of the Comitia Centuriata, which Mommsen assigned to his censorship, is perhaps earlier. Alone of the senators, he supported the *Lex*

Claudia (see CLAUDIUS 7). His election to a second consulship in 217 was a popular criticism of the Senate's conduct of the Hannibalic war. He guarded the Western Apennines at Arretium; when Hannibal passed, he hastened south (probably to join his colleague Servilius with whom it was alleged he refused to co-operate) but fell into Hannibal's ambush at Lake Trasimene, where his army was destroyed and he himself met a hero's death, a fate which hostile tradition attributed to his disregard of the customary religious ceremonies.

K. Jacobs, *Gaius Flaminius* (1938; written in Dutch). H. H. S.

FLAVIUS (1), GNAEUS, son of a *libertus* of Appius Claudius (q.v. 4) Caecus, was a jurist and author of a dissertation *De usurpationibus*, on interruptions of the *usucapio*. He was Appius' secretary. Pomponius relates that he purloined a manuscript of Appius' containing the *Legis actiones* and published it. This publication, the first on this subject, gave the people knowledge of the Civil Law and of the forms of procedure which had been the monopoly of the pontiffs. For this service Flavius became *tribunus plebis*, senator, and *aedilis curulis* in spite of his humble origin. His formulary was known under the name *Ius civile Flavianum*. In his aedileship (304) he exhibited in the forum the list of court-days on which the *legis actio* was admissible. A. B.

FLAVIUS (2) FELIX; his verses, often unclassical in quantities, are preserved with Florentinus' verses in the *Anthologia Latina* (ed. Riese, 254).

FLAVIUS, see also CLEMENS, DOMITIAN, FIMBRIA, SABINUS, TITUS, VERGINIUS, VESPASIAN.

FLEVO LACUS, the Zuyder Zee. In Roman times it was a lake (whose name is preserved in Vlieland), with an island of the same name; most of the Frisian Islands were then part of the mainland. The Vecht flowed into Lake Flevo, and its outlet to the sea was a narrow stream, now the Vlie channel. These waterways were used by the Roman fleets in the wars of Drusus, Tiberius, and Germanicus; and Drusus canalized the Vecht for navigation from the Rhine to the sea. The Zuyder Zee retained this configuration substantially until the great inundations of the twelfth and thirteenth centuries.

O. B.

FLORA (Oscan *Flusia*: Conway, *Ital. Dial.* nos. 46; 175a; L 24), an Italian goddess of flowering or blossoming plants. The antiquity of her cult in Rome is proved by the existence of a *flamen Floralis* (cf. FLAMINES), but her festival is not in the 'calendar of Numa' (*see* CALENDARS), and therefore was movable (*conceptiuae*). In 238 B.C., by advice of the Sibylline books, she was given a temple (Pliny, *HN* 18. 286; cf. Platner–Ashby, 209 f.). Its dedication day was 28 April, and games (*ludi Florales*) began to be celebrated then annually in 173 B.C. (Ov. *Fast.* 5. 329 f.). These included farces (*mimi*) of a highly indecent character (Ov. ibid. 331 and Frazer ad loc.). Foreign, probably Greek influence accounts for this non-Italian feature (Aphrodite Ἀνθεία?).

See Wissowa, *RK* 197. H. J. R.

FLORENTIA, the modern *Florence*, probably was not an Etruscan foundation. It may have been in existence by the time of the Civil Wars (Florus 2. 8: text doubtful and certainly exaggerated), and possibly received a colony under the Triumvirs (*Lib. Colon.* 213). In Tiberius' reign a Florentine mission to Rome asked that the Clanis be not diverted into the Arnus (Tac. *Ann.* 1. 79). Otherwise Florentia played no recorded part in history until late Imperial times. In the fifth century it was a considerable fortress (Procop. *Goth.* 3. 5. 6); by Lombard times apparently the capital of a duchy.

L. A. Milani, *Monumenti Antichi* vi (1896); E. Pucci, *Short History of Florence* (Florence, 1939); G. Maetzke, *Florentia* (1941). E. T. S.

FLORENTINUS (*Anth. Lat.* (Riese) 376), *see* FLAVIUS FELIX.

FLORIANUS, MARCUS ANNIUS, praetorian prefect and half-brother of the Emperor Tacitus, accompanied him to the East in A.D. 276 and defeated the Goths in the north of Asia Minor. On the death of Tacitus at Tyana he seized the Empire 'quasi hereditarium' and was recognized everywhere except in Syria and Egypt, which set up Probus. Probus took the field against him at Tarsus and, by cleverly delaying the campaign, tired out and demoralized Florianus' troops. Florianus was put to death by his own men, after a short 'dream of Empire' lasting some ninety days (*c.* June 276). H. M.

FLORUS (*Lucius Annaeus F.* in Cod. Palat. 894 and most editions, *Julius F.* in Cod. Bamberg.) is generally held to be identical with F. the poet-friend of Hadrian and with P. Annius F., author of the imperfectly preserved dialogue *Vergilius orator an poeta* (*see infra*). The dialogue states that he was born in Africa and in boyhood took part unsuccessfully in the Capitoline competition under Domitian; he afterwards settled at Tarraco in Spain, but returned to Rome in Hadrian's time. His chief work is entitled *Epitome bellorum omnium annorum DCC.* He states (Introd. § 8) that he is writing 'not much less than 200 years after Caesar Augustus'; if these words mean the beginning of Augustus' career (27 B.C.), '200 years' is a slight exaggeration.

2. WORKS. The *Epitome* is an abridgement of Roman history with special reference to the wars waged up to the age of Augustus. Some manuscripts describe it as an epitome of Livy; but it is sometimes at variance with Livy. The author also made use of Sallust, Caesar, and the elder Seneca; and there are reminiscences of Virgil and Lucan. It is planned as a panegyric of the Roman people. Of the two books the first traces the rise of Rome's military power, the second its decline, the line of division being drawn in the Gracchan age.

3. Of the dialogue only a fragment of the introduction survives. It was probably written about A.D. 122 (F. Schmidinger, 'Untersuchungen über Florus', *Neue Jahrb. f. Philol.* xx, Supplement 6, pp. 781–816. E. Woelfflin (*Arch. für latein. Lexikogr.* vi (1889)) shows that its diction closely resembles that of the *Epitome*.

4. *Poems*. The lines on Hadrian beginning 'Ego nolo Caesar esse', had the honour of a retort from him (S.H.A. *Hadr.* 16. 3). Other fragments are preserved (Riese, *Anth. Lat.* i. 1, nos. 87–9 and 245–52). They are not sufficient to enable judgement to be passed on the author's poetry and hardly justify the theory that the famous *Pervigilium Veneris* is his work (H. O. Müller, *de P. Annio F. poeta et Pervig. Ven.* (1855)).

5. Florus in the *Epitome* shows a certain literary gift, marred, however, by a strong tendency to rhetoric. His brevity often entails obscurity, though he sometimes produces a felicitous epigram. He has irritating habits of inserting exclamatory remarks and repeating favourite words. As an historian he is often inaccurate in both chronology and geography, but the work as a whole achieves a limited success as a rapid sketch of Roman military history. It was a favourite school-book in the seventeenth century.

BIBLIOGRAPHY

LIFE AND WORKS. Schanz–Hosius, § 539; Teuffel–Schwabe–Kroll–Skutsch, § 348; J. Wight Duff, *Lit. Hist. Rome, Silver Age,* 644 ff.; P. Monceaux, *Les Africains* (1894), 193 ff.; F. Eyssenhardt, *Hadrian u. Florus* (1882); F. Schmidinger, *Untersuch. über Fl.* (1894); O. Hirschfeld, *Anlage u. Abfassungszeit d. Epitome d. Fl.* (1899); S. Lilledahl, *Florusstudien* (1928).

TEXTS (*Epitome* and *Dialogue*). Teubner (Jahn, Halm, Rossbach).
COMMENTARIES. Salmasius and Gruter (1609); Freinsheim (1632); Graevius (1680); Duker (1744); Seebode (1821).
TRANSLATIONS. *Epitome*: E. S. Forster with text (Loeb, 1929). *Poems*: J. W. and A. M. Duff, with text (Loeb: *Minor Latin Poets*, pp. 426 ff., 1934). E. S. F.

FOEDUS means a treaty, solemnly enacted, which established friendly association, *pia et aeterna pax*, and alliance between Rome and another State or States for perpetuity. *Foedus* is distinct from *indutiae*, which ended a state of war and were limited in duration up to a century. It might be *aequum* or *iniquum*. The former kind set both parties on equality, and provided for military assistance in defensive wars. The latter marked out Rome as *in foedere superior*, the second party being bound to assist Rome in offensive wars also, and to respect the dignity of Rome, *maiestatem populi Romani comiter conseruare*. This attempt to express the spirit of the law in the letter indirectly limited the allies' sovereignty, placing them in the relationship of client to patron (*see* SOCII). Special conditions were not normally added to the treaty, being out of place in *foedus aequum* and unnecessary in *foedus iniquum*, until the later Republic. Treaties were usually limited to establishing the general alliance, with arrangements for agreed alterations and the usual sanctions. The earliest known *foedus aequum* is the treaty of Spurius Cassius (q.v. 1). *Foedera iniqua* were commonest in Italy and stressed the Roman hegemony (*see* SOCII). *Fetiales* (q.v.) or consuls usually officiated, but other military commanders also could make treaties, which then needed ratification at Rome. They were published on bronze and kept on the Capitol. Exceptional forms appear in the first two Carthaginian treaties, which are of non-Roman type, and the *foedus Gabinum* which mediated the incorporation of Gabii in Rome (6th c. B.C.).

For bibliography *see* SOCII.   A. N. S.-W.

FOLK-SONGS, GREEK. The Greeks, like other peoples, had their folk-songs, though it is impossible to give dates to them or to construct a history. They may be roughly classified as follows: (1) to gods (*Carm. Pop.* 46–53); (2) ritual songs (ibid. 31–2); (3) occupational (ibid. 29–31); (4) averting songs (ibid. 42); (5) love-songs (ibid. 43–4).

Cf. J. M. Edmonds, *Lyra Graeca* (Loeb) iii, pp. 488–549.
C. M. B.

FOLK-SONGS, LATIN. Folk-songs are to be distinguished from lilting folk-saws and other folk-lore, as well as from so-called 'popular songs' which have not originated among the people and hence are not natural expressions of the people's spirit. Genuine folk-songs may be classed according to their favourite themes; (*a*) love-songs; (*b*) occupational songs; (*c*) carols; (*d*) ballads or songs on historical themes (see collections of English and American folk-songs by Cecil Sharp). No doubt there were Latin folk-songs also on these themes, but we can only repeat Cicero's words (*Brutus* 75) 'utinam exstarent illa carmina!' A connexion may be claimed between folk-songs or folk-ditties and the religious *carmina* such as those of the *Salii* and the *arvales* (*see* CARMEN), and also forms such as the Fescennine (q.v.) verses, *satura* (q.v.), triumph-songs, *epithalamia* (q.v.) or marriage-songs, *neniae* (q.v.), and those in 'Saturnian' metre (q.v.). The 'ancient lays' sung at banquets by 'modest boys' or by the banqueters themselves in honour of great men of the past, referred to by Varro and Cato, may be embellished versions of folk-songs. The *versus populares* upon prominent men in later days are probably to be classed rather as topical songs. The rhythms (e.g. trochaic tetrameter) of the folk-poetry appear to have survived throughout the period when art-poetry was using Greek metres exclusively, and reappeared at a later date. For occupational songs, see Varro ap. Non. 56; Victorin. *Gramm. Lat.* 6. 122.
A. L. P.

FOLK-TALES. Only one *märchen*, told as such, has come down to us from antiquity, and that in a literary form, Apuleius' story of Cupid and Psyche (*Metam.* 4.

28 ff.; this is Stith Thompson C 421). Tertullian names two more, *adv. Valent.* 3. But numerous folk-tale themes are to be found scattered up and down classical legends, though the chronological question whether the theme or the legend is the older often cannot be decided. Examples are the external soul (Meleager, q.v.); the husband who returns just in time to stop his wife, who supposes him dead, marrying another (Odysseus, q.v.); the unwitting killing by Aëdon (q.v.) and Themisto (*see* ATHAMAS) of their own children (essentially the story of Tom Thumb and the ogre); Home-Comer's Vow, the tale of the man who, like Jephtha, vows to sacrifice the first thing which meets him on his return, or otherwise to destroy or dispose of it, and is met by his own child. This is told of Idomeneus (q.v. 1). At least one Greek tale, that of Odysseus and Polyphemus (*see* CYCLOPES), is found as far away as Lapland (see Qvigstad, *Lappiske Eventyr og Sagn* ii (1928), 448–9). The vast popularity of Homer makes it no wise incredible that we have here simply Homer's story (source unknown). That several of the longer cycles of story, as the legends of Perseus and of the Argonauts (qq.v.; for the latter, see S. Hartland, *Legend of Perseus*, and Halliday, op. cit. infra (2), pp. 21 ff.), are packed with details found in various folk-tales in and out of Europe is common knowledge.

For one common form of (Oriental?) folk-tale, the beast-fable, Greece has been a great distributing centre, owing to the collections popularly associated with the name of Aesop. From the earlier oral or written versions (see Halliday (1), pp. 101 ff.; (2), pp. 143 ff.) these apologues have spread, first into Latin (Phaedrus, 'Romulus', etc.), thence into modern languages, meanwhile never ceasing to be repeated among the later Greeks themselves. In all cases it is necessary to remember the reciprocal action between literary and popular compositions. Supposing, for example, what is likely in itself, that the beast-fable was originally popular and oral, we find it at very varying levels. It is used by serious authors to point grave morals (Hesiod, *Op.* 202 ff.; Pindar, *Pyth.* 2. 72 ff.; Aeschylus, fr. 139 Nauck). It was a popular form of after-dinner story (Ar. *Vesp.* 1259 f.). It was used as edifying reading for children (Babrius, *praef.*), and for first exercises in composition (Quint. *Inst.* 1. 9. 2). Finally, it became a popular chapbook, and so found its way back into oral or quasi-oral circulation. Thus the simple, popular tale may always be a worn-down form of the elaborate and literary one, not its predecessor. Caution is therefore necessary in tracing connexions such as those suggested above.

W. R. Halliday, *Greek and Roman Folklore*, U.S.A. 1927 ('Halliday (1)'); *Indo-European Folk-Tales and Greek Legend*, Cambridge, 1933 ('Halliday (2)'); Rose, *Handbook of Greek Mythology*, ch. 10, where some further references are given. *See also* FABLE.   H. J. R.

FOLLIS, the bag in which coins were collected for large payments; then the coins themselves.

Follis seems to be applied only to coins of bronze or silvered bronze, but not to be restricted to any one denomination. Under Diocletian it may have denoted the common 'Genius Populi Romani' piece. Under Julian six *folles* are the price of a pound of pork. St. Augustine knows the *follis* as a tiny fraction of the *solidus*. In Byzantine times the *follis* was pre-eminently the piece of 40 *nummia*. The *Historia Augusta* is very doubtful authority for the use of the word in the third century A.D.

E. Babelon, *Traité des monnaies grecques et romaines* (1901) i. 615 ff., 761 ff.   H. M.

FOODSTUFFS. Of all the departments of ancient life revealed to us in literature we know more of food than of any subject, and that although the Athenians of the fifth and fourth centuries B.C. were conspicuously frugal in their tastes. The simplest classification of food we owe to the Athenians, for whom there were only two kinds: (a) bread—σῖτος, (b) anything consumed with bread—ὄψον. We shall consider in turn cereal foods, fish, vegetables and fruit, game, poultry, and meat.

2. Of cereal foods there were many varieties. Both in Greece and at Rome porridge (μάζα, alica, polenta) was in use before bread. Wheat, barley, and (more rarely) rye and millet were all used for making loaves, but at Athens a wheaten loaf—ἄρτος—was a luxury, and normally barley and oats supplied material both for porridge and bread. The grain was ground into flour by hand-mills, and the product was far more nutritious than our machine white. Leaven was occasionally used; the loaves were square and flat; and they were sometimes flavoured with honey or cheese.

3. There were 150 species of fish, most of them edible, known to the Greeks and Romans; at Athens a piece of fish, fresh, dried, or pickled, was so frequently the accompaniment of bread that it is often synonymous with ὄψον. The Romans were equally fond of a fish diet, and under the Empire immense sums were paid for the choicer and larger kinds, such as sturgeon and turbot. Lampreys and mullet were often reared on meat in fish-ponds, and oysters fattened in the Lucrine Lake were served with a special fish-sauce, garum.

4. For ordinary folk vegetables, fruit, and nuts were even more important than fish. Beans, peas, lettuce, carrot, radish, marrows, beet, onion, garlic, are only a few items in the long catalogue given by Theophrastus. In fruit, however, the Greeks had a more restricted choice. Apples, pears, mulberries, figs, and grapes and nuts grew in their own country, and dates were imported from Phoenicia. The Romans had in addition peaches, apricots, and cherries, which they transplanted from the Near East. But of what they had they made full use, and Galen tells us of people who for two months of the year lived well on bread, grapes, and figs.

5. Poultry, game, and eggs played a large part in Roman cookery. Geese, duck, and farmyard fowls were all reared for the table, where they appeared together with pheasants, partridges, quails, and every kind of small wild bird. Hares were a familiar delicacy, and the rich feasted on peacocks, flamingoes, and cranes. But of butchers' meat there was comparatively little, if we except pork in all its forms and an occasional joint of veal. In cooking, condiments and sauces were freely used; mustard, salt, pepper, vinegar, and innumerable herbs and spices, together with the famous silphium from Cyrene which served as many purposes as our ginger.

6. The Greeks and Romans used honey instead of sugar, and olive oil in place of butter; and the goat rather than the cow was their chief milking animal. They lacked potatoes, tomatoes, oranges, bananas; strawberries, raspberries, gooseberries were not cultivated. Of more substantial food beef, mutton, and lamb were seldom eaten. They had no distilled beverages, and no infusion drinks like our tea and coffee; and unlike other ancient peoples they did not brew beer. See also MEALS.

Hippocrates, Περὶ διαίτης; Theophrastus, History of Plants; Galen, Περὶ τροφῶν δυνάμεως; Athenaeus, Deipnosophists. E. Fournier, Dar.-Sag. s.v. 'Cibaria'. F. A. W.

FORDICIDIA (this is the pure Latin form; Sabine Hordicidia, cf. Conway, Ital. Dial. i. 385): Roman festival of Tellus on 15 April, when a forda (cow in calf) was sacrificed to her (Ovid, Fasti 4. 630 ff.). See further Frazer, Fasti of Ovid, iii. 317; add Pausanias 2. 11. 4 (pregnant ewes sacrificed to the Eumenides). H. J. R.

FORGERIES, LITERARY. I. GREEK. Forgeries differ from other pseudepigrapha (works wrongly attributed to authors) in two respects. With a true forgery the attribution must be made by the real author himself, and there must be intention to deceive. On both points we are frequently left in doubt. If Lobon (q.v.) wrote

the Hymn to Poseidon attributed to Arion, Lobon is not necessarily responsible for the attribution; and the authors of the later Theognidea certainly took no pains to pass off their work as that of Theognis. Again, the Anacreontea, though they bear the superscription of Anacreon, and often refer to his darling Bathyllus as living, make no serious claim to be Anacreon's work (cf. 1, and 60 B τὸν Ἀνακρέοντα μιμοῦ). The poems are only fathered on the old poet by a fanciful pretence, not even consistently maintained. Similarly, we cannot say that the composers of letters attributed to eminent Greek authors or personages (e.g. the famous Epistles of Phalaris) meant in every case to deceive the public (see LETTER). On the other hand, it is certain that from desire for gain, fame, or a cachet for philosophical doctrines some deliberate forgeries were perpetrated, e.g. the Orphica of the neo-Pythagoreans and much Jewish-Greek literature. Heraclides Ponticus, according to Aristoxenus, wrote tragedies which he attributed to Thespis; and pseudo-Democritea (see Diels's Vorsokratiker) are numerous. The music to part of Pindar's first Pythian, published by Kircher in 1648, is an almost certain example of forgery by a modern scholar. The invention of sources, e.g. by Ptolemaeus Chennus (and see DIONYSIUS (13) SCYTOBRACHION), may also be mentioned here. J. D. D.

II. **LATIN.** Suetonius (p. 47 Reiffersch.) relates that there had come into his hands certain elegi and a prose letter addressed to Maecenas purporting to be by Horace. He rejected them, however, because the elegies were commonplace and the letter even obscure. False, too is the so-called Sulpiciae satira (ed. Unger, 1887), a poem of seventy hexameters in dialogue form lamenting the tyranny of Domitian and prophesying his fall. Earlier attributed to the poetess Sulpicia, it is unquestionably a late forgery. For Latin versions of fourth or fifth century A.D. based on Greek sources of some two centuries earlier professing to be by two participants in the Trojan War see DARES and DICTYS. Other late forgeries are the four poems and fragments of Gallus first edited by Manutius in 1590, while an epigram addressed to Augustus begging him not to allow the Aeneid to be destroyed is also falsely attributed in some manuscripts to Gallus. In 1510 a work by A. D. Fiocchi, De magistratibus et sacerdotiis Romanorum, was published under the name of the historian Fenestella, and the De progenie Augusti Caesaris attributed to Valerius Messala first saw the light of day in the fifteenth century. In still later times Guez de Balzac published thirty verses (Indignatio in poetas Neronianorum temporum) purporting to come from an ancient manuscript, and though they appeared among his own works as ficta pro antiquis, they were attributed by Wernsdorf to the poet Turnus. Active as a forger was C. Barth (1587–1658), who published various Latin poems, among which some were alleged to be by Vestricius Spurinna. Nodot's publication at Paris in 1693 of alleged portions of Petronius was fraudulent.

See also PSEUDEPIGRAPHIC LITERATURE. L. R. P.

FORMULA, see LAW AND PROCEDURE, II. 3.

FORNACALIA, a movable festival, celebrated not later than 17 Feb. (Quirinalia), which day was hence called also stultorum feriae, because, as Ovid explains (Fast. 2. 531–2; from Verrius Flaccus, cf. Festus, pp. 304. 5 ff.; 418. 33 ff.; 419. 5 ff. Lindsay), those who were too stupid to know to what curia they belonged kept the festival then instead of on the proper day, proclaimed by the curio maximus (Ov. ibid. 527–8). It was, then, celebrated by the curiae, not the people as a whole; it consisted of ritual either to benefit the ovens, fornaces, which parched grain, or to propitiate the doubtful goddess Fornax who presided over them, ibid. 525.

See Frazer ad loc.; Wissowa RK, pp. 158, 399. H. J. R.

FORTIFICATIONS in the Mediterranean area were from the first closely related to physical conditions. 'Praeruptis oppida saxis' are typical of the whole area, and it was the fortified acropolis, the oldest type, which was naturally productive of revetted slopes or terrace-walls, i.e. stone ramparts containing a filling of beaten earth or rubble. In Greece, Tiryns, Mycenae, and Gla (on Lake Copais) afford excellent pre-Hellenic examples in advanced development, exhibiting casements and bastions at Tiryns, gates with enfilading bastions at Mycenae (cf. TROY I), and vantage-courts at Gla. Hittite towns and citadels exhibit improved enfilading, and a combination of rectangular and semicircular towers, as at Zindjirli II (c. 900 B.C.). All these devices were translated bodily to Greek architecture in the fifth century B.C., when masonry town-walls on a large scale began to develop, and the tactical device of the Long Walls (Megara c. 460, Athens 457, Argos 417) converted the city-state into the city-fortress. Theory was formulated in the fourth century by Philo Byzantinus, and put into practice at such sites as Messene (371) and Ephesus. By this time improved methods of attack were demanding new defensive developments, also long anticipated in Asia Minor. The movable siege-tower (ἑλέπολις) called for wide ditches or moats to prevent its approach and for the catapult, invented in 399 (Diod. Sic. 14. 42), to smash it. Syracuse and Selinus (397–383; cf. *Antiquity* vi. 261–75) provide remarkable instances of modifications in their fortifications designed for defence of this kind. Siege-artillery came later, but its development belied its promise, and Greek military architecture stood still. *See* ARTILLERY; SIEGECRAFT, GREEK.

The Italic tradition had an early development partly akin to that of Greece, but was less dependent upon the acropolis, being early modified by dissociation of the fortified bank, or *agger*, from hill-sides, as at Ardea or at Rome itself (*murus terreus*, Varro, *Ling.* 5. 48), and the revetment of such earth-banks in stone, creating earth-filled walls. The progressive development of such a wall has been traced at Pompeii (*Mon. Ant.* xxxiii (1930), pt. 2), beginning in 520–450 B.C.; it was enlarged in Italic style, as a revetted *agger* with rearward slope, in the fourth and third centuries B.C., and only hellenized, by the addition of towers, in 120–89 B.C. Meanwhile Rome had been experimenting with a masonry wall of partly Hellenistic type (*see* WALL OF SERVIUS), such as was adopted in her colonies of Ostia and Minturnae (qq.v.). But Hellenistic practice was not introduced wholesale until Sulla's day, as at Tarracina and Ostia II, though artillery casemates, as at Perusia and Rome, had been introduced somewhat before this. Vitruvius presents the intermediate stage (*De Arch.* 1. 5) between Sullan work and the eclecticism of the Augustan age. Another strain in Roman military architecture had already been introduced by military field-work, developed on a scale hitherto quite unknown, and predominant in all frontier provinces until the latter half of the first century A.D. There are notable works in earth and timber at Xanten, Haltern, Oberaden, and Alteburg in lower Germany, at Margidunum and Fendoch in Britain. This tradition of military building, combining simplicity and strength, was not ousted until the Flavian period in legionary fortresses, and under Trajan on the frontiers. Thenceforward masonry building takes first place, though never completely deserting the earthwork tradition. The fortified frontier, in which a wall, rampart, or palisade, patrolled from watch-towers, connected a chain of forts, is also a Roman invention (*see* LIMES). The town-walls of the later Roman Empire and occasional forts, like Altrip, culminating in the double walls and artillery defences of Constantinople, combine the best Greek theory with Roman resource, and remained unsurpassed until the invention of gunpowder created entirely new defensive problems.

See G. L. Bell, *The Palace and Mosque of Ukhaidir* (1914), 106–10; K. Humann, *Ausgrabungen in Sendschirli* II, *Mitt. aus den orientalischen Sammlungen, königliche Museen zu Berlin*, Heft xii (1898). Schultze, *Bonner Jahrbücher*, Heft 118; A. Schulten, *Numantia* iii and iv; W. Fischer, *Das römische Lager*; for Haltern, *Westfälische Mittheilungen* v. 87–100; I. A. Richmond, 'Trajan's Army on Trajan's Column', *BSR* xiii; 'The Agricolan Fort at Fendoch', *Proc. Soc. Ant. Scot.* lxxiii; 'Das römische Kastell in Altrip', *Neue deutsche Ausgrabungen, Deutschtum und Ausland*, Heft 23–4 (1930); I. A. Richmond, *City Wall of Imperial Rome* (1930); A. Blanchet, *Les Enceintes de la Gaule romaine* (1907). I. A. R.

FORTUNA or FORS (Ennius ap. Cic. *Off.* 1. 38), in full Fors Fortuna (Terence, *Phorm.* 841), an Italian goddess identified in classical times with Tyche (q.v.). There is, however, good evidence that she was in the native cult not a deity of chance or luck, but rather the 'bringer', as her name signifies (*ferre*), of fertility or increase. She is praised by gardeners (Columella 10. 316), and her ancient temple in the Forum Boarium at Rome (see Platner–Ashby, p. 214; ibid. 212 ff., for her other Roman shrines) had the same dedication-day as that of Mater Matuta (*see* MATUTA), viz. 11 June (Ov. *Fasti* 6. 569). These facts suggest a deity potent for the fruits of the earth and the life of women, cf. her titles Muliebris (Festus, p. 282. 21 Lindsay; this shrine was 4 miles from Rome, and only women living in a first marriage might approach the goddess) and Virgo (Varro ap. Non. p. 189. 19). However, her titles are so numerous (see especially Plutarch, *Quaest. Rom.* 74, and Rose ad loc.) that too much should not be made of these.

It is regularly said that her cult was introduced into Rome by Servius Tullius (Plutarch, ibid., and many other passages), and this is true in the sense that she has neither a *flamen* nor a feast-day belonging to the oldest list. How old her cult is in other parts of Italy is unknown, but certainly older than at Rome, whither it came from some place outside. Of the other Italian centres of her worship, one of the most interesting is Praeneste, where a number of archaic inscriptions throw light on the cult. One is a dedication 'nationu cratia', 'for offspring' (*CIL* xiv. 2863), which furthermore calls the goddess 'Diouo filea primocenia', i.e. 'Iouis filia primigenia', the one instance in Italian cult which makes one deity the child of another, unless, as suggested in Rose, *Roman Questions of Plutarch*, p. 83 f., a very old error underlies the title. Equally interesting is the fact that she had an oracular shrine there. The method of consultation was for a boy to draw at random one of a number of billets of oak-wood (*sortes*), inscribed with sentences (one was 'Mars shakes his dart', at a similar oracle at Falerii, Livy 22. 1. 11) which the consultant might apply to his own case (Cicero, *Div.* 2. 85–6, and Pease ad loc.). A temple was built to the Praenestine goddess on the Quirinal (Livy 29. 36. 8; 34. 53. 5). This was in 194 B.C. At Antium a plurality of Fortunae was worshipped (Macrob. *Sat.* 1. 23. 13), and these also gave oracles, apparently by movements of the statues (Macrob. ibid.). Cf. NORTIA.

Wissowa, *RK* 256 ff.; Drexler in Roscher's *Lexikon* i. 1503 ff. (exhaustive account of her titles, identifications, representations in art, etc.). H. J. R.

FORTUNATAE INSULAE ('Blessed Islands') were originally, like the 'Gardens of the Hesperides', the mythical winterless home of the happy dead, far west on Ocean shores or islands (Homer, *Od.* 4. 563 ff.; Hesiod, *Op.* 171; Pindar, *Ol.* 2. 68 ff.). They were later identified with Madeira (Diod. 5. 19–20; Plut. *Sert.* 8), or more commonly with the Canaries, after their discovery (probably by the Carthaginians). The Canaries were properly explored by King Juba II (c. 25 B.C.–c. A.D. 23), who described apparently six out of the seven. From the meridian line of this group Ptolemy (*Geog.* passim) established his longitudes eastwards.

Cary–Warmington, *Explorers*, 52 ff., 100. E. H. W.

FORTUNATIANUS, *see* ATILIUS (4).

FORTUNATUS, see VENANTIUS.

FORUM AUGUSTUM or AUGUSTI, dedicated in 2 B.C., is the vast precinct (125 metres by 90 metres) of Mars Ultor in Rome, vowed by Octavian at Philippi. Its long axis is based upon the equestrian statue of the avenged Dictator in the *Forum Caesaris*, whence it opened eastwards. The octostyle peripteral temple, in Corinthian style, stood upon a lofty bronze-plated podium, and its deep porch gave access to a sanctuary with aisles and apsidal nave which housed colossal statues of Mars and Venus. Caesar's sword was kept there. The apse was set against the high precinct wall of fire-resisting peperino, here irregular in plan owing to rising ground and the difficulties of buying out private property in the populous Subura. The temple lies between broad walks, leading from the Subura by flights of steps and spanned by triumphal arches, dedicated to Drusus and Germanicus in A.D. 19. Beyond the walks lay two-storied façades of lateral galleries, the northern one containing a colossal statue, probably of Divus Iulius. Out of either gallery opened an *exedra*. All these buildings were embellished with niches containing statues of eulogized *triumphatores*. In this *Forum* youths were admitted to manly estate, here provincial governors ceremonially departed or returned. Behind the northern *exedra* a group of apartments, centred upon an *atrium*, may have housed the Salii, priests of Mars.   I. A. R.

FORUM BOARIUM, see CAMPUS MARTIUS; COMMERCE, para. 4; HERCULES.

FORUM CAESARIS or IULIUM, dedicated by Julius Caesar in 46 B.C., on land bought about eight years earlier for over 60 million sesterces (Cic. *Att.* 4. 16. 8). The area (115 metres long by 30 metres wide), was surrounded by a colonnade, behind which lay *tabernae* on east and west; an irregular plot of land to north was systematized by an *exedra*, while on the south and in the south-west corner lay Caesar's new *curia* (q.v.) and its appendages. In the centre of the *Forum* lay the peripteral octostyle temple of Venus Genetrix, mythical foundress of the Julian *gens*. In front of the temple stood an equestrian statue of the Dictator. While the *tabernae* are Caesar's work, the existing entablature of the temple is Domitianic.   I. A. R.

FORUM HOLITORIUM, see CAMPUS MARTIUS.

FORUM IULII, modern *Fréjus*, presumably founded by Julius Caesar as a market town (*forum*). A colony was settled here probably by Augustus, who dispatched here the warships captured at Actium, so that Forum Iulii became a naval base as well (*Colonia Octavanorum Pacensis Classica*). The fleet was still here in A.D. 69, but the harbour, now quite dry, was perhaps already silting up. Very extensive remains of the port and colony survive. Forum Iulii was the birthplace of C. Julius Agricola and probably of C. Cornelius Gallus.

A. Donnadieu, *Fréjus* (1927); Grenier, *Manuel* i. 298–314; *Carte arch. de la Gaule rom.* ii. 1–19.   C. E. S.

FORUM NERVAE or TRANSITORIUM, 120 metres long by 40 metres wide, was built in Rome by Domitian and dedicated by Nerva in A.D. 97. It converted the Argiletum, which approached the *Forum Romanum* between *Forum Augustum* and *Forum Pacis*, into a monumental avenue: hence the name *Forum Transitorium*. At its east end, against the south *exedra* of *Forum Augustum*, stood a temple of Minerva, Domitian's patron goddess; reliefs illustrating her cult and legends decorated the frieze and attic of the peperino precinct wall, which is divided into fifteen shallow bays by detached marble columns. Alexander Severus placed here colossal statues of the *Divi*. At the east end traffic from the Subura

entered on the south side of the temple only; at the west end, towards the *Forum Romanum*, were twin monumental gates.   I. A. R.

FORUM PACIS or VESPASIANI was the precinct of the Temple of Peace at Rome, dedicated by Vespasian in A.D. 75. The enclosure, bounded by a fire-wall of peperino lined with marble, was 145 metres long and about 100 metres broad. It contained, in addition to the temple, the *bibliotheca Pacis*, housing treasures from Jerusalem and, at its south-east end, the famous Marble Plan of Rome. After the fire of Commodus it was restored by Severus, and the Marble Plan shows traces of a Diocletianic restoration.   I. A. R.

FORUM ROMANUM, the chief public square of Rome, surrounded by monumental buildings, occupied a swampy trough between the Palatine, Oppian, Quirinal, and Capitol. The edges of the marsh, of which Lacus Curtius was a survival, were covered with cemeteries of prehistoric settlements, until the area was drained in the sixth century B.C. by the Cloaca Maxima (q.v.). Memorials of this early state are the Regia, Aedes Vestae, Lacus Iuturnae, the *tabernae*, and *comitium* (q.v.). The earliest dated monuments are the temples of Saturn (497 B.C.: Livy 2. 21), Castor (484 B.C.: Livy 2. 20, 42), and Concordia (336 B.C.: Plut. *Cam.* 42). The *rostra* (q.v.) were decorated by Maenius (338 B.C.), whose civic sense gave balconies (*maeniana*) to the *tabernae veteres* and *argentariae novae*, the latter associated with the shrine of Venus Cloacina, and decorated in 310 B.C. with Samnite *clipei*. Butchers and fishmongers were relegated to the *macellum* and *forum piscarium*. *Basilicae* were introduced in 184 B.C. by Cato (Livy 39. 44), and of this stage in the Forum's development Plautus (*Curc.* 468–81) gives a racy sketch. Cato's work was soon imitated by the *basilica Aemilia* (179 B.C.) behind the *tabernae novae*, and *basilica Sempronia* (170 B.C.) screened by the *tabernae veteres*.

2. The growing official importance of the *Forum* is emphasized by the transfer thither of the *comitia tributa* in 145 B.C., with the consequent change in direction of the *rostra*. In 121 Opimius restored the temple of Concord, and built a new adjacent *basilica*, while the first triumphal arch, to Fabius Maximus Allobrogicus (*CIL* vi. 1303–4), spanned the Sacra Via. The temple of Castor was rebuilt in 117 (Cic. *Scaur.* 46). Much of the present setting, however, is due to Sulla (*JRS* xii. 1 ff.), who planned the erection of the Tabularium (q.v.), new *rostra*, and a new *basilica Aemilia*, paving much of the area and altering many minor monuments to suit his new plan.

3. Caesar, working through Aemilius Paulus (Cic. *Att.* 4. 16. 14), rebuilt the *basilica Aemilia* and planned a new *basilica Iulia*, to replace the old *basilica Sempronia*, which like the *curia* (q.v.) was finished by Augustus. His repaving of the *Forum* is marked by the series of galleries (*cuniculi*) below it. After Caesar's assassination a column was erected to mark the site of his pyre and later (29 B.C.) replaced by the *aedes divi Iuli*. Caesar's *rostra* (q.v.) were also rebuilt by Augustus, who received an arch (19 B.C.), while his *viri triumphales* restored the Regia (36 B.C.), the *basilica Aemilia* (14 B.C.), and the temples of Saturn (42 B.C.), Castor (A.D. 6), and Concord (A.D. 10). Minor Augustan monuments were the *porticus Iulia*, the *milliarium aureum*, the repair of *fons Iuturnae*. Under Tiberius came an *arcus Tiberii* (A.D. 16), the repair of *basilica Aemilia*, the *templum divi Augusti*, and the *schola Xantha* (*CIL* vi. 30692).

4. The Flavians made their impression on the *Forum*. The temple of Vespasian (ibid. 938; 1019) was built in 81, and Domitian also restored the *curia* (q.v.), the temple of Castor and of *divus Augustus*. His equestrian statue occupied the centre of the open space in 91.

5. Later monuments were the Trajanic sculptures from the *rostra*, commemorating *alimenta* for Italy and taxation-reliefs for the provinces, the *templum divae Faustinae* (A.D. 141: ibid. 1005), the *arcus Severi* (A.D. 203: ibid. 1003), the Diocletianic columns in front of *basilica Iulia* (*Röm. Mitt.* 1938), the columns for the *decennalia* and *vicennalia* (*CIL* vi. 1203; 1204), the *templum divi Romuli* (A.D. 307), the *basilica* of Maxentius, completed by Constantine, the *equus Constantini* (ibid. 1141), the *statio aquarum* at *fons Iuturnae* (ibid. 36951). Last of all come the monuments to Stilicho (ibid. 1187), the *rostra Vandalica* (*see* ROSTRA), and the column of Phocas (ibid. 1200).

C. Hülsen, *The Roman Forum* (tr. Carter, ed. 2, 1909); G. Lugli, *Roma antica: il centro monumentale* (1946), 55 ff.; P. Marconi, *Il foro romano* (1935); T. Ashby, *Topographical Dictionary of Ancient Rome* (1929).   I. A. R.

FORUM TRAIANI or ULPIUM.

Of all *fora* in Rome this huge colonnaded square, of which the fourth side is occupied by the Basilica Ulpia, most resembles provincial *fora*, though on the vaster scale paid for by Dacian spoils. The *Forum*, apparently begun by Domitian, was completed for Trajan by the architect Apollodorus of Damascus in A.D. 114. It lies between the Capitol and Quirinal, impinging upon the slopes of both by immense *exedrae*. It has a single portico to the south, where its main entrance, adorned by a triumphal arch in A.D. 116, faced the *Forum Augustum*; the lateral porticoes were double. The *basilica*, with broad nave, double aisles, and two very large apsidal *tribunalia*, occupied the north side of the *Forum*. Behind it lay Greek and Latin libraries, flanking a colonnaded court, modified to contain Trajan's Column, 38 metres high. The column was decorated with spiral reliefs illustrating the Dacian Wars and was at first crowned by an eagle. Later Trajan's statue surmounted it, and it contained his and Plotina's ashes. The inscription on the column asserts that its purpose was to show the height of the cutting required for the *Forum*: this refers to the scarping of the Quirinal, where the elaborate *exedra*, separated from the *Forum* by fire-wall and street, screens a terraced rock-face ingeniously adapted to streets and staircases and crowned by an interesting market-hall. The libraries and column originally marked the end of the group of buildings, but Hadrian added the *templum Divi Traiani* beyond them.   I. A. R.

FORUM VESPASIANI, see FORUM PACIS.

FOSSAE MARIANAE, see CANALS.

FOUR HUNDRED, THE,

were a council set up at Athens in 411 B.C., after the failure of the *probouloi* (q.v.) to retrieve the situation after the disaster in Sicily (*see* PELOPONNESIAN WAR). Many saw the need for a change in the constitution to secure greater efficiency, and the oligarchs realized their chance of a radical change. Alcibiades (q.v.) offered to win Persia over to alliance with Athens, on condition that an oligarchy be established and he himself return. Both moderates and oligarchs prepared the way, the latter by murder of prominent democrats, the former by urging the need for economy and for restricting the franchise to some 5,000 'able in their persons and their wealth to aid the State', a vague phrase that in practice meant the exclusion of all *thetes* and many *zeugitai* (qq.v.) from government. The negotiations with Alcibiades broke down, and the fleet, then at Samos, manned largely by *thetes*, stood firm for democracy; but the Ecclesia at Athens was finally persuaded or terrorized into electing five men who would (indirectly) select 400 to act as a Boule and into ceding their own powers to the 5,000 (May 411). Under the influence of its extremist members the 400 dispensed with the 5,000; but they failed to win over the

fleet at Samos, and when the Peloponnesians attacked Euboea, the squadron they hastily sent in its defence was defeated with disgrace. By this time, too, many of their leaders were intriguing with Sparta to surrender. Theramenes (q.v.), who had been a prominent revolutionary in the spring, now led the moderates, and the 400 were overthrown (Sept. 411). The 5,000 were now instituted; but after the victory at Cyzicus (410) the full democracy was restored. *See also* ANTIPHON, PEISANDER (2), HETAIRIAI.

Thuc. bk. 8 (a record of the actual course of events); Aristotle, *Ath. Pol.* chs. 29–33 (supported by documents, which, however, express the political ideas of the reformers rather than the realities of the revolution).   A. W. G.

FRANKS,

a name ('freemen') assumed in the third century by a coalition of German tribes on the middle and lower Rhine. They are prominent in attacks on Gaul and Spain between A.D. 253 and 276. A violent incursion in 355 was subsequently defeated by Julian, who granted the Salian Franks a large area for settlement (Toxandria). Frankish relations with the empire were fairly good after this, and Franks (e.g. Count Arbogastes) rose to high positions in the empire. *C.* 425, however, the Salians under Chlodio broke out from Toxandria, and the Franks of the middle Rhine crossed into Gaul. Both were checked by Aetius, but succeeded after his death in extending their power southward and westward. With the defeat of Syagrius in 486 or 487 by the Salian Clovis at Soissons, the last remains of Roman power in Gaul disappeared, and in the ensuing century the Merovingian house of the Salian Franks made itself supreme in the whole area of modern France (*Francia*).

L. Schmidt, *Geschichte der Deutschen Stämme*[1] ii. 433–614; *CAH* vol. xii; J. B. Bury, *Invasion of Europe by the Barbarians* xii, xiii (1928).   C. E. S.

FRATRES ARVALES,

an ancient priestly college in Rome, mentioned under the Republic only by Varro, *Ling.* 5. 85, and restored by Augustus before 21 B.C. We owe our detailed knowledge of this brotherhood to the survival of substantial remains of their records (*Acta Fratrum Arvalium*) in inscriptions, some found in various places in Rome, but most on the site of the sacred grove of the brethren at the fifth milestone on the *Via Campana* outside the *Porta Portuensis* (now the settlement *La Magliana* on the Rome–Pisa railway, near the station). The first in a long series of discoveries was made there in 1570; systematic excavations carried out in the years 1867–71 almost doubled the number of fragments.

The college consisted of twelve members chosen from the most distinguished senatorial families by co-optation; the reigning emperor was always a member. The president of the college (*magister*) and his assistant (*flamen*) were elected annually. The most important ceremony of the brotherhood took place in May in honour of the goddess Dea Dia to whom the grove was dedicated. The rites of this agricultural cult belong to an early stage of Roman religion. The Acts of the year A.D. 218 have preserved the famous song of the Arval Brethren, the *Carmen Arvale* (q.v.), which originated in the fifth century B.C., and traces of Greek influence have been seen in its construction and form.

While the brotherhood's worship was directed to Dea Dia and other traditional deities, divus Augustus was added after his consecration, and one of the explicit intentions of that worship was the well-being of the imperial house. Numerous events in the history of that house received commemoration, and these commemorations, being dated, are a very important source for the chronology of the Empire. The preserved records begin in 21 B.C. and end in A.D. 241 (*ILS* 9522), but the cult still existed in 304 (*Not. Scav.* 1919, pp. 105 f.). *See also* AMBARVALIA.

For the history of Latin script in Rome the *Acta Fratrum Arvalium* are of unique significance.

Fundamental editions: W. Henzen, *Acta Fratrum Arvalium* (1874); *CIL* vi. 2023-119, 32338-98, 37164 f. New fragments: *Not. Scav.* 1914, 464-78; 1919, 100-6; 1921, 49-51; *Bull. Com. Arch.* lv (1927/8), 275-80. Selections: H. Dessau, *ILS* 229-30, 241, 451, 5026-49, 9522; G. McN. Rushforth, *Latin Hist. Inscript.*² (1930), pp. xvi, 78, n. 66. For the *Carmen Arvale* see now Ed. Norden, 'Aus altrömischen Priesterbüchern', *Acta Reg. Soc. Hum. Litt. Lund.* xxix (1939), 109-280. Generally cf. A. D. Nock, *CAH* x (1932), 475. A new edition of the *Acta*, which will contain photographs and an English translation, is being prepared by H. Bloch.
                                                                                H. B.

FREE WILL AND DETERMINISM, *see* FATE.

FREEDMEN. In Greece freedmen (ἀπελεύθεροι or ἐξελεύθεροι) were less numerous and influential than at Rome. A slave could buy his freedom, though the master was not obliged to accept the ransom offered; sometimes masters gave gratuitous freedom. Manumission was done at a temple and before witnesses, and many manumission records survive (*IG* ii². 1553-78; 340-320 B.C.). Freedmen ranked among metics (q.v.). They might be bound by contract, embodied in their manumission deed, to give services for specified periods, without pay or for a percentage of the wages. Most freedmen remained in humble positions as shopkeepers, labourers, craftsmen, carriers; more rarely as landworkers. Some, however, attained to position and wealth (e.g. the banker Pasion (q.v.) or Mylias who managed the armoury of Demosthenes). Numerically freedmen were few compared with slaves: the State was not interested in manumission, for slave labour was needed and the Greeks believed that barbarians were by nature slaves. The Greeks did not develop any theory or practice of progress from slavery to citizenship and office, as the Romans did.

2. In Rome the freedman (*libertus*, implying citizenship, or *libertinus*, a general word including Latin freedmen) owed deference and service to his manumitter as patron. He could not bring an action unless with a magistrate's leave; if he died intestate or without heir, his property reverted to his patron. He was not eligible for certain positions (e.g. magistracy in Rome or the *municipia*, or the higher orders, or the army), but his son born after manumission was *ingenuus* and a full citizen.

3. In the Republic there was no limit to manumission, and large numbers of unsuitable slaves were turned into citizens. The enrolment of freedmen in the tribes became an important political issue, since on this depended their political influence (see the laws of Aemilius Scaurus (115 B.C.), Sulpicius (88), and Sulla). Following the liberal attitude of his day Caesar proposed to place freedmen on a level with *ingenui* in the *municipia*. Augustus, however, realized that unrestricted manumission was dangerous, and his social legislation was designed to allow only the best elements to attain full freedom (*see* LATINI IUNIANI).

4. For many freedmen freedom must have differed little from the best form of slavery. They carried on their previous work or gained slightly more responsible positions; they were generally artisans, traders, shopkeepers, copyists, bailiffs, secretaries, teachers. Most lived humbly, a few won fortunes and influence, gaining often a reputation for ostentation and vulgarity (cf. Juvenal and Petronius passim). Tacitus (*Ann.* 13. 26, 27) records a proposal to give patrons a right to revoke freedom, to such lengths had the insolence of freedmen gone. While on the whole the literature presents the worst aspects of the freedmen, the inscriptions show that they were devoted benefactors of the townships, spending money on public works and holding office as *seviri Augustales*. (In this connexion, see Pliny, *Ep.* 7. 32.)

5. When Augustus turned his household into a State

department, his freedmen became officials. Under his successors freedmen obtained secretaryships (named, e.g. *ab epistulis, a rationibus, a libellis*) which carried much political power and gave possibilities of great wealth (*see* PALLAS (3), NARCISSUS (2), NYMPHIDIUS). There were also thousands more in the service of the central government or the *municipia*. Some emperors, notably Claudius, relied too much on freedmen. *See also* MANUMISSION, SLAVES, SLAVERY (LAW OF).

A. M. Duff, *Freedmen in the Early Roman Empire* (1928); H. Last, *CAH* x, ch. 14 on the social legislation of Augustus; R. H. Barrow, *Slavery in the Roman Empire* (1928) (chs. 7 and 8 for social and legal aspects); S. Dill, *Roman Society from Nero to Marcus Aurelius* (1905), 100-37, 196-286.
                                                                                R. H. B.

FRIGIDARIUM, *see* BATHS.

FRISII, a German tribe on the Zuyder Zee and the coast from Vecht to Ems. They allied with Rome in 12 B.C., and their territory was used as a base in certain of the German campaigns. They paid taxes of ox-hides, but in A.D. 28 they revolted against oppressive taxgatherers. Corbulo defeated them in 47; in 70 they joined Civilis. Their subsequent status is not clear, but *cunei Frisiorum* served in Britain in the third century (*ILS* 2635; 4761). Throughout the period they carried on a lively trade with the neighbouring Roman provinces, as numerous Roman objects in the Frisian 'terpen' show. In 294-5 Constantius repelled a Frisian incursion. Though driven from some of their lands by the Franks, they maintained themselves on their coasts and later on occupied land east of the Ems vacated by the Saxons.

L. Schmidt, *Geschichte der deutschen Stämme. Die Westgermanen*² (1938), 71 ff.
                                                                                O. B.

FRONTINUS, SEXTUS JULIUS (c. A.D. 30–104), was *praetor urbanus* in 70 and *consul suffectus* in 73; after his consulate he was appointed governor of Britain (probably 74–8), where he subdued the Silures (q.v.). He was probably the founder of the legionary camp at Isca (q.v.).

Frontinus' writings are essentially practical, dealing with professional subjects in a straightforward style admirably suited to his purpose. Of his two-volume work on land-surveying, published under Domitian, only excerpts survive. A theoretical treatise on Greek and Roman military science (*De re militari*), used by Vegetius (1. 8; 2. 3), has perished; but the *Strategemata*, also of Domitian's reign, a more general manual of historical examples illustrating Greek and Roman strategy for the use of officers (bk. 1, *praef.*) survives in four books. The first three are closely related (stratagems before, during, and after battle; during sieges), but bk. 4, where critics detect differences of style and structure, collects instances more ethical in character (Discipline, Justice, etc.) and has been attributed to a later 'Pseudo-Frontinus'. Its authenticity remains doubtful.

Appointed *curator aquarum* by Nerva (A.D. 97), Frontinus began for his own and his successors' guidance a two-volume account of the water-supply of Rome (*De aquis urbis Romae*), completed under Trajan. This describes the aqueducts and their history, with complete technical details as to quantity and distribution of supply, and examines the regulations governing the system and its public and private use. The sources include personal inquiry, engineers' reports, State documents and plans, and senatorial decrees, as well as previous technical writers.

BIBLIOGRAPHY

ON HIS CAREER: Kappelmacher, *PW* x. 591-606; Collingwood-Myres, *Roman Britain*, 110-11.

ON HIS WRITINGS: Texts. Surveying: excerpts in C. Lachmann, *Röm. Feldmesser* (1848); C. Thulin, *Corpus Agrimensorum Rom.* i. 1 (1913). *Strategemata*: G. Gundermann (1888). *De aquis*: F. Bücheler (1858); F. Krohn (1922). Text and translation: *Strat.* and *De aq.*, C. E. Bennett, M. B. McElwain (Loeb, 1925).

On 'Pseudo-Frontinus': C. Wachsmuth, *Rh. Mus.* xv (1860)

(bk. 4 spurious); P. Esternaux, *Die Kompos. v. Frontins Strategemata* (1899) (bk. 4 authentic); G. Bendz, *Die Echtheitsfrage des vierten Buches der Frontinschen Strategemata* (1938) (convincing defence).
On *De aquis*: R. Lanciani, *Topografia di Roma antica; i comentarii di Frontino intorno le acque e gli acquedotti* (1880); C. Herschel, *The Two Books on the Water-supply . . . of . . . Frontinus* (U.S.A., 1899); T. Ashby, *Aqueducts of Ancient Rome* (1935).

C. E. S. and G. C. W.

FRONTO, MARCUS CORNELIUS (*c.* A.D. 100–*c.* 166), born at Cirta, Numidia, became the foremost Roman orator of his day. After passing through the *cursus honorum* (*CIL* viii. 5350) he was *consul suffectus* in 143. Some years earlier he had been appointed tutor in Latin rhetoric to the future emperors M. Aurelius and L. Verus, and he continued in their service till his death in 166 or soon after.

In the pages of Aulus Gellius F. makes several appearances as the centre of a philological coterie. Later writers speak highly of his oratory, mentioning him in the same breath with Cato, Cicero, and Quintilian; the author (Eumenius?) of the *Panegyricus Constantio dictus* (14) even calls him 'Romanae eloquentiae non secundum sed alterum decus'. Except for a doubtfully ascribed treatise *De Differentiis Vocabulorum* there was no basis for testing these judgements till early in the nineteenth century, when palimpsests at Milan and Rome were found to contain the greater portion of his correspondence with M. Aurelius and others. Its publication so disappointed the expectations of historians that F. became the victim of much intemperate criticism. The correspondence has indeed little bearing on history, though it does something to rehabilitate the characters of Verus and of the elder and younger Faustina, and clearly pictures the *bourgeois* home life of the Antonines. It is, however, of considerable interest as a personal record, as a literary by-product, and as a document for the study of rhetoric and language. The mutual affection of Fronto and M. Aurelius is unquestionably sincere, and is the more remarkable since the author of the *Meditations* so obviously preferred philosophy to rhetoric and Greek to Latin. They write to each other as close friends, with just that touch of self-consciousness which is inevitable between master and pupil, but with no thought of having to run the gauntlet of posterity. Much of their correspondence is the merest small-talk, but it is also largely concerned with the study of rhetoric, and F.'s views on this subject are amply documented, though it remains impossible to estimate his achievement in oratory either from his precepts or from the few rhetorical exercises which survive with the correspondence. As a teacher F. employed the traditional rhetorician's technique, and reposed an excessive faith in similes. His favourite prose reading consisted of Cato, C. Gracchus, Sallust, and Cicero's letters; Seneca was his abomination. He deprecated the purism which would confine literary Latin to the vocabulary of Cicero's orations, and by drawing partly on early poets and partly on the *sermo cotidianus* he devised the *elocutio novella*. This euphuistic attempt to revitalize a decaying language is best illustrated in his own writings and those of his fellow-countryman Apuleius, but left its mark on most of the Latin prose written after his time.

Text: S. A. Naber (Leipzig, 1867). With translation: C. R. Haines (Loeb, 1919–20). Critical essays, text and translation of selected letters, and full bibliography to date: M. D. Brock, *Studies in Fronto and his Age* (1911).
R. G. C. L.

FRONTONIANI (Sid. Apoll. *Ep.* 1. 1. 2), followers of Fronto (q.v.) in his archaizing theories of a style, *elocutio novella* (q.v.), calculated to displace both Silver Age mannerisms and Quintilian's veneration for Cicero by a return to the old-fashioned and largely discarded language of Ennius, Cato, and the Gracchi as models. *See* ARCHAISM.

M. D. Brock, *Studies in Fronto and his Age* (1911); E. S. Bouchier, *Life and Letters in Roman Africa* (ch. 5, Fronto and his Circle) (1913).
J. W. D.

FRONTONIANUS, *see* PALMA.

FUCĬNUS LACUS, a large lake at the centre of Italy. It lacked a visible outlet, but legend stated that the river Pitonius from the Paeligni country traversed it without their waters mingling, the Pitonius reappearing near Sublaqueum to supply the Aqua Marcia (Pliny, *HN* 2. 224; 31. 41; Lycoph. *Alex.* 1275). The lake sometimes overflowed (Strabo 5. 240: exaggerated). Claudius, employing 30,000 men for 11 years, executed Caesar's plan to drain the lake: an *emissarium* was excavated 3½ miles through a mountain ridge to carry the lake waters to the Liris (Suet. *Iul.* 44; *Claud.* 20 f.; 32). But Claudius' efforts were not entirely successful. Even repairs to his *emissarium* by Trajan and Hadrian proved vain (Dio Cass. 60. 11. 33; Dessau *ILS* 302; S.H.A. *Hadr.* 22). Drainage attempts recommenced in A.D. 1240, but were unsuccessful until the nineteenth century, when practically the whole lake-bed was reclaimed.

E. Agostinoni, *Il Fucino* (1908).
E. T. S.

FUFIUS CALENUS, QUINTUS, who, as praetor, had supported Caesar in 59 B.C., was one of his lieutenants in the Civil War. On Caesar's return to Rome in July 47, he was elected consul, with Vatinius, for the remainder of the year. After Caesar's death he led the senatorial opposition to Cicero and early in 43 proposed that a conciliatory embassy be sent to Antony. On the formation of the Second Triumvirate, Calenus was given a military command in Italy; and when the triumvirs divided the Empire, he was left in Gaul, as Antony's representative, with eleven legions. He died not later than 40 (Dio Cassius 48. 20).
J. M. C.

FULGENTIUS, FABIUS PLANCIADES, a native of the province Africa, wrote probably about the end of the fifth century A.D. a number of works, of which four survive: *Mitologiarum libri tres*, *Expositio Vergilianae continentiae secundum philosophos moralis*, *De Aetatibus mundi et hominis*, and *Expositio sermonum antiquorum*. The first is a dialogue between the Muse Calliope and the author, professing to discover the true sense of various old myths. The conclusions are sometimes based on fancy etymologies and seem to be derived mainly from scholia; the work is in general careless. In the second the Virgil of the *Aeneid* is alone regarded, the Muses and Virgil himself being introduced in dialogue. The work is a rather silly allegory. The third is based principally on Bible history, but that of the world in general is covered in fourteen books and twenty-three periods: the whole production is worthy of the others. The fourth is a study of a number of rare Latin words, illustrated by references to authors who used them, but here also carelessness rules. It is fairly widely held that this Fulgentius is to be identified with the bishop of Ruspe, from whom various theological works of considerable importance have come down to us. *See also* MYTHOGRAPHERS (ad fin.).

Ed. R. Helm (Teubner, 1898); Christian works: Migne *PL* lxv; O. Friebel, *Fulgentius der Mythograph u. Bischof* (1911), on the language.
A. S.

FULLING. Both in Greece and Rome, the fuller—κναφεύς, *fullo*—played the part of our laundryman. His business was to collect the soiled woollen garments which were the common wear, clean them, raise the surface with a carding comb, and finally dress them with fuller's earth. The ancients had no soap, and the cleaning process was sometimes performed by using various alkalis—νίτρον, κονία—but more often by urine. The garments were trodden under foot in a bath of this liquid, and on removal were purified with sulphur.
F. A. W.

FULVIA, the daughter of M. Fulvius Bambalio and wife of (1) Clodius, (2) Curio, and (3) Antony (45 or earlier). She played an active part in the political campaign against Octavian which resulted in the Perusine War. After the fall of Perusia she escaped to Greece, where she died in the same year (40 B.C.). Fulvia was an ambitious woman of strong character, a precursor of the imperial women of the succeeding epoch. Among her five children were Antyllus and Iullus Antonius (q.v. 7 and 8).

Cicero, *Letters* and *Philippics*; Plutarch, *Antony*; Appian, *BCiv.* bks. 3–5; Dio Cassius, bks. 45–8. Drumann–Groebe, *Gesch. Roms,* ii. 310–13.   G. W. R.

FULVIUS (1) FLACCUS, QUINTUS, as consul I (237 B.C.) fought against the Gauls in north Italy; censor(231); consul II (224) he temporarily subdued the Boii; *praetor urbanus* in 215 and again *extra ordinem* in 214 to guard Rome; *magister equitum* (213). As consul III (212) he captured Hanno's camp near Beneventum, thus cutting off supplies from Capua, which he then besieged and captured as proconsul (211); proconsul in Campania (210); consul IV (209), he won over some Lucanian hill-towns. He served again as proconsul (208–207), opposed Scipio's African expedition (205), and died soon after-wards.   H. H. S.

FULVIUS (2) NOBILIOR, MARCUS (*cos.* 189 B.C.), the victor over Aetolia, was curule aedile in 196, praetor in 193 in Spain, subduing Oretania and Car-petania (193–192), and as consul in 189 defeated the Aetolians, capturing Ambracia and sending its art treasures to Rome. In 188 he won Cephallenia, taking Same, and intervened between the Achaeans and Sparta. He triumphed, despite complaints about Ambracia, building the temple of Hercules Musarum. Censor in 179 with M. Aemilius Lepidus, he reformed the *Comitia Centuriata* and carried out a large building programme. A patron of Greek culture (Ennius accompanied him to Aetolia), he was attacked by Cato. One son was consul in 159, another consul in 153 at Numantia.

Livy 35. 7 and 22; 37. 50; 38; 39. 4–5; 40. 45–6 and 51–2; Polyb. 21. 25 ff.; De Sanctis, *Stor. Rom.* iv. 1, pp. 210, 456, 605.
                                                                              A. H. McD.

FULVIUS (3) FLACCUS, QUINTUS (*cos.* 179 B.C.), son of (1) above, was curule aedile in 184. As praetor in Spain in 182 he opened the campaigns against the Celtiberians (182–180) which led to the settlement of Ti. Sempronius Gracchus. Consul in 179 in Liguria, he became censor in 174, repatriating Latins in Rome and controlling the *equites*. In 173 he dedicated a temple to Fortuna Equestris, after despoiling the temple of Hera Lacinia in Croton. He committed suicide in 172. It is doubtful whether he built the Via Fulvia. A fine general and conservative senator, his career marks the Fulvian predominance after Scipio Africanus.

Livy 40; 41. 27; 42. 2 and 10; Appian, *Hisp.* 42. De Sanctis, *Stor. Rom.* iv. 1, pp. 420, 460, 608; F. Münzer, *Röm. Adelsparteien und Adelsfamilien* (1920), 199.   A. H. McD.

FULVIUS (4) FLACCUS, MARCUS (*cos.* 125 B.C.), a nephew of (3) above, was a prominent member of the Gracchan reform-party. Little is known of his career till he became a member of the Gracchan Agrarian Commission (130). As consul in 125 he unsuccessfully brought forward the first proposal to admit the Italians generally to the Roman franchise, and was sent to help Massilia against the Ligurians, over whom he triumphed. He went in 122 to help C. Gracchus in colonizing Carthage. In the final struggle against Opimius, he was the most violent of the Gracchan leaders; he and his son were killed in the popular rising.   M. H.

FULVIUS, *see also* MACRIANUS, PLAUTIANUS.

FUNDANIUS, GAIUS, unrivalled in witty comedy according to Horace, *Sat.* 1. 10. 40–3 (cf. Porphyr. ad loc.). Belonging to Maecenas' circle, he is imagined to describe Nasidienus' dinner (*Sat.* 2. 8. 19).

FUNDITORES, *see* ARMS AND ARMOUR (ROMAN).

FUNERARY PRACTICE, *see* DEAD (DISPOSAL OF).

FURIAE, Latin equivalent of Erinyes (q.v.), perhaps a translation (*furere*=ἐρινύειν, to rage like an Erinys). There is no proof of their existing in cult or unprompted popular belief; sometimes they are identified with the obscure goddess Fur(r)ina(q.v.), as Cicero, *Nat. D.* 3. 46.
                                                                              H. J. R.

FURIUS (1) ANTIAS (i.e. of Antium), AULUS (fl. 100 B.C.), friend of Lutatius Catulus (Cic. *Brut.* 132), epic poet influenced by Ennius and in turn influencing Virgil and Statius, cf. his 'pressatur pede pes' with Verg. *Aen.* 10. 361 and Stat. *Theb.* 8. 399). From his *Annales,* a national poem, Gellius (18. 11) quotes some hexameters.
Baehr. *FPR*; Morel, *FPL*.   J. W. D.

FURIUS (2) PHILUS, LUCIUS, the friend of Scipio Aemilianus, was consul in 136 B.C., commanding in Spain in the Numantine War; he handed over Mancinus (q.v.) to the Numantines. A prominent member of the Scipionic Circle, he may be the author of a work, probably antiquarian, including sacral formulae; he appears in Cicero's *De Republica*. His excellent Latin and literary style in speaking were noted.
Appian, *Hisp.* 83; Cicero, *Brut.* 108; *De Or.* 2. 154; Macrob. *Sat.* 3. 9. 6.   A. H. McD.

FURIUS, *see also* BIBACULUS, CAMILLUS, SCRIBONIANUS, TIMESITHEUS.

FURNITURE. Little Greek furniture has survived, owing to the perishable nature of the material, but the forms can be recovered from representations in art. They are few in number, the principal being: the throne (θρόνος), a high-backed chair for occasions of state; the chair (κλισμός) of lighter build, without arms, in general domestic use; the stool (δίφρος), four-legged, boxed, or folding (δίφρος ὀκλαδίας); the footstool (θρῆνυς), which might be square or oblong; the table (τράπεζα), always small and portable, on three legs and oblong or circular (τρίπους); the couch (κλίνη), used for dining as well as for sleeping; and the chest (κιβωτός, λάρναξ), in which clothes and bedding were stored. Rugs were used on the couches; in the fifth century their use as floor-coverings was considered effeminate, though the practice was known to Homer and became common in Hellenistic times. Utensils were piled on the floor or hung on the walls; lamps stood on shelves or in niches. The general effect to our eyes would be one of bareness and simplicity.

The Greek types are the basis of Etruscan and Roman furniture, and the greater luxury of these nations is evinced more in costliness of material than in novelty of form. Etruria introduced a new type of chair with rounded back resembling the modern arm-chair, and high candelabra of metal on which clusters of candles could be placed. Rome adapted these as lamp-stands. The Roman throne (*solium*), chair (*cathedra*), and stool (*sella*), follow Greek models; the couch (*lectus*) was either of Greek shape or was provided with a back, like a sofa. Sideboards and cupboards with drawers, sometimes used as book-cases, appear in Imperial times, together with new forms of the table (*mensa*) which was the typical object of domestic ostentation: Cicero gave a million sesterces for a table of citron wood.

G. M. A. Richter, *Ancient Furniture* (U.S.A. 1926); W. Deonna, *Délos,* fasc. xviii: *Le Mobilier délien* (1938).   F. N. P.

FURRINA (this form is preferable to **FURINA**), a divinity belonging to the earliest stratum of Roman religion; she possessed a grove, an annual festival (*Furrinalia,* 25 July), and a *flamen*, but as early as the last decades of the Republic her very name was forgotten save by a few individuals. The interpretation as *Furia* (in spite of Altheim, *History of Roman Religion*, 116 f.) rests upon a false analogy; the term *Nymphae Furrinae* appears to be late, although Furrina may have been a divinity of a spring or of springs. The location of her grove, on the slopes of the Janiculum near the Pons Sublicius, is indicated by the account of the death of C. Gracchus in 121 B.C. (Plut. *G. Gracch.* 17; Auctor, *De Vir. Ill.* 65; less precisely, Orosius 5. 12. 8), and fixed by epigraphical and other discoveries (P. Gauckler, *Le Sanctuaire syrien du Janicule*, 1912); these have established the existence of springs and the fact that under the Empire the traditional worship became almost totally ousted by Oriental cults. Cicero, *QFr.* 3. 1. 4, mentions another shrine near Arpinum.   A. W. Van B.

FURTUM. In the developed Roman law this term embraced different actions qualified as theft according to the elastic definition in Paul. *Dig.* 47. 2. 1. 3. (= *Inst. Iust.* 4. 1. 1): 'contrectatio (handling) rei fraudulosa lucri faciendi gratia', where *res* is understood also in the sense of possession or use of another's goods (as e.g. when a depositee uses the deposit). The penalties prescribed in the XII Tables, which combined the customary system of private justice with voluntary composition, were differentiated according to the gravity of the act and the age of the thief: they allowed a thief to be killed by night, but by day only when the wrong-doer made use of arms. The ancient distinction between *furtum manifestum* (when the thief was caught in the act) and *nec manifestum* remained in the law of the Republic and the Principate, in spite of praetorian reforms which dealt with the *furtum* as a private delict (*see* LAW AND PROCEDURE, ROMAN, III), and exposed the thief to a twofold prosecution: (*a*) for a penalty (the double or the quadruple of the value of the stolen object), by means of an *actio furti*, which might be initiated by any interested person (e.g. the *bonae fidei* possessor); (*b*) for restitution of the stolen object, whether by the normal procedure for the protection of property or by a special action, *condictio furtiva*.

P. Huvelin, *Études sur le furtum* i (1915); H. F. Jolowicz, *Digest* xlvii. 2, *De Furtis* (1940).   A. B.

FUSCUS, CORNELIUS, of a senatorial family, adopted the equestrian career, 'quietis cupidine', though of a dashing and adventurous character (Tac. *Hist.* 2. 86). He was a partisan of Galba in A.D. 68 and was rewarded by him with the procuratorship of Illyricum, in which function he actively helped the Flavian generals to invade Italy. Later, as Prefect of the Guard he was entrusted with the conduct of the war against the Dacians; he crossed the Danube and penetrated into Dacia (86 or 87), but met with a signal defeat and lost his life (Dio 67. 6; Jordanes, *Getica* 13. 76). The altar at Adam-Klissi (q.v.) has been connected with him, without much reason (cf. *CAH* xi. 670).

R. Syme, *AJPhil.* 1937, 7.   R. S.

G

GABII, an ancient Latin city twelve miles east of Rome (Strabo 5. 239), nowadays *Castiglione*. Prehistoric finds do not contradict the story of its foundation by Alba Longa (Verg. *Aen.* 6. 773). Its resistance to Tarquin, separate treaty with Rome, and special role in augural practices prove its early importance (Livy 1. 53 f.; Dion. Hal. 4. 53; Varro *Ling.* 5. 33). After 493 B.C. Gabii appears as Rome's ally but was possibly sacked in the Latin War (Livy 3. 8; 6. 21; Macrob. *Sat.* 3. 9. 13). By 50 B.C. it had become a village (Cic. *Planc.* 23. Record of Sulla's colony is suspect: *Lib. Colon.* p. 234). Nevertheless the poets exaggerate its desolation. Under the Empire Gabii was a prosperous *municipium* with celebrated baths and ornate Hadrianic buildings (*ILS* 272). Although still a bishopric in the ninth century, to-day only a temple (third century B.C.) remains. The Romans reputedly derived from Gabii the *cinctus Gabinus*, a particular mode of wearing the *toga* which was used in certain ceremonial rites (Serv. on *Aen.* 7. 612; Livy 5. 46).

T. Ashby, *BSR* i (1902), 180; G. Pinza, *Bull. Com. Arch.* xxxi (1903), 321.   E. T. S.

GABINIANUS, *see* JULIUS (6).

GABINIUS (1), AULUS, the grandson of a slave, served under Metellus in Macedonia in 149 B.C. Tribune in 139, he introduced the secret ballot in elections, against the influence of senatorial houses over their clients' votes.

Cicero, *Leg.* 3. 16. 35; Livy, *Epit. Oxyrh.* 193-4.   A. H. McD.

GABINIUS (2) AULUS, tribune 67 B.C., legislated usefully on provincials' rights, and after transferring Bithynia and Lucullus' legions to Glabrio, sponsored the *Lex de piratis persequendis* (*see* POMPEY), threatening to depose Trebellius, a fellow tribune who attempted veto. He served Pompey as legate in the East and in 58 as consul, when he incurred Cicero's lasting hatred by scorning his appeals for help. Clodius had bribed him with the province of Syria, which he administered competently, reorganizing Judaea and setting Antipater in power. But in 55 he restored Ptolemy Auletes, for a large bribe; in return for this, and for his alienation of the *publicani* (perhaps through his leniency to the provincials—Cic. *Prov. Cons.* 10), he had to face three prosecutions on his return in 54. Cicero called his acquittal for *maiestas* a 'lex impunitatis', but next month was shamefacedly defending him for *repetundae*; this time, however, Gabinius was condemned and went into exile, a third charge, for *ambitus*, being dropped. Recalled by Caesar, he fought for him in Illyricum (winter 48–47), but was besieged by barbarian tribes in Salonae, where he died. He was a typical *popularis* of the period, in character probably quite unlike the 'calamistratus saltator' persistently depicted by Cicero.

SOURCES (*a*) 67 B.C.: Cic. *Att.* 5. 21. 12; 6. 2. 7; *QFr.* 2. 11. 3; Plut. *Pomp.* 25; Dio 36. 23; Asconius, 63 KS; Cic. *Leg. Man.* 44; 52.
(*b*) LATER LIFE: Cicero passim, and esp. *Red. Sen.*, *Sest.*, *Prov. Cons.*, *Rab. Post.*, and the letters of 54–53; [Caesar] *BAlex.* 42–3; Strabo 796.   G. E. F. C.

GADES, the oldest extant urban settlement in Spain, on a promontory south of the Baetis (*Guadalquivir*) estuary. The traditional foundation by Tyrian colonists *c.* 1100 B.C., and its early relations with Samian and Phocaean traders, are open to doubt. In the sixth century B.C. it appears as a Phoenician rival and eventual successor of the native town of Tartessus (q.v.). Gades served as the base of Hamilcar Barca's conquest of Spain, but later fell to the Romans (206 B.C.). As an ally of Rome it was permitted to continue its Phoenician coinage. Gades was associated with Metellus, who campaigned against Sertorius, and with Caesar, who started his Atlantic naval expedition from its harbour. Made an *oppidum civium Romanorum* by Caesar, Gades flourished for over three hundred years. Its wealth, proved by the five hundred citizens of equestrian rank in the first century A.D., was derived from trade. Tin from the north, minerals from the upper Baetis, olive-oil, wine, wool, and fish were exported. Its most famous citizens were the Cornelii Balbi and Columella. J. J. Van N.

GAEA (Γαῖα) or **GE** (Γῆ), the Earth, conceived as a vaguely personal goddess. It may be that in the earliest times she, like Tellus (q.v.), was simply the power or *mana* resident in that parcel of earth which the particular group of worshippers tilled or otherwise used; but as far back as our records go she is the Earth in general, or a goddess resident in and governing it. Her cult can be traced in a number of places, though in most of them she has been superseded by a more definitely personal power, chthonian or other. At Delphi she was the original holder of the oracular shrine (Aesch. *Eum.* 2), a statement which there is no reason to doubt, as it is supported by sundry other traditions and by the fact that Apollo is said to have killed Python, a serpent and therefore a creature of earth (he actually gave the oracles, Hyg. *Fab.* 140. 1), before he could take over the holy place; cf. APOLLO. Her well-supported identity or close connexion with Themis (q.v.; Aesch. loc. cit. and *Prom.* 209-10) is to be explained by that goddess's original nature as simply 'the fixed or firm one' and not an abstraction (see Farnell, op. cit. inf. 12 ff.). For more or less probable identifications of her with other figures, see ibid. 19 ff. One of her most characteristic functions is as a witness to oaths (as *Il.* 3. 278), because she must know what is done on her surface.

In mythology she is the offspring of Chaos, or at least comes into being after it. Heaven (Οὐρανός) is her child and husband, and their offspring, besides such things as seas and mountains, are the Titans, Cyclopes, and Hecatoncheires (qq.v.). After her separation from Uranus (cf. KRONOS) she bore the Erinyes and Giants (qq.v.), being fertilized by the blood from his mutilation; later she produced Typhon (q.v.), whose father was Tartarus (Hesiod, *Theog.* 117 ff.; 820 ff.). This is a systematized account of the wedding of Sky and Earth; there are many legends ultimately to the same effect, e.g. the union of Zeus and Semele (*see* DIONYSUS) and many more children of Earth, as Erichthonius (*see* ATHENA), and Python in some accounts.

Apart from actual cult of Earth as a goddess, antiquity had its share of beliefs concerning her, as, e.g., the source (probably) of the life of new-born children, hence the Roman custom of placing them on the ground; the author of the potency ascribed to sundry herbs, and so forth. See, in general, A. Dieterich and E. Fehrle, *Mutter Erde*³ (1925); for herbs, A. Delatte, *Herbarius*² (1938).

Farnell, *Cults* iii, pp. 1 ff. (cult); Drexler in Roscher's *Lexikon*, s.v. (mythology, etc.). H. J. R.

GAETULICUS, *see* LENTULUS (9).

GAISERIC, *see* VANDALS.

GAIUS(1), the Emperor, 'Caligula' (GAIUS JULIUS CAESAR GERMANICUS; A.D. 12-41), son of Germanicus and Agrippina, born at Antium on 31 Aug. A.D. 12. In 14-16 he was on the Rhine with his parents and, because of the military boots which he wore, was nicknamed Caligula ('Baby Boots') by the soldiers. In 18-19 he was with his parents in the East and, after Germanicus' death in 19, lived in Rome with his mother until her arrest in 29, then successively with Livia and Antonia minor, until 32, when he joined Tiberius on Capreae. After the death of his brother Drusus in 33 he was the only surviving son of Germanicus and, with Tiberius (q.v. 2) Gemellus—Claudius' claims not being considered seriously—next in succession to the Principate. He was elected *pontifex* in 31 and was *quaestor* two years later,

but received no other training in public life. Tiberius appointed Gaius and Tiberius Gemellus joint heirs to his property, having already indicated in language typically obscure that he expected Gaius to succeed to the Principate. Strongly supported by Macro, prefect of the Praetorian Guard, Gaius was acclaimed emperor (16 March 37), Tiberius' will being declared invalid by the Senate, so that Gaius might inherit the whole of his property. In the early months of his rule Gaius honoured the memory of his mother, father, and brothers and spoke abusively of Tiberius. Antonia, a restraining influence, died on 1 May 37. In October Gaius was seriously ill, and it is possible that Philo (*Leg.* 14; 22) is right in thinking that his mind was unhinged as a result (see, however, Balsdon, op. cit. inf., 212 ff.). On recovering he executed, some time before 24 May 38, both Macro and Tiberius Gemellus. In Jan. 39 Gaius quarrelled seriously with the Senate, revised his attitude to Tiberius' memory, and became more autocratic. The autumn and winter of 39-40 he spent in Gaul and on the Rhine; at Moguntiacum he forestalled a conspiracy against his life, whose leader, Cn. Cornelius Lentulus Gaetulicus, was executed. It is possible that at this time two new legions were raised (XV and XXII Primigeniae) and that Gaius had intended to invade Germany or Britain. The intention, if serious, was abandoned, either because of military indiscipline or because of Gaius' instability of character (Suetonius 24. 3; 39; 43-9; Dio Cass. 59. 21-3; 25. 1-5; cf. Balsdon, op. cit. 58-95 and *JRS* xxiv. 13-18). After his return to Rome (in ovation, on 31 Aug. 40) Gaius was in constant danger of assassination, governed with much cruelty, and was murdered in the Palace on 24 Jan. 41. His (fourth) wife, Milonia Caesonia, and daughter (his only child) were also murdered.

The government of Gaius was more autocratic than that of earlier emperors. He was consul four times, in 37 (suffect), 39, 40 (sole consul), 41; on the first occasion for two months, on the last two for a few days only. In many respects he appears to have deserted the Augustan form of principate in favour of monarchy of the Hellenistic type; this, at least, is the easiest explanation of his treatment of his sisters, especially Drusilla, with whom he was suspected of committing incest and whom he consecrated after her death. For himself he accepted extravagant honours, which came close to deification, and, though in face of opposition he desisted from his intention to set up a statue of himself in the temple at Jerusalem, he was responsible for serious unrest among the Jews both in Alexandria and in Judaea.

ANCIENT SOURCES. Books 7 and 8 of the *Annals*, in which Tacitus described the principate of Gaius, being lost, we depend on Suetonius, *Gaius Caligula*, Dio Cassius, bk. 59, and Josephus *AJ* 18. 6. 8. 205-19. 2. 5. 111 (with a detailed account of the murder of Gaius and an estimate of his character and principate, probably derived from Cluvius Rufus: see M. P. Charlesworth, *Camb. Hist. Journ.* iv (1933), 105-19). For detailed knowledge of Gaius' relations with the Jews of Alexandria we have contemporary evidence in Philo, *Contra Flaccum* (edited by H. Box, 1939), and *Legatio ad Gaium* (Philo was himself a member of the embassy to Gaius which he describes). See also, on the sources, A. Momigliano, *Rend. Linc.* serie sesta, viii (1932), 293-336.

MODERN LITERATURE: J. P. V. D. Balsdon, *The Emperor Gaius (Caligula)* (1934), with full bibliography; M. P. Charlesworth, *CAH* x. 653-66. J. P. B.

GAIUS (2) (2nd c. A.D.), one of the most renowned Roman jurists, though little is known of his personality. His gentile name and cognomen are unknown, likewise his origin (perhaps a Greek province) and studies. Born under Hadrian, he lived at Rome as a teacher and writer (about 100 books) without having the *ius respondendi* or any official charge. A determined follower of the Sabinian School (*see* SABINUS 2), he sometimes rejects their point of view and takes into consideration opinions of the opposite school. In his own times he was not much appreciated: it is a striking fact that he was never cited by the later jurists, not even by Paulus and Ulpian who must have known and used his works. On the other hand, Justinian's compilers excerpted him freely, for his authority had been officially established by the Law of Citation (A.D. 426). Justinian seems to have had a special predilection for Gaius, for he frequently calls him 'Gaius noster', and by his order Gaius' standard work, the *Institutes*, was used as the basis for the composition of the imperial *Institutiones*.

WORKS: *Ad edictum provinciale*, a long commentary in thirty-two books, which has led some scholars to believe that he was a provincial jurist; *Ad edictum praetoris urbani*; *Ad legem XII tabularum*; *De verborum obligationibus*; *Res cottidianae sive Aurea*; *Liber singularis regularum*; and several monographs. His principal work, which procured him great renown, was his *Institutionum commentarii quattuor*, written about 161. Until they were discovered (1816) on a *codex rescriptus* at Verona (probably of the 5th c.), the *Institutes* were known only by a score of fragments in the *Digest* and the *Lex Romana Visigothorum*. The Veronese manuscript containing the fourth book of the *Institutes* (till then unknown) furnished quite new details on the Roman formulary procedure. The genuineness of the Veronese text has been severely attacked in recent years, but without sufficient reasons. The manuscript may be corrupt and completed here and there by additional notes (glosses) by later users of the work, but unquestionably the criticism applied to the text of Gaius by some modern authors, by which a gloss is discovered in nearly every paragraph, is carried much too far. The new fragments of the *Institutes* found in Egypt in 1933 on a few parchment sheets, and belonging apparently to the fourth century, confirm this opinion. It should not be forgotten that the text-book of Gaius, being destined for beginners, had not to be so perfect in its composition as his modern critics demand; on the other side Gaius' qualities as a writer suffice to explain the deficiencies and defects of the work. Being more of a compiler than an original author, now and then rather superficial and generally not of an independent mind, he was a faithful copyist and reporter of other jurists' opinions; but his language is clear and smooth (in spite of not infrequent grecisms), his formulations are elegant and clear, his exposition plain and perspicuous, and the few mistakes in historical discussions cannot diminish the high educational value of the work, which will always remain unique as a source of our knowledge of classical Roman law.

B. Kübler, *PW*, s.v. 'Gaius'; H. Fitting *Alter und Folge der Schriften röm. Juristen*[2] (1908), 49 ff.; F. Kniep, *Der Rechtsgelehrte Gaius* (1910); Arangio-Ruiz, *Storia del diritto rom.* (1937), 271 ff., 285 ff.
Editions of the *Institutes*: G. Studemund and P. Krüger (1923); B. Kübler 7th ed. in Huschke's *Iurispr. anteiust.* (1935); G. Baviera in the Italian ed. of *Fontes iuris rom. anteiust.* (1st ed. 1909, 2nd ed. 1940).
The new Gaius (MS. now in Florence): First edition, V. Arangio-Ruiz, *Papiri della Soc. Ital.* xi (1933), no. 1182; cf. *Bull. Ist. Dir. Rom.* xlii (1935), 571 ff.; E. Levy, *Sav. Zeitschr.* liv (1937), 258 ff.; Fr. de Zulueta, *JRS* xxiv (1934), 168 ff., xxv (1935), 19 ff., with copious citations of the newest literature; W. W. Buckland, 'Reflections suggested by the new fragments of Gaius', *Juridical Review* 1936, with admirable observations on the authenticity of the Veronese Gaius. A. B.

GALATEA (Γαλάτεια, perhaps 'milk-white'), name of a sea-nymph, first in Homer (*Il.* 18. 45); her legend was apparently first told by Philoxenus (see Bergk, *PLG*[4] iii. 609 ff.). Polyphemus (*see* CYCLOPS) loved her, and wooed her uncouthly; the story is a favourite especially with pastoral writers (Theocr. 11; cf. 6. 6 ff.; Bion, fr. 12 Wilamowitz-Moellendorff, Ἐπιτάφιος Βίωνος, 58 ff.; Verg. *Ecl.* 9. 39 ff.; cf. 2. 19 ff.; 7. 37 ff.; but particularly Ov. *Met.* 13. 738 ff.). In this, the earliest surviving passage which adds anything important to the story, Galatea loved a youth, Acis, son of Faunus (Pan?) and a river-nymph. Together they listened in hiding to Poly-

phemus' love-song, but when he had finished he rose to go and caught sight of them. Galatea dived into the sea, but Polyphemus pursued Acis and hurled a huge rock at him. As it fell on him and crushed him, Galatea turned him into a river, which bore his name ever after. The whole may well be a local Sicilian tale. The resemblance between Galatea's name and Γαλάτης, a Gaul, seems to underlie a less-known version in which she finally accepted Polyphemus' attentions and had by him a son, Galas or Galates, ancestor of the Gauls (see App. *Ill.* 2)—mere pseudo-historical or pseudo-mythical aetiology. H. J. R.

GALATIA is used, when applied to territory in the East, in two senses. (1) As the name of a territory in central Asia Minor, comprising parts of what was formerly Phrygia and Cappadocia, occupied and settled by a Celtic people which crossed the Hellespont in 278 B.C., and after much raiding and plundering were finally penned in an area stretching from the Sangarius to east of the Halys by Attalus I of Pergamum in 230. Here they continued to harass their neighbours; after the battle of Magnesia Rome sent Manlius Vulso to subdue them, and afterwards used them as a check on Pergamum. In the Mithridatic Wars they remained faithful to Rome. Their territory was organized on the Celtic tribal basis, the three tribes Tolistobogii, Tectosages, and Trocmi occupying separate areas around their respective capitals Pessinūs, Ancyra, and Tavium, and each tribe being divided into four parts under tetrarchs. The council of the three tribes met at a place called Drynemetum, and tried cases of murder. The Galatians maintained their Celtic character throughout the Imperial period, and when visited by St. Jerome were still speaking a Celtic language.

(2) As the name of a Roman province, formed in 25 B.C., incorporating the kingdom of Amyntas, which comprised besides Galatia proper parts of Phrygia, Lycaonia, and Pisidia, and possibly Pamphylia. Other territories in Paphlagonia and Pontus were afterwards added to the province, which was normally governed by a praetorian *legatus* until about A.D. 72, when Cappadocia and Armenia Minor were united with Galatia, and the combined province was put under a *legatus* with consular rank. Galatia was reduced in size, and again put under a praetorian *legatus*, by Trajan, and still further diminished about A.D. 137. Under Diocletian the province shrank to the size of Galatia proper, with a strip of Lycaonia. The two principal cities of the province Galatia were Ancyra (the metropolis) and Pisidian Antioch.

It is disputed whether the 'Galatia' of St. Paul's Epistle to the Galatians refers to Galatia proper (the 'North-Galatian theory') or to the province Galatia, in whose Lycaonian and Phrygian regions St. Paul founded the churches mentioned in Acts (the 'South-Galatian theory').

Jones, *Eastern Cities*, ch. 4; F. Stähelin, *Geschichte der kleinasiatischen Galater*[2] (1907). W. M. C.

GALBA (1), the Emperor (SERVIUS SULPICIUS GALBA, *c.* 3 B.C.–A.D. 69), son of C. Sulpicius Galba and Mummia Achaica, was adopted by Livia Ocellina, second wife of his father. He was highly esteemed by Augustus and Tiberius, and was a favourite of Livia, as afterwards of Gaius and Claudius. Governor of Aquitania, consul (A.D. 33), legate of Upper Germany, proconsul of Africa (45), and from 60 governor of Hispania Tarraconensis, he had an exceptionally brilliant record to his credit, when in 68 Vindex invited him to replace Nero. He made his troops proclaim him only a legate of the Senate and of the Roman people. He had one legion and enrolled another of provincials (afterwards VII Gemina). The dangers inherent in the fall of Vindex were removed by Nero's death. Nymphidius (q.v.) Sabinus with the praetorians declared for Galba, who took the title of Caesar and went to Rome with Otho, governor of

Lusitania. Subsequent threats from Nymphidius Sabinus and Clodius (q.v. 2) Macer were removed. Galba had the mind of an honest, but suspicious, administrator: 'omnium consensu capax imperii nisi imperasset'. His avarice was notorious. He did not pay the donative promised to the soldiers. A commission was appointed to recover Nero's presents. He was unwise in sending his Spanish troops to Pannonia. Early in Jan. 69 the troops of the Rhine declared against him. He adopted a certain L. Calpurnius Piso Frugi Licinianus as his successor, and offended Otho, who had hoped for that position. Otho organized a conspiracy among the praetorians, and Galba was killed on 15 Jan. 69.

SOURCES: Tacitus, *Historiae*; Suetonius, *Galba* (ed. G. W. Mooney, 1930); Plutarch, *Galba* (ed. E. G. Hardy, 1890); Dio Cassius, bks. 63-4; Josephus, *BJ* 4. Tacitus, Suetonius, Plutarch mainly follow the same author (the usual identification with the Elder Pliny is very doubtful).

MODERN LITERATURE: Fluss, *PW* iv A. 772; B. W. Henderson, *Civil War and Rebellion in the Roman Empire* (1908); G. H. Stevenson, *CAH* x. 808; P. Zancan, *La crisi del principato nell' anno 69 d. C.* (1939).
A. M.

GALBA (2) **MAXIMUS**, PUBLIUS SULPICIUS, was elected consul for 211 B.C. without having held any curule magistracy. He defended Rome against Hannibal's surprise attack. As proconsul (210-206) in Greece he conducted the First Macedonian War against Philip of Macedon, leading the first Roman fleet into the Aegean, where he captured Aegina (210); he achieved little else, and the main burden of war was gradually transferred to Rome's Greek allies. As consul II (200) he conducted the Second Macedonian War. Landing at Apollonia he planned to invade Macedonia from the west. He worsted Philip at Ottolobus and forced the pass of Banitza, but retired to Illyria for the winter (199); this campaign, though marked by no great military success, led the Aetolians to support Rome. Galba served as legate to Flamininus (197), as one of the ten senatorial commissions appointed to help Flamininus settle Greece (196), and later as ambassador to Antiochus (193). H. H. S.

GALBA (3), SERVIUS SULPICIUS, military tribune in 168 B.C., opposing Aemilius Paullus' triumph in 167, was praetor in 151 in Further Spain, where in subduing the Lusitanians he treacherously massacred a number who had sued for peace (151-150). A prosecution against him in 149, supported by Cato, failed. He was consul in 144. His oratory set new rhetorical standards in emotional effect.

Livy 45. 35 ff.; *Per.* 48-9; Appian, *Hisp.* 58-60; Cicero, *Brut.* 22. 86. De Sanctis, *Stor. Rom.* iv. 1. 480; H. Malcovati, *Or. Rom. Frag.* i. 76, 108, 203, 229.
A. H. McD.

GALBA (4), GAIUS SULPICIUS (son of (3) above), an orator whose peroration (*Epilogus*) defending himself on trial for mismanagement in the Jugurthine War was a choice specimen to be committed to memory in Cicero's boyhood (*Brut.* 127).

GALBA (5), SERVIUS SULPICIUS (grandson (?) of (3) above), was legate of Caesar in Gaul. He conducted a not entirely successful campaign (Caes. *BGall.* 3. 1) to open up the road leading from the Valais into Italy (57 B.C.). Candidate for the consulship of 49, he was not elected. Conspirator in 44 against Caesar, in 43 he fought in the battle of Forum Gallorum, which he described to Cicero (*Fam.* 10. 30).

F. Münzer, *PW* iv A. 769.
A. M.

GALBA (6), GAIUS SULPICIUS, grandfather of the Emperor Galba, wrote an historical work cited by Juba.

Peter, *HRRel.* ii. 41.

GALEN of Pergamum (A.D. 129-? 199) in a spectacular career rose from gladiator-physician in Asia Minor to court-physician in the Rome of Marcus Aurelius. Well educated in his native town, he travelled later, studied in Greece and Alexandria, started practising in Pergamum in 157, and went to Rome in 162. He had become very famous when he left there in 166, only to return again from Pergamum in 169. He then stayed in Rome until his death. Writing all his life, he began with philosophical treatises and ended with medical books.

As philosopher and as physician Galen was an eclectic dogmatist. Plato and Hippocrates were his gods; Aristotle he held in sincere respect. But in spite of his belief in authorities he was anxious to form his own judgements, and his personality, therefore, takes the foreground in all his actions and writings. His knowledge was equally great in theory and practice; he excelled in diagnosis and prognosis and was a remarkably good teacher. His system is the ambitious effort to comprise the whole of medicine, the usual specialization of that time being rejected. Yet Galen realized that the physician has to deal with individuals, and that medicine can never be expressed adequately in general statements.

Galen was particularly productive as anatomist and physiologist. Performing dissections carefully in all their details, he collected and corrected the results of earlier generations and added many new facts. His physiological research based on experiment was masterly, particularly in the field of neurology; he proved that the arteries as well as the veins carry blood. His pathology was founded on the doctrine of the four humours; here he was most strongly influenced by speculative ideas. His pharmacological and dietetic doctrines were the codification of what had been accomplished in these fields.

Galen's monotheistic views, his ardent belief in teleology, his religious attitude—even anatomy to him was praise and veneration of God—foreshadow the coming Middle Ages. Yet his dominant influence on later generations, comparable only to that of Aristotle, is really due to his having made accessible through his work, as he had claimed, all parts of medicine, just as Trajan had made accessible through his roads all parts of Italy. *See* ANATOMY AND PHYSIOLOGY, paras. 12-21; MEDICINE, § 2.

BIBLIOGRAPHY

TEXTS. *Opera omnia*, C. G. Kühn, i-xx (1821-33), the only complete edition, unreliable text. Published by Teubner: *Scripta minora* i-iii (1884-93); *Institutio logica* (1896); *De victu attenuante* (1898); *De temperamentis* (1904); *De usu partium* (1907-9); *Historia Philosophica* in Diels, *Doxographi Graeci* (1879). Modern editions of various writings in dissertations etc. listed, F. Überweg-K. Praechter, *Die Philosophie d. Altertums* (1926), 558, and A. Rehm-K. Vogel, *Exakte Wissenschaften*, Gercke-Norden ii. 5 (1933). E. Wenkebach, *Optimus medicus philosophus*; H. Schöne, *De septimanis, Quell. u. Stud. z. Gesch. d. Naturw. u. d. Med.* (1933); for *De septimanis*, cf. R. Walzer, *Riv. degli Studi Orient.* (1935); E. Wenkebach, *Protrepticus, Quell. u. Stud. z. Gesch. d. Naturw. u. d. Med.* (1935) and *De parvae pilae exercitio, Archiv f. Gesch. d. Medizin* (1938). In preparation *CMG*, published V. iv. 1+2; ix. 1+2; x. 1, 2 (1+2); Suppl. 1, 2. Fragments, Kühn, i, p. clxxii. Translation from Arabic into German cf. Rehm–Vogel, loc. cit.; besides M. Meyerhof–F. Schacht, 'Über die medizinischen Namen'. *Berl. Abh.* (1931); cf. also *Galen on Medical Experience*, ed. and tr. R. Walzer (1944).

TRANSLATIONS. With text, *On Natural Faculties* (A. J. Brock, Loeb). Ch. Daremberg, *Œuvres anatomiques, physiologiques et médicales* i-ii (1854-6).

WORKS. List of writings, Christ-Schmid, ii⁶ (1925), s.v. 'Galen'; cf. H. Diels, *Sitz. Berl.* 1908. In Arabic: R. Walzer, *Sitz. Berl.* 1934. Spurious books, Kühn, i, p. clviii; M. Meyerhof, *Sitz. Berl.* 1928. Epitome of works, J. R. Coxe, *The Writings of Hippocrates and G.* (U.S.A., 1846). Chronology of writings, J. Ilberg, *Rh. Mus.* 1889 and 1897.

LITERATURE: General: J. S. Prendergast, *Enc. Brit.*¹⁴ s.v. 'Galen'; J. Mewaldt, *PW* vii. 578; W. A. Greenhill, *Dict. of Greek and Roman Biography and Mythol.* (1846), s.v. 'Galen'. Life. M. Meyerhof, *Arch. f. Gesch. d. Med.* 1929. Influence on G.'s writings, J. Walsh, *Annals Med. Hist.* 1927 f. G. as critic, L. O. Bröcker, *Rh. Mus.* 1885. G.'s philosophy, Überweg-Praechter (1926), 177 ff. Medical views, T. C. Allbutt, *Greek Medicine in Rome* (1921). Anatomy, F. Ullrich, *Die anatomische u. vivisektorische Technik d. G.*, Diss. Leipz. (1919). Physiology, Th. Meyer-Steineg, *Arch. f. Gesch. d. Med.* 1911; T. C. Allbutt, *CR* 1917. Biology, H. O. Taylor, *Greek Biology and Medicine* (1922), Ch. Singer, *A Short History of Biology* (1931). Gynaecology, J. Lachs, *Abh. z. Gesch. d. Med.* (1903). Laryngology, Gordon Holmes, *History of Laryngology* (1885). Practice, J. Ilberg, *Neue Jahrb.* 1905.
L. E.

GALERIUS(1), the Emperor (GAIUS GALERIUS VALERIUS MAXIMIANUS), was chosen as Caesar of the East by Diocletian in A.D. 293 and put away his wife to marry Diocletian's daughter, Valeria. Placed in charge of Illyricum and the north of Asia Minor Galerius spent a long and hard apprenticeship, beating back the barbarians and reclaiming land on the Danube. After settling the Carpi in Pannonia, he was called East to a greater task, the defence against Narses of Persia. Defeated at first near Carrhae, Galerius was treated with studied scorn by Diocletian, but given opportunity to repair his error. With strong reinforcements from the Balkans, he invaded Armenia, and gained a complete victory over Narses, capturing his concubines. A peace entirely favourable to Rome followed (298). Narses had lost the will to fight, and Diocletian discountenanced the large annexations that Galerius was disposed to make.

Galerius now began to insist on fuller recognition of his great labours and services. It was he above all others who drove Diocletian to persecute the Christians (303) and, during the illness of Diocletian in 304, intensified the persecution. Succeeding as Augustus of the East in 305, Galerius was nominally second to Constantius, actually superior, as both Caesars, Severus and Maximinus Daia were his men. When Constantius died (306) Galerius reluctantly accepted Constantine as Caesar of the West, but declined to recognize Maxentius and sent Severus, now Augustus of the West, against him. After the defeat and capture of Severus, he himself invaded Italy, but was forced to beat an ignominious retreat. Summoning Diocletian from his retirement, he made a new settlement of the Empire at Carnuntum (308), appointing Licinius Augustus and declaring Maxentius a public enemy. But Constantine and Daia refused the offered rank of 'filii Augustorum' and assumed the full imperial title. Falling ill in 309 Galerius relented so far as to issue an edict of partial toleration to the Christian Church. He died the year following, leaving the Church on the edge of triumph and the system of Diocletian on the brink of dissolution.

H. Mattingly, *CAH* xii, ch. 9. 329 ff.; Parker, *Roman World*, 229 ff., 272, 292 f., 308.   H. M.

GALERIUS (2) **TRACHALUS** (*cos.* A.D. 68), a recent orator mentioned by Quintilian. His lofty and lucid style were enhanced by a voice and delivery 'that would have done credit to the stage' (*Inst.* 10. 1. 119; 12. 5. 5 and 10. 11). The Emperor Otho employed him to compose speeches (Tac. *Hist.* 1. 90).   J. W. D.

GALERUS, *see* APEX.

GALINTHIAS (Γαλινθιάς, Anton. Liber. 29), or **GALANTHIS** (Γαλανθίς, Ov. *Met.* 9. 307), in mythology, a friend or servant of Alcmene (q.v.). When the latter was bearing Heracles, Eileithyia (and the Moirai) sat with hands clasped (and knees together), magically preventing delivery. Galinthias, perceiving this, ran out crying that Alcmene had borne a son; the goddess(es) leaped up in surprise and the charm was broken. In anger, they turned Galinthias into a lizard (Ovid) or weasel (Ant. Lib.).   H. J. R.

GALLI, *see* EUNUCHS, RELIGIOUS.

GALLIA, *see* GAUL.

GALLIC WARS is the name usually given to the campaigns by which Caesar completed the Roman conquest of Gaul (58–51 B.C.). It is uncertain whether this conquest had been premeditated by Caesar; but appeals for his intervention on behalf of one Gallic tribe against another, or against German intruders, involved him in campaigns beyond the existing Roman province in south Gaul, and drew him as far as the Rhine (*see*

AEDUI, ARIOVISTUS, HELVETII). At the end of 58 Caesar took up winter-quarters in north-east Gaul, an act foreshadowing a permanent Roman occupation of all Gaul. In 57 accordingly he had to meet preventive attacks by the tribes of northern Gaul (*see* BELGAE, NERVII); by his victories over these he brought northern France and Belgium under Roman control. In 56 Caesar had evidently resolved on the complete subjugation of Gaul, for in this year he forced the submission of the peoples on the Atlantic seaboard (*see* VENETI 2). It is uncertain whether the tribes of central Gaul at this time came to terms with him; but these were now ringed off within the Roman area of occupation, and Caesar at this stage considered the pacification of Gaul as complete.

In this belief Caesar spent the campaigning seasons of 55 and 54 in Germany and Britain. But sporadic revolts in northern Gaul kept him occupied throughout the winter of 54–53 and the following summer, and in 52 he was confronted by a formidable coalition of tribes in central Gaul under the leadership of Vercingetorix (q.v.). The duel between Caesar and Vercingetorix was the most critical event in the Roman conquest of Gaul. After repeated marches and counter-marches across central Gaul the issue still remained undecided, when Vercingetorix allowed Caesar to invest him in the fortress of Alesia (q.v.). The reduction of Alesia by famine and the capture of Vercingetorix finally broke Gallic resistance, and the local rebellions which flared up here and there in 51 strained Caesar's patience more than his resources.

The conquest of Gaul was accomplished by Caesar at a surprisingly low cost of men. The Gauls lost heavily in men and in treasure; but the estimate of Plutarch (*Caesar*, ch. 15), that their casualties amounted to one million killed and two millions captured, need not be taken literally. For the results of the conquest *see* GAUL.

Caesar, *De Bello Gallico commentarii* 1–7; Hirtius, *De Bello Gallico commentarius octavus*; Plutarch, *Caesar*, chs. 15–27.
T. Rice Holmes, *Caesar's Conquest of Gaul*[2] (1911); C. Jullian, *Histoire de la Gaule*, ii[4] (1921); iii[2] (1920); G. Veith, *Geschichte der Feldzüge C. Iulius Caesars* (1906); C. Hignett, *CAH* ix, ch. 13, and bibliography.   M. C.

GALLICUS, *see* RUTILIUS.

GALLIENUS, PUBLIUS LICINIUS EGNATIUS, son of Valerian, appointed Augustus by the Senate in A.D. 253. While his father lived, he commanded in the West and fought a series of successful campaigns against German tribes on the Rhine. In 258 he checked an invasion of Italy by the Alamanni at Milan. After the capture of Valerian (late 258?), the full burden fell on the son. Leaving the East to Macrianus, Ballista, and Odenathus, Gallienus successfully crushed two rebels, Ingenuus and Regalianus, in Illyricum (258–9). The revolt of Postumus (early 259?) detached Gaul and the West, and Saloninus, younger son of Gallienus, who had succeeded his brother Valerian II as Caesar in 257, was put to death. In 260 the Eastern armies revolted. But the two Macriani were destroyed, as they marched West, by Aureolus in Thrace, and Odenathus then defeated Quietus and Ballista in Emesa (261). The rising of Aemilium was crushed in Egypt, a military revolt in Byzantium was suppressed, and Gallienus celebrated his 'decennalia' with great pomp. An attempt to recover Gaul failed: Gallienus won a victory, but Aureolus did not press the pursuit. In the East, Odenathus of Palmyra made a successful attack on Persia, taking Ctesiphon, and was recognized by Gallienus as his vicegerent, but fell victim to a domestic plot in 267. Zenobia defeated the general, Heraclianus, whom Gallienus sent against her.

The great barbarian invasions, by land and sea, of Asia and Illyricum recommenced, after some years' interval, in 267. Gallienus gained a brilliant victory over the Goths at Naissus, but was recalled to Italy by the revolt of Aureolus, backed by Postumus. Gallienus defeated Aureolus and besieged him in Milan, but was murdered by his own staff, who chose Claudius to succeed him. A massacre of the friends of Gallienus in Rome followed.

The reign of Gallienus is notable for several reasons. By excluding senators from military commands, he broke the power of the *ordo* and earned its relentless hate. He developed a field army and an independent cavalry corps, based on Milan. He reversed his father's policy of persecution and granted recognition and peace to the Christian Church.

Later tradition has blackened his character and made of him the typical tyrant, cruel, lascivious, and inefficient. In point of fact, he brought the Empire, without complete disaster, through a grim succession of crises, and showed a sound understanding of the essential requirements of his age.

A. Alföldi, *CAH* xii, ch. 6; Parker, *Roman World*, 167 ff.   H. M.

GALLIO: Lucius Junius Novatus, brother of the philosopher Seneca, was adopted by the senator L. Junius Gallio, by which name he was then known. As proconsul of Achaea *c.* A.D. 52 (*SIG* ii³. 801) he refused to consider the case put by the Jews against St. Paul (Acts xviii. 12). He was consul at some unknown date. Seneca dedicated some works to him. After his brother's ruin he was compelled to commit suicide.

O. Rossbach, *PW* i. 2236; F. Jackson and K. Lake, *Beginnings of Christianity* v (1933), 462; E. Groag, *Röm. Reichsbeamten von Achaia* (1939), cols. 32 ff.   A. M.

GALLUS (1), Gaius Lucretius, praetor commanding the Roman fleet against Perseus in 171 B.C., destroyed Haliartus and captured Thisbe. He oppressed the Greek allies, e.g. Chalcis, and requisitioned corn, e.g. from Athens. Returning to adorn Antium with spoil, he was convicted and fined.

Livy 42. 48 and 63; 43. 4 and 6–8.   A. H. McD.

GALLUS (2), Gaius Sulpicius, the Roman astronomer, as military tribune under Aemilius Paullus, predicted the eclipse of the moon on 21 June 168 B.C., before Pydna. Consul in 166, in Liguria, he was envoy to Pergamum in 164. He wrote, or adapted, an astronomical work from Greek sources (Pliny, *HN* 2. 53 and 83).

De Sanctis, *Stor. Rom.* iv. 1. 369.   A. H. McD.

GALLUS (3), Gaius Cornelius (*c.* 69–26 B.C.), poet and politician, friend of Augustus, was born at Forum Iulii, possibly of a native Gallic family. He is said to have saved the farm of his friend Virgil. Servius' allegation that a first draft of Georgic 4 contained a eulogy of him is doubtful; but the tenth Eclogue is dedicated to him. In the war against Antony and Cleopatra, as general of Octavian, he guarded Africa, occupied Paraetonium, and contributed most to the victory. He was in consequence the first governor of Egypt, where he crushed two rebellions. He advanced beyond the First Cataract, received envoys of the Ethiopian king, and appointed a vassal-prince in the buffer-state of Triakontaschoinos. But his administration was bad, and his vanity is attested by an inscription at Philae (*ILS* 8995). Some other obscure reason contributed to his recall. He was condemned to banishment and committed suicide (26 B.C.).

Of Gallus' poetry only part of a line survives (Morel, *FPL* 99), unless we accept, as several scholars have done, the theory of F. Skutsch (*Aus Vergils Frühzeit*, 1901, and *Gallus und Vergil*, 1906) that he wrote the *Ciris* (see APPENDIX VERGILIANA). But whether that is his work or not, Gallus was outstanding among the *neoterici* (q.v.) of his age for his development of the love elegy. He wrote after the Alexandrian manner of Euphorion and according to Servius translated into Latin some of his epyllia. Imbued with the traditions of pastoral elegy and influenced by the love-stories of Parthenius, he

transferred the theme of wounded love from mythological or bucolic settings to the real and personal sufferings of a deserted lover (cf. Verg. *Ecl.* 10). In his four lost books of love elegies 'Lycoris' (i.e. the coquette mime-actress 'Cytheris', a stage-name for Volumnia) was the heroine (Ovid *Am.* 1. 15. 29–30; *Tr.* 2. 445; Serv. ad Verg. *Ecl.* 10 ad init.). Echoes of his poems are woven by Virgil into the tenth Eclogue, where it is felt poetically appropriate to introduce him as an Arcadian shepherd. In *Ecl.* 6. 64–73 the obeisance of the Muses and the presentation to him of the reed pipes are designed to mark his eminence in pastoral poetry. *See* ELEGIAC POETRY *and* EPYLLION.

PIR², C 1369; E. Norden, *Sitz. preussisch. Akad.* 1934, 627; R. Syme, *CQ* 1938, 39; A. Rostagni, *La letteratura di Roma repubblicana ed augustea* (1939), 306; 348–51; Schanz-Hosius, §§ 270–2; J. Hubaux, *Les Thèmes bucoliques dans la poésie latine* (1930), 87 ff.   A. M. and J. W. D.

GALLUS (4), Marcus Aelius, Prefect of Egypt after Gallus (3) above and before C. Petronius. Influenced by prevalent and exaggerated reports of the wealth of Arabia Felix, Augustus instructed him to invade that land. The expedition, which lasted two years (25 and 24 B.C.), was a complete failure; the blame was conveniently laid upon the treachery of the Nabatean Syllaeus. Aelius Gallus wrote upon medical topics and was a personal friend of Strabo the geographer. It is highly probable that he adopted the son of the distinguished Roman knight L. Seius Strabo (*see* SEJANUS).   R. S.

GALLUS (5), Gaius Asinius, son of C. Asinius Pollio, was consul in 8 B.C. and proconsul of Asia two years later. Augustus judged him ambitious enough to aim at the principate (Tac. *Ann.* 1. 13). Tiberius disliked him, perhaps because of his marriage with Vipsania (*see* AGRIPPINA 1)—a marriage which produced at least five sons—after Tiberius had been forced, against his will, to divorce Vipsania in 12 B.C. His behaviour in the Senate was designed to provoke the anger of Tiberius when emperor, and Gallus was arrested in A.D. 30, perhaps as an associate of Sejanus (so Dio Cass. 58. 3, but cf. Tac. *Ann.* 4. 71), and died of starvation after three years' imprisonment.

For coin-portrait see M. Grant, *From Imperium to Auctoritas* (1946), 387.   J. P. B.

GALLUS (6), Aulus Didius (*cos. suff. anno incerto*), a prominent Claudian senator. When legate of Moesia *c.* A.D. 46 he conducted an expedition to the Cimmerian Chersonesus and established Cotys as king of Bosporus, for which service he received the *ornamenta triumphalia*. He was also *curator aquarum* and proconsul of Asia or Africa. Legate of Britain from 52 to 58, Didius made no noteworthy advance, though interfering with the Brigantians, and was able to maintain the conquests of his predecessors. The fragmentary inscription *ILS* 971 (Histonium) may be referred to him.   R. S.

GALLUS (7), Appius Annius, *consul suffectus* between A.D. 62 and 69, was dispatched as general by Otho against Vitellius in 69. In 70 he was legate of Germania Superior against Civilis.

Klebs, *PW* i. 2268; *PIR²*, A 653.

GALLUS, *see also* FADIUS, TREBONIANUS.

GAMES. One of the earliest games played in Greece, if we may believe Athenaeus, was marbles. According to his story the suitors of Penelope shot their alleys in turn against another marble, which represented the queen; the first one to hit had another turn, and if he were successful again he was considered to be the presumptive bridegroom. A favourite game at Athens was draughts (πεσσοί). The board was divided into thirty-six squares, and on them the oval pieces were moved;

the centre line was called ἱερὰ γραμμή, perhaps because when you crossed it you were on the enemy's ground. A tablet somewhat resembling a backgammon board has been found in the Palace of Cnossos. More popular still was the 'Wine-throw' (κότταβος), especially at the end of dinner. The players, reclining on their left elbow, had to throw with their right hand the last drops of wine from their cups into a basin set in the middle, so that none was spilt. This was the simplest form; alternatively the basin was filled with water on which saucers floated, and the game was to sink the saucers with the wine; in a third variety the wine had to fall into a scale suspended over a small figure—Manes—so that the two came into contact.

At Rome the two favourite games were 'Twelve Lines' (*duodecim scripta*) and 'Robbers' (*ludus latrunculorum*). The first resembled our backgammon or race-game. The other, also played on a board, had pieces of different value, *calculi, latrones, mandrae*, and the object was either to take or check—*ad incitas redigere*—your opponent's pieces. There were also two games, common to Greeks and Romans, whose names explain themselves, 'Odd and Even', and 'How many fingers do I hold up?' *See also* ASTRAGALUS, ATHLETICS, BALL-GAMES, DICING, LUDI.

Athenaeus, 15. 2–7; *Panegyricus in Pisonem*, 180–200.

F. A. W.

GAMES, PUBLIC, (1) in Greece, *see* FESTIVALS and the names of the particular games, OLYMPIC, PYTHIAN, etc.; (2) at Rome, *see* LUDI, SECULAR GAMES.

GAMES, SECULAR, *see* SECULAR GAMES.

GANYMEDES (Γανυμήδης: probably not Greek, but suggesting to a Greek ear γάνος or a cognate, cf. *Etym. Magn.* s.v.; older Latin *Catamitus*). Son of Tros (*Il.* 5. 265; 20. 232; later authorities, from the *Little Iliad* on, make him son of one of the other Trojan princes), carried off by the gods to be Zeus' cup-bearer, his father being given in exchange a marvellous breed of horses (*Il.* loc. cit.) or a golden vine (*Little Iliad* ap. schol. Eur. *Or.* 1392, *Tro.* 821). The older authorities say nothing definite of the manner of his carrying off, though the reason given is his beauty, and Zeus, who gives the horses or the vine, is clearly the prime mover. In the *Homeric Hymn* to Aphrodite it is a storm-wind, ἄελλα, which takes him (208), but at some unknown date, probably not early, it was said that he was snatched up by an eagle (Verg. *Aen.* 5. 255), or Zeus himself in that shape (Ov. *Met.* 10. 155 ff.). The eagle, in the former version, was turned into the constellation Aquila, Ganymedes himself becoming Aquarius (*Homil. Clement.* 5. 17; [Eratosth.] 26; 30). The earlier versions also imply simply that the gods wanted a handsome cup-bearer; the later ones (from Theognis 1345) make him Zeus' minion. His childishly pretty figure is a favourite in Hellenistic and later literature and art. See for examples Drexler in Roscher's *Lexikon*, s.v.

H. J. R.

GARDENS. Minoan and Helladic pottery, wall-paintings, and artistic objects, evincing manifest pleasure in decorative flowers, anticipate the Homeric appreciation of wild and planted flora, notably trees (cf. *Il.* 6. 419; *Od.* 5. 64), including the imported date-palm (*Od.* 6. 162), and prepare for palace gardens like that of Alcinous (*Od.* 7. 112 ff.). The emphasis, however, is upon vegetables and fruit. Cultivated roses are first mentioned in 648 B.C., though the appreciation is much older in Homeric epithets. Royal parks (παράδεισοι) derive from Persia, and Hellenistic examples are described in the *Geoponica*, a work containing extracts from earlier writers compiled by Cassianus Bassus in the tenth century A.D. (10. 1; 11. 23; 3. 13), by Longus (4. 2), and Achilles Tatius (1. 15). Closely connected are the sacred groves (ἄλσοι), as at Antioch–Daphnae. A wide range of

plants is mentioned by Theophrastus (passim), while private gardens occur in Alciphron (fr. 6. 1–9).

In Rome also the *hortus* is old, but primarily a kitchen garden, part of the *heredium*. Flower-gardens, however, soon grew up in the *xystus* or *viridarium* of the courtyard house. But the word for gardener (*topiarius*) is of the late Republic, and so is the formal garden, with topiary work (Plin. *HN* 12. 13) and *ambulationes* of given sizes (*CIL* vi. 29774, 29975). Wall-paintings give a vivid picture of the scope of Roman gardening, from formalism to landscape-gardening (cf. *Röm. Mitt.* v (1890), 783; *JDAI* 1904, 103). Much attention was paid to irrigation. Large pleasure gardens are very late, the earliest in Rome being the *horti Lucullani*, and they always remained the privilege of emperors, aristocrats, and wealthy freedmen. Sacred groves were no less frequent than in Greece.

P. Grimal, *Les Jardins romains* (1943).

I. A. R.

GARGANUS, MONS, *see* APENNINES, APULIA.

GARGILIUS MARTIALIS, QUINTUS, wrote on gardens (*De hortis*), probably in the third century A.D.; Galen is already quoted by him. The remnants preserved in late excerpts do not allow a judgement about the book as a whole; they show, however, that Gargilius relied on his own experience as well as on a carefully discriminating study of the literature. The book apparently was very famous, since Servius, in commenting on Virgil (*G.* 4. 147–8): 'haec . . . praetereo atque aliis post me memoranda relinquo', tersely remarks: 'aliis: Gargilium Martialem significat'. Cassiodorus recommended Gargilius' work, like those of Hippocrates and Galen. If this Gargilius is identical with the Gargilius who wrote on the diseases of oxen, both treatises may have been part of a book on agriculture. The identification with the otherwise unknown historian Gargilius who wrote about Alexander Severus is as uncertain as is that with the statesman G., mentioned in inscriptions of the same time.

TEXT: V. Rose (Teubner, 1875), together with Plinius Secundus, *De Medicina*; *Curae Boum*, in Vegetius, E. Lommatzsch (Teubner, 1903); other fragments, V. Rose, *Anecdota Graeca* ii.
MODERN LITERATURE: H. Stadler, *PW* vii. 760; A. Thomas, *Rev. Phil.* 1907; G. source of Palladius (?), M. Wellmann, *Hermes* 1908.

L. E.

GAUL (Transalpine). Geographically, the territory bounded by the Alps, the Rhine, the Ocean, the Pyrenees, and the Mediterranean forms a unity, and most of its history has been a sequence of unifying cultural developments, followed by catastrophes. Such a cultural unity was achieved in respect of religious feeling in the neolithic period (c. 2000 B.C.), when megalithic tombs are found spread over the area, and maintained itself more or less till disrupted by the invasions of the Celts across the Rhine. Commencing perhaps as early as 900, these spread with varying thickness a layer of Celtic culture over the country, represented from c. 500 by the artistic style of La Tène. An 'erratic' in this picture is the Phocaean colony of Massilia, founded c. 600, which established trading-posts along the Mediterranean, and spread Hellenism in the hinterland.

2. Rome's interest in Transalpine Gaul was at first confined to the security of communications with Spain, and these were guarded by her old ally Massilia. When Massilia, however, was threatened by a Celtic coalition, Rome intervened (121) and annexed a belt of territory between the Cévennes and the Alps. Threat to the *status quo* in the shape of Helvetian and German inroads led to the campaigns of Julius Caesar (58–51), by which all Transalpine Gaul was annexed.

3. Formal settlement came with Augustus. The earlier conquests, called Gallia Narbonensis from their capital Narbo (q.v.), became senatorial; the remainder

(Gallia Comata) became imperial, and was eventually divided into three provinces, cutting deliberately across ethnological divisions.

4. Narbonensis (the *provincia* above all others, its inhabitants 'provinciales') had an Italian air. There were five military colonies; the important native towns enjoyed Latin rights, and eventually the name, and, in some cases at least, the full privileges of a Roman colony. Throughout the country *tria nomina* (the badge of citizenship) are as normal as they are rare in Gallia Comata, and legionary soldiers with Narbonensian domiciles are numerous.

5. In Gallia Comata, Lugdunum, Augusta (*Augst*), Noviodunum (*Nyon*), and subsequently Cologne are the only Roman colonies. Native towns enjoying at later date the title of colony are also rare (e.g. Trier, Avenches), as is possession of the citizenship or entry into the legions. Under Claudius Aeduan nobles were admitted to the Senate (A.D. 48). Local government was based on the old tribes (now *civitates*) with their subdivisions of *pagi* and *vici*.

6. Romanization proceeded apace with construction of new towns in place of hill-forts, public buildings (temples, theatres), and roads; the expense of the process indeed provoked local revolts (A.D. 21), which were easily suppressed by the troops of the Rhine. Here eight legions with auxiliaries were stationed in two commands, intended as much to overawe Gauls as to repel Germans; and a rebellion in 68 against Nero was similarly suppressed by them; while a national movement started by the Treveri under cover of disturbances in the frontier garrisons (69–70) failed not least owing to the lukewarmness of the Gauls, who were realizing the advantages of the Roman connexion.

7. Roman ideas were introduced by the application of Roman names to native gods, which often maintained, however, extraordinary shapes (e.g. horned, cross-legged Cernunnus); and by the imperial cult, which may have been utilized to supplant Druidism (suppressed by Claudius). The centres of worship were Narbo and the river-junction below Lyons, itself the financial centre of the Comata. To the latter the sixty Celtic *civitates* sent deputies to form a provincial parliament.

8. Gaul developed a vigorous if somewhat upstart culture, and was famous for good foodstuffs (and good eating). Its pottery industries, undertaking orders of thousands of mass-produced pieces, competed successfully even in the Italian market. Inroads on capital wealth and a series of devastating barbarian invasions (notably 253 and 276) crippled its prosperity, which was but partially restored in the fourth century. Studded with fortresses and posts connected with State supplies, with its towns huddled into a fraction of their former area behind walls made of the debris of temples, with brigands (Bagaudae) abroad, Gaul had a sad look. Christianity, however, which was becoming important in the second century, had firm hold by the fourth, and was responsible, incidentally, for extinguishing the Gaulish language: its development stimulated the Gallic taste for story-telling (Sulpicius Severus) and vigorous rhetoric (Hilary of Poitiers, Salvian). The later Empire shows a veritable Indian summer of interesting if rather mediocre literary figures (Ausonius, Paulinus of Nola, Sidonius).

9. The withdrawal of Roman garrisons in the fifth century, and the slow development of federate barbarian settlements into independent kingdoms, mark the end of the Roman Empire in Gaul. But though there are decisive dates (e.g. the cession of Auvergne in 475, the victory of Clovis in 486 or 487), the process was gradual. Of formal movements of independence there were virtually none; indeed, even the 'regnum Galliarum' (260–70) was a device of military expediency rather than a separatist movement. Gaul through all its history remains a document of the success of romanization.

INSCRIPTIONS. Latin: Narbonensis, *CIL* xii and E. Espérandieu, *Inscriptions romaines de la Narbonnaise*; Comata, *CIL* xiii. Greek: G. Kaibel, *Inscriptiones Graecae Siciliae et Italiae*, 2427–547. Celtic: C. Dottin, *Langue gauloise* (1920).
SCULPTURE: E. Espérandieu, *Recueil général des bas-reliefs, statues et bustes de la Gaule romaine* (1907–28).
COINS: A. Blanchet, *Traité des monnaies gauloises* (1905); R. Forrer, *Keltische Numismatik* (1908).
NOMENCLATURE: A. Holder, *Altceltischer Sprachschatz* (1891–).
MAP: A. Blanchet and others, *Carte archéologique de la Gaule romaine* (in progress).
BIBLIOGRAPHY: C. E. Ruelle, *Bibliographie générale des Gaules* (1880–6); R. Montandon, *Bibliographie générale des travaux paléthnologiques et archéologiques* (in progress); R. de Lasteyrie and others, *Bibliographie générale des travaux historiques et archéologiques publiés par les sociétés savantes de France* (in progress). Yearly summaries in *Revue des études anciennes* (C. Jullian and A. Grenier); *Pro Alesia* (J. Toutain) and *Revue celtique* (J. Vendryès).
GENERAL WORKS: J. Déchelette, *Manuel d'archéologie* (1911–14); E. Desjardins, *Géographie de la Gaule* (1886–93); A. Grenier, *Manuel d'archéologie gallo-romaine* (in progress); 'Gaul' in Frank's *Economic Survey*, vol. iii; C. Jullian, *Histoire de la Gaule* (1908–26).
C. E. S.

GAVIUS (1) **BASSUS**, contemporary with Cicero, wrote *De Origine Verborum et Vocabulorum* and other works quoted by Gellius and Macrobius; see H. Funaioli, *Gram. Rom. Fragmenta*, pp. 486–91; also *PW* s.v.

GAVIUS (2) **SILO**, an orator to whose eloquence in pleading cases Augustus testified when he heard him at Tarraco 26 B.C. (Sen. *Controv.* 10 *praef.* 14).

GAVIUS, *see also* PONTIUS (1).

GE, *see* GAEA.

GELA (Γέλα), a Dorian colony, founded by Cretans and Rhodians (690 B.C.) on fertile Sicanian territory in southern Sicily, was the celebrated 'metropolis' of Acragas (q.v.) and scene of Aeschylus' death (456). Its earliest personalities are tyrants: Cleander (505–498) and Hippocrates (498–491), who made Gela temporarily Sicily's strongest State. Gelon, however, soon depeopled Gela by seizing Syracuse and transporting Geloans thither (c. 485). Hieron of Syracuse exiled many others. When the refugees returned after 466 Gela began to prosper: it recolonized Camarina (q.v.) and supported Syracuse against Athens (415). However, Carthage sacked it (405) and Gela never fully recovered: Timoleon's efforts to revive it (338) were undone by Agathocles' massacre of 4,000 Geloans (312). Finally, in 280, Phintias of Acragas transferred Gela's inhabitants to his new city of Phintias; thereupon the Mamertini razed Gela, which thus disappeared (reject Pliny, *HN* 3. 91). The *Gelenses* mentioned by Cicero (*Verr.* 3. 103; 192; 4. 73) inhabited Phintias.

Sources. 690–413 B.C.: Hdt. 7. 153 f.; Thuc. bks. 6 and 7; 413–280 B.C.: Diod. bks. 13–23. See, too, Strabo 6. 272; Arist. *Pol.* 5. 12; Paus. 8. 46. 2; 9. 40. 4; Verg. *Aen.* 3. 701 f. L. Pareti, *Per la storia e la topografia di Gela* (1910); J. Bérard, *Bibliogr. topogr.* (1941), p. 53.
E. T. S.

GELLIUS (1) **POPLICOLA**, LUCIUS (*cos.* 72 B.C.), *homo novus* and friend of C. Papirius Carbo (consul 120 B.C.), was praetor in 94. As governor (of Macedonia?) in 93 he tried to reconcile the rival schools of philosophers in Athens. As consul (72) he defeated Spartacus. He was censor (70) and legate of Pompey (67–66). In 63 he warmly supported Cicero. In 59 he opposed Caesar's agrarian law.
A. M.

GELLIUS (2), GNAEUS, the Gracchan annalist, whom Cato attacked in defence of L. Turius, wrote *annales* from the origins of Rome to at least 146 B.C., reaching the Sabine Rape in bk. 2, the year 389 in bk. 15, and the year 216 in bk. 33 (or 30); a reference to bk. 97 is incorrect. His work is fuller than the previous annals; the reason is probably the publication of the *annales maximi* and the first use of Hellenistic methods in elaborating source material. Dionysius used his work.

H. Peter, *HRRel.* i² (1914), pp. cciv, 148; K. J. Beloch, *Röm. Gesch.* 103–4; M. Gelzer, *Hermes* 1934, 55; 1935, 269.

A. H. McD.

GELLIUS (3), AULUS (c. A.D. 123–c. 165), born perhaps in Rome (18. 4. 1), studied literature (*grammatica*) there with eminent teachers, and was intimate with Fronto (19. 8. 1). He went to Athens for at least a year, hearing Calvisius Taurus on Plato and Aristotle, and enjoying the hospitality of Herodes Atticus. At Rome he was appointed judge in private cases (14. 2. 1), probably after his return from Greece; the requisite age was 25 (*Digest* 42. 1. 57; 50. 4. 8), and some legal experience may be assumed. He continued practice at the bar to the end of his life (*Praef.* 23–4), keeping up his interest in general learning.

WORK. *Noctes Atticae* in twenty books (lacking beginning and end, and bk. 8 except chapter-headings and brief fragments): discussion of points of law, grammar, antiquities, history and biography, textual and literary criticism, and other topics. G. began to collect material during the winter nights in Attica (*Praef.* 4), to assemble it under Antoninus Pius, and had partly finished bk. 20 in the principate of Marcus Aurelius.

Little is known about G. except from his writings; all the dates of his career are uncertain; he was of good family and some means, well educated, generally conscientious and accurate, but of moderate ability. He gave considerable thought to the composition of the *Noctes*, devising ingenious methods of introducing his discussions, but not always using them or carrying them through consistently. His defects are largely those of his period: he sometimes refers to original sources when he got his information at second hand, and tries to pass off the learning of others as his own; but his book is of real interest and value, and it preserves extracts from Greek and Roman writers (275 are named), whose works are otherwise wholly, or in great part, lost. He gives it additional interest by accounts of excursions to famous places (2. 21. 1), of monthly dinners with his fellow-students (15. 2. 3), and of visits to the villas of Atticus and others. He was used by many later writers (a full list in Hertz, ed. mai., pp. v ff.), especially Nonius Marcellus and Macrobius, and is highly praised by Augustine (*De Civ. D.* 9. 4) and Erasmus (*Adagiorum Chilias*, 1. 4. 37). As a rule he is easy reading, but his style is that of his age and is sometimes made obscure by unusual and archaic words and expressions, in spite of his own remarks on that subject (11. 7; cf. 1. 10). See ARCHAISM.

BIBLIOGRAPHY

LIFE AND WORKS. Nettleship, *Lectures and Essays* i. 248 ff. (= *AJPhil.* 4. 39 ff.); Introdd. to Commentary and Translations.
TEXTS. M. Hertz (1883–5); Teubner (Hertz, Hosius).
COMMENTARY. H. M. Hornsby (1936; Book I).
TRANSLATION. J. C. Rolfe, with text (Loeb, 1927–8).
STYLE AND DICTION. Nettleship, op. cit., p. 276. Introdd. to Commentary and Translation.
SPECIAL STUDIES. P. Faider, 'Gellii Praefatio' in *Musée belge* xxxi (1927); L. Damasso, 'Aulo Gellio Lessicografo', in *Riv. Fil.* li (1923).

J. C. R.

GELLIUS, see also EGNATIUS.

GELLO (Γελ(λ)ώ), a female daemon that steals children, in ancient, medieval, and modern Greek belief, from Sappho (fr. 104 Diehl) on. According to Suidas, s.v. Γελλοῦς παιδοφιλωτέρα, she was a woman who died untimely, ἄωρος, notoriously a dangerous kind of ghost. Cf. Leo Allatius, *De Graec. hodie quorundam opinationibus*, 3; B. Schmidt, *Volksleben der Neugriechen*, 139 f.; P. Perdrizet, *Negotium Perambulans in Tenebris* (1922).

H. J. R.

GELON (Γέλων) (c. 540–478 B.C.), son of Deinomenes. He became commander of cavalry to Hippocrates (q.v. 1), tyrant of Gela, whom he succeeded by dispossessing his sons (probably in 491). In 485 he restored the expelled Gamori of Syracuse and made himself tyrant (possibly, but not certainly, with the title of στρατηγὸς αὐτοκράτωρ). He handed over Gela to his brother Hieron. Under his rule Syracuse became a large and strongly fortified city of great wealth. Being allied with Theron of Acragas (q.v.), he constituted the greatest Greek power of the time. Therefore, in 480, Athens and Sparta asked his help against Xerxes. According to Herodotus, G. offered to send a big army and fleet, but drew back when they refused to appoint him commander-in-chief. In fact, he could not afford to leave Sicily defenceless. Some months later, simultaneously with Xerxes' attack on Greece, if not in concert with it, a great Carthaginian army under Hamilcar invaded Sicily, but was entirely defeated by Gelon and Theron at Himera. G. now became lord of almost all Sicily, and lived two more years as a great and popular ruler, though idealized by later tradition.

Hdt. bk. 7; Diod. bk. 11. Hackforth, *CAH* iv. 369 ff.; M. Scheele, Στρατηγὸς αὐτοκράτωρ (1932), 23 ff.

V. E.

GEMINUS of Rhodes, a Stoic philosopher and a pupil of Posidonius, wrote (about 73–67 B.C.) a treatise on the scope of the mathematical sciences entitled Περὶ τῆς τῶν μαθημάτων τάξεως or θεωρίας, in at least six books, citations from which are made by various writers, especially Proclus and the scholiasts on Euclid bk. 1, including the Arabian an-Nairīzī (c. A.D. 990), who also drew on Simplicius. The treatise included a classification of the mathematical sciences, arithmetic, geometry, mechanics, astronomy, optics, geodesy, *canonic* (musical harmony) and *logistic* (practical calculation), an examination of the first principles, definitions, postulates, axioms, and of the whole structure based upon them (bk. 6 dealt with conic sections). Geminus also classified 'lines' (including curves), from 'simple' lines (straight lines and circles) to higher curves, e.g. the conics, the cissoid, 'spiric' curves and the cylindrical helix; so also with surfaces. Geminus gave a proof of the special property of 'uniform' lines (the straight line, the circle, and the cylindrical helix). Simplicius (*in Phys.* 991–2 D.) quotes from a commentary by Geminus on Posidonius' *Meteorologica*. An extant work attributed to Geminus, an *Introduction to Phenomena* (Εἰσαγωγὴ εἰς τὰ φαινόμενα), edited by Manitius (Teubner 1898), may be only a compilation by a later editor based on an original εἰσαγωγή; it is an elementary treatise on astronomy suitable for teaching purposes, setting out the most important doctrines of Greek astronomy from the standpoint of Hipparchus. It deals with such subjects as the motions of the sun, moon, and planets, the circles on the heavenly sphere, the milky way, risings and settings, the calendar, the lengths of months and years, and the various 'cycles'.

On Geminus generally see K. Tittel, *De Gemini Stoici studiis mathematicis* (1895), and *PW* vii. 1026.

T. H.

GEMINUS, see also TANUSIUS.

GEMS. Precious stones were valued in antiquity as possessing magical and medicinal virtues, as ornaments, and as seals when engraved with a device. Such engravings (intaglios) in soft mediums like steatite or ivory are found in Early Minoan days (see SEALS); the use of hard stones dates from the Middle Minoan Age. Late Minoan and Mycenaean gems have a rich repertory of human and animal designs; the favoured shapes are the lenticular (round) and glandular (sling-stone). In sub-Mycenaean and Geometric times the art of working hard stones was largely lost. A revival in the seventh century B.C. is usually associated with the island of Melos, and the commencement of classical gem engraving in the sixth century is marked by the introduction of the scarab (beetle) form of seal from Egypt. This was soon abandoned in Greece for the scaraboid, which omits the beetle-back. The late fifth and fourth centuries mark the climax of Greek gem engraving. In Hellenistic times the choice of subjects grows restricted, but excellent work was done in portraiture. In Italy the Etruscans used the scarab until the third century; gems of the later Roman Republic show a wide range of subjects, combined with clumsiness of execution. With Augustus begins the large series of 'Graeco-Roman' gems with few local characteristics. A period of decadence in the middle Empire is succeeded by a revival under Constantine.

Cameos, in which the design is in relief, are for ornament only; apart from some experimental developments of the scarab in the fifth century, they are not older than the Hellenistic period, and the finest are of the early Empire.

Several gem-engravers are recorded in literature, e.g. Pyrgoteles, who worked for Alexander the Great; others are known from their signatures on extant stones, though many signatures are false.

C. W. King, *Antique Gems* (1866); A. Furtwängler, *Die antiken Gemmen* (1900); H. B. Walters, *Catalogue of the Engraved Gems and Cameos, Greek, Etruscan, and Roman, in the British Museum* (1926). F. N. P.

GENETHLIACON, a birthday poem. We do not know of such poems at Rome before the last century of the Republic. Though there were Greek antecedents in the conception of the δαίμων, in the rhetorical handling of natalician themes, and in epigrams of the Anthology, yet the typical birthday poetry of Rome was so intimately associated with the worship of the Genius, that as a separate genre it made one of the original features in Latin literature. Virgil's fourth Eclogue stands apart as a mystical herald of an expected birth. The birthday poetry of Tibullus and in the *Corpus Tibullianum* shows more independence of Hellenic mythology than Propertius does, and more devotion to Roman religious tradition. Propertius' single example (3. 10) greets Cynthia with an anticipation of banquet and festivity. In him and in Horace (*Carm.* 4. 11, invitation to Phyllis to celebrate Maecenas' birthday) there is formal excellence, but a sincerer human note marks Tibullus and Ovid. Ovid pours out his personal feelings: *Tr.* 3. 13 deplores the melancholy birthday of an exile for whom there is no white robe or altar ceremony; and 5. 5 expresses his sympathy with his innocent wife on her birthday.

Persius in his second *Satura* turns birthday congratulations into a homily on praying aright; and Statius in *Silv.* 2. 7, addressed to Lucan's widow on the dead poet's anniversary, blends birthday elements with those of the *laudatio funebris* and *consolatio*. Martial proves the importance attached to birthdays: he celebrates a friend's anniversary, which he loves like his own (9. 52; cf. 10. 24; 12. 60); he sends three epigrams to Lucan's widow recalling *his* anniversary (7. 21; 22; 23); another is on Virgil's (12. 67), which Pliny (*Ep.* 3. 7. 8) says Silius kept more strictly than his own birthday; others are bantering pieces, on being passed over for a birthday feast, on being asked for the day after, on a man of 'no birth' who entertains the highest society on his birthday, on one who, as he does not want gifts on the day, might oblige Martial with a gift instead (7. 86; 11. 65; 10. 27; 8. 64; 9. 53). The last pagan poem in this class is Ausonius' address to his grandson entering his sixteenth year (*Idyll.* 5), where the Genius no longer counts. Christian poets break the ancient tradition by their faith that death is a new birthday, though in structure poems of the sort by Sidonius Apollinaris, Ennodius, and Julianus are indebted to classical rules.

See E. Cesareo, *Il carme natalizio nella poesia latina* (1929). J. W. D.

GENIUS, literally 'the begetter', cf. *ludius*, 'player'. In classical and pre-classical Latin the attendant spirit of every man, a sort of guardian angel, whose activities were apparently directed largely towards fostering the natural desires and their satisfaction; 'suom defrudans genium' (Terence, *Phorm.* 44) means living very parsimoniously; 'genio indulgere' is to enjoy oneself. Although in common parlance every male, bond or free, seems to have a *genius*, in family cult only one *genius* was honoured in each household, that of the *paterfamilias*, particularly on the occasion of his marriage, as Festus, p. 83. 23 Lindsay ('genialis lectus, qui nuptiis sternitur in honorem genii'), but also in the ordinary worship at the *lararium*, see, e.g., Boyce in *Am. Ac. Rome* xiv, plate 17. 1 (one large serpent, bearded and therefore male, a well-known art-convention, underneath a scene of sacrifice); 18. 1 (two such serpents, one beardless, i.e. female, presumably the *iuno* of the *materfamilias*, cf. JUNO). It is quite conceivable (see Rose in *CQ* xvii (1923), 57 ff.) that originally the *genius* is the life-force of the family or clan, always in the guardianship of the *paterfamilias* for the time being and passing on at his death to his successor.

Be that as it may, in classical times the *genius* seems to have been thought of as exactly equivalent to the ἴδιος δαίμων (cf. BIRTHDAY); Horace even says that it is mortal (like its possessor: *Epist.* 2. 2. 188), though adding 'in unum quodque caput', which might imply that it passes to another person on the death of the first one. By a curious extension, gods are said to have a *genius* (first in 58 B.C., *CIL*[1] i. 166 = Bruns 90, line 16). It is more understandable that corporations and places are said to have each its *genius* (Wissowa, 178). The fact that occasionally the *genius* of a dead person is mentioned (examples in De-Marchi, 71) is certainly Greek; cf. the occasional dedications to the *daimon* of the departed. It is the divine guardian who still watches over him in another world.

A. De-Marchi, *Il culto privato di Roma antica* i (1896), 69 ff.; Wissowa, *RK* 175 ff., and the larger classical dictionaries s.v. H. J. R.

GENOS, a family in the widest sense, e.g. Eumolpidae in Athens, or Aegeidae in Sparta (with branches in Thebes and Cyrene); narrower than the *phratria* (q.v.) of which it formed part, wider than the ἀγχιστεῖς (or συγγενεῖς) (see ANCHISTEIS). Its members were γεννῆται. The *genos* in Athens was a corporate body, and could hold property; a member introduced his legitimate male children to the *gennetai* as a body, who accepted or rejected them (cf. PHRATRIAI); if they were rejected, an action could be brought in the dicastery to prove legitimacy and so compel acceptance. Membership of a *genos* was not, however, necessary for citizenship (at any rate after Solon); and most scholars now believe that the *gene* were all aristocratic families (cf. EUPATRIDAE), i.e. that most citizens were not members of any *genos*. It is not, however, necessary to assume that all the members of a *genos* were noble or rich; the *gene* might include nobles at the head and many poor peasants and artisans as well, like the Scottish clans; and the influence in early times of powerful *gene* like the Eumolpidae and Philaïdae was probably largely due to this.

Some *gene* at Athens had a hereditary right to certain priesthoods, as the Eumolpidae and the Kerykes, a right not disturbed in the democratic constitution of Cleisthenes. The names of some ninety Athenian *gene* are known. A. W. G.

GENS (etymologically related to *gignere*) indicates a Roman clan, or a group of families linked together by a common name and their belief in a common ancestor. Beside this, purity of blood, personal liberty, descent from free-born parents, and freedom from any shameful punishment implying *deminutio capitis*, were held the essential claims to membership of a *gens*. Theories that the *gentes* existed before the State, or were set up by law, or originated from an artificial partition of the community, have been refuted by anthropologists and historians, who have rightly emphasized how the rapid economic improvement of the wealthier classes in a predominantly agrarian State would soon lead to a marked distinction between upper and lower classes, and later to the establishment of an order with a narrow family organization. Yet the *gentes*, despite their political and social importance, never fulfilled any specifically public or political duties, apart from the superintendence of several cults and ceremonies. The privacy of the *gentes* and the fact that their members (*gentiles*) neither recorded nor worshipped their founders confirms their relatively late origin. A further proof that the gentile assemblies were not regarded as legally capable of passing resolutions binding on the whole community is that the annalists never mention any public enactment carried in these assemblies, although they often record measures taken by the *gentes* (cf. Livy 6. 20. 14). Although the *gentes* played little part in Roman constitutional and political history they greatly influenced the development of law and religion, even after the prohibition of intermarriage between the orders, which caused the early collapse of several patrician *gentes*, had been abrogated by the *Lex Canuleia* (*see* CANULEIUS). When social equality was attained, the wealthiest plebeian families had already organized themselves on the model of the patrician *gentes*, to which some of them probably gained admission. This, rather than a supposed original difference of race, settlement, or nationality, explains best the existence of both plebeian and patrician families within the same *gens*, and both *minores* and *maiores gentes*. If a member of a *gens* died intestate, his *gentiles* inherited all in default of direct agnates; this fact supports the view that in early times land-property was based on the principle of family, rather than individual, ownership. The gentile assemblies dealt with questions concerning testaments and bequests, *adrogatio*, adoption, emancipation, guardianship of minors, and appointment of *curatores* for insane or spendthrift members; their resolutions had to come twice a year before the *comitia calata* which also had to ratify resolutions referring to the *detestatio sacrorum* and the consequent *transitio ad plebem*. Clients and servants of the *gentiles* shared in their worship and ceremonies, and were often buried in their masters' family tombs. These *sacra gentilicia* mainly consisted in honouring the guardian divinities of the *gens*. They frequently came to be worshipped by the whole community; so, for instance, faith and flattery transformed Apollo, the 'private god' of the *gens Iulia* and of Augustus, into the most honoured god of imperial Rome.

Mommsen, *Röm. Staatsr.* iii³. 9 ff.; B. Kübler, *PW* s.v.; A. H. J. Greenidge, *Roman Public Life* (1911), 9 ff.; G. De Sanctis, *Stor. Rom.* i. 229 ff.　　　　　P. T.

GENUA, the modern *Genoa*, although presumably always Liguria's chief town, is not mentioned until 218 B.C. when already under Roman control (Livy 21. 32). After its destruction in the Hannibalic War Rome restored Genua and used it as a base against the Ligurians (Livy 30. 1; 32. 29; Val. Max. 1. 6. 7). A boundary quarrel between Genuates and Veiturii Langenses was settled by Roman adjudicators in 117 B.C. (*ILS* 5946). Although an important harbour and road-centre, ancient writers seldom mention Genua. For its exports and imports see Strabo 4. 202.　　　　　E. T. S.

GENUCIUS, LUCIUS, tribune of the plebs in 342 B.C., is credited with three laws of which only the first has historical support: (1) forbidding the lending of money on interest as a temporary measure (which was soon

disregarded) to relieve social troubles, caused by debts, usury, and a military rebellion; (2) fixing a ten-year interval before a second tenure of the same office (this was seldom observed and its attribution to Genucius is doubtful); (3) according to Livy (7. 42. 2) allowing both consuls to be plebeian, or more probably making one plebeian consulship obligatory.

G. Billeter, *Gesch. d. Zinsfusses* (1898), 135 ff.; F. Klingmüller, *Sav. Zeitschr.* 1902, 72 ff.; G. Niccolini, *Fasti dei tribuni della plebe* (1934), 66 ff.　　　　　P. T.

GEOGRAPHY (γεωγραφία, 'delineation of land'). It was the Greeks who created geography as a science (the Romans being merely their pupils). The Greeks based their geography on fewer adjunct sciences than modern geographers, and throughout they lacked good technical appliances, and therefore could not obtain technical accuracy. Their knowledge of the globe covered but a fraction of the Old World; and scientific study merged with imaginative speculation and *a priori* deduction about the unknown. Within these limitations, however, their achievements in mathematical and descriptive geography were considerable.

2. In Homer and Hesiod the earth was a round ocean-girt plane, symmetrically vaulted by heaven above and Tartarus below. In the following centuries the gradual discovery of the Mediterranean basin and of the adjacent lands not only gave wider knowledge of geographical details, but stimulated the Ionian philosophers (from *c.* 625 B.C.) to investigate the real causes of the earth's structure and to map the earth and heavens more systematically. The Pythagoreans (after *c.* 525 B.C.) put forward the theory that the earth was a sphere, and Aristotle proved it. Heraclides Ponticus (*c.* 388–315) declared that the earth revolved round its axis, Aristarchus of Samos (*c.* 310–230) stated that it might also be revolving round the sun. But only the theory of the earth's sphericity won general acceptance, and after 450 the 'universal' geography of the Greeks tended to be replaced by a more narrow study of the οἰκουμένη or inhabited land-mass of the earth.

3. Geographic elucidation of the οἰκουμένη, progressing continually with geographic discovery, was expressed in a literature comprising the following classes:

A. WORKS ON PARTICULAR REGIONS. (*a*) Reports of discoveries. These were partly official, e.g. the reports of Hanno on north-west Africa, and of Nearchus (embodied in Arrian's *Indica*) on the Asian coast from Indus to Euphrates. Some of Caesar's chapters are geographical, e.g. *BGall.* 5. 12–13, 6. 25. A surviving unofficial specimen is the *Periplus of the Erythraean Sea* (see PERIPLOI).

(*b*) Reports of surveyors. Of this class we possess fragments from Alexander's surveyors in Asia, and the *Parthian Stations* of Isidorus of Charax. These were in the nature of road-books, giving the important halts on the routes described.

(*c*) Manuals for travellers, sometimes based on first-hand information. A large proportion of these consisted of coastal descriptions for practical navigators (περίπλοι, παράπλοι, ἀνάπλοι). Fragments of an early example (*c.* 500 B.C.) are reproduced in Avienus; an almost complete specimen survives in the so-called 'Periplus of Scylax' (*c.* 350). We also have large pieces of Arrian's *Periplus of the Euxine Sea*, and of the *Stadiasmus Maris Magni* (3rd c. A.D.), detailing landmarks, harbours, and waterpoints of the Mediterranean coasts, with distances in stades. To this class also belong the surviving Itineraries (q.v.).

(*d*) Maps (q.v.), issued in connexion with the above works, or published independently.

B. GENERAL TREATISES OF DESCRIPTIVE GEOGRAPHY. These comprised comprehensive surveys (γῆς περίοδοι or περιηγήσεις), with or without maps, coupled with descriptions of separate lands and land-groups (χωρο-γραφίαι), or of particular places (τοπογραφίαι). They sometimes included physical geography and ethnography. The Γῆς περίοδος of Hecataeus (c. 510–490) described towns and peoples as well as geographic features; the geographic insertions in Herodotus' *History* contain much ethnological material. Of two fourth-century historians who included geography Ephorus attempted ethnography and historical geography, and devoted entire books to descriptive geography. Timaeus dealt largely with the general geography of western Europe. The contemporary historians of Alexander contained much useful geographical material. The description of India by Ctesias (c. 400) was overloaded with fable, but that of Megasthenes (c. 295) gave a good description of the Ganges valley, of which he had personal knowledge.

The opening up of the Near East by Alexander's successors was reflected in Agatharchides' description of the Red Sea coasts (c. 110—partly extant), and in the geographical chapters of Diodorus Siculus (c. 100–20), that of western Europe by the Romans in the geographical excursuses of Polybius and of Posidonius. A general resumptive work on Mediterranean and Near Eastern geography was composed by Artemidorus (c. 100). This was eclipsed a century later by the treatise of Strabo, which includes topography, physical, historical, political, and also mathematical geography. The only other descriptive geography of scientific value was the *Descriptio Orbis* of Agrippa, containing a commentary to his map of the world. Other works of this class were bks. 2–6 of the *Natural History* of Pliny (little more than a gazetteer); a description of Africa by Juba II (25 B.C.–c. A.D. 24); a versified description of the whole known world by Dionysius Periegetes (c. A.D. 300?); and school primers like that of the versifier miscalled 'Scymnus' (c. 100 B.C.?) and of Pomponius Mela (c. A.D. 43).

C. MATHEMATICAL GEOGRAPHIES. Scientific analysis of the earth's surface and a more accurate plotting of maps became possible when Aristotle demonstrated the earth's sphericity, Eratosthenes made a reasonably exact measurement of the earth's circumference, and latitudes were determined by means of shadow-sticks or by calculation from the length of a solstitial day. Aristotle introduced the general principle of dividing the globe into zones. Dicaearchus (c. 310) laid down a basic line of latitude from Gibraltar to the Himalayas; Eratosthenes drew several parallels of latitude and longitude to a main line of latitude and a meridian intersecting at Rhodes; Hipparchus (c. 150) divided Eratosthenes' main parallel of latitude into 360 degrees, drew parallels of latitude computed from the duration of the longest day, and proposed to plot all places on the map by latitude and longitude. A comprehensive attempt to apply the principles of mathematical geography was made in the Γεωγραφικὴ ὑφήγησις of Ptolemy (c. A.D. 150–60). Though the greater part of his geographical data was not actually determined by astronomical observation, he systematically expressed them in reference to curved lines of latitude measured northwards from the Equator, and curved meridians measured eastwards from the Canary Islands. Unfortunately the works of the mathematical geographers and of Strabo did not command the attention which they deserved; the erroneous beliefs of older writers were preserved by tradition, and the authors of later date than Ptolemy were for the most part mere compilers from variegated and incongruous sources. *See also* ITINERARIES, MAPS, PERIPLOI, and articles on the persons mentioned above.

E. H. Bunbury, *History of Ancient Geography* (1879); H. Berger, *Geschichte der wissenschaftlichen Erdkunde der Griechen*[2] (1903); H. F. Tozer, *History of Ancient Geography*[2] (1935); Cary–Warmington, *Explorers* (1929); E. H. Warmington, *Greek Geography* (1934).
E. H. W.

GERMANI. The earliest home of the German race was south Scandinavia, Jutland, and the north German coast from the Weser to the Oder. In the long period from the last glaciation to the Iron Age many different immigrant groups arrived from south-west, south, and east, and the mixed ancestry of the race is further shown by the earliest skeletal remains, which exhibit differing anthropological characteristics. From c. 1000 B.C. Germans expanded southwards and westwards, so that by 600 there were Germanic elements in the lowlands around the lower Rhine mixing with the peoples already established there. As the Germans moved southwards they came into contact with the Celts, who held the belt of highlands from the Ardennes to Bohemia against them for some centuries to come. In the third century German pressure became serious, and a fresh horde crossed the lower Rhine, while others pushed into the Westerwald and Taunus region of the middle Rhine and crossed to the Moselle, where they brought a Germanic strain into the Treveri. A new invasion west of the lower Rhine brought in the *Germani cisrhenani* known to Caesar, and some of the mixed population was driven down into the Marne–Aisne basins (*see* BELGAE). The migration of the Cimbri and Teutoni followed shortly after 120, and the Helvetii south of the Main, already suffering from the pressure of tribal movements, retreated into Switzerland. This general falling-back of the remaining trans-Rhenane Celts was hastened when early in the first century B.C. a new German host, the Suebi, moved south-west to the Main and Rhine.

2. Corresponding expansion took place among the Germans to the East. Those of the Baltic coast had spread over a wide area before the second century B.C., but were pushed away from the sea by the arrival of successive tribes from Scandinavia (q.v.), Vandals from Jutland, Burgundians from Bornholm, the Langobardi from Gotland, the Rugii from south Norway, and the Goths from south Sweden. The vanguard of the east Germans were the Bastarnae, who appeared on the borders of Thrace c. 200 B.C. By the first century A.D. the Vandals, with the Lugii, occupied Silesia, the Burgundians were behind them astride the Warthe, and the Langobardi had moved in the wake of the Cimbri and Teutoni to the lower Elbe, leaving the Rugii on the Pomeranian coast, while the Goths held the lower Vistula.

3. The origin of the name *Germani* is explained in Tacitus, *Germania*, 2. One of the tribes or tribal groups taking part in the great offensive along the lower Rhine of the third century B.C. had been called *Germani*, and this name was adopted by the Gauls to designate the whole race (cf. the analogous case of *Alamanni* and *Allemands*).

4. The Germans themselves believed that they were descended from the god Tuisto, born of the earth; his son Mannus (Man) had three sons, the ancestors of the three west German groups, Ingaevones (northern and north-western tribes), Istaevones (Westphalian and Rhenish tribes), Herminones (Suebi, Chatti, Cherusci, etc.). The absence of the east Germans from this classification points to its originating in a period before they became differentiated. They worshipped Woden (Mercury), Donar or Thor (Hercules), Ziu or Tiu (Mars). Goddesses were as a rule less important, though notable exceptions like Nerthus and Tamfana are known, both the central deities of important religious federations. Though there were no temples in the classical sense, there were from an early age places—most commonly sacred groves—set apart for the worship of the gods.

5. German society of the time of Tacitus was aristocratic, and consisted of chiefs, freemen, and slaves. The kings were generally elected from one princely house in each tribe, but on occasion special leaders were elected for special campaigns. Great chiefs maintained a *comitatus* which lived by warfare. A rudimentary law had already been developed and was generally dispensed by the priests. Women were under the guardianship of father or husband and had no independent legal or political rights, but they exercised considerable influence in religious matters. Agriculture had been practised from very early times and the Germans lived in settled communities.

Tacitus, *Germania*, ed. Anderson (1938); L. Schmidt, *Gesch. d. deut. Stämme—Die Ostgermanen*[2] (1934), 40–85; G. Ekholm, *CAH* xi, ch. 2 (with bibliography). O. B.

GERMANIC RELIGION, see RELIGION, TEUTONIC.

GERMANICUS JULIUS CAESAR (15 B.C.–A.D. 19, before adoption, NERO CLAUDIUS GERMANICUS ?), son of Drusus (q.v. 3) and husband of Agrippina (q.v. 2). His name Germanicus was inherited from his father. In A.D. 4 he was adopted by Tiberius, whom he accompanied against the Pannonians and the Germans. Sent again to the Rhine as a commander (A.D. 13), he faced a mutiny upon the death of Augustus and substantially met the legionaries' demands. His popularity became well established. He was sensitive, gentle, and ambitious. Like his father, he was considered Republican in his sentiments. The unpopularity of Tiberius worked in his favour. He hoped to emulate his father and conquer a large part of Germany. He successfully led the repentant soldiers over the Rhine against the Marsi. In 15 he rescued Segestes from Arminius (q.v.), against whom his army advanced in three divisions. He reached the Teutoburgian Forest, where he paid the last honours to Varus, and pursued Arminius eastwards. After an indecisive battle he suffered heavy losses on his return. For the campaign in 16 a great fleet was prepared. The troops apparently landed on the western bank of the Ems and then had to cross the Weser in the face of the enemy. After a battle at Campus Idistaviso and a second engagement Germanicus returned to his base without any result. He had vainly tried to starve the enemy and to overcome transport difficulties by approaching from the sea; a winter residence in Germany, indispensable to victory, proved impossible. Tiberius recalled Germanicus, wishing to use him in the East. Germanicus celebrated a triumph in Rome (A.D. 17). The whole of the Eastern provinces were assigned to him with a *maius imperium*. In 18 he was consul with Tiberius and travelled to Asia. He crowned Zeno, son of Polemo I, king of Armenia, and reduced Cappadocia and Commagene to the status of provinces. In 19 he offended Tiberius by travelling unauthorized to Egypt, which his romantic curiosity prompted him to visit. On his return to Syria the enmity between him and Cn. Piso, whom Tiberius had unhappily appointed governor of Syria with the intention of controlling him, became intolerable. Shortly after, he died at Antioch, convinced that Piso had poisoned him. His mysterious death enhanced his popularity. He translated into Latin and revised the *Phaenomena* of Aratus (see ARATEA) and compiled another work which modern critics call *Prognostica* (mainly lost). The Emperor Gaius and Julia Agrippina, Nero's mother, were among his nine children.

CAH x, passim; G. Kessler, *Die Tradition über Germanicus* (1905); F. Knoke, *Die Kriegszüge des Germanicus in Deutschland*[2] (1922); L. Schmidt, *Geschichte der deutschen Stämme* i[2] (1938), 111; cf. M. Gelzer, *PW* x. 435. For the portrait, H. Fuchs, *Röm. Mitt.* 1936, 212. A. M.

GEROUSIA, the Council of Elders at Sparta, consisting of twenty-eight γέροντες of over sixty years of age, together with the two kings. Elected similarly to the ephors (q.v.), by acclamation of the citizens (a childish system, Arist. *Pol.* 2. 1271[a]), the *gerontes* held office for life, but at some later date the office was made annual, and under the Roman Empire re-election became a frequent practice. Possessing both deliberative and judicial functions, they considered questions of public policy and prepared business for the Apella (q.v.), whose decisions, in early times at least, they were competent to reverse, in conjunction with the kings. They heard cases involving death, exile, or ἀτιμία, and could try even the kings; when the ephors laid charges before them they joined them in passing sentence. In spite of its wide powers and high prestige the Gerousia was not free from drawbacks inherent in old age, in the greater readiness of the ambitious or rich to seek election, and in the opportunities afforded for corruption in its judicial capacity.

Gerousia was also a common name for city councils of an aristocratic or plutocratic type, whether survivals of the Homeric Councils of Elders, or new creations, as in the Greek towns of Asia Minor in Hellenistic or Roman times. A. M. W.

GESORIACUM (**Bononia** under the later Empire), modern *Boulogne-sur-Mer*, and almost certainly the Portus Itius (i.e. 'channel harbour') of Caesar; under the Empire the normal port of embarkation for Britain and station of the *Classis Britannica*. Its lighthouse was constructed by Caligula. Carausius' fleet was blockaded here in A.D. 292.

A. E. E. Desjardins, *Géographie hist. et admin. de la Gaule romaine* (1875–93) i. 346–80; T. Rice Holmes, *Ancient Britain*, 552–95. C. E. S.

GESTURES. Since the peoples of southern Europe notoriously make more use of gesture than the northerners, it is not surprising that gesticulation was frequent and lively among the ancients. (*a*) The natural signs of the emotions were less restrained than with us. Thus, to jump for joy would appear to be no mere metaphor nor confined to children and excitable young people; Q. Cicero says he did it on receiving good news (*Fam.* 16. 16. 1). Angry or troubled people bite their nails or their fingers (Hor. *Epod.* 5. 48; Persius 5. 162). Achilles, disturbed by bad news, smites his thighs (*Il.* 16. 125), and so do many after him, but it was too violent a gesture for an orator till Cleon introduced it (Quint. *Inst.* 11. 3. 123). One or two gestures are strange to us, as the angry or perplexed scratching of the ear or cheek (Apul. *Met.* 6. 9; Heliodorus 2. 8 (p. 44. 29 Bekker)). (*b*) Orators and actors naturally made a study of gesture. The former were at first very restrained, particularly at Athens, where it was not good form till after Pericles to withdraw the hand from under the mantle (Aeschin. 1. 25); later they elaborated, keeping, however, within narrower limits than those of the stage (Quint. loc. cit., 89; see the whole passage for oratorical usage). Concerning actors we are not so well informed, especially for tragedians of the classical Greek period, who cannot have gesticulated freely in their heavy costume. Of New Comedy we can say a little more, owing to the descriptions by characters of their own movements, e.g. Plaut. *Capt.* 794 ff., where Ergasilus runs about the stage, shouldering through an imaginary crowd. In farce and pantomime much could be conveyed by gesture (e.g. Suet. *Nero* 39; Lucian, *Salt.* 37 ff.). (*c*) Religious and magical gestures: the most common gesture of prayer was to look up, or down, according as a celestial or infernal power was invoked, holding the hands palm upwards, or downwards (*Il.* 3. 275; 24. 307; Picard in *Rev. Hist. Rel.* 1937, 137 ff.). In the latter case the ground might be struck or stamped upon (as *Il.* 9. 568; Cic. *Tusc.* 2. 60), which perhaps is why the latter is not very common as a mere sign of irritation. Kneeling or prostration were not usual in Greece (Theophr. *Char.* 16. 5, where see H. Bolkenstein, *Theophrastos' Charakter der Deisidaimonia*), quite common in Rome. Kissing statues was common (Cic. *Verr.* 2. 4. 94), also blowing kisses to them (Min. Fel. *Oct.* 2. 4). In human relationships a friend kissed the face, a suppliant the hand (Sittl, op. cit. infra, 79, 166); handshaking was more solemn. The most common magical gesture (to avert the evil eye, etc.) was to hold the hand so as to imitate the *pudenda* of one or the other sex, Sittl, 101 ff.

It is not surprising that there grew up a sign-language, ranging in signification from rudeness (Pers. 1. 58–60) to arithmetical calculations and even a sort of deaf-and-dumb alphabet (Bede, *De computo vel loquela digitorum*; critical text in Sittl, 256 ff.).

C. Sittl, *Die Gebärden der Griechen und Römer* (1890). T. Elworthy, *The Evil Eye* (1895), *Horns of Honour* (1900), contain much but inaccurate and unsystematic information.   H. J. R.

GĔTA (1), LUCIUS SEPTIMIUS, younger son of Septimius Severus and brother of Caracalla, became Caesar in A.D. 198 and Augustus in 209. During the Scottish campaigns he was left as governor of Britain at York. The mutual hatred of the two brothers was intensified after their father's death, especially as Geta was popular with the soldiers. On their return to Rome they lived in different parts of the Palace. After some vain attempts at reconciliation by their mother, Geta was assassinated by his brother in 212. *See* AURELIUS (2).   H. M. D. P.

GETA (2), HOSIDIUS (2nd c. A.D.), contemporary with Tertullian (*De praescr. haeret.* 39), patched together from lines or phrases of Virgil a cento (q.v.) to form dialogue and choruses of a tragedy *Medea*, probably identical with that in *Anth. Lat.* (codex Salmasianus).

Text: Baehr. *PLM* iv. 219 ff. Cf. Teuffel, 370. 5; O. Delepierre, *Littérature du Centon* i. 37 ff.   J. W. D.

GETAE, a Thracian tribe situated on the lower Danube (*see* THRACE). The name was subsequently applied by Greek and Latin writers to the Goths, with whom the Getae had nothing in common.

GIANTS, a mythological race of monstrous appearance and great strength. According to Hesiod they were sons of Ge (Earth) from the blood of Uranus which fell upon earth; he describes them as valiant warriors (*Th.* 185). Homer considers them a savage race of men who perished with their king Eurymedon (*Od.* 7. 59). The prevailing legend of the fight of the gods and the G. was formulated in archaic epics and was embroidered by many later writers. A substantial account is given by Apollodorus (1. 34 ff.) When the gods were attacked by the G. they learned that they could win only if they were assisted by a mortal. They called in Heracles, who killed the giant Alcyoneus and many others with his arrows. Zeus, who led the gods, smote with his thunderbolt Porphyrion who attempted to ravish Hera; Athena killed Pallas or Enceladus; Poseidon crushed Polybotes under the rock that became the island of Nisyrus (Strabo p. 489); Apollo shot Ephialtes; Hermes slew Hippolytus; Dionysus killed Eurytus and many other giants besides who were caught in his vine; and Hephaestus aided the gods, throwing red-hot iron as missiles. The G. were defeated and were believed to be buried under the volcanoes in various parts of Greece and Italy, e.g. Enceladus under Aetna. Bones of prehistoric animals were occasionally believed to be bones of giants.

The Gigantomachy was one of the most popular myths in Greece and accordingly the names of participants and the episodes of the battle vary from writer to writer and from representation to representation. Zeus, Heracles, Poseidon, and later Athena, are the usual protagonists. In its early stage the myth seems to represent a variation of the popular motif of the tribe that attempted to dethrone the gods; in a more advanced stage of culture the myth was interpreted as the fight of civilization against barbarism.

In art the giants are first shown as warriors or wild men (Hanfmann, *Art Bull.* 1937), later as snake-legged monsters. (Waser, *PW* Suppl. iii, s.v. 'Giganten'). The

most famous sculptural renderings are found on the archaic treasury of the Siphnians and on the Hellenistic altar of Pergamum.   G. M. A. H.

GLABRIO (1), MANIUS ACILIUS (*cos.* 191 B.C.), a *novus homo*, tribune in 201 B.C., plebeian aedile in 197, rose under the aegis of Scipio Africanus to the praetorship in 196, crushing an Etruscan slave revolt, and became consul in 191 in the Syrian War. He defeated Antiochus at Thermopylae and began operations against the Aetolians; he extended the Delphic sanctuary. After triumphing (190) he stood for the censorship, but withdrew under a charge of peculation supported by Cato in opposition to the Scipionic group. In 181 his son dedicated a temple to *Pietas* vowed at Thermopylae. The *Lex Acilia de intercalando* belongs to his consulship.

Livy 33. 36; 36. 14 ff.; 37. 57. De Sanctis, *Stor. Rom.* iv. 1, 158, 376, 586; G. Daux, *Delphes au IIᵉ et au Iᵉʳ siècle* (1936), 225; R. Flacelière, *Les Aitoliens à Delphes* (1937), 356; A. H. McDonald, *JRS* 1938, 162.   A. H. McD.

GLABRIO (2), MANIUS ACILIUS, husband of Mucia (daughter of Q. Scaevola 'Augur') and supporter of the Gracchi, was the author, as tribune (probably 123 B.C.), of the *Lex Acilia Repetundarum*, excluding senators from the juries, and providing a choice in procedure between conviction at the first hearing and a second hearing (*see* AMPLIATIO). Mommsen's identification of this law with the partly extant *Lex Repetundarum* is generally accepted.

E. G. Hardy, *Roman Laws and Charters*, no. 1; H. Last, *CAH* ix. 892 ff.; J. P. Balsdon, *BSR* 1938, 98 ff.   M. H.

GLABRIO (3), MANIUS ACILIUS, consul with M. Ulpius Traianus in A.D. 91, when he was compelled to fight in the arena and was exiled. In 95 he was executed. The cause is uncertain (Christian faith?). He or his family is connected with the catacombs of Priscilla.

PIR², A 67; P. Styger, *Die römischen Katakomben* (1933), 100; H. Leclercq, *Dict. d'Arch. Chrétienne* vi. 1259. K. Friedmann, *Atene e Roma* (1931), 69.   A. M.

GLADIATORS. Gladiatorial combats, in which armed men fought one another, were borrowed by the Romans from Etruria, where originally they may have been part of the ceremonies at a chief's funeral. The first recorded instance of their appearance in Rome was at the funeral games given by his sons in honour of M. Brutus, 264 B.C. On that occasion only three pairs of gladiators were engaged, but in 174 B.C. at the funeral games of T. Flamininus thirty-seven pairs fought, and finally at private celebrations, such as these funerals, 100 pairs became common. At the games given by Julius Caesar as aedile 320 pairs fought. Under the Empire the numbers steadily mounted, and Trajan exhibited 5,000 pairs in his triumph over Decebalus.

Gladiators were usually prisoners of war, slaves bought for the purpose, or condemned criminals. They were trained in a school—*ludus*—under very harsh discipline by a professional—*lanista*—who either owned the establishment himself or was employed by the State or private persons. The town of Capua was a favourite training-ground for gladiators; a gladiatorial school has also been discovered at Pompeii. Under the Empire these slaves were often joined by free men who being reduced to poverty hired themselves to a *lanista* at a wage, and were bound by an oath—*auctoramentum gladiatorium*—to serve for a fixed period. The last stage was reached when men and women of rank entered the arena and fought, either of their own accord or at the Emperor's bidding.

Gladiators were of four main types. The Mirmillo and the Samnite were heavily armed with oblong shield, vizored helmet, and short sword. The Thracian had a round buckler and a curved scimitar. The Retiarius fought almost naked, with a net and trident as his only weapons. Defeated combatants were usually dispatched by the victors; but their lives were sometimes spared at the instance of the onlookers, who would wave their handkerchiefs as a signal of pardon.

Friedländer ii. 41–60; Lafaye, Dar.-Sag., s.v. 'Gladiatores'; L. Robert, *Gladiateurs dans l'Orient grec.* (1940). F. A. W.

GLADIUS, see ARMS AND ARMOUR, ROMAN.

GLASS (ὕαλος, *vitrum*). The art of producing a vitreous surface on clay, frit, or quartz (faience) was known in predynastic Egypt and passed to Crete, where plaques and figurines from the Palace of Cnossos illustrate the high level attained in the second millennium B.C. Faience objects are common on Greek sites of the archaic period, some of them Egyptian imports, others probably made locally. In Hellenistic and Roman times Egypt and Asia Minor were centres of fabrication, and St. Rémy-en-Rollat in southern France produced vases during the Early Empire.

Objects composed entirely of glass paste begin to appear in Egypt about 1500 B.C., when two allied processes seem to have been in use: modelling molten glass about a core of sand, and pressing it into an open mould. The chief Mycenaean glass is κύανος, of dark blue imitating lapis lazuli, used for beads, inlays, and architectural ornaments. In the sixth century small vases made by the sand-core process became known in Greece; they have opaque blue or white bodies decorated with polychrome bands formed by fusing coloured threads rolled round the body. Their place of origin is unknown, though the Greek character of the shapes suggests native production. In the Hellenistic period bowls made in moulds come into fashion; these were mainly produced in Egypt. Here the tradition of opaque polychrome glass was continued far into Roman times with the *millefiori* vases (identified by some with the *murrina vasa*, q.v.), in which coloured patterns were fused into the vase. In the same tradition are the vases in two layers of which one is carved like a cameo: the Portland Vase in London is the best-known example.

The invention of glass-blowing in the first century B.C. (probably in Syria) wrought a profound change in the glass industry which, hitherto limited to luxury articles, now became capable of cheap mass production. Under the Roman Empire glass largely replaced pottery for domestic use and funeral furniture. Foundries have been located in many provinces; like the *terra sigillata* potteries, the manufacture tended to move away from the Mediterranean towards the borders of the Empire. Thus in the later Empire, Belgic Gaul and Germany had taken the place of Italy and southern Gaul. The vases, even when plain, show much variety of form, and there are several styles of decoration—tooling or applying relief ornament to the surface when warm, cutting or engraving when cold. Window glass, made by a primitive process of rolling, was known at Pompeii, and later became common; in the late Empire also begins the use of glass for mirrors.

A. Kisa, *Das Glas im Altertume* (1908); Morin-Jean, *La Verrerie en Gaule* (1913); M. L. Trowbridge, *Philological Studies in Ancient Glass* (U.S.A. 1930); D. B. Harden, *Roman Glass from Karanis* (U.S.A. 1936). F. N. P.

GLAUCIA, GAIUS SERVILIUS, leader of the *Populares* during the period of Marius' rise to power. Low-born, and an effective demagogue, he obtained the support of the *Equites* as well as of the plebs. As tribune (presumably soon after 106 B.C.; but see Greenidge and Clay, *Sources*, p. 225 for another view), by his law *De Repetundis*, he restored the jury-courts to the *Equites*, and made compulsory the procedure of *comperendinatio*, an adjournment or division of a trial into two parts. As praetor, Glaucia took a leading part in the democratic agitation

of 100. He hoped to be chosen consul for 99, but was killed in the disorders which followed the murder of his rival C. Memmius.

F. Münzer, *PW* ii. A. 1796; J. P. Balsdon, *BSR* 1938, 98 ff. M. H.

GLAUCUS, in mythology, (1) a Lycian, son of Hippolochus, second in command of the Lycian contingent before Troy (*Il.* 2. 876 and often). He encounters Diomedes (q.v.), and exchanges armour with him in sign of friendship when told that they are hereditary ξένοι, getting the worse of the bargain, since his is gold and that of Diomedes bronze (*Il.* 6. 234–6; proverbial later). Wounded by Teucer (12. 387–8), healed by Apollo (16. 527 ff.), he rallies the Lycians after the death of Sarpedon. Killed, over the body of Achilles, by Aias son of Telamon (Quint. Smyrn. 3. 278 ff.), Apollo caused the winds to snatch his body from the pyre and take it to Lycia, where the Nymphs made the river of like name to spring up about his grave (ibid. 4. 4 ff.). (2) Of Anthedon in Boeotia. He somehow (Ov. *Met.* 13. 920 ff. is but one of several versions; see Drexler in Roscher's *Lexikon* i. 1679–80) became immortal by a magic herb (or a magic bath, schol. on Pl. *Resp.* 611 c) and then for some reason leaped into the sea and became a sea-god. He was renowned for his prophecies (schol. ibid. and often); vainly wooed Scylla (1) (q.v.; Ov. ibid.). (3) Of Corinth (*Il.* 6. 154), son of Sisyphus and father of Bellerophon (qq.v.), therefore great-grandfather of Glaucus (1) (Bellerophon–Hippolochus–Glaucus). His most famous legend is connected with Potniae in Boeotia, where he kept a stud of mares and fed them on human flesh (or they ate a herb which drove them mad, or Aphrodite was angry with Glaucus because he would not let them mate), till they devoured him at the funeral games over Pelias, whereupon he became a Taraxippos (horse-frightener) which scared the teams at the Isthmus (Verg. *G.* 3. 267, Servius and 'Probus' ad loc., Pausanias 6. 20. 19; *Etym. Magn.* 685, 41). That the name belongs to these and some dozen other persons (Drexler, op. cit.) is due to it being (*a*) an epithet of the sea, (*b*) an adjective appropriate to the 'bright' eyes of a vigorous man.

H. J. R.

GLAUCUS (4) of Chios (or Samos, according to some late authors), to whom is ascribed the invention of welding iron (σιδήρου κόλλησις; not of soldering, which is a modern process), made for Alyttes of Lydia (reigned 617–560 B.C.) a stand of iron, supporting a silver bowl; this was for Herodotus (1. 25) 'worth seeing above all the other offerings at Delphi'. In the time of Pausanias (10. 16. 1) the bowl had disappeared, but the stand remained, tower-shaped with an upward taper, the sides of openwork with crossbands, and decorated with figures and animals (Ath. 5. 210). F. N. P.

GLAUCUS (5) of Rhegium (*c.* 400 B.C.) wrote an important work *On the Ancient Poets and Musicians* (used by [Plut.] *De mus.*), which began the ancient study of the history of lyric poetry. His comments on Homer and his discussion of the plots of Aeschylus may have formed part of this work. The name Glaucus has been thought to be a pseudonym of the sophist Antiphon.

FHG ii. 23 f.; E. Hiller, *Rh. Mus.* 1886. J. F. L.

GLOSSA, GLOSSARY (Greek). In Greek literary criticism γλῶσσαι meant any words or expressions (not being mere neologisms or metaphors) ἃ οὐδεὶς ἂν εἴποι ἐν τῇ διαλέκτῳ (Arist. *Poet.* 1458ᵇ32), i.e. belonging not to the spoken language familiar to the critic (1458ᵇ6), but to a dialect, literary or vernacular, of another region or period (1457ᵇ4). The interpretation of Homeric γλῶσσαι, misunderstood already by Hesiod, fell, no doubt, from the first, to schoolmasters (cf. Ar. *Daitaleis*) and rhapsodes, and it appealed to sophistic interest in language: cf. Democritus, Περὶ Ὁμήρου ἢ ὀρθοεπείης καὶ γλωσσέων. The living dialects were early used for the purpose (cf. Arist. *Poet.* 1461ᵃ12), but, apart from Aristarchus, Alexandrian commentators, no less than the Pergamenes, usually preferred to explain by etymology, as did Neoptolemus of Parium in Περὶ γλωσσῶν Ὁμήρου. Interest in dialects was fostered by fifth-century linguistic speculations, and in the next two centuries by Peripatetic studies, not least in natural history and its vocabulary, and by monographs based on personal knowledge of local dialects before the levelling operation of the κοινή. The spirit of Alexandrianism in literature further encouraged search for linguistic oddities. Sometimes literary glosses were collected with only sporadic dialectal illustration, as the Homeric Glosses of Philetas and Simmias. Some specifically dialectal collections were devoted to Homer, Alcman, the Old Comedy, etc.; others were not so related to particular authors or styles, e.g. the Φρύγιαι φωναί of Neoptolemus, the Ἐθνικαὶ λέξεις of Zenodotus (perhaps not the Alexandrian), and the Αἰολικαὶ γλῶσσαι of Antigonus of Carystus. The Ὀνομαστικόν, often with dialectal variants, also became common: e.g. Callimachus compiled names of winds, fishes, and months; Dionysius Iambus had a chapter on fishermen's terms, and Eratosthenes other vocational vocabularies. Aristophanes of Byzantium excelled all in the scope and diversity of his lexicographical labours (cf. Ael. *NA* 7. 47). In his footsteps followed his pupil Artemidorus (on Doric, and cookery), Philistides (on names of family relationships), and many others, notably, in the first century B.C., Cleitarchus of Aegina, who proved a fertile source of dialect glosses under the Empire. The Περὶ τῶν ὑποπτευομένων μὴ εἰρῆσθαι τοῖς παλαιοῖς of Aristophanes is a prototype of the 'Atticist' lexica which were common in the first century A.D. and still more in the following centuries. The first professed Atticist was Eirenaeus of Alexandria (end of 1st c. B.C.), and the ultimate sources of most later Atticists are also Alexandrian. As to glosses of all kinds, in the first century B.C. compilation largely displaces independent research, and almost exclusively prevails under the Empire; to the latter period, down to Constantine, the extant scholiasts and lexicographers are directly or indirectly indebted; but the sources thus absorbed have generally perished.

K. Latte, *Philol.* lxxx (1925), 136; R. Reitzenstein, *Geschichte d. Gr. Etymologika* (1897); *see also under* GRAMMAR, ETYMOLOGY.
P. B. R. F.

GLOSSA, GLOSSARY (Latin). The need for marginal or interlinear interpretations of difficult or obsolete words (γλῶσσαι) is coincident with the serious study of literature. The earliest reference to Latin glosses is in Varro (*Ling.* 7. 10: ' "tesca" aiunt sancta esse qui glossas scripserunt'). Some of the work of Republican scholars like Opilius and Ateius was of a glossographical kind, and Verrius Flaccus was indebted to collections of glosses on Plautus, Ennius, Lucilius, etc.

2. The extant Latin glossaries (generally named from their first item, e.g. Abstrusa, Abavus, or from the home of their chief MS., e.g. St. Gall, Erfurt) cannot be traced back farther than the sixth century A.D. They arose from the needs of monastery teachers who in the first instance gathered together (as *glossae collectae*) and arranged in a roughly alphabetical order the trivial marginalia from copies of the Bible, Terence, Virgil, Orosius, etc., in their own or neighbouring libraries; only rarely did such marginalia contain any scholarly comment, and few glossary compilers had access to e.g. Festus or the *Etymologiae* of Isidore from which to borrow. Copies of a glossary thus constructed sometimes had a wide circulation and formed the basis for larger derivative compilations; for example, Abstrusa (which contained material from a good Virgil commentary) and Abolita (which contained Festus items and Terence and Apuleius glosses) form the foundation for Abavus, Affatim, etc.,

and above all for the huge (early 9th c.?) encyclopaedic *Liber Glossarum* or *Glossarium Ansileubi* (which also includes long passages from Jerome, Ambrose, Gregory, Isidore, etc.). The value of such glossaries is threefold: (*a*) their interpretations often contain Late Latin or Early Romance words; (*b*) they sometimes contain latent evidence for readings in the text of an author; (*c*) occasionally they transmit some fragment of ancient learning.

3. Amongst later collections of glosses the best known are those of Salomon (10th c.) and Papias (11th c.), both of which rely on the *Liber Glossarum*.

4. Of bilingual glossaries may be mentioned: (*a*) the (6th-c.?) Cyrillus glossary (Greek with Latin interpretations) wrongly attributed to the fifth-century patriarch of Alexandria and not yet fully published; (*b*) the Philoxenus glossary (Latin with Greek interpretations) wrongly attributed to the consul of A.D. 535; (*c*) the *Hermeneumata* (Greek with Latin interpretations) wrongly attributed to Dositheus; (*d*) glossaries with Anglo-Saxon, Celtic, or Germanic interpretations.

BIBLIOGRAPHY

J. Tolkiehn, s.v. 'Lexikographie', and G. Goetz, s.v. 'Glossographie', in *PW*; Schanz–Hosius § 1119: Fr. Lammert in *Bursian*, vol. cclii; W. M. Lindsay in *Journ. Phil.* xxxiv. 255 ff. and 267 ff.; in *AJPhil.* xxxviii, 349 ff.; in *CQ* xi. 119 and 185; in *CR* xxxi. 158 and 188; W. M. Lindsay and H. J. Thomson, *Ancient Lore in Medieval Latin Glossaries* (1921); J. F. Mountford, *Quotations from Classical Authors in Medieval Latin Glossaries* (1925). Vol. i (1923) of the *Corpus Glossariorum Latinorum* (ed. G. Goetz), entitled *De origine et fatis glossariorum latinorum*, consists entirely of prefatory material; vols. ii–v give apographs of the oldest MS. of the chief early medieval glossaries (with readings of other MSS. in the app. crit.): ii (1888) contains Latin-Greek (= Philoxenus) and Greek-Latin glossaries; iii (1892) contains the pseudo-Dositheus *Hermeneumata*; iv (1889) contains Abstrusa+Abolita (under the name *gloss. cod. Vat. lat. 3321*) and short derivative glossaries; v (1894) contains the Placidus glossary, excerpts from the *Liber Glossarum*, etc.; vols. vi and vii (1899–1901), entitled *Thesaurus Glossarum Emendatarum*, present the items of vols. ii–v in alphabetical and corrected form. The series *Glossaria Latina* (ed. W. M. Lindsay and others) gives critical editions of the chief glossaries with the fullest possible indication of the source of each item: vol. i (1926) contains the purely glossary material of the *Lib. Gloss.* in its entirety; vol. ii (1926) contains the Arma, Abavus, and Philoxenus glossaries; vol. iii (1926) contains Abstrusa and Abolita; vol. iv (1930) contains Placidus (and an ed. of Festus based on glossary material); vol. v (1931) contains the Abba and AA glossaries. Of Latin–Anglo-Saxon glossaries, the Leyden glossary has been edited by J. H. Hessels (1906), the Corpus glossary by W. M. Lindsay (1921). Latin-Celtic glossaries were edited by Whitley Stokes and John Strachan, *Thesaurus Palaeohibernicus* (1901–3) two vols. with Supplement (1910); cf. R. Thurneysen, 'Irische Glossen' (Zeitschrift für Celtische Philologie xxi); and Latin–Germanic by E. Steinmeyer and E. Sievers (*Die Althochdeutschen Glossen*, 4 vols. 1879–98).
J. F. M.

GLYCON (1), poet of unknown date and place to whom the Γλυκωνεῖον or glyconic metre is attributed by Hephaestion (p. 33, 12). Nothing else is known about him. The epigram in *Anth. Pal.* 10. 124 on the unreason of the universe is thought to be by a different poet of later date, since it appears with other late poems.

S. Leichsenring, *De Metris graecis quaestiones onomatologicae* (1888).
C. M. B.

GLYCON (2), sculptor, of Athens; known from signature of Farnese Heracles (Winter, *KB* 333. 4) in Naples. The statue was found in the baths of Caracalla, and is proved by the ancient inscription on another example in Florence to be a copy of a Heracles by Lysippus (q.v. 2). Nothing in the copy suggests a date later than the first century B.C.

G. Lippold, *Kopien und Umbildungen* (1923), 56.
T. B. L. W.

GLYCONIC, see METRE, GREEK, III (8).

GNIPHO, MARCUS ANTONIUS, a scholar of the Ciceronian age. He taught in the home of Julius Caesar and had a school of his own. His lectures on rhetoric were attended by Cicero during his praetorship (66 B.C.). He is said (by his pupil Ateius Philologus) to have composed only two books *De sermone latino*; but there is evidence that he wrote a commentary on the *Annales* of Ennius.

Cf. Teuffel, § 159. 5; Schanz-Hosius, § 195. 3.
J. F. M.

GNOME (γνώμη). From the root-meaning 'expression of opinion' various specialized meanings spring, one of which is 'pregnant utterance', the pithy expression of a general thought. The sense is something like 'epigram' (in the commonest modern sense of that word), or, when the epigram has become current coin, 'proverb'. Man must have begun to think of gnomes almost as soon as he was capable of making general propositions. At any rate we meet them on the threshold of Greek literature; for Homer's αὐτὸς γὰρ ἐφέλκεται ἄνδρα σίδηρος (Od. 16. 294) is a gnome. The famous γνῶθι σεαυτόν and μηδὲν ἄγαν are unsurpassable for brevity. Hesiod is full of gnomes, and so, centuries later, is Euripides, in whose day the cult of the gnome in intellectualist circles is satirized by Aristophanes (see L. & S., s.v. γνωμίδιον, γνωμοτυπέω, and cognate words). In prose, the gnomic tendency is strongly marked in Heraclitus (q.v., and e.g. fr. 43), and even more so in Democritus (q.v.). The use of the gnome as not merely an ingredient in poetry or prose but as a literary form in itself can be traced back to Phocylides and Theognis (qq.v.) in the middle of the sixth century B.C., and Democritus (c. 460–370 B.C.) himself talks of his works as γνωμέων (fr. 35). For the collection of gnomic sayings into anthologies, see CHREIA. See also SENTENTIA.

PW, Suppl. vi. (1935), pp. 74–90 (Horna and v. Fritz).

J. D. D.

GNOSTICISM is a modern term applied to a group of sects and theosophical writers, most if not all of whom broke with Christianity to set up eclectic systems which rivalled Catholicism, not in points of detail, but in their total outlook on life. The most important of these were Simon Magus, the Ophites, Marcion, Valentinus, Basilides, and Mani. Not all Gnostics advocated the same varieties of worship, some give no evidence of interest in cultus at all; but many groups formed sects of their own, the ceremonies and theology of which were, at least in theory, community secrets.

2. The beginnings of these radical heresies may perhaps be seen in Paul's opponents at Colossae, but the period of their greatest success was in the second and third centuries A.D. They were disseminated throughout the Empire, but exhibit a tendency to rise in and return to the Orient. Their imagery and religious temper were Oriental, and it is no accident that the first and last of the great Gnostics were Simon in Syria and Mani in Persia. Their philosophy, however, was Greek, a feature characteristic of the Hellenistic cultural tradition of which they were the last and most decadent religious product.

3. In the religion of the Hellenistic age special importance was attached to knowledge which enabled men to understand and control the forces conditioning their destiny and to adapt themselves effectively to their demands and restrictions. Confidence in the last of the great classic epistemologies, that of Chrysippus, was shattered by Carneades, and philosophy in the first century B.C. entered upon a phase of intuitionism and mysticism, playing with various combinations of Platonism and Stoicism of which the most successful was the system of Posidonius. The material and phenomenal worlds were connected by a middle ground in which intermediate dynamic forces were released in dramatic interplay. These forces could be unified as the activities of the divine mind (logos) to which man had immediate and intuitive access, or personalized and imagined as the background of cult legends. Plato's Timaeus and the early chapters of Genesis lent themselves easily to this treatment and we have examples of non-Christian gnosticism in Philo and in Hermetic literature, and relatively orthodox Christian parallels in Clement of Alexandria and Origen. To popular apprehension this knowledge was communicated by revelations contained in sacred books and dramatized in esoteric rites. The books gave accounts of the origin and history of the universe and of the life and death of a god who offered salvation to his followers; the rites involved participation of the imagination and feelings in the heroic events of the god's career and a share in their supernatural benefits which included security (soteria) from the ruthlessness of fate and the hostility of demons and men, and the assurance of a happy life after death.

4. To the educated adherents of these cults of salvation through knowledge the mythical revelations symbolized an abstract philosophy; to the uneducated they became the vehicles of superstition and undisciplined living. Astral speculation found a ready reception into this mixed world of thought and fancy and Marcus' eucharistic hocus-pocus, and the text regarded by Dieterich as a liturgy of Mithras shows its magical aspects, while an inscriptional record of a vision of Mandulis Aion strikingly illustrates the underlying zest for revelations.

BIBLIOGRAPHY

SOURCES. Greek and Latin: Justin Martyr, Irenaeus, Clement of Alexandria, Origen, Hippolytus, Alexander of Lycopolis, Epiphanius, Serapion of Thmuis, Titus of Bostra; Tertullian, Filastrius, Augustine.
COPTIC TEXTS: C. Schmidt, Texte und Untersuchungen viii. 1–2 (1892); Griech. christl. Schriftsteller, 13; Pistis Sophia (1925); C. Baynes, A Coptic Gnostic Treatise (1933); and the new Manichaica, C. Schmidt, and J. Polotsky, 'Ein Mani-fund in Aegypten', Sitz. Berlin 1933 i, which are in process of publication.
SYRIAC: Ephraim Syrus; Bardesanes, F. Nau, Le Livre des lois des pays (1899) (cf. H. H. Schaeder, 'Bardesanes', in Zeitschrift für Kirchengeschichte li (1932), 21 ff.; A. A. Bevan, 'Hymn of the Soul', Texts and Studies, v. 3). Mani, in Theodore Bar Konai (cf. F. Cumont, Recherches sur le Manichéisme i (1908), H. H. Schaeder, 'Urform und Fortbildungen des manichäischen Systems', in Vorträge der Bibliothek Warburg, 1924–5 (published 1927)).
ARMENIAN: Eznik of Kolb, Contra Haereses iv (a Marcionite source, cf. Casey, J. Biblical Literature lii 1938), 185).
Gnostic influences have been detected in some of the apocryphal gospels and acts.
GENERAL WORKS: E. de Faye, Gnostiques et gnosticisme² (1925); H. Leisegang, Die Gnosis (1924); A. Hilgenfeld, Ketzergeschichte des Urchristentums (1884); R. P. Casey, JTS xxxvi (1935), 45 ff.; W. Bousset, Hauptprobleme der Gnosis (1907); A. D. Nock, Gnomon xii (1936), 605 ff.; F. C. Burkitt, Church and Gnosis (1932).
PARALLEL TEXTS: Philo (q.v.) Hermetica (see HERMES TRISMEGISTUS); Mandulis Aion (A. D. Nock, Harv. Theol. Rev. xxvii (1934), 53); A. Dieterich, Eine Mithrasliturgie (1903); ed. 3 by O. Weinreich, 1923). For another pagan parallel, cf. W. Kroll, 'De oraculis Chaldaicis' (Bresl. phil. Abh. vii. 1, 1894). R. P. C.

GODS, RIDER-, RIVER-, WIND-, see RIDER-GODS, RIVER-GODS, WIND-GODS.

GOLD (χρυσός, aurum). Gold is a rare metal in Greece, and the source of the rich treasures found in tombs of the Bronze Age (Mycenae, etc.) is unknown. The island of Siphnos prospered in the sixth century B.C. by its gold production; later the mines were flooded. Mines on Thasos, opened by the Phoenicians, were working in Thucydides' day. Macedonia and Thrace had a large auriferous area, where the mines of Mt. Pangaeus were working before 500 B.C. More fruitful than the home supplies were probably those from overseas. Nearest at hand were Mysia, Phrygia, and Lydia; their fame as gold-bearing lands is attested by the stories of Midas, Croesus, and the river Pactolus. Colchis also furnished gold, and Scythians brought supplies from inner Asia. Yet there was a scarcity of gold in Greece until the conquests of Alexander made available the hoards of Persia.

Early Etruscan tombs show a wealth of gold furniture comparable to that of Bronze Age Greece. Traces of early mining are found in several districts of Italy, in particular the Pennine Alps. At Rome the metal long remained rare; it probably first became common through war indemnities. Under the late Republic and early Empire the main source of supply was Spain, where the north-west and Baetica yielded immense quantities. Gold was also mined in southern France and dredged from rivers in other parts of Gaul; there are also workings in south Wales. After the first century the western gold-fields were largely superseded by those of the Balkans, Noricum, and Dacia. When the supply from these fell off during the third century a shortage of the metal appears to have been generally felt.

O. Davies, *Roman Mines in Europe* (1935). For the technical processes involved in making gold jewellery see F. H. Marshall, *Catalogue of Jewellery in the British Museum* (1911), Introduction.
F. N. P.

GONATAS, ANTIGONUS, *see* ANTIGONUS II.

GORDIAN. GORDIAN I (MARCUS ANTONIUS GORDIANUS), Roman emperor, A.D. 238, was descended on his father's side from the Gracchi, while his mother was a relative of Trajan. When proconsul of Africa he was at the age of eighty-one invited to become emperor by some young nobles who had conspired against Maximinus. From a mixture of fear and ambition he accepted, and assumed his son, GORDIAN II, as colleague. The Senate and most of the European provinces acknowledged him, but Capellianus, governor of Numidia, rebelled and moved on Carthage. Gordian II opposed his legionary army with a volunteer militia, and when he was killed his father committed suicide after a reign of twenty-two days (238).

GORDIAN III, son of Gordian I's daughter Maecia Faustina, was, after the murder of Balbinus and Pupienus (*see* BALBINUS) in A.D. 238, saluted emperor by the Praetorians at the age of 13. The conduct of affairs was at first in his mother's hands, but in 241–4 it passed to the praetorian prefect Timesitheus (q.v.). In 242 Timesitheus accompanied Gordian to the Danube to repel an invasion of Goths, and the next year defeated the Persians at Rhesaena. But while a campaign against Ctesiphon was being planned he died of an illness. In his place Gordian appointed an Arab called Philippus, who soon showed his imperial aspirations. Profiting by a food shortage he appealed to the soldiers who wanted a man, not a boy, as their ruler. Gordian was murdered at Zaitha in 244 (*see* PHILIPPUS I).

For bibliography *see* MAXIMINUS (1). H. M. D. P.

GORGIAS (1) of Leontini (*c.* 483–376 B.C.), sophist and rhetor, who won renown at Athens (427) by his eloquence, wrote a philosophical treatise, in which he despaired of attaining positive knowledge, and then devoted himself to revealing the power of λόγος and the value of artistic form in prose speech. The treatise (*Π. φύσεως ἢ π. τοῦ μὴ ὄντος*) is lost, but it is known to have maintained three theses—that nothing exists; that if anything exists, it is unknowable; that if anything can be known, the knowledge cannot be communicated by language. The chief philosophical influences which G. came under seem to have been Empedocles and Zeno the Eleatic. The *Ἑλένης ἐγκώμιον* and *Παλαμήδης* have survived, as well as a few fragments of his speeches (*Πυθικός, Ὀλυμπικός, Ἐπιτάφιος*). He wrote no τέχνη, and his teaching is gathered from his writings and from the remarks of Plato and others. He aimed at a prose which should rival poetry in its effects. Hence his advocacy of (1) poetic words, metaphors, coinages, (2) figures embodying parallelisms and musical effects (anti-thesis, parisosis, paromoiosis, assonance, rhyme), as substitutes for metre. He also pointed out the effects of propriety, brevity, prolixity (αὔξησις), and other devices (Kroll, *Rhet.* § 6). As the founder of artistic prose he made the teaching of style an essential part of rhetoric.

Testimonia and frs. in Diels, *Vorsokr.*⁵ 2. 271–307. P*W* vii. 1598.
J. W. H. A.

GORGIAS (2) (1st c. B.C.), Athenian rhetor of Atticist tendencies (Sen. *Controv.* 1. 4. 7), who taught Cicero's son 44 B.C.) and wrote *Π. σχημάτων* (lost), which was illus-trated by examples drawn from classical and Asiatic orators and was translated into Latin (abridged) by P. Rutilius Lupus (Halm, *Rhet. Lat. Min.* 3–21). J. W. H. A.

GORGO or **MEDUSA**, a terrible monster in Greek mythology. G. was the daughter of the marine deities Phorcys and Ceto. She had a round, ugly face, snakes instead of hair, a belt of the teeth of a boar, sometimes a beard, huge wings, and eyes that could transform people into stone. She had two immortal sisters, who in art are also shown in the shape of Gorgons, Sthenno ('the Strong') and Euryale ('the Wide Leaping'), with whom she lived in the far West, where Poseidon loved her. Perseus went in search of the G., killed her with the aid of Athena, and escaped (Hes. *Theog.* 270). The head of G. adorned the aegis (q.v.) of Zeus and also that of Athena (*Il.* 5. 738). From the body of the G. blood sprang forth; from one vein blood that Asclepius used to revive the dead, from the other blood which he used to harm men (Apollod. 3. 120). In the moment of her death Gorgo-Medusa gave birth to Pegasus and Chrysaor.

The myth of Gorgo-Medusa as known in classical Greece contained religious and folkloristic elements of diverse origin. The head of Gorgo, buried under the Agora of Argos (Paus. 2. 21. 5), seems to indicate that the Gorgoneion was originally an independent embodi-ment of apotropaic power. Medusa again may have been originally an independent earth goddess (L. Malten, *JDAI* 1914, 184; 1925, 121 ff.). In art, Perseus killing Gorgo and pursued by Gorgons is a popular subject during the archaic period; Gorgo alone, a running winged daemon, is also frequently shown, especially in Corinthian art. In the Classical period G. is humanized, and Hellenistic representations develop a definitely beautiful type of head for the dying maiden Gorgo (cf. Cic. *Verr.* 4. 124). Her head always remained a popular apotropaic symbol.

Cl. Hopkins, *AJArch.* 1934; H. Besig, *Gorgo und Gorgoneion* (1937); J. M. Woodward, *Perseus* (1937). G. M. A. H.

GORTYN, one of the most important towns of Dorian Crete, was situated in the southern central plain of the island. Many ruins have been excavated, and many inscriptions found, among them the famous 'Code of Gortyn', containing large parts of a supplementary codification (probably *c.* 450 B.C.). It included many older laws, or referred to them; some of these are also preserved in other inscriptions. The code contains rules of civil law only, but some facts of public law are men-tioned. The laws, lacking systematic order, deal with the family and family-property, with slaves, surety, donations, mortgage, procedure in trials, and other items. Generally in accordance with what we know about early Greek and Indo-European legal usage, the code of Gortyn is a mixture of primitive and developed regula-tions. Most interesting is the position of the slaves, who had certain rights for their protection; they were also allowed to have their own property, and even to marry free women. There was a clear distinction, especially in matters of hereditary right, between family and private property. There were detailed and rather liberal regula-tions on adoption and sole heiresses. Criminal law was still closely connected with family law, but in many cases money penalties had replaced previous forms of punish-ment, and frequently the fines were payable to the State. Self-defence was forbidden. Witnesses and compurga-tors, and the oath of the party, served to establish a case; but the judge decided at his own discretion. On the whole, the laws of Gortyn are the most important source of pre-Hellenistic Greek law, and reveal rather a high standard of juristic conceptions.

J. Kohler and E. Ziebarth, *Das Stadrecht von Gortyn* (1912); R. Dareste, B. Haussoullier, Th. Reinach, *Recueil des inscriptions juridiques grecques* (1891) i, 352 ff. Date: M. Guarducci, *Riv. Fil.* lxvi (1938), 264 ff. V. E.

GOTHS, a German tribe which had migrated from its original home, Götaland in south Sweden, to the lower Vistula by the first century B.C. In the second century A.D. they began to displace tribes farther south, and by the third century their advance-guard was settling in south-west Russia, whence they transmitted the influence of Graeco-Sarmatian culture to the Germanic north and west. *C.* A.D. 238 they began to raid the Roman Empire. They harried Greece and Asia Minor as well as the Danube provinces; successive emperors failed to drive them out until the victories of Claudius Gothicus (268–70) stemmed the tide. The division into Ostrogoths and Visigoths now began to form; the Visigoths made good their hold on a large part of the old province of Dacia, and Constantine, after much warfare, made a treaty with them. He also refortified the Danube frontier, and the peace was maintained in general for thirty-five years. Many Goths served with the Roman armies. The Ostrogothic kingdom between Dnieper and Don became large and powerful under Hermanric (mid-fourth century), but was brought to a sudden end by the invasion of the Huns (370), and the Ostrogoths were driven in the wake of the Visigoths to seek asylum in the Empire. In 376 the Visigoths had entered Moesia, and in the resultant war Valens was defeated and slain at Adrianople (378). Theodosius was able to subdue them, but allowed them to remain. Under Alaric they invaded Italy and sacked Rome (410); they were finally diverted to Gaul, where they founded the kingdom of Toulouse (419) and extended their dominion over Spain. The Ostrogoths entered Italy later and set up a kingdom under Theodoric (493). In the middle and later fourth century Christianity was penetrating among the Goths, through the efforts of missionaries such as Ulfilas, but the majority of them embraced Arianism, which embittered their subsequent conflicts with the Empire.

Iordanes, *de Getis*; Ammianus; Zosimus. L. Schmidt, *Geschichte der deutschen Stämme—Die Ostgermanen*[2] (1934), 195–528. O. B.

GRACCHUS (1), TIBERIUS SEMPRONIUS (*cos. I* 215 B.C.), curule aedile (216) and *magister equitum* to Junius Pera after Cannae, commanded two legions of *volones*, slaves enrolled after Cannae. As consul he thwarted Hannibal at Cumae, as proconsul (214) near Beneventum he defeated Hanno who was trying to join Hannibal from south Italy. Consul II (213); as proconsul in 212 he was surprised and killed probably in Lucania. H. H. S.

GRACCHUS (2), TIBERIUS SEMPRONIUS, the censor, was augur in 204 B.C., accompanied the Scipios to the East in 190, negotiating with Philip V, and as tribune at the time of the prosecution of L. Scipio saved him from imprisonment. Envoy to Greece in 185, he became curule aedile in 182, and as praetor in 180 succeeded Q. Fulvius Flaccus in Spain. Here he completed the reduction of the Celtiberians by systematic operations and a liberal settlement (180–179), founding Gracchuris and giving peace for a generation. Consul in 177, he ruthlessly subjugated Sardinia (cf. Livy 41. 28. 8–10). Censor in 169, with C. Claudius Pulcher, he intervened in the levies, opposed the *publicani*, and restricted the rights of freedmen; his austerity became famous. He served on embassies to the East (165, 161), was again consul (163), and died in 154. A man of high character and liberal thought, a fine strategist and great colonial governor, he dominated the policy of foreign consolidation and internal restoration towards the middle of the century. He married Cornelia, daughter of Scipio Africanus, and his twelve children included Tiberius and Gaius Gracchus.

Livy 37. 7; 38. 52 ff.; 39. 24 and 33; bks. 40–5; Polyb. bks. 25 and 31–2; Appian, *Hisp.* 43; Gellius 6. 19; Cicero, *Prov. Cons.* 8. 18. A. Schulten, *Numantia* i (1914), 329; De Sanctis, *Stor. Rom.* iv. 1, 240, 440, 463, 596, 611; J. Carcopino, *Autour des Gracques* (1928), 47; A. H. McDonald, *JRS* 1938, 163, *Cambr. Hist. Journ.* 1939, 135, 138; R. M. Geer, *TAPA* 1938, 381. A. H. McD.

GRACCHUS (3), TIBERIUS SEMPRONIUS, tribune in 133 B.C., the great reformer and founder of the party of the *Populares*, was the son of Gracchus (2) and of Cornelia (q.v. 1), and the husband of Claudia, daughter of App. Claudius (q.v. 9), *cos.* 143. Educated, like his brother, by Greek philosophers, he was apt to apply Greek democratic conceptions and methods in Roman politics, just as contemporary Roman jurists introduced Greek practices and ideas into the Law. He served under his sister's husband, Scipio Aemilianus, at Carthage in 146; as quaestor, in 137, he took part in the Numantine War, and after the defeat of Mancinus (q.v.) negotiated terms which the Senate rejected; hence perhaps arose his later bitterness against the *Optimates*. We may trust his brother's testimony that the sight of the *latifundia* (q.v.) of Etruria, on Tiberius' journey to Spain, inspired him to proceed with the agrarian scheme of C. Laelius 'Sapiens'.

Tiberius' Agrarian Law aimed at recovering the vast tracts of public land from its *possessores* (each of whom could, however, retain 500 *iugera*, plus an extra 250 *iugera* for each of 2 sons). On the land thus made available, poor citizens were to be settled as tenants, paying rent to the Treasury. Tiberius thus hoped to restore the old yeoman-farmer population which had always been the backbone of the Roman armies. The board of IIIvirs appointed to carry out this plan consisted of Tiberius' father-in-law, Appius Claudius, and of the brothers Tiberius and Gaius Gracchus. Though the proposal roused intense opposition from large landowners, including most of the Senate, it was supported by such influential men as the jurist, P. Mucius Scaevola (*cos.* 135) and his brother Crassus Mucianus, Gaius' father-in-law. To obtain funds for equipping the new settlers Tiberius introduced a plebiscite ordering that some part of the legacy of Attalus III of Pergamum should be devoted to this end; Tiberius thus invaded the Senate's field of financial control and possibly also of foreign policy.

When Octavius (q.v. 2) suddenly vetoed the Agrarian Bill, Tiberius created a constitutional crisis by insisting, on Greek principles, on the deposition of Octavius. The Bill was then passed, but a further crisis followed when Tiberius presented himself for re-election as tribune, for which there was no recent precedent. Tiberius was killed on the day of the elections by his cousin Scipio (q.v. 12) Nasica.

Many of Tiberius' partisans were executed in 132 (*see* POPILLIUS LAENAS): but the work of the IIIvirs continued successfully, as is shown by the census-lists.

Sources: Greenidge and Clay, *Sources* 1–10, cf. F. B. Marsh, *Hist. Roman World*, 378–80. Modern works: A. H. J. Greenidge, *A History of Rome* i, chs. 1–5; H. Last, *CAH* ix, ch. 1; J. Carcopino, *Autour des Gracques* (1928); G. Cardinali, *Studi Graccani* (1912); D. Kontchalowski, *Rev. historique* cliii (1926), 161 ff. M. H.

GRACCHUS (4), GAIUS SEMPRONIUS, husband of Licinia (daughter of Crassus Mucianus), was the great organizer of the reform-party founded by his elder brother Tiberius. He proceeded vigorously, after Tiberius' death, with the work of the Agrarian Commission; and, returning specially from service in Sardinia, was elected tribune for 123 B.C. with a well-prepared series of reforms. The exact order of these measures, and even their distribution between the years 123 and 122, is uncertain; but their underlying aim was clearly to undermine the Senate's authority by uniting permanently with the plebs the rich business class (later known as the *Equites*). By the *Lex Acilia* (probably 123) the *Equites* were given control of the jury-courts for *res repetundae* (q.v.); by Gaius' own enactment they were favoured by the arrangement that the censors should sell, at Rome, the lucrative contracts for the tithes of the province of Asia. Gaius also enabled them to enrich themselves, while serving the State by their ability.

through contracts for carrying out his big plans for road-building in Italy, and for providing warehouses and wharves in connexion with his improvement of the corn-supply of Rome. Gaius attracted various elements among the poorer plebeians by providing corn at reasonable prices, by re-enacting Tiberius' Agrarian Law (restoring the judicial powers which the IIIvirs had lost in 129), and by a large programme of colonization both in Italy and overseas, including Tarentum and Carthage (to be named Junonia). A declaratory law was also passed (under which Popillius (q.v. 2) was exiled); it insisted that capital courts could only be established by the people. Gaius, however, was prevented by his mother from passing a law, aimed at Octavius (q.v. 2), precluding men deprived of office by the people from standing for further offices.

In Gaius' second tribunate (122) resistance hardened; the counter-proposals of Drusus (q.v. 1) may have attracted the plebs, and the *volte-face* of Carbo (q.v. 1) was perhaps symptomatic of a feeling among moderate reformers that Gaius' plans were too revolutionary. The most far-reaching (and far-seeing) of Gaius' proposals, in which he followed the aims of Fulvius (q.v. 4) Flaccus for the extension of the Roman citizenship to Latins and Italians, was not passed; and he failed to obtain re-election to a third tribunate. A riot followed, in which Flaccus and the extremists carried matters beyond the wishes of Gaius himself. The consul Opimius was called by the Senate's *Ultimum Decretum*, then first used, to defend the State; and Gaius was killed in the struggle. The resultant legacy of bitter hatred led directly to the violent party-strife of the Marian period—and, in due course, to the fall of the Republic.

Greenidge and Clay, *Sources*, 19–36. For modern works see above, s.v. GRACCHUS (3), esp. H. Last, *CAH* ix, ch. 2.   M. H.

GRAECINUS, JULIUS, quoted by Columella (e.g. 1. 1. 14; 4. 3. 6) for his work on vines; probably son of the Graecinus addressed by Ovid, *Am.* 2. 10, *Pont.* 1. 6, and father of Julius Agricola (Tac. *Agr.* 4), whose name may allude to farming tastes. Agricola's father was executed A.D. 39 or 40.   J. W. D.

GRAIAE (*Γραῖαι*), in mythology, daughters of Phorcys and Ceto, by name Pemphredo, Dino, and Enyo, sisters of the Gorgons (Hes. *Theog.* 270 ff.); they were three (Aesch. *PV* 794 ff.). They are an incarnation of age, grey-haired from birth (Hesiod), with one eye and one tooth left (Aesch.). Perseus (q.v.) stole their eye and so made them tell him the way to the Gorgons (Pherecydes ap. schol. Apoll. Rhod. 4. 1515); or threw it away (Aesch. ap. [Eratosth.] 22) and left them blind and unable to help their sisters.   H. J. R.

GRAMMAR, GRAMMARIANS (Greek). Linguistic analysis and classification begin, in Greece, with the fifth-century sophists. Their phonetic studies are reflected in the title of a lost work of Democritus 'On euphonious and cacophonous letters', and in a fragment of Euripides' *Palamedes* ἄφωνα καὶ φωνοῦντα συλλαβὰς τιθείς ... Plato (*Cra.* 424 c; cf. *Tht.* 203 b) mentions a classification of the alphabetic sounds as (*a*) voiced (the vowels), (*b*) ἄφωνα but not ἄφθογγα (the ἡμίφωνα of Aristotle), and (*c*) ἄφωνα καὶ ἄφθογγα (the largest class): the last are the ἄφωνα of the Alexandrians, who followed Aristotle in dividing them into δασέα, ψιλά, and μέσα (χ θ φ, κ τ π, and γ δ β), and used σύμφωνα (consonants) to include both second and third classes, (*b*) and (*c*) above.

2. Plato notices two distinctions of accentual intonation, 'acute' and 'grave' (*Cra.* 399 b), Aristotle also a third, intermediate, our circumflex (*Poet.* 1456ᵇ33). In Ps.-Arcad. at p. 186—probably a sixteenth-century interpolation—Aristophanes of Byzantium is said to have invented signs for the accents (and other marks); but

earlier work in this subject was eclipsed by that of Aristarchus.

3. Grammatical classification of words begins with Protagoras, who first distinguished γένη ὀνομάτων as ἄρρενα, θήλεα, and σκεύη. Aristotle has the same terms, but sometimes uses μεταξύ for σκεύη, and notes that many σκεύη are ἄρρενα or θήλεα. Later, οὐδέτερον (neuter) came into use, and κοινόν (common) was added, and ἐπίκοινον (i.e. of one gender but used of both sexes).

4. Plato (*Soph.* 261 d) makes a practical discrimination between examples of two classes of words, ῥήματα and ὀνόματα, distinguished by their potential functions as predications and designations respectively, in a sentence. Aristotle (*Poet.* 20) names and defines ὄνομα, ῥῆμα, σύνδεσμος, and ἄρθρον; but as to the two last the text is disputed as to both definitions and examples. These four, however, with στοιχεῖον, συλλαβή, πτῶσις, and λόγος (composite statement—possibly without verbs) Aristotle calls parts of speech. He includes under πτώσεις all forms of the noun (which comprises also our pronoun, adjective, and adverb) other than the κλῆσις, our nominative, and all verb-forms except the present indicative (ῥῆμα in the narrowest sense). These flexions, whether nominal or verbal, have no separate names. Subject and predicate are distinguished as ὑποκείμενον and κατηγορημένον.

5. The stages leading up to Stoic grammar are obscure. There is evidence that Chrysippus discriminated τὰ προσηγορικά, perhaps as a class of noun. Diogenes Babylonius recognized five parts of speech—Aristotle's with the addition of προσηγορία (common noun). His pupil, Antipater of Tarsus, added a sixth, named by him μεσότης (as allied to noun and verb), by others πανδέκτης, but excluded from the final Stoic classification, which was the same as that of Diogenes. The terminology of inflexion—as of most phenomena—was greatly developed by the Stoics. In Chrysippus, *On the Five Cases*, the fifth was almost certainly the adverb (cf. Aristotle); for the Stoics did not reckon the vocative a case. The nominative they called ὀρθή or εὐθεῖα; the others (πλάγιαι, oblique) were γενική, indicating a γένος, δοτική, used after verbs of giving, and αἰτιατική, denoting the αἰτιατόν, the result caused. A tense (χρόνος) present (ἐνεστώς) or past (παρῳχημένος), might be ἀτελής (sometimes called παρατατικός), imperfect, or τέλειος (or συντελικός), perfect; a past tense might be described as ἀόριστος, undefined in respect of this distinction. The future tense was named ὁ μέλλων (χρόνος). Predications by finite verbs (κατηγορήματα or συμβάματα—ῥῆμα being, in contrast, restricted to the infinitive) were classified as active (ἐνεργητικά), passive (παθητικά, including reflexives, ἀντιπεπονθότα), and οὐδέτερα (neuter, e.g. ζῶ); or, on another basis, as complete (our intransitive) and incomplete (our transitive —requiring an object), with other refinements as to παρασυμβάματα (e.g. μέλει μοι).

6. From their predecessors the Alexandrians adopted ὄνομα (but not, as an independent part of speech, προσηγορία), ῥῆμα, σύνδεσμος, and ἄρθρον; also the adverb (including our interjections), under a name, ἐπίρρημα, the history of which is obscure. To these they added ἀντωνυμία (personal and possessive pronouns only) and πρόθεσις—a term which Chrysippus used, but in what sense does not appear; the later Stoics had a class of προθετικοὶ σύνδεσμοι. The eighth part was created by separating the μετοχή (participle) from the verb; and some proposed, in vain, to give the infinitive and possessive adjective a like status. These eight were known to Aristarchus, and were standardized by the text-book of his pupil, Dionysius (q.v. 16) Thrax.

7. Systematic syntax made little progress until the first century A.D. (*see* HABRON *and* THEON 1): the next century saw, however, the great and original work of Apollonius (q.v. 15) Dyscolus.

For the history of kindred studies, *see* GLOSSA (GREEK) *and* ETYMOLOGY.

J. E. Sandys, *Hist. of Class. Schol.* i (1903); L. Lersch, op. cit. (1838–41, unreliable); H. Steinthal, *Geschichte d. Sprachwissenschaft b. d. Gr. und Römern* (no index); Christ–Schmid–Stählin. The most important Greek grammarians have been, or are to be, published in Teubner's *Grammatici Graeci* and *Lexicographi Graeci*.
P. B. R. F.

GRAMMAR, GRAMMARIANS (Latin).

The Romans' interest in formal grammar was stimulated, even if not first aroused, by Crates of Mallos (*c.* 169 B.C.). The Greek influence on Roman grammatical theory was permanent and is clearly indicated by the Latin terminology, e.g. *casus* (πτῶσις), *accentus* (προσῳδία), *coniugatio* (συζυγία). It was the doctrines of the Stoic scholars of Pergamum in their τέχνη περὶ φωνῆς (a part of the theory of διαλεκτική), and not (as is sometimes asserted) the work of Dionysius Thrax, which afforded the model for Roman grammatical treatises. The short school grammar, no less than the large comprehensive expositions, had three essential sections: (*a*) on *vox, littera, syllaba*, with an introduction defining *ars* and *ars grammatica*; (*b*) on the parts of speech with details of declensions, conjugations, etc.; (*c*) on the *vitia* and *virtutes orationis*. When fully expanded, section (*b*) treated each of the eight *partes orationis* according to their *accidentia*: thus, nouns (including adjectives) were subdivided according to *qualitas* (*propria* or *appellativa*), *genus* (= gender), *figura* (*simplex* or *composita*, as *felix : infelix*), *numerus*, and *casus*; verbs according to *qualitas* (as *perfecta, inchoativa*, etc.), *genus* (*activum, passivum, neutrum, deponens*), *figura* (*simplex* or *composita*), *persona, numerus, modus, tempus, coniugatio*. Section (*c*) included discussions of *barbarismus, soloecismus, cetera vitia* (e.g. *pleonasmus, tapinosis*), *tropi* (e.g. *metaphora, onomatopoeia*), *metaplasmus, schemata lexeos*, and *schemata dianoeas*. Syntax was treated incidentally in sections (*a*) and (*b*), but sometimes (as in Priscian) a further section *de constructione* was appended. The later grammars frequently included other sections: *de orthographia, de differentiis, de idiomatibus* (i.e. divergencies between Greek and Latin usage, e.g. *sequor te* : σοι ἕπομαι), *de metris* (in which all metres were frequently derived by *additio* and *detractio* from the dactylic hexameter and the iambic trimeter); but these topics were often the subjects of separate treatises.

2. Interest in grammatical matters is first attested in the ninth book of Lucilius. In the second century B.C. Aelius Stilo, in the first century B.C. Gnipho, Opilius, Cosconius, Ateius, Nigidius Figulus, and Santra are known as writers on grammar; but it is Varro's grammatical system (included in bk. 1 of his lost *Libri disciplinarum* and implicit in his *De Ling. Lat.*) which is the earliest we can reconstruct with any fullness. He distinguished only four parts of speech: nouns (including adjectives and pronouns), verbs, participles, and particles (including adverbs). The genitive, dative, and ablative cases he called *casus patricus, casus dandi*, and *casus sextus* (the last of which persisted for centuries alongside of *ablativus*); and nouns he grouped according to the ending of the nominative singular. The terms *declinatio* and *modus* were apparently not used by him, nor were the conjugations clearly defined.

3. No complete grammatical work of the first century A.D. is extant (if we except the very interesting sketch in Quintilian 1. 4–8), but the *Ars* of Remmius Palaemon, known to Quintilian and quoted by later writers, was clearly a work of great importance. Planned on a large scale, it brought a new clarity into grammatical exposition. The eight parts of speech are now satisfactorily differentiated, the ending of the genitive singular becomes the basis for classification into declensions, and the four conjugations (I, II, III *correpta*, III *producta* [= IV]) are distinguished by the final syllable of the second person singular present active indicative. Furthermore, the practice of illustrating points by quotations from standard authors is firmly established.

4. Except for the *De Orthographia* of Velius Longus and a similar work of Terentius Scaurus, nothing remains of second-century A.D. grammatical work, though both these writers, like Flavius Caper, seem to have written comprehensive grammars. Of the third-century writers, Julius Romanus is known only by fragments, and the relatively short work of his contemporary Sacerdos (which omits the *vitia et virtutes orationis* and includes a section on metre) remains as our oldest extant Latin grammar. Possibilities of originality and innovation were apparently exhausted by the fourth century; for, apart from short grammars of the school-book type (e.g. Aelius Donatus), authors either boldly copied out with minor modifications large sections of their predecessors' work (e.g. Charisius) or fashioned a minute mosaic of borrowed phrases and ideas (e.g. Diomedes); in either case they achieved a fictitious novelty by their combination of sources and their illustrative quotations. To this century belong, besides those mentioned, Albinus, Cominianus, Marius Victorinus, Servius (who expanded the *ars* of Donatus), and the bilingual Dositheus. From the fifth century have been preserved the treatises of Asmonius, Cledonius, Consentius, Phocas, Pompeius, and Rufinus, none of which is of major importance; but the early sixth century witnessed the publication of the vast grammar of Priscian (in eighteen books) which remained a standard work of reference for grammatical matters in the Middle Ages.

H. Keil (and others), *Grammatici Latini*, 8 vols. (1855–78), contains all the extant treatises of third to sixth centuries A.D. (but for Charisius the standard ed. is now that of Karl Barwick, 1925; for Dositheus, that of J. Tolkiehn, 1913); G. Funaioli, *Grammaticae Romanae Fragmenta* (1907), gives the remains of Republican and early Imperial grammarians. A. Gudeman, s.v. 'Grammatik' in *PW*; K. Barwick, *Remmius Palaemon und die römische ars grammatica* (1922; = *Philologus*, suppl. xv, ii), especially pp. 215–68; J. E. Sandys, *History of Classical Scholarship* i² (1906). J. F. M.

GRAMMATEIS,

secretaries, of various kinds; generally not responsible magistrates, though like them elected (mostly by lot), and serving for a year only. They are found in most Greek States (sometimes called γραμματισταί or γραφεῖς). In Athens the *grammateus* of the Boule was, until *c.* 367 B.C., an elective official; but he served for a prytany only. After this the Boule had two secretaries, both elected by lot (but not from the *bouleutae*) and serving for one year. The γραμματεὺς τῆς βουλῆς performed the general secretarial duties. The γραμματεὺς κατὰ πρυτανείαν supervised the copying, registering, and preserving of all State documents, and (at first) arranged for their publication when this was ordered; his name was normally put at the head of a published document as a guarantee of its accuracy. The γραμματεὺς τῷ δήμῳ or τῆς πόλεως read out dispatches, etc., to the Ecclesia. The *prytaneis* (q.v.) also had a *grammateus* (one of their own number); and collegiate magistracies, as the Eleven, the *Hellenotamiai*, the *Thesmothetai*, had theirs—the last chosen from the *phyle* not represented by the nine archons, and performing some duties for his *phyle*.

A more important official, though serving for a year only, was the γραμματεὺς τοῦ κοινοῦ or τῶν συνέδρων of Federal States, such as the Aetolian and Achaean Leagues. He generally ranked next after the higher military officers. A. W. G.

GRAMMATICUS

in rhetoric has a wider meaning than 'grammarian', and implies a professor of literature, who carried on the elementary work of the *litterator* and trained a student for advanced rhetoric or even trenched on its province (Quint. *Inst.* 2. 1. 4–6). The Greek γραμματικός supplanted the Latin *litteratus*: *grammatici* were *poetarum explanatores* (Cic. *Div.* 1. 116) and expounders of a still more extensive field of knowledge (Cic. *De Or.* 187). Suetonius (*Gram.* 4) gives an instructive summary. *See* EDUCATION, III. 3.　　J. W. D.

GRANIUS LICINIANUS wrote a handbook of Roman history in annalistic arrangement going back ultimately to Livy, but including antiquarian material, e.g. signs and wonders, anecdotes, and curiosities. The remains, preserved in a London palimpsest, come from bks. 26 (?), 28, 33 (?), 36, referring to events of 165, 105, 78 B.C. The work, which shows archaism in style, an interest in Sallust, and the aim of school use, was written after Hadrian's completion of the Olympieum in Athens, and may be Antonine in date.

Editions: G. Camozzi (1900); M. Flemisch (1904). O. Dieckmann, *De Gran. Lic. fontibus et auctoritate* (1896); M. Flemisch, *Gran. Lic.* (1898).　　A. H. McD.

GRAPHE (γραφή) in Athenian practice was a public suit in which the plaintiff could be a volunteer (ὁ βουλόμενος), whereas in a private suit (δίκη) no one but the party concerned could be plaintiff. The injured party could always bring a criminal action in his own behalf. The designation γραφή indicates that the indictment was written, while a δίκη was initiated orally. A plausible reason for this distinction is that commonly the plaintiff was a stranger whose name should be recorded at the inception of the prosecution. The γραφή was doubtless a device of Solon (G. Calhoun, *Growth of Criminal Law* (1927), 104). When the court fixed the penalty (ἀγὼν τιμητός) a second trial was held forthwith to decide between the penalty asked by the plaintiff and that suggested by the defeated defendant.　　R. J. B.

GRAPHE PARANOMON (γραφὴ παρανόμων) was an action at law which might be taken under the Athenian democracy in order to annul a resolution of the Boule or Ecclesia, on the ground that it contravened an existing statute, or that it had been passed by an improper procedure. It was usually directed against the person who had moved the resolution or had put it to the vote, and the dicastery which tried the case might impose upon him any penalty at its discretion. After the lapse of twelve months from the passing of the resolution, an action might no longer be taken against the mover or the presiding magistrate, but the measure itself might be submitted to a dicastery for confirmation or annulment; in this case the Ecclesia appointed advocates (σύνδικοι) to plead in its defence. The date at which the *Graphe Paranomon* was instituted is uncertain: it is first mentioned in connexion with the Revolution of the Four Hundred (411 B.C.). In the fourth century it was frequently used as a means of obstruction by rival politicians; but it probably served a useful purpose as a check upon precipitate action by the Boule or Ecclesia.　　M. C.

GRATIAE, *see* CHARITES.

GRATTIUS 'FALISCUS' (less correct 'Gratius', Buecheler, *Rh. Mus.* xxxv (1880), 407: *CIL* vi. 19–117 ff.; his connexion with Falerii, based on 1. 40 and the epithet 'Faliscus' reported from a lost MS., are not universally accepted), Augustan poet contemporary with Ovid before A.D. 8 (*Pont.* 4. 16. 34), has left one work in about 540 hexameters, the *Cynegetica*. In it he treats of the chase and especially the management of dogs for hunting. It is difficult to decide whether he owes anything to Xenophon (or pseudo-Xenophon) and Plutarch; for his list of breeds of dogs he may have used an Alexandrian source. The Latin influence most operative upon him is that of Virgil's *Georgics*; borrowings from the *Aeneid* are less certain. Authorities differ as to his influence on the similar poem by Nemesianus, third century. *See* DIDACTIC POETRY, LATIN.

The earlier part of his work, after a proem, deals with equipment for capturing game (nets, snares, spears, and arrows); the remaining and longer part (150–541) deals with huntsmen, dogs, and horses. Here, the allotment of nearly 300 lines to dogs (their breeding, points, and ailments) justifies his title. Fortunately for a reader's interest, G. diversifies his theme by the introduction of episodes. There is pleasant relief in these digressions— a eulogy on the chase, the accounts of two clever huntsmen (Dercylus and, considerably later, Hagnon), the homily on the deleterious effects of luxurious fare on human beings (somewhat amusingly juxtaposed with plain feeding for dogs), and two descriptive passages, a Sicilian grotto and a sacrifice to the huntress deity Diana. The concluding portion on horses is mutilated. Good scholars have praised the elegance of Grattius' hexameters; his alliterations may imply imitation not only of Virgil but of earlier Latin poets.

BIBLIOGRAPHY

TEXTS. M. Haupt, *Ovidii Halieutica, Gratii et Nemesiani Cynegetica* (1888); E. Baehrens, *PLM* i (1898); G. Curcio, *Poet. Lat. Min.* (1902); J. P. Postgate, *CPL* ii (1905); F. Vollmer, *PLM* ii. 1 (1911).
COMMENTARY. P. J. Enk, *Gratti Cynegeticon quae supersunt* (proleg. etc.; 1918).
TRANSLATION. J. Wight Duff and A. M. Duff in *Minor Latin Poets* (Loeb, 1935; with text, introd., bibliography).
SPECIAL STUDIES. M. Fiegl, *Des Gr. Cynegetica, seine Vorgänger u. seine Nachfolger* (1890); F. Vollmer, *PW*, s.v.　　J. W. D.

GREECE (*Geography*). Greece constitutes, in regard to its land-forms, the terminus of the central mountain structure of southern Europe. From the central Alps a southern extension of mountain ridges, the Dinaric Alps, runs south-east; over the Greek frontier Mt. Olympus and the main range of Pindus and the central Greek mountains that divide Epirus from Thessaly constitute the concluding portion of this Dinaric Alpine projection. The three prongs of the Peloponnese are its final terminations, except where it emerges again as the island of Crete and swings due eastwards to link up with the Taurus range in Anatolia. Crete is definitely the end of the curve of this submerged mountain ridge, for the depth of water on the south side of Crete is the greatest in the Mediterranean (2,000 fathoms to the west and 1,350 to the east). The Cyclades are the emergent subsidiary and minor peaks of the sunken mountain terminus. It seems that the whole southern extension of this main mountain mass acquired an inclination on the south that led to its submergence. There is no high ground in Africa which resumes the system. Asia Minor is largely independent of this main structure, belonging as it does to the Asiatic systems, which run mainly west–east. The Aegean probably formed a depression in the land between Greece and Asia Minor.

2. Geologically, Greece is composed of rocks mainly Tertiary, consisting principally of grey-blue limestone. In places Cretaceous formations are known, as in Crete and Cephalonia, where a soft yellow rock prevails. Granite emerges in certain places such as Delos, or on the Thracian coast. The blue limestone mountains have, in some places, been metamorphosed under great pressure into crystalline forms, and the upper parts of many mountains and islands are thus of marble. Thasos in the north, Paros and Naxos in the Cyclades, and Mt. Pentelicus at Athens were all sources of white marble. Coloured marbles are found at Tenos in the Cyclades (red), at Skyros (variegated), Euboea (green striated), and Thessaly (*verde antico*). These were always sources of income to Greece. Some mountains, like Mt. Hymettus, are only partly metamorphosed, and consist of grey marble with a slight crystalline structure.

3. The soil of Greece is mostly rich in iron and reddish, consisting of decomposed limestone. It is good for vines and olives, but inferior for crops, which require a

blacker and more carbonized earth. The only exceptions are the volcanic regions, such as Thera and Melos; an active volcano in the former and an extinct or dormant volcano in the latter have provided a very rich soil.

4. In almost all regions of Greece the heavy winter rainfall washes down earth to the lower parts of the mountains, but also washes away in the rivers much earth from the plains. This steady process of enrichment and denudation almost balances, though the plains often suffer undue erosion. This is particularly evident north of the Corinthian Gulf, where the rivers wash down an enormous silt to the sea. The Alpheus in the Peloponnese also heavily denudes the valleys of Arcadia. The Achelous in the north is its equivalent.

5. The principal centres of extensive cultivation in Greece are few. The plain of Thessaly is by far the largest and richest. The Spercheus valley north of Thermopylae and the Cephisus valley and plain in Boeotia are the only cultivable land in central Greece. In the west the plain of Ambracia and the southern parts of Acarnania are cultivable. In Attica the plains of Eleusis and Athens, and the Mesogaia, provide an arable area, but insufficient for the inhabitants. In Peloponnesus the plain of Elis is rich, and the coastal flatlands of Messenia productive, and small areas of fairly good land lie behind the modern Kalamata, in the Vale of Sparta, and in the Argolid. But without proper irrigation all these tend to become barren. In comparison the coastal plains of Asia Minor are unbelievably fertile and well watered. The wealth of the Ionian cities was due to the wider extent of cultivable land and to its essential excellence.

6. Mountains in Greece are not high, the highest being Olympus, about 9,000 feet. Nowhere is there permanent snow except in the unlit valleys of the highest mountains, and even Olympus is clear of snow by August. The rivers mostly run dry, or nearly so, in summer. The northern rivers, the Vardar, the Strymon, and the Hebrus, are deep and constant. To the south only the Peneus, the Alpheus in Peloponnesus, and the Cephisus in Boeotia are non-periodic.

7. Greece is thus essentially a land where life is organized on the periphery of mountain masses and on the coast, so that sea communication is essential for survival. An inter-island life developed and is continued to-day with hardly any change in its main economy. Ancient modes of life can therefore be closely compared with modern. Greek colonization is the essential consequence of a rise in population in a land where the limits of possible population are quite clearly defined.

S. Casson, *Ancient Greece* (1922); Y. Béquignon, *Grèce* (Guides Joanne, 1935); C. Bursian, *Geographie von Griechenland* (1862–72); C. Neumann and J. Partsch, *Physikalische Geographie von Griechenland* (1885).
S. C.

GREECE (*History*). I. Greek history is generally taken to begin at the point when the northern invasions which broke down the prehistoric civilization of Greece came to an end, and when the colonization of the west coast of Asia Minor, partly by refugees from the northern invaders, and partly by the invaders themselves, was completed (roughly *c.* 1000 B.C.). The elements out of which the Greek people of historic times was composed were now all assembled in Greece, and an age of migrations was followed by a period of settlement.

In the first stage of the period of settlement the Greeks (as the inhabitants of Greece may henceforth be called) lived in village communities and were bound together by a loose tribal organization. Within each tribal State a hereditary king (βασιλεύς) discharged the functions of a war-lord and chief priest, and exercised a voluntary jurisdiction (*see also* MONARCHY). A nobility, consisting of the chief landowners of the community, advised the king in council (γερουσία). The common people were occasionally convened in a folk-moot (ἀγορά, ἐκκλησία), but this assembly carried less weight than the Council of Nobles. The details of early tribal organization are very imperfectly known, and the relations of the tribe to its sub-groups, the *phyle*, *phratria*, and *genos* (qq.v.), are uncertain. But it is clear that the authority of the tribal kings was precarious, despite their hereditary position and their claim to divine descent, and that they lacked the power to suppress private warfare within the community. For this reason, and because of the prevalence of inter-tribal wars and forays, life in the early period of settlement remained very insecure, and the foundations for a high civilization had not yet been laid.

II. In the eighth century a new turn was given to Greek history by the growth of cities, which in most parts of Greece replaced the village as the ordinary unit of settlement (*see* POLIS, SYNOECISMUS). The early Greek cities were mostly situated on an easily defensible site, at some distance from the sea, and their original purpose was to provide security against raiders and pirates; but the convenience of towns as centres of government was soon recognized, and the city-state came to replace the tribal State in most parts of the Greek world. In some districts, as in Attica and Laconia, one city (Athens, Sparta) absorbed an entire tribal State or several such States, and controlled a territory of a thousand square miles. More commonly the tribal State was split into several city-states, each of which, as a rule, had only some hundred square miles attached to it and counted not more than five thousand citizens.

Between 750 and 500 B.C. another movement of population took place, which led to the foundation of numerous Greek colonies in the north Aegean area, in the Black Sea district and its approaches, in Cyrenaica, Sicily and south Italy, and at other isolated points of the Mediterranean lands (*see* COLONIZATION, GREEK). This colonial expansion, which probably had its chief cause in the scantiness of cultivable land in Greece proper, but was partly due to political discontents and the growing pains of the city-state (see below, III), was the other main event of early Greek history. It gave the Greek people a large frontage on the Mediterranean seaboard, it provided them with a sufficiency of land, and it stimulated their industry and commerce. But the colonies, with rare exceptions, became fully independent States, and the consequent large increase in the number of these complicated the problem of Greek political union.

III. In the meantime, and partly as a result of the colonial movement, the internal development of the city-states proceeded at a rapid, and sometimes at a revolutionary, rate. The government of the cities was in the first instance monarchical; but after 700, and almost universally before 500, the city-kings were supplanted by the nobles, who combined their forces against the monarch (*see* ARISTOCRACY). The aristocracies abolished the right of private war and compelled the reference of disputes to their courts of law; but they incurred unpopularity by using their power to exploit and in some cases to enslave the peasantry.

With the growth of industry and commerce the ascendancy of the nobles was challenged by a new class of artisans and traders, and was undermined by a loss of solidarity among the ruling class. In some towns the ensuing struggle between nobles and commons ended in a peaceful compromise, like the Conflict of the Orders at Rome; in others the aristocracies were forcibly ejected from power, and were replaced by tyrannies (q.v.) exercising autocratic rule. The tyrants generally sought to conciliate the commons and introduced a more enterprising government. They adorned their cities with public buildings, they patronized art and literature, they entered foreign alliances and carried out schemes of colonization. But it was never long before they became 'tyrannous' in the modern sense and succumbed to a counter-revolution. The first tyranny was set up (at Sicyon) *c.* 650; by 500 this form of government had almost everywhere been abolished.

After the fall of the tyrants most Greek cities reverted to some form of government by a privileged class, for which the magistracies and the seats on the Council were reserved (*see* OLIGARCHY). But these oligarchies were based on wealth rather than on birth, so that enriched families could from time to time bring fresh blood into the ruling class; and in some cities they allowed the commons an ultimate control over the affairs of State. This control was exercised by an Ecclesia (q.v.), which usually obtained the right of deciding important issues like those of peace and war, and sometimes also elected the magistrates and revised their judgements on appeal. By 500 most of the Greek cities had established a strong but responsible government, and one which gave the ordinary citizen a sufficient share in the affairs of State to draw him out and make him a keen student of politics.

IV. But the patriotism which the city-states fostered was apt to become perverted. Participation by the commons in political affairs whetted their appetite for a larger share of power, which the ruling class was reluctant to concede. A perpetual conflict thus arose between democratic and oligarchic parties within each city, and feeling at times rose so high that democrats would use armed force to overthrow the oligarchs, and vice versa. The history of many city-states was therefore punctuated with revolutions, in which now one party and now the other killed its opponents and confiscated their property. Although *stasis* (party rancour) was vigorously denounced by the best Greek minds, it went on asserting itself so long as the Greeks retained their political freedom.

Again, the legitimate pride which the Greeks felt in their cities was apt to degenerate into aloofness or even hostility in their relation to other towns. It is true that by 600 the Greeks had become conscious of their common nationality; the poetry of Homer, religious institutions such as the oracle of Delphi and the athletic festival at Olympia, and increasing contacts between themselves and non-Greek peoples, had made the Greeks aware of their common culture, and they had accordingly applied to themselves the national name of 'Hellenes'. The recognition of Greek nationality also brought with it the beginnings of political co-operation. Cities sometimes facilitated mutual commerce by means of consuls (*see* PROXENOI), or by entering into treaties for the peaceful regulation of trade disputes (*see* SYMBOLA); they occasionally referred disputes of a territorial or political character to a third city for arbitration (q.v.); and in a few cases they combined into a rudimentary federation (*see* FEDERAL STATES). But more substantial progress towards political union was hindered by the geographical barriers which divide Greece internally, and more especially by an exaggerated municipal pride, which insisted that each city should possess not only the right to make its own laws and administer its internal affairs (*see* AUTONOMY), but complete and sovereign independence.

V. The more usual method of settling political disputes was therefore a resort to war. The inter-city wars of the Greeks, it is true, were fought under certain decent conventions (*see* WAR, RULES OF), and seldom resulted in heavy casualties; but they kept alive ill-feeling and created 'hereditary enemies'.

The only practical remedy for this state of things was that one city should outstrip all the others in power and use its strength to enforce a general peace, in the same way as the 'pax Romana' was subsequently established by Rome. By 500 two such potential leaders of a united Greece had emerged, Sparta and Athens. Of these two States Sparta had undergone a development which was almost unique among the Greek cities. In order to keep down its serf population (*see* HELOTS), it had constituted itself as a totalitarian military State, whose citizens gave their whole time to training for war. But the Spartan army developed from a means of defence into an instrument of conquest. By 500 the greater part of Peloponnesus had been brought together in a permanent military alliance under Spartan control (*see* PELOPONNESIAN LEAGUE), and all Greece recognized in Sparta the predestined *hegemon* or war-leader in the event of national danger.

Athens had a more normal development, except that it made slow progress until 600 and then went ahead rapidly. It possessed large natural assets—rich silver-mines (*see* LAURIUM), clay beds and marble quarries, and a capacious and centrally situated harbour (*see* PIRAEUS). In the sixth century its tyrant Pisistratus (q.v.) fostered its material development; its legislators Solon and Cleisthenes (qq.v.) gave it a constitution which conferred large political powers upon the common people and strengthened their public spirit. Finally, Themistocles (q.v.) provided it with a war-fleet far surpassing that of any other Greek city.

VI. The political development of the Greek people and its colonial expansion were favoured by the absence of any foreign pressure upon it during its early history. But after 650 a regrouping of foreign Powers to east and west checked its expansion and endangered its independence. Between 650 and 550 the Greeks of Asia Minor were attacked, and for lack of any concerted resistance were subdued one by one, by the kings of Lydia. Soon after 550 they were absorbed with the rest of the Lydian kingdom into the empire of Persia, and an attempt at rebellion on their part in 499–493 (the 'Ionian Revolt') was suppressed. The Persians followed up their victories in Asia by invading the Greek mainland in 490 and again in 480–479. The former expedition, which was aimed primarily at Athens, was beaten off single-handed by the Athenians at Marathon. In the second invasion King Xerxes brought to Greece an army and fleet of unprecedented size, but had to face a coalition of Greek States under Spartan leadership. He overran Greece as far as the Isthmus of Corinth, but his navy was eventually defeated at Salamis, and his land forces at Plataea. During the next thirty years (478–449) the Athenians led the Aegean Greeks in a counter-attack which resulted in the liberation of the Asiatic Greeks (*see* PERSIAN WARS).

In the western Mediterranean the Carthaginians opposed further Greek expansion after 600; by 500 they had almost confined the Greek colonists to Sicily and southern Italy, and in 480 they made a determined attempt to conquer all Sicily. The Sicilian Greeks, who had been forcibly united under the rule of a military tyrant, Gelon (q.v.) of Syracuse, beat off this attack, but they did not recover any of the lost ground in the west.

VII. The Greeks ever after regarded their victory in the Persian Wars as their greatest national achievement. They rightly emphasized the superiority of morale which they, as a self-governing people, had shown over the subjects of the Persian autocrat; but they did not sufficiently appreciate the important part which unity of command on the Greek side had played, and they did not adequately recognize the need of continued co-operation. or at least of the avoidance of further inter-city warfare. It is true that the Athenians induced most of the Aegean Greeks (including the Asiatic Greeks whom they had freed from Persia) to enter into a permanent alliance (the Delian League, q.v.), whose object was to maintain a durable peace on the Greek seas. Though the Athenians presently gave grounds for complaint to their allies by needless interference in their internal affairs, the Delian League, while it lasted, was the chief stabilizing agency in Greek politics. At the same time the Athenians, under the guidance of Pericles (q.v.), carried out a series of bold constitutional experiments, by which almost the entire administration of the city was placed in the hands of the common people. As the pioneer of democracy, Athens became the rallying-point of the many Greek cities in which the democratic movement was gaining strength at this time. After the Persian Wars, moreover, Athens acquired commercial supremacy in the Greek world and was becoming its intellectual centre. The city was now marked out as the future leader of Greece.

In the meantime Sparta had been content to revert to its former position as head of the Peloponnesian League, and offered no sustained opposition to the growth of Athenian power. But in 431 the two chief cities of Greece were involved through a series of small incidents in a war that drew in behind them the greater part of the Greek world (see PELOPONNESIAN WAR). In this Greek 'World War', which lasted twenty-seven years, the Athenians threw away the advantage of a stronger fleet and greater financial resources in ill-advised adventures. In the later stages of the conflict they also had to contend with Persia, which gave the Spartans support, on condition of receiving back the Asiatic Greeks. The war therefore ended in a decisive defeat for Athens.

VIII. The hegemony of Greece was now resumed by the Spartans, who had acquired control, by conquest or alliance, over most of the mainland and the Aegean area. But the benefits of the Spartan peace were, in the opinion of the Greeks, outweighed by the harshness of Sparta's dominion over them, for the Spartans now made a general practice of imposing unwelcome oligarchic governments upon them, and enforced their authority in many towns by means of garrisons. In 395 the next four strongest States in Greece, Argos, Athens, Corinth, and Thebes, combined in an attempt to shake off the Spartan yoke, and they received support from the Persians, whom the Spartans had offended by going back on their bargain about the Greek cities of Asia. Eventually the Spartans won back the Persians to their side by fulfilling their previous compact, and by the 'King's Peace' of 386 they confirmed their hold upon the Greeks of the mainland. But by repeating their former political mistakes they provoked fresh rebellions, and in 371, at the battle of Leuctra, they sustained a resounding defeat at the hands of a Theban general named Epaminondas (q.v.), who greatly improved upon the conventional Greek tactics. In the general uprising that followed this defeat Sparta finally lost her ascendancy, both in the rest of Greece and in Peloponnesus. The Thebans, however, made but a half-hearted attempt to substitute their dominion for that of Sparta, and in the peace settlement of 361 they reverted to the principle of autonomy for all the mainland cities, and hegemony for none. In the meantime the Athenians had enrolled some of the Aegean Greeks in a second maritime confederacy, but this always lacked vitality and by 350 it was visibly falling to pieces.

IX. In the fourth century Persia, though still alert to snatch advantages from Greek disunion, no longer had the strength or the will to undertake a new invasion of Greece. In the west the Carthaginians persisted in their attempts to conquer Sicily, but the Greeks in that island were saved in spite of themselves by a succession of fresh tyrants in Syracuse, who forcibly rallied the other cities and beat off several Carthaginian attacks (see DIONYSIUS I; AGATHOCLES).

But to the north of Greece, where weak tribal monarchies had kept each other in play since the beginnings of Greek history, a new conquering power arose in 359, when Philip II (q.v.) of Macedon created a centralized realm and trained up an army which was more than a match for the Greek hoplites (see WAR, ART OF). Against the encroachments of Philip the Greeks offered no

combined resistance, until the Athenian orator Demosthenes (q.v.) brought about a coalition of Athens, Thebes, and a few other cities. But the scratch force which the allies put into the field was irretrievably defeated by Philip at the battle of Chaeronea (338), and the Greek homeland now accepted his rule. The Macedonian king used his authority to impose upon the Greeks a federal union which obliged them to settle their disputes in future by arbitration in place of war, and to send delegates to a regular Hellenic parliament at Corinth. Though nominally the Greek confederacy was on a basis of alliance with Macedon, in fact Philip, who kept garrisons at Corinth and other key points of Greece, could dictate his terms to it, and he had himself appointed captain-general of a national Greek army which was to co-operate with the Macedonians in an attack upon Persia.

X. By the sudden death of Philip the command of the joint forces devolved upon his son Alexander III (q.v.), who overran and annexed the whole Persian Empire (334–325). The empire thus formed by Alexander was the largest which the world had yet seen; but after his premature death in 323 it broke into pieces, and during the next forty years Alexander's chief officers (mostly Macedonian noblemen) fought one another for its fragments. By 275 three new dynasties had been established: the Antigonids held Macedonia, with a few outlying dependencies in Greece (notably Corinth); the Seleucids had acquired most of Alexander's Asiatic possessions; the Ptolemies ruled Egypt, together with southern Syria, Cyprus, and Cyrenaica. The Greek homeland, after passing through the hands of successive Macedonian overlords, for the most part recovered its independence, but the federal constitution with which Philip had presented it was allowed to lapse. Athens and Sparta again became disconnected city-states. Athens, though still acknowledged as the intellectual centre of the Greek world, had lost much of its commercial importance and soon renounced all hopes of hegemony in Greece. Sparta still nursed ambitions of renewed leadership, but never realized them.

The rest of the Greek homeland was for the most part incorporated into two sectional confederacies, of which the Aetolian League came to comprise most of central Greece, and the Achaean League the greater part of Peloponnesus. More important than this redistribution of political power was the fact that continual contact between Greeks and Macedonians brought about a peaceful conquest of victorious Macedonians by the vanquished Greeks. By 200 the Macedonians, acknowledging the superior culture of the Greeks, had become fully hellenized.

XI. Between 275 and 200 the Greek world was again distracted by continuous sectional wars. Of the three new dynasties, the Ptolemies repeatedly came into conflict with the Seleucids over the possession of Syria, and they endeavoured to keep the Antigonids in play by fomenting movements against them on the Greek mainland and in the Aegean area. At the end of the century the territory of the Ptolemies had undergone little change, but that of the Seleucids had been enormously reduced. Unable to form a front against the Ptolemies, and at the same time to hold down the vast masses of their Oriental subjects, they allowed most of these to slip out of their grasp. By 200 they retained little else besides Mesopotamia, northern Syria, and southern Asia Minor; in western Asia Minor they acquiesced in the formation of yet another Greek monarchy, which the Attalid dynasty set up round the city of Pergamum. The Antigonids on the other hand gradually increased their hold on the Greek homeland. In 225 an attempt by the Spartans to recover control of Peloponnesus led to an alliance between the Antigonids and the Achaean League. At the battle of

Sellasia (222) King Antigonus Doson finally destroyed Sparta's hopes of hegemony; at the same time he reduced the Achaean League to a position of virtual dependency, and thus acquired an authority in Greece not unlike that which Philip and Alexander had secured for themselves.

XII. The conquests of Alexander had imposed upon the Greeks (under which term the Macedonians may henceforth be included) the problem of administering vast territories with non-Hellenic populations. Alexander's scheme for the government of his empire appears to have been based upon the amalgamation of Macedonians and Persians in the first instance, and a more general fusion of his European and Asiatic subjects to follow. But his plan for the 'marriage of Europe and Asia' was deliberately rejected by his successors. During the first century at least of their rule both Seleucids and Ptolemies sought to maintain a sharp distinction between Greeks and Orientals; they reserved the more important administrative posts for the Greeks, and they recruited their armies principally from the Hellenic settlers in their kingdom.

In Egypt the Ptolemies, following the tradition of the Pharaohs, set up a highly centralized government, entailing a large staff of professional administrators. Their special interest lay in the collection of a large revenue, and to this end they exercised a close control over the economic activities of their subjects and imposed a highly complicated system of taxation upon them. The Seleucids, whose territory was more extensive and less homogeneous, maintained the Persian system of devolving authority to their district governors, and they accorded a considerable measure of self-government to the numerous Greek cities which they founded in the Nearer East (see COLONIZATION, HELLENISTIC).

In the Greek homeland the Achaean and Aetolian Leagues (qq.v.) devised a system of federal government which adequately safeguarded the autonomy of the constituent cities and prevented the larger towns from acquiring a dangerous preponderance over the rest. But they failed to provide an adequate substitute for the Hellenic federation of Philip and Alexander, or to prevent the recrudescence of sectional warfare in Greece.

XIII. After 200 the history of Greece becomes progressively merged in that of Rome. The intrusion of Rome into Greek affairs was in the first instance due to Antigonus Doson's successor Philip V, who offended the Italian republic by intervening in the Second Punic War, and also came to blows with the kingdom of Pergamum and the city of Rhodes. An appeal for help from these two States brought the Romans into the field against Philip and gave them their first victories on Greek soil (200–196). For the time being they attempted no more than to guarantee the liberty of the lesser Greeks against the Antigonids; but they again became embroiled with the Antigonids, and the Greek cities endeavoured to shake off their protectorate. After further forcible interventions they annexed Macedonia (148) and dissolved the Aetolian and Achaean Leagues, so as to reduce the political power of the Greek homeland to a nullity (146). Henceforth the Greek cities enjoyed an almost unbroken peace, but the people lost their interest in politics and left their municipal government in the hands of the wealthier classes.

About 200 a revival of Seleucid power was achieved by King Antiochus III, who temporarily recovered most of the lost eastern provinces and captured Syria from the Ptolemies. But by an ill-judged intervention in the affairs of the Greek homeland he was drawn into conflict with Rome (192–189), and at the battle of Magnesia he sustained a defeat which shattered Seleucid authority in Asia. Within the next sixty years the eastern Seleucid provinces finally secured their independence, while the Jews set up a free State in Palestine. By 100 B.C. the Parthian monarchy had seized Mesopotamia, and the Seleucid realm had shrunk to a small principality in Syria. During the second century Rome's former allies, Pergamum and Rhodes, and the Ptolemaic kingdom (which had always cultivated friendly if somewhat distant relations with Rome) gradually lapsed into the condition of dependent allies. The final settlement of the Greek East by Pompey, Caesar, and Augustus accomplished little more than to give Roman authority a more definite shape.

While the Macedonian conquest had the paradoxical effect of giving the Greeks extended power, the Roman domination definitely reduced them to subject status. But under Roman rule the Greeks still enjoyed a large measure of autonomy, and their culture continued to spread in the Near East. A Greek-speaking Byzantine monarchy was therefore able to rule the Near East for many centuries after the fall of the Roman Empire.

BIBLIOGRAPHY

(a) For the ancient sources of Greek history see HISTORIOGRAPHY (GREEK), EPIGRAPHY (GREEK), COINAGE (GREEK), PAPYROLOGY, OSTRACA. Modern source-books: G. F. Hill, *Sources for Greek History between the Persian and the Peloponnesian Wars*[2] (1903); M. Cary, *The Documentary Sources of Greek History* (1927).

(b) GENERAL TEXT-BOOKS. Among older works the *Histories of Greece* by G. Grote (1888 ed., 10 vols.) and A. Holm (Engl. Transl., 4 vols., 1896–8) may still be consulted with profit. Of recent works by single authors the most important are: J. B. Bury, *History of Greece*[2] (1913); M. Rostovtzeff, *History of the Ancient World*, vol. i[2] (1930); id., *Hellenistic World* (1941); A. W. Gomme, in E. Eyre, *European Civilization*, vol. i (1935); E. Cavaignac, *Histoire de l'antiquité* (3 vols., 1913–17); R. Cohen, *La Grèce et l'hellénisation du monde antique*[2] (1938); E. Meyer, *Geschichte des Altertums* (to 350 B.C.: vols. ii and iii in the 2nd ed., 1928–37; vols. iii–v in the 1st ed., 1901–2); G. Busolt, *Griechische Geschichte* (to 404 B.C.: 3 vols., vol. iii in 2 parts, 1893–1904); K. J. Beloch, *Griechische Geschichte*[2] (4 vols. in 2 parts each, 1916–27); U. v. Wilamowitz-Moellendorff, *Staat und Gesellschaft der Griechen und Römer*, pt. i[2] (1923); G. Busolt, *Griechische Staatskunde* (2 vols., 1920–6); G. De Sanctis, *Storia dei Greci* (to 403 B.C.: 2 vols., 1939).

The following are the principal composite works: *The Cambridge Ancient History*, vols. ii–ix (1924–32); The *Methuen Series of Ancient History*, vol. ii, 478–323 B.C., by M. L. W. Laistner (1936); vol. iii, 323–146 B.C., by M. Cary (1932); G. Glotz, R. Cohen, and P. Roussel, *Histoire grecque* (3 vols., i–iv pt. i, 1925–38).

(c) SPECIAL PERIODS. (1) *To 500 B.C.* J. L. Myres, *Who Were the Greeks?* (U.S.A., 1930); T. D. Seymour, *Life in the Homeric Age* (U.S.A., 1907); A. R. Burn, *Minoans, Philistines and Greeks* (1930); A. F. H. Jardé, *The Formation of the Greek People* (1926); P. N. Ure, *The Origin of Tyranny* (1922).

(2) *500–323 B.C.* A. E. Zimmern, *The Greek Commonwealth*[5] (1931); G. Glotz, *The Greek City* (1929); T. R. Glover, *From Pericles to Philip* (1917); H. Francotte, *La Polis grecque* (1907). See also s.vv. ATHENS, SPARTA, PERSIAN WARS, PELOPONNESIAN WAR, PHILIP II, and ALEXANDER III of Macedon.

(3) *The Hellenistic Age.* W. W. Tarn, *Hellenistic Civilization*[2] (1929); W. S. Ferguson, *Greek Imperialism* (1913); P. Jouguet, *L'Impérialisme macédonien et l'hellénisation de l'Orient* (1936); P. Roussel, *La Grèce et l'Orient* (1928); J. Kaerst, *Geschichte des Hellenismus*[2] (2 vols. 1926–7). See also s.vv. MACEDONIA, PERGAMUM, PTOLEMY, SELEUCUS.

(4) *The Roman Period.* G. F. Hertzberg, *Geschichte Griechenlands unter der Herrschaft der Römer* (1868); G. Finlay, *History of Greece* (ed. Tozer, 1877), vol. i; S. Accame, *Il dominio Romano in Grecia dalla guerra Achaica ad Augusto* (1946).

(d) SPECIAL DISTRICTS. R. Carpenter, *The Greeks in Spain* (1925); E. A. Freeman, *History of Sicily* (4 vols., 1891–4); E. Ciaceri, *Storia della Magna Grecia* (2 vols., 1926–7); S. Casson, *Macedonia, Thrace and Illyria* (1926); M. Rostovtzeff, *Iranians and Greeks in South Russia* (1922); W. W. Tarn, *The Greeks in Bactria and India* (1938).

(e) SPECIAL TOPICS. (1) *Chronology.* H. F. Clinton, *Fasti Hellenici* (1834–51), though out of date, has not been superseded.

(2) *Statistics of population.* K. J. Beloch, *Die Bevölkerung der griechisch-römischen Welt* (1886).

(3) *Economics.* J. Toutain, *The Economic Life of the Ancient World* (1930); G. Glotz, *Ancient Greece at Work* (1926); H. Michell, *The Economics of Ancient Greece* (1940); P. Guiraud, *La Propriété foncière en Grèce* (1893); H. Francotte, *L'Industrie dans la Grèce ancienne* (2 vols., 1900–1); Rostovtzeff, *Hellenistic World.* See also s.vv. AGRICULTURE, INDUSTRY, COMMERCE.

(4) *Finance.* A. M. Andreades, *A History of Greek Public Finance*, vol. i (U.S.A., 1933).

(5) *Warfare.* See s.vv. ARMIES, NAVIES, WAR (ART OF).

Fuller general bibliographies will be found in the *Cambridge Ancient History*.

For annual reports on recent publications, see *The Year's Work in Classical Studies*; J. Marouzeau, *L'Année philologique*; C. Bursian, *Jahresbericht über die Fortschritte der classischen Altertumswissenschaft*.

M. C.

GREEK LANGUAGE, see DIALECTS, GREEK.

GRILLIUS (5th c. A.D.), grammarian. Extracts from his *Commentum in Ciceronis libros de inventione* are extant (ed. Halm, *Rhet. Lat. Min.* 596–606). Cf. Teuffel, § 445. 7; Schanz-Hosius, § 1122.

GROMATICI, land-surveyors, from *groma* (derived, through Etruscan, from γνώμων or γνῶμα), an instrument for taking bearings to fix lines of orientation; the name survived as a professional title, beside the commoner *agrimensores*, after the instrument was obsolete. They formed a special profession to which we find reference made as early as in Plautus (*Poen.* 48). Their services were used for the plotting of camps (*castrametatio*), the planning of colonies, and the measurement and division of estates, by subdivision into rectangles, and for census. During the land assignations of the last century of the Republic the demand for surveyors was probably met by private enterprise; under the later Empire official surveyors formed a highly organized branch of the civil service. Military surveying, which in Caesar's army was done by the centurions, became a specialized profession, and inscriptions show that each legion had *mensores* attached. Besides the practical work of measuring and dividing land, public or private, and producing plans (*formae*) and schedules (*commentarii*), the *gromatici* also acted as arbitrators or as expert assessors in private land-disputes (*controversiae*). The combination of mathematics, practical advice, and law which we find in Roman writings on this subject, does not occur in Greece, although the mathematical basis is Greek.

The technical literature of the profession is represented by a collection of miscellaneous treatises, ranging in date from the first to the fifth century, and dealing with the technique of mensuration, boundary-marking and map-making, and the rules of land-tenure as they concern the surveyor. The collection has come down to us in an edition of the sixth century, in which the original matter has suffered much from corruption and interpolation. Besides excerpts from Frontinus (q.v.), embedded in a commentary by Aggenius Urbicus, it contains works ascribed to Hyginus, Junius Nipsus, Siculus Flaccus, and Innocentius (see these names), some shorter treatises, anonymous or ascribed to unknown authors, notes on geometry, and extracts from official registers of surveys. The wide differences in date between the parts are reflected in their latinity; the writing is crabbed, often to the point of obscurity, and devoid of literary merit.

The only complete edition is *Die Schriften der Römischen Feldmesser*, by F. Blume, K. Lachmann, and A. Rudorff (two vols. 1848, 1852); vol. ii contains essays by Lachmann, Rudorff, and Mommsen which are still valuable. Of the Teubner edition by C. Thulin (*Corpus Agrimensorum Romanorum*) only vol. i, part i (1913) has appeared, containing Frontinus, Aggenius Urbicus, Hyginus, and Siculus Flaccus. Teuffel-Schwabe, *Hist. of Lat. Lit.*[4], Engl. Transl., Index (s.v.); *PW* vii. 188 b.; H. Stuart Jones, *Companion to Roman History* (1912), 13 ff.; F. Haverfield, *Ancient Town-Planning* (1913), passim. C. J. F. and K. O. B.

GUARDIANSHIP. (*a*) GREECE. The development of the law of guardianship in Greece and Rome was influenced by the change in the conception of guardianship itself, which began as a right of preserving and protecting the ward's property in the interest of the whole kin (as contingent heir of the ward), but became gradually a duty of the guardian in the interest of the ward himself. This explains the restrictions imposed upon the guardian with regard to his control over the child's property, and the increasing supervision of public authorities over his activity as guardian. The Greek guardian was either ἐπίτροπος of boys and girls until their majority—eighteen years in the case of boys—and registration in the citizen list, or κύριος of women for lifetime or until marriage. Guardians were appointed by the father's will; failing testamentary appointment the next relatives (brother or uncle), being the most

likely successors, were entitled to claim the guardianship; in the absence of these an official (the Chief Archon in Athens) appointed the guardian. The guardian had to provide for the ward's education, attend to all his interests, and represent him in legal transactions: in general he was required—as Plato, *Leg.* 11. 928 recommends—to act on his behalf with the same solicitude as for a child of his own. The administration of property by the guardian, especially of landed property, was submitted to the control of magistrates. Action for damages caused by the guardian might be brought against him by the ward within five years of the end of the guardianship. The principles of guardianship of women were analogous; but a woman could dispose freely of objects of lesser importance, without the help of her *kyrios*.

2. (*b*) ROME. Roman law distinguished between *tutela* and *cura* as types of guardianship of persons *sui iuris*, not subject either to *patria potestas* or *manus* (qq.v.). *Tutela* concerned children below the age of puberty (*impuberes*: boys under 14, girls under 12) and women; *cura* comprehended *puberes* under twenty-five (*minores*), lunatics (*furiosi*), and spendthrifts (*prodigi*). The XII Tables admitted the appointment of a tutor by a *pater familias* to his child (who by the parent's death became *sui iuris*). In the absence of a testamentary tutor, the next agnate became *tutor legitimus* as appointed by law. In default of a *tutor legitimus*, the guardian was appointed by the competent magistrate (at Rome there was for a long period a special *praetor tutelaris*).

3. The whole institution of guardianship was in ancient law intended to keep the property within the agnatic family; therefore both *tutela mulierum* and *cura furiosi* and *prodigi* passed likewise to the nearest agnates. Under the developed law guardianship became a public duty (*munus*), depending more and more on the magistrate. Persons duly appointed might, however, refuse to assume the burden of guardianship, on the ground of high office, advanced age, ill health, a certain number of children or guardianships, etc.

4. In the ancient law the *tutor* stood *domini loco* in regard to the ward's property. The effects of all his transactions primarily concerned himself, and he could not oblige the ward. But before long the capacity of *impuberes* to conclude transactions with *auctoritas* of his tutor was recognized. This *auctoritas* was at first a formal act, but later informal. The classical law gave greater scope to the supervision of the tutor by the magistrate. He might be compelled to give security; alienation or hypothecation of landed property could be operated only with authorization of the magistrate, etc. For misconduct the guardian could be removed from his trust. Another remedy, originating also in the XII Tables, was available in case the tutor embezzled the child's property. A later action, *actio tutelae*, served for the recovery of damages, in case of any intentional or negligent breach of duty by the tutor. Since his responsibility rested on the principle of *bona fides*, it was susceptible of a wide interpretation; condemnation involved infamy.

5. The *tutor* of an adult woman did not administer her property; his authorization was required for more important transactions only. In the last century of the Republic *tutela mulierum* fell into decay.

6. The latest type of *cura* was created exclusively in the interest of minors. By reason of the *Lex Plaetoria* (*c.* 200 B.C.) and the praetorian remedy *in integrum restitutio*, transactions with a *minor sui iuris* (originally freely admitted) might be impugned, if his inexperience was misused to his detriment; therefore dealings with him became risky, and his right to administer his estate was practically illusory. For this reason a *cura minorum* was introduced, so that the co-operation of the *curator* might protect transactions with the minor. *Curatores* were appointed by the magistrate on demand of the minor, originally only for one affair, later for more general purposes. By later development the rights of permanent curators were considerably enlarged to the detriment of the minor's independence. In post-classical and Justinian's law *tutela* and *cura* were largely assimilated, but remained distinct.

(*a*) GREECE: O. Schulthess, *Vormundschaft nach griechischem Recht* (1886); Beasley, *CR* 1906, 249 ff.; J. H. Lipsius, *Attisches Recht und Rechtsverfahren* ii. 2 (1912); L. Mitteis, *Grundzüge der Papyruskunde* (1913), 248 ff.
(*b*) ROME: S. Solazzi, *La minore età* (1913); 'Tutele e curatele' (*Rivista ital. per le scienze giuridiche*, 1914); *Istituti tutelari* (1919); R. Taubenschlag, *Vormundschaftsrechtliche Studien* (1913); P. Bonfante, *Corso di diritto romano* i (1925); O. Lenel, *Sav. Zeitschr.* 1914; A. Berger, *PW*, s.v. 'Minores'. *See also* LAW AND PROCEDURE, ROMAN, I. A. B.

GUILDS, *see* CLUBS.

GYES, *see* HECATONCHEIRES.

GYGES, king of Lydia (*c*. 685–657 B.C.), founded the Mermnad dynasty by murdering King Candaules and marrying his widow; attacked Miletus and Smyrna, captured Colophon, and sent offerings to Delphi. He sought protection from Assyria against the Cimmerians, but lost it later by helping Psammetichus of Egypt, and was killed in a new Cimmerian invasion. He was the first ruler to be called 'tyrant', possibly a Lydian word. To the Lydia of Gyges belongs the momentous invention of coins.

Herodotus, bk. 1; Plato, *Republic*, 359 d; Archilochus, fr. 19. Geo. Smith, *Assurbanipal* (1871), 64–8; G. Radet, *La Lydie* (1893), 151–86; P. N. Ure, *Origin of Tyranny* (1922), 127–53. P. N. U.

GYLIPPUS, Spartan general, was sent in 415 B.C. to help Syracuse against Athens. By his very arrival he encouraged the besieged Syracusans; he organized their resistance with activity and courage, and he succeeded in turning the scales and vanquishing the Athenians. But his honesty was not beyond doubt; later on (after 405) he was convicted of having taken public money and had to escape from Sparta.

Thucydides, bks. 6 and 7; Diodorus 13. 105; Plutarch, *Nicias* passim. V. E.

GYMNESIAE, *see* BALEARES INSULAE.

GYMNASIARCHOS. This official appears in Egypt under the Ptolemies as a functionary of Greek type, charged with the supervision of gymnasia in towns or villages where there was a hellenized community; the office was probably a voluntary one. The Roman authorities seem to have allowed an organization of the Graeco-Egyptian population to subsist under officials with Greek titles, of whom the gymnasiarch ranked as the chief; his duties, judged by the evidence of papyri, were extended from the gymnasia to all kinds of public works. The office thus became in practice a liturgy. At first the normal tenure was apparently a year; as the impoverishment of the Graeco-Egyptian class increased two men might share the burden; in the third century several are found acting together or for short periods. As even children have been named as gymnasiarchs, the title would seem to have been given to any person of means who could be asked for money. The only place where the gymnasiarchs played a part of more than local importance was Alexandria; in the time of Strabo they were not of sufficient standing there to be named as city officers, but half a century later they were the leaders of the Nationalist opposition to Rome, and reappeared as such on occasion till the end of the second century.

B. A. van Groningen, *Le Gymnasiarque des métropoles de l'Égypte romaine* (1924). J. G. M.

GYMNASIUM. The Greek γυμνάσιον was a sports ground, usually outside the city walls; a public institution, and open to all citizens. Its main feature was a running-track, but it usually also contained a *palaestra* (q.v.). The site was often a sacred grove beside a stream, as was the case with the three gymnasia at Athens, the Lyceum on the banks of the Cephisus, the Academy and the Cynosarges by the Eridanus and the Ilissus. The two first of these were large enough for riding lessons and cavalry parades, and besides the running-track there were jumping-pits and ranges for throwing the discus and javelin. The buildings included bathrooms, undressing-rooms, an oil store, a dust-room where the athletes powdered themselves before exercise, a room for ball games, and a room for practising boxing with hanging punch-balls of different sizes. The gymnasia were especially frequented by the *ephebi* (q.v.). At Athens they were managed by a board of ten *Sophronistae*, in other cities by an honorary magistrate, the gymnasiarch, who employed and paid professional trainers, the *gymnastai* and *paidotribai*. *See* EDUCATION, III. 2.

E. N. Gardiner, *Athletics of the Ancient World* (1930), 72 ff. F. A. W.

H

HABRON, of Phrygia and Rhodes (1st c. A.D.), a Greek grammarian at Rome. His Περὶ ἀντωνυμίας is cited, sometimes with approval, by Apollonius Dyscolus.

Fragments: R. Berndt, *B.phil.Woch.* xxxv (1915).

HADAD, *see* ATARGATIS.

HADES (Ἅιδης, Epic Ἀΐδης, 'the Unseen'), one of the sons of Kronos (q.v.), lord of the lower world, 'the House of Hades'; the name is always that of a person, never of a place, in classical Greek, the dead going ἐς Ἅιδου. He has next to no mythology, except the story of his wedding with Persephone (*see* DEMETER). Personally, he is represented as grim, unpitying, a severe punisher of wrongdoers (in those pictures of the lower world which find room for a Hell or a Purgatory), but never as evil; Greek mythology has no Satan. Nor does he appear as the actual tormentor of the wicked dead, that being the business of the Erinyes (q.v.).

Under his own name he has almost no cult, the one exception being his precinct at Elis (Paus. 6. 25. 2). But under various titles he is heard of here and there. Of these the best known is Pluton (Πλούτων), i.e. the Rich One, obviously connected with Plutus (q.v.). For example, at Byzantium there was a temple of Pluton (Dionysius Byzant. fr. 9 Müller; *GGM* ii. 23). For others *see* CLYMENUS, EUBULEUS; more examples in Farnell, op. cit. inf. 281 ff. He is quite often called Zeus, with some distinguishing title. It seems reasonable to recognize three motives at work: (*a*) reluctance to name anyone so ill-omened as the god of the dead, to which may be added a feeling that he has little to do with the living, save in so far as they are solicitous for the condition of their dead kin; (*b*) confusion of such a god, as lord of the depths of the earth, with deities concerned with its fertile surface (cf. DEMETER); (*c*) comparatively developed theological ideas, which extended the activity of Zeus beyond his proper sphere of the sky and air.

Farnell, *Cults* iii. 280–8 and refs. H. J. R.

HADRIAN (Publius Aelius Hadrianus), Roman Emperor A.D. 117–38, son of P. Aelius Hadrianus Afer and of Domitia Paulina of Gades, was born A.D. 76, probably at Italica. His paternal grandfather (a senator) had married Ulpia, aunt of Trajan. Left fatherless in 85, Hadrian became the ward of Trajan and of P. Acilius Attianus (q.v.) and took a regular place in Trajan's childless household. He became tribune successively of Legio II Adiutrix, probably at Aquincum (95), V Macedonica in Lower Moesia (96), and XXII Primigenia under L. Julius Ursus Servianus in Upper Germany (*ILS* 308). Thence, in 99, he accompanied Trajan (now emperor) to Rome, marrying Vibia Sabina (q.v.) in 100. He became imperial quaestor (101); staff-officer in the First Dacian War (101–2); senatorial archivist; plebeian tribune (105); commander of Legio I Minervia in the Second Dacian War (105–6), and simultaneously praetor (106); governor of Lower Pannonia (107); suffect consul (108, June); member of priestly colleges. He was in high favour with Trajan and Plotina and friendly with the chief court-officers; though, lacking any public mark suggesting that he would succeed Trajan, he was perhaps viewed askance by some of the more senior men. Nevertheless, in 111 or 112 he was elected archon of Athens—a significant honour—and in 114 (less probably 117) he was appointed governor of Syria (S.H.A. *Had.* 4. 1) during Trajan's Parthian war, being designated *cos.* II in 117.

2. Trajan died in Cilicia on 8 August 117. On the 9th it was announced at Antioch that he had adopted Hadrian as his successor, and, on the 11th (Hadrian's *dies imperii*), that he was dead. The circumstances were unfortunate, even ambiguous. Trajan had not advertised his dynastic intentions (but see *B.M. Coins, Rom. Emp.* iii, pp. lxxxvi, 124); men like Neratius (q.v.) Priscus and Servianus were senior in experience; Plotina was known to favour Hadrian; Trajan's swift death denied the formal investigations which Rome might have seen. The ancient biographers regarded the 'adoption' as fictitious, forgetting that Hadrian was given the key-position in Syria during Trajan's absence in the East—the culmination of a life of intimacy and advancement under Trajan, who would hardly leave the succession a matter for armed contention, still less for senatorial decision. The fact of the adoption may be accepted.

3. A formal declaration of accession to the Senate (with guarantees of senatorial privilege) and a double military donative preceded Hadrian's journey to Rome in 118. There he held a Parthian triumph in Trajan's name. Called quickly to Moesia, he subdued the Sarmatae and Roxolani, and gave unified command of Dacia and Pannonia to Q. Marcius Turbo (q.v.), displacing Lusius (q.v.) Quietus from honour. Thus he perhaps brought to a head the disaffection of the 'old guard', in the conspiracy of the four 'consulars': Quietus, A. Cornelius Palma, L. Publilius Celsus, and C. Avidius (q.v.) Nigrinus were said to have plotted against Hadrian's life, and were swiftly executed by the Senate in his absence. Returning to Rome (118), he attributed full responsibility to Attianus, now praetorian prefect, and by favours (an extra public largesse, remission of accession-gifts for Italy, a week's gladiatorial show, reform in the postal services, grants to the *alimenta*, financial assistance to poor senators, and especially a ceremonial cancellation of 900,000,000 HS. worth of debts to the State) sought to placate a suspicious public opinion. Orthodox circles, however, cannot have relished his prompt abandoning of Trajan's imperialist policy in the East. Nor could senatorial sentiment welcome Hadrian's development of the Imperial Civil Service, now enlarged and staffed by graded and salaried knights (headed by the praetorian prefects), or of the imperial *consilium* (q.v.). But senatorial prerogative was not sensibly diminished (S.H.A. *Had.* bk. 8; Dio 69. 5. 7).

4. Various reasons prompted Hadrian to tour his provinces: military organization and defence; administrative co-ordination; the need to recognize—and guide—provincial aspirations by showing himself as their common symbol; and his own desire to learn provincial conditions, especially in the hellenized areas. He deliberately advertised his policy by coins (cf. *B.M. Coins, Rom. Emp.* iii, pp. clxxi ff.). In 120 or 121 he travelled to Gaul, and thence to the Rhine, where, living a simple soldierly life, he instituted stricter regulations for legionary discipline. Crossing from Holland to Britain in 121 or 122 (cf. *CIL* iii. 4279; a previous detour by Raetia and Noricum is very unlikely), he established the triple *limes* (see WALL OF HADRIAN). Returning to Gaul (where he commemorated Plotina's death by a temple at Nîmes), he reached Spain in 122; his personal intervention in the Mauretanian campaign (S.H.A. *Had.* 12. 7) is very doubtful. In 123 he sailed from Spain, and toured Asia, the Troad, Propontis, and Phrygia, founding or restoring or favouring communities, until he left for Greece in 125, returning to Rome in 127 by way of Sicily. Next year he visited Africa, to review the troops (*CIL* viii. 2532, 18052) and to revise conditions of land-tenure on imperial domain-lands (ibid. 10570). After a few weeks in Rome he left (late 128) to winter in Athens, where he dedicated the Olympieum, himself—the new Zeus Panhellenios—accepting the title 'Olympius'. In 129 he travelled to Caria, Cilicia, Cappadocia, and Syria; in 130 he journeyed up the Nile (there to lose Antinous, q.v.), and returned to Rome in 131.

5. These travels influenced a foreign policy which aimed at peaceful economy and secure defence, as witness the restoration of the Flavian *status quo* in the East, the building of the British 'sentry-walk', the consolidation of Dacia (the contemplated destruction of the Danube bridge deserves no credence), and the demarcation of a customs-palisade on the German-Raetian frontier. Risings in Britain and Mauretania called for purely punitive measures. Only in Judaea was his policy questionable: the building of a shrine to Jupiter Capitolinus on the site of the Temple at Jerusalem (itself to be renamed Colonia Aelia Capitolina), with or without the prohibition of circumcision, precipitated a revolt (132–5) which perhaps drew Hadrian to Antioch for a time. After a siege of Jerusalem and widespread repressive measures Judaea became *Syria Palaestina*, under a consular legate with two legions; and the new colony and temple were established. To Christianity as such Hadrian's attitude was that of Trajan.

6. His general administrative policy was unsensational. There was reorganization in the army; the *alimenta* continued in Italy; the system of *curatores* was developed to supervise local finance; provincial extortion was rare; and conditions of slavery were ameliorated. In jurisdiction there was real progress, of which the appointment of four consular circuit-judges to administer law in Italy was but a symptom. By 129 one consolidated code had been drawn up by L. Salvius (q.v.) Julianus. It may be noted that Hadrian allowed no treason charges.

7. Spanish-born and Greek-inspired, intellectual critic and connoisseur, littérateur, accomplished executant in music and the arts, Hadrian enjoyed from 131 to 138 the mature pleasures of peaceful life at Rome. Government was enlightened centralization, in which his debt to the gods was plain (cf. *B.M. Coins, Rom. Emp.* iii, p. clxiv f.). The succession must be made clear, especially if plotting now began: Servianus and his grandson Fuscus were both executed in 136. Hadrian, weakening in health, in the same year adopted L. Aelius (q.v.); after Aelius' death (138) he turned to Antoninus (q.v.) Pius. In 138, consumptive and dropsical, he died, aged sixty-three, with now famous verses on his lips. Buried in the Mausoleum which he had built, he was deified at length by a Senate perhaps alienated, perhaps apathetic, but not above the prompting of Antoninus.

BIBLIOGRAPHY

ANCIENT SOURCES. (a) Literary authorities. The garbled biography in the Historia Augusta contains a few statements from Hadrian's lost Autobiography and from Marius (q.v.) Maximus (see B. W. Henderson, Life and Principate of the Emperor Hadrian, A.D. 76–138 (1923), 274 f.). Cf. also fragments of Dio Cassius, bk. 69, and brief references in Aurelius Victor and Eutropius.
(b) Inscriptions. E. de Ruggiero, Diz. Epigr. s.v. 'Hadrianus' (G. Mancini and D. Vaglieri); PIR², A 184.
(c) Coins. H. Mattingly, B.M. Coins, Rom. Emp. iii (1936); H. Mattingly and E. A. Sydenham, The Roman Imperial Coinage ii (1926); P. L. Strack, Untersuchungen zur römischen Reichsprägung des zweiten Jahrhunderts ii (1933).
MODERN LITERATURE. (a) Source-criticism. See bibliography in CAH xi (1936), 894.
(b) General. B. W. Henderson, op. cit.; W. Weber, Untersuchungen zur Geschichte des Kaisers Hadrianus (1907); W. Weber in CAH xi (1936), ch. 8; O. Th. Schulz, Leben des Kaisers Hadrians (1904); W. D. Gray, 'A Study of the Life of Hadrian prior to his Accession', in Smith College Studies in History iv, pt. 2 (1919), pp. 141 ff.; P. von Rohden, PW, s.v. 'Aelius (64)'.
(c) Special. J. Dürr, Die Reisen des Kaisers Hadrian (1881); R. H. Lacey, The Equestrian Officials of Trajan and Hadrian, etc. (Diss. Princeton, 1917). The new Hellenism in Hadrianic art: J. Toynbee, The Hadrianic School (1934).   C. H. V. S.

HADRUMETUM (modern *Sousse*), a seaport 60 miles south of Carthage. Phoenician emigrants settled there in the ninth century B.C. Hannibal made Hadrumetum his base for the Zama campaign. It joined the Romans in 146 B.C., and was made a *civitas libera et immunis*. In 46 B.C. it opposed Caesar; he planned a colony there which was probably carried out in 42–40 (M. Grant, *From Imperium to Auctoritas* (1946), 227). Under Trajan it was entitled *Colonia Concordia Ulpia Traiana Frugifera*. Hadrumetum grew very prosperous from agriculture, horse-breeding, and shipping. Later it became capital of the Byzacene and an important Christian centre with extensive catacombs.   W. N. W.

HAEMON (Αἵμων), (1) eponym of Haemonia, i.e. Thessaly, and father of Thessalus (Rhianus, fr. 25 Powell). (2) Grandson of Cadmus (q.v.); leaving Thebes on account of homicide, he came to Athens, and his descendants went successively to Rhodes and Acragas; Theron, tyrant of the latter city, claimed him as an ancestor (schol. Pind. *Ol.* 2. 16). (3) Son of Creon (q.v. 3). For his legend as usually told *see* ANTIGONE; but according to Apollodorus (3. 54) he was killed by the Sphinx (cf. the *Oedipodia* ap. schol. Eur. *Phoen.* 1760). Homer makes him father of Maeon, one of the Thebans who ambushed Tydeus (*Il.* 4. 394).   H. J. R.

HAIR-DRESSING, see TOILET.

HALICARNASSUS, a town of Caria, situated on a promontory of the Ceramic Gulf. It received Greek settlers from Argolis (Troezen and perhaps Argos) c. 1000 B.C., but retained a native Carian element, which was subsequently reinforced by Mausolus (q.v.). As a vassal of Persia it was ruled by tyrants, one of whom, Artemisia (q.v.), accompanied Xerxes on his invasion of Greece. After the expulsion of the tyrants (460–455) Halicarnassus joined the Delian League. In the fourth century it fell into the hands of the Carian dynasts Hecatomnus and Mausolus, the latter of whom made it into his residence (c. 362). His tomb, the Mausoleum (q.v.), built by his widow Artemisia in the centre of the theatral area in which the town stood, made Halicarnassus into one of the show-towns of the ancient world. The city was captured and partly destroyed by Alexander, after a stout defence by the Persian garrison (333). Under the rule of the Ptolemies (c. 280–200) and the Romans it had little importance. Its ring-walls are fairly well preserved, but nothing remains *in situ* of the Mausoleum.

C. T. Newton, *Travels and Discoveries in the Levant* (1865) iv, chs. 35–41, 45.   M. C.

HALIRRHOTHIUS, in mythology, son of Poseidon; for the usual legend about him *see* ARES. There is, however, another account, according to which he was sent by his father to cut down Athena's sacred olives, but his axe missed the trees and mortally wounded him (schol. Ar. *Nub.* 1005, cf. Servius on Verg. *G.* 1. 18).   H. J. R.

HALTERES (ἁλτῆρες) were heavy pieces of iron shaped and gripped like our dumb-bells. They were especially used in the standing long-jump, where they were swung to and fro until sufficient momentum had been gained for the leap. They were also employed in various gymnastic exercises and in musical drill.   F. A. W.

HALYS (the 'Salt River', so called from the salt springs in its upper course), the longest river in Asia Minor, rises in Antitaurus near the Armenian border and flows first south-west through Cappadocia and then in a northerly direction past Phrygia (later Galatia) and through Paphlagonia to join the Euxine west of Amisus. In the time of Croesus it divided the Lydian Kingdom from the Persian Empire; hence 'Croesus by crossing the Halys destroyed a great empire'. Herodotus knew of a bridge across it, and, probably in error, made the Royal Road from Sardes to the Cilician Gates cross the Halys.   W. M. C.

HAMARTIA, *see* FATE, para. 3 and bibliography.

HAMILCAR (1) (5th c. B.C.), Carthaginian general, son or grandson of the great Mago (q.v.). He commanded a large army against the Sicilian Greeks. At the hard-fought battle of Himera he was completely beaten and probably killed by Gelon (q.v.) (480 B.C.).

Hdt. 7. 165 f.; Diodorus 11. 20 ff.   V. E.

HAMILCAR (2) **BARCA,** a great Carthaginian general of the time of the First Punic War. As commander of the Carthaginian fleet, Hamilcar ravaged the coast of Bruttium (247 B.C.). Landing in Sicily he seized Hercte (q.v.), where he held the Romans at bay by frequent skirmishes, again raiding the Italian coast as far as Cumae. In 244 he advanced to Mt. Eryx (q.v.), but failed to relieve the siege of Drepana. After the Punic defeat at Aegates Insulae he negotiated the terms of peace and laid down his command. When attempts to suppress the subsequent revolt of the mercenaries failed, Hamilcar was reappointed commander-in-chief (241). He thrice defeated the mercenary leader Spendius; then, co-operating with Hanno, his old enemy, he defeated the other leader Matho and reduced Utica (238), thus ending the revolt. In 237 he was sent to Spain with his young son, Hannibal. Based on Gades he conquered southern and eastern Spain, advancing the frontier to Cape Nao and building a fortress at Alicante. To a Roman protest, prompted by Massilia, he replied that his conquest was designed to secure money to pay his country's war indemnity (231). While withdrawing from the siege of Helice (? *Elche*) he was drowned (229–228). The anti-Barcid tradition, found in some Roman writers, that he conquered Spain against the will of the Carthaginian government, is tendentious and designed to shift the responsibility of the Hannibalic war on to the Barca family and to represent it as a personal war of revenge not countenanced by the home government. The immediate purpose of Hamilcar's conquest was to add the mineral wealth and man-power of Spain to his country's empire, which had lost Sicily and Sardinia; whether he ultimately hoped to invade Italy is uncertain, but each of his three sons, Hannibal, Hasdrubal, and Mago, attempted this adventure.   H. H. S.

HANNIBAL, the great Carthaginian general, born in (late) 247 B.C., was the eldest son of Hamilcar (q.v.) Barca. After making Hannibal swear eternal hatred to Rome Hamilcar took him in 237 to Spain, where he served until he assumed command in 221 on the death of

Hasdrubal (q.v.). Although he married a Spanish princess from Castulo, he reverted to his father's warlike policy by attacking the Olcades (Upper Guadiana). In 220 he advanced Carthaginian arms beyond the Tagus, defeating the Vaccaei and Carpetani. He then besieged Rome's ally, Saguntum, which fell after an eight months' blockade (219). Although his action may have broken no formal agreement with Rome, he knew that it involved the risk of war.

2. Hannibal intended to win the war, which he had precipitated, by a bold invasion of Italy before Rome was prepared. He would sacrifice his base in Spain, cross the Alps recruiting *en route*, and seek a new base on the northern plain of Italy, where he could encourage the Italian allies of Rome to revolt. Leaving Carthago Nova in April 218 with some 35,000–40,000 men he reached the Rhône. Thence by a heroic effort, made more difficult by early autumn snow, he crossed the Alps (somewhere between the Little St. Bernard and Mt. Genèvre passes: the perennial problem of the exact route does not admit of a definite solution) and reached Turin, but with only 26,000 men. After defeating P. Scipio in a cavalry engagement at Ticinus, he won a great victory at Trebia over the combined forces of Scipio and Ti. Sempronius Longus, thanks to his outflanking tactics combined with an ambush (Dec. 218). In May 217 Hannibal crossed the Apennines, ravaged Etruria and entrapped the army of Flaminius (q.v.) in a defile between the hills and lake of Trasimene: nearly two Roman legions were destroyed. But as no towns revolted to him Hannibal marched to Apulia and then into Campania, where he failed to force Fabius (q.v. 5) to an open battle and was thus compelled to retire to Apulia for the winter. In 216 at Cannae (q.v.) he inflicted on the Romans the worst defeat they had known. Capua and many towns in Campania and south Italy went over to him, but as the Romans refused to acknowledge defeat and central and northern Italy remained loyal to them, he had to devise a wider strategy to force them to dissipate their strength (*see* PUNIC WARS), while in Italy he vainly tried to provoke another pitched battle.

3. While the Romans held the line of the Volturnus Hannibal wintered in Capua, where it was alleged (falsely?) that luxurious quarters undermined the discipline of his troops. The failure of his attacks from Mt. Tifata on Cumae, Nola, and Puteoli (215–214), which were parried by Marcellus, Gracchus, and Fabius (qq.v.), forced him to abandon his offensive in Campania. He won over Tarentum and other Greek cities in 213, but after failing to force the Romans to relax their siege of Capua (started in 212) by a vain march against Rome itself (211), he retired to Apulia. Ever pressed farther south, Hannibal suffered a setback in the Roman capture of Tarentum (209), while his hope of reinforcements was sadly diminished when his brother Hasdrubal (q.v. 2) was defeated at Metaurus (207). Forced to withdraw, unaided and undaunted, to Bruttium, he lost Locri in 205 and held on desperately like a lion at bay until ordered to return to Africa to defend Carthage (autumn 203). After sixteen years in enemy country he withdrew his unconquered army and advanced to final defeat by Scipio Africanus at Zama (qq.v.) in 202. He escaped to Carthage and counselled peace.

4. As suffete (between 197 and 195; probably 196) Hannibal weakened the power of the oligarchs at Carthage by constitutional reforms; he also reorganized the revenues and encouraged commerce and agriculture. His political enemies replied by telling Rome that Hannibal was intriguing with Antiochus of Syria. When a Roman commission of inquiry arrived in Carthage, Hannibal fled, ultimately to Antiochus, whose hostility to Rome he is alleged to have encouraged. He was ready, it was said, to stir up the Carthaginians against Rome and even to invade Italy if given an army by Antiochus.

In fact he took only a small part in the subsequent war: he was defeated in a small naval engagement off Side in Pamphylia by the Rhodian fleet under Eudamus (190). After Antiochus' defeat at Magnesia Hannibal fled to Crete and then to Prusias of Bithynia whom he supported against Eumenes of Pergamum (184). He took his own life to avoid a Roman extradition order (183 or 182).

5. Adjudged by common consent one of the world's greatest soldiers, Hannibal was the disciple of Alexander and Pyrrhus as well as of his father Hamilcar. He developed the Hellenistic system of combining infantry and cavalry till he could surround and annihilate the enemy. But beside extraordinary tactical skill and a wide and bold conception of strategy he possessed a capacity for leadership which commanded the loyalty of mercenary troops amid danger and defeat. His strategical plans and his reforms at Carthage should win for him the name of statesman. Above all it is his character (which remains unsullied despite accusations of perfidy and cruelty deriving from Roman propaganda) that counts and that has given to the Hannibalic war its epic quality and invested his name with an undying glamour (see, e.g., Polybius 9. 21–6, 10. 32–3, 11. 19, 23. 13 and Livy 21. 4).

For bibliography *see* PUNIC WARS; fundamental for his campaigns are the works of J. Kromayer and G. De Sanctis there cited (cf. De Sanctis in *Enc. Brit.* s.v.). For his statesmanship: E. Groag, *Hannibal als Politiker* (1929).   H. H. S.

HANNO (1), Carthaginian, sent to west Africa before 480 B.C., founded Thymiaterium (*Mehedia*), Carian Fort (*Mogador*), Acra (*Agadir*), etc., beyond Soloeis (*C. Cantin*), and river Tensift. After staying by river Lixus (*Draa*) and founding Cerne (*Herne*?), H. reached river Chretes (*Senegal*), the Guanches, and C. Verde, river Gambia, West Horn (*Bissagos Bay*), God's Chariot (*Mt. Kakulima*?), S. Horn (*Sherbro Sound*), where gorillas (dwarfs? apes?) were caught, and Sierra Leone. Of his report, written in Punic, a Greek translation survives.

GGM i. 1–14 (later refs. to H. are confused). Translations: M. Cary and E. Warmington, *Anc. Explorers* (1929), 47 ff.; Warmington, *Greek Geography* (1934), 72 ff.   E. H. W.

HANNO (2), a Carthaginian commander, surnamed the Great, who raised supplies in Africa for the First Punic War. A good organizer, but a poor general, he helped after failures and quarrels with Hamilcar Barca to crush the rebel mercenaries (241–238 B.C.). He represented the landed nobility who wished to maintain good relations with Rome and to exploit the Carthaginian land empire in Africa. He thus disapproved of the Hannibalic War and argued for peace after Cannae (216). He may be identified with a Hanno who participated in the peace negotiations after Zama.   H. H. S.

HARBOURS. The first steps in harbour improvement must be connected with the increase of commerce during the Greek age of colonization and the development of trade routes centring on certain cities. Beginning with Delos in the eighth century, the more prosperous communities guarded their natural harbours with moles of rough stone and built quays, to which ships, now larger, tied up. Harbour works increased steadily in magnitude, carefulness, and complexity. Whereas the earlier port had often been some distance from the city, to assure neutrality of commerce and to protect the city itself (cf. Arist. *Pol.* 7. 5), by the fifth century the importance of commerce and of the grain trade demanded that the urban walls should contain at least one harbour, and many cities possessed two. The moles were fortified and ended in lofty towers, the ancestors of the lighthouse (q.v.), between which chains could be strung to close the entrance. Within the harbour were storehouses for warcraft, and the market, with a sales hall, grain hall, and other buildings. Such a complex as the Piraeus (q.v.), with its three harbours, Cantharus, Zea, and

Munychia, all enclosed by walls and connected by the famous Long Walls with Athens itself, possessed a greater unity and self-sufficiency than our modern harbour.

The new ports of the Hellenistic period were built on a more regular plan which took less account of natural protection. In the Roman Empire military and commercial harbours were separated for the first time, and architects gained complete independence of nature. The great Claudian harbour at Ostia, measuring over 170 acres—the largest in antiquity—was constructed on a bare shore by extensive excavation and the sinking of a large ship as artificial island breakwater.

Strabo 17. 1. 6–10 (Alexandria); Pliny, *Ep.* 6. 31 (Centumcellae). K. Lehmann-Hartleben, 'Die Antiken Hafenanlagen des Mittelmeeres', *Klio*, Beiheft 14 (1923).   C. G. S.

HARMODIUS, Athenian tyrannicide, *see* ARISTOGITON.

HARMONIA, *see* ARES.

HARMOST (Ἁρμοστής) was the title borne by officials sent by Sparta after the downfall of Athens in 404 B.C., usually in command of a garrison to govern subject cities of her empire. It was also applied to commanders controlling large areas with stronger forces, e.g. Thibron in Asia Minor (Xen. *Hell.* 3. 1. 3; 4. 2. 5), Teleutias in Chalcidice (ibid. 5. 2. 18 and 37). A Ἁρμοστής is attested in Cythera by an inscription (*IG* v. 1. 937, ? 4th c. B.C.); but it is uncertain whether such officials regularly governed the towns of the *Perioeci* in Laconia.   A. M. W.

HARPALUS (*c.* 355–323 B.C.), a Macedonian noble and a close friend of Alexander from earliest youth. A cripple, and hence no soldier, he accompanied Alexander to Asia as paymaster, but gave early evidence of his unreliability by a sudden flight to Greece, of which the occasion is unknown. Alexander reinstated him, and later (331) entrusted him with the central treasury of the Empire at Babylon. During Alexander's absence in India (327–5) Harpalus was guilty of gross extravagance and malversation, if not of positive treason, and when Alexander returned he decamped with money and soldiers. He sought refuge in Athens, and probably bribed various Athenian politicians, including Demosthenes; but failing of his purpose he took his force to Crete, where he was killed by one of his officers.

Berve, *Alexanderreich*, no. 143.   G. T. G.

HARPALYCE, in mythology, (1) *see* ALASTOR, CLYMENUS. (2) Daughter of Harpalycus, king of the Amymonei in Thrace. Her mother dying, her father brought her up as a warrior, and on one occasion she saved his life in battle. After his death she became a brigand, but at last was caught and killed. At her tomb rites were celebrated which included a sham fight (Hyg. *Fab.* 193; Servius on *Aen.* 1. 317). Cf. Verg. loc. cit. (earliest mention); his Camilla is modelled upon her.   H. J. R.

HARPOCRATES, *see* HORUS.

HARPOCRATION, VALERIUS, of Alexandria, lexicographer. His date is not known: some place him under Tiberius; others identify him with the teacher of Verus named by Capitolinus. It has been held that he wrote not long after Athenaeus, the latest author used by him, from whose *Deipnosophistae* H. apparently drew some of his information on cups and hetaerae. His *Lexicon of the Ten Orators* is preserved in an early abridgement and in a longer form, closer to the original but not free from corruptions. It is based mainly on works of the Imperial age, e.g. by Didymus, Dionysius of Halicarnassus, and Dionysius son of Tryphon, but cites also Aristophanes of Byzantium, Aristarchus, οἱ γλωσσογράφοι, and many historical and antiquarian

sources such as Hecataeus, Hellanicus, Theopompus, Ister, and Apollodorus. The contents are words (including proper names) and phrases, mainly from the Orators, in alphabetical order, generally assigned to their sources, with explanations of points of interest or difficulty. Some of the entries are drawn from non-oratorical literature, and in his explanations throughout H. quotes, from time to time, nearly every important Greek writer, from Homer downwards. Besides stylistic details he has valuable notes on architectural, religious, legal, constitutional, social, and other antiquities.

Editions: I. Bekker, 1833; W. Dindorf, 1853. C. Boysen, *De H. lex. fontibus*, 1876.   P. B. R. F.

HARPYIAE, HARPIES (Ἅρπυιαι), supernatural winged beings, apparently winds in origin, who 'snatch', as the name implies, and carry off various persons and things. They have at the same time some characteristics of ghosts, and, as the ideas of wind and spirit are closely allied (cf. the etymology of the words in Greek, Hebrew, Latin, and other tongues), it is perhaps most correct to say that they are spirit-winds. Their names are Aello, Ocypete, and Celaeno (Hesiod, *Theog.* 267, who says that they and Iris, q.v., are daughters of Thaumas and Electra daughter of Ocean). They appear in *Od.* 20. 77 as carrying off the daughters of Pandareus, apparently to the other world, since they are given as servants to the Erinyes (q.v.). Much later (Ap. Rhod. 2. 188 ff.) they plague Phineus (q.v.) by carrying off his food and defiling what they leave with their excrement. Whence this detail comes is not known; it is an ingenious suggestion (W. R. Dawson, *Bridle of Pegasus*, p. 27) that Apollonius had heard of the voracious and filthy fruit-eating Indian bat. Virgil (*Aen.* 3. 210 ff.) follows Apollonius in part, but describes them as birds with women's faces, in this agreeing with their ancient representation, as on the Harpy-tomb from Xanthus in Lydia.   H. J. R.

HARUSPICES. This word, variously spelled (*haru-, aru-, hari-, ari-, are-*) and probably cognate with χορδή, Latin *hira*, etc. (Walde-Hofmann, *Lat. etym. Wörterb.*[3], s.v.) and the root of *specio*, was applied to diviners imported into Rome from Etruria (where an *haruspex* was called *netśvis*; *CIL* xi. 6363). Appearing, according to Livy 1. 56. 4–5, in the reign of Tarquinius Superbus, *haruspices* increased in importance from the Second Punic War, and though long regarded as barbarous (Cic. *Nat. D.* 2. 11), gradually encroached upon the field of the augurs. From the late Republic on they formed an *ordo haruspicum LX*, headed by a *summus, primarius*, or *maximus haruspex*, while others served in Italian municipalities. The art was practised to the time of Theodosius (*Cod. Theod.* 16. 10), and still seriously discussed as late as Laurentius Lydus (6th c.) or later. The principles were contained in priestly books (Cic. *Div.* 1. 72), which legend derived from Tages (q.v.; also Cic. *Div.* 2. 50 and Pease's n.), and some of which were translated into Latin by L. Tarquinius Priscus (C. Thulin, *Ital. sakrale Poesie u. Prosa* (1906), 1–5).

This *Etrusca disciplina* sought to interpret three types of phenomena (Cic. *Div.* 1. 12, 2. 26): *exta, monstra* (*ostenta, portenta, prodigia*), and *fulgura*. Significant for the *exta* were the size, shape, colour, and markings of the vital organs, especially the livers and gall-bladders of sheep, changes in which were believed by many races to arise supernaturally (cf. Pl. *Tim.* 71 a ff.; Cic. *Div.* 1. 118; Iambl. *Myst.* 3. 16) and to be susceptible of interpretation by established rules. Models of the liver—e.g. from Piacenza (Etruscan), Boghazkeui (Hittite), and Babylonia—were probably intended for instruction in extispicy. *Monstra* (from *moneo*) or prodigies (*see* PRODIGIA) included teratological or otherwise unusual births or growths and abnormal meteorological phenomena.

Fulgura were interpreted by their frequency, the precise one of the sixteen Etruscan divisions of the heavens in which they were seen, and by their physical effects. Of these three types of divination that through the *exta* was deliberately sought (*impetratiuum*), but those by *monstra* or *fulgura* were considered divinely sent (*oblatiua*) and hence usually demanding some expiation (*procuratio*). *See also* ETRUSCANS, para. 4; RELIGION, ETRUSCAN.

For bibliography *see under* DIVINATION.   A. S. P.

HASDRUBAL (1), leader of the democratic party in Carthage and son-in-law of Hamilcar (q.v. 2) Barca, whom he accompanied to Spain (237 B.C.). Later he reduced a Numidian rising in Africa and according to Fabius Pictor (Polyb. 3. 8) schemed to overthrow the Carthaginian constitution. He succeeded to the command in Spain on Hamilcar's death (229) and achieved more by diplomacy than force of arms. He married an Iberian princess and founded Carthago Nova (q.v.), whence he advanced to the Ebro, which was later recognized as the boundary of Carthaginian and Roman spheres of influence in a treaty with Rome (226). In 221 he was murdered by a Celtic slave. The view of Fabius that Hasdrubal ruled as viceroy in Spain independent of his home government is improbable.   H. H. S.

HASDRUBAL (2) (BARCA), son of Hamilcar (q.v. 2) and younger brother of Hannibal, was left in command in Spain (218 B.C.). Repulsed by Cn. Scipio (218), he launched a combined land and sea attack which terminated in a naval defeat off the Ebro (217). Reinforced and with his rear secured by his defeat of the Turdetani (216), Hasdrubal took the offensive with the ultimate hope of joining Hannibal in Italy, but was defeated at Ibera on the Ebro owing to the failure of his enveloping tactics (215). Recalled to Africa, where he crushed the rebellious Syphax, he returned to Spain (212) and defeated Cn. Scipio at Ilorci (211), so that Carthaginian control was extended to the Ebro. Tactically outwitted by P. Scipio at Baecula, he withdrew his army from complete defeat and reached Gaul through the western Pyrenees (208); crossing the Alps, perhaps by the pass used by Hannibal, he raised his forces to 30,000 and moved south to join Hannibal (207). Unexpectedly faced by two consular armies through the arrival of Claudius Nero (q.v. 2) he could not force the coast road and so withdrew along the Metaurus (q.v.) valley by night, either to retire to north Italy or more probably in a desperate attempt to reach central Italy. Overtaken and defeated in a decisive battle, he died fighting. A good organizer and a fairly competent soldier, his generalship did not match his courage (Polyb. 11. 2).   H. H. S.

HASDRUBAL (3) (son of Gisgo) commanded a Carthaginian army in Spain 214–206 B.C. With Mago he compassed the destruction of P. Scipio (211), but later was driven from his base Orongis to Gades (207) and was completely defeated with Mago at Ilipa by Scipio Africanus (206). He fled via Gades to Africa, where as commander-in-chief he relieved the siege of Utica (204), but his camp was burnt by Scipio and his newly raised army was defeated at Campi Magni (203). After some guerrilla warfare he was accused of treason and committed suicide before Zama.   H. H. S.

HASDRUBAL (4) (2nd c. B.C.), commanded the Carthaginian forces against Masinissa and was defeated in 150 B.C. Although condemned to death, he escaped and was reinstated in his command at the outbreak of the Third Punic War. He organized resistance first in the country-side (149), twice repulsing the Romans at Nepheris, and then, on the arrival of Scipio Aemilianus, in Carthage itself during the siege (148–146). In this he showed more ability than Polybius' unflattering

characterization might suggest (38. 1–2), but when the city was doomed Hasdrubal surrendered, later to grace Scipio's triumph, while his wife and children preferred death to capture.   H. H. S.

HASTA, HASTATI, see ARMS (ROMAN) and LEGION.

HATĔRIUS, QUINTUS (*cos. suff.* 58 B.C.), Augustan orator and declaimer, of senatorial family, noted for facility of improvisation and impetuous delivery (Tac. *Ann.* 4. 61; Sen. *Ep.* 40. 10), which called forth Augustus' remark 'Haterius needs a brake' (Sen. *Controv.* 4. *pr.* 6–11). He died A.D. 26, nearly 90 years old.   C. J. F.

HEATING for cooking or warmth was primarily supplied in the classical world by charcoal stoves: hence the importance of charcoal-burning. The stoves took the form of chafing-dishes, gridirons, or braziers, elaborated in the Hellenistic world into jacketed vessels heated by fire or boiling water, of which magnificent examples for table use have been discovered at Pompeii. Equally old is the oven, extending from baker's shop to field-army, without a flue and heated by blazing wood withdrawn upon exhaustion of the air within. The use of hot water for bathing is as old as Homer (*Od.* 8. 249, 253) and precedes him at Cnossos, while Herodotus (4. 75) mentions sweat-baths, traditionally assigned to Sparta (Strabo 3. 154; Mart. 6. 42. 16) and warmed with heated stones, as in Lusitania. In Italy, where public bathing was widely introduced by the third century, heating was revolutionized by the introduction of the heated floor or hypocaust (q.v.). *See* BATHS.   I. A. R.

HEBE (Ἥβη, i.e. adolescence, youthful beauty), daughter of Hera (q.v.) and Zeus, sister of Ares and Eileithyia (qq.v.) (Hesiod, *Theog.* 922). She is unimportant in cult (temple at Phlius, Paus. 2. 13. 3, where she had been anciently called Ganymeda, cf. GANYMEDES), but occasionally associated with other deities (Heracles at Cynosarges, Paus. 1. 19. 3; Aphrodite, Farnell, *Cults* ii. 624, 744). In mythology she is the cup-bearer of the gods, as *Il.* 4. 2 and often later. Heracles has her to wife from *Od.* 11. 603 (a doubtfully genuine passage) onwards, and she appears now and again in a scene of Olympian domesticity, e.g. she bathes Ares after his encounter with Diomedes (*Il.* 5. 905), as a sister might an earthly brother in Homeric society. She intervenes to make the aged Iolaus young again, Eur. *Heracl.* 349 ff.; according to Ovid (*Met.* 9. 401–2) Heracles induced her to make him young again. See von Sybel in Roscher's *Lexikon*, s.v.   H. J. R.

HECABE, see HECUBA.

HECALE or **HECALINE,** a goddess worshipped with Zeus Hecalos in the deme Hecale; said to have been an old woman who entertained Theseus.

Callimachus, *Hecale* (see CALLIMACHUS); Plutarch, *Theseus,* 14; Deubner, *Attische Feste,* 217.

HECATAEUS (1), son of Hegesandrus, of Miletus, was active in the Ionian Revolt, 500–494 B.C., travelled in Egypt and elsewhere, and wrote in 'pure Ionic' dialect two works, each the first of its kind: (1) Γενεαλογίαι ('Ηρωολογία, 'Ιστορίαι), a collection of family traditions and pedigrees, including his own (Hdt. 2. 143), without chronological scheme; beginning with scornful reference to current 'stories many and absurd', and offering unorthodox and rationalist views; seldom quoted later. (2) Περιήγησις (Περίοδος), a 'journey round the world' in two parts, 'Europe' and 'Asia' (with Egypt and Libya); long popular, though later criticized; pre-Alexandrian silence probably reflects sophistic superiority. Callimachus attributed 'Asia' to some 'islander', but Eratosthenes accepted it; a fourth-century forgery (Cobet,

Sieglin, Wells) is unlikely (Diels). Among geographers, Hecataeus stands next to Anaximander (q.v.); Aristagoras may have used his map (Hdt. 5. 49); Heraclitus distrusted his judgement; Strabo compared him with the poets. Herodotus, profoundly influenced, quotes him as 'the λογοποιός' (2. 143), correcting and amplifying; and was accused of wholesale borrowing (Euseb. *Praep. Evang.* 10. 3. 16 and 23); demonstrable loans are all from Egypt. Copious fragments (333) refer to peoples and places, from Tartessus to India, but mainly Mediterranean; frs. 284, 286–7, 291–2 are descriptive, fr. 324 is narrative.

FHG i. 1–31, iv. 627 b; *FGrH* i. 1–373; *PW*, s.v.; Diels, *Hermes* xxii (1887), 411–44; Wells, *JHS* xxix (1909), 41–52; L. Pearson, *Early Ionian Historians* (1939), ch. 2 (bibliography pp. 106–8). *See* LOGOGRAPHERS.   J. L. M.

HECATAEUS (2) of Teos. His history of Egypt (Αἰγυπτιακά) under Ptolemy I, c. 300 B.C. popularized the theory of Egypt as the source of civilization, and was the basis of Manetho's more official account.

FHG ii. 384.

HECATE, an ancient chthonian goddess (a kind of fish, τρίγλη, is sacrificed to her, Apollodorus ap. Ath. 325 a, and fish are a typical offering to under-world powers, cf. F. J. Dölger, Ἰχθύς, *passim*), of obscure origin and early history. She is frequently confused with Artemis (q.v.), whose functions overlap to some extent with hers, also with Selene, the theory that she is a moon-goddess being supported also by many modern authors, though without justification, as no cult of the moon is to be found in Greece; however, a goddess of women, such as she was, tends to acquire some lunar features. Her associations with Artemis are so close and frequent that it is not always easy to tell to which of them a particular function or title belongs originally (Farnell, *Cults* ii. 516 ff.).

Hecate is not mentioned at all in Homer, but comes into sudden prominence in a sort of hymn to her in Hesiod, *Theog.* 411 ff., a passage whose genuineness has been much disputed. There she is daughter of Coeus and Phoebe, other authors giving other genealogies in a way which suggests that her connexion with Greek, or even pre-Greek and Titanic, deities was precarious. Zeus honours her exceedingly, giving her power and honour on earth and sea and also in the heavens, and taking away none of her original rights. If a man invokes her, she can benefit him in all manner of ways, for she is powerful in courts of law and in assemblies, can grant victory in war and athletics and success in horsemanship, in fishing, and cattle-breeding; she is also a nurturer of children (κουροτρόφος, a title likewise of Artemis). No other passage rates her so high, and this one must reflect the enthusiasm of a strong local cult, Boeotian or other, of which no more is known. Generally she is associated with uncanny things and the ghost-world. For this reason she is worshipped at the cross-roads, which seem to be haunted the world over. Hence her statues, of which the most famous was by Alcamenes, often have three faces or three bodies, less commonly four.* Here the notorious 'Hecate's suppers' were put out monthly for her (Ar. *Plut.* 594 ff. with schol.). It was a rite of purification, and one of its common constituents was dogs' flesh (Plutarch, *Quaest. Rom.* 290 d); cf. EGGS. Hecate is herself a formidable figure, Ἀνταία (see Hesychius s.v.), i.e. a bogy which 'meets' and frightens wayfarers. Hence it is not remarkable that she is associated with sorcery and black magic, from at least the tragic Medea (Eur. *Med.* 394 ff.) onwards. Thus we find her invoked to go away and take an obsessing spirit with her

* The typical cross-road is a place where a side path joins a main road; for particulars see Roscher in his *Lexikon,* i. 1904 ff., to which add *Hymn. Magic.* 5. 22 Abel (in his *Orphica*); Preisendanz, *PGM* iv. 2817–18; Lydus, *Mens.* 3. 8, p. 41. 20 Wünsch, for her fourfold aspect.

(Sophron, new frag.; see Festa in *Mondo classico* ii. 476 ff. for recent text); to help a dangerous love-charm which may bring destruction on the person it is aimed at (Theoc. 2. 12 ff.); and very often in magical papyri, etc. However, a more respectable cult of her seems also to have continued, see Farnell, *Cults* ii. 501 ff., 596 ff.

For bibliography see references in the text.   H. J. R.

HECATOMPEDON, *see* ACROPOLIS.

HECATON (Ἑκάτων) of Rhodes, a Platonizing Stoic, pupil of Panaetius, wrote chiefly on ethics, and was, next to Panaetius and Posidonius, the most influential member of the middle Stoic school. Works: Περὶ ἀγαθῶν, Περὶ ἀρετῶν, Περὶ παθῶν, Περὶ παραδόξων, Περὶ τελῶν, Περὶ τέλους, Χρεῖαι, Περὶ καθήκοντος. Cicero preserves some of his arguments with regard to conflict of duties, from which he seems to have been interested in casuistry.

PW vii. 2797. H. Gomoll, *Der Stoische Philosoph Hekaton* (1933).
                                                            W. D. R.

HECATONCHEIRES, hundred-handed monsters, Cottus, Briareos, and Gyes, sons of Heaven and Earth (Hes. *Theog.* 147 ff.); aided Zeus against the Titans (713 ff.). Briareos (called Aegaeon by men) was brought by Thetis to protect Zeus against Hera, Poseidon, and Athena (*Il.* 1. 396 ff.).

HECTOR, in mythology, eldest son of Priam and Hecuba (qq.v.), and the bravest of the Trojan champions; husband of Andromache (q.v.) and father of Astyanax (*Il.* 6. 394 ff.). His name appears to be Greek ('holder', 'stayer'), and it is possible that he is the invention either of Homer or of some earlier poet. In the *Iliad* he first appears leading the Trojans out to battle (2. 807 ff.); he reproaches Paris for avoiding Menelaus (3. 38 ff.), and arranges the truce and the single combat between the two (85 ff.). He takes a prominent part in the fighting of bks. 5 and 6, but in the latter leaves the field for a while to advise the elders to make offerings to the gods. He thus sees Andromache for the last time and returns with Paris to the battle. In bk. 7 he challenges any Greek to single combat, and is met by the greater Aias, who has somewhat the better of it; they part with an exchange of gifts. In the next book he drives the Greeks back to their camp and bivouacs with his army on the plain. In the long battle of bks. 11–17 he takes a prominent part, leading the chief attack on the fortification of the camp and being struck down with a stone by Aias (14. 409 ff.), but restored by Apollo at the command of Zeus (15. 239 ff.). He dispatches Patroclus (16. 818 ff.). After the appearance of Achilles at the trench he again bivouacs in the open, against the advice of Polydamas (18. 249 ff.). After the rout of the following day he refuses to enter Troy (22. 35 ff.), but waits for Achilles, despite the entreaties of his parents. At Achilles' approach he flees, but after a long chase halts, deceived by Athena into thinking that Deïphobus has come to his aid. In the subsequent fight he is killed and his body dragged behind Achilles' chariot to the ships. After the burial of Patroclus, Priam ransoms his body (24. 188 ff.), and his funeral ends the *Iliad*. Later poets add nothing of importance to Homer's account.

Hector had a hero-cult in several places, notably at Troy and at Thebes, his supposed bones having been brought to the latter city at the bidding of an oracle (Julian, *Ep.* 79 Bidez-Cumont; Lycophron, 1205 ff. and schol. there; Paus. 9. 18. 5). See Halliday in *Liverpool Annals* xi, pp. 3 ff.

Farnell, *Hero-Cults,* 328 f.; the larger dictionaries **s.v.**
                                                            H. J. R.

HECUBA (Ἑκάβη, Lat. *Hecuba*), in mythology, chief wife of Priam (q.v.), daughter of Dymas king of the Phrygians (*Il.* 16. 719; but later writers, as Eur. *Hec.* **3,** call her father Cisseus). Who her mother was was a problem of mythologists in Tiberius' time (Suet. *Tib.* 70). She was the mother of Hector (q.v.) and eighteen others of Priam's fifty sons (*Il.* 24. 495–7), the most noteworthy being Paris (q.v.).

In Homer she is a stately and pathetic figure, coming only occasionally into the foreground, as in the lament for Hector (*Il.* 24. 747 ff.). In Tragedy she is more prominent. Euripides (*Hecuba*) tells the following story of her last days. Her son Polydorus (q.v.) had been murdered by the Thracian Polymestor, to whom he had been entrusted; the discovery of his body came as a final blow to Hecabe after the sacrifice of her daughter Polyxena (q.v.). By a desperate appeal to Agamemnon, she got permission to revenge herself and, enticing Polymestor into her tent, she and her women killed his children and blinded him. He then foretold that she should turn into a bitch before her death, the place Cynos Sema getting its name from her tomb. In Eur. *Tro.* 969 ff., she so convincingly accuses Helen that Menelaus promises to kill her on reaching home, one of Euripides' curious departures from tradition. In several plays no longer extant, e.g. Ribbeck *TRF, incert.*, 5, from some Greek model, she was represented as dreaming, while carrying Paris, that she brought forth a torch, which burned all Troy (Apollod. 3. 148). All these legends appear in numerous variants, with rationalizations, more or less fanciful additions, and so forth, as is usual with much-handled themes. H. J. R.

HEDYLUS (fl. 270 B.C.), Greek epigrammatist, has three excellent poems in the *Anthology*, and several others are quoted by Athenaeus. He belonged to the gay poetic circle at Samos which was headed by Asclepiades and Posidippus, and he imitates and answers their poems.

R. Reitzenstein, *Epigramm und Skolion* (1893), 87; U. v. Wilamowitz-Moellendorff, *Hellenistische Dichtung* (1924), i. 144. G. H.

HEGEMON of Thasos, parodist, described 'by some' as a poet of Old Comedy (Ath. 1. 5 b. But Ath. 15. 699 a γέγραφε δὲ καὶ κωμῳδίαν εἰς τὸν ἀρχαῖον τρόπον ἣν ἐπιγράφουσι Φιλίνην suggests a later date for him). For Aristotle (*Poet.* 2. 1448ᵃ12) Hegemon is ὁ τὰς παρῳδίας ποιήσας πρῶτος, in that Hegemon raised Parody (already cultivated by others, *see* PARODY) into an independent genre with a separate place of its own in competitions. A passage of Hegemon (21 vv.) is quoted by Athenaeus (15. 698 f.) from Polemon: Hegemon's verses claim for his performance 50 drachmae, the second prize, and Polemon attests the victory of Hegemon at Athens with his *Gigantomachia* and other parodies.

For two verses of the *Philine* see *CAF* i. 700. Brandt, *Corp. poes. ep. Graec. lud.* 37 ff.; *FCG* i. 214 f. W. G. W.

HEGESANDER of Delphi (2nd c. B.C.) wrote at least six books of *Memoirs* (Ὑπομνήματα: Ath. 162 a), an ordered collection of unreliable anecdotes concerning Hellenistic kings, parasites, courtesans, philosophers, etc.; references mainly in Athenaeus (*FHG* iv. 412–22).

HEGESIAS (1) of Cyrene, head of the Cyrenaic school between Paraebates and Anniceris in the time of Ptolemy Soter (who died 283 B.C.); nicknamed Πεισιθάνατος because in his Ἀποκαρτερῶν he advocated suicide. He was expelled from Alexandria because of the scandal caused by his lectures.

PW vii. 2607. W. D. R.

HEGESIAS (2) of Magnesia (fl. *c.* 250 B.C.) wrote speeches and a *History of Alexander* of which a few passages survive (Gorgias Π. σχημ., Dion. Hal. *Comp.* 4, and Strabo 10. 396). Long recognized as the arch-corrupter of style, he was the chief representative of the earlier Asianism. His style, based on that of Charisius, accentuated the worst Gorgian faults, and his short jerky

sentences, his unnatural word-order, bold metaphors, and the rest were severely condemned by Dion. Hal. and others. *See further* ALEXANDER (3), Bibliography, Ancient sources. J. W. H. A.

HEGESIPPUS (1) (d. not earlier than 325 B.C.), son of Hegesias of Sunium, Athenian orator, contemporary of Demosthenes. He is believed by Libanius and many modern scholars to be the author of [Dem.] *De Halonneso* (342). If this is correct, Hegesippus had in 357 prosecuted Callippus of Paeania in connexion with the affairs of Cardia. A vigorous supporter of the anti-Macedonian policy (he is called by schol. on Aeschin. 1. 64 μισοφίλιππος), he opposed the peace of Philocrates (346) and was the head of an embassy sent to Philip to discuss modifications of the treaty (343; Dem. 19. 331). In 342 he accompanied Demosthenes and Lycurgus on a tour of the Peloponnese for the purpose of raising opposition against Philip (Dem. 9. 72). He was nick-named κρώβυλος ('top-knot') because he affected the old fashion of wearing his hair in a roll on the top of his head (Aeschin. 3. 118).

The speech *De Halonneso* is a retort to Philip's offer to give to Athens an island which was of little value to either side. The national party at Athens insisted that he was only restoring to them what was really their own.

Dionysius of Halicarnassus, who believed the speech to be by Demosthenes, pointed out that it is in many ways unworthy of him, and recalls the manner of Lysias; there is no attempt to avoid hiatus, and certain tricks of style recur with monotonous frequency. J. F. D.

HEGESIPPUS (2), New Comedy poet, who, like others in this period, mentions Epicurus (fr. 2). In fr. 1 a vainglorious cook expatiates upon his art.

FCG iv. 479 ff.; *CAF* iii. 312 ff.

HEGESIPPUS (3) (fl. 300 B.C.), a professional writer of epigrams: eight of his poems are in the *Greek Anthology*, most of them authentic inscriptions for tombs and votive tablets. His language is noticeably formal, archaic, and impersonal.

HEGESIPPUS (4) of Mecyberna, *see* NOVEL, GREEK.

HEIMARMENE, *see* FATE.

HEKTEMOROI (ἑκτημόροι), 'sixth-parters', in Athens before Solon's legislation, men who worked another's land, paying or receiving for it (for ancient authorities and modern scholars are divided) a sixth part of the produce; paying one-sixth would be a very moderate rental, five-sixths severe but not unparalleled. The *hektemoroi* had been free peasants, but in hard times they had first mortgaged their lands and then their persons and their children to their rich neighbours—so as to become tied serfs. Solon (q.v.) freed them once and for all by his *seisachtheia*. A. W. G.

HELEN (Ἑλένη), daughter of Zeus and Leda, or Nemesis (qq.v.). She is one of the most plausible examples of a 'faded' goddess, i.e. one whose original deity has been forgotten, and consequently made into a mortal woman in mythology. This is not proved by her having had a cult at Sparta and elsewhere (Farnell, *Hero-Cults*, p. 323); we may compare, for instance, the much more widely spread worship of Heracles (q.v.). But her non-Greek name, her association with trees (Δενδρῖτις at Rhodes, Paus. 3. 19. 10, with a story that she was hanged on a tree, cf. Artemis Ἀπαγχομένη, ibid. 8. 23. 6–7; 'Helen's tree' at Sparta, Theoc. 18. 43 ff.), and her connexion with birds (she is born from an egg and Zeus takes bird-form to visit her mother; cf. Nilsson, *Minoan-Mycenaean Rel.*, ch. 10, for epiphanies of Minoan gods in bird-shape) all fit an ancient, pre-Hellenic goddess, probably connected with vegetation and fertility, better than a dimly remembered princess, or even a purely imaginary human member of an ancient royal family. It is in no wise impossible that an old deity traditionally worshipped by the pre-Dorian population of Laconia had been taken, long before Homer, for an ancestress of their kings. Even in Homer she has something daemonic about her, e.g. the mere fact of being her husband is Menelaus' passport to Elysium (*Od.* 4. 569).

In the *Iliad* and *Odyssey* she is the human wife of Menelaus, who has been carried off to Troy by Paris (q.v.). She is, while at Troy, Paris' wife, not his mistress, but feels deeply the anomalous position of being the legal wife of two different men in different places (see *Il.* 3. 139–40, 443 ff.; 24. 763 ff.). Her sympathies are on the whole with the Greeks, but on occasion she is decidedly pro-Trojan, as *Od.* 4. 274 ff. There seems to have been no difficulty about a reconciliation between her and Menelaus after the war, and in the *Odyssey* she is living happily with him at Lacedaemon. Her carrying off by Paris is the cause of the war (*Il.* 3. 87 and often).

Later authors, not realizing that Agamemnon was overlord of Mycenaean Greece, elaborate the reasons for the war. Besides the original plan of Zeus (cf. NEMESIS, and add Hesiod, fr. 96. 58 ff. Rzach), she was wooed by the noblest men in Greece, and they all swore to support the rights of her husband, whoever he might be (authorities and variants in Rose, *Handb. Gk. Myth.* 249, note 7). Others tell the story of her earlier and later life. She was carried off when a mere child by Theseus (Plut. *Thes.* 31 and elsewhere; cf. DIOSCURI). At the sack of Troy Menelaus was at first disposed to kill her (see Robert, *Bild und Lied*, 76 ff.; cf. HECUBA). She never went to Troy at all, but Paris carried off a phantom of her, Stesichorus (J. Vürtheim, *Stesichoros' Fragmente* (1919), 64 ff.). She appears as St. Elmo's fire (schol. Eur. *Or.* 1637, Pliny, *HN* 2. 101). *See also* ACHILLES.

Farnell, *Cults* ii. 675; *Hero-Cults*, 323 ff.; and the dictionaries and handbooks of mythology. H. J. R.

HELENUS, in mythology, son of Priam, warrior and prophet. In the *Iliad* he gives prophetic advice to Hector (6. 76, 7. 44), and is wounded by Menelaus at the battle of the ships (bk. 13). Captured by Odysseus, he prophesied the fall of Troy if Philoctetes was brought there with his bow (Soph. *Phil.* 604–13). After the fall of Troy he was carried off by Neoptolemus, who gave him Andromache as his wife (Eur. *Andr.* 1243). They settled in Epirus and made 'a little Troy'; there they were visited by Aeneas, to whom Helenus prophesied his future wanderings (Verg. *Aen.* 3. 294–505). C. B.

HELIAEA (ἡλιαία, Doric ἁλιαία, Public Assembly; see Bonner and Smith, *Administration of Justice*, i. 157, n. 5) was originally an Athenian court of appeal instituted by Solon (Lys. 10. 16). The word ἡλιαία and its derivatives survived both in official documents and in everyday speech as the equivalent of δικαστήριον after the disappearance of the Solonian court. The dicasts oath continued to be called ὅρκος ἡλιαστικός or τῶν ἡ'λιαστῶν ὅρκος. In the oath itself there appears ἡλίασις. Religious conservatism doubtless accounts for the continued use of ἡλιαία (Dem. 23. 97), in the curse with which the herald opened the meetings of the Assembly, 'accursed be he who in speech deceives ἢ βουλὴν ἢ δῆμον ἢ τὴν ἡλιαίαν'.

When the Solonian appeal was abandoned and a number of dicasteries (q.v.), divisions of the ἡλιαία, were substituted for the whole body, one of the new courts was called the ἡλιαία of the *thesmothetai*. This was due to the fact that this court met in the commodious quarters of the old ἡλιαία. They were needed because sometimes several panels of 500 each assembled for the trial of important cases. On one occasion the entire group of 6,000 dicasts sat on a case (Andoc. 1. 17).

The court was used also for other legal purposes. Arbitrations involving members of the tribes of Oeneus and Erechtheus and possibly others were held there.

See also DICASTERIES, and the bibliography there. R. J. B.

HELICON, the largest mountain of Boeotia (5,868 feet), between Copais and the Corinthian Gulf; and particularly the summit behind Thespiae, which contained the sanctuary of the Muses in a glen. There are remains of an Ionic temple, theatre, and statues of the Muses; games were held every fourth year in their honour. On its slopes lay Ascra, the home of Hesiod. The spring Hippocrene, struck by Pegasus' foot from the rock, the inspiration of poets (Prop. 3. 3; legend and function are Hellenistic), is a little below the summit.

Paus. 9. 28–31; Bölte, Mayer, and Fiehn, *PW* viii. 1 ff., 1853 ff.; xvi. 696 ff., 821; *see also* THESPIAE. T. J. D.

HELIODORUS (1) of Athens wrote (c. 150 B.C.?) Ἀναθήματα (title varies), fifteen books on artistic works on the Athenian Acropolis, with historical and other digressions.

Ath. 6. 229 e; 9. 406 c; 2. 45 c (?); Pliny 1. 34–5; *FHG* iv. 425–6; *PW* viii. 15–18.

HELIODORUS (2), a metrist who flourished in the middle of the first century A.D. He edited Aristophanes' comedies with a colometry (division of the text into cola), with metrical signs (σημεῖα) and a running commentary. Much of his labours is preserved in the scholia to Aristophanes. He was the principal authority used by Juba (q.v. 3). J. D. D.

HELIODORUS (3), a popular surgeon of the time of Juvenal (who lived c. A.D. 60–140; cf. Juv. 6. 373), probably from Egypt. He belonged to the pneumatic school. Works: (1) Χειρουργούμενα (principal work, chiefly known from Oribasius); (2) ? Περὶ ἄρθρων πραγματεία or Ἐπιμήχανος; (3) Περὶ ὀλισθημάτων πραγματεία; (4) Περὶ ἐπιδέσμων (on bandages); (5) Περὶ μέτρων καὶ σταθμῶν; (6) *Epistula phlebotomiae* (Lat. transl.). *See* SURGERY, para. 6.

PW viii. 41. W. D. R.

HELIODORUS (4), author of a Greek novel called the *Aethiopica* or *Theagenes and Charicleia* (Τὰ περὶ Θεαγένην καὶ Χαρίκλειαν Αἰθιοπικά), says that he was a Phoenician of Emesa, son of Theodosius, of the race of the Sun. Emesa, famous for a cult of Helios with which the last statement implies some family connexion, was included in Syria Phoenike already in the reign of Elagabalus and reached the height of its glory in that period. H., a pagan influenced by Sun worship and Neo-Pythagorean thought, may have written soon after the publication of Philostratus' *Life of Apollonius of Tyana* (c. A.D. 220), which he seems to have known; but the tradition that he later became a Christian and bishop of Trikka in Thessaly (Socrates, *Hist. Eccl.* 5. 22) has not been disproved.

Summary: Charicleia, white daughter of the king and queen of Ethiopia, was exposed at birth by her mother. She was rescued and passed into the care of a Greek priest who took her to Delphi, treating her as his own daughter. She and Theagenes meet, fall in love, and with the help of Calasiris, a visiting Egyptian priest, escape from Delphi and after some adventures reach the coast of Egypt in the hands of pirates. Fortune separates them, but later all three meet again at Memphis, where Calasiris dies. The lovers, sometimes masquerading as brother and sister, survive many threats to their lives and honour and finally come to Meroe as prisoners of the Ethiopians, then at war with Persia. Recognition and reconciliation just save them from being sacrificed as the first-fruits of victory, and their marriage is then blessed by Charicleia's parents.

A summary does less than justice to H., who diversifies his main plot with subsidiary, but relevant, stories and develops it with unusual skill. In style he is rhetorical, but rarely ridiculous; he shows himself to be a man of considerable culture, well acquainted with classical literature. Though not free from the faults inherent in the literary form, he is the most successful of the extant novelists, and when translated in the sixteenth century he exercised some influence not only on romance but also on drama.

BIBLIOGRAPHY

TEXTS. Teubner (Bekker); A. Colonna (1938). With translation (French), Budé (Rattenbury, Lumb, Maillon).
COMMENTARY. O. D. Coraes (Modern Greek; Paris, 1804).
TRANSLATIONS. Th. Underdowne (1587, etc.); French, J. Amyot (1559, etc.).
STYLE AND DICTION. R. M. Rattenbury and A. Colonna (see TEXTS above); H. Dörrie, De Longi Ach. Tat. Heliodori memoria (1935).
LIFE AND WORK. R. M. Rattenbury and J. Maillon (see TEXTS above); M. Oeftering, Heliodor und seine Bedeutung für die Literatur (1901).
See also under NOVEL, GREEK.   R. M. R.

HELIOGABALUS, see ELAGABALUS (2).

HELIOPOLIS (modern *Baalbek*) was the religious centre of the Ituraean tetrarchy, after whose dissolution it was incorporated in the territory of Berytus (17 B.C.). Septimius Severus made it a separate colony, with *ius Italicum*. The huge temple of Jupiter, begun by Antoninus Pius and completed under Caracalla, the adjacent temple of Venus, and another small circular temple are among the most impressive monuments of the Syrian school of Hellenistic architecture.

T. Wiegand, *Baalbek* (1921–5).   A. H. M. J.

HELIOS, the Sun-god. The general attitude towards the heavenly bodies in Greece seems to have been that although undoubtedly gods (cf. the indignation at Athens over Anaxagoras' announcement that the sun was a material body, Diog. Laert. 2. 12; and Nilsson's comments, *Harv. Theol. Rev.* 1940), they were no concern of mankind, or at most were beings to be saluted with due reverence on occasion (Plato, *Leg.* 887 e), not to receive a regular cult, as did those gods who dwelt in the cities or country-side, like Athena or the Nymphs, or at farthest on hill-tops, like Zeus. Hence the traces of sun-cult in Greece proper are few and often uncertain (see Farnell, *Cults* v. 419 f.). Rhodes, however, had a vigorous cult of Helios, which is one of several non-Greek features in its classical culture. He appears to have been the chief national god (Diod. Sic. 5. 56. 4), and the local legend (Pind. *Ol.* 7. 54 ff.) makes the island his peculiar property, chosen by him before it rose to the surface of the sea, and his sons its chief early inhabitants, after whom the leading towns were named; their mother was the eponymous nymph of the country, Rhodos. His festival was the Halieia (Nilsson, *Griechische Feste*, 427); it was celebrated with much splendour and included important athletic contests, though never rising to the level of the Great Games. Outside of actual cult, Helios is often appealed to as a witness of oaths and the like, as *Il.* 3. 277, because, as there stated, he sees and hears everything.

He has not much mythology; for the most interesting story about him *see* PHAETHON. He is regularly conceived as a charioteer, who drives daily from east to west across the sky. The question how he got back again during the night was evidently discussed very early, and the quaint solution evolved that he floated around the earth by the stream of Ocean in a huge cup (references collected in Athenaeus, 469 c ff.).

In later times the theological importance of Helios increased considerably, owing to the growing tendency to identify him with other gods. In the case of Apollo (q.v.), this is as early as the fifth century B.C., and doubtless the allegorizing tendency of the Stoics, who very commonly sought a physical explanation of myths, made its contribution a century or so later; but the strongest impetus in this direction was given by the late imperial increase of actual cult of the Sun, culminating in making him in some sense the principal god of the Empire from Aurelian on. The *locus classicus* is Macrobius, *Sat.* 1. 17. 2 ff., where by a series of ingenious arguments the proposition is supported that all the gods, 'dumtaxat qui sub caelo sunt', i.e. with the omission of the transcendental powers outside the material universe, are powers or activities ('uirtutes', 17. 4) of the sun; but Macrobius' own quotations, beginning with Verg. *G.* 1. 6, show that the theory had been long growing.

Farnell, *Cults*, v. 417 ff.; Rapp in Roscher's *Lexikon*, art. 'Helios'; Cumont, *Religions orientales*, see index s.v. 'Soleil'; Nilsson, *ARW* xxx (1933), 141 ff.; Cumont, *Mélanges Bidez* (1934), 141 f.
                                                                 H. J. R.

HELLANICUS, son of Andromenes, of Mytilene was born in 500 B.C. (Ol. 70. 1 Eusebius) or later; in 497 if he was 65 in 432 (Aul. Gell. 15. 23); not before 491 if he mentioned Arginusae (406, schol. Ar. *Ran.* 694) and died at 85 (Lucian, *Macr.* 22). Dionysius Halicarnassensis (*Thuc.* 5) groups him with Charon (q.v.) and Herodotus; Thucydides (1. 97) thought his Athenian history slight and ill-dated. He is quoted, under twenty-five titles (both prose and verse), on myths and primitive history, and on many countries and cities; on the *Priestesses of Hera in Argos*, and on the *Carneian Victors*. Suidas ranks him as 'successor' to Hecataeus (q.v.), but as an historian he was soon superseded. His unorthodox conjectures, etymologies, identifications of sites, and duplications of personages were distrusted by Strabo (10. 2. 6; 11. 6. 2; 12. 3. 21; 13. 1. 42) and by Josephus (*Ap.* 1. 16), but his mythology was used freely by Dion. Hal. (especially for the early West) and by Apollodorus, *Bibliotheca*. His style was undistinguished (Hermog. *Id.* 2. 12; Cic. *De Or.* 2. 12. 53).

FHG i. 45, iv. 630–2; *FGrH* i. 41; L. Pearson, *Early Ionian Historians* (1939), ch. 5.   J. L. M.

HELLANODIKAI were the judges of the Olympian Games (q.v.). They were chosen from the ruling families of Elis, to whom also the revenues of the festival accrued. Dressed in purple robes, they had special seats, presented the victors with their crowns, and presided over the banquet which ended the festival. They exercised disciplinary authority over the athletes and imposed fines for breaches of their rules.   F. A. W.

HELLE, see ATHAMAS.

HELLEBORE, see ANTICYRA.

HELLEN (Ἕλλην), eponymous ancestor of the Hellenes, son or brother of Deucalion (q.v.; Thuc. 1. 3. 2; schol. Pind. *Ol.* 9. 68). His sons were Dorus, Xuthus (q.v.), and Aeolus (q.v.; Hesiod, fr. 7 Rzach); i.e. the Dorians, Ionians, and Aeolians have a common ancestry. This is not mythology, but early ethnological theory cast in the traditional mythological form of a genealogy. H. J. R.

HELLENES (Ἕλληνες), the national name of the Greeks. Originally it was confined, as well as the territorial name of Hellas, to a small tribe in south Thessaly (Hom. *Il.* 2. 683 f.). Perhaps these were in some way related to the Selloi or Helloi of Dodona (though these were a priesthood, not a tribe); the surroundings of Dodona were called Hellopia (cf. Arist. *Mete.* 1. 352ª 31 ff.). The name of 'Hellenes' wandered southwards, probably in connexion with the migration of the Dorians and the western tribes. We do not know how the name spread farther. In order to give it a general meaning, more or less covering the whole Greek people, the form of 'Panhellenes' was introduced. It is confirmed by linguistic research that, in this sense, 'Panhellenes' was earlier than 'Hellenes'. Homer, who only once (in the Catalogue of Ships, *Il.* 2. 530) mentions 'Panhellenes and Achaeans', generally calls the Greek people Achaeans, Argives, or Danai. Hesiod and Archilochus (both *c.* 700 B.C.) were, as a later Greek writer put it, 'the first to know that all Greeks were called Hellenes as well as Panhellenes'. For their eponymous ancestor, Hellen, father of Dorus, Aeolus, and Xuthus (whose sons were Ion and Achaeus), see the preceding article. The name of the judges at the Olympian Games (*Hellanodikai*, q.v.), the earliest testimonial of which is an inscription of *c.* 600 B.C., proves that during the seventh century the name of Hellenes had been generally acknowledged as that of the Greek people.

A. R. Burn, *Minoans, Philistines and Greeks* (1930), 123; V. Ehrenberg, *Ost und West* (1935), 54 ff., 215 f.   V. E.

HELLENICA OXYRHYNCHIA, see OXYRHYNCHUS HISTORIAN.

HELLENOTAMIAI ('Treasurers of the Greeks') were the financial overseers of the Delian League, with their office in Delos from 477 to 454 B.C., thereafter in Athens; from the first, however, they were Athenian officials. They were ten in number, perhaps elected by vote, normally one from each *phyle*. They received, through the *apodektai* (q.v.), the tribute from the cities of the League, subject to audit by the *logistai* (q.v.). They had general management of the tribute for the year, paying out sums on the instruction of the Ecclesia, chiefly to *strategi*, sometimes for other purposes (such as the Acropolis buildings). After 411 they received wider powers (see KOLAKRETAI); with the fall of the Athenian Empire in 404 the office was abolished.   A. W. G.

HELLESPONT, the narrow strait dividing Europe from Asia at the final exit of the waters of the Black Sea and Marmara into the Aegean—the modern Dardanelles. It was crossed by the Persian army under Xerxes between Sestos and Abydos, at the narrowest part near the modern Nagara Point. It was again crossed by Alexander the Great in 334 B.C. A strong current runs out from the Hellespont into the Aegean. Callipolis (*Gallipoli*), Lampsacus, Sestos, and Abydos are on its shores, with the sites of Troy and Dardanus on the Asiatic side. All cities alike derived much of their wealth from the fisheries, and from the passage of people and armies from Europe to Asia and vice versa. The name Hellespont is connected with the legend of Phrixus and Helle (see ATHAMAS). S. C.

HELOTS (εἵλωτες), the name applied to the serfs of the Spartans both in Laconia and Messenia, appears to be related to ἁλίσκομαι and thus to designate captives. Though the helots spoke Doric, they must have belonged largely to the pre-Doric stock. They far outnumbered their masters and were a constant threat, always ready to revolt. To keep them in check a secret police of young men was organized (*krypteia*), while any overt act could be justified by the declaration of war issued annually by the ephors. Yet many helots must have been trustworthy, for helots accompanied Spartiates in the field and in addition, particularly during the Peloponnesian War and later, considerable numbers were used in the army and rewarded for their services by grants of freedom, thus becoming *neodamodeis*. Yet the precise status of the helots is difficult to define. Our sources frequently call them δοῦλοι and so fail to differentiate them from slaves, but there are a few more precise statements. The remark that they occupied a middle position between slave and

free (Pollux 3. 83) justifies their classification as serfs, while the reference to them as in a sense State slaves (Ephorus in Strabo 8. 365; cf. Paus. 3. 20. 6) shows that they were the property of the State. It also is clear that only the State could set them free. They were assigned to definite estates and paid a fixed quota of the products. In addition to helots the Spartans had regular slaves, and the manumission of individuals recorded in inscriptions must refer to the latter.

G. Gilbert, *The Constitutional Antiquities of Sparta and Athens* (1895), 30–5; A. H. J. Greenidge, *Greek Constitutional History* (1896), 83–6; G. Busolt, *Griechische Staatskunde* ii (1926), 667–71 et passim. U. Kahrstedt, *Griechisches Staatsrecht* (1922), 57–70, maintains that the helots were the only servile class of Sparta and were private property.   J. A. O. L.

HELVETII, a Celtic tribe originally located in south Germany, which migrated gradually *c.* 200 B.C. to an area between the Rhine, the Jura, and the lake of Geneva. Part of the tribe joined the Cimbri *c.* 111, and a mass migration (263,000 persons; Caes. *BGall.* 1. 29. 1) in 58 was defeated by Caesar, who sent the remnants home, allowing them, however, the privilege of a *foedus*. Under Augustus they formed part of *Gallia Belgica*, with the normal organization of a cantonal senate at the capital, Aventicum (*Avenches*), and *pagi*. The region paid dearly for opposition to Vitellius (A.D. 69); Vespasian, however, restored Avenches with the title of colony, and a period of prosperity began. From *c.* A.D. 260, when the *Limes* was abandoned, the region was exposed to the attacks of Alamanni and was heavily fortified. By 460 it was under the control of Burgundians and Alamanni.

F. Stähelin, *Die Schweiz in Römischer Zeit*[2] (1931).   C. E. S.

HELVIDIUS PRISCUS, son of a *centurio primipilaris*, was *tribunus plebis* in A.D. 56, praetor in 70. He married Fannia, daughter of Paetus Thrasea (q.v.), and when the latter was forced to commit suicide in 66 Helvidius was exiled; but Galba recalled him in 68. A keen follower of the Stoic sect, his own exile and the murder of Thrasea turned him into a fanatic. He appeared in 70 as the spear-head of senatorial opposition to Vespasian and eventually preached out-and-out republicanism. His activities, which even extended to the mob, became so dangerous that Vespasian was forced to exile him and finally to have him executed (? 75).

PIR[1], H 37.   R. L. J.

HELVIUS, see CINN (4), PERTINAX.

HEMINA, see CASSIUS (2).

HEMITHEA, see TENES.

HENDEKA. The Eleven (ἕνδεκα) at Athens as executive officials had charge of prisons and executions; as judicial officers they presided at the trial of various classes of thieves known as κακοῦργοι. As a board they had themselves the right to try and convict confessed κακοῦργοι.   R. J. B.

HENIOCHUS, Middle Comedy poet. One of his plays was named Πολύευκτος, not necessarily after the well-known partisan of Demosthenes: it was a common name. From the prologue of a piece (fr. 5), perhaps entitled Πόλεις, 18 verses are spoken by a deity or abstraction who introduces the assembled States; they have come to Olympia to make thank-offerings for freedom, but the disturbing influence of Δημοκρατία and Ἀριστοκρατία thwarts their purpose. This probably refers to the time of the Corinthian alliance under Philip, 338 B.C.

FCG iii. 560 ff.; *CAF* ii. 431 ff.   W. G. W.

HEPATOSCOPY, see DIVINATION, para. 5, HARUSPICES, and RELIGION, ETRUSCAN.

HEPHAESTION (1) (*c.* 356–324 B.C.), son of Amyntor, a Macedonian noble, became a friend of Alexander the Great from childhood, and remained his closest companion. His military career after 330 was distinguished, and he was evidently a competent commander, though probably not the equal of Craterus, Nearchus, or Ptolemy (or others who proved themselves later). His value to Alexander, however, apart from personal affection, lay in his sympathetic understanding of his dearest plans for the empire. Alexander revived for him the Persian office of 'chiliarch' (vizier), which, with other honours, marked him out as his first subordinate (324). Hephaestion seems to have been of an arrogant and possessive nature, and he was not universally popular, but his death (by fever) caused Alexander great grief, and he was mourned extravagantly.

Berve, *Alexanderreich*, no. 357.   G. T. G.

HEPHAESTION (2), metrist, probably to be identified with the tutor of Verus (A.D. 130–69). His treatise Περὶ μέτρων, originally written in forty-eight books, was reduced by successive abridgements to an ἐγχειρίδιον in one book, in which form it is extant. Ancient commentaries on H. sometimes enable us to reconstruct the earlier, fuller, versions; and parts of the extant treatise appear to belong to one of these versions, not to the final abridgement (Π. σημείων and Π. παραβάσεως), while others may not come from H. at all (Π. ποιήματος, Π. ποιημάτων). The work is divided into the following parts: (1) on long and short syllables; (2) on συνεκφώνησις (synizesis); (3) on feet, in general; (4) on catalexis; (5)–(13) on the various feet, including the antispast (∪−−∪); (14) on cola composed of heterogeneous feet; (15) on ἀσυνάρτητα (combinations of two cola separated by diaeresis, e.g. the Archilochean dicolon); (16) on πολυσχημάτιστα (cola which assume varying forms). There follow appendixes dealing with the building of a poetic structure out of lines and cola (Π. ποιήματος, Π. ποιημάτων) and with notation for elucidating that structure (Π. σημείων). Besides the *Encheiridion* various other works on metre are ascribed to H. by Suidas.

Hephaestion belonged to the school of metrists who sought to explain metre by analysing it into its primary elements (μέτρα πρωτότυπα), that is, the feet, as opposed to others who derived all metres from the Homeric hexameter and the iambic trimeter. His treatment of lyric metre is almost confined to solo lyric and comedy, and he rarely tries his hand on the more difficult measures of choral poetry and tragedy. His procedure is extremely mechanistic, and we learn little from him directly of the true nature of Greek metric. But he has preserved many fragments of lost poems which are of great value to metrical science.

Text: M. Consbruch (Teubner, 1906). Commentary: T. Gaisford (2nd ed. 1855).   J. D. D.

HEPHAESTUS (Ἥφαιστος), god of fire and especially of the smithy fire. It is, however, extremely unlikely that this was his original character. Examination of the distribution of his cult (facts in L. Malten, s.v. 'Hephaistos', in *PW*) shows that it spreads from the volcanic regions of Asia Minor via Lemnos, which is also volcanic. This decidedly indicates that he was originally an Asianic deity of volcanic fire; that he is associated with volcanoes in Greek mythology (his forge is under Aetna, or one of the neighbouring islands, Callim. *Dian.* 47; Verg. *G.* 4. 170 ff., *Aen.* 8. 416 ff.) is less cogent, as such a notion might have grown up independently, to explain the eruptions of the mountain, considered as a huge chimney. But there is no doubt that for the Greeks he was a craftsman's god and himself a divine craftsman; hence the distribution of his cult in Greece itself, where it is practically confined to the most industrialized regions, being particularly prominent at Athens and partly displacing the old native worship of Prometheus.

His mythology is what might be expected from his development into a smith-god, which had taken place before Homer. He is lame (in an early community a lame man with strong arms would naturally become a smith, being handicapped for farming, fighting, or hunting), and consequently awkward in his movements and somewhat ridiculous (*Il.* 1. 597 ff.). He is constantly employed in making marvellous works of all sorts (as *Il.* 18. 373 ff.; *Od.* 7. 91 ff.), clearly magical (a smith is often a magician also). He makes various famous objects, as Achilles' armour, Harmonia's necklace (*see* CADMUS), Agamemnon's sceptre (*Il.* 2. 101 ff.). His workmen are the Cyclopes (q.v.), though not in Homer (see Callimachus and Virgil, locc. cit. supra). He makes Pandora, the first woman (Hesiod, *Op.* 70 ff.), or mankind in general (Lucian, *Hermot.* 20); cf. PROMETHEUS. His parents are Zeus and Hera (Homer), or Hera alone (Hes. *Theog.* 927), but he was cast out of heaven by Hera, because he was misshapen (*Il.* 18. 395 ff.), or by Zeus, because he defended Hera against him (*Il.* 1. 590 ff.). A comic story of his return was told by Epicharmus in his Κωμασταί (see Hyg. *Fab.* 166 and Rose ad loc.). His wife is Charis (*Il.* 18. 382) or more usually Aphrodite (as *Od.* 8. 266 ff.), which is little more than an allegory, Craftsmanship allied to Grace or Beauty.

Malten, op. cit.; Rapp in Roscher's *Lexikon*, s.v.; Farnell, *Cults* v. 374 ff. Cf. ATHENA.   H. J. R.

HERA (Ἥρα, Epic Ἥρη), an ancient, pre-Hellenic goddess. Her Greek name seems to be a title, 'lady', fem. of ἥρως; her native name is unknown. She is regularly said to be wife of Zeus, his numerous connexions with other goddesses being explained away by making them either former wives or mistresses. But the natural suggestion that she is the earth, a common consort of the sky-god, lacks cogent evidence (see Farnell, op. cit. infra, 181 ff.). She is rather a deity of marriage and of the life, especially the sexual life, of women. Her connexion with Zeus is perhaps best explained by supposing that the Greeks on arrival found her cult too strong to be suppressed or ignored, supposing that they wished to do so, and made room for her by making her the wife (and sister) of their own principal god. It seems conceivable that the persistent stories of the quarrels of the divine pair (e.g. *Il.* 1. 540 ff.) reflect a faint memory of a time when the two cults were not fully reconciled. That in pre-Hellenic belief she should be very prominent and have either no male partner or none of any importance is quite in accord with what is known of early, especially Cretan, religion.

2. Mythologically, she is one of the children of Kronos and Rhea (e.g. Hes. *Theog.* 454); later versions differ only in details, as Hyg. *Fab.* 139, where Hera has not been swallowed by her father (cf. KRONOS) and saves Zeus from him. She is the mother of Ares, Eileithyia, Hebe, Hephaestus, and, in one account, of Typhon (qq.v.). Beyond these points her story consists mainly of her hostility to Troy, and consequently in later authors, such as Virgil, to Aeneas (q.v.), and generally her bitterness against her numerous rivals and their offspring, *see*, e.g., LETO, SEMELE. In the story of the Argonauts (q.v.) she appears in all accounts as the friend and helper of Jason (q.v.). For her part in the Judgement of Paris, *see* PARIS.

3. Her most ancient place of worship seems to be Argos, hence her very common title of Ἀργεία. But Samos certainly worshipped her from very early times also (references in Farnell, p. 253 f.), and there is abundant evidence for cults of her, many certainly old, all up and down the Greek world, both alone and with Zeus. Perhaps her most characteristic rite is the sacred marriage (q.v.), whereof more or less clear evidence can be had for eight places (Farnell, p. 185). She is also connected with the ritual of ordinary human marriage, as at Ceos (Callim. *Aet.* 3, fr. 1. 4 Mair), at least in legend. To her functions as marriage-goddess several of her titles refer, as Zygia, Gamelia, and so forth; for her remarkable surnames at Stymphalus *see* EPITHETS, para. 2. She is also frequently connected with birth and the nurture of children; not only is she mother of Eileithyia (q.v.), but she is called Eileithyia herself (Hesychius s.v. (Argos), Farnell, p. 247, note 28 c (Attica)).

4. At some places, especially Argos and Samos, she rises to the status of a city-goddess, a not unnatural development, considering the vital importance of increase to any State; but not many of her titles bear witness to a civic side of her activities (Farnell, p. 196 f.).

5. Associations with deities other than Zeus are occasionally to be found; for example, she is paired with Aphrodite, q.v. (Paus. 3. 13. 9; Sparta, where an ancient statue of her was called Hera Aphrodite), and once or twice elsewhere.

6. Her ritual for the most part is not remarkable; at Argos she is connected with the ancient ceremonial of the Shield. At her festival, the Heraia, a shield was the prize at the athletic contests which took place, and an armed procession was a prominent feature. The latest discussion of this somewhat unusual proceeding for the cult of a goddess (I. R. Arnold in *AJArch.* 41, 436 ff.) would associate it with the Minoan-Mycenaean sacred shield and shielded goddess.

7. Hera was commonly identified with Juno (q.v.), occasionally with other foreign goddesses.

Farnell, *Cults* i. 179 ff.; Nilsson, *Minoan-Mycenaean Religion*, Index s.v.; Roscher in his *Lexikon*, s.v.　　H. J. R.

HERACLEA (Ἡράκλεια) (1), nowadays *Policoro*, a Tarentine foundation in Lucania (Diod. 12. 36; Strabo 6. 264; Livy 8. 24), scene of Pyrrhus' costly victory over Rome, 280 B.C. (Plut. *Pyrr.* 16). By granting Heraclea an exceptionally favourable treaty Rome detached it from Tarentum *c.* 278 B.C. (Cic. *Balb.* 21 f.; *Arch.* 6 f.). The so-called *Lex Iulia Municipalis* (*see* LEX, LEGES) was found here (Dessau, *ILS* 6085).

J. Bérard, *Bibliogr. topogr.* (1941), 55.　　E. T. S.

HERACLEA (2) (ἡ πρὸς Λάτμῳ) was a small town at the top of the Latmian Gulf, some 10 miles east of Miletus. Its ring-wall, constructed *c.* 300 B.C. by Cassander's brother Pleistarchus, is the finest surviving example of Hellenistic fortifications.

F. Krischen, in Th. Wiegand, *Milet* iii. 2 (1922).　　M. C.

HERACLEA (3) **PONTICA,** a Megarian and Boeotian colony founded *c.* 560 B.C. among the Mariandyni, whom the colonists reduced to serfdom, but agreed not to sell outside the city territory. Heraclea at one time controlled much of the coast as far as Cytorus; it founded two colonies, Callatis and Chersonesus, and was active in Euxine trade, its people being among the chief navigators there in the days of Xenophon. Civil discord led to tyranny, which lasted eighty-four years (until 281 B.C.), and is said, when at its height, to have been the town's best period. The rise of the Bithynian and Pontic kingdoms and the settlement of the Galatians in the interior steadily weakened the city. Taken and sacked by the Romans in the Third Mithridatic War, it finally lost its prosperity, and the colony which Caesar founded there did not endure. Heraclea became a metropolis of the Pontic *Koinon* in the second century A.D.

Memnon, in *FHG* iii. 525 ff.; Xenophon, *Anab.* bks. 5–7; Strabo, pp. 542–3.　　T. R. S. B.

HERACLEA (4) **TRACHINIA,** a Spartan colony founded in 426 B.C. in a strong position about 5 miles from Thermopylae, as a halting-place for armies marching to Chalcidice and also as a naval base. Owing to misgovernment by Spartan officials and raids by local tribes the colony scarcely fulfilled expectations. In the Corinthian War Heraclea was captured by Boeotians and Argives, who expelled the Peloponnesians. After a brief revival of Spartan control, Jason of Pherae dismantled the fortifications and handed the city over to the Oetaeans. Heraclea was forced to join the Aetolian League in 280 and was sacked by the Romans in 191.

Y. Béquignon, *La Vallée du Spercheios* (1937).　　H. D. W.

HERACLES (Ἡρακλέης, Ἡρακλῆς). Many details must remain obscure for us concerning this, the most popular and widely worshipped of Greek heroes. In the first place, we have lost all the older continuous accounts and also Plutarch's Life of him, which no doubt contained much valuable information, and are reduced to patching together many scattered references, with such late documents as [Apollodorus] 2. 61 ff., Hyginus, *Fab.* 29–36 as our basis. However, the following conclusions may be accepted as fairly certain.

2. He is a hero, not a god, although occasionally worshipped as a god (Farnell, op. cit. infra, 97; on his cult see also Ch. Picard, *BCH* xlvii (1923), 241 ff., H. Seyrig, ibid. li (1927), 185 ff. and 369 ff.), for his name is theophoric, and no Greek deity is thus named from another. Heracles (cf. 'Diocles') 'Hera's glory', i.e. probably 'glorious gift of Hera (to his parents)', is a typically human name. Behind all the rest of the story, then, must lie a man, real or, less likely, imaginary, the son of a Hera-worshipping people. This fits excellently with the constant tradition that he was an Argive, or rather a Tirynthian, apparently of a younger branch of the Perseid dynasty (cf. *Il.* 19. 105), related to Eurystheus of Argos, for whom he performed the Labours. If the real Heracles was prince or baron of Tiryns, the king of Argos (or Mycenae) might well have been his overlord, and it seems possible that distinguished service in some forgotten war or other exploit may have laid the first foundations of his vast reputation for strength and courage, though the stages by which he rose to his unique position in popular favour remain unknown. But his Argive nationality is supported by the geography of his Labours, six of them belonging to the Peloponnesus. By all accounts, these were (1) The Nemean Lion. For authorities see Rose, *Handbk. Gk. Myth.* 211, note 113; it may be remarked that in the earliest versions the beast was apparently not invulnerable (O. Berthold, *Die Unverwundbarkeit* (1911), 2–5). (2) The Hydra of Lerna. (3) The Boar of Erymanthus. (4) The Hind of Ceryneia. (5) The Birds of Stymphalus. (6) The Stables of Augeas (authorities, Rose, ibid., note 117 ff.). Nor are the other six Labours inconsistent with Argive origin and residence. The seventh, the Cretan Bull, and the eighth, the Horses of Diomedes (q.v. 1), are in or near the Greek world, but the other four are quite outside it, and so about equally remote wherever we suppose Heracles' home to have been; they are (9) The Girdle of the Amazon (q.v.), (10) Geryon, (11) Cerberus, (12) The Apples of the Hesperides. All these last three are variants of one theme, the conquest of Death. The hero must go to an island in the extreme west, Erytheia (q.v.), and there overcome a triple-bodied monster, Geryon, and his attendants and take his cattle; or he must descend to the House of Hades and steal the infernal watch-dog; or, finally, he must pluck the golden apples from the dragon-guarded tree at the world's end (further details and references in Rose, op. cit. 214 ff.). All these are manifestly more elaborate forms of the simple and ancient tale that on one occasion Heracles met Hades and worsted him (*Il.* 5. 395 ff., cf. Pind. *Ol.* 9. 33). The fact that they are variants one of another indicates that the cycle of the twelve Labours is artificial, made up to the round number, familiar anywhere in the wide region which used the Babylonian sexagesimal counting, by including duplicates.

3. But the story is complicated by an attempt on the part of Thebes (already known to Homer, *Il.* 19. 99) to acquire Heracles; cf. ALCMENE, AMPHITRYON. The only legend of his birth and early adventures which we have is laid in Thebes, and in this connexion we must notice that he is often called Alcides, a name explained by that of the father of Amphitryon, Alcaeus (Apollod. 2. 50). As a matter of fact, Ἀλκαῖος and Ἀλκείδης are variants, respectively Boeotian, as we may suppose, and a translation from it into a more normal Greek patronymic, of a name which meant no more than Valiant; and it is a reasonable guess that this Alcaeus was a Theban hero, with whom Heracles became identified by local zeal. To Alcaeus we may attribute the little group of Boeotian adventures, the conquest of Orchomenus (Apollod. ibid. 67 ff.), the killing of the lion on Mt. Cithaeron (ibid. 65), which suspiciously resembles the Nemean labour, and the episode of the daughters of Thespius, all fifty of whom the hero enjoyed while the guest of their father (ibid. 66).

4. Finally, an attempt was made by the Dorians to acquire him, with some success, since it was for a time a dogma of modern researchers that he was a Dorian hero. *See* AEGIMIUS, HERACLIDAE.

5. The Athenians were content to model their national hero upon him; *see* THESEUS.

6. So far we have dealt with him simply as a hero; it is to be noted that he was on occasion identified with foreign gods. The story that he was sold into slavery to Omphale, queen of Lydia (Soph. *Trach.* 252; Apollod. ibid. 131–3), probably has behind it some myth of an Oriental goddess and her inferior male consort. At the other end of the Mediterranean the famous temple of 'Heracles' at Gadeira (*Cadiz*), in a region under Carthaginian influence and with its Semitic-sounding tabu on swine (Silius Italicus 3. 22–3), is no doubt a shrine of Melqart (cf. Arrian, *Anab.* 2. 16. 4). In Egypt, Herodotus identifies him with one of the native deities (2. 43). The ancients themselves had noticed the diversity of these identifications, and early evolved a theory that Heracles was not one person but several (Herodotus and Arrian, locc. cit.).

7. Outside the cycle of the Labours, the chief events of his life, as generally told, are as follows. Hera pursued him from childhood with implacable enmity; here we may see a stock feature of the myths of Zeus' children imported into a legend where, to judge by the hero's name, it is little in place. She first attempted to destroy him by sending serpents to attack him in his cradle (Pind. *Nem.* 1. 39 ff., and many later passages). These he strangled. Later, when for his services to Thebes he had been given Megara, daughter of Creon (q.v. 2), to wife and she had borne him children, he murdered (her and) them in a fit of madness sent by Hera (Eur. *HF*, which puts this after the Labours; Apollod. ibid. 72, makes them the penance prescribed by Delphi for his purification). In addition, incidentally to the Labours, he had a vast number of other adventures, traditionally classified into the πράξεις, or independent exploits, and the πάρεργα, which merely happened as incidents in the Labours proper. Of these only a few examples can be given. For the former, we may instance his dealings with Laomedon king of Troy, whom he killed and sacked his city, sparing, however, his son Podarces, later known as Priam (q.v.). This arose out of a πάρεργον; on his return from the ninth Labour, bringing the girdle of Hippolyte, queen of the Amazons, he touched at Troy and found the city in distress as a result of Laomedon's treacherous dealings with Apollo and Poseidon, whom he cheated of their wage when they built the wall of his city. A sea-beast was ravaging the country and must be appeased by the sacrifice of Hesione, Laomedon's daughter. Heracles promised to kill the monster and save her if Laomedon would give him his famous horses; he

fulfilled his part of the bargain, but Laomedon would not keep his, hence the campaign later (see Apollod., ibid. 103–4, 134–6). For his second marriage and death *see* DEIANIRA; it is noteworthy that the manner of his death, by burning on a pyre on Mt. Oeta, when he found Nessus' poison overcoming him, is an interpolation into his original story, though an early one, due to the desire to find an *aition* for the ancient fire-ceremony there (Nilsson, *Hist. Greek Rel.* 63 f.; to the refs. there add *Nordisk Tidskrift* (1923), 125). He is an intruder into the Argonautic story, hence perhaps the dropping of him early in the adventure, cf. HYLAS. One of the most singular ramifications of his legend is the story of Heracles the Dactyl (Paus. 8. 31. 3, statue at Megalopolis; 5. 7. 6 ff., foundation of the Olympian Games by him and not, as generally said, by Heracles son of Alcmene). No plausible connexion between the hero and this gnome-like being has ever been suggested.

8. Something has incidentally been said of his cult. Details are given in Farnell, chap. 5. It is interesting that, especially in private worship, he was commonly appealed to as warder-off of evils and victor over them (ἀλεξίκακος, καλλίνικος). Naturally, his sundry identifications with other deities and his ambiguous status (mostly worshipped as a hero but occasionally as a god) led to very great local varieties in his ritual. The Cynic and Stoic schools seized on his reputation for hardiness, simple living, and valour in the service of mankind to idealize him into the exemplar of the follower of their doctrines.

See also STONES, SACRED.

Farnell, *Hero-Cults*, 95 ff.; Preller-Robert, *Griechische Mythologie*[4] ii. 422 ff.

H. J. R.

HERACLIDAE (Ἡρακλεῖδαι). The Dorians, who seem to have little mythology of their own, having tried to make Heracles (q.v.; cf. AEGIMIUS) a kind of connexion of theirs and his eldest son Hyllus a Dorian by adoption, formed the adventures of his sons into a legend legitimizing their conquest of the Peloponnesus by making their kings descendants of the Perseidae. After sundry adventures, in which the sons of Heracles were persecuted by Eurystheus and defended by Athens (Eur. *Heracl.*), they inquired of Delphi when they might return, and were told to do so at 'the third harvest'. Hyllus supposed this to mean the third year, but failed and was killed in single combat against a Peloponnesian champion at the Isthmus. A hundred years later his descendant Temenus again inquired, and got the same reply, which was now interpreted for him as meaning the third generation. The Dorians therefore tried again, in three companies, led by Temenus, Cresphontes, and the sons of Aristodemus, Eurysthenes, and Procles. They entered by Elis, taking, again by oracular advice, the 'three-eyed man' for their guide; he turned out to be Oxylus of Aetolia, whose mule, or horse, had but one eye. Conquering the Peloponnesus, they divided it into three parts, whereof Cresphontes took Messenia, Temenus Argos, and the sons of Aristodemus Lacedaemon, thus founding the dual kingship of Sparta. In the fighting Tisamenus, son of Orestes and grandson of Agamemnon, was killed, thus ending the line of the Pelopidae.

See Apollodorus 2. 167 ff.; Pausanias 1. 41. 2; 3. 1. 6; 5. 3. 5 ff.; 8. 5. 1; Herodotus 9. 26. 4 ff.

H. J. R.

HERACLIDES (1) (Ἡρακλείδης) of Heraclea on the Pontus (Black Sea), called **PONTICUS** (Diog. Laert. 5. 86), Academic philosopher and writer, c. 390–310 B.C. (see Voss, 16 f.). He was the son of one Euthyphron, of a noble and rich family. When he came to Athens, probably during Plato's second voyage to Sicily (367–365), he became Speusippus', and later Plato's, pupil (D.L. loc. cit.). On Plato's request he tried to collect copies of Antimachus' poems in Colophon (Procl. *In Ti.*

1. 90 Diehl). He is referred to as 'joint editor' of Plato's lectures 'On the Good' (Simpl. *In Phys.* p. 453 Diels). The testimonies calling him a pupil of Aristotle and the Pythagoreans (D.L.) are likely to have been deduced from the character of his writings. H. was left in charge of the school during Plato's third Sicilian journey (361–360; Suid. s.v.). On Speusippus' death (338) he competed with Xenocrates and Menedemus for the mastership of the Academy. Xenocrates being elected, H. returned to Heraclea (*Acad. index Herc.* col. 6. 39), where he opened a school of his own.

There is no book of H. preserved. An incomplete catalogue of his numerous writings, classified as ethical, physical, grammatical, musical, rhetorical, and historical, is given by Diogenes Laertius (5. 88).

Heraclides' most important contributions to science are his molecular theory, which purports to overcome the mechanical character of Democritus' atomic doctrine (Diels, *Dox. Graec.*, Index, s.v.), and his astronomical discoveries. Taking the views of the Pythagorean Ecphantus as a starting-point, he taught that the so-called lower planets Mercury and Venus circulate round the sun, not round the earth (Chalcid. *In Tim.* 176 Wrobel). He even put forward the hypothesis that the sun rests without motion in the centre of the universe and the earth circulates around it, i.e. the later so-called Aristarchian or Copernican system (Simpl. *In Cael.* p. 444; 541 Heib.).

Heraclides was not a scientist in the strict sense of the word. He believed strongly in supernatural and occult knowledge, to which he devoted many writings. He also inaugurated the romantic belief in Pythagoras' divine wisdom which greatly influenced later centuries. Subjects like these he discussed in dialogues whose literary and artistic character rendered them famous throughout antiquity.

In life H. appears to have shown a similar sense for mystery and a lofty dignity (D.L. 86, 89 f.).

Müller, *FHG* 2. 197; O. Voss, *De Heraclidis Pontici vita et scriptis*, thesis, Rostock 1896 (good collection of the frs.); E. Zeller, *Plato*, etc., Engl. Transl., 606 f.; T. Gomperz, *Greek Thinkers*, Engl. Transl., I. 121 f.; 4. 13 f.; Ueberweg–Praechter, *Grundriss*[12], 345; *PW* viii. 472; T. L. Heath, *Aristarchus of Samos*, 259–83. K. O. B.

HERACLIDES (2) of Cyme, author of a Persian history (Περσικά) written *c.* 350 B.C. One of Plutarch's sources for the life of Artaxerxes II.

FHG ii. 95.

HERACLIDES (3) **LEMBUS** of Callatis or Alexandria became an Egyptian civil servant at Oxyrhynchus, and was living at Alexandria in 170 B.C. Works:(1) Ἱστορίαι, a mythological and historical commonplace-book, only known by five frs.; (2) Λεμβευτικὸς λόγος, perhaps about Homer. (3) The Epitome of the Lives of Satyrus, and (4) the Epitome of the Διαδοχή of Sotion. These two collections of biographies of the Greek philosophers were much used by Diogenes Laertius. (5) A life of Archimedes in Eutocius, *In Arch. circ. dim.*, may be by him. (6) A selection from Aristotle's Πολιτεῖαι.

Frs. in Müller, *FHG* iii. 167. *PW* viii. 488. W. D. R.

HERACLIDES (4) of Tarentum (fl. *c.* 75 B.C.), physician. He was trained in the Herophilean school, but later became more empirical in his methods and, indeed, the most important empirical physician of antiquity. He is highly praised by Galen for his technical skill and for his objectivity in the pursuit of truth. He seems to have practised dissection of human bodies, and this makes it probable that he worked in Alexandria. The names of fourteen works by him are known, and fragments of some of them are preserved in Galen; his most important work was done on pharmacology, therapeutics, and dietetics.

PW viii. 493. W. D. R.

HERACLIDES (5) **PONTICUS the Younger,** grammarian, from Heraclea Pontica, pupil of Didymus, later taught at Rome under Claudius and Nero, and wrote three books in Sapphic hendecasyllables (Ath. 649 c) called Λέσχαι, which may have influenced Statius' *Silvae*. These were erudite and obscure (*Etym. Gud.* 297, 50, Artem. 4. 63) in the style of Lycophron. He also wrote epic poems and *Pyrrichae* of which nothing is known.

Susemihl, *Gesch. gr. Litt. Alex.* ii. 196. C. M. B.

HERACLITUS (Ἡράκλειτος) (fl. *c.* 500 B.C.), son of Bloson of Ephesus, probably came of royal blood and surrendered the (nominal) kingship voluntarily to his brother. He is said instead of publishing his λόγος or treatise (written *c.* 500 B.C.) to have deposited it in the temple of Artemis.

Following Anaximander, H. conceived the universe as a conflict of opposites controlled by eternal Justice. In this conflict he found at once the apparent relativity of nature and her hidden unity. 'The damp dries itself, the parched grows moist', so that the same thing is (e.g.) both moist and dry together and is called one or other only from a partial standpoint. 'Men do not understand how what is at variance agrees with itself; it is an attunement of opposite tensions like that of bow and lyre' (fr. 51 Diels). Unlike his predecessors H. disbelieved in the genesis of the world from an original element, and the Stoics thought wrongly that he believed in a periodic world-conflagration. All particular things are 'an exchange for Fire, as goods for gold'; but the world-order (κόσμος) itself 'was not made by god or man, but always was, is, and will be everliving Fire being kindled and quenched in due measures' (fr. 30). The order discovered in the world by the soul (ψυχή) he does not distinguish from the soul's discourse upon it; both are the Logos which is 'the same for all men', and is, amid the conflict and streaming change of creation, itself eternal. Nature becomes, the Logos is.

Heraclitus' challenge to mankind is to learn to understand (ξυνιέναι) the discourse of nature, i.e. to know the right use of language or discourse (λόγος, λέγειν) as such. Wisdom lies not in much learning but in the awakening of the entire soul from the slumber of its private wants and opinions to consciousness of the world-order which is 'one and the same for those who are awake'. Thus all knowledge is self-knowledge (he says of his own philosophy 'I sought for myself') and morality and understanding coincide. 'The dry soul is wisest', for it resembles more the divine Fire which (like Anaximander's Infinite) governs the universe. Nevertheless, compared with God man is a child in wisdom, his speech at best a lisping version of the divine discourse. Accordingly H. writes consciously in the oracular style of Delphi, aiming 'neither to say nor conceal but to indicate' the truth.

Heraclitus' physics and astronomy are elementary. His achievement is that he is the first Greek writer to explore the nature of knowledge and the soul. By finding the intelligible principle of the Universe not only (like Anaximander) in an external order, but primarily in the depths which the philosophic soul discovers within itself, he became the first mental philosopher.

I. Bywater, *Heracliti Ephesii Reliquiae* (1877); Diels, *Vorsokr.*[5] i. 139–90; R. Hercher, *Epistulae*, in *Epistolographi*, 280; Burnet, *Early Greek Philosophy*[4], 130–68; O. A. Gigon, *Untersuchungen zu Heraklit* (1935); B. Snell, 'Die Sprache Heraklits' (*Hermes* lxi (1926), 353 f.); Zeller, *Philosophie der Griechen*[6] i. 783–939; *PW* viii. 504. A. H. C.

HERAEUM, *see* ARGOS (1).

HERALDS (κήρυκες) in Homeric times were important aids of the kings used for a multiplicity of tasks such as maintaining order in meetings, making proclamations, and bearing messages. They were under the protection of Hermes, were inviolable, and carried a herald's staff as a symbol of authority. In later Greece they retained much of their importance, assisting magistrates in assemblies and law courts and bearing messages to other States. In this capacity they are to be distinguished from ambassadors, who were authorized not only to transmit messages but also to negotiate. The Roman public crier (*praeco*) was a more humble attendant of magistrates.

E. Saglio, Dar.-Sag., s.v. 'Praeco'; J. Oehler, *PW*, s.v. 'Keryx'.

J. A. O. L.

HERCTE (Ἕρκτη, Εἵρκται), a mountain near Panormus (*Palermo*) in Sicily, seized and held by Hamilcar Barca (247–244 B.C.) in order to strike at the rear of the Roman armies besieging Drepana and Lilybaeum and to threaten Panormus. Its identification with Monte Pellegrino has been maintained by De Sanctis (*Stor. Rom.* iii. 1. 181) against J. Kromayer (*Antike Schlachtfelder* iii. 1), who identifies it with Monte Castellaccio north-west of Palermo.

Polybius, 1. 56. H. H. S.

HERCULANEUM was built on a spur projecting from the lower slopes of Vesuvius, *c.* 5 miles from Naples, on the coast road to Nuceria Alfaterna; it covered *c.* 26 acres. Strabo (5. 4. 8.) says that it was settled, like Pompeii, successively by Oscans, Etruscans, Pelasgians, and Samnites; but the Greek character of the town plan suggests Greek colonization (6th c.?) and the influence of Naples. During Samnite occupation Herculaneum was in the league headed by Nuceria, but Roman intervention in Campania (326–307 B.C.) brought the town into the Roman confederacy. In the great Italian rebellion Herculaneum joined the rebels, was reduced in 89 B.C., and became a Roman *municipium*; her *meddix tuticus* was superseded by *duoviri*. Though small (*c.* 4,000) the town was wealthy; in the early Empire her public buildings were richly ornamented, and her upper classes lived elegantly. The earthquake of A.D. 63 did serious damage (Seneca, *QNat.* 6. 1. 2); the eruption of Vesuvius in A.D. 79 was fatal. Herculaneum was buried deep under heavy volcanic ash; the covering solidified to a form of tufa. As a result the buildings have collapsed more completely than at Pompeii, but, having been more completely sealed, their furnishings are better preserved.

In the eighteenth century excavation began in search of works of art. By shaft and tunnel the theatre and, later, the basilica were reached and robbed. In the nineteenth century tunnelling was abandoned in favour of complete excavation; systematic work was resumed in 1927. Herculaneum differs profoundly from Pompeii. The Greek town plan is completely regular. The streets show no signs of heavy traffic, there are no stepping-stones for pedestrians, no painted notices on the walls; shops are less obtrusive. Herculaneum was a residential, not a commercial town, the main industry being fishing. The houses show great variety in construction and plan, more modern than Pompeii. The principle of lighting from inner court and windows is freely used; upper stories are built with confidence. Most of the houses show taste and refinement as well as wealth, notably those that overlook the sea, with their terraces and gardens. In contrast is the *Casa a graticcio*, lightly built of rubble in a timbered frame, with small apartments separately accessible.

Luxurious villas were common in the neighbourhood, and the Villa of the Papyri, north-west of the town, excavated in the eighteenth century, yielded numerous statues and an Epicurean's library of papyrus rolls, mainly the work of Philodemus of Gadara.

Inscriptions, *CIL* x. 156–70; M. Ruggiero, *Storia degli scavi di Ercolano*; J. Beloch, *Campanien* (1890), 214–38; C. Waldstein and L. Shoobridge, *Herculaneum: Past, Present, and Future* (1908); E. R. Barker, *Buried Herculaneum* (1908); A. Maiuri, *Ercolano* (1936); R. Carrington, *Pompeii* (1936), 180–7; Comparetti and de Petra, *La Villa Ercolanesi* (1883). R. Meiggs.

HERCULES, Roman pronunciation of Heracles (q.v.). His is perhaps the earliest foreign cult to be received in Rome, the Ara Maxima (see Platner–Ashby, 253), which was his most ancient place of worship, being within the *pomerium* of the Palatine settlement. It was probably desired to make the Forum Boarium, in which it stood, a market-place under the protection of a god better known than the local deities. The theory of some ancients (as Propertius 4. 9. 71 ff.) that he is identical with Semo Sancus Dius Fidius (q.v.), although revived in modern times by Preller (Preller–Jordan, *Römische Mythologie*³ ii. 272 ff.) is untenable, and seems ultimately to rest on nothing better than the interpretation of *Dius Fidius* as *Iovis filius*. His cult had become very popular with merchants, no doubt because of his supposed ability to avert evil of all kinds (*see* HERACLES) and the long journeys involved in his Labours and other exploits. It was common to pay him a tithe of the profits of an enterprise (see, e.g., Eliz. C. Evans, *Cults of the Sabine Territory* (U.S.A. 1939), 70 ff.); this was not confined to commercial dealings but included spoils of warfare.

His worship at the Ara Maxima had some interesting features. No other god was mentioned (Plut. *Quaest. Rom.* 90, citing Varro); no women were admitted (Propert. ibid. 21 ff.); dogs were excluded (Plut. loc. cit.). The ritual was originally in the hands of two *gentes*, the Potitii and Pinarii, of whom the former were senior (Plut. ibid. 60, Veranius ap. Macrob. *Sat.* 3. 6. 14); in the censorship of Appius Claudius Caecus, 312 B.C., it passed to the State (Asper ap. Macrob. ibid. 13). It was performed in Greek fashion (Varro ap. Macrob. ibid. 17). The exclusion of women is found also in his cult at Lanuvium (Tert. *Ad nat.* 2, 7).

For his numerous other places of worship at Rome, see Platner–Ashby, ibid. Identification or comparison with him was common among the later emperors, as Commodus (S.H.A. *Comm.* 1. 8. 5), Maximinus (*Maxim.* 18. 4. 9; 6. 9).

Wissowa, *RK* 271 ff. J. Bayet, *Les Origines de l'Hercule romain* (1926). H. J. R.

HERCYNIAN FOREST, German mountains, properly the wooded heights of Thuringia and Bohemia. Originally put near the Pyrenees (schol. ad Dionys. Per. 286) or among Celts (schol. Ap. Rhod. 4. 640) near the Northern Ocean (Diod. 5. 21, etc.), Aristotle (*Mete.* 1. 13) placed it in north Europe, Timaeus found the Danube's sources in it ([Arist.] *Mir. Ausc.* 105). Caesar (*BGall.* 6. 24. 5) heard that it was more than nine days' journey wide, sixty days' travel long from the Black Forest along the Danube's northern bank, and thence turned north. Strabo (7. 290) extends it from Lake Constance and Danube sources to the north frontier of Bohemia and Moravia. After the exploratory conquests of Tiberius and Drusus the Hercynian Forest was clearly distinguished from the Alps and was identified with the heights extending round Bohemia and through Moravia to Hungary (Plin. *HN* 4. 80, 100; Tac. *Germ.* 28, 30). In Ptolemy (*Geog.* 2. 11. 7) the name is restricted to a range between the Sudetes and the Carpathians. E. H. W.

HEREDIA, see CENTURIA.

HERENNIUM, RHETORICA AD, see RHETORICA.

HERENNIUS DEXIPPUS, PUBLIUS, *see* DEXIPPUS.

HERENNIUS SENECIO (1st c. A.D.), a native of Hispania Baetica, was its quaestor and afterwards supported Pliny the Younger in the prosecution of Baebius Massa, an oppressive governor of Baetica (A.D. 93). He wrote the life of Helvidius Priscus and was put to death by Domitian. His memory was attacked by M. Aquilius Regulus. A. M.

HERILLUS of Carthage, pupil of Zeno of Citium and founder of a separate Stoic sect. He seems to have treated knowledge as the supreme end, the life of moral virtue as a subordinate end (ὑποτελίς), and to have added that the subordinate end differs in detail for different men according to their circumstances; the natural goods of life, in distinction from knowledge and virtue, he treated as strictly indifferent. The sect of the Ἡρίλλειοι seems not to have survived 200 B.C.

Testimonia in von Arnim, *SVF* i. 91–3. *PW* viii. 683. W. D. R.

HERMAE were marble or bronze pillars surmounted by a bust and given a human semblance by the addition of the genitals in the case of a male. Usually two beam-shaped projections near the shoulders were added to hold wreaths. Originally *Hermae* represented only the god Hermes, but later they served for portrait busts or for other deities. The herm was not known in sculpture before the fifth century. Alcamenes made a famous herm of Hermes Propylaeus at the entrance to the Acropolis at Athens. He may have originated the type. *Hermae* stood in large numbers in the streets and squares of Athens and other cities. The defacement of the *Hermae* at Athens in 415 B.C. was a sacrilegious act which led to the banishment of Alcibiades (q.v.). S. C.

HERMAGORAS of Temnos (*fl. c.* 150 B.C.) wrote Τέχναι ῥητορικαί (6 bks.), in which he revived rhetorical theory (neglected by Asianists and denounced by philosophers) and gave to it new direction. His teaching (cf. Quint. 3. 6; Hermogenes passim) was confined to forensic oratory and to a treatment of εὕρεσις. He claimed for rhetoric the right to deal with all non-technical matters (πολιτικὰ ζητήματα), whether particular causes (ὑποθέσεις) or general questions (θέσεις), thus meeting the attacks of contemporary philosophers. By his στάσις (Lat. *status*) theory—according to which, στάσεις (i.e. questions to be considered in all disputes) were of two main kinds, logical or legal (Susemihl, *Gesch. gr. Litt. Alex.* 2. 471 ff., Kroll, *Rhet.* § 26)—he introduced some sort of system into the study. On actual practice he had little influence; nor was he interested in either stylistic or philosophical matters. His doctrines, with modifications, became the basis of all school-teaching; and with them began that scholastic hair-splitting associated with later phases of rhetorical study. J. W. H. A.

HERMAPHRODITUS or Aphroditus. The concept of this bisexual divinity is perhaps due originally to certain marriage rites in which the sexes exchange clothing; the god was then fashioned to fit and explain the rite. Aphroditus (Hesych. s.v.; Macrob. *Sat.* 3. 8. 2) is found at Amathus in Cyprus. A unique dedication, of the early fourth century B.C., attests the cult of H. in Attica (*Ath. Mitt.* 1937, 7–8; cf. Theophr. *Char.* 16. 10; Alciphr. *Epist.* 3. 37). Fourth-century art portrayed H. as a beautiful youth with developed breasts; later art as an Aphrodite with male genitals. Ovid (*Met.* 4. 285–388) relates the myth of the union in one body of H., the son of Hermes and Aphrodite, and the nymph Salmacis.

M. P. Nilsson, *Griechische Feste* (1906), 369–74. F. R. W.

HERMARCHUS of Mytilene, Epicurean, studied under Epicurus in Mytilene before the school was moved to Lampsacus in 310 B.C., and in 270 he succeeded Epicurus as head of the school. Epicurus' will enjoins his heirs to put part of the revenues of his estate at Hermarchus' disposal for the maintenance of the school, and bequeaths to him the whole of Epicurus' library. With Epicurus, Metrodorus, and Polyaenus, Hermarchus was treated as representing the authoritative form of the Epicurean doctrine. Works: Πρὸς Πλάτωνα, Πρὸς Ἀριστοτέλην, Ἐπιστολικὰ περὶ Ἐμπεδοκλέους, Περὶ τῶν μαθημάτων, all of them polemical works.

PW viii. 721. K. W. G. Krohn, *Der Epikureer Hermarchos* (1921). W. D. R.

HERMEIAS (1), tyrant of Atarneus (in Mysia, opposite Lesbos) *c.* 355 B.C. A former student of the Academy (though he never met Plato), he introduced a more moderate régime, admitting the Platonists Erastus and Coriscus of Scepsis to a share in his power and encouraging them to found a new philosophical school at Assos. There they were joined on Plato's death (348) by Aristotle, Xenocrates, and Callisthenes, and later by Theophrastus. Aristotle became an intimate friend of Hermeias and married his niece and adopted daughter Pythias. Hermeias possessed a formidable naval, military, and financial power, and was virtually independent of the Persian Empire. He negotiated, with Aristotle's assistance, an understanding with Macedonia. In 341, however, he was treacherously arrested at a conference with Mentor, and sent captive to the Great King, who vainly tried to coerce him into revealing Philip's plans and executed him.

W. Jaeger, *Aristotle* (1934), 105; D. E. W. Wormell, *Yale Studies in Classical Philology* v (1935). D. E. W. W.

HERMEIAS (2), choliambic poet, of Curion, not before the third century B.C., reviled the Stoics (Ath. 563d).

J. U. Powell, *Collectanea Alexandrina* (1925), 237; G. A. Gerhard, *Phoinix von Kolophon* (1909), 213.

HERMES (Ἑρμείας, Ἑρμῆς), one of the younger gods in myth, for in reality he is probably one of the oldest and most nearly primitive in origin. The most plausible explanation of his name is that it is connected with ἕρμα, and signifies the daemon who haunts or occupies a heap of stones, or perhaps a stone, set up by a roadside for some magical purpose (examples of such in Frazer, *GB*, see index s.v. 'Stones' and art. STONES (SACRED) herein). Tradition and cult facts combine to make him Arcadian; he was son of Zeus and Maia daughter of Atlas, born on Mt. Cyllene on the fourth day of the month (*Hymn. Hom. Merc.* 19; four is Hermes' number). He was cunning from birth, and on the first day of his life invented the lyre, stole Apollo's cattle, impudently denied the theft, and was reconciled to his elder brother. The merry tone of the hymn is characteristic. Hermes never had much concern with the higher moral or philosophical developments of religion: the writings ascribed to Hermes (q.v.) Trismegistus have nothing to do with the Greek Hermes but are the result of fathering on the Egyptian Thoth, who was identified with him, certain late mystical philosophizings. For the most part, H. occupies a subordinate part in myth, being rather a messenger of the greater gods, and especially of Zeus, than an independent actor. Hence the shape he takes when represented in fully human form is that of a herald, equipped for travelling with a broad-brimmed hat and a stout pair of sandals and carrying the *kerykeion* (Lat. *caduceus*) or herald's staff (to be distinguished from the magic wand which also he bears on occasion, see de Waele, *The Magic Staff*, The Hague, 1927). But he was from early times shown, and continued to be so represented, as a mere stock or stone, a herm, having generally a human head carved at the top and a phallus half-way up it. The latter is, indeed, a characteristic emblem of this god, who was always interested in fertility; which perhaps is why we find him occasionally united with a goddess connected with fertility, Aphrodite (mother by him of Hermaphroditus, Ovid, *Met.* 4. 288; of Priapus, q.v., see Hyginus, *Fab.* 160, cf. H. Herter, *De Priapo*, 64), Hecate (q.v.), or Brimo (schol. Lycophron, 1176, cf. Propert. 2. 2. 11–12), Herse daughter of Cecrops (Ovid, *Met.* 2. 708 ff.). One of his most striking functions may also derive in part from his connexion with fertility, though his occupation as messenger probably has something to do with it. He is the Guide of Souls, from Homer (or at least *Od.* 24. 1 ff., be that genuinely Homeric or not) onwards. In this respect he is unique among the gods, unless we count the Dioscuri (qq.v.) as originally divine; for the others belong either to the upper or the lower world, the peculiar position of Persephone, for whom *see* DEMETER, not constituting a real exception. It is in this connexion especially that his magic wand (see above) becomes prominent (e.g. Verg. *Aen.* 4. 242 ff., where see the further material collected by Pease ad loc., and add Wilamowitz-Moellendorff, *Glaube der Hellenen* ii. 147, note 2). Such a wand is the characteristic implement of a necromancer. It is not particularly remarkable that he is the god of merchants and others who use roads, including thieves, though the latter characteristic illustrates his non-moral nature (for illustrations see Ar. *Plut.* 1155, with schol., Plut. *Quaest. Graec.* 55, with Halliday's note). In Crete we find him associated with a piece of ritual topsy-turveydom, for which cf. KRONOS, SATURNUS. At the Hermaea there (city not specified) masters waited on their slaves as they feasted (Ath. 639 b). For a deity with chthonian associations he has very little to do with divination and oracles; Apollo grants him an obscure minor form of divining, in the Homeric Hymn, 550 ff., and he had an oracle at Pharae (Paus. 7. 22. 2–3). Here the consultant, after paying his respects to the god, stopped his ears till he got beyond the market-place where the temple stood; the first words he heard when he unstopped them were the answer to any question he had asked of Hermes. This is no more than a systematization of one of the most usual forms of omen, the κληδών or unintentionally significant utterance.

Two other functions show a longer development from the old daemon of the roadside, if that is what he originally was. A herald must of course state his business plainly and on occasion plead the cause of those who sent him. Hence from a fairly early date Hermes is associated with oratory. When to this is added the invention, already told, of the lyre, we can see how he became in time a general patron of literature, Horace even calling those who follow it 'Mercuriales uiri' (*Carm.* 2. 17. 29–30). It is less evident why he is constantly regarded, in classical times, as the patron of young men and their exercises, and himself represented in statuary as a young man. The stages are perhaps as follows: fertility easily passes into the notion of luck or good fortune; luck is needed by those who engage in athletic contests (cf. HECATE); but the most regular practitioners of such things are the younger men, whose athletic training formed an important part of their education in every normal Greek State.

Farnell, *Cults*, v. 1 ff., for his worship generally; Nilsson, *Griechische Feste*, 388 ff., for his non-Attic, Deubner, *Attische Feste*, 217, for his (unimportant) Attic cult; cf. the larger dictionaries s.v. H. J. R.

HERMES TRISMEGISTUS, a clumsy translation of Egyptian 'Thoth the very great', with the adj. emphasized by repetition (W. Scott, *Hermetica* i. 5, note 1). When so named, Thoth is the reputed author of the philosophico-religious treatises known collectively as *Hermetica* (*see* GNOSTICISM), also of sundry works on astrology, magic, and alchemy. These are invariably late, Egyptian in the sense of being produced in Egypt by men of Greek speech and (except for the astrological books: Nock, *Gnomon* 1939, 359 ff.) contain little or nothing of native Egyptian doctrine or custom. Their attribution to the Egyptian god of letters is a result of the then prevalent enthusiasm for the supposed ancient wisdom of Egypt and of the older Oriental cultures generally.

W. Scott–A. S. Ferguson, *Hermetica* (1924–36); edition by A D. Nock and A. J. Festugière i– (1946); A. J. Festugière, *La Révélation d'Hermès Trismégiste* i– (1944). H. J. R.

HERMESIANAX of Colophon, probably born *c.* 300 B.C., was a pupil of Philetas (schol. Nic. *Ther.* 3). His mistress's name, which he took as title for his collection of elegies, was Leontion (Ath. 13. 597 b).

WORKS. The *Persica* (schol. Nic. *Ther.* 3) may have contained the story of Nanis and Cyrus (Parth. 22 = fr. 6). The *Leontion* was in three books. One line describing Polyphemus gazing out to sea is definitely cited from bk. 1. This suggests a treatment of the Polyphemus-Galatea story, cf. fr. 7. 69–74, and two other bucolic love-stories (frs. 2 and 3) may have been narrated in this book. Bk. 2 contained the tale of Arceophon and Arsinoe, the rejected suitor and the callous maid, who is punished by being turned into stone (Ant. Lib. *Met.* 39), possibly also the story of Leucippus' incest with its tragic sequel (Parth. 5). From bk. 3 Athenaeus (13. 597 b) has preserved a 'catalogue of love-affairs'. In the manner of contemporary Peripatetic biographers, e.g. Chamaeleon, H. details the loves, unrequited or otherwise unlucky, of a series of poets, starting with Orpheus and ending with Philetas, and of philosophers (Pythagoras, Socrates, Aristippus). Three times in the fragment the poet addresses Leontion herself, but it is unlikely that he used this device throughout the poem. Of the remaining fragments (8–11) one is cited from an 'Elegy on the Centaur Eurytion'.

The loss of most early Alexandrian poetry has given to the long fragment from the *Leontion* an importance which it hardly merits. It is true that H. illustrates many features found in later representatives of that poetry, e.g. a fondness for 'glosses', an interest in love, especially if it be unhappy, and in aetiology, but, though he is a tolerable metrist despite his monotonous habit of ending the first half of a pentameter with an adjective and the second with the substantive which it qualifies, he possessed, to judge by what remains of his poetry, a very mediocre brain.

Texts: J. U. Powell, *Collectanea Alexandrina* (1925), 96–106; E. Diehl, *Anth. Lyr. Graec.* vi (1924), 214–20. General literature: Heibges, 'Hermesianax (2)', in *PW* viii. 823–8. E. A. B.

HERMIONE, in mythology, daughter of Menelaus and Helen (qq.v.; *Od.* 4. 14 and often in later authors). Possibly she was originally a goddess, as her name occurs as a title of Demeter and Persephone (Hesychius s.v.). She was at various times (details differ in different authors, see Weizsäcker in Roscher's *Lexikon*, s.v.) betrothed to Orestes and Neoptolemus (qq.v.). According to Eur. *Or.* 1655 Neoptolemus never married her, but in Eur. *Andr.* he did so, was murdered by Orestes while at Delphi inquiring why Hermione was childless, and she was carried off by Orestes. All authors, save schol. Pind. *Nem.* 10. 12, citing Ibycus, who says she married Diomedes, agree that she became Orestes' wife and mother (Paus. 2. 18. 6) of his son Tisamenus. H. J. R.

HERMIPPUS (1) (5th c. B.C.), Athenian comic poet; brother of Myrtilus, also a writer of comedies. His first victory at the Dionysia was in 435 B.C. (E. Capps, *Hesperia*, xii). The Ἀγαμέμνων (*Lex. Mess.* 283. 15) may have been a parody of Aeschylus, and it is clear that parody (cf. Ath. 15. 699 a) played a large part in H.'s plays: e.g. fr. 63, a parody of Homer occurring in the Φορμοφόροι ('The Porters', between 430 and 424 B.C.). The Ἀθηνᾶς γοναί must have been a mythological burlesque of the type common in Middle Comedy, cf. Nicophron's Ἀφροδίτης γοναί, Araros' Πανὸς γοναί, etc. The Ἀρτοπώλιδες (421–418 B.C.) (Ar. *Nub.* 551–7, and schol.) was a violent attack on Hyperbolus and his mother, whose low birth and bad Greek (fr. 11) are satirized. The Μοῖραι (*c.* 430 B.C.) contained a violent attack on Pericles and his Fabian tactics. The Στρατιῶται had a similar theme, and some have supposed it a διασκευή of the Μοῖραι. H. did not confine his hostility to the stage, but actually brought an action against Aspasia for ἀσέβεια (Plut. *Per.* 32) in which he attacked Pericles also (ibid. 33). That H. was essentially a 'political' dramatist is seen from his attacks on Peisander (fr. 9), Cleon (fr. 42), and others.

FCG ii. 380 ff.; CAF i. 224 ff.; Demiańczuk, Suppl. Com. 53. M. P.

HERMIPPUS (2) of Smyrna (*fl.* 3rd c. B.C.), Peripatetic biographer and follower of Callimachus, wrote a vast work (descending to his own time) on famous writers, philosophers, and law-givers, which Plutarch used. H. deliberately falsified history, revelling in sensationalism, particularly in death scenes. Fragments in Diog. Laert. Perhaps H. also wrote Φαινόμενα.

FGH iii. 35-54; additional frs. listed by Heibges, PW, s.v.
F. W. W.

HERMOCRATES (5th c. B.C.), Syracusan statesman and general. His anti-Athenian policy first became manifest at the conference of Gela (424 B.C.), where he achieved a pan-Siceliote alliance. In 415 he failed to unify Sicily against the Athenian invasion. Next year, as general, he fought without success, but he supported Gylippus (q.v.) in organizing the Syracusan resistance, and, by a stratagem, he caused the final disaster of the Athenians (413). He insisted on carrying the war to the East, and took part in the Aegean campaigns of 412-410; after the loss of the fleet at Cyzicus he was banished, but still fought on the Spartan side as a mercenary leader. In 408 he returned to Sicily, but in spite of considerable successes he was not allowed to enter Syracuse, his opponent being the democratic leader Diocles, and he was killed in trying to force his entry (407). His daughter was married to Dionysius I.

Thuc. bks. 6-8; Xen. Hell. bk. 1; for the last years Diod. Sic. bk. 13. Lenschau, PW, s.v. 'Hermokrates'.   V. E.

HERMOGENES (1) (*c.* 200 B.C.), a Greek architect. His only known works are the temple of Dionysus at Teos and the temple of Artemis Leucophryene at Magnesia-on-Maeander, both in the Ionic Order. From these, and from his books about them, Vitruvius (q.v.) derived some of the principles of proportion included in his own book. But the remains of the two temples do not exactly agree with the precepts he attributes to Hermogenes; nor was the octastyle pseudodipteral type of temple invented by Hermogenes as he states. He also includes Hermogenes among those architects who objected to the use of the Doric Order in sacred buildings because of the complications arising from the spacing of the triglyphs. Strabo praises the Magnesian temple, and it is probable that Hermogenes' influence on Roman architecture of the Augustan period was considerable.

Vitruvius 3. 3; 4. 3; 7 praef.; Strabo 14. 1. 40 (c. 647). H. W. R.

HERMOGENES (2) of Tarsus (b. *c.* A.D. 150), sophist, a famous orator in his youth. His technical writings, forming a complete course in school rhetoric, include Προγυμνάσματα, Π. τῶν στάσεων, Π. εὑρέσεως, Π. ἰδεῶν, and Π. μεθόδου δεινότητος. In Π. ἰδεῶν, which owed much in form and detail to Ps.-Aristides' τέχναι (see ARISTIDES 5), he tried to arrive at the laws of style by an analysis of the qualities of ancient writers. He divided his subject into (1) λόγος πολιτικός, (2) λόγος πανηγυρικός; distinguished seven main ἰδέαι or forms, σαφήνεια, μέγεθος, etc.; established Demosthenes and Plato as models; and recommended a blending of Demosthenes' qualities for the highest eloquence (δεινότης) (Kroll, Rhet. § 40). With the philosophical treatment of rhetoric he was not concerned; he limited himself mainly to the elaboration of unending distinctions and oversubtle rules, which rendered rhetoric fixed and sterile. Yet by this work, and by his στάσις-teaching, he achieved lasting fame in the schools, from the fifth century onwards, and especially in Byzantine times his influence was considerable.

Text, L. Spengel, Rhet. ii (1854), 3-426; H. Rabe (Teubner, 1913).
J. W. H. A.

HERMOPOLIS (mod. *Ashmunein*) in Graeco-Roman times marked the boundary between Middle and Upper Egypt, where dues were collected on goods passing along the Nile. The mounds there have yielded many papyri, but the buildings described by Jomard (c. 1800) have almost disappeared. Recent excavations have disclosed important religious and sepulchral structures in the western quarter, with interesting Graeco-Egyptian wall-paintings. The papyri give useful information about the organization of the town under the Romans.

E. Jomard, Description de l'Égypte, Antiq. ch. 14, pl. 50-2; G. Méautis, Hermoupolis-la-grande (1918) (chiefly on papyri); S. Gabra in Illustrated London News 4. 3. 1933, 21. 4. 1934, 8. 6. 1935, 12. 6. 1937, 2. 7. 1938 (excavations).   J. G. M.

HERNICI inhabited the Trerus valley and hills north of it in Italy (Strabo 5. 231: inaccurate). Their treaty with Rome in regal times is possibly apocryphal (Dion. Hal. 4. 49; Festus, p. 476 L.). But they certainly signed a defensive alliance with Rome *c.* 486 B.C., and in the subsequent wars against Aequi and Volsci fought staunchly (Dion. Hal. 8. 64 f.; Livy 2. 41, etc.: untrustworthy). Later, in 387 and 362, the Hernici opposed Rome but renewed the old alliance in 358 (Livy 6. 2 f.; 7. 6 f.). After remaining loyal in the Latin War the Hernican cities, except Ferentinum, Aletrium, and Verulae, were led into war against Rome in 306 by Anagnia, but were easily conquered and granted partial, later full, citizenship (Livy 9. 42 f.; Festus, p. 262 L.). Hernican territory became part of Latium and the Hernici were so completely latinized that their own language cannot be discovered. It may have been Oscan (q.v.), but more probably belonged to the Latinian group (J. Whatmough, Foundations of Roman Italy, 262).

R. S. Conway, Italic Dialects, i (1897), 306.   E. T. S.

HERO ('Ηρώ) and **LEANDER** (Λέανδρος), a pretty love-story of apparently Alexandrian origin (earliest surviving authorities Ov. Her. 18 and 19, where see Palmer's note, and Verg. G. 3. 258 ff.). Hero was priestess of Aphrodite at Sestos; Leander lived at Abydos, saw her at a festival, fell in love with her, and used nightly to swim the Hellespont to see her until a storm put out the light by which she guided him across and he was drowned; she threw herself into the sea after him. Cf. Strabo 13. 1. 22.   H. J. R.

HERO-CULT, the worship, as being superhuman, of noteworthy dead men and women, real or imaginary, normally at their actual or supposed tombs. The nature of the cult did not differ appreciably from that given to other chthonian powers (black victims, generally not shared by the worshippers, evening or night rather than day for the ritual, blood and other liquids poured into a trench, hearth, or low altar, ἐσχάρα, rather than the high Olympian altar, βωμός), except that it was seldom practised at more than one place, or if at more, usually because several places claimed to possess the bones of the hero or heroine. The most noteworthy exception, Heracles (q.v.), was on his way to become a god and, indeed, received divine honours in some places. Hero-cult must be distinguished from the ordinary tendance of the dead, i.e. the performance of certain rites, including offerings of food and drink, intended to make them comfortable in the next world, for this did not involve worship.

Hero-cult is not found in Homer, where the word ἥρως means simply 'gentleman, noble'; Iliad 2. 550-1, supposing it genuine, is proof rather that Erechtheus (q.v.) was regarded as a god than that hero-worship was then practised. But in classical and post-classical Greece it is exceedingly common, and its typical objects are the traditional ἥρωες of Homer and other writers of saga, though this is not the only category, see below. It is therefore likely that it began after the Dorian migration, when the ancient chieftains had become legendary figures, idealized because native and not belonging to the new invading aristocracy. Whatever its origin, it spread to include many persons who had never existed save in the imagination of their worshippers.

These imaginary figures may be considered as a class in themselves; for more elaborate classification, see Farnell (op. cit. infra). It includes the so-called 'faded gods', that is to say figures originally divine, which for one reason or another had come to be considered dead men, and their places of worship tombs. Many such are of course doubtful, see ASCLEPIUS, HELEN, IPHIGENIA, for examples. Others are practically certain, as Hyacinthus (q.v.), Trophonius, and Agamedes (see TROPHONIUS), who, although they have a characteristic folk-tale told of them concerning their prowess as master-builders and master-thieves (Paus. 9. 37. 5 ff.), have no other existence except that the former is the possessor of a famous oracle. Generally the following characteristics may be looked for in a 'faded' figure. The name often, if Greek, is significant of something directly connected with the ritual; Trophonius seems to be the 'feeder', a natural enough name for a chthonian power, but odd for a human being. The legend, if one exists, is generally irrelevant to the cult altogether, as in the case of Hyacinthus, or explains some detail of it only, as with Glaucus (q.v. 3), whose connexion with the Taraxippos at the Isthmus is obviously secondary. The connexion with a genealogy is non-existent, fluctuating, or artificial (Hippolytus may be a case in point, see Farnell, p. 64 ff.; Aeneas, perhaps an offshoot of Aphrodite to begin with, becomes an ancestor by suspicious processes, cf. Farnell, p. 55, and Cults, ii. 638 ff.). Finally, the ritual generally contains something alien to normal worship of the dead, as the curious performances connected with the Delphic 'heroine' Charila (Plut. Quaest. Graec. 12).

The more normal heroes, i.e. those who, if they ever really existed, were human, are simpler. Many naturally are worshipped by their descendants or former subjects; indeed, this is the ordinary case, as with Theseus (q.v.) at Athens and the Tritopatores (q.v.) in the same city. Many, again, are characters from the epic poems, and here ancestral connexion, although desirable (presumably the alleged fetching by the Spartans of Orestes' bones from Tegea, Hdt. 1. 67. 3 ff., had to do with their adoption of the house of Agamemnon as in some sense theirs) was not necessary; the Thebans who imported the bones of Hector (q.v.) did not claim to be descended from him, nor the Athenians from Oedipus (q.v.); the mere presence in the land of the bodies of such men was a blessing, however they came there. Others, though regarded as ancestors, are transparent inventions, made up from the name of the city or its people, as Messene (see Farnell, p. 360). Finally, a considerable number were fully historical, heroized because of some notable action or even mere strangeness, as Brasidas at Amphipolis (Thuc. 5. 11. 1) and the homicidal lunatic Cleomedes at Astypalaea (Paus. 6. 9. 6 ff.). (See also EUTHYMUS.)

Theological speculation busied itself with the possibility of heroes ultimately becoming gods (see Plutarch, De def. or. 415 b), not the least interesting part of the common Hellenistic and later belief that men could turn into gods if sufficiently virtuous.

See also RELICS. Older standard work E. Rohde, Psyche (1907); completest, with many references to ancient and modern literature, L. R. Farnell, Greek Hero-Cults (1921). On the ritual cf. W. S. Ferguson and A. D. Nock, Harv. Theol. Rev. xxxvii (1944). See CITY FOUNDERS, RIDER-GODS.   H. J. R.

HEROD (1) THE GREAT (c. 73–4 B.C.), on his father Antipater's murder (43 B.C.), succeeded jointly with his elder brother Phasael to his position of vizier to Hyrcanus II. Phasael was killed in the Parthian invasion, but Herod escaped to Rome, where Antony nominated him king

of Hyrcanus' ethnarchy with Idumaea. Despite the intrigues of Cleopatra, who coveted his kingdom, he retained Antony's confidence and was in 30 B.C. confirmed by Octavian, who added to his dominions several cities and later (in 24 and 20) large parts of the Ituraean (q.v.) tetrarchy. Herod was an able king. He relentlessly enforced order and greatly developed the economic resources of the country, building for it a new port (Caesarea, q.v. 2). He also endeavoured to promote hellenization, celebrating games in Jerusalem and refounding several cities within his dominions, as well as bestowing lavish gifts on many without them. These activities increased the hatred of the Jews towards him, and his power was based on his fortresses and his mercenary barbarian army, his secret police, and a centralized bureaucracy. He ruthlessly crushed the old aristocracy, building up in its stead a new nobility of service, many of them Greeks, and a subservient priesthood, drawn in part from the Dispersion, from which he filled the Sanhedrin and the high-priesthood, now held during the king's pleasure. Till late in his reign he secured the acquiescence of the Pharisee party, but neither his effective championship of the rights of the Dispersion nor even his magnificent new temples won him popularity. His family life was embittered by intrigues fomented by his sister Salome, later assisted by his eldest son, Antipater, against his favourite wife Mariamne (executed 29 B.C.) and her sons, Alexander and Aristobulus (executed 7 B.C.); he finally executed Antipater shortly before his own death. At first respected by Augustus and Agrippa, he later lost the former's confidence owing to his savagery to his family and his highhanded conduct in a dispute with the Nabataeans.

Ancient sources: Josephus, BJ 1. 203–673; AJ 14. 158–17. 192. Modern accounts: W. Otto, PW, Suppl. ii (1913), cols. 1–158; A. Momigliano, CAH x. 316–37; A. H. M. Jones, The Herods of Judaea (1938), 28–155.   A. H. M. J.

HEROD (2) ANTIPAS, on the death of his father (Herod the Great, q.v.), was appointed tetrarch of Galilee, where he founded two cities, Sepphoris and later Tiberias (q.v.), and of Peraea, where he built the town of Livias (later Julias). He was a trusted friend of Tiberius, who in A.D. 36 gave him the task of mediating between Rome and Parthia. He divorced his first wife, a daughter of Aretas IV (who in revenge invaded Peraea in 37), in favour of his niece Herodias. Incited by her, he petitioned Gaius for the title of king, but was deposed on a charge of treason trumped up by his nephew Agrippa I (39).   A. H. M. J.

HEROD AGRIPPA, see AGRIPPA I.

HERODAS (HERONDAS?), a third-century B.C. writer of mimiambi, literary mimes in iambic scazons. A papyrus containing eight of his pieces was discovered in 1890; they are short, subtle, realistic presentations of typical mime-themes, perhaps intended for solo performance. 1. *The Bawd*. Metriche, whose lover (husband?) has gone to Egypt, is visited by old Gyllis, who urges her to transfer her affections to a young athlete, Gryllus. She refuses with refreshing firmness and politely dismisses Gyllis with a cup of wine. 2. *The Pimp*. Battarus delivers a harangue in court against a trader for house-breaking and attempted abduction of one of his slave-girls. The vulgar, unctuous, menacing yet entirely mercenary pimp is perhaps the author's masterpiece. There is much parody of legal forms. 3. *The Schoolmaster*. The voluble Metrotime, exasperated by poverty and the pranks of her incorrigible son Cottalus, brings him to the dry schoolmaster, Lampriscus, for a flogging, which is duly administered. 4. *The Women Worshippers*. Cynno, her friend Coccale, and the maid (mute) bring their humble offering to the temple of Asclepius at Cos. The matter-of-fact, short-tempered mistress Cynno, the naïve

Coccale, lost in admiration at the temple-statues, and the oily sacristan are effectively portrayed. 5. *The Jealous Mistress*. Bitinna, furious at discovering the infidelity of Gastron, her slave-paramour, orders him off for flogging, in spite of his entreaties; then she hastily sends her maid Cydilla to fetch him back for branding; finally Cydilla wheedles her into granting a provisional pardon. 6. *The Private Conversation*. Metro calls on Coritto to ask for certain information, and the two dear friends converse with admirable cynicism. 7. *The Shoemaker*. Metro introduces some prospective lady-customers to the fashionable shoemaker Cerdon, an outstanding portrait of the salesman, alternately oily and truculent. 8. *The Dream*. A farmer (clearly Herodas himself) relates his dream of how his goat was torn limb from limb by certain worshippers of Dionysus, and how, in the subsequent contest, he won the prize. Herodas is evidently referring to the harsh treatment of his works by his critics, and his hopes of ultimate recognition as the successor of Hipponax.

Annotated editions: J. A. Nairn (1904); W. Headlam and A. D. Knox, with translation (1922); O. Crusius (2nd ed., by R. Herzog, 1926); A. D. Knox (Loeb, with Theophrastus' *Characters*).   W. B.

HERODES ATTICUS of Marathon (A.D. 101–77), famous sophist and patron of learning, who did much by his benefactions, his eloquence, and his culture to enhance the glory of Athens. Of his writings, including letters, diatribes, and ἐφημερίδες (a literary diary), a fragment of a diatribe against Stoic teaching (Gellius 19. 12, Latin transl.) and one μελέτη (Π. πολιτείας) alone have survived. The latter is based on a harangue of Thrasymachus, and its style is modelled on that of Critias.   J. W. H. A.

HERODIAN(1)(AELIUS HERODIANUS), son of Apollonius Dyscolus, of Alexandria, grammarian at Rome under M. Aurelius. He wrote works on the accentuation of the *Iliad* and *Odyssey*, and of Attic. These he afterwards included in his Καθολικὴ προσῳδία, reviewing the accentuation of (it is said) some 60,000 words. It was in twenty-one books: 1–19 contained rules of accentuation, the 20th dealt with quantities and breathings, and the last with enclitics, synaloepha, and some other points concerning words in combination. This immense work survives only in later citations, and in extracts such as those by Theodosius and Ps.-Arcadius. It was largely based on Aristarchus and his successors in this field. Two of Herodian's other works are extant—Περὶ μονήρους λέξεως (on anomalous words) and Φιλέταιρος, a short Atticist lexicon. He disagrees, however, with his father's extreme doctrines of ἀναλογία, expressly repudiating such forms as ἵμι (see APOLLONIUS DYSCOLUS). Of his many other works the titles of about thirty survive, together with extracts and quotations by later scholars: they cover many departments of grammar, including, e.g., treatises on various parts of speech, figures, declensions, conjugations, defective verbs, and some anomalous words such as ὕδωρ. Herodian ranks with his father as one of the greatest, as he is the last, of original Greek grammarians.

Editions: Φιλέταιρος: Pierson, 1739; Π. μον. λέξ.: Dindorf, 1823; Π. μον. λέξ., Π. 'Ιλιακῆς προσῳδίας, Π. διχρόνων, Lehrs, 1848. *Herodiani Reliquiae* (much conjectural reconstruction) Lentz in Teubner's *Gramm. Gr.* C. A. Lobeck's *Pathologiae Gr. sermonis elementa* (1852–63), is based on Herodian.   P. B. R. F.

HERODIAN (2) of Syria, a subordinate official in Rome early in the third century A.D., wrote Τῆς μετὰ Μάρκον βασιλείας ἱστορίαι in eight books from M. Aurelius to Gordian III (A.D. 180–238). Moralizing and rhetorical, his work is superficial, although his value increases with his contemporary knowledge.

Texts: L. Mendelssohn (1883); K. Stavenhagen (1922); E. Baaz, *De Herodiani fontibus et auctoritate* (1909).   A. H. McD.

HERODICUS of Babylon (perhaps late 2nd c. B.C.), author of Κωμῳδούμενοι (persons satirized in Comedy, see AMMONIUS 1), Σύμμικτα ὑπομνήματα, and Πρὸς τὸν φιλοσωκράτην.

M. Müller, *De Seleuco Homerico* (1891), 10 ff.; J. Steinhausen, Κωμῳδούμενοι (1910); A. Dittmar, *Aischines von Sphettos* (1912), 56–7.   J. D. D.

HERODORUS OF HERACLEA, see LOGOGRAPHERS.

HERODOTUS (1), son of Lyxes, of good family in Halicarnassus, and related to Panyassis, a 'reviver of epic', was born 'a little before the Persian War, and lived till the Peloponnesian War' (Dion. Hal. *Thuc.* 5): in 468 B.C. he was 'well known' (Gell. 15. 23); in 432 he was fifty-three (Eusebius, *Chronica*); he records events of 431–430; and his preface was parodied in 425 (Ar. *Ach.* 513 ff.). In civil strife at Halicarnassus Panyassis was killed by the tyrant Lygdamis, grandson of Artemisia (q.v.), and Herodotus withdrew to Samos. By 454 Halicarnassus was pacified and a Delian tributary; but if H. returned, he did not remain; for he had travelled, and lectured in Greece, and visited Athens, before he joined the Athenian colony at Thurii (founded 443). Here his tomb and epitaph were shown. He was described as 'of Thurii' until the third century, when Halicarnassus reclaimed him, erecting a statue and figuring him later on coins.

2. TRAVELS. Besides acquaintance with Samos (3. 60), Athens (5. 79), and south Italy (4. 14. 99), H. records travels—(a) in Egypt, to Elephantine, during the Nile flood and ebb, after the Persian reconquest (449), perhaps also before the revolt of 460–454; (b) to Gaza (3. 5), Tyre (2. 44), and down the Euphrates (1. 185) to Babylon (1. 178–83); (c) in Scythia, to Olbia (4. 16) and up the Borysthenes (4. 81), and in the north Aegean from Bosporus (4. 87) to Thasos (6. 47). For inland Asia Minor and for Persia there is no 'eyewitness'; Cyrene (4. 156–203) was on a sea-route to Egypt. Some of these visits were deliberate, in search of information (2. 3. 44), and were supplemented by inquiries (2. 29) from natives of over forty places. At Delphi especially tradition was corroborated by monuments (1. 14. 50, 9. 51). Silence about western journeys suggests that the main motive was not geographical but historical, and that the visit to Athens was a crisis in life and outlook: acquaintance with Sophocles, who wrote him verses (*Anth. Lyr. Graec.* 1. i², p. 81), interest in Pericles and Alcmaeonid house-lore, in Cimon's ancestors (4. 137–8; 6. 34 ff., 103 ff.), and in topographical details (5. 77, 8. 53) enhance the significance of his eulogy and vindication of Athenian aims and achievements (7. 139). From the Athenians he is said to have received a gift of ten talents; for a literary reward the amount is without parallel. Allusions to events about 431 are consistent with a return from Thurii to Athens, but do not prove it; it is an independent question when and why the book achieved its actual form.

3. OTHER SOURCES. Besides his own travels and inquiries H. has wide geographical, historical, and literary knowledge. Among many other writers he quotes Homer and Hesiod, discusses the authorship of the *Cypria* (2. 117), notes suspect or misapplied oracles (7. 6; 8. 20, 43), and defends genuine ones (8. 77); dissents from current Ionian theories (2. 15, 20, 143; 4. 36; 6. 137), and expressly criticizes and derides Hecataeus, from whom, however, he borrows freely. Other anonymous loans may be presumed, as H. rarely quotes individual sources, though he frequently mentions Argives and other peoples.

4. TEXT. There are a few lacunae, and the account of the Pyramid kings (2. 124–36) should follow 2. 99. An unfulfilled reference to 'Ασσύριοι λόγοι (1. 184) indicates that a Mesopotamian counterpart to the description of Egypt has been lost, or was not written.

5. PLAN AND SCOPE. The plan of the *History* is stated in its opening words (1. 1). Great deeds have value in retrospect, whether done by Greeks or by others (and H.'s portraits of Persians are masterly), and it is reasonable to ask, of the Great War, 'what they fought each other for'. Current theories explain nothing; peoples and States must be studied objectively. Blame for clash of Persians with Greeks is on Croesus, whose headstrong attack on Cyrus ruined Lydia (1. 6). The story of that 'middle kingdom' (1. 7–94) is interrupted characteristically by a pair of digressions (1. 59–68) explaining why neither Athens nor Sparta helped Croesus. The rise of the Medes, their subjection by Cyrus, and a sketch of him and his Persians (1. 95–140) lead to his conquest of the Asiatic Greeks (1. 141–77). The story of the Empire under Cyrus, Cambyses, and Darius (1. 178 to 5. 27) includes a long account of Egypt (bk. 2) which balanced the lost 'Assyrian story' (1. 181). The accession and reforms of Darius (3. 61–87, 150–60) are interleaved with his first oversea success, against Polycrates of Samos (3. 39–60; 120–49), and followed by pendant narratives of his aggressions in Thrace and Scythia (4. 1–144; 5. 1–27) and in Libya (4. 145–205). After all this retrospect comes the Ionic Revolt (5. 28–38), its suppression (5. 97–6. 42), and the consequent Marathon campaign (6. 94–120), similarly alternated with events in Greece, involving Sparta (5. 39–54; 6. 51–84) and Athens (5. 55–96; 6. 85–93, 121–40) in resistance to Persia. In bks. 7, 8, 9 the accession of Xerxes, and his choice between policies (7. 1–19), lead to pendant narratives of preparation, Persian (7. 20–131) and Greek (7. 131–75). Then the sea-fight at Artemisium (7. 175–95) and the land-battle at Thermopylae (7. 196–239), with their sequels (8. 1–23, 24–39), prepare for the crucial struggle at Salamis (8. 40–112) and its aftermath, the return of Xerxes (8. 113–32), and the winter parleys (8. 133–44). Finally, the land-battle of Plataea (9. 1–89) and naval operations at Mycale (9. 90–106) are the counterpart of Artemisium and Thermopylae.

6. The *History* has been regarded as unfinished; but the brief epilogue (9. 107–22) elaborately displays Persian demoralization, contrasted with initial hardiness. If H. meant to go beyond the capture of Sestus (9. 117–21), it was to be a fresh 'account' of new aims and events; and it is where our text of Herodotus ends that Thucydides begins his retrospect (1. 89) of τὰ μετὰ τὰ Μηδικά. The clumsy division of the work into nine 'Muses' is some librarian's fancy: H. himself cross-refers to this or that λόγος.

7. LITERARY ART. Within this broad design the main story is clearly distinguished from 'additions' (προσθῆκαι 4. 30; παρενθῆκαι 7. 171) large and small, some composed for their place, some utilizing earlier drafts. Such digressions have Epic precedent, and those of Herodotus—for which he apologizes (2. 13)—are deliberate. His literary art must be compared with Pindar's notions of relevance, and with the tragedians' use of choral odes, annotating rather than interrupting the development of the plot. Like the dramatists, too, H. chooses a hero—Croesus, Polycrates, Cleomenes, Mardonius—and traces his response to events and persons, in success and in disaster. Through *peripeteia* and *catastrophe* the question—δι' ἣν αἰτίην—answers itself: only rarely need H. intervene, chorus-like, to point a moral; for his public, like the audience of a tragedy, knew the story. Hence economy of detail, significant hearsay without guarantee of veracity; Aeschylean word-painting, Pindaric allusiveness, Aristophanic humour, above all, Sophoclean irony; a new literary art and expository skill, applied in lucid prose to a fresh field of research—the causes of 'men's deeds'—which establish Herodotus as the 'Father of History'.

8. HISTORICAL METHOD. Like earlier writers of λόγοι (*see* LOGOGRAPHERS), H. professes to record things seen and heard. His book results from his journeys; yet it is no mere περίοδος γῆς or ἐπιδημίαι, but ἱστορίης ἀπόδεξις, the outcome of research. Eyewitness (ὄψις 2. 99, 147; 4. 81; cf. 5. 59), hearsay (ἀκοή 2. 99–106; 6. 81; 7. 30), and written authority (poets, oracles, Ionian travellers, and theorists) are to be supplemented and verified by inquiry (ἱστορίη 2. 19, 44, 75, 113, 118; 6. 96) and criticized by common sense (γνώμη 2. 24; 5. 3). He states alternative versions and views with discreet reticence (2. 3, 46–7), and reserves judgement or offers conjecture (εἰκασίη 2. 24; 4. 11–12; 7. 22) when evidence fails. Ethnographical and historical interests have outrun (but not extinguished) physical and geographical. Historical facts have intrinsic value and rational meaning. Patriotism is tempered by comparison of régimes and customs, and by respect for age-long Oriental experience: Plutarch calls H. φιλοβάρβαρος. In Egypt he believed that he had received mystic teaching; but he reveals nothing, because 'all men know equally about divine things' (2. 3).

9. PERSONALITY. His personality is written in his book. Explorer, observer, and listener, he combines encyclopaedic interest and curiosity—about deeds rather than ideas—with humane sympathy and goodwill. Childlike, he loves wonders and secrets, enjoys a tale and a joke, and tells them vividly. Devoid of race-prejudice and intolerance, he venerates antiquity and is fascinated by novelties; and in these things trusts informants overmuch. Without linguistic skill, he extracts information from all; without military insight, he has recorded a great war. For a philosophy he has common sense, moral honesty, and piety. In a world regulated by fate (μοῖρα) but deranged by chance (τύχη), the gods (or 'the divine') maintain righteousness and punish wrongdoers. They can warn, but they cannot prevent, though they intervene to punish arrogance. Amid these external forces, and with the guidance of law and usage, man, using experience and reason, has freedom of choice and is responsible (αἴτιος) for his acts.

10. Of such work, criticism was immediate and persistent. H. himself replies to critics (6. 43); Thucydides (1. 20) challenges statements (6. 43; 9. 53); Aristophanes parodies the preface (*Ach.* 513 ff.); Ctesias contradicts; Plutarch (*De Malignitate Herodoti*) imputes unfairness and perversion of facts; Christian writers make charges of plagiarism, which Sayce (1883) has repeated and amplified. But closer study and better acquaintance with the resources, equipment, and literary custom of ancient writers have restored Herodotus' reputation for industry and honesty, while noting mistakes and omissions. J. L. M.

11. Herodotus' style probably owes little to the early logographers, whose scanty fragments hardly reveal any style at all—an impression confirmed, on the whole, by Dion. Hal. *Thuc.* 5 and 23. To Homer he undoubtedly owes much, in cast of thought as well as in language (Norden, *Antike Kunstprosa* i. 40). What other literary influences may have gone to the moulding of him it is hard to say. Nor is it easy to analyse the surpassing beauty of his prose, for H. has no mannerisms. Sometimes it is traceable to a subtle disposition of long and short words, as in the majestic proem (comparable, in this respect, to the openings of Sappho's *Ode to Aphrodite* and Lucretius' poem) and in 1. 45, ad fin.; sometimes to other technical means (1. 119, unobtrusive word-echoes; 1. 45, loc. cit., hyperbaton; 1. 32, asyndeton and initial assonance). But hardly a single technical device can be said to be characteristic of H. Each is used when, and when only, it is needed, as the period, for example, is reserved for great moments (e.g. 1. 45, 86). The first book is peculiarly rich in noble passages: Solon and Croesus (29–33, with the unforgettable solemnity of τὸ θεῖον πᾶν ἐὸν φθονερόν τε καὶ ταραχῶδες and πᾶν ἐστι ἄνθρωπος συμφορή, and 86–90); Harpagus eating his children's flesh (119, with the master-stroke at the close, where the historian is transformed into the hushed, yet curious, spectator). Such passages are the perfection of tragedy, as Don't-care Hippocleides pirouetting on his head is the perfection of comedy. They reveal a side of H. not always perceived by modern readers or by ancient critics, who praise his sweetness and beauty, but find him lacking in emotional power (e.g. Cic. *Orat.* 39 'quasi sedatus amnis fluit'; Quint. *Inst.* 10. 1. 73 'dulcis et candidus et fusus H.'; Dion. Hal. *Pomp.* 3 and *Thuc.* 23 (comparisons with Thuc.); Ath. 3, p. 78 e (μελίγηρυς)). Hermogenes, however (*Id.* 2, p. 421), does recognize H.'s grandeur and emotional power. H. has suffered the fate which befell Mozart. His charm, wit, and effortless ease have diverted attention from the note of profound sadness and pity sounded not seldom in his History. J. D. D.

BIBLIOGRAPHY
(A fuller list, *CAH* x. 520–2)
LIFE AND WORKS. Dion. Hal. *Pomp.*, *De Imit.*; Plut. *Mor.* 855–75 (*De Malignitate H.*); Lucian, Ἡρόδοτος ἢ Ἀετίων; Suidas.
H. IN EGYPT. A. Wiedemann, Bk. 2 (1890); W. Spiegelberg, *Die Glaubwürdigkeit d. H. Beschr. v. Aeg.* (1926; Engl. transl. A. M. Blackman, 1927).
TEXTS. J. C. E. Bähr (1856); H. Stein (1856; 1901); C. Hude (O.C.T. 1908).
COMMENTARIES. G. Rawlinson (1858; 1876³); H. Stein (1869; 1901⁶); A. H. Sayce (bks. 1–3, 1883); R. W. Macan (bks. 5–6, 1895; 7–9, 1908); W. W. How and J. Wells (1912; 1928²).
TRANSLATIONS. G. Rawlinson (1858; ed. A. W. Lawrence 1935); G. C. Macaulay (1890); A. D. Godley (Loeb, 1921).
STYLE AND DICTION. W. Dindorf, *Commentatio de dialecto H.* (in Didot ed., 1886); J. E. Powell, *Lexicon to H.* (1938).
LITERARY AND HISTORICAL. A. Kirchhoff, *Entstehung d. H. Geschichtswerke* (1878); A. Bauer, *Entst. d. H. Gesch.* (1878); A. Hauvette, *Hérodote* (1894); E. Meyer, *Forschungen* (i, 1892; ii, 1899); G. B. Grundy, *The Great Persian War* (1901); F. Jacoby, *Herodotos*, PW Suppl. ii (1913); T. R. Glover, *Herodotus* (1924); M. Pohlenz, *Herodot* (1937); J. E. Powell, *The History of Herodotus* (1930). J. L. M.

HERODOTUS (2), pupil of Agathinus and adherent of the pneumatic school of medicine, in the Flavian period (A.D. 70–96), wrote Ἰατρός and Περὶ βοηθημάτων (lost); Διάγνωσις περὶ τῶν ὀξέων καὶ χρονίων νοσημάτων (extant).

PW viii. 990.

HERON of Alexandria (date uncertain), known as ὁ μηχανικός, was also an able mathematician. In geometry he wrote *Metrica* (mensuration of figures), three books; other titles are *Definitions, Geometrica, Geodaesia, Stereometrica, Mensurae, Liber Geëponicus*; no doubt these collections are in part by others who borrowed Heron's name. Of his *Commentary on Euclid's Elements* a few extracts are given by Proclus and an-Nairīzī. Heron's other works are: *Mechanica*, three books (but for some extracts by Pappus, only an Arabic version exists), *Pneumatica*, two books, *On Automaton-making* (Περὶ αὐτοματοποιητικῆς), *On the Dioptra, Belopoeica, Cheirobalistra, Catoptrica* (*On Mirrors*) known in a Latin translation only.

In the *Metrica* we have the mensuration of regular polygons up to the hendecagon, circles, cones, pyramids, etc. Heron solves quadratic equations arithmetically, approximates to square roots of non-square numbers, and to cube roots. In the *Mechanics* we find the parallelogram of velocities, problems on centres of gravity, etc., Heron's solution of the problem of the two mean proportionals, motion on an inclined plane, the five mechanical powers, the mechanics of daily life. The *Pneumatica* treats of such things as siphons, penny-in-the-slot machines, 'Heron's fountain', a fire-engine, a water-organ, and many contrivances operating by means of compressed air, water, or steam. *See* PHYSICS, para. 5.

Heronis Opera, 5 vols. (Teubner, 1899–1914); F. Hultsch, *Heronis Alexandrini geometricorum et stereometricorum reliquiae* (1864); and, for the *Belopoeica* and *Cheirobalistra*, Thévenot, *Veterum mathematicorum opera* (1693); C. Wescher, *Poliorcétique des Grecs* (1867); V. Prou, *Notices et Extraits* xxvi. 2 (1877). The latest ed. of the *Belopoeica* is that of H. Diels and E. Schramm in *Abh. Berl. Akad.* (1918). PW viii. 992. T. H.

HEROPHILUS of Chalcedon, one of the leading dogmatic physicians, lived in Alexandria in the first half of the third century B.C.; his school was still flourishing at the end of the first century B.C. Herophilus stressed the importance of experience no less than that of reasoning. Though a great scholar, his work seems primarily determined by the practical task of the physician; health he went so far as to consider the indispensable foundation of all physical and intellectual happiness. His greatest original contributions were his anatomical inquiries based on the human cadaver; he probably wrote a systematic outline of anatomy (particularly famous was his study of the brain—to him the organ of the soul, of the liver, the eye, the sexual organs). He discovered the rhythm of the pulse and formulated a mathematical law of its systole and diastole. Much interested in the aetiology of diseases, he explained their origin through humours. In therapy he paid careful attention to prognostics and used drugs abundantly; but he was also an authority on dietetics and gymnastics. Through his books, in which practical questions were emphasized, he exercised a considerable influence. *See* ANATOMY AND PHYSIOLOGY, para. 7.

Text. Fragments: K. F. H. Marx (1838); Marx, *De vita, scriptis*, etc. (1842). List of writings: Susemihl, i. 787. Translation and Commentary: J. F. Dobson, *Proceedings of the Royal Society of Med.*, Section Hist. of Med. (1925), indispensable translation and interpretation of the more important fragments. Literature: the handbooks on history of medicine. Pupils of H.: H. Gossen, PW viii. 1104. L. E.

HESIOD, son of an unsuccessful citizen of Cyme in Aeolis, who with two sons, Hesiod and Perses, migrated to Greece and settled at Ascra on the slopes of Helicon. Some time after the father's death Perses, who had already obtained more than his share of the estate, tried with the help of the rulers (βασιλῆες) to obtain still more. It is not known how the dispute was settled, but it appears to have led H. to begin a series of moral admonitions in hexameter verse which afterwards resulted in the poem *Works and Days* (see DIDACTIC POETRY). The above account of his life is derived from H. himself (*Op.* 27–41, 633–8; cf. 650–62 and *Th.* 22–35). We are told also that he contended with Homer (Schol. Pind. *Nem.* 2. 1 = fr. 265 Rzach), whence arose the *Agon* (see *Agon Homeri et Hesiodi*), and that he met a violent death (Thuc. 3. 96) which legend made him to deserve (e.g. Plutarch, *Conv. sept. sap.* 19. 162). It is impossible to determine his date exactly; the general opinion in the fifth and fourth centuries B.C. was that H., like Orpheus, Musaeus, and Homer, was one of the earliest teachers and civilizers of man (Ar. *Ran.* 1032 ff.; Pl. *Ap.* 41 a). Herodotus (2. 53) makes him contemporary with Homer, but later antiquity was uncertain. Modern opinion generally regards him as later than Homer, but there is no agreement about his date. T. W. Allen (*Homer: the Origins and Transmission* (1924), ch. 4) would put him as early as 800 B.C.

WORKS

1. *Works and Days* (Ἔργα καὶ ἡμέραι). The composition may have been spread over a long period, but though many ancient sayings have been incorporated (e.g. in 286–382, 706–64), there is no reason to suspect wholesale interpolation, with the possible exception of the *Days* (765–828). H. addresses himself to his brother Perses on the subject of their dispute (see above) and preaches the need for every man to work for his living. He supports this thesis with a myth (the punishment of the presumptuousness of Prometheus), and elaborates it with an account, partly historical, of the Five Ages of the World. After a series of moral precepts follows the famous description of a year's farm-work (383–617). H., having expounded first the necessity for work, then its righteousness, now explains its performance. Emphasis is laid on the proper time for various operations

and this is indicated in various ways, e.g. by the positions of constellations and by the migrations of cranes and other movements of animals. Advice is given on farm labour and implements, on feeding and relaxation, and on clothing, especially in winter. Indeed, the lines (504–63) on the month Lenaeon, though suspected by some, are justly famous; not even Homer has surpassed this unforgettable picture of mid-winter in a bleak mountain homestead. There follow advice on navigation and much other proverbial lore, then finally (765–828) an account of days lucky or unlucky for various operations, chiefly but not entirely agricultural. Their genuineness has been suspected (M. P. Nilsson, *ARW* xiv. 439 n.), but not in antiquity (Heraclitus ap. Plut. *Cam.* 138 a); Herodotus, too (2. 82), alludes to this part of H.'s work.

2. The *Theogony* (Θεογονία) is the first piece of conscious religious writing in Greek. Here, too, H. is gathering ancient material; he attempts to bring traditions concerning the gods into a consistent connexion with each other and with his conception of the Universe as a whole. Zeus is the supreme god, but he is a latecomer, and neither he nor any other being is named Creator. Creation meant procreation. So, starting from Chaos and Gaea, with Eros to unite them, the genealogy of the gods is deduced—Uranus, Kronos, Zeus. The other offspring of Uranus and their descendants are listed; the myth, not in Homer, of the mutilation of Uranus by Kronos is told, and finally how Zeus overthrew Kronos, Titans, and Giants, and assumed the overlordship of the gods. Then follows an account of Zeus' numerous offspring, and another of the progeny of goddesses in union with mortals. The last two lines indicate that there was to follow a list of mortal women, presumably the lost *Ehoiai*.

In spite of Pausanias 9. 31 (story that H. was author only of the *Erga*), there is no good reason for doubting that H. was the author, and the mention of his name (22) is to be regarded as a σφραγίς. Hdt. 2. 53 is very definite. Like the *Works and Days* it is something of a medley, but there is more apparent unity of subject-matter. The long prooemium and the digressions should probably be regarded as characteristic of the poetical practice of the time rather than as evidence of multiple authorship.

3. The *Shield* ('Ασπίς) begins with the catalogue formula ἤ οἵη ('or like her who'), and the first fifty-six lines refer to Alcmene. The opening formula suggests, and it is stated in the 'Argument', that lines 1–56 are an extract from the Hesiodic *Catalogue of Women* ("Η οἷαι, *Ehoiai*). For the rest (the fight between Heracles and Cycnus and the description of Heracles' shield), the opinion of Aristophanes of Byzantium (cited in the Argument) is generally accepted—that it is not by H. 'but by some other person who had the notion of imitating the Homeric Shield' (*Il.* 18. 478–609). Its date is uncertain, but some of the scenes depicted (e.g. 215–17) appear to resemble those on vases of the late seventh and early sixth centuries (J. M. Woodward, *Perseus*, p. 46; R. M. Cook in *CQ* xxxi (1937), 204).

4. *Lost Works.* Numerous fragments exist both in ancient citations and in papyri of H.'s *Catalogues* (Κατάλογοι), of which the *Ehoiai* seem to have formed a part. Some fragments exist of the following works, which are of doubtful authenticity: 'Αστρονομία, Δάκτυλοι 'Ιδαῖοι, Αἰγίμιος, Κήϋκος Γάμος, Μελαμπόδεια (divinations of Melampus), Χείρωνος ὑποθῆκαι (gnomic), Μεγάλαι ἠοῖαι, Μεγάλα ἔργα, but nothing remains of the 'Ορνιθομαντεία attested by Proclus on *Op.* 828.

BIBLIOGRAPHY

GENERAL. Schmid–Stählin, *Gesch. der griech. Lit.* (1. i); F. Leo, *Hesiodea* (Progr. 1894); F. Dornseiff, *Die Archäische Mythenerzählung* (1933), ch. 3; M. R. Dimitrijević, *Studia Hesiodea* (1899); C. Buzio, *Esiodo nel Mondo Greco* (1938).
TEXTS. Teubner, Rzach ed. minor 1913 and, with full critical notes and references, ed. major, 1902.
COMMENTARIES WITH TEXT. Goettling–Flach[2] (1878); Paley[2] (1883); Sittl (Mod. Gk.; 1889); Scholia in Gaisford *Poet. Min. Graec.* vol. iii. **Works and Days:** Van Lennep (1847); Mazon (1914); Wilamowitz (1–764) (1928); Sinclair (1932). **Theogony:** Van Lennep (1843); Schoemann (1868); Jacoby (1930).
TRANSLATIONS. Mair (1908); Evelyn White (Loeb, 1914); Mazon (Budé, 1928).
STYLE AND DICTION. Rzach, *Der Dialekt des Hesiodos* (1876); J. Paulson (*Index Hesiodeus*), 1890; I. Sellschopp, *Stilistische Untersuchungen zu Hesiod* (1934).
STUDIES OF PARTICULAR WORKS. **Works and Days:** C. F. Ranke, *De Hes. Op. et Di.* (1838); P. Waltz, *Hésiode et son poème moral* (1906); E. Meyer, in *Genethliakon Carl Robert* (1910). **Theogony:** F. Schwenn, *Die Theogonie des Hesiodos* (1934). T. A. S.

HESIONE ('Ησιόνη), in mythology, (1) an Oceanid, wife of Prometheus (Aesch. *PV* 560). (2) Wife of Nauplius and mother of Palamedes (q.v.), Oeax, and Nausimedon (Apollod. 2. 23). (3) Daughter of Laomedon (q.v.; ibid. 3. 146). After her rescue from the sea-monster by Heracles (q.v.), she was taken prisoner by him when he captured Troy, given as the prize of valour to Telamon, and granted leave to save any prisoner she chose; she therefore bought (ἐπρίατο) her brother Podarces for a nominal price, and he was henceforth called Πρίαμος. By Telamon she became mother of Teucer (q.v.; Apollod. 2. 136; 3. 162). H. J. R.

HESPERUS ("Εσπερος Lat. *Vesper*, *Vesperugo*), the Evening Star; shown in art as a boy carrying a torch. Father of the Hesperides (*see* HERACLES 2) or their mother Hesperis (Diod. Sic. 4. 27. 2–3; Serv. on *Aen.* 4. 484).

HESTIA, goddess of the hearth, etymologically identical with Vesta (q.v.), and not unlike her in cult, though less important and not having her virgin priestesses. In early times, when it was a difficult and slow process to make fire, to keep a hearth burning continually was very advisable, and it would seem that in communities of that age, both in Greece and in Italy, the hearth of the chief or king was especially important, probably for practical reasons and certainly also from magico-religious motives; it seems to have been considered in some sense the life of the people (the equation 'fire = life' is very widespread). Hence the cult of the communal or sacred hearth was apparently universal, but the goddess never developed, hardly even achieving anthropomorphization. She therefore has next to no mythology. Homer never mentions her, the word ἱστίη meaning simply a fire-place; Hesiod and later authors after him make her daughter of Kronos (q.v.) and Rhea (*Theog.* 454), and the *Homeric Hymn* to Aphrodite says (21 ff.) that she 'liked not the works of Aphrodite', and so refused to marry either Poseidon or Apollo, but swore to remain a virgin, and she accordingly granted her sundry honours, especially to 'sit in the midst of the house taking the fatness'. Of her private cult not much is known; swine or, on occasion, cows were offered to her, no doubt according to the means of the household (Ar. *Vesp.* 844 and schol.; Callim. *Cer.* 109). At the Amphidromia (Plato, *Theaet.* 160, schol. there and lexicographers s.v.), when the five-days-old child was received into the family and named, part of the ceremony was to run with it around the hearth, but it does not appear that the goddess was thought present in any personal way. Publicly, she has 'the council-houses (*prytaneia*) for her portion' (Pind. *Nem.* 11. 1), confirmed by the public hearth in the *prytaneia* of many cities (Farnell, op. cit. inf. 348). Since the senate-house often had a sacred hearth also, Hestia is not infrequently called Βουλαία, 'she of the Senate'. She commonly received the first of the sacrifice, or a preliminary sacrifice for herself, was named first in prayers and first or nearly so in oaths (Preuner in Roscher, 2616 ff.; Farnell, 346, 349; Rose in *Harv. Theol. Rev.* xxx (1937), 172.

Farnell, *Cults*, v. 345 ff.; Preuner in Roscher's *Lexikon*, s.v. (cf. his *Hestia-Vesta*, 1864); Diehl, *Anthologia lyrica*[1] ii. 301 f. (hymn of Aristonous at Delphi). H. J. R.

HESTIASIS, *see* LITURGY.

HESYCHIUS of Alexandria, lexicographer. If the Eugenius to whom he addresses the introductory epistle of his lexicon is E. ὁ σχολαστικός, H. (like Eugenius) probably belongs to the fifth century A.D. The comprehensive scope of his design is indicated both in that epistle and in the title, Συναγωγὴ πασῶν λέξεων κατὰ στοιχεῖον. The work, H. says, was based on the specialist lexica (*see* GLOSSA, GREEK) of Aristarchus, Heliodorus (1st c. B.C.), Apion, and Apollonius, son of Archibius (pupil of Apion), and on Diogenianus and Herodian; H. seems to have added the interpretations of a number of proverbs which are included. The lexicon is known only from a fifteenth-century MS., badly preserved, and in many places interpolated (even obliterated) by expansions and other notes made by the first editor, Marcus Musurus (1514). Bentley showed that the Biblical Glosses in H. are interpolations; less successful attacks have been made on the Latin and Atticist items. The original, as H. says, included the sources of the rare words listed. The sources, however, have disappeared in the severe abridgement which has reduced the lexicon to a glossary, copious though that remains. H. often preserves correct readings for which easier synonyms have been substituted in our extant MSS. of Greek literature. His dialectal items are sometimes imperfect: he writes ϝ either as B (less often Y) or as Γ (less often T), as, e.g., Γοῖδα· οὐκ οἶδα [sic cod.], Γιογόν [sic cod.]· ἴσον. Nevertheless, he is of the greatest value for the study of Greek dialects and the interpretation of inscriptions.

Editions: Alberti, 1746–66; Schmidt, 1858–68; ed. minor, 1867; A. von Blumenthal, *Hesychiosstudien* (1929).   P. B. R. F.

HETAIRIAI (ἑταιρίαι) (1) in Crete. In many Cretan cities all male citizens were grouped into *hetairiai* as part of the military system; the members fed in common in *andreia* very similar to the military messes at Sparta.

(2) In Athens *hetairiai* may have been social clubs at the outset; but since *c.* 425 B.C. they appear as political associations of oligarchic character. They served primarily for mutual assistance in the dicasteries, but under the influence of extreme oligarchs like Antiphon (q.v.) they became instruments of revolution, and they were principally responsible for the movement of the Four Hundred (q.v.).   A. W. G.

HETAIROI (ἑταῖροι, Companions), first applied to the 2,500 Myrmidons of Achilles in the *Iliad*, this title in classical times was peculiar to Macedonia. Anaximenes (fr. 4 Jacoby *FGrH*) ascribed the institution of *hetairoi* and *pezetairoi* to Alexander. Probably the *hetairoi*, as Cavalry-Companions, had existed for centuries before the *pezetairoi* or Infantry-Companions were formed; since Macedonia was not economically emancipated until the fourth century, the *pezetairoi* system may be ascribed to Alexander II (369–368 B.C.). By adopting the nobles of Upper Macedonia and able Greeks into the Companions, Philip II welded together his expanding State on a military basis. The *hetairoi*, to whom Philip granted estates of conquered land, numbered 800 *c.* 340 B.C. (Theopompus fr. 225 Jacoby). Alexander the Great increased their number, and late in his life enrolled Asiatics even in the royal bodyguard who served as his Council. In war the *pezetairoi*, equipped by Philip with *sarissa* and *pelta*, formed the defensive phalanx, and the *hetairoi*, equipped with a thrusting spear, delivered the offensive, usually from the right wing; they formed the core of the invincible army led by Alexander the Great. After his death Seleucus commanded the survivors of the *hetairoi* in one hipparchy, which later split up among the Successors. Further references in Arrian, *Anab*.

N. G. L. H.

HIATUS, the gap that occurs when a word ending with a vowel is immediately followed by a word beginning with a vowel.

I. HIATUS IN GREEK VERSE

For hiatus at end of line or colon *see* METRE, GK. I (4).

Hiatus within line or colon, (1) without shortening of the first vowel, (2) with shortening:

(1) Hiatus without shortening is common in Homer, at certain points in the line, and, after certain words, in Comedy. Elsewhere it is rare, except that post-Homeric poets allow themselves some epic freedom in hexameters. Broadly speaking, the post-Homeric examples fall into the following classes:

(i) Where the second word is digammated (e.g. ἄναξ, ἔπος, ἴον), hiatus cannot be truly said to exist in the case of poets (e.g. Alcman, Pindar, Bacchylides, Epicharmus) for whom the digamma was a living letter. Further, memory of the digamma makes tolerable such juxtapositions as δέ οἱ (dative) in Sophoclean lyric. Hiatus is also tolerated (ii) before certain proper names in lyric poetry (e.g. Ἰσθμός, Pind. *Isthm.* 1. 9 and 32); (iii) often in drama after, or between, exclamations: e.g. ἐλελεῦ ἐλελεῦ (Aesch. *PV* 877), αἰαῖ, ἱκνοῦμαι (Soph. *El.* 136), ὦ Ἡράκλεις, often in Comedy. Even in tragic trimeters, ὦ οὗτος (Soph. *OC* 1627). Similarly with quasi-interjectional expressions: ἴθι ἴθι (Soph. *Phil.* 832), παῖ, ἠμί, παῖ (Ar. *Ran.* 37); (iv) after τί, occasionally in tragic trimeters, very frequently (and also after ὅτι, ὅ τι) in Comedy, especially in such phrases as τί ἐστι; τί οὖν; (v) εὖ οἶδα (ἴσθι, ἴστε) very occasionally in tragic, more frequently in comic, trimeters; (vi) in Comedy, often after περί, occasionally after πρό and μέχρι (ἄν); (vii) οὐδὲ (μηδὲ) εἷς (ἕν), occasionally in Old Comedy, very often in Middle and New Comedy; (viii) in the phrase μὴ ὥρας, ὥρασι (Comedy).

It will be noticed that in drama hiatus is mainly found within a more or less closely unified word-group, where the *concursus vocalium* seemed hardly more objectionable than within a single word (e.g. ἄοκνος). Perhaps, therefore, the freer toleration of hiatus (as of crasis) in Comedy is a consequence of a delivery more rapid, and less articulated, than that employed in Tragedy.

(2) Hiatus with shortening, sometimes called 'Epic correption' because of its commonness in epic (and elegiac) verse, is found in the dactylic cola of the early lyric poets (e.g. Sapph. fr. 116 οἶον τὸ γλυκύμαλον ἐρεύθεται ἄκρῳ ἐπ’ ὕσδῳ), and is frequent in the dactylo-epitrites of Pindar and Bacchylides. In the lyrics of Tragedy, Sophocles uses it far more frequently (e.g. *El.* 162–70) than Aeschylus or Euripides (who in his later plays almost banishes it). It is found in the anapaestic dimeters of Tragedy and Comedy (in the resolved arsis as well as in the thesis), and in the catalectic anapaestic tetrameters of Comedy (much more often in earlier than in later Aristophanes). A monosyllabic thesis does not admit correption; consequently all cases in dochmii, and the few cases in lyric iambics, occur in resolved arses (e.g. Soph. *Aj.* 349 μόνοι ἐμῶν). The shortened syllable is much more frequently a diphthong (especially, perhaps, an accentually short diphthong in -αι or -οι) than a single vowel.

See J. Descroix, *Le Trimètre iambique* (1931), 26–9 and for bibliography see E. Kalinka in Bursian, *Jahresb.*, 250, pp. 402–6.
J. D. D.

II. HIATUS IN GREEK PROSE

1. *Theory.* Isocrates (Τέχνη) deprecates hiatus generally; Hermogenes and his scholiast and Longinus accept this ruling (Walz, iii. 289; vi. 102–3; ix. 560). [Arist.] *Rh. Al.* 1435[ab] probably concerns ambiguous elision, not hiatus. Dionysius distinguishes: the austere style (Thucydides) allows hiatus freely; the middle style (Demosthenes) allows a little; the smooth style avoids

it carefully—Isocrates and Theopompus too carefully (*Comp.* 22–3; *Dem.* 4, 38, 40, 43; *Isoc.* 2; *Pomp.* 6). Plutarch satirizes Isocrates' scrupulousness (*Mor.* 350 e). Demetrius thinks marked hiatus desirable in the grand style, but too dignified for the simple style (*Eloc.* 68–74, 207, 299–301). Cf. also Cic. *Orat.* 77, 150–2, *De Or.* 3. 171–2; Quint. 9. 4. 33–7.

2. *Practice.* Marked avoidance of hiatus first appears in Thrasymachus, then in Gorgias (*Pal.*) and Alcidamas (*Soph.*); there is moderate avoidance in Antisthenes and Lysias; little in Andocides; none in Antiphon. (Benseler assumes that pre-Isocratean writers cannot have avoided hiatus, and rejects as spurious those works which show avoidance.)

3. Isocrates is the pattern of the technique of avoidance, in securing which he relies little on crasis, elision, or pauses, but much on word-order and word-choice; hence some hyperbaton and such plurals as ταῖς ἀληθείαις, σεμνότησιν. His few licences are chiefly before ἄν, οὖν, and after καί, περί, πρό, ὦ. He avoids long vowels in hiatus (especially η) more strictly than short. His judicial speeches show rather more freedom than the rest.

4. Demosthenes, though careful, allows hiatus also before ὡς and after εἰ, ἤ, ὅτι, μή, and the article; at pauses within and after sentences; and with proper names and set phrases (ἐν τῷ ἐμῷ ὕδατι εἰπάτω). He often elides.

5. Further, hiatus is avoided carefully: by Lycurgus, Dinarchus, Demades, Theopompus, Polybius, Philodemus; by Isaeus and Plutarch sometimes; by Plato in his latest works and in *Phdr.* and *Menex.*; by Aristotle in *Pol.* and *Metaph.* 1. It is tolerated by Aeschines and Hyperides, and freely allowed by Herodotus, Thucydides, and usually Xenophon.

G. E. Benseler, *De hiatu in oratoribus Atticis* (1841; detailed, dogmatic); F. Blass, *Attische Beredsamkeit*[2] (1887–98); S. Skimina, *Études sur le rythme de la prose grecque I* (1937).   W. H. S.

III. HIATUS IN LATIN VERSE

There are three groups of fairly homogeneous cases:

(1) 'Epic correption' *in or before Greek words* from Cicero to Horace: etesiǣ Cic. *Aratea* (*Phaen.*) fr. 24 (marked by himself, *Orator* 15. 2) and Lucr. 6. 716, *Peliŏ Ossam* Verg. *G.* 1. 281 (imitated—Ov. *Met.* 1. 155), *insulǣ Ionio Aen.* 3. 211; cf. *Ecl.* 6. 44, *G.* 1. 437, 4. 461, *Aen.* 5. 261, Ov. *Am.* 2. 13. 21. *Without a Greek word*: valě Verg. *Ecl.* 3. 79 (imitated—Ov. *Met.* 3. 501); cf. lectulŏ, Catull. 57. 7. This licence is of Greek origin and conditioned by metrical necessity.

(2) Hiatus without shortening is not infrequent in Virgil, e.g. *pecori,* | *apibus G.* 1. 4, *dea.* | *ille Aen.* 1. 405 (cf. Hor. *Epod.* 5. 100, *Carm.* 1. 28. 24). In some of these cases Greek technique is obviously imitated, e.g. *Glauco* | *et Panopeae G.* 1. 437, *castaneae* | *hirsutae Ecl.* 7. 53 (cf. Hor. *Epod.* 13. 3, Ov. *Met.* 3. 184, 5. 625).

(3) Cases like *qui a*(*mat*), *dum ab*(*est*) = ᴗᴗ(ᴗ). They are frequent in dramatists (especially Plautus) and Lucretius (see Munro on 2. 404), and occur sporadically in Catullus (55. 4), Virgil (e.g. *Ecl.* 8. 108), Horace (*Satires*), etc., but not in Ovid or later. This phenomenon is not of Greek origin and its prosodical character is doubtful, disyllabic and monosyllabic pronunciation being both possible.

Apart from these three groups there are some hundreds of cases of hiatus in Plautus, many of them complicated by problems of prosody or textual criticism. Some scholars think that hiatus in the caesura is legitimate in Plautus; but it has not yet been proved that hiatus is more frequent in the caesura than it would be if it was legitimate at any place in the line.

Literature: Luc. Mueller, *De re metr.*[2] 368–79. Kalinka in Bursian's *Jahresb.* ccl (1935), 407–11.   P. M.

HIBERNIA (᾽Ιέρνη), Ireland, first known to the Greeks through Massiliote mariners (*c.* 525 B.C.) as being 'five days' sail from Brittany, near the Albiones' island'. Eratosthenes (*c.* 235), probably through Pytheas' circumnavigation of Britain (*c.* 310–306), placed Ireland correctly on his map. Strabo (4. 201) says that, oblong in shape, it lay near and *north* of Britain and contained greedy incestuous cannibals. Mela (3. 6. 53) makes Ireland nearly as large as Britain, oblong, with pastures that caused the cattle to burst, and savage untrustworthy husbandmen. Pliny gives as its area 800 × 100 miles. Agricola may have reconnoitred Ireland. Ptolemy (*Geog.* 2. 2) shows fair knowledge of the whole coast, giving sixteen peoples of counties Wicklow, Kildare, Waterford, Wexford, Kerry, Dublin (Eblana), Connaught province; rivers Shannon, Barrow, Lagan, Avoca, Boyne. Solinus added the detail that Ireland has no snakes. The older tendency to place Ireland between Britain and Spain was due probably to early direct voyages from Spain.

Cary–Warmington, *Explorers*, 29 ff.; Orpen, *Journ. R. Soc. Antiqu. of Ireland*, June 1894 (Ptolemy); MacNeill, *New Ireland Rev.*, Sept. 1906.   E. H. W.

HICETAS of Syracuse, Pythagorean, probably the teacher of Ecphantus and younger than Philolaus, is said to have been the first to teach that the earth moves in a circle (also ascribed to Philolaus). His view probably was that the earth rotates on its own axis while the heavenly bodies are at rest.

Testimonia in Diels, *Vorsokr.*[5] i. 441–2. *PW* viii. 1597. W. D. R.

HIEMPSAL, see NUMIDIA.

HIEROCLES, Stoic of the time of Hadrian (A.D. 117–38), wrote (1) an 'Ηθικὴ στοιχείωσις (*Elements of Ethics*) which may have been an introduction to (2) a work on ethics, frs. of which are preserved in Stobaeus. The former was a scientific work dealing with the instinct of self-preservation (πρώτη οἰκείωσις) as the starting-point of the Stoic ethics, and with self-consciousness as the foundation of this instinct. The latter was a work of edification dealing with duties, Περὶ καθηκόντων. The teaching in both works followed the orthodox doctrine of the early Stoics.

Ed. H. von Arnim, *BKT* 4 (1906). *PW* viii. 1479.   W. D. R.

HIERODOULOI, a relatively late term (first in 3rd-c. B.C. papyri), though temple-slaves, performing the menial tasks, existed from early times in Greece as elsewhere (cf. Martiales at Larinum, Cic. *Clu.* 43). The word *hierodouloi* can designate such chattels of a god; it can also bear certain special connotations. In Ptolemaic Egypt the *hierodouloi* take minor roles in the ceremonies, tend the sacred cats (*PSI* 440), or collect temple revenues (*PHib.* 35). In Asia Minor they may be the serfs, rather than actual slaves, attached to the great temple estates (Strabo, bks. 11–12, passim). The religious prostitutes of Comana Pontica (Strabo 559) and Corinth (Athen. 573–4; Strabo 378) are called *hierodouloi*, and the term has hence been mistakenly applied to all sacred prostitution (q.v.). In Oriental cults a devotee might consider himself the slave of a divine master (cf. δοῦλος τοῦ θεοῦ in Christian inscriptions); the κάτοχοι of Egypt (cf. SARAPIS) and some of the ἱεροί in Anatolia may fall in this category. In the Hellenistic period arose the custom of manumitting slaves through a fictitious sale (or occasionally dedication) to a god, who thus became the guarantor of their freedom; persons thus freed were occasionally called *hierodouloi* (A. Cameron, *Harv. Theol. Rev.* 1939, 154–5, cf. 149).

See METRAGYRTES.   F. R. W.

HIEROMNEMONES, religious officials, found in many Greek States. Aristotle (*Pol.* 1321[b]), classifies them with the civil registrars of public and private documents, and temples frequently served as record offices. Their functions varied widely: some appear as archivists, others as financial officers, some managed the festivals or controlled temple properties, and in several cities, e.g. Issa and Byzantium, they were the eponymous magistrates. They usually formed a college, and the position was one of responsibility and honour. Best known are the *hieromnemones* who represented their States in the Delphic-Pylaean Amphictiony. Their number was normally twenty-four, but varied considerably under the Aetolian domination (c. 290–191 B.C.). Their exact relationship to the other delegates, the *pylagorai* (in the Aetolian period called *agoratroi*), is not clear. The duties of the *hieromnemones* are set forth in a law of 380 (*IG* ii². 1126). Their tenure of office varied from State to State: in the fourth century the Thessalian *hieromnemones* served for several years, the Athenians one year, while the Malians sent different *hieromnemones* for each of the semi-annual meetings; a Chian decree of 258–254 (*SIG* 443) stipulates that their delegate should serve one year and be ineligible for reappointment. For *hieromnemon* as a functionary of a private cult association see *AJArch.* xxxvii (1933), 254. The term was sometimes used to translate the Latin *pontifex*.   F. R. W.

HIERON (1) I was appointed ruler of Gela when his brother Gelon (q.v.) became master of Syracuse. He succeeded in Syracuse in 478 B.C. and successfully overcame the counter-claims of his brother Polyzelus. Free from immediate Carthaginian menace, he intervened in south Italy, helping Sybaris and saving Locri from destruction by Anaxilas of Rhegium (477). In 474 he saved Cumae and destroyed Etruscan sea-power by a great naval victory (for dedicated helmet, see Tod, no. 22). To maintain this influence Hieron founded a short-lived colony in Pithecusae (Ischia). Meanwhile he tried to strengthen his power in Sicily by refounding Catana under the name of Aetna with 10,000 new settlers (475). His alliance with Acragas broke down and he destroyed the tyranny there (472). His court was open to poets and philosophers—Aeschylus, Pindar, Bacchylides, Simonides, Xenophanes, Epicharmus; his victories in the Games extended his prestige. He died in 467/6.

Sources: Diodorus, bk. 11 (from Timaeus). Cf. Pindar and Bacchylides, *Odes*, 3–5. Modern literature: Th. Lenschau, *PW* viii. 1496; R. Hackforth, *CAH* v; U. v. Wilamowitz-Moellendorff, *Hieron und Pindaros*, *Sitz. Preuss. Akad. Berl.* 1901, 1273 (cf. *Pindaros*, 1922). See also under SICILY, SYRACUSE.   A. M.

HIERON (2) II (c. 306–215 B.C.), of an unimportant family, later claimed descent from Gelon. He was appointed commander of the Syracusan army c. 275. Severely defeated by the Mamertines (q.v.), he later defeated them at the river Longanus and was saluted as king (265?). When they held Messana with Carthaginian help, Hieron broke with tradition and joined the Carthaginians when the Romans seized Messana. Driven back by Roman forces, he concluded a peace with Rome (263) by which he became Rome's ally, retained about half his territory, provided ships and supplies for Rome during the Punic Wars, paid 100 talents, and promised an annual tribute of 25 talents for fifteen years. This last was remitted when the alliance was renewed in 248. Under Roman protection and Hieron's mercantile policy Syracuse became wealthy and magnificent. He maintained a good fleet to police the seas (for his enormous ship see Athenaeus 5. 40) and utilized the genius of Archimedes in the defence of the city. The *Lex Hieronica*, which regulated the tithe-system, shows Hellenistic influences. He himself wrote books on agriculture. He remained Rome's loyal ally till his death (215).

Polybius 1. 8; 7. 7; Diodorus, bks. 22–6; Justin 23. 4. G. De Sanctis, *Stor. Rom.* iii. 1, p. 90; J. Carcopino, *La Loi de Hiéron* (1919); Th. Lenschau, *PW* viii. 1503; A. Schenk von Stauffenberg, *König Hieron der Zweite von Syrakus* (1933). See also under SICILY, SYRACUSE, THEOCRITUS.   A. M.

HIERON (3), admiral of Alexander the Great, *see* ARABIA.

HIERONYMUS (1) of Cardia, the contemporary and trustworthy historian of the period from the death of Alexander (323 B.C.) to the death of Pyrrhus (272), or perhaps as far as 263, the year of the treaty between Antigonus Gonatas and Alexander of Epirus. He appears first in the service of Eumenes of Cardia, fighting for him against Perdiccas and Antigonus until Eumenes' execution by the latter after the battle of Gabiene (316). H. entered the service of Antigonus, was appointed harmost of Boeotia (293) by his son Demetrius Poliorcetes, and assisted Antigonus at the battle of Ipsus (301). He retained the friendship of Antigonus Gonatas until his death (c. 250). His account of this period, perhaps entitled Αἱ περὶ Διαδόχων Ἱστορίαι, was the most important source behind Arrian (Τὰ μετὰ Ἀλέξανδρον) and Diodorus (bks. 18–20), and the later books were Plutarch's chief authority for his life of Pyrrhus.
FHG ii. 450.   G. L. B.

HIERONYMUS (2) of Rhodes, philosopher and historian of literature, lived at Athens c. 290–230, under the protection of Antigonus Gonatas. Trained in the Peripatetic school, he left it when it was declining under Lycon's headship, and founded an eclectic school. Works: Περὶ ἐποχῆς; Περὶ μέθης; Συμπόσιον; a work on ethics; Περὶ ἀοργησίας; Περὶ ποιητῶν; Ἱστορικὰ ὑπομνήματα; Σποράδην ὑπομνήματα; Περὶ Ἰσοκράτους; Ἐπιστολαί. The extant frs. illustrate chiefly his love of literary gossip.
PW viii. 1561.   W. D. R.

HIERONYMUS (3), EUSEBIUS (SOFRONIUS) (c. A.D. 348–420), generally known as ST. JEROME, is the most important to the classical student of all the Fathers. Born at Stridon, in Dalmatia, he was taken early to Rome; it was his good fortune to be taught by the greatest teacher in that age, Aelius Donatus. The best training in rhetoric followed. There he was baptized, but this did not prevent him from indulging in immorality. After his studies he proceeded to Trèves (Trier), and dedicated himself to religion. Later, at Antioch, he laid the foundations of his theological training, and mastered Greek. The ascetic life had a growing attraction for him, and he visited the Chalcis desert (375 to 378), where he learned Hebrew with great difficulty. The theological disputes of Antioch brought him no peace. He decided to return to Rome. He received priest's orders from the Bishop of Antioch. On his way westwards, at Constantinople, about 381, he made the acquaintance of the great Greek theologian Gregory of Nazianzus. His stay in Rome lasted from 382 to 385. It was then that Pope Damasus compelled him to revise the old Latin texts of the Gospels, in view of the variety of such texts then in existence. The revision took two directions: first, the Latinity was made more literary; second, the underlying Greek texts were brought into accord with the type of Greek text closely related to that in the Codex Sinaiticus, now in the British Museum. Several ladies of the Roman nobility found in him a valued religious adviser. The death of Damasus (384) made things difficult for Jerome, as he was suspected of aspiring towards the papal chair. He left Rome, Aug. 385, and travelled by Antioch to Jerusalem, then to Egypt to see ascetic life at close quarters, and subsequently with some like-minded friends to Palestine and Bethlehem. There, 389, he founded a religious house and spent his days in study and writing. He died 30 Sept. 420.

Of all Christian Latin writers Jerome most closely approaches the standard of classical purity, when writing his best. He had so absorbed Cicero, Virgil, Horace, and other Latin writers that we hear constant echoes of them in his works. Though he tried hard to 'declassicize' himself, he could not succeed. His pagan master was Cicero; his Christian was Origen. His most important works are his *Chronicle* (partly based on Suetonius) translated from Eusebius and expanded (380–1), a leading authority for dates of ancient historical events; *De Viris Inlustribus* (392), short notices of 135 Christian writers; his revision and translation of the Latin Bible (called since 9th c. *Vulgata [editio]*), and his correspondence, full of interest to students of scripture and to historians of morals. His controversial works are characterized by the foulest abuse. His reputation is due to his immense services to the study of Scripture in the West rather than to saintliness of character.

Migne, *PL* xxii–xxx; newly discovered works, ed. G. Morin, *Anecdota Maredsolana*, vol. iii (3 parts) (Maredsous, 1895–1903); *Chronicle* (J. K. Fotheringham, 1923; R. Helm, 1913). See H. Goelzer, *Étude lexicographique et grammaticale de la latinité de Saint Jérôme* (1884); lives by G. Grützmacher and F. Cavallera.　A. S.

HIEROPHANTES, head of the Eleusinian cult, was the most revered priest in Attica. He was chosen for life from the hieratic family of the Eumolpidae (*see* EUMOL-PUS). He was distinguished by a head-band (στρόφιον) and a long purple-dyed robe ornamented with embroideries. His principal duty was to preside over the Mysteries. Before the celebration he sent forth *spondo-phoroi* to proclaim truce for the period of the Mysteries. He opened the ceremonies with a proclamation that barbarians, murderers, and those defiled must keep away, and he had the right to refuse admittance to others. To the initiates he revealed the secrets of the Mysteries; for this purpose it was necessary that a man of impressive voice should be selected for the office. He was assisted by the *daduchos* (δαδοῦχος, torch-bearer) and hiero-phantess (ἱεροφάντις). He also took part in other State festivals and had several minor public duties. In the Imperial period his only legal name was Hierophantes; on entering office he performed the ceremony of casting his old name into the sea.

J. Joeppfer, *Attische Genealogie* (1889), 44–66; P. Foucart, *Les Mystères d'Éleusis* (1914), 168–91; P. Stengel, *Griechische Kultus-altertümer* (1920), 177–9; G. Méautis, *Les Mystères d'Éleusis* (1934), 35 f. See F. Cumont, *AJArch.* xxxvii (1933), 243 f. on the use of this title in the cults of Dionysus.　J. E. F.

HIEROPOIOI, *see* DELOS, para. 3.

HILARY (*Hilărius*) of Poitiers (d. A.D. 366), after receiving the complete pagan education, in which he failed to find satisfaction for his soul, was converted by Scripture study. He became a protagonist in the conflict with Arianism. Being banished to Asia, he used the opportunity to increase his knowledge of Greek literature. He wrote commentaries on Matthew and on the Psalms, and a 'liber mysteriorum', but the greatest of his works is his *De Trinitate* (in twelve books). He was also the author of three Latin hymns, the earliest we have.

Ed. Migne, *PL* ix–x; partly in *CSEL* xxii (1891), lxv (1916); tr. E. W. Watson, *Post-Nicene Fathers*; A. S. Walpole, *Early Latin Hymns* (1922).　A. S.

HILDESHEIM TREASURE, a collection of Roman silver plate found in 1868 at Hildesheim in south Hanover and now in Berlin; assigned to the Augustan age and possibly booty from the camp of Quintilius Varus in the Teutoburger Wald (A.D. 9). The principal piece is a mixing-bowl covered with floral relief resembling that of the Ara Pacis; there is also a series of drinking-bowls with embossed designs of Minerva, Hercules and the snakes, reliefs of Cybele and Men-Attis, and Bacchic emblems.

E. Pernice and F. Winter, *Der Hildesheimer Silberfund* (1901).　F. N. P.

HIMATION, *see* DRESS, para. 2.

HIMERA (Ἱμέρα), Stesichorus' birthplace, the only independent Greek city on Sicily's northern coast, was founded by Zancle (= Messana), 648 B.C., with mixed Chalcidian and Dorian settlers. Here Theron of Acragas and Gelon of Syracuse overwhelmed the Carthaginians, traditionally on the day of the battle of Salamis (480). After 461 Himera flourished until the vengeful Carthaginians literally obliterated it (408). Thermae (mod. *Termini Imerese*), Agathocles' birthplace, 7 miles to the west, replaced Himera. Although founded by and subject to Carthage, Thermae acquired Himera's refugees and became completely Greek, sometimes even being called inadvertently Himera. It came under Roman dominion after the First Punic War; Augustus made it a *colonia*. Himera lay on a similarly named river (nowadays *Fiume Grande*), which together with another R. Himera (nowadays *Fiume Salso*) long separated Greek from Carthaginian Sicily.

Strabo 6. 272; Hdt. 7. 165 f.; Thuc. bks. 6 and 7; Xen. *Hell.* I. 1. 37; Diod. bks. 11, 13, 14; Cic. *Verr.* 2. 35. J. Bérard, *Bibliogr. topogr.* (1941), pp. 57, 112.　E. T. S.

HIMILCO (1), Carthaginian navigator who explored north-wards four months from Gades but not beyond Brittany (probably before 480 B.C.). His complaints about calms, shoals, tangled seaweeds, which held ships back, have been taken to indicate that he reached also, or was blown to, the Sargasso Sea. But he may never have gone out of sight of Spain and France. Whether he ever visited Britain is unknown.

See Pliny 2. 169; Avienus, *Ora Maritima*, 114–34, 380–9, 406–15; Cary–Warmington, *Explorers*, 31–3; Warmington, *Greek Geography* (1934), 75–7.　E. H. W.

HIMILCO (2), a Carthaginian general. In 406 B.C. he conquered and destroyed Acragas, Gela, and Camarina, but pestilence among his troops forced him to conclude peace, albeit a very favourable one for Carthage. In 397 he resumed operations in Sicily with a small force; in 396 he brought up a big army, and succeeded in conquering the whole western and northern coast. He founded Lilybaeum (q.v.). After a naval victory by his admiral he blockaded Syracuse. But again a dreadful plague broke out in the Carthaginian army. Himilco could not resist the attack of the Syracusans, and was entirely beaten. By agreement with Dionysius he managed to save his citizen-soldiers. After returning home he committed suicide.

Diod. bks. 13, 14. Lenschau, *PW*, s.v. 'Himilkon'; J. B. Bury, *CAH* vi, ch. 5.　V. E.

HIPPALUS (probably 1st c. B.C.), a Greek merchant who discovered the full use of monsoon-winds to and from India. Becoming aware of the general shape of the Arabian Sea and the southward projection of India and the existence of regular winds between Aden Gulf and north-west India, one summer he sailed across from Ras Fartak to the Indus. This resulted in cross-sea voyages even to south India and back by Greeks and vast increase in commerce with India. Hippalus' name was given to the south-west monsoon, to an African cape, and to part of the Arabian sea.

Peripl. M. Rubr. 57; Pliny, 6. 100–6, 172; Ptolemy, *Geog.* 4. 7. 12; *It. Alex.* 110; Warmington, *Indian Commerce*, 44 ff.; W. W. Tarn, *The Greeks in Bactria and India* (1938), 369; J. Thiel, *Eudoxus Van Cyzicus* (in Dutch, 1939); W. Otto and H. Bengtson, *Abhandlungen d. bayerischen Ak. d. Wissenschaften, philosophisch-historische Klasse* 1938, 194 ff.　E. H. W.

HIPPARCHUS (1), younger son of Pisistratus of Athens by his first wife; constantly associated with his elder brother Hippias, under whom he acted as patron of literature and art. Anacreon and Simonides came to Athens at his invitation, and the artistic movements of Pisistratid Athens, which included the first great developments of red-figured vase-painting and corresponding activities in sculpture and architecture, owed much to this frivolous and amorous but cultured prince. His personal vices led to his murder by Harmodius and Aristogiton in 514 B.C.

For bibliography, see HIPPIAS. P. N. U.

HIPPARCHUS (2) (*fl. c.* 260 B.C.), New Comedy poet and (probably) actor. In frs. 1 and 3 foreign drinking-cups (κόνδυ, λαβρώνιος) are mentioned, and in Ζωγράφος, fr. 2, the painter praises professional skill.

FCG iv. 431 f.; *CAF* iii. 272 ff.

HIPPARCHUS (3), greatest of Greek astronomers, born at Nicaea in Bithynia about 190 B.C., made observations between 161 and 126 (the best of them at Rhodes). We possess his commentary *In Eudoxi et Arati phaenomena* (ed. Manitius 1891); but his matured astronomy takes its definitive form in Ptolemy's *Syntaxis*. Hipparchus adhered to the geocentric system, accounting for the movements of the sun, moon, and planets by the hypotheses of epicycles and eccentric circles and combinations of the two. He is the first person known to have made systematic use of trigonometry in his work. He compiled a Table of Chords in a Circle, equivalent to trigonometrical sines. He made great improvements in the instruments used for observations, and compiled a catalogue of 850 stars or more (see F. Boll, *Sphaera* 1903, 83). He gave improved estimates of the sizes and distances of the sun and moon, and calculated the tropic year at 1/300th part of a night and day less than 365¼ days. His calculation of a 'great year' gives for the mean lunar month a figure differing by less than one second from the present accepted figure. His greatest discovery was no doubt that of the Precession of the Equinoxes (Ptol. *Alm.* 7. 1). He wrote a *Geography* (Πρὸς Ἐρατοσθένην), which is lost, as also a book *On things borne down by their weight* (Simpl. *in Cael.* 264 f.). Arabian writers attribute to him a work 'on the art of algebra', which subject he may easily have learnt from Babylon.

PW viii. 1666. T. H.

HIPPASUS, an early Pythagorean, treated fire as the substance out of which the world is made and into which it is from time to time resolved. He is said to have discovered the harmonic mean (the arithmetical and the geometrical mean being already known).

Testimonia in Diels, *Vorsokr.*⁵ i. 107–10. *PW* viii. 1687. W. D. R.

HIPPEIS, Cavalry. Only a few districts in Greece being suitable for horse-breeding, cavalry was rare in the Greek States, and played a very restricted part in warfare. Thessaly produced the best horses, and its ruling aristocracies relied mainly on their cavalry; Boeotia had the next largest force, but one quite subordinate to its infantry. About 450 B.C. Athens organized a body of 1,000 horse, which played an occasional part in warfare; as the men provided their own horses it was a rich man's corps. Like the infantry, they were divided into ten regiments, one from each *phyle*, commanded by *phylarchoi*; at the head of the whole corps were two *hipparchoi*.

In Athens it was also the name of the second of the four census-classes into which the citizens were divided —men possessing property productive of between 500 and 300 *medimnoi* of corn or the equivalent in other produce or money. As the minimum—300 *medimnoi*—was not a high one, many, and probably most, of the citizens in this class served as *hoplitai* (q.v.). See also PENTACOSIO-MEDIMNOI, ZEUGITAI, THETES.

There was a body of 300 *hippeis* at Sparta; but by the sixth century this corps had become an *élite* of infantry. A. W. G.

HIPPIAS (1), tyrant of Athens 527–510 B.C., eldest son and successor of Pisistratus; associated with his brother Hipparchus, he continued his father's policy both at home and abroad, sending out Miltiades II to the Chersonese. But after Hipparchus' murder (514) his rule became harsher, while the Persian conquests in Thrace deprived him of one root of his tyranny, his revenues from the Pangaeum mines, whence perhaps his alleged attempt to devalue the drachma. Attacked by the Spartans under the influence of the Alcmaeonidae, Hippias first defeated them, but when King Cleomenes occupied Athens he retired to Sigeum and Lampsacus, and thence to the court of Darius. He was with the Persian forces at Marathon.

Herodotus, bks. 1, 5, and 6; Thucydides, bks 1 and 6; Aristotle, *Ath. Pol.* C. T. Seltman, *Athens* (1924). P. N. U.

HIPPIAS (2) of Elis, sophist, a younger contemporary of Protagoras (who lived *c.* 481–411), is vividly depicted in Plato's *Hippias Major* and *Hippias Minor*. He acquired great fame and wealth by travelling all over Greece as a teacher and orator, claiming competence in mathematics, astronomy, grammar, poetry, music, and the history of the heroic age, as well as in various handicrafts, and was frequently employed on State business by his native city. That his claims had a solid basis is indicated by the fact that he can probably be identified with the Hippias who discovered the *quadratrix*, the first curve other than the circle to be recognized by the Greek geometers. It was probably discovered in the attempt to solve the problem of trisecting the angle, but was subsequently used in the attempt to square the circle. Of his immense output, the following works are known by name: an elegy on the drowning of a chorus of boys from Messenia; a συναγωγή (probably archaeological in its contents); a Τρωικὸς λόγος; an Ὀλυμπιονικῶν ἀναγραφή; Ἐθνῶν ὀνομασίαι.

Testimonia and frs. in Diels, *Vorsokr.*⁵ ii. 326–34. *PW* viii. 1706. W. D. R.

HIPPIATRICI are veterinarians, more strictly those who treat animals of the farm (Varro, *Rust.* 2. 7. 16: 'De medicina vel plurima sunt in equis et signa morborum et genera curationum . . . itaque ab hoc in Graecia potissimum medici pecorum ἱππιατροί appellati'). The *Hippiatrici* gave medical and surgical treatment in more difficult cases; ordinary diseases were handled by the farmers themselves. The so-called *Corpus Hippiatricorum Graecorum*, collected in the ninth century A.D., has preserved only excerpts dealing with horse-medicine, hardly any of them earlier than the Christian era. The authors mentioned (Apsyrtus, Eumelus, Theomnestus, Anatolius, Hierocles, etc.) are only names. Of older books nothing is known. The treatise of the Athenian Simon (5th c. B.C.) and Xenophon's Π. ἱππικῆς are written by gentlemen-amateurs, interested in horse-breeding or the selection of horses; Ps.-Aristotle, *Historia Animalium* 8. 21 f., treats of animal diseases from a more theoretical point of view.

Within the *Corpus Hippiatricorum* the semeiotics of diseases plays an important part; for 'animals cannot speak'. Cures consist in drugs and diet; the prevention of diseases is considered even more important than their treatment. Magical remedies are rejected, at least by physicians (for farmers cf. *Geoponica* xvi). All these features are reminiscent of human medicine; in fact, conclusions based on the observation of men seem valid for animals and vice versa. The great achievement of veterinary art is certainly dependent on the fundamentally agrarian character of ancient life and the resulting close contact with animals, but also on the fact that animal anatomy had been practised continuously since the fifth century B.C.

TEXTS. *Corpus Hippiatricorum Graecorum*, E. Oder–C. Hoppe (Teubner, 1924–7). Latin translation, *Mulomedicina Chironis*,

E. Oder (Teubner, 1901), the original written about A.D. 400; MSS., G. Björk, *Rev. Ét. Grec.* (1935).

MODERN LITERATURE. General survey, Sir Fr. Smith, *The Early History of Veterinary Literature* i (1919), antiquated in its literary data; survey on literature, G. Sarton, *Isis* (1937). Date of collection not tenth century, as formerly assumed, Hoppe, op. cit. ii, xv; relative chronology of authors, ibid. vi; cf. Björk, *Uppsala Universitets Arsskrift* 1932, 1944, who also proves that Heraclides Tarentinus (2nd c. B.C.) did not write on veterinary medicine. *PW* viii. 1713. **L. E.**

HIPPO, *see* HIPPON.

HIPPO REGIUS (near modern *Bône* in Algeria), a seaport of great antiquity. A quay of megalithic stones marks the site of the original harbour. An early centre of the Numidian kings, it passed to the suzerainty of Carthage and later Rome. It became a *municipium* under Augustus, and later acquired colonial rights. Its fortifications checked Gaiseric's Vandals; its bishop, St. Augustine, inspired the defence. **W. N. W.**

HIPPOBOTUS (*fl.* late 3rd c. B.C.) wrote a philosophico-historical Περὶ αἱρέσεων and Φιλοσόφων ἀναγραφή, used by Diog. Laert. (Frs. catalogued by v. Arnim, *PW*, s.v.)

HIPPOCOON (Ἱπποκόων), in mythology, son of the Spartan or Amyclaean hero Oebalus, and elder brother of Tyndareos (q.v.). He and his many sons drove out Tyndareos and his other brother Icarius from Sparta (Apollod. 3. 124). Later Heracles, offended at some action of Hippocoon, attacked and killed him and his sons (Alcman fr. 15 Bergk). **H. J. R.**

HIPPOCRATES (1), tyrant of Gela, succeeded his brother Cleander (*c.* 498 B.C.). He conquered several cities of east Sicily. In 493 when Samian refugees were invoked by Anaxilas (q.v.) of Rhegium to occupy Zancle, which was under his supremacy, he did not help the Zanclaeans, but came to an agreement with the Samians. He defeated the Syracusans, but was prevented from capturing their city by the intervention of Corinth and Corcyra. Soon after he died in a battle against the Sicels (probably 491). He was the true precursor of the great Sicilian tyrants.

Hdt. 6. 23; 7. 154 f. **V. E.**

HIPPOCRATES (2), the Asclepiad of Cos, a contemporary of Socrates (469–399), though the most famous Greek physician, is yet the one least of all known to posterity. That he was of small stature, that he travelled much, that he died at Larissa is probable; more about his life and his personality cannot be ascertained.

According to Plato, Hippocrates claimed that one cannot understand the nature of the body without understanding the nature of the whole. That means, Plato adds, that one must ask whether the body is simple or multiform and, whatever the answer, then determine what is its power of acting on or being acted upon by other things. Thus, Hippocrates considered the body an organism; medical practice he based on the knowledge resulting from the comprehension of the scattered particulars into one concept and the division of the whole in turn into its natural species, in Platonic language, on dialectic. Diseases he explained, as Aristotle's pupil Meno relates, by assuming that if food is not digested air is excreted from the remnants, invades the body, and causes illness.

Such a conception of medicine is not to be found in any of the so-called Hippocratic books, though these writings, dealing with all subjects of medicine, with prognostics, dietetics, surgery, pharmacology, with health and diseases, show the most widely different attitudes towards medicine. Being inconsistent in themselves they were never attributed to Hippocrates in their entirety; moreover, there is not a single book the authenticity of which was not disputed already in antiquity. Only fractions, and always different fractions, were ascribed to Hippocrates by later centuries according to their constantly varying conception of Hippocrates as a philosopher or a mere practitioner, a dogmatist, an empiric, a sceptic, a believer in the four humours or in the pneuma-theory, a surgeon or a theoretical scientist.

It seems likely that none of the books preserved under the name of Hippocrates is genuine. Their content does not agree with the pre-Alexandrian testimonies. Moreover, the authenticity of hardly any of them seems to be attested by good tradition; in this case one would expect unanimity of the critics at least in regard to one or a few books. It is probable rather that the writings came to Alexandria as the remnants of medical literature which had circulated in the fifth and fourth centuries, but that they were anonymous, as technical literature of that era commonly was. Philological criticism then attributed them to Hippocrates on the basis of what was considered Hippocratic doctrine in the various periods. But since the proof of genuineness depended on logical argument alone, not on tradition or testimonies, no general agreement could be reached.

All that can be said of the identity of Hippocrates, then, is that he is a physician whose works are lost, though he is not a mere name; his method and doctrine are known; he is the founder of scientific medicine in the Platonic sense; moreover, his fame has been recognized since Plato's time. If one asks what Hippocrates meant to the Greeks, the Middle Ages, the Renaissance, what he means even to-day, the answer is that by a complicated historical process he has become the embodiment of the ideal physician. See the references under HIPPOCRATIC COLLECTION.

BIBLIOGRAPHY

TESTIMONIES. Plato: *Phaedrus* 270 c–d; *Anon. Lond. ex Aristotelis Menoniis et aliis medicis eclogae*, H. Diels, Suppl. Arist. iii. 1 (1893), v. 35 f. The meaning of these testimonies is much disputed. The above interpretation is maintained by L. Edelstein, *Problemata* iv (1931); *PW*, Suppl. vi, 1317.

The opposite theory: K. Deichgräber, *Abh. Berl.* (1933); H. as representative of meteorological medicine, pneuma-theory, M. Pohlenz, *Hippokrates* (1938); reviewed L. Edelstein, *AJPhil.* 1940.

WORKS. Corpus Hippocraticum, *Œuvres complètes d'H.*, E. Littré, i–x (1839–61); Opera omnia i–ii, J. Ilberg–H. Kühlewein (Teubner, 1894–1902), not complete; I. L. Heiberg, *CMG* i. 1 (1927); *CMG* to be continued. Separate editions: H. Gossen, *PW* viii. 1811. Besides, Περὶ καρδίης, F. C. Unger, *Mnemosyne* (1923); Περὶ σαρκῶν, K. Deichgräber–E. Schwyzer, *Hippokrates, Über Entstehung u. Aufbau d. menschlichen Körpers* (1935); Ὅρκος, W. H. S. Jones, *The Doctor's Oath* (1924); Ἐπιστολαί, W. Putzger (Gymnasium Wurzen 1914), cf. H. Diels, *Hermes* 1918.

TRANSLATIONS. French: with text, E. Littré. Ch. Daremberg, *Œuvres choisies d'Hippocrate* (1855). English: with text, *Selected Works*, i–iv (Loeb); F. Adams, *The Genuine Works of Hippocrates*, i–ii (1849). German: R. Kapferer, *Die Werke des Hippokrates* (1934 f.).

LITERATURE. Introductions to editions of Littré, Daremberg, Loeb Series. Ch. Singer, *Enc. Brit.*[14], s.v. H.; cf. also Ch. Singer, *Greek Biology and Greek Medicine* (1922). J. Hirschberg, *Vorlesungen über Hippokratische Heilkunde* (1922). More recent literature collected in A. Rehm–K. Vogel, *Exakte Wissenschaften*, Gercke–Norden ii. 5 (1933). **L. E.**

HIPPOCRATES (3) of Chios (*c.* 470–400 B.C.), mathematician, the first person to compose a book of *Elements of Geometry*; his work anticipated much of Euc. bk. 3, as well as some later parts of Euclid. He contributed (*a*) to the problem of squaring the circle, by succeeding in squaring three out of the five 'lunes' which can be squared by means of the straight line and the circle; (*b*) to the problem of doubling the cube by reducing it to the finding of two mean proportionals.

PW viii. 1780. **W. D. R.**

HIPPOCRATIC COLLECTION, *see* HIPPOCRATES (2), ANATOMY AND PHYSIOLOGY, para. 3, MEDICINE, §§ II, IV, V, VI, VII, *and* SURGERY, paras. 2 and 3.

HIPPOCRATIC OATH, *see* MEDICINE, para. 10.

HIPPODAMIA, see PIRITHOUS.

HIPPODAMUS (5th c. B.C.) of Miletus, a Greek architect and town-planner, chiefly celebrated for his association with the introduction into European Greece and Italy of 'gridiron' methods of planning towns. He designed Pericles' Panhellenic colony at Thurii (443 B.C.), and remodelled Piraeus at about the same period. *See* TOWNS.   H. W. R.

HIPPODROME, see CIRCUS.

HIPPOLYTUS ('Ἱππόλυτος, i.e. 'loosed horse', query wild driver or rider?), in mythology, son of Theseus by the Amazon Hippolyte (cf. AMAZONS). Hippolyte being dead, Theseus married Phaedra daughter of Minos (q.v.). Her character varies in Tragedy. Apparently in the (lost) Ἱππόλυτος καλυπτόμενος of Euripides and certainly in the *Phaedra* of Seneca she was a lustful and wholly unscrupulous woman; in the surviving *Hippolytus* of the former she is much more interesting, having intense natural desires but a strong sense of modesty. Theseus being long absent (on his journey to the lower world, according to Euripides), Phaedra conceived a passion for Hippolytus, but he, being honourable (Euripides makes him anti-sexual), repulsed her. She thereupon hanged herself, leaving behind a letter which accused him. Theseus returned, read the letter, and would not believe Hippolytus' protestations of innocence. He banished Hippolytus and used one of the three wishes which his father (Poseidon, in this version; cf. AEGEUS) had given him in asking for his death. Poseidon sent a sea-monster which frightened Hippolytus' horses as he was driving away, and he was thrown from his chariot and dragged to death; Theseus learned the truth from Artemis too late.

In cult Hippolytus is associated with Aphrodite, who had a shrine ἐφ' Ἱππολύτῳ on the Acropolis at Athens; while at Troezen, the place of his death, he had a ritual including laments for him and offerings of hair from girls about to marry (Eur. op. cit. 1423 ff., Paus. 2. 32. 1); the local legend said that he did not die as above described but became the constellation Auriga, but this clearly is not early. Whether he was originally god or hero is disputed (Farnell, *Hero-Cults*, 64 ff.).

The story that Asclepius restored him to life is as old as the *Naupactica* (Apollod. 3. 121); it led to his identification with Virbius (*see* DIANA) at Nemi (see Verg. *Aen.* 7. 765 ff., and Servius on 761).   H. J. R.

HIPPOLYTUS, alternative title for Seneca's tragedy *Phaedra*.

HIPPON, also called **HIPPONAX,** natural philosopher of the Periclean age, probably came from Samos. He treated water or the moist as the principle of all things, reasoning chiefly from observation on the semen of animals. He considered the soul (seated in the brain) to be derived from the semen and to be itself moist, and devoted special attention to the development of the human body from the embryonic state to maturity. Aristotle describes him as a second-rate thinker, probably because of his materialistic bias.

Testimonia and frs. in Diels, *Vorsokr.*[5] i. 385–9. *PW* viii. 1889.   W. D. R.

HIPPONACTEUM, see METRE, GREEK, III (10).

HIPPONAX (*fl.* 540–537 B.C.; Plin. *HN* 26. 11), iambic poet, of Ephesus, whence he was banished and went to Clazomenae. By making the iambic trimeter end with a spondee he invented the σκάζων or χωλίαμβος, and in this metre he wrote satirical, colloquial verse. Some of his fragments are concerned with his love for Arete (frs. 15–22), others with his quarrel with the two sculptors Bupalus and Athenis. The story was that they made a statue which caricatured him and were so distressed by his lampoons that they committed suicide (Suidas s.v. Ἱππῶναξ, cf. frs. 1, 13, 15, 20). He also fell foul of the painter Mimnes (fr. 45). Polemon credited Hipponax with the invention of parody (Ath. 698 b), and frs. 77–8 show the existence of a poem in mock-heroic verse on the adventures of the glutton Eurymedontiades. Hipponax has a vivid, terse style and drew for his vocabulary on life.

Text: E. Diehl, *Anth. Lyr. Graec.* i. 3, pp. 74–98.   C. M. B.

HIPPONAX, see also HIPPON.

HIPPOTHOON, in mythology, son of Poseidon and Alope daughter of Cercyon (Hyg. *Fab.* 187, who calls him Hippothous); eponym of the Attic tribe Hippothoontis (Paus. 1. 5. 2; Harpocration s.v. Ἀλόπη; Hesychius s.v. Ἱπποθοῶντειον).

HIPPOTROPHIA, see LITURGY.

HIRTIUS, AULUS (*cos.* 43 B.C.), since *c.* 54 B.C. an officer of Caesar, who sent him as envoy to Pompey in Dec. 50. In the Civil Wars he served in Spain and the East; in 46 he was praetor and next year governed Gaul. After Caesar's murder he was consul designate, and Cicero induced him to take arms against Antony (43). With Octavian he raised the siege of Mutina, but was killed in the victory, receiving with his colleague Pansa (q.v.) a public funeral. Hirtius added to Caesar's *De Bello Gallico* an eighth book, the preface to which, supported by linguistic arguments (cf. A. Klotz, *Cäsarstudien*, 1910, pp. 180 ff.), proves him author as well of the *Bellum Alexandrinum* (q.v.); his correspondence with Cicero, published in nine books, and the draft for Caesar's *Anticato* have not survived. His writings show little sign of military experience, and suggest that Caesar admired Hirtius, an agreeable epicure, for his literary gifts alone.

O. Seel, 'Hirtius', *Klio*, Beiheft 1935.   G. E. F. C.

HISPANIA, see SPAIN.

HISTIAEUS, tyrant of Miletus, rendered service to Darius during the Scythian campaign (*c.* 512 B.C.). He was presented with Myrcinus near the later city of Amphipolis, but Darius growing distrustful invited him to Susa, where he was kept in honourable confinement. Meanwhile his son-in-law Aristagoras (q.v.) ruled Miletus. They both seem to have co-operated in preparing the Ionian Revolt; the details given by Herodotus, however, are not trustworthy. After the destruction of Sardes (498) he was sent on his own request to pacify Ionia, but tacking between both sides he was unsuccessful. He settled at Byzantium as a mere pirate, and fought on his own account on the islands and in Asia Minor. In 494 or 493 he was captured and crucified. He probably was no more than a restless adventurer and had no large political ideas.

Hdt. bks. 4–6. Swoboda, *PW*, s.v. 'Histiaios'. Cary, *CAH* iv, 213 ff.   V. E.

HISTORIA AUGUSTA, a collection of the lives of thirty Roman emperors from Hadrian to Numerian (A.D. 117–284), dealing also with the Caesars and Usurpers; a gap must have contained the lives of Philip, Decius, Gallus, Aemilian, and part of Valerian (244–53). Whether the lives of Nerva and Trajan have been lost cannot be ascertained, as we do not possess the preface to the work. Aelius Spartianus, Julius Capitolinus, Vulcacius Gallicanus, Aelius Lampridius, Trebellius Pollio, and Flavius Vopiscus appear as the authors, who ostensibly wrote between 284 and 337, as several lives are dedicated to Diocletian, several to Constantine the Great. This date, though defended by H. Peter and by M. Schanz (*Geschichte der römischen Literatur*, iv. 1², 1914, 51 ff.), cannot be accepted, since it has been proved by decisive arguments that the *Historia Augusta* must be of later date. Different results have been obtained by different scholars: thus Mommsen dated it to the time of Diocletian and Constantine, yet believed the collection had been revised twice, first *c.* 330, later in the time of Valentinian and Theodosius; H. Dessau, whose contribution to the problem was great, dated it *c.* 380–95; O. Seeck suggested 409–10; A. von Domaszewski, later sixth century. The whole question has been put on a new level by N. Baynes, who in a careful investigation almost certainly has established that the *Historia Augusta* was written in 362–3 as propaganda for Julian the Apostate.

The *Historia Augusta* must be divided into two groups of different historical value, the first mostly relying on Latin, the second on Greek sources. Group I (till Caracalla), in which an annalistic and a biographical source can be traced, shows, except in the lives of the Co-regents and Usurpers, a good knowledge of the public administration (cf., e.g., the first chapters of *Vit. Hadr.* and *ILS* 308). Group II, which besides Greek sources used the so-called 'Kaiserchronik' of Enman, freely invented facts where reliable information was not obtainable. Thus a great many obviously forged documents (as imperial letters, senatorial decrees) have been incorporated into group II, which is only to be used with the utmost caution; nothing which lacks independent proof must be taken as reliable. The *Historia Augusta* directly utilized the *Caesares* of Aurelius Victor (A.D. 360) but did not consult Eutropius (369–70); only the latter's source, the 'Kaiserchronik', was used. Whether one or more writers composed the *Historia Augusta* cannot be decided upon with certainty; the identity of Pollio and Vopiscus has been established by E. Hohl. The hypothesis was advanced by Baynes (op. cit. 146 f.) that an author (Capitolinus?), perhaps incited by the success of Aurelius Victor, conceived the plan of group I and completed the draft, while another author (Vopiscus?) planned a propaganda book in favour of Julian. After joining forces, they then completed the collection more or less hurriedly, perhaps aided by some friends.

EDITIONS. D. Magie, i–iii (Loeb, 1922–32) with full bibliography; E. Hohl, 2 vols. (Teubner, 1927).

GENERAL LITERATURE. E. Diehl in *PW* (1913), s.v. 'Historia Augusta'; A. Rosenberg, *Einleitung und Quellenkunde zur röm. Geschichte* (1921); N. Baynes, *The Historia Augusta. Its Date and Purpose* (1926); E. Hohl, 'Bericht über die Literatur zu den SHA für die Jahre 1906–15' in Bursian, *Jahresb.* clxxi. 95–144; for 1916–23, cc. 167–216; for 1924–35, cclvi. 127–56. The view of N. Baynes (see above) has been accepted by E. Hohl (*Klio* 1934, 149 ff.) and defended by W. Ensslin (*Klio* 1939, 90 f.) against A. Alföldi (*Röm. Mitt.* 1934, 109 ff.; cf. *Diss. Pan.*, Ser. ii, fasc. 7, 1937, p. 46 n. 104). W. Hartke, 'Geschichte und Politik im spätantiken Rom; Untersuchungen über die Scriptores Historiae Augustae', *Klio*, Beiheft XLV, 1940 (attempts to date S.H.A. to A.D. 394).   F. A. W. S.

HISTORIOGRAPHY, GREEK. The most progressive Greek towns began to keep records from *c.* 700 B.C., which were later embodied in local histories, and to compile lists of kings, eponymous magistrates, etc.; yet it was not from annalistic sources that Greek historiography arose. Historical writing only came into being with the awakening of the Greek mind under the influence of science and rationalism. Following the example of the Ionian physicists and geographers, the so-called *logographoi* (prose writers, as opposed to epic poets) assumed a critical attitude towards the traditions of poetry and mythology, and thus created historical science. The greatest of the *logographoi* to our knowledge, the Milesian Hecataeus, was the first to submit tradition to the test of reason.

2. The followers of Hecataeus (Xanthus, Hellanicus, Scylax, etc.) either confined themselves to local history, or wrote general history (not Greek history exclusively) from a Persian standpoint. A noticeable exception was a contemporary of Hecataeus, Antiochus of Syracuse, who wrote a history of the Greek colonies in southern Italy and Sicily. Herodotus also may be styled a disciple

of Hecataeus. He felt such admiration for the achievements of the Persian kings that he planned to write both a history of the wars they had waged and a geographical survey of their empire. Only at a later stage, when he fell under the spell of the Athenian democracy, did he realize the greatness of the victory of Greece over Persia, and made this the chief subject of his narrative. Even so, his account showed so much sympathy with the vanquished that later Greek writers, probably influenced by Isocratean panhellenism, did not hesitate to brand Herodotus as a friend of the barbarians (cf., for instance, Plutarch's treatise 'On the Malignity of Herodotus').

3. The immediate success of Herodotus was great; but his history was too discursive to satisfy the literary taste of succeeding generations, and too remote from the problems of party politics and of Athenian imperialism which took the place of the Persian Wars as the centre of Greek political interest. These problems produced two new kinds of historical writing: (1) an objective and scientific account of the Peloponnesian War by Thucydides; (2) a violently biased propaganda on the part of Greek conservatives, who cast their programmes into the mould of an idealized or merely fictitious past, and published pamphlets against the Athenian democracy (Pseudo-Xenophon) and its leaders (Stesimbrotus), as well as schemes of fantastic constitutions (Critias, Theramenes, etc.). Meanwhile, a new branch of historical writing, the memoir, was created by Ion of Chios and others.

4. In the fourth century Greek historiography was influenced by the prevailing dissatisfaction with public life, the growing detachment from politics, and a renewed interest in foreign Powers (Persia and, later, Macedonia) which showed signs of becoming the deciding factor in Greek politics. It was the Asiatic Greek Ctesias who was chiefly responsible for the revival of interest in Persian history and civilization. Thucydides himself had prepared the way for these tendencies, for in the final draft of his *History* he had emphasized the bearing of moral ideas on history, and had shown that the subject of historical writing could not be confined to politics alone. His continuators, however, neglected his method of research and his accuracy and obeyed new masters, Socrates, Plato, and Isocrates. The latter, besides imposing new rules of style, taught the principles of panhellenism, while both Socrates and Plato laid down principles of morality as standards of political judgement. Xenophon, Theopompus (both of whom started at the point in the Peloponnesian War where Thucydides had left off), and Ephorus combined the two methods and created a new form of historical writing. Xenophon inaugurated a literary fashion in associating historical memoirs and romance (in the *Anabasis* and the *Cyropaedia*); his political partisanship and eulogistic rhetoric appealed to every class of reader and secured for his *Hellenica* a wholly unmerited influence. Ephorus envisaged the history of the Greek peninsula as a unity, and was the first to write a complete account from the mythical age down to Philip of Macedon. The success of his work, which was to become the 'vulgate' of Greek history, is best attested by the fact that it was never repeated. In his principal work, the *Philippica*, Theopompus accomplished something unique in ancient historical writing. Psychological insight into his protagonist, Philip, whom he saluted as the creator of a new age, moral and political discussions, geographical digressions in which he boasted that he had surpassed Herodotus, made of the *Philippica* the crowning achievement of classical and the forerunner of Hellenistic historiography.

5. A more scientific if less ambitious school of historiography was founded in the fourth century by Cleidemus and Androtion, who wrote local histories of Attica (Ἀτθίδες) based on documentary evidence, and by Aristotle and Philochorus, who also collected and published records of public and religious institutions, games, and literary competitions. These research historians laid the foundations of Hellenistic scholarship and antiquarianism. But the principal historians of the Hellenistic age, disregarding documentary evidence and technique of historical writing, aimed, as a general rule, not at being accurate and learned, but readable. The political and military accounts of the expedition of Alexander the Great written by official authors such as Aristobulus, Nearchus, and Ptolemy (on whom Arrian is chiefly dependent) were soon superseded by the highly rhetorical and romantic stories of Callisthenes, Onesicritus, and Cleitarchus, who founded the 'vulgate' tradition represented by Diodorus and Plutarch, as well as by Justin and Curtius.

6. In the third and second centuries the field of historiography was similarly divided between men of political and military experience, such as Hieronymus, Aratus, and Polybius, and writers who sought to entertain or to excite their readers by a pathetic or realistic style of narrative (Duris, Phylarchus). The latter school was more generally read; because of the prominence which it gave to outstanding personages, it was largely utilized by biographers and ultimately became the chief source of Plutarch.

7. Since no Hellenistic historian, with the exception of Polybius, survived the change in Greek taste and mentality towards the end of the first century B.C., Plutarch is indisputably the author who provides the best survey of the methods, peculiarities, and defects of Hellenistic historiography. Plutarch established the principle that history is the product, not of dry abstractions, such as economics, parties, climate, environment, etc., but of the will and the passions of individuals. Another feature of Plutarch's biographies, the equal measure of importance which he attached to Greek and to Roman personages, illustrates the readiness with which Hellenistic historians perceived the significance of the Roman conquests and influenced Roman culture and historical writing. Greek authors were the first to realize the problem and importance for world-history of the Roman Empire, and through them the Romans became conscious of the mission they were called on to fulfil. A far-sighted interest in the beginnings of Roman history was shown by Timaeus, a Sicilian Greek of the early third century, who coupled the history of his native island with that of Greece and Italy. Polybius, taking up the story where Timaeus left off, at the beginning of Rome's Punic Wars, made it the object of his work to bring home to his compatriots the military, political, and moral advantages which gave the Romans their victory and guaranteed its permanence. The providence of God had imposed on Rome the task of building an empire, and this empire was actually working out to the material and moral benefit of its subjects. This idea Polybius' continuator, Posidonius, also sought to convey; in his view, apparently, the commonwealth of God was reflected in the world-wide Roman republic, and the unity of history was realized in the unity of the Roman Empire. The immense influence exerted by Posidonius is attested by the revival of historical feeling which he promoted. Not only did he become the model and the chief source of universal historians and epitomizers, such as Diodorus and Nicolas of Damascus, and of geographers such as Strabo, but he also suggested inquiries into less familiar fields. It was under his spell that interest in primitive or non-European races was felt and satisfied. In the Augustan age the literary critic, Dionysius of Halicarnassus, turned to explore the origins and early history of Rome. In a similar spirit Flavius Josephus, proceeding along the path paved by Philo, wrote under the Flavians a history of the Jews, in order to show the similarity of their civilization with that of the Greeks and Romans.

8. It is with Plutarch and Arrian, in the first half of the second century A.D., that Greek historiography properly comes to an end. No later author showed any creative power, or interest in philology, or (despite Lucian's treatise 'How to write history') insight into historical technique. But the work of epitomizers, such as Appian of Alexandria, who related the wars of the Republic down to the Augustan Principate, and Dio Cassius, who narrated at length the history of the Republic and Empire down to the dynasty of the Severi, was of importance, for it was through them, and others like them, that knowledge of Greek and Roman antiquity reached Byzantine scholars (e.g. Procopius), and the methods of Greek historiography (either directly or through the mediation of Latin authors, such as St. Augustine and Orosius) were bequeathed to Western thinkers, as elements of a new conception of history which Christianity was called on to promote. See also the articles on individual historical writers and the bibliographies attached.

TEXTS. The fragments of the lost Greek historians are collected (with a Latin translation) in C. Müller, *Fragmenta historicorum graecorum (FHG)*, 5 vols. (1841 ff.), and F. Jacoby, *Die Fragmente d. griech. Historiker (FGrH)* (with German introductions and commentary, 1923 ff.). The papyrus fragments (with the exception of the Hellenica Oxyrhynchia—*see* OXYRHYNCHUS HISTORIAN) have been collected by F. Bilabel (1923).

GENERAL LITERATURE. C. Wachsmuth, *Einleitung in das Studium d. alten Gesch.* (1895); U. v. Wilamowitz-Moellendorff, *On Greek Historical Writing* (1908; the enlarged German text republished in *Reden u. Vorträge* ii², 1926); J. B. Bury, *The Ancient Greek Historians* (1909); B. Croce, *Theory and History of Historiography* (1921), 181 ff.; E. Schwartz, *Charakterköpfe aus der antiken Literatur* (1903); J. Bruns, *Die Persönlichkeit in der Geschichtsschreibung der Alten* (1908); P. Scheller, *De hellenistica historiae conscribendae arte* (1911); B. Lavagnini, *Saggio sulla storiografia greca* (1933); M. Braun, *History and Romance in Graeco-Oriental Literature* (1938); L. Pearson, *The Early Ionian Historians* (1939); G. De Sanctis, *Storia dei Greci* (1939).   P. T.

9. MODERN STUDIES. The study of Greek history as an independent branch of Greek scholarship was a product of the new aesthetic interest in the Greek world evoked by Winckelmann, and of the political interest aroused by the French Revolution. The aesthetic school of Greek historiography was founded by K. O. Müller (*Geschichte der griechischen Stämme und Städte*, 1820), and had its most finished exponent in E. Curtius (*Geschichte Griechenlands*, 1857). The political lessons of Greek history were first set forth systematically by two severe critics of democracy, J. Gillies (*History of Ancient Greece*, 1786) and W. Mitford (*History of Greece*, 1784–1818). Neither of these works attained a high standard of scholarship. Before a truly scientific history of Greece could be written much systematic sifting of evidence was still required. The most important products of this spade work were H. F. Clinton's *Fasti Hellenici* (1824), which laid the foundations of modern Greek chronography, A. Boeckh's *Staatshaushaltung der Athener* (1817), which paved the way for the study of Greek economics, and his *Corpus Inscriptionum Graecarum* (1828 ff.). The *Histories of Greece* by C. Thirlwall (1835–44) and G. Grote (1846–56) were the first to attain modern standards of scientific exactitude; Grote's work, though not free from democratic bias, definitely fixed the main outlines of modern Greek historiography. Hellenistic history (until recently the Cinderella of modern historiographers) first came by its own in the epic narratives of J. G. Droysen (*Geschichte Alexanders des Grossen*, 1833; *Geschichte des Hellenismus*, 1836–43). The general place of Greece in world history was first set forth clearly by Ed. Meyer (*Geschichte des Altertums*, 1884 ff.).

For more recent works, see the bibliography s.v. GREECE (HISTORY).   M. C.

HISTORIOGRAPHY, ROMAN. The foundations of Roman historical writing lie not solely in the pontifical tradition but in Hellenistic historiographical theory. The first Roman historians, Fabius Pictor, Cincius Alimentus,

Postumius Albinus, and C. Acilius, wrote in Greek to justify their free institutions and confederate policy to the Greek world upon which they were imposing their protection. Their work thus comes under the class not of annalistic chronicles but of the Hellenistic episodic histories. Political writers, not professional historians, *narratores*, not *exornatores rerum*, they fell short of Cicero's Isocratean standards (*De Or.* 2. 51–2; *Leg.* 1. 5), but their quality is reflected in the ἐπιστόλια of Scipio Africanus (Polyb. 10. 9) and Scipio Nasica (Plutarch, *Aem.* 15 ff.). Their tradition inspired Polybius to analyse and set in its perspective the imperial rise of Rome, and their work was continued in Latin, in its same form, by Cato in his *Origines* (*see* ANNALS).

2. It was Cato, after Ennius, who inspired national historiography in Rome. The 'early' annalists, Cassius Hemina and Calpurnius Piso, began the systematic reconstruction of Roman history; and the study of pontifical law, cult and constitutional antiquities, public and private law, reflects the growth of historical consciousness, influenced by Stoic thought, which led to the publication of the *annales maximi* (*c.* 123 B.C.). This definitive work of documentary reconstruction and formal arrangement founded the annalistic historiographical γένος; the influence of Hellenistic theory furthered its development. Cn. Gellius probably first applied the rhetorical Isocratean methods to elaboration of the records; certainly the Sullan annalists, Valerius Antias and Claudius Quadrigarius, by free legalistic reconstruction and conventional rhetorical elaboration, fully established the literary form, which was accepted by Livy and adapted by the Imperial annalists and Tacitus.

3. In contemporary historiography Polybius' work was continued by Posidonius, and his methods followed by Sempronius Asellio. Aemilius Scaurus and Rutilius Rufus wrote autobiography, Catulus and Sulla left ὑπομνήματα. Coelius Antipater introduced the historical monograph and Asianic style; Hellenistic biography grew on the tradition of the *laudatio funebris* (q.v.). It may be said that all the Hellenistic historiographical γένη were established in Rome, with increasing literary independence, by the time of Sulla.

4. Sisenna practised the dramatic Peripatetic art of Cleitarchus in his work on Sulla. Annalistic history continued with Macer, the democrat, and Tubero, the Caesarian. Contemporary history is represented by names from Cn. Aufidius to Tanusius Geminus. Antiquarian studies flourished with Nigidius Figulus and Varro, and Cornelius Nepos shows the advance of biography. Caesar's *commentarii* represent the Hellenistic military ὑπομνήματα in Latin. The Caesarian and anti-Caesarian writings, the *Catones* and *Anticatones*, mark the maturity of political propaganda.

5. It is in this setting that Sallust wrote and Cicero defined the tasks of Roman historiography. Sallust represents an Atticist standpoint, associating Catonian archaism with Thucydidean *severitas*, and joining to rhetorical device the syntactical aggressiveness of his style. Cicero held the Hellenistic view that history, an 'opus oratorium maxime', should be based on the rhetorical Isocratean canons represented by Theopompus. These theoretical principles reflect their different historical purpose, Cicero justifying the tradition with dignity, Sallust attacking present corruption against the background of the past. The issue in thought and in mode was defined, and Livy's Augustan idealism could follow Cicero, Tacitus draw inspiration from Sallust.

6. Augustan historiography marks the balance of Roman tradition and Hellenistic influence. Memoirs dealing with the end of the Republic are common, from Augustus himself to Tiro. Asinius Pollio represents Atticist theory. Livy, on the one side, glorified the Republican tradition; Pompeius Trogus, on the other, set Rome in her Hellenistic perspective. To the Isocratean rules Livy adds elaborate rhetorical and Peripatetic effects, practising the fine psychological interpretation which had come to maturity in Rome from Hellenistic studies. Poetical colour makes his opening books the prose epic of Rome; the later books enshrine the annalistic tradition and adapt the form to contemporary history. Trogus used Peripatetic methods, avoiding direct rhetoric.

7. The Augustan achievements were final in their own field. Fenestella might add antiquarian interest, L. Arruntius Sallustian style to the annalistic tradition, but Livy was followed, after Velleius Paterculus, only by the Epitome and its dependent writers. Trogus, unchallenged, was joined by Curtius Rufus, but Thallus, L. Cornelius, Bocchus, and Vibius Maximus led merely to Justin's Epitome. After the Republican work of Cremutius Cordus, however, the Imperial annalists appear: Aufidius Bassus, the Elder Pliny continuing his work, the Elder Seneca, and Bruttedius Niger; then Cluvius Rufus, Vipstanus Messalla, and Fabius Rusticus. Imperial rule increased biography, not only of the emperors but of their administrators, and memoirs were common. *Exempla* were published by Valerius Maximus and Hyginus. Ethnography and geography entered into history. Rhetorical theory developed in declamation; style passed through an Asianic stage to Atticism; and historical drama, perhaps, strengthened the appeal of dramatic historiography.

8. Thus the Roman historiographical γένη took on fresh life in this century, and Tacitus adapted them in unity of conception and stylistic mastery. Historical in his treatment of rhetorical theory, biography, and ethnography, he pressed these in their turn into the service of history. Roman in his central theme, traditional in accepting the annalistic conventions, he strove for dramatic concentration, pathetic and horrific description, and psychological depth, in the full maturity of Peripatetic art; to rhetorical effect he added the *severitas* and syntactical aggressiveness of Sallust. Drawing on historical tradition and historiographical technique, he created a work of original genius.

9. Imperial biography attained its highest point with Suetonius, but after Marius Maximus degenerated to the *Historia Augusta*. Only Greek historiography now had life; Roman historiography entered the age of epitome and chronicle, and style became archaistic. The handbooks of Ampelius and Julius Obsequens, chronographical work, the *breviaria* of Florus, Granius Licinianus, Aurelius Victor, Eutropius, and Festus, lead to Hieronymus and Orosius. Ammianus Marcellinus alone shows historical quality in his continuation and imitation of Tacitus, but his technique and style, for all their power, betray his historiographical isolation. Yet the Gothic history of Cassiodorus, himself a chronicler, shows that historiography might revive under fresh historical inspiration.

BIBLIOGRAPHY

See ANNALS and the various writers mentioned; and HISTORIOGRAPHY, GREEK, for Hellenistic influences.
G. De Sanctis, *Stor. Rom.* i. 16; H. Peter, *Wahrheit und Kunst, Geschichtsschreibung und Plagiat im klass. Altertum* (1911); F. Leo, *Gesch. der röm. Lit.* i (1913), 259; A. Rosenberg, *Einleitung und Quellenkunde zur röm. Geschichte* (1921); E. Norden, *Die Antike Kunstprosa* (2nd ed. 4th reprint, 1923); W. Kroll, *Studien zum Verständnis der röm. Literatur* (1924), 331; T. Frank, *Life and Literature in the Roman Republic* (1930), 169; M. Gelzer, *Hermes* 1934, 46; F. Altheim, *Epochen der röm. Geschichte* ii (1935), 305; F. W. Walbank, *CQ* 1945, 15.   A. H. McD.

10. MODERN STUDIES. The systematic study of Roman history first arose out of the interest of the Roman Church for the Roman Empire. Its first notable product was the *Histoire des empereurs romains* by a Jesuit scholar, Lenain de Tillemont (1700–38). This treatise was based on a full and critical use of the ancient literature, but contented itself with a bald narrative of events. Tillemont's book served as a foundation for E. Gibbon's *History of the*

Decline and Fall of the Roman Empire (1776–88), a work which remains unsurpassed in its firm grasp and clear exposition of Late-Roman politics and culture. The French Revolution diverted interest to Rome's republican beginnings. The early history of Rome (to *c.* 250 or 200 B.C.) was studied in a sympathetic but critical spirit by B. G. Niebuhr (*Römische Geschichte*, 1811–12), who made the first serious attempt to sift fact from legend in the ancient sources, and by T. Arnold (*History of Rome*, 1838–40). The Republican period as a whole received an authoritative exposition in the *Römische Geschichte* of T. Mommsen (1854–6), which rivalled Gibbon's *Decline and Fall* in its penetrating and comprehensive analysis of Roman life and politics, and in its brilliance of narrative. Mommsen subsequently produced innumerable researches on points of detail, and several systematic treatises on special aspects of Roman History, notably the *Römisches Staatsrecht* (1871–87) and the *Römisches Strafrecht* (1899), which remain fundamental for the study of Roman public law. In addition, he initiated and directed the international enterprise of the *Corpus Inscriptionum Latinarum* (1863 ff.), and in *The Provinces of the Roman Empire from Caesar to Diocletian* (Engl. Transl. 1886) he laid the foundation of regional study of the Empire's component parts. All later writers on Roman History are disciples of Mommsen. The only large field in which he left much pioneer work to be done was that of economics. This field has recently undergone systematic exploration by T. Frank (*Economic History of Rome*[2], 1927) and M. Rostovtzeff (*Social and Economic History of the Roman Empire*, 1926).

For more recent works, see the bibliography **s.v.** ROME (HISTORY).
M. C.

HISTRIA, *see* ISTRIA (2).

HOMER. The Greeks, with insignificant exceptions, believed that both the *Iliad* and the *Odyssey* were composed by Homer, but they had no certain or accepted facts about his life. His date was very variously given, as contemporary with the Trojan War (Tzetz. *Chil.* 12. 183), soon after it ([Plut.] *Vit. Hom.* A 5), at the time of the Return of the Heraclidae (? Crates Theb. ap. Tatianum *Ad Gr.* 31), at the time of the Ionian wandering (Philostr. p. 194. 9), in the middle of the ninth century (Hdt. 2. 53), and 500 years after the Trojan War (Theopomp. Hist. ap. Clem. Al. *Strom.* 1. 117). This great divergence indicates that external evidence was lacking and that the Greeks knew little more than we do. If we try to date the poems by internal evidence, some facts emerge. Archaeology gives ambiguous results, but forbids an early date, since the sitting statue of *Il.* 6. 302–3 cannot be earlier than the eighth century, the shield of Agamemnon in *Il.* 11. 19 ff. may be even later, and the use of the phalanx in warfare (*Il.* 13. 131 ff.) may be later still. Even if we regard these passages as later corrections or additions, the *Iliad*, though it contains echoes of much earlier times in the *Shield of Achilles*, certainly does not describe the culture of the Mycenaean age as a contemporary document should. Literary evidence gives at least a *terminus ad quem* in the seventh century, when Terpander is said to have recited Homer at Sparta and echoes of him are to be seen in Tyrtaeus (frs. 6–7, 21–8 from *Il.* 22. 71–6, fr. 8. 29–34 from *Il.* 16. 215–17), Semonides (fr. 29 from *Il.* 6. 146), and Alcman (fr. 1. 48 from *Il.* 9. 124, fr. 73 from *Il.* 3. 39). We may even place the date earlier than this, since Archilochus (*c.* 700 B.C.) seems also to give variations on Homeric phrases at fr. 65 (*Od.* 22. 412), fr. 41 (*Od.* 14. 228), fr. 38 (*Il.* 18. 309), and though the date of Hesiod is not known, he seems to be later than Homer, since *Op.* 159–60 may owe something to *Il.* 12. 23 and *Th.* 340 ff. to *Il.* 12. 20 ff. We may then perhaps place Homer before 700 B.C., though we must admit that there is always a possibility of his text having been altered and the indications of date being additions. But Theopompus

may not have been far from the truth in making Homer a contemporary of Archilochus.

2. His place was a matter of dispute in antiquity. Of the different possibilities Chios and Smyrna are best supported. Chios was regarded as his home by Semonides of Amorgos (fr. 29), and it was there that the Homeridae lived and maintained his memory (schol. Pind. *Nem.* 2. 1), while Smyrna was supported by Pindar (fr. 279). The predominance of Ionic elements in Homeric language points to Ionia as Homer's home, and this is supported by hints in the poems, notably by similes which mention the Cayster (*Il.* 2. 459 ff.), the Icarian Sea (ibid. 144 ff.), and a Maeonian or Carian woman (*Il.* 4. 141–2), and by a certain geographical acquaintance with the Troad, the weeping Niobe on Sipylus (*Il.* 24. 614 ff.), and the towns of the Aeolic peninsula. Since in certain places (*Il.* 9. 4–5, 11. 305–8) he implies a shore facing west, he may have the Asiatic coast in his mind. On the other hand, in the *Odyssey* there is certainly some, not always exact, information about the islands round Ithaca and the Peloponnese, which may be due to personal acquaintance or simply to hearsay. He seems on the whole to have lived in Ionia, since his apparent ignorance of the Dorians in the Peloponnese indicates that he knew little of it.

3. Other traditions of his life, embodied in the ancient *Lives*, are almost without value. The episodes in them are usually to be traced back to episodes in the *Iliad* and *Odyssey*. The tradition that he was blind is better founded, since bards were often blind and the Homeric *Hymn to Apollo* 172 speaks of a blind poet in Chios and may refer to him. His condition may well have resembled that of the bards in the *Odyssey* who earned a livelihood by singing lays at the courts of princes. In the *Iliad* and *Odyssey* the poet says next to nothing about himself. This may imply that he was of a social position inferior to that of his patrons, and belonged to the class of δημιοεργοί (*Od.* 17. 383). His tastes may to some extent be seen in his similes, which are drawn from contemporary life and show an interest in humble people quite unlike the heroes and heroines of his poems, in handicrafts and agricultural pursuits, in animals and birds.

4. Our ignorance of Homer's date, place, and life has led to scepticism about his existence. It has been thought that the poems are collections of lays put together from different sources, or original poems much expanded and altered, or single examples of poems of which many different variants existed. The early arguments for such views, based on the belief that no man could have composed poems of such a length before writing was known, have now been dispelled by our knowledge of what memory can do when writing is not familiar. Other arguments, such as the presence of repetitions and inconsistencies, are less powerful when we realize that such poems were meant not to be read but to be heard, and that in such conditions the poet cannot be so exact about details as he can when he is helped by a written text. Still other arguments based on the varying treatment of the gods, of moral questions, of history and mythology, do not necessarily prove variety of authorship, since it is at least possible that Homer belonged to an old tradition which provided him with a very mixed collection of materials, on which he drew freely and not always critically.

5. On the other hand, the *Iliad* and the *Odyssey* each shows in itself the marks of a controlling and unifying poet. In the *Iliad* the whole poem hangs on the wrath of Achilles, and though many other episodes are introduced, this gives a unity to the whole. The last book picks up the themes of the first and shows the end of the wrath with which the poem began. The *Odyssey* shows what Ithaca was before Odysseus returned and then his return with his triumphant conduct of it. In each poem the characters are admirably consistent, convincing, and even elaborated—a trait unlikely if many hands have been at work. In each poem the language, rich, complex, and traditional though it is, seems to show no real differences between one section and another. The use of abstract nouns, of the digamma, of Aeolic forms, of patronymics, all seem to be spread equally through the whole work. Any serious omission of a long passage from either poem in the belief that it is a later addition seriously impairs the structure and makes the plot less easy to understand. In both poems devices such as similes are used on a consistent plan, revealing the individual tastes of the poet and providing a variety where it is most needed in the narrative. Each poem shows that it is a whole and suggests that even if many hands have gone to its making, most of the poets preceded the actual author, who made use of their work but harmonized it according to his own ideal of composition.

6. These considerations do not prove that the *Iliad* and *Odyssey* were necessarily composed by the same poet. This has been doubted even by some who believe that each is itself the work of a single man. The Alexandrian grammarians who held this view were known as the 'Chorizontes'. There are certainly differences between the two poems, though not all are equally important. Much may be explained by differences of theme and of setting. The *Iliad* deals with war, the *Odyssey* with peace; therefore the social structure of life at Troy is different from that at Ithaca. The *Iliad* with its long accounts of battles is more monotonous than the *Odyssey*; therefore it uses many more similes to diversify its narrative. Many words appear in one poem and not in the other, but that is to be expected from two stories so different. The *Odyssey* has an element of fairy-tale almost lacking in the *Iliad*, but that is natural in telling of a man's wanderings at the ends of the world. It places its emphasis on wits, while the *Iliad* places its on courage, but that does not mean that the poems were written in different ages; for a heroic age may well admire cunning as much as bravery, and in any case the cunning of Odysseus is already manifest and admired in the *Iliad*.

7. The *Odyssey* certainly looks as if it were composed to be a sequel to the *Iliad*. The events which fall between the two stories, the Wooden Horse, the sack of Troy, the returns of the Achaeans, the murder of Agamemnon, are all introduced, so that we have in effect a continuous narrative. Important characters of the *Iliad* who have no essential part in the story of Odysseus—Helen, Menelaus, Nestor, even Achilles and Aias—appear at one point or another, before or after death, in the *Odyssey*. The *Odyssey* closes with a second νέκυια in which the great ghosts of Troy make their last bow on the stage as if to make a finale to both poems. Moreover, these characters preserve their individuality from one poem to the other; Odysseus, though depicted on a far greater scale, is recognizably the same man that he was in the *Iliad*, Nestor is no less garrulous and reminiscent, Helen still shows wisdom learned in suffering. Both poems, too, are similar in structure, though the *Odyssey* shows an advance in its treatment of events which take place contemporaneously. In both we find similarities of technique, such as the way in which an action is first suggested and then postponed, the abrupt transition from one episode to another, the rapidity with which the final crisis comes when it comes, the slackening of tension after the crisis, and the quiet end. In both we find repeated lines and even passages which suggest that the poet, well instructed in his formulae, felt no qualms about using them when they suited his need. Compared even with Hesiod or the *Homeric Hymns* the *Iliad* and *Odyssey* seem to belong to a world of their own and suggest that they are the work of a single poet.

8. On the other hand, there are, undeniably, serious differences between the two poems. The *Odyssey*, at least in its second half, seems to lack the rapidity and force of the *Iliad*. The poet does not lead to his crisis with the same directness, and in the handling of it there is not the same immediacy of effect. The difference may of course be due to advance of years; Homer may have begun to fail in his later poem (as [Longinus] suggests, *Subl.* 9). Again, in the *Odyssey* the gods are not what they were in the *Iliad*. Certain episodes show the old gay touch, but their position is, on the whole, different, and in the relations between Odysseus and Athene we may perhaps see a new view of the ways of the gods with men. Finally, the *Odyssey* seems to take a different view of life from the *Iliad*. The Suitors are lower characters than anyone except Thersites, and their end, deserved though it may be, is conceived in a harsher and less tragic temper than that in which Achilles revenges the death of Patroclus on Hector. These differences can be explained either as the result of passing years on a single poet or as the work of a second poet who admired and imitated the poet of the *Iliad* but did not see eye to eye with him on all points. The first alternative seems more likely because the differences are outweighed by the similarities and are at least explicable if we assume the *Odyssey* to be the later of the two poems.

9. Even if we admit that a single poet composed both poems, we must also admit that he owed a very great deal to tradition. The extent of his debt may be seen in the many stories which he mentions but does not elaborate, showing that they were already known, in his use of standard epithets for his characters, who have often grown beyond them, in his inconsistent treatment of the gods, now as real moral forces, now as figures of comic relief, in the episodic character of his narrative, a survival from the method of short narrative lays, in his language, which was never a spoken tongue, but, being drawn from different dialects and full of archaisms, artificial lengthening, synonyms, and alternative forms, shows the marks of many years given to its making. Above all, this traditional character is apparent in the important fact that Homer composes not with words but with groups of words or formulae. In almost every line we find a set of words that occurs elsewhere, often many times. This technique belongs to improvised verse. The poet who improvises must learn formulae before he can practise his art, and though there is no reason to believe that the *Iliad* and *Odyssey* were ever improvised, it is clear that their technique is derived from improvisation. Of these formulae many must have existed before Homer, and at times we may see traces of his indebtedness when a phrase is not perfectly suited to its context. But such formulae were no doubt altered and new formulae invented, and there is no reason to think that Homer took over all his from other poets. In fact the success of many parts of his poetry is unthinkable if he confined himself entirely to traditional phrases. So, too, in his plots we may find hints of an earlier treatment which is not his. In the poems which lay behind the *Iliad* Achilles seems actually to have mutilated Hector, but Homer avoids this and makes his hero give back the dead body to Priam. In the stories of Odysseus there must have been variants of the means by which he was recognized; in the *Odyssey* these are combined and worked into a single story. These earlier versions were obliterated by Homer and quite forgotten, but it seems next to certain that he used them and improved on them.

10. Even if Homer composed the *Iliad* and *Odyssey*, we cannot assume that we have them just as he left them. There are certainly interpolations in them. Some are not serious; others, like passages in *Od.* 11, may easily be detected. But it is quite possible that there are still others, though there is no sure way to mark them. The language, too, has certainly been altered from its first appearance, notably by the substitution of Attic forms due to the recitation of the poems at Athens and to the fact that Athens was the centre of the Greek book-trade. Other changes are due to the misunderstanding of archaic words and their distortion or replacement by others. And the text may have suffered more than this. If it was preserved, as is possible, in the oral tradition of the Homeridae, it cannot but have suffered seriously in the centuries between Homer's death and the appearance of the first texts in the time of Pisistratus. Even if it was written down much earlier and preserved with reverence as a sacred book, it may still have suffered serious changes. In any case it is not as we have it that the author left it, and we cannot confidently restore it to its original purity.

For the allegorical interpretations of Homer, *see* ALLEGORY.

BIBLIOGRAPHY

TEXT. Iliad, ed. T. W. Allen (1931), with prolegomena and full apparatus; Odyssey, ed. T. W. Allen (O.C.T., 1906).
COMMENTARY. Iliad. W. Leaf² (1900–02); Odyssey, bks. 1–12, W. W. Merry and J. Riddell (1886), 13–24, D. B. Monro (1901).
CRITICISM. F. A. Wolff, *Prolegomena ad Homerum²* (1876); K. Lachmann, *Betrachtungen über Homers Ilias²* (1874); P. Cauer, *Grundfragen der Homerkritik²* (1921–3); E. Drerup, *Das Homerproblem in der Gegenwart* (1921); G. Finsler, *Homer* (1914–18); C. Rothe, *Die Ilias als Dichtung* (1910); id., *Die Odyssee als Dichtung* (1911); U. von Wilamowitz-Moellendorff, *Die Ilias und Homer* (1916); J. A. Scott, *The Unity of Homer* (Univ. of California Press, 1921); C. M. Bowra, *Tradition and Design in the Iliad* (1930); W. J. Woodhouse, *The Composition of Homer's Odyssey* (1930); S. E. Bassett, *The Poetry of Homer* (Univ. of California Press, 1938).   C. M. B.

HOMERIC HYMNS, *see* EPIC POETRY, GREEK, para. 6.

HOMERIDAE, rhapsodes, who spread the knowledge of Homer's poems in Greek lands. The title was originally confined (Acusilaus and Hellanicus cited by Harpocration, s.v. Ὁμηρίδαι) to Homer's descendants, who recited his poems by hereditary right, but was afterwards extended to others who were not related to him (schol. Pind. *Nem.* 2. 1). They were supposed to have special knowledge of Homer (Pl. *Resp.* 599 e; Isocr. 218 e; cf. Pl. *Ion*, 530 c), sometimes contained in esoteric verses, ἀπόθετα (Pl. *Phdr.* 252 b–c). Analogy with other Greek families and guilds confirms the early and reliable authorities against critical doubts, ancient and modern.

T. W. Allen, *Homer, the Origins and Transmission* (1924), 42–50.   W. F. J. K.

HOMERUS LATINUS, *see* ILIAS LATINA.

HOMICIDIUM, *see* PARRICIDIUM.

HOMONOIA, agreement or concord between the members of a community. The bitter experience of faction in Greek States led to much theoretical praise of concord, also from early Hellenistic times to a certain amount of cult (altar at Syracuse, Livy 24. 22. 13; at Olympia, Paus. 5. 14. 9; inscriptional dedications, see Stoll in Roscher's *Lex.* i. 2701, 30 ff.), also quite common occurrence on coins (ibid. 2702, 31 ff.), which may or may not connote actual cult in the States issuing them. Hence the cult was occasionally projected into remote antiquity, as Apoll. Rhod. 2. 717 ff., where the foundation of a shrine of Homonoia is ascribed to the Argonauts (q.v.). No doubt some of the dedications, etc., refer at least equally to Concordia (q.v.).

Cf. in general Eiliv Skard, *Euergetes-Concordia* (1932), 67 ff.; W. W. Tarn, *Alexander the Great and the Unity of Mankind* (1933).   H. J. R.

HONESTIORES were persons belonging to the upper classes of Roman society. A definition of this term is not to be found in the works of Roman jurists, nor is there a list of the categories of citizens possessing this distinctive qualification. Their counterpart were the *plebei, humiliores, tenuiores*. In Imperial times, especially from the third century onwards, they enjoyed a privileged position in criminal law, as being subject to milder forms of punishment for some crimes, in particular where the lower classes and slaves were liable to capital punishment. The *poena capitis* was applied to them only in quite exceptional cases, and could never be carried out by crucifixion or *bestiis obicere*. There was the same restriction on corporal punishment (*fustibus non subiciuntur*), heavy forced labour in mines (*in metallis*), torture in criminal procedure, and the like. They had also some privileges in procedure on appeal. These exceptional rules were applied in some cases to all *honestiores* generally, in others only to certain classes, (*decuriones, veterani*, etc.).   A. B.

HONESTUS of Corinth, author of ten epigrams in the Anthology and eleven lately discovered in inscriptions in Boeotia, was contemporary with the Emperor Gaius (c. A.D. 40). The inscriptions are polite ceremonial greetings: the others are mild, faintly pedagogic (*Anth. Pal.* 11. 230) conceits.

C. Cichorius, *Röm. Stud.* viii. 11 (1922).   G. H.

HONEY (*mel*, μέλι), the chief sweetener known to the ancients, who understood apiculture (cf. Varro, *Rust.* 3. 16) and appreciated the honey-producing qualities of flowers and localities. Hymettus honey was famed for pale colour and sweet flavour; Sicilian (particularly Hybla) as proverbially good; Corsican, harsh and bitter; Pontic, poisonous, inducing madness. Honey was used in cookery, confectionery, and medicine, and valued for its preservative qualities. Its religious associations derive from the notion that it is a *ros caelestis*, which bees gather in the upper air as well as from flowers (cf. Aristotle, *Hist. An.* 5. 22, p. 553ᵇ29). Poets repeat the fancy that it dripped from trees in the Golden Age. As celestial it possesses mystic virtues, was used in libations for the dead (see S. Eitrem, *Opferritus*, 1915, passim), and in literature is given to infants to impart numinous qualities, as wisdom or eloquence (see H. Usener, *Kleine Schriften* iv (1913), 398–417). Bees fed the infant Plato with honey (Cicero, *Div.* 1. 78: cf. A. S. Pease, ad loc.), and Zeus was called Melissaios from a similar legend of his Cretan birth. And see W. H. Roscher, *Nektar und Ambrosia* (1883); W. Robert-Tornow, *De apium mellisque apud veteres significatione et symbolica et mythologica* (1893); W. Telfer, *JTS* xxviii (1927), 167 ff. *See also* BEE-KEEPING, MELISSA.   W. T.

HONORARIUM, *see* ADVOCATUS.

HONOS and VIRTUS. These abstractions had three temples in Rome; one outside the Porta Collina (Cicero, *Leg.* 2. 58), to Honos; one *ad portam Capenam*, dedicated originally to Honos by Q. Fabius Maximus Verrucosus in 234 B.C., then enlarged into a double temple to both by M. Marcellus (Livy, 25. 40. 2–3; 27. 25. 7–9; 29. 11. 13), because two deities could not be worshipped in one *cella*; one somewhere near the Capitolium, built by Marius after defeating the Cimbri and Teutones (Platner–Ashby, p. 259, q.v. for further particulars); cf. Wissowa, *RK*, 149 ff.   H. J. R.

HOPLITES (ὁπλῖται) were the regular type of heavy-armed infantry in the Greek city States. Citizens who could not maintain horses, yet had sufficient property to equip themselves with full personal armour, were required to serve as hoplites. In the later fifth century at Athens the hoplite qualification was regarded as equivalent to the old Solonian class of the *zeugitai* (q.v.). The body-armour of the hoplite consisted of a helmet with nasal and cheek pieces, a breastplate, and greaves of bronze. The heavy bronze shield was his chief defence; it was elliptical in shape and was usually secured on the left arm and hand by leather bands (ὄχανα). The iron sword was short and straight; the spear, some 9 feet long, was held in the hand for thrusting. When in proper formation on their appropriate terrain hoplites were able to sustain effectively the assaults of archers or cavalry. But they were slow and heavy in attack, and when in difficult country or scattered they were easily defeated in detail.

J. Kromayer and G. Veith, *Heerwesen und Kriegführung der Griechen und Römer* (1928), 50 ff.   H. W. P.

HORACE, see HORATIUS (2) FLACCUS.

HORAE, goddesses of the Seasons in Greek mythology. In Homer the Horae roll aside the veil of clouds from the gate of Olympus (*Il.* 5. 749; 8. 393), which is perhaps a mythological expression of the belief that H. could give rain or heat. Hesiod (*Th.* 900) makes H. daughters of Justice and gives to them individual names, *Eunomia* (Good Government), *Dike* (Right), and *Eirene* (Peace). Commonly H. are, however, regarded as goddesses who come with the changes of seasons and make flowers and plants grow. Their names and number vary from region to region. In Attica these names were *Thallo, Karpo,* and perhaps *Auxo,* referring to growth, flowering, and ripeness of vegetation (C. Robert, *Comment. in hon. Mommsen,* 143). These H. of fertility had a place on the lips of peasants (Ar. *Pax* 1168). The Hesiodic H., who stand for ethical and political ideas, are mentioned in some later inscriptions (Kaibel, *Epigr. Gr.* 1110). Because H. have the power to make things and beings grow and because the gifts of H. are pleasant, they are welcome guests at marriages and births of Olympians and heroes (Hes. *Op.* 73; *Hymn. Hom. Ven.* (vi), 1; Pind. *Pyth.* 9. 60; Paus. 2. 13. 3; Moschus 2. 164). When Hellenic religion develops to a more unified and intellectual state, the Seasons, whether three or four, are also called *Horae.* Spring, Summer, Autumn, Winter all bring their proper blessings and are depicted in art with appropriate attributes. The regularity of seasons was a favourite argument of Greek philosophers for the existence of a divine world order (Plato, *Epin.* 977 b; Von Arnim, *SVF* i, no. 499; cf. Aratus, *Phaen.* 550). Seasons appear in Roman houses and on Roman tombs (F. Cumont, *Rev. Arch.* 1916, ii, p. 1). H. are associated with many deities, e.g. Demeter, Kora, Pan, Apollo, Dionysus, Aphrodite, and Helios, but only as subordinate companions. Philochorus describes some details of the cult of H. in Athens (ap. Athen. 2. 38; 14. 656). They were worshipped also in Argos and Olympia. In art, Horae are first shown on the François vase, without any individualizing attributes, whereas the later Season-Horae are carefully distinguished from each other by attributive plants and animals.

P. Herrmann, *De Horarum figuris* (1887); J. A. Hild in Dar.-Sag., s.v.; A. Merlin, *Monuments Piot* 1934, 133; M. P. Nilsson, *Primitive Time Reckoning* (Lund, 1920); L. R. Farnell, *The Cults of Greek City States* iv (1907), 130.   G. M. A. H.

HORATII were, according to a popular tradition (probably independent of Greek literary influence), three Roman brothers, two of whom were killed in combat with the Curiatii, three Alban brothers, while the survivor was tried, but acquitted on appeal, for the murder of his sister Horatia. An ancient ritual celebrated at the *Tigillum sororium* and traditionally explained as a commemoration of Horatia probably gave rise to the story, unless it was invented as a precedent for the institution of the *provocatio ad populum* (see PROVOCATIO).   P. T.

HORATIUS (1) COCLES, a Roman who traditionally held back the Etruscans from the wooden Sublician bridge until it could be demolished, and then, despite his wounds, swam across the Tiber to safety. Polybius, however, records (6. 55) that Horatius was drowned. The story is probably an aetiological myth. Opposite the Sublician bridge, in the area consecrated to Vulcan,

there stood an ancient statue of a lame, one-eyed man, erected traditionally to Horatius. In fact, however, it represented not the wounded Horatius but Vulcan (one-eyed as a sun god, and lame like the Greek Hephaestus, or rather because the primitive sculptor could not express the movement of the legs). The earliest allusion to the story is probably in a recently discovered passage of Callimachus' *Aetia* (Διηγήσεις, ed. Norsa–Vitelli, v. 26 ff.).

G. De Sanctis, *Riv. fil.* 1935 (contra, G. Pasquali, *Stud. Ital.* 1939).   P. T.

HORATIUS (2) FLACCUS, QUINTUS **(HORACE)** was born on 8 Dec. 65 B.C. at Venusia in Apulia. His mother is nowhere mentioned. His father was a freedman, probably of Italian stock, and as collector of dues had amassed sufficient money to purchase a small farm. Being a man of ambition, he refused to send his son to the local school and had him educated by Orbilius at Rome along with sons of knights and senators. When about twenty, H. removed to Athens for further study, but in autumn 44 joined Brutus' army as *tribunus militum.* Returning to Rome 'with clipped wings' after Philippi (42), he found that his father was dead and his farm confiscated. He therefore purchased the post of *scriba quaestorius,* and poverty, as he tells us, drove him to write verses. About this time he made the acquaintance of Virgil and Varius, who secured him an introduction to Maecenas; and in 38 he was finally admitted to the circle of M.'s friends. This event not only marked the beginning of a lifelong friendship but was a turning-point in H.'s career. It introduced him to the society of the leading poets and statesmen of Rome; it won his sympathies for the cause, and later for the régime, of Augustus; and it freed him from financial worries and brought him, five years later, the gift of his beloved Sabine farm. Henceforth he devoted himself to the writing of poetry, declining Augustus' offer of a private secretaryship; and after Virgil's death in 19 he was virtually a Poet Laureate. He died on 27 Nov. 8 B.C., only a few months after Maecenas.

Horace was short and stout in appearance, of delicate health, and prematurely grey. In character he was independent, tactful, kindly, and sensitive. He never married.

WORKS

1. Epodes (*iambi*): a collection of seventeen poems composed between 41 and 31 B.C. and published in 30. H. claims that in them he first introduced the Parian iambics of Archilochus to Latium (*Epist.* 1. 19. 23–5): eleven employ a purely iambic metre (1–10, couplets of trimeter and dimeter; 17, trimeters throughout); the other six have various combinations of iambics and dactyls. The subject-matter is threefold: (*a*) Lampoons, especially on the witch Canidia (5 and 17). These are at times both coarse and bitter despite H.'s claim (loc. cit.) that he reproduced Archilochus' spirit and metres but not his themes and venomous invective. Perhaps his animosities were less personal than those of A., for he describes himself as a watch-dog of society (6). (*b*) Political: 1 and 9 are connected with Actium, at which H. was apparently present. 16 expresses the disillusionment caused by the Perusine War in 41 B.C. and suggests that the Romans should migrate to the shores of Ocean where they will enjoy a new Golden Age. Virgil's 4th Eclogue is probably an answer to this Epode. (*c*) Erotic and miscellaneous: the love-poems (11 and 15) have some merit, and in 2 a Roman money-lender gives a charming eulogy of country-life.

The *Epodes* are experimental and immature, but in parts (especially 13 and 16) show considerable poetical power.

2. Satires. H. calls them *satirae* (miscellanies) or, jointly with the Epistles, *sermones* (discourses). Hexameter poems in two books: Book I (10 poems) was published *c.* 35 B.C., Book II (8 poems) *c.* 30 B.C. They are modelled on Lucilius and show the diversity of topics traditional in Roman satire. Some are homilies on conduct, literature, and even gastronomy (2. 4) and legacy-hunting (2. 5): others are descriptions of various incidents, e.g. H.'s journey to Brundisium (1. 5), his encounter with a bore (1. 9), Priapus and the witches (1. 8), Nasidienus' dinner (2. 8). The following elements are noteworthy: (*a*) Autobiography: H. gives us many details about his early career—his debt to his father, his education, his relations with Maecenas, his life in town and country. There is also much frank self-revelation of character: like Lucilius, H. 'entrusted his secrets to his writings' (2. 1. 30–4). (*b*) Moralizing: H. had acquired an early and lasting interest in practical ethics from his father (1. 4. 105 ff.); and satire which, as successor to the Cynic diatribe (cf. *Epist.* 2. 2. 60), purveyed popular philosophy to the Roman world, gave this full scope. He discourses on avarice, contentment, tolerance, etc., but does not profess any of the current creeds. In Book I he is, on the whole, Epicurean in sympathies and ridicules the Stoic paradoxes that all sins are equal and that the Wise Man is king (especially 3). Book II reveals the increasing appeal of Stoic earnestness: 3 and 7 are Stoic sermons on the madness and inconsistency of mankind. (*c*) Literary criticism (esp. 1. 4 and 10; 2. 1): H. discusses the nature of satire and distinguishes it from true poetry. He demands that the satirist should vary his tone, and declares that humour is a more effective weapon than sarcasm. Above all he insists on the necessity for finish, criticizes Lucilius for slovenliness, and defends the moderns against the ancients.

Written in racy, conversational style, the *Satires* provide many vignettes of scenes and characters, and present a varied and intimate picture of contemporary life. Satire in the modern sense is rare; H.'s humour is genial, and is directed against types rather than individuals, foibles rather than vices. Book I contains some very early work (e.g. 7, *c.* 43 B.C.) and is less finished, though livelier, than Book II; unlike the latter, it also prefers monologue to dialogue. With H. Roman satire first became great literature.

3. Odes (*Carmina*): four books containing 103 lyrical poems varying in length from 8 to 80 lines and modelled chiefly on Sappho and Alcaeus. The commonest metres are Alcaics, Sapphics, and Asclepiads, but there are occasional experiments in other metres (*see* LYRIC POETRY, LATIN). Except in 4. 8 (probably spurious in part), the number of lines is always divisible by four. The *Odes* were written to be read and not sung, but a musical accompaniment is occasionally assumed as a literary convention. The poems are carefully arranged within their books to give variety of metre and subject-matter, but an exception is provided by the six Alcaic 'Roman Odes' (3. 1–6) which naturally stand together.

The *Odes* were published in two collections:

(1) Books I–III, 23 B.C., containing poems written from 31 onwards. H. apparently regards this as his greatest achievement. In the prologue he confesses his ambition to be ranked among 'lyric bards' (1. 1. 29–36); in the epilogue he proudly claims that he has completed his 'monumentum aere perennius' (3. 30).

(2) Book IV, *c.* 13 B.C. This owed its inception to Augustus' command that H. should celebrate the Alpine campaigns of Drusus and Tiberius in 15 B.C. Poems 4 and 14 are devoted to this, and 5 and 15 extol Augustus' government. These four official Odes are good of their kind; the remainder show little loss of lyric power.

Each Ode normally has (*a*) an addressee, e.g. Augustus, Lydia, Apollo, the Roman people, the ship of State, a wine-jar, the fountain of Bandusia; (*b*) an occasion, real or imaginary, e.g. a great flood, Virgil's departure for Greece, a banquet, a wintry day, the death of Quintilius, the defeat of Cleopatra. Within this framework there is an almost infinite variety of theme and treatment. The subjects range from love and wine to the greatness of Rome and the character of the ideal citizen. In some poems the tone is light and playful (e.g. 1. 22, 2. 4, 3. 9); in others there is the high seriousness of the moralist, the patriot, and the 'priest of the Muses' (e.g. 1. 35, 2. 1, 3. 1–6 and 29, 4. 9). Many contain quick changes of mood, and perhaps the most typical of H.'s genius are those which contrast the beauty and permanence of Nature with the shortness of man's life (1. 4, 2. 3, 4. 7). The incomparable grace, economy, and inevitability of H.'s language in the *Odes* and his complete success in 'adapting Aeolian song to Italian measures' are universally recognized; but some of their charm is also due to his selection of beautiful material and to his skilful use of mythology and proper names. According to Quintilian (10. 1. 96), he is practically the only Latin lyric poet worth reading.

4. Carmen Saeculare: a Sapphic hymn to Apollo and Diana written by the command of Augustus for the Secular Games in 17 B.C. and sung by a chorus of 27 boys and 27 girls.

5. Epistles I: nineteen familiar letters and an envoi, written in hexameters and published in 20 B.C. They are in essentials a development of the *Satires*, and the scholiasts comment on the similarity of metre, diction, and subjects. Some are personal, e.g. 4 comforting Tibullus; 9 introducing Septimius to Tiberius; 7 tactfully informing Maecenas that H. cannot resign his independence. One (19) rebuts charges of unoriginality in his *Odes* and defends his poetic ideals. The majority, however, are strongly philosophical in tone and contain genial reflections and advice on life and conduct. In 1 H. states his position: though now a Stoic, now a Cyrenaic, he swears allegiance to no school, but seeks to work out his own rule of life. In this task he finds more help in Homer than in the professed philosophers (2). He concludes (6) that peace of mind depends on the attitude of will which refuses to set store by external goods ('nil admirari'). True happiness is within us: change of place avails nothing without change of heart (11), but the simple life of the country approaches closely to the ideal of 'living in harmony with nature' (10; 14). Though he describes himself as 'Epicuri de grege porcum' (4. 16), his growing seriousness inclines him rather towards Stoicism (cf. 16).

There is some justification for those who hold with Lehrs that 'the real H. is never found in his *Odes*' and that *Epistles* I is his greatest achievement. The *Epistles* gave full scope to his peculiar qualities—his sympathetic and penetrating outlook on life, his philosophy of moderation in all things, his humour which could laugh at himself as well as others. His moral homilies are enlivened by anecdote and fable, and made palatable by confession of his own faults. As compared with the *Satires*, the *Epistles* show a greater mellowness and depth, and a more perfect command of the varied tones of the hexameter.

6. Epistles II: two long letters in hexameters chiefly concerned with literary criticism. 1, which is addressed to Augustus (*c.* 13 B.C.), upholds the standards of Augustan poetry against its detractors; describes the social function of poetry; enumerates the difficulties which confront a would-be writer of tragedy at Rome; and incidentally gives many interesting (if hardly profound) criticisms on the development of Roman poetry and the earlier Roman poets (Livius, Ennius, Plautus, etc.). 2 is to Florus, the young poet of *Epist.* 1. 3, and was probably written between 20 and 17 B.C. After describing his education and early life, H. discusses style and the proper use of archaisms and neologisms.

7. Ars Poetica (*Epistula ad Pisones*): a discussion of poetry in a long hexameter letter to a certain Piso and his two young sons ('iuuenes', *Ars P.* 24). If Piso be identified with Cn. Piso (*cos.* 23 B.C.), its composition falls roughly between 23 and 20; if with L. Piso (*cos.* 15 B.C.), it belongs to the last few years of H.'s life. The second identification is supported by Porphyrion, who also states that the poem embodies the literary precepts of Neoptolemus of Parium (3rd c. B.C.); and it is perhaps significant that the writings of Philodemus from which we derive our knowledge of Neoptolemus were discovered in L. Piso's villa at Herculaneum. The title *Ars Poetica*, which first occurs in Quintilian (8. 3. 60), is misleading: the poem is not a systematic treatise but a series of rather desultory precepts, and its marked preoccupation with tragedy and the satyr-play seem to connect it with a deliberate attempt to revive Roman drama. Though H. may have owed to Neoptolemus many of his maxims and his general framework (*poesis, poema, poeta*), most of the content is the fruit of his own experience. The chief topics are: artistic unity; style and vocabulary; metre and the genres; originality and imitation; the proper end of poetry; genius and art; the uselessness of mediocrity and the need for taking infinite pains. The *Ars* is the only piece of serious Latin criticism written by one who was also a great poet; and its literary influence, especially in the seventeenth and eighteenth centuries, has been immense (*see* LITERARY CRITICISM, LATIN, para. 3).

Augustus' conviction that H.'s writings would be immortal ('mansura perpetuo') has been justified by time. He was, like Virgil, a school classic by A.D. 100 (Juv. 7. 226); he was commented on by various ancient scholars (notably Acron and Porphyrion); and in modern times he has been repeatedly edited, imitated, and translated. His popularity springs from three principal sources: (1) He reveals his personality in his works (esp. *Sat.* and *Epist.*) to a degree hardly paralleled in any other ancient poet; and his frankness, his tolerance, his sanity, his kindly humour tinged with melancholy make him somehow seem an intimate friend (cf. Pers. 1. 116–17). (2) He displays, alike in his descriptions and his musings, a truthfulness to perennial human nature which gives them an abiding interest. Though lacking profundity of thought and intensity of passion, he is a shrewd critic of life on its ordinary levels, and as poet of the 'golden mean' and of the average man he is perhaps unique. (3) His perfection of form gives charm even to his slighter pieces. Subtle in structure and 'sparing of his strength', he prefers the allusive touch and swift transition to the painstaking elaboration which 'oppresses the weary ears' (*Sat.* 1. 10. 9–14). In his consummate mastery of metre and diction he illustrates the principles of Classicism and of the 'limae labor et mora' which he preached; and if many of his famous phrases are now hackneyed, it is because his 'curiosa felicitas' gave perfect expression to the thought once and for all. *See* LYRIC POETRY, LATIN, para. 5.

BIBLIOGRAPHY

LIFE. H.'s own writings (passim). Suetonius: *Vita*.

TEXTS. O.C.T. (E. C. Wickham, revised H. W. Garrod) 1912; Teubner (F. Vollmer) 1912; O. Keller and A. Holder (ed. maior) 1899–1925.

SCHOLIA. Porphyrion: A. Holder (1894). 'Pseudoacron': O. Keller (1902–4).

EDITIONS. R. Bentley (1711); Orelli–Baiter–Mewes–Hirschfelder (1886–92); E. C. Wickham (1874–91); A. Kiessling, revised R. Heinze (1914–30). Odes: T. E. Page (1895); F. Plessis (1924). Satires: A. Palmer (1883); P. Lejay (1911). Epistles: A. S. Wilkins (1892).

TRANSLATIONS. (1) Prose: E. C. Wickham, *H. for English Readers* (1903). Odes, Epodes: A. D. Godley (1898); C. E. Bennett (Loeb). Sat., Epist., Ars P.: H. R. Fairclough (Loeb). (2) Verse: J. Conington (1905). Odes: W. S. Marris (1912).

GENERAL. O. Keller, *Epilegomena zu Horaz* (1879–80; textual criticism); A. W. Verrall, *Studies in H.* (1884); H. Nettleship, *Lectures and Essays* (1885); W. Y. Sellar, *H. and the Elegiac Poets* (1892); J. F. D'Alton, *H. and His Age* (1917); A. Y. Campbell, *H. a New Interpretation* (1924); L. P. Wilkinson, *H. and his lyric poetry* (1945).   T. E. W.

HORATIUS BARBATUS, MARCUS, *see* VALERIUS (2).

HORNS OF CONSECRATION, *see* RELIGION (MINOAN–MYCENAEAN), para. 1.

HOROLOGIUM, *see* CLOCKS.

HORSE AND CHARIOT RACES. Horse-racing was as popular in Greece and Rome as it is in our own country, but the horses were usually harnessed to chariots, two or four abreast, instead of having a rider on their back. In the four Panhellenic Festivals there were races both of driven and of ridden horses, and Pindar gives us the name of one race-horse, Pherenikos, belonging to Hieron of Syracuse, which won the race for single horses both at the Olympian and at the Pythian Games. This race, however, was only a sprint of under 6 furlongs, and was held of far less importance than the four-horse chariot-race which was the chief event of the day. The Hippodrome was a long rectangle of about 600 yards, with pillars at each end round which the horses turned. The chariots were light two-wheeled cars with a rail in front and at the sides; the driver wore a long white robe girt at the waist, and held a whip in his right hand, the reins in his left. The fields were large, forty teams sometimes starting, but the distance was twelve laps, nearly 9 miles, and as accidents at the turning-points were frequent it is probable that few teams finished.

From the Greeks chariot-races passed on to the Romans, who found an ideal site for a race-course in the centre of Rome in the level space between the Palatine and Aventine hills. This *Circus Maximus* they gradually surrounded with permanent stands, which in the fourth century A.D. could hold over 200,000 spectators. Down the length of the course there ran a low wall—*spina*—ornamented with two obelisks, seven stone dolphins, and seven stone eggs. At one end were the twelve closed stalls—*carceres*—from which the chariots started when the presiding magistrate gave the signal; at the other was a wide semicircle where the chariots turned, the race being usually seven laps, and twenty-four races forming a full day's programme. The chariots were drawn by two, three, or four horses, the most important horse being that in the left-hand traces. The driver wore a short tunic, with the reins fastened round his body and a knife in his girdle to cut them in case of need, together with a cap bearing the colour of the faction which he represented. These factions were a Roman development; in Greece chariot-racing had been possible only for rich men, in Rome it passed into the hands of companies. There were four of these, distinguished by their colours, white, red, blue, and green, the last two of which gradually absorbed the others. The Roman onlooker displayed his favourite colour and betted on it, and the rivalry between the blues and the greens became so intense that at Constantinople it led to the famous Nika riot.

Friedländer, ii. 19–40. For other literature *see* ATHLETICS.

F. A. W.

HORSES. From the beginning of history two separate species of horse were known to the ancients. There was the primitive horse of Europe and Asia, an animal with ugly head, large joints, dun colour shading to white, tail set low on croup, bad-tempered, and driven with a bit. There was also the so-called Arab or blood horse, a different species from the European-Asiatic, developed in north Africa; slightly built with small joints, fine head, tail set high, bay colour, often with white star on forehead and white bracelets on legs, skin blue-black, temper so gentle that it could be ridden with a nose-band only. These Libyan horses were used by the early kings of Egypt and by Solomon, and the best breeds known to the Greeks and Romans were the results of a cross between them and the European stock. In Thessaly there was a good strain from which Alexander got the mounts for his cavalry; in Sicily there was another which won many prizes for the Sicilian tyrants at Olympia; the horses sent from Africa by Hasdrubal gave Hannibal his most effective arm against the Romans; and the Gallic black and grey cobs known as *manni* were found very serviceable as carriage horses. The ordinary Athenian horse was a poor creature, often both lazy and vicious, so that it is not surprising that the young Athenians did not usually ride for pleasure. The average price of horses seems to have averaged between 20 and 50 pounds; Bucephalus (q.v.) is said to have cost 4,000. Horses were sometimes branded, either with letters *sanpi* and *koppa* or with devices such as a bull's head.

Xenophon, *On Horsemanship*; Vergil, *Georgics* 3. 72–208; W. Ridgeway, *Origin and influence of the Thoroughbred Horse* (1905).
F. A. W.

HORTENSIUS (1), QUINTUS, was appointed dictator *c*. 287 B.C., despite his obscure descent, to reconcile the Orders after debts and usury had provoked the final secession of the plebs to the Janiculum. He carried a *Lex Hortensia* by which *plebiscita* were to be binding on the whole community and the Senate had to recognize such measures as legal before they were put to the plebeian assembly. Another *Lex Hortensia* (probably 287) provided that lawsuits should take place on the *nundinae*, when the peasants, taking advantage of the country-holiday, came to Rome on business.

Mommsen, *Röm. Staatsr.* iii³. 153, 372 f.; G. W. Botsford, *The Roman Assemblies* (1909), 313 ff.; E. Costa, *La 'lex Hortensia de plebiscitis'* (1912); V. Costanzi, *Riv. fil.* 1914. P. T.

HORTENSIUS (2) HORTALUS, QUINTUS (114–50 B.C.), was for many years the great forensic rival of Cicero; he first crossed swords with him in the trial of P. Quinctius (81 B.C.) and later in that of Verres, whom he defended. He was consul in 69 B.C., and as a staunch supporter of the supremacy of the Senate he opposed the proposals of Gabinius and Manilius (67; 66). Later he co-operated with Cicero in the defence of C. Rabirius (63), L. Murena (63), P. Sulla (62), L. Flaccus (59), and P. Sestius (56). In 57 he pressed the claims of the consul Lentulus to the Egyptian command, and in 52 he opposed the *Lex Pompeia de vi*. He married (i) Lutatia, daughter of Q. Catulus (q.v. 2), who bore a son Quintus (who was at first a Caesarian, but later helped Brutus and fell at Philippi), and (ii) Marcia, also wife of Cato Uticensis.

Hortensius' fame rests mainly on his oratory; his influence is shown by the order of speaking in the Senate in 61, where he ranked fourth after Piso, Cicero, and Catulus. He was the leader of the 'Asianic' school, which relied for its effect on florid ornament and verbal conceit. The rapid and high-pitched flow of his speeches was convincing, but easily degenerated into bombast (Cic. *Brut.* 228–30, 301–29). He was also a prominent art-collector (Pliny, *HN* 34. 48; 35. 130). J. M. C.

HORUS, called Harpocrates (Horus the child) by the Greeks, was originally a god of lower Egypt. His characteristics and his unique qualities as they were known to the Greeks came almost entirely from his role in the myth of Osiris. The myth is given in a late, hellenized form by Plutarch in his essay concerning Isis and Osiris. After the murder of Osiris Isis gave birth to a son, Horus, who, after many trials, succeeded in punishing the wicked Set (Typhon). Egyptian mythology dealt at length with the obstacles which the untried youth had to overcome, and, in later times, Horus the child drew the affections of the Greeks and Romans. There are a few dedications to Horus outside Egypt, and he is sometimes represented as a mounted warrior with the head of a hawk. In unnumbered instances, however, he appears as Harpocrates and is represented as a chubby infant with his finger held to his mouth. He is frequently represented within Egypt and outside as a baby being suckled by his mother Isis, less frequently as a youth with pomegranate or a child on a lotus flower. Harpocrates is usually found as a member of the cult of the Egyptian deities, along with Isis and Sarapis, his mother and father. Representations of him are almost innumerable, from rings and amulets to life-size statues of him as a youth. In his various forms he is at times identified with Heracles, Eros, and Apollo.

A. Erman, *Die Religion der Ägypter* (1934); P. Roussel, *Les Cultes égyptiens à Délos* (1916); F. Cumont, *Les Religions orientales dans le paganisme romain* (1929); G. Lafaye, *Histoire du culte des divinités d'Alexandrie* (1884); P. Perdrizet, *Terres cuites de l'Égypte gréco-romaine* (1921); W. Weber, *Die ägyptisch-griechischen Terrakotten* 2 vols. (1914). T. A. B.

HOSIDIUS GĔTA, see GETA.

HOSTIA, see PROPERTIUS.

HOSTILIUS MANCINUS, GAIUS, as consul (137 B.C.) campaigned against Numantia. After several defeats he was surrounded with 20,000 men, but obtained peace through his quaestor, Ti. Gracchus. But the Senate, influenced by Scipio Aemilianus, would not recognize the pact and delivered Mancinus as a scapegoat, bound and naked, to the enemy, who refused to accept him. A law restored to him his civil rights. He was subsequently praetor again. A. M.

HOSTIUS, the epic poet, followed a well-established tradition in writing about a Roman war, the *Bellum Histricum* of 129 B.C. Perhaps he dealt with contemporary events as Naevius and Ennius had. Scanty fragments survive.

Morel, *FPL* 33 f.

HOUSEHOLD WORSHIP, see WORSHIP, HOUSEHOLD.

HOUSES (Greek). The ordinary Greek house of the classical period was modest in appearance and irregular in plan. The Hellenistic house which developed from it was more luxurious, but similar in essentials. The fundamental features were the *andrōn* (men's room) and the *gynaikōn* (women's room). When possible these were approached through an *aule* (courtyard), often small in towns, probably larger in the country. In all but the humblest houses secondary rooms (*thalamoi*) for sleeping, storage, and other special uses were built along the sides of the *aule*, which was often entirely surrounded except for a vestibule (*thyroreion*) inside the street door or recess (*prothyron*) outside it. Most of the room doors opened into the *aule*, and so did most of the windows (*thyrides*), though street windows were not rare. The plan-system was *radial* rather than *axial*; exact mirror symmetry of the whole plan about a major axis-line was exceptional even in Hellenistic times. The smaller sorts of unit were combined into a larger sort, *the court surrounded by buildings*, an inward-looking quadrangle, not necessarily rectangular, which could be fitted to all kinds of sites and, on occasion, doubled. The *aule* was the 'hub' of the plan; shady and cool in summer, sheltered and sun-trapping in winter, it formed an invaluable overflow area, especially for the women. In better-class houses loggias (*exedrai*) were formed by omitting the inner wall from one of the secondary rooms. Threshold areas, always favourite sitting-places, were sheltered by porch (*prostas, pastas, parastas, prothyron*) and colonnade (*prostoa*), which also protected the walls and rooms behind from damp and heat. In Hellenistic times these rooms and sheltered colonnade-walls were often decorated with brightly coloured frescoes; as early as the fifth century a few Athenian houses had painted walls. Colonnades were at first restricted to one or two, or at most three sides of the *aule*, but in the third century the complete *peristylon* begins to occur, a feature which in its more contracted form closely resembled the larger sorts of Roman *cavaedium*. Two-storied colonnades, like those used in the *stoa* and hypaethral temple-cell, were sometimes used in two-storied houses.

2. The palatial 'Greek House' of Vitruvius (q.v.) has two 'quadrangles', each with its own colonnaded *aule* and street door. The first, called *gynaeconitis*, contains all the more private and indispensable rooms and is, in fact, the house proper. The second, called *andronitis*, is a luxurious reception-suite for the men, with richly decorated *peristylon* surrounded by large dining-rooms (*triclinia*) opening externally on gardens, and by loggias (*exedrae*), and even libraries (*bibliothecae*) and picture-saloons (*pinacothecae*); small private suites (dining-room, bedroom, store) are provided for guests from abroad— an improvement on the earlier practice of bedding them in the porch or colonnade. Even in one-quadrangle houses there was some kind of *gynaeconitis*; sometimes in an upper story, like the Homeric *hyperōion*.

3. Upper stories were in common use from 600 B.C. onwards. In Hellenistic times they were sometimes planned as independent 'flats' with front doors of their own. Pitched roofs and flat terraces were both common. Latrines, slop-flushed and discharging into the gutter outside, were sometimes placed near the street door. In large houses the entry might be flanked by a porter's lodge and stables. Gardens were fairly frequent at the back. Water-supply was from public fountains or private wells or underground rain-water-cisterns; artificial lighting by torches and oil lamps; heating by *escharai* (hearths), internal and external, and *anthrakia* (chafing-dishes). Smoke escaped through smoke-holes (*kapno-dochai*) and through doors and windows.[*]

See also ARCHITECTURE, PALACES, TEMPLES, TOWNS.

[*] Architectural terms were very loosely used by classical writers The meanings indicated above are the most usual ones.

Vitruvius, *De Architectura* 6. 7; B. C. Rider, *The Greek House*; D. S. Robertson, *Greek and Roman Architecture* xviii; T. Homolle, etc., *Exploration archéologique de Délos*, fasc. viii (1922 and 1924); T. Wiegand and H. Schrader, *Priene*.   H. W. R.

HOUSES (Italian). TYPES. Two types of town-house coexisted in Italy. One type had as its main feature an *atrium*, i.e. an unroofed or only partially roofed area with rooms round about, which were lighted from it and arranged along a central axis in a more or less stereotyped order (viz. the *tablinum* and its flanking rooms at one end, the *alae* separating the *tablinum* end from the rest, and small rooms on each of the sides and also flanking the door, which lay opposite the *tablinum*). The other was a combined shop and dwelling—a shop facing the street and living quarters either above or behind it. *Atrium*-houses, self-contained and secluded, were the homes of the well-to-do; shop-houses, usually placed one against another in rows, were the homes of humble artisans and shopkeepers. The former tended to be spacious and one-storied, the latter to be cramped and many-storied. Architecturally the two types of house developed more or less independently.

2. ATRIUM-HOUSE. The origin of the *atrium*-house is uncertain. The triple division of the *tablinum* and its flanking rooms is possibly related to the triple division of the *cella* of an Etruscan temple, and the whole house may derive from the Etruscans. The earliest extant examples are found at Pompeii, e.g. the Casa del Chirurgo (4th to 3rd centuries B.C.). This house, when first built, had no *impluvium* (a basin in the floor designed to catch rain-water). This feature is not found earlier than the second century, but thereafter became normal. In the absence of an *impluvium*, it is not known if the *atrium* of the Casa del Chirurgo was roofed. A century later this type of house had grown more imposing in size and design (e.g. Casa di Sallustio at Pompeii). The *atrium* had an

impluvium, which implies that except for the *compluvium* (a rectangular opening in the centre of the roof) the area was roofed. The darkening of the *atrium*, which was a consequence of the roofing, was offset by large windows in the *tablinum* and adjoining rooms, which opened on a portico running round the outside wall and overlooking a garden. The rooms on the street-side were converted into shops, an innovation inspired by the plan of the shop-house.

3. SHOP-HOUSE. Shop-houses in their more complex forms were typical of large cities like Ostia and Rome. At least three types are known, viz. (i) a single row of shops facing the street, with living-quarters behind or above. At Ostia in the late-Republican and early-Imperial age such rows of shops reached an imposing dignity, having upper balconies or porticoes over the pavement of the street; (ii) a double row of shops built back to back; (iii) rows of shops surrounding a central area. The shops might face on the street or might be in a double series, one facing outwards, the other facing into the courtyard. In its most elaborate form (e.g. the Casa di Diana at Ostia) this type of dwelling formed a huge, many-storied *insula*. All three types can be seen at Ostia and in the *Forma Urbis Romae*, and the first and the third at Pompeii also.

4. HYBRID TYPES AND FOREIGN INFLUENCE. The *atrium*-house and the shop-house were gradually modified, partly through importations from the Greek and Hellenistic East. (*a*) As early as the third to second centuries B.C. at Pompeii (Casa di Sallustio) shop-houses were inserted in the façade of the *atrium*-house. From the first century B.C. onwards, when the use of brick-faced concrete became common and, owing to its solidity, made high buildings easier to construct, the growing popularity of these shops—with living-rooms above and often with external balconies and separate entrances from the street—made the *atrium*-house almost unrecognizable. (*b*) In the *atrium*-house the most striking Hellenistic importation was the use of a peristyle surrounding a courtyard, which either (i) was incorporated as an additional feature behind the *atrium*, or (ii) led to the insertion of rows of columns round the edge of the *impluvium* to support the roof, thus giving to the *atrium* the appearance of a small peristyle, or (iii) superseded the *atrium* altogether.

5. In shop-houses Greek influence is apparent in type iii (e.g. Casa del Triclinio, Casa di Diana, Casa del Tempio Rotondo at Ostia). Behind façades of shops lies an open area with entrances from the street, surrounded by narrow corridors on several floors with rooms opening off them and on one side a large, high room, sometimes with two columns supporting the lintel. In these *insulae* the façades and the multiplicity of floors are Roman, the internal arrangement is Greek and can be paralleled at various times during the fifth to third centuries B.C. from the Palace at Vouni, from Olynthus, Priene, and Delos.

6. In the first century A.D. the *atrium*-house fell out of use in towns. The shop-house, however, especially in the elaborate form of the *insula*, was typical of Imperial cities, and was destined to hand on many of its characteristics to the great *palazzi* of medieval Italy, and, through them, to the modern world. *See also* VILLA.

BIBLIOGRAPHY
On the question of origins G. Patroni, *Rendiconti della Reale Accademia dei Lincei* xxi (1912), 260 ff., and R. C. Carrington, 'Some Ancient Italian Country-Houses', *Antiquity* 1934, 261 ff. A. Maiuri, 'Contributi allo studio dell' ultima fase edilizia pompeiana', *Atti del Primo Congr. Naz. di Studi Romani* i (1929), 161 ff.; A. Boethius, 'Remarks on the Development of Domestic Architecture in Rome', *AJArch.* 1934, 158 ff.; 'Das Stadtbild im Spät-republikanischen Rom', *Acta Instituti Romani Regni Sueciae* 1935, 164 ff.; 'Appunti sul carattere razionale e sull' importanza dell' architettura domestica di Roma imperiale', *Scritti in onore di B. Nogara* (1937), 21 ff.; P. Harsh, 'The Origins of the *Insulae* at Ostia', *Am. Ac. Rome* 1935, 9 ff.   R. C. C.

HUNTING (κυνηγεσία, *venatio*) was practised by the Greeks and Romans, but, except in Homeric times, not in a very sporting spirit. In Homer the animals hunted have a fair chance of escape and the hunter incurs a certain amount of danger, as Odysseus did when faced by the wild boar (*Od.* 19. 429–46). But in classical Greece the hunter ran little risk; hunting, as Xenophon tells us, meant chiefly pursuing hares on foot, with dogs and nets placed to catch the quarry, which was then dispatched with a club. In hunting the roe deer nets were used and snares in the form of a wooden clog, which caught the deer's foot and hindered its escape; another method was to catch a fawn and to entice the dam into the open—'that is the moment to set the hounds on and ply the javelins'. In hunting the wild-boar caution comes first: 'Provide yourself with Indian, Cretan, Locrian, and Laconian hounds, boar-nets, javelins, spears, and cal-trops; also a company of hunters, for the task of cap-turing the beast is no light one.' The Romans followed the same methods; but under the Empire the hunting of big game for the arena became an important business. (*See* VENATIONES, DOGS.)

Xenophon, *Cynegeticus*; Oppian, *Cynegetica*; Nemesianus, *Cynegeticus*. F. A. W.

HYACINTHUS, a pre-Hellenic god worshipped at Amyclae. In historical times his cult was subordinate to that of Apollo, and a story was told that he was a beautiful boy whom the god loved, killed accidentally with a discus (in one version Zephyrus, who was Apollo's rival, blew the discus aside so that it struck Hyacinthus on the head), and mourned for, in token of which the flower of the same name, a sort of iris, sprang from the boy's blood and is marked αἰαῖ ('alas, alas!'; cf. AIAS 1). But the ritual of the festival, the Hyacinthia (Ath. 139 d ff.), the representation in local art of Hyacinthus as bearded (Paus. 3. 19. 4), the name of Artemis Ὑακυνθο-τρόφος, and the pre-Greek *-nth-* of the name, all point to the truth. Various Dorian cities had months named after Hyacinthus.

See Rose, *Handbk. of Myth.* 142, 160; Farnell, *Cults* iv. 125, 264 ff., *Hero-Cults*, 22, 27; Nilsson, *Minoan-Mycenaean Religion*, 485 ff. Machteld J. Mellink, *Hyakinthos*, diss. 1943. Chief ancient references, besides those already given: Nic. *Ther.* 902 ff. and schol.; Apollod. 1. 16–17; 3. 116; Palaephatus, 46 (47). H. J. R.

HYADES (Ὑάδες, 'the rainers'), a group of five stars in Taurus, so named because their acronychal rising and setting (respectively 17 Oct. and 12 Apr. according to Eudoxus) are at rainy times of the year; absurdly called Suculae in Latin, as if from ὗς. Mythologically they were nurses of Dionysus (q.v.; see Hyg. *Fab.* 182. 2 and Rose ad loc.); but the story, which seems to go back to Pherecydes, is very confused in the forms which we have. Another account (Hyg. *Poet. Astr.* 2. 21; schol. *Il.* 18. 486; Eustath. p. 1155. 45 ff.) is that they are sisters who cried themselves to death when their brother Hyas was killed hunting. H. J. R.

HYDROSTATICS, see PHYSICS, para. 4.

HYGIEIA (Ὑγίεια), personified Health, usually said to be daughter of Asclepius (q.v.), and associated with him in cult. She is the most important of his attendants, having a cult at Titane (Paus. 2. 11. 6), apparently almost as honoured as his. In the Hippocratic oath her name follows immediately on his and before that of Panacea (Kühn, p. 1), and Licymnius (fr. 4 Diehl) addresses her as 'mother most high', curiously, for she is usually said to be virgin. The word occurs also as a title of Athena (q.v.; Plut. *Pericles*, 13), earlier than the introduction of Asclepius to Athens. H. J. R.

HYGINUS (1), GAIUS JULIUS; a Spaniard (according to another account, an Alexandrian brought to Rome by Caesar), a freedman of Augustus, appointed by him librarian of the Palatine Library (Suet. *Gram.* 20). A pupil of Alexander Polyhistor, he was himself a teacher and was a friend of Ovid, who addresses him in *Tr.* 3. 14. His writings, now lost, covered a wide range of scholar-ship: (*a*) a treatise *De Agricultura*, perhaps including the *De Apibus* cited by Columella, who calls him 'Virgil's teacher' (1. 1. 13); (*b*) a commentary on Virgil, cited by Gellius and Servius, apparently both exegetical and critical; (*c*) historical and archaeological works—*De familiis Troianis, De origine et situ urbium Italicarum, De vita rebusque illustrium virorum, exempla*; (*d*) works on religion—*De proprietatibus deorum, De dis penatibus.*

See H. Peter, *HRRel.*; Funaioli, *Gramm. Rom. Fragm.* See also SCHOLARSHIP, LATIN, IN ANTIQUITY. C. J. F.

HYGINUS (2), *gromaticus*, of Trajan's time; author of treatises (1) on boundaries, (2) on types of land-tenure, (3) on land-disputes. He refers to another work not extant, a handbook of imperial land-regulations. A treatise *De limitibus constituendis* to which his name is attached is generally assigned to a later author. C. J. F.

HYGINUS (3). Two extant Latin works are attributed to a H. who cannot be identified with Augustus' freedman or with the *gromaticus*.

(*a*) *Genealogiae*, a handbook of mythology, compiled from Greek sources, probably in the second century A.D. Abbreviated, perhaps for school use, the work has suffered later accretions; its absurdities are partly due to the compiler's ignorance of Greek. The usual title *Fabulae* is due to the *editio princeps* of Micyllus (Basle, 1535), now the only authority for the text; the manu-script which he used is lost. See MYTHOGRAPHERS (ad fin.). Critical ed.: H. J. Rose, Leiden 1934.

(*b*) A manual of astronomy, based on Greek sources, possibly by the same author. C. J. F.

HYLAS. Theiodamas king of the Dryopes attacked Heracles because the latter had seized and eaten one of his plough-oxen. After a desperate struggle in which even Deianira took part, Theiodamas was defeated and killed. Heracles spared his young son Hylas and made him his page. They went together on the voyage of the Argo-nauts (q.v., para. 2), till the landing at Cios. There Hylas went to fetch water, found a spring, and was pulled into the water by its nymphs, who were in love with his beauty. Heracles stayed to look for him and the rest, after some discussion, went on without him; cf. DIOSCURI. It would seem that this story connects with a local cus-tom, for Apollonius says (1354) that in his day the people of Cios still looked for Hylas. Ritual search for a deity, perhaps of vegetation, is not unfamiliar in the Greek world, see Athenaeus, 619 f (Bormos among the Marian-dyni), Rose, *Handb. Gk. Myth.* 118 (Britomartis). See Ap. Rhod. 1. 1177 ff. and schol.; Theocr. 13. H. J. R.

HYLLEIS, see DORIANS.

HYLLUS, in mythology, eldest son of Heracles (q.v.) by Deianira (Soph. *Trach.* 55, etc.) or Melite (schol. ibid. 54). See HERACLIDAE.

HYMENAEUS. It was customary at Greek weddings to cry Ὑμὴν Ὑμέναι' ὦ or ὦ Ὑμὴν Ὑμέναιε (Ar. *Pax.* 1334 ff.; Catull. 61. 4, etc.; 62. 5, etc.). Rightly or wrongly, this was understood as an invocation of a being called Hymen or Hymenaeus, and various stories were invented of him, all to the effect that he was a very handsome young man who either married happily or had something happen to him on his wedding-day. See Sauer in Roscher's *Lexikon*, s.v. H. J. R.

HYMNS. A ὕμνος is any metrical address to a god, originally sung. The word is of doubtful origin, possibly non-Greek. It occurs once in Homer (*Od.* 8. 429), and a choral hymn to Apollo is described in *Il.* 1. 472–4.

Hesiod speaks of winning a prize for a ὕμνος (*Op.* 651 ff.). Hymns were both lyric and hexametric, and Callim. *Lav. Pall.* may be based on earlier elegiac models. Although all choral lyric poetry seems religious in origin, and hymns were written by the well-known early lyrists (e.g. Alcaeus), the hexameter was in antiquity considered the earlier form. (Cf. esp. Pausanias, who knows of Olen, Pamphus, Orpheus, Musaeus, and Homer as hymn-writers.) The content was usually an accumulation of names and epithets of the god (suggesting an original element of magical compulsion), and recital of his deeds, followed by a short prayer. Hymns written to invoke a local god on special occasions must have existed from very early times. An example survives in the Elean invocation of Dionysus (Diehl. *Anth Lyr. Gr.* ii, p. 206). Hexametric hymns mentioned by Pausanias have the same local and ritual nature, and were sometimes written for private mystical groups, e.g. the Lycomid *genos* (Paus. 9. 30. 12). The Homeric Hymns (8th to 6th cc.; *see* EPIC POETRY, GREEK, para. 5) are literary rather than devotional, and the myth is the chief feature. The ascription to Homer suggests the aristocratic epic tradition, and they were probably delivered in competition by professional rhapsodes at festivals (cf. *Hymn. Hom. Ven.* (vi) 19). Geographically they are widely scattered. Lyric hymns tended to displace the hexametric (cf. Pindar's Ὕμνοι and Παιᾶνες, and in the sphere of cult the paean to Asclepius found in four copies, J. U. Powell, *Collectanea Alexandrina*, 137 f.), but the hexameter survived for purposes of cult. (For ritual hymns in the classical period see also F. Adami in *Jahrb. f. cl. Phil. Suppl.* xxvi (1901), 215 ff.) Hymns were sung at Symposia (Plato, *Symp.* 176 a), as—according to his accusers—was Aristotle's paean in honour of Hermeias (Diehl I². i. 117–19; for its literary *genre* see C. M. Bowra in *CQ* xxxii (1938), 182 ff.). The Hellenistic period provides the elegiac hymns of Callimachus and many cult-hymns from inscriptions, e.g. the paean of Isyllus to Apollo and Asclepius (Wilamowitz, *I. von Epidauros*, 1886; cf. J. U. Powell and E. A. Barber, *New Chapters in the History of Greek Literature* (1921), 46 f.). Some found at Delphi have musical notation, a valuable addition to the scanty evidence for Greek music. Epigraphical material increases in the Graeco-Roman age, especially from Asia Minor, telling, e.g., of guilds of ὑμνῳδοί and their performances. The Palaikastro hymn to the Cretan Zeus, with interesting magical element (Diehl ii. 279 f.), is recorded in a copy made not earlier than A.D. 200, but reproduces a Hellenistic or earlier composition. In a series of pregnant prose sentences, which were reworked by later writers into hexametric and iambic form, the goddess Isis recounts her own virtues (W. Peek, *Der Isis-Hymnos von Andros und verwandte Texte*, 1930), illustrating the age's craving for revelation. From Imperial times we have the prose hymns of Aristides, the directions of the rhetorician Menander for the writing of such compositions, and the hexametric hymns of 'Orpheus' (ed. E. Abel, 1885), syncretistic and with a flavour of popular Stoicism, which were almost certainly written for a cult-society on the coast of Asia Minor (O. Kern in *Hermes* xlvi (1911), 431 ff.).

From Cleanthes onwards appears the philosophico-religious hymn, beloved of the Neoplatonists. Finally the growth of superstition brought back the magical hymn in elaborate forms.

R. Wünsch s.v. 'Hymnos' in *PW*; E. Norden, *Agnostos Theos* (1913), and, for early Roman hymns, *Aus altrömischen Priesterbüchern* (1939, including, pp. 271 ff., a discussion of the Palaikastro hymn).
                                                                    W. K. C. G.

HYPERBOLUS (d. 411 B.C.), Athenian demagogue of humble origin. During the Archidamian War he was a prominent member of the radical war-party and became its leader after the death of Cleon. In 417 an ostracism was held by which Hyperbolus expected to secure the removal of Alcibiades or Nicias, but they secretly allied against him, and he was himself ostracized. He went to Samos, where he was murdered by oligarchical revolutionaries. He is condemned by Thucydides in unusually violent terms (8. 73); but, since he was the constant butt of comic poets, his influence must have been considerable.
                                                                    H. D. W.

HYPERBOREANS. A legendary race of Apollo-worshippers living in the far North, highly revered by the Greeks. (Earliest mention is *Hymn. Hom. Bacch.* 28–9; for their blessed existence see esp. Pind. *Pyth.* 10.) In Delphic legend Apollo spent the winter months with the H. Offerings from them arrived at the Delian shrine (Hdt. 4. 33), not brought by the H. themselves (a myth gives the *aition* for this), but passed 'from city to city' until brought to Delos by the men of Tenos. 'The Greek stages are given carefully, but the Northern ones are unknown' (How and Wells). The name has been variously interpreted as 'beyond the North wind', 'beyond the mountains', and 'carriers round or over' (cf. the περφερέες, officials at Delos, Hdt. loc. cit.). W. K. C. G.

Various historical substrata to the legend of the Hyperboreans have been sought by modern scholars. Some have suggested that the line of stations by which the offerings of the Hyperboreans reached Delos was an actual trade route for amber in Herodotus' day. But no finds of amber have been made on this route, and we know from Callimachus that the offerings were ears of wheat (*Del.* 283–4). A more plausible theory is that the wheat was sent as first-fruits to Apollo by some lost Greek colony in the cornlands of the lower Danube (C. T. Seltman, *CQ* 1928, 155). But the route by which the offerings travelled cannot be traced back beyond Epirus; their place of origin must remain conjectural.
                                                                    M. C.

HYPERIDES (Ὑπερείδης) (389–322 B.C.), son of Glaucippus, an Athenian of good family, shared the political views of his contemporary Lycurgus. At first a professional speech-writer, he made a name later as a prosecutor in public trials. In 360 he impeached the general Autocles on a charge of treason, and in 343 prosecuted Philocrates. As a delegate to the Amphictionic Council he staunchly supported the policy of Demosthenes. After Chaeronea he proposed extreme measures, including the manumission of slaves, for the public safety, and was impeached by Demades for illegality. Shortly before this he had proposed a decree to honour Demosthenes, but later he was one of the prosecutors of Demosthenes in the affair of Harpalus (q.v.), 324 B.C. After the death of Alexander, H. was chiefly responsible for the Lamian War, and pronounced the funeral oration on the Athenian dead. The general Leosthenes, who was among the fallen, was his personal friend, and the speech deals mainly with him. After the battle of Crannon, Antipater demanded that H., together with Demosthenes and others of the war-party, should be surrendered to him. H. was arrested and put to death (322).

WORKS. Except for a few fragments H.'s work was unknown to the modern world until 1847. Between that year and 1892 papyri were discovered containing several of his speeches, in whole or in part. The speech *Against Athenogenes* gives an interesting picture of Athenian life. It concerns an attempt to invalidate a contract made for the purchase of slaves. In the *Lycophron* (fragments) a cavalry commander is impeached for a moral offence. In the *Philippides* H. charges Philippides with making an illegal proposal. *For Euxenippus*: a hill in the territory of Oropus, restored to Athens by Philip, was assigned to two Athenian tribes, but the question was raised whether it was already sacred to Amphiaraus. Euxenippus and two others spent a night in the shrine of the hero in the hope that he might appear and tell them the truth. One Polyeuctus impeached Euxenippus for giving a false report of the vision; Lycurgus prosecuted and H. defended. *Against Demosthenes* (fragments) was delivered in the trial of Demosthenes in connexion with the Harpalus scandal. For the *Funeral Oration* see EPITAPHIOS.

Hyperides was a pupil of Isocrates, whose influence may be traced in the exalted style of the *Epitaphios*, but in general tone he is more akin to Lysias. He borrowed words and phrases from Comedy, thus bringing his language into touch with the speech of everyday life. Linguistically his speeches have been studied in relation to the rise of the κοινή. [Longinus] *On the Sublime* draws attention to his wit, his suavity and persuasiveness, his tact and good taste. He can be sarcastic and severe without becoming offensive; his reproof often takes the form of humorous banter. He speaks with respect of his adversaries, and avoids scurrilous abuse. Ancient opinion ranked him second only to Demosthenes as an orator.

For general bibliography *see* ATTIC ORATORS. Text: O.C.T. (Kenyon, 1907); Teubner (Jensen, 1917). Text and translation: Colin (Budé). Special studies: L. Gromska, *De Sermone Hyperidis* (1927); V. Pohle, *Die Sprache des H. in ihren Beziehungen zur Koine* (1928). Index: H. Reinhold (in Teubner text).   J. F. D.

HYPERION, a Titan, husband of his sister Theia and father by her of the Sun, Moon, and Dawn (Hes. *Theog.* 371 ff., cf. 134 f.). Often the name is used as an epithet of the Sun himself, as *Od.* 12. 133.

HYPNOS, the god of sleep in Greek mythology. H. is fatherless, son of Nyx and brother of Thanatos (Hes. *Theog.* 211, 756). According to Hesiod he lives in the underworld and never sees the sun, but in contrast to his brother he comes softly and is sweet for men. In Homer, however, H. lives on Lemnos and gets from Hera the Charis Pasithea as wife. He is human at first, but changes into a bird of the night before he makes Zeus fall asleep (*Il.* 14. 231 ff.). Throughout antiquity H. was usually thought of as a winged youth who touches the foreheads of the tired with a branch or pours sleep-inducing liquid from a horn (Verg. *Aen.* 5. 854). Myths about H. are few: he helps to bury Sarpedon (*Il.* 16. 672) and is said to have fallen in love with Endymion whom he made to sleep with open eyes (Ath. 13. 564 c). He had a cult in Troezen (Paus. 2. 31. 3). In art, H. carried by Nyx was shown on the chest of Cypselus; on vases, H. and Thanatos carry Memnon, Sarpedon, and human warriors to the grave. A beautiful Hellenistic statue known through several copies shows H. gliding over the ground and pouring sleep-bringing liquid from his horn.

B. Sauer in Roscher, *Lex.* s.v.; Paus. ed. Frazer, iii, 600; H. Schrader, *Winckelmannsprogramm Berlin* 1926; E. Pottier, 'Étude sur les lécythes blancs', *Bibl. Éc. Franç.* xxx (1883).   G. M. A. H.

HYPOCAUST (ὑπόκαυστον, *hypocaustum*), a raised floor heated from below by a furnace (ὑπόκαυσις), a device applied *c.* 100 B.C. to baths (Val. Max. 9. 1. 1; Pliny, *HN* 9. 168) and occurring also in private houses by the time of Vitruvius (5. 10). During the first century A.D. box-tiles (*tubuli*) were introduced into walls and roof, permitting the development of Roman bathing from the simple Greek sweat-bath (*laconicum*) to an elaborately graded system (Celsus, *Med.* 1. 4; 2. 17). Heat was conveyed by radiation, the floors being carried upon many thin pillars, while walls were continuously jacketed. The furnace might also carry hot-water boilers (*ahena*, Vitr. 5. 10). A second type, the channelled hypocaust, employed charcoal to heat large masses of masonry intersected by channels, and warmed the room above by air introduced through the heated channels (Pliny, *Ep.* 2. 17. 23). While Pliny's Italian villa boasted few hypocausts, they were common in colder lands for heating living-rooms ('diaetarum hypocaustarum', *Dig.* 32. 1. 55).

See Macdonald, *Proc. Soc. Ant. Scot.* lxiii, 446 ff.; G. Fusch, *Über Hypokausten-Heizungen und mittelalterliche Heizungsanlagen* (1910).   I. A. R.

HYPODOCHMIUS, *see* METRE, GREEK, III (7).

HYPORCHEMA, *see* DANCING.

HYPOTHECA, *see* SECURITY.

HYPOTHESIS (Greek). (1) Prefixed to plays. Very few Greek plays lack a hypothesis, and some have several. Many hypotheses are in iambics; Soph. *OC* III is in elegiacs. The word strictly means 'subject', and some hypotheses give no more than a résumé, sometimes very brief, of the plot. In others we find further information of the kind to be met with in a modern introduction. Points regularly mentioned are the date and scene of the play, the composition of the chorus and identity of the prologist, the names of the other prize-winners and the other plays produced simultaneously by the author; occasionally also the name of the choregus or the principal actor. The treatment of the legend by other authors, especially dramatists, is often touched on; also, particularly in the case of comedies, the historical background, sometimes the intention or moral of the play (Soph. *Aj.*, exposure of the dangers of ambition; Ar. *Ach.*, pacifism; *Ran.* IV, σκοπὸς τοῦ παρόντος δράματος). Attention is called to points of interest about the production of plays (διασκευή of *Clouds*, repetition of *Frogs*, posthumous production of *OC*, *Plutus* the last play produced in Ar.'s own name), and to incidents in the authors' lives (Soph. a demesman of Colonus, and elected general on the strength of the *Ant.*). Titles and names of characters are explained (*OT*, *Lys.*, *Plut.*). There is a good deal of literary criticism. Sometimes a play is simply styled 'good' (*OC* θαυμαστὸν δρᾶμα). The *Andromache* is 'second-class', though certain passages are commended. *Alcestis* and *Orestes* 'approximate to satyric drama and comedy'. The *Phoenissae* is 'painful (περιπαθὴς ἄγαν), has a lot of characters, and is full of fine γνῶμαι; there are fine stage effects, but parts are patched on inorganically.' The *Orestes* 'acts well, but all the characters except Pylades are bad'. We learn why the prologist in the *Ajax* has to be Athena, and why Electra in the *Orestes* sits at her brother's feet, not his head.

The date and authorship of these hypotheses have been much debated. Two are assigned by the copyists to late authors (*OC* IV, *Ran.* III), *Alc.* I (by the copyist of the Laurentian MS.) to Dicaearchus, many to Aristophanes of Byzantium. Dicaearchus is said to have written hypotheses to Sophocles and Euripides, and ὁ Γραμματικός (presumably Ar. Byz.) to have based his hypotheses on the *Pinakes* of Callimachus. The metrical hypotheses to *OT* and many comedies of Aristophanes ascribed to Ar. Byz. are almost certainly to be considered spurious on grounds of versification and diction. But many of the prose hypotheses to tragedies and comedies —including some not bearing his name—may be wholly or partly his work. (Körte holds that Symmachus is the source of the hypotheses to Aristophanes' comedies.)

Cohn in *PW* ii. 998-9; Körte, *Hermes* xxxix (1904), 481-98 (on the hyp. to Cratinus' *Dionysalexandros*, contained in a papyrus of the late 2nd c. A.D.); Achelis, *Philol.* lxxii-lxxiii (1913-14).

(2) Hypotheses to the speeches of Demosthenes, written by Libanius for the proconsul Montius, an enthusiastic admirer of Demosthenes.

(3) A particular case propounded for discussion in rhetorical schools, contrasted with a general question (θέσις) discussed in dialectical schools. The distinction is, however, not always observed.

H. Thom, *Die Thesis* (1932), 61-2.

(4) *See* MIMUS.   J. D. D.

For *Hypothesis* in Latin Literature, *see* ARGUMENTUM.

HYPSAEUS, *see* PLAUTIUS (2).

HYPSICLES of Alexandria (second half of 2nd c. B.C.) is known as the author of 'Book xiv' added to Euclid's *Elements* (see Heiberg, *Euclidis opera omnia* v. 2-36), which has some interesting propositions regarding the regular dodecahedron and icosahedron inscribed in one sphere. He gave also a definition of a polygonal number quoted by Diophantus (1. 470). He was the reputed author of the Ἀναφορικός, on the times taken by signs of the zodiac to rise, in different conditions (ed. Manitius, Dresden, 1888); the tract may be only a clumsy reproduction of an original work. We find in it the first occurrence in Greek of the division of the zodiac circle into 360 degrees. It distinguishes the 'time degree' (μοῖρα χρονική) from the 'degree in space' (μοῖρα τοπική). T. H.

HYPSICRATES (probably 1st c. B.C.), historian, may be identified with the grammarian Hypsicrates of Amisus; he may have served Caesar, who freed Amisus in 47 B.C., as Theophanes served Pompey. His work was perhaps rather a history of the times than a local chronicle or Ποντικά, and was possibly Strabo's source for Bosporan affairs.

FGrH ii, B, p. 923; BD, p. 618. A. H. McD.

HYPSIPYLE. The women of Lemnos having neglected the rites of Aphrodite, the goddess plagued them with a foul odour. Their husbands left them in disgust and took to themselves concubines from Thrace; whereat the women planned to murder all the males on the island. The massacre was successful; but Hypsipyle, daughter of King Thoas the son of Dionysus, hid her father and managed to convey him out of the country. She governed Lemnos and received the Argonauts (q.v.) when they came. She and her women now mated with them (nothing more is heard of Aphrodite's curse), and Hypsipyle had two sons (see EUNEOS) by Jason. Some time after their departure she was captured by pirates and sold to Lycurgus king of Nemea, whose wife employed her as nurse to her child Opheltes or Archemorus. For the sequel, see ADRASTUS.

Authorities: Euripides, Hyps.; Apollonius Rhodius 1. 609 ff., and schol. there; Statius, Theb. 4. 715 ff.; 5. 28 ff.; Apollod. 1. 114 f.; 3. 64 f.; Hyginus, Fab. 15; 74. H. J. R.

HYPSISTOS was, like Hypatos, a not uncommon title in Greece of Zeus as the supreme god, or as a mountain or sky god; it was popular in Macedonia. Theos H. seems generally to have been an unofficial synonym for Zeus H. In the Orient H. was applied under the Empire to various native gods of Asia Minor and to the local Baals of Syria, many of whom were mountain divinities. Numerous bilingual inscriptions of Palmyra equate Zeus H. and the anonymous god 'whose name is blessed forever'. This cult was pagan but shows clear signs of Jewish influence (H. Seyrig, Études syriennes (1934–8), i. 98 f. = Syria 1933, 249 f.). The epithet is frequent in Hellenistic Judaism, and hellenized Jews and Gentile sympathizers could meet in a common cult of Theos H., as at Gorgippia and Tanais. A Jewish background appears also in dedications and prayers for vengeance to Theos H. at Delos. But except where Jewish influence is indicated, its presence need not be assumed, and in general the term implies only a tendency to exalt one god to a pre-eminent position.

A. B. Cook, Zeus ii, Appendix B; C. Roberts, T. C. Skeat, A. D. Nock, Harv. Theol. Rev. 1936. F. R. W.

HYRCANIAN SEA, see CASPIAN SEA.

HYRCANUS, see JEWS, para. 2.

HYRIEUS, see ORION.

I

For Greek and Latin proper names whose standard English form begins with J, such as *Janus, Jason, Javolenus, Jaxartes, Julius, Juno, Jupiter,* see under J.

IACCHUS (Ἴακχος). A minor deity (τῆς Δήμητρος δαίμονα, Strabo, 10. 3. 10) associated with the Eleusinian deities and probably in origin a personification of the ritual cry ἴακχ᾽ ὦ ἴακχε (Ar. Frogs 316); cf. Hymenaeus (q.v.). The deity, the song of which these words apparently formed the refrain, and the day (Boedromion 19) on which his image was fetched to Athens from Eleusis with other holy things were all called by the same name, Ar. op. cit. 320, Hesychius s.v. Ἴακχος; cf. MYSTERIES, PROCESSION. Iacchus was variously said to be the son of Demeter, of Persephone, and of Dionysus, or the consort of Demeter (refs. in Höfer, see below); in art he is seen torch in hand (cf. Ar. op. cit. 340 ff.) conducting the mystics, Deubner, plate 5. 1 (pinax of Ninnion). But, owing to the resemblance between his name and Βάκχος, the title of Dionysus, he is often identified with the latter, not only in literature (e.g. Eur. Cyc. 69, Verg. G. i. 166, Strabo, loc. cit.), but to some slight extent in cult; at the Lenaea, when the daduchus said 'Invoke the god' the congregation answered Σεμελήι᾽ Ἴακχε πλουτοδότα (Schol. on Ar. op. cit. 479). In Italy he was on occasion identified with Liber (q.v.), as in the temple of Ceres on the Aventine, where Ceres Liber and Libera are Demeter Iacchus and Kore.

L. Deubner, Attische Feste (1932), pp. 73–4; Höfer in Roscher's Lexikon, s.v. 'Iakchos'. H. J. R.

IACULUM, see ARMS AND ARMOUR, ROMAN.

IALMENUS, in mythology, son of Ares and Astyoche; leader, with his brother Ascalaphus, of the contingent from Aspledon and Orchomenus at Troy (Iliad 2. 511 ff.).

IAMBELEGUS, see METRE, GREEK, III (15).

IAMBIC POETRY, GREEK. The word ἴαμβος, of unknown but probably Asiatic origin, is first used by Archilochus (fr. 20) and seems to refer to his own satirical verse written in the iambic metre. It is possible that he was not the first so to use it, since Aristotle (Poet. 4) regards the Homeric Margites as the first work in which it appeared. He considers that its use for such purposes as satire and ridicule was due to its nearness to common speech. Archilochus' debt to the Margites may be seen in his use of a line from it (fr. 103), but he certainly developed iambic satire in his own way and used it especially to portray his own likes and dislikes. So, too, he used iambic epodes and the trochaic tetrameter for similar purposes. He probably influenced Semonides of Amorgos, who used the simple iambic trimeter, and seems both to have shown less personal spite and to have been more dependent on traditional fables than Archilochus was. Hipponax, however, follows the Archilochean tradition in giving full vent to his hatreds and in using everyday language. His chief innovation was the substitution of the σκάζων for the true iambic, but this did not alter his essential similarity to Archilochus.

Satirical iambics were also written in the sixth century by Anacreon, though his fundamental good nature does not seem to have left him except in his lines on Artemon (fr. 54) which are not strictly iambic in metre, though their temper is violently satirical. These poets all belong to Ionia, and iambic verse, as they practised it, was characteristic of free Ionian life. Elsewhere it took rather different forms. In Syracuse the ἰαμβισταί were a choir who carried *phalli* in honour of Dionysus (Ath. 181 c) and may have sung abusive songs, while the use of trochaics by Epicharmus in his early dramatic pieces indicates that he may have owed something to this tradition, while it must be to him and his kind that Attic comedy owed its use of iambic and trochaic verse. In Athens the iambic and trochaic measures were used from about 600 B.C. by Solon to answer his critics and justify his political decisions. He shows little rancour or abuse, and his temper is quite unlike that of the Ionian iambic poets, but he probably owed the form to them. It was the best means available for personal controversy, and that, no doubt, was why he used it. His example does not seem to have inspired many followers in Athens, and though such work is attributed to Euenus of Paros, its real influence is to be seen in Comedy. A possible follower of Solon is Chrysogonus (*fl.* 408 B.C.), whose poem Πολιτεία was wrongly ascribed to Epicharmus (Ath. 648 d).

In the Hellenistic age the satirical iambic was revived with some success. Some oddities appeared, like Castorion's *Hymn to Pan*, in which each dipody in the trimeter ended with the end of a word (Ath. 454 f), and the riddles attributed to Panarces (Diehl, *Anth. Lyr. Graec.* i. 3, p. 70), but the traditional use may be seen in Alcaeus of Messene's political diatribes against Philip of Macedon (Euseb. *Praep. Evang.* 10. 3. 23) and the philosophical invectives of Timon of Phlius, Heraclides Ponticus, and Hermeias of Curion. In this kind the most important practitioner was Callimachus, who wrote iambic, choliambic, and trochaic verses in the character of a new Hipponax, into whose mouth some of the verses are put. But he is less bitter than his predecessor, and the remains indicate that his *Iambi* were quite mild and humorous, with plentiful fables and discursions on varied topics. He seems to have widened the scope of topics for which the iambic metre was used, and his influence may be seen on Cercidas, whose scazons deal with topics of popular morality and make fun of pretentious speculations, and on Phoenix of Colophon, who wrote on such different matters as Ninus and the song of beggars in Rhodes. More primitive were the verses of Sotades, which belong essentially to this tradition and were famous for the scurrility and impropriety of their abuse. A new turn was given to iambic verse by Menippus of Gadara, who is best known through Varro's Latin adaptations and wrote criticisms of all manner of men and things, set his situations in fantastic backgrounds, and mixed verse with prose. In the Roman period iambic verse was put to new uses, some of them instructive, as when 'Scymnus' wrote his geography, Diodotus about plants, and Simylus about literature.

Texts: E. Diehl, *Anth. Lyr. Graec.*; J. M. Edmonds, *Elegy and Iambus* (Loeb).   C. M. B.

IAMBIC POETRY, LATIN. The use of iambic metres for personal invective and the censure of contemporaries is not widespread in Latin poetry, where the spirit of Archilochus and Hipponax is most often enshrined in Phalaecean hendecasyllabics and elegiac couplets (cf. Catullus, Ovid's *Ibis*, and Martial). The iambic senarius of the Republican dramatists (cf. METRE, LATIN) was, indeed, used occasionally for non-scenic purposes, as by Pacuvius and others for epitaphs and by Volcacius Sedigitus for literary criticism; yet Lucilius (like Horace, Persius, and Juvenal) preferred the dactylic hexameter

for satire and included senarii in his 28th and 29th books only. In the first half of the first century B.C. Cn. Matius introduced the scazon (limping iambic) in his *mimiambi* (in imitation of Herodas), and Laevius in his *Erotopaegnia* experimented with iambic dimeters, scazons, hendecasyllabics, and other metres; Varro also achieved a mastery of the iambic trimeter in his *Menippeae*. The scazon found some favour with Catullus, Cinna, Calvus, and Bibaculus; and of the eight poems of Catullus in this metre, all except no. 31 contain some personal criticism or abuse. Horace avoids the metre, but it occurs twice in the *Appendix Vergiliana* (*Catal.* 2 and 5, both critical of *rhetores*) and occasionally in the salacious Priapea. Martial was not strongly attracted to the metre, though he employed it in seventy-seven of his poems with epigrammatic effect. The iambic trimeter appears in Catullus in three poems only—nos. 4 (not scurrilous), 29, and 52; and when (in hendecasyllabic poems: nos. 36, 40, 54, and frag. 1) he mentions his 'iambi', he probably has in mind the critical spirit of his attacks rather than the exact metres (trimeter or scazon) in which a few of them were made. Horace's claim (*Epist.* 1. 19. 23) to have been the first to introduce *Parii* (= Archilochean) *iambi* into Latin is therefore not unjustified; for all his *Epodes* (in which abuse, friendship, moralizing, and patriotism provide the themes) have iambic elements used in the manner of Archilochus; in nos. 1–10 the couplets consist of a trimeter followed by a dimeter, 11–16 show iambic and dactylic elements variously combined into couplets, and 17 is entirely in trimeters. In this type of poetry Horace had no real successor. In the *App. Verg.* three poems (*Catal.* 6, 10, and 12) are in trimeters and one (no. 13) in iambic couplets; all except no. 10 (a parody of Catullus 4) are vituperative. In the first century A.D. Phaedrus used iambics for his fables; but his 'trimeters' (like those of the maxims of the mimographer Publilius Syrus, 1st c. B.C.) admit spondees in the 2nd and 4th feet and so are nearer to the dramatic senarius than to the stricter forms employed by Horace. Seneca, who in his tragedies uses elegant trimeters in the dialogue and some dimeters in the lyric parts, is far removed from the spirit of the ἴαμβος; Martial, who might have made powerful use of iambics, almost entirely neglects the dimeter and trimeter; and the apotheosis of the iambic metres (especially the dimeter) is found in Christian poets such as Prudentius (*Cathemerinon* and *Peristephanon*) and the author of 'Veni creator spiritus'.

Texts of minor authors and fragments in: E. Baehrens, *PLM*; W. Morel, *FPL*; F. Bücheler, *Carmina Lat. Epigraphica* (in A. Riese's *Anthologia Latina*).   J. F. M.

IAMBLICHUS (1) (*fl. c.* A.D. 160), born in Syria, wrote a Greek novel called the *Babyloniaca* or *Rhodanes and Sinonis*. An abstract by Photius and a few fragments preserved by Suidas suggest that while it was less probable in incident and more discursive than the extant novels, it shared their general characteristics. *See also* NOVEL, GREEK.

Text: R. Hercher, *Erotici Scriptores Graeci* i (Teubner).   R. M. R.

IAMBLICHUS (2) (probably *c.* A.D. 250–*c.* 325), Neoplatonist philosopher, born at Chalcis in Coele Syria, studied under Porphyry in Rome or Sicily; later he founded his own school in Syria (? at Apamea). Extant writings: (1) Περὶ τοῦ Πυθαγορικοῦ βίου (*Vit. Pyth.*); Λόγος προτρεπτικὸς εἰς φιλοσοφίαν (*Protrept.*); and three treatises on mathematics (see bibliography: the authorship of Θεολ. ἀριθμ. is disputed). These five formed part of a semi-popular encyclopaedia of Pythagoreanism. *Protrepticus* is a *catena* of extracts from earlier writers, and valuable as a source-book. (2) The 'Reply of Abammon to Porphyry's *Letter to Anebo*', a defence of ritualistic magic, generally known as *De mysteriis*, is attributed in our best manuscript to Iamblichus, on the authority of a lost work of Proclus. The ascription, which Zeller doubted, is probably right (C. Rasche, *De I. libri . . . de myst. auctore*, 1911). Though ill-written and philosophically worthless, the book is a curious guide to the superstitions of its age. Iamblichus' lost writings include a Περὶ ψυχῆς (excerpts preserved in Stobaeus); a Περὶ θεῶν, used by Macrobius and Julian; an elaborate exposition of 'Chaldaean' theology; and a number of highly tendentious commentaries on Plato and Aristotle, much quoted by Proclus.

Iamblichus' extant works are superficial; but his successors credit him with important contributions to the architecture of the Neoplatonic system. On the other hand, he corrupted Plotinus' teaching by introducing theosophical fantasies from alien sources; and his tendency is to substitute magic for mysticism, θεουργία for the Plotinian θεωρία.

TEXTS: Vit. Pyth., L. Deubner (1937); Protrept., H. Pistelli (1888); Περὶ τῆς κοινῆς μαθηματικῆς ἐπιστήμης, N. Festa (1891); Εἰς Νικομάχου ἀριθμητικὴν εἰσαγωγή, H. Pistelli (1894); Θεολογούμενα τῆς ἀριθμητικῆς, V. de Falco (1922); De myst., G. Parthey (1857), Germ. trans. and comm. Th. Hopfner (1922).
IDEAS AND INFLUENCE: K. Praechter in *Genethliakon Robert* (1910), 108 ff.; J. Bidez, *Rev. Ét. Gr.* 1919; E. R. Dodds, *Proclus' Elements of Theology* (1933), xix ff.; *PW* ix. 645 ff. Cf. bibliography under NEOPLATONISM.   E. R. D.

IAMUS, legendary son, by Apollo, of Evadne (q.v. 1). She bore him while alone and left him in a bed of (?) gillyflowers (ἴα, hardly violets, for they were yellow and red, Pindar, *Ol.* 6. 55). Aepytus, her guardian, learning at Delphi what had happened, had the baby searched for, and found that he had been fed with honey by serpents. From the flowers he was called Iamus. Coming to young manhood, he prayed to Poseidon and Apollo, and the latter bade him go to Olympia; there he became a prophet and ancestor of the clan of the Iamidae, which continued at Olympia well into the third century A.D. (L. Weniger, *ARW* xviii (1915), 53 ff.).   H. J. R.

IAPETUS, in mythology, son of Earth and Heaven, father by Clymene the Oceanid of Prometheus, Epimetheus, Atlas, and Menoetius (Hes. *Theog.* 134, 507 ff.). His name yields no plausible Greek etymology, and it is far from unlikely that it is to be connected with that of Japhet son of Noah, both probably going back to some very old figure of Asianic mythology, variously handled by Greek and Hebrew tradition.   H. J. R.

IAPYGES, see MESSAPII.

IAPYGIA, the name given by the Greeks to Calabria (q.v.).

IARBAS, see DIDO.

IASUS, IASIUS. These names seem to be etymologically identical, are perpetually confused, and occasionally are confounded with Iasion, Demeter's lover (see DARDANUS, DEMETER). Apart from Dardanus' brother, they are borne by a number of persons, all totally insignificant and uninteresting, e.g. two early kings of Argos, Arcadian and also Boeotian heroes, etc.; list given by Höfer in Roscher's *Lexikon* ii. 88–9.   H. J. R.

IBERIA, (1) one of the ancient names for Spain (q.v.); (2) the name of the mountain-girt land (roughly coincident with mod. *Georgia*) south of the Caucasus, north-east of Armenia, between the Black Sea and the Caspian. Its chief river was the Cyrus (*Kur*). The Greeks, after Pompey's exploration in 65 B.C., knew four entrance-passes: from Colchis by Scharapani; from the north by the Caucasian Gates (*Darial Pass*); from Albania by Derbent Pass; from Armenia through Kars. The people, organized in four classes (chiefs, priests, fighter-tillers,

slaves), were subject probably to Persia and certainly to Mithridates VI. They were not included in the Roman Empire except occasionally as 'clients'.
Strabo 11. 491–2, 497, 500–1, 528; Ptol. *Geog.* 5. 9. 27 ff.; 8. 18. 2; 19. 1. 5.   E. H. W.

IBYCEAN, see METRE, GREEK, III (5).

IBYCUS, son of Phytius, of Rhegium, lyric poet of the sixth century B.C., whose *floruit* is given by Suidas as 564–561 B.C. and by Eusebius–Jerome as 536–533 B.C. He seems to have begun by writing lyrical narratives in the style of Stesichorus, and fragments indicate that he told of the Funeral Games of Pelias (Ath. 4. 172 d), the Sack of Troy (fr. 16), and the Calydonian boar-hunt (fr. 28). He also wrote about Ortygia (fr. 21) and told Sicilian stories (Ael. *NA* 6. 51). He left Sicily because, it was said, he refused to become a tyrant (Diogenian. 1. 207) and went to Samos, where he worked at the court of Polycrates (Suid. s.v. Ἴβυκος). To this period may belong his most striking fragments, notably those about love when he is getting old (frs. 6 and 7), and the lines to Euryalus. *POxy.* 3 has been attributed to him, since it mentions Polycrates, but the attribution is uncertain. If it is his, it is more probably concerned with the tyrant's son than with the tyrant himself, and seems to be a playful leave-taking of his earlier manner for the erotic poetry in favour at Samos. His works were collected in seven books and seem to have consisted largely of choral poems, of which some were *encomia*, and personal love-songs, written in a great variety of metres. He has a rich and brilliant style, a vivid imagination, a great capacity for describing the emotions, especially love, and a real love of nature (frs. 9, 11, 13, 21). He is said to have been killed by robbers, who were brought to justice by birds who saw the murder (Plut. *Garr.* 14; Antip. Sid. ap. *Anth. Pal.* 7. 745), and was buried at Rhegium (*Anth. Pal.* 7. 714).
TEXT: Diehl, *Anth. Lyr. Graec.* ii, pp. 48–60.
CRITICISM: U. von Wilamowitz-Moellendorff, *Sappho und Simonides* (1913), 121–8; C. M. Bowra, *Greek Lyric Poetry* (1936), 248–83.   C. M. B.

ICARIAN SEA, see AEGEAN SEA.

ICARIUS or ICARUS (but the latter name is usually that of Daedalus' son (see DAEDALUS)), in mythology, (1) an Athenian who received Dionysus hospitably when he came to Attica, and was given the vine. He made wine and gave some to his neighbours, who on feeling the effects concluded that they were poisoned and killed him. His daughter Erigone was guided by their dog Maera to his body and hanged herself for grief. In memory of her the festival of the Aiora was instituted, in which swinging played a part, and Aristaeus propitiated the shade of Icarius; in consequence, a pestilence on Ceos which had followed their reception of the murderers of Icarius ceased. Icarius became the constellation Boötes; Erigone, Virgo; the dog, Canicula (Procyon). See schol. *Il.* 22. 29; Hyginus, *Fab.* 130 and Rose ad loc.; *Poet. Astr.* 2. 4. (2) Father of Penelope (q.v.; *Od.* 1. 329 and often). Tyndareus induced him to give Penelope to Odysseus in return for the latter's good advice to make Helen's wooers take the oath (see HELEN). Icarius tried to induce them to remain with him in Lacedaemon, but, on the choice being left to her, she indicated that she would follow her husband to Ithaca (Apollod. 3. 132; Paus. 3. 20. 10).   H. J. R.

ICILIUS, LUCIUS, a plebeian hero, betrothed to Verginia and leader of the second secession, has little claim to historical existence, but the *Lex Icilia de Aventino publicando* (traditionally dated 456 B.C.), the text of which was still preserved in Augustus' time in the Aventine temple of Diana (Dion. Hal. 10. 32. 4), is indisputably a genuine document of *c.* 450. The law provided allotments on the Aventine to the plebs either as agricultural or (very probably) as building land. It was later attributed to Icilius merely because of his renown as a popular hero. P. T.

ICTINUS (*fl.* after 450 B.C.), a Greek architect. His best-known work was the Parthenon (q.v.), in which he was assisted by Phidias and Callicrates (qq.v.), and about which, according to Vitruvius (7 *praef.*), he and a certain Carpion wrote a book, since lost. According to Pausanias (8. 41), he was the architect of the temple of Apollo Epicurius at Bassae, which was noted for beauty in its day and, like the Parthenon, had several unusual features (*see* BASSAE). According to Vitruvius (7 *praef.*), Ictinus also rebuilt the Telesterion at Eleusis on a greatly enlarged scale. H. W. R.

ICTIS, probably *St. Michael's Mt.* by Penzance. Diodorus (5. 22. 2, 4) records that the people of Belerium (*Land's End*) brought tin in wagons at ebb-tide to the adjacent island Ictis. Pliny (4. 104 from Timaeus) puts Ictis six days' sail inwards from Britain, perhaps confusing it with Vectis (*Isle of Wight*) or the Scillies. E. H. W.

IDAEAN DACTYLS (Δάκτυλοι Ἰδαῖοι), literally the Fingers of Ida, but whether the Phrygian or the Cretan Ida and whether their name refers to craftsmanship, dwarfish size, or something else, the ancients were in doubt. The oldest mention surviving is in the *Phoronis*, ap. schol. Apoll. Rhod. 1. 1129, which says they were called Celmis, Damnameneus, and Acmon, that they were big and powerful, wizards, servants of 'Adresteia of the mountains', presumably the same as Cybele or Rhea, Phrygians, and inventors of smithcraft. But Apollonius (ibid.) says they were Cretans, sons of a nymph Anchiale, who grasped handfuls of dust in her birthpains, or (the language is ambiguous) produced them by throwing handfuls of dust. More and divergent accounts of them in the schol., ibid., and still more collected by Lobeck, *Aglaoph.* 1156 ff.; von Sybel in Roscher's *Lexikon*, s.v. 'Daktyloi'. For their dwarfish size cf. Paus. 8. 31. 3, and for their connexion with Heracles *see* HERACLES. *See also* MAGIC, para. 4. H. J. R.

IDAEUS, 'connected with Ida', and so (*a*) a title of Zeus (*Iliad* 16. 605 (Trojan) and on Cretan coins and (usually in a dialect form) inscriptions); (*b*) a stock name for sundry little-known Trojans or Cretans (list in Stoll in Roscher's *Lexikon* ii. 95). (*c*) Magic name for a finger, perhaps the index (*PMG* iv. 455). H. J. R.

IDAS, in mythology, son of Aphareus and brother of Lynceus. He was 'the strongest of men' (*Iliad* 9. 558), and drew his bow against Apollo (ibid.). The reason, according to later authorities (Chest of Cypselus in Paus. 5. 18. 2; Apollod. 1. 60–1), was that after he had won his bride Marpessa from her father Euenus, son of Ares (add Bacchylides 19), Apollo in turn carried her off; Idas fought him and Zeus made peace by giving Marpessa her choice between them; she preferred Idas. He was one of the Argonauts (q.v.; Ap. Rhod. 1. 152 and often), valiant but hot-tempered. He also took part in the Calydonian boar-hunt (Apollod. 1. 67), as was natural, for Meleager (q.v.) was his son-in-law (*Il.* 9. 556). Though his final encounter with the Dioscuri (q.v.) is variously told, Pindar (*Nem.* 10. 60) makes Idas kill Castor, while Lynceus, whose sight was preternaturally sharp, looks out for the approach of the twins. H. J. R.

IDMON, 'the knowing one', name of several skilful persons, especially a seer, son of Apollo or Abas (Ap. Rhod. 1. 139 ff. and schol.), who accompanied the Argonauts (q.v.) although he foreknew he would not return alive (ibid. and 2. 815 ff.); he was killed by a boar in the country of the Mariandyni. H. J. R.

IDOMENEUS (1), in mythology, leader of the Cretan contingent before Troy (*Iliad* 2. 645); of distinguished valour although older than most of the warriors (13. 210 ff., 361 ff.). He was of Minos' race and one of Helen's suitors (Hesiod, fr. 96. 16 ff. Rzach). The story of Homecomer's Vow (Stith Thompson, S241) is told of him (Servius on *Aen.* 3. 121); in a storm he vowed to sacrifice to Poseidon the first thing which met him on his return. This was his son; fulfilling or trying to fulfil the vow he was forced to leave Crete for Italy because a pestilence broke out. H. J. R.

IDOMENEUS (2) (*c.* 325–*c.* 270 B.C.), biographer and politician of Lampsacus, and friend of Epicurus (cf. Usener, *Epicurea*, frs. 128–38).
WORKS (*FHG* ii. 489–94). (1) Περὶ τῶν Σωκρατικῶν (Diog. Laert. 2. 20): fragments on the Socratic Aeschines. (2) Περὶ δημαγωγῶν in at least two books; fragments in Plutarch and Athenaeus concern leading Athenian politicians. (3) Ἱστορία τῶν κατὰ Σαμοθράκην, cf. Suidas s.v. 'Idomeneus'. Following the Peripatetic, anecdotal method, I. reproduced much unreliable scandal, perhaps attacking politicians whose ideas he disliked; after Hermippus he was not used. F. W. W.

IDUMAEA. The Edomites, pushed westwards by the Nabataeans, occupied the arid country (henceforth known as Idumaea) south of Judaea in the fourth century B.C. They were conquered and forcibly converted to Judaism by John Hyrcanus (*see* JEWS), but detached from Judaea and organized as the two cities of Adora and Marisa (both prominent commercial towns since the 3rd c. B.C.) by Pompey in 63 B.C. Idumaea was granted to Herod in 40 and became a toparchy of his kingdom. Early in his reign an Idumaean noble, Costobar, tried to revive the national cult of Kose, but the mass of the people were fanatical adherents to the Jewish faith. A. H. M. J.

IDYLL, *see* PASTORAL POETRY, GREEK.

IGUVINE TABLETS, *see* TABULAE IGUVINAE.

ILIAS LATINA (*Homerus Latinus*), a version of the *Iliad* in 1,070 hexameters. The ascription of the work (entitled merely 'Homerus') to Silius Italicus on the grounds of two acrostics is untenable; but the author may be a Baebius Italicus. The allusion to the Julian house in 899 ff. precludes a date of authorship later than A.D. 68. Though important for its perpetuation of the *Iliad* during centuries ignorant of Greek, the work is in general a meagre epitome devoid of artistic merit, characterized by free and uneven treatment, a straightforward style thickly embellished with Virgilian and Ovidian echoes, and careful versification.
Texts: F. Vollmer, *PLM* ii². 3 (1913); F. Plessis (1885). Cf. J. Tolkiehn, *Homer u. die römische Poesie*, 1900. A. H.-W.

ILIAS PARVA, *see* EPIC CYCLE.

ILIONA (Ἰλιόνη), in mythology, eldest daughter of Priam and Hecabe (qq.v., Verg. *Aen.* 1. 653–4). Wife of Polymestor (*see* HECUBA), she saved the life of Polydorus by passing him off as her son, Polymestor thus murdering his own child (Hyginus, *Fab.* 109, cf. Pacuvius, frs. of *Iliona*). H. J. R.

ILIU PERSIS, *see* EPIC CYCLE.

ILIUM, an Aeolian foundation, established in the seventh century B.C. on the site of ancient Troy. Its importance derived from the famous temple of Athena (visited by Xerxes and Alexander), the centre, from the fourth century onwards, of a religious synedrion. The landing of Livius Salinator (190) inaugurated cordial relations with Rome (though Ilium was sacked by Fimbria's unruly troops in 85); and the emperors followed Julius Caesar's example in patronizing Ilium and its temple, because of the legend that the founders of Rome were of Trojan origin.

A. Brückner, in Dörpfeld's *Troia und Ilion* (1902), ii. 549.

D. E. W. W.

ILLYRICUM, the territory of the Indo-European Illyrians, was a geographical notion of varying extent. According to the Greeks Illyricum was bounded by the Adriatic, the Eastern Alps, the Danube, the Shar-Dagh, and the Ceraunian Mountains. In the sixth and following centuries the coast was partly colonized by the Greeks, who may have been attracted by the mines of the interior. But the difficulty of access to the inland and the reputation of the natives for piracy retarded the opening up of the country. The great number of independent tribes delayed the formation of a national kingdom until the third century B.C., when in the south the kingdom of Scodra arose. Against this the Romans fought in the First and Second Illyrian Wars (229–228, 219 B.C.), for they then considered the Adriatic their sphere of interest. In 167 B.C., after the defeat of Genthius, Illyricum (sc. *regnum*) was divided into three parts under Roman control. As the Roman conquest, especially of the Dalmatians, progressed, so Illyricum became a more clearly defined geographical expression, the southern districts together with Apollonia and Dyrrhachium being allotted to Macedonia in 148–147. First administered by consuls from Italy, later (since Sulla?) Illyricum was connected either with Macedonia (cf. the governorship of M. Brutus) or with Gallia Cisalpina (cf. Caesar's governorship). In the Civil War some tribes surrendered to Caesar in 46, but soon fighting was renewed (*see* DALMATIA). It was finally subdued by Octavian in the Illyrian War (35–33), in which first the Iapudes and Pannonii and later the Dalmatians were conquered (cf. N. Vulić, *JRS* 1934, 163 ff.). In 27 B.C. Illyricum became a senatorial province, but was put under imperial administration again (? 11 B.C.), no doubt because of the operations against the Pannonii which had begun in 13. The subdued tribes were added to Illyricum, which thus was extended to the Danube and was reorganized in 11 B.C. (A list of the legates between 8 B.C. and A.D. 6 is given by R. Syme, *JRS* 1934, 130.) After or even during the Pannonian-Illyrian revolt (A.D. 6–9), which was repressed by Tiberius, Pannonia was disconnected from Illyricum, the remaining part of Illyricum sometimes being called *superior provincia Illyricum*, till later the name 'Dalmatia' (q.v.) prevailed, whereas Illyricum meant the great customs-area of the *portorium Illyricum* covering Raetia, Noricum, Dalmatia, Pannoniae, Moesiae, and Dacia (cf. Marquardt, *Röm. Staatsverw.* ii². 273; i². 295 f.; M. Rostovtzeff, *Geschichte der Staatspacht in der röm. Kaiserzeit* (1904), 393 f.; Ruggiero, l.c. inf. 25 ff.). From the time of Diocletian Illyricum denoted two dioceses, namely *Illyricum orientale* or *dioecesis Moesiarum*, and *Illyricum occidentale* or *dioecesis Pannoniarum*.

Vulić, *PW*, s.v. 'Illyricum'; Fluss, *PW* Suppl. v, s.v. 'Illyrioi'. Patsch, *Sitz. Wien*, 214 i (1932); 215 iii (1933). Ruggiero, *Diz. Epigr.* iv/1 (1924), 20 ff.; J. M. F. May, *JRS* 1946, 48 ff. R. L. Beaumont, *JHS* 1936, 159 ff. on Greek colonization, influence, and trade in Illyrium before the fourth century B.C. J. V. Antwerp Fine, *JRS* 1936, 24 ff. on the early Roman wars. F. A. W. S.

ILUS, in mythology, (1) son of Dardanus (q.v.; Apollod. 3. 140). (2) His grand-nephew, son of Tros and father of Laomedon (qq.v.). He founded Ilium, being guided to the site by a cow (cf. CADMUS) and received the Palladium from heaven (ibid. 141–3).

IMAGINES, the death-masks of distinguished ancestors at Rome, where the *ius imaginum* belonged to families numbering curule magistrates among their forebears. These masks, of wax or more durable material, were kept in cupboards in the *alae* of a Roman house, and on the death of a similarly qualified member of the family they were worn by actors in the funeral procession. The custom originated in magical observance, but acquired an ethical and later a social significance. Outside Italy death-masks occur in the shaft graves of Mycenae and occasionally throughout classical Greece.

Polybius 6. 53. Annie Zadoks-Jitta, *Ancestral Portraiture in Rome* (Amsterdam, 1932). F. N. P.

IMAGINES, *see also* SIGNA MILITARIA.

IMBREX, *see* LICINIUS.

IMMORTALITY, *see* AFTER-LIFE.

IMMUNITAS. Under the Roman Republic exemption from taxation was granted to the States of the Italian Confederacy and to the few provincial cities possessing a treaty or *libertas*. There is some doubt as to whether tribes and kings with whom Rome concluded treaties possessed *immunitas*: probably the practice varied. Possibly before the end of the Republic, and certainly in the Principate, *libertas* did not involve *immunitas*, which was regarded as a separate privilege that could be granted to communities or to individuals (Suet. *Aug.* 40). Many 'free' cities normally paid tribute under the emperors (Tac. *Ann.* 2. 47; 12. 63). When Nero gave *libertas* to the cities of Greece he explicitly granted ἀνεισφορία as well (*SIG.* 814). The most important Gallic tribes were termed *foederata* or *libera*, and they certainly paid taxes. *Immunitas* might be granted (usually for a fixed period) to cities of any type. Provincial *coloniae* and *municipia* were not necessarily *immunes*. The most valuable form of immunity was the *ius Italicum*, which exempted a community from the payment of the *tributum soli* as well as the *tributum capitis*. It is probable that *immunitas* of the ordinary type exempted only from the latter (*Dig.* 50. 8. 7). G. H. S.

IMPERATOR (αὐτοκράτωρ), a generic title for Roman commanders, became a special title of honour. After a victory the general was saluted *imperator* by his soldiers. He assumed the title after his name until the end of his magistracy or until his triumph. Sometimes the Senate seems to have given or confirmed the title. The origin of this form of honour is unknown, but some religious meaning is possible (cf. the formula *Iuppiter imperator*). The first certainly attested *imperator* is L. Aemilius Paullus in 189 B.C., as the evidence about Scipio Africanus is uncertain. The title was assumed especially by proconsuls and gained new importance through Sulla before he was appointed dictator. The increasing influence of the army in the late Republic made *imperator* the symbol of the military authority. Pompey emphasized that he was saluted *imperator* more than once. Caesar first used the title permanently, but it is doubtful whether in 45 B.C. he received from the Senate a hereditary title of *imperator* (as Dio Cass. 43. 44. 2 states). Agrippa in 38 B.C. refused a triumph for victories won under Octavian's superior command and established the rule that the *princeps* should assume the salutations and the triumphs of his legates. Henceforth, apparently, Octavian used *imperator* as praenomen (*imperator Caesar*, not *Caesar imperator*), perhaps intending to emphasize the personal and family value of the title. Thus the title came to denote the supreme power and was commonly used in this sense. But, officially, Otho was the first who imitated Augustus. Vespasian definitively converted the name *imperator* into a praenomen of the *princeps*. The formula *imperator Caesar* was sometimes extended to members of the family of the *princeps* who were associated with him in power. On the death of a *princeps*, or during a rebellion, the *salutatio* of a general as an *imperator* by an army indicated that he was the candidate of that body to the imperial dignity.

The use of the praenomen did not suppress the old usage of *imperator* after the name. After a victory the emperor registered the *salutatio imperatoria* after his name (e.g.: Imp. Caesar . . . Traianus . . . imp. VI). From the second half of the third century the emperor was deemed to receive a *salutatio* every year. The number of the salutations became practically identical with the number of the years of the reign.

Theoretically, governors of senatorial provinces, having their own *auspicia*, could assume the title of *imperator*. But the last instance of such a *salutatio* is that of Junius Blaesus, proconsul of Africa in A.D. 22 (Tac. *Ann.* 3. 74).

D. McFayden, *The History of the Title Imperator under the Roman Empire* (U.S.A. 1920); M. A. Levi, *Riv. Fil.* 1932, 207; G. De Sanctis, *Studi in onore di S. Riccobono* (1932), ii. 57; J. Carcopino, *Points de vue sur l'impérialisme romain* (1934), 127; J. Stroux, *Die Antike* 1937, 197; H. Nesselhauf, *Klio* 1937, 306; A. v. Premerstein, *Vom Werden und Wesen des Prinzipats* (1937), 245; E. Peterson, 'Christus als Imperator', in *Zeuge der Wahrheit* 1937, 54; M. Grant, *From Imperium to Auctoritas* (1946). A. M.

IMPERIUM was the supreme administrative power, involving command in war and the interpretation and execution of law (including the infliction of the death penalty), which belonged at Rome to the kings and, after their expulsion, to consuls, military tribunes with consular power (from 445–367 B.C.), praetors, dictators, and masters of the horse. It was held later in the Republic by members of certain commissions (e.g. boards for the distribution of land, Cic. *Leg. Agr.* 2. 28) and by proconsuls and propraetors, who were either ex-magistrates or *privati*, on whom a special command had been conferred. Its application was increasingly restricted; first, when two consuls replaced the king, by the principle of *collegium*. Secondly, by the *Leges Valeriae*, traditionally assigned to 509, 449, and 300 B.C., and the *Leges Porciae*, probably of the second century B.C., magistrates were not allowed to execute Roman citizens at Rome without trial, a prisoner at Rome having the *ius provocandi ad populum*. This right of appeal was extended, probably by convention and not by legal enactment, to Roman citizens on service with the armies and in the provinces (A. H. J. Greenidge, *The Legal Procedure of Cicero's Time* (1901), 410 ff.; *CR* 1896, 225–33; 1897, 437–40, against J. L. Strachan-Davidson, *Problems of the Roman Criminal Law* (1912), i. 115 ff.). Thirdly, the *imperium* of pro-magistrates both legally and conventionally, and of magistrates by convention, was restricted to the bounds of their *provinciae* (*see further* PROVINCIA). *Imperium* needed ratification by a *lex curiata*—a convention which persisted to the end of the Republic (Cic. *Leg. Agr.* 2. 26; *Fam.* 1. 9. 25). To a pro-magistrate or a *privatus cum imperio*, *imperium* was granted for a year at a time, or until his commission was achieved. Grants of *imperium* for a specified term of several years occur only at the end of the Republic, the earliest being the grant of *imperium* to Pompey for three years by the *Lex Gabinia* of 67 B.C.

2. Octavian held *imperium*, *pro praetore* and later as consul in 43 B.C., as triumvir from 42 to 33 B.C., and as consul in 31–23 B.C. When in 27 B.C. he was given the administration of a large number of provinces and their armies for ten years, he was given *imperium* for their government. In 23 B.C., when he resigned the consulship, his constitutional power rested on the *tribunicia potestas* and on the *imperium*, which was *imperium proconsulare maius* (so E. G. Hardy, *Studies in Roman History* (1910), 283 ff., and most historians, against Pelham, *Essays on Roman History* (1911), 65–71, who thought it was *imperium consulare*). By virtue of this right Augustus was entitled in an emergency to interfere in the public provinces, as is proved conclusively by the Cyrene Edicts (*JRS* 1927, 34–8, 42 ff.: cf. Dio Cass. 53. 32. 5 and Ulpian in *Digest* 1. 16. 8); he was also by special dispensation allowed to exercise his *imperium*

from within the city of Rome (Dio Cass. l.c.). *Imperium* was granted to him for ten-year periods in 27 and 8 B.C. and A.D. 3 and 13, and for five-year periods in 18 and 13 B.C. It was voted to succeeding emperors at their accession by the Senate (Dessau, *ILS* 229, at Nero's accession), though the senatorial decree was probably ratified formally by a *lex curiata* (Gaius, *Inst.* 1. 5, 'lex de imperio'). The *imperium proconsulare* should be dissociated from the *praenomen imperatoris*. This was used by Augustus; though refused by Tiberius, Gaius, and Claudius, it appears frequently in inscriptions, and from the Flavian period onwards it was in common use. It is probable that this *praenomen* was inherited by Augustus from Julius Caesar, who used *Imperator* as *cognomen*.

3. *Imperium* was recorded in a different sense in the titles which followed the emperor's name. Under the Republic a general, after winning a victory and being saluted by his troops, adopted the official title *Imperator* (q.v.) until he celebrated his triumph. Under the Empire the whole army fought under the emperor's *auspicia*, and he, rather than the general who was his deputy (*legatus*), was accorded the *salutatio*. Emperors therefore recorded, among the titles which followed their names, the number of salutations which they had received, the first being the acclamation at the time of their accession. Claudius, for example, at the end of his life was *Imperator xxvii*.

4. *Maius imperium* was sometimes conferred on others besides the emperor, for the creation of a single military command—in this way it was granted to Germanicus in the East in A.D. 17 (Tac. *Ann.* 2. 43) and to Corbulo in A.D. 63 (Tac. *Ann.* 15. 25). If given for no such specific purpose, its recipient was indicated as a suitable successor to the Principate; in this sense it was granted to Agrippa in 18 B.C. (Dio Cass. 54. 12) and to Tiberius in A.D. 13 (Vell. Pat. 2. 121; Tac. *Ann.* 1. 3).

Mommsen, *Staatsr.* and A. H. J. Greenidge, *Roman Public Life* and passim. On the Republic, the articles mentioned above, and J. P. V. D. Balsdon, *JRS* 1939, 57 ff. On the Empire, Mason Hammond, *The Augustan Principate* (U.S.A. 1933); E. Kornemann, *Doppel-prinzipat und Reichsteilung im Imp. Rom.* (1930); A. von Premerstein, *Vom Werden und Wesen des Prinzipats* (1937); M. Grant, *From Imperium to Auctoritas* (1946); H. Wagenvoort, *Roman Dynamism* (1947), 59 ff.; H. Last, 'Imperium Maius', *JRS* 1947. J. P. B.

INACHUS, an Argive river and river-god, father of Io (q.v.). He was made judge between Poseidon and Hera when both claimed Argos, and decided in favour of Hera, whose cult he introduced (Apollod. 2. 13; Paus. 2. 15. 4–5); Poseidon therefore dried up his waters. He is often represented as a mortal, ancestor of the Argive kings. H. J. R.

INARIME, *see* AENARIA.

INCENSE, *see* SACRIFICE, PRAYER.

INCUBATION denotes the practice common among the Greeks and Romans of sleeping within the precincts of a temple for the purpose of receiving a vision, revelation, or relief from disease or pain. All gods could speak in dreams, but not all were thought capable of being induced by specific means to give an answer or perform a function. Some deities made a profound impression of their power upon the mind of the visitor. At the oracle of Trophonius at Lebadea, for instance, one received a memorable emotional experience by descending into the earth and visiting the god (Paus. 9. 39). The technique of incubation was generally used for producing cures, although it could be used to regain lost articles or to discover some important item of information. The technique, in a way, was akin to magic in that it brought performance on the part of the deity when one used the proper procedure. Incubation was most widely used in the temples of Asclepius. The practice is attested for the cult of this deity at Epidaurus (*IG* iv². 121–7); Pergamum and Smyrna (Aristides, *Sacred Orations*); Rome (*CIG* 5980); Lebene (Hamilton, *Incubation* 69); Cos (Pliny, *HN* 29. 4, Strabo, 14. 2. 19). The cult of Amphiaraus (q.v.) also fostered the practice, especially at Oropus (*Hermes* xxi. 91 ff. = *IG* vii. 235; Paus. 1. 34), and Strabo (14. 1. 44) mentions the practice at the three Plutonia in Asia Minor. The ability to heal was attributed to Isis, and Sarapis was widely acclaimed as a deity who communicated cures in dreams. Usually there was a regular ritual to be followed in practising incubation. The incubant frequently sacrificed an animal and slept on the animal's hide. Previously, very likely, he had been purified by lustration, and had fasted or abstained from certain foods. Incubation, as described in the record of cures from Epidaurus, involved mainly faith-healing, since medical remedies are not often mentioned. In the later inscriptions and literary works, especially in the *Orations* of Aristides, a medical prescription is usually given by the god. In some instances at least, the cure is regarded as having been produced by a combination of faith and drugs. Votive offerings frequently testify to cures produced by dream-revelations, and long inscriptions were often set up which detailed at some length the miraculous cures ascribed to the deity. In some temples (in the temple of Sarapis at Delos for instance) there were official interpreters of dreams as well as aretalogists whose duty it was to sing the praises of the god. Many of the dreams and the miracles which they wrought had no connexion whatever with cures or disease, though there must have been many cures recorded, especially cures of nervous ailments and mental complaints (*see* MIRACLES).

ANCIENT SOURCES: in addition to the sources cited, for the early period see Aristophanes, *Plut.* 658 ff., and Paus. 2. 27. 3. For the later period: A. D. Nock, 'A Vision of Mandulis Aion', *Harv. Theol. Rev.* 1934; *POxy.* 1381; P. Roussel, *Les Cultes égyptiens à Délos* (1916).

MODERN LITERATURE: L. Deubner, *De Incubatione* (1900); Mary Hamilton, *Incubation* (1906); W. H. D. Rouse, *Greek Votive Offerings* (1902).　　　　　　　　　　　　　　　　　　　J. A. B.

INCUBO, *see* FAUNUS.

INDIA. This country had early trade connexions with east Africa; but it remained unknown to Mediterranean peoples until the extension of the Persian Empire to the Indus and the voyage of Darius' admiral Scylax down the Kabul and Indus rivers and round Arabia to Suez (Hecataeus, frs. 244–9 Jacoby; Hdt. 3. 98 ff.; 4. 44). Even so, India remained a land of fable and wonders (as in the *Indica* of Ctesias, *c.* 400 B.C.); it was believed to lie in the Farthest East, yet Indians were confused with Ethiopians, and in popular belief India and Ethiopia formed one country. The conquests of Alexander (327–325) brought accurate knowledge of north-west India as far as the river Hyphasis (*Beas*), and vague information about the Ganges valley and Ceylon; and the voyage of Nearchus (q.v. 2) opened up a sea connexion with the Persian Gulf. Seleucus I perhaps penetrated to the river Jumna, but in 302 he relinquished India to the Mauryan king Chandragupta. He kept a resident named Megasthenes at Chandragupta's court in Patna, who published much detail about India (*see* MEGASTHENES, PALIBOTHRA); and King Asoka (264–227) sent embassies to the Hellenistic kings. In the second century north-west India was reoccupied by the Greco-Bactrian rulers (*see* DEMETRIUS (9), MENANDER (2)); but the rise of the Parthian Empire separated India from the Greek lands, and invaders from Central Asia (*c.* 80–30 B.C.) obliterated the Greek principalities in the Indus valley. In the first century A.D. Chinese silk reached the Roman dominions through India, but land-communications with India remained irregular. The chief routes to India were (1) via Meshed and the Bolan or Mula passes, (2) via Merv, Balkh, Kabul, and Peshawur.

2. Sea communications between India and the Persian Gulf were probably maintained by the Seleucids, but were interrupted under Parthian rule. Direct travel from Egypt to India was impeded for long by the Arabs of Yemen, whose monopoly of trade was not seriously challenged by the Ptolemies, and the voyages of Eudoxus (q.v. 3) to India proved abortive. The Arab obstruction was removed by the imperious appetite of Rome for Eastern luxuries in the prosperous days of Augustus, and by the discovery of open-sea routes from Africa to India. In the first century B.C., or soon after, the periodicity of the monsoons in the Indian Ocean and the right seasons for navigation were discovered by Hippalus (q.v.), and direct crossings to various points of the western coast were subsequently established (Pliny 6. 96–100). Augustus received Indian envoys (Dio Cass. 54. 9), and Greek merchants organized a regular trade from Egypt. In Augustus' day 120 ships sailed to India every year, and under his early successors the drain of Roman money to pay for Indian imports caused passing anxiety (Pliny 6. 101; 12. 84). The principal imports to Rome were perfumes, spices (especially pepper), gems, ivory, pearls, Chinese silk. The Romans exported linen, coral, glass, base metals, etc., and also sent much gold and silver (and later copper) coin, of which large hoards have been found in south India.

3. The chief marts on the west coast were Barbaricon (*Bahardipur*) and Barygaza (*Broach*) and, above all, the Tamil towns Muziris (*Cranganore*) and Nelcynda (*Kottayam*). Beyond Cape Comorin the Greeks visited Colchoi (*Kolkai*), Camara (*Kaviripaddinam*), Poduce (*Pondicherry?*), and Sopatma(*Madras*); a few reached the Ganges mouth and brought news of Burma, Malaya, and of the Thinae or Sinae (in S. China—*see* SERES). Greek traders figure in Tamil literature as residents in many of the inland centres (A.D. 70–140). The Maldives and Laccadives were now discovered, Ceylon was circumnavigated (*see* TAPROBANE); and one Alexander, taking advantage of the Bay of Bengal monsoon, sailed past Burma and Malaya to Cochin China and even to China proper (Ptolemy 7. 1–2). Nevertheless, Greek geographers always underrated the extent of India's southward projection and exaggerated the size of Ceylon. From *c.* A.D. 200 direct Graeco-Roman trade declined, communications with India passed into the hands of intermediaries (Arabians, Axumites, Sassanid Persians), and India again became a land of fable to the Mediterranean world. The founders of Christian settlements in India were mostly Persians.

V. A. Smith, *The Early History of India* (1924; embodying Indian records); H. Rawlinson, *Intercourse between India and the Western World* (1926); Warmington, *Indian Commerce* (1928); W. W. Tarn, *The Greeks in Bactria and India* (1938).　　　　　　　E. H. W.

INDICTIO, a prescribed charge or impost, especially a levy in kind (*annona*, q.v.) as opposed to precious metals. The *indictio* can be traced from the early Empire, especially in Egypt, but as an occasional and irregular charge. It assumed a new meaning and importance in A.D. 297 when Diocletian established the *indictio* as the schedule of rate of tax to be raised on *capita* and *iuga* for a period of fifteen years, divided into three census-periods of five years. If more was needed, a *superindictio* was added. The *indictio* was now applied to the whole Empire and was freely used as a method of dating, though there is some doubt whether the first *indictio* began in A.D. 297 or 312. The latter date is supported by E. H. Kase, *A Papyrus Roll in the Princeton Collection* (U.S.A. 1933), 25.　　　H. M.

INDIGETES or -ITES, INDIGITAMENTA. Both words, also the corresponding verb *indigitare*, are fairly common and there is no doubt that they mean respectively a class of Roman gods, a list of gods and their titles, and to address by the proper name or title. Concerning their more exact meaning and relation to one another three views have been held. (1) Peter in Roscher's

Lexikon, s.v., explains the *indigetes* as the *di minuti* (*Sondergötter*), deities of extremely limited function, as Cunina, who looks after the child in the cradle, Cinxia, who sees to the bride's girdle, etc. (2) G. Wissowa, *Gesammelte Abhandlungen*, 175 ff., refuted this. The *indigitamenta* contain names of other gods, including Apollo (Macrob. *Sat.* 1. 17. 15) and the Bona Dea (q.v.; ibid. 12. 21). Furthermore (Wissowa loc. cit. 304 ff.), the lists of the *di minuti* show many features suggesting late grammatical learning, not early priestly lore. He explained the *di indigetes* as native gods, from *indu*+rt. *gen*, an impossible etymology, but the latter half of the word could be explained (Th. von Grienberger, *Indogerm. Forsch.* xxiii. 337 ff.) as from root of *agere*, 'dwell'. *Indigitamenta* Wissowa supposed to be from *indu*+rt. *agh*, 'say'. Modifications of Wissowa's view are proposed by E. Goldmann (*CQ* xxxvi. 43) and H. Wagenvoort (*Imperium*, 1941, 85). Both understand *indiges* as 'active within', though they interpret this differently. (3) C. Koch, *Gestirnverehrung im Alten Italien* 1933, 78 ff., points out the absence of any sort of proof that the *indigetes* were native as distinct from foreign gods, or even an important class of deities. Starting from the cult of Sol Indiges he takes the epithet to mean 'ancestral' (but his proof is very unconvincing, see Rose in *Harv. Theol. Rev.* xxx (1937), 165 ff.) and makes *indigitare* mean 'treat as an *indiges*', i.e. worship, *indigitamenta* the formulae of address in such worship. At present *indiges* seems of doubtful meaning, but the connexion of it with the other two words likely.   H. J. R.

INDUSTRY (Greek and Roman). Craftsmanship in wood, bone, shell, earth, stone, and leather, as well as use of colour for painting and of fire for cooking purposes, and the preparing of primitive tools are palaeolithic, craftsmanship in textiles, pottery, architecture, flint-mining, and ship-building neolithic. Metal-work and glass production began with the Bronze Age, and rationalization of craftsmanship by written prescriptions, exact measures, and weights in the Ancient Oriental towns. The Indo-European and Semitic tribes of the Neolithic and Cuprolithic Ages had wandering craftsmen who performed the more difficult work of larger households. The crafts of smiths originated in the Bronze Age, representing the first village artisan, with his own workshop in some places. The Ancient Oriental, the Minoan, and Mycenaean metal-workers, potters, ship-builders, brewers, weavers, leather-workers, artists, and doctors occupied more often special workshops, mostly provided for them by kings, temple-rulers, and wealthy owners.

2. Homer and Hesiod mention a considerable variety of craftsmen. But only the smiths had their own workshops, a standard which was gradually reached by potters and, perhaps, ship-builders in Corinth, Athens, and other towns during the eighth and seventh centuries B.C. The money economy of the sixth century produced the *ergasterion*, a workshop able to produce for the needs of expanding markets, with a number of slaves and free workers under the control of foremen. *Ergasteria* of potters, leather-workers, and smiths are known from paintings of sixth-century Attic vases. Many other branches of craftsmanship followed during the fifth and fourth centuries, primarily those producing for export and the military and naval requirements of the Athenian Empire and other States. Craftsmanship in metal, leather, wood, bone, and pottery therefore reached a higher economic and social standard, and was specialized to a higher degree. Craftsmen of the branches of leather manufacture (Cleon, Anytus, Lysias father of Iphicrates), pottery (Hyperbolus), and of work in metal, wood, and bone (Cleophon, the fathers of Sophocles and of Demosthenes) could reach political and social honours in democratic Athens. Here we find shops with at least 20 to 30 slaves (owned by Demosthenes' father), yielding

annually from *c.* 15 to 30 per cent. of the invested capital. Division of labour is known in *ergasteria* which produced metal-work and from potters' shops, but was not usual everywhere. The craftsmen of Athens and other big towns seem to have sold more of their products to merchants and traders than to private customers. Only a few wandering craftsmen may have existed even in rural districts of Greece during the Classical period, the only exception being artists who roamed from town to town and from court to court. On the other hand, there existed wandering Greek metal-workers in the Persian Empire, in South Russia, Italy, and the Alps, who immigrated for longer or shorter periods and produced Greek merchandise on the spot. Specialized crafts of metal- and leather-workers, potters, dyers, musicians, and *fabri* (primitive all-round craftsmen), are ascribed by tradition to Rome under the kings. These craftsmen were organized in *collegia*, which were originally institutions with military obligations, but later of political and economic importance as well.

3. The Hellenistic age, and that of the later Roman Republic, produced a growth of the Greek *ergasterion* system which spread throughout the whole civilized world, and was introduced into textile and food production. Glass-blowing was invented; several glass producers of the first century B.C. and a potter, Aristion, of *c.* 200 B.C., seem to have had workshops in different towns. The Ptolemaic Empire combined the craftsmanship of the whole of Egypt in its industrial enterprises. The baths of Egypt, the production of papyrus rolls, oil, perfumes, textiles (perhaps not woollen goods), and beer became government monopolies. The craftsmen of these trades became State employees, who were controlled by tax-farmers and government officials, received salaries and, in the oil production, a share of the profit for their work. The State issued a production schedule each year and provided the workshops with tools and raw materials. Privileges were granted to temples and to distinguished owners who combined large estates with commercial, industrial, and banking enterprises; but State control was even there not completely removed. Large enterprises for fish-curing, for the production of metal-work and of bricks, also belonged to the Ptolemaic State, which might be considered the greatest trust organizer in the Ancient World.

4. Craftsmanship in Republican Rome developed on Greek lines during the second and first centuries B.C., periods of a considerable specialization and expansion of slave *ergasteria* throughout the whole of industry. The petty craftsmen often combined general retail trade with the sale of their own products. Another characteristic of Roman craftsmanship was the prevalence of great capitalistic enterprises which united different branches of industry with banking, commerce, and agriculture, and gave their slaves and freedmen the necessary capital for half-independent workshops. Among persons of this type we need mention only the elder Cato, the publisher Pomponius Atticus, and Rabirius Postumus with his big *terra sigillata* workshops.

5. Organizations of craftsmen were more common during these centuries than in the Classical period. Those of the city-states had almost exclusively social and religious intentions. They were tools of the Ptolemaic Government for orders and concessions throughout the Egyptian country-side. The Roman *collegia* mixed so much in politics that they had to be dissolved or strictly controlled (*see* CLUBS).

6. The period of the Roman Principate saw craftsmanship of the Greek and Roman type with its specialization, *ergasteria*, and great capitalistic enterprises, spreading over the provinces of the Empire. The Egyptian monopolies were broken up or changed into monopolistic concessions for small districts farmed out to independent craftsmen. Nevertheless, remains of controlled economy were found throughout the whole Empire as a Hellenistic heritage, especially in mining districts, temples, and public domains. Gradually the craftsmen of public and private estates began to furnish the local markets of provincial districts with bricks, coarse pottery, cheap leather- and metal-work, *terra sigillata*, cheap textiles, etc., and even to supersede town craftsmen. A regulated economy began to grow in many small regions from the second century A.D. Finally the State built up its own workshops for the needs of army, court, and administration, or commandeered private corporations of craftsmen for State purposes, and used them for the farming out of concessions and monopolies. During the crisis of the third century A.D. the craftsmen of whole regions became dependent on orders of the administration.

7. The Late Roman period, which begins with Diocletian, made this organized compulsion final. It did not mean a breakdown of technical knowledge; but the number of independent workshops decreased everywhere, and estate workshops and union between craftsmen and traders became the rule in the country-side of the Late Roman world. The State provided for its own requirements by establishing factories in all provinces and by regulating the more important *collegia* of craftsmen throughout the Empire. Sons had to follow their fathers' trade, and large taxes in merchandise had to be paid collectively by the corporations, which thus gained a new economic unity. Gradually they received privileges (especially during Justinian's reign), which enabled them to influence prices, to buy raw materials cheaply for all members, to regulate production and sale, workshop capacity, and the number of their members. The guilds of Byzantium, which are known from the tenth century A.D. and preserved a fundamental nucleus of Graeco-Roman technique and craftsmanship, originated directly from these earlier corporations, and the Christian, Jewish, and Islamic guilds of the Middle Ages are doubtless either in historic connexion with Byzantine institutions or, what is more likely in some cases, with Late Roman and similar Sassanian corporations of the periods before the Germanic and Arabic conquests in West and East. *See* ARCHITECTURE, DYEING, FULLING, METALLURGY, MINES, MONOPOLIES, POTTERY, SPINNING, WEAVING.

H. Blümner, *Technologie und Terminologie der Gewerbe und Künste der Griechen und Römer* i², ii–iv (1879–1912); M. N. Tod in *CAH* v, ch. 1; T. Frank, ibid. viii, ch. 11; F. Oertel, ibid. x, ch. 13; xii, ch. 7; H. Francotte and H. Gummerus, *PW*, s.v. 'Industrie und Handel'; H. Francotte, *L'Industrie dans la Grèce ancienne* i, ii (1900–1); T. Frank, *Economic History of Rome²* (U.S.A., 1927); *Economic Survey of Ancient Rome* i–v (U.S.A., 1933–40); G. Glotz, *Le Travail dans la Grèce ancienne* (1920); F. M. Heichelheim, *Wirtschaftsgeschichte des Altertums* (1938), index s.v. 'Handwerk'; Cl. Préaux, *L'Économie royale des Lagides* (1939); M. Rostovtzeff, *Social and Economic History of the Roman Empire* (1926); *Social and Economic History of the Hellenistic World* (1941); G. Mickwitz, *Die Kartellfunktionen der Zünfte* (1936); *Vierteljahrschrift für Sozial- und Wirtschaftsgeschichte* 32 (1939), 17 ff.; E. P. Wegener, *Mnemos.* iii (1936), 232 f.; H. Michell, *The Economics of Ancient Greece* (1940). F. M. H.

INFAMIA, condemnation for certain private delicts (e.g. theft, fraud) or in civil actions, where the defendant was guilty of breach of confidence (e.g. in case of *fiducia*, deposit, partnership, or guardianship), entailed for the condemned person diminution of his personal dignity (*existimatio*): he became *infamis* in the same manner as those who exercised certain shameful professions. Dishonourable or unseemly actions and bankruptcy involved *infamia*. The praetorian edict contained a long list of persons 'qui notantur infamia' (*Dig.* 3. 2); Justinian considerably extended this. *Infamia* entailed different disabilities for persons subject to it: incapacity to act for another at law; *intestabilitas* in some cases (*see* TESTIMONIUM); exclusion from offices and dignities (e.g. that of a judge); and so forth.

A. H. J. Greenidge, *Infamia in Roman Law* (1894); E. Levy, in *Studi Riccobono* ii; L. Pommeray, *Études sur l'infamie* (1937). A. B.

INFERI, *see* AFTER-LIFE, para. 8.

INHERITANCE, LAW OF. (*a*) GREECE. In Greek law (as at Athens and Gortyn) intestate succession was favoured. The sons and male descendants of the deceased came first in order of succession. In default of them his brothers and their descendants inherited, and in the third place the sons of his grandfather and their male descendants. Ascendants were excluded if their descendants were living: a brother of the deceased excluded the father, an uncle the grandfather. Adoptive sons were treated on the same footing as natural ones. The claims of sons and male descendants could not be set aside by testamentary dispositions. In general, males excluded females in the same group of kinship. A daughter inherited only if no sons or male descendants of predeceased sons existed; she was obliged to marry the man to whom her father had destined her either in his lifetime or by will. Failing such disposition the next collateral could claim the daughter, together with her father's fortune. But if a son remained, the daughter had no right to succeed and could demand only a dowry, to be determined at her brother's discretion.

2. Wills (introduced into Attic law by Solon) were allowed only when the testator had no sons; disinheritance was unknown. But testamentary provisions for the division of the inheritance were admitted, and legacies might be left. The institution of an heir was possible only when combined with adoption. No special forms such as setting down the will in writing were prescribed; it was usual to declare the will before witnesses. Legitimate sons could take possession of the inheritance without any formality, and they had no right to refuse it; other relatives needed an official authorization.

3. (*b*) ROME. The legal order of succession came into force only in cases of intestacy. The validity of a *testamentum* depended upon the appointment of an heir (*heres*), to whom the rights and duties of the testator passed as a whole. The ancient testamentary forms were subject to the supervision of the people assembled in *comitia*, or in military array (if war was imminent). A later form of merely private character was *testamentum per aes et libram*: the testator mancipated his estate to an intimate friend, obliging him to distribute it after his death according to his directions. The ancient forms soon fell out of use, and the mancipatory will became the normal form in classical times. The testator usually delivered his instructions on wax tablets to the fiduciary trustee, accompanying this action with a solemn oral declaration (*nuncupatio*). By a further development the praetor granted possession of the inheritance (*bonorum possessio*) to the successor designated in tablets sealed by seven witnesses (just the number of persons assisting at *mancipatio*, q.v.), irrespective of *nuncupatio*. This was the origin of the praetorian will, which was more convenient and more widely applicable than the quiritary forms. Thus there originated a dualism between civil and praetorian law, since the praetor preferred the successor appointed by such a simplified will to one who claimed the inheritance on intestacy in the absence of a civil will. Post-classical forms of wills had a partly public character, being entered on the rolls of a court or imperial chancellery or deposited in public archives. Justinian adopted a form which was legalized by a constitution of A.D. 439, and required the presence of seven witnesses and their seals and signatures in addition to the testator's.

4. There was also a contrast between civil and praetorian law on intestacy. The former entitled only agnatic relatives (i.e. people being in the same *patria potestas*, q.v.): in the first place, the descendants subject directly to *patria potestas* of the deceased, who became *sui iuris* by his death (*sui heredes*, males and females equally, natural and adoptive, the wife *in manu* being considered

as a daughter); in the second place, the next agnates (brothers, sisters from the same father). The praetorian law took into consideration blood relationship (*cognatio*) independent of *potestas*, and granted *bonorum possessio* to a group of persons neglected by *ius civile*, such as emancipated sons and their children, cognates up to the sixth and sometimes the seventh (partly) degree, adopted children, and many others. An important praetorian reform was the admission of further relatives when the successors of a foregoing class or nearer degree refused the succession, a practice unknown in the civil law. Lastly, when no blood relatives existed or all of them refused, *bonorum possessio* was given to husband or wife reciprocally; this was of particular importance in marriage without *manus*. After various subsequent innovations the succession in cases of intestacy was reformed by Justinian (*Novels* 118 and 127), who established the order of succession of descendants, ascendants, and collaterals on the cognatic principle.

5. Roman law recognized the claims of some next relatives even against the testator's will. *Sui heredes* of the *ius civile* could not be passed over in silence in a will, and must be formally excluded from inheritance, otherwise the will was void; similar provisions were introduced by the praetor with regard to all children. If disinheritance was not made correctly, *bonorum possessio* was given to the person omitted, contrary to the will. Later legislation, however, required a material provision in favour of such relatives and excluded an express disinheritance, unless there was a just cause for it. If the exclusion was not justified, the privileged successor could obtain by a special remedy (*querela inofficiosi testamenti*) a fourth part of what he would get on intestacy. *See also* LAW AND PROCEDURE, ROMAN, 1, and ADOPTIO.

(a) GREECE. F. Schulin, *Das griechische Testament* (1882); K. Hermann–Th. Thalheim, *Lehrbuch der griechischen Rechtsaltertümer* (1895); L. Beauchet, *Histoire du droit privé de la république athénienne* iii (1897); J. H. Lipsius, *Attisches Recht und Rechtsverfahren* ii, 1 (1912).
(b) ROME. C. Fadda, *Concetti fondamentali di diritto ereditario romano* i–ii (1900, 1907); V. Scialoja, *Diritto ereditario romano* (1914); G. La Pira, *La successione ereditaria intestata* (1930); S. Solazzi, *Diritto ereditario romano* i–ii (1932, 1933). A. B.

INHUMATION, *see* DEAD, DISPOSAL OF.

IN IURE CESSIO, *see* DOMINIUM.

INIURIA, *see* LAW AND PROCEDURE, ROMAN, III. 6.

INNOCENTIUS, *gromaticus*. An *agrimensor* of this name is known in A.D. 359 (Amm. Marc. 19. 11. 8), but the obscure treatise ascribed to I. in the *corpus gromaticorum*, apparently an exercise in map-reading, is of later date.

INNS were common in Greece and later throughout the Roman Empire. They had in general a bad reputation, though Strabo mentions that there were good inns in Egypt, and no doubt comfortable hotels existed in the larger towns and at watering-places. Wealthy men usually put up at *deversoria* of their own or in the houses of friends, but even they might have to content themselves with *cauponae*, as Maecenas did on his journey with Horace to Brundisium. Some inns were managed by the slaves or freedmen of the owner of a neighbouring villa. In the remoter parts of the Empire official resting-places (*praetoria*) were built by the government for its travelling officials, and accommodation could no doubt be secured in the *mansiones* of the *cursus publicus*.

Friedländer i. 290–3; W. A. Becker, *Gallus* (Engl. Transl. 1898), 351 ff. G. H. S.

INO, *see* ATHAMAS, LEUCOTHEA.

INSTITUTIONES were elementary text-books of Roman law. The most renowned work of this kind is the *Institutiones* of Gaius (q.v.). The same title was given

to an introductory part (*totius legitimae scientiae prima elementa*) of Justinian's codification published on 21 Nov. 533 shortly before the *Digest*, with which it contemporarily came into force six weeks later. This work, which was chiefly based on Gaius' *Institutes* and their system (*personae*, *res*, *actiones*), on his *Res cottidianae*, and on the *Institutiones* of other jurists (Marcian, Florentinus, Paulus), was compiled by Tribonianus (q.v.) and the eminent scholars Theophilus and Dorotheus, known also as collaborators in the *Digest*, to which they often refer. A considerable part of the book refers to Justinian's reforms. Numerous historical reminiscences and comparisons with earlier law increase its value.

C. Ferrini, *Opere* (1929), vol. i; A. Zocco–Rosa, *Justiniani Institutionum Palingenesia* (2 vols., 1908). A. B.

INSUBRES lived north of the Po. The most powerful people in Cisalpine Gaul, they frequently exercised dominion over the neighbouring Taurini, Salassi, etc. Their capital was Mediolanum (Strabo 5. 213). Livy (5. 34) represents them as Aedui who entered Italy via the Mont Genèvre Pass; but his account is untrustworthy. These Gauls, however, certainly established themselves about the Ticinus c. 400 B.C., and were henceforth called Insubres—probably a pre-Celtic name. C. 232 B.C. they clashed with Rome. At Clastidium (222) Marcellus stripped the *spolia opima* from their king. In 218 the new Latin colony at Cremona and Hannibal's arrival incited them to fresh efforts, until finally they were subjugated in 194 (Polyb. 2. 17 f.; Livy, bks. 21–34). Subsequently they disappeared as a separate nation. Insubrian districts obtained Latin rights in 89, full citizenship in 49 B.C. For bibliography *see* CISALPINE GAUL. E. T. S.

INSULAE, *see* HOUSES (ITALIAN).

INTERCESSIO was the right of the magistrate to veto a motion carried by another magistrate, provided the former was invested with *maior* or *par potestas*. A dictator's measures could not be vetoed as his authority was supreme. *Intercessio* arose from the idea of magisterial collegiality, and was reputed to be a necessary precaution against any abuse of their power by magistrates. The same principle was later applied to municipal administration. A particular form of *intercessio* was the right of the tribunes (*intercessio tribunicia*) to veto any measure which they held to be contrary to the interests of the plebs or the whole community. As, however, every tribune possessed this right, every one of them could veto any of his colleagues' measures. *Intercessio* was valid only within the sphere of civil legislation and within Rome, and fell into disuse when it was conferred upon the emperors, as a part of their *tribunicia potestas*. *See also* COLLEGIUM.

Mommsen, *Röm. Staatsr.* i³. 258 ff.; ii³. 290 ff. P. T.

INTERCIDONA, *see* PILUMNUS.

INTERDICTUM, *see* LAW AND PROCEDURE, ROMAN, II. 11.

INTEREST, RATE OF. The rate of interest in Greece and Rome is known from the fifth century B.C., throughout which the temple of Delos gave loans at 10 per cent. The Roman Republic fixed interest at 8⅓ per cent. (*fenus unciarium*) in 357 B.C. A *Lex Genucia* of 342 forbade usury completely; but this law, though re-enacted several times during the fourth, third, and second centuries, fell into disuse because it was economically impossible.

During the fourth century the interest of town mortgages in Athens amounted to c. 8 per cent., and of country mortgages to c. 6–12 per cent. Other loans brought from 10 to 33⅓ per cent., and on the average c. 12 per cent. A contemporary Delphic law fixed the interest of normal loans at 9 per cent., of small short-term loans at, perhaps, 25 per cent. Safe investments in the Greek motherland brought 6 to 10 per cent. during the third century, 24 per cent. in the Hellenistic East of the same period, from 5 to 10 per cent. in Egypt during the later second century.

The maximum rate of interest introduced by Lucullus and Cicero for their Asiatic provinces was 12 per cent.; Sulla decreed in 88 B.C. a maximum of 8¾ per cent., and the Roman Senate in 51 B.C. 12 per cent., a regulation valid throughout the Roman Empire for centuries. Interest in Rome during the first century B.C. was normally *c.* 6 to 10 per cent. for safe investments, while loans in kind brought up to 50 per cent.

The maximum rate of interest was increased to 12½ per cent. during the fourth century A.D. More capital seems gradually to have accumulated during the following centuries, and Justinian was able to fix the ordinary interest at 6 per cent., that for trade investments at 8 per cent., and that which senators might demand at 4 per cent. Bottomry loans (q.v.) were excepted from these and earlier regulations.

H. Billeter, *Geschichte des Zinsfusses im griechisch-römischen Altertum bis auf Justinian* (1898); T. Frank, *Economic Survey of Ancient Rome* i–iv (U.S.A. 1933–8), Indexes; E. Grupe, *Sav. Zeitschr. Röm. Abt.* 46 (1926), 26 f.; F. M. Heichelheim, *Wirtschaftsgeschichte des Altertums* (1938), Index s.v. 'Zins'. F. M. H.

INTERNATIONAL LAW, *see* LAW, INTERNATIONAL.

INTERPRETATIO ROMANA, literally, 'Roman translation' (Tacitus, *Germ.* 43. 3); the use of a Latin divine name, as Mercurius, to signify a foreign god, as Odin. This is merely a particular case of the assumption that all peoples worshipped the same gods; thus the Greeks regularly call Minerva Athena, and the Romans speak of Zeus as Iuppiter. Foreign divine names were hardly used unless no native equivalent could be found, as Apollo in Rome, or a foreign cult (e.g. Isis, Mithra) was adopted.

G. Wissowa in *ARW* xix (1916–19), 1 ff.; cf. H. J. Rose, *Roman Questions of Plutarch*, 53 ff. H. J. R.

INTERREX was originally the magistrate appointed by the senators on the death of a king to exercise provisional authority. On the simultaneous death, illness, or resignation of both consuls, an *interrex* was successively appointed from each of the senatorial *decuriae* for five days, until the auspices were taken and the new consuls elected. The *interrex* had to be a patrician and a senator. He exercised all the functions of the consulship, and was escorted by twelve lictors. The last known example of *interregnum* occurred in 43 B.C. *Interreges* also held temporary office in cities of Latin Italy until the dawn of the Imperial age.

Mommsen, *Röm. Forsch.* i. 218 ff.; *Röm. Staatsr.* i³. 647 ff. P. T.

INUUS, *see* FAUNUS.

INVULNERABILITY. Such stories of invulnerable men or beasts as are found in classical mythology mostly conform to the Sigurd type, in which there is one vulnerable spot (*see* ACHILLES, AIAS (1)), or the Balder type, in which there is one thing which can wound (Nemean lion; own claws, Theoc. 25. 277. Caeneus, q.v.; (?) wooden pikes, Hyg. *Fab.* 14. 4 and Rose ad loc.).

O. Berthold, *Die Unverwundbarkeit* (1911); and *see* MESSAPUS. H. J. R.

IO, in mythology, priestess of Hera at Argos; usually said to be daughter of Inachus (q.v.). Zeus loved her, but to conceal her from Hera gave her the shape of a heifer. Hera asked to be given the heifer, which Zeus could hardly refuse; she set Argos (q.v. 3) to watch her. On his being killed by Hermes Hera plagued Io with a gadfly, which drove her out of the country. After long wanderings she came to Egypt, where Zeus restored her

with a touch of his hand; hence the son which she bore him was called Epaphus (from ἐφάπτειν). For his descendants *see* DANAUS. See especially Aesch. *PV* 561 ff.; Ov. *Met.* 1. 583 ff.; Apollod. 2. 5 ff. Io was identified with Isis (q.v.; Apollod. 9); this is in turn due to Isis' identification with Hathor, who has bovine shape. Rationalizations of the story were current early, as Hdt. 1. 1. 4–5 (she was kidnapped by Phoenicians); Ephorus ap. schol. Ap. Rhod. 2. 168 (she was kidnapped and the Egyptians sent Inachus a bull for compensation). It has been suggested that she was originally a moon-goddess (hence the cow-horns), or a form of Hera (q.v.); see Engelmann in Roscher's *Lexikon* ii. 269; Farnell, *Cults* i. 200; Eitrem in *PW* ix. 1732 ff. H. J. R.

IOCASTA, *see* OEDIPUS.

IOLAUS, *see* IPHICLES.

ION (1), eponymous ancestor of the Ionians; his legend as we have it seems to be Attic in all its forms. He is the son of Creusa (q.v. 1), but his father, in the tradition followed by Euripides, is Apollo (Patroös); elsewhere, as in Apollod. 1. 50, he is Xuthus, son of Hellen (q.v.). After the death of Erechtheus, Xuthus, Ion, and his brother Achaeus (q.v. 1) have adventures which vary from author to author and obviously have more to do with early ethnological theory than real tradition (see Stoll in Roscher's *Lexikon*, s.v., for particulars), but regularly Ion settles sooner or later in Athens and divides the people into the four traditional Ionian tribes, Hopletes, Geleontes, Argadeis, and Aigikoreis (named after his four sons, Eur. *Ion* 1575 ff.). H. J. R.

ION (2), of Chios, but equally at home in Athens, Greek poet, was probably born about 490 B.C. He was on friendly terms with Cimon, whom he met, with Themistocles, at a dinner party in Athens about 475, and whose sociability he contrasted with the aloofness of Pericles; and in 462 he heard Cimon speak in the Assembly in favour of assisting Sparta when hard-pressed by her neighbours (Plut. *Per.* 5, *Cim.* 9, 16). Anecdotes record his meeting with Aeschylus at the Isthmian Games (Plut. *De prof. virt.* 8), with Sophocles at Chios in 441–440, when the latter was a general in the Samian War (Ath. 13. 603 e), and possibly with Socrates (Diog. Laert. 2. 23). He was fond of his wine and other pleasures—the satyric element which, as he said, virtue, no less than tragedy, needed to complete it (Plut. *Per.* 5). He died before 421 (Ar. *Pax* 835 and schol.). His first appearance as a tragic poet was about 451 B.C. (Suidas, s.v.); in 428 he was defeated by Euripides when the latter produced the *Hippolytus* (Arg. Eur. *Hipp.*), but on another occasion he won the first prize at the Great Dionysia for both tragedy and dithyramb, and in his delight made a present of Chian wine to every Athenian citizen (Ath. 1. 3 f.). The number of his plays was variously given as 12, 30, or 40 (Suidas, s.v.). The known titles include, from the Heraclean cycle of legend, *Alcmene, Eurytidae,* and the satyric *Omphale*; from the Trojan, *Agamemnon, Laertes, Teucer, Φρουροί* (dealing with Odysseus' entry into Troy as a spy); and besides these, *Argivi, Phoenix* or *Caeneus,* and *Μέγα Δρᾶμα* (a title unparalleled for a Greek tragedy); but fragments are few and insignificant (*TGF*, pp. 732–46). The Alexandrian critics admitted him to the *Canon* —their select list of outstanding tragic poets (Cramer, *Anecd. Par.* 4. 197, etc.); Aristarchus and Didymus wrote commentaries on his plays (Ath. 14. 645), and Baton (2nd c. B.C.) a monograph on him (Ath. 10. 436). In the treatise *On the Sublime* (23) he is described as a faultless and perfectly finished writer in the 'smooth style', but without the force and fire of Pindar and Sophocles. In addition to his tragedies he composed elegiac poems, epigrams, encomia, paeans, hymns, scolia, possibly a comedy, at least one cosmological work in prose, a history of the founding of Chios (of which Pausanias 7. 4. 8 made use), and memoirs (perhaps of several kinds) in which there were personal reminiscences of a number of famous men. (The exact meaning of the titles Ἐπιδημίαι and Συνεκδημητικός is uncertain. The former may have given an account of the visits of distinguished persons to Chios, as Bentley suggested, or of his own travels; the latter may have been a 'travelling companion'. The title Ὑπομνήματα probably covers both: cf. Ath. 13. 603, schol. Ar. Pax 835, Pollux 2. 88, etc.)

See A. von Blumenthal, Ion von Chios (1939); T. B. L. Webster in Hermes lxxi (1936), 263 ff.; F. Jacoby in CQ xli (1947), 1 ff.
A. W. P.-C.

IONIAN SEA (Ἰόνιος, Ἰώνιος κόλπος), a name used alternatively with 'Adriatic Sea' for the waters between the Balkan Peninsula and Italy; no clear line of demarcation can be drawn between the two seas. The name 'Ionian', like that of 'Adriatic', was sometimes extended to include the sea to east of Sicily.
M. C.

IONIANS (Ἴωνες, Ἰάϝονες), a section of the Greek people mentioned but once by Homer (Il. 13. 685, Ἰάονες ἑλκεχίτωνες), but important later, after the central part of the west coast of Asia Minor (still non-Greek in Homer) had become known as Ionia.

Ionia was colonized, according to early traditions, by refugees from the Greek mainland, flying before the Dorians and other tribes from north-west Greece (Mimnermus in Strabo, p. 634; Hdt. 1. 145–8; Thuc. 1. 12). Herodotus (1. 146–7) speaks of the mixed blood of the colonists, and adds that some of them took the women of the conquered Carians. All were, however, reckoned as Ionians 'who trace their descent from Athens and keep the Apaturia' (q.v.).

The claim of Athens to be the mother-city of all Ionians will not hold, as Herodotus himself says; and the eponymous ancestor Ion (q.v.) could only artificially be worked into the Athenian genealogies, themselves extremely artificial. But the Athenian claim to be the 'eldest land of Ionia' was as old as Solon, and long preceded any Attic claims to political predominance (Arist. Ath. Pol. ch. 5); and it receives some confirmation from the reappearance of the four ancient 'tribes' of Attica—the Aigikoreis, Hopletes, Geleontes, and Argadeis—in inscriptions of Delos, Teos, Ephesus, Perinthus (a Samian colony), Cyzicus, and Tomi (Milesian colonies). There may be truth in the Athenian claim to have organized the emigrants.

The Ionic dialect, first known to us from Homer, was spoken (with local variations) in a compact region comprising the Cyclades, Ionia proper, Euboea, and Attica. The fact that inscriptions from Chios show some forms akin to the adjacent Aeolic and the surviving Aeolicisms in Homer—mostly metri gratia (εἷος, λαός, for ἕως, λεώς, etc.), but also gratuitously (e.g. Ναυσικάα, ὁράᾳτο) —suggest that Ionic arose after the migrations, among the States whose culture-centre was at Delos. Its area was subsequently expanded by colonization.

A mixed race, inheriting something of the Aegean civilization, and highly 'selected' amid the turmoil of the migrations, the Ionians, from about 800 B.C., developed precociously (see the brilliant picture in the Hymn to the Delian Apollo). Indeed, the whole achievement of Greek colonization (q.v.) and Greek rationalism belongs to them and to those neighbouring Greeks who came within their orbit. Throughout the East 'Yawani' (Javan: Genesis x. 2) became the generic term for 'Greek' (cf. Frank, Feringhi). They were, however, exposed to attack from the Lydian and Persian monarchies, and the effort to throw off the despotic though beneficent yoke of Darius ended in ruin after a heroic struggle of six years (494). Then came Athenian overlordship and the unmerited depreciation of Ionians as unmanly (Hdt. 1. 143; 5. 69; Thuc. 5. 9; 6. 77; 8. 25). To fifth-century Greek

theory 'Dorian' and 'Ionian' corresponded to 'Nordic and 'Mediterranean' in modern Europe (Hdt. 1. 56). The generalization that credited the former with more steadfastness, the latter with more intelligence, is in each case open to numerous exceptions: contrast the sobriety of Ionian Olbia or Massilia (Strabo 179–80; Dio Chrys. Borysthenite Discourse) with the unstable brilliance of Dorian Syracuse and Tarentum in Thucydides and Livy.

D. G. Hogarth, Ionia and the East (1909); CAH iii, ch. 21. See also CHIOS, EPHESUS, MAGNESIA, MILETUS, PHOCAEA, PRIENE, SAMOS.
A. R. B.

IONIC, see DIALECTS, GREEK.

IONIC, MAJOR and **MINOR,** see METRE, GREEK, III (13).

IOPHON, son of Sophocles, competed with frequent success, sometimes with his own tragedies, sometimes, it was suspected, with his father's (or at least with his father's help) (Ar. Ran. 73 ff. and scholia). He won the second prize in 428, Euripides being first and Ion third (Arg. Eur. Hipp.). The story that he tried to obtain control of his father's property by accusing him of senile decay, and that Sophocles disproved the charge by reading from the Oedipus Coloneus, is very doubtful (Vit. Soph., etc.). He wrote an epitaph for his father's monument after his death (Val. Max. 8. 7. 2). He was credited with fifty plays (Suidas, s.v.).

TGF 761.
A. W. P.-C.

IPHIANASSA, see AGAMEMNON, ad fin.

IPHICLES, in mythology, twin brother of Heracles (q.v.), also called Iphiclus. He was Heracles' companion on some exploits and father of Heracles' better-known companion Iolaus. Two other children of his were killed by Heracles in his madness (Apollod. 2. 61 ff.; schol. on Lycoph. 38 and Od. 11. 269; Nic. Dam. fr. 13 Jacoby).
H. J. R.

IPHICRATES (c. 415–353 B.C.), Athenian general. A man of humble origin, he first won fame by commanding a company of peltasts who annihilated a Spartan division (390). During the Corinthian War he led successful raids from the Isthmus, and afterwards (386) took service as a mercenary commander in Thrace, where he married Cotys' daughter, and in Syria against the Egyptian rebel kings. After returning to Athens (373) he was sent to relieve Corcyra from a Spartan invasion. He succeeded, but caused dissatisfaction by failing to prevent Epaminondas from invading the Peloponnese (369). He led the Athenian attempts to recover Amphipolis (367–364), but on his failure ceased to be στρατηγός and retired to Thrace. With his son Menestheus he commanded the Athenian fleet at Embata (355), and was afterwards prosecuted by his colleague, Chares, but acquitted. Two forensic speeches, now lost, were cited under his name (Dion. Hal. Lys. 12).

Iphicrates was notable as the general who first established the importance of peltasts (q.v.). He also had a reputation for strictness of discipline and the ingenuity of his stratagems.

Xenophon, Hellenica, and Diodorus, bks. 14–16 (passim); Nepos' Life (poor); C. Rehdantz, Vitae Iphicratis, etc. (1845); U. Kahrstedt, PW, s.v. 'Iphikrates'; Prosop. Att. 7737.
H. W. P.

IPHIGENIA (Ἰφιγένεια), perhaps a by-form of Artemis (A. Iphigeneia at Hermione, Paus. 2. 35. 1; Ἰφιγένεια ἡ Ἄρτεμις, Hesychius) (q.v.), but in mythology a daughter of Agamemnon. For some reason he was obliged to sacrifice her, either because he had vowed to sacrifice the fairest thing born in a particular year, and she was born then, or because he had offended Artemis by an impious boast (Eur. IT 20 ff., cf. IDOMENEUS; Soph. El. 569, whereon see Jebb). She enforced this by delaying the fleet at Aulis with contrary winds until the sacrifice was made (Aesch. *Ag.* 184 ff. and elsewhere; the story is from the *Cypria*). Iphigenia was therefore sent for to Aulis, under pretext that she was to be married to Achilles before the fleet sailed (*Cypria*; Eur. *IA*), and led to the altar. Aeschylus (loc. cit.) implies that she was actually killed; but the story in the *Cypria*, followed by Euripides, *IT*, is that Artemis snatched her away, substituting a hind for her, and brought her to the country of the Tauri. There, according to the version followed by Euripides, she was Artemis' priestess, and by the local rite she had to superintend the sacrifice to the goddess of all strangers caught in the country. At length Orestes (q.v.) came there with Pylades, having been instructed that he could finally get rid of the Erinyes if he brought to Greece the Taurian image of Artemis. Both were taken prisoner, but during the preparations for sacrifice Iphigenia discovered who they were and under pretence of purificatory rites got them and the image away from the temple to the sea-shore, whence they escaped with the help of Athena. The image was duly brought to Halae in Attica (cf. ATTIC CULTS), where Iphigenia continued to be priestess, the goddess was given the title of Tauropolos, and a pretence of human sacrifice (a slight cut made in a man's throat) was kept up.

The local legend of Brauron said that the sacrifice of Iphigenia took place there, and that a bear, not a hind, was substituted for her (schol. Ar. *Lys.* 645, an interesting example of adaptation of a Panhellenic story to particular purposes; for the rite which it purports to explain, *see* ARTEMIS). Antoninus Liberalis, 27, says the surrogate was a calf, and that Iphigenia finally was made immortal and married to Achilles (q.v.) on Leuce.

P. Clément in *Antiquité classique* iii (1934). H. J. R.

IPHIS, in mythology, (1) father of Eteoclus, one of the Seven against Thebes, and of Euadne, wife of Capaneus (q.v.). (2) A young Cypriot, who loved Anaxarete, a noblewoman of that island. She would have none of him, and he finally hanged himself at her door; she looked, unmoved, from her window, and was turned by Aphrodite into stone. The resulting image was called Aphrodite *prospiciens* (ἐκκύπτουσα?).

See Ovid, *Met.* 14. 698 ff., cf. Ant. Lib. 39 (from Hermesianax). H. J. R.

IRIS, the goddess of the rainbow, and for the most part hardly distinguishable from the natural phenomenon itself. She appears to have had no cult at all, being simply, when thought of as in human form, a messenger of the greater gods, presumably because the rainbow seems to touch both sky and earth. In Hesiod (*Theog.* 266 ff.) she is daughter of the Titan Thaumas and Electra the Oceanid, and sister of the Harpyiae (q.v.). According to Alcaeus (fr. 13 b Diehl, from Plutarch, *Amat.* 765 e) she is the mother by Zephyrus of Eros, a conceit which means no more than that in moist spring weather men feel amorous; a few later writers catch it up. As messenger of the gods she is specialized to Hera in many of the later poets, e.g. Callimachus, *Del.* 228 ff., where she sleeps under her throne like a dog; Homer represents Zeus as her usual employer. H. J. R.

IRON. The earliest specimens are mainly of meteoric origin, though smelted iron belonging to the third millennium has been found in Mesopotamia. Probably meteoric iron was used for Mycenaean jewellery, and Homer mentions it as a valuable metal. In the thirteenth century it was mined in Hittite territory. It appears suddenly as the material for weapons in Greece in perhaps the eleventh century. The change was probably due to the failure of bronze-supplies, as in other countries the replacement was gradual. It was hardly an advance, as early iron was of uncertain quality. Homer speaks of an iron knife, but has no explicit reference to iron swords.

Greece possesses small iron-deposits, but the main sources in classical times were Elba and the Chalybes country behind Trapezus. The manufacture of iron articles was concentrated at Athens and the Isthmus States. As geographical knowledge extended, other sources became available. The magnetite sands of Thrace were used at an early date. Spanish iron was prized under the Roman Republic, and from about 40 B.C. Rome drew on the deposits of Noricum. The mines of inner Dalmatia are of later date. In many parts of Gaul are enormous slag-heaps, and British iron was used locally. Indian iron is mentioned, but cannot have been of economic importance.

The furnaces of the ancients could not normally produce cast iron. Statues were made by chasing pure wrought iron. Weapons were of mild steel. Quenching to harden is known as early as Homer, and certain waters were thought (without real reason) to be particularly suitable. The Romans understood intentional carburization and annealing, and by complicated damascening they produced blades which would not snap. They did not use water-power, and all iron-working was by hand. Semi-nomadic natives often reduced the ore in the mountains, and sold the blooms at cities or at military forts, where they were forged into tools.

O. Davies, *Roman Mines in Europe* (1935). O. D.

ISAEUS (1) (*c.* 420–350 B.C.). Nothing is known with certainty about the life of this orator; it is even doubtful whether he was an Athenian by birth, and some ancient authorities call him a Chalcidian. Traditionally he was a pupil of Isocrates and a teacher of Demosthenes. His political views, if he had any, were never allowed to intrude into his speeches, which were all composed for delivery by others. All the extant speeches are concerned directly or indirectly with questions of inheritance. The earliest of these, if we follow Jebb (*Attic Orators* ii. 350), is *Or.* 5, which he assigns to the year 390 B.C., but a later date (372) is possible, in which case the earliest is 377. The date of the latest is *c.* 353.

WORKS. Of fifty speeches which the biographer (Ps.-Plutarch) considered genuine we possess eleven and the fragment of a twelfth. Six deal with disputed inheritance. Three refer to prosecutions for false witness in testamentary cases. *On the estate of Hagnias* throws light on the Athenian law of collateral succession. In the *Euphiletus* the speaker appeals to have his name restored to the roll of his deme. Dionysius quotes a fragment from the *Eumathes* for comparison with the style of Lysias.

Isaeus is our chief authority for the laws of inheritance, in which he was an expert. In addition to his minute legal knowledge, he possessed a singular skill in stating a case, so that the most complicated pleadings assume, under his treatment, the appearance of lucidity. His language is comparable to that of Lysias for simplicity, but he uses a certain number of words which have a poetical association, and some few colloquialisms. Dionysius considered him artificial in comparison with Lysias, but the examples which the critic gives do not make this statement obvious. His efficiency is beyond question; to read his speeches is a fine intellectual exercise; but he makes no appeal to the senses.

For general bibliography *see* ATTIC ORATORS. Text: Teubner (Thalheim, 1903). Commentary: W. Wyse (1904). Text and Translation: E. S. Forster (Loeb); P. Roussel (Budé). Index: W. A. Goligher (in *Hermathena* li–liii; in progress). J. F. D.

ISAEUS (2) (1st c. A.D.), Syrian rhetor, famous in Trajan's time at Rome for improvisation and for impassioned and epigrammatic utterance (Plin. *Ep.* 2. 3; Juv. 3. 74).

ISAGOGIC LITERATURE denotes didactic compositions addressed to particular recipients and intended as an introduction (εἰσαγωγή) to the knowledge of a science or to the practice of an art or of an activity, administrative or political. The word is used in Latin under its Greek form or latinized, *isagoga* (Gell. 1. 2. 6; 14. 7. 2; 16. 8. 1). Sometimes it is rendered by *institutio* or *introductio*. An author occasionally employs the method of question and answer, and often divides his work into two principal parts, *ars* and *artifex*: e.g. Quintilian bks. 2–11, *ars oratoria*; bk. 12, *orator*. Conformably with Roman practical inclinations, isagogic literature had a wide range at Rome.

We may cite as specifically isagogic: Cato, Varro, Columella, their treatises on agriculture; Cicero, *Partitiones Oratoriae*; Q. Cicero, *Commentariolum petitionis*; Horace, *Epistula ad Pisones*; Vitruvius, *De Architectura*; Celsus, *De Medicina*; Frontinus, *De Aquis*; Quintilian, *Institutio oratoria*; Vegetius, *Epitoma rei militaris*.

L. Mercklin, 'Die isagogischen Schriften der Römer', *Philol.* iv (1849); Jahn, 'Über römische Encyclopädien', *Berichte der sächs. Gesellsch. der Wissensch.* ii (1850); E. Norden, 'Die Poetik des Horaz als isagogische Schrift', *Hermes* xl (1905), 508.

C. F., transl. J. W. D.

ISAURIA was the inland face of the central chain of Mt. Taurus, corresponding to Pamphylia on the seaward slope. Its inhabitants were notorious for brigandage. They evaded attempts to reduce them until the Roman general Servilius (q.v. 2) Isauricus systematically captured their strongholds, chief among them Isaura Vetus and Isaura Nova (76–75 B.C.). Isauria was included by Augustus in the province of Galatia. Though pacified, it was little developed; Isaura Vetus, the chief stronghold, was the only place to attain municipal status. M. C.

ISAURICUS, *see* SERVILIUS (2) and (3).

ISCA, British river-name, hence applied to sites on rivers so called:

(1) Ptolemy's Isca (2. 3. 3), where he fixes the Second Legion (ibid. 14) is apparently a site on the Axe (Bradley, *Archaeologia* xlviii. 390), and there are traces of the Second Legion near its mouth (*Eph. Epigr.* ix. 1268 a).

(2) Modern Exeter on the Exe was occupied as a military post under Claudius and became a walled town, the capital of the Damnonii (or Dumnonii), with trading connexions (cf. *Numismatic Chronicle*⁵ xvii. 1–12). See Shortt, *Sylva Antiqua Iscana* (c. 1840); publications of the Devon Archaeological Exploration Society.

(3) Modern Caerleon on the Usk was probably from c. A.D. 75 the fortress of Legio II Augusta. Originally consisting of timber buildings surrounded by a clay bank, it was gradually rebuilt in stone, and its bank fronted with a stone revetment from 99–100 (*JRS* xviii. 211). During periods of reduced occupation in the second century its buildings decayed; but a complete overhaul occurred under Severus and his successors; a partial rebuilding is recorded 254–60 (*ILS*, 537). The legion left Isca towards the end of the century. Christian martyrs Aaron and Julius may be realities (Gildas, 10), but an archbishopric is fabulous. Administrative buildings (including a hospital?), barrack-blocks, and, of extramural works, an amphitheatre and baths have been excavated.

Archaeologia Cambrensis lxxxiv–lxxxvii, xc; *Archaeologia* lxxviii, 111–218 (Amphitheatre); R. G. Collingwood, *Archaeology of Roman Britain* (1930), 22–4, 104. C. E. S.

ISIDORUS (1), a Greek of Charax, near Tigris mouth, wrote c. A.D. 25 on Parthia and its pearl-fisheries (Ath. 3. 93 d), and, to judge from Pliny, a general geographical work, a portion perhaps of which is the extant Σταθμοὶ Παρθικοί, a meagre description of 'stations' from Zeugma on the Euphrates through Seleuceia, Ecbatana, Rhagae, Caspian Gates; Hyrcania, Parthia, etc., to Alexandria (*Kandahar*).

GGM i, lxxx ff., 244 ff.; W. Schoff, *The Parth. Stations of I. of C.*; *PW* ix. 2064–8. E. H. W.

ISIDORUS (2) **HISPALENSIS,** bishop of Seville (A.D. 602–36), one of the most important links between the learning of antiquity and the Middle Ages. His chief works were: (1) *Chronica*, a history extending to his own times; (2) *Historia Gothorum*, preserved in two editions; (3) *De natura rerum*, (4) *Differentiae*, in two books, (5) *Quaestiones in vetus Testamentum*; (6) *Etymologiae* or *Origines* (now divided into twenty books), a widely used encyclopaedia which deals not only with the seven liberal arts but also with geography, law, medicine, natural history, prodigies, gems, foods, drinks, etc. (*See* ENCYCLOPAEDIC LEARNING.) Though Isidore does not often mention his sources, it is clear that he gathered his information from a wide range of authorities (including Pliny and Suetonius). His works are printed in J. P. Migne's *Patrologia Lat.*, vols. lxxxii–lxxxiv, and the *Etymologiae* are separately edited by W. M. Lindsay (2 vols., 1911).

Cf. Teuffel, § 496; M. Manitius, *Geschichte der Lat. Lit. des Mittelalters* i. 52–70. J. F. M.

ISIGONUS of Nicaea (1st c. B.C. or 1st c. A.D.), a writer of *paradoxa* (see PARADOXOGRAPHERS), who probably drew to some extent on Varro, and was himself drawn upon by Pliny the Elder.

A. Westermann, *Paradoxographi* (1839), 162–3; *FHG* iv. 435–7.

ISIS, in Egyptian religion, was the wife of Osiris and the mother of Horus. In addition to her position as a national deity in Egypt, Isis acquired in the Hellenistic age a new rank as a leading goddess of the Mediterranean world. Her worship was established in Piraeus by the fourth century by Egyptians residing there. Most of the foundations of her cult in the Aegean area during this period, however, included her as a member of the new Hellenistic cult of the Egyptian (q.v.) deities along with Sarapis, Harpocrates, and Anubis (qq.v.). Many of these cults in the Greek cities soon became public ones and were managed by priests who were magistrates of the State. Yet one finds attached to some of these public cults such groups as the *melanephoroi*, a fact which indicates that there probably was some sort of periodic ritual or ceremony carried on. While we know of relatively few temples of Sarapis in Egypt during the Ptolemaic era, most of the priests in Greece are known as priests of Sarapis or of Sarapis and Isis. In Egypt, however, even in the city of Alexandria, Isis seems to become very soon the more important of the two deities. The inscriptions written by Greeks in Egypt mention the cults and festivals of Isis more frequently than those of Sarapis, and the name of Isis usually appears ahead of that of Sarapis. The cult of these gods was highly Hellenized, at least in externals: the statues and temples are frequently Greek in design and execution, the priests, in Greece at least, are usually civic functionaries, and the language of the cult is Greek. The practices of the cult, such as incubation, the interpretation of dreams, festive banquets, and cult societies, have a Hellenic character, though there are Egyptian analogies for many of them. Herodotus had identified Isis with Demeter, but in the early Hellenistic age she is identified, via Hathor, with Aphrodite, with Arsinoë II the wife of Ptolemy II, and with later Ptolemaic queens. The plastic representation of her in Greece is almost uniformly Hellenic in character, portraying her with the ancient Egyptian head-dress, in a long garment with a characteristic knot of drapery on the breast. In her most Hellenic form she is shown with serene, ideal, and typically Greek features, with no head-dress, but a curl or braid of hair hanging down each side of her face. Isis came more and more to mean all things to all men. In the great hymns which celebrate her manifold accomplishments, virtues, and miracles, she is addressed as 'O Thou of countless Names', and is identified with many and varied goddesses. Although the cult of Isis had, in many instances in Greece, the external appearance of a typical public city-state cult, it had also, to some extent in Greece and in the West, the characteristics of a mystery cult as well. The range of experience involved in participation in the cult runs all the way from individual initiatory rites to the elaborate cult drama which celebrated the old myth of the death and resurrection of Osiris. At Rome, Pompeii, near Corinth, and probably at other places the elaborate mysteries of Isis were carried out. At the numerous other temples of Isis which we know in the Graeco-Roman world it is frequently difficult to say just what form the ritual of the cult assumed. Prominent among the characteristics of the cult of Isis which distinguished it from ordinary Greek and Roman cults were the appearances of an Egyptian professional priesthood, the regular ritual, the use of sacred water from the Nile, elaborate processions, penitents, dances, and the use of musical accompaniments. Certain festivals were of especial importance, one of the most significant being the Ploiaphesia which marked the opening of the season of navigation. That these Mysteries and their attendant ritual could awaken a deep religious emotion is testified by the conversion of Lucius which Apuleius describes (*Met.* bk. 11). Of all the temples of Isis known to us, the one at Pompeii is most perfectly preserved. Here we find at the top of a flight of steps a high platform upon which sacred rites were performed, a cistern for holding Nile-water, homes or cells for the priests, and many of the other arrangements necessary for the celebration of the worship. Although Sarapis and other deities of the group associated with Isis were worshipped in her temples, it is she who appears as the chief deity, occupying the place that Sarapis had frequently held in the public cults of Greece. The goddess Isis as she was presented in the Mysteries, however, must have drawn a more devoted and significant type of worship than was ever inspired by a civic deity. Not only are the statues and monuments of her worship found in all parts of the Roman Empire and her symbols quite commonly used on rings, gems, pins, and other jewellery, but many grave reliefs and tombs show representations of her symbols, particularly the *sistrum* and the *situla*. The deceased, if a woman, was frequently portrayed on the funeral monument in the costume characteristic of the deity.

ANCIENT SOURCES: W. Peek, *Der Isishymnus von Andros und verwandte Texte* (1930). For other sources *see under* SARAPIS *and* EGYPTIAN DEITIES.

MODERN LITERATURE. In addition to the literature cited under SARAPIS and EGYPTIAN DEITIES the following are important: A. Erman, *Die Religion der Ägypter* (1934); W. Drexler, art. 'Isis' in Roscher's *Lexikon*; A. D. Nock, in *CAH* xii (1939).   T. A. B.

ISLES OF THE BLEST, *see* AFTER-LIFE.

ISMENE, *see* ANTIGONE (1).

ISOCRATES (436–338 B.C.), Athenian orator, is reputed to have studied under Prodicus and Protagoras, to have visited Gorgias in Sicily, and to have been a friend of Socrates. His family estate having been dissipated in the course of the Peloponnesian War, he adopted the profession of rhetoric. He at one time conducted a school of rhetoric in Chios—perhaps in 404–403 (Jebb). Owing to nervousness and the poorness of his voice he never appeared in court, but between 403 and 392 he composed numerous speeches for others. About the latter date he opened a school at Athens, and continued his work as a teacher till after 351. The last period of his life was mainly occupied in writing: his intellect remained unimpaired to the end, for at the age of ninety he published one of his most important works, the *Philippus*; and between 342 and 339 he wrote the *Panathenaicus*. His last composition was a letter congratulating Philip of Macedon on his victory at Chaeronea (338). He died a few days later.

2. Isocrates, apart from his technical skill, is important for his views on education and his political theories. (*a*) He may himself be described as a sophist in the older and honourable sense of educator. He used the speech-form as Plato used the dialogue, where modern practice uses the essay. Most of his speeches and some of his letters are simply tracts. *On the Sophists* is directed not against the profession as a whole, but against those members of it who betray their high calling; they are dishonest, for they promise more than they can possibly perform. Only the first half, composed c. 390, is extant, and it contains only destructive criticism; but the speech *On the Antidosis*, c. 355, contains I.'s *apologia* for his own life and profession. His 'Philosophy' is distinguished from abstract speculation, from 'eristic', from literary work *per se*, and from the practical rhetoric of the law courts. It is, in fact, a laborious training for practical political life.

(*b*) Isocrates was a patriot, but beyond the narrow limits of life in a city-state he could look out on a Hellenism which was to civilize the world. In 380 he composed the *Panegyricus* for recitation at the Olympic festival. He saw no way to establish peace and unity unless some common cause could teach the Greeks to regard themselves as a nation. He suggested that Sparta and Athens should make a compromise in their claims to leadership and head a union of all States in a national war against Persia. His hopes were dashed by the rise of Thebes to supremacy, but in 368 he suggested to Dionysius of Syracuse that he should come forward as a national champion. Again disappointed, he appealed in 356 to Archidamus, king of Sparta, to put an end to civil war and curb the insolence of the barbarians. Finally, in 346, I. directed a masterly appeal to Philip of Macedon to take the lead and unite the four principal cities in a great expedition to conquer the East. After the battle of Chaeronea he may well have thought that his hopes could at last be realized.

3. WORKS. (*a*) Educational. *Against the Sophists* (390 B.C.). *On the Antidosis* (355 or 353)—the forensic form, though suggested by the fact that I. had been respondent in a case for *antidosis* in 355, is not maintained throughout.

(*b*) Political. *Panegyricus* (c. 380). *Plataicus* purports to be a speech for delivery in the Ecclesia on the occasion of the destruction of Plataea by the Thebans in 373. *On the Peace* (355) includes strong criticism of Athens' present politics and of the treatment of her allies under the old Empire. *Areopagiticus* (355) supplements the *De Pace* and contrasts the conditions of life under Solon and Cleisthenes with those of I.'s own days. *Philippus* (346 B.C.), see supra. *Archidamus*, an imaginary speech by the Spartan king discussing proposals of peace made by Thebes (366).

(*c*) Exhortations. *To Demonicus* and *To Nicocles* (374) concern the duties of a monarch, *Nicocles* (372) the duties of subjects.

(*d*) Epideictic Speeches. The *Busiris* (391) and *Encomium of Helen* (370) show how legendary subjects should be treated (*see* ENCOMIUM). The *Evagoras* (c. 365) is a panegyric on the late king of Salamis. The *Panathenaicus* (342–339) deals mainly with the historical aspect of the greatness of Athens.

(*e*) Forensic Speeches. I. considered this type of speech unworthy of him. We possess six examples of such early work. The *De Bigis* (No. 16) is spoken by the younger Alcibiades against Tisias, who asserts that the father of A. robbed him of a team of horses.

(*f*) Letters. A number of letters, mostly addressed to kings, are ascribed to I. Their authenticity, often disputed, is defended by Blass (*Att. Ber.* ii. 326–31).

4. The works of Isocrates represent Attic prose in its most elaborate form. Dionysius (*Comp.* 23) compared it to 'closely woven material', or 'a picture in which the

lights melt imperceptibly into shadows'. He seems, in fact, to have paid more attention to mere expression than any other Greek writer. He was so careful to avoid hiatus that Dionysius could find no single instance in the whole of the *Areopagiticus*; he was very sparing even in the elision of short vowels, and crasis, except of καί and ἄν, occurs rarely. Dissonance of consonants, due to the repetition of similar syllables in successive words, and the combination of letters which are hard to pronounce together, is similarly avoided. These objects are attained without any perceptible dislocation of the natural order of words. Another characteristic of the style is the author's attention to rhythm; though avoiding poetical metres, he considered that prose should have rhythms of its own, and approved of certain combinations of trochee and iambus. His periods are artistic and elaborate; the structure of some of the longer sentences is so complex that he overreaches himself; he sacrifices lucidity to form, and becomes monotonous. His vocabulary is almost as pure as that of Lysias, but while the simplicity of Lysias appears natural, the smoothness of Isocrates is studied.

For general bibliography *see* ATTIC ORATORS. Text: Teubner (Benseler–Blass, 1879), with App. Crit. E. Drerup (vol. i, 1906). Text and Transl.: Norlin and Van Hook, 3 vols. (Loeb); Mathieu and Brémond (in progress—Budé). Commentaries: *Cyprian Orations*, E. S. Forster (1912); *De Pace* and *Philippus*, Laistner (1927); *Trapeziticus*, Bongenaar (1933). Special Studies: *Les Idées pol. d'I.*, G. Mathieu (1923); *Evagoras*, J. Sykutris (in *Hermes* 1927). Index, S. Preuss (1904). J. F. D.

ISOPOLITEIA is a term that probably originated in the practice of granting citizenship to new citizens on terms of equality with older citizens and thus means practically the same as *politeia*. The word was used frequently in grants to individuals but also became a technical term, used both in documents and literature, for grants to the entire citizen body of a State and particularly for reciprocal grants between two States. This use of the term occurs first in the second half of the third century, though the institution existed earlier; a unilateral grant occurs as early as 405/4 B.C. (Athens to the Samians), and there were several reciprocal grants in the fourth century. Cities connected by *isopoliteia* were not merged but remained distinct; in fact *isopoliteia* is included in several treaties of alliance. Instead, the citizens of one State became potential citizens of the other; to become active citizens it was necessary to establish residence and be registered. For the others there were such privileges as *enctesis* (the right to own land), *epigamia* (the right to contract a marriage), and the right to trade without paying import and export duties. *Isopoliteia* was used extensively by Miletus and the Aetolians.

ANCIENT SOURCES. Examples of documents: *SIG* 116, 172, 421, 472, 522, 633; *GDI* 4940, 5039–40, 5075, 5183–5; *Milet* i, pt. 3, nos. 136–7, 141–3, 146.
MODERN LITERATURE: C. Lécrivain in Dar.–Sag., s.v.; *J.* Oehler, *PW*, s.v.; E. Szanto, *Das griechische Bürgerrecht* (1892), ch. 2; G. Busolt, *Griechische Staatskunde*, index. J. A. O. L.

ISTER was the name given by the Greeks to the lower Danube. From a knowledge of its estuary, where they established a colony before 600 B.C. (*see* ISTRIA 1), the Greeks drew conclusions as to the size of the Danube. Hesiod mentioned it as one of the four great streams of the world (*Theog.* 337). Herodotus regarded it as the largest river of Europe and a northern counterpart to the Nile (4. 47–51). He correctly stated that it had a constant volume of water, but mistakenly assumed that its last bend was to the south and was quite in the dark as to its source. In the third and second centuries the Greeks probably ascended as far as the Iron Gates, but they remained ignorant as to the river's upper course; perhaps misled by a vague inkling of the river Save, and by the name of the Histri in the hinterland of Trieste, they imagined that the Ister threw off an

arm into the Adriatic. This error was corrected by the Roman advance from Italy into the Danube basin after 200 B.C.; the identity of the Ister with the Danuvius was probably established during Octavian's Illyrian campaign in 35 B.C. (Sall. *Hist.* fr. 79). *See also* DANUVIUS.
M. C.

ISTER of Cyrene (*c.* 250–200 B.C.), pupil of Callimachus. His chief work was concerned with the mythical period of Attica in some sixteen books, quoted under various titles, Συναγωγή τῶν Ἀτθίδων, Ἀττικά, etc. Contrary to the practice of the other atthidographers, Ister in none of the fragments refers to the historical period, and there is no trace of any chronological arrangement. Accounts of festivals and cults appear in widely different books, which suggests a subject system, perhaps by kings or localities. It was a compilation from the earlier atthidographers dealing only with the mythical period, and the last in the series of Ἀτθίδες.

FHG i. 418. G. L. B.

ISTHMIA. The Isthmian Games were athletic competitions held at Corinth in honour of Poseidon, the prize being a crown of wild celery. According to one legend they were founded by Sisyphus, king of Corinth, to commemorate his kinsman the sea-god Melicertes Palaemon. The Athenians preferred the story that they were established by Theseus after he had killed the robber chief Sinis. This was one reason why the Athenians especially patronized the Isthmian Games, but there were others: the journey was easily made, Corinth was the pleasure city of Greece, and, although there was less parade, there were more amusements at the Isthmian than at the other three festivals. They were definitely organized, as an international festival held in every second year, in 581 B.C. F. A. W.

ISTRIA (1) or **ISTRUS**, a Milesian colony, founded between 650 and 600 B.C. on an island south of the Danube estuary. Originally a fishing-village, it soon became a trading centre for the lower Danube basin, where it distributed Ionian, Corinthian, and (after 525 B.C.) Attic pottery. It maintained a factory near modern Braila, and its coins had a wide currency. In the third century it forwarded Greek wines (especially those of Thasos and Rhodes) as far as the Iron Gates, and withstood attempts by Lysimachus to curtail its independence (315), and by the Byzantines to control its commerce (260). After 200 Istria was often attacked by the hinterland peoples; in 72 M. Lucullus made it into a Roman dependency.

V. Pârvan, *Dacia* (1928), 81–93. M. C.

ISTRIA (2) or **HISTRIA**, a peninsula at the northeastern extremity of the Adriatic, lying between Venetia and Illyricum and extending inland towards the Julian Alps. The Illyrian Istri inhabited the peninsula, eastwards to the plateau of the Cicceria and Monte Maggiore, and to the river Arsia; the western strip of the Istrian Peninsula was inhabited by the Liburni. The Istri were known as pirates, but the Romans did not interfere before 221 B.C., when the Istri seized a ship carrying corn. How far they were subdued then is not known, for the Second Punic War must have hindered the Romans from establishing their power in Istria. As the Istri showed a hostile attitude when Aquileia was founded, the Romans conquered them after capturing their chief settlement (178–177). Though under Roman supremacy, the Istri did not cease threatening Aquileia, as is shown by Livy 43. 1. 5 (171 B.C.). In 129 the Istri and Iapudes were defeated by C. Sempronius Tuditanus (cf. *CIL* i². 652 and addit., p. 725). In 52 the Istri attacked Tergeste (*Trieste*), to whose aid Caesar sent troops; this probably was the reason for their siding with Pompey in the Civil War. In the west their territory must once have reached the

Timavus (Strabo 5. 9, 215 c), but the Formio was made the frontier in the first century B.C., no doubt because the Celtic Carni had occupied the territory round Tergeste. Istria, which was part of Illyricum during the Republic, became part of Italy under Augustus, and with Venetia formed *regio* X.

Weiss, *PW*, s.v. 'Histria'; H. Nissen, *Italische Landeskunde* ii. 1 (1902), 237 ff.; A. Gnirs, 'Forschungen über antiken Villenbau in Südistrien', *JÖAI* xviii (1915), 99–164; A. Gnirs, *Istria praeromana* (1925); archaeological reports in *Not. Scav.*; A. Degrassi, 'Istria archaeologica (1918–32)' in *Aevum* vii (1933), 279 ff.; 'Notiziario archeologico' in *Atti e Mem. d. Soc. Istriana d. Arch. e Stor. patria* 1928 ff. F. A. W. S.

ISYLLUS of Epidaurus, author of six poems found inscribed at Epidaurus in a hand of about 300 B.C. Nos. I and III are dedications, the first in trochaic tetrameters, the other in an elegiac couplet followed by three hexameters. II is a hexameter poem in which the poet praises himself for the introduction of a procession to Phoebus and Asclepius to Epidaurus. IV is a paean to Apollo and Asclepius, and V a hymn in hexameters to Asclepius, in which the poet thanks the god for defending Sparta from the attack of King Philip, and which may refer to the war of 338 B.C. The poems have little poetical merit.

J. U. Powell, *Collect. Alexandr.* 132–6. C. M. B.

ITALIC DIALECTS, *see* DIALECTS, ITALIC.

ITALICA (nowadays *Santiponce* near Seville) was founded by Scipio Africanus as an outpost against the Lusitanians (206 B.C.). It received municipal status, probably from Augustus, and contributed to Rome three emperors, Trajan, Hadrian (who made it a *colonia*), and Theodosius I. Its wealth is attested by the remains of the fourth largest amphitheatre of the Roman world, and by its coins, statues, mosaics, etc. (Seville Museum). The magnitude of its oil exports is indicated by the fragments of amphorae from Italica in the Monte Testaccio at Rome.

Conde de Aguiar, *Italica* (1929). J. J. Van N.

ITALY. The name *Italia*, probably a graecized form of Italic Vitelia (= 'calf-land'), was originally restricted to the southern half of the 'toe' but was gradually extended. By 450 B.C. it meant the region subsequently inhabited by the Bruttii (q.v.) (Theophr. *Hist. Pl.* 5. 8); by 400 it embraced Lucania (q.v.) as well (Thuc. 6. 4; 7. 33). Campania (q.v.) was included after 325, and by Pyrrhus' day Italia as a geographical expression meant everything south of Liguria and Cisalpine (q.v.) Gaul (Zonar. 8. 17); this area, however, only acquired political unity after the Social War. Cisalpine Gaul was not officially incorporated until Augustus' time when, accordingly, Italy reached its natural Alpine frontiers. Unofficially, however, whatever the administrative divisions, the whole country south of the Alps has been called Italy from Polybius' time onwards. The Augustan poets also call Italy *Hesperia* (= 'the western land'), *Saturnia* (= strictly Latium), *Oenotria* (= strictly SW. Italy), *Ausonia* (= 'the land of the Ausones', *Opica* to the Greeks: strictly Campania).

2. Italy's greatest length is roughly 700 miles; the greatest breadth of the peninsula proper is some 150 miles. Its long coast-line possesses comparatively few, mostly indifferent, ports, Genoa, Spezzia, Naples, Tarentum, Brundisium, Ancona, and Pola being noteworthy exceptions. In compensation, however, Italy could exploit its central position to build a Mediterranean empire. Mountains, valleys, and plains in juxtaposition feature the Italian landscape. On the north are the Alps, a natural but not impassable frontier: the Carnic Alps pass is not formidable and the Brenner from time immemorial has been used by invaders attracted by Italy's pleasant climate, fertility, and beauty; the Alps actually are steeper on the Italian side. Between Alps

and Apennines lies the indefensible North Italian plain watered by the Padus (q.v.). The Apennines (q.v.) traverse peninsular Italy, impeding but not actually preventing communications; the ancients' belief that they abounded in minerals was erroneous, since Italy only possessed some alluvial gold, copper (Etruria), iron (Elba), and marble (Liguria).

3. Despite fertile upland valleys the mountain districts usually permitted only a frugal existence. The plains, however, were amazingly productive, being enriched partly by volcanic activity (Euganean district in the north, Alban Hills in Latium (q.v.), Mons Vultur in Apulia (q.v.), the still-active Vesuvius in Campania), partly by fertilizing silt carried down by numerous rivers which in winter contained adequate amounts of water. (Northern Italy also possessed important lakes, but not central and southern Italy apart from Trasimenus, Fucinus, and water-filled craters like Albanus and Avernus.) Italy's natural products were consequently abundant and varied: olives, various fruits, cereals, timber, etc., even though some typically Italian products of to-day, e.g. oranges, were unknown in antiquity. The variety is explained chiefly by the varied climate, which is temperate if not cold in the mountains and northern Italy and warm if not hot in southern Italy. Possibly the ancient climate was slightly more equable; malaria was certainly less prevalent. Italy contained excellent pasturage; in many districts ranching supplanted agriculture. Also its seas abounded in fish.

4. Italy was thus well adapted to support human life and attract invaders, and actually did so from very early times. Traces of Neanderthal not to mention palaeolithic man have been found, while remains of neolithic people, chalcolithic *terramaricoli* (*see* TERREMARE), and iron-using Villanovans (q.v.) are copious. Long before the rise of Rome Italy was well populated and civilized from end to end. On the east coast were Illyrian immigrants: Veneti, Picenes, Messapii (qq.v.); these occasionally penetrated to the west. Hardy Sabelli (q.v.) and the related Umbrians and Volsci (qq.v.) held and tended to expand from the mountainous central regions. The southern coast-lands comprised Magna Graecia (q.v.). In the north Gauls began to settle c. 400. Various peoples inhabited the west: Ligurians, who were possibly of neolithic stock and originally held a wider area; Etruscans; Latini and the related Falisci and Hernici (qq.v.); Aurunci-Ausones and Oenotri (= Sicels?). These various peoples differed greatly from one another in race, language, and civilization, and Italy's mountainous configuration accentuated and perpetuated their mutual divergencies.

5. But ultimately they were united under the hegemony of Rome. Her political unification of Italy, however, was a protracted task finally accomplished only in Augustus' day. The romanization of Italy took much longer and, indeed, was never fully achieved.

6. After unifying Italy Augustus divided it into eleven administrative districts:

   i. Latium, Campania, Picentini district.
  ii. Apulia, Calabria, Hirpini district.
 iii. Lucania, Ager Bruttius.
 iv. Region inhabited by Samnites, Frentani, Marrucini, Marsi, Paeligni, Aequiculi, Vestini, Sabini.
  v. Picenum, Praetuttii district.
 vi. Umbria, Ager Gallicus.
vii. Etruria.
viii. Gallia Cispadana.
 ix. Liguria.
  x. Venetia, Istria, Cenomani district.
 xi. Gallia Transpadana.

This arrangement lasted almost unaltered until Constantine's time, when the islands were customarily included in Italy.

BIBLIOGRAPHY

ANCIENT SOURCES: Strabo's detailed description (bks. 5 and 6) is good; *inter alia* it corrects Polybius' assertion (2. 14) that Italy is triangular. Pliny's account (*HN* 3. 38–132) is based on Augustus' *Commentaries*. Pomponius Mela (2. 58–73), Ptolemy (bk. 3), and the *Liber Coloniarum* are less important. Amongst others Varro (*Rust.* 1. 2. 1 f.), Virgil (*G.* 2. 136 f.), Dionysius of Halicarnassus (1. 36 f.), Propertius (3. 22. 17 f.), Pliny (*HN* 37. 201 f.), and Rutilius Namatianus (2. 17 f.) extol Italy's beauty and fertility. Roads are described in the Itineraries, especially the Antonine Itinerary (4th-c. copy of a work of *c.* A.D. 212) and Peutingerian Table which is probably based on Castorius' world-map of A.D. 366. See, too, the separate articles: VIA APPIA, etc.

For epigraphic finds, see *CIL* xi and *Inscriptiones Italiae* (Italy: 1932–); for archaeological, *Notizie degli Scavi, Monumenti Antichi*, and *Forma Italiae* (1928–).

MODERN LITERATURE: (i) *General.* H. Nissen, *Italische Landeskunde* (2 vols. 1883, 1902); A. v. Hofmann, *Land Italien u. seine Geschichte* (1921); F. Sabin, *Classical Associations of Places in Italy* (U.S.A. 1928); P. Ducati, *Italia Antica* (1932; illustrated).

(ii) *Special.* Economics: A. Sambon, *Monnaies antiques de l'Italie* (1903); T. Frank, *Economic Survey of Ancient Rome*, vols. i, v (U.S.A. 1934, 1940; documented). Ethnography: J. Whatmough, *Foundations of Roman Italy* (1937; documented). Maps: *Edizione Archeologica della Carta d'Italia* (1 : 100,000). Maps of Istituto Geografico Militare (Florence). Bibliographies for Italian cities: Mau–von Mercklin–Matz, *Katalog der Bibliothek des deutsch. arch. Inst. in Rom* (1914–32). *Italia Romana: municipi e colonie* (1939–). R. Thomsen, *The Italic Regions from Augustus to the Lombard Invasions* (Copenhagen, 1947). E. T. S.

ITERDUCA, see JUNO.

ITHACA was the name given by the Greeks in historical times to the small island east of Cephallenia (mod. *Thiaki*). This island conforms generally to the description of Homer's Ithaca, but ancient writers found a difficulty in *Od.* 9. 21–7, and especially in ll. 25–6, where Ithaca is described as the outermost and westernmost of the Ionian isles, which Thiaki is not; and Strabo (10. 454–5) was not successful in explaining this passage away. The problem was recently restated by W. Dörpfeld, who identified Homeric Ithaca with Leucas and sought to prove his case by excavation. Others defend the claims of Thiaki, and British scholars have excavated several sites on Thiaki. On both islands remains of the appropriate (Late Helladic) date have been found, but nothing decisively Homeric has come to light. The question therefore remains an open one.

For recent summaries of either theory, see W. Dörpfeld, *Alt-Ithaka* (1927), and Sir Rennell Rodd, *Homer's Ithaca* (1927); also Bürchner in *PW* xii. 2240–57. M. C.

ITHOME, a prominent and easily fortified mountain rising isolated in the Messenian plain (2,646 feet), was the rallying point of the Messenians in their struggles for independence against Sparta. In the first Messenian War they held it for twenty years; on its fall they lost their freedom. In 464 the revolted helots fortified it, and maintained it against all assaults. Epaminondas founded the town of Messene on its west side, fortifying it with some of the finest extant Greek walls, which include Ithome as an acropolis.

Tyrtaeus; Thuc. 1. 101–3. T. J. D.

ITHYPHALLIC VERSE, see METRE, GREEK, III (2).

ITINERARIES were in the form of *itineraria adnotata* (road-books) and *itineraria picta* (maps). Much of the information used by the compilers of such productions was originally derived from the map of the Roman Empire set up in Rome under Augustus by Agrippa (Plin. *HN* 3. 17), but with the development of the road-system the amount of detail available was greatly increased. The most important surviving example of an *itinerarium adnotatum* is the so-called Antonine Itinerary, which probably dates from the early third century A.D. but contains later additions. It covers almost the whole of the Empire, but its arrangement is so unsystematic that it can scarcely be an official publication. It is, however, of great value in establishing the sites and names of Roman towns. Other itineraries are the *Itinerarium Maritimum*, which gives distances by sea in the Mediterranean, and the Jerusalem Itinerary, composed in the fourth century for pilgrims to the Holy Land. The latter follows the roads from Bordeaux to North Italy, Sirmium, and Constantinople, and then through Asia Minor, and gives two alternative routes for the return journey. The only extant example of the *itinerarium pictum* is the so-called Peutinger Table. As it is in the form of a strip of 21 feet by 1 it is not a map in the modern sense: it gives not only distances but representations of natural features. Itineraries were regarded as of special value to generals operating in unfamiliar country.

H. F. Tozer, *History of Ancient Geography*[2] (1935), 306 ff.; W. Kubitschek, s.v. 'Itinerarien' in *PW*; G. Parthey and M. Pinder, edition of Antonine Itinerary (1848). G. H. S.

ITINERARIUM AETHERIAE ABBATISSAE, *see* PEREGRINATIO AD LOCA SANCTA.

ITURAEA. The Ituraeans, a predatory Arab people, occupied the Libanus, Antilibanus, and Hermon, and the Massyas, where lay Chalcis their capital and Heliopolis (q.v.) their religious centre. In the early first century B.C., under their tetrarch and high-priest Ptolemy, they almost captured Damascus, having conquered most of the country north and south of it. Ptolemy was confirmed by Pompey (64); his son Lysanias was killed by Antony (35), who granted his dominions to Cleopatra. The tetrarchy was restored by Octavian (30) to Zenodorus, who was, however, soon deprived of most of it owing to his depredations (24). Parts were granted to Berytus, Sidon, and Damascus; part became the tetrarchy of Abilene; Batanaea, Trachonitis, and Auranitis went to Herod, who on Zenodorus' death in 20 received Paneas and Gaulanitis also. Herod's Ituraean dominions passed to his son Philip (4 B.C.–A.D. 34), Agrippa I (37–44), who from 41 also ruled Abilene, and Agrippa II (53–*c.* 93), who ruled Abilene and in addition Arcene, an Ituraean tetrarchy in northern Libanus which had never belonged to the main principality. Chalcis formed a kingdom for Herod, brother of Agrippa I (41–8) and Agrippa II (50–3). The Ituraeans were gradually broken of their predatory habits, but remained a primitive people, living in villages. Famed as archers, they contributed three cohorts and an *ala* to the imperial army.

A. H. M. Jones, *JRS* 1931, 265–72; *Eastern Cities*, 255 ff. A. H. M. J.

ITYLUS, see AËDON.

ITYS, see PHILOMELA.

IUDEX. In the Roman civil procedure (*see* LAW AND PROCEDURE, ROMAN, II), with its bipartite arrangement in two stages *in iure* and *apud iudicem*, the *iudex* was a private person taken from the higher social classes (senators and, later, *equites*). No special juridical education was legally required; only persons with physical defects, women, and *minores* were excluded. For a particular trial the judge was designated by both parties, or, in default of such agreement, by choice from a panel of qualified jurors (*album iudicum*). Normally the plaintiff proposed the judge, but the defendant could reject persons whose impartiality seemed to him suspect. The parties' choice, approved by the magistrate *in iure*, was binding for the *iudex*, who was unable to refuse the commission conferred upon him by the magistrate's *iussum iudicandi*, except when he could adduce motives for exemption such as old age, a numerous family, or a privileged profession (philosopher, physician, rhetorician). For the proceedings *apud iudicem* see the article quoted above. The functions of the *iudex*, assisted during the trial by juridical advisers (*consilium*), ended with the sentence pronounced by him orally in the presence of the litigants. He could, however, refuse to pass a sentence when the matter did not appear to him quite cleared up, in which case the trial was repeated before another *iudex*. In classical times the *iudex* had full discretion in appraising the evidence and was not bound by previous decisions in similar cases. Nevertheless, judicial sentences (*res iudicatae*) tended to acquire authority in later times (*Dig.* 1. 3. 38) and were not without influence on the evolution of the law. The *iudex* was responsible to the wronged party for an unjust decision passed by unfairness or negligence. The XII Tables punished by death the judge convicted of bribery; the praetorian edict introduced a special civil remedy against the careless or corrupt judge (*qui litem suam fecit*). In special cases the judge was called *arbiter* (being more expert than *iudex*), where the matter at dispute required more professional knowledge, or estimates and technical calculations, as in the division of property or inheritance. His discretion was larger than that of *iudex*. As a rule a single judge was provided (*unus iudex*), but there were also courts composed of several persons, *recuperatores*, *centumviri* (qq.v.), and *decemviri stlitibus iudicandis* (*see* VIGINTISEXVIRI).

In the *cognitio extra ordinem* the judge was appointed by the imperial law officer alone or later by the emperor, independently of the parties. He was now called *iudex datus*, *pedaneus*, or *specialis*, and his competence (final decision or only a partial cognition of the case) depended on his commission. Under the late Empire the use of the term *iudex* became much larger: each official endowed with jurisdictional or administrative power was so called. Therefore '*iudex*' was often interpolated in classical texts in place of judicial magistrates. Justinian's constitution, *Cod.* 3. 1. 14. 1, demonstrates the wide application of the term.

For the bibliography, see the article quoted above. A. Steinwenter, *PW*, s.v. 'iudex' (vol. ix and Suppl. v); J. Mazeaud, *La Nomination de unus iudex* (1933); P. Collinet, *Le Rôle des juges* (Recueil d'études F. Gény i, 1935).   A. B.

IUDICIA POPULI. An old Roman rule sanctioned by the XII Tables prescribed that only the people assembled in *Comitia Centuriata* could pass sentence of death on a Roman citizen. Hence each capital sentence passed by the competent magistrate (except the dictator) was subject to revision in a trial before the people (*iudicium populi*), judging in second instance on account of the appeal (*provocatio ad populum*) of the condemned. Appeal was also admitted when the magistrate imposed a fine (*multa*) exceeding the legal maximum (thirty oxen and two sheep or about 3,000 *asses*); such matters were brought before the Tribal Assembly.

The proceedings before the magistrate in cases where a *iudicium populi* was obligatory (only on appeal from a citizen) were peculiar in that the investigation by the magistrate was made *in contione*, i.e. before the assembled people, who subsequently judged by what they heard, as repetition of the evidence was not prescribed. The people had no option but wholly to confirm or to quash the magistrate's sentence; alteration was not admissible. The case was decided by a majority of votes; voting was by word of mouth until 107 B.C., by ballot after that date. A magisterial acquittal was final. The activity of the *iudicia populi* diminished with the increase of criminal jurisdiction by *quaestiones* (q.v.). As a manifestation of civic liberty they could not survive the Republic.

Mommsen, *Röm. Strafr.* (1899); C. H. Brecht, *Sav. Zeitschr.* lix (1939), 261 ff.; E. G. Hardy, *JRS* 1913, 25 ff.   A. B.

IUDICIUM, *see* LAW AND PROCEDURE, ROMAN, II. 6.

IULUS, *see* ASCANIUS.

IUNO, *see* JUNO.

IUPPITER, *see* JUPITER.

IURIDICUS was a judicial functionary of praetorian rank in Italy (except Rome and its environs), nominated by the emperor. The first mention of *iuridici* is in A.D. 163. By introducing them Marcus Aurelius imitated the *consulares* created by Hadrian but abolished by Antoninus Pius. The field of their competence (confined to civil cases) was one or more districts, *regiones*; the procedure was *cognitio extra ordinem*. The *iuridici* disappear under Diocletian; later uses of this title (as in the *Digest*) are to be referred to the *iuridicus Alexandreae*, a high jurisdictional officer in Egypt, known also from the Greek papyri as δικαιοδότης. In other imperial provinces there were *legati iuridici* (called in some inscriptions simply *iuridici*), also appointed by the emperor, with a limited jurisdictional competence.   A. B.

IUS CIVILE. This term appears in different senses. Its original signification, derived from the definition 'ius quod quisque populus ipse sibi constituit', was the proper law of and for Roman citizens. The earliest *ius civile* was called *ius Quiritium*. In contradistinction to *ius honorarium* or *praetorium*, which comprehends the law introduced by the magistrates and especially by *praetores* (*see* EDICTUM) in order to support, amplify, or correct the *ius civile*, the latter includes the law originating in other sources (*Dig.* 1. 1. 7), such as legislation of the *comitia* (*leges*) or *concilia plebis* (*plebiscita*), *senatus consulta*, authority of jurists, and imperial constitutions (*see* CONSTITUTIONES). Another contrast is between *ius civile* (in its widest sense, including the law in all its appearances arising from all recognized legal sources) and *ius naturale*, a vague conception influenced by Greek philosophy, not elaborated by the Roman jurisprudence as a legal notion and far from being a real source of law. Its content is all 'quod naturalis ratio inter omnes homines constituit' (Gaius), and therefore it is always *aequum et bonum* (*Dig.* 1. 1. 11), and in this sense it coincides (by a false terminology) with *ius gentium*, as a law common to all peoples, 'ius quo omnes gentes utuntur'. For the contrast between *ius civile* and *ius gentium*, wherein *ius civile* signifies the law applied exclusively to Roman citizens, *see* IUS GENTIUM.   A. B.

IUS GENTIUM. This term has two main senses: (1) legal rules concerning relations between two independent States in times of peace and war corresponding to the modern international law; (2) the complex of legal institutes and rules which, originating in commercial and other contracts between Romans and foreigners, infiltrated and fertilized the Roman private law. Originally the relations between Romans and foreigners were based solely on reciprocal trust, as the formal institutions of the old *ius civile* and the procedure of *legis actiones* were inaccessible to *peregrini* acting generally according to the laws of their own State. The development of international trade made it necessary to recognize some institutions of other legal systems, which, being free from the rigid formalities of Roman law, were applied profitably in commercial relations, and to admit foreigners to the legal protection of Roman courts and specific Roman institutions (adapted, e.g., by using the foreigner's language in the *stipulatio*). From this arose—especially after the creation of *praetores peregrini*, who had occasion to adopt legal principles and ideas from the law of other nations in trials between Romans and *peregrini*—a new mass of legal rules which grew continuously with the subjection of other nations and acquisition of new provinces. This *ius gentium* represents in the development of Roman private law a later stratum of highest importance, in that it was equally applied to Romans and non-Romans.

It exercised a special influence on the law of contracts,

whilst the law of family and succession preserved more faithfully its national character. The final result was the complete fusion of the old *ius civile* and the new *ius gentium* into one system, some parts of which retained more elements of the former, whilst others retained more of the latter. After the *Constitutio Antoniniana de Civitate*, when the same law was applied to Romans and *peregrini*, the distinction between *ius civile* and *ius gentium* was only an historical reminiscence. *See* IUS CIVILE.

A. B.

IUS ITALICUM represents the legal quality of the territory of a Roman colony in Italy or, later, of Italian ground in general: the land is free from *tributum soli* and can be possessed in full ownership *ex iure Quiritium*; the inhabitants are not liable to *tributum capitis*. The distinction arose when colonies were founded outside Italy, from which such privileges might be withheld. Under the Empire this was the highest privilege obtainable by a provincial municipality. Augustus only gave it to genuine citizen colonies, mostly his eastern foundations. Later it was granted along with colonial rights to Roman municipalities, but, for fiscal reasons, sparingly. Severus, however, distributed it not only to three municipalities of Africa, his native province, but, after their co-operation in the civil war, to several Greek cities. This development typified the assimilation of East and West, which the *Constitutio Antoniniana* completed (*see* CITIZENSHIP, ROMAN).

For bibliography, *see* COLONIZATION, ROMAN.   A. N. S.-W.

IUS LATII. The Latin rights of the Empire were a continuation of the rights enjoyed by the Latin Name (*see* LATINI) of the Republic, which were derived from the social and political ties existing between the original *populi Latini*. Latins after 338 B.C. shared *conubium* and *commercium* (q.v.) with Rome, and possessed the *ius mutandae civitatis* together with the closely associated *ius exsilii*. Hereby individual Latins settling permanently in Rome acquired the Roman citizenship, and vice versa. Later, when this encouraged the depopulation of the Latin States, the more limited *ius civitatis per honorem adipiscendae* was substituted for it (*c.* 150 B.C.?). This gave Roman citizenship to Latins holding the magistracies of their local communities. Less important was the right of Latins temporarily resident in Rome to vote in the *concilium plebis*. The *ius provocationis* was possibly added in 122 B.C. There were no different kinds of Latin rights, although sometimes special regulations might be included in the charter establishing a Latin colony or group of colonies. In 89 B.C. Latin rights were conferred *en bloc* upon the Transpadane Gauls. Their communities were remodelled on the pattern of the earlier Latin colonies, adopting Latin language and law. When in 49 B.C. the Transpadanes received Roman citizenship, *ius Latii* was extended to many parts of *Gallia Narbonensis* and *Hispania Ulterior*, and thus became an intermediate, temporary stage—henceforth stereotyped —in the promotion of *peregrini* to Roman citizenship. Under Hadrian *Latium maius* appeared, whereby *decuriones* (q.v.), as well as magistrates, received the citizenship *per honorem*.

For bibliography, *see* LATINI.   A. N. S.-W.

IUS PRIMAE RELATIONIS. When in 23 B.C. Augustus ceased to hold the consulship, certain compensatory rights and powers were voted to him by the Senate in order that his position might not be weakened, among them the *ius primae relationis* (Dio Cass. 53. 32. 5). His *tribunicia potestas* gave him the right to introduce business in the Senate: the *ius primae relationis* either allowed him to submit proposals to the Senate in writing (so Mommsen, *Staatsr.* ii(3), 899) or, far more probably, gave him, for one piece of business at each meeting of the Senate, the prior right of reference that would otherwise

have belonged to the consuls (so H. F. Pelham, *Essays in Roman History* (1911), 74–7). This right is specified as 'relationem facere' in the *Lex de imperio Vespasiani* (Dessau, *ILS* 244). Later the number of items of business for which the emperor was given precedence was raised as high as five (*Vita Alexandri* 1).   J. P. B.

IUS TRIUM LIBERORUM, a privileged status which was conferred by the *Lex Papia Poppaea* (A.D. 9) upon the fathers of three children at Rome, of four children in Italy, and of five children in the provinces. Other persons (e.g. Pliny the Younger) obtained this status by special grant of the emperor. Persons possessing the *ius trium liberorum* were exempted from various charges (e.g. that of guardianship), and had a prior claim to magistracies.   M. C.

IUSIURANDUM. In some trials the oath of a litigant could terminate litigation already *in iure*, when the plaintiff offered an oath (*deferre*) to the defendant and the latter swore that he did not owe anything to the plaintiff. He might, however, offer back the oath (*referre*) to the plaintiff, who in this case was obliged to swear to his claim. Refusal entailed loss of the case. In some special cases a *iusiurandum calumniae* was admitted: on demand of a litigant his adversary was compelled to swear to the good faith of his claim or defence. Justinian made it likewise obligatory for the parties' advocates. In the proceedings *apud iudicem* the oath served only for evidence or assessment of the value of the object at issue.

Except in the matter of procedure the oath had but restricted application. An extra-judicial oath of a party affirming the truth of his claim gave occasion to a special action based solely on this fact.   A. B.

IUSTITIA, Roman equivalent of Dike (q.v.); mostly in poetry, but had a temple from 8 Jan. A.D. 13 (Ovid, *Pont.* 3. 6. 25, *Fasti Praen.* under 8 Jan.; see further Wissowa, *RK*² 333). In inscriptions she sometimes has the title Augusta.

IUSTITIUM (from *iuris stitium* = *ius sistere*), temporary suspension of all jurisdictional activity of magistrates, *iudices*, and courts, in civil and criminal matters, on account of events disturbing the whole of public life, as in the case of great national calamities, riots, and the like. A *iustitium* could be proclaimed by the Senate; it produced immediate suspension of *iurisdictio* and inhibition of *iudicia* (Cic. *Har. Resp.* 26. 55).   A. B.

IUVENES (or **IUVENTUS**—i.e. *Equestris ordinis iuventus*, Val. Max. 2. 2. 9). When, usually at the age of fourteen, a Roman boy adopted the *toga virilis*, he became a *iuvenis*. At the age of seventeen those who intended to follow an equestrian or a senatorial career started the military service which Augustus made a necessary preliminary to those careers. In the interval the *iuvenes* of fourteen to seventeen years of age who were *equites* (whose number included the sons of senators) served at Rome their *tirocinium*, a preparation for military service. They practised physical exercises and riding, paraded at great festivals, and held their own games, the *ludi sevirales* (the *lusus Troiae* being celebrated by those who were still *pueri*). This institution, which had precedents in the Roman Republic (Cic. *Cael.* 11), was thoroughly organized by Augustus, with a view to invigorating the youth of the upper classes at Rome (cf. Maecenas' speech, Dio Cass. 52. 26). It was extended also, for free-born youths, in the *municipia* of Italy and, by the second century A.D., had spread widely through the western provinces of the Empire. Nero held games called *Iuvenalia* and organized a body of picked youths, perhaps known as *Iuvenes Augustiani*. A *collegium iuvenum Augustianorum* was established later, perhaps by Domitian.

Iuventus was also used in a wider sense to indicate at Rome the whole body of *equites equo publico* (i.e. *equites* under the age of thirty-five who were still 'iuniores' technically, and sons of senators under the age of twenty-five who had not yet held a senatorial magistracy), organized in six *turmae* and parading, for inspection by the emperor, under the *seviri equitum* at the *recensio equitum*. This is the sense of *iuventus* in the courtesy title 'Princeps Iuventutis' (q.v.).

M. Rostovtzeff, 'Römische Bleitesserae', *Klio*, Beiheft iii (1905), 59–93.   J. P. B.

IUVENTAS, goddess, not of youth or youthful beauty in general, but of the *iuvenes*, or men of military age (contrast HEBE). She had a shrine in the vestibule of Minerva's *cella* in the Capitoline temple (Dion. Hal. *Ant. Rom.* 3. 69. 5), and is said to have been there before the temple was built, she and Terminus (q.v.) refusing to leave (ibid. and Livy 5. 54. 7). When any young man took the *toga virilis*, a contribution was made to her temple chest (Dion. Hal. 4. 15. 5).

Cf. Wissowa, *RK*² 135 f.   H. J. R.

IUVENTUS, see IUVENES.

IXION, the Greek Cain, the first to murder one of his kin (Pindar, *Pyth.* 2. 31 f.); as other accounts (e.g. schol. Apoll. Rhod. 3. 62, quoting Pherecydes) make the victim his father-in-law Eïoneus, whom he killed to avoid paying bride-price, either Pindar is speaking loosely or Eïoneus was also his blood-relation. Zeus purified him, but he attempted the chastity of Hera; consequently he was first deceived with a cloud-image of her, on which he begat the Centaurs (q.v.) or their father, and afterwards attached to a revolving wheel. Pindar, ibid. 21 ff.; scholiasts on Pindar and Apollonius (above).

Weizsäcker in Roscher's *Lexikon* ii. 766 ff.; A. B. Cook, *Zeus* i. 198 ff.   H. J. R.

IYNX (ἴυγξ 'wryneck') was in legend a nymph, daughter of Peitho or Echo, who by magic spells won the love of Zeus for herself (or for Io), and was turned to a bird by Hera. The legend may be due to the use of the wryneck, spread out on a wheel, as a love-charm, which Pindar says (*Pyth.* 4. 214) Aphrodite invented to enable Jason to obtain the love of Medea. The iynx used by Simaetha in Theocr. *Id.* 2 was probably a simple wheel, pierced with two holes, and threaded with string, the twisting of which caused the wheel to rotate (see Gow, *JHS* liv. 1–13). C. B.

J

JANICULUM, the prominent ridge on the west bank of the Tiber at Rome, some 3½ miles long. The name was anciently connected with Janus, but the only trace of his cult on the hill is the shrine of his son Fons or Fontus. The place was early a defensive outpost (Livy 1. 33) and was later enclosed in a great salient of Aurelian's Wall. Here lay the Lucus Furrinae, scene of the death of C. Gracchus and later occupied by the temple of the Syrian cults favoured by Commodus and the Severi and restored by Julian.

The district was primarily industrial, with mills driven by the Aqua Traiana (*CIL* vi. 1711), and nurseries for sacred fish fed from the same source.

P. Gauckler, *Le Sanctuaire syrien au Janicule* (1912); F. Cumont, *CRAcad. Inscr.* 1917, 275–84; Darier, *Les Fouilles du Janicule à Rome* (1920).   I. A. R.

JANUARIUS NEPOTIANUS, author of a loose and imperfect epitome of Valerius (q.v. 17) Maximus before the sixth century A.D. It was inferior to that by Julius Paris.

JANUS. The word properly means a gate or barbican (Livy 1. 19. 2 and often); especially the monument there named, the *Ianus geminus* in the Forum 'ad infimum Argiletum', though other structures of a like kind were so called also. They were mostly free-standing, not part of a city or other wall, and used originally for ceremonial purposes,* and it is very probable that such *iani* as that in the Forum were used for the formal setting out of an army or other party, to make sure that they began in the proper way. Hence *ianua*, the outer door of a house, and the god Janus, who is the *numen* of both it and the arch. But to enter house or city one must pass through the gate or the door; hence Janus tended to become a god of beginnings. He is named at the beginning of any list of gods in a prayer, even before Jupiter (as Livy 8. 9. 6); the first month of the reformed calendar, Ianuarius, is his and his festival comes in it (*see* AGONIUM). His priest is the *rex sacrorum*, his proper

* There is a right and a wrong way to march out through a gate (Livy 2. 49. 8); the Fabii go out to war 'infelici uia, dextro iano [arch] portae Carmentalis'.

offering a ram, and the place the Regia (Varro, *Ling.* 6. 12; Ovid, *Fasti* 1. 318)—perhaps some ancient piece of ritual connected with the king's door. All this seems to have given rise to the notion that he was a very great god ('diuom deus', hymn of the Salii ap. Varro, op. cit. 7. 27), and finally a sky-god or cosmic god (e.g. Ovid, ibid. 101 ff., where see Frazer's note for modern adaptations of this theory). When represented otherwise than by the gate, his symbol was a double-faced head, a very old art-type, sometimes awkwardly joined to a body. The closing of the *Ianus geminus* signified peace (i.e. no need for war-magic).

Wissowa, *RK* 103 ff.; Platner–Ashby, p. 275 ff.   H. J. R.

JASON (1) (Ἰάσων), in mythology, son of Aeson and leader of the Argonauts (q.v.). Apart from his adventures on the voyage the chief events in his life are as follows. On the usurpation of Pelias his parents smuggled him out of Iolcus, under cover of a mock funeral and a report of his death, and gave him to Chiron to bring up. On reaching young manhood he returned to claim his heritage, and arrived in the city with but one sandal, having lost the other in crossing a torrent. Pelias, who knew that the man with the one sandal was to be fatal to him (or in general, that one of the Aeolidae should overthrow him), managed to induce him to go for the Golden Fleece (Pindar, *Pyth.* 4. 71 ff., for earliest surviving account). The episode of the lost sandal is variously explained, the most interesting story being that Hera disguised as an old woman met him and asked to be taken across the river, in struggling through which he lost his shoe in the mud. It seems possible that originally Pelias did not neglect to sacrifice to her (Ap. Rhod. 1. 14) but refused to carry her across. See in general Apollonius, loc. cit. and schol.; Γένος Ἀπολλωνίου; Hyginus, *Fab.* 12 and 13. After the return from the voyage the chief incident is his desertion of Medea (q.v.; cf. CREON 1); thereafter there is nothing interesting save the manner of his death (foretold Eur. *Med.* 1386–7, whereon see schol.): as he slept under the stern of the Argo, part of it fell on him and killed him.   H. J. R.

JASON (2), tyrant of Pherae *c.* 380–370 B.C., probably son of Lycophron. He sought to gain control of all Thessaly, and finally gained his object in 374 by winning over Pharsalus. Elected *tagus* (q.v.), he modernized the organization of the Thessalian State and extended his influence over northern Greece. He maintained friendly relations with Athens and allied himself to the Thebans, who summoned him to Leuctra immediately after their victory (371). He refused to use his well-trained mercenaries on their behalf and negotiated an armistice between them and the Spartans. In 370 he caused alarm in Greece by mobilizing the entire Thessalian army at the time of the Pythian Games, but he was assassinated before the completion of his preparations, and their object remained unknown.

The success of Jason in uniting a potentially strong people, long weakened by inter-city feuds and external intervention, affords proof of his ability. His ambition to establish a Thessalian hegemony over Greece remained far from accomplishment, but his methods foreshadowed, and may in some degree have suggested, those adopted by Philip of Macedon.

Xenophon, *Hellenica* 6. 1. 2–19 and 4. 20–32; Diodorus, bk. 15. F. Stähelin, *PW*, s.v.; H. T. Wade-Gery, *JHS* 1924, 51; H. D. Westlake, *Thessaly in the Fourth Century B.C.* (1935), chs. 4–6. H. D. W.

JASON (3), a hellenized Jew of Cyrene, wrote a history of the exploits of Judas Maccabaeus in five books, of which 2 Maccabees is an epitome; he was probably a contemporary (2 Macc. ii. 23).

JAVOLENUS PRISCUS, a prominent Roman jurist, born before A.D. 60, died after 120. He held high official and military appointments, governed as *legatus consularis* the provinces of Britannia, Germania Superior, and Syria, and became proconsul of Africa (cf. *CIL* iii. 2864, pp. 1062, 1965). He enjoyed a high reputation among his contemporaries and was chief of the Sabinian School; but posterity did not cite him very frequently. This may be explained by the fact that his literary production consisted mainly of epitomes of the works of elder jurists (*libri ex Cassio, ex Plautio, ex Posterioribus Labeonis*), in which the personal view of the editor is manifested only by short phrases of approval or dissent. This last work, an edition of posthumous writings unique in legal literature, was published only once (not twice, as has been generally affirmed till now), and is rather a commentary than an extract. His most mature and most important work is his *Epistulae* (in 15 books), freely excerpted by Justinian's compilers. The *Epistulae* reveal fine, independent legal thinking on the author's part, and prove that he was a sagacious respondent and not only a critical and judicious epitomator. He was a renowned teacher: the great Salvius (q.v.) Julianus was his disciple.

A. Berger, s.v. 'Octavius Javolenus' (*PW* xvii. 1830 ff.); *Bull. Ist. dir. rom.* xliv. 92 ff. (1937). A. B.

JAXARTES, Asiatic river (*Syr Darya*, flowing into the Aral Sea). Though known perhaps to Herodotus by repute, it was discovered by Alexander, who founded Alexandria Eschate (*Khodjend*?) on it. The Greeks thought that it flowed into the Caspian (which perhaps was once true—*see* CASPIAN SEA), and sometimes confused it with the Araxes (*Aras*). Ptolemy gives geographical details of tribes on its banks.

Strabo 11. 507 ff.; Ptol. *Geog.* 6. 12–14. E. H. W.

JERUSALEM ('Ιεροσόλυμα), GREEK AND ROMAN, the capital of Palestine. The town, after the Babylonian captivity, was reoccupied by the Jews in 538 B.C., and the second Temple dedicated in 516; the walls were rebuilt in 445. It became a city, under the name of Antioch, early in the reign of Antiochus IV, who later (167) dedicated the Temple to Zeus Olympius, building a citadel (the Acra) to dominate it. The Temple was rededicated to Jehovah in 164, and from 152 Jerusalem became the capital of the Maccabee kings, who in 142 demolished the Acra. Jerusalem was captured in 63 by Pompey, who demolished the walls; they were rebuilt by Caesar's permission in 47. In 37 the town was again stormed by Sosius, who handed it over to Herod. Herod adorned it with many buildings, a theatre, hippodrome, and amphitheatre, a palace protected by three famous towers (the Mariamne, Phasael, and Hippicus), the fortress of Antonia, and the magnificent third Temple, which was severely damaged in the riots following his death, and slowly repaired by the Roman procurators. Agrippa I began to fortify the northern suburb Bezetha; Agrippa II paved the streets. Jerusalem was at this time a large and prosperous town, frequented by thousands of pilgrims. In the First Jewish War it was the centre of resistance and was razed by Titus in A.D. 70, becoming the camp of Legio X Fretensis. Reoccupied by Barcochba in the Second War, it was rebuilt by Hadrian in 135 ('Colonia Aelia Capitolina'), and was peopled with aliens, no Jew being allowed to enter it. Though immune and ruling a large territory, Aelia never flourished greatly, till the rise of Christianity revived the pilgrim traffic. Of the Herodian city there survive one of the three towers ('the Tower of David') and parts of the containing wall of the Temple platform (including 'the Wailing Wall'); of Aelia the east gate ('Pilate's Arch').

G. A. Smith, *Jerusalem* (1907–8); H. Vincent, F. M. Abel, *Jérusalem* (1922–6). A. H. M. J.

JEWISH GREEK LITERATURE. By the beginning of the second century B.C. the Greek language and Greek civilization were widely diffused over Judaea, and continued to flourish there up to the fall of Jerusalem. The revolt of the Maccabees against the extreme hellenization attempted by Antiochus Epiphanes (175–164 B.C.) stopped the spread of Greek religion, but not that of Greek culture; and Herod the Great (37–4 B.C.) was an enthusiastic Philhellene. But the Jews of the Diaspora were naturally more influenced by Hellenism than the Jews of Judaea. Jews were numerous in Egypt, particularly in Alexandria, the centre of Hellenistic-Judaic literature. Here the Septuagint (q.v.) translation of the Bible was made in the third and second centuries B.C. for the benefit of the Jews of the Diaspora, to whom Hebrew was largely an unknown tongue, and formed the foundation of Hellenistic-Judaic literature. This literature was largely apologetic and propagandist in aim, being designed to show that the Jews possessed all that was most valuable in Greek thought, an orientation which inevitably led to a certain hellenization of Jewish ideas.

The literary forms were sometimes Jewish (Hebraic histories, collections of wise sayings, prophetic books, etc.). At other times they were taken over from the Greeks—philosophy (*see* PHILON (4) *and* ARISTOBULUS (2)), sometimes in dialogue form, imaginary letters, epic, and tragedy, but no comedy. The first writer of Jewish history in Greek was the Jew Demetrius (end of 3rd c. B.C.), who wrote simply and did not hellenize the great figures of Jewish history. Eupolemus (q.v.) was freer in his treatment of the biblical tradition. The greatest of these historians were Josephus and Justus of Tiberias (qq.v.). *See also* JASON (3) and *FHG* iii. 211–30.

Three Jewish authors treated themes from Jewish history in the forms of Greek poetry. Philo the Elder (? *c.* 200 B.C.) wrote an epic, Περὶ τὰ 'Ιεροσόλυμα, of which 24 lines in an obscure style survive (A. Ludwich, *De P. carmine graeco-iudaico*, 1900); Theodotus (date unknown) a Π. 'Ιουδαίων, another epic of which 47 lines in a clear and simple style survive (A. Ludwich, *De T. carmine graeco-iudaico*, 1899). Ezechiel (date unknown) wrote a drama 'Εξαγωγή, describing the Exodus from Egypt; 269 trimeters survive, in simple Euripidean Greek

(A. Kuiper, *Mnemos.* xxviii (1900), 237–80). Among *pseudepigrapha* (see PSEUDEPIGRAPHIC LITERATURE) may be mentioned the fictitious letter of Aristeas about the Septuagint translation (Engl. Transl. H. St. J. Thackeray, 1917) and the *pseudo-Phocylidea*, probably of the first century A.D. (M. Rossbroich, *De pseudo-Phocylideis*, 1910). See, in general, E. Schürer, *Geschichte des jüdischen Volkes im Zeitalter Jesu Christi* iii⁴ (1909).

J. D. D.

JEWS (in Greek and Roman times). A. JUDAEA. Early in Antiochus IV's reign the hellenized priestly aristocracy, led by Jason, who usurped the high-priesthood from his brother Onias, obtained from the king permission to establish a gymnasium and the ephebate, and to incorporate Jerusalem as the 'city of Antioch'. Misunderstanding this movement, Antiochus in 167 B.C. dedicated the Temple to Zeus Olympius and endeavoured to suppress Judaism, building a citadel in Jerusalem and occupying it with royal troops. The result was a profound religious reaction, which expressed itself in the formation of the Pharisee party, and a popular revolt, led by Judas Maccabaeus, a priest of the house of Hashmon. In 164 the regent Lysias allowed the Temple to be re-dedicated to Jehovah, but the hellenizing aristocracy remained in power and the revolt went on. Judas was killed in 160, but his brother Jonathan continued the fight, and was in 152 appointed high-priest by Alexander Balas, who sought his support against Demetrius I. In 150 he was rewarded with the governorship of Judaea, to which Demetrius II added three toparchies of Samarcitis. Jonathan was treacherously killed by Tryphon in 143, but his brother Simon in 142 expelled the Seleucid garrison and was confirmed as high-priest by a national assembly; he later conquered Joppa and colonized it with Jews. His son John Hyrcanus (134–104) was subdued by Antiochus VII, but after that ruler's death conquered the Samaritans and Idumaeans, forcibly converting the latter to Judaism. His elder son Aristobulus (104–103) took the title of king and conquered and judaized the Ituraeans of Galilee. His younger son Alexander Jannaeus (103–76) judaized the Peraea and captured and destroyed many cities on the coast and in the northeast.

2. But as it grew in military strength the dynasty lost touch with the people. John quarrelled with the Pharisees, and Alexander faced several popular revolts, which he quelled with his Pisidian mercenaries. His widow Alexandra Salome (76–69) reversed his policy, reigning peacefully with Pharisee support. On her death her younger son Aristobulus, supported by the discontented military leaders, expelled his brother Hyrcanus, who, incited by an Idumaean noble, Antipater, fled to Aretas III of Arabia. Aretas was besieging Aristobulus in Jerusalem when Pompey intervened, stormed the city, and appointed Hyrcanus high-priest of an ethnarchy comprising Galilee, Samarcitis, Judaea, and Peraea; all the conquered cities, including Adora and Marisa in Idumaea, were made independent (63). Gabinius split the ethnarchy into five autonomous communes, leaving Hyrcanus only his spiritual powers (57). In 48 Antipater (Hyrcanus' vizier since 63) gave important aid to Caesar at Alexandria, and Hyrcanus was in recompense reinstated as ethnarch and granted Joppa. Antipater was murdered in 43 but succeeded by his sons, Phasael and Herod. In 40 the Parthians installed Antigonus, son of Aristobulus, as king; Hyrcanus was carried off to Babylonia and Phasael was killed, but Herod escaped to Rome, whence he returned as king (for his reign *see* HEROD 1).

3. On Herod's death his kingdom was divided. Antipas (q.v.) ruled Galilee and Peraea till 39. Samarcitis, Judaea, and Idumaea were, after Archelaus' brief reign (4 B.C.–A.D. 6), annexed and ruled by Roman procurators, under whom there was much unrest; the Zealot party

(founded in A.D. 6) aimed at national independence. In 39–40 Gaius almost provoked a rebellion by his attempt to place his statue in the Temple, and Claudius thought it wise to make Agrippa I (q.v.) king of the whole country. On Agrippa's death (44) the kingdom was annexed and, under the often tactless rule of the procurators, discontent, increased by famines, developed into guerrilla warfare, led by the *Sicarii*, a terrorist organization. Under Gessius Florus the masses, despite the efforts of the priestly aristocracy and Agrippa II to restrain them, broke into an open rebellion (66); this was crushed by Vespasian and Titus, who in 70 destroyed Jerusalem. Temple worship was abolished, and the two-drachma tax which every Jew had paid to the Temple funds was diverted to Jupiter Capitolinus.

4. Despite this blow, Judaism, now centred in the synagogues, flourished in Palestine, and a famous school of Rabbis established itself at Jamnia. At the end of Trajan's reign there was unrest in Palestine, quelled by Lusius Quietus. Under Hadrian a serious rebellion broke out under the leadership of Barcochba, which was ruthlessly crushed by Julius Severus (135). Another revolt was crushed under Antoninus Pius, and yet another under Septimius Severus. As a result of these wars the highlands of Judaea seem to have been almost depopulated; Jews were, however, still thick on the coastal plain and in Galilee, where Tiberias became the chief centre of rabbinical studies. The Palestinian Jews resisted hellenization, and their literature was written in Aramaic, the language of the people.

Sources: Maccabees i and ii; Josephus *BJ*; *AJ* 11. 313–20. Cassius Dio 70. 12–14; Eusebius, *Hist. Eccl.* 4. 6. Modern authorities: E. Schürer, *Geschichte des jüdischen Volkes im Zeitalter Jesu Christi* i⁴ (1901), ii–iii³ (1898); Mommsen, *The Provinces of the Roman Empire* (1886) ii. 160–231; A. Schlatter, *Geschichte Israels von Alexander dem grossen bis Hadrian³* (1925); E. R. Bevan, *CAH* viii, ch. 16; ix, ch. 9; A. Momigliano, *CAH* x, chs. 11, 25, §§ 4, 5.

B. THE DISPERSION. A great number of Jews never returned to Jerusalem, but remained in Babylonia. In the Hellenistic age many migrated from Babylonia and from Palestine to all the eastern Mediterranean lands. The kings, who found in the Jews loyal and industrious subjects and good soldiers, sometimes actively promoted the movement, and generally encouraged it by granting special privileges to them. By the first century B.C. almost every city in the eastern half of the Empire had its Jewish community, and the larger towns of the west were beginning to be invaded. The Jews had by now, owing to their exclusiveness, become thoroughly unpopular with their pagan neighbours, but the Roman government —notably Caesar and Augustus—upheld their privileges, such as the right to hold assemblies and collect and send money to Jerusalem, and protected them and their synagogues from violence. Gaius' dislike of the Jews, who refused to worship him, encouraged local pogroms, the most serious of which was at Alexandria, but Claudius reaffirmed Jewish privileges. The revolt of 66 was the signal for further pogroms, especially in Syria, but Vespasian still maintained the liberties of the Jews except that he appropriated to Jupiter Capitolinus the tax formerly sent to Jerusalem. In 115–16 the Jews of Cyprus, Cyrenaica, and Egypt raised a bloodthirsty revolt, and those of Cyrenaica and Egypt rose again at the time of the Barcochba revolt. Hadrian retorted with severe penal laws, prohibiting circumcision, but these laws were allowed to lapse by Pius, and henceforth the Jews enjoyed toleration. They were from the second century subject to the spiritual jurisdiction of a hereditary patriarch resident in Palestine, who collected dues from them and appointed synagogue officers. The Jews of the Dispersion early forgot Hebrew and adopted Greek (except for liturgical purposes), using a translation of the Scriptures—the Septuagint—which was begun at Alexandria under Ptolemy II.

J. Juster, *Les Juifs dans l'empire romain* (1914).   A. H. M. J.

JOCASTA, see OEDIPUS.

JOSEPHUS (b. A.D. 37–8), a priest of aristocratic Jewish family and a Pharisee, was in 66 appointed by the Sanhedrin joint governor of Galilee, where he paid more attention to curbing the zeal of the insurgents than to organizing them. In 67 he was besieged in Iotapata and captured, but saved his life by prophesying that Vespasian would become emperor. When this prophecy was fulfilled he was released, but remained in attendance on Titus till the fall of Jerusalem. He then settled in Rome, where he was granted Roman citizenship and a pension. He first wrote a history of the war in Aramaic for the benefit of Mesopotamian Jews. This he next translated into Greek with the aid of collaborators who seem, to judge by its smooth style, to have rewritten the entire work. The *de Bello Judaico* (Ἱστορία Ἰουδαϊκοῦ πολέμου πρὸς Ῥωμαίους) appeared in 75–9; it comprises seven books, of which the first and half the second are an introduction, recording Jewish history from the Maccabee revolt. Josephus next wrote the *Antiquitates Judaicae* (ἡ Ἰουδαϊκὴ Ἀρχαιολογία), which appeared in 93–4. It is a history of the Jews from the Creation to A.D. 66 in twenty books; its laboured style suggests that Josephus composed it himself in Greek. His last works are his autobiography (*Vita*) and two essays in which he vindicates the Jewish race against the aspersions of Apion, an anti-Semite Alexandrian scholar (*Contra Apionem*). Josephus' principal sources are for the earlier history the Old Testament, for the period 175–174 B.C. Nicolaus of Damascus (and, in the *Antiquities*, 1 Maccabees), for the war his own contemporary notes and the *commentarii* of Vespasian and Titus. Politically Josephus was pro-Roman, and he had no sympathy with extreme Jewish nationalism; but he was a zealous defender of the Jewish religion and culture.

Texts: B. Niese (1887–9); S. A. Naber (1888–96). Text and translation: H. St. J. Thackeray (1926–30; *Vit., Ap., BJ, AJ,* bks. 1–4); R. Marcus, 1934–7 (*AJ,* bks. 5–11). Discussions: G. Hölscher, *PW* ix. 1934–2000; R. Laqueur, *Der jüdische Historiker Flavius Josephus* (1920); H. St. J. Thackeray, *Josephus the man and the historian* (1929). A. H. M. J.

JUBA (1) I (Ἰόβας) (d. 46 B.C.), king of Numidia, succeeded to the domains of his father Hiempsal II. He supported the Senate in the Civil War, because of his *paternum hospitium* with Pompey and his personal grievances against Caesar and Curio (Caesar, *BCiv.* 2. 25). His decisive defeat of Curio (q.v. 2) in 49 gave him two years' respite in which to build up a strong army. In the campaign of 47–46, notwithstanding a diversion by the Mauretanian king Bocchus in Numidia, Juba himself came to the aid of Metellus Scipio, the Pompeian commander-in-chief. He was not present at the battle of Thapsus, as Scipio had divided his forces. The victorious Caesar then turned against Juba, but he had already fled to his capital of Zama, where he killed himself. Most of his realm was made into a Roman province. Juba's ruthless cruelty and arrogance were notorious; he remained faithful to Pompey because he dared not hope for forgiveness from Caesar.

Sources: Caesar, *BCiv.*; Appian, *BCiv.* bk. 2; Dio, bks. 41–2.
J. M. C.

JUBA (2) II (c. 50 B.C.–c. A.D. 23), king of Mauretania and son of Juba (1) of Numidia, was sent to Rome for Caesar's triumph of 46 and brought up in Italy; he received Roman citizenship, and accompanied Octavian on his expeditions. Perhaps first reinstated in Numidia, he was then transferred (25 B.C.) to Mauretania. He married first Cleopatra Selene, Antony's daughter, and secondly Glaphyra, daughter of Archelaus, king of Cappadocia. An insurrection of Gaetuli compelled him to call in Roman help. He was above all a man of learning, who endeavoured to introduce Greek and Roman life into his kingdom. The city of Iol was transformed into Caesarea (q.v. 3). His collections of artistic treasures were remarkable. He wrote many books (now lost) in Greek:

a history of Rome; works about Libya, Arabia, and Assyria; grammatical and literary researches; a treatise on the plant Euphorbia, which he discovered and named after his doctor Euphorbos; and Ὁμοιότητες, chiefly a comparison of Greek and Latin antiquities. Plutarch and Pliny the Elder used his writings.

Fragments in C. Müller, *FHG* iii. 464; *FGrH* iii A (1940), 127 ff.; G. Funaioli, *Gramm. Rom. Fragm.* i. 451. Cp. F. Jacoby, *PW* ix. 2384; S. Gsell, *Histoire anc. de l'Afrique du Nord* viii (1929), 206; J. Carcopino, *Le Maroc antique* (1943); M. Durry, *Études d'archéologie romaine* (1937), 111. A. M.

JUBA (3), of Mauretania (2nd c. A.D.), wrote a treatise (now lost) on metric, which later grammarians used. Unlike Varro and Caesius Bassus, Juba followed the Greek Heliodorus and did not derive all metres from the dactylic hexameter and iambic trimeter.

Cf. Teuffel, § 373 a, 5; Schanz-Hosius, § 606. J. F. M.

JUCUNDUS, see CAECILIUS (5).

JUDAEA, see JEWS (§ A).

JUGURTHA was a grandson of Masinissa (q.v.), whose successor Micipsa adopted him and educated him with his own sons, Hiempsal and Adherbal. In 134 B.C., commanding the Numidian contingent at Numantia, Jugurtha took the measure of the Roman aristocracy, and (relying on senatorial venality) aimed, after Micipsa's death in 118, at uniting Numidia under his own rule. In a complicated series of intrigues and struggles, Hiempsal was murdered and Adherbal defeated; but in the sack of the capital, Cirta, many Italian business men met their death (112). This enabled tribunes like Memmius to stir up a popular agitation, so that the Senate dispatched an army to Africa under L. Calpurnius Bestia, who was soon persuaded by Jugurtha to cease operations (111). After further tribunician agitation Jugurtha was summoned to Rome under safe conduct in order to explain the situation, but he was forbidden to speak by another tribune; after murdering a cousin he left Rome, *urbs uenalis*. War was resumed but a Roman army under A. Spurius Albinus capitulated (110). After the establishment of a court of inquiry (see MAMILIUS 3) the Senate sent out an efficient commander, Q. Metellus, but Jugurtha's skill and personality prolonged the struggle even after Metellus, in two vigorous campaigns (probably 109 and 108), had driven him from Numidia proper—where, however, he still retained many strongholds until Marius, Metellus' successor, with a larger force made a systematic 'drive' throughout the country (probably 107 and 106). There were always many Numidians ready to join Rome, though Jugurtha had nearly succeeded in making Numidia into a nation-state. In the later phases of the war Jugurtha showed his mastery of guerrilla warfare, as long as his treasures enabled him to hire Gaetulian nomads; and even after he had been deprived of this resource by Marius' capture of his stronghold near the Muluccha, he made an all-but-successful effort, near Cirta, to defeat Marius in the field, with the help of his father-in-law Bocchus of Mauretania (Orosius, 5. 15. 10–17). Finally he took refuge with Bocchus, who was induced by Sulla's daring diplomacy to surrender him; he was strangled in the Tullianum after Marius' triumph (104).

Sallust, *Bellum Iugurthinum* (tendentious); S. Gsell, *Hist. anc. de l'Afrique du Nord* vii (1928); M. Holroyd, *JRS* 1928; H. Last, *CAH* ix, ch. 3. M. H.

JULIA (1), daughter of Caesar and Cornelia, betrothed to Q. Servilius Caepio, but married in April 59 to Pompey, whom her affection bound more strongly to her father. In 55 the sight of Pompey returning from the *comitia* bespattered with blood caused a miscarriage; and next year she died in childbirth, the child dying a few days later. On the people's insistence, she was buried in the Campus Martius, and in 46 Caesar held magnificent shows over her tomb. G. E. F. C.

JULIA (2) **MAJOR** (39 B.C.–A.D. 14), daughter of Augustus, was married to her cousin Marcellus (25) and after his death to Agrippa (21), to whom she bore five children (Gaius Caesar, Julia, Lucius Caesar, Agrippina, and Agrippa Postumus). She accompanied Agrippa to the Eastern provinces in 16–13. Her third marriage, with Tiberius (11), is said to have been happy at first, but estrangement followed, and Julia's licentious conduct may have contributed to the decision of Tiberius to retire to Rhodes. In 2 B.C. Augustus had her banished for adultery (to Pandateria; later she was allowed to live in Rhegium). Anecdotes attest her culture and wit, and Macrobius contrasts her licentiousness with her 'mitis humanitas minimeque saeuus animus'.

Velleius 2. 100; Seneca, *Ben.* 6. 32; Dio Cassius, bks. 48 and 53–6; Macrobius, *Sat.* 2. 5.   G. W. R.

JULIA (3) **MINOR** (c. 19 B.C.–A.D. 28), daughter of Agrippa and Julia, married (c. 4 B.C.) L. Aemilius Paullus (*cos.* A.D. 1). She was banished for immorality to the island of Trimerus in the Adriatic (c. A.D. 8).

Pliny, *HN* 7. 149; Tacitus, *Ann.* 3. 24 and 4. 71; schol. ad Juv. *Sat.* 6. 158.

JULIA (4) **DOMNA**, a native of Syria, was the second wife of Septimius Severus. Outwitted in the political world by Plautianus, she collected about her a large coterie of men of learning (e.g. Galen and Philostratus), and exercised a wide influence over them. Cultured, witty, and beautiful, she combined oriental credulousness with a ratiocination derived from philosophical study, and was not undeservedly called ἡ φιλόσοφος Ἰουλία. She accompanied her husband to Britain in 208, and after his death endeavoured unsuccessfully to support the claims of Geta against Caracalla. She died in A.D. 217 at Antioch.

J. Réville, *La Religion à Rome sous les Sévères*; T. Whittaker, *Apollonius of Tyana and other Essays* (1906). *See also* SEPTIMIUS SEVERUS.   H. M. D. P.

JULIA (5) **MAESA,** daughter of Bassianus and sister of Julia Domna, was the wife of Julius Avitus, by whom she had two daughters, Julia Soaemias and Julia Mamaea. After Caracalla's death she returned from Rome to Emesa. She assisted in the proclamation of the Emperor Elagabalus and accompanied him to Rome, becoming Augusta and 'mater castrorum et senatus'. Later she induced Elagabalus to adopt his cousin Alexianus. She died after Elagabalus' murder and was consecrated as Diva.

G. Herzog, *PW* x. 940. Coins: H. Mattingly, etc., *The Roman Imperial Coinage* iv. 2 (1938), 62, 101.   A. M.

JULIA (6) **SOAEMIAS BASSIANA,** daughter of Julia (5) Maesa, spread the report that Elagabalus was her son by Caracalla; she followed him to Rome and took part in political life. She is said to have intervened in the deliberations of the Senate. She was slain with Elagabalus (A.D. 222).   A. M.

JULIA (7) **MAMAEA,** daughter of Julia (5) Maesa, was, unlike her sister Soaemias, a woman of refined tastes and noble ideals. She directed the early education of her son Severus Alexander, secured his acceptance by the Praetorians, and after her mother's death virtually ruled the Empire. Her fear of malign influences upon her son, however, drove her to an almost possessive domination. She chose his wife and later from jealousy had her exiled. Finally her attempts to dictate foreign policy alienated the army and led to the murder of herself and her son (235; *see* SEVERUS ALEXANDER). For bibliography *see* SEVERUS ALEXANDER.   H. M. D. P.

JULIANUS, FLAVIUS CLAUDIUS ('Julian the Apostate'), the younger son of Julius Constantius (half-brother of Constantine I), and Basilina, was born in A.D. 332. In 337 the soldiers rose and destroyed most of the house of Constantine, in order to secure the succession to his three sons. Julian and his brother, Constantius, were almost the only survivors. From 337 to 351 the boys were brought up quietly at Nicomedia and, later, in Cappadocia. But when Constantius II in 351, shaken by the death of Constans and the rebellions of Magnentius and Vetranio, called Constantius Gallus to be his Caesar, Julian obtained freedom to move as he pleased. Gallus was a sorry failure and was put to death in Italy in 354. But the emperor still needed a Caesar of his own house, and after much vacillation nominated Julian (November 355) and gave him his daughter, Helena, in marriage. Julian was sent to Gaul, and, by bold and resolute strategy, relieved the province from the Alamanni and Salian Franks who beset it. He was less successful in his relations with his staff, whom he suspected, perhaps unjustly, of hampering his policy. When Constantius in 360 demanded Gallic troops for the Persian War, a movement of the army, not seriously checked by Julian, raised him to the throne (at Lutetia Parisiorum). Constantius refused any compromise, and civil war was inevitable. Julian struck first and had already reached Naissus, when the death of Constantius left him undisputed emperor.

2. Julian proved himself a friend of the Senate, a vigorous reformer, and a stern enemy of the Christian Church. But, above all, he was resolved to re-establish Roman reputation in the East. In 363 he invaded Persia and reached Ctesiphon in triumph. But he refused offers of peace and, becoming entangled in a difficult campaign, died in June 363, near the little village of Maronga. Jovian, chosen to succeed him, patched up a peace and marched home.

3. Great soldier as he was, Julian is even better known as the 'Apostate', who attempted to reverse the Christian revolution. Educated as a Christian and baptized, Julian rebelled against the faith of the men who had butchered his kindred. His own strong religious instincts, fostered by pagans like Libanius and Maximus, turned to the old paganism and, in particular, to the sun-worship which was hereditary in his family. While not an actual persecutor, Julian encouraged divisions in the Church and forbade Christian children to receive the old 'Greek' education. What is more, he attempted to improve the organization and morale of the pagan priesthood. But this noble visionary was sadly out of touch with his time, as his bitter quarrel with the people of Antioch shows. It is probable that the 'Historia Augusta' preserves much of the attitude to religion and history characteristic of his reign. As a reformer, he set his face against the eunuch régime of Constantius, fought against high prices, and reformed the coinage.

4. Julian was a voluminous and vigorous writer. Of his surviving works we may mention encomia of Constantius II and his wife Eusebia, addresses to King Helios and to the Mother of the Gods, the Συμπόσιον or Καίσαρες, a highly satirical sketch of the princes who had sat on the imperial throne, and the Μισοπώγων, a bitter retort to the Antiochenes, who had mocked his philosopher's beard. Of his lost works, some dealt with his campaigns in Gaul. Another, which we would fain possess, was a definite attack on the Christian Church. Intolerant of any nonsense that was not his own, he exposed, from intimate knowledge, all that he found weak or unsound in the Christian teaching and practice. He was probably hardly conscious himself of the bitter prejudice which controlled him.

Works: *Juliani imperatoris epistulae, etc.*, edited by J. Bidez and F. Cumont (1922); W. C. Wright (Loeb). J. Geffcken, *Kaiser Julianus* (*Das Erbe der Alten* viii, 1914); A. Rostagni, *Giuliano l'Apostata* (1919); J. Bidez, *Vie de Julien* (1930).   H. M.

JULIANUS, *see also* SALVIUS JULIANUS.

JULIUS (1) **AFRICANUS**, a speaker of the first century A.D., ranked by Quintilian, who knew him, alongside of Domitius Afer and admired for his force (*Inst.* 10. 1. 118; 12. 10. 11).

JULIUS (2) **AFRICANUS**, a Christian philosopher of Aelia Capitolina, went *c.* A.D. 220 on an embassy to Elagabalus which secured city rank and the title of Nicopolis for Emmaus, and established a library in the Pantheon for Severus Alexander. His principal works were the *Chronographies* in five books, a synchronization of sacred and profane history from the Creation to A.D. 221, which was the basis of Eusebius' *Chronicle*, and Oἱ Kέστοι in twenty-four books, a miscellany of information, chiefly relating to magic, on various topics ranging from medicine to tactics. He also wrote a letter to Origen, in which he questioned the authenticity of the story of Susannah, and a letter to a certain Aristides, in which he harmonized the two genealogies of Christ.

H. Gelzer, *Sextus Julius Africanus*, 1880–98; W. Reichardt, *Die Briefe des Sextus Julius Africanus an Aristides und Origenes*, 1909.
　　　　　　　　　　　　　　　　　　　A. H. M. J.

JULIUS (3) **CANUS** or **KANUS**, a philosopher whose uncompromising reproaches offended Caligula and led to his execution (Sen. *Dial.* 9. 14. 4–9).

JULIUS (4) **CEREALIS**, epic and pastoral poet friendly with Martial (11. 52. 1 and 16–18).

JULIUS (5) **EXSUPERANTIUS**, in his *opusculum*, preserved in a Sallust manuscript, describes the civil war of Marius and Sulla to the death of Sertorius. The dependence upon Sallust (*Jugurtha* and *Histories*) in subject-matter, without understanding of Republican institutions or personalities, and in style, without feeling for phraseology, points to the fourth to fifth century A.D., when Sallust was in fashion.

Edited by C. Bursian (1868); G. Landgraf–C. Weyman, *Archiv für lat. Lex.* xii (1902), 561.　　　　　　A. H. McD.

JULIUS (6) **GABINIANUS**, SEXTUS, mentioned in Suetonius' list of rhetors, was an eminent teacher in Gaul in the Flavian age (Hieron. *Ab Abr.* 2092 = A.D. 76; Tac. *Dial.* 26. 11).

JULIUS (7) **MODESTUS**, freedman of Julius Hyginus (Augustus' *libertus*), followed his patron's broad treatment of grammar (Suet. *Gram.* 20).

JULIUS (8) **OBSEQUENS** (probably 4th c. A.D.) composed tables of prodigies from 249 to 12 B.C. (extant for 190–12 B.C.; the earlier part and perhaps an introduction lost). Based on the epitomized Livian tradition, further 'contaminated', or on consul lists to which Livian details of prodigies were added, it represents late heathen justification of the forms of the old faith.

Edited by O. Jahn (1853); O. Rossbach (1910), with Livian *Periochae*.　　　　　　　　　　　　A. H. McD.

JULIUS (9) **PARIS** (4th c. A.D.), epitomator of Valerius Maximus; Teuffel 279. 9: cf. JANUARIUS NEPOTIANUS.

JULIUS (10) **ROMANUS** (3rd c. A.D.) wrote an extensive grammatical work entitled Ἀφορμαί, of which considerable fragments are preserved by Charisius (q.v.).

Cf. Teuffel, § 379. 3; Schanz–Hosius, § 603.

JULIUS (11) **SECUNDUS**, among recent orators specially mentioned by Quintilian (*Inst.* 10. 1. 118; 3. 12). Like M. Aper, another of the *personae* in Tacitus' *Dialogus*, he came from Gaul. A quiet and refined speaker, he also wrote a biography of Julius (q.v. 1) Africanus.　　　　　　　　　　　　J. W. D.

JULIUS (12) **TIRO** (full name *CIL* ii. 3661 *Q. Iulius C.f. Gal. Tiro Gaetulicus*), given in Suetonius' list of rhetors next after Quintilian's name (Reifferscheid wrongly emended to M. Tullius Tiro). Pliny mentions a case about his will (*Ep.* 6. 31. 7).

JULIUS (13) **VALERIUS ALEXANDER POLEMIUS** (3rd–4th c. A.D.) composed a Latin version of a Greek novel on Alexander the Great by 'Aisopos' or 'Pseudo-Kallisthenes'. Its linguistic peculiarities betray his alien extraction. He was perhaps also author of the *Itinerarium Alexandri* (on Alexander's eastern campaigns), presented to Constantine's son, Constantius.
　　　　　　　　　　　　　　　　　　　J. W. D.

JULIUS (14) **VICTOR**, GAIUS (4th c. A.D.), author of an *ars rhetorica* largely and closely based on Quintilian.

C. Halm, *Rhet. lat. min.* 373.

JULIUS, *see also* AGRICOLA, ATTICUS, AUGUSTUS, CAESAR, CALLISTUS, CIVILIS, CLASSICIANUS, EURYCLES, FRONTINUS, GERMANICUS, GRAECINUS, MAXIMINUS, NERO (4), PAULUS, PHILIPPUS, PHILOPAPPUS, SACROVIR, SEVERUS (3), SOLINUS, TIBERIUS, VINDEX.

JUNIUS (1) **CONGUS**, MARCUS, a friend regarded by Lucilius as a reader to whom he would have his satires appeal (595 f. Marx). A satire in bk. 26, possibly, indeed, the whole book, was addressed to him. He wrote a legal treatise *de potestatibus* and perhaps an historical work (Cichorius, *Unters. zu Lucilius*, 121 ff.).　　J. W. D.

JUNIUS (2) **OTHO**, rhetor, praetor A.D. 22; formerly an elementary schoolmaster, he owed his advancement to Sejanus (Tac. *Ann.* 3. 66). A master of innuendo, he wrote four books of *colores*, 'complexions to be put on cases' (Sen. *Controv.* 2. 1. 33).

JUNIUS (3) **NIPSUS**, MARCUS (perhaps 2nd c. A.D.), *gromaticus*; author of treatises on mensuration, replacement of boundaries, and surveying of rivers.

JUNIUS, *see also* ARULENUS, BRUTUS, GALLIO, SILANUS.

JUNO, an old and very important Italian goddess, in functions resembling Hera (q.v.), with whom she was anciently identified. There is no doubt that she was closely connected with the life, especially the sexual life, of women (hence indirectly with the moon, and therefore theorists ancient and modern have made her a moon-goddess; see Roscher in his *Lexikon* ii. 578 ff., cf. *Juno und Hera*, (1875), p. 1 ff.). This is shown among other things by the fact that she either assimilates the minor deities Lucina, who makes the child see the light of day, Opigena, who brings help to women in childbirth, Cinxia, *numen* of the bride's girdle, Iterduca, who brings her to her new home, and several other such vague figures, or else these are titles of hers which tended to assume independent existence as goddesses attendant on women (references in Roscher, *Lex.* 579 ff.). But she developed wider functions and became a great goddess of the State (probably for the same reason as Hera), notably at Lanuvium, where she was worshipped as Sospita or Sispes and shown armed and wearing a goatskin cloak, and, under the Etruscan kings, at Rome also, where as Juno Regina she forms one of the Capitoline triad with Jupiter and Minerva (qq.v.); see Wissowa, *RK* 187 ff. Concerning her origin there is much doubt. Wissowa (ibid. 181) would derive her name from the root of *iuvenis, iunix*, etc., with the meaning 'young woman', 'bride', and her functions from the individual *iuno* who is to a woman what the *genius* (q.v.) is to a man ('iuno mea', Petron. *Sat.* 25. 4; cf. Lygdamus 6. 48; Seneca, *Ep.* 110. 1). Others, notably J. Whatmough (as in *Foundations* *of Rom. Italy* (1937), 159 f.), suppose the individual *iuno* secondary and late and support a derivation of the name from the same root as that of *Iuppiter*, despite the difficulty that no such forms as *Diuno, *(D)iouno ever occur, as would be expected. The views are not wholly exclusive of each other; the *numen* which watches over women and their functions might from the beginning have been thought of now as appearing in each individual woman, now as forming a great reservoir of power on which all women drew, and these have developed respectively into the individual *iunones* and the great goddess.

Her most interesting festival is the Nonae Caprotinae, *see* CAPROTINA. It was commonly alleged in antiquity that she was connected with the Lupercalia (see Wissowa, op. cit. 185, but *contra*, Rose in *Mnemos*. xl. 389 f.). The Kalends of every month were sacred to her (Macrob. *Sat.* 1. 15. 18), and in the old ceremony of announcing at the new moon the date of the Nones (Varro, *Ling.* 6. 27, whereon see Goetz and Schoell) she was addressed as Juno Covella, showing some connexion with the moon. An important festival was the Matronalia of 1 Mar., also the foundation-day of the temple of Juno Lucina (Wissowa, ibid.). Cf. MONETA.   H. J. R.

JUNO MONETA, TEMPLE OF, *see* CAMILLUS (2) *and* CAPITOL *and* COINAGE, ROMAN, para. 11.

JUNONIA, *see* CARTHAGE, para. 8, *and* COLONIZATION, ROMAN.

JUPITER (*Iuppiter*), the Italian sky-god, *Diou-pater*, the first member of the name being etymologically identical with that of Zeus (q.v.), and the god himself an inheritance from pre-ethnic days among the Wiro-speaking population. Primitively it would appear that he was simply the power (*numen*) of the sky, manifesting itself in various ways. As Iuppiter Lapis (see Gellius 1. 21. 4; Livy 1. 24. 8, cf. FETIALES; 30. 43. 9; Festus, p. 102. 11 Lindsay; Rose in *Custom is King* (1936), 56 ff.) he was incorporated in one or all of sundry stones used in taking oaths and presumably supposed to be thunder-bolts; they were probably neolithic implements. As Iuppiter Feretrius he appears to have been a holy tree (Livy 1. 10. 5–7; Dion. Hal. *Ant. Rom.* 2. 34. 4; Rose, op. cit. 54 ff.). How old his association with the Ides of every month may be (Macrob. *Sat.* 1. 15. 15) we cannot say, but it probably is very ancient; he is naturally wor-shipped at the time of full moon, when the light from the sky is most powerful. Like Zeus he is also associated with rain (Iuppiter Elicius originally, perhaps, see Wissowa, *RK* 121, but regularly spoken of as connected with the ritual of thunderstorms, see Valerius Antias, fr. 6 Peter; Ov. *Fasti* 3. 291 ff.). It is also as sky-god that he was worshipped at the Vinalia (Rustica) on 19 Aug., when the flamen Dialis (*see* FLAMINES) offered a ewe-lamb to him and cut the first grapes 'inter exta caesa et porrecta' (Varro, *Ling.* 6. 16). His development into a personal and to some extent anthropomorphic god seems to have been more complete in the rest of Italy than in Rome, and it is also outside Rome that signs are to be found of an early association with Juno (q.v.), and of connexions with the underworld (cf. Zeus Chthonios, etc.); see C. Koch, *Der römische Juppiter* (1937) and cf. Rose in *Gnomon* xiv. 255 ff. In Rome, apart from Greek and Etruscan influence, he remains almost purely a sky-god and not very sharply personal.

2. His festivals, besides the Vinalia, not only Rustica but Meditrinalia on 11 Oct., where his connexion with the goddess Meditrina is obscure (see Varro, ibid. 21; Festus, p. 110. 21 Lindsay; *Fasti Amiternini* on 11 Oct.; Wissowa, op. cit. 115), and Priora, 23 Apr. (Varro 16; Pliny, *HN* 18. 287; Ov. *Fasti* 4. 863 ff., whereon see Frazer), include the *nundinae* or market-days, when the

flaminica Dialis sacrificed a ram to him (Macrob. *Sat.* 1. 16. 30); also the very obscure Poplifugia on 5 July (see Rose in *CQ* xxviii. 157) and an unnamed festival on 23 Dec. (Macrob. 1. 10. 11 and *Fasti Praenestini* on that date), apparently because the winter solstice occurs about then. His oldest associates in Roman cult are Mars and Quirinus, e.g., 'Numa' ap. Fest., p. 204. 13 ff. Lindsay; the first *spolia opima* go to Jupiter, the second to Mars, the third to Quirinus.

3. The Etruscan kings introduced (shortly before their fall according to tradition, supported by the fact that the oldest calendar-festivals do not include those of the Capitol) the cult of Iuppiter Optimus Maximus, i.e. the best and greatest of all Jupiters, in which the god, in his Capitoline temple, built in the Etruscan manner and with three *cellae*, was associated with Juno and Minerva (qq.v.), apparently a purely Etruscan grouping. From then on his cult became more splendid. The oldest games, *Ludi Capitolini* (15 Oct., Plut. *Rom.* 25; see, further, Wissowa, ibid. 117), are indeed connected with Iuppiter Feretrius and have peculiarities in their celebration which may be pre-Etruscan; but the *Ludi Romani* (which seem to have originated from games cele-brated on the occasion of a triumph; see below) of 4–19 Sept., the *Ludi Plebei* of 4–17 Nov., and the attendant *epula Iouis* (cf. EPULONES) were among the greatest feasts of the year. To this temple also came the triumphs, in which the general, in the full costume of a king (and so in that of Jupiter, whom he did not impersonate) drove at the head of his army to do honour to the god (see Marquardt, *Staatsverw.* ii². 582 for references).

4. In the moral and political sphere Jupiter was associated not only with war but with treaties and oaths of all kinds, a development, as the cult of Iuppiter Lapis shows (see above), from his functions as sky-god and wielder of thunderbolts, wherewith he can punish the perjurer; cf. ZEUS, and *see also* FETIALES. Hence it is that he seems to be connected in some way with Fides (q.v.); cf. also SEMO SANCUS.

5. For his Roman shrines see Platner–Ashby, 291 ff. Outside Rome, but within her sphere of influence in historical times, his most noteworthy solemnity was the *feriae Latinae*, celebrated yearly, but not on a fixed date, on the Alban Mount. Here he bore the title Latiaris, in his capacity as god of the Latin League. The ritual was in some respects archaic, milk and not wine being used for libation (Cicero, *Div.* 1. 18, whereon see Pease for further details); the chief Roman magistrate for the time being was in charge, and representatives of all the cities of the League were present to claim their share of the sacrificial meat (*carnem petere*) and take part in the ritual, which as usual must be exactly observed (Livy 41. 16. 1–2).

Jupiter is the *interpretatio Romana* (q.v.) of a number of foreign sky-gods.   H. J. R.

JURISPRUDENCE. *Iurisprudentia* was, according to Ulpian's definition (*Dig.* 1. 1. 10. 2), 'diuinarum huma-narumque rerum notitia, iusti uel iniusti scientia'. The first part of this definition refers to ancient times, when knowledge of law and of its practical application was a monopoly of the patrician pontifical board, the second defines the later jurisprudence, when knowledge of law was secularized by the publication of the XII Tables (*see* TWELVE TABLES), by *ius Flavianum* (*see* FLAVIUS 1), and in larger measure by public legal teaching, exercised at first by Tib. Coruncanius (q.v.). The activity of the jurists was very extensive: drafting legal forms for legal transactions, wills, etc. (*cavere*), assisting litigant parties in procedural questions and forms (*agere*), and giving opinions (*responsa*) on questions of law addressed to them by private individuals, magistrates, or judges. *Responsa* were given by writing or orally; some jurists combined responding activity with teaching, discussing in public the practical cases submitted to their opinion. From the time of Augustus *respondere* acquired an official character: it could be practised by jurists authorized by the emperor (*ius respondendi*). *Responsa* delivered henceforth *ex auctoritate principis*, in writing and sealed, had actually (if not legally) a decisive authority in the trial for which they were issued; but under Hadrian they definitely received binding force, even those issued in similar cases by defunct jurists. If different opinions were produced the judge had a free hand.

Jurisprudence remained for a long time a vocation of the nobility: the Republican jurists belonged to senatorial families and occupied the highest offices (as pontiffs, consuls, praetors); under the Principate the prominent offices in the administration of Rome and the provinces were often occupied by jurists, who always enjoyed high authority in public life. Jurisprudents had a wide influence on the development of law, as members of the *consilia* of magistrates, especially of the praetors, whom they advised in the composition of new edicts and *formulae* and, later, as legal advisers of emperors. As counsellors of *iudices* (q.v.) they controlled jurisdiction in large measure, and as teachers and writers they promoted the evolution of legal science—a distinguished achievement of Roman culture which was wholly wanting in Greece. The writings of the jurists were of different types: comprehensive treatises on the law as a whole (*Digesta*), on the *ius civile*, or on the praetorian edict; collections of *responsa* or practical cases discussed in school (*Quaestiones*, *Disputationes*); text-books for beginners (*institutiones*); concise manuals (*regulae*, *sententiae*); notes to (*libri ad . . .*) or epitomes from (*libri ex . . .*) works of other jurists; monographs on statutes, *senatus consulta*, or single institutes or magistracies. The scientific elaboration of the law began at the end of the Republic: the first systematic treatise of private law, by Q. Mucius Scaevola (q.v. 4), was the model followed by later jurists. Augustus founded a legal library in the temple of Apollo on the Palatine, which became a centre of law-teaching (*instituere* for beginners, *instruere* for advanced scholars). The schools produced rivalry and controversies which furthered the evolution of law and legal science. With the last representatives of the schools of Sabinians and Proculians (*see* SABINUS (2), MASURIUS), Celsus, and Salvius Julianus (qq.v.), Roman legal science reached the height of its development under Trajan and Hadrian. The literary production of the jurists was mostly based on practical experience: they were always in contact with actual legal practice, and had a keen eye for its requirements, as is proved by the innumerable decisions of practical cases, which take up more room in their works than mere theoretical or doctrinal deliberations. The number of known names of jurists is less than a hundred. For individual jurists see the special articles; for the influence of jurisprudence on the development of the law *see* LAW AND PROCEDURE, ROMAN, I, DIGESTA, TRIBONIANUS.

The decay of the Roman jurisprudence began *c.* A.D. 250. A revival of legal science came in the fifth century from the schools in the Eastern part of the Empire, especially that of Berytus; but its importance was far inferior to that of the classical Roman legal science (from Augustus till the Severi).

For bibliography *see* LAW AND PROCEDURE, ROMAN, I. A. Berger, *PW*, s.v. 'Iurisprudentia'; S. Riccobono, *Jurisprudentia* (Nuovo Digesto Italiano vi, 1938); B. Biondi, *Obbietto e metodi della scienza giuridica romana* (Scritti in onore di C. Ferrini. University of Pavia, 1943); F. Schulz, *History of Roman Legal Science* (1946).

A. B.

JUSTINIAN (FLAVIUS PETRUS SABBATIUS IUSTINIANUS), Roman Emperor of the East, A.D. 527–65. Justinian was called by his uncle, the elderly Emperor Justin, to assist him in 518 and, after a short period of joint rule, succeeded without question in 527. His wife, Theodora, was crowned with him.

2. Justinian had a strong sense of his imperial rank and mission. In the East his policy was not aggressive, but he held Persia in check by a war fought in Syria and Mesopotamia, 527–32, and by further campaigns from 540 onwards, centring largely round the district of Lazica near the Black Sea. In the Balkans he had to deal with a succession of threats from the barbarians—Huns, Slavs, Bulgars, and, finally, Avars. At home his authority was shaken in 532 by the famous 'Nike' riots, when the two circus factions, the Greens and the Blues, combined to set up a rival emperor, Hypatius. Theodora moved the wavering Justinian to a final effort when all seemed lost and the revolt was drowned in blood.

3. But it was in the West that the ambitions of Justinian found their full scope in the resolve to reassert the majesty of the Empire, where necessary by force of arms. First came Africa. Hilderic, king of the Vandals, was driven out by Gelimer and appealed to Justinian in 531. The great general Belisarius, with a small but efficient army, consisting mainly of cavalry, captured Carthage and won the battles of Decimum and Tricamarum. After a series of revolts Africa remained in the firm possession of the Empire. Next came the turn of the Ostrogoths. Belisarius occupied Sicily (535), took Naples and Rome (536), and defended the capital against Witigis, successor of Theodahad (537–8). Jealousies between Belisarius and other generals, notably the eunuch Narses, hazarded success, but in 540 Witigis surrendered at Ravenna and the West was re-won.

4. The gallant prince Totila revived the Gothic cause (541–52), and Belisarius, hampered by rivalries and insufficient support, could gain no decision. Victory finally fell to Narses at the battles of Taginae and Mount Vesuvius (552). Franks and Alamanni were driven from the north, Narses as imperial exarch at Ravenna ruled Italy, and even a part of eastern Spain resumed its allegiance to Constantinople.

5. Justinian's financial administration, notably under John of Cappadocia, was terribly oppressive. He built on the grand scale; the Church of Hagia Sophia is his great monument. He aspired to impose peace on the Church, vexed by the monophysite heresy, and found a formula of unity at the Council of Chalcedon. But his supreme achievement was the great codification of Roman law (*Digesta* or *Pandectae*, *Institutiones*, and *Novellae*, qq.v.), carried out under Tribonian (530–4).

6. The long reign of Justinian ended in gloom, with storms gathering and plague ravaging the Empire. In his personality there was a sinister and unlovely element that antagonized his contemporaries, but he had a grand conception of his office and translated much of it into fact.

Stein, *PW*, s.v.; *Cambr. Med. Hist.* ii.   H. M.

JUSTINUS, MARCUS JUNIAN(I)US (Justin), made an epitome in Latin of Pompeius Trogus' *Historiae Philippicae*, probably in the third century A.D. It is an unequal work, but preserves the main lines of the original (cf. the report of Mithridates' speech in 38. 4–7). The epitome was widely read in the Middle Ages.

Editions: F. Ruehl (1886), E. Pessonneaux (1903) with notes, M. Galdi (1923), O. Seel (1935). L. Castiglioni, *Storie Filippiche di Giustino* (1925); M. Galdi, *L'epitome nella lett. lat.* (1922), 108.

A. H. McD.

JUSTITIA, *see* IUSTITIA.

JUSTUS, a hellenized Jew of Tiberias, an opponent of Josephus when the latter was commander of Galilee (A.D. 66–7). He fled to Agrippa II, who protected him against charges of rebellion and later appointed him his secretary, but eventually dismissed him for forgery. After Agrippa's death Justus published a history of the war, which Josephus criticizes severely in his autobiography. It is possible that this history formed part of a work entitled Ἰουδαίων βασιλέων τῶν ἐν τοῖς στέμμασι, which covered Jewish history from Moses to the death of Agrippa II. He also wrote commentaries on the Scriptures.

Joseph. *Vita* 336 ff.; Phot. *Bibl.*, cod. 33; H. Luther, *Josephus und Justus von Tiberias* (1910); F. Jacoby, *PW* x. 1341–6.
A. H. M. J.

JUTURNA, *see* CASTOR AND POLLUX.

JUVENAL (DECIMUS IUNIUS IUVENALIS), greatest of Roman satiric poets, wrote with relentless impersonality and was little known during his lifetime, so that no detailed account of his career is possible. He came from Aquinum (3. 319). Shortly after A.D. 100, when he published his first extant satires, he was middle-aged (1. 25, 49); and he was writing at least as late as 127 (13. 17; 15. 27): so that he was born between 45 and 65, probably about A.D. 50. All his extant poems were published under Trajan and Hadrian. Like Martial—who knew him well (Mart. 7. 24, 91; 12. 18)—he was miserably poor (cf. *Satires* 1, 3, 5, 7), lived in Rome as a client of the rich, and acquired a small competence in later life (cf. 11, 12). He is mentioned by nobody else until the fourth century, and never writes as if he knew any distinguished contemporary.

2. He says nothing of his youth; but the scholia have a tradition that he was banished for lampooning a court favourite. His terror of satirizing living persons (1. 155 f.), his tone of fierce, hopeless, indiscriminate rancour, his penetrating hatred of Domitian, and the mildness of his later work make it probable that Domitian, if anyone, exiled him. Since any property he had would be confiscated, when he returned in 96 he would be as poor as he appears in his early poems. On a votive tablet from Aquinum (*CIL* x. 5382) the broken name '. . . nius Iuvenalis' is found. If the poet dedicated it, he was once a magistrate of Aquinum and a knight in the imperial service. Perhaps his failure to obtain promotion led him to write the lampoon which ruined him. Certainly the chief impetus to his satire was a bitter sense of failure and injustice, reminiscent of the exiled Swift; focused on Domitian's principate, it gradually faded in intensity with advancing years.

3. WORKS. Juvenal left sixteen hexameter satires, in five books averaging 750–800 lines each and apparently arranged in the order of publication. The last two books are noticeably weaker and vaguer than the rest. In book I, 1, the introduction, explains that J. cannot help writing satire when he sees the corruption of Rome, but that for safety he will attack only the dead; 2, beginning with gibes at hypocritical moralists, broadens into a savage polemic against sodomy; 3 shows why J.'s friend Umbricius is leaving Rome, where honest Romans cannot earn a living and poverty entails frightful discomfort and danger; 4 tells how Domitian summoned his council to discuss the cooking of a monster turbot; 5 describes the client's dinner at his patron's home, where insolent slaves serve him cheap food while his host laughs to see him squirm.

Book II (after A.D. 115, cf. 6. 407 f.) consists of 6, a vast, ruthless diatribe against immoral and affected women.

In book III (date unknown) 7, after complimenting some literary-minded emperor (Hadrian?), exposes the misery of littérateurs lacking patrons; 8 reproaches the aristocrat who thinks nobility superior to virtue; 9 is a repulsive dialogue in which a catamite expounds the troubles of his vocation.

Book IV (date unknown) contains 10, a magnificent declamation on the folly of men in desiring hurtful things instead of courage, health, and sanity; 11, an invitation to dinner, contrasting decent moderation with contemporary extravagance and archaic austerity; 12, relating a friend's escape from shipwreck, with reflections on false and true friendship.

In book V (incomplete; about A.D. 127) 13 is a cynical consolation to a friend cheated of some money; 14 discusses the influence of parents' sins upon children, emphasizing the danger of greed; 15 describes an Egyptian lynching, adding disquisitions on man's inhumanity to man; 16 is a fragment ironically expounding the advantages of being a soldier.

4. Although J. speaks as a moralist, he poses not as a philosopher but as an ordinary man (1. 30, 79; 13. 21, 120) who feels that the world is out of joint, and writes satire as a protest rather than a remedy. His denunciations of folly, meanness, vulgarity, and vice gain enormous force from the fascinated accuracy with which he describes their practitioners and victims. His bitterness often seems to be dictated by literary fashion or exaggerated by personal rancour. Yet (despite Tac. *Ann.* 3. 55) there can have been no great change in the morality of the Roman plutocracy since it was attacked by Seneca and others. Domitian's moral crusade and Martial's callous frankness show that J. told the truth, even if he confined himself to its blacker side.

5. He retained the variety characteristic of satire, adding a more lofty and sustained tone of invective. His memorable epigrams have seldom been surpassed, and he is an amusing, though cruel, parodist. In his vast vocabulary, colloquialisms and queer foreign words jostle the big phrases of epic and rhetoric. His poems, often condemned for structural laxity, have at best quite as clear a pattern as is compatible with the quasi-improvisatory tone of satire. He is the last Roman poet to use the full range of the hexameter, which he adapts to every mood, although his rhythm is graver than that of earlier satirists. His work had a profound influence in the Middle Ages, and is the model for most modern verse-satirists.

BIBLIOGRAPHY

LIFE AND WORKS: H. Nettleship, *Lect. and Essays*, 2nd ser., v (1895); C. Martha, *Les Moralistes sous l'emp. rom.* vi (1900); S. Dill, *R. Society from Nero to M. Aurelius* I. ii (1911); P. de Labriolle, *Les Sat. de J.* (1932); J. Wight Duff, *R. Satire*, viii (1937); G. Highet, *Life of J.* (*Trans. Am. Phil. Ass.* 1937).
TEXTS: O.C.T. (Owen); Cambridge (Housman) ed. 2; Weidmann (Jahn, Buecheler, Leo).
COMMENTARIES: complete, L. Friedlaender (1895); omitting 2 and 9, J. D. Duff (1898); omitting 2, 6, 9, J. E. B. Mayor (1889–93), H. L. Wilson (U.S.A. 1903).
TRANSLATIONS: B. Holyday (1673); J. Dryden (1, 3, 6, 10, 16; 1693); W. Gifford (1802); G. G. Ramsay (1918).
STYLE AND STRUCTURE: L. Kiaer, *Sermonem J. certis legibus astrictum* (1875); E. Strube, *De rhetorica J. disciplina* (1875); L. Bergmüller, *Quaestiones Juvenalianae* (1886); J. Streifinger, *Der Stil des Satirikers J.* (1892); W. Stegemann, *De J. dispositione* (1913).
SUBJECT-MATTER: F. Strauch, *De personis J.* (1869); R. Schütze, *J. ethicus* (1905); J. de Decker, *J. declamans* (1913); F. Gauger, *Zeitschilderung und Topik bei J.* (1936).
METRE: G. Eskuche in Friedlaender's ed.; K. Smith in Wilson's ed.; A. Kusch, *De saturae R. hexametro* (1915).   G. H.

JUVENCUS, GAIUS VETTIUS AQUILINUS, a Spanish presbyter of high rank, about A.D. 330 took the Gospel narrative (especially the Matthew Gospel) as he found it in an Old-Latin text, and turned it into an epic in four books of hexameters (*Evangeliorum libri IV*, an average of 800 lines to each book), in which Virgil's influence is everywhere evident.

Best ed., I. Huemer, *CSEL* xxiv (1891).   A. S.

JUVENTAS, *see* IUVENTAS.

JUVENTIUS CELSUS, PUBLIUS, *see* CELSUS (3).

K

For Greek proper names beginning with K *see under* C.

KAIROS, personified Opportunity. He had an altar at Olympia (Paus. 5. 14. 9), and Ion of Chios (cited there) called him the youngest son of Zeus (i.e. opportunity is god-sent) in a hymn possibly composed for this cult. That he was a little more substantial than most personifications is perhaps indicated by Antimachus, fr. 32 Wyss, where Kairos is one of Adrastus' horses. He has no mythology, but was a favourite subject in art, especially from Lysippus onwards. Then or later he was shown with a long forelock, but bald behind (Posidippus in *Anth. Plan.* 4. 275; see Sauer in Roscher's *Lexikon*, s.v.). Hence, by a gross mistranslation of his name, our phrase 'to take time by the forelock'.

Material in A. B. Cook, *Zeus* ii. 859 ff.   H. J. R.

KANEPHOROI (κανηφόροι) were usually young women who bore baskets or vessels (κανᾶ) in religious processions. In the Panathenaic procession the young women were chosen from noble houses, and were required to be of good family (Harpocration, Photius, Hesychius s.v.), unmarried, and of unsullied reputation; hence 'to be fit to carry the basket' is to live chastely (as Menander, *Epit.* 221 Allinson), and to reject a candidate was a grave insult (Thuc. 6. 56. 1). They were dressed in splendid raiment; hair and garments were decked with gold and jewels; they were powdered with white barley-flour and wore a chain of figs (ἰσχάδων ὁρμαθός). They carried vessels of gold and silver, which contained all things needed in the sacrificial ceremony: first-fruits, the sacrificial knife, barley-groats (ὀλαί), and garlands. Erichthonius was said to have introduced Kanephoroi at the Panathenaea. Certainly the institution was very old, and its object was doubtless to secure the efficacy of the sacrificial materials by letting them touch nothing that was not virginal and therefore lucky and potent.

Kanephoroi are also found in other Attic cults, e.g. those of Apollo, Dionysus, and Isis, and in the cult of Zeus Basileus at Lebadea.

E. Pfuhl, *De Atheniensium pompis sacris* (1900), 20–3; Mittelhaus, *PW* x. 1865–6; L. Deubner, *Attische Feste* (1932) 25.
                                          J. E. F.-H. J. R.

KANUS or **CANUS**, *see* JULIUS (3).

KAPELOS (κάπηλος), *see* COMMERCE, paras. 2 and 11.

KARNEIA, *see* CARNEA.

KASIOS (Κάσιος, less correctly Κάσσιος), ZEUS. An oriental god, possibly Semitic, but the etymology of the name is uncertain. He is plainly connected with Casius, a mountain near Antioch on the Orontes, and also one near Pelusium, on both of which he had a cult. He was also worshipped (owing to the similarity of the names?) at Cassiope in Corcyra. The evidence for his worship, which is Hellenistic and Imperial, is largely archaeological, and his original nature is conjectural. He may have been a mountain- or weather-god, thus leading to his identification with Zeus.

See further Roscher, *Lex.* ii. 970–4; *PW* x. 2265–7; A. B. Cook, *Zeus* ii. 906, 981, 1191.   H. J. R.

KERES, malignant spirits, the bringers of all sorts of evil. They pollute and make unclean (Plato, *Leg.* 937 d, like the Harpies), cause blindness (Eur. *Phoen.* 953), other diseases (Soph. *Phil.* 42), old age and death (Mimnermus fr. 2. 5 f. Diehl), spiritual blindness (ἄτη), misfortune, and troubles in general (cf. Emped. fr. 121

Diels, Semon. 1. 20 Diehl). In its most frequent sense of death or death-bringer K. is used almost as a common noun. Sometimes it must be rendered 'fate', as when Achilles is given the choice between two Keres (*Il.* 9. 411), but it is never neutral or favourable in sense. K. can also mean the souls of the dead, as in the cry at the all-souls festival (end of the Anthesteria, q.v.) θύραζε κῆρες, οὐκέτ᾽ Ἀνθεστήρια (the only certain instance—but see R. Cranszyniec in *Eranos* 45, 100 ff.: the weighing of Keres in *Il.* 22. 210 ff. may reflect an earlier weighing of souls (Malten in *PW*, Suppl. iv. 895; M. P. Nilsson, *Homer and Mycenae*, 267 f., fig. 56)). From this use earlier writers (Crusius, Rohde) posited 'ghosts' as the original meaning of K., but this is convincingly denied by Malten (*PW*, Suppl. iv, s.v.). Malten concludes that K. is originally a predicative word (like θεός, Wilamowitz, *Platon* i. 348) meaning harmful (√ κηραίνειν, ἀκήρατος). As to their form, literary descriptions suggest birds of prey, similar to Harpies or Sirens; it is hard to identify any figures on monuments as Keres.

                                          W. K. C. G.

KERYX (κῆρυξ), *see* HERALDS.

KEYS AND LOCKS. The primitive Greek door-fastening was a horizontal bolt working in staples behind the door (μοχλὸς θύρας, ὀχεύς, sera, claustrum). From the outside the bolt was drawn by a strap passing through a hole in the door; it was withdrawn by inserting through a second hole a bar (κλείς, clavis) bent twice at right angles, so that its end engaged in a groove in the bolt. This bar is the 'temple key' of Greek art. Subsequently a slot was cut in the bolt, into which a vertical peg (βάλανος) fell as the bolt moved forward; then a βαλανάγρα had to be employed to hook up the peg before the bolt could move back. This seems to be the 'lock of Penelope' (*Od.* 21. 46); it remained long in use, with growing complexity of the slots and correspondingly of the prongs of the key. The *clavis Lacedaemonia* of Pliny, with three teeth, is probably one of these variants. The modern form of lock in which the key rotates the bolt on a pivot is not found before Roman times, but is then common, as are movable padlocks. The key in art is often a symbol of power, as when Hecate holds the key of Hades (κλειδοῦχος, clavigera); to give or take back the household keys was a Roman form of divorce.

British Museum Guide to Greek and Roman Life, s.v. 'Keys'; R. Vallois, Dar.-Sag., s.v. 'Sera'.   F. N. P.

KIBOTOS (κιβωτός), *see* FURNITURE.

KNOSSOS, *see* CNOSSOS.

KOINE, *see* DIALECTS (GREEK).

KOLAKRETAI (κωλακρέται, probably from κῶλον and ἀγείρειν, 'collectors of legs' of sacrificial animals for distribution among kings and priests), an old-established financial magistracy in Athens (known also at Cyzicus). They became later overseers of the State-treasury. They paid out money for shipbuilding, for public buildings, for the pay of dicasts (Ar. *Vesp.* 695), and for some religious purposes. The office was seemingly abolished in the revolution of 411 B.C., and not re-established, its general duties being handed over to the *Hellenotamiai*

KOLLEMATA (κολλήματα), *see* BOOKS, I. 4. (q.v.).   A. W. G.

KOMOS (κῶμος), see COMEDY (GREEK), ORIGINS OF.

KORDAX, see COMEDY (GREEK), ORIGINS OF, para. 2, and DANCING.

KORE, see DEMETER, PERSEPHONE, MYSTERIES.

KRONOS, youngest son of Heaven and Earth and leader of his brethren the Titans (q.v.). By advice of his mother he castrated his father, who therefore no longer approached Earth but left room for the Titans between them. Kronos then married his sister Rhea, and there were born to them Hestia, Demeter, Hera, Hades, Poseidon, and Zeus, all of whom (or all the males), save the last, he swallowed, because he was fated to be overcome by one of them. Rhea, by counsel of her parents, wrapped a stone in swaddling-clothes when Zeus was born, and hid him away in Crete (cf. CURETES, ZEUS); Kronos swallowed the stone, thinking it to be his son. Later, by the contrivance of Earth, Kronos vomited up all those he had swallowed, and was overcome by them after a desperate struggle (Hes. *Theog.* 137–8, 154 ff., 453 ff., and many later authors, who differ only in minor details).

This story is so extraordinary and so unlike normal Greek mythology that it is pretty certainly pre-Hellenic; Andrew Lang long ago pointed out (*Myth, Ritual and Religion* (1887), chap. 10) its resemblance to the Maori myth of Tane Mahuta; for legends of swallowing see Stith Thompson, F 913. Another group of stories represents Kronos as king of the Golden Age (ὁ ἐπὶ Κρόνου βίος; Hes. *Op.* 111) or of a distant wonderland (ibid. 169, if genuine; Pind. *Ol.* 2. 70; Plut. *De def. or.*

420 a, etc.). Hence, through his identification with Saturnus (q.v.), his position as civilizer of Italy.

It is therefore very likely that Kronos is a god of the pre-Hellenic population. His festival, the Kronia, was celebrated at Athens and elsewhere (Deubner, *Attische Feste*, 152 ff.; Farnell, op. cit. infra, p. 20) at harvest-time, masters and slaves feasting together; here and there, as at Olympia (Paus. 6. 20. 1), we find him with a priest-hood and a sacrifice. He may have been a god of agriculture; this is not inconsistent with the human sacrifice to him in Rhodes (Porphyry, *Abstin.* 2. 54), even if that is not an Oriental rite, since human sacrifices in connexion with agricultural ceremonies are well attested (see Frazer, *GB*³, index under *Sacrifices, human*). At all events he had a somewhat grim reputation, leading to his being identified with foreign gods of formidable character (e.g. [Plato], *Minos* 315 c, Dion. Hal. *Ant. Rom.* 1. 38. 2).

Literature. Cult: Farnell, *Cults of the Greek States* i. 23 ff. Mythology: M. Mayer in Roscher's *Lexikon*, art. 'Kronos'; M. Pohlenz in *PW*, art. 'Kronos'. H. J. R.

KRYPTEIA, the Spartan secret police, in which young Spartiatae, selected for their intelligence, were authorized by the ephors to patrol the remoter parts of Laconia and to murder secretly helots reputed dangerous to the State. To justify this conduct, the ephors on entering office declared war unconditionally on the helots. Plutarch, who is reluctant to follow Aristotle in ascribing the *Krypteia* to Lycurgus, believes that it dated from after the helots' revolt of 464 B.C., and quotes the murder of 2,000 helots in 424 B.C. (Thuc. 4. 80) as typical of its methods.

Plut. *Lyc.* 28. A. M. W.

KTISTAI (κτίσται), see CITY-FOUNDERS.

L

LABEO, ATTIUS (1st c. A.D.), an unscholarly ('indoctus') translator of both *Iliad* and *Odyssey* into Latin hexameters (Pers. 1. 4 and 50 with the scholia).

LABEO, see also ANTISTIUS (2), CORNELIUS (4).

LABERIUS, DECIMUS (c. 115–43 B.C.), together with Publilius Syrus elevated to literary standards the popular southern Italian *mimus* (q.v.), in Rome called also *fabula riciniata*. The surviving 43 titles and 155 lines (Ribbeck, *CRF*) do not offer enough material to let us understand the value of his work or of this type of play, in which women were allowed to act for the first time in Rome. Unfortunately his fame has been connected with two things which do not throw any light upon the development of his dramatic art, viz. the performance requested by Caesar (Macrob. *Sat.* 2. 7), and the grammarians' interest in his uncommon words.

See G. Malagoli, 'Cavaliere e Mimo', *Atene e Roma* viii (1905), 188–97; H. Reich, *Der Mimus, Ein Litterarentwickelungsgeschicht-licher Versuch* (1903). R. M.

LABIENUS (1), TITUS (c. 100–45 B.C.), served under Servilius (q.v. 2) as *tribunus militum* in Cilicia (c. 78–74). In 63 as *tribunus plebis* he conducted the prosecution of C. Rabirius for *perduellio*, and obtained the re-enaction of the *Lex Domitia* sanctioning election to priesthoods (*see* LEX, LEGES). Appointed *legatus* of Caesar, he acted as his principal subordinate in Gaul (58–51), taking full command in his absence, and he was entrusted with the independent conduct of important operations (e.g. against the Treveri 54–53 and Parisii 52—the latter a strategical and tactical masterpiece). Caesar may have intended him for consul in 48 (a very doubtful inference from *BGal.*

8. 52. 2), but at the beginning of 49 he deserted to Pompey. There is reason to believe that Labienus was always a partisan of Pompey, also of Picenian origin (R. Syme, *JRS* xxviii. 113–25). He fought at Pharsalus and in the African campaign, and died in the final campaign of Munda.

Münzer, *PW* xii. 259–70. C. E. S.

LABIENUS (2), QUINTUS, son of (1) above, was sent to Parthia by Cassius to solicit help against Antony and Octavian. Philippi marooned him in Parthia; but in winter 41–40 B.C. he invaded Syria with Parthian help and defeated Antony's governor, Decidius Saxa; with Saxa's troops he overran part of Asia Minor, and put on his coins the shameful title 'Parthicus Imperator'. In 39 he was defeated and killed by Ventidius (q.v.). W. W. T.

LABIENUS (3), TITUS, Augustan orator who combined an older eloquence with a modern vigour in furious invectives which earned him the nickname of 'Rabienus' (Sen. *Controv.* 10. praef. 4 ff.). When his books, like those of Cassius (q.v. 9) Severus, were burned by senatorial decree, L. refused to survive them. Caligula restored their works to circulation (Suet. *Cal.* 16).

See H. Peter, *HRRel.*; *Prosop. Rom. s.v.* J. W. D.

LABYRINTH (λαβύρινθος, probably derived from a pre-Greek word), a building of complicated plan, constructed by Daedalus for King Minos of Crete, from which nobody could escape. The original labyrinth was located at Cnossos (Cleidemus in Plut. *Thes.* 19), but some later writers identified it with a quarry near Gortyn. The Minotaur lived in the labyrinth and was killed there by Theseus (Catull. 64). By extension Greeks called all kinds of architectural mazes labyrinths, especially, in Egypt, the funeral temple of Amenemhet III (Hdt. 2. 148; H. Kees in *PW* xii. 324). An inscription found in Rome records the construction of a labyrinth in the reign of Septimius Severus (Kaibel, *Epigr. Gr.* 920).

A dance with complicated figures performed in Delos and at Cnossos in memory of the delivery of Athenian youths and maidens from the Minotaur is said to have been an imitation of the labyrinth (Plut. *Thes.* 21).

The labyrinth is represented on coins of Cnossos, on Greek vases, and in Roman mosaics (L. Shear, *AJ Arch.* 1923). Even on the walls of a house in Pompeii we find a graffito of the labyrinth inscribed: 'hic habitat Minotaurus'.

R. Eilmann, *Labyrinthos* (1931); W. F. J. Knight, *Cumaean Gates* (1936). G. M. A. H.

LACERNA, *see* DRESS, para. 4.

LACHARES, Athenian general after Ipsus (301 B.C.), friend of Cassander. In 298–297 he used his mercenary troops to crush an attempted usurpation by his colleague Charias, but shortly after employed them to make himself tyrant. He abolished compulsory military service at Athens and stripped the gold from Athena's statue to pay his troops. His opponents rallied against him in the Piraeus and in 296–295 besieged Athens with the aid of Demetrius Poliorcetes. After a determined resistance he fled to Boeotia, leaving Athens in Demetrius' hands (294). Of his later adventures nothing certain is known.

G. De Sanctis, *Riv. fil.* 1928, 1936 (chronology as above); W. S. Ferguson, *CPhil.* 1929 (Lachares tyrant from 300; fall of Athens 295). F. W. W.

LACHESIS, *see* FATE.

LACONIA ('Η Λακωνικὴ [γῆ or χώρα], and *Laconica* are the usual forms; these are derived from Λάκων, a short and unofficial, but convenient, version of Λακεδαιμόνιος), the south-eastern district of the Peloponnese, bounded on the north by Argolis and Arcadia, on the west by Messenia, and on the south and east by the Aegean Sea. The land-frontiers gave rise to prolonged disputes with Argos, in the seventh and sixth centuries over possession of Thyreatis, with Arcadia at various points and dates, and with Messenia over the *Ager Dentheleatis* (on the W. foot-hills of Taygetus, cf. Tac. *Ann.* 4. 43, etc.; *IG* v. 1, 1431).

Geographically it is a mountainous limestone-region, comprising in the eastern portion the chain of Mt. Parnon, rising to nearly 6,000 ft. near the Argive frontier, which runs south-south-east and sends off subsidiary spurs extending towards Cape Malea, and in the western portion Mt. Taygetus, which runs nearly north to south and forms a high ridge (culminating in a peak of *c.* 7,800 ft. overlooking the plain of Sparta), and continues southward at a lower elevation to form the promontory ending in Cape Taenarum (*Matapan*). Between these masses lies the valley of the Eurotas, which flows into the Laconian Gulf; its principal tributary, the Oenus, coming from the north-east, joins it just above the Sparta, and smaller streams flow from Taygetus through the Spartan plain to join it farther south.

By far the most fertile region is the plain of Sparta, lying between Taygetus and the Eurotas, dominated at its north end by the low hills on which stood Sparta (q.v.). This plain, together with the rest of the Eurotas valley down to the sea and the adjoining coastal plains, as well as a fertile region west of Gytheum, the harbour and arsenal of Sparta, formed the territory of the *Spartiatai*, cultivated for them by their helots. The remainder of Laconia, which includes a few smaller fertile areas, both coastal and inland, was the territory of the *perioikoi*. After 146 B.C. the great majority of their communities were incorporated to form a κοινὸν τῶν Λακεδαιμονίων, which was transformed by Augustus into the Κοινὸν τῶν ᾿Ελευθερολακώνων, independent of Sparta; the latter comprised twenty-four members, which had dwindled to eighteen by the Antonine age (Paus. 3. 21. 7). A. M. W.

LACTANTIUS (*Caecilius Firmianus qui et Lactantius*, A.D. ?250–?317), 'the Christian Cicero', a pupil of Arnobius (q.v.) and native of the province Africa, became a Christian in mature years. He received an appointment as professor of rhetoric from Diocletian, and held it for a considerable time before the persecution broke out which brought an end to his tenure. Part of his life was spent at Nicomedia in Bithynia, and when very old he was appointed by Constantine to educate the Prince Crispus in Gaul.

His works include: *De Opificio Dei*, which contains a description of the body and soul of man, and is a sort of supplement to the fourth book of Cicero's *De Re Publica*; *Divinae Institutiones* (A.D. 304–13), greatest of all his works, which was written against two opponents of Christianity and is a comprehensive survey of all the arguments then available in favour of the new religion (after 314 an epitome was issued, composed by Lactantius himself); *De Ira Dei*, an able discussion of the problem with which it deals, correcting the false conclusions of the chief philosophical schools. Doubts have been cast on the authenticity of the *De Mortibus Persecutorum*. The work deals with the Diocletian persecution, which was abortive, and is historically valuable, whether L. or some contemporary be the author. A quaint poem *De ave Phoenice*, a medley of heathen and Christian elements, is generally believed genuine.

Ed. J. L. Bünemann (1739); S. Brandt and G. v. Laubmann (*CSEL* xix, xxvii, 1890-3–5); R. Pichon, *Lactance* (1901); *Phoenix* (with trans.), J. W. and A. M. Duff, *Minor Latin Poets* (Loeb, 1934). A. S.

LACYDES of Cyrene succeeded Arcesilaus as head of the Middle Academy in 241–240 B.C., and held the position till at least as late as 224–223, after which the headship was probably in commission till Carneades became head; Lacydes died in 206–205. He is sometimes described as founder of the New Academy, but in truth he simply emphasized the scepticism which was already well developed in Arcesilaus. He seems to have made no important contribution to philosophy.

PW xii. 530. W. D. R.

LAELIUS (1) (MAJOR), GAIUS, a *novus homo* who owed his political advancement to his commander and friend Scipio Africanus. In Spain (210–206 B.C.) he commanded the fleet at New Carthage and fought at Baecula and Ilipa. He shared in Scipio's African campaign (204–202), defeating Syphax (q.v.), capturing Cirta, and commanding one wing at Zama. He was plebeian aedile (197), praetor in Sicily (196), consul with L. Scipio (190), proconsul in Gaul (188), and ambassador to Perseus (174) and to some Celtic tribes (170). He lived to meet Polybius (160), to whom he was a valuable source of information about Scipio Africanus, even if his memory of Scipio's early life was somewhat dimmed by age.

H. H. S.

LAELIUS (2) (MINOR), GAIUS, named *Sapiens* for his Stoic learning, the friend of Scipio Aemilianus, accompanied Scipio against Carthage, and, as praetor in 145, fought in Spain. Consul in 140, he proposed land settlement on *ager publicus*, presumably in a Scipionic scheme of reform, but withdrew before the landowners' opposition. He rejected Tiberius Gracchus' policy, opposed the re-election of tribunes, and pronounced the *laudatio* over Scipio Aemilianus. A leader in the Scipionic Circle, he was cultured and eloquent.

Cicero, *Rep.*; *Amic.*; *Off.* 2. 40; Appian, *Pun.* 126–7; Plutarch, *Ti. Gracch.* 8; H. Malcovati, *ORF* i. 102, 224. A. H. McD.

LAELIUS (3) **ARCHELAUS**, a friend of Lucilius, who, like Vettius Philocomus, lectured and commented on Lucilius' satires.

Suet. *Gram.* 2.

LAESTRYGONES, a race of cannibal giants encountered by Odysseus (q.v. *and see* ANTIPHATES). In their country the night is so short that men going out with the flocks to pasture meet those coming back (*Od.* 10. 82 ff.), apparently a vague echo of some traveller's tale of northern conditions in summer (cf. Crates in schol. ibid. 86). Their city, Laestrygonia, is described as the 'lofty town of Lamos', a name suggesting Lamia (q.v.), i.e. their royal family is descended from King Bogey. The ancients, as usual, tried to locate the country in the neighbourhood of Magna Graecia, either in Sicily (Thuc. 6. 2. 1) or at Formiae (Cic. *Att.* 2. 13. 2), when they did not suppose it completely fabulous, as it is.

H. J. R.

LAEVINUS, *see* VALERIUS (5).

LAEVIUS, MELISSUS (? Suet. *Gram.* 3), early in the first century B.C. wrote *Erotopaegnia* (*fantaisies galantes*). Other titles seem to refer to the same work or sections of it, but opinions differ. Surviving fragments suggest a cleverish, rococo, unlatin latinity. Ignored apparently for two centuries, Laevius was then desultorily read and admired by archaizing illuminati. Morel, *FPL. See* ALEXANDRIANISM *and* LYRIC POETRY, LATIN, para. 3.

E. P. B.

LAMACHUS (d. 414 B.C.), Athenian general. He was *strategus* as early as *c.* 435 and was a well-known member of the war-party before 425, when he appears as a blustering soldier in the *Acharnians* of Aristophanes. In 415 he was appointed with Alcibiades and Nicias to conduct the expedition to Sicily. He advocated an immediate attack on Syracuse, but was overborne by his colleagues. The rapid progress of the Athenian blockade in 414 was largely due to his energetic leadership and terminated abruptly when he was killed in a skirmish. Aristophanes in later plays pays tributes to his heroism.

Thucydides, bk. 6.　　　　　　　　　　　　　　H. D. W.

LAMBAESIS (modern *Lambèse*), a Roman camp in Numidia north of the Aurès range. Trajan moved the Third Augusta Legion there to control the route which led north from the Sahara through Vescera (*Biskra*) and Calceus Herculis (*El Kantara*). Military roads enabled the legate to reinforce the auxiliaries in Numidia and the Mauretanias. Hadrian visited Lambaesis (A.D. 128); his address to the troops was inscribed on a column, and much of it survives (Dessau, *ILS* 2487 and 9133–5). The legion was disbanded by Gordian III (238), but Valerian restored it to its old quarters (253).

Lambaesis is the finest example of a Roman fortified camp extant. It contains an *arcus quadrifons* (usually called the *praetorium*), legionary head-quarters, offices, storerooms, chapels, messrooms, baths, and latrines. Platforms along the walls served as artillery emplacements, and at the four corners are rounded re-entrant towers. An amphitheatre was built outside the walls, and married-quarters were erected after Septimius' army reforms; these grew into a substantial town with its own baths, arches, and temples.　　　　　　　　　　W. N. W.

LAMENT, *see* DIRGE, EPICEDIUM.

LAMIA, a child-stealing nursery bogey, Ar. *Vesp.* 1035= *Pax* 758 (where she is apparently bisexual) and often. The schol. on *Pax* says she was daughter of Belus and Libya (*see* DANAUS), whose children Hera destroyed because Zeus was her lover, whereat she became savage with grief; more refs. in Roscher's *Lexikon* ii. 1819. For a later conception of her see Philostr. *VA* 4. 25. H. J. R.

LAMIA, the principal city of Malis, situated near the Malian Gulf. Its strong acropolis commanded the chief route from Thessaly to central Greece. Lamia perhaps was not founded until the close of the fifth century, but it soon dominated Malis and developed rapidly, especially after Spartan control of Heraclea (q.v. 4) terminated. In the Lamian War Antipater was blockaded in Lamia for some months (323–322). In the third century the city prospered under Aetolian hegemony, but in 190 it was sacked by Acilius Glabrio.

Y. Béquignon, *La Vallée du Spercheios* (1937). H. D. W.

LAMPADIO, GAIUS OCTAVIUS, a Roman scholar of the second century B.C., prompted by the influence of Crates of Mallos to take a literary interest in early Latin poets (Suet. *Gram.* 2). He arranged in seven books the *Bellum Punicum* of Naevius.

LAMPOON (GREEK). The tradition of abusive and satirical verse seems to have been indigenous to the Greeks. An early example can be seen in the verses with which Archilochus assailed Lycambes, or later those with which Hipponax attacked Bupalus. The form was recognized by the word ἴαμβος, used for any poetry which abused (cf. Procl. ap. Phot. *Bibl.* 321 a 28, Ael. *VH* 3. 40, Poll. 2. 54). Hence it was applied to the satirical verses of Xenophanes and Timon. *See also* ALCAEUS (3) OF MESSENE. C. M. B.

LAMPOON (LATIN). The lampoon, which in Italy grew out of the *opprobria rustica* of the *versus Fescennini* (Hor. *Epist.* 2. 1. 145 ff.), was employed as a prophylactic against the evil eye at weddings and in the *carmina triumphalia* of the soldiers. Apart from such privileged occasions, the *carmen famosum* was forbidden by a law of the XII Tables (Bruns, *Font.*[7] 28 f.). But, in spite of the law, political and personal enmity often found vent in such poems. The poet Naevius was imprisoned for his lampoons on the Metelli; Catullus and Bibaculus were famous for their lampoons (Tac. *Ann.* 4. 34); the Emperor Augustus was not above writing them himself (Macrob. *Sat.* 2. 4. 21). During the Empire the writing of political lampoons was punished under the law of *maiestas*, while the pseudonymous private lampoon in various metres was raised to the position of a literary genre by Martial. The favourite metre for the popular lampoon was the trochaic tetrameter: an example may be found in Bücheler, *Carmina epigraphica* 231 (*CIL* iv, 1939, tab. 23, 10) from a wall in Pompeii. R. M. H.

LAMPROCLES (early 5th c. B.C.), Athenian musician and poet, teacher of Damon (schol. Pl. *Alc.* 118 c), exponent of the mixo-Lydian mode (Plut. *De mus.* 16), composer of dithyrambs (Ath. 491 c) and of a famous hymn to Athene quoted by Aristophanes (*Nub.* 967).

Text: E. Diehl, *Anth. Lyr. Graec.* ii, pp. 123–4. Criticism: U. von Wilamowitz-Moellendorff, *Textg. d. gr. Lyr.* (1900), pp. 84–5. C. M. B.

LAMPS (λύχνος, *lucerna*) were used not only to illumine interiors and, more rarely, exteriors, but as votive offerings to deities and as tomb-furniture. The commonest materials were bronze and clay. Primitive lamps are known in neolithic Greece and the Minoans and Mycenaeans used them freely. Later their use died out; Homer has only a single reference to lamps (*Od.* 19. 34). About 600 B.C. they were reintroduced into Greece from the East, where a simple 'cocked-hat' form is found throughout the early Iron Age. In Italy outside the Greek cities the use of lamps, apart from some isolated Etruscan examples, does not begin before the third century. The earliest Greek lamps in clay are wheel-made in the form of open saucers; later the body is deepened and the top covered. After 200 most lamps are moulded and have decoration in relief. Hellenistic lamps are rounded or oval and limit the decoration to the rim. The typical lamp of the early Roman Empire is circular with decoration on the top; in the later Empire the oval shape reappears. More elaborate specimens with many nozzles are not uncommon, while the forms of the metal lamps are extremely varied.

H. B. Walters, *British Museum Catalogue of Lamps* (1914); O. Broneer, 'The Terracotta Lamps' in *Corinth* iv. 2 (U.S.A., 1930); S. Loeschcke, *Lampen aus Vindonissa* (1919). F. N. P

LAMPSACUS, a Phocaean foundation in the northern Troad with a good harbour. Its strategic position guarding the eastern entrance to the Hellespont explains the city's economic prosperity and historical significance. Hence, too, sprang its attempt to check the elder Miltiades' domination of the Chersonese. In the sixth and fifth centuries Lampsacus passed successively under Lydian, Persian, Athenian, and Spartan control. It was assigned by Artaxerxes I to Themistocles, whom it supplied with the wine for which it was famous. Its tribute of twelve talents as a member of the Delian Confederacy, and its gold coinage in the fourth century, attest its commercial well-being. Attempts to assert its independence against Persia and Athens were quickly repressed, but in the fourth century Lampsacus enjoyed lengthy periods of self-government. Its prosperity continued during the Hellenistic age and under the Roman Republic (Cic. 2 *Verr.* 1. 24. 63) and Empire.

W. Leaf, *Strabo on the Troad* (1923), 92. D. E. W. W.

LANA, see APEX.

LANISTA, see GLADIATORS.

LANUVIUM, nowadays *Lanuvio*, an ancient Latin city in the Alban Hills (Cato fr. 58 P.; Strabo 5. 239). In 338 B.C. Rome dissolved the Latin League, granted Lanuvium Roman citizenship, and officially adopted its famous cult of Juno Sospes (Livy 8. 14; Cic. *Nat. D.* 1. 83: for ancient remains, G. Bendinelli, *Monumenti Antichi* 1922, 292). Although it suffered in the Civil Wars (App. *BCiv.* 5. 24), Lanuvium, unlike many Latian towns, continued to flourish even in Imperial times (however, reject *Lib. Colon.*, p. 235). Milo, Roscius, and Antoninus Pius were born there (Cic. *Mil.* 27; *Div.* 36; S. H. A. *Ant. Pius* 1; *Comm.* 1). Lanuvium was often confused with Lavinium: hence its medieval name *Civita Lavinia*.

G. B. Colburn, *AJArch.* xviii (1914); A. E. Gordon, *Cults of Lanuvium* (U.S.A. 1938). E. T. S.

LAOCOÖN, a legendary Trojan prince, brother of Anchises and priest of the Thymbraean Apollo or (in some accounts) of Poseidon. Of his story as it was told by Arctinus in the *Iliupersis*, by Bacchylides, and by Sophocles in a tragedy bearing his name we know little. According to the generally accepted tale (Verg. *Aen.* 2. 40–56, 199–231; Apollod. *Epit.* 5. 17–18), he protested against the proposal to draw the Wooden Horse within the walls of Troy, and two great serpents coming over the sea from the island of Tenedos killed him and his two sons (in Arctinus one son, in Quint. Smyrn. 12. 444–97 Laocoön himself escaped). According to Hyginus (*Fab.* 135. 1) the serpents were sent by Apollo to punish him for having married in spite of his priesthood,* in Quint. Smyrn. and Virgil, by Athena on account of his hostile attitude to the Horse. The story is famous not only from the dramatic pathos of Virgil's rendering, but as the subject of one of the most famous examples of ancient sculpture, the marble group now in the Vatican which depicts father and two sons in their death-agony. This, a masterpiece of the Pergamene school, was the work of three Rhodian sculptors, Agesander, Polydorus, and Athenodorus, of the second half of the first century. In

* But see Rose's note there.

Roman times it was exhibited in the palace of the Emperor Titus, and in Pliny's view (*HN* 36. 37) surpassed all other works of painting and sculpture. Lessing made it the text for his famous essay of 1766 on the difference between poetry and the fine arts. R. A. B. M.

LAODAMEIA, see PROTESILAUS.

LAODICE (1), in mythology, a stock name for women of high rank, meaning 'princess' (cf. CREON, CREUSA), e.g. (*a*) a daughter of Priam, see ACAMAS, DEMOPHON, (*b*) a daughter of Agapenor, q.v.; she founded the temple of Paphian Aphrodite in Tegea (Paus. 8. 53. 7, cf. 5. 3); (*c*) daughter of Agamemnon (*Il.* 9. 145), later replaced by Electra (q.v.). H. J. R.

LAODICE (2), probably a niece of Antiochus I, married her cousin Antiochus II, by whom she had two sons and two daughters. Antiochus repudiated her and her children in favour of Berenice (daughter of Ptolemy II), whose son (born 251 B.C.) became heir-apparent. The result, when Antiochus died, was a war of succession, in which Egypt supported Berenice's son ('Third Syrian', or 'Laodicean War', 246–241). Tradition gives Laodice a great share in inspiring and organizing the resistance (especially in Asia Minor) which enabled her eldest son to succeed as Seleucus II. G. T. G.

LAODICEA AD LYCUM (Λαοδίκεια ἐπὶ Λύκῳ, also called Λ. τῆς Ἀσίας), a city founded by Antiochus II (261–246 B.C.) and called after his wife Laodice (q.v. 2). It occupied the site of an older city on a flat hill overlooking the valley of the Lycus a few miles east of its junction with the Maeander; its territory was bounded by the rivers Λύκος and Κάπρος, symbolized as Wolf and Boar on its coins. It lay on a great trade-route and was one of the most prosperous cities in Asia; it was the head of a *conventus* and one of the 'Seven Churches' of the Apocalypse. Diocletian made it the *metropolis* of the province of Phrygia. W. M. C.

LAOMEDON, legendary king of Troy, for whose genealogy *see* DARDANUS. For his relations with Heracles *see* HERACLES; for his dealings with Apollo and Poseidon *see* ibid. Apart from this he has little place in mythology, the most interesting feature of his legend being the story of his grave, which lay over the Scaean Gate and ensured the safety of the city so long as it was undisturbed (Servius on *Aen.* 2. 241, cf. Plautus, *Bacch.* 955; see W. F. J. Knight in *CJ* xxviii. 257 ff.). This undoubtedly refers to some kind of magical precaution, whether or not originally associated with Troy. H. J. R.

LAPIS MANALIS, see STONES, SACRED.

LARCIUS (? LARGIUS) LICINUS (1st c. A.D.) wrote a *Cicero-mastix*. Its reprehensible audacity in criticizing the orator is coupled by Gellius (17. 1. 1) with that of Asinius Gallus.

LARENTALIA, see ACCA LARENTIA, LARES.

LARES (older **LASES,** Arval hymn; Henzen, *Acta Arualium*, p. cciv. 33). The etymology and consequently the connexion, if any, with the names Larentia (Acca, q.v.), Larunda, Lara, and Etruscan Lasa and Larth are very uncertain (Boehm, op. cit. infra, 806 f.). As to their origin there are two principal theories, supported respectively by Samter and by Wissowa and W. Warde Fowler. (1) They are the ghosts of the dead. Samter starts from the *Lar Familiaris*, and supposes him closely connected with the cult of the dead, because (*a*) if a bit of food falls on the floor during a meal, it is proper to burn it before the Lares (Pliny, *HN* 28. 27; see X. F. M. G. Wolters, *Antique Folklore* (1935), 96 ff., but *contra*, Rose in *Gnomon* xii. 390). Now the floor is a notorious haunt of ghosts; the food, therefore, has gone to the ghosts' region and so is formally given to the ghosts. (*b*) At the Compitalia, or festival of the cross-roads (cross-roads being again a favourite place for ghosts, cf. HECATE), it was the custom to hang up a male or female puppet for each free member of a household, a ball for each slave (Festus, p. 272. 15 Lindsay, cf. pp. 108. 27; 273. 7), that the Lares, says Festus, might spare the living and take these surrogates instead. This is a quite reasonable precaution against ghosts. (*c*) The connexion, which he assumes, with Larentia and the Larentalia definitely connects them with chthonian ritual.

(2) Wissowa points out that the Roman dead are honoured not in the house but at their graves; the hearth is the place of Vesta and the *di Penates* (qq.v.), and the *Lar* (*familiaris*), a later intruder. The ceremonial at the cross-roads is easily enough explained when it is remembered that a *compitum* is properly and originally the place where the paths separating four farms meet (Gromatici, p. 302. 20 ff., Lachmann; schol. Pers. 4. 28). This has no ghostly associations, but it regularly had a chapel of the Lares. That the *Lar familiaris* (Lar of the servants, rather than of the household generally, in origin) was brought into the house by the farm-slaves is likely, cf. Warde Fowler, *Roman Essays*, p. 61.

The Lares, then, are originally deities of the farm-land. From this, and from the secondary cult in the houses, they expand (apart from purely theoretical developments of the use of their name to signify ghost or *daimon*) (1) into guardians of any cross-way, including one in a city. Hence grew up in Rome the *collegia compitalicia*, associations of small people, mostly freedmen, who tended the shrines, and their festival. These are somewhat doubtfully said to have been restored by Augustus, after having been suppressed by Julius, with the addition of his own Genius (q.v.; Ov. *Fasti* 5. 145, whereon see Frazer, but see L. Delatte in *Ant. class.* vi (1937), 103 ff.); (2) into guardians of roads and wayfarers, *Lares uiales*, including travellers by sea, *Lares permarini*; (3) into guardians of the State in general, *Lares praestites*; see especially Wissowa, *Ges. Abh.* 274 ff.; Ovid, ibid. 129 ff., and Frazer thereon.

Like all Roman deities the Lares have no mythology. Ovid (*Fasti* 2. 599 ff.) has a story of their begetting by Mercurius on Lara, manifestly a late invention and quite possibly his own. For another alleged mother *see* MANIA. In one version (Pliny, *HN* 36. 204) of the wonderful birth of Servius (q.v.) Tullius his father is the *Lar familiaris*; a late anthropomorphizing (for a different one see Ovid, *Fasti* 6. 627) of an old folk-tale, that he or some other remarkable person was born of a woman fertilized by the fire.

Since the cult of the *Lar familiaris*, whatever its origin, became universal, see for many examples in popular art Boyce in *Am. Ac. Rome* xiv, lar or lares is used, like *penates*, by metonymy for 'home', 'house'; *lararium* is 'private chapel'.

Good conspectus, with bibliography, Boehm in *PW*, s.v. H. J. R.

LARGUS, *see* SCRIBONIUS (3).

LARISSA, the principal city of Thessaly, dominating the fertile plain of Pelasgiotis, with an acropolis on a low hill protected by the river Peneus. It was the first Thessalian city to strike coins, and its earliest issues, struck on the Persian standard, reflect both the medism of the Aleuadae (q.v.) and their influence over the Larisseans. *C.* 400 B.C. Larissa was weakened by party struggles, and although it formed the centre of aristocratic opposition to the tyrants of Pherae, its efforts were seldom successful without external support. Jason won Larissa before 374, but it resisted his successors by enlisting aid first from Thebes and later from Philip of Macedon. This policy led to the Macedonian annexation

of Thessaly, and Larissa remained in Macedonian hands until liberated by Rome in 196, after which it became the capital of the new Thessalian League and enjoyed considerable prosperity.

F. Stählin, *Das hellenische Thessalien* (1924), 94–9. H. D. W.

LARNAX (λάρναξ), *see* FURNITURE.

LARUNDA, an extremely obscure Roman goddess, said to be Sabine (Varro, *Ling.* 5. 74, cf. E. C. Evans, *Cults of the Sabine Territory* (1939), 227 ff.), and generally supposed to be chthonian (Wissowa, *RK* 234). The quantity of the first syllable (known from Ausonius, *Technop.* 8. 9 (p. 161 Peiper), 'nec genius domuum, Larunda progenitus Lar') suggests a possible connexion with Acca Larentia (q.v.). The ancients equate her with Lăra, said by Ovid (*Fasti* 2. 599 ff.) to be mother of the Lăres (see Frazer ad loc.; Lactantius, *Div. Inst.* 1. 20. 35). The quantity, however, is against this. Probably this identification is meant by Philoxenus, p. 225 (LA 66), Lindsay–Laistner, *Larunda*: δαιμόνων μήτηρ, cf. [Placidus], p. 66 (L 15) Lindsay–Pirie, 'Larunda: quam quidam Maniam dicunt', but the reading is doubtful. If right, cf. Varro, *Ling.* 9. 61, 'uidemus enim Maniam matrem Larum dici'. For the Mother of the Lares cf. Henzen, *Act. Arval.* 145, and add Dessau, *ILS* 9522, on which see L. R. Taylor in *AJArch.* 29 (1935), 299 ff.; E. Tabeling, *Mater Larum* (1932). The most probable explanation of the occurrence of this un-Roman genealogy in a sacral document is that it had been affected by the theories mentioned above. H. J. R.

LASUS (b. *c.* 548–545 B.C., Suidas), son of Charminus, of Hermione, lived at the court of Hipparchus, where he disclosed the forgeries of Onomacritus (Hdt. 7. 6). Rival of Simonides (schol. Ar. *Vesp.* 1410), he composed hymns (Ath. 467 a, 624 e) and dithyrambs, of which he was a pioneer in Athens (schol. Pind. *Ol.* 13. 25; schol. Ar. *Av.* 1403; Clem. Al. *Strom.* 1. 16).

Text: E. Diehl, *Anth. Lyr. Graec.* ii. 60. C. M. B.

LATERANUS, *see* PLAUTIUS (6).

LATIFUNDIA. It was a characteristic of ancient Oriental large estates that commercial, industrial, and lending enterprises were interrelated with agriculture. The primitive serf estates of archaic Greece and Italy were broken up, except in backward countries like Thessaly, as a consequence of democratic movements. Imitation of the *ergasterion* (*see* INDUSTRY) produced the slave estate of classical Greece, which was larger than the normal peasant holdings, used scientific handbooks on agriculture, and produced with a view to high profit. The Hellenistic large estates and the Italian *latifundia* originated in a blending of Oriental and Greek estate systems in Hellenistic and, perhaps, Carthaginian territories. The division of labour and the wide economic activities of Oriental estates were preserved, and very cheap labour became most important. Hellenistic estates like the *dorea* ('concession') of Ptolemy II's minister Apollonius (q.v. 3) used more free workmen than slaves, in spite of being actively engaged in the slave trade. The West exploited cheap slave labour with an unrivalled mercenary spirit and cruelty.

The Roman *latifundium* originated in distributions of the *ager publicus* in the early second century B.C., as soon as the wealth of the Roman upper class had sufficiently increased to imitate Eastern landlords. The *villa* with its slave *familia* was much stronger economically than the surrounding peasants, because only large owners had capital for introducing new crops and breeds. In consequence, a large number of peasants in Italy and even in the provinces lost their homesteads. *Latifundia*, with *villa urbana, villa rustica, instrumentum vocale*

(= slaves), *semivocale* (= cattle), and *mutum* (furniture and implements) became characteristic of all Roman provinces.

A change came as soon as slave labour ceased to be cheap, and the *familia* gave way to the *colonus*, who learned all the methods of *latifundium* agriculture useful to him. A new Late Roman type of large estate arose, which later became a model for the Middle Ages. Most of the soil was in the hands of *coloni*, who cultivated small tracts in accordance with the teachings of Cato, Varro, and Columella (qq.v.), as far as the economic situation permitted. Enterprises in trade, craftsmanship, and banking, as well as small garrisons, remained on the estates. These Late Roman estates, together with State and Church institutions, remained as islands of classical culture and experience during the difficult times of the Germanic, Slavic, and Islamic conquests. *See* AGRICULTURE, PASTURAGE.　　　　　　　　　　　　　F. M. H.

LATIN LANGUAGE. Latin was originally the language of the city of Rome and the Latian plain, and it was only as Rome's power extended that her language spread itself over the ancient Western world. It belongs to the Italic branch of the Indo-European family of languages and is thus akin to Greek, Germanic, Celtic, etc.; within Italy its nearest relative is Faliscan, and next are the Italic dialects proper, Oscan and Umbrian (qq.v.). When and whence Italic came into Italy cannot be stated exactly, but it must have come over the Alps and Apennines from somewhere in Europe before the eighth century B.C. Besides the numerous Italic dialects there were in Italy also Greek in the south and on the coast, Celtic in the north, and the non-Indo-European language of Etruria. All these exerted more or less influence upon Latin. Borrowings from Celtic were confined to a few words, e.g. *petorritum, gaesum, carrus*, and the Greek influence, though considerable, did not come in till late. From Etruscan came names such as *Sulla, Casca*, and many with an *-n*-suffix, e.g. *Perpenna, Sisenna, Maecenas*. Etruscan also are technical terms such as *histrio, subulo, persona, puteal, camillus*, and perhaps even such common words as *urbs* and *amare* (infinitive). The substitution of breathed for voiced sounds in words like *sporta* (<σπυρίδα), *catamitus* (<Γανυμήδης), the aspirate in names like *Gracchus, Cethegus*, and the weakening or disappearance of syllables which resulted from the shifting of the word-accent as in Pollux (<Πολυδεύκης) are probably due to Etruscan. This theory receives support from the Etruscan names of the old Latin tribes, *Ramnes, Tities, Luceres* (cf. *lucumo*), and it is now generally accepted that the Latin alphabet is derived not directly from Greek but is partly of Etruscan origin.

2. Outside Italy the Italic group (including Latin) has its closest affinity with Celtic, and the number of morphological innovations which both groups share gives much plausibility to the theory that their pre-ethnic speakers must have lived in close association after the separation of the Indo-European peoples. Both groups show

(*a*) extension of the abstract-noun stems in *-ti-* by an *-n*-suffix, e.g. *men-ti-on-em*;

(*b*) superlative formation in *-smmos*, e.g. *aegerrimus* (<*aegr-ismmos*);

(*c*) genit. sing. of *-o*-stems in *-ī*: e.g. *filī*, O. Ir. *magi*;

(*d*) medio-passive formation in *-r*: *sequitur* = Ir. *sechedar*;

Both Celtic and Italic are divided into two sub-families, a Goidelic and a Brythonic, and an Oscan-Umbrian and a Latin-Faliscan respectively, which differ in the same way in their treatment of Indo-European *q*. Thus Latin has *quod, quinque* while Oscan has *pod, pompe*: Irish has *coic* (five), Welsh *pump*; Gaelic has *Mac* (e.g. MacDonald), Welsh *Ap* (e.g. Powell < Ap Howell).

3. The most striking feature of Latin is its accentuation. In Indo-European the accent was predominantly *musical* and was unrestricted. In the historical period of Latin, while remaining *musical*, it was restricted by the trisyllabic law dependent on the quantity of the penult. In the intervening period, however, it became strongly *stress* and shifted to the first syllable of the word. This resulted in the transformation of words by

(*a*) syncope: *ardere, audere* (cf. *aridus, avidus*);

(*b*) umlaut: *teneo, capio* (cf. *retineo, retentum*; *incipio, inceptum*);

(*c*) iambic shortening: *benĕ, vidĕ* (cf. *rectē, audē*).

Thus all short vowels in open position in medial syllables either disappeared or were narrowed to *i* or *ĕ*, and diphthongs became monophthongs, e.g. *caedo, claudo* (cf. *occīdo, exclūdo*).

4. Other vocalic changes were the reduction of (accented) diphthongs *ai, ei, oi, eu*, e.g. *aedes* (αἴθω), *dīco* (δείκνυμι), *ūnus* (οἴνη), *iumentum* (ζεῦγος).

5. Of the consonants original *i* and *u* were lost very early, the former between any two vowels (e.g. *trēs* <*treies*), the latter between two similar vowels if the first was accented, e.g. *audiī* < *audīvi* (but not in *amāvi* or *avārus*). Where *i* occurs between vowels it equals *ii*, e.g. *Maia*. Initially *du-* became *b-*, e.g. *bis* (cf. *duo*). In the second century A.D. Latin *v* (pronounced *w*) came to be sounded like English *v* (cf. *vox*, Fr. *voix*), and Latin *b* in certain positions developed the same sound (cf. *habere*, Fr. *avoir*). Hence late spellings like *Bictorinus, birtus*. Between 450 and 350 B.C. intervocalic *-s-* became *-r-*, e.g. *gero: gestum*. Therefore, words such as *rosa, miser* are non-Latin, while in *causa, fīsus* there was originally not *-s-* but *-ss-*.

6. The chief innovations in morphology are:

(*a*) loss of the dual number;

(*b*) new forms of genitive singular and nominative plural in *-o-* and *-ā-* stems;

(*c*) new adverbial forms in *-ē-, -m, -iter*;

(*d*) rise of the so-called 5th declension;

(*e*) confusion of consonantal stems with stems in *-ī* and the disuse of the *u* declension in adjectives, e.g. ἡδύς but *suavis*;

(*f*) confusion of primary and secondary personal terminations in the verb;

(*g*) almost complete disappearance of non-thematic conjugations;

(*h*) fusion of aorist and perfect forms and of active and middle endings in what we call the perfect;

(*i*) complete fusion of conjunctive and optative into one mood.

7. Latin syntax has restricted case-usage more sharply than Greek except in the ablative, which combined ablative, locative, and sociative-instrumental uses from which developed the characteristically Latin ablative absolute. In the verb there is great extension of the subjunctive, particularly in dependent clauses, and a very complex and strict system of *oratio obliqua* and sequence of tenses.

8. As a vehicle of literature Latin, unlike Greek, appears at first as crude and unpolished in both verse and prose. The pioneer efforts of Ennius, however, to graft on Latin the artistic excellences of Greek were ably seconded by Lucretius and Catullus and culminate in the full glory of Latin poetry in the *Aeneid* of Virgil and of prose in the resonant periods of Cicero and the rich smoothness of Livy. The rhetorical style reaches its height in the Ovidian elegiac and the brilliant epigram of Tacitus. In the hands of the greatest masters Latin was shown to be the worthy vehicle of the thought of a great imperial race.

A. Meillet, *Esquisse d'une histoire de la langue latine*[4] (1938); Stolz–Schmalz, *Lateinische Grammatik*, 5th ed. by Leumann–Hofmann (Müller's Handbuch, 1928); J. Marouzeau, *Le Latin*[2] (1927).　　　　　　　　　　　　　　　　　　　　　P. S. N.

LATIN, SILVER. The period of Silver Latin is broadly from A.D. 17 to 130, but the literary decline which marks it began even before Livy's death. The loss of political liberty and the practice of barren declamation led to a striving after novelty in which forced expression, exaggerated emphasis, antithesis, and epigram were cultivated for the express purpose of winning applause. Though the diction of Seneca is still fairly classical, all these faults abound in his works, and thereafter the same vein of rhetoric runs through the literature, reaching its height in Tacitus, the greatest of Silver writers. Quintilian has well summarized its faults when he says (bk. 8 proem) 'nihil iam proprium placet, dum parum creditur disertum, quod et alius dixisset' and 'tum demum ingeniosi scilicet, si ad intelligendos nos opus sit ingenio'. The chief features of Silver Latin are:

(1) words borrowed for prose from the poets, especially Virgil;

(2) words in new (frequently poetical) meanings;

(3) new formations of agent-nouns in -*tor*, -*sor*, and abstracts in -*sus*, -*ura*, -*mentum*;

(4) as in poetry, use of simple instead of compound verbs;

(5) freer use of cases, e.g. dative of purpose, ablative of separation without preposition, ablative of duration of time, instrumental ablative even of persons, etc.;

(6) present and perfect subjunctive in *oratio obliqua* after secondary tenses;

(7) subjunctive of indefinite frequency and its extension to relative conjunctions;

(8) interchange of *quin* and *quominus*;

(9) *quamvis*, *quanquam* with subjunctive even when denoting facts;

(10) *tanquam*, *quasi*, *velut* to express, not comparison, but alleged reason.   P. S. N.

LATIN, SPOKEN. Colloquial Latin (*sermo cotidianus*) means the easy everyday Latin of cultured people in which, as Quintilian says, 'cum amicis, coniugibus, liberis, seruis loquimur'. The plays of Plautus and Terence are written mostly in this style, just as in a modern comedy of manners the language is the ordinary speech of polite society. Thus Cicero tells us that the speech of nobly born Roman ladies, e.g. Laelia, was strongly reminiscent of the language of Plautus, and Terence has always been considered a model of familiar, but elegant, latinity. Particularly important are the letters of Cicero, especially those written to his 'second-self' Atticus, or, e.g., to Paetus, to whom he says: 'Quid tibi uideor in epistulis? nonne plebeio seimone agere tecum? epistulas uero cotidianis uerbis texere solemus.' Characteristic features of this style are (1) the frequency of diminutives; (2) interjections; (3) very free syntax; (4) use of Greek words and tags, as we nowadays use French; (5) wide use of forms intensified by *per*- or weakened by *sub*-, e.g. *subinuidere*. The same style in verse is found in Horace's *Satires* and *Epistles*, and there are occasional lapses into colloquialism in other writers, e.g. Catullus. On a somewhat lower level are the *Bellum Africanum* and *Bellum Hispaniense*, while in the *De Architectura* of Vitruvius we have what might be called the Latin of business life. Very important, too, is the *Satyricon* of Petronius with its descending scale of urbanity from the cultured familiarity of Encolpius to the coarse vulgarity of Echion and Habinnas.

J. B. Hofmann, *Lateinische Umgangssprache*, 1925 (2nd ed. with additions 1936).   P. S. N.

LATIN, VULGAR. Vulgar Latin is that form of the Latin language which was used by the uneducated classes in Italy and the provinces. We know it from (1) inscriptions, (2) a few texts such as the *Satyricon* of Petronius, *Peregrinatio Aetheriae*, *Mulomedicina Chironis*, *Appendix*

Probi, and (3) the early development of the Romance languages. It differs from classical Latin mainly in a disregard of seemingly unnecessary distinctions, a desire for greater regularity in word-form, and a striving after emphasis. Vowels are slurred and confused, final -*m*, -*s*, -*t* are dropped, *b* is confused with *v*, *s* with *x*; hence forms like *oli*, *plevis*, *milex*. Analogy creates *nura*, *aprus*, *acrum*, and syncope *veclus*, *oclus*, *virdis*, *frigda*. *Caelus* and *caelum* are pronounced *caelo*, whence confusion of gender (e.g. *vinus*, *fatus*); and the break-up of declension leads to a greatly increased use of prepositions (e.g. *ab*+*ante*, *de*+*intus*). The infinitive and accusative construction disappears in favour of clauses with *quia*, *quoniam*, *ut*; and new perfect and future tenses are formed by auxiliary verbs, *habere*, *debere*, e.g. *qui nasci habent* (= *nascentur*). There is great activity in word-composition, especially diminutives of nouns (e.g. *ossucula*, *oricla*, *audaculus*) and frequentatives and intensives of verbs (e.g. *ausare*, *contenebricare*). Many common words become obsolete and are replaced by others, e.g. *magnus*, *ĕdere*, *ludus*, *senex*, *ignis*, *ferre*, *emere* by *grandis*, *manducare*, *iocus*, *vetulus*, *focus*, *portare*, *comparare*. Finally, the word-order of Vulgar Latin is simpler and more rational, e.g. 'Haec est autem vallis ingens et planissima, in qua filii Israhel commorati sunt his diebus, quod sanctus Moyses ascendit in montem Domini' (*Peregrinatio Aetheriae*, 2. 2).

Report on literature of 1925-36 by T. Boegel, Bursian *Jahresb.* 270 (1940), 256-405.   P. S. N.

LATIN LEAGUE, *see* LATINI *and* LATIUM.

LATIN LITERATURE, HISTORY OF, *see* APPENDIX at the end of this work.

LATIN NAME, *see* LATINI *and* IUS LATII.

LATINI. The inhabitants of the plain of Latium—a people of mixed stock, predominantly 'cremators' but including a late wave of 'inhumators'—lived originally in numerous small communities, *populi*, which gradually coalesced or were forcibly amalgamated between the sixth and fourth centuries B.C. into larger States, the greatest of which was Rome. The *populi* formed confederations for religious purposes. The largest was the cult-group of Jupiter Latiaris on the Alban Mount, the presidency of which passed early to Rome but was of no political significance. The 'league of Ferentina', based on a shrine of Diana in the territory of Aricia, was from the sixth to the fourth century the political centre of all Latium, where the representatives of the independent *populi* deliberated on equal terms, elected federal officers, and decided on joint policy. These conditions, interrupted by the partial ascendancy of the Etruscan kings of Rome, were reaffirmed by the Cassian treaty (*see* CASSIUS (1)) and continued during the troubled period of the fifth century till, in the fourth, Rome began to encroach seriously on her neighbours. Eventually, in 338, Rome incorporated the smaller States and reduced the larger to subject allies. The characteristics of the later Latin Name were fixed in this early period by the continuous tradition of social and political equality between the Latins. Even the establishment of federal colonies drawn from all the Latin peoples, and the sharing of booty won in federal wars, persisted unchanged after 338 (*see* IUS LATII, COMMERCIUM). Henceforth the Latin Name consisted of the few remaining *populi Latini* and an ever-growing number of Latin colonies, of which the man-power was increasingly drawn from Rome. These colonies were autonomous States subject to Rome only in foreign policy, but dependent for their existence upon the Roman law establishing them. This autonomy remained unchallenged even when Rome in the second century assumed the supervision of all Italy, since her edicts were only advisory. The Latin

Name provided Rome with numerous troops *e formula togatorum*, and garrisoned Italy at strategic points with loyal colonies. The Latins by their origin and special social position formed an intermediate category between Romans and the foreign *socii Italici* (*see* socii), and were commonly associated by Rome in many material privileges with Roman citizens. Though in 209 twelve colonies objected to the strain of continuous military service and were later punished (but not by diminution of civic rights), the Latins remained continuously loyal till the abuse by Roman commanders of their *imperium* at the expense of individual Latins led to a demand for the *ius provocationis*, which, after the rebellion of Fregellae (125), may have been granted by the tribune Drusus in 122; for the Latins took no major part in the Social War, accepting the Roman citizenship by the *Lex Iulia*. After 89 B.C. *Latium* became a purely legal concept (*see* ius latii).

ANCIENT SOURCES: Livy and Dion. Hal. *Antiquities*, passim, are basic, but retroject Roman supremacy to earliest period. Scattered references in Cato, Cicero, Gellius, Pliny *HN*, Varro, etc. Also Gaius, *Digest*.
MODERN LITERATURE: (*a*) Republic: K. J. Beloch, *Der italische Bund* (1880); *Röm. Gesch.* (1926); G. De Sanctis, *Stor. Rom.*; T. Frank, *Roman Imperialism*; M. Gelzer, 'Latium' in *PW*; Mommsen-Marquardt, *Manuel* vi. 2 (*Röm. Staatsr.* iii. 1), especially for legal aspects; E. T. Salmon, *JRS* 1936, for second century; A. Rosenberg, *Hermes* liv (1939). A. N. Sherwin-White, *The Roman Citizenship* (1939). (*b*) Empire: E. G. Hardy, *Six Roman Charters*; Hirschfeld, *Kl. Schr.* xxii; H. M. Last, *CAH* xi, ch. 11. *See also* MUNICIPIUM.
A. N. S.-W.

LATINI IUNIANI were a class of Latins who originated with the *Lex Iunia* (probably 17 B.C.). Previously a private arrangement between *dominus* and *servus* gave actual liberty to slaves but left them legally in bondage; the *Lex Iunia* gave statutory freedom to slaves informally manumitted, and defined their rights. They had *ius commercii* (*see* COMMERCIUM); but they could not receive legacies or make a will, and on death their property reverted to their patron. Their children were free-born Latins and so enjoyed *Latinitas* which might lead to Roman citizenship. Manumissions which did not comply with certain conditions of the *Lex Aelia Sentia* (A.D. 4), e.g. about the age of the slave or the manumittor, conferred only *Latinitas Iuniana*; but repetition (*iteratio*) of manumission when the conditions could be fulfilled gave citizenship. By the same law a Junian Latin could obtain citizenship for himself and his wife when his child became one year old. *Latinitas Iuniana* was abolished by Justinian in A.D. 531.

See Gaius 1. 29. 30; 3. 63; *Inst. Iust.* 3. 7. 4. *CAH* x 429, 434, 450; R. H. Barrow, *Slavery in the Roman Empire* (1928), 184–6; A. M. Duff, *Freedmen in the Early Roman Empire* (1928). R. H. B.

LATINUS, eponymous hero of the Latini (q.v.). Hesiod (*Theog.* 1011–16) makes him the son of Circe and Odysseus and king of the Tyrrhenians. Timaeus first connects him with Aeneas, whose daughter Rhome Latinus married and had as sons Rhomus (in Roman tradition Remus) and Romulus, founders of Rome. Cato's version (probably also that of Naevius and Ennius) is that Latinus betroths his daughter Lavinia to Aeneas; Turnus, to whom she was formerly promised, makes war with Latinus on Aeneas, Latinus is killed, and Aeneas becomes king of the Latins. In Livy's version (1. 2) Latinus is killed fighting with Aeneas against Turnus. Virgil (*Aen.* bks. 7–12) in the main follows Cato's version, but makes Latinus son of Faunus and the nymph Marica. Latinus, a weak and vacillating character, takes no part in the war and only emerges from his palace to propose concessions to Aeneas (bk. 11) and to arrange the single combat of Turnus and Aeneas (bk. 12). C. B.

LATIUM, lying between the Apennines and the Tyrrhenian Sea in western Italy, originally was a small area about the Albanus Mons (q.v.). By 500 B.C., however, it stretched from the Tiber to the Circeian promontory (*Latium Vetus*). Subsequently Latium embraced Volscian, Auruncan, and Hernican territories, and by Strabo's time included Mons Massicus and Sinuessa (*Latium Adiectum*). Augustus amalgamated Latium with Campania, and after A.D. 292 the name Campania prevailed; consequently Latium is still called *Campagna*. Eastern Latium (the Apennine slopes and Trerus valley) and Central Latium (an undulating plain embracing the Alban Hills and Pomptine Marshes) supported large herds; subterranean drainage channels, excavated apparently in pre-Roman times, aided flourishing agricultural operations. Western Latium contained extensive forests. Latium was well watered and possessed sulphur springs, abundant volcanic building-materials (tufas, travertine, basalt, pozzolana), and a road network (ultimately developed into Viae Latina, Appia, etc.). Human habitation commenced *c*. 1150 B.C. The prehistoric Aborigines (= Ligurians? or Sicels? Ciaceri identifies the two) apparently did not speak Latin. In historical times Latium was peopled by Latini, traditionally a mixed race and presumably an amalgam of Aborigines and various Bronze and Iron Age invaders: 'Southern Villanovans' (who probably introduced Latin into Latium), Sabelli, Etruscans, and apparently Picenes (= Illyrians). The Latini inhabited mutually independent settlements on knolls or mountain slopes, but from early times grouped themselves together for religious, and ultimately for political, purposes. There were several Latin federal sanctuaries (at Albanus Mons, Ardea, Aricia, Lavinium, and elsewhere) and therefore probably several Latin Leagues, although tradition is explicit about only one— that led by Alba Longa (q.v.). When Rome destroyed Alba (*c*. 600 B.C.) she allegedly succeeded her as leader of this league. However, when the Roman monarchy fell (508 B.C.) the Latini (led apparently by Tusculum, Aricia, Lanuvium, Lavinium, Cora, Tibur, Pometia, Ardea: Cato, *Orig.* fr. 58 P.) threw off any predominance Rome possessed, but failed to subordinate her to themselves (*see* REGILLUS LACUS). In 493 B.C. Rome and the Latin League signed a defensive alliance (*foedus Cassianum*) against threatening Volsci and Aequi. For Rome's subsequent relations with the Latini *see* LATINI, IUS LATII.

Depopulation of Latium began *c*. 300 B.C., caused chiefly by the centripetal pull of Rome, various wars (Pyrrhic, Hannibalic, Civil), the growth of *latifundia*, and malaria (which, however, reached its full virulence much later). The Augustan poets mention, and exaggerate, the desolation of Gabii and other places; Pliny, significantly, records towns that had utterly disappeared. Other towns (e.g. Tibur, Praeneste, Antium) undoubtedly became fashionable resorts, and in Imperial times Latium contained numerous opulent villas. In general, however, its towns failed to revive. Pasturage ousted agriculture (Pliny, *Ep.* 2. 17) and, after the Barbarian Invasions, Latium assumed that derelict appearance which it bore until recently.

ANCIENT SOURCES: Livy, bks. 1–8; Dion. Hal. bks. 1–11; Diodors *Römische Annalen* ed. Drachmann; Verg. *Aen.* bks. 7–12; Strabo 5. 228 f.; Pliny *HN* 3. 54 f.; Mela 2. 4. 70.
MODERN LITERATURE: M. Zoeller, *Latium und Rom* (1878); T. Ashby, *Roman Campagna in Classical Times* (1927); T. Frank, *Economic History of Rome*[2] (1927); H. M. Last, *CAH* vii 333, 400 (with bibliography); G. Lugli, *I santuari celebri del Lazio antico* (1932); G. Säflund, *Opuscula Archaeologica* i (1934); A. Blakeway, *JRS* 1935, 129; H. Rudolph, *Stadt und Staat im römischen Italien* (1935); J. Whatmough, *Foundations of Roman Italy* (1937); E. Ciaceri, *Le Origini di Roma* (1937); A. W. Van Buren, *Bibliographical Guide to Southern Etruria and Latium*[4] (Rome, 1938); B. Tilly, *Vergil's Latium* (1947). *See also* LATINI. E. T. S.

LATRO, see PORCIUS.

LATRUNCULI, see GAMES.

LAUDATIO FUNEBRIS, the funeral oration, originally part of the rites of the Roman *gens*, developed into a public *laudatio*, pronounced by a magistrate, later over women as well as men, e.g. Catulus' mother. It retained its traditional character, linking praise of the deceased with glorification of his ancestors, covering public and (probably) private life, and describing outstanding events. The encomiastic treatment, when the *laudationes* were published, tended to falsify history (Livy 8. 40. 4; 27. 27. 13; Cicero, *Brut.* 16. 62). The occasion gave rise to propaganda, e.g. the *Catones* and *Anticatones* on the younger Cato. The *laudatio* played an important part in the rise of Roman biography.

Polyb. 6. 53–4. F. Vollmer, *Laud. fun. Rom. historia et rel. editio* (1892); F. Leo, *Die griech.-röm. Biographie* (1901), 225; D. R. Stuart, *Epochs of Greek and Roman Biography* (1928), 209.
A. H. McD.

LAUREA, MARCUS TULLIUS, one of Cicero's freedmen, wrote an epigram on the hot springs which burst out at Cicero's villa soon after his death (Plin. *HN* 31. 7–8): see Baehrens, *FPR* 316; Morel, *FPL* 80.

LAURIUM, near Cape Sunium in Attica, was one of the largest mines in the Greek world. Silver was mainly sought, but other minerals, especially lead, were also produced. The mine was probably discovered in the early Iron Age; it flourished in the fifth century B.C., richer deposits having been tapped about 483. Here first scientific exploitation was developed, assisted by the simplicity of the geological formation. Narrow shafts, furnaces, cisterns, and washing-tables are visible. It was worked less actively in the fourth century B.C., but revived about 320. In the third century it suffered under the low prices of silver, but in the second century it was exploited ruthlessly until the revolt of the slave workers in 103. A few tailings were reworked in the first century A.D., and the mine closed soon after; but an attempt was made to reopen it in the fourth century.

E. Ardaillon, *Les Mines du Laurion* (1897); O. Davies, *Roman Mines in Europe* (1935), 246.
O. D.

LAUS (or **LAUDATIO**) **PISONIS,** a panegyric in 261 respectable hexameters, is addressed by a poet under twenty (ad fin.) to a Calpurnius Piso, best identified with the conspirator of A.D. 65. He is praised as an impressive speaker in law courts and Senate, accomplished in music and athletics, and a 'draw' when playing the game of *latrunculi*. Such qualities suit Tacitus' description (*Ann.* 15. 48) of the figure-head in the plot against Nero, and the last point strongly suggests identity with Juvenal's 'Piso bonus' (5. 109), whose renown in *latrunculi* the scholiast records. Hubaux (*Les Thèmes bucoliques*, p. 185), however, maintains that the poem concerns L. Calpurnius Piso, consul with Nero in 57.

The authorship is uncertain. Among several authors advocated Lucan belongs at least to the right period. Haupt at one time claimed the work for Calpurnius Siculus; more recently Ferrara (op. cit. infra), using metrical and other evidence, held this ascription to be impossible.

The poet pleads poverty, but feels confident of fame if he wins Piso—even Virgil needed a Maecenas (230–5). He promises to immortalize his patron (246–58); and the absence in Calpurnius Siculus of any fulfilment of this promise tells against the belief that he wrote the *Laus Pisonis*.

Text: E. Baehrens, *PLM* i; Gladys Martin, *Laus Pisonis* (introd., notes, U.S.A. 1917). Translation: J. W. and A. M. Duff, *Minor Latin Poets* (Loeb, 1934). Special Study: G. Ferrara, *Calp. Siculo ed il panegirico a Calp. Pisone* (1905).
J. W. D.

LAVINIUM, nowadays *Pratica di Mare*, an ancient Latin city (often confused with Lanuvium). Its inhabitants were called Laurentes, later Laurentes Lavinates (Livy 1. 14; Dessau, *ILS* 1371). Lavinium was a member of the Latin League. The Romans revered it for its Aeneas traditions, its Venus temple common to all Latins, its cults of Vesta and Penates (O. Seeck, *Rh. Mus.* 1913, p. 11), and its loyalty in the Latin

War. However, like most Latian towns, Lavinium fell into decay. Apparently there was no town of Laurentum at *Tor Paterno*, *Castel Fusano*, or elsewhere, although Lavinium was called Laurolavinium in late times. However, see G. Bendz, *Opus. Archaeol.* i (1934).

Strabo 5. 232; Cato, *Orig.* fr. 58 P.; Livy 1. 1; 8. 11. R. Lanciani, *Mon. Ant.* (1903), 133; (1906), 241; J. Carcopino, *Virgile et les origines d'Ostie* (1919), 171 ff.; B. Tilly, *Vergil's Latium* (1947), 54 ff.
E. T. S.

LAW AND PROCEDURE, ATHENIAN, see AN-CHISTEIS, AREOPAGUS, DICASTERIES, DRACO, EISANGELIA, EPHETAI, GRAPHE, GRAPHE PARANOMON, HELIAEA, NAUTO-DIKAI, PARAGRAPHE, SYCOPHANTS, SYMBOLON.

LAW AND PROCEDURE, ROMAN. I. CIVIL LAW. The beginning and end of the historical development of Roman law are marked by two legislative works, both unique in universal legal history, though diametrically opposed in origin, nature, and structure—the XII Tables and Justinian's Codification. In the intervening thousand years the Romans did not produce any codification; the XII Tables were never officially abolished and remained operative (although in a restricted measure) even until the legislation of Justinian. The XII Tables, a collection of the principal rules of the oldest Roman law, originated in ancient customs (*mores maiorum*): they are the germ from which the Roman civil law was evolved. This evolution was promoted and influenced by the increase in the political importance of the State, its new economic and social structure, its spiritual progress (contact with Greece and its civilization), and finally its constitutional organization and administration, all of which reacted on the legal institutions, customs, and doctrines. Three main periods may be distinguished in the history of Roman law, coinciding roughly with three constitutional stages: (*a*) from the XII Tables to the end of the Republic, ending in a century of rapid development after 150 B.C. (at which date accordingly some scholars fix the beginning of the next period); (*b*) from Augustus to Diocletian: in this period Roman law reaches the summit of its development, thanks chiefly to the co-operation of legal science, to which it owes its influence on modern codifications; (*c*) the Late Empire, under which the evolution of law took a new turn in spite of the decadence of legal science. In Justinian's code Roman law was unified.

2. The most characteristic mark of the oldest law was its rigorous formalism: in transactions as well as in judicial proceedings, legal effect could as a rule be given only by the use of solemn, oral, inflexible forms; the will of the parties, if not expressed in the set form, was without any effect. The poverty of primitive economic and social life was accurately reflected in the scantiness of legal forms: two institutions, *mancipatio* and *stipulatio* covered, in their different and always extending applications, most of the exigencies of legal business. The small rustic community excluded foreigners from participation in the institutions and forms of the *ius Quiritium* (citizen law); the ancient Roman family, under the unlimited control of the *pater familias*, preserved its exclusive organization.

3. In later times, however, the narrow and rigorous norms of the law no longer met needs arising out of commercial contact with other peoples, which grew considerably with the occupation of new territories and dominion over the Mediterranean world. Commercial relations with foreign nations imperatively required the abolition of a cast-iron formalism which took into account only the spoken word (XII Tables: 'uti lingua nuncupassit, ita ius esto !'); the will of the parties could no more be disregarded. The hard formalistic provisions descending from ancient Roman tradition now produced many unjust decisions: this is the sense of the famous saying of Cicero (*Off.* 1. 33): 'summum ius summa iniuria'. Hence informal contracts, indispensable in commercial

relations, such as *emptio-venditio, mutuum, pignus, societas,* and the like, were gradually introduced; *stipulatio* was extended to transactions with foreigners; special courts (*recuperatores*) were constituted for controversies with non-citizens, and a new magistrate (*praetor peregrinus*) was appointed to protect their interests. This new stratum of private law, common to all free persons, exempt from burdensome forms and governed by equity, which dominated procedure and the judge's decision in controversial cases (*iudicia bonae fidei*), brought about a rejuvenescence of the law, the more so as Roman jurisprudence contributed considerably in its own way to an amalgamation of the new views and constructions, the *ius gentium* with those of the old *ius civile*.

4. Another factor which contributed materially to the release of private law from the fetters of the ancient formalism was the *ius praetorium* (*honorarium*; *see* IUS CIVILE). The reform of the civil procedure initiated by the *Lex Aebutia* empowered the directing magistrate with procedural prerogatives, authorizing him to instruct the judge to take into consideration particulars of the matter at dispute, not recognized by the *ius civile*. Ordinary and extraordinary praetorian remedies (various *exceptiones, actio doli, actiones in factum, restitutio in integrum,* and so on) served to exclude a rigorous application of the inexorable *ius civile*, when it appeared too iniquitous, or to fill up its deficiencies and even, if necessary, to correct it with the object of basing the decision on principles of equity, unknown to the ancient law. The praetorian law, continuously modernized by the mechanism of *edicta*, profited in a large measure by the activity of jurists: the suggestions by the legal advisers, members of the *consilia* of the praetors on the one hand, and *responsa* by the jurists on the other, often led on to general innovations in *edicta* or to the application of a special remedy in a particular trial. In practice, this activity of the praetors signified the recognition of new types of agreements or facts which otherwise could not be taken into consideration. Thus arose a dualism between two systems: some fundamental institutions of the *ius civile* (e.g. wills, successions *ab intestato,* ownership) acquired a counterpart in an analogous institution of the praetorian law depending on other forms and rules. A less important part was played in the Republican period by the legislative activity of *comitia* and *concilia plebis*: a few statutes dealt merely with particular points of some parts of the private law (guardianship, inheritance, or the like), others only introduced limits into existing institutions (*usucapio,* interest, donation). The *Lex Aquilia,* with its detailed provisions concerning damage to property, is an exceptional case. The contribution of *senatus consulta* to private law was no larger.

5. Under the Principate the legislative activity of the assemblies soon came to an end: a series of *Leges Iuliae,* promoted by Augustus, was the last instance of comitial legislation. On the other hand, the Senate developed a greater activity. Several reforms, especially in the law of inheritance, modernized the ancient norms in a sense more appropriate to the necessities of practical life. A large part of the senatorial legislative activity must be put to the account of the emperors, whose initiative in legal matters increased more and more, until finally the Senate's decisions became a simple approval of imperial motions. But the emperors did not content themselves with this indirect legislative activity: their constitutions exercised an important direct influence on the development of the law. Their decisions in particular trials, though relating in the first instance to special cases, subsequently acquired general force, either directly, if the emperor enlarged them into a general rule, or indirectly by virtue of their high authority, being observed as binding precedents by imperial officials, or recognized as such by the emperor (or his delegates) in his later decisions. In the same way the imperial rescripts, though

legally limited on particular questions, when submitted to the decision of the emperor, became not infrequently *de facto* the source of important substantial innovations in the law.

6. This happened particularly in the *cognitio extra ordinem,* where the imperial judges adopted the principles of the new law created by the emperors, and, not being bound either by the *ius civile* or by the *ius honorarium,* had full discretion in giving effect to the demands of justice and equity. After the codification of the praetorian edict under Hadrian, jurisdiction by *cognitio* took over the innovatory function previously discharged by the praetors, but without having at its disposal their organ of publicity (*edicta*). New norms concerning the *patria potestas,* the patrimonial capacity of the *filius familias,* the protection of slaves against their *domini,* the *fideicommissa,* were introduced by the operation of the new proceedings. The influence of *cognitio* on the progress of the law was doubtless very considerable not only in this period, but also in later times, for by its operation new legal ideas were applied in legal practice. But if the period of the Principate is called the period of *classical* Roman law, it is above all because of its scientific elaboration by the jurisprudents. The direct influence of the jurists on legal evolution, already established in the preceding period, did not diminish in this one: they were members of the emperor's *consilium* and of the Senate, and from the time of Augustus their *responsa* probably acquired official and binding character. But the law of this period owes its description as 'classical' to legal science and literature. The works of the jurists had not only an instructive and educative influence on generations of jurists, and contemporarily an influence on all legislative and judicial activity; the jurisprudents also undertook the task of levelling the discrepancies which existed between the different coexisting strata of legal norms, *ius civile, gentium,* and *honorarium,* and of preparing gradually their simplification and fusion. Starting from practical cases, the Roman jurists arrived at theoretical problems, from single decisions at the formulation of general rules, from the analysis of legal facts and forms at the construction of legal categories. The questions in which legal science was most influential were: recognition of informal bindings and agreements, together with the abolition of abstract (formal) transactions in respect of agreements endowed with *causa,* regard to the intention of the parties (*voluntas, mens, animus*) in transactions *inter vivos* and in wills, promotion of the validity of written documents, elaboration of the conception of *dolus* and *culpa,* extension of the sphere of contracts governed and interpreted by ethical principles (equity), changes in the organization of the family, and so forth.

7. New problems arose from the conquest of provinces to which the Romans conceded from the first the right of organizing their legal life according to their own laws. Only the persons upon whom Roman citizenship was conferred (individually, regionally, or by groups) were obliged to observe in their legal relations the Roman *ius civile.* Differences between the various legal systems gave rise to misunderstandings which were submitted to the decision of the emperor, who decided not infrequently in favour of the provincial law. (Diocletian's tendency to repress provincial customs and bring the old civil law into universal operation was not followed by his successors, least of all by Justinian.) The general bestowal of Roman citizenship by Caracalla (A.D. 212) simplified the legal situation, but unavoidably some conceptions of local law penetrated the law of the Empire and vice versa, a phenomenon which is brought into particularly clear view in Egypt by the Graeco-Egyptian papyri which illustrate legal practice in this province.

8. The last period, the Late Empire, brought about essential transformations in the law-making agencies: disappearance of the praetors and *ius honorarium* in all its manifestations, cessation of the *responsa prudentium*, the decay of jurisprudence and the consequent drying up of this source of legal ideas, so exuberant in the foregoing period, and the abolition of the classical system of civil proceedings with all its marvellously organized mechanism of remedies. The entire legislative activity was now concentrated in the hands of the emperors. The imperial constitutions, now commonly called *leges* (the previous term for statutes created by the people), assume the character of general binding norms, without territorial restriction. On the other hand, the works of the classical jurisprudents constituted a body of law (now simply called *ius*, to distinguish it from the *leges*), from which *cognitio* drew the rules for its decisions. Their importance grew even greater, since their official character as a source of law was recognized by the 'Law of citations' of Theodosius II. The legal schools which arose in this period in the West and East (where that of Beyrout enjoyed a particularly high reputation) were not able to continue the tradition of the classical jurists, however meritorious they might be in the training of practising lawyers. Their contribution to the progress of legal development was, so far as can be proved, rather insignificant, though efforts have been made by some scholars to exalt it.

9. But this period of more than two centuries was not an age of stagnation. The frequently changing imperial legislation produced a temporary state of chaos in some parts of the law; but a comparison of the classical law with the law crystallized in Justinian's work shows essential differences not only in particular points, but also in general rules and doctrines. All this cannot be merely a result of Justinian's reforms. The formation of Justinian's law is one of the most discussed problems in the latest romanistic literature. The question is not only which innovations belong to Justinian and which are post-classical, but also what factors influenced the reforms introduced by Justinian or any others of post-classical times. The solution depends above all on a just separation of the classical law from later innovations. This usually involves the difficult problem of correctly appraising the genuineness or spuriousness of the texts collected in Justinian's codification, and of determining whether the alterations effected in them are legislative measures of Justinian or merely a recognition of a legal state, of doctrines and views which existed already before the Emperor's compilation. It cannot be denied that the interpolations are innumerable, but a moderate and methodically unassailable criticism, free from exaggerations and fantasy, shows that apart from alterations which were necessary in consequence of the new imperial legislation, such as the abolition of obsolete forms, institutions, and conceptions, and the reform of civil procedure, and apart from interpolations of merely formal or paraphrastic and not substantial character, and from more or less harmless glosses which Justinian's compilers found in the manuscripts excerpted by them—a great deal of pretended Byzantine innovations originated in ideas suggested and developed by classical jurists. If the post-classical innovations and those of Justinian are reduced to their right limits, the character of the whole codification acquires another aspect: there is no necessity to see in the emperor's work the result of foreign influence.

10. If the law wears another appearance in the period from Constantine to Justinian, this is the effect of a spontaneous, organic, and natural development. The fusion of the different legal orders, already initiated in the classical period by the jurisprudents, was now completed in the practice of the courts, without any intervention or co-operation of foreign forces. *Cognitio extra ordinem* applied in its judicial activity the most recent and advanced views, at the cost of the ancient *ius civile*, which was thus condemned to disappear. Symptoms of this process of fusion, or of the replacement of institutions of the old *ius civile* by modern ones, created or developed by *ius honorarium, gentium,* or the *cognitio* can be observed in different fields of private law: agnatic and cognatic inheritance, *bonorum possessio* and *hereditas, legata* and *fideicommissa,* civil and praetorian ownership and possession, fusion of modes of constituting servitudes, *tutela* and *cura,* development of *stipulatio* into a written transaction, whereby only the assent of the parties is pronounced orally as a mere formality, and so forth.

11. It is self-evident that the law could not remain untouched by reactions of a political, economic, social, and cultural character (Greek civilization, philosophy, and late rhetoric). The theory of the spontaneous and organic evolution of the Roman law is contested by some scholars in favour of Hellenistic influences, which by a gross over-estimation are considered sufficient to qualify this period of Roman law as Graeco-Oriental. Undoubtedly some institutions of the Hellenistic East appear in the latest law and with Justinian (e.g. *arrha sponsalicia, donatio propter nuptias,* appointment of a woman as a *tutor, manumissio in ecclesia*). A contact with Greek legal ideas and customs existed in the history of Roman law from early times, and tendencies to assimilate it to provincial law, especially that of the Greek East, are already discernible in the preceding period. The fourth and subsequent centuries favoured these tendencies, since the centre of gravity of the Empire had been transferred to the East. But all this does not justify us in speaking of an orientalization of Roman law. Roman law conserved its national character in this period and in Justinian's codification, as it did before in spite of multiple and sometimes fundamental alterations to which it had to submit in the course of several centuries.

12. One new factor, however, impressed its mark on some institutions of the latest Roman law: Christianity. Its most notable influence appears in the law of marriage (divorce), of family (restriction of *patria potestas*), and of slavery, in the protection of the weak, in the attenuation of the individualistic rigidity of the Roman ownership, and an increasing regard for social interests. The conception of equity, considered before as the tendency to the realization of plain justice, in conformity with the common legal conscience, became a larger one under the influence of Christian charity; it was now governed by humanity and benignity. But the influence from this quarter also failed to alter the structure and physiognomy of Roman law as a whole. In his great codification Justinian simplified all the different legal orders which came into being during the centuries of the mighty expansion of Rome to a unitary system. He made it in a singular manner, which has sometimes been criticized too harshly by posterity; but his work, composed of old but indestructible material, fortunately did not completely cover the phases in the evolution of the Roman civil law, which was destined to become the foundation of most codifications of the world up to the present.

For particulars on sources *see* CODEX, CONSTITUTIONES, DIGESTA, EDICTUM, INSTITUTIONES, IUS CIVILE, IUS GENTIUM, JURISPRUDENCE, TRIBONIANUS, TWELVE TABLES; for the private law: COMMUNIO, CONTRACT, DAMNUM, EMPHYTEUSIS, FIDEICOMMISSUM, GUARDIANSHIP, INHERITANCE, MANCIPATIO, MARRIAGE, NEXUM, POSSESSIO, SECURITY, SERVITUTES, SLAVERY, STIPULATIO, VINDICATIO. *See also below,* II. 'Civil procedure'.

P. Krüger, *Geschichte der Quellen*[2] (1912); Th. Kipp, *Geschichte der Quellen*[4] (1919); B. Kübler, *Geschichte des römischen Rechts* (1925); H. Siber, *Römisches Recht* i, ii (1925-8); S. Perozzi, *Istituzioni di diritto romano,* i, ii[2] (1928); E. Cuq, *Institutions juridiques des Romains*[2] (1928); S. Riccobono, 'Dal diritto romano classico al diritto moderno' (*Annali Sem. Giur. Palermo* iii, iv, 1917); id., *Mélanges Cornil* ii (1926); id., *Annali Palermo* xii (1928); P. De Francisci, *Storia del diritto Romano* i-iii (1926-38); P. F. Girard, *Manuel élémentaire de droit romain*[8] (1929); P. Bonfante, *Corso di diritto romano* i-iii, vi (1925-30); i-ii[4] (1936); L. Chiazzese, *Introduzione allo studio del dir. rom. privato* (1931); W. W. Buckland, *Text-*

book of Roman Law² (1932); H. F. Jolowicz, *Historical Introduction to the Study of Roman Law* (1932); A. Berger, 'Le XII Tavole e la codificazione giustinianea' (*Atti Congresso Intern. di Diritto Romano* i, 1934); F. Schulz, *Principles of Roman Law* (1936); P. Jörs, W. Kunkel, *Römisches Recht²* (1935); E. Weiss, *Grundzüge der römischen Rechtsgeschichte* (1936); Arangio-Ruiz, *Storia del diritto romano³* (1942); id., *Corso di istituzioni di diritto romano⁵* (1941); E. Volterra, *Diritto romano e diritti orientali* (1937); R. Monier, *Manuel élémentaire de droit romain* i⁴ (1943), ii³ (1944); S. Di Marzo, *Istituzioni di diritto romano* (1938).   A. B.

II. CIVIL PROCEDURE. The Roman civil trial from earliest times showed a characteristic feature: the division into two stages. The first took place before a magistrate, *in iure* (*ius* signifies here the place of magisterial jurisdiction), who conducted the proceedings from the beginning to their culminating point, *litis contestatio.* This was a formal agreement concluded between the litigants under the magistrate's supervision and with his co-operation, and contained a formulation of the principal points of the question at issue, which had to be examined and decided in the second stage by the *iudex* (q.v.). He was a private person empowered to investigate the case and to pass the sentence by a special order (*iussum iudicandi*) of the magistrate delivered by consent of both the parties. This bipartite division of the trial (whose origin is much disputed) was an ingenious combination of official jurisdiction and private arbitration, from which it differs in that the *iudex* was obliged to accept the commission conferred upon him by the magistrate and the litigants, and was bound by their agreed definition of the matter in dispute. Only in the first stage, *in iure*, were certain formalities observed; the second stage, *apud iudicem*, was conducted without any prescribed form. Two systems are to be distinguished in the proceedings before the magistrate: *legis actiones*, the earlier one, and *formulae.*

2. *Legis actio* was a solemn procedure of a rigidly formal character, wherein the plaintiff (*is qui agere vult*; after the *litis contestatio* he was called *actor*) and the defendant (*is cum quo agitur, reus*) had to assert their rights in oral forms prescribed by law or custom. This system was known already in the time of the XII Tables, which dealt with it at length, as has been confirmed by the newly discovered fragments of Gaius (q.v. 2). There were five types of *legis actiones.* The most usual, applicable to claims of ownership and to claims originating in obligations, was the *legis actio sacramento*, proceedings combined with a kind of wager between the parties, who both deposited a fixed sum of money (*sacramentum*, q.v.). The winner (the party whose assertion was declared right by the judge) received his *sacramentum* back, while the loser's *sacramentum* was forfeited to the State. The other types were (1) *per iudicis postulationem* for claims based on *stipulatio* (q.v.) or for disputes about the division of property belonging to several persons; (2) *per condictionem* (of later date) for recovery of *certa pecunia* or *certa res* in particular cases. These were of greater simplicity and did not require a *sacramentum.* The last two *legis actiones* were methods of execution: the one (*per manus iniectionem*) against the person of the condemned debtor, the other (*per pignoris capionem*) against his property.

3. *Legis actiones* were supplanted by the formulary system, in which the matter in dispute was defined in a written document (*formula, concepta verba*) in place of the oral forms of the *legis actio.* But the written *formula* was rather elastic and adaptable to the particular details of the case, though its structure was based on some permanent essential parts: the *intentio* (concise formulation of the plaintiff's claim) and the *condemnatio*, by which the judge was authorized to condemn or to discharge the defendant, if it appeared from the results of the evidence produced that the defendant ought, e.g., to pay a certain sum to the plaintiff, or if a particular matter of fact, on which the plaintiff based his claim,

was verified. To suit the complexities of each case the *formula* might be extended by additional clauses, e.g. by a *demonstratio*, which served to determine more precisely the matter at issue when the *intentio* was indefinite (*incerta*); or by an *exceptio*, a clause on behalf of the defendant excluding his condemnation, if he should make a statement which would make the condemnation appear unjust. The composition of the *formula*, which was variously worded to suit each case and might contain special clauses, was not easy; but model *formulae* were published in the praetor's edict. The parties, therefore, were often forced to consult jurisprudents, the more so as the reforming activity of judicial magistrates introduced more and more new forms or modifications in existing forms. The praetors were authorized to admit the application of a new form in cases which previously had not been recognized by the law and appeared worthy of judicial protection. The development of the system of *formulae* and their mechanism was of the highest importance for the development of private law.

4. The formulary process was introduced officially by a statute, *Lex Aebutia* (probably after 150 B.C.), the details of which are unknown. It was not obligatory for all kinds of lawsuits, but became so by an amending law of Augustus (*Lex Iulia iudiciorum privatorum*). In trials assigned to the centumviral court (*see* CENTUMVIRI) proceedings by *legis actio* remained untouched. The origin of the formulary system was not purely Roman; written forms seem to have been used before the passing of the *Lex Aebutia* in international issues wherein the Senate had to adjust differences between Greek communities and in trials before the *praetor peregrinus.* In actions between *peregrini* the *legis actio* was not practicable and the magistrate had a larger liberty in conducting the trial; the whole proceedings depended on his *imperium.* On these elements is based the distinction between *iudicium legitimum* (where the parties and the private judge, *unus iudex*, were Roman citizens and the proceedings took place within a mile of Rome) and *iudicium quod imperio continetur.* In the latter, whereat the above-mentioned conditions were not fulfilled, the course of the trial was left to the discretion of the magistrate invested with *imperium*; there was no protection of the parties against the arbitrary action by the magistrate, who decided the case either in his own person or by a delegate on whose appointment the parties had no influence.

5. This unlimited authority of the judicial magistrate became predominant in the third and last system of Roman civil procedure, *cognitio extra ordinem* (sc. *iudiciorum privatorum*) or *extraordinaria*, which was unlike the normal bipartite proceedings with a private judge. This system was first applied in exceptional cases in which the place of the private *iudex* was taken by a public functionary as delegate of the magistrate or of the emperor. It came into regular use under the Late Empire, though it continued to be called 'extraordinary', even when the older systems had disappeared. The transition to the new system was gradual, and externally some institutions of the classical procedure were maintained for a long while, as for instance the bipartition, or the written *formula.* But the fundamental characteristic feature was always the same: the whole proceeding was official; the same functionary held the trial in his hands till its final decision by sentence, and if he delegated the trial and passing of sentence to another person, this deputy depended only on him. With the increase of absolutism the former democratic institutions of the classical process were condemned to disappear.

6. Roman juridical language had two expressions for a civil lawsuit: *actio* and *iudicium.* Both terms originally had separate meanings, which were enlarged by the development of the procedure, so that from early times they overlapped, particularly when used to indicate a special kind of action by its technical name (e.g. *doli, mandati, tutelae, communi dividundo, in factum,* and so on). *Actio* signified originally the activity of the plaintiff who initiated the trial, but subsequently came to denote the whole proceedings, and especially their first stage *in iure.* But *actio* had also a material sense. A famous definition (*Dig.* 44. 7. 51) qualifies *actio* as 'ius quod sibi debetur, iudicio persequendi', where the difference between the material *actio* and the formal *iudicium* is evident. *Iudicium* signifies generally the second stage of the classical law-suit, connected with the *iudex,* but it is often used to indicate the entire trial or only its final act, the sentence; frequently it refers to the written *formula.* In the language of the compilers *iudicium* acquired a very wide application and was often interpolated in the place of classical mentions of the first stage, *in iure,* after the bipartition had been abolished.

7. The classical trial began with an extra-judicial private act, *in ius vocatio,* by which the plaintiff personally summoned the defendant to follow him before the magistrate. The XII Tables contained detailed provisions for cases in which the defendant disobeyed the summons on grounds of physical disability. It is note-worthy that they began merely by stating the absolute duty of the party summoned to go with the plaintiff immediately: 'si in ius uocat, ito.' The only manner of avoiding an immediate appearance before the magistrate (which could be enforced in case of resistance) was for the summoned party to give a guarantor (*vindex*). In the formulary system summons remained a mere private act, the plaintiff being obliged to announce to the defendant the claim and the form which he wished to apply against him. In the extraordinary procedure the summons was issued in writing with the assistance of an official. Finally the summoning was performed exclusively by a judicial functionary without any co-operation of the plaintiff.

8. The magistrate began by trying some preliminary questions such as the competence of the court, the personal capacity of the litigants, and their legitimation to be plaintiff or defendant in the intended lawsuit. A negative result of this examination made further litigation superfluous; *denegatio actionis* by the magistrate put an end to the trial. Other cases where the litigation was finished *in iure* were: acknowledgement of the plaintiff's claim by the defendant (*confessio*) or his oath (in special matters only) that he did not owe anything to the plaintiff. Normally, however, the stage *in iure* was devoted to the concluding of an agreement between the litigants (approved by the magistrate) about the matter in dispute to be submitted to the decision of the judge. In the formulary process there might often be long discussions about the composition of the *formula,* especially when the case and the appropriate form were not provided in the praetor's edict and the plaintiff tried to obtain the protection of his right by a new form adapted to the particularities of the case (*actio in factum*). The contractual character of the *litis contestatio* required the co-operation of both the parties; neither of them could frustrate the achievement of this act by repeated refusal of the other's proposals, the plaintiff being exposed to *denegatio actionis,* the defendant to an executive measure applied by the magistrate on behalf of the plaintiff (*missio in possessionem*).

9. The *litis contestatio,* as the name declares, was performed in the presence of witnesses. After its completion another trial on the same claim was debarred, and the judge's sentence was determined by the condition of the case at the moment of the *litis contestatio,* especially in regard to the fruits or the alienation of the object at issue and the like.

10. The second stage of the trial was governed by the private *iudex.* This was occupied by the pleadings of the parties and their advocates (*see* ADVOCATUS) and citation of evidence, the assessment of which depended wholly

on the discretion of the judge. The classical Roman procedure did not provide for an appeal against the judge's sentence; it was the *cognitio extraordinaria* which broke this principle (*see* APPELLATIO). If the defendant lost the case, he was obliged to carry out his obligations under the sentence within a fixed term (thirty days according to the XII Tables; various in later development; extended to a maximum of four months by Justinian). But a sentence could be annulled by an extraordinary remedy such as *restitutio in integrum.* If the condemned debtor did not carry out the terms of the sentence the creditor could proceed to a forcible execution of his rights, which always took place with the co-operation of public officials. Personal execution (*manus iniectio*) was the rule; real execution on objects forming part of the property of the debtor (*pignoris capio*) was admitted only for distraints of a sacral or public character. Real execution eventually became prevalent, but not exclusive. The formulary procedure comprised a special *actio iudicati* for execution of the sentence, wherein a contumacious debtor risked a condemnation on the double value of the object in dispute and an immediate authorization of the creditor to seize his property. The *cognitio extraordinaria* softened the rigid earlier forms of execution by restricting it to single objects instead of the whole property. This development in post-classical times was in conformity with the new tendencies of the civil procedure under the Late Empire. Other innovations were the admission of appeals to the emperor's jurisdiction and of claims addressed directly to him (giving rise to a new form of proceedings to be determined by imperial rescripts), the introduction of new procedures for abbreviating the trial and reducing its costs. All these and other reforms gave a new character to the latest Roman procedure. Some features of this new procedure as it existed in Justinian's time outlasted a series of centuries and passed into modern legislations.

11. A strange procedural institution, partly of administrative character, was provided in classical Roman law by the *interdicta.* These were orders or prohibitions issued by the magistrate without long investigations and addressed as a rule to a particular person. Their object was to give immediate protection to menaced or violated interests of the plaintiff. If the defendant ignored the interdict, the case was tried under conditions highly unfavourable to him. The private interests protected by *interdicta* were such as were requisite for the maintenance of public order, for instance possession, rights of succession, mortgage, servitudes, some personal rights, and the like. *Interdicta* could be applied for a direct protection of public interests, for instance with regard to roads and rivers. The interdictal proceedings were a kind of magisterial cognition; eventually the fundamental differences between *actio* and *interdictum* became effaced.

See ADVOCATUS, APPELLATIO, CENTUMVIRI, EDICTUM, IUDEX, IURIDICUS, IUSIURANDUM, IUSTITIUM, RECUPERA-TORES, SACRAMENTUM, TESTIMONIUM.

Older works on Roman civil procedure, e.g. A. M. Bethmann-Hollweg, *Der römische Civilprocess* i–iii (1864–6); F. L. Keller, *Der römische Civilprocess*[6] (1883), are still useful though out of date. Chief modern works: M. Wlassak, *Röm. Prozessgesetze* i, ii (1888, 1891); *Die Litiskontestation im Formularprocess* (1889); *Zum römischen Provinzialprocess* (1919); *Der Judikationsbefehl der römischen Prozesse* (1921); *Die klassische Prozessformel* (1927). The last three works have been published in the *Sitz. Wiener Akad. der Wissenschaften* cxc, cxcvii, ccii. P. F. Girard, *Histoire de l'organisation judiciaire des Romains* (1901); C. Bertolini, *Appunti didattici di dir. rom. Il processo civile* i–iii (1913–15); A. H. J. Greenidge, *The Legal Procedure of Cicero's Time* (1901); J. Partsch, *Die Schriftformel im röm. Provinzialprocess* (1905); E. Costa, *Profilo storico del processo civile* (1918); L. Wenger, *Institutionen des röm. Zivilprozessrechts* (1925), the best modern text-book with complete bibliography; an Italian translation (by R. Orestano, 1937) and an English translation (by Otis H. Fisk, U.S.A., 1940) have been revised and supplemented by the author. O. Lenel, *Edictum perpetuum*[3] (1927); B. Biondi, in

Studi Bonfante iv (1930); id., *Conferenze per il XIV Centenario delle Pandette* (1931); id., *Atti Congreso intern. di Diritto Romano*, ii (1935); P. Collinet, *La Procédure par libelle* (1935); A. Berger, *PW*, s.v. 'Interdictum'; Suppl. vii, s.v. 'Lex Aebutia'; P. W. Duff, *Personality in Roman Private Law* (1938).   A. B.

III. Criminal Law and Procedure. In the evolution of Roman criminal law we can distinguish three phases governed by different fundamental ideas not unknown in criminal law of other ancient nations. The older phase is characterized by the principle of private revenge; then followed the period of composition between offended and offender, first voluntary and sporadic, later obligatory. But even in this phase the beginnings of a new system can be observed: intervention of the State in punishing some crimes, especially those directed against the structure or existence of the community (a characteristic feature of the last phase). The State now takes in its hands the repression of offences, not only those which menace the public order or interest directly, but also those affecting private property or interests. The separate systems cannot be distinguished by exact dates, as none of them was completely replaced by the next one, but generally speaking the first phase falls in the Regal period, the XII Tables represent a combination of the first two systems, while in the advanced Republic the intervention of the State, hitherto exceptional, becomes more and more common. Under the Principate it gains dominance, and under the Late Empire and Justinian it becomes exclusive, having absorbed nearly the whole field of private criminal law. A survival of the idea of vengeance is found in the *noxae deditio*, the surrender of the wrongdoer (slave or child under *patria potestas*) to the person wronged.

2. The Romans did not create an organic body of statutes relating to criminal law. The XII Tables are, as the fragmentary remains of Tables VIII and IX show, a mosaic of various penal provisions but not a code. They were restricted to such criminal matters as interested a primitive peasant community, and therefore could not suffice for the State in its further development. The copious legislation of the Republic did not solve the problem, as these *leges* dealt only with single crimes, and it is noticeable that some offences were even treated by several *leges* voted within a relatively short period of time, e.g. the *crimen repetundarum (see* REPETUNDAE) or *ambitus* (q.v.). The various *Leges Corneliae* (of Sulla) and *Iuliae* (of Caesar and Augustus; it is not always certain which of them was the author) with their different courts and proceedings for particular crimes were as far from a systematic treatment or a coherent code as the later legislation of the Empire, which, though creative in particular details, made no attempt to codify. Extensive interpretation of earlier statutes to cover new facts (wherein the Senate co-operated as long as it remained active), or modification of penalties in the direction of greater or lesser severity, constitutes all the legislative activity of these times in substantive criminal law. The procedure *extra ordinem*, it is true, caused the introduction of new ideas into the general doctrines of penal law; and imperial constitutions applied some novel conceptions; but all these, being sporadic and exceptional, did not give an impulse to systematic and comprehensive elaboration.

3. The jurists of the second century A.D.—the best period of classical jurisprudence—did not contribute to the development of criminal law in so great a measure as to that of civil law. A compilation analogous to the *Edictum perpetuum* in civil law would certainly have roused their interest in criminal matters; and it is very instructive to learn how fertile was their contribution to doctrines of private delicts, with which the praetorian edict dealt (cf. the excellent elaboration of *iniuria*, *Dig.* 47. 10), in comparison with their modest part in public criminal law. The effect of the interpretative work of all

these more or less authoritative elements (imperial rescripts and edicts, *senatus consulta*, practice of *cognitio extra ordinem*, jurisprudence) was that offences quite different from those which were described and made punishable in Republican statutes were subjected to the statutory penalties. Thus (1) Sulla's *Lex Cornelia testamentaria (nummaria*, called also *de falsis)*, which originally dealt with falsification of wills and of coins, was extended not only to the forgery of documents and the assumption of false names, titles, or official rank, but even to corruption in litigation, as when a juror, accuser, witness, or advocate was bribed, in which case both giver and receiver were punishable. Even a juror who *constitutiones principum neglexit* was punished according to this statute. (2) The penalties of the *Lex Cornelia* against murderers and poisoners were extended in later times to magistrates, jurymen, and witnesses who contributed to an unjust capital sentence. (3) The *Lex Iulia de ambitu* was applied to cases of pressure exercised on a juryman by the accuser or the accused, though the original field of the statute was electoral corruption.

4. Under the Late Empire criminal legislation is directed more to penalties than to the doctrinal treatment of offences. The punishableness of some delicts varied under the influence of political or religious points of view; the creation of new categories of crimes in this long period is restricted to abduction and offences against the Christian religion after its recognition by the State. The profession of Christianity had at one time been prosecuted as *crimen maiestatis (see* PERDUELLIO). Justinian's legislative compilations show the first endeavour to collect the scattered provisions of public and private criminal law into a systematic whole. The *Digest*, books 47–9, and the *Code*, book 9, give a well-arranged design of criminal law, procedure, and penalties. The compilers, of course, found some help in works of the latest classical jurists, who in just appreciation of the difficulties created by this fluctuating and uncertain state of criminal legislation dealt with these matters in monographs: *de iudiciis publicis* (Marcianus, Macer, Paulus), *de poenis* (Paulus, Saturninus, Modestinus), *de cognitionibus* (Callistratus). But all these and similar works, though doubtless meritorious and useful, aimed rather at collecting material than at creative criticism or presentation of new ideas. Even the terminology distinguishing different categories of offences does not show that stability and precision which is so excellent a feature of Roman legal language. The terms most used are *crimen, delictum, maleficium*; but it can hardly be affirmed that these expressions had a particular exclusive sense, though generally *crimen* indicates more serious offences directed against the State or public order, whilst *delictum* is rather used for delicts against private property or personal integrity and of no great harmfulness. The meaning of *maleficium* as a general term is still less technical, especially as it was used for designating sorcery and magic arts. All endeavours to bring order into classical texts by allotting to these terms an exclusive technical sense and removing all inconvenient texts as interpolated break down because of the indiscriminate use of these terms in texts not suspected of interpolation.

5. For the distinction between public and private offences we likewise lack any precise definition or statement of distinguishing marks; and yet it was of fundamental importance for Roman criminal law. This distinction rested upon a practical rather than a doctrinal differentiation of offended interests, and found its visible consequences in the fields of procedure and penalties, which differed greatly in the two spheres. The Roman jurists dealt more with *iudicia publica* and private *actiones poenales* than with the distinction between the interests violated as public or private, and the post-classical and Justinian classification into *delicta privata, crimina extraordinaria*, and *iudicia publica (Rubr. Dig.* 47. 2;

47. 11; 48. 1) was also made from a procedural point of view.

6. The private delicts form a group apart: the wrong-doer is exposed to an action by the person wronged, the effect of which is that he must pay a pecuniary penalty to the plaintiff (to be distinguished from another *actio* by which the restitution of the *res* or compensation is claimed—*rei persecutio*). The procedure was that of private suits; the State as such did not show any interest in the prosecution of these offences. The principal forms were theft(*furtum*, q.v.), robbery (*rapina*, theft combined with violence), damage to property (see DAMNUM), and physical assault (*iniuria*). The XII Tables already recognized this kind of offence, by laying down fixed penalties, e.g. double or triple the value of the stolen object in some cases of theft, and in the case of *iniuria* a tariff of 25 to 300 *asses* in proportion to the seriousness of the assault. Some Republican statutes (e.g. the *Lex Aquilia* for damage to property, *Lex Cornelia* for *iniuriae*) continued the work; praetorian reforms and subsequently the jurists contributed considerably to the perfection of the law on the subject. Praetorian reforms took into account new types of *iniuria* committed by infractions of the moral integrity of a person, such as insult or defamation, and new forms of offences, such as threats (*metus*), deceit (*dolus*), malicious corruption of other people's slaves, and the like. Praetorian law also introduced a category of actions for misdemeanours which, though less serious, affected public interests, e.g. damage to the *album* (q.v.) of magistrates, violation of sepulchres, and pouring liquids or throwing things out into the streets. In such cases anyone, *quivis ex populo* (hence the name *actiones populares*), could be plaintiff and claim the penalty. The private prosecution of offences was in later times greatly restricted in favour of *cognitio extra ordinem*, to which more serious cases were assigned till finally it was absorbed by public prosecution.

7. The special domain of criminal law is, however, the second group of crimes prosecuted by public organs in *iudicia publica*. The oldest law knew the intervention of the State, as avenger of offences against its security or against public order, only in exceptional cases such as treason (*perduellio*, q.v.), desertion to the enemy, or special forms of murder (*parricidium*, q.v.). For the evolution of this group the series of criminal *leges* of the last century of the Republic (*Corneliae*, *Iuliae*, see supra) were of the greatest importance. They instituted special criminal courts for particular crimes, extending in large measure the competence of the State to the prosecution and punishment of criminal acts. A survey of the various kinds of crimes allotted to the *quaestiones perpetuae* shows that they comprehended not only offences against the State, its security and organization, or public order in the widest sense of the word, but also the more serious offences against life, personal integrity, private interests (falsification of wills and documents, serious injuries), and morality (adultery). (For the procedure before these courts see QUAESTIO.)

8. However, even with the help of the Senate, imperial constitutions, and the jurists, this legislation covered only part of the offences needing repression. Furthermore, the *quaestiones* operated only at Rome and tried Roman citizens only (not women or slaves or *peregrini*). Augustus introduced juries into some provinces (see the Cyrene Edicts), but they had no jurisdiction over Roman citizens. These and other deficiencies were made good by a new kind of procedure called *extra ordinem*, as not being subordinated to *ordo iudiciorum*. The trials in these *iudicia publica extra ordinem* were always conducted by public officials. Jurisdiction was exercised—apart from political offences and senatorial matters reserved for the Senate—chiefly by the emperor and the prefects, in the provinces by *praesides* and *procuratores* as his delegates. The sphere of *cognitio extra*

ordinem became, thanks to the emperor's policy, more and more extensive and superseded the *quaestiones*, which are not mentioned after Alexander Severus. On the strength of new legislative provisions new forms of offences arose (called later *crimina extraordinaria*), e.g. fraud (*stellionatus*), participation in illicit corporations, displacing of boundary stones, special types of theft (*fures balnearii, nocturni*), and the like. Whilst in *quaestiones* only the penalty laid down by the statute could be pronounced, the imperial judges had discretion in grading the penalty according to their appreciation of all the facts of the case. From the earliest times the intention of the wrongdoer was taken into consideration; even the legendary law of Numa on parricide (see PARRICIDIUM) required that the murderer had acted *sciens dolo*; the analogous expression in Republican laws was *sciens dolo malo*.

9. More adequate differentiation between different states of mind was developed in the practice of the *cognitio extra ordinem*, influenced also by imperial constitutions. In appreciating the atrocity of the act and depravity of its author the judge considered the intensity and persistence of the delinquent's will (*dolus*), the question whether the act had been committed with premeditation or on sudden impulse, whether it had been provoked by a moral offence (e.g. murder of an adulterous wife when caught in the act) or was due to drunkenness ('per uinum'). A late classical jurist, Claudius Saturninus, known only by a treatise on penalties, distinguished seven points to be taken into consideration in determining the punishment: reason, person, place, time, quality, quantity, and effect (*Digest* 48. 19. 16.). Judicial liberty, however, gave occasion for arbitrariness: the third century, with the decline of imperial authority, brought anarchy into criminal jurisdiction. Under the Late Empire the absolute determination of the penalties—now more severe than formerly—was restored, the discretion of the judge in the infliction of punishment having been abolished. But in contrast to the trial before *quaestiones* appeal was admitted *extra ordinem*. From the third century onwards a distinction was made between *honestiores* (q.v.) and *humiliores*, the latter being punished more severely than distinguished persons. There is no further trace of the old Republican principle of equality of all citizens in the eyes of the criminal law which had been expressed in the rule 'priuilegia ne inroganto' ascribed by Cicero to the XII Tables.

10. The magistrates invested with *imperium*, acting personally or by delegates, were in general the organs of criminal justice. From early times their power of punishment was restricted by the rule that a sentence *de capite civis* could be passed only by decision of the people assembled in *comitia* (see IUDICIA POPULI). The magistrate could, however, apply by informal procedure coercive measures(*coërcitio* in a narrower sense) against disobedient or recalcitrant citizens, e.g. prison, castigation, and fines (*multae*); foreigners, slaves, and women were also subjected to *coërcitio*. The oldest stage of criminal proceedings before the magistrate was governed by the inquisitorial principle: the magistrate initiated the prosecution at his discretion; he controlled the investigation and production of evidence, he passed the sentence. During the struggle of the orders the jurisdiction of *tribuni plebis* in criminal matters was established especially for political offences and abuses committed by patrician magistrates. Sulla's reform, however, aimed at superseding the jurisdiction of *comitia* and plebeian tribunes and completed the new system of *quaestiones*. This procedure was a compromise between the former criminal proceedings (the jury now representing the popular element) and principles of civil procedure, as the accused had a voice in the choice of jurymen. But the criminal trial preserved its own forms, distinct from the bilateral, contractual character of civil proceedings. The *quaestiones*

brought about a restriction of the magistrates' prerogatives, because the prosecution depended now upon the necessary intervention of an accuser. This accusatory system was, however, abolished in the trials *extra ordinem*, where the imperial jurisdictional official regained the full initiative in prosecuting criminal acts and conducted the trial from beginning to end. Accusation was sometimes admitted and even, when successful, rewarded, but the accuser was simply an informer without any substantial procedural rights.

11. The Roman penal system was peculiar in its distinction between public and private penalties, reflecting the division into public and private offences. The private penalty was originally a substitute for private vengeance and retaliation (*talio* = infliction on the delinquent of the same injury as that done by him). Pecuniary composition between the parties (*pacisci*), always permissible, had become compulsory. The private penalty consisted in payment of a sum of money to the person wronged, and is to be distinguished from *multa*, a fine inflicted as a coercive measure by a magistrate and paid to the State. The public penalty originated, as in other primitive systems, in the idea of public revenge, or religious expiation for crimes against the community, or religious conceptions ('sacer esto'), and could not be other than the death of the delinquent. The death-penalty (*poena capitis*), known already in the XII Tables for several crimes, was inflicted in different ways, varying with the times: decapitation (with *gladius*, applied to military persons), gallows (crucifixion, *furca*), burning (in case of arson; application of the talio-principle), drowning in a sack (*culleus*), precipitation *de saxo Tarpeio*, and the like. The most severe form, *bestiis obicere*, was practised under the Empire till Justinian. In the Republican times the execution (and even the sentence) could be avoided by voluntary exile of the wrongdoer (*see* EXSILIUM). Banishment was later applied as an independent penalty in various forms: *relegatio* (q.v.), *deportatio*, and condemnation to heavy work in mines (*metalla*) or public works (*opus publicum*) or to the gladiatorial training-schools (*in ludos*). These penalties were normally combined with loss of citizenship; *damnatio in metalla* (considered as *morti proxima*), with loss of liberty and flagellation; an accessory penalty was the total or partial confiscation of property. It is noticeable that the Romans applied imprisonment only as a coercive or preventive measure, not as a penalty (*see* PRISON): the Roman conception of penalty laid more stress upon its vindictive and deterrent nature than on correction of the delinquent.

For particular topics *see* ADULTERY, AMBITUS, AMPLIATIO, APPELLATIO, DAMNUM, DIVINATIO, EXSILIUM, FURTUM, HONESTIORES, INFAMIA, IUDICIA POPULI, PARRICIDIUM, PERDUELLIO, PRISON, QUAESTIO, RELEGATIO, REPETUNDAE, TORTURE.

W. Zumpt, *Criminalrecht der röm. Republik* i, ii (1865–9); Mommsen, *Röm. Strafr.* (1899); C. Ferrini, *Diritto penale romano* (1899); 'Esposizione storica e dottrinale del dir. rom. penale' (*Encicl. del dir. penale italiano, diretta da E. Pessina*, 1902); J. L. Strachan-Davidson, *Problems of the Roman Criminal Law* i, ii (1912); M. Wlassak, 'Anklage und Streitbefestigung im Kriminalrecht der Römer', (*Sitz. Akad. Wien* clxxxiv (1917); cxciv (1920)); E. Costa, *Crimini e pene da Romolo a Giustiniano* (1921); E. Levy, 'Röm. Kapitalstrafe' (*Sitz. Akad. Heidelberg*, 1930–1); H. F. Jolowicz, 'The assessment of penalties in primitive law', *Cambridge Legal Essays* (1926), 203 ff.; id., *Historical Introduction to the Study of Roman Law* (1932); M. Lauria, 'Accusatio-Inquisitio', *Atti Accad. Napoli* lvi (1934); H. Siber, *Analogie, Amtsrecht und Rückwirkung im Strafrecht des röm. Freistaates* (1936); E. Albertario, 'Delictum e crimen'[2] in *Studi di dir. rom.* iii, 141 ff. (1936); M. Lauria, *Studia et documenta historiae et iuris* (1938), 182 ff.; V. Arangio-Ruiz, *Storia del dir. rom.*[3] (1942); U. Brasiello, *La repressione penale in dir. rom.* (1937); E. Levy, 'Gesetz und Richter im kaiserlichen Strafrecht' (*Bull. Ist. Dir. Rom.* xlv (1938)). For monographs from 1928 to 1935 see Albertario, l.c., p. 146. Modern literature has contributed much to a correct appreciation of Roman criminal law and procedure. Mommsen's masterpiece if re-edited would now assume quite a different appearance.   A. B.

LAW, INTERNATIONAL. Under this heading law must be taken in its widest sense to include customary, religious, and moral law. Some approach to statutory law can be seen in the Amphictionic laws, the decrees of the Congress of Plataea of 479 B.C., and the King's Peace, not to mention that the relations of States to each other were regulated by treaties. Nevertheless, international law remained essentially customary and, in contrast to the laws of individual States, which also had once been customary, was never officially recorded or codified. The importance of religion is seen in the Amphictionic oath, the *fetial* rites, and the practice of ratifying treaties by oath.

2. Public international law was relatively well developed by Homeric times, when heralds and ambassadors were considered inviolable and the sanctity of sworn agreements was recognized. Similar evidence is supplied for early Italy by the *fetial* code with its demand that every war be a just war. Greek law was soon expanded by the Amphictionic oath and the truces for the Panhellenic Games.

3. In both countries treaties were negotiated at an early date. The Greek treaties (σπονδαί, ὅρκοι, συνθῆκαι) obviously were descended directly from the compacts of Homeric times, while the Roman organization of Italy indicates extensive use of treaties relatively early. Omitting armistices, the chief classes were treaties of peace, of alliance, and of friendship. The lack of treaties need not mean hostility. Thus, though Rome had treaties of friendship (*amicitia*) with several States, friendly relations often existed without such a treaty. Though permanent treaties probably were made at an early date, the oldest Greek treaties preserved in detail were made for a limited period, and treaties 'for all time' did not become the rule before the fourth century. The short-term treaties of peace probably were not looked upon as interrupting a natural state of war by a temporary rest, but as imposing additional obligations for the period of their duration. Many Greek treaties contained clauses providing for the arbitration of disputes, and even in their absence arbitration was frequently offered. The system was used with some success and continued to be used under Roman supervision in the second and first centuries B.C.

4. Private international law developed more slowly. At first piracy, private seizure, and enslavement of foreigners were common. In fact, the theory of the complete absence of rights for foreigners not protected by special arrangements was retained by Roman jurists (*Dig.* 49. 15. 5). The foreigners in question are not enemies, so that the theory does not involve the doctrine that all strangers are enemies. On the other hand, there was a high regard for the sanctity of suppliants and for hospitality. Out of this grew hereditary exchanges of private hospitality and later the institution of *proxenoi*, to which the Roman *hospitium publicum* roughly corresponded. Outright piracy soon was widely condemned, and the feeling developed that private seizure should be used only as a reprisal for wrongs suffered. Its use sometimes was further regulated and limited by treaties. Courts, too, began to give protection to foreigners, sometimes when no treaties existed, but probably more frequently on the basis of commercial treaties (σύμβολα). These, at least at Athens, were ratified by a jury-court and so probably were regarded as contracts of a less sacred nature—but not less binding—than other treaties. More extensive rights were granted through treaties of *isopoliteia*. Related to this for Rome was the frequent grant of *commercium*.

5. The regard for what was customary or morally right applied to many points not so far mentioned, for instance to the rules of war. Such a basis for law meant that the standards varied from time to time and from place to place. Everyone is familiar with the lowering of standards which, according to Thucydides, resulted from the Peloponnesian War, while the accusation of piracy constantly made against the Aetolians implies that their standard was lower than those of other States. Nor were all foreigners treated alike, but barbarians were shown less consideration than closely related States. Yet there was always a line which could not be overstepped without incurring censure.

6. Roman expansion, at first glance, seems to leave less scope for development of international law in Rome than in Greece. It must not be forgotten, however, that Rome's early organization of Italy was based on international law and that the existence of free and allied cities also outside Italy and the control of States not formally annexed caused the Roman Empire to be governed for long largely by a modified form of international law.

See also AMPHICTIONIES; ASYLIA; FETIALES; HERALDS; ISOPOLITEIA; PROXENOS; SYMBOLON; SYMMACHIA; WAR, RULES OF.

C. Phillipson, *The International Law and Custom of Ancient Greece and Rome* (1911); F. E. Adcock, 'Some Aspects of Ancient Greek Diplomacy', *Proceedings of the Classical Association* 1924; M. N. Tod, *International Arbitration amongst the Greeks* (1913); E. Täubler, *Imperium Romanum* (1913); A. Heuss, *Die völkerrechtlichen Grundlagen der römischen Aussenpolitik in republikanischer Zeit* (1933), and his discussion of treaty-making in *Klio* 1934; V. Martin, *La Vie internationale dans la Grèce des cités* (1940).
J. A. O. L.

LAW, *see also* ARBITRATION, LEX, etc.

LEAD. Metallic lead was discovered early, but little used in primitive cultures. Even at Laurium much was thrown away; but the Romans needed for water-pipes all that they produced. Lead was extensively used for desilvering pyritical ores and for alloying with copper to save tin, both processes being known in pre-Roman times.

Lead mines were mainly exploited for silver, the lead being regarded as a by-product. Of the various deposits in Greece the most important were at Laurium (q.v.). There were extensive workings in Anatolia. Of pre-Roman origin are the mines of Sardinia and Etruria. Spain, Gaul, and Britain were exploited actively by the Romans, and many stamped Roman pigs have been found there. In the Late Empire mines were opened in the Balkans; the workings in Africa are of doubtful date.

E. Ardaillon, *Les Mines du Laurion* (1897); W. Gowland, *Archaeologia* lxix (1917–18), 121; M. Besnier, *Rev. Arch.* Ser. V, x (1919), 31; xii (1920), 211; xiii (1921), 40; G. C. Whittick, *JRS* 1931, 256; O. Davies, *Roman Mines in Europe* (1935).
O. D.

LEAGUES, *see* ACHAEAN LEAGUE, AETOLIAN LEAGUE, PELOPONNESIAN LEAGUE, FEDERAL STATES.

LEARCHUS, *see* ATHAMAS.

LECTISTERNIUM. A Roman version of the Greek customs of κλίνη and θεοξένια, q.v. A god or gods were made guests at a meal, couches being prepared for them as for human banqueters. This might be (*a*) in a private house (e.g. Varro ap. Serv. on *Aen.* 10. 76); (*b*) at some shrine, when the *lectus* may but need not be identical with the *pulvinar* (q.v.; Agnes H. Lake in *Quantulacumque* (1937), 243 ff.); (*c*) simultaneously to several gods, first in 399 B.C. (Livy 5. 13. 6). The gods might be represented by statues or *capita deorum*, i.e. bundles of herbs (Festus, pp. 56, 12; 473, 4 (cf. 410, 6) Lindsay; H. Wagenvoort, *Roman Dynamism* (1947), 21.

See Wissowa in *PW*, s.v. H. J. R.

LECTUS, *see* FURNITURE.

LECYTHION, *see* METRE, GREEK, III (2).

LEDA, in mythology, daughter of Thestius king of Aetolia, wife of Tyndareus, and mother of the Dioscuri and Helen (qq.v.), but see below. Zeus approached her

in the shape of a swan (a very favourite subject in art, see Höfer–Bloch in Roscher's *Lexikon* ii. 1925 ff.) and begat Helen and Polydeuces (Apollod. 3. 126); Castor was begotten by Tyndareus the same night (ibid.). Hyginus (*Fab.* 77) adds Clytaemnestra (*see* CLYTEMNESTRA), whose name has perhaps fallen out of the text of Ps.-Apollodorus; but the whole story is told in a number of different ways, Helen being regularly daughter of Zeus (but of Tyndareus, Hyg. 78. 1), the Dioscuri both his sons in Homer. The most noteworthy variant (Apollod. ibid. 127) is that Helen was daughter of Zeus and Nemesis; both parents having been transformed into birds, Nemesis (q.v.) laid an egg, of which Leda took care; when Helen was hatched out from it she passed for Leda's daughter. This is obviously a reconciliation of two conflicting stories. Leda is everywhere mother of Clytaemestra, and frequently, as [Eur.] *IA* 1–2, she has a third daughter, called there Phoebe, Timandra in Apollod. loc. cit. and elsewhere, even a fourth (Apollodorus), Phylonoe, who was made immortal by Artemis. Again, Helen was hatched from an egg laid by Leda, not Nemesis (Eur. *Helena*, 257–9, a doubtfully authentic passage, but the earliest mention surviving, if genuine). The egg is, indeed, a central feature in the story, and was alleged to be preserved in Sparta down to Pausanias' time (Paus. 3. 16. 1); it may therefore be conjectured to go back to some very old tale of deities in bird-shape (Minoan-Mycenaean? cf. Nilsson, *Minoan-Mycenaean Religion*, ch. 10). It may well be older than Homer and the lack of mention of it in his poems due to his dislike of the grotesque; later Greeks disbelieved the story (Eur. *Hel.* loc. cit.) or made fun of it (Cratinus in Athenaeus, 373 e).

The latest literature is S. Eitrem in *PW*, s.v. H. J. R.

LEGATI. During the last two centuries of the Roman Republic provincial governors and generals were authorized by the Senate, and in exceptional cases by law (e.g. *Lex Gabinia* for Pompey in 67 B.C.), to choose *legati* to serve on their staff. These *legati*, whose number seems to have varied from two to fifteen, were regularly senators and often experienced officers, but had no fixed range of duties. Thus the elder Scipio accompanied his brother as *legatus* to the war against Antiochus, and Marius in his old age functioned in a similar capacity. Caesar was the first to employ *legati* as commanders of individual legions or detachments, and this experiment provided a precedent for Augustus.

In the imperial army of the first two centuries A.D. each legion (except those in Egypt) was with its *auxilia* commanded by a *legatus legionis*, who was normally of praetorian but sometimes of quaestorian status. If there was more than one legion in a province, the supreme command lay with the governor, who was regularly a *legatus Augusti pro praetore* of consular status; where the garrison was a single legion its commander was also the provincial governor.

When Septimius Severus raised his three new legions he gave the command of each, not to a *legatus*, but to an equestrian *praefectus*. Gallienus removed senators from all military commands.

Legati Augusti pro praetore was also the title of commissioners appointed to undertake some special work, such as the census or a levy of recruits.

A. von Domaszewski, *Die Rangordnung des römischen Heeres* (1908); H. M. D. Parker, *The Roman Legions* (1928). H. M. D. P.

LEGATUM (legacy), *see* FIDEICOMMISSUM.

LEGION. 1. EARLY REPUBLIC. Although the origin of the legion may be as old as the Republic, its early history is very uncertain. The first trustworthy account is that of Polybius, which reflects the conditions of the third century B.C. In addition to 300 cavalry each of the four legions composing the two consular armies contained 4,200 infantry, drawn up in three lines of *hastati*, *principes*, and *triarii*, the two former 1,200 and the latter 600 strong, while 1,200 poorer citizens provided the light-armed troops (*velites*). The legion was divided into 30 maniples, 10 to each line, and 60 centuries. The commanding officer was the consul, who had under him 6 military tribunes and 60 centurions. Inside the legion the tactical unit was the maniple, which had a *signum* and was commanded by the senior of its two centurions. During the Punic Wars the legions were greatly increased in size and number.

2. MARIUS TO CAESAR. By the Marian reforms (*a*) eligibility for service was extended to the *capite censi* and the legions became volunteer forces of professional soldiers; (*b*) each legion, now 6,000 strong, received an *aquila*; (*c*) the cohort permanently superseded the maniple for tactical purposes. The cavalry and *velites* were abolished.

There were no changes in the junior commands, except that Caesar began to appoint *legati* of his own choosing to command separate legions in his army.

3. THE PRINCIPATE. Out of the forces of the triumvirs Augustus established a standing legionary army of a size requisite for imperial defence and pacification. In 15 B.C. the number of legions, each comprising some 5,000 foot-soldiers and a mounted bodyguard 120 strong, was 28, which, by the loss of 3 in A.D. 9, was reduced to 25. In the next two centuries additions were made and losses sustained, but the total did not exceed 30 (i.e. about 150,000 men) till Septimius Severus raised 3 new legions. Each legion bore a number, which was not infrequently duplicated, and a title honorific to itself or its creator.

The commander was a senatorial *legatus*, except in Egypt, where an equestrian *praefectus* was employed. This latter practice was extended by Severus to his new legions, and Gallienus eliminated senators from the army.

In the Julio-Claudian period the legions were enlisted mainly from Italy and Gallia Narbonensis. As citizenship became more widely extended the provinces provided the greatest number of recruits, till in the late second century local recruiting became the rule. The period of service was fixed by Augustus first at 16 and then at 20 years *sub aquila*, with an additional 4 and 5 years respectively *sub vexillo*. The Flavians abolished the veteran corps and made 25 years the total legionary service. The legionary received pay rising from 225 *denarii* under Augustus to 750 under Caracalla, and on his discharge a pension from the *aerarium militare*.

4. CONSTANTINE. Legions were now included both in the Field and Garrison armies. The units, composed entirely of foot-soldiers, were only 1,000 strong, and in status ranked below the cavalry *vexillationes* and picked auxiliary contingents of infantry.

See also ALAUDAE, CENTURIO, COHORS, LEGATI, MANIPULUS, PRAEFECTUS, PRIMIPILUS, SACRAMENTUM, SIGNA MILITARIA, STIPENDIUM, TRIBUNI MILITUM, VEXILLUM.

E. Ritterling and W. Kubitschek, *PW*, s.v. 'Legio'; H. M. D. Parker, *The Roman Legions* (1928). A. von Domaszewski, *Die Rangordnung des römischen Heeres* (1908). H. M. D. P.

LEGIS ACTIO, *see* LAW AND PROCEDURE, ROMAN, II. 2.

LELEGES (Λέλεγες), a tribe mentioned, *Il.* 10. 428, 21. 86, as allied with Troy and occupying Pedasus in the Troad. Later writers give them a wide distribution. In Herodotus (1. 171) Carians 'formerly called Leleges' occupied the Islands and manned King Minos' navy. Philip of Theangela (in Caria) says that Leleges were to Carians as helots to Spartans (Ath. 6. 272). Hesiod located Leleges as aborigines in Locris, and Aristotle in Acarnania, Aetolia, Boeotia, and Megaris (Strabo pp. 321–2). Pausanias (3. 1. 1) makes Lelex the first king of Laconia. Like the Pelasgi (q.v.) they seem to have been extensively postulated as 'aborigines'. We cannot associate them with any particular archaeological discoveries. A. R. B.

LEMNOS, an island of the north-east Aegean. The lava from its volcano (reputed to be the forge of Hephaestus, but extinct in historical times) gave it high fertility, and it grew considerable wheat crops. In the *Iliad* it figures as a victualling centre for the Achaeans at Troy, but it is doubtful whether it had a Greek population before the sixth or fifth century. According to Herodotus (6. 137–40) its early inhabitants were 'Pelasgians', and an undeciphered inscription (*IG* xii. 8. 1; probably of the 6th c.), which seems to have affinities with Etruscan, suggests a settlement of proto-Etruscans from Asia Minor. Lemnos received Athenian colonists after its seizure by the younger Miltiades in his capacity as ruler of the Thracian Chersonese, c. 500 B.C. It was organized as an Athenian cleruchy c. 450, and after a brief period of Spartan domination (404–393) was recovered by Athens. From the time of Philip II of Macedon it passed occasionally into the possession of various Hellenistic dynasts, but it was again in Athenian hands from 307 to 295 and from 281 to 202. In 166 it was definitely attached to Athens by the Romans. M. C.

LEMURIA, 9, 11, 13 May, on which days apparently kinless and hungry ghosts, *lemures* (Wissowa's doubts, *PW*, s.v. 'Lemuria', col. 1932, that such a word originally existed seem unjustifiable), were supposed to prowl about the houses. Ovid (*Fasti* 5. 419 ff.) describes the ritual of feeding and getting rid of them, but his assertion (443) that they were addressed as *manes paterni* is incredible.

See Rose in *Univ. of California Pubs.* in *CPhil.* 1941, 89 ff., and AFTER-LIFE, para. 8. H. J. R.

LENAEA, a Dionysiac festival celebrated in Athens on the 12th day of the month Gamelion (Jan.–Feb.), which in other Ionian calendars is called Lenaeon. The name is derived from λήνη, maenad. The official Athenian name, Διονύσια τὰ ἐπὶ Ληναίῳ, proves that it took place in this sanctuary, which is believed to have been situated west of the Acropolis. Very little is known of the rites. There was a procession and it is said that the *dadouchos* of Eleusis officiated in the Lenaean ἀγῶνες. The chief importance of the festival lies in the dramatic performances; it seems that originally comedy was preferred to tragedy. The attempt to connect with the Lenaea vase pictures, representing the mixing of the wine and (occasionally) a dance of Maenads, is to be rejected; they belong to the Anthesteria.

M. P. Nilsson, *Studia de Dionysiis atticis* (1900), 109 ff.; L. Deubner, *Attische Feste*, 123 ff. Much has been written on the so-called 'Lenäenvasen'; the last paper by Deubner, *JDAI* xlix (1934), 1 ff. M. P. N.

LENAEUS, POMPEIUS, a learned freedman of Pompey's, taught in Rome and, loyal to his patron's memory, attacked the character and style of Sallust who had described Pompey as 'oris probi, animo inuerecundo' (Suet. *Gram.* 15). He wrote also on pharmacology (Pliny, *HN* 25. 5). Della Corte, *La poesia di Varrone ricostituita* (1938), 33, bases the spelling *Lenius* on manuscripts of the elder Pliny. J. W. D.

LENTULUS (1), LUCIUS CORNELIUS, served under Scipio Africanus in Spain, where he remained from 206 to 201 B.C. as a *privatus* with proconsular imperium, which was constantly prolonged, despite his election as curule aedile for 205. He claimed a triumph in defiance of precedent, but received an *ovatio*. He served in north Italy as consul (199) and proconsul (198). In 196 he was sent on an ineffective diplomatic mission to Antiochus III to mediate on behalf of Egypt. H. H. S.

LENTULUS (2), PUBLIUS CORNELIUS, legate in Greece (172–171 B.C.), curule aedile (169), envoy to Perseus after Pydna, became praetor in 166 or 165, reorganizing the *ager Campanus*, and consul *suffectus* in 162. In 156 he negotiated with the kings of Asia Minor. *Princeps senatus* from 125, he opposed C. Gracchus.

Livy 42. 37 and 47; 45. 4; Granius Licinianus 28, p. 9; Cicero *Leg. Agr.* 2. 30. 82; Polyb. 32. 16. A. H. McD.

LENTULUS (3) **CLODIANUS**, GNAEUS CORNELIUS, *cos.* 72 B.C. with L. Gellius Poplicola, legitimized grants of citizenship made by Pompey. In the war against Spartacus he was defeated more than once. Censor with Poplicola in 70, he ejected from the Senate sixty-four members. He was Pompey's legate against the pirates (67) and supported the *Lex Manilia* (66).

F. Münzer, *PW* iv. 1380. A. M.

LENTULUS (4) **SURA**, PUBLIUS CORNELIUS, was expelled from the Senate shortly after his consulate (71 B.C.), but was elected to a second praetorship in 63. His personal ambition led him to join the conspiracy of Catiline, and after the latter's flight from Rome he became the ringleader in the city. His overtures to some Gallic envoys who played him false provided Cicero with documentary proof of his guilt. He was arrested with four of his associates (3 Dec. 63) and was compelled to lay down his office. Two days later, after a historic debate in the Senate, the five prisoners were strangled on Cicero's orders.

J. M. C.

LENTULUS (5) **SPINTHER**, PUBLIUS CORNELIUS, an agreeable aristocrat, lavish in his aedileship (63 B.C.) and praetorship (60), who was active as consul (57) in promoting Cicero's recall. Next year Cicero vainly tried to preserve for Spinther as governor of Cilicia the right, procured during his consulate, of restoring Ptolemy Auletes. Before leaving Cilicia in 53 Spinther was saluted *imperator*, and he triumphed in 51. In 49 he fled from Asculum before Caesar's advance, and surrendered at Corfinium with Domitius; he abused Caesar's clemency and was executed after Pharsalus.

G. E. F. C.

LENTULUS (6) **MARCELLINUS**, GNAEUS CORNELIUS, was *patronus* of the Sicilians against Verres (70 B.C.) and legate of Pompey (67). In 61 he opposed Clodius. In 60 he was praetor and then governor of Syria; in 57 he supported the restoration of Cicero's property. As consul (56) he opposed the triumvirs and prevented a war for the restoration of Ptolemy XI Auletes.

F. Münzer, *PW* iv. 1389. A. M.

LENTULUS (7) **CRUS**, LUCIUS CORNELIUS, consul 49 B.C., and a determined advocate of civil war. Later in 49 he administered Asia, and thence brought two legions to Dyrrhachium; after Pharsalus he fled to Egypt, and arrived to meet his death the day after Pompey's. It is possible (though *see* BALBUS (2)) that, after fighting against Sertorius, Lentulus gave Balbus Roman citizenship and his name Cornelius; in any case they were close friends, and Balbus persistently begged Lentulus to keep the peace. But Lentulus, according to Caesar, was made desperate by debt; and all authors, including Cicero, whom he had befriended in 58 and 49, describe him as lazy, luxurious, and pretentious.

Cicero, *Att.* 6. 1. 23; 8. 9. 4; 11. 6. 6; *Fam.* 8. 4. 1; *Brutus*, 268; Caesar, *BCiv.* 1. 4. 2; 3. 96. 1; Velleius, 2. 49. 3, 51. 3.

G. E. F. C.

LENTULUS (8), GNAEUS CORNELIUS. A Lentulus of this name, either the consul of 18 B.C. or the consul of 14 B.C. (probably the latter), operated at an unknown date against Sarmatians and Dacians. One or other of them was accused in A.D. 24 of conspiracy against Tiberius, but he was not prosecuted, and died in 25.

PIR[2], C 1378–9; R. Syme, *The Roman Revolution* (1939), 400. A. M.

LENTULUS (9) **GAETULICUS**, GNAEUS CORNELIUS, was consul in A.D. 26 and legate of Upper Germany, possibly in succession to his brother, in 30–9. As a lax disciplinarian he was popular with his own army and also with the Lower German legions, commanded by L. Apronius, his father-in-law. An attempt to indict him in 34 as an associate of Sejanus failed. In 39 he appears to have led a conspiracy by which the Emperor Gaius was to be murdered at Moguntiacum. Gaius was forewarned of the plot and Gaetulicus was executed. He was an erotic poet, regarded by Martial (1 *praef.*) as one of his models. Nine epigrams in the *Greek Anthology* may be by him.

Baehr. *FPR*, p. 361. J. P. B.

LEOCHARES, sculptor, probably Athenian. Pliny places his *floruit* in 372 B.C., but Leochares is mentioned in a letter of Plato written after 366 as 'young and good'. Selected works: *dated*, (1) Isocrates, dedicated by Timotheus presumably before his banishment in 356 (the surviving bust (Winter, *KB* 317. 5) derives from a later statue). (2) Signature from the Acropolis, about 350. (3) West side of Mausoleum, after 351. Slabs 1020, 1021 of the Amazonomachy (Winter, *KB* 304. 2) with tall, slim, dramatic figures are probably by Leochares. (4) Gold and ivory group of Philip, Alexander, Amyntas, Olympias, and Eurydice in the Philippeum at Olympia, dedicated after Chaeronea, 338. (5) (with Lysippus, q.v.) Alexander's lion hunt, bronze, after 321. *Undated*, (6) Ganymede. Pliny's description of the eagle 'parcentem unguibus etiam per uestem puero' fits the marble group in the Vatican (Winter, *KB* 299. 1), which must therefore be the basis of attribution to Leochares. *Attributed*, (7) Apollo Belvedere in the Vatican (Winter, *KB* 299. 2–4), Roman adaptation of fourth-century original (Leochares made an Apollo in Athens). (8) Artemis of Versailles (Winter, *KB* 312. 3). (9) Hypnos (Winter, *KB* 299. 6). Nos. 3, 6–9 are all theatrical compositions of tall, slim figures.

Overbeck, 508. 1177–8, 1301–16, 1491; F. Winter, *JDAI* 1892, 164; P. Wolters and J. Sieveking, *JDAI* 1909, 171; O. Deubner, *Hellenistische Apollogestalten*, 46. T. B. L. W.

LEON (1) of Byzantium, prominent as one of the leaders of his city who claimed Athenian support against Philip of Macedon. He conducted the successful resistance to Philip's siege, 339 B.C., but when the city later made terms Philip secured his death. If he died *c.* 338 various historical works on Philip, the Sacred War, and Alexander should probably be assigned to a later Leon.

FHG ii. 329. G. L. B.

LEON (2) of Pella (? late 4th c. B.C.), wrote a book on the Egyptian gods, in the form of a letter from Alexander the Great to his mother, in which the gods are represented as in origin human kings, the discoverers of agriculture and other means of human subsistence.

FHG ii. 331–2; *PW* xii. 2. 2012–14.

LEONIDAS (1), king of Sparta, succeeded his elder brother Cleomenes (whose daughter Gorgo he married) *c.* 487 B.C. In 480 he was commissioned to hold Thermopylae with 4,000 Peloponnesians and contingents from Thebes and central Greece, apparently as a vanguard of the entire Peloponnesian levy. He held the main pass for two days, but his Phocian allies fled before a Persian corps advancing by the mountain path of Anopaea and allowed Leonidas to be outflanked. The other Greek forces dispersed, but Leonidas and 300 companions remained to cover the retreat of the fleet from Artemisium and, after inflicting heavy losses, fell fighting. Forty years later Leonidas' body, which Xerxes is alleged to have maltreated, was buried at Sparta. Simonides' epigram and *threnos* inaugurated a long series of eulogies on the heroes of Thermopylae.

Ch. Lenschau, *PW*, s.v.; G. De Sanctis, *Riv. fil.* 1925, 122 ff.; F. Miltner, *Klio* 1935, 228–41. P. T.

LEONIDAS (2) of Tarentum, one of the greatest Greek epigrammatists, led a poor wandering life in the early third century B.C. The Anthology contains about a hundred of his epigrams, three-quarters of which are dedicatory poems or epitaphs, usually artificial—e.g. epitaphs on a drunkard, on a diver half-eaten by sharks. There are no real love-poems, no convivial poems. Almost all his poetry deals with the life of the very poor, among whom he reckons himself (*Anth. Pal.* 7. 302, 736); nevertheless it is highly elaborate, full of grand compound words and odd technical terms, and the flow of the sentences within the verse is mannered and rhetorical. This contrast may be decadent, but it is fascinating. L. took many themes and patterns from his predecessors, but enlarged and enriched them all. The Romans greatly admired him, he was imitated by Propertius (3. 7. 7) and Virgil (*Ecl.* 7. 29), and all later epigrammatists use some of his devices.

J. Geffcken, *Jahrb. f. Philol.* suppl. xxiii (1896), is fundamental; B. Hansen, *de L. Tarentino* (1914); E. Bevan, *Poems of L. translated* (1931).   G. H.

LEONIDAS (3) of Alexandria, an astrologer who turned poet and was patronized by Nero, Vespasian, and Domitian. His datable poems fall between A.D. 55 and 85. There are over forty of them in the Anthology—thirty being *isopsepha*, so composed that the letters in each couplet, if read as numbers ($a = 1$, $\beta = 2$, etc.), make the same sum. Both these and his other epigrams are negligible except for the ingenuity characteristic of what Juvenal calls 'the hungry Greekling'.

K. Radinger, *Rh. Mus.* 1903; P. Perdrizet, *Rev. Ét. Grec.* 1904; C. Cichorius, *Röm. Stud.* c. viii. 12 (1922).   G. H.

LEONNATUS (c. 358–322 B.C.), a Macedonian noble related to the royal house, accompanied Alexander to Asia, became one of his personal 'Bodyguard' in 332 and (after 328) a prominent general, distinguishing himself in an independent command on the return from India. As satrap of Hellespontine Phrygia (323) he reinforced Antipater in the Lamian War; but he was defeated and killed in Thessaly by the Greek insurgents. His character lacked moderation and stability, and he would probably have fared badly against cooler heads in the age of the 'Successors'.

Berve, *Alexanderreich*, no. 466.   G. T. G.

LEONTIADES, Theban oligarch. After surrendering the Cadmea to Phoebidas in the midst of peace (382 B.C.), he caused the Spartans to execute the democratic leader Ismenias. At the liberation of Thebes in 379, he was killed immediately.

Xen. *Hell.* bk. 5; Diod. bk. 15; Plut. *Pel.*   V. E.

LEONTINI was founded by Naxos in fertile Sicel territory in eastern Sicily (729 B.C.). Although at first independent and prosperous, Leontini in the fifth century became subject, first to Gela, but soon to Syracuse, traditional enemy of the Chalcidian cities. It remained under Syracusan domination except for occasional interludes until Hieron's death (216). Provoked by an incident here, the Romans attacked Syracuse (215) and made Leontini a *civitas censoria* which later suffered in the Servile War (104: hence Cicero's exaggerated description 'misera ciuitas atque inanis'). Leontini was traditionally the abode of Homer's Laestrygones, the place where wheat first grew, the realm of Panaetius (Sicily's earliest tyrant), and the birthplace of Gorgias the sophist. Saracens finally destroyed it (A.D. 848).

Polyb. 7. 6 (excellent description); Strabo 6. 272 f.; Thuc. bk. 6; Diod. bks. 11–23; Cic. *Verrines*. J. Bérard, *Bibliogr. topogr.* (1941), 59.   E. T. S.

LEOSTHENES (d. 322 B.C.), an Athenian, perhaps general at Athens in 324–323, having probably served as captain of mercenaries in Asia previously (Tarn, *GAH*

vi. 455). With acute political insight he organized the return and maintenance at Taenarum of mercenaries disbanded by Alexander's satraps (324); he negotiated secretly with Athens and (later) Aetolia for their employment in an anti-Macedonian war. The Lamian War (323–322) was his opportunity. He commanded the Greek army and inspired its devotion, and his death at the siege of Lamia was a heavy blow to the Greek cause.

Berve, *Alexanderreich*, no. 471.   G. T. G.

LEOTYCHIDES, king of Sparta c. 545–469 B.C., succeeded the exiled Demaratus (c. 491 B.C.) with aid of Cleomenes I (q.v.). In the Aeginetan War he apparently secured the granting of a truce to Athens and delivery of hostages by Aegina. In 479, as commander-in-chief of the allied fleet, he fomented the revolt of Chios and Samos, and decisively defeated the Persians in a land and sea battle at Mycale. He led another combined Greek force on a punitive expedition against the medizing aristocracies in Thessaly (c. 477). He took Pagasae and perhaps Pherae, but failed to capture Larissa. He was tried at Sparta on a charge of bribery (probably c. 476), but he escaped condemnation by retiring to Tegea. An earlier namesake (with whom Leotychides has often been confused) subdued Messenia in the Second Messenian War (see MESSENIA).

K. J. Beloch, *Griech. Gesch.*[2] (1912 ff.), i, pt. 2, 179 ff.; ii, pt. 2, 190 ff.; J. Johnson, *Hermathena* 1931; J. Kroymann, *Sparta und Messenien*, 3 ff. (1937); L. R. Shero, *Trans. Am. Phil. Ass.* 1938, 516 ff.   P. T.

LEPIDUS (1), MARCUS AEMILIUS, the censor of 179 B.C., appears first on the embassy to Greece, Syria, and Egypt in 200, delivering the Roman ultimatum to Philip V. Curule aedile (193), praetor in Sicily (191), he became consul (187), constructing the Via Aemilia, and as triumvir (183) founded Mutina and Parma. Pontifex Maximus (180) and censor (179) with M. Fulvius Nobilior, he reformed the Comitia Centuriata and carried out a large building programme, including the Basilica Aemilia. Consul again (175) in Liguria, he was decemvir for land settlement there (173). From his censorship to his death in 152 he was *princeps senatus*. Well-born and handsome, combining liberal culture with observance of tradition, he was pre-eminent in the Senate, and his name marks the pacification of Cispadane Gaul.

Polyb. 16. 34; Livy 31. 18; 38. 42 ff.; 39. 2; 40. 45–6, 51–2. F. Münzer, *Röm. Adelsparteien und Adelsfamilien* (1920), 170; De Sanctis, *Stor. Rom.* iv. 1, 609; H. Mattingly, *Roman Coins* (1928), 76; A. H. McDonald and F. W. Walbank, *JRS* 1937, 192, 195; A. H. McDonald, *JRS* 1938, 162.   A. H. McD.

LEPIDUS (2), MARCUS AEMILIUS, elected consul for 78 B.C. with the young Pompey's assistance, despite the opposition of Sulla, sought while Sulla yet lived to revive the *populares*. He proposed the restoration of confiscated lands, recall of exiles, and eventually the restoration of tribunician authority. Raising an army in Cisalpine Gaul, whose resources he was the first to realize, he marched on Rome to enforce his programme and obtain a second consulship, but was driven out of Italy by the proconsul Catulus with the help of Pompey and the *S.C. ultimum* to Sardinia, where he died. His supporters joined Sertorius in Spain, but were later pardoned.

Rice Holmes, *Roman Republic* i. 363–9. *See also under* SULLA.
A. N. S.-W.

LEPIDUS (3), MARCUS AEMILIUS, the Triumvir, son of (2), was *praetor urbanus* in 49 B.C., governor of Hither Spain in 48, consul in 46, and Caesar's *magister equitum* in 45 and 44. He supported Antony after the murder of Caesar, but shortly left Rome for Gallia Narbonensis and Hither Spain. In the War of Mutina he eventually joined Antony, took part in the conference near Bononia, and was appointed Triumvir with Antony and Octavian, receiving the additional province of Further Spain. In

42 (consul II) he remained in charge of Italy. After Philippi he was deprived of his provinces by his colleagues, who contemplated ousting him from the Triumvirate on the allegation of intrigues with Sextus Pompeius, but he supported Octavian in the Perusine War and was given Africa and Numidia. He played an independent part in the campaign of 36 against Sextus Pompeius, and laid claim to Sicily, but Octavian won over his army and compelled him to retire into private life. He was Pontifex Maximus from 44 till his death in 13 (or 12) B.C.

Lepidus lacked the character and energy to use the opportunities which high birth and Caesar's favour placed in his way. His wife was Junia, sister of Brutus.

Ancient sources: Cicero, *Letters* and *Philippics*; Velleius, bk. 2; Plutarch, *Caesar* and *Antony*; Appian, *BCiv.* bks. 2–5; Dio Cassius, bks. 41–50 and 54. Modern literature: F. Brüggemann, *De M. Aem. Lepidi Vita*, Diss. Münster (1889); Drumann–Groebe, *Gesch. Roms* i. 9–17. G. W. R.

LEPIDUS (4), MARCUS AEMILIUS, son of the Triumvir (3) and Junia (sister of Brutus). In 30 B.C. (less probably 31) he conspired to assassinate Octavian but was detected by Maecenas and executed. His wife Servilia committed suicide.

Velleius 2. 88; Appian, *BCiv.* 4. 50. Drumann–Groebe, *Gesch. Roms* i. 17. G. W. R.

LEPIDUS (5), MARCUS AEMILIUS, consul in A.D. 6 and son of L. Aemilius Lepidus Paullus, was legate of Tiberius in the war against the Dalmatians (9). In 14 he governed Hispania Citerior, in 21 Asia. He was father of Aemilia Lepida, wife of Drusus, Germanicus' son. Augustus probably described him as 'capax imperii, sed aspernans' (Tac. *Ann.* 1. 13).

Rohden, *PW* i. 562; *PIR*², A 369; R. Syme, *The Roman Revolution* (1939), 433 n. 4. A. M.

LEPIDUS (6), MANIUS AEMILIUS, consul A.D. 11, was a friend of Augustus and Tiberius, and was celebrated by Tacitus for his dignity. In 21 he declined the proconsulate of Africa, and in 26 he accepted that of Asia. He died in 33.

Rohden, *PW* i. 551; *PIR*², A 363.

LEPTIS (or LEPCIS) **MAGNA**, an African port, easternmost of the Three Cities of Tripolitania. Sidonian sailors founded Lebqi about the sixth century B.C. in rich agricultural country. It traded in goods brought from the Fezzan through Garamantian territory, and exported corn and oil. The Leptitans were usually on bad terms with their Tyrian neighbours at Oea (q.v.); as late as A.D. 70 Oea combined with the Garamantes to attack its rival. Septimius Severus beautified Leptis, his native city, with ornate public buildings. It was very prosperous in the third century, but was sacked by raiding tribes from the Fezzan in the fourth. Refortified by the Byzantines, it was soon destroyed by Berbers.

The ruins of Leptis Magna are the most extensive and imposing in Roman Africa. They include a hippodrome with seating for 50,000, the harbour, baths, palaestra, forum, theatre, amphitheatre, and Septimius' *arcus quadrifons*.

P. Romanelli, *Leptis Magna* (1925); R. Bartoccini, *Le Terme di Lepcis* (1929); S. Aurigemma, *I Mosaici di Zliten* (1926). W. N. W.

LESBIAN, *see* DIALECTS, GREEK.

LESBONAX of Mytilene (2nd c. A.D.), sophist, author of probably the earliest collection of love-letters extant, and of three declamations (imaginary addresses to 5th-c. Athenians) embodying reminiscences of Thucydides and written in spirited and figurative style (Norden, *Ant. Kunstpr.* i. 390). J. W. H. A.

LESBOS, the largest of the islands off the coast of Asia Minor, lying athwart the entrance to the Gulf of Adramyttium, roughly triangular in shape, but with two

landlocked bays cutting deep into the hills on the southern side. The fertile soil and mild climate supported five cities: Mytilene (overshadowing but never completely dominating her neighbours), Methymna, Eresus, Antissa, and Pyrrha. The Aeolian immigrants, who formed the chief element in the population, turned to the sea, as well as to agriculture, for a livelihood, as their secondary colonization and their participation in founding the Hellenium at Naucratis show. This widening of horizons must have helped to stimulate the intense intellectual and cultural life among the aristocratic classes during the Golden Age of the late seventh and early sixth centuries B.C., represented by the poets Arion, Sappho, and Alcaeus, and the statesman Pittacus. Lesbos later had a distinguished philosophical tradition: Theophrastus came from Eresus, and in the fourth century Aristotle and Epicurus, in the first century Cratippus, resided for a time on the island.

Longus, *Daphnis and Chloe* (a vivid picture of life on Lesbos in the third century A.D.). L. Bürchner, *PW*, s.v. 'Lesbos'. D. E. W. W.

LESCHES of Mytilene (?7th c. B.C.), epic poet, to whom the *Ilias Parva* is almost universally attributed. *See* AGON HOMERI ET HESIODI *and* EPIC CYCLE.

EGF, pp. 3, 36–48.

LETO (Λητώ, Lat. **LATONA**), a Titaness, daughter of Coeus and Phoebe, 'gentle to men and to the deathless gods' (Hesiod, *Theog.* 404 ff.). She is one of the few Titans who have a cult in historical times, although generally it is together with her children (see Sauer in Roscher's *Lexikon* ii. 1966 ff.), and some of her temples had pious legends connected with them, see Semos of Delos in Athenaeus, 614 a (the Letoön on Delos), Nicander in Ant. Lib. 17, cf. LEUCIPPUS (the Letoön at Phaestus). The etymology of her name is quite obscure, though Wilamowitz-Moellendorff (cf. APOLLO) would connect it with Lycian *lada*, 'woman' (*Apollo* (Oxford, 1908), p. 31). It is almost certainly not Greek. (For her cult in Lycia, cf. W. H. Buckler, *JHS* lv (1935), 78; in Phrygia, L. Robert, *Villes d'Asie mineure* (1935), 128.) But her chief importance is as mother of Apollo and Artemis (qq.v.). Homer (*Il.* 24. 605 ff.) and Hesiod (*Theog.* 918–20) merely say she bore them and give no details; we may conjecture that many famous shrines of one or both deities claimed to be the birthplace, but for some reason, perhaps not unconnected with the great 'Homeric' hymn to the Delian Apollo, Delos imposed its claims on nearly the whole Greek world, other legends, as those of Tegyra in Boeotia (Plutarch, *Pelopidas*, 16), Zoster in Attica (Semos in Steph. Byz. p. 611, 5 Meineke, cf. Paus. 1. 31. 1), and even Delphi (Naevius in Macrob. *Sat.* 6. 5. 8), fading into obscurity.

According to the Hymn Leto was delivered of Apollo (but not Artemis, 16) 'leaning against Cynthus' mountain' in Delos (26; her gigantic size needed this huge prop), for none of the other islands dared to let so terrible a god be born in it, and even Delos was afraid till reassured by an oath of Leto (83 ff.) that Apollo would make his temple there. But Leto was in labour nine days and nights, because Hera would not let Eileithyia go to her (97 ff.) till the other goddesses sent her word and promised her a great fee; she then came without Hera's knowledge or consent and Leto was delivered. Callimachus in his fourth Hymn follows a somewhat different account; Hera forbade any land to afford Leto refuge and set Ares and Iris to see that they did not, but at last Delos ventured to disobey (202 f.), and was forgiven because she was once the nymph Asteria (q.v.). A later story (Hyginus, *Fab.* 160, 3) makes Poseidon overreach Hera; the waves were washing over Delos, therefore it was not land.

A curious legend is preserved by Aristotle (*Hist. An.*, 580ª15 ff.). Leto, as mother of the 'wolf-god' (cf.

APOLLO), took the form of a she-wolf to deceive Hera, and so journeyed from the Hyperborean country to Delos in twelve days. Therefore there are but twelve days of the year in which she-wolves bring forth.

Besides the literature cited in the text see the art. 'Leto' in *PW* and the handbooks of mythology.   H. J. R.

LETTERS (Greek). We may distinguish four kinds of letter:

(1) Purely personal communications, almost exclusively represented by papyri. These are valuable as evidence both of the language commonly spoken and written in Hellenistic and later ages and of contemporary social and economic conditions.

(2) Letters written by, or attributed to, persons of note, statesmen, orators, philosophers, etc., which have survived because they possessed an interest not confined to their actual addressees. Few are even doubtfully genuine. The spurious letters are sometimes real forgeries; more often they are school exercises or inventions intended to illustrate the characters of famous men. The deliberate forgeries belong mostly to the last two centuries B.C., and may have been partly due, as Galen asserts of literary forgeries in general, to the eagerness of the Attalids and Ptolemies to acquire, and pay for, additions to their libraries. The second sort is chiefly the product of the age 100 B.C.–A.D. 200; amongst the oldest are those of Anacharsis (which imposed on Cicero), Hippocrates, and Diogenes the Cynic. The famous letters of Phalaris, exposed by Bentley, may be as late as fifth century A.D.

The most important surviving collections are those of Isocrates, Plato, and Demosthenes: some at least of these—in the case of Plato the majority—have strong claims to authenticity. Many of them are 'open' letters: this is probably true of all Isocrates' letters (in v he speaks explicitly of 'readers', though the actual addressee is Alexander); the largest and most important of Plato's (vii and viii), sent to the friends of Dion, are in the main a defence *urbi et orbi* of his participation in Syracusan politics; on the other hand, vi and xiii are real private letters of first-rate interest. Of the six letters of Demosthenes all except v belong to his exile (324–323 B.C.); the two longest (ii and iii) have the best claim to authenticity. Each letter in such collections must be judged separately, for a genuine nucleus may attract spurious accretions.

The practice of collecting letters is specially characteristic of the philosophical schools; those of Aristotle were much admired in antiquity, but they cannot have included the six printed in Hercher. We know also of collections by Theophrastus, Epicurus, Arcesilaus, and Carneades. Of genuine letters in later antiquity the most important are those of Julian and Libanius.

(3) The letter as a medium of philosophic or scientific exposition, or of literary criticism: e.g. the three long letters of Epicurus, and the three 'literary' letters of Dionysius of Halicarnassus. The practice may have originated in the schools of philosophy, when the head wished to instruct absent pupils. The long 'hortatory' letters of Isocrates (*Or.* 2 and 3) belong, at least from one point of view, to this type. Writers adopting this form for scientific exposition include Archimedes and Eratosthenes.

(4) 'Imaginative' letters, designed to entertain readers by recreating the lives and manners of real or imaginary persons of a bygone age. The master of this style is Alciphron (end of 2nd c. A.D.); it owes much to the New Comedy, and is the germ of the historical novel, and of such works as Richardson's *Pamela* and *Clarissa*.

R. Bentley, *A Dissertation upon the Epistles of Phalaris* (1699); F. Blass, *Die Attische Beredsamkeit*[2] (1887–98), pt. iii, 439–55 (Demosthenes); J. Harward, *The Platonic Epistles* (1932); R. Hercher, *Epistolographi Graeci* (1873; new edition in preparation by J. Sykutris); R. C. Jebb, *The Attic Orators*[2] (1893), ii. 239–58 (Isocrates); F. Novotny, *Platonis Epistulae* (1930); K. Münscher, 'Isokrates' in *PW*; Valentin Rose, *Aristotelis Fragmenta* (Teubner, 1886), 411–21; J. Sykutris, 'Epistolographie' and 'Sokratikerbriefe' in *PW*; *Die Briefe des Sokrates und der Sokratiker* (1933); F. Susemihl, *Gesch. griech. Litt. Alex.* (1892), ii. 579–601; V. Weichert, Introd. to Demetrius Τύποι ἐπιστολικοί (Teubner, 1910); U. von Wilamowitz-Moellendorff, *Unechte Briefe* in *Hermes* xxxiii (1898), 495 ff.   R. H.

LETTERS (Latin). Letter-writing was, next to Satire, Rome's most distinctive legacy to the world's literature. In the self-contained communities of independent Greece there was comparatively little need or scope for correspondence; but as Rome became the hub of the Mediterranean world written communication gained in importance. Landowners visiting their estates in Italy, senators on military or administrative service in the provinces, merchants and tax-farmers, students and exiles, all needed to be kept in touch with the capital, and every traveller went laden with letters he had been asked to deliver, often in return for letters of introduction to influential persons (*epistulae commendaticiae*), such as are found among Cicero's extant correspondence (*Fam.* 13). Men of wealth and position in Cicero's time had among their slaves couriers (*tabellarii*) who could cover fifty Roman miles a day, and the companies of tax-farmers had their own postal service (*publicanorum tabellarii*). Later Augustus, in order to maintain close contact with his provincial governors, instituted a system of post-couriers along the main routes of the Empire, but there was still no organized postal system for private correspondence.

2. Letters were normally written with a reed pen (*calamus*) and ink (*atramentum*) on papyrus (*charta*). Pages were pasted together, as in the case of books, to form a roll which was tied with thread and sealed. Notes written off-hand to persons at no great distance were sometimes scratched with a *stilus* on wax-covered folding tablets (*codicilli*); the recipient could erase the message and use the same tablets for his reply (Cic. *Fam.* 6. 18. 1; Plin. *Ep.* 6. 16. 8). To Atticus, his most intimate friend, Cicero generally wrote in his own hand ('suo chirographo') unless for some special reason (*Att.* 2. 23. 1, 8. 13. 1); but it was usual for persons of rank to employ an amanuensis (*librarius* or *servus ab epistulis*). Cicero's secretary, Tiro, appears to have kept copies of letters dictated to him (*Fam.* 7. 25. 1), and to have pasted together in rolls (*volumina*) those which Cicero thought best worth keeping. It is no doubt to this practice that we owe the preservation of Cicero's *Epistulae ad Familiares*, though his intention, expressed in 44 B.C. (*Att.* 16. 5. 5), of revising and publishing a selection of letters remained unfulfilled. His letters to Atticus and to his brother Quintus were preserved by their recipients, and the former probably remained unpublished for a century after his death (see CICERO).

3. Cicero himself (*Fam.* 2. 4) classified letters under three heads, news-letter, 'genus familiare et iocosum', and 'genus seuerum et graue'. To the first of these categories belong his letters to Atticus, which, more than any other document of antiquity, show history in the making, and discuss with absolute frankness all that is in the writer's mind; also the vivid and somewhat cynical letters of M. Caelius Rufus, seventeen of which are preserved (*Fam.* 8). The second type is well represented by Cicero's letters to C. Trebatius Testa, M. Fadius Gallus, and L. Papirius Paetus (*Fam.* 7. 6–27, 9. 15–26); the third perhaps best of all by the letter of condolence addressed to Cicero, on the death of his daughter Tullia, by Sulpicius Rufus (*Fam.* 4. 5). This last, together with such letters as those in which Cicero asks the historian Lucceius to immortalize his consulship (*Fam.* 5. 12), or expresses his distaste for the *Ludi* exhibited by Pompey in 55 B.C. (*Fam.* 7. 1), may be taken as representing the type of letter which was to serve as a model for the younger Pliny. Close on a hundred letters from other correspondents are preserved along with Cicero's; of these

perhaps the most distinctive in character and style are those of Q. Metellus Celer (*Fam.* 5. 1), M. Cato (*Fam.* 15. 5), M. Antonius (*Att.* 10. 8 a), P. Vatinius (*Fam.* 5. 9–10), C. Asinius Pollio (*Fam.* 10. 31–3), and C. Matius (*Fam.* 11. 28), and the letter in which Cicero's son, writing to Tiro, gives a glimpse of student life at Athens (*Fam.* 16. 21).

4. The correspondence of Augustus was extant in the time of Suetonius (*Aug.* 71, 76; *Claud.* 4, etc.), and Macrobius (*Sat.* 1. 24. 11) quotes a letter of Virgil. But the Augustan age has left us only the verse epistles of Horace and Ovid, and from the Claudian and Flavian dynasties we possess only the *Epistulae Morales* of the younger Seneca (q.v.). With these authors the epistolary form is a mere literary convention, and although Seneca was undoubtedly influenced by the recently published *Epistulae ad Atticum*, his letters to Lucilius are essentially the ramblings of a philosopher; their ancestry should be sought rather in the epistles of Epicurus.

5. That life under the Empire afforded neither the material nor the freedom of expression for letter-writing in the true Ciceronian tradition is evident even when we come to the second great collection of Latin letters, published under the liberal rule of Trajan. The letters of Pliny the Younger (q.v.) resemble Cicero's in that they cover a wide range of topics and reflect the life, interests, and personality of their author; but they do so deliberately and selectively. Their writing belongs, not to the urgent business of living, but to the tranquil detachment of literature. The tenth book, consisting of letters exchanged between a responsible official and his emperor, stands alone as representing the practical side of Pliny's activities. Certain of Statius' *Silvae* are poetical epistles.

6. The correspondence of Fronto (q.v.) with Marcus Aurelius and others owes nothing to the literary tradition of Seneca or Pliny. Much of its subject-matter is purely academic, but the affectionate exchanges of gossip between master and pupil have something of the unselfconscious intimacy of Cicero's letters to Atticus, and their style and diction, quaintly compounded of colloquialism and pedantry, add both to their interest and to their charm.

7. The literary epistle reappears in the fourth century with Symmachus, last of the pagan prose-writers, and Ausonius, first of the Christian poets, some of whose *Epistles* are in prose. In a long list of letter-writers extending through the two following centuries the outstanding names are those of Ambrose, Jerome, Paulinus of Nola, Augustine, Sidonius Apollinaris, and Cassiodorus.

Cf. H. Peter, *Der Brief in d. röm. Lit.* (1901). R. G. C. L.

LEUCAS, an island of the Ionian Sea, opposite the coast of Acarnania. It derived its name from the white limestone cliffs on its west coast. Its south-west promontory, C. Leucatas, has a sheer drop of 2,000 ft.; suspected criminals were hurled from it, and if they survived the ordeal were rescued in boats (Strabo 10. 452). The shallow waters between its north-east coast and the mainland were liable to be closed to navigation by the formation of a sand-bar. The early Corinthian colonists cut through this spit (Strabo, ibid.), but in the fifth century ships had to be hauled across it (Thuc. 3. 81, 4. 8). Leucas was occupied by Corinthian settlers under the tyrant Cypselus. In the Persian Wars it furnished contingents to the Greek fleet at Salamis and to the army at Plataea, and it gave active assistance to Corinth in the Peloponnesian War. After a brief alliance with Athens against Philip of Macedon it passed into the hands of various Hellenistic rulers (Cassander, Agathocles, Pyrrhus), but c. 250 it joined the Acarnanian League, of which it became the capital. The Romans besieged and captured it in 197; in 167 they detached it from Acarnania and constituted it a free city.

Bürchner and 'Maull, *PW*, s.v. Leukas'. M. C.

LEUCE COME (Λευκὴ Κώμη, 'White Village'), on the Red Sea, probably *Sherm Wehj*, possibly *El Haura*. Nabataean Arabs here received in small ships Eastern wares for Petra and the West. A due (25 per cent.; *Peripl. M. Rubr.* 19) was levied there (perhaps under Roman control: in 25 B.C. Aelius Gallus, on an expedition to S. Arabia, landed there). It seems to have declined after Nabataea became a Roman province (A.D. 106). It may be Ptolemy's *Aὔαρα*.

Strabo, 16. 780–1; *Peripl. M. Rubr.* 19; Plut. *Ant.* 51; Cosmas 2. 143; Warmington, *Indian Commerce*, 16, 334–5. E. H. W.

LEUCIPPUS, 'person who keeps white horses', hence 'rich man, noble'. Name of fifteen mythological characters, see Stoll in Roscher's *Lexikon*, s.v., but especially (1) father of Hilaeira and Phoebe, cf. DIOSCURI; (2) a young Cretan, turned from a girl into a boy by a miracle of Leto (Anton. Lib. 17).

LEUCIPPUS (3) (*fl. c.* 440 B.C.), originator and joint author with Democritus (q.v.) of the Atomic theory, a native of Miletus (not Elea or Abdera, as suggested ap. Diog. Laert. 9. 30). He may have visited Elea after 450: he is associated with Parmenides in philosophy in spite of their views appearing to be directly opposed (Theophrastus ap. Simpl. *in Phys.* 28. 4), and he 'heard' Zeno (D.L. ibid.). There is no evidence that he visited Abdera or settled there. His existence was denied by Epicurus (ap. D.L. 10. 13), but the authority of Aristotle, who mentions him repeatedly, should dispose of any doubts.

WORKS. Two in the Democritean *corpus* are attributed to him: (1) *The Great World System* (Μέγας διάκοσμος); (2) *On Mind* (Περὶ νοῦ). From (2) comes the sole fragment (quoted by Aëtius): 'Naught happens for nothing, but all things from a ground and of necessity.'

For the Atomic theory *see* DEMOCRITUS. The main outlines are due to L., the detailed working out to Democritus. Attempts by Diels, Dyroff, Burnet, and Bailey to separate their respective contributions reveal few major differences. Aristotle suggested the metaphysical derivation of Atomism from Eleaticism (see *Gen. Corr.* 324[b] 35 f. and cf. *Phys.* 187[a]1 f.), convincingly demonstrated by Burnet (*EGP*[4] 333 f.). L.'s atoms, apart from their infinity and mobility, have the other characteristics of Parmenides' One Being. Diogenes Laertius (9. 31 f.) preserves an interesting account of L.'s cosmology, the formation of a 'world' from an initial vortex (δίνη), an occurrence repeated innumerable times throughout infinite space. In other respects L. is a reactionary, and follows Anaximander's tradition of a drum-shaped earth.

Leucippus' importance in the history of thought is immense. This Milesian gave the final Greek answer to Thales, and by pure speculation anticipated modern theories of matter.

1. Ancient sources: Diels, *Vorsokr.*[5] (Kranz, 1934–7); Ritter and Preller[10] (1934). 2. Modern Literature. (i) General: Zeller-Nestle, *Philosophie der Griechen* i. 2[7] (1922) (Engl. Transl. 1881); Th. Gomperz, *Greek Thinkers* i (1901); J. Burnet, *Early Greek Philosophy*[4] (1930) and *Greek Philosophy, Part* i. *Thales to Plato* (1914); L. Robin, *La Pensée grecque*[2] (1932); H. Cherniss, *Aristotle's Criticism of Pre-Socratic Philosophy* (U.S.A., 1935). (ii) Special: A. Dyroff, *Demokritstudien* (1899); C. Bailey, *The Greek Atomists and Epicurus* (1928); A. Brieger, *Die Urbewegung der Atome und die Weltentstehung bei Leucipp und Demokrit* (1884); H. C. Liepmann, *Die Mechanik der Leucipp-Democritischen Atome* (1885); O. Hamelin, *La Pesanteur de l'atome dans le système de Démocrite* (1888); L. Mabilleau, *Histoire de la philosophie atomistique* (1895). *PW* xii. 2266. A. J. D. P.

LEUCON, writer of Old Comedy who lived during the Peloponnesian War (Suid.). In his Φράτερες he attacked Hyperbolus (fr. 1)—probably as a βάρβαρος who had no clansmen (φράτερες).

FCG ii. 749–50; *CAF* i. 703–4.

LEUCOS LIMEN (Λευκὸς Λιμήν, 'White Haven'), *Kosseir*, Egyptian port on the Red Sea, was connected with Coptus on the Nile by a track with stations and intervisible beacons, but was less important in Oriental trade than Berenice and Myos Hormos (qq.v.).

LEUCOTHEA (probably 'white goddess', perhaps 'runner on the white [foam]'), a sea-goddess identified early (*Od.* 5. 333–5) with Ino daughter of Cadmus, for reasons unknown. For her story *see* ATHAMAS. It is an old suggestion (see Farnell, *Cults* ii. 637) that she has Semitic connexions (through the 'Phoenician' Cadmus) and her son Melicertes is Melqart; but this is unproved and unnecessary, for his name may be Greek, 'Honey-cutter', i.e. a minor deity of bee-keeping. He is also called, or identified with, Palaemon ('the Wrestler'), again for uncertain reasons. Children are said to have been sacrified to him (schol. Lycoph. 229).

Eitrem in *PW*, s.v.; L. R. Farnell, *JHS* 36 (1916), 36 ff.   H. J. R.

LEX (1), (cf. *ligare*, to bind) signifies an agreement binding on the contracting parties. *Lex privata* means a contract signed by private individuals. *Lex publica* is an agreement between two parties of whom at least one is invested with magisterial authority and represents the State. Two types of *lex publica* must be distinguished according to the procedure followed and the authority enacting the law: a *lex rogata* results from the co-operation of the magistrate and the people, a *lex data* proceeds from the unilateral action of the magistrate. The *leges regiae*, of which the extant fragments are in all likelihood forgeries of the Republican age, were probably *leges datae*, but the laws of the early Republic were indisputably *leges rogatae*, despite the small share of the lower classes in legislation. *Plebiscita*, too, were formally *leges rogatae*, since they were passed in assemblies summoned and presided over by a plebeian magistrate, although in practice they could hardly be regarded as laws until the right of the plebeians to legislate for the whole community was recognized. After the *Lex Hortensia* (c. 287 B.C.) (*see* HORTENSIUS 1) the terms *lex* and *plebiscitum* were used indiscriminately. The *lex rogata* was divided into four categories: (1) a *lex perfecta* invalidated an act prohibited by the terms of the law itself; (2) a *lex minus quam perfecta* penalized any person performing an act which the law forbade, but did not invalidate; (3) a *lex plus quam perfecta* both invalidated an act which it prohibited and penalized the offender; (4) a *lex imperfecta* neither invalidated an act which it prohibited nor punished the offender.

2. In order to be valid a *lex rogata* had to pass through three stages: (1) *legislatio* or public announcement by a magistrate of the draft of the *lex* (*promulgatio*), and the summoning by him of an assembly to debate it at a date not earlier than a *trinundinum* (q.v.) after the *promulgatio*; (2) *rogatio*, or the polling in the assembly, where debate, not amendment, was allowed; (3) *publicatio*, or the publication of the Bill in due form and time. Copies of laws enacted had to be kept in the *aerarium* (q.v.), engraved on wooden, and later bronze, tablets. Any enactment could be legally abrogated by subsequent legislation.

3. A *lex data* was issued by a Roman magistrate, and depended on his authority only, provided that senatorial approval was previously secured. It generally concerned either aliens (individuals and communities), or statutes issued by the Roman Republic, which the new law was intended to amend. In Republican times *leges datae* were mainly concerned with provincial administration and municipal statutes. They were issued by magistrates *cum imperio*, appointed to organize a province, or to reform its administration (*see* PROVINCIA), or as municipal statutes granted (also by a magistrate *cum imperio*) to cities both inside and outside Italy.

4. Laws conferring unlimited power upon dictators (e.g. on Sulla and Caesar) or on triumvirs *rei publicae constituendae*, were also *leges datae*, as the reformers thus appointed could legislate without the people's co-operation or approval. Moreover, they were exempted from the obligations and restrictions of ordinary legislation. These exceptional legislative measures therefore mark an intermediary stage between Republican and Imperial legislation. The theory and practice of the Hellenistic monarchies, and the political philosophy of Cicero and his age, tended to make belief in leaders and emperors as the living source of law widespread. Consequently the emperors were regarded as *legibus soluti* and as alone competent to give laws to their subjects. From Tiberius onwards the comitia were no longer summoned for legislation, and the distinction between *lex data* and *lex rogata* thus ended. The imperial constitutions finally covered all the field originally covered by the *leges datae* (grants of citizenship, municipal statutes, founding of new cities, enfranchisement of slaves, etc.).

5. *Lex* also indicated a contract between the State and a private individual (e.g. a middleman) to whom the State leased the exploitation of public land (e.g. a mine, estate), or the collection of the provincial taxes, etc. Similarly the regulations affecting a locality, or building, reputed to be holy (e.g. a wood, common, temple, altar) were termed *leges*.

Mommsen, *Röm. Staatsr.* iii². 308 ff.; É. Cuq, in Dar.-Sag. iii. 1107 ff.; E. Weiss, *PW*, s.v.   P. T

LEX (2), **LEGES.** Individual Roman laws are generally treated in this work under the name of the magistrate who introduced them. The following list contains cross-references and occasional explanation. For a detailed list and discussion see G. Rotondi, *Leges publicae populi Romani* (1912).

ACILIA
 (1) *de intercalendo* (191 B.C.), *see* GLABRIO (1).
 (2) *de repetundis* (123 B.C.), *see* GLABRIO (2).
 (3) (*Acilia*) *Calpurnia de ambitu* (67 B.C.) imposed perpetual incapacity to hold office as a penalty for electoral corruption.

AEBUTIA
 (1) *de magistratibus extraordinariis* (? 154 B.C.) prohibited the election to an extraordinary magistracy of the man who had proposed its institution.
 (2) *de formulis* (*de legis actionibus*), *see* LAW AND PROCEDURE, ROMAN, I. 4; II. 4.

AELIA
 (1) *Aelia et Fufia* (c. 150 B.C.), two separate but similar laws of uncertain content. They regulated the use of auspices by magistrates and probably established the right of magistrates and tribunes to obstruct the holding of assemblies through the announcement of unfavourable auspices (*obnuntiatio*). They probably forbade the holding of legislative assemblies in the interval between the announcement of consular elections and the elections themselves. See W. F. McDonald, *JRS* 1929, 164 ff.; S. Weinstock, *JRS* 1937, 215 ff.
 (2) *Aelia Sentia* (A.D. 4) regulated the manumission of slaves and completed the work begun by the *Lex Fufia Caninia*. Cf. *CAH* x. 433–4. *See* SLAVERY, LAW OF.

AEMILIA of M. Aemilius Scaurus (consul 115 B.C.), of uncertain content, which concerned the distribution of freedmen among the tribes.

ANTONIA
 (1) *de Termessibus* of a tribune C. Antonius and his colleagues (? 71 B.C.; cf. *CAH* ix. 896) concluded an alliance between Rome and the Pisidian city of Termessus. Dessau, *ILS* 38.
 (2) *leges Antoniae*, a variety of measures passed by the triumvir M. Antonius (q.v. 4), included laws to abolish dictatorship, to readjust provincial commands (*de permutatione provinciarum*), to confirm Caesar's *acta*, and to grant *provocatio* to those convicted *de maiestate* and *de vi*.

APPULEIA: various *leges* of Saturninus (q.v. 1) in 103 and 100 B.C.

AQUILIA, *de damno*, see LAW AND PROCEDURE, ROMAN, I. 4; III. 6.

ATERNIA-TARPEIA (454 B.C.) fixed the maximum fine which magistrates could impose (Gell. 11. 1).

ATINIA, *de tribunis plebis in senatum legendis* (before 102 B.C.) (Gell. 14. 8. 2).

AURELIA
(1) *de tribunicia potestate* (75 B.C.), see COTTA (1).
(2) *iudiciaria* (70 B.C.), see COTTA (3).

BAEBIA, *de praetoribus* (? 181 B.C.), enacted that four and six praetors should be elected in alternate years (Livy 40. 44. 2); it was not long observed. Cf. De Sanctis, *Stor. Rom.* iv. 504 ff.

CAECILIA DIDIA (98 B.C.), see DIDIUS (1) *and* COMITIA.

CAELIA, *tabellaria* (107 B.C.), of the tribune C. Caelius Caldus, extended vote by ballot to cases of *perduellio* which had been excepted in the *Lex Cassia*.

CALPURNIA
(1) *de repetundis* (149 B.C.) established a permanent court to try cases of extortion. Cf. W. G. Ferguson, *JRS* 1921, 86. See REPETUNDAE *and* PISO (1).
(2) *de civitate sociorum* (89 B.C.), of uncertain content, perhaps empowered generals to grant citizenship for distinguished military service. (Sisenna, frs. 17, 120 Peter).
(3) *de ambitu*, see LEX ACILIA, no. 3, above.

CANULEIA, *de conubio patrum et plebis* (445 B.C.). See CANULEIUS.

CASSIA
(1) *tabellaria* (137 B.C.), of the tribune L. Cassius Longinus, introduced vote by ballot in the *iudicia populi*, except in cases of *perduellio*. See VOTING *and cf.* LEX CAELIA above.
(2) *de plebeis in patricios adlegendis* (45 B.C.) empowered Caesar to create patricians (Tac. *Ann.* 11. 25). *See* PATRICIUS.

CINCIA, *de donis et muneribus* (204 B.C.), of the tribune M. Cincius Alimentus, forbade gifts which might defeat justice and certain donations above a given amount. *See* ADVOCATUS, PATRONUS.

CLAUDIA, *de nave senatorum* (218 B.C.). See CLAUDIUS (7).

CLODIAE: various *plebiscita* proposed by P. Clodius (q.v. 1), tribune in 58 B.C.

CORNELIAE
(1) Various *leges* passed by Sulla (q.v.). *See also* LAW AND PROCEDURE, ROMAN, III. 3.
(2) Laws of Cinna (q.v. 1), consul in 87 B.C., including the distribution of the new citizens in the thirty-five tribes.
(3) *Cornelia Pompeia de comitiis centuriatis et de tribunicia potestate* (88 B.C.). App. *BCiv.* I. 59; Livy, *Epit.* 77.

DOMITIA, *de sacerdotiis* (104 B.C.), of the tribune Cn. Domitius Ahenobarbus, virtually abolished co-optation for the priestly colleges and substituted election by seventeen tribes. It was abrogated by Sulla, but renewed by a *lex* of Labienus in 63 B.C.

FANNIA, *sumptuaria* (161 B.C.), limited the sums to be spent on entertainments.

FLAMINIA, *agraria*. See FLAMINIUS.

FUFIA CANINIA, *de manumissione* (2 B.C.), limited the number of slaves a master might liberate by will. Cf. *CAH* x. 432. *See* SLAVERY, LAW OF. *See also* LEX AELIA (2) above.

GABINIA
(1) *tabellaria* (139 B.C.) introduced ballot in the election of magistrates.
(2) Various *leges Gabiniae* (67 B.C.) of the tribune Gabinius (q.v. 2), which included the establishment of a command against the pirates (for Pompey), the forbidding of the lending of money to provincials in Rome, and *de senatu legatis dando*, which fixed February as the month of audience for foreign *legati* to the Senate.

GENUCIAE, *see* GENUCIUS.

HIERONICA was not strictly a *lex*. *See* HIERON II.

HIRTIA (? 46 B.C.) gave Caesar the right of making peace and war.

HORTENSIA, *see* HORTENSIUS (1).

ICILIA, *see* ICILIUS.

DE IMPERIO VESPASIANI is the name given to the content of a bronze inscription (*ILS* 244) of which only the end survives. It is part of an enactment which conferred powers on Vespasian. Although the phrasing suggests a *senatus consultum*, it is, however, a *lex rogata*; the People who passed it into law allowed the formulation of the preliminary *S.C.* to stand. The surviving fragment enumerates specific privileges. The problem is to deduce what the missing part contained, whether it conferred on Vespasian (*a*) *imperium*, i.e. is a *lex de imperio* (Ulpian records that Vespasian received his *imperium* by a *lex regia*), (*b*) *tribunicia potestas* (this is unlikely), (*c*) all his powers (the jurists of the second and third centuries conceived that all imperial power had been bestowed on Augustus by a single enactment), or (*d*) 'a consolidated grant of miscellaneous rights additional to those which formed the main basis of the imperial position', i.e. the right to do what Vespasian's predecessors had done by virtue of either special enactment or their own *auctoritas* (so H. Last, *CAH* xi. 404 ff.).

IULIAE. It is doubtful whether certain *leges Iuliae* were enacted by Caesar or by Augustus.
(1) *de civitate Latinis et sociis danda* (90 B.C.), see CAESAR (2).
(2) *Leges* of Julius Caesar (q.v.) in 59 B.C. (*agraria, de publicanis Asiae, de actis Pompeii, de Ptolemaeo Aulete, de pecuniis repetundis* (cf. *PW* xii. 2389), *de provinciis*), and in 49–44 B.C. measures which included *de pecuniis mutuis* (to relieve debtors); *de civitate Transpadanis danda; frumentaria* (reducing the number of recipients of free corn); *de collegiis* (see CLUBS, ROMAN); *iudiciaria* (see TRIBUNI AERARII); *sumptuaria; de maiestate* (see MAIESTAS); *de re pecuaria* (that at least one third of Italian herdsmen should be freemen); *de provinciis* (limiting provincial promagistracies to one year for ex-praetors, to two years for ex-consuls); *Lex Iulia municipalis* (so-called; it was a collection of various statutes, drafted by Caesar and later incorporated in one general bill and carried by Antony. Cf. E. G. Hardy, *Roman Laws and Charters* i. 136 ff.).
(3) *Leges* of Augustus included *de maiestate* (see MAIESTAS *and* PERDUELLIO); *de vi; de ambitu* (18 B.C.; excluding from office for five years men convicted of bribery; *see also* LAW AND PROCEDURE, ROMAN, III. 3); *de adulteriis coercendis* (18 B.C.; cf. *CAH* x. 443 ff.; *see* ADULTERY); *de maritandis ordinibus* (18 B.C.; cf. *CAH* x. 448 ff.; *see* MARRIAGE); *de senatu; de vicesima hereditatum* (A.D. 6; levied a 5 per cent. tax on legacies which was paid into the *aerarium militare*); *de magistratibus* (12 B.C.); *de collegiis* (see CLUBS, ROMAN); *de tutela; de iudiciis*

privatis (see LAW AND PROCEDURE, ROMAN, II. 4); *de iudiciis publicis* (A.D. 7; see QUAESTIO).

(4) *Iulia Papiria* (430 B.C.) is said to have introduced payment for fines in bronze instead of in sheep or oxen. See COINAGE (ROMAN), para. 1.

IUNIA

(1) *de peregrinis* (126 B.C.) of the tribune M. Junius Pennus, expelling from Rome all non-citizens.
(2) *de manumissione* (? 17 B.C.), see LATINI IUNIANI, SLAVERY (LAW OF).
(3) *Iunia Licinia* (62 B.C.) ordered the deposition in the Aerarium of a copy of promulgated laws.

LICINIA

(1) *rogatio Licinia agraria* (c. 145 B.C.) proposed some land settlement.
(2) *Licinia Mucia* (95 B.C.), proposed by L. Licinius Crassus and Q. Mucius Scaevola, expelled Latins from Rome. See CRASSUS (3).
(3) *Liciniae Pompeiae*, two measures passed by Crassus and Pompey: (*a*) *de tribunicia potestate* (70 B.C.), which restored full competence to the tribunate, and (*b*) *de provincia Caesaris* (55 B.C.), which prolonged Caesar's Gallic command for five more years (until ? 13 Nov. 50 or 1 March 49).
(4) *Liciniae Sextiae* (367 B.C.), see STOLO.

LIVIAE, see DRUSUS (1) and (2).

MAENIA, *de patrum auctoritate* (q.v.).

MAMILIA

(1) *de coniuratione Iugurthina* (110 B.C.) established a court of inquiry. See MAMILIUS (3).
(2) *Mamilia Roscia Peducaea Alliena Fabia* (Bruns, *Fontes*[7], 15) perhaps belongs to Caesar's land legislation of 59 B.C. or is more probably a later supplement to it (55 B.C.). Cf. M. Cary, *JRS* 1929, 113 ff. It has also been assigned to the tribune Mamilius (109 B.C.).

MANILIA, see MANILIUS (2).

MINUCIA, *de liberis* (before 90 B.C.), established that sons of parents who had not *conubium* should take the status of the inferior parent.

MUNATIA AEMILIA (42 B.C.) authorized the Triumvirs to grant citizenship and exemption from taxes.

OCTAVIA, *frumentaria* (? c. 120 B.C.), modified the *Lex Sempronia frumentaria* by raising the prices.

OGULNIA, see OGULNIUS.

OPPIA, see OPPIUS (1).

ORCHIA, *sumptuaria* (181 B.C.), limited the number of guests at entertainments.

OVINIA, see OVINIUS.

PAPIA (64 B.C.) made all non-citizens liable to eviction from Rome.
Papia Poppaea (A.D. 9) completed the *Lex Iulia de maritandis ordinibus*.

PAPIRIA

(1) *tabellaria* (131 B.C.) carried by Carbo (q.v. 1), who also proposed a *rogatio de tribunis plebis reficiendis*.
(2) *semunciaria* (89 B.C.) of the tribune C. Papirius Carbo, made the *as* semiuncial.

PETRONIA, *de servis* (?A.D. 61), forbade masters arbitrarily to send their slaves to fight wild beasts.

PINARIA FURIA (472 B.C.) regulated the quadrennial period of intercalation.

PLAETORIA, *de circumscriptione adolescentium* (c. 193–192 B.C.), see GUARDIANSHIP.

PLAUTIA

(1) *de vi* (between 78 and 63 B.C.).
(2) *de reditu Lepidanorum*. For date see *CAH* ix. 896.
(3) *Plautia Papiria* (89 B.C.), see PLAUTIUS (1).

POETELIA, see POETELIUS.

POMPEIA

(1) *de Transpadanis* (89 B.C.). See STRABO (1).
(2) various *leges* of Pompeius Magnus, which included *de parricidio* (q.v.); *iudiciaria* (55 B.C.?; limiting the magistrate in the choice of *iudices*); *de vi* (52 B.C., simplifying the procedure and increasing the penalty of the *lex Plautia*); *de ambitu* (52); *de provinciis* (52, prescribing a five-year interval between a magistracy and a provincial command); *de iure magistratuum* (52, renewing the obligation for candidates to register in person). See also LEGES LICINIAE POMPEIAE, above.

PORCIAE, *de provocatione* or *de tergo civium*. Three laws— see J. Carcopino, *La Rép. romaine* ii. 144; A. H. McDonald, *JRS* 1944, 19.

(1) The tribune P. Porcius Laeca extended the right of *provocatio* in capital cases to Roman citizens in Italy and the provinces (199 B.C.).
(2) M. Porcius Cato, as praetor (198) or less probably as consul (195), prohibited the scourging of citizens without appeal.
(3) Military officers were deprived of the right of summary execution by the consul L. Porcius Licinus (184) or more probably later (c. 150–135).

PUBLILIAE, see PUBLILIUS (1) and (2) *and* PATRUM AUCTORITAS.

PUPIA, *de senatu diebus comitialibus non habendo*. See SENATUS, 1 *b*.

QUINCTIA: proposed by T. Quinctius Crispinus, consul 9 B.C., for the preservation of aqueducts (Bruns, *Fontes*[7], no. 22).

ROSCIA

(1) *theatralis* (67 B.C.), see ROSCIUS (2).
(2) *de civitate Transpadanorum* (49 B.C.) mentioned in *Tab. Atestina* (Bruns, *Fontes*[7], p. 101); its content is uncertain.

RUBRIA

(1) A bill of the tribune Rubrius in 122 or possibly 123 B.C. to found a colony at Carthage. An attempt to repeal it in 121 led to disorder and C. Gracchus' death; it was repealed soon afterwards.
(2) A partly extant law of uncertain date, which regulated jurisdiction in Cisalpine Gaul and may be supplementary to Caesar's Transpadane law. See E. G. Hardy, *Roman Laws and Charters* i. 110 ff.

RUPILIAE, *de iure Siculorum*, *de re frumentaria*, etc., were *leges datae* of the proconsul P. Rupilius, regulating the condition of Sicily in 131 B.C.

SAENIA, see PATRICIUS.

SCRIBONIAE, *rogationes* of Curio (q.v. 2), tribune 50 B.C.

SEMPRONIAE of Tiberius and Gaius Gracchus. See GRACCHUS (3) and (4).
Sempronia de pecunia credita (193 B.C.), of M. Sempronius Tuditanus, extended to *socii* and the *nomen Latinum* the laws about loans (Livy 35. 7).

SERVILIA

(1) *iudiciaria*, see CAEPIO (1).
(2) *de repetundis*, see GLAUCIA.
(3) *rogatio Servilia agraria*, see RULLUS.

SULPICIAE of Sulpicius Rufus 88 B.C. See RUFUS (1).

TERENTIA

(1) *de libertinorum liberis* (189 B.C.), *see* CULLEO.

(2) *Terentia Cassia frumentaria* (73 B.C.), *see* CASSIUS (4).

THORIA, *agraria*. Sp. Thorius was, according to Appian (*BCiv.* 1. 27), the author of a measure (of 119 B.C.; cf. Cic. *Brut.* 136) which (*a*) abolished the land commission established by the Gracchi, (*b*) granted perpetual tenancy to *possessores* of *ager publicus*, and (*c*) reimposed rent on this. More probably Thorius was the author of the agrarian law of 111 B.C. (Cic. *Brut.* 36, 136) which has been partially preserved on the back of a bronze tablet with the *Lex Acilia*; this laid down (*a*) that all public land dealt with by the Gracchan commissioners should become the private property of its occupants, (*b*) the abolition of rent, (*c*) all colonies and municipia were given security of tenure in *ager publicus* which had been granted to them, (*d*) the system of *possessio* was abolished, (*e*) lands in Africa and at Corinth were dealt with. Cf. *AJPhil.* 1935, 232.

TITIA, *de IIIviris reipublicae constituendae* (27 Nov. 43 B.C.), gave legal status to the Second Triumvirate.

TREBONIA, *de provinciis consularibus* (55 B.C.), *see* TREBONIUS.

TULLIAE of Cicero in his consulship (63 B.C.)

(1) *de ambitu* forbade anyone to exhibit a public show for two years before he was a candidate, and extended the penalty established by the *Lex Calpurnia* to ten years.

(2) *de legationibus liberis* limited the privilege of *libera legatio* to one year.

VALERIAE

(1) of Valerius Poplicola (509 B.C.), *see* VALERIUS (1).

(2) *Valeriae Horatiae* (449 B.C.), *see* VALERIUS (2).

(3) *de provocatione* (300 B.C.) of the consul M. Valerius Corvus. *See* PROVOCATIO.

(4) *de aere alieno* (86 B.C.), *see* VALERIUS (8).

VARIA, *de maiestate* (90 B.C.), instituted a *quaestio extraordinaria* against those who had aided the rebel allies.

VATINIAE of the tribune P. Vatinius (q.v.) in 59 B.C., including the conferring on Caesar of the Gallic command.

VIBIAE. The consul C. Vibius Pansa (42 B.C.) carried some *leges* (confirming Caesar's *acta*, founding colonies, and abolishing the dictatorship) to replace similar laws of Antony which had been abrogated.

VILLIA, *annalis* (180 B.C.), *see* VILLIUS.

VISELLIA (A.D. 24) granted full citizenship to Junian Latins who served in the *Vigiles* for six years and debarred all who were not *ingenui* from gaining municipal magistracies unless supported by the Princeps.

VOCONIA, *de mulierum hereditatibus* (169 B.C.). Cf. *PW* xii. 2418.   H. H. S.

LEX CURIATA DE IMPERIO (the term probably being a part of the official wording) was the measure by which the Comitia Curiata conferred *imperium* on magistrates who could not enter office unless and until their election was thus ratified (except censors, whose election was ratified by the Comitia Centuriata). The traditional view that in the regal period *imperium* was conferred upon the king by a *lex curiata de imperio* is probably, whether the Roman monarchy was hereditary or elective, an anticipation of Republican times. The *lex curiata* was carried soon after the election, e.g. not later than 1 March for magistrates appointed at the beginning of the year.

The Comitia Curiata, however, soon ceased to be summoned, and thirty lictors were chosen to act as representatives of the thirty tribes. With the introduction of proconsular and propraetorian *imperium* the *lex curiata* soon became a pure formality. Towards the end of the Republic it was often disregarded or suspended, and it ceased to be in force in the Imperial age.

Mommsen, *Röm. Staatsr.* i³. 609 ff.; W. Liebenam, *PW* iv. 1826 ff.; G. W. Botsford, *The Roman Assemblies* (1909), 188 ff.
                                                                 P. T.

LEXICA SEGUERIANA, so named from a former MS.-owner, or Bekkeriana, from the editor (*Anecd. Bekk.* i), are I, Phrynichus the Atticist (excerpts); II, Anonymus Antatticista; III, Περὶ συντάξεων; IV, Δικῶν ὀνόματα; V, Λέξεις ῥητορικαί; VI, Συναγωγὴ χρησίμων λέξεων. Of the last Bekker prints only *A*: Bachmann adopts this and edits the rest (*B*, etc.) in his *Anecd.* i.   P. B. R. F.

LIBATIONS, *see* WORSHIP (HOUSEHOLD), SACRIFICE.

LIBELLUS was a petition to the emperor by a party to a judicial suit at Rome. It was answered by a *subscriptio* appended to it, which the emperor himself signed (S.H.A. *Comm.* 13). The official who dealt with *libelli* was the *a libellis*, who was a personal secretary of the emperor. The post of *a libellis* no doubt existed from the time of Augustus, but it is prominent first under Claudius, when it was held at first, perhaps, by Polybius (Seneca, *Consolatio ad Polybium* 6. 5) and then by Callistus. It was in the hands of freedmen until the reign of Hadrian, after which its holders were *equites* (S.H.A. *Hadr.* 22). The jurists Papinian and Ulpian (qq.v.) held the post.
                                                                 J. P. B.

LIBER PATER, Italian god of fertility and especially of wine, commonly identified with Dionysus (q.v.). Concerning his origin and relation to Jupiter (I. Liber) divergent views have been held, see Wissowa, *RK*², p. 138; Altheim, *Hist. Rom. Rel.* 125, 149. But it is certain that he was an independent god when the festival calendar was completed, for it contains his feast, the Liberalia of 17 Mar. He had, however, no temple, or none of any importance, in Rome (see Platner–Ashby, pp. 316, 321). This may be explained by the fact that his feast would be chiefly rustic and have little to do with the city. According to Verg. *G.* 2. 385 ff. it was a merry occasion, and characterized by crude songs, doubtless traditional, and the use of masks, which apparently were hung on trees; they may have been intended to scare away evil influences.

Liber had, however, an important cult in Rome along with his partner Libera as associate of Ceres on the Aventine (cf. CERES); but we have too little information about the ritual there to say anything definite about the manner of his worship. It appears to have been Greek in origin, like everything about that temple.

By a sort of play on words (*Liber—liberi*) the Liberalia became a favourite day for boys to put on the *toga virilis* (Ov. *Fast.* 3. 771). It was a day of feasting (Wissowa, op. cit. 299), but the native and Greek elements are not easily dissociated.

He has no mythology of his own, simply taking over that of Dionysus.   H. J. R.

LIBERALIA, *see* LIBER PATER.

LIBERTAS, the personification of personal liberty, the condition of a free man. She was given a temple in or about 238 B.C. by Ti. Sempronius Gracchus, consul in that year, on the Aventine (Livy 24. 16. 19); it was restored by Augustus (*Mon. Ancyr.* 4, 6; 10, 11 of the Greek version). Here, as commonly, she was associated with Jupiter, like Liber (q.v.): (*aedem*) *Iouis Libertatis* (Augustus ibid., but cf. Platner–Ashby, p. 296 f.). How old her cult is we do not know, but certainly later than the 'calendar of Numa', which contains no mention of her. Under the Empire *libertas* comes to mean political liberty, not only in republican declamations, as Lucan 7. 432 ff., but in official language, to signify constitutional government, especially as opposed to usurpation or tyranny (see Wissowa, *RK* 139).   H. J. R.

LIBERTUS, *see* FREEDMEN.

LIBITINA, Roman goddess of burials, which were registered at her grove; Dion. Hal. *Ant. Rom.* 4. 15. 5, cf. Plutarch, *Quaest. Rom.* 23. Both identify her with Venus (q.v.), a mere confusion with Lubentina.

LIBO, *see* SCRIBONIUS.

LIBRA, *see* WEIGHING-INSTRUMENTS.

LIBRARIES. I. GREEK. In the article on *Books* it is noted that writing was probably available from the date of the composition of the Homeric poems downwards, but in these primitive ages books probably existed only for the use of rhapsodists, actors, singers, and the like. There is no trace of a reading public until about the end of the fifth century. Athenaeus (1. 4) names Polycrates of Samos and Pisistratus as traditional owners of collections of books. Euripides owned books (ibid.), and Socrates refers to the accessibility of books (Pl. *Ap.* 26 d, *Phd.* 97 b, 98 b; Xen. *Mem.* 1. 6. 14), but evidently reading and the ownership of books were far from common, and provided the basis of Aristophanic jests at 'highbrows' (Denniston, *CQ* xxi. 117). Aristotle is said (Strabo 13. 1. 54) to have been the first collector of books, and to have taught the kings of Egypt to set up libraries. In the fourth century Aristotle (*Rhet.* 1413^b 12) recognizes the existence of authors whose works were intended to be read (ἀναγνωστικοί) rather than recited, naming the dramatist Chaeremon and the lyric poet Licymnius. Beyond doubt the foundation of the Library at Alexandria marks an epoch in bibliographical history. It appears to have been founded, in connexion with the Museum, by Ptolemy I, under the direction of Demetrius of Phalerum, but greatly extended by Ptolemy II, whom some regarded as the real founder. It is variously said to have contained from 100,000 to 700,000 volumes (Aristeas, ed. Thackeray ap. Swete, *Introduction to the O.T. in Greek*, p. 520; also ed. P. Wendland (Teubner) and Meecham (1935); Tzetzes ap. Ritschl, *Opusc.* i. 8, *Die alexandrinische Bibliotheken*; Gell. 6. 17; Amm. Marc. 22. 16); but book-counting is notoriously an inexact science. At its head were placed a series of distinguished scholars, Zenodotus, Eratosthenes, Aristophanes of Byzantium, Aristarchus; Callimachus and Apollonius Rhodius worked there, but were apparently not chief librarians. It became the great centre of literature in the Hellenistic world, and the practice of its copyists was probably decisive in the forms of book-production. Classified catalogues (πίνακες) of its contents were drawn up under the direction of Callimachus, and no doubt continued by his successors. A second, smaller library was established at the Serapeum.

According to Plutarch (*Caes.* 49) the great library was burnt when Caesar was besieged in Alexandria. Dio Cassius (42. 38), however, says only that the 'storehouses of corn and books' were so destroyed. Later legend magnified this into the total destruction of the great Library, or of both libraries (Sen. *Tranq.* 9; Oros. 6. 15; Gell. 6. 17); but this is very improbable.

The chief rival of the Alexandrian Library was that of Pergamum, founded by Eumenes II (*see* BOOKS). This is said to have contained 200,000 volumes when Antony presented it to Cleopatra (Plut. *Ant.* 58). Perseus of Macedon had a library (Plut. *Aem.* 28); and no doubt there were also libraries in the other principal Hellenistic towns.

Of private libraries there is little mention. The discoveries of literary papyri in Egypt is proof of private collections of books; but no particulars are on record. A third-century papyrus from the Fayum contains a fragment of an inventory of a library, comprising 132 rolls of philosophy (100 opisthograph) and 296 of medicine (*Arch. Pap.* 11. 277). With the beginning of the Hellenistic age the habit of reading set in, and libraries, public and private, seem to have become common.

II. LATIN. At Rome, apart from archives of official documents, there is no trace of libraries before the first century B.C. Lucullus is recorded to have possessed a large library, which he made freely accessible, especially to Greeks (Plut. *Luc.* 42). Atticus and Cicero had considerable collections of books. Caesar commissioned Varro to assemble a library for him (Suet. *Iul.* 44), but the project was not consummated. The first public library in Rome was founded by C. Asinius Pollio (Plin. *HN* 7. 30; 35. 2); but the decisive impulse was given by Augustus, who founded two libraries, one (the Porticus Octaviae) in the Campus Martius, the other on the Palatine. Both were connected with temples and comprised separate Greek and Latin libraries and a hall or reading-room in which conversation was possible (Gell. 13. 19). This model was generally followed. Tiberius, Vespasian, and Trajan built libraries in Rome, and Hadrian at Athens, all in connexion with temples. Eventually there are said to have been twenty-six in Rome alone, and the gift of a library to a provincial town was a recognized form of public munificence. The younger Pliny gave one to Como (*Ep.* 1. 8. 2), and remains of libraries, also the result of private benefactions, have been found at Ephesus and Timgad.

Private libraries also became so fashionable that Seneca (*Tranq.* 9) declares that a library is considered as essential to a house as a bath, and that the idlest people fill their houses with books from mere ostentation. Suidas (s.v. 'Epaphroditus') mentions a private library of 30,000 volumes. A specimen of a private library was found in the excavation of Herculaneum in 1752. It was a room about 12ft. square, lined with bookcases ornamented with inlaid woods. In the middle was a table for readers. In the presses (*plutei, armaria*) of such libraries the rolls lay on shelves or in pigeon-holes (*nidi, foruli*), or stood in boxes (*capsae, scrinia*) with projecting *tituli*. Portraits of authors were often inserted in the woodwork of the presses, or stood as busts upon them. The younger Pliny had a book-case let into the wall of his bedroom (*Ep.* 2. 17. 8), a fashion afterwards followed in medieval monasteries.

J. W. Clark, *The Care of Books* (1909), ch. 1; Dziatzko in *PW*, s.v. 'Bibliotheken'; F. G. Kenyon, *Books and Readers in Ancient Greece and Rome* (1932); H. Stuart Jones, *Companion to Roman History* (1912), 138–41.   F. G. K.

LIBRI LINTEI, *see* BOOKS, II. 1.

LIBUM, *see* CAKES.

LIBYA was the Greek name for the continent Africa. The relation of Libya to Asia was at first in dispute. Until *c.* 500 B.C. it was regarded as part of Asia; when it came to be regarded as a separate continent its frontier was drawn along the Nile, or to west of Egypt, but after Herodotus it was fixed at Suez.

The north coast was opened up by the Phoenicians, and a Carthaginian, Hanno (*c.* 490?), followed the Atlantic coast to Sierra Leone (or perhaps Kamerun). The east coast was known to the early Egyptians as far as Somaliland; in the first two centuries A.D. Greek pioneers sailed to C. Delgado. The story that Phoenicians had circumnavigated Libya (Hdt. 4. 42) found little credence, and the attempt by Eudoxus (q.v.) to sail round ended in failure.

Inland exploration was carried on under the Ptolemies by way of the Atbara and Blue Nile to Abyssinia; some Roman soldiers under Nero reached the swamps of the White Nile to the south of Khartoum. But these obstructed further advance, and it was probably by journeys from the east coast that knowledge was obtained of the 'Mountains of the Moon' (Kilimanjaro and Ruwenzori?) and lakes (Victoria and Albert Nyanza) of central Africa, and of the Nile's sources. The Sahara was traversed *c.* 500 B.C. by some natives from Tripoli, who found the Niger near Timbuctoo (Hdt. 2. 32–3); a Roman officer, Julius Maternus (*c.* A.D. 100?), reached the Sudanese steppe, probably near Lake Chad. But there is little evidence of trans-Saharan trade before the Middle Ages.

In the general opinion of the Greeks Libya was a right-angled triangle (with the right angle at Suez); it lay wholly north of the equator (its southernmost parts being too hot to inhabit), and it was water-girt. But later exploration of the east coast suggested the theory (accepted by Ptolemy), that east Africa was joined by land to SE. Asia.

Cary–Warmington, *Explorers*, 45 ff., 62 ff., 86 ff., 165 ff. E. H. W.

LICENTIUS, of Tagaste, friend and (probably) relation of St. Augustine, to whom (A.D. 395) he addressed 154 hexameters, declaring himself unable to understand Varro's encyclopaedia without St. Augustine's guidance, and asking for a copy of the latter's work *De Musica*. The poem is preserved with St. Augustine's reply (Aug. *Ep.* 26 g). It hardly justifies St. Augustine's description of Licentius as 'poeta paene perfectus', its language being unoriginal and often obscure; its prosody, however, is fairly correct (shortening of final *o*, as is usual in late poetry; actual mistakes 'Pelōpum', 'Maeŏtidum'), and the hexameter is built with care (no spondee word in the fifth foot, etc.).

See Baehrens, *FPR* 413–19; Zelzner, *De carmine Licentii* (diss. Breslau, 1915). O. S.

LICINIANUS, see LICINIUS (1), VALERIUS (20).

LICINIUS (1), VALERIUS LICINIANUS, a comrade-in-arms of Galerius, came into sudden prominence at Carnuntum in A.D. 308, when he was raised directly to the rank of Augustus. On the death of Galerius in 310 he prepared to contest the inheritance with Maximinus, but concluded peace on the Hellespont on the basis of *uti possidetis*. In 312 he formed a close alliance with Constantine, marrying his sister, Constantia, and, after Constantine had destroyed Maxentius, himself conquered Maximinus (313). In 315 he quarrelled with Constantine, lost a sharp but indecisive war, ceded part of Illyricum, and allowed his nominee, Valens, to fall. His infant son, Licinius, was made Caesar beside Crispus and Constantine II. From *c.* 320 new difficulties arose. Licinius withdrew his favour from the Christians and revived the persecution. In 323 Constantine attacked and won decisive victories on land and sea. Licinius was sent into retirement at Thessalonica, then accused of plotting and put to death (324). His colleague, Martinian, fell with him.

CAH xii. 348 ff.; Parker, *Roman World*, 257 ff., 307 f. H. M.

LICINIUS (2) **IMBREX,** Latin poet, called by Gellius 'an old writer of comedies', whose *palliata* entitled *Neaera* he cites (13. 21. 16; 15. 24).

LICINIUS, see also CRASSUS, GALLIENUS, LUCULLUS, MACER, MUCIANUS, MURENA, STOLO, SURA, VALERIANUS.

LICIN(I)US PORCIUS, see PORCIUS LICINUS.

LICINUS, LARCIUS (?LARGIUS), see LARCIUS.

LICTORES (cf. *licere*, to call) formed a corporation, divided into several *decuriae*, of attendants on magistrates, whom they accompanied continuously both in Rome and abroad. They were of low birth, sometimes freedmen. In the town they wore the toga; out of it, and in the triumphal procession, a red coat (*sagum*); at funerals, a black mourning-dress. They preceded their particular magistrate in single file, the one nearest to the magistrate being styled lictor *proximus* or *summus*. They announced the approach of the magistrate and removed everyone, except Vestal Virgins and *matronae*, from the path. Each lictor bore a bundle of *fasces* (q.v.). Originally lictors often acted as executioners. Their number varied according to the rank of the magistrate. Each consul had six lictors until *c.* 300 B.C. and thereafter twelve. A dictator had originally twelve and subsequently twenty-four, since he united in his person the power of both consuls. The *praetor urbanus* had two lictors. The emperors were attended by twelve lictors, until Domitian doubled the number. Their *fasces* were *laureati* (i.e. bound with branches of laurel) like those displayed by the victorious generals (*imperatores*) of the Republican armies. The institution of lictors goes back to the regal period, and probably was of Etruscan origin.

Mommsen, *Röm. Staatsr.* i³, 355 f., 374 ff.; G. De Sanctis, *Riv. fil.* 1929, 1 ff.; C. Lécrivain, Dar.-Sag., iii. 2, 1239 ff.; B. Kübler, *PW*, s.v. P. T.

LICYMNIUS (1), in mythology, brother of Alcmene and uncle of Heracles (q.v.). He was the only son of Electryon to escape the Taphii (see AMPHITRYON), and when Amphitryon and Alcmene left for Thebes he accompanied them (Apollod. 2. 55. 57). He met his death when an old man at the hands of Tlepolemus (q.v.; *Il.* 2. 661–2). The reason is variously given. Pindar (*Ol.* 7. 27 ff.) says Tlepolemus struck him in anger 'as he came from the bowers of Midea', whether that means the town or his mother, Electryon's concubine; the reason for the quarrel is not given. Others, as Diod. Sic. 5. 59. 5, say it was an accident; but all agree that Tlepolemus left for Rhodes, where he founded the Dorian settlement, led his people before Troy (Homer, loc. cit.), and was killed by Sarpedon (*Il.* 5. 628 ff.). H. J. R.

LICYMNIUS (2), of Chios, dithyrambic poet and rhetorician, teacher of Polus (Pl. *Phdr.* 267 c). Aristotle says that his works were better to read than to hear (*Rh.* 1413ᵇ14). Also wrote on language (ibid. 1414ᵇ15).

Text: Diehl, *Anth. Lyr. Graec.* ii. 131–2.

LIGARIUS, QUINTUS, a Sabine by extraction, was legate in Africa of the governor C. Considius Longus in 50 B.C.; remaining with the Pompeians, he fought in 49 and 46. After Thapsus he was banished. When Caesar was about to pardon him he was accused by Q. Aelius Tubero, whose father he had not acknowledged as governor of Africa in 49, on account of his conduct there. Cicero defended him and obtained acquittal. He joined the conspirators in 44, however, and died soon after, probably not in the proscriptions. A. M.

LIGHTHOUSES. Although the Piraeus had been indicated at night by open fires on columns in the fifth century B.C., and the use of towers as day beacons began in the Hellenistic age, the first true lighthouses seem a result of the growing commerce in the Roman Empire. The Pharos at Alexandria bore a lantern by the reign of Nero, and subsequently towers at the mouths of numerous harbours and on some dangerous coasts, as at Sestos, were crowned by lanterns or open fires within a wall. The largest such tower, the Alexandrian Pharos, built about 300–280 B.C. by Sostratus of Cnidos (Strabo 17. 1. 6) 'for the safety of sailors', rose 300 feet to the top of the crowning statue, and was composed of three stories, respectively square, hexagonal, and round. Other light-houses, apart from the Colossus at Rhodes, imitated this arrangement to some extent. The stump of a Roman lighthouse may be seen inside Dover Castle.

H. Thiersch, *Der Pharos von Alexandria* (1909); M. de Asin and M. L. Otero, *Proc. Brit. Acad.* xix (1933), 277–92, with four plates.
C. G. S.

LIGHTING. The ancients knew two methods: the burning of oil in a lamp (*see* LAMPS), and the combustion of a solid substance. In Minoan and in classical times lamps were preferred for indoor illumination, and in the Roman Empire they were sometimes employed for streets and on exteriors of buildings. The torch (λαμπάς) was more generally used out of doors and also for interiors during the early Iron Age. The Greek torch was generally of wood (δαΐς), a branch or a bundle of twigs (δετή). The Italians preferred candles of tallow (*candela*) or wax (*cereus*), and the abundance of these materials explains the late adoption of the lamp in Italy. Lanterns were also freely used, candles or lamps enclosed within horn or (in Imperial times) glass. Torches were also used for signalling in warfare. F. N. P.

LIGURIANS. The Ligures of classical times lived on the eastern half of the French Riviera and along the north-west coast of Italy around Genoa. They were divided from the Iberians by the Rhône and from the Etruscans by the Arno. Ancient writers and modern anthropologists and archaeologists, however, suggest that they once occupied a much wider area. The accepted theory is that they migrated from north Africa in neolithic times and passed by way of Spain to France and Italy. Their path is traced by graves and habitations. Brizio's theory, that Ligurians were the originators of Lake-dwellings and of Terramare, has been generally discarded.

Of the language nothing has survived except a few place-names; these are consistent with the view that it was pre-Aryan. Terminations such as -*asc*-, -*esc*-, -*usc*-, frequent over a wide area of France and Italy, are claimed as Ligurian. Instances are 'Giubiasco', 'Cerinasca', 'Veraglasca'. Some inscriptions from the Italian lakes are not necessarily Ligurian (Rhys, *Proc. Brit. Ac.* 1913). Rude stelae of men and women found near Spezia are not earlier than the first century B.C., but many of the rock-drawings of the Maritime Alps (copies in Bordighera Museum) belong to the Bronze Age; they represent men, oxen, weapons, implements, ploughs, probably with a religious motive. A colony of Ligurians settled near Bellinzona about 600 B.C. and acted as transport agents in the traffic between Italy and the upper Rhine. The Ligurians probably nowhere rose above a state of quite rude barbarism. The chief tribes were the western Salluvii and Oxybii, the eastern Ingauni and Apuani. Roman campaigns (238–230 B.C.) resulted in the partial submission of the Apuani, the occupation of Luna, and the freeing of Pisa, which the Ligurians had seized from the Etruscans. After Ligurian support of Mago (q.v. 2) sporadic fighting occurred until the Romans reduced the Ingauni (181) and Apuani (180); 40,000 Apuani were deported to Samnium. The desire to win easy 'Ligurian triumphs', rather than strategic needs, probably caused some further fighting. In securing the coast road to Massilia and Spain the Romans repulsed the Oxybii who had raided Massiliote ports (154). Liguria formed one of the Augustan *regiones* of Italy.

T. E. Peet, *The Stone and Bronze Ages in Italy* (1909); Ebert's *Real-Lexikon*, svv. 'Ligurer' and 'Felsenzeichnung'; C. Bicknell, *Prehistoric Rock-engravings of the Italian Alps* (1902).
D. R.-MacI.

LILYBAEUM (nowadays *Marsala*), the westernmost city of Sicily, founded in 396 B.C. by Carthage to replace Motya (q.v.), which Dionysius had sacked. Its

excellent harbour had been used earlier; but Diodorus' statement (11. 86) that Lilybaeum already existed in 454 is erroneous. Lilybaeum quickly became a great military and commercial stronghold, impregnable alike to Pyrrhus (276) and the Romans, whose protracted but vain siege of it is famous (250–242). Rome, however, acquired Sicily by treaty, and with it Lilybaeum, which she apparently made a *civitas decumana*, the seat of a quaestor. As the principal port of communication between Sicily and Africa Lilybaeum was a flourishing place, a 'ciuitas splendidissima' during Cicero's quaestorship there (*Verr.* 5. 10). It became a *municipium* under Augustus and a *colonia* under Septimius Severus (?), and remained an important port until the sixteenth century, when its harbour was blocked with boulders.

Polyb. 1. 41 f.; Diod. 13. 54; 22. 10; Strabo 2, p. 122; 6, p. 265 f.
E. T. S.

LIMES originally meant a pathway, especially the strip of open land along which a column of troops advanced into enemy territory. Hence it came to mean a military road, with fortified posts and signal-towers, and finally a frontier. The Roman Republic had no proper frontiers. Only the boundaries of the old province of Africa were marked by a ditch—a Carthaginian heritage. The foundations of a frontier system were laid by Augustus, but Domitian was the first to organize permanent defences on some frontiers. After the conquest of the Wetterau he constructed along the new German frontier a series of small earth forts and wooden signal-towers. An earth rampart of the Dobrudja with forts is perhaps of the same period. Hadrian was responsible in Germany as in Britain for the construction of a continuous barrier. In Germany it took the form of a palisade; in Britain the Wall of Hadrian (q.v.) probably had been preceded, under Trajan, by a *limes* corresponding to the Stanegate. A *limes* of Trajanic-Hadrianic times has been traced in the Dobrudja. The *limes*, besides its military purpose, helped to bring barbarians under fiscal control. This system of fortifications was employed on other frontiers during the second century A.D., and assumed forms corresponding to the varying geographical and military conditions. In Africa and along most of the Danubian frontier the forts were never linked by ramparts. Antoninus Pius advanced the frontier both in Germany and in Britain. A new palisade was erected between Miltenberg and Haghof in Germany, where the wooden towers had gradually been replaced by stone ones. In Britain the new Wall of Antoninus (q.v.) did not totally supersede Hadrian's Wall. About the time of Caracalla a great earth wall and ditch were built in Upper Germany and a stone wall in Raetia. In Germany the palisade was retained as an essential part of the scheme; the forts of the German *limes* were a few hundred yards behind the watch-tower line, while the line of the palisade was determined by the watch-towers. The troops employed on the *limes* were generally auxiliary cohorts or *numeri*. The cohorts were on an average 1¾ miles apart on the Antonine Wall, 4¼ miles apart on Hadrian's, 7 in Germany, between 10 and 20 in Syria. The *limes* gradually deprived the Roman army of the idea of offensive and did not prove sufficient, as a rule, to check serious attacks. The German *limes* was abandoned under Gallienus. In Britain, though the Antonine Wall was abandoned under Commodus, Hadrian's Wall was occupied until the time of Magnus Maximus. The Syrian *limes* was thoroughly reorganized by Diocletian and his successors, especially to check cavalry-attacks, and lasted until the Arab invasion. For the late developments of frontier defence *see* LIMITANEI.

E. Fabricius, *PW*, s.v. *Il Limes romano* (1939) is a survey of unequal value. For Germany, etc., see O. Brogan, *Arch. Journ.* 1935, p. 1; B. W. Henderson, *Five Roman Emperors* (1927), ch. 6; and the standard works by E. Fabricius and others: *Der obergermanische-rätische Limes* (1894 ff.); *Der römische Limes in Oesterreich*

(1900 ff.). Good plates in *Germania Romana, Ein Bilder-Atlas*[a] (1924). For Syria: A. Poidebard, *La Trace de Rome dans le désert de Syrie* (1934); R. Monterde and A. Poidebard, *Le Limes de Chalcis, organisation de la steppe en haute Syrie romaine* (2 vols. 1945). For N. Africa: J. Guey, *Mélanges d'arch.* 1939, 177–248. For Britain *see under* WALL OF HADRIAN, WALL OF ANTONINUS.

For new research: *Germania*; *JRS*; *Berichte der röm.-germ. Kommission.*   A. M.

LIMITANEI (or *Riparienses*) was a generic term for Constantine's Frontier Army, which was stationed permanently in garrison outposts. It comprised cavalry (*cunei equitum, equites*) and infantry (*legiones, cohortes*), and was commanded by *duces*. It later developed into a local militia whose members farmed the frontier lands.

R. Grosse, *Römische Militärgeschichte*, 63–70.   H.M.D.P.

LINDUM (*Lincoln*) lay in the territory of the Coritani, whose capital was Ratae (*Leicester*). It began as a fortress for Legio IX Hispana soon after A.D. 43 (*CIL* vii. 183, 188; *Eph. Epigr.* ix. 1111), and its *munimenta* are presumably referred to by Tacitus (*Ann.* 14. 32). Tombstones of Legio II Adiutrix (of A.D. 71–86/8) are also known there (*CIL* vii. 185, 186). Soon after 71 Legio IX Hispana was advanced to Eboracum (q.v.) and Lindum became a colony, perhaps contemporary with Glevum (*Gloucester*), founded by Nerva. The new town, with colonnaded main streets, small *insulae*, and noble gates (*JRS* xxviii. 182), occupied the hill-top north of the river Witham, and doubled its size in Roman times. The river was probably a trade-route (*JRS* xi. 102). Lindum was an important road-centre and perhaps the seat of a bishopric (F. Haverfield, *Arch. Ael.*, 1918, 24; S. N. Miller, *Eng. Hist. Rev.* xlii. 79–80).   I. A. R.

LINGUISTICS, COMPARATIVE, *see* PHILOLOGY, COMPARATIVE.

LINUS (*Λίνος*). An old and apparently mournful-sounding song (*Il.* 18. 570, which shows that it was not always sung on mournful occasions, for there it is at a vintage; but it may be a lament for the 'death' of the grapes, a custom widely paralleled, see Frazer, *GB* vii. 216 and the whole chapter) contained the sounds αἴλινον, interpreted as meaning 'alas for Linus'. The song was called a Linus (Homer, ibid.), and the question was asked who Linus was and why he should be bewailed. Argos said he was a son of Apollo and Psamathe, a local princess; she exposed him, he was devoured by dogs, and the city plagued by Apollo till satisfaction was made (Paus. 1. 43. 7–8). In central Greece, Linus was son of Amphimarus and Urania, killed by Apollo for saying he was as good a singer as the god (Paus. 9. 29. 6). A third variant made him Heracles' music-teacher, whom his pupil killed with a blow from a cithara (Apollod. 2. 63). A favourite modern explanation (Frazer, loc. cit.) is that αἴλινον is Phoenician, *ai lanu*, 'woe to us!' This is not impossible, cf. LITYERSES.   H. J. R.

LIPARA, *see* AEOLIAE INSULAE.

LITAI, *see* PERSONIFICATIONS.

LITERARY CRITICISM IN ANTIQUITY. I. GREEK. Literary criticism is concerned with literature on its aesthetic side, and consists of attempts at theorizing, legislating, judging, and appreciating. In Greek literature it is represented by a series of pronouncements, inspired by various causes and assuming different forms, which embody doctrines of intrinsic and historical value, and thus form an important chapter in the history of Greek thought and taste (*see* RHETORIC). The beginnings of Greek criticism date from the sixth century B.C., when the philosophers Xenophanes and Heraclitus condemned Homer on moral grounds, and Theagenes and Anaxagoras in defence advocated an allegorical interpretation. Then in the fifth century speculation on poetry tentatively emerged, traces of poetic theory being found in Pindar, in Sophistic philological writings, and in the *encomia* of Gorgias. Meanwhile literary judgements were appearing in comedy; and with Aristophanes' shrewd estimates of Aeschylus and Euripides in the *Frogs* serious judicial criticism had also begun.

2. In the century following, a new phase of critical activity was inaugurated by Plato. Viewing literature in its relation to social and political life, he treated incidentally in his *Dialogues* of current literary abuses, discussed the place of poetry in an ideal State, and dealt with many aspects of poetic theory. His censures of contemporary literature, often in parody form, are of considerable interest. Of interest, too, is his much-discussed rejection of poets from his commonwealth (*Resp.* 607 a)—a perplexing pronouncement in the light of all the evidence, best understood perhaps, not as dogmatic and final, but as a challenge made, on behalf of philosophy, to the place hitherto held by poetry as the main avenue to truth. Most valuable, however, is his positive and constructive theorizing, in which he appears as a pioneer of lasting and beneficent influence. In his pages were first set forth basic doctrines concerning the nature and art of poetry, consisting of earlier theories reinterpreted and transformed, besides original and daring suggestions, which reveal, often intuitively, the innermost spirit and the technique of art. Working from first principles and applying psychological methods in his discussions, he began that larger and more philosophical criticism which gave inspiration and direction to later effort.

3. On the foundations thus laid Aristotle in his *Poetics* built, modifying and developing the teaching of Plato on rational and systematic lines, with a view to including the study in his philosophical scheme. Basing his doctrines on an analysis of existing Greek poetry, and making use of psychological and historical methods, he sets forth a comprehensive theory of the poetic art, concluding with an exposition of sound methods of forming literary judgements. On poetry in general he throws light from various angles, pointing out, for instance, its element of universal truth, its aesthetic function, and its emotional value, revealing at the same time basic principles of the literary art, while also imparting much studio-wisdom in the form of practical hints for the poet. And this he supplements by an illuminating treatment of the various forms or 'kinds' of poetry. Dealing mainly with tragedy as the representative form, he submits canons of the dramatic art, principles relating mostly to plot and characterization; and in addition he supplies notes on comedy and the epic, all of which retain in some measure their validity. Hardly less significant, however, is the guidance he gives in judicial criticism, when, condemning contemporary judgements based on verbal details or on tests of morality, reality, and the like (cf. Zoïlus Ὁμηρομάστιξ), he further maintains that aesthetic criteria are all that matter, and illustrates his teaching by reasoned appreciations of Homer and the great dramatists. Of the value of the work and its far-reaching influence there can be no question; though it has obscurities and defects and is devoid of literary grace. In literary history it represents the first 'Apology' and the first *Art* of poetry; but it is in its seminal quality that it stands unrivalled. In establishing original and profound doctrines of poetry, and in inaugurating new and effective methods of both theorizing and judging, it opened men's eyes to more fruitful conceptions of art and made aesthetic judgement possible. Its importance in the history of criticism can scarcely be overrated.

4. Under the changed conditions of the Hellenistic period critical activities assumed a new form, which, while representing a decline from earlier efforts, was yet to influence subsequent developments at Rome. The outstanding feature was the abandonment of the philosophical approach to literature for one of a scholastic

kind; and the main business now became the systematizing of poetic technique for school purposes, though the textual and historico-critical labours of Alexandria and Pergamum were in the meantime preparing the way for sounder criticism. The nature of the new system may roughly be gathered from the *Poetics* of Neoptolemus of Parium (3rd c. B.C.)—a work now lost, but partly reconstructed from the Περὶ ποιημάτων of Philodemus of Gadara—in which poetry was treated schematically under the heads of ποίησις, ποίημα, ποιητής, and a static view of literature was taken, according to which earlier poetic forms were regarded as fixed genres and models, each with its distinctive formal characteristics. Certain problems were also discussed, namely, whether native endowment (φύσις) or technical training (τέχνη) was more important for the poet, whether thought or form constituted the essence of poetry, and, again, whether the poet's aim was to teach or to delight. Of these problems (all handed down as unfinished controversies to later generations) one in particular influenced later discussions, as a result of the supreme value attached to artistic form by Heracleodorus, Andromenides, Crates of Mallos, and others. Nevertheless, the system of poetics thus forming did not emerge unchallenged. Callimachus, under Alexandrian influences, was already urging a break with classical forms, while stressing the prime importance of neat and careful workmanship; and his doctrine found expression in the later verses of Simylus (q.v. 1). Nor was the period without its advance in judicial criticism, though the irrational methods condemned by Aristotle still held the field. From Eratosthenes, however, and more especially from Aristarchus, came sounder estimates of Homer; and further evidence of increasing interest in aesthetic matters was supplied by appreciations of earlier poets in the *Greek Anthology*.

5. Towards the close of the first century B.C. Greek criticism underwent further and more substantial developments. Owing to the rapid hellenization of Rome, and the desire of Romans to emulate the ancient literature of Greece, Hellenistic teaching was now subordinated to the larger purpose of clarifying contemporary views concerning Greek classical ideals and standards; and in the Augustan period and the following century Caecilius, Dionysius of Halicarnassus, 'Longinus', and Demetrius took up the task, treating primarily of style—the then current problem—but revealing at the same time many important principles of literature. Now, for the first time since the days of Aristotle and Theophrastus, the subtleties of Attic prose were explored under the guidance of those earlier authorities; such matters as the effects of an artistic word-order, the euphonious qualities of words in isolation or in combination, or the reasoned use of figures, being discussed in original and illuminating fashion. This teaching was illustrated by appreciations of Greek writers (both of poetry and prose), which threw further light on the form and spirit of classical literature. Equally significant, however, was the advance in critical achievement bound up with these activities, and seen most clearly in the works of Dionysius of Halicarnassus and 'Longinus'. By Dionysius, for instance, a return was made to Aristotle's inductive theorizing; perspective and weight were added to literary judgement by his use of historical and comparative methods; while to the actual appreciation of literature he made substantial and lasting contributions, of which his penetrating judgements of Lysias, Thucydides, and Demosthenes are examples. Yet greater was the performance of 'Longinus', whose unfailing insight into the essentials of literature opened up a new world of critical possibilities. Apprehending clearly the imaginative and emotional effects of all great literature, he succeeded in capturing the spirit of Greek art; and with his grasp of principle, his wide-ranging tastes, his infectious enthusiasms, and, not least, his suggestive comments on literature

and literary criticism itself, he made of criticism not only a stimulating study but also the most potent of instruments for the appreciation of the literary art.

6. In the meantime the last effective phase of Greek criticism was represented by the efforts of Plutarch and Dio Chrysostom to interpret Greek culture—and incidentally Greek literature—for Imperial Rome, as a result of the Hellenic revival towards the end of the first century A.D. The main interest of their critical work is of an historical kind: it bore witness to the persistence of Hellenistic traditions, and to the fact that classical ideals were already fading. This is seen, for instance, in Plutarch's ethical theory of poetry, and yet more clearly in his judgements of Homer, which (like those of Dio) perpetuated Alexandrian methods and standards. Both, however, were interested in aesthetic questions, and whereas Plutarch's main effort was directed to restoring poetry to its former place as a prime factor in education, Dio's greatest achievement was his masterly appreciation of Aeschylus, Sophocles, and Euripides in his *Comparison*. Apart from this but little criticism of value was forthcoming, rhetorical displays of the Second Sophistic movement absorbing all attention. Lucian made war on the literary impostures of his day; Philostratus (q.v. 3) threw fresh light on aesthetic theory in defining the artistic process as being, not 'imitation', but 'creative imagination' (φαντασία). For the rest, however, literary comment now fell under the sterile treatment of rhetoricians, grammarians, and philologians, and was ultimately silenced in the dark days that followed.

E. Egger, *Essai sur l'histoire de la critique chez les Grecs* (1885); B. Bosanquet, *History of Aesthetic* (1892); S. H. Butcher, *Aristotle's Theory of Poetry and Fine Art* (1895); G. Saintsbury, *History of Criticism* (1900); J. E. Sandys, *History of Classical Scholarship* (1903); Lane Cooper, *Aristotle on the Art of Poetry* (1913); C. Jensen, *Philodemus Über die Gedichte* (1923); J. D. Denniston, *Greek Literary Criticism* (1924); C. S. Baldwin, *Ancient Rhetoric and Poetic* (1928); W. R. Roberts, *Greek Rhetoric and Literary Criticism* (1928); E. E. Sikes, *The Greek View of Poetry* (1931); J. W. H. Atkins, *Literary Criticism in Antiquity* (1934).

II. LATIN. Latin literary criticism consists of that running commentary on literature and literary matters to which, in various forms, Roman writers contributed from the second century B.C. onwards. As yet an occasional by-product of contemporary literary activities, though ultimately the result of aesthetic interests inspired by earlier philosophical, rhetorical, and grammatical studies, this criticism nevertheless constitutes a considerable body of literary theorizing and judgements which throw valuable light on contemporary thought and taste. Its immediate causes, apart from earlier Greek teaching, were certain urgent questions which arose from time to time; and to their solution Cicero, Horace, the elder Seneca, Tacitus, and Quintilian were the main contributors.

2. Already in the Scipionic circle the critical spirit had appeared. Terence's replies to detractors and his searching comments on dramatic technique were among the first-fruits; and they were followed by Lucilius' remarks on poetic diction and satire, together with fragments of Hellenistic teaching. More far-reaching was the criticism evoked by the clash of styles in Republican oratory, which led to Cicero's exposition of rhetorical principles (*see* RHETORIC), his pronouncement on the Asianist-Atticist problem, and his illuminating survey of the development of oratory. Animated throughout his dialogues by a reasoned admiration for the doctrine and practice of the classical Greeks, he condemns the Asianist excesses of Hortensius and the colourless correctness of Calvus and Brutus; and indicating the limitations of Lysias and Thucydides as models, he commends Demosthenes as the supreme guide in style. Equally significant was his judicial criticism where he reveals his reverence for Ennius and his dislike for the neoterics (q.v.). Using comparative and historical methods, he submits appreciations of Greek and Roman orators, and inculcates a sense of the continuity of literature. With him thus begins a classical reaction in literary theory, accompanied by wider conceptions of the critical function.

3. Further developments were witnessed under Augustus, when the main problem became that of creating a great national poetry; and Horace, amidst the confused counsels of the archaizing and Alexandrian schools, prescribed the poetic forms and standards of classical Greece. In his *Satires* he incidentally expounds his theory of satire, in his *Epistles* (Book 2) he outlines his programme of reform, and in the *Ars Poetica* (based on the *Poetics* of Neoptolemus of Parium) he submits principles and rules for the guidance of poets. What he advocates is an imitation of ancient Greek masterpieces; by which he meant, not a slavish copying, but a process of re-creation, the evolution of something new, by adapting Greek measures to the Roman lyre. His doctrines, though coloured by his experience, are primarily derivative in kind; he does not arrive at his theories by an analysis of actual literature. Alexandrian influence, moreover, is seen in his work, notably in his demand for careful workmanship and polish. But among the principles he propounds are many that treat of essentials; he commends his teaching in memorable phrase, and his lasting achievement was the establishment of classicism in poetic theory.

4. With the decline of literature (1st c. A.D.) critical effort assumed new functions, turning naturally to a consideration of the nature and causes of that decline. A valuable commentary on contemporary oratory was forthcoming in the specimens collected by the elder Seneca, which, apart from the light it throws on Augustan declaimers and declamations, embodies many sound judgements, condemns all departures from simplicity and good taste, and commends Cicero as the model for Roman orators. Persius followed, waging war on the affectations and insincerities of contemporary poets; and Petronius in his *Satyricon* attacked Lucan for his choice of an historical subject and his omission of epic machinery from his *Civil War*. Meanwhile not without interest were the attempts made to account for the decline by viewing literature in its relation to social life. Thus the two Senecas attributed it to the decay of morality; Petronius to debased taste fostered by declamation in the schools; while Velleius Paterculus in his history explained it as a natural sequel to a period of great literary achievement.

5. Nor was criticism of a more constructive kind wanting, though petty but futile attacks on Virgil continued throughout the century. Manilius, for one, had proposed fresh themes for poetic treatment, and Petronius had recalled the part played by imagination and passion in the poetic process. Martial, again, advanced claims for a realistic treatment of life, commented on the epigram as a literary genre, and condemned the growth of antiquarianism; while the younger Pliny in his *Letters* reflected contemporary literary tastes. More significant was the contribution of Tacitus in his *Dialogue*, where he commended the oratory of the Ciceronian age, but suggested also that changed conditions called for expression more lively, less formal. He further maintained that oratory had declined because of the cessation of Republican strife; and these shrewd comments marked a new phase of literary theorizing. With him criticism ceased to be dogmatic and final; and in upholding the relativity of literary standards he successfully challenged a more rigid classicism. Similar tendencies had been seen in Quintilian's *Institutio*; in his doctrine of a modified classicism, his sense of the need for literary development, his enlightened conception of Imitation, and his wide-ranging survey of literary history, limited though it was in aesthetic appreciation. In him culminated the movement begun by Cicero, the effort to

maintain, amidst shifting and conflicting influences, the highest artistic standards then known. The attempt, it is true, was only partially successful; for with Fronto and Gellius came later one of the periodic revivals of archaism. But many good things had meanwhile been said, and the way prepared for future critical activities.

Special studies: G. Saintsbury, *History of Criticism* (1900); J. Wight Duff, *Lit. Hist. Rome to Golden Age* (1909); id., *Silver Age* (1927); E. E. Sikes, *Roman Poetry* (1923); W. Kroll, *Studien zum Verständnis der römischen Literatur* (1924); J. W. H. Atkins, *Literary Criticism in Antiquity* (1934).   J. W. H. A.

LITERARY PATRONAGE, *see* PATRONAGE.

LITERATURE, GREEK and **LATIN,** HISTORY OF, *see* APPENDIX at the end of this work.

LITERNUM, a Roman citizen colony on the Campanian coast, founded in 194 B.C. but soon derelict (Livy 34. 45): nowadays *Torre di Patria*. The disillusioned Scipio Africanus Maior retired and possibly was buried there (Livy 38. 52, 53, 56; Seneca, *Ep.* 86). Later the Via Domitiana, like the modern railway, somewhat increased its importance.   E. T. S.

LITTERATOR, chiefly used of the elementary instructor in reading and writing whose teaching was continued by the *doctrina* of the *grammaticus* (q.v.). See EDUCATION, III. 3.

LITTERS (*lecticae*) were introduced into Rome from the east: Cicero (*Verr.* 5. 27) associates them with the kings of Bithynia. They are first mentioned in the second century B.C. and were common in the following century. They were provided with curtains and sometimes with glass windows (Juv. 3. 239). They were carried on poles by slaves, of whom as many as eight might be required. At first they were used in the city only by women and invalids, but later they were freely employed by both sexes in the city and outside. Restrictions on their use were sometimes imposed by the government (Suet. *Iul.* 43, *Claud.* 28).   G. H. S.

LITTLE ILIAD, *see* EPIC CYCLE.

LITURGY. At Athens in the fifth and fourth centuries B.C. certain public functions were compulsorily conferred upon the richer citizens and metics. Of these liturgies some, like the trierarchy (q.v.), were occasional, others were imposed regularly, according to a fixed order of rotation. These included the *choregia* (q.v.: the production of a chorus at the musical and dramatic festivals), the gymnasiarchy (q.v.), ἑστίασις (the provision of a banquet for a tribe at festivals), ἀρχιθεωρία (the leadership of a public delegation to a foreign festival), ἱπποτροφία (the maintenance as a knight of a horse). To some liturgies nominations were made by a magistrate, e.g. by the archon to the tragic *choregia*, to others by the tribes, e.g. to the cyclic *choregia* and ἑστίασις. A person nominated might challenge another whom he considered better able to bear the expense, and the latter might either undertake the liturgy or exchange properties with his challenger, or appeal to the courts (*see* ANTIDOSIS). A liturgy involved the holder both in personal service (though he might employ a deputy) and in expense. In some cases the State made an allocation, but this did not by any means cover the costs.

In the Hellenistic age no clear line was drawn between ἀρχαί and λειτουργίαι. Both were filled by popular election; neither imposed any obligatory expenditure in theory, but both in fact often involved a heavy personal outlay; both might in the last resort be compulsorily imposed. Immunity was in this age often granted, not only from liturgies, but from magistracies, and the term 'liturgy' came to denote minor offices, which were onerous but did not carry much authority

In Roman municipal law a sharp distinction was drawn between *honores* and *munera*; *honores* qualified their holder for a seat on the council; the *immunitas* conferred by the Roman government meant exemption from *munera*. These rules were also applied in the Greek East, and offices must therefore have been definitely classified into ἀρχαί and λειτουργίαι. In time the distinction became blurred; immunity (ἀλειτουργησία) by the early third century included exemption from magistracies. By this time the most important and onerous liturgies were imperial, such as the collection of tribute.

In Egypt a liturgy meant a compulsory State office. Compulsion was little used in the Ptolemaic or early Roman period, but from the latter part of the first century A.D. became commoner, till every post below the rank of στρατηγός or βασιλικὸς γραμματεύς became a liturgy. Qualified persons were nominated by the scribes of the *metropoleis* and villages to be *strategi*, who themselves appointed to lower posts, and for higher posts submitted the names to the *epistrategus*, who drew lots between them. When councils were instituted in the *metropoleis*, many of the more important officers were elected by them.

V. Thumser, *De civium Atheniensium muneribus eorumque immunitate* (1880); J. Oehler, *PW*, s.v. 'Leitourgia'; F. Oertel, *Die Liturgie, Studien zur Ptolemäischen und Kaiserlichen Verwaltung Aegyptens* (1917).

A. H. M. J.

LITYERSES. 'Some say that he was a son of Midas, and that he challenged all and sundry to a contest in reaping, and maltreated those who were overcome by him. But, encountering a stronger reaper, he met his death. Some say that it was Heracles who killed him' (Pollux 4. 54, who says that Lityerses is the Phrygian reapers' song). His source is uncertain, cf. Crusius in Roscher's *Lexikon*, s.v. It would seem, therefore, to be a traditional song with a story to explain it, cf. LINUS. H. J. R.

LIVIA (58 B.C.–A.D. 29), daughter of M. Livius Drusus Claudianus, married Tiberius Claudius Nero (q.v. 3), whom she accompanied in his flight after the Perusine War. Nero divorced her in 38 to enable her to marry Octavian (Augustus), whose affection and esteem she retained till his death in A.D. 14. Her beauty, dignity, intelligence, and tact well fitted her for her high position. Augustus valued her counsel, and she appears to have exercised a restraining influence upon him. A natural fondness for power may explain allusions to friction between her and Tiberius, but suggestions that she had any part in the deaths of Marcellus, Gaius Caesar, Lucius Caesar, or Germanicus do not deserve serious consideration. Livia bore two sons to her first husband—Tiberius (later emperor) and Drusus (q.v. 3). She became 'Julia Augusta' under the will of Augustus.

Velleius, bk. 2; Tacitus, *Ann.* bks. 1–5; Dio Cassius, bks. 48 ff. Modern literature: V. Gardthausen, *Augustus u. seine Zeit* (1891 etc.); H. Willrich, *Livia* (1911). G. W. R.

LIVILLA (*Livia*), daughter of Drusus (q.v. 3) and Antonia minor and granddaughter of Livia (q.v.), born *c.* 13 B.C., was married to Gaius Caesar (grandson of Augustus), and after his death to Drusus, son of Tiberius. She was executed in A.D. 31 on evidence of complicity in the murder of her husband.

Tacitus, *Ann.* bk. 4; Dio Cassius 57. 22 and 58. 11. G. W. R.

LIVIUS (1) ANDRONICUS, LUCIUS (*c.* 284–*c.* 204 B.C.), early Latin poet, a Greek (?) born at Tarentum, was brought a slave to Rome in 242, was manumitted, and took his master's names Lucius Livius; he became a teacher of Greek and Latin literature, then also an actor, stage-manager, and writer of *saturae*, 'medleys', for the stage, then of stage-plays. By public request, 240 B.C., he composed and acted in the first Latin comedy and the

first Latin tragedy, both having Greek models and metres (*see* DRAMA, ROMAN, para. 1). Others followed, ousting the old *saturae* into literature for reading only. Failure of L.'s voice caused the institution of the *cantor* to sing *cantica* to an actor's gestures. In 207 L. officially composed an expiatory hymn (the first real lyric in Latin), and the *collegium* of playwrights and actors was founded.

Livius' works, popular at first, were later regarded as rough though impressive. Fragments: (i) about forty-six lines (early work) of the first Latin epic the *Odissia*, a rude prosy paraphrase-translation, into Latin saturnians, of Homer's *Odyssey*. (ii) About forty lines from tragedies on Greek models—*Achilles, Aegisthus, Aiax Mastigophorus, Andromeda, Danae, Equos Troianus, Hermiona, Tereus.* (iii) Lines from *comoediae palliatae*.

Text of fragments: E. H. Warmington, *Remains of Old Latin* ii (Loeb, with translation); H. de la Ville de Mirmont, *Ét. s. l'ancienne poés. lat.* (1903), 5–201; G. Pascoli, *Epos* (Livorno; 2nd ed. 1911; *Odiss.* pp. 1–6); O. Ribbeck, *Scaen. Romanorum Poesis Fragmenta* (2nd ed.; 3rd ed. Teubner. Plays). E. H. W.

LIVIUS (2), TITUS (Livy) (59 B.C.–A.D. 17), the Roman historian, was born in Patavium (Padua) at the height of the old Venetic city's prosperity and fame; the circumstances of his early years may well have influenced the growth of his character. We know little of his life. His daughter married a rhetorician, Magius, and his son may have been a writer, followed by Pliny. He himself wrote philosophical dialogues, historical in tendency, and his advice on rhetoric to his son (Quint. 10. 1. 39) shows his place in the Ciceronian tradition. At Rome he entered the Imperial literary circle, gave readings of his work, and won Augustus' interest in his historical task (4. 20. 7) and appreciation of his republican sentiment (Tac. *Ann.* 4. 34); he encouraged Claudius in his historical studies (Suet. *Claud.* 41). His work reflects knowledge of the Empire, presumably gathered in travel, but he must have spent most of his time at work in Rome or in Padua, where he died.

2. The history of Rome (*ab urbe condita libri*), which he began at thirty and continued for forty years, was composed in 142 books. Bks. i–v covered from the origins to the Gallic sack of Rome, vi–xv reached the beginning of the Punic Wars, xvi–xx treated the First Punic War, xxi–xxx the Second Punic War, xxxi–xlv the Macedonian and Syrian Wars. As the work grew under his hand the pentad and decade arrangement had to be modified. The destruction of Carthage appeared in bk. li, Ti. Gracchus in lvii, the defeat of the Cimbri in lxviii, the opening of the Social War in lxxi, Marius' death in lxxx, Sulla's death in xc, Caesar's consulship in ciii, Pharsalus in cxi, Caesar's death in cxvi, Actium in cxxxiii, the death of Drusus (9 B.C.) in cxlii. Bks. cix–cxvi were entitled *belli civilis libri.*

3. The proemium reflects the situation after Augustus' proposed social legislation in 28 B.C.; bk. i. 19. 3 was published after 27 B.C. and before 25 B.C.; bk. xxviii. 12 presupposes Agrippa's Spanish campaign of 19 B.C. Bk. lix followed Augustus' quotation of Metellus' speech on marriage in 18 B.C. If bk. cxxi was published after Augustus' death (A.D. 14), it was presumably accompanied by several subsequent books, since Livy could scarcely have written twenty-one books in the three years before his death. He probably died pen in hand, the work closing with Drusus' death.

4. Of this immense work only thirty-five books are extant: i–x, xxi–xlv. For the lost books we have a palimpsest fragment of bk. xci, cited fragments and excerpts, and the epitomized, perhaps slightly 'contaminated' tradition of the *Periochae* (q.v.) and the Oxyrhynchus Epitome of bks. xxxvii–xl, xlviii–lv; also, in basis, the work of Florus, Granius Licinianus, Aurelius Victor, Eutropius and Festus, Orosius and Cassiodorus, Julius Obsequens.

5. Livy stood at the peak of annalistic historiography, and was able to develop the work of the Sullan annalists. Valerius Antias from the beginning, and Claudius Quadrigarius from the Gallic sack (bk. vi), appear to have provided the basis of composition; they are cited throughout the work. The set annalistic arrangement allowed easy transition from source to source and the incorporation of episodic material; in bks. i–x Licinius Macer, Aelius Tubero, and (indirectly) Fabius Pictor and Calpurnius Piso, in bks. xxi–xxx Coelius Antipater and Polybius, in xxxi–xlv Polybius, supplement Valerius Antias and Claudius Quadrigarius; afterwards Posidonius, and perhaps Sulpicius Galba, Sisenna, Caesar, and Augustus' *Memoirs,* among others, were used in the same way.

6. In accordance with contemporary historiographical practice, Livy does not cite his authorities, except in cases of dispute or doubt, and often, e.g. in the comparison of casualty figures, this may be conventional. As a rule he adapted the source material with scarcely more than literary and stylistic elaboration, apparently without 'contamination', if we may judge from his reproduction of Polybius and the common inconsistency of the annalistic narrative. There is always a certain negligence in his treatment of context, with obvious discrepancies, repetitions, and chronological divergences; this is most striking in his use of Polybius, where the Olympiad yearly divisions are forced within the narrative based on the Roman year. The reason appears to lie in his undue dependence upon narrative form in constructing his work, beginning with the Sullan histories. This acceptance of the annalistic tradition in both matter and form largely explains his lack of source criticism; the authority of the *annales maximi,* persisting in its literary development, limited criticism to detail, and here Livy, with characteristic sincerity and restraint, refused to argue on grounds of mere probability or rationalize without full evidence.

7. Yet, even granting this, he falls short in critical methods, except perhaps in the discussion of figures and finance. His defective treatment of the problem of Cossus' *spolia opima* (4. 19), his neglect of the *libri lintei* when two sources cited the same passage differently (4. 23), not to mention again the inconsistencies in his narrative, reflect his subservience to written authority, and show literary procedure over-simplifying the task of historical composition. Livy had little knowledge of Roman institutions. His inexperience in military matters affects his description of battles: his ignorance of the phalanx, for example, is unpardonable; he is, however, better on ships. He does not falsify events, but his literary elaboration often makes his narrative conventional and misleading. His ignorance of conditions in early Rome and in the East leaves blemishes on his historical reconstruction, which is always coloured by his Augustan idealism. In the later books, no doubt, his increasing command over his material and his better understanding of events raised the critical level of his work.

8. Yet Livy's purpose in the first instance was not to analyse the process of history in the light of institutions or circumstances. He set himself to give Rome a history that in conception and style should be worthy of her imperial rise and greatness, and in influence lend understanding to the Augustan moral recovery. He depicted in general the life and character, the policies and personalities of the past and the later decay of discipline; in particular, the social morale of early Rome, the 'integra atque immobilis uirtus' against Hannibal, the policy of Republican freedom against the Hellenistic monarchies, and the consequences of luxury and avarice in the later age. His patriotism and sense of Roman dignity dominate his narrative, without excluding wider sympathy or appreciation.

9. His genius lay in his power of vivid historical reconstruction, visualizing scenes and people, and conveying his impression by description and interpretation. His natural historical feeling developed under the influence of Hellenistic psychological knowledge, now established in Rome, and his literary talent was trained in Hellenistic historiographical theory and Roman rhetoric; the annalistic tradition gave him material and form. Cicero had defined his task, and the patriotic inspiration of Augustus gave life to his composition. In his first books his narration, fitting the subject-matter, has poetical colour and style: it is the prose epic of Rome, ranking with the *Aeneid.* The later books take on a more regular prose form, but show equally brilliant conception of events, understanding of personal and mass psychology, and careful literary presentation. The feeling for atmosphere, as well as the principle of variation, allowed the set appearance of formal notices and prodigy tables.

10. In detail Livy's composition followed the Isocratean canons of brevity, economy, and verisimilitude, with the devices of literary elaboration, characterizing speeches, and the dramatic Peripatetic technique. The style conformed to the Ciceronian requirements of 'uarietas colorum, collocatio uerborum', and 'tractus orationis lenis et aequabilis' in historical narration (e.g. for the sake of homogeneity, Livy (27. 37) would not quote Livius Andronicus); but composition and style had their own varying character, suitable to the different elements in the annalistic tradition. Livy's 'clarissimus candor' and 'lactea ubertas' reflect the lucidity and continuity of his thought, but the style is not purely periodic: it corresponds to the mode of the passage, poetic or formal, elaborate or plain, expository or rhetorical, depending on the complexity of ideas or rhythm of the narrative. Even stylistic irregularity or strained word usage may occur to convey a nuance, departing from the pure Latinity of the capital. This may justify the charge of 'Patavinitas', if Pollio's jibe was not directed at the moral and romantic tone of Livy's work.

11. The command of his theme and its expression, the love of truth where it could be found, the deep seriousness and wide humanity, give life to Livy's historical achievement: his work captures the imagination and moves the spirit. It is Augustan, with the faults as well as the merits of the time, and it falls below modern critical standards. Yet it reproduces tradition faithfully, without the defective rationalization practised in both ancient and modern times; for this modern criticism may be grateful. In his presentation of persons and events, the flesh and blood of history, he ranks among the great historians.

12. His success was immediate and lasting. His work was used by historians and epic poets; an epitome had appeared for common use by the time of Martial (14. 190); his speeches were collected. In the Middle Ages, Dante praised 'Livio che non erra'. The Renaissance saw him in high favour, and printing made him a popular author. Machiavelli discoursed on the First Decade. Niebuhr and Lewis began the critical examination of his early tradition, and historical study has continued it. Our new knowledge of Hellenistic historiography has revealed the secrets of his composition, and syntactical study is throwing light on his style.

BIBLIOGRAPHY

EDITIONS: A. Drakenborch (1738–46; 1820–8); J. Th. Kreyssig (xxxiii; 1839); C. F. S. Alschefski (i–x, xxi–xxiii; 1841–6); M. Hertz (1857–64); A. Luchs (xxvi–xxx; 1879; xxi–xxx; 1888–9); W. Weissenborn–M. Müller–W. Heraeus (2nd ed. 1860; 1881 ff. Teubner); A. Zingerle (1883–1908); J. N. Madvig–J. L. Ussing (1861 ff.; 4th ed., 1886 ff.); R. S. Conway–C. F. Walters–S. K. Johnson (i–x; xxi–xxx; 1914–35, O.C.T.); C. Giarratano (xli–xlv; 1933); P. Bayet (i and ii, Budé, 1941–). *Periochae*: O. Jahn (1853); O. Rossbach (1910).

COMMENTARIES: W. Weissenborn–H. J. Müller–O. Rossbach (2nd ed. 1867 ff.).

TRANSLATIONS: W. M. Roberts (1912–24); B. O. Foster-E. T. Sage-A. C. Schlesinger (1919 ff.).

LEXICONS: A. W. Ernesti, *Glossarium Liv.* (1827); F. Fügner, *Lex. Liv.* i (A–B, 1897).

MANUSCRIPTS: E. Chatelain, *Paléographie des classiques latins: T.-L.* (1895); Th. Mommsen and W. Studemund, *Analecta Liv.* (1873); J. N. Madvig, *Emend. Liv.* (2nd ed.; 1877); L. Traube, *Paläograph. Forsch.*, Part iv (Abh. Bayr. Ak. III. xxiv. 1; 1904); R. S. Conway-C. F. Walters-S. K. Johnson, *praef.* O.C.T.; C. Wessely, *Codex Vindobonus* photographed (1907).

SOURCE CRITICISM: H. Nissen, *Krit. Unters. über die Quellen der IV und V Dekade des L.* (1863); G. F. Unger, *Philol.*, Suppl. vol. iii, pt. 2 (1878); H. Hesselbarth, *Hist. krit. Unters. zur III Dekade des L.* (1889); W. Soltau, *Livius' Geschichtswerk* (1897); G. De Sanctis, *Storia dei Romani*, vols. i–iv, pt. 1 (1907–23); U. Kahrstedt, *Gesch. der Karthager* (Meltzer, vol. iii, 1913); *Die Annalistik von L., B. 31–45* (1913); A. Klotz, *Hermes* 1915, 481; M. Zimmerer , *Qu. Claudius Quadrigarius* (1937), 22; V. Wiehemeyer, *Proben hist. Kritik aus L.* xxi–xlv (1938).

COMPOSITION: H. Nissen, op. cit.; *Rh. Mus.* 1872, 539; H. Dessau, *Festschr. O. Hirschfeld* (1903), 465; *Hermes* 1906, 142; C. Cichorius, *Röm. Stud.* (1922), 261.

HISTORICAL AND LITERARY CRITICISM: H. Taine, *Essai sur T.-L.* (1856; 8th ed. 1910); K. Witte, *Rh. Mus.* 1910, 270, 359; W. Kroll, *Stud. zum Verständnis der röm. Literatur* (1924), 351; Fr. Klingner, *Antike* 1925, 86; R. Ullmann *La Technique des discours dans Salluste, T.-L. et Tacite* (1927); R. Heinze, *Vergils Epische Technik* (4th ed. 1928), 333; *Augusteische Kultur* (1930), 91; T. Frank, *Life and Lit. in the Roman Republic* (1930), 169; A. Reichenberger, *Stud. zum Erzählungsstil des T. L.* (1931); G. De Sanctis, *Problemi di storia ant.* (1932), 225; H. Bornecque, *Tite Live* (1933); E. Burck, *Die Erzählungskunst des T. L.* (1934); H.-G. Plathner, *Die Schlachtschilderungen bei L.* (1934); *Studi Liviani* (1934); W. Aly, *Livius und Ennius* (1936); H. Bruckmann, *Die röm. Niederlagen im Geschichtswerk des T.-L.* (1936); R. Syme, *The Roman Revolution* (1939), 463, 485; F. Hellmann, *Livius Interpretationem* (1939); Latte, *Class. Phil.* xxxv (1940), 56–60; Hoffmann, *Hermes*, Einzelschriften, Heft VIII (1942); P. Zancan, *Tito Livio* (1940); Catin, *En lisant Tite-Live* (1944).

STYLE AND LANGUAGE: E. Wölfflin, *Liv. Kritik und Liv. Sprachgebrauch* (1864); L. Kühnast, *Die Hauptpunkte der liv. Syntaxe* (2nd ed. 1871); O. Riemann, *Études sur la langue et la grammaire de T.-L.* (2nd ed. 1885); S. G. Stacey, *Die Entwicklung des liv. Stiles* (Archiv. für lat. Lex. x, 1898, p. 17); E. Norden, *Die antike Kunstprosa* (4th impr. 1923); Kroll, op. cit. p. 366; R. Ullmann, *Étude sur le style des discours de T.-L.* (1929). (See M. Schanz-C. Hosius, *Gesch. der röm. Literatur* ii (1935), 297.)   A. H. McD.

LIVIUS, see also DRUSUS, SALINATOR.

LOBON of Argos (perhaps 3rd c. B.C.) was a literary forger, author of a work (perhaps in verse) on poets (Diog. Laert. I. 34. 112), in which he ascribed verses fabricated by himself to the Seven Sages and works in prose to early poets, e.g. Aristeas, Semonides, Pindar. His treatise seems to have been extensively used by Suidas.   J. F. L.

LOCI COMMUNES, see COMMUNES LOCI.

LOCKS, see KEYS.

LOCRI EPIZEPHYRII (Λοκροὶ Ἐπιζεφύριοι), a Dorian city in the 'toe' of Italy, was founded c. 700 B.C., apparently by Opuntii (East Locrians), although its settlers probably included Ozolae (West Locrians), fugitive slaves, and Lacedaemonians. Oenotri (= Sicels?) previously inhabited the site. Locri's oligarchy, The Hundred Houses, reputedly governed excellently: the town possessed Europe's earliest written legal code (attributed to Zaleucus, q.v.). Locri defeated Croton at the Sagras battle (6th c.), founded its own colonies (Hipponium, Medma; before 450), and usually was friendly with Syracuse who supported it against its rival Rhegium (q.v.). Bruttian, Pyrrhic, and Hannibalic Wars caused some decline, but Locri was still a considerable town, allied to Rome, in Polybius' day; Polybius knew it intimately (12. 5 f.). Apparently Saracens finally destroyed it.

Strabo 6. 259 f.; Pindar *Ol.* 10 and 11; *Pyth.* 2; Thuc. bks. 3–8; Diod. bks. 12 and 14; Justin 20. 2; Livy bks. 22 and 29. W. A. Oldfather in *PW* xiii. 1289 f. (1927); D. Randall-MacIver, *Greek Cities of Italy and Sicily* (1931), 37 f.; J. Bérard, *Bibliogr. topogr.* (1941), 62.   E. T. S.

LOCRIS. Eastern Locris, comprising the mainland coast of the Euboean Straits from Thermopylae to Larymna, and Western Locris, comprising the valley of Amphissa and the northern coast of the Corinthian Gulf from Naupactus to near Crisa, were separated from one another by Doris and Phocis, probably the results of an invasion through an early Locrian State occupying central Greece. As late as the fifth century B.C. the two divisions of Locris, known as 'Opuntian' and 'Ozolian', possessed a joint franchise. Their territory being mainly infertile and hemmed in by stronger States, the Locrians played little part in history. Opuntian Locris united round a centre at Opus, where the assembly of the Thousand drawn from noble families met, founded Locri in south Italy, and began to coin in the fourth century B.C. But Ozolian Locris remained backward and without unity (Thuc. 1. 15). Both areas were curtailed by their neighbours, Opuntian Locris losing Thermopylae to the Thessalians and Daphnus to the Phocians, whereby Eastern Locris split into Hypocnemidian and Opuntian Locris, and Ozolian Locris losing Naupactus to Athens. The valley of Amphissa, traversed by the route from Doris to the Corinthian Gulf, was of strategic importance and became involved in the Sacred Wars (q.v.).

W. A. Oldfather, *AJArch.* 1916.   N. G. L. H.

LOCUSTA (LUCUSTA), a noted poisoner of Gallic origin, was employed by Agrippina to poison Claudius and by Nero for Britannicus. Nero took with him on his flight a poison prepared by her. Galba executed her.

LOGAOEDIC, see METRE, GREEK, III (5).

LOGIC. For the history of Greek logic the following works may be consulted: C. Prantl, *Geschichte d. Logik im Abendlande* (4 vols., 1855–70); L. Rabus, *Logik u. Metaphysik*, vol. i (1868); F. Ueberweg, *System d. Logik u. Geschichte d. logischen Lehren*[3] (1874, Engl. Transl. 1871); R. Adamson, *A Short History of Logic* (1911); T. Zieher, *Lehrbuch d. Logik* (1920); H. W. Blunt, art. 'Logic' in *Enc. Brit.*; Herbertz, *Das Wahrheitsproblem in d. griechischen Philosophie* (1913); E. Hoffmann, *Die Sprache u. d. archäische Logik* (1925); W. Lutoslawski, *The Origin and Growth of Plato's Logic*[2] (1905); N. Hartmann, *Platons Logik d. Seins* (1909); J. Stenzel, *Studien z. Geschichte d. platonischen Dialektik von Sokrates zu Aristoteles*[2] (1931, Engl. Transl. 1940); H. Maier, *Die Syllogistik d. Aristoteles* (3 vols., 1896–1900).   W. D. R.

LOGISTAI, Athenian magistrates: (1) A body of ten chosen by lot from their own members by the Boule; its duties were to examine the accounts of magistrates in each prytany, and thus to prepare for the final *euthyna*. (2) A body of thirty (later ten) chosen by lot from all citizens. They conducted the examination of accounts at the end of the magistrates' term of office (see EUTHYNA). They also assisted the *Hellenotamiai* (q.v.) in checking the contributions of the allies in the Delian League, and calculating the one-sixtieth part set apart for Athena.   A. W. G.

LOGOGRAPHERS. Until the late sixth century B.C., historical and biographical traditions were oral, like the 'myths' about sacred rites and cults, and other ancedotes, romances, folk-tales, and proverbial lore. Epic verse, Homeric and Hesiodic, had canonized much. The first prose transcripts from this fluid folk-memory are ascribed, in natural knowledge to Thales and Anaximander (qq.v.), in human affairs to Hecataeus, also of Miletus, whom Herodotus describes (2. 143) like Aesop (2. 135) as λογοποιός, Homer being ἐποποιός (2. 120) and Sappho μουσοποιός (2. 135). Later critics distinguish these early λογογράφοι, as mere compilers, from the first 'historians', Herodotus and Thucydides, who recomposed and interpreted similar sources to illustrate such larger themes as the Persian or the Peloponnesian War. Hecataeus (fr. 1), like Herodotus and Thucydides, derides contemporary 'Greek stories', and like Hesiod (*Th.* 24–8) professes veracity; yet Heraclitus (fr. 40 Diels) couples him with Pythagoras and Xenophanes as a man of more knowledge than judgement.

Principal types of such compilation are: (1) *Genealogies*, especially of families which 'went up to a god' like that of Hecataeus himself (Hdt. 2. 143). Like Hesiod's *Theogony* they codified aristocracies at a time when social prerogatives of birthright were challenged. (2) *Chronologies*, cross-referring pedigrees to official lists; kings of Sparta and of Athens, priestesses of Hera at Argos, Olympic and Carneian victors. (3) *Periegeseis* or *Periodoi*, descriptions of particular regions and especially of Greek cities with their institutions, resources, and local events, from their reputed foundations (Κτίσεις). (4) *Histories* only begin when (*a*) the rise of Persia needed explanation, and Persian conquest linked regional descriptions together into Περσικά; (*b*) Persian aggression drew Greek cities into concerted resistance and counter-attack, worthy of record in Ἑλληνικά. (5) Eventually, Herodotus (q.v.) explicitly includes both Greek and alien deeds (1. 1) in a single *History* and seeks the cause of the quarrel. Fragments in *FHG* i and *FGrH*; L. Pearson, *Early Ionian Historians* (1939), full bibliography.

Principal *logographers* are Acusilaus, Charon, Damastes, Hecataeus, Hellanicus, Pherecydes, Scylax, Xanthus; see these. The first author of town-histories was Cadmus of Miletus; Dionysius of Miletus wrote Περσικά, the first general survey of Oriental history; Eugeon (Euagon) of Samos wrote a chronicle of his own city; Herodorus of Heraclea Pontica, a contemporary of Hecataeus, wrote on Heracles, Orpheus and Musaeus, the Argonauts, and the Pelopids. *FHG* ii. 27, 28, 30; *FGrH* i. 31. Of a few others little is known but their names. J. L. M.

LOGOS, in its origin a psychological idea ('thought' and 'thought-as-expressed'), acquires a metaphysical meaning in Greek philosophy, as the self-actualizing rational principle of the universe. In Heraclitus (Bywater 1, 2, 23, 71, 92, 93; Diels 115, 126 a) it is the rationality of the world-process, the law of change, which comes to self-consciousness in the philosopher. Fructified by Aristotelian teleology, the Logos becomes in Stoicism the dynamic rational principle active in the world-whole and its parts (λόγος σπερματικός, λόγοι σπερματικοί), and the ethical ὀρθὸς λόγος common to gods and men and the medium of communion with the Divine; the conception becomes religious in popular Stoicism and Hellenistic syncretism (Hermes-Logos, etc.). In Philo it is both the active intelligent world-principle, as in Stoicism, and the sum of the Platonic Ideas, which for Philo are thoughts in the mind of God; both the Divine Thought-thinking and the Divine Thought-thought, the instrument and the plan of God, and the unique mediator between God and His creatures; in its soteriological aspect it is equated with the Jewish Wisdom and Word of God, and typified by a great variety of Old Testament figures (cf. especially Quisrer. div. her. 42, *CW.* 205–6). For Philo, as for the Greeks, the Logos is neither personal nor impersonal; the assertion of its hypostatic distinction from God (δεύτερος θεός, etc.) has always reference to the limitations of human knowledge (so Bevan, against Heinze); in the last resort the Logos is God Himself in His relative aspect (so Drummond and Lebreton). In Neoplatonism Logos is subordinate to Nous. But the second-century Apologists, notably Justin Martyr, equate the conception with the pre-existent and incarnate Christ in their presentation of Christianity as the revealed philosophy, and so establish its long association with Christian theology.

GENERAL LITERATURE. M. Heinze, *Die Lehre vom Logos in der griechischen Philosophie* (1872); A. Aall, *Der Logos, Geschichte seiner Entwickelung in der griechischen Philosophie und der christlichen Litteratur* (2 vols. 1896–8); J. Lebreton, 'Les Théories du Logos au début de l'ère chrétienne', *Études* (*Revue de la Compagnie de Jésus*) *vol. cvi* (1906); R. P. Lagrange, 'Le Logos d'Héraclitie' and 'Vers le Logos de Saint Jean', *Révue Biblique* 1923. SPECIAL SUBJECTS. (Stoicism) A. Schmekel, *Die Philosophie der mittleren Stoa*, 1892. (Hellenistic syncretism) E. Krebs, 'Der Logos als Heiland im ersten Jahrhundert', *Freiburger Theologische Studien* 1910. (Philo) J. Drummond, *Philo Judaeus* (2 vols. 1888); H. A. A. Kennedy, *Philo's Contribution to Religion* (1919); and especially E. R. Bevan, essay on 'Hellenistic Judaism' in *The Legacy of Israel* (1927). (Justin Martyr) E. R. Goodenough, *The Theology of Justin Martyr* (Jena 1923). J. L. MATTHEWS.

LOLLIA PAULINA was a woman of distinguished ancestry and very great wealth. She was forced to abandon her marriage with P. Memmius Regulus in order that she might marry the Emperor Gaius in A.D. 38. Divorced by him in the following year, she was an unsuccessful candidate for the hand of Claudius after Messalina's death in 48. Agrippina secured her banishment (on the charge of consulting astrologers) in the following year, and she was driven to suicide. J. P. B.

LOLLIUS (1) PALICANUS, MARCUS, tribune in 71 B.C., obtained from Pompey the restoration of the powers of the tribunate. He supported the *lex iudiciaria* of Aurelius Cotta. His humble Picene origin and political sentiments prevented his election to the consulship in 67. A. M.

LOLLIUS (2), MARCUS (*cos.* 21 B.C.), a *novus homo* and prominent partisan of Augustus, praised by Horace (*Carm.* 4. 9) for conspicuous integrity, but described by Velleius as crafty, corrupt, and rapacious. He was the first legate of Galatia (25), active in Macedonia, probably as proconsul (*c.* 19–18) and then in Gaul, where German raiders inflicted a defeat, capturing the eagle of a legion, but hardly causing a serious disaster. In 1 B.C. he was chosen to be counsellor and overseer of C. Caesar in the East. A bitter enemy of Tiberius, he influenced the young prince against the exile. As a result of quarrel or intrigue, however, he fell from favour, was accused of taking bribes from the Parthian king, and died before long, perhaps by suicide (A.D. 2). Lollius left enormous wealth.

R. Syme, *Roman Revolution* (1939), see Index. R. S.

LOLLIUS (3) BASSUS of Smyrna has about a dozen epigrams in the *Greek Anthology*, of which one (7. 391) is a pompous reflection on the death of Germanicus, and another (9. 283 Plan.) a comment on his German expedition (A.D. 14–16). The rest of the poems are uninteresting, except for one joke (11. 72) in the manner which Martial was to perfect seventy years later.

C. Cichorius, *Röm. Stud.* c. viii. 7 (1922) G. H.

LOLLIUS (4) URBICUS, QUINTUS, governor of Britain from A.D. 139 until after 142 (*JRS* xii. 66) and formerly legate of Legio X Gemina and governor of Lower Germany, built the Wall of Antoninus (q.v.) (S.H.A. *Pius* 5. 6; *CIL* vii. 1125; *Eph. Epigr.* ix. 1390). Inscriptions commemorating the erection of buildings under Urbicus come from Corstopitum (*JRS* xxvi. 264; *Eph. Epigr.* ix. 1146), and from High Rochester (*CIL* vii. 1041). He later became governor of Africa (Apul. *Apol.* 2) and *praefectus urbi* (*CIL* viii. 6705, 6706). I. A. R.

LONDINIUM (perhaps denoting 'place of Londinos', 'the fierce one'), originally stood on the eastern of two hillocks bounding the Walbrook at the mouth of the Thames. Tacitus states that at the time of Boudicca's revolt (61) it was an important trading-centre (*Ann.* 14.

33) and that at the principal towns, Londinium, Verulamium, and Camulodunum, 70,000 persons perished. Early vestiges have been found, but authority inclines against a pre-Roman origin for this considerable community.

Though originally merely a *vicus* of the Cantii (Ptolemy, 2. 3, 12), it soon became the financial centre of the province (*CIL* vii. 30 and *JRS* xxvi. 264–5), and eventually the capital, probably of Britain, certainly of one of the provinces into which Britain was subsequently divided. It was the principal road-centre, and is mentioned as a key-point in official activities. In *c.* 290–326 and 383–8 it was the seat of a mint, and a treasury official was stationed there (*Not. Dign. Occid.* xi. 37). The Council List of Arles calls it a 'ciuitas' and assigns it a bishop. It received at an unknown date (?326–65) the title of Augusta. Of its local divisions, a *vicinia* is known (*CIL* vii. 20).

The principal remains are subsequent to Boudicca's destruction, after which the settlement spread to the western hill. About 80 a vast *basilica* (500 feet long) and *forum*, enclosing perhaps an official temple, were built; *c.* 120 the town wall was built of squared stones and brick-bonders with bank and ditch or ditches. It enclosed an area of *c.* 330 acres, making Londinium the fifth largest town in the west. Traces of stone and timber foundations, mosaics, etc., are found with frequency within the walls, and there was a suburb on the south bank connected by a bridge. A serious fire seems to have occurred *c.* 120–30, and at various late dates bastions were added to the town wall, the river section of which was built (or rebuilt).

How far Londinium survived the Saxon invasions is the subject of controversy (see R. E. M. Wheeler, *Antiquity* viii. 290–302, ix. 443–7; *Antiquaries Journal* xiv. 254–63; *London and the Saxons*; J. N. L. Myres, *Antiquity* ix. 437–42; *JRS* xxvi. 87–92). Wheeler has ingeniously postulated a dual settlement, each community (Saxons and Romano-Britons) occupying one of the hillocks, a state of affairs for which Trier furnishes a parallel. But Londinium was certainly a town without a bishop in the seventh century (Bede, *Hist. Eccl.* ii. 3).

Complete account in *Royal Commission on Historical Monuments, London (Roman)* (1928); subsequent discoveries summarized in *JRS*. See also T. D. Pryce and F. Oswald, *Archaeologia* lxxviii (1928), 73 (the beginnings of Roman Britain).   C. E. S.

LONG WALLS, THE (τὰ μακρὰ τείχη or σκέλη),
were built between 461 and 456 B.C. to connect Athens with her ports, Phalerum and Piraeus. About 455 the Phaleric wall was replaced by a third, parallel to the north or Piraeus wall. They were destroyed by the Spartans to flute music in 404 but rebuilt by Conon in 393. The walls to Piraeus were about 4 miles long and *c.* 200 yards apart; the traces visible a century ago have now almost entirely disappeared. The course of the Phaleric wall is uncertain. The main road from Piraeus to Athens lay outside, the road inside being primarily military. The Long Walls were used in the Peloponnesian War to make Athens into an isolated fortress, in which most of the population of Attica could live on sea-borne provisions. The example of Long Walls was followed elsewhere, notably at Megara.

W. Judeich, *Topographie von Athen*² (1931), 155 ff. (his course for the Phaleric wall is improbable); T. Lenschau, *PW* xix, 88–9; R. L. Scranton, 'The Fortifications of Athens at the opening of the Peloponnesian War', *AJArch.* 1938, 525 ff.   T. J. D.

'LONGINUS' (*Ps.-Longinus*) is the name commonly
assigned to the unknown author of *On the Sublime* (Π. ὕψους), owing to its long but mistaken association with Cassius Longinus. Author of two works (lost) on σύνθεσις (39. 1) and one (lost) on Xenophon (8. 1) the unknown, in the light of his consistent treatment of first-century problems, was probably a first-century rhetor (*fl.* A.D. 80?), with Theodorean sympathies (3. 5),

who endeavoured in Π. ὕψους to supplement Caecilius' early teaching on 'distinction' in style (1. 1; 8. 2). The work (despite gaps) is one of the greatest of all critical achievements. An illuminating dissertation on style, accompanied by many penetrating judgements, as well as suggestive pronouncements on critical standards and principles, the treatise is unique in its interpretation of the classical spirit, its compelling enthusiasms, its sanity, its freshness, and its unerring insight into the essentials of art. *See* LITERARY CRITICISM IN ANTIQUITY, I. 5.

Texts, etc.: *On the Sublime*, ed. W. Rhys Roberts (1899); ed. W. H. Fyfe (Loeb, 1927): see also J. W. H. Atkins, *Lit. Crit. in Antiquity*, 2. 210 ff.   J. W. H. A.

LONGINUS, CASSIUS (*c.* A.D. 213–73), eminent rhetori-
cian, who taught (Porphyrius was one of his pupils) at Athens, and later (*c.* 268) became counsellor to Zenobia, queen of Palmyra, in whose service he was executed by Aurelian for rebellion. Of his philosophical writings (in Greek), Π. τέλους and Π. ἀρχῶν, a fragment of the former alone remains. He wrote also a τέχνη, of which three sections have survived (Spengel, *Rh. Gr.* i. 299–328), treatises on Homer and Homeric Problems, and the Φιλόλογοι ὁμιλίαι, upon which his fame as a critic rested. To him in later times the famous Π. ὕψους was falsely attributed.   J. W. H. A.

LONGINUS, *see also under* CASSIUS (4), (5), and (6).

LONGUS, author of a Greek pastoral romance called
Daphnis and Chloe (Ποιμενικὰ τὰ κατὰ Δάφνιν καὶ Χλόην), was probably a native of Lesbos, which is the scene of his story and which has provided inscriptional evidence for his peculiar but unjustly suspected name. On the strength of style and supposed imitations he has been assigned to every century from the second to the sixth; if there is any relation between him and Alciphron, L. is more likely to be the model, and on general grounds his most probable date is the third century A.D.

Daphnis and Chloe, exposed in infancy and found in remarkable circumstances, pass their childhood together tending their foster-parents' goats and sheep. An idyllic existence, broken by occasional mishaps and adventures, is at once inspired and distracted by the bitter-sweets of love, of which in their innocence they know neither the meaning nor the remedy. Daphnis is taught the remedy, but only experiments on Chloe when they are married with the blessing of their true parents, who prove to be rich Mytileneans.

The story is exceptional both for its pastoral setting and for its maintenance of the unity of place; nevertheless L. contrives to introduce many of the incidents characteristic of the Greek Novel—piracy, war, the attentions of unwelcome suitors. The descriptions of pastoral life and country scenes are often charming, and the studied artificiality which lies behind the apparent simplicity is well concealed. Compared with the other Greek novels the tone is decadent, but the elegance of the composition has justly earned it praise and popularity.

BIBLIOGRAPHY
TEXTS: A. Kaïris (Athens, 1932). With translation: Edmonds (Loeb); Dalmeyda (Budé).
TRANSLATIONS: G. Thornley (1657, etc.); G. Moore (1922). French, J. Amyot (1559, etc.).
COMMENTARY: Villoison (1778).
STYLE AND DICTION: the editors named above under *Texts*; G. Valley, *Über den Sprachgebrauch des Longos* (1926); L. Castiglioni, *Rendiconti della R. Ist. Lomb. di scienze e lettere* (1928); H. Dörrie, *de Longi Ach. Tat. Heliod. memoria* (1935).
LIFE AND WORK: the editors named under *Texts*; G. Dalmeyda, *Mélanges Glotz* i (1932); H. Reich, *de Alciphronis Longique aetate* (1894).
See also bibliography under NOVEL, GREEK.   R. M. R.

LONGUS, *see also* VELIUS.

LORICA SEGMENTATA, *see* ARMS, ROMAN.

LOTOPHAGI, a fabulous people, living on the lotus (flower?), the effect of which is to make the eater forget his own country and desire to live in Lotus-land (*Od.* 9. 82 ff.).

LUA MATER. Cult-partner of Saturnus, Gellius 13. 23. 2 (Luam Saturni; cf. SATURNUS). Her name may be connected with *lues* and mean something like 'baneful'; she is one of the deities to whom captured arms may be dedicated and burned (Livy 8. 1. 6; 45. 33. 2).

LUCA, nowadays *Lucca*, a town in Liguria (later incorporated in Etruria) on the river Ausar (Strabo 5. 217). Both notices of the town before 100 B.C. are suspect (Livy 21. 59; Vell. Pat. 1. 15: preferably read Luna (q.v.) in each case). Luca was a border town of the Cisalpine province and became famous when Caesar, Pompey, and Crassus met there for their conference in 56 B.C. (Suet. *Iul.* 24, etc.). Under the late Republic Luca was a *municipium* (Cic. *Fam.* 13. 13), under the Empire a *colonia* (Pliny *HN* 3. 50). But, although a fairly important station on the Via Clodia, it is rarely mentioned until late Imperial times.   E. T. S.

LUCAN (MARCUS ANNAEUS LUCANUS, A.D. 39–65) was born at Corduba (modern *Cordova*), 3 Nov. A.D. 39. His father, M. Annaeus Mela, was a Roman knight and a brother of the philosopher Seneca. Mela migrated to Rome when his son was about eight months old. There Lucan received the ordinary liberal education, ending with the school of rhetoric, where he was a great success; there is also good reason to believe that he studied philosophy under the famous Stoic Cornutus. He continued his studies at Athens, but was recalled by Nero, who admitted him to his inner circle and conferred on him the offices of quaestor and augur. In A.D. 60, at the first celebration of the games called Neronia, he won a prize with a poem in praise of Nero. In 62 or 63 he published three books of his epic on the Civil War. Growing enmity between him and Nero, for which various reasons are given, finally caused the emperor to debar him from further exercise, or at least from public display, of his literary talent. Lucan recklessly joined the conspiracy of Piso, and on its disclosure was compelled to put an end to his life (30 Apr. 65). The story that he sought to win leniency by accusing his mother of complicity in the plot is probably a malicious fabrication (see F. Plessis, *La Poésie latine* (1909), 547–50).

WORKS. Lucan was a voluminous writer from early years. The titles of many of his works, both in prose and in verse, have come down to us, but nothing more than a few lines remains of any of them except the *Bellum Civile* (the title *Pharsalia* is due to a misunderstanding of 9. 985). It is in ten books, the last being unfinished. Beginning with the causes of the war between Caesar and Pompey, it carries the story beyond the death of Pompey until it breaks off with Caesar's occupation of Pharos in Egypt. The battle of Pharsalia is related in bk. 7. In all probability Lucan intended to continue the narrative to the death of Caesar, if not farther. His principal historical authority was undoubtedly Livy, but he probably consulted others, including Caesar. It is not his purpose to give a full account of the war. Several events are omitted, others receive only a brief perfunctory mention. He dwells at length on particular episodes, not solely for their intrinsic importance, but largely because they appealed to his emotions or offered scope for a display of his powers. There are a few glaring departures from historical truth, as when he makes Cicero, who was not present at Pharsalia, deliver a harangue to Pompey on the eve of the battle; but apart from instances of carelessness, his perversions of the facts consist mostly of a false colouring due to his Stoic and Republican bias. On the other hand, he shows some notable instances of penetrating insight.

Recent history is ill suited to be the subject of a sustained epic poem, and Lucan, by discarding (wisely, it is true) the traditional apparatus of divine interventions, made his task doubly hard. All the resources of rhetoric are enlisted to impress the reader; vehement declamation and brilliant epigrammatic utterances (*sententiae*) are everywhere in evidence. There are numerous digressions, many of them making a display of curious learning. In bk. 6, for example, we find 80 lines on Thessaly and 136 on witches, in bk. 9, 115 lines on serpents and their bites, in bk. 10, 138 lines on the Nile. In general Lucan shows an excessive fondness for the purple patch. There is much exaggeration, often absurd; bizarre effects and far-fetched paradoxes abound. Nevertheless, the poet's feeling is strong and sincere. The horrors of civil war stirred his heart, and as the poem proceeded (and especially after his estrangement from Nero) his detestation of Caesarism and of its founder became a ruling passion. But with all his prejudice he cannot entirely conceal, even from himself, the greatness of Caesar, and the attempt to exalt the unheroic Pompey above such a colossus was foredoomed to failure; he does, however, succeed in making Pompey a truly tragic figure and in evoking sympathy both for him and for his cause. The portrayal of Cato, the unflinching Stoic, arouses at best a qualified admiration without much appeal to the heart. The language of the poem, though not without vigour and occasional novelty, lacks the richness and colour of Virgil. The verse is deficient in flexibility and variety; the comparative rarity of elision and the great fondness for the 'hephthemimeral jerk' are conspicuous features. But with all its faults the work is a remarkable achievement for so young a writer. Permeated though it is, and often marred, by rhetoric, it soars at times to those higher regions where poetry and oratory meet, where vision, imagination, and emotion commingle and find noble utterance. Even where this has not been achieved, there are many passages whose stirring trumpet-tones vibrate in the memory and whose unsurpassed epigrams, incisive and often strangely thrilling, have become part of the world's literary heritage. Lucan had a great vogue in the Middle Ages, and his influence is often seen in the poetry and drama of the seventeenth century. In later times he has found more critics than admirers, but Shelley drew inspiration from him, and, like Southey, at first preferred him to Virgil. Macaulay considered him one of the most remarkable men that ever lived. *See also* EPIC POETRY, LATIN, para. 2.

Critical texts by Hosius² (1913) and (with much valuable exegesis) by Housman (1926, 1927). Commentaries by Oudendorp, Cortius and Weber, Lemaire, Haskins (with good introduction by Heitland). Text and prose translation: J. D. Duff (Loeb, 1928); verse translation, E. Ridley³ (1919). Cf. R. Pichon, *Les sources de Lucain* (1912); E. Trampe, *De Lucani arte metrica* (1884).   W. B. A.

LUCANIA, a mountainous region of southern Italy; recently its ancient name has replaced the medieval *Basilicata*. Its earliest recorded inhabitants are Oenotri (= Sicels?) and Chones (= Illyrians). *C.* 700 B.C. Greeks commenced colonizing its fertile coastlands. *C.* 420 Sabelli (q.v.), the pugnacious Lucani, began to subjugate the Greeks; by 390 they held all Lucania and were partly hellenized (Polyaen. 2. 10; Diod. 14. 91–102; Strabo 5. 253 f.). Lucanian communities had an official known as *meddix*; a generalissimo led their confederation in war (Strabo 6. 254). In the fourth century Tarentum was their chief enemy; apparently their decline began after her mercenary captain Alexander defeated them (326). Thereupon they prudently sought a Roman alliance (Livy 8. 24, 27; 10. 11; Diod. 20. 104). Later, however, Lucani opposed and were conquered by Rome in the Pyrrhic, Hannibalic, and Social Wars. These struggles completely ruined Lucania; malaria appeared and is only now being eradicated (Zonar. 8, 3 f.; Livy 22. 61; App. *BCiv.* 1. 90 f.). Sulla massacred both

Lucani and Samnites, and the Lucani as a separate nation disappeared. Chief towns: coastal Greek colonies and Grumentum, Atina, Potentia, and perhaps Bantia.

R. S. Conway, *Italic Dialects* i (1897), 11; K. J. Beloch, *Röm. Gesch.* 544, 591.   E. T. S.

LUCCEIUS, LUCIUS, a senator who figured in the political moves of 64 B.C. Caesar, who was presiding over the *quaestio de sicariis*, encouraged the prosecution of two of Sulla's agents on a charge of murder (Suet. *Iul.* 10) in order to challenge the legality of his act of indemnity. Thereupon Lucceius brought a similar charge against Catiline, whom Caesar and Crassus were supporting for the consulship (Asconius 81). Catiline was eventually acquitted; but thereafter Sulla's agents were left in peace. Lucceius unsuccessfully stood for the consulship with Caesar in 60; later he devoted himself to history (Cic. *Fam.* 5. 12).   J. M. C.

LUCIAN (Λουκιανός) of Samosata (b. *c.* A.D. 120), author of some eighty pieces, chiefly in Dialogue form. For details of his career we have to depend largely on his writings. He received a sufficiently good education to become, first a pleader (Suidas), and later a travelling lecturer; he practised the art of Sophistic rhetoric as far afield as Gaul (Δὶς κατηγορούμενος 27). About the age of 40 (Ἑρμότιμος 13), when he moved to Athens, he deserted rhetoric for 'philosophy'. From then onwards he proceeded to develop the special variety of Dialogue which made him famous. He later resumed the habit of public recitation and accepted a post under the Roman administration in Egypt. He died later than A.D. 180 (Ἀλέξανδρος 48).

Of his writings, certain μελέται, or exercises on set themes (e.g. Φάλαρις), probably belong to his early period; so also his first essays in Dialogue (e.g. Θεῶν διάλογοι). His προλαλίαι ('introductions') and certain epideictic pieces (Μυίας ἐγκώμιον, Περὶ τοῦ οἴκου) may belong to any part of his career. The strongest influence in his development was the Cynic humour of Menippus of Gadara (Δὶς κατ. 33); it was supplemented by that of the Mime, Attic Comedy (notably the Old), and in his later works the Platonic Dialogue. In his typically Menippean period he aimed his satire at such objects as popular religious ideas (Ἰκαρομένιππος, Θεῶν ἐκκλησία), human vanity (Χάρων, Νεκρικοὶ διάλογοι), and philosophic pretensions (Βίων πρᾶσις). Contact with the Platonic Dialogue produced a series of pieces, some late in his life, in which he introduces himself as Λυκῖνος (Ἑρμότιμος, Πλοῖον, Εἰκόνες). Beside the Dialogue form he adopted the epistolary, either direct (Πῶς δεῖ ἱστορίαν συγγράφειν), or as a setting for Dialogue (Νιγρῖνος). Notable among his productions in this style are Περεγρῖνος and Ἀλέξανδρος, the castigation respectively of a religious maniac and of a charlatan. His most famous narrative is Ἀληθὴς ἱστορία; the authorship of Λούκιος ἢ ὄνος is questioned.

Lucian compares favourably with his contemporaries, not merely in the variety of his literary resources and in his skill in handling them, but in the reality of his objects. He uses his Atticism, in which he yields to none of them, as a means rather than as an end. He illustrates contemporary life and manners; his comments on art, in particular, are more helpful than those of some professed critics. He cannot, however, be called either a great original literary artist or a profound thinker. His stock of ideas, except when he is dealing with topical subjects, is drawn either from classical literature or from the popular philosophy of the preceding age; he has no genuine philosophic position, but is essentially an opportunist, σπουδαῖος ἐς τὸ γελασθῆναι (Eunapius). At the same time, though he derived his forms from earlier models, the Satiric Dialogue as he ultimately developed it is a worthy addition to Greek literature of the second rank.

A certain adroitness of appeal to the less reflective side of human nature has preserved his work in spite of contemporary disregard.

Ancient sources: Suidas; Eunap. *VS prooem.* 9; Photius, *Bibl.* cod. 128. Editions: J. Sommerbrodt (1886–99); C. Jacobitz (1896); Nils Nilén (1907–). Scholia: H. Rabe (1906). Complete studies: M. Croiset, *Essai sur L.* (1882); R. Helm, *L. und Menipp.* (1906). Articles and notices: R. C. Jebb, *Essays and Addresses* (1907); E. J. Putnam, *Class. Phil.* 1909. E. Norden, *Antike Kunstprosa* (1909) (style). W. Schmid, *Atticismus* i (1887) (language).   W. M. E.

LUCĪLIUS (1), GAIUS (*c.* 180–*c.* 102 B.C.), Latin satirist, born at Suessa Aurunca, was a well-educated friend of Greek philosophers, and possessed estates in Italy (possibly elsewhere). Coming to Rome after 160, he made political friends, especially Scipio Aemilianus, with whom he served in Spain 134–133, returning thence to live in a fine house at Rome. In 131 he completed books now numbered 26–7 (*septenarii*), 28 (*septenarii*, *senarii*, hexameters), 29 following *c.* 129 B.C. About 125 bk. 30 was written wholly in hexameters—henceforth his fixed metre. A new series began *c.* 123 with bk. 1, others following to bk. 21 between 125 and 120. Meanwhile he closely watched Roman politics (he was perhaps not a citizen), journeyed to south Italy (and Sicily and Sardinia?), suffered some ill health, and, being now a prominent man, made more friends (especially Junius Congus, C. Laelius, Q. Laelius Archelaus, Vettius Philocomus) and enemies (especially Metellus Macedonicus, Lentulus Lupus, Mucius Scaevola Augur, Lucius Opimius). In 105 he retired to Naples, where perhaps he wrote little elegiac poems (bks. 22–5) on his slaves and freedmen, and died *c.* 102.

Surviving fragments (less than 1,300 lines) come from thirty books. Those now numbered 26–30 formed one volume *c.* 124 B.C., while bks. 1–21 were published in a second volume *c.* 106, bks. 22–5 later. New grouping, with present numbering, took place before the Imperial period, and resulted in books 1–21 (mature work in hexameters), 22–5 (occasional? elegiacs), 26–30 (various metres; early work). The fragments reveal a free-and-easy, not a fanatical, man, acquainted with country-life but living in a city where he watched society and politics —a man carelessly casting his thoughts into metre without much poetic art; recording bits of his own and others' lives in the first really extensive literary presentation of *satura* or medley (thus establishing a specially Roman form of literature, owing little to Greece except its metres) including politics, social life, and their problems; a journey; letters to friends; literary criticism (especially of Ennius, Pacuvius, and Accius and their heavy diction in tragedies); even rules of spelling. Posterity remarked on his satiric powers, how he lashed the city, tore away the mask of respectability, and scared the guilty; and called him variously harsh, bitter, agreeable, graceful, witty, learned, and so on. He first made Satire satiric, but of later satirists was more like gentle Horace, who imitated him, than fiery Juvenal.

Fragments (chiefly from Nonius): F. Marx, *C. Lucili Carminum Reliquiae*, Teubner, 1904 (text), 1905 (Latin commentary); E. H. Warmington, *Remains of Old Latin* iii (Loeb, 1938; with translation). Important modern studies: C. Cichorius, *Untersuchungen zu Lucilius*; G. C. Fiske, *Lucilius and Horace* (U.S.A., 1920); N. Terzaghi, *Lucilio* (1934); J. Wight Duff, *Roman Satire* (U.S.A., 1936).   E. H. W.

LUCILIUS (2) IUNIOR, GAIUS, Seneca's friend and the recipient of *De Providentia*, *Naturales Quaestiones*, and *Epistulae Morales*, was born at Pompeii, apparently in Augustus' last decade, without wealth or prospects. Ambition, energy, and personality gained him distinguished connexions and raised him to equestrian rank. He survived, under Gaius, a friendship with Gaetulicus and, under Claudius, Messalina's displeasure; appears to have held procuratorships in Illyricum and Africa; and is last seen about A.D. 63–4, still dissatisfied and deploring his handicaps, as procurator of Sicily. His unofficial interests were philosophy and poetry. Seneca's estimate of his work was high: we cannot check it, as nothing survives but three verses, the attribution of the *Aetna* to him lacking substance. E. P. B.

LUCILLA, ANNIA (AURELIA GALERIA) (b. *c.* A.D. 148), daughter of M. Aurelius (q.v.), and married at Ephesus to L. Verus (q.v.) *c.* 164, with the title 'Augusta'. On Verus' death (169) M. Aurelius immediately married her —an unwilling bride—to Ti. Claudius (q.v.) Pompeianus. About 182 she conspired unsuccessfully against her brother Commodus (q.v.); exiled to Capreae, she was subsequently put to death.

See *under* AURELIUS (1), MARCUS, *and* VERUS; also *PIR*[2], A 707. Coinage struck in her name: H. Mattingly and E. A. Sydenham, *The Roman Imperial Coinage* iii (1930). C. H. V. S.

LUCILLIUS (Λουκίλλιος) was the author of some 120 Greek epigrams in the *Anthology*. He was patronized by Nero (*Anth. Pal.* 9. 572), just as Martial (whom he closely resembles) was by Domitian. His poems are almost all exaggerated jokes on curious or repulsive people, many being extremely funny: thus we have the thief who stole everything, including the detective (*Anth. Pal.* 10. 177), and the thin man who had to wear a sinker when diving (10. 100). L. was one of the first poets to emphasize the climactic point in the last line of the epigram, and to make it exclusively a humorous point. The influence of Latin satire is obvious—he was contemporary with the *Apocolocyntosis* and the satire of Petronius.

E. Pertsch, *De Martiale Graecorum poetarum imitatore* (1914); K. Prinz, *Martial und das griech. Epigramm* (1914); C. Cichorius, *Röm. Stud.* c. viii. 13 (1922); A. Linnenkugel, *De Lucillo Tarrhaeo* (1926), identifies him with a distinguished scholar of the same period. G. H.

LUCILLUS of Tarrha, *see* PAROEMIOGRAPHERS.

LUCINA, *see* JUNO.

LUCRETIA, the wife of Tarquinius (q.v.) Collatinus, according to legend was outraged by Sextus, son of Tarquinius Superbus; having told her husband, she took her own life. This incident resulted in a popular rising led by Junius Brutus (q.v.) against the Tarquins, and their expulsion from Rome. While the story of Lucretia arose from popular poetry, independent of Greek literary influence, her father Lucretius (q.v. 1) was invented by annalists who elaborated the legend. P. T.

LUCRETIUS (1) TRICIPITINUS, SPURIUS, the father of Lucretia (q.v.). When the annalists associated her with the fall of the monarchy, they placed Lucretius among the founders of Republican freedom by alleging that he had been appointed prefect of Rome by the last king, and had retained that office under the Republic. The tradition that he was consul in 509 is disproved by Livy (2. 5). P. T.

LUCRETIUS (2) (TITUS LUCRETIUS CARUS), poet and philosopher, probably 94 to 55 B.C. Jerome gives the date of his birth as 94 and says that he died in his 44th year, i.e. in 51 or 50. Donatus in his Life of Virgil states that Virgil assumed the *toga virilis* on 15 Oct. 55, and adds that 'it happened that on that very day Lucretius the poet died'. Cicero (*QFr.* 2. 9. 3), writing in 54, implies that both he and his brother had read the poem, but it is clear from its unfinished state that it was not published till after the poet's death. His death should therefore probably be placed in 55; if Jerome is right as to his age, he was born in 99.

2. Of Lucretius' life almost nothing is known. It is natural to assume that he was a member of the aristocratic Roman family of the Lucretii, whose names occur in the Fasti as holders of magistracies. This view has lately been contested on the ground that Carus was not a cognomen of noble families, but of slaves and freedmen, and was possibly a romanized version of a Celtic name; Lucretius would then be a freedman attached to the house of the Lucretii. But inscriptions show Carus as a cognomen of free men. A more recent theory is that Lucretius was a Campanian—a landowner near Pompeii —and learned his Epicureanism at Naples, but the evidence is slender.

3. The only certain fact of his life is that he was a friend—or possibly dependant—of the aristocrat C. Memmius, the patron of Catullus and Cinna, to whom the poem is dedicated. A 'Life' prefixed to the Editio Veneta in the British Museum and written in the hand of Girolamo Borgia, secretary of Pontanus, states that he was intimate with Atticus, Cicero, Cassius, and Brutus, but this 'Life' is of doubtful authority. Jerome makes the famous statement that Lucretius was poisoned by a love-philtre, wrote the poem in his lucid intervals, and ultimately committed suicide. The attack on the passion of love in bk. 4 might be held to support this, but the poem itself does not show signs of insanity; it may be that the poet was of a melancholy disposition and that a love-philtre led to suicide. Jerome also says that Cicero 'emended' the poem, but this need mean no more than that he suggested corrections, not that he edited it for posthumous publication.

4. Lucretius' only work is the *De Rerum Natura*, a didactic poem in six books, in which the poet expounds the physical theory of Epicurus (q.v.) with a view to abolishing superstitious fears of the intervention of the gods in the world and of the punishment of the soul in an after-life. This he accomplishes by demonstrating that the world is governed by the mechanical laws of nature ('foedera naturai') and that the soul is mortal and perishes with the body. The bulk of the poem is occupied in setting out in detail the atomic view of the universe, which Epicurus adopted with modifications from the Atomists Leucippus and Democritus (qq.v.). Lucretius also touches from time to time on Epicurus' moral theory that pleasure is the end of life, and his thought is regulated throughout by Epicurus' rules of procedure (*Canonica*), which are to some extent expounded in bk. 4. The root-idea is that of atoms infinite in number moving in space infinite in extent and by their combinations bringing about the creation of things. Lucretius' philosophy is thus purely material, but not, like that of Democritus, deterministic; for he postulates free-will for man and corresponding to it a certain spontaneity of movement in the atoms (2. 216–93).

5. Book 1, after an introductory address to Venus as goddess of creation, starts from the principle of the permanence of matter and demonstrates the existence of matter in the form of 'first-bodies' or particles, and of void as empty space. L. then shows that the first-bodies are 'atoms', solid, indivisible, and eternal. In a digression he refutes the rival physical systems of Heraclitus the monist and Empedocles the pluralist, and the homoeomeria of Anaxagoras; and in conclusion shows that the universe and its components, the atoms and space, are infinite.

Book 2 opens with a poem on the blessings of philosophy and deals first with the motions of the atoms, then with their shapes and the effects of difference in their shapes on compounds. L. then argues that the atoms do not possess secondary qualities, colour, heat, sound, taste, and smell, or sensation, and concludes with a section on the many worlds and their formation and destruction.

Book 3 deals with the soul. After a preliminary laudation of Epicurus, L. discusses the atomic formation of the soul and its relation to the body. There follows a long series of proofs of its mortality, drawn from its atomic structure and from the phenomena of disease and its cure. The book ends with a triumph-hymn on the mortality of the soul and the folly of the fear of death.

Book 4, which opens with a picture of L.'s mission, treats mainly of the psychology of sensation and thought. L. demonstrates that sight is effected by means of 'images' coming off from things and entering the eye. He then discusses the nature of sensation and thought, and deals with false inferences of the mind based on sensation, which is itself infallible. In the end of the book he treats of certain functions of the body and especially of the passion of love, which he violently condemns.

Book 5 is devoted to the phenomena of our world. After another hymn of praise to Epicurus and an attack on the theological view, he shows that the world had a beginning and will have an end, describes its formation, and discusses certain problems of astronomy. He then speaks of the origin on the earth of vegetable and animal life, of the creation of man and the early development of civilization.

Book 6, whose proem is once more a laudation of Epicurus, deals with miscellaneous phenomena, celestial and terrestrial. Among the former L. discusses thunder, lightning, and thunderbolts, waterspouts, clouds, and rain; among the latter earthquakes, volcanoes, the Nile, infected lakes and hot springs, the magnet, and pestilences. The last leads to a description of the plague at Athens, with which the poem closes.

6. Lucretius regarded himself primarily as a philosopher and only secondarily as a poet (1. 931-4); posterity has been inclined to reverse this judgement. As a thinker he followed scrupulously in the steps of Epicurus, setting out his doctrine without alteration, though there is evidence that he avoided some of the more abstruse of his master's discussions. His mind was visual rather than logical, and modern editors have erred in endeavouring by transposition, lacuna, and the assumption of passages written by the poet but not adjusted to their place, to establish a strictly logical sequence in the poem. On the other hand he adorned the dry exposition of Epicurus with a wealth of illustration and imagery, derived from a vivid observation of the world, which shows him as the true poet. Cicero (*QFr.* 2. 9. 3) recognized in him both 'high lights of genius' ('lumina ingenii') and 'artistry' ('ars'), and both elements are abundantly evident. In style L. represents a moment of transition between the cruder work of the older Latin poets and the polish of the Augustan age, but he attached himself to the school of Ennius rather than to his Alexandrianizing contemporaries. He used alliteration and assonance, archaic forms and constructions, and many compound adjectives; verbs fluctuate between conjugations and substantives between declensions. He complains of the poverty of his native tongue and does not hesitate to invent words as he wants them. His hexameters, judged by the standard of Virgil, are rough and sometimes clumsy, and exhibit certain licences which later taste spurned. As philosopher he accomplished an amazing feat in expounding atomism in verse, and as poet his lines have a weight and majesty, and often a depth of passion and feeling, which have caused critics to rank him as the equal of Virgil, if not his superior. *See also* DIDACTIC POETRY, LATIN.

BIBLIOGRAPHY

EDITIONS: C. Lachmann (1850, 1855, showed the superiority of the MSS. O and Q—and laid the foundation of all modern criticism of the text); H. A. J. Munro (1860, 1886); A. Brieger (Teubner, 1894, 1909); C. Giussani (1896-8); C. Bailey (O.C.T. 1898, 1921); W. A. Merrill (U.S.A. 1907, 1917); A. Ernout (Budé, 1920); H. Diels (1923); J. Martin (Teubner, 1934); C. Bailey (1947).
COMMENTARIES: Munro, Giussani, Merrill, Ernout, and I. Robin (1925); C. Bailey (1947); C. Pascal (bk. 1, 1904, revised by L. Castiglioni 1928); R. Heinze (bk. 3, 1897); M. Patin (bk. 5, 1884).
TRANSLATIONS: Verse: W. E. Leonard (U.S.A. 1916); Sir R. Allison (1919); A. S. Way (1933); R. C. Trevelyan (1937). Prose: Munro; Bailey (1910, 1921); W. H. D. Rouse (Loeb, 1924); T. Jackson (1929).
Index Lucretianus: J. Paulson (1911).
LIFE AND POEM: Munro; Mewaldt (*PW*); O. Regenbogen, *Lukrez, seine Gestalt in seinem Gedicht* (1932); G. Della Valle, *Tito Lucrezio Caro e l'Epicureismo Campano* (1933).
CRITICISM: Giussani, *Studi Lucreziani* (1896); C. Martha, *Le Poème de Lucrèce*⁶ (1869); C. Pascal, *Studi critici sul Poema di L.* (1903); J. Masson, *L., Epicurean and Poet* (1907, 1909); E. E. Sikes, *Lucretius* (1936).
SPECIAL STUDIES: Life: F. Marx, *Neues Jahrbuch* 1899; G. Giri, *Il Suicidio di L.* (1895). Composition: J. Mussehl, *De Lucretii Libri Primi Condicione ac Retractatione* (1912); K. Büchner, *Beobachtungen über Vers und Gedankengang bei Lukrez* (1936).
GRAMMAR: F. G. Holtze, *Syntaxis Lucretianae Lineamenta* (1868); A. Cartault, *La Flexion dans Lucrèce* (1898).
INFLUENCE: G. D. Hadzits, *L. and his Influence* (U.S.A. 1935).

C. B.

LUCRETIUS, *see also* GALLUS (1), OFELLA.

LUCULLUS (1) LUCIUS LICINIUS, consul 151 B.C. and founder of the *nobilitas* of his family, commanded in Hispania Citerior. Finding peace with the Celtiberians already established, he turned against the Vaccaeans and afterwards the Lusitanians without any successes except a treacherous massacre at Cauca. On his return he was prosecuted, but not condemned, and erected a temple to Felicitas.

F. Münzer, *PW* xiii. 373. A. M.

LUCULLUS (2) LUCIUS LICINIUS (*c.* 117-56 B.C.), born of a noble plebeian family, was Sulla's quaestor in 87. After raising a fleet from Egypt and Syria he campaigned successfully in the Aegean; when peace came he remained in Asia as proquaestor of Murena until 80 B.C. Thanks to Sulla's influence he was elected aedile for 79 and praetor for 78. After three years as propraetor of Africa he was consul with M. Aurelius Cotta in 74 when the Eastern question came to the fore; Lucullus secured an extraordinary command to carry on the war against Mithridates and left for the East in the same year.

After relieving Cyzicus in 73 Lucullus prepared to invade Pontus. He advanced up the Lycus valley towards Mithridates' capital of Cabeira, and after prolonged skirmishing defeated the king's forces so decisively that he fled to Tigranes (71). Lucullus spent the winter in the administration of Asia, where his firm and just settlement of a financial crisis saved the province from insolvency and ensured for him the hostility of the *Equites*. Advancing into Armenia, he defeated Tigranes at Tigranocerta and made for his capital Artaxata (69-68), but the disaffection of his troops compelled him to retreat. Meanwhile his eastern command had been gradually reduced in scope, and by the *Lex Manilia* (66) Pompey was entrusted with the further conduct of the war. Lucullus returned to Rome humiliated to celebrate a belated triumph in 63. The remainder of his life he devoted mainly to the art of elegant living.

Lucullus was a good strategist and a sound administrator. His failure was due partly to the intrigues of the *Equites* and the popular leaders at Rome, and partly to his own inability to inspire the affection of his soldiers.

ANCIENT SOURCES: fragments of Sallust's *Histories*; Plutarch's *Life* (largely founded on Sallust; perhaps also on Lucullus' own memoirs); scattered references in Cicero (esp. *De Imp. Cn. Pomp.*); Appian's *Mithridatica*; Dio Cassius is of use from 68 B.C.
MODERN LITERATURE: G. Ferrero, *The Greatness and Decline of Rome* (Engl. transl., 1907-8); W. Drumann-P. Groebe, *Geschichte Roms* iv (1908); J. M. Cobban, *Senate and Provinces, 78-49 B.C.* (1935). *See also* MITHRIDATES. J. M. C.

LUCULLUS (3), MARCUS TERENTIUS VARRO, brother of Lucullus (2) and adopted son of a M. Terentius Varro, rendered Sulla valuable service during the Civil War. In 73 B.C. he was, as consul, partly responsible for the *Lex Terentia Cassia* which authorized the distribution of cheap corn on a limited scale. As governor of Macedonia in 72 he reduced the country between Mount Haemus and the Danube, and pressed on to the Black Sea. Returning home for his triumph, he arrived at Brundisium in time to check the retreat of Spartacus. In 67 he served on the senatorial commission which was sent to organize Pontus. (Cic. *Att.* 13. 6. 4.)   J. M. C.

LUCUSTA, *see* LOCUSTA.

LUDI. The chief uses of the word touch diverse fields of Roman culture:

1. Formal sports and representations, generally with religious origin, motivation, and sanction, and counting as religious rites just as did sacrifices and processions; commonly annual, sometimes *ad hoc*. First, *L. Circenses*: the evolutions of the contestants suggested, eventually if not originally, the movements of the planets about the centre of the heavens—a form of sympathetic magic conceivably thought to promote the orderly progress of the seasons. Then, the gladiatorial and other displays in the fora and amphitheatres, a survival from the funeral games of the Etruscans and Campanians—whether their original purpose was to send the spirits of the brave as companions to the souls of the deceased, to satisfy the craving of the departed spirit for blood, or to release a high degree of emotion in replenishment of the vitality of the dead man, or perhaps something more vague or confused. Further there were priestly games like the dances of the Salii (q.v.), and these constituted an older type under the control of priests as contrasted with others, including the *Circenses*, which were under the control of magistrates. *L. Scaenici* were associated with literature, music, and the dance; they were held especially at the Apollinare in the Prata Flaminia (*L. Apollinares*) and at the temple of the Magna Mater on the Palatine (*L. Megalenses*), but every city in the Empire possessed at least one theatre as well as an amphitheatre. *Ludi*, part sport, part pre-military drill, entered into the routine of the Juventus (*see* IUVENES), probably an early Italic institution for the training of youth, revived by Augustus; they included the *Lusus Troiae* (Verg. *Aen.* 1. 545–603; E. Norden, *Aus altrömischen Priesterbüchern* (1939), 188 f.). There were eventually over forty different varieties of *ludi* in Rome itself, religious, votive, or commemorative, with specific names: *Magni* (regularized as *Ludi Romani*), *Florales*, etc.

2. Informal games, of which the Romans had fully as many varieties as the moderns, retaining the practice of some of them even in mature years; the Campus Martius contained a 'multitude of those exercising themselves with ball and hoop and in the sports field' (Strabo 5. 236). They are attested by numerous toys, dice, tablets, etc., in the museums; also by 'gaming-boards' scratched upon ancient pavements. The games of chance led to grave abuses, as the Church Fathers realized.

3. Schools of instruction, also training-schools for gladiators. Grammatical and literary instruction was largely in the hands of Greeks; training for the law and politics was acquired through apprenticeship until the schools of rhetoric replaced the old tradition (Quintilian; Tac. *Dial.*).

4. Buildings for housing *ludi* in the third sense: a school building has been identified with probability at the north-west end of the forum of Pompeii, scratched inscriptions testify to school-teaching in a hall adjoining the Forum of Julius Caesar in the Capitol, and the *L. Magnus* (recently discovered) and *L. Matutinus* in the Third Region of Rome served for the practice of the gladiators who were to perform in the Amphitheatre.

See also SECULAR GAMES, LUDI SCAENICI.

Wissowa, *RK²* 449 ff.; Habel, *PW* Suppl. v. 608 ff.
                                                                A. W. Van B.

LUDI CAPITOLINI, PLEBEII, *see* JUPITER, para. 3.

LUDI SCAENICI, theatrical shows, first added to the *Ludi Romani* in 240 B.C. (*see* LIVIUS ANDRONICUS); in 200 the *Stichus* was produced at the *Plebeii*; in 194 the scenic *Megalenses* were instituted; in 169 the *Thyestes* was performed at the *Apollinares*; in 160 the *Adelphoe* was performed at the funeral games of Paullus. Under the Empire performances chiefly consisted of mime and pantomime. The cost was usually shared between State and presiding magistrates. Admission free; certain seats reserved; women and slaves admitted (Prologue, *Poenulus*).

Dar.–Sag., s.v. 'Theatrum'.   W. B.

LUDI SEVIRALES, *see* IUVENES.

LUGDUNUM (1) (earlier Lugudunum, perhaps = 'bright hill'), modern *Lyons*. The Roman colony, founded in 43 B.C. by L. Munatius Plancus, occupied the hill of Fourvière, west of the Rhône. It was the capital of the Augustan province of Lugdunensis, and the financial centre of Gallia Comata. It owed its importance primarily to its geographical position, which caused it to become the centre of the Roman road-system. Its dominant situation was recognized by the location here *c.* 15 B.C. of the principal mint for Imperial coinage with a *cohors urbana* to protect it. The mint was closed in A.D. 38 on the opening of the imperial mint at Rome, but was reopened at times as a subordinate mint (Mattingly–Sydenham, *Roman Imperial Coinage*, i. 3–9). At the junction of Rhône and Saône, Drusus founded in 12 B.C. the altar of Rome and Augustus 'ad confluentem', the centre of the Imperial cult for Comata, from which a provincial Gallic assembly developed.

The colony (*Colonia Copia Claudia Augusta Lugdunum*) enjoyed the *ius Italicum* (*Dig.* 1. 15. 3. § 1), but it seems, like Alexandria, to have had no organ of local self-government.

Lugdunum flourished in the first and second centuries A.D., not however without crises, such as the fire of 65 and the disturbances of 68, when it suffered for its fidelity to Nero. A theatre, terraced *exedrae* climbing the hill, and aqueducts in fine preservation attest material prosperity to which the favour of Claudius (born here 10 B.C.) may have contributed; a Christian community developed from the numerous Oriental settlers, and the documents of its persecution in 177 are authentic. Lyons suffered severely in the rebellion of Albinus (197) and seems never to have recovered. It became the centre of the Burgundian kingdom *c.* 460.

Allmer et Dissard, *Inscriptions de Lyon* ii. 135–334; CIL xiii. 248; O. Hirschfeld, *Kleine Schriften*, 133–85; G. de Montauzon, *Aqueducs antiques de Lyon* (1909); C. Jullian, *Hist. de la Gaule* vi. 515–27; A. Grenier, *Manuel* i. 329–32.

(2) Capital of the Convenae (*St. Bertrand-de-Comminges*). Alleged to have been settled by Pompeius with Spaniards conquered in the Sertorian War (71 B.C.). Styled colony by Ptolemy (2. 7. 13); important remains of public buildings, forum, and temple have been recently uncovered.

R. Lizop, *Convenae* (1931) Lavedan, Lizop & Sapène, *Fouilles de St. Bertrand* (1922–29).

(3) Town of the Batavi, near modern Katwijk (not Leyden). J. H. Holwerda, *Nederlands vroegste Geschiedenis²* (1925), 190.   C. E. S.

LULLABY, *see* CHILDREN'S SONGS, LATIN.

LUNA, Roman moon-goddess. Varro (*Ling.* 5. 74) names her among a number of deities introduced by Titus Tatius and therefore of Sabine origin. The latter statement may be doubted, but the existence of an early cult of Luna remains likely, though Wissowa (*RK²* 315), objects that no trace of it is to be found. This may be mere accident; in historical times she certainly had a cult and more than one temple (ibid. p. 316; cf. C. K. ch, *Gestirnverehrung im alten Italien* (1933), 27).   Ho. JR.

LUNA, a town in Liguria on the river Macra, the boundary with Etruria, a district still called *La Lunigiana* (Strabo 5. 222). The Romans early used its harbour (= the Bay of Spezzia? or the mouth of the Macra?), but the first certain reference to a town is in 177 B.C., a Roman citizen colony, which in 168 quarrelled with Pisae (q.v.) over boundaries (Livy 34. 8; 41. 13; 45. 13; Ennius fr. 1, 2 Steuart). Subsequently Luna became a *municipium* (derelict by 49: Lucan 1. 586). The triumvirs colonized it anew (*Lib. Colon.* p. 223), but it never became a place of consequence. The neighbouring Carrara marble quarries were extensively worked under the Empire.

L. Banti, *Luni* (1937). E. T. S.

LUPERCALIA, a Roman festival held on 15 Feb. After the sacrifice of a goat or goats and a dog, a rite generally in ancient and commonly in modern times thought to be directed to the god Faunus, at the Lupercal, a cave below the western corner of the Palatine, youths, naked except for girdles made from the skins of the victims, ran about the bounds of the Palatine city, striking those whom they met, especially women, with strips of the goat-skins, a form of fertility magic combined with the ritual beating of the bounds and with purificatory rites. Their name, *Luperci*, suggests aversion of wolves or propitiation of a wolf god, and the whole ceremony reflects the needs of a small pastoral community. It is described by Dion. Hal. 1. 80. 1; Ovid, *Fasti* 2. 19–36, 267–452 (see Frazer's commentary); Plut. *Ant.* 12, *Rom.* 21, *Caes.* 61; and elsewhere. At the Lupercalia of 44 B.C. the consul Marcus Antonius, being one of the Luperci, offered an enwreathed diadem to Caesar. Augustus added dignity to the ceremony (Suet. *Aug.* 31; Mommsen, *Staatsr.* iii 566 f.).

See *PW*, s.v., and especially, L. Deubner, *ARW* xiii (1910), 481–508; H. J. Rose, *Mnemos.* lx (1933), 385 ff.; for another view, F. Altheim, *History of Roman Religion*, 206 ff. A. W. Van B.

LUPUS, see RUTILIUS (2).

LUSCINUS, see FABRICIUS.

LUSCIUS LANUVINUS (? LAVINIUS), Latin poet (attacked in prologues by Terence, whom he blamed for departing from Greek models and for 'contaminatio'—fusion of several plots into one), translated Menander's *Phasma* and (Menander's?) *Thesaurus*.

O. Ribbeck, *CRF²* 83 (3rd ed. Teubner). (Ter. *Ad.* 1; *And.* 15; *Eun.* 9–10; *Hau.* 16; *Ph.* 1.) E. H. W.

LUSITANIA, a province of Imperial Roman Spain named from the most vigorous native tribe, the Lusitani. First mentioned in 193 B.C., the Lusitani submitted to Rome in 139 after the assassination of their greatest leader, Viriathus (q.v.), and a military demonstration by D. Junius Brutus (q.v. 2). At the close of the Republican period the entire western littoral had been occupied by the armies under the governors of Farther Spain from the Anas (Guadiana) to the Bay of Biscay. Augustus organized the territory as an imperial province, Lusitania, probably in 27 B.C. Between 7 and 2 B.C. the northern segment (Gallaecia and Asturia) was assigned to Hither Spain. Lusitania suffered in reputation from its proximity to wealthy Baetica. Its chief cities were Augusta Emerita (q.v.), Olisipo (*Lisbon*), Scallabis (*Santarem*), Pax Iulia (*Beja*); its chief exports were horses, pigs, and metals. The bridge at Alcantara and the regulations of the Vipasca (*Aljustrel*) mining district are the most noteworthy remains.

Remoteness from the Mediterranean and relative paucity of natural resources, especially in the eastern marches, probably account for the separation by Augustus and the development of a modern State independent of Spain. J. J. van N.

LUSIUS QUIETUS, a Libyan Moor, was *praefectus alae Maurorum* under Domitian, by whom he was dismissed. With his cavalry he served successfully in Trajan's Dacian and Parthian campaigns, capturing Singara and later recovering northern Mesopotamia from Parthian attack. In 116 he ruthlessly quelled a revolt of Mesopotamian Jews. Raised to the consulship, in 117 he became governor of Judaea, where he stamped out revolt. Un-Roman, impetuous, and cruel, though loyal and capable, he was replaced after Hadrian's accession, and killed after the Conspiracy of the Four Consulars (118).

E. Groag, *PW*, s.v. 'Lusius (9)'; *PIR*, L 325; J. Carcopino, *Istros* i (1934), 5 ff. C. H. V. S.

LUSTRATION. A *lustrum* is a purificatory ceremony conducted every five years by the censors (q.v.) at Rome; *lustrare* is to perform this or a like ceremony and *lustratio* is the performance of such ritual. The ultimate etymology of the words is uncertain, especially the connexion (recently defended by C. Koch, *Gestirnverehrung im alten Italien*, 1933, 25 f.) with *lustrare*, to illuminate. In all cases the general form of the ceremonial seems to have been the same, whether the object to be purified was a body of people (*lustratio exercitus, populi*), a piece of land (*see* AMBARVALIA), a city (*see* AMBURBIUM), or some other object. Plautus (*Amph.* 775–6) clearly knows of a like process for ridding a mad person of his disease or possession: 'quin tu istanc iubes pro cerrita circumferri?' The essential was to carry or lead materials having supposedly magical virtues around the object to be benefited; the speaker, believing Alcumena ('istanc') to be insane, proposes that this should be done to her.

Normally such a process would require a procession of some kind, small or great; hence the not uncommon use of *lustrare*, to move slowly around something, like a procession (Warde Fowler, *Anthrop. and the Classics*, p. 169 ff.; *Rel. Exper.*, p. 209; qq.v. for his discussion of the words and ideas involved). This is shown by the passages quoted s.v. AMBARVALIA, especially by Verg. *G.* 1. 345 ff.; the farmers go around the farm (or *pagus*), taking with them a *felix hostia*, that is a beast proper to be sacrificed to the gods and so full of good luck; they accompany this by a loud invitation to Ceres to come into the barn. In Cato, *Agr.* 141, the victims are three, *suouitaurilia*, and the prayer is to Mars (q.v.) to keep away all manner of evil from the land and its inhabitants. Ceres might fittingly be invited into a place thus made pure and lucky. In the case of the censors' *lustratio populi* it is not unlikely that the ceremony concluded with the burial or other disposal of the materials used; cf. the phrase *lustrum condere*. In an *amburbium*, the State clergy formed the procession (Lucan 1. 592 ff.); this could be reinforced by sacrifices at the gates, as at Iguvium (*tab. Iguvin.* vi A f.; i A f.; see I. Rosenzweig, *Ritual and Cults of pre-Roman Iguvium*, 26 ff., and s.v. 'Tabulae Iguvinae'). The Lupercalia (q.v.) were an early and peculiar expression of the like idea (see Rose in *Mnemos.* 60, pp. 385 ff.). In all cases the ceremonial keeps evil out and puts good in. H. J. R.

LUSUS TROIAE, see IUVENES, LUDI.

LUTATIUS, see CATULUS.

LUTETIA (or Lutecia), modern *Paris*. Originally a marshy island (*c.* 25 acres) in the Seine, and capital of the Parisii, it was burnt by them in Labienus' campaign (52 B.C.). Under the Empire it spread up the Mont Ste. Geneviève on the S. bank, where vestiges of important public buildings still exist. The town was laid out in irregular *insulae*. In the third century the island alone was inhabited, surrounded by a wall of re-used stones. It was a favourite residence of Julian, who was proclaimed Augustus here in 360. Lutetia (from the 3rd c. called Parisii) fell to Clovis *c.* 493.

F. de Pachtère, *Paris à l'époque gallo-romaine* (1912). C. E. S.

LUXORIUS of Carthage (5th c. A.D.), an imitator of Martial in elegiacs and hendecasyllabics. His *Epithalamium Fridi* is a Virgilian cento (Buecheler–Riese, *Anth. Lat.* 18).

Baehr. *PLM* iv.

LYCANTHROPY. It was occasionally believed in antiquity that a man might turn into a wolf. Plato (*Resp.* 565 d) knows a story that in the worship of Zeus Lycaeus a man is sacrificed and whoever tastes of his flesh becomes a wolf (cf. SACRIFICE). Pliny (*HN* 8. 34) has a circumstantial tale of a whole clan, one of whose members in each generation becomes a wolf for nine years. A sorcerer could turn himself into a wolf (Verg. *Ecl.* 8. 97; Petronius, *Sat.* 61–2). Cf. also LYCAON. Wolves are among the shapes into which Circe (q.v.) changes men (Verg. *Aen.* 7. 18).

R. P. Eckels, *Greek Wolf-Lore* (Philadelphia, 1937), 32 ff. H. J. R.

LYCAON, in mythology, (1) Son of Priam (q.v.) and Laothoe; killed by Achilles (*Il.* 21. 34 ff.). (2) Father of Pandarus (q.v.; *Il.* 2. 826–7). (3) Son of Pelasgus (q.v.), king of Arcadia, first mentioned in Hesiod, *fr.* 44 Rzach. According to Apollodorus (3. 96 ff.), who seems to follow Acusilaus, he had fifty sons, but accounts vary, partly owing to attempts to provide Arcadian towns with founders going back to remote antiquity (e.g. Halipherus and Mantineus, eponyms of Haliphera and Mantinea, in Apollod.; Phigalus, of Phigalia, Paus. 8. 3. 1). His character is an odd mixture of piety and extreme impiety. He founded the cult of Zeus Lycaeus (Paus. ibid.), but sacrificed a child on his altar, and therefore was turned into a wolf (for this story cf. R. P. Eckels, *Greek Wolf-Lore* (Philadelphia, 1937), 49 ff.). He tried to murder Zeus, also to trick him into eating human flesh (Ovid, *Met.* 1. 222 ff.), thus provoking the deluge, cf. DEUCALION.
H. J. R.

LYCAONIA. The original home of the Lycaonians was the mountainous country around Laranda (on the north side of Mt. Taurus), but they were already under Persian rule raiding and settling in the plain to the north, which came to be called Lycaonia. Subdued by Perdiccas in 322 B.C., they were subject to the Seleucids (280–189) and Attalids (189–133). Lycaonia became, it is uncertain when, a *conventus* of the province of Cilicia; the southern mountainous area was, however, ruled by a dynast, Antipater (50–36 at least). The plain, with Iconium as capital, was granted by Antony to Polemon in 39, and in 36 was transferred to Amyntas, who conquered Antipater. From 25 B.C. the plain was part of Galatia and Cappadocia-Galatia. The mountainous country was probably ruled by Archelaus I and II, and certainly by Antiochus IV, till A.D. 72, when it (Lycaonia Antiochiana) joined Cappadocia-Galatia. Trajan on dividing this province probably allotted the plain to Galatia, Antiochiana to Cappadocia. Under Antoninus Pius most of Lycaonia (excluding Iconium and Laodicea) was added to Cilicia, within which it was a κοινόν. The Lycaonians were a backward people, still speaking their native language in the first century A.D. Most of their cities issued no coins till Antoninus Pius' reign.

Sir W. M. Ramsay, *BSA* xi (1901), 243, *JÖAI* 1904, Beiblatt 57. A. H. M. J.

LYCIA was subdued by the Persians in 546 B.C. Though the Lycians were freed by Cimon *c.* 468 and paid tribute to Athens in 446, they reverted to Persian rule, being governed first by their own princes, from *c.* 362 by

Mausolus and his successors, till they submitted voluntarily to Alexander. During the third century they were subject to the Ptolemies, under whom they abandoned their native language and script for Greek. Conquered by Antiochus III in 197, they were given by the Roman Senate in 189 to Rhodes, whose rule they bitterly resented. After three revolts they were freed by the Senate in 169. Their native federal institutions now attained full development. The League gave proportional representation to the cities, which varied greatly in size. There were twenty-three cities, of which six exercised three votes each, some two, the rest one; actually one vote was sometimes shared by a *sympoliteia* of the smallest cities. The members of the federal council and assembly were elected on this basis; the latter body, which elected the principal officers, declared war, and ratified treaties, seems to have consisted of a limited number of elected delegates. Contributions to the federal treasury were paid and the federal itinerant courts were composed in the same proportion. The coinage, whether issued by the League, its districts, or individual cities, was uniform. The freedom of the Lycians was confirmed by Sulla and Antony, taken away by Claudius in A.D. 43, restored probably by Nero, and finally revoked by Vespasian. The league survived as a 'κοινόν of Lycia-Pamphylia', and, though the military offices (nauarch and hipparch) lapsed, the federal courts still functioned and federal officers (*archiphylakes*) collected the imperial tribute.

O. Treuber, *Geschichte der Lykier* (1887); G. Fougères, *De Lyciorum communi* (1898); W. Ruge *PW*, s.v. 'Lykia'; Jones, *Eastern Cities*, 96–110. A. H. M. J.

LYCON (302/299–228/225 B.C.; cf. Diog. Laert. 5. 68), Peripatetic philosopher. He was born in Troas, son of Astyanax (D.L. 65). When thirty years of age he succeeded Strato in the presidentship of the school, which he held for forty-four years (D.L. 68).

Lycon confined himself mainly to ethics and rhetoric. From the time of his presidentship the school loses its philosophic and scientific vigour and begins to decline. As a man L. must have been attractive (cf. D.L. 67).

U. von Wilamowitz-Moellendorff, *Antigonos von Karystos* 78 f.; *PW* xiii. 2303. K. O. B.

LYCOPHRON (1), tyrant of Pherae *c.* 406–390 B.C. He may have established his tyranny by championing a democratic element against the aristocracy, for he was opposed by the nobles of Larissa and other cities, whom he defeated in 404. He allied with Sparta and in 395 fought against Medius of Larissa. Medius, who captured Pharsalus with support from Boeotia and Argos, perhaps won a temporary advantage over Lycophron, but this does not appear to have been maintained. Lycophron's ambition to dominate Thessaly was achieved by Jason (q.v. 2), who was probably his son.

U. Kahrstedt, *PW*, s.v. 'Lykophron (3)'. H. D. W.

LYCOPHRON (2) (b. *c.* 320 B.C.), of Chalcis in Euboea, as a young man frequented the philosopher Menedemus at Eretria. *C.* 285–283 he went to Alexandria and was entrusted by Ptolemy Philadelphus with the *diorthosis* (preliminary sorting-out) of the comedies collected for the Library. He was included in the *Pleiad* of Tragic Poets. According to Ovid, *Ibis* 529–30, L. was killed by an arrow.

WORKS. (1) *Verse*: Tzetzes credits L. with 64 or 46 tragedies, and Suidas gives the titles of 20. The *Cassandreis* must have been historical and based on recent events, since Cassandreia was founded *c.* 316. The only fragment (4 lines) is from the *Pelopidae* (*TGF* 818). L.'s satyric drama, the *Menedemus* (*TGF* 817–18), depicted the high thinking and low living of Menedemus' circle. Suidas further credits L. with 'the Alexandra, the obscure poem'. This survives, a dramatic monologue in 1474 tragic iambics, in which the slave set to watch

Alexandra (Cassandra) reports her prophecies to Priam. Apart from prologue (1–30) and two epilogues (1451–74) the poem falls into three sections, 31–364 Destruction of Troy and crime of Ajax, 365–1282 Returns of the Greeks, 1283–1450 Struggle between Europe and Asia. At one time or another the poem touches on nearly all the themes of the Epic Cycle, but the central idea, the Greek sufferings as compensation for the Trojan, was probably suggested by Euripides' *Troades*. In 365–1282 the author devotes most space to early Greek and Trojan colonization of the West and here draws extensively on Timaeus. In 1226–80 Cassandra foretells Aeneas' arrival in Latium and the future glories of Rome. This passage and 1446–50, where the precise reference is disputed, raised doubts even in antiquity (cf. the scholia on 1226) about L., the tragic poet, being the author of the *Alexandra*. Since the two passages show no stylistic differences from the rest of the poem, excision is unjustified. Some see a reference to Pyrrhus in 1446–50 and attribute the recognition of Rome's power to her victory in the Tarentine war. On this view the poem was composed by the tragedian L., probably *c.* 273, when the Romans sent an embassy to Alexandria. Others refer 1446–50 to T. Quinctius Flamininus, who defeated Philip V at Cynoscephalae in 197. These date the poem not long after that event and suppose the author to have been a namesake, perhaps descendant, of the tragedian. General grounds favour the later dating. The obscurity of the *Alexandra* exceeds that of any other Greek poem. This is due to the recondite material, to the blending of inconsistent myths, but above all to the language. Of about 3,000 words used in the *Alexandra* 518 are found nowhere else and 117 appear for the first time (Scheer). Of the rest many are 'glosses' from Epic and Tragedy, especially Aeschylus. Neologisms too are frequent, and there are some modernisms and vulgarisms. The syntax is characterized by extravagant use of the figures of speech and rhetoric. The real names of gods and men occur rarely, and, when they do, usually refer to another character, e.g. Zeus means Agamemnon and vice versa. Normally the gods appear under some obscure cult-title, the heroes under the names of animals or disguised by a riddling periphrasis. Countries are indicated by some little-known town, mountain, or river situated in them. In metre the author is strict. There are few resolutions and the rule of the final cretic is uniformly observed. The explanation of the numerous coincidences between the *Alexandra* and the poems of Euphorion depends on the dating of the former. The first explicit reference to the poem is in Statius (*Silv.* 5. 3. 157), but soon after this Clement of Alexandria, Lucian, and Artemidorus all mention it, and later the lexicographers and Stephanus of Byzantium cite it frequently. Theon (*fl. c.* 40 B.C.) wrote a *hypomnema* on the *Alexandra*, and some of the material contained in the scholia and in the commentary of Tzetzes probably goes back to this scholar.

(2) *Prose*: The only known work of L. is a lexical compilation Περὶ κωμῳδίας in at least nine books (Ath. 11. 485 d). This treatise, presumably a by-product of his labours in the Library, was much criticized by later workers in this field.

TEXTS: E. Scheer, *Lycophronis Alexandra*, i, Text (1881); ii, Scholia (1908); C. von Holzinger, *Lykophron's Alexandra* (1895); A. W. Mair, in *Callimachus, Lycophron, Aratus* (Loeb, 1921).
GENERAL LITERATURE: K. Ziegler, 'Lykophron (8)', *PW* xiii. 2316–81; G. W. Mooney, *The Alexandra of Lycophron* (1921).   E. A. B

LYCORTAS, father of Polybius and friend of Philopoemen, represented with these the Megalopolitan policy of Achaean independence in a unified Peloponnese with Egyptian support. Hipparch in 192–191 B.C., he defended Philopoemen's pressure on Sparta before the Senate (189–188), and, after visiting Egypt(186), renewed alliance with Ptolemy Epiphanes as General in 185–184. General *suffectus* in 182, after Philopoemen's death, he suppressed

the Messenian revolt and received Sparta again into the League. Possibly General in 182–181, he was prevented by Epiphanes' death from going to Egypt in 180. Against the pro-Roman Callicrates he failed to gain Achaean neutrality in the Third Macedonian War or help for Egypt against Syria in 168.

Polyb. bks. 22–4; 28–9; Livy bks. 38–9. G. Colin, *Rome et la Grèce* (1905), 203; De Sanctis, *Stor. Rom.* iv. 1, pp. 245, 347, 405; A. Aymard, *Les Premiers rapports de Rome et de la Confédération achaïenne* (1938).   A. H. McD.

LYCURGUS (1) a mythological personage, according to Homer, *Il.* 6. 130 ff., a son of Dryas, who attacked Dionysus (q.v.), driving him and his nurses before him till the god took refuge in the sea; thereafter Lycurgus was blinded and died soon. This is vaguely placed on Mt. Nysa. Later, as in Aeschylus (Nauck, *TGF* 19 ff.), he is an Edonian; he and others elaborate the story in various ways. Apollodorus (1. 35) and Hyginus (*Fab.* 132) say Dionysus drove him mad, and further embroider the story of his sufferings and death; their sources are uncertain. For details, see Rapp in Roscher's *Lexikon*, s.v., Marbach in *PW*, s.v.   H. J. R.

LYCURGUS (2), the traditional founder of the Spartan constitution and military system. The earliest mention of him is in Herodotus, where he appears as the author of the Gerousia and Ephorate (qq.v.). Greek writers of the fourth century, from Xenophon onward, ascribed to him almost everything that was peculiar in Spartan institutions. The prevalent belief was that Lycurgus' legislation had been suggested or at any rate approved by the oracle at Delphi. But the widest diversity of opinions obtained as to the date of Lycurgus (which ranged between 1100 and 600 B.C.) and as to the circumstances under which he became a legislator. These discrepancies, and the comparative lateness at which his name first appears in Greek literature, have led modern scholars to doubt whether Lycurgus was an historical character; and the archaeological evidence from Sparta, which has established that many of its peculiar customs were not introduced until after 600 (*see* SPARTA), has left little scope for a great legislator of earlier date. Some scholars still accept Lycurgus as a real person who may have assisted in the constitutional changes of the eighth or seventh century. Others identify him with a god of the same name who was worshipped in various parts of Peloponnesus and had a cult at Sparta itself, and suggest that the institutions of Sparta, though really the product of a long development, were fastened upon him in the sixth or fifth century. The fact that Lycurgus received worship as a god and not as a hero tends to confirm the view that he was a deity before he became a legislator.

Herodotus 1. 65–6; Plutarch, *Lycurgus*. J. Wells, *Studies in Herodotus* (1923), 44–51; V. Ehrenberg, *Neugründer des Staates* (1924), 1–54.   M. C.

LYCURGUS (3) (d. 324 B.C.), son of Lycophron, was a political ally of Demosthenes, came into prominence after the battle of Chaeronea, and was one of the ten statesmen whose surrender Alexander demanded in 336. In 338 he was appointed to an important financial office; the pseudo-Plutarch calls him 'Steward of the public revenues'. He brought the finances of the city into a sound condition, and was responsible for improving the harbour of Piraeus and the arsenal, and adorning the city with statues of the poets. He had an official copy made of the works of the great tragedians; this was borrowed by Ptolemy Philadelphus for the library of Alexandria, and never returned. L. was never a paid speech-writer, but as a man of strict probity and ardent patriotism he many times appeared as a public prosecutor of officials charged with corrupt practices, and was nearly always successful. He died a natural death in 324. According to a story contained in a letter ascribed to Demosthenes he was accused by his successor Menesaechmus of having left a deficit; his sons were condemned to repay the money, and were imprisoned when unable to do so. They were released on the appeal of Demosthenes.

WORKS. Of fifteen speeches known in antiquity, the only one extant is *Against Leocrates*, who fled after the battle of Chaeronea and about 332 B.C., on returning to Athens, was prosecuted as a traitor.

The ancient opinion that Lycurgus was mercilessly severe in his prosecutions is supported by the study of his extant speech. His literary style was influenced by that of Isocrates, but he is a much less careful writer, being often negligent in the matter of hiatus, and in-artistic in the composition of his sentences. Evidently he cared more for matter than style. His disregard of proportion is shown by his inordinately long quotations from the poets.

General literature: see ATTIC ORATORS. Text: Blass (Teubner ed. maior 1899; ed. minor 1912). Commentary: A. Petrie (1922). Text and translation: Durrbach (Budé, 1912). Special study: F. Durrbach, *L'Orateur Lycurgue* (1890); P. Treves, *Licurgo* (1934). Index: see ANDOCIDES. J. F. D.

LYCUS of Rhegium (*fl.* 300 B.C.), second in importance to Timaeus for his history of Sicily (Περὶ Σικελίας), and one of Timaeus' sources. The history of Libya (Ἱστορία Λιβύης) was a separate work.

FHG ii. 370.

LYDIA was a territory in the west of Asia Minor, centred in the lower Hermus and the Caÿster valleys, bordered on the north by Mysia, on the east by Phrygia, on the south by Caria; the Phrygian and Carian borders were indeterminate, and the coastal cities (Cyme, Smyrna, Ephesus, etc.) were reckoned sometimes to Lydia, sometimes to Aeolis or Ionia. Lydia contained much natural wealth, and lying astride and along the two main routes from the coast to the interior of Asia Minor it was an entrepôt of trade and lay open both to Greek and to Oriental influences, and both are reflected in its civilization, art, and cult. Under the Mermnad dynasty (*c.* 700–550 B.C.) Lydia was a powerful kingdom which by the time of its last king Croesus had incorporated all the plateau of Asia Minor up to the Halys (q.v.). After the defeat of Croesus Lydia became the chief Persian satrapy, with its head-quarters at Sardes; this satrapy was in close political relations with the Greek States throughout the Persian period. The conquest by Alexander threw Lydia open to Graeco-Macedonian settlement; after the battle of Magnesia in 190 it became Attalid territory and passed to Rome with the rest of the Attalid kingdom in 133. It remained part of the province Asia till Diocletian made it a separate province, with Sardes as *metropolis*.

Lydian civilization and art were influenced by and reacted on Greece; Lydia was the first State to use coined money and was an innovator in music. The racial affinities of the Lydians are obscure; their language is carved on about 50 inscriptions of the fourth century B.C. excavated from the temple of Artemis—in Strabo's day it was still spoken on the border of Lycia.

G. Radet, *La Lydie* (1893); L. Bürchner and J. Keil, *PW*, s.v. 'Lydia'. W. M. C.

LYDIA, see APPENDIX VERGILIANA.

LYDIADAS (d. 227 B.C.), son of Eudamus (*SIG* 504), was Megalopolitan commander against Sparta in 251 (Paus. 8. 10. 5) and assumed the tyranny *c.* 243. Threatened by Achaea, he abdicated, brought Megalopolis into the Achaean League (235), and was elected general in 234, 232, and 230. He was a constant rival of Aratus and disobeyed his orders in the battle of Ladocea against Cleomenes III, when he charged with the cavalry and was killed (227). He was ambitious and generous, but was eclipsed by Aratus.

Plut. *Aratus, Cleomenes*; K. J. Beloch, *Griech. Gesch.* iv (1928); F. W. Walbank, *Aratos of Sicyon* (1933). F. W. W.

LYGDAMUS (b. *c.* 43 B.C.), an amateur poet of the Messalla circle and author of six frosty elegies which constitute bk. 3 of the Tibullus collection. Lygdamus is chiefly influenced by Tibullus, Propertius, and Ovid. He lacks, however, the inspiration of the two former and the technical skill of the last. He appeals in his elegies to Neaera, a lady of rank, whose love he wishes to win back. Like Neaera, the name of Lygdamus is also pseudonymic; attempts to identify him with Ovid's brother, with Propertius, with Ovid himself, and with others remain fruitless. That he was a Roman of distinction is evident from his connexion with Messalla's circle and from the presence of his work in the Tibullus collection.

Text in editions of Tibullus; commentary in the older editions by Heyne and Dissen; see also G. Némethy, *Lygdami Carmina, etc.* (1906), and Postgate, *Selections from Tibullus*². Cf. Schanz–Hosius, *Gesch. röm. Lit.* ii (1935), and 'Lygdamus' in *PW*. J. H.

LYNCEUS (Λυγκεύς), see IDAS.

LYRE, see MUSIC, § 9.

LYRIC POETRY, GREEK. Lyric poetry, in the sense of song accompanied by a musical instrument which is normally but not necessarily the lyre, must have existed both as monody and as choral song from an early age in Greece. Homer hints at monody in the Linus Song which a boy sings (*Il.* 18. 570), and he knows of several kinds of choral song which were later to be practised by known poets, notably the Dirge (*Il.* 18. 50–1, 314–16, 24. 746–7), the Paean (ibid. 1. 472–4), the *Hymenaeus* (ibid. 18. 493), the *hyporchema* or song accompanied by mimetic dancing (*Od.* 13. 256–65), and the Maiden-Song (*Il.* 16. 182–3). In all these the procedure seems to be the same; there is a choir and a leader, each belongs to a definite occasion, and each is accompanied by music and dancing. These characteristics survived for centuries, and the different types of song known to Homer were standard parts of Greek life. Poets wrote words and music for them, so that all five kinds are, for instance, included in the different types of poetry written by Pindar. The earliest example of such a poem comes from Alcman's Maiden-Song (fr. 1), written in the seventh century. Its chief characteristics belong to its kind and lasted long after it. First, there is the attention paid to the gods at whose festival it is sung. Secondly, there are the moral maxims which the poet makes. Thirdly, there are remarks about the persons who take part in the festival. Fourthly, there is the myth or story, from which, in this case, the poet draws an emphatic moral. These main elements are to be found in Pindar and Bacchylides and seem to be essential to the choral ode as such. Of them the only one that needs some comment is the myth. In origin its presence must have been due to the song's being sung in honour of some god, and no doubt the myth told something about him. But even in Alcman the connexion of the myth and the festival is not clear, and in Pindar the myth might be introduced for different reasons, though often it gave an example of some law about god and man which the poet wanted to emphasize.

2. Another early type of choral song was the *Prosodion* or Processional Song. Homer does not mention this, but it was already in existence in the middle of the eighth century, when Eumelus of Corinth wrote one for the Messenian choir which was sent to Delos (Paus. 4. 4. 1). Only a little later came the Dithyramb, which, after being an unorganized song to Dionysus, was reduced to order by Arion and made like other choral songs in the seventh century. It is possible that some of Stesichorus' poems and a fragment of Alcman (fr. 37) were also of this kind, though its heyday came when it was made a subject for competition at Athens in the last quarter of the sixth century, and was written by Lasus, Simonides, Pindar, and Bacchylides. Later than this came songs which were

addressed not to gods but to pre-eminent men. Their development probably belongs to the age of the tyrants, and an early example may perhaps be seen in Ibycus' lines to Polycrates (fr. 3), in which all centres round the boy whom the poet wishes to honour. Encomia were written for distinguished persons like Scopas by Simonides, Hieron and Xenophon of Corinth by Pindar, Alexander of Macedon by Bacchylides. Similar to the *Encomium* in origin was the Epinician, a song written for a victor in one of the great games. This might be sung at the place where he won or at his home after his return. It came into prominence under Simonides, who seems to have treated it in a light-hearted way, but its real exponent was Pindar, who gave to it most of the characteristics of the formal hymn by writing for occasions when the victor was welcomed at the feast of some god in his home. It may be doubted whether earlier Epinicians had this religious character.

3. These different types survived into the middle of the fifth century, and even later, since Euripides wrote an Epinician for Alcibiades and Sophocles a Paean for Asclepius. But with the rise of tragedy and the decay of the Greek aristocracies the choral hymn seems to have declined. The best poets seldom wrote them, and the occasions which required them were no longer as important as before. The only popular choral poetry of the later fifth and the fourth centuries was the Dithyramb, which underwent considerable changes, becoming less formal than before, more concerned with music than with words, more artificial in its language. Closely allied to it was the *Nomos*, an astrophic composition, like Timotheus' *Persae*, which aimed at sensational effects in words and music.

4. Outside this main stream of development other types may be observed. Monody grew to great distinction *c.* 600 B.C. in Lesbos, where Sappho and Alcaeus produced a personal poetry concerned with the emotions and interests of their own lives; they were followed a generation later by Anacreon in Ionia, and the example of all three may have helped Athenian aristocrats to produce their σκόλια or drinking-songs at the turn of the sixth and fifth centuries. But this art, like that of choral poetry, declined as the fifth century advanced, and σκόλια seem to have ceased to be composed. Quite separate from these was the poetry written by women for women in different parts of Greece. Corinna in Boeotia, Telesilla in Argos, and perhaps Praxilla wrote a special kind of traditional verse which in simple language told of local myths.

5. In the fourth century the old divisions of forms began to be confused. Aristonous wrote a Paean (proper to Apollo) to Hestia, Philodamus to Dionysus; Aristotle used the form of the Paean as a memorial hymn for his dead friend Hermeias and addressed it to the abstract power Ἀρετά. This confusion persisted into the Hellenistic age, when Paeans were addressed to human beings, and the form of the folk-song was used by Hermocles for the entry of Demetrius Poliorcetes into Athens. But the lyric tradition survived both in the real Paeans which were still composed for Apollo and in other new types of monody, of which the most distinguished are the Serenade, the Lovers' Dialogue from Marisa (Powell, *Coll. Alex.* p. 184), simple songs of work like that of the Nile Boatmen (ibid. p. 195), while more elaborate forms existed like Mesomedes' hymns to Nature and Isis, and the beautiful anonymous *Teliambi* (ibid. p. 197). There were still imitations of earlier poets like the Aeolic poems of Theocritus based on Alcaeus, and the sapphics of Melinno, who seems to have lived in South Italy and used the form of personal monody to praise the grandeur of Rome.

Text: E. Diehl, *Anth. Lyr. Graec.*; J. M. Edmonds, *Lyra Graeca* (Loeb). Commentary: H. W. Smyth, *Greek Melic Poets* (1900). Criticism: C. M. Bowra, *Greek Lyric Poetry from Alcman to Simonides* (1936).   C. M. B.

LYRIC POETRY, LATIN. Latin lyric poetry, unlike Greek, is meagre in quantity and (excepting Catullus and Horace) mediocre in quality. The practical Roman temperament seems generally to have lacked the lyrical note, and to have found in the *sermo* a more congenial vehicle for the expression of personal thoughts and feelings. Lyrics were commonly regarded as *lusus* or *nugae*; Cicero (Sen. *Ep.* 49. 5) condemned the lyric poets as flippant triflers ('ex professo lasciuiunt'), and declared that, even with a double span of life, he would not find time to read them. Latin lyric poetry also differs from classical Greek lyric in that it followed the new Alexandrian tradition and was written to be read or recited instead of sung to music as solo or in chorus (cf. Plin. *Ep.* 7. 17. 3). The official *Carmen Saeculare* of Horace is the only certain exception to this rule.

2. The rudimentary beginnings of Latin lyric may perhaps be found in the primitive Saturnian *carmina*, e.g. the songs in honour of the dead, the religious chants of the Salii and Arval Brothers, and the intercessory hymn composed by Livius Andronicus in 207 B.C. (Livy 27. 37). These early efforts, however, were 'rough and unpolished' (loc. cit.); and it was only under Greek influence that Latin lyrics attained the rank of literature.

3. The first Roman poet to write lyrics on the Greek model was Laevius (*fl. c.* 100 B.C.), who treated mythological and erotic subjects in at least six books of *Erotopaegnia*. A precursor of Alexandrianism at Rome, he experimented not only in language but also in metre; and his scanty fragments contain various lyrical metres popular at Alexandria, e.g. anapaests, dactylic tetrameters, and ionics. His historical importance appears to have been greater than his literary merit.

4. Catullus composed five poems in lyrical metres (11 and 51 in the sapphic strophe; 34 and 61 in stanzas of 3 and 4 glyconics respectively + 1 pherecratean; 30 in the greater asclepiad). Following the freedom of his Greek models, he admits trochees, spondees, and iambs as base in his glyconics and pherecrateans, and a short fourth syllable in the first three lines of the sapphic stanza. Caesura is not rigid, and elision and division of words between lines are sometimes bold. Many of C.'s poems in other metres (e.g. 5 in hendecasyllables and 31 in scazons), though not technically lyrics by ancient reckoning, display an intensity of feeling, beauty of language, and mastery of metre which entitle them to rank as great lyric poetry in the wider modern meaning.

5. The four books of Horace's *Odes*, which followed his early lyrical experiments in the *Epodes*, are the chief contribution to Latin lyric poetry (Quint. 10. 1. 96). H.'s purpose was to give Rome a body of lyric poetry which would bear comparison with that of Greece, and he claims (*Carm.* 3. 30. 1) that he has succeeded. Modelling himself upon Sappho and Alcaeus, he employed chiefly the alcaic and sapphic stanzas and the various types of asclepiad; he also experimented in archilochians, the greater sapphic, ionics, the alcmanian and the hipponactean. In 'adapting Aeolian song to Italian measures' he modified Greek metrical practice to suit the greater proportion of long syllables in Latin and the delicate problem of reconciling accent and ictus. In general he admits only a long syllable where in Greek a short was a permissible variant. The alcaic anacrusis is normally long in bks. 1–3 (published 23 B.C.), and invariably in bk. 4 (published *c.* 13 B.C.). The rules of caesura are strict: the masculine caesura is general, but bk. 4 shows an increasing use of the feminine in sapphics. Synapheia is usually observed. The Odes take many forms (hymn, prayer, exhortation, serenade, triumph song, etc.), and contain great variety of style and theme. Some have the simplicity of Aeolian monody, others are complex and enigmatic like Pindar's choral lyric. In the great 'national' Odes (esp. 3. 1–6) the Latin lyric attains a new seriousness and dignity.

6. Lyrics continued to be written in the first century A.D., but, although Quintilian (loc. cit.) praises Caesius Bassus and 'certain living poets', their work has not survived. We have, however, an alcaic and a sapphic Ode by Statius (*Silv.* 4. 5 and 7); and Annianus, Serenus, and other second-century 'neoterici' made many experiments in Alexandrian lyric metres to which Ausonius later was considerably indebted. The final development of Latin lyric poetry is the Christian hymn as written by Prudentius, Ambrose, and their successors; in this the quantitative system was gradually replaced by the accentual.

T. E. W.

LYSANDER (d. 395 B.C.), Spartan general and statesman. Appointed admiral for 408–407, he restored the efficiency of the Peloponnesian fleet, gained the friendship and support of Cyrus, and won a victory at Notium which caused the withdrawal of Alcibiades (q.v.). After the battle of Arginusae he resumed command, and, transferring his fleet to the Hellespont, destroyed the Athenian navy at Aegospotami (405). He conducted the blockade of the Piraeus and after the surrender of Athens (spring, 404) supported the establishment of the Thirty. In most of the States hitherto allied to Athens he set up 'decarchies' of his oligarchical partisans, reinforced by Spartan harmosts. His arrogance and unscrupulousness estranged the Spartan government, which reversed his policy by assisting in the restoration of the Athenian democracy and modifying his system of decarchies. Attempts to regain his autocratic position proved unsuccessful: his plot to introduce an elective monarchy at Sparta miscarried, and after he had secured for Agesilaus the kingship and supreme command in the war against Persia he found himself discarded by his protégé. At the outbreak of the Corinthian War he invaded Boeotia from Phocis, but before he could establish contact with Pausanias he was surprised and killed at Haliartus.

Xenophon, *Hellenica*, bks. 1–3; Diodorus, bks. 13–14; Plutarch, *Lysander*. W. S. Ferguson and M. Cary, *CAH* vols. v, ch. 12, and vi, ch. 2; U. Kahrstedt, in *PW*, s.v. 'Lysandros (1)'.   H. D. W.

LYSANIAS of Cyrene (*fl.* 2nd c. B.C.), Alexandrian philologist, taught Eratosthenes, wrote Περὶ ἰαμβοποιῶν and Homeric studies (frs. listed by Gudeman, *PW*, s.v.).

LỸSIAS (*c.* 459–*c.* 380 B.C.), son of Cephalus (a Syracusan whom Pericles persuaded to settle in Athens), went, with his brothers Polemarchus and Euthydemus, to Thurii, where they lived for some years. Returning to Athens in 412, they carried on a prosperous business at the Piraeus as manufacturers of shields. The evidence of Plato (*Resp.* i ad init.) makes it clear that they moved in the best intellectual society at Athens. In 404 they were proscribed by the Thirty, partly on the ground of their democratic sympathies, but chiefly because of their wealth; L. was arrested, but escaped to Megara; Polemarchus was put to death, and their funds were confiscated. While in exile L. still showed himself a true friend of the democracy and on his return in 403 the Ecclesia conferred on him the rights of citizenship. Owing to some informality this decree was pronounced illegal and L. lost his new privilege. Between this time and his death he is said to have composed over two hundred forensic speeches. As a *metoikos* he could not appear in court himself, but he could appeal to a far wider audience by his *Olympiac* speech of 388 B.C., which contained a solemn warning against the dangers of internal discord.

2. WORKS. In addition to the *Olympiacus*, an *Epitaphios*, and a fragment (*Or.* 34) of a deliberative speech, the following are preserved:

(i) *Speeches in public causes*: *Or.* 20, on a charge of subverting the democracy, which, if by L., is his earliest extant work (*c.* 407 B.C.); 27, 28, and 29, dealing with embezzlement and the betrayal of Greek cities in Asia;

21, a charge of taking bribes; 30, negligence in performing public duties; 22, prosecution of the public corn-dealers for making excessive profits; 16, 25, 31, cases concerning δοκιμασία; 1, 12, 13 murder-charges, of which 12 (*Against Eratosthenes*) provides first-hand evidence about the reign of terror under the Thirty, and 1 (*On the Murder of Eratosthenes*) throws an interesting light on the domestic life of the middle classes; 3 and 4, charges of malicious wounding; 5 and 7, sacrilege; 14 and 15, charges of (*a*) desertion, (*b*) evasion of military service, against the son of the great Alcibiades; 17, 18, 19, claims on confiscated property; 9, non-payment of a fine; 24 (*For the Cripple*), an excellent speech in defence of a man charged with receiving a state-pension under false pretences.

(ii) *Speeches in private causes*: *Or.* 32 against Diogiton, a dishonest guardian, is admirable for its character-drawing, its clear exposition of a complicated story, and the dramatic touches which enliven the narrative; 10 is in an action for defamation; in 23 the charge is not stated; 8 is a trivial declamatory exercise; 6 (*Against Andocides*) is probably spurious.

3. Lysias, by his exceptional mastery of idiom, turned the spoken language of everyday life into a literary medium unsurpassed for its simplicity and precision. He possesses a felicity of expression which is based on art skilfully concealed. He avoids rare and poetical words, striking metaphors, and exaggerated phrases, with the result that at times he may seem to lose in force what he gains in smoothness. His blameless style and unimpassioned tones may seem monotonous to some readers who would prefer a diction that rises above the level of conversation; to others his smoothness may seem more telling than the vigour of Antiphon or the solemnity of Demosthenes. Even when his own personal feelings are deeply concerned he is always moderate. The character of the Thirty is brought out by the calm narration of their actions rather than by denunciation. In the structure of sentences he passes without effort from a running style to the use of the period, which he employs with skill and moderation.

4. Lysias did not, any more than other orators, vary his language to suit his characters, but he succeeds, by subtle *nuances* of thought rather than of language, in suggesting their personality. We cannot fail to sympathize with the young Mantitheus (*Or.* 16)—ambitious and unaffectedly pleased with himself, he seems to have some ground for his harmless conceit; the 'Cripple' (*Or.* 24) strikes us as a plausible rogue. In the construction of his speeches L. is no less simple than in his language: they regularly consist of preface, narrative, proof, and epilogue—a form approved by Isocrates, but seldom adopted with such regularity as by L. It is noted, as a proof of his versatility and good taste, that he never used the same exordium twice, or borrowed from current collections of Prefaces (*see* PROOEMIUM).

For general bibliography *see* ATTIC ORATORS. Texts: O.C.T. (Hude, 1912); Teubner (Thalheim; ed. maior 1913; ed. minor 1928). Text and translation: Gernet and Bizos (Budé). Commentary: E. S. Shuckburgh, *Select Orations* (1882); Index: D. H. Holmes (1895).   J. F. D.

LYSIMACHUS (*c.* 360–281 B.C.), companion and successor of Alexander. His father was probably a Thessalian Greek who migrated to Macedonia. He was one of Alexander's bodyguards, and in one of Alexander's lion-hunts he killed a beast at close quarters, though wounded himself. (This feat gave rise to the absurd story that Alexander had caged him with a lion.) After Alexander's death he received a province consisting of Thrace and the north-west of Asia Minor. In 315 he joined the coalition of Cassander and Ptolemy against Antigonus, but was mainly occupied with the consolidation of his power in Thrace, where he founded a new capital at Lysimacheia (on the neck of the Thracian Chersonese).

In 306 he assumed the royal title. Four years later he drew Antigonus into Asia Minor and held him on successive prepared lines until Seleucus, coming from the eastern provinces, could join hands with him. In 301 he helped Seleucus to defeat Antigonus at Ipsus, and received northern and central Asia Minor as his share of the spoil. Crossing the Danube in 292, he was captured by a Thracian chief, but obtained his speedy release. In 285 he won Macedonia and Thessaly from Demetrius and thus became the strongest of the successors in man-power. But he was disliked for his high-handed administration and oppressive taxation, and was distracted by family quarrels. In 281 he was attacked by his former ally Seleucus and completely defeated in a battle at Corupedium (near Magnesia ad Sipylum), where he fell fighting. His kingdom was broken up after his death.

G. B. Possenti, *Il re Lisimaco di Tracia* (1901); Berve, *Alexanderreich*, no. 480; F. Geyer, in *PW*, s.v. 'Lysimachos'. M. C.

LYSIPPUS (1), poet of Old Comedy. Won prizes in 435 and 410–409 B.C. (*IG* xiv. 1097). His Βάκχαι contained an attack on the seer Lampon (fr. 6).

FCG ii. 744 ff.; *CAF* i. 700–3.

LYSIPPUS (2), sculptor, of Sicyon; Pliny places his *floruit* in 328 B.C. (because of Alexander). Athenaeus connects him with the founding of Cassandreia (316). Selected works:

Dated: (1) Troïlus, Olympic victor, 372; the statue probably later. (2) Coridas, Pythian victor, probably in 342. (3) Statues of Alexander, from about 340. Alexander allowed Lysippus alone to figure him because he preserved his lion-like and manly look as well as the turn of his neck and the softness of his eyes. Herm of Alexander in the Louvre has ancient inscription attributing it to Lysippus (Winter, *KB* 334. 1–2); bronze statuette in the Louvre (Winter, *KB* 334. 3) and head in the British Museum are near in style. Bronze statuette in Grado best fits Plutarch's description of Alexander with spear. (4) Agias of Pharsalus, epigram and signature preserved. The epigram without signature recurs under the Agias (Winter, *KB* 331. 3) of a group erected at Delphi by Daochus, tetrarch of Thessaly, 338–334; this Agias is probably a contemporary marble copy of the Pharsalus Agias. (5) Equestrian group, commissioned by Alexander after Granicus, 334. (6) Socrates, probably erected by

Lycurgus, 338–326. Has been reconstructed by combining the Louvre bust (Winter, *KB* 317. 1) with seated body in Copenhagen. (7) Signatures from Corinth and Thermon, about 330. (8) Chilon, who fell at Lamia, after 322. (9) (with Leochares, q.v.) Alexander's lion hunt, erected by Craterus' son after his death in 321. Reflected in relief in the Louvre (Winter, *KB* 334. 8). (10) Seleucus, probably after 312. (11) Signature from Megara, about 300. Probably from base of Zeus and Muses.

Undated: (12) Colossal bronze Zeus at Tarentum. (13) Chariot of the Sun for Rhodes. (14) Eros at Thespiae. Lysippan Eros survives in copies (Winter, *KB* 332. 2). (15) Satyr in Athens. Borghese satyr may be copy (Winter, *KB* 343. 1). (16) Kairos in Sicyon. Reproduced on reliefs and gems. (17) Colossal bronze seated Heracles at Tarentum, later in Rome and Constantinople. Described by Nicetas. (18) Heracles Epitrapezius. Statuette described by Statius (*Silv*. 4. 6) and Martial. Copies are preserved. (19) Heracles at Sicyon. Original of Farnese Heracles by Glycon, q.v. (Winter, *KB* 333. 4). (20) Polydamas, Olympic victor. Base has been discovered. (21) Apoxyomenos. Copy in the Vatican (Winter, *KB* 331. 1–2).

Attributed: from likeness to 18, 22, seated Hermes (Winter, *KB* 333. 1); from likeness to 19, 23, Satyr with infant Dionysus in the Louvre; from likeness to 21, 24, athlete tying sandal (Winter, *KB* 332. 1).

Lysippus was famed for the new and slender proportions of his figures (although he called the Polyclitan Doryphorus his master), his representation of momentary appearance, the precision of his detail. The tridimensionalism of the Apoxyomenos is in advance of any earlier statue. His influence lasted into the Hellenistic period through his pupils, e.g. Eutychides (q.v.).

Overbeck, 903, 954, 1443–1516; F. P. Johnson, *Lysippus* (1927); F. Poulsen, *Delphi* (1920), 265; *Iconographic Studies* (1931), 31; F. von Lorentz, *Röm. Mitt*. 1935, 333. T. B. L. W.

LYSIS (1) of Tarentum, a Pythagorean who migrated to Achaea and then to Thebes and became the teacher of Epaminondas. It is uncertain whether he wrote anything.

Testimonia in Diels, *Vorsokr*⁵. i. 420–1. *PW* xiv. 64.

LYSIS (2) (*fl. c.* 300 B.C.), originator of λυσιῳδία, and probably from Magnesia in Ionia, like his predecessor Simus, inventor of σιμῳδία. *See* MAGODIA.

M

MÂ, *see* BELLONA.

MACAR, sometimes called Macareus (q.v.), in mythology a Lesbian king (*Il*. 24. 544), but usually a son of Helios and so a Rhodian (schol. Pind. *Ol*. 7. 135); for various accounts of his parentage and adventures, see Schirmer in Roscher's *Lexikon*, s.v. His name, very strange for a mortal because a stock divine epithet, has been interpreted as corrupted from Melqart. H. J. R.

MACAREUS, when not identical with Macar (q.v.), is usually the name of a son of Aeolus (q.v. 2, for his incestuous love of his sister Canace). Several minor figures have the same name, e.g. a son of Lycaon (q.v.; Apollod. 3. 97); a Lapith (Ovid, *Met*. 12. 447). H. J. R.

MACCABEES, THE, *see* JEWS, A.

MACCUS, the clown in *Atellana* (q.v.).

MACEDONIA. By its geographical position Macedonia forms the connecting link between the Balkans and the Greek peninsula. Three important routes converge on the Macedonian plain: from the Danube via the Morava and Vardar (Axius) valleys, from the Adriatic via Lake Ochrida, and from Thrace via Mygdonia. In climate Macedonia is intermediate between Europe and the Mediterranean. Contact with the south is made by sea or by the narrow vale of Tempe into Thessaly. Macedonia proper consisted of the coastal plain of the Thermaic Gulf, which has been formed by the rivers Haliacmon, Lydias, and Axius; these rivers, draining the wide plateaux of Upper Macedonia, cut the mountain-ring of the Macedonian plain at Beroea, Aegae, and the defile of Demir Kapu respectively. Of the cantons of Upper Macedonia Orestis occupied the upper and Elimiotis the middle Haliacmon valley, Lyncestis the upper valley of the Erigon (tributary of the Axius), Paeonia the upper valley of the Axius, and Eordaea the basin of Lake Ostrovo west of Aegae. The Macedonian plain comprised Bottiaea between the lower Haliacmon and Axius, Pieria south of the Haliacmon mouth, Almopia in the upper Lydias valley, Mygdonia in the Lake Bolbe basin leading towards the Strymon valley, Krestonia and Anthemus north and south respectively of Mygdonia. Upper Macedonia is girt by high mountain-ranges traversed only by the three important routes mentioned above; when united, it had strong natural defences. The Macedonian plain is vulnerable from the sea and from Mygdonia, but the defiles leading into Upper Macedonia are easily defensible. The natural products were horses, cattle, sheep, crops, wine, fruit, timber, and silver (at Mt. Dysoros between Krestonia and the Strymon valley), the last two being exported in antiquity.

2. Prehistoric Macedonia, occupied from neolithic times, possessed a uniform culture in the Bronze Age, little influenced by Mycenae, and was invaded c. 1100 B.C. by a northern people, who may also have provoked the Dorian invasion. Of the Dorian peoples some known as Macedni (Hdt. 1. 56) came from south-west Macedonia; a remnant of these perhaps formed the nucleus of the classical Macedonians. The tradition of the Macedonian royal house, the Argeadae (Hdt. 8. 137 f.; Thuc. 2. 99 f.), suggests that from the upper Haliacmon valley they conquered Eordaea, occupied Aegae, and captured the Macedonian plain c. 640 under Perdiccas I, the first in the Macedonian list of kings; while these Macedonians were probably of Dorian blood, the tribes of Upper Macedonia appear to have been composed of Greek, Illyrian, and Thracian elements. Until the reign of Philip II Macedonia struggled with the semi-independent principalities of Upper Macedonia, with the Odrysian kingdom in Thrace, with the Greek States in Chalcidice, with Persia, Athens, and Sparta. Hellenization began with Alexander I (q.v.), who claimed descent from Argos and issued State coinage, and urbanization followed in the fourth century B.C.

3. When Philip II incorporated Upper Macedonia and annexed the Strymon valley and Chalcidice, he created a State superior in military and economic strength to any Greek city-state; the military genius of Philip and Alexander raised Macedonia to a world power, but imposed a severe strain upon the nation, which was accentuated by the Wars of the Successors, and resulted in its collapse before the expanding power of Rome (167 B.C.). Disintegrated into four republics by Rome, Macedonia was annexed as a province in 146, and its history merged with that of the Roman Empire.

4. During its acme Macedonia, a national territorial State with an enlightened monarchy, was the intermediary between Greek and Hellenistic culture, being herself a fusion of Greek and barbarian elements and transmitting a fused culture which long survived under the Roman Empire.

W. A. Heurtley, *Prehistoric Macedonia* (1939); S. Casson, *Macedonia Thrace and Illyria* (1926); F. Geyer, 'Makedonien bis zur Thronbesteigung Philipps II' (*Historische Zeitschrift*, Beiheft 19, 1930); U. Wilcken, *Alexander the Great* (1932).   N. G. L. H.

MACEDONIAN CULTS. There are two distinct elements in the religion of early Macedonia. The first is the original worship of the dominant Μακεδόνες; the second, pre-existing cults of the regions conquered by the Argead kings.

(1) The religion of the Μακεδόνες was Greek, as is demonstrated by the names of the Macedonian months. Its emphasis seems to have been patriarchal and monarchic. Cults of most of the chief Hellenic deities are sufficiently attested for the early period. To Zeus, father of Μακεδών, and Heracles, progenitor of the royal house, the Macedonians were particularly devoted.

(2) Cults, largely Thracian, indigenous to the regions occupied by the Macedonians, were received and preserved. Such was the βέδυ, the water-air spirit worshipped

at Edessa-Aegae, the capital. Sileni (σαυάδαι) and Bacchae (Κλώδωνες and Μιμάλλονες) illustrate the worship of Dionysus-Sabazius (see SABAZIUS). Deities such as Ζειρήνη (equated with Aphrodite) and Artemis Γαζωρία, both stated to be Macedonian, were in fact Thracian and took their names from localities east of the Strymon first conquered by Philip II. In western Macedonia Illyrian elements appear.

The Hellenistic and Roman periods show few developments peculiar to Macedonia. Only now is there evidence for the cults of Zeus Hypsistos (q.v.) and Heracles Κυναγίδας, which, however, are very early and are specifically Macedonian. The Egyptian triad and the Syrian Goddess appear by 200 B.C. By far the most popular cult in the Roman period was that of the Dioscuri-Cabiri (see CABIRI).

W. Baege, *De Macedonum sacris* (1913); C. Edson, *Harv. Stud.* xlv (1934), 226 ff.; O. Hoffman, *Die Makedonen, ihre Sprache und ihr Volkstum* (1906), 92 ff.; A. D. Nock, *Harv. Theol. Rev.* xxix (1936), 60 ff.   C. F. E.

MACER (1), GAIUS LICINIUS, the Roman annalist, tribune in 73 B.C., when he agitated for popular rights (cf. Sallust, *Hist.* 3. 48), praetor in 68 or 67, was convicted of extortion in 66 and committed suicide. His history of Rome, in at least sixteen books, began with the origins; Pyrrhus appeared in bk. 2; its closing point is unknown. It reflected democratic and family bias (Livy 7. 9. 5) and was rhetorically composed. At the same time, it rationalized legends and quoted original authorities, particularly the *libri lintei* (Livy 4. 7. 12; 4. 20. 8; 4. 23. 2). The discrepancy with Tubero (Livy 4. 23. 2) shows error, but the accusation of deliberate falsifying is scarcely proven. Livy and Dionysius used his work.

H. Peter, *HRRel.* i² (1914), pp. cccl, 298; W. Soltau, *Livius' Geschichtswerk* (1897); G. Scaramella, 'L'annalista C. Lic. Macro', in *Annali Scuola norm. sup. Pisa* 1897; K. J. Beloch, *Röm. Gesch.* pp. 1, 105.   A. H. McD.

MACER (2), AEMILIUS, of Verona, was an Augustan poet, older than Ovid (*Tr.* 4. 10. 43–4). A few lines of his didactic poems *Ornithogonia*, *Theriaca*, and *De Herbis* remain (Morel, *FPL*). In ancient times he was held in high esteem. Ovid mentions him first amongst recent 'bards' whom he worshipped (*Tr.* 4. 10. 41–56); and Quintilian (10. 1. 56, 87; 12. 11. 27) couples his name with that of Virgil and Lucretius. See DIDACTIC POETRY, LATIN.   R. M.

MACER, see also CLODIUS (2).

MACHAON (Μαχάων) and **PODALIRIUS** (Ποδαλείριος), sons of Asclepius (q.v.), *Iliad* 2. 731–2, where they are described as physicians, but also as leaders of the contingent from Tricca, Ithome, and Oechalia. Whatever may be the character of their father, their names have no hieratic meaning; Machaon is 'Warrior', Podalirius apparently 'Lily-foot'. Machaon heals Menelaus (4. 200 ff.), but is also active as a fighter and is wounded by Paris (11. 505 ff.); Podalirius is too busy in the battle to tend Eurypylus (11. 836). Their further adventures consist mostly of healing (Machaon, or both, cure Philoctetes (q.v.), Soph. *Phil.* 1333, where see Jebb) and fighting (Machaon killed by Eurypylus, *Little Iliad*, fr. 7 Allen; Podalirius survives the war and settles in one of several places, see Türk in Roscher's *Lexikon* iii. 2588–9). They had a cult, both separately (Machaon at Gerenia, Paus. 3. 26. 9; Podalirius at Drion in Daunia, Strabo 6. 3. 9, p. 284) and together, generally with their father (references in Farnell, *Hero-Cults*, 420). There seems no reason for supposing them originally gods.   H. J. R.

MACHON (Μάχων), New Comedy poet, born at Corinth or Sicyon and resident in Alexandria, where he staged his comedies in the second half of the third century B.C.

From his epitaph by Dioscorides (Ath. 6, p. 241 f., *Anth. Pal.* 7. 708)—'O city of Cecrops, sometimes on the banks of the Nile too the pungent thyme of poesy grows'—it has been inferred that he revived the keen invective of Old Comedy in Alexandria, but the two extant fragments of two plays belong to the type of New Comedy, which was not devoid of δριμύτης (pungency).

In another genre Machon composed χρεῖαι (*see* CHREIA) or *bons mots* in iambic verse of the sayings and doings of notorious Athenian courtesans, parasites, etc. (462 verses, preserved by Athenaeus, bk. 13).

Fragments of comedies in *FCG* iv. 496 f.; *CAF* iii. 324 f.
W. G. W.

MACRIANUS, TITUS FULVIUS JUNIUS, commissariat officer of Valerian, who, after the latter's capture, joined with Ballista in rallying the Roman forces in the East, and then, in A.D. 260, in revolting against Gallienus. The two sons of Macrianus, Macrianus II and Quietus, were proclaimed emperors, and the two Macriani marched west to wrest the throne from Gallienus. Met by his generals, Aureolus and Domitianus, in Thrace, they both fell in battle, and the whole cause soon collapsed (261). Macrian II and Quietus had won general recognition in the East before they hazarded all on one desperate stroke.
H. M.

MACRINUS, MARCUS OPELLIUS, a native of Africa, became praetorian prefect under Caracalla and from motives of personal safety contrived his assassination (A.D. 217). Saluted Augustus by his troops, he was the first Roman emperor who was not a senator. He quickly alienated the Senate by assuming the imperial titles before they had been decreed, and, more serious, he did not retain the soldiers' confidence. Macrinus was no general and patched up an inglorious peace with Artabanus. His subsequent retrenchments in pay and the retention of the European legions in Syria made the army ready to transfer its allegiance. Through the agency of Julia (q.v.) Maesa the story was put about that her grandson Bassianus, priest of the Sun-god at Emesa, was Caracalla's natural son. The soldiers of Legio III Gallica saluted him emperor (218), and disaffection spread till Macrinus was routed in a battle near Antioch and subsequently captured and put to death (*see* ELAGABALUS).

Herodian 4. 14–5. 4; Dio Cassius bk. 78; S.H.A. Parker, *Roman World*, 96–101; M. Besnier in Glotz, *Histoire Romaine* iv. 76–80; *CAH* xii, ch. 1, § 6.
H. M. D. P.

MACRO, NAEVIUS SERTORIUS, was Tiberius' agent in the overthrow of Sejanus in A.D. 31 and was Sejanus' successor as sole commander of the Praetorian Guard. He exerted strong influence in Rome in the last six years of Tiberius' life and was largely responsible, in 37, for the ease with which Gaius succeeded to the Principate. Unable to tolerate so powerful a minister, Gaius first promoted him to be Prefect of Egypt but, before he sailed, early in 38, forced him, together with his wife Ennia, to commit suicide.
J. P. B.

MACROBIUS, AMBROSIUS THEODOSIUS (*fl. c.* A.D. 400), 'uir clarissimus et illustris' (MSS.), is possibly the Macrobius mentioned in the Codex Theodosianus (16. 10. 15; 8. 5. 61; 11. 28. 6; 6. 8.1) as *praefectus praetorio Hispaniarum* (399), *proconsul Africae* (410), *praepositus sacri cubiculi* (422). His works show no trace of the Christianity that *may* be implicit in the last title. He was foreign to Italy (*Sat.* I *praef.* 11, 12), perhaps African.

WRITINGS. (1) *De differentiis et societatibus Graeci Latinique uerbi*: fragments (excerpts made by Johannes Scottus, 9th c.) in Keil, *Gramm. Lat.* v. 599 ff.; cf. Manitius i, pp. 331, 338.

(2) *Commentarii in Somnium Scipionis*, a Neoplatonist work in two books, attached to Cicero's *Somnium Scipionis* in several manuscripts. Plato's *Timaeus* is often mentioned; perhaps M. used Porphyry's commentary.

Popular with medieval scholars (e.g. Dungal, Helperic, Hadoard), the book is important for the study of the twelfth-century philosophical poets of France.

(3) *Saturnalia*, a symposium in seven books, possibly imitating Athenaeus: 'praesens opus non eloquentiae ostentationem sed noscendorum congeriem pollicetur' (I *praef.* 4). It is rich in philological, historical, and antiquarian lore; among its miscellaneous topics are dancing, drunkenness, indigestion, fishes. The central theme is Virgilian criticism, with interesting parallels from Homer, Ennius, Lucilius, Lucretius. Virgil appears as the perfect rhetorician, and there now begins that tradition of his omniscience which ends only with Dante. Among M.'s sources are Varro, Gellius, and Plutarch. The interlocutors include Servius (then a youth), Avienus, and Symmachus.

Macrobius admits that, as a foreigner, he cannot write with native elegance; however, his style, though somewhat artificial, possesses some vigour and individuality; in the *Commentarii* he is much more involved than in the *Saturnalia*. His dialogue-form is unconvincing, and the flimsiness of his transitions is seldom redeemed by artistry. The *Saturnalia* (where, unlike Gellius in his similar work, M. employs orderly arrangement) contains valuable material for the scholar, besides throwing light on social conditions. M.'s attitude to Virgil has importance for the medieval tradition; James Henry (*Aeneidea* passim) accords his criticism some respect.

Text, F. Eyssenhardt (Teubner, 1893). T. R. Glover, *Life and Letters in the Fourth Century* (rp. U.S.A., 1924), ch. 8; T. Whittaker, *Macrobius* (1923); M. Schedler, *Die Philosophie des M.* (1916); D. Comparetti, *Vergil in the Middle Ages* (transl. E. F. M. Benecke, 1895; rp. 1929), ch. 5.
R. G. A.

MADAUROS in Numidia was ruled successively by Syphax and Masinissa (qq.v.). It was occupied by the Romans to dominate the powerful Musulamii. Under the Flavians its Berber-Phoenician population was supplemented by time-expired legionaries, and it received colonial rank. It was noted for its olives and its schools. Apuleius was born at Madauros; Augustine, as bishop, closed its pagan temples. It was a hotbed of religious strife between Donatists, Catholics, and worshippers of the old Berber and Phoenician gods.

S. Gsell and C.-A. Joly, *Khamissa, Mdaourouch, Announa* (1914–22).
W. N. W.

MAEANDER (Μαίανδρος), a river which rises in several sources, including the Marsyas, in and near Celaenae-Apamea in Phrygia, and flows through the Peltene plain to engage itself first in a narrow valley and then in a canyon 1,500 feet deep, sunk in the western flank of the Anatolian plateau, whence it emerges to join the Lycus near Colossae, Laodicea, Hierapolis, and Tripolis. Thence to the Sinus Latmius it flows through a flat-bottomed, fertile valley, here dividing Lydia from Caria, and passing among other cities Tralles and Magnesia ad Maeandrum. In this part of its course it winds much, and the Greeks described it as σκολιός and used its name to describe a winding pattern. The sand it carries has silted up much of the Latmian Gulf; the harbour of Miletus is now landlocked, and Lade, the scene of the naval battle of 494 B.C., is no longer an island.
W. M. C.

MAECENAS, GAIUS (d. 8 B.C.), a scion of the ancient Etruscan aristocracy, was a trusted friend, counsellor, and diplomatic agent of Octavian (Augustus). He accompanied him in the campaign of Philippi, negotiated his marriage with Scribonia, represented him in the discussions which preceded the treaty of Brundisium, undertook a diplomatic mission to Antony (38), and helped to negotiate the treaty of Tarentum. His luxurious habits and apparent indolence concealed his capacity for vigilance and firmness, and though he never held public office he was called upon on critical occasions to represent Octavian in Rome—during the campaign against Sextus

Pompeius in 36 and during or after that of Actium, when he detected the conspiracy of Lepidus. Of great importance to the Augustan Principate was the influence of Maecenas as a patron of literature: he was the friend and benefactor of Horace, and Virgil wrote the *Georgics* at his suggestion. His marriage with Terentia was temporarily disturbed by the attentions which Augustus paid to her, and in later years the emperor's friendship is said to have lost its earlier cordiality. Maecenas bequeathed his extensive property, including a magnificent house and gardens on the Esquiline, to Augustus. There is no good authority for the tradition that his full name was C. Cilnius Maecenas.

Horace, *Odes, Epodes,* and *Satires; Elegiae in Maecenatem;* Velleius 2. 88; Appian, *BCiv.* bks. 3 and 4; Dio Cassius, bks. 49–55. There are frequent references in the poets, especially Propertius and Martial. V. Gardthausen, *Augustus u. seine Zeit* (1891, etc.).
G. W. R.

MAECIANUS, Lucius Volusius, a Roman jurist of the second century A.D. His official career is now fully known by two inscriptions discovered in 1930 at Ostia (*CIL* xiv. 5347–8). Some of his official posts (*procurator bibliothecarum, praefectus vehiculorum, adiutor operum publicorum, praefectus fabrum*), are not known to have been held by any previous jurist. He was also *praefectus annonae, a libellis et censibus* under Antoninus Pius, and *praefectus Aegypti* about 160. He instructed Marcus Aurelius when he was heir to the throne, and was a member of the imperial *consilia* under Antoninus Pius and Marcus Aurelius. From the *Digest* we know the following works of Maecianus: a voluminous treatise on *fideicommissa* (16 books), *De iudiciis publicis* (14 books), and a monograph written in Greek on the *Lex Rhodia*. A booklet entitled *Assis distributio* and dedicated to Marcus Aurelius is preserved almost complete; it contains the terms used to denote fractions, particularly with reference to inheritance.

Best edition: E. Seckel and B. Kübler, in Huschke, *Jurispr. anteiust.* i⁶ (1908). A. B.

MAELIUS, Spurius, was a rich plebeian who is alleged to have relieved a food shortage and courted popularity by distributing corn at his own expense (440–39 B.C.); suspected of aiming at a tyranny he was killed (? by C. Servilius (q.v.) Ahala. Many modern critics have questioned his historicity and undoubtedly many features are late Republican inventions, but the story was told by Cincius (q.v.) Alimentus and is thus of the pre-Gracchan period when there was less reason to invent it, while the circumstances of the corn-shortage cannot easily be rejected (*see* MINUCIUS 1). H. H. S.

MAENADS, also **Bacchae** or **Thyiades,** women inspired to ecstatic frenzy by Dionysus. Adorned with wreaths of ivy, oak, or fir, and draped with skins of animals they celebrate the power of Dionysus in song, music, and dance. They roam through mountains and woods and lead the life of animals. They are beyond all human concerns, conventions, and fears. Dionysus inspires them with strength so that they can uproot trees and kill strong animals. They also hunt animals and devour their raw flesh, an action which must be connected with the Dionysiac ritual *omophagia* (*see* DIONYSUS).

In mythology Maenads accompany Dionysus on his triumphal journey from Lydia or Phrygia to Thrace and Greece. The women of Thebes who follow Dionysus also become Maenads (Eur. *Bacch.* 329, 1021). They destroy his enemies Pentheus and Orpheus (Ov. *Met.* 11. 22; M. P. Nilsson, *Harv. Theol. Rev.* 1938, 190). M. form a contingent in the army of Dionysus during his campaign in India. But they are also associated with the peaceful aspect of Dionysus as inventor of wine and are frequently shown gathering grapes or preparing wine.

In literature Aeschylus (q.v.) had given a powerful picture of M. in his lost plays *Edonoi, Bassarides, Xantriai,*

and *Pentheus,* but the classic description of Dionysiac ecstasy of M. was drawn by Euripides in the *Bacchae.* This was the model of later accounts by Lycophron, Accius, Pacuvius, ps.-Theocritus (26), Ovid (*Met.* 3. 511), and Nonnus.

From the middle of the sixth century B.C. onwards M. are distinguished in art from other Dionysiac female figures. Greek vase-painters delight in depicting their revelries in the *thiasus,* their amorous meetings with satyrs and sileni, their nocturnal dances, their sacrifices to Dionysus, and their assaults on Pentheus and Orpheus. In classical and later art they are sometimes shown in more subdued mood, with Aphrodite and her circle, with Eirene, and even with Muses. Two fine types of statues show dancing M. The first (Dresden) is commonly assigned to Scopas, the other is a Hellenistic creation.

The Maenads of tragedy and myth are an idealized, mythological reflection of human Bacchantes modelled on the behaviour of women in the orgiastic worship of Dionysus in Thrace. More than any other figure of the Dionysiac worship they represent the complete liberation from conventions of daily life, the awakening of primeval instincts, and the union with nature achieved in the cult of Dionysus.

Theocritus 26; Catullus 63. 24; Ovid, *Met.* 3. 511, 11. 1; Nonnus 45. 273; Ps.-Eratosthenes xxiv, ed. Robert. Marbach in *PW*, s.v.; J. E. Sandys, *The Bacchae of Euripides* (1900); L. Lawler, *Am. Ac. Rome* 1927; H. Philippart, *Rev. belge phil. hist.* 1930, 35; E. R. Dodds, *Harv. Theol. Rev.* 1940. G. M. A. H.

MAENIUS, Gaius (*cos.* 338 B.C.), the only Maenius to reach the consulship. As consul he conquered the Antiate fleet and subjugated the Latins; his statue was erected in the Forum, and the captured ships' beaks (*rostra*) adorned the speaker's platform (henceforth called *rostra*) (Livy 8. 13 f.). The *columna Maenia* in the forum, however, probably did not celebrate him; apparently it was a column of the Basilica Porcia supporting a projecting balcony (*maenianum*) erected by a descendant (M. Lehmann-Hartleben, *AJPhil.* 1938, 290). Later Maenius was censor (318) and the first certainly attested plebeian dictator (314). An earlier dictatorship (320: *Fasti Cap.*) is apocryphal. E. T. S.

MAEOTIS was the ancient name for the Sea of Azov. Greek colonists from Miletus and other Ionian towns were attracted by the fisheries at its mouth (the 'Cimmerian Bosporus'), and here founded Panticapaeum (q.v.). They subsequently founded a city named Tanais (q.v.) at the upper end of the sea, but they do not appear to have explored its interior systematically. Greek geographers (Herodotus, Scylax, Strabo, Ptolemy) greatly exaggerated its size and were very hazy about the river Tanais (q.v.). But they noted the shallowness of the sea and prophesied that it would eventually be silted up. M. C.

MAERA, *see* ICARIUS (1).

M(A)EVIUS belonged to a group of poetasters who criticized Horace and Virgil and incurred their contempt and enmity (*Ecl.* 3. 90). Undoubtedly he was conspicuous enough to induce Horace to write the whole tenth Epode against him.

MAGI, *see* MAGIC; RELIGION, PERSIAN.

MAGIC is commonly defined as the art of influencing the course of nature by occult practices characteristic of uncivilized peoples or of a more or less primitive state of mind. There is always some sort of constraint in all magic (unlike prayer and sacrifice to the official gods).

2. The word (μαγική, sc. τέχνη, or μαγεία, Latin *magia*) originally means the science of the *magi*, the members of the Persian priestly clan; later it covered all

sorts of magic, whether indigenous or foreign (φαρμακεία, properly the science of plants and simples, 'drugs'; γοητεία, often just 'charlatanry'). Designating as it does the practices of a foreign religion, the word tended to be equivalent to something secret or illicit, at any rate difficult to control, therefore anti-social and in opposition to the official religion. As a fact, magic exists everywhere at all times, and magical elements appear even in the most developed forms of religion. It therefore is often a question of orthodoxy whether a rite or a formula is to be termed magical or religious. As regards Greek and Roman civilization we may state that the growth of purified religious belief, the increasing insight into the laws of nature—physical and intellectual—inaugurated by the leading Greek philosophers, and finally the criticisms of Sceptics, Cynics, and Epicureans gradually undermined the use of magic and the belief in it in the upper social strata (this disesteem of magicians is already conspicuous in the 5th c. B.C.).

3. Our earliest examples of Greek magic come from Homer, but we may presume that the Greek invaders a long time before had taken over much pre-Greek magic (connected, e.g., with agriculture, navigation, and useful arts). An incantation can stop the flow of blood from the wounded Odysseus. Circe effects the most wonderful transformations by means of potions, salves, and a magic wand (which we also find in the hands of Hermes and Athena); she is also able to teach Odysseus how to summon the ghosts from the nether world. In the Homeric epics the great Olympian gods generally do not practise any witchcraft. Hermes, however, still preserves traits which remind us of the old magician; he presents the 'moly' to Odysseus, who by this means is able to outdo Circe. In Hesiod's *Opera et Dies* we get glimpses of agricultural and everyday usages, and his *Theogony* contains a unique glorification of Hecate (q.v.), elsewhere the protectress of all witches, as the greatest and most beneficent of all deities.

4. Greek myth affords still more material. We hear of the Telchines (q.v.; perhaps pre-Greek), skilful but malignant smiths, hostile to gods and fearful to men, well versed in magic; cf. the Curetes (q.v.) and Dactyli (*see* IDAEAN DACTYLS), the latter especially known as masters of medical charms and music (the same combination recurs in Chiron). Orpheus the magician, Musaeus, Melampus, Autolycus (Hesiod fr. 136 Rzach) are other well-known names; but the female sex seems in literature as elsewhere to predominate, the most renowned enchantress through all antiquity being Medea. She commands all nature, puts the dragon at Colchis to sleep, makes warriors invulnerable and old men young. She also has the Evil Eye, terrible to all living things (*see* TALOS). Magic brings her victory, but love is her tragedy (*see* MEDEA); so far she remains a prototype for the jilted witch of later literature (cf. Canidia in Horace). The Thessalians claimed that she had lost her box of drugs on their fertile soil, and their wonder-working plants were just as widely known as their witches (see the equally brilliant *Metamorphoses* of Ovid and Apuleius).

5. Later literature gives us further evidence of the interest taken in magic and magicians by poets and writers, Greek as well as Latin. New fragments of Sophron give a vivid picture of a piece of Hecate-magic (the prototype of Theoc. 2), but we are still waiting for more of Sophocles' 'The female Herbalists' and Menander's 'Thessalian Woman', where the popular Thessalian feat of 'drawing down the moon' was mentioned. The dramatists on the whole were fully alive to the scenic possibilities of a *necyomantea*, the first description of which we find in Homer's *Odyssey* (cf. Aeschylus' *Persae*, Aristophanes' *Frogs*, Seneca's *Oedipus*). Homer again inspired Virgil (*Aeneid* 6), and Seneca (*Apocolocyntosis*) as well as Lucian used it as a welcome satirical theme. Virgil and Horace have a specialist's insight into love-charms,

popular—and feared—in their time, and Lucan in his epic gave an illustration of Thessalian witchcraft which for completeness and gruesome description remains unrivalled. The keen interest felt in the theme is excellently illustrated by Apuleius' *Apologia*.

6. A clear insight into the whole magical technique of a syncretistic character, its practices, prayers, and faith in demons and demonic powers is furnished by the many finds of magical papyri in Egypt, now easily available in Preisendanz's collection, *Papyri Graecae magicae*. Thus we can now also measure the distance between ancient witchcraft in real life and the literary treatment of the subject.

7. From a sociological point of view we may divide the vast field of magic (of positive and negative *mana*) into *official* and *private* practices, but their mutual interpenetration is evident. A number of official Greek and Roman festivals, concerned with, e.g., the fertility of soil and man (*hieros gamos*: see MARRIAGE, SACRED), rain-making, war, etc., where public welfare is at stake, have preserved their old magic character. On the other hand, many apotropaeic ceremonies to purify and avert, having an obviously magical character, were used in a public and in a private way; so likewise prayers (cf. HYMNS, PAEAN) and curses (*see* CURSES); even sacrifices offered to the gods on behalf of the State or the single family were magical in much of their ritual (cf. the use of fire and water, circumambulation), still more so the offerings to the dead. All the main events in man's life (birth, marriage, death, etc.) and the emotional force of such events called for supernatural help and defence.

8. Theoretically the division into *sympathetic* (*homoeopathic, similia similibus*) and *contagious* magic (*pars pro toto*) is of great help. You make an image of a person whose love you desire or whose death you wish, you melt it at a fire, you pierce it with nails, etc., and the person in question suffers correspondingly—this is a homoeopathic procedure (cf. Plato, *Leg.* 933 b, Theoc. 2, Verg. *Ecl.* 8, Ovid, *Her.* 6. 91). If, when burning the image, you throw some of the victim's hair or a bit of his cloak (Theoc. 2. 53 ff.) or anything else that has been his (Verg. *Aen.* 4. 494 ff.) into the fire, you simultaneously make use of contagious magic. The combination naturally gives you a stronger hold upon the victim. Further we may call the transmission of disease into another person or beast (e.g. when stung by a scorpion you whisper into the ear of an ass: 'A scorpion has stung me', Pliny, *HN* 28. 155) *direct* magic, as contrasted with the *indirect* where gods, demons, or spirits are at work (cf. *devotio*). Direct are, e.g., the apotropaeic efficacy of rings and crowns of amulets (the phallus, *fascinum*, vulva, the Gorgoneion on wine-cups, etc.), the 'binding' practices (δέω σε, *ligo te*; κατάδεσις, *defixio*, cf. R. Wuensch, *Defixionum tabellae Atticae* (1897); A. Audollent, *Defixionum Tabellae*), the use of the wryneck (ἴυγξ) in homoeopathic love magic, a host of medical charms, preserved in so many works of popular medicine (Marcellus, *De medicamentis*, Aëtius, Alexander of Tralles, etc.), innumerable concoctions, incantations (ἐπῳδαί) and formulas to be found in the papyri (in Egyptian and Greek), magical sounds and tunes, finally the power of the spoken word and the name, the 'great name', of god or demon. We find an early example of *indirect magic* in the Homeric description of a *necyomantea*, the evocation of the spirits of the dead (*Od.* 11, cf. the witch of Endor in the O.T. and the definition of γοητεία in Cramer, *Anecd. Ox.* iv. 240). The necromancers (ψυχαγωγοί) were a definite class of magicians (popular also in Etruria), and corresponding official oracles existed, cf. the incubation (q.v.), officially sanctioned at Asclepiea and elsewhere. Compare also the ὀνειραιτητά of *PGM*. The introduction of foreign demons (and rites), characteristic of ancient magic from early times, culminated in the 'syncretistic' period after Alexander the Great. A wider outlook on all sorts of magic and on the powers of the supernatural world now made possible the synthesis of magic and *theurgia* which the Alexandrian philosophic speculation attempted (cf. the magico-religious Gnosticism: *see* GNOSTICISM). Accordingly, the prescriptions for consecration and prayer, for the material to be used (e.g. plants, stones, extensive use of lead), and for the ritual fitness of the persons became more and more complicated.

9. As civilization developed, the lawgivers in Greece as in Italy (where the Marsi and Paeligni were famous indigenous magicians) became more and more interested in repressing magic (so far the division into beneficent and mischievous witchcraft often materially coincides with public and private magic; cf. the later white and black magic). Already in Ancient Egypt a magician could be prosecuted, and the Homeric hymn to Demeter (228) contains a hit at witchcraft. Plato wants the abuse of magic (φαρμακεία) to be punished, and the Roman *decemviri* really did so. New laws under the Roman emperors repressed the new growth of magical influence (cf. Julius Paulus, *Sent.* 5. 23, 14 ff.; *Cod. Theod.* 9. 10; 16. 10; *Cod. Iust.* 9. 18). In spite of all criticisms magic is, if not 'the mother of freedom and truth' (Frazer), at least in many respects the mother of science, owing to its keen observations and bold experiments. *See* ASTROLOGY, CURSES, DIVINATION, SACRIFICE.

H. Hubert, art. 'Magia' in Dar.-Sag.; Hopfner, art. 'Mageia' in *PW*; K. F. Smith, art. 'Magic, Greek and Roman' in Hastings, *ERE*; J. G. Frazer, *The Magic Art* (=GB³ i–ii); Lynn Thorndike, *A History of Magic and Experimental Science*, i–ii² (1929); J. Bidez et F. Cumont, *Les Mages hellénisés—Zoroastre, Ostanès et Hystaspe*, i–ii (1938); S. Eitrem, 'Magische Papyri' (*Münchener Beiträge zur Papyrusforschung* xix (1933), 243–63). S. E.

MAGISTER EQUITUM, or the master of the horse, was a subordinate official, nominated by every dictator on appointment, originally to control the cavalry, but, in later practice, to represent the dictator either on the field of battle or at Rome. He held derivatory *imperium* from the dictator and ranked with the praetors. His commission ended with that of his dictator. A notable but unsuccessful attempt was made in 217 B.C. to equate the *magister equitum* with the *dictator* as a colleague (*see* MINUCIUS 2). A similar though permanent magistracy is found in the municipalities of Italy, known as *magister iuventutis* or *magister iuvenum*. *See also* MAGISTER MILITUM.

For bibliography *see* DICTATOR. A. N. S.-W.

MAGISTER MEMORIAE, the successor in the period after Diocletian of the *a memoria* of the early Empire, who, in the second and third centuries, had drawn a salary of 300,000 HS, with the rank of 'uir perfectissimus'. The *scrinium memoriae*, receiving materials prepared by other offices, dealt with all petitions, drafted official letters and speeches, and edited official reports. The essential function of the head of the office, the *magister memoriae*, was to receive from the emperor the decisions taken and to communicate them to the public. H. M.

MAGISTER MILITUM. Constantine deprived the praetorian prefects of their military functions, and in their place appointed two generals, the *magister peditum* and *magister equitum*, the former with supreme command over the infantry, the latter over the cavalry of the Empire. Despite the precedence of cavalry over infantry, the *magister peditum* was always the senior officer. Later the number of *magistri* was enlarged, and the limitation of their command to either infantry or cavalry was removed. By A.D. 350 two *magistri militum praesentales* are found at either imperial headquarters.

R. Grosse, *Römische Militärgeschichte*, 180–91. H. M. D. P.

MAGISTER OFFICIORUM. From the time of Diocletian all *officia*, public bureaux, were organized on military lines, though kept distinct from military service proper. The *officiales* were free from such obligations as those of the local *curiae* (*see* CURIA 1) and were subject to the principle of hereditary succession. They received payment mainly in kind, though money payments were added later. The lower assistants attached to the *officia* were organized in *scholae*.

The *Magister* (originally the *tribunus*) *officiorum* was in general charge of all *officia*, having under him the *scrinia* of correspondence, petitions, 'memoriae', 'dispositionum', 'admissionum', etc., and later also the 'agentes in rebus' (q.v.); from the latter he drew his own special *officium*.

Boak, *PW*, s.v. 'Officium'. H. M.

MAGISTRACY, GREEK. Magistracy in Greek city-states was the heir of the old monarchy. According to Greek tradition, which, however, sometimes tends to over-emphasize the regularity of the process, firstly one or a few magistrates, elected by the ruling class, governed the State for life; these were mostly derived from the former assistants of the king. At an early stage military, judicial, and religious functions were separated, part of the religious duties being transferred to an official who preserved the royal title. Next the duration of office became limited, and official power was distributed among several colleagues. By a procedure which varied in each city the leaders of the State gradually became mere executive instruments. The number of officials was gradually increased. Besides the leading political and military magistrates there were officials needed for special tasks, e.g. finance or public works. But it was never usual to elect men with special qualifications, except to military offices. Officials were elected by the full citizens out of their own body. They received no salary and some magistracies were open to men of great wealth only. After their period of administration, all officials had to render account (εὔθυνα). In democracies the number of magistracies underwent a large increase, and their power accordingly diminished. Boards of three, five, or more colleagues were far more common than single officials. Their term of office never exceeded one year and they could not be re-elected. Some technical offices excepted, election was by lot (*see* SORTITION). Most of the lower officials received small daily salaries. Under such conditions Greek magistracy represented no political leadership whatsoever. It expressed the participation of all citizens in politics, and their equality; therefore all magistracies were of the same rank, and there existed no hierarchy or 'cursus honorum'.

In the Hellenistic monarchies magistrates were on a quite different footing. They were professionals, paid by the king in money, natural products, or gifts of land. The higher magistracies were occupied by Macedonians or Greeks, the lower mostly by natives, who did not rise to high positions before the second century B.C. Greek was the official language. The members of the central government resided in the chief city, but there were numerous higher and lower officials in every part of the realm. The most important provincial officials were generally called *strategi*. The administration was strictly centralized in Egypt, but entirely decentralized in the Seleucid Empire. In all cases there was a compact hierarchy, well organized and rather bureaucratic. Lower officials were often personally dependent on the higher, as the higher were on the king.

Besides the books on Greek political institutions, see F. Leifer, *Klio*, Beiheft 23 (1931); U. Kahrstedt, *Untersuchungen zur Magistratur in Athen* (1936). V. E.

MAGISTRACY, ROMAN. Magistracy was one of the three basic elements of the Roman Republic, the other two being the Senate and the people. In the regal period magistracy was embodied in the person of the king, and the other executive officials were merely his representatives. But under the Republic magistrates were regarded as the representatives of the whole State, for they were invested with rights, duties, and executive power (*potestas*) by the joint authority of the Senate and the people, although the latter's share was confined to confirming the election of patrician candidates. During the fifth century a new board was created in opposition to the senatorial magistrates, called *magistratus plebeii*; but it soon lost its revolutionary character, since a process of compromise, beginning c. 366 B.C., led by the middle of the third century to the admission of plebeians to all the patrician magistracies and to the absorption of the plebeian offices within the sphere of authority of the Senate. Even earlier, however, excessive magisterial power had been successfully checked by several limitations. The *imperium* (q.v.) was restricted to the military sphere (*imperium militiae*), and thus was exercised only beyond the walls of Rome (*extra pomerium*); while the *imperium domi*, although, like the *imperium militiae*, it still included *iurisdictio* and *coercitio*, was considerably limited by the right of appeal (*provocatio*). Moreover, the principle of collegiality always made it impossible for a magistrate to start any revolutionary movement (until the age of Sulla and Caesar, when magistrates came to be commanders in chief of professional, mercenary armies). Magistrates became progressively more dependent on the Senate, with whom they were compelled to collaborate, especially when the Senate became a closed assembly of magistrates and ex-magistrates, from whose ranks alone the candidates for magistracies were mostly taken. As Polybius observed, it was this compromise between the Senate, conceived as the administrative power, and the magistrates invested with the executive, that assured the stability and continuity of the Roman constitution. To maintain the correct balance, measures were taken to guarantee the regular succession of magistrates, and the alternate and balanced exercise of authority by colleagues. The *leges annales* determined both the age-limits required for candidature and the intervals of time between the tenure of magistracies: this *certus ordo magistratuum* remained essentially undisturbed from 180 B.C. (*Lex Villia*; *see* VILLIUS) until the Augustan age. Similarly the principle, emphatically maintained by Cicero, that public office and service was a civic duty, was observed until the end of the Republic. Since public service was never regarded as a profession, no remuneration was given to Roman magistrates, except for journeys, special celebrations, military commands and expenses, etc. This purely honorary aspect of magistracy was confirmed by regulations concerning the escort of lictors (q.v.) and their number, the dress to be worn, the use of the *sella curulis* (q.v.), different forms of homage due to magistrates, etc. These formalities were observed even under the Empire, at least down to the end of the fourth century A.D., when magistracies lost any independence and political significance. Imperial magistrates, being appointed by the emperor, were in fact reduced to the condition of civil and military subordinates.

Mommsen, *Röm. Staatsr.* i³ (abridged in *Abriss d. röm. Staatsrechts*, 1893, 82 ff.); B. Kübler, *PW* xiv. 400 ff. P. T.

MAGISTRI. A common title for the head of a religious or semi-religious organization in Rome was *magister*. This official was primarily not a priest, though he generally had some sacral duties, but rather a president (see De-Marchi, *Culto Privato* ii. 146 f.). Thus the *fratres Aruales* elected a *magister* annually to serve from one Saturnalia to the next (e.g. *Acta Arualium* for 19 May, 87, p. cxix 30, Henzen; at the same time a different person was made *flamen*, ibid. 32). When Augustus restored, if he did, the worship of the Lares Compitales (*see* LARES), he apparently organized it under *magistri uicorum*, perhaps on the analogy of the *magistri pagorum* or presidents of the rural districts (see

De-Marchi, i. 230; cf. Marquardt–Wissowa, *Staatsverw.* iii². 204–7).

For other uses of the term, and in particular for that revealed in Jotham Johnson, *Excavations at Minturnae* ii (Rome and Philadelphia, 1933), see Nock, *AJPhil.* lvi (1935), 86 ff. H. J. R.

MAGNA GRAECIA comprised the flourishing but mutually quarrelsome Greek cities of south Italy. Their inhabitants, the Italiotes, developed an amphictiony, Olympic champions, schools of philosophy, etc. Internecine strife started their decline (c. 500 B.C.); malaria and neighbouring barbarians accelerated it. By 280 B.C. Tarentum alone remained comparatively powerful.

Polyb. 2. 39; Strabo 5. 251 and 6. 277; Pliny, *HN* 3. 95. *CAH* iv. 113 (P. N. Ure); vi. 127 (J. B. Bury); p. 299 (R. Hackforth); vii. 638 (T. Frank); E. Ciaceri, *Storia della Magna Grecia* (3 vols., 1927–32); A. Olivieri, *Civiltà Greca nell' Italia Meridionale* (1931); A. Blakeway, *BSA* xxxiii (1932–3), 170; J. Bérard, *La Colonisation grecque de l'Italie méridionale et de la Sicile dans l'antiquité* (1941), and *Bibliographie topographique des principales cités grecques de l'Italie et de la Sicile dans l'antiquité* (1941). E. T. S.

MAGNES, one of the earliest writers of Old Comedy (Arist. *Poet.* 3. 1448ᵃ34). Born at ? Athens (Anon. Περὶ κωμ. 5) about 500 B.C. Victorious in 472 (*IG* ii². 2318). His later plays were unsuccessful (Ar. *Eq.* 520 ff.). He won eleven victories (Anon. Περὶ κωμ.)—a figure substantiated by *IG* ii². 2325 and by Aristophanes (loc. cit.), who says that of all comic writers M. had πλεῖστα τροπαῖα to his credit. Aristophanes adds: πάσας δ' ὑμῖν φωνὰς ἱεὶς καὶ ψάλλων καὶ πτερυγίζων | καὶ λυδίζων καὶ ψηνίζων καὶ βαπτόμενος βατραχείοις | οὐκ ἐξήρκεσεν. These participles have no doubt given rise to the list of M.'s plays as given in Suidas and schol. Ar. *Eq.* 522: Βαρβιτισταί (the *Harpers*), Ὄρνιθες, Λυδοί, Ψῆνες (the *Gall-flies*), Βάτραχοι. Fragments of the Λυδοί only survive. We further possess fragments of Διόνυσος α' and β' and of a ? Τιτακίδης.

FCG ii. 9–11; *CAF* i. 7–9. M. P.

MAGNESIA AD MAEANDRUM (Μαγνησία πρὸς (or ἐπὶ) Μαιάνδρῳ), an Ionian city on a tributary of the Maeander, inland from Ephesus. Colonized by the Magnetes (q.v.), it and Magnesia ad Sipylum (q.v.) were the only Greek cities out of sight of the sea in pre-Hellenistic Asia Minor. Successively subject to Lydia and Persia, it was presented by Artaxerxes to Themistocles, whose female relatives were priestesses of the local goddess Artemis Leucophryene. Like Magnesia ad Sipylum it sided with Rome against Mithridates, and was made a *civitas libera* by Sulla when he reorganized the province of Asia. W. M. C.

MAGNESIA AD SIPYLUM (Μαγνησία πρὸς Σιπύλῳ) a city of Lydia lying in the fertile Hermus valley at the point where the roads from the interior and the Propontis converge on the way to Smyrna, the scene of the decisive battle between Antiochus and the Scipios in 190 B.C. *See also* MAGNESIA AD MAEANDRUM.

MAGNETES, a tribe occupying the mountain-systems of Ossa and Pelion on the eastern border of Thessaly. They became *Perioikoi* to the invading Thessalians and had to surrender the coastal district round Pagasae, which became the port of Pherae, but they retained their two votes on the Amphictionic Council. Pagasae was restored to the Magnetes when Philip expelled the tyrants of Pherae, but they lost the limited autonomy which they had previously enjoyed and became subjects of Macedonia. Their chief towns were Meliboea, Homolion, and Rhizus. In 293 Demetrias (q.v.) was founded through a 'synoecism' of the Magnetes.

F. Stählin, *PW*, s.v. 'Magnesia (1)'. H. D. W.

MAGNETISM, *see* PHYSICS, para. **8.**

MAGO (1), the founder of the military power of Carthage as well as of the influence of his family, according to Justin (18. 7. 19; 19. 1. 1), flourished *c.* 520 B.C.

S. Gsell, *Histoire anc. de l'Afrique du Nord* i² (1921), 480; ii (1918), passim; V. Ehrenberg, *PW* xiv. 495.

MAGO (2) was youngest brother of Hannibal, under whom he served in Italy (218–216 B.C.), fighting at Trebia and Cannae. He fought in Spain from 215 till his defeat at Ilipa (206). After failing to seize Carthago Nova and to re-enter Gades he attacked the Balearic Isles (Mahon in Minorca perpetuates his name) and in 205 landed in Liguria. After lengthy recruiting he advanced into the Po valley, where he was defeated by the Romans (203). He successfully re-embarked his army for Africa, but died of wounds on the voyage.   H. H. S.

MAGODIA, a type of low-class mime or lyric, sub-literary (like *hilarodia*, *simodia*, and *lysiodia*), about which the ancient tradition (Ath. 14. 620 f., Strabo 14. 648) is far from clear. *Magodia* is defined as ὄρχησις ἀπαλή (Hesych.); the actor, accompanied by kettledrums and cymbals, represented in comic style the drunken lover and other low characters. The best example of a possible libretto of such a performance is the *Alexandrian Erotic Fragment* (ed. Grenfell, 1896) or *The Forsaken Maiden's Lament*, found on an Egyptian papyrus of the second century B.C. (see Powell and Barber, *New Chapters in Grk. Lit.* i (1921), 54 f.).

Maas, in *PW*, s.v. σιμῳδοί; A. Dieterich, *Pulcinella* (1897) 29; H. Reich, *Mimus* (1897) i. 230–7.   W. G. W.

MAHARBAL, Hannibal's chief cavalry officer, defeated a Roman cavalry squadron near Assisi after the battle of Lake Trasimene (217). After Cannae (216) he is alleged to have urged Hannibal to march on Rome ('for in five days we shall dine on the Capitol'), and when Hannibal wisely refused he added 'uincere scis, Hannibal, uictoria uti nescis.'   H. H. S.

MAIA, (1) Μαῖα, mother of Hermes (q.v.) by Zeus and daughter of Atlas; she is one of the Pleiads (*Od.* 14. 435, where she is called Maias; Hesiod, *Theog.* 938, fr. 275, 3 Rzach). Her name means simply 'mother' or 'nurse' (cf. M. P. Nilsson, *AJPhil.* lix (1938), 392 on the Attic sacrifice mentioned in a text published by W. S. Ferguson, *Hesperia* vii (1938), 5, 65 f.), and apart from her son she has little existence. (2) A Roman goddess, associated with Volcanus (Gellius 13. 23 (22). 2); on 1 May the *flamen Volcanalis* sacrificed to her (Macrob. *Sat.* 1. 12. 18), further confirming the association, which, however, is quite unexplained, since he is undoubtedly a fire-god (*see* VOLCANUS), while her name appears to come from the root *mag* and signify growth or increase; cf. the by-form Maiesta (Piso in Macrob. ibid.) and the month-name, appropriate to a time of year when all plants are growing. By a natural confusion with (1) she was associated with Mercurius (q.v.) and worshipped also on 15 May, the *natalis* of his temple, apparently under the title of *inuicta* ('Maiae inuict.', *Fasti Antiates* on that date).

Wissowa, *RK* 229, 304.   H. J. R.

MAIESTAS. Every State must safeguard itself not only against external enemies but against traitors within. In early Rome treason was *perduellio* (q.v.): the traitor was 'hostili animo aduersus rem publicam animatus' (*Dig.* 48. 4. 11). Later, when tribunes were exalting the people's sovereignty, since *maiestas* 'residet proprie in p. R.', anyone 'qui de dignitate aut amplitudine aut potestate p. R. aut eorum quibus populus potestatem dederit derogat' could be accused of lowering the *maiestas* of the State, and Saturninus (q.v.) introduced in 103 B.C., against incompetent generals, the *Lex Appuleia de maiestate*. Sulla (q.v.) established a permanent *quaestio*; henceforward, *inter alia*, for a governor

to leave his province, begin war, or invade territory, 'iniussu p. R. aut Senatus' would be treasonable (Cic. *Pis.* 21. 50; cf. Tac. *Ann.* 1. 72). The constitutional changes of Julius Caesar and Augustus naturally involved new meanings for *minuta maiestas*, since the *maiestas* of the State became slowly embodied in the *maiestas* attaching to the *princeps* (Phaedrus, 2. 5. 23; Pliny, *HN* 25. 4). The *quaestio de maiestate* remained; before it came men accused of plotting Augustus' murder (Dio 54. 3), of making war without leave (ibid.), of adultery with a member of the *princeps'* family (Tac. *Ann.* 3. 24), or of publishing 'procacia scripta' (ibid. 1. 72). A man who had removed from a public square a statue bearing Augustus' name was detained at Augustus' pleasure (Cyrene Edicts, Malcovati, *Caes. Aug. Imp. operum fragm.*, p. 42), and the treatment of statues always provided difficult questions (e.g. Tac. *Ann.* 1. 74; *Dig.* 48. 4. 5). Definition being incomplete, at the beginning of Tiberius' reign informers, eager for rewards, brought all manner of frivolous charges, hoping to gain condemnation (Tac. *Ann.* 1. 73 and 74), but the good sense of Tiberius rejected them. Some trials provided genuine cases (e.g. Piso's: Tac. *Ann.* 3. 10–19), but sinister abuse began when Sejanus employed treason-trials to eliminate enemies. After Tiberius' death the hearing of charges of *maiestas* was abolished, but in 62 the law was invoked again for 'probrosa aduersus principem carmina' (Tac. *Ann.* 14. 48–9), and Nero used it frequently against suspected persons. Vespasian and Titus had no need for it, but Domitian found it a useful weapon for terrorization. We hear little of it under 'the good emperors', and those of the third century had a shorter way with their enemies.

The dangers in any law of treason are lack of precise definition and abuse for political terrorism; the Romans 'do not seem to have attained even a moderate degree of precision in the matter, and trials for *maiestas* were decided mainly on political considerations' (Jolowicz, *Hist. Intro. to the Study of Roman Law*, 324). A secure government does not need to use it, and Trajan wisely declared his policy 'non ex metu nec terrore hominum aut criminibus maiestatis reuerentiam nomini meo adquiri' (Pliny, *Ep.* 10. 82).

Digest 48. 4 is devoted to the *Lex Iulia de maiestate*, and Tacitus' *Annals* recount cases under Tiberius and Nero. In general see Mommsen's *Strafrecht*. For cases under Tiberius see R. S. Rogers, *Criminal Trials and Criminal Legislation under Tiberius* (1935); E. Ciaceri, in *Processi Politici* (1918), 249–308; M. P. Charlesworth, *CAH* x. 626–41.   M. P. C.

MAIORCA, see BALEARES INSULAE.

MALACA (nowadays *Malaga*), a Phoenician foundation on the southern coast of Spain, was an emporium for the opposite African shore. Its trade and industry (chiefly fish-curing) were not interrupted when it became an ally of Rome. This status it held until Vespasian conferred Latin Rights upon it. The remnants of the charter, issued by Domitian, are a valuable source for the study of Roman municipal administration.

Dessau, *ILS* 6089; Bruns, *Fontes*⁷, p. 147, no. 30.   J. J. Van N.

MALEA, south-eastern promontory of Laconia, and of the whole Peloponnesus, a dangerous corner for shipping, chiefly because of the sudden veering of the winds off a harbourless coast. It was denounced on this account from Homer down to Byzantine writers. But in part this perilousness was a literary tradition, and there was always much traffic through the narrow strait between Malea and Cythera.

Bölte, *PW*, s.v.   V. E.

MALLIUS THEODORUS (*cos.* A.D. 399) wrote a *De metris* (ed. Keil, *Gramm. Lat.* 6. 585–601). His philosophical and astronomical works are lost.

Cf. Teuffel, § 442, 3; Schanz–Hosius, § 1085.

MAMERTINES. A body of Campanian mercenaries, enlisted by Agathocles, treacherously seized Messana on his death (289 B.C.). Calling themselves *Mamertini* or Sons of Mars, they dominated and plundered north-east Sicily, although temporarily checked by Pyrrhus, until defeated on the Longanus river by Hieron of Syracuse (? 265). Tiring of a protective Carthaginian garrison which they had invited in, they appealed to Rome, thereby precipitating the First Punic War. When Rome accepted the alliance, they ejected the Carthaginian garrison and called in Appius Claudius (q.v. 5) Caudex, who drove back both Carthaginians and Hieron. H. H. S.

MAMERTINUS, see CLAUDIUS (16).

MAMILIUS (1) TUSCULANUS, OCTAVIUS, is said to have been the son-in-law of Tarquinius Superbus, and to have assisted the exiled king in his attempt to return to Rome by force. At the battle of Lake Regillus, in which he commanded the army of the Latin League, he was defeated and killed. Though Livy's account of him (2. 18. 3 ff.) ultimately may depend on popular ballads, this does not disprove his historical character.
P. T.

MAMILIUS (2), LUCIUS, dictator of Tusculum, is praised by tradition for the voluntary help which he brought to the Roman Republic when its safety was menaced by the Sabine Appius Herdonius, who had entrenched himself on the Capitol (460 B.C.). Mamilius is said to have been rewarded with the Roman citizenship (458).
P. T.

MAMILIUS (3) LIMETANUS, GAIUS. In the democratic agitation during the Jugurthine War, Mamilius (tribune in 110 B.C.), by a special *quaestio* set up (with M. Scaurus as chairman) to inquire into the conduct of various Roman commissions, secured the condemnation of a number of Optimate leaders, including Sp. Albinus, L. Bestia, C. Cato, C. Galba, and L. Opimius.
M. H.

MAMURRA of Formiae, *praefectus fabrum* under Caesar in Spain (61 B.C.) and Gaul, where he accumulated great wealth. His extravagance aroused ill feeling, and Catullus (29, 41, 43, 51), who had personal reasons for disliking him, coupled his name scandalously with Caesar's.
Münzer, *PW* xiv. 966–7.
C. E. S.

MANCINUS, see HOSTILIUS.

MANCIPATIO was a solemn transaction ending in the use of *aes et libra* (copper and scales, see NEXUM); it served for the transfer of ownership of *res mancipi*. This category included the most important objects in a primitive agricultural economy, such as land (*solum Italicum*), slaves, and beasts of draught and burden. By a declaration in prescribed form (Gaius 1. 119) the recipient announced his ownership of the property; the act acquired a kind of publicity by the presence of five citizens as witnesses and the *libripens* holding the balance. *Mancipatio* was mentioned already in the XII Tables; its field of application gradually expanded: it was used for making a gift, for the constitution of a dowry or mortgage, for some acts of family law, such as *adoptio*, *emancipatio* (qq.v.), *coemptio* (see MANUS), and for a will, called *testamentum per aes et libram*, in which the testator bequeathed his entire property.
A. B.

MANCIPIUM, see PATRIA POTESTAS, EMANCIPATIO.

MANDATUM, see CONSTITUTIONES.

MANES, the spirits of the dead. The most generally accepted derivation is that from the old Latin adjective *manus*, 'good'; the appellation may be euphemistic. (i) In early times the dead were thought of as an undifferentiated mass with a collective divinity expressed in *Di Manes*; Cicero (*Leg.* 2. 9. 22) quotes the ancient ordinance 'deorum manium iura sacra sunto'. Graves were dedicated to them in the formula DIS MANIBUS SACRUM, and they were worshipped at the festivals of the Feralia, Parentalia, and Lemuria (qq.v.). From this primary sense there are two derivatives: (*a*) *manes* is used by the poets in a topographical sense for the realm of the dead, e.g. Verg. *Aen.* 11. 181. (*b*) *Manes* was applied to the Graeco-Roman underworld gods, Dis, Orcus, Persephone, etc., e.g. Verg. *Aen.* 10. 39. (ii) Later in a special, though still collective sense, the *Di Manes* were identified with the *Di Parentes*, the ancestors of the family, e.g. Ov. *Met.* 9. 407. (iii) Still later *manes* came to be used of the soul of individual dead persons. The first recorded instance is Cic. *Pis.* 16 'coniuratorum manes', and in Augustan writers the usage is frequent, e.g. Liv. 3. 58. 11 'manes Verginiae'; and so in the famous line of Virgil, *Aen.* 6. 743, 'quisque suos patimur manes'. From the beginning of the Empire it became customary on grave inscriptions to add to DIS MANIBUS SACRUM the name of the dead person in the genitive or dative case. *See also* AFTER-LIFE, para. 9.
C. B.

MANĔTHO (*fl.* 280 B.C.), Egyptian high-priest in Heliopolis under the first two Ptolemies, who dedicated to Ptolemy II a history of Egypt (Αἰγυπτιακά) from mythical times to 323. His claim to have consulted the lists of kings (ἱερὰ γράμματα) implies that his version was more official than that of Hecataeus of Teos. The three-fold division of the thirty-one dynasties corresponds with the recognized division into old, middle, and new kingdoms. Frequently used by Jewish and Christian writers to establish biblical chronology.
FHG ii. 511.
G. L. B.

MANIA, Roman goddess of whom nothing certain is known except her name. This apparently means 'the good one', cf. *manes*, and may be a euphemism for a death-goddess. By way, it would appear, of the theory that the Lares (q.v.) are ghosts, ancient speculation made Mania their mother (Varro, *Ling.* 9. 61), and this affects late cult (Henzen, *Acta Arvalium*, p. 145; add Dessau, *ILS* 9522).
Cf. Altheim, *Hist. Rom. Rel.* 117–18, 133.
H. J. R.

MANĪLIUS (1), MANIUS. After a not very successful praetorship in Spain (154 or 155 B.C.) Manilius as consul in 149 commenced the siege of Carthage in the Third Punic War, his colleague L. Marcius Censorinus co-operating by sea. After two expeditions to Nepheris (south-east of Tunis) had been saved from disaster by Scipio Aemilianus, Manilius was superseded in 148. In 133 he tried to check Tiberius Gracchus. He was introduced by Cicero as one of the speakers in the *De Republica*. He was a famous jurist, one of three who 'fundauerunt ius ciuile' (Pomponius). His works included *Monumenta* and forms for contracts of sale (*venalium vendendorum leges*); a few of his *actiones* and *responsa* survive (see Huschke, *Iurisprud. Anteiust.*[6] 1. 5–7).
H. H. S.

MANILIUS (2), GAIUS, on the last day of 67 B.C. carried as tribune a law distributing freedmen through all the tribes; this the Senate annulled next day for non-observance of the *trinundinum*. Manilius then (66) conferred on Pompey the command against Mithridates and Tigranes, with *imperium* over all the provinces of Asia Minor. On laying down his tribunate he was prosecuted for *repetundae* by Pompey's enemy Cn. Piso, but the case was dropped amid the disturbance of January 65, to which date Cicero, praetor for 66, had reluctantly postponed it. But Manilius was soon prosecuted for *maiestas* and condemned.
Asconius, 53, 57 ff.; Schol. Bob. *Cic. Mil.* 284 Or.; Dio, 36. 42. 4; Plut. *Cic.* 9.
G. E. F. C.

MANILIUS (3), Marcus, author of the *Astronomica*, a didactic poem on astrology, wrote under Augustus and Tiberius. (Book 1. 899 mentions Varus' defeat in A.D. 9, while in 384–6, etc. Augustus (who died in August A.D. 14) is still alive, as he is in 2. 508–9; in 4. 763–6 and 773–7 Tiberius is the reigning *princeps*.) Of the man himself we know nothing else whatever. Of his work we have five books. Book 1 (926 lines) describes the creation, the arrangement of the starry heavens, and the circles which mark them out; bk. 2 (970 lines) the signs of the zodiac, their characteristics, mutual aspects, and subdivisions; bk. 3 (682 lines) their division into twelve *sortes*, methods of determining the place of the horoscope, etc.; bk. 4 (935 lines) their influence on men born under them, their divisions as combined in decads, and other technicalities; bk. 5 (745 lines) the risings of the other signs and their effects on children born on each occasion. Thus many essential parts of the subject are omitted, for instance any discussion of the movements and influence of the planets; but whether the work is incompletely preserved or was never finished we cannot tell. Manilius writes as an enthusiast for his subject, anxious to make converts and to provide practical instruction for their use, but his poem even if complete would not serve as a technical treatise. He is not seldom inaccurate and sometimes appears to have misunderstood his sources; what these were is unknown, for much of what he tells us appears nowhere else. He is not a great poet, but his literary gifts are by no means negligible. If sometimes feeble or obscure, his language is correct, often forcible, and sometimes eloquent, and he writes with an easy mastery of the technique of hexameters; his skill in doing sums in verse is worthy of Ovid. Much of the poem is condemned by its subject to find few readers, but the non-technical books 1 and 5, and the proems to the others, deserve to be better known. To students of Latin he will always appeal as the object of some of the best work of three great latinists, Scaliger, Bentley, and Housman.

See also ASTROLOGY.

Text and commentary: A. E. Housman, 5 vols. 1903–30 (with Latin notes); text only, 1932. Book 2 (with English notes and translation) H. W. Garrod, 1911. R. A. B. M.

MANIPULUS. With the introduction, perhaps during the fourth century B.C., of the *pilum* or throwing spear, the legion ceased to be a phalanx and was organized for open-order fighting. It was subdivided into thirty maniples, which in the Polybian period varied in strength from 120 to 200 men. Each maniple comprised two centuries, was commanded by the centurion of the right-hand century, and had its own standard (*signum*). For tactical purposes the maniples were normally drawn up in three lines with the rear units covering off the intervals in the line in front. After the introduction of the cohort the maniple was retained as a constituent unit. *See* COHORS. H. M. D. P.

MANLIUS (1), Marcus, according to Roman tradition defeated the Aequi as consul in 392 B.C., held the Capitol against the Gauls, and repulsed a night attack after being awakened by the cackling of the sacred geese (387); hence he was surnamed *Capitolinus*. It is not unlikely that he or his kinsmen rendered distinguished service against the Celts, but the above story in its present form is probably an aetiological myth invented to explain the surname *Capitolinus* borne by a branch of the Manlii, because they lived on the Capitol even before the sack of Rome. In the crisis that followed the Gallic catastrophe Manlius probably supported the poor against Camillus, and may have made an abortive attempt at revolution, in which he fell. The traditional account was greatly elaborated by late annalists, who read back into the story of Manlius the aims and policy of the plebs in and after the Gracchan period.

Mommsen, *Röm. Forsch.* ii. 179 ff. P. T.

MANLIUS (2) **TORQUATUS**, Titus. Popular tradition and annalistic speculation made Manlius a striking embodiment of Roman virtue. He reputedly killed a gigantic Celt in a duel and despoiled him of his collar (*torques*), thereby winning the *cognomen* Torquatus (361 B.C.); the story is probably an aetiological myth invented to explain the surname Torquatus borne by a branch of the Manlii. Manlius' piety was displayed in saving his father from prosecution, and his stern justice in sentencing his son to death, while he was consul for the third time, as the son engaged the enemy against his father's orders. We may believe the accounts of Manlius' successful campaign as dictator against Caere (*c.* 353), and against the Latins, whose subjugation, the main object of his policy, he secured by the battle of Trifanum (340). P. T.

MANLIUS (3) **VULSO LONGUS**, Lucius, as consul (256 B.C.) with Regulus (q.v.) won the naval battle of Ecnomus and led the expeditionary force to Africa. He returned to Rome to receive a triumph, leaving Regulus in sole command in Africa. As consul II (250) he blockaded Lilybaeum. H. H. S.

MANLIUS (4) **TORQUATUS**, Titus, as consul (235 B.C.) served in Sardinia. He closed the Temple of Janus, a symbol of restored peace, on the only occasion between Numa and Augustus. Censor 231, but *vitio creatus*. Consul II (224), he defeated the Boii, crossed the Po, and attacked the Insubres. He deprecated ransoming Roman prisoners after Cannae. He defeated a Carthaginian expeditionary force in Sardinia (215), celebrated games as dictator (208), and died in 203. H. H. S.

MANLIUS (5) **VULSO**, Gnaeus, curule aedile in 197 B.C., praetor in Sicily in 195, succeeded L. Scipio as consul in 189 in the East, concluding the peace with Antiochus and subduing the Galatians in defence of law and order in Asia Minor; the campaign was also profitable in booty. In 188 he settled Asia and returned through Thrace, suffering losses. His triumph in 187 was opposed by L. Furius Purpurio and Aemilius Paullus, probably as part of Scipionic criticism of his policy. Tradition made him introduce luxury to Rome, and certainly the effects of Eastern spoil became apparent with the close of the Syrian War.

Livy 38; 39. 6; Polyb. bk. 21; Appian, *Syr.* 39 ff.; Pliny, *HN* 34. 8; 37. 6. De Sanctis, *Stor. Rom.* iv. 1, 217; A. H. McDonald, *JRS* 1938, 161. A. H. McD.

MANLIUS (6), Gaius, a centurion under Sulla, was financially ruined, and became a follower of Catiline. He collected troops for him in Etruria and in October 63 openly proclaimed his rebellion. In the battle of Pistoria he commanded the right wing of Catiline's army and was killed. A. M.

MANTINEA lay in a plain of south-east Arcadia, to the north of Tegea (q.v.). The two States were constantly at war over boundaries and the control of the swallow-holes which drained the plain (Thuc. 5. 65); their rivalry often prevented the Arcadians from uniting against Sparta. Mantinea was synoecized from five villages (Strabo, p. 337), probably *c.* 500 B.C., when its coinage began. It became a moderate democracy *c.* 450 B.C. (for date of synoecism and democracy, not necessarily related, see *PW* xiv. 1318 ff.). Mantinea withdrew from the anti-Spartan movement after the Persian Wars (Hdt. 9. 35) and supported Sparta in the helot revolt (Xen. *Hell.* 5. 2. 3); but under the democracy it grew in power and joined Sparta's enemies in 420. It was the scene of a decisive Spartan victory in 418. After the peace of 387 the Spartans obliged the Mantineans to dismantle their walls and live in villages, but after the battle of Leuctra (371) the city was restored. In 362 Epaminondas won his last victory over the Spartans here. The city was destroyed by the Achaean League in 223 and refounded under the name of Antigonea. Unlike most fortified Greek cities, Mantinea stood in the middle of a plain.

IG v. 2, 46 ff. G. Fougères, *Mantinée et l'Arcadie Orientale* (1898); Bölte, *PW* xiv. 1290 ff.; W. J. Woodhouse, *King Agis of Sparta* (1933) (battle of 418 B.C.). T. J. D.

MANUBIAE (or *manibiae*, as in inscriptions. From *manus* and *habeo*, or rather perhaps from an old verb *manuo* = to grasp). The original meaning of this term has been variously defined, (1) (Mommsen) as the revenue raised from the public sale of booty (Gell. 13. 25. 28: 'pecunia per quaestorem populi Romani ex praeda uendita contracta'), or, (2), more probably (Karlowa), as the portion of the booty reserved for the victorious general, of which he could dispose at his discretion (Ps.-Asc. in Cic. *Verr.* 2. 1. 54: 'manubiae . . . sunt praeda imperatoris pro portione de hostibus capta'). Although legally he could not be prosecuted for any use to which he put his share of the booty, the commander generally devoted it to works of public utility (temples, roads, forums, theatres, etc.), or, to avoid popular resentment, he shared it or the proceeds of its sale with his officers and men. Thus the distinction between *praeda* and *manubiae* was easily forgotten or ignored, especially when the emperors compelled their officials to contribute a certain amount of their *manubiae* to the emperor's privy purse.

Mommsen, *Röm. Forsch.* ii. 443 ff. (cf. J. Marquardt, *Röm. Staatsverw.* ii. 277 f. and F. Lammert in *PW*, s.v.); O. Karlowa, *Röm. Rechtsgesch.* ii. 1, 5 ff. (cf. Ph. Fabia, Dar.–Sag. iii. 2, 1582 ff.). P. T.

MANUMISSIO, see SLAVERY, LAW OF.

MANUS signified the power of the husband over the wife in a marriage accompanied by *conventio in manum*. Such a marriage could be made either by *confarreatio*, the earliest form, a religious ceremony in the presence of ten witnesses (requiring the assistance of a pontiff and the utterance of *sollemnia verba*, and obligatory for marriages of patricians), or by *coemptio* (sale of the wife through *mancipatio* (q.v.) to her husband). *Manus* was also acquired by *usus*, which took effect if in informal matrimony the partners lived together as man and wife in the husband's house uninterruptedly for a year. By a rule of the XII Tables if the woman was absent for three successive nights, the *usus* was interrupted.

In consequence of the *conventio in manum* the woman left her own agnatic family and entered that of her husband, in which she was *filiae loco*. The legal effects of *manus* were similar to those of *adoptio* and *capitis deminutio minima* (qq.v.).

Matrimony without *manus*, which even in the time of the Republic tended more and more to displace marriage with *manus*, did not have these effects: the woman remained in her agnatic family. *See also* MARRIAGE, LAW OF. A. B.

MANUSCRIPTS, see BOOKS, PALAEOGRAPHY.

MAPS (πίνακες). For measuring distances the Greeks and Romans counted the steps of a pedestrian or estimated the length of a sea-journey on a basis of 500 stades (*c.* 55 statute miles) by sea. Lacking the compass, they determined direction by the sun or stars. For latitude they used sticks that projected their shadow into a bowl (πόλοι, introduced from Babylon by Anaximander). For longitude they were reduced to guesswork, since their sand- or water-clocks were useless for synchronizing. In spite of this primitive equipment, the Greeks achieved considerable proficiency in cartography. Their first world-maps, constructed in the sixth century by Anaximander and Hecataeus (qq.v.), showed a plane landmass of circular contour round the Mediterranean basin. Herodotus (esp. 4. 36–40) derided these 'compass-drawn'

maps and had a rudimentary idea of meridians. Local maps had become familiar in the fifth century (Ar. *Nub.* 200 ff.).

The foundations of scientific cartography were laid when Aristotle (*Cael.* 293^b ff., *Mete.* 362^a ff.) confirmed the sphericity of the earth (previously assumed by Pythagoras) and defined more closely the five zones of Parmenides. Parallels of latitude were established by Pytheas (q.v.), and Dicaearchus (*c.* 310 B.C.) laid down a median line from Gibraltar to the Himalayas. Eratosthenes (*c.* 200) made a scientific and accurate computation of the earth's circumference, and drew two main axes of latitude and longitude intersecting at Rhodes, with corresponding parallels. His world-map was the first to achieve tolerable accuracy. Hipparchus (*c.* 140) divided Eratosthenes' main parallel of latitude into 360 degrees and drew 12 parallels of latitude (with details of longest days), dividing the land-mass into 'climata' or zones. Crates constructed a large globe (with three imaginary land-masses besides the known one).

The results of Greek cartography were combined with data from Roman road-makers by Artemidorus, and especially by Agrippa (Plin. *HN* 3. 17), who set up a large globe at Rome. Strabo discussed the principles of map-making on plane and sphere (3. 116–17, 120). Lastly, Ptolemy constructed a plane world-map, using a modified method of conical projection (with curved lines of latitude and longitude), and furnished delusively accurate calculations of latitude north of the Equator and of longitude east of the Canaries. Copies of his map survive in his manuscripts. Other extant maps are a street-plan of Rome (*Forma Urbis Romae*) *c.* A.D. 200; the Peutinger Table (q.v.); and various road-maps (*see* ITINERARIES). *See also* GEOGRAPHY.

E. H. Bunbury, *History of Ancient Geography* (1907), with maps; E. H. Warmington, *Greek Geography* (1934), 234 ff.; H. Berger, *Geschichte der wissenschaftlichen Erdkunde der Griechen*² (1903); W. Kubitschek, *PW*, s.v. 'Karten'. E. H. W.

MARATHON, a deme on the north-east Attic coast, lay in a fertile plain near a small, deep bay, at the end of the two major roads from Athens to the sea over Mt. Pentelicus and along the river Cephisus. It was the capital of an ancient religious confederacy (the Tetrapolis), and the base from which Pisistratus recovered Athens (*c.* 545 B.C.). Here the Greeks gained their first victory over Persia (490). It was the birthplace of Herodes Atticus (q.v.). It is perhaps to be identified with the village of Vrana or with the ruins on the east slope of Mt. Agrieliki.

Wrede, *PW*, s.v. P. T.

MARBLE. Under μάρμαρος, *marmor*, the ancients included granites, porphyries, and all stones capable of high polish. In Greece the island marbles were employed in the third millennium B.C. for Cycladic sculpture, and later the Minoans had a liking for coloured Lacedaemonian marbles, breccias, and other variegated stones. After the archaic period marble largely supplanted the softer limestones in monumental architecture, while in the late seventh century the coarse-grained island marbles, grey Naxian and white Parian, began to be used for statuary. Parian was the usual sculptural marble of Greece. Attic marbles were the fine-grained Pentelic, used in the Parthenon and other fifth-century buildings, and the inferior Hymettian.

Marble came slowly into use in Rome, and Augustus boasted that he found the city of brick and left it of marble. Owing to the cost of transport, Roman buildings were rarely built wholly of marble, which was usually applied as facing to brick. Under the Empire the provinces were ransacked to provide rare stones, and many quarries passed into imperial control under a special office, the *ratio marmorum*. The storehouses of the foreign marbles have been discovered on the Tiber. The chief statuary marble was the white Luna (Carrara), first worked by the Etruscans and introduced into Rome in 48 B.C.

G. Lafaye, Dar.-Sag., s.v. *'marmor'*.   F. N. P.

MARCELLINUS (1) (probably 2nd c. A.D.), author of an extant work Περὶ σφυγμῶν, borrowed very largely from Hippocrates.

Ed. H. Schöne, *Festschrift zur 49 Versammlung deutscher Philologen und Schulmänner*, 1907. PW xiv. 1488.

MARCELLINUS (2), biographer of Thucydides (best text, C. Hude's ed. of *Thuc.*, 1898–1901). His 'Life' contains three sections, of which A (ch. 1–45) is probably the 'Life of Thucydides' from [Proclus'] *Chrestomathia*, worked over by a schoolmaster, and B by a contemporary of Dion. Hal. (perhaps Caecilius), whose main interest was Thucydides' style. To these Zosimus (5th c. A.D.) added C to make the introduction to his edition of scholia on Isocrates, Demosthenes, and Thucydides. Marcellinus was probably the scholar who, shortly after Justinian, isolated the Thucydidean scholia and gave the composition his name. Its main value lies in the biographical parts, where the deductive method is employed to reach sound conclusions.   F. W. W.

MARCELLINUS, *see also* LENTULUS (6).

MARCELLUS (1), MARCUS CLAUDIUS, served in the First Punic War and was augur, aedile, and praetor. As consul (222 B.C.) he campaigned successfully against the Insubres, relieving Clastidium and winning the *spolia opima* (q.v.) by killing the Gallic chief Viridomarus in single combat. As praetor II he thwarted Hannibal's attack on Nola (216). He was either appointed *consul suffectus* for 216 or else, being consul designate for 215, withdrew when objection was raised to the election of two plebeian consuls. In 215 and as consul III in 214 he followed a Fabian strategy from his base at Castra Claudiana near Suessula, whence he parried two further thrusts by Hannibal on Nola; in 214 he stormed Casilinum. From the autumn until 211 he served in Sicily. He sacked Leontini, commenced the blockade of Syracuse by land and sea (213), stormed Epipolae (212), and finally took Syracuse despite the engineering skill of Archimedes (211). After routing a Carthaginian force near Himera he returned to Rome and celebrated an *ovatio*. As consul IV (210), proconsul (209), and consul V (208) he skirmished cautiously but successfully against Hannibal until he was killed while reconnoitring near Venusia. Named the Sword of Rome, he had shown an energy which set him above most of his contemporaries, while the exaggerations which embellish the annalistic accounts of his exploits against Hannibal are a tribute to his vigorous personality. His faith was exemplified in his dedication of temples to Honos and Virtus, his appreciation of Greek culture by the artistic treasures which he shipped from Syracuse to Rome. For his appearance see coin, *CAH*, Pl. IV, 57.   H. H. S.

MARCELLUS (2), MARCUS CLAUDIUS, eldest son of (1), tribune (204 B.C.), curule aedile (200), praetor in Sicily (198), became consul in 196, crushing the Insubrians near Comum; he was legate in Gaul (193). Censor in 189 with T. Flamininus, he restored census rights to the Campanians. He died in 177.

Livy 33. 25 and 36–7; 35. 4–8; 38. 28 and 36. De Sanctis, *Stor. Rom.* iv. 1, pp. 414, 587.   A. H. McD.

MARCELLUS (3), MARCUS CLAUDIUS, tribune in 171 B.C., was praetor in 169, when, after intervening in the levies, he commanded in Spain (169–168); he became consul in 166 in Liguria. He was consul again in 155 in Liguria, and for a third time in 152, within the ten years' interval, on account of the war in Spain. He subdued

the Celtiberians and negotiated a peace in the liberal tradition of Sempronius Gracchus (152–151); the Scipionic tradition (in Polybius) depreciates his achievement. He was drowned in 148 on an embassy to Africa.

Livy, bk. 43; *Per.* 46, 48, 50; Polyb. 35. 2–3; Appian, *Hisp.* 48–50. A. Schulten, *Numantia* i (1914), 345; De Sanctis, *Stor. Rom.* iv. 1, pp. 420, 471.   A. H. McD.

MARCELLUS (4), MARCUS CLAUDIUS, consul 51 B.C., proposed a motion, declared illegal by the Caesarians, probably to recall Caesar on 1 Mar. 50. Pompey resisted this, but in October Marcellus carried various resolutions which, though some were vetoed, ensured that the question be discussed on the ensuing 1 March. He also declared invalid the *Lex Vatinia* on Novum Comum, and flogged a citizen of Comum to prove that he was not a Roman. After Pharsalus Marcellus retired to Mytilene, but in Sept. 46 Caesar allowed his return; Cicero in gratitude delivered the *pro Marcello*. But in May 45 Marcellus was murdered at the Piraeus, and Caesar, unjustly according to Cicero, was suspected of complicity.

Sources: (a) the *Relatio* of 51: [Hirtius], *BGall.* 8. 53. 1; Suet. *Iul.* 28; Dio, 40. 59. 1; App. *BCiv.* 2. 25; Cic. *Att.* 8. 3. 3; (b) the flogging: E. G. Hardy, *Problems in Roman History* (1924), 126 ff.
                                                             G. E. F. C.

MARCELLUS (5), GAIUS CLAUDIUS (d. 40 B.C.), owes his historical importance to his consulship in 50. Frustrated in his efforts to procure a decree of the Senate for Caesar's recall, he took the responsibility of commissioning Pompey to command the two legions stationed at Capua and to raise troops (2 Dec.). He remained in Italy, however, after the outbreak of war and obtained Caesar's pardon. His wife Octavia bore him a son (M. Marcellus) and two daughters.

Cicero, *Letters*; Plutarch, *Pompey*, 58–9; Appian, *BCiv.* 2. 26–31; Dio Cassius 40. 59 and 64–6. Drumann–Groebe, *Gesch. Roms* ii. 335–7.   G. W. R.

MARCELLUS (6), GAIUS CLAUDIUS, consul of 49 B.C., was brother of (4) and cousin of (5); he supported Pompey and held a naval command. He probably died before the battle of Pharsalus.

F. Münzer, *PW* iii. 2736.

MARCELLUS (7), MARCUS CLAUDIUS, son of (5) above and of Octavia, sister of Augustus, was born in 42 B.C. He was betrothed to a daughter of Sex. Pompeius, but in 25 he married Augustus' daughter Julia. In 25 he accompanied the emperor to Spain; in 23, as aedile, he gave magnificent games. As the supposed heir of Augustus he incurred the rivalry of Agrippa (q.v. 3). He died in 23 and was buried in the Mausoleum of Augustus. Octavia named a library after him and Augustus a theatre. He was celebrated by Virgil (*Aen.* 6. 860) and Propertius (3. 18).

Gaheis, *PW* iii. 2764; *PIR*², C 925.   A. M.

MARCELLUS (8), MARCUS POMPONIUS (early 1st c. A.D.), grammarian, notorious for pedantic purism in diction. Nothing of his work remains.

Cf. Teuffel, § 282, 2; Schanz–Hosius, § 475 a.

MARCELLUS (9) of Side, physician and poet, lived under Hadrian (117–38) and Antoninus Pius (138–61) and wrote 42 books of Ἰατρικά in heroic metre (lost); Περὶ λυκανθρώπου; a poem Περὶ ἰχθύων (frs. preserved); *Epigrammata* written in 160 for Herodes Atticus' *Triopion*.

Ed. M. Schneider, *Commentationes philologae quibus O. Ribbeckio ...congratulantur discipuli* (1888), 115. *PW* xiv. 1496; M. Wellmann, *Marcellus von Side als Arzt* (1934).

MARCELLUS (10), ULPIUS, a Roman jurist of the second half of the second century A.D. An acute, independent thinker and no mere compiler, he often argues

with success against the opinions of earlier jurists (even those of Julianus), and is cited with predilection by his successors. His main work was the *Digesta* (31 books), a partly casuistic, partly dogmatic treatise, which was extensively transcribed by later jurists (particularly by Ulpian in his commentary to the Edict), and was also discussed in special commentaries by Ulpian and Scaevola. Marcellus also wrote *notae* to the *Digesta* of Julian (very valuable) and to Pomponius' *Regulae*, and besides this a collection of *Responsa*, a commentary *Ad legem Iuliam et Papiam*, and five books *De officio consulis*.
A. B.

MARCELLUS, *see also* EPRIUS, NONIUS.

MARCIA, a freedwoman, was mistress of Quadratus and, after his execution, of Commodus (q.v.). Friend and helper of the Christians, she co-operated in the murder of Commodus. She later married Eclectus and was killed by Didius Julianus.

MARCIANUS, AELIUS, one of the last classical Roman jurists, was active in the period after Caracalla. He was the author of voluminous manuals (*Institutiones, Regulae*) and some monographs, chiefly in the domain of criminal procedure, and apparently addressed to the new citizens created by the *Constitutio Antoniniana* for the purpose of instructing them in Roman Law. His writings are not lacking in original thoughts which may quite well be authentic and must not be regarded as post-classical or Byzantine additions. We owe to him our knowledge of numerous imperial rescripts of the period A.D. 198–211. It is probable that he held office in the imperial chancery.

W. W. Buckland, *Studi Riccobono* i (1932). A. B.

MARCIUS (1) is the eponymous author of a number of miscellaneous oracular sayings current in Rome in early days. During the Punic Wars certain *carmina Marciana*, similar to the Sibylline oracles, succeeded in obtaining sufficient authority to give rise to the Ludi Apollinares celebrated in 212. This may have been due partly to war-time conditions, and partly to the collection of scattered oracular sayings and prophecies ordered to be made by the Senate in the previous year. There seem to have been two diverging views about their authorship. According to Cicero (*Div.* 1. 115; 2. 113), whose view is supported by Servius in his commentary on *Aeneid* 6, there were *Marcii fratres*, men of noble birth, who wrote prophecies and oracular sayings. According to Livy, however, and several later writers, there was one only, *vates Marcius*; and it seems impossible to determine the truth more exactly.

Of an ancient collection of *praecepta* under the name of Marcius three Saturnian quotations survive, which may be dated at latest as of the second century B.C. It is uncertain whether they have any connexion with *Marcius vates*.

See Morel *FPL* 63. A. L. P.

MARCIUS (2), ANCUS, traditionally the fourth king of Rome (642–617 B.C.), is probably an historical figure and not an annalistic reduplication of the portrait of Numa. To surmise, from the connexion of Marcius' name with Mars, that he was a god, or that his acts are mere duplications of achievements by members of the *gens* Marcia, is quite gratuitous. He did not build the Aqua Marcia (cf. MARCIUS 5) or capture and colonize Ostia (q.v.), but indubitably he seized from the Etruscans a territory near the salt-pits at the Tiber mouth, he enlarged Rome, and he built the Pons Sublicius.

J. Carcopino, *Virgile et les origines d'Ostie* (1919), 18 ff.; H. Last, *CAH* vii. 377 ff. P. T.

MARCIUS (3) **RUTILIUS,** GAIUS, four times consul and the first plebeian dictator (356 B.C.?) and censor (351). His repulse of an Etruscan invasion in 356, for

which despite patrician opposition Marcius was granted a triumph, led to the foundation of the first Roman settlement at Ostia. By a natural confusion this settlement was subsequently attributed to King Ancus Marcius (q.v. 2). P. T.

MARCIUS (4) **PHILIPPUS,** QUINTUS, praetor in Sicily in 188 B.C., as consul in 186 suppressed the Bacchanalian 'conspiracy' and suffered defeat in Liguria in the *saltus Marcius*. In 183 he was envoy in the Peloponnese, checking the Achaean League. He influenced the preliminaries of the Third Macedonian War, persuading Perseus in 171 to accept a truce which allowed Rome more time for preparations. Consul in 169, he penetrated into Pieria, clearing the way for Aemilius Paullus' Pydna campaign. He was censor with Paullus in 164–163.

Livy bks. 39–40, 42–4; Polyb. bks. 24, 27–8. T. Frank, *CPhil.* 1910, 358; De Sanctis, *Stor. Rom.* iv. 1, pp. 274, 300, 419, 565, 613; F. W. Walbank, 'A Note on the Embassy of Q. Marcius Philippus', *JRS*, 1941. A. H. McD.

MARCIUS (5) **REX,** QUINTUS, praetor in 144 B.C., built a famous aqueduct (Aqua Marcia). His imperium was prolonged after a dispute in order that he might complete it.

MARCIUS (6) **PHILIPPUS,** LUCIUS (*cos.* 91 B.C.), was perhaps grandson of (4) above and father of (8), Augustus' stepfather. An influential politician, he succeeded in living at Rome, unmolested by either side, through the struggles of the Marian and Sullan period. He began as a democrat, proposing a land-law in 104 B.C. as tribune (asserting that there were not 2,000 men of property in the State). In 100 he followed Marius in turning against Saturninus and the extremists; in his consulship (91) his opposition perhaps turned the scale against Drusus' reforms, which he declared invalid. He was censor in 86, when he defended the young Pompey. After Sulla's death he resisted Lepidus' attempted revolution in 78, and advocated sending Pompey to check Sertorius in Spain, 'non pro consule sed pro consulibus'. M. H.

MARCIUS (7) **REX,** QUINTUS, was consul (68 B.C.) with L. Caecilius Metellus. As his colleague died soon, and the suffect also, he was consul alone. After superseding his brother-in-law Lucullus in Cilicia and meeting King Philip II of Syria at Antioch (67), he was himself replaced by Pompey (66). He patrolled Etruria against the Catilinarian conspirators (63).

F. Münzer, *PW* xiv. 1583; G. Downey, *CPhil.* 1937, 144. A M.

MARCIUS (8) **PHILIPPUS,** LUCIUS, son of the censor of 86 B.C., was praetor (62), governor of Syria (61–60), and consul (56). He married Atia, Caesar's niece and C. Octavius' widow, and thus became stepfather of Octavian. He took no prominent part in the Civil Wars and went as an emissary of the Senate to Antony (43). The *porticus Philippi* probably was built by his son (tribune in 49 and *cos. suff.* in 38).

F. Münzer, *PW* xiv. 1568. A. M.

MARCIUS, *see also* CORIOLANUS, TURBO.

MARCOMAN(N)I (Stat. *Silv.* 3. 3. 170 scans Marcomāni), a West-German (Suebic) tribe, the name meaning inhabitants of a border country, are first mentioned by Caesar. Stirred up by the Cimbri and Teutones, the Marcomanni left Saxony and Thuringia (*c.* 100 B.C.) and settled down on the upper and middle Main; they joined Ariovistus' expedition against Gaul. Attacked by the elder Drusus (9 B.C.), they emigrated to Bohemia (*c.* 8 B.C.). There Maroboduus (q.v.) established a powerful kingdom, which Augustus considered a danger and wanted to destroy, but was hindered by the Pannonian-Illyrian revolt. Weakened by a war against Arminius,

Maroboduus was expelled by Catualda (A.D. 19), who in turn was overthrown by Vibilius (20), the following kings being more or less dependent on Rome. After wars under Domitian and Nerva peace prevailed till the great Marcomannic wars (166–72; 177–80) under M. Aurelius. The Marcomanni must have played their part in the subsequent wars on the middle Danube, though they are not very frequently mentioned. After 500 they left Bohemia and occupied Bavaria.

Franke, *PW*, s.v.; J. Klose, *Roms Klientel- und Randstaaten am Rhein und an der Donau* (1934); R. Heuberger, *Klio* 24 (1931), 89 ff.; L. Schmidt, *Geschichte der deutschen Stämme bis zum Ausgang der Völkerwanderung. Die Westgermanen*[2] (1938).   F. A. W. S.

MARDONIUS, Persian general, nephew of Darius, whose daughter he married *c.* 493 B.C., probably co-operated in crushing the Ionian revolt. He successfully commanded an expedition to Thasos, Thrace, and Macedon (492), notwithstanding heavy losses in Thrace and in a storm off Mt. Athos. Though he was not the chief and the evil counsellor of Xerxes (as Aeschylus and Herodotus assert), he was probably the author of the plan of campaign in 480–479. His outstanding ability is revealed in the co-ordinated land and naval operations in 480. As commander of the forces kept in Greece after Salamis, Mardonius made two vain attempts to detach Athens from the Greek alliance by offers of peace. In 479 he was forced to withdraw from Attica by the Greek land forces and was routed by them at Plataea, where he fell fighting (479).

G. B. Grundy, *Great Persian War* (1901), 148 ff.; K. J. Beloch, *Griech. Gesch.* ii[2]. 2, 83 ff.; E. Obst, *PW*, s.v. 'Mardonios'.   P. T.

MARINUS (*c.* A.D. 130), anatomist, often mentioned by Galen, perhaps lived in Alexandria. Works: (1) Ἀνατομικαὶ ἐγχειρήσεις; (2) an Anatomy in 20 books; (3) a book on the roots of the nerves; (4) an Anatomy of the muscles; (5) a commentary on aphorisms.

PW xiv. 1796.   W. D. R.

MARIUS (1), GAIUS (157–86 B.C.), was born near Arpinum; as a country-side Italian he could scarcely hope for a rapid rise to office. He served with credit in the Numantine War. As tribune in 119 he opposed a popular proposal for cheap corn, but persisted, in spite of Optimate opposition, in a plan for improving election procedure; he thus showed political impartiality. He married Julia (daughter of the consul of 91, Sextus Caesar, and the aunt of Julius Caesar). After his praetorship (115) as propraetor (114) he pacified Further Spain. In 109 he went to Africa as legate of Metellus. Aided by the *Equites*, many of whom had commercial interests in Africa, he won the consulship (107) and ousted Metellus, who had been his patron, from the command against Jugurtha, which was transferred to him by the interference of the People against the wishes of the Senate—a dangerous precedent. Marius broke with tradition when he raised volunteers for his African campaign from the *capite censi*, who previously were unqualified for legionary service. The war against Jugurtha (q.v.) was ended by Marius (107–105) with his greatly increased forces and with some luck (as at Cirta, where the weather robbed Jugurtha and Bocchus of almost certain victory). The reputation which Marius thus gained made him the indispensable leader against the Teutones and Cimbri who were now threatening northern Italy. Though a *novus homo* Marius was elected consul year after year (104–101); he trained his army and finally defeated the Teutones at Aquae Sextiae (102) and with Catulus (q.v. 2) the Cimbri on the Campi Raudii near Vercellae (101). These victories were largely due to the army reforms which Marius had introduced: these included, besides the new basis of recruitment, the arming of all ranks alike, the abolition of the old three lines (*hastati, principes,* and *triarii*), the supersession of the maniple by the cohort,

an improved *pilum*, and, as a result of the work of Rutilius (q.v.) Rufus, greater individual training in arms drill.

2. In the years of his repeated consulships there was a working agreement between Marius and the extremist democrats. The colonial laws of Saturninus (q.v. 1) in 103 and 100, giving land to Marius' veterans, were obviously necessary despite the Optimate opposition. Lacking political aptitude and needing land for his troops and a fresh military command for himself, Marius allied himself with Saturninus and Glaucia and entered on his sixth consulship (100); but when these extremists insisted on pressing their programme too far, Marius, with the *Equites*, abandoned them. With the death of his former allies Marius lost his popularity with the people and his influence with the Senate. He left Rome to travel in Asia, preparing himself for the command against Mithridates. Later he returned and served in the Social War, when he defeated the Marsi (90).

3. Meanwhile the alliance between the *Optimates* and *Equites*, established in 100, had broken up in the later nineties. The claims of Marius to command in the war against Mithridates were supported by the democrats against those of Sulla, whose exploits in the Social War had outshone those of Marius. In 88 Sulla's appointment to the Eastern command was challenged in Marius' interest by Sulpicius. When Sulla, refusing defeat, marched on Rome, Marius fled after many adventures to Africa. After Sulla's departure for the East, Marius landed in Etruria, collected a force, and marched on Rome to join hands with Cinna (87). Together they forced the capitulation of the consul Octavius (q.v. 3) and occupied the capital, where Marius massacred all his enemies in a reign of terror. Marius appointed himself to his seventh consulship (86), but died a few days later (13 Jan.). His ashes were later scattered in the Anio by Sulla.

4. Thus the mutual jealousy of Marius and Sulla, combined with the bitterness of party feeling, led to the first great Civil War at Rome. Marius' career, therefore, though he does not seem to have had any special policy, is significant of the extent to which purely personal questions came to dominate Roman politics: he is the precursor of the great *principes*, Pompey, Crassus, and Caesar, whose rivalries caused the downfall of the Republic. And the military changes associated with Marius, who saved his country from the Northern peril and created a semi-professional army which looked to its commander as well as to the State to protect its interests, were themselves of vital importance in determining the course of the Revolution. *See also* JUGURTHA; ARMIES, ROMAN; WAR, ART OF, ROMAN.

Greenidge and Clay, *Sources*; A. Passerini, *Athenaeum* 1939 (for inscriptions relating to Marius); H. Last, *CAH* ix, ch. 3; A. Passerini, 'Caio Mario come uomo politico', *Athenaeum* 1934; F. W. Robinson, *Marius, Saturninus und Glaucia* (Bonn, 1912); S. Accame, *Riv. Fil.* 1936, on Marius' first consulship; W. Schur, *Klio*, 1938, on his sixth consulship. Germanic invasions: C. Jullian, *Histoire de la Gaule* iii[2] (1920); M. Clerc, *La Bataille d'Aix* (1906); S. Accame, *Riv. Fil.* 1935 on Vercellae.   M. H.

MARIUS (2), GAIUS, adopted son of the great Marius (1), was chosen consul in 82 B.C. at the age of 27, with Cn. Carbo. He was defeated at Sacriportus, on the borders of Latium, by Sulla (who had returned to Italy in 83). He withdrew into the fortress of Praeneste, where Ofella besieged him, and whence he sent orders to L. Brutus, at Rome, for the massacre of Sulla's supporters in the Senate. Sulla's victory at the Colline Gate, following the failure of various efforts to relieve Praeneste, drove him to suicide.   M. H.

MARIUS (3) **GRATIDIANUS**, praetor 86 B.C. (?), won fame by anticipating a decision taken by his colleagues and devising an 'ars probandi denarios', to separate out the good from the bad money. He received something like divine honours from the common people, but was brutally murdered by Catiline in the Sullan terror.

His 'ars' probably consisted in affixing to the *denarius* certain small stamps that would reveal any underlying base metal. After such a scrutiny (*spectatio*) bags of money would be labelled with one of those *tesserae nummulariae* that still survive.   H. M.

MARIUS (4), SEXTUS, was a very wealthy owner of mines in Spain. He was accused unsuccessfully in A.D. 25, but in 33 he was charged with incest and thrown from the Tarpeian rock. His mines were confiscated.

MARIUS (5) **MAXIMUS**, a biographer of the emperors from Nerva to Elagabalus inclusive, a 'continuator' and imitator of Suetonius. He was a main source of the 'Historia Augusta', but receives a very bad character—'homo omnium uerbosissimus qui et mythistoricis se uoluminibus implicauit'—from Vopiscus. His work was arranged, on the model of Suetonius, by subjects and not by dates; it seems to have drawn largely on the *acta urbis* and certainly included quotations from documents. Pretenders were handled under the reigns of the emperors against whom they rose.

What adds interest to the work is the very high probability that he was himself a man of affairs—the Marius Maximus who went through a long career of military and senatorial posts, governed Syria, Africa, and Asia, and was *praefectus urbi* in A.D. 217 (Dessau, *ILS* 2935 f.). He must have died soon afterwards. It is strange that such an experience left him so uncritical.

Miltner, *PW*, s.v.   H. M.

MARMOR PARIUM, an inscribed marble stele, originally about 6 ft. 7 in. high, 2 ft. 3 in. broad, and 5 to 6 in. thick, set up at Paros. Two fragments survive, one of which, brought from Smyrna to London in 1627, is now preserved in the Ashmolean Museum, Oxford (save the upper part, which perished during the Civil War), while the other, discovered at Paros in 1897, is now in the Museum there. The compiler of the inscription, whose name is lost, claims to have 'written up the dates from the beginning, derived from all kinds of records and general histories, starting from Cecrops, the first king of Athens, down to the archonship of Astyanax (?) at Paros and Diognetus at Athens', i.e. 264/3 B.C. The text is written continuously, but comprises a number of items (80 on the first fragment, 27 on the second), each containing one or more events, dated by the number of years separating it from 264/3 and by the name of the Athenian king or archon then in office; the first fragment covers the period from 1581/80 to 355/4; the second that from 336/5 to 299/8. The events commemorated form a curious medley, drawn chiefly from political, military, religious, and literary history.

The best editions are those by F. Jacoby, *Das Marmor Parium* (1904), and *FGrH* ii, no. 239; and by F. Hiller von Gaertringen, *IG* 12 (5), 444; Cf. Jacoby, *Rh. Mus.* lix. 63 ff.; R. Laqueur, *PW* xiv. 1885 ff.   M. N. T.

MARO, cognomen of Virgil (P. Vergilius Maro).

MAROBODUUS, a prince of the Marcomanni, persuaded his tribe to migrate from southern Germany to Bohemia (soon after 9 B.C.), where he built up a kingdom and extended his power over the Germans of Saxony and Silesia. His army was large and well trained. Confronting Roman armies of invasion from the west and from the south in A.D. 6, he was saved from destruction by the outbreak of a rebellion in Illyricum. He refused to help Arminius three years later. In A.D. 19, however, as the result of troubles fomented by the Romans, Maroboduus was expelled from his kingdom, sought refuge on Roman territory, and was interned at Ravenna, where he lived on for nineteen years.   R. S.

MARON, a legendary priest of Apollo, son of Euanthes, of Ismarus in Thrace, who gave Odysseus the wine with which he made Polyphemus drunk (*see* CYCLOPES), along with other presents, for sparing him and his family (*Od.* 9. 197 ff.). Later writers connect him with Dionysus, e.g. Euanthes is Dionysus' son (schol. *Od.* ibid.).

H. J. R.

MARPESSA, *see* IDAS.

MARRIAGE, LAW OF. I. GREEK

1. Greek marriage was monogamous; indeed, monogamy was believed to be a distinguishing feature of Greek as opposed to barbarian usage (Eur. *Andr.* 172 ff.). The oldest form of contracting marriage was the purchase of the bride by the future husband from her father or guardian (κύριος); her consent was not necessary, for she was the object of the sale. On this occasion the bridegroom gave to the father a consideration (ἕδνα), which, after having been originally a real purchase-price, became later a fictitious one, since the father delivered it to the wife, or the husband gave it directly to her without intervention of the father. In classical Attic law the conclusion of a marriage was preceded by an informal agreement between the same persons as had been parties to the ancient marriage by purchase (ἐγγύησις). Its legal nature is very problematical, for it is not certain whether *engyesis* was a betrothal only or a definitive marriage-contract. At any rate *engyesis* as a preliminary act to a future marriage, for the validity of which no further ceremony or legal form was required, was followed (immediately or some time after) by the conveyance of the bride to the house of the husband (ἔκδοσις), an act similar to the Roman *in domum deductio* (see below). *Engyesis* might include stipulations (also informal) about the dowry (προίξ), which came into use by the fifth century B.C. But dowry was not necessary for the validity of a marriage, nor was there a legal duty on the wife's father or guardian to provide one.

2. Greek marriage being, like the Roman, a mere matter of fact, could easily be dissolved by divorce. Divorce at first was possible on the initiative of the husband only, who could expel his wife from the house; under the later law, the wife also was free to break off the marriage.

3. A peculiarity of Greek law was the right of the husband to dispose in his will of the future marriage of his wife, obliging her to marry a certain man in case of her widowhood.

II. ROMAN

4. According to the celebrated and more ethical than legal definition given by the jurist Modestinus (*Dig.* 23. 2. 1) Roman marriage was considered in the classical epoch as 'coniunctio maris et feminae, consortium omnis uitae, diuini et humani iuris communicatio'. Its main element was the living together of man and woman with intention of being husband and wife, of procreating children, and of forming a lasting union of life. This *affectio maritalis* is not a momentary *consensus* but a continuous state of mind, of which Justinian still says (*Nov.* 117. 3): 'ex solo affectu potest consistere matrimonium.' Roman marriage was strictly monogamous. Requirements of a valid marriage (*iustae nuptiae, iustum matrimonium; legitimum matrimonium* in Justinian's language)—the only one which created the father's *patria potestas* over his children (see PATRIA POTESTAS)—were the *ius conubii*, the capacity of civil marriage, *uxoris iure ducendae facultas*. In early times the Roman citizens only had this right; later it was granted to Latins and *peregrini* by general or personal concession. A *lex*, called *Canuleia* (445 B.C.), allowed marriage between patricians and plebeians, formerly prohibited. Other reasons of exclusion from *conubium* were of a relative character, such as near relationship (natural or adoptive), affinity

and moral or political considerations, and, finally (cf. Gai. 1. 59–63), difference of social rank, religious natural capacity (limit of age: 14 years for males, 12 for girls). The marriage of soldiers seems to have been prohibited till the third century A.D. Special prohibitions were introduced in the Principate: the *Lex Iulia de maritandis ordinibus* prohibited persons of senatorial rank from marrying *libertinae* and actresses; but it admitted the marriage of freeborn with freed persons; an imperial constitution forbade marriage between a *tutor* and his *pupilla*. Augustus' legislation with its various prohibitions was the point of departure for a rapid development of the concubinate (*concubinatus*), a union of man and woman, similar to matrimony, but without *affectio maritalis* and *honor matrimonii*. The concubinate was tolerated by the earlier emperors; its legal recognition followed later, owing to the legislation of Christian emperors, especially of Justinian.

5. In the early law there was a clear distinction between a marriage accompanied by *in manum conventio* and that without *manus* (q.v.). Special legal forms were not required for the conclusion of marriage; the ceremonies and feasts on this occasion had no legal character; its validity depended only on life in common based on the *affectio maritalis*. Hence a *deductio in domum mariti* was a requisite part of the marriage ceremony. Externally matrimony was manifested by the participation of one consort in the rank and social dignity of the other (*honor matrimonii*).

6. Marriage was usually, but not necessarily, preceded by a betrothal, *sponsalia*. In the early law this reciprocal promise of marriage was made on behalf of the future consorts by their fathers in the solemn form of a *sponsio* (hence the nomenclature *sponsalia, sponsus, sponsa*); later it became informal and was not binding, and even a *stipulatio poenae* in case of breach was without effect. In course of time some legal effects of secondary importance, similar to those of marriage, were ascribed to the *sponsalia*. In the fourth century A.D. an institution of Oriental origin, the *arrha sponsalicia*, or earnest money in guarantee of the fulfilment of the promise of marriage, came into use. The betrothal could be broken off by mutual consent or even by simple declaration of one party (*repudium*).

7. The constitution of a dowry, *dos*, was known already in early times. It made no difference to the dowry whether a marriage was with *manus* or without, because the woman, when *alieni iuris*—and this was the rule—had no property of her own which could pass to the husband in consequence of the *manus*. Therefore the woman brought into her husband's household a *dos*, the purpose of which was *ad ferenda onera matrimonii*. The *dos* became originally—according to the prevalent doctrine—the property of the husband; but its purpose gave rise to considerable limitations on his power of disposal. On the dissolution of a marriage the *dos* had normally to be returned to the woman and could be reclaimed by her by means of an *actio rei uxoriae*. The ownership of the husband over the *dos* became more and more of a fiction, being reduced finally to a mere usufruct.

8. It was at Rome a moral duty, especially for the father, to endow a daughter with a dowry, for it was considered dishonourable to a *mulier* to enter into a marriage *indotata*. Justinian changed this moral obligation into a legal one. The *dos* could be constituted either by the actual delivery to the husband of the property of which it consisted (*dotis datio*) or by a promise. The earlier form of promise was *dotis dictio*, a unilateral declaration made in solemn words by the woman herself, her father, or her debtor, the later a simple *stipulatio (dotis promissio)*. After A.D. 428 no special form was required and *qualiacumque verba* sufficed. Particular agreements were admitted concerning the return of the *dos* in case of divorce or the husband's decease during the marriage,

pacta dotalia; written documents for the same end, *instrumenta dotalia*, were a later creation.

9. Apart from the will of the parties, a marriage was dissolved when one of them died or lost *conubium* (through loss of *libertas* or *civitas*); with their will it ceased to subsist when the *affectio maritalis* no longer existed in both or in one consort, because in default of this element there was no matrimony. The external sign of this state of things was the definitive interruption of common life as man and wife. Divorce (*divortium*), therefore, did not require any formality; a simple oral notification, or one *per litteras* or *per nuntium*, sufficed; a unilateral declaration for this purpose was called *repudium*, as in the case of *sponsalia*. But in the earlier period when an *in manum conventio* had intervened, a husband could not release his wife from *manus* except by an act contrary to that by which the marriage had been concluded: *diffarreatio* or *remancipatio*.

10. The Roman law of marriage was thoroughly reformed in the Later Empire, and finally by Justinian under the influence of Christianity and the law and customs of the Oriental provinces. *See also* ADULTERY, MANUS (where the legal forms of Roman marriage are set forth).

GREECE: J. H. Lipsius, *Attisches Recht* ii. 2 (1912), 468 ff.; W. Erdmann, *Ehe im alten Griechenland* (1934); O. Schulthess, *PW*, s.v. Φέρνη; F. Bozza, 'Il matrimonio nel dir. attico', *Annales Seminarii giur. Catania* (1934); H. J. Wolff, 'Marriage Law and Family Organisation in ancient Athens' (*Traditio* ii, 1944). A copious literature exists on the law of marriage in Greco-Roman papyri, especially on the very controversial matter of γάμος ἔγγραφος and ἄγραφος, cf. F. Bozza, *Aegyptus* xiv (1934); W. Erdmann, *Die Ehe im alten Griechenland* (1934).

ROME: P. Bonfante, *Corso di dir. rom.* i (1925); E. Levy, *Hergang der römischen Ehescheidung* (1925); P. E. Corbett, *The Roman Law of Marriage* (1930); H. J. Wolff, 'Zur Stellung der Frau im röm. Dotalrecht', *Sav. Zeitschr.* liii (1933); W. Kunkel, s.v. 'Matrimonium', *PW* xiv; A. Erhardt, s.v. 'Nuptiae', ibid. xvii; J. B. Thayer, *On Gifts between Husband and Wife* (1929); S. Solazzi, 'Studi sul divorzio', *Bull. Inst. Dir. Rom.* xxxv (1925); M. Lauria, 'La dote romana', *Atti Accad. Napoli* lviii (1938); E. Volterra, 'Arrha sponsalicia', *Riv. Ital. Scienze Giurid.* vols. ii, iv, v (1927, 1928, 1930); 'Ricerche intorno agli sponsali', *Bull. Inst. Dir. Rom.* xl (1932); Aem. Hermann, *Schliessung der Verlöbnisse im just. Rechte* (1935); H. J. Wolff, 'Written and unwritten Marriages in Hellenistic and Post-classical Roman Law' (*Amer. Philol. Assoc., Philological Monographs* ix, 1939). The newest monographs are mentioned by S. Di Marzo, *Istituzioni di dir. rom.* (1938).   A. B.

MARRIAGE, SACRED (ἱερὸς γάμος), the sexual union of two persons, both divine or one divine and the other human but in some way sacral. The supposed result would appear to be increase of fertility, animal or vegetable, or of prosperity in general. An interesting example is the union on the day of the Choes (see ANTHESTERIA) of Dionysus with the wife of the Basileus at Athens (cf. DIONYSUS). Here one partner only is divine, there being no sufficient reason to suppose that an Attic queen was regarded at any date as other than human. No doubt, however, while the monarchy lasted both she and her husband had some priestly functions. Both partners are divine at the Daedala (references under BOEOTIA, CULTS), viz. Zeus and Hera; for a main feature of it was the bringing of a wife for Zeus. She was represented by a wooden image and came on a carriage, like a Boeotian bride (cf. Plut. *Quaest. Rom.* 29), accompanied by a brideswoman (νυμφεύτρια, Paus. 9. 3. 7).

                                        H. J. R.

MARRIAGE CEREMONIES. The marriage ceremonies of the Greeks and Romans were in most respects similar, the only important difference being in connexion with betrothal (q.v.). There were, however, some minor points in which Greek usage varied. In Greece marriages usually took place in the winter, preferably in the month Gamelion; on the morning of the wedding-day sacrifices were made to Zeus and Hera, the tutelar gods of marriage; before the ceremony bride and bridegroom bathed in the water of some sacred fountain, at Athens Callirrhoe

Enneakrounos. Otherwise an account of a Roman wedding will in most ways hold for Greece.

2. The proceedings began in the evening at the rising of the star Hesperus, when the bride was solemnly conducted from her father's to her husband's house (*deductio*). At Athens the bridegroom drove the bride home in a mule cart, but at Rome she was escorted by a torchlight procession of relatives and friends, among them the *pronubae*, matrons who had only been married once, who afterwards attended the bride in the nuptial chamber. Among the company were flute-players and singers, often a double choir of maidens and youths who chanted the marriage song 'Hymen, O Hymenaee, Hymen'. The bride, who was often no more than fourteen to sixteen years old, laid aside her girl's dress and dedicated her toys to Artemis or the household Lar shortly before the wedding-day. She was dressed in a long white robe with a woollen girdle fastened in a Hercules knot. Her veil was of a bright saffron colour, her hair-net and shoes were of the same auspicious hue, and her hair was dressed in the fashion of the Vestal Virgins so as to show three curls hanging down on each side of her face. When the bridegroom's house was reached the bride anointed the door with oil and placed woollen fillets on the doorposts; and as she was carried over the threshold the onlookers cried 'Talassio', a word of unknown meaning but connected by the Romans with the rape of the Sabine women.

3. In the strictest form of marriage, *confarreatio*, a number of symbolical acts followed the bride's entrance, performed in the presence of ten witnesses under the direction of the Flamen Dialis. The auspices were taken, and the couple, sitting on two chairs placed side by side and covered with one sheepskin, ate bread together and clasped hands in sign of union. The marriage contract was then read and sealed by the witnesses, and the marriage feast began. At its conclusion nuts, sweet-meats, and sesame cakes were showered among the guests, in token of the plenty which would attend the happy pair; and then to avert the evil eye the company sang the Fescennine Songs, a mixture of raillery and abuse. And so at last the bride was led to the nuptial couch, *lectus genialis*, placed in the *atrium* opposite to the entrance door.

Catullus, *Carmen* 61; W. Erdmann, *Die Ehe im alten Griechenland* (1934). For other literature *see* WOMEN. F. A. W.

MARRIAGE SONG, *see* EPITHALAMIUM.

MARS (Mavors, Mamers, Etr. **Maris;** reduplicated **Marmar**), next to Jupiter (q.v.) the chief Italian god. Months were named after him at Rome (Martius, mod. Engl. March), Alba Longa, Falerii, Aricia, Tusculum, Lavinium, and among the Hernici, Aequiculi, Paelignians, and Sabines (Ovid, *Fasti* 3. 89–95, presumably from Verrius Flaccus). At Rome his festivals came in March and October, with the exception of the first Equirria (27 Feb.). They were the *feriae Marti* on 1 Mar. (old New Year's Day), second Equirria (14 Mar.), *agonium Martiale* (17 Mar.), Quinquatrus (19 Mar.; afterwards extended to five days and supposed to be a festival of Minerva, q.v.), and Tubilustrium (23 Mar.). All these may be reasonably explained, so far as their ritual is known, as preparations for the campaigning season, with performance of rites to benefit the horses (Equirria), trumpets (Tubilustrium), and other necessaries for the conduct of war. On 1, 9, and 23 Mar. also, the Salii, an ancient priesthood belonging to Jupiter, Mars, and Quirinus (Servius on *Aen.* 8. 663), danced a sort of war-dance in armour of the fashion of the Bronze Age and sang their traditional hymn, addressed apparently to all the gods, not to these three only. This is intelligible as further preparation for war. In October the Equus October came on the ides (15th). A horse-race took place in the Campus Martius; the off horse of the winning team was sacrificed and his head contended for by the inhabitants of the Sacra Via and the Suburra. On the 19th was the Armilustrium, presumably the purification of the soldiers' arms before putting them away for the winter. In this month again the Salii performed their dances ('arma ancilia mouent', the *ancilia* being archaic shields shaped like the figure 8). Before commencing a war the general shook the sacred spears of Mars in the Regia, saying 'Mars uigila'; it is most probable that these were the original embodiments of the god. His priest is the *flamen Martialis* (*see* FLAMINES) and his sacred animals the wolf and woodpecker (see Wissowa, *RK* pp. 141 ff., 555 ff.). It is therefore not remarkable that he is usually considered a war-god and was equated with Ares (q.v.). But it has been pointed out (summary in Bailey, *P. Ouidi Nasonis fastorum lib. iii*, pp. 33 ff., cf. Frazer, *Fasti of Ovid* iii. 1 ff.) that he has agricultural functions also (Cato, *Agr.* 141. 2 ff.; hymn of Arval Brethren, Henzen, *Acta Arvalium*, p. cciv), and that some at least of his feasts (see above) can be interpreted as agricultural from their date and the ceremonial. Three explanations seem possible. (*a*) He was originally a war-god, and therefore called upon to guard the fields of his worshippers from enemies physical and spiritual. (*b*) He was originally a chthonian deity, hence a god of death and hence of war (cf. ARES), though originally connected with the fertility of the soil. (*c*) He was the high god, little differentiated as to function, of a people often engaged in war and having agriculture for their staple industry and food-supply. All of these have been maintained by various scholars.

His mythology is almost entirely borrowed from Ares, the only exception being the comic tale of how he was deceived into marrying Anna Perenna (q.v.; Ovid, ibid. 675 ff.), probably a folk-tale applied (by Ovid?) to deities treated after the Alexandrian manner. Under Augustus he obtained an important new title, Ultor, in connexion with the recovery of the standards from the Parthians (Platner–Ashby, p. 329 f., q.v. for his other places of worship). H. J. R.

MARSI inhabited mountains and strategic passes in central Italy near the Fucine Lake. Their chief town was Marruvium (Strabo 5. 241). They were probably Sabelli (q.v.), although their early latinization makes proof of this impossible. They were allied, ethnically and politically, with Marrucini, Vestini, and Paeligni, but from early times were friendly to Rome (cf. Appian, *BCiv.* 1. 46). In 340 B.C. they gave Roman troops passage through their territory and remained friendly in the Second Samnite War (Livy 8. 6, 29; 9. 13; Diod. 20. 44, 101. Records of Marsic hostility are suspect: K. J. Beloch, *Röm. Gesch.*, 403; Livy 9. 41, 45; 10. 3 probably confuses Marsi with Aequi). The Marsi were loyal against Hannibal (Livy 28. 45) but took the initiative in demanding Roman citizenship in the Social War (hence often called Marsic War: Vell. Pat. 2. 21). When this demand was granted, the separate nation of Marsi disappeared. Marsic magicians were famous for miraculous snake-bite cures; Angitia, a local deity of healing, was appropriately worshipped in their territory (Verg. *Aen.* 7. 750 f.).

R. S. Conway, *Italic Dialects* (1897) i. 289. E. T. S.

MARSUS, *see* DOMITIUS (6), VIBIUS (1).

MARSYAS (1), a satyr or silenus, generally associated with the river of that name, a tributary of the Maeander, but also with other streams (Jessen in Roscher's *Lexikon* ii. 2439, q.v. for the legend and its representation in art). He was a musician and inventor of a form of music for flute or oboe, the μητρῷον αὔλημα, Pausanias 10. 30. 9, which passage also shows that at Celaenae he was the subject of local myths and regarded as a guardian deity. He is therefore pretty certainly a Phrygian or at all events Asianic figure. In the Greek handling of his story, the origins of which are obscure, he is associated with Athena and Apollo (qq.v.) as follows. Athena, having invented the oboe (αὐλός), threw it away because it distorted her face to play it. Marsyas picked it up and soon learned to play on it (*Frag. Trag. Adesp.* 381 Nauck; Melanippides and Telestes in Ath. 616 e ff.; and later authors). He now challenged Apollo to a contest in music; Apollo, having defeated him, took advantage of an agreement that the winner should do as he liked with the loser and flayed him alive (Apollod. 1. 24). The river sprang from his blood or the tears of his mourners.   H. J. R.

MARSYAS (2) of Pella, relative and afterwards admiral of Antigonus I, wrote on Alexander. *See* ALEXANDER (3), Bibliography, Ancient Sources.

MARTIAL (MARCUS VALERIUS MARTIALIS), born at Bilbilis in Spain *c.* A.D. 40 (1. 61. 12), died *c.* 104. His cognomen records his birth on 1 Mar. (9. 52; 10. 24 and 92. 10; 12. 60). H. Lucas (*CQ* xxxii. 1, 1938) argues against taking this literally; but references to other birth-days seem to mark actual anniversaries rather than adjacent kalends (e.g. 3. 6; 11. 65). Educated in Spain, he proceeded in 64 to Rome, where intimacy with his fellow Spaniards Seneca and Lucan was soon cut short by their fate in the Pisonian conspiracy. Celebrating at Rome his 57th birthday (10. 24. 4), he had spent 34 years there (10. 103. 7–10, i.e. in a poem probably of A.D. 98, but this depends on whether it belongs to the first or second edition of bk. 10). Before his *Spectacula* (80) we know little of his career. It was one mainly of poverty-stricken dependence on patrons not over-generous in return for complimentary verses. For a time he had to be content with a three-stair-high lodging in the sweltering city (1. 117. 7); acquisition of a small farm at Nomentum afforded a welcome relief. By degrees his social influence, but not his wealth, increased. He received an honorary military tribunate and, though he never married, the *ius trium liberorum* (q.v.) (3. 95. 5). Brought into contact with all classes from emperor and court downwards, he chronicled succinctly every sort and condition of men and women. With his chief literary contemporaries, except Statius, he had friendly relations. These included Frontinus, Juvenal, Silius Italicus, Quintilian, and the younger Pliny. His early works attracted notice, but his real fame rests on the amazing versatility which marks his epigrammatic depiction of life in the volumes issued from 86 (bks. 1, 2) to 98 (bk. 11). Then, under Nerva, he recognized that indecency and flattery were no longer acceptable. The younger Pliny paid for his return to his never entirely forgotten home-land, and he settled on a rural property presented by a patroness Marcella. Three years later his final book was complete and in a letter which can be dated *c.* 104 Pliny regrets his recent death.

2. WORKS. A.D. 80. *Liber Spectaculorum* commemo-rated the opening by Titus of the Flavian Amphitheatre ('Colosseum'). Its 33 surviving pieces record contests in the arena without as yet full mastery of style.

A.D. 84–5. (*a*) *Xenia* (now bk. 13), mottoes for 'guest-gifts', 127 pieces, all except three in elegiac couplets, and, with four exceptions, on eatables and drinkables—an extended list indicative of Roman dinners like the fuller *menus* in some of M.'s invitations (10. 48; 11. 52). (*b*) *Apophoreta* (now bk. 14), mottoes for 'gifts to take home', 223, all, except two, couplets, originally perhaps paired to suit the purse of rich and poor alternately, and forming an instructive catalogue of presents.

Of his twelve *Epigrammaton libri* most appeared at intervals of about a year from 86, when he issued a revised edition of bks. 1 and 2 together. Book 3 came out during a temporary retreat to Cisalpine Gaul. From bks. 10 and 11 he made for Nerva an expurgated anthology. Book 12 occupied him for three years after he left Rome in 98. The division into books was his own (2. 93; 5. 2 and 15; 7. 17, etc.). Prose prefaces of literary significance are given to bks. 1, 2, 8, 12, and a few lines of prose introduce the poem prefixed to bk. 9.

3. Of his 1,561 poems the most by far, 1,235, are in elegiac metre, where Ovid's influence unites with that of Catullus; 238, hendecasyllabic; 77, choliambic; a few are in iambics and hexameters. His three chief metres are frequently, though not exclusively, used satirically; but he can employ limping iambics for telling description or personal grief (3. 58, a farm; 10. 30, beach at Formiae; 5. 37, lament for Erotion: cf. the beautiful one in elegiacs 5. 34); while hendecasyllables can be realistic, as in 4. 64 (a view), or semi-personal, 4. 55 (pride in Spain). M. regards as his Latin exemplars Catullus, Domitius Marsus, Pedo Albinovanus, and Gaetulicus (2. 77; 5. 5. 6). The last-named may be the Γαιτυλικός of the *Greek Anthology*, and recalls its influence, which Martial never mentions. But Greek epigrams contributed to his literary skill and some (e.g. those by Lucillius, q.v.) suggested subjects, though M.'s great repertory lay in the Roman world around and though his fame was largely won by the suspension of point or sting to the close of an epigram—a feature comparatively rare in Greek.

4. Martial's predominant interest centred in his fellow human beings: 'hominem pagina nostra sapit' (10. 4. 10). He denounces mythology as remote from life (4. 49); and in his pictures of Roman society, high and low, rich and poor, virtuous and vicious, he is a spectator writing with a sort of Spanish detachment. His *métier* was no deep system of thought, but extraordinarily keen observa-tion and sharply condensed expression. Much of his work is therefore that realism in a nutshell which fits Coleridge's definition of an epigram as 'a dwarfish whole: its body brevity and wit its soul'. He often calls his poems *nugae* or *ioci*, yet he maintains they are not mere flippancies. They reflect life as in a mirror (10. 4. 8). Conscious of contemporary fame (5. 15; 6. 60; 7. 88), he is sure that he will survive, and no century, medieval or modern, has failed to remember him.

5. Where M. most repels is in his undisguised mime-like obscenity, parallel to the naked licence of the Floralia, and in that grotesque adulation of Domitian which tempts him into artificial conceits foreign, as a rule, to his genius. The method in his satiric epigrams is one of concealed personalities, using invented names (2. 23), 'to spare the sinner but denounce the sin' (10. 33. 10). He thus regards his sportive attacks as harmless ('ludimus innocui', 7. 12), but recognizes that, to avoid insipidity, epigrams need a drop of gall (7. 25). His poems of friendship and of mourning over young lives cut short are a winning testimony to the warm affections of the most many-sided of all epigrammatists. Privations rather than any theoretical Stoicism taught him endurance as a health of soul. He has little sympathy for the theatrical exit from the world affected by some Stoics (1. 8. 5–6): 'contempt for life is easy in distress' (11. 56. 15). This is one of the brave traits in him. Without profound philo-sophy, he yet had the roots of his writings in his manifold experience of life and penetrating insight into humanity.

See also EPIGRAM, I. 3 and II, *and* LITERARY CRITICISM IN ANTIQUITY, II. 5.

BIBLIOGRAPHY

LIFE AND WORKS. L. Friedlaender's ed. (*infra*), introd.; *Sit-tengeschichte Roms* (ed. 9, posthumous, by Wissowa) iv. 209 ff.
TEXTS: W. Heraeus (1925); W. M. Lindsay, O.C.T. (1929).
COMMENTARY: L. Friedlaender, *Martialis Epigrammaton Libri* (1886).
TRANSLATIONS: The Bohn translation (prose) adds many examples of verse translations including some by W. Hay, 1755.   W. C. A.

Ker (prose with text; Loeb, 1919–20). J. A. Pott and F. A. Wright, *Twelve Books* (London and New York 1926).
    STYLE AND DICTION: E. Wagner, *De Martiale poetarum Augusteae aetatis imitatore* (1888); K. Prinz, *M. u. die griech. Epigrammatik* (1910); J. Wight Duff, *Lit. Hist. Rome* (*Silver Age*) (1927), 498–529; *Roman Satire* (U.S.A. 1936), 126–46; 'Varied Strains in Martial', *Studies in Honor of E. K. Rand* (U.S.A. 1938); O. Autore, *Marziale e l'epigramma greco* (1937).
    STUDIES: C. Giarratano, *De M. re metrica* (1908); O. Weinreich, *Studien zu M.* (1928); P. Nixon, *M. and Modern Epigram* (U.S.A.).   J. W. D.

MARTIANUS CAPELLA or *Felix Capella*, of Carthage, after A.D. 410 (Alaric's sack of Rome) and before the Vandal conquest of north Africa (429), wrote what Fulgentius in 520 calls *Liber de nuptiis Mercurii et Philologiae*, but which he may himself have called *Disciplinae*. It is a *Satura* of mixed prose and verse influenced by Varro's *Menippeae*, in style largely based on Apuleius, and metrically so nearly correct that Dick, in his edition, favours a date a century earlier. The opening allegory covers the first two books. Mercury, desiring to marry, is introduced by Apollo to Philologia, who is raised to heaven while the Muses celebrate the marriage. The seven remaining books celebrate the seven bridesmaids, Grammar, Dialectic, Rhetoric (the later *Trivium*), Geometry, Arithmetic, Astronomy, Music (the later *Quadrivium*); but in these the myth disappears, and a handbook based on Varro is epitomized. The work had an amazing vogue for eight centuries. It was revised by Felix (*c.* 535), mentioned by Gregory of Tours (d. 595), expounded by Scotus Erigena (d. 875), commented on by Remi of Auxerre (900), translated into German by Notker (d. 1028). Not till the school of Chartres (Bernard of Chartres, William of Conches, and John of Salisbury) went back to the classical texts did the late Middle Ages get better *pabulum* than this dry mixture of fancy and pedantry (*see* ENCYCLOPAEDIC LEARNING *and* SCHOLARSHIP, LATIN). Its style, perversely mannered in avoidance of plain expression, may be characterized by the author's own words (bk. 3 *ad init.*) 'paginam uenustans multo illitam colore'.
    Manuscripts (mostly unexamined) are numerous: at one time no important monastic library lacked a copy.

    Editions: princeps, Vicenza 1499. F. Eyssenhardt, (Teubner, 1866). The edition by A. Dick (Teubner, 1925) is criticized by Wessmer (*PW*).   G. C. R.

MARULLUS. At his rhetorical academy the elder Seneca and Porcius Latro were fellow-students (Sen. *Controv.* 1 *praef.* 22).

MARY THE JEWESS, *see* ALCHEMY, para. 4.

MARYANDYNOI, *see* SERFS.

MASCHALISMOS (μασχαλισμός), a practice adopted by man-slayers, literally to prevent the ghost from walking or otherwise manifesting itself. The hands and feet of the corpse were cut off and tied under the armpits (μασχάλαι). See Aesch. *Cho.* 439; Soph. *El.* 445, with schol. there, which, however, is confused; Jebb's note and appendix ad loc. quote the other authorities, all apparently going back to Aristophanes of Byzantium, and analyse them usefully.   H. J. R.

MASINISSA (so Latin writers; Polybius gives Μασσανάσσης) (*c.* 240–149 B.C.), son of Gaia king of the eastern Numidian Massyles, was brought up at Carthage and served with the Carthaginians against the Romans in Spain from 212 until 206, when he was won over by the diplomacy and friendship of Scipio. Dynastic troubles following Gaia's death forced Masinissa to flee from his kingdom, which was partially overrun by Syphax (q.v.). After many adventures Masinissa joined the Romans when they landed in Africa (204), and fought in the

night attack on the enemies' camps and at Campi Magni, after which he defeated Syphax and reoccupied Cirta, where he met Sophonisba (q.v.) in 203. His cavalry played a decisive part in Scipio's victory at Zama (202). Thereafter as Rome's faithful ally Masinissa was complete master of all Numidia, while Carthage was by treaty unable to resist when he gradually advanced his frontiers at her expense, filching the Emporia on the Syrtis and finally (*c.* 155) Tusca near Campi Magni. To Carthaginian complaints Rome merely replied by sending out boundary commissions which decided in Masinissa's favour or left the question unsettled (e.g. in 193, 182, 174, 172, 153). Finally, helped by a party within Carthage, Masinissa goaded the Carthaginians to break their treaty with Rome by attacking him; he defeated them (150). When the Roman army arrived he was treated somewhat coldly by the Romans, who feared his ambitions (*see* PUNIC WARS). He died soon afterwards (149), and his kingdom was divided between his sons.
    Of great physical strength even in extreme old age, Masinissa was a brave soldier, a skilful diplomatist, and a creative statesman. He not only extended his empire until it embarrassed Rome, but he revolutionized its economic and social life, making 'nomads into farmers and welding them into a State' (Strabo 17. 833), and turning local dynasts into feudal barons owning large estates and loyal to the throne; Punic art, language, and culture penetrated inner Numidia, urban life was encouraged, and Masinissa, following the pattern of Hellenistic monarchy, became Numidia's greatest king. He created a nation and by widening the basis of Punic civilization enabled it to survive to influence the Africa of the Roman Empire.   H. H. S.

MASSILIA (Μασσαλία), modern *Marseilles*, a colony of the Phocaeans founded *c.* 600 B.C. on Ligurian territory. The site was recommended by the remarkable harbour Lacydon (*Vieux-Port*). In spite of warfare with its neighbours, Ligurian and Gallic, Massilia gradually became a centre for the diffusion of Hellenism, and founded colonies along the coast from Antipolis (*Antibes*) to Emporia (*Ampurias*). Victories were won over Carthaginian fleets (6th c. and *c.* 400 B.C.); in the fourth century Pytheas (q.v.) visited Britain, while Euthymenes explored the Guinea coast. A treasury at Delphi maintained contact with distant Hellas, while friendly connexions were established early with Rome, and Massiliot seamen played an important part in the Second Punic War. Subsequently Rome's power overshadowed her ally's, which was much harassed by Celtic pressure. In answer to its appeal Rome intervened in Gaul (123), but by establishing the Provincia weakened Massiliot commercial power still further; and for its courage in standing a siege against Caesar (49) Massilia, while keeping the federate relation, lost almost all its territory. Under the Empire Massilia, though maintaining a reputation for Hellenism even to the fifth century, became barely distinguishable from an ordinary Roman municipality. Maximian, attempting to regain the purple, defended himself behind the walls (rebuilt under Nero by the successful physician, Crinias) against Constantine (A.D. 307). The town came under Visigothic control *c.* 476.

    M. Clerc, *Massalia* (1929).   C. E. S.

MASTARNA, a legendary hero of Etruria, was identified with Servius Tullius by the Emperor Claudius or his informant (Dessau, *ILS* 212; A.D. 48). According to another, purely Etruscan, version (attested by the famous wall-paintings from Vulci), Mastarna came to power at Rome after rescuing his comrade Caeles Vibenna, and murdering a king Tarquinius. He must therefore be identified not with the Servius Tullius of the Roman tradition, but with the Servius Tullius of the Etruscan version, or with Porsenna (q.v.), or with both. In any case, although he may be a purely mythical figure, Mastarna represents an Etruscan master of Rome.

L. Pareti, *Studi etruschi* (1931), 154 ff.; A. Momigliano, *Claudius* (1934), 11 ff., 84 ff. P. T.

MATERNUS, *see* CURIATIUS, FIRMICUS.

MATHEMATICS. The Greeks, acquiring their first mathematical ideas from Egypt, were the first to think of making mathematics a demonstrative science. *Thales* 'proved' certain elementary propositions in geometry and used the properties of similar triangles. *Pythagoras* and the Pythagoreans laid down definitions and first principles in geometry, studied numbers geometrically (figured numbers), established a theory of proportion and *means* (including the 'harmonic'). Pythagoras himself discovered the dependence of the musical intervals on arithmetical ratios, gave a formula for finding squares which are the sum of two squares, and proved the corresponding property of the right-angled triangle (Eucl. 1. 47). The *Pythagoreans* invented the method known as the 'application of areas' (equivalent to solving geometrically the general quadratic equation) and discovered the incommensurable (in the diagonal of a square); they found successive arithmetical approximations to the value of $\sqrt{2}$.

By the middle of the fifth century the Greeks had advanced beyond the Elements. *Democritus* wrote on Irrationals and touched on infinitesimals (volumes of cone and pyramid). *Hippocrates* of Chios reduced the duplication of the cube to the finding of two mean proportionals, and squared three sorts of 'lunes'; *Hippias* discovered a higher curve which served for trisecting any angle and squaring the circle ($\tau\epsilon\tau\rho\alpha\gamma\omega\nu i\zeta o\upsilon\sigma\alpha$, *quadratrix*). *Archytas* of Tarentum (*fl. c.* 400–365 B.C.), the friend of Plato, found the two mean proportionals by a construction in three dimensions, and wrote on mechanics. *Theodorus* of Cyrene and *Theaetetus* investigated more surds, $\sqrt{3}$, $\sqrt{5}$, $\sqrt{17}$; Theaetetus classified further irrationals, discovered the octahedron and icosahedron, and wrote on all five regular solids. *Plato* was intensely interested in mathematics, especially definitions (e.g. of line, straight line, circle, 'figure') and methods, analysis, synthesis, and—with *Leon*—the $\delta\iota o\rho\iota\sigma\mu\delta\varsigma$ (determination of conditions and limits of possibility of solutions of problems). Meantime *Leon* and *Theudius* wrote books of elements. *Eudoxus* (408–355 B.C.) discovered the general theory of proportion set out in Euclid 5–6 and the 'method of exhaustion', the classical method of dealing with the area and content of curvilinear plane and solid figures respectively. *Menaechmus*, a pupil of Eudoxus, discovered the conic sections, which later became the subject of *Aristaeus*' 'Solid Loci' and Euclid's *Conics*. The geometry of the sphere (*Sphaeric*) now emerges in *Autolycus* (on the moving sphere) and Euclid's *Phaenomena*. *Euclid* (fl. 300 B.C.) wrote the immortal *Elements* and works on higher geometry, 'Porisms', 'Surface-Loci', etc.; he wrote too on Optics and the Elements of Music. *Archimedes*' use of the 'method of exhaustion' brings geometry to its highest point, in measurements of the circle, parabola, sphere and cylinder, conoids and spheroids, anticipating the integral calculus. Archimedes wrote the first scientific work on statics, solved difficult problems of finding centres of gravity, and invented the whole science of hydrostatics (*On Floating Bodies* 1, 2); he also devised a system for expressing large numbers which substituted 100,000,000 as the base instead of 10. With *Apollonius* of Perga, the 'great geometer', author of the great treatise on Conics in eight books and other works the golden age of Greek geometry ends. His successors are mainly known for discovering special curves—*Diocles* (the cissoid), *Nicomedes* (the conchoid), *Perseus* (the 'spiric' curves). Trigonometry and spherical

trigonometry are developed by *Hipparchus*, *Menelaus*, and *Ptolemy*, the elementary theory of numbers by *Nicomachus* and *Theon* of Smyrna, applied mathematics (mechanical powers, pneumatics, engines of war) by *Philon* of Byzantium and *Heron*. Algebra, with the first approach to an algebraic notation, appears in *Diophantus*' *Arithmetica*, containing problems in semi-determinate analysis which inspired Fermat. There remain commentators, the greatest of whom is *Pappus* (3rd c. A.D.), to whose $\sigma\upsilon\nu\alpha\gamma\omega\gamma\dot\eta$ we are indebted for precious descriptions of lost works in higher geometry and some remarkable things of his own (area cut off by a spiral on a sphere, a theorem later known as 'Guldin's theorem', and 'Pappus' Problem', which inspired Descartes).

T. H.

MATIUS (1), GNAEUS, in Sulla's time translated the *Iliad* into Latin hexameters. Gellius admired his learning. He introduced scazons into Latin light verse from the *mimiambi* of Herodas.

Baehr. *FPR* 281; Morel, *FPL* 48.

MATIUS (2), GAIUS, Cicero's learned friend and Caesar's partisan, helped the former in his relations with the latter, especially in 49 and 48 B.C. He presided over the games which Octavian exhibited in honour of Caesar (44). Augustus' friend, C. Matius, who published three books about gastronomy, was probably his son.

A. M.

MATRALIA, *see* MATUTA.

MATRES, *see* DEAE MATRES.

MATRIMONIUM, *see* MARRIAGE, LAW OF.

MATRIS of Thebes (3rd c. B.C. ?), rhetor, who wrote an $'E\gamma\kappa\dot\omega\mu\iota o\nu$ $'H\rho\alpha\kappa\lambda\dot\epsilon o\upsilon\varsigma$ with Asianist characteristics.

MATRON of Pitane (late 4th c. B.C.), parodist, wrote a poem called $\Delta\epsilon\hat\iota\pi\nu o\nu$ $'A\tau\tau\iota\kappa\delta\nu$, quoted by Athenaeus (4. 134–7), beginning $\Delta\epsilon\hat\iota\pi\nu\dot\alpha$ $\mu o\iota$ $\dot\epsilon\nu\nu\epsilon\pi\epsilon$, $Mo\hat\upsilon\sigma\alpha$, $\pi o\lambda\dot\upsilon$-$\tau\rho o\phi\alpha$ $\kappa\alpha\dot\iota$ $\mu\dot\alpha\lambda\alpha$ $\pi o\lambda\lambda\dot\alpha$.

P. Brandt, *Corpusc. poes. ep. graec. ludibundae* i. 53–95.

MATRONALIA, *see* JUNO.

MATUTA, MATER, a Roman goddess of growth (Varro ap. August. *De Civ. D.* 4. 8: '[praefecerunt frumentis] maturescentibus deam Matutam'). Lucretius (5. 656), followed by many moderns, makes her a goddess of dawn, but this is hardly possible, since she is a figure of cult, not poetry or myth, which the dawn seems never to be. For her temple in the Forum Boarium see Platner–Ashby, p. 330 f. Her festival, the Matralia, 11 June, is included in the 'calendar of Numa'. The ritual was conducted by women, apparently *uniuirae* (Tertullian, *De Monog.* 17), and they prayed only for their sisters' children (Ovid, *Fasti* 6, 559; Plut. *Quaest. Rom.* 267 e, *De frat. amor.* 492 d, the ultimate source being probably Verrius Flaccus). This being both well attested and absurd, it seems probable that they prayed for *pueri sororii*, i.e. adolescent children; Rose in *CQ* xxviii. 156 f. H. J. R.

MAURETANIA, the land of the Moors, stretching from the Ampsaga to the Atlantic and embracing the western half of the Atlas range. Most of the country is high and rocky, supporting sheep and producing a little wine; corn and olives grew on the coast, in the Mulucha valley, and on the plains of Volubilis (q.v.) and Sala. The chief exports were ebony, precious woods, and purple dyes.

There seems to have been communication with Spain from early days, binding Europe and Africa by piracy and colonization. The bulk of the population belonged to the Moorish branch of the Berber race; there was an admixture of negro blood in the south, and numerous Phoenician trading-stations were established on the Mediterranean and Atlantic coasts.

By the second century B.C. the small Moorish tribes had formed kingdoms; their rulers, Bocchus and Bogud, played important parts in the Jugurthine and Civil Wars. Roman law and Greek art spread during the reign of Juba II. The murder in Rome of Ptolemy, his son and successor (A.D. 23–40), led to disturbances. Mauretania was pacified by Suetonius Paulinus (41–2) and Hosidius Geta. Before 44 Claudius constituted two Mauretanian provinces, ruled by procurators with capitals at Tingi and Caesarea (q.v. 3). Moorish cavalry served in the Roman armies, and the Moor Lusius Quietus won distinction under Trajan. But large tracts of country remained under Moorish chieftains; there were serious rebellions. Mauretania Tingitana was attached to the diocese of Spain by Diocletian.

S. Weinstock, *PW*, s.v.; L. Chatelain, *Inscriptions latines du Maroc* (1942) and *Le Maroc des Romains* (1944); R. Roget, *Index de topographie antique du Maroc, Publicat. du service des antiquités*, fasc. 4 (1938); S. Gsell, *Histoire ancienne de l'Afrique du Nord*, esp. vol. viii (1928); J. Carcopino, *Le Maroc antique* (1940). *See also* VOLUBILIS. W. N. W.

MAUSOLEUM, the Tomb of Mausolus (q.v.), satrap of Caria, built of white marble by his widow, Artemisia *c.* 353 B.C. at Halicarnassus, the architect being Pythius (q.v.). An earthquake caused its collapse before the fifteenth century. In 1857 the site was excavated by Sir C. Newton, who brought many pieces to the British Museum, including some fine friezes and the colossal statues of Mausolus and Artemisia, nearly intact. The monument was described by Pliny and was regarded as one of the seven wonders of the ancient world. Many restorations have been attempted (most recently by A. W. Law, *JHS* 1939, 92 ff.). All agree in showing a rectangular arrangement of the Ionic order, with thirty-six columns, standing on a high base and carrying a stepped pyramid surmounted by a four-horsed chariot (*quadriga*); the total height being about 134 feet.

A. H. Smith, *Catalogue of Sculpture in the British Museum* ii (1900), 65; W. R. Lethaby, *Greek Buildings represented by Fragments in the British Museum* (1908), 37. T. F.

MAUSOLUS, satrap of Caria 377/6–353 B.C. in virtual independence of Persian control. His early relations with the Great King were cordial and in 365 he co-operated with Autophradates in suppressing Ariobarzanes. Subsequently, however, he embarked on an expansionist policy symbolized by the substitution of Halicarnassus for Mylasa as the seat of government, and in 362 he became involved in the Satraps' Revolt, though he diplomatically deserted the losing side at the right moment. Left in undisturbed possession of his satrapy, he resumed his advance at the expense of Lycia and Ionia. The conflict of his interests with those of Athens resulted in the Social War of 357, when Rhodes, Cos, Chios, and Byzantium revolted on a promise of support from Mausolus. Athens' attempts at reasserting her control proved unsuccessful, and Rhodes and Cos became appendages to his kingdom. His marriage to his sister Artemisia, the fortress-like palace with its private harbour at Halicarnassus, his philhellenic patronage of literature and the arts, and the monumental tomb (*see* MAUSOLEUM) which he planned but did not live to complete, foreshadow the rule of the Ptolemies.

W. Judeich, *Kleinasiatische Studien* (1892), ch. 6. D. E. W. W.

MAVORTIUS (perhaps not the consul of A.D. 527) wrote two Virgilian centos, *Iudicium Paridis* and *De Ecclesia* (Baehr. *PLM* iv. 198 f., 214 ff.; K. Schenkl, *CSEL* xvi, 1887).

MAXENTIUS, MARCUS AURELIUS VALERIUS, son of Maximian (q.v.) and Eutropia, was passed over in A.D. 305 and was living in retirement at Rome, when Constantius died and Constantine was proclaimed. The Praetorian guard and the city of Rome, both bitter over lost privileges, raised him to the throne, and called in Maximian from his retirement in Lucania to assist him. Severus marched against Rome, but was driven to surrender after retreating to Ravenna, while Maximian went to Gaul and won over Constantine. Galerius, invading Italy, was likewise forced to retire, but Maximian, perhaps vexed at the unjust execution of Severus, tried to depose his son and, failing, fled to Constantine. Declared a public enemy at Carnuntum (308), Maxentius yet maintained himself in Italy and soon recovered Africa when it revolted under Alexander (309–10). But trouble now arose with Constantine, who represented himself as a deliverer from tyranny, while Maxentius resented the execution of his father. Constantine invaded Italy with a small army of fine quality, won the north, and, pushing on to Rome, destroyed Maxentius at the battle of the Mulvian Bridge. Maxentius had failed to establish a dynasty, since his young son, Romulus, died in 310. Personally without ability or character, Maxentius only had significance as the champion of the old privileges and the old faith of the capital.

CAH xii. 344 ff.; Parker, *Roman World*, 242 ff. H. M.

MAXIMIAN (MARCUS AURELIUS VALERIUS MAXIMIANUS), a comrade of Diocletian, called by him in A.D. 285 to assist him as his Caesar. Sent against the Bagaudae in Gaul, he soon dispersed their irregular bands and was promoted to be Augustus, early 286. Against Carausius, who revolted to escape punishment for neglect of his duties against the pirates, Maximian was less successful. A first expedition by sea failed and Carausius received peace and recognition (289).

Maximian, charged with Italy and the West, was heavily engaged on the lower Rhine and in Raetia, against the Chaibones, in 289. Though acting in close accord with Diocletian, he only met him once in three years, at Milan (winter of 289–90).

Constantius, appointed Caesar of the West in 293, took charge of a new attack on Carausius. He took Boulogne, and, after the death of Carausius, recovered Britain from his murderer Allectus in 296. Maximian came up in person to secure the Rhine frontier, and in 297 settled the Salian Franks in the 'insula Batauorum'. He then defeated the Quinquegentanei in Africa and visited Rome. He shared in the persecution of the Christians (303) and retired with Diocletian, 1 May 305, abdicating at Milan.

Maximian returned from retirement in Lucania to support the rising of his son, Maxentius, 306. He forced Severus to surrender at Ravenna and then won over Constantine, giving him his daughter, Fausta, in marriage. In 307, after the failure of Galerius against Rome, Maximian tried in vain to depose his son and fled to Gaul. Required to abdicate again at Carnuntum, 308, Maximian could not settle down to a life of honourable inactivity. He led a revolt against Constantine, but was captured at Massilia and died by his own hand (310). An able soldier, he lacked humanity and statesmanship.

CAH xii. 327 ff., 345 ff.; Parker, *Roman World*, 225 ff., 237 ff. H. M.

MAXIMINUS (1), GAIUS JULIUS VERUS (Roman emperor A.D. 235–8), a Thracian peasant who had been promoted centurion by Septimius Severus because of his physical strength and powers of endurance, was the first Roman emperor who rose from the ranks. When saluted emperor at Mainz he was, like Macrinus, of equestrian rank but, unlike him, had held no civil appointments. A rough, uneducated man, he had no administrative talents, but as a soldier was fearless and untiring. After quelling two mutinies he ravaged Germany and won a victory in a swamp in Württemberg (235). After two years' fighting on the Danube a rebellion in Africa, caused by the unscrupulousness of one of his procurators, led to the proclamation of Gordian I and his son (qq.v.) as emperors, and the Senate declared Maximinus a public enemy (238). He immediately invaded Italy, but his progress was arrested by the stout resistance of Aquileia. His troops became enfeebled and disheartened, till the soldiers of II Parthica sought an end of civil war by murdering Maximinus and his son (see GORDIAN 1–3; BALBINUS).

Herodian, bks. 7–8; S.H.A. G. M. Bersanetti, *Studi su Massimino il Trace* (1940); L. Homo, *Revue Historique* 1919, ii. 209 ff. and iii. 1 ff.; Parker, *Roman World*, 141–51; *CAH* xii, ch. 2, § 3.
H. M. D. P.

MAXIMINUS (2), GAIUS GALERIUS VALERIUS, surnamed *Daia* (or *Daza*), an uneducated lad, a kinsman of Galerius, was made Caesar of the East in A.D. 305. Entrusted with the government of Syria, Egypt, and the south of Asia Minor, Maximinus served Galerius faithfully but, in 308, refused the offered title of 'filius Augusti' and was 'compelled by his troops' to assume the rank of Augustus, already conferred on Licinius. When Galerius died in 310, Maximinus occupied Asia Minor up to the Hellespont, but made peace with Licinius, who contested the crossing to Europe. Maximinus now drew closer to Maxentius, to balance the alliance of Constantine and Licinius, but after the fall of Maxentius was unable to withstand Licinius' attack; he lost two battles and died, a fugitive, at Tarsus. He had tried in vain to win the hand of Valeria, widow of Galerius.

Maximinus was a noted persecutor—in some ways the most interesting of them all. Not content with repression of the Christians, he tried to revive and reform the paganism of his subjects. He encouraged cities to petition against the Christians, and strove to improve the organization and raise the morale of the pagan priesthood.

CAH xii. 342 ff.; Parker, *Roman World*, 239 ff., 253 ff. H. M.

MAXIMUS (1), PAULLUS FABIUS (*c.* 46 B.C.–A.D. 14), an intimate friend of Augustus, was consul in 11 B.C., governor of Asia, and *legatus Augusti* in northern Spain (3–2 B.C.). He was an orator and advocate and a friend of Horace and Ovid. The story that he accompanied Augustus on a visit to Agrippa Postumus and committed suicide because his wife Marcia revealed the secret to Livia is improbable.

OGI 458 (rescript to the κοινὸν τῆς 'Ασίας); Horace, *Carm.* 4. 1; Ovid, *Pont.* (e.g. 1. 2; 3. 3); Seneca, *Controv.* 2. 4; Quintilian, *Inst.* 6. 3. 52; Tac. *Ann.* 1. 5. For coin-portrait see M. Grant, *From Imperium to Auctoritas* (1946), 387. G. W. R.

MAXIMUS (2), SEXTUS QUINCTILIUS VALERIUS, born in Alexandria Troas, received the *latus clavus* from Nerva and served as *legatus Augusti ad ordinandum statum ciuitatium liberarum* in Achaea, probably not after A.D. 108–9. An Epicurean, he was a friend of Pliny the Younger (*Ep.* 8. 24).

M. N. Tod, in *Anatolian Studies presented to W. H. Buckler* (1939), 333; E. Groag, *Die röm. Reichsbeamten von Achaia* (1939), cols. 125 ff. A. M.

MAXIMUS (3) of Tyre (*c.* A.D. 125–85), sophist, the author of forty-one extant Διαλέξεις (lectures), lived the life of an itinerant lecturer; he is known to have lectured in Athens, and the extant lectures were delivered in Rome, apparently in the reign of Commodus (180–92). He was well read in Greek literature, but apparently not in Greek philosophy except in Plato, of whom he claimed to be a follower. His lectures show no philosophical originality, and are simply eloquent exhortations to virtue decked out with quotations, chiefly from Plato and Homer; he belongs to the same genus as the sophists, though his views have no affinity with theirs, being borrowed from Cynicism and Platonism.

Ed. H. Hobein (1910); *PW* xiv. 2555. W. D. R.

MAXIMUS (4) (probably 2nd c. A.D.), author of the extant astrological poem Περὶ καταρχῶν, part of which later passed under the name of Orpheus. Suidas calls the author an Epirote or Byzantine, but identifies him with Julian's teacher Maximus, who came from Ephesus; this, however, seems improbable, as the poem is quite unphilosophical.

Ed. A. Ludwich (1877); *PW* xiv. 2573. W. D. R.

MAXIMUS, *see also* VALERIUS (17), VIBIUS (4), VICTORINUS.

MEALS. The times and the names of meals in Greece varied at different periods. In Homeric times breakfast (ἄριστον) was taken soon after sunrise, followed by a mid-day meal (δεῖπνον), with a supper (δόρπον) in the early evening. At Athens these three meals were reduced to two, a light lunch (ἄριστον) in the forenoon and a dinner (δεῖπνον) in the evening. The Hellenistic Greeks went back to three meals, a breakfast (ἀκρατισμός), a lunch (ἄριστον), and a dinner (δεῖπνον); and in this they were followed by the Romans of the Empire.

The Roman began his day early, and broke his fast with a very light meal (*ientaculum*). This usually consisted of a piece of bread and some fruit. Next came a slightly more substantial lunch (*prandium, merenda*), taken late in the forenoon, of fish, eggs, and vegetables, together with wine and water. This comparative frugality was atoned for at dinner (*cena*), which began normally in the late afternoon and was often continued well into the night. Dinner consisted of three parts:

(1) *Gustatio*, the hors d'œuvre, eggs, shell-fish, salad, washed down with *mulsum*, honeyed wine.

(2) *Fercula*, prepared dishes; generally in three, five, or seven courses, the chief item coming in the middle. A typical menu would be this: a dish of lampreys, a huge turbot, a roast boar served whole, a roast peacock, a joint of roast veal.

(3) *Mensae secundae*, pastry and sweetmeats of all kinds, fresh and dried fruits, and wine.

(*See* FOODSTUFFS.) F. A. W.

MEALS, SACRED. To eat together is everywhere a sort of communion, varying in different cultures from a mere mark of friendliness to a close and binding connexion. If a god is present at the meal, it becomes sacred, and the human participants are his hosts or guests and so in association with him. Hence every meal in an ancient household which kept up the old customs was sacred, for the household gods were present(cf. CHILDREN, WORSHIP, HOUSEHOLD; 'sacrae adsistere mensae', Juvenal 6. 365. O. 4, is to be present at a family meal). This is true also of the normal Olympian sacrifice, where the god and the sacrificers both partake of the victim, and equally of such rites as the *lectisternium* (q.v.), at which the god is a guest. It is most of all true of those rites in which the god himself is devoured (see DIONYSUS). In the Hellenistic mystery-cults this idea seems to have been strongly developed, ritual feasts, at which apparently the bond between god and worshippers was renewed, being a regular feature of them. These also served to mark the tie uniting initiates of a common cult; see for examples Cumont, *Rel. or.*[4], pp. 37, 65, 192, with p. 219, note 43; dining-rooms formed a regular part of Syrian temples, p. 256, note 52. It is therefore natural that such feasts were imagined as the portion of the blessed hereafter (ibid. pp. 57, 61, 202 f.; 309, note 51). More examples will be found by consulting Cumont's index, s.vv. 'Banquet', 'Festin', 'Repas'. Nock in *Essays on the Trinity and the Incarnation* (1928), 124 ff., *Harv. Theol. Rev.* xxix (1936), 77 ff.; *see also* BIRTHDAY, EPULONES, THEOXENIA. H. J. R.

MEASURES. I. MEASURES OF LENGTH. **1.** Measures of length were based primarily on parts of the human body. Homer is acquainted with the foot-standard, but the length of his foot is unknown. In historic Greece many standards are found. The Olympic, said to have been taken from the foot of Heracles, was of 320·5 mm. but may originally have been longer; it is surpassed by other standards, e.g. the Aeginetan of 333 mm., the Pergamene of 330 mm., while a Samian foot may have reached 350 mm. The Aeginetan and Pergamene standards correspond with the *pes Drusianus* of Gaul and Germany in the first century B.C. (330 mm.) and seem to be derived from a people of bigger build than the Athenians, whose foot is only 295·7 mm.; this is comparable with the Roman foot of 296 mm. and the English of 301 mm. Subdivisions of the foot are taken from the fingers: thus

2	finger-breadths, δάκτυλοι	= 1 κόνδυλος,	middle joint of finger
4	,,	,,	= 1 παλαστή (Homeric δῶρον), palm
8	,,	,,	= 1 διχάς or ἡμιπόδιον, half-foot
10	,,	,,	= 1 λιχάς, span of thumb and first finger
12	;;	,,	= 1 σπιθαμή, span of all fingers
16	,,	,,	= 1 πούς, foot.

2. Higher dimensions are taken from the arms; thus

18	δάκτυλοι	= 1 πυγμή, short cubit, elbow to start of fingers
20	,,	= 1 πυγών, short cubit of Homer and Herodotus, elbow to end of knuckles of closed fist
24	,,	= 1 πῆχυς, normal cubit, elbow to tips of fingers.

For longer distances:

2½ feet = 1 βῆμα, pace
6 feet = 1 ὄργυια, fathom, stretch of both arms
100 feet = 1 πλέθρον, breadth of the γύης, acre.

Beyond this Homer uses phrases such as the cast of a stone or quoit or spear. The later Greek unit, the στάδιον, originally the distance covered in a single draught by the plough, contained 600 feet, no matter what the length of the foot might be, and its exact length is therefore often doubtful. The παρασάγγης of 30 stadia was adopted from Persia.

3. The Roman foot (*pes*) of 296 mm. was generally divided into 12 inches, corresponding to the division of the *libra* into 12 *unciae*; the names of the subdivisions are the same and are given under WEIGHTS. There was also a division into 16 *digiti*, similar to the Greek system and possibly derived from it.

For higher distances:

5 pedes = 1 *passus*, pace
125 paces = 1 *stadium*
1,000 ,, = 1 mile, about 95 yards less than the English mile.

4. II. MEASURES OF AREA. Measures of area in both Greece and Rome were based on the amount ploughed in a day by a yoke of oxen. The Greek unit is the πλέθρον, measuring 100 × 100 = 10,000 feet. Another unit, the μέδιμνος, found in Sicily and in Cyrenaica, represented the amount of land that could be sown by a *medimnus* of wheat. The Romans employed the *actus quadratus*, a square of 120 feet, two of which formed the *iugerum* of 28,800 square Roman feet = 5/8ths of an acre. Two *iugera* formed a *heredium*, 100 *heredia* a *centuria*.

5. III. MEASURES OF CAPACITY. Measures of capacity fall into two divisions, dry and wet (μέτρα ξηρά, μέτρα ὑγρά), corresponding to the primary products, corn and wine, of ancient agriculture. The lower units are common to both divisions, the higher denominations diverge. In Greece there are numerous local systems, but most are based on the gourd, κύαθος = 0·04 litre or approximately 0·07 of an English pint. Then

1½	kyathoi	= 1 ὀξύβαφον
3	,,	= 1 ἡμικοτύλιον
6	,,	= 1 κοτύλη
12	,,	= 1 ξέστης.

The systems now fall apart; for dry measures:

4	kotylai	= 1 χοῖνιξ, at Athens a day's corn ration for a man
4	choinices	= 1 ἡμίεκτον
8	,,	= 1 ἑκτεύς or μόδιος
6	modioi	= 1 μέδιμνος, which in Attica contained 51·84 litres, in Sparta 71·16 to 77·88 litres.

For liquid measures the table continues:

6	kotylai	= 1 ἡμίχους
12	,,	= 1 χοῦς
12	choes	= 1 μετρητής.

The *metretes* is the measure of the large wine-amphora and contained 864 *kyathoi* = 38·88 litres.

6. The Roman system is similar to the Greek; the spoonful, *cochlear* or *ligula* (= 0·02 pint or 1·14 centilitres), is the lowest unit.

Then 4 *cochlearia* = 1 *cyathus*

6	,,	= 1 *acetabulum*
12	,,	= 1 *quartarius*
24	,,	= 1 *hemina* (= Gr. κοτύλη)
48	,,	= 1 *sextarius*.

For dry measures the higher denominations are:

8 *sextarii* = 1 *semodius*, nearly an English gallon
16 ,, = 1 *modius*.

For liquid measures:

12 *heminae* = 1 *congius*
8 *congii* = 1 *amphora*
20 *amphorae* = 1 *culleus*, tun of 120 gallons.

The *amphora*, or quadrantal, by which the burden of ships was determined, was the volume of a cubic Roman foot, 25·79 litres.

O. Viedebantt, 'Forschungen zur Metrologie des Altertums' (*Abh. d. phil.-hist. Klasse der k. Sächs. Gesell. d. Wissensch.* XXXIV, iii) (1917); P. Tannery, Dar.-Sag. s.v. 'Mensura'; F. Hultsch, *Reliquiae Scriptorum Metrologicorum* (1882). F. N. P.

MECHANICS, *see* PHYSICS, para. 3.

MEDDIX *tuticus* or *summus*, assisted by a *meddix minor*, was the senior magistrate among the Oscan-speaking peoples. His authority differed from that of the Romano-Latin *praetura*, to which some communities, notably Bantia, tended to assimilate the office, in being non-collegiate and yet lacking the absolute character of *imperium* (q.v.), though supreme in jurisdiction and administration. The relation of *m. minor* to *m. tuticus* recalls that of *magister equitum* to *dictator* (q.v.).

A. Rosenberg, *Staat der alten Italiker* (1913); J. Whatmough, *The Foundations of Roman Italy* (1937). A. N. S.-W.

MEDEA (Μήδεια), 'the cunning one', in mythology, daughter of Aeetes king of the Colchians and his wife Eidyia ('the knowing'), grand-daughter of Helios and niece of Circe (q.v.). She is universally said to have been a witch, but shows a certain tendency to pass into a goddess (ἀθανάτου στόματος, Pindar, *Pyth.* 4. 11, meaning the mouth of Medea; cf. Athenagoras, *Leg. pro Christ.* 14, a corrupt passage but sufficient to show that according to him she was worshipped somewhere). In the story of the Argonauts (q.v.) as we have it she plays a prominent part; when Aeetes sets Jason a seemingly impossible task, Medea, being in love with him, helps him to perform it by magic. In other words, she is that common figure of folk-tale, the Ogre's Daughter (Stith Thompson, G 530. 2). But the Argonauts have in many cases highly specialized characteristics, as wonderful sight (Lynceus), extraordinary speed (Euphemus), power of flight (the Boreadae) (Ap. Rhod. 1. 153, 182, 219); hence it is clear that there was another form of the story, whether older or not, in which they and not Medea helped Jason (cf. Grimm, *Kinder- u. Hausmärchen*, no. 246). Her love is elaborately motivated by Apoll. Rhod. 3. 7 ff., but this would not be original, though it may belong to the earliest literary form of the story (cf. Pindar, *Pyth.* 4. 213 ff.). Having helped Jason, Medea escapes with him in all known variants, and is regularly pursued; either her brother Apsyrtus leads the pursuit and she contrives his murder (so Ap. Rhod. 4. 410 ff.), or he is a child whom she takes with her, kills, and scatters his limbs in the way of Aeetes, thus delaying him (Cicero, *Leg. Man.* 22, and elsewhere). Returning to Iolcus, she renewed the youth of Aeson, Jason's father, by boiling him with virtuous herbs (fullest description in Ovid, *Met.* 7. 162 ff., but earliest reference in *Nostoi*, fr. 6 Allen). This done, she persuaded the daughters of Pelias to attempt the like on their own father, but was careful to give them inefficacious herbs, thus rendering them guilty, technically, of his death. This story is as old as the fifth century (Pind. *Pyth.* 4. 250 calls Medea Pelias' slayer, cf. Pherecydes in the schol. there, and both Sophocles and Euripides wrote on it, respectively in the Ῥιζοτόμοι and the *Peliades*), but doubtfully part of the oldest form of the legend, since Hesiod (*Theog.* 997 ff.), represents her and Jason as settled in Iolcus and her child Medeus as born there.

Her connexion with Corinth seems due to the Corinthian school of epic poets, who traded on the ambiguity of the name Ephyra (a town in Thesprotia where Jason and Medea lived, schol. *Od.* 1. 259, or Corinth). For her dealings with Creon see s.v. (1); after the murder of him, his daughter, and her children, she took refuge with Aegeus (q.v.) in Athens. After her banishment from that city, a late story (Hyginus, *Fab.* 27) represents her as bringing about the death of Perses, Aeetes' brother and enemy, with the help of her son by Aegeus, Medus; the country was thereafter called Media.

See also MAGIC, para. 4. H. J. R.

MEDIA, the mountainous country south-west of the Caspian Sea which was for a century the centre of the Median Empire. The Medes, an Indo-European people ethnologically and linguistically akin to the Persians, appear as a group of tribes, some nomadic, some settled in fortified villages, against whom the Assyrians waged war. They were possibly in the neighbourhood of L. Urmia as early as the second millennium B.C.

Deioces, whom Herodotus (1. 96–100) accounts the founder of the Median Empire, appears in the Assyrian records only as a local chieftain. The real unifier of the Medes seems to have been Phraortes (Khshathrita, *c.* 675–653 B.C.). His son Cyaxares (Uvakhshatra, 625–585 B.C.) conquered neighbouring territories and, in alliance with Nabopolassar of Babylon, defeated the Assyrians; Nineveh fell in 612 B.C. His empire included most of Iran, the northern territory once subject to Urartu, and Cappadocia as far as the river Halys. Of its organization little is known. Astyages (Ishtumegu, 585–550 B.C.) extended his boundaries at the expense of Babylonia, but was defeated by his vassal Cyrus, and the Median Empire passed to the Persians.

E. G. Klauber, *Politisch-religiöse Texte aus der Sargonidenzeit* (1913); F. W. König, *Älteste Geschichte der Meder und Perser, Alte Orient* xxxiii 3/4 (1934); J. V. Prášek, *Geschichte der Meder und Perser* (1906–10); *see also* PERSIA. M. S. D.

MEDICINA PLINII, an extant compilation made (probably A.D. 300–50) from Pliny's account, in bks.

20–32 of the *Naturalis Historia*, of the plants and animals used for medicinal purposes. Marcellus Empiricus describes it as being the work of a second Pliny. This work has to be distinguished from a work commonly but falsely ascribed to Plinius Valerianus, of which the first three books are a garbled version (6th or 7th c.) of the earlier work, while the last two books come from a different source. W. D. R.

MEDICINE. I. NON-RATIONAL ELEMENTS. Historians of Greek Medicine rightly stress its scientific character. This goes far back, for there are traces of science in the medical practice of the Homeric poems and the very earliest scientific works are medical. Nevertheless throughout antiquity and in every part of the ancient world other and lower types of Medicine were prevalent. No cultural element is so transmissible as irrational beliefs and practices concerning disease. These are susceptible neither of logical arrangement nor of true historic treatment, nor can their sources be entirely separated from each other. Such material can only be discussed under artificial headings based on mere convenience.

(*a*) References to practices on a very low anthropological level are scattered through the literature of classical antiquity. Sympathetic, contagious, and imitative magic, the influence of rulers, priests, and the dead upon disease, and the various elements with which folklore deals are all represented. They were long ago collected and analysed by Sir J. G. Frazer in *The Golden Bough*.

(*b*) Peculiar rites and beliefs are associated with the gathering of herbs in both early and late literature. There are collections of them attached to the *Inquiry into Plants* of Theophrastus and embedded in the *Natural History* of Pliny. Some of these customs are comparable to those in the Sanskrit Vedas. A fair case can be made for the existence of a stream of Indo-Germanic Medicine associated specially with herb remedies. Some of these practices persist among European peasants. (*See* BOTANY, THEOPHRASTUS, PLINY THE ELDER.)

(*c*) The Medicine of the New Testament is mainly that of possession by evil spirits. There is only a trace of demonism in the Old Testament and it is not prominent in classical writings until Christian times. Its presence often indicates Persian contacts. It is well illustrated in the writings of Philostratus. Its main source is probably Mesopotamian. (*See* POSSESSION.)

(*d*) All deities, both Chthonic and Olympian, had healing powers. There was also, among the Greeks and later among the Romans, a tendency to the formation of cults ascribing such powers to deceased physicians. The most prominent of these cults was that of Asclepius. A whole family of supernatural healers became associated with him. His history has an extraordinarily close parallel in Egyptian civilization. (*See* ASCLEPIUS.)

(*e*) Essential to Asclepian rites was 'Incubation', the temple-sleep and its accompanying dream. This, however, neither originated with nor was peculiar to the cult. Throughout antiquity advice concerning disease and preservation of health was drawn from dreams which were held to be sometimes curative. The *Oneirocritica* of Artemidorus (2nd c. A.D.) is an exposition of this. (*See* INCUBATION.)

(*f*) Dedication of votive models of affected parts, especially in Asclepian shrines, was a common practice. The model may bear a representation of the disease or an invocation to the deity or an indication of the remedy desired. Similar votives are found in all civilizations. Modern votives are often indistinguishable from ancient. (*See* VOTIVE OFFERINGS.)

(*g*) Amulets and periapts, inscribed with prayers, invocations, charms, or signs of power, were suspended or tied to the person to ward off evil or effect cure. Specially common in the Western Empire was the ocular cachet—

an inscribed clay tablet to be applied to the diseased eye. Identical practices still persist. (*See* AMULET.)

(*h*) Magical incantations of syncretic origin were used against disease. Characteristic of these is the inclusion of foreign words of power, especially names of foreign divinities. Most records come from the later classical period. (*See* MAGIC.)

(*i*) A peculiarity in Roman practice, not easily paralleled, was the association of bodily parts and even sensations, symptoms, and diseases with their own specific deities. These tutelary beings needed propitiation according to the part or function affected.

(*j*) There is an important body of herb-lore that is irrational but unassociated with 'superstitious' practices. Such is the drug list of Dioscorides. Only a minute percentage of his hundreds of herbs have the activities he ascribes to them. Yet these drug lists remained in use for centuries and generated the ancient herbals and the medieval and modern pharmacopoeias. (*See* BOTANY, DIOSCORIDES 2.)

(*k*) Apart from superstitious practices, Medicine in classical antiquity retained throughout certain relations to the current higher religion. (See § II.)

2. II. RELATION TO RATIONAL RELIGION AND PHILOSOPHY. Celsus calls Hippocrates 'the first who separated medicine from philosophy'. In fact the works of the Hippocratic Collection that date from the fifth and fourth centuries B.C. have definite philosophical affinities. Moreover, religion entered largely into the practice of healing. Thus the references to these topics are of great significance.

3. Among the ancients there were those, such as Anaxagoras, who took the 'practical' scientific attitude towards phenomena, regarding them as devoid of any divine element. This was not the common view. Nearly all the ancients—and specifically the ancient physicians—considered that there were at least some bodies and forces, and specifically the heavenly bodies and the 'winds', that could not be treated on the merely phenomenal level. For this reason, among others, any translation into a modern language of the basic terminology of Greek Medicine is liable to be misleading. Thus, for example, the classic presentation of the 'naturalist' view, the *Sacred Disease* of the Hippocratic Collection, has the key-sentence: 'This disease has the same *cause* (πρόφασις) as others that come and go from the body—cold, sun, and changing restlessness of *winds* (πνεύματα). These are *divine* (θεῖα). No need to put this disease in a special class as more divine than others; all are divine, and all *human* (ἀνθρώπινα). Each has its own *nature* (φύσις) and *power* (δύναμις).' None of the italicized words adequately renders the original, but the general sense of the passage will indicate to the reader that it is not legitimate to interpret all terms descriptive of 'natural processes' as normally devoid of religious content. Notably two of these words, *pneuma* (= wind) and *physis* (= nature), are not only untranslatable but carry a highly complex religious content. These words recur again and again in Greek medical literature.

4. The general view of antiquity, including that of the physicians, is that 'nature' must be conceived as permeated in some way or other by God. We think to-day of the great forces of nature as comparable on a large scale to the operations in our test-tubes. Greek physicians, without the resources of experimental science, thought of the forces of nature as of a different order from the minor mechanics of their own more intimate world. In what degree, then, was man a mere machine—that is a product of these minor mechanics—in what degree were his visitations 'natural', in what degree divine?

5. Three types of answer were given. One regarded as divine only those events which seem 'spontaneous', that is without immediate discoverable exciting cause; all else

is 'natural', man being linked with nature and God treated as a separate entity. This is the method, for example, of *Decorum* in the Hippocratic Collection. A second type of answer identified God with nature as in the *Sacred Disease* quoted above. A third made three independent categories of events, those originating in nature, those human, and those divine. This is the method of *Prognostic* and *Diseases of Women* of the Hippocratic Collection. There are variations and degrees of these solutions.

6. There was thus no unity of outlook among the earlier physicians, no 'primitive Hippocratic doctrine', for which historians of Greek Medicine, following Galen, have vainly sought. From Hellenistic times, however, the philosophic differences that divided the medical world, though no more profound than before, are certainly more clearly visible. They are conventionally and somewhat artificially treated under four 'schools', known as the Dogmatists, Empirics, Methodists, and Pneumatists, corresponding roughly to the philosophic sects Stoics, Epicureans, Sceptics, and Eclectics respectively.

7. Galen (129–99), summator of ancient Medicine, borrowed ideas from all four medical schools and all four philosophic sects, inclining most to the Dogmatists and Stoics. Being not only a selective but also an extremely voluminous writer, it is not surprising that he was not always consistent. His inconsistency did not, however, lessen his influence and in his *Uses of the bodily parts of man* he reached conclusions that determined medical thought for nearly a millennium and a half. He claims in that work that the organs are so well constructed, and in such perfect relation to the functions to which they minister, that it is impossible to imagine anything better. Following Aristotle's dictum that 'nature makes naught in vain', he seeks to justify the form and structure of all the organs, and of every part of every organ, with reference to the functions for which he believes they are destined. Moreover, he considers that he can discover the end served by every part and requiring it to be constructed as it is.

8. Galen was the last active scientific intellect of antiquity. His teleological message, delivered in a world of Stoic determinism, carried the implication of the worthlessness of research. His doctrine demanded *a priori* solutions of all the problems of physiology. Galen himself was among the pioneers of this teleological view. It was a relatively novel presentation of the world that it was worth exploring only to verify the hypothesis. He explored it, but his theory removed the motive for further exploration (*see* ANATOMY AND PHYSIOLOGY). His view fitted well with the Christian attitude and works by Galen were studied and respected throughout the Dark and Middle Ages.

9. The writings of the ancient physicians before Galen had no association with the lower religious elements. This cannot be said for all the derivative works which appear after him. But there was one earlier cult which had a general relation to the practice, if not to the theory, of Medicine. It was by no accident that Asclepius became god of doctors as well as of patients. His worship, in its best presentation, stood for rational religion in opposition to demonic and magical rites and purifications. It contained, moreover, a psychological element that was of great value to rational practice. The physician's attitude to Asclepius and that of Asclepius to Medicine is indicated in the famous Hippocratic *Oath*. It is not misleading to say that the normal relation of Medicine to the best side of the Asclepian cult was fairly near what it is to the current practice of religion in a settled modern society.

10. III. MEDICAL STATUS AND ORGANIZATION. The status of the Greek physician was at first not much above that of the higher craftsman. He carried his skill from town to town, establishing in each a workshop or surgery (ἰατρεῖον). As nurses and assistants he had pupils bound by agreement, one form of which is the Hippocratic *Oath*. This was not a legal but a private contract; for there was no licenciation. Medical status was raised by the Alexandrian school, where for the first time there was systematic instruction. At Rome Medicine was originally the work of slaves or subordinates. In 46 B.C. Julius Caesar gave citizenship to all who practised there. Thus status rose further and way was made for such physicians as Galen, the friend of emperors.

11. The earliest scientific teacher in Rome, who founded the first regular school there, was Asclepiades of Bithynia (*c.* 40 B.C.). But schools, at first mere personal followings, combined at the beginning of the Christian era in the use of a meeting-place on the Esquiline. State-paid professors with public *auditoria* were available at Rome from the time of Vespasian (70–9). Subsidiary teaching centres were founded in other Italian towns and later in such transalpine centres as Marseilles, Bordeaux, Arles, Nîmes, Lyons, and Saragossa.

12. State physicians existed in the time of Herodotus. We know little of their terms or duties. District physicians were early appointed in Italy and the custom spread to the provinces, beginning with the army and associated first with military *valetudinaria*. Inscriptions show that such men were held in respect. In the army itself, however, the medical staff had only status equivalent to that of higher non-commissioned officers.

13. From the military *valetudinarium* it was no great step to the construction of similar institutions for the numerous imperial officials and their families in the provinces. Motives of benevolence came in and public hospitals were founded in many localities. The idea passed to Christian times. The pious foundation of hospitals for the sick and outcast in the Middle Ages is to be traced back to the Roman *valetudinaria*. The first charitable institution of this kind concerning which we have clear information was established at Rome in the fourth century by a Christian lady of whom we learn from St. Jerome.

14. IV. CLINICAL THEORY. There are sufficient common features in the practice of antiquity to make possible a general sketch, despite differing individual doctrinal allegiances throughout, and changes in the different periods.

15. First of all, and without any theory, there comes to every physician the duty of observation. His first question must be 'How ill is this patient?' We see the ancient physician at this task of observation in his records of actual cases. The most remarkable of these are the forty-two in the Hippocratic Collection, evidently from a practitioner's day-to-day note-book. They are models of succinct record, and are without any attempt at diagnosis or prognosis. Among them the modern physician can discern clearly a case of diphtheria, and examples of the 'typhoid state', and of 'Cheyne-Stokes breathing'. All forty-two cases were gravely ill and the majority died.

16. An outstanding feature of ancient Medicine is stress on foreknowledge of the course of the sickness. 'It is most excellent for a physician to cultivate *pronoia*. Since he foreknows and foretells the past, present, and future . . . men would have confidence to entrust themselves to his care. . . . By an early forecast in each case he can tend aright those who have a chance to survive and by foreseeing who will die . . . he will escape blame' (*Prognostic*). *Pronoia* is not quite our prognosis, which, however, it includes. It means knowing things about a patient without being told them. A great *pronoia* is the immortal description of the signs of death, known still as the *Hippocratic facies*:

'The physician should observe thus in acute diseases: First, the face of the patient, if it be like to those in health, and especially to itself, for this would be the best of all; but the more unlike to this, the worse; such would be these: sharp nose, hollow eyes, collapsed temples;

ears cold, contracted, and with their lobes turned out; skin about the forehead rough, distended, and parched; colour greenish or dusky. If it be so at the beginning and if this cannot be explained by other symptoms, inquiry should be made whether he has been sleepless; whether he be purged; whether he is suffering from hunger. If any of these be admitted the danger may be reckoned so far the less and it may be judged in a day and a night if the appearance proceed from these. But if none of these exist and the symptoms do not subside in that time, be it known for certain that death is nigh' (*Prognostic*).

17. After his *pronoia* the physician must consider the nature of the condition he is to treat. Most ancient medical works pass lightly over theories of disease. Nevertheless treatment to be rational must have some theoretical basis. The usual doctrine was simple. Just as matter was made of the four elements, so the human body was made of their surrogates, the four cardinal fluids or humours, Blood, Phlegm, Yellow Bile, and Black Bile (melancholy). Health meant that the humours were blended harmoniously; sickness that they were in disharmony. A determinant of health was the *innate heat*, which was greatest in youth, when most fuel is needed, and declined with age. Its abdication is death. The supporter of the innate heat is the pneuma (or pneumata) which circulates in the vessels. (*See* ANATOMY AND PHYSIOLOGY.)

18. Disease must be treated by rectifying any disharmony of the humours. Happily these have a natural tendency to equilibrium and, left to themselves, are likely to reach that state. This is the 'Hippocratic' doctrine of *Nature as the healer of diseases*, νούσων φύσις ἰητρός, the *Vis medicatrix naturae* of the later Latin writers and of the present day. It was ridiculed by the more active—and more dangerous—practitioners as a 'meditation on death'.

19. The actual process by which the humours come into harmony is *pepsis* (Latin *coctio*, later elaborated as a series of 'digestions'). The turning-point at which *pepsis* is complete is the *crisis*, a term which still bears some of its original medical meaning. The crisis was expected on certain days. The physician must bring his remedies to bear especially at the critical time.

20. V. TREATMENT. Disturbance in the balance of the humours was, however, only the immediate cause of disease. There were more remote factors which the physician needed to study. Injudicious modes of life, exposure to climatic changes, and the like could be directly corrected. For such disturbances as could not be healed on these preventive lines various therapeutic measures were available.

21. After rest and quiet the central factor in treatment is dietetics, concerning which there are exceedingly elaborate details. An entire book is devoted to the preparation and uses of barley-water! The general principles of dietetics, especially related to fevers, are substantially those of the present day. The physician also had at his disposal a variety of physical remedies—baths, inunctions, clysters, etc. He employed cupping and bleeding too frequently.

22. Until later times the ancient physician was no great user of drugs except, we may note, in the treatment of diseases of women; from works on these the greater part of the 300 constituents of the pharmacopoeia of the Hippocratic Collection are derived. At first drugs were given by themselves—they were 'simples'. From Alexandrian times onward prescriptions were liable to become very elaborate. The prescription of a Theriac by Andromachus, physician to Nero and the first to bear the title *Archiater*, was one of the longest on record. About one-third of the herbs employed in a modern pharmacopoeia were known to the Greek physicians.

23. The general line of treatment—surgery excepted—was not very unlike that of an intelligent and rather conservative English country practitioner of about a century and a half ago. (For surgical resources of the ancients *see* SURGERY.) The ancient physician was, perhaps, a little less confident than his eighteenth-century successor, a little more cautious, a little more conscious of his helplessness.

24. No medical work has had the influence of the great *Aphorisms*, a series of very brief generalizations by a highly experienced physician many of whose conclusions have been confirmed by later ages, some passing into medical commonplaces, others becoming popular proverbs. The work is included in the Hippocratic Collection but cannot be even approximately dated. The meaning of the first Aphorism is misrepresented by its usual truncated quotation. In depressing completeness it runs: 'Life is short and the Art long, the occasion urgent, experience deceptive, and decision difficult; yet not only must the physician be ready to do his duty but patient, attendants, and circumstances must co-operate if there is to be a cure.'

25. VI. MATERIAL AND LITERARY SOURCES. Of material remains the most impressive are Asclepian sites excavated at Epidaurus, Cos, Pergamus, Athens, Rome, and elsewhere. There is a doctor's house and nursing-home at Pompeii. Numerous instruments have been found at Pompeii and at many other places. Vase-paintings have yielded much information, especially for hygiene, bathing customs, athletics, etc. Sanitation is superbly represented by the aqueducts, water-supply, and drainage-systems of Rome. There are remains of military hospitals in the Empire, of which the best known are those at Novaesium and Vetera (*Neuss* and *Xanten* on the Rhine frontier) in lower Germany and at Aquae Helveticae (*Baden* in Switzerland). In the latter numerous instruments were found. Many inscribed stone stamps used for impressing ointments, especially for diseases of the eyes, with name of maker and directions for use have been found in the western provinces.

26. The fund of Greek manuscripts is very large and is inadequately explored. Latin manuscripts containing versions and translations from Greek also yield information. The papyri are disappointing, but among them is a substantial fragment of the otherwise unknown historical work of Menon, pupil of Aristotle, giving views of some pre-Hippocratics. There are also papyri illuminating the herbal tradition. Information is accumulating of works lost in the original but surviving in versions in Arabic, Hebrew, and Syriac manuscripts.

27. Light is cast on practice by innumerable allusions in literary texts. Here we consider only technical literature, which is so extensive that no one would claim to have studied the whole closely; there are modern critical editions of only about a half. Best explored is the Hippocratic Collection, but it is complete in no edition after Littré's (1839–61) and for many of its members we still depend on this. Of Galen's writings and pseudepigrapha only a small percentage is critically edited, and we still depend substantially upon an inferior edition completed in 1833.

28. For the earliest stratum of rational Medicine we have only the fragments of the pre-Socratic philosophers, notably those of Pythagoras, Alcmaeon, Empedocles, Heraclitus, Democritus, and Anaxagoras. For the fifth century there are several works in the Hippocratic Collection and fragments of several other medical writers. For the fourth century there is the bulk of the Hippocratic Collection, one work in which can be ascribed to Polybus, son-in-law of Hippocrates. There are also many relevant passages in the works of Plato, Aristotle, and Theophrastus. Specially interesting are fragments of the physician Diocles, contemporary with or a little older than Aristotle.

29. Of the earlier Alexandrian period there are fragments of Herophilus and Erasistratus, the poems on drugs by Nicander, and fragments of a number of herbalists and others. The later Alexandrians are more happily represented by Celsus *On medical matters* (in Latin from a Greek original), by finely illustrated texts of the herbal of Crateuas (*c*. 80 B.C.), of a commentary on the *Dislocations* of the Hippocratic Collection (*c*. A.D. 50), of Dioscorides *On materia medica* (*c*. A.D. 60), and of Soranus *On fractures and bandaging* and *On obstetrics* (*c*. A.D. 60). There are also fragments of the first Greek practitioner in Rome, the Methodist Asclepiades of Bithynia, and others.

30. Writers after Galen were numerous and mostly inferior. Important historically are the fourth- and fifth-century Latin translations of Dioscorides and of works both of the Hippocratic and of the Galenic corpus. Interesting for the soundness of its physiology is Nemesius, Bishop of Emesa, *On the nature of man* (*c*. 400). Solid derivative source-books are those of Oribasius (325–403), Aëtius (*c*. 550), Paul of Aegina (625–90), and Alexander of Tralles (525–605). The last still shows some spark of originality but much superstition.

31. Of Latin works that *On acute and chronic diseases* by Caelius Aurelianus, a Numidian of the fifth century, is interesting both linguistically and as the only complete Methodist work. Among the more bizarre survivals are the medical verses of Quintus Serenus Sammonicus which introduce that word of power *Abracadabra*; the popular, irrational but also non-superstitious herbal of 'Apuleius Platonicus Madaurensis' known in scores of early illustrated manuscripts; and the disgusting Sextus Placitus Papyriensis *On drugs from animals*. On the lowest level is Marcellus Empiricus of Bordeaux (*c*. A.D. 400), whose semi-insane assembly of folly and superstition is a happy hunting-ground for folk-lorists.

32. VII. MODERN CRITICISM. Nineteenth-century scholarship produced an account of the origin and course of ancient Medicine that accorded substantially with the views of the ancient physicians from the third century onward as to the history of their art. The ancient tradition was modified but not fundamentally altered. Despite the difficulty in identifying the 'genuine' works of Hippocrates it was persistently held that from the older elements in the Hippocratic Collection a fairly coherent doctrinal system could be deduced, which was treated under the (sometimes admittedly conventional) name of 'Hippocrates'. The figure and part of the personal history of the 'Father of Medicine' were substantially retained.

33. Work of the last three decades calls for a fundamental change in this attitude. A middle way is impossible. The controversy turns primarily on the figure of Hippocrates (*c*. 400 B.C.) and upon the question of his share in the so-called 'Hippocratic Collection', which took its first form in the third century B.C. (*See* HIPPOCRATES.)

34. The 'Hippocratic' works, even of the older stratum in that collection, contain differences in outlook as great as those between Socrates and Anaxagoras. Parts of the 'Collection' are separated from each other by centuries in time and were written under widely different social and geographical conditions. To attribute all or many of their doctrines, or of the works that contain them, to a conventionalized 'Hippocrates' conserves nothing but confusion. Moreover, archaeological, textual, and historical investigation combine to render untenable the traditional account of the life of the 'Father of Medicine' even in a greatly modified form.

35. It has been assumed in this article that scientific Medicine did not take shape first with Hippocrates; that it was not originally connected with Cos or with the cult of Asclepius either at Cos or elsewhere; that we know almost nothing of Hippocrates except the approximate period of his life, and that he was regarded by his immediate successors as one—but only one—of several distinguished physicians of his age; that we have no evidence of the existence of any work by Hippocrates, and that we have some evidence that no work by him exists. These are negative conclusions; the positive are incorporated in §§ III, IV, and V. This critical attitude affects neither the value of the Greek picture of the ideal physician, nor the view that such qualities were to be found among the ancients, nor the inspiration and beauty of the 'Hippocratic' mode of life.

BIBLIOGRAPHY

For the complete Hippocratic Collection and Galenic writings the reader must still rely on the editions of E. Littré (10 vols., 1831-62) and C. G. Kuhn (20 vols., 1821-33). The collection of general information on Greek Medicine in F. Adams, *The Seven Books of Paul of Aegina* (3 vols., 1844-7), is still unexcelled. The best modern Hippocrates, by W. H. S. Jones and E. T. Withington (Loeb Library, 4 vols., 1922-31), is imperfect, as is H. Kühlwein and J. Ilberg, *Hippocratis Opera Omnia* (2 vols., 1894-1902). The *Corpus Medicorum Latinorum* contains several useful volumes. The progress of the *Corpus Medicorum Graecorum* is negligible. Works of other individual authors are given in the articles under their names.

General material in Charles Singer, *Greek Biology and Greek Medicine* (1922), and in *The Legacy of Rome* (1924); L. Edelstein in *Bulletin of the Institute of the History of Medicine* (U.S.A. 1937 and 1939); Werner Jaeger, *Diokles von Karystos* (1938); J. J. Walsh, *Galen's Writings and the Influences inspiring them*, 'Annals of Medical History' (1934-9); E. Nachmanson *Erotianstudien* (1917).

§ II. L. Edelstein, 'Greek Medicine in Relation to Religion and Magic', *Bull. of the Inst. of Hist. of Med.* v (U.S.A. 1937), p. 201, and 'Hippocrates' in *PW*, Supplt. to Bd. vi a (1935), 1290; W. A. Heidel, *The Heroic Age of Science* (U.S.A. 1933); M. Neuburger, *History of Medicine* (2 vols., 1910-25); O. Weinreich, *Antike Heilungswunder* (1909); A. Abt, *Die Apologie des Apuleius und die antike Zauberei* (1908); W. A. Jayne, *The Healing Gods* (1925); M. Hamilton, *Incubation* (1906). E. J. and L. Edelstein, *Asclepius* (2 vols., Baltimore, 1946). See also references in § iv and bibliography under HIPPOCRATES (2), etc.

§ III. W. Müri, *Arzt und Patient bei Hippokrates* (1936); W. H. S. Jones, *The Doctor's Oath* (1924); T. Meyer, *Geschichte der römischen Aerztestandes* (1907); H. E. Sigerist, 'Notes and Comments on Hippocrates', *Bull. of the Inst. of Hist. of Med.* ii (U.S.A. 1934), p. 190; F. H. Garrison, *Notes on the History of Military Medicine* (U.S.A. 1922); 'History of Drainage', *Bull. of New York Acad. of Med.* v (U.S.A. 1929), p. 887; T. Puschmann, *A History of Medical Education* (1891). Still useful are R. Briau, *L'Assistance médicale chez les Romains* (1869), and *L'Archiatrie romaine ou la médecine officielle dans l'empire romain* (1877), and M. Albert, *Les Médecins grecs à Rome* (1894).

§ IV. Ch. Daremberg, *La Médecine, histoire et doctrine* (1863), is still the best book on the subject. T. Clifford Allbutt, *Greek Medicine in Rome* (1921); A. J. Brock, *Greek Medicine* (1929), and *Galen on the Natural Faculties* (Loeb, 1916); O. Temkin, *The Falling Sickness* (Baltimore, 1945); Charles Singer and C. Rabin, *A Prelude to Science* (1946).

§ V. J. H. Dierbach, *Die Arzneimittel des Hippokrates* (1924), is still useful; J. Berendes, *Des Pedanios Dioskurides Arzneimittellehre* (1902), and *Die Pharmacie bei den alten Culturvölkern* (2 vols., 1891); H. Schelenz, *Geschichte der Pharmazie* (1904); Theodor Meyer, *Theodorus Priscianus und die römische Medizin* (1909); K. Sudhoff, *Aus dem antiken Badewesen* (2 vols., 1910); E. N. Gardiner, *Athletics of the Ancient World* (1930); G. F. Still, *History of Paediatrics* (1931); C. Tsintsiropoulos, *La Médecine grecque depuis Asclépiade jusqu'à Galien* (1892); P. Pansier, 'Repertorium oculariorum inter Graecos Romanosque', *Janus* x and xi (1905-6); I. Fischer, *Geschichte der Gynäkologie* in J. Halban and L. Seitz, *Biologie und Pathologie des Weibes* (1926).

§ VI. Eugen Holländer, *Plastik und Medizin* (1912), is the largest collection of minor material remains. The magnificent work of A. Defrasse and H. Lechat, *Épidaure*, contains many good restorations. For other Asclepian sites see ASCLEPIUS. For the legionary and other hospitals see the *Bonner Jahrbücher* cxxxviii-cxxxix. 54 ff. and F. Stähelin, *Die Schweiz in römischen Zeit* (1931), and cf. *Proc. Soc. Ant. Scot.* lxxiii. 132. H. Diels, *Die Fragmente der Vorsokratiker* (3 vols., 1934-7) is indispensable in its field. The early references to medicine in general literature are usefully collected by M. Mollet, *La Médecine chez les grecs avant Hippocrate* (1906); Ch. Daremberg, *La Médecine dans Homère* (1865), has not been displaced.

For Hippocratic and Galenic Collections see above.

Important communications between 1911 and 1919 are listed by F. E. Kind in C. Bursian's *Jahresbericht über die Fortschritte der klassischen Altertumswissenschaft* for 1919, and after that in the bibliographies of *Isis* and the *Mitteilungen zur Gesch. der Med. und der Naturwissenschaften*.

The Greek MSS. are indicated in H. Diels, *Die Handschriften der antiken Aerzte* (2 vols., 1905-6).

Most of the medical illuminations that are of ancient origin are discussed or reproduced in J. Ilberg, *Die Ueberlieferung der Gynäkologie des Soranus von Ephesos* (1910), and *Sorani Gynaeciorum Libri IV, De signis fracturarum, De fasciis* (1927). E. Howald and H. E. Sigerist, *Antonii Musae de Herba Vettonica*, etc. (1927); Charles Singer, 'The Herbal in Antiquity', *JHS* 1927; H. Schöne, *Apollonius von Kitium, illustrierter Kommentar zu den hippokratischen*

Schrift ΠΕΡΙ ΑΡΘΡΩΝ. Illustrations of Roman surgery are given by Charles Singer in *The Legacy of Rome* (1924). For Pompeian and other surgical instruments see J. S. Milne, *Surgical Instruments in Greek and Roman Times* (1907), T. Meyer-Steineg, *Chirurgische Instrumente des Altertums* (1912), and Cagnot and Chapot, *Manuel d'archéologie romaine* (1920) ii. 513 ff.

§ VII. Max Pohlenz, *Hippokrates und die Begründung der wissenschaftlichen Medizin* (1938). L. Edelstein, *ΠΕΡΙ ΑΕΡΩΝ und die Sammlung der hippokratischen Schriften* (1931), and article 'Hippocrates' in *PW*, Supplt. to Bd. vi a, 1290; H. E. Sigerist, 'Notes and Comments on Hippocrates', *Bull. of the Inst. of Hist. of Med.* ii (U.S.A. 1934), 190; O. Temkin, 'Geschichte des Hippokratismus' in *Kyklos* iv. 1, 19 and 'Doctrine of Epilepsy in the Hippocratic writings', *Bull. of the Inst. of Hist. of Med.*, i (U.S.A. 1933), 277; M. Wellmann, *Die hippokratische Schrift περὶ ἑβδομάδων* (1933); H. Diller, *Die sogenannte 2ᵗᵉ Fassung des 19 Hippokratesbriefes* (1933). C. S.

MEDIOLAN(I)UM, nowadays *Milan*, founded *c.* 396 B.C. on or near the site of Etruscan Melpum (Pliny, *HN* 3. 125) by the Insubres, came under Roman control temporarily in 222, permanently in 194 B.C. (Polyb. 2. 34; Livy 5. 34; 34. 46). It obtained Latin rights in 89, Roman citizenship in 49 B.C. Under the Empire, as *municipium* and later as *colonia*, it grew steadily. The principal north Italian road-centre, Mediolanum ultimately became the capital of the Western Empire. The frequent presence of the imperial court, especially in the fourth century, contributed to its prosperity; but, centrally situated in the fertile plain of Cisalpine Gaul, it was independently important. After 300 Mediolanum was the seat of the governor of Liguria, the praetorian prefect, and the vicar of Italy. Attila (452), Odoacer (476), Theodoric (493), Uraia who sacked it (539), and Alboin (569) successively captured Mediolanum. Its famed bishop Ambrose (374-7) established its ecclesiastical independence. The Emperors Didius Julianus and Geta were born there.

Strabo 5. 213; Eutrop. 9. 27; Aur. Vict. *Caes.* 39; Procop. *Goth.* 2. 8. A. Colombo, *Lombardia Romana* (1939). E. T. S.

MEDON (*Μέδων*), name of several mythological persons, the only one of importance being the herald in the *Odyssey*, who warns Penelope of the suitors' plot against Telemachus (4. 677 ff.) and is spared by Odysseus (22. 357 ff.).

MEDUSA, see GORGO.

MEFITIS, Italian goddess of sulphurous vapours arising from the ground (Verg. *Aen.* 7. 84 and Servius there); hence her temple at Cremona was outside the walls (Tacitus, *Hist.* 3. 33), though in Rome her grove was on the Esquiline (Varro, *Ling.* 5. 49). There are indications that her cult extended throughout Italy, but especially in the central (the most volcanic) regions.

See Wissowa, *RK* 246.

MEGACLES, son of Alcmaeon, of the Alcmaeonidae (q.v.) family at Athens. He was the successful suitor of Agariste, daughter of Cleisthenes, tyrant of Sicyon (*c.* 575 B.C.). He led the moderate party, his rivals being Lycurgus (a narrow oligarch) and Pisistratus. When the latter as democratic leader made himself tyrant, Megacles at first combined with Lycurgus against him, but later helped Pisistratus, who agreed to marry his daughter. The marriage, however, led to a further quarrel and Pisistratus was again driven out; but on his final return (*c.* 543) Megacles went into exile. Nothing later is recorded of him. A. W. G.

MEGALESIA, see CYBELE.

MEGALOPHANES, see DEMOPHANES.

MEGALOPOLIS (ἡ μεγάλη πόλις: the compound form is Latin) was founded by Epaminondas between 370 and 362 B.C. as the centre of the Arcadian League. Most of the Arcadians (excluding the NE. and E. Arcadian towns) and the Scirites of the Laconian borderland became its citizens; forty villages were completely or partially abandoned (Paus. 8. 27. 3–4). It lay in a plain, through which the headwaters of the Alpheus and Eurotas flow, and was therefore a centre of communications. It was one of the largest cities of Peloponnesus, and many of its buildings have been excavated, including the Thersilion, where the Arcadian federal assembly met.

Megalopolis was often hard pressed by Sparta, and suffered from the lukewarmness or hostility of other Arcadian cities and the centrifugal tendencies of the mountaineers. It consistently took the Macedonian part in the fourth century. In 235 its tyrant Lydiadas (q.v.) abdicated and introduced Megalopolis into the Achaean League (Polyb. 2. 44. 5), in which it subsequently played a leading part under Philopoemen. The last great Megalopolitan was Polybius the historian. In Roman times Megalopolis became an ordinary provincial town (Strabo, p. 388).

Paus. 8. 27. 30–2; Diod. 15. 72. *Excavations at Megalopolis, 1890–1* (British School at Athens); E. Fiechter, *Das Theater in Megalopolis* (1931).   T. J. D.

MEGARA was a town on the isthmus of Corinth, situated in a fertile but narrow plain between Mts. Geranea, Cithaeron, and Cerata, which separated it from Corinthia, Boeotia, and Attica respectively. Its communications with the Corinthian Gulf were difficult, but it had good harbours on the Saronic Gulf, and it was of some importance as a land of passage between Peloponnesus and central Greece.

Between 730 and 550 B.C. Megara displayed considerable colonizing activity. Its chief daughter-cities were Megara Hyblaea in Sicily, Chalcedon and Byzantium on the Bosporus, and Heraclea Pontica in Bithynia. To this period we may also assign the rise of its extensive woollen industry. But c. 600 B.C. it came under the rule of a tyrant (see THEAGENES), and it subsequently fell a prey to domestic strife. Consequently it lost its western region, the Peraea Chora, to Corinth, and Salamis to Athens. Shortly before 500 it joined the Peloponnesian League, and it played its full part in the Persian Wars. After 460 it became a bone of contention between Athens and Corinth, and an attempt by Pericles to starve it into surrender by the 'Megarian Decree', which laid an embargo upon its Aegean and Pontic trade (432), was an important contributory cause of the Peloponnesian War. In the fourth century it generally contrived, despite its position, to remain detached from the inter-city warfare of the period, and it recovered its early prosperity. It allied with Athens against Philip, but in the Hellenistic period it relapsed into obscurity. Megara was the temporary seat of the Socratic school of philosophers and is commonly believed to have been the home of the poet Theognis (q.v. 1).

E. L. Highbarger, *The History and Civilisation of Ancient Megara* (U.S.A. 1927); Ernst Meyer, *PW*, s.v.   M. C.

MEGARIAN SCHOOL, THE, founded at an uncertain date by Eucleides (q.v. 1) of Megara, the companion of Socrates and a somewhat older contemporary of Plato's. It is not known what form the school took, but it seems probable that it was not a corporate body and it does not appear to have survived as a school for long after the immediate successors of Eucleides. It adopted the doctrines of Parmenides and the Eleatics. Its members seem to have used this doctrine primarily as a basis for criticism of other schools. They developed a reputation for their skill in dialectical argument and were known for the invention of some ingenious sophisms. There are some indications also of contributions to ethical theory, but the exact nature of these is uncertain.

Histories of Ancient Philosophy, Zeller, ii. 1³. 244–75; Gomperz (Engl. Transl. ii. 170–208); Robin (Engl. Transl. 162–5); G. C. Field, *Plato and his Contemporaries* (1930), ch. 12.   G. C. F.

MEGASTHENES (*fl.* 300 B.C.), an Ionian who wrote on the topography, religion, and customs of India ('Ινδικά). Served on several embassies, 302–291, sent by Seleucus I to the court of the Indian king, Sandrocottus. His Greek background in philosophy and myth made him an unreliable observer, inventing parallels between two quite different cultures. The chief source of Arrian's 'Ινδικά.

FHG ii. 397.   G. L. B.

MEGELLUS, *see* POSTUMIUS (2).

MEIDIAS, potter, in Athens, late fifth century B.C. The 'Meidias painter' who painted for him has a sweet, rich style, often used white for flesh, and added gold for ornaments.

J. D. Beazley, *A.V.* 459; W. Hahland, *Die Vasen um Midias* (1930).

MEILICHAI (μειλίχαι), *see* BOXING.

MELA, LUCIUS (?) ANNAEUS, youngest son of Seneca the Rhetorician, and father of Lucan, was *eques* and financier. Claiming Lucan's property after his death in the Pisonian conspiracy of A.D. 65, he was himself implicated and committed suicide.   E. P. B.

MELA, *see also* POMPONIUS (4).

MELAMPUS (Μελάμπους) (1), prophet, missionary of Dionysus (post-Homeric tradition), and ancestor of the prophetic clan of the Melampodidae. Three principal stories are told of him. (*a*) Serpents licked his ears, and he became able to understand the speech of all creatures (schol. *Od.* 11. 290; Eustath. p. 1685, 25). (*b*) His brother Bias wished to marry Pero, whose father Neleus demanded as bride-price the cattle of Iphiclus son of Phylacus, which had been taken by him from Neleus' mother Tyro. Melampus undertook to get them, was caught and imprisoned, but so impressed his jailer by foreseeing the fall of a roof, which he had heard of from the wood-worms, that Iphiclus, hearing of it, promised him the cattle if Melampus could discover why he was childless. By questioning a vulture, Melampus discovered that Iphiclus' father had unwittingly worked a charm of impotence against him. All was thus settled satisfactorily (*Od.* 11. 287 ff. and scholia). (*c*) He cured the daughters of Proetus (q.v.) of their madness.

See further Wolff in Roscher's *Lexikon*, s.v., Pley in *PW*, s.v., and art. DIVINATION.   H. J. R.

MELAMPUS (2), author of two extant works on divination, Περὶ παλμῶν μαντική (ed. H. Diels, *Abh. Berl. Akad.* 1907) and Περὶ ἐλαιῶν τοῦ σώματος (ed. J. G. F. Franz, *Scriptores Physiognomoniae Veteres*, 1780).

PW xv. 399.

MELANIPPIDES, dithyrambic poet, of Melos. Suidas distinguishes two poets of the name, but there was probably only one, who was active from c. 480 B.C. to his death at the court of Perdiccas of Macedon (Suid. s.v. Μελανιππίδης). His fame is attested by Xenophon (*Mem.* 1. 4. 3). He altered the structure of the Dithyramb by introducing ἀναβολαί, or lyric solos, instead of the antistrophe (Arist. *Rh.* 3. 9) and is mentioned by Pherecrates (fr. 145) as the first corrupter of the art of music (*see* MUSIC, § 10). His scanty remains are of a *Danaides*, a *Marsyas*, in which Athene flings away her flute in disgust because of its effect on her cheeks (fr. 3), and a *Persephone*. Meleager included some poems of his in his *Garland* (*Anth. Pal.* 4. 1. 7) and calls them Hymns.

Text: E. Diehl, *Anth. Lyr. Graec.* ii. 153–4. Criticism: A. W. Pickard-Cambridge, *Dithyramb, Tragedy, and Comedy* (1927), 55–8.   C. M. B.

MELANIPPUS, in mythology, one of the Theban champions opposed to the Seven (cf. ADRASTUS; Aesch. *Septem*, 414 and often). He was one of the Sparti (cf

CADMUS) by descent (ibid.); in Aeschylus he defends the Gate of Proetus against Tydeus (q.v.). His father was Astacus. He succeeded in wounding Tydeus mortally, but the latter with a final effort killed him and, in dying, asked for the head of his opponent. This was brought him by Amphiaraus, who hated him, or Capaneus, and he gnawed it. Thereupon Athena, who had intended to make him immortal for his valour, turned away in horror and Tydeus died.

See Apollod. 3. 75–6; Statius, *Theb.* 8. 716 ff. For Melanippus' cult see Farnell, *Hero-Cults*, p. 335. H. J. R.

MELANTHIUS (1) (5th c. B.C.), a minor tragic poet of Athens, who wrote an elegiac poem in honour of Cimon. The comic poets attack his gluttony, effeminacy, and other defects (Ath. 8. 343 c). One of his plays was a *Medea*.

TGF 460. A. W. P.-C.

MELANTHIUS (2) (4th c. B.C.), painter. Pupil of Pamphilus (q.v.), whom he probably succeeded as head of the Sicyonian school. The picture of Aristratus in his victorious chariot was painted by 'all those about Melanthius' including Apelles; no other work by him is mentioned. Apelles admitted his superiority in composition. He wrote on painting, and said that works of art, like characters, should show a certain stubbornness and harshness (in contrast to Apelles' boasted 'charm').

T. B. L. W.

MELANTHIUS (3) (4th c. B.C.), an atthidographer who also wrote on the Eleusinian mysteries.

FHG iv. 444.

MELEAGER (Μελέαγρος) (1), in mythology, son of Oeneus (q.v.), or of Ares (Hyginus, *Fab.* 14. 16; 171. 1), and the former's wife Althaea. His story is told in two different forms, the Homeric and the non-Homeric; the former is typical epic, the latter typical folk-tale with the motif of a life-token (Stith Thompson, E 765. 1. 2). In the former he is a valiant warrior, whose aid is desperately needed when the Curetes (q.v.) attack Calydon. Being angry with his mother, who had cursed him 'for the slaying of her brother' (*Iliad* 9. 567; see the whole passage), he refused to defend the city, till at last he yielded to the entreaties of his wife Cleopatra, daughter of Idas (q.v.) and Marpessa. Homer also says (ibid. 533 ff.) that Oeneus forgot to sacrifice to Artemis, and she therefore sent a great wild boar to ravage the country; Meleager then gathered huntsmen and hounds from many cities and killed the boar. Elsewhere (*Il.* 2. 642) it is mentioned in passing that he was dead by the time of the Trojan War, but nothing is said of the manner of his death. In the *Ehoiai* (fr. 135, 12 Rzach) Meleager is killed by Apollo in battle with the Curetes; the text is very fragmentary, but cf. Paus. 10. 31. 3. This, then, continues the Homeric or normal heroic tradition. The other story cannot be traced further back than Phrynichus the tragedian (q.v. 1; fr. 6 Nauck, from Paus. ibid. 4). As told by later writers (e.g. Apollod. 1. 65 ff.; ultimately from Euripides' *Meleager*?) it runs thus. When the boar-hunt began, Atalanta (q.v.) was the first to wound the beast. Meleager, who loved her, adjudged her the spoils when he himself killed the boar. His mother's brothers tried to take them from her and Meleager killed them. Althaea then had recourse to her power over his life. Shortly after his birth, the Moirai had come to the room and said that he should live until a brand then on the fire burned away; this is a theme which might be found in a modern Greek story, the belief in these spirits of birth being still prevalent. Althaea quenched the brand and put it in a chest; now, hearing of the death of her brothers, she took it out and burned it, and Meleager died.

Bacchylides (5. 93 ff.) combines the two versions; the Curetes and Aetolians fought over the boar's spoils (as in Homer, op. cit. 547 ff.); in the mêlée Meleager accidentally killed his uncles, but Althaea did not reflect that it was an accident, and so brought about his death by means of the brand.

Since the name of the guinea-fowl, μελεαγρίς, suggests that of Meleager, a story grew up (see Thompson, *Gloss. Gk. Birds*[2], p. 199) that his sisters turned into them.

MELEAGER (2) (c. 140–c. 70 B.C.), poet and philosopher, lived mainly in Tyre and Cos. His Menippean satires, Cynic sermons in prose mingled with verse, are lost. But he was also a master of the epigram and constructed the first large critical anthology of epigrams, calling it his *Garland*—see his charming introduction, likening each poet to an appropriate flower (*Anth. Pal.* 4. 1). In the *Anthology* there are some 130 of M.'s own epigrams, nearly all on love. Their ornate diction and complex style are akin to the flamboyant rhetoric of Asia Minor; they introduce every traditional erotic image and vary and interchange them with astonishing skill, yet not without true emotion. *See* ANTHOLOGY, EPIGRAM, § 1, para. 3, *and* CYNICS.

K. Radinger, *Meleagros v. Gadara* (1895); F. A. Wright, *Poems of M. translated* (1924). G. H.

MELETUS (1) (5th c. B.C.), an Athenian tragic poet, attacked by contemporary comic poets for his dullness (Suidas, s.v., schol. Ar. *Ran.* 1302, etc.), his immorality, and his starveling appearance, composed a tetralogy on the Story of Oedipus (schol. Plato, p. 839 a 14, quoting the Διδασκαλίαι of Aristotle); probably identified wrongly with the accuser of Socrates in 399 B.C. (see art. 'Meletus' in *PW* xv. 503). A. W. P.-C.

MELETUS (2), probably son of (1) above; the titular accuser of Socrates in 399. But he was then quite young, and was probably the tool of Anytus, who was Socrates' real opponent. The story that he was later put to death by the Athenians is doubtful. He is apparently not identical with the Meletus who in 399 accused Andocides of impiety.

PW xv. 503. W. D. R.

MELICERTES, see ATHAMAS, LEUCOTHEA.

MELINNO, authoress of a poem in five sapphic stanzas on the world-power of Rome, quoted by Stobaeus (3. 7), who calls her a Lesbian. Her dialect is Doric, and it is more likely that she came from some town of Magna Graecia which had been conquered by the Romans. Her date is much disputed. Some think that the similarity of her sentiments to those of Horace and the cult of 'Roma aeterna' point to the Imperial age, while others claim that the absence of any mention of a *princeps* points to Republican Rome, even so early as the Punic Wars. There is no need to assume that she was influenced by Latin poetry.

Text: E. Diehl, *Anth. Lyr. Graec.* ii. 315–16. Criticism: F. G. Welcker, *Kleine Schriften* (1845) ii. 160–8. C. M. B.

MELISSA (Μέλισσα, Bee). Like its Hebrew equivalent Deborah, this is occasionally found as a proper name, also as a title, especially of priestesses of Demeter (according to schol. Pind. *Pyth.* 4. 104); of Artemis (Aesch. fr. 87 Nauck); of Rhea (Didymus quoted below), besides the Asianic cult of the Ephesian Artemis, whose regular symbol is a bee; that, however, her priestesses were called *melissai* is not quite certain, see Ch. Picard, *Éphèse et Claros*, 183 f. One or two minor heroines of mythology are so named, the least unknown being the sister of Amalthea (q.v.); both were daughters of Melisseus king of Crete, who was the first to sacrifice to the gods. While her sister fed the infant Zeus with milk, she provided honey for him, and was afterwards made the first priestess of the Great Mother, meaning presumably Rhea (Didymus in Lactant. *Divin. Inst.* 1. 22, from his commentary on Pindar, the source probably of the above scholion). Columella (*De Re Rust.* 9. 2. 3) mentions a 'very beautiful woman Melissa whom Iuppiter turned into a bee', generally taken to refer to the same story. *See* HONEY.

H. J. R.

MELISSUS (1) of Samos commanded the Samian troops against Athens in 442-440 B.C., and after defeating Pericles was himself defeated. He was the last member of the Eleatic school of philosophy, differing from Parmenides in maintaining the spatial infinity of the universe. The extant fragments of his work Περὶ φύσεως ἢ περὶ τοῦ ὄντος defend Eleaticism against Empedocles' doctrine of the four elements, against the Atomists' belief in a void, against Anaximenes' derivation of the world from its original matter by rarefaction and condensation, and against Anaxagoras' assumption of the reality of heat and cold. Testimonia and frs. in Diels, *Vorsokr.*[5] i. 258-76.

PW xv. 530. W. D. R.

MELISSUS (2), GAIUS, Maecenas' freedman, invented a form of light drama in the *fabula trabeata*, whose characters were equestrian. He compiled a book of jests (*ineptiae*, Suet. *Gram.* 21) and was possibly the Melissus quoted several times by Pliny on natural history.

MELISSUS (3), AELIUS, contemporary with Gellius, who cites his *De loquendi proprietate* (18. 6. 1).

MELITA, nowadays *Malta*, a strategically situated island between Sicily and Africa with interesting megalithic monuments and excellent harbours. Phoenicians colonized Melita shortly after 1000 B.C. Later (6th c. B.C. ?) Carthage acquired it, only to lose it in 218, when Melita became a Roman ally administered by the governor of Sicily. Subsequently, although Phoenician was still spoken, Melita acquired Roman citizenship. Despite its barren and waterless condition Melita has always enjoyed industrial and commercial prosperity. Hannibal was possibly born and St. Paul was shipwrecked here.

Strabo 6. 277 (inaccurate); Pliny, *HN* 3. 92; Diod. 5. 12; Livy 21. 51; Cic. *Verr.* passim. A. Mayr, *Die Insel Malta im Altertum* (1909); T. Zammit, *Malta* (Malta, 1926); L. Viviani, *Storia di Malta* (2 vols., 1933-4); C. Seltman, *Num. Chron.* 1946, 81. E. T. S.

MELOS, with Thera, the most southerly of the Sporades. The island was celebrated in neolithic times for its monopoly of obsidian, which was exported all over the Aegean area. There was a rich deposit at Phylakopi, where successive sites were occupied from the Early Minoan period; the examination of these sites has thrown most light on the early history of the Cyclades. When the demand for obsidian in the Bronze Age decreased the wealth of Melos declined. In the Dorian migration it was colonized from Laconia. In 480 the inhabitants sent a contingent of ships to Salamis. They were not, however, members of the Delian Confederacy, and remained neutral at the outbreak of the Peloponnesian War. Nicias attacked them in 426, and ten years later they were brutally enslaved by the Athenians, who established a cleruchy on the island.

Thuc. 5. 87-111. Bursian, ii. 496 ff.; C. Smith, etc., *Excavations at Phylakopi in Melos* (1904), *BSA* iv; cf. ibid. xvii. 1 ff. W. A. L.

MEMBRANA, in sense of parchment, *see* BOOKS, II, paras. 2 and 4.

MEMMIUS (1), GAIUS, a prominent democrat, who as tribune (111 B.C.) led the agitation against the Optimate leaders, many of whom (e.g. Bestia) had shared in Opimius' severities of 121. He carried a proposal to send L. Cassius Longinus, then praetor, to Numidia to induce Jugurtha to visit Rome under a safe-conduct. He was praetor during the period of coalition of *Equites* and *Populares* (104), and as candidate for the consulship of 99 was a rival of the extremist Glaucia. Saturninus had him murdered, and thus precipitated the crisis that led to his own destruction. M. H.

MEMMIUS (2), GAIUS, husband of Sulla's daughter Fausta Cornelia, opposed the demand of L. Lucullus for a triumph (66 B.C.). In 58 he was, as a praetor, hostile to Caesar. In 57, as propraetor in Bithynia, he took with him the poets C. Helvius Cinna and Catullus. To him the *De Rerum Natura* of Lucretius is dedicated. In 55 he divorced Fausta and supported Caesar, but was compromised in the electioneering scandal of 53 and was exiled. In 49 he returned to Italy. A. M.

MEMMIUS (3) **REGULUS,** PUBLIUS (*cos.* A.D. 31), of undistinguished ancestry. He governed Moesia, Macedonia, and Achaea from 35 until the early years of Claudius' principate. In 38 he was compelled to divorce his wife, the wealthy Lollia Paulina, in order that Gaius might marry her. He was proconsul of Asia under Claudius and died in 61. J. P. B.

MEMNON (1), a mythical king of Ethiopia, was the son of Eos and Tithonus. He went to Troy to the aid of his uncle Priam, killed Antilochus, and was himself slain by Achilles, after which Zeus rendered him immortal. The legend of Memnon was probably first set forth in the *Aethiopis*, one of the lost poems of the Trojan cycle. The myth is mentioned in the *Odyssey* and by Hesiod, Alcman, and Pindar. Several of the dramatists treated the legend in plays now lost, and other writers refer to it frequently. Aeschylus associates Memnon with Susa, as does Herodotus, while Diodorus (using Ctesias) relates that Memnon was sent by Teutamus king of Assyria with a force of Ethiopians and Susans to the aid of Priam. Strabo and Pausanias likewise, following Herodotus, regard Susa as the city of Memnon. On his march to Troy Memnon was said to have left several great *stelae* along his route, and Herodotus notes that this has caused him to be confused with Sesostris. In spite of reference to Susa and the 'Ethiopians of Asia', there are unmistakable traces of Memnon's being localized in Egypt and Ethiopia. There was a Memnoneion in Thebes which gave its name to a part of the city, and another at Abydos, the latter really a temple built for Osiris by Seti I. During the Ptolemaic period incubation was practised in the Memnoneion at Abydos and *katochoi* attached to the worship of Isis and Sarapis resided there. In Roman times a peculiar cult and oracle of Bes had its location there. The colossi of Memnon whose stones, before the restoration of the statues, were said to sing at dawn, once stood before the temple of a king and are inscribed with the name of Amenhotep III. There have been many attempts to interpret the legend of Memnon. Several modern authorities believe him to have been a Hittite leader.

R. Holland, art. 'Memnon' in Roscher's *Lexikon*; P. Perdrizet, G. Lefebvre, *Les Graffites grecs du Memnonion d'Abydos* (1919); A. Wiedemann, *Herodots Zweites Buch* (1890). T. A. B.

MEMNON (2), a Rhodian of the 4th c. B.C., began his career as a mercenary leader with his elder brother Mentor (q.v. 2). After the failure of Artabazus' revolt (353 B.C.) Memnon stayed with Mentor, and after his death he married his widow Barsine (later Alexander's mistress) and succeeded him as Persian general in Asia Minor. In 336 he fought successfully against Philip's generals. In 334 his ingenious plan to retire before Alexander, to waste the country, and to fight on sea, was rejected by the satraps. He took part in the battle of Granicus and escaped. Appointed commander-in-chief by Darius, he organized the maritime war and occupied several Greek islands, hoping to make the Greeks revolt (333). He died suddenly, a severe loss for Persia.

Arrian, *Anab.* bks. 1 and 2; Diod. bks. 16 and 17. H. W. Parke, *Greek Mercenary Soldiers* (1933); Berve ii, no. 497. V. E.

MEMNON (3) of Heraclea Pontica, after Caesar and probably before Hadrian, wrote the history of his city in at least sixteen books, perhaps following Nymphis; bks. 9–16 are substantially preserved by Photius. Book 13 had a long digression on the rise of Rome, and in general the wider issues in which the city was involved were treated. The remains allow study of the methods and style of Hellenistic local chronicle.

FHG iii. 525. A. H. McD.

MEMOIRS, see BIOGRAPHY.

MEMOR, ?SCAEVA (?*Scaev*(*i*)*us*), a writer of tragedies (lost), contemporary with Martial, who composed an elegiac distich on his statue. His brother Turnus was a well-known satirist (Mart. 11. 9 and 10).

MEMPHIS, the traditional centre of Lower Egypt, was naturally the scene of Alexander's installation; it continued populous till the Roman conquest, being ranked by Strabo second to Alexandria. The fortification of Babylon, across the river, as a legionary camp under Augustus probably started its decline, and it sank to a provincial metropolis. Its importance under the Ptolemies was due largely to the cult of the Serapeum, which the religious policy of Augustus would not favour. There are few remains of Graeco-Roman buildings; the walls of the camp of Babylon stand amongst the houses of Old Cairo.

U. Wilcken, 'Das Serapeum von Memphis', *UPZ* i. 7; A. J. Butler, *Babylon of Egypt* (1894). J. G. M.

MEN (Μήν), a Phrygian god, worshipped throughout Anatolia (cf. Strabo 557, 577, 580). He frequently bears a crescent moon behind his shoulders, or the crescent alone may represent him. The native form of his name was Man(n)es, and his lunar associations, if not original, may be due to a confusion with the Greek μήν. In some respects he seems merely the counterpart of Attis. Both celestial (Οὐράνιος) and chthonic (Καταχθόνιος), he was invoked also as Lord (Τύραννος) and by numerous titles, such as *M. Ἀσκαηνός, M. Κάρου, M. Φαρνάκου, M. Τιάμου* (perhaps = Καταχθόνιος), found chiefly in restricted localities. He was a healing god, a protector of tombs, and a giver of oracles. Metics or slaves worshipped M. in Attica from the fourth or third century B.C., but elsewhere in Greece only isolated inscriptions of Rhodes, Delos, and Thasos attest his cult. At Rome and Ostia a series of inscriptions to Attis Menotyrannus have been found.

In addition to the general articles (s.v.) in Roscher, *Lex.* and *PW,* see the accounts of the shrine at Pisidian Antioch in *JHS* 1912 and *JRS* 1913 and 1918. F. R. W.

MENAECHMUS (*fl. c.* 350 B.C.), pupil of Eudoxus and friend of Plato, discovered the three conic sections and with the help of two of them solved the problem of doubling the cube. None of his works are extant.

PW xv. 700.

MENANDER (Μένανδρος) (1) (342/1–291/90 B.C.), of Athens, 'star' of the New Comedy. His parents were of distinguished class—Diopeithes of Cephisia and Hegesistrate; he was trained in philosophy by association with Epicurus (his συνέφηβος) and initiated by Alexis (q.v.) into the art of comedy-writing. For some thirty years after his first play, Ὀργή, 321 B.C., Menander produced a series of over 100 comedies (few to be exactly dated—as Ἴμβριοι, 301 B.C.), of which about 98 (including Νέμεσις and Χρηστή—see Körte, *Men. Rel.* i. 150) are known by name. His comedies (like those of Philemon, q.v.) were

revived on the Athenian stage after his time (e.g. Φάσμα 167 B.C.) and held a place upon the Roman stage.

2. No complete comedy is extant, but on papyrus we have recovered several connected scenes of different plays, from which Menander's dramatic technique may be estimated. Of Ἐπιτρέποντες, *The Arbitration*—an example of Menander's mature art—we possess nearly two-thirds, and in spite of lacunae the essential features of plot and characterization are known. Of *Perikeiromene, The Rape of the Ringlets* (c. 313 B.C.), about two-fifths survive, and some details of the treatment remain uncertain. Of *Samia* (an early comedy) we have 341 verses from the second half of the play, which reveal much of the plot. Of *Hērōs* little more than one scene is known and the outline of the plot; and plots can be partially sketched of *Fabula Incerta, Γεωργός, Θεοφορουμένη* (*The Maiden Possessed*), Κιθαριστής, Κόλαξ, Κωνειαζόμεναι (*Women Drinking Hemlock*), Μισούμενος (*The Hated Lover*), Περινθία, Φάσμα, and another unnamed play, *PSI* ii. 126, 'the Florentine Comedy'. For discussion of these plots see Körte, *PW*, s.v. 'Menandros', and *Men. Rel.* i. praef.; G. Norwood, *Greek Comedy*; G. Murray, in *Aristophanes*.

3. In the Latin adaptations of Plautus (*Stichus, Bacchides, Cistellaria*; probably *Poenulus* and *Aulularia*) and especially of Terence (*Adelphoe, Andria, Heauton Timoroumenos, Eunuchus*) it is mainly Menander's technique that is seen, despite the Roman poets' interpolations and alterations.

4. The influence of Euripides is manifest in Menander's work: see COMEDY, NEW, and for direct quotations from Euripides see *Epit.* 765 f. Körte and *Com. Flor.* 82 f.

5. Unlike his contemporaries, Menander renounced the treatment of mythological subjects: his plays mirror the life of his own time (Manilius 5. 476, 'qui uitae ostendit uitam chartisque sacrauit'; and cf. Aul. Gell. 2. 23, of a passage in Πλόκιον, *The Necklace*, which Gellius ranked high above the imitation by Caecilius, 'illud Menandri de uita hominum media sumptum, simplex et uerum et delectabile'). Hence the diction must be that of contemporary Athens.

6. The love-plot is the only theme, but with endless variations, leading to one, two, or three marriages at the close. Ingenuity was shown in varying and elaborating the obstacles to the lovers' union (cf. the plot of Φάσμα, *The Apparition*), and desire for novelty led sometimes to extreme complication of plot (Γεωργός). Yet occasionally comedies were very similar (*Andria* and *Perinthia*; see Ter. *Andr. prol.*); and a play might appear in two recensions, α' and β' (Ἀδελφοί, Ἐπίκληρος).

7. Menander's varied and delicate characterization raises him above his contemporaries: his dramatis personae develop as the action proceeds. In the *Epitrepontes* Charisius, Pamphila, Habrotonon are strikingly human in their behaviour, reacting to the situations in which they are placed. Menander vitalizes the traditional roles: his characters usually deviate in certain qualities from the ordinary types. Smicrines (*Epit.*) is more than the conventional miser: where money is not concerned he gives an honest judgement. Polemon (*Perik.*) differs widely from the merely swaggering soldier beloved in Comedy. Davus (*Heros*) is a slave in love, but with noble, self-sacrificing intentions.

8. Menander's easy, natural style (well displayed in fine passages among the old fragments, e.g. fr. 481) is rich in dramatic qualities: speech is adapted to each individual speaker (Plutarch, *Comp. Ar. et Men.* 2. 2). His humour depends either upon the situation as a whole or upon the speaker's character; he uses comic irony (Smicrines in *Epit.*) and farcical humour (e.g. in *Samia*), but of verbal humour there is little—rather the whimsical expression of ideas (frs. 85, 283).

9. Menander's humanity appears in many passages: Menandrean comedy is the fruit of an equable philosophy and a large-hearted sympathy. In the narrow field of domestic tragi-comedy M. with admirable breadth of tolerance displayed the failings and foibles, as well as the nobility, of common men and women, and attained a universality which has influenced the literatures of Rome and of modern Europe.

BIBLIOGRAPHY

LIFE AND WORKS: A. Körte, 'Menandros' in *PW* (1931).
TEXTS: Papyrus fragments: A. Körte, *Menander, Reliquiae*² i (1938). (With commentary) van Leeuwen, *Menandri Fabularum Reliquiae* (1919). (Text of *Epitrepontes*, with commentary) Wilamowitz, *Das Schiedsgericht* (1925). Old fragments in *FCG* iv. 3–374; *CAF* iii. 4–272, with additions in Demiańczuk, *Suppl. Com.* 54–63. Text and translation, F. G. Allinson (Loeb).
CRITICISM: G. Norwood, *Greek Comedy* (1931), ch. 7; G. Murray, *Aristophanes* (1933; chapter on Menander); A. W. Gomme, in *Essays in Greek History and Literature* (1937); Powell and Barber, *New Chapters* i. 66–98 (T. W. Lumb), iii. 167–75 (M. Platnauer).   W. G. W.

MENANDER (2), general of Demetrius of Bactria, married his daughter Agathoclea after his death, successfully withstood Eucratides, and to his own death (*c.* 150–145 B.C.) ruled all Greek India, except the Paropamisadae, from Mathurā to Kathiawar. He carried on Demetrius' policy, and in Indian eyes was a Chakravartiu, a supreme ruler. He was the only successor of Alexander, except Cleopatra VII, who acquired a legend: Buddhists transferred to him stories told of Buddha and Asoka, and the Milindapañha made him a great Buddhist monarch. Certainly he stood close to Buddhism—a political necessity; but almost certainly he was not a Buddhist. *See* DEMETRIUS (7) of Bactria.   W. W. T.

MENANDER (3) of Ephesus compiled from native records, which he translated into Greek, 'the actions which took place under each of the kings [of Phoenicia?] both among the Greeks and the barbarians'. His Tyrian history is cited by Josephus (*AJ* 8. 144–6, *Ap.* 1. 116 ff.).

MENANDER (4) of Laodicea (3rd c. A.D.) wrote commentaries on Hermogenes and Minucianus, also the first of two treatises (Π. ἐπιδεικτικῶν) still extant (Spengel, *Rhet.* iii. 329–446) and associated with his name. He there treats of the kinds of epideictic discourse—hymns to the gods, eulogies of cities, etc.—while the second treatise is concerned with ceremonial addresses to the emperor and other officials.   J. W. H. A.

MENARIA, *see* BALEARES INSULAE.

MENDES, a he-goat represented usually on monuments as a ram, and identified by Herodotus and other Greeks with Pan, was worshipped in the Egyptian city of Mendes. The cult attained national prominence in the Ptolemaic period. The great Mendes stele (*Zeitschrift für ägyptische Sprache und Altertumskunde* xiii (1875), 33–40) refers to Ptolemy II 'son of the great living goat of Mendes' as having visited the temple 'as the kings before him had done'. The deceased queen Arsinoë II is called 'Arsinoë Philadelphus beloved by the goat', and her deification throughout the land is described. The stele also notes that the province of Mendes paid no taxes to the king but used its revenues for the worship of the god. The completion of the temple and the attendant celebration, the discovery of a new sacred animal, and various feasts and processions are mentioned.   T. A. B.

MENECRATES (1) of Xanthus, a fourth-century writer of the history of Lycia (Λυκιακά) in Ionic.

MENECRATES (2) of Ephesus, probably born *c.* 340, wrote a didactic poem called *Erga* in imitation of Hesiod, and probably another poem on Apiculture (*Melissurgica*).

Texts: H. Diels, *PPF* (1901), 171–2. Göbel, 'Menekrates (16)', in *PW* xv. 800

MENEDEMUS (1) of Eretria (*c.* 319–*c.* 265 B.C.; Beloch, *Griech. Gesch.* iv. 2². 461 f.), statesman and founder of the Eretrian philosophical school. He was a pupil of Stilpo, and later of Phaedon's followers in Elis (Diog. Laert. 2. 216). When he returned to Eretria he founded a school of his own and henceforward taught and took part in the administration of his city. At the age of 74 he is believed to have committed suicide from grief at his native town's loss of freedom. As a philosopher M. pursued the methods and doctrines of the Megarian School.

C. Mallet, *Histoire de l'école de Mégare*, etc. (1845); E. Zeller, *Socrates*³, Engl. Transl., 282; U. von Wilamowitz, *Antigonos von Karystos*, 86, 142 f.; Ueberweg-Praechter, *Grundriss*¹², 158; *PW* xv. 788.   K. O. B.

MENEDEMUS (2), Cynic philosopher of the third century B.C., from western Asia Minor, first a pupil of Colotes the Epicurean, later of Echecles the Cynic, both of Lampsacus. He is best known from Colotes' polemic against him.

PW xv. 794.

MENELAUS (1) (Μενέλαος, Μενέλεως), younger brother of Agamemnon (q.v.) and husband of Helen (q.v.). In all literature, beginning with Homer, Paris' kidnapping of his wife causes the Trojan War. In the *Iliad* he appears prominently in 3. 21 ff. (Paris avoids him, 96 ff.; he agrees to settle the dispute by a duel with Paris, defeats him, but is prevented by Aphrodite from killing him). In 4. 86 ff. Athena instigates Pandarus (q.v.) to wound him, in order to prevent the war from ending; he is slightly hurt, but cured by Machaon (q.v.). In 17. 1 ff. he distinguishes himself in the fighting over the body of Patroclus; elsewhere he is usually rather in the background, being inferior to Agamemnon in prowess and deliberately holding back (10. 121 ff.) so as not to seem to thrust himself before his greater brother. In the *Odyssey* he is seen safe at home with Helen after a long series of adventures on his return (4. 1 ff.) and is promised Elysium (4. 561 ff.).

Post-Homeric accounts supply details of his life before and after the period covered by the Homeric poems. He had previously met Paris (q.v.) at Delphi, and the oracle had warned them, but they had not understood (schol. *Il.* 5. 64). He was in Crete when Helen was carried off, and was warned by Iris of what had happened, *Cypria* (Photius). For his reunion with Helen after Troy fell see the same source. In Euripides' *Helena*, which follows Stesichorus' version of the story, Menelaus comes with the phantom Helen to Egypt, is shipwrecked, and meets the real one outside the palace of Theoclymenus, son of Proteus, who has been humanized into a Pharaoh. She has taken refuge at Proteus' tomb to avoid being forced to marry Theoclymenus. After a half-comic scene in which Menelaus realizes the situation, they plot with Theonoë, Theoclymenus' sister, to escape. Helen tells the king Menelaus is drowned, and gets the use of a ship to perform funeral rites at sea. Menelaus' men overpower the crew and sail away with him and her, the Dioscuri forbidding Theoclymenus to pursue.

For his cult as hero and occasionally as god see Farnell, *Hero-Cults*, 322 f.   H. J. R.

MENELAUS (2), sculptor, working in the first century A.D. Known from signature on group of Orestes and Electra in the Terme (Winter, *KB* 394. 4), for which he has adapted motives of the fourth century B.C., but Orestes wears his cloak Roman fashion. He called himself pupil of Stephanus, who signed a statue of a youth in the style of the early fifth century (Winter, *KB* 394. 3). Stephanus was the pupil of Pasiteles, a south Italian Greek sculptor who became a Roman citizen in 89 B.C. and wrote a book on notable works of art. M. has been identified with M. Cossutius Menelaus who signed a lost statue. The Cossutii had a workshop of long standing in Paros, and another of their freedmen, M. Cossutius Cerdo, made the two Polyclitan Pans in the British Museum.

G. Lippold, *Kopien und Umbildungen* (1923), 40; O. Rubensohn, *JDAI* 1935, 56. T. B. L. W.

MENELAUS (3) of Alexandria, mathematician and astronomer, made an observation in Rome, A.D. 98, which is mentioned by Ptolemy (vol. ii, p. 30 Heib.). His *Sphaerica* in three books is extant in Arabic; it was translated by Gerhard of Cremona (1114–87), edited by Halley (1758), and is now adequately reproduced in Björnbo's *Studien über Menelaos' Sphärik*, (*Abh. z. Gesch. d. Math.* xiv, 1902). In it we find the first conception and definition of a 'spherical triangle' (τρίπλευρον), 'Menelaus' Theorem' for the sphere, and the solution of spherical triangles by means of it. Book 1 gives the main propositions about spherical triangles corresponding to Euclid's about plane triangles. Book 3 contains spherical trigonometry. Menelaus wrote also six books on Chords in a Circle.

T. L. Heath, *History of Greek Mathematics* ii. 260–73. T. H.

MENENIUS AGRIPPA reputedly appeased the plebeians and brought them back to Rome after the first secession by telling them the parable of the Belly and the Limbs (494 B.C.). Menenius and the story are fictitious, but it is difficult to explain the origin and date of the legend, which is either a fable common to the peoples of Aryan stock or the adaptation of an allegorical tale elaborated by Greek sophists.

Ed. Meyer, *Kl. Schriften* i² (1924), 358 ff.; W. Nestle, *Klio* 1927, 350 ff.; E. Skard, *Avhandl. Akad. Oslo* 1931, no. 2, 88 ff. P. T.

MENESTOR, a Greek writer on botany much quoted by Theophrastus. He applied the Pythagorean theory of the opposition of the warm and the cold to plants, dividing these into those which by their warm nature can grow even in water or in the cold parts of the earth, and those which from their cold nature need a warm climate. It has been much discussed whether his explanation of evergreenness by the doctrine of 'warm plants' or that of Empedocles by means of pores is the older, but on the whole it seems that he can be dated between Empedocles and Theophrastus. He may fairly be called the first Greek who made an inductive study of plants.

Testimonia in Diels, *Vorsokr.*⁵ i. 375–6. *PW* xv. 853. W. D. R.

MENEXENUS of Athens, pupil of Socrates, was one of those present at the conversation in prison related in Plato's *Phaedo*. He plays a considerable part in the *Lysis*, and a less prominent one in the dialogue called after him.

PW xv. 858.

MENIPPE, name of a Nereid in Hesiod, *Theog.* 260, and of two or three insignificant heroines, as the mother of Eurystheus (schol. *Iliad* 19. 116, which also gives her several other names); the mother of Orpheus (q.v.), generally a Muse (Tzetzes, *Chil.* I. xii. 306).

MENIPPEAN SATIRE, distinguished by Quintilian (*Inst.* 10. 1. 95) as a separate sort of satire. Ultimately founded on Menippus (q.v. 1), it was characterized by its mixture of prose and verse. In Latin it is represented by Varro, Seneca, and Petronius, and descends to the pedantic fantasia by Martianus Capella (5th c.) and to the French *Satyre Ménippée*.

See J. Wight Duff, *Roman Satire* (1937), ch. 5. J. W. D.

MENIPPUS (1) of Gadara (first half of 3rd c. B.C.), a slave at Sinope, became pupil of the Cynic Metrocles, bought his freedom, and acquired the Theban franchise. Originator of the serio-comic style (σπουδογέλοιον), in which humorous expression was given to philosophical views. His works include Νέκυια (in which he imitated Crates), Διαθῆκαι, Ἐπιστολαὶ κεκομψευμέναι ἀπὸ τοῦ τῶν θεῶν προσώπου, Διογένους πρᾶσις, Συμπόσιον. His prose was interspersed with verses, whether quoted or original is uncertain. He influenced Meleager of Gadara and Lucian, and Varro's *Saturae Menippeae* are adapted from him. *See* IAMBIC POETRY, GREEK.

Diog. Laert. 6. 29, 95, 99–101; C. Wachsmuth, *Corp. poes. ep. graec. lud.* ii. 78–85; R. Helm, *Lucian und Menipp.* (1906). J. D. D.

MENIPPUS (2) of Pergamum (*fl. c.* 20 B.C.), Greek author of Περίπλους τῆς ἐντὸς θαλάσσης (Mediterranean), abridged, corrected, and augmented by Marcian. Bk. 1, Euxine, Sea of Marmora; 2, Mediterranean, north side; 3, south; Palestine, Asia Minor. It gave chiefly names and distances.

GGM I. cxxxv ff., 563 ff.; *PW* xv. 862, 888. E. H. W.

MENO, pupil of Aristotle, author of a doxographical compendium of the older Greek medicine—Ἰατρικὴ συναγωγή. A selection from it is contained in a London papyrus; ed. H. Diels (1893).

PW xv. 927.

MENODORUS (or **MENAS**) was a freedman of Pompey (less probably of Sextus Pompeius) and may previously have been a pirate. He captured Sardinia for Sextus in 40 B.C., but surrendered it to Octavian in 38, was rewarded with equestrian rank, and fought under Calvisius Sabinus in the battle off Cumae. In 36 he returned to Sextus, but being treated with suspicion again deserted. He was killed in the Illyrian campaign of 35.

Appian, *BCiv.* bk. 5; Dio Cassius, bks. 48 and 49. G. W. R.

MENODOTUS (1) of Perinthus, author of a history (Ἑλληνικαὶ πραγματεῖαι) probably beginning *c.* 217 B.C. as a continuation of the histories of Psaon of Plataea or Phylarchus.

FHG iii. 103. *FGrH* ii. 82.

MENODOTUS (2), Samian Greek (?identical with M. of Perinthus, Diod. Sic. 26. 4), wrote (i) Τῶν κατὰ τὴν Σάμον ἐνδόξων ἀναγραφή and (ii) Περὶ τῶν κατὰ τὸ ἱερὸν τῆς Σαμίας Ἥρας.

FHG iii. 105; *FGrH* ii. A. 189.

MENODOTUS (3) of Nicomedia (*fl.* probably *c.* A.D. 120), follower of Pyrrhon, pupil of Antiochus of Ascalon, and leader of the empirical school of medicine. He was a voluminous author, and is often referred to by Galen.

PW xv. 901.

MENOECEUS (Μενοικεύς), in mythology, (1) father of Creon (q.v. 3; Sophocles, *Ant.* 1098 and elsewhere). (2) Creon's son, whose story is best known from Eur. *Phoen.* 905 ff. Tiresias revealed that Thebes could not survive the assault of the Seven unless atonement were made for the killing of the dragon by Cadmus (q.v.); the victim must be one of the Sparti, and unmarried, and no other was available. Menoeceus, despite his father's attempts to save him, killed himself over the dragon's lair. H. J. R.

MENOETIUS (Μενοίτιος), father of Patroclus (q.v.; *Il* 9. 202 and elsewhere). Of what country he was seems to have been uncertain even to Homer: see *Il.* 11. 765–6; 23. 85.

MENS, personified right thinking ('Mens Bona', Propertius 3. 24. 19 and elsewhere; it was her title at Paestum, Wissowa, *RK*² 314). She was vowed a temple, by advice of the Sibylline books, in 217 B.C. after Trasimene (Livy 22. 9. 10; 10. 10; cf. Platner–Ashby, p. 339); it was dedicated two years later (Livy 23. 32. 20). H. J. R.

MENSA, see FURNITURE.

MENTHE (μένθη) or **MINTHE** (μίνθη), i.e. mint. According to Strabo 8, 3. 14, p. 344 (more authorities given by Peter in Roscher's *Lexikon*, s.v.) she was Hades' mistress (a Naiad, daughter of Peitho, Photius s.v.), and Persephone trampled her underfoot, whereat she became the plant named after her, which smells the sweeter when trodden upon.   H. J. R.

MENTOR (1), in mythology, an old Ithacan, friend of Odysseus, who left his household in his charge (*Odyssey* 2. 225 ff.). Athena takes his shape to help Telemachus (ibid. 401 and elsewhere; cf. 24. 548).

MENTOR (2), Rhodian mercenary leader, brother-in-law of the satrap Artabazus (q.v.), whose service he and his brother Memnon (q.v.) entered. He married his niece Barsine, Artabazus' daughter. Both brothers took part in the Satraps' Revolt (362–360 B.C.) and received some territory in Troas. In 353 they fled with Artabazus. Mentor went to Egypt, entered again the king's service, and was general at the conquest of Egypt (343). He rose high in Persian service and was ordered to quell the dynasts of Asia Minor. Among them was Hermeias (q.v.), whom he put to death (342). He had previously obtained the recall of Artabazus and Memnon. He probably died soon after.

Dem. 23. 150 ff.; Diod. 16. 42 ff.; H. W. Parke, *Greek Mercenary Soldiers* (1933).   V. E.

MERCATORES, see COMMERCE, paras. 7 and 11.

MERCENARIES (GREEK AND HELLENISTIC).
(1) *From the earliest times till the Peloponnesian War* (431 B.C.) mercenaries play a small part in Greek warfare, being few in number and not clearly distinguishable from voluntary helpers. They are most frequently mentioned as forming the bodyguards of tyrants. But the early tyrants were often content to enrol citizens and, except in Sicily, did not maintain large armies of professional soldiers. Before the Persian conquests Greek mercenaries were employed to some extent in Egypt and Mesopotamia; afterwards they were mainly used as bodyguards for the satraps of Asia Minor and were largely recruited from Arcadia.
(2) *Till the King's Peace* (386 B.C.). During the Peloponnesian War there grew a demand for auxiliary troops to supplement the ordinary hoplite. These were drawn especially from the backward parts of Greece and from Thrace. The end of the war released many soldiers for professional service, from whom Cyrus raised an army of more than 10,000 hoplites for his attempt on the Persian throne. In the Corinthian War Iphicrates (q.v.), leading a force of peltasts (q.v.), achieved such success that this type of soldier was established as an independent unit. Meanwhile in Sicily Dionysius I was founding an outstandingly powerful tyranny on a large professional army.
(3) *Till Chaeronea* (338 B.C.). The possibilities of using mercenaries were now fully exploited. The Persian satraps hired large armies to oppose the Great King, who replied by employing the same material. In Greece the city-states used mercenaries in their struggles with each other or remodelled their citizen-armies on a professional pattern. Many tyrants of a militaristic type arose, and in the Third Sacred War (356–346) Phocis showed how even a small State could be dominant so long as it had large financial resources. Philip II of Macedon, however, relied on mercenaries only as a supplement to the main body of his citizen army.
(4) *Till Ipsus* (301 B.C.). Alexander employed mercenaries mostly for garrison duty and settlement abroad, and on separate expeditions away from his main column. The Persians until Arbela formed the bulk of their heavy infantry from Greeks. The Diadochi made the nucleus of their armies out of Macedonians, but the bulk of the troops were mercenaries, who were ready to change sides according to the fortunes of war.
(5) *Till Pydna* (168 B.C.). Warfare gradually depended less on foreign soldiers. In the Hellenistic kingdoms a small standing army of professional soldiers was maintained, but newly hired mercenaries were not used to form the main phalanx. In time of need they could reinforce it in other directions. Even barbarians were thus employed with their native equipment.

H. W. Parke, *Greek Mercenary Soldiers from the earliest times to the Battle of Ipsus* (1933); G. T. Griffith, *The Mercenaries of the Hellenistic World* (1935).   H. W. P.

MERCENARIES (ROMAN). Contact with foreign Powers such as Carthage and Macedon exposed Rome's weakness in cavalry and light-armed troops. This deficiency she remedied by obtaining contingents outside Italy which, in contrast with the Italian *Socii*, were called *Auxilia*. Some came from independent allies like Masinissa, others were raised by forced levies or paid as mercenaries. Gallic *Auxilia* served in the First Punic War, 600 Cretan archers fought at Lake Trasimene, Numidian cavalry turned the scale at Zama. During the next two centuries the number and variety of *Auxilia* increased. Spain was a favourite recruiting-ground because of the superiority of the native over the Roman weapons, while Caesar obtained his cavalry from Gaul and Germany, and his archers and slingers from Crete and the Balearic Islands. Under the Principate the *Auxilia* became part of the standing army. *See* AUXILIA.

W. Liebenam, *PW*, s.v. 'Exercitus'.   H. M. D. P.

MERCURIUS (Merqurius, Mirqurios, Mircurios), the god of traders, Roman equivalent of Hermes; indeed, it is highly probable that he is Hermes (q.v.) introduced under a name, or title, suggestive of his commercial activities (cf. *merx, mercari*). He does not appear in the 'calendar of Numa', nor has he a flamen or any other indication of primitive Roman (or Italian) cult. On the other hand, his temple is *extra pomerium*, being on the Aventine overlooking the Circus Maximus (see Platner–Ashby, p. 339); he is worshipped there with a goddess who is in essence the Greek, not the Roman Maia (q.v.), and its dedication day, 15 May, became a festival of merchants (Festus, p. 135, 4 Lindsay). From all this it is generally supposed that his cult is an early example of Greek, or hellenizing, commercial influence, comparable to that of Ceres, Liber, and Libera (*see* CERES); the date of the temple is 495 B.C. Altheim, however, seeks by an ingenious combination to prove that he is an old Graeco-Etruscan deity comparable in functions to the Genius (q.v.; *Griechische Götter*, 39 ff.), and supposes the connexion of the name with *merces* to be a false etymology. It is generally agreed that his ultimate origin is Greek, by whatever route and under whatever circumstances his cult reached Rome; his connexion with trade is equally undoubted. Under the Empire he, like many gods, sometimes takes the title Augustus (see Steuding in Roscher's *Lexikon* ii. 2818; cf. also Nock, *JHS* 48 (1928), 33 f., 41 f.). His identifications with foreign gods (Steuding, 2826 ff.; *see* RELIGION, CELTIC) result from his equivalence with Hermes, also his mythology, save for one or two tales, probably Latin literary inventions.   H. J. R.

MERMNADAE, see LYDIA.

MEROBAUDES, FLAVIUS, a Spaniard, distinguished as soldier and poet. His works include thirty hexameters in praise of Christ, a panegyric on Aëtius, of which fragments contain a prose speech on his second consulship (A.D. 437), and a poem on his third (446). He imitated earlier Spanish writers and Statius' *Silvae*.

Ed. F. Vollmer (1905).   A. S.

MEROË, the 'island' between the junction of the Bahr-el-Abiad with the true Nile and that of the Atbara with the Nile. The city Meroë (*Bakarawiga*), the southern and later the sole capital of the Kings of Napata, was known by hearsay to Herodotus. In the time of Ptolemy II the kingdom became partly hellenized. Despite further exploration of the Nile in Ptolemaic and Roman times (*see* NILE), even Ptolemy knew little beyond Meroë and falsely made the land a true island.

For excavations at Meroë see: E. Budge, *Egyptian Sudan* (1907) and *History of Ethiopia* (1928); J. Garstang, *Meroë* (1911); H. Kees, *PW*, s.v.   E. H. W.

MEROPE (Μερόπη), in mythology, (1) a Pleiad, wife of Sisyphus (q.v.); she is the nearly invisible star of the group, for she hides her face for shame at having married a mortal, while all her sisters mated with gods (see Apollod. 1. 85; Hyg. *Fab.* 192. 5). (2) Wife of Cresphontes king of Messenia; *see* AEPYTUS. (3) Wife of Polybus of Corinth, Oedipus' foster-father (Soph. *OT.* 775); *see* OEDIPUS. (4) Daughter of Oenopion (*see* ORION; Apollod. 1. 25). For more Meropae see Stoll in Roscher's *Lexikon*, s.v.   H. J. R.

MERULA, LUCIUS CORNELIUS, was appointed colleague by the consul Cn. Octavius after the deposition of Cinna (87 B.C.). On Marius' return he resigned the consulship and, anticipating his condemnation, committed suicide.

F. Münzer, *PW* iv. 1407.

MESOPOTAMIA, the country between the Tigris and the Euphrates. The name is generally used to include the whole alluvial country south of the mountains, and the deserts on either side, i.e. the ancient kingdoms of Assyria and Babylonia, modern 'Iraq. Classical writers usually regarded Mesopotamia as excluding Babylonia.

As an important political and commercial link between Syria and Babylonia, Mesopotamia was colonized extensively by the Seleucids. It was a frequent battle-ground of Roman and Parthian armies, and the prosperity of the Greek cities diminished under the Arsacids. Mesopotamia was conquered by Trajan and constituted a Roman province (114–17) but was promptly abandoned by Hadrian. It was again overrun by L. Verus (162–5) and Septimius Severus (197–9) but was not permanently occupied. *See also* OSROËNE.

V. Chapot, *La Frontière de l'Euphrate* (1907); Jones, *Eastern Cities*, ch. 9; H. Schachermeyr, *PW*, s.v.   M. S. D.

MESSAL(L)INA (1), VALERIA, a woman of good family, married Claudius (at some time before his accession in A.D. 41) and bore him a daughter, Octavia, and a son, Britannicus. The influence which she exercised on Claudius' public policy has probably been exaggerated by ancient historians. Her profligacy was notorious in Rome, but apparently unknown to Claudius until, in 48, she celebrated a formal marriage with her paramour, C. Silius. The marriage was no doubt part of a plot against Claudius. The conspiracy was detected by Narcissus (q.v. 2) and Messalina was put to death.   J. P. B.

MESSAL(L)INA (2), STATILIA, third wife of Nero (A.D. 66), who put to death her fourth husband Atticus Vestinus, was perhaps daughter of T. Statilius Taurus (*cos.* 44). She received some divine honours. After Nero's death she maintained a brilliant position. Otho contemplated marriage with her.   A. M.

MESSALLA, see VALERIUS (4), (14), (15), (16).

MESSALLINUS, see VALERIUS (16).

MESSANA (nowadays *Messina*), a Greek colony originally called Zancle, was founded *c.* 725 B.C. on Sicel territory in north-east Sicily with Chalcidian colonists from Cumae, Naxos, and Euboea. Zancle allegedly founded Mylae (717?) and Himera (648); otherwise its early history is virtually unknown. *C.* 493 Samian refugees, backed by Anaxilas of Rhegium, seized Zancle, which was then renamed Messene (Anaxilas is said to have soon replaced these Samians with Messenians). After 461 Messana (the Doric form henceforth prevails), becoming independent of Rhegium, flourished greatly until destroyed by Carthage (396). Rebuilt by Dionysius, it became subject successively to Dion, Hippon, Timoleon, Agathocles. In 288 Agathocles' Campanian mercenaries, Mamertini, seized Messana (which consequently was often called Mamertina) and, when threatened by Hieron, sought aid desperately from Rome and Carthage. Both responded and the ensuing imbroglio provoked the First Punic War. When Rome annexed Sicily Messana became a privileged *civitas foederata* ('maxima et locupletissima' according to Cicero: *Verr.* passim). In Imperial times, although rarely mentioned, Messana was apparently a *municipium* (Pliny, *HN* 3. 88) and, owing to its strategic situation and fine harbour (Charybdis' whirlpool being fortunately outside the shipping lanes), was undoubtedly important. Messana was Euhemerus' birthplace.

Strabo 6. 268 f.; Hdt. 6. 22 f.; 7. 164; Thuc. bks. 4, 5, 6; Paus. 4. 23. 6; Diod. bks. 11–16, 19, 22, 23; Polyb. 1. 7 f. R. Giacomarzi, *Storia dei Mamertini* (1935); J. Bérard, *Bibliogr. topogr.* (1941), 67.   E. T. S.

MESSAPIA = CALABRIA (q.v.).

MESSAPII immigrated into Calabria (q.v.) in the Early Iron Age. Probably they were Illyrians, not Cretans (despite M. Mayer in *PW* xv. 1175 f.). They undoubtedly spoke an Illyrian language: over 200 inscriptions, written *c.* 450–50 B.C. in a Tarentine-Ionic alphabet, survive (J. Whatmough, *Prae-Italic Dialects* ii. 258 f.). The civilized Messapii, strictly speaking neighbours of Tarentum, are scarcely distinguishable from the Calabri (who dwelt near Brundisium) and Sal(l)entini (who inhabited the 'heel' proper); the Apulian Peucetii (= Poediculi) and Daunii, although they supported Tarentum against the Messapii (Strabo 6. 281), also spoke Messapic. These peoples were collectively called Iapyges (Polyb. 3. 88). In 473 B.C. the Messapii defeated Tarentum (Hdt. 7. 170) and in 413 under King Artas supported Athens against Syracuse (Thuc. 7. 33). In 338 they helped to defeat Tarentum's mercenary, Archidamus, but in the Pyrrhic War supported Tarentum and were consequently subjugated by Rome (266: *Acta Triumph.*). Although only casually mentioned thereafter, they were never completely assimilated. Chief towns: Uria, Rudiae, Caelia, Brundisium, Uzentum.

J. Whatmough, *Foundations of Roman Italy* (1937), 111 (with bibliography).   E. T. S.

MESSAPUS, (1) eponym of Messapia in south Italy (Strabo 9. 2. 13). (2) Son of Neptune, an Etruscan, invulnerable to fire and steel, one of Turnus' allies (Verg. *Aen.* 7. 691 ff.; cf. 9. 523; 12. 128).

MESSENE was founded in 369 B.C. to be the capital of Messenia (q.v.). Situated on the western slopes of Mt. Ithome in the lower Messenian plain, its natural strength was reinforced by city-walls (largely preserved) which furnish the finest example of fourth-century fortification on the Greek mainland. Important traces of other public buildings can be seen near the modern village of Mavromati. Attacked unsuccessfully by Demetrius (q.v. 6) of Pharos (214 B.C.), by Philip V of Macedon, and by Nabis of Sparta, it was captured by the forces of the Achaean League under Lycortas (182 B.C.) in revenge for the Messenians' execution of Philopoemen (q.v.). It retained considerable importance under the Roman Empire.   A. M. W.

MESSENIA, the south-west region of Peloponnesus, bounded on the north by Elis, along the lower course of the river Neda, and Arcadia, and on the east by Laconia, where the frontier follows at first the main ridge of Taygetus, but farther south runs to the west of it, and terminates at the river Choerius a few miles south of the head of the Messenian Gulf. (For the disputed territory of the Ager Dentheliates in this region *see* LACONIA.) Whilst west Messenia is a bleak, mountainous region, dominated by Mt. Aegaleos, with its few settlements along the coast (Cyparissia, Coryphasion-Pylos, Mothone, Asine, Corone), the central and eastern region watered by the river Pamisus and its tributaries was more populous, and the lower plain, Μακαρία, was renowned for its fertility.

Recent finds, particularly of beehive tombs, indicate extensive occupation in Late Helladic (Mycenaean) times, on the west coast and in the valley north-west of the upper (Stenyclarus) plain, where a walled town of the same period has been explored. The great palace discovered near Pylos in 1939, with its huge hoard of inscribed clay tablets of Cretan type (*JHS* 1939, 195), may prove to be the house of Nestor, who appears in Homer as lord of west Messenia (the remainder being perhaps ruled by Menelaus).

After the Dorian conquest Messenia came under Cresphontes, whose youngest son Aepytus evicted and slew the usurper Polyphontes and gave his name to the Messenian royal line. After the First and Second Messenian Wars in the eighth and seventh centuries, associated with the heroic but unavailing leadership of Aristodemus and Aristomenes respectively (qq.v.), such inhabitants as had not left the country were, apart from a few communities of *perioeci*, reduced to the status of helots, and their lands occupied by the Spartan nobility. The Third Messenian War, after the great earthquake of 464 B.C., terminated, like the first war, in the surrender of the stronghold of Ithome after a long siege. Granted a safe-conduct, many of the survivors (of the *perioeci* only?) were settled by the Athenians at Naupactus (455). During the Peloponnesian War the Messenian helots were encouraged to sporadic revolts by the Athenian garrison established at Pylos after the victory at Sphacteria (425), in which Messenians from Naupactus played a decisive part. In 369 Messenia recovered its independence with the help of the Theban general Epaminondas. Its subsequent history is bound up with that of its new capital Messene (q.v.).

C. A. Roebuck, *A History of Messenia from 369 to 146 B.C.* (U.S.A. 1941). A. M. W.

MESSENIA (CULTS AND MYTHS). Since the Messenians were in a condition of serfdom between the Third Messenian War and 369 B.C., their religious and mythical traditions were disturbed to a very considerable extent. In their capital the cults as seen by Pausanias suggest partly foreign influence, partly deliberate attempts at revival. He found (4. 31. 6 ff.) temples of Poseidon and Aphrodite, such as any Greek city might have; a cult of Artemis Laphria, imported from Naupactus; shrines of Eileithyia, the Curetes (to whom holocausts of all manner of victims were offered), Demeter, Asclepius, and the local eponymous heroine Messene; also of the national hero Aristomenes, while Zeus was worshipped on Mt. Ithome under the local title Ithomatas. Some of these cults had peculiar legends connecting them with the country and polemizing against myths which claimed them for other regions. Outside the capital the most famous cult, which, however, is of Hellenistic date, is the Mysteries of Andania (Kern, *Relig. der Griechen* iii. 188 ff., and refs.). For a list, with references, of other cults, see Reincke in *PW* xv. 1241 (also ATARGATIS for cult of Syrian goddess).

Most of the legends of the country have come down to us in an excerpt by Pausanias of Rhianus' (q.v.) epic on the Messenian Wars (Paus. 4. 6. 1), mingled with material from other authors, as Myron of Priene (ibid.) and inquiries of his own. It is thus impossible to say how much of what he tells us is really Messenian tradition and how much Rhianus' learned imagination or the conjectures of some antiquarian. The central figure is Aristomenes, and the historical kernel nearly undiscoverable. H. J. R.

MESSIUS, *see* ARUSIANUS and DECIUS (4).

METABUS, *see* CAMILLA.

METAGENES (*fl.* not earlier than 410–400 B.C.; *IG* ii². 2325), writer of Old Comedy. His Φιλοθύτης had a parabasis (fr. 14), which points to a comparatively early date. The Ὅμηρος ἢ Ἀσκηταί mentions (fr. 10) Lycon's betrayal of Naupactus to the Spartans in 400 (Diod. Sic. 14. 34. 2; Paus. 4. 26. 2; 10. 38. 10).

FCG ii. 751 ff.; *CAF* i. 704–10. M. P.

METALLURGY. After extraction from the mine ore must be crushed. The use of grooved stone hammers was common in the west in early Roman times, though iron hammers replaced them slowly. The broken pieces of rock were roughly sorted, all poor and sterile material being rejected. If washing was practised, the ore had to be finely milled. From Egypt there are stone rollers operated on saddle-querns, and the latter occur in Wales and the Balkans; more common and of later date are rotary millstones. Sieves were used to reduce the particles to equal size. Ore, especially when markedly denser than the gangue, can be profitably enriched by washing. This applies especially to gold, whether from placers or veins, and to lead-ore, but was used for ochre and is feasible for pyrites. Washing was often carried out in wooden bowls or cradles. Gold may be caught on rough cloth or fleece, a method attested on the Rhine, and in Colchis, where it gave rise to the Golden Fleece legend. The washing-tables at Laurium were well built and cemented, with several tanks to catch the ore. The washing process would normally be repeated several times.

Sulphide and hydrated ores are best roasted before smelting. Direct evidence for roasting has seldom been found, but certain furnaces are too large for smelting and may have served this purpose. The most primitive smelting-furnaces were banked-up bonfires or holes in the ground. The blast was at first introduced over the rim, but in Gaul some bowl-furnaces have a hole near the base and their height was raised by courses of stones round the lip. This led to the shaft-furnace, a structure often partially sunk in the ground. Vase-paintings of Greek smithies show a high-built shaft whence the bloom was extracted at the base, while the blast was introduced at the back. The shaft-furnace spread fairly rapidly through the west; some in the Jura are thought to be pre-Roman. They probably did not reach England until after the Roman period. Most shaft-furnaces have only one hole at the base, for blast and tapping, though a few in central Europe have six. Whereas in a bowl-furnace only one charge can be smelted at a time, a shaft-furnace admits of continuous production. Fuel and ore can be added down the chimney, and the metal and slag can be tapped at the base. In fact, however, they were probably cooled and demolished frequently. Slag, unless fluxes are skilfully added, will clog the tapping-hole. Only those metals which were liquefied could be tapped. An iron-bloom could be extracted only by destroying the furnace, and the great number of furnaces at some sites shows that each was used only once. The fuel was charcoal, occasionally coal or peat.

After smelting, iron had to be purified by reheating and hammering. During this process it would become slightly steeled. Lead would be cupelled to extract silver; the Romans knew bone-ash cupels, though the more primitive method of skimming the oxidized metal from the surface was used earlier. Copper would be purified and then alloyed and cast into the forms required.

O. Davies, *Roman Mines in Europe* (1935); U. Täckholm, *Studien über den Bergbau der römischen Kaiserzeit* (1937); C. Zschocke and E. Preuschen, *Das urzeitliche Bergbaugebiet von Mühlbach-Bischofshofen* (1932); H. Blümner, *Terminologie und Technologie* iv. 140, 222–7, 330; *Archaeologia* lvii (1900), 113.   O. D.

METAMORPHOSIS.

Though the word itself is not early, it describes a kind of tale quite common in Greek from Homer on, that of a magical or miraculous transformation into a new shape. The origin of such stories may perhaps be sought partly in real or fancied resemblances between inanimate and animate objects (e.g. the snake which in *Iliad* 2. 319 turns to stone may have as its origin a stone which looked like a snake, perhaps a fossil of some kind), partly in resemblances between the movements or cries of a bird or beast and those of human beings (the nightingale's song, for instance, *see* AËDON, PHILOMELA). An aetiological story would then grow up around it. Magicians, moreover, are very commonly supposed to be able to change their own shapes and those of others, and for a like power to be ascribed to gods is quite natural. In some cases we can point to the actual object which started the legend; Pausanias (1. 21. 3) says he has seen the Niobe (q.v.) of Mt. Sipylon (apparently a rock-formation, but see Frazer ad loc.) mentioned in *Il.* 24. 614 ff.; cf. also Paus. 8. 2. 7. Collections of such legends seem to have become popular in Alexandrian times; we know, for instance, of the Ἑτεροιούμενα of Nicander, several times quoted by later writers, and Ovid's surviving *Metamorphoses* draws almost entirely on Greek sources. Hence in the later versions of many legends (see, for instance, AIAS 1) a metamorphosis of some kind is added of which earlier accounts have no trace.

C1. S. Eitrem, *PW* vi A. 893 ff.   H. J. R.

METANIRA (Μετάνειρα), in mythology, wife of Celeus, king of Eleusis; she received Demeter hospitably, but spoiled her plan to make Metanira's child immortal by screaming when she saw him laid on the fire; *see* DEMETER. She had a cult in Eleusis (Paus. 1. 39. 2) near the well where Demeter sat; cf. Athenagoras, *Leg. pro Christ.* 14.

METAURUS, a river in Umbria flowing into the Adriatic Sea, famous as the site of a victory which was Rome's Crowning Mercy of the Hannibalic War (207 B.C.). In this valley Hasdrubal (q.v. 2), who had hoped to join his brother Hannibal, was forced to fight by the Romans, who rolled up his line.

Polybius 11. 1–3; Livy 22. 46–9. Kromayer-Veith, *Antike Schlachtfelder* iii. 424 ff.   H. H. S.

METELLUS (1), LUCIUS CAECILIUS (*cos.* 251 B.C.), thwarted a Carthaginian attack on Panormus, capturing the dreaded enemy war-elephants (250). The elephant was commonly portrayed on coins struck by the Metelli. Metellus was *magister equitum* in Sicily (249), consul II (247), Pontifex Maximus (243–221); he was blinded when saving the Palladium from the burning Temple of Vesta (241) and died in 221.   H. H. S.

METELLUS (2), QUINTUS CAECILIUS (*cos.* 206 B.C.), an orator of note, pronounced a funeral eulogy on his father, Metellus (1) above (Pliny, *HN* 7. 139; Malcovati, *ORF* i. 151). He was an enemy of the poet Naevius (q.v.) and a supporter of Scipio Africanus.

METELLUS (3) **MACEDONICUS,** QUINTUS CAECILIUS (*cos.* 143 B.C.), son of (2) above, fought at Pydna (168 B.C.). Praetor in 148, he crushed Andriscus and began operations against the Achaean League, defeating Critolaus. As consul he suppressed a slave revolt at Minturnae

and opened the Numantine War successfully against the Celtiberians and Vaccaeans (143–142). In 138 he defended L. Aurelius Cotta against Scipio Aemilianus. He first supported Tiberius Gracchus' agrarian policy, but rejected his demagogy. Censor in 131, he proposed compulsory marriage in a celebrated speech *de prole augenda*, quoted by Augustus (Livy, *Per.* 69). In 121 he followed Opimius against Gaius Gracchus. A fine soldier, great senator, and political rival of Scipio Aemilianus, his death in 115 was honoured by four distinguished sons, M. Metellus (*cos.* 115), Q. Balearicus, C. Caprarius (*cos.* 113), L. Diadematus (*cos.* 117). He built the marble temples of Jupiter Stator and Juno Regina and the Porticus Metelli (147).

G. Colin, *Rome et la Grèce* (1905), 609; A. Schulten, *Numantia* i (1914), 353–5; F. Münzer, *Röm. Adelsparteien und Adelsfamilien* (1920), 247; H. Malcovati, *ORF* i (1930), 97, 220.   A. H. McD.

METELLUS (4) **BALEARICUS,** QUINTUS CAECILIUS (*cos* 123 B.C.), a son of (3) above, was censor in 120. He derived his surname from the conquest of the Balearic Isles in 123–121 (*see* BALEARES INSULAE).

METELLUS (5) **DELMATICUS,** LUCIUS CAECILIUS (*cos.* 119 B.C.), son of L. Metellus Calvus (*cos.* 142) and grandson of Metellus (2) above, was father of Caecilia, wife of Sulla. As consul Metellus provoked a war with the Illyrians, one of the few clear cases of 'triumph-hunting'. He vainly opposed the passage of Marius' ballot bill. He was censor (115) with Cn. Domitius Ahenobarbus. In 114, when the *Populares* launched their assault against the *Optimates* by accusing Vestals of unchastity, Metellus as Pontifex Maximus condemned Aemilia but acquitted Licinia and Marcia; whereupon the investigation was transferred to severer hands.   M. H.

METELLUS (6) **NUMIDICUS,** QUINTUS CAECILIUS (*cos.* 109 B.C.), brother of (5) above, was a distinguished commander and leading Optimate. As consul he took command against Jugurtha, after the failure of the brothers Albinus; in two years' campaigns he largely restored the prestige both of Rome and of the Optimate party. After the battle of the River Muthul (probably 109), Jugurtha took to the desert, though certain strongholds in Numidia remained in his officers' hands. Nevertheless, Metellus was replaced in command by his legate and *protégé* Marius (q.v. 1), probably early in 107. This, however, did not prevent Metellus' triumph from improving the Optimates' situation, and their candidate Caepio was elected consul for 106. As censor Metellus tried to exclude Glaucia and Saturninus from the Senate (102). In 100 Metellus went into exile rather than take the oath to maintain Saturninus' Agrarian Law; he was recalled in 99. He is probably the Metellus who is said to have been poisoned in 91 by the tribune Varius.

G. De Sanctis, *Problemi d. stor. antica*, 215 ff.   M. H.

METELLUS (7) **PIUS,** QUINTUS CAECILIUS (*cos.* 80 B.C.), who accompanied his father, Metellus (6), in Numidia and was surnamed Pius for his effort to recall him from exile, was praetor (89 B.C.) and legate in the Social War. Recalled to Rome to fight Marius, he refused to replace the consul Cn. Octavius when invited by the soldiers. Unable to resist Marius, he went to Africa and thence to Liguria. As Sulla's best general, he gained the decisive victory over the Marians at Faventia (82). He was consul with Sulla (80) and campaigned successfully against Sertorius (q.v.) in Spain (79–72), where his movement northwards can be traced in places named after him: Metellinum (*Medellin*), Castra Caecilia (near *Cáceres*), and Vicus Caecilius (north of the Tagus). He 'triumphed' (71), was Pontifex Maximus, and died c. 64.

F. Münzer, *PW* iii. **1221.**   A. M.

METELLUS (8) **CRETICUS,** Quintus Caecilius (*cos.* 69 B.C.), grandson of (3) above and son of C. Metellus Caprarius (*cos.* 113), was a supporter of C. Verres at his trial in 70. In 68–66 he effected the conquest of Crete, which had become an important pirate base. After a set battle near Cydonia he systematically besieged and captured the Cretan towns. His excessive severity to the Cretans provoked an appeal to Pompey (then engaged on his general drive against the Mediterranean pirates), who sent an officer to arrange their amicable surrender. Disregarding Pompey's lieutenant, and even using force against him, Metellus completed the reduction of the Cretan towns. On Pompey's return to Rome Metellus joined the opposition against him, thus driving him into the arms of Caesar.

Drumann–Groebe, *Geschichte Roms* ii (1902), 41–5.   M. C.

METELLUS (9) **CELER,** Quintus Caecilius (*cos.* 60 B.C.), grandson of Metellus (4) above, son of Q. Metellus Nepos (*cos.* 98), and husband of the notorious Clodia. As *praetor urbanus* in 63 he played a prominent part in the trial of Rabirius (q.v. 1) and in the military operations against Catiline. After governing Cisalpine Gaul he was elected consul for 60, when he constantly obstructed the designs of Pompey and his agent the tribune Flavius (Dio 37. 50). Appointed governor of Transalpine Gaul, he died before he reached his province (59). For his relations with Cicero see Cic. *Fam.* 5. 1. 2.   J. M. C.

METELLUS (10) **NEPOS,** Quintus Caecilius (*cos.* 57 B.C.), brother of (9), was a *legatus* of Pompey in the East, and came to Rome as his agent in 63. As tribune (62) he inaugurated a campaign against Cicero's 'unconstitutional' behaviour. Despite the veto of his fellow-tribune Cato, he pressed his proposal that Pompey be recalled from the East to restore order, and was only deterred by the passing of the *senatus consultum ultimum*. He was praetor in 60 and consul in 57, and then proceeded to Hither Spain. Continued unrest in his province provided an excuse for his supersession by Pompey in 55 (Dio 39. 54).   J. M. C.

METELLUS (11) **PIUS (SCIPIO),** Quintus Caecilius (*cos.* 52 B.C.), son of Nasica, adopted by Metellus Pius (*cos.* 80 B.C.), was candidate at the abortive consular elections for 52. Pompey, who then became sole consul and had recently married Scipio's daughter, rescued him from a bribery charge and made him his colleague. Thenceforward Scipio led the attack on Caesar and proposed the decisive motion in Jan. 49. The Senate granted him Syria, whence in 48 he brought two legions to Thessaly; he commanded the centre at Pharsalus. He escaped to Africa and became supreme general in the Bellum Africum. Caesar tried to bribe Scipio before Pharsalus, but detested him, and wrote a brilliantly bitter passage on his activities in Syria (*BCiv.* 3. 31–3). Cicero despised him as a man ignorant of his family tradition (*Att.* 6. 1. 17). But his dying words in reply to the Caesarian soldiers who sought him out after Thapsus, 'Imperator se bene habet', passed into 'Republican' legend (cf. Livy, *Epit.* 114).   G. E. F. C.

METEMPSYCHOSIS, see TRANSMIGRATION.

METEOROLOGY. Although nature and natural phenomena had already been considered at length by the pre-Socratic philosophers, and though the word μετεωρολογία occurs in Plato (*Phdr.* 230 a), it was left to Aristotle to give an exact definition of what was comprised in the subject. In his four epoch-making books on meteorology he distinguished the respective spheres of meteorology and general natural science with great accuracy, confining the term meteorology to the study of the processes, conditions, and phenomena of the atmosphere. Aristotle's work was continued by Theophrastus and the Epicureans,

to whom Lucretius is greatly indebted for the meteorological sections of his poem. Lucretius also made extensive use of Posidonius, who, looking upon meteorology as the doctrine of the structure of the outer and upper world, had fitted it into a system of thought uniting harmoniously matter and spirit. It is still possible to reconstruct Posidonius' meteorological system, since his book was the main source of the two most important contributions to post-Aristotelian meteorology that have survived, namely the *Naturales quaestiones* of Seneca and the poem *Aetna*. After the first century A.D. students of meteorology confined themselves to summarizing and popularizing the discoveries of their forerunners, which, through the Graeco-Byzantine commentators on Aristotle, came to be known to, and to exercise a beneficent influence upon, the scientific achievements of the Arabs.

TEXTS: Aristotle, *Meteorologicorum Lib. IV*, ed. F. H. Fobes (1919); *Aetna*, ed. S. Sudhaus (1898); Alexander Aphrodisiensis' and Johannes Philoponus' commentaries on Aristotle, ed. M. Hayduck (1899, 1901). Useful selections are given in Sir T. L. Heath, *Greek Astronomy* (1932).

GENERAL LITERATURE: O. Gilbert, *Die meteorologischen Theorien des griech. Altertums* (1907); W. Capelle, *PW* Supplt. iv. 315 ff.; H. Strohm, *Untersuch. z. Entwicklungs-Gesch. d. aristot. Meteorologie* (1935); G. Bergsträsser, *Neue meteor. Fragm. d. Theophrast (Sitz. Heidelberg,* ix (1918)).   P. T.

METICS. In Greek States metics (μέτοικοι) were resident aliens who had acquired a definite status distinguishing them from other foreigners and giving them a recognized place in the community. There were commonly three groups of foreigners: temporary visitors, more permanent residents who had not attained the status of metics, and metics. Among the latter, in turn, some were distinguished by grants of special privileges. Metics were found in many States, but those of Athens are best known. There each metic must have a citizen as sponsor (*prostates*), must be registered in the deme in which he resided, and must pay an annual head tax (*metoikion*) amounting to twelve drachmas for a man and six for a woman not a member of the household of a husband or son. They could also be called on to assume liturgies—though not the trierarchy—and contributed to the *eisphorai*, probably more in proportion than citizens. Metics could not contract legal marriages with citizens and could not own houses or land unless they had received *enktesis* through a special grant. In return they had a share in the life of the community and received the protection of the courts, though the exact role of the *prostates* in court procedure remains a matter of dispute. Metics served in the army in separate divisions and were also used as oarsmen in the fleet. The privileges sometimes granted included *enktesis*, remission of financial burdens, equality with citizens in financial matters, and the right to serve alongside of citizens in the army. Metics were important chiefly in commerce and industry.

A. E. Zimmern, *The Greek Commonwealth*[5] (1931), index; M. Clerc, *Les Métèques athéniens* (1893), and *De la condition des étrangers domiciliés dans les différentes cités grecques* (1898); Hommel, *PW*, s.v. 'Metoikoi'.   J. A. O. L.

METIS (Μῆτις), counsel personified. She was the consort of Zeus (Hesiod, *Theog.* 886 ff.) and wisest of gods and men. By the advice of Earth and Heaven Zeus beguiled her into letting him swallow her when she was pregnant, since he knew she would first bear Athena and then another child, very mighty, who should become ruler of the universe. Having swallowed her, he had her always with him to advise him, and Athena (q.v.) was in due time born from his head (924 ff.). The story would seem to be an early and crude blend of myth and allegory.   H. J. R.

METON (Μέτων) of Athens (*fl. c.* 433 B.C.), best known as having introduced, in place of former cycles of eight and of sixteen years, a cycle of nineteen years designed to correlate the lunar month with the solar year by intercalating a 13th lunar month in the 3rd, 5th, 8th, 11th, 13th, 16th, and 19th years of the cycle, and making 110 of the months in the nineteen years 'hollow' months of 29 days, and 125 of them 'full' months of 30 days: $(110 \times 29) + (125 \times 30) = 6940$ days $= 19 \times 365\frac{5}{19}$. The first of these cycles began with the summer solstice of 432 B.C. It is often stated that this calendar was at once generally adopted in Greece, and lasted down to the adoption of the Julian calendar in Imperial times; but its official adoption at Athens can be proved only for the period 338–290. Meton is caricatured in the *Birds* (414 B.C.) with reference to his scheme for geometrical town-planning.

PW xv. 1458. W. D. R.

METRAGYRTES (*Μητραγύρτης*), a mendicant servitor of Cybele. *Metragyrtai* travelled in bands, begging, dancing, and prophesying. They were known to fifth-century Athens, and Cicero (*Leg.* 2. 22 and 40; cf. Dion. Hal. *Ant. Rom.* 2. 19) implies that these *famuli* were tolerated at Rome. They were generally eunuchs (q.v.), the Galli. Similar *agyrtai* (cf. Plato, *Resp.* 364 b) existed in other cults, chiefly Oriental, and Apuleius (*Met.* bks. 8–9) gives a lively picture of those of the *dea Syria*. An inscription of Syria (*BCH* 1897, 59, no. 68) records the collections made on his travels by one such *δοῦλος* of Atargatis (cf. *SEG* vii. 358, 801). *See* ANATOLIAN DEITIES.

H. Graillot, *Le Culte de Cybèle* (1912), ch. 8; L. Ziehen, *Leges Graecorum Sacrae* ii (1906), 301–3, no. 116. F. R. W.

METRE, GREEK

I. GENERAL PRINCIPLES

(1) The ancient metricians, of whom Hephaestion (q.v.) is the chief, do not help us greatly towards an understanding of Greek metric, and it is unlikely that they represent a tradition dating back to the classical period. We are thus mainly dependent on what we can ourselves discover from the poetry. A full appreciation of the Greek metres is rendered extremely difficult for us by the fact that we are accustomed in English verse to rhythms based on stress (which is solely determined by the sense), the differentiation between long and short syllables being virtually obliterated. Greek verse, on the other hand, whether it contained an element of stress or not (see below), is based principally upon a precise differentiation of time values, without the least relation to the sense of the words; and for this there are parallels in the verse of eastern nations. It is very doubtful if our ears, accustomed from childhood to stressed verse, are capable of being trained to a full appreciation of quantitative verse. Further, in two fundamental matters we are left in uncertainty. (*a*) Was there a verse stress (*ictus*) on the 'arses'?* (*b*) To what extent, if any, were the time values inherent in the syllables altered by the music in lyric (sung) verse?

(2) *Ictus.* The case for ictus is mainly based on (*a*) the alleged inconceivability of verse—particularly verse

* In Greek metric long elements, *longa* ('syllables' is an unsuitable term, since we are concerned with the parts of a verse-form, not with the parts of a word), usually alternate with short elements, *brevia*, or with pairs of *brevia* (sometimes, as in the dactylic hexameter and anapaestic dimeter, fused into single long elements, – – for ∪ ∪ or ∪ ∪ –), or with elements in which either a short or a long syllable is allowed, *ancipitia* (e.g. the first element of the iambic metron ⌣ – ∪ –). In the ionic (∪ ∪ – –) and dochmius (∪ – – ∪ –) two *longa* are juxtaposed. In many cases a *longum* may be 'resolved' into two *brevia*, and substitution of ∪ ∪ for *anceps* and *breve* is sometimes allowed (e.g. ∪ ∪ – for ⌣ – or ∪ – in iambics). The Lesbian poets, Sappho and Alcaeus, do not allow the resolution of *longa* or the fusion of *brevia* except in dactylic hexameters.

The term 'arsis', applied to the *longa*, originally (probably) signifies the lifting of the foot, 'thesis', applied to the elements (*brevia* or *ancipitia*) between the *longa*, its placing on the ground. Arsis should therefore mean the weak beat, thesis the strong beat—if such a distinction existed. I follow the modern terminology, which has inverted the meanings of the two terms. Wrong as it is, it has (at least in England) become canonical.

associated with dancing, marching, and other movements of the body—without ictus, (*b*) the alleged difficulty of differentiating between – ∪ ∪ dactyl and – ∪ ∪ anapaest and between long, or between short, elements in a series of longs or of shorts, without ictus, and (*c*) the fact that certain lengthenings of short syllables occur in Homer far more often in arsis than in thesis. The opponents of ictus answer that verse without ictus is found in certain Eastern nations, and that (*b*) may be disposed of by assuming slight variations in the values of long and of short elements. They also point out that there is no evidence in ancient theory for ictus, since this and other terms denoting striking (e.g. *percussio*) were used simply for the marking off of the parts of a verse by beating time, and they infer from this that ictus did not exist—an argument *ex silentio* which is hardly conclusive. Kalinka (Bursian, *Jahresb.* 250. 332–9) sums up the evidence. It is impossible to decide with any certainty between the contending views.

(3) In lyric iambics and trochaics a short element often seems to be omitted, ∪ – ∪ – appearing alongside of – ∪ – or ∪ – – and – ∪ – ∪ of – ∪ – or – – ∪. E.g. Aesch. *Ag.* 385 *βιᾶται δ' ἁ τάλαινα πειθώ*; Eur. *Phoen.* 1025 *χαλαῖσί τ' ὠμοσίτοις*. Sometimes this occurs in two consecutive feet, so that we have – – instead of either ∪ – ∪ – or – ∪ – ∪. E.g. Eur. *Phoen.* 1039 *βροντᾷ δὲ στεναγμός* (– – | – ∪ – ∪). Similarly, by omission of the last long element, we find ∪ ∪ – among minor ionics (∪ ∪ – –). This dropping of an element ('syncopation') is particularly common at the close of a colon, where it is termed 'catalexis' (e.g. ∪ – ∪ – | ∪ – – and – ∪ – ∪ | – ∪ –), 'brachycatalexis' when two elements are omitted (e.g. ∪ – ∪ – | – – and – ∪ – ∪ | – –). Catalexis is common in spoken, as well as in sung, iambics and trochaics. Further, the anapaestic dimeter ∪ ∪ – ∪ ∪ – | ∪ ∪ – ∪ ∪ – has its catalectic form ∪ ∪ – ∪ ∪ – | ∪ ∪ – –, in which *two* short elements are omitted.

Was the time value of the suppressed short element, or elements, actually missing? Or was it supplied by the compensatory lengthening of the following, or preceding, long element? In general, to what extent, if any, did the music alter the time values? These questions cannot be answered with certainty. The remains of ancient Greek music (*see* MUSIC, §§ 11–13) almost all have metrical as well as pitch signs, but they are extremely scanty, and only one, the music to a few dochmiacs from Euripides' *Orestes*, may go back to the fifth century B.C. This records no musical alterations of the metrical values. On the other hand the Seikilos inscription (not earlier than 2nd c. B.C.) provides clear examples of long elements protracted after† missing shorts both in catalexis and earlier in the colon, and the hymns attributable to Mesomedes (early 2nd c. A.D.?) give similar evidence as regards catalexis. (The Berlin paean goes much farther in altering the metrical values of the elements.) Statements of ancient metrists about protraction after missing short elements are thus corroborated for the first century A.D. We have no proof, though the assumption is a reasonable one, that protraction was employed in the fifth century B.C. and earlier.

(4) *Line and colon.* Modern verse is built up of a succession of 'lines', the ending of a line being marked by the end of a word. Greek epic and elegiac verse and the spoken metres of tragedy and comedy are constructed on the same principle. The last element of the line is always a *longum*. For the pause at the end of the line makes the prosodic length of the final syllable indifferent, and thus a short syllable can fill a long element (*syllaba brevis in elemento longo*).

Greek lyric verse, though sometimes built on the

† It may be noted that protraction *after* a missing element is alien to our modern rhythmic instinct. We rhythmize 'A captain bold from Halifax, who dwelt in country quar-ar-ters', not 'quar-ter-ers'.

repetition of a line (κατὰ στίχον composition, see IV), far more often consists of a varied combination of shorter entities termed 'cola', which are neverthleess long enough (about eight elements) to possess a definite character as metrical entities. These cola sometimes consist of homogeneous parts (e.g. two iambic metra or four dactyls), sometimes of heterogeneous parts (e.g. the glyconic). In places they are divided off from each other by hiatus or *syllaba brevis in elemento longo*, which clearly mark a pause in the rhythmic flow. In other places they are linked together by 'enjambement', the run-over of a word from one colon into the next. In many places there is only diaeresis,* which may or may not indicate a pause. If we are to use the word 'line' at all in such cases, we can only use it of the whole series of cola between one pause and the next; and modern texts of Pindar are in fact printed in such long 'lines'. In the lyrics of drama, where a metrical system is seldom repeated more than once, we have often not sufficient data on which to determine the pauses and to divide up the structure into its lines. (These pauses do not invariably coincide with the ends of sentences or clauses, which in fact often end in quite different places in strophe and antistrophe; and the view that the tolerance of hiatus is in any way dependent on punctuation is untenable.) See further under IV.

II. The metres of Epic, Elegiac, and dramatic dialogue

The lines are divided at fixed places by word-endings, either caesura or diaeresis.

(1) The dactylic hexameter, used by epic, didactic, and pastoral poets, consists of six feet,† the last of which must be a spondee. The first four are either dactyls or spondees, and the fifth, while almost always a dactyl, is occasionally a spondee. The line is divided by caesura somewhere near the middle. The commonest caesuras are (i) 'penthemimeral' (after 5/2 feet), μῆνιν ἄειδε, θεά: (ii) after the trochee of the third foot, ἄνδρα μοι ἔννεπε, Μοῦσα. (iii) The 'hephthemimeral' caesura (after 7/2 feet), ὅς κε θεοῖς ἐπιπείθηται, is rarer. Diaeresis after the fourth foot (which then must be a dactyl) is particularly characteristic of the pastoral poets, and is hence termed 'bucolic'. The ending of a word after the third foot without caesura in that foot is strictly avoided. After the trochee of the fourth foot it is rare in Homer and Hesiod and nearly excluded afterwards.

(2) The elegiac couplet consists of a dactylic hexameter followed by a dactylic pentameter (or rather 2 × 2½ metra, i.e. two *hemiepe*; see III. 5). The first half of the pentameter allows, the second does not allow, the substitution of spondees for dactyls. Diaeresis is invariably observed between the two halves.

(3) The iambic trimeter is used by the iambographers and is the main metre of dramatic dialogue. It consists of 6 feet (3 metra). There is normally caesura either in the 3rd foot (Soph. *Ant.* 8) or in the 4th (*Ant.* 1). In tragedy spondees are allowed in the 1st, 3rd, and 5th feet, tribrachs (resolved iambi) in the first four and occasionally in the 5th, dactyls (resolved spondees) in the 1st and 3rd, and anapaests (sparingly) in the 1st. Resolved feet become increasingly common in Euripides' later plays. Where a word ends before – ⏑ at the end of the line the preceding syllable is always (or almost always) short (Porson's law), but, e.g., αὖθίς μοι φράσον (Eur. *Hel.* 471) and ἐκ δεμνίων (Eur. *Tro.* 495) are allowed, since in the former case the enclitic μοι looks back, in the latter the preposition looks forward. The comic

* Diaeresis means division between words at the end of a foot or colon; caesura, division within a foot.

† In dactyls the *metron*, or unit of measurement, is the foot; in iambics, trochaics, and anapaests it is the dipody, consisting of two feet. The term foot is somewhat misleading when applied to these last three metres, implying as it does that there is a division after the second element; but its use is convenient for practical purposes.

trimeter allows anapaests in all feet but the last, and is not bound by Porson's law. The *scazon* or *choliambus* ('Limper') is a form of iambic trimeter used by Hipponax and other iambographers, having a spondee in the last foot.

(4) Occasionally, especially in moments of excitement (e.g. Aesch. *Ag.* 1649–73), tragedy employs the trochaic tetrameter catalectic,‡ – ⏑ – ⏓ | – ⏑ – ⏓ | – ⏑ – ⏓ | – ⏑ –, which, according to Arist. *Poet.* 1449ᵃ 21, was the original metre of dialogue. It is also employed in comedy. Always in tragedy, usually in comedy, there is diaeresis after the second metron.

The dialogue metres of comedy are more numerous, and looser, than those of tragedy. The following are peculiar to comedy.

(5) Iambic tetrameter catalectic, ⏓ – ⏑ – | ⏓ – ⏑ – | ⏓ – ⏑ – | ⏑ – –, usually with diaeresis after the first dimeter. Closely connected with this is the *Pnigos* ('Suffocator', a patter metre), of iambic metra, ending with a catalectic dimeter. E.g. Ar. *Ran.* 971–91, following catalectic tetrameters. There is often *enjambement* between dimeters (Ar. *Eq.* 911–40).

(6) The anapaestic tetrameter catalectic, ⏖ – ⏖ – | ⏖ – ⏖ – | ⏖ – ⏖ – | ⏑ ⏑ – –, is a dignified metre. The Just Argument and Aeschylus use it (*Nub.* 961 ff., *Ran.* 1006 ff.), while the Unjust Argument and Euripides use the less noble iambic tetrameter catalectic (*Nub.* 1036 ff., *Ran.* 907 ff.). Spondees, and also dactyls, can take the place of anapaests; but anapaest following dactyl (producing ⏑ ⏑ ⏑ ⏑) is avoided. Diaeresis occurs after the second metron.

(7) The eupolidean consists of a 'polyschematist' choriambic dimeter (⏓̿ ⏓̅ – ⏓ | – ⏑ ⏑ –, see III. 12. ii), followed by ⏓̿ ⏓̅ – ⏓ – ⏑ –. See White, *Verse of Greek Comedy* §§ 508, 528. E.g. Ar. *Nub.* 518–62. This appearance of polyschematism in spoken verse is certainly remarkable.

(8) Anapaestic dimeter, ⏖ – ⏖ – | ⏖ – ⏖ –. Spondee and dactyl may be substituted for anapaest, but only very rarely does an anapaest directly follow a dactyl, producing a series of four shorts. Diaeresis separates the metra. At frequent intervals the series of acatalectic dimeters is broken by a catalectic one, ⏑ ⏑ – ⏑ ⏑ – | ⏑ ⏑ – –, called a 'paroemiac' because proverbial expressions (παροιμίαι) are often contained in cola of a similar type. Only after a paroemiac is 'pause' (see I. 4) allowed.

III. The Metres of Lyric Verse

Some Greek lyric metres are, like the metres discussed under II, formed by the regular repetition of a single measure, iambic, dactylic, etc.; others, e.g. the glyconic and choriambic dimeter, by the combination of diverse entities within the limits of the colon. In some, e.g. the archilochean dicolon and dactylo-epitrites, the basis of the rhythm is formed by two diverse cola.

The principal metres of Greek lyric poetry are as follows.

(1) *Iambics.* At times dimeters and trimeters are well defined. At others, the iambics run on continuously for a considerable stretch without obvious breaks (e.g. Aesch. *Ag.* 768–70). Resolutions are allowed, as in spoken iambic trimeters, producing tribrachs and dactyls. The anapaest is rare in lyric iambics, but should perhaps be recognized, e.g. at Soph. *Phil.* 141. Syncopation (see I. 3) is common in tragedy, e.g. Aesch. *Supp.* 138–40 ⏑ – – | – ⏑ – | ⏑ – ⏑ – | – – | ⏑ ⏑ –. Certain combinations of syncopation are frequent, e.g. the trimeter ⏑ – – | – ⏑ – | ⏑ – – (Aesch. *Ag.* 376, etc.). At *El.* 504–15 Sophocles produces a beautiful effect by combining resolutions and syncopations. Often a choriamb (– ⏑ ⏑ –)

is substituted for an iambic metron ('choriambic ana-clasis'), e.g. Aesch. *Supp.* 783.

(2) *Trochaics* are frequent in the lyrics of comedy (e.g. Ar. *Ran.* 589–604), rare in tragedy. The catalectic dimeter goes back to Alcman's *Partheneion*, and is called 'lecythion' because identical (in its resolved form, – ⏑ ⏓ ⏑ – ⏑ –) with ληκύθιον ἀπώλεσεν (Ar. *Ran.* 1208 ff.): series of lecythia at Eur. *Phoen.* 239–245. The brachycatalectic dimeter (see I. 3) is termed *ithyphallic* (– ⏑ – ⏑ – –). Aesch. *Ag.* 160–6 and Eur. *Hel.* 348–59 illustrate resolution and syncopation (– – ⏑ and – – for trochaic metron). Cf. also Eur. *Cyc.* 608–23.

(3) *Cretics* are common in comedy (e.g. Ar. *Eq.* 304–10, with first paeon*), rare in tragedy. But Aeschylus turns the fourth paeon to magnificent account at *Eum.* 328–9, and for the first paeon cf. *Supp.* 418–22. Two hymns of the second century B.C. (Diehl, *Anth. Lyr. Graec.* ii. 303–9) are written in cretics and paeons.

(4) *Anapaests.* Lyric (or 'threnodic') anapaests, frequent in passages of a dirge-like character, differ from the normal anapaests of II. 8 in the frequency of paroemiacs (cf. the series in *Carmina popularia* 18, Diehl, *Anth. Lyr. Graec.* ii), the preponderance of long syllables, and the occasional neglect of diaeresis between metra. Ar. *Ran.* 372–7 (a slow march); Eur. *Ion*, 859–922 (a lament). Resolution of the long syllable (giving ⏑ ⏑ ⏑ ⏑, 'proceleusmatic') is allowed.

The close combination of iambics with trochees (e.g. Pind. *Ol.* 2. 1 ⏑ – ⏑ – | – ⏑ – –) and with anapaests (Eur *El.* 586, 588, 590) is sometimes found. The swing from iambics to trochaics is capable of charming effects (Eur. *Hel.* 361–3) and humorous ones (Ar. *Ran.* 209–68).

(5) *Dactyls.* Continuous hexameters are occasionally found (e.g. Sappho's *Epithalamia*, frs. 115 ff., Soph. *Trach.* 1010–14, Ar. *Ran.* 1528–33). Cratinus and other comic poets often use them for burlesque. But the tetrameter is far commoner. (As in the hexameter, an admixture of spondees is allowed.) Alcman and Anacreon wrote 'whole strophae and songs' in tetrameters (Heph. cap. 7; cf. Alcm. fr. 49), and Sophocles loves them, constantly mixing them with other metres with beautiful effect (*El.* 124–36). Pentameters and dimeters (called *adonei*, from the cry ὦ τὸν Ἄδωνιν) are found, also catalectic cola of varying lengths. For the trimeter see *hemiepes* below. Aeschylus frequently composes dactyls in a continuous stream, with no perceptible division into cola (e.g. *Pers.* 882–6, with ithyphallic clausula). Purely, or mainly, dactylic systems are Aesch. *Ag.* 104–21, Soph. *OT* 151–8, Eur. *Phoen.* 784–800. For the association of dactyls with iambics, cf. Archil. fr. 104, Eur. *Hipp.* 1120–30; with trochaics, Eur. *Cyc.* 608–23, Ar. *Lys.* 1279–90, and *Eccl.* 1168 ff. (the salad song).

'Aeolic', or 'lesbian', dactyls (Sappho, Alcaeus) have a free first foot of two syllables and a cretic close: e.g. the 'fourteen-syllable sapphic' in which Sappho wrote her second book (Heph. cap. 7, p. 23), ⏓⏓ – ⏑ ⏑ – ⏑ ⏑ – ⏑ ⏑ – ⏑ –.

The 'ibycean', – ⏑ ⏑ – ⏑ ⏑ – ⏑ –, is perhaps to be explained as a dactylo-trochaic tetrapody catalectic (Ibyc. fr. 6. 1–3, followed by normal dactylic tetrapodies). But in the lyrics of drama the same combination of elements is probably nothing else than a glyconic with dactylic opening.

The dactylic trimeter catalectic and acatalectic, – ⏑ ⏑ – ⏑ ⏑ – and – ⏑ ⏑ – ⏑ ⏑ – –, or *hemiepes* (τὸ ἡμιεπές, Marius Victorinus and Sacerdos), often occurs in dactylic systems, and forms one of the two parts of the dactylo-epitrite (see below). It is sometimes repeated in a series, either one form being used throughout, or the

two in combination: Aesch. *Pers.* 584–90; Soph. *Trach.* 113–15; Eur. *Tro.* 1094–8.

(6) The placing of ⏑, –, or ⏑ ⏑ before the two types of hemiepes, as a spring-off, produces the *prosodiac*, ⏓⏓ – ⏑ ⏑ – ⏑ ⏑ –, and *enoplion*, ⏓⏓ – ⏑ ⏑ – ⏑ ⏑ – –. For ⏑ ⏑ in the first and second dactyls – and ⏑ are sometimes substituted. *Rhes.* 895–8, two prosod.+ithyphallic+enopl.: *Med.* 435–7, enoplia, cf. 849–53.

(7) The *dochmius* ('slanter'), of which the basic form is ⏑ – – ⏑ –, is rarely found before the tragedians, by whom it is much used in agitated lamentations (e.g. Aesch. *Sept.* 78–180). The first and fourth elements may be long (– – – – among spondaic anapaests, Eur. *Hec.* 182, 190, 193). Resolutions are frequent, but the rhythm is easily felt through all the multiplicity of the transformations. Dochmiacs are often associated with iambics, anapaests, and cretics (Aesch. *Ag.* 1156–66, *PV* 574–88, Eur. *Ion* 1445–67). ⏑ – – ⏑ – (Eur. *Hel.* 657, 680–1) is perhaps a syncopated dochmius (⏑ – –[⏑]–).

The *hypodochmius*, or 'anaclastic' dochmius, inverts the first two elements, – ⏑ – ⏑ – (Soph. *OT* 1208–10, Eur. *Or.* 992–4).

(8) *Glyconics* are first found in Sappho, Alcaeus, and Anacreon. The metre is ⏓⏓ – ⏑ ⏑ – ⏑ –. The catalectic form, *pherecratean*, ⏓⏓ – ⏑ ⏑ – –, usually comes after every few glyconics. (But at Ar. *Thesm.* 359–66 there is a long series of glyconics, at Aesch. *Sept.* 295–300 a series of pherecrateans.) The metre may perhaps be, in origin, a form of aeolic dactyls, manifesting the same freedom in the first foot. (Sapph. fr. 99 has an aeolic dact. pent. cat. among glyconics.) Pindar has many glyconics. In drama Aeschylus has few (apart from short stanzas at the end of a system, e.g. *Ag.* 381–4), Sophocles, Euripides, and Aristophanes have many (e.g. Soph. *OC* 1211–18, Eur. *Andr.* 501–14, Ar. *Eq.* 973–84). The penultimate syllable is occasionally long (e.g. Eur. *Hipp.* 141). A tribrach (resolved trochee) at the opening is rare in Sophocles, common in Euripides.

(9) The *telesilleion*, or 'acephalous' glyconic, is a glyconic docked of its first element† (Telesilla, fr. 1, Soph. *OC* 1044–6, Ar. *Av.* 1731–4). An acephalous pherecratean (⏓ – ⏑ ⏑ – –) forms the metre of the Rhodian *Swallow Song*, ἦλθ' ἦλθε χελιδών (*Carm. Pop.* 32), and is common in Pindar and drama. It is sometimes called a *reizianum* after the German scholar Reiz, and the same name is applied to the acephalous choriambic dimeter (see (12)) catalectic ([–]⏑ ⏑ – | ⏑ – –). For the two forms cf. Eur. *Alc.* 908–10. The term *reizianum* has also been stretched to include the colon ⏓ – ⏑ – –.

(10) The glyconic may be extended† to various lengths. The *hipponacteum* (Eur. *Bacch.* 902, 904, 906) has one extra element at its end. The *phalaecean hendecasyllable* adds ⏑ – – to the glyconic: e.g. the first two lines of the Harmodius scolium metre, ἐν μύρτου κλαδὶ τὸ ξίφος φορήσω (*scol. anon.* 12) and Soph. *Aj.* 697, 700. This ⏑ – is probably a syncopated iambic metron: cf. Soph. *Ant.* 816 glyc.+spondee. Sometimes, again, a full iambic metron follows or precedes the glyc. (Alc. fr. 54, Soph. *Aj.* 600–1, 624–5).

(11) The minor asclepiad (⏓⏓ – ⏑ ⏑ – – ⏑ ⏑ – ⏑ –, e.g. Alc. fr. 50. 1 ἦλθες ἐκ περάτων γᾶς ἐλεφαντίναν) has sometimes been explained on the assumption that a glyconic = ⏓⏓ + – ⏑ ⏑ – + ⏑ –, and that therefore an

---

* The paeon is a cretic with one long syllable resolved. The 'first' paeon is – ⏑ ⏑ ⏑, the 'fourth', ⏑ ⏑ ⏑ –. The 'second' and 'third' exist in theory only.

† This is a convenient way of putting the matter. It cannot, however, be assumed by any means certain that the 'acephalous' cola described in this section actually came into existence through such a process of decapitation, or the longer cola by a process of extension.

extra choriamb can be inserted in the middle. A more natural method is to explain it as a fusion of two short cola which are often found, $\overline{\underline{\cup}}\cup-\cup\cup-$ and $-\cup\cup-\cup-$. But some colour is lent to the first view by the existence of the major asclepiad, or 'sixteen-syllable sapphic' ($\overline{\underline{\cup}}\underset{\cup}{\cup}-\cup\cup--\cup\cup-\cup-\cup-$, e.g. Alc. fr. 94, Soph. *Phil.* 175–6), which is not easy to explain except on the assumption that *two* choriambs are inserted.

(12) The *choriambic dimeter* assumes, broadly speaking, two forms:

(i) A strict form, in which the first or the second half is a choriamb, the other an iambic metron (Soph. *Trach.* 116–21, Ar. *Eq.* 551–8: cf. Anacr. fr. 54).

(ii) A free form, styled 'polyschematist' ('of many shapes'), in which the first half usually consists of four elements ($\overline{\underline{\cup}}\underset{\cup}{-}\cup-\circlearrowright$), sometimes increased to five or six by resolutions of long elements, while the second half is a choriamb. This form of dimeter is probably to be explained as dactylo-trochaic, the first half being a trochaic metron $-\cup-\underline{\cup}$, with free variations of quantity in the first two elements as in the glyconic and in aeolic dactyls. It is already found in Corinna, who makes much use of it, and in Pindar, also in Sophocles (*El.* 121–2, *Phil.* 204–8). Euripides has a great liking for it, combined with glyconics, and Aristophanes probably parodies this in the cento at *Ran.* 1309–22. Not infrequently the first half consists of only three elements. Systems consisting mainly of glyconics and polyschematist dimeters are found, e.g., at Eur. *Hel.* 1301–18, *Phoen.* 202–13.

The characteristic features of the metres described in paras. 8–12 are the juxtaposition of dactyl and trochee and (in most of them) free variation in the quantities of the first two elements. They are generally known as 'aeolic', owing to their prominence in the poetry of Aeolian Lesbos (Sappho and Alcaeus).

(13) The *minor ionic* (metron $\cup\cup--$) is found in the lyric poets (Alcman, Sappho, and Alcaeus wrote whole songs in it, Heph. cap. 12, pp. 37–8, cf. Alcm. fr. 34, Sapph. fr. 86) and is particularly associated with certain dramas (Aesch. *Supp.* 1018 ff., and *Pers.* 65 ff.; Eur. *Supp.* 42 ff., and *Bacch.* 64 ff.; Ar. *Ran.* 324 ff.). The syncopated form ($\cup\cup-$) is frequent (e.g. *Pers.* 100–1. The *anacreontic* ($\cup\cup-\cup-\cup--$) is often combined with Ionics (e.g. Anacr. fr. 44) and is the metre of the late *Anacreontea*. The view (Heph. cap. 12, p. 39. 15) that the anacreontic is derived from the ionic dimeter by the interchange of the final long of the first metron with the opening short of the second ('anaclasis') does not account for cola of the form $\cup\cup--|-\cup--$ (e.g. Ar. *Ran.* 330). The alternation of iamb. dim. cat. and anacreontic in Sapph. fr. 114 suggests that the anacreontic may be in origin an iamb. dim. cat. with anapaestic opening.

The *major ionic* is $--\cup\cup$. According to Hephaestion (cap. 11, p. 36. 15) one form of it, the Αἰολικόν, was much used by Sappho. He cites frs. 63–4 $\underline{\cup}-\cup\cup|$ $--\cup\cup|--\cup\cup|-\cup--$ (where, as with minor ionics, we have the metron $-\cup--$). But here, as often in other places in lyric and tragedy where major ionics have been detected, choriambic scansion, with a jumping-off element ('anacrusis') at the start ($-|-\cup-\cup-$, etc.), is possible. Major ionics are far less well attested than minor ionics.

(14) The *archilochean dicolon* consists of enoplion and ithyphallic. Archilochus fr. 107 Ἐρασμονίδη Χαρίλαε, χρῆμά τοι γελοῖον. It is not infrequent in tragedy. Sometimes (Heph. cap. 15, p. 47. 16) the division is $\underline{\cup}-\cup\cup-\cup\cup-\|\underline{\cup}-\cup-|\cup--$ (prosodiac and iamb. dim. cat.).

(15) *Dactylo-epitrites* are formed of dactylic cola (hemiepes, $-\cup\cup-\cup\cup-$ or $-\cup\cup-\cup\cup--$) and 'epitrites',

trochaic metra with long final element($-\cup--$, i.e. the ratio of 3:4, λόγος ἐπίτριτος, taking the length of a *breve* as the standard). Often a long element (very rarely a short one) precedes the dactylic colon or the epitrite, and the epitrite is often catalectic, becoming a cretic. There are many other occasional variations. The metre is first found in Stesichorus, and is very often used, in a strictly regularized form, by Pindar and Bacchylides. It occurs in tragedy, especially in certain plays (Aesch. *PV* 526 ff., 887 ff., Eur. *Med.* and *Andr.*), even in comedy (Ar. *Eq.* 1264 ff.). It is one of the easiest Greek metres to grasp.

Dicola of a similar type are the *iambelegus* ($\underline{\cup}-\cup--|$ $-\cup\cup-\cup\cup-$), the *encomiologicum*($-\cup\cup-\cup\cup-|\underline{\cup}-\cup--$), and perhaps the *praxilleion* ($-\cup\cup-\cup\cup-\cup\cup-\cup--$). The *archebulean* is a praxilleion preceded by one or two short elements or one long one ($\underline{\cup}-\cup\cup-\cup\cup-\cup\cup-\cup--$).

IV. The Architecture of Greek Lyric Verse

The principal building materials have been described above. It remains to consider how these are combined into organized structures. In modern verse we are familiar with the stanza form of, say, four lines. Such stanzas play a relatively small part in Greek verse. The following deserve mention.

(1) *Sapphic stanza*, $-\cup-\underline{\cup}-\cup\cup-\cup--$ (possibly = polyschematist dimeter$+\cup--$) thrice and $-\cup\cup--$ (*adoneus*).

(2) *Alcaic stanza*, $\underline{\cup}-\cup-\underline{\cup}-\cup\cup-\cup-$ (probably $\underline{\cup}+$ trochaic metron+the colon $-\cup\cup-\cup-$, for which see III. 11) twice:$\underline{\cup}-\cup-\underline{\cup}-\cup--(\underline{\cup}+$ troch. dim.):$-\cup\cup-\cup\cup-\cup--$ ('Alcaic ten-syllable'), a colon often used, especially as a clausula, in the lyrics of tragedy).

(3) *Scolion metre* (e.g. the *Harmodius Song*, Diehl, *Anth. Lyr. Graec.* ii, 184–5), phalaecean hendecasyllable twice: an enigmatical colon, $\cup\cup-\cup--\cup\cup-$ (perhaps a form of choriambic dimeter, with anapaest for iambus at the opening): $-\cup\cup-\cup-$ twice.

Sappho, Alcaeus, and Anacreon constructed their solo songs for the most part either (1) by the repetition of a single metrical unit, composition κατὰ στίχον (e.g. Sappho's second and third books were written in the '14-syllable' and '16-syllable sapphic' (see III. 5 and 11) respectively, and cf. Alc. frs. 54, 94: or (2) in stanzas, sapphic or alcaic, and cf. Sapph. frs. 96, 98, Alc. fr. 43, Anacr. fr. 5: Anacr. fr. 2 is a little more elaborate in structure, but equally simple in its constituents. There is, broadly speaking, no *enjambement* (contrast Anacreon's way of writing glyconics with Ar. *Eq.* 973–96), though Sappho runs the third line of her stanza into the closing Adoneus, and cf. fr. 98. The colon is usually a line, in the modern sense of the term, and a modern reader feels that he is treading familiar ground. In contrast, choral lyric is, from the first, more complicated. Alcman's *Partheneion* (fr. 1) is a highly organized, though readily intelligible, structure: lec.+enopl. four times, 2 troch. trim., 2 troch. dim., dact. tetr., alc. 10-syll. (answering dact. tetr. cat.). Hiatus and *syllaba brevis in elemento longo* occur frequently, while *enjambement* is eschewed.

Pindar's odes are extremely elaborate. The general character of the dactylo-epitrites is easily grasped, but the remainder, which are virtually all written in 'aeolic' metres (see III. 12, ad fin.), present numerous and formidable difficulties. The constituent cola, among which the shorter forms ($\overline{\underline{\cup}}\underset{\cup}{-}\cup\cup-$ and reizianum) are prominent, are interspersed with shorter entities (iambic monometers, cretics, etc.) and with non-aeolic cola. A colon is seldom repeated in juxtaposition. The whole structure has the elaborate intricacy of a tessellated pavement. The 'lines', marked by the presence of hiatus or *syllaba brevis in elemento longo*, occasionally consist of a single colon, but are normally longer, though seldom more than some 25 elements. *Pyth.* 1 str. 6 (dactylo-epitrites) runs to 30 elements. The contrast between short and long lines is well illustrated by *Ol.* 1 str. 3–6, where three separated cola are followed by a long combination at 6. Cf. also *Nem.* 2 str. 1 and 4.

In tragedy we find long lines e.g. at Aesch. *Pers.* 882–5, Eur. *Heracl.* 615–17, *Hipp.* 771–5, *Bacch.* 383–6. The dramatists, unlike Pindar, tend to repeat the same colon many times in succession; and they do this in such a manner that the cola are in one place linked, in another separated. E.g. Aesch. *Supp.* 171–4, where 171–2 are linked, 173–4 separated; Soph. *OT* 1202–3, *OC* 1215–18; Ar. *Thesm.* 360–4. The division of a passage into its constituent cola (colometry, κωλισμός) is often subject to doubt, particularly in aeolic systems. Where, as often, diaeresis coincides in strophe and in antistrophe, it is natural to take this as a guide. On this principle Soph. *OC* 668–80 = 681–93 would be regarded as constructed of a great variety of aeolic cola, while alternatively it can be analysed into more homogeneous elements if we assume frequent *enjambement* between cola.

On the whole, the lyrics of tragedy stand between the complexity of Pindar and the simplicity of Lesbian solo-song. Ionic and dochmiac systems are, it is true, very regular in character; and there are many homogeneous iambic systems (e.g. Aesch. *Ag.* 238–47, and often in the *Oresteia*; Soph. *Trach.* 132–40; Eur. *Tro.* 551–67). Other simple systems are Soph. *OT* 1186–96 (tel., glyc., pher., with reiz. clausula), *Trach.* 113–21 (hemiep. and chor. dim.), Eur. *Heracl.* 608–17 (dactyls), *Andr.* 501–14 (glyc., pher.), *Supp.* 971–9, and *Phoen.* 226–38 (glyc., pher., and chor. dim.). Against these we may set the elaboration of some of the lyrics in the *Alcestis*, and the great difficulty of *Bacch.* 135–67 and 576–603. The metres of comedy are in general far simpler than those of tragedy: e.g. Ar. *Eq.* 1111–30 and *Pax* 1329–57 (tel. and reiz.), *Av.* 1553–64 (troch. dim. and lec.), *Ran.* 1251–60 (glyc. and pher.); though even in comedy complicated systems are to be found (e.g. Ar. *Lys.* 1247–70 and, naturally, many parodistic passages). The beginner will be well advised to start with Sappho, Alcaeus, Anacreon, and comedy, and feel his way through tragedy to the complexities of Pindar.

V. Strophic Response

Most Greek choral poetry is 'strophic'. That is to say, a metrical system is repeated, the first occurrence being termed 'strophe', the second 'antistrophe'. In tragedy there is only one repetition, in satyric drama and comedy sometimes more (Eur. *Cyc.* 495 ff., Ar. *Pax* 346 ff.). The oldest extant piece of Greek choral poetry, Alcman's *Partheneion*, repeats the system many times, as does Pindar in his more elaborate odes. Pindar adds an epode to strophe and antistrophe, and then repeats the whole 'triadic' structure. (Triadic structure is already clearly present in Ibyc. fr. 3. There is no good ground for assuming it in Alcman's *Partheneion*. Suidas, s.v. τρία Στησιχόρου, ascribes its invention to Stesichorus.) Epodes are also often found in drama (e.g. Aesch. *Pers.* 897–906, Soph. *Ant.* 876–82). In the κομμός in the *Choephoroe* (315–475) the structure is highly elaborate, and the antistrophes do not immediately follow the strophes: cf. Soph. *Trach.* 1004–42. Some passages are 'astrophic', the system not being repeated (e.g. Soph. *Trach.* 205–24, Eur. *Hel.* 515–27; particularly in the monodies and duets of Eur.'s later plays). In an *Ephymnion* (refrain) words, as well as metrical form, are repeated: e.g. Aesch. *Supp.* 117–75, *Ag.* 1455–1550.

Strophic response is usually very close, and often undeviatingly precise, syllable by syllable, for long stretches. The main divergencies from strictness are the response of – and ∪ in many metres. A syncopated iambic metron probably sometimes corresponds to a full metron (e.g. Eur. *El.* 1185=1201). A few surprising responsions occur, notably that between polyschematist dimeter and glyconic*(Corinna, fr. 5, passim, and several times in Euripides, e.g. *El.* 146 = 163). For loose response in comedy see Wilamowitz, *Verskunst*, 470–86.

* The explanation seems to be that a monosyllabic thesis corresponds to a disyllabic one and vice versa: ×× – ∪ – ∪ – ∪ – (×× standing for the two variable syllables at the opening).

BIBLIOGRAPHY

U. v. Wilamowitz-Moellendorff, *Griechische Verskunst*, 1921 (the great work, and not an unduly difficult one); K. Rupprecht, *Einführung in die griech. Metrik²* (1933; a useful handbook); P. Maas, in Gercke–Norden, *Einleitung in die Altertumswissenschaft*, i. 7 (1929); O. Schroeder, *Grundriss d. griech. Versgeschichte* (1930), *Aeschyli Cantica²* (1916), *Soph. C.²* (1923), *Eur. C.²* (1928), *Ar. C.²* (1930) (scansions of all lyrics in the plays); J. Descroix, *Le trimètre iambique* (1931); W. R. Hardie, *Res Metrica* (1920); G. Thomson, *Greek Lyric Metre* (1929); W. J. W. Koster, *Traité de Métrique grecque* (1936); J. W. White, *The Verse of Greek Comedy* (1912). E. Fraenkel, 'Lyrische Daktylen', *Rh. Mus.* lxxii. (1917–18), 161–97, 321–52; E. Kalinka in Bursian's *Jahresbericht*, 250, 256, and 257 gives a full account of recent literature.

J. D. D.

METRE, LATIN. Except for the Saturnian metre (q.v.) and (possibly) the trochaic 'uersus quadratus' used in popular ditties (e.g. rex erit qui recte faciet, qui non faciet non erit) all Latin metres were deliberately borrowed from Greek. This borrowing was complicated by three important differences between the two languages: (1) the sequences of long and short syllables inherent in Latin words and terminations (cf. Cicero, *Orat.* 189) were not always readily adaptable to foreign metres, and the poet's choice of diction was consequently fettered (e.g. Ĭmpĕrātor is impossible in dactylic verse); (2) it is virtually certain that stress, not pitch, predominated in the Latin accent, and therefore the relation between word-accent and rhythmical beat (ictus) created problems unknown apparently to Greek; (3) the phonetic tendency of 'breuis breuians' (q.v.) in popular Latin speech, though it might offer some prosodical freedom, introduced an element of caprice and really meant that many Latin syllables had no fixed quantity. As in Greek, attenuation ('elision', synaloepha) of a final vowel before the initial vowel of a succeeding word was the common practice, and syllables ending in -*m* were similarly treated; but whereas Latin elides long final vowels more freely than Greek (yet not unrestrictedly), it rarely halves their quantity (e.g. an quī amant, Verg. *Ecl.* 8. 108). Hiatus is tolerated only at fixed places in certain metres, for special effects (e.g. femineō ululatu, *Aen.* 9. 477), or as a bold licence (e.g. Neptunō Aegaeo, *Aen.* 3. 74). Obsolete quantities are occasionally revived by later poets (e.g. velīt, labōr); a few lengthenings are due to Greek models (e.g. liminaquĕ laurique dei, *Aen.* 3. 91). In Republican poets final -*s* after a short vowel may be neglected before a following consonant (e.g. rationĭs potestas, Lucr.). In dactylic and lyric metres the Romans often subject themselves to stricter rules than did the Greeks. The development of accentual metres in late Latin falls outside the scope of this article.

I. Metres of Republican drama, introduced by Livius Andronicus, are fully represented in the comedies of Plautus and Terence; fragments of the tragedians are meagre. In general, these metres have three common features: (1) popular pronunciations based on 'breuis breuians' (e.g. bŏnĭs as ∪ ∪) or synizesis (e.g. ēorum) are freely admitted; (2) word-accent and ictus often coincide, and it is possible that the effects of enclisis (e.g. patér-meus) may have made such coincidences more frequent than appears from a printed text; (3) where two short syllables are used as the resolution of one long, the first short syllable is usually an accented one; this principle embraces and may be the basis of many minor 'rules'. (A) Dialogue metres: (i) The iambic senarius is the commonest (e.g. nunc huc | ad Vĕnĕ|ris fa|num uĕnĭ|o ui|sere, Plaut. *Rud.* 94). Unlike the Greek comic trimeter, which allowed spondees (and dactyls) for ◡ ◡̄ only in the first, third, and fifth feet, the Latin line admitted ×– (= ◡◡ ◠◠) in every foot except the last (◡ –); hence the line is felt to be not three *metra* but six feet (cf. Hor. *Ars P.* 251–62). There is caesura usually in the third foot, sometimes in the fourth; at the caesura hiatus is admitted (rarely in Terence). 'Porson's law' (cf. METRE, GREEK, II. 3) does not operate. As in other dialogue metres, resolutions of any long syllable are common (especially in comedy), but proceleusmatic feet (◡ ◡ ◡ ◡) are restricted in use. (ii) The iambic septenarius (a catalectic tetrameter, sometimes called 'laughing metre') is confined to comedy (e.g. nam quom | modo ex|ibat | foras || ad por|tum se ai|bat i|re, Plaut. *Rud.* 307). The seventh foot is generally a pure iambus and must be so if a monosyllable follows. The fourth foot must be iambic if, as usually happens, diaeresis follows. All other feet are ×–. Hiatus is permitted at the diaeresis; failing diaeresis, there is caesura in the fifth foot. (iii) The iambic octonarius has a pure iambus as its last foot; its fourth foot is also pure if, as is usual, diaeresis follows. The other six feet are ×–. Hiatus is found at the diaeresis; failing diaeresis, there is caesura in the fifth foot. (iv) The trochaic septenarius (or catalectic tetrameter) is widely used (e.g. exi e | fano | natum | quantumst || hŏmĭnum | săcrĭle|gissu|me, Plaut. *Rud.* 706). It keeps only its seventh foot pure (– ◡) and so differs from the Greek metre, which kept the first, third, and fifth feet also pure. Diaeresis (with hiatus permitted, though not in Terence) is common after the fourth foot; failing diaeresis, there is caesura in the fourth foot. (B) The metres of cantica (i.e. lyrical monodies or duets, rare in Terence) are mainly iambic, trochaic, anapaestic, bacchiac, and cretic dimeters and tetrameters (catalectic and acatalectic); choriambic, glyconic, and ionic metres are occasionally used; to these must be added the *colon reizianum* (× –́ × ◡◡́), which, when preceded by an iambic dimeter, gives the *versus reizianus*. The relation between word-accent and ictus, the extent to which popular pronunciations, resolutions, and hiatus are used, and the admission of impure feet differ with the metre employed. For example: conflict of accent and ictus is usual in anapaests, though shortening by 'breuis breuians' is common; in bacchiacs and cretics popular pronunciations are avoided, but accent and ictus generally coincide; in bacchiacs the first part of the foot may be ◡, or ◡ ◡, or –, but it is rare for both long syllables of a foot (× – –) to be resolved; yet cretics normally have the form ◠◠ ◡ ◠◠, rarely ◠◠ × ◠◠. Some cantica are composed in a single metre. In others the metre changes with the emotions expressed or when a new topic is introduced; in such passages the division into cola is sometimes uncertain. In a number of cantica it is possible to discern a metrical structure of strophe and antistrophe, especially when a general theme is followed by a particular application (e.g. Plaut. *Amph.* 633–44).

II. Dactylic verse, introduced by Ennius. (i) The hexameter is used with considerable variety of treatment as the metre of epic, narrative, didactic, and satiric poetry, and forms the first line of the elegiac couplet. Its first four feet may be dactyls or spondees, its fifth is regularly a dactyl, its sixth a spondee or trochee. A spondaic fifth foot (an Alexandrian mannerism) is frequent only in Catullus (but cf. cara de|um subo|les mag| num Iouis | incre|mentum, Verg. *Ecl.* 4. 49). Except for some cretic words in Ennius, no use is made of shortening by 'breuis breuians' and synizesis is rare. Ennius, Ovid, and Imperial poets are sparing with elisions; Lucilius, Lucretius, and Virgil (especially in *Aen.*) employ them more frequently. The commonest caesura is after the long syllable of the third foot (penthemimeral); it is often accompanied by another masculine caesura in the fourth foot (hephthemimeral) or in the second foot (trihemimeral), or by both; if there is not a masculine caesura

in the third foot, both hephthemimeral and trihemimeral are usual (e.g. o pas|si graui|ora, da|bit deus | his quoque | finem, Verg. *Aen.* 1. 199). The comparative infrequency of a feminine caesura in the third foot is a striking contrast to the Greek hexameter. In the fifth foot, however, feminine caesuras are more frequent than masculine. Monosyllables are avoided where they would create diaeresis near a main caesura. After Ennius they are progressively less frequent at the end of a line (where a disyllabic or trisyllabic noun, verb, or adjective is preferred); in Virgil they are used only for special reasons (e.g. restituis rem, *Aen.* 6. 846, imitating Ennius); in Horace's *Satires* conversational tone is achieved by final monosyllabic adverbs and particles. Diaeresis with a clear break in the sense at the fourth foot (the so-called 'bucolic caesura') is a conspicuous but not common mannerism (e.g. Pollio et | ipse fa|cit noua | carmina: || pascite | taurum, Verg. *Ecl.* 3. 86). In general, there is conflict between word-accent and ictus in the first half of the hexameter, harmony in the second. Whether Latin poets sought this alternation and arranged their caesuras to ensure it, or whether it is the inevitable result of their preference for certain masculine caesuras, is a matter of controversy. It is also disputed whether the Romans read hexameters with normal prose accentuations, neglected them in favour of ictus, or in some way made both audible. By skilfully varying their caesuras, elisions, and sense pauses, and employing all the delicate resources of alliteration and assonance, the great Roman poets made the hexameter a sonorous but flexible instrument for the expression of all human emotions. (ii) The pentameter consists of two catalectic dactylic cola (*hemiepes*, – ◡ ◡ – ◡ ◡ –) separated by diaeresis. In the first colon spondees may be substituted for either dactyl, but not usually for both; no spondees are permitted in the second colon. A monosyllable before the diaeresis is avoided unless another monosyllable or a pyrrhic (◡ ◡) word precedes; the final syllable is usually long. Ovid and later writers normally end the line with a disyllable (though 'es' and 'est' are allowed), but earlier elegists admit polysyllables. Except in Catullus elision is restricted and is generally avoided at the diaeresis, in the second half of the line, and especially in the last dactyl. A symmetrical arrangement of words (e.g. aspicio *patriae* tecta relicta *meae*, Ovid) is a common feature of the best writers, and each couplet is normally complete in sense.

III. *Lyric metres.* Latin lyric verse is smaller in quantity and less complicated in form than Greek. The chief writers are Catullus, Horace, Martial, and Seneca (in his tragedies). Apart from iambic, trochaic, dactylic, and anapaestic lines of various lengths, the principal metres are glyconics, pherecrateans, asclepiads, phalaecean hendecasyllabics, scazons (limping iambics), and the elements of the sapphic and alcaic stanzas (cf. METRE, GREEK); ionics (e.g. Hor. *Carm.* 3. 12) and the controversial galliambic (in Catull. 63) are rare. Popular pronunciations are virtually excluded and there is considerable strictness in matters of caesura, elision, and liaison (synaphea) between successive lines (for details see standard editions). The iambic and trochaic lines of lyric (excluding the 'trimeters' of Publilius Syrus and Phaedrus) are metrically purer than those of comedy, since they are based on dipodies of the forms ◡̄ – ◡ – and – ◡ –́ ◡̣; resolutions of long syllables also are comparatively fewer, though Seneca admits them in his iambics more freely than Horace. Some of the metres (e.g. iambic dimeters and trimeters, hendecasyllabics, asclepiads) are used in continuous passages; but more frequently lines of different length or metre are combined into couplets (e.g. Hor. *Carm.* i. 7; *Epod.* 16) or four-line stanzas. Horace is especially fond of the alcaic and sapphic stanzas and combinations of asclepiads, glyconics, and pherecrateans, in all of which he restricts himself by rules unknown to Greek (e.g. in sapphics and alcaics he uses an epitrite (– ◡ – –) where Greek may have a ditrochee (– ◡ – ◡)).

W. M. Lindsay, *Early Latin Verse* (1922); W. A. Laidlaw, *Prosody of Terence* (1938); E. Fraenkel, *Iktus und Akzent* (1928) and 'Die Vorgeschichte des Versus Quadratus' (*Hermes* 1927, 357–70); H. Drexler, *Plautinische Akzentstudien* (2 vols., 1932); O. Skutsch, *Prosodische u. metrische Gesetze der Iambenkürzung* (1934); F. Curtius, *Römische Metrik* (1929) and 'Die Responsion in den Plautinischen Cantica' (*Philol.* Suppl. xxi. 1, 1929); E. Norden, *Aeneis Buch VI* (Anhänge) (1926); A. W. de Groot, 'Wesen u. Gesetze der Caesur' (*Mnemos.* 1935, 81–154); L. Müller, *De re metrica* (1894); J. P. Postgate, *Prosodia Latina* (1923); W. R. Hardie, *Res Metrica* (1920); F. Vollmer, 'Römische Metrik' in Gercke–Norden's *Einleitung* i, 8; W. Meyer, *Gesammelte Abhandlungen zur Mittellat. Rhythmik* (3 vols., 1905–36); summary of literature in Bursian's *Jahresberichte* vols. 250, 256, 257 (E. Kalinka), and annual reports in *Glotta*.   J. F. M.

METRODORUS (1) of Chios, pupil of Democritus, lived in the 4th century B.C. His Περὶ φύσεως seems to have attempted to combine Atomism with the Eleatic denial of the reality of change; he occupied himself mainly with the explanation of meteorological and astronomical phenomena. He also wrote historical works—a Τρωικά and perhaps also an Ἰωνικά.

Testimonia and frs. in Diels, *Vorsokr.*⁵ ii. 231–4. *PW* xv. 1475.
                                                          W. D. R.

METRODORUS (2) of Lampsacus (331/330–278/7 B.C.) was one of the four καθηγεμόνες of Epicureanism, and the most important after Epicurus; Epicurus dedicated to him his *Eurylochus* and his *Metrodorus*, besides writing letters to him and mentioning him often in his works. He reckoned him not among original thinkers, but as first among those who could reach the truth with the help of others, and ordered that Metrodorus' memory as well as his own should be celebrated on the 20th of every month. The list of Metrodorus' writings is a long one, and considerable fragments remain, largely occupied with polemic against other schools, and confirming Epicurus' judgement as to his lack of originality. *See* ALLEGORY, GREEK.

Ed. A. Körte, *Jahrbücher für Classische Philologie, Suppl.* 17. 529 (1890); *Papyrus Herculanensis* 831, ed. A. Körte, ib. 571 ff. *PW* xv. 1477.   W. D. R.

METRODORUS (3) of Stratonicea, an adherent first of the Epicurean school, then of that of Carneades (Diog. Laert. 10. 9, Cic. *De Or.* 1. 45).

PW xv. 1480.

METRONOMOI, overseers of weights and measures in Athens; five for the city, five for the Piraeus, elected by lot for one year. In other States their duties were carried out by the *Agoranomoi* (q.v.).

METROPOLIS, (*a*) the mother-city of a colony; (*b*) in Roman times an honorary title granted usually to the capitals of provincial κοινά, sometimes to other important cities; (*c*) in Egypt the administrative capital of a *nomos* (q.v.). Under the Ptolemies the *metropoleis*, though they usually had many Greek residents, possessed no official communal organization. Augustus placed on a special register the hellenized residents of the *metropoleis* (οἱ ἀπὸ μητροπόλεως), and these henceforth formed a hereditary class, paying poll-tax at a lower rate. He also established in each metropolis a body of magistrates (ἄρχοντες), who managed the gymnasium and the ephebic training, the market and corn supply, and the Greek temples. These were chosen—in theory probably by popular election from a hereditary class styled ἡ ἀπὸ γυμνασίου. Septimius Severus established in each metropolis a council (βουλή), which co-opted its members and nominated the magistrates and the principal officials of the *nomos* except the στρατηγός and βασιλικὸς γραμματεύς (who were appointed by the prefect). The *metropoleis* officially became cities probably in A.D. 297, perhaps ten years later.

P. Jouguet, *La Vie municipale dans l'Égypte romaine* (1911); Jones, *Eastern Cities*, ch. 11.   A. H. M. J.

METTIUS POMPUSIANUS, a victim of Domitian's tyranny, because he had made a volume of extracts of speeches by kings from Livy.

MEZENTIUS, king of Caere in Etruria, whose aid was invoked by Turnus against the invading Aeneas. According to the earlier story, told in Cato's *Origines*, Turnus and Aeneas alike fell in the subsequent conflict, and Mezentius was later killed or forced to submit in single combat with Ascanius. (Some authorities, e.g. Ovid, *Fasti* 4. 877–900, say he demanded payment to himself of the first-fruits of the vintage.) Virgil in *Aen.* bks. 7–10 develops him into a full-blooded, atheistical tyrant, killed by Aeneas after the death in his defence of his attractive son Lausus.   R. A. B. M.

MICIPSA, *see* NUMIDIA.

MICON (Μίκων) (5th c. B.C.), painter and sculptor, of Athens. He painted (1) in the Theseum (soon after 475): Theseus and Minos; probably also Amazonomachy and Centauromachy. (2) In the Stoa Poikile (soon after 460) Amazonomachy. The Amazonomachies and Centauromachy are reflected on vases; one Amazon is named Peisianassa after Peisianax, who built the Stoa; one Centauromachy is very like the centre of the west pediment at Olympia, on which Micon *may* have worked as sculptor. (3) In the Anakeion: Argonauts. He painted Butes (in the Amazonomachy?) so that only head and eye appeared above a hill; analogies can be found on contemporary vases. His painting was closely connected with Polygnotus, but Polygnotan ἦθος is never attributed to him. He made a statue in Olympia of Callias, victor in 472; the Mariémont warrior may reproduce an original by him.

Overbeck, 1058, 1080–93; Pfuhl, 688, 716, 732; J. D. Beazley *AJArch.* 1933, 366; F. Dornseiff, *Der sogenannte Apollon von Olympia* (1936).   T. B. L. W.

MIDAS (1), a legendary Phrygian king, of whom several stories are told, the most famous being the following.

Midas had a garden which a Silenus or satyr used to visit. Midas had a curiosity to learn his wisdom, and so mixed wine with the water of a spring in the garden; the Silenus was thus made drunk and caught. What he told Midas seems to have been a subject for learned conjecture; according to Aristotle ap. [Plut.] *Cons. ad Apoll.*, 115 b, he said that life was a penance and it was a misfortune to be born; Aelian (*VH* 3. 18) puts into his mouth a lecture on geography. The place of the garden also varies: see Herodotus 8. 138. 4 (somewhere in Macedonia), Xenophon, *An.* 1. 2. 13 (near Thymbrium in Cilicia), Bion in Athenaeus 45 c (name given as Inna, between Thrace and Paeonia).

Having to judge a musical contest between Apollo and Pan (or Marsyas, q.v., Hyginus, *Fab.* 191. 1), Midas voted against Apollo, who therefore bestowed ass's ears on him. He managed to hide these from most people with his head-dress, but was obliged to tell his barber; the latter, bursting with the secret, found relief by whispering it into a hole in the ground; reeds grew over this when he refilled it, and whispered the tale whenever the wind blew through them (Ovid, *Met.* 11. 153 ff.).

Midas was very hospitable to a Silenus, whom his people had found wandering drunk and captured (a variant of the first story, probably). Dionysus therefore offered him anything he wished; he asked that all he touched might become gold. Soon after, he found that this applied to his food and prayed to lose the gift; by Dionysus' advice he bathed in Pactolus, which ever since has had golden sands (Ovid, ibid. 90 ff.).

Whether any facts of cult or history lie behind the story of Midas is doubtful.

Cf. S. Eitrem, *PW.* xv. 1526 ff.   H. J. R.

MIDAS (2), an historical king of Phrygia 738–696 B.C. (Eusebius). He was the first barbarian king to make presents to Delphi (Hdt. 1. 14); married the king of Cyme's daughter, who first struck coins in her native city (Heraclides, *FHG* ii. 216, Pollux 9. 83); and drank bull's blood when the Cimmerians overthrew his kingdom (Strabo 1. 61). In Assyrian records he appears as Mita, joins a confederacy against King Sargon (717), but becomes his vassal (707). His history anticipates that of the Lydian Gyges (q.v.). P. N. U.

MIDDLE PLATONISM. The period of Platonism beginning with Arcesilaus (q.v. 1) c. 265 B.C.; it lasted for about a century, and was terminated by Carneades (q.v.), the founder of the Third Academy. *See* ALBINUS, APULEIUS, PLUTARCH.

MILESTONES, though not an invention of the Romans, were used most frequently by them. The earliest surviving milestone (*ILS* 5801) dates from c. 250 B.C. Under the Republic they bear the names of consuls or other officials connected with the construction or repair of roads, but in the Principate the name and titles of the emperor invariably appear, though the names of provincial governors and others are sometimes added. The inscriptions frequently give important information as to the date and payment for the costs of construction of new roads (e.g. *ILS* 208, 5834). In Italy the distance from Rome is usually given; in the provinces the distances recorded are usually those from the nearest important town. In Gaul from the time of Trajan distances were reckoned by *leugae* (1,500 paces). Milestones were cylindrical pillars, generally about 6 feet high.

ILS 5800 ff.; Schneider, *PW*, Suppl. vi, s.v. 'miliarium'. G. H. S.

MILETUS, southernmost of the great Ionian cities of Asia Minor, claimed partly Cretan origin (Paus. 7. 2. 5). In Homer it was occupied by 'barbarous-tongued' Carians who fought for Troy. Ionians from Athens under Nileus descendant of Nestor (probably c. 1100 B.C.) seized Miletus and married Carian wives. During the eighth, seventh, and sixth centuries Miletus founded many colonies on the Black Sea and its approaches (including Abydos, Cyzicus, Sinope, Trapezus, Dioscurias, Panticapaeum, Theodosia, Olbia, Borysthenes, Istrus, Odessus), led the way in Greek penetration of Egypt (Milesians' Fort and Naucratis; Necho's offering to the temple at Didyma after Megiddo, 608 B.C.), and had close contacts with Sybaris till its destruction in 510.

2. Miletus' sea-power and colonies were partly cause, partly result of her long struggle with the kings of Lydia. Alyattes made terms with Miletus (then under a tyrant Thrasybulus, the friend of Periander), which apparently kept a privileged position when Croesus subdued Ionia (both Alyattes and Croesus sent offerings to the temple of the Branchidae at Didyma), and when Persia conquered Croesus' dominions in 546. In 499 Miletus, instigated by its ex-tyrants Histiaeus and Aristagoras (qq.v.), started the Ionian revolt. After the naval disaster at Lade the city was captured, the temple at Didyma was burnt, and the Milesians were sold into slavery (494).

3. Lade ended for Miletus a long period of great prosperity, interrupted by intervals of party struggles; to this period belong the Milesian philosophers Thales, Anaximander, and Anaximenes, the chronicler and mapmaker Hecataeus, and the seated statues from Didyma (British Museum, *Catalogue of Sculpture*, I. i, plates VI–XV). Whether the archaic pottery generally known as Rhodian was really Milesian remains uncertain. Milesian woollen goods were world-famous.

After the Persian defeat at Mycale (479) Miletus joined the Delian League, being assessed at 10 talents in 450, and at 5 in 443. In 412 Miletus revolted from Athens, only to fall under Persia. In the fourth century it passed under the vassal kings of Caria, Hecatomnus and (377–353) Mausolus. Among Milesians of this later period were Aspasia of Periclean fame, Hippodamus, town-planner of the Piraeus, and the dithyrambic poet Timotheus (c. 447–357). Miletus was conquered and rebuilt by Alexander.

4. Hellenistic monarchs of the houses of Seleucus, Antigonus, Lysimachus, Ptolemy, and Attalus successively held Miletus and erected great buildings there. After becoming part of the Roman province of Asia (129 B.C.) Miletus lived on its past glories. St. Paul visited it; Apollo performed a miracle at Didyma when the Goths assaulted the city in A.D. 205; but its decline was assured by the silting up of its harbour.

Herodotus; Thucydides, bk. 8; Xenophon, *Hell.* bk. 1; Strabo, esp. pp. 632–6; *SIG* 57, 58, 272, 322. B. Haussoullier, *Études sur l'Histoire de Milet et du Didymeion* (1902); T. Wiegand, *Milet, Ergebnisse der Ausgrabungen und Untersuchungen seit 1899*. P. N. U.

MILK (γάλα, *lac*). A considerable use was made of milk in religious ceremonies of classical date, and there is reason to think that it was once much commoner, having been in many cases superseded by wine. It is a natural drink-offering from a people largely pastoral, and also an obvious sort of first-fruits. The Greeks often retained it in the conservative rustic cults, e.g. that of the Nymphs (Theoc. 5. 53) and the tendance of the dead (as Aesch. *Pers.* 611 ff.), though wine might be added (ibid. 614 f.; wine was, however, forbidden in the ritual of the Erinyes, Aesch. *Eum.* 107). Roman rituals provide more instances; see Varro, *Rust.* 2. 11. 5 (Rumina), Ovid, *Fasti* 4. 745–6 (Parilia); cf. BONA DEA, JUPITER.

Herzog–Hauser in *PW*, s.v. 'Milch', and references. H. J. R.

MILO, TITUS ANNIUS, of Lanuvium, tribune 57 B.C. Originally Pompey's man, he actively promoted Cicero's recall and organized gladiators against those of Clodius (q.v.). Their riots, which continued over five years, were varied by prosecutions for *vis*: in 57 Milo twice sued Clodius, who escaped by being elected aedile; in 56 a prosecution of Milo was also dropped, and he became praetor in 55. Late in 54 he inaugurated, with games costing 1,000,000 HS, a candidature for the consulate of 52 against Hypsaeus and Metellus Scipio; but disorder was still preventing the elections when Milo murdered Clodius near Bovillae 18 Jan. 52. Pompey then became sole consul and had Milo prosecuted before a court so heavily guarded that Cicero did not dare to defend him (though he subsequently published his speech *Pro Milone*). Milo retired to exile at Massilia, thanking Cicero that his reticence allowed him to enjoy the mullets there. But in 48 he answered Caelius' appeal to recreate disorder and was captured and executed at Cosa. (On the lawsuits of 57–56 cf. Ed. Meyer, *Caesars Monarchie²* (1919), 109, n. 3.) G. E. F. C.

MILON, an athlete from Croton of the later sixth century B.C.; six times victor in wrestling at the Olympian Games, six times at the Pythian. He is said to have carried a heifer down the course, killed it with one blow, and eaten it all in one day. Trying to rend a tree asunder he was caught in the cleft and eaten alive by wolves. F. A. W.

MILTIADES (c. 550–489 B.C.) belonged to the noble Athenian family of the Philaïdae, and was sent c. 524 by Hippias to continue the policy of Athenian hegemony in the Thracian Chersonese which Miltiades' namesake and paternal uncle had inaugurated under Pisistratus (c. 555) and probably at his prompting. Miltiades ruled as absolute king over the natives, but he encouraged Athenian settlers and, after freeing Lemnos from Persia (c. 500), he handed it over to Athens. He had previously been a vassal of Darius and accompanied him on the

Scythian expedition (c. 513), but his later claim to have proposed the breaking down of the Danube bridge is disproved by the fact that Darius left him unmolested. He married Hegesipyle, daughter of the wealthy Thracian king Olorus, who bore him Cimon. His other children (including the ill-famed Elpinice) were by a previous marriage with an Athenian lady. After a short exile caused by a Scythian invasion Miltiades was restored by the Thracians (496). At the end of the Ionian Revolt, in which he had participated, he fled from the Persians and returned to Athens (493). Here he survived an accusation of 'tyranny' in Thrace and became the most influential politician. As general in 490 he won the support of Callimachus (q.v. 1) and most of his colleagues for engaging the Persians at Marathon, where he won a decisive victory. Inaugurating a policy of naval expansion, he led an expedition to Paros (early spring 489), which he was unable to capture. On the accusation of Xanthippus (q.v. 1) Miltiades was fined 50 talents for having deceived the people, and soon afterwards succumbed to a wound sustained at Paros.

E. Obst, *PW*, s.v.; W. W. How, *JHS* 1919; J. Wells, *Studies in Herodotus* (1923), 112 ff.; E. Cavaignac, *Rev. Phil.* 1929; A. Passerini, *Milziade e l'occupazione di Lemno* (1935); H. Berve, *Miltiades* (1937); V. Ehrenberg, *Eunomia* i (1939), 13 ff., 28 ff.; H. Bengtson, *Sitz. der Bayrischen Akademie, philos.-historische Abt.*, 1939, Heft 1. P. T.

MIMNERMUS, elegiac poet and musician (Strabo 643) of Colophon (ibid.) and Smyrna (Paus. 9. 29. 4). His *floruit* is given as 632–629 B.C. by Suidas; this suits his interchange with Solon (fr. 6 and Sol. fr. 22). The eclipse of the sun to which he referred (Plut. *Mor.* 931 e) gives no help, as it may be either 648 or 585 B.C. His elegies were collected in two books (Porph. ad Hor. *Epist.* 2. 2. 101), one of which was called *Nanno* after the flute-girl he is said to have loved (Hermesianax ap. Ath. 597 f., Strabo 643). This seems to have been a collection of poems on very different themes, such as mythology about Tithonus (fr. 4), the Sun's magic bowl (fr. 10), and history about the foundation of Colophon (fr. 12, Strabo 633). The same book may have contained his account of the war between Smyrna and Gyges (fr. 13, Paus. 9. 29. 4). His other fragments are concerned largely with the pleasures of youth and the horrors of old age (frs. 1–3). But he tempers his hedonism with a respect for truth (fr. 8) and for warlike qualities (frs. 12–13). He seems to have written a *Smyrneis*, or historical poem on Smyrna, which may have been contained in the *Nanno*. He is remarkable for his musical use of the elegiac, his brilliant sustained images, the directness of his emotional appeal, and his love of pleasure.

Text: E. Diehl, *Anth. Lyr. Graec.* i. i. 50–7. Commentary: T. Hudson-Williams, *Early Greek Elegy* (1925), 90–9. Criticism: U. von Wilamowitz-Moellendorff, *Sappho und Simonides* (1913), 276 ff.; C. M. Bowra, *Early Greek Elegy* (1936), 17–35. C. M. B.

MIMUS (μῖμος), an imitative performance or performer.
I. GREEK. In Greece, as elsewhere, the instinct for imitation found its expression in the mimetic dance. From early times solo performers, by play of gesture, voice, and feature, gave imitations of neighing horses, etc. (Plato *Resp.* 396 b), and small companies, called in Sparta δεικηλίκται (? 'masked men'), elsewhere αὐτοκάβδαλοι ('improvisers') or in Italiot towns φλύακες, presented short scenes from daily life (e.g. 'The Quack Doctor') or mythology, probably on a hastily erected stage in the market-place or in a private house; such performers belonged to the social class of acrobats, etc. Xenophon (*Symp.*) tells of a mime 'of Dionysus and Ariadne', danced at a private banquet by a boy and girl; we note the connexion with Syracuse, the musical accompaniment, the use of dialogue, and the fact that the girl is also a sword-dancer and the concubine of the Syracusan dancing-master. In the fifth century Sophron of Syracuse wrote 'men's' and 'women's' mimes in

Dorian rhythmic prose; the language was popular and included frequent proverbs; the surviving titles (e.g. 'The old fishermen', 'The women quacks', 'The women visitors to the Isthmia') indicate stock mime themes. Of the mimes of Sophron's son, Xenarchus, virtually nothing is known. In the third century the taste for realism brought the mime to the fore; Theocritus dressed traditional themes in his courtly hexameters (Idyll 2: the deserted heroine resorts to magic; 15: two Syracusan women visit the festival of Adonis in Alexandria; 21: two old fishermen converse; 14 is also dramatic in form); these pieces, like those of the more realistic Herodas (q.v.), were probably intended for semi-dramatic recitation. Meanwhile the popular mime invaded the theatre; it now took the form either of παίγνια (? slight, often vulgar, performances) or of ὑποθέσεις, 'plots' (Plut. *Quaest. conv.* 7. ή. 4, p. 712 e), taken over from drama proper and presented in mimic fashion by the μαγῳδοί (Ath. 621 c) or μιμολόγοι (the meaning of the various terms for performers, whether they suggest spoken or musical delivery, is uncertain); cf. the third-century Athenian lamp with its representation of three maskless performers and the inscription 'Mimologi; hypothesis: Stepmother'. The 'Alexandrian erotic fragment' is perhaps a sung mime: theme, the deserted heroine. In *POxy.* 413 we have (a) a prose farce, based on the plot of *Iph. Taur.* (?): a Greek girl, named Charition, aided by her brother, escapes from an Indian king and his followers by making them drunk; the barbarians speak pseudo-Indian; there is a low clowning part; (b) a prose mime: theme, the jealous mistress (cf. Herodas v), who tries to poison her husband and make love to her slaves; there are six or seven short scenes and seven roles, all unimportant except that of the archimima; here, as always, the interest of the mime is in character and situation rather than in action. In the Marissa wall-inscription we have a song-dialogue between a hetaera and the *exclusus amator*. (See Herodas, ed. Crusius, 1914, for the text of all these pieces).

II. ROMAN (known also as *fabula riciniata*). Before the end of the third century B.C. the barefooted *planipes* appeared on the stage at Rome. The undatable epitaph of Vitalis (*Minor Latin Poets*, J. W. and A. M. Duff; Loeb, pp. 636–9) points to solo, maskless displays; Cicero refers to extempore troupe performances of improbable themes like 'The Beggar turns Millionaire' (*Phil.* 2. 65). A popular feature at the Floralia was the appearance of the *mimae* (alias *meretrices*) naked. Sulla patronized the mime; soon it rivalled the *Atellana* as an after-piece; Dionysia received 200,000 sesterces yearly, and we read of a company of 60 *mimi* under an *archimimus*. Associated with Julius Caesar were the mime-writers Laberius, Syrus, and Matius. Favoured by the emperors, beloved by the rabble, still topical, farcical, and indecent, the mime (with the pantomime) practically monopolized the stage; a typical *mimus* was the close-cropped fool, dressed in the patch-work *centunculus*. Domitian had a real crucifixion inserted in a mime; Heliogabalus ordered mimic adulteries to be performed realistically; in the person of Theodora a *mima* reached the throne. Unsubdued by their losing battle with the Church and even by the barbarian invasions, the strolling companies, it is claimed, have survived as the wandering *jongleurs* of the Middle Ages.

H. Reich, *Der Mimus* (1903); *PW* (1932), s.v. 'Mimos'; J. R. A. Nicoll, *Masks, Mimes and Miracles* (1931; well illustrated). W. B.

MINDARUS, Spartan admiral, 411/10 B.C. Mistrusting Tissaphernes (q.v.) and relying on support from Pharnabazus (q.v.), he transferred the main Peloponnesian fleet to the Hellespont. The Athenians defeated him off Cynossema and again off Abydos (autumn, 411), thereby safeguarding the passage of their corn-ships. Early in 410 Mindarus recaptured Cyzicus, but he was there surprised by a superior fleet under Alcibiades and fell in a vain attempt to save his ships from capture. Though out-generalled by Alcibiades, he showed more enterprise and ability than his predecessors.

Thucydides 8. 99–107; Xenophon, *Hell.* 1. 1. 2–18; Diodorus 13. 38–51.   H. D. W.

MINERALOGY. Although the Greeks and Romans had a practical knowledge of metals, precious stones, and building materials, and were always familiar with their use, they never made outstanding discoveries in the science of mineralogy. The passages in Homer and Hesiod which refer to mines and stones are of no scientific importance, and the same may be said of most of the incidental remarks made by geographers and historians, e.g. Strabo. Even so practically minded a man as the author of the treatise on Revenues generally attributed to Xenophon, although he deals at length with the exploitation of the Laurian silver mines, shows no appreciation of the truly technical problems of mineralogy. Plato's *Ion* is evidence that among his contemporaries the theory of the attractive power of the loadstone was widely known, but neither the philosopher himself nor his disciples were interested in this branch of science. Theophrastus' work Περὶ λίθων (On stones) gives only a brief survey of marbles, pointing out their peculiar qualities, and where they are to be found; but here too mineralogy is treated not as an independent field of research or as a study of scientific value, but as of merely practical utility. For instance, one looks in vain for any exposition of the chemical properties of stones and minerals. Nevertheless, Theophrastus' work had a deep influence on Roman writers, especially Lucretius, Vitruvius, and Pliny the Elder. The last gave even more attention to mineralogy than Theophrastus himself had done, but from an essentially geographical and architectural point of view, while a contemporary of Pliny, Dioscorides, approached it from the standpoint of the physician and physiologist. His five books Περὶ ὕλης ἰατρικῆς (On materia medica) exerted a wide influence upon Graeco-Byzantine science, and it was from Dioscorides that knowledge of ancient mineralogy, scanty as it was, passed through the channel of Arabian alchemy into medieval Europe.

Texts: A useful selection, with a German translation, is given by H. O. Lenz, *Mineralogie d. alten Griechen u. Römer* (1861). Theophrastus' Περὶ λίθων (ed. Wimmer, Teubner) was translated into English by Sir J. Hill (1774). Dioscorides has been edited by M. Wellmann (Weidmann series, 1906–14), and there exists a German translation and commentary by J. Berendes (1902). General literature: E. v. Lippmann, *Abhandlungen u. Vorträge z. Gesch. d. Naturwissenschaften* (1906), 1 ff.   P. T.

MINERVA (archaic **Menerva**), an Italian goddess of handicrafts, widely worshipped and regularly identified with Athena (q.v.). Altheim (*PW*, s.v.; cf. *Hist. Rom. Rel.*, p. 235 and note 34; *Griechische Götter*, p. 142, note 4) believes her actually to be Athena, borrowed early through Etruria; but most scholars think her native, and connect her name with the root of *memini*, etc. At all events there is no trace of her cult in Rome before the introduction of the Capitoline Triad, where she appears with Jupiter and Juno (qq.v.) in an Etruscan grouping. Apart from this she was worshipped in a shrine on Mons Caelius under the name of Minerva Capta, after the taking of Falerii in 241 B.C. (Ovid, *Fasti* 3. 835 ff., where see Frazer; cf. Platner–Ashby, p. 343 f.). A much more important cult lay *extra pomerium* on the Aventine (Platner–Ashby, p. 342), but its age is unknown; it was the headquarters of a guild of writers and actors during the Second Punic War (Festus, p. 446, 26 ff. Lindsay) and seems to have been generally the centre of organizations of skilled craftsmen. Minerva's worship spread at the expense of Mars (q.v.) himself, the Quinquatrus coming to be considered her festival, apparently because it was the *natalis* of her temple (Ov. ibid. 812); it was also

extended to five days, from a misunderstanding of the meaning ('fifth day after' a given date; see Frazer ad loc.) 13 June was called the *Quinquatrus minusculae* and was the peculiar feast-day of the professional flute-players (*tibicines*; cf. Ov. *Fasti* 6. 651 ff., and Frazer ad loc.).   H. J. R.

MINES. Though ore had been extracted (both opencast and underground) at other places much earlier, systematic exploitation was first developed at Laurium. The simple geological strata there made it easy to learn to prospect where no indications appeared on the surface. This experience was utilized by the Romans, who were able to test dipping veins, though complex problems such as faulting defeated them.

2. Ancient shafts and galleries are normally small, as they were cut with hand-tools and it was desirable to obviate propping. Siliceous rocks were broken by firesetting, a method known in the Bronze Age in Austria. Placer-mines were worked by panning, and for largescale enterprises (in Spain and at Dolaucothy in Wales) water was brought by aqueducts for hushing (i.e. breaking down of softer beds by rush of water). Iron tools were normal in classical times, though stone hammers survived in many districts for crushing ore.

3. The miners were mainly slaves, both in the larger Greek mines and in the centralized workings of the Roman Empire. Overseers and engineers were also slaves; in the Empire legionaries were sometimes used. Later, criminals were employed at a few mines and quarries. The Romans sometimes kept their workmen permanently below ground. Some mines the Roman Government exploited directly; at others small concessions were leased, but both technically and socially the mining community was controlled by a procurator. Large lessees, individuals and companies, subject to little control, were common in the Republic but rare later, save at iron-mines. At Laurium concessions were leased to citizens; they were usually large enough to employ several slaves, but sometimes the lessee would himself work underground. In Egypt state-exploitation was the rule.

4. A developed mining-royalty never existed, though the State claimed dues from miners and authorized mining on other men's property. In earlier times the State *de facto* owned most mines. The idea of royalty was probably developed by the German kingdoms.

5. The chief difficulties of ancient miners were ventilation and drainage. The former was poor owing to narrow galleries and the use of naked lights, and the various artificial improvements were seldom successful. The best was to drive intercommunicating adits at different levels. The influx of water often caused mines to be abandoned. The Romans used various drainage-machines, such as the screw-pump and perhaps the chain-pump (1st c. A.D.), the water-wheel (2nd c.), and the suction-pump (late Empire); but these devices, being worked by human power, were expensive, and could be used only where the ore was profitable. Batteries of water-wheels superimposed to a depth of 75 metres have been found at Ruda. No machines were sufficiently powerful to reclaim a mine once abandoned. Where the ground-formation permitted, drainage was secured by adits, which were sometimes driven through a mile of sterile rock. The ore was hauled to the surface on trays or in sacks, often by boys, who could move quickly in narrow galleries.

Ancient sources: scattered references in Pliny, Strabo, etc. Technique: O. Davies, *Roman Mines in Europe* (1935); U. Täckholm, *Studien über den Bergbau der römischen Kaiserzeit* (1937); detailed studies in E. Ardaillon, *Les Mines du Laurion* (1897), C. Zschocke and E. Preuschen, *Das urzeitliche Bergbaugebiet von Mühlbach-Bischofshofen* (1932). Legal position: *Lex Metalli Vipascensis* (Dessau, *ILS* 6891), and references in *Codex Theodosianus*; E. Schönbauer, *Beiträge zur Geschichte des Bergbaurechts*.

Mining personnel: inscriptions quoted in general works; the most informative Christian source is *Passio IV Coronatorum*. Drainage-machines: E. Treptow, *Beiträge zur Geschichte der Technik und der Industrie* viii (1918), 155; R. E. Palmer, *Trans. Institution of Mining and Metallurgy* xxxvi (1926/7), 299; *Archaeologia Cambrensis* (1936), 51; T. A. Rickard, *Engineering and Mining Journal* cxxiii (1927), 917. Fire-setting: Holman, *Trans. Institution of Mining and Metallurgy* xxxvi (1926/7), 219.   O. D.

MINOAN (derived from *Minos*, q.v.), a term used to denote the Bronze Age civilization of Crete; its successive stages are known as Early, Middle, and Late Minoan (E.M., M.M., L.M.). The archaeological evidence of the greatness of Cnossos (q.v.) is held to support the historical basis of the tradition. Minos' overlordship of Athens is reflected in Cretan influence on the Greek mainland during the first two phases of the Late Bronze Age (1600–1400 B.C.). The tradition of Minos the thalassocrat, and the frequent occurrence of Minoa as a place-name in the Aegean, are believed to be reflected in the Minoan pottery found in the islands, on the Syrian coast, in Cyprus, and in Egypt. Some think that Cretans under Minos conquered and colonized part of the Greek mainland and that Mycenae was a Minoan colony. Mycenae, however, has no legendary connexion with Crete, and Minoan influence on the mainland was no stronger than Greek influence in Etruria in historical times. Middle Minoan objects occur in the Cyclades (Melos, Thera), in Cyprus, at Byblus, and in Egypt, but in Late Minoan times in Melos, Cyprus, Syria, Palestine, and Egypt the mainland pottery is far more frequent than Cretan. The pottery in Sicily thought to be Cretan and to confirm the legend of Minos' death there is not Cretan, but comes from some centre of Mycenaean culture.
                                                        A. J. B W.

MINORCA, *see* BALEARES INSULAE.

MINORS, *see* GUARDIANSHIP.

MINOS (*Μίνως*), a king of Crete; the traditions concerning him preserve faint reminiscences of the might of the civilization now called Minoan (q.v.), and 'Minos' may be a dynastic name or title. See, e.g., Thucydides 1. 4 for a tradition of his sea-power. It is conceivable at least that the evil character given him in Attic legends, but not in the main stream of Greek tradition ([Plato], *Minos*, 318 d–e), has behind it a real contest between prehistoric Attica and Crete; cf. below.

He is consistently said to be son of Zeus and Europa (q.v.), and to have married Pasiphaë, daughter of Helios (Apollod. 3. 7, followed here unless the contrary is stated). Her name, 'all-shining', has been interpreted as that of a moon-goddess, which is unnecessary, as it fits a fully human child of the sun-god (cf. Phaëthon); but that both the kings and queens of Minoan Crete were regarded as partly or wholly divine is quite possible. To settle the question whether Minos or another should be king, Minos prayed to Poseidon to send a bull from the sea for him to sacrifice. Poseidon did so, thus confirming his right to rule, but the bull was so handsome that Minos would not kill it. Poseidon therefore caused Pasiphaë to fall in love with it.* By the help of Daedalus (q.v.) she was disguised as a cow and attained her end; consequently she bore a creature half-man, half-bull, 'Minos' bull', *Μίνω ταῦρος*, the 'Minotaur(us)' of Latin and English. Daedalus constructed a maze, the labyrinth,† to hide it in.

Minos made war on Megara and Athens. As regards the former, for the legend of Minos, Nisus, and Scylla,

* Minos' power is derived from Zeus in *Odyssey* 19. 178–9, an obscure passage; Aphrodite causes Pasiphaë's passion, e.g. in Hyginus, *Fab.* 40. 1, more appropriately.
† The word is pre-Hellenic, connected with λάβρυς, a double axe, the well-known Cretan religious symbol; a rite involving the use of a maze may underlie the story; see Knight, *Cumaean Gates*, ch. 8.

see NISUS. At Athens he was provoked by the murder of his son Androgeos, and so made peace only on terms of receiving a yearly tribute of youths and maidens, whom he shut up with the Minotaur (Plutarch, *Thes.* 15; *see* THESEUS).

Minos' death was due to treachery. Daedalus having escaped, he pursued him to Sicily, where he found him by a stratagem in the house of Cocalus, king of Camicus. He demanded his surrender, and Cocalus pretended to agree, received Minos with show of hospitality, and handed him over to his daughters to be bathed in the Homeric fashion. They killed him by pouring boiling water (or pitch instead of water) on him (Hdt. 7. 170. 1; Apollod. *Epit.* 1. 13–15).

Besides the larger dictionaries s.v., see Cook, *Zeus* ii, 939 ff.
                                                        H. J. R.

MINOTAUR, *see* MINOS.

MINT (at Rome), *see* AERARIUM, COINAGE, MONETA.

MINTURNAE was a town of the Aurunci, situated midway between Formiae and Sinuessa on the Via Appia. The original town and the sixth-century shrine of the sea-goddess Marica lay on the north bank of the Liris and consisted of a small, rectangular fortification with pseudo-polygonal walls and angle-towers. To this was added, on the west, a Roman colony in 295 B.C. (Vell. 1. 14; Livy 8. 11), which was restored by Augustus (Pliny, *HN* 3. 59). The *capitolium* and *forum* of this colony have been excavated, and its houses lie buried below later Imperial buildings. When the Imperial *forum* was built the old one became a portico behind the Augustan theatre, while the *capitolium* was eclipsed by three new temples, one embodying manumission records of the Sullan period. The west town-gate (*JRS* xxiii. 155) embodies an aqueduct-*castellum* or distribution-chamber. The ancient *forma* of the field-system, figured by the Agrimensores (*Corpus Agrimens. Rom.* i. 1, fig. 81, p. 21), is discussed by A. Schulten (*Hermes* xxxiii. 537–40), though with erroneous assumptions about the earliest site and the Liris.

J. Johnson, *Excavations at Minturnae* (U.S.A. 1933), i, ii.
                                                        I. A. R.

MINUCIANUS the Elder (2nd c. A.D.), rival of Hermogenes, wrote Προγυμνάσματα, a τέχνη (treating of στάσις theory), and a commentary on Demosthenes. The Π. ἐπιχειρημάτων (Spengel, *Rhet.* i. 417–24) is probably by a third-century namesake. In rhetorical theory Minucianus, influenced by Aristotle and Theodorus, stood for philosophic, as opposed to Sophistic, rhetoric; and he challenged without success the innovations of Hermogenes.
                                                        J. W. H. A.

MINUCIUS (1), LUCIUS, figures in two famous legends. He is said to have been rescued by Cincinnatus (q.v.) from defeat by the Aequi on Mount Algidus (458 B.C.), and to have been a member of the second decemvirate. In 439 he dealt with a famine and a revolutionary attempt by Sp. Maelius. Although the traditional account was much elaborated by annalists of the Gracchan period, who invented his *transitio ad plebem* and vested him with a chronologically impossible *praefectura annonae*, Minucius was probably an actual public benefactor during a fifth-century famine. He need not be explained away either as a god, corresponding to Hercules μηνυτής, or as the eponymous builder of the Porticus Minucia, which was not built before *c.* 106 or used for corn distributions until Claudius, while Cincius Alimentus shows that the story of Minucius was known already in his time.

A. Momigliano, *Studia et documenta historiae et iuris* ii (1936).
                                                        P. T.

MINUCIUS (2) **RUFUS**, Marcus (*cos.* 221 B.C.), helped to reduce the Istri. After the battle of Trasimene (217) he was appointed *magister equitum* to Fabius (q.v. 5) Cunctator by the Comitia, not by the dictator himself as was customary. Minucius disobeyed Fabius' orders and in his absence attacked Hannibal at Gerunium with considerable success. The People then appointed Minucius co-dictator with Fabius, an undermining of the nature of the office. The aristocratic tradition records that he was rescued from an attack by Hannibal only by the timely arrival of Fabius. He fell at Cannae (216).
H. H. S.

MINUCIUS (3) **AUGURINUS**, Gaius, a tribune (*c.* 187 B.C.), who, after the attack of the Petilii (q.v.), accused L. Scipio of refusing to render an account of monies received from Antiochus; he imposed a fine and a demand for surety, but was prevented by his colleague Gracchus (q.v. 2) from enforcing his demands.
H. H. S.

MINUCIUS (4) **RUFUS**, Quintus or M. (*cos.* 110 B.C.), brother of M. Rufus who as tribune in 121 proposed the repeal of C. Gracchus' legislation, triumphed in 106 for victories as consul over the Scordisci and Triballi in Macedonia. He erected the Porticus Minucia, where corn was publicly distributed during the early Empire. M. H.

MINUCIUS (5) **FELIX**, probably a native of the Roman province Africa, who lived at some period between the middle of the second and the middle of the third century A.D. He has left one work, a dialogue called *Octavius* (from the name of one of the interlocutors), the scene of which is laid at Ostia. The work is of relatively high literary quality, and belongs to the class of 'apologetic' literature, being concerned with the defence of Christianity.

Ed. H. A. Holden (1853); J. P. Waltzing (Teubner, 1912); J. Martin (Bonn, 1930); A. D. Simpson (U.S.A., 1938). Transl. J. H. Freese (SPCK, 1918). J. P. Waltzing, *Lexicon Minucianum* (1909). A. S.

MINUCIUS PACATUS, see EIRENAEUS.

MINYANS (Μινύαι), a prehistoric tribe, whose chief branches inhabited the Boeotian Orchomenus (*Il.* 2. 511) and Iolcus in Thessaly (ibid. 712). To the latter belong the legends of Athamas and Jason (qq.v.). There were also families claiming Minyan descent in Laconia (the Aegeids), Thera, and Cyrene; a Minyan tribe round Lepreum, destroyed by the Eleans *c.* 475 B.C.; and legends of former Minyans in Lemnos, descended from the Argonauts (Pindar, *Pyth.* 4; Hdt. 4. 145–8, who combines all these facts and legends into one story).

The fine wheel-made pottery, of 'soapy' surface, known as 'Grey Minyan', was so called by Schliemann because first found at Orchomenus. It first appears *c.* 2000 B.C., and has no probable connexion with the Minyae of legend. *See* MINYAS. A. R. B.

MINYAS (Μινύας). Founder of Orchomenus and eponym of the Minyae (Pindar, *Isthm.* 1. 56); his 'treasury', shown at Orchomenus in Pausanias' time (Paus. 9. 38. 2), was a Mycenaean beehive-tomb, as was proved by Schliemann's investigations. He is also in some sense ancestor of the Argonauts (q.v.), they being commonly called Minyans, as Pindar, *Pyth.* 4. 69; the reason given by Apoll. Rhod. 1. 230 ff., that most of them were descended from his daughters, does not agree with the surviving lists but may have with the primitive form of the story. His legend, if ever he had one (the lost epic *Minyas* may have had something to say of him), has vanished, and we know of him chiefly as a member of several genealogies, mutually inconsistent and connecting him with Orchomenus, Thessaly (Iolcus), and several

other regions. These are conveniently assembled by Fiehn in *PW* xv. 2015–8; see the whole article for ancient and modern literature. H. J. R.

MIRACLES. Wonderful stories of the power of gods were common at all periods of antiquity, and many of them were attached to particular shrines. For instance, there is the very pretty tale of the ugly child miraculously made beautiful by Helen (Hdt. 6. 61; shrine at Therapnae); another local legend told how Poseidon miraculously smote an impious intruder into his temple at Mantinea (Paus. 8. 10. 3). In Rome tales of this sort perhaps clustered most thickly around Vesta. For example, there is the legend of the Vestal Aemilia, during whose service of the goddess the holy fire went out. It being by no fault of hers, she prayed to Vesta to prove her innocence, and flung a strip of her robe upon the altar, which at once blazed to confirm her innocence (Dion. Hal. *Ant. Rom.* 2. 68. 3). One of Martial's flatteries of Domitian is the story of how a man who violated his 'sacred' fishpond was blinded, a regular form of divine punishment (Mart. 4. 30. 8 ff.; cf. Sauter, *Kaiserkult bei Martial u. Statius*, 110 f.). The cult of Asclepius (q.v.), produced a vast quantity of miracles of healing, by no means all confined to his shrines (see, e.g., Suidas s.v. Θεόπομπος). But miracles are more prominent in Hellenistic times, and especially in connexion with foreign gods, such as Isis and Sarapis. Among these international gods there was necessarily competition. Hence many stories of the manifestation of, e.g., Sarapis' power to convince the sceptical, prove his deity, and so on; examples in Nock, *Conversion*, index under 'Miracles'. H. J. R.

MISE (Μίση), an obscure goddess, first mentioned in Hero(n)das 1. 56, where the name of the festival, κάθοδος, suggests chthonian ritual. The forty-second Orphic hymn says she is bisexual and seems to identify her with both Dionysus and Demeter; she may well be Asianic. H. J. R.

MISENUM, the northern headland of the Bay of Naples, with a similarly named town and harbour, reputedly the burial place of Aeneas' trumpeter Misenus (Verg. *Aen.* 6. 234). Cumae early used the harbour, but until Imperial times Misenum was merely a villa resort (Octavian, Antony, and Sextus Pompeius signed their Treaty of Misenum at Puteoli, 39 B.C.: *Rev. Arch.* xxii (1913), 253). Agrippa made the harbour Rome's chief naval station (31 B.C.), and the town subsequently became a *colonia* (Dessau, *ILS* 6335). The Elder Pliny was stationed here and perished when Vesuvius erupted, A.D. 79 (Pliny, *Ep.* 6. 16. 20). The harbour fell into disuse *c.* 400, and finally the Saracens destroyed Misenum. Remains exist of Marius' villa, later the property of Lucullus and the emperors.

K. Lehmann-Hartleben, *Die Antiken Hafenanlagen des Mittelmeeres* (1923), 176. E. T. S.

MISENUS, a follower of Aeneas, best known from Verg. *Aen.* 6. 162 ff.; he was a trumpeter, formerly a follower of Hector, and was drowned by an envious Triton. Cape Misenum (q.v.) was named from him.

MISERICORDIA. Hyginus, *praef. Fab.* 1, makes Misericordia one of the children of Night and Erebus, but the passage is too corrupt to draw any definite conclusions.

MITHRAS (Μίθρας, -ης), an ancient Aryan (Indo-Iranian) god; in Zoroastrianism (*see* RELIGION, PERSIAN; ZOROASTER) one of the good powers, of the party of Ahura-Mazda and closely associated with light, hence easily understood as a sun-god, whatever his original character may have been. His cult was important in

Asia (cf. the common occurrence of the name Mithridates), and his existence known to Greeks at least as early as Herodotus (I. 131), who, however, imagines him to be a goddess. But in passing west from Iran his worship absorbed many foreign, especially Mesopotamian, elements, including a strong tincture of astrology. He is said (Plutarch, *Pomp.* 24) to have been introduced into the West by the Cilician pirates overthrown by Pompey the Great, but if so his worship remained obscure, perhaps confined to foreigners and the lowest of the native population, till much later. The first clear mention of him in surviving literature is late in the first century A.D. (Statius, *Theb.* I. 719–20), and Plutarch (*Mor.* 369 e) gives a curious account of him as an intermediary between the good and evil powers, which is hardly consistent with what is otherwise known of him. The mysteries of Mithras become really important about the time of the Flavians and increase rapidly in influence during the following centuries (Cumont, op. cit. infra, i. 245 ff.). The main channel of their propagation in the Roman Empire (Greece did not welcome them) was the army; foreign, especially Asianic, merchants were also devotees. Hence the monuments of the cult are almost confined to the sites of garrisons and large sea-ports.

The ritual, being secret and confined to men, so far as is known, remains largely obscure, little light being thrown on it by texts, and the figured monuments from the shrines being often of doubtful interpretation. It appears, however, that Mithras' legend included a miraculous birth in primeval times from a rock (Jerome, *Adv. Iovinian.* I. 7; Cumont, i 59 ff., and refs.). Adored, it would seem, by shepherds (one of several curious resemblances to Christianity, between which and Mithraism there are certainly influences, perhaps reciprocal), the god embarked on a series of adventures whereof two were of outstanding importance.

The first was some kind of trial of strength with the Sun-god, resulting in friendship and alliance between the two. This, while showing that Mithras is not himself the Sun, does not prevent the two from being often identified, not only in literature (as Statius, loc. cit.), but in dedications, which constantly call him *Sol inuictus Mithras*. The second exploit was the capture of a mysterious bull, which after some minor episodes was sacrificed by Mithras. The sculptures representing this (Mithras Tauroctonus) are the most characteristic of Mithraic monuments; the expression on the god's face indicates strongly that it is a painful duty. Composition and technique are plainly Greek in origin. From the bull's body came all manner of useful plants and so forth.

The ritual of Mithras was carried out in artificial caves, *spelaea*, evidently meant to represent real ones; a characteristic sanctuary (e.g. that at Ostia) is oblong, like the nave of a church, having at one end a sort of altar-piece, with Mithras and the bull for the central figures and other sculptures around this. Along the sides of the structure run shallow benches fixed to the walls. The details are little known; we have evidence, however, that there was a kind of sacramental meal (Cumont, i. 146 f.); that the candidate for initiation went through certain ordeals, one of which seems to have been a pretended homicide (S.H.A., *Commodus* 9. 6); that there was a rite of baptism, a mark of some kind made on the forehead of initiates, and a ceremony in which the candidate, having had a garland put on his head, took it off, saying 'Mithras is my garland' (Tertullian, *De Bapt.* 5; *De praescr. haeret.* 40; *De Corona* 15). We also know that there were seven grades, doubtless having each its own ceremonial of initiation. These were: Corax (crow), Cryphius (Gryphus? Nymphius? see E. Wüst and O. Weinreich in *ARW* xxxii. 211 ff.), of uncertain meaning and reading, Miles (soldier), Leo (lion), Perses (Persian), Heliodromus (sun-runner, possibly messenger of the Sun-god), and finally Pater (father; this was no doubt the highest rank,

but we have no proof that the rest are listed in ascending order). See Jerome, *Ep.* 107. 2. 2. It is not accidental that the number is that of the traditional planets. There was other astrological symbolism (Origen, *c. Cels.* 6. 21) and doubtless an eschatology, but concerning this we have hardly more than conjectures based on what is known of Persian and other teachings.

Literature: chief work, Fr. Cumont, *Textes et monuments figurés relatifs aux mystères de Mithra* (2 vols., 1896 and 1899). See also same, *Les Mystères de Mithra*[3] (1913); also English and German transl.); *Les religions orientales dans le paganisme romain*[4] (1929); A. D. Nock in *JRS* xxvii. 108–113. H. J. R.

MITHRIDATES. The name of several kings of Pontus.

(1) MITHRIDATES I of Cios, a member of a Persian family which claimed descent from one of the six associates of Darius the Great, founded the Pontic dynasty in 337–336 B.C. (the coin era of the realm). He was put to death in 302 by Antigonus I, who had become suspicious of his loyalty.

(2) MITHRIDATES II, son or nephew of (1), escaped from Antigonus I and soon won Pontus, making Amaseia his capital. He took the royal title in 281, and joined Nicomedes of Bithynia in settling the Galatians in Phrygia. He died about 266, and was succeeded by Ariobarzanes, who died about 250 while engaged in a war with the Galatians.

(3) MITHRIDATES III terminated the Galatian war. He married Laodice, sister of Seleucus II, but his interest in weakening the Seleucid power led him to assist Antiochus Hierax in driving Seleucus beyond Mt. Taurus. He gave one daughter in marriage to Achaeus and another to Antiochus III (c. 223). He made gifts to Rhodes after the earthquake (227), but his attempt on Sinope in 220 was defeated with Rhodian help. He died about 185. (*See* PHARNACES I.)

(4) MITHRIDATES IV succeeded his brother Pharnaces I, with his sister Laodice as queen. He became a friend and ally of Rome and supported Attalus II of Pergamum against Prusias II of Bithynia in 156–154. He probably died c. 150 B.C.

(5) MITHRIDATES V, probably son of Pharnaces I, followed a philo-Roman and hellenizing policy while striving to enlarge his kingdom. He aided Rome against Carthage in 149–146 and against Aristonicus in 132–129, and received Phrygia as a reward from Aquilius. He had already gained control of Galatia, was named the heir of Pylaemenes of Inner Paphlagonia, and brought Cappadocia under his influence through the marriage of Ariarathes VI with his daughter Laodice. He was murdered at Sinope, his capital, in 120, and a suspiciously convenient will named his wife Laodice and his two minor children, Eupator and Chrestus, as his successors.

(6) MITHRIDATES VI, EUPATOR DIONYSUS ('the Great'), son of Mithridates V, fled from his mother and led a fugitive existence for seven years, then suddenly captured Sinope, imprisoned his mother, killed his brother, married his sister Laodice (the first member of a large harem), and resumed his father's policy of expansion. He first acquired the north shore of the Euxine, from which he drew large revenues and many soldiers. He then occupied Lesser Armenia, eastern Pontus, and Colchis. Attempts (in alliance or rivalry with Bithynia) to secure control of Inner Paphlagonia and Cappadocia were foiled by Rome, and an attempt to expel Nicomedes IV from Bithynia was equally unsuccessful. Raids on Pontic territory in 88 by Nicomedes led to the First Mithridatic War. Mithridates occupied most of Asia Minor, where Roman exactions made him welcome as a deliverer, the islands of the Aegean except Rhodes, and (with Athenian help) much of Greece. Sulla's victories drove him out of Greece and led to a reaction against him in Asia, which he met by severe reprisals. He made peace at Dardanus in 84 on Sulla's terms, giving up all conquered territory. He easily repelled the raids of

Sulla's lieutenant Murena in 81 (the Second Mithridatic War), and used the next years to tighten his hold on the Pontic coast, to foster close relationships with the pirate leaders, and lay up stores of treasure and supplies. Rome's decision in 74 to annex Bithynia precipitated the Third Mithridatic War. Mithridates occupied Bithynia, but the resistance of Cyzicus enabled Lucullus to cut off his army from supplies and destroy it. He was expelled from Pontus by Lucullus (72), and although a mutiny of the Roman army allowed Mithridates to recover much of his territory (67), he had not enough strength left to stand against Lucullus' successor Pompey. Defeated at Nicopolis, he fled to Colchis, sending orders for the massacre of his harem, and made his way to the Crimea. Here the sacrifices which he demanded for a new fleet and army raised his subjects in revolt, led by his son Pharnaces. Driven to bay, he found that a diet of pro-phylactics had made him immune to poison, and died by the sword of a guard at the age of 68. In cunning, courage, and organizing ability Mithridates was Rome's stoutest Oriental antagonist, but he failed in the arts of a strategist, and could not keep the loyalty of his sub-ordinates. His portraits show that he copied Alexander in personal appearance. He was a true representative neither of the Hellenism which he affected nor of the Iranians who formed the most important element among his people.

Appian, *Mith.*; Plutarch, *Luc.* and *Pomp.* Th. Reinach, *Trois royaumes de l'Asie Mineure* (1888); *Mithridate Eupator* (1890); M. Rostovtzeff, *CAH* ix, ch. 5; H. A. Ormerod and M. Cary, ibid., ch. 8. T. R. S. B.

MITYLENE, *see* MYTILENE.

MNASALCES (not 'Mnasalcas'), of the deme Plataeae in Sicyon, seems to have flourished *c.* 250 B.C. A satirical epitaph for him (perhaps composed while M. was alive) by Theodoridas (*Anth. Pal.* 13. 21) refers to him as ὁ ἐλεγγοποιός, which, however, may mean 'epigram-matist', and derides his plagiarisms and bombast. The first charge is to some extent supported by the extant epigrams; the second may refer to lyric compositions now lost. A few of M.'s epigrams, e.g. *Anth. Pal.* 6. 128, 264; 7. 242, justify Meleager's description (*Anth. Pal.* 4. 1. 16) of them as 'the sharp needles of Mnasalces' pine', but most are devoid of originality.

J. Geffcken, 'Mnasalkes (2)', in *PW* xv. 2247-8. E. A. B.

MNASEAS (3rd c. B.C.), Greek traveller of Lycia (*POxy.* xiii, no. 1611, pp. 127 ff.), published geo-graphical and antiquarian details uncritically in (i) Περίπλους, (*a*) Εὐρώπη; (*b*) Ἀσία; (*c*) Λιβύη. (ii) Δελ-φικῶν χρησμῶν συναγωγή.

FHG iii. 149 ff.; iv. 659 ff. *PW*, s.v.

MNEMONES, *see* ARCHIVES.

MNESICLES, a Greek architect of the fifth century B.C. and designer of the gate-porches called 'Propylaea' (q.v.) to the acropolis at Athens.

MNESIMACHUS, a Middle Comedy writer (Ath. 7. 329 d). Victorious *c.* 365-360 B.C. (*IG* ii². 2325). Wrote Ἀλκμέων and Βούσιρις (clearly mythological burlesques), Ἱπποτρόφος, Ἰσθμιονίκης, Δύσκολος, and Φαρμακο-πώλης (comedies of everyday life), and Φίλιππος (a political play).

FCG iii. 567 ff.; *CAF* ii. 436-42. M. P.

MNEUIS, the sacred bull of the city of Heliopolis, who was worshipped there in the temple of Ra. His cult is similar in most respects to that of Apis at Memphis, although not so important in Greek and Roman religion. The cult of Mneuis was combined with that of Apis in the temple at Memphis.

A. Erman, *Religion d. Ägypter* (1934). T. A. B.

MODERATUS of Gades (*c.* A.D. 50–100), wrote Πυθαγορικαὶ σχολαί in eleven books. He tried to derive the main principles of Plato's metaphysics from Pytha-gorean teaching, and treated the Pythagorean theory of number as a symbolic representation of metaphysical doctrine, the monad being the principle of rest and har-mony, the dyad the principle of change and multi-plicity. Ancient references show him to have played a great part in the formation of Neoplatonic doctrine.

PW xv. 2378. W. D. R.

MODESTINUS (3rd c. A.D.) has left a short piece in hexameters on Cupid Asleep (J. W. and A. M. Duff, *Min. Lat. Poems*, 1935).

MODESTUS, *see* JULIUS (7).

MOERIS, an Atticist lexicographer, to be dated (prob-ably) not long after Phrynichus, and author of the extant Λέξεις Ἀττικῶν καὶ Ἑλλήνων κατὰ στοιχεῖον (sometimes called Ἀττικιστής): κατὰ στοιχεῖον here means only that words beginning with the same letter are grouped together under that letter without further attempt at arrangement within the group. The work deals with sundry points of grammar (accidence and syntax) and, mainly, with diction—the choice of words and their correct, 'Attic', forms and proper meanings. It is based on Aelius Dionysius, Phrynichus, Philemon, and the *Synonyms* of Herennius Philon of Byblus. Moeris recognizes the distinction between Old and New Attic; as models he accepts Plato, Aristophanes, Thucydides, Xenophon, the orators, Herodotus, and Homer, but, unlike Phrynichus, none of the tragedians. In the nature, merits, and limitations of his work he resembles Phryni-chus (q.v. 3).

Editions: Hudson, 1712; Pierson, 1759; Bekker, 1833. P. B. R. F.

MOERIS, a lake in a basin on the west of the Nile valley, fed by the floods at high Nile. When Herodotus visited Egypt most of the basin was under water, though some land had been reclaimed in Pharaonic times; Ptolemy Philadelphus built dikes and canals to control the inflow, and so recovered about half the area of the lake. This created the Arsinoite nome, which was largely peopled by foreign settlers and flourished till the decay of the third century A.D. ruined the irrigation system. The lake is now known as the Birket el-Kurûn.

B. P. Grenfell and A. S. Hunt, *Fayûm Towns* (1900). J. G. M.

MOERO (or **MYRO**) of Byzantium (*c.* 300 B.C.), epic poetess; mother of the tragic poet Homerus; wrote poems of various kinds, including a *Curses* (Ἀραί), a genre subsequently used by Euphorion and Valerius Cato.

F. Susemihl, *Gesch. griech. Litt. Alex.* (1891-2) i. 381.

MOESIA was in the first instance the country of the Moesi, a Thracian tribe situated on the lower Danube in present-day Serbia. Little is heard of the Moesi before 29 B.C., when they were defeated and subdued by M. Crassus. They were placed for the time being under a *praefectus* and loosely attached to the province of Macedonia or of Illyricum. The date at which Moesia was constituted a separate province is uncertain. It probably had on some occasions a governor of its own since A.D. 6, but its definite organization as a province seems to have been deferred until 44. Henceforth Moesia extended along the lower Danube from the river Drinus to the Black Sea; its southern frontier ran roughly along the main Balkan range. The governor of Moesia also had under his supervision the Black Sea coast to the Straits of Kertch, and from the time of Vespasian, if not before, a *Classis Moesica* patrolled its northern waters. Under Domitian Moesia was split into two provinces, Superior and Inferior, with the river Ciabrus as the boundary, and the defences of the latter province were strengthened by an earthen wall across the Dobrudja. After the Dacian Wars of Trajan Moesia Superior was extended to comprise the plain between the Danube, the lower Theiss, and the Maros; Moesia Inferior was enlarged so as to overlap Dacia on the east bank of the Aluta.

Moesia always remained a military borderland. Apart from the old-established Greek cities on the Black Sea coast and from Naissus on the upper Morava, all its chief towns grew out of the Roman camps on the Danube —Singidunum (*Belgrade*), Viminacium, Ratiaria, Oescus, Novae, Durostorum (*Silistria*), and Troesmis. Under Hadrian, or soon after, these places were constituted colonies or *municipia* of Italian pattern. Under the Roman peace the wheat and orchard lands of the lower Danube valley were well developed, and the Latin language obtained a firm hold among the native population, which had received repeated increments by transplantation of Dacians and kindred peoples across the Danube. During the invasions of the third century Moesia became a principal storm-centre, but its cities at any rate were held until the sixth or seventh century.

M. Fluss, in *PW*, s.v.; R. Syme, *JRS* 1934, 113–37; V. Parvan, *Dacia* (1928), passim; A. Stein, *Die Legaten von Moesia* (1940).
M. C.

MOGUNTIACUM (*Mainz*) commanded several important routes into the heart of Germany, and under Augustus a fortress was built here to hold two legions and as a base for the invasion of Germany. The first earth and wood structure was destroyed in A.D. 69–70 and replaced by a stone fortress, which was reduced after the rebellion of Saturninus (89) to hold a single legion. The city which grew up between the fortress and the Rhine was large and important, being the capital of Upper Germany, but it never acquired the commercial pre-eminence of Cologne or Trèves. The fortress was given up after 260 and the town was fortified, the bridge being protected by a new fortified bridgehead on the site of an old auxiliary fort at Castel. Excavation has produced many fine Roman objects, including sculptures and numerous tombstones; some piers of the Roman aqueduct are still standing, and also the core of an imposing structure, probably the monument to Drusus mentioned by Eutropius (7. 13). The early Christian quarter (Mainz was a bishopric) seems to have lain round the port, north of the walls.

K. Schumacher, *Siedelungs- und Kulturgesch. der Rheinlande* ii. (1923). O. B.

MOIRA, *see* FATE.

MOLIONES (Μολίονε), the twin sons of Molionē (originally 'Siamese' twins, in the opinion of Schweitzer, *Herakles* (1922), 19; see *contra* Farnell, *Hero-Cults*, 208, who makes this form of the legend Hesiodic and so comparatively late). Certainly in Homer (*Il.* 11. 750 ff.) they are normal and mortal, though sons of Poseidon; their names are Cteatus and Eurytus and they are married and have sons (2. 621). In the former passage they are enemies of the Pylians; elsewhere (Apollod. 2. 139–40) they attack Heracles' men and are afterwards ambushed and killed by him. They are often (as in Homer) called Ἀκτορίωνε, Actor being their mother's mortal husband.
H. J. R.

MOLOSSI, *see* EPIRUS.

MOMOS (Μῶμος), fault-finding personified, a literary figure, hardly mythological (though he occurs in Hesiod, *Theog.* 214, among the children of Night) and quite divorced from cult. Callimachus makes use of him (*Dian.* 113 and fr. 70 Schneider) as the mouthpiece of views

which he opposes, while in Lucian (as *Iupp. Trag.* 19 ff.) he amusingly voices the author's satires on the conventional (popular Stoic) theology, or otherwise makes fun of his fellow-gods. He is a figure in a fable, also cited by Lucian (*Nigr.* 32; cf. *Hermot.* 20, *Ver. Hist.* 2. 3).
H. J. R.

MONA (1) The Isle of Man (Caesar, *BGall.* 5. 13. 3).

(2) Anglesey. As a centre of Druidism it was attacked by Suetonius Paulinus (A.D. 61), who was baulked of success by Boudicca's revolt. It was presumably reduced *c.* 75. It shows scant traces of romanization, but copper-mining and the *pax Romana* increased the quality and quantity of its village life. A late Roman fort exists at Holyhead. Welsh tradition speaks of an Irish invasion (5th c.), repelled by Cunedda, whose descendants ruled here.

Royal Commission on Historical Monuments (Wales), Anglesey, lxvii–xc. C. E. S.

MONARCHY (βασιλεία). Greek monarchy includes several entirely separate institutions. The kingdom of 'heroic' times denotes the Mycenaean lordship as well as the Homeric and legendary kingdom. Its core was military leadership, but the Mycenaeans seem to have been rather autocratic monarchs 'by the grace of the Gods': Agamemnon was more than a simple 'war lord'. But in the period of renewed migrations the king was the military chief of the tribe again; the Spartan, and even more the Macedonian, kings were survivals of this type. It was a hereditary kingship, acknowledged by the assembly of the armed people, and its power was limited by other 'kings', i.e. the heads of the aristocracy, and their council. The second type was what the Greeks called tyranny (q.v.), an individual and democratic rulership arising from the aristocratic *polis*. The third species of Greek monarchy was more theoretical. Usually Greeks of the fifth century B.C. knew monarchy only as barbarian despotism. But the political philosophy of the Sophists and the Socratic Schools, fighting against democracy, established the ideal of the rule of the strongest or of the best man, of the ruler 'by nature' (φύσει). Some of the writers of the fourth century, especially Xenophon and Isocrates, became rather impressed by some real attempts to found monarchies, e.g. the younger tyranny in Syracuse, the rules of Jason of Pherae, of the kings of Cyprus, of Mausolus of Caria; and the conflict between the Greek city-states and Philip of Macedon found its reflection in the antithesis of democratic and monarchic ideas. The reigns of Alexander and his successors ended the theoretical controversies. Hellenistic monarchy combined the popular kingship of Macedon, the individual ambitions of Greek 'royal men', and Oriental traditions of theocratic despotism. Its characteristic features were: rule over a large territory, dynastic government and succession, cult of the dead and sometimes also of the living kings. This monarchy was supported by the philosophical idea of the rule of the truly wise man. It exercised a marked influence on Roman monarchy and imperial administration.

V. Bartoletti, *Studi ital. di filol. class.* N.S. xii (1935), 185 ff.; E. R. Goodenough, *Yale Class. Studies* i (1928); W. Schubart, *Arch. Pap.* xii (1926), 1 ff.; *Die Antike* xiii (1937), 272 ff. V. E.

MONETA, a title of Juno (q.v.). The name is probably connected with the root of *monere* ('mindful', 'reminder') and hence is used occasionally (Livius Andronicus, in Priscian, 2, p. 198 Keil; Hyginus, *praef. Fab.* 3 and 27) to translate Mnemosyne. There is no indication, however, that any cult of a goddess so named, independent of Juno, ever existed. Her temple stood on the Arx (see Platner-Ashby, p. 289 f.), having been vowed in 345 B.C. and dedicated the next year (Livy 7. 4–6), apparently replacing an older shrine where the sacred geese had been kept (Plut. *Cam.* 27). Cicero (*Div.* 1. 101) explains the title by a story that a warning voice was heard from it directing the proper sacrifice after an earthquake. It became the mint of the Roman State for some time (Livy 6. 20. 13; cf. Platner–Ashby, loc. cit. and p. 345 f.); hence *moneta* came to mean 'mint', and so passed into modern languages.   H. J. R.

MONEY. In Minoan Crete (as in all Ancient Oriental cultures) metal measured by weight seems to have been used as money. The usage persisted in non-Hellenic Italy until finally superseded by Roman coinage. Cattle was used as money in the early Iron Age (Homeric Greece and Italy). Tools also were passed as tokens, the form and not the weight or metal purity being of importance for exchange. In the time of Homer money chiefly took the form of axes, which occur in finds and (perhaps) in Minoan inscriptions. Written sources and finds point to the use in early Greece and prehistoric Europe of tripods, cauldrons, rings, anchors, metal 'cakes', and scales for weighing (the 'talent' of Homer, unless this was a bar of gold). *Oboloi* also (iron spits), which later gave the name to a small Greek coin, are well known, both by tradition and from finds and an early inscription. This primitive 'tool' money was connected with public sacrifices and religion.

2. The invention of coinage took its rise in Asia Minor, where East and West met, and was perfected in the Greek motherland, where small silver coins replaced local 'tool' money. It combined the principle that the exterior of any medium of exchange should be of conventional type and unalterable form, with the Ancient Oriental preference for bars of a given weight and metal content.

3. Changes in the price of bullion, of course, influenced the policy of Greek and Roman mints. The ratio of silver to gold was 1 : 13 or 13⅓ in the Lydian and Persian Empires of the sixth century; 1 : 14–17 in the later years of Pericles; 1 : 10 in Athens during the Peloponnesian War; 1 : 11–12 in Greece and Persia in the early fourth century; 1 : 10 from the later years of Philip; 1 : 13⅓ *c.* 280 B.C.; 1 : 10 *c.* 189 B.C.; 1 : 12 under Augustus; 1 : 8–11 in the early third century A.D., and 1 : 10 in the early fourth century.

4. The ratio of bronze to silver was 1 : *c.* 110 in the fifth century; 1 : 50–70 from Alexander's time to the third century A.D. (Italy of the third and earlier second centuries B.C. was perhaps an exception to this decline in value of the more precious metal); 1 : 125 in A.D. 396 and 1 : 100 in A.D. 538. The decline in value of the precious metals during Alexander's campaigns, and their rise in consequence of the economic crisis in the third century A.D., can clearly be seen from these figures.

5. By a law of Constantine (A.D. 325) the Imperial treasury had to accept both minted and unminted gold at the same rate, and gold coins had to be valued according to their actual weight. The Greek preference for coined money was not to the same extent shared by the Late Roman world, which had seen the terrible inflation of the third century A.D. and reverted of necessity to a more primitive currency system. *See* COINAGE (GREEK, ROMAN).

A. R. Burns, *Money and Monetary Policy in Early Times* (1927); G. F. Hill, in *CAH* iv, ch. 5; F. M. Heichelheim, *Wirtschaftsgeschichte des Altertums* (1938), Index s.v. 'Geld'; K. Regling, s.v. 'Geld' in *PW*, and in Ebert, *Reallexikon der Vorgeschichte*; J. G. Milne, *Greek and Roman Coins and the Study of History* (1939); L. C. West and A. C. Johnson, *Currency in Roman and Byzantine Egypt* (1944).   F. M. H.

MONOPOLIES. The earliest Greek State monopolies (for certain crafts in Sparta and Epidamnus) were political rather than economic. A later stage of progress in public administration is represented by the State currency control of the Attic Empire in the fifth century B.C. and of Olbia after 400; monopolies for the production of silphium in Cyrene, of alum in Lipara, and of salt in Rome, as well as others for the import or export of certain products in Athens, Clazomenae, Heraclea, Lampsacus, and Selymbria; of banking in Byzantium; and of trade and craftsmanship in the camp of the Persian satrap Datames (early 4th c.).

Hellenistic monopolies—in striking contrast to the Classical period—were more concerned with the State's own citizens than with foreigners. We find ferry control in Delos and Miletus; salt control in the empire of Lysimachus; control of salt, oil, and perhaps parchment, perfumes, and public baths in parts of the Seleucid Empire. A complete monopoly system in the Ptolemaic Empire covered the production, sale, and import of oils, textiles, beer, leather, perfumes, papyrus, the output of mines and quarries, currency and banking, hunting, fishing, meat sales, goose-breeding, and the management of public baths. This system included gigantic commercial and industrial enterprises, for which schedules regulating production were issued annually, wholesale and retail prices were fixed, and prohibitive customs duties imposed, very few enterprises escaping notice.

The monopolies of the Roman Principate were nothing more than exclusive local concessions to private capitalists. We know of such in Roman Egypt, controlling salt, oil, perfumes, baths, dyeing, kiln-dried bricks, alum, the goldsmith's trade, the wool trade, ferries, some Indian imports from the Red Sea, and (perhaps) beer, papyrus, and painting. Other sources mention control of banks in Mylasa and Pergamum, ferries in Myra, bakeries in Ephesus; a salt-monopoly in Palmyra, a complete regional sales' control in Baetocaece (in Syria); a monopoly of balsam in Palestine, of purple in Tyre, of wood in the Lebanon. The *metallum Vipascense*, a mining district in Spain, had public monopolies which covered banking, auctioning, fulling, leather production, baths, and the barber's trade. Late Roman monopolies for salt, silk, purple, production of arms, and the various monopoly experiments of Justinian should also be mentioned. *See* AGRICULTURE, BANKS, COMMERCE, FINANCE, INDUSTRY.

A. M. Andreades, *A History of Greek Public Finance* (U.S.A. 1933), Index, s.v.; E. Bikerman, *Les Institutions des Séleucides* (1938), 106 ff.; F. E. Brown, *AJArch.* xlii (1938), 607 f.; F. M. Heichelheim in *PW*, s.v. 'Monopole'; F. M. Heichelheim, *Economic History* (1938), 1 ff.; A. van Groningen, *Aristote, Le second livre de l'Économique* (1933); R. H. McDowell, *Univ. of Michigan Studies. Hum. Series.* xxxvi (1935); Cl. Préaux, *L'Économie royale des Lagides* (1939); M. Rostovtzeff, *Yale Classical Studies* iii (1932), 1 ff., and *Social and Economic History of the Hellenistic World* (1941); T. Frank, *Economic Survey of Ancient Rome*, ii–iv (U.S.A. 1936–8).
                                                          F. M. H.

MONOTHEISM. Apart from the influence of developed Judaism and Christianity, no such thing as monotheism, i.e. the refusal to use the predicate 'God' of any but one Being, existed in classical antiquity; even theistic philosophers acknowledged the existence of subordinate deities besides the supreme one. But a tendency towards it may be detected at any rate in Greek popular religion as interpreted by non-philosophical authors. This takes the form of an increasing supremacy of Zeus. Even in Homer (*Il.* 8. 18–27) he is much stronger than all the other gods put together; later authors tend to use 'Zeus', 'the gods', 'God' indiscriminately, e.g. Hesiod, *Op.* 42 and 47, where the same act is ascribed, first to 'the gods', then to Zeus. To Aeschylus (*Ag.* 160 ff.) Zeus is the supreme moral governor of the universe, though even there the existence of other gods is clearly recognized (169 ff.). Hellenistic writers favour vague phrases like τὸ θεῖον, τὸ δαιμόνιον.   H. J. R.

MONS SACER, a hill near Rome just beyond the Anio on the Via Nomentana. In 494 and 449 B.C. the plebeians left Rome, returning only when the patricians granted concessions guaranteed by a *lex sacrata*. The Mons Sacer, for obvious aetiological reasons, was represented as the destination of the seceding plebeians (Livy 2. 32; 3. 52; Festus, p. 422, 423 L.).   E. T. S.

MONTANUS, *see* VOTIENUS.

MONUMENTUM ANCYRANUM. The so-called Monumentum Ancyranum is one of the four documents written by Augustus which were deposited with the Vestal Virgins and were read in the Senate after his death. It was 'a record of his enterprises (*index rerum a se gestarum*), which he wished to be engraved on two bronze tablets placed outside his Mausoleum' (Suet. *Aug.* 101). The proper title is consequently *Index rerum gestarum*. Neither a manuscript copy nor the original inscription near the Mausoleum is preserved. But copies were set up in some, if not all, of the provinces. The greater part of the text has been recovered from a copy found in 1555 at Ancyra (q.v.) in Galatia, on the walls of a mosque which had been the temple of Rome and Augustus. It consists of the original Latin text and a Greek translation. Another copy, far more fragmentary, has been found at Apollonia in Pisidia. The Greek translation is here the same as in the text of Ancyra, which proves its official inspiration. A third fragmentary copy of the Latin text was found at Antioch in Pisidia in 1914 (so-called Monumentum Antiochenum). As Antioch was a Roman colony, it was probably considered unnecessary to add a Greek text.

2. The Monumentum Ancyranum contains four parts: (1) the *honores* received by Augustus (chs. 1–14); (2) a statement of the money spent on public objects from his private means (chs. 15–24); (3) the *res gestae* proper, an account of his victorious expeditions and conquests (25–33); (4) a concluding statement about his position in the Roman State. A short appendix, written after his death, follows.

3. The document represents itself as composed in Augustus' last year, apparently after 27 June A.D. 14 (cf. chs. 4 and 8), but since the *Res Gestae* were already mentioned in the testament of Augustus, which was written on 3 April A.D. 13, the text obviously has been retouched either by Augustus himself or by the editor. Further, possibly the document was written by Augustus many years before his death and then revised more than once. Yet no certain evidence of successive stages has been discovered.

4. The document has a clear internal unity. Part 1 demonstrates Augustus' exceptional position in the State and his fundamental respect for Roman liberty. In parts 2 and 3 Augustus justifies his position by what he achieved with his own private money and under his own military command. The concluding sentences state again that he restored the Republic and consequently obtained a superior authority and the qualification of *pater patriae*. The style is that of the Roman texts concerning triumphs. The content gives us a profound insight into the way in which Augustus wished to be appreciated.

EDITIONS AND COMMENTARIES: by Mommsen (2nd ed. 1883); E. G. Hardy (1923); W. M. Ramsay and A. v. Premerstein, 'Monumentum Antiochenum', *Klio*, Beiheft 19 (1927); J. Gagé (1934; the best); J. D. Newby, *Numismatic Commentary on the Res Gestae of Augustus* (U.S.A. 1938).
RECENT STUDIES: H. Dessau, *Klio* xxii (1929), 261; U. Wilcken, *Sitzungsb. Preuss. Akad.* 1931, p. 772; 1932, p. 225; W. Ensslin, *Rh. Mus.* 1932, 335; W. Weber, *Princeps* i, 1936 (cf. E. Hohl, *Philol. Wochenschrift* 1937, 374; id. *Klio* xxx (1937), 323 and W. Kolbe, *Gött. Anz.* 1939, 152); J. Gagé, *Rev. Ét. Lat.* 1939, 33; A. Ferrabino, *Augustus. Studi in occasione del bimillenario augusteo* (1938), 48.
A. M.

MOPSUS, a diviner, or two diviners of the same name, for the legend is quite irreconcilable with the mythological chronology. In one set of authorities (e.g. Pind. *Pyth.* 4. 191) he is the Argonauts' prophet and therefore is contemporary with the generation before the Trojan War; he is son of Ampyx or Ampycus (Ap. Rhod. 1. 1083) and he dies on the journey (4. 1502 ff.), bitten by a serpent in Libya. In another (as Paus. 7. 3. 2) he is son of Manto, daughter of Tiresias (q.v.), by Rhacius

the Cretan; he is connected with the oracle at Claros, and there meets Calchas (q.v.) and causes his death by outdoing him in a contest of divination; this was after the Trojan War. Probably several stories gathered independently around one famous figure, or the name tended to be used of any prophet. See Kruse in *PW*, s.v.

H. J. R.

MORMO (Μορμώ; also Μορμολύκη, Μορμών), a figure like Empusa, Gello, and Lamia (qq.v.), and equated with the last two by schol. on Theoc. 15. 40; he says she was a queen of the Laestrygonians (q.v.) who lost her own children and so tries to kill those of others. Her name is sometimes a mere interjection (Theoc. loc. cit.; Ar. *Eq.* 693). See Tamborino in *PW*, s.v.
H. J. R.

MORPHEUS. Three of the sons of Sleep, Morpheus, Ikelos or Phobetor, and Phantasos, send respectively visions of human forms (μορφαί), beasts, and inanimate objects (Ovid, *Met.* 11. 633 ff.).

MORSIMUS, son of Philocles and grand-nephew of Aeschylus, oculist and tragic poet, a 'frigid' or uninspired writer, often ridiculed by comic poets of the fifth century (Suidas, s.v.; Ar. *Pax* 803 and schol.), though he may have had his admirers (Ar. *Ran.* 151).

MORYCHUS (Μόρυχος). Lexicographers and paroemiographers (q.v.) explain a saying 'sillier (μωρότερος) than Morychus, who neglects inside affairs and sits outside' as alluding to a statue of Dionysus in Sicily, surnamed Morychus, which was outside his temple; their authority is Polemon.
H. J. R.

MOSAIC. While examples of mosaic as architectural decoration occur at an early date in Mesopotamia, the Egyptians and Minoans apparently restricted its use to the minor arts. In Greece mosaic pavements of natural pebbles are known from 400 B.C.; the designs, in light silhouette on dark ground, include patterns and mythological subjects. In the Hellenistic period shaped stones replace pebbles and the use of mosaic becomes general.

There were several techniques. *Opus sectile* covered the surface of walls and pavements with thin slabs cut into patterns. Of Eastern origin, it was at first restricted to few colours and to geometric patterns, but under the Empire its range was enlarged. In *Opus tessellatum* the slabs of *sectile* were replaced by small cubes (*tessellae*) of uniform size; *tessellatum* was regarded as a cheaper form of *sectile* and at first obeyed the same conventions of colour and pattern. *Opus vermiculatum* similarly employed *tessellae*, but these were irregularly shaped and adapted to the field. Derived from the inlay of Egypt, this was a painter's technique, and its range of colour and material was unlimited. *Opus musivum* was wall-decoration in *tessellae* applied to vaults, domes, and curved surfaces (it is disputed whether flat walls were thus decorated before the Christian period). Lapis lazuli or blue glass representing the sky and, after A.D. 200, gold for the sun were the principal colours. *Lithostroton* is believed to have meant an irregularly paved, patternless floor. *Opus signinum* was used of a cement floor reinforced with tiles or pebbles.

Hellenistic pavements were distinguished by use of the *emblema*, a picture executed in *vermiculatum*, as a central feature to which the rest of the floor was subordinated. In the Augustan age the simpler colours and the all-over patterns of *sectile* and its derivative *tessellatum* came into favour. By the Antonine period the two traditions had blended; the distinction between *vermiculatum* and *tessellatum* disappeared and pavements combined the varied colouring of one with the all-over designs of the other. Figured pavements, very popular in the late Empire, disappeared in the sixth century, when the wall or ceiling was considered more suitable for the sacred subjects then preferred.

P. Gauckler, Dar.-Sag., s.v. 'musivum opus'; R. P. Hinks, Introduction to the *Catalogue of Paintings and Mosaics in the British Museum* (1933); E. Pernice, *Die hellenistische Kunst in Pompeii* vi, 'Pavimente und figürliche Mosaïken' (1938).   F. N. P.

MOSCHION, tragic poet, probably of the fourth century B.C., wrote a *Telephus* and two historical plays, the *Themistocles* and the *Men of Pherae*, the theme of which was perhaps the death of Alexander of Pherae. A long fragment on the origins of civilization recalls in some points Aeschylus, *PV* 436 ff., and his style, though uneven, shows greater boldness than that of most of the late tragic poets.

TGF 812.-16.   A. W. P.-C.

MOSCHUS of Syracuse, described by Suidas as a pupil of Aristarchus, must have flourished *c.* 150 B.C. This agrees with Suidas' further statement that the chronological order of the three Bucolic poets was Theocritus, Moschus, Bion. The same authority calls M. a grammarian, but no traces of such activity survive unless we identify M. with the Moschus mentioned by Athenaeus (11. 485 e) as author of a work on Rhodian Words.

WORKS. Three extracts (respectively thirteen, nine, and eight hexameters) are preserved by Stobaeus from M.'s *Bucolica*. The first contrasts the pleasures of the countryman with the hard lot of the fisher. The two others are erotic *paegnia*, having little or no connexion with Bucolic. The three extracts are probably complete, as it were epigrams in hexameters. Similar in kind are two other pieces, twenty-nine hexameters entitled 'The Runaway Love' and an epigram (*Anth. Plan.* 4. 200) on Eros as Ploughman. Finally several manuscripts of the Bucolic Corpus assign to M. an epyllion in 166 hexameters with the title *Europa*, in which the Rape of Europa by Zeus is gracefully narrated. The disproportionate space (25 lines) given to the description of Europa's basket is in the Alexandrian manner, as is also the introductory dream. M.'s style is sometimes too sugared, but he has the merit of using a fairly simple vocabulary. Metrically the fragments and the *Runaway Love* conform to Callimachus' rules, but the *Europa* is less strict, a fact which has led some to dispute M.'s authorship. M. is also credited in some sources with the *Lament for Bion* and the *Megara*. The former must be by some disciple of Bion (q.v.); the latter, a duet in hexameters between Heracles' mother and wife (who gives her name to the piece), in which they vie with each other in bewailing the anxieties caused by his long absence, may be a product of M.'s muse in a tearful mood, but may equally well belong to some other late Hellenistic poet.

Texts: U. von Wilamowitz-Moellendorff, *Bucolici Graeci²* (1910), 91, 106, 120, 131, 138; Ph. Legrand, *Bucoliques grecs* ii (1927), 135–83. General literature: P. Maas, 'Moschos (2)', in *PW* xvi. 355–6.   E. A. B.

MOSCHUS, *see also* VOLCACIUS (2).

MOTORIA sc. *fabula* (contrast *stataria*), *see* FABULA.

MOTYA (nowadays *S. Pantaleo*), an islet which an artificial causeway joined to western Sicily. Originally a Phoenician trading-post among the Elymi, Motya subsequently became a Carthaginian city; its strategic position, indeed, made it one of the three great military and commercial strongholds of Carthaginian Sicily (Panormus and Soloeis being the other two). It remained Carthaginian until Dionysius of Syracuse sacked it after a memorable siege, 397 B.C. Motya was never subsequently resurrected, the Carthaginians preferring to colonize nearby Lilybaeum (q.v.).

Thuc. 6. 2; Diod. 14. 47 f. (inaccurate); Pausanias' elaborate description (5. 25. 5) confuses Motya with Motyka. J. I. S. Whitaker, *Motya* (1921).   E. T. S.

MOUNTAIN CULTS. There is no classical Greek or Italian cult of a mountain as such, but several indications that such cult may once have existed. Mountains are fairly prominent in Greek myths; thus Atlas (q.v.), at once mountain and Titan, although classically placed in Africa (the Atlas range), probably was originally a mountain of Arcadia. Helicon and Cithaeron contend for a prize of song (Corinna, fr. 4 Diehl), and Helicon is represented by a wild-looking figure (*Bull. Corr. Hell.* xiv, plates ix, x; cf. Kern, *Rel. d. Griech.* i. 42). Earth brings forth the mountains in Hesiod (*Theog.* 129), though they are not said to be gods but haunts (ἔναυλοι) of the gods. This is in accordance with much that is told of various deities, Pan (*Hymn. Hom.* 19 Allen, 7), the Nymphs (Eur. *Bacch.* 951, and often; the next line mentions Pan also), Rhea (Eur. *Hel.* 1301 ff., where she is curiously identified with Demeter), and above all Zeus, among whose best-known titles are Olympius and Lycaeus. It is quite possible (see Kern, ibid.; cf. p. 77) that Zeus, who as 'cloud-gatherer' may be seen at work on the tops of hills, absorbed or displaced many ancient cults of mountain gods: for his mountain-cults cf. A. B. Cook, *Zeus* ii. 868 ff., and art. HYPSISTOS). Of cults on mountains of gods other than Zeus who are certainly not themselves mountains personified there is abundant evidence, from the familiar Cretan representation (see Harrison, *Prolegomena*, p. 498, for one of many reproductions) of a goddess standing on top of a conventionalized hill onwards, as in the case of all the deities mentioned above. *See* TMOLUS.

For Italy, the clearest example of a mountain cult is perhaps Soranus (identified in historical times with Apollo or Dis Pater, Verg. *Aen.* 11. 785; Servius ad loc.), the god of Mt. Soracte; the legend, connected as it is with a cave on the mountain (Servius ibid.) suggests a divine power which actually lives in Soracte and does not simply choose to roam on the sides or summit. See Wissowa, *RK* 238.   H. J. R.

MUCIA TERTIA, daughter of Q. Mucius Scaevola (*cos.* 95 B.C.), was connected with the Metelli. She was wife of Pompey, by whom she had two sons (Gnaeus, Sextus) and a daughter (Pompeia), but was divorced for unfaithfulness (62). She next married M. Aemilius Scaurus. In 39 she tried to mediate between Sextus Pompeius and Octavian.   A. M.

MUCIANUS, GAIUS LICINIUS (*cos. anno incerto, cos.* II *suff.* A.D. 70, *cos.* III *suff.* 72), legate of Syria in 69. Reconciled with Vespasian after earlier disagreements, he encouraged his designs and secured the allegiance of Syria. Leading the Flavian army through Asia Minor and the Balkans, he was anticipated by Antonius Primus in the invasion of Italy and defeat of the Vitellians, but was able on the way to repel a Dacian incursion into Moesia. He arrived in Rome a few days after its capture, repressed the ambitions of Primus, and controlled the government for Vespasian, whose chief adviser he remained. He is said to have urged that emperor to banish the philosophers from Rome. Mucianus possessed various accomplishments (for a pointed sketch of his character, cf. Tacitus, *Hist.* 1. 10). He wrote a book of geographical *mirabilia*, largely used by Pliny the Elder.   R. S.

MUCIUS, *see* SCAEVOLA.

MULOMEDICINA is the Latin equivalent for *Hippiatrike*. The subject was dealt with by all agriculturalists (Cato, Varro, Columella, Celsus, Gargilius Martialis, Palladius), but also by poets who wrote on country life (Verg. *G.* 3. 295) and by naturalists (Pliny, bk. 8). The earliest special treatises preserved are those of Pelagonius and Vegetius (4th c. A.D.).

Latin writers, if physicians, accept semeiotics and

cures and reject magic, in accordance with their Greek sources. Yet Latin literature seems not only dependent but also original. The fact that Latin authors were translated into Greek (e.g. Pelagonius) indicates that 'the barbarians' held views of their own. They were interested in veterinary medicine from a business point of view (Varro, *Rust.* 2. 5. 11), cattle being the most valuable property (*pecunia*). The insistence on the segregation of sick animals from the healthy stock, first mentioned by Columella and demanded long before any such segregation of human beings was thought of, may well be Roman; in the time of Vegetius it was under State control. *See also* SURGERY, para. 10.

TEXTS: Pelagonius, M. Ihm (Teubner, 1892); Vegetius, E. Lommatzsch (Teubner, 1903); Palladius, Book 14, J. Svennung (1926); cf. G. Björck, *Mnemos.* 1938. LITERATURE: Cf. article HIPPIATRICI; also K. Hoppe, *PW* xvi A. 503 (interdependence of authors); J. Svennung, *Untersuchungen zu Palladius*, etc. (1935). L. E.

MUMMIUS ACHAICUS, LUCIUS (*cos.* 146 B.C.), commanded as praetor in Spain in 153 B.C. against the Lusitanians, whom after an unsuccessful opening he decisively checked, celebrating a triumph in 152. As consul he succeeded Metellus in command against the Achaean League, and after crushing Diaeus took Corinth, which he sacked and destroyed, and dissolved the League. He shipped the treasures of Corinth to Italy, apparently less appreciative of their artistic value than would have been expected from his association with the Scipionic circle. He was censor with Scipio Aemilianus in 142, modifying his severity against Ti. Claudius Asellus.

Livy, *Per.* 52; Polyb. bk. 39; Appian, *Hisp.* 56–7; Pausanias 7. 16; Cicero, *De Or.* 2. 66. 268; *Brut.* 25. 94; Vell. 1. 13. 4; G. Colin, *Rome et la Grèce* (1905), 628; De Sanctis, *Stor. Rom.* iv. 1, 467. A. H. McD.

MUNATIUS, *see* PLANCUS.

MUNDUS (etymology unknown), a ritual pit (*see* PITS, CULT). (1) The traditional site in the Comitium where Romulus in founding the city dug a pit, put in firstfruits, and earth from each country from which his followers came, afterwards filling it up and putting an altar upon it (Ovid, *Fasti* 4. 821 ff.; Plut. *Rom.* 11). (2) The *mundus Cereris*, a structure of unknown site, vaulted, divided into two parts, and with a cover which was removed on 24 Aug., 5 Oct., and 8 Nov., which days were *religiosi* and the way supposed open to the lower world (Festus pp. 144, 145 Lindsay, quoting Cato and Ateius Capito; Varro ap. Macrob. *Sat.* 1. 16. 18). These have only the name in common.

Weinstock in *Röm. Mitt.* 45, pp. 111 ff.; Rose in *SMSR* 7, pp. 3ff.; Kroll in *PW*, s.v. H. J. R.

MUNICHIA (or MUNYCHIA) was the citadel of Piraeus, a steep hill on its east part (284 ft.) with a small well-fortified harbour below it on the east, and a larger, land-locked harbour to the south-west (Zea). Hippias began to fortify it in 510 B.C. (*Ath. Pol.* 19. 2). It was the scene of street-fighting in 403, when Thrasybulus took Piraeus, and the chief seat of the Macedonian garrison which controlled Athens, with interruptions, from 322 to 229. Its especial goddess was Artemis. *See also* PIRAEUS. T. J. D.

MUNICHUS (Μούνιχος), (1) eponym of the Attic harbour Munichia, Photius s.v. Μουνυχία (an inferior spelling of the name), who says he was a king of Attica). (2) A pious seer, son of Dryas, king of the Molossians. He and his family, attacked by robbers and in danger of being burned alive in their fortress, were changed by Zeus into birds (Anton. Lib. 14). H. J. R.

MUNICIPIUM. *Municipium* originally meant an Italian community (*see* SOCII, CIVITAS) which accepted *civitas sine suffragio*. This denoted not an inferior citizenship but a kind of alliance whereby the *municipium* and Rome exchanged social rights, *conubium* and *commercium* (q.v.). Such *municipes* retained full local autonomy, except in foreign policy, and provided Rome with troops (*see* MUNUS). They became Romans only by settling in Rome. *Municipium* thus resembled *ius Latii*. *Municipia* were liable to occasional, and eventually annual, visits of Roman judicial authorities—*praefecti*—and were sometimes called *praefecturae* (q.v.). The first *municipes*, from Campania and Volscium (*c.* 338 B.C.), were willing allies. Later this status was given to conquered peoples, notably the Sabines and Picenum, and was eventually regarded as a limited, inferior franchise, mediating the incorporation in the Roman State, by the grant of *ius suffragii*, of Italian peoples, which were then called *municipia civium Romanorum*. First the Sabines were thus incorporated (257 B.C.), others later (Arpinum, Fundi, Formiae in 188 B.C.), but some *municipes* remained *sine suffragio* till 90 B.C. Latin States incorporated by Rome, though properly known as *oppida civium Romanorum* before 90 B.C., were sometimes called *pro municipiis*. The magistrates of the early incorporated boroughs were known as aediles, dictators, praetors, or *octoviri*. After 89 B.C. all the communities of Latins and *socii Italici* except the Transpadanes became *municipia civium Romanorum*. A uniform system of *quattuorviri* was substituted for their diverse magistracies. Between 89 and 44 B.C. new and old *municipia* and *oppida civium Romanorum* were assimilated to one another (*see* OPPIDA). Lands once organized on a village system were divided up into artificial *municipia* (*see* CONCILIABULUM, PAGUS, VICUS). Henceforth *municipium* meant any self-governing Italian borough irrespective of origin, apart from colonies (q.v.). In the Principate citizen rights were extended to provincial communities, when sufficiently italianized, in a similar fashion. Latin rights were usually given first (q.v.). Thereby a native *civitas* became a *municipium Latini iuris*, with a municipal charter of Roman type. Later it was granted full citizen rights, without further change of constitution. The whole population, both of town and country-side, was affected: a *municipium* was not a purely urban municipality, though life centred in the towns. *Municipia* spread thus throughout the Western Empire, rapidly in the Mediterranean regions—Narbonensis, the Spains, Africa, and Mauretania—slowly in the German and Balkan provinces (except Dacia), still more slowly in northern Gaul and Britain, where *municipia* were exceptional, their place being taken by the non-urban, pre-Roman cantons (*see* CIVITAS). In and after the second century municipal ambition, centred on the imitation of Rome, caused provincial municipalities to apply for colonial rights (*see* COLONIZATION, ROMAN; IUS ITALICUM). Local government rested with the councils (*see* DECURIONES) and the magistrates. The *quattuorviri* introduced in 89 B.C. developed into two *quattuorviri* or *duoviri iuri dicundo* and two *quattuorviri* or *duoviri aedilicia potestate*, or two aediles. The duoviral system was normal in the provinces. Quaestors sometimes existed for finance, and there were municipal priesthoods. Every five years the upper magistrates, as *duoviri quinquennales*, etc., held a general census for the central government. The municipal system declined in the third and fourth centuries with the general economic collapse of the Empire (*see* DECURIONES).

ANCIENT SOURCES: Cicero; Festus (esp. s.v. *municipium, praefecturae, vicus*); Pliny, *HN*; Strabo, passim; *Digest* esp. 50. Inscriptions: *CIL* and *ILS* passim, esp. *Lex* (*Rubria*) *de Gallia Cisalpina, Lex Tarentina, Tabula Heracleensis, Lex Malacitana*, and *Lex Salpensana*. MODERN VIEWS: (*a*) Republic: Abbott and Johnson, *Municipal Administration in the Roman Empire*; K. Beloch, *Der Italische Bund* and *Röm. Geschichte*; E. G. Hardy, *Roman Laws and Charters*; Z. Z. Konopka, *Eos* xxxii (Origins of *Civitas sine suffragio*); E. Kornemann in *PW*, s.v. 'Municipium', 'Conventus'; *Klio* 1905, 'Πόλις und Urbs'; Mommsen, *Staatsr.* iii. 1; A. Rosenberg, *Staat der alten Italiker* (1913); H. Rudolph, *Stadt und Staat im römischen*

Italien (1935, over-schematic); E. Täubler on *tribus*, *Sitz. Heid.* 1930; A. N. Sherwin-White, *The Roman Citizenship* (1939). (*b*) Empire: Above and W. Liebenam, *Städteverwaltung im. r. Kaiserreiche*; Mommsen, *The Provinces of the R.E.*; J. S. Reid, *The Municipalities of the Roman Empire*; Rostovtzeff, *Roman Empire*; M. Grant, *From Imperium to Auctoritas* (1946). *See* particular provincial histories, esp. T. S. R. Broughton, *The Romanization of Africa Proconsularis.* H. M. Last, *CAH* xi, ch. 11.   A. N. S.-W.

MUNUS meant originally the duty of a Roman citizen to the State. The chief *munus publicum* in the Republic was military service. With the abolition of compulsory service this fell into neglect, and the *munus* came to mean simply the obligations of an individual to his municipality, the *munera municipalia*. These were of diverse kinds, and concerned the maintenance of roads, waterworks, and buildings, and especially the payment of taxes. The municipal system worked smoothly as long as the local magistrates saw to it that the *municipes* performed their *munera*, according to their various degrees of liability, which were determined by wealth and position. In the late Empire the *munus publicum* reappeared, in effect, in the liability of the municipal councillors for the imperial taxes, with disastrous results for the municipal system; for the magistracies themselves came to be regarded as burdensome *munera* (*see* DECEMPRIMI, DECURIONES).

For bibliography *see* MUNICIPIUM.   A. N. S.-W.

MURENA, LUCIUS LICINIUS, served under his father, who as propraetor of Asia in 84 B.C. had provoked the Second Mithridatic War. In the third war against Mithridates he served with distinction as *legatus* of Lucullus (74–*c.* 68). After holding the praetorship in 65 he governed Transalpine Gaul. After his election to a consulship in 63 he was charged with bribery by Cato and Sulpicius. His guilt was obvious, but it was not expedient that the consul-elect should be condemned during the Catilinarian crisis. Cicero therefore defended him, and secured his acquittal by cleverly ridiculing the pedantry of the accusers.

Cicero, *pro Murena* (edited by W. E. Heitland, 1874).   J. M. C.

MURENA, *see also* VARRO (4).

MURRINA VASA, cups and bowls made from a mineral substance obtained in small quantities from Parthia (in particular from Carmania). They were introduced into Rome by Pompey and in Pliny's time were cherished articles of luxury, for which fabulous prices were paid. The material is described as scented, fragile, and prized for its colouring, which was purple, white, or flame-coloured, sometimes iridescent, sometimes opaque or knobbed. The identification of this *murra* is still disputed, though opinion inclines to some variety of fluorspar or jade. There were imitations in glass of the true murrine ware (*see* GLASS).

Pliny, *HN* 37. 2. 7 and 8.   F. N. P.

MUSAEUS (1), a mythical singer, closely related to Orpheus, by others connected with Eleusis. Aristophanes (*Ran.* 1032–3) make the distinction that Orpheus taught mysteries and abstinence from flesh, Musaeus taught cures of diseases and oracles. Oracles attributed to him were in circulation, and Onomacritus was driven out by Hipparchus, the son of Pisistratus, for having added a forged oracle to his collection. Plato speaks of him together with Orpheus and calls both descendants of Selene and the Muses (*Resp.* 364 e). Musaeus is a 'descriptive' name; his personality is pale and thoroughly mythical.

M. P. Nilsson, *Harv. Theol. Rev.* xxxviii (1935), 192; O. Kern, *Orphicorum fragmenta* (cf. index viii).   M. P. N.

MUSAEUS (2) of Ephesus (? Alexandria), epic poet; author of a *Perseid* and poems in honour of Eumenes and Attalus I of Pergamum.

MUSAEUS (3) **GRAMMATICUS** (? late 5th c. A.D.), epic poet, author of *Hero and Leander*, a Greek poem of some competence and romantic grace, which influenced Marlowe. *See* EPIC POETRY.

Text: A. Ludwich (1912).

MUSCULUS, *see* SIEGECRAFT, ROMAN.

MUSES, Greek deities of poetry, literature, music, and dance; later also of astronomy, philosophy, and all intellectual pursuits. Throughout antiquity the prevailing conception of Muses follows Hesiod (*Th.* 25 ff.). Muses approach the poet on Helicon and give him sceptre, voice, and knowledge. Hesiod is also responsible for the canonical number of nine and the traditional names of the Muses. In late Roman times the M. were differentiated according to their function (*Anth. Pal.* 9. 504, 505). Calliope is M. of the heroic epic, Clio of history, Euterpe of flutes, Terpsichore of lyric poetry (dance), Erato of lyric poetry or hymns, Melpomene of tragedy, Thalia of comedy, Polyhymnia of the mimic art, and Urania of astronomy. These functions and names vary considerably and names of other Muses are known.

Daughters of Zeus and Mnemosyne, the M. sing and dance at the festivities of Olympians and heroes, often led by Apollo. They have few myths of their own. The Thracian poet Thamyris, who competed against the M., lost his sight and song (*Il.* 2. 594). They were judges in the contest of Apollo and Marsyas (q.v.). The Sirens tried once to compete with the Muses; defeated, they lost their wings and jumped into the sea (Steph. Byz. s.v. Ἄπτερα).

The most ancient cults of the M. were in Pieria and Ascra, but smaller cults existed throughout Greece. Pythagoreans, Plato, and Aristotle organized their schools as associations for the cult of Muses (*thiasoi*). Thus Museum (Alexandria) came to mean a place of education and research. An interesting private cult of Muses was established by Epicteta in Thera (*IG* xii. iii. 330).

The M. are among the most lovable and most influential creations; personifications of the highest intellectual and artistic aspirations, they yet retained a personal character. Poets, scientists, and philosophers from Homer (*Od.* 8. 488) to Ausonius (Auson. 20) and from Heraclitus to Proclus celebrate the M. as bringing to humanity the purifying power of music, the inspiration of poetry, and divine wisdom.

P. Boyancé, *Le Culte des Muses chez les philosophes grecs* (1937). O. Bie in Roscher, *Lex.*, s.v. 'Musen'.   G. M. A. H.

MUSEUM (Μουσεῖον), originally a place connected with the Muses (q.v.) or the arts inspired by them. Euripides speaks of the μουσεῖα of birds, the places where they sing. When a religious meaning was attached an altar or a temple was built to mark the spot. But the predominant significance of the word was literary and educational. Thus Mount Helicon had a Museum containing the manuscripts of Hesiod and statues of those who had upheld the arts (*Ath.* 14. 629 a). Almost any school could be called 'the place of the Muses' (Libanius). There was a Museum in Plato's Academy and in Aristotle's Lyceum.

By far the most famous Museum was that of Alexandria, founded by Ptolemy Soter *c.* 280 B.C. on the advice of Aristotle's pupil, Demetrius of Phalerum, to counterbalance the anti-monarchical Athenian schools and the socialist movements that arose in opposition to the capitalist *bourgeoisie* of the Hellenistic world. It was distinct from the Library. Both were near the palace, but the exact site of neither is clearly identifiable. The Museum housed a band of about 100 research scholars, drawn from all parts of the Mediterranean. They were supported by a generous salary granted by the Ptolemies and later by the Caesars, who appointed a President (ἐπιστάτης) or Priest (ἱερεύς) as head of the institution. Lectures were secondary to research, but there were many discussions in which the kings joined. Dinners or symposia, illuminated by witticisms, epigrams, and the solution of problems, were frequent and characteristic. The philosophy of the Museum seems to have been mainly Aristotelian. Learning was held in repute and many literary prizes were given. The papyri show how great was the influence of the Museum on the smaller towns. The buildings, splendidly furnished by the Ptolemies, included a communal dining-hall, an *exedra* for discussions and lectures, a *peripatos* planted with trees.

Circa 146 B.C. political upheavals caused learned men, including the great Aristarchus, to flee from Alexandria, which was henceforth rivalled by Pergamum as well as by Athens, Rhodes, Antioch, Berytus, and Rome. The Museum suffered in reputation, but Cleopatra, the last of the Ptolemies, still took part in its discussions. According to a doubtful tradition Mark Antony gave the Pergamene library to Alexandria to make up for loss by fire during Caesar's siege, 47 B.C. Renewed prosperity came under the Pax Augusta. The early emperors visited the Museum and extended its buildings, and Hadrian bestowed special care on it. The Museum was visited by famous litterati like Plutarch, Dio Chrysostom, Lucian, and Galen. In A.D. 216 it suffered under the tyranny of Caracalla. It was destroyed, probably by Zenobia, in 270, but seems to have resumed its activities. It suffered by the foundation of a library at Constantinople, whither many scholars fled to avoid the theological controversies of Alexandria. Suidas gives the last member of the Museum as Theon, the father of Hypatia (c. A.D. 400). In the first century the Museum was famous for philology and history; in the second century for the New Rhetoric; in the third century for Neoplatonism. In the fourth century Ammianus (22. 16) reports scientific activity, but admits a decline.

Müller–Graupe, *PW*, s.v. 'Museion'. Jacques Matter, *Histoire de l'école d'Alexandrie²* (1840). T. J. H.

MUSIC. 1. IN GREEK LIFE. When the embassy from Agamemnon visited Achilles in his tent and found him playing on a lyre and singing lays about heroes (Hom. *Il.* 9. 186–9), they expressed no astonishment that a hardy warrior should seek relaxation in music of his own making. That is symbolic of the Greek attitude to an art which was woven into the very texture of their lives. It was an important feature of many public religious observances, of marriage and funeral rites, and of harvest and vintage festivals; banquets and convivial gatherings were not complete without it. At the Pythian Games, attended by crowds of competitors and spectators from every Greek State, musical contests had been instituted alongside of the athletic ones from the very beginning; and though such contests were not established at the Nemean and Isthmian Games until comparatively late (and apparently never at the Olympic Games), there were many other festivals, such as the Panathenaea at Athens and the Carnea at Sparta, where prizes were offered for singing to the accompaniment of cithara or aulos (κιθαρῳδία, αὐλῳδία) or for instrumental solos (ψιλὴ κιθάρισις, ψιλὴ αὔλησις). The victors in these contests were honoured no less than the athletes (cf. Pindar, *Pyth.* 12).

It is particularly important to recall that Greek poetry was much more frequently associated with music than is our own. Even the poems of Homer were sometimes chanted or recited by rhapsodes to the accompaniment of a lyre or cithara. In the compositions of the lyric poets the tune was scarcely less essential than the words; the personal monodies of Sappho and Alcaeus, no less than the choral odes of Pindar, Bacchylides, and the tragic poets, were inspired by a Muse who held sway over the sister arts of music and poetry.

This wealth of music was far from being the preserve of professional performers. The more elaborate kinds, especially of instrumental music, were, indeed, left to professional musicians; but in classical times instruction in singing and lyre-playing was a regular part of the education of the freeborn citizen. There thus existed a musically educated public which could not only judge between good and bad performances but could itself take its part in singing hymns, paeans, dithyrambs, and dramatic choruses.

2. MUSIC AND THE PHILOSOPHERS. A philosophic sanction was first given to the study of music by the Pythagoreans. The founder of the school is said to have discovered that the chief concordant intervals (συμφωνίαι) could be represented by simple numerical ratios: the Octave (τὸ διὰ πασῶν, sc. χορδῶν) by the ratio 2 : 1, the Fifth (τὸ διὰ πέντε) by 3 : 2, and the Fourth (τὸ διὰ τεσσάρων) by 4 : 3. If a lyre string were stopped midway by a movable bridge, either half would give a note an octave higher than the note of the whole string; if the string were stopped at a point a third of the distance from one end, the remaining two-thirds would give a note a fifth higher than the whole string. It was thus demonstrated that music, more directly than the other arts, brought men into contact with Number, which for the Pythagoreans was the ultimate reality; music, or at least the study of music, was thereby justified in the eyes of serious men.

Plato's attitude to music is that the art is capable not merely of affecting the emotions temporarily but of permanently influencing the character. This point of view is clearly seen in his discussion of the musical education which would be suitable for the virtuous citizens of his ideal State (*Resp.* 398 c–399 d). He rejects types of music (ἁρμονίαι, scales) which are plaintive (Mixolydian and Syntonolydian) or effeminate (Ionian and Lydian), and leaves only the Dorian and Phrygian, which represent (μιμοῦνται) courage and sobriety. In his later work, the *Laws* (653 d–673 a; 795 a–812 e), his opinion is still unchanged that the training of the young in good and carefully selected music will contribute to the attainment of virtue.

Aristotle also regards music as important and discusses its uses in his *Politics* (8. 1339ᵃ–1342ᵇ). Less puritanical than Plato, he would allow all types of music for purposes of relaxation; but he holds that rhythms and melodies are representations (μιμήματα) of moral qualities and as such have an effect on the soul. For educational purposes, therefore, only the 'most ethical' types of music (ἁρμονίαι ἠθικώταται) should be used. At the same time he criticizes Plato for including the Phrygian, and would himself apparently confine instruction to the Dorian, which for him is the golden mean in music.

It is impossible to pass these opinions over as idle fancies when they are not only attested by two such different minds as Plato's and Aristotle's, but are implicit in many of the references to music in other writers (e.g. Aristophanes). The direct ethical effect of music may, indeed, have been exaggerated, as Aristoxenus hinted (*Harm.* p. 31) and as the Epicureans seem to have contended (cf. the *De musica* of Philodemus, 1st c. B.C.). Quite probably conventions and associations with poetic texts had much to do with the attribution of ἦθος to the modes; but at least it is evident that the Greeks associated their various ἁρμονίαι with distinctive feelings and emotions; and the keenness with which they felt the differences between the modes is well illustrated by the story of Philoxenus (Arist. *Pol.* 8. 1342ᵇ), who tried to compose his dithyramb 'The Mysians' in the Dorian but had to return to the appropriate ἁρμονία, which was the Phrygian. Furthermore, this attitude of respect for the power of music found expression in an artistic conservatism. In Argos, for instance, the purity of music was regulated by law; and at Sparta venturesome innovators had their instruments destroyed.

3. THE ROMAN ATTITUDE. If any music different in kind from that of Greece was indigenous in the Italian peninsula, all trace of it has disappeared; in musical matters Rome was the unenterprising pupil of Greece. The Romans were content to leave the cultivation of music largely in the hands of professional musicians. Cato voiced the feeling of his age when he adduced as a final proof of the worthlessness of an opponent the fact that he sang ('praeterea cantat'); and too great a proficiency in lyre-playing is mentioned as a fault in Sempronia, one of Catiline's associates. Music was not an essential part of a boy's education during the Republic, and even when it was included in a semi-Greek curriculum it seems to have consisted of little more than a simple theoretical outline. Cicero, for example, speaks with surprise of those who can recognize a theatre melody after the first few notes have been played (*Acad.* 2. 20). Furthermore, the forms of poetry which were most favoured by the Romans were just those which could most easily dispense with music; and Horace's *Carmen Saeculare* is the only extant lyric poem in Latin which we know to have been sung.

In the whole range of Latin literature we find only the most common-place and conventional references to music, and though gifted amateurs (including Nero) were more frequent in Imperial times, nowhere is there any indication that the Romans regarded music as anything more than a tolerable adjunct of civilized life. Unlike Achilles, Aeneas did not find his solace in music, and the nation he founded never acquired a passion for it.

4. EVIDENCE FOR GREEK MUSIC. For knowledge of Greek music we may turn to: (i) actual fragments of musical scores; (ii) remains of musical instruments; (iii) later types of music supposed to be descended from the Greek; (iv) ancient treatises. (i) The musical scores are few in number and very fragmentary; only one is claimed to be classical; and all depend for their interpretation upon a knowledge of the ancient musical notations (see § 11). (ii) Even if any citharas remained, they would be useless without their strings at the original tension; the few surviving auloi have lost their mouthpieces and very specialized knowledge and expert skill in playing are required before they can begin to yield up their secrets. The most recent attempt to utilize this type of evidence is in K. Schlesinger's *The Greek Aulos*. (iii) It is reasonable to suppose that Greek folk-song and Byzantine music retain some elements which are derived from the ancient art and there is a tradition that the music of the Roman liturgy owes a debt to Greece. But all these types of music have been subjected through the centuries to so many influences that it would be extremely hazardous to attempt to define those features which may be due to Greek inheritance. (iv) The easiest and most definite line of approach is provided by the treatises on music.

Of these theoretical books the earliest is the *Harmonics* (Ἀρχαί and Στοιχεῖα) of Aristoxenus (q.v.), which is of fundamental importance. Part of bk. 11 and the whole of bk. 19 of the ps.-Aristotelian *Problems* (Προβλήματα) are concerned with music, and Euclid's *Division of the Monochord* (Κατατομὴ κανόνος) contains a series of mathematically formulated propositions about musical intervals. Next in date comes the work *On Music* (Περὶ μουσικῆς), attributed by the manuscripts to Plutarch (1st c. A.D.), which contains much historical material, derived partly from Aristoxenus. To the second century A.D. belong the *Introduction to Harmonics* (Εἰσαγωγὴ ἁρμονική) of Cleonides (formerly attributed to Euclid), which gives a valuable outline of Aristoxenian theory; Theon of Smyrna's *Mathematics useful for reading Plato* (Τὰ κατὰ τὸ μαθηματικὸν χρήσιμα), which includes excerpts from Archytas and other reputable authorities; Claudius Ptolemy's *Harmonica* (Ἁρμονικά),

in three books, which is indispensable; the *Handbook of Harmonics* (Ἁρμονικὸν ἐγχειρίδιον) of Nicomachus of Gerasa; and the *Introduction to Harmonics* (Ἁρμονικὴ εἰσαγωγή) of Gaudentius. To the third century A.D. probably belong the three books *On Music* (Περὶ μουσικῆς) of Arstides Quintilianus and the *Introduction to Music* (Εἰσαγωγὴ μουσική) of a certain Alypius, which is our chief source of information for the musical notations. To the fourth century A.D. belongs the *Introduction to the Art of Music* (Εἰσαγωγὴ τέχνης μουσικῆς) by an otherwise unknown Bacchius (Βακχεῖος). In Latin the chief works are the *De musica* of Boethius and the ninth book of the *De nuptiis Philologiae* of Martianus Capella.

It is obvious that most of these treatises are far removed in date from classical Greek music; and though much of their doctrine is traditional, we cannot always be sure that the writers are relying upon older authorities. Unfortunately their testimony is not unanimous in a number of important matters and they are silent about some topics on which information is desirable.

5. ANCIENT AND MODERN MUSIC. (i) The most striking difference between the music of the Greeks and that to which western Europeans are accustomed is that the ancient art made use of a large number of scales or modes, which differed from each other in the sequence of the intervals composing them and in tonality. It was to these modes that the Greeks attributed the varying ethical effects of music. Our Major and Minor scales are often called modes, but they give only a poor idea of modal music; for though the sequence of intervals is different and the Minor is distinguished from the Major by the flattening of its third and sixth notes, both scales have a common tonic or key note (actually the lowest note of the scale), in relation to which the importance and function of the other notes is determined. A better, though still imperfect, idea of the ancient modes may be obtained from Gregorian music, in which the tonal centre does not occupy the same relative position in every scale.

(ii) The second difference lies in the size of the intervals used in the modes. Our scales consist only of tones and semitones; the semitones (on the pianoforte at least) are made as nearly equal as possible, and twelve of them complete an octave. In Greek music tones and semitones were not all equal and the enharmonic *diesis* (δίεσις, sometimes translated as 'quarter-tone') was smaller than any interval with which we are familiar. Neither modern nor Gregorian music can afford us any example of this wide variety of intervals; we must listen to Indian, Arabian, or Chinese music if we wish to gain some impression of intervals different from our 'tempered' tone and semitone. Indeed, it is very probable that if we could hear a piece of ancient Greek music accurately performed, we should regard it as bizarre, uncouth, and possibly barbaric.

(iii) The third great difference is of a less technical nature: Greek music was predominantly melodic. Choruses sang in unison (or in octaves if men and boys were performing together); to this practice there seems to have been no exception (cf. [Arist.] *Pr.* 19. 18). There is evidence (Plut. *De mus.* 1137 b) that an instrumental accompaniment played by a professional musician did not always follow the melodic line of the vocal part and sometimes included notes which made dissonances with the voice. How wide a liberty was permissible in such an accompaniment (ἑτεροφωνία, cf. Plato, *Laws* 812 d) is unknown; but there is no reason to suppose that the instrument provided more than an embellishment. It is indisputable that neither in vocal nor in instrumental music was there anything like a counterpoint of mutually independent but congruous parts, and no harmonic structure in the sense in which we understand the term. The Greeks did not evolve the prototype of an eight-part motet or of an orchestral symphony.

6. THE ARISTOXENIAN THEORY. (*a*) *Tetrachords and systems.* The simplest approach to an understanding of the details of Greek music is from the theoretical expositions of Aristoxenus and his followers (especially Cleonides). As a starting-point we shall take the diatonic tetrachord such as may be found between the notes *E* and *A* on a pianoforte. In ascending order—if we may neglect the downward progression which is generally favoured by the Greek theorists—its intervals are: semitone, tone, tone (S, T, T, or $\frac{1}{2}$, 1, 1). Two such tetrachords could be combined to form a scale or *system* (σύστημα) either (i) by conjunction (συναφή), when the top note of one tetrachord was identical with the bottom note of the other; or (ii) by disjunction (διάζευξις), when an interval of a tone (τόνος διαζευκτικός) was inserted between the two:

Conjunct system: E F G A B♭ C D   *or* S T T S T T

Disjunct system: E F G A B C D E   *or* S T T T S T T

There are three particularly important *systems* thus constructed from tetrachords: (i) the Lesser Perfect System (σύστημα τέλειον ἔλασσον), which consisted of three conjunct tetrachords with an added note called *proslambanomenos* (προσλαμβανόμενος, sc. φθόγγος) at the bottom. This *system*, with the technical names of its notes (originally derived from their position on a simple lyre, see § 9 (i)) and of its tetrachords, may be represented as follows (though it should be clearly understood that a pianoforte will give a very imperfect idea of the intervals even of a diatonic scale):

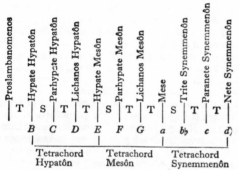

(ii) The Greater Perfect System (σύστημα τέλειον μεῖζον) consisted of the Proslambanomenos and four tetrachords grouped in conjunct pairs:

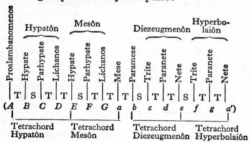

(iii) The combination of the Lesser and Greater Perfect Systems gave the Immutable System (σύστημα ἀμετάβολον) which can be regarded as the Greater Perfect System with the addition of the tetrachord Synemmenôn from the Lesser Perfect System.

(b) *Octave species.* Within the Greater Perfect System there were seven different types or *species* of octave (εἴδη τοῦ διὰ πασῶν) which could be distinguished by their different interval sequences. Each had its own distinctive name:

Mixolydian: Hypate Hypatôn—Paramese (*B–b*)
Lydian: Parhypate Hypatôn—Trite Diezeugmenôn (*C–c*)

Phrygian: Lichanos Hypatôn—Paranete Diezeugmenôn (*D–d*)
Dorian: Hypate Mesôn—Nete Diezeugmenôn (*E–e*)
Hypolydian: Parhypate Mesôn—Trite Hyperbolaiôn (*F–f*)
Hypophrygian: Lichanos Mesôn—Paranete Hyperbolaiôn (*G–g*)
Hypodorian: Proslambanomenos—Mese (*A–a*) *or* Mese—Nete Hyperbolaiôn (*a–a′*).

(c) *Transposition scales, Keys, or Tonoi.* The Perfect Immutable System could as a whole be played at various pitches without any alteration of the internal interval sequence, just as our modern Major or Minor scale can be taken at various pitches. When associated with a given pitch the Perfect Immutable System had a distinctive name and was called a *tonos* (τόνος). According to Aristoxenus himself there were thirteen such *tonoi*, to which later theorists added two more (the Hyperaeolian and the Hyperlydian). On the commonly accepted equation of Greek and modern pitch the fifteen *tonoi* in ascending order were:

Hypodorian	commencing on	F
Hypoionian	,,	,, F♯
Hypophrygian	,,	,, G
Hypoaeolian	,,	,, G♯
Hypolydian	,,	,, A
Dorian	,,	,, B♭
Ionian	,,	,, B
Phrygian	,,	,, C
Aeolian	,,	,, C♯
Lydian	,,	,, D
Hyperdorian *or* Mixolydian	,,	,, E♭
Hyperionian	,,	,, E
Hyperphrygian	,,	,, f
Hyperaeolian	,,	,, f♯
Hyperlydian	,,	,, g

It will be noted that the names of the lowest five include the prefix Hypo- (ὑπο-) and the names of the highest five have the prefix Hyper- (ὑπερ-); the middle five have simple ethnic designations. The range from the lowest note of the Hypodorian to the highest of the Hyperlydian was rather more than three octaves, and so corresponded to the combined capabilities of normal male and female voices. Though Aristoxenus is silent on the point, it is reasonable to suppose that the original purpose of the *tonoi* was to bring the various octave *species* within the same vocal range. That is why the pitch order of the *tonoi* is the reverse of the pitch order of the *species* of the same names; the higher is the pitch of a *species* in the Greater Perfect System, the lower is the homonymous *tonos*. Claudius Ptolemy (*Harm.* 2. 9) points out quite legitimately that since there are only seven *species* of the octave, only seven *tonoi* were really necessary. It is also worth noting that the use of the tetrachord Synemmenôn in the Immutable System provided a means of modulation from one *tonos* to another *tonos* a fourth higher; for the conjunction between the tetrachords Mesôn and Synemmenôn could be treated as if it were the conjunction between the tetrachords Hypatôn and Mesôn of another *tonos*: thus:

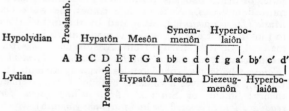

(d) *Genera and 'colours'.* So far we have been concerned only with tetrachords containing no other interval than a tone or semitone. The structure of the tetrachords themselves, however, admitted a number of variations known as *genera* (γένη) and 'colours' (χρόαι). The two extreme notes of a tetrachord were regarded as fixed (φθόγγοι ἑστῶτες), while the position of the two inner notes (φθόγγοι κινούμενοι) was variable; and the two lowest intervals of the tetrachord were together called a *pycnum* (πυκνόν) if their sum was less than the remaining interval of the tetrachord. The *genera* were three in number: the diatonic (γένος διατονικόν), the chromatic (γ. χρωματικόν), and the enharmonic (γ. ἐναρμόνιον). The diatonic itself was subdivided in the Aristoxenian theory into two 'colours', the High (σύντονον) and the Soft (μαλακόν); and the chromatic into three 'colours', the Tonic (τονιαῖον), the Hemiolic (ἡμιόλιον), and the Soft (μαλακόν). If we take the tone as a unit, the intervals constituting the various kinds of tetrachords can be set out as follows:

High (σύντονον) diatonic	½	1	1
Soft (μαλακόν) ,,	½	¾	1¼
Tonic (τονιαῖον) chromatic	½	½	1½
Hemiolic (ἡμιόλιον) ,,	⅜	⅜	1¾
Soft (μαλακόν) ,,	⅓	⅓	1⅚
Enharmonic	¼	¼	2

When we make allowances for the fact that this doctrine of *genera* is only a theoretical systematization of the actual practice of musicians, it becomes obvious that a Greek composer had a great wealth of subtle intonations at his disposal, and that Greek melodies must have had a delicacy and fineness of outline to which the melodies of modern music can offer no parallel.

7. THEORY AND PRACTICE. The predecessors of Aristoxenus in musical theory were the Pythagoreans and the Harmonists (ἁρμονικοί). The Pythagoreans, however, were more interested in tracing numerical relationships in concordant intervals than in establishing a comprehensive theory; and it is significant that the dying Pythagoras was reputed to have adjured his followers to study the monochord, which was a piece of scientific apparatus and not a musical instrument at all. As a whole, the school devoted its attention to the Dorian scale; and intervals whose ratios they evaluated were considered satisfactory only if they conformed to one or other of the favourite Pythagorean formulae, such as *x* : *nx* or *x* : *x* + 1. The Harmonists, on the other hand, were much more interested in the practical art; but it is evident from what Aristoxenus himself tells us about their work (*Harm.* pp. 2, 6, 36, 37, 40) that they were not capable of organizing their knowledge into a really homogeneous system of theory. They did not analyse all the scales, but restricted their study to the enharmonic ones whose compass was an octave; they interested themselves in the search for a small unit of measurement (cf. Plato, *Resp.* 531 a), the *diesis*, which they used in the construction of diagrams of close-packed intervals (καταπύκνωσις), without any regard for melodic or unmelodic sequences; and they were at variance with one another in their pronouncements about the order of the *tonoi* and the intervals which separated them.

The homogeneity of the system of Aristoxenus cannot be denied. It seems to provide a means whereby any melody, when reduced to its elements, might be related to a scale whose 'colour', *genus*, *species*, and *tonos* could be defined. But apart from the fact that no theory can profess to give more than the osteology of an art, the Aristoxenian theory, as it has come down to us, is unsatisfying.

(i) Underlying it all is the idea that sound can be regarded as a line, at any point of which the voice could rest (though not at all in succession); and that an interval, since it may be thought of as a linear distance between two such points, can be subdivided exactly into any given number of equal parts. But the Pythagoreans had

already laid the foundations of a true acoustic science when they demonstrated that the size of an interval can properly be expressed only by a numerical ratio. There is, in fact, no such interval as a semitone, if by that term we mean an interval which taken twice will produce a 9 : 8 tone, for the ratio involved (3 : 2 √2) is irrational. The intervals 18 : 17 and 17 : 16 can be called semitones, and 36 : 35, or 35 : 34, or 34 : 33, or 33 : 32 may be called 'quarter-tones'; but when Aristoxenus speaks of a ἡμιτόνιον or a δίεσις, his vague description does not give us sufficiently precise information about Greek intonations.

(ii) In Plato and Aristotle and other writers we read of ἁρμονίαι most of which had ethnic names: Ionian, Lydian, Dorian, Phrygian. The word itself, when used in this musical sense, is most easily explained by the assumption that each ἁρμονία involved a new tuning of the lyre. Though Aristoxenus (*Harm.* p. 36) refers to those 'who confined their attention to the seven octave scales (ἑπτὰ ὀκταχόρδων Westphal; ἑπταχόρδων MSS.) which they called ἁρμονίαι', he himself does not use the plural ἁρμονίαι in a technical sense. His octave scales are called *species* (εἴδη τοῦ διὰ πασῶν), and their names are not identical with those used for the ἁρμονίαι. There is amongst them no Ionian or Syntonolydian; and the names of three of them include the prefix Hypo- (ὑπο-) which is not found in earlier writers. Even if we identify the *species* with the ἁρμονίαι and equate, for instance, the Syntonolydian and Lydian of Plato with the Aristoxenian Lydian and Hypolydian respectively, it is quite impossible to believe that the ἁρμονίαι had their origin as *species* within a two-octave scale which itself evidently belongs to a comparatively advanced stage of musical development. It would be worth much to know what modifications, if any, had to take place before the ἁρμονίαι could be theoretically treated as octave *species*.

(iii) A further obscurity, and one of considerable importance, concerns the form of the *species* in the chromatic and enharmonic *genera*. The problem is simple in the case of the Dorian *species* which is bounded by fixed notes (φθόγγοι ἑστῶτες) of the Greater Perfect System; for its enharmonic form would be: ¼ ¼ 2 1 ¼ ¼ 2. The enharmonic form of the Lydian, however, which is bounded by movable notes (φθόγγοι κινούμενοι) would appear to be: ¼ 2 ¼ ¼ 2 1 ¼; and it is scarcely credible that such a sequence was ever a musical possibility.

(iv) Nothing is said by Aristoxenus about the tonality either of the Greater Perfect System or of the individual octave *species*. Yet if these *species* were virtually the old ἁρμονίαι or a developed form of them, we cannot understand them fully until we know what note had the function of a tonal centre in each. One of the ps.-Aristotelian Problems (19. 20) states that all the best melodies make a frequent use of Mese, and we may conjecture that this note was in fact a tonic. But unfortunately it is not clear whether the writer meant the Mese of the Greater Perfect System (i.e. a Mese κατὰ δύναμιν) or the fourth note ascending (i.e. a Mese κατὰ θέσιν) of any octave *species*.

So far we have mentioned only those deficiencies of the Aristoxenian theory which are evident from an examination of the system itself. Further problems arise when we try to relate it to other evidence. (i) Aristides Quintilianus (pp. 21-2) gives an account (possibly derived from some work of Aristoxenus himself) of the six ἁρμονίαι mentioned by Plato in the *Republic*. Of the scales which Aristides describes, only one (the Lydian) is identical with an Aristoxenian *species* (the Hypolydian); the Phrygian and Mixolydian have an internal structure somewhat different from the corresponding Aristoxenian εἴδη; the Dorian has an additional tone at the bottom; and the Ionian and Syntonolydian are less than an octave in compass. Several of them seem to involve a mixture of *genera*. There is no reason to reject in its entirety the evidence of Aristides, which, so far as concerns the Mixolydian, is confirmed by a passage of Plutarch (*De mus.* 1136 d); and the truth would appear to be that the old ἁρμονίαι were not parts of a homogeneous musical system. (ii) There is other evidence also for defective and anomalous scales used by Olympus and Terpander and analysed by Philolaus (Plut. *De mus.* 1134 f–1135 b, 1137 b–d; [Arist.] *Pr.* 19. 32; Nicom. p. 253 Jan.). (iii) In connexion with the older types of music, prominent mention is made (Plut. *De mus.* 1134 f, 1141 b; Aristid. Quint. p. 28) of intervals called σπονδειασμός (a rise of three *dieses*), ἔκλυσις (a fall of three *dieses*), and κέβολή (a rise of five *dieses*). Intervals of these magnitudes have a very unimportant place in the system of Aristoxenus (cf. his μαλακόν diatonic, § 6). (iv) Claudius Ptolemy (*Harm.* 2. 14) has preserved the evaluations for the *genera* made by his predecessors and has added some of his own. The size of the tone is given as 11 : 10, 10 : 9, 9 : 8, and 8 : 7. The smaller intervals of the enharmonic vary from 46 : 45, which is less than a quarter-tone, to 24 : 23, which is larger than a third of a tone; the chromatic intervals vary between 28 : 27 and 12 : 11. Though the enharmonic usually has an interval of ratio 5 : 4 (a major third) at the top, and the chromatic an interval of 6 : 5 or 7 : 6 (a minor third) at that place, in both *genera* the two lower intervals are of varying sizes; and it seems that the distinction between the *genera* is not as clear or as definite as the Aristoxenian theory postulates. (v) The Greek musical notations seem on analysis to conflict with the theory of the *tonoi* and their tetrachordal structure. Where we should expect an identity of notation there is divergence, and variety where we should expect identity (see K. Schlesinger, *The Greek Aulos*, 527–30). (vi) Though the widely varying dates (see § 12) of the fragments of Greek music warn us not to press their evidence too far, it is noteworthy that they exhibit a number of melodic progressions which violate the doctrines of Aristoxenus.

8. THE LIMITS OF DOUBT. Despite the defects of the Aristoxenian system which have just been mentioned and the conflicting evidence from other sources, it would be generally accepted that, in the earlier stages, Greek music made use of a number of modal scales which, because they involved separate tunings of the lyre, were called ἁρμονίαι. As the compass of the lyre and cithara was extended, the relations between the ἁρμονίαι were more clearly apprehended and, at the expense perhaps of the elimination of some apparent anomalies, they came to be regarded as segments of a single two-octave scale based upon homogeneous tetrachords. On the other hand, we know nothing, apart from the evidence of Aristides Quintilianus and Plutarch, about the original structure of the ἁρμονίαι. We cannot say whether each of them had a diatonic, chromatic, and enharmonic form or whether the various *genera* and 'colours' were in practice associated with particular ἁρμονίαι. Nor can we make any positive assertion about the tonality of the ἁρμονίαι or of the octave *species*; the theoretical treatises are almost silent on the point and the musical fragments are not decisive.

9. INSTRUMENTS. Musical instruments (ὄργανα) of many types were known to the Greeks; it was therefore by definite preference that only the lyre and cithara among strings and the aulos among wind-instruments ever attained artistic importance. The lyre or cithara predominated in lyric poetry, though the aulos shared in the accompaniment of Pindar's odes and monopolized the dithyramb and the dramatic choruses; the lyre prevailed in education, the aulos had its place in social and military life; both were prominent in cult.

(i) *Strings* (ἔντατα). The *lyre* (λύρα, κιθαρίς, φόρμιγξ) and the *cithara* (κιθάρα) were characterized by strings of equal length, vertically strung and sounded by plucking.

They thus differed from: (*a*) bowed types, which were unknown to Greece; (*b*) harps, with strings of unequal length, known but not employed in serious music (e.g. ψαλτήριον, τρίγωνον, σαμβύκη). Pitch was regulated by the tension (and perhaps the thickness) of the strings. In the absence of a fret-board, each string would normally provide one note only; but we cannot rule out the possibility of (*a*) obtaining the octave-harmonic by stopping the string at its middle point (διάληψις), or (*b*) of shortening the string by finger-pressure near the top to raise its tone by a small interval.

The cithara, which came into use for public performance about the time of Terpander (*c.* 675 B.C.), was an elaborated form of the lyre, from which it differed mainly in size and sonority. The sound-box of the lyre was formed of the carapace of a tortoise (or a wooden structure of similar shape) with ox-hide stretched over its concavity (cf. *Hom. Hymn. Merc.* 41 ff.); from it rose two slender curved side-pieces (πήχεις, κέρατα) of wood or horn. The body of the cithara was of wood and more solidly and squarely built, the arms forming a substantial prolongation of the sound-box. In both instruments the strings (χορδαί, νευραί), of gut or sinew, were stretched from a holder (χορδότονον) fixed to the body over a bridge to the cross-bar (ζυγόν) which joined the two side-pieces. Here there was an apparatus of thongs or pegs (κόλλοπες) by which the strings could be tuned; but how the tuning was done is not clear.

The traditional number of strings for the lyre was seven, and it is doubtful if the cithara had more than eight till the fifth century, when strings were added by e.g. Phrynis and Timotheus (see § 10); but the evidence for details is confused. Timotheus himself refers (*Persae* 242) to the eleven strings of his cithara; he is said to have added a twelfth also (Pherecrates ap. Plut. *De mus.* 1141 f). It is unlikely that the number was ever increased to fifteen or eighteen (as late theorists imply) and uncertain how many strings the lyre ultimately had. The strings were plucked by the left hand directly, following the vocal melody (ψάλλειν, *intus canere*), or by the right hand with the aid of a plectrum (πλῆκτρον), to provide such independent accompaniment, preludes, interludes, etc., as there may have been (πλήσσειν, κρούειν, *foris canere*; cf. Apul. *Flor.* 2. 15, Ascon. in Cic. *Verr.* 2. 1. 53). The cithara rested against the body of the performer and was supported in position by a belt (τελαμών), the strings of lowest pitch being farthest from him (cf. the nomenclature of notes: ὑπάτη, νήτη).

The *barbitos* (βάρβιτος, -ον), the instrument of Sappho and Alcaeus, seems to have differed little from the lyre, except that its strings, being longer, gave notes of lower pitch. As to the πηκτίς and μαγαδίς, it is uncertain whether they were distinct from one another and whether they belonged to the class of harp or lyre. They had many strings, and so made playing in octaves possible; hence came the term μαγαδίζειν, for doubling a vocal part at the octave.

(ii) *Wind* (ἐμπνευστά). The αὐλός, commonly mistranslated 'flute', was akin rather to the clarinet or oboe. The exact nature of the vibrator is, despite a passage of Theophrastus (*Hist. Pl.* 4. 11. 4), a matter of uncertain inference, since the instruments preserved lack mouthpieces; but it was probably a double-reed (ζεῦγος, γλῶττα, γλωττίς). This was inserted into a cylindrical pipe, and the extrusion of the reed was partially hidden by one or more bulbs (ὅλμοι). K. Schlesinger, however, in *The Greek Aulos* (a mine of information about the behaviour of reed pipes) maintains that the double-reed gave place at a certain stage to a single-reed. The pipe, of reed, wood, bone, or ivory, was open at the lower end and pierced with lateral holes. Of these the early aulos had probably no more than three or four, which, in conjunction with the βόμβυξ or note of the whole pipe, would seem to provide a very limited range. The question is complicated, however, by the fact that auloi were generally played in pairs (contrast μόναυλος, a single pipe, and cf. the Latin *tibiae*). The suggestion that one of them provided a drone is supported by no evidence; and the commonly accepted view that the right-hand pipe played the melody, the left-hand pipe the accompaniment (κροῦσις), suggests a hardly credible degree of polyphony, if both pipes spoke together. If, however, there was some device (of which we know nothing) to allow the pipes to speak separately, the two instruments may have combined to produce a more extended scale. The pipes were not always of the same length. In the Phrygian auloi they were of exceptionally small bore, and the left was longer and consequently deeper in tone. Of such a type, probably, were the *tibiae impares* of the Roman *palliata*.

In the early period a separate pipe (or pair of pipes) was required for each mode (ἁρμονία). Later the potentialities of the instrument were greatly enlarged, particularly by Pronomus and the Theban school of the fifth century. Length and the number of holes were increased (the longest of surviving auloi has 15 or 16, the shortest 6), and a device was introduced by which the holes not required for a particular scale could be closed by a perforated metal ring operated by a small projection (κέρας). In this way it was possible to play a number of different modes on one pair of auloi; and instruments were no longer classified according to mode, but by general range of pitch. Aristoxenus (ap. Ath. 634 e) distinguishes five types (in descending order of pitch): παρθένιοι, παιδικοί, κιθαριστήριοι, τέλειοι, ὑπερτέλειοι; and he states (*Harm.* 20) that between them they embraced a range of more than three octaves. Furthermore, a practitioner of the highly individualistic art of aulos-playing had at his disposal many professional tricks such as overblowing, cross-fingering, partial obturation of holes, regulation of the reed and of his own breath, whereby he could extend the capabilities of his instrument.

The transverse flute finds no parallel in Greece (for the πλαγίαυλος was an aulos in which the reed was introduced obliquely by a lateral tube). But an instrument of the flute *type* was the syrinx (σύριγξ). Blown directly at the upper end, like a flageolet, it might consist of a single pipe (σ. μονοκάλαμος) or of a structure of pipes of graded length bound side by side (σ. πολυκάλαμος). The latter, the high-pitched Pan's Pipes, beloved of shepherds, was part-ancestor of the water-organ (ὕδραυλίς: invented by Ctesibius of Alexandria in the 3rd c. B.C.), in which rows of graduated auloi were supplied with air hydraulically.

Brass instruments (with bone mouthpiece) were primarily employed for military purposes. Both the straight (σάλπιγξ, *tuba*) and curved (κέρας, *cornu*) varieties of trumpet were known. In the Roman *lituus* the curvature was probably confined to the extremity.

(iii) *Percussion*. Tambourines (τύμπανα) and cymbals (κύμβαλα) belonged rather to the cults of, e.g., Dionysus and Cybele than to serious music.

10. HISTORY. The history of Greek music overlaps the history of Greek poetry, for the main function of music was to accompany poetic texts. Thus the principal types of musical composition correspond largely to the types of poetry, and our scanty sources mention as leading composers many who are better known to us as poets: Archilochus (evidently an important influence), Sappho, Pindar, Sophocles; unfortunately, no detailed account of the musical side of their work can be given. There are others, however, known primarily as musicians; and we know of types of performance that were primarily musical.

Musical history really begins in the seventh century with Terpander and Archilochus. In the background

are folk-song, work-song, song (personal or choral) occasional to the principal events of human life, and above all cult-song. In the background is the epic tradition: a Phemius or Demodocus singing epic verse to the lyre. In the background is also an elusive foreign influence; for Greek music was not racially pure. Recent research into Egyptian, Babylonian, and Palestinian music has shown possible points of similarity; indeed, the Greek tradition itself avowed an influence from the Orient, not only in the names of certain modes, but in the legendary figure of Olympus the Mysian. But the contrast is not a simple one, and Olympus himself is a composite figure, representing a fusion of the Hellenic and the Oriental. Nor was the instrument with which he is chiefly connected, the aulos, new to Greece, for it was already associated with traditional cults; and the antithesis of Hellenic lyre and Asiatic aulos needs to be used with great caution. Probably new styles and techniques were introduced from the East in the eighth century, but we are not in a position to separate the new from the old.

Terpander (*fl. c.* 675) came from Antissa in Lesbos, but his activity is associated with Sparta. His chief claim to fame is that he first impressed his individuality upon the traditional νόμοι κιθαρῳδικοί so that they were handed down as his personal compositions. Styles, rather than definite melodies, in origin (see Sachs, *Musik d. Altertums*, p. 64), these νόμοι, which were vocal solos accompanied by the cithara, became the subjects of competition. The texts were for the most part epic, with a prelude written by the composer-executant; the melody was severe and eschewed modulation. About the same time the obscure *Clonas* (of Tegea?) performed the same service for the analogous νόμοι αὐλῳδικοί. But more famous names connected with the aulos are those of *Polymnestus* of Colophon and *Sacadas* of Argos. The former's fame was recognized by Pindar (fr. 188), and Plutarch speaks of him as an innovator who, nevertheless, did not depart from the severe style. Sacadas was the most famous executant of the sixth century. For not only was he singer-composer of νόμοι αὐλῳδικοί, but player-composer of the famous αὐλητικὸς νόμος Πυθικός (a purely instrumental piece, dealing with Apollo's victory over the Python) in which he won in 586 the first of three successive victories at the Pythian Games. The accounts that late authorities give of the structure of this piece reveal an element of 'programme-music'. It is interesting too that purely instrumental music (ψιλὴ αὔλησις) should have won and kept an important place in a Greek festival at all; even solo cithara-playing (ψιλὴ κιθάρισις), which would seem a bleak entertainment, found its way into the Pythian and other festivals.

Doubtless the main triumphs of Greek music in this period were in choral lyric, an indissoluble complex of poetry, melody, and dance, which culminated with Pindar, Simonides, and the early tragedians. To later —and moralizing—theorists this was the epoch of the 'educative' style, in contrast to the 'theatrical' or 'popular' style that developed in the fifth century. The process of transition cannot be traced in detail. An important factor may have been the evolution of the aulos (see § 9), which increased the available range of melody and facilitated modulation. String-players, too, envious of the freedom of their fellows, added strings to the cithara (see § 9). Furthermore, the balance of importance between choir and instrumentalist began to change. The chief factor, however, was mental rather than technical. Individualism was in the air and convention suspect; and the interpreter of a tradition intimately associated with religion became a virtuoso bent upon giving pleasure to an audience. Thus variety (ποικιλία) took the place of simplicity: the melodic range was extended, modulation (and perhaps vocal and instrumental embellishments) cultivated; rhythmical structure became freer; the poetry mattered less in comparison with the melody.

The types of music especially affected were the dithyramb and the νόμος κιθαρῳδικός. The latter was revolutionized by *Phrynis* of Mytilene (*fl. c.* 450). The former, under *Melanippides* and *Cinesias*, broke away from strophic structure into free verse (cf. A. W. Pickard-Cambridge, *Dithyramb, Tragedy, and Comedy*, 53 ff.). *Timotheus* of Miletus (*c.* 450–360) was a master of both forms; and, indeed, the distinction between them was blurred, for while Timotheus seems to have introduced a choral element into the νόμος, *Philoxenus* (his contemporary) introduced *soli* into dithyramb. The impure poetic style favoured by composers of νόμοι and dithyramb alike can be judged from the *Persae* of Timotheus, a νόμος, which has in great part survived. The rhythms are varied but uninteresting; the diction is turgid, obscure, and undistinguished. But the work is a libretto rather than a poem; and we should not condemn the music unheard, though we may suspect that lack of taste was not confined to the poetic text. How far the new style affected other types of music it is hard to say. Certainly it was not unchallenged in the fourth century; and, when we come to the earliest of our substantial fragments, the Delphic Paeans, we find a strong archaizing tendency.

11. THE NOTATIONS. (i) *Melodic.* To note their melodies the Greeks used alphabetic forms, written, in the case of poetic texts, above the syllables. Two systems of notation for the fifteen *tonoi* are recorded in ancient authorities (notably Alypius), who also assert that one was used for vocal, the other for instrumental melody (σήματα τῆς λέξεως, τῆς κρούσεως). This is confirmed by the Berlin papyrus, where both notations are so employed. It should be observed, however, that (*a*) we have no certain case of the employment of both together; (*b*) the second Delphic Hymn is noted in the instrumental notation, which suggests that, where vocal and instrumental melody were identical, the notations might be employed indifferently.

The history of the notations is obscure and their interpretation controversial. It is unlikely that Pindar and Aeschylus had no means of writing down their melodies; but the vocal notation can hardly have preceded the general adoption, towards the end of the fifth century, of the Ionic alphabet on which it is based; the instrumental notation, the origin of whose forms is uncertain, may well be earlier, but, being designed for a system of *tonoi*, it implies a developed theory. That system was not, however, the fifteen *tonoi* of Alypius. For instance, in both notations the signs above Dorian *nete hyperbolaiōn* repeat those an octave below with the addition of an acute accent and probably did not belong to the original scheme; at the lower end the instrumental notation has adapted the forms below Hypolydian *proslambanomenos* from the vocal notation. It would seem, then, that the original scope of the instrumental notation was two octaves and a tone, and that it was designed for five (or six) *tonoi*, having a range of a twelfth (or eleventh) only.

The instrumental notation is characterized by triads, in which the same form appears in three positions (e.g. F ⊔ ⅂), representing the three notes of an enharmonic *pycnum* (see § 6 *d*). Thus the highest note is a semitone above the lowest, and the highest and lowest notes of the various triads combine to form a semitonal series of fixed pitch. But this notation as applied to the chromatic and diatonic shows some peculiarities: all three *genera* have a common sign for *parhypate*, despite its varying pitch; and, while the sign for diatonic *lichanos* correctly implies an interval of 1½ tones from *hypate*, chromatic *lichanos* is distinguished from the enharmonic only by a diacritical mark. There were thus two conflicting

principles at work, those of absolute pitch and relative function; and it is to this conflict, and to the adaptation of the original scheme to additional *tonoi*, that many of the much-canvassed anomalies are due: namely, the employment of the same sign with different values, of different signs with the same value. (Sachs, in *Zeitschrift f. Musikwissenschaft* vi, proposing a radically new interpretation, relates the instrumental notation to a pentatonic tuning of the lyre.) The vocal notation corresponds to the instrumental note for note, but replaces the triads by a continuous alphabetic series. Most of the letters of the alphabet are employed (in descending order) within the range of the central octave of the Dorian *tonos*, which was the kernel of the whole system; above and below are altered forms of the same series.

(ii) *Rhythmical.* Symbols were used, when necessary (see § 13), to elucidate the rhythm. (*a*) The signs —, ⌐, ⌐⌐, ⊔ placed over a note indicated that its length was that of two, three, four, and five time-units (or χρόνοι πρῶτοι) respectively. (*b*) A rest (χρόνος κενός), or a protraction of the preceding note, was indicated by Λ or ⌒, which might be used in conjunction with the signs of quantity: e.g. ⊼. (*c*) Dots (στιγμαί) might be used to distinguish the structure of the metrical foot, and ancient authority states that the function was to mark the *arsis* (ἄρσις). On the whole our fragments confirm this, but the evidence is complicated (see Powell and Barber, *New Chapters* ii. 160 ff.). (*d*) A subscript curved hyphen might be used to bind together notes sung to the same syllable.

12. THE FRAGMENTS. The following constitute the corpus of surviving Greek melody.

A. In papyri. (i) A musical setting of Euripides' *Orestes* 338–44, found among the Rainer papyri, may be Euripidean, since the poet's own score was extant in the time of Dionysius of Halicarnassus. (ii) A Zenon papyrus of *c.* 250 B.C. contains a brief fragment, possibly from a tragedy, though the date of composition is unknown. (iii–vii) These five fragments from a Berlin papyrus were written down later than A.D. 156, but may have been composed earlier: (iii) twelve lines of a Paean in a Hellenistic manner; (iv) three lines of melody for instrument only; (v) four lines of an address to the suicide Ajax, possibly excerpted from a tragedy; (vi) three lines of melody for instrument; and (vii) half a line of lyric. The instrumental pieces iv and vi have no discernible connexion with the vocal fragments they follow; all five make elaborate use of rhythmical notation. (viii) The setting of a Christian hymn, found in an Oxyrhynchus papyrus of the third century A.D., is in Greek notation, but it is doubtful whether it affords evidence of the adaptation of Greek melody to the new worship (cf. E. Wellesz, *CQ* 1945).

B. On stone. (ix–x) The most extensive fragments of Greek music that survive are two paeans, both seriously incomplete, found in 1893 during French excavations at Delphi. The second can be dated 128–127 B.C. and ascribed to a certain Limenius; the first may well have the same date and authorship. Both are written in paeonic or cretic metre, which, in the absence of rhythmical notation, suggests 5/8 time. The second paean is followed by a brief prosodion in an Aeolic metre. Melodically, these two paeans strikingly illustrate the Aristoxenian scale-system, tetrachordal structure being clearly marked and the 'standing-notes' emphasized (see § 6 *d*). (xi) An inscription of the second century B.C. or later, found at Aidin near Tralles, presents us with a brief but intact and attractive melody, commonly known as the 'Epitaph of Seikilos'. The words are a kind of skolion in free iambics, the rhythm being elucidated by notation.

C. In manuscript. (xii–xv) Four melodies have come down among the manuscripts of the ancient treatises. (xii–xiii) The Hymn to the Muse should in fact be regarded as two separate pieces, both of uncertain date. (xiv) The Hymn to Nemesis is attributable to Mesomedes, a contemporary of Hadrian. (xv) Similarity of style suggests the same authorship for the Hymn to the Sun. (xvi) Short snatches of melody occur in Bellermann's *Anonymus* (§§ 97–101, 104). Their apparent purpose is to illustrate types of rhythm.

Musical analyses of these fragments are given in Powell and Barber, *New Chapters* ii. 167–78 and R. P. Winnington-Ingram, *Mode in Ancient Greek Music*, 30–47. The melody to the opening lines of Pindar's first Pythian ode, published by A. Kircher in his *Musurgia Universalis* (1650), is under such grave suspicion of being a forgery that its evidential value is negligible (see *CPhil.* xxxi. 120 ff.).

13. MELODY, RHYTHM, AND THE GREEK LANGUAGE. Two important principles of composition emerge from a consideration of the fragments. Both in melody and in rhythm, a Greek composer had less apparent freedom in setting words than his modern successors. This is explicable from the nature of the Greek language: (a) by virtue of its pitch-accent, it possessed, even when spoken, an inherent melody—in the phrase of Aristoxenus, λογῶδές τι μέλος; (b) it possessed clearly marked long and short vowels, which formed the basis of quantitative metres.

(a) In the majority of extant compositions this word or sentence melody is respected: an accented syllable is set to a note which is not lower and is frequently higher than other syllables of the same word (for details see Powell and Barber, *New Chapters* ii. 165). Yet this principle is not observed by all the vocal fragments or by all equally. They fall into three groups: (1) in iii, ix, x, xi, xii, xiii exceptions are absent or negligible; (2) in i and v the accent seems to be altogether disregarded; (3) viii, xiv, xv show the influence of the accent, but with more frequent exceptions. The phenomena of (3) may reflect the gradual break-down of the pitch-accent which was taking place during the period of their composition. This explanation will not, however, account for (2), which includes the *Orestes* fragment; but it should be observed that i is strophic, v may well be; and, if (as is probable) strophe and antistrophe were sung to the same melody, the accent was then bound to be disregarded.

(b) The rhythms of Greek music were practically identical with the metres of Greek poetry; and, where the natural quantities of the syllables are distorted, such a distortion is also a concern of the metrist. Some of our fragments (e.g. ix, x, xii–xv) are without rhythmical notation, presumably because the natural lengths of syllables were a sufficient guide; only in the Berlin Paean (where – – – is rhythmized as, e.g., ♩ ♪♪) is there a considerable divergence between rhythm and metre. In judging this apparent restriction of the musician's freedom, however, it must be remembered that the Greek lyric metres themselves were elaborate partly because they were musical and choreographic as well as poetic rhythms.

BIBLIOGRAPHY

ANCIENT SOURCES: (a) *Theoretical works.* (i) *Collections*: M. Meibomius, *Antiquae Musicae Auctores Septem* (2 vols., Amsterdam, 1652; containing: Aristoxenus, Euclid with Cleonides, Nicomachus, Alypius, Gaudentius, Bacchius, Aristides Quintilianus, Martianus Capella). C. von Jan, *Musici Scriptores Graeci* (1895; containing: Aristotelis loci, ps.-Arist. Problems, Euclid, Cleonides, Nicomachus, Bacchius, Gaudentius, Alypius). (ii) *Separate authors*: Aristoxenus, ed. P. Marquard (1868), R. Westphal (1893), H. Macran (1902); ps.-Aristotelian Problems, ed. F. A. Gevaert and J. C. Vollgraff (1903); Plutarch, *De mus.*, ed. R. Volkmann (1856), R. Westphal (1866), H. Weil and Th. Reinach (1900); Theon of Smyrna, ed. E. Hiller (1878); Ptolemy, ed. J. Wallis (1682 and, with the commentary of Porphyrius, in *Opera Math.* iii, 1699), I. Düring (Göteborg, 1930); Porphyrius, ed. I. Düring (Göteborg, 1932); Aristides Quintilianus, ed. A. Jahn (1882); Philodemus, *De mus.*, ed. J. Kemke (1884). Add also F. Bellermann's *Anonymus de musica* (1841) and H. A. J. Vincent's *Notice sur trois MSS grecs* (= vol. 16, 2 of *Notices et Extraits des MSS du Roi*, 1847).

(b) *Fragments of music.* Incomplete collection in C. von Jan's *Musici Scriptores Graeci, Supplementum* (1899). For Delphic Hymns add J. U. Powell's *Collectanea Alexandrina* (1925); for Christian Hymn add *POxy.* xv, No. 1786, Th. Reinach in *Revue Musicale* (1922), and R. Wagner in *Philologus* (1923); for Berlin fragments add W. Schubart in *Sitz. Preuss. Akad. Berl.* (1918) and R. Wagner in *Philol.* (1921); for Cairo fragment add J. F. Mountford in *JHS* (1931).

MODERN LITERATURE: H. Abert, *Lehre vom Ethos* (1899) and article in Adler's *Handbuch der Musikgeschichte* (1924); Dar.-Sag. s.v. 'Lyra', 'Tibia', etc.; I. Düring, *Ptolemaios u. Porphyrios über die Musik* (Göteborg, 1934); M. Emmanuel in Lavignac's *Encyclopédie de la musique* i (1924); F. A. Gevaert, *Histoire et théorie de la musique de l'antiquité* (1875–81), *La Mélopée antique* (1895); C. del grande, *Espressione musicale dei poeti greci* (1932); F. Greif in *Rev. Ét. Gr.* (1909–14); A. A. Howard, The Αὐλός in *Harv. Stud.* iv (1893); L. Laloy, *Aristoxène de Tarente* (1904); H. Macran, introd. to ed. of Aristoxenus (1900), and article in Grove's *Dictionary of Music*⁴; D. B. Monro, *The Modes of Ancient Greek Music* (1894); J. F. Mountford in *JHS* (1920), *CQ* (1923), and 'Greek Music in the Papyri and Inscriptions' (in Powell and Barber, *New Chapters* ii, 1929); G. Reese, *Music in the Middle Ages* (1940), 11–53; Th. Reinach, *La Musique grecque* (1926); H. Riemann, *Handbuch d. Musikgeschichte*³ (1923); C. Sachs, *Musik des Altertums* (1924), *The History of Musical Instruments* (1940), *The Rise of Music in the Ancient World* (1943); K. Schlesinger, *The Greek Aulos* (1938); W. Vetter in *PW*; R. Westphal, *Griechische Harmonik u. Melopoie* (1886), *Theorie d. musisch. Künste d. Hellenen*³ (1885), *Aristoxenos* (1883–93); R. P. Winnington-Ingram, *Mode in Ancient Greek Music* (1936) and articles in *Cambr. Companion to Gk. Studies*⁴ (1931) and in *CQ* (1928 and 1932). Reviews of modern Literature: Bursian vol. 104 (von Jan), 118 (Graf), 144 (Abert), 193 (Abert), 246 (Fellerer).
J. F. M. & R. P. W.-I.

MUSIC IN WORSHIP.

Both in Greece and Italy music, vocal and instrumental, formed an important part of worship at all periods. To begin with Homer, the embassy sent to Chryse in *Iliad* 1. 472–4 spend the whole day after their arrival singing a hymn (παιήων) to Apollo, who is pleased with it. This paean remained typical of his worship, and the quintuple rhythm characteristic of it was named after it. In like manner the dithyramb was appropriated to Dionysus (q.v.). Neither of these, however, was exclusively the property of Apollo or Dionysus; e.g. paeans were composed to Asclepius (see Powell, *Coll. Alex.* 133 ff.). The singing of some kind of hymn (q.v.) appears regularly to have accompanied any formal act of worship, and instrumental music (strings and wind) also is commonly mentioned: cf. SACRIFICE.

Much the same is true for Italy. Hymns are continually met with, some traditional, as those of the Salii (see MARS) and Arval Brothers (Henzen, *Acta Arualium*, p. cciv). Instrumental music was so regular and necessary an accompaniment of ritual (e.g. Cicero, *Har. Resp.* 23, the proceedings are vitiated 'si . . . tibicen repente conticuit') that the *collegium tibicinum et fidicinum qui sacris publicis praesto sunt* formed an ancient and important gild with a holiday of its own, cf. MINERVA. One reason for this was doubtless to drown any slight noises which might be of ill omen.

Very little is known of the style of this music, but it is fairly certain that there was no prohibition of the introduction of new forms.
H. J. R.

MUSONIUS RUFUS, GAIUS, of Volsinii, Stoic, seems to have been born before A.D. 30 and to have died before 101/2. About A.D. 60 Rubellius Plautus was banished by Nero to Asia Minor, and Musonius followed him. After Rubellius' death he returned to Rome, but in 65–6, on the discovery of the Pisonian conspiracy, he was banished to Gyaros. He returned to Rome, probably under Galba. He was again banished by Vespasian, but returned again in the reign of Titus. We do not know of his having written books, but many of his apophthegms and discourses have been preserved. Among his pupils were many philosophers (notably Epictetus) and many leading Roman citizens.

Ed. O. Hense (1905); one letter in R. Hercher, *Epistolographi Graeci*, 401–4. PW xvi. 893.
W. D. R.

MUTILUS, see PAPIUS.

MUTINA, a prosperous wool-trading town in Cisalpine Gaul, controlling important roads and passes (Strabo 5. 218); nowadays *Modena*. Although Boian and possibly Etruscan settlements existed here from early times, Mutina is first mentioned in 218 B.C. when already a Roman stronghold (Polyb. 3. 40—inexact; Livy 21. 25). Rome apparently held Mutina uninterruptedly, making it a citizen colony in 183 which Ligurians sacked in 177; the Romans immediately restored it (Livy 39. 55; 41. 16). Mutina is famous for its successful resistance to Pompey in 78 and to Antony in 43 (the *bellum Mutinense*) (Plut. *Pomp.* 16; App. *BCiv.* 3. 49 f. etc.). Subsequently it is rarely mentioned. E. T. S.

MYCENAE (*Μυκῆναι, Μυκήνη*), lies in the north-east corner of the Argive plain, 6 miles from Argos and 9 from the sea, among the foothills guarding the road to Corinth. The name Mykene is not Greek. The city was first inhabited at the opening of the Bronze Age (3000–2800 B.C.) by people akin to the pre-hellenic population of the Islands and Crete, and possibly that called 'Carian' by the Greeks. Its power increased during the Middle Bronze Age (*c.* 2100–1600), when it was occupied by people who probably belonged to the first wave of Greek-speaking folk in Greece, for tombs and pottery of this period are common on the site. In the transition from the Middle to the Late Bronze Age Mycenae rose to greatness under a dynasty of kings whose remains and treasures were found by Schliemann in the Shaft Graves in the Grave Circle within the Lion Gate. These royal graves were succeeded in the second and third phases of the Late Bronze Age by the nine beehive tombs. During the first two phases (*c.* 1600–1400) of the Late Bronze Age the citadel was fortified and contained a palace, but reconstruction at the opening of the third phase destroyed all but a few traces. This third phase (1400–1150) was the great age of Mycenae. Then were built the citadel walls with the Lion and Postern Gates, the palace, and the greatest beehive tomb, the Treasury of Atreus, probably that of the king responsible for this great architectural activity. To a later stage belong the extension of the citadel to the north-east with a sally-port and the secret approach to the subterranean cistern and the last of the beehive tombs, that of Clytemnestra. At the close of this age Mycenae was destroyed by fire. It was reoccupied in the Early Iron Age, and in the archaic period a temple associated with early sculptured reliefs was built over the ruins of the palace. In the Persian Wars it sent a contingent to Plataea, but *c.* 470 B.C. it was captured and dismantled by Argos. In Hellenistic days Mycenae revived as a dependency of Argos. The acropolis was repaired, the temple rebuilt, and a wall erected round a lower town to the west including a theatre. This town gradually decayed and by the time of Pausanias was deserted.

The citadel of Mycenae was a fortified royal residence with quarters for the court, the officials, and the necessary guards and servants. The civilian population lived in open townships around. The extent of the cemeteries of the Late Bronze Age shows that it was well populated and prosperous. The theory that the contents of the Shaft Graves were originally in the beehive tombs and later moved within the citadel for safety is open to serious objections. It assumes that the finest beehive tombs, the Treasury of Atreus and the Tomb of Clytemnestra, date from the close of the Middle Bronze Age. This is contrary to the archaeological evidence as well as to the logical idea that the construction of such tombs evolved parallel with other arts, and separates the most developed beehive tombs from the great age of Mycenae in art and architecture in the third phase of the Late Bronze Age.

H. Schliemann, *Mycenae* (1878); Ch. Tsountas, *Πρακτικά* (1886); *Ἐφ. Ἀρχ.* 1887, 1888, 1891, 1896, 1897, 1902; Ch. Tsountas and J. I. Manatt, *Mycenaean Age* (1897); A. J. B. Wace, *BSA* xxiv, xxv (1922, 1925), *Chamber Tombs at Mycenae* (1933), *JHS* 1939; *Illustrated London News*, 16 and 23 Dec., 1939. A. J. Evans, *Shaft Graves and Beehive Tombs* (1929); G. Karo, *Schachtgräber v. Mykenai* (1930). A. J. B. W.

MYGDON (*Μυγδών*). In *Iliad* 3. 184 ff. Priam relates that he went as an ally to a Phrygian army gathered under Mygdon and Otreus to fight the Amazons on the Sangarius. The Coroebus of Verg. *Aen.* 2. 407 was Mygdon's son, [Eur.] *Rhes.* 539. Mygdon is apparently the eponym of the Thracian or Phrygian Mygdones. H. J. R.

MYIA, said to have been daughter of Pythagoras, is mentioned in Clem. *Strom.* 4. 19. 121, p. 224 as a Pythagorean philosopher. A letter purporting to be by her is printed in R. Hercher, *Epistologr. Gr.* 608.
PW xvi. 1002.

MYLITTA, a goddess, certainly akin to Ishtar and perhaps specially concerned with childbirth, worshipped at Babylon, and identified by Herodotus (1. 131) with Aphrodite. In honour of M. every Babylonian woman, once in her lifetime, had to prostitute herself to a stranger: she sat in the temple area, and remained there till accosted by a stranger in the name of the goddess. The fee offered might be of any amount, and was dedicated to M. (Hdt. 1. 199; cf. LXX, *Epist. Jerem.* 42–3 perhaps [*c.* 300 B.C.]). *See* PROSTITUTION, SACRED. F. R. W.

MYLLUS. Suidas and Zenobius (5. 14) mention him as a writer of Old Comedy. But he may be merely one of the typical figures of farce = 'The Squinter': cf. Cratinus, fr. 89.

MYOS HORMOS, 'Mussel-Harbour', *Abu Scha'ar* on the Egyptian coast of the Red Sea, was founded by Ptolemy II (274 B.C.) and connected with Kenah on the Nile by a well-equipped desert-trade. Very important for Oriental trade, it was later surpassed by Berenice.
Warmington, *Indian Commerce*, 6 ff.; Kees, *PW*, s.v. E. H. W.

MYRO, see MOERO.

MYRON (*fl. c.* 480–445 B.C.), Greek sculptor, a native of Eleutherae and reputed pupil of the Argive artist Ageladas. Primarily a worker in bronze, his main contribution to the art of sculpture was to create entirely new compositions and attitudes which the relatively new process of bronze-casting made possible. He emancipated the artist from the conventions of composition of the preceding generation. Two of his major works survive to us in copies—the Discobolus, of which the 'Lancelotti' copy is the best of many, and the 'Athena and Marsyas'. The latter is illustrated by coin-designs for the general attitude and by Roman copies for the figures in detail. The Athena is best represented by a copy at Frankfurt, the Marsyas by a copy in the Lateran gallery. The group as a whole appears on a relief on a marble vase at Athens. Two small-scale Roman copies (in the Boston Fine Arts Museum and in the Ashmolean Museum, Oxford) representing a Hercules at rest are generally considered to derive from a statue by Myron, on grounds of style. As a stylist Myron seems to have been extremely individual. His facial type is of great distinction and beauty. S. C.

MYRONIDES, Athenian general in 458/7 and 457/6 B.C., known by his victory at Oenophyta. He is probably not identical with the ambassador Myronides, sent with Cimon and Xanthippus to Sparta in 480, and one of the Athenian generals at Plataea. Comic poets praised Myronides as a representative of the 'good old times'. Eupolis in his *Demoi* puts him on the stage; he seems to have died shortly before the performance of this comedy (412).
Ehrenberg, *PW*, s.v., Suppl. vii (superseding vol. xvi); J. M. Edmonds, *Mnemos.* 1939. V. E.

MYRRHA, see ZMYRNA.

MYRSILUS of Methymna (*fl. c.* 250 B.C.), author of a history of Lesbos (*Λεσβικά*) who was interested in early folk movements.

FHG iv. 455.

MYRTILUS, poet of Old Comedy, son of Lysis and brother of the comic poet Hermippus (Suid.), victorious in 427 B.C. (*IG.* ii². 2325). Suidas mentions *Τιτανόπανες* (probably an attack on paederasty) and *Ἔρωτες* (perhaps merely another name for *Τιτανόπανες*).

FCG ii. 418 ff.; *CAF* i. 253–4.   M. P.

MYRTIS, Boeotian poetess, said to have been the teacher of Corinna (Suidas s.v. *Κόριννα*) and of Pindar (id. s.v. *Πίνδαρος*). Corinna (fr. 15) blames her for competing with Pindar. No fragment of her work survives, but Plutarch (*Quaest. Graec.* 40) gives an abstract of her poem on the Boeotian hero Eunostus.

J. M. Edmonds, *Lyra Graeca* iii, pp. 2–5.   C. M. B.

MYRTOAN SEA, see AEGEAN SEA.

MYSTERIES were secret cults which generally include mystic ideas. Their characteristic is that certain initiations were needed for admission. It has been suggested that this is due to the fact that the old mysteries of Greece, at least for a part, go back to an emotional pre-Greek religion which survived in secret societies. In regard to certain mysteries, e.g. those of Eleusis and Phlya, it is also to be taken into consideration that they were family cults to which the head of the family admitted whom he pleased.

2. The gods with whom the old Greek mysteries are connected were Demeter and Dionysus and the Eleusinian Mysteries are the most famous of all. In origin they were an agrarian cult, akin to the Thesmophoria and celebrated in Boedromion (Sept./Oct.) on the occasion of the sowing. After the union of Eleusis with Athens, some time before 600 B.C., the Athenian State took charge of the mysteries. The *mystai* gathered at Athens where an announcement was made excluding murderers and those who spoke a foreign language. The *mystai* bathed in the sea, and the sacred things which previously had been brought to Athens were brought back to Eleusis in the great Iakchos procession (Iakchos is a personification of this procession, and was assimilated to Dionysus). In the evening the mystery rites began in the mystery hall at Eleusis which was illuminated by many torches. In spite of many ingenious hypotheses the chief rites are unknown. We hear of *λεγόμενα, δεικνύμενα, δρώμενα,* (1) things recited, from which the Eumolpidae, 'those who sing beautifully', have their name; (2) things shown, from which the chief priest, the *ἱεροφάντης* (*see* HIEROPHANTES), has his name; (3) things performed, whether by the priests or the *mystai* we do not know. There were three stages, *μύησις,* initiation, *τελετή,* the preliminary, and *ἐποπτεία,* the highest rite, to which the *mystai* were admitted the year after; the name indicates that the *epoptai* saw something. The Homeric hymn to Demeter, composed before Eleusis was united with Athens, gives some information concerning the preliminary rites, the fast, the sitting on a chair decked with a ram's skin, the drinking of the *kykeon.* The information concerning the highest rites which is found only in ecclesiastical authors, in particular what relates to sexual symbols by which the *mystes* became a son of the goddess, a matter of which modern scholars have made much, is to be regarded with caution; the statement that the highest mystery shown was a corn-ear is perhaps more trustworthy.

3. We shall do better to turn to the deities and the myths. The rape of Kore-Persephone by Pluto is the central subject of the hymn, and it has been suggested that in the mysteries this rape and the bringing back of Kore to Demeter were dramatically represented. There were two pairs of deities: the Mother and the Maid and Pluto and Persephone, who is identical with Kore. To the former pair Triptolemus, the hero of agriculture, was added and to the latter Eubuleus (q.v.: *see also* THESMOPHORIA). The myth that during four months of the year Kore was absent, dwelling with Pluto, and then was reunited with her mother and dwelt eight months in the upper world is to be referred to the seed-corn which, from the harvest in June to the sowing in October, was stored in subterranean silos and was brought forth at the festival of the sowing: the Corn-maiden was reunited with the Corn-mother. She was also wife of Pluto, the god of the wealth, i.e. the corn store, and Lord of the Underworld. The hymn ends by promising, to those initiated, wealth and a happy life in the Underworld, of which other authors speak confidently: the *Frogs* of Aristophanes proves that this happiness consisted in the continued celebration of the mysteries in the Underworld. Moral notions came to be associated with the mysteries, and righteousness and gentleness were added to ritual purity. At the end of the sixth century B.C. the conception of agriculture as the foundation of a civilized and peaceful life arose; Triptolemus was its hero. Since the end of the fifth century B.C. individual edification came more to the front. The Eleusinian Mysteries had no fixed doctrine; they consisted in rites which might be interpreted variously and thus were able to conform to the religious needs of every age. They were so impressive that to the end of paganism they were the most venerated part of Greek religion.

4. There were other mysteries of Demeter, the mysteries at Agrae near Athens which were joined to the Eleusinian, the mysteries at Phlya in Attica, which were old but remodelled according to the ideas of a later age, the mysteries at Andania in Messenia which were revived (or instituted) after the liberation of Messenia. The orgia of Dionysus (*see* DIONYSUS) which were celebrated only by women were mysteries in a certain sense. Dionysiac religion lent itself readily to mystical ideas, but the Dionysiac mysteries mentioned in Greece, e.g. those of Lerna and the Herois at Delphi, seem to be late creations. In the Hellenistic age Dionysiac mysteries developed and flourished; Ptolemy IV regulated them by an edict and the repression of the Bacchanalia (q.v.) by the Roman Senate is well known. Many Dionysiac mystic cults are recorded from the Roman age. The Orphic Mysteries (*see* ORPHISM) are an offshoot of the Dionysiac religion, at least in a certain sense. The mysteries of the Phrygian god Sabazius, who was akin to Dionysus, are found at Athens at the time of Aristophanes and at that of Demosthenes, a sign of the growing propensity for foreign and mystic cults: another is the popularity of the mysteries of the Cabiri at Samothrace. The Cabiri were especially venerated as the protectors of seafarers, but we know very little of the cult; in the Cabirion near Thebes it seems to have been influenced by Orphic ideas. The propensity for mystic cults grew in the Hellenistic age and still more in Roman times and was satisfied by cults introduced from the Orient, those of the Great Mother and Attis, Isis and Osiris, Mithras. We cannot here discuss details (see the respective articles), but may note certain general features. These mysteries were in a certain measure bound up with syncretism; the supporters of paganism in its last days were often initiated into various mysteries. Religion was detached from the old ties, the family and the State, and was individualized; man was able to choose his gods. The adherents of a certain cult (especially foreign) formed associations, sometimes headed by professional priests, an Oriental feature. The religious precepts were

more detailed and binding than before. There were sacred symbols and rites with magical efficacy, purifications, asceticism, baptisms, sacraments. The adherents were sometimes divided into two classes; sometimes there were several grades of these. The highest promise of the mysteries was a happy after-life. The rise of dualism which considered the corporeal world as evil stressed the need of salvation which was conferred by participation in the mysteries: they promised even the deification of man. The myth was a symbolic expression of the doctrine and the god was the prototype of man, suffering, dying, and rising to a new life. *See also* AFTER-LIFE.

The literature is copious. References may be found in R. Pettazzoni, *I misteri*; O. Kern, *Die griech. Mysterien der klassischen Zeit*; P. Foucart, *Les Mystères d'Éleusis*; M. P. Nilsson, *Gesch. d. griech. Religion* i. 440 ff., 619 ff.　　　　　M. P. N.

MYTHOGRAPHERS. Since mythology was much studied in antiquity, at least to the extent of collecting and systematizing the traditional stories, and commenting on them in the light of rather crude and shallow theories (as that the myths were philosophical allegories, or had arisen from misunderstandings of ambiguous phraseology, tendencies exemplified by Heraclitus and Palaephatus respectively, see below), we hear of a number of writers on the subject and the works of a few survive fairly complete. The movement may be said to start with the school of Hesiod (q.v.; *Theogony* and *Ehoiai*). It certainly may properly be taken to include sundry of the early logographi, such as the two or three writers called Pherecydes, Acusilaus of Argos, Hellanicus, and Herodorus (see Rose, *Handb. Gk. Lit.* 296 ff.), for although their aim was generally to write history, they used of necessity for the earlier periods the only material available, namely myths. Later, the voluminous writings of Callimachus (b. *c.* 310 B.C.) and other Alexandrian scholars included many treatises more or less purely mythological in content; foreign mythologies also were discussed by Berosus and Philon of Byblos (Rose, op. cit. 367).

The composition, however, of compendia of mythology is relatively late, although some semi-philosophical works, such as the absurd treatise of Euhemerus (q.v.) and the rationalizing essay of Palaephatus (Rose, p. 369), might be considered a sort of annotated handbooks of the subject; they are related in their way to Heraclitus' little book on Homeric allegories and Cornutus' Stoic treatise on the inner meaning of myths (ibid. 355, 411). All the surviving works fall not earlier than the time of Augustus, and most are later. One, the *Bibliotheca* of the so-called Apollodorus, of whose personality nothing is known, is valuable from the good information possessed by the author and his not infrequent citations of his sources, direct or indirect. It consists of three books; the rest is lost, though something is preserved in an epitome surviving in two forms. This work was an attempt at a complete mythical history of Greece; the other surviving treatises specialize. Parthenius, the earliest (contemporary and friend of Cornelius Gallus), collects love-stories, primarily as poetic material for Gallus to work up. The pseudo-Eratosthenes, epitomizing, it would seem, a treatise of the real one (b. *c.* 275 B.C.), is himself much later; his subject is catasterisms, i.e. the metamorphoses of terrestrial persons and objects into constellations. Antoninus Liberalis, whose name shows him not earlier than the second century A.D., collects metamorphoses, but not those into stars. The trashy author of the *Parallels* which have come down under the name of Plutarch finds, or more commonly invents, Roman stories which are parallel to Greek ones. He is earlier than Clement of Alexandria, and therefore about second century also.

Latin has not left us many such works, though not a few were written, e.g., by C. Julius Hyginus, Augustus'

librarian (Rose, *Handb. Lat. Lit.* 446). The author known as Hyginus who wrote the *Fabulae* (more properly *Genealogiae*) whereof we have a late and bad series of extracts may have been contemporary with the Antonines (ibid.); his so-called *Poetica Astronomica*, if it is his, largely depends on the genuine Eratosthenes, probably not directly. The *Mitologiae* of Fulgentius (three books) may be of about the end of the fifth century; the three miscellaneous collections known as the Mythographi Vaticani (ed. Bode, 1834) are medieval, but contain, amid many blunders, some scraps of material not found elsewhere.　　　　　H. J. R.

MYTHOLOGY. Although etymologically the word means no more than the telling of tales, it is used in modern languages to signify a systematic examination of the traditional narratives of any people, or all peoples, with the object of understanding how they came to be told and to what extent they are or were believed, also of solving various other problems connected with them, such as their connexion with religion, their origin (popular or literary), the relations, if any, to similar stories told elsewhere, and their chronology, relative or absolute. The examination of folk-tales (*Märchenforschung*) is really a branch of mythology, but has grown to such proportions, owing to the abundance of material, that it may be regarded as a separate discipline and will receive only brief mention here.

2. The most characteristic object of mythological study is the myth proper. This may be defined as a prescientific and imaginative attempt to explain some phenomenon, real or supposed, which excites the curiosity of the myth-maker, or perhaps more accurately as an effort to reach a feeling of satisfaction in place of uneasy bewilderment concerning such phenomena. It often appeals to the emotions rather than the reason and, indeed, in its most typical forms seems to date from an age when rational explanations were not generally called for. For example, it was commonly said (Hdt. 7. 129. 5) that the gorge of the Peneus had been created by Poseidon (q.v.) cleaving the mountain-chain which formerly closed in Thessaly on that side. To Herodotus himself, this was merely a picturesque way of saying that the gorge had been formed by an earthquake, a solution very like the 'cataclysmic' school of geological theory once popular in modern Europe. But it seems far more probable that the originator of the story had a vivid mental picture of the gorge, which to his eye suggested a great cut, being hewn out by a gigantic and powerful being, and that, finding the picture satisfactory to his imagination, he was not troubled with any question as to its probability. This is not to say that no myth contains intellectual features, for many of them do; to take a crude example, the originator of the quaint tale of the deceiving of Zeus by Prometheus (Hesiod, *Theog.* 535 ff.) must have asked himself why those parts of a victim which were burned on the altars of the celestial gods were the least valuable. Late myths often show signs of elaborate speculation, e.g., the identification of Virbius (*see* DIANA) with Hippolytus (q.v.) in Verg. *Aen.* 7. 761 ff. clearly arises from a sophisticated and learned explanation of the facts that Diana was worshipped at Aricia along with a male being and that horses were not allowed in her grove. The only male associated with and subordinate to Artemis, with whom Diana had long been identified, was Hippolytus; now he had been brought to life by Asclepius after being killed by his own team; he must therefore be Diana's attendant and the taboo on horses must arise from his, and her, reluctance to have anything more to do with such dangerous creatures.

3. Myths therefore deal principally with the doings of gods, their ritual and their relationships to one another, or else with natural phenomena in some way striking, and they are characteristically aetiological, having for

their aim to furnish an explanation of something. If the main characters of the story are human, or supposedly so, and the tale concerns their doings in battles or other adventures, it is usual to speak, not of myth but of saga or legend. Here the mental process giving rise to the story seems to be different. A real event of some kind, such as a raid or a great and dangerous hunt, impresses those who take part in it and also their contemporaries; it continues to be told from generation to generation, often getting into the hands of a professional maker (finally a professional writer) of such narratives, and so acquiring all manner of additions, modifications, and re-handlings intended to make it a better story. Nevertheless, it regularly has behind it the original fact, which may obtrude itself in curious ways (e.g. in the ballad of Chevy Chase, which springs from the historical Battle of Otterbourne, the Scots are divided into three parts and attack from higher ground, though the rest of the fighting has been changed almost past recognition). Even if the story is pure fiction, it will be modelled upon real semi-historical narratives, and may then be conveniently called pseudo-saga.

4. The *Märchen* (see FOLK-TALES; neither that nor 'fairy-tale' is a wholly satisfactory equivalent) seems always to have been told for pure amusement, with no basis in speculation or fact.

5. Finally, it must be realized that any two, or all three, of the above forms may be almost inextricably blended in any given story; thus the tale of the Argonauts (q.v.) has manifest elements of *Märchen*, and the adventures of Heracles (q.v.) have also laid myths under contribution.

6. In order to reach such conclusions as the above, it is necessary to have a sufficient body of material, carefully examined to show its age and origin; else the investigator will perpetually be misled into taking a late or foreign story for the genuine product of the people he is studying, e.g. such a narrative as that in Ovid, *Fasti*, 2. 305 ff., either for a genuine part of the Greek tradition concerning Heracles or a native Italian story throwing light on the nature of Faunus, instead of what it is, a typical Alexandrian humorous aetiology, perhaps Ovid's own invention. We may therefore look upon K. O. Müller (1797–1840) as in some sense the father of modern mythology, owing to his consistent emphasis on the historical origins of Greek traditions, i.e. the time and place, so far as they could be discovered, when the earliest form of each tale appeared. With him may be bracketed a slightly earlier investigator, C. A. Lobeck (1781–1860).

7. Hardly less important for the researcher in any given branch of mythology, e.g. that of Greece, is a knowledge of similar stories told elsewhere, especially among peoples likely to have influenced those he is studying. Here a great service was performed by Max Müller, whose use of Sanskrit material led investigators in the late nineteenth century to examine Greek (and other) material against a comparative background, thus getting a perspective such as earlier researchers had not had. It needed only to widen the scope of comparison, and this was done chiefly by Andrew Lang.

Some account of the progress of the subject is given in any good modern manual of classical mythology. For some methodological considerations see Rose, *Modern Methods in Classical Mythology* (1930). For light thrown on Greek myths by art see especially C. Robert, *Bild und Lied* (1881).   H. J. R.

MYTILENE (or **MITYLENE**; the former was the official form), the chief city of Lesbos, situated in the south-east of the island, with a fine double harbour, and facing the Anatolian mainland. The population was predominantly Aeolian—both Sappho and Alcaeus resided in Mytilene. In the sixth century B.C. overseas expansion led directly to war with Athens, indirectly to *stasis*, only relieved by the mediation of Pittacus. Under Persian control Mytilene participated in the forlorn hope of the Ionian Revolt. Its two secessions from the Delian Confederacy (428 and 412) resulted in the loss of its fleet, its fortifications, and much of its land, and brought it to the verge of destruction. During most of the fourth century, however, it was a faithful ally of Athens. In 333 it fell to Memnon, but was soon retaken by the Macedonian fleet. After Alexander's death Mytilene passed successively under Antigonus', Lysimachus', and the Ptolemies' rule. Through tactful diplomacy it kept on good terms with Rome, becoming a favourite holiday resort. Its revolt against excessive taxation following the Mithridatic War led to the storming of the city by Minucius Thermus (80), but Pompeius restored its freedom, and this privilege, though suspended by Vespasian, was confirmed by Hadrian.

R. Herbst, *PW*, s.v. 'Mytilene'.   D. E. W. W.

N

NABATAEANS were a people of northern Arabia (though their inscriptions are Aramaic). They were in occupation of Petra (q.v.) by 312 B.C., when Demetrius, son of Antigonus, unsuccessfully attacked them. A commercial people, they expanded along the caravan routes radiating from Petra. Northwards their first known king, Aretas I (169), already held Moabitis, and despite defeats by Alexander Jannaeus they pushed on till Aretas III in 85 occupied Damascus for a brief while. Westwards Aretas II nearly took Gaza in 96, but was prevented by Alexander; the Nabataean power, however, extended over all the Sinai peninsula, save the northern coast, to Pelusium. Southwards they occupied the once Ptolemaic port of Aela and in the late first century B.C. held the east coast of the Red Sea to Egra. Unsuccessfully attacked by Scaurus in 62 the Nabataeans were admitted to the alliance of the Roman People and henceforth ranked as a client kingdom, regularly sending troops to assist the Roman armies. The kingdom was divided into a large number of districts, ruled by hereditary *strategi*. It was annexed by Trajan in A.D. 105, becoming the province of Arabia.

A. Kammerer, *Pétra et la Nabatène* (1929–30); R. E. Brünnow and A. von Domaszewski, *Die Provincia Arabia* (1904–9).   A. H. M. J.

NABIS, son of Demaratus, probably descended from the Spartan king of the latter name (q.v.), followed Machanidas in 207 B.C. as guardian of the young Spartan king, Pelops, and on Pelops' death (of which he was accused) seized the crown. Forming a mercenary guard, he drastically restored the revolutionary programme of Cleomenes (q.v. 2) in alliance with the Cretan pirates. In 204–3 he raided Megalopolis, but was in 201 repelled from Messene and in 200 defeated by Philopoemen. In the Second Macedonian War he gained Argos, betrayed to him by Philip V, but went over to Flamininus, only to find himself in 195 charged with tyranny and forced to give up Argos and the Laconian ports. In 193, attempting to regain the ports, he was subdued by Philopoemen and Flamininus. He was assassinated in

192 in an Aetolian *coup d'état* in Sparta. A revolutionary type, his career and policy have suffered unduly in the Megalopolitan tradition of Polybius.

Polyb. 13. 6–8; 16. 13; 16–17; Livy, 29. 12; 31–5; Plutarch, *Flamininus*; *Philopoemen*. T. Homolle, *BCH* 1896, 502; J. Mundt, *Nabis, König von Sparta* (1903); De Sanctis, *Stor. Rom.* iii. 2, 436; iv. 1, pp. 42, 72, 104, 132; M. Holleaux, *Rome, la Grèce et les monarchies hellénistiques* (1921), 262; A. Aymard, *Les Premiers rapports de Rome et de la Confédération achaienne* (1938); F. W. Walbank, *Philip of Macedon* (1940), see index.   A. H. McD.

NAENIA, *see* NENIA.

NAEVIUS, GNAEUS, plebeian (?) Latin poet, born (in Rome?) *c.* 270 B.C., having served in the First Punic War (264–241), began writing plays in Rome 235 B.C., especially *comoediae palliatae* but also *togatae*. After 222 he invented the *fabula praetexta(ta)* or historical Roman play. In *togatae*, possibly also in *palliatae*, he attacked Roman statesmen, even Scipio Africanus, but especially the Caecilii Metelli, so that, after threats from Q. Metellus, 206 B.C., he was put in prison. There he wrote plays (*Ariolus, Leo*) in which he apologized. He was freed, then exiled from Italy. He went to Utica in north Africa, where he died *c.* 201. He was a truly Latin poet, an outspoken Roman citizen, and imbued with national spirit, writing probably independently of any profession. While his *palliatae* were famous, it was probably his *Punic War* (see below) which impressed Romans most, though its defects were not missed.

Fragments survive: (i) About 130 lines from *palliatae* on Greek models: *Acontizomenos, Agitatoria, Agrypnuntes, Apella, Carbonaria= Clamidaria, Colax* (adapted from Menander), *Corollaria, Dementes, Demetrius, Dolus, Figulus, Glaucoma, Gymnasticus, Lampadio, Leo, Pellex, Personata, Proiectus, Quadrigemini, Stalagmus, Stigmatias, Tarentilla, Technicus, Testicularia, Triphallus, Tunicularia*; also five lines from *Ariolus*, a *togata*. (ii) About sixty lines from tragedies on Greek models: *Andromacha, Danae, Equos Troianus, Hector Proficiscens, Hesione, Iphigenia* (from Euripides' *'I. ἐν Ταυροῖς*), *Lycurgus* (*c.* 35 lines). (iii) Lines from two *praetextae*: *Clastidium* (dramatizing the campaign of 222 B.C. in Cisalpine Gaul by Marcellus and Scipio) and *Romulus*. (iv) About forty-five lines from unknown plays. (v) A line from *Satura*; a line against the Metelli; and N.'s own epitaph. (vi) About sixty-five lines from *Bellum Poenicum*, in saturnians, on the First Punic War, with an account of the origins and growth of Rome (and Carthage?). This work was a national epic in a national metre, but was prosy and wooden. Yet it greatly influenced Ennius and Virgil. *See also* DRAMA, ROMAN, para. 2.

Fragments: (w. transl.) E. H. Warmington, *Remains of Old Latin* ii (Loeb, 1936); G. Pascoli, *Epos* i² (1911. *Bellum Punicum*); O. Ribbeck, *Scaenicae Romanorum Poesis Fragmenta*, 2nd ed. (3rd ed. Teubner. Plays); E. Klussmann, *Cn. Naevii ... reliquias collegit* (1843). Cf. Thelma de Graff, *Naevian Studies*.   E. H. W.

NAISSUS (to-day *Nisch*) in Moesia (after Diocletian in Dardania), first visited by Roman troops in 75/72 B.C., was probably the earliest permanent military camp in Moesia. Though of great strategic importance, little is known of its history: it became a *municipium* under M. Aurelius or later. Here Claudius II decisively defeated the Goths in A.D. 269. Frequently visited by Roman emperors, especially by Constantine the Great, who was born at Naissus, it was destroyed by the Huns in 441, but was partially restored. Under Justinian Naissus flourished anew, but was seriously threatened by the Slavs. It was destroyed or at least sacked by the Avars in 596, but continued to exist as a Slav town.

Fluss, *PW*, s.v.   F. A. W. S.

NAMATIANUS, RUTILIUS CLAUDIUS, author of the *De Reditu Suo*, the most elaborate itinerary in Latin literature, was the last Roman poet. Of Gallo-Roman extraction, hailing probably from Toulouse, this archpagan held in Christian but tolerant Rome the offices of *magister officiorum* (A.D. 412) and *praefectus urbi* (414) under Honorius. Biographical and self-revealing, his poem comes to us in two books, the first of which begins abruptly, while the second is a fragment (68 lines). In September 416, much against his will, he left Rome to look after his estates in Gaul, which, like Italy, suffered terribly from barbarian invasions. In two months, by the safer sea route, he reached Luna and here the poem breaks off. He probably reached Gaul, as the poem could not have been composed in its present form during the journey. Besides presenting lively topographical observations on the coastal scenery of Etruria, the poem mirrors both contemporary events and the author's soul—as well as the minds of the pagan nobility whose solitary spokesman he is and with whom he shared the belief in Dea Roma and Rome's glorious mission. That he would resent opposition to paganism is clear. Hence his invectives against Judaism, monasticism, and Stilicho, the barbarian general (then dead) who burned the Sibylline books; for to N. and his class antipaganism and the barbarians were the forces that tended to undermine ancient institutions and disintegrate the Empire. Far from being a cold declaimer (Gibbon), he writes with charm and feeling. His lucid, though rhetorical, Latinity and his graceful elegiacs reveal him a keen student of the best models in Latin literature.

For the period: Bury, *Hist. of Later Roman Empire*; Dill, *Roman Society in Last Century of Western Empire*; Hodgkin, *Italy and Her Invaders*. Editions: Ch. H. Keene (1907; English verse translation; commentary); G. Heidrich (1912); V. Ussani (1921); R. Helm (1933; commentary); J. Vessereau and F. Préchac (1933; Fr. transl.); J. W. and A. M. Duff (Engl. transl.), in *Minor Latin Poets* (Loeb, 1934); P. van de Woestijne, Antwerp, 1936 (index verborum). See R. Pichon, *Les Derniers écrivains profanes* (1906), 243–69; *PW*, s.v. 'Rutilius (13)'; E. S. Duckett, *Latin Writers of the Fifth Century* (U.S.A. 1930), 35–44; A. B. Hawes, *Citizens of Long Ago* (U.S.A. 1934), 162–83; O. Schissel-Fleschenberg, *Claud. Rut. Namatianus gegen Stilicho* (1920), and articles of de Labriolle and Carcopino in *Rev. Ét. Lat.* vi (1928), 30–41 and 180–200.   J. H.

NAMES. The Greeks distinguished two types of proper names: (1) θεοφόρα ὀνόματα, names etymologically connected with the name of a god, e.g. Apollonius (see the following article); (2) ἄθεα, names etymologically connected with magisterial or professional titles, with virtues, qualities moral or physical, omens, etc., and with names of places (e.g. Λακεδαιμόνιος). Since it was customary to give a child one name only (the first-born son bore the name of his paternal or, less frequently, maternal grandfather), men's names at Athens were generally followed by that of their father (in the genitive), and of their deme (q.v.). Romans of the regal and early Republican period probably bore two names, as can be seen from the list of kings and other evidence. But by *c.* 300 B.C. the custom prevailed in the highest order of society of bearing three names, the *praenomen, nomen* or name of the *gens*, and *cognomen* or family name (e.g. 'Marcus Tullius Cicero'). In the late Imperial age the use of the nickname (*signum*) in the form of *sive* or *qui et* led to a rapid decay of the traditional custom. Greek and Roman women and slaves regularly bore but one name, followed, if necessary, by that of the person (father, husband, master, etc.) on whom they legally depended. Freedmen generally kept their original, mostly Graeco-Oriental, names as a *cognomen*, adopting that of their master as a *nomen*. After the age of Sulla a similar process was followed in the case of adopted children, who had previously retained their family name transformed into an adjective (e.g. Scipio Aemilianus).

Ch. Morel, Dar.–Sag. iv. 1, 88 ff.; Ernst Fraenkel, *PW*, s.v. 'Namenwesen'. Greek: A. Fick–F. Bechtel, *Griechische Personennamen*² (1894); F. Bechtel, *Attische Frauennamen* (1902). Roman: Mommsen, *Röm. Forsch.* i. 1 ff.; W. Schulze, *Zur Geschichte lateinischer Eigennamen* (1904); B. Doer, *Die römische Namengebung* (1937).   P. T.

NAMES, THEOPHORIC PERSONAL (GREEK).

Theophoric personal names reflect the cult interests of the parents, interests which in some clear instances were carried on by the offspring; but among the names of 1,324 persons interested in Egyptian deities, the names of only 28 derive from the Egyptian deities. Names of ill omen, e.g. Anubis, were generally avoided. No feeling against naming a boy after a goddess or a girl after a god is discernible. Locality mattered: in Phrygia, among 1,500 theophoric names, 233 are from Men, none is from the (foreign) deity Isis. Theophoric names provide an index rather of a given deity's true popularity (plus suitability for being a name-god) than of his formal prestige in cult or myth: names e.g. from Poseidon are few and late. Caution is needed: nothing prevented the name Demetrios, despite underworld associations, from being popular, but an unknowable degree of the popularity was due to the fame of Poliorcetes.

Before the middle of the second century B.C. the pressure to use names traditional in the family was felt so strongly that (theophoric names being uncommon to start with) only some 6 to 15 per cent. of all names are theophoric in Athens; Sparta appears to have had fewer still. Hence an Isigenes of Rhamnus, born *c.* 400, and an Isidorus, ephor of Sparta in 410/409, are significant. For Asklepios no known Athenian was named until a generation after the adoption of his cult in 420, and only six in the fourth century, six again in the third century; but fifty-five in the second or early first, and 202 under the Empire. No foreign deity adopted by Athena *ante* 150 B.C. provided more names in that period.

After about 150 B.C. the general relaxation of traditions, the spread of the foreign cults, and the ever-present tendency to find novel names, raised the proportion of theophoric names to 30 per cent. of all names in Athens (at Alexandria it is apparently even higher). Hence not much more than whim may account for a name such as Ῥαδάμανθυς Ἀττίνου. The naming a child Isigenes is less significant *c.* 100 B.C. than *c.* 400 B.C.: by 100 B.C. the name may be a mere heritage. But the total figures for Athens are impressive: under the Empire 301 names recorded in Athens are from Isis; 48 from Sarapis (less popular now, as earlier); only one each for Adonis, Attis, Bendis; four for Mithras (only one known earlier); 45 for Helios, 116 for Men, 63 for Meter, 40 for Eros. Clearly there was discrimination, and there were real influences. Isis alone threatened the supremacy of the older gods: Apollo 334, Zeus 258 (a marked decrease), Dionysos 514 (a marked increase), all of whom have large figures earlier; and Aphrodite 383 (Ἐπαφρόδιτος, which could mean *felix*, accounts for 108 of these), though *ante* 30 B.C. her total was 19. Their status relatively to each other had changed, but the Olympians were by no means dead.

Founded by Letronne over a century ago, this subject has been studied only sporadically: full account in pp. 1–10 of the important study by E. Sittig *De Graecorum nominibus theophoris* (Diss. Philol. Halenses, vol. xx, pars 1, 1911). Add for names in -δωρ- and -γεν-: W. Froehner, *ARW* xv (1912), 380–7; for Thasos, M. Seyrig, *BCH* li (1927), 229; for Thera, I. Braun, *Theräische Kulte*, 66; for Alexandria, C. E. Visser, *Götter und Kulte in ptolemäischen Alexandrien* (1938, reprinted in *Allard Persson Stichting*, No. V, 1938), pp. 45–7 and ref.; for Athens, S. Dow, *Harv. Theol. Rev.* xxx (1937), 216–24.   S. D.

NAOS, *see* TEMPLE.

NARBO,
modern *Narbonne*. The name, which originally denoted the hill-fort of Montlaurès, appears in Hecataeus (*c.* 500 B.C., *FGrH* 54). It became the centre of a Celto-Iberian kingdom (coins NERONC) which was absorbed by the Volcae. In 118 the *colonia Narbo Martius* was founded in the plain, and Montlaurès was dismantled *c.* 71. Caesar's tenth legion was settled in the new town, which became the capital of Narbonensis,

the seat of the imperial cult and an important trading-centre. Enlarged by Claudius, its full title was *Colonia Iulia paterna Claudia Narbo Martius decumanorum*. Damaged by fire in the second century, it declined in prosperity, and apparently lost its position as capital to Nemausus. In 462 it fell finally to the Visigoths.

C. H. Benedict, *A History of Narbo* (U.S.A. 1941); P. Héléna, *Origines de Narbonne* (1937); G. F. Hill, *Coins of Narbonensis* (1930); *CIL* xii. 521; Grenier, *Manuel* ii. 483–92.   C. E. S.

NARCISSUS
(1), in mythology, a beautiful youth, son of Cephisus (the Boeotian river) and Liriope, a nymph. He loved no one till he saw his own reflection in water and fell in love with that; finally he pined away, died, and was turned into the flower of like name. The story may arise from the magical danger of seeing one's own image in a mirror (see Frazer, *GB*[3] iii. 94), but Ovid gives an explanation (his own?) of it; Narcissus was punished for his cruelty to Echo (q.v.). Hera had deprived her of normal speech because her chatter prevented the goddess catching Zeus at his amours with the other nymphs; she could only repeat what others said. She tried to make love to Narcissus with fragments of his own speech, but he repulsed her and she so wasted away with grief that there was nothing left of her but her voice (Ovid, *Met.* 3. 342 ff.). Other explanations, Paus. 9. 31. 7–8; Conon, 24.   H. J. R.

NARCISSUS
(2). As private secretary (*ab epistulis*) to Claudius, this freedman acquired prodigious wealth (400 million sesterces, it was said) and exercised large political influence. He was even sent to the north of Gaul in A.D. 43 to expedite the embarkation of the expeditionary force to Britain and received *quaestoria ornamenta* in 48 as a reward for the exposure of Messalina's plotting. His power was afterwards eclipsed by that of Pallas and Agrippina, whose marriage with Claudius he had not favoured, and he was unsuccessful in seeking to promote the interests of Britannicus. After the murder of Claudius in 54 he was immediately arrested and driven to suicide.   J. P. B.

NARRATIO,
rhetorical statement of a case (following the *exordium*), a feature stressed as vitally important by Apollodoreans (q.v.) and by Quintilian (*Inst.* 4. 2).

For three *genera* of *narrationes*, *Rhet. Her.* 1. 8. 12; for requisite brevity, perspicuity, plausibility, Cic. *De Or.* 2. 326 ff., *Orat.* 124.

NASICA, *see* SCIPIO (6), (10), and (12).

NAUARCHOS
(ναύαρχος), admiral. The geographical conditions of Greek warfare, with its demand for 'amphibious' operations, discouraged the separation of naval from military commands: thus, Athenian fleets were always commanded by *strategi* (q.v.). *Nauarchos* was a general term for the commander of a navy, of a squadron however small, even of a single ship. As an official title it appears comparatively late, the outcome of a greater specialization in certain States, mostly such as lacked an established naval tradition. The most important were Sparta (*c.* 430–360 B.C.), Syracuse under Dionysius I and II, Ptolemaic Egypt (and probably Macedonia, Pergamum, and the Seleucid kingdom), the Achaean League, and Rhodes. Everywhere (except perhaps at Pergamum) the *nauarchos* was admiral-of-the-fleet, with no colleague, his tenure varying from the single year (usually) of Greek republican admirals to the long commands of admirals (e.g. in Syracuse and Egypt) who served a monarch.

Strack, *PW*, s.v. 'Nauarchos'.   G. T. G.

NAUCRATIS,
on the Canopic branch of the Nile, was a Greek 'treaty port' which under Saite Pharaohs became the chief centre of cultural relations between Greece and Egypt. According to Herodotus it was the sole

emporium for Greek traders, who received concessions (τεμένη) from Amasis. The chief of these, established jointly by the Ionian cities of Chios, Teos, Phocaea, Clazomenae, the Dorian Rhodes, Cnidos, Halicarnassus, Phaselis, and Aeolian Mytilene, was called the Hellenium and appointed magistrates of the mart; Aegina, Samos, and Miletus had separate concessions. Excavations by Petrie and Gardner (1884–6) and Hogarth (1899, 1903) have produced abundant potsherds (many with dedications to 'the gods of the Greeks', Hera, Apollo, and also Aphrodite and the Dioscuri) dating from the latter years of the seventh century onwards, and show that the history of Greek Naucratis did not begin with Amasis' charter. According to Strabo Naucratis was founded by Milesians who, in the reign of Psammetichus, had founded the 'Milesians' Fort' near the Bolbitine mouth of the Nile. Sappho's brother Charaxus travelled to Naucratis on business. The city continued to flourish through the classical period.

After Alexander's conquest of Egypt, the trade of Naucratis passed to Alexandria: some references in the correspondence of Zenon suggest that there was still some business done there in the middle of the third century, and inscriptions show that buildings were erected under the earlier Ptolemies; also, about the time of the conquest it struck the only civic silver and bronze coins known in Egypt. It was allowed to retain its Greek constitution by the Romans, and this served as a model for the constitution of Antinoopolis in the reign of Hadrian. But there is no record of any active life there.

Herodotus, bk. 2; Strabo, bk. 17; Sappho (ed. Lobel), pp. 2, 3. W. M. Flinders Petrie and E. A. Gardner, *Naukratis* i, ii (1886–8). *BSA* v. 26 f.; D. G. Hogarth, *JHS* 1905, 105 ff.; E. R. Price, ibid. 1924, 180 ff.; R. M. Cook, ibid. 1937, 227 ff. (with references to earlier literature).   P. N. U. & J. G. M.

NAUKLEROS, *see* COMMERCE, para. 2.

NAUKRARIAI (from ναύκραρος, shipmaster) were local divisions of Attica, twelve to each of the pre-Cleisthenic *phylae*. Originally it seems that each naucrary had to finance one warship and its crew; subsequently it took on other financial duties. Cleisthenes raised their number to fifty (five to each *phyle*) and made them responsible for ship-building, like the later symmories (q.v.). But according to Aristotle their administrative duties were transferred to the *demoi*, and in 483 B.C., when the State took over the building of warships, the *naukrariai* disappeared. (*See also* TRIERARCHIA.)

Herodotus (5. 71. 2) says that at the time of Cylon (q.v.) the presidents of the *naukraroi* administered the State; an exaggeration, but they were doubtless powerful.
                                                                      A. W. G.

NAUMACHIA. The word is used both of a sham fight in the water, such as was given first by Julius Caesar at Rome in 46 B.C., and also in a local sense for any flooded arena, especially for the huge circus excavated by Augustus under the Janiculum. For it water was brought from Lake Alsietinus about twenty miles from Rome by a new aqueduct, the Alsietina, and one of the first spectacles given in it was apparently a representation of the Battle of Salamis. The most famous *naumachia* was exhibited by Claudius in A.D. 52 on the Fucine Lake; 19,000 men took part. The combatants were usually prisoners and condemned criminals. *Naumachiae* were apparently held in provincial towns, since arrangements to flood the amphitheatres at Capua and Nîmes can be traced.

Friedländer, ii. 74 ff.   F. A. W.

NAUMACHIUS (perhaps as early as the 2nd c. A.D.), author of a poem on wifely dutifulness, of which Stobaeus (68. 5, 74. 7, 93. 23) cites portions.

NAUPACTUS, in western (Ozolian) Locris, with an excellent harbour and small coastal plain cut off from the interior by mountains, commands the narrowest entrance of the Corinthian Gulf; its least difficult land-contacts are with Amphissa and eastern Greece. A legend, probably derived from the name of Naupactus ('ship-construction'), records that the Dorians crossed into the Peloponnese from Naupactus. Its value as a naval base was appreciated by the Athenians, who seized it and peopled it with exiled Messenians (456 B.C.). During the Peloponnesian War it was the main Athenian station in the west. After Sparta had expelled the Messenians (399), Achaea colonized and held it, until Philip captured it and gave it to Aetolia (338). With the collapse of the Aetolian League, Naupactus lost its importance.

W. J. Woodhouse, *Aetolia* (1897), 311 f.   N. G. L. H.

NAUPLIUS, (1) eponym of Nauplia; son of Poseidon and Amymone (q.v.). (2) His descendant (Nauplius I–Proetus (q.v.)–Lernus–Naubolus–Clytoneus–Nauplius II, Ap. Rhod. 1. 134–8), father of Palamedes (q.v.) and Oeax. He was an Argonaut (Ap. Rhod. loc. cit.) and plays a part in two other well-known stories. Auge (*see* TELEPHUS) was entrusted to him after her delivery to sell overseas; he gave her to Teuthras, king of Teuthrania, who married her (Apollod. 2. 147). He was instrumental in wrecking the Greek fleet on its return from Troy (his namesake had been a wrecker also, Apollod. 2. 23; indeed, the two are identical, *Nostoi*, quoted there), for to avenge the death of Palamedes he lit false lights at Caphareus in Euboea (Eur. *Hel.* 767 ff., 1126 ff., and many later authors).

Wagner in Roscher's *Lexikon, s.v.*   H. J. R.

NAUSICAA, daughter of Alcinous (q.v.; *Od.* 6. 15 ff.). The night of Odysseus' landing in Scheria (*see* ODYSSEUS), she was moved in a dream by Athena to go down to the washing-place at the river-mouth and wash the family linen with her handmaids. Having done so the next morning, she and her maids played ball, and a cry from one of them woke Odysseus. He improvised a loin-cloth from a branch, came out of the hollow under trees where he had spent the night, and appeared before the girls. The maids ran away, but Nausicaa, given courage by Athena, stood her ground. He then made known his wants to her and she gave him food, drink, and clothing and showed him the way to the city, modestly directing him to walk the last part of the distance alone, lest the gossips should see them together and accuse her of husband-hunting. This very charming episode was handled in the lost *Nausicaa* of Sophocles and a few other post-Homeric works; Hellanicus, in Eustathius on Homer, p. 1796, 42 ff., says she married Telemachus and had by him a son Perseptolis, an obvious next-best to marrying Odysseus, as Alcinous wished on their first meeting (*Od.* 7. 311 ff.).   H. J. R.

NAUSIPHANES of Teos (b. *c.* 360 B.C.), Atomist, studied under Pyrrhon of Elis, probably while they were fellow soldiers in Alexander's campaigns, and before the end of these campaigns established himself as a teacher at Teos, where Epicurus studied under him *c.* 324. He was essentially a follower of Democritus, and was the channel through which Democritus' physics and theory of knowledge passed to Epicurus. He departed from Democritus' ethical views by insisting that the philosopher should take part in public life, and devoted himself largely to the exposition of a theory of rhetoric, which was later bitterly attacked by Philodemus.

Testimonia and frs. in Diels, *Vorsokr.*[5] 2. 246–50. *PW* xvi. 2021.
                                                                      W. D. R.

NAUTIKOS TOKOS (ναυτικὸς τόκος), *see* BOTTOMRY LOANS.

NAUTODIKAI were Athenian officials who presided at the trial of commercial suits (δίκαι ἐμπορικαί) between merchants native and foreign. They were probably instituted when Athens became an important commercial centre after the Persian wars. They presided also in citizenship suits involving foreigners who filed suits as citizens. In the time of Demosthenes both types of suit came before the *thesmothetai* (J. H. Lipsius, *Das Attische Recht*, 86).   R. J. B.

NAVICULARII, see COMMERCE, para. 7.

NAVIES (Greek and Roman). Apart from the Homeric fleets, which served only for transport, the construction of navies followed closely upon the expansion of Greek commerce in the age of colonization. The first recorded sea-battle took place between Corinth and Corcyra in 664 B.C. (Thuc. 1. 13. 4). The new commercial States found warships especially necessary to guard their coasts, to check piracy, and later to assure the free flow of grain and other vital products; also, their growing prosperity permitted maintenance of a fleet more easily. The expense, however, remained an impediment to large-scale, protracted naval operations throughout the Greek and Hellenistic periods, especially when mercenaries replaced citizen rowers (after 400 B.C.). Until the Roman Empire, the peace-time navy of a State consisted usually of a number of hulls, with rigging and oars, laid up in the docks of the harbour (q.v.), from which the galleys were launched only in need. Sporadic piracy in consequence flourished; great expeditions in war-time required extra construction and levies of sailors.

2. The peculiarities of the ancient war galley (see NAVIGATION) also influenced the character of naval power. It was impossible to keep up successfully a lengthy blockade, inasmuch as the galleys suffered in storms and furnished but cramped quarters to their crews. Thus, even the most heroic attempt, that of Bibulus to keep Caesar's reinforcements from crossing the Adriatic in the winter of 48 B.C. (Caesar, *BCiv.* 3 passim), eventually failed. The simple construction of the warship made it much easier for the so-called naval powers suddenly to be challenged by a State previously without a fleet, as by Sparta at various times in the Peloponnesian War (e.g. Thuc. 3. 26 ff.) and by Thebes under Epaminondas in 364 B.C. (Diod. 15. 78–9). The general object of naval strategy was to protect one's own coast and commerce, to destroy the opponent's fleet and commerce, and to assist land invasions by feints, transport of troops, and acquisition of bases.

3. Early navies were composed chiefly of *pentekontors* in small numbers, the forty triremes of Polycrates of Samos (Hdt. 3. 44) forming one of the largest squadrons before the fifth century. The Persian Wars brought great changes. Fleets grew in size; the trireme (q.v.) became the standard galley; naval tactics improved greatly. Athens benefited chiefly, under the leadership of Themistocles, who secured the construction of 200 triremes at Athens before 480 (see TRIERARCHY); thereafter, apart from a short period after the Peloponnesian War, it remained the pre-eminent naval power in Greece until 322, when its fleet of 170 galleys was destroyed at Amorgos by a Macedonian fleet of 240 ships.

4. Although navies in the Hellenistic age did not surpass the size of these two fleets, they entailed an immensely greater expense, which lay beyond the resources of the small States. The standard vessel was now the quinquireme (q.v.), with a crew twice as large as that of the trireme, and after the time of Alexander even larger vessels were built. Throughout this period Macedonia generally held the Aegean and Egypt the rest of the eastern Mediterranean, but the balance of naval power shifted frequently. By 188 B.C. all had yielded to Rome. Although Rome had possessed some previous

naval organization (see DUOVIRI NAVALES), its first great naval effort came in the First Punic War, during most of which the Romans maintained a fleet of over 200 quinqueremes. Unskilled in naval warfare, they relied upon their soldiery and used boarding tactics exclusively; ships were built in heavy fashion, the number of marines, small on Greek vessels, was increased, and the *corvus*, a grapnel, was extensively used (Polyb. 1. 20 ff.). The classical tactics of manœuvre, with the *diekplus* (q.v.), steadily gave way as the Romans overcame first Carthage, the chief naval power in the western Mediterranean, and then the Hellenistic States.

5. After 167 B.C. Rome permitted her fleets to decay and, in emergencies, conscripted ships and crews from her Greek allies. In the civil wars the contestants again built up huge squadrons, which were merged at last into the fleets of Antony and Octavian. To the campaign of Actium the former brought 500 warships and the latter 400. After his victory Octavian organized part of these into the first permanent fleet the Mediterranean had known (Tac. *Ann.* 4. 5). Based on Misenum and Ravenna, with auxiliary squadrons off Syria, Egypt, and Mauretania, and on the Black Sea, Rhine, Danube, and English Channel, the Roman imperial navy eradicated Mediterranean piracy for the first and last time previous to the nineteenth century. During the third and fourth centuries this navy vanished, but the Byzantine navy in part perpetuated the Graeco-Roman naval tradition.

Ancient Sources: Thucydides (1. 13 ff.) and Herodotus (bks. 6 ff.) reveal most clearly the nature of ancient navies. Modern literature: Camille de la Berge, 'Étude sur l'organisation des flottes romaines', *Bulletin épigraphique* vi (1886); F. W. Clark, *The Influence of Sea-power on the History of the Roman Republic* (U.S.A. 1915); J. Kromayer and G. Veith, *Heerwesen und Kriegführung der Griechen und Römer* (1928); F. Miltner, *PW*, s.v. 'Seekrieg'; H. A. Ormerod, *Piracy in the Ancient World* (1924); C. G. Starr, *The Roman Imperial Navy* (U.S.A. 1941); W. W. Tarn, *Hellenistic Military and Naval Developments* (1930); J. H. Thiel, *Studies on the History of Roman Sea-power in Republican Times* (Amsterdam, 1946).   C. G. S.

NAVIGATION. The Mediterranean, tideless, broken by numerous peninsulas and islands, calm in summer, has always furnished encouragement to the seafarer, and to none more than the Greeks, whose experience became the basis of Graeco-Roman naval knowledge. The progress of navigation, however, was impeded by the lack of instruments for determining direction and distance, such as the compass, sextant, and log. Ships, also, were generally small, and, although they could sail within a few points of the wind, their sails, tackling, and steering apparatus were deficient.

2. The season of sailing was accordingly limited to the months when visibility was good and the sea mild; when storm clouds veiled the stars, the sailor sought the shore or some harbour. Hesiod (*Op.* 663 ff.) would restrict navigation to fifty days in midsummer, and usual practice placed its limits at March and October. As confidence and experience grew, and ships (q.v.) increased in size and stability, the period of sailing could be extended. Martial (6. 80) mentions Egyptian roses at Rome in winter, and other evidence from the Roman Empire (e.g. Tac. *Ann.* 12. 43) indicates some seafaring in winter by the more hardy travellers.

3. Although the Romans themselves were not seafarers, the Roman Empire marked the height of ancient navigation. The scourge of piracy was eliminated; traffic by sea increased enormously. Ships, moreover, tended to stand farther out from land. As late as 400 B.C. the route from Greece to the west lay by Corcyra and thence to Italy; in like manner, the importance of Rhodes in the Hellenistic period was partly the result of its key situation on the route from Egypt and Syria to the Aegean via Cyprus and Caria. Under the Empire, travellers to the east usually went straight to Alexandria from Puteoli, rather than cross Macedonia as under the

Republic (Philo, *In Flacc.* 5. 26–7). Alexandrian merchants at this time, after the discovery of the monsoon winds, voyaged directly to India, but Mediterranean craft never sailed regularly about Spain to Gaul and Britain.

4. The speed of vessels did not rise greatly in the ancient world. The average speed for cargo ships was approximately three to four knots; voyages of eight days from Puteoli to Alexandria and of six days from Gades to Ostia were records (Pliny, *HN* 19. 3–4). Seasonal winds were often employed, as by the Alexandrian grain fleet under the Empire, which sailed to Puteoli in June and caught the etesian winds back to Alexandria in August. Systematic descriptions of coasts (*Periplus*) appeared in the Hellenistic Age, a period in which physical aids to navigation such as harbours (q.v.) and lighthouses (q.v.) were constructed. This work continued under the Roman Empire.

Acts xxvii–xxviii; Lucian, *The Ship*; A. Köster, *Das antike Seewesen* (1923); H. J. Rose, *The Mediterranean in the Ancient World* (1933); H. de Saussure, 'De la Marine antique à la marine moderne', *Rev. Arch.* 1937.   C. G. S.

NAXOS (1), the largest and most fertile of the Cyclades (q.v.), famous for its wine and worship of Dionysus. Tradition represents Carians, Thracians, and Cretans as its early inhabitants. Naxos was mistress of the Cyclades in the late sixth century. For its concern with the Ionian revolt the city was sacked by the Persians in 490 B.C. After the Persian wars Naxos joined the Delian Confederacy, revolted and became tributary to Athens, and a cleruchy was established about 450. As a member of the second Athenian Confederacy, the island again revolted without success. In the third century Naxos was a member of the Islanders' League; subsequently it was of little importance.

Bursian, ii. 489 ff.   W. A. L.

NAXOS (2), nowadays *Capo Schisò*, Sicily's earliest Greek colony, was founded by Chalcis in Sicel territory on the east coast (735 B.C.). Naxos quickly colonized Leontini, Catana (729), and allegedly Zancle (= Messana), but never became really powerful. Its traditional enemy, as of the other Chalcidian States, was Syracuse: Hieron even attempted to doricize Naxos (476). After 461, however, Naxos prospered and supported the anti-Syracusan movements of Leontini (427) and Athens (415), until finally (403) Dionysius of Syracuse razed it and gave its site to Siculi who then founded Tauromenium near by. Naxos was never recolonized (reject Pliny, *HN* 3. 91), its refugees ultimately settling at Tauromenium (q.v.).

Strabo 6. 267 f.; Thuc. bks. 3, 6, 7; Hdt. 7. 154; App. *BCiv.* 5. 109; Diod. bks. 11–14. P. Rizzo, *Naxos Siceliota* (1904); J. Bérard, *Bibliogr. topogr.* (1941), p. 77; H. A. Cahn, *Die Münzen Naxos* (1944).   E. T. S.

NAZARIUS (*fl.* A.D. 320), see PANEGYRIC.

NEANTHES of Cyzicus (3rd c. B.C.), historian, pupil of Philiscus of Miletus. His extensive writings included an *Hellenica* (Ἑλληνικά), annals of Cyzicus (Ὧροι Κυζικηνῶν), and a series of biographies (Περὶ ἐνδόξων ἀνδρῶν) notable for the first recorded literary treatment of the life of Timon the misanthrope. His reliability for accurate knowledge is small. The history of Attalus I of Pergamum, 241–197 B.C. (Τὰ περὶ Ἄτταλον), usually ascribed to him, is by a younger Neanthes.

FHG iii. 2; FGrH ii. 84 and 171.   G. L. B.

NEAPOLIS, nowadays *Naples*, was founded in fertile territory by Cumae *c.* 600 B.C. Its early history being unknown, ancient authors invented the tale that its original name was Parthenope. Neapolis became the chief Greek centre of Campania (*c.* 425) and received refugees from Cumae (q.v.) into its suburb Palae(o)polis. In 327 the anti-Roman policies of these Palaeopolitans

constrained Rome to capture Neapolis. Palaepolis disappeared; Neapolis became a favoured allied State that furnished Rome naval help and repulsed Pyrrhus and Hannibal. In Republican times Puteoli outstripped Neapolis, but by Cicero's day, despite a treacherous massacre of its inhabitants in 82 (App. *BCiv.* 1. 89), Neapolis was a flourishing *municipium* where Virgil and others, seeking beauty or Hellenic culture, sojourned. Subsequently Neapolis became a *colonia* but retained its Greek institutions and language until the late Empire. In the Gothic Wars it suffered severely (Procop. *Goth.* 1 and 3), but was always important. Here Statius was born and Romulus Augustulus, last Western emperor, virtually imprisoned.

Strabo 5. 246; Livy 8. 22 f.; 35. 16. A. Sambon, *Monnaies antiques de l'Italie* i (1903), 171, 283; F. E. Adcock, *CAH* vii. 595; J. Bérard, *Bibliogr. topogr.* (1941), 71.   E. T. S.

NEARCHUS (1), potter and vase-painter, in Athens. Known from four signatures on small black-figure vases of about 550 B.C. and dedication of Antenor Kore (about 530). His sons Tleson and Ergoteles signed 'little master' cups.

G. M. A. Richter, *AJArch.* 1932, 272; A. Rumpf, *Sakonides* (1937), 19.   T. B. L. W.

NEARCHUS (2) of Crete, Alexander's friend, commanded the fleet which circumnavigated the coast from the Indus to the Tigris. His honest and trustworthy chronicle, written before 312 B.C., was not a history of Alexander, but gave an account of India, which Strabo and Arrian used, and of his voyage, which is reproduced in Arrian's *Indike*. After the death of Alexander Nearchus played a subordinate part under Antigonus I and Demetrius I. He was probably killed at the battle of Gaza (312 B.C.). *See* ALEXANDER (3), Bibliography, Ancient Sources.   W. W. T.

NECESSITAS, *see* FATE.

NECHEPSO, titular author with Petosiris of a comprehensive astrological work, the basis of the later astrology. He probably invented the astrological significance of the signs of the zodiac, as well as making many other innovations. 'Nechepso and Petosiris' may have been the pseudonym of a single author, and his date may be placed *c.* 150–125 B.C.

Ed. E. Riess, *Philol.* 6 Suppl. (1891–3), 325–94. *PW* xvi. 2160.   W. D. R.

NECROMANCY, *see* MAGIC, III.

NECTAR, *see* AMBROSIA.

NECYOMANTEA, *see* MAGIC, II and III, ORACLES.

NEGOTIATORES, *see* COMMERCE, paras. 7 and 11.

NELEUS (Νηλεύς) and **PELIAS** (Πελίας), in mythology, sons of Tyro, daughter of Salmoneus (q.v.) by Poseidon; he approached her in the shape of the river-god Enipeus, whom she loved (*Od.* 11. 235 ff.). Here (237) she is apparently already married to Cretheus (for the relationships *see* AEOLUS); later, as in Apollodorus (1. 90), he is her guardian. Apollodorus also says that she exposed the children, who were picked up by a horse-herder. Tyro was ill-used by Sidero, her step-mother, till her sons grew up, recognized her, and pursued Sidero into a temple of Hera, where Pelias killed her at the altar. For the rest of his story *see* JASON, MEDEA. Neleus married Chloris, daughter of Amphion of Orchomenus (*Od.* 11. 281 ff.), who bore Nestor and other sons, also Pero, cf. MELAMPUS. But Heracles attacked Pylos, Neleus' kingdom, because Neleus would not purify him from the blood-guilt of Iphitus (*Iliad* 11. 690 ff., Hesiod, *fr.* 14 ff. Rzach; schol. *Il.* 2. 336), and killed all his sons save Nestor (q.v.). His own death is variously told, see Weizsäcker in Roscher's *Lexikon* iii. 110.   H. J. R.

NEMAUSUS, town in Gallia Narbonensis (modern *Nîmes*), originally a La Tène stronghold, capital of the Volcae Arecomici. In 16 B.C. it was laid out with walls enclosing *c.* 550 acres and given the title of *Colonia* with Latin rights and an extensive *territorium*. A crocodile on its coins suggests a partly oriental population (? Antony's veterans). Very important remains of public buildings exist: amphitheatre, precinct of *Deus Nemausus*, and a temple erected by Agrippa (16 B.C.) and re-dedicated to C. and L. Caesar (the 'Maison Carrée'). The Pont-du-Gard forms part of its aqueduct. Perhaps in the second century it became the capital of Narbonensis.

F. Heichelheim and E. Linckenheld, *PW* xvi. 2286–310; R. Neumann, *Quellbezirk von Nîmes* (1937). C. E. S.

NEMEA was an open valley on the north borders of the Argolid, in the territory of Cleonae. It was the scene of Heracles' encounter with the lion, and of the Nemean Games (q.v.). The fourth-century temple of Zeus, the great altar, palaestra, and gymnasium have been excavated. Nemea is also the name of the river flowing north and forming the boundary of Corinth and Sicyon, the scene of the first battle of the Corinthian War (394; Xen. *Hell.* 4. 2. 13 ff.).

C. W. Blegen, 'Excavations at Nemea', *Art and Archaeology* xix (1925), 175 ff.; *AJArch.* 1927, 421 ff.; N. Clemmensen and R. Vallois, *Le Temple de Zeus à Némée*, *BCH* 1925, 1 ff. T. J. D.

NEMEAN GAMES, THE, according to one legend were founded by Adrastus of Argos, when he led the Seven against Thebes; according to another by Heracles after he had slain the Nemean lion: but we know little of them until 573 B.C., when they became a Panhellenic festival. They were held in the sanctuary of Nemean Zeus (*see* NEMEA), and were at first managed by the people of Cleonae, afterwards by Argos. The games were conducted on the same lines as those at Olympia, the prize was a crown of wild celery, and they took place every second and fourth year in each Olympiad. F. A. W.

NEMESIANUS, MARCUS AURELIUS OLYMPIUS, from Carthage, late in the third century A.D. composed four pastorals (long ascribed to Calpurnius, q.v.), and an incomplete didactic poem in 325 verses on the chase. But he also distinguished himself in poetic contests and meditated an epic on the deeds of the imperial brothers Numerianus and Carinus (Vopiscus, *Carus, Numer. et Carinus*, 11; *Cyn.* 63–78). His *Cynegetica* is best dated between the death of the emperor Carus, 283, and that of Numerianus, 284. It seems to refer to his pastorals as lighter productions which had preceded (58–62).

WORKS (1) **Eclogae**: these four short poems, 319 lines in all, show the influence of Virgil and Calpurnius. In I the shepherd Timetas' threnody on Meliboeus recalls the praises of Daphnis in Verg. *Ecl.* 5; in III the song demanded from Pan is a parallel to that of Silenus in Verg. *Ecl.* 6. IV (62–72) borrows magical ideas which Virgil in *Ecl.* 8 drew from Theocritus: here too Nemesianus restores the pleasant music of the refrain which was part of the Theocritean tradition in Virgil. His diction and metre gain by his Virgilian imitations, though his period accounts for shortenings like *laudandŏ, devotiŏ, exercetŏ* (*Ecl.* 2. 80, *Cyn.* 83, 187). From Calpurnius he borrows freely, especially in eclogue III.

(2) **Cynegetica**: 102 lines are introductory; then, departing from the order in Grattius (whom he probably had read), he devotes 223 lines to indispensable preliminaries for hunting—dogs (rearing, training, diseases, breeds), horses, nets, and traps. The poem breaks off on the verge of the chase—'uenmur dum mane nouum'.

(3) **De Aucupio**. Two fragments on birdcatching (28 hexameters) are ascribed to N.

His style, though unoriginal, is agreeable. He at least declares his independence of mythology (*Cyn.* 15–47) and certain notes of enthusiasm in him lend colour to the almost conventional claim to be breaking new ground (8–14) in his didactic poem; while in his feeling for pastoral environment there are suggestions of the open air in spite of his book-borrowings. He is rather less inclined to lose himself in details of the essentials for the chase than Grattius is. *See* DIDACTIC POETRY, LATIN; PASTORAL POETRY, LATIN, para. 5.

BIBLIOGRAPHY

TEXTS: (a) Eclogues: E. Baehrens, *PLM* iii; H. Schenkl (w. Calp. Sic.; 1885) and in Postgate's *CPL* (1905); C. H. Keene (w. Calp. Sic., introd., comm.; 1887); C. Giarratano (w. Calp. Sic.; 1910); Turin (Paravia, 1924); J. Wight Duff and A. M. Duff in *Minor Latin Poets* (Loeb, 1934).
(b) Cynegetica: E. Baehrens *PLM*. iii; J. P. Postgate, *CPL* (1905); D. Martin, (w. comment.; U.S.A. 1917); J. W. and A. M. Duff in *Min. Lat. Poets* (Loeb).

SPECIAL STUDIES: M. Fiegl, *Des Grattius Cynegetica: seine Vorgänger u. seine Nachfolger* (1890) [argues that N. borrowed from G.: supported by Enk (ed. Grattius), opposed by Curcio (ed. Grattius)]. P. Monceaux, *Les Africains: étude sur la littér. latine d'Afrique* (1894); J. Hubaux, *Les Thèmes bucoliques dans la poésie latine* (1930). J. W. D.

NEMESIS (1). One of the most puzzling of Greek goddesses, owing to the wide divergence between her mythology and her position in cult and morals. Her best-known shrine was at Rhamnus in Attica, where she appears to have been a deity of the type of Artemis (q.v.; see Farnell, *Cults* ii. 488 ff.). Zeus pursued her amorously, and to avoid him she took all manner of non-human forms, especially those of fish (*Cypria*, frs. 6 and 7 Allen). Finally (Apollod. 3. 127, continuing what seems to be the same story) she changed into a goose, he into a swan, and so she laid the egg which a shepherd found and gave to Leda (q.v.). This is the sort of story which might be told of almost any minor goddess or nymph. The fact that in Smyrna (Paus. 9. 35. 6) there were statues of the Charites in her temple, of old workmanship ascribed to Bupalus, would suggest that there at least she had something to do with the fertility of the soil.

But in the vast majority of cases she is nothing but retribution or righteous indignation, particularly that of the gods at human presumption, personified. This identification extends to her Attic cult, cf. Catullus 66. 71 (64. 395 seems to make her a war-goddess, but he may mean that she appeared to rouse men fighting in a good cause); and a local worship in Boeotia, apparently of Nemesis Adrasteia, was said to have been founded by Adrastus (q.v.), because of the resentment he felt against the Thebans (Antimachus, fr. 53 Wyss). Adrasteia is certainly the 'unescapable' power before which all must bow (προσκυνεῖν τὴν Ἀδράστειαν, Aesch. *PV* 936, Plato, *Resp.* 451 a). But she in turn is, or is identified with, a goddess of the Phrygian Ida, associated with the Dactyli q.v. (*Phoronis* in schol. Ap. Rhod. 1. 1129). Possibly in this case some accidental resemblance of a foreign to a Greek word has come into play; Nemesis of Rhamnus may have been originally the goddess who deals or distributes, νέμει, appropriate gifts to her worshippers, and afterwards made abstract, a process like that which Fors Fortuna (q.v.) seems to have undergone. It does not appear that her statue, for which see Rossbach in Roscher's *Lexikon* iii. 153–4 (see the whole art. for good discussion and literature and cf. Herter in *PW*, s.v.), had the characteristic pose of later representations of her (see Volkmann in *ARW.* 26, pp. 296 ff., 31, pp. 57 ff. for this and other points), which are shown spitting into the breast-fold of her robe (cf. Theocr. 6. 39). For her later developments in cult and literature, which last to the days of Theodosius, see Rossbach. H. J. R.

NEMESIS (2) succeeded 'Delia' in the affections of Tibullus (2. 3. 51; 5. 111; Ov. *Am.* 3. 9. 31; Mart. 8. 73. 7).

NENIA (less approved, *naenia*), our knowledge here is limited by the sometimes contradictory evidence of antiquity. The word may derive from νηνίατον [Φρύγιον]

(Pollux 4. 79 [80]), but, as *nenia* goes back to times preceding foreign influence, it is more likely a Latin onomatopoeia. Usually *nenia* means a dirge containing lamentation and praise of a deceased person (Diomedes, Keil, *Gramm. Lat.*, i. 485: 'cum lamentatione'; Festus, 158 Lindsay: 'carmen quod in funere laudandi gratia cantatur ad tibiam'). It was sung to a flute accompaniment by a hired mourner (*praefica*), whose assistants made responses (Serv. *ad Aen.* 6. 216) before the house of mourning, during the funeral procession, and beside the pyre. It never became a literary *genre*. No example has reached us: we have only an anapaestic parody (Sen. *Apocol.* 12). *Nenia* is also the goddess of the dying; she had a temple at Rome.

Because of its primitive character, *nenia* soon fell into discredit (Plautus, *Asin.* 808). This explains why it may be a synonym for children's songs (Hor. *Epist.* I. 1. 63), a magical litany, a senseless rigmarole (*nugae*). In Ausonius it signifies *epicedium* (q.v.); in Sidonius Apollinaris, a metrical epitaph.

H. de la Ville de Mirmont, *Revue de philologie* xxvi (1902), 263 and 335; W. Kroll, *PW*, s.v. C. F. (Transl. J. W. D.)

NEODAMODEIS, see HELOTS.

NEOKOROI, see TEMPLE OFFICIALS.

NEOPHRON, of Sicyon, was said by Dicaearchus and in the pseudo-Aristotelian ὑπομνήματα to have written a *Medea* which was adapted by Euripides in his play of that name (Argum. Eur. *Med.*), but the truth of this is very doubtful and the three extant fragments are almost certainly later than Euripides (see D. L. Page, Euripides, *Medea*, pp. xxx ff.). Suidas says that he wrote 120 tragedies and was the first to introduce into his plays 'paedagogi and the torture of slaves'—perhaps an inference based on his supposed priority to Euripides; such priority is inconsistent with Suidas' further statement that he associated with Alexander the Great, who put him to death with Callisthenes (Suidas elsewhere calls Alexander's victim Nearchus).

TGF 729–32. A. W. P.-C.

NEOPLATONISM, the revived Platonism—really a new synthesis of Platonic, Pythagorean, Aristotelian, and Stoic elements—which was the dominant philosophy of the pagan world from the middle of the third century A.D. down to the closing of the pagan schools by Justinian in 529, and strongly influenced medieval and Renaissance thought. The following phases may be distinguished in its history. (1) A long period of preparation, extending from the time of Antiochus (d. *c.* 68 B.C.) and Posidonius (d. *c.* 50 B.C.) down to that of Plotinus, during which we can trace the movement towards a comprehensive synthesis. In the work of such second-century writers as the Neopythagorean Numenius and the Middle Platonist Albinus (q.v.) there is much that foreshadows Plotinian Neoplatonism. (2) The oral teaching of Ammonius Saccas at Alexandria (early 3rd c.), of Plotinus at Rome (244/5–269/70), and of Plotinus' immediate pupils Porphyry and Amelius. Plotinus' *Enneads* (published posthumously, *c.* 300–5) gave Neoplatonism its abiding shape, and are incomparably its most important philosophical product. *See* PLOTINUS, PORPHYRY. (3) The period of diffusion in the fourth century when Neoplatonism becomes the fashionable creed of the pagan reaction, with its chief teaching centres in Syria and later at Pergamum, while it also begins to influence Christian thought through Augustine. To this period belong Iamblichus (q.v.); Sallustius, author of the *De diis et mundo*, a curious popular handbook of Neoplatonic religion (ed. and transl. A. D. Nock, 1926); Eunapius, who made out of the lives of his Neoplatonic teachers a pagan hagiology (*Vitae Sophistarum*, ed. and transl. W. C. Wright, Loeb,

1922); and the Latin Neoplatonists Chalcidius (Commentary on Plato's *Timaeus*, ed. Wrobel, 1876), Marius Victorinus, and Macrobius (ed. Eyssenhardt², 1893). (4) The Athenian School (Syrianus, Proclus, Simplicius, etc.) and the Alexandrian (Hypatia, Synesius, Olympiodorus, etc.), belonging mainly to the fifth and sixth centuries, fall outside the limits of date of this dictionary; as does the survival of Neoplatonism in writers like 'Dionysius the Areopagite' and John the Scot, and its revival by Psellus at Byzantium in the eleventh century and by Pico and others at the Renaissance.

BIBLIOGRAPHY

GENERAL: T Whittaker, *The Neoplatonists²* (1918); J. Simon, *Histoire de l'école d'Alexandrie* (1845); J. Geffcken, *Der Ausgang des griechisch-römischen Heidentums²* (1929); Zeller, *Phil. d. Gr.⁴* iii. 2. See also bibliography to PLOTINUS, PORPHYRY, IAMBLICHUS. Selections: E. R. Dodds, *Select Passages illustrating Neoplatonism* (text 1924, transl. 1923).
ORIGINS: W. W. Jaeger, *Nemesios v. Emesa* (1914); W. Theiler, *Die Vorbereitung des Neuplatonismus* (1930); F. Heinemann, *Hermes* 1926; E. R. Dodds, *CQ* 1928; R. E. Witt, *CQ* 1930, 1931, and *Albinus and the History of Middle Platonism* (1937). E. R. D.

NEOPTOLEMUS (1), in mythology, son of Achilles and Deidameia; *see* ACHILLES. After his father's death he was sent for to Troy by the Greeks, because his presence was one of the necessary conditions for taking the city (Soph. *Phil.* 114 f., 345 ff.), Odysseus acting as messenger (*Od.* 11. 508–9; Soph. ibid. 344 adds Phoenix). Arrived there, he showed himself a notable warrior and wise counsellor (*Od.* ibid.), killing among others Eurypylus, son of Telephus. He was one of the chosen party who manned the Wooden Horse, and came through that and the other dangers of the war unharmed. So far Homer (Sophocles' details presumably are from some cyclic epic, however); later authors do little more than enlarge and embroider. After the war, Homer says no more of him than that he returned safely and Menelaus sent Hermione to be married to him (*Od.* 3. 188–9; 4. 5 ff.). For the sequel of this marriage *see* HERMIONE. There is, however, a curious double version of the story of his visit to Delphi, which has left its mark on Pindar. In the sixth Paean it is said (100 ff.) that Neoptolemus, having been fetched from Scyros and taken Troy, incurred the wrath of Apollo by killing Priam at the altar of Zeus Herceius (cf. Verg. *Aen.* 2. 513 ff.); the god therefore swore that he should never reach home. Consequently, he was killed at Delphi in a dispute with 'the servants', presumably of the shrine. This seems to have given much offence in Aegina; therefore in *Nem.* 7. 33 ff. Pindar retold the tale with a different emphasis. Neoptolemus did go to Delphi and was killed there in a quarrel; but he went with the best of intentions (for details see Farnell's commentary), and the ultimate reason of his death was that one of the Aeacidae must needs enjoy heroic honours at that spot. He never returned to Scyros or Phthia, but, being driven by winds off his course, made his way to the Molossian territory, the kings of which country claimed descent from him through his son by Andromache (q.v.), Molossus; hence the name Pyrrhus borne by the most famous of them, that being the alternative name of Neoptolemus (e.g. *Cypria*, fr. 14 Allen, which says Pyrrhus was his original name; Neoptolemus means 'young warrior'). His cult at Delphi is a historical fact, but it practically dates from the Gaulish invasion, according to Pausanias (1. 4. 4); earlier than that his tomb had been held in no honour, but it was thought that he had been seen fighting alongside the Hyperborean heroes against the attackers.

See the larger dictionaries s.v.; Farnell, *Hero-Cults*, 311 ff. H. J. R.

NEOPTOLEMUS (2) of Parium (3rd c. B.C.; earlier than Aristophanes of Byzantium, probably later than Eratosthenes), Greek writer. His works included poems (Διονυσιάς, Τριχθονία), literary criticism (Π. ἐπιγραμμάτων,

Π. ἀστεϊσμῶν, and a *Poetic*), and a treatise *Π. γλωσσῶν Ὁμήρου*, on the strength of which he was dubbed *γλωσσογράφος*. In the *Poetic*, largely drawn upon, according to Porphyry, by Horace for his *Ars Poetica*, N. defined the aim of poetry as *τέρπειν τε καὶ ὠφελεῖν*. He seems to have followed the tradition of the earlier Peripatos, without being exactly a Peripatetic. *See also* GLOSS, GREEK; LITERARY CRITICISM, GREEK, para. 4.

A. Rostagni, *Arte poetica di Orazio* (1930); *PW* xvi. 2. 2465–70.
J. D. D.

NEOPYTHAGOREANISM, the revived Pythagorean school, or rather direction of thought, which appeared at Rome and Alexandria in the first century B.C. and persisted until it was merged in Neoplatonism. It combined in varying proportions a small amount of early Pythagorean tradition with elements derived from Platonic, Peripatetic, and Stoic sources, the whole being accommodated to contemporary religious tendencies. Neopythagorean writers appear to have been interested mainly in theological speculation, in the symbolism of numbers, and in glorifying Pythagoras as the founder of a way of life and author of a religious revelation. There is little trace of a systematic body of philosophical doctrine held in common by them: some of them were Stoicizing monists, others Platonizing dualists. The historical importance of Neopythagoreanism lies chiefly in the influence which it exercised (*a*) on Neoplatonism, especially in the post-Plotinian period; (*b*) on Jewish thought through Philo and Christian thought through Clement of Alexandria. For individual Neopythagoreans *see* NIGIDIUS FIGULUS, APOLLONIUS (14) OF TYANA, NUMENIUS.

(*a*) Ancient sources: Alexander Polyhistor (*c.* 80 B.C.) ap. Diog. Laert. 8. 24 ff. (cf. M. Wellmann, *Hermes* 1919); two accounts in Sext. Emp. 10. 261 ff. (Platonizing), 281 ff. (Stoicizing); Photius *cod.* 249 (cf. O. Immisch, *Sitz. Heid. Ak.* 1919); 'Ocellus Lucanus', ed. R. Harder with Germ. comm. (1926); fragms. of Nigidius, A. Swoboda (1889); of Numenius, E. A. Leemans (1937); of other Neopythagoreans, Mullach, *Fragm. Phil. Graec.* (*b*) Modern discussion: Zeller iii. 2⁴; A. Schmekel, *Philosophie der mittleren Stoa* (1892), 403 ff.; A. Delatte, *Études sur la littérature pythagoricienne* (1915); F. Cumont, *Recherches sur le symbolisme funéraire des Romains* (1942).
E. R. D.

NEOTERICI, οἱ νεώτεροι (Cic. *Att.* 7. 2. 1), 'poetae noui' (Cic. *Orat.* 161), 'cantores Euphorionis' (Cic. *Tusc.* 3. 19. 45), a coterie of younger poets, who, eschewing Ennius, turned to Alexandria, especially to Euphorion of Chalcis, for their models of *epyllia* and amatory or satirical epigrams and elegies. Catullus to some extent (64; 66) followed the movement; thus his *Peleus and Thetis* has an immoderate use of the σπονδειάζοντες which Cicero (*Att.* 7. 2. 1, Nov. 50 B.C.) parodies in his 'flauit ab Epiro lenissimus Onchesmites'. 'Cantores E.' is not well rendered by 'warblers of Euphorion': it suggests tiresome reiteration of Alexandrian characteristics. The 'summus grammaticus', Valerius Cato, led the coterie. Other members were Cinna, who accompanied Catullus to Bithynia and took nine years for his epyllion *Zmyrna*, Calvus, Catullus' close friend, better known as an orator, Furius Bibaculus, like Catullus anti-Caesarian, and Ticidas, a Caesarian, as was Cinna, if identical with the tribune who met a tragic end in 44 B.C. Cornelius Gallus (q.v. 3) also belongs to the group. In Ovid's list (*Tr.* 2. 427–38) other names occur too shadowy to mention. By Ovid's time the fame of Virgil and Horace had almost consigned the Neoterics to oblivion, and Horace expresses contempt for them (*Sat.* 2. 5. 41; cf. Mart. 10. 21. 4). In youth, Asinius Pollio had relations with them: Cinna wrote him a *Propempticon*.

There were later 'neoterici' in Hadrian's age. *See* ALEXANDRIANISM, LATIN.
G. C. R.

NEPOS, *see* CORNELIUS (2), METELLUS (10), PLATORIUS.

NEPTUNUS, Italian god of water (not of the sea, though his identification with Poseidon, q.v., extended his cult in this direction; it was then purely Greek in form, the *exta* being thrown raw into the sea, Livy 29. 27. 5; it is in virtue of this capacity that the absurd identification of Consus with 'Neptunus Equester', i.e. Poseidon Hippios, takes place, Livy 1. 9. 6). The etymology of his name is quite uncertain; in Etruscan it is Neθun(u)s. His festival is of the oldest series (Neptunalia, 23 July); we know concerning its ritual only that arbours, *umbrae*, of boughs were commonly erected (Festus, p. 519, 1 Lindsay), but it may be conjectured that its object was to obtain sufficient water at this hot and dry time of year. His cult-partner is Salacia (Gellius 13. 23. 2); she may be the goddess of 'leaping', i.e., springing water (*salire*), but was identified with Amphitrite as he was with Poseidon.

For his temples see Platner–Ashby, p. 360 f. Cf. Wissowa, *RK* 225 ff.; L. Delatte in *Ant. Class.* iv (1935), 45 ff. H. J. R.

NERATIUS PRISCUS, LUCIUS, a considerable Roman jurist of the age of Trajan and Hadrian; born at Saepinum in Samnium. He was *praefectus aerarii Saturni*, suffect consul (under Domitian), *legatus Augusti pro praetore* of Pannonia. Trajan estimated him highly and even wished to make him his successor (but *see under* HADRIAN). Neratius was together with Celsus the last head of the School of Proculians. He is the author of some important publications freely excerpted by his successors: *Membranae* (which illustrate well his penetration as a jurist); *Regulae*; *Epistulae*; and a dissertation *De nuptiis*.
PIR¹, N 46. A. B. & C. H. V. S

NEREUS, an old sea god, son of Pontus and father by the Oceanid Doris of the Nereids. He lives with the Nereids in the depths of the sea (*Il.* 1. 358; Hes. *Th.* 233 ff.), particularly in the Aegean Sea (Ap. Rhod. 4. 771 f.). Hesiod and Pindar extol his righteousness. To give fair praise to an enemy's achievement is quoted as an advice of a sea god, presumably N., by Pindar (*Pyth.* 9. 94). Like other 'Old Men of the Sea' N. has great wisdom and even the gift of prophecy (Hor. *Carm.* 1. 15). These abilities bring him into a strenuous contest with Heracles. Bacchylides and Pherecydes relate that Heracles had to catch Nereus unawares in order to learn the whereabouts of the Golden Apples. Panyassis (Ath. 11. 469 d) makes N. give the cup of the Sun to Heracles. When Peleus wrestles with Thetis, N., his future father-in-law, looks on. Later N. attends the wedding of Peleus (François Vase) and brings presents. In his contest with Heracles N. transforms himself into fire, water, and many other shapes (Apollod. 2. 5. 11). In addition to his fifty or hundred daughters, the Nereids, he is said by Lucian (*Trag.* 87) to have educated Aphrodite. It is uncertain whether a small cult in Gythium belonged to N. or to some other sea god (Paus. 3. 21. 9). The earliest representations of N. in art go back to the early sixth century B.C. In an Athenian pediment and on vases he watched Heracles fight Triton. As a dignified spectator N. is a great favourite with vase-painters, but sometimes he is also shown wrestling with Heracles. Only the inscription referring to N. survives on the famous Hellenistic frieze of Pergamum.

Pindar, *Pyth.* 9; *FGrH* i. 65 (Pherecydes); L. Bloch in Roscher, *Lex.* s.v.; E. Buschor, *Ath. Mitt.* 1921/2, 56. G. M. A. H.

NERIO, *see* BELLONA.

NERO (1) (NERO CLAUDIUS CAESAR), Roman emperor A.D. 54–68, was born in 37 of Cn. Domitius Ahenobarbus (*cos.* A.D. 32) and the younger Agrippina (q.v.). For the circumstances of his accession *see* CLAUDIUS (1).

2. To strengthen his doubtful claim stories were spread of his miraculous childhood (Suet. *Nero*, 6; Tac. *Ann.* 11. 11), and stress laid on his descent from the divine Augustus. In his inaugural speech he promised

to rule 'ex praescripto Augusti' (Tac. *Ann.* 13. 4). He showed modesty by declining an honour with the phrase 'cum meruero', *pietas* by consecrating Claudius and by gratitude to Agrippina ('optima mater'), and clemency by his unwillingness to sign a death-warrant—'quam uellem nescire litteras'. His enthusiasm for art made flatterers hail him as Apollo.

3. Between artistic son and imperious mother trouble was likely: Otho (q.v.) encouraged Nero to free himself. Agrippina retorted by sympathy for the dispossessed Britannicus (q.v.): Britannicus was poisoned (55), and Agrippina went into retirement. Poppaea (q.v.), Otho's ambitious wife, wishing to marry Nero, planned to eliminate both Agrippina and Nero's wife Octavia. Though Nero preferred literary pursuits or amusement, there was some good legislation (Tac. *Ann.* 13. 51) and able governors—Galba, Suetonius Paulinus, Vespasian, and Corbulo—were sent to the provinces: here the credit should probably be ascribed to Seneca and Burrus (q.v.), the Prefect of the Praetorians, who apparently controlled serious policy.

4. But Nero soon became his own master. In 59 he had Agrippina murdered, while the death of Burrus (who was replaced by two Prefects, Tigellinus and Faenius Rufus) and the retirement of Seneca (62) left him uncontrolled. Octavia was divorced and murdered. Now Poppaea could marry Nero: in 63 she bore him a daughter who lived three months.

5. Nero's emancipation meant free rein for his artistic passions. His enthusiasm for art and horsemanship seem genuine enough; he wanted to lead Rome from gladiatorial shows to humaner things. He founded games: the *Juvenalia* (59), where nobles were encouraged to compete, and the *Neronia* (61); he opened a *gymnasium*, and distributed free oil to competitors 'Graeca facilitate'. He eagerly displayed his own powers in public, to the scandal of traditionalists. His voice, 'exigua et fusca' (Suet. *Nero*, 20), hailed by his admirers as divine, may have been passable; his poetry, modernistic and laborious, was probably his own, for Suetonius had seen his note-books with their erasures (ibid. 52). At Naples his *première* brought thunderous applause from trained Greek bands; Greeks alone deserved to hear him, and he resolved on a Greek tour.

6. Meanwhile his extravagance, vanity, and fear, coupled with sense of power—'negauit quemquam principum scisse quid sibi liceret' (ibid. 37), made him unpopular. His helpers and associates were low-born, or Greek and Oriental freedmen, avaricious and arrogant. The expense of wars in Britain and Armenia compelled him to depreciate the coinage and rob the rich. The law of *maiestas* (q.v.) was revived (62); wealthy nobles, Faustus Sulla, Rubellius Plautus, and Torquatus Silanus, were executed on suspicion. A fire that ruined one-half of Rome (64) increased his unpopularity, as he seized the opportunity to build himself the colossal *Domus Aurea* (q.v.); rumours circulated that he had instigated the fire, and recited his own poems over the burning city, and Nero tried to make the Christians scapegoats (*see* PERSECUTIONS). By the end of 64 all classes had good reason to hate or fear him.

7. Hence a conspiracy to assassinate Nero and make C. Calpurnius Piso (q.v. 9) emperor. The scheme was betrayed (65); Piso and his accomplices, Faenius Rufus, Seneca, Lucan, knights, tribunes, and soldiers were executed. But Nero now suspected all, and after Poppaea's death (66) more judicial murders followed, including Ostorius Scapula, C. Petronius, *arbiter elegantiae*, and the Stoics Paetus Thrasea and Barea Soranus. In 66 Tiridates, kneeling, received the diadem of Armenia from him, but a Jewish revolt forced him to send Mucianus to govern Syria and Vespasian to pacify Judaea. During 67 he actually left a freedman, Helius, to govern Rome, while he competed in the great Greek games, invincibly; in

gratitude he proclaimed 'Freedom for Greece' at Corinth: 'Other emperors have freed cities, Nero alone a whole province' (*SIG* iii. 814). Yet amid this buffoonery he ordered the successful general Corbulo and two popular governors of Germany, the 'fratres Scribonii', to commit suicide (Dio 63. 17).

8. It was the last straw: in spring 68 C. Julius Vindex (q.v.), governor of Lugdunensis, rose against Nero; Galba in Spain declared himself 'legatus S.P.Q.R.', and in Africa Clodius Macer revolted. The situation might have been saved by military action, but Nero could only conceive fantastic schemes of revenge or of reducing his enemies to penitent tears by his art (Suet. *Nero* 43). The Praetorians, bribed to acclaim Galba, deserted Nero, who fled from Rome and on 9 June 68 committed suicide.

9. A vicious ancestry and repressed childhood, followed by absolute power, made Nero vain, egotistic, and assertive. Yet his devotion to art was real. Some good he achieved, yet mainly where (as in the solution of the Armenian problem, or the rebuilding of Rome with wider streets) it was grandiose and involved glorification of himself. Jealous fear of all eminence—noble, military, or literary—forced him to persecution and murder; his crimes alienated all, nobles, people, and soldiery, while his phil-Hellenic outlook and theatrical performances shocked Roman sentiment. Greek longing for him is reflected in the mysterious belief that he would 'return'; for the rest the tribune's verdict holds good—'odisse coepi, postquam parricida matris et uxoris, auriga et histrio et incendiarius extitisti' (*Ann.* 15. 67).

BIBLIOGRAPHY

ANCIENT SOURCES: Tacitus, *Ann.* 13-16, supplemented by Suetonius, *Nero*, and Dio Cassius 61-3. Three speeches and letters of Nero are published in M. P. Charlesworth, *Documents illustrating the reigns of Claudius and Nero* (1939).

MODERN LITERATURE: Analysis of sources: E. Ciaceri, 'Claudio e Nerone nelle storie di Plinio', in *Processi Politici* (Rome, 1918), and A. Momigliano, 'Osservazioni sulle fonti per la storia di Caligola, Claudio, Nerone', *Rend. Linc.* 1932, 293. Works on Nero: *CAH* x. 702-42; B. W. Henderson, *The Life and Principate of the Emperor Nero* (1903); A. Boethius, 'The Neronian "nova urbs"', in *Corolla Archeologica* 1932; Ph. Fabia, *Néron acteur* (1906); C. Pascal, *Nerone nella storia aneddotica e nella legenda* (1923); G. Schumann, *Hellenistische und griechische Elemente in der Regierung Neros* (1930). M. P. C.

NERO (2), GAIUS CLAUDIUS (*cos.* 207 B.C.), after serving under Marcellus in 214 B.C., took part in the siege of Capua as praetor (212) and propraetor (211). After the defeat of the elder Scipios he was sent to Spain, where he secured the land north of the Ebro (210). He again served under Marcellus in Italy (209). As consul in 207 with his former enemy M. Livius Salinator (q.v.) he took up his command against Hannibal in south Italy. When Hasdrubal's dispatches to Hannibal were intercepted, Nero boldly led part of his army by forced marches (traditionally 240 miles in six days) to join Livius. At the battle of Metaurus the two consuls defeated Hasdrubal, Nero turning the tide of battle by a skilful tactical movement. Nero reported his victory to Hannibal by flinging Hasdrubal's head into his camp. When Nero held the censorship with Livius in 204 the old enmity was renewed. He probably served on the embassy which delivered the Senate's ultimatum to Philip in 200. H. H. S.

NERO (3), TIBERIUS CLAUDIUS, father of Tiberius and Drusus (q.v. 3), commanded Caesar's fleet as quaestor in the Alexandrine War, conducted colonies to Gallia Narbonensis, and was praetor in 42 or 41 B.C. He supported L. Antonius in the Perusine War, attempted to foment an insurrection in Campania, and escaped with his wife Livia and infant son. Reinstated by the Treaty of Misenum, he divorced Livia to enable Octavian to marry her. He died *c.* 33 B.C.

B Alex. 25; Velleius 2. 75-9; Suetonius, *Tib.* 4-6; Dio Cassius 44. 40; 48. 15 and 44. G. W. R.

NERO (4), JULIUS CAESAR, the eldest of the three surviving sons of Germanicus and Agrippina, was, after the death of Tiberius' son Drusus in A.D. 23, at the age of seventeen, next in succession to the Principate. Twice commended to the Senate by Tiberius, he held the quaestorship, probably in 26, but in 29 Tiberius, believing the accusations of Sejanus against him and his mother, denounced him in a dispatch to the Senate. He was deported to Pontia and put to death there in 31.

J. P. B.

NERVA (1) (MARCUS COCCEIUS NERVA), Roman emperor (A.D. 96–8), grandson of M. Cocceius Nerva (q.v. 3), was born at Narnia, probably A.D. 30, on 8 November. He was praetor designate in 65, receiving *ornamenta triumphalia* on the suppression of the Pisonian conspiracy. Not discredited by his friendship with Nero (who admired his verses), he was *consul ordinarius* in 71 (with Vespasian), and again (being by now a lawyer of distinction) in 90, with Domitian. The report of his temporary exile in Domitian's last years may be doubted.

On Domitian's death (16 Sept. 96) he was proclaimed emperor (and *Pater Patriae*) by a Senate which regarded him as the pattern of its ideals—nobly born, eloquent, peaceful, just, a guardian of the constitution. But Nerva lacked administrative experience and capacity to command, particularly in face of a soldiery angered at Domitian's murder. General opinion, however, reacted violently: Domitian's memory was damned, his *acta* were annulled, his statues destroyed; and informers were attacked. Nerva failed to check the spirit of vendetta, itself encouraged by his own 'reformist' programme, which abolished treason-charges and was reflected in such coin-legends as *Libertas Publica, Salus, Aequitas, Iustitia*. Above all, he lacked military support (hence the wishful *Concordia Exercituum* coins; unrest in the frontier armies was disturbing (cf. Plin. *Ep.* 9. 13. 11; Philostratus, *VS* 1. 7. 1) and the opposition of the Praetorians dangerous. The latter in 97 disregarded Nerva's refusal to surrender Domitian's assassins. His prestige ruined, himself childless and infirm, he formally adopted Trajan (q.v.), giving him full powers (autumn 97). On 25 Jan. 98 he died, after 16 months of morally blameless rule; he was consecrated, and his ashes were placed in Augustus' Mausoleum.

Nerva's administration, if hampered by financial difficulties, was enlightened and progressive, though it chiefly favoured Rome and Italy. Most important was the 60 million sesterces spent on land-allotments for poor citizens and the system of poor relief (see ALIMENTA). The cost of postal services in Italy was taken over by the government. In Rome granaries were built; the system of corn-distribution and the aqueducts (q.v.) received attention. Legislation was just and humanitarian. Foreign policy was uneventful, being disturbed only by a brief Suebic war (Plin. *Pan.* 8; cf. *ILS* 2720).

With the pendulum swinging sharply back from autocracy to constitutionalism, *libertas* and *principatus* ('res olim dissociabiles') were reconciled, and Rome could recapture the ideals of government, vindicate the right of free speech, and recognize the principle of dynastic adoption. Nerva's short reign, narrow though its imperialism was, was in many ways wise and beneficial. But without military support Nerva could not uphold the complex burden of power—'imperium ruens super imperatorem'. 'Prouidentia Senatus' required 'Concordia Exercituum' for its fulfilment.

BIBLIOGRAPHY

ANCIENT SOURCES: 1. Literary: Dio Cassius, 67–8; Pliny, *Pan., Ep.*; references in Suetonius, *Dom.*, Eutropius, bk. 8, Aurelius Victor, *Caes.* 12–13, *Epit.* 12.
2. Inscriptions: see A. Stein, *PW*, s.v. 'Cocceius (16)'; *PIR²*, C 1227.
3. Coins: H. Mattingly, *B.M. Coins, Rom. Emp.* iii 1936);

H. Mattingly and E. A. Sydenham, *The Roman Imperial Coinage* ii (1930); A. Merlin, *Les Revers monétaires de l'empereur Nerva* (1906); and W. Kubitschek in *Anz. d. Akad. d. Wissensch. in Wien* lxx (1933), 4 ff.
MODERN LITERATURE: A. Stein, *PW*, loc. cit.; R. P. Longden, *CAH* xi, ch. 5; B. W. Henderson, *Five Roman Emperors* (1927), ch. 8; R. Paribeni, *Optimus Princeps* i (1926), ch. 5. On finance see R. Syme, *JRS* 1930, 55 ff.; C. H. V. Sutherland, *JRS* 1935, 150 ff.
C. H. V. S.

NERVA (2), LUCIUS COCCEIUS, was sent by Octavian to Antony (in Syria) in 41 B.C., returned with him in 40, and helped to negotiate the treaty of Brundisium. In 38 (or 37) he accompanied Maecenas on another diplomatic mission to Antony.

Horace, *Sat.* 1. 5; Appian, *BCiv.* 5. 60–4. G. W. R.

NERVA (3), MARCUS COCCEIUS, lawyer, grandfather of the Emperor Nerva and friend of Tiberius, was *consul suff., curator aquarum* (A.D. 24), and committed suicide at Capri (33). As Labeo's pupil he greatly contributed to the formation of the Proculian school (see SABINUS 2).

O. Lenel, *Palingenesia Juris Civilis* i (1889), 787; C. Arno, *Tijdschrift v. Rechtsgesch.* iv (1922), 210. A. M.

NERVII, a mixed Celto-German tribe, occupying parts of Hainault and Flanders. They were defeated by Caesar after a desperate struggle (57 B.C.). Under the Empire the capital (Bagacum, mod. *Bavay*) became an important centre, and Nervian merchants traded in the Rhineland. Pottery works and numerous villas attest prosperity. The Nervii contributed six auxiliary cohorts to the army.

Caesar, *BGall.* 2. 15–28; T. Rice Holmes, *Caesar's Conquest of Gaul²* (1911), 456–8, 671–7; C. Jullian, *Hist. de la Gaule* (1908–26) v. 462–4; pro *Nervia*, 1922– . C. E. S.

NESIOTES, *see* CRITIUS.

NESSUS, *see* CENTAURS.

NESTOR (1) (Νέστωρ), in mythology, surviving son of Neleus (q.v.), who lived to a great age (he is more than two generations old in *Iliad* 1. 250 ff., i.e. over sixty, schol. ad loc., not two hundred odd years, as Ovid, *Met.* 12. 187 f., makes him), retaining some mental vigour and bodily strength long after his youth was passed. The *Iliad* gives a humorous, kindly portrait of an old and respected but rather ineffective man, full of advice generally either platitudinous or unsuccessful, the really useful counsellors being Odysseus and at times Diomedes (qq.v.). His tactics are archaic (*Il.* 4. 301 ff., cf. Lang, *World of Homer*, p. 58); he loads the embassy to Achilles with suggestions (9. 179), and when it fails has nothing more to say, except 10. 204 ff., where he advises sending a scout to discover what the Trojans are doing. He is very fond of long narratives of his early successes in war (as 11. 670 ff.) or sport (23. 626 ff.); a particularly delightful touch is his long speech of advice to his son Antilochus (23. 306 ff.), which he himself admits the younger man does not need. In the *Odyssey* he is safe at home in Pylos (3. 4 ff.), and there entertains Telemachus (q.v.). For the death of his son *see* ANTILOCHUS. His return was due to his realization that things were being ill-conducted after the fall of Troy and disaster impended (*Od.* 3. 165 ff.); at Achilles' funeral he stops the panic of the Greeks at the wailing of Thetis and her attendants (24. 50 ff.). Later works do no more than add details; it is he who settles the dispute over the arms of Achilles by suggesting that Trojan prisoners should be asked whether Aias or Odysseus was more to be dreaded (Quint. Smyrn. 5. 157, cf. 318; cf. schol. *Od.* 11. 547). So far as we know, there was no tradition of when or how he died; his grave was shown in Pausanias' day (Paus. 5. 36. 2).

H. J. R.

NESTOR (2) of Laranda, lived in the reign of Septimius Severus (A.D. 193–211), and wrote, among other works, an Ἰλιὰς λειπογράμματος, in each of the twenty-four books of which one letter of the alphabet did not appear, and Μεταμορφώσεις (*Anth. Pal.* 9. 129, 364). His son was the epic poet Peisander (q.v. 3) of Laranda.

PW xvii. 125–6. J. D. D.

NEXUM, a transaction of the oldest Roman law, was presumably a form of loan, contracted solemnly with copper and scales (*per aes et libram*), in presence of five witnesses and *libripens* carrying the scales. Because of the ambiguity of our literary sources (Varro, Livy), the nature and effects of this institution are obscure. It remains doubtful whether *nexum* resulted in immediate execution (without judgement) against the debtor, if he did not repay at the appointed term, or whether it was a kind of self-sale (*mancipatio*) or self-pledge by which the debtor enslaved himself to the creditor to guarantee him the payment of the debt. *Nexum* is mentioned in the XII Tables, but it fell out of use when *Lex Poetelia Papiria* (c. 326 B.C.) prohibited bondage and enchainment for private debts.

F. de Zulueta, *Law Quarterly Review* xxix (1913); H. Lévy-Bruhl, *Quelques problèmes du très ancien droit romain* (1934); R. Düll, *PW*, s.v. 'Nexum'; A. Berger, ibid. (Suppl. vol. vii), s.v. 'Lex Poetelia Papiria'. A. B.

NICAENETUS (probably second half of 3rd c. B.C.), of Samos or Abdera (perhaps born at Abdera but migrated early in life to Samos). Athenaeus in quoting from N.'s *Epigrams* calls him 'the Epic Poet' and refers to his treatment in various works of Samian history. N. also wrote a *Catalogue of Women* (Ath. 13. 590 b), and an epyllion called *Lyrkus* (Parth. 1), describing the adventures of that hero. The most attractive of the epigrams is that preserved by Athenaeus (15. 673 b), an invitation to a picnic at Hera's temple in Samos. *Anth. Pal.* 6. 225 is probably a literary reminiscence of Callimachus (fr. 126) and Apollonius Rhodius (*Argon.* 4. 1309, 1323, 1358).

Texts: J. U. Powell, *Coll. Alex.* (1925), 1–4. General literature: E. Diehl, 'Nikainetos (2)', in *PW* xvii. 245–6. E. A. B.

NICANDER, of Colophon. N. describes himself as 'reared by the snowy burg of Clarus' (*Ther.* 958), and as 'seated by the Clarian tripods of the Far-Shooter' (*Alex.* 11), and was apparently hereditary priest of Apollo of Clarus (*Vita*, citing Dionysius of Phaselis). His date is variously given. The confusion may be due in part to the existence of another Nicander, son of Anaxagoras, mentioned as an epic poet in an inscription of Delphi (*SIG* 452), which is best assigned to 258. The internal evidence of the two extant poems favours a date in the second century.

2. WORKS. Two didactic poems in hexameters, the *Theriaca* and *Alexipharmaca*, survive complete. The first is an account of various snakes and other poisonous creatures and the best remedies for their bites. The second enumerates vegetable, mineral, and animal poisons and their antidotes. The matter of both poems is taken from the prose-treatise of Apollodorus the Iologus (early 3rd c.). *Thebaica, Oetaica, Europia* (?), *Sicelia, Cimmerii* were all apparently Epics. Better known is the *Heteroioumena* (Metamorphoses), since it was used by Antoninus Liberalis and Ovid. The *Georgica*, on which Cicero (*De Or.* 1. 69) cites a flattering opinion of the *docti*, had some influence on Virgil. So perhaps had his *Melissurgica* (*On Apiculture*). More in the vein of the two extant poems were the *Prognostica* and *Collection of Cures*. The former was a versification of the (pseudo-) Hippocratean treatise on this subject (Suidas). All the above seem to have been in hexameters, but the *Ophiaca* (schol. *Ther.* 377), which recounted legends connected with snakes, was probably in elegiacs, cf. frs. 31–2, as also was perhaps a poem on Hunting (frs. 97–100). Of

three other works, *Aetolica, Colophoniaca*, and *About Poets* or *About Poets from Colophon*, it is not established whether they were in prose or verse. A collection of Glosses and a treatise on Temple Utensils were certainly in prose.

3. Suidas describes N. as 'grammarian, poet, and doctor'. The last is probably a false inference from the nature of many of his writings, but the order of the first two is significant. As Suidas later puts it, N. was a *metaphrastes*, i.e. converter into verse, of any topic that came to hand, whether a medical dissertation or a collection of *paradoxa*. To judge by the *Theriaca* and *Alexipharmaca*, N. had little gift and, indeed, little inclination for enlivening his arid themes with flights into real poetry. Digressions are few and similes almost non-existent. But neither was N. a scientist. He took over from his sources the bad with the good and thus we find in his poems absurd errors due to popular superstition alongside exact descriptions of plants and medical prescriptions so detailed and precise that the remedy could be made up to-day. But a grammarian of a sort N. undoubtedly was. He describes himself (*Ther.* 957) as *Homereius* and he can at least claim the title as being one of the most diligent seekers after Homeric glosses among the Alexandrians. Like Euphorion and the author of the *Alexandra* he has no scruples about altering the meanings of words nor about playing fast and loose with normal grammar. In metre his handling of the hexameter conforms in general to the rules laid down by Callimachus.

4. N. was read and cited by a certain number of later writers on the subjects with which he had dealt, but he received more attention from professional scholars drawn to him by the obscurity of his language and style. Theon wrote a *hypomnema* on him, as did Plutarch, and the names of other students are mentioned in the Scholia. The result is that the latter, especially those on the *Theriaca*, often contain valuable material.

Texts: O. Schneider, *Nicandrea* (1856). General literature: W. Kroll, 'Nikandros' (10) and (11) in *PW* xvii. 250–65. E. A. B.

NICANOR (1) of Stagirus (c. 360 (?)–317 B.C.), perhaps shared with Alexander the tuition of Aristotle, whose daughter he married. He may have commanded Alexander's Greek fleet, but he is first identified for certain in 324, when he brought to Greece several rescripts of Alexander, including the decree for the return of exiles. In 319 he commanded Cassander's garrison at Munychia, and from this position he soon secured the Piraeus also. He next commanded Cassander's fleet and defeated Cleitus (q.v. 2) near the Bosphorus (318); but he quarrelled with Cassander, who had him condemned to death for treason by the Macedonian army-assembly. G. T. G.

NICANOR (2) of Alexandria (2nd c. A.D.), wrote on the punctuation of the *Iliad*, of the *Odyssey*, and of Callimachus; also a general work Περὶ στιγμῆς. He recognized three kinds of full stop, three of the comma, and two of the colon. In punctuation he dominates the Homeric scholia as Herodian does in accentuation, Aristonicus in Aristarchan textual criticism, and Didymus in erudition.

Fragments: Ἰλ. στιγμῆς, Friedlaender (1850); Π. Ὀδ. στ., Carnuth (1875). P. B. R. F.

NICANOR, *see also* SAEVIUS.

NICARCHUS, one of the sourest of Greek epigrammatists, lived at Alexandria; to judge from close resemblances in tone and themes, he was nearly contemporary with the epigrammatist Lucillius (*fl.* A.D. 55–85). The *Anthology* contains some forty of his jesting epigrams: the edge of their humour is blunted by roughness and dirt.

P. Sakolowski, *de Anth. Pal. quaestiones* (1893); F. Brecht, *Philol.* suppl. xxii (1930). G. H.

NICETA OF REMESIANA (*Bela Palanka*, Old Serbia), *c.* A.D. 400, missionary bishop to the Goths and friend of Paulinus (q.v.) of Nola, wrote *De Psalmodiae Bono*, *De Vigiliis*, and other works, above all the great Church hymn, *Te Deum laudamus*.

A. E. Burn, *Niceta of R. Life and Works* (1905). Authorship of *Te Deum*: cf. G. Morin, *Revue Bénédictine* 1894, 49 ff.   A. S.

NICIAS (1) (*c.* 470–413 B.C.), Athenian politician and general. Though very wealthy, he was not an oligarch, but led a moderate democratic party which, composed of landowners and peasants, aimed at peace with Sparta on favourable terms and abhorred the aggression of Cleon and the war-party. He frequently held the *strategia* and conducted expeditions competently, if with little enterprise. He was largely responsible for the armistice concluded in 423, and the Peace of 421 appropriately bears his name.

His schemes for cautious retrenchment were shattered by Alcibiades (q.v.), who involved Athens in the Peloponnesian movement against Sparta in 420–418 and later advocated an expedition to Sicily. Despite his disapproval Nicias was appointed with Alcibiades and Lamachus (q.v.) to conduct this enterprise. Alcibiades was soon recalled, and little was accomplished in 415, but in 414 Syracuse was invested and almost reduced to capitulation. The death of Lamachus, the arrival of the Spartan Gylippus, and the inactivity of Nicias, now seriously ill, transformed the situation, and in spite of the efforts of Demosthenes (q.v. 1), who brought reinforcements in 413, the Athenians were themselves blockaded. Nicias, who refused to withdraw by sea until too late, led the vanguard in a desperate attempt to escape by land. His troops were overwhelmed at the river Assinarus, and he was subsequently executed.

Thucydides, bks. 3–7; Plutarch, *Nicias*. A. B. West, *CPhil.* 1924, 124–46 and 201–28; R. Cohen, *Mélanges Glotz* (1932), 227–329; G. Reincke *PW*, s.v. 'Nikias'.   H. D. W.

NICIAS (2), painter, pupil of Antidotus (pupil of Euphranor), Athenian. Pliny dates 332 B.C. He painted statues for Praxiteles (about 340) and refused to sell a picture to Ptolemy (after 306). His works included Nemea (signed as encaustic), Necyomantea (after *Iliad* bk. 11), Alexander, Io, Andromeda. The Io and Andromeda are reflected in versions in Pompeii and Rome (Pfuhl, 646–7) which have a similar colour scheme to the fourth-century Alexander sarcophagus (Winter, *KB* 336–7). He advised the choice of large subjects such as cavalry and sea battles (contrast Pausias, q.v.). His treatment of light and shade made his figures stand out. According to Rumpf, 'diligentissime mulieres pinxit' means that he was the first to represent women plastically; monumental evidence supports this.

Overbeck, 1109, 1726, 1810–26; Pfuhl, 821; A. Rumpf, *JDAI* 1934, 6.   T. B. L. W.

NICIAS (3) of Nicaea, author of philosophic διαδοχαί ('successions' of philosophers), which have been thought to be the basis of Diogenes Laertius' work.

NICOCHARES, one of the later Old Comedy writers; an Athenian, son of the comic poet Philonides. Most of his plays may with confidence be attributed to the fourth century. Suidas mentions ten plays. Of these all except Λάκωνες and Κρῆτες seem to have been mythological burlesques.

FCG ii.842 ff.; *CAF* i.700–4; Demiańczuk, *Supp. Com.*, 64–6. M.P.

NICOLAUS OF DAMASCUS, born of distinguished Greek family about 64 B.C. and liberally educated, became the adviser and court historian of Herod the Great, perhaps before 20 B.C., certainly from 14 to 4 B.C., accompanying him twice to Rome. Returning to private life after Herod's death, he re-emerged to represent Herod Archelaus in Rome, but did not resume court life.

Besides dramatic composition (tragedies and comedies) and writings on philosophy and natural science of a Peripatetic character, he published an autobiography, a panegyrical biography of Augustus' youth, and a Universal History in 144 books from the earliest times to the death of Herod the Great. It reached the Persian Empire in seven books (preserved in excerpts), treated the Mithridatic Wars in bks. 96–110, and with bks. 123–24, preserved in Josephus' *Jewish Antiquities* 14–17, came to Herod and described in full contemporary events to 4 B.C.; the introduction to Josephus' *Jewish War* is also based upon this work. The early narrative reproduced ultimately, among others, the tradition of Xanthus, Ctesias, perhaps Dinon and Hellanicus, Ephorus, Posidonius, Caesar; the whole work, the greatest World History since Ephorus, followed the rationalistic, rhetorical Ionic historiography of Ctesias, using also, especially in the dramatic treatment of Herod's family circumstances, the Peripatetic technique which marked his biographical writing.

FGrH ii, A, p. 324; C, p. 229; W. Witte, *De Nicolai Dam. frag. Rom. fontibus* (1900).   A. H. McD.

NICOMACHUS (1), son of Aristotle; to him, according to an ancient account, Aristotle dedicated the *Nicomachean Ethics*; but possibly the name is due to his having edited the work, as Eudemus may have edited the *Eudemian Ethics*.

PW xvii. 462.

NICOMACHUS (2), New Comedy poet, whom Suidas confuses with a tragedian of the same name. Fr. 1 describes a cook magnifying his art.

FCG iv. 583 ff.; *CAF* iii. 386 ff.

NICOMACHUS (3) of Gerasa (*c.* A.D. 100), arithmetician, wrote: (1) *Introductio arithmetica*, giving the Pythagorean theory of numbers (classification of numbers, odd, even, prime, etc., 'perfect' and 'friendly' numbers, 'polygonal' and 'pyramidal' numbers, arithmetical and geometrical progressions, means, etc., sum of the series of cube numbers); (2) Ἐγχειρίδιον ἁρμονικῆς, edited by Meibom, 1652; (3) Θεολογούμενα ἀριθμητιχῆς, on mystical properties of numbers. The work under the latter title edited by Ast with the *Introductio* in 1817 is not the original, but contains extracts from it, with others from Speusippus and Anatolius. (2) and (3) can be read in C. Jan, *Musici Scriptores Graeci* (1895). For the *Introductio arithmetica* see Hoche's edition (Teubner, 1866) and the English translation by M. L. D'Ooge with essays by Robbins and Karpinski (New York, MacMillan, 1926).

PW xvii. 500.   T. H.

NICOMEDES, the name of several kings of Bithynia.

(1) NICOMEDES I, son of Zipoetes, succeeded to the kingdom and to his father's war with Antiochus I *c.* 279 B.C. He purchased the help of Heraclea by ceding some Paphlagonian land, and engaged by treaty the Galatian hordes then in Thrace to fight his battles against the Seleucids, assisting them to settle in Phrygia. He founded the city of Nicomedia in 264–262.

(2) NICOMEDES II went on an embassy to Rome, to secure the release of his father Prusias II from war indemnities. Learning that death would be the penalty of failure, he revolted with the aid of Pergamum, drove his father to sanctuary, and ordered his death (149 B.C.). He assisted Rome against Aristonicus in 133–129, but his request for Phrygian territory was refused in favour of Mithridates V of Pontus. He died *c.* 128.

(3) NICOMEDES III EUERGETES, son of the above. His answer to Marius' request for military aid against the Cimbri, that most of his men had been seized by Roman tax-farmers and sold into slavery, led to a senatorial decree to secure their freedom. His attempt to share

Paphlagonia with Mithridates and win Cappadocia by a matrimonial alliance was foiled by Roman intervention. He died in 94. He is sometimes confused with his son of like name, though Appian (*Mith.*) distinguishes three successive kings named Nicomedes.

(4) NICOMEDES IV was ousted from his kingdom by Mithridates in favour of his brother Socrates, but was restored by Rome in 92. Under pressure from his Roman creditors he raided Pontic territory, thus bringing on the First Mithridatic War (88). Restored once more by the Romans in 84, he ruled thereafter in such peace as Roman officials and business men allowed him. He received a visit from young Julius Caesar in 80–79. At his death in 74 he bequeathed his kingdom to Rome.

App. *Mith.*; references in Diodorus and Memnon, *OGI* 340–6; Wilhelm, *JÖAI* xi (1908), 75 ff.; Th. Reinach, *Trois royaumes de l'Asie Mineure* (1888); *Mithridate Eupator* (1890); M. Rostovtzeff, *CAH* ix, ch. 5; H. A. Ormerod, ibid., ch. 8.   T. R. S. B.

NICOMEDES (5), mathematician, probably lived at Pergamum, in the second century B.C.; he was the discoverer of the cochloidal or conchoidal curves, by means of which he solved the problem of trisecting the angle and that of doubling the cube.

PW xvii. 500.

NICOMEDIA (Νικομήδεια) was founded by Nicomedes I *c.* 264 B.C. to replace Astacus (on a more northerly site). It became the capital of the kingdom and of the Roman province of Bithynia. In 29 B.C. Augustus authorized a provincial temple to himself at Nicomedia which became the meeting-place of the provincial assembly. It accumulated titles of honour, and in the third century A.D. was styled 'greatest metropolis, leading city of Bithynia and Pontus, Hadrianic Severianic Nicomedia, twice *neocorus*, sacred asylum, friend and ally of the Roman people'. It suffered from frequent earthquakes, and in 258 was sacked by the Goths; but it received favours from several Roman emperors and became the eastern capital of Diocletian. Its prosperity depended on an extensive and fertile territory, a good harbour, and its location on the trunk road from the Danube provinces to the eastern frontier. Nicomedians appear in almost every province of the Empire. In spite of these advantages Pliny's letters yield evidence of disordered finances and social discontent.

P. Ruge, *PW*, s.v. 'Nikomedeia'; C. Bosch, *Die kleinasiatischen Münzen der römischen Kaiserzeit*, teil II, band i, *Bithynien*.   T. R. S. B.

NICOPHON, Athenian comic poet; much younger than Aristophanes, but won victories in the last decade of fifth century B.C. (*IG* ii². 2325). Suidas mentions Ἐξ Ἅιδου ἀνιών, Ἀφροδίτης γοναί, Πανδώρα, Ἐγχειρογάστορες (? Χειρογάστορες; possibly = 'The Workmen', possibly the Cyclopes), Σειρῆνες (depicting, like many Middle Comedies, the Golden Age).

FCG ii. 848 ff.; *CAF* i. 775–80.   M. P.

NICOPOLIS was the name of several towns with a Greek-speaking population, built to commemorate Roman victories. (1) *Nicopolis of Pontus*, see following article. (2) *Nicopolis ad Istrum*, on the main axial road through Thrace from Philippopolis to the Danube, founded by Trajan after the Dacian Wars. (3) *Nicopolis in Epirus*, on the isthmus of the Bay of Actium. Augustus created this town by sweeping into it the population of the neighbouring Greek communities. It secured much of the former trade of Ambracia and was the scene of the 'ludi Actiaci', a quadrennial festival of equal rank with the Olympian Games, under Spartan stewardship. Its theatre is well preserved.

Strabo 10. 325.   M. C.

NICOPOLIS of Pontus, the site of Pompey's victory in 66 B.C. over Mithridates, where he settled a mixed colony of veterans, wounded, and natives; the scene also

of Pharnaces' victory over Caesar's lieutenant Domitius in 47. Being a strategic point in the system of frontier roads it grew in importance under the Empire, received *ius Italicum*, and finally became the metropolis of Lesser Armenia.

F. Cumont, *Studia Pontica*, ii. 302–30 (1906); H. Grégoire, *BCH*, xxxiii (1909), 31–9; Jones, *Eastern Cities*, pp. 152, 172.   T. R. S. B.

NICOSTRATUS (1), Middle Comedy poet, said to be the son of Aristophanes. Some of the titles known may be of comedies by N. (2). N. (1) mentions the parasite Chaerephon (fr. 25) and the impostor (πλάνος) Cephisodorus (fr. 24): he (or N. (2)) quotes Euripides (fr. 28), but his chief topics are victuals and meals.

FCG iii. 278 ff.; *CAF* ii. 219 ff.; iii. 739; Demiańczuk, *Suppl. Com.*, p. 66.   W. G. W.

NICOSTRATUS (2), New Comedy poet, mentioned in a list of Lenaean victors after Menander, Diphilus, and Philippides, and probably as winner of the second prize in 311 B.C. He is named with Philemon and Ameinias as a comic poet of 280 B.C.

See reference under NICOSTRATUS (1).   W. G. W.

NIGER, *see* VALERIUS (14).

NIGHT, *see* NYX.

NIGIDIUS FIGULUS, PUBLIUS (praetor 58 B.C.), a learned man who wrote comprehensive works on grammar, theology, and various branches of natural science. His love for the abstruse and the exceptional worked against his influence, and he was quite superseded by his contemporary Varro. In politics he was a thorough conservative and an active supporter of Pompey, in philosophy a Pythagorean. A considerable number of fragments of his works have been recovered from later writers, such as Gellius and Servius. Some of these have been collected by A. Riccobonus (Basle, 1579) and others, the latest edition being by A. Swoboda, *P. Nigidii Figuli operum reliquiae* (1889). *See also* SCHOLARSHIP, LATIN.

See Kroll, *PW*, s.v.   A. S.

NIGRINUS, *see* AVIDIUS.

NIKE, the goddess of Victory in Greek religion. N. is first mentioned by Hesiod (*Th.* 383) as daughter of the Titan Pallas and of Styx, and as sister of Zelos, Kratos, and Bia (Rivalry, Strength, and Force). With these she was honoured by Zeus because she fought on the side of the gods against the Titans (q.v.). She is here an abstraction or symbol of decisive victory for the gods. The poets of athletic contests see N. in vivid terms. Bacchylides (11. 1 Kenyon) depicts her standing next to Zeus in Olympus and adjudging the award for 'areta' to gods and men. The victorious athlete sinks into the arms of N. (Pind. *Nem.* 5. 42). Here N. is already victory of an athletic, not only a military, contest. She rules over all contests. She is invoked by the chorus of Aristophanes (*Eq.* 581) and on vases she crowns women of victorious beauty or craftsmen of extraordinary skill.

Statues of Nike begin in the archaic period with the famous N. from Delos. Some scholars have connected this statue with the base inscribed by Archermus, the sculptor who is said to have first represented N. as winged (schol. Ar. *Av.* 374). The Persian Wars resulted in a great popularity of N. The Athenians dedicated her statue in Delphi after the battle of Salamis (Hdt. 8. 121) and she becomes very frequent on vases. She decorates a trophy, writes on the helmet, aids in preparations for the fight, the battle, or the athletic or musical contest, and brings the sacrifice after the victory. She stands on or flies over the chariot of the victorious mortal charioteer (Bacchyl. 3. 5) or serves as charioteer for Heracles on his way to Olympus. The invention of this type of small flying Nike enabled the artists to use her as an attribute. Thus she appeared in Phidias' images of Athena Parthenos and of Zeus of Olympia. These masterpieces are lost as well as the later paintings of Nicomachus and Apelles (Pliny, *HN* 35. 108. 93), but the famous N. by Paeonius found in Olympia, the balustrade of the temple of Athena Nike in Athens (R. Carpenter, *The Sculpture of the Nike Temple Parapet*, U.S.A. 1929), and the Hellenistic N. of Samothrace show the fire and enthusiasm with which Greek artists conceived the goddess.

As befits a race fond of competition the Greeks invoked N. in most flattering terms and she had cults in Olympia (Paus. 5. 14. 8), Ilion, Tralles, and elsewhere. She enjoyed favour with Hellenistic rulers and as Victoria was worshipped by the Romans. As symbol of Victory over death N. was a favourite motif of Roman allegorical art.

Baudrillart, *Les Divinités de la Victoire* (1894); H. Bulle in Roscher, *Lex.*, s.v.   G. M. A. H.

NILE, Egypt's river (explored by ancient Egyptians to the Upper Blue Nile and the confluence of the Bahr-el-Gazal with the White Nile), was known to Homer as 'Aegyptos river', to Hesiod first as Νεῖλος. It was opened to westerners after 665 B.C. Cambyses the Persian (*c.* 525 B.C.) reached the desert south of *Korosko*, but Herodotus knew little beyond Meroë. None knew the cause of summer-time flooding; Aristagoras' conclusion (melting snows) was good guess-work. Ignorant folk believed that the Nile was joined to the Indus, until Alexander's explorations disproved this. False ideas about the flooding continued, though Aristotle guessed correctly. The foundation of Alexandria and Ptolemaic trading up the river and through the Red Sea changed matters. The *White Nile* (Astapous), the Blue Nile, and the sources of the Astaboras (*Atbara*) became known, and flooding by waters from Abyssinian heights was confirmed. According to Juba, the Nile rose in Mt. Atlas and emerged in east Sudan after two journeys underground. Explorers sent by Nero passed the confluence of the *Sobat* with the White Nile, but were blocked by sudd (masses of decayed plants). Later, the Blue Nile was further explored. Lastly, *c.* A.D. 100 a traveller named Diogenes (Ptol. *Geog.* 1. 9. 3–4, etc.) reported from the E. African coast that inland 'Mountains of the Moon', snow-capped, supplied two lakes; from each flowed a stream uniting into the Nile. This vaguely indicates Lakes Victoria and Albert, the Ruwenzori Range, and Mts. Kenya and Kilimanjaro.

Cary–Warmington, *Explorers*, 165 ff.; E. H. Warmington, *Greek Geography* (1934), index.   E. H. W.

NIMBUS, a circular cloud of light which surrounds the heads of gods, emperors (Serv. *Aen.* 2. 616; 3. 587), and heroes. The belief that light radiates from a sacred or divine person is a common one and the nimbus only a special form which was developed in classical religion and art. Assyrian art, for instance, represents some gods with rays around their shoulders (Th. Dombart, *Journ. Soc. Oriental Research Toronto* 1932, 38) and Greek art shows deities of light, such as Helios, with a radiate crown. Greek vases and Etruscan mirrors of the fifth century afford the earliest examples of nimbus, often combined with the crown of rays; under the Roman Empire the nimbus becomes very common. The temple of the Palmyrene gods in Palmyra has an early dated example (A.D. 32). Almost all pagan gods of any importance are occasionally represented with a nimbus in Pompeian wall paintings, African mosaics, and the painting and reliefs of Palmyra and Dura. In late ancient art emperors, consuls, and other dignitaries, and sometimes even portraits of dead commoners have the nimbus. In Christian art only Christ was represented with nimbus at first, but it was soon extended to the Virgin, the major saints, and angels.

Cabrol–Leclercq, *Dict. ant. chrét.* xii. 1272. G. M. A. H.

NINNIUS CRASSUS (? early 1st c. B.C.), author of a translation of the *Iliad*.

Baehr. *FPR* 283; Morel, *FPL* 51.

NIOBE (Νιόβη), in mythology, daughter of Tantalus and wife of Amphion (qq.v.). They had a large family, six sons and six daughters (Homer, *Il.* 24. 604, the oldest mention of her, which seems to imply that the story was already well known and she a stock type of bereavement), or seven of either sex (Ovid, *Met.* 6. 182–3); the number varies in different accounts (see for this and other details Apollod. 3. 45 ff. and Sauer in Roscher's *Lex.*, s.v.). She boasted that she was at least equal to Leto (q.v.), who had borne but two children, Apollo and Artemis. Thereupon the two children of Leto killed all the children of Niobe. According to Homer, Zeus also turned all the people into stone; Niobe lived long enough to eat at least one meal when 'wearied with tear-shedding', and then became a stone which is still on Mt. Sipylon. The gods buried the children on the tenth day. These details, except Niobe's own metamorphosis, do not appear in later accounts. The stone, according to Pausanias (1. 21. 3), was a natural formation looking somewhat like a woman; cf., however, modern opinions in Frazer ad loc. *See* METAMORPHOSIS.

It is fairly evident that the story, the kernel of which must be very old, has been modified in the interests of genealogy. It can hardly be that the daughter of Tantalus of Sipylon was originally married to Amphion of Thebes, of whom Telesilla (ap. Apollod. loc. cit. 47) gets rid again by making him perish with the children. Again for genealogical reasons the pathos is modified by making a son and a daughter survive (ibid. 46 f.).

In art the deaths of the children and the grief of their mother at the sight are a common and favourite subject.

See Roscher's *Lex.*, s.v.   H. J. R.

NIPSUS, *see* JUNIUS (3).

NIREUS (Νιρεύς), in mythology, the commander of a small party (three ships) from Syme (*Iliad* 2. 671 ff.); he was the son of Charops and Aglaia and the handsomest man in the Greek army except Achilles, but a weakling. He was killed by Eurypylus, son of Telephus (Quint. Smyrn. 6. 368 ff.).   H. J. R.

NISUS. (1) Legendary king of Megara, whose life together with the fate of the city depended on a lock of red hair on his head. His daughter Scylla cut this off and betrayed the city to Minos king of Crete who was besieging it, either for a bribe (Aesch. *Cho.* 613–22) or for love of him (Ov. *Met.* 8. 1–151). Nisus was turned into a sea-eagle, Scylla into a bird *ciris** pursued by him. The story is told at length in the pseudo-Vergilian poem *Ciris*. See also Ov. *Met* 8. 6 ff., Strabo 8. 6. 13, Stith Thompson, K 976. Cf. AMPHITRYON.

(2) Son of Hyrtacus, hero of a famous episode in Verg. *Aen.* 9. 176–502; also prominent in the foot-race in 5. 286–361.

(3) Roman grammarian of the second half of the first century, used by Suetonius and Velius Longus; his works are now lost.

*See D'A. W. Thompson, *Gloss. of Gk. Birds*³, s.v.; Hyginus, *Fab.* 198. 4, calls it a fish.   R. A. B. M.

NOMEN LATINUM, *see* LATINI *and* IUS LATII.

NOMENCLATOR, *see* CANDIDATUS.

NOMOPHYLAKES (νομοφύλακες). We are told that this magistracy existed in Athens by 462 B.C., but we hear nothing of its activity—they were possibly archivists. They reappear *c.* 326–323, seven in number, and were of some importance under Demetrius (q.v. 2) Phalereus, as supervisors of magistrates and to some extent controlling meetings of the Boule and Ecclesia, at which they had the right of sitting with the presidents. They disappear with Demetrius.

They are found in many Greek States, including Sparta, in the third and second centuries, but we can say little of their importance. A. W. G.

NOMOS (1) (νομός) was the Greek name for the ancient administrative districts of Egypt; under the Seleucids the term is also found in Palestine, where it was probably introduced by the Ptolemies. The Egyptian *nomoi* probably numbered thirty-six in the third century B.C., but by the third century A.D. had increased to nearly sixty. They were subdivided into toparchies, and these into villages. Each was governed by a στρατηγός, who completely over-shadowed the old native governor (νόμαρχος). He was assisted by many departmental officials. Of these only the royal scribe (βασιλικὸς γραμματεύς) retained any importance under Roman rule. The *nomoi* were abolished *c.* A.D. 300, becoming the territories of the *metropoleis* (q.v.).

H. Gauthier, *Les Nomes d'Égypte depuis Hérodote jusqu'à la conquête arabe* (1935). A. H. M. J.

NOMOS (2). The word νόμος, applied originally to a tune, was applied especially to a type of melody invented by Terpander as a setting for texts taken from the epic (Procl. ap. Phot. *Bibl.* 320 a, 32 ff.). Such νόμοι could be used for the flute or for the lyre. Later the word was used for a choral composition constructed astrophically like Timotheus' *Persae.*

Cf. U. von Wilamowitz-Moellendorff, *Timotheos: Die Perser,* 89 ff. C. M. B.

NOMOTHETAI (νομοθέται). This word had a special use in legislative procedure in Athens in the fourth century. In 403/402 B.C. 500 *nomothetai* were appointed to revise and publish, with the Boule, the fundamental laws of the democracy; and thereafter they played a regular part. Whenever the Ecclesia decided that changes in the law were desirable, the proposed additions or amendments (which any citizen might put forward) were referred to a body of 501 or 1,001 *nomothetai* selected from the dicasts. The procedure of this court, which acted under a time limit, resembled that of a trial in a dicastery. The decision of the majority was final, unless the new law was attacked under the *graphe paranomon* (q.v.), in which case the verdict of the dicastery which tried the case was conclusive.

Nomothetai also pronounced on inconsistencies and irregularities in the law-code submitted to them by the *thesmothetai* (q.v.). A. W. G.

NONIANUS, see SERVILIUS (4).

NONIUS MARCELLUS (early 4th c. A.D.), lexicographer and grammarian. The first twelve books of his *De compendiosa doctrina* (ed.W. M. Lindsay, 3 vols.,1903) deal with points of grammar (e.g. *de numeris et casibus*), bks. 13 to 20 (but bk. 16 is lost) with miscellaneous information (e.g. *de genere nauigiorum*). The material is arranged with more or less strictness in alphabetical order and each topic is illustrated by quotations. The foundation of the work seems to have been Nonius' own excerpting from a range of authors which included many Republican poets. These authors he used in a stereotyped order of his own. In addition he had access to some work like that of Flavius Caper from which he took other citations. For many fragments of early writers, and especially of Varro's poetry, N. is our chief authority.

Cf. Teuffel, § 404a; Schanz–Hosius, § 826; W. M. Lindsay in *CR* xx. 440; and for N.'s sources and methods of citation, F. della Corte, *La Poesia di Varrone ricostituita* (1938). J. F. M.

NONNUS of Panopolis in Egypt (5th c. A.D.), epic poet, author of a *Paraphrase of St. John's Gospel* and a *Dionysiaca*, describing the god's triumphal progress to India, which is valuable for mythological learning, but as poetry very variously judged. His versification, in contrast with the carelessness of some of his predecessors, is accurate, and has been called pedantically precise. It is sometimes influenced by the stress accent of Greek as pronounced in his day, and sometimes it makes forceful use of assonance. *See* EPIC POETRY, GREEK, para. 9.

Texts: A. Scheindler (1881); A. Ludwich (1909, 1911). Text and translation: W. H. D. Rouse, 1940 (Loeb). Criticism: P. Friedländer, *Hermes* xl (1912), 43–59. W. F. J. K.

NORBANUS (1), GAIUS, *tribunus plebis* in 104 B.C., successfully prosecuted Q. Servilius Caepio (q.v. 1). He himself was charged *ob maiestatem minutam* by P. Sulpicius Rufus (prob. *c.* 98), but was defended by M. Antonius and acquitted (Cic. *De Or.* 2. 48, 199–50, 203). He was praetor in Sicily and defeated the remaining Italian rebels in south Italy near Rhegium (88 or 87). A partisan of Marius and consul in 83, he opposed Sulla's return, but was routed by him near Casilinum and blockaded in Capua. In 82 he took command in north Italy, but was defeated by Metellus Pius at Faventia. He fled to Rhodes, where he committed suicide. H. H. S.

NORBANUS (2), A. LAPPIUS MAXIMUS, defeated L. Antonius Saturninus, legate of Upper Germany, who was attempting to raise a rebellion, supported by Germans, against Domitian (A.D. 89). Norbanus was probably legate of Lower Germany. The most probable conjecture would place the battle near Andernach, between Coblenz and Bonn. The four legions of Lower Germany were honoured with the title Pia Fidelis Domitiana, but this may have been merely a reward for rejecting the overtures of Saturninus. Norbanus won great fame for destroying the private papers of Saturninus before Domitian's arrival, thus shielding others who were in the plot from the Emperor's vengeance. Our only other information about Norbanus is that he was twice consul.

CAH xi. 172 ff. R. L. J.

NORICUM, a Roman province in the Alps, south of the Danube, between Raetia and Pannonia. The root of the word is Illyrian, as are pre-Roman finds in the interior and the east. This Illyrian element, however, was celticized from the south (3rd/2nd c. B.C.) and from the Danube (2nd/1st c. B.C.). Though the Celtic Taurisci were the chief tribe, Noricum (apparently derived from the Celtic *Norici* dwelling round *Noreia*, the ancient capital) became in the first part of the second century B.C. the name of the Celtic federal State, which had its own coinage. It was of considerable importance in Caesar's time, as shown by the fact that Caesar accepted aid from Noricum in 49 B.C., and that Ariovistus' second wife was the daughter of the king of Noricum. To secure the northern frontier of Italy, the Taurisci north of the Ocra were made tributary (35 B.C.), and then the kingdom of Noricum was peaceably incorporated into the Roman Empire by P. Silius Nerva, governor of Illyricum (16 B.C. or later). Perhaps for some time under a *praefectus civitatum*, Noricum was put under an equestrian governor who resided at Virunum and commanded the *auxilia* and the *iuventus Noricorum*. The first known governor is A. Trebonius (*CIL* iii. 4810; cf. *JÖAI* xxix (1935), Bbl. 261). Owing to the Marcomannic wars the newly raised Legio II Italica was quartered in Noricum (first at Albing, before 191 at Lauriacum), and its commander became the governor of Noricum as a *legatus Augusti pro praetore*, residing at Ovilava; the financial *procurator* remained at Virunum. After Gallienus had eliminated senators from military command, Noricum was put again under equestrian administration (cf. the governor *Ael(ius) Restutus v(ir) p(erfectissimus) a(gens) v(ices) p(raesidis)*, *RLÖ* xi (1910), 151 f. no. 42). Under Diocletian Noricum was divided into two parts under *praesides*: *N. Ripense* on the Danube and *N. Mediterraneum* in the south, the former also having a *dux* as military commander. In the fifth century Noricum was overrun by German tribes and was occupied after 493 by Goths, by Franks (c. 536), by Langobards (568), and shortly before 600 by Slavs and Avars.

Inscriptions: *CIL* iii (1873–1902) and V. Hoffiller and B. Saria, *Antike Inschriften aus Jugoslavien*, Heft I, *Noricum und Pannonia Superior* (1939); E. Polaschek, *PW*, s.v.; U. Täckholm, *Studien über den Bergbau der römischen Kaiserzeit* (Uppsala 1937), 108 ff. On the site of Noreia, see E. Polaschek, *PW*, s.v.   F. A. W. S.

NORTIA, an Etruscan goddess, the native form of whose name is uncertain. Her chief place of worship was Volsinii (Livy 7. 3. 7, cf. Wissowa, *RK* 288, for archaeological evidence). The most remarkable rite was the periodical driving of a nail into the wall of the temple, Livy loc. cit., certainly not, as he there supposes, merely to serve as a record of time, one nail being driven each year, but rather (cf. ibid. 3–4; Warde Fowler, *Roman Fest.* 234 f.) to nail down evil and make it harmless (here an epidemic; perhaps at Volsinii all the ill of the past year). Another ancient interpretation was that it signified the unchanging fixedness of destiny; hence Nortia was identified with Fortuna (schol. on Juvenal 10. 74), and by implication with Necessitas (Horace, *Carm.* 1. 35. 17 ff.).   H. J. R.

NOSSIS, Greek poetess, lived in south Italian Locri about 290 B.C. A dozen of her Doric epigrams, mostly inscriptional, are in the Anthology. Nearly all relate to a cult of Aphrodite in which she was official poetess. She compares herself therefore with Sappho (*Anth. Pal.* 7. 718), but her extant poetry is far cooler and shallower.

R. Reitzenstein, *Epigramm und Skolion* (1893), 137; U. von Wilamowitz-Moellendorff, *Hellenistische Dichtung* i (1924), 135.
                                                              G. H.

NOSTOI, see EPIC CYCLE.

NOTAE TIRONIANAE, see TACHYGRAPHY.

NOTITIA DIGNITATUM. The document that has come down to us in two sections, 'Notitia dignitatum omnium, tam ciuilium quam militarium, in partibus Orientis, in partibus Occidentis', is famous as the one survivor of its kind; but in ancient times similar official lists of the chief functionaries of the Empire must have been regularly turned out from the offices of the *primicerii notariorum*. The arrangement is simple and uniform. First comes a summary list of high officials, then each high official with his staff; under the military, the various corps are detailed, each at its station. The whole work is illustrated with the insignia of the various officers, the badges of the military units and figures of provinces, though part of this illustration is thought to have been added later. Included are the praetorian prefects, the prefects of Rome and Constantinople, the *vicarii*, the chief governors and *duces*, the *magistri militum* and *peditum*, and such central officers as the quaestors of the palace, the *magistri officiorum*, and the *comites largitionum* and *privatarum*.

The *Notitia* is valuable to-day for several different reasons. It adds precision to our general knowledge of the chief imperial functionaries, it preserves information, otherwise not available, about their insignia, and gives the names and stations of many military units otherwise unknown. It would be interesting if it could be determined with certainty whether our document comes from an Eastern or a Western source, but both views have been maintained and no final decision can yet be given. Even

more important is the question of date; for if that can be determined, we have invaluable evidence for the exact conditions of the Empire at a precise moment of history. It is generally held that the conditions represented are in the main those of the end of the reign of Theodosius I (c. A.D. 395), but that certain entries must be assigned to dates as late as 425 or even 433. A very interesting problem now arises, especially in reference to the Danube countries and Britain. In both cases the *Notitia* preserves details of an organization in detail, which on general grounds of history and archaeology is thought to have been obsolete before those final dates. In Britain, for example, units are still found strung across the line of the wall. J. B. Bury has claimed the *Notitia* as evidence that Britain, in the official view, had not been abandoned in 425, and that any withdrawals yet made were treated as provisional only. Others consider that the *Notitia* had only been very imperfectly revised after 395 and that its evidence, therefore, must not be overstressed.

Edited by O. Seeck, *Notitia Dignitatum* (1876). E. Polaschek, *PW*, s.v.; J. B. Bury, *JRS* 1920; F. S. Salisbury, *JRS* 1929 and 1933; F. Lot, *Rev. Ét. Anc.* 1936.   H. M.

NOVAESIUM (*Neuss*), at a point where important roads from Gallia Belgica reached the Rhine, appears to have been selected during the Augustan wars for a military post, and by A.D. 40 the twentieth legion from Cologne was stationed there. Its fortress was destroyed in 70 and rebuilt, but the legion was withdrawn before 107. Gallienus installed an *ala* at Novaesium which, however, remained there only until 270; but the civil settlement persisted and was provided with walls which were repaired by Julian. The legionary fortress was fully excavated by C. Koenen (*Bonner Jahrbücher* cxi–cxii, 1904).   O. B.

NOVATIAN(US), Roman presbyter, anti-pope (A.D. 251), and founder of the *Novatiani* (or καθαροί), a dissident sect which, persisting for about three centuries, held intransigent views concerning ecclesiastical purity. He apparently suffered martyrdom under Valerian. The first Roman Christian to write exclusively in Latin, he composed several works, few of which survive, viz. *De Trinitate* (ed. W. Y. Fausset, 1909), two letters to Cyprian (*Ep.* 30 and 36 in the Cyprian collection), *De Cibis Iudaicis* (ed. G. Landgraf and C. Weyman, *Archiv f. lat. Lex.* 11, 1900, p. 226), and perhaps [Cyprian] *De Spectaculis* and *De Bono Pudicitiae*. N. possessed eloquence, philosophic knowledge, and an exceptional sense of style.   A. H.-W.

NOVEL, GREEK, a romantic composition in rhetorical prose. Five complete examples, two summaries, and some fragments are extant. Of the authors of the complete novels (ACHILLES TATIUS, CHARITON, HELIODORUS, LONGUS, XENOPHON OF EPHESUS) none is likely to have written before the second century A.D.; but the theory that the literary form was a creation of this period has been disproved by the fragments, preserved on papyrus, some of which must and others may represent work of an earlier age. Most important are the fragments of the Ninus Romance, which perhaps belongs to the first century B.C. These and others which include the names of historical or legendary characters suggest, in view of the tendency of the later novelists to set their fiction against an historical background, that the romantic novel was developed from the semi-historical, semi-mythical accounts of legendary heroes and famous men which were popular in the Alexandrian age. Alexander the Great probably received such treatment not long after his death, though the extant Alexander Romance (PSEUDO-CALLISTHENES) is mostly of a much later date. Among classical authors there is nothing strictly comparable; there is a romantic element in Xenophon's *Cyropaedia*, but the scope and treatment are very different. To judge from meagre fragments, the same seems to be true of several Alexandrian historians, e.g. Hegesippus of Mecyberna, Andriscus, etc. (*see* PARTHENIUS).

The extant novels, even the *Daphnis and Chloe* of Longus, of which the pastoral setting is exceptional, show similarities of matter and style which, with the supporting evidence of the summaries and fragments, may be called characteristic. Psychological subtlety is absent, though a wealth of rhetoric does something to conceal the poverty of thought; but there is positive merit in the plots, which, however stereotyped their general lines, are often ingeniously developed and include a variety of incident which, with an appeal to the eye rather than to the mind, would be suitable material for film scenarios. The central figures are a young man and his betrothed or bride whose moral rectitude and physical courage are tested by a prolonged series of adventures which ultimately lead them to the bliss for which they crave. During their wanderings, which cover wide areas, they meet friends and enemies who tend to have little individuality and are sometimes reminiscent of the stock types which people New Comedy, but whose experiences permit the inclusion of shorter stories within the wider framework. Such stories perhaps belong to the more ancient and more durable tradition exemplified by the Milesian Tales as well as by Petronius and Apuleius. The erotic element leads to tedious sentimentality but rarely to pornography, and though Love (Ἔρως) supplies the motive power, the greater part of every novel is devoted to adventure. The authors delight in elaborate descriptions of battles, storms, and other exciting events; some are also eager to parade a pseudo-scientific outlook which is responsible for the grossest irrelevancies.

The absence of contemporary references to Greek novels and the character of their material suggest that they were not esteemed by the educated classes; but the language is more literary and the style more elaborate than would seem suitable for popular fiction. Hackneyed quotations from Homer and other classical writers may have been as commonplace and as popular as our own biblical or Shakespearian quotations, but there are at times more obscure literary allusions which argue some erudition not only in the authors but also in their readers. The Byzantines admired the Greek novelists; Photius, who is loud in his praises, summarized Heliodorus and Achilles Tatius as well as the works, now lost, of IAMBLICHUS and ANTONIUS DIOGENES; and others imitated them. Some of the novels, when translated in the sixteenth century into modern European languages, earned a temporary fame and importance. Though essentially artificial, they seemed natural and realistic to a public which was at length tiring of the Romance of Chivalry, and they were read, esteemed, and even imitated by writers of greatly superior talents.

BIBLIOGRAPHY

(For translations, and for texts, etc. of individual authors see separate articles.)
TEXTS: *Erotici Scriptores* (1) ed. G. A. Hirschig (Didot), (2) (without Heliodorus) ed. R. Hercher (Teubner); *Eroticorum Graecorum Fragmenta Papyracea*, ed. B. Lavagnini (Teubner); *Griechische Roman-Papyri und verwandte Texte*, ed. F. Zimmermann (1936; commentary and bibliography).
ADVERSARIA CRITICA: H. Richards, *CR* 1906; J. Jackson, *CQ* 1935.
LITERARY HISTORY: E. Rohde, *Der griechische Roman* (1914); O. Schissel von Fleschenberg, *Entwickelungsgeschichte des gr. Rom. im Altertum* (1913); A. Calderini, *Le avventure di Cherea e Calliroe* (Prolegomeni) (1913); B. Lavagnini, *Le origini del romanzo greco* (1921); R. M. Rattenbury in J. U. Powell's *New Chapters in the History of Greek Literature*, third series (1933), and in *Year's Work* 1938 (bibliography); F. Garin, *Stud. Ital.* 1909; S. Gaselee, Appendix to the Loeb *Daphnis and Chloe* (1916; select bibliography); S. L. Wolff, *The Greek Romances in Elizabethan Prose Fiction* (U.S.A. 1913); J. S. Phillimore, *English Literature and the Classics* (1912). R. M. R.

NOVEL, LATIN. In spite of two great names, there is no continuous tradition of prose fiction among the Romans as there was with the Greeks. The Atellane farces, closely connected with mimes, seem to have been in verse, and we hardly reach fiction, and then only in the form of short stories, before L. Cornelius Sisenna (119–67 B.C.), otherwise known as an historian, translated into Latin the Μιλησιακά of Aristides (2nd c. B.C.). These were 'broad' (Plutarch, *Crassus* 32; [Lucian], *Amores* 1) and Sisenna when translating them heightened their obscenity (Ovid, *Tr.* 2. 443).

In a different line of descent are the adaptations by M. Terentius Varro (116–27 B.C.) of the satires of Menippus of Gadara (2nd c. B.C.), a Syrian writing in Greek, in mixed prose and verse: they are of the nature of 'character-sketches', and are under the influence of the Epicurean (and Cynical) tendency of their Greek originals. We have plentiful but fragmentary remains, which hardly seem to us very amusing, though some titles are ingenious and funny. This literary form was employed before A.D. 66 by Petronius (q.v.), whose long and amusing novel was in a mixture of prose and verse; but it consisted of a continuous narrative, not of short sketches. Petronius introduced at least two Μιλησιακά—the stories of the Widow of Ephesus and of the Quaestor's Son at Pergamum.

Far more use of them was, however, made by Apuleius (q.v.) about the middle of the second century, whose *Metamorphoses* began 'At ego tibi sermone isto Milesio uarias fabulas conseram'; and his romance is, indeed, a series of them strung on the thread of a plot—the change of Lucius into an ass and his adventures in animal form—which is sometimes lost sight of for long periods. We know from Capitolinus (11. 7; 12. 12) on Clodius Albinus (d. A.D. 197, the rival of Septimius Severus for the imperial power) that he too tried his hand at this form.

At the very end of the classical period we have the anonymous *History of Apollonius, King of Tyre*, perhaps written in Greek in the third century and translated into Latin, christianized, and adapted in other ways about the sixth century; it belongs rather to the tradition of Greek than of Latin fiction, and is chiefly interesting to us as the ultimate source of Shakespeare's *Pericles, Prince of Tyre*.

Fragments of Sisenna and of Varro's *Menippean Satires* in Bücheler's *Petronius* ed. min. There are no very satisfactory editions of *Apollonius of Tyre*: best by Riese (1871 and 1893); by M. Ring (1888). Students should consult Klebs's careful study, *Die Erzählung von A. v. T.* (1899). S. G.

NOVELLAE, see CODEX.

NOVENSIDES, a group of Roman deities of totally unknown function. According to the second explanation of the Indigetes (q.v., and see references there), they are to be etymologized as *nou-en-sides*, the 'newly settled in' gods, i.e. comparatively recent borrowings from non-Roman sources, such as Minerva and Apollo; but this view stands or falls with the etymology of *indiges* (s.v. INDIGETES). The *nouensides* seem to be the more important class, to judge from their being mentioned before the *indigetes* in the formula of *deuotio* (Livy 8. 9. 6), where the name is written 'Nouensiles', a characteristic Italian variation of *d* and *l*. Wagenvoort (*Dynamism*, p. 83) would connect the first syllable with *nuere* and for the suffix compares *ut-ensilis*: hence 'mobile, active' deities. The ancients generally connected the name with *nouem*, occasionally with *nouus*, see Arnobius, *Adv. Gent.* 3. 38–9 (p. 136, 19 ff. Reifferscheid). H. J. R.

NOVIOMAGUS, a Batavian settlement near Nymwegen (perhaps the *oppidum Batauorum* of Tac. *Hist.* 5. 19). It was destroyed in A.D. 70, and the Romans established a legionary fortress (garrisoned until *c.* 100) near by. The civil population settled on lower ground to the west, where an important commercial town developed, which traded extensively with Britain and the north and was raised to colonial status by Trajan. It suffered badly in the invasions of the third century and was practically deserted after 260. Pottery finds persist beyond the fourth century, but by then a new fortified settlement was growing up farther east which survived the Dark Ages.   O. B.

NOVIUS (*fl. c.* 95–80 B.C.), Latin composer of *fabulae Atellanae*, which he and his older contemporary Pomponius (q.v.) made literary. Forty-three titles show the four stock Atellan characters (fool, boaster, old driveller, old sly-boots), country-bumpkins, rustic and other occupations, literary allusions and parodies; in popular language with broad jokes.

Fragments: O. Ribbeck, *CRF²* 254 (3rd ed. Teubner 1897).
                                                    E. H. W.

NOVUS HOMO, the term applied to one attaining curule office without being *nobilis*, i.e. without *commendatio maiorum* but *per se cognitus*, had a double usage. The strict use, seen in the charge of *novitas generis* against Murena, whose family for three generations had contained praetors, in references to Cn. Octavius (*cos.* 165 B.C.) and Mummius (*cos.* 146) as *novi homines*, although their fathers had been praetors, and in the mention of *novi homines praetorii* (Q. Cicero, *Comment. pet.* 13), based *nobilitas* on the attainment of consular rank; these *nobiles* formed the inner circle of the Senate. The popular and literary use, with a looser conception of the senatorial order, based *nobilitas* on the attainment simply of curule office; thus Cicero might claim to be the first *novus homo* since C. Coelius Caldus (*cos.* 94).

The distinction, based on political *honos*, grew up with the patrician-plebeian nobility. *Novi homines* were usually from the equestrian order, rising through the patronage of a noble house; the outstanding figures were Cato, Marius, and Cicero.

M. Gelzer, *Nobilität der röm. Republik* (1912); J. Vogt, *Homo Novus* (1926); W. Schur, *Bonner Jahrb.* 1930; H. Strasburger, *PW* xvii, s.v. 'nobiles', col. 785; 'novus homo', col. 1223; A. Afzelius, *Classica et Mediaevalia*, 1938, 40 ff.; 1945, 150 ff.   A. H. McD.

NOXA, *see* PATRIA POTESTAS.

NUMANTIA, a strategical site on the upper Durius (*Douro*) in Spain, occupied in the Bronze age, in the Hallstatt period, and by the Celts. Built anew by the Celtiberians *c.* 300 B.C., Numantia played a heroic role in the Celtiberian resistance to Rome, repelling attacks by Cato (195), Q. Fulvius Nobilior (153), Marcellus (152), Q. Pompeius (141), and Popillius Laenas (139–8); the capitulation of Hostilius (q.v.) Mancinus (137) crowned a series of shameful incidents. Finally, after an eight-month blockade Numantia's 4,000 citizens capitulated to the overwhelming forces of Scipio Aemilianus in 133 B.C., a date which marks the end of organized resistance to Rome in Spain. Marius, Jugurtha, and Polybius witnessed Numantia's destruction. Thorough excavations have uncovered the city, Scipio's works of circumvallation, and thirteen Roman camps at Numantia or in the neighbourhood (one each of Marcellus and Pompeius, two of Cato and Nobilior, and seven of Scipio). Although rebuilt by Augustus, Numantia gradually sank to the level of a way-station on the Asturica-Caesaraugusta highway.

A. Schulten: *Numantia* (4 vols. and atlas, 1914–31), and a shorter sketch, *Geschichte von Numantia* (1933).   J. J. Van N.

NUMA POMPILIUS, the second king of Rome (traditionally 715–673 B.C.), is probably an historical figure, although most of the reforms ascribed to him were the result of a very long process of religious and cultural development. His name, which has often been wrongly connected with Etruria, suggests a Sabine origin. Numa is not the personification of the river Numicus or any other Latin deity. There is no means of deciding whether Numa really organized the priestly colleges and reformed the calendar by fixing the dates of the festivals and adding two months to a primitive ten-month year, or whether he built the Regia (q.v.), which was traditionally assigned to the regal period. Later legends recount that he received counsel from the nymph Egeria and, in defiance of chronology, make him a disciple of Pythagoras (q.v.) to account for similarities between early Roman religion and Greek cults in southern Italy.

H. Last, *CAH* vii. 374 ff.   P. T.

NUMBERS. I. GREEK NUMERICAL NOTATION.
There were two systems:

(1) The 'Attic' or 'Herodianic' (from Herodian, a grammarian of the 2nd c. A.D.), represented by Attic inscriptions from 454 to 95 B.C. but used outside Attica also. Apart from I, the unit, the signs were initial letters, Γ ($\pi\acute{\epsilon}\nu\tau\epsilon$), Δ ($\delta\acute{\epsilon}\kappa\alpha$), H for $\acute{\epsilon}\kappa\alpha\tau\sigma\nu$, X ($\chi\acute{\iota}\lambda\iota\iota$), M ($\mu\acute{\upsilon}\rho\iota\iota$), repeated where necessary, and combined with Γ for intermediate numbers, e.g. $\boxed{\Delta} = 50$, $\boxed{X} = 5,000$.

(2) The alphabetical system originating in Ionia and using the ordinary Greek letters together with F or $S = 6$, $\varphi = 90$, T or $\lambda = 900$; first found in a Halicarnassus inscription of about 450 B.C. but may have started earlier in Miletus or Caria; not used officially in Greece proper before the 3rd c. B.C.

The two systems went on side by side till about 50 B.C. See Friedlein, *Die Zahlzeichen und das elementare Rechnen der Griechen* (1869); Larfeld, *Handbuch der griechischen Epigraphie* i (1907); Keil in *Hermes* 29 (1894). M. N. Tod, 'Three Greek Numerical Systems' in *JHS* 1913, 27–34, cites from inscriptions some variations in the signs used on the 'Herodianic' system.

Archimedes, in his lost ᾿Αρχαί and in the *Sand-reckoner* (*Psammites*), sketched a system for expressing very large numbers going by powers of a myriad myriads (100,000,000 or 10^8). The first *order* consists of numbers from 1 to 10^8, the second *order* those from 10^8 to 10^{16}, and so on, up to the 10^8 *order* concluding the first *period*. Other *periods* follow *ad lib.* This system amounts to taking 100,000,000 in place of 10 as the base of a scale of notation. Apollonius of Perga formulated a 'position-value' system going by powers of 10,000, i.e. with 10,000 substituted for 10 as the base (see Pappus I, 8 f.).

Fractions. At first the Greeks, following the Egyptians, preferred to express fractions as submultiples and the sums of such, using for the submultiple the sign for the number with an accent ($\gamma' = \frac{1}{3}$), with special signs L' for $\frac{1}{2}$ and ω' for $\frac{2}{3}$. Proper fractions could be expressed by the word (or the sign) for the numerator and the accented letters for the denominator, e.g. $\delta\acute{\upsilon}o\ \mu\epsilon' = \frac{2}{45}$ (Aristarchus of Samos), $\theta\ \iota\alpha' = \frac{9}{11}$ (Archimedes), or (better) expressions like $\delta^{\omega\nu}\varsigma = \frac{8}{4}$, $\nu\ \kappa\gamma^{\omega\nu} = \frac{50}{23}$ (Diophantus). Most convenient of all was the practice, regular in Diophantus, and occasional in Heron, of placing the denominator *above* the numerator, e.g. $\frac{\phi\mu\beta}{\beta\upsilon\nu\varsigma} = \frac{2456}{512}$ (Diophantus).

II. THEORY OF NUMBERS. This began with the Pythagoreans. Plato is held by some to have extended the notion of number to include incommensurables and irrationals; there is, however, no sign of such an idea in Euclid's bk. 10, though that book owed much to Theaetetus; the irrationals in the book are all *straight lines* or *areas*. Euclid's bks. 7–9 contain the elementary theory of numbers; bk. 8. 11–21 include the 'Platonic' theorem that there is one mean between squares and two (in continued proportion) between cubes. Besides Nicomachus and Iamblichus, Theon of Smyrna has some propositions in the theory of numbers; but it is Diophantus who gives the most, some purporting to be contained in his 'Porisms' (lost), e.g. *Arith.* 5. 16, 'the difference of two cubes is also the sum of two cubes'.   T. H.

NUMBERS, SACRED. Most nations have sacred or magical numbers. Some of these are explicable (e.g. seven is the traditional number of the planets), and of others it may be conjectured that they are the last term of some very old and primitive system of counting, or an important term in such a system (e.g., five perhaps because it is the number of the fingers of one hand); others are entirely obscure. For Greece the following may be noted, apart from Pythagorean mysticism and the divinatory calculations given below. Three is very commoŋ in all ritual, especially magical; the dead are invokeɗ thrice (Ar. *Ran.* 1175–6); gods are frequently invoked in threes, as Zeus, Athena, and Apollo often in Homer, or grouped in threes, as the Charites (generally); charms are commonly repeated thrice, Theocr. 2. 43; other magical actions, Theocr. 6. 39. Hence nine is of importance (nine Muses usually, sometimes nine Corybantes and nine Curetes), being 3 × 3. Four is Hermes' number, being his birthday (*Hymn. Hom. Merc.* 19), perhaps explaining why it is a holy day (Hesiod, *Op.* 770). Seven is Apollo's number (see Rose, *Handb. Gk. Myth.* p. 135, cf. Hesiod, ibid. 771). This is without doubt oriental; twelve, though traditionally the number of the signs of the Zodiac, need not be Eastern (twelve gods, see Weinreich in Roscher's *Lexikon*, art. 'Zwölfgötter'; twelve labours of Heracles, q.v.). Finally there is a tendency to round larger numbers off to fifty (see W. H. Roscher, 'Die Zahl 50 in Mythus', etc., *Abh. sächs. Ges. Wiss.*, 1917). The numerical values of letters of the alphabet are the basis of an elaborate system of divination, see Bouché–Leclercq,*Hist. de la divin.* i. 261 ff.; for an attempt to find a like system in early times see Eisler, *Orpheus the Fisher* and *Weltenmantel und Himmelszelt*. Numbers which exceed a familiar 'round' number by one, e.g. 13 (12+1), are occasionally of importance, see O. Weinreich, *Triskaidekadische Studien* 1916 (*RGVV* xvi. 1).

In Italy triads of gods are common, not only under Etruscan influence (as the Capitoline triad), but outside it (Jupiter, Mars, and Quirinus are native Roman). Four is of significance (a prayer said four times, Ovid, *Fasti* 4. 778); five appears to have had some sacral connotation, see Wissowa, *Gesammelte Abhandl.* 166, cf. Plutarch, *Quaest. Rom.* 1 and Rose ad loc. Other numbers seem to be Greek.

The references in the text may be supplemented by Keith in Hastings, *ERE* ix. 407 ff., and bibliography, p. 413. **H. J. R.**

NUMENIUS of Apamea (*c.* A.D. 150–200), Platonist or Pythagorean, is the immediate precursor of Neoplatonism. He combined his philosophy with a great interest in Eastern religions, and especially in Judaism; he described Plato as Μωυσῆς ἀττικίζων. He treated the philosophies of Pythagoras and Plato as at bottom identical; his own originality lies chiefly in his maintaining that there are three Gods—the Father, the Creator, and the Created World.

Ed. and tr. K. S. Guthrie (U.S.A. 1929). **W. D. R.**

NUMERI was the title given to units of cavalry and infantry recruited from provinces recently conquered or little romanized. Owing to their character they were normally employed in areas distant from those in which they had been raised (e.g. *numeri Brittonum* in Germany). They are found in existence between the time of Trajan and Constantine; they were probably organized in cohorts and commanded by *praefecti*.

In the Constantinian army *numerus* was the generic title of a unit of the Field Army (e.g. *vexillatio* or *legio*).

A. von Domaszewski, *Die Rangordnung des römischen Heeres* (1908). **H. M. D. P.**

NUMERIANUS, MARCUS AURELIUS, younger son of Carus, was appointed Caesar in A.D. 282 and shared in the campaign against Persia. After the death of Carus,

July 283, Numerian had no thought but to bring his army back from Ctesiphon. Marching slowly, the army did not reach Nicomedia till the autumn of 284. There the alarming discovery was made that the young prince, who had travelled in a closed litter to spare his sore eyes, was a putrefying corpse. The army chose Diocles (later Diocletian), commander of the guard, to avenge the murder, and he struck down the guilty Aper, praetorian prefect and father-in-law of Numerian. Famed as orator and poet, Numerian showed no capacity for command.

H. M.

NUMIDIA, originally the country of the Numidae or African Nomads, lying west and south of Carthaginian territory. Later the title was given to a Roman province, covering a triangle broadening out from its apex on the Mediterranean coast north of Cirta across the High Plateaux (Atlas Mountains) down to the Saharan *limes*. This Numidia was bounded by Mauretania Caesariensis on the west and the province of Africa on the east. Though not as fertile as the latter, Numidia produced corn, wine, and olives on the plains, and bred horses, cattle, and sheep on the uplands.

The original Berber inhabitants were nomad herdsmen, who sometimes practised a primitive agriculture. Those on the coast came under the influence of Utica, Carthage, and the other Phoenician colonies, and there is some evidence of Jewish settlement. By the time of the Second Punic War their small clans had coalesced into the tribal confederacies of the Masaesyli under Syphax and the Massyli under Masinissa (q.v.). Their cavalry were formidable, but their national custom of Sof or civil disunion made them difficult allies politically. Under Masinissa nomadism was abandoned for agriculture, and town life developed. Masinissa was followed by Micipsa (148–118 B.C.), Adherbal (118–112), Jugurtha (q.v., 118–106), Hiempsal (106–60), and Juba I (60–46). As Numidia supported Pompey (47–46), the native dynasty was overthrown. It was established as the province of Africa Nova (46), then (30–25) made a client kingdom under Juba II (q.v.), and later united with the old province of Africa until separated by Septimius Severus.

When the frontiers of Africa Proconsularis were placed on the river Ampsaga (*Rummel*), the Third Augustan legion moved into Numidia under its legate, and was stationed successively at Theveste and Lambaesis (qq.v.). Military colonies were founded at Thamugadi, Madauros (qq.v.), and elsewhere; cereals and olives were cultivated largely; the slave-trade with the Sahara increased. Traffic moved along the great roads which radiated from Theveste to be shipped from Carthage, Hadrumetum, Taparura, and the Syrtic ports. The richest parts of Numidia were in the Tell (*see* ATLAS MOUNTAINS) and round Cirta (q.v.).

On its southern frontier Numidia was protected by the forts of the *limes*, which ran from the Tunisian shotts or salt lakes westward and north-west to Aumale. Between the military roads were districts ruled by native chieftains, who occasionally rebelled. The frontier held till the end of the fourth century A.D., when Saharan raiders took advantage of the quarrels of Donatists, Catholics, and Circumcellions to burn Vescera (*Biskra*), Calceus Herculis (*El Kantara*), and Thamugadi.

For bibliography *see* AFRICA, ROMAN. **W. N. W.**

NUMITOR, *see* ROMULUS.

NUMMULARII, quoted in inscriptions as subordinate officers at the mint, but probably not technical workmen, who are properly called *officinatores*. The *nummularius* of Martial (12. 57. 7) disturbs sleep by thumping the heavy *sestertii* of Nero on his dirty table, in the intervals of business ('otiosus'). He is a money-changer. So was the *nummularius*, whose hands Galba cut off, 'non ex fide uersanti pecunias' (Suetonius, *Galba* 9); he had cheated over the exchange. This passage shows that the *nummularii* were under official control; they may even have been directly employed by the mint to put on the market the new coin as it was struck.

The passage in Petronius, *Satyricon* 56, where Trimalchio asks 'quod autem putamus secundum litteras difficillimum esse artificium? ego puto medicum et nummularium', does not necessarily imply the meaning of 'moneyer'.

R. Herzog, *PW*, s.v. H. M.

NUPTIAE, *see* MARRIAGE.

NUX ELEGIA, 'The Nut-tree's Complaint', *see* OVID.

NYMPHIDIUS SABINUS, GAIUS, son of a court freedwoman, claimed to be the son of Caligula. We know nothing of his early career, though he may have served in Pannonia (Dessau, *ILS* 1322). In 65 he was given the *consularia ornamenta* by Nero and made *praefectus praetorio* with Tigellinus. In 68 he swore allegiance to Galba, but had designs upon the principate himself. He forced his colleague Tigellinus to resign, and intended to demand from Galba the praefecture for life without colleague. But he met with unexpected opposition from the Praetorians, and was slain by them.

PIR[1], N 200. R. L. J.

NYMPHIS of Heraclea in Bithynia, statesman and historian. Enough remains of his history of Heraclea (in Memnon's epitome) to show how good it was; this and his character as a politician suggest that his lost history of Alexander and his successors (after 247 B.C.) may be a real loss. *See* ALEXANDER (3), Bibliography, Ancient Sources. W. W. T.

NYMPHODORUS (*fl. c.* 335 B.C.), Syracusan Greek, wrote (i) Ἀσίας περίπλους, (ii) Περὶ τῶν ἐν Σικελίᾳ θαυμαζομένων, and possibly (iii) *On strange things in Sardinia* (Ath. 6. 265 c; 13. 588 f., 609 c; Ael. *NA* 16. 34).

FHG ii. 378; *PW* xvii. 1625-7.

NYMPHS, female spirits of nature representing the divine powers of mountains, waters, woods, and trees, and also of places, regions, cities, and States. As the word νύμφη, young unmarried woman, implies, nymphs were thought of as young and fair. They like dancing and music and can inspire mortals with poetry and prophetic power. In contrast to gods nymphs are mortal (Ovid, *Met.* 8. 771), although Hesiod endows them with extreme longevity. They are daughters of Zeus.

Since nymphs are called after that part of nature in which they dwell, or after their functions, or after the specific geographic locality where they reside, there is an infinite variety of nymphs known. Alseides, Napaeae, and Dryades are nymphs of forests and groves (the last were originally nymphs of the oak but came to stand for nymphs of the woods in general). Hamadryades, the tree nymphs proper, were believed to die when their tree decays (Serv. on Verg. *Ecl.* 10. 62), for the nymph is the life spirit of the tree. Orestiads are the nymphs of the mountains, Leimoniads those of the meadows. All kinds of waters are inhabited by nymphs, such as the Naiads, the Potameids, the Creneids, and the Hydriads. The difference between these broader classifications of nymphs and the nymphs representing a locality was recognized by the ancients (*Myth. Vat.* 2. 50). Examples of local nymphs are the Acheloids, named after the river Achelous, or the Nysiads, named after the mountain Nysa where Dionysus was born. Many local goddesses are brought under this category of nymphs and married to founders of the cities.

Most of the nymphs are benevolent to mankind. They bring flowers to gardens and meadows, watch with Apollo and Hermes over the flocks, and frequently, as patronesses of healthful springs, aid the sick. Such nymphs are often associated with Asclepius. As goddesses of woods and mountains they give success to hunters. Yet nymphs also partake of the wilder aspects of nature. They are akin to Satyrs (q.v.) and Sileni, and associate with Pan. They range with Artemis over the mountains and take part in the Dionysiac *thiasus*. Folk-lore tales, similar to those attaching to fairies and mermaids, are told about some of the nymphs. Those of the woods scare travellers. A man who sees nymphs becomes 'possessed by nymphs'. They take mortals whom they love with them as they did Hylas and Bormus (Theocr. 13. 44 and schol., Athen. 14. 619 f). The drowning of a girl in the Nile was associated with them (*SEG* viii. 473). They punish unresponsive lovers as did the nymphs who blinded Daphnis (Diod. 4. 84).

The cult of nymphs was widely spread through Greece from Homeric times on (*Od.* 13. 356; 17. 205), and extended over the Roman provinces under the Empire. Nymphs were often worshipped in caves; an interesting example is the cave in Vari which was transformed into a sanctuary of the nymphs by their faithful devotee Archedemus (*AJArch.* 1903, 263). In art nymphs are represented on a vase of Sophilus and on the François vase as undistinctive draped females. A special type of votive relief for the nymphs was developed in Attica in the late fifth and the fourth centuries B.C. The dancing nymphs are led by Hermes, while Pan and Achelous look on (R. Feubel, *Die attischen Nymphenreliefs* (1935)); sometimes a cave and an altar indicate the rustic sanctuary. Shepherds often dedicated these humble votives.

L. Bloch in Roscher, *Lex.*, s.v. 'Nymphen'; J. E. Harrison, *Prolegomena to the Study of Greek Rel.*, 288. G. M. A. H.

NYX. Naturally enough, Night is frequently personified by the Greek poets as by those of other peoples. But the significance of Nyx in Greek mythology goes far beyond this. She was a great cosmogonical figure, feared and respected even by Zeus (Hom. *Il.* 14. 259). In Hesiod she is born of Chaos and mother of Aether, Hemera, and lesser powers. Frequent touches in the description recall her nocturnal aspect, but this is scarcely seen in the Orphic theogonies, where her influence over creation is immense (cf. ORPHIC LITERATURE, ORPHISM). In the Rhapsodies she is born of Phanes and succeeds to his power. When in turn she hands the sceptre to her son Uranus she continues to advise the younger generations, Uranus, Kronos, and especially Zeus, in the task of world-making. Her influence is due to her oracular powers, exercised from a cave. There are signs that in an earlier Orphic version Phanes was absent and Nyx the primal power. The theogony of the Birds (Ar. *Av.* 693 ff.) makes her prior to Eros (= Phanes), and this supposition suits the awful dignity of Nyx which Homer and 'Orpheus' alike emphasize, and the vague reference of Aristotle (*Metaph.* 1071[b]27) to *theologoi* who derive everything from Night. Nyx was primarily a mythographer's goddess, with little cult, but one may mention her connexion with oracles (not confined to Orphic literature, see Plut. *De sera* 22; schol. Pind. *Pyth. Argum.*) and a dedication to her in the temple of Demeter in Graeco-Roman Pergamum (*SIG* 1148 n. 2).

W. K. C. G.

OASIS, the name by which the Greeks called any watered and habitable land in deserts, particularly in north Africa. Though really depressions, they were regarded as elevations. They were of some importance as trading-stations and sources of alum, and several of them were garrisoned by the Ptolemies, and later by the Romans. The oases of the Sahara were described by Herodotus (4. 181–5) as a chain extending from east to west, about ten days' journey apart. The most renowned of them, near Egypt, were (i) the 'Ammonium' (*El Siwah*), 6 mls. × 3, 20 days from Thebes and 12 from Memphis, famed for springs, salt, old Egyptian temples, and the oracle of Ammon (q.v.); (ii) 'Oasis Magna' (*El Khargah*), 80 mls. × 8–10, 7 days from Thebes, with a Greek and Roman population. (iii) 'Oasis Minor' (*El Dakkel*), south-east of the Ammonium, a source of wheat under the Roman Empire. (iv) 'Oasis Trinytheos' (*El Bakhariah*), north of Oasis Magna, with artesian wells and alum deposits.

For the oasis of Palmyra see PALMYRA.   E. H. W.

OBELUS, *see* SCHOLARSHIP, GREEK, IN ANTIQUITY.

OBNUNTIATIO, *see* CONTIO.

OBSEQUENS, *see* JULIUS (8).

OCEANUS (mythological), son of Uranus (Sky) and Ge (Earth), husband of Tethys, and father of the Oceanids and River gods (Hes. *Th.* 133. 364). In Homer O. is the river encircling the whole world and accordingly is represented as a river by Hephaestus on the rim of the shields of Achilles (*Il.* 18. 607) and Heracles ([Hes.] *Sc.* 314). From O. through subterranean connexions issue all other rivers. Styx, the river of Hades, is part of O. (Hes. *Th.* 786). O. begins at the columns of Heracles, borders on the Elysian fields and Hades, and has its sources in the west where the sun sets. Monsters such as Gorgons, Hecatonchires, Hesperides, Geryoneus, and Eurytion, and outlandish tribes such as Cimmerians, Aethiopians, and pygmies, live by the waters of Oceanus (*Od.* 1. 22; 11. 13; *Il.* 3. 3). Those regions of O. are the land where reality ends and everything is fabulous.

In Greek theories of the world O. is conceived as the great cosmic power, θεῶν γένεσις (*Il.* 14. 201, 246, 302; W. Jäger, *Paideia* 1 (1934), 207), the water, through which all life grows, and in Greek mythology as a benign old god. Sometimes the elemental, sometimes the personal, aspect is more emphasized. The belief that sun and stars rise and set in the ocean is expressed mythologically in the statement that stars bathe in O. (*Il.* 18. 489), and the Sun traverses O. in a golden bowl by night to get back to the East (Mimnermus in Ath. 11. 470 a–b). The rise of rational geographical investigation in Herodotus, Eratosthenes, and others narrowed the significance of O. down to the geographical term of 'Ocean'.

Oceanus never became quite personal enough to accumulate many myths. Pherecydes supplied a humorous sequel to the myth of Sun in the golden bowl: when Heracles set out across the Ocean in the same golden bowl in which the sun used to cross, O. began to rock. Heracles threatened him with his arrows and O. was frightened (Ath. 11. 470 c).

In art O. appears early (François vase), is represented on the famous Gigantomachy of Pergamum, and becomes really common in Roman times, especially on sarcophagi, with Earth as a counterpart.

P. Weizsäcker, s.v. in Roscher, *Lex.* iii.   G. M. A. H.

OCEANUS (geographical). Expeditions outside the Straits of Gibraltar by Phoenicians and (after *c.* 630 B.C.) by Greeks, and exploration of the Red Sea and Persian Gulf under Darius I, showed that the Oceanus of mythology (see preceding article) was a salt-water 'ocean' indented with seas (so Herodotus). But erroneous notions persisted. Poets tried to relegate the river Oceanus beyond the newly found Outer Sea. Hecataeus believed that Oceanus flowed from east to west (Hdt. 4. 8), and the Caspian Sea (q.v.) was commonly regarded as one of its inlets. After the voyage of Pytheas (q.v.) in the Atlantic the action of the Ocean tides came to be understood, though the early Roman navigators in Atlantic waters were puzzled by them. As the sphericity of the earth became known (since *c.* 350 B.C.), geographers imagined that eastern Asia might be reached by sailing westward from Europe, and *c.* 120 B.C. Eudoxus (q.v. 3) of Cyzicus attempted the circumnavigation of Africa. But the belief that the Ocean extended all round the inhabited earth was never proved. Some geographers conjectured that the southern Ocean contained another continent, or that it was a vast land-locked sea (so Ptolemy); the northern Ocean was supposed to be frozen or too shallow or glutinous for navigation.

See also GEOGRAPHY, HANNO (1), HIMILCO (1), HIPPALUS, INDIA, LIBYA.   E. H. W.

OCELLUS (or Occelus) of Lucania occurs in Iamblichus' list of Pythagoreans (testimonia in H. Diels, *Vorsokr.* i. 440–1), but the work Περὶ τῆς τοῦ παντὸς φύσεως bearing his name and known as early as the first century B.C. is undoubtedly spurious. It shows considerable traces of Aristotelian influence, and may probably be dated about 150 B.C.

Ed. R. Harder (Berlin, 1926). *PW* xvii. 2361.   W. D. R.

OCTAVIA (1) *major*, half-sister of Augustus, was the daughter of C. Octavius and his first wife Ancharia. She married Sextus Appuleius (*ILS* 8783. Plutarch, *Antony* 31, confuses her with Octavia minor). Her son Sextus was consul in 29 B.C.

OCTAVIA (2) *minor* (d. 11 B.C.), sister of Augustus and wife of Antony, whom she married after the death of her first husband, C. Marcellus, in 40. She spent the winters of 39–38 and 38–37 with Antony in Athens, and in 37 was instrumental in bringing about the Treaty of Tarentum. In 35 she set out for the East with supplies and 2,000 picked men for Antony's army, but was forbidden to proceed beyond Athens. She rejected her brother's advice to leave Antony's house, and when he divorced her (in 32) contrived to care for her stepchildren. Octavia's nobility, humanity, and loyalty won her universal esteem and sympathy. She bore a son and two daughters to Marcellus and two daughters to Antony.

Plutarch, *Antony*; Suetonius, *Caesar* and *Augustus*; Appian, *BCiv.* bks. 3–5; Dio Cassius, bks. 47 ff. Drumann–Groebe, *Gesch. Roms* iv. 250–8.   G. W. R.

OCTAVIA (3) (b. A.D. 40?), daughter of Claudius and Messallina, was betrothed to Domitius Ahenobarbus (Nero) in 49 and married to him in 53. Nero, who disliked and neglected her, divorced her in 62 in order to marry Poppaea, and sent her to live in Campania under military surveillance. When a rumour that she had been reinstated evoked demonstrations of popular approval she was banished to Pandateria (on a fictitious charge of adultery and treason) and then murdered.

[Seneca], *Octavia*; Tacitus, *Annals* 11–14; Suetonius, *Nero*; Dio Cassius, bks. 60–2. B. W. Henderson, *Life and Principate of the Emperor Nero* (1903).   G. W. R.

OCTAVIA, the one extant *praetexta*, dramatizes in 983 lines the fate of Nero's neglected empress. Seneca is brought in as a character to protest against the emperor's barbarity, and Agrippina's ghost comes to foretell Nero's doom in words so true to fact as to show that they were written after the event of A.D. 68. Commonly printed with Seneca's tragedies, it is not by him, but by someone who wrote in his manner soon after Nero died. There is too much melancholy repetition and too little epigram for Seneca, and there are metrical differences.

See J. Wight Duff, *Lit. Hist. Rome* (Silver Age); Schanz–Hosius; J. Schmidt, *PW*; V. Ciaffi assigns *Octavia* to L. Annaeus Cornutus, *Riv. Fil.* N.S. xv (1937). Text: edns. of Seneca's tragedies, e.g. F. Leo. With notes, C. L. Thompson (U.S.A. 1921); C. Hosius (1922). J. W. D.

OCTAVIANUS, see AUGUSTUS.

OCTAVIUS (1), GNAEUS, curule aedile, a member of the embassy assuring Greek allied rights in 170/169 B.C., was praetor in 168, commanding the Roman fleet against Perseus, whom he captured at Samothrace. He celebrated a naval triumph, and from spoil built the *Porticus Octavia.* Consul in 165, he led the embassy to the East in 162 which attempted to settle Syria in Roman interests after the death of Antiochus Epiphanes, destroying ships and elephants, and was murdered in a patriotic riot at Laodicea.

Polyb. bk. 31; Appian, *Syr.* 46 ff.; Justin. 34. 3, 6. B. Niese, *Gesch. der griech. und maked. Staaten* iii (1903), 243; P. V. M. Benecke, *CAH* viii. 285; E. R. Bevan, ibid. 518. A. H. McD.

OCTAVIUS (2), MARCUS, perhaps a son of (1), was tribune in 133 B.C. and a friend of Tiberius Gracchus, but he was persuaded to veto his Agrarian Bill—and accordingly deposed from his tribunate. Gaius Gracchus prepared a Bill to prevent persons thus deposed from standing for further office, but was persuaded by his mother Cornelia not to press it. M. H.

OCTAVIUS (3), GNAEUS, an Optimate, was consul with Cinna in 87 B.C., when Sulla left for the East. He resisted Cinna's proposed revival of Sulpicius' plan to distribute the new citizens throughout the thirty-five tribes, and drove Cinna from Rome. But he failed to hold Rome against the renewed attack and siege by Cinna and Marius and fell with the city (the so-called *Bellum Octavianum*). M. H.

OCTAVIUS (4), GAIUS, belonged to a wealthy equestrian family of Velitrae, rose to the praetorship (61 B.C.), and governed Macedonia with conspicuous ability. He died shortly after his return (59 or 58). Octavius was twice married and left two daughters and a son (later Augustus).

ILS 47; Suetonius, *Augustus* 2–4. G. W. R.

OCTAVIUS, see also AUGUSTUS, TITINIUS (2).

OCYPETE, see HARPYIAE.

ODAENATHUS, SEPTIMIUS, a Palmyrene noble of consular rank, on the capture of Valerian assumed the title of king and at the head of local troops inflicted a severe defeat on Sapor (A.D. 260). Gallienus rewarded him with the post of *dux* and, it would seem, *corrector totius orientis*, and Odaenathus on his behalf crushed the usurper Quietus at Emesa. From 262 to 267 he led the Roman army of the East and his own Palmyrene troops against Persia, reconquering Mesopotamia, but failing to capture Ctesiphon; he was rewarded with the title of *imperator*. In 267 he and his eldest son were murdered. Odaenathus' main interest was to protect the Eastern trade of his own city against the Persians, and he was content to acknowledge the suzerainty of Gallienus, since his nominal submission gave him command over the Roman army of the East.

J. G. Février, *Histoire de Palmyre* (1931), 70–102. A. H. M. J.

ODEUM (ᾠδεῖον), a small theatre or roofed hall for musical competitions and other assemblages. The earlier Athenian Odeum, which according to Plutarch (*Pericles*) was built by Pericles, was a building of a different kind. Plutarch's description, 'many-seated and many-columned', suggests a resemblance to the Telesterion at Eleusis—a square building—and his description of the roof as conical or pyramidal (said to have been copied from the tent of Xerxes) also seems to imply approximate equality of length and breadth. Recent excavations, however, appear to indicate a plan of *c.* 208 by 62 feet, and the relationship of the tent-shaped roof to this remains doubtful. Vitruvius (5. 9) states that Pericles ornamented the building with stone columns and with the masts and spars of ships captured from the Persians, and that it was destroyed by fire during the Mithridatic war and rebuilt by king Ariobarzanes.

H. W. R.

ODYSSEUS ('Οδυσσεύς, Lat. *Vlixes*, a dialectical form, not Ulysses), son and successor of Laertes king of Ithaca, husband of Penelope and father of Telemachus (qq.v.). Like Achilles (q.v.) he comes from a fringe of the Achaean world and is a favourite of Homer. Throughout the *Iliad* he is both brave and sagacious; he gives prudent counsel (e.g. 19. 154 ff.); he is enterprising and so chosen by Diomedes as his companion in the night expedition (10. 242 ff.); he displays great valour in battle, especially 11. 312 ff., where he and Diomedes stop the rout of the Greeks and Odysseus continues to fight after Diomedes is wounded till he himself gets a flesh wound and Menelaus and the greater Aias (qq.v.) rescue him. He is one of the three envoys sent to carry Agamemnon's offer to Achilles in bk. 9. In the funeral games of Patroclus he wins the foot race, Aias the Locrian coming in second (23. 778–9); he draws a wrestling match with the greater Aias (708 ff.).

2. He is the central figure of the *Odyssey*, which, by direct narrative of the poet and his own tale of his adventures in bks. 9–12, covers his career from the fall of Troy till ten years later. Leaving the Troad, he attacked the Cicones, but was beaten off with loss (9. 39 ff.); he was then caught by a storm, visited the country of the Lotophagi (q.v.), and wandered thence to the land of the Cyclopes (q.v.). Escaping from Polyphemus, he next visits Aeolia, the home of Aeolus (q.v. 1), who gives him a sack containing all the winds save the one which will bring him home. But while Odysseus sleeps his crew untie the sack, a storm arises and blows them from the coast of Ithaca back to Aeolia, where Aeolus refuses to have anything more to do with them (10. 19 ff.); after six days' sailing they reach the Laestrygonians (q.v.), and Odysseus barely escapes with his own ship and crew. He reaches Aeaea, the home of Circe (q.v.), and is told by her that he must, in order to reach home, go to Hades and consult the ghost of Tiresias (q.v.). This he succeeds in doing, sees many of the ghosts, and is told by Tiresias that after reaching home he is to sacrifice to Poseidon in a place where salt is unknown and an oar mistaken for a winnowing-fan, thus appeasing the god's anger for the blinding of his son Polyphemus. He will then find an easy death 'from the sea' (11. 134) in old age. Returning to Aeaea, he is given directions for his further voyage; by means of these he passes the Sirens (q.v.), runs between Scylla and Charybdis (qq.v.) with the loss of six men to the former, and comes to the island where the cattle of the Sun pasture. Here his men insist on landing, but, being windbound and short of provisions, they eat of the cattle. Helios demands revenge, and when they leave the island the ship is caught in a gale and destroyed by a thunderbolt; Odysseus alone escapes, and drifts to the island of Calypso (q.v.). Seven years later she lets him go by order of Zeus (5. 43 ff.) on a boat of his own making

Poseidon wrecks him, he swims ashore at Scheria and there is relieved by Nausicaa (q.v.) and sent home, after munificent entertainment, by Alcinous (q.v.). Meanwhile Telemachus has returned from his search for news of his father; Odysseus, disguised as a beggar by Athena, enters his own palace and disposes of the suitors of Penelope with the help of his son and the two faithful thralls, Eumaeus and Philoetius (21–2). He is reunited to Penelope, and an attempt by the kinsmen of the suitors to take vengeance is stopped by Athena, who makes peace between the two parties after the father of Antinous (q.v.) has been killed by old Laertes (24. 523).

3. The lost *Telegonia* continued the story. Odysseus performs his pilgrimage, meeting some subsidiary adventures; Telegonus, his son by Circe, sets out to look for him, lands in Ithaca and starts to plunder it; in the succeeding fight he kills Odysseus. Circe then makes the survivors immortal; she marries Telemachus and Penelope Telegonus.

4. Later authors, especially the tragedians, tend to blacken Odysseus' character. In Homer he is cunning and lies fluently on occasion; in some of the later legends he is a cowardly rascal. As early as the *Cypria* he tries to avoid coming to Troy, but is outwitted by Palamedes (q.v.), and he and Diomedes murder him (fr. 21 Allen). The same pair steal the Palladium, and Odysseus tries to murder Diomedes on the way back, to get all the credit himself (*Little Iliad*, fr. 9). In the surviving *Philoctetes* of Sophocles and apparently in that of Aeschylus also (see Rose, *Handb. Gk. Lit.* 169) his cunning is contrasted with the straightforwardness of Diomedes, or Neoptolemus, who accompanies him.

5. Odysseus had occasional worship as a hero in historical times, though, curiously enough, not in Ithaca (see Farnell, *Hero-Cults*, 326). There is no sufficient reason to suppose him other than a real local chieftain originally, though no doubt his actual doings are hopelessly overlaid with details of Homer's imagination or that of later writers. The plot of the *Odyssey* in particular is a folk-tale, as was pointed out by Nilsson (*Mycenaean origin of Gk. myth.*, U.S.A. 1932, p. 96; the motif is Stith Thompson K 1815. 1).

6. By the most probable theory the scene of his wanderings is outside known territory, however much vague reports of foreign lands may have helped to provide details (see, however, V. Bérard, *Les Phéniciens et l'Odyssée*, 1902–3). But during and after the period of colonization numerous identifications of places in the *Odyssey* with those in or on the way to Italy and Sicily became very popular. Of these perhaps the most plausible is that of Scheria with Corcyra; for some account of this see A. Shewan, *Homeric Essays* (1935), 242 ff. The site of Ithaca itself has been hotly disputed (ibid. 1 ff.), though the traditional place, the modern Thiaki, is probably the one Homer means.

Besides the literature cited in the text, J. Schmidt in Roscher's *Lexikon*, s.v., gives much useful material. H. J. R.

OEA (modern *Tripoli*), a port on the Syrtic Sea, was founded by Tyrian colonists about the seventh century B.C. With Sabratha and Leptis (q.v.) it constituted the African Tripolis, which acknowledged the suzerainty of Carthage and Masinissa's house in turn. Trade jealousy resulted in hostilities with Leptis, which continued even when both had been included in Proconsular Africa. Oea's relations with Sabratha were friendlier; both supplied Rome with grain, and Sabratha maintained a guild-house at Ostia. An *arcus quadrifons* survives to testify to Oea's prosperity under M. Aurelius.

W. N. W.

OEBALUS, an early Spartan king, who had a hero-shrine at Sparta (Paus. 3. 15. 10). He has no legend, merely a place in several mutually contradictory genealogies, for which see Wörner in Roscher's *Lexikon*, s.v.

Hence *Oebalius*, *Oebalides*, etc., in Latin poetry often mean Spartan, and the name itself is now and then used for some minor character of Spartan or Peloponnesian origin (as Verg. *Aen.* 7. 734). H. J. R.

OECLES (*Οἰκλῆς*) or **OECLEUS** (*Οἰκλέους*), in mythology, father of Amphiaraus (q.v.; Aesch. *Sept.* 609 and often). He has neither a consistent place in genealogy nor a legend of the smallest importance.

OEDIPUS (*Οἰδίπους*, anciently, and probably correctly, taken to mean 'swell-foot'), in mythology, son of Laius king of Thebes and his wife Iocasta (Epicaste in Homer, *Od.* 11. 271 ff.). The story is told there that he married his mother unwittingly, and when it was found out she hanged herself, but he continued to be king. He afterwards fell in battle and had a great funeral feast (*Il.* 23. 679 f.). Hesiod says (*Op.* 162–3) that some men of the heroic age fell before Thebes fighting for the flocks of Oedipus; he may therefore have been killed in warding off a raid. Clearly this is inconsistent with his later story, dating in essentials from the cyclic epics *Thebais* and *Oedipodia* but best known from the tragedians.

Laius had been warned by Apollo that if he begot a son that son would kill him (Ar. *Ran.* 1184–5). This was his punishment for sinning against Pelops (q.v.), who had been his host while he was in exile from Thebes; he had carried off Pelops' son Chrysippus (Soph. *OT*, argument). Nevertheless, he neglected the warning (Aesch. *Sept.* 842; Soph. *OT* 711 ff.); a son was born and Laius exposed him, running a spike through his feet (to prevent his ghost walking?). The infant was found by a shepherd of Polybus king of Corinth, who was herding on the summer pastures of Mt. Cithaeron; Polybus, who was childless, adopted him and passed him off as his own, naming him Oedipus from the state of his feet. But Oedipus, being taxed in young manhood with being a supposititious child, went to Delphi to ask who his parents were. He was told that he should kill his father and marry his mother. Determining never to revisit Corinth, he wandered to Thebes, killing Laius in a chance encounter by the way. Arrived at Thebes, he found the city plagued by the Sphinx, a monster which destroyed those who could not solve a riddle she asked. He guessed it and she killed herself; or he overcame her in fight (Robert, op. cit. infra, ch. 2). His reward was the hand of the widowed queen. They had four children, Eteocles and Polynices, Antigone (q.v.) and Ismene (the *Oedipodia*, fr. 1 Allen, made a second wife, Euryganeia, their mother after Iocasta's death). But the secret of the relationship came out; Iocasta hanged herself, Oedipus either blinded himself or (Euripides, fr. 541 Nauck) was blinded by Laius' servants. Thus he ceased to be king, going into exile or retirement. The former is Sophocles' version, the latter that of the lost epics, followed by Euripides (*Phoenissae*) and Statius (*Thebais*). His death is variously told, corresponding to his various cults (see Farnell, *Hero-Cults*, 332 ff.). The Attic version of his disappearance from earth at Colonus is told by Sophocles, *OC*.

But two explanations of the story seem possible. Either Oedipus is a real person, about whom fabulous details had gathered, following on the whole the lines of well-known folk-tales (so Rose, *Modern Methods in Class. Myth.* (1930), 24 ff.), or he is pure *Märchen*, taken up by epic (so Nilsson in *Gnomon* 8, p. 18). See, however, M. Delcourt, *Œdipe ou la légende du conquérant*, 1944.

The classical work and best collection of facts is C. Robert, *Oidipus* (1915). H. J. R.

OENEUS (*Οἰνεύς*), in mythology, king of Calydon, husband of Althaea and father or reputed father of Deianira and Meleager (qq.v.). The names of husband and wife ('Wine-man' and 'Healer') and the story that Dionysus was the real father of Deianira (Hyg. *Fab.* 129, and Rose ad loc.) suggest that they were originally wine-gods. Oeneus is also connected with Ares, who is his grandfather in Nicander ap. Anton. Lib. 2, Meleager's father in Hyg. *Fab.* 171. 1. Periboea, daughter of Hipponous or Olenus, whom he married after the death of Althaea and who was the mother of Tydeus, is variously said to have been with child by Ares, Oeneus, or a certain Hippostratus (Apollod. 1. 74 f.; Diod. Sic. 4. 35. 1–2). In his old age he was robbed of his kingdom by his brother Agrius, but restored by Diomedes (q.v.) or Tydeus (Hyg. *Fab.* 175 and Rose ad loc.; Pherecydes in schol. *Iliad* 14. 120). An obscure story apparently from Ps.-Apollod. (see Wagner's Teubner ed., p. 186) says that Agamemnon and Menelaus (qq.v.) were put in his charge for a time to escape Thyestes. H. J. R.

OENOMAUS (Οἰνόμαος) (1), see PELOPS.

OENOMAUS (2) of Gadara (c. A.D. 120), Cynic philosopher. Works (of which a few frs. remain): Περὶ κυνισμοῦ; Πολιτεία; Περὶ τῆς καθ᾽ Ὅμηρον φιλοσοφίας; Περὶ Κράτητος καὶ Διογένους καὶ τῶν λοιπῶν; Γοήτων φώρα (= Κατὰ χρηστηρίων); Κυνὸς αὐτοφωνία; and tragedies. The fragments of Γοήτων φώρα show it to have been a lively attack on the belief in oracles, an attack resting in part on the belief in freewill. He aimed at a Cynicism which did not follow slavishly either Antisthenes or Diogenes, and defined Cynicism as 'a sort of despair, a life not human but brutish, a disposition of soul that reckons nothing noble or virtuous or good'.
PW xvii. 2249. W. D. R.

OENONE (Οἰνώνη), a nymph of Mt. Ida, loved by Paris (q.v.). When he deserted her for Helen she was bitterly jealous, and on learning that he had been wounded by Philoctetes (q.v.) with one of Heracles' arrows, she refused to cure him. Relenting too late, she came to Troy and found him already dead, whereat she hanged herself or leapt upon his funeral pyre.
Apollodorus 3. 154–5; Parthenius 4; Quintus Smyrnaeus 10. 259 ff., all with small variations. H. J. R.

OENOPIDES of Chios (*fl. c.* 450–425 B.C.), astronomer and mathematician, discovered the obliquity of the ecliptic, and introduced improvements in elementary geometry; he may have been the first to require that only the ruler and the compasses should be used in the solution of simple problems.
PW xvii. 2258. W. D. R.

OENOPION (Οἰνοπίων), see ORION.

OENOTROPE (Οἰνοτρόποι), in mythology, daughters of Anius (q.v.).

OFELLA, QUINTUS LUCRETIUS, a Roman *eques*, deserted from Marius to Sulla. He successfully conducted the blockade of Praeneste (82 B.C.), held by the younger Marius. In 81 in defiance of Sulla's law he presented himself as a candidate for the consulship, although he had not yet been quaestor. Sulla had him murdered by a centurion.
F. Münzer, PW xiii. 1686 and xvii. 2039; R. Gardner, *Journ. Phil.* 1919, p. 1. A. M.

OFONIUS, see TIGELLINUS.

OGULNIUS, QUINTUS (*cos.* 269 B.C.), as tribune of the plebs together with his brother Gnaeus, in 300 carried a law (*Lex Ogulnia*), despite the opposition of patricians and Appius Claudius Caecus (q.v.), by which plebeians became eligible for the highest priesthoods, and gained the majority in the college of the augurs. Possibly (so Beloch, *Röm. Gesch.* 350 f.) the *Lex Ogulnia* was passed in 296, when the Ogulnii were aediles. In this year

they set up near the *Ficus Ruminalis* a figure of the wolf suckling Romulus and Remus. In 292 Q. Ogulnius headed the delegation sent to Epidaurus to bring Asclepius to Rome, which in 293 had been visited by a pestilence. In 273 he officially visited Alexandria.
F. Münzer, PW, s.v.; F. Altheim, *Hist. of Roman Religion* (1938), 283 f. P. T.

OGYGUS (Ὤγυγος, etymology and meaning uncertain), a primeval king, generally of Boeotia (as Paus. 9. 5. 1), but of Lycia, Steph. Byz. s.v. Ὠγυγία; of Egyptian Thebes, schol. Lycophr. 1206; of the Titans, Theophilus, *ad Autol.* 3. 29. The first Deluge was in his time, Eusebius, *Praep. Evang.* 10. 10. 7. H. J. R.

OIKISTAI (οἰκισταί), see CITY-FOUNDERS.

OIL, USE OF. Greek gods being anthropomorphic for the most part, it was only natural that they should be supposed to use olive-oil as men did, in food, as ointment, and for light, though hardly as medicine. Hence the occasional use of it for libations, ἐλαιόσπονδα (Porphyry, *Abst.* 2. 20). To oil a cult-object is one of the commonest acts of worship (e.g. Paus. 10. 24. 6; Theophrastus, *Char.* 16. 5; Prudentius, c. *Symm.* 1. 204). For the oiling of the doorposts in a Roman marriage see Rossbach, *Röm. Ehe*, p. 365. For full references to the sacral use of oil see Pease in PW, s.v. 'Oleum', 2466–9. H. J. R.

OINTMENTS served for medical purposes, mere pleasure, and religious ceremonies. The medical application, of course, was determined only by the expediencies of treatment. Half-way between remedy and luxury was the use of ointments in the gymnasium and as stimuli. To the side of luxury belonged, in spite of climatic conditions in the Mediterranean, the use of ointments before, during, and after the bath, at dinner, at almost any time of day or night. Neither the reprobation of the moralists nor governmental restrictions could check this indulgence; people liked ointments, elaborate mixtures, the attribute of Aphrodite, rather than pure oil, that of Athena. Moreover, the use of ointments was a sign of nobility and distinction and therefore was important also in the veneration of the gods and in burial ceremonies.

Material for the fabrication of ointments came from all over the world. Both wholesale trade and retail business were considerable, and hardly of any detrimental effect on the economic life as has been claimed; rather they provided a good tax revenue.

The receptacles in which ointments were kept, vases of various shapes and boxes, are among the most refined objects of art. Dry ointments were also wrapped in papyrus; to serve this purpose was the final destination of many an ancient book.
Hug, PW i B. 1851, s.v. 'Salben'; A. Schmidt, *Drogen u. Drogenhandel im Altert.* (1924). Economic implications correctly evaluated, M. Rostovtzeff, *Social and Economic History of the Roman Empire* (1926). Handbooks on Greek and Roman antiquities. Archaeological material ('Lekythos', 'Aryballos', 'Alabastron', 'Pyxis', 'Plemochoe') surveyed by G. M. A. Richter and M. J. Milne, *Shapes and Names of Athenian Vases* (1935), with bibliography. L. E.

OKNOS, delay or hesitancy personified; a figure of Greek folk-lore. For some reason he is associated with the lower world (Plut. *De tranq. anim.* 473 c; cf. Paus. 10. 29. 1, Polygnotus' picture of Hades). He is always making a straw rope, which an ass eats as fast as he twines it (cf. the futile labour of the Danaids, q.v.; this may explain his infernal associations). Another version seems to be that he loads the ass with sticks, which fall off as fast as he puts them on (Apuleius, *Met.* 6. 18); perhaps the rope is to tie them.
See Höfer in Roscher's *Lexikon*, s.v. H. J. R.

OLBIA, a colony of Miletus, situated near the mouth of the Hypanis (*Bug*), and within easy reach of the estuary of the Borysthenes (*Dnieper*). Its traditional foundation-date, *c.* 645 B.C., is confirmed by finds of Ionian pottery. It was a fishing-centre and the terminal point of a trade-route up the Hypanis into central Europe; but its main importance lay in its export of wheat from the 'Black Earth' area of south-west Russia, much of which it bought for resale from the Scythian hinterland. Olbia enjoyed its highest prosperity in the sixth century and until the middle of the fifth, at which time it was visited by Herodotus. It apparently had no share in the grain trade with Athens after 450, and in the third century it suffered from the growing insecurity of its hinterland (*SIG* 495—a record of frequent danegelds paid to marauding chieftains by a wealthy citizen). It was sacked *c.* 60 B.C. by the Dacian king Burebistas, and the rebuilt city appeared to Dio Chrysostomus (*c.* A.D. 80) impoverished and half-barbarized, though its inhabitants professed a passionate regard for Homer. It recovered some of its prosperity when Hadrian gave it a garrison, but it was destroyed by the Alans in the third century.

Dio Chrys. *Or.* 36; E. H. Minns, *Scythians and Greeks* (1913), 451–89.　　M. C.

OLEN, mythical epic poet, before Musaeus (q.v.); a Hyperborean or Lycian; said to have brought the worship of Apollo and Artemis from Lycia to Delos, where he celebrated their birth among the Hyperboreans in hymns which continued to be recited there (Hdt. 4. 35; Callim. *Del.* 304–5; Paus. 1. 18. 5; cf. *eund.* 8. 21. 3). *See* HYMNS.
　　W. F. J. K.

OLIGARCHY, the 'rule of the few'; on its connexions with the old nobility and its growth out of aristocracy *see* ARISTOCRACY. The chief difference consisted in the replacement of birth by wealth as the decisive qualification: oligarchy was plutocracy. There were many conflicts between the old nobility and the 'nouveaux riches', but finally 'money made the man' (Alcaeus and Theognis, passim). This also meant a victory of urban over tribal organization. In assuming political power the wealthy classes took over the economic burdens of the State.

In oligarchy political power was confined to a minority of the citizens; the majority had citizenship, but without full political rights. The method of selecting the 'few' varied extremely, according to the economic conditions of each city. In most States the landowners predominated for a long time. In addition, the ruling few might be limited to a fixed number which differed greatly in the different States, often rising to the 'rule of the Thousand'. Sometimes there was a scale of several citizen classes distinguished by wealth and accordingly by political rights (timocracy). In his classification of oligarchies (*Pol.* 6. 1292ª38 ff., 1293ª11 ff.) Aristotle differentiates between aristocracy and oligarchy rather than the actual forms of oligarchy. Political power in oligarchies was generally concentrated in the council. But formally the final decision was left to the assembly of all citizens, i.e. of full citizens, and in cases where the number of citizens was very small, the assembly could preserve a real activity. It is difficult sometimes to distinguish the assembly from the council, e.g. the 600 in Massilia. Sometimes, as in the case of the Areopagus (q.v.), the Council was composed of retired high officials formerly elected by the assembly. Some characteristic features of oligarchy appear in Sparta, always its champion. But Sparta represented a particular form of State, and its institutions must not be considered as typically oligarchic.

L. Whibley, *Greek Oligarchies* (1896); G. Glotz, *The Greek City* (1929).　　V. E.

OLIVE CULTURE. We know from finds that olives were grown in the Mediterranean area and Minoan Crete during the neolithic age. Plantations are mentioned by Homer, and oil was exported from Attica in the time of Solon. As soon as it became possible by imports of corn to satisfy most of the requirements of the Greek people, crops such as olives and grapes took the place of corn and were very widely cultivated in Greece during the classical age. There was a similar increase of olive cultivation in Italy after the Punic Wars. From the later first century A.D., exports of oil and wine from Italy being no longer able to compete with the increased local production of the Roman provinces, a more equable cultivation became a characteristic of the Mediterranean areas.

Methods of cultivation were much improved from the classical Greek period to the early Principate, bringing about a world-wide interchange of varieties. Two hundred trees, for example, were exported from Attica to Egypt under Ptolemy II. At least twenty-seven varieties were known, and improved mills and presses increased production. The grafting of olive-shoots on fig-trees and vines was successfully performed, and wild olives were grafted on the cultivated stocks to improve production (*terebratio*). Cheap labour, mostly servile, was used for the harvest. Olives were more remunerative to the large owner than to the small peasant, as it might take fifteen years to ensure a profitable return on an investment in a new plantation. In Cato's time the average profit was *c.* 6 per cent. on the capital invested. A model plantation of 160 acres described by Cato employed a slave overseer, his wife, five slave labourers, three ox-drivers, one ass-driver, a swineherd, a shepherd, with its oil mills, cattle, and working implements. Rome seems to have occasionally restricted cultivation in the provinces to protect Italian growers. Olive cultivation in the ancient world created a tradition in most Mediterranean countries which has never been completely lost until to-day.

A. S. Pease, *PW*, s.v. 'Ölbaum', 'Oleum'; J. Hörle, ibid., s.v. 'Torcular', 'Trapetum'; A. B. Drachmann, 'Ancient Oil Mills and Presses' (*Dansk Videnskab-Selskab, Archeologiske Meddelelser* i, 1932); B. Laum, *Rev. Arch.* Sér. v, 27 (1928), 233 f.　　F. M. H.

OLYMPIA, the main sanctuary of Zeus in Greece, was situated in a rich and lovely tract of Elis, in a hollow between the low hills that flank the river Alpheus. Strabo states that its fame was first derived from an oracle of Earth, like that at Delphi, and a pre-Hellenic occupation of the site is proved by the discovery of pottery and houses of the Bronze Age at the foot of Kronos Hill; but there does not seem to have been a Mycenaean occupation. According to Pindar the Olympic festival was founded by Heracles, and this tradition was also held at Elis; but the local belief was that Pelops originated it after his victory over Oenomaus. The games were said to have started in the ninth century, but the first Olympiad was dated 776 B.C.

The sanctuary of 'Altis' was a walled enclosure, which came into full occupation soon after the Dorian Invasion. The oldest shrine was that of Pelops. There were two temples, that of Hera, dating from the early seventh century and originally constructed of wood, and that of Zeus, completed in 457. On the north side, under Kronos Hill, lay eleven Treasuries (q.v.) of various Greek States in a row. The only building on the east side, other than a portico, was the circular 'Philippeum', built by Philip II of Macedon to commemorate himself. Innumerable statues of athletic victors stood in the Altis. Outside it were many large buildings of various dates: the Palaestra, a hostelry known as the Leonidaeum, of fourth-century date, used by officials, a Prytaneum, and a Bouleuterium.

Olympia was excavated by German archaeologists in 1881, although an earlier expedition from France in 1829 had secured parts of the sculptured metopes of the temple of Zeus, now in the Louvre. The German excavators found the remaining metopes and almost 80 per cent. of the pedimental sculptures. Among other notable discoveries were the head of Hera from the Heraeum, the Victory of Paeonius, the Hermes and

Dionysus, and a bronze head of a boxer attributed to Silanion. Renewed German excavations are now revealing the stadium, which was built of earth, without stone seats. An edict of the Emperor Theodosius, enjoining the destruction of all pagan shrines, made an end of Olympia as a show-site.

E. N. Gardiner, *Olympia. Its History and Remains* (1925). S. C.

OLYMPIAS, daughter of Neoptolemus of Epirus, married Philip II of Macedon in 357 B.C. and bore him two children, Alexander (in 356) and Cleopatra. Passionate and mystical, she gave her son these qualities; but his practical and imaginative mind was not hers. Her relations with the polygamous Philip became strained, but the story that she was his real murderer was only Cassander's propaganda. Devoted as Alexander always remained to her, he wisely refused to let her exercise any power, and he supported his governor in Macedonia, Antipater, against her. In 331 she quitted Macedonia for Epirus, which for years she virtually ruled. After Alexander's death she waged a propaganda war against Antipater's house, until in 317 Polyperchon invoked her help against Antipater's son Cassander in Macedonia. Macedonians regarded Alexander's mother as sacred; she mastered Macedonia without a blow, murdered Philip III, and made her grandson (Alexander IV) sole king. But her unbridled passions, displayed in an orgy of murder, ruined her chances and brought Cassander back; she had to surrender, and Cassander's army condemned her to death. But even so they dared not touch her themselves; she was finally killed by relatives of her victims.

G. H. Macurdy, *Hellenistic Queens* (1932), 22-45; *see also* ALEXANDER (3). W. W. T.

OLYMPIC GAMES. According to tradition the Olympic Games, held once every four years, were founded in 776 B.C., and a list of the winners from that year to A.D. 217, drawn up by Julius Africanus, has been preserved for us by Eusebius. In A.D. 393 (or 426) they were abolished by the Emperor Theodosius I. At first they were confined to one day and the contests consisted only of running and wrestling; but in the early years of the seventh century B.C., perhaps under the influence of Pheidon, tyrant of Argos, they were reorganized and enlarged, with races for chariots and single horses as the chief events. The Spartans, who till then had supplied the majority of the winners, thereupon withdrew and their place was taken by the Sicilian and Italian Greeks.

The games were in honour of Olympian Zeus. In his precinct, the Altis, lying between the rivers Alpheus and Cladeus, stood his temple, together with the statues of victorious athletes (*see* OLYMPIA). The first of the five days, to which the games in 472 were extended, was spent in sacrifices and general festivity, while the competitors and judges took the oath of fair dealing. On the second morning the herald proclaimed the names of the competitors, and the day passed in chariot- and horse-races together with the pentathlon competition for men. The boys' contests came on the third day; the men's foot-races, jumping, wrestling, boxing, and pankration on the fourth, the last event being the race for men in armour. On the fifth day there were sacrifices, and in the evening a banquet at which the victors were entertained. The prizes consisted of chaplets of wild olive.

E. N. Gardiner, *Olympia* (1925). For other literature *see* ATHLETICS. F. A. W.

OLYMPIEUM, the temple of Zeus Olympius at Athens; begun by Antistates, Callaeschrus, Antimachides, and Porinus, architects employed by Pisistratus, but abandoned after the latter's death, and not resumed until Antiochus Epiphanes employed the Roman architect Cossutius to continue the work. It was completed at the order of Hadrian (Vitruv. 7 *praef.*). The Pisistratean building was planned as an Ionic temple. Cossutius changed the order to Corinthian, but in general seems to have adhered to the original plan, dipteral at the sides, tripteral at the ends. The cella was of the open-roofed type called 'hypaethral' (Vitruv. 3. 2). The stylobate measured *c.* 135 by 354 feet, and the Corinthian columns were nearly 57 feet in height. H. W. R.

OLYMPIODORUS (1) (*fl.* 307-280 B.C.), democratic Athenian commander, secured Aetolian help against Cassander (*c.* 306), whom he subsequently repulsed from Elatea. He gave support to Lachares (q.v.), but subsequently headed the opposition against him at Piraeus (Paus. 1. 26. 3) and after the recapture of Athens by Demetrius Poliorcetes became virtually tyrant, holding the archonship for two successive years (294-292). In 287 he led the insurrection against Macedon, seizing the Museum; later he helped Demochares to take Eleusis.

W. S. Ferguson, *Hellenistic Athens* (1911); W. B. Dinsmoor, *Archons of Athens* (1931); G. De Sanctis, *Riv.fil.* 1936. F. W. W.

OLYMPIODORUS (2) of Gaza, sceptical philosopher, pupil of Carneades (who lived 214-129 B.C.). See Zeller, *Phil. d. Griechen* 3⁴. 1. 544.

OLYMPIODORUS (3) of Thebes in Egypt, *see* ALCHEMY, para. 4.

OLYMPUS (1), a mountain of nearly 9,600 feet, on the borders of Macedonia and Thessaly. Being the highest peak in the Greek peninsula, it was regarded as the home of the gods. The huge massif covers a large area extending inland from the coast of Pieria, and it therefore served to shield Greece on the north-east, since invaders must either force the narrow defile of Tempe (q.v.) or use the mountain-passes of Petra and Volustana to the west of Olympus. It also contributed to the isolation of Thessaly by cutting it off from Macedonia and the Thermaic Gulf. H. D. W.

OLYMPUS (2), in Cyprus (mod. *Troodos*), rises to 6,000 feet and constitutes the main mountain mass of the south-west part of the island. It was reputed to have held on its summit a temple of Aphrodite Acraea, which women were not allowed to enter. On the lower slopes are modern mines of asbestos, and in antiquity there were said to have been gold mines. It is used to-day as a summer resort. S. C.

OLYNTHUS, a city north of Potidaea on the mainland of the Chalcidic peninsula. Originally Bottiaean, it became a Greek city after its capture by Persia (479 B.C.) and repopulation from Chalcidice; its position and mixed population made it the natural centre of Greek Chalcidice against attacks from Athens, Macedonia, and Sparta. In 433 the city was strengthened by further migration and received territory from Macedon (Thuc. 1. 58), and it soon became the capital of a Chalcidian League issuing federal coinage; by 382 the growth of the League aroused the enmity of Sparta, which reduced Olynthus after a two-year siege and disbanded the League (Xen. *Hell.* 5. 2. 11 f.). When Sparta collapsed, Olynthus re-formed the League and resisted Athenian attacks on Amphipolis; when that city fell to Philip II of Macedon Olynthus allied with him against Athens (Diod. 16. 8), expelled the Athenian cleruchy from Potidaea, and received Anthemus from Philip (357-356). Alarmed by the growing power of Philip, Olynthus intrigued with Athens, harboured rivals to the Macedonian throne, and with Athenian assistance defied Philip; the city fell by treachery (Dem. 19. 266 f.) and was destroyed (348).

A. B. West, *The History of the Chalcidic League* (U.S.A. 1919); D. M. Robinson, *Excavations at Olynthus* (U.S.A. 1929-38). N. G. L. H.

OMENS, *see* AUGURES, AUSPICIUM, DIVINATION.

OMOPLATOSCOPY, *see* DIVINATION, para. 6.

OMPHALE, in mythology, a Lydian queen, daughter of Iardanus (Apollod. 2. 131, which see for the story, which is much older, perhaps going back to Creophylus and mentioned in Tragedy, e.g. Soph. *Trach.* 248 ff.). Heracles (q.v.), having killed Iphitus son of Eurytus of Oechalia, could find no one to purify him (cf. NELEUS) and applied to Apollo. The god would give him no answer till Heracles started to carry off his tripod, saying he would found an oracle of his own. Zeus stopped the quarrel with a thunderbolt, and Apollo said he could be purified and rid of the madness which afflicted him if he was sold as a slave and the price given to Eurytus. Hermes arranged the sale and Omphale was the buyer. According to Apollodorus, she set him labours of the usual type, against brigands, etc., none of which has a Lydian setting or geography; Alexandrian poets (see, e.g., Ovid, *Her.* 9. 53 ff.) make great play with the theme of her setting him to women's work. The length of the slavery varies (one year in Soph., three in Apollod.), and it is commonly said he had a son, Lamus, by Omphale (Ovid, loc. cit.).

See further Tümpel and Sieveking in Roscher's *Lexikon*, s.v.; W. R. Halliday, *Plutarch's Greek Questions* (1928), 187. H. J. R.

OMPHALOS, the navel, a name given to objects, especially stones, of navel shape. Such stones were cult-objects in the most primitive religion of the Aegaean region. They remained attached to several cults when a higher level of religion had been reached. The most famous omphalos was that in the adytum of Apollo's temple at Delphi (q.v., *and see* APOLLO, para. 4). Late and untrustworthy authors call it the tomb of Python or of Dionysus; this raises the question of the relation of the omphalos to omphaloid tombs and omphaloid altars. In any case, if the small limestone block inscribed ΓΑΣ, found in the adytum, is actually the omphalos, it could at most have been the marker of a tomb. Two other omphaloi have been found at Delphi, manifestly copies, one being the marble omphalos seen by Pausanias before the temple. Its surface is covered with a sculptured network that represents the woollen fillets placed around the true omphalos.

Any centrally located place was called the omphalus of its region, as Phlius of the Peloponnesus. So Delphi's omphalos was thought to mark the centre of the earth. The story was that Zeus, desiring to find the centre of the earth, started two eagles of equal speed at the same moment, one from the eastern edge of the world, one from the western; they met at Delphi. This story led to the placing of two golden eagles beside the omphalos, which were taken by Philomelus in the Sacred War.

J. H. Middleton, *JHS* xix (1899), 225–44; J. G. Frazer, *Pausanias* (1913), 314–20; W. H. Roscher, 'Omphalos', *Sächsische Gesellschaft der Wissenschaften, Abh. Phil.-Hist. Kl.* (1913), no. 9; id. 'Neue Omphalosstudien', ibid. (1915), no. 1; L. B. Holland, *AJArch.* xxxvii (1933), 201–14. The articles of Roscher and Holland are venturesome. See A. B. Cook, *Zeus* ii (1925), Plate ix for photographs of the Delphic omphalos. J. E. F.

ONAGER, *see* SIEGECRAFT, ROMAN.

ONASANDER ('Ονάσανδρος, the preferable spelling), whom tradition makes a Platonic philosopher, wrote his Στρατηγικός under Claudius. It is a treatise on the duties of a commander, a dull exposition of commonplace military and ethical principles, for which the author disclaims any originality; it was enormously popular during the Renaissance.

A. Köchly, 'Ονοσάνδρου Στρατηγικός (1860); Illinois Greek Club, *Onasander* (Loeb, 1923), with full bibliography. W. W. T.

ONESICRITUS of Astypalaea, seaman, Cynic, and Alexander-historian, was with Alexander in India; he steered Alexander's ship down the Jhelum, and was Nearchus' lieutenant on his voyage. He has left a reputation as a liar, but his book did not profess to be history; it was an historical romance resembling Xenophon's *Cyropaedia*, with Alexander as a Cynic hero and culture-bringer. It formed an element in the vulgate, and Strabo and Pliny used it for natural history; but it exercised little direct influence.

See ALEXANDER (3), Bibliography, Ancient Sources. W. W. T.

ONOMACRITUS, *see* MUSAEUS (1).

ONOMARCHUS, Phocian commander in the Third Sacred War (q.v.). After the Phocian defeat at Neon (354 B.C.) he was elected *strategos autokrator* and employed the temple funds at Delphi to bribe Thessaly into neutrality and to hire mercenaries. Defeating the Locrians and Boeotians, he refounded Orchomenus in Boeotia, and forced Philip II of Macedon to evacuate Thessaly (late 353). All-powerful from Olympus to the Corinthian Gulf, Onomarchus hoped with Athenian and Spartan aid to crush Thebes; but he was drawn northwards by Philip's invasion of Thessaly. Marching towards his ally, Lycophron of Pherae, probably in co-operation with an Athenian squadron, Onomarchus was defeated and killed at the battle of the Crocus Field (352). An able and unscrupulous individualist, Onomarchus made Phocis a first-class power; gambling on the dwindling assets of Delphian monies, he came near to success. N. G. L. H.

OÖSCOPY, *see* DIVINATION, para. 6, *and* EGG.

OPELLIUS, *see* MACRINUS.

OPHELLAS, Macedonian officer under Alexander; sent by the satrap Ptolemy to subdue Cyrene (322 B.C.). He became governor there; but we know nothing certain of his attitude in the Cyrenean revolt of 313/312, nor whether he was concerned with the constitutional reforms of that period (*see* CYRENE). At any rate, he became almost independent. There is little information about his relations to Carthage. But he took part in Agathocles' (q.v.) campaign to Africa, when, overestimating his forces, he hoped to subdue Carthage, and to found an African realm. Having assembled a large body of Greek soldiers and colonists, he lost many of his men during the march through the desert. Eventually the two Greek generals joined forces. But soon after (probably 309), Ophellas was murdered by Agathocles, who incorporated his troops. Almost all the colonists perished.

V. Ehrenberg, *Riv. Fil.* lxvi (1938). V. E.

OPHELTES, *see* HYPSIPYLE.

OPHION ('Οφίων), Orphic god, husband of Eurynome and ruler of the universe before Kronos (q.v.); Apoll. Rhod. 1. 503 ff.; Kern, *Orphicorum fragmenta*, p. 98, no. 29.

OPHTHALMOLOGY was greatly advanced by the Greeks. Twenty operations were devised; until the beginning of the eighteenth century only four were added. The treatment of more than thirty diseases was not essentially changed until the beginning of the seventeenth century. This great achievement, mostly due to the Hellenistic physicians, was closely connected with the development of human anatomy and probably with that of mathematical optics. Other factors may have contributed to a special interest in the subject and thereby to the amazing success: the frequency of eye diseases in the Mediterranean world, the importance of sight for every human being, the valuation of sight peculiar to the Greeks.

As regards anatomy, the fabric of the eye was almost entirely unravelled. Seven membranes were distinguished, the optic nerve was accurately described. The theories of vision were less satisfactory, depending too much on the various philosophical conceptions; Galen assumed that a sight-spirit proceeds from the brain along the nerves, envelops the object seen, and then returns to the crystalline humour, thus completing the act of vision. The explanation of diseases, in spite of all anatomical knowledge, was based mainly on humoral conceptions. The therapy consisted in certain dietetic measures and also in the local application of collyria, the great variety of which is attested by the innumerable seals of Roman oculists. As for surgery, it suffices to refer to the astounding operations for cataract, as described by Celsus and as practised by Antyllus (2nd c. A.D.).

TEXTS: Celsus, bks. 6 and 7; Aetius, bk. 7; the only Greek treatise preserved: Th. Puschmann, 'Nachträge z. Alexander Trallianus', *Berl. Stud. f. class. Philol. u. Archaeol.* v. 2 (1886). Medieval compilations, probably based on ancient material now lost: P. Pansier, *Collectio ophthalmologica Veterum Auctorum* (1903), (fasc. vii Ps.-Galen, *De oculis*). Fragments of the canon of ophthalmology, written by the Herophilean Demosthenes (1st c. A.D.) and dependent on Herophilus' book on eye diseases, collected J. Hirschberg, *Arch. f. Gesch. d. Med.* (1918–19); concerning a medieval translation of this work, M. Wellmann, *Hermes* 1903. Translation of Antyllus, M. Meyerhof, *Die Antike* 1933.

LITERATURE: General survey, J. Hirschberg, *Gesch. d. Augenheilkunde im Altertum, Handbuch der gesamten Augenheilkunde* xii² (1899); cf. also V. Deneffe, *Les Oculistes gallo-romains au III siècle* (1896). Galen's theory of vision, H. Cherniss, *AJPhil.* 1933. Operations, J. Ilberg, *Arch. Pap.* (1908). Instruments, J. St. Milne, *Surgical Instruments in Greek and Roman Times* (1907). Seals, *CIL* xiii. 3, 10021. L. E.

OPIGENA, see JUNO.

OPIL(L)IUS, AURELIUS (early 1st c. B.C.), a freedman who wrote on philosophy, rhetoric, and grammar, and was cited as an authority by Varro and Verrius Flaccus. One of his works in nine books was entitled *Libri Musarum*. He interested himself in determining the canon of the genuine works of Plautus, an author whom he frequently cited in his explanations of the meanings of words.

Cf. G. Funaioli, *Gramm. Rom. Frag.*, 86–95; Teuffel § 159. 4; Schanz–Hosius, § 195. 2. J. F. M.

OPIMIUS, LUCIUS, was a leading Optimate in the Gracchan period. As praetor (125 B.C.) he subdued the revolt of Fregellae. As consul in 121 (he failed to be elected for 122) he led the opposition to Gaius Gracchus; and in the final struggle, supported by the *Ultimum Decretum* of the Senate—then first used—took arms against the Gracchans. Gaius, with Flaccus and others, lost their lives. Opimius then set up a special *Quaestio* to try Gracchus' supporters, over 3,000 of whom were executed. In 120, Opimius was tried before the people for executing citizens *iniussu ciuium*; Carbo, then consul, defended him, and he was acquitted. But the democrats were revenged on him in 110, when the Mamilian commission condemned him, with other Optimates, for having received bribes from Jugurtha; he died in poverty at Dyrrhachium. M. H.

OPISTHOGRAPH, see BOOKS, I. 6.

OPPIAN of Cilicia (late 2nd c. A.D.), author of Greek hexameter poetry, the *Cynegetica*, for each verse of which Caracalla gave him a piece of gold, and possibly also the *Halieutica*, which may, however, be by another Oppian, of Syria, early third century A.D.; the poems do not contain much new scientific knowledge on their subjects, but have some grace and power of expression.

Text: A. W. Mair (Loeb, 1928). W. F. J. K.

OPPIDUM means not a community—*civitas, pagus, municipium*, or *colonia* (qq.v.)—but the town centre of such a community, or else any urban agglomeration in Italy or the provinces to which no territory was juridically attached. In Roman territory before 89 B.C. the chief *oppida* were those of the ex-Latin incorporated States. In them was centred the local administration of their former *territorium*. The towns of the indigenous Romans, known as *fora* and *conciliabula*, had less authority, if any, over the locality. All these *oppida* were, however, assimilated to *municipia* between 89 and 44 B.C., becoming the centre of self-government for the adjacent territory. In the provinces regular communities of Roman citizens (Italian immigrants or enfranchised natives) were at first called *oppida civium Romanorum*, whether administered like villages by boards of *magistri*, or with a fuller constitution. Later these were assimilated to the Italian *municipia* by the grant of charters based on the Italian model.

See the works cited in the bibliography under MUNICIPIUM (Modern Views, (a) Republic). A. N. S.-W.

OPPIUS (1), GAIUS, a tribune of 215 B.C. who carried a war-time sumptuary measure (*Lex Oppia*) forbidding women to own more than half an ounce of gold, wear multi-coloured dresses, or ride in two-horsed vehicles in Rome. It was repealed despite the fierce opposition of Cato in 195.

Livy 34. 1–8. H. H. S.

OPPIUS (2), GAIUS, Caesar's friend of equestrian rank and manager, with L. Cornelius Balbus, of his affairs. He corresponded with Cicero and helped Octavian. He wrote many biographies: certainly of Scipio Africanus and Cassius, probably of Caesar. He wrote a pamphlet to prove that Caesarion was not the son of Caesar by Cleopatra. Some ancient critics wrongly attributed to him the *Bellum Alexandrinum, Africum, Hispaniense* (qq.v.).

H. Peter, *HRRel.* II, p. lxiii; Schanz–Hosius, *Röm. Literatur*, i. 350; R. Syme, *The Roman Revolution* (1939), see index. A. M.

OPRAMOAS of Rhodiapolis in Lycia is famous for the huge inscription (*IGR* iii. 739) engraved on his temple tomb, which records the honours decreed to him by the Lycian League between A.D. 124 and 152, and the letters of the procurators and legates of Lycia Pamphylia and of the Emperor Antoninus Pius relative to these decrees. He gave more than 600,000 denarii to the League and its constituent cities for games, buildings, distributions, etc., and perhaps hoped by bringing his munificence to the Emperor's notice to achieve senatorial rank. He lived to see his great-grandchildren senators.

A. H. M. J.

OPS, Roman goddess, of obscure functions. Her festivals (Opalia, 19 Dec.; Opiconsivia, 25 Aug.) suggest by their dates and the title of the latter association with Consus (q.v.; Consualia, 15 Dec. and 19 Aug.), but the December festival also a connexion with Saturnus, (q.v.; Saturnalia, 17 Dec.), and, indeed, she is regularly associated with him by the ancients, he being identified with Kronos and she with Rhea. Her oldest place of worship was a small chapel in the Regia (Varro, *Ling.* 5. 21; Festus, p. 202, 20 Lindsay); for her other shrines, see Platner–Ashby, p. 372; Rohde, 750 ff. Her titles are Consiva and Opifera, Festus ibid. and *Fast. Arval.* on 23 Aug. (Volcanalia, where she is one of a group of deities receiving sacrifice).

See Rohde in *PW*, s.v. H. J. R.

OPTATIANUS PORFYRIUS, PUBLILIUS (4th c. A.D.), poet. From exile he sent (before A.D. 325) a verse panegyric to Constantine and after his recall he became *praefectus urbi*. His poems (ed. E. Kluge, 1926) are full of ingenuities, such as acrostics and deliberate limitations of the kind of words employed; some are arranged to have the shape of altars, water-organs, etc.

Cf. Teuffel, § 403, 1–3; Schanz-Hosius, §§ 783–4.   J. F. M.

OPTICS, see PHYSICS, para. 6.

OPTIMATES, a conservative political group in the later Roman Republic. They were neither a nobility of blood nor a political party, but merely the members of the few families which, owing to their wealth, influence, and ability, had succeeded in exercising control over public finances and administration. Membership of the Senate enabled the *Optimates* to distribute magistracies and commands to candidates of their own choice and class, thus keeping a narrow political leadership, which only a century of revolution could overthrow.

M. Gelzer, *Die Nobilität d. röm. Republik* (1912), and in *Neue Jahrb.* 1920; F. Münzer, *Röm. Adelsparteien u. Adelsfamilien* (1920).
P. T.

ORACLES (*oracula, μαντεῖα, χρηστήρια*). The primary meaning of *oracle* is the response of a god to a question asked him by a worshipper. It may also indicate either the body of priests that administer an oracular shrine or the shrine itself. There were many established oracular shrines in the ancient world, several of which had widespread fame. In each the god was consulted by a fixed mode of divination. At the most primitive oracles the god's will was revealed by the casting of lots or by the observation of signs: the movements of objects thrown into a spring, the movements of the god's image when carried, the markings of the entrails of victims sacrificed upon the god's altar, the rustle of the leaves in the god's sacred oak. At healing-oracles, after the performance of preliminary rites, the consultant slept all night in the shrine (*see* INCUBATION) and received a dream-vision. At the most highly developed oracles the god spoke through the mouth of a man or woman. Such was the method at Delphi, which is typical of all inspirational oracles. The prophetess spent several days in purificatory preparation and then entered into a trance, during which she heard the consultant's question. Her answer, no doubt unintelligible to the untrained auditor, was interpreted by the attendant priests and transformed by them into intelligible verse or prose.

At the major oracles the consultants had to go through preliminary rites of sacrifice and purification, and were admitted to consultation only if all signs were favourable. Usually their questions were submitted in writing, and the answer was returned to them in writing. Only at the simplest oracles did the consultant approach the god directly. Usually, whatever the mode of divination, the consultant addressed the god through the cult-functionaries.

Many of the gods spoke oracles at some of their sanctuaries, but Apollo was most esteemed as an oracular god. He had many oracles of the inspirational type: the world-famous Delphi, Didyma, and Claros, and numerous shrines in Lycia, Troad, and Boeotia. Zeus, also esteemed as an oracular god, spoke through signs at Dodona and Olympia. Asclepius at Epidaurus, Rome, and elsewhere, and Amphiaraus at Oropus sent healing visions. Trophonius at Lebadea had the most famous of hero-oracles.

The great oracles were Greek (except that of Ammon, q.v.), but there were oracular establishments in Syria, Egypt, and Italy. Worthy of mention among Italian oracles are the oracle of the dead (*νεκυομαντεῖον*) at Avernus, the incubation-oracle of Faunus at Tibur, and the lot-oracle of Fortuna at Praeneste.

See APOLLO, CLAROS, DELPHIC ORACLE, DIDYMA, DODONA, EPIDAURUS.

ANCIENT SOURCES: (a) Cicero, *De Divinatione*; Plutarch, *De Pythiae oraculis, De defectu oraculorum*; Eusebius, *Praep. Evang.* 3–6; Iamblichus, *Myst.* 3. 11. (b) For collections of oracles see R. Hendess, *Oracula graeca quae apud scriptores Graecos Romanosque exstant* (Halle, 1877); E. Cougny, *Anthologia epigrammatum graecorum. Appendix nova* (1890), 464–533. For inscriptions containing oracles see Michel, *Recueil*, 840–56; *SIG* 1157–66.
MODERN LITERATURE: A. Bouché–Leclercq, *Histoire de la divination dans l'antiquité* (1879–82); W. R. Halliday, *Greek Divination* (1913); P. Stengel, *Griechische Kultusaltertümer*³ (1920), 66–78; H. W. Parke, *A History of the Delphic Oracle* (1939). See the articles on the individual oracles for further bibliography.   J. E. F.

ORBILIUS PUPILLUS, LUCIUS, of Beneventum, teacher and grammarian (Suet. *Gram.* 9), migrated to Rome aged fifty (63 B.C.). His pupils included Horace (*Epist.* 2. 1. 69), who calls him *plagosus* ('Whacker') from thrashings administered during lessons on Andronicus' translation of Homer's *Odyssey*. He wrote embittered criticisms of contemporary characters and conditions.
G. C. W.

ORCADES, *Orkney* and *Shetland Islands*, were probably discovered by Pytheas (q.v.), and were visited by the fleet of Agricola (q.v.), who temporarily subdued them. Pomponius Mela gave their number as 30–40; Ptolemy mentioned some by name, but placed them incorrectly.

Mela 3. 54; Tac. *Agr.* 10; Ptol. *Geog.* 2. 3. 31.   E. H. W.

ORCHOMENUS. (1) Eponym of the Boeotian Orchomenus, a vague genealogical figure. He is son of Zeus and the Danaid Isonoe (schol. Ap. Rhod. 1. 230; obviously late, cf. DANAUS) and father of Minyas (q.v.); son of Minyas (Paus. 9. 36. 6 and elsewhere); his brother, and so son of Eteocles (not the Theban) (schol. Pind. *Isthm.* 1. 79). (2) Eponym of the Arcadian Orchomenus (Paus. 8. 36. 1).   H. J. R.

ORCHOMENUS, the name of an Arcadian and a Boeotian town. Boeotian Orchomenus stood on a promontory on the north of the Copaïc plain. It was an important neolithic and Bronze Age site and had a Late Bronze Age palace and beehive tomb. It was the northernmost Mycenaean fortified town and was associated by Homer and Greek tradition with the Minyans; its wealth implies that the Copaïs was then drained. It was among the first Boeotian cities to coin (*c.* 550 B.C.), and appears then not to have belonged to the Boeotian League. It declined continually, as a result of the hostility of Thebes and the flooding of Lake Copaïs, and was destroyed by the Boeotian League in 364. The Nymphs were especially worshipped there (Pindar, *Ol.* 14).

H. Schliemann, *Orchomenos* (1881); H. Bulle and E. Kunze, *Orchomenos* i–iii (1907–34); A. de Ridder, *Fouilles d'Orchomène*, *BCH* 1895, 137 ff. (archaic period; cf. Frazer on Paus. 9. 38).
T. J. D.

ORDERS, ARCHITECTURAL, see ARCHITECTURE, I. 3 and 4, II. 1 and 3.

OREITHYIA, see BOREAS.

ORESTES, in mythology, son of Agamemnon and Clytemnestra (qq.v.). In all accounts he avenged the death of his father, but the story is variously told in authors of different ages.

(1) Homer says that when Orestes reached manhood he killed Aegisthus (q.v.), and implies that he also killed Clytemnestra; it was a most laudable and exemplary deed, for which he won great reputation. No details are given, save that till the vengeance was accomplished Orestes was in exile (he came from Athens, *Od.* 3. 307), as indeed he must have been to escape. It is a straightforward telling of a quite possibly real event, and no regrets are expressed by anyone at his having to kill his mother; she was 'hateful' (*Od.* 3. 310), and in any case Orestes, as head of the family, would be her only possible

judge and executioner. See *Od.* 1. 29 ff.; 298 ff.; 3. 310; 4. 546–7; 11. 458 ff.

(2) Stesichorus (we may neglect the shadowy and perhaps fabulous Xanthus of Sicily, Aelian, *VH* 4. 26) told a slightly different and much more elaborate story in his *Oresteia* (see Vürtheim, *Stesichoros' Fragmente und Biographie*, 45 ff.). The scene was transferred to Sparta, an interesting reflection of the political situation; Sparta is Menelaus' kingdom, not Agamemnon's, in Homer. Here Simonides (schol. Eur. *Orest.* 46) and Pindar (*Pyth.* 11. 16) followed him. Orestes was apparently a baby when his father was killed, for his nurse rescued him (fr. 8 Vürtheim), whereas in Homer only eight years intervene between the murder and the revenge. Whether Stesichorus said that he was sent to Strophius of Phocis and that the latter's son Pylades became his close friend and helper (Pindar, ibid. 15. 35) does not appear from the scanty remains; but Clytemnestra was put on her guard by a boding dream (fr. 9) and, most important of all, Orestes was haunted after her death by the Erinyes and given a bow by Apollo with which to keep them away (fr. 7). See further ELECTRA.

(3) The tragedians elaborate three points especially: the manner of the return, the characters of Orestes and his sister, and the consequences of the deed. In Aeschylus (*Choephoroe*) he returns by strict command of Apollo, gets access to the palace as a stranger, bringing news of his own death, can scarcely bring himself to kill Clytemnestra, and is at once haunted by the Erinyes, of whom he is rid in the sequel (*Eumenides*). Sophocles (*Electra*) brings him into contact with his mother by a like stratagem, but otherwise has a Homeric atmosphere, with no Erinyes and no remorse, only a little natural hesitancy, which Electra does not share. Euripides modernizes the whole setting (*Electra, Orestes*) and makes brother and sister hateful monomaniacs. He also, following local legends (cf. IPHIGENIA), makes the ridding of Orestes from the Erinyes (who are purely subjective phantoms of his disordered conscience) a long process, involving a journey to the land of the Tauri (*Iphigenia in Tauris*).

(4) Later and less known versions of the story elaborate sundry minor points and tell parts of the adventures of Orestes and his companions differently. Some of the accounts we have may be due to lost tragedies, while others are local traditions; others are seen, by the date of the vases and other works of art by which we know them, to be old, although our literary authorities say nothing about them. See C. Robert, *Bild und Lied* (1881), pp. 149 ff.; Höfer in Roscher's *Lexikon*, s.v. For example, Pausanias was shown (1. 28. 5) an altar which Orestes set up in commemoration of his being freed from the Erinyes by verdict of the Areopagus (as in Aeschylus), a stone at Trozen (2. 31. 4) on which he had been purified, and another at Gythium where he was cured of madness (3. 22. 1); also a place near Megalopolis in Messene where he had bitten off a finger in his madness and so been cured (8. 34. 1–3). In Hyginus, *Fab.* 122. 3, Orestes kills Aletes son of Aegisthus, but Artemis rescues Aegisthus' daughter Erigone from him. *See also* ANDROMACHE, HERMIONE, NEOPTOLEMUS.

Of his death there is no consistent account. His childhood has no real legend, but he is introduced as a subsidiary figure into one or two stories, see, for instance, TELEPHUS.

For literature see references in the text. H. J. R.

ORESTHEUS, in mythology, a king of Aetolia, grandfather of Oeneus and son of Deucalion (qq.v.). He had a bitch which brought forth a stick; this he buried and from it sprang a vine. From its branches, ὄζοι, the Ozolian Locrians were named, and Orestheus called his son Phytios, 'Plant-man'. Athenaeus, 35 a–b + Pausanias, 10. 38. 1 (= Hecataeus of Miletus). For the connexion of the family with wine cf. OENEUS. H. J. R.

ORGEONES (ὀργεῶνες), at Athens, were members of groups, other than kin-groups, for purpose of common worship (ὄργια, rites). As there was a law compelling the *phratriai* (q.v.) to admit *orgeones* as members, it is probable that they originally consisted largely of the new citizens admitted by Solon and Pisistratus, and that the law belongs to the sixth century, or perhaps to a time shortly after Cleisthenes, who left the phratries undisturbed. A. W. G.

ORIENTATION is the placing of any person or thing so as to front a definite point, generally a quarter of the compass, as north or south. This was not infrequently done in building ancient temples. In Greece they commonly faced more or less due east (e.g. the Parthenon), although examples of other positions are not wanting (e.g. Apollo at Bassae has the long axis N.–S.). This may be a consequence of the east being the lucky quarter, that from which light comes. If so, the same motives were at work in determining the position of a Greek augur, who regularly faced north and counted lucky those omens which appeared on the right (e.g. *Iliad* 12. 237 ff., where 'right' and 'east' are explicitly identified). Contrast, however, Hippocrates, Περὶ διαίτης ὀξέων, 8 (Kühlwein), which says the left is the lucky side in some cases; cf. Psellus (ed. Hercher) in *Philol.* viii (1853), p. 167, 23 ff. To curse one turned west (Lysias 6. 51), and occasionally the dead were buried facing west (Plut. *Solon* 10; cf. Rose in *CR* xxxiv (1920), 141 ff., for suggestions). In Italy the common augural position and the correct direction for an Etruscan temple were facing south; for the former, however, there was also an eastward position (Livy 1. 18. 6; cf. Rose in *JRS* 13 (1923), 82 ff.). In general a *templum* had two axes, N.–S. and E.–W. Racial differences may have something to do with this. Sporadic examples of Italian graves apparently oriented have been found (F. von Duhn, *Italische Gräberkunde* i (1924), index under 'Orientierung'). H. J. R.

ORIENTIUS, a Gaul of the fifth century A.D. who composed an elegiac exhortation to a Christian life (Teuffel, § 464).

ORIGEN (ORIGENES ADAMANTIUS) (probably A.D. 185 or 186 to 254 or 255; Euseb. *Hist. Eccl.* 7. 1, Hieron. *De Vir. Ill.* 54) was born at Alexandria of Christian parents. His life is known to us chiefly from Eusebius, who devoted the greater part of the sixth book of his *Ecclesiastical History* to him, collected many of his letters (now lost), and joined with O.'s pupil Pamphilus in writing an *Apology for Origen*, of which one book is extant in a translation by Rufinus (Migne, *PG* xvii. 521–616). O. received his education from his father Leonides (who perished in 202 in the persecution under Septimius Severus) and later in the Catechetical School of Alexandria under Pantaenus and Clement (q.v.). He became a teacher and was so successful that, though still a layman, he was recognized, at first informally then in 203 officially, as head of the School. In order better to understand pagan thought he attended the Neoplatonic lectures of Ammonius Saccas. He also visited Rome. Literally applying the precept in Matthew xix. 12, he underwent castration (Euseb. *Hist. Eccl.* 6. 8). His career as a teacher was interrupted in 215 by the massacre of Alexandrians known as the Fury of Caracalla. O. withdrew to Palestine, but after a time was recalled by his bishop Demetrius. He now engaged in extensive literary work and acquired such personal influence in the Eastern Church as to become its unofficial arbiter. On a journey to Greece in this capacity he allowed himself, without the consent of his bishop, to be ordained priest by the bishops of Caesarea and Jerusalem (c. 230). This irregularity caused umbrage to Demetrius, who may also have taken exception to certain elements in O.'s teaching. O. was banished from Alexandria and deposed from the presbyterate, on what precise grounds is not known; but the decision was disregarded in Palestine, and O. in 231 settled at Caesarea where he continued his labours. In the Decian persecution (250–1) he was repeatedly tortured. His health gave way and he died at Tyre at the age of 69.

WORKS

Origen's writings were voluminous and their range wide, but only a small proportion has survived. He was a pioneer in textual criticism of the Bible, in exegesis, and in systematic theology.

(1) *Critical.* His chief work in this sphere was the *Hexapla*, begun before 231 and not completed till 244–5. In it were set out in six columns (*a*) the Hebrew text of the O.T., (*b*) the same transliterated in Greek characters, (*c*) and (*d*) the two Greek versions thereof by Aquila and Symmachus, (*e*) the *LXX*, (*f*) the revision of this by Theodotion. Only a few fragments of the work are extant. Origen's critical work led him into controversy with Julius Africanus; his *Letter to Africanus* survives.

(2) *Exegetical.* He wrote commentaries on the greater part of Scripture. Some of these took the form of scholia on obscure passages; others of homilies on numerous books of the O.T. and N.T., many of which homilies are preserved in the original or in Latin translations by Jerome or Rufinus; others again, τόμοι or volumes, are elaborate commentaries on divers books of the O.T. and on the Gospels of St. Matthew and St. John (fragments or considerable parts of some of these are extant). O.'s method of exegesis was allegorical, seeking out a moral as well as a mystical sense in the literal words.

(3) *Doctrinal.* The *De principiis* (Περὶ ἀρχῶν) is a remarkable exposition of Christian dogma written before O. left Alexandria. Setting out from certain points of doctrine given by the tradition of the Church, he proceeds by speculation to show how these can 'be arranged as a whole by the help either of statements of Scripture or of the methods of exact reasoning' (*DCB* iv. 119). Considerable fragments of the original Greek survive; and the work is preserved in full in a 'translation', frequently adjusted in the interests of orthodoxy, by Rufinus.

(4) *Apologetic.* A certain Celsus, a Platonist and 'an enlightened advocate of the reformed paganism' (Bigg), had, probably in 176, in his Λόγος ἀληθής written an elaborate indictment of Christianity. O.'s reply, *Contra Celsum*, written *c.* 249, which survives, deals with this point by point.

(5) *Devotional.* Two of O.'s works in this category have come down to us, *De Oratione* (Περὶ εὐχῆς) and *Exhortatio ad martyrium* (Προτρεπτικὸς πρὸς μαρτύριον). The former, written probably *c.* 231, treats of prayer in its various aspects. The latter was written *c.* 235 to his friends Ambrosius and Proctetus, who suffered in the persecution under Maximin.

The *Philocalia* is a collection of excerpts from O.'s writings by Gregory of Nazianzus and Basil. It preserves the original text of many passages known otherwise only in Latin translations and is interesting as showing what in the fourth century were regarded as characteristic points in O.'s teaching.

Origen exerted great influence and left important schools of followers; but the venturesome nature of his speculations aroused controversy, and he himself came repeatedly under ecclesiastical condemnation.

TEXTS: *Opera omnia*, C. de la Rue (Paris, 1733–59); C. H. E. Lommatzsch (1831–48); Migne, *PG* xi–xvii; *Origenes Werke*, in *Die griechischen christlichen Schriftsteller* (1899 ff. [not quite complete, 1941]). *Origenis Philocalia*, ed. J. A. Robinson (1893).
GENERAL LITERATURE: Eusebius, *Hist. Eccl.* bk. 6; Jerome, *De Vir. Ill.* 54; B. F. Westcott in *DCB*, s.v.; C. Bigg, *The Christian Platonists of Alexandria* (Bampton Lectures, 1886); O. Bardenhewer, *Geschichte der altkirchlichen Lit.* ii² (1914), 96–194; B. J. Kidd, *History of the Church to A.D. 461* (1922) i, ch. 15; E. de Faye, *Origène, sa vie, son œuvre, sa pensée*, 3 vols., 1923–8.

ORIGENES, Neoplatonist, next to Plotinus the most important pupil of Ammonius Saccas. He shared Plotinus' general standpoint, but did not distinguish the supreme being, the One, from Nous. He was much inferior to Plotinus in philosophical power. Works: Περὶ δαιμόνων, Ὅτι μόνος ποιητὴς ὁ βασιλεύς (that the supreme being is also the creator—in opposition to Apuleius and Numenius).

See Zeller, *Phil. d. Griechen* iii. 2⁴. 513–16. *PW* xviii. 1033.
W. D. R.

ORION (Ὠ(α)ρίων), in mythology, a gigantic hunter, identical, at least in name, with the constellation as early as Homer (*Il.* 18. 486, cf. *Od.* 11. 572–5), an unprecedentedly early star-myth. He was Eos' love and killed by Artemis (*Od.* 5. 121–4); bigger and handsomer even than the Aloadae (q.v.; *Od.* 11. 309–10). A part of his story in later authors is evidently astral; he pursued the Pleiads, or Pleïone their mother (schol. Pind. *Nem.* 2. 16), a clear reference to the relative position of the constellations.

There is some reason for saying that he is Boeotian. A rather late legend (Aristomachus in Hyginus, *Poet. Astr.* 2. 34; see Frazer on Ovid, *Fasti* 5. 494) says that Hyrieus, eponym of Hyriae, asked for offspring from three gods (their names vary) whom he had hospitably received. They made water (οὔρησαν) on a bull's hide and bade him bury it; in time a child was born, which he called Urion, the name afterwards becoming Orion. For more Boeotian legends about him see Rose, *Handb. Gk. Myth.* 116; Küentzle in Roscher's *Lexikon* iii. 1028 ff. He is also connected with Chios. He loved Merope, daughter of Oenopion ('Wine-face'), king of that island, but Oenopion disapproved, made him drunk, and blinded him. He therefore waded through the sea (in one version he is Poseidon's son, and has the power to walk through water) till he came to the farthest east, and there got his sight back from the sun's rays. He was finally killed by Artemis for insulting her, or by a scorpion sent by Earth, because he boasted that he would kill all animals. The story varies greatly in detail; see Küentzle's art., cited above.

Cf. S. Eitrem in *Symb. Osl.* vii. 53 ff. H. J. R.

ORMENUS, (1) father of Ctesius king of the island Syrie and grandfather of Eumaeus (*Od.* 15. 414). (2) Name of two Trojan warriors, *Il.* 8. 274 and 12. 187. (3) Eponym of the city Ormenion on the Gulf of Pagasae (Demetrius of Scepsis in Strabo 9. 438, cf. *Il.* 9. 448). H. J. R.

ORNAMENTA were insignia of a magisterial rank (*quaestoria, aedilicia, praetoria, consularia*), which were conferred by the Roman emperors and entitled the recipients to the courtesies of that rank. This honour was sometimes conferred upon men outside the *senatorius ordo*. Tiberius gave *praetoria ornamenta* to *praefecti praetorio, quaestoria* to a *praefectus vigilum*, and Claudius accorded them even to freedmen. Grants of this kind were usually made by decree of the Senate, but they did not include a seat in the Senate. *Ornamenta triumphalia* were conferred upon successful generals under the Empire as a substitute for the *triumphus* (q.v.) of Republican times. J. P. B.

ORODES II (*c.* 56–38 B.C.), son of Phraates III of Parthia and brother of Mithridates III (Dio Cass. 39. 56), with whom he disputed the throne in a struggle lasting many years, and finally gained sole control. In 53, when Parthia was threatened by a Roman invasion, Orodes marched against Rome's ally Armenia, while his general Suren opposed Crassus in Mesopotamia. After the Roman defeat at Carrhae, Orodes' son Pacorus invaded Syria. Profiting by the Roman civil wars, Orodes occupied nearly all the Asiatic possessions of Rome (*c.* 40 B.C.), but was dispossessed by M. Antonius and P. Ventidius (38). He died soon after. M. S. D.

OROMASDES, see RELIGION, PERSIAN.

OROPUS, on the north-east frontier between Boeotia and Attica, belonged geographically to Boeotia, of which 't was originally part. In the fifth century it was annexed to Attica, but not incorporated; it was lost in 412, and changed hands repeatedly later, being most often Boeotian. It was the landward end of the nearest Athenian route for supplies from Euboea (Thuc. 8. 28; [Dicaearchus] 1. 6, in *FHG* ii. 256). In the territory of Oropus was the Amphiareum, where the earth had opened to receive Amphiaraus (cult and legend are Theban importations of the late fifth century). Oracles were given by the interpretation of dreams and cures effected. The chief remains are of the third century, theatre, stoa, and temple.

Paus. 1. 34 and Frazer ad loc.; E. Fiechter, *Das Theater in Oropos* (1930). T. J. D.

OROSIUS, PAULUS, was a Spaniard. A presbyter at an early age, he fled before the Vandals to Africa, A.D. 414. There he became a pupil of Augustine (q.v.). His *Commonitorium de errore Priscillianistarum et Origenistarum* led Augustine to address to him a work on the subject. But his chief title to fame rests on his *Historiae* in seven books. This work, completed probably in 418, was written after Orosius returned from the East, where at Jerusalem in 415 he had prosecuted Pelagius (q.v.) for heresy. The work is an 'apologetic' history whose interest now is that Orosius used lost portions of an epitome of Livy and of Tacitus' *Histories* as 'sources'. Its aim was very much that of Augustine's *City of God*—to rebut the charge that the fall of Rome to Alaric in 410 was due to Christianity.

Ed. K. Zangemeister (Teubner, 1889); *CSEL* xviii for *Commonitorium*: Cf. H. Svennung, *Orosiana* (1922). A. S.

ORPHEUS, the founder of Orphism, generally said to be a Thracian. His fame in Greek myth as a singer is due to the poems in which the Orphic doctrines and myths were set forth. A metope of the treasure house of the Sicyonians at Delphi represents him (the inscription reads ’Ορφᾶς) on board the Argo with a lyre in his arms. The first mention in literature is found in Ibycus or perhaps in Alcaeus. Aeschylus and Euripides say that he attracted trees and wild beasts and even stones and was able to charm whom he wished. In vase and wall paintings, even in the Catacombs, he is often represented singing. The Christians referred the representation to the Prince of Peace of whom Isaiah speaks. The best-known myth tells how his wife Eurydice was killed by the bite of a snake, and Orpheus went down to the Underworld and persuaded its lord to allow him to bring her back on the condition that he should not turn round and look at her before he reached the upper world. According to the earlier myth the ending was happy. The common tradition that he was not able to fulfil the condition is later, but existed probably in the fifth century B.C. The myth is probably connected with some Orphic poem called the 'Descent into the Underworld'. Another myth, also represented in vase paintings, tells that Orpheus was killed and dismembered by Thracian women or Maenads. His severed head floated singing to Lesbos. This myth was the subject of Aeschylus' tragedy *Bassarae*. Some scholars think that Orpheus in fact may have been a real personage, the founder of Orphic religion, others take him to be purely mythical; to Kern he is a projection of the Orphic sect. The question must be left undecided.

J. E. Harrison, *Proleg. to the Study of Greek Religion* (1903; ed. 3, 1922), 453 ff.; O. Kern, *Orpheus* (1920); M. P. Nilsson, *Harv. Theol. Rev.* xxviii (1935), 186 ff.; W. K. C. Guthrie, *Orpheus and Greek Religion* (1935), 25 ff.; Alcaeus as restored in E. Diehl, *Anth. Lyr. Graec.* i², fr. 80, p. 129. M. P. N.

ORPHIC LITERATURE. Many poems were in circulation at an early date under the name of Orpheus (q.v.). Euripides and Hippias hint at their existence, Plato is the first to quote verses from them, and Aristotle speaks of the 'so-called Orphic epics'. The fame of Orpheus as a singer is due to these poems. It is said that Onomacritus, who lived at the court of Pisistratus, wrote Orphic poems. A few fragments preserved show that they contained a cosmogony and an anthropogony and that they were dependent on Hesiod. A list of Orphic poems and authors, due to an Alexandrian scholar, Epigenes, is preserved in Clement of Alexandria and Suidas. The majority of these poems are *pseudepigrapha*. The dates and personalities of the alleged authors are unknown to us and were unknown to Epigenes himself. The most important poem was the *Rhapsodic Theogony*, from which Neoplatonic writers quote many passages. Its age is controversial; most probably it is a compilation, not very much earlier than the authors who quote it, but it may have incorporated earlier elements. Under the name of Orpheus are preserved some late poems: the *Argonautica*, which is dependent on Apollonius Rhodius, the *Lithica* (on precious stones), which has hardly anything to do with Orphism, and a number of Hymns to various gods, probably composed in Asia Minor in the Roman age. The poems are edited together with the fragments by E. Abel, *Orphica* (1885). As regards the fragments this defective edition is superseded by the fundamental work of O. Kern, *Fragmenta Orphicorum* (1922); idem, 'Die Herkunft des orphischen Hymnenbuchs' in *Genethliakon C. Robert* (1910), pp. 89 ff. M. P. N.

ORPHISM, a religious movement originating in the archaic age, the first Greek religion which had a founder (see ORPHEUS) and laid down its doctrines in texts (see ORPHIC LITERATURE). The early poems being lost, our knowledge of the Orphic system depends on late sources. It comprised a cosmogony and an anthropogony. At the head of the cosmogony was Chronos, the Time which never grows old; of him were born Aither (q.v.), Chaos, and Erebus. Chronos formed an egg in the Aither and from this Phanes (q.v.) sprang forth, the creator and first king of the gods. His daughter Night assisted him and bore to him Uranus and Gaea. Then follows the common myth of Kronos and Zeus. Zeus was praised as the beginning, the middle, and the end of all; the contradiction thus implied to the creation by Phanes was solved by the statement that Zeus swallowed Phanes and all was created anew. By Demeter Zeus had the daughter Kore-Persephone who bore Dionysus, who was also named Zagreus. Zeus wanted to hand over his royal power to the child, but the wicked Titans lured it to them with toys, tore it to pieces, and devoured its limbs. Yet Athena saved its heart and brought it to Zeus, who ate it, and of him a new Dionysus, the son of Semele, was born. The Titans were struck by the lightning of Zeus and burned to ashes from which man was formed.

The important question is how much of this belongs to the old Orphism of the sixth and even the seventh centuries B.C. in which it spread abroad, especially in Attica and south Italy. Plato quotes an Orphic verse referring to the six generations of Orphic cosmogony, and Aristophanes in his *Birds* (685 ff.) expounds a cosmogony which is justly taken for Orphic; it does not essentially differ from that quoted above. It begins with Chaos, Night, Darkness, and Tartarus, adding that neither earth, nor air, nor heaven existed. Black-winged Night bore a wind-egg in the bosom of Darkness and from this emerged Eros (who takes the place of Phanes), gold-winged and like the swift whirlwinds. The high-sounding epithets betray the imitation of hieratic poetry. A little later Isocrates testifies to the fact that Orpheus more than others told crude and immoral stories of the gods. So far Orphism was dependent on old cosmogonic myths, embodying crude folk-tale motives, and especially on Hesiod, but enlarged them and developed them in a speculative sense.

The anthropogony is in fact the original contribution of Orphism to the development of religious thought. The killing of Dionysus-Zagreus is not mentioned in the classical age, except for a reference in Pausanias to an Orphic poem attributed to Onomacritus; he says that Onomacritus took over the name of the Titans from Homer and instituted orgia for Dionysus and invented the story that the Titans caused the sufferings of Dionysus. The authenticity of this information can hardly be doubted, for Plato speaks of the 'Titanic nature' of man as a proverbial saying in the sense of his innate evil nature, which can only be understood as referring to the crime of the Titans as told by the Orphics. Because man had been formed of the ashes of the Titans who had devoured the Divine Child, he contains within himself something of the divine and something of the evil Titanic nature. Further, Plato says that the followers of Orpheus called the body ($\sigma\hat{\omega}\mu\alpha$) a tomb ($\sigma\hat{\eta}\mu\alpha$), because the soul is punished for that for which it is punished and it seems to have this covering—the likeness of a prison—in order that it may be kept in custody. First it is to be noted that evidently the body is the evil and the soul the divine part of man. Abstinence from killing animals and eating their flesh was the best known feature of Orphic life, noted, e.g., by Euripides and Plato. The reason for this prohibition may be found in the uncleanness of the body or in the crime of the Titans or most probably in the belief in metempsychosis (see TRANSMIGRATION). This belief is not expressly ascribed to the Orphics, but it is to be remembered that Orphism is no isolated religious phenomenon but is in various ways related to the mystic movements and beliefs of the archaic age which it took up and systematized. Plato tells of sorcerers who produced books by Musaeus and Orpheus and through sacrifices according to these and pastimes called initiations promised deliverance and purification from guilt and from pains in the after-life: the righteous were to be rewarded by a symposium in the Nether World. The Orphics had appropriated the belief in punishments in the Underworld. Though it was not peculiar to them it had a special note: whosoever had not undergone the purifications in this life was to lie in the mire in the Nether World; the initiated and righteous were to live in happiness. This belief appealed to the broad public and was important for Orphic practice. In the words quoted from Plato the soul is apparently punished by being imprisoned in the body. In the archaic age there was a tendency, opposed to general Greek ideas, to scorn this life and to attribute a higher value to the other life in which the soul is freed from the fetters of the body. This is consistent with Orphism. Gold leaves from the Hellenistic age, found in tombs in south Italy and Crete, contain verses to be spoken on arrival in the Underworld, in which the dead man presents himself as a child of Earth and Heaven and asks for a drink from the Lake of Memory; it is also said that he has escaped from the sorrowful wheel.

Although Dionysus is the chief god of the Orphics, there is an apparent hostility between the adherents of Orpheus and those of Dionysus. This is understandable from the fact that the Orphics transformed the central sacred rite of the orgia, the omophagy, into the primeval crime of the Titans. On the other hand, Orpheus is connected with Apollo; he is even sometimes said to be his son. The reason is that both laid stress on purifications and righteousness. Orphism implied legalism of ritual and life, mysticism of cult and doctrine, a speculative cosmogony and an anthropogony which emphasized the mixture of good and evil in human nature; it contributed to the transformation of the Underworld into

a place of punishment. It made the individual, in his relationship to guilt and retribution, the centre of its teaching. But its high ideas were mixed up with crude myths and base priests and charlatans misused them in practice. In the classical age it was despised; only Pindar and Plato understood its great thoughts. It sank down to rise again with the recrudescence of mystic ideas in a later age. *See also* AFTER-LIFE.

C. A. Lobeck, *Aglaophamus* (1829); J. E. Harrison, *Proleg. to the Study of Greek Religion*, 455 ff.; W. K. C. Guthrie, *Orpheus and Greek Religion* (1935); I. M. Linforth, *The Arts of Orpheus* (1941); M. P. Nilsson, 'Early Orphism and Kindred Religious Movements', *Harv. Theol. Rev.* xxviii (1935), 181 ff.; *Gesch. d. griech. Rel.* i. 642 ff.; O. Kern, *Orphicorum fragmenta* (1922).
M. P. N.

ORTYGIA, old name of Delos ('Quail Island'); its nymph was identified with Asteria (q.v.). But as some half-dozen other places were called Ortygia, it is by no means certain that all references (e.g. *Od.* 5. 123) are to Delos. See Höfer in Roscher's *Lexikon*, s.v.

OSCAN, *see* DIALECTS, ITALIC.

OSCANS ('$O\pi\iota\kappa o\iota$), whom the Greeks sometimes reckoned identical with Italici generally, were strictly the inhabitants of Campania (q.v.): (Thuc. 6. 2; Pliny, *HN* 29. 1; cf. Juv. 3. 207). These Campanians, when Rome first encountered them, spoke the language of the Sabelli (q.v.), which the Romans consequently always called Oscan (Livy 10. 20; Festus, p. 121 L.). Central Italian coins reveal that a more correct name would be Safine (etymologically identical with Latin *Sabinus*). Safine was spoken by Paeligni, Marrucini, Vestini (and probably by Aequi, Marsi, and Sabini) (North Oscan), Frentani, Samnites, Campani (Central Oscan), Apuli, Lucani, Bruttii, Mamertini (South Oscan). The numerous inscriptions, few earlier than 300 or later than 90 B.C., are meticulously written, usually in a modified Etruscan alphabet. Oscan with Volscian and Umbrian forms one group of Italic languages, Latin and Faliscan forming the other. It differs greatly from Latin in sound changes, word forms, and vocabulary, less in syntax (see DIALECTS, ITALIC). Official and educated classes in Italy long continued to use Oscan; but the Social War ensured its ultimate displacement by Latin. Strabo (5. 233) makes the astonishing statement that Atellane farces, the only Oscan literary form known to us, were performed in Oscan *at Rome* in his day. Certainly the language was still spoken at Pompeii in A.D. 79 and in country districts survived even longer.

R. S. Conway, *Italic Dialects* i (1897), 1–266; C. D. Buck, *Grammar of Oscan and Umbrian* (U.S.A. 1928); J. Whatmough, *Foundations of Roman Italy* (1937), 110, 301 (with bibliography).
E. T. S.

OSIRIS represented the deceased Pharaoh. He died, was brought to a new life, and reigned in the Underworld. He was associated with fertility, and in Herodotus (2. 144) is identified with Dionysus. The Egyptians believed that men (and sacred animals as well) were identified with Osiris, hence Osirified, in the next life. In Hellenistic times, although the name and character of Sarapis indicate his relationship to Osiris, the latter appears sometimes in the cult of the Egyptian deities along with Sarapis, Isis, Anubis, and Harpocrates. In Egypt Osiris remained primarily the god of the Underworld. With the construction of the elaborate mysteries of Isis and their spread throughout the Roman Empire, Osiris travelled along with Isis as a central figure in the liturgical and ritual drama.

Ancient sources (Greek and Latin): Th. Hopfner, *Fontes Historiae Religionis Aegyptiacae* (1922–5). Modern literature: A. Erman, *Die Religion der Ägypter* (1934); F. Cumont, *Les Religions orientales dans le paganisme romain* (1929); G. Roeder, art. 'Usire' in Roscher's *Lexikon*.
T. A. B.

OSROËNE, kingdom in north-west Mesopotamia, bounded on three sides by the Khabûr and Euphrates, and on the north by Mt. Masius. In the second century B.C. it broke away from Seleucid control and formed a separate kingdom with Edessa (q.v.) as its capital. Its kings bore Semitic names, and the population was mainly Aramean, with an admixture of Greeks and Parthians. As a Parthian vassal State Osroëne played a prominent rôle in the struggle between Rome and Parthia. After the campaigns of L. Verus it became a Roman dependency, later a province. Long coveted by the Sassanids, it was at last conquered by the Arabs (A.D. 637).

M. S. D.

OSSA, a mountain of nearly 6,500 feet in Thessalian Magnesia. On the north it is separated from the massif of Olympus by the defile of Tempe (q.v.), but on the south it forms with Pelion an almost unbroken wall which shuts off the interior of Thessaly from the sea.

OSTIA. The site of Ostia, commanding the Tiber mouth some 16 miles from Rome, was of natural importance, but its traditional colonization by Ancus Marcius has not yet been confirmed by excavation. Walls of the first known settlement (c. 350–300 B.C.) are built of tufa quarried near Fidenae and enclose some 5½ acres; the four gates of the rectangle are flanked by strong towers. Ostia was thus one of the maritime colonies designed to protect Italy's west coast, and probably, like the others, had 300 colonists.

2. Ostia later became an important naval base, especially during the Second Punic War. She soon spread beyond her walls and assumed growing commercial importance. Goods from Spain and the West and the vital corn supply came to the Tiber's mouth, and so up-river to Rome. This made the town a major objective in the fighting between Marians and Sullans. Marius sacked the town. Under Sulla new walls were built and now enclosed over 170 acres. A new town-plan was also laid down, which needed little subsequent change.

3. Ostia was sacked by pirates (c. 68 B.C.), but under Augustus a period of vigorous building began, including the construction of a theatre, behind which was laid out a great colonnade, where representatives of overseas trade could rent offices. Under Gaius wells were replaced by an aqueduct. The development of the town was due partly to imperial generosity, largely to increasing trade; but the Tiber's mouth was silting up and proving dangerous, especially to the corn transports. Caesar had contemplated work here, but it was left to Claudius to build a completely new harbour some three miles to the north. Two moles and a lighthouse were built, and connexion was made with the Tiber by canal. For greater security Trajan added a hexagonal inner basin.

4. Ostia had developed steadily during the Julio-Claudian and Flavian periods, but the building of Trajan's harbour was followed by a more intensive expansion, especially under Hadrian. Though granaries and offices were built round the harbours, the old town remained the centre of the workers' guilds and her government controlled the new settlements. Large areas were rebuilt, including the dock-quarter, with its granaries and market, and an imposing Capitolium to crown it. To protect the granaries Hadrian stationed at Ostia a detachment of *vigiles*. Already the Pompeian type of house was giving way to a more modern pattern, to meet the increasing population: in Hadrian's rebuilding the tall brick-built blocks, well lit by rows of large windows, became universal. In the business quarters the blocks were designed to be let in single apartments or flats, with separate access to the upper stories; in the more residential parts of the town, particularly towards the coast, the houses were no doubt more luxurious and less compact.

5. Under the Antonines the new harbour system, which now eclipsed Puteoli, was the receiving port of the largest consuming centre in the world, and trade attracted men from all parts. The profits of trade rapidly increased the number of knights, and the governing classes were generous. The common people found satisfaction in their numerous guilds of builders, boatmen, bakers, etc., with their patrons, officers, guild-houses, and banquets. For recreation they had more than six sets of public baths, a theatre, and possibly an amphitheatre. Ostia also provided good sea-bathing.

6. The town's religious life changed with her growing cosmopolitanism, though Vulcan remained Ostia's *patrius deus*. There were temples to Roma et Augustus (Julio-Claudian) and to Magna Mater (? Claudian); Isis and, from the second century, Mithras were freely worshipped. Christianity is not certainly found until c. A.D. 200, but by 250 Ostia had her own bishop.

7. Decay set in before A.D. 200. New building became rare, the financial office of quaestor became ominously important, men seldom held magistracies (an expensive honour) more than once, the population dropped rapidly. This decline was hastened when Constantine made the harbour settlement, Portus, independent.

8. While Portus was worth protecting, Ostia became a prey successively to Goth, Hun, and Saracen. Attack and the growth of malaria gradually made the site a desert. In the Middle Ages it became a quarry for the builder, in the Renaissance and later for the collector. Systematic and continuous excavation on the site began only in 1907. By 1938 roughly a quarter of the area was cleared and the pace was then quickened in order to expose the whole town for the projected International Exhibition of 1942.

Ostia's inscriptions are collected in *CIL* xiv and supplement. A second supplement arranges the inscriptions topographically. Excavation reports in *Notizie degli Scavi*, especially 1908 f. L. Paschetto, *Ostia: Colonia Romana* (1912); J. Carcopino, *Virgile et les origines d'Ostie* (1919); id., *Ostie* (1929); G. Calza, *Ostia: guida storico-monumentale* (1929) (also in English); id., *La necropoli del Porto di Roma nell' isola sacra* (1940); F. H. Wilson, 'Studies in the Social and Economic History of Ostia', *BSR* xiii. 41–68; xiv. 152–62.

R. MEIGGS.

OSTORIUS SCAPULA, PUBLIUS, of equestrian family, *consul suffectus* before A.D. 47, when he succeeded Plautius as governor of Britain. He seems to have built the Fosse Way (*JRS* xiv. 252–6) and a forward line (modern *Ryknild Street*) as *limites* against the Britons of the Highland zone, with Viroconium (*Wroxeter*) as an advanced point and his rear secured by a *colonia* at Camulodunum (*Colchester*). Attempts at the offensive against Highland tribes were less successful: an advance to the Irish sea proved premature; and though Ostorius defeated Caratacus, who had fled thither, he was unable to subdue the Silures and Ordovices of Wales, and died worn out in A.D. 56.

Tacitus, *Ann.* 12. 31–9; *PIR*, O 112; Collingwood–Myres, *Roman Britain*, 91–7; F. N. Pryce in *Antiquaries Journal* xviii. 29–48.

C. E. S.

OSTRACA. Potsherds were not habitually used for writing in Greece, except as voting tablets at Athens. In Egypt such use began after the Greek conquest; the first dated example is of 274 B.C. Nearly all early Ptolemaic ostraca are tax-receipts; later, orders and lists are common, and letters, school exercises, magical spells, and religious texts, pagan or Christian, were inscribed on them. The Thebaid is the most prolific source of ostraca of all periods, especially Thebes itself, with Hermonthis and Crocodilopolis; a fair number have come from Elephantine and Coptos; a single group is recorded from Pselcis in Nubia, another from Tentyra. Oxyrhynchus has produced some hundreds, nearly all Byzantine. In the Fayûm they are rare before Roman times; one lot from Philadelphia is the only considerable find of Ptolemaic date; under the Empire they occur on most town-sites till *c.* A.D. 400. No ostraca have been reported from the Delta. Outside Egypt Latin ostraca have been found near Carthage. Except in the Fayûm, few have been obtained by scientific excavation: they are usually found in ancient rubbish-mounds or in house-ruins.

U. Wilcken, *Griechische Ostraka aus Aegypten und Nubien* (1899); [mainly Thebaid] A. H. Gardiner, H. Thompson, and J. G. Milne, *Theban Ostraca* (1913); P. M. Meyer, *Griechische Texte aus Aegypten* (1916); P. Viereck, *Ostraca aus Brüssel und Berlin* (1922); id., *Ostraca der Bibliothek zu Strassburg* (1923); L. Amundsen, *Ostraca Osloensia* (1933); Claire Préaux, *Ostraca grecs au Musée de Brooklyn* (1935); [Fayûm] B. P. Grenfell, A. S. Hunt, and D. G. Hogarth, *Fayûm Towns and their Papyri* (1900); P. Jouguet, *Ostraka du Fayoum* (1902); P. Viereck and F. Zucker, *Papyri ostraka und Wachstafeln aus Philadelphia* (1926); L. Amundsen, *Greek Ostraca in the University of Michigan Collection* (1935); [Oxyrhynchus] *E. E. Fund Arch. Reports* 1903/4, p. 16; 1904/5, p. 15; 1905/6, p. 14; 1906/7, p. 9; [Tentyra] J. G. Milne, *Arch. Pap.* vi (1913), 125 ff.; [All districts] J. G. Tait, *Greek Ostraca in the Bodleian Library etc.* i (1930); [Carthage] R. Cagnat and A. Merlin, 'Ostraka latins de Carthage' (*Journ. Sav.* N.S. ix (1911), 514). Publications of texts in periodicals are mostly reproduced in Preisigke-Bilabel, *Sammelbuch griechischer Urkunden aus Aegypten.* J. G. M.

OSTRACISM (ὀστρακισμός), at Athens, banishment without disgrace and without loss of citizen rights or property for ten years. It was, we are told, instituted by Cleisthenes, 'because Pisistratus as popular leader and strategus had made himself tyrant'—an altogether trustworthy account: the new democracy feared lest another popular leader might make himself too powerful (without having committed a crime against the State) and establish a second tyranny. It was first used in 487–485 B.C. against relatives and suspected friends of the tyrant. Thereafter, as the democracy became firmly established, it tended to become an instrument of party warfare. Among its victims were Xanthippus, Aristides, Themistocles, Cimon, and Thucydides son of Melesias (qq.v.). It was not used again till 417, when, by an intrigue between Nicias and Alcibiades, Hyperbolus, a minor demagogue, was ostracized; this was the last occasion.

Once a year a preliminary vote was taken whether a vote of ostracism should take place. If there was a majority in favour, the second vote took place shortly after. As for all νόμοι ἐπ' ἀνδρί, i.e. the application of a law to an individual by the Ecclesia, voting was by *phylae* and secret; and a quorum was necessary. It is not clear whether only a total of 6,000 was necessary, or 6,000 against any individual. Strongly in favour of the first view is the general regulation about νόμοι ἐπ' ἀνδρί; in favour of the second is our best authority (Philochorus), and the fact that, if only a total of 6,000 votes was necessary, if 3,001 were given against A and 2,999 against B, A would be ostracized, whereas if 5,999 were given against A and no other vote was given at all, there would be no ostracism. In other νόμοι ἐπ' ἀνδρί there was no conflict between individuals; perhaps it was so in this case too, the individual against whom a vote was to be taken having been decided at the preliminary vote.

The name of the individual to be ostracized was cut by the voters on *ostraca*, broken pieces of pottery. Several hundred such ostraca have been found, and on them the names of all those known to have been ostracized.

Similar institutions are known at Argos and (for a short period *c.* 450 B.C.) at Syracuse, where the names were written on olive-leaves (*petala*: hence the vote was called *petalismos*).

G. Busolt-H. Swoboda, *Griechische Staatskunde* (1920–6), 884–6; R. J. Bonner, *CPhil.* viii. 223 ff.; J. Carcopino, *L'Ostracisme athénien*[2] (1935). A. W. G.

OTACILIUS CRASSUS, TITUS, praetor in 217 and 214 B.C., served in Sicily 216–211, raiding the African coast (215 and possibly in 212) and commanding a fleet at the siege of Syracuse. His exploits in 212 (Livy 25. 31) and his election to the consulship before his death in 211 are doubtful. H. H. S.

OTHO, MARCUS SALVIUS (A.D. 32–69), whose father received patrician rank from Claudius, was husband of Poppaea Sabina and friend of Nero. As Nero fell in love with his wife (afterwards divorced), he was sent to Lusitania as governor in 58 and remained there until Nero's death (68). He supported Galba and hoped to be his heir. Disappointed, he organized a conspiracy among the Praetorians and was hailed emperor (15 Jan. 69). He tried to appear as the legitimate successor of Nero. Egypt, Africa, and the legions of the Danube and the Euphrates declared for him. But the legions of the Rhine had already chosen Vitellius (q.v. 1), to whom he made unsuccessful advances. He was attacked in Italy and could oppose only an inferior army. He had to arm 2,000 gladiators. He dispatched his generals Annius Gallus and Vestricius Spurinna to hold the line of the Po (March 69), but remained idle in Rome until April. A body of troops, which was sent by sea to Gaul, achieved nothing. The decisive battle was fought at Bedriacum, *c.* 22 miles east of Cremona. Notwithstanding some help from Illyricum, Otho was decisively beaten and his army surrendered. He committed suicide (April 69). Tradition reasonably represents him as an incapable and profligate man.

Sources: Plutarch, *Otho* (commentary by E. G. Hardy, 1890); Suetonius, *Otho* (commentary by G. W. Mooney 1930), etc. See further s.v. GALBA (1); cf. L. Paul, *Rh. Mus.* 1902, 76; Nagl, *PW* i A, 2035; A. Passerini, 'Le due battaglie presso Betriacum', *Studi di antichità classica offerti a E. Ciaceri* (1940). A. M.

OTHO, see also JUNIUS (2), ROSCIUS (2).

OTUS, see ALOADAE.

OURANOS, see GAEA.

OVATIO was a minor form of *triumphus* (q.v.). It might be granted to a general who could not claim a full triumph, e.g. if his victory had not involved the destruction of a large number of the enemy or if he had handed over his army to a successor. He entered Rome on foot or horseback, wearing a wreath of myrtle instead of laurel, and the procession was much less spectacular. H. H. S.

OVID (PUBLIUS OVIDIUS NASO, 43 B.C.–A.D. 17?) was born at Sulmo, a town of the Paeligni. He prided himself that he was of equestrian rank by birth, not through property or service (*Tr.* 2. 110 ff.; 4. 10. 7; *Am.* 3. 15. 3). He was educated at Rome in law and rhetoric under Arellius Fuscus, whose redundant manner he reflected, and Porcius Latro, whose style was more restrained. Ovid's heart, however, was not in pleading but in poetry. His prudent father tried to dissuade him from that unprofitable pursuit. For a time he followed this advice. He completed his education at Athens (*Tr.* 1. 2. 77), and travelled in Sicily and Asia Minor with a poet-friend, the younger Macer. On reaching manhood he assumed the *angustus clavus*, as he did not aspire to a senatorial public career. He served in the centumviral court, acted as arbitrator (*Tr.* 2. 93–6; *Pont.* 3. 5. 23), and on the board of *tresviri capitales*, in charge of prisons and executions (*Tr.* 4. 10. 34; Owen, *Tr.* ii, p. 140). He was married three times. He had a daughter probably by his second wife. His third wife was a dependant of Paullus Fabius Maximus, and intimate with his wife Marcia (*Pont.* 1. 2. 136–8). He speaks of her with affection, praising her loyalty. She was a widow, with one daughter Perilla (Wheeler, *AJPhil.* xlvi. 28). He had attended *recitationes* by the didactic poet Macer, Horace, and Propertius his personal friend. Virgil he saw only (*Tr.* 4. 10. 51). His friendship with Tibullus was cut short by that poet's death, which he lamented in exquisite verse (*Am.* 3. 9). He knew many of the younger poets.

2. With comfortable means he lived in Rome devoting himself to society and poetry. The *Amores* at once

brought him celebrity. The fair frail idol of his verse, called by the fictitious name Corinna, was no real person, but the creation of his fancy, the epitome of many women. The *Heroides* won fresh applause. In his fortieth year he produced his masterpiece of witty impropriety, the *Ars*, which marked him as the chief of erotic poets. The publication of the *Ars* followed closely on the banishment of Augustus' daughter Julia, whose profligacy was a grave blow to her father's moral reforms. Augustus was angered by the pernicious influence of the *Ars*, and it was the contributory cause of O.'s banishment.

3. Ovid's brilliant talent was now acknowledged and his social position assured when, in the island of Elba (*Pont.* 2. 3. 84), he learned that he was sentenced (A.D. 8) to banishment to a place prescribed (*relegatio*); he retained his property, and the possibility of pardon was not excluded. The charges were two, his poem and a mistake of conduct ('duo crimina, carmen et error', *Tr.* 2. 207). The 'error' was the more serious. He had concealed something he had seen which affected the Emperor and his family. Ovid never dared to disclose what this offence was. There have been many guesses as to its nature. It may have been concerned with some scheme regarding the popular prince Germanicus which clashed with the dynastic aims of Livia and Tiberius, who obdurately refused to pardon the poet. Ovid departed into exile Nov. A.D. 8, reaching Tomis in spring or summer of A.D. 9.

4. Tomis (not Tomi, cf. MSS. *Tr.* 3. 9. 33; *Pont.* 4. 14. 59), a frontier fortress on the Euxine, now *Constanza*, was inhabited by half-bred Greeks and barbarian Getae, expert horsemen, who constantly went armed. Life was insecure, harassed by raids from wild tribes beyond the Danube. The severe winter cold is vividly described by O. in terms not overdrawn. The languages (Latin was almost unknown) were corrupt Greek, but chiefly Getic and Sarmatian, which tongues O. learned. At Tomis he lived, busy with verse-making and poetical epistles. He was abstemious, slender and not strong (*Pont.* 1. 5. 51; 10. 29), genial and lovable (Sen. *Controv.* 2. 2. 8). He won the goodwill of the Tomitae, who exempted him from taxes (*Pont.* 4. 9. 101). Even his native Sulmo, he says, could not have been kinder (*Pont.* 4. 14. 49). He died in exile according to Jerome in A.D. 17. A reference to the restoration by Tiberius of the temple of Janus (*Fasti*, 1. 223–6) suggests that he may have lived till 18.

5. WORKS

(1) **Amores,** love poems which, except in the lament for Tibullus, show little real feeling. Ed. 1 (five books) appeared soon after 16 B.C. (1. 14. 45); ed. 2 (rearranged in three books: cf. epigram prefixed to bk. 1) shortly before the *Ars* (*Ars Am.* 3. 343).

(2) **Heroides** (so cited by Priscian, Keil, *Gramm. Lat.* ii. 544, referred to as *Epistulae* by O., *Ars Am.* 3. 345), mostly letters addressed by noble ladies of the legendary past, in *Ep.* 15 by the poetess Sappho, to absent husbands or lovers. The idea of the fictitious love-letter may be derived from Propertius 4. 3 (letter of Arethusa); but O.'s claim to originality holds good, since Propertius dealt with contemporary fact, O. with mythological past.

The last six letters, in pairs, were suggested by the replies composed by O.'s friend Sabinus to six of the *Heroides* (*Am.* 2. 18. 27). Encouraged by the popularity of the original issue (1–15), O. added the pair letters in the complete edition. He testifies that he wrote a letter of Sappho (*Am.* 2. 18. 26). But the genuineness of the *Ep. Sapph.* (15), also of 16–21, has often been questioned on insufficient grounds. Loss of sheets in the archetype may explain the absence from its place of *Ep.* 15 in the chief manuscripts and of the conclusion of *Ep.* 21.

(3) **Medicamina faciei femineae,** a fragment in elegiacs, is a handbook of cosmetics for the female toilet.

(4) **Ars Amatoria,** three books. O. as professor of Love ('praeceptor amoris', 1. 17) presents Love as a science in didactic mockery of current text-books, *ars grammatica* and such. It is concerned not with respectable women but with the demi-monde; therefore O. argued it was not immoral (*Tr.* 2. 247). Books 1 and 2 instruct men how to find and keep a mistress, bk. 3 contains corresponding instruction for women. Beautiful narrative episodes enliven the work. Allusions to the naumachia of 2 B.C. (1. 171) and the Parthi (1. 179) indicate that it appeared soon after 1 B.C.

(5) **Remedia amoris,** one book, followed soon after the *Ars* (155), the wantonness of which had roused disapproval. O. replies that erotic poetry must be erotic; his aim is renown; this the *Ars* has brought him. The specifics for escape from irregular entanglements are obtained chiefly by 'converting' the rules of the *Ars*.

(6) **Metamorphoses,** fifteen books in hexameters, a collection of stories mainly Greek, some Roman, involving changes of shape, from the change of chaos into order down to that of Julius Caesar into a star. In combining, like Callimachus in the *Aitia*, short stories into a continuous whole, O. followed Alexandrian precedent. The subject of transformations was treated by Alexandrian poets. The Ὀρνιθογονία of Boios was adapted by Aemilius Macer. O. had heard Macer recite, and thence possibly conceived his idea (*Tr.* 4. 10. 43). He draws mainly from Greek dramatists and poets, towards the end from Virgil. When he was banished, the *Met.* lacked his final revision. He burnt it in disgust, but it was preserved in copies possessed by friends (*Tr.* 1. 7. 13).

A storehouse of mythology, this great poem has inspired medieval and later painters, sculptors, and poets, among them Chaucer and Shakespeare. O.'s proud confidence of immortality (15. 871) has been amply justified.

(7) **Fasti,** six books, a poetical calendar of the first six months of the Roman year, a book allotted to each month, arranged under three heads, astronomical, historical, religious. The risings and settings of constellations are expounded, with remarks about the weather. Legendary and historical events connected with dates are sketched. Festivals and religious rites are recorded with minute information. Six out of twelve projected books were completed when O. was banished. These at his death he had incompletely revised, prefixing the dedication to Germanicus (1. 3). They were issued posthumously, the original dedication to Augustus being retained at 2. 3–18. The last six books were too unfinished to be published.

The aetiological conception of the *Fasti* comes from Callimachus' *Aitia*, though the poems of Propertius on legends (bk. 4) may have influenced O.

(8) **Tristia,** five books (A.D. 8–12), letters addressed to persons whose names are generally suppressed, lest connexion with the disgraced poet might injure them. Where that was not feared, names are given, in three letters to Augustus, six to his wife, and in that to his stepdaughter Perilla. These 'mournful numbers' are pathetic, often servile supplications, pleading for mitigation of his sentence. The defence of himself (bk. 2) is interesting, especially the survey of Greek and Latin poets, and the summary of games.

(9) **Epistulae ex Ponto,** four books, letters of the same sort, except that names of recipients are given. Books 1–3 were written A.D. 12–13: book 4 was published posthumously. The latest chronological reference (4. 9. 4) is to the suffect consulship of Graecinus A.D. 16.

(10) **Ibis,** a comprehensive curse, expressed by recondite allusions, imprecating disaster and death of every conceivable kind on an enemy who persecutes the poet's wife and attempts to deprive him of his property. This person, whom O. calls Ibis, has been identified with the man referred to in *Tr.* 1. 6. 14; 3. 11. 2 and 20; 4. 9. 15 ff. Title and idea were borrowed from the lost poem

in which Callimachus attacked Apollonius Rhodius under the name Ibis, a bird seen everywhere in Alexandria, of dirty habits (Strabo, p. 823). Ovid's adaptation was written at Tomis (*Ib.* 11 ff.; 637), later than *Pont.* 4. 14. 44, where he says that he had written no poem of personal attack.

(11) **Halieutica,** in hexameters, a fragment on fishes. Pliny, who gives the title, paraphrases it (*HN* 32. 11), and concludes that certain fishes recorded here only were peculiar to the Euxine, where O. began this poem at the end of his life. It was published posthumously, unrevised. This accounts for metrical and other blemishes, which have caused its genuineness to be impugned unnecessarily (Owen, *CQ* viii. 267).

(12) **Nux,** the lament of a nut-tree over its sufferings from stones thrown at it by passers by. Written probably towards the end of O.'s life, it is allegorical, the innocent victim of persecution representing the poet. The compliment to the Emperor, who brought peace (143–6), supports this interpretation. It is an expansion of an epigram by Antipater (*Anth. Pal.* 9. 3), or some such work. Its genuineness, often questioned, was established by Ganzenmüller.

(13) **Lost poems.** To the early period belong the unfinished (entirely lost) *Gigantomachia* (*Am.* 2. 1. 11–16; Owen, *Tr.* ii. 63) and the tragedy *Medea* (*Tr.* 2. 553) (of which two lines survive), praised by Quintilian (*Inst.* 10. 1. 98) and ranked by Tacitus (*Dial.* 12) with the *Thyestes* of Varius.

Besides one *Priapeum* (*Priap.* 3) fragments exist of epigrams, of a shortened adaptation of Aratus' *Phaenomena* (Lactantius *Inst.* 2. 5. 24), and others of uncertain location.

Nothing but the titles remain of the following: (1) *Liber in malos poetas* (Quint. *Inst.* 6. 3. 96). (2) Epithalamium for Paullus Fabius Maximus (*Pont.* 1. 2. 131). (3) Epicedium on M. Valerius Messalla Corvinus (*Pont.* 1. 7. 30). (4) Panegyric on the Pannonian Triumph of Tiberius (*Pont.* 3. 4. 3). (5) Epicedium on Augustus (*Pont.* 4. 6. 17; 9. 131). (6) Poem praising the imperial house, written after Augustus' death, in the Getic language (*Pont.* 4. 13. 19–36).

The fragments are collected in Owen, *Tristia*, etc., O.C.T., Lenz, *Halieutica*, etc., Paravia.

6. A poet by instinct, Ovid lacked the dignity and earnestness which the loftiest poetry demands. His one tragedy has perished and cannot be assessed. By his own confession he abandoned epic as beyond his powers. But as an interpreter of his age he is a master. He reflects its spirit, grateful subserviency to the ruler who had established peace, and enthusiastic appreciation of its blessings. His message was to the cultured society of the capital; his mission to cheer, give pleasure, and amuse. His success is due to his vivacity and sparkling wit. He is deeply sensitive to beauty, the physical beauty of youth and strength, the beauties of nature, of scenery and the gay tints of flowers, idealized with peculiar richness of terms for glowing colour. Having a fertile and creative imagination, he is unrivalled in the ease and liveliness with which he conceives and describes scenes and incidents. His style is brilliant and lucid. The variety of his metaphors and polished similes, the dexterity with which he enlivens his diction by introducing legal phrases and formalities, and the many new words with which he enriched the language add peculiar charm. He was learned, but carried his learning lightly. He had an extensive knowledge of Greek literature, especially of the Alexandrians, from whom he drew much, and of the Latin poets, both predecessors and contemporaries. With striking originality he enlarged the slender range of the elegiac couplet. In this metre having perfected the artistic form of the Roman love-elegy, he used the couplet in the *Heroides* for psychological studies of the fluctuating moods of women; in

the *Ars Amatoria* for didactic poetry; in the *Fasti* for sustained serious effort; in the *Ibis* for vituperation; during his exile for personal letters which, though monotonous from their circumstances, are always neat and ingenious. His most ambitious work, the *Metamorphoses*, though epic in form, is in fact a new creation. It is not a concrete whole, but a string of stories of love and adventure, a wonderland of fancy, passing from grave to gay. In this great poem, intensely modern in its appeal through its vivacity and swiftness of narrative shifting from scene to scene, O. stands forth as the forerunner of romance. His faultless precision of metre gave its final polish to the elegiac couplet, and added fluidity to the stately hexameter of Virgil. His faults, to some of which he was not blind and which were deliberate (Sen. *Controv.* 2. 2. 12; Quint. *Inst.* 10. 1. 88), are frivolity and irreverence, lapses into bad taste, want of restraint in describing what decency should have forbidden, and redundancy of language. But though shocking he is not prurient; though redundant he is not diffuse.

See ALEXANDRIANISM; DIDACTIC POETRY, LATIN; ELEGIAC POETRY, LATIN; EPYLLION.

BIBLIOGRAPHY

LIFE AND WORKS: Martini, *Einleitung zu O.* (1933); Owen, *Tristia* ii (1924).
TEXTS: Teubner (Merkel, Ehwald, Levy); O.C.T., *Tr. Ib. Pont. Hal. Fragmenta* (Owen).
EDITIONS WITH APPARATUS CRITICUS: Heroides Sedlmayer, w. Prolegg. (1878, 1886); Met. Magnus (1914); Slater, *Towards a text of M.* (1927); Fasti, Merkel (1841); Tr. Owen (1889); Pont. Korn (1868); Pont. Ib. Hal. Fragmenta, Nux, Lenz (Paravia).
COMMENTARIES: Complete works, Heinsius–Burman (1727). Separate works: Am. (1907), Rem. (1921), Tr. (1913), Pont. (1915), Supplement (1922) Némethy; Am. (1911), Ars (1902) Brandt; Heroides, Palmer (1898); Ep. Sapph. De Vries (1888); Comparetti, *Sull' autenticità della Ep. Ovid. di Saffo a Faone* (1876); Medic. Kunz (1881); Met. Haupt-Ehwald (1916–25); Magnus (1885); Fasti, Peter (ed. 4, 1907), crit. append. (1889); Sir J. G. Frazer (1929); Tr. i, Owen (ed. 3, 1902), ii (1924); Pont. i, Scholte (1933); Ib. Ellis (1881); Hal. Birt, *de Hal. falso Ov. adscriptis* (1878); Nux, Ganzenmüller, *Die Elegie Nux u. ihr Verfasser* (1910).
TRANSLATIONS: With text, Loeb, Budé (French) Series. Planudes (Greek) Her. in Palmer's ed.; Met. Boissonade (Lemaire 1822). In verse, Am. Marlowe (c. 1599); Ars, Wright, *Lover's Handbook* (Broadway); Met. Golding (1567), used by Shakespeare.
CRITICISM, STYLE, AND DICTION: F. W. Lenz, *Parerga Ovidiana* (1938); Owen, 'A Manuscript of O.'s Heroides' (i) *CQ* 1936, 155; (ii) *CQ* 1937, 1; A. Zingerle, *Ovidius u. s. Verhältniss z. d. Vorgängern* (1869–71); Martials Ovidstudien (1877); E. Linse, *De O. vocabulorum inventore* (1891); J. v. Iddekinge, *De insigni in O. romani iuris peritia* (1811); N. G. McCrea, 'On O.'s use of colour etc.', *Class. Studies in hon. of H. Drisler* (1894); J. A. Washietl, *De similitudinibus imaginibusque Ovidianis* (1883); Owen, 'O.'s use of the simile', *CR* 1931, 97; W. Y. Sellar, *Roman Poets of Augustan Age* (1892); É. Ripert, *O. poète de l'amour, des dieux et de l'exil* (1921); E. K. Rand, *O. and his Influence* (1925); G. Lafaye, *Les Métamorphoses d'O.* (1904); T. F. Higham, 'O. some Aspects of his Character and Aims', *CR* 1934, 105; Owen, 'O. and Romance' in *Eng. Lit. and the Classics* (1912); W. Brewer, *O.'s Metamorphoses in European Culture* (1933). S. G. O.

OVINIUS, as tribune of the plebs proposed a resolution (the *Lex Ovinia* or *plebiscitum Ovinium*, probably passed between 318 and 312 B.C.) by which the right of enrolling members of the Senate was transferred from the consuls and military tribunes to the censors. It directed the censors to enrol 'optimum quemque ex omni ordine' (Festus, p. 246), which probably means only ex-magistrates, not 'the best men of every rank', so as to counteract individual authority or family influence. As a result membership of the Senate depended on the conduct of the magistrate while in office.

P. Willems, *Le Sénat de la république romaine* i. 153 ff.; i². 668 ff.; Mommsen, *Röm. Staatsr.* i³. 418 f. P. T.

OXUS (Ὦξος, mod. *Amu Darya*). This river was known by name to Herodotus and Aristotle, but was apparently confused by them with the Araxes (q.v.). It was discovered by Alexander, and some Indian merchandise was known to come by it, and thence by the Caspian and the rivers Cyrus and Phasis to the Euxine. But later information about it was from hearsay only, and the belief persisted that it flowed into the Caspian—which may have been true of prehistoric times. Its efflux into the Aral Sea was never located by Greek geographers.

Strabo 11. 514–18; Ptol. *Geog.* 6. 9–18; Cary-Warmington, *Explorers*, 133–56; Warmington, *Indian Commerce*, 26–7, p. 337, n. 70. E. H. W.

OXYRHYNCHUS (*Behnesa*) is now represented only by extensive mounds beyond the Bahr Yusuf to the west of the Nile, which have proved the richest source of papyri in Egypt yet discovered. The first scientific exploration of the site was by Grenfell and Hunt in 1897; since their last campaign there in 1906 other diggers, official and unofficial, have reaped good harvests. The proportion of Ptolemaic papyri is small: most are Roman and Byzantine. Apart from the information derived from these papyri, practically nothing is known of the history of the town. J. G. M.

OXYRHYNCHUS, The historian from. In 1906 some 900 lines of a lost Greek historian were discovered at Oxyrhynchus in Egypt. The writer dealt in consider-able detail with events in the Greek world, 396–395 B.C., and was an authority of the first importance. The papyrus indicates a strict chronological arrangement by summers and winters, competent criticism and analysis of motives, a first-hand knowledge of the topography of Asia Minor, and certain details found in no other work on the period. It was probably a continuation of Thucydides beginning with the autumn of 411, was written between 387 and 346, and its elaborate scale suggests that it covered only a short period, perhaps to the battle of Cnidos, 394.

Its authorship has been much discussed. Grenfell and Hunt preferred an attribution to Theopompus (q.v. 3), later strongly supported by E. Meyer; the case for Ephorus was ably argued by E. M. Walker, in spite of his previous advocacy of the shadowy Cratippus, and more recently F. Jacoby has argued for Daimachus (q.v.). The close resemblance of the text with Diodorus bk. 14 coupled with significant divergencies indicates that Diodorus' source, Ephorus, had P, as the editors termed the author of the papyrus, before him for his universal history. The question of authorship does not yet admit of a definite solution.

Hellenica Oxyrhynchia, O.C.T.; E. Meyer, *Theopomps Hellenika* (1909); E. M. Walker, *The Hellenica Oxyrhynchia* (1913); G. L. Barber, *The historian Ephorus* (1935), ch. 3; H. Bloch, *Harv. Stud.*, Supp. Vol. 1940. G. L. B.

P

PACATUS, MINUCIUS, *see* EIRENAEUS.

PACATUS DREPANIUS, LATINUS (*fl.* A.D. 390), Gallo-Roman orator; *see* PANEGYRIC, LATIN.

PĀCŬVIUS, MARCUS (220–*c.* 130 B.C.), tragedian and painter, nephew of Ennius, born at Brundisium; he died at Tarentum. We are told that as a tragedian he equalled Accius in moral elevation and surpassed him in learning, if inferior in native force; further that he was a polished metrist but that his latinity was poor. The extant titles (only about a dozen, with one *praetexta*, *Paulus*) and the fragments (about 400 lines) suggest that he was a painstaking if slow worker, original in choice of subject (e.g. *Armorum Iudicium*) and in treatment (cf. the stoicizing of Ulysses' death-agonies in the *Niptra*, translated from Sophocles, to suit Roman *gravitas*), fond of complicated plots (Medus, son of Medea, pretends to be Hippotes; Medea, wishing to injure the supposed Hippotes, accuses him of being—Medus!), debates (Amphion and Zethus, in the *Antiopa*, discuss the artistic versus the practical life), and pathetic scenes (e.g. the famous appeal by the ghost of the murdered Deiphilus to his mother Iliona). Command of metre and sound-effect is shown in the words of the old nurse in the *Niptra*:

> manibus isdem, quibus Ulixi saepe permulsi, abluam
> lassitudinemque minuam manuum mollitudine,

or in the bitter words of Telamon to Teucer:

> segregare abs te ausu's aut sine illo Salaminam ingredi . . .?

pictorial power in the descriptions of calm or storm at sea; rationalism in the attack on divination in the *Chryses*. Word-forms like *monerint* (= *monuerint*) and compounds like *incuruiceruicum* perhaps support Cicero's charge of bad latinity.

Text: E. H. Warmington, *Remains of Old Latin* ii (Loeb, 1936). W. B.

PADUS (Ligurian *Bodincus*, Greek Ἠριδανός, nowadays *Po*): Italy's longest river with numerous tributaries. It rises in the Cottian Alps, flows over 400 miles east-ward through Cisalpine Gaul, and enters the Adriatic near Ravenna. Its valley was inhabited in prehistoric times by *terramaricoli* (*see* TERREMARE), and from Etruscan days dikes have protected its reclaimed riparian lands. In antiquity navigation as far as Turin was possible but hazardous owing to the swift current. Since ancient times floods and the silt carried down have considerably altered its lower course and delta.

Polyb. 2. 16; Strabo 4. 203 f.; 5. 212, 217; Pliny, *HN* 3. 117–22. C. Jacini, *Il Viaggio del Po* (1937) with full bibliography. E. T. S.

PAEAN. The Paean seems originally to have been a hymn addressed to Apollo in his rôle as Healer (*Il.* 1. 473; schol. Ar. *Plut.* 636), but it was early used for other purposes, such as (1) military, as in *Il.* 22. 391, Aesch. *Sept.* 635, schol. Eur. *Phoen.* 1102; (2) sympotic, when all the guests sang it in unison after the libations and before the symposium, as in Alcman fr. 71, Aesch. *Ag.* 247, Ath. 149 c, Pl. *Symp.* 176 a, Xen. *Symp.* 2. 1; (3) on public occasions such as the ratification of peace (Xen. *Hell.* 7. 4. 36; Arr. 7. 11); (4) in the Hellenistic age Paeans were addressed to successful individuals, such as Lysander (Plut. *Lys.* 18) and Titus Flaminius (Plut. *Flam.* 16). Paeans were by no means confined to Apollo, but were also sung to Zeus (Xen. *An.* 3. 2. 9), Poseidon (id. *Hell.* 4. 7. 4), Dionysus, Asclepius, and Hygieia. *See also* HYMNS. C. M. B.

PAEDAGOGUS, *see* EDUCATION, III. 1.

PAENULA (vellum cover), *see* BOOKS, II. 2; (cloak) *see* DRESS, para. 3.

PAEONIUS, Greek sculptor, native of Mende in Thrace, known mainly for his Victory of Olympia, now in the Olympia Museum. His full inscription on the base informs us that the statue was dedicated by Messenians. This is confirmed by Pausanias. The occasion of the dedication was almost certainly the battle of Sphacteria in 424 B.C. It is now known that the statue at Olympia is a contemporary version in marble of a bronze original that stood at Delphi, where its base has been found. Paeonius is said by Pausanias to have been the sculptor of the east pediment of the temple of Zeus at Olympia. Our knowledge of the sculptor's style makes this view untenable. But Paeonius did, as his inscription tells us, make acroterial figures for the temple. s. c.

PAESTUM (*Ποσειδωνία*), coastal town of Lucania famous for its roses and pottery (Strabo 5. 251); nowadays *Pesto*, with excellently preserved walls and temples. Founded with Doric-speaking colonists by Sybaris c. 600 B.C., it became a flourishing town by 540 (Hdt. 1. 167). Early attacked by Lucani, Paestum was under their domination from c. 390 until 273 when Rome made it a Latin colony (Ath. 14. 632; Vell. Pat. 1. 14). Paestum loyally resisted Hannibal (Livy 27. 10). Under the Empire its municipal life continued, but the neighbouring marshes made it increasingly unhealthy. Finally Paestum was deserted.

D. Randall-MacIver, *Greek Cities of Italy and Sicily* (1931), 9; A. D. Trendall, *Paestan Pottery* (Rome, 1936); J. Bérard, *Bibliogr. topogr.* (1941), 79; see too bibliography s.v. MAGNA GRAECIA. E. T. S.

PAETUS, LUCIUS CAESENNIUS (cos. A.D. 61), was sent by Nero in 61 or 62 to defend Armenia as a legate of Cappadocia. He failed and capitulated on disgraceful terms in his camp at Rhandeia. Dismissed, but unpunished, in 70 he was appointed governor of Syria by Vespasian (whose relative he probably was) and annexed the kingdom of Commagene.

*PIR*², C 173. A. M.

PAETUS, see also AELIUS (1), AUTRONIUS, THRASEA.

PAGANALIA, Roman festival of the *pagi*, or village communities. They were *sacra publica* (Festus, p. 284, 20 Lindsay), but not *pro populo*, because not on behalf of the people as a whole. They are also called *paganicae feriae*, Varro, *Ling.* 6. 16, who says they were 'agri culturae causa susceptae'; *Paganalia*, Macrob. *Sat.* 1. 16. 6, who lists them among *feriae conceptiuae*, or movable feasts. H. J. R.

PAGANUS, an inhabitant of a *pagus* (q.v.). Hence, by Imperial times (as Tacitus, *Hist.* 3. 24, where Antonius derisively calls the Praetorians *pagani*, cf. Julius Caesar's *Quirites*, Suet. *Divus Iulius* 70; Pliny, *Tra.* 86 b), one who stays at home, a civilian. Hence, in Christian use, one who is not a *miles Christi*, a heathen (*fides pagana*, Tert. *De Corona* 11, and so often; used also of non-Jews, cf. Augustine, *Retract.* 2. 43, who says it is the usual term for polytheists). Some authors (as Orosius 1, prol. 9, Prudentius, *c. Symm.* 1. 449) imply that this use is derived from the sense of 'rustic', 'uncultured', rather than 'civilian'. H. J. R.

PAGASAE, the principal harbour-town of Thessaly. Originally Magnesian, it was appropriated by the Thessalians at an early date and became the port of Pherae. Since it commanded the only convenient outlet from the Thessalian plain to the sea, it virtually monopolized the export of corn, meat, and slaves, thus contributing largely to the rise of the Pheraean tyranny. Philip captured Pagasae in 353 B.C. and subsequently terminated its dependence upon Pherae.

The walls, dating from c. 350, are impressive, but the site was ill chosen, and Pagasae was later supplanted by Demetrias (q.v.).

F. Stählin and E. Meyer, *Pagasai und Demetrias* (1934), a detailed archaeological and historical account. H. D. W.

PAGUS, an area of land with its population as distinguished from the *oppidum* or *vicus* (qq.v.) which housed the inhabitants, was the smallest unit of the Italian territorial system. Every community, tribal or urbanized,

consisted of a group of *pagi*, which thus persisted after the municipalization of Italy. Within the Roman State before 90 B.C. the *pagi* of those parts where the municipal system was undeveloped were the only intermediaries between the *populus Romanus* and the individual citizens. In the provinces agricultural immigrants from Italy settled in *pagi*, whereas groups of Romans in provincial towns were known as *conventus*. Such *pagi*, which were usually attached to the nearest Roman municipality, assisted the spread of Roman civilization in the neighbouring native *civitas*, whose *oppidum* the *pagus* might share, and with which it was eventually united as a *municipium* or *colonia* (qq.v.). The provincial communities also, especially the great cantons of Gaul, were sometimes subdivided into *pagi*. The administrative powers of a *pagus* varied with its comparative independence. In Italy they had boards of three or four aediles or *magistri*; Roman or peregrine *pagi* in the provinces might form a miniature *res publica*.

For bibliography *see* MUNICIPIUM (Modern views (a) Republic). A. N. S.-W.

PAIDOTRIBES, see EDUCATION, III. 2.

PAIGNION, a title, of which *jeu d'esprit* is a rough equivalent, applied to various very different types of literature. It was used of the satirical poems of Crates the Cynic and of poems of Philetas and Theocritus, and generally of effusions of a light character (L. & S., s.v. *παίγνιον*, III. 3). Gorgias (fr. 11. 21) similarly designates his *Helena*, the prototype of later essays in lighthearted whitewashing and denigration composed by Isocrates (*Helena*) and later by Asiatic rhetoricians; cf. Polyb. 12. 26 b *Ἐγκώμιον Θερσίτου, Ψόγος Πηνελόπης. See also* MIMUS *and* TECHNOPAIGNIA. J. D. D.

PAINTING. Except for a few clay plaques and stone stelae little ancient painting survives that is earlier than the Roman period. The sources are references in literature, vase-painting (q.v.; until c. 400 B.C. often of the highest quality), Etruscan tomb-painting (7th to 4th c.), and occasional copies of earlier pictures in painting and mosaic.

2. *Before the fifth century.* The scenes on geometric vases are in silhouette with filling ornament; the artist shows all the essential parts of figures and objects disregarding spatial relations (e.g. the corpse is placed above the bier on his side to show both arms and legs). From about 750 the silhouette changes partially into outline, and a more normal two-dimensional representation is adopted; but figures are still composed of typical views of each part—head profile, frontal eye, frontal body, profile legs (cf. particularly Proto-Attic and Melian vases). Corinth was early famous for painting; her claim is justified by the clay metopes from Thermon representing Perseus, etc., the elaborate battle scenes on Proto-Corinthian vases (both 650–620), and the later Amphiaraus vase (560). From c. 625 the black-figure style predominates in Athens for vases and plaques; the red-figure style begins c. 530. After 540 forms are more rounded and clothing more decorative and elaborate (*see* EXECIAS, ANDOCIDES). Ionian pictures of c. 525 are echoed by the Caeretan hydriae (Embassy to Achilles, Busiris, etc.). From c. 515 painters experiment with uneven stance, back views, frontal faces, etc., which later become common (*see* EUPHRONIUS, EUTHYMIDES; cf. Pliny on Eumarus of Athens, 'figuras omnis imitari ausum').

3. *Fifth century.* Three-quarter faces and varied expressions, ascribed to Cimon of Cleonae, appear on the vases of the Cleophrades painter and his contemporaries; the frontal eye gradually changes into the profile eye. Between 470 and 460 further advances were made by Micon and Polygnotus (qq.v.); in their large pictures the surface of the wall was divided by undulating lines representing hillocks, which supported or partly hid the serious figures of men 'better than ourselves', arranged in groups united by a common emotion. The use of perspective was greatly developed by Agatharchus (q.v.), painting c. 470–430, and shading by Apollodorus (q.v.), c. 430. Parrhasius (q.v.), painting from c. 450, achieved plastic effects by his outline; he also developed further the painting of facial expression. Aglaophon (c. 420) painted in the rich, sweet style known from the vases of the Meidias painter (q.v.). Zeuxis (q.v.) united the romantic, emotional, and realistic tendencies of the late fifth century, the art which Plato rejected in the *Republic*. Copies of late-fifth-century painting have been seen in paintings on marble from Herculaneum.

4. *Fourth century.* The Sicyonian school (see PAM-PHILUS *and* MELANTHIUS) in revolt against the colour effects of Zeuxis, etc., insisted on line, composition, and severity; their art influenced mirrors, ivories, and Kertch and Tarentine vases. Aristides (q.v.) continued the emotional tradition of Parrhasius, etc.; he 'first painted soul, feelings, and passions'. Encaustic (q.v.), of which Pausias (q.v.) was the first great master, made greater realism possible; Nicias, who unlike Pausias chose large subjects, made his figures stand out from the canvas (copies of his Io and Andromeda have been recognized). Of Apelles (q.v.), the most renowned painter of antiquity, nothing survives; the charm (χάρις) of his works distinguished him both from the austerity of the Sicyonians and from the over-elaboration of Protogenes (q.v.). The earliest interior scenes to receive mention are the late-fourth-century 'Alexander and Roxane' by Aetion (q.v.) and 'Boy blowing the fire' by Antiphilus. Philoxenus (q.v.) painted a 'Battle of Alexander with Darius' (the Issus mosaic in Pompeii is a copy), a brilliant composition of crowded figures in a shallow strip of space.

5. *Hellenistic.* Literary sources are less informative and the contributions of different schools are difficult to assess. The enucleation and dating of the originals behind frescoes and mosaics at Pompeii, etc., are largely conjectural. To the third century may be assigned the stele of Hediste from Pagasae and the original of the Pharmaceutriae by Dioscorides (mosaic; c. 100 B.C.); both have shallow interior scenes. Hediste is a realistic portrait; the Pharmaceutriae and its companion, the 'Street Musicians', represent the Hellenistic genre tendency. The original of the 'Arcadia and Telephus' from Herculaneum should from the subject be Pergamene, second century; the diagonal composition gives the picture considerable depth; the basket of fruit in the foreground is a still life, a descendant of Pausias' (q.v.) flowers, an ancestor of Sosus' 'Drinking doves' and many small pictures in Pompeii.

6. *Roman period.* Timomachus of Byzantium, the last great painter recorded, painted in the time of Julius Caesar a Medea and an Iphigenia; reflections in Pompeii show that his figures derived from the fourth century or earlier. The Aldobrandini marriage may also be an eclectic original of c. 50 B.C. The Second Style of wall-painting begins in Pompeii, Delos, and Athens early in the first century B.C.; the simple architecture leaves room for large pictures of great spatial depth such as the ritual scenes of the Villa Item, the illusionistic buildings and gardens of the Boscoreale villa (cf. Vitruvius on Apaturius of Alabanda), and the Odyssey pictures from the Esquiline, as well as the smaller landscapes in the house of Livia (cf. Pliny on Studius). The painted architecture of the Third Style (20 B.C.–A.D. 20, perhaps contemporary with the later stages of the second style) is elaborate and fantastic, and frames academic groups set against a landscape backcloth. The pictures of the Fourth Style (extending into the Flavian period) are also set in fantastic architecture; the composition is often based on diagonals, and the painting is often impressionistic (cf. the putto in the catacomb of Domitilla). The earliest of the mummy portraits from Egypt belong to the first century A.D.; the series lasts into the fourth century; most of the portraits are in the encaustic (q.v.) technique, and many are excellent pictures. After the austerity of the Trajanic period and the softer, more impressionistic style of the second century, the spirituality of Early Christian art begins to appear, as in the apostles from the tomb of the Aurelii and the best drawings on gold glass.

Recent works. General: E. Pfuhl, *Malerei und Zeichnung der Griechen* (1923); J. D. Beazley and B. Ashmole, *Greek Sculpture and Painting* (1932); M. H. Swindler, *Ancient Painting* (1929); R. P. Hinks, *Catalogue of Paintings and Mosaics in the British Museum* (1933), ix. Special (*see also* VASE-PAINTING and individual vase-painters and painters): J. Overbeck, *Antiken Schriftquellen* (1868; literary sources); A. Rumpf, *JDAI* 1934, 8 (plaques and marble copies); O. Broneer, *Hesperia* 1938, 224 (plaques); F. Poulsen, *Etruscan Tomb-paintings* (1922); W. Hahland, *Corolla L. Curtius* (1938), 121 (geometric); H. G. H. Payne, *Necrocorinthia* (1931), 96 (Thermon); R. G. Steven, *CQ* 1933, 149 (Plato); H. Bulle, *Eine Skenographie* (1934), 23 (Sicyonian painting); G. E. Rizzo, *La Pittura Ellenistico-Romana* (1929); L. Curtius, *Die Wandmalerei Pompejis* (1929); H. Beyen, *Über Stilleben* (1928); *JDAI* 1927, 41; H. Diepolder, *Röm. Mitt.* 1926, 1 (treatment of space); F. Matz, *Arch. Anz.* 1932, 278 (composition); A. Maiuri, *Villa dei Misteri* (1931); F. Wirth, *Römische Wandmalerei* (1934); P. Styger, *Die Römischen Katakomben* (1933); H. Drerup, *Datierung des Mumienporträts* (1933); R. Kömstedt, *Vormittelalterliche Malerei* (1929); C. Albizzati, *Röm. Mitt.* 1914, 240 (gold glass). T. B. L. W.

PALACES. That the abodes of kings in Greek and Hellenistic times were like extra large houses seems probable. There are scant evidences of palaces comparable in size or magnificence with those of Minoan Crete or Assyria. Unfortunately the palace of the Ptolemies at Alexandria has completely disappeared, nor is it likely that Antioch will yield much of the palaces of the Seleucid kings. The fortress town of Pergamum (*see* TOWNS), the best preserved of the major Hellenistic sites, was too constricted to permit a palace of great extent. The most hopeful site so far has been Palatitza, in Macedonia, where valuable evidences of grandiose entrance planning have been disclosed, and further research may prove even more clearly the importance of this link between Hellenistic and Roman palace planning. The entrance buildings at Palatitza led to a spacious pillared forecourt, and all the evidences from Pergamum and Miletus point to palace buildings as an assemblage of such courts with rooms on two stories opening into the pillared loggias which surrounded them: an enlargement of ideas which are evident from the houses at Priene and Delos.

Of Roman palaces in the times of the earlier Caesars the evidences are also comparatively scanty. Eastern conceptions of the segregation of women no doubt had some effect: the House of Livia on the Palatine Hill, which has well-preserved elements, points to separate quarters for royal ladies and their retinue. In Roman palaces, however, it is evident that assemblages of units were more fully mastered than in Greek and Hellenistic times, and Roman constructive possibilities gave increased scope to grandiose planning (*see* BATHS). By far the most complete Roman palace in existence, that of Diocletian at Spalato—invaluable to the architectural historian for many reasons—shows a fortified building planned with characteristic simplicity and practicality of outlook. It was guarded by strong walls with gates and soldiers' quarters on the three land sides, and on the sea side, where were the emperor's quarters, with a continuous terrace raised above a vaulted passage (*cryptoporticus*), the temples being planned with some dignity between the front and the middle region containing courtiers' quarters.

Anderson, Spiers, and Dinsmoor, op. cit. under ARCHITECTURE, p. 185; Anderson, Spiers, and Ashby, op. cit. ibid., p. 133. T. F

PALAEMON, in mythology, *see* ATHAMAS, LEUCOTHEA.

PALAEMON, Quintus Remmius, a manumitted slave who under Tiberius and Claudius won a reputation for his evil life, arrogance, and unusual learning. Martial (2. 86. 11) pours scorn on his verses. He was the first Roman to write a really comprehensive grammatical treatise (see GRAMMAR) which influenced all subsequent writers (e.g. Charisius, Diomedes, Priscian). The extant *Ars Palaemonis* (ed. Keil, *Gramm. Lat.* v. 533; cf. also vi. 206) is spurious.

See SCHOLARSHIP, LATIN, IN ANTIQUITY and cf. Teuffel, § 282. 3; Schanz–Hosius, § 475; K. Barwick, *Remmius Palaemon und die römische ars grammatica* (1922) = *Philol.* Suppl. xv. 2.   J. F. M.

PALAEOGRAPHY is the science that studies writing upon papyrus, wax, parchment, and paper, while Epigraphy deals with inscriptions carved in hard materials; it teaches us to read old writings and to observe their changes particularly for criteria of date and place. It is also concerned with the layout of the written leaf and the form of the book. We here confine ourselves to Greek and Latin writing and refer to the articles on Papyrology, Greek and Latin, for those branches of the subject. In both languages carved and written letters start by being identical, but the written change more quickly under the influence of three forces: the first, the desire to make letters with less labour, and the second, the need of being legible, oppose each other; the third, regard for beauty, whether in the individual letter, the line as a whole, or the page, tends to careful work, but sometimes the scribe, forcing the letters into one mould to attain a pleasant regularity, makes them hard to distinguish.

2. Writings may be classed as *Book-hands* and *Cursives* or everyday hands: both have existed side by side as far as our documents go back; the book-hand is conservative, but the cursive may change very quickly; its forms tend to invade the book-hand. Hands are also divided into *Majuscules* and *Minuscules*: in Majuscules, comprising *Capitals*, *Uncials*, and early Cursives, the letters lie in the main between two parallel lines, though, e.g., Φ in Greek or F in Latin Capitals and several letters in Latin Uncials (e.g. h and q) project above and below them. *Uncials* is the name given to the earliest book-hand deviating from Capitals, marked by certain rounded forms. It means 'inch-high', being taken from Jerome's attack upon the elaborate letters in gold and silver on purple parchment fashionable in his day: it matters not that really they were never more than $\frac{5}{8}$ in. high. Later Cursive both in Greek and Latin developed many tall and tailed letters and these passed into the book-hands derived from it. Such hands are called *Minuscules*, scripts in which the bodies of the letters lie between two inner lines but the 'ascenders and descenders' reach out towards two outer lines above and below; only one line is actually ruled, upon which the letters stand, or from which in Greek after A.D. 1000 they hang.

3. The *Materials* that receive writing deeply influence its development; as against papyrus and paper, parchment encourages a more careful and heavier style; wax produced in letters special deformations that have left their mark on all subsequent Latin writing, e.g. in d, g, f. Papyrus was the general material from classical times till the fourth century A.D., after which it was, save in Egypt, a mere survival; the latest papyrus is a Papal bull of the eleventh century. In the fourth century parchment, hitherto rare though of very ancient use, won a sudden victory. Paper, adopted from China by Islam, spread through Europe in the thirteenth to fifteenth centuries. Wax was used from at least the fifth century B.C. until the Renaissance.

4. Papyrus (see PAPYROLOGY), which did not stand folding well, was mostly used in the form of a roll, the text being in narrow columns; the criss-cross structure of papyrus guided the scribe in keeping these vertical and his lines regular. The bound book arose in Egypt in the second century A.D.; though at first made of papyrus, it suited parchment better; its form was perhaps suggested by that of the wax codex of joined tablets. Its rise was probably associated with the spread of Christianity (see BOOKS). Writing on parchment involves elaborate cutting and folding of the double leaves which make up the quires, and laborious pricking and ruling to guide the scribe. The methods of doing this, now being studied, may furnish indications of date and place of writing.

5. The *Ink* used on papyrus is finely divided carbon and gum ('Indian ink'), chemically very stable but sensitive to damp. That used on parchment is a solution of oak-galls and iron, not always satisfactory chemically. Pens were of reed and in medieval times of quill. Writing on parchment was often erased and a new text written over it: this is called a *Palimpsest* (q.v.). The older writing may be read by the application of ammonium sulphide, or better if it is photographed under ultra-violet rays. Study of manuscripts is largely dependent on photographs; these are cheaper when taken white on black (*rotographs* or *photostats*), or still cheaper as *microfilms* which can be read by using a projector. The difficulty of reading manuscripts, apart from bad preservation, is due to the unfamiliar forms of the letters, the non-division of the words, and the use of abbreviations. The first trouble is much increased by the presence under cursive influence of *ligatures*, i.e. combinations in which two or more letters are knotted together and lose their original shapes, e.g. &, a combination of Є and Ϲ.

6. *Abbreviations* are divided into *suspensions*, in which the first letter or the beginning of a word is given but not the ending (sign: a dot or a transverse stroke); *contractions*, giving the first letter, generally some of the middle of a word and always the last letter (sign: a *tittle* or horizontal stroke above); and *specific signs* denoting particular words, syllables, or letters. These largely go back to ancient shorthand, e.g. in Latin to the *Notae Tironianae* (see TACHYGRAPHY). Numerals are marked by tittles, so sometimes foreign words, or by flanking signs, also used for 'quotes'. A letter wrongly written may be dotted above or, more usually, below.

7. These difficulties tend to increase as time goes on, save that later manuscripts begin to divide the words. Division into paragraphs is at first rare and inconspicuously marked; later it is indicated by the methods still in use. Punctuation too is at first scarce and irregular, and never becomes very helpful.

8. A scribe sometimes is good enough, especially in later times, to add at the end of a manuscript a note, called a *Colophon*, giving his name with place and date of writing: the Greek era runs from 5508 B.C. We also find *subscriptiones* (q.v.), notes by readers who have corrected a manuscript, and these are sometimes dated.

9. The study of the decoration of manuscripts and of miniatures does not really concern classical students: the ancient book until its very latest stage was practically devoid of ornament.

10. *Greek Writing* has a simple history: starting with epigraphic capitals it soon adopted rounded shapes for Є, Ϲ, ω and made small changes in some other letters. The *Uncial* thus established continued as the only book-hand until the ninth century, the cursive meanwhile developing independently. The uncial changes very little until parchment encouraged scribes to make the vertical strokes thick and gradually arrive at a heavy style (miscalled 'Slavonic') too elaborate for ordinary books. Accents and breathings, hitherto sporadic, and used mostly in difficult texts, now become general. About A.D. 800 scholars in Constantinople got right away from the heavy uncial (which lingered on for another three centuries in liturgical use), and deliberately

designed a new book-hand, a *Minuscule*, founded on the cursive: this was the vehicle of Greek literature until the introduction of printing, but it degenerated steadily through the centuries, admitting capricious forms and abbreviations and complicated ligatures combining the letters with the accents; these survived into printing, but have now been eliminated.

11. The *Latin Book-hand* is like the inscriptions until the fifth century, having the same two varieties, the rare *Square Capital* and the more usual *Rustic* made quickly with a slanting pen. Only school-books and law-books seem to have been produced in an easier style with an admixture of cursive forms. This contributed to the Latin *Uncial*, which became the regular book-hand from the fourth to the eighth century, its characteristic letters are ᴀ, ᴅ, ᴇ, ʜ, ʟ, ᴍ, ǫ, ᴜ; it sometimes admits ʙ and ᴅ. When more cursive letters, ᴀ, ᴢ, m, p, ɼ, ſ, are used (but N remains), the script is called *Half-uncial*: books written in it are few, but it is the ancestor of the script called *Insular*, developed by the Irish in the fifth and sixth centuries and taught by them to the English and in many monasteries on the Continent. We gave up its use for Latin in the tenth century, but retained it for Anglo-Saxon. The Irish used it for Latin till the fifteenth century and still keep it for their own language.

12. Meanwhile, from the sixth century, the cursive, which was developing upon wax and papyrus, began to be used for books, and by A.D. 800 had been made tolerable in every Latin-using country save 'Insular' Ireland and England; south and north Italy, Spain, Gaul, and Germany each had fair '*National*' hands labelled *Lombardic*, *Visigothic*, and *Merovingian*, but they are all still disfigured by ligatures. In the late eighth century book-production was systematized at Tours under Charles the Great; in these books Square and Rustic Capitals, Uncial and Half-uncial, were used for headings, prefaces, initials, etc., and a Minuscule called *Caroline* or *Carolingian*, eliminating most of the ligatures, was designed for the text. Caroline quickly superseded the various forms of Merovingian and the Lombardic in north Italy, and in the eleventh century the Visigothic, but south Italy and Dalmatia retained their beautiful writing, now called *Beneventan*, until the end of the twelfth century. Caroline is the main vehicle of Classical literature; manuscripts in capitals are not more than twenty, half of them Virgils: few Uncials are classical; of the other scripts only Insular and Beneventan have any importance for the classics. For most authors a ninth- or tenth-century Caroline manuscript is the best authority; the Caroline scholars copied the ancient manuscripts, which then went out of use and perished; they did their best to produce a good text but had not the necessary scholarship. Of a few authors, e.g. Catullus, the Caroline has been lost and we have only later copies. In other cases later copies derived from a lost Caroline may preserve good readings not found in extant Carolines.

13. Caroline changed very little till the twelfth century; then it developed, first of all in north France, into the angular hand we call *Gothic* or *Blackletter*; this came to vary greatly in style in different countries; it can be very handsome, but suffers from the letters being very much alike, and from innumerable abbreviations.

14. In the fifteenth century the Italian scholars revived the Caroline, thinking it to be the writing of the ancient Romans, and used it with singular elegance. Manuscripts and printing in this *Humanistic* or *Roman* hand gradually spread over Europe, and likewise the cursive derived from it. Only Germany retained till the other day the Blackletter derived from France.

BIBLIOGRAPHY

E. Maunde-Thompson, *Introduction to Greek and Latin Palaeography*, 1912 (still the best summary, with bibliography and list of MSS. completely reproduced down to 1912, facsimiles inadequate). SCRIBES AND BOOK-MAKING: W. Wattenbach, *Das Schriftwesen im Mittelalter*[3], 1896 (best survey of materials, forms of books, and habits of scribes). T. Birt, *Das Antike Buchwesen*, 1882 (standard, but out of date). F. G. Kenyon, *Books and Readers in Ancient Greece and Rome*, 1932. B. L. Ullman, *Ancient Writing and its Influence*, Philadelphia, London, 1932. (These two books bring Wattenbach up to date.) F. W. Hall, *Companion to Classical Texts*, 1913 (summary of book-lore and lists of chief MSS. of each author). A. C. Clark, *The Descent of MSS.*, 1918 (interesting but not always convincing).

GENERAL SERIES OF FACSIMILES. Palaeographical Society, *Facsimiles of Ancient MSS. and Inscriptions*, Series I and II, 1873–94. New Palaeographical Society, Series I and II, 1903–29 (unrivalled series). A. Monaci, *Archivio Paleografico Italiano*, 1881 (10 vols.). G. Vitelli e C. Paoli, *Collezione Fiorentina di Facsimili Paleografici*, 1884–97 (2 vols.). A. Chroust, *Monumenta Palaeographica*, 1899–1917 (6 vols.).

Many manuscripts have been reproduced in full (v. Maunde Thompson, p. 581), especially in two great series: *Codices e Vaticanis selecti phototypice expressi*, Milan and Rome, 1899– . Scato de Vries, *Codices Gr. et Lat. phototypice depicti*, 1897– . A useful *Album Palaeographicum*, selected from the earlier issues, came out in 1909.

GREEK. B. de Montfaucon, *Palaeographia Graeca*, Paris, 1708 (still useful). V. Gardthausen, *Griechische Palaeographie*[2], 1911 (standard). P. Maas, 'Griechische Palaeographie' in Gercke-Norden, *Einleitung in die Altertumswissenschaft*, Bd. I, Heft 9 (1924), 69–81. T. V. Allen, *Notes on the Abbreviations in Greek MSS.*, 1889 (useful). G. Ph. Ts'ereteli, 'Abbreviations in Greek MSS.', suppl. to *Mém. (Zapiski) de la Soc. Imp. Archéol. Russe, Sect. Classique*, iii, St. Petersburg, 1904 (in Russian, but plates can be used). L. Traube, *Nomina Sacra, Versuch einer Gesch. d. christlichen Kürzung*, 1907 (clears up contraction, first in Greek and then in Latin, etc.).

Facsimiles. W. Wattenbach et A. von Velsen, *Exempla Codicum Graecorum Litteris Minusculis Scriptorum*, 1878. W. Wattenbach, *Scripturae Gr. Specimina*, 1883 (poor facsimiles but largely classical). H. Omont, *Facs. des MSS. grecs datés de la Bibliothèque Nationale du xe au xiv 's.*, Paris, 1891 (with list of other facs. of dated Gr. MSS. up to 1891). Id. *Facs. des plus anciens MSS. grecs de la Bibl. Nle. . . . du ive au xiie s.*, 1892. Id., *Facs. des MSS. grecs . . . des xve et xvie s. de la Bibl. Nle.*, 1887 (still the best collection of late hands). P. F. de' Cavalieri et J. Lietzmann, *Spec. Codd. Gr. Vaticanorum*, 1910 (convenient and cheap, mostly theological). A. Sobolevski et G. Ph. Ts'ereteli, *Exempla Codd. Gr. Litteris Uncialibus Scriptorum*, 1913. Id. *Ex. Codd. Gr.*, I. *Codd. Mosquenses*; II. *Codd. Petropolitani*, Moscow, 1911–13 (contain some very important documents). Kirsopp and Silva Lake, *Dated Greek Minuscule MSS. to the year 1200*, U.S.A. 1934–41, 10 vols. (comprising all known dated minuscules).

LATIN. F. Steffens, *Lateinische Palaeographie*[3], 1929; in French, Paris, 1907–9 (varied contents, best moderately priced book). A. Cappelli, *Dizionario di Abbreviature Lat. ed Ital.*[3], 1929 (most convenient). W. M. Lindsay, *Notae Latinae*, Cambridge, 1915 (deals with abbreviations till about A.D. 900); D. Bains, *A Supplement to N.L.*, 1936 (brings them down to 1100).

Facsimiles. W. Wattenbach et C. Zangemeister, *Exempla Codd. Lat. Litteris Majusculis Scriptorum*, 1876–9 (still very useful). E. Chatelain, *Paléographie des classiques latins*, 1884–1900 (the standard collection, almost complete for French libraries). Id., *Uncialis Scriptura Codd. Lat. novis exemplis illustrata*, 1902 (the standard collection for uncial). W. Arndt u. M. Tangl, *Schrifttafeln zur Erlernung d. lat. Paläographie*, 3 parts, 1904–7 (a very varied and interesting collection). F. Ehrle et P. Liebaert, *Specimina Codd. Lat. Vaticanorum*, 1912 (best cheap collection of varied facsimiles). E. A. Lowe, *Codices Latini Antiquiores*, Oxford, 1934– (will give a description and specimen of every Latin manuscript up to the year 800 with a bibliography of each. Incomparable). J. Mallon, R. Marichal, C. Perrat, *L'Écriture latine de la capitale romaine à la minuscule*, 1939 (a convenient series of facsimiles).

SPECIAL SCRIPTS. *Uncial.* E. A. Lowe and E. K. Rand, *A VIth Century Fragment of the Letters of Pliny the Younger*, U.S.A. 1922.

Half-uncial. E. A. Lowe, 'A Handlist of Half-uncial MSS.', *Misc. Ehrle*, iv. 34–61, Rome, 1924. *Codices Lugdunenses Antiquissimi*, Lyon, 1924.

Dark-age writing. L. Traube, *Vorlesungen u. Abhandlungen*, 3 vols., 1909–20. W. M. Lindsay, *Early Irish Script, Early Welsh Script*, and the journal *Palaeographia Latina*, all publications of St. Andrews University, 1922–9. No complete account of Insular exists.

Beneventan. *Paleografia Artistica di Monte Cassino*, 1876–81 (coloured plates). E. A. Lowe, *The Beneventan Script*, 1914 (best study of any hand). Id., *Scriptura Beneventana*, 1929 (facsimiles).

Visigothic. P. Ewald et G. Loewe, *Exempla Scripturae Visigoticae*, 1883. E. A. Lowe, 'Studia Palaeographica', *Sitz. Bayer. Akad., Phil.-hist. Kl.*, 1910 (important for all National Hands). J. M. Burnam, *Palaeographica Iberica*, U.S.A. 1914 (good facsimiles). Z. G. Villada, *Paleografía Española*, 1923 (with album). R. P. Robinson, 'MSS. 27 and 107 of the Municipal Library at Autun', *Am. Ac. Rome*, xvi, 1939 (redates all early Visigothic).

Caroline. E. K. Rand, 'The Vatican Livy and the script of Tours', *Am. Ac. Rome*, i, 1919 (very important for transmission of classical texts). Id., 'Studies in the Script of Tours', 1, 3, *Medieval Acad. of Amer.* 3, 20, 3, Cambridge, Mass., 1929, 1934. P. Lauer, 'La Réforme carolingienne de l'écriture latine', *Mém. Acad. Inscr. et Belles-Lettres*, 1924 and 1933. L. W. Jones, 'The Script of Cologne', *Med. Acad. of Amer.* 10, 1932.

E. H. M.

PALAEPHATUS wrote (? in the late 4th c. B.C.) a *Π. ἀπίστων*, extant only in an excerpt, in which myths are rationalized. It had considerable influence in the Byzantine period. The name Palaephatus is perhaps a pseudonym.

N. Festa, *Mythographi Graeci* iii. 2 (1902); J. Schrader, *Palaephatea* (1893).　J. D. D.

PALAESTRA (*παλαίστρα*), was a low building with a central courtyard in the interior covered with fine sand, and rooms about it for undressing and washing. It was frequently the private property of a schoolmaster, and was especially used by boys who were there taught the rules of wrestling. *See* EDUCATION, III. 2; GYMNASIUM; BATHS.
　　　　　　　　　　　　　　　　　　F. A. W.

PALAMEDES (*Παλαμήδης*, 'the handy or contriving one'), a proverbially (cf. Ar. *Ran.* 1451) clever hero, son of Nauplius (q.v.). His chief distinctions are the invention of letters and his cunning while serving with Agamemnon. These respectively bring him into competition with Cadmus and Odysseus (qq.v.). For the former sundry accounts divide the invention of the alphabet between them, e.g. Hyginus, *Fab.* 277. 1 (see Rose ad loc.). For the latter, tradition, from the Cypria, makes them rivals and enemies; Odysseus pretended to be mad to avoid going to Troy and Palamedes detected him by a stratagem (see, e.g., Hyginus, *Fab.* 95. 2 and Rose ad loc.). In revenge Odysseus forged a letter from Priam to Palamedes, arranging for him to betray the Greeks, and hid a sum of gold in his tent; on this evidence Palamedes was found guilty and put to death by the army (Hyg. *Fab.* 105). See Lewy in Roscher's *Lexikon*, s.v.　　　　　　　　　　　　　　　　H. J. R.

PALATINE, the chief of the seven hills of Rome, traditionally (Varro, *Ling.* 5. 164; Tac. *Ann.* 12. 24; Dionys. Hal. 1. 87; Livy 1. 7, etc.) the site of the oldest settlement there. The etymology is disputed, and the ritual reasons usually given for the early choice of the hill for settlement are probably archaistic inventions, like the legend of *Roma quadrata* (*Phil. Wochenschr.* 1903, 1645). Tradition assigns fortifications to the hill, but their reality is still in need of sound archaeological confirmation. Early settlement is represented by two archaic cisterns and rock-cut post-holes. Indigenous deities included Aius Locutius (390 B.C.), Viriplaca, Luna Noctiluca, and Febris. Later came the temples of Victoria, near the *clivus Victoriae* (294), the Magna Mater (191), and possibly Jupiter Victor (see *Bull. Com. Arch.* 1917, 84–92). The hill was also the seat of many houses, from at least 330 onwards (Livy 8. 19. 4; 20. 8), famous owners being Fulvius Flaccus, Lutatius Catulus, Cicero, Crassus, Milo, P. Sulla, M. Antony, Livius Drusus, and Hortensius. The house of Hortensius became the *domus Augusti* (Suet. *Aug.* 72) and is still visible. A new palace was built near it, in association with a temple of Apollo (Vell. Pat. 2. 81), the latter being identified with a large Augustan temple-platform south of the *domus Augusti* (*JRS* 1914, 201–8). An Augustan triumphal arch was erected on the *clivus Victoriae* (*AJArch.* 1923, 400). Tiberius built a large palace, *domus Tiberiana* (Tac. *Hist.* 1. 27) on the Cermalus, or northwest summit, to which Gaius added a vestibule contiguous with the temple of Castor. Nero built yet another sumptuous palace, *domus transitoria*, covering Republican houses, and itself covered in turn by the foundations of his *domus aurea* (q.v.; Suet. *Nero* 31). Domitian was responsible for the Flavian state-apartments and gardens (*hippodromus*), by the architect Rabirius, and also extended the *domus Tiberiana* towards the *nova via*, as did Hadrian still further. Severus built out towards the south-east, masking his work with the Septizonium (q.v.). The

palaces continued to be used until the sixth century, when they were repaired by Theodoric and Athalaric.

Not. Scav. 1904, 43–6; C. Hülsen–H. Jordan, *Topographie der Stadt Rom* (1907), 29–111; Hülsen, *Forum und Palatin* (Berlin 1926, U.S.A. 1928); G. Lugli, *Roma antica* (1946).　　I. A. R.

PALATINI, in origin the troops forming the Palace Guard, became the senior branch of Constantine's field army. Like the *Comitatenses* they were commanded by the *magistri militum* and comprised cavalry (*vexillationes*) and infantry (*legiones* and *auxilia*) in that order of precedence. *See* COMITATENSES.　　　　　　　H. M. D. P.

PALES, see PARILIA.

PALFURIUS SURA, an able orator (Suet. *Dom.* 13) and active *delator* under Domitian, is mentioned in Juvenal, 4. 53–5, as an upholder of the emperor's unlimited claims over property. After Vespasian expelled him from the Senate he turned Stoic.

PALIBOTHRA (*Pataliputra*, now *Patna*), situated on the Royal Road from the river Beas down the Ganges valley, was the capital of the Mauryan kings of north India (*c.* 300 B.C.). The Seleucid kings kept Greek residents, Megasthenes (q.v.) and Deimachus, at the court of Kings Chandragupta and Vindusara. In his account of India Megasthenes gave an accurate account of the city's fortifications, a stockade and a moat. It remained an important royal seat, though little noticed by later Greek or Roman visitors to India.

Strabo 2. 70, 15. 702; Plin. *HN* 6. 63; Ptol. *Geog.* 1. 12. 9, etc.
　　　　　　　　　　　　　　　　　　E. H. W.

PALICI (*Παλικοί*), twin gods of the pool now known as *Lago Naftia* or *Fetia*, more learnedly as *L. dei Palici*, in Sicily, which still sends up a considerable amount of natural gas. Of the bulky ancient literature we have left some extracts in Macrobius, *Sat.* 5. 19. 15 ff., also Diod. Sic. 11. 88. 6 ff., Servius on *Aen.* 9. 581. For some modern writers see Bloch in Roscher's *Lexikon* iii. 1281. Their legend was that a local nymph, Thalia, being with child by Zeus, begged to be swallowed up in the earth to escape Hera; this was granted her, and when she bore twins they made their way up through the pools known as Delloi. The most noteworthy thing about their worship was that a suspected person might go to the pools and swear he was innocent; if he lied, he lost his life by the power of the gods (the gases are in fact somewhat poisonous); if not, he returned safe and might claim damages from his accuser.　　　　　　H. J. R.

PALIMPSEST (*παλίμψηστος*), a term applied to manuscripts in which the original text has been scraped or washed away, in order that another text may be inscribed in its place. As the term properly implies scraping, it must have originally been applied to such materials as leather, wax, or vellum, and only by analogy to papyrus, which could be washed, but not scraped. The term seems to occur first in Catullus (22. 5); cf. Plut. 2. 504 d, 779 c, where it is treated as synonymous with ἔκπλυτος. When vellum was scarce (especially, it seems, about the ninth century) early manuscripts were not infrequently treated thus; and since the removal of the original writing was seldom complete, valuable texts of the Bible, Cicero, Plautus, Gaius, Licinianus, etc., have been recovered from such palimpsests.

V. Gardthausen, *Gr. Paläographie²* (1911) i. 103–9; E. M. Thompson, *Introd. to Gr. and Lat. Palaeography* (1912), 64–66.
　　　　　　　　　　　　　　　　　　F. G. K.

PALINODE, see STESICHORUS.

PALLA, see DRESS, para. 3.

PALLADAS of Alexandria (*fl.* A.D. 400), Greek epigrammatist, was a schoolmaster, miserably poor; he was also a pagan in the age of rising Christianity. The *Anthology* contains over 150 epigrams of his, deeply melancholy in tone. He is the Juvenal of epigrammatists: even his jokes are bitter as wormwood—see those on matrimony in *Anth. Pal.* 9. 165 ff., and those on fortune and human life in *Anth. Pal.* 10. 77 ff. He has no great verbal dexterity, but the depth and strength of his emotion are remarkably impressive.

P. Sakolowski, *De Anth. Pal. quaestiones* (1893); A. Franke, *De P. epigrammatographo* (1899). G. H.

PALLADIUM, an ancient sacred image of Pallas (Athena), said to have been sent down from heaven by Zeus to Dardanus, the founder of Troy (Arctinus ap. Dion. Hal. 1. 69), or to his descendant Ilus (Ov. *Fasti* 6. 419–22). It was believed that the protection of the city depended on its safe custody. Greek legend told that Diomede and Odysseus, at the instigation of Calchas or Helenus, carried off the Palladium and thus made possible the sack of Troy (Serv. ad *Aen.* 2. 166, Sil. Ital. 13. 36–50). Virgil adopts this legend (*Aen.* 2. 162–79), but adds that the theft was followed by the displeasure of the goddess. The more common Roman tradition was that the Palladium was rescued from the burning Troy by Aeneas, who brought it to Italy, where it was ultimately placed in the *penus Vestae* as a pledge of the safety of Rome (Dion. Hal. l.c.; cf. Cic. *Phil.* 11. 24). The Palladium was believed to have saved Rome from the attack of the Gauls in 390 B.C. (Sil. Ital. 13. 79–81), and when the temple of Vesta caught fire in 241 B.C., it was rescued by the Pontifex Maximus, L. Caecilius Metellus (Ov. *Fasti* 6. 436–54, Cic. *Scaur.* 48). These two legends are clearly inconsistent; Ovid (*Fasti* 6. 433–5) is content not to judge between them, but stories were invented to reconcile them, such as that the image stolen by the Greeks was only a copy (Dion. Hal. l.c.), or that Diomede brought the Palladium to Italy and handed it over to Aeneas at Lavinium (Sil. Ital. 13. 51–78). The truth probably is that many cities possessed such talismans, which owing to the fame of the Trojan image all came to be known as Palladia; in Greece Argos and Athens claimed the Palladium, and in Italy not only Rome but Lavinium and Luceria and the Graeco-Roman city of Heraclea in Lucania (Strabo 6. 1. 14). C. B.

PALLADIUS, RUTILIUS TAURUS AEMILIANUS (4th c. A.D.), a practical farmer, wrote an *Opus agriculturae* in fourteen books, arranged according to the farmer's year. The last, on grafting, is in elegiac verse: a prose 'book XIV', *de ueterinaria medicina*, probably authentic, has recently been discovered and published by Svennung (*Eranos*, Göteborg, 1926). P. follows Columella, Gargilius Martialis, Vitruvius, and unnamed 'Graeci', besides personal observation; phrases such as 'quod expertus sum' constantly occur. Medieval scientists, notably Albertus Magnus, used him extensively. His prose style is jejune; his verses are metrically faultless, but monotonous and of limited vocabulary.

Teubner text (J. C. Schmitt, 1898); H. Widstrand, *Palladiusstudien* (1926); J. Svennung, *Untersuchungen zu Palladius* (1935); H. Fischer, *Mittelalterliche Pflanzenkunde* (1929). R. G. A.

PALLAS, (1) Παλλάς, -άδος, title of Athena (q.v.). A late legend, Philodemus, *De piet.* p. 6 Gompertz, Apollod. 3. 144 (spurious), says she was a friend of Athena whom the goddess accidentally killed and made the Palladium (q.v.) to commemorate her. (2) Πάλλας, -αντος, (*a*) a Titan (Hesiod, *Theog.* 376); (*b*) a giant, killed by Athena (Apollod. 1. 37); (*c*) an Attic hero who with his sons opposed Aegeus and was overcome by Theseus (qq.v.; Plut. *Theseus* 13; Apollod. 3. 206); (*d*) the son of Evander the Arcadian, an ally of Aeneas, killed by Turnus (Verg. *Aen.* 9. 104, 514 ff.; 10. 441 ff.); (*e*) son of Hercules and Evander's daughter (Dion. Hal. *Ant. Rom.* 1. 32. 1). H. J. R.

PALLAS (3), freedman of Antonia and financial secretary (*a rationibus*) of her son, the Emperor Claudius. His wealth, success, and arrogant temper made him deservedly unpopular. Devoted to Agrippina and alleged to be her lover, he successfully promoted her candidature in the competition after the execution of Messalina; he also hastened Claudius' adoption of her son. The Senate voted him *ornamenta praetoria* and a sum of money: he refused the money and received public commemoration for virtue and frugality (Tacitus, *Ann.* 12. 53; cf. Pliny, *Ep.* 7. 29. 2; 8. 6. 1, who indignantly quotes the senatorial decree inscribed on the tomb of Pallas on the Via Tiburtina). After the accession of Nero, Pallas, like Agrippina, was gradually and firmly thrust aside from power. Compelled to resign his office, he stipulated that no questions should be asked, that his accounts be regarded as balanced. Finally he was put to death by Nero, because of his wealth, it is said (A.D. 62). R. S.

PALLIATA, see FABULA *and* DRAMA, paras. 2 ff.

PALMA FRONTONIANUS, AULUS CORNELIUS (*cos.* I, A.D. 99), governor of Tarraconensis (*c.* 101), became governor of Syria *c.* 104. Operating with Legio VI Ferrata, he annexed Nabataea and formed it into a province by 106; the conquest was easy and coins commemorated *Arabia adquisita*. Palma was honoured with *ornamenta triumphalia* and was *cos.* II (*ordinarius*) in 109. Rich and influential, he apparently gave offence to Hadrian in Trajan's lifetime, being put to death after the Conspiracy of the Four Consulars (118).

E. Groag, *PW*, s.v. 'Cornelius (279)'; *PIR*², C 1412. C. H. V. S.

PALMARIUM, see ADVOCATUS.

PALMYRA (Aramaic *Tadmor*) owed its wealth to its position as an oasis between Syria and Babylonia. Owing to the disturbed condition of Mesopotamia in the first century B.C. it captured the trade between these two countries, organizing caravans direct across the desert, which it policed from the Euphrates to Damascus. The city was formed by the amalgamation of about twenty-five tribes, four of which held a dominant position. It was slightly hellenized, Aramaic being regularly used (sometimes with a Greek version added) in the inscriptions, which cover the first two and a half centuries A.D. Palmyra was raided by Antony. It was probably annexed in A.D. 17 by Germanicus; the tenth legion occupied it about this date, and Pliny's statement (in Titus' reign) that it was an independent buffer State is certainly false, for Vespasian built a road from Palmyra to Sura in 75. It retained much independence, however, maintaining its own army till the reign of Septimius Severus, who made it a Roman colony, and collecting for its own use the frontier customs: a tariff of the reign of Hadrian survives. Under Odaenathus and Zenobia (qq.v.) it ruled the Eastern Empire for a brief space, but after its reduction by Aurelian in 273 it never fully recovered. The ruins, which include the great temple of Bel, colonnaded streets, and triumphal arches, are impressive. The necropolis, with its curious tower tombs, has produced many examples of the local, and markedly oriental, school of sculpture.

History: J. G. Février, *Histoire de Palmyre* (1931). Monuments: T. Wiegand, *Palmyra* (1932). A. H. M. J.

PAMPHILA of Epidaurus, a scholar and historian (of literature) at Rome under Nero. Her chief work, Σύμμικτα ἱστορικὰ ὑπομνήματα, was summarized by Favorinus.

PAMPHILUS (1) (4th c. B.C., painter, of Amphipolis. Pupil of Eupompus of Sicyon (contemporary of Parrhasius); teacher of Apelles, Pausias, Melanthius (qq.v.). He painted a 'Battle at Phlius' (probably 367 B.C.) and the Heraclidae, referred to by Aristophanes (*Plut.* 385: before 388 B.C.). His pupils paid him a talent for a course lasting twelve years. He insisted on a knowledge of arithmetic and geometry, and had drawing introduced in Sicyon as a school subject. T. B. L. W.

PAMPHILUS (2) of Alexandria (*fl.* A.D. 50), lexicographer. He wrote a Τέχνη κριτική, Φυσικά, Περὶ βοτανῶν, and, in ninety-five books, a great lexicon—Περὶ γλωσσῶν ἤτοι λέξεων—which absorbed many previous specialist collections (cf. GLOSSA, GREEK). It was used by Athenaeus, and abridged by Vestinus. Cf. DIOGENIANUS (2). P. B. R. F.

PAMPHOS, mythical pre-Homeric writer of hymns.

PAMPHYLI, *see* DORIANS.

PAMPHYLIA was traditionally colonized by a mixed multitude of Greeks led by Amphilochus and Calchas (or Mopsus); the local dialect, which is related to Arcadian, confirms this tradition. The name in early times denoted all the coast from Phaselis to Coracesium, but was later restricted to the plain where lay Magydus, Perga, Sillyum, Aspendus, and Side. Despite Cimon's victory on the Eurymedon these cities remained under Persian rule till they surrendered to Alexander. Though occupied by Ptolemy I and III Pamphylia was generally subject to the Seleucids till 189 B.C. when it was ceded to Rome by Antiochus III; most of the cities were received into the Roman alliance by Cn. Manlius, and the Attalids gained only the strip of coast where they founded Attaleia. Pamphylia was probably part of the province of Cilicia from 102 till *c.* 44, when it was transferred to Asia. In 36 it was granted by Antony to Amyntas, who coined in Side, and from 25 B.C. was part of Galatia till in A.D. 43 Claudius formed Lycia-Pamphylia. Reattached to Galatia by Galba (the Lycians having been freed), it was reunited to Lycia by Vespasian, remaining a separate κοινόν.

Jones, *Eastern Cities*, 124 ff.; R. Syme, *Klio* xxvii (1934), 122 ff., xxx (1937), 227 ff. A. H. M. J.

PAN (Πάν), a god native to Arcadia (q.v.). His name, of which a form Πάων also exists, is probably to be derived from the root found in Lat. *pa-sco*, and interpreted 'the Feeder', i.e. herdsman. Since Arcadia was not rich in large cattle the goat was its characteristic beast, and Pan is half-goatish in shape (human body to the loins, goat's legs, ears, and horns). A vague deity, he is not unheard of in the plural, Panes. The ancients regularly associated his name with πᾶς or πᾶν (see *Hymn. Hom. Pan.* 47; Pl. *Crat.* 408 c); hence in late theologizings he becomes a universal god (see Kern, *Relig. d. Griechen* iii. 127 ff.). This, however, has nothing to do with either his native worship or any normal developments of it.

He is regularly son of Hermes, the only other Arcadian deity of importance ('Homer' and Plato, locc. citt., and often); but his mother varies. He has little mythology, hardly more than a couple of late stories of his love affairs, *see* ECHO, SYRINX; another is that he loved Pitys the nymph of the fir-tree, who ran away from him and changed into her tree-shape (Nonnus, *Dion.* 42. 258 ff.). In general he is amorous, as is natural in a god whose chief business it was to make the flocks fertile. When they did not increase a primitive rite was resorted to of flogging his statue with squills (Theoc. 7. 106 ff., where one of the scholia says it was when hunting was unsuccessful). This was no doubt meant at once to arouse the god and to strike fresh vigour into him. He was also on occasion formidable; it is well to be quiet at noonday (still a haunted time in Greece, see, e.g., Schmidt, *Volksleben d.*

Neugriechen, 94), because he is asleep then and will be angry if disturbed (Theoc. 1. 15 ff.). He can induce 'panic' terror (like that of a frightened and stampeding flock or herd) among men, as Polyb. 20. 6. 12 Büttner-Wobst (the actual word is not pre-Hellenistic). He sends nightmares (Artemidorus, 2. 37, p. 139, 18 Hercher), but not all dreams of him are bad (ibid. 12 ff.). In general, he is thought of as loving mountains, caves, and lonely places (i.e. the regular haunts of flocks in hilly country) and as musical, his instrument being the pan-pipe (still used by shepherds; cf. SYRINX).

He has few relations with other gods. On Mt. Lycaeon he and Zeus both had shrines (Paus. 8. 38. 5). Selene was one of his loves, and he trapped her by attracting her attention to a fine fleece (Verg. *G.* 3. 391 ff., and Servius ad loc.), or bribed her with sheep ('Probus', ad loc.).

His cult began to spread beyond Arcadia early in the fifth century B.C. Pindar, whose piety embraced quite minor deities, wrote him an ode (frs. 85–90 Bowra). Athens adopted him and gave him a cave-shrine on the Acropolis in the year of Marathon, when he was supposed to have promised and given help against the Persians (for the legend of his appearance to the runner Philippides see Herodotus 6. 105. 2–3). There were yearly sacrifices and torch-races in his honour (ibid. 4); L. Deubner, *Attische Feste* (1932), p. 213, doubts the latter, which, indeed, are hard to connect with Pan. Elsewhere he is not testified before the fourth century (Farnell, op. cit. infra, 432).

Of higher developments he has none. Aeschylus (*Ag.* 56) makes him an avenger of wrongs done to beasts; Plato (*Phdr.* 279 b–c) includes him among the gods to whom Socrates prays for inward beauty; pastoral poets make him a kind of divine patron of their literature; but these have nothing to do with his cult.

Farnell, *Cults* v. 431 ff., and the larger dictionaries s.v. H. J. R.

PANACEA (Πανάκεια), 'All-Healer', daughter of Asclepius (q.v.; Pliny, *HN* 25. 30 and often).

PANAENUS (*fl.* 448 B.C., Pliny), painter, brother (or nephew) of Phidias (q.v.), Athenian. He helped Phidias with the colouring of the Olympian Zeus and painted mythical scenes on screens between the legs of the throne. In the temple of Athena in Elis he put on a plaster mixed with saffron (for fresco?), and painted the inside of the shield of Colotes' Athena. The best sources ascribe to him, rather than to Micon or Polygnotus, the 'Battle of Marathon' in the Stoa Poikile (soon after 460); on the left, equal combat, with Miltiades urging on the Athenians and Plataeans; in the centre, Persians fleeing into the marsh; on the right, the fight round the ships with Cynegeirus and Callimachus; attendant gods and heroes, Theseus rising from the ground.

Overbeck, 696, 698, 1054, 1083, 1094–1108; Pfuhl, 717. T. B. L. W.

PANAETIUS (*c.* 185–109 B.C.), son of Nicagoras of Rhodes, Stoic philosopher. He attended the lectures of Crates of Mallos at Pergamum and then went to Athens, where he became a disciple of Diogenes the Babylonian, then head of the Stoa, and of his successor Antipater of Tarsus. Between 170 and 150 he must have returned to Rhodes for a short time, since he became priest of Poseidon Hippios at Lindus. In about 144 he went to Rome and soon joined the circle which gathered around P. Scipio Aemilianus. In 141 he accompanied Scipio on his travels in the Orient. After that he lived alternately in Rome and in Athens. In 129 he succeeded Antipater as head of the Stoa; and he held this position until his death in 109.

In spite of his Stoic creed Panaetius was an admirer of Plato and Aristotle and adopted the Peripatetic doctrine of the eternity of the universe. He tried to adapt

Stoic ethics to the requirements of the life of the Roman *grands seigneurs* with whom he associated, by putting into the foreground the more active and brilliant virtues of magnanimity, benevolence, and liberality as against the more passive virtues of fortitude (*not* to be disturbed in danger) and justice (*not* to do wrong), preached by his predecessors. His work Περὶ τοῦ καθήκοντος was used by Cicero in his *De Officiis*.

Panaetii et Hecatonis fragmenta, ed. H. N. Fowler (1885); R. Philippson, *Rh. Mus.* lxxviii (1929), *Philol.* lxxxv (1930), 357–413; B. N. Tatakis, *Panétius de Rhodes* (1931); L. Labowsky, *Die Ethik des Panaetius* (1934); M. van Straaten, *Panétius, sa vie, ses écrits et sa doctrine avec une édition des fragments* (1946). K. von F.

PANATHENAEA, an Athenian festival celebrated every year, and every fourth year with much greater pomp (the Great Panathenaea), on the 28th Hecatombaeon (July/Aug.), which was considered to be the birthday of Athena. It comprised a procession, sacrifices, and games. Citizens, maidens carrying sacred implements, youths conducting the sacrificial animals, metics, chariots which were to take part in the contests, and the cavalry figured in the procession. A famous representation is found on the frieze of the Parthenon. An embroidered peplos, hoisted on the mast of a ship set on wheels, was brought to the goddess. The flesh of the numerous victims was distributed among the people. The prize of the games was oil from the holy olives, stored in amphorae with a representation of Athena brandishing the spear and of one of several kinds of games.

E. Pfuhl, *De Atheniensium pompis sacris* (1900), 3 ff.; L. Deubner, *Attische Feste* (1932), 22 ff.; G. von Brauchitsch, *Die panathenäischen Preisamphoren* (1910). M. P. N.

PANCHAIA, *see* EUHEMERUS.

PANDAREOS (Πανδάρεως), name of either one or two obscure mythological persons, the father of Aëdon (q.v.), and, if this is not the same Pandareos, the father of two daughters whose story is told *Od.* 20. 66 ff., whereon see the ancient commentators. Their names were Cleothera and Merope, and they were left orphans (the scholiast says Zeus killed their father and mother because Pandareos had stolen his dog from Crete). Hera, Athena, Artemis, and Aphrodite befriended them, brought them up and gave them all manner of good qualities; but while Aphrodite was visiting Zeus to arrange their wedding, the Harpyiae (q.v.) carried them off and gave them to be servants to the Erinyes (q.v.). Cf. Roscher, *Lexikon*, s.v. H. J. R.

PANDARUS, a Trojan, son of Lycaon (*Iliad* 2. 826–7), and an archer favoured by Apollo. At the instigation of Athena, he broke the truce between the Greeks and Trojans by shooting at and slightly wounding Menelaus (q.v.; 4. 88 ff.); wounded Diomedes (5. 95 ff.), and was killed by him (290 ff.). H. J. R.

PANDORA, *see* PROMETHEUS.

PANEGYREIS, *see* FESTIVALS.

PANEGYRIC (πανηγυρικός), **GREEK**, properly a speech composed for a general gathering (πανήγυρις), such as the Olympic festival. Gorgias delivered such a speech (the *Olympiacus*), of which the theme was the necessity of union among the Greek States; Lysias in his *Olympiacus* followed similar lines. The best-known discourses of this kind are those of Isocrates, viz. the *Panegyricus*, composed, probably, for Olympia, in which he urged that Athens and Sparta should unite against Persia, and the *Panathenaïcus*, in which he did not deal with contemporary politics, but enlarged on the glories of Athens through the ages. Thus the *panegyric* is hardly

distinguishable from an *encomium* (q.v.), and in Roman times the word was particularly used of speeches in praise of the emperor, e.g. Pliny's *Panegyric of Trajan* and that of Aelius Aristides on Marcus Aurelius. A collection of *Panegyrici Veteres* was edited by E. Baehrens, 2nd ed. by G. Baehrens (Teubner, 1911). J. F. D.

PANEGYRIC, LATIN. The origins of Latin panegyric are to be sought in the ancient institution of the *laudatio funebris*. Such speeches of Cicero as the *Ninth Philippic*, the *Pro Lege Manilia*, and the *Pro Marcello* show developments and extensions of eulogy in relation both to deceased and to living persons. The *Pro Marcello* combines *laudatio* and *gratiarum actio*. In the Imperial age the *gratiarum actio*, formerly addressed to Senate or People, was delivered in honour of the emperor. A *senatus consultum* passed under Augustus required newly elected consuls to return thanks publicly to gods and emperor, but by Pliny's time the emperor's praise had supplanted that of the gods. This consular *gratiarum actio* provided the model for panegyrics addressed to the emperor or his representative on various occasions.

A collection of such speeches was found by Aurispa, 1433, in a Mainz manuscript (now lost) under the title of *XII Panegyrici Latini*. Its contents are (numeration according to W. A. Baehrens' ed. 1911): I. Pliny's (q.v. 2) *gratiarum actio* to Trajan on Pliny's elevation to the consulship. II. Latinus Pacatus Drepanius' panegyric to Theodosius. Pacatus (q.v.), a Gaul, had been sent to Rome to congratulate Theodosius on his victory over Maximus. III. Claudius (q.v.) Mamertinus' *gratiarum actio* to Julian, at Constantinople, on Mamertinus' elevation to the consulship. IV. Nazarius' panegyric to Constantine (in his absence) on an important imperial anniversary. V. Anonymous Gallic orator's *gratiarum actio* to Constantine, at Trèves, for benefits conferred on Autun. VI. Anonymous Gallic orator's panegyric to Constantine, at Trèves. VII. Anonymous orator's panegyric to Maximian and Constantine, at Trèves, in celebration of Constantine's marriage to Fausta. VIII. Anonymous Gallic orator's panegyric to Constantius, at Trèves, after the death of Allectus and the recovery of Britain. IX. Eumenius' (q.v.) *Pro Instaurandis Scholis Oratio*, in honour of all four emperors, at Autun, in presence of a provincial governor. X. Panegyric of an anonymous *magister memoriae* (unjustifiably named Mamertinus in the editions) to Maximian, in Gaul, on Rome's birthday. XI. *Panegyricus Genethliacus* to Maximian by the author of X. XII. Anonymous orator's panegyric to Constantine, at Trèves, after the defeat of Maxentius.

Although Pliny's speech is prefaced to the collection as the model of later panegyrists, the later speeches are much shorter, the longest, by Pacatus, being less than half as long as Pliny's. Otherwise there is considerable similarity, and Pliny's methods of adulation are imitated with progressive exaggeration. Former emperors, historical and mythological heroes, the gods, and nature herself are disparaged in favour of the emperor, whose most neutral and even unpraiseworthy actions and characteristics are eulogized with fantastically ingenious artificiality. The authors' outstanding virtue is the purity of their latinity, which is almost Plinian, if scarcely Ciceronian. The speeches are by no means equal in quality: they contain frequent passages of real beauty and eloquence, in spite of their general tawdriness. *Pro Instaurandis Scholis* is a pleasing speech, to whose author some of the anonymous panegyrics have been attributed. The *panegyrici* are of considerable historical interest, and throw much light on fourth-century Gaul.

Examples of panegyric not included in this collection are Ausonius' *Gratiarum Actio* and Ennodius' *Panegyricus*, addressed to Gratian and Theodoric respectively.

Verse panegyric is represented by the pseudo-Tibullian *Panegyricus Messallae*, the anonymous *Laus Pisonis*, Statius' *Silvae* 5. 2, and the panegyrics of Claudian and Apollinaris Sidonius (qq.v.). Its methods resemble those of prose panegyric.

Texts: Teubner (E. Baehrens, W. A. Baehrens). Style, diction, etc.: R. Pichon, *Les Derniers écrivains profanes* (1906); Schanz–Hosius–Krüger, *Gesch. röm. Lit.* iii (1922; for authorship problems).
W. S. M.

PANEGYRICUS MESSALLAE, aptly characterized by Sellar as 'a strange specimen of a fly preserved in amber', a tasteless and bombastic eulogy of Valerius (15) Messalla Corvinus in 212 hexameters, which opens the fourth book of the collection of Tibullian poetry. That is why it survives. Fruitless attempts have been made to identify the unknown author with Tibullus, Propertius, and Ovid. Once wealthy, but now vexed by 'the sense of loss', he tries hard, by celebrating Messalla's exploits, to find favour in his eyes—and to secure a reward. The piece was composed between 31 and 27 B.C.

Text in editions of Tibullus; with commentary, in the older editions by Heyne and Dissen; G. Némethy, *Lygdami Carmina, acc. Panegyr. in Messalam* (1906). See F. Hankel, *De Panegyrico in Messallam Tibulliano* (1874); H. Hartung, *De Panegyrico ad Messallam Pseudo-Tibulliano* (1880); R. S. Radford, 'The Juvenile Works of Ovid' (*Trans. Am. Phil. Ass.* li); (most exhaustive) S. Ehrengruber, *De Carmine Panegyrico Messalae Pseudo-Tibulliano* (1889–99); cf. Schanz–Hosius, *Gesch. röm. Lit.* ii (1935). J. H.

PANGAEUS, a mountain of southern Thrace, rising steeply to 6,000 feet, and important by reason of its timber supplies and the gold and silver mines at its base. The mines were first exploited by Thracian chieftains or by private Greek concessionaires. But the city of Thasos had acquired partial possession of them by 500 B.C.; the Athenians gained access to them in 437 (*see* AMPHIPOLIS); and in 358–357 Philip of Macedon occupied the main auriferous region to the east of Pangaeus, where he founded the town of Philippi (q.v.). The mines brought to Philip an annual revenue of 1,000 talents, but after 300 their productivity declined.

S. Casson, *Macedonia, Thrace, and Illyria* (1926), esp. 63–6; P. Perdrizet, *Klio* 1910, p. 1. M. C.

PANKRATION (παγκράτιον). In this event boxing and wrestling were combined with kicking, strangling, and twisting. It was a dangerous sport, but strict rules were enforced by umpires who closely watched the combatants. Biting and gouging were forbidden, but nearly every manœuvre of hands, feet, and body was permissible. You might kick your opponent in the stomach; you might twist his foot out of its socket; you might break his fingers. All neck holds were allowed, the favourite method being the 'ladder-grip', in which you mounted your opponent's back, and wound your legs round his stomach, your arms round his neck.
F. A. W.

PANNONIA, a Roman province south and west of the Danube, was originally the land of the warlike Pannonians, who were Illyrians, only to a small degree celticized, and split up into many tribes. The southern part of Pannonia was subdued by Octavian in 35 B.C., but in 16 South Pannonian tribes invaded Istria, and in 14 a revolt had to be repressed in Pannonia. In 13 B.C. Roman troops commanded by M. Vinicius and M. Agrippa successfully took the offensive. After Agrippa's death the resistance of the Pannonians stiffened; Tiberius became commander-in-chief and conquered them (12 and 11), with the result that the whole of Pannonia up to the Danube came under Roman rule and was added to Illyricum. After a revolt in 8 B.C., put down by Sex. Appuleius, peace prevailed till A.D. 6, when the well-prepared Illyrian-Pannonian revolt broke out: Pannonians, Illyrians, and Dalmatians, led by two chiefs named Bato (q.v.), desperately fought for independence, until their country was reconquered by Tiberius by

A.D. 9 (see R. Rau, *Klio* 1924; C. Patsch, *Sitz. Wien,* 214. i, pp. 110 ff.). Shortly afterwards or even during the revolt, Pannonia was separated from Illyricum, and organized as an imperial province under a *legatus Augusti pro praetore* (a list of the governors is given by E. Ritterling, *Arch.-Epigr. Mitt. Österr.* xx (1897), 1–40; cf. R. Egger, *JÖAI* ix (1906), Bbl. 63 f.). Shortly after A.D. 103 (perhaps in 106) it was divided into *P. Superior,* containing the northern and western parts, under a consular *legatus Augusti pro praetore,* and *P. Inferior,* covering the southern and eastern parts, under a praetorian *legatus Augusti pro praetore,* the latter being replaced by a consular *legatus* under Caracalla. Inscriptions (Dessau, *ILS* 2457 and 545) show that from the time of Gallienus *P. Inferior* was put under equestrian administration, which must also be presupposed for *P. Superior.* Under Diocletian both provinces were subdivided, *P. Superior* into *P. Prima* in the north (capital probably Savaria) under a *praeses* and a *dux,* and *P. Ripariensis* or *Savia* in the south (capital: Siscia) under a *dux*; *P. Inferior* into *Valeria* in the north (chief places: Aquincum and Sopianae) under a *praeses* and a *dux,* and *P. Secunda* in the south (capital: Sirmium) under a *consularis* and a *dux* (cf. *Rh. Mus.* xlv (1890), 203 ff. and *JÖAI* ix (1906), 63 ff.). In the fourth century Pannonia was increasingly threatened by the barbarians. Unable to hold it, the Romans recalled the garrisons and gradually relinquished Pannonia after 395. The view (of Alföldi) that Pannonia was officially surrendered to the Huns in A.D. 406 is improbable (see W. Ensslin, *Phil. Wochenschr.* 1927, 848).

BIBLIOGRAPHY

INSCRIPTIONS: *CIL* iii (1873–1902). V. Hoffiller and B. Saria, *Antike Inschriften aus Jugoslavien,* Heft I, *Noricum und Pannonia Superior* (1939). A. Dobó, *Inscriptiones extra fines Pannoniae Daciaeque repertae ad res eandarum provinciarum pertinentes* (1940).
GENERAL LITERATURE: A. Graf, *Übersicht der antiken Geographie von Pannonien* (1936); C. Patsch, *Sitz. Wien,* 214. i (1932); A. Alföldi, *Der Untergang der Römerherrschaft in Pannonien* i (1924), ii (1926); Alföldi, 'Bibliographia Pannonica II' in *Pannonia* ii (1936), 143 ff., 309 ff. Further cf. *Dissertationes Pannonicae,* ser. I, fasc. 1 (1932)–12 (1946), and ser. II, fasc. 1 (1933)–21 (1946); O. Davies, *Roman Mines in Europe* (1935), 182 ff.; U. Täckholm, *Studien über den Bergbau der röm. Kaizerzeit* (Uppsala, 1937), 108 f.
SPECIAL SUBJECTS: On the distribution of legions see E. Ritterling, *PW* xii. 1362 ff. On the romanization of Pannonia, A. Alföldi, *Studi romani nel mondo* ii (1935), 265 ff. On the influence of Pannonians in the Roman Empire, Alföldi, *25 Jahre Röm. German. Kommission* (1930), 11–51. On Roman–Pannonian decorative painting, L. Nagy, *Rh. Mus.* xli (1926), 79–131. On Pannonian art, culture, etc., A. Hekler, *Strena Buliciana* (1924), 107 ff.; M. Lang, *JÖAI,* xix–xx (1919), Bbl. 207–60; L. Hampel, *Arch. Ért.,* 1907, 289–341; 1910, 311–44. On the Ostrogoth settlement, Ensslin, *Byzant. Neugriech. Jahrb.,* 1928, pp. 160 ff. On the etymology of the word Pannonia, K. Kerényi, *Glotta,* 1934, 31 ff. F. A. W. S.

PANNYCHIS, an all-night festival or vigil in honour of a deity, e.g. Demeter at the Haloa (Deubner, *Attische Feste,* 62); Artemis at the Tauropolia (ibid. 208). Since these were on occasion made an excuse for illicit love-affairs (see Menander, *Epit.* 234 ff. Allinson), it is not surprising that Pannychis appears as an attendant of Aphrodite (see Höfer in Roscher's *Lexikon,* s.v.). It was also a common name for a hetaera, as in Lucian, *Dial. Meret.* 9 (name of a speaker). H. J. R.

PANORMUS (nowadays *Palermo*), despite its name, was never Greek. Originally a Phoenician settlement in northern Sicily, it subsequently became Carthaginian; its spacious and beautiful harbour made it the capital of Carthaginian Sicily, an important naval and military base (so, e.g., in the Himera campaign, 480 B.C.). Except for its temporary loss to Pyrrhus (276), Panormus remained continuously in Carthaginian hands until captured by Rome (254). Carthage, despite valiant efforts by Hamilcar Barca from neighbouring Hercte (q.v.), never recovered it. Under Rome Panormus was a privileged *civitas libera et immunis,* acquired the status of *colonia* (*c.* 20 B.C.), and was recolonized under Vespasian and Hadrian (*Lib. Colon.* p. 211). It has, indeed, never ceased to be a flourishing, populous, commercial centre.

Strabo 6. 272; Thuc. 6. 2; Diod. 11. 20; 14. 48; 15. 17; 22. 10; Polyb. 1. 21, 24, 38, 56 f.; Cic. *Verr.* passim.   E. T. S.

PANSA, GAIUS VĪBIUS, defended Caesar's interests as tribune in 51 B.C., governed Cisalpine Gaul in 45, and was designated consul for 43. Pansa was attached to Cicero. In March 43 he led four legions of recruits by the Via Cassia to join Hirtius (q.v.) against Antony. He was wounded in a preliminary engagement at Forum Gallorum, 8 miles from Mutina, and after the battle of Mutina he died. Gossip alleged that Octavian had poisoned him.   G. E. F. C.

PANSPERMIA, *see* FIRST FRUITS.

PANTHEON, a temple in the Campus Martius built with Baths and water-gardens by M. Agrippa in 27–25 B.C. and twice destroyed by fire. The existing building, repaired by Septimius Severus (*CIL* vi. 896), is by Hadrian (S.H.A. *Hadr.* 19) with Agrippa's dedication retained (*CIL* ibid.). It is a rotunda (43·20 m. in internal diameter) of brick-faced concrete, stuccoed externally to imitate masonry, with a portico (34 m. wide and 13·60 m. deep) of Corinthian columns, eight in front and two groups of four behind, facing north. Below the portico lies a rectangular foundation (43·76 m. wide and 19·82 m. deep) with porch (21·26 m. wide) opening southwards on a circular enclosure concentric with Hadrian's rotunda. Hadrian's building, evidently an entire remodelling, was largely screened by unconnected structures, including a large hall to south. The rotunda is 43·20 m. high, with central skylight 9 metres in diameter; its wall (6·20 m. thick) contains four rectangular and three semicircular alcoves. The door, breaking the circle, is flanked by niched buttresses, a common structural device also occurring in the body of the wall, which is converted by semicircular chambers into eight piers built as niches, all vertically linked by a very elaborate system of relieving arches extending to the haunch of the richly coffered dome. This covers a sumptuous interior, decorated in marble, framed by an entablature above the columned alcoves and canopied statue-bases. A flat panelled attic, with shallow rectangular niches, then prepares us for the dome, of which the upper structural system remains unknown. The bronze doors still remain.

G. Beltrani, *Il Panteon* (1898); J. Durm, *Ant. Baukunst,* 550–73; T. Ashby, W. J. Anderson, and R. P. Spiers, *Architecture of Ancient Rome*[2] (1927).   I. A. R.

PANTHOUS (Πάνθοος, Πάνθους), a Trojan elder (*Iliad* 3. 146). Apollo protects his son, Polydamas (q.v.; 15. 521–2), whence some said he was a Delphian (schol. ibid.). In Verg. *Aen.* 2. 318 ff. he is a pious priest of Apollo, killed by Aeneas' side at the storming of Troy.

PANTICAPAEUM, a colony of Miletus, on the west side of the Cimmerian Bosporus (*Straits of Kertch*), founded probably *c.* 600 B.C. It throve on the fisheries of the Straits, on the trade along the river Tanais, and especially on the export of wheat from the Crimea. It was ruled successively by two dynasties, the Archaeanactids (probably a line of Greek tyrants), and the Spartocids (q.v.), who gained power in 438. The gold coinage of Panticapaeum and the magnificently furnished rock tombs of its chief citizens attest its wealth in the fourth and third centuries. It subsequently (*c.* 115) became the capital of Mithridates VI's territory in south Russia, and was the seat of the local Crimean dynasty founded by his descendants under Roman sovereignty. In the third century A.D. it fell to the Sarmatians and Goths.

E. H. Minns, *Scythians and Greeks* (1913), 503–6.   M. C.

PANTOMIMUS, a dancer who represented traditional themes in dumb show, supported by instrumental music and a chorus. (The apparent meaning is 'one who imitates everything', but the distinctive quality of pantomime was that the chief performer did everything by imitation.) This type of performance (the Greeks called it the 'Italian dance') was created at Rome in 22 B.C. by Pylades of Cilicia and Bathyllus of Alexandria. 'To dance the shepherd Cyclops' in tragic mask and buskins was nothing new (Hor. *Sat.* 1. 5. 64); Pylades' innovation, according to himself (Macrob. *Sat.* 2. 7), was to add the orchestra and chorus. Bathyllus seems to have specialized in light themes, akin to comedy or satyric drama, with a rustic setting—e.g. Pan revelling with a satyr (Ath. 1. 20; Plut. *Quaest. conv.* 7. 711 f.; Sen. *Con. Ex.* 3. pref. 10 and 16; cf. Lucian, *Salt.* 74 and Libanius iii, p. 392, Reiske); Pylades' style is said to have been 'high flown, passionate, melancholy' and more akin to tragedy; but these comparisons with drama look artificial; the immediate origins of pantomime do not appear to have been dramatic; its themes, whether erotic or otherwise, are taken from mythology or (occasionally) remote history as presented by the poets, whether dramatic or epic. It was a highly sophisticated type of entertainment, demanding much from both performers and spectators; though demoralizing, it was not coarse, like the mime.

Performances took place on the public stage or in private houses. The pantomimus, usually a handsome, athletic figure, wore a graceful silk costume (long tunic and cloak, Suet. *Calig.* 54), which allowed of free movement, and a beautiful mask with closed lips (Lucian, *Salt.* 29, A. Baumeister, *Denkmäler des klassischen Altertums* (1885–8), figs. 1351–2). Behind him stood the chorus, the players of flutes, pipes, cymbals, etc., and the *scabillarii,* who beat time by pressing with the foot on the *scabillum,* a wooden or metal instrument fastened underneath the sandal (see Baumeister, fig. 1350). Beside the pantomimus there sometimes stood an assistant—perhaps an actor with a speaking part (ὑποκρίτου εὐφωνίαν, Lucian 68). Lucian tells (83) of a pantomimus who overacted the part of 'mad Ajax': he tore the clothes of one of the scabillarii, snatched a flute from an instrumentalist and with it struck the triumphant 'Odysseus' a blow which would have been fatal but for Odysseus' traditional head-dress (the πῖλος); then, springing down into the body of the theatre, he seated himself between two alarmed ex-consuls —all this to the delight of the rabble, who thought it the perfection of acting. Better performers were more subtle: Pylades, when the chorus uttered the words τὸν μέγαν Ἀγαμέμνονα, expressed the monarch's greatness by assuming an air of statesmanlike reflection (Macrob. l.c.). The dancer might in one piece have to appear in five different roles, each with its own mask (Lucian 66; change of costume seems unproved; cf. *eodem pallio,* Fronto, p. 57, 3, ed. Naber—but Arnobius, *Adv. Gent.* 7. 33, seems to speak of a special costume for the part of Adonis). To convince an unbeliever, a pantomimus acted single-handed the love-tale of Ares and Aphrodite—Helios bringing his tidings, Hephaestus setting his snare, the gods coming one by one to look at the entrapped lovers, the confusion of Aphrodite, the abject alarm of Ares (Lucian 63; Lucian adds a story of a foreigner from the Pontus on a visit to Rome who, though he could not follow the song of the chorus because of his lack of Greek, found the pantomime's performance so lucid that he wished to take him home as an interpreter). The dancer's power to convey his meaning by steps, postures, and above all gestures (Quint. *Inst.* 11. 3. 88) was aided by certain conventions, e.g. there was a traditional dance for 'Thyestes devouring his children', which one pantomimus unfortunately performed when wishing to represent Kronos devouring *his* children.

The songs of the chorus were of secondary importance

(Libanius p. 381); such fragments as we possess are in Greek. Lucan and Statius wrote libretti for pantomimes —a degrading (Sen. *Suas.* 2. 19), if lucrative, occupation (Juv. 7. 87). That the chorus also expounded the narrative in recitative, while the dancer was changing for his next role, seems to be merely a guess of Friedländer. The music, like the whole performance, was enervating (Plin. *Pan.* 54).

For the popularity of the pantomimi (and pantomimae), the faction-fights of their supporters, the effect of their performances on public morality and the efforts of the government to deal with the problem, see Friedländer, *Rom. Life* (Engl. Transl.) ii. 100–17, and consult Daremberg et Saglio, Lübker, and esp. Smith's *Dict. Ant.*, s.v. 'pantomimus'. W. B.

PANYASSIS of Halicarnassus (5th c. B.C.), epic poet, uncle of Herodotus; revived epic poetry; author of a *Heraclea*; classed by some critics second to Homer; discussed by Quintilian (*Inst.* 10. 1. 54); said to have plagiarized a poem of Creophylus. *See* EPIC CYCLE.

EGF 253–65. W. F. J. K.

PAPAS, *see* ATTIS.

PAPHLAGONIA, a territory of north Asia Minor, which included the mountainous coastal region between Bithynia and Pontus and extended inland to the plateau. It was noted for its ship timber and cabinet woods. In social structure it was similar to Pontus. Villages predominated, organized in administrative districts, and temple territories were numerous. Greek settlements dotted the coast from Heraclea to Sinope, but in Persian times the native population remained largely autonomous. After Alexander Paphlagonia was broken up, part falling to Bithynia and part to Pontus; and either then or at the fall of the Pontic kingdom the coastal cities acquired extensive territories. From the third century B.C. a portion south of Mt. Olgassys, called Inner Paphlagonia, kept its independence under native kings. Occupied in turn and divided by the kings of Bithynia and Pontus, and entrusted at first by the Romans to various dependent kings, this portion was attached by Augustus to the province of Galatia (6 B.C.). Diocletian revived Inner Paphlagonia as a province under a *corrector*. The chief town was Gangra-Germanicopolis.

Strabo 12. 542–4; R. Leonhard, *Paphlagonia* (1915); Jones, *Eastern Cities*, 148 ff. T. R. S. B.

PAPHOS was a city situated a short distance inland from the west coast of Cyprus, and settled by colonists from Greece in the Mycenaean period. It contained a famous temple of Aphrodite, who was believed to have risen from the sea near Paphos. The sanctuary was reputed to have been founded by Cinyras, a contemporary of Agamemnon, whose descendants combined the priesthood of Aphrodite with the royal authority in Paphos down to the time of the Ptolemies. After the fall of the Cinyrad dynasty the upper city was superseded by its port town (situated some 7 miles away), which became an assize centre and perhaps the seat of the proconsul under Roman rule. In Roman times the name of Paphos was reserved for the port town, the upper city being known as Old Paphos (Παλαίπαφος).

D. G. Hogarth, *Devia Cypria* (1889), ch. 1. For the temple of Aphrodite see M. R. James, *JHS* ix. 175 ff.; C. Blinkenberg, *Le Temple de Paphos* (1924). M. C.

PAPINIANUS, AEMILIUS, one of the greatest classical Roman jurists. His origin (Syria?, Africa?) is uncertain; some peculiarities of his language do not suffice to establish his Oriental origin. He was seemingly a pupil of Cervidius Scaevola (q.v. 5). His official career was brilliant and in A.D. 203 he became *Praefectus Praetorio*.

He was executed in 212 by order of Caracalla for having disapproved of the murder of the emperor's brother Geta. Papinian owes his high reputation principally to his collective works, mostly of casuistic character: *Quaestiones* (37 bks.), completed before 198, and *Responsa* (19 bks.). Neither of these works, however, is uniform: the *Quaestiones* are not free from doctrinal discussions and contain numerous citations of earlier jurists, while the other work does not consist merely of *responsa*, being more casuistic than *responsa* normally were, and containing *responsa* of other jurists, decisions pronounced in the emperors' and prefects' *auditoria* and even in imperial constitutions. *Notae* to both these works were written by Paulus, to the *Responsa* also by Ulpian. Other writings of Papinian: *Definitiones, De adulteriis*. He did not publish any comprehensive systematical work.

Papinian was highly appreciated by posterity. In the Law of Citations (426) his pre-eminence was recognized by the provision that, failing a majority of jurists cited on one side or the other, Papinian's view should be decisive. The exclusion of Paulus' and Ulpian's notes on Papinian is likewise a tribute to his personal value. Justinian said justly of him: 'acutissimi ingenii uir' and 'merito ante alios excellens' (*Cod.* 6. 42. 30). The quotations from him are among the most instructive, though sometimes difficult on account of the conciseness of his style. The independence of his judgement and the sagacity of his mind led him not infrequently to original solutions which are not governed by a rigid technical process, but left room for equity, and to ethical and moral arguments. The logic of his thought is incontestable, his criticism is deliberate, yet without prejudice or harshness. He is not averse to changing his opinion when another appears to him to be right (cf. *Dig.* 18. 7. 6. 1: 'nobis aliquando placebat . . ., sed in contrarium me uocat Sabini sententia').

E. Costa, *Papiniano* (1894–9); H. Fitting, *Alter und Folge der Schriften röm. Juristen*[2] (1908), 71 ff. On P.'s language: Leipold, *Sprache des Juristen Aemilius Papinianus* (1891); W. Kalb, *Roms Juristen* (1890), 111 ff. A. B.

PAPINIUS, *see* STATIUS.

PAPĪRIANUS (5th c. A.D.), grammarian, from whose *De Orthographia* excerpts are preserved by Cassiodorus (ed. Keil, *Gramm. Lat.* vii. 158–66). Cf. Teuffel, § 472. 5; Schanz–Hosius, § 1108.

PAPĪRIUS (1) **CURSOR,** LUCIUS, Roman hero of the Second Samnite War, consul in 326, 320, 319, 315, 313 B.C.; dictator in 325, 309. The details of his military career, especially in the years immediately after the Caudine Forks disaster (321), are untrustworthy (cf. Livy 9. 15). But his Samnite victory and triumph in 309 stamp him as a great general, a fit match for Alexander the Great according to Livy (9. 16; 9. 38 f.). Rhetorical accounts are also given of his eating, drinking, and running abilities, while his alleged attempt to execute the other patrician hero of the age, Fabius (q.v. 3) Rullianus, for fighting against orders illustrates his strictness and severity (Livy, bks. 8 and 9; [Aur. Vict.] *De Vir. Ill.* 31; Eutrop. 2. 8; Zonar. 7. 26). Possibly Cursor was partly responsible for the law which virtually terminated enslavement for debt (H. Last, *CAH* vii. 545). E. T. S.

PAPIRIUS (2) **CURSOR,** LUCIUS, son of (1), twice consul with Spurius Carvilius: in 293 B.C. when he defeated specially consecrated Samnite levies at Aquilonia (Livy 10. 38–42: numbers exaggerated); and in 272 when he ended the Pyrrhic War by subduing Lucani, Bruttii, and Tarentines (Zonar. 8. 6). He erected the first sundial at Rome (Pliny, *HN* 7. 213). E. T. S.

PAPIRIUS, *see also* CARBO, FABIANUS.

PAPIUS MUTILUS, Gaius, Samnite, was an Italian leader in the Social War. He invaded Campania in 90 B.C., and took many towns, but was repulsed by the consul Sex. Caesar, losing 6,000 men. Sulla defeated him in 89. He may be the Mutilus who perished in Sulla's proscription (82).   M. H.

PAPPUS of Alexandria (*fl. c.* A.D. 300), a distinguished mathematician, wrote commentaries (1) on the *Elements* of Euclid, fragments of which are quoted by Proclus and others, while the section on bk. 10 has come down in Arabic; (2) on Ptolemy's *Syntaxis*; bks. 5 and 6 of this survive (edited by A. Rome, *Biblioteca Apostolica Vaticana*, 1931); (3) on Ptolemy's *Planisphaerium* and the *Analemma* of Diodorus (lost). But his great work is the *Synagoge*, 'Collection', edited by F. Hultsch 1876–8, invaluable for its accounts, (a) of Greek achievements in higher geometry, notably works (now lost) by Euclid, Aristaeus, and Apollonius belonging to the 'Treasury of Analysis' (Τόπος ἀναλυόμενος); (b) of works by Autolycus, Theodosius, and Menelaus belonging to the 'Little Astronomy' (Μικρὸς ἀστρονομούμενος), Euclid's *Optics* and *Phaenomena*, and Aristarchus' *On the sizes and distances of the sun and moon*; (c) of various solutions of the problem of the two mean proportionals, a method of inscribing the five regular solids in a sphere, Archimedes' spiral, Nicomedes' 'cochloids', and the *quadratrix*; (d) of Archimedes' semi-regular solids, and of the subject of *Isoperimetry*, or the comparison of the areas and volumes of different figures with equal contours and equal surfaces respectively, including the volumes of the five regular solids which have their total surfaces equal; (e) of works on theoretical and practical mechanics by Archimedes, Philon of Byzantium, Heron, and Carpus. Pappus supplies many lemmas, etc., to the treatises elucidated, and important additions of his own, e.g. an extension of Eucl. i. 47 to *any* triangle, proof of the constancy of anharmonic ratios, measurement of the superficial area bounded by a spiral on a sphere, an anticipation of the theorem called by the name of Guldin, and 'Pappus' Problem', which was taken up by Descartes.   T. H.

PAPPUS (πάππος), the old grandfather in *Atellana* (q.v.).

PAPYROLOGY, GREEK. Papyrus (*see* BOOKS), a marsh plant that grew abundantly in the Nile valley and elsewhere (though the Egyptian variety alone was manufactured into paper), was the normal writing material of the ancient world from the classical age onwards. Yet with few exceptions, of which the chief are (a) the Epicurean papyri from Herculaneum, (b) the papyri found at Dura-Europos on the Euphrates and the unpublished find from south Palestine, (c) the Ravenna and papal documents of the early Middle Ages, all our papyri come from Egypt south of the Delta, where the rainless climate favours their survival. A few have been found placed in tombs, some have been extracted from the wrappings of mummies; but the great majority come from the ruined buildings and rubbish heaps of the towns and villages of Upper Egypt, abandoned when the irrigation level receded; hence the fragmentary condition of so many of our texts. From 1788 onwards miscellaneous papyri (including some rolls of Homer and of the lost speeches of Hyperides) were acquired by travellers and made their way into European collections; excavations of Graeco-Roman sites did not begin till a century later. The most successful of these were carried out by B. P. Grenfell and A. S. Hunt, in particular at Oxyrhynchus (q.v.) which, with the Fayûm, the ancient Arsinoite nome, has proved the most fertile source of papyri.

2. We have no papyri certainly anterior to Alexander's conquest of Egypt in 332 B.C., though it is likely that our oldest literary papyrus, the *Persae* of Timotheus, dates from the middle of the fourth century; our earliest dated document is a marriage contract of 311 B.C. from Assuan, the latest documents extend well beyond the Arab conquest of A.D. 642. Under the first two Ptolemies settlers from all parts of the Greek world flocked into Egypt, and in the first century of Greek rule the country was steadily hellenized. Greek was the official language of the country and remained so throughout the Roman and Byzantine periods; for a large part of the population it was also the language of business and of everyday life. Of this civilization—Hellenistic, Roman, Byzantine—the papyri are the record; of it, thanks to their endless variety, which includes ephemeral matter such as private letters, school exercises, prayers and charms as well as literary texts and public and legal documents, we can form a picture in singular detail. The number of published texts, varying enormously in size, condition, content, and value, is approximately 20,000. The extent of the material as yet unpublished is unknown.

3. Papyrology, which is strictly the decipherment and study of anything written on papyrus, is not a unified subject except in as far as all the papyri represent the different activities of a single civilization. The most obvious division is between literary and documentary texts. We owe the former, about 1,500 in number, in part to the fact that a knowledge of the Greek classics, in particular of Homer, was the staple of education throughout the period. Among them the new texts slightly outnumber those already known to us, though in the later centuries new texts become rare; yet the Byzantine papyri have given us the codex of Menander and a poem of Sappho's. The new texts include, besides those mentioned, various fragmentary manuscripts of the lyric poets, Bacchylides, much of Callimachus (notably the *Aitia* and the *Iambi*), Herodas, the *Ichneutae* of Sophocles, and many other fragments of the dramatic poets, including Aeschylus, Aristotle's *Constitution of Athens*, and the *Hellenica Oxyrhynchia*, an historical work probably from the hand of Ephorus.

4. Of the papyri of extant Greek authors more than half are texts of Homer, the *Iliad* appearing more frequently than the *Odyssey*. The later Homeric papyri add very little to what we know from our medieval manuscripts, but the 'eccentric' papyri of the earlier Ptolemaic period, with their numerous additions and omissions and variant readings, even if the text they present is an inferior one, yet enable us to appreciate the work of the Alexandrian scholars in standardizing the text. For the textual criticism of other authors the papyri have often been of great value. They are almost invariably not only older than the medieval manuscripts (in the case, e.g., of Xenophon or Lysias by as much as 1,000 years) but are also older than the families into which the manuscripts are commonly divided. There are not a few instances of new and improved readings contributed by, a few of emendations confirmed by, the papyri; but on the whole they bear witness to the general soundness of our tradition, by showing that the text as known to the Graeco-Roman world differed little from that we already possess. These papyri are, as a rule, from the standpoint of our medieval manuscripts, 'eclectic'; they agree now with one manuscript, now with another, and not infrequently the readings of the later and less valued manuscripts have been found in papyri, with the result that textual criticism relies less than formerly on the testimony of a single, ancient manuscript and takes more into account the evidence of the later, inferior manuscripts.

5. Besides the strictly literary papyri there are others which may be termed 'quasi-literary'; these include the scientific, in particular the medical, texts, the astrological and the magical; texts of these last two classes are of value for social and religious history. But more important than any of these are the Christian literary texts.

Here the papyri of texts already known are hardly, if at all, less important than the new texts; the Chester Beatty papyri, which consist of extensive portions of eleven papyrus codices, take our knowledge of the text of the Greek Bible back to the second century A.D., while the Rylands Library at Manchester has some fragments of Deuteronomy dating from the second century B.C. Here again, in spite of important modifications in the history of the text at various points for which we are indebted to the papyri, its general soundness is confirmed. Among the new texts the most sensational discoveries have been those of the Oxyrhynchus *Sayings of Jesus* and the Unknown Gospel in the British Museum of the second century; there are other fragments of apocrypha and of liturgical, theological, and hagiological works—of the last class the lengthy *Acta Pauli* is the best representative. Evidence of Christianity can also be found in some of the documents, notably in the *libelli* (certificates of sacrifice) of the Decian persecution and in private letters; of the latter the small archive of letters relating to the Meletian schism (A.D. 330-40) is particularly noteworthy.

6. The great mass of the papyri is roughly classified under the heading of documents—official, legal, and private papers of every description. Their value to the historian lies less in the direct information about events of historical importance which they convey (though texts of this character are extant, e.g. decrees of the Ptolemaic kings, the letter of the Emperor Claudius to the Alexandrians, the imperfect text of the *Constitutio Antoniniana* of A.D. 212 announcing the extension of the Roman *civitas* throughout the Empire) than in the indirect evidence about the historical background; such evidence may be all the more valuable because it was not deliberately selected for the benefit of posterity. Their contribution, apart from that to such specialist studies as metrology and numismatics or chronology, belongs to economic and social history in the widest sense and to the history of Greek and Roman law. In the Ptolemaic period, for example, we can observe in detail the nature and methods of Greek colonization of an Eastern Mediterranean country and its adaptation to the local conditions, and the growth of a bureaucracy which set the precedent for that of Rome; in the Roman age we see at close quarters what the Roman system of government meant to the governed and the exploitation of the country in the interests of Rome; in the Byzantine period there is the change-over to a quasi-feudal system, the growth of the great estates, the decay of Greek culture and its final disappearance before the Arab invaders.

7. The history of Greek culture and education in Egypt is partly to be found in the literary texts, their frequency, their geographical distribution, and their contents, partly in the private letters relating to education, and not least in the language of the documents themselves. Of this language, the Egyptian *Koine*, there is not one variety but many in the documents; not only does the clear, straight-forward Greek of the Ptolemaic documents differ from the cumbrous, half-understood periphrases of the Byzantine age, but in a given century the language of the official document will differ from that of a business document or that of a private letter of an educated writer, and these again from the illiterate documents closest to the spoken tongue. The language of the documents has been of the greatest value for the study of the contemporary works of the New Testament both in syntax and vocabulary, and provides a link connecting the language of the classical age with that of Byzantine and modern Greece.

BIBLIOGRAPHY

The only general work that deals with the whole subject is still W. Schubart's *Einführung in die Papyruskunde* (1917); for the historical and legal documents the *Grundzüge und Chrestomathie der Papyruskunde* (1912: 4 vols., with briefly annotated editions of

882 texts) of L. Mitteis and U. Wilcken is indispensable; for the legal papyri cf. also P. M. Meyer, *Juristische Papyri* (1917). For essays on some of the new literary texts see J. U. Powell and E. A. Barber, *New Chapters in Greek Literature* (three series, 1921–33); for a survey of the literary texts, new and extant and including the Christian, see J. G. Winter, *Life and Letters in the Papyri* (U.S.A. 1933: includes chapters on social life).

The list of published volumes of papyri is too long to give here; the most up-to-date list is that in A. Calderini, *Manuale di Papirologia* (1938). Of English publications the Oxyrhynchus series (ed. B. P. Grenfell, A. S. Hunt, H. I. Bell, vols. i–xvii, 1898–1927; in progress) is the most representative. For a selection of the documents see A. S. Hunt and C. C. Edgar, *Select Papyri* (Loeb, 2 vols., 1932–4). For publication of new books, texts, etc., on all branches of the subject see the annual bibliography of Graeco-Roman Egypt in *The Journal of Egyptian Archaeology*.   C. H. R.

PAPYROLOGY, LATIN. Latin papyri (with parchments, waxed tablets, and ostraca) are less numerous and valuable than Greek papyri: they are found not only in Egypt but at Herculaneum and at Dura-Europos on the Euphrates. In Roman Egypt Latin did not supplant Greek, but was employed in official documents, legal and military, and in education.

CLASSIFICATION

(1) Legal documents: imperial rescripts, ἀπογραφή, wills, birth-certificates, deed of appointment of guardian to woman.

(2) Military documents: Registers of cohorts, accounts, receipt for loan of money, birth-registration; private letters, e.g. recommendation to military tribune, *Select Papyri* (Loeb) i. 122. Cf. *The Excavations at Dura-Europos*, Prel. Rep. of fifth season, ed. M. I. Rostovtzeff (U.S.A. 1934), pp. 295–303, pl. xxx–xxxi.

(3) Scholastic work: (Cicero) see 'Latin Exercises from a Greek Schoolroom', *CPhil.* xix (1924), 317; (Virgil, with Greek translation) *PRyl.* iii. 478 (4th c. A.D.); (Babrius, with Latin translation) *PAmh.* ii. 26 (3rd–4th c. A.D.); (Q. Remmius Palaemon, *Ars Grammatica*) Milne, *Cat. Lit. Pap.* 184 (2nd c. A.D.). Graeco-Latin lexica: *PLund* 5 (2nd c. A.D.), *PLondon* ii. 481, p. 321 (4th c. A.D.).

(4) Literary texts (less trustworthy than Greek texts on papyrus): (a) new authors: (from Herculaneum) C. Rabirius (?), *Carmen de Bello Aegyptiaco* (*Actiaco*, Lowe, *Codd. Lat. Antiq.*; 70 hexameters), Baehrens, *PLM* i. 212, I. Ferrara, *Poematis latini rell. ex vol. Herculanensi* (1908). Anonymous histories, e.g. *POxy.* xvii. 2088 (2nd c. A.D.; on Servius Tullius, perhaps by L. Aelius Tubero, Cicero's friend, author of *Annales*).

(b) New parts of known authors: Sallust, *Histories* (*PRyl.* iii. 473, 2nd–3rd c. A.D.); Livy, *Epit.* 37–40, 48–55 (*POxy.* iv. 668: E. Kornemann, *Klio* 1904, 2. Beiheft).

(c) Texts already known: Sallust, *Catilina, Jugurtha*: Cicero (the best represented Latin author), *Verr.* 2. 2, *PIand.* v. 90, time of Augustus—the oldest Latin papyrus and the oldest manuscript of Cicero; Virgil, *Aeneid, POxy.* viii. 1098 (4th–5th c. A.D.), *PFouad* i. 5 (4th–5th c. A.D.), *POxy.* i. 31 (5th c. A.D.), *PSI* i. 21 (5th c. A.D., with accents and marks of long quantity); Livy bk. 1; Lucan; Juvenal 7. 149–98 (parchment, *c.* A.D. 500), *JEg.Arch.* xxi (1935), 199 (line 156 *fronte* with four less important manuscripts).

Facsimiles of Latin literary papyri in British collections: E. A. Lowe, *Codices Latini Antiquiores*, ii (1935).

(5) Liturgical fragment, *PRyl.* iii. 472 (3rd–4th c. A.D.).

(6) Legal texts, e.g. Gaius (Teubner, 1935) and the *Digest* (*PRyl.* iii. 479).

Medieval Latin papyrus books include Paris Homilies of St. Avitus (6th c. A.D.), Paris and Geneva Sermons and Letters of St. Augustine (7th c. A.D.), the Vienna Hilary, the Milan Josephus: see Preisendanz, *Papyrusfunde u. Papyrusforschung* (1933), 18.

BIBLIOGRAPHY

M. Ihm, 'Lateinische Papyri', in *Zentralblatt für Bibliothekswesen* xvi (1899), 341 ff.; W. Schubart, *Klio* xiii (1913), 27 ff.; A. Stein,

Untersuchungen zur Geschichte u. Verwaltung Ägyptens unter röm. Herrschaft (1915), 207 ff.; P. Jouguet, 'Les papyrus latins d'Égypte', *Rev. Ét. Lat.* iii (1925), 35 ff.; U. Wilcken, 'Über den Nutzen der lat. Pap.', *Atti del IV. Congresso di Pap.* 1936, 101 ff.; A. Calderini, *Manuale di Papirologia* (1938; p. 174 Latin authors (pagan)).

W. G. W.

PARABASIS, see COMEDY, ORIGINS OF, para. 2; COMEDY, OLD, para. 8.

PARACHOREGEMA (παραχορήγημα), see COMEDY, OLD, para. 9.

PARADISI (παράδεισοι), see GARDENS.

PARADOXOGRAPHERS. Interest in the marvellous and out-of-the-way, as such (παράδοξα, θαυμάσια), is prominent in the *Odyssey*, the histories of Herodotus, Theopompus, and Ephorus, and other Greek writings. Paradoxography came into existence, as a distinct literary genre, early in the Alexandrian age, and continued to be practised for many centuries. The Seven Wonders of the World (τὰ ἑπτὰ θεάματα, or θαύματα), that is, the temple of Zeus at Olympia, the Colossus of Rhodes, the hanging gardens of Semiramis, the walls of Babylon, the Pyramids, the Mausoleum, and the temple of Artemis at Ephesus (or the Delian altar of Apollo), seem to have been canonized in Alexandrian times. Callimachus' contemporary, Bolus, who wrote Περὶ τῶν ἐκ τῆς ἀναγνώσεως τῶν ἱστοριῶν εἰς ἐπίστασιν ἡμᾶς ἀγόντων, and Callimachus himself, one of whose Ὑπομνήματα was entitled Θαυμάτων τῶν εἰς ἅπασαν τὴν γῆν κατὰ τόπους ὄντων συναγωγή (so Suidas), may perhaps be regarded as the founders of paradoxography. Archelaus composed Ἰδιοφυῆ (epigrams on 'peculiarities') for Ptolemy Euergetes (247–221 B.C.), and Antigonus (q.v. 4) of Carystus wrote on similar themes at about the same time. Callimachus' pupil, Philostephanus of Cyrene, wrote, like Archelaus in verse, on Παράδοξοι ποταμοί and κρῆναι. Prominent among the paradoxographers of the Roman period are Isigonus and Phlegon (qq.v.). After Phlegon paradoxography seems to have declined in popularity. But as late as the sixth century A.D. Philo of Byzantium wrote Π. τῶν ἑπτὰ θαυμάτων. The paradoxographers often took some particular country as their field, Sicily, Scythia, etc. Natural phenomena, especially rivers, attracted them greatly. But zoology, history, and social customs also came within their purview.

A. Westermann, *Paradoxographi* (1839); O. Keller, *Rerum naturalium scr. gr. minores* (1877). J. D. D.

PARAGRAPHE (παραγραφή). In Athens this corresponded roughly to demurrer in Anglo-American practice. Upon the expulsion of the Thirty Tyrants in 403 B.C. an amnesty between their adherents and their opponents was arranged. A law sponsored by Archinus was enacted that if a defendant claimed the protection of the amnesty, he could enter a special plea (παραγραφή) that the case was not actionable, and he was permitted to speak first in an action to determine the validity of his plea. If the defendant won, the original case was dismissed; otherwise it went to trial. Early in the fourth century the procedure was extended to practically all civil suits. It is now established that the law of Archinus applied only to civil suits.

G. Calhoun, *CPhil.* 1918, 169 ff. R. J. B.

PARAKLAUSITHURON, a serenade or lover's complaint sung at his mistress's door (Plut. *Aem.* 8). A good example comes from a Tebtunis papyrus (J. U. Powell, *Coll. Alex.*, 177–80).

PARASITE (παράσιτος), originally 'guest' with no invidious meaning, had associations especially with one of the local cults of Heracles: see Diodorus of Sinope fr. 2. 23 (*CAF* ii. 421), cf. article CRITON, and writers cited by Athenaeus 6. 234 ff. (from Epicharmus onwards).

From contemporary life Comedy early adopted the parasite, 'sponger', or man-about-town, as a regular character. In Eupolis, Κόλακες, parasites doubtless form the chorus. Plays of Middle Comedy are entitled Παράσιτος (Antiphanes, Alexis; also, later, Diphilus) from their chief character; and in New Comedy the parasite is the satellite of the swaggering soldier, playing upon his vanity (Menander, Κόλαξ: Terence, *Eunuchus*).

Notorious parasites in real life are described in Comedy, e.g. Chaerephon (Menander, *Sam.* 258), who belonged to the generation before Menander and wrote the first book on Dining; and a parasite nicknamed Ζωμός, 'soup', because he was always there at the beginning of dinner.

Outside Comedy, but indebted to it, are the studies of parasites in Lucian, Περὶ παρασίτου, and Alciphron, *Epistles*.

See O. Ribbeck, *Kolax, Abh. sächs. Ges. Wiss.* 9 (1883). W. G. W.

PARCAE, see FATE.

PARCHMENT, see BOOKS, I, paras. 12, 13.

PARENTALIA, Roman feast of All Souls, on the *dies parentales* (13–21 Feb.), the last of which was a public ceremony, the Feralia (q.v.), while the rest were days reserved for private celebrations of the rites to the family dead (cf. *di parentum*, or *parentes*). They were *dies religiosi* (cf. DIES FASTI) during which the magistrates did not wear the *praetexta*, temples were closed and no weddings celebrated, but not all *nefasti* (Lupercalia, 15th, Quirinalia, 17th, 18th–20th all *comitiales*).

Ovid, *Fasti* 2. 532 ff., and Frazer ad loc. H. J. R.

PARILIA, festival of the god and goddess Pales (cf. *Palibus II, fast. Antiates* on 7 July, and the varying gender of the name in literature), held on 21 April. As they were the patrons of flocks and herds, their feast was one of purification of the beasts, herdsmen, and stalls. The Vestals distributed *februa*, in this case ashes of the calf of the Fordicidia, blood of the October Horse (see MARS), and bean-straw. The beasts were sprinkled with water at dawn, the stalls swept out and decked with branches and wreaths; sulphur and other purifying agents were used to fumigate the beasts, and bonfires lighted through which the celebrants jumped three times. A prayer to Pales was recited four times, facing east (Ovid, *Fasti* 4. 721 ff., with Frazer's notes). For some unknown reason it was supposed by Cicero's time (*Div.* 2. 98; Varro, *Rust.* 2. 1. 9) that it was the foundation-day of Rome (*natalis urbis*).

Cf. Wissowa, *RK* 199 ff. H. J. R.

PARIS (Πάρις) or **ALEXANDER** (Ἀλέξανδρος), in mythology, son of Priam and Hecuba (qq.v.). Homer introduces him as a well-known character and merely alludes to his doings before the *Iliad* begins. He had insulted Hera and Athena (24. 28–30), an earlier equivalent of the Judgement (see below); he had carried off Helen from Lacedaemon (3. 443 ff.). He takes part in the fighting with some distinction, especially as an archer, but shrinks from Menelaus (q.v.; 3. 16 ff.), and though he afterwards challenges him to a duel to decide the war, he gets much the worst of it and is only rescued by Aphrodite (67 ff., 340 ff.). His death is implied but not mentioned in the *Odyssey* (see DEÏPHOBUS).

The Cypria gave a more detailed account (Proclus, in Photius). After the incident of the 'apple of Discord' (see ERIS), Hera, Athena, and Aphrodite are brought by Hermes to Paris to judge which is the most beautiful; bribed with a promise of Helen, he prefers Aphrodite. This incident is not later than the seventh century, see *Artemis Orthia* (*JHS* supp. vol. v, p. 223 and pl. cxxvii; cf. Reinhardt, *Das Parisurteil* (1938), p. 6.) An ivory from Sparta shows Paris seated, holding the apple, as the goddesses approach him. It is essentially a folk-tale of choice (which is best, kingship, warlike prowess, or love?), comparable to the Hebrew story of the choice of Solomon (1 Kings iii. 5 ff.; wisdom, long life, riches, destruction of enemies). How it came to be attached to the (possibly) historical Paris is not known. As a result, the Cypria continued, he built ships by advice of Aphrodite, went to Sparta, and so carried off Helen (q.v.). He was killed, according to the *Little Iliad* (Proclus), by Philoctetes (q.v.); cf. OENONE.

His early adventures cannot now be traced farther back than the tragedians, though they may have been told in some quite lost part of the Cypria, or other epic. As the tragedies also are lost (Soph. and Eur., *Alexandros*), our remaining sources are the mythographers. Hyginus, *Fab.* 91, says that he was one of the younger children of his parents, and Hecuba while pregnant dreamed that she brought forth a torch from which serpents issued. The dream-interpreters ordered her child to be destroyed, but the servant charged with killing him exposed him instead; he was rescued by shepherds, grew up, and made a pet of a bull which Priam's servants carried off for a prize at funeral games. Paris, to recover it, entered Troy, took part in the games, won all his events, and was recognized and restored. Something like this must have been the plot of the lost plays, especially that of Euripides, see the frs., Nauck 42–64. Apollodorus (3. 148 ff.) makes him the second son, says he was suckled by a she-bear, and omits the incident of the games.

For his slaying of Achilles *see* ACHILLES. He does not appear to have had any hero-cult (correct Farnell, *Hero-Cults*, p. 412, note 97; the passage there cited refers to Alexander of Abonuteichos, q.v.).

Convenient summary of literature in Türk's art. 'Paris' in Roscher's *Lexikon*; some later refs. in text.   H. J. R.

PARIS, *see also* JULIUS (9).

PARMA, *see* ARMS AND ARMOUR, ROMAN.

PARMENIDES of Elea is said to have legislated for his native city and (c. 450 B.C.) to have visited Athens in his sixty-fifth year (Pl. *Prm.* 127 b). His didactic poem, in prosaic but trenchant hexameters, survives in large fragments. It opens with an allegory describing his chariot-journey from the House of Night to that of Day, where he is greeted by a goddess whose welcoming address forms the remainder of the work.

There are three ways of thought, that It is, that It is not, and that It is and is not (the last being that of Heraclitus). The two latter she denounces, the first, which Parmenides has just travelled, she describes in detail; it is a rigorous deduction of the characteristics of what is from the premiss that it is. What is is without beginning or end, single, motionless, continuous, determinate, like a sphere.

It follows that the diversity of nature exists only in name; and the goddess now, starting afresh and rejecting explicitly the monism of earlier physicists, derives our acceptance of experience as true from an original convention to 'name' two contrasting 'forms' (Light and Darkness), and unfolds a cosmology which is no longer her own divine revelation but an historical account of the world according to human belief.

Parmenides' account of the ways of thought is the earliest discussion of method in philosophy; his rejection of the third way the discovery of the Law of Contradiction; his distinction of the object and method of thought (νοῦς) from that of belief (δόξα) the separation of philosophy from physics; his journey along the Way of Persuasion the discovery of the possibility of cogent logical proof.

Diels, *PPF* 48–73; *Vorsokr.*⁵ i. 217–46; Burnet, *EGP*⁴, 169–96; K. Reinhardt, *Parmenides und die Geschichte der griechischen Philosophie* (1914); G. Calogero, *Studi sull' eleatismo* (1932); W. Jaeger, *The theology of the early Greek philosophers* (1947), ch. vi.
                                                                          A. H. C.

PARMENION (1) (c. 400–330 B.C.), son of Philotas, a Macedonian noble, became the best general of Philip II, though few details are known of his activities at this time. He accompanied Alexander to Asia as second-in-command of the army, and besides holding independent commands was present at all the great engagements of the first three years; at Issus and Gaugamela he commanded the left (defensive) wing. He was left at Ecbatana to guard the Persian treasure and the lengthening communications when Alexander himself moved east (330); but the trial and execution for treason of his son Philotas made him an obvious danger to Alexander, who promptly had him murdered.

Parmenion was certainly no accomplice to the alleged treason of Philotas. But he was not in sympathy with Alexander's bold ideas for the conquest (still less the government) of the Persian Empire: he represented the older school among the Macedonian officers ('Philip's men'), in contrast to Alexander and his intimates. He was certainly a good general, but the view (K. J. Beloch, *Griechische Geschichte*², iv. 2, pp. 290 ff.) that his was the brain directing Alexander's victories is fantastic.

Arrian, *Anabasis*, bks. 1–3; H. Berve, *Alexanderreich*, no. 606.
                                                                          G. T. G.

PARMENION (2) of Byzantium (1st c. B.C.), one of the last original dialect-lexicographers. *See* GLOSSA (GREEK).

PARMENISCUS, pupil of Aristarchus and defender of his texts against Crates of Mallos, wrote Πρὸς Κράτητα, Περὶ ἀναλογίας (recognizing eight noun declensions), and some commentaries.

PARMENO, of Byzantium, author of *Iambi*, i.e. choliambi. The fragments exhibit P. as a realist with a turn for moralizing. He was probably contemporary with Phoenix of Colophon, i.e. first half of third century B.C.

Texts: J. U. Powell, *Collectanea Alexandrina* (1925), 237–8; A. D. Knox, *Herodes, Cercidas, and the Greek Choliambic Poets* (Loeb, 1929), 272–3. General literature: G. A. Gerhard, *Phoinix von Kolophon* (1909), 211–13.   E. A. B.

PARNASSUS, outlying spur of the Pindus range, running south-east and rising to 8,200 feet. It separates the Cephissus valley from that of Amphissa and runs into the Corinthian Gulf at Cape Opus. Its limestone mass is mostly barren, but its lower slopes are well-watered; they carry the Phocian towns on its eastern flank and the plain of Crisa with the high valley of Delphi on the south. The best ascent is from Daulis; the passes, which cross its spurs, run from Cytinium to Amphissa and from Daulis to Delphi via the σχιστὴ ὁδός, where the latter is joined by the route from Lebadea. A sacred mountain especially to the Dorians.   N. G. L. H.

PARODOS, *see* TRAGEDY, para. 14. In the structural sense *see* THEATRES.

PARODY, GREEK (παρῳδία). A cartoon exaggerates a prominent feature of the subject and presents him in incongruous dress and surroundings. Parody uses the same means, exaggeration and incongruity, either together or singly. Much ancient and modern parody contents itself with describing trivial things in the language of high poetry. The subtler task of bringing into bolder relief, by exaggeration, the salient features of an individual's style was seldom attempted by the Greeks. Aristophanes achieves it brilliantly in the Glyke song in the *Frogs* (1331–63), with a bathetic subject (the stolen cock) to add to the fun; and Plato's parodies, unaided by bathos, are perhaps as near to their originals as Max Beerbohm's

Meredith in *Seven Men*. Aristotle (*Poet.* 1448ᵃ12) mentions Hegemon as ὁ τὰς παρῳδίας ποιήσας πρῶτος, but Athenaeus (15. 699 a) says, more precisely, that he was the first to enter τοὺς θυμελικοὺς ἀγῶνας and win contests at Athens for parody. (For similar contests cf. an Eretrian inscription of *c.* 400 B.C., Ἐφημερὶς Ἀρχαιολογική (1902, pp. 98 ff.).) Athenaeus (15. 698b), following Polemon, regards Hipponax as the real inventor of the genre, and quotes from him four burlesque hexameters on a parasite. In the same vein are some of Simonides' iambics on women (fr. 7. 83–93). But we can go farther back than any of these poets. The *Margites*, generally attributed to Homer in antiquity, was known to Archilochus (8th–7th c. B.C.). It described the adventures of a Simple Simon, and had iambics mixed up with its hexameters. Virtually nothing of it or of the *Cercopes* remains. The extant *Batrachomyomachia* (*Battle of the Frogs and Mice*), written perhaps during the Persian Wars, is a mildly amusing piece. Athena, impartially detesting the mice who gnaw holes in her Peplus and the frogs who keep her awake in the small hours (178–96), is entertaining, and the dying mouse (65–81) rather pathetic as well. The tradition of Homeric parody runs through comedy from Cratinus to Diphilus, the gastronomists (Matron, Archestratus, etc.), and the Sillographers (*see* TIMON 2).

2. Epicharmus' mythological burlesques must have contained much parody, but little of it survives (frs. 42–3. 10–11, 229). In Old Attic Comedy Hermippus seems to have been fond of parody and in Middle Comedy Eubulus had a flair for it. Fr. 10 (a Euripidean epilogue) is excellent; in fr. 64 even the well-worn theme of the 'Lady of Copais in her robe of beet' amuses; and there is freshness in fr. 75. Parody survives sporadically in Diphilus and Menander (Diph. frs. 30, 126; Men. pp. 150, 188, 267, 402, 414, 477–8, Loeb); but by this time the poet sometimes has to warn his audience that he is parodying.

3. In Aristophanes the rise and fall of style is almost as persistent as in Wodehouse. Noble and ignoble words rub shoulders, 'guts and glory' at *Eq.* 200, 'poniards and piles' at *Vesp.* 1119. *Lys.* 715 descends precipitately to Rabelaisian frankness, set off (as often in Ar., cf. *Eq.* 1242) by the smoothest of tragic rhythm. Mnesilochus–Palamedes, writing his letter (*Thesm.* 781), momentarily forgets the dignity of his rôle and curses 'that rotten rho'. Often comic tails are appended to well-known passages. *Ran.* 931 'Oft in the stilly night, ere slumber's chain has bound me, I lie wondering what on earth a brown horse-cock is'. *Eq.* 1250–2 the farewell of Cleon–Alcestis. The apostrophe to the soul (Eur. *Med.* 1057) takes unexpected turnings (*Ach.* 450 ff., *Eq.* 1194, *Vesp.* 756 (!)). In other passages the contrast is given by two characters talking in contrasted styles, as in the dialogue between Lamachus and Dicaeopolis at the end of the *Acharnians*. In this vein nothing can beat *Thesm.* 808: 'Why live I still?'—'The crows don't know their job.'

4. Sometimes, again, the parody is concerned, not with poetical or tragic style in general, but with some particular feature of tragedy (a prologue, a messenger's speech, a recognition scene), or of religious, political, or forensic procedure (*Eq.* 1316–34, *Vesp.* 892–1008, *Ran.* 738–55, and passages in *Thesm.* 332–432, *Eccl.* 151–65). Then there are parodies of situation, Odysseus under the ram's belly (*Vesp.* 177 ff.), Bellerophon mounted on Pegasus (*Pax* 76 ff.), Palamedes, Helen, and Andromeda (*Thesm.* 769–1135), which give us an idea of what a mythological burlesque was like (*see* COMEDY *and* PHLYĀKES).

5. Aristophanes also parodies the styles of particular authors, especially Euripides. The tragedian's supposed passion for enigmatical epigram is satirized at *Ach.* 397, *Thesm.* 5–8, *Ran.* 1443–4. In the Glyke song (*Ran.*

1331–63) the points are (over and above metrical and musical considerations which are hard to assess) certain idiosyncrasies of diction, such as ὄρφνα and compounds in -φαής (cf. *Ach.* 460, *Vesp.* 1484, *Thesm.* 881, 1075 κλῇθρα χαλάσθω, ἐξώπιος, ὀχληρός), incessant repetitions of words (often parodied elsewhere), and the 'wings of a dove' motif (1352); in the cento (1309–22), excessive affection for the polyschematist dimeter (*see* METRE, GREEK, III. 12), a licentious anapaest (1322), the use of melisma (1314), and perhaps the constant references to animal life. In other places Aristophanes takes off the jargon of philosophical and other cliques (see *CQ* 1927, 113–21, and cf. Damoxenus fr. 2). But many of Aristophanes' poetic flights (cf. *Nub.* 1005–8, *Ran.* 154–7) cannot justly be described as parodistic. They are gay, enchanting lyrics, light as air, which he wrote to delight himself and us. Such parody as they contain consists in the lightest touches, and we are seldom brought down to earth with a bump. Of such a kind are *Eq.* 551–64, 581–94, *Nub.* 563–74, 595–606 (though there the Socratic-Euripidean deity Αἰθήρ is meant to look out of place among the Olympians), and many lyrics in the *Birds*. There is gentle irony in the beauty with which the frogs invest their surroundings (*Ran.* 209–69), but the beauty matters more than the irony. At the same time, the style absorbs a word like κραιπαλόκωμος without incongruity. Aristophanes resembled Shakespeare more than any Greek tragedian in his power to bring homeliness within the compass of beautiful or passionately serious verse (e.g. *Lys.* 1122–61).

6. Plato deftly hits off the manner of Prodicus, distinguishing between apparent synonyms (*Prt.* 337 a–c), and Polus with his assonances (*Grg.* 448 c). At *Resp.* 452 d, for no apparent reason, he breaks off into an amusing skit on the Antiphontine manner. If the *Menexenus* is his, the funeral speech it contains is a parody—for he cannot have meant it seriously. Best of all is the parody of Agathon in the *Symposium* (194 e–197 e); little as we have of Gorgias, the Gorgianic touches are unmistakable here.

7. Lucian's parodies are not on the level of Aristophanes, but his rollicking humour is irresistible. In the *Timon* (9) Zeus' thunderbolt has gone for repairs; he hurled it at Anaxagoras, but missed, and it hit a temple instead. The *Prometheus* has a good law-court speech (7–19). There are some clever touches in the *Deorum Dialogi*: 1. 2 Zeus' ignorance of Caucasian geography; 5. 4 Hephaestus, the grubby waiter; 9. 1 Zeus bears children all over his body; 10. 2 the Sun-god, ordered to arrange a Νὺξ Μακρά, grumbles that 'there weren't goings on like this in old Kronos' time; day was day then, and night night'. Best of all is 20, the Judgement of Paris; Zeus is a benign father, Hermes a charming guide, and the three goddesses admirably catty to each other. Ζεὺς Τραγῳδός has some amusing passages; Τραγῳδοποδάγρα and Ὠκύπους are pretty dull.

H. Täuber, *De usu parodiae apud Aristophanem* (Progr. 1849); W. H. S. Bakhuyzen, *De parodia in comoediis Aristophanis* (1877); A. T. Murray, *On parody and paratragoedia in Aristophanes* (Berlin, 1891).   J. D. D.

PARODY, LATIN. The two types of literary parody— (*a*) pastiche, which caricatures the manner of an original without adherence to its actual words, and (*b*) parody proper, in which an original, usually well known, is distorted, with the minimum of verbal or literal change, to convey a new sense, often incongruous with the form —are both found in Latin, though less often than in Greek; they occur more often in verse than in prose. The former type demands some measure of literary appreciation in the reader, while the latter generally aims at a simpler comic effect.

Examples of (*a*) occur sporadically in comedy, when the grandiose language of tragedy is burlesqued. This type is sometimes used as a vehicle of literary criticism;

so some lines of Lucilius parody the clumsy solemnity of Ennius and the tragic bombast of Pacuvius. Some parts of the poem on the Civil War recited, as a model for epic, by Eumolpus in the *Satyricon* of Petronius (119–24) read like a pastiche on Lucan.

The only extant example of sustained parody of type (*b*) is the tenth poem of the *Catalepton* (see APPENDIX VERGILIANA) in which poem 4 of Catullus, addressed to a yacht, is turned, with remarkable dexterity, into an address to a parvenu magistrate. The *Antibucolica* of Numitorius seem to have been parodies of the 1st and 3rd Eclogues of Virgil, but only the opening lines are preserved by Donatus; in these the point of the parody turns on alleged liberties taken with language by Virgil.

C. J. F.

PAROEMIAC, *see* METRE, GREEK, II (7).

PAROEMIOGRAPHERS. The Proverb (παροιμία), or concise saying in common and recognized use, often summarizing experience or embodying practical wisdom, is a constant feature in Greek literature, both prose and verse, from Homer onwards. It not only provided an ingredient calculated to please the ordinary hearer, but contributed not a little to the formulation of moral philosophy. It might be in prose or metrical form, and gave its name to the Paroemiac (*see* METRE, GREEK, II (7)). Paroemiography, or the making of collections of proverbs for specific purposes, may be said to have begun with Aristotle in a work entitled Παροιμίαι (Diog. Laert. 5. 26); he was followed in this by his pupil, the Peripatetic Clearchus of Soli, and later by the Stoic Chrysippus; Theophrastus also wrote Π. παροιμιῶν. So far such collections were made for the purposes of philosophy. In the Alexandrian age collections for literary purposes began to be made by such writers as the antiquarian Demon (Π. παροιμιῶν, of which a fragment has been recovered); Aristophanes of Byzantium, who made prose and metrical collections; Didymus (13 books); and Lucillus of Tarrha (in Crete). The later sophistic movement led to a great demand for the proverb as an ornament of style, as may be seen, for example, in the works of Lucian (W. Schmid, *Atticismus* i. 411) and Libanius. The origins of the existing *Corpus Paroemiographorum* go back to Zenobius, a sophist of the time of Hadrian; he made an Epitome in three books of the collections of Didymus and Lucillus Tarrhaeus (Suidas, Ζηνόβιος), obliterating their book-divisions in the process; they appear to have been already arranged according to literary genres. The Corpus in its original form, as constituted in the early Middle Age, consisted of (i) the work of Zenobius, arranged alphabetically for scholastic purposes; (ii) a collection of *Proverbs of Plutarch used by the Alexandrians*, probably deriving from Seleucus of Alexandria (Suidas, Σέλευκος); and (iii) an alphabetical list of *Popular Proverbs*, derived from the same sources as Zenobius, ascribed to the lexicographer Diogenianus (time of Hadrian), but probably the work of an anonymous writer. From these were formed later the collections of Gregory of Cyprus (13th c.), Macarius (14th c.), and Apostolius (15th c.); these have no independent value.

Editions: T. Gaisford (1836); E. v. Leutsch and F. G. Schneidewin (1839). Criticism: A. and M. Croiset, *Hist. Lit. Gr.* (1899) v. 981 f.; O. Crusius and L. Cohn, *Philol.* Suppl. 6 (1891–3) (sources and MS. tradition); O. Crusius, *Analecta critica ad Paroem. gr.* (1883); *Paroemiographica, Sitz. Münch. Ak.* 1910; P. Tschaikanowitsch, *Quaestionum paroem. cap. sel.* (1908). W. M. E.

PAROS, the second largest of the Cyclades, a centre of Aegean trade, and famous for its marble. Early in the seventh century the Parians colonized Thasos. In 490 the island furnished a trireme to the Persians under Datis, for which the Athenian Miltiades later besieged the town without success. In 480 the Parians played a double game, and after the battle of Salamis were compelled by Themistocles to pay an indemnity. Paros was a member of the Delian Confederacy, also of the second Athenian Confederacy, but later revolted, and lost importance before the establishment of Macedonian authority. Here was found the Marmor Parium (q.v.).

Bursian ii. 483 ff.; Rubensohn, *Ath. Mitt.* xxv–xxvii; xlii (archaeological exploration). W. A. L.

PARRHASIUS, painter, son and pupil of Evenor of Ephesus, later Athenian. Pliny dates Evenor 420 B.C. and Parrhasius 397 (with Zeuxis, q.v.); but he made designs for Mys' reliefs on the shield of the Athena Promachus (before 450). He was arrogant and wore a purple cloak and a gold wreath. He painted a 'rose fed' Theseus (i.e. in the rich style; Pliny attributes 'elegantiam capilli, uenustatem oris' to him), Demos, 'Healing of Telephus', Philoctetes, 'Feigned madness of Odysseus'. Such pictures displayed the details of expression, 'argutias uoltus', which he discusses with Socrates in the *Memorabilia* of Xenophon. He wrote on painting. He was famed for subtlety of outline (cf. white lecythi, e.g. Pfuhl, figs. 543, 552); therefore perhaps did not use shading (contrast Apollodorus, q.v.). His gods and heroes became types for later artists; his drawings on parchment and wood were used by craftsmen (probably metal workers) in Pliny's time.

Overbeck, 637, 1130, 1649, 1680, 1692–730; Pfuhl, 750; A. Rumpf, *JDAI* 1934, 23; G. Rodenwaldt, *Arch. Anz.* 1933, 237; E. Bielefeld, *Archäologische Vermutungen* (1938). T. B. L. W.

PARRICIDIUM. The word *paricidas* (whose original meaning is much discussed) first occurs in a law attributed to Numa (Festus, s.v. 'Parricidium') in which it denotes the intentional—*dolo sciens*—murderer of a free man. In later terminology *parricidium* meant the murder of near relations (e.g. in the *Lex Pompeia de parricidiis, c.* 70 B.C.); it retains this meaning in classical texts and in Justinian's codification, which defines precisely for this purpose the circle of persons considered as near relations (*Dig.* 48. 9). *Parricidium* was, together with *perduellio* (q.v.), the first crime prosecuted by the State: the *quaestores parricidii* are mentioned in the XII Tables. A wider general sense was given to the term *homicidium* (rarely used in earlier texts, but more frequent in the legislation of the later Empire). In ancient times the parricide was drowned in the sea, tied up in a sack (*culleus*). In the later legislation the penalty was differentiated according to the gravity of the act, but the death-penalty remained the normal sanction.

Mommsen, *Röm. Strafr.* (1899); C. Ferrini, 'Dir. penale romano' (*Encicl. del dir. penale ital.* Pessina, 1902). Cf. the literature mentioned in H. F. Jolowicz, *Historical Introduction* (1932), 324 and S. Riccobono, *Fontes iuris Romani anteiust.* i² (1941), 13 n. 4 and Add. p. xvi. A. B.

PARTHENIUS of Nicaea (1st c. B.C.), enslaved during the Third Mithridatic War, was taken to Italy, where he was freed. Of his poetry, mostly elegiac, for which he was well known in antiquity, only a few fragments remain. Extant is a collection of prose outlines of love-stories (Ἐρωτικὰ παθήματα) culled from poets, historians, etc., and intended for the use of Cornelius Gallus, the Roman elegist. P., with the elegist's predilection for unhappy endings, has little or no connexion with the tradition of the Greek Novel, but his extracts illustrate the romantic tendency of much Alexandrian literature.

Text: E. Martini, *Mythographi Graeci* ii. 1 (Teubner); with translation, Loeb (Edmonds). *See also on the* NOVEL, GREEK. R. M. R.

PARTHENON, the most renowned Greek temple, the culmination of Doric proportion and refinement without loss of strength, exhibiting all of the various subtleties of building expression more or less prevalent from sixth to fourth centuries B.C.; carried out under Pericles (q.v.) in 447–432 by Ictinus and Callicrates (qq.v.), and the sculpture by Phidias (q.v.) or his school, and still remarkably preserved, after an explosion in 1687, on the Athenian Acropolis (q.v.), south side, though most of the sculpture is in the British Museum. Executed entirely in Pentelic marble, it stands on the foundations of an earlier temple, also of Athena Parthenos, and is peripteral octastyle (columns 8 × 17), measuring 228 ft. × 101 ft. on top step of stylobate. There were great doors at each end of the cella and metal grilles between the columns entirely enclosed the pronaos and opisthodomus (*see* TEMPLES). The shorter (western) part of the cella had four columns, probably Ionic; the longer (eastern) part had the arrangement usual in large temples—two rows of double-tiered columns forming central and side compartments; but the Parthenon was unique, not only in the great relative width of the 'nave' but in the return of the colonnades round its western end. Well in front of this return is the foundation of the great pedestal, about 26 ft. × 13 ft., which carried the colossal chryselephantine statue of Athena, by Phidias. Other Ionic features were the carving of two moulded members (in antae capitals and external frieze), and the continuous frieze in low relief representing the Panathenaic Procession, within the peristyle at the top of the cella wall. The metopes (panels between triglyphs) of the external entablatures contained high relief sculptures of combats between centaurs and lapiths. The pediments were fully sculptured in the round, representing east, the birth of Athena, and west, the contest between Athena and Poseidon for the Attic land.

M. L. D'Ooge, *The Acropolis of Athens* (1908); F. C. Penrose, *Principles of Athenian Architecture*² (1888).   T. F.

PARTHENOPAEUS (Παρθενοπαῖος), in mythology, one of the Seven against Thebes (cf. ADRASTUS). In earlier tradition, he is a brother of Adrastus and an Argive; in later, an Arcadian, son of Atalanta (q.v.). See Wilamowitz-Moellendorff, *Aeschylos Interpretationen*, p. 100 f., with schol. on Aesch. *Sept.* 547, Soph. *OC* 1320, Eur. *Phoen.* 150 (Antimachus, fr. 17 Wyss).

H. J. R.

PARTHIA has recently assumed an increasingly important place in the story of Asia. The people whom Greeks and Romans called Parthians were traditionally Parni, members of the semi-nomad Dahae Confederacy north of Hyrcania. They occupied the Seleucid satrapy called Parthia (*Parthava*), traditionally in 248–247 B.C., whence their Greek name; later they ruled from the Euphrates to the Indus, with Ecbatana as their capital. They were never more than a land-owning military aristocracy. The king was feudal superior of his nobles, including the seven great Pahlavi families who were almost kings in their territories, Seistan, Atropatene, etc. There were other vassal kingdoms, but Parthia never assimilated Persis, which ultimately overthrew her, while before the Christian era the Surens (q.v.) in Seistan became independent and gradually created an Indo-Parthian kingdom.

2. The Parthians spoke Parthian Pahlavi, a North Iranian dialect akin to Sogdian; they adopted popular Iranian Mazdaism, but tolerated every other religion. They were a silent and easy-going race, fond of hunting, not bad rulers. They were the supreme imitators of the ancient world; they stepped into a ready-made Greek kingdom, and just copied the Seleucids. They utilized Greek science, Greek secretaries, Greek methods of administration and Court titles, wrote on parchment, and had Greeks on their Council; they even flirted with Greek king-worship, and Seleuceia struck their coins for them with Seleucid dating instead of their own Arsacid era (from 248/7), itself an imitation. They imitated Bactria by turning the Seleucid eparchies into satrapies; later, an occasional Parthian reached China, and there imitated the Chinese by becoming a Chinese scholar. But in war they were original and competent; before

Carrhae they discarded Greek notions and employed cavalry only; the nobility fought as cataphracts, mailed knights with enormous spears, and their retainers as horse-archers, and they bred the Nesean horses into magnificent chargers for the cataphracts. Their Greek cities had perhaps rather more autonomy than under the Seleucids, and there was an outburst of Greek literature in the East; never was communication across Asia less trammelled, and Seleuceia, centre of all routes, dominated Asia's trade.

3. A change came in A.D. 10 when a collateral branch from Atropatene replaced the old Arsacid line. There was an Iranian reaction against the former Philhellenism; Mazdaism was emphasized; Seleuceia revolted for seven years, whereupon the capital was shifted to Ctesiphon and subsequently Vologasia was founded (near Babylon), in an attempt to divert from Seleuceia the increasingly important trade between China and Roman Syria; Parthia realized her lucrative position as middleman and now prevented direct communication between the two empires. The influence of 'Parthian' art—a revived Iranian art of many branches, which utilized and sometimes misapplied Greek elements—spread far and is historically interesting.

M. Rostovtzeff, *CAH* xi, ch. 3; W. W. Tarn, ibid. x, ch. 14; (full bibliographies); N. C. Debevoise, *A Political History of Parthia* (U.S.A. 1938).   W. W. T.

PASION (*d.* 370 B.C.) was the wealthiest banker and manufacturer of his time in Athens. He began his career as a slave with a banking firm, becoming a freedman and later an Athenian citizen. We learn much of his business activity from the speeches of Demosthenes and the *Trapeziticus* of Isocrates. The revenue derived from his bank and a shield workshop amounted to 120–60 minae after his death, the bank alone bringing in 100 minae. He left a fortune of 40 talents.

J. Kirchner, *Prosopographia Attica* (1903), no. 11,672; J. Hasebroek, *Hermes* lv (1920), 118 f. passim; T. R. Glover, *From Pericles to Philip* (1917), ch. x.   F. M. H.

PASIPHAË, *see* MINOS.

PASSENNUS PAULUS, a contemporary *eques* whom the younger Pliny (*Ep.* 6. 15) praises for his *elegi* as being, like his actual descent, Propertius.

PASSIENUS (*d.* 9 B.C.), Augustan orator, a distinguished representative of the old style (Sen. *Controv.* 3 *pr.* 14, 10 *pr.* 11).

PASTORAL (or BUCOLIC) POETRY, GREEK (βουκολικά). Ancient authorities (e.g. *Proleg. scholl. ad Theocr.*; Diomedes, 486 K.; Probus *in Verg. Ecl.* 2. 8 K.; Servius, *praef. in Ecl.*), who derive Bucolic from religious ritual, deserve little credence. Modern theories of the same sort (R. Reitzenstein, *Epigramm und Skolion* (1893), 193–263) are equally unconvincing. Pastoral song, accompanied by the flute, doubtless existed in all Greek lands from an early date (cf. *Il.* 18. 525–6), and especially (Diod. Sic. 4. 84) in Sicily, the home of Daphnis, the bucolic hero. This popular origin accounts for certain features, e.g. singing-match, refrain, strophic arrangement, which are found in later bucolic. But the intermediate steps are obscure. Aelian (*VH* 10. 18) makes Stesichorus the founder of bucolic, but probably Stesichorus merely described Daphnis' unhappy love and death. Athenaeus (14. 619 a, b) regards a Sicilian herd, Diomus, as the founder and says that Epicharmus (fr. 105 K.) mentioned him in two plays. Diomus is probably mythical, like Daphnis, but Epicharmus perhaps dramatized bucolic themes, and some of Sophron's *Mimes* dealt with the life of rustics and fishermen. In Greece itself legend (Hermesianax, frs. 2, 3) connects Daphnis and Menalcas, another bucolic figure, with Boeotia and Euboea, and the dimeter (μακραὶ δρύες, ὦ Μενάλκα), repeated by the despairing Eriphanis in search of Menal-cas, is assigned by Athenaeus (14. 619 d) to a pastoral song. In literature bucolic matter was handled in satyr-plays (Euripides, *Cyclops*), in the dithyramb (Philoxenus, *Cyclops*), and by Peloponnesian epigrammatists (Anyte of Tegea, but this does not wholly explain Arcadia as the later bucolic paradise). Bucolic love finds expression in the lyric of Lycophronides (*c.* 350) (cf. Diehl, *Anth. Lyr. Graec.* 2. 1, p. 157). All this would suffice to explain the creation of full-blown bucolic by Theocritus, but the facts of his life and the peculiar character of much of his pastoral poetry suggest that the immediate inspiration came rather from a school already existing at Cos when he first visited the island. In *Id.* 7 he describes a bucolic masquerade at Cos, in which he and his friends took part, and, while the evidence for Philetas' writing bucolic is disputable, Hermesianax' treatment of bucolic themes is certain. Theocritus' reaction to this apparently romantic form of the Coan school was twofold. In some Idylls (1, 3, 6, 7, 11) he complies with the mode and its idealization of bucolic life, though even in these poems many details come from first-hand observation. In others (4, 5, 10) he adopts a more realistic tone without altogether eschewing topical allusions (4. 31; 5. 105). The metre of Theocritus' Bucolics is the hexameter, except that 8. 33–60 are in elegiacs, which is one argument against Theocritean authorship of that poem, but various devices modify the 'heroic' character of the verse. The dialect, a literary Doric, may result from the accident of Theocritus' Syracusan birth, but was well suited to the genre and was adopted by Theocritus' successors, Moschus and Bion. These, to judge by the scanty fragments, added little or nothing to bucolic as such.

The word εἰδύλλιον (Idyll) is a diminutive of εἶδος, and Pindar's lyric odes were called εἴδη, according to some because the εἶδος ἁρμονίας in which they were to be sung was written over each. Hence εἴδη came to mean separate poems (cf. Suidas, s.v. Σωτάδης) and εἰδύλλια short separate poems (cp. Pliny, *Ep.* 4. 14. 9). The full description in Greek of a pastoral is εἰδύλλιον βουκολικόν.

G. Knaack, 'Bukolik' in *PW* iii. 998–1012; Christ-Schmid-Stählin, *Gesch. der Griech. Litt.* ii. 1⁶ (1920), 181–98; Ph. Legrand, *Étude sur Théocrite* (1898), 141–72; R. J. Cholmeley, *The Idylls of Theocritus*² (1919), Introduction.   E. A. B.

PASTORAL POETRY, LATIN.

Latin Pastoral poetry, if viewed as extant bucolics on the Theocritean model, consists of Virgil's ten eclogues, Calpurnius Siculus' seven, two Einsiedeln eclogues, and four by Nemesianus (qq.v.). But this is not the full reckoning. Other pastorals, long since lost, were written, such as those by Cornelius Gallus which influenced or, some would say, inspired Virgil (F. Skutsch, *Aus Vergils Früh-zeit* (1901)); and pastoral motifs entered into other genres. Fragments of Roman epigrammatists early in the first century B.C. who introduced pastoral colour into their short poems give cause for regretting their loss. Virgil's claim, indeed, to have first adapted Theocritus to Latin verse (*Ecl.* 6. 1) must be qualified as in itself an echo of Callimachus, and in any case does not gainsay the previous employment of bucolic themes by Latin poets who did not follow the Theocritean norm. Even a sketch must spare a few glances for these poets.

2. The so-called *Elegia in Messallam* (*Catalepton* 9. 13–20), unless with Hubaux we date it as Neronian, indicates that M. Valerius Messalla was a pioneer in Greek imitations of Theocritus which the unknown author of the poem translated into Latin. Among four love-lyrics cited by Antonius Julianus (Gell. *NA* 19. 9) one from Porcius Licinus ('custodes ouium . . .') typically combines bucolic with erotic elements of a sort in favour with Roman literary circles about 90 B.C. The welcome by Lutatius Catulus to young Archias led to the com-position of similarly erotico-bucolic epigrams. If the

two poems *Dirae* and *Lydia* could be decisively credited to Valerius Cato, their blends of idyll and elegy might be regarded as in a sense preludes to Virgil's *Eclogues*. The *Culex, Moretum, Copa* of the *Appendix Vergiliana* all contain pastoral ingredients, and the conclusion to be drawn from many pieces of evidence is that there was at Rome a group of bucolic poets of which Virgil was the chief but not the only representative. Fontanus' 'Naids beloved by Satyrs' (Ovid, *Pont.* 4. 16. 35) may or may not imply bucolic poetry. Pollio presumably wrote bucolics and influenced Virgil; and the question how far pastoral themes appeared in the poems of Virgil's con-temporaries Codrus (questionably identified with Helvius Cinna), Valgius Rufus, Varius, Bavius, Mevius, and others is discussed by Hubaux (*Les Thèmes bucoliques*, 66 ff.). It is likely that Domitius Marsus, continuing the epigrammatic tradition, wrote short poems at once erotic and bucolic.

3. Among extant Latin bucolic poets Virgil reigns supreme in literary power and influence. His debt to Theocritus is deep: he adapts and combines themes, he translates (even mistranslates), he paraphrases. His shepherds are 'Arcades' (*Ecl.* 7. 4; 10. 31–33), but their Arcadia is mixed with north Italian scenery, where 'Mincio fringes his green banks with waving reeds' (*Ecl.* 7. 12–13). Here is an Arcady whose frontiers can be infinitely extended in imagination: from rural sur-roundings an escape may be made at will into themes of epic dignity, although the Sicilian muses are still invoked (*Ecl.* 4. 1). Or a break-away may be made when the poet's own sufferings from land-confiscations are disguised under a thin allegory. Virgil's realism depends not merely on his knowledge of the country-side and country life, but on his allusions to contemporary events like the military expropriation of land and to contem-porary figures, political or poetical, like Caesar, Pollio, Gallus. The call to sing of themes 'paulo maiora' was Virgil's great transformation of bucolic poetry. Theo-critus' poetry, perfect in form, had as a rule presented rustics busy with their loves or songs; but Virgil's famous 'Pollio' opened up a world of enchanted hopes: its Age of Gold remained a *locus communis* for subsequent bucolic writers and exerted influence outside the bucolic field on Tibullus and Ovid.

4. Except for the 'Messianic' presages of *Eclogue* 4 Virgil's bucolics turn partly on his personal experiences (1, 6, 9, and 10), partly on elegiac or erotic motifs, in which 'omnia uincit amor'. Propertius' welcome to the forthcoming *Aeneid* (3. 34. 65 ff.) specially mentions the love-melodies of Virgil's rustics. Their warm feeling and sweet cadences are suggestive now of rural peace, now of poetic learning. Horace (*Sat.* 1. 10. 44) significantly uses one of Virgil's frequent epithets when he stresses his impressionable vivacity ('molle atque facetum'), implying his openness to beauty around him and his grace of expression. One may listen to his shepherds singing as though they should never grow old.

5. In the Neronian age, Calpurnius and the Einsiedeln Eclogues have an eye not only for shepherds but also for the times. The Alexandrian notion of a beneficent ruler as a saving deity (σωτήρ, θεὸς ἐπιφανής) was familiar to Virgil, and this soteriologic idea reappears in the Golden Age associated with the early part of Nero's reign. The Virgilian and Theocritean sources of Calpurnius are illustrated by E. Cesareo (*La Poesia di Calpurnio Siculo*, 1931). Both influences acted on the pastorals by Neme-sianus of Carthage in the third century. Nemesianus was, besides, a sedulous pillager of the text of Cal-purnius, but he deserves credit for restoring the pleasant music of the refrain.

6. Even in Christian poems on pastoral subjects by St. Paulinus the classic forms of paganism kept their vitality. In Endelechius' *De Mortibus Boum*, where Tityrus has saved his herd from plague by the Sign of

the Cross, the elegant asclepiads make an innovation, but the names Aegon and Tityrus and the manner of the dialogue descend from Virgil.

7. Later still, during the Renaissance, in different countries, the Virgilian tradition remains operative on such pastoral authors as Baptista Mantuanus (called by Erasmus 'Christianus Maro'), Sannazaro, Geraldini, Andrelinus, Arnolletus, and Cayado (edns. of these by W. P. Mustard, U.S.A.).

For differences among Virgil's imitators see Calpurnius, Einsiedeln Eclogues, and Nemesianus in J. W. and A. M. Duff's *Minor Latin Poets* (Loeb, 1935). Cf. J. Hubaux, *Le Réalisme dans les bucoliques de Virgile* (1927); and *Les Thèmes bucoliques dans la poésie latine* (1930); G. Knaack, 'Bukolik', *PW* iii. 998–1012.
J. W. D.

PASTURAGE. Cattle was the main source of wealth of the Greek and Roman peasants from earliest times. Horses were reared by the wealthier owners, horned cattle by the less well-to-do, and small cattle by the smaller peasants. Selection in cattle-breeding dates back to archaic Greece and Italy. Stall-feeding is mentioned in Homer (*Od.* 18. 367). Herdsmen formed one of the typical very early crafts of ancient agriculture. Poultrybreeding also flourished during the Classical and Hellenistic periods, and in Italy under the Republic. The horses of Thessaly, the cattle of Epirus, and the Milesian sheep, famous throughout the world, were exported to all countries where scientific agriculture flourished during the period from Alexander to Augustus.

There was not enough natural pasturage for all the cattle of the Mediterranean world. Grazing-grounds were therefore sown by governments and private owners. Many States reserved pasture rights (*epinomia*) for their own citizens; for an alien to receive it was a great honour. Some States (e.g. Delos and Teos) introduced pasture taxes. The Ptolemaic government owned large herds and claimed the right to requisition all cattle in the country for agricultural purposes. For the use of the royal pastures as well as for protection while grazing high fees were imposed.

The Roman *latifundia* developed stock-breeding economy to its highest pitch, often converting cornlands to pasture and so diminishing the population of the country-side. The largest pasture estate mentioned in any ancient source (S.H.A., *Aurelian*, ch. 10) fed 2,000 cows, 1,000 horses, 10,000 sheep, and 15,000 goats, with 500 slaves to work it. Development ended with the breakdown of the ancient slave economy, but the strains developed in ancient times persisted throughout the Middle Ages and are in the main the ancestors of our modern stocks.

For bibliography *see under* AGRICULTURE. Also O. Brendel, *Die Schafzucht im Alten Griechenland* (1933); M. Cobianski, *Aegyptus* xvi (1936), 91 f.; A. Hauger, *Zur römischen Landwirtschaft und Haustierzucht* (1921); A. Hörnschemeyer, *Die Pferdezucht im klassischen Altertum* (1929); O. Keller, *Die antike Tierwelt* i, ii (1909–1913); F. Vincke, *Die Rinderzucht im alten Italien* (1931); H. Winkelstern, *Die Schweinezucht im klassischen Altertum* (1933); K. Zeissig, *Die Rinderzucht im Alten Griechenland* (1934).
F. M. H.

PATAVINITAS, the provincial smack of Livy's native Patavium declared by Asinius Pollio (Quint. *Inst.* 1. 5. 56; 8. 1. 3) to mark or mar the style of Livy (q.v.). Pollio, as governor of Cisalpine Gaul, might claim to recognize northern expressions in contrast with true Roman *urbanitas*. His charge against Livy excited the indignation of Morhof (1639–91) who retorted on Pollio's 'Asinity' in *De Patavinitate Liviana* (1685).

See Whatmough, 'Quemadmodum Pollio reprehendit in Livio Patavinitatem' in *Harv. Stud.* xliv (1933).
J. W. D.

PATAVIUM, a city situated near celebrated springs in a fertile part of Cisalpine Gaul (Strabo 5. 212 f.; Pliny, *HN* 2. 103); nowadays *Padua*. The Veneti, but certainly not Antenor, probably founded Patavium. It became their capital, successfully resisting a Spartan attack in

301 B.C. (Livy 10. 2). By 174 it was subject to Rome, but retained local autonomy (Livy 41. 27). Asinius Pollio temporarily oppressed Patavium, probably because it opposed Antony, 43 B.C. (Macrob. 1. 11. 2; Cic. *Phil.* 12. 10). But in general it prospered. It was a roadcentre, and canals connected it with the sea. Its flourishing woollen industries made Patavium the wealthiest north Italian city in Augustus' time. Later Mediolanum and Aquileia outstripped it, but Patavium always remained important even after Huns (452) and Lombards (601) sacked it. Its most famous sons were Livy, Asconius, and Thrasea Paetus (Tac. *Ann.* 16. 21).

C. Foligna, *Story of Padua* (1910); E. Ghislanzoni and A. De Bon, *Romanità del territorio padovano* (1938).
E. T. S.

PATER PATRATUS, see FETIALES.

PATER PATRIAE. After the execution of the Catilinarian conspirators in 63 B.C., Cicero was hailed in the Senate as *Parens Patriae* or *Pater Patriae*, and after Munda the title *Parens Patriae* was accepted by Julius Caesar (*CAH* ix. 720). Augustus was given the title *Pater Patriae* by 'the Senate, the equestrian order and the whole Roman people' in 2 B.C. The title was not held by the short-lived emperors, Galba, Otho, Vitellius, and was refused by Tiberius and by Gaius. On inscriptions it is found for Augustus before 2 B.C., and for Tiberius and Gaius. Nero accepted it late in his reign, and so did Claudius and Hadrian, who here copied Augustus' action.
J. P. B.

PATERCULUS, see VELLEIUS.

PATRAE (modern *Patras*), situated in Achaea outside the narrows of the Corinthian Gulf, had an unimportant early history. It supported Athens in the Peloponnesian War (Thuc. 5. 52), took the lead with Dyme in expelling the Macedonians and reforming the Achaean League (c. 280 B.C.), but ceased to be inhabited as a city at some date before the Roman occupation. Augustus planted a Roman colony there, attaching to it the neighbouring Achaean towns (Paus. 10. 38. 9). As the port where travellers from Italy landed, it attained an importance which it still keeps.

Paus. 7. 18 ff.; W. M. Leake, *Travels in the Morea* (1830), ii. 123 ff.
T. J. D.

PATRIA POTESTAS. At the head of the Roman family, which was the main pillar of the Roman social constitution, was the *pater familias*, who exercised a sovereign authority over all members of the family (his wife, if the marriage was with *manus* (q.v.), his children, the wives of his sons subject to the same condition, the children of his sons, and so on). The absolute character of the *patria potestas* in its original form offers some analogies (both in name and in fact) with the *imperium* (q.v.) in the early Roman State. *Familia* signified originally all persons living together under the *potestas* of the *pater familias*, the house with all its inmates; in its later meaning the term embraced the totality of persons and things (the whole property) which were placed under the legal power of the *pater familias*. The members of the family united under a single *patria potestas* were connected by the agnatic tie (*agnatio*), as opposed to the relationship by blood, *cognatio*. The Roman family was especially noteworthy for the peculiar position of the *pater familias* and for the *patria potestas* which was 'proprium ius ciuium Romanorum' (Gai. 1. 55).

2. The autocratic character of the *patria potestas* manifested itself not only in the father's right to punish but also in his *ius vitae necisque* which he had over his children, with all its consequences (killing the new-born, exposure of children), though custom, sacred law, and the family council composed of relatives and friends had a restraining influence on it. The *pater familias* had a

full right of disposal over his children, as over slaves and things; he might sell them into slavery *trans Tiberim*; but if he sold them to a citizen they came to be *in mancipio* (a status analogous to slavery) to the purchaser, and on manumission reverted to the *potestas* of the father; only after three such sales did the son become finally free of the father by a provision of the XII Tables. The son also passed *in mancipii causam*, if he was surrendered (*in noxam deditus*) by the father to an injured person on account of a delict committed by the son. The father could, however, when sued by an *actio noxalis*, avoid handing over the son by paying the damages.

3. It was an old rule that the 'filius familias nihil suum habere potest'. What he acquired (by inheritance, legacy, or transaction *inter vivos*) he acquired for his father, but he could not involve him in any liabilities. The praetorian law, however, admitted a suit against the *pater familias* for his son's debts under special circumstances (when the son had a particular authorization from his father or when he had received from the father a personal fund (*peculium*) for free administration). The *peculium* remained, however, the property of the father. On the other hand, the *peculium castrense* (everything that the son gained in or on account of his military service) was his own from the time of Augustus, as was also in later days the *peculium quasi castrense* (the son's acquisitions in some public employments and professions). From the time of Constantine the ownership of the son was extended to inheritance from his mother, and later to other acquisitions from the mother's side. Justinian finally set up the general rule that all the son's acquisitions (except those *ex substantia patris*, and *peculium castrense* or *quasi-castrense*) belonged to him as his *bona adventicia*, on which the father retained only the usufruct or life interest. Together with this gradual recognition of the son's capacity to have a fortune of his own proceeded the development of his capacity to be a party to a civil lawsuit.

4. The father acquired the *patria potestas* over his children begotten in *iustae nuptiae* (see MARRIAGE), if he himself did not stand under his father's *patria potestas*. Artificially *patria potestas* arose from *adoptio* (q.v.) and *adrogatio*. *Patria potestas* over the whole family was terminated by the death or *deminutio capitis* (even *minima*) of the father. It was also extinguished over individual children if a son underwent *emancipatio* (q.v.) or became *flamen Dialis*, and if the daughter was married with *conventio in manum* or became a *virgo Vestalis*.

Very few vestiges of the ancient *patria potestas* remained in Justinian's law: it dwindled into a simple domestic authority. This development was influenced partly by Christianity, partly by the legal conceptions of Hellenistic provinces.

Ancient sources: Gaius 1. 55; 2. 86–7; *Inst. Iust.* 1. 9; 2. 9; *Dig.* 1. 6; 49. 17; *Cod.* 8. 46; 6. 61; 12. 30. 36. Modern literature: P. Moriaud, *De la simple famille paternelle* (1909); E. Weiss, *PW*, s.v. 'Kinderaussetzung'; L. Wenger, 'Hausgewalt und Staatsgewalt im römischen Altertum', in *Miscellanea Fr. Ehrle* ii (1927); P. Bonfante, *Scritti giuridici* i (1916), 64 ff., *Corso di diritto rom* i (1925), 69 ff.; M. Roberti, *Studi in mem. di A. Albertoni* i (1933); C. W. Westrup, *Family property and p.p.* (Copenhagen and London 1936); M. Kaser, *Sav. Zeitschr.* lviii (1938). On the *patria potestas* in Greek papyri: R. Taubenschlag, ibid. xxxvii (1916). A. B.

PATRICIUS. Patricians were the privileged class of Roman citizens. Their name is probably connected with *pater*, meaning 'member of the Senate', as exemplified by certain technical phrases such as 'patrum auctoritas', 'auspicia ad patres redierunt'. There is no reason to believe that the patrician *gentes* were the whole citizen body of primitive Rome. In the distinction between patrician 'gentes maiores' and 'minores' there is probably a trace of the gradual formation of the patriciate. We have furthermore some hints of the admission of new families in early times: e.g. of the *gens Claudia* at the beginning

of the Republic. The same *gens* could probably develop plebeian and patrician branches; this would explain the apparently plebeian names of some of the kings (Hostilius, Marcius), if these kings are not antecedent to the creation of a patriciate (see PLEBS).

Until 445 B.C. *patricii* were not allowed to marry plebeians. *Confarreatio* (q.v.) was perhaps a special form of marriage for the patricians. The patricians were the holders of the magistracies and of the most important religious offices. They served in the cavalry, and six centuries were probably reserved to them. The diminution of their political influence (see PLEBS) corresponded to a certain extent with the diminution, absolute and relative, of their numbers: about 50 patrician *gentes* are known in the fifth century, 22 (with 81 families) *c.* 367 B.C., only 14 (with 30 families) at the end of the Republic. Only a patrician could become *rex sacrorum, interrex*, and perhaps *princeps senatus*. The *patrum auctoritas* (q.v.) was confined to the patrician senators.

The patricians could renounce their status by a special public act (*transitio ad plebem*) or by simple *adoptio* or *adrogatio*. Caesar (by a *Lex Cassia*, 45 or 44 B.C.) and Octavian (by a *Lex Saenia*, 30) were empowered to admit new members to the patriciate. The later emperors conferred the rank on the strength of their censorial powers. In the senatorial *cursus* the patricians were *quaestores Augusti* in the quaestorship and passed directly from the quaestorship to the praetorship. The patriciate apparently disappeared in the third century A.D.

The new dignity of *patricius* created by Constantine was a personal title, conferred for faithful service to the Empire.

Mommsen, *Röm. Forsch.* i (1864), 69; id., *Röm. Staatsr.* iii (1887), 3; P. Willems, *Le Sénat de la République romaine*² (1885). For the patricians under the Empire, C. Heiter, *De patriciis gentibus quae imperii romani saec. I–II–III fuerint* (1909). For the late Empire, O. Hirschfeld, *Kleine Schriften* (1913), 662; G. B. Picotti, 'Il patricius nell' ultima età imperiale e nei primi regni barbarici d'Italia', *Arch. Storico Italiano*, N.S. ix (1928). *See also* GENS, PLEBS. A. M.

PATRIMONIUM CAESARIS, the fortune of Augustus, as kin to the line of the Caesars, and of his successors in the imperial office. *Patrimonium* denotes the property of a *pater familias*, and the *patrimonium Caesaris*, in origin, differed little from other *patrimonia*, except in its extent. It was a private, not a public, chest, and the procurators who administered it were much like those of any private individual. The public revenues of the emperor were administered by the *fiscus*. It cannot be determined with certainty where the line was drawn between the two chests, but the *patrimonium* was mainly fed by the immense private fortunes bequeathed to the emperor; the estates of Agrippa in the Hellespont will serve as an example.

Though private in origin, the *patrimonium Caesaris* was far too important to be detached from the imperial office and passed from emperor to emperor. A *patrimonium privatum* was therefore separated off to deal with the emperor's own private fortune. Some emperors made over their fortune to the State: Antoninus Pius settled his on his daughter, Faustina the younger, but devoted its yield to public ends. A new private chest, the *res privata* (q.v.), was created by Septimius Severus and soon came to overshadow the *patrimonium*.

O. Hirschfeld, *Die kaiserlichen Verwaltungsbeamten bis auf Diocletian*² (1905); H. Mattingly, *The Imperial Civil Service of Rome* (1910). H. M.

PATROCLES, Greek commander at Babylon after 312 B.C. under Seleucus I, whom he assisted against Demetrius. Under Seleucus and Antiochus I, he governed lands from the Caspian towards India, gathering reliable geographical material including north-west India. *C.* 285 he was sent to explore the Caspian, voyaged up its western and then its eastern sides, learnt about Indian trade down the Oxus, but mistakenly asserted that the Oxus and Jaxartes flowed into the Caspian. His reports confirmed the belief that this sea opened into the nearby Northern Ocean.

Strabo 2. 68–70, 74; 11. 508–9; 15. 689. Cary–Warmington, *Explorers*, 51–2; Warmington, *Greek Geography* (1934), 67–9; W. W. Tarn, *JHS* xxi. 10 ff.　　　　　　　　　　　　　E. H. W.

PATROCLUS, in mythology, son of Menoetius (q.v.). Having accidentally killed a playfellow, the young Patroclus took refuge with Peleus (q.v.; *Iliad* 23. 85 ff.). He and his father were kindly received, and Patroclus, who was somewhat older than Achilles (11. 787), was assigned to him as a personal attendant. For the rest *see* ACHILLES.　　　　　　　　　　　　　　　　　H. J. R.

PATRONAGE, LITERARY.
I. IN GREECE. Literary patronage in Greece, formally an extension of the duty of ξενία, is due to the tyrants who attracted to their courts the leading representatives of the arts. The Pisistratids at Athens, Polycrates in Samos, the tyrants of Corinth and especially those of the Greek cities in Sicily, surrounded themselves with men of letters; and poets such as Arion, Alcman, Pindar, Bacchylides, and Simonides were patronized by all of them in turn. Anacreon on the fall of Polycrates went to Hipparchus in Athens; Simonides from Athens to the Scopadae in Thessaly and then to Hieron of Syracuse. In Athens the patronage of the Pisistratids was in part taken over by Cimon and Pericles; but here official and public competitions on the whole replaced individual patronage. Aeschylus ended his days under the protection of a Sicilian court and Euripides died in the home of a Macedonian tyrant, Archelaus, who had collected at his court a literary coterie including Agathon and Timotheus, and in whose honour Euripides wrote an *Archelaus*. In Hellenistic times the literary patronage of the tyrants was carried on by the successors of Alexander, notably the Ptolemies, the first of whom founded the Museum of Alexandria, which supported and housed a brilliant succession of poets and men of letters. Similar patronage was exercised in Asia Minor notably by the kings of Pergamum.

W. Jaeger, *Paideia* i. 292 ff.; M. Cary, *A History of the Greek World from 323 to 146 B.C.*, 318 ff.

II. AT ROME. Literary patronage at Rome was an extension of the ordinary social relation between *patronus* and *cliens*, and was fostered by the fact that so much of the early literature was due to freedmen (e.g. Livius Andronicus) or to Italians of non-Roman origin (Plautus, Naevius, Ennius), whose social and legal position but for such protection might have been precarious. But, while the relation was formally that between *patronus* and *cliens*, the actual relations between the patron and the man of letters varied according to the character of both and the social conventions of the period: e.g. while Livius Andronicus was probably in the position of a *libertus* to the family of the Livii, P. Terentius Afer, on the other hand, stood apparently in a different relation to his patrons of the 'Scipionic circle' (q.v.). Ennius accompanied his literary patron M. Fulvius Nobilior on his expedition to Aetolia and obtained Roman citizenship. As acquaintance with the work of Greek historians and philosophers increased, these also were drawn into the range of Roman literary patronage, and the 'Scipionic circle' embraced Polybius and Panaetius as well as Terence; the same is true of Q. Lutatius Catulus and his 'circle', and towards the end of the Republic the flow of Greek men of letters to Rome increased in the hope of the patronage to be expected there. In the Augustan age the emperor himself, as well as Maecenas, Asinius Pollio, and others, carried on the tradition. This was the Golden Age of Roman literary patronage. Virgil and Horace were both *amici* to their patrons rather than

clientes: each was given a small property which ensured his independence, and Horace's manly letter to Maecenas (*Epist.* 1. 7) is a striking testimony to the character of the relations between the poet and his 'pater et rex'. During the first century A.D. this tradition was on the whole maintained. Nero, Titus, and Domitian (in his early years) wished to be known as patrons of literature; Vespasian established Quintilian in Rome. Many wealthy men and imperial officials adopted the role of Maecenas. Some of these (e.g. Silius Italicus) wrote poetry themselves and were the patrons of humbler poets. To writers of the Flavian period we are indebted for most of our knowledge of the nature and extent of imperial literary patronage: Statius in his *Silvae* claims as his *amici* his wealthy *patroni*, as does Martial in his epigrams, though the latter is full of complaints of the stinginess of many professed patrons. While Juvenal in his *Satires* is full of bitter complaints derived from his earlier experience under the Flavians, he professes hopes of better things from their successors.

L. Friedländer, *Roman Life and Manners* (Engl. Transl.) i. 195 ff., iii. 47 ff.; R. Büttner, *Porcius Licinus und der litterarische Kreis des Q. Lutatius Catulus* (1893); Abbé Reure, *Les Gens de Lettres et leurs Protecteurs à Rome* (1891); D. M. Schullian, *External Stimuli to Literary Production in Rome, 90–27 B.C.*, Chicago diss. (1932).　　　　　　　　　　　　　　　　　　　R. M. H.

PATRONUS, at Rome, was a man who agreed to protect another person, Roman or non-Roman, by making him his client. Several types of *patroni* may be distinguished.

(1) In the early days of Rome the members of the ruling families attached to themselves a number of poorer citizens to whom they gave financial or legal assistance in return for political services or social deference. The bond between patron and client probably could not be enforced by legal sanctions, but by long custom it acquired a quasi-religious force.

(2) With the growth of slavery and the increasing frequency of emancipation, the relation between a slave-owner and his freedman developed into a special type of patronage which was clearly defined by law (*see* FREEDMEN). The patron retained a certain amount of domestic jurisdiction over his freedmen-clients. Patrons and freedmen were often buried together, and epigraphic evidence (especially since the 2nd c. A.D.) indicates that a genuine feeling of friendship often subsisted between them.

(3) Under the later Republic the function of legal assistance by *patroni* was extended to include cases where practised forensic speakers supported litigants in return for a fee. Though a *Lex Cincia* of 204 B.C. forbade the payment of *patroni*, this statute was frequently circumvented. The forensic *patronus* is to be held distinct from the technical legal adviser or *advocatus* (q.v.).

(4) Roman generals assumed a general patronage over peoples conquered by them, and this patronage was transmitted to their descendants. As early as 278 B.C. C. Fabricius took the Samnites as his clients, while the Claudii Marcelli undertook to look after the interests of the province of Sicily (conquered in 210 B.C. by Claudius Marcellus, q.v. 1). The patronage of Pompey extended widely over the Empire; in 83 B.C. he raised three legions of clients in Picenum and his son Sextus could still get help in Spain and Asia from the clients of his family. It is probable that a patronage of this type was one of the elements that went to make up the *auctoritas* of the emperors.

(5) A similar form of patronage, which became common under the Empire, originated in the action of Roman municipalities, which appointed one or more influential Romans to defend their interests in Rome and to serve as channels of communication between themselves and the emperors (cf. the *tabula patronorum* of Canusium— *ILS* 6121).

(6) Under the Roman emperors many *collegia* or clubs appointed *patroni* similar to those of the municipalities.

(7) Under the emperors men of wealth kept large numbers of merely parasitic clients for the sake of ostentation. *See* CLIENS.

For the political *patronatus*, Fustel de Coulanges, *Histoire des institutions politiques de l'ancienne France* (1892), 205; M. Gelzer, *Die Nobilität der römischen Republik* (1912), 43; R. Syme, *The Roman Revolution* (1939); A. v. Premerstein, *Vom Werden und Wesen des Prinzipats* (1937). For the *municipia*, Mommsen, *Lex Coloniae Genetivae, Juristische Schriften* i. 188; A. v. Premerstein, *Sav. Zeitschr.* (1922), 124. For the *collegia*, J. P. Waltzing, *Étude historique sur les corporations professionnelles* i (1895), 425; ii (1896), 367. A. M.

PATRUM AUCTORITAS was the consent given by the *patres* to the deliberations and to the elections of the popular assemblies in Rome. The conditions under which this consent was given are uncertain. It was probably the prerogative of the patrician senators, not of the whole Senate (Livy 6. 42. 10; Sall. *Hist.* 3. 48. 15; Cic. *Dom.* 14. 38; Gaius 1. 3). As the Senate became mostly plebeian, the *patrum auctoritas* was reduced to a matter of form. A *Lex Publilia* of 339 B.C. (Livy 8. 12) established that it must be given to new laws before the voting of the Comitia. The rule was extended by a *Lex Maenia* of the third century (Cic. *Brut.* 14. 55) to elections. The *patrum auctoritas* affected the Comitia Curiata and Centuriata and (probably) the Comitia Tributa.

Mommsen, *Röm. Forsch.* i (1864), 233; id., *Staatsr.* iii. 155, 1036; P. Willems, *Le Sénat de la République romaine* ii (1885), 33; De Sanctis, *Stor. Rom.* ii (1907), 220. A. M.

PAULINUS OF NOLA (MEROPIUS PONTIUS PAULINUS), born at Bordeaux *c.* A.D. 353, was a favourite pupil of Ausonius (q.v.), and entered on a brilliant career in the State service, attaining the consulship quite early. In Italy he was baptized and dedicated himself to a monastic life, as did his wife Therasia. Paulinus' letters, among them those to Ausonius, number over fifty. The remainder of his works are thirty-three poems, which about equal the letters in bulk. The letters are in part addressed to Augustine, and the poems are in various metres; the subjects of both are definitely Christian.

Ed. W. v. Hartel (*CSEL* xxix, xxx, 1894). A. S.

PAULLUS (1), LUCIUS AEMILIUS (*cos.* I 219 B.C.), brilliantly defeated Demetrius of Pharos in the Second Illyrian War. In 218 he was on the embassy to Carthage opening the Second Punic War. Consul again in 216 he shares, despite the senatorial tradition, in the strategical responsibility for the disaster of Cannae; he fell on the battlefield. Aemilius Paullus (2) Macedonicus was his son; his daughter, Aemilia Tertia, married Scipio Africanus. A distinguished figure, his memory was preserved in the Scipionic Circle and is glorified in Polybius.

Polyb. 3. 16–19; 106 ff.; Livy 21. 18; 22. 35 ff. M. Holleaux, *CAH* vii. 848; De Sanctis, *Stor. Rom.* iii. 2, pp. 1, 55. Cf. J. Van Antwerp Fine, *JRS* 1936, 30 ff. A. H. McD.

PAULLUS (2) **MACEDONICUS**, LUCIUS AEMILIUS (*cos.* I 182 B.C.), curule aedile in 193 B.C., augur by 192, was praetor in 191 in Further Spain, where after initial failure he subdued the Lusitanians (190–189); note the decree for *turris Lascutana* (Dessau, *ILS* 15). On the commission for settling Asia, he opposed the triumph of Cn. Manlius Vulso. Consul in 182, he subjugated the Ligurian Ingauni in 181. In 171 he was patron in the inquiry into extortion in Spain. Consul again in 168, he ended the Third Macedonian War at Pydna; a monument remains at Delphi. His settlement of Greece, including the sack of Epirus, carried out the Senate's policy. Of the spoil he kept only Perseus' library. His triumph was clouded by the death of his two younger

sons. Censor in 164, he died in 160; the *elogium* is partly preserved (*CIL* i², 194). His elder sons, by Papiria, were Q. Fabius and P. Scipio Aemilianus; a daughter married Cato's son.

Aemilius symbolizes the union of Roman tradition with Hellenism. Cultured yet conservative, a fine soldier and just administrator, strict in religious observance, he played an honourable and authoritative part in public and private life in Rome.

Livy 37. 46 and 57; 38. 44 ff.; 40. 25–8; 43. 2; 44–5; Polyb. 18, 35; 29–32; Plutarch, *Aemilius Paullus*. On sources: H. Nissen, *Krit. Unters. über die Quellen der IV und V Dekade des Livius* (1863), 280; W. Schwarze, *Quibus fontibus Plut. in vita L. Aem. Paull. usus sit* (1891); historical commentary in Dutch: C. Liedmeier (1935). De Sanctis, *Stor. Rom.* iv. 1, pp. 315, 419, 457, 613; A. H. McDonald, *JRS* 1938, 163; H. H. Scullard, *JRS* 1945, 58. A. H. McD.

PAULLUS (3), LUCIUS AEMILIUS (*cos.* 50 B.C.), son of Lepidus (q.v. 2) and brother of the triumvir, accused Catiline *de vi* (63 B.C.). While quaestor in Macedonia he was accused (absurdly) by the informer Vettius of conspiracy against Pompey (59). As aedile he began to rebuild the Basilica Aemilia (55). Consul in 50, he was bought by Caesar with 1,500 talents, which he wanted for the Basilica. In 43 he declared his brother a public enemy and was later proscribed, but allowed to escape. He passed over to Brutus, and continued to live at Miletus, although pardoned.

Klebs, *PW* i. 564. A. M.

PAULLUS (4), LUCIUS AEMILIUS LEPIDUS, son of (3) above, commanded a fleet for Brutus in 42, subsequently became a supporter of Octavian, and was *consul suffectus* in 34 and censor in 22. He completed the Basilica Aemilia begun by his father.

Propertius 4. 11; Velleius 2. 95; Dio Cassius 49. 42; 54. 2 and 24. G. W. R.

PAULLUS (5), LUCIUS AEMILIUS, son of (4) above, and husband of Julia (q.v. 3), was consul with C. Caesar (A.D. 1). He entered into a conspiracy against Augustus and was executed. (Date uncertain. Dessau, *ILS* 5026 is attributed to his son.)

V. Rohden, *PW* i. 580; *PIR*², A 391; E. Hohl, *Klio* 1937, 339. A. M.

PAULUS (1), JULIUS (*fl. c.* A.D. 200), one of the most prominent representatives of the classical Roman jurisprudence. The place and date of his birth and of his death are unknown. A disciple of Cervidius Scaevola (q.v. 5), he began his juridical activity as a practising advocate, was assessor of Papinian when he was *praefectus praetorio*, then *magister memoriae*, and member of the imperial *consilium* of Severus and Caracalla. Banished by Elagabalus, he was soon recalled by Alexander Severus and nominated *praefectus praetorio*, an office which he probably held with his younger contemporary Ulpian. It is strange that they do not cite one another in their works.

Paulus was in great demand as a respondent jurist; he was a celebrated teacher, and several of his works are of an educational character (*Institutiones, Manualia, Regulae, Sententiae*; his authorship of this last collection is denied by several authors). He was a very voluminous writer (nearly 320 books, written in the period between Commodus and Alexander Severus). We find among his works a long commentary on the Edict (80 bks.), an extensive exposition of *ius civile* (*Ad Sabinum*, 16 bks.), extracts from and commentaries on the works of older jurists (Plautius, Neratius, Vitellius, Labeo, and Alfenus), a commentary on Papinian, his contemporary and as it seems also a pupil of Scaevola; a long series of monographs on *leges, senatus consulta*, imperial constitutions, and on various topics of private, criminal, fiscal, and constitutional law.

Paulus was highly esteemed by the ancient authors, jurists, and emperors; less favourable opinions were passed upon him in the modern Romanist literature of the nineteenth century, which criticized him severely, not only for his language and want of clarity, but also for faults of character (alleged intolerance of other men's views) and lack of legal insight. The Romanists of this century judge him very differently, many texts of Paulus which gave occasion for attacking him having been demonstrated as interpolated. Paulus is neither an uncritical copyist nor a compiler; he is rather a critical and original thinker who knows how to examine with penetrating logic what others say, and to present his own opinion. The best proof of his sound method, precision in exposition, mastery of his subject, and cogency in demonstration lies in the circumstance that his texts in particular have been used by the Compilers of the *Digest* who plentifully excerpted him (nearly one-sixth of the *Digest* is composed of his works) for completing the expositions of other authors, especially those of Ulpian.

H. Fitting, *Alter und Folge der Schriften röm. Juristen*[2] (1908) 81 ff.; P. Krüger, *Gesch. der Quellen und Literatur des röm. Rechts*[2] (1912), 227 ff.; A. Berger, s.v. 'Julius Paulus' *PW* x, 690–752; B. Kübler, *Gesch. der röm. Rechts* (1925), 283 ff. Literature on the question of genuineness of Paulus' *Sententiae*: E. Volterra, *Rivista di storia del dir. ital.* viii (1935), who gives a list of glosses and interpolations inserted in the literature on the *Sententiae*. Editions of *Sententiae*: P. Krüger, *Collectio librorum iuris anteiust.* ii (1878); E. Seckel-B. Kübler in Huschke's *Jurisprud. anteiust.*[6] v. 2 (1911); G. Baviera, *Fontes iuris romani anteiust.* ii (1st ed., 1909; 2nd ed., 1940); E. Levy, *Pauli Sententiae A Palingenesia* i (1945). A. B.

PAULUS (2), entitled *Silentiarius*, 'private secretary', was a high official at Justinian's court *c.* A.D. 560 and a close friend of the epigrammatist Agathias. Some eighty of his epigrams are in the *Greek Anthology*—forty are erotic and twenty aesthetic fancies inspired by pictures, gardens, etc. His love-poems, though all imitated from classical models (*Anth. Pal.* 5. 275 = Propertius 1. 3), are bright and vivid. He also wrote an elaborate ἔκφρα-σις (*see* EKPHRASIS), or poetical description, of the restored church of St. Sophia—the work is interesting archaeologically, but not poetically.

B. L. Gildersleeve, *AJPhil.* 1917, on the epigrams; P. Fried-länder, *Johannes v. Gaza und P. Silent.* (1912), text of the St. Sophia poem, with commentary. G. H.

PAULUS, *see also* PASSENNUS.

PAUSANIAS (1), son of the Spartan king Cleombrotus I (d. 480 B.C.), and nephew of Leonidas. In 479 he commanded the combined Greek forces at Plataea and was largely responsible for the Greek victory by meeting the Persian onset with a counter-attack. In 478 he captured Byzantium at the head of an allied Greek fleet, but provoked a mutiny by his arrogant behaviour and fell under suspicion of treasonable negotiations with the king of Persia; it was said that he offered to enslave Greece to Persia in return for the hand of a Persian princess. Recalled to Sparta for trial on this charge, he escaped conviction and returned to Byzantium, where he established himself with a private army. Expelled from Byzantium by Cimon (*c.* 475), he maintained himself at Colonae in the Troad and was believed to be continuing his negotiations with Persia. He was again recalled and tried *c.* 470, only to be once more acquitted. But he now came under further suspicion of fomenting a helot revolt; to escape arrest by the ephors he took sanctuary in a temple, where he was starved out. At the last moment he was taken out of the sanctuary to expire on unconsecrated ground. Whatever the truth about his earlier plots, it is probable that he finally planned a coup against the ephorate.

Herodotus, bk. 9; Thucydides 1. 95, 131–4; Aristotle, *Pol.* 1307[a]4. M. C.

PAUSANIAS (2), grandson of (1), king of Sparta 445–426 and 408–394 B.C. His first reign (after the temporary deposition of his father Pleistoanax) was merely nominal, as he was a minor. He resumed the kingship after his father's death. In 403 he was sent to replace Lysander at the head of the Spartan forces engaged in besieging Thrasybulus and the Athenian democrats in the Piraeus. Reversing Lysander's policy, he procured the return of the democrats to Athens and the removal of the remnant of the Thirty Tyrants (q.v.). In 395 he was sent to co-operate with Lysander in an invasion of Boeotia, but failed to join hands with him and retired without a battle. For this failure he was sentenced to death, but he lived on in exile.

Xenophon, *Hell.* 2. 4. 29 ff.; 3. 5. 6. 21–5. M. C.

PAUSANIAS (3) of Lydia (?) (*fl. c.* A.D. 150), Greek traveller and geographer, knew Palestine, Egypt, Italy, and Rome, but especially Greece, and wrote Περιήγησις τῆς Ἑλλάδος, 'Description of Greece'. I. Attica, Megara. II. Argolis, etc. III. Laconia. IV. Messenia. V–VI. Elis, Olympia. VII. Achaia. VIII. Arcadia. IX. Boeotia. X. Phocis, Delphi.

Generally, P. sketches the history and then the topography of important cities, and of their surroundings, often including worships and superstitious customs, mythology, and the like. Descriptions of scenery are uncommon, but he dwells on natural phenomena, and in later books we get glimpses of products and social life. He loves all religious and historical remains, as at Olympia and Delphi, the older glories of Athens, and historic battlefields and memorials, but above all, artistic monuments, on which he writes plainly and honestly. His accuracy herein is confirmed by existing remains.

J. G. Frazer, Pausanias' *Description of Greece*, text, translation, and commentary, 6 vols. 1898; W. Gurlitt, *Über P.* (1890); R. Heberdey, *Die Reisen des P.* (1894). Text and transl., H. L. Jones (and R. Wycherley), 5 vols. (Loeb). E. H. W.

PAUSANIAS (4) and **AELIUS DIONYSIUS** (q.v. 3) were important Atticists at Rome in the second century A.D. From Aristophanes of Byzantium, Didymus, Pamphilus, and others they compiled Attic Lexica, used by Photius and Eustathius.

D. et P. fragmenta: E. Schwabe, 1890. P. B. R. F.

PAUSIAS (4th c. B.C.), painter, son and at first pupil of Bryes, then of Pamphilus, a Sicyonian. Restored painting by Polygnotus at Thespiae. According to Pliny was the first to paint ceiling-panels (some, however, survive from the fifth-century Nereid monument). He liked small pictures of boys and flowers (thereby influencing Gnathia vases and later decoration), but also painted a Sacrifice with a frontal view of an ox, painted in black without high light, and Methe (in the Tholos at Epidaurus, about 350 B.C.) drinking from a glass cup through which her face could be seen. Such subjects displayed the encaustic technique of which he was the first great master.

Overbeck, 1062, 1726, 1760–5; Pfuhl, 796. T. B. L. W.

PAUSILYPUS MONS, named after Vedius Pollio's care-dispelling villa (παύσων λύπην), separates Puteoli from Naples: nowadays *Posilipo*. Two ancient tunnels pierce the hill: the *Grotta di Sejano* built *c.* 37 B.C., and the *Grotta di Posilipo*, near Virgil's reputed tomb, probably built by Claudius.

Dio Cass. 54. 23; Pliny, *HN* 9. 167; Strabo 5. 245. R. T. Guenther, *Pausilypon* (1913). E. T. S.

PAX, the personification of (political) peace, cf. EIRENE. Scarcely heard of before Augustus, she comes (as Pax Augusta) to represent one of the principal factors which made the Imperial government both strong and popular, the maintenance of quiet at home and abroad (cf. Tacitus, *Ann.* 1. 2. 1: 'cunctos dulcedine otii pellexit'). The most famous, but not the only, monuments of the cult were the Ara Pacis Augustae (see Platner–Ashby, 30 ff.) erected by the Senate in 9 B.C. (voted 13 B.C.) and the Flavian Templum Pacis (op. cit. 386 ff.), erected A.D. 75.

Cf. Wissowa *RK*² 334 f.   H. J. R.

PECULIUM was the private property of a slave which from humble beginnings (tips, wages, perquisites, savings of food, produce of a plot of land) might increase greatly and include property, businesses, ships, slaves (*vicarii*), rights, and claims, which, however, his master would have to help him to enforce. In law the *peculium* was the property of the master, but was often regarded as the slave's; it enabled a third party to deal with the slave, for it guaranteed his good faith. For the business enterprises of the slave the master was liable to the extent of the *peculium*. The slave could neither 'donate' his *peculium* nor dispose of it by will (though slaves in the service of the State could bequeath half of it). On the sale of a slave the *peculium* was not included. On manumission in the lifetime of the master the slave retained his *peculium* (unless expressly reserved), but not on manumission by will unless the will so enjoined. *See also* PATRIA POTESTAS, para. 3.

R. H. Barrow, *Slavery in the Roman Empire* (1928), 100–4.
                                                          R. H. B.

PECUNIA TRAIECTICIA, see BOTTOMRY LOANS.

PEDIUS, QUINTUS, son (less probably grandson) of Caesar's elder sister. He served in the Gallic War, suppressed Milo's rising when praetor in 48 B.C., was sent to Spain (probably as governor of Hispania Citerior) in 47, and fought in the campaign of Munda. Pedius put the property which he inherited from Caesar at Octavian's disposal, was elected consul with him in 43, and carried a law providing for the trial of Caesar's murderers. He died apparently from overstrain due to the commencement of the Proscription.

Appian, *BCiv*, bks .3 and 4, and Dio Cassius, bks. 43 and 46.
                                                          G. W. R.

PEDIUS (2), SEXTUS, a Roman jurist who lived perhaps between A.D. 50 and 120. He wrote a commentary on the praetorian and aedilician Edict, which is often quoted by the later commentators, Paulus and Ulpian, but which is not represented in the *Digest* by any direct excerpt. He was an original thinker who frequently asserts his own doctrines. He wrote also a dissertation *De stipulationibus*.   A. B.

PEDO ALBINOVANUS, see ALBINOVANUS.

PEGASUS (1), in mythology, winged horse who carries the thunderbolt of Zeus (Eur. fr. 312). The dying Medusa gave birth to him (Hes. *Theog.* 280). When P. was drinking at the fountain Pirene he was caught and tamed by the hero Bellerophontes, with the aid of Athena Chalinitis or of Poseidon (Paus. 2. 4. 1). He helped Bellerophon to fight the Chimaera, the Amazons, and the Solymi (Hes. *Th.* 325, Pindar, *Ol.* 13. 86), but when Bellerophon attempted to fly to heaven P. threw him. In another story Bellerophon flung Anteia or Stheneboea from Pegasus (Eur. *Stheneboea*). P. was said to have stamped many famous sources out of the earth with his hoof.

The ending -ασος shows that P. is of pre-Greek origin and his legend probably goes back to pre-Greek inhabitants of Asia Minor. P. became early a favourite of Greek artists and poets; proto-Corinthian vases show P. in action against the Chimaera (H. Payne, *Necrocorinthia* (1931), 133, cf. pl. 4, 1) and his birth is represented in the early archaic pediment of Corcyra. He also appears on early coins of Corinth, the city with which he is most closely connected by legends. P. has no

connexion with poets in ancient sources beyond the fact that he created Hippocrene (Paus. 9. 31. 3). In Roman times P. becomes a symbol of immortality.

L. Malten, *JDAI* 1925, 138 ff.; J. Aymard, *Mélanges École franç. Rome* 1935, 143 ff.; F. Cumont, *Études syriennes* (1917), 91 ff.; M. Launy, *Mon. Piot* (1935), 32, 47.   G. M. A. H.

PEGASUS (2), a Roman jurist of the time of Vespasian; he was consul and *praefectus urbi*; successor of Proculus in the leadership of the Proculians' School. He was considered very erudite ('liber, non homo'). He passes for the author of the *senatus consulta* mentioned by Gaius 1. 31 and 2. 254 f. (the latter is called *SC Pegasianum*).   A. B.

PEISANDER (Πείσανδρος) (1) of Cameirus in Rhodes (7th or 6th c. B.C.), epic poet, author of a *Heraclea*, perhaps the most important poem so named; the first to represent Heracles with a club; said to have plagiarized the *Heraclea* from Pisinus; other poems attributed to him were spurious (Suid.). *See* EPIC CYCLE *and* QUINTUS SMYRNAEUS.

EGF 248–53.   W. F. J. K.

PEISANDER (2), Athenian politician, *floruit* between 430 and 411 B.C. Often attacked in comedy for corruption and cowardice, and ridiculed for extreme fatness. He was the principal actor in the negotiations between the oligarchic faction and Alcibiades in 412, and in the overthrow of the democracy in 411. He made the proposal in the assembly at Colonus for the appointment of a new Boule of 400, and of the '5,000' to take the place of the Ecclesia. On the overthrow of the oligarchs he fled to the Spartans and was condemned for treason in his absence.   A. W. G.

PEISANDER (3) of Laranda (early 3rd c. A.D.), epic poet, author of a long Greek poem on world history under the title Ἡρωικαὶ θεογαμίαι.

PEISISTRATUS, see PISISTRATUS.

PEITHO (Πειθώ), persuasion personified, Lat. *Suada*. Although, in the great majority of cases where she is mentioned, she is no more than a poetical or rhetorical figure, she has a slight hold on cult and mythology. Peitho is a cult-title of Aphrodite in a few places (Farnell, *Cults* ii. 664; Fischer, *Nereiden und Okeaninen*, Diss. Halle 1934, 31); it is a curious fact that she is daughter of Ocean in Hesiod, *Theog.* 349 (attempted explanation, Fischer, p. 32). She is a marriage-goddess in the opinion of the theologians cited by Plut. *Quaest. Rom.* 2. As an attendant on Aphrodite she appears constantly in art and literature; see Weizsäcker in Roscher's *Lexikon*, s.v.
                                                          H. J. R.

PELAGIUS (*fl.* A.D. ? 360–? 425), either British or Irish. Between 405 and 409 he wrote in Rome his *Expositions of Thirteen Epistles of St. Paul*, the earliest surviving work from the British Isles. His denial of 'original sin' caused bitter controversy and his excommunication. The value of his works nevertheless led to their being preserved either anonymously or under other names. He wrote also an *Epistula ad Demetriadem*, which had great vogue. His literary style is of high quality.

Expositions, ed. A. Souter (3 vols. 1922–31), who discovered the original form in 1906; G. de Plinval, *Pélage, ses écrits, sa vie et sa réforme* (1943).   A. S.

PELASGIANS (Πέλασγοι = ? Πελαγ-σ-κοι, Sea-people?) a tribe mentioned by Homer (*Il.* 2. 840; 17. 301) as Trojan allies, 'from Larisa, afar' (apparently in Thrace). In Greece, Achilles' domain includes 'Pelasgian Argos' (*Il.* 2. 684), perhaps named after former inhabitants, and Achilles worships 'Pelasgian Zeus' of Dodona (16, 233). In *Od.* 19. 177 Pelasgi are among the motley population of Crete. In historic times the district round Thessalian Larisa was still called Pelasgiotis. Herodotus (1. 57) records surviving Pelasgian villages east of Cyzicus, and 'beyond the Tyrsenians' at Creston in Chalcidice; they preserved a common non-Greek language.

The Pelasgi seem to have been primarily a North-Aegean people, uprooted (to judge from their scattered distribution) by Bronze Age migrations. The Greeks, however, soon came to use their name for all 'aboriginal' Aegean populations (see PELASGUS). To Herodotus (1. 57) 'Pelasgian' stands for all 'pre-Aryan' and 'Mediterranean' elements in Greece.

J. L. Myres, *JHS* xxvii; J. A. R. Munro, *JHS* liv.   A. R. B.

PELASGUS, eponym of the Pelasgi (see PELASGIANS), the pre-Hellenic inhabitants of Greece. Hence the name is given to mythical ancient princes of various districts whose inhabitants claimed to be autochthonous, or at least of very long residence: Arcadia (Asius in Pausanias, 8. 1. 4; he was son of Earth); Argos (Aesch. *Supp.* 251; Hyginus, *Fab.* 145. 2; contemporary with the rape of Persephone, Paus. 1. 14. 2); Thessaly (schol. *Il.* 2. 681; grandson of Thessalos, eponym of Thessaly). Generally speaking, he is either Peloponnesian (and if so, either Arcadian or Argive), or else Thessalian. Weizsäcker in Roscher, s.v.   H. J. R.

PELEUS (Πηλεύς), in mythology, son of Aeacus (q.v.), and therefore an Aeginetan; but as his name seems to mean 'man of Pelion' and his chief adventures are in that neighbourhood, it is highly likely that there has been an early conflation of two genealogies (Achilles is already an Aeacid in Homer), for some reason quite unknown. His transference from one district to the other is explained by the story that he and Telamon killed their half-brother Phocus (Apollod. 3. 160), whereat their father banished them both. Peleus then went to Phthia, was purified by Eurytion, and married his daughter Antigone; but at the Calydonian boar-hunt he accidentally killed Eurytion and was again exiled. This time he reached Iolcus, where Acastus son of Pelias purified him, and he took part in Pelias' funeral games. But Astydameia, Acastus' wife, fell in love with him. As he was unwilling, she sent word to Antigone that Peleus was to marry Sterope, Acastus' daughter, whereat Antigone hanged herself; Astydameia then lied to Acastus much as Phaedra did to Theseus (see HIPPOLYTUS). Acastus thereupon took him out hunting on Pelion, hid his sword as he slept (for the sword cf. Ar. *Nub.* 1063, and schol. there, who says Hephaestus made it and the gods brought it to Peleus when he was left defenceless), and left him to be attacked by the Centaurs; but Chiron brought him the sword again, he escaped, and took vengeance upon Astydameia, capturing Iolcus and cutting her to pieces (Apollod. 173, who says he led his army between the pieces, a ritual of purification, cf. Livy 40. 6. 1; Plut. *Quaest. Rom.* 290 d). Finally, for his virtue, he was given Thetis (q.v.) to wife; from the Chest of Cypselus on (Paus. 5. 18. 5) he had to win her by wrestling with her, while she took all kinds of shapes (Apollod. 170). She left him because he interfered when she tried to make Achilles immortal by burning his mortality away in a fire (ibid. 171, cf. Lycophron, 178–9). Finally he was reunited to her and made immortal (Eur. *Andr.* 1253 ff.).   H. J. R.

PELIADES (Πελιάδες), the daughters of Pelias; see MEDEA.

PELIAS, see NELEUS, MEDEA.

PELION (τὸ Πήλιον ὄρος), a mountain of over 5,300 feet in Thessalian Magnesia. The mountain system of Pelion with that of Ossa cut off the plain of Pelasgiotis from the Aegean. On the east the steeply rising coast was harbourless, but beneath its fertile south-western slopes were good harbours on the Gulf of Pagasae.   H. D. W.

PELLA (mod. *Alaklissi*) capital of Macedonia *c.* 400–167 B.C., situated in a strong natural position beside the lake of the river Lydias, which was navigable from Pella to the sea (Livy 44. 46; Strabo 7. fr. 20). Known to Herodotus (7. 123) and Thucydides (2. 100. 4), it became the capital of Archelaus and the largest Macedonian city (Xen. *Hellenica* 5. 2. 13), until replaced in importance by Thessalonica in 146 B.C. Pella was later a Roman colony.   N. G. L. H.

PELOPIDAS was born about 410 B.C. of a distinguished Theban family. He must have attached himself prominently to the democratic party of Ismenias before the seizure of the Theban citadel by the Spartans (382), when he took refuge in Athens. He led the *coup d'état* by which the oligarchy was overthrown and the citadel recovered (winter 379/378), and became notable at once as a statesman and general. In 378 he was a Boeotarch, and in the war with Sparta won great fame by his leadership of the Sacred Band (q.v.), especially at Tegyra (375) and Leuctra (371). He accompanied Epaminondas on his first invasion of the Peloponnese (winter 370/369). But after that he turned his attention to Thebes' northern enemies, Alexander of Pherae and Macedon. On his second expedition (368) he was made prisoner by Alexander, but was rescued by Epaminondas. On an embassy to the Great King he persuaded him to withdraw his diplomatic support from Sparta (367). He defeated Alexander of Pherae at Cynoscephalae, but died in action (364).

Pelopidas' energy and leadership were of great service in the advancement of Thebes. He showed less originality than Epaminondas, but equal capacity.

Nepos' and Plutarch's *Lives*; G. Reincke, *PW*, s.v. 'Pelopidas'.   H. W. P.

PELOPONNESIAN LEAGUE, the earliest known, and likewise the most long-lived and influential Greek *symmachia* (q.v.). The name is modern, the usual Greek term being 'the Lacedaemonians and their allies'. After an earlier period of separate treaties between Sparta and individual States the League was organized shortly before 500 B.C. as a permanent offensive and defensive alliance under the presidency of Sparta, who held the command in war and summoned and presided over the assembly of allies. Only after the majority of this body, in which each allied State cast one vote, had ratified a proposal to go to war could Sparta demand the support of all members. She herself probably cast no vote in the Assembly but exercised great influence over its decisions by her power to refuse to call a meeting except to consider proposals that had her own approval. When no League war was in progress, the members were free to carry on separate wars even with other members. Thus the League could not support every allied State in war; even to secure defence against aggression from the League as such it was necessary to convince first Sparta and next the Assembly. Athens, at the time of her surrender in 404, and later other allies, were forced to accept treaties promising complete obedience on questions of peace and war. In other ways, too, a tendency to transform the League into an empire was shown. This process was not completed before the collapse of the power of Sparta and the dissolution of the League in 366 B.C.

Ancient sources: Herodotus, Thucydides (especially bk. 1); Xenophon, *Hell.* For modern literature *see under* SYMMACHIA. The origin and constitution of the League are discussed by Larsen in *CPhil.* 1932, 1933, and 1934. An interpretation differing on many points is given by U. Kahrstedt, *Griechisches Staatsrecht* (1922).   J. A. O. L.

PELOPONNESIAN WAR (431–404 B.C.). The cause of the war, according to Thucydides, was that the Athenian Empire had destroyed the autonomy of some Greek States and threatened many more. There was a general fear of Athens, particularly on the part of Corinth which was hemmed in both on east and west, and goodwill towards her enemies who were to be the 'liberators of

Greece'. Nothing, however, in Thucydides' opinion, would have come of this if Sparta had not feared for her own position. Thucydides, well aware of the economic factor in the *conduct* of the war, does not consider it as a cause. Athens was morally the aggressor, but her enemies began the war. Military victory was therefore a necessity for the Peloponnesians; a draw meant victory for Athens.

2. The main lines of strategy were simple. A superior hoplite force was at that time irresistible on land; it could master an enemy's territory, depriving him of supplies, and if necessary besiege the city. But in the absence of effective siege-engines a besieged city could normally be reduced by famine only, and Athens had countered this risk by her Long Walls (q.v.), which provided a refuge space for her country population, and secured her connexion with the sea. On land she could not muster a force half as strong as her enemies (among whom the Spartans and Boeotians were the finest soldiers in Greece); but she was overwhelmingly strong at sea, in numbers, skill, and morale. She could thus temporarily sacrifice her land without sacrificing her people, and she could neither be taken by assault nor reduced by starvation. At the same time she could harry her enemies' trade (the Peloponnese depending partly on imported food, though not at all to the same extent as Athens) and their coasts. Pericles therefore persuaded his countrymen to transfer themselves and all their movable goods within their walls. The one advantage the Peloponnesians had at sea was that they could concentrate their forces to secure a local superiority; but this was neutralized by their lack of skill and confidence, and by their financial weakness. In available wealth, indispensable for the fleet and for overseas supplies, Athens had a decided advantage.

3. In autumn 433 a quarrel between Corinth and her colony Corcyra gave Athens the opportunity to secure in Corcyra an ally with a considerable fleet and Athenian intervention robbed Corinth of the fruits of a naval victory over Corcyra. In Naupactus she already possessed an important naval base in the Corinthian Gulf. Next year Potidaea revolted from Athens, and Corinth unofficially sent help. In the autumn the Peloponnesian League voted for war. In May 431 war was declared and the Peloponnesians invaded Attica, ravaged the deserted land for about a month, and retired. The first year went according to Pericles' plan: Athens was undamaged and the issue depended on Athenian patience and morale; and so it continued for six years. In 430 a devastating pestilence broke out among the crowded people within the walls (where no proper provision had been made for their housing), and Athens lost more than a quarter of her population, a blow from which she never fully recovered; and Pericles died (429), the one man with enough influence to carry out a consistent policy. But Potidaea was forced to capitulate, Phormion gained two brilliant naval victories over superior forces off Naupactus (429), a revolt in Lesbos was crushed, the Peloponnesian fleet failing to help the island (428–427), and Demosthenes gained a decisive victory over the Peloponnesians in Acarnania (426). In 425 Pylos on the west coast of Messenia was captured, which gave Athens not only a permanent post in the enemy's country in a vulnerable spot—for helots could be encouraged to revolt—but a number of Spartan prisoners. Sparta was being hemmed in; fearful for her prisoners and of leaving her territory now, she gave up the annual invasions of Attica and sued for peace. Pericles' strategy had triumphed.

4. But the Athenians, at the instance of Cleon, a demagogue who had made capital out of the victory of Pylos, refused the peace. In 424 a brilliant Spartan, Brasidas, first saved Megara from capture by Athens, then slipped through Thessaly, and with support from Perdiccas II of Macedon won over several Athenian dependencies in the Thraceward region, including the important Amphipolis. At the same time an ambitious attempt by Athens to overthrow Boeotia was decisively defeated at Delium. A year's truce was concluded (423); in the autumn of 422 Cleon took a force to Thrace, but after some successes was decisively defeated at Amphipolis; both he and Brasidas fell. Brasidas had been unable to extend his successes; and peace was now made between Sparta and Athens, practically on the basis of the *status quo ante bellum*. This was in effect a victory for Athens, the more so because her enemies were divided, Corinth and Boeotia refusing to sign the peace; the united forces of the rest of Greece had been unable seriously to weaken the Athenian Empire.

5. But again the ambition of a politician wrecked the peace: Alcibiades intrigued against Sparta in the Peloponnese, and a coalition was formed against her—Argos, Elis, Mantinea, and Athens. But Athens sent half-hearted help, and Sparta recovered herself at Mantinea (418). Athens suddenly attacked and destroyed the unoffending Melos (416), because it was an island not subject to her, and then launched the grandiose expedition to Sicily (415–413), championed by Alcibiades and opposed by Nicias. The finest force that ever left Greek shores went to Sicily; but Alcibiades was soon recalled to answer charges to which his lawless private life had exposed him, and he promptly went over to the enemy; and the irresolute Nicias allowed initial successes to be turned into defeat. Large reinforcements under Demosthenes were sent; but finally the whole force was utterly destroyed (Oct. 413).

6. Meanwhile Sparta had renewed the war in Greece and occupied Decelea in Attica as a permanent base (spring 413). Athens had lost almost all her fleet, and though she began to rebuild she no longer had trained crews. Persia provided money for a Peloponnesian fleet, which crossed the Aegean, and the subject States began to revolt; Athenian food-supplies from the Bosporus and from Egypt were endangered. Further, there was political strife in Athens, ending in the revolution of the Four Hundred and the loss of Euboea (411). But the new fleet, led by Alcibiades, who had been recalled, gained several victories in the Hellespont, secured the food-supply, and recovered many revolted allies (411–408). However, Lysander with Persian help recreated the Peloponnesian fleet. Almost exhausted, Athens won the costly battle of Arginusae (406). But once more politics destroyed what the fleet had saved: a new peace offer was rejected and the victorious generals were tried and executed for failure to rescue the crews of waterlogged ships. In 405 the last Athenian fleet was surprised and destroyed at Aegospotami in the Hellespont. Besieged by sea and land, Athens capitulated in April 404.

7. The Peloponnesian War had been, as Thucydides says, the greatest 'disturbance' in Greek history. Methods of warfare, never gentle in Greece towards prisoners and non-combatants, became more cruel; the only hopeful attempt at Greek unity was defeated; and the old autonomy was not won back, but an incompetent imperialism substituted for an enlightened one. Greece hardly recovered from the war.

ANCIENT SOURCES. For the first twenty years Thucydides is our authority; for the last seven the less adequate Xenophon (*Hellenica*, 1–2. 2). Diodorus' history (12. 30–13. 107; probably only an epitome of Ephorus) covers the whole war, but contains little of value. Of the subsidiary sources, Aristophanes gives incomparable pictures of Athens in war-time. Several speeches of Antiphon, Andocides, and Lysias, and the partisan pamphlet on the *Constitution of Athens* (falsely ascribed to Xenophon) also throw light on contemporary feeling. Plutarch's *Lives* of Pericles, Nicias, Alcibiades, and Lysander add much biographical detail. For inscriptions see *IG* i (ed. minor, 1924); M. N. Tod, *Greek Historical Inscriptions*[2] (1946), containing a valuable selection of indispensable official documents.

MODERN WORKS. Besides the general histories of Greece (of which Busolt's, which gives the sources throughout, is most useful), see G. B. Grundy, *Thucydides and the History of his Age*[2] (1948). See also the separate articles on most of the individuals mentioned above.

A. W. G.

PELOPONNESUS, 'Isle of Pelops', the large peninsula of south Greece, connected with the mainland only by the Isthmus of Corinth. The name Peloponnesus, mentioned for the first time in the Cypria (fr. xi Allen) and the Homeric Hymn to Apollo, proves that the whole territory was considered an island, a separate part of Greece. Ancient geographers knew about its peculiar shape, comparing it to the leaf of a plane-tree; the medieval name Morea is said to have been taken from the mulberry.

The area of Peloponnesus, including the islands except Aegina and Cythera, amounts to about 8,430 sq. miles (cf. Sicily 9,960, Cyprus 3,580 sq. miles). The number of the population can scarcely be estimated. The civic population may have been about 500,000 or 600,000 in 400 B.C. (1928: 1,053,300).

Although virtually an island, and indented by deep gulfs, Peloponnesus had but little communication with the sea, for the few good harbours (mostly in Argolis) had almost no hinterland. Arcadia, the central, nearly inaccessible district, did not touch the sea at all; the surrounding divisions (Laconia, Messenia, Elis, Achaea, Isthmus, Argolis, qq.v.) were separated from one another by mountains, which also were a great hindrance to intercourse by land.

The parallel mountain chains of central Peloponnesus running to south-south-east once formed part of the huge arc stretching from Albania through middle Greece and Crete to Asia Minor. This original system was destroyed by the subsidence which created the large gulfs and most of the plains in the interior. In the Isthmian province and Argolis the predominant direction of the ranges is west to east, as in the eastern parts of middle Greece. The western and southern divisions of Peloponnesus are characterized by larger plains, forming a kind of counterweight to the smaller ones of east and north. And as the mountain-ranges seem to radiate from Arcadia, the Peloponnesus, in spite of its heterogeneous geological formation, gives the impression of a peculiar system, with a centre surrounded by other districts.

There are plains fit for agriculture; by far the largest part of Peloponnesus, however, is mountainous, uncultivable, and poor. About 50 per cent. of the surface, consisting of chalk and limestone, provides only pasture for sheep and goats, the oak-woods also for swine. Flora and climate depend, of course, upon the geographical and geological conditions, which vary greatly. Arcadia and the east are almost entirely continental, while the western parts are subject to maritime influences.

Most important sources: Strabo 8. 335–89; Pausanias, bks. 2–8; E. Curtius, *Peloponnesos* (1851); A. Philippson, *Der Peloponnes* (1892) (with good maps); E. Meyer, *PW*, s.v. Area and population: J. Beloch, *Bevölkerung der griech.-röm. Welt* (1886), 109 ff. V. E.

PELOPS (Πέλοψ), in mythology, son of Tantalus (q.v.). His chief adventures are: (1) In childhood he was killed and cooked by his father, who served his flesh to the gods to see if they could tell that it was not that of a beast. Demeter inadvertently ate part of his shoulder; the other gods brought him to life again, replacing the lost part by ivory. See especially Pindar, *Ol.* 1. 46 ff. (controverts ordinary account); schol. ibid. 40; Apollod. *Epit.* 2. 3 ff. (2) By favour of his lover Poseidon he became possessed of wonderful horses and great skill in driving. On reaching manhood he wooed Hippodameia daughter of Oenomaus of Pisa. This king had an incestuous love for his daughter, or had been warned that her husband would kill him (Apollod. ibid. 4). He therefore let it be known that anyone who wished might carry her off, on condition that he might pursue, and spear the suitor if he caught him. Thirteen suitors had already perished when Pelops appeared. He bribed Myrtilus, Oenomaus' charioteer, to take out the linchpins of his master's chariot (the details vary in different authors; see Roscher's

Lexikon, arts. 'Myrtilos', 'Oinomaos'). Oenomaus was thus thrown and killed and Pelops carried off his bride. But, either because he was ashamed to owe his victory to Myrtilus (Hyginus, *Fab.* 84. 5), or because Myrtilus loved Hippodameia and Pelops was jealous (Apollod. ibid. 8), he cast him into the sea which was afterwards called Myrtoan. Myrtilus, or Oenomaus, cursed Pelops in dying, and the curse was efficacious, the more so as they were both sons of gods, Hermes and Ares respectively; see, for the later fortunes of his family, ATREUS, AGAMEMNON. However, for the time being Pelops prospered greatly and had six sons by his wife (various lists in schol. Pind. ibid. 144). But various stories of his offspring were current, see Bloch in Roscher iii, 1872. He was supposed (falsely, for the 'barrow' contained no burial) to be buried at Olympia. H. J. R.

PELTASTS (πελτασταί) were Greek soldiers, named from their small round shield (πέλτη). Originally they had no body-armour and their chief weapons were light throwing-spears (ἀκόντια). They are first recorded as derived from Thrace, and were imported into Greece in the later fifth century B.C. to act as skirmishers. Their style of equipment was adopted in Greek armies, and achieved numerous successes, especially under Iphicrates (q.v.) and Chabrias. To Iphicrates are attributed the changes whereby the length of their spears was increased by a half, and the size of their swords almost doubled. The object of these alterations was to enable the peltasts to act as regular troops and not mere skirmishers. After the rise of the Macedonian armies apparently they fell into disuse.

Aristotle, fr. 498 (Rose), and Diod. 15. 44 (on their equipment). O. Lippelt, *Die griechischen Leichtbewaffneten bis auf Alex. d. Gr.* (1910); J. Kromayer and G. Veith, *Heerwesen und Kriegführung* (1928), 88 ff.; H. W. Parke, *Greek Mercenary Soldiers* (1933), 17 ff. and 79 ff. H. W. P.

PELUSIUM, a city at the eastern mouth of the Nile. Renowned for its flax, it was especially important as a frontier fortress towards Palestine. Near it Cambyses defeated the Egyptians (525 B.C.). In 374 Pharnabazus and Iphicrates were balked here by floods; but the position was carried in 343 by Artaxerxes III, in 333 by Alexander, in 169 by Antiochus IV, in 55 by Gabinius and M. Antonius, and in 30 by Octavian (against Antonius). Under the Roman Empire it was a station on a route to the Red Sea. E. H. W.

PEMPHREDO, see GRAIAE.

PENATES, DI, 'the dwellers in the store-cupboard (*penus*)', cf. *Aquinas, Arpinas*. These guardian *numina* of the family larder were worshipped in close conjunction with Vesta (q.v.), also with the Lares (q.v.), properly the Lar Familiaris. It was the chief private cult of every Roman household, especially in early times. It would seem, however, that the royal *di penates*, like the royal Vesta, were reckoned of especial importance to the community; this at least is the most reasonable explanation of the cult of the *Penates Publici*. This was attached to Vesta's temple (Tacitus, *Ann.* 15. 41. 1), but there was also a separate shrine, of unknown but fairly early date, on the Velia (see Platner–Ashby, p. 388). Speculation was rife as to who these Penates originally were, and it was generally supposed that they were the Dioscuri (q.v.). But, since the latter were commonly identified with the Samothracian gods also, and the Penates were called *di magni*, like the Cabiri (q.v.), it was held, not later than Cassius Hemina (see Servius on *Aen.* 3. 12; Cassius Hemina, fr. 5 Peter), that the Roman, and other Italian, *Penates Publici* owed their origin to Samothrace, having been brought by Aeneas (Klausen, *Aeneas und die Penaten*).

Wissowa, *RK* 161 ff. H. J. R.

PENELEOS (Πηνέλεως; also Πηνέλαος, *Etym. Magn.* 670. 50 Sylburg, but reading uncertain; Peneleus, Hyginus, *Fab.* 81, cf. Πηνέλεον, read by Aristophanes in *Iliad* 13. 92), son of Hippalcimus or Hippalcus (Diod. Sic. 4. 67. 7; Hyginus, *Fab.* 97. 8); one of the Boeotian leaders (*Iliad* 2. 494); killed by Eurypylus (Quint. Smyrn. 7. 104); wooed Helen (Apollod. 3. 130); an Argonaut (ibid. 1. 113).　　　　　　　　　　　　　　　　H. J. R.

PENELOPE (Πηνελόπη, Epic Πηνελόπεια), in mythology, daughter of Icarius, brother of Tyndareos (q.v.), and wife of Odysseus (q.v.). In the *Odyssey* she faithfully awaits his return, although pressed to remarry one of her numerous suitors, the local nobles. She puts them off for a while by pretending that she cannot marry until she has finished weaving a shroud for Laertes, Odysseus' father. This she unravels every night, so that the work is never finished, but after three years she is betrayed by one of her maids and compelled to complete it (*Od.* 2. 93 ff.; 19. 137 ff.; 24. 128 ff.). At last, ten years after the fall of Troy and twenty after the departure of her husband, she is at her wits' end and determines to give herself in marriage to whoever can bend Odysseus' bow. This is at Athena's prompting (*Od.* 21. 1) and is used by Odysseus to get hold of the weapon and kill the wooers with it. Later writers add very little, save some particulars concerning her father's adventures and the statement (in the *Telegonia*) that she married Telegonus after Odysseus' death.

There is, however, another story of Penelope so different from that of the epic tradition that it seems possible that we have here to do with a different figure (nymph or minor local goddess?) of the same name. This is that she was the mother of Pan. Tzetzes, who mentions the tale that she and Hermes were his parents, is already of this opinion (schol. Lycophron, 772, cf. Apollod. *Epit.* 7. 38). It of course produced sundry reconciliations and rationalizations, the most notorious, that of Duris of Samos in Tzetzes, ibid., being simply an indecent pun. But possibly the whole legend is no more than an etymological fancy, a connexion of Πάν with Doric or Doricized Πανελόπα. For more details see J. Schmidt in Roscher's *Lexikon*, s.v.　　　　H. J. R.

PENESTAE, see SERFS.

PENIA (Πενία), poverty personified, a literary figure, perhaps also popular (see Hdt. 8. 111. 3), and so appearing in various allegorical contexts (pleads her cause against Wealth, Ar. *Plut.* 489 ff.; mates with Abundance to produce Eros, Plato, *Symp.* 203b f.; humorously said to guard a poor man's house, *Anth. Pal.* 9. 654), not in cult.
　　　　　　　　　　　　　　　　　　　　　　H. J. R.

PENTADIUS (3rd c. A.D.) has left elegiac poems in 'echoic' verse on Fortune, Spring, Narcissus, besides several epigrams. Text and translation: J. W. and A. M. Duff, *Minor Lat. Poets* (Loeb, 1935).

PENTAKOSIOMEDIMNOI, the richest of the four census classes at Athens with a (comparatively low) minimum rating of 500 *medimnoi* of corn, or their equivalent in other produce or money. By the constitution of Solon (q.v.) they alone could be elected archons or *tamiai*. This privilege was preserved by Cleisthenes (q.v.), but it was abolished soon after. *See* HIPPEIS, ZEUGITAI, THETES.　　　　　　　　　　A. W. G.

PENTATHLON, *see* ATHLETICS, paras. 2 and 3.

PENTECONTAETIA, the 'period of fifty years' between the Persian and Peloponnesian Wars, is treated by Thucydides, but not so called, in his first book, chs. 89–118. It did not comprise exactly fifty years, being merely the period from autumn 479 (Sestos) until spring 431 (attack on Plataea). The detailed chronology of the Pentecontaetia is highly controversial.　　　V. E.

PENTHESILEA (Πενθεσίλεια), in mythology, queen of the Amazons who came to the aid of Troy after the death of Hector (q.v.), *Aethiopis*, fr. 1 Allen. According to this poem (see Proclus and cf. Quint. Smyrn. 1. 18 ff.) she was daughter of Ares (cf. AMAZONS) and did valiantly until finally overcome and slain by Achilles. She was buried by the Trojans, and Achilles, by a touch of un-Homeric sentimentality, grieved over her so that Thersites (q.v.) reviled him for being in love with her, whereat Achilles slew him and consequently quarrelled with Diomedes (q.v.), his kinsman in this version (Thersites was son of Agrius (*see* OENEUS) and so first cousin once removed to Diomedes, Quint. Smyrn. 1. 770 ff.). The reason for her being willing to help Priam was that after Theseus married Phaedra, Hippolyte (*see* HIPPOLYTUS) roused the Amazons against him and in the ensuing battle was accidentally killed by her own comrade Penthesilea. The latter then obtained purification from her blood-guilt at the hands of Priam (Apollod. *Epit.* 5. 1). This is plainly a secondary addition to the story, and in fact Apollod. ibid. gives two other accounts of Hippolyte's death.

Like all Amazons, Penthesilea is a common and favourite subject in art.　　　　　　　　　　H. J. R.

PENTHEUS (Πενθεύς), in mythology, son of Agave, daughter of Cadmus (q.v.), and her husband Echion. When Dionysus returned to Thebes from his conquests in the East, Pentheus denied his deity and refused to let him be worshipped. But the supernatural strength of the women who had gone out to worship Dionysus was too much for his soldiers, and he consequently (by advice of a mysterious stranger, the god in disguise or another) went out to spy upon them. He was detected and torn in pieces, his mother, who in her frenzy took him for a beast, leading the rest. It is possible that this goes back to some ritual killing, cf. DIONYSUS. See especially Euripides, *Bacchae*, whence Ovid, *Met.* 3. 511 ff., Nonnus, *Dion.* 44–6, chiefly derive.　　　　　H. J. R.

PERDICCAS (1) **I**, the first king of Macedon (Hdt. 8. 139), who probably conquered the Macedonian coast *c.* 640 B.C.

PERDICCAS (2) **II**, king of Macedon *c.* 450–413 B.C. By astute diplomacy Perdiccas survived rebellions in Upper Macedonia, invasion by Sitalces (q.v.), and intervention by Athens and Sparta, and succeeded in uniting Macedonia and diminishing the Athenian control of his coast. In alliance with Athens until she founded Amphipolis in 436, he subsequently promoted the revolt of Potidaea and the Chalcidians, whom he advised to concentrate at Olynthus. The Athenians aided by Derdas, prince of Elimiotis, and by Philip, exiled brother of Perdiccas, captured Therme before they came to terms with Perdiccas in order to invest Potidaea. Perdiccas assisted Potidaea until Sitalces negotiated a treaty for him with Athens, who ceded Therme (431); probably Derdas also submitted to Perdiccas. In 429 the invasion of Sitalces was repelled by the Macedonian cavalry, and a marriage-alliance was contracted; in 425 Perdiccas allied with Brasidas to oust Athens and to reduce Arrabaeus, prince of Lyncestis, but when the campaign in Lyncestis failed, allied with Athens (422). Allying in 417 with Sparta and Argos, he allied again with Athens when attacked in 415, and died *c.* 413.

F. Geyer, *Historische Zeitschrift, Beiheft* 19 (1930). N. G. L. H.

PERDICCAS (3) (d. 321 B.C.), son of Orontes a Macedonian noble, accompanied Alexander to Asia as 'taxiarch' commanding a brigade of Macedonian infantry. He was promoted 'Bodyguard' (member of Alexander's personal staff; 330), and thereafter often held independent commands. Craterus' return to Europe and Hephaestion's death (324) made him Alexander's second-in-command.

and when Alexander died he became in effect, if not in name, regent of the empire (323–2), an arrangement which alarmed Antipater and Craterus in Europe, and the insubordinate satraps Antigonus (Phrygia, etc.) and Ptolemy (Egypt). In the ensuing war Perdiccas tried to invade Egypt, but Ptolemy's skilful defence and propaganda incited his Macedonians to mutiny, and they killed him. Able, brave, and loyal, but unpopular because of his arrogance, Perdiccas is the type of a Macedonian nobleman and general who just missed greatness.

H. Berve, *Alexanderreich*, no. 627; W. W. Tarn, *CAH* vi, ch. 15.
G. T. G.

PERDUELLIO (from *perduellis* = *hostis*) signified in the ancient Roman law all kinds of hostile activity against the State, especially collusion with the enemy. It was the first crime to be prosecuted by the State, which exercised justice by means of special *duoviri perduellionis*. The penalty was death at all times; the same sanction is mentioned in the XII Tables for cases of treason, even for the act of *civem hosti tradere*. *Perduellio* was absorbed at later times in the wider conception of *crimen maiestatis* (sc. *imminutae*) including all offences against the security, independence, or honour of the Roman people. Augustus' *Lex Iulia maiestatis*, to which Justinian dedicated the first title dealing in the *Digest* with public crimes (48. 4), embraced a long series of criminal acts classified as *crimen maiestatis*, which was enlarged considerably by the classical jurisprudence. The profession of Christianity was classified also as *crimen maiestatis*.

Besides the text-books of Criminal Law (q.v.), E. Pollack, *Majestätsgedanke im röm. Recht* (1908); F. Vittinghoff, *Der Staatsfeind in der röm. Kaiserzeit* (1926); C. H. Brecht, *Perduellio* (1938).
A. B.

PEREGRINATIO AD LOCA SANCTA, strictly *Itinerarium Aetheriae abbatissae*, discovered in a fragmentary state in a Monte Cassino manuscript at Arezzo, was first published by Gamurrini, 1887. He believed that he had found a work by one Silvia, but the lady's name was Silvania, and Férotin made it clear in 1903 that the guess was false. The work, when complete, consisted of letters sent by the head of a nunnery to the nuns under her charge. She was one of the early pilgrims to the Holy Land, and describes in rather colloquial Latin her journeys to Egypt, Palestine, Asia Minor, and Constantinople. She is interested in all biblical sites, liturgical practice, and monastic life. The date is uncertain; whereas much points to the latter part of the fourth century A.D., the religious and literary atmosphere is much like that of Gregory of Tours and the sixth century, to which the high authority of Löfstedt assigns the book.

Ed. W. Heraeus (3rd ed. 1929); commentary by E. Löfstedt, *Philol. Komm. zur Peregrinatio Aetheriae* (1911). A. S.

PEREGRINI, meaning the citizens of any State other than Rome, implied membership of a definite community. Some non-Romans were distinguished from *peregrini*, notably the *Latini* (q.v.). The *socii Italici* remained *peregrini* till 89 B.C., and all provincial peoples enjoying any form of local autonomy were *peregrini* (*see* CIVITAS, DEDITICII). They sometimes enjoyed *conubium* or *commercium*, but could not receive the Roman citizenship unless they surrendered their own sovereignty. In practice, however, the grant of Roman status to an individual *peregrinus* meant, by the end of the Republic, that he was automatically freed from liability to the civic duties of his native *civitas*, while enjoying its amenities; for no Roman could be a citizen of two States. This led to abuses, as Roman citizenship spread abroad, which were rectified by a decree of Augustus affirming the liability of such Roman citizens to their local *munera* (q.v.).

For bibliography *see* SOCII; MUNICIPIUM; CITIZENSHIP, ROMAN.
A. N. S.-W.

PEREGRINUS (with the nickname *Proteus*) of Parium in Mysia (c. A.D. 100–65), Cynic. Our knowledge of him comes almost entirely from Lucian Περὶ τῆς Περεγρίνου τελευτῆς. He was suspected of murdering his father, and to avoid the scandal travelled in Palestine, where he became a Christian. For his activities in this connexion he was imprisoned. On being released he returned to Parium, but soon resumed his travels. He quarrelled with the Christian community, and betook himself to Egypt, where he studied under the Cynic Agathobulus. From there he went to Italy, and then to Greece, as a wandering preacher. His reputation became such that by some he was classed with Epictetus, but Lucian has no high opinion of his character. In 165 he committed suicide by throwing himself on the flames at the Olympic Games.

PW xix. 656. W. D. R.

PEREMNIA, *see* AUSPICIUM.

PERGAMUM, a city of Mysia, in the fertile Caicus valley c. 15 miles from the sea, must have been inhabited from early times, though we hear nothing of it before 401 B.C. Its true history begins only in the third century B.C., when under the so-called Attalid dynasty it became the capital of a Hellenistic kingdom inferior in importance only to Macedonia, Egypt, and the Seleucid realm. For the political history of this development, *see* PHILETAERUS, EUMENES, ATTALUS, ARISTONICUS.

Although the original Greek population of the city cannot have been large, it possessed the constitution of a Greek city-state even under the Attalids, who assumed, however, wide powers of interference at will. They also ruled directly the native population in the surrounding country under their control, and with the expansion of the kingdom and broadening of their political aims, they became increasingly like the great Hellenistic kings, relying on a Greek bureaucracy and a semi-professional army also predominantly Greek, though less elaborate than the Seleucid and Ptolemaic systems based on permanent military settlements. The expansion of Pergamum was due to a skilful exploitation of its natural wealth, which included silver-mines, but also an annual surplus from agriculture (corn) and stock-breeding, with its dependent industries of woollen textiles and parchment. The wealth of the country can perhaps be judged best from its unhappy fate later as the Roman province of Asia.

The Attalids were not great founders of cities, but they made Pergamum itself one of the greatest and most beautiful of all Greek cities. The public buildings, laid out in terraces on a hill-side and culminating in the palace and fortifications of the acropolis, were a splendid example of Hellenistic town-planning. With her famous school of sculpture, her library second only to that of Alexandria, and her kings who were philosophers at least in their spare time, Pergamum became a leader of the Greek world in culture even more than in politics and commerce.

ANCIENT SOURCES. Inscriptions: *Altertümer von Pergamon* viii (M. Fränkel, 1890–5); see also *CAH*. ix, bibliography to ch. 19; *Abh. Berliner Akademie*, 1932. For the period 220–168 B.C. Polybius and Livy (bks. 30 ff., using Polybius) are the most important.
MODERN LITERATURE. Hellenistic period: G Cardinali, *Il regno di Pergamo* (1906); M. Rostovtzeff, *Hellenistic World* (1941); id., *CAH* ibid.; E. V. Hansen, *The Attalids of Pergamon* (1947). Roman period: Jones, *Eastern Cities*, 58 ff., 82 ff. G. T. G.

PERIANDER (Περίανδρος), tyrant of Corinth c. 625–585 B.C., and son of Cypselus (q.v.). He recovered Corcyra, founded Potidaea and probably Apollonia and Epidamnus, thus controlling the Damastium silver-mines and what was later the Via Egnatia. He deposed his father-in-law Procles of Epidaurus and seized his dominions; propitiated Delphi and Olympia, had dealings with Thrasybulus of Miletus and Alyattes of Lydia; and arbitrated between Athens and Mytilene in their dispute for Sigeum. Contacts on his part with Egypt are indicated by Egyptian objects found at Perachora and by the Egyptian name of his nephew Psammetichus. Arion the dithyrambic poet came to his court from Lesbos and sailed from it in a Corinthian ship to tour Italy and Sicily. The scene of Plutarch's *Septem Sapientum Convivium* is Periander's court. Arts and crafts, industry and commerce flourished exceedingly under him, witness the ruins of the Apollo temple and the Peirene fountain at Corinth and the Gorgon pediment at Corcyra. The famous chest of Cypselus at Olympia was probably a dedication of Periander. The potteries increased their output. Periander is said to have built triremes and plied both seas, to have forbidden idleness and luxury, and to have continually found employment for his subjects. His vivid and passionate character left a deep impression, of which we have a picture in Herodotus' dramatic tale of his relations with his son Lycophron. His sons all predeceased him and he was succeeded by his nephew Psammetichus (Cypselus II), whose murder shortly after ended the seventy-three years of the tyranny of the house of Cypselus.

Herodotus, bks. 1, 3, 5 (with How and Wells' *Commentary* ii. 340–2); Nic. Dam. frs. 59, 60; Pausanias 5. 17. H. G. Payne, *Necrocorinthia* (1931), 54, 85, 240–4, 350–1. *See also* CYPSELUS *and* CORINTH.
P. N. U.

PERIBOEA, *see* OENEUS.

PERICLES (*c.* 495–429 B.C.), Athenian statesman, was the son of Xanthippus (q.v.) and of Agariste, niece of Cleisthenes (q.v.) and granddaughter of Agariste of Sicyon and Megacles (q.v.). He was *choregus* when Aeschylus' *Persae* was produced in 472; but first came into prominence as one of the State prosecutors of Cimon (q.v.) in 463. In 462–461 he joined with Ephialtes (q.v.) in the attack on the Areopagus. According to Plutarch he became popular leader and the most influential man in Athens after Ephialtes' death and the ostracism of Cimon. But little is recorded of him for some years, and we do not know his attitude to the Egyptian war (459–454) and to the campaigns of 457 which resulted in the Athenian domination of Boeotia, Phocis, and Locris. He perhaps initiated the building of the Long Walls (q.v.; 458–456). In domestic politics he proposed payment for the dicasts, and perhaps instituted the theoric fund (q.v.)—in rivalry with Cimon for the popular favour, we are told, and therefore probably after the latter's recall, which he proposed in person. In 451–450 he proposed the law restricting the citizenship to children both of whose parents were citizens. In 454 or 453 he was *strategus* and campaigned in the Corinthian Gulf against Sicyon and Oeniadae. After the truce with Sparta (451 or 450) he led an expedition which restored Delphi to the Phocians (448?). He is said to have opposed the rash expedition of Tolmides which ended in the defeat of Coronea (447) and to have bought off the invading Peloponnesians in 446. He reduced Euboea, which had revolted from the League, to submission; and in the winter of 446–445 he secured Sparta's recognition of the Athenian empire in the Thirty Years' Peace. In 440–439 Pericles reduced the insurgent island of Samos after a nine months' siege.

2. Meanwhile his great influence had been shown in other directions. He initiated many cleruchies (q.v.) to strengthen the empire, especially in the Hellespont, and he established an important colony at Thurii (q.v.) to spread Athenian influence in Italy. He called, perhaps in 448–447, a general congress of all Greek States to consider the rebuilding of the temples destroyed by the Persians, the freedom of the seas for all, and peace—but nothing came of it, owing to the opposition of Sparta. He was building commissioner for the Parthenon (begun

in 447) and the other great buildings of this time. His bitter enemy at home in this imperial policy was Thucydides (q.v. 1), son of Melesias, who was at last ostracized in 443; henceforth Pericles had no eminent opponent, and he was elected *strategus* every year till his death. In 437 he founded a colony at Amphipolis (q.v.), and about this time he led an expedition to establish Athenian influence in the Black Sea.

3. When war with the Peloponnesians threatened, Pericles determined to resist their demands. He doubtless counselled the alliance with Corcyra in 433, and he was the author of the decree against Megara in 432. When war broke out the whole of the Athenian strategy was devised by him (*see* PELOPONNESIAN WAR). The invasion of Attica provoked indignation and excitement in the city, but he remained supreme till the ravages of the pestilence in 430 momentarily broke Athenian morale. He was now driven from office, tried for embezzlement, and fined. Soon after (probably spring 429) he was again elected *strategus*; but he too had been attacked by the pestilence, and he survived only another six months.

4. Pericles' long eminence was due to his incorruptible character, a consistently intelligent policy, and remarkable powers as an orator. He was reserved and even haughty in demeanour, with nothing democratic about him (unlike Pisistratus, with whom he was often compared). He was intimate with many of the leading philosophers and artists, especially Anaxagoras, Sophocles, and Phidias. His first marriage was unhappy and ended in divorce; but *c.* 450–445 he formed a lasting union with Aspasia (q.v.). Commonplace minds resented his distant superiority; scandalous and ridiculous stories were spread about him; and finally prosecutions were begun against his friends, Phidias and Anaxagoras, and against Aspasia, who was acquitted. These attacks, however, did not affect Pericles' ascendancy.

We have comparatively good and contrasted sources for Pericles' life—Thucydides' detailed account of political events from 433 to 429 and summary of his character and policy (1. 24 to 2. 65), and Plutarch, who adds much biographical detail, mostly from contemporary sources.
A. W. G.

PERICLYMENUS, in mythology, (1) son of Poseidon (and Chloris daughter of Tiresias, schol. Pind. *Nem.* 9. 57, but cf. (2)). Defended Thebes against the Seven, killing Parthenopaeus (q.v.; Eur. *Phoen.* 1157); pursued Amphiaraus (q.v.; Pind. *Nem.* 9. 26). (2) Son of Neleus (or Poseidon, Seneca, *Med.* 635) and Chloris daughter of Amphion; Argonaut; killed by Heracles (q.v.) while in the form of a fly, Poseidon having given him power to assume any shape when fighting (Ap. Rhod. 1. 156 ff., and schol.).
H. J. R.

PERIGUNE, *see* SINIS.

PERIOCHAE, the summaries in the Roman epitomizing treatment of long, usually chronographical, works, represent in particular the abridgement of Livy, an epitome of whose history is mentioned by Martial (14. 190). The epitomized Livian tradition appears in the *Periochae* (for all 142 books except 136–7, with two *periochae* of bk. 1) and in the Oxyrhynchus Epitome (for bks. 37–40, 48–55), 'contaminated' with further chronological, anecdotal, and antiquarian data, perhaps including *exempla* and reference to Livy's full text.

E. Kornemann, 'Die neue Liviusepitome aus Oxyrhynchus', *Klio*, Beiheft 2 (1904); G. Costa, *I fasti consolari Romani* i (1910); A. Klotz, *Hermes* 1913, 542; *Philol.* 1936, 67; M. Galdi, *L'epitome nella letteratura latina* (1922).
A. H. McD.

PERIOIKOI (περίοικοι, *perioeci*), 'those that dwell round about', was the name used to describe groups of subjects or half-citizens, normally with local self-government. They formed parts of or were subject to various Greek States without having a share in their government.

Perioikoi were found in Argolis, Crete, Elis, Thessaly, and elsewhere, but those of Sparta are best known. These, like the Spartiates, were counted as Lacedaemonians, served in the Lacedaemonian army, were on a par with Spartiates in the payment of taxes, and so were citizens with lesser rights. Nevertheless, though such government never is described, they clearly formed communities with local self-government. Thus the entire complex resembled a federal State with the federal government delegated to the Spartiates, though the emphasis on military service caused it also to resemble an alliance. In Laconia the perioecic towns along the coast and in the mountains roughly formed a circle around the Spartiate land; in Messenia they were less numerous, particularly on the west coast. To them must have fallen what industry and commerce there was, but it seems that the *perioikoi* that served in the army and controlled their communities were landholders. The proportion of Dorians and pre-Dorians among them is unknown and cannot be determined by their dialect, for Spartiates, *perioikoi*, and helots spoke the same language. As in Sparta, so in Crete and Elis, the *perioikoi* appear as citizens with lesser rights, while in Thessaly they are described as subject allies.

G. Gilbert, *The Constitutional Antiquities of Sparta and Athens* (1895), 35–7; A. H. J. Greenidge, *Greek Constitutional History* (1902), 78–83; Larsen, *PW*, s.v. 'Perioikoi'. These works refer to other literature and the scattered sources; the Lacedaemonian *perioikoi* are discussed—with emphasis on their citizenship—by F. Hampl in *Hermes* 1937. J. A. O. L.

PERIPATETIC SCHOOL. The name of Aristotle's school is Peripatos (περίπατος = covered walking-place in a gymnasium; school) or Lyceum (Λύκειον). After the name Peripatos had become popular, members of the school were called Peripatetics (οἱ ἀπὸ or ἐκ τοῦ Περιπάτου: Περιπατητικοί). The name is rather insignificant, like Epicurus' 'garden'. Since early Hellenistic times its meaning has often been misunderstood and connected with the ancient method of teaching while walking (περιπατεῖν = to walk), which is by no means characteristic of Aristotle (wrong, e.g. Hermipp. ap. Diog. Laert. 5. 2; id. 1. 17; right, Hesych. in *Menagii Vita Aristot.* p. 10. 12 R. = Suid. s.v. Ἀριστ.).

There are two main periods of the school. In the first the Peripatos has its widest influence under Theophrastus and becomes rather specialized under Straton. This was a time of lively scientific research, in which the basis for most of the branches of European scholarship was laid. Metaphysical speculation, however, loses ground after Aristotle. The second great era of the school dates from Andronicus (1st c. B.C.). Although it cannot be compared with the vigour and scope of the earlier period, it is in some respects more important for the development of philosophy. For the new school rediscovered Aristotle as the metaphysician and logician who had been almost forgotten during the Hellenistic age. Peripatetics now prepared editions of Aristotle's difficult speculative writings, worked out commentaries, and moreover, framed a system of Aristotelian philosophy which became an important part of Neoplatonism and of scholastic philosophy in the Middle Ages. The most important figure of this school of systematizers and commentators was Alexander of Aphrodisias (c. 200 A.D.).

E. Zeller, *Philos. d. Griechen* ii b², 806 f.; iii a⁴, 641 f., 804 f. Ueberweg-Praechter, *Grundriss*¹², §§ 52, 66, 71, 85; K. O. Brink, art. 'Peripatos' in *PW*, suppl. vol. vii. K. O. B.

PERIPETEIA, *see* TRAGEDY, para. 15.

PERIPHETES (Περιφήτης, 'famous', 'notorious'), name of several minor mythological figures, see Höfer in Roscher s.v., and especially of a brigand, also called Corynetes (Κορυνήτης 'club-wielder'), killed by Theseus (q.v.) on his way to Athens. He was son of Hephaestus and Anticleia, Apollod. 3. 217, who adds that he lived in

Epidaurus, was weak in the legs (or feet, πόδας) and killed all passers-by with an iron club. This Theseus took from him and afterwards carried (another resemblance between Theseus and Heracles). Hyginus (*Fab.* 38. 1) says he was son of Poseidon; no other author mentions his mother. See further Höfer, op. cit., and literature of THESEUS. H. J. R.

PERIPLOI (περίπλοι, 'circumnavigations') were (*a*) reports of navigations by pioneers along unexplored coasts, (*b*) manuals for the use of navigators, which collected and systematized the information of previous travellers. The term primarily referred to sailings round an enclosed basin like the Mediterranean and Black Seas, but was also applied to continuous navigations along any kind of coast, even a straight coast (thus partially replacing the more appropriate terms παράπλοι, ἀνάπλοι). Some Periploi contained, in addition, descriptions of the adjacent lands and peoples.

Periploi of the former class include (1) an account of the outer coast of Spain, with references to Britain and Ireland, by a Massilian captain (c. 525 B.C. ?), quoted by Avienus. (2) A description (extant in Greek) of the west African coast by Hanno (c. 500 ?). (3) The narrative of Nearchus' cruise from Indus to Euphrates (325–324), reproduced by Arrian. (4) Pytheas' account of his Atlantic voyage (late 4th c.), quoted by Strabo and others. (5) Arrian's extant *Periplus of the Euxine Sea* (c. A.D. 132).

The Periploi of the latter class comprise (1) the survey of the Mediterranean and Black Seas compiled c. 325 B.C. (?) under the name of Scylax. (2) Agatharchides' description of both Red Sea coasts (c. 110 B.C.), partly reproduced in Diodorus and Photius. (3) *The Periplus of the Erythraean Sea* (1st c. A.D.), describing the coastal routes from Egypt to India and along E. Africa, with copious information for navigators and traders. (4) The *Stadiasmus Maris Magni* (4th c. A.D. ?), an excellent sailing direction, with details of harbourage and waterspots, and of distances from point to point. (5) Marcianus' description of the 'Outer Sea' (Indian and Atlantic Oceans; c. A.D. 400 ?), a poor compilation from Ptolemy.

Texts in *GGM*. Text of the *Periplus of the Erythraean Sea* by Frisk; translation and notes by W. H. Schoff (1912). F. Gisinger, *PW*, s.v. 'Periplus'. *See also s.v.* AVIENUS, HANNO, NEARCHUS, etc., in the present work. E. H. W.

PERONE (περόνη), *see* FIBULA.

PERPERNA (1), MARCUS, of Etruscan origin, was the first of his family to reach the consulship (in 130 B.C.). He served in 135, as praetor, in the Sicilian Slave-War; and bore the brunt of the war in Asia against Aristonicus (130–129). He died near Pergamum.

PERPERNA (2) **VENTO** (or perhaps **VEIENTO**), MARCUS, a son of the consul of 92 B.C., was a partisan of Marius and praetor in Sicily (82 B.C.), but managed to escape, probably to Liguria. In 78 he joined Lepidus; after their failure they sought refuge in Sardinia. On Lepidus' death (77) Perperna joined Sertorius in Spain with the rest of the army and the treasure. According to tradition, he intended to carry on the war on his own account, but was compelled by his soldiers to submit to Sertorius, with whom he served for five years without distinction. In 76 he failed to hold the Ebro against Pompey. When the fortune of Sertorius declined, Perperna murdered him and assumed command (72). Defeated and captured, he offered Pompey the papers of Sertorius, which compromised many aristocrats, but Pompey burnt them unread and killed Perperna. A. M.

PERRHAEBI, a tribe occupying a mountainous district on the northern border of Thessaly and commanding passes from Macedonia. Oloosson, the tribal capital, and Phalanna were situated in fertile plains, but remained insignificant. The Perrhaebi, who had been thrust northwards by the invading Thessalians, were reduced to the status of *perioeci*. Though liable to a war-tax, they enjoyed some degree of autonomy whenever the Thessalian κοινόν was weak, and they held two votes on the Amphictionic Council. Philip of Macedon severed Perrhaebia from Thessaly, and it remained under Macedonian control until liberated by Flamininus in 196.

F. Stählin, *Das hellenische Thessalien* (1924), 5–39; B. Lenk, *PW*, s.v. 'Perrhaebi'.   H. D. W.

PERSAEUS (*c.* 306–*c.* 243 B.C.), son of Demetrius of Citium in Cyprus. He was brought up at Athens in the house of his fellow-countryman Zeno, founder of the Stoic school, became his disciple, and later taught philosophy under his guidance. In 277, when Zeno declined the invitation of Antigonus Gonatas to come to his court at Pella, Persaeus was sent in his stead. He became the educator of Antigonus' son Halcyoneus and acquired great political influence. In 244 he was made commander of Acrocorinthus, but lost the town and citadel to Aratus in 243, whereupon he committed suicide. He defended orthodox Stoicism against the heretics Ariston and Herillus, and elaborated on the doctrine of the philosopher king.

WORKS: *On Kingship, Polity of the Lacedaemonians, Dialogues*, and others (cf. Diog. Laert. 7. 1. 36.). Fragments: von Arnim, *SVF* i. 4. 96 ff.

PW xix. 926.   K. von F.

PERSECUTION. The Romans, the most religious of peoples, lived under the sense of divine protection. The Senate, as guardian of the common weal, maintained traditional worships, fended off Eastern philosophies and religions, and occasionally suppressed such a subversive cult as the *Bacchanalia* in 186 B.C. The Empire, faced with new problems, kept the same spirit. A 'Roman interpretation' was extended to the miscellaneous cults of the provinces. The worship of the emperor became a bond of union. The Jews, religiously intolerant themselves, were treated with great tolerance in matters purely religious. It was political discontent added that brought tragedy here.

2. The Christian Church presented a new problem. Originally known only as a troublesome sect of the Jews, it first came into prominence in A.D. 64, when Nero found in the hated Christians scapegoats for the Great Fire of Rome. Domitian too persecuted the Church, perhaps in connexion with his merciless scrutiny of the Jews. Pliny, in A.D. 112, writes from Bithynia to Trajan, asking how to deal with the rapidly growing Church there. Trajan is unwilling to persecute—'non sunt exquirendi' —but he admits the principle that persistence in Christianity after challenge is punishable with death. For long this continued to be the official position. Clement emperors, like Hadrian, discouraged denunciation, while Christian apologists tried to commend their religion to the authorities. Under Marcus, in A.D. 177, there was a great persecution at Lugdunum. Commodus was lenient, Septimius more harsh, but his dynasty was on the whole favourable. Persecution of the Church as a body, perhaps planned by Maximinus I, was set on foot by Trajan Decius, who enforced sacrifice on all his subjects. Many fell away, but the persecution, continued by Valerian, was ended in 259 (?) by Gallienus, who granted peace to the Church. This peace, threatened for a moment by Aurelian, lasted till *c.* 296, when Diocletian began to purge army and civil service of Christians. In 303 he was led on by Galerius to open persecution, which became harsher and more bloody, till it threatened to destroy the Church. Buildings were destroyed, books burnt, leaders arrested. Yet by 311 Galerius admitted defeat and granted a grudging toleration. Constantine took up the cause of the Christians and to toleration added marked favour. From thenceforward the Church grew and paganism declined.

Julian's apostasy stopped short of actual persecution and ended with him. Under Theodosius the revolution was complete: Christianity had become the official religion of Rome.

3. To the Roman government the Christians at first were simply an affair of the police—an obscure and turbulent sect, suspected of cannibalism, incest, and a general 'hatred of their fellow-men'. As a society not protected by charter they had no status under law. Hence arose 'persecution for the name', apart from crimes supposed to adhere to it. As the Church grew in numbers and quality, authority tended to treat it with consideration; persecution usually arose out of local embitterment. In the third century came a change of tone. The State was racked and strained, the Church grew in power and pretensions, its loyalty was on some points questionable. Hence the official attempt to crush it, ending in the acceptance of it as the official religion.

4. Rome certainly never persecuted for theological reasons—always for social or political. Yet the Roman State and religion were so closely related that this distinction made little difference. The Christian, refusing to sacrifice to the Genius of the Emperor and to curse Christ, knew himself a martyr to his religion; to the Roman official he was a troublesome and contumacious citizen. The Church, in accepting the protection of Constantine, surrendered much of its power of attack.

Bibliography in *CAH* xii. 775 ff., 794 ff. Cf. especially E. G. Hardy, *Christianity and the Roman Government*[2] (1906); H. Last, 'The Study of the Persecutions' in *JRS* 1937, 80 ff.; W. M. Ramsay, *The Church in the Roman Empire before A.D. 170*[7] (1903).   H. M.

P[H]ERSEPHONE, PERSEPHASSA or -ATTA (Περσεφόνη, Φερσ-, Περσέφασσα, -αττα) or **KORE** (Κόρη); in Latin *Proserpina*, a simple mispronunciation, to which a false etymology from *proserpere* came to be attached (Augustine, *De civ. D.* 4. 8, from Varro), with the absurd explanation that she was the deity who made food-plants germinate. The varying forms of the name and the presence in one of the well-known pre-Hellenic suffix -*ss*- suggest that she is a very old native goddess of the Greek peninsula, taken over by the invaders and identified with the 'virgin daughter' (Kore) of their own corn-goddess. For the story of her carrying off by Hades *see* DEMETER.

Another and very remarkable story in which she bears a part is the Orphic myth of Zagreus (cf. ORPHISM). The earliest reasonably certain mention of this is in Pindar (fr. 133 Bergk, 127 Bowra), where the poet states that those in the other world 'at whose hands Phersephona accepts satisfaction for her ancient grief' return in the ninth year to this world and become kings or otherwise distinguished men, later passing to the status of heroes. The 'grief' seems to mean the death of her child Zagreus (Rose in *Greek Poetry and Life* (1936), 79 ff.). For the story itself see Kern, *Orphicorum fragmenta*, nos. 209 ff.; it is fully told only in late authors, as Firmicus Maternus, *De Errore*, 6; Nonnus, *Dionys.* 6. 155 ff. Zeus, in serpent form, approached Persephone and begat Zagreus, to whom he intended to give all power in the universe. But the Titans, incited by the jealous Hera, attracted the child's attention with toys, set upon him, tore him in pieces, and devoured him. Athena saved his heart, which Zeus swallowed, being thus enabled later to beget Dionysus. He destroyed the Titans with thunderbolts, and from their ashes sprang mankind.

In cult Persephone has little place save with her mother, when she is more commonly called Kore (e.g. at Eleusis). For a list of places where the two goddesses are worshipped together see Bloch in Roscher's *Lexikon* ii. 1288 ff. It does not appear (see Paus. 6. 25. 2) that she shared the unique cult of Hades (q.v.) at Elis, although they are continually associated in literature and art. *See* MYSTERIES.   H. J. R.

PERSEPOLIS, in Persis, residence of the Achaemenid kings. Alexander in 331 B.C. took and looted Persepolis and set fire to the palaces (Diod. 17. 71–2). The royal quarters, built on a hill-terrace, contained two palaces, consisting in either case of a forecourt, a large colonnaded reception-hall which apparently had no outer wall, and a storehouse and armoury.

Excavations on the site have revealed that Darius I levelled the rock-terrace and built the great *apadana* (audience-hall), the main palace-buildings, and the harem. These were completed by Xerxes; Artaxerxes finished the Hall of a Hundred Pillars and built his own palace. Around the whole complex was a fortification wall, and a great gate and stairway led up to the terrace. The bas-reliefs of these palaces are among the finest extant examples of Achaemenid art. The graves of the Achaemenid kings are nearby.

J. H. Breasted, 'The Oriental Institute' (*Univ. of Chicago Survey* xii. 310 ff.); E. Herzfeld, *Archäologische Mitteilungen aus Iran* i (1929); *Journ. Royal Asiatic Soc.* 1934, 226 ff.; F. Sarre and E. Herzfeld, *Iranische Felsreliefs* (1910); Erich F. Schmidt, *The Treasury of Persepolis* (Chicago, 1939); F. Stolze, *Persepolis; die achämenid. und sassanid. Denkmäler und Inschriften* (1882). *PW*, s.v. 'Persepolis' (J. Sturm). M. S. D.

PERSEPTOLIS, see NAUSICAA.

PERSES of Thebes, whose first datable poem is of 316 B.C., has eight or nine simple epigrams in the *Anthology*. Unlike many contemporary epigrams, they are genuine inscriptions: two of them actually describe the reliefs beneath which they were carved (*Anth. Pal.* 7. 445, 730). They are in poetry what the beautifully restrained and impersonal Attic tombstones are in sculpture. G. H.

PERSES, see also HESIOD.

PERSEUS (1), a mythological hero. The following, founded on Apollod. 2. 34 ff., is the usual legend; for variants, etc., see the larger works on mythology. Acrisius, brother of Proetus (q.v.), being warned by an oracle that his daughter Danaë's son would kill him, shut her in a bronze chamber. Zeus visited her there in a shower of gold. Acrisius, learning that she had borne a son, whom she called Perseus, put both in a chest and set it afloat. It drifted to Seriphus, where mother and child were received by the king Polydectes. When Perseus was grown the king contrived to send him to fetch the head of the Gorgon Medusa. This he did by the help of Athena (cf. GRAIAE). After rescuing and marrying Andromeda (q.v.) he returned to Seriphus, where he used the Gorgon's head to turn Polydectes and his followers into stone for persecuting Danaë. He now gave the head to Athena and returned his flying shoes and the wallet in which he had carried the head, also the Cap of Darkness which had made him invisible, to Hermes. With his wife and mother he then came to Argos to see his grandfather, whom he at length found in the Pelasgiotis. Here he contended in some funeral games and, throwing the discus, accidentally struck and killed Acrisius, thus fulfilling the oracle. Leaving Argos to the son of Proetus, he became king of Tiryns and founder of the dynasty of the Perseidae. H. J. R.

PERSEUS (2), king of Macedon 179–168 B.C., the elder son of Philip V and legitimate heir despite the tradition of slave birth, was born about 213/212. He fought against Rome (199) and the Aetolians (189). Representing his father's Antigonid imperialism against the Roman sympathies and royal aspirations, with Roman favour, of his brother Demetrius, he intrigued against him from 183 until Philip ordered Demetrius' death in 181. Polybius' description, reproducing a partisan version (cf. Livy 41. 23–4), does scant justice to the realities of the political struggle.

Succeeding Philip in 179, he renewed his treaty with Rome, and continued consolidating Macedon, declaring an amnesty. He extended influence in Thrace, Dardania, and Illyria, the northern field of Macedonian imperialism. In Greek diplomacy he married Laodice, daughter of Seleucus IV, gave his sister to Prusias, and was honoured by Rhodes; he influenced the social struggles in Thessaly and Aetolia, subdued Dolopia, and visited Delphi with his army. This challenge to the predominance of Pergamum sent Eumenes to Rome and brought on the Third Macedonian War (171–168). Yet the tradition of his warlike designs against Rome may be discounted; his policy, based on the north, aimed at prestige, not war, in Greece.

His military strategy of defence on the Macedonian frontiers was at first successful. But Roman reinforcements and the collapse of his ally Genthius, opening up Macedonia from the west, forced a decision at Pydna. The charge of the phalanx was his last stroke, failing before Aemilius Paullus' experienced generalship. He was captured at Samothrace, and adorned Paullus' triumph, dying two years later at Alba Fucens.

Vigorous in campaigning, he lacked tactical initiative. His alleged miserliness often rather reflects caution in policy. The charge of cowardice at Pydna is to be rejected. Sound in diplomacy and generalship, he yet lacked in both the virtuosity necessary to reconcile Antigonid aims with the Roman protectorate over Greece.

Livy, bks. 38–45; Polyb. bks. 22, 25, 27–30; Plutarch, *Aemilius Paullus*; Diod. bks. 29–31; Appian, *Mac.* 11–16. P. Heiland, *Unters. zur Gesch. des Königs Perseus* (1913); De Sanctis, *Stor. Rom.* iv. 1, pp. 251, 270; C. F. Edson, *Harv. Stud.* 1935, 191; F. W. Walbank, *Philip V of Macedon* (1940, see Index). A. H. McD.

PERSEUS (3) (2nd c. B.C.), mathematician. Proclus describes him as the discoverer of the sections of the σπεῖρα (tore or anchor-ring).

PW xix. 1021.

PERSIA, in its widest geographical sense, includes all the great Iranian plateau bounded on west and east by the valleys of Tigris and Indus, and on the north by the Armenian mountains, the Caspian Sea, and the steppes of south Russia—an area of c. 1,000,000 sq. miles. The high mountain ranges lie at the edges of the plateau, so that it resembles a basin. These mountains abound in mineral wealth, gold, silver, copper, lapis-lazuli and other prized stones; the numerous rivers carry down silt and cultivation is possible in the valleys. The interior of the plateau is a waste of salty lakes and marshes, with wide tracts of desert. In spite of this Persia has always had importance as the bridge between east and west Asia, and the ancient trade-routes are still used.

The Aryan Persians probably entered Iran from the north-east; the date at which they reached their final home is unknown. In the ninth century the Assyrians mention Parsua, a northern country adjoining Median territory. If this was for a time their home, they moved southward, for Teispes the Achaemenid was king of Anshan and Parsa, the country later to be known as Persia proper (Persis, mod. *Fars*). It was from this southerly kingdom that Cyrus II set out to conquer western Asia; Susa remained the administrative capital of the Persian Empire.

The organization of this empire was begun by Cyrus, and completed by Darius. It was a great advance on any previous imperial system, combining local autonomy with the centralization of authority in a supreme controlling power. The country was divided into provinces, each governed by a satrap (q.v.), who might be the local ruler, or a Persian of one of the six privileged noble families. Within his province the satrap had absolute authority, but the presence of military and civil officials responsible only to the king, and of travelling inspectors, constituted a check on his power. Each satrapy had to contribute a fixed amount to the royal treasury and furnish levies for the army. Local forms of government were preserved as far as possible, e.g. in the Phoenician and Greek city-states religion, language, and local custom were not interfered with. Royal inscriptions are written in the three official languages, Persian, Elamitic, and Babylonian. A universal gold coinage, introduced by Darius, and the building of highways facilitated trade, and a royal messenger post linked the farthest corners of the empire with Susa.

Religion played an essential part in the life of the Persians. The Achaemenid kings were Zoroastrians, worshippers of Ahura Mazda, whose vicegerents they regarded themselves (see ZOROASTER). The Magian sect, who specialized in ritual observances, acted as the priests of Mazdaism. Popular religion was syncretistic, including the worship of the elements, especially fire, and that of more ancient deities.

Achaemenid art owes much to Babylonia and Assyria, and something to Greece and even Egypt, but it is by no means merely derivative, as the palaces at Persepolis (q.v.) and elsewhere, with their delicate bas-reliefs and impressive architecture, show.

Classical sources for Achaemenid Persia: Herodotus; Ctesias, *Persica*; Xenophon, *Cyropaedia, Anabasis*, etc.; Strabo bks. 11–17. Cuneiform: F. H. Weissbach, *Keilschriften der Achämeniden* (1911). Archaeological: E. Herzfeld, *Archäologische Mitteilungen aus Iran*. Modern works: *CAH* iv, ch. 1, 9, 10; vi, ch. 12; P. M. Sykes, *History of Persia* i (1930); A. Godard, *L'Art de la Perse ancienne* (1930); PW, arts. on individual kings. *See also* ACHAEMENIDS, ARSACIDS, SASSANIDS.   M. S. D.

PERSIAN WARS.
(1) CAUSES. Economic causes played a comparatively small part in bringing on the Persian Wars. The Ionian Revolt which constituted their first phase may have been prompted by commercial losses among the Asiatic Greeks, consequent upon the Persian conquest of the Levant and a possible increase of Phoenician trade competition; but any deficit on this score would be offset by the increased security of communications and wider commercial facilities, which King Darius made available to all his subjects in the reorganization of the Persian Empire. In any case the expansion of Persia did not hinder the commercial activities of the Greek homeland, and the intervention of European States like Athens in the Ionian Revolt was from the Persian point of view an act of aggression justifying reprisals upon Greece proper. But for reasons of a political order the Greeks both in Asia and in Europe regarded Persia with aversion and alarm. Darius upheld tyranny among his Asiatic Greek subjects, and by affording hospitality to fugitive despots from the Greek homeland such as Hippias (q.v.) he kept alive the fear that he might reinstate these forcibly. Though the Persian régime honestly strove to promote the welfare of the subjects and to respect local customs, the Greeks not unnaturally regarded it as the negation of their own system of government and the enemy of the very idea of liberty as understood by them. The ultimate cause of the Persian Wars therefore lay in the anxiety of the Asiatic Greeks to recover their autonomy, and of the European Greeks to preserve theirs.

(2) THE IONIAN REVOLT. Its immediate author was the Milesian Aristagoras (q.v.), who laid down his 'tyranny' and brought about a general expulsion of tyrants among the cities of Ionia (499 B.C.). The rebel cities formed a league which directed the war and issued a federal coinage. Aristagoras secured a reinforcement of twenty ships from Athens and of five from Eretria, but for one campaigning season only, and he obtained no assistance from Sparta, which shrank from overseas expeditions and was preoccupied with an impending war against Argos; yet success in the revolt depended on support from Greece. In 498 the insurgent army captured and burnt Sardes (thus giving the Persians a good

pretext for retaliating upon Greek cities); the fleet spread the rebellion along the coast from Byzantium to Cyprus, and in 497 defeated a Phoenician squadron off Cyprus. But disunion and insubordination among the Greeks allowed the Persians to recover Cyprus despite a naval defeat, and Aristagoras withdrew from the scene of war. After two years' deadlock the Greek fleet, weakened by rivalries and treason, was crushed at Lade (494). Miletus and other cities were destroyed, but Darius eventually imposed a lenient settlement.

(3) THE CAMPAIGN OF MARATHON. In 492 Mardonius (q.v.) prepared the way for Xerxes' later expedition by the definite reduction of Thrace and Macedonia. In 490 Datis and Artaphernes conducted a punitive expedition by sea against Athens and Eretria. Obtaining the surrender of the Cyclades *en route*, they carried Eretria by treachery and made a landing on Attica at Marathon (probably on the advice of Hippias). An appeal to Sparta for help was conveyed by Pheidippides (q.v.) in record time, but the Spartan forces arrived too late, and the Athenians, some 10,000 strong, with 1,000 Plataeans only to assist them, had to encounter the far stronger Persian army. Under the leadership of Miltiades (q.v.) the Athenians routed the Persians with heavy loss (c. 6,000 men) and by a prompt return march to Athens they thwarted an attempt by the Persian fleet to take the city by surprise. The battle of Marathon made Athens safe for democracy and strengthened her alliance with Sparta —and only by a united front could the Greeks hope to resist the main Persian attack, which befell ten years later.

(4) THE EXPEDITION OF XERXES (480). This was planned as a co-ordinated invasion by land (c. 100,000 soldiers) and sea (1,000 ships); but (notwithstanding the statement of Ephorus) it was not made in concert with the simultaneous Carthaginian attack upon the Greeks of Sicily. By a preliminary diplomatic offensive Xerxes won over Thessaly, most of central Greece, Argos, and the oracle of Delphi. But meantime the Athenians had acquired a powerful fleet (see THEMISTOCLES), and at a Panhellenic congress held at the Isthmus (autumn 481) they combined with Sparta to resolve internal feuds in Greece and to organize a national league of common defence. Sparta held the chief command, but the plan of campaign was mainly by Themistocles. The Greeks abandoned the Thessalian frontier after a mere inspection, and posted their army and fleet at the interdependent positions of Thermopylae and Artemisium (qq.v.). The fleet held the Persians in a three days' battle, but insufficient forces at Thermopylae, combined perhaps with treason, allowed the Persians to circumvent the pass, in which the Spartans and their king Leonidas (q.v.) perished to the last man. All central Greece was now lost to the Greeks, Athens was hastily evacuated before Xerxes occupied and sacked it, and the Greek fleet withdrew to Salamis. The Peloponnesians now advocated passive defence on the Isthmus of Corinth, but Themistocles, supported by the Spartan commander Eurybiades (q.v.), forced a naval decision in the narrows of Salamis, by which the Greeks gained definite command of the sea. Xerxes now retired to Asia with the remnant of his fleet, but Mardonius was left to winter in Thessaly and to carry on the campaign by land.

(5) THE CAMPAIGN OF 479. After two vain attempts in the next spring to detach Athens with the offer of a separate peace Mardonius fell back to Boeotia, where his superior cavalry forces severely harassed an oncoming army of c. 40,000 Peloponnesian and Athenian hoplites. During a retreat to higher ground near Plataea the Spartan commander Pausanias (q.v. 1) was set upon by the Persians, but repelled and routed them; Mardonius fell, and the remnant of his army evacuated Greece. Meanwhile a Greek fleet under the Spartan king Leotychides (q.v.) cut out and destroyed the remains of the Persian fleet in a land battle off C. Mycale. This victory

started a new revolt by the islanders and the Asiatic Greeks.

(6) THE GREEK COUNTER-ATTACK. In support of this rebellion the Greeks cleared the entrance to the Black Sea, and in 478 a fleet under Pausanias started a revolt in Cyprus and captured Byzantium. Friction between Pausanias and the Spartan government led to the recall of the Spartan and Peloponnesian contingents; but the Athenians, assuming command of the liberated Greeks in the Aegean islands and Asia Minor, and enrolling them in the Delian League (q.v.), carried on the war. Their operations (of which little is known) were probably not continuous, but c. 469 Cimon (q.v.) made a bold advance to Pamphylia and Cyprus, and destroyed a Persian army and fleet at the river Eurymedon. He did not follow up this success, but c. 459 Pericles sent 200 ships to support a rebellion in Egypt. Difficulties of communication and the outbreak of war in home waters prevented the timely dispatch of reinforcements, and after some early successes, in which the Persians were driven up the Nile, the Greek fleet succumbed to a strong counter-attack and was destroyed near Memphis (c. 454). Another expedition was sent c. 450 to resuscitate the Egyptian rebellion and to safeguard Cyprus against a Persian counter-attack; but in spite of a victory off Cyprian Salamis it abandoned the island, and the death of its commander Cimon left Pericles a free hand to come to terms with Persia. In 449/448 an agreement (whether a formal treaty or simply a non-aggression pact) was negotiated by Callias (q.v. 1), which secured the independence of the Asiatic Greeks (save those of Cyprus) and closed the Aegean to Persian warships.

(7) RESULTS OF THE WARS. The Persian Wars facilitated the undisturbed development of the Greek system of city-state government, which found its characteristic expression in the democracy of Athens, the Delian League, and the autonomy of the Asiatic Greeks. They gave the Greeks a greater confidence in the city-state and a more vivid consciousness of their common nationality and of the value of their national freedom. Yet they did not bring about the development of the Greek war-coalition into a permanent organ of national government. The wars further brought home to them the superiority of their culture over that of the barbarians—a belief which finds clear expression in Aeschylus, Pindar, and Herodotus—but the medism of Delphi disturbed belief in traditional religion.

SOURCES. By far the most important is Herodotus. For the operations after 479 see Thucydides i. 93–112. The chief other ancient sources are Diodorus bk. 11 (reproducing Ephorus), and Plutarch, *Themistocles*, *Aristides*, *Cimon*, and *De malignitate Herodoti*. These are of occasional value only. On source-criticism see G. Busolt, *Griechische Geschichte* ii² (1895), 600 ff.
MODERN WORKS. See the general histories of Greece. For military details: G. B. Grundy, *The Great Persian War* (1901); H. Delbrück, *Geschichte der Kriegskunst* i³ (1920); J. Kromayer, *Antike Schlacht-felder* iv. 1 (1924); G. De Sanctis, *Riv. Fil.* 1925–6, 1930, 1931.
P. T.

PERSIUS FLACCUS, AULUS (A.D. 34–62), born in Etruria. Rich and well connected, he knew Lucan, Thrasea Paetus, and most of the Stoic 'opposition' to the Principate. His intimacy with the Stoic philosopher L. Annaeus Cornutus began when he was sixteen, continued until his death, and was (cf. *Sat.* 5) the strongest influence on his character. After his death Cornutus prepared his poems for publication: they had immediate success.
WORKS. His satires form one *libellus* of 650 hexameters and a brief choliambic apologia. 1, the introduction, derides the fashionable admiration for smooth mytho-logical poetry, and calls for readers with robust taste. 2 attacks the popular conception of prayer, mocking those who ask heaven for external goods rather than virtue. 3 is a quasi-medical description of the effects of chronic vice on the sick soul. 4 urges the popular young statesman Alcibiades (= Nero?) to examine his own soul, dis-regarding public admiration. 5, eulogizing Cornutus, develops into a general indictment of mankind, slaves to vice, who could be freed by virtue. 6 preaches the wisdom of living as comfortably as one's means allow.

Persius will never be popular, because his thought, though sincere, is contorted, and his language, though vigorous, is obscure. He strains and even breaks the thread of his argument by digressions, forced emphases, and answers to hypostasized objections. Always striving to impress, he writes in a grotesque mixture of forced metaphors, cryptic allusions, and harsh colloquialisms; and he converts every abstract disquisition into a series of realistic pictures which seldom harmonize with one another (cf. 5. 115–18). Yet he rarely describes real life: many of his phrases and most of his characters are taken from Lucilius and Horace; so that his work has what he himself (1. 106) calls 'the taste of bitten nails'. His use of sound and rhythm, however, is extremely skilful (e.g. 1. 92–102, 3. 34, 3. 84, 5. 132 f.).

BIBLIOGRAPHY

LIFE AND WORKS: biography by Probus; F. Villeneuve, *Essai sur P.* (1918); J. Wight Duff, *Roman Satire* vi (1937).
TEXTS: O.C.T. (Owen); Weidmann (Jahn, Buecheler, Leo).
COMMENTARIES: J. Conington & H. Nettleship (1893); F. Ville-neuve (1918).
TRANSLATIONS: J. Dryden (1693); J. Conington (in his ed.); G. G. Ramsay (1918); J. Tate (1930).
STYLE: J. Sorn, *Die Sprache des P.* (1890); H. Küster, *De P. elocutione* (1894–7); A. Eichenberg, *De P. saturarum natura* (1905); V. d'Agostino, *Riv. indo-greco-italica di filol.* 1928–30.
SPECIAL STUDIES: G. C. Fiske, *Harv. Stud.* 1913; A. E. Hous-man, *CQ* 1913; R. Kukula, *P und Nero* (1923); G. L. Hendrickson, *CPhil.* 1928.
G. H.

PERSONIFICATIONS of abstract ideas play an important part in the worship, the literature, and the art of the Greeks and Romans. Between the objects of actual popular worship and the literary devices of a poet the line is often hard to draw; at one pole stands the cult of Tyche (q.v.), at the other pole the description of Fama (*see* PHEME) by Virgil (*Aen.* 4. 173–88). A single figure, such as Ate, varies from passage to passage and from poet to poet, being now a physical or psychological phenomenon, now a moral force, now a full-fledged divinity with family connexions (*Il.* 9. 505–7; 19. 91–6, 126–33; Hes. *Op.* 216, 231, 352, 413; Aesch. *Ag.* 355). Even a given poet within a single work often vacillates between the genuine personification of a vividly charac-terized abstraction and 'grammatical apotheosis' (the illuminating phrase is that of Bouché-Leclercq), to the despair of modern editors who would like to be consistent in the matter of capital letters. So within sixty lines of the *Philoctetes* of Sophocles one encounters the fully personified Hypnos (827), the barely personified Thanatos (797), the hardly personified Phthonos (776) and Kairos (837). Complete personification may be said to exist where an abstraction is the recipient both of cult and of a substantial amount of characterization in literature or art.

2. The way in which abstractions came to receive worship is often doubtful; no single formula will fit all cases. Some hardly personified beings, corresponding to passing phenomena (e.g. Fear), may have been wor-shipped at a very early time. Both in Greece and in Italy an abstraction that had some independent validity was capable of attachment to a major divinity as *paredros* or satellite or epithet. In Homer abstractions play a relatively small part. War spirits, such as Phobos and Eris, and Hypnos and Thanatos receive hardly more than mention; Aidos, Nemesis, and Moira do not achieve real personality. But Ate, devastating daughter of Zeus, and the wrinkled 'Prayers' are conceived as real persons (*Il.* 9. 502–12), though a far more complete projection of a moral or intellectual event is to be found in the appear-ance to Achilles of the fully anthropomorphic Athene

(*Il.* 1. 188–222). The Hesiodic *Theogony* is peopled in part with shadowy abstractions, many of them certainly pre-Hellenic, chthonian beings, whose relationships are set forth: the 'Children of Night' include Moros and Ker and Nemesis, as well as the Moirai, who are now three in number and have names; but the latter appear also as daughters of Zeus and Themis, along with Eunomia and Dike (q.v.) and Eirene (q.v.) (*Theog.* 211–25, 901–6). Hesiod's *Works and Days* more success-fully moralizes such abstractions; if the two kinds of Eris are almost lifeless (11–24), Aidos and Nemesis, who in the Iron Age gather their white garments about them and leave earth for Olympus (197–200), seem on the verge of coming alive; while Dike, daughter and assessor of Zeus, champions justice among men (219–24, 256–62). She, like other moral abstractions, was to play her part in the religious and philosophic thought of later Greece: e.g. Dike in Parmenides and in Orphic literature; Philotes and Neikos in Empedocles; Chronos and Eros in Pherecydes of Syros; Eros and Ananke in Plato (*Symp.* 203 b–e; *Rep.* 616 c–621 a); Heimarmene (*see* FATE) in the Stoics; Themis (q.v.) and Moira passim. Such use of personification made easier the allegorical interpretation of literature from the fifth century on; for the anthropomorphic deities of mythology could be regarded as concrete expressions of moral and psycho-logical phenomena, as indeed they sometimes were.

3. Lyric poetry, and still more tragedy, appropriated the personification of earlier poetry, Aeschylus most fully and Euripides next, Sophocles somewhat less. But by the latter half of the fifth century such exploitation was less the result of vivid poetic imagination or personal conviction than of a rhetorical tendency. This is due in part to sophistic influence, and has little to do with religion. The 'Choice of Heracles' between Arete and Kakia in the moral apologue of Prodicus (Xen. *Mem.* 2. 1. 21–34), or the appeal of the Laws to Socrates in Plato's *Crito* (50 a–54 c) imply nothing as to cult. The literary tendency was carried still further in comedy; Aristophanes em-ployed such characters as Plutus, Penia (qq.v.), Demos, and Basileia, and presented the rivalry of Dikaios Logos and Adikos Logos. The mention of these names indicates how far the older religion was being superseded by intellectual, economic, and political ideas—in a word, by humanism.

4. In the Greek world cult and poetry had thus far in general kept pace together. Pausanias records the dedica-tion at Athens of altars to Eleos, Aidos, Pheme (q.v.), and Horme; to his list may be added Eukleia, Eunomia, and Pistis, abstractions with a political significance, as are many of those which we first encounter during the fifth century and later. There are evidences of cults at Sparta of Phobos, Thanatos, and Gelos; at Corinth of Bia, Ananke, and the Moirai; and in other regions of Nemesis (q.v.; notably at Rhamnus, in Attica), Soteria, Kairos, Metameleia, Hygieia Dike, Peitho (once associated with Aphrodite, later also with political significance), Homo-noia, Eirene, Demos (and even Democratia), Themis (cf. the Hymn of the Kouretes, J. E. Harrison, *Themis*, p. 8), and Tyche. Naturally cult called into being works of art, so that many personifications appear on vases and coins, as well as in sculpture. Well known is the form of the child Plutus carried in the arms of Eirene, as also the various representations of Nike, usually winged and with floating drapery. The ideals thus fostered in the fourth century were particularly Victory (Nike, earlier associated with Zeus or with Athena), Peace (Eirene, first given a cult at Athens after the Battle of the Eury-medon, *c.* 468 B.C.), Wealth (Plutus), and Concord (Homonoia, a concept of increasing political and philo-sophic importance in the period of the Peloponnesian War and afterwards). And in this twilight of the elder gods, amid the decay of the *polis*, the power that came more and more to take the place of the gods was Fortune

(Tyche). Unknown to Homer, she appears in the lyric poets, in tragedy, and in historical and philosophic thought; she represents the capriciousness and the inevitability of events and man's lack of responsibility for them. Devoid of moral content at first, she is often worshipped as a power that may bring good fortune, as Agathe Tyche (sometimes associated with Agathos Daimon); embodying the good fortune of a *polis* or of its ruler, she receives a cult as *Tyche Poleos* (or with the proper name substituted).

5. Despite the Roman gift for abstract thought, the worship of personifications in Rome came comparatively late, seldom appearing in cult before the third century B.C. In time they played a very important part, though they never achieved vivid personalities or were subjects of myths. Cicero suggests (*Nat. D.* 2. 23) that the good things given by the gods come in time to be worshipped in their own right, and seeks to purify the list of un-worthy conceptions. His roster includes Fides, Mens, Virtus, Honos, Ops, Salus, Concordia, Libertas, Victoria. It is only a step from Cicero's view to the view that deified abstractions achieved divinity by separation from the gods to whom they had been attached; thus Fides, Good Faith, may well have been detached from (Jupiter) Dius Fidius. Some personifications, however, must have had a different career; Ops (q.v.), for example, is simply the deified fullness of the grain, and finds a place in the oldest Roman calendars. Salus (q.v.), at first any kind of safety, especially military or political, presently was identified with the Greek Hygieia. (Fors) Fortuna (q.v.), who may well be in origin an Italic birth-goddess, became, like the Greek Tyche, the representative of Chance, and received famous cults at the oracular shrines at Praeneste (here as Fortuna Primigenia) and Antium; still later she was associated, again like Tyche, with the fortunes of cities and of the emperor. Libertas, possibly detached from Jupiter Liber, represented personal, and later political, liberty. The worship of certain abstractions dates from events that called them into being: the temple of Concordia, dedicated in 367 B.C., marked the new political accord that was to follow the Licinian Laws; Spes received a temple after the First Punic War; the Ara Pacis Augustae, dedicated *c.* 9 B.C., commemorated the return of peace to a long-troubled world. The epithet Augustus was often added during the Empire to words indicating qualities which the emperor was supposed to possess, such as Clementia. The altar of Victoria, who had presided over success in battle, chanced in the late fourth century to become a precious symbol of dying paganism in its last stand, under Q. Aurelius Symmachus, against Christianity, championed by St. Ambrose, though Christian emperors usually tolerated the worship of abstractions which could be interpreted as attributes of the true God.

6. Latin poetry mirrors Roman cult, and adds much in the way of merely literary use of personifications. Fortuna, Salus, and Spes are conventional, as Plautus uses them; when Terence quotes 'Fortes Fortuna adiuuat' (*Phorm.* 203), or Pacuvius moralizes on Fortune (Ribbeck, *TRF* i. 124–6), they are not thinking of the goddess of Praeneste. Virgil introduces abstractions sparingly: Justitia (*G.* 2. 474, a Hesiodic echo), Fides (*Aen.* 1. 292), Fama (*Aen.* 4. 173–88, an effective concep-tion, often imitated), the ghostly forms at the threshold of the Lower World (*Aen.* 6. 273–81). Prominent in Tibullus is Pax (1. 10. 45 and 67), and his poems reflect the feeling of the Ara Pacis Augustae. Horace can personify on his own responsibility: 'Post equitem sedet atra Cura' (*Carm.* 3. 1. 40) is as vivid as Keats's 'Joy, whose hand is ever at his lips | Bidding adieu'; whereas in the ode to Fortuna (1. 35) Horace uses the accepted attributes of the goddess of Antium and her associates as the occasion of his own reflections. Later poets duly perpetuate the personifications of their predecessors.

7. Finally it should be noted that the personifications of classical paganism find a place in late Orphic, Neoplatonist, Gnostic, and Hermetic literature: Dike, Tyche, Ananke, Aion or Chronos, and now Physis (in an Orphic hymn) are among the agents in the later as in the earlier cosmologies.

BIBLIOGRAPHY

Roscher, *Lexikon* iii. 2068–169 (L. Deubner); *PW* iii. 1120–3 (Kruse); xix. 1042–58 (F. Stössl); O. Kern, *Die Religion der Griechen* (1926–38), i. 255–72; iii. 78–84; F. Allègre, *La Déesse grecque Tyche* (1889); G. Wissowa, *RK* 327–38; W. W. Fowler, *The Religious Experience of the Roman People* (1911), 153–64, 282–8; H. L. Axtell, *The Deification of Abstract Ideas in Roman Literature and Inscriptions* (U.S.A. 1907); K. Latte, *ARW* xxiv (1926), 244–58; O. Weinreich, ibid. xxxv (1935), 307 ff.; G. Downey, *Trans. Am. Phil. Ass.* lxix (1938), 349 ff.   W. C. G.

PERSPECTIVE in painting, *see* AGATHARCHUS.

PERTINAX, PUBLIUS HELVIUS, who had distinguished himself as a general under Marcus Aurelius in Raetia and under Commodus in Britain, was after the latter's assassination (A.D. 193) proclaimed emperor by the Praetorian Guard on the proposal of the prefect Laetus and through the promise of a large donative. During his rule of three months he attempted to restore the Augustan principles of government and revived for himself the title of *princeps senatus*, while refusing the titles of Augustus and Caesar for his wife and son. An excessive eagerness for reform, however, caused discontent in the Senate, and the sale of State offices undermined confidence in his economic policy. At the same time his failure to pay the promised donative aroused the resentment of the Praetorians, and after an abortive conspiracy to make the consul Falco emperor, Laetus urged the Praetorians to invade the Palatine. Pertinax, deserted by all his retinue except Eclectus, fell a victim to the spear of a Tungrian soldier (28 March A.D. 193). Upon his tombstone might fittingly be inscribed Tacitus' epitaph for Galba 'capax imperii nisi imperasset'.

Herodian 2. 1–5; Dio Cassius bk. 73; S.H.A.; Parker, *Roman World*, 55–8.   H. M. D. P.

PERUSIA, nowadays *Perugia*, an ancient Italian hill city with interesting walls and Etruscan tombs. Originally perhaps Umbrian, Perusia first appears in history as an Etruscan city. In 295 B.C., despite a treaty, it fought against Rome, then submitted and signed a lengthy truce (Serv. ad *Aen.* 10. 201; Diod. 20. 35; Livy 10. 30, 31, 37). Thereafter it remained loyal, e.g. against Hannibal (Livy 23. 17; 28. 45). When Perusia sheltered L. Antonius in 41 Octavian besieged, captured, and plundered it (Perusine War: App. *BCiv.* 5. 32–49). Subsequently called *Augusta Perusia*, Perusia always flourished but is rarely mentioned before the sixth century.

Strabo 5. 226; Pliny, *HN* 3. 52. W. Heywood, *History of Perugia* (1910); C. Shaw, *Etruscan Perugia* (U.S.A. 1939).   E. T. S.

PERVIGILIUM VENERIS is a poem of ninety-three trochaic verses of unknown date and authorship, but written not earlier than the second century A.D. and perhaps nearer to the fifth than the second. The poet, who was a man of culture and learning, combines material for a hymn to Venus with a description of spring; the latter is interrupted with explanation why the coming festival is appropriate at that time, and the festival itself, set in Sicily, is the theme of thirty lines in the middle of the poem which ends on a mysterious and unexpected note of private sadness introduced by the line: 'illa [the nightingale] cantat, nos tacemus: quando uer uenit meum?' Detailed interpretation is a little difficult because of uncertainty about the proper order of the verses. Whatever may be the exact date of this bright and lively poem, which has as a refrain 'cras amet qui numquam amauit, quique amauit cras amet',

the warmth of its description and its delight in passion set it between two worlds and make it the prologue of the Middle Ages.

Standard edition (introd., text, transl., facsimiles, commentary, full bibliography) by Sir Cecil Clementi (1936), the only one making use of all three manuscripts in which the poem is preserved. D. S. Robertson, *CR* lii (1938), 109–12, argues on historical grounds that it was written about A.D. 307 by a poet belonging to the circle of Romula, mother of Galerius.   G. B. A. F.

PESCENNIUS NIGER JUSTUS, GAIUS, came of an equestrian family. Enrolled by Commodus into the Senate, he was consul in A.D. 190 and next year governor of Syria, where after the murder of Pertinax he was proclaimed emperor by his legions. Unable to forestall Septimius' advance upon Rome, he attempted to secure his position from Byzantium, which voluntarily surrendered to him. Defeated at Perinthus, Cyzicus, and Nicaea (winter of 193–4), he withdrew to Antioch and was routed at Issus. Fleeing towards the Euphrates he was overtaken and executed. *See* SEPTIMIUS SEVERUS.
                                                              H. M. D. P.

PETALISMOS, *see* OSTRACISM.

PETASOS, *see* DRESS (para. 4) *and* EPHEBI.

PETIL(L)IUS. Two cousins named Q. Petillius, *tribuni plebis* in 187 B.C., initiated the attack on L. Scipio (q.v. 7). Livy, following Valerius Antias, wrongly states that they accused Africanus also. One is probably Q. Petillius Spurinus, the praetor who burnt the forged writings of Pythagoras discovered in 181 (Livy 40. 29) and campaigned in Liguria as consul (176).   H. H. S.

PETILLIUS, *see also* CERIALIS.

PETOSIRIS, *see* NECHEPSO.

PETRA (Aramaic *Selah*, 'the Rock') was the capital of the Nabataeans by 312 B.C. After A.D. 105 it ceased to be the administrative centre but remained the religious metropolis of Arabia. The town lies in a hollow surrounded by mountains; the only access is by narrow gorges. The ruins of the town itself, though extensive, comprising several temples, two theatres, baths, markets, gymnasium, etc., are not impressive. The rock-hewn temples and tombs in the surrounding hills are most magnificent, ranging in style from a primitive blend of Egyptian, Assyrian, and Greek motifs to a highly developed Hellenistic with strong baroque tendencies.

R. E. Brünnow and A. von Domaszewski, *Die Provincia Arabia* i (1904), 125–428; G. Dalman, *Petra und seine Felsheiligtümer* (1908); T. Wiegand, *Petra* (1921); Sir A. Kennedy, *Petra* (1925).
                                                              A. H. M. J.

PETREIUS, MARCUS, probably son of Cn. Petreius Atinas, a Marian *primipilaris*, was already 'uir militaris' of thirty years' service in 63 B.C. (Sall. *Cat.* 59. 6), when as propraetor in Northern Italy he defeated Catiline at Pistoria. From 55 he governed Hispania Ulterior as Pompey's legate, and in 49 brought his two legions to the Ebro, where he proved more stubborn than Afranius in the retreat from Ilerda. In 48 he was in Peloponnesus, but he joined the Pompeians in Africa, where early in 46 he won a success over Caesar. After Thapsus, by compact with King Juba, he killed the king and then himself.   G. E. F. C.

PETRONIUS (1), PUBLIUS (*cos. suff.* A.D. 19 with M. Junius Silanus), passed some laws in favour of slaves (e.g. the *Lex Junia Petronia*, which provided that if the *iudices* were equally divided the judgement had to be in favour of liberty). He was proconsul of Asia and in 39 legate of Syria. Commanded to erect a statue of Gaius in the temple of Jerusalem, he desisted because of Jewish opposition. Gaius' order to commit suicide arrived after the news of the emperor's death. A connexion between the *Lex Junia Petronia*, the *Lex Petronia* of *Dig.* 48. 8. 11. 2, and the *praefecti (iure dicundo) lege Petronia* (*ILS* 6125, 6359, 6518) is very doubtful.

W. W. Buckland, *The Roman Law of Slavery* (1908) 36, 654, 664; J. Marquardt, *Röm. Staatsverwaltung* i.² 170; G. Rotondi, *Leges publicae populi Romani* (1912), see index.   A. M.

PETRONIUS (2) **ARBITER.** The main question about Petronius Arbiter (his *praenomen* is uncertain, being given as Titus by the elder Pliny and Plutarch (Plin. *HN* 37. 20, Plut. *Mor.* 60 d), and as Gaius by Tacitus) is whether the author of the fragmentary novel that has come down to us is identical with the Petronius described by Tacitus (*Ann.* 16. 18) as once the *elegantiae arbiter* of Nero's Court but later fallen into disfavour and enjoying an elegant suicide. The style and language of the novel are perfectly consonant with the second half of the first century A.D., and arguments designed to bring him to the second or third century, whether linguistic or historical, seem quite unsuccessful. As to the character and intellect of the writer and the courtier, it is almost inconceivable that there should be two people of the same name, of the same age, so alike in genius and sentiment.

2. Petronius had proved his worth as proconsul of Bithynia and then as *consul suffectus* when he rose in Nero's favour and became a Master of the Emperor's pleasures—a delicate voluptuary, lending a certain elegance to the corrupt court, whose distractions lacked refinement. In A.D. 66 the all-powerful Tigellinus (Ofonius) saw in him the possibility of a dangerous rival, and turned Nero's mind against him, by suborning a slave to defame him and by alleging his friendship with Scaevinus, the leading figure in Piso's conspiracy. The court was in Campania, and Petronius was hurrying thither to justify himself, but at Cumae learned that his position was hopeless, and determined to end matters by suicide: he opened his veins and bound them up again, rewarded some slaves and punished others, broke a murrhine vase that the tyrant might not have the pleasure of it, and destroyed his signet-ring for fear that misuse of it should bring other people into trouble. Instead of making a will full of flattery of Nero or his favourite, he wrote a document denouncing the imperial vices with the names of his accomplices, and then passed from life to death. This denunciation has nothing to do with the literary remains of Petronius that have come down, though it was natural that it should be believed in the medieval period, and even in the Renaissance, that we have here fragments of the famous document recorded by Tacitus.

3. Of his literary work we have all too little: fragments of the fifteenth and sixteenth books of a romance of which we do not know the whole extent. An epitomator has sadly cut down even what has come to us, though the *Cena Trimalchionis* is almost intact. The book is unique in Latin literature—and it probably had no Greek model —as a picaresque novel, its nearest succession being Apuleius' *Metamorphoses*, in which, however, there is a mystical and magical element absent from Petronius. It seems to have been little known or appreciated in antiquity: we have bare references to it in Terentianus Maurus and Sidonius Apollinaris, the latter giving him a connexion with Marseilles which has confirmation, though the circumstances are unexplained, in our fragments. In the Middle Ages he was mostly known from the Florilegia, but John of Salisbury (d. 1180) had a better acquaintance with his works, and even quoted from a part of them which was only rediscovered some five hundred years later.

4. The novel recounts the adventures, mostly in southern Italy, of three disreputable young persons of the freedman class, Encolpius (the narrator), Ascyltus, and Giton. They have much trouble with the authorities, many love-affairs, and occasional good times, as at Trimalchio's Feast, in the course of which we have an unexampled store of 'Vulgar Latin' from the lips of the diners—there is nothing to compare with it except the Pompeian wall-inscriptions—who are all of the lowest stratum of Italian society. The form of the work is 'Menippean'—i.e. prose interlarded with occasional verse, and it contains some anecdotes of the type of the Milesian Fables (*see* NOVEL), among which is the famous *Widow of Ephesus*. Our remains include two longer poems, a *Troiae Halosis* which may or may not be a parody of Seneca, and a *Poem on the Civil War*, which is almost certainly an enlightened and penetrating criticism of Lucan's treatment of the same theme.

5. Petronius has also left to us a small collection of lyric and elegiac poems which look back to Ovid and forward to Martial, some of considerable merit; but he will live in the world's literature as the master novelist of low and adventurous life. *See also* LITERARY CRITICISM, LATIN, paras. 4 and 5.

BIBLIOGRAPHY

[There is a fairly complete bibliography down to 1909 by S. Gaselee, *Transactions of Bibliographical Society*, 1910.]

TEXTS: Ed. princ., Milan (*c.* 1482) in *Panegyrici Veteres*. Text improved by J. Sambucus (Antwerp, 1565); Jean de Tournes (Lyons, 1575); P. Pithou (Paris, 1577); J. Dousa (Leyden, 1585). 1st ed. of *Cena Trim.* (Trau fragment), Giovanni Lucio (Amsterdam, 1670). The whole work appeared in an important 'variorum' ed. by P. Burman (2 vols., Utrecht, 1709). The beginning of modern criticism of Petronius is the ed. maior by Fr. Buecheler (Berlin, 1862): his editiones minores still hold the critical field. See also E. Sage, New York, 1929 (critical and explanatory notes). On MSS. C. Beck (U.S.A. 1863) remains useful; S. Gaselee, facsimile of Codex Traguriensis (1915). *Cena Trim.* Best commentary by L. Friedländer (1891², 1906). See also W. D. Lowe (1905); W. B. Sedgwick (1925).

POEMS: E. Baehrens, *PLM* iv; H. E. Butler in Loeb Petronius (1913).

ENGLISH TRANSLATIONS: Burnaby (1694); John Addison (1736); M. Heseltine (Loeb, 1913); J. M. Mitchell (1922). Of *Cena* only, H. T. Peck (U.S.A. 1898); M. J. Ryan (1905).

STYLE AND DICTION: I. Segebade et E. Lommatzsch, *Lexicon Petronianum* (1898); W. Heraeus, *Die Sprache des Petronius und die Glossen* (1899).   S. G.

PETRONIUS (3) **TURPILIANUS**, PUBLIUS (*cos.* A.D. 61), succeeded Suetonius Paulinus as governor of Britain. His policy was one of peace. In 63 he was *curator aquarum* in Rome. He contributed to the repression of the Pisonian conspiracy. In 68 Nero entrusted to him the command against the rebels. His conduct is uncertain (Dio 63. 27. 1; Plut. *Galba* 15, 17). He was killed by Galba.   A. M.

PETS. An ancient house sheltered many more domestic pets than would normally be found in a modern dwelling. The tame mullets of Lucullus were a rich man's fantasy, but hares, monkeys, and serpents were quite usual pets. The hare was a favourite present from lovers in Greece; monkeys both in Greece and Rome contributed to the gaiety of family life; serpents in Rome would creep about the dinner-table and eat from the master's hand. Birds also of every kind moved freely around the house; small birds such as pigeons, doves, quails, and partridges, and larger kinds such as geese and ducks. Parrots were a late introduction from India; cats and caged birds were very rare. The commonest pet of all was the small Maltese dog, with its sharp nose and bushy tail, which frequently had a special attendant and was sometimes buried in a marble tomb. *See* DOGS.

Catullus 2 and 3; Ovid, *Am.* 2. 6; Martial i. 109.   F. A. W.

PEUCESTAS (b. *c.* 360 B.C.), son of an Alexander, a Macedonian noble, accompanied Alexander the Great to Asia, but held no high command till after the Indian expedition, on which he saved Alexander's life (325). He was then promoted to Alexander's personal staff ('Bodyguard'), and to the important satrapy of Persis (325–324). Alone of the important Macedonians he learned Persian and adopted Persian dress, which pleased Alexander and the Persians greatly, and in equal measure displeased the Macedonian soldiers. In the disorders after Alexander's death he probably took the lead among the eastern satraps, but in the war of Antigonus and Eumenes he chose the losing side, and though his life was spared by Antigonus he disappears from history thereafter (316).

H. Berve, *Alexanderreich*, no. 634; W. W. Tarn, *CAH* vi, ch. 15.
G. T. G.

PEUTINGER TABLE, a world-map of the third or fourth century A.D., copied from a lost original by a monk of Colmar (A.D. 1265) and acquired in the sixteenth century by a scholar named Peutinger. It is a long narrow strip, in twelve sections, and was intended to serve as a portable road-map. All distances are greatly elongated (from east to west), and the only features systematically marked on it are rectilinear roads, towns, and the chief mountains and rivers. It extends from Britain to the Ganges mouth, but most of Britain, all Spain, and west Mauretania are missing.

K. Miller, *Die Weltkarte des Castorius* (1888), *Itineraria Romana* (1916); J. Wartena, *Inleiding op een Uitgave der Tabula Peutingeriana* (1927).
E. H. W.

PHAEA (Φαιά, Φαῖα), the name, according to Plut. *Thes.* 9, and other authors, of a monstrous sow (a boar, Hyginus, *Fab.* 38. 6, with some support from art, see Höfer in Roscher, iii 2203, 20), killed by Theseus (q.v.) at Crommyon in Attica (Bacchylides 17. 23 and later writers). Apollod. *Epit.* 1. 1 says that Phaea was the name of the old woman who kept the sow.
H. J. R.

PHAEACIANS, see ALCINOUS, SCHERIA.

PHAEAX (Φαίαξ), Athenian politician and opponent of Alcibiades (Plut. *Alc.* 13). As ambassador to Italy and Sicily in 422 B.C. he tried to stir up anti-Syracusan feeling (Thuc. 5. 4). According to Theophrastus (Plut. *Nic.* 11) Phaeax, not Nicias, joined Alcibiades in promoting Hyperbolus' ostracism. His oratory is mentioned by Eupolis and Aristophanes (*Eq.* 1377 ff.). The attribution of the speech *Against Alcibiades* (see ANDOCIDES (1), § 4) to Phaeax is improbable (Jebb, *Attic Orators* i. 136).
Prosop. Att. n. 13921.
H. H. S.

PHAEDON (Φαίδων) of Elis (b. *c.* 417 B.C.), founder of the philosophical school of Elis. He was brought as a slave to Athens but later set free. He became one of Socrates' most devoted pupils, and Plato named after him the dialogue in which Socrates' last hours are depicted. His own teaching seems to have been confined to ethics. Of the dialogues ascribed to him *Zopyrus* and *Simon* were probably genuine.
PW xix. 1538.
W. D. R.

PHAEDRA, see HIPPOLYTUS.

PHAEDRUS (1) of Athens (*c.* 450–400), Socratic philosopher, a character in Plato's *Prt.* and *Symp.* as well as in the *Phdr.* He was a member of the Socratic circle though not precisely a pupil. His personality appears in Plato's dialogues as enthusiastic and rather naïve.
PW xix. 1555.
W. D. R.

PHAEDRUS (2)(*fl.* 300–270 B.C.), of the deme Sphettus, Athenian statesman, joint leader of the moderate, anti-democratic party after Ipsus (301). He served as general under Lachares (296/5), but joined Demetrius Poliorcetes when he recovered Athens (294), and headed the government on the death of Stratocles (293). When Demetrius finally lost his hold on Athens (288), Phaedrus was debarred from office, but he recovered favour when Demetrius' son Antigonus rose to power (277), and in

Xenophon's archonship (probably 274) he was general ἐπὶ τὰ ὅπλα πρῶτος. A decree in his honour was passed some time later than 263 (*IG* ii² 682; wrongly dated in *SIG* 409).

W. S. Ferguson, *Hellenistic Athens* (1911); *Athenian Tribal Cycles* (1932).
F. W. W.

PHAEDRUS (3)(*c.* 140–70 B.C.), Epicurean philosopher, perhaps an Athenian by birth, was in Rome, where Cicero heard him lecture, before 88. He was head of the Epicurean school in Rome for a short time. He appears in Cicero as one of the most respected Epicureans of the time, but perhaps more for his character than for his philosophic ability. Cicero refers to his work Περὶ θεῶν. He is hardly mentioned except by Cicero, and does not seem to have been an independent philosopher.
PW xix. 1557.
W. D. R.

PHAEDRUS (4) (or possibly **PHAEDER**; *c.* 15 B.C.–*c.* A.D. 50), the Roman fabulist. His works, which provide the only details of his life, show that he was a native of Macedonia, came early to Italy, there received a good education, and became a freedman of Augustus. Under Tiberius, by suspected references in his fables, he offended Sejanus and suffered punishment of a nature unknown. The last book was the work of his old age. Scarcely noticed by Roman writers (being passed over by both Seneca and Quintilian in their references to fable), he is first mentioned by Martial (3. 20. 5 'improbi iocos Phaedri', the meaning of which is obscure, 'shameless' being scarcely appropriate to the extant works, and possibly some unknown mime-writer is referred to), and next by Avianus (*praefat.*). Prose paraphrases of his fables, entitled 'Romulus', were subsequently made, and in the Middle Ages, when P. himself was forgotten, exercised an immense influence.

The fables form five books which are clearly incomplete and to which certainly belong thirty other fables (*Appendix Perottina*) included in Perotti's epitome of fables (*c.* 1465). In addition, about twenty new fables, undoubtedly going back to P., are contained in the paraphrases of 'Romulus'. The importance of P., who is very proud of his achievement, lies in his elevation of the fable into an independent genre of Roman literature. His fables, written in iambic senarii, consist of beast-tales based largely on 'Aesop' as well as jokes and instructive anecdotes taken not only from Hellenistic collections but also from his own personal experience. Added weight is sought for his work by borrowings from the χρεία and διατριβή. Besides his professed purpose of providing amusement and counsel, P. also satirizes contemporary conditions both social and also, to an extent difficult to determine, political (e.g. the *delatores*). Retorts to his detractors are frequent. The presentation is, in general, marked by vivacity, charm, and a brevity of which P. is rightly proud, but which sometimes leads to obscurity. Eagerness, however, to emphasize the moral, which is sometimes misunderstood, often mars the effect. Departures from his originals are seldom happy. In his outlook P. displays resignation rather than the gloomy pessimism sometimes ascribed to him, but offers no profound philosophy. In language, skilfully adapting the *sermo urbanus*, he shows an admirable purity (apart from an unclassical use of abstract nouns and occasional vulgarisms), clearness, and a simplicity that is in refreshing contrast to the turgid rhetoric of his day. His iambic senarius is modelled on that of the early comic writers and is very regular. P. is not a great creative artist, yet in the history of the fable he occupies an important place. *See also* FABLE.

Editions: L. Havet (1895 and, with notes, 1896, 14th ed. 1923); J. Gow, *Corp. Poet. Lat.* ii (1905); J. P. Postgate, O.C.T. (1920); A. Brenot (Budé, text and translation, 1924). Cf. L. Hervieux, *Les Fabulistes latins* i²–ii² (1893); H. Vandaele, *Qua mente Phaeder fabellas scripserit* (1897); J. W. Duff in *Lit. Hist. Rome* (Silver Age, 1927); *Roman Satire* (U.S.A. 1936), ch. 6.
A. H.-W.

PHAENIAS of Eresus (*fl.* 320 B.C.), a pupil of Aristotle who inherited the Peripatetic interest in literary and historical research. Amongst various writings may be noted Τυράννων ἀναίρεσις ἐκ τιμωρίας, an expansion of Aristotle, *Pol.* 1311ᵃ25, marked by moral judgements characteristic of the period, and Περὶ τῶν ἐν Σικελίᾳ τυράννων.

FHG ii. 293. G. L. B.

PHAESTUS stands on a hill at the west end of the Messara plain in south Crete, 3½ miles from the sea. The earliest habitation was of the Neolithic Age, and the site increased in importance in the Early Bronze Age, when neighbouring sites show Egyptian contacts. The palace was founded early in the Middle Bronze Age; it consisted of a series of buildings grouped round courts. It was enlarged during the Middle Bronze Age, a shrine was built, and flights of steps added to the north side of the west court made it resemble the theatral area at Cnossos. In the last phase of the Middle Bronze Age the palace was entirely remodelled. It resembled Cnossos with its light wells, magazines, and propylaea, but the peristyle of the central court, a feature which occurs too at the neighbouring villa of Hagia Triada, had no Cnossian parallel. Phaestus did not suffer from the earthquakes which affected Cnossos towards the end of the Middle Bronze Age; but except for inevitable alterations, it retained the same form, till it too perished in the universal catastrophe at the end of the second phase of the Late Bronze Age (c. 1400 B.C.). It was reoccupied during the third phase and in the Early Iron and Archaic Ages. In Classical times it was a well-known city, with a temple on the site of the ruined palace. It survived till Roman times, when it was overshadowed by its neighbour Gortyn.

L. Pernier, *Il Palazzo Minoico di Festos* (1935); J. D. S. Pendlebury, *Archaeology of Crete* (1939). A. J. B. W.

PHAETHON (Φαέθων), in mythology, son of Helios (q.v.) and the heroine Clymene. Learning who his father was, he set out to the East to find him, and arriving at his palace, asked him a boon. The Sun granting him in advance anything he liked, he asked to guide the solar chariot for a day. But he was too weak to manage the immortal horses, which bolted with him and were likely to set the world on fire till Zeus killed Phaethon with a thunderbolt. He fell into the Eridanus, and his sisters, mourning for him, turned into amber-dropping trees. See Eur. frs. of *Phaethon*, with Nauck's notes. H. J. R.

PHALAECEAN, see METRE, GREEK, III (10).

PHALANX, infantry in order of battle. It was used of the common soldiers by Homer, and in the classical period of Greek hoplites generally; but modern usage applies it particularly to the Macedonian infantry after the reform ascribed to Philip II (Diodorus 16. 3. 1 f., under the year 359 B.C.; it may really have been earlier). The new phalanx owed its great successes under Philip, and later under Alexander, to its numbers (Macedonia could produce at least 25,000 men for this service), to its unusually long pike (*sarissa*; about 13 feet), to its superior training which made it comparatively mobile and flexible when disposed in depth (up to sixteen deep), and to the splendid cavalry which guarded its flanks and rear, where every phalanx was vulnerable. Inside it the tactical unit was the brigade (*taxis*: about 1,500 men), subdivided into companies (*lochoi*) and sections (*dekades*).

Alexander's conquests made this phalanx, or imitations of it, a primary instrument of Hellenistic strategy, and the problem of man-power became acute. Alexander had planned a mixed phalanx of Macedonians and Asiatics. The 'Successors', unable to get enough Macedonians, used Greeks. The Ptolemies and Seleucids in particular based their army-systems upon military settlers, mostly Greek mercenaries by origin, who received land and became a hereditary soldier class. The Seleucid phalanx lasted well (numerically), mustering 20,000 at a review in 166. Technically, however, the phalanx deteriorated, even in Macedonia, mobility and individual skill being sacrificed to depth and weight and a longer *sarissa* (up to 21 feet). When it met Roman legions it was long past its best (Cynoscephalae 196; Magnesia, 189; Pydna, 168); and Pyrrhus in Italy (280–275) had few Macedonians.

W. W. Tarn, *Hellenistic Military and Naval Developments* (1930), 1 ff.; J. Kromayer in *Heerwesen und Kriegführung der Griechen und Römer* (1928), especially pp. 95 ff. and 136 ff. G. T. G.

PHALARIS, tyrant of Acragas (c. 570–554 B.C.), notorious for cruelty, especially for the hollow brazen bull in which his victims were confined and roasted alive. This practice, recalling the ritual of Phoenician cults, 'appears to be better authenticated than the nature of the story would lead us to presume' (Grote). Polyaenus records that Phalaris became tyrant after being entrusted with the building of a temple and arming his workmen. He was finally overthrown by Telemachus, ancestor of Thero. The letters bearing his name were written by a sophist, perhaps of the second century A.D. (proved by Bentley in 1697). V. E.

PHALERUM, the harbour of Athens until the early fifth century (see PIRAEUS) was the nearest point to Athens on the coast, at or near the modern Old Phaleron. There is little shelter here; the early port was an open beach. A cemetery of the eighth and seventh centuries on the marshy ground west of Old Phaleron has been excavated.

Σ. Πελεκίδης, Ἀνασκαφαὶ Φαλήρου, Ἀρχ. Δελτ. 2. 13 ff.; J. Day, Cape Colias, Phalerum and the Phaleric Wall', *AJArch.* 1932, 1 ff. T. J. D.

PHALLUS, a model or image of the male organ of generation, used (a) in certain rites connected with fertility, e.g. at the rural Dionysia, Ar. *Ach.* 243 (see DIONYSIA), cf. 265 ff., for a song in honour of a daimon Phales, a sort of personification of the symbol (Herter, *de dis Atticis Priapi similibus*, 42 ff.); (b) as an attribute of some gods, notably Hermes (q.v.) on herms and Priapus (q.v.). H. J. R.

PHANES, a god of the Orphic cosmogony, born from an egg fashioned by Chronos in the Aither, also called Protogonos, the First-born. He is the creator of all, bisexual, radiant with light, gold-winged, and has the heads of various animals. His daughter is Night, who bore Gaea and Uranus to him. He is also called Eros, Metis, and Erikapaios. See ORPHIC LITERATURE, ORPHISM.

W. K. C. Guthrie, *Orpheus and Greek Religion*, 80 and 95. M. P. N.

PHANOCLES, Greek poet (place and date of birth unknown). The six fragments from his verse seem all to come from one elegiac poem, the title of which is given by Clement of Alexandria as Ἔρωτες ἢ Καλοί. This was a catalogue-poem and dealt with the affection of gods (e.g. Dionysus) and heroes (e.g. Orpheus, Tantalus, Agamemnon) for beautiful boys. Probably each episode began with a stereotyped ἢ ὡς in the Hesiodic manner, cf. frs. 1 and 3. The longest fragment, in which P. describes the death of Orpheus and its sequel, proves that the author possessed considerable skill in narration. The language is simple and well chosen and the versification melodious, though, like Hermesianax, P. is too prone to the arrangement of the pentameter by which an adjective closes the first half and the noun with which it agrees the second. It is possible that the *Erotes* was intended as a male counterpart to the *Leontion* of Hermesianax, but P. is more interested in aetiology than Hermesianax, cf. frs. 1, 5, 6. A rationalistic interpretation of myth appears in fr. 4. Apollonius Rhodius (*Argon.* 4. 903) seems to

imitate an unusual scansion found in Phanocles, fr. 1. 1.
If this is correct, P. lived in the first half of the third
century B.C. He was perhaps a younger contemporary of
Hermesianax.

Texts: J. U. Powell, *Collectanea Alexandrina* (1925), 106-9;
E. Diehl, *Anth. Lyr. Graec.* vi (1924), 225-7. General literature: v.
Blumenthal, 'Phanokles' in *PW* xix. 1781-3.   E. A. B.

PHANODEMUS of Athens, born in the first quarter of
the fourth century B.C. and probably father of the historian Diyllus. Since his identification by Ad. Wilhelm
(*Anz. d. Wien. Akad.* 1895, 45) with the Phanodemus
who played a prominent part in the public life of Athens
after the Peace of Philocrates (346), we have inscriptional
evidence for his activities in four decrees. Three of these
(*SIG*³ 227, 287, 298) record the granting of civic crowns as
a reward for his services to the Boule and Demos between
343 and 329, and show his strong interest in the festivals
of Dionysus and Amphiaraus. In 329 he was elected to
assist in conducting the latter's festival, and a fourth
decree (ibid. 296) mentions his appointment as ἱεροποιός
to Delphi in 330. His interest in Attic cults and myths
found expression in an *Atthis* of at least nine books. He
also wrote an account of the island of Icus, which was
probably one of Callimachus' sources for his *Αἴτια*.

FHG i. 366.   G. L. B.

PHAON, a legendary ferryman in Lesbos, made so
handsome or given such a potent charm by Aphrodite,
that Sappho among others fell desperately in love with
him, finally jumping off the Leucadian rock for his sake.
The story apparently is a comedian's invention (see
Ovid, *Her.* 15, with Palmer's notes).   H. J. R.

PHARMAKOS, a kind of human scapegoat or embodiment of ill-luck. In Ionia a *pharmakos* was used when
some disaster (as famine) befell a community. He was
chosen for his ugliness, led to a certain place (presumably
outside the city), and there burned in pretence or reality
(Tzetzes, *Chil.* 5. 726 ff., with Hipponax, frs. 6 ff. Diehl,
quoted there). A like custom existed at Massilia (Petronius in Servius on *Aen.* 3. 57). In Athens, at the
Thargelia (q.v.), there were annually two *pharmakoi*,
one for the men and one for the women, called also
sybakchoi; they were sent out of the city, but no one
says they were killed (Harpocration and Photius s.v.).
Details are obscure.

See L. Deubner, *Attische Feste* (1932), p. 179 ff.; V. Gebhard, *Die
Pharmakoi in Ionien* (Munich Diss. 1926).   H. J. R.

PHARNABAZUS, satrap of Dascyleum *c.* 413-370
B.C. He co-operated with Sparta against Athens at
Abydos, Cyzicus, and Chalcedon, but in 408 encouraged
the Athenians to open negotiations with Darius, though
these broke down through the pro-Spartan sympathies
of Cyrus. In 404, at Lysander's request, he caused the
refugee Alcibiades to be assassinated. In the war with
Sparta which followed Cyrus' downfall Dascyleum was
ravaged by Dercyllidas (398) and again by Agesilaus,
whose famous meeting with Pharnabazus (Xen. *Hell.*
4. 1. 29 ff.) occurred in 395. He strongly supported the
revival of Persian sea-power, and shared the command
with Conon at Cnidos and in the later naval operations.
Recalled to Susa in 392, he was entrusted with the
reconquest of Egypt, but failed in two attempts (385-383
and 374), and died shortly afterwards.

T. Lenschau, *PW*, s.v. 'Pharnabazos (2)'.   D. E. W. W.

PHARNACES (1) **I**, king of Pontus, succeeded Mithridates III *c.* 185 B.C. He captured Sinope (*c.* 183) and
made war on Eumenes II of Pergamum. He refused to
come to terms at the instance of a Roman commission,
but he was defeated by a combination of kingdoms
and cities against him and compelled to surrender most
of his conquests (179). However, he kept Sinope and
united her colonies Cerasus and Cotyora to form the city

of Pharnacia. His diplomatic relations with cities and
principalities of south Russia show that he anticipated
Mithridates Eupator's dream of a Pontic empire (*IPE* i².
402); and an Attic decree attests his gifts to Athens. He
died in 169.

For bibliography *see* MITHRIDATES.   T. R. S. B.

PHARNACES (2) **II**, son of Mithridates the Great, led
the revolt that drove his father to death, and was granted
the Bosporan kingdom by Pompey. This he reduced to
order and enlarged. During the war between Caesar
and Pompey he seized Colchis, Lesser Armenia, and
some of Cappadocia, defeated Calvinus, Caesar's lieutenant, and overran much of Pontus, but was defeated
at Zela by Caesar himself, who announced his victory
with the words 'Veni, vidi, vici'. He escaped to his
kingdom but was killed in a rebellion.   T. R. S. B.

PHARSALUS, a city of Thessaly, dominating the tetrad
of Phthiotis (q.v.) and situated on the main road from
Larissa to central Greece. A hill overlooking the well-
watered plain supplied an impressive acropolis. The
Echecratidae of Pharsalus were among the most powerful
baronial houses of Thessaly, but they were expelled in
457 B.C. In the struggle between the Pheraean tyranny
and the rest of Thessaly, Pharsalus was several times
occupied by a garrison. Yet, thanks to the policy of its
leaders in furthering the intrigues of Philip, it became
the strongest city of Thessaly under the Macedonian
régime, and Pharsalian cavalry served Alexander well in
Asia. In the Lamian War, however, the Pharsalians
attempted to throw off the yoke of Macedon and paid
dearly for their failure.

In the neighbourhood were fought three important
battles, the victories of Pelopidas (364 B.C.) and Flamininus (197) at Cynoscephalae, and that of Caesar over
Pompey (48).

F. Stählin, *Das hellenische Thessalien* (1924), 135-43.   H. D. W.

PHASELIS, a Greek colony in Lycia, was founded
early in the seventh century B.C. by Rhodes. It was a
member of the Delian League (454-417 B.C.), surrendered
to Alexander, was ruled by the Ptolemies from 309 to
197, when it was captured by Antiochus III. From 169
it seems from its coinage to have been a member of the
Lycian League, but it seceded before the first century
B.C. began. In about 78 it was mulcted of its territory by
Servilius Isauricus for abetting the pirate king Zenicetes.
Under the Roman emperors it belonged to the Lycian
League.   A. H. M. J.

PHAYLLUS (1), an athlete from Crotona in south
Italy who gained three victories in the Pythian Games and
also fought at Salamis (480 B.C.) in a ship which he fitted
out at his own expense. He is said to have jumped 55
feet, but this is certainly a poetical exaggeration.
                                                 F. A. W.

PHAYLLUS (2), brother of Onomarchus (q.v.) and
Phocian commander in the Third Sacred War (q.v.).
He was defeated by Philip II of Macedon in Thessaly
(353 B.C.), but succeeded Onomarchus upon his death
in 352. Realizing Philip's intention to march south,
Phayllus united the Phocian people, occupied Thermopylae with a Phocian and mercenary army, and received
assistance from Sparta, Achaea, and Athens. After
Philip's withdrawal, Phayllus was able to concentrate on
the war with Thebes. In 351 he invaded the Peloponnesus
to assist Sparta against Thebes. He died of illness, and
was succeeded in his command by Phalaecus.
                                                 N. G. L. H.

PHEGEUS (Φηγεύς), in mythology, father of Arsinoë,
wife of Alcmaeon (q.v.); his sons murdered Alcmaeon
when he remarried (cf. CALLIRHOE; Apollod. 3. 87 ff.).

An undatable but probably late story (*Certam. Hom. et Hes.*, p. 249 Rzach) says Hesiod stayed for some time at his court and was put to death by his sons, who suspected him of seducing their sister.   H. J. R.

PHEIDIAS, *see* PHIDIAS.

PHEIDIPPIDES (so the best MSS. of Herodotus) or **Philippides** was the Athenian courier dispatched to solicit Spartan help upon the news of the Persian landing at Marathon (490 B.C.). He is credited with the exploit (which need not be regarded as fictitious) of having covered the distance (*c.* 150 miles) in two days. Legend connected him with the establishment of the Athenian cult of Pan.   P. T.

PHEIDON, king of Argos, changed the kingship into a tyranny (Aristotle, *Pol.* 1310^b). He made their measures (*metra*) for the Peloponnesians and interfered at Olympia (Hdt. 6. 127). Later writers add that he struck in Aegina the first Greek coins and dedicated to Hera the spits previously current, and recovered the 'lot of Temenus', the Dorian conqueror of north-east Peloponnesus, from whom they make him variously sixth, seventh, or tenth in descent (i.e. between 900 and 700 B.C.). Pausanias (6. 22. 2) dates the interference at Olympia Olympiad VIII (748), but a plausible emendation proposes XXVIII (668), and an earlier date is scarcely possible. Herodotus mentions a 'son' of Pheidon *c.* 575, and even if 'son' is loosely used it favours a date for Pheidon not earlier than early seventh century, the period of the first Aeginetan coins. The statements about Pheidon's striking them are probably genuine tradition, preserved perhaps in the Argive Heraeum, where a bundle of spits has been discovered which may be Pheidon's dedication. Herodotus' story of an occupation of Aegina by Argos that resulted in both adopting the distinctive standard of Aeginetan coins (5. 82–9) may be a distorted version of Pheidon's achievements. He would thus be the immediate predecessor of the tyrant dynasties of Corinth and Sicyon, whose rise *c.* 660–650 meant his own collapse (Nic. Dam. fr. 41).

Strabo 8. 358, 376, 355; Marmor Parium, 30; *Etym. Magn.* s.v. ὀβελίσκος. P. N. Ure, *Origin of Tyranny* (1922), 154 f.; H. T. Wade-Gery, *CAH* iii. 539 f., 761 f.; T. Lenschau, *PW*, s.v. 'Pheidon'.   P. N. U.

PHEME (φήμη), a rumour of unknown origin which springs up among the people at large; unprompted and unguided popular opinion. It is a god (Hesiod, *Op.* 763–4) and is never quite in vain (οὐ ... πάμπαν ἀπόλλυται).

PHERAE, a city of Thessaly, strategically situated on the southern verge of the plain of Pelasgiotis. When in possession of Pagasae (q.v.), Pherae controlled the export of Thessalian corn. Though prominent in mythology, it remained politically insignificant except during the half-century (*c.* 406–352 B.C.) when it was ruled by the family of Jason (*see* LYCOPHRON (1), JASON (2), ALEXANDER (5)). Philip of Macedon expelled the tyrants and terminated the prosperity of Pherae by depriving it of Pagasae.

Excavation has disclosed a badly preserved temple, apparently of Zeus Thaulios, dating from the sixth century but reconstructed in the fourth.

F. Stählin, *Das hellenische Thessalien* (1924), 104–7; Y. Béquignon, *Recherches archéologiques à Phères de Thessalie* (1937).   H. D. W.

PHERECRATEAN, *see* METRE, GREEK, III (8).

PHERECRATES, writer of Old Comedy. Anon. *Περὶ κωμ.* 8 says he began as one of Crates' actors and was afterwards his rival. Dramatic *floruit* about 430–410 B.C. (*IG* ii². 2325). The Ἄγριοι (420; cf. Pl. *Prt.* 327 d) seems to have depicted (?) two Athenian citizens who, tired of city life, retire to some uncivilized country. A

mention (fr. 19) of the faithlessness of Argos in the Αὐτόμολοι probably assigns that play to 417. The Δουλοδιδάσκαλος seems to have pictured a model household (Ath. 6. 262 b). The Κοριαννώ (named from a *meretrix*) satirized the drinking habits of prostitutes and contained a quarrel between a father and a son over one of them. The scene of the Κραπάταλοι ('Hell's pennies'; cf. Poll. 9. 83) was laid in Hades (schol. Ar. *Pax* 749). The Μυρμηκάνθρωποι contained the story of Deucalion's flood, and Zeus' repopulation of the earth by turning ants into men—a conflation of the Flood myth with the story of Zeus' repeopling by that method of Aegina after a plague (schol. Pind. *Nem.* 3. 13). The Πέρσαι contained an ἀγών between Wealth and Poverty. The Τυραννίς may have had a plot similar to that of Ar. *Eccl.* It also attacked the female toping (fr. 143). The Μεταλλῆς ('The Miners'; reference to mines at Laurium as entrance to Hades) depicts a woman returned from Hades and singing the praises of the life there. The Χείρων contains a conversation between Achilles, a pupil of Chiron, and Odysseus. The Ἰπνὸς ἢ παννυχίς may probably be assigned to 414.

Pherecrates, comparatively early though he was, seems to mark the transition to Middle Comedy in his avoidance of personal satire, and to have been inventive in plots (εὑρετικὸς μύθων; Anon. *Περὶ κωμ.* 8).

FCG ii. 252 ff.; CAF i. 145 ff.; Demiańczuk, *Suppl. Com.* 66 ff.   M. P.

PHERECYDES (1) of Syros (*fl. c.* 550 B.C.), mythologist and cosmologist, one of the earliest writers of Greek prose. Author of Ἑπτάμυχος, a work in which is described the origination of the world by three primal deities—Zeus (the supreme god and the upper heaven), Chronos or Kronos (the second god and the lower heaven), and Chthonie (the earth-goddess). Testimonia and frs. in Diels, *Vorsokr.*⁵ i. 43–51.

PW xix. 2025.   W. D. R.

PHERECYDES (2) of Athens, 'the genealogist' (later confused with (1), wrote copious *Histories* mythical and genealogical, commended by Dion. Hal. *Ant. Rom.* 1. 13. 1. Eusebius' date is 456 B.C. (*Ol.* 81. 1).

FHG i. 70, iv. 639b; FGrH i. 3.

PHIDIAS (Φειδίας), Athenian sculptor, born probably *c.* 490 B.C., and a reputed pupil of Hegias and of Ageladas. When he first became known is uncertain. But a recently published inscription (B. Meritt, *Hesperia* 1936, 355 ff.) proves that one of his most famous works, the Athena Promachos, was made in 460–450. This statue, in bronze, stood on the Acropolis near the Propylaea and rose to a height of some 30 feet. Part of its base survives, but there is no extant copy of the statue. It was the largest metal statue ever made at Athens.

Soon after its construction Phidias seems to have made another bronze, the Athena Lemnia, for colonists at Lemnos in 451–448. A fine Roman copy of an Athena without a helmet consisting of a head at Bologna and a body at Dresden has been identified as this statue. This attribution is most probable.

Our main knowledge of the style of Phidias rests in the marble sculptures of the Parthenon (constructed in 447–432). He was commissioned to design these by Pericles, and was responsible for the design of the sculptures and their composition. He made the models for the actual sculptors, who worked under him. Being primarily a bronze-worker, he almost certainly made models of clay and plaster, which were exactly reproduced by his sculptors. This close dependence of stone-carving on a clay or plaster model profoundly affected the development of Greek sculpture and made carving subordinate to modelling. It enabled sculptors to embark on highly elaborate adventures in the carving of drapery; and it is probably this new approach to carving which gave to

Phidias his reputation as an innovator. Certainly sculpture throughout Greece after 450 adopted the manner and style of Athenian sculpture, and all the regional styles vanished with the exception of the Peloponnesian (on which see POLYCLETUS). *See also* AGORACRITUS.

Phidias acquired much of his fame from his skill at chryselephantine statues. His Athena Parthenos survives to us in several tolerable copies, but his equally famous Zeus of Olympia is only a memory. As the Athena Promachos was finished by 450 and the Parthenon was built in 447–432 Phidias must have gone to Elis after 432. He went there in exile owing to political charges against him by the opponents of Pericles, and he died either there or in Athens some fifteen years later. He is said to have returned to Athens to stand his trial.

No work from his hand survives, but the Parthenon sculptures can be taken as representing his style correctly.

S. C.

PHILADELPHIA (1) (Φιλαδέλφεια), in the north-east of the Fayûm, was founded by Ptolemy II Philadelphus in connexion with the reclamation of the Moeris basin. The site, now *Darb Gerze*, was partly excavated for the Berlin Museum in 1908/9; the plan showed the normal Ptolemaic scheme of rectangular *insulae*, mainly of private houses, with a temple and possibly an official bureau. Considerable finds of papyri and small objects were secured by the excavators; others, before and after them, by native diggers, among these being the papers of Zenon (see APOLLONIUS 3). The cemetery, lying to the east, has produced many mummy-portraits: one was found in a house. The town seems to have been abandoned in the fourth century.

P. Viereck, *Philadelpheia* (1928), gives a full description and bibliography. J. G. M.

PHILADELPHIA (2), a city in Lydia, founded by Attalus II Philadelphus (159–138 B.C.) in the valley of the Cogamus, near the pass which carries the principal road from the Maeander to the Hermus valley, now *Alashehir*. It lies in a volcanic district, which produces excellent vines, and it has suffered much from earthquakes—for some time after A.D. 17 it lay in ruins. It was one of the 'Seven Churches' of the Apocalypse.

W. M. C.

PHILAE, see ELEPHANTINE.

PHILAMMON (Φιλάμμων), a musician, either wholly fabulous or so ancient as to be much overlaid with mythical details. Son of Apollo (Hesiod, fr. 111 Rzach + Pherecydes in schol. *Od.* 19. 432); invented maiden choirs (ibid.); first to celebrate the birth of Leto's twins and institute choruses at Delphi ([Plut.] *De mus.* 1132 a).

H. J. R.

PHILARGYRIUS, JUNIUS (5th c. A.D.), a commentator on Virgil; but there is some doubt about his real name (Filagrius?). His *Explanatio in Bucolica* is extant (ed. H. Hagen in Thilo's Servius, III. ii) in a longer and a shorter version, both of which contain Celtic glosses. The Berne scholia to the *Eclogues* and *Georgics* (ed. H. Hagen, *Jahrb. für class. Phil. Suppl.* 4, 1867, 749 ff.) which mention 'Iunilius Flagrius' as one of their sources, and the *Brevis expositio Georgicorum* (ed. H. Hagen in Thilo's Servius, III. ii) probably owe a great deal of their material to Philargyrius.

Cf. G. Funaioli, *Esegesi Virgiliana Antica* (1930); Teuffel, § 472, 9; Schanz-Hosius, § 248. 6. J. F. M.

PHILEMON (1) (Φιλήμων), in mythology, a good old countryman, who lived with his wife Baucis in Phrygia. Zeus and Hermes, coming to earth to test men's piety, were refused hospitality elsewhere but received by them.

The gods revealed their deity and warned them to climb a mountain. On arrival near the summit, they saw the district covered by a flood. They then became priest and priestess and finally were turned into trees.

Ovid, *Met.* 8. 618 ff.; cf. W. M. Calder in *Discovery* 1922, 207 ff.; J. E. Fontenrose in *Univ. of Cal. Pub. in Class. Phil.* 1945, 93 f.
H. J. R.

PHILEMON (2) (c. 361–262 B.C.), New Comedy poet, Menander's successful rival, of Syracuse (or of Soli in Cilicia—Suidas). The grant of Athenian citizenship to P. is attested by inscriptions (*IG* ii². 3073, 4266). In a long life (Suidas says 99 or 101 years), spent partly at Alexandria, he wrote ninety-seven comedies, of which sixty-four titles (including Λιθογλύφος, not in either Meineke or Kock) are known. Only two titles indicate mythological burlesque (Μυρμιδόνες, Παλαμήδης)—surprisingly few, for Apuleius (*Flor.* 16) designates P. 'a writer of Middle Comedy'. It seems that P.'s early plays (from c. 341 B.C., Λιθογλύφος) were in the Middle style, and only after Menander had gradually developed the type of New Comedy did P. write in the New style. Contemporary judgement awarded P., although of foreign origin, frequent victories over the Athenian Menander; but the final verdict of ancient critics ranked P. inferior to Menander (Quint. *Inst.* 10. 1. 72). Well over 200 fragments survive, illustrating P.'s thought and style, e.g. fr. 73, uselessness of tears; fr. 89, varieties of character; fr. 93, animals happy as compared with man; fr. 118, a god that hideth himself—cf. fr. 166. Like Menander, P. has many gnomic lines and couplets, often lacking Menander's terse precision (but cf., e.g., fr. 147). P. differs from Menander in detail—he uses less varied metres (only one certain passage in trochaic tetrameters, fr. 213), but more examples of the old dative in -οισι, -αισι.

Of P.'s technique in complete plays Latin adaptations by Plautus furnish evidence—*Mercator* (from Ἔμπορος), *Trinummus* (from Θησαυρός), *Mostellaria* (from Φάσμα). Certain additions by Plautus are recognizable, but doubt exists about others, e.g. the prologue by Luxuria and Inopia (Philemon's Ἀήρ, fr. 91, is a real prologue, whereas Luxuria expressly disclaims such a role, v. 16). *Mostellaria* probably gives the clearest impression of a comedy of the best period of Philemon (Φάσμα, later than 289 B.C.).

Like other comic poets, P. had a great admiration for Euripides: see the new fragment—Εὐριπίδης πού φησιν οὕτως, ὃς μόνος | δύναται λέγειν (life of Euripides by Satyrus), and cf. fr. 130.

In Athens P.'s comedies were revived after his death; in the second century A.D. a statue was erected there in his honour. But as an index of diminished popularity as compared with Menander, there are far fewer quotations from Philemon, and no papyrus certainly assigned to P. has been recovered in Egypt (*PSI* x. 1176 is possibly by P.).

FCG iv. 3 ff.; *CAF* ii. 478 ff., iii. 747 ff.; Demiańczuk, *Suppl. Com.* 71 ff. See C. A. Dietze, *De Philemone Comico* (1901).
W. G. W.

PHILEMON (3) **the Younger,** son of the celebrated Philemon (2), and himself a New Comedy poet; wrote fifty-four plays (none known to us by name) and won six victories.

FCG iv. 68; *CAF* ii. 540.

PHILEMON (4). A fourth Philemon, whether of the same family as (2) and (3) or not, is known from didascalic inscriptions as author of Μιλησία (*CAF* ii. 540), 183 B.C.

PHILEMON (5). In the middle of the fourth century B.C. lived a fifth Philemon, an actor, mentioned by Aeschines (1. 115) and Aristotle (see ANAXANDRIDES).

PHILEMON (6) of Aixonae (an Attic deme) (probably early 2nd c. B.C.), grammarian, edited Homer and compiled Ἀττικαὶ γλῶσσαι.

PHILEMON (7) of Athens (c. A.D. 200), an Atticist grammarian, wrote Σύμμικτα and Περὶ Ἀττικῆς ἀντιλογίας (? ἀναλογίας) τῆς ἐν ταῖς λέξεσιν.

PHILETAERUS (1), Middle Comedy poet, said by Suidas to be the son of Aristophanes, but this was disputed; however, allusions assign him to the earlier period of Middle Comedy. Of twenty-one comedies (Suidas) thirteen titles are preserved, four or five being mythological burlesques. Many references to living contemporaries.

FCG iii. 292 ff.; CAF ii. 230 ff. W. G. W.

PHILETAERUS (2) (c. 343–263 B.C.), son of Attalus of Tios and a Paphlagonian mother. First an officer of Antigonus (before 302), and next commander of Pergamum for Lysimachus, who kept a large treasure there, he deserted opportunely to Seleucus (282), and henceforth was ruler of Pergamum under Seleucid suzerainty. He may have enlarged his territories somewhat in his last years, but his best work was in defending Pergamum from the Galatian invaders of Asia Minor (278–276), and in founding the Attalid dynasty, which he did by adopting his nephews, one of whom (Eumenes) succeeded him. He was himself said to be a eunuch. G. T. G.

PHILETAS (rather than **Philitas**) of Cos, son of Telephus, born not later than 320 B.C., became tutor of Ptolemy II Philadelphus (born in Cos 309/8). Other pupils of P. were Zenodotus, Hermesianax, and (probably 275–271) Theocritus. Since P. is described as suffering from bad health and abnormally thin, it is unlikely that he lived to a great age. Certainly he was dead when Theocritus (after 270) wrote Id. 7. His grave seems to have been in Cos, where the Coans put up a bronze statue of him (Hermesianax, fr. 7. 75–8 Powell).

WORKS. (1) Verse. According to Suidas (s.v.) P. wrote 'Epigrams and Elegies and other works'. The sources cite five titles: Demeter, Hermes, Telephus, Epigrammata, Paegnia. The Demeter was a narrative elegy, recounting the goddess's wanderings, among them perhaps her visit to Cos (cf. schol. Theocr. 7. 5–9 f.). The Hermes was an epyllion, in which P. narrated the intrigue of Odysseus with the Aeolid Polymele (Parth. 2). The emotions of Polymele formed the central theme, but Odysseus told Aeolus the tale of his wanderings, though not in the Homeric order. The Telephus included a reference to the marriage of Jason and Medea. It is uncertain whether Paegnia (frs. 10 and 11) and Epigrammata (frs. 12 and 13) were separate works or alternative titles for one collection. Among the unassigned fragments fr. 22, a reference to the Bougonia of bees, has been thought to prove that P. anticipated Theocritus' treatment (7. 78–89) of the Comatas legend. In any case Theocritus acknowledged P. as his master (7. 39–41).

(2) Prose. Thirty fragments survive from a work entitled Miscellaneous Glosses or Miscellanea (Ἄτακτοι Γλῶσσαι, Ἄτακτα). This was a lexical compilation explaining rare words drawn from Homer (Aristarchus wrote a brochure 'Against Philetas') and various dialects, and also technical terms. The book became famous almost at once, being referred to in the Phoenicides of Straton (Ath. 9. 382 c). This passage already figures in a school anthology of c. 220, cf. Guéraud and Jouguet, Un Livre d'écolier du IIIᵉ siècle avant J.-C. (1938). [Strabo] 3. 168 assigns to P. a work with the title Ἑρμηνεία (? Interpretation) and quotes from it an elegiac couplet (fr. 17). If this was a prose work, the lines were cited by P. as an illustration and need not be by him.

Though Aelian (VH 10. 6) calls P. 'the poet of

hexameters', it was as an Elegist that he won lasting fame. He was included in the Canon of Elegists and, according to Quintilian (Inst. 10. 1. 58), in the opinion of most came second to Callimachus. Propertius and Ovid several times allude to him as their model in Elegy. In two passages (Tr. 1. 6. 2; Pont. 3. 1. 57–8) the latter refers to one Battis or Bittis as having been sung by P. This is confirmed by Hermesianax, fr. 7. 77–8, where the name is Bittis. It is uncertain whether this lady was P.'s wife or mistress, and in what kind of verse P. celebrated her charms. It is unlikely that P. wrote subjective love-elegies in the Roman manner, but tributes to Bittis may have been included in the Epigrams or Paegnia. P.'s great reputation as a poet among his younger contemporaries—besides Hermesianax and Theocritus, Callimachus too mentioned him in the preface to his Aetia and probably in fr. 254—may have been influenced by his position as the inaugurator of the scholar-poet tradition which the Alexandrians continued.

Texts: J. U. Powell, Collectanea Alexandrina (1925), 90–6; E. Diehl, Anth. Lyr. Graec. vi (1924), 209–14; A. Nowacki, Philitae Coi fragmenta poetica (1927); G. Kuchenmüller, Philetae Coi Reliquiae (1928). The last includes the prose fragments. General literature: v. Blumenthal, 'Philetas (1)', in PW xix. 2165–70; H. E. Butler and E. A. Barber, The Elegies of Propertius (1933), xxxix–xliv, xlvi–xlviii; A. A. Day, The Origins of Latin Love-Elegy (1938), 14–19. E. A. B.

PHILICUS (not Philiscus), of Corcyra, was one of the 'Tragic Pleiad' under Ptolemy II Philadelphus, also Priest of Dionysus at Alexandria and possibly Eponymous Priest of Alexander (Schubart from PHib. 30. 23). In the procession of 275–274 he marched at the head of the technitai (Ath. 5. 198 c, from Callixenus). Suidas credits P. with forty-two tragedies but no certain title or fragment survives (cf. TGF 819). As a lyric poet P. claimed in his Hymn to Demeter (Diehl, Anth. Lyr. Graec. vi. 296) to have invented the metrum Philicium (catalectic choriambic hexameters) used in that poem. Fragments from a Hymn to Demeter written in this metre have been published (by M. Norsa in Stud. Ital. N.S. v (1927), 87 ff.) from a papyrus and plausibly identified as belonging to P.'s poem. The fragments testify to the author's skilful craftsmanship and power of realistic description.

F. Schramm, Tragic. Graec. hellenist. aetatis fragmenta (1929); M. Gabathuler, Hellenistische Epigramme auf Dichter (1937), 16; Powell and Barber, New Chapters, Series I, 107; Series II, 61–2; Series III, 195–200; Stoessl, 'Philiskos (4)' in PW xix. 2379–81. E. A. B.

PHILINUS (1) of Cos (fl. c. 250 B.C.), a pupil of Herophilus, was called the founder of the Empirical School of Medicine. He wrote about difficult words in Hippocratic books and rejected any diagnosis based on the pulse— that is all the information which the fragments yield, except a few pharmacological precepts. If Philinus' doctrine is identical with that of his school—and the Empirical system, according to ancient sources, remained essentially unchanged—he must have denounced inquiry into hidden causes, explanation of physiological processes, systematic study of anatomy in dead or living bodies, and general theories concerning diseases. Relying only on his own experience and that of others, and on the conclusions resulting therefrom by analogy, he must have paid attention to factors which evidently influence illness and to the individual differences of people and localities.

Fragments, K. Deichgräber, Die Gr. Empirikerschule (1930). Galen on Medical Experience, ed. and transl. by R. Walzer (1944); review The Philosophical Review (1947), historical background and philosophical dependence of empiricism. H. Diller, PW xix. 2193. L. E.

PHILINUS (2) of Acragas, pro-Carthaginian historian of the First Punic War, writing probably in monograph form, was used by Polybius (1. 13–64) with Fabius Pictor, and perhaps by Diodorus (23–4).

FGrH ii, B, p. 897, BD, p. 598; F. W. Walbank, CQ 1945, 1 ff.

PHILIP (1) **II,** king of Macedon 359–336 B.C., laid the foundations of Macedonia's greatness. Internally, he unified Macedonia by removing the semi-independent principalities of upper Macedonia and incorporating territorial divisions in the army system, by favouring Greek culture, and by promoting urbanization and trade. The capture of Pydna, Methone, and Amphipolis, the exploitation of the Pangaeum mines (yielding 1,000 talents annually), and the alliance with the Chalcidian League favoured the economic growth of Macedonia; by incorporating Thrace, Chalcidice, and Thessaly under the royal mint he created an economic power capable of supporting a standing army and launching the expedition of Alexander. Under the stress of long warfare Philip forged a professional army with national spirit, which became the Grande Armée of Alexander; he developed siegecraft, trained the Macedonian infantry in the novel phalanx formation, employed the tactic of offensive and defensive wings, and bequeathed an able staff to Alexander. At Chaeronea the Macedonian power created by Philip overwhelmed Greece as decisively as it later overwhelmed Persia.

In the rise of Macedon Philip displayed diplomatic genius by exploiting the enmity between Athens and Chalcidice, the Social and Sacred Wars, and the dissension in Thrace and Thessaly. By making peace with Athens in 358 he covered his attack on Amphipolis and Pydna, and by allying with the Chalcidian League in 356 he captured Potidaea and defeated a Balkan coalition organized by Athens. By marriage alliances with the Molossian royal house and the Aleuadae of Larissa, and by annexing western Thrace he acquired sufficient strength to intervene in the Sacred War. He defeated Onomarchus, organized Thessaly, and penetrated to Thermopylae (352). He invaded and annexed Chalcidice, instigating a revolt against Athens in Euboea to synchronize with it (349–348). After these successes he concluded peace and alliance with Athens, and terminated the Sacred War (346). Invited by Isocrates to lead Greece against Persia, Philip endeavoured to conciliate Athens, until the opposition hardened under Demosthenes' leadership; frustrated at Perinthus and Byzantium by Athenian and Persian help, he used a diplomatic opening offered by the Delphic Amphictiony to force the issue at Chaeronea. He used his victory to give Greece a federal constitution under his leadership as elective Hegemon (the League of Corinth), and to ally it with Macedonia. He was assassinated at the age of 46, when about to lead the forces of Macedonia and Greece against Persia.

Of his contemporaries the nationalist Demosthenes saw in Philip a perfidious despot, the Panhellenist Isocrates and Ephorus a leader of Greece, and the individualist Theopompus the greatest man Europe had known. Modern scholarship, while divided in interpretation of his personality, is unanimous in appreciating his statesmanship, diplomacy, and generalship.

ANCIENT SOURCES: Diodorus, bk. 16, following Ephorus and Duris (A. Momigliano, *Rendiconti Istituto Lombardo* 1932), or Ephorus and Diyllus (N. G. L. Hammond, *CQ* 1937–8); Theopompus frs.; Isocrates, *Philippus*; passages in Attic Orators; Polyaenus; Justin, bks. 7–9; Hicks and Hill, *Greek Historical Inscriptions* (1901) no. 125 f.; Ἀρχ. Ἐφ 1925/6, 76; *Trans. Am. Phil. Ass.* 1934, 105; Seltman, *Greek Coins* (1933), ch. 12; West in *Num. Chron.* 1923, 169.
MODERN LITERATURE: D. G. Hogarth, *Philip and Alexander of Macedon* (1897); A. W. Pickard-Cambridge, *CAH* vi (1933), chs. 8–9; A. Momigliano, *Filippo il Macedone* (1934); K. J. Beloch, *Griech. Gesch.²* iii. 1, ch. 7 f.; U. Wilcken, *Alexander der Grosse* (Engl. Transl. 1932), ch. 2; J. Kromayer, *Schlachtenatlas* iv, with Text 36 f. (1926); N. G. L. Hammond, *Klio* 1938, 186 f.; F. Hampl, *Der König von Makedonien* (1934); F. R. Wüst, *Philipp II u. Griechenland 346–338 B.C.* (1938).   N. G. L. H.

PHILIP (2) **ARRHIDAEUS** (c. 358–317 B.C.), son of Philip II of Macedonia and Philinna of Larissa; his correct title was Philip III of Macedonia. Practically nothing is known of his life under Philip and Alexander, except that he was feeble-minded. His election as king,

jointly with Alexander's posthumous son Alexander IV (323), gave him no real power, but he was steered skilfully through the early struggles of the 'Successors' by his wife Eurydice, his name and authority being used by (successively) Perdiccas, Antipater, Polyperchon, and Cassander. He was ultimately captured and killed by Olympias, who desired the full succession for Alexander's son.
                              G. T. G.

PHILIP (3) **V** (238–179 B.C.), king of Macedon, son of Demetrius II and Phthia (Chryseis), was adopted by Antigonus III, and succeeded in summer 221. The Social War (220–217), in which the Hellenic Confederacy opposed Aetolia, Sparta, and Elis, brought him considerable renown, notwithstanding the intrigues of his ministers, headed by Apelles (executed 218), against Achaea. After the Peace of Naupactus (217), instigated by Demetrius of Pharos, he took up arms against Rome in Illyria, first by sea, later, after losing his fleet (214), by land; his treaty with Hannibal (215) defined spheres of operation. His brutal attacks on Messene in 215–214 alienated Achaea. An Aetolian alliance (211) and Attalus of Pergamum's collaboration now gave Roman forces in Greece an advantage; but Philip held out, and when they retired in 207, he sacked Thermum and forced terms on Aetolia (206). The war concluded with the favourable Peace of Phoenice (205). Philip then turned eastward: he employed a pirate, Dicaearchus, to obtain resources, and in 203/2 combined with Antiochus of Syria to plunder the possessions of the infant Ptolemy V. His terroristic methods, however, aroused Rhodes and Pergamum, who in 201 defeated him by sea off Chios, and by alarmist reports persuaded the Senate to declare war on him. This declaration Philip received at Abydos (200), after a campaign against Athens and the Thracian Chersonese; by September a Roman army was in Illyria. After two campaigns in Macedonia (199) and Thessaly (198) the Romans under Flamininus defeated him decisively at Cynoscephalae in Thessaly (197); and the subsequent peace settlement confined him to Macedonia, and exacted 1,000 talents indemnity, almost his whole fleet, and hostages, including his younger son, Demetrius. Until 189 Philip collaborated with Rome, and having sent help against Nabis (195) and Antiochus and Aetolia (192–189), made acquisitions in Thessaly. For facilitating the Scipios' advance through Macedon and Thrace he had his tribute remitted and Demetrius restored (190). Henceforward he concentrated on consolidating Macedon: finance was reorganized, populations were transplanted, mines reopened, central and local currencies issued. Accusations from his neighbours, however, led to constant Roman interference; and in 185 adverse decisions convinced him that his destruction was intended. In three campaigns (184, 183, 181), therefore, he extended his influence in the Balkans; meanwhile Demetrius' pro-Roman policy led to a quarrel with the crown-prince Perseus, and his own execution for treason (180). In 179, amidst an ambitious scheme for directing the Bastarnae against the Dardani, Philip died at Amphipolis.

A brilliant soldier, Philip was handicapped in politics by his unbalanced temperament. He maintained popular loyalty while combining the protection of his northern frontiers with expansionist programmes elsewhere; but he lacked a consistent constructive policy, hence his main significance is as a figure in the history of Roman expansion.

Ancient sources: Polybius; Livy, bks. 23–40; otherwise scattered. Modern literature: M. Holleaux, *Rome et la Grèce* (1921); *CAH* vii and viii; A. H. McDonald and F. W. Walbank, *JRS* 1937; F. Geyer, *PW*, s.v. 'Philippos V'; F. W. Walbank, *Philip V of Macedon* (1940).   F. W. W.

PHILIPPI, a town in the plain east of Mt. Pangaeus. Founded by Philip II of Macedon in 358/7 B.C., it replaced a former Thasian settlement named Crenides, and became the chief mining-centre in the Pangaeus goldfields. In 42 B.C. it was the scene of the double battle in which Antony defeated M. Brutus and Cassius. After the battle of Actium Octavian constituted it as a colony for partisans of Antony evicted from Italy. Philippi was the first European town to hear a Christian missionary (St. Paul). For the battle see Appian 4. 105–31 (good description of the site); Dio Cass. 47. 42–9.

P. Collart, *Philippes* (1937).   M. C.

PHILIPPIDES, New Comedy poet, an Athenian, who won a victory in 311 B.C. Of forty-five comedies (Suidas) we know fifteen titles—one a mythological burlesque, Ἀμφιάρεως. As a friend of Lysimachus, king of Thrace, P. possessed great influence, and boldly denounced the sacrilege of Demetrius Poliorcetes (fr. 25, *c.* 300 B.C.). Fr. 9, the ways of *nouveaux riches*; fr. 18, Euripides quoted for consolation in trouble.

FCG iv. 467 ff.; *CAF* iii. 301 ff.   W. G. W.

PHILIPPIDES, *see also* PHEIDIPPIDES.

PHILIPPOPOLIS, a city of Thrace, commanding the main road from Macedonia to the Black Sea. It was founded by Philip II of Macedon in 342 B.C., and reoccupied by Philip V in 183, as a military outpost beyond Mt. Rhodope; but in either case it soon reverted to native rule. Under Roman rule it served as the meeting-place of the provincial parliament of Thrace, and as a stronghold against Gothic invaders (A.D. 250–70). From the mixed character of the population which Philip II settled there it obtained the nickname of 'Poneropolis' ('Crookham').   M. C.

PHILIPPUS (1), JULIUS VERUS, Roman emperor A.D. 244–9, a native of Arabia, succeeded Timesitheus as Praetorian Prefect and connived at Gordian's assassination (*see* GORDIAN III). After concluding peace with Persia he reached Rome with his son in 244, where he established good relations with the Senate. A great victory over the Carpi in 247 was followed by the elevation of his son to the rank of Augustus and by the celebrations in the ensuing April of the thousandth birthday of Rome. But in the summer the Goths invaded Moesia and pretenders arose in the Balkans and the East. Decius was appointed to the Danubian command and his popularity with the troops led to his acclamation as emperor. Despite assurances of loyalty Philip mistrusted Decius' sincerity. He and his son were killed in a battle at Verona.

Later tradition honoured Philip as the first Christian emperor, but it is questionable whether his indulgence to the Faith entailed his conversion.

Zosimus 1. 19–22; Zonaras 12. 19; Salisbury and Mattingly, *JRS* xiv; E. Stein, *PW*, s.v. 'Julius Philippus'; Parker, *Roman World*, 150–7; *CAH* xii, ch. 2, § 5.   H. M. D. P.

PHILIPPUS (2) of Opus (*fl. c.* 350 B.C.), mathematician and astronomer, pupil of Plato. An ancient tradition (D.L. 3. 37) describes him as having edited Plato's *Laws* for publication and written the *Epinomis*. It is still in doubt whether the latter was the work of Plato or of a pupil.

PW xix. 2351; H. C. G. Friedrich, *Stylistische Untersuchung d. Epinomis d. Philippos von Opus* (1927).   W. D. R.

PHILIPPUS (3) of Thessalonica, who lived in Rome, and was probably a rhetor, published about A.D. 40 a *Garland* of Greek epigrams written since Meleager, with a shockingly dull preface imitating him (*see* ANTHOLOGY). Some eighty of his own survive in the *Anthology*, mostly imitated from earlier authors; his vocabulary is rich and affected, and he tends to cultivate point at all costs.

C. Cichorius, *Röm. Stud.* ch. viii. 9 (1922), dating the *Garland*.
                                                      G. H.

PHILIPPUS, *see also* MARCIUS.

PHILISCUS (1) (*c.* 400–325 B.C.), rhetorician from Miletus, who came to Athens and studied under Isocrates. His works included a Μιλησιακός and an Ἀμφικτυονικός (probably political brochures) and a life of the orator Lycurgus.

PW xix. 2. 2384–7.

PHILISCUS (2), Middle Comedy poet, to whom Suidas assigns six plays (five being mythological burlesques; fourteen lines in a papyrus, *PSI* x. 1175, are doubtfully attributed to Διὸς γοναί).

FCG iii. 579 f.; *CAF* ii. 443 f.

PHILISCUS (3) of Aegina (4th c. B.C.), came under the teaching of Diogenes of Sinope at Athens and joined the Cynic school. He is said to have taught Alexander the Great, but this is doubtful. Seven tragedies were ascribed to him in antiquity, and the ascriptions may well be correct.

PW xix. 2. 2382.   W. D. R.

PHILISCUS (4) of Thessaly (*c.* A.D. 190–220), rhetorician, professor of rhetoric at Athens under Caracalla.

PW xix. 2. 2887.

PHILISCUS, *see also* PHILICUS.

PHILISTION of Locri, physician, a contemporary of Plato (*c.* 427–347), according to Callimachus the teacher of Eudoxus, illustrious in his art according to Plutarch, was the main representative of the Sicilian School of medicine. Like Empedocles he assumed four elements, fire, air, water, earth, which he equated with the qualities hot, cold, moist, dry, and considered responsible for all bodily processes. Respiration he regarded as the cooling of innate heat. His interest in anatomy may be inferred from the fact that the name ἀετοί for certain veins was attributed to him. In the physiology of drinking he agreed with Plato, as Plutarch relates (2. 1047 c). Diseases he explained by the excess or deficiency of the four elements, by external causes like wounds, climate, nourishment, or by changes in the bodily constitution, especially by difficulties of breathing, which he believed to occur all over the body. His book on dietetics must have been famous (half of the fragments preserved come from it, 9–16).

Fragments, M. Wellmann, *Die Fragmente d. Sikelischen Ärzte* (1901). Influence of P., Wellmann, *Hermes* (1900). Influence on Plato, A. E. Taylor, *A Commentary on Plato's Tim.* (1928), 9, 599, n. 1; cf. F. Cornford, *Plato's Cosmology* (1937), 334; W. Jaeger, *Diokles v. Karystos* (1938), 9 f.; 212, n. 1 (P. identical with the Philistion mentioned in the second Platonic Letter?). H. Diller, *PW* xix. 2405.   L. E.

PHILISTUS of Syracuse, Sicilian historian who in his youth saw Gylippus rescue Syracuse (414 B.C.), and took a prominent part in supporting Dionysius I and II. He assisted the former to become general and tyrant(405), and served as his counsellor and governor of Syracuse, but later quarrelled with him and was banished. Recalled by Dionysius II, he expelled Dion (366), and was appointed admiral. He failed to intercept Dion's expedition from Greece (357), and committed suicide after a naval defeat by Dion (356).

The history (Σικελικά) was written during his exile. There were at least twelve books, of which the first seven dealt with Sicilian affairs from the earliest times until 406. Philistus was a competent historian and imitator of Thucydides. The charge of flattery of the tyrants should be discounted in view of the characteristic Greek refusal to recognize their achievements.

FHG i. 185.   G. L. B.

PHILO, *see* PHILON, PUBLILIUS (2), JEWISH GREEK LITERATURE.

PHILO JUDÆUS, *see* PHILON (4).

PHILOCHORUS of Athens, the most famous of the atthidographers. Sprung from a distinguished family, he held the official positions of μάντις καὶ ἱεροσκόπος in 306 B.C. The *Atthis* reached 261/260, and P. was executed shortly afterwards by Antigonus Gonatas as a partisan of Ptolemy II Philadelphus.

Philochorus' religious duties implied a close knowledge of Athenian festivals and cults, and this was linked with an interest in the myths and history of Attica. His large literary output was mostly concerned with books on religious antiquities and customs, and is sparsely represented in the extant fragments. His most important work was an *Atthis* in seventeen books. Unlike most atthidographers, and perhaps because the material had already appeared in other works, he dealt summarily with early Athenian history (bks. 1–2), passed on to the constitutional problems of Solon and Cleisthenes (bk. 3) and the fifth century (bk. 4), and devoted some two-thirds of his narrative to a detailed survey of contemporary politics. The last seven books are almost entirely lost, probably because they had no interest for Alexandrine scholars, who used him chiefly in explanation of the Attic orators.

The style of the *Atthis* is plain and unattractive, but its chronological arrangement by kings and archons and the evidence of an eyewitness who was also interested in genuine research established P.'s position as an historian. He produced an abridged version which may be identical with the 'Atthis against Demon', a polemical treatise criticizing the earlier atthidographer.

FHG i. 384. G. L. B.

PHILOCLES, nephew of Aeschylus, wrote 100 plays and defeated Sophocles on the occasion when the latter produced the *Oedipus Tyrannus* (Suidas s.v., Arg. Soph. *OT*), but is frequently attacked by the comic poets (e.g. Ar. *Vesp.* 461; *Thesm.* 168; Cratin. fr. 292). His unpleasant style earned him the nicknames Χολή (Gall) and Ἁλμίων (son of Brine). His plays included a tetralogy, the Πανδιονίς, on the story of Tereus (schol. Ar. *Av.* 281).

TGF 759–60. A. W. P.-C.

PHILOCOMUS, *see* VETTIUS (1).

PHILOCRATES, an Athenian statesman who initiated the peace negotiations with Philip II of Macedon after the fall of Olynthus (348 B.C.). He headed the first peace embassy and secured a place on it for Demosthenes, who had defended him in court (347–346). On the embassy's return Philocrates proposed, and finally carried, a peace and alliance with Philip. He headed a second embassy to obtain Philip's signature, returned to carry a proposal to implement the alliance, despite Demosthenes' opposition, and served on two more embassies to Philip. Prosecuted in 343 for corruption in the peace negotiations, Philocrates absconded and was condemned to death; his prudent policy had become unpopular. N. G. L. H.

PHILOCTETES, in mythology, son of Poeas (*Od.* 3. 190) and leader of the seven ships from Methone and other towns of that region (*Il.* 2. 718), but left behind in Lemnos suffering from a snake-bite (ibid. 722–3). Homer says no more of him but that he returned safely from Troy (*Od.* ibid.); the *Cypria* (in Proclus) add that while the Greeks were on their way to Troy they sacrificed in Tenedos and there Philoctetes was bitten and left behind because of the stench of his wound. The *Little Iliad* continues the story. Odysseus captured Helenus, the Trojan prophet, and learned from him that Troy could not be taken unless Philoctetes was present; he therefore went to Lemnos with Diomedes and brought him. Tragedy (the *Philoctetes* of Sophocles survives, and plays on the subject were written also by Aeschylus and Euripides) gives further details. Philoctetes had the bow and arrows of Heracles (q.v.) given him (Soph. op. cit.

801 ff.) or his father (Apollod. 2. 160) for lighting the pyre on Mt. Oeta. Without these Troy could not fall. He was therefore persuaded or tricked into coming (in Soph. Odysseus' companion is Neoptolemus, q.v., and his honesty produces complications in the plot), healed on arrival by Machaon (q.v.; *Little Iliad*), and there killed Paris. Since he had hero-cults in more than one place (near Sybaris and at Macella, Lycophron, 919 ff., cf. [Aristotle] *Mir. Ausc.* 107) it was naturally said that he had wandered to Magna Graecia after leaving Troy and founded cities there; cf. Apollodorus in Strabo 6. 254.

H. J. R.

PHILODAMUS, of Scarphea, author of a Paean to Dionysus discovered at Delphi. The poem, of some 150 lines in Aeolic metres, describes the birth and early travels of Dionysus and gives directions for his cult. Date 335–334 B.C.

Text: E. Diehl, *Anth. Lyr. Graec.* ii. 252–7; J. U. Powell, *Coll. Alex.* (1925), 165–71. Criticism: H. W. Smyth, *Greek Melic Poets*, 525 ff.; Powell and Barber, *New Chapters* i. 42–3. C. M. B.

PHILODEMUS (c. 110–c. 40/35 B.C.), born at Gadara, died probably at Herculaneum; he came to Rome c. 75 B.C. as a consequence of the First Mithridatic War and enjoyed there the favour and powerful friendship of the Pisones. One of them, L. Calpurnius Piso Caesoninus (*cos.* 58), who was probably his disciple, presented him with a magnificent villa at Herculaneum. Cicero's somewhat ironical praise of Philodemus (*Pis.* 28. 68 ff.) shows that he was already well known in 55 B.C. His connexions with Piso brought Philodemus the opportunity of influencing the brilliant young students of Greek literature and philosophy who gathered around him and Siron at Herculaneum and Naples. In 44/43 B.C. he strongly opposed the policy of Antony, and aroused republican feelings in several of his disciples, as is shown by Varius' *De morte*, Virgil's *Appendix*, and the military career of Horace. Although his prose work was dull and colourless, Philodemus greatly surpassed the average literary standard of the Greek Epicureans. In his elegant but often indecent love epigrams, some twenty-five of which are preserved in the *Anthologia Palatina*, he displays taste and ingenuity worthy of his fellow-citizen Meleager. The success of these poems is proved by the allusions to, and imitations of, them in several passages of Horace and Ovid. Although Cicero seems to imply that Philodemus' main activity was poetry, he devoted himself chiefly to the task of popularizing Greek philosophy, which he dealt with systematically and historically (in his treatise σύνταξις τῶν φιλοσόφων, comprising an outline of the doctrines of Greek thinkers viewed from the standpoint of Epicureanism, in ten or more books). His work covered a wide field, including psychology, theology, logic, ethics, aesthetics, and rhetoric. Particularly remarkable was his theory of art, which he conceived as an autonomous activity of the mind, independent of morals and logic, and determined not by its content, but by its aesthetic value. Though scarcely original as a philosopher, Philodemus achieved his great ambition of influencing the most learned and distinguished Romans of his age. No prose work of Philodemus was known until several rolls of papyri, charred but partly legible, containing fragments of his writings, were discovered among the ruins of Piso's villa at Herculaneum.

TEXTS: No complete edition of Philodemus has hitherto been published. His epigrams were edited with a commentary by G. Kaibel (1885). His prose works, apart from the general editions of the Herculaneum papyri, in part appeared in the Teubner series (Sudhaus, Olivieri, Jensen, Kemke, Wilke), and in part were edited elsewhere by Gomperz (*Herk. Stud.* i–ii, 1865–6), Crönert (*Kolotes u. Menedemus*, 1906), Diels (*Abh. Berl. Akad.*, 1915–16), Jensen (1923, Weidmann series), and A. Vogliano in *Epicuri et Epicureorum Scripta* (1928). A lexicon Philodemeum (I) is being published by C. J. Vooys (1934).
GENERAL LITERATURE: F. Susemihl, *Gesch. Griech. Litt. Alex.* ii. 267 ff.; Ueberweg-Praechter, *Grundriss*, 12. 439 ff.; R. Philippson,

PW xix, 2444 ff.; W. Crönert, *Memoria Graeca Herculanensis* (1903); C. Cichorius, *Röm. Studien* viii. 1 (1922). For Philodemus' life and villa, D. Comparetti, *Mélanges Chatelain* (1910), 118 ff.; for his theory of art, A. Rostagni, *Atene e Roma* (1920); *Riv. Fil.* 1923–4; introduction to Rostagni's commentary on Horace's *Ars* (1930); *PW* xix. 2444.   P. T.

PHILOLAUS of Croton, Pythagorean contemporary with Socrates. Works: Περὶ φύσιος, Βάκχαι (possibly the same work). The authenticity of the frs. has been much discussed, and the question cannot be regarded as settled.

See Zeller–Mondolfo, *Filosofia dei Greci* ii. 304–8, 367–82. Testimonia and frs. in Diels, *Vorsokr.*⁵ i. 398.   W. D. R.

PHILOLOGUS, see ATEIUS.

PHILOLOGY, COMPARATIVE, or, as it is now better named, Comparative Linguistics, is a modern study. The Greeks were little interested in languages other than their own, and without comparison with other languages but little progress could be made even in Greek. The Sophists, and later Plato, dabbled in language and made attempts at etymology that were crude and often ridiculous. The Stoics, with their special interest in the *etymon*, also pursued this study, which in due course was taken up by the Romans, notably Aelius Stilo and Terentius Varro. But no certain principles of linguistic development were yet laid down; there was no phonetic, no clear discrimination between root, stem, and termination, and no proved method in etymology (q.v.). Thus *vulpes* is derived from *volo*+*pes*, i.e. 'flying-foot', and *lepus* from *levi-pes*, i.e. 'light-foot', although *ped-*, the stem of *pes*, is not present in *vulpes -is* or *lepus -oris*. Other fantastic etymologies in Varro's *De Lingua Latina* are *cervi* (<*gervi*: 'quod gerunt cornua'), *aper* (<*asper*), *aries* (<*ara*), *pecus* (<*pes*). Another type is the famous *lucus a non lucendo*: cf. 'caelum a celando quod apertum est'. Sometimes they even assumed hybrid formations e.g. *caelebs* (<*caelum*+βίος; i.e. a bachelor has a heavenly life!).

2. The Romans, then, scarcely improved upon the Greeks and throughout the Middle Ages (see Isidore's *Etymologiae*) linguistic study remained just as the Romans had left it. The rediscovery of learning at the Renaissance and the greatly increased travel made possible by geographical exploration extended the knowledge of languages, but no real advance was made in the understanding of linguistic development and relationships. There was much speculation about the original language of mankind and because of scriptural tradition it was commonly believed that man's original language was Hebrew, from which by some process of unexplained change and decay all other tongues were derived. But in the eighteenth century, when the British occupation of India made Sanskrit known to Western scholars, linguistic studies were revolutionized; for Sanskrit was particularly suited both by its structure and its ancient grammatical tradition to reveal even upon a cursory examination its relationship to the languages of Europe. In 1786 Sir William Jones in a paper to the Asiatic Society of Bengal declared that both in the roots of verbs and in grammatical forms Sanskrit bore a stronger affinity to Greek and Latin than could possibly have been produced by accident, and probably Gothic and Celtic were similarly connected also. He further suggested that they were all derived from 'some common source which, perhaps, no longer exists'. Here in embryo is what is now called the Indo-European family of languages, and it has been the task of succeeding scholars to fill in the outlines and extend the limits of the sketch presented by Jones. They no longer admit the possibility that original Indo-European exists or even that it can be reconstructed, as Schleicher attempted, but ever since Jones's pronouncement they have been working out in detail the historical developments and the comparative relationships not merely of the many members (and their

dialects) of the Indo-European family but of the other great linguistic families, the Semitic, the Finno-Ugrian, etc., as well.

3. While the German Franz Bopp (1791–1867) has often been called 'the father of Comparative Philology', the first of the great specialists in this study was undoubtedly the Dane, Rasmus Rask (1787–1832). In 1811 the Danish Academy of Science held a prize competition on the origin of the ancient Scandinavian language and its relation to the Germanic dialects, and in his brief essay entitled *Investigation on the Origin of Old Norse* Rask clearly showed that Germanic, Baltic, Greek, Latin, Armenian, 'and probably Indian and Iranian' are related languages, while Eskimo, Celtic, Basque, Finno-Ugrian, and Semitic are unrelated. The Napoleonic Wars had cut England off from the Continent and impeded the study of Sanskrit, and, when Rask wrote, Sanskrit and Avestan were still practically unknown in western Europe; hence his doubts about Indian and Iranian. He was wrong in excluding Celtic; but by 1818 he corrected that, though he still excluded Albanian, which, however, had been so badly preserved that it was not established as Indo-European until the end of the century by Gustav Meyer (1850–1900). It is also Rask's great triumph that he clearly perceived and enunciated the sound-changes that exist between the classical and the Germanic languages and also the later consonantal changes in High German, a discovery which is usually ascribed to Jacob Grimm (1785–1863), who has had the honour of having it named Grimm's Law. But Rask's essay, written in Danish, was not easily accessible to scholars, and so the first detailed Indo-European grammar came to be written by Bopp, who in 1816 published a short treatise on *The Verbal Inflection of Sanskrit compared with Greek, Latin, Persian, and Germanic*. Bopp had the great advantage of really knowing Sanskrit, and his analyses of verbal morphology were a tremendous advance, in spite of the fact that he thought he could find some part or trace of the verb 'to be' in all verbal terminations. Thus in all *-s* endings he sought the root *es- s-* (Latin *es-t, s-unt*). In phonology Bopp was much inferior to Rask; but just as Sanskrit with its clear structure separating root, stem, and termination had brought about the admirable clarity of Indian grammar, so it produced Comparative Grammar when it became widely known among European scholars. Bopp's work provided a great stimulus to further study such as Rask's without a real knowledge of Sanskrit could not do, and in that sense Bopp is the founder of Comparative Philology.

4. Two periods are clearly discernible in modern Comparative Philology, the earlier stretching from Rask to Schleicher (1821–68), and the later commencing in 1876 and continuing until the present day. August Fick (1833–1916) shares in both; for his earlier work belongs to the pre-Brugmann era, while his later work participates in the new method and outlook. Next to Rask comes Grimm, whose great contribution was his *German Grammar*, a vast work in which he made a detailed comparison of all the Germanic dialects and by which he became 'the father of historical grammar'. In it he formulated with copious examples the sound-changes which bear his name. In 1833 Bopp began to follow up his first success by a *Comparative Grammar of Sanskrit, Zend, Greek, Latin, Lithuanian, Gothic, and German*, and in a subsequent edition he included also Celtic and Albanian. But his treatment of sounds was still very weak and the next advance in phonology was made by August Pott (1802–87) in his *Etymologische Forschungen*, a comparative Indo-European grammar with the emphasis on phonology. Pott displays real understanding of sound-change and insists on the historical character of sound-laws. But like his predecessors he has no idea that these laws, when properly formulated, admit of no exceptions. In this he was followed by Georg Curtius

(1820–85), Schleicher, and Fick. They all proclaim their strict adherence to sound-laws; but Curtius differentiated between 'regular sound-changes' and 'sporadic sound-changes', while Schleicher's laws were sufficiently flexible to enable him to follow some of Bopp's worst mistakes. Curtius did his best work as a teacher in making Comparative Philology known to a wider public; but he also succeeded in breaking down Grimm's triad of three original vowels *a, i, u*, and showing that *e* was also Indo-European and that *e* of Latin *ĕdo* was older than *a* of Sanskrit *admi*. More important than Curtius was Schleicher, who, besides doing valuable work in Slavonic and Baltic, brought organization into linguistic study by his excellent *Compendium of Comparative Indo-European Grammar* (1861–2, 4th ed. 1876). Unlike Bopp, Schleicher is strong in phonology and his grammar is clearly written and well arranged. But a decisive change was approaching both in outlook and method; and Fick, the last of the scholars of the earlier period, overlaps into the later. The decisive year for the transformation in Indo-European linguistics was 1876. Schleicher was already dead, and Curtius steadfastly opposed, but in vain, the new ideas; but Fick, whose *Wörterbuch der indogermanischen Sprachen* first appeared in 1868 and shows the old standpoint, had by the time of the fourth edition in 1890 been won over completely to the new.

5. The difficulty before 1876 had been the great uncertainty and irregularity of the same vowels and consonants as represented in the various languages; but a series of brilliant discoveries in the seventies by the Italian Ascoli (1829–1907), the Danes Thomsen (1842–1927) and Verner (1846–96), the Frenchman de Saussure (1857–1913), and the German Brugmann (1849–1919) brought order out of chaos. In 1870 Ascoli attacked the *k* problem which had baffled both Bopp and Schleicher and showed that there was not only one *k* series in the parent language but three quite distinct series represented, for example, in the initial sounds of Latin *centum, caecus, quis*. Ascoli, however, wrongly thought that the Sanskrit palatals were original: so his discovery was retarded and only two of his series were accepted, and the existence of three had to be proved again in 1890 by Bezzenberger (1851–1922) and Osthoff (1847–1909). In 1875 Verner published his famous article wherein he established Verner's Law, which explains the apparent exceptions to Grimm's Law. In the following year Brugmann in defiance of Curtius published his epoch-making article on Sonant Nasals (e.g. Gk. τατός, Lat. *tentus*<Ind. Eur. *tṇtós*; Gk. δέκα, Lat. *decem*<Ind. Eur. *dekṃ*; Gk. πόδα, Lat. pedem<Ind. Eur. *pe/odṃ*). This article greatly advanced the knowledge of Vowel Gradation or Ablaut, which received its most inspired treatment in de Saussure's 'Treatise on the primitive vowel-system of the Indo-European languages' in 1879. Brugmann's work was strongly opposed by Curtius and others; and thence arose the furious struggle on the strictness of Phonetic Laws to which Brugmann and his followers, nicknamed the Junggrammatiker, declared that there were no exceptions. The two great forces operating in linguistic change are Phonetic Law and Analogy, and for long it was so strongly held that the former admitted of no exceptions that in recent years the extreme position of Brugmann's school has been again challenged by Hermann's penetrating *Lautgesetz und Analogie* (1931). To Brugmann we also owe the authoritative survey of Indo-European linguistics, the *Grundriss* (2nd ed. 1897–1911). In this vast work the Syntax was undertaken by Delbrück (1842–1922), whose contribution in this sphere has been quite outstanding. Another excellent work on syntax, particularly of Latin and Greek, is the *Vorlesungen über Syntax* (1924–8), of Wackernagel, who is also the author of the first *Comparative Sanskrit Grammar*. In the study of Meaning or Semasiology the pioneer work is the *Essai de Sémantique* (4th ed. 1908) of Michel Bréal (1832–1915), a study which now has a journal of its own, *Wörter und Sachen* (1909–). An interesting offshoot of Indo-European Comparative Philology is Indo-European Prehistory, which deals with the original habitat and civilization of the undivided Indo-European community. Outstanding on this subject is the *Sprachvergleichung und Urgeschichte* (3rd ed. 1907) of Otto Schrader (1855–1919). On the general principles of language the standard work is the *Prinzipien der Sprachgeschichte* (5th ed. 1920) of Hermann Paul (1846–1921).

6. In this brief sketch little has been said of phonetics, inscriptions, or linguistic geography, and many famous scholars have not been mentioned. But an excellent account of their work is contained in *Linguistic Science in the 19th Century* by Pedersen and Spargo (Harvard University Press, 1931).

7. For the classical languages the reader should consult A. Meillet, *Introduction à l'étude comparative des langues indo-européennes*[8] (1937); A. Meillet and J. Vendryes, *Traité de grammaire comparée des langues classiques*[2] (1927); C. D. Buck, *Comparative Grammar of Greek and Latin* (U.S.A. 1937). P. S. N.

PHILOMELA (Φιλομήλα). Pandion king of Athens had two daughters, Procne (Πρόκνη) and Philomela, of whom the former was married to his ally, Tereus king of Thrace, son of Ares. Tereus, pretending that Procne was dead, asked that Philomela might be sent to him, and on her arrival raped or seduced her and then cut out her tongue to prevent her telling. She contrived to send her sister a piece of embroidery on which she had woven her story. Procne found her and took revenge on Tereus by serving him at a meal with the flesh of his and her child Itys. Finding this out, he pursued the women, but the gods turned him into a hoopoe, Procne into a nightingale, and Philomela into a swallow (a later tradition, represented in Latin authors, reverses these last two).

Apollod. 3. 193 ff.; Ovid, *Met*. 6. 424 ff. H. J. R.

PHILOMELUS, Phocian commander in the Third Sacred War (q.v.). Elected *strategos autokrator* of Phocis at the threat of war, he seized Delphi (summer 356 B.C.), raised 5,000 mercenaries, defeated the Locrians and Boeotians in the winter, and allied Phocis with Athens and Sparta. In autumn 355, when the Amphictiony declared a Sacred War on Phocis, Philomelus used temple funds to raise 10,000 men; in 354 he defeated the Thessalians and defended southern Phocis until he was defeated and committed suicide near Neon (late autumn 354). An able diplomatist and general, he based Phocian power on mercenaries and the Delphic monies.

N. G. L. H.

PHILON (1) of Eleusis (4th c. B.C.), architect. He designed the arsenal at Piraeus, and added a porch to the Telesterion at Eleusis. The former building was destroyed by Sulla, and no vestiges of it have been identified; but we possess a detailed specification (*IG* ii. 1054). His books on the arsenal, and on the proportions of sacred buildings (Vitruv. 7 praef.), have not survived. H. W. R.

PHILON (2) of Byzantium (early 2nd c. B.C.), mechanician, followed in the footsteps of Ctesibius, and his works were used by Heron. He wrote a Μηχανικὴ σύνταξις; a fragment on engines of war is preserved (ed. H. Diels and E. Schramm in *Abh. Berl. Akad.* 1918, 19), and, in Arabic and a Latin translation from the Arabic, some chapters on *Pneumatica* (V. Rose, *Anecdota graeca* ii. 299–313; Heron, *Opera* 1. 458 f.). Heron in his *Automata*, c. 20, alludes to a setting by Philon of the 'Nauplius story', which presumably came from *Automata* by Philon; Philon's explanations were apparently not much in advance of Aristotle's standpoint; the theoretical basis is much better put by Heron. Philon is credited with a solution of the problem of finding two mean proportionals; it has a slight variation from, but is equivalent to, solutions attributed to Apollonius and Heron.

T. H.

PHILON(3) of Larissa in Thessaly (Stob. *Ecl.* 2. 38, etc.) (160/59–80 B.C.), founder of the so-called fourth Academy (Sext. Emp. *Pyr.* 1. 220; etc.). He succeeded Clitomachus as president of the Academy 110/9. On the outbreak of the Mithridatic War in 88 he fled to Rome (Cic. *Brut.* 306) where he became famous, and taught important pupils and hearers, amongst whom was Cicero (*Acad. Index Herc.* col. 33. 3 f.).

Philon held that things were not comprehensible in the Stoic sense but that they were knowable in themselves (Sext. Emp. op. cit. 235). So he led Academic scepticism a step farther away from Carneades towards the teaching of his pupil and opponent Antiochus of Ascalon.

E. Zeller, *Eclectics*, Engl. Transl., 75 f.; A. Goedeckemeyer, *Gesch. des Skeptizismus*, 103 f.; Ueberweg-Praechter, *Grundriss*[12], 469 f.; *PW* xix. 2535. K. O. B.

PHILON (4) commonly known as **Philo Judaeus** (*c.* 30 B.C.–A.D. 45), spent all his life in his native city of Alexandria and became head of its Jewish community, which he represented on the delegation sent to Rome in A.D. 39–40 to ask exemption from the duty of worshipping the emperor. This is the only incident from the life of P. of which anything is known; it is related at length in his pamphlet *Legatio ad Gaium*. Here and in his *In Flaccum*, a similar treatise of earlier date, P. tries to show that God is mindful of His people and punishes with death their persecutors (i.e. the Roman prefect of Egypt and the emperor). These works exerted a lasting influence upon early Christian literature, e.g. upon the *De mortibus persecutorum*; the latter took over from P. the idea that persecutors themselves are responsible for evoking the inevitable punishment which, by God's judgement, eventually overwhelms them. P. cannot, however, be considered as an enemy of Hellenistic and Roman civilization merely because he was opposed to the worship of the Emperor Gaius; for besides speaking of Augustus and Tiberius in very high terms of praise, and adapting formulas of the Hellenistic ruler-cult to the praise of the Jewish patriarchs, he casts the traditions of Judaism into the literary forms of Greek allegory. Modern scholars have often overestimated the extent of P.'s. indebtedness to Judaism, especially to the Alexandrian school. In fact, he owes far more to Greek philosophy, and his very efforts to demonstrate a substantial similarity between Hellenic and Jewish doctrines are a proof of his Hellenistic character. His main sources were indisputably Plato, Aristotle, and the Stoics, above all Posidonius; the extent of his indebtedness to Neopythagoreanism, although great, is now difficult to estimate. Despite his scanty originality as a philosopher, P. played a very important role in the history of ancient thought as a mediator between Hellenistic philosophy and both Christianity and Neoplatonism. Not only did the author of the *De mortibus persecutorum* and Plotinus borrow from him, but St. Augustine probably derived from P. his theory of the two cities, which is merely an application of P.'s dualism to the realm of politics. Nevertheless, P. did not bridge the gulf between the world of God and the world of matter, since, had matter been created by God, the existence of evil would be inexplicable. To establish an artificial connexion between the two worlds P. introduced intermediary beings representing the different aspects of God's existence and thought. With these God communicates only through an intermediary, which P. calls Logos and is careful to distinguish from God himself: the word Logos refers to God in so far as His existence is conceived as

pure thought, while the word God merely indicates His essence as pure Being. Man's duty is to conform to the will of God, not only by living according to His law, but by 'seeing' Him. This supreme achievement, the discovery of the essence of God, can be reached only by means of 'ecstasy', which P. thinks of as an act of grace. But worship and purity of life and mind enable man to succeed in achieving communion with God in His existence as thought. In P.'s system the soul of man is ultimately dependent on the grace of God and cannot enjoy communion with Him also by a spontaneous activity of love unassisted by grace.

Texts: Best complete edition: Cohn, Wendland, Reiter (*ed. major*, 7 vols., 1896–1930; *ed. minor*, 6 vols., 1896–1915). Ed. T. Mangey (London, 2 vols., 1742). English Translation: Loeb (9 vols., 1929 ff.). Frs., ed. J. Rendel Harris (1886). The *In Flaccum* edited with an historical commentary by H. Box (1939).

A full bibliography (by H. L. Goodhart and E. R. Goodenough) in appendix to E. R. Goodenough, *The Politics of Philo Judaeus* (1938). Most important works on Philo: J. Drummond, *Philo Judaeus* (2 vols., 1888); É. Herriot, *Philon le Juif* (1898); J. Martin, *Philon* (1907); É. Bréhier, *Les Idées philosophiques et religieuses de Philon*[2] (1925); T. H. Billings, *The Platonism of Philo* (1919); I. Heinemann, *Philos. griech. u. jüdische Bildung* (1932). P. T.

PHILON (5) of Byblos (A.D. 64–161) composed in Greek a learned work of euhemeristic character in which for the Phoenician religion he cites at length, as he alleges, from the Phoenician Sanchuniathon, who had devoted a treatise in his own language to theogony, cosmogony, and the origins of civilization. Extensive fragments of Philon have been preserved by Eusebius in his *Demonstratio evangelica* (1. 9; 22–10; 28); with a parallel in Theodoret. These fragments have now been critically republished, along with translation, extensive essays, and full bibliography, by C. Clemen, 'Die phönikische Religion nach Philo von Byblos', *Mittheilungen d. vorderasiatisch-aegyptischen Gesellschaft* xlii, pt. 3 (1939). Over Philon's alleged translation there has been long dispute, distinguished scholars like Baudissin regarding it as a fraud. But the extraordinary recent discoveries at Ras Shamra, ancient Ugarit, on the Syrian coast north of Laodicea–Latakia, of fourteenth-century B.C. documents, in alphabetic cuneiform script, and of Hebraic language, containing lengthy mythological texts, epic, choric, etc. (published for the most part in *Syria* since 1929), have proved conclusively that Sanchuniathon is doubtless a verity in view of the many correspondences between him and these fresh texts and of the picture of the lush development of Phoenician mythology by the middle of the second millennium.

See O. Eissfeldt, *Ras Schamra u. Sanchuniathon* (1939), esp. 79 ff. J. A. M.

Philon also wrote a ʿΡηματικόν (paradigm of verb-flexions), and a dictionary of synonyms (the probable source of the Byzantine Pseudo-Ammonius). He was much used by Hesychius of Miletus. *See also* SANCHUNIATHON. P. B. R. F.

PHILONIDES, an older contemporary of Aristophanes, various of whose plays he produced. First victorious *c.* 410 B.C. (*IG.* ii². 2325). Suidas mentions Κόθορνοι (an attack on Theramenes (cf. Ar. *Ran.* 534 ff.)), Φιλέταιρος, and Ἀπήνη.

FCG ii. 421 ff.; *CAF* i. 254 ff.; Demiańczuk, *Suppl. Com.* 73. M. P.

PHILOPAPPUS, Syrian prince, Roman consul (A.D. 109), and Athenian archon. His sepulchral monument, erected between 114 and 116, stands at Athens on the top of the Museum Hill. His full name was C. Julius Antiochus Epiphanes Philopappus, his grandfather being Antiochus IV, the last king of Commagene.

OGI 409–13. *PIR* ii¹. 166, 99; ii². 262, 1086. V. E.

PHILOPATOR, Stoic, probably of the time of Hadrian (A.D. 117–38). See Zeller, *Phil. d. Griechen*, iii. 1⁴. 169, 714.

PHILOPOEMEN of Megalopolis (c. 253–182 B.C.), the Achaean soldier and statesman, was trained from his youth in arms and taught by the patriotic Megalopolitan philosophers, Ecdemus and Demophanes. He resisted Cleomenes (223) and won praise from Antigonus Doson at Sellasia. After ten years' mercenary soldiering in Crete, he became Hipparch of the Achaean League in 210/9 and General in 208/7, reforming the army, and in 207 defeated Machanidas of Sparta at Mantinea. General again in 206/5 and 201/200, he repelled Nabis in 202–200. In the Second Macedonian War, favouring neutrality, he lost influence and returned to Crete (199/8). Reappearing after the Roman evacuation to find war with Nabis, he became General (193/2) and blockaded Sparta. Flamininus made a settlement, but on Nabis' assassination (192) Philopoemen incorporated Sparta in the Achaean League. In annexing Messene and Elis (191) and as General in 191/90 or 190/89 and in 189/8 he dominated policy; finally, in 188, on an ambiguous ruling of the Senate, he demilitarized Sparta and abolished the Lycurgan institutions. General again in 187/6 and 183/2, he was captured during the revolt of Messene and given poison (182). A great soldier and patriot, 'the last of the Greeks', he remained in politics the Megalopolitan, narrow and rancorous, pressing Flamininus' and the Senate's acquiescence in Achaean rights to dominate the Peloponnese, when wider statesmanship was needed to strike a balance with Roman power in Greece.

Polybius 2. 40; 2. 67–9; bks. 10–11, 16, and 20–4; Livy bks. 35–9; Plutarch, *Philopoemen; Flamininus.* G. Niccolini, *La Confederazione Achea* (1914); De Sanctis, *Stor. Rom.* iii. 2, pp. 427, 443; iv. 1, pp. 57, 133, 169, 229, 238, 402–6; A. Aymard, *Les Premiers rapports de Rome et de la Confédération achaienne* (1938). On *strategiae*, De Sanctis, op. cit. iv. 1, p. 402; cf. A. Aymard, *Rev. Ét. Anc.* 1928, p. 1.   A. H. McD.

PHILOSOPHY, HISTORY OF. Aristotle often gives in the introductions to his works a survey of the history of the problem he is going to treat. The scope is more systematic than historical; the treatment is rather polemical. He advised his pupils, however, to write similar works of their own, not as introductions but as separate and autonomous books. Thus Theophrastus wrote a history of Physics and Metaphysics (the fragments and the later history of which are treated in a masterly way by H. Diels, *Doxographi Graeci*, 1879), Eudemus histories of Theology, Astronomy, Geometry, and Arithmetic. In these works history prevails over systematic philosophy, although they follow the order of problems, not of time, and contain some criticism. They are the basis of all later work in this field. In the same generation another Aristotelian, Aristoxenus, became the first writer of philosophical biography.

Scholars in Alexandria found an external principle of unification by arranging the extensive material under 'successors' (διάδοχοι). They made up lineages of teachers, pupils, and pupils of the pupils, many of whom became presidents and successors of their respective schools. This also is the scheme of the only complete ancient history of philosophy which has been preserved, that of Diogenes Laertius. In this work, as was often the case, biography and doxography are combined.

The standard general work (which takes account of Roman as well as of Greek philosophers) is E. Zeller, *Philosophie der Griechen*: 1⁴ (1919–20), the Pre-Socratics (Engl. Transl. 1881); 2. 1⁴ (1889) (E.T.), Socrates and the Socratics, 1868, Plato and the Older Academy, 1888; 2. 2⁴ (1921), Aristotle and the Earlier Peripatetics (E.T. 1897); 3. 1⁴ (1909), Stoics Epicureans and Sceptics (E.T.² 1880); 3. 2⁴ (1903), Eclectics (E.T., 1883). An Italian transl., with extensive additions, by R. Mondolfo (1932–8), comes down to the Pythagoreans (inclusive). There is a shorter work by Zeller, *Grundriss der Geschichte der griechischen Philosophie*¹³ (1928) (E.T. 1892).

A shorter but still fairly full treatment and an excellent bibliography will be found in F. Ueberweg, M. Heinze, and K. Praechter, *Grundriss der Geschichte der Philosophie*, 1¹² (1926).

The chief collections of fragments are: F. G. A. Mullach, *FPG* (Paris, 1860, 1867, [1879]); H. Diels, *Fragmente der Vorsokr.⁵* (1934, 1935, 1937); H. von Arnim, *Stoicorum Veterum Fragmenta* (1905, 1903, 1903, 1924). H. Ritter and L. Preller, *Historia Philosophiae Graecae*¹⁰

(1934), is a useful collection of leading passages, with notes. H. Diels, *Doxographi Graeci* (1879), is the standard edition of the Doxographers.

Other books are mentioned under the various schools and philosophers.   K. O. B. and W. D. R.

PHILOSTEPHANUS of Cyrene (3rd c. B.C.), pupil or friend of Callimachus, wrote: (1) geographical works, full of marvels and fables (Ath. 7. 297 f, 8. 331 d; Aul. Gell. 9. 4. 2; Harpocr. svv. Βούχετα, Στρύμη; schol. Pind. *Ol.* 6. 77); (2) a mythological and antiquarian treatise *Notebooks* (Ὑπομνήματα) (schol. Ap. Rhod. 2. 124); (3) *On Discoveries* (Clem. Al. *Strom.* 1. 308 a).   J. F. L.

PHILOSTRATI. Four members of this family, which was of Lemnian origin, are probably to be distinguished. (I) Verus, a sophistic writer of the second century A.D., none of whose works survive. (II) Flavius P., son of Verus, born c. A.D. 170. He studied at Athens, and later joined the philosophical circle patronized by Septimius Severus and his wife Julia Domna. At her instance he wrote the *Life of Apollonius of Tyana*, a philosophizing mystic of the first century A.D.; the Ἡρωϊκός, a dialogue concerned with the cult of Protesilaus, probably belongs to the same period. After returning to Athens he wrote Βίοι σοφιστῶν, chiefly interesting for notices of his contemporaries. He is probably also the author of a few of the Philostratean Ἐπιστολαὶ ἐρωτικαί, of the protreptic Γυμναστικός, of the second of the two Διαλέξεις, and of the dialogue Νέρων, wrongly attributed to Lucian. He died in the reign of Philippus Arabs (A.D. 244–9) (Suidas). (III) P. Lemnius (Βίοι σοφ. 2. 27), born c. A.D. 191; a great-nephew of P. I, and son-in-law of P. II. He wrote the earlier Εἰκόνες, purported descriptions of pictures in a Neapolitan collection; probably also the second Διάλεξις (see LITERARY CRITICISM IN ANTIQUITY, 1. 6). (IV) A grandson of P. III (Εἰκ. B. prooem.), who wrote the later Εἰκόνες.

The *Life of Apollonius* is not uninteresting on account of the mystical and orientalizing tendencies which it illustrates; the Ἡρ. shows similar characteristics. But P. II finds his happier vein in the Βίοι σοφ., a work which throws valuable light on the habits and personalities of the Second Sophistic. It is written in the affectedly simple and unmethodical style. The earlier Εἰκ., though they add to our knowledge of Hellenistic art, are hardly, in spite of their subsequent popularity, to be accepted as a serious contribution to criticism; they are exemplary exercises in the art of rhetorical description. The later Εἰκ. are distinctly inferior to them.

Suidas (confused notice). Editions: C. L. Kayser (1844–53; comment.); (1870–1, Teubner); J. Jüthner (1909; Γυμν.); O. Benndorf and C. Schenkl (1893; Εἰκ. A.); C. Schenkl and A. Reisch (1902; Εἰκ. B). Text and translation: *Life of Apollonius*, F. C. Conybeare (Loeb, 1912); Βίοι σοφιστῶν, W. C. Wright (Loeb, 1922); Εἰκόνες, A. Fairbanks (Loeb, 1931). Translation: *Life of Apollonius*, J. S. Phillimore, 1912. Criticism: K. Münscher, *Philol. Suppl.* x (1907) (authorship, etc.). W. Schmid, *Atticismus* iv (1896) (P. II, language).   W. M. E.

PHILOTAS (c. 360–330 B.C.), a Macedonian noble, son of Parmenion (q.v.), and the commander of the ἑταῖροι or Guards Corps in the early campaigns of Alexander the Great. He was distinguished among Alexander's marshals by his gallant bearing and liberality, but gradually became alienated from the king himself. This estrangement may have been due to Philotas' resentment of the disfavour shown by the king to Parmenion, or of Alexander's tendency to disregard Macedonian custom and to adopt oriental habits. In 330 he was accused of conspiracy by Alexander before the Macedonian army, which found him guilty and executed him with a volley of javelins. Philotas was clearly convicted of connivance at a plot against Alexander, but it is uncertain whether he was an active conspirator. The story that under torture he incriminated his father may be dismissed as a later embroidery.

Arrian, *Anab.* 3. 26; Plutarch, *Alex.* 48–9. Berve, *Alexanderreich*, no. 802.   M. C.

PHILOXENUS (1) of Cythera (436/5–380/379 B.C., *Marm. Par.* 82), dithyrambic poet. He lived at the court of Dionysius of Syracuse, who sent him to the quarries (Ael. *VH* 12. 44). His most famous work was his *Cyclops*, in which the Cyclops sang a solo to the lyre—a great innovation (schol. Ar. *Plut.* 290). The work is parodied in *Plut.* 290 ff. *See* MUSIC, § 10.

Text: E. Diehl, *Anth. Lyr. Graec.* ii. 132–4. Criticism: A. W. Pickard-Cambridge, *Dithyramb, Tragedy, and Comedy* (1927), pp. 61–4.   C. M. B.

PHILOXENUS (2), author of poem *The Banquet* quoted by Plato Comicus (ap. Ath. 6 d), which described a feast in full dithyrambic language (Ath. 146 f). He may be the same as Philoxenus son of Eryxis (Ar. *Ran.* 932 ff.).

Text: J. M. Edmonds, *Lyra Graeca* iii. 340–63. Criticism: U. von Wilamowitz-Moellendorff, *Textgesch. d. griech. Lyr.* (1900), 85–8.   C. M. B.

PHILOXENUS (3), painter of Eretria, pupil of Nicomachus (dated by Pliny 330 B.C.). Painted for Cassander (after 306?) a 'Battle of Alexander and Darius'. A mosaic in Pompeii (Pfuhl, fig. 648), probably of the third century, is proved by likeness to the Alexander sarcophagus (Winter, *KB* 336–7) to represent faithfully a fourth-century original, probably the picture by him; the half-hidden figures illustrate his 'breuiores compendiarias' (Pliny).

Overbeck 1775, 1777; Pfuhl 828; H. Fuhrmann, *Philoxenos von Eretria* (1931).   T. B. L. W.

PHILOXENUS (4) of Alexandria (1st c. B.C.) wrote on the text of Homer, accents, metre, verbs, and Atticism, and compiled important (lost) lexica of Homeric and other dialects. *See* ETYMOLOGY.

Funaioli, *Gramm. Rom. Fragm.* i. 443 ff.

PHILUMENUS of Alexandria, member of the eclectic school of medicine, c. A.D. 180. An excerpt from his work *De Venenatis Animalibus* (on poisonous animals), the basis of the 13th bk. of Aelian, has been edited by M. Wellmann in *CMG* (1908). He also wrote a book on diseases of the bowels (only part extant, in a Latin tr., ed. Michaeleanu, 1910), and one Περὶ γυναικείων (on gynaecology, not extant).   W. D. R.

PHILUS, *see* FURIUS (2).

PHILYLLIUS, Athenian comic poet(*fl. c.* 410–390 B.C.), victorious ?400 (*IG* ii². 2325). The titles suggest a preference for mythological burlesque, e.g. Αἰγεύς, Ἀταλάντη, Αὔγη, Ἑλένη, Ἡρακλῆς, Πλύντριαι ἢ Ναυσικάα.

FCG ii. 857 ff.; *CAF* i. 781 ff.; Demiańczuk, *Suppl. Com.*, pp. 73–4.   M. P.

PHILYRA, i.e. linden-tree; in mythology an Oceanid loved by Kronos (q.v.), who, being surprised by Rhea while with her, turned himself and Philyra into horses. Her child was the centaur (q.v.) Chiron, and she was so horrified at his monstrous shape that she prayed to change her own form, and so became the tree called after her.

Hyginus, *Fab.* 138.   H. J. R.

PHINEUS. The best known of several mythological persons so named was a Thracian king. For some offence, he was plagued by the Harpies (q.v.); since they stole or defiled all his food, he was nearly starved to death by the time the Argonauts arrived at his land (Salmydessus, Soph. *Ant.* 970). He made a compact with them; if they would deliver him from the Harpies, he would prophesy to them the further course of their adventures. The sons of Boreas therefore (*see* CALAIS) attacked them, followed them through the air, and finally meeting Iris, received a pledge through her that Phineus should no longer be troubled. They then turned back from the islands afterwards known as the Strophades (Islands of Turning); Ap. Rhod. 2. 178 ff.

What the offence was is a question variously answered. The best-known account, which does not in all versions lead up to the story of his rescue, and so probably is not originally connected with it, is the following. He married Cleopatra, daughter of Boreas (q.v.), and had sons by her. The marriage coming to an end, by her death or otherwise, he remarried, and the stepmother so slandered her stepsons that Phineus either blinded them himself or let her do so (Soph. loc. cit. and schol. there); the latter records a variant that Cleopatra herself blinded them, in anger at being cast off by Phineus. The name of the second wife, those of the sons, and the reason for their ill-treatment all vary in different sources. Another sin attributed to Phineus was betrayal of divine secrets which he had learned through his prophetic powers (Ap. Rhod. loc. cit. 180 ff.); this obviously suits his delivery by the Boreadae much better. For more details and authorities see Jessen in Roscher's *Lexikon*, s.v.   H. J. R.

PHLEGON of Tralles, a freedman of Hadrian, author of *Olympiades* (a history reaching from the first Olympiad to A.D. 140), Π. θαυμασίων, and Π. μακροβίων.

A. Westermann, *Paradoxographi* (1839), 197–212; O. Keller, *Rerum natural. script. graec. min.* (1877), 57–105; *FHG* iii. 602–24.

PHLEGYAS, eponym of the Phlegyae, a Thessalian people, son of Ares (Apollod. 3. 41 and elsewhere; his mother's name varies). He is also represented as living near Lake Boebeis (Pindar, *Pyth.* 3. 34), or in Orchomenus (Paus. 9. 36. 1), while the Epidaurian legend (Paus. 2. 26. 4) brings him to the Peloponnesus. He was father of Coronis, the mother of Asclepius (q.v.; Pindar, ibid. and elsewhere); of Ixion (q.v.; Eur. fr. 424 Nauck). Verg. *Aen.* 6. 618, whereon see Servius, puts him in Tartarus.   H. J. R.

PHLYĂKES. Farces (also called ἱλαροτραγῳδίαι) which were performed by 'phlyakes' in south Italy and at Alexandria in the fourth and third centuries B.C. The chief authors of these ludicrous scenes from daily life or from mythology are Rhinthon, Sciras, and Sopater of Paphos (qq.v.).

A. Olivieri, *Frammenti della Comedia Greca e del Mimo nella Sicilia e nella Magna Grecia*; *CGF* 183–97.   W. G. W.

PHOCAEA, the most northerly of the Ionian cities in Asia Minor, occupying a site with twin harbours midway between the Elaitic and Hermaean Gulfs. She pioneered in the exploration and colonization of the western Mediterranean, though Lampsacus was almost her only contribution to the opening-up of the Euxine. In the sixth century B.C. her trading stations were strung along the route linking Magna Graecia with Spain, where Arganthonius, king of Tartessus, was her friend; and the foundation of Massilia gave the Greeks access to southern Gaul. In 540, when Phocaea was besieged by a Persian army, most of the citizens preferred emigration to submission, and finally found refuge at Elea in Italy. Phocaea never recovered from their loss. Dionysius, the generalissimo of the Greek fleet in the Ionian Revolt, was a Phocaean, but his city contributed only three ships.

M. Cary and E. H. Warmington, *The Ancient Explorers* (1929), 22.   D. E. W. W.

PHOCAS (5th c. A.D.), grammarian, author of an *Ars de nomine et verbo* (ed. Keil, *Gramm. Lat.* v. 410–39) and a *Vita Vergilii* in hexameters (often published, e.g. in Baehrens, *PLM* v. 85). A *De aspiratione* attributed to him (ed. Keil, *Gramm. Lat.* v. 439–41) is apocryphal. Cf. Teuffel, § 472. 4; Schanz-Hosius, § 1106.   J. F. M.

PHOCION (4th c. B.C.), Athenian general and statesman. Although contemptuous of the people's fickleness and of popular leaders, Phocion commanded constant respect and was elected general forty-five times. Making his military reputation in the service of Persia (350 and 344 B.C.), he distinguished himself by campaigns in Euboea (348 and 341), by defending Megara (343) and Byzantium (339), and by repelling a Macedonian attack on Attica in the Lamian War (322). In politics Phocion supported Eubulus, Aeschines, and Demades against Demosthenes and Hyperides. Realizing the military strength of Macedonia, Phocion advised Athens to treat for terms when outmanœuvred before the battle of Chaeronea. After her defeat he assisted Demades in preserving peace with Philip and Alexander, opposed Harpalus, and sought to prevent Athens joining in the Lamian War, after which he acted as envoy to Antipater and sponsored with Demades the limitation of the franchise at Athens. By an error of judgement he allowed Cassander's general Nicanor to seize the Piraeus. When the democracy was restored, Phocion was condemned to death (318). Prudent, patriotic, and responsible, he controlled Athens by a force of character which is portrayed in Plutarch's *Life of Phocion.* N. G. L. H.

PHOCIS, a country of central Greece comprising the middle Cephissus valley and the valley of Crisa, which are linked loosely by passes over the southern spurs of Mt. Parnassus. Both areas were fertile, the former possessing pasture and agricultural land, and the latter olives, vines, and corn. In the sixth century B.C. Phocis was organized in a strong federation, issuing federal coinage and levying a federal army. Her internal unity enabled her to resist the aggression of her neighbours, who coveted the control of Delphi and of the route to northern Greece via the Cephissus valley and the pass of Elatea to Thermopylae, and she showed skill in her diplomacy. Deprived of Delphi and the Crisaean plain in the first Sacred War (c. 596) and overrun by Thessaly, her ambition was to regain her outlet to the sea; checked from expanding at the expense of Doris by Sparta, the Phocians allied with Athens (457), seized Delphi, and were confirmed in their control by an expedition under Pericles (448), to whom a Phocian alliance was valuable for encircling Boeotia. After the battle of Coronea (447) Phocis joined Sparta, was loyal to her during the Peloponnesian War and in the early fourth century, until Boeotia impressed her into her Central Greek League. Her bid for independence in the Third Sacred War broke Theban power but exhausted Phocis. *See* PHILOMELUS, ONOMARCHUS.

L. B. Tillard, *BSA* 1910–11. N. G. L. H.

PHOCUS (Φῶκος), in mythology, son of Aeacus (q.v.) by the nymph Psamathe, who took the shape of a seal, φώκη, hence the name of her son (Apollod. 3. 158). He proved a distinguished athlete, which aroused the jealousy of the legitimate sons, Peleus and Telamon (qq.v.); they drew lots to see which should kill him, and Telamon, to whom the task fell, murdered him while they were exercising; Aeacus found out and banished them both (ibid. 160).

H. J. R.

PHOCYLIDES (*fl.* 544–541 B.C., Suidas), elegiac and hexameter poet of Miletus. His work is of a gnomic character. He sometimes begins his lines with the formula καὶ τόδε Φωκυλίδου, writes about traditional matters such as the virtues of husbandry (fr. 7), the badness of women (fr. 2), the Mean (fr. 12), protecting spirits (fr. 16); he disbelieved in noble birth (fr. 3) and liked club-life (fr. 14).

Text: E. Diehl, *Anth. Lyr. Graec.* i. 1. 58–62. C. M. B.

PHOEBE (Φοίβη), a Titaness, daughter of Heaven and Earth (Hesiod, *Theog.* 136); wife of Coeus and mother of Leto (q.v.; ibid. 404 ff.). She is thus grandmother of

Artemis. But her name, 'the bright one', is not infrequently used for the Moon (e.g. Statius, *Theb.* 1. 105), though never in an early author; and therefore also for Artemis and Diana, as identical with the Moon (e.g. Stat. *Silv.* 1. 3. 76). Of several other mythological figures who bear this name, the only well-known one is a daughter of Leucippus, *see* DIOSCURI. The schol. Strozziana on Germanicus, *Aratea*, p. 175, 3 Breysig, says Hesiod called one of the Heliades Phoebe. H. J. R.

PHOENICIANS (Φοίνικες, *Poeni*) are said by Herodotus (1. 1; 2. 44; 7. 89) to have migrated from the Persian Gulf (c. 2750 B.C.). At this date, under Sargon of Akkad, Mesopotamian traders and armies certainly were reaching Syria and Cappadocia. Byblus was a very early Phoenician port.

2. Phoenician seafaring, however, began only about 1250. The only sea-people known to the Eighteenth Dynasty in Egypt were Keftiu—Minoans or Cilicians. Minoan, too, are the prehistoric remains at Thebes, traditionally founded by 'Cadmus the Phoenician'; and as the name 'Phoinix' is pure Greek (cf. Φοίνιος, φοινός, φόνιος), we infer that the name 'Red Men' was applied by the presumably fairer early Hellenes to any copper-skinned Mediterraneans. 'Phoenician' in Greek myths, then, usually = Minoan Cretan.

3. Homer, however, knows Phoenicians well, as craftsmen and traders. Sidon is their great city; Tyre is not mentioned (*Il.* 6. 290–1; *Od.* 13. 272 ff., 14. 288 ff., etc.). The rise of sea-power among these Semites, who called themselves *Chna*, Canaanites (Hecataeus, fr. 272, *FGrH*), probably resulted from the strong Aegean influence, from c. 1400 onwards, revealed by excavations at Ras Shamra and elsewhere (Schaeffer, *Antiquity*, 1930). After the Philistine migrations (c. 1200) there arose a new Phoenicia, nautical and cosmopolitan; its art was a weird mixture of Egyptian, Mesopotamian, and other elements; and it possessed a hieratic literature (Virolleaud, *Antiquity*, 1931). Their scripts included, besides cuneiform, the new Phoenician Alphabet (q.v.).

4. Stimulated by the collapse of Minoan carrying trade, the Phoenicians now explored the whole Mediterranean, winning footholds in Cyprus, Sicily, Africa, and Spain. The foundation of Cadiz (Gaddir, 'the Walled Place') c. 1100 and Utica, in Tunis, c. 1087 (Velleius 1. 2; [Aristotle], *Mirabilia* 134) is inherently probable. The Phoenicians took no land and traded for their food with the natives, with whom consequently, unlike the Greeks, they remained on excellent terms. Even Carthage paid rent until after 550 for the very site of the city (Justin, bk. 18).

5. Tyre now took the lead, though from ancient custom Ethbaal, King of Tyre, is still called in an eighth-century inscription from Cyprus (*Corp. Inscr. Semit.* i. 5) 'King of the Sidonians'.

6. Of Phoenician annals from c. 970 to 772 we have a summary in Josephus (*AJ.* 8. 5. 3, *Ap.* 1. 17, 18) derived from Menander of Ephesus. This includes the story of Dido and Pygmalion.

7. From the ninth century onwards the cities were repeatedly attacked and held to ransom by Assyrians, and later by Babylonians; but Tyre on its island site was impregnable, and Phoenician trade continued to flourish. The *locus classicus* for its character is Ezekiel xxvii, which, reduced to prose, describes the export of Asiatic manufactures against metals and minerals from overseas, and a local trade with the hinterland for food and raw materials (cf. 1 Kings v. 9; Acts xii. 20). There was also a slave-trade in both directions (Joel iii. 4 ff.; Amos i. 6). Phoenicia, like Israel, sometimes flirted unsuccessfully with Egypt; and Phoenicians are credibly reported to have circumnavigated Africa for Pharaoh Necho (Hdt. 4. 42).

8. With the beneficent imperialism of Persia Phoenicia soon came to terms. Phoenician squadrons under native

kings formed the backbone of Persian navies. From 535 to 335 the cities had peace and prosperity at home, and the Persian wars with Athens, as recent Syrian excavations show, seldom interrupted their brisk trade with that city. Trade with Carthage and Spain continued, though there is no evidence that Phoenicians from Tyre or Sidon reached Cornwall. The desperate resistance of Tyre to Alexander the Great shows well in what light it regarded the change of masters.

G. Contenau, *Les Phéniciens* (1926); A. R. Burn, *Minoans, Philistines and Greeks* (1930). See also CARTHAGE, SIDON, TYRE.

A. R. B.

PHOENICIDES, New Comedy poet. Fr. 1 refers to a peace made in 287 B.C. In fr. 4 a ἑταίρα bids farewell to the gay life, describing her experiences with various lovers.

FCG iv. 509 ff.; *CAF* iii. 333 ff.

PHOENIX, in mythology, (1) son of Amyntor king of Hellas (in the old sense of the word), who left home when young on account of a quarrel with his father. The latter had a concubine of whom his wife, Phoenix' mother, was jealous; she induced her son to corrupt the woman and thus make her lose Amyntor's favour. The old man, finding this out, cursed his son with childlessness, and Phoenix, despite his relations' attempts to stop him, escaped and went to Phthia, where Peleus (q.v.) received him kindly and made him a sort of tutor to the young Achilles (q.v.). He accompanied his charge to the Trojan War, where he was one of the ambassadors sent to bring Agamemnon's offers of reconciliation (*Iliad* 9. 168 ff.); Euripides, in his lost *Phoenix*, followed a version in which Amyntor blinded Phoenix and the latter was finally healed by Chiron (see Nauck, *TGF*, p. 621 ff.).

(2) Son of Agenor and brother of Cadmus (q.v.); like Cadmus, he was sent to look for Europa, did not return home, and founded a people, the Phoenicians, who were named after him (Eurip. fr. 819, etc.). He is a shadowy figure whose story, such as it is, varies in different authors, see Türk in Roscher's *Lexikon* iii. 2401 ff.

H. J. R.

PHOENIX (3) of Colophon, iambic poet of third century B.C., author of moralizing choliambics and of a poem *Coronistae* based on a Rhodian beggars' song. *See* IAMBIC POETRY (GREEK).

Text: E. Diehl, *Anth. Lyr. Graec.* i. 3. 104–10: J. U. Powell, *Collectanea Alexandrina* (1925), 231–6. Text and translation: A. D. Knox, *Herodes, Cercidas, and the Greek Choliambic Poets* (Loeb, 1929), 242 ff.

PHOENIX, 170 lines (elegiac) on the fabulous bird whose resurrection to life through death made appeal to both pagan and Christian thought. Many critics have endorsed its ascription to Lactantius (q.v.).

Text and transl. (with bibliog.) J. W. and A. M. Duff, *Minor Lat. Poets* (Loeb, 1935).

PHOLUS, *see* CENTAURS.

PHORBAS, name of several mythological persons, all obscure. (1) A Thessalian (Lapith), son of Lapithes, the eponym of the Lapiths, or of his son Triopas (Paus. 5. 1. 11; *Hymn. Hom. Ap.* 211). His home, according to various accounts, is Thessaly, Elis, Argos, or Rhodes; see Höfer in Roscher's *Lexikon* iii. 2424 ff. This may be the Phorbas who takes part in the fight of the Lapiths and Centaurs (Ovid, *Met.* 12. 322). (2) A Phlegyan, living at Panopeus, who challenged pilgrims on their way to Delphi to box with him and so killed them, till he was killed by Apollo in human disguise (schol. *Il.* 23. 660, cf. Ovid, *Met.* 11. 414, Philostratus, *Imag.* 2. 19). (3) An Athenian hero, said to have been an attendant on Theseus, schol. Pind. *Nem.* 5. 89. A shrine, the Phorbanteion, belonged either to him or to (4), an ally of Eumolpus (q.v.), killed by Erechtheus (Harpocration, s.v. Φορβαντεῖον).

H. J. R.

PHORCYS, in mythology, son of Nereus and Earth (Hesiod, *Theog.* 237). Marrying his sister Ceto, he became father of the Graiae and Gorgons (qq.v.; ibid. 270 ff.). Other children are ascribed to him in various sources, as Thoosa, mother of Polyphemus (q.v.; *Od.* 1. 71); the Sirens (q.v.; Sophocles in Plut. *Quaest. conv.* 745 f.). In general he is the father or leader of sea-monsters, such as the Tritons (q.v.; Verg. *Aen.* 5. 824).

H. J. R.

PHORMION, Athenian admiral, first mentioned in 440 B.C. before Samos. In the next years he proved an excellent military leader in Acarnania, at Potidaea, and in Chalcidice. In 430 he blockaded Corinth from Naupactus; and next summer, by brilliant tactics, he defeated two superior Peloponnesian fleets, thus restoring Athenian influence in Acarnania. After his return (428), he is said to have been sentenced for peculation (schol. Ar. *Pax* 347). Probably he died at this time.

Thuc. bks. 1 and 2; *Prosop. Att.* 14958; Adcock, *CAH* v, passim.

V. E.

PHORMIS (or **PHORMUS**), writer of Dorian comedy. Aristotle (*Poet.* 5. 1449^{b}6) calls him a contemporary of Epicharmus. Suidas agrees, adding that he was tutor to the sons of Gelon (d. 478 B.C.). He further attributes to P. the invention of long cloaks for his actors and curtains for his stage. Of the seven plays mentioned by Suidas all have historico-mythological titles.

CGF 148; A. W. Pickard-Cambridge, *Dithyramb, Tragedy, and Comedy*, p. 413 f.

M. P.

PHORONEUS (Φορωνεύς), a very ancient ancestral figure of Argive tradition. He was older than Deucalion's flood (Plato, *Tim.* 22 a), husband of the Argive Niobe, the first earthly love of Zeus, cf. Hyginus, *Fab.* 145. 1, who makes her his daughter. He was son of Inachus (q.v.; ibid. 124, cf. Apollod. 2. 1, where his descendants are given). He has no legend, except that he was one of the judges between Hera and Poseidon for possession of the country (Paus. 2. 15. 5), but he had a cult (ibid. 20. 3).

H. J. R.

PHOROS, *see* FINANCE, GREEK, para. 7.

PHOSPHORUS (Φωσφόρος = Ἑωσφόρος; Lucifer), the morning star, personified son of Eos and Astraeus (Hes. *Th.* 381) or Cephalus (Hyg. *Poet. Astr.* 2. 42; cf. Hes. *Th.* 986–91), sometimes represented as a youth bearing a torch. As a cult name P. was applied to Hecate, Artemis (cf. Diana Lucifera), and, more rarely, to other divinities. The *deus bonus puer P.* is the Syrian god, Aziz.

F. R. W.

PHOTIUS, the best of the Byzantine scholars and (A.D. 858–67, 878–86) Patriarch of Constantinople. 'At the pressing intreaty of the Caesar (Bardas), the celebrated Photius renounced the freedom of a secular and studious life, ascended the patriarchal throne, and was alternately excommunicated and absolved by the synods of the East and West. By the confession even of priestly hatred, no art or science, except poetry, was foreign to this universal scholar, who was deep in thought, indefatigable in reading, and eloquent in diction' (Gibbon, ch. 53). His most important work is the *Bibliotheca* (or *Myriobiblion*), 'a living monument of erudition and criticism' (Gibbon, l.c.). It is a hastily compiled, ill-arranged critical account (in 280 chapters, with numerous extracts) of 280 prose works read by Photius in the absence of his brother, Tarasius, for whose information, and at whose request, the work was composed, at some date before A.D. 858. Theology and history predominate, oratory, romance, philosophy, science, medicine, and lexicography also come within its scope. Besides its intrinsic value (the criticisms are often felicitous and acute), it has a considerable adventitious importance as the best or sole source of our information about many notable lost works. The *Lexicon*, which is an earlier work, is a glossary based ostensibly and in fact indirectly upon Aelius Dionysius, Pausanias, and Diogenianus, but immediately drawn from such later compilations as Timaeus' Platonic lexicon, and chiefly from the Συναγωγή (*see* LEXICA SEGUERIANA). The *Lexicon* was long known only from the *Codex Galeanus* at Cambridge, now supplemented by a manuscript at Athens and one at Berlin, from which last Reitzenstein edited the lost beginning (*A—Ἄπαρνος*), *Der Anfang d. Lexicons d. Photios*, 1907.

Editions: *Bibl.* Bekker, 1824–5; Migne, *PG* (1860), vol. 103. *Lexicon*: Naber, 1864–5. Criticism: E. Orth, *Photiana* (1928), *Stilkritik d. P.* (1929).   P. B. R. F.

PHRAATES IV (*c.* 38–2 B.C.), king of Parthia. He secured the succession by murdering his father Orodes II (q.v.) and many Parthian princes and nobles (Plut. *Ant.* 37, Dio Cass. 49. 23). He soon had to face a Roman invasion, when M. Antonius penetrated into Media Atropatene, but Phraates' general Monaeses forced him to retire with great loss. From 31 to 25 B.C. Phraates had to contest his throne with the rebel Tiridates (q.v. 1). His embassy to Augustus led to better relations between Rome and Parthia, and the standards captured from Crassus and Antony were restored to Rome. He was assassinated in a harem intrigue.   M. S. D.

PHRATRIAI, 'brotherhoods' or kinship groups whose members were called φράτερες (*fratres*). They occur in Athens and many other States (in others, again, we find πατραί or πατριαί, which were probably of similar origin and function). At Athens they held property, and had their own cults and officials (*phratriarchoi*) and priests. They were smaller than the *phylae*, more comprehensive than the *gene*. All alike worshipped Zeus Phratrios and Athena Phratria, and the Apaturia (q.v.) was their common festival. They made their own regulations at meetings of all the *phrateres*. Soon after birth a child (boy or girl) was entered by its father into his phratry, which scrutinized its legitimacy. Admission to a phratry was good proof of citizenship. This was the religious recognition of citizenship, as the entry into the deme (*see* DEMOI) was the secular recognition; but whether every citizen must belong to a phratry is doubtful. A phratry could subsequently eject a member, but apparently he did not thereby lose his citizenship, as he did if ejected from his deme; and some phratries seem to have had stricter laws of membership than others. It was, however, certainly normal for citizens to be members; and a judgement of a dicastery that a man was a legitimate son of a citizen compelled a phratry to accept him. A foreigner on receiving citizenship was entered in a phratry as well as a deme.

IG ii². 1237, *SIG* 921; Wilamowitz, *Aristoteles und Athen* (1893), ii. 260 ff.; Wade-Gery, *CQ* xxv (1931), 129–43.   A. W. G.

PHRIXUS, *see* ATHAMAS.

PHRYGIA, a country comprising part of the central plateau and the western flank of Asia Minor. The conquest of central and western Asia Minor by the European Phryges took place towards the end of the second millennium B.C., and was still remembered when the Trojan saga was taking shape (*Iliad* 3. 184 ff.); it extended farther to the north and west than the Phrygia of the Greek and Roman periods. The limits of the original Phrygian conquest were driven in on the west by the emergence of the Lydian Kingdom, and in the north by subsequent invasions from Europe of Mysians and Bithynians, and, much later, Galatians; in the Roman period the northern boundary of Phrygia lay well south of the northern mountain parapet and far from its early

maritime base on the Sea of Marmara. On the east and south the later boundaries still represent the extreme limit of the original Phrygian permanent settlement, which appears not to have crossed the Halys or penetrated beyond Iconium or Pisidian Antioch or south of the Maeander basin.

In Phrygia the European invaders absorbed the older population and founded a kingdom, associated in Greek legend with the names of Midas and Gordius, whose memorials survive in the rock-cities and sculptured façades, some of them inscribed, of the 'Phrygian Monument Country' south of Dorylaeum. After its conquest by Lydia Phrygia never again appears as an independent State; the old warrior stock was merged in the peasant population, and to the classical Greeks 'Phrygian' was equivalent to 'slave'. Phrygia was subject in turn to the Persians, Seleucids, and Attalids; in 116 B.C. the greater part of it was absorbed in the province Asia (q.v.), and in 25 B.C. the remaining eastern portion became a region of the province Galatia. The Phrygian religion, whose male god Papas took his place beside the old Anatolian Mother goddess, and the Phrygian language survived until the early Byzantine period. Diocletian made Asian Phrygia a separate province, which Constantine subdivided into two, Prima or Pacatiana and Secunda or Salutaris, administered from Laodicea and Synnada respectively.

W. M. Ramsay, *Cities and Bishoprics of Phrygia* (1895–7).   W. M. C.

PHRYNICHUS (1), an Athenian tragic poet, coupled by some ([Plato], *Minos* 320 e) with Thespis as one of the originators of tragedy. His first victory is dated 511 B.C. (Suidas, s.v.). He produced a play dealing with the taking of Miletus by the Persians in 494, and was fined for reminding the Athenians too vividly of the misfortunes of their friends (Hdt. 6. 21). Another historical play, the *Phoenissae* (probably identical with his Πέρσαι), related to the Persian War just ended; the scene was laid in Persia and opened with a servant setting seats for the Persian nobles (Arg. Aesch. *Persae*). In 476 Themistocles was his choregus at the Great Dionysia (Plut. *Them.* 5), and this may have been the date of the *Phoenissae*. Among his mythological plays were the *Pleuroniae* (from the story of Meleager and Oeneus); the *Aegyptii* and *Danaides*; the *Antaeus* and the *Alcestis* (probably a satyric play) from the Heraclean cycle, and the *Actaeon*. He was remembered for the beauty of his lyrics (Ar. *Vesp.* 220, *Av.* 748 ff.) and the many varieties of dance which he invented (Plut. *Quaest. conv.* 8. θ. 3); Aristophanes admired him greatly (see also *Thesm.* 165 ff., *Ran.* 1298 f.), though he hints (*Ran.* 910 ff.) that Phrynichus' audiences did not exact too high a standard of art. He was said (Suidas, s.v.) to have been the first tragic poet to employ a feminine mask, i.e. to introduce a female character. The few fragments suggest that he employed metaphors freely.

TGF 720–5.   A. W. P.-C.

PHRYNICHUS (2), Athenian comic writer, dramatic activity roughly 430–400 B.C.; constantly confused by ancient authorities with (1) the tragedian, (2) the actor, and (3) the politician of the same name. Anon. Περὶ κωμ. 10 gives his first production as 430, and the victors' list (*IG* ii². 2325) puts the first of his two victories as 428. Plays: Ἐφιάλτης (variously explained, probably = *The Nightmare*; cf. Crates' Λάμια). A Κόννος (Socrates' music-master) is attributed to Ameipsias also, but it is possible that there was only one play of this name, P. giving it to Ameipsias to produce as his own. Similarly with the Κωμασταί. Ameipsias produced a Κωμ. in 414 (arg. 1 Ar. *Av.*) and P. his Μονότροπος. The Κωμασταί probably dealt with the hermocopid scandal, the Μονότροπος with the life of some misanthrope (fr. 18, ζῶ δὲ

Τίμωνος βίον). The *Μοῦσαι* contained an *ἀγών* between Sophocles and Euripides, in which Sophocles seems to have been victorious (Schol. Soph. *O.C.* 17). The *Μύσται* may probably be dated 407.

CFG ii. 580 ff.; *CAF* i. 369 ff.; Demiańczuk, *Suppl. Com.* 74 ff.
M. P.

PHRYNICHUS (3) **ARABIUS,** of Bithynia, Atticist, rhetorician, and lexicographer under M. Aurelius and Commodus. He compiled *Σοφιστικὴ προπαρασκευή*, a lexicon of 'Attic' words in 37 books, preserved only in a summary by Photius and in fragments; also *Ἀττικιστής* (*περὶ κρίσεως καλῶν καὶ δοκίμων ὀνομάτων*), extant in an abridgement, our *Ἐκλογή*. They were based on Eirenaeus and Aelius Dionysius. Phrynichus criticizes Pollux (q.v.) for his laxity in the choice of words, and, with Moeris, ranks among the strictest of the 'Atticists'. His models are Plato, the Ten Orators, Thucydides, Aeschines Socraticus, Critias, Antisthenes, Aristophanes, Aeschylus, Sophocles, and Euripides. Nor would he accept the usage of even the best of these without cavil. In the letter to the Imperial Secretary, Attidius Cornelianus, which introduces the *Ἐκλογή*, he reprobates those who try to justify their diction by citing the impeached words from classical authors: *ἡμεῖς δὲ οὐ πρὸς τὰ διημαρτημένα ἀφορῶμεν, ἀλλὰ πρὸς τὰ δοκιμώτατα τῶν ἀρχαίων*. Such critical scrutiny, however, if at all possible, would demand a clearer perception than the Atticists ever had of the nature and relations of spoken and literary Attic, and of the diverse sources from which the language of the poets was drawn. Nevertheless, Phrynichus' work contains many acute and accurate observations.

Editions. *Σοφ. προπ.*: (Summary) Bekker, *Anecd.* i; (Fragments) H. von Borries, Teubner, 1911. *Ἐκλογή*: C. A. Lobeck, 1820. W. G. Rutherford (*The New P.*), 1881; M. Naechster, *De Pollucis et Phrynichi controversiis* (1908). P. B. R. F.

PHRYNIS, *see* MUSIC, § 10.

PHTHIOTIS, a district of Thessaly. In mythology, when it was the realm of Achilles, and in Roman times it included Achaea Phthiotis and extended from Cynoscephalae to the border of Malis. In the intervening period, however, Phthiotis denoted only the neighbourhood of Pharsalus (q.v.) and formed one of the tetrads of Thessaly proper, whereas Achaea Phthiotis belonged to the Perioecis and owed allegiance to Thessaly, particularly to Pharsalus.

Achaea, a mountainous district including the Othrys range, has a coastal plain on the Bay of Pagasae. Its principal towns were Phthiotic Thebes, Larissa Cremaste, Melitaea, and Halus. The Achaeans rarely enjoyed freedom from external intervention. When liberated from Alexander of Pherae they were forced to join the Boeotian League, and when Philip detached the Perioecis from Thessaly they became subjects of Macedonia. An Achaean League apparently existed in the third century B.C.

G. Kip, *Thessalische Studien* (1910), 53–64; F. Stählin, *Das hellenische Thessalien* (1924), 135–44 and 150–91. H. D. W.

PHYLACUS, in mythology, (1) father of Iphiclus, for whose story *see* MELAMPUS, son of Deion and so grandson of Aeolus (q.v.; Apollod. 1. 86). (2) Son of Iphiclus and grandson of (1) (Eustath. *Il.* p. 323, 42). (3) A local hero of Delphi (Hdt. 8. 39. 1). He appeared with Autonous, another local hero, and helped to drive off the Persian raiders in 480 B.C. (ibid. 38). H. J. R.

PHYLAE (*φυλαί*), the largest political divisions of a Greek State. There is no evidence of their existence in Thessaly or Boeotia, but they are found or may be inferred in all the Dorian and most of the Ionian States. In all Dorian States the same three *phylae*—Hylleis, Dymanes, and Pamphyli—recur, though in cities like Argos and Sicyon, which contained a non-Dorian element, other *phylae* might be added: the three *phylae* were therefore anterior to the Dorian Invasion. The original four *phylae* of Athens—Geleontes, Hopletes, Argadeis, and Aegicoreis—recur in some Ionian States (though seldom all in one State), together with other *phylae* for the non-Ionian population. The *phylae* were kinship groups, comprising the entire citizen-body. They were corporate bodies with their own priests and officials (*φυλοβασιλεῖς* at Athens); but they were also administrative and military units of the city. In Athens, at least, they were also local divisions, like the three *trittyes* (q.v.) and the twelve *naukrariai* (q.v.) into which they were subdivided. The *phylae* of a city were liable to be reorganized, following a change in the citizen-body or the constitution.

2. In Sparta, it seems, the three Dorian *phylae* were replaced by five local *phylae* (perhaps in the 8th c.), which formed the five *lochoi* or regiments of the Spartiate army and elected the five ephors. A similar change was made by Cleisthenes (q.v.) at Athens, where the old *phylae* had been dominated by the nobles, and excluded many new citizens, admitted under the legislation of Solon and by the tyrants. For these he substituted ten new *phylae* (the old surviving for a few sacred cults only). To break up not only the old ascendancy of the nobles but the more recent division in the State between the Pedieis, Parali, and Diacrii (*see* PISISTRATUS), he divided each *phyle* into three *trittyes* (q.v.), one from each of the main territorial divisions of Attica—the town (*τὸ ἄστυ*, including Piraeus and Phaleron, and part of the plain of Athens), the coast, and the interior. Membership of these new *phylae* (as of the *trittyes* and of the *demoi*, q.v.) depended on residence at the time of the reform. It was not broken by a subsequent change of residence, but was transmitted by descent. The *phylae* were not units of local government—each had its headquarters in the city. The new State administration was based on them: magistracies (the nine archons and their secretary, the *strategi*, etc.) were mostly in colleges of ten, one from each *phyle*; the ten prytanies of the Boule each represented a *phyle* (*see* PRYTANIS); the ten regiments of hoplites and (later) ten squadrons of cavalry were recruited from the separate *phylae*. The *phylae* were also represented as such by choruses and *choregi* (q.v.) in the dithyrambic contests at festivals. Their names and official order were: Erechtheis, Aegeis, Pandionis, Leontis, Acamantis, Oeneis, Cecropis, Hippothontis, Aeantis, Antiochis.

In Hellenistic and Roman times new *phylae* were occasionally added (by a redistribution of the citizens) in honour of powerful princes, as Antigonis Demetrias, Attalis, Ptolemais, Hadrianis. The usual number was twelve. A. W. G.

PHYLARCHUS of Athens, the most important historian of the period between Pyrrhus' death, 272, and the defeat of Cleomenes by Antigonus Doson, 220 B.C. His history (*Ἱστορίαι*), one of a number of works, ran to twenty-eight books. Its arrangement cannot be ascertained, but it was not based on a chronological scheme. The few definite facts of books 6–14 all refer to the east, the remainder to Greece. P. was Plutarch's chief authority for the lives of Agis and Cleomenes. His moralizing digressions and bias against Macedon throw suspicion on his reliability.

FGrH ii. 81. *FHG* i. 334. G. L. B.

PHYLAS, name of four minor mythological persons, the least unknown being a king of the Dryopes. He sinned against the shrine at Delphi, and consequently Heracles (q.v.) overthrew him and gave his people to Apollo as serfs. Many of them, either escaping or being sent by Apollo's command, went to the Peloponnesus, where they settled at Asine and other places. Heracles had by Phylas' daughter a son Antiochus, after whom the Attic tribe Antiochis was named (Diod. Sic. 4. 37; Paus. 1. 5. 2; 4. 34. 9–10). H. J. R.

PHYSICA ET MYSTICA, *see* ALCHEMY, para. 4.

PHYSICS. Until the time of Plato and Aristotle physics was a part of philosophy. Occupied with the study of nature and cosmogony, the first philosophers knew only a few isolated facts in physics discovered by experience (cf. Thales on the property of the lode-stone, and Pythagoras' discovery of the musical intervals); they had no general theories, except that of transmutation of elements by rarefaction and condensation (cf. the upward and downward courses in Heraclitus), or the eternal mixing and unmixing of them, combined with the indestructibility of matter (Empedocles). Perhaps the first attempt to state a law was Heraclitus' Πάντα ῥεῖ. On the other hand, centrifugal force is postulated by Anaxagoras, and we have Empedocles' declaration that light travels and takes time to pass from one place to another. Anaxagoras and Empedocles both realized the corporeal quality of air; Empedocles, by an experiment with a water-clock, showed that water can enter a vessel only as air escapes. The first to make systematic experiments was apparently Democritus, whose theory of atoms approaches nearer to the most modern views than any other that has been held before or since. Important also is the declaration of Leucippus that 'nothing comes into being for nothing; everything happens on a rational ground and by the pressure of necessity'.

2. Aristotle made a point, in his treatises, of summarizing all that was so far known in each subject, with a view to adapting it to his own philosophical system. His views on physical subjects are spread over the *Physics, De Caelo, De Generatione et Corruptione,* and the *Meteorologica.* Physics is for him one of the theoretical sciences; it deals with natural bodies having in them a source of movement or rest. Aristotle discusses such things as matter and form, the four causes, three kinds of 'motion' (increase and decrease, change, and locomotion), 'place', and space, the void, the continuous, the infinite, the laws of motion, e.g. the dependence of speed on the weight of the object moved and on the density of the medium through which it moves, natural and forced movement and the prime mover, the application of the theory to the heavenly sphere, the movement of the elements (including the 'aether') to their 'natural places'. Among the things bearing on mechanics we find the germ of the principle of 'virtual velocities' and a statement very like Newton's 'First Law of Motion'; in a void, if a thing is in motion, 'no one can say why it should stop anywhere; for why here rather than there? hence it will either remain at rest or it must move *ad infinitum* unless something stronger prevents it' (*Phys.* 4. 8. 215ᵃ20–2). The *Mechanica*, containing mechanical problems, is not by Aristotle, but it retains many ideas which are found in Aristotle's works. It contains the 'parallelogram of velocities' (ch. 2) and the principle of the lever (ch. 3), which it applies extensively to the explanation of many mechanical devices, e.g. the balance, interacting pulleys, etc.

3. But, for mechanics, the scientific foundation was laid by Archimedes in his proof of the principle of the lever and his investigation of the position of the centre of gravity in a number of bodies (*Plane Equilibriums* I, II, and the *Method*, in which he makes full use of the 'moment' about a fixed point)—to say nothing of his machines for moving a great weight by a small force (δός μοι ποῦ στῶ, καὶ κινῶ τὰν γᾶν), his water-screw, etc.

4. Archimedes further initiated the whole science of *hydrostatics* (Περὶ ὀχουμένων, *On Floating Bodies*), laying down the principles that a body floating in a fluid will take a position in which its weight is equal to that of the portion of the fluid which it displaces, and that a body weighed in a fluid will be lighter than its true weight by the weight of the displaced portion of the fluid. He further lays it down that the upward force exerted by the fluid on the floating solid will act along the line perpendicular to the surface of the fluid which passes through the centre of gravity of the displaced portion of the fluid. With these principles, Archimedes works out fully the positions of rest and stability of (1) any segment of a sphere and (2) a right segment of a paraboloid of revolution floating in a fluid either way up.

5. On the mechanical side Archimedes' work was continued by Ctesibius, Philon, and Heron. Only Heron's works survive in any completeness, but we find there the recognition of the elasticity of air and the force of steam; his engines include a thermoscope, a forcing air-pump, siphons, a fire-engine, and the first steam-engine, in which the recoil of steam issuing in jets from four tubes, the open ends of which are perpendicular to the tubes, while the tubes issue from a centre, forming a cross (like the *swastika*), makes a ball or a wheel revolve.

6. *Optics.* Until the time of the Atomists it was supposed that sight resulted from visual rays proceeding in straight lines from the eye and impinging on the object seen. The Atomists postulated atoms constantly proceeding from the object and carrying, as it were, copies of it to the eye. Aristotle, too, regards the eye as a receptive organ only; the object acts on the eye through a transparent medium (*De Anima* 2. 7, *De Sensu* ch. 2). Aristotle gave an explanation of the rainbow and the halo in the *Meteorologica* (3. 2–6). The first systematic treatise on geometrical *Optics* was by Euclid and survives in a version by Theon. The law of reflection was known before Euclid. Heron (*Catoptrica*) bases it on the assumption of a *minimum path.* Ptolemy wrote *Optica*, in which occurs the first attempt to discover a law of *refraction.* The hypothesis of atmospheric refraction appears in Cleomedes (*De motu circulari*, ch. 6).

7. *Acoustics.* The dependence of the musical intervals on numerical ratios was discovered by Pythagoras. There were many writers on harmonics, e.g. Archytas, Aristoxenus, Euclid, Ptolemy. The κατατομὴ κανόνος included in the *Musici Scriptores* may be partly based on the *Elements of Music* by Euclid.

8. *Electricity and Magnetism.* Thales is said to have discovered the attractive power of the lode-stone (Arist. *De An.* 1. 2). Theophrastus mentions the *Lyncurion* as having still stronger force, and notes the necessity of rubbing the lode-stone (Περὶ λίθων). Pliny's data in the *Natural History* 37. 13 and 2. 37 rest on legend and are of no scientific value.

In the Platonic *Ion* 533 we are told that the lode-stone not only attracts bits of iron, but communicates to them the same power: apparently the first hint of magnetic induction.   T. H.

PHYSIOGNOMONICI, writers who try to divine the true character of man by comparing him to certain types of animals or races, the moral nature of which they suppose to be known ([Aristotle], *Phgn.* 805ᵃ20), or by inferring a person's idiosyncrasy from movements, gestures of the body, colour, characteristic facial expressions, the growth of the hair, the smoothness of the skin, the voice, conditions of the flesh, the parts of the body, and the body as a whole (ibid. 806ᵃ26). Such observations of necessity result from any social and political contact; they are, therefore, already contained in early Greek literature (Simonides, fr. 7); later, after physiognomy, based on the theory of the interdependence of body and soul (Aristotle, *An. Pr.* 70ᵇ7), had been developed by philosophers, especially by Socratics and Stoics (Posidonius), the results influenced in ever-increasing measure painters, writers, orators, and actors. In medicine physiognomical signs had been valued from the beginning. They were particularly emphasized by the gymnasts of the second century A.D., probably in connexion with the codification of physiognomical studies by Polemon. But at no time in antiquity does physiognomy seem to have been nearly as important as during the Middle Ages and the Renaissance.

TEXTS: R. Förster, *Scriptores Physiognomonici* i–ii (Teubner 1893), containing Ps.-Aristotle, Polemon (2nd c. A.D.), Adamantius (4th c. A.D.), Anonymi, *De physiognomia*, *Secreta secretorum* (cf. also Roger Bacon, V, ed. R. Steele (1920)). References in Greek and Latin authors collected, Förster ii. 237. Additional material, R. Asmus, *Philol.* (1906); J. Jüthner, *Philostratos über Gymnastik* (1909); R. A. Pack, *AJPhil.* (1935). New MS. readings, Förster, *Rh. Mus.* 1900.
LITERATURE: Förster, i, introduction (history of Ph., tradition, etc.). Best survey, Förster, *Die Physiognomik d. Griechen* (1884); E. Rohde, *D. griech. Roman³*, 160; cf. also A. Macalister, *Enc. Brit.* (11th ed.), s.v. 'Physiognomy'; E. C. Evans, *TAPA* (1941); R. A. Pack, op. cit. *PW* xx, s.v. 'Physiognomik'. L. E.

PHYSIOLOGUS ('the Naturalist'), a collection of some fifty fabulous anecdotes from natural, mostly animal, history, of a moralizing and symbolical character. The date and place of its production are uncertain; Christian writers towards the end of the fourth century A.D. (more doubtfully Origen in the third century) knew and used it; it was translated into Latin about this time. The subject-matter is largely drawn from traditional Christian commentary on Scriptural passages; in general spirit the work may be said to belong to the class of popular descriptions of the marvels of nature, real or imaginary, which tended increasingly to usurp the place of legitimate natural science after Theophrastus. The work as it stands appears from internal evidence, including that of translations, to have taken shape in Egypt; its ultimate source may be the pseudo-Democritean writer Bolus of Mendes (2nd c. B.C.). The *Physiologus* enjoyed great subsequent popularity; it was translated into the principal languages of Europe and the Near East; its material continued to be reproduced in the medieval Bestiaries. Many traditional religious symbols, such as the Pelican and the Phoenix, derive from it.

F. Lauchert, *Gesch. des Physiologus* (Greek text), 1889; M. Goldstaub, *Philol. Suppl.* 8 (1899–1901); K. Krumbacher, *Gesch. der byzantinischen Litteratur²* (1897); M. Wellmann, *Philol. Suppl.* 22 (1930); Christ-Schmid-Stählin⁶, 2. 2 (1924). W. M. E.

PHYSIOLOGY, see ANATOMY AND PHYSIOLOGY.

PHYTALUS, eponym of the Phytalidae, an Attic clan having certain duties in the worship of Theseus (q.v.; Plut. *Thes.* 23). According to what is no doubt the clan-legend, Phytalus received Demeter in his house when she visited Attica, and she gave him the fig-tree, whereof he is apparently the presiding hero or daimon, hence his name, 'planter', and his descendants welcomed Theseus. Paus. 1. 37. 2 and 4. H. J. R.

PICENES. Picenum is that part of the Adriatic coast which is contained between Ancona and the river Sangro. Linguistic and archaeological evidence connect the Picenes very closely with the opposite coast of Illyria and have suggested a definite Illyrian immigration of doubtful date and magnitude. The view, however, that this region continued to be inhabited principally by descendants of the original neolithic stock must be given due weight. Less important is the probable intermingling of Picene-speaking Italic tribes. The name Picenes may be considered in archaeology as a regional term to include the inhabitants of the whole district on the east of the Apennines from Rimini to Vasto. This constitutes a homogeneous cultural province contrasting in every respect with its northern and western neighbours. These 'Picenes', in the broader sense, preserve the burial custom of inhumation, unlike the Villanovans. The earlier phases of their civilization are bound up with Istria and the Balkans, while the later and richer developments after 600 B.C. depend on land-trade with Magna Graecia.

Material for study is rare before 800 B.C. Some large eighth-century cemeteries demonstrate the remarkably war-like character of the Picenes; every man's grave contains weapons, among which many are of Balkan types. Dress and ornaments are well represented in graves of the sixth century; the similarity to objects found round Como (q.v.) betrays the existence of definite trade-routes. The prodigal use of amber points to the head of the Gulf of Venice (*see* AMBER). In the sixth and fifth centuries carvings in amber and ivory, figured bronzes of Ionic style, and fine bronze bowls and censers are evidence of a lively trade through Apulia with Tarentum. Apulian painted pottery is occasionally found in Picene graves. Many works of art remain unpublished in the museum of Ancona.

D. Randall-MacIver, *The Iron Age in Italy* (1927); and in brief summary, *Italy before the Romans* (1928). For the linguistic side, J. Whatmough, *The Foundations of Roman Italy* (1937). D. R.-MacI.

PICTOR, see FABIUS (6).

PICUMNUS, see PILUMNUS.

PICUS, properly the woodpecker, sacred to Mars (q.v.), but rationalized into an early king of the Italians (for his identification with Zeus in Diod. Sic. 6, frag. 5, see Halliday in *CR* xxxvi (1922), 110 ff.). Ovid (*Met.* 14. 320 ff.) gives an explanation, perhaps his own, of how he came to be changed into bird-form. H. J. R.

PIETAS is the typical Roman attitude of dutiful respect toward gods, fatherland, and parents and other kinsmen (Cic. *Nat. D.* 1. 116: 'est enim pietas iustitia aduersum deos'; Cic. *Inv. Rhet.* 2. 66: 'religionem eam quae in metu et caerimonia deorum sit appellant, pietatem quae erga patriam aut parentes aut alios sanguine coniunctos officium conseruare moneat'). Pietas, personified, received a temple in Rome (191 B.C.); she is often represented in human form, sometimes attended by a stork, symbol of filial piety; during the Empire, Pietas Augusta appears on coins and in inscriptions. Some Romans adopted as cognomen the term Pius; Virgil's 'pius Aeneas' significantly expresses the Roman ideal in his religious attitude, in his patriotic mission, and in his relations with father, son, and comrades. W. C. G.

PIGNUS, see SECURITY.

PIGRES, Carian poet; brother of Artemisia wife of Mausolus; said to have interpolated pentameters into the *Iliad*, and to have written the *Margites*.
EGF 65.

PILATUS, see PONTIUS (4).

PILUM, see ARMS AND ARMOUR, ROMAN.

PILUMNUS and **PICUMNUS.** By Roman custom, when a woman was delivered, three persons kept off Silvanus (q.v.) from her by chopping, sweeping, and pounding with a pestle; the deities Intercidona, Deverra, and Pilumnus were supposed to preside over these actions (Varro in Aug. *De civ. D.* 6. 9). More puzzling is the statement of Varro in Nonius (p. 528 M), which associates Picumnus with Pilumnus as marriage-gods. H. J. R.

PILUS, see CENTURIO, PRINCIPILUS.

PINDAR (*Πίνδαρος*) (518–438 B.C.), lyric poet, of Cynoscephalae in Boeotia, born in the Pythian year of the 65th Olympiad, i.e. 518 B.C. (Suidas, s.v. *Πίνδαρος*, fr. 183). Nothing is known of his parents, Daiphantus and Cleodice, but they must have belonged to an aristocratic family, since Pindar himself claims to be a member of the Aegeidae, an international clan with high connexions in Sparta, Thera, and Cyrene (*Pyth.* 5. 75, with scholl., cf. Hdt. 4. 149). He learned his craft first from his uncle Scopelinus, later at Athens from Apollodorus and Agathocles, who was also the teacher of Damon (Pl. *La.* 180 d). His earliest known poem is *Pyth.* 10, written in 498 for a young protégé of the powerful Thessalian Aleuadae. In 490 he made the acquaintance of Theron's brother, Xenocrates, and celebrated his chariot-victory with *Pyth.* 6, while *Pyth.* 12, written in the same year for a Sicilian flute-player, is probably due to the same connexion. In 486 he wrote *Pyth.* 7 for the ostracized Alcmaeonid Megacles. To the same years may belong *Ol.* 14, and *Paean* 6 and *Nem.* 7, which show a curious conflict between him and his Aeginetan patrons; they seem to have thought that in the first poem he had libelled their hero Neoptolemus, and in the second poem he maintains his position against them. In the Persian Wars of 480-479 Pindar seems to have accepted the Theban policy of neutrality (fr. 99), but without satisfaction, as *Isthm.* 8, written soon after, shows, while *Isthm.* 5 shows his appreciation of Aeginetan courage at Salamis. In 476 he went to Sicily, where he produced *Ol.* 1 in honour of Hieron's victory in the horse-race and *Ol.* 2 and 3 in honour of Theron's in the chariot-race. *Ol.* 2 is an important and intimate document about life after death, and shows the influence of Orphic ideas, which were prevalent in Sicily. *Nem.* 1 and 9, also written for Sicilian patrons, may belong to the same period. On his return Pindar probably wrote his famous Dithyramb for Athens (frs. 64-5), and it is possible that in *Pyth.* 9 (474 B.C.) he defends himself before a Theban audience against the charge of undue partiality for Athens. *Pyth.* 11 may belong to the same year, but the alternative date of 454 cannot be entirely disregarded. Though he did not return to Sicily, he maintained his connexion with Hieron. *Pyth.* 3 is a poetical letter, sent probably about 474 as a consolation to the suffering tyrant; it refers to the cult of Pan, for which Pindar wrote a Hymn (frs. 85-90). *Pyth.* 1 celebrates both Hieron's chariot-victory of 470 and the official foundation of his new town of Aetna under his son Deinomenes. *Pyth.* 2, a dark and unhappy poem, may have been written in 468, when Hieron won the chariot-race at Olympia, but asked Bacchylides instead of Pindar to celebrate his victory for him. At the same time Pindar sent a *Hyporchema* (fr. 94) to Hieron. *Ol.* 6, written for a friend of Hieron's, probably belongs to the same year. At this period Pindar numbered patrons in many different parts of Greece. He wrote an Encomium for Alexander of Macedon (fr. 106), a Paean for Abdera (fr. 36), poems for Sparta (frs. 101, 189), *Ol.* 7 for a Rhodian in 464, and *Ol.* 13 and fr. 107 for a Corinthian in the same year. The height of his achievement in these years were *Pyth.* 4 and 5, written for the King of Cyrene in 462-461. In the first of these Pindar enters high politics and appeals to the king to recall his exiled kinsman Damophilus. Before 460 Pindar shows no hostility to Athens, but after it he seems to have been shocked and pained by the policy of the Athenian imperialists. At first he maintained his personal loyalties to Athenians such as Melesias (*Ol.* 8 in 460), but in *Isthm.* 7, which seems to have been composed after Oenophyta (*c.* 456 B.C.), he combines a quietist attitude in himself with a conviction that the gods punish the presumptuous. His latest known poems are *Pyth.* 8, written in 446 for a young Aeginetan at a time when it seemed possible that Aegina might free herself from Athens, and *Nem.* 11 and fr. 108 for the boy Theoxenus of Tenedos, who is said to have been with Pindar at his death. He died at the age of eighty in 438.

Pindar's works were collected in seventeen books, Hymns, Paeans, Dithyrambs (2), Processional Songs (2), Maiden-Songs (2), other Maiden-Songs Hyporchemata (2), Encomia, Dirges, and Epinicians (4). The Epinicians have by an accident survived complete; despite their peculiar character they are probably typical of all Pindar's work, and new fragments of Paeans and Dithyrambs show little difference of style and thought. Pindar seems to have made the rejoicing over victory a religious occasion on which he demonstrated the power of men to find, temporarily, a happiness like that of the gods by displaying their ἀρετά. This ἀρετά was itself partly inborn and due to men's having divine blood in their veins. His Epinicians are usually choral hymns in which the victor is presented to some god, and they have the traditional characteristics of such hymns,—moral maxims, a myth, and praise of the gods. Into this frame the victor's own achievements are fitted, not always easily. In his maxims Pindar sometimes achieves a great beauty and insight. His myths, inserted for varying reasons, tend to stress elements in a story rather than to tell a straight tale. In them Pindar often improves on his originals in the interests of morality, notably in *Ol.* 1, where he rejects the story that Pelops' shoulder was eaten. Sometimes, as in the great Argonautic saga of *Pyth.* 4, the myth is told for its own sake; more often it has a moral, as in *Pyth.* 3 and *Ol.* 1. Some of the shorter Epinicians were sung at the place of victory, notably *Ol.* 11 and *Pyth.* 7, but more usually a longer poem was sung when the victor came home. The other types of poem show a similar high style and temper, though the Maiden-Songs may have been more simple. Pindar's language is an elaborate poetical creation, made of several dialects, with many echoes and variations from Homer. His poems are written in regular stanzas, either in a series of strophes on the same plan or in a series of triads, each consisting of strophe, antistrophe, and epode. Except for *Isthm.* 3 and 4, which may be the same poem, no two poems are the same metrically. Pindar uses three main classes of metre, Dorian or 'dactylo-epitrite', Aeolian built up from such elements as the glyconic, choriambic dimeter, etc., and paeonic as in *Ol.* 2. Pindar was a great conservative in politics, morals, and religion, but the glory of his poetry lies largely in his sense of joy and honour. He was capable of deep emotion and, at times, of a sublimity to which there is no parallel.

BIBLIOGRAPHY

TEXT: O. Schroeder, *Pindari Carmina* (1900); C. M. Bowra *Pindari Carmina*[2] (1947).
COMMENTARIES: A. Boeckh (1811-32); T. Mommsen (1864); W. Christ (1896); B. L. Gildersleeve, *Olympian and Pythian Odes* (2nd ed., 1890); J. B. Bury, *Nemean Odes* (1890), *Isthmian Odes* (1892); L. R. Farnell (1932).
CRITICISM: C. Gaspar, *Chronologie Pindarique* (1900); U. von Wilamowitz-Moellendorff, *Pindaros* (1922); F. Dornseiff, *Pindars Stil* (1921); H. Gundert, *Pindar und sein Dichterberuf* (1935).
C. M. B.

PINDARUS, a name in medieval manuscripts for Homerus Latinus (see ILIAS LATINA), due perhaps to the possible use of 'Thebanus' as an epithet for Homer.

J. W. Duff, *Lit. Hist. Rome* (Silver Age), 344.

PIRACY was an endemic plague in the ancient Mediterranean. From prehistoric times this sea was the world's chief highway of traffic, and most of the traffic proceeded by regular routes (usually near the coast), which lay open to observation. Ancient merchantmen were slow and unhandy, and therefore fell a ready prey to the pirate cutters, whose crews, lurking in the numerous gulfs and coves of the Mediterranean, or behind off-shore islands, and making full use of their knowledge of local winds and currents, could often spring a surprise on passing traffic. The social and political conditions of the ancient world favoured the growth of piracy. The institution of slavery made kidnapping profitable; lack of land, spells of unemployment for mercenary soldiers or rowers, and political revolutions with their harvests of broken men, provided a constant stream of recruits to the corsairs. Ancient city-states encouraged privateering in war (see SYLE), and the less scrupulous towns acted as receivers for the pirates: in the first century B.C. Delos became notorious as a slave mart where no awkward questions were asked. The Mediterranean was full of pirate haunts (though the Moroccan Riff did not yet possess its later evil reputation). In western waters Liguria and the Baleares, Ischia and the Aeolian Isles, and, above all, the Illyrian coast were regular stations for corsairs. In the Aegean area the islands off Thessaly, the channel of Cythera, and (more especially) Crete served as bases. In the Black Sea, the Crimea and the Caucasus foreshore were infested. But the most extensive pirate base was the rugged coast of south Asia Minor.

2. In prehistoric times the Aegean Sea was cleared of corsairs by the sea-kings of Crete. In the Homeric age, after the breakdown of the Minoan thalassocracy, piracy was not only common but almost respectable (Thuc. 1. 5). Hence early Greek cities were usually built some distance inland, harbours were fortified, and watch-towers set along the coast. In the eighth and following centuries piracy was checked by the institution of city-state navies, until the tyrant Polycrates (q.v.; c. 525 B.C.) used his war-fleet for systematic plunder. After the Persian Wars the Athenian navy regularly policed the Aegean Sea, which now became safer than ever in Greek history. But a scheme of Pericles to establish a pan-Hellenic patrol-fleet miscarried (Plut. Per. 17), and in the Peloponnesian War privateering became a serious scourge. In the fourth century piracy again became rife (Isoc. Paneg. 117); the restored Athenian navy was not wholly successful in repressing it; and the plan of Philip II of Macedon (renewed by Demetrius the Besieger—SEG i. 75, l. 22) to create a pan-Hellenic naval police was not carried into effect. After the death of Alexander the intensified warfare of the Diadochi gave a fresh fillip to piracy, but the Ptolemaic and Rhodian fleets rendered good service in protecting shipping.

3. In the western Mediterranean the Greeks had to contend not only with regular pirates but with the privateering attacks of their Carthaginian and Etruscan trade-rivals; and the fleets of Syracuse made only desultory attempts to safeguard Greek shipping. In the fourth and third centuries better protection was given by the Romans, who destroyed the pirate base at Antium in 338, instituted a small patrol fleet in 311 (see DUOVIRI NAVALES), and made two pirate-drives in the Adriatic (229 and 219). But in the second century the Republic disbanded its navy, and the Hellenistic States followed suit. Consequently Mediterranean piracy reached its height in the first century B.C. Regular flotillas of war-ships, based on Crete and south Asia Minor, were organized for the plunder of entire towns, and entered into league with the enemies of Rome, Mithridates VI and Sertorius. After spasmodic attempts to cope with this danger in 102 and 78–68 (see ANTONIUS 1 and 2, METELLUS 8, SERVILIUS 2), the Romans commissioned Pompey to make a comprehensive drive against the pirates, and by a series of excellently organized operations the Mediterranean Sea was all but cleared in three months. After a temporary recrudescence of piracy under Sextus Pompeius (q.v. 5), Augustus instituted patrol fleets which kept the Mediterranean and the west European seaboard safe for some 250 years; but the Black and the Red Seas were left unprotected. After A.D. 250 the Goths and in the fifth century the Vandals infested Mediterranean waters, and from the third century Saxon pirates frequented the North Sea and the Channel.

H. A. Ormerod, *Piracy in the Ancient World* (1924); E. Ziebarth, *Seeraub und Seehandel im alten Griechenland* (1929), chs. 2–4.
M. C.

PIRAEUS (Πειραιεύς) is a promontory four miles from Athens, with a landlocked harbour on the west (Kantharos or μέγας λιμήν) and two small harbours on the east (Zea and Munichia, q.v.). Themistocles fortified it from the time of his archonship (493–492 B.C.); it grew first as a naval harbour, with docks and ship-houses, and fortifications narrowing the harbour-mouths so that they could be closed with chains; then as a commercial harbour, with quays and warehouses on the great basin. It grew rapidly, and after the Persians had destroyed Athens was suggested as the capital of Attica. C. 450 Hippodamus of Miletus laid it out on a rectangular plan.

The inhabitants were the radical party of Athens, attached by interest to navy and empire; they included many foreigners, who introduced strange cults (e.g. Bendis; Plato, Resp. 327 a). It was joined to Athens by the Long Walls (q.v.); its fortifications were destroyed in 404 but rebuilt by Conon in 393. The chief event in its later history was its siege and destruction by Sulla (87–86). Considerable parts of the walls remain; also ships' houses at Zea and Munychia, and two theatres.

W. Judeich, *Topographie von Athen*[2] (1931), 144 ff.; 430 ff.
T. J. D.

PIRENE (Πειρήνη), see PEGASUS.

PIRITHOUS (Π[ε]ιρίθοος or -θους), in mythology, a Lapith, son by Zeus of Ixion's wife Dia (Il. 14. 317–18; Pherecydes in schol. Ap. Rhod. 3. 62). Homer knows of him as fighting the Centaurs (Il. 1. 263 ff.), presumably in the quarrel mentioned Od. 21. 295 ff., and a doubtfully genuine verse (Od. 11. 631) mentions him in Hades. In the first and last of these passages he is associated with Theseus (q.v.), whose close friend he is in later authors. Hence, as our mythological tradition is largely Attic, he tends to appear as little more than the pendant of his friend. He is actually an Athenian in schol. Il. 1. 263.

One of the few adventures which are his rather than Theseus' is his wedding-feast. Marrying Hippodamia daughter of Butes (Il. 2. 742 and schol. on 1. 263), he forgot, according to one account, to include Ares among his guests (Servius on Aen. 7. 304). For that or some other reason (the simplest is that they were very drunk, cf. Od. 21. 295, where one Centaur is responsible for the disturbance) the Centaurs abused his hospitality by offering violence to Hippodamia, and a great fight began (Ovid, Met. 12. 210 ff.; the earlier accounts of a story which the Parthenon metopes show to have been well known in the fifth century, if not before, have not survived), ending in the victory of the Lapithae.

For the rest, Pirithous took his share in the carrying off of Helen, the war against the Amazons, and finally Theseus' descent to Hades, which, indeed, in one account (Hyginus, Fab. 79. 2) was undertaken to get Persephone as wife for Pirithous, in return for his services in the matter of Helen. Theseus in most accounts escapes; Pirithous generally does not (but cf. Hyginus, ibid. 3).

Weizsäcker in Roscher's *Lexikon*, s.v. H. J. R.

PISA was the district round Olympia; it probably never contained a town, but the Pisatans were in early times a power independent of the Eleans. After Pheidon's usurpation of the Olympic Games (668 B.C.) they held the presidency until c. 580, under the tyranny of the house of Pantaleon. Their claim was revived by the Arcadians in 364 (Xen. Hell. 7. 4. 28).

H. T. Wade-Gery, *CAH* iii. 544 ff. T. J. D.

PISAE, nowadays *Pisa* on the Arno, an Etruscan, possibly originally a Ligurian, town (it was certainly not founded from Pisa in Elis: Serv. ad Aen. 10. 179; Dion. Hal. 1. 20). Although presumably important earlier, it is first mentioned in 225 B.C. when the Romans used its harbour (Polyb. 2. 16 f.; Livy 21. 39). Pisae served as a frontier fortress for Rome against the Ligurians and in 180 offered territory for a Latin colony (Livy 33. 43, etc.; 40. 43). Apparently this colony never materialized, although in 177 neighbouring Luna (q.v.) received a citizen colony. Later Pisae became a prosperous Augustan *colonia* but, despite its importance, is seldom mentioned (Strabo 5. 222; Dessau, *ILS* 139 f.).

N. Toscanelli, *Pisa nell' antichità*, 3 vols. (1933–4). E. T. S.

PISIDIA, a mountainous district of south Asia Minor, at the western extremity of the Taurus chain. It was inhabited by predatory tribes which evaded all attempts by the Persian kings and their Hellenistic successors to subdue them effectively, though they made temporary submission to Alexander, and were partly held in check by the neighbouring Seleucid colony of Antioch (q.v. 2). The Pisidians apparently escaped invasion by Servilius (q.v. 2) Isauricus in 75 B.C., and they beat off an attack by the Galatian king Amyntas (25); but they were finally reduced by Sulpicius Quirinius and incorporated in the province of Galatia. The earliest urban centres of Pisidia were at Selge and Termessus; under Roman occupation, especially in the second century A.D., many prosperous small cities sprang up.

Strabo 569–77. Jones, *Eastern Cities*, 125–47. M. C.

PISISTRATIDS, see HIPPIAS, HIPPARCHUS.

PISISTRATUS (Πεισίστρατος), tyrant of Athens 560–527 B.C., claimed descent from the Neleids of Pylos and Pisistratus, archon 669/8 B.C. His mother was related to Solon. As polemarch (c. 565) he distinguished himself in war against Megara. During the subsequent faction fights he raised a third party called *Hyperakrioi, Diakrioi,* or *Epakrioi* (of which, though all explanations are speculative, the nucleus was probably the free mining population of the Laurium district adjacent to Sunium, ἄκρον Ἀθηνῶν), and in 560 made himself tyrant with a body-guard granted him by the Athenian people (*CAH* Plates I. 284). After five years he was expelled by a coalition of the Plain and Coast parties, but an understanding with the Alcmaeonids soon led to his peaceful restoration. (On the story of his restoration by Athena see *PW* xix. 163.) The new entente soon broke down and Pisistratus withdrew to Macedonia and the Mt. Pangaeus mining district; here he made money, raised mercenaries, and fostered alliances with Thessaly, Thebes, Eretria, Naxos, and Argos, and after ten years returned to Attica. He defeated his opponents at Pallene, and firmly based his tyranny on mercenaries and money derived partly from the Strymon district, partly from Attica. He died of sickness in 527.

Pisistratus retained the forms of the Solonian constitution, remaining to the end affable and benevolent. He encouraged small farmers and aimed at keeping them content to pay a moderate tax on their produce: hence the district judges instituted by him and his frequent journeys about the country. He succeeded in placating many of the nobles; only the very greatest left Attica, either to establish a tyranny elsewhere under a friendly understanding, like Miltiades I in the Thracian Chersonese (opposite Pisistratus' own outpost at Sigeum), or in definite opposition, like the Alcmaeonids at Delphi. In his day Attic black-figured pottery became the foremost fabric in the Greek world, and Attic coinage one of its foremost currencies. His building programme included the Enneakrounos fountain and the temple of Olympian Zeus. The large industrial population implied by these developments was essentially urban, and the tyrant's good-humoured but determined efforts to keep the farmers out of the city is sufficient evidence that it was the basis of his power. Only at the great festivals of the Panathenaea and Dionysia did all Athenians assemble to celebrate the glory of their city. Apollo was placated by a solemn purification of Delos.

The levelling tendency of the Athenian tyranny prepared the way for the equalitarian democracy of the succeeding century, but Pisistratus' personal pliability and the way he repeatedly bowed to the storm only to return triumphant were also momentous in Athenian history, if they suggested to Cleisthenes the possibility of a government which might be in word the rule of the leading citizen but in fact a democracy.

Herodotus, bks. 1, 5, 6; Thucydides, bk. 3; Aristotle, *Ath. Pol.* 13–16; Plutarch, *Solon* 29–31, *Moralia* 763, 805; Pausanias 1. 14. C. T. Seltman, *Athens* (1924); P. N. Ure, *Origin of Tyranny* (1922), 32 f., 307 f. P. N. U.

PISO (1) **FRUGI,** Lucius Calpurnius (*cos.* 133 B.C.), the Roman annalist, was tribune in 149, carrying his *Lex de pecuniis repetundis*, consul in 133, and censor, probably in 120. His *Annales* covered from the origins of Rome to his own times in at least seven books, the year 158 in bk. 7, the latest date 146; antiquarian and mythological fragments are also attributed to him. He rationalized the legends and, presumably under Cato's influence, set the ancient virtues against contemporary vices. Plain in style, although with lively anecdotes, he did not elaborate his material, and his authority was recognized by Cicero, Varro, Livy, Dionysius, and Pliny; Gellius quoted him for his archaism.

H. Peter, *HRRel.* i² (1914), pp. clxxxi, 120; W. Soltau, *Livius' Geschichtswerk* (1897), exaggerating Livy's use of Piso; T. Frank, *Life and Literature in the Roman Republic* (1930), 172. A. H. McD.

PISO (2), Gaius Calpurnius, as consul (67 B.C.) opposed the Gabinian law and proposed a *Lex Acilia Calpurnia de ambitu*. He governed Gallia Narbonensis (66–65). In 63 he was defended by Cicero against a charge *de repetundis* brought at Caesar's instigation. In revenge he vainly attempted to accuse Caesar of conspiracy with Catiline.

F. Münzer, *PW* iii. 1376; E. Ciaceri, *Cicerone* i (1926); W. McDonald, *CQ* 1929, 196; J. A. O. Larsen, *CPhil.* 1931, 127; H. Last, *CAH* ix. 341. A. M.

PISO (3), Gnaeus Calpurnius, an unscrupulous and dissipated friend of Caesar and Crassus, formed with Catiline in 66 B.C. the so-called first conspiracy. Sent out of the way to Hispania Citerior as *quaestor propraetore*, he was murdered in 64 by the natives.

F. Münzer, *PW* iii. 1379. A. M.

PISO (4), Marcus Pupius (*cos.* 61 B.C.), a Calpurnius adopted by M. Pupius, married Cinna's widow, Annia, whom he divorced when he went over to Sulla. He was propraetor in Spain and Pompey's legate. As consul, in the case against P. Clodius (q.v.) he proposed that the praetor should select a special jury from the then existing panels of judges. But Pupius obstructed his own proposal, and a modified plan was adopted, the *Lex Fufia*.

A. H. J. Greenidge, *The Legal Procedure of Cicero's Time* (1901), 387; J. L. Strachan-Davidson, *Problems of the Roman Criminal Law* ii (1912), 40. A. M.

PISO (5) **CAESONINUS,** Lucius Calpurnius, father-in-law of Caesar, was consul with Gabinius (58 B.C.). He supported the proposals of Clodius (q.v.), and in return he was granted the province of Macedonia, with extraordinary powers, by a direct vote of the assembly. On his return in 55 he wrangled bitterly with Cicero, who had already attacked him in his speeches *Pro Sestio* and *De provinciis consularibus* (56) and now, in the *Oratio in L. Pisonem*, charged him with peculation, misgovernment, and neglect of the safety of his province. Through Caesar's influence he was appointed censor in 50; he followed Pompey to Capua in 49, but soon returned to Rome to join his son-in-law. J. M. C.

R. Syme, *Roman Revolution* (1939), see Index.

PISO (6) **FRUGI,** Lucius Calpurnius (*cos.* 15 B.C.), called 'the *pontifex*' to distinguish him from the *augur* (no. 8). Born in 48, son of no. 5, Piso inherited a prudent nature and philhellenic tastes: he was the patron of the poet Antipater of Thessalonica. (According to Porphyrio on Horace, *Ars P.* 1, that poem was dedicated to the sons of this Piso.) Attested in Pamphylia in 13 B.C. (Dio 54. 34. 6), presumably as consular legate of the province of Galatia, he was summoned to Thrace to put down a serious insurrection, which task took three years and earned him the *ornamenta triumphalia* (Dio 54. 34. 6 ff.; Velleius 2. 98). Soon after this he may have been appointed proconsul of Asia (cf. *Anth. Pal.* 10.

25. 3 f.). Piso died in A.D. 32, after having been *praefectus urbi* for twenty years (Tacitus, *Ann.* 6. 11, if correct). He had enjoyed the unbroken confidence of Tiberius; and his notorious convivial habits impaired neither his efficiency nor his reliability (Seneca, *Ep.* 83. 14).

PIR², C 289. R. Syme, *Roman Revolution* (1939), see Index.

R. S.

PISO (7). GNAEUS CALPURNIUS (*cos.* 7 B.C.), who inherited from his father (*cos. suff.* 23 B.C.) a Republican independence of temper, was appointed governor of Syria in A.D. 17, for the avowed purpose of lending counsel and assistance to Germanicus Caesar when he journeyed to the East. After reciprocal bickering and open quarrel, Germanicus broke off his 'amicitia' with Piso. Germanicus' death (19) was attributed by his friends to magical devices or poisoning by Piso and his wife Plancina. Returning to Rome, Piso was prosecuted in the Senate, but took his own life before the trial was terminated, protesting his innocence and his loyalty to Tiberius.

R. S.

PISO (8), LUCIUS CALPURNIUS, consul (1 B.C.) and proconsul of Asia, pronounced in A.D. 16 a famous speech against the corruption of public life. Accused of *maiestas* in 24, he died before trial.

E. Groag, *PW* iii. 1383; PIR², C 290.

PISO (9), GAIUS CALPURNIUS (d. A.D. 65), came of a wealthy and distinguished family. He was exiled by Gaius, who compelled his wife Livia Orestilla to leave her husband in favour of himself and then accused the pair of adultery (probably A.D. 40). Under Claudius Piso became *consul suffectus*, but he showed no real ambition. He lived in magnificent style and was one of the most popular figures in Rome, with his charming manners and oratorical gifts, which he put at the service of rich and poor alike. It is surprising, therefore, to find him at the head of the 'Pisonian' conspiracy against Nero in 65. When the plot was betrayed, Piso, together with his associates, was compelled to suicide. His irresolution at the end, and the cringing flattery of Nero which he displayed in his will, reveal Piso as a man whom accident made famous.

PIR², C 284.

R. L. J.

PISO (10), LUCIUS CALPURNIUS, consul in A.D. 57 with Nero, whose adviser he was, served as proconsul in Africa (69). Suspected in 70 of aspiring to the throne, he was murdered by Valerius Festus, who was in touch with Licinius Mucianus in Rome.

E. Groag, *PW* iii. 1385; PIR², C 294.

PISO (11), CALPURNIUS, a contemporary of the younger Pliny (*Ep.* 5. 17), chose a Greek title κατασterισμοί for his elegiac poem on Constellations. His identification by Mommsen with the consul of A.D. 111 is doubtful.

PITHECUSAE, see AENARIA.

PITHOEGIA, see ANTHESTERIA.

PITHOLAUS, see VOLTACILIUS.

PITS, CULT. Apart from a *mundus* (q.v.), pits were dug in ritual for two principal reasons. (*a*) In rites of invocation of the dead, and in their tendance generally, liquid offerings were often poured into a pit, βόθρος, apparently by way of getting them underground into their realm; e.g. *Od.* 11. 517; Lucian, *Charon*, 22. (*b*) Consecrated objects, when worn out or useless (e.g. broken ornaments, bones and ashes of sacrifice, etc.), being still sacred, were often buried in a pit (Lat. *fauissa*) in the temple precincts.

H. J. R.

PITTACUS of Mytilene (*c.* 650–570 B.C.), statesman and sage. He commanded in the war against Athens for Sigeum, on which Periander of Corinth later arbitrated; helped to overthrow the tyrant Melanchrus, and after further party struggles in Mytilene was elected *aesymnetes* (q.v.) for ten years. He died ten years after laying down office. His best remembered law doubled the penalty for all offences if committed under the influence of drink. A moderate democratic reformer like his contemporary Solon, Pittacus was violently attacked by his younger fellow-citizen Alcaeus, whose family had helped to overthrow tyranny but wished to restore the old aristocracy.

Strabo 13. 617; Diogenes Laertius 1. 4; Suidas, s.v. 'Pittacus'; Plato, *Protagoras* 26 ff.; Plutarch, *Septem Sapientium Convivium*; C. M. Bowra, *Greek Lyric Poetry* (1936), ch. 4.

P. N. U.

PITYOCAMPTES, see SINIS.

PIUS CESTIUS, see CESTIUS.

PLACENTIA, a north Italian town near the confluence of Po and Trebia, nowadays *Piacenza*. Placentia is first mentioned as a Latin colony successfully established despite Boian opposition (218 B.C.). Military mention of Placentia is frequent: it harboured Romans after the Trebia battle, resisted Hasdrubal, rose again after Gallic and Ligurian devastations (200–190), witnessed Civil War battles and Aurelian's Marcomannic defeat (Polyb. 3. 40. 66; Livy 27. 39. 43; 31. 10. 21; 34. 22. 56; 37. 46 f.; App. *Hann.* 7; *BCiv.* 1. 92; Suet. *Otho* 9; S.H.A. *Aurel.* 21). Otherwise, although always a prosperous *municipium* or *colonia* on the Via Aemilia, it is seldom mentioned (Cic. apud Asc. p. 3 Cl.; Tac. *Hist.* 2. 19).

E. T. S.

PLACIDUS (1), grammarian of fifth or sixth century A.D. The glossary extant (in several versions) under his name is a compilation from two separate works, one of which (now called pseudo-Placidus) was based on marginal notes in copies of Republican poets. The ed. of J. W. Pirie and W. M. Lindsay (*Glossaria Lat.* iv. 12–70) supersedes that of G. Goetz (*Corp. Gloss. Lat.* v. 3–158).

Cf. Teuffel, § 482. 6; Schanz–Hosius, § 1120.

J. F. M.

PLACIDUS (2), LACTANTIUS (6th c. A.D.?), a grammarian under whose name is extant a collection of scholia on the *Thebais* of Statius (ed. R. Jahnke, 1898). He is not identical with the glossographer.

Cf. Teuffel, § 321. 10; Schanz–Hosius, § 408.

PLACITA PHILOSOPHORUM, see AËTIUS.

PLAGIARISM. I. GREEK. The charge of plagiarism was freely bandied about by Greek authors. Aristophanes accused Eupolis of 'vilely turning his *Knights* inside-out in the *Maricas*' (*Nub.* 553–4) and other comic poets of stealing his 'images' (ibid. 559), and Phrynichus Comicus was similarly accused (Scholl. Ar. *Av.* 750, *Ran.* 13). Isocrates said that some of his rivals made a living out of copying his writings (12. 16, cf. 5. 94). Among philosophers, Democritus is reputed (Favorinus ap. Diog. Laert. 9. 34) to have charged Anaxagoras with 'filching' (ὑφῃρῆσθαι) astronomical theories from someone else. Plato was said to have taken the idea of the *Republic* from Protagoras (Diog. Laert. 3. 37), and Epicurus to have plagiarized from his teacher Nausiphanes (id. 10. 7 and 14). Heraclides accused Apollonius of Perge of appropriating Archimedes' unpublished work on conic sections.

Investigation of plagiarism formed a part of Alexandrian scholarship. Aristophanes of Byzantium wrote Παράλληλοι Μενάνδρου τε καὶ ἀφ' ὧν ἔκλεψεν ἐκλογαί. Such studies enjoyed a great vogue in the first century

A.D. *Mimesis*, conscious imitation of good models, was recommended by the Atticists of that period to the aspiring writer, who was urged to say to himself, 'How would Homer, Plato, Demosthenes, or Thucydides have expressed this?' ([Longin.] *Subl.* 14.) Such imitation may lead to direct plagiarism, and Longinus (ibid. 13) is careful to distinguish between μίμησις and κλοπή. How freely plagiarism was discussed in the first century A.D. is shown by the list of authors who wrote, mainly in that century, περὶ κλοπῆς, preserved by Porphyry (ap. Euseb. *Praep. Evang.* 10. 3. 12).

So much Greek literature has been lost that it is seldom possible to say whether the charge is strictly maintainable in a particular case. But it must be remembered that the Greeks laid less stress than we do on originality of material. Originality of style was what mattered in their eyes. Further, in so far as historical works are concerned, writers were unwilling to break the flow of their style by constant references to authorities, until the conscientious Aristotle set the precedent, followed by Alexandrian writers, for extensive documentation. Herodotus often uses Hecataeus, but never names him except to disagree. Ephorus uses Herodotus, Plutarch (in his life of Coriolanus) Dionysius of Halicarnassus, without mentioning their sources. But the absence of an acknowledgement is not, of itself, sufficient ground for a charge of plagiarism.

E. Stemplinger, *Das Plagiat in der griechischen Literatur* (1912).
J. D. D.

II. LATIN. When Roman literature came under Greek influence, the Greeks themselves had fallen under the spell of their own past and found the royal road to authorship in imitating the best models. Thus Cicero (*De Or.* 2. 90), Horace (*Ars P.* 268 f.), and Quintilian (*Inst.* 10. 2) merely follow Greek theorists when they urge imitation on the young author. So it is not surprising to find that the Romans did not insist on originality as the prime literary virtue, but, freely acknowledging their debt to Greek models, made it a proud boast to have been the first to introduce a particular Greek genre into Latin poetry. Thus study preceded composition. Catullus can write no poem, he says, without his library and Horace must warn Albinovanus Celsus against borrowing too many plumes from the Palatine library. Indicative of the Roman attitude is Terence, who when accused of lifting certain characters from Naevius and Plautus defended himself on the ground that he had taken them straight from Menander—the virtue of original theft. Macrobius, too, apropos of Afranius' confession of promiscuous theft, remarks that both Greeks and Romans plundered one another. Ennius borrowed from Naevius and Lucretius from Ennius, while Virgil incorporates in his poems, often with striking improvements, many turns of phrase from his Latin predecessors. On the other hand, the occurrence of a line recalling the frivolous *Coma Berenices* in the passage describing the meeting between Aeneas and Dido (*Aen.* 6. 460) must surely be an unfortunate unconscious reminiscence.

We must mention, too, the habit of quoting another author's poems as a form of literary compliment. Thus Virgil includes in his tenth eclogue some four verses by his friend Cornelius Gallus. L. R. P.

PLANCINA, MUNATIA, was in Syria with her husband, Cn. Calpurnius Piso, governor of the province, when Germanicus and Agrippina were in the East (A.D. 18–19). By temperament no less domineering than Agrippina, she was, moreover, a friend of Livia. It was inevitable, therefore, that she should quarrel with Agrippina, and when Germanicus died in 19 Agrippina accused her of murder. Livia's intercession saved her life when Piso was condemned in 20. Accused again in 33, she committed suicide. J. P. B.

PLANCUS (1), LUCIUS MUNATIUS (*cos.* 42 B.C.), served under Caesar in the Gallic and Civil Wars, was *praefectus urbi* in 46 B.C., and subsequently governor of Gallia Comata (44–43), where he founded veteran colonies at Lugudunum and Raurica. He joined Antony before the end of the War of Mutina, was consul in 42, commanded an Antonian force in the Perusine War, and governed Asia (from 40) and Syria (*c.* 35) as Antony's *legatus*. Opposing Cleopatra's intended participation in the campaign of Actium, he went over to Octavian in 32. Plancus was the proposer of the title of Augustus for Octavian (27), was censor in 22, and restored the temple of Saturn.

Cicero, *Letters*; Velleius, bk. 2; Appian, *BCiv.* bks. 3–5; Dio Cassius, bks. 46–54. Modern literature: E. Jullien, *Le Fondateur de Lyon* (1892); F. Stähelin, *Munatius Plancus* (1900); Drumann-Groebe, *Gesch. Roms.* iv. 223–9; Tyrrell and Purser, *Correspondence of Cicero* vi² (1933), pp. lxxvi–lxxxiv. G. W. R.

PLANCUS (2) BURSA, TITUS MUNATIUS, brother of (1) above, promoted riots after Clodius' death and strongly favoured Milo's condemnation. After his tribunate (52 B.C.) he was accused by Cicero *de vi* and was condemned. He escaped to Caesar and returned in 49. In the campaign of Mutina he fought for Antony and was defeated near Pollentia. A. M.

PLANTS, SACRED. Plants are associated with many deities, the reason being sometimes quite clear. Thus, corn is sacred to Demeter and Ceres alike, it being their province (mythologically the gift of the former; of the latter we have no legends). Similarly, vines belong to Dionysus (q.v.), since he is among other things a winegod. In other instances we may reasonably conjecture that the plant is associated with the deity because used for some medical or magical purpose which falls within his or her province. Thus, wormwood is called Artemis' herb (*artemisia*), hence in some sense sacred to her; but she is a woman's goddess, and the herb was used to cure some diseases of women (Pliny, *HN* 25. 73), apparently those arising out of childbirth or pregnancy, for it is especially Artemis Eileithyia whom Pliny mentions in this connexion. Laurel had a reputation for purging from other than bodily ills (Festus, p. 104. 23 Lindsay); hence it is natural enough that Apollo, the divine specialist in purification, should be its patron. It should not, however, be assumed without further examination that the medical or magical use of the plant comes first and the association with the god is secondary, for the reverse may be true. Often the reason for the association is quite unknown and the ancients invented fantastic explanations; thus, no one can tell why the wreaths in Britomartis' festival must be of pine or mastic, and why myrtle (Aphrodite's especial plant) must not be used (Callimachus, *Dian.* 200 f.). H. J. R.

PLANUDES, *see* ANTHOLOGY (para. 6).

PLATAEA, a town in south Boeotia between Mt. Cithaeron and the river Asopus, was influenced by its geographical position and by Theban enmity to collaborate constantly with Athens from 519 B.C. onwards. It joined the latter at Marathon (490) and suffered heavily from Mardonius (q.v.), who encamped near by (479). Plataea was the scene of the Greek victory over Mardonius, and a four-yearly festival (the *Eleutheria*) was instituted there to commemorate the battle. The town was attacked by Thebes in 431, and besieged by the Spartans (429–427). The inhabitants received asylum and isopolity at Athens, until their restoration by Sparta in 386. Plataea was again razed by the Thebans *c.* 373 for its fidelity to Athens (cf. the *Plataicus* of Isocrates). Philip restored the exiles (*c.* 338), and Alexander helped to reconstruct it (*c.* 331). But Plataea never recovered its fifth-century prosperity.

G. B. Grundy, *Great Persian War* (1901), 455 ff. P. T.

PLATO (Πλάτων) (1) (c. 429–347 B.C.), son of Ariston and Perictione, both Athenians of distinguished lineage. His writings show the enormous influence that Socrates had upon him both by his life and by his death. He relates in his *Seventh Letter* that the spectacle of contemporary politics, during the ascendancy of his own associates as well as under the democracy, gradually weakened his original intention to become a statesman and drove him to the paradox that there was no hope for cities until philosophers became rulers or rulers philosophers. After the execution of Socrates in 399 he retired for a time to Megara with other Socratics. In the next twelve years he perhaps travelled to many places, including Egypt. At any rate he visited Italy and Sicily in 387, where he met Dionysius I and initiated lifelong friendships with Dion of Syracuse and the Pythagorean Archytas of Tarentum. On his return he was perhaps captured and ransomed at Aegina. It was probably only a few months later that he began formal and continuous teaching at a place near the grove of Academus about a mile outside the wall of Athens (*see* ACADEMY). This was his chief occupation almost without interruption for the remaining forty years of his life; but he made two more visits to Syracuse. Dionysius I died in 367; and Dion thereupon summoned Plato to try to realize the philosopher-king in the person of Dionysius II, and also to strengthen Dion's declining influence at court. Plato felt bound to try; but the new ruler's suspicion of Dion was soon reinforced by jealousy of his friendship with Plato. He banished Dion and sought to retain Plato. Some years later Plato was obliged to visit Syracuse for the third and last time, because Dionysius had promised to 'do as you wish about Dion' if he came, and to do nothing of the sort if he did not. Dionysius not merely broke his promise, but practically confiscated Dion's money and kept Plato a prisoner until the influence of Archytas procured his release. In 357 Dion re-entered Syracuse by force and expelled Dionysius. A few years later Dion was assassinated by persons who seem to have had something to do with Plato. The *Seventh Letter* was written to Dion's party after his death, ostensibly to urge moderation and constitutional procedure, but more to explain and justify Plato's own part in the whole miserable affair.

2. His PUBLICATIONS, which are all preserved, consist of some twenty-five dialogues and the *Apology*. There are also thirteen letters whose genuineness is much debated; but even those who reject them appear to think the *Seventh* reliable in its history. The precise order of these works is unknown; but stylometric and other inferences permit a rough division into three periods, of which the early certainly includes *Apology, Laches, Charmides, Euthyphro, Crito, Hippias Minor*, the middle certainly includes *Phaedo, Symposium, Republic*, and the late certainly includes *Sophist, Statesman, Philebus, Timaeus, Laws*. (For Plato's poetry *see* ELEGIAC POETRY, GREEK.)

3. THE EARLY DIALOGUES aim primarily at portraying a character. Plato's Socrates is ugly in body but magnetic in mind; convivial and erotic, yet Spartan in habits and of enormous physical endurance. The most striking thing about him is his conversation, to which he devotes his whole life. At first appearing absurdly simple and homely, it soon becomes intensely impressive. Its main tone is great moral earnestness, often paradoxically strict; but this is seasoned with paradoxes of another sort (as that pleasure is the only good in *Protagoras*) and with an apparently mischievous treatment of his interlocutor. The main doctrine to which he tends is that virtue is knowledge. He usually does not specify what it is knowledge of, but on the whole seems to mean: of the individual's happiness or good. Hence, since real knowledge is supremely effective in practice, no one willingly does wrong; and so-called incontinence is

ignorance. Hence, also, virtue should be teachable; and Socrates wonders why great statesmen have not taught it to their sons. Hence, lastly, Socrates holds it his duty to shatter the false conceit of knowledge wherever it occurs. He asks questions to which there is only one answer; and when these admissions are put together they entail the contradictory of the answerer's original assertion. He explains in Plato's *Apology* that this bewildering elenchus is an essential preliminary to the acquisition of real knowledge and virtue; but neither there nor elsewhere does he justify his sly and mischievous manner of conducting it. The search for knowledge appears to him mostly as a question in the form: 'What is *X*?' When offered examples he says he wants 'not many *X*'s but the one *X*', '*X* itself', the 'form' or 'idea' or 'essence'. He regards this question as prior to all others, and even as answerable apart from any examples of *X*. Yet he cannot himself produce any answer, and all those proffered by others are dissolved by his elenchus. The typical form of an early Platonic work is therefore a dialogue which raises the question 'What is so and so?', refutes all suggested answers, and ends in ignorance.

4. The typical work of THE MIDDLE PERIOD is a narration of an earlier conversation, and Plato makes magnificent use of the opportunity to describe the external scene. The elenchus now yields to a blaze of positive doctrine; and the combination of artistic and philosophic excellence thus achieved makes the *Republic* a very great book. Instead of pursuing some particular 'form', Socrates is now represented as concerned about the nature of a 'form' as such, about the whole collection of 'forms' as such, and about the consequences of the hypothesis that there are such entities. 'We are accustomed to posit some one form concerning each set of things to which we apply the same name', *Resp.* 596 a. This form is the very thing itself meant by the name. Being invisible, it is grasped by thought and not by sense. It is absolutely and perfectly what it is, independent of all else, changeless, divine. The 'forms' constitute a second class of existences, more real than the changing animals and things around us. The 'form' of the Good has a unique status among them, being 'even beyond essence'; it has some of the characteristics the Christian ascribes to God, but Plato distinguishes it from God and regards all the 'forms' as quite independent of Him. He leaves the relations between 'forms' and things somewhat vague; but the 'forms' are certainly causes of things, both in that each 'form' causes the things named after it and, apparently, in that the 'form' of the Good helps to cause all things. The relation of a 'form' to its namesake is represented as that of the original to the copy, but also as that of what is shared in to what shares; and Plato apparently thought the two accounts compatible. Modern interpretations of these 'forms' as 'concepts' or 'hypotheses' are wholly mistaken; and even the terms 'substances', 'universals', and 'ideals' can be applied only with careful distinctions and reservations. The 'forms' were 'separate' in that they were independent and self-sufficing and not parts or elements of things; but they were 'unseparated' in that Plato meant his spatial language about them to be taken metaphorically, and in that he really believed that things 'shared' in them and could not have been what they are if there had been no 'forms'.

5. As the 'forms' are absolutely distinct from things, so our apprehension of them, which is knowledge, is absolutely distinct from opinion, which is a faculty set over things. There can be no true knowledge of the changing. Opinion is changeable, fallible, irrational, and the result of persuasion; knowledge is enduring, infallible, rational, exact, clear. Knowledge comes from teaching rather than persuasion, but from recollection rather than teaching; it is our recollection of the 'forms' we saw with the mind's eye before the body imprisoned and confused us. The things we see now remind us of the 'forms' they imitate (*Phd.*); and the love of a beautiful person can lead us to the love of wisdom and of the 'form' of beauty itself (*Symp.*). In other places Plato seems to allow no part at all to sense in the creation of knowledge. Knowledge is by nature practical and commanding; for ἐπιστήμη and τέχνη are identical. For the method by which it advances *see* DIALECTIC.

6. The hypothesis that there are 'forms' has among its consequences that soul is immortal; and this is elaborately argued in the *Phaedo*. Within the human soul Plato finds three parts, the natural appetites, the spirit or resolution by which we can if we will resist the appetites, and the reason that determines when we should resist (*Resp.* bk. 4). Virtue is the proper functioning of these three. The man is wise if his reason decides rightly, brave if his spirit carries out the decision firmly, temperate and just if the better part rules the worse and each confines itself to its own business. Vice is necessarily unhappy because it is disorder and anarchy among these parts. Analogously, the ideal city will separate from the mass a small class of soldiers, living together without private property or family, and rendered by their education completely devoted to the protection of the city. They will perpetuate themselves mostly by procreation, but occasionally by enlisting a common citizen of superior metal. Within this 'spirit' of the city a higher education in mathematics and dialectic, and a series of examinations, will gradually elevate a few philosophic souls to an understanding of the 'form' of the good; and this will give them the duty though not the desire to rule. Plato's main political principle is that government is a science and requires expert knowledge. To this he adds a constitutional love of neatness and order. Both lead him to the strongest condemnations of democracy.

7. With the *Parmenides* and the *Theaetetus* Plato's late period approaches. In the latter he explicitly abandons narrated dialogue as cumbrous (143); in the former Socrates is for the first time a subordinate character. The *Parmenides* consists first of an apparently extremely damaging critique of the 'forms', and secondly of a sustained piece of abstract and self-contradictory dialectic. Undoubtedly Burnet and Taylor are mistaken in believing that the first part is really directed against the existence not of the 'forms' but of the sensibles. Undoubtedly also the 'forms' here attacked are those of Plato's own middle dialogues. But beyond this all is uncertain; and interpretations of the second part range from finding it a parody of some fallacious kind of reasoning to finding it an exposition of superrational truth.

8. The *Theaetetus*, applying the Socratic question to the concept of ἐπιστήμη, examines three likely answers with great thoroughness and insight. The first, that knowing is perceiving, is developed into an elaborate relativist theory of perception and knowledge, based on Protagorean and Heraclitean notions, before being abandoned because (1) it cannot deal with the undeniable difference between the layman and the expert, and (2) being or οὐσία is grasped by 'the soul herself by herself' and not through the senses. The second, that knowledge is true opinion, is quickly dismissed, but gives occasion for a digression on false opinion, in which Plato compares the mind to a waxen tablet and to an aviary. The third, that knowledge is true opinion with λόγος, allows him to examine the meanings of λόγος, and to consider the theory that knowledge is the analysis of compounds into their unknowable elements.

9. The *Sophist*, where the leader is an unnamed Eleatic, is Plato's most intense study in metaphysics. Sophistry entails falsehood, which entails 'not-being', which seems self-contradictory. 'Being' is no better; it raises difficulties alike for pluralists, monists, materialists, and immaterialists; it is neither rest nor motion, yet everything must either rest or move. The solution is

the doctrine of 'communication'. Some things communicate with each other, so that we can sometimes truly say '*A* is *B*'. Some things do not communicate with each other. Some things communicate with everything else; e.g. otherness, for each thing is other than each other thing. Not-being therefore exists and has being as otherness; while being itself 'is not' myriads of things. Using this discovery, Plato finds an explanation for falsehood and error.

10. Inquiring about the *Statesman*, Plato reiterates that government like medicine is a job for experts, and infers that the perfect ruler should be completely irresponsible to the people and unfettered by any inviolable constitution. Law is a second-best, useful only when science is lacking. The best constitution is simply the rule of the expert; but, failing that, we have, in order of diminishing goodness, law-abiding monarchy and aristocracy and democracy, and then lawless democracy and oligarchy and tyranny. In this dialogue, and in *Phaedrus*, *Sophist*, *Philebus*, much space goes to the method of διαίρεσις and συναγωγή. Διαίρεσις is occasionally analysis into elements (*Phdr.* 270–1), but oftener distinction, and especially the 'carving' of a 'form' into component 'forms', which seems to be an ancestor of Aristotle's 'genus and species'. By repeated carving until we reach an 'atomic form', Plato expects to reach a definition for any 'form', and also, apparently, to 'demonstrate' its truth. By συναγωγή he understands 'seeing the one in the many', which probably includes both our 'universal in the particulars' and our 'genus in the species' (*Phlb.* 16–18).

11. The *Philebus*, weighing the claims of pleasure and knowledge to be the good, and undertaking a close analysis of the former, rejects both, but sets knowledge nearer to that unity of 'beauty and symmetry and truth' which makes a thing good. It is hard to say whether Plato considered this a termination of the *Republic*'s quest for the 'form' of the good.

12. The *Timaeus*, devoted to natural science, describes how the creator made the world a single spherical living thing, having both soul and body, modelled upon 'the living creature that truly is', peopled with gods visible and invisible and with men. Tradition declares that this creator is only a mythical device for exhibiting the *rationality* inhering in the world, which has always existed and always will. Plato goes on to exhibit the complementary element, *necessity*. Besides the world and its model there is a third thing, the receptacle in which the copy becomes. The four elements can be analysed into the regular solids. The dialogue then deals at length with man, his various perceptions, the irrational part of his soul, his body, his diseases, and his health. This study, being directed towards things and not 'forms', cannot achieve infallible or even perfectly consistent results (29 c); but it will be as good as possible if we take care always to pursue both kinds of cause, reason and necessity (48 a).

13. The *Laws*, Plato's longest and perhaps last dialogue, takes up again the question of the best constitution for a city. Though reaffirming the *Republic*'s doctrine that the ideal is perfect unity achieved through communism (739), Plato now writes in a different temper and plans a different city. Extremes are bad, whether of despotism or of freedom; so let us have a mixed constitution. The citizens shall be 5,040 persons, each supporting his family by the cultivation of two inalienable parcels of land. Trading and teaching shall be practised exclusively by resident foreigners. There shall be an 'Assembly' and 'Council'. A long panel of officers culminates in the thirty-seven 'lawguards', for whom Plato gradually accumulates a multifarious set of duties; their authority, constitutional from the beginning, is further limited in the last book by the institution of 'Examiners' and of a 'Nocturnal Council' to revise the laws. Contrary to the *Republic* and the *Statesman*, this work values law very highly, institutes 'preambles' to the laws by which the legislator adds persuasion to command, and is chiefly remarkable for its immense wealth of detailed enactments, regulating every part of public and private life. Furthermore, dialectic and philosophy, which the *Republic* emphasized as the coping-stones of the constitution, here yield almost entirely to religion. The reality of the divine can be proved both from the soul and from the stars, which are gods. Plato infers that everyone should be taught astronomy, and that atheists should be converted or killed.

14. Aristotle in his *Metaphysics* attributes to Plato doctrines not stated in the dialogues, especially that (1) there is a class of entities intermediate between 'forms' and things, immutable like 'forms' but plural like things, and these are what mathematics studies; (2) the 'forms' are numbers, composed of 'inassociable' units; (3) these number-forms are not ultimate, but result from the action of 'the One' upon 'the indefinite Dyad of the Great and Small'; thus produced, they in turn act upon this Dyad to produce the world of changing things. This report of Aristotle's cannot be wholly mistaken or fictitious; and something of these doctrines was probably delivered in Plato's famous lecture on the Good, for the Good and the One were apparently identical. Plato's view on the inefficiency of writing (*Phdr.* and *Letter* 7) is sufficient explanation of their not being found in the dialogues.

15. Burnet's edition of the *Phaedo* (1911) urged that Plato must have meant this dialogue to be essentially a true account of what was said on Socrates' last day. It would follow that Socrates had studied physics in his youth, that he believed in immortality and the 'forms', and that Plato was not the inventor of the 'forms'. Burnet and Taylor have since developed this theory into the general principle that Plato aimed at historical accuracy, ascribed to famous persons only the sort of view they had really held, and expressed himself only through such characters as the 'Eleatic stranger'. The extreme consequence, that the *Timaeus* is a minute reconstruction of the state of science several decades earlier, is brilliantly drawn in Taylor's commentary; and it constitutes an adequate disproof of Burnet's hypothesis by reduction to impossibility.   R. R.

16. Plato's style possesses infinite variety. He can write easy, graceful, charming narrative, lit up with flashes of humour (openings of *Protagoras* and *Republic*, *Symp.* 217 a–21 c) or infused with the noblest pathos (end of *Phaedo*). In another vein he is capable of the gorgeous pageantry of the *Phaedrus* myth (245 c ff.), the passionate religious fervour of the address to the young atheist (*Leg.* 904 e–6 c), and the solemnity of the last paragraph of the *Republic*. Once or twice he recalls the statuesque grandeur of the pre-Socratics (*Phdr.* 245 c–e, *Resp.* 617 d–e), perhaps the only literary influence definitely traceable in him.

His language has a lavish fullness, sometimes amounting to redundancy. In structure he ranges from the simplest λέξις εἰρομένη (*Resp.* 328 b–c) to very long periods, often straggling and anacoluthic (*Resp.* 488 a–e), but sometimes even more powerful than those of Demosthenes, though quite different from them (*Criti.* 120 b–c and the tremendous period at *Leg.* 865 d–e). He fully appreciated the potentialities of a very short clause, closing a period or immediately following it (*Leg.* 727 c βλάπτει γάρ: *Phdr.* 238 c ἔρως ἐκλήθη). His language, as the ancient critics noted, is often deeply tinged with poetry. It is packed with metaphors (sometimes dead metaphors revived), especially from music. He will go back to a metaphor, as a dog goes back to a bone, when one thinks he has done with it. Much of the *Sophist* is cast in the form of an extensive metaphor, the elusive Sophist, so hard to define, being represented as a hunted animal eluding chase. In his

later years P.'s style shows traces of mannerism—a trick of interlacing the order of words, and some affectations of assonance (*Leg.* 657 d ἡμῖν ἡμᾶς, cf. 659 c; *figura etymologiae*, *Leg.* 868 c), including the pun, which fascinated P., though he laughed at it in others. But all in all, from the earliest works to the latest, no other author reveals as Plato does the power, the beauty, and the flexibility of Greek prose.

Dion. Hal. *Comp.* 18, *Pomp.* passim: [Longin.] *Subl.* 12–13, 32. For an admirable discussion of P.'s style and ancient criticisms of it see E. Norden, *Antike Kunstprosa* (1898) i. 104–13. J. D. D.

The following works, arranged in a probable chronological order, may be confidently accepted as genuine: *Hippias Minor*; *Laches*; *Charmides*; *Ion*; *Protagoras*; *Euthyphro*, *Apology*, *Crito* (comm. J. Burnet, 1924); *Gorgias* (comm. W. H. Thompson, 1894); *Meno* (comm. E. S. Thompson, 1901); *Lysis*; *Menexenus* (c. 386); *Euthydemus*; *Cratylus*; *Symposium* (c. 384); *Phaedo* (comm. J. Burnet, 1911); *Republic* (comm. J. Adam, 1902, etc.; tr. A. D. Lindsay, 1908, etc.); *Parmenides* (c. 370, tr. A. E. Taylor, 1934); *Theaetetus* (c. 368, comm. L. Campbell, 2nd ed. 1883); *Phaedrus* (comm. W. H. Thompson, 1868); *Sophist* (360 or later) and *Statesman* (comm. L. Campbell, 1867); *Philebus* (comm. R. G. Bury, 1897); *Timaeus* (A. E. Taylor comm. 1928, tr. 1929); *Critias*; *Laws* (comm. E. B. England, 1921; tr. A. E. Taylor, 1934).

The following are doubtfully genuine: *Hippias Major* (comm. D. Tarrant, 1928); *Clitopho*; *Epinomis* (tr. with notes J. Harward, 1928); *Letters* 2–13 (comms. F. Novotny, 1930, and G. Morrow, *Illinois Univ. Studies in Lang. and Lit.* xviii, 1935; tr. L. A. Post, 1925).

The following may be confidently rejected as spurious: *Letter* 1; *Alcibiades* 1 and 2; *Hipparchus*; *Amatores*; *Theages*; *Minos*; *De Justo*; *De Virtute*; *Demodocus*; *Sisyphus*; *Eryxias*; *Axiochus*; *Definitions*.

For various aspects of Plato's doctrine and writings, *see also* ACADEMY, AFTER-LIFE, ANATOMY AND PHYSIOLOGY, ASTRONOMY, LITERARY CRITICISM IN ANTIQUITY, I. 2, MATHEMATICS, MUSIC.

BIBLIOGRAPHY

LIFE: Plato, *Letter* 7; Diogenes Laertius, bk. 3; G. C. Field, *Plato and His Contemporaries* (1930); and the general studies below.
TEXT: O.C.T. (Burnet).
SCHOLIA: C. F. Hermann, *Platonis Dialogi*, vol. i.
COMMENTARIES: Stallbaum-Wohlrab (1836–77); and the special commentaries above.
TRANSLATIONS: B. Jowett (all the probably genuine works, inaccurate but charming); and the special translations above.
GENERAL STUDIES: G. Grote, *Plato and the Other Companions of Socrates* (1888); C. Ritter, *Platon: Sein Leben, seine Schriften, seine Lehren* (1910–23), esp. for stylometry; J. Burnet, *Greek Philosophy* (1914), 205–351; U. v. Wilamowitz-Moellendorff, *Platon* (1920); A. E. Taylor, *Plato, The Man and His Work*[2] (1927); P. Friedländer, *Platon* (1928–30); P. Shorey, *What Plato Said* (1933), esp. for bibliography.
SPECIAL STUDIES: H. Jackson, 'Plato's Later Theory of Ideas', in *Journ. Phil.* 10–11 (1882–3), 13–15 (1885–6); F. M. Cornford, *Plato's Theory of Knowledge* (1935), *Plato's Cosmology* (1937), *Plato and Parmenides* (1939); J. Stenzel, *Plato's Method of Dialectic* (D. J. Allan, tr. 1939), *Zahl und Gestalt bei Platon und Aristoteles*[2] (1933); L. Robin, *La Théorie platonicienne des idées et des nombres d'après Aristote* (1908); R. Robinson, *Plato's Earlier Dialectic* (1941). R. R.

PLATO (2), Athenian comic writer. First play, *Ζεὺς κακούμενος*, (?) 428 B.C.; last datable reference 389. Wrote twenty-eight comedies (Suid. and anon. *Περὶ κωμ.*) both Old and Middle, many on political themes. Such are *Νῖκαι* (ref. to Peace of Nicias); *Περιαλγής* (c. 420, possibly dealt with sufferings of Athens under Hyperbolus); *Συμμαχία* (possibly produced by Cantharus, q.v.); *Πείσανδρος* (possibly attacked the politicians whose machinations resulted in the rule of the Four Hundred); Ἑορταί (c. 414; attacked Dieitrephes (cf. Ar. *Av.* 798, 1442)); Ἑλλὰς ἤ Νῆσοι (? dealt with the break-up of the Athenian Empire); *Κλεοφῶν* (405 (hyp. 1 Ar. *Ran.*)); *Πρέσβεις* (? ref. to embassy sent to Persia after Cnidos).

He also wrote mythological burlesques: Ζεὺς κακούμενος; Ξάντριαι ἢ Κέρκωπες; Νὺξ μακρά (all three dealt with the Heracles saga); Ἄδωνις; Δαίδαλος (possibly really by Aristophanes, q.v.); Λάϊος; Μενέλεως; Φάων (depicting the loves of Aphrodite and Phaon; a long fragment (174) shows the goddess acting as *leno* to her favourite). A third class of his plays treated of social subjects: e.g. Αἱ ἀφ' ἱερῶν; Λάκωνες ἢ Ποιηταί (possibly dealt with recall of one or more of the old school of poets from Hades); Σκευαί (? = 'Accoutrements of Tragedy'); Σοφισταί (parodies Eur.; a play probably on the lines of Ar. *Nub.*). The few ancient criticisms on Plato we possess comment on his elegance and his scurrility. The fragments show a prevalence of erotic motive.

FCG ii. 615 ff.; CAF i. 601 ff.; Demiańczuk, *Suppl. Com.* 76 ff.
M. P.

PLATONISM, MIDDLE, see MIDDLE PLATONISM.

PLATONIUS (of uncertain date) wrote *On the Difference between Comedies*, i.e. between Old, Middle, and New Comedy, and *On the Difference of Types*, in which he discussed the characteristics of individual comic poets. The extant fragments, prefixed to editions of Aristophanes, are brief but valuable.   J. F. L.

PLATORIUS NEPOS, AULUS, consul in A.D. 119 and governor of Lower Germany, was legate of Britain from July 122 (*JRS* xii. 65; xx. 21) until after Sept. 124 (*CIL* vii. 1195 = xvi, p. 64, no. 70). He was a personal friend of and possible successor to Hadrian (S.H.A. *Hadr.* 4. 2; 15. 2) whom he apparently accompanied to Britain (122), bringing Legio VI Victrix from Lower Germany. He built the milecastles (*CIL* vii. 660–3; *JRS* xxv. 16) and forts (*JRS* xxvii. 247; xxviii. 201) of Hadrian's Wall (q.v.).
I. A. R.

PLAUTIANUS, GAIUS FULVIUS (*cos.* A.D. 203), was, like Septimius Severus, a native of Africa, and is said to have been exiled by Pertinax for treason. The origin of his relationship with Septimius is unknown, but by the time of the Second Parthian War he had won his confidence and vigorously persecuted the adherents of Niger. Appointed Praetorian Prefect, he came to exercise an almost autocratic power, and while retaining the Emperor's trust amassed a private fortune. In A.D. 202 he reached the zenith of his career by the marriage of his daughter Plautilla to Caracalla. Next year he was consul with Geta and thus held at the same time the two highest appointments open to senators and knights. His influence over the Emperor was resented by Julia Domna, and when he caused his own statue to be placed among those of the imperial family he fell from favour (203). But his disgrace was short-lived, and for another year he continued to enjoy the indulgence of the Emperor. His final downfall was due to Caracalla, who was disappointed in his marriage and induced his father to believe that the prefect was plotting his assassination (205).

For bibliography *see* SEVERUS (1).   H. M. D. P.

PLAUTIUS (1) **SILVANUS,** MARCUS, a moderate *popularis* of obscure origin, as tribune in 89 B.C. was responsible with C. Papirius Carbo for the *Lex Plautia Papiria* which, supplementing the *Lex Iulia* of 90, offered the citizenship to insurgents who withdrew straightway from the revolt, and to folk not covered by the previous law, in particular to certain persons who, though attached to the *municipia* incorporated in 90 as *adscripti*, were then resident not in their municipality but at Rome or elsewhere in but not outside Italy. Such persons were to apply to the *praetor urbanus* within sixty days.

Plautius also modified the *quaestio Variana*, which was trying the friends of Livius Drusus and other sympathizers with the insurgents, by a *lex iudiciaria* which introduced mixed instead of equestrian juries.

Asconius, *Corn.* p. 79; Cicero, *Arch.* 4. 7. A. N. Sherwin-White, *The Roman Citizenship* (1939), 132.   A. N. S.-W.

PLAUTIUS (2) **HYPSAEUS,** PUBLIUS, was Pompey's quaestor in the East and consular candidate in 53 B.C. with Q. Caecilius Metellus Scipio against Milo. He contributed to the riots of the year. After Clodius' murder he and Scipio attacked the *interrex* M. Aemilius Lepidus in his house in order to obtain election. But Pompey was appointed sole consul and abandoned Plautius, who was condemned for bribery.

T. Rice Holmes, *The Roman Republic* ii (1923), 164.   A. M.

PLAUTIUS (3) **SILVANUS,** MARCUS, consul in 2 B.C. with Augustus, was proconsul of Asia, and probably legate of Galatia. He probably fought the mountaineers of Isauria (A.D. 6) and certainly commanded troops in the Pannonian War. His mother Urgulania was a friend of Livia, his daughter Urgulanilla married the future Emperor Claudius.

PIR, P 361; E. Groag, *JÖAI* xxi–xxii (1922–4) Beibl. 445; R. Syme, *Klio* 1934, 139; id., *Anatolian Studies Presented to W. H. Buckler* (1939), 332.   A. M.

PLAUTIUS (4), AULUS (*cos. suff.* A.D. 29), governor of Pannonia in 43, when he was appointed by Claudius to command the British expedition. He defeated the sons of Cunobellinus in battles (probably at the Medway and at the Thames), and took the Belgic capital, Camulodunum. Before his departure (47) he seems to have conquered Britain up to the oolitic ridge on the Cotswolds–Lincoln Edge line. On his return he received the honour of an ovation. In 57, 'according to ancient custom,' he himself conducted an inquiry into charges of 'externa superstitio' against his wife—and acquitted her.

Dio Cass. 60. 19–21; Tac. *Ann.* 13. 32; PIR, P 344; Collingwood-Myres, *Roman Britain*, 78–91.   C. E. S.

PLAUTIUS (5) **SILVANUS AELIANUS,** TIBERIUS (*cos. suff.* A.D. 45, *cos.* II 74), is barely known to history save for the long inscription recording his career and exploits, still extant at the Mausoleum of the Plautii near Tibur (*ILS* 986). The precise degree of his relationship to M. Plautius (3) Silvanus is uncertain. Silvanus served as a legate in the conquest of Britain, clearly enjoying the favour of the Emperor Claudius (whose first wife, Plautia Urgulanilla (*see* PLAUTIUS 3), belonged to his family). After being proconsul of Asia (c. A.D. 57) Silvanus was appointed legate of Moesia, in which function he conducted diverse operations, and made the frontier safe, though his army was weakened by the dispatch of troops to the East for Corbulo's campaigns. He prevented a disturbance among the Sarmatians, relieved the siege of Chersonesus, transplanted more than 100,000 natives to the southern bank of the Danube, and sent a copious supply of corn to Rome. For these services, however, he got no honour from Nero; Vespasian subsequently granted him the *ornamenta triumphalia*. After governing the province of Hispania Tarraconensis (70–73?), he was appointed *praefectus urbi* by Vespasian.

L. Halkin, *Ant. Class.* 1934, 121.   R. S.

PLAUTIUS (6) **LATERANUS,** a Roman senator, deprived of his rank in A.D. 48 as a lover of Messalina, was restored by Nero (55). Consul designate (65), he took part in the Pisonian conspiracy and was executed.

PIR, P 354.

PLAUTIUS (7), a Roman jurist of the time of Vespasian, not directly excerpted in the *Digest* and known only through commentaries entitled *ad Plautium* and written by Neratius, Javolenus, Pomponius, and Paulus. This interest of posterity in Plautius' work, which apparently dealt mostly with the praetorian law, though its title is unknown, proves his high reputation. His original work seems to have played the same important part as the *Libri iuris civilis* of Sabinus in relation to later treatises on private law.   A. B.

PLAUTUS, Titus Maccius (so the name is given by the Ambrosian palimpsest, in the subscriptio to the *Casina*; references in the text are usually to *Plautus*, but *Merc.* 10, where the MSS. read *mactici, mattici*, presumably corruptions of *Macci Titi*, and *Asin.* 11, where the nominative appears as *Maccus*, throw a doubtful light on the subject; Festus-Paulus derives *Plautus* from *plotus*, 'flat-footed'), is stated by Cicero (*Brut.* 60) to have died in 184 B.C.; the date of his birth appears to have been not later than 251, as he was already 'senex' (Cic. *Sen.* 50) when the *Pseudolus* was produced in 191 (didasc.). The other details are filled in by Jerome (who unfortunately gives the year of his death as 200) and Gellius (3. 3. 14), who claims to be quoting Varro: they are that he was born at Sarsina in Umbria, that after acquiring some capital in the service of the theatre he lost it in trade, and that, when forced by poverty to work as a labourer in a flour-mill, he wrote the *Saturio*, the *Addictus*, and another play. Leo (*Plautinische Forschungen*) unconvincingly (?) argues that these statements are mere inferences from passages in lost plays; Marx (*Z. für die öst. Gym.*, 1898) accepts the traditional account. We can be certain that the *Stichus* was produced in 200 (didasc.); the references in *Miles Gloriosus* (211–12) to the imprisonment of Naevius would suggest that this play was produced soon after 206. P. was a highly popular dramatist, and his plays continued to be produced long after his death (*Cas.* prol.); imitators seem to have tried to pass off their work as his, with the result that 130 plays were in later times attributed to him (Gell. 3. 3. 11 ff.). Varro drew up a list of twenty-one which were universally regarded as Plautine (Gell. 3. 3. 3); these must be the twenty-one which have come down to us: *Amphitruo, Asinaria, Aulularia, Bacchides, Captivi, Casina, Cistellaria, Curculio, Epidicus, Menaechmi, Mercator, Miles Gloriosus, Mostellaria, Persa, Poenulus, Pseudolus, Rudens, Stichus, Trinummus, Truculentus, Vidularia*. Varro assigned other plays also to Plautus on stylistic grounds, and we may note that Terence ascribes to Plautus the *Colax* (*Eun.* 25) and *Commorientes* (*Ad.* 7), neither of which plays has reached us. Terence's words, however, may imply that the *Colax* was partly the work of Naevius, and Gellius (l.c.) states that Plautus was in the habit of touching up plays written by other writers: here we have, perhaps, the explanation of the confusion which seems to have prevailed from an early time as to which plays were the work of Plautus.

2. Unlike his predecessors, Plautus confined his activities to one branch of literature, the translation of works of the Greek New Comedy. That he treated his originals with considerable freedom is evident not only from the puns and topical allusions which occur frequently in his plays, but from Terence's general reference to his 'neglegentia' (*An.* 20) and Terence's explicit statement (*Ad.* 9, 10) that he omitted a whole scene in Diphilus' Συναποθνῄσκοντες. We may well believe that he lost no opportunity of raising a laugh, that he expanded or inserted passages which would appeal to the rough taste of his audience, and that as a result there is much in his plays which jars upon our sense of dramatic propriety; but attempts to ascertain more precisely the nature of Plautus' methods as a translator are rendered nugatory by the fact that we possess scarcely a line of any of his originals, and that no play of New Comedy has come down to us complete (*see* CONTAMINATIO). From Menander he took the *Cistellaria* (cf. 89 ff. with Meineke, *Menandri et Philem. Reliquiae*, Berl. 1823, *Incert. fabb.* 32), the *Stichus* (didasc.), and the *Bacchides* (line 817 is a translation of a line of the Δὶς ἐξαπατῶν preserved by Stobaeus); from Philemon the *Trinummus* (l. 19) and *Mercator* (l. 10) but *not* the *Mostellaria* (see Terzaghi's edition 1929, pp. xxi ff., and A. Ernout, *Plaute* v, p. 13); from Diphilus the *Casina* (l. 32) and *Rudens* (l. 32); from Demophilus the *Asinaria* (l. 11);

the statements made by modern writers about the authors of the other originals are little more than guesses. The dates of production of the *Pseudolus* and *Stichus* are known from the didascaliae; the *Miles* seems to have appeared soon after the imprisonment of Naevius (see above); the *Cistellaria* during or soon after the Hannibalic War (ll. 197–202); the *Truculentus*, like the *Pseudolus*, was a work of Plautus' old age (Cic. *Sen.* 50); the *Bacchides* was subsequent to the *Epidicus*, to which it contains a reference (214–15); further than this we have no sure evidence, though it has been plausibly argued that, e.g., the *Mercator* is early and the *Trinummus* late. The argument of Sedgwick (*CQ* xxiv. 102–5) that Plautus increased the lyrical element in his plays as he gained skill must be regarded as a mere hypothesis, though a not unreasonable one.

3. The plays of Plautus vary widely in tone. If we can judge from his own expression of liking for the *Epidicus* (*Bacch.* 214–15) and Cicero's remark (see supra) that Plautus was much attached to the *Pseudolus* and the *Truculentus*, we may infer that his favourite type of play was one of lively, complicated, and somewhat shady intrigue; but against this we must set the unexceptionable sentiments expressed in the *Trinummus*, the nobility and pathos of the *Captivi*, and the heroic figure of Alcumena in the *Amphitruo*. There is enough obscenity to suggest that its comparative rarity was not due merely to police supervision; it is mostly of a trivial character. The conscious rectitude of the prologue and epilogue to the *Captivi* is not typical; the general tone is one of genial cynicism. Among the most noteworthy plays are the *Aulularia*, with its powerful if exaggerated portrait of Euclio, who is something between a miser and a worthy poor man whom the sudden acquisition of wealth has made wretched; the *Menaechmi*, an entertaining 'Comedy of Errors' (and the source of Shakespeare's play); the *Miles*, the richest portrait of the swaggering poltroon so popular on the stage of Hellenistic times; the *Mostellaria* with its high-spirited intrigue and its hero Tranio, most engaging of all the *servi callidi*; and the *Rudens* with its unusual setting and interesting plot.

4. The language of Plautus is all his own; here his claims to greatness are undeniable. No one ever exploited more fully the resources of Latin for expressions of endearment and abuse, for animated dialogue and effective repartee. For him words had an interest in themselves: we see this in the frequent assonance, word-play, and comic compounds. Connected with his command of language is his command of metre, e.g. the solemn senarii of Arcturus' utterance (prologue to the *Rudens*), the vigorous cretics in which Sosia describes the battle (*Amph.* 223 ff.), above all, perhaps, the varied uses of the trochaic septenarius.

5. *Prosody*. The prosody of the early Latin dramatic poets corresponds to the facts of pronunciation more closely than does the artificial verse of the Augustan period. Many syllables (especially final) were still long which afterwards became shortened; final -*s* was still so faintly sounded that it could be disregarded in scansion before an initial consonant. A combination of mute and liquid can be, and was, pronounced with the following vowel ($\check{a}$-*gros*); therefore it is nowhere allowed by Plautus to give the preceding syllable length by position. Hiatus may legitimately occur at a pause in the sense, e.g. when the speaker is deciphering a letter. The words are so arranged that the recurrent beat of the verse (*ictus*) corresponds *as far as possible* with the stressed syllables:

qui'st imperátor díuom et hóminum Iúppiter.

A rigid classification of syllables into longs and shorts does not do justice to the flexibility of speech, especially in a stress-accent language. In Plautus we find certain syllables scanned now long, now short; many such cases are covered by the so-called law of *breuis breuians* (q.v.), or iambic shortening, which may be stated thus: an unaccented syllable, normally long by quantity or position, which is immediately preceded by a short syllable and immediately (a) preceded or (b) followed by an accented syllable ((a) $\cup - $ (b) $\cup - \acute{x}$) is so weakened in pronunciation that it *may* be scanned as a short. The position and value of the accent itself is not quite fixed, but depends to some extent on the arrangement of the words and on the sense.

6. The *Prologues*. There seems no good reason for regarding these as post-Plautine, except *Cas.* 1–20 (written for a revival performance after the death of Plautus), the opening lines of the *Menaechmi* (3, 'adporto uobis Plautum'), and perhaps the brief Prologue to the *Pseudolus* (2):

> Plautina longa fabula in scaenam uenit.

Certainly many of the criteria by which critics have pronounced other prologues spurious (e.g. clumsiness, tautology, references to a seated public) are of doubtful validity; see Lindsay's edition of the *Captivi*, pp. 113–15. (Lindsay does, however, find some linguistic evidence that the prologue to the *Captivi* is in parts post-Plautine. No doubt the prologue would be the part of the play most exposed to alteration by producers of a later age.) In many cases Plautus must have translated his prologues from the Greek (though we may well suppose that here he took even more than his usual liberties); the postponed prologue of Auxilium in the *Cistellaria* (translated from Menander) is in position and form not unlike the prologue of Ἄγνοια in the Περικειρομένη. If Plautine, the prologues throw light both on the outlook of the dramatist and on the character of the turbulent crowds before whom his pieces were performed.

See also DRAMA, para. 3.

BIBLIOGRAPHY

MANUSCRIPTS: (a) the fifth-century Ambrosian palimpsest, discovered in 1815, now indecipherable and only to be studied in the apograph of W. Studemund (1889), which cost the author his sight; (b) the Palatine family—tenth or eleventh century. See W. M. Lindsay, *An Introduction to Latin Textual Emendation* (1896).

TEXT: This was first put on a sound basis by F. Ritschl, whose first volume appeared in 1848. His pupils, G. Götz, G. Löwe, F. Schöll, completed his work in their authoritative edition, with full apparatus (1871–94, since partly re-edited). J. L. Ussing's text (1875–86) contains a Latin commentary; Fr. Leo's edition (1895–6) is ingenious and important, but arbitrary; W. M. Lindsay's Oxford Text (1903) and A. Ernout's Budé edition (below) are more conservative.

(The scene-division is based on the manuscripts; the act-division is the work of Renaissance editors.)

EDITIONS OF SEPARATE PLAYS: Specially important are Lindsay, *Captivi* (1900); E. A. Sonnenschein, *Rudens* (1901) and *Mostellaria* (1922); F. Marx, *Rudens* (1928); Brix-Niemeyer, *Menaechmi* (1929), *Captivi* (1930), and *Trinummus* (1931), and P. J. Enk, *Mercator* (1932).

TRANSLATIONS WITH TEXT: P. Nixon (Loeb, 1928–38), in general accurate and lively; A. Ernout (Budé, 1932– , not yet completed).

GENERAL: The most readable and reliable work is perhaps that of G. Michaut (*Plaute*, 1920). P. Lejay (*Plaute*, 1925) gives special attention to music. Other well-known works are Ph. É. Legrand's *Daos, Tableau de la comédie grecque* (1910), which lays scarcely sufficient emphasis on P.'s originality, E. Fraenkel's *Plautinisches im Plautus* (1922), and G. Jachmann's *Plautinisches und Attisches* (1931), which go perhaps too far in the attempt to distinguish between Greek and Latin elements.

PROSODY, METRE, ETC.: W. M. Lindsay, ed. of *Captivi* (above) and *Early Latin Verse* (1922); E. Fraenkel, *Iktus und Akzent* (1928); H. Drexler, *Plautinische Akzentstudien* (1932).

SYNTAX: W. M. Lindsay, *Syntax of Plautus* (1907). Fuller bibliography in Schanz-Hosius, *Röm. Lit.* i (1927), 55–86.   W. B.

PLEBISCITUM was a resolution passed by the plebs. As only the *populus* (q.v.) was originally allowed to carry a law, plebiscites could bind only the group that had issued them in the *concilia tributa plebis* (from the first decades of the 5th c. B.C.). Many plebiscites, however (e.g. the *Lex Canuleia* in 445 B.C.), must have obtained a *de facto* recognition from the whole community, before the *Lex Hortensia* (c. 287) gave plebiscites the force of law. Sulla made them again dependent on the approval of the Senate, but Pompey and Crassus as consuls in 70 re-enacted the *Lex Hortensia*.

Mommsen, *Röm. Forsch.* i. 177 ff.; *Röm. Staatsr.* iii². 150 ff.
                                                                                        P. T.

PLEBS was the name given to the general body of Roman citizens, as distinct from the privileged *patricii*; it is perhaps related to πλῆθος. The contrast between it and the *patricii* no doubt arose through the differentiation of certain wealthier and more influential families into a separate class. The modern hypothesis that the plebs was racially distinct from the *patricii* is not supported by ancient evidence; and the view of some ancient writers (Cic. *Rep.* 2. 16; Dion. Hal. 2. 9; Plut. *Rom.* 13) that the plebeians were all clients of the patricians in origin can be true only in the sense that the clients were plebeians. The plebeians were originally excluded from religious colleges, magistracies, and the Senate, and by a law of the XII Tables they were debarred from intermarriage with patricians. But they were enrolled in the *gentes*, *curiae*, and *tribus*; they served at all times in the army and could hold the office of *tribunus militum*. It is very doubtful whether it is legitimate to speak of plebs for the period of monarchy. A sharp distinction between the two classes seems to have developed only in early Republican times.

The 'Conflict of the Orders', by which the plebs achieved political equality with the patricians, forms part of the general history of Rome. The victory of the plebs was essentially due to the fact that it organized itself into a separate corporation, which held its own assemblies (*concilia plebis*), appointed its own officers, the *tribuni* and *aediles plebis* (usually selected from the wealthier members of their order), and instituted its own Record Office (in the temples of Diana and of Ceres on the Aventine). It secured inviolability for the persons of its officers by a collective undertaking to protect them, and at times of special crisis it withdrew *en masse* from Rome (see SECESSIO). After two centuries of struggle the plebs attained all its political objects by 287 B.C. Under the later Republic the name 'plebeian' acquired in ordinary parlance its modern sense of a member of the lower social orders. In Imperial times those who did not belong to the senatorial and equestrian orders, or to the *ordo* of the *municipia*, were often called plebeians.

Mommsen, *Röm. Staatsr.* iii (1887); G. De Sanctis, *Stor. Rom.* i. 224; J. Binder, *Die Plebs* (1909); A. Rosenberg, *Hermes* 1913, 359; H. J. Rose, *JRS* 1922, 106; H. Stuart Jones, *CAH* vii. 413; F. Altheim, *Lex Sacrata, Die Anfänge der plebeischen Organisation* (1940); H. Last, *JRS* 1945, 30. *See also* TRIBUNI PLEBIS; PATRICIUS.
                                                                                        A. M.

PLEBS FRUMENTARIA, *see* CONGIARIUM.

PLEIAS, *see* TRAGEDY, para. 21.

PLEMINIUS, QUINTUS, propraetor in 205 B.C., under Scipio Africanus recaptured Locri from Hannibal. Left in charge of a garrison Pleminius plundered Locri, including the treasury of Persephone. After an inquiry by Scipio he retained his command and continued to oppress the Locrians until they appealed to the Senate. He was arrested by a senatorial commission of inquiry and perhaps held in prison until his death (195?).
                                                                                        H. H. S.

PLINY (1) THE ELDER (GAIUS PLĪNIUS SECUNDUS) (A.D. 23/4–79), born at Comum, came to Rome as a boy for education. Following the military career appropriate to his equestrian family, he served as cavalry officer in Germany 47–57, to which last year is usually ascribed his *castrense contubernium* (*HN praef.* 3) with the future Emperor Titus. He practised also as a pleader, but during Nero's reign devoted his time to literature; under Vespasian, with whom he was intimate, 'he held various successive procuratorships with the highest integrity' (Suet. *Vita*), in Gallia Narbonensis, Africa, Hispania Tarraconensis, and Gallia Belgica. The claim (Mommsen, *Hermes* xix. 644) from a restored inscription (*CIG* iii. 4536) that he was on the staff of Titus in the Jewish War of 70 is controverted. His last post was as admiral at Misenum, whence, fired by scientific zeal, he sailed to get a closer view of the eruption of Vesuvius, 24 Aug. 79. His nephew, the Younger Pliny, describes his last hours, before he succumbed to asphyxiation on the sea-shore at Castellammare.

WORKS (Nos. 1–6 are lost):

1. **De iaculatione equestri**, on the javelin as a cavalry weapon, written as *praefectus alae* in Germany, *HN* 8. 162.

2. **De vita Pomponi Secundi**, a biography in two books of his early friend and literary preceptor, *HN* 14. 56.

3. **Bellorum Germaniae libri xx**, a narrative of all Roman wars with Germans, intended to rescue the memory of Drusus from oblivion, and used by Tacitus (*Ann.* 1. 69).

4. **Studiosi**, in three books, each of two parts, on rhetorical training from childhood, and containing specimens from declamations. Quintilian (3. 1. 21) recognized it as pedantically careful.

5. **Dubius Sermo**, eight books, published A.D. 67, when technical subjects like grammar were alone safe, *HN praef.* 28. Pliny took a middle position between analogists and anomalists.

6. **A fine Aufidi Bassi**, thirty-one volumes, a history of his own times from the point where Aufidius Bassus left off, probably the close of Claudius' reign. Written with scrupulous care, it was left for publication posthumously.

7. **Naturalis Historia**, sole extant work of Pliny's 102 volumes. Though dedicated to Titus by a preface of 77, revision still proceeded at Pliny's death; in its final form it consisted of the preface, a book containing tables of contents and lists of authorities (who were also given with each book) 'to facilitate handling and acknowledge indebtedness to sources', and thirty-six books of subject-matter. The topics are: ii, the Physical Universe; iii–vi, Geography and Ethnology; vii, Anthropology and Physiology; viii–xi, Zoology; xii–xxvii, Botany; xx–xxvii, Botany in relation to Pharmacology; xxviii–xxxii, Zoology in relation to Pharmacology; xxxiii–xxxvii, Mineralogy and Metallurgy and their use in the arts. Included were 20,000 matters worthy of attention, gathered from 2,000 books and 100 principal authors, who cannot be disentangled from the 146 Roman and 327 foreign authors in the indexes. For each topic he probably depended on a few main authorities (thus, for Physics, Varro, behind whom lay Posidonius), and added a mosaic of excerpts from his 160 note-books, mingling Roman examples with material basically Greek.

Pliny had a disinterested love of knowledge but was not a scientific observer. With an encyclopaedist's superficiality he introduces many avoidable inaccuracies and lacks constructive criticism ('prodenda quia sunt prodita', *HN* 2. 85). His style is the most formless among contemporary writers; with a dry catalogue of facts in abrupt sentences he mingles vivid periodic descriptions of considerable power, and plentiful rhetorical devices. His vocabulary has poetical elements and many borrowings from Greek, but is not extensively colloquial.

BIBLIOGRAPHY

LIFE AND WORKS: Own writings; Pliny, *Ep.* 3. 5; 5. 8; 6. 16 and 20; fragment of Suetonius' *Vita*. H. N. Wethered, *The Mind of the Ancient World: A Consideration of Pliny's N.H.*, 1937.

TEXTS: D. Detlefsen (1866–73); Jan's Teubner, 2nd edition (Mayhoff). The numbering by short sections is modern, but there is an older twofold division into chapters, the second of which was made by Hardouin in the Delphin edition (1685); see his preface, vol. i. *Dubii Sermonis Reliquiae*, Teubner (J. W. Beck), 1894.

COMMENTARIES: L. Urlichs, *Chrestomathia Pliniana* (1857); K. Jex-Blake and E. Sellers, *Chapters on History of Art* (1896); K. C. Bailey, *Chapters on Chemical Subjects*, 2 vols. (1929–32); *HN* bk. 2, D. J. Campbell (1936).

TRANSLATIONS: Philemon Holland (1601); J. Bostock and H. T. Riley, Bohn, 6 vols.; Loeb vol. i, etc., H. Rackham.

STYLE: Joh. Müller, *Der Stil des älteren P.* (1883).

SOURCES: H. Brunn, *De auctorum indicibus Plinianis disputatio isagogica* (1856); F. Münzer, *Beiträge zur Quellenkritik der Naturgesch.* (1897); W. Kroll, *Die Kosmologie des ält. P.* (1930) and *PW*, s.v.

Recent literature to 1927, Fritz Krohn, Bursian 231.   D. J. C.

PLINY (2) THE YOUNGER

(A.D. 61 or 62–before 114), born at Comum, was a son of L. Caecilius Cilo, and nephew of Pliny the Elder (q.v.). His father's early death brought him under the guardianship of the distinguished soldier Verginius Rufus; later, on adoption by his uncle, he changed his name from P. Caecilius Secundus to C. PLINIUS CAECILIUS SECUNDUS. At Rome he studied under Nicetes Sacerdos and Quintilian, began his career as a pleader at 18, and became a specialist in disputes concerning property. His wealth and the influence of his guardian secured him early preferment, and his discretion enabled him to retain Domitian's favour, though several of his friends fell victims to the reign of terror (*Ep.* 3. 11). The chronology of his career has been much disputed (Mommsen, *Hermes* iii. 31; W. Otto, *Sitz. Bayer. Akad.* 1919, 1923), but it is known that besides fulfilling the *cursus honorum* he was appointed *praefectus aerarii militaris* by Domitian, *praefectus aerarii Saturni* by Nerva, and by Trajan *augur* and *curator alvei Tiberis et riparum et cloacarum urbis*. As *consul suffectus* in 100 he addressed to Trajan the customary *gratiarum actio*, and later published the elaborate rhetorical essay which survives as the *Panegyricus*, based on this speech (*Ep.* 3. 18), but considerably expanded (see Durry's ed., p. 9; for disputed date of publication, ibid. pp. 9–15). To the modern reader this epideictic oration may seem fulsome and tedious, but its reputation in antiquity can be judged from its position as the earliest, by two centuries, of the *XII Panegyrici*. Rightly interpreted, it appears not as mere unctuous flattery but as an admonitory tract (cf. 45. 6, 62. 9). We possess none of the forensic orations on which P. relied for fame. He figured in several important political trials, first as prosecutor, his most notable success being the impeachment of Marius Priscus in 100, and later as counsel for the defence of two senatorial ex-governors accused of maladministration in Bithynia (104 and 106). The knowledge thus acquired, together with his treasury experience, made P. the obvious choice when Trajan decided to place Bithynia under an imperial legate with special powers to overhaul its finances. P. certainly spent two winters in Bithynia, and his term of office overlapped that of Calpurnius Macer, who is known to have been governing Moesia Inferior in 112 (Plin. *Tra.* 42, etc.; *CIL* iii. 77). Beyond this his governorship cannot be dated with precision, nor is it known whether he ever returned to Italy; that he died before 114 is inferred from an inscription (*CIL* v. 5262) on stone erected after his death, in which Trajan is mentioned without the title *Optimus*, assumed in that year.

The first nine books of P.'s correspondence belong to the years 97–109, and were published during his lifetime, probably in groups of three (H. Peter, *Der Brief in d. röm. Lit.* (1901), 107 ff.). Unlike Cicero's letters, they were written, or rewritten, with a view to publication. Each letter is a self-contained causerie on some one topic, with no allusion left unexplained; even in an affectionate letter to his wife (6. 4.) P. is careful to inform the reader of the reason for her absence from home, which must have been known to herself. In spite of their self-conscious artistry the letters have considerable charm, and present a richly varied picture of the life of the more cultured Romans under the Empire. P. himself is revealed as a man of great kindliness and generosity, though vain and self-complacent. As a writer he possesses great descriptive powers, and among his most famous letters are the description of his Laurentine villa (2. 17) and his account of the eruption of Vesuvius in which his uncle perished (6. 16 and 20). P.'s correspondents included the historians Tacitus and Suetonius; himself a dabbler in verse (7. 4), he patronized the poets of his day (1. 13), including Martial (3. 21).

There also survives a tenth book consisting of letters exchanged between P. and Trajan, mainly concerned with the administration of Bithynia. Strictly practical in scope, these show P. as a conscientious and fair-minded administrator, though Trajan's replies to his requests for advice sometimes imply that he might well have been more self-reliant. These letters are, with the *Panegyric*, among the main historical sources for Trajan's ill-documented reign; especially celebrated are those dealing with the Christians (*Tra.* 96–7; *see* TRAJAN). *See also* LETTERS (LATIN).

Text: R. C. Kukula (1908, 1912); *Epistles* only, E. T. Merrill (Leipzig, 1922); M. Schuster (1933); *Ep.* with W. Melmoth's transl. revised by W. M. L. Hutchinson (Loeb, 1921–7). Text with commentary: *Paneg.*, M. Durry (Paris, 1938); *Ep. ad Tra.*, E. G. Hardy (1889); *Ep.* bk. 3, J. E. B. Mayor (1880); *Select Letters*, E. T. Merrill (1903). R. G. C. L.

PLOTINA, POMPEIA, who married Trajan (q.v.) before his accession, was famous for her simplicity, dignity, fidelity, and virtue. Refusing the title 'Augusta' A.D. 100, she accepted it only in 105; from 112 she enjoyed an honorific coinage (her *Vesta* type emphasized the purity of family ties). She bore no children. Present at Trajan's death in Cilicia, she probably facilitated the succession of Hadrian (q.v.), long her favourite. Hadrian honoured her on the coinage of 117–18. Dying *c.* 121–2, she was consecrated: Hadrian commemorated her by a temple at Nemausus and another, dedicated to Trajan and Plotina, in the Forum Traiani.

Dio Cassius 68. 5; 69. 1 and 10; S.H.A. *Hadrian*; Aur. Victor, *Epit.* 42. 21; Pliny, *Pan.* 83; *PIR*, P 509; H. Mattingly, *B.M. Coins, Rom. Emp.* iii (1936); H. Mattingly and E. A. Sydenham, *The Roman Imperial Coinage* ii (1930). C. H. V. S.

PLOTINUS (Πλωτῖνος) (A.D. 205–269/70). The main facts of his life are known from Porphyry's memoir (prefixed to editions of the *Enneads*). His birthplace, on which Porphyry is silent, is said by Eunapius and Suidas to have been Lyco or Lycopolis in Egypt, but his name is Roman, while his native language was almost certainly Greek. He turned to philosophy in his 28th year and worked for the next eleven years under Ammonius (q.v.) Saccas at Alexandria. In 242–3 he joined Gordian's unsuccessful expedition against Persia, hoping for an opportunity to learn something of eastern thought. The attempt was abortive, and at the age of 40 he settled in Rome as a teacher of philosophy, and remained there until his last illness, when he retired to Campania to die. At Rome he became the centre of an influential circle of intellectuals, which included men of the world and men of letters, besides professional philosophers like Amelius and Porphyry. He interested himself also in social problems, and tried to enlist the support of the Emperor Gallienus for a scheme to found a Platonic community on the site of a ruined Pythagorean settlement in Campania.

2. WRITINGS. Plotinus wrote nothing until he was 50. He then began to produce a series of philosophical essays arising directly out of discussions in his seminars (συνουσίαι), and intended primarily for circulation among his pupils. These were collected by Porphyry, who classified them roughly according to subject, arranged them rather artificially in six *Enneads* or groups of nine, and eventually published them *c.* 300–5. From this edition our manuscripts are descended. An edition by another pupil, the physician Eustochius, is known to have existed (schol.

Enn. 4. 4. 30); and it has been argued by some scholars (Henry, *Recherches etc.*, *see* Bibliography) that the extracts from Plotinus in Eus. *Praep. Evang.* are derived from this Eustochian recension. Save for the omission of politics, Plotinus' essays range over the whole field of ancient philosophy: ethics and aesthetics are dealt with mainly in *Enn.* 1, physics and cosmology in *Enns.* 2 and 3; psychology in *Enn.* 4; metaphysics, logic, and epistemology in *Enns.* 5 and 6. Though not systematic in intention, the *Enneads* form in fact a more complete body of philosophical teaching than any other which has come down to us from antiquity outside the Aristotelian corpus. Plotinus' favourite method is to raise and solve a series of ἀπορίαι: many of the essays give the impression of a man thinking aloud or discussing difficulties with a pupil. Owing to bad eyesight, Plotinus never revised what he wrote (Porph. *Vita Plot.* 8), and his highly individual style often reflects the irregular structure of oral statement. Its allusiveness, rapid transitions, and extreme condensation render him one of the most difficult of Greek authors; but when deeply moved he can write magnificently.

3. PHILOSOPHICAL DOCTRINE. In the nineteenth century Plotinus' philosophy was often dismissed as an arbitrary and illogical syncretism of Greek and oriental ideas. Recent writers, on the other hand, see in him the most powerful philosophical mind between Aristotle and Aquinas or Descartes; and in his work a logical development from earlier Greek thought, whose elements he organized in a new synthesis designed to meet the needs of a new age. These needs influenced the direction rather than the methods of his thinking: its direction is determined by the same forces which resulted in the triumph of the eastern religions of salvation, but its methods are those of traditional Greek rationalism. Plotinus attached small value to ritual, and the religious ideas of the Near East seem to have had little direct influence on the *Enneads*, though Bréhier would explain certain parallels with Indian thought by postulating contact with Indian travellers in Alexandria. To Christianity Plotinus makes no explicit reference; but *Enn.* 2. 9 is an eloquent defence of Hellenism against Gnostic superstition.

4. Plotinus holds that all modes of being, whether material or mental, temporal or eternal, are constituted by the expansion or 'overflow' of a single immaterial and impersonal force, which he identifies with the 'One' of the *Parmenides* and the 'Good' of the *Republic*, though it is strictly insusceptible of any predicate or description. As 'the One', it is the ground of all existence; as 'the Good', it is the source of all values. There is exact correspondence between degrees of reality and degrees of value, both being determined by the degree of unity, or approximation to the One, which any existence achieves. Reality, though at its higher levels it is non-spatial and non-temporal, may thus be pictured figuratively as a series of concentric circles resulting from the expansion of the One. Each of these circles stands in a relation of timeless dependence to that immediately within it, which is in this sense its 'cause'; the term describes a logical relationship, not an historical event. Bare Matter (ὕλη) is represented by the circumference of the outermost circle: it is the limiting case of reality, the last consequence of the expansion of the One, and so possesses only the ideal existence of a boundary.

5. Between the One and Matter lie three descending grades of reality—the World-mind (νοῦς), the World-soul (ψυχή), and Nature (φύσις). The descent is marked by increasing individuation and diminishing unity. The World-mind resembles Aristotle's Unmoved Mover: it is thought-thinking-itself, an eternal lucidity in which the knower and the known are distinguishable only logically; within it lie the Platonic Forms, which are conceived not as inert types or models but as a system of interrelated forces, differentiations of the one Mind

which holds them together in a single timeless apprehension (νόησις). The dualism of subject and object, implicit in the self-intuition of Mind, is carried a stage farther in the discursive thinking characteristic of Soul: because of its weaker unity, Soul must apprehend its objects successively and severally. In doing so it creates time and space; but the World-soul is itself eternal and transcends the spatio-temporal world which arises from its activity. The lowest creative principle is Nature, which corresponds to the immanent World-soul of the Stoics: its consciousness is faint and dreamlike, and the physical world is its projected dream.

6. Man is a microcosm, containing all these principles actually or potentially within himself. His consciousness is normally occupied with the discursive thinking proper to Soul: but he has at all times a subconscious activity on the dreamlike level of Nature and a superconscious activity on the intuitive level of Mind; and his conscious life may lapse by habituation to the former level or be lifted by an intellectual discipline to the latter. Beyond the life of Mind lies the possibility of unification (ἔνωσις), an experience in which the Self by achieving complete inward unity is momentarily identified with the supreme unity of the One. This is the Plotinian doctrine of ecstasy. Plotinus was not its originator; but the essays in which he expounds it, on the basis of personal experience, show extraordinary introspective power and are among the classics of mysticism. It should be observed that for Plotinus unification is independent of divine grace; is attainable very rarely, as the result of a prolonged effort of the will and understanding; and is not properly a mode of cognition, so that no inference can be based on it.

7. Plotinus also made important contributions to psychology, particularly in his discussion of problems of perception, consciousness, and memory; and to aesthetic, where for Plato's doctrine that Art 'imitates' natural objects he substitutes the view that Art and Nature alike impose a structure on Matter in accordance with an inward vision of archetypal Forms. His most original work in ethics is concerned with the question of the nature and origin of evil, which in some passages he attempts to solve by treating evil as the limiting case of good, and correlating it with Matter, the limiting case of reality.

BIBLIOGRAPHY

TEXTS: R. Volkmann (Teubner, 1884); H. F. Müller (1880); E. Bréhier (Budé, 1924-38). Critical edition by P. Henry and H. R. Schwyzer in preparation.
COMMENTARIES: G. F. Creuzer (Oxford, 1835, unsatisfactory); R. Harder (in preparation).
TRANSLATIONS: S. MacKenna and B. S. Page (1917-30). French: E. Bréhier (with text, see above). German: R. Harder (1930-7, the most trustworthy).
MSS. AND HISTORY OF TEXT: P. Henry, Recherches sur la 'Préparation Évangélique' d'Eusèbe et l'édition perdue des œuvres de P. publiée par Eustochius (1935); Lès États du texte de P. (1938); Les Manuscrits des Ennéades (1941).
PHILOSOPHY: (a) General: T. Whittaker, The Neoplatonists² (1918); E. Bréhier, La Philosophie de P. (1928); W. R. Inge, The Philosophy of P.² (1929, brilliant but over-emphasizes kinship with Christian mysticism); F. Heinemann, Plotin (1921, attempts to trace development in Plotinus' thought).
(b) Special problems: R. Arnou, Le Désir de Dieu dans la philosophie de P. (1921); E. Schröder, P.'s Abhandlung Πόθεν τὰ κακά; (1916); G. Nebel, P.'s Kategorien der intelligiblen Welt (1929); C. Schmidt, P.'s Stellung zum Gnosticismus und kirchlichen Christentum (1901); A. H. Armstrong, The Architecture of the Intelligible Universe in the Philosophy of P. (1940). E. R. D.

PLOTIUS TUCCA, a friend of Virgil (*Catal.* 1) and Horace (*Sat.* 1. 5. 40) and a member of Maecenas' literary circle. He assisted Varius (q.v.) Rufus as literary executor to Virgil, whose initial instructions to burn the *Aeneid* were rejected, the poem being published at Augustus' command without additions after merely superficial revision (Donat. *Vita Verg.* 39; Serv. *Praef.* 2. 12 Th.). G. C. W.

PLOTIUS, *see also* SACERDOS.

PLUTARCH (Πλούταρχος) (*c.* A.D. 46–after 120), son of Autobulus of Chaeronea, Academic philosopher and biographer. When Nero visited Greece (A.D. 66) P. was at Athens (*Mor.* 385 b) studying physics, natural science, and rhetoric; but his enthusiasm was for ethics. Public duties sent P. to Rome, where his many friends included the philosopher Favorinus; he may have held a consulship (Suidas) and under Hadrian was procurator of Achaea and an Athenian citizen. P. visited Sparta, Corinth, Patrae, Sardes, and Alexandria, but resided mainly at Chaeronea, where he kept a private school. He was in close touch with Delphi (holding a priesthood for life from A.D. 95) and may have assisted the renewed vogue of the oracle under Trajan. P. lived until perhaps A.D. 127 (*Mor.* 380 b: cf. Juv. *Sat.* 15). His wife Timoxena bore him four sons, and a daughter who died in infancy.

WORKS

The so-called Lamprias catalogue, containing 277 works by P. (not all authentic) is incomplete; no detailed chronology yet exists.

A. *Moralia*: P's ethical, religious, physical, political, and literary studies are cast as Dialogues or Diatribes.

Dialogues: these vary from a series of speeches to informal conversation-pieces with occasional narrative-matter; characters usually from P.'s family circle; time and place rarely indicated.

1. *Convivium septem sapientium* (Τῶν ἑπτὰ σοφῶν συμπόσιον) and *De genio Socratis* (Περὶ τοῦ Σ. δαιμονίου), early works: the latter is staged among the conspirators who seized the Cadmea.

2. *De sollertia animalium* (Πότερα τῶν ζῴων φρονιμώτερα, τὰ χερσαῖα ἢ τὰ ἔνυδρα) and *Bruta ratione uti* (*Gryllus*) (Περὶ τοῦ τὰ ἄλογα λόγῳ χρῆσθαι), also early, contain Pythagorean elements and attack the Stoic denial of reason to animals; *Gryllus* is staged on Circe's island.

3. The two dialogues *De esu carnium* (Περὶ σαρκοφαγίας) draw the vegetarian moral.

4. *De musica* (Περὶ μουσικῆς) defends simple musical forms; probably early.

5. *Non posse suaviter vivi secundum Epicuri praecepta* (Ὅτι οὐδ' ἡδέως ζῆν ἔστιν κατ' Ἐπ.) attacks Epicureanism, stating P.'s ideals; Academic sources.

6. *De communibus notitiis* (Περὶ τῶν κοινῶν ἐννοιῶν πρὸς τοὺς Στωικούς), *De Stoicorum repugnantiis* (Περὶ Στ. ἐναντιωμάτων), and *Stoicos absurdiora poetis dicere* (Σύνοψις τοῦ ὅτι παραδοξότερα οἱ Στ. τῶν ποιητῶν λέγουσιν), the last highly satirical, attack the Stoics.

7. *De facie in orbe lunae* (Περὶ τοῦ ἐμφαινομένου προσώπου τῷ κύκλῳ τῆς σελήνης), also anti-Stoic, elaborates a cosmology and contains physical speculation.

8. *Amatorius* (Ἐρωτικός) discusses Eros, favouring heterosexuality.

9. *De tuenda sanitate praecepta* (Ὑγιεινὰ παραγγέλματα), on dietetics.

10. *De ira cohibenda* (Περὶ ἀοργησίας) contains Peripatetic and Stoic material.

11. *De sera numinis vindicta* (Περὶ τῶν ὑπὸ τοῦ θείου βραδέως τιμωρουμένων), staged in Delphi, justifies the postponement of divine justice to allow time for repentance.

12. Three Pythian dialogues, late works: *De defectu oraculorum* (Περὶ τῶν ἐκλελοιπότων χρηστηρίων), of wide scope, including prophecy and demonology: links the decline of the oracle with that of the population. *De E apud Delphos* (Περὶ τοῦ ΕΙ τοῦ ἐν Δ.), interprets the word ΕΙ at the temple-entrance. *De Pythiae oraculis* (Περὶ τοῦ μὴ χρᾶν ἔμμετρα νῦν τὴν Π.) discusses why the oracle no longer answers in verse, seeks to restore belief; influenced by Posidonius.

13. *Quaestiones convivales* (Συμποσιακὰ προβλήματα), in nine books, each containing about ten problems. The scenes are elaborate, the subjects wide: but the treatment is superficial, nor are original solutions attempted.

Diatribes: simpler and more vigorous, many showing Menippean influence.

14. *De fortuna Alexandri* (Λόγοι περὶ τῆς Α. τύχης ἢ ἀρετῆς), *De fortuna Romanorum* (Περὶ τῆς P. τύχης), and *De gloria Atheniensium* (Πότερον Ἀθ. κατὰ πόλεμον ἢ κατὰ σοφίαν ἐνδοξότεροι) are early works, rhetorical and artificial; so, too,

15. *Aqua an ignis utilior* (Περὶ τοῦ πότερον ὕδωρ ἢ πῦρ χρησιμώτερον).

16. *An virtus doceri possit* (Εἰ διδακτὸν ἡ ἀρετή) is superficial.

17. *De virtute morali* (Περὶ τῆς ἠθικῆς ἀρετῆς) outlines the task of virtue in subordinating the unreasonable to the reasonable side of the soul, an idea developed in fifteen succeeding works containing many examples from the lives of the famous, some wise observations, but little originality.

18. *De fraterno amore* (Περὶ φιλαδελφίας), *De amore prolis* (Περὶ τῆς εἰς τὰ ἔκγονα φιλοστοργίας), and *Praecepta coniugalia* (Γαμικὰ παραγγέλματα) treat the virtues of family life.

19. *De liberis educandis* (Περὶ παιδῶν ἀγωγῆς),—authenticity doubtful,—*Quomodo adulescens poetas audire debeat* (Πῶς δεῖ τὸν νέον ποιημάτων ἀκούειν), and *De recta ratione audiendi* (Περὶ τοῦ ἀκούειν) discuss educational problems; influential during the Renaissance.

20. *De malignitate Herodoti* (Περὶ τῆς Ἡ. κακοηθείας), a piece of unscientific, Boeotian local-patriotism; *Comparatio Aristophanis et Menandri* (Σύγκρισις Ἀ. καὶ Μ.) prefers Menander on moral grounds.

21. With the formal *Consolatio ad uxorem* (Παραμυθητικὸς εἰς τὴν γυναῖκα τὴν αὑτοῦ), on their daughter's death, goes the *De Exilio* (Περὶ φυγῆς); the *Consolatio ad Apollonium* (Παραμυθητικὸς πρὸς Ἀ.) is probably by a contemporary.

22. *Praecepta reipublicae gerendae* (Πολιτικὰ παραγγέλματα) and *An seni respublica gerenda sit* (Εἰ πρεσβυτέρῳ πολιτεύτεον), both written after A.D. 115, give P.'s political views: the former contains a collection of precepts, often from the *Lives*, the latter urges Euphanes of Athens, though old, to continue his public work. *De unius in republica dominatione* (Περὶ μοναρχίας καὶ δημοκρατίας καὶ ὀλιγαρχίας) shows P. a monarchist. Stoic ideas appear in the short *Ad principem ineruditum* (Πρὸς ἡγεμόνα ἀπαίδευτον) and fragmentary *Maxime cum principibus viris philosopho esse disserendum* (Περὶ τοῦ ὅτι μάλιστα τοῖς ἡγεμόσι δεῖ τὸν φιλόσοφον διαλέγεσθαι).

23. Among works attacking Epicurean and Stoic doctrines are *Adversus Coloten* (Πρὸς Κωλώτην) and *De latenter vivendo* (Εἰ καλῶς εἴρηται τὸ λάθε βιώσας); P. mentions a defence of Plato against Chrysippus, and 'Lamprias' catalogues studies of the early philosophers.

24. Of P.'s extensive work on Plato survive *De animae procreatione in Timaeo* (Περὶ τῆς ἐν Τ. ψυχογονίας), a commentary on Plato, *Tim.* p. 35 a, and *Platonicae quaestiones* (Πλατωνικὰ ζητήματα), surveying superficially ten problems of Platonic metaphysics.

25. *Quaestiones naturales* (Αἴτια φυσικά) discuss natural history topics; so, too, *De primo frigido* (Περὶ τοῦ πρώτου ψυχροῦ), dedicated to Favorinus.

26. The early *De superstitione* (Περὶ δεισιδαιμονίας) reveals a hatred of superstition, *De Iside et Osiride* (Περὶ Ἰ. καὶ Ὀ.) (contemporary with the Pythian dialogues) a mystical approach to religion.

27. Of various collections of anecdotes and apophthegms claimed for P., *De mulierum virtutibus* (Γυναικῶν ἀρεταί) may be genuine: many are spurious.

28. *Quaestiones Romanae* (Αἴτια Ῥωμαϊκά) and *Quaestiones Graecae* (Αἴτια Ἑλληνικά) are aetiological studies.

B. *Historical works*: In later years P. composed his biographies of soldiers and statesmen, mainly in pairs, first a Greek, then a Roman and a comparison. Twenty-three such pairs survive (including the tetrad *Agis*, *Cleomenes*, and the *Gracchi*), also four single *Lives*; four comparisons are missing. With variations the *Lives* follow the scheme of 'peripatetic' biography—birth, youth and character, deeds, death with circumstances; frequent ethical reflections occur. Details, however, vary with the sources, which cover a wide field, including peripatetic anecdote-mongers, historians proper, and memoir-writers. P. prefers Greek sources, and often takes material at second-hand. His real concern is with the form: he seeks first to please, next to provide his reader with examples of political and moral virtues. The *Lives* probably appeared in A.D. 105-15. The order in which P. wrote them is undetermined; their present order follows the chronology of the Greek characters.

The following works are of doubtful authenticity: *Consolatio ad Apollonium* (see A. 21 above); *De liberis educandis* (see A. 19 above); *De mulierum virtutibus* (see A. 27 above); *De placitis philosophorum*; *De vita et poesi Homeri*; *Narrationes amatoriae*; *Parallela minora*; *Proverbia Alexandrinorum*; *Vitae decem oratorum*.

Plutarch has achieved perennial popularity by treating concrete human problems without raising disquieting solutions. Ambling pleasantly along the surface, he sacrifices literary form to a wealth of anecdote; he employs a not purely Attic, but simple, style, reflecting the colour of his sources. P.'s youthful rationalism yielded to mysticism: his philosophy was an eclecticism which grafted on to the Academy shreds from the middle Stoa and Pythagoras. Like Seneca he revelled in ethical problems: and he accepted uncritically both Greek superiority and the meritoriousness of the Empire. In private life P. was quiet, humane, and affectionate; he combined imperial office with a full civic life in Chaeronea. A foe to extremes, he succeeded, for all his mediocre talent, in illuminating the cultural darkness of first-century Greece. *See also* HISTORIOGRAPHY, GREEK, para. 7, *and* LITERARY CRITICISM IN ANTIQUITY, I. 6.

BIBLIOGRAPHY

GENERAL: Suidas, s.v.; R. Volkmann, *Leben, Schriften u. Philosophie des P.'s von Chaeronea* (1869); R. Hirzel, *P.* (1912); J. J. Hartman, *De P. script. et philos.* (1916).
TEXTS: Moralia: Teubner (Bernardakis (1888-96), new ed. by Wegehaupt and others in progress). *Pyth. Dial.*, W. R. Paton (1893). Vitae: Teubner (Lindskog-Ziegler, 1914-35).
COMMENTARIES: Moralia: D. Wyttenbach (1795-1830: unfinished); *Quaest. Rom.*, H. J. Rose (1924); *Quaest. Graec.*, W. R. Halliday (1928). Vitae: Teubner (O. Siefert - F. Blass); select. *Lives*, 1909); *Gracchi*, K. Ziegler (1911); *Aem.*, C. Liedmeier (1935); *Arat.* W. H. Porter (1937); *Gracchi* (1885), *Sulla* (1886), *Nicias* (1887), *Timoleon* (1889), *Themistocles* (1892), *Demosthenes* (1893), *Pericles* (1894), H. A. Holden; *Galba and Otho*, E. G. Hardy (1890); *Lysander*, J. Smits (1939); *Cato maior*, J. H. W. Strijd (1941).
TRANSLATIONS: Moralia: Philemon Holland (1603); W. W. Goodwin (1870); T. G. Tucker-A. D. Prickard (2 vols. select. 1913-18); Loeb (F. C. Babbit: H. N. Fowler: W. C. Helmbold, 1927- (in progress)). Vitae: Sir T. North (from French, 1579); Loeb (B. Perrin: 1914-26).
SPECIAL ASPECTS: R. M. Jones, *The Platonism of P.* (U.S.A. 1916); K. M. Westaway, *The Educational Theory of P.* (1922); A. Weizsäcker, *Untersuch. ü. P.'s biog. Technik* (1931); *see* BIOGRAPHY, GREEK (bibliog.).
PARTICULAR WORKS: See Bursian, vol. clxxxvii (1921: F. Bock, Moralia), vol. ccli (1936: A. Hauser, Vitae); *De fac.*, *De gen.*, W. Hamilton (1934); *De lat. viv.*, G. H. Luttanzi (*Riv. Fil.* 1932); *Quom. adulesc.*, A. Benzoni (*Il Mondo Classico* 1933); *Marc.*, A. Klotz (*Rh. Mus.* 1934); *Caes.*, A. Klotz (*Mnemos.* 1934); *Flam.*, A. Klotz (*Rh. Mus.* 1935); *Tim.*, *Pel.*, H. D. Westlake (*CQ* 1938-9); *Cat. mai.* and other Roman lives (*CQ* 1940), *Flam.* (*CQ* 1944), R. E. Smith; *Alex.*, J. E. Powell (*JHS* 1939).   F. W. W.

PLUTEUS, *see* SIEGECRAFT, ROMAN.

PLUTON (Πλούτων), *see* HADES.

PLUTUS (Πλοῦτος), Wealth, originally and properly abundance of crops, hence associated with Demeter (q.v.) at Eleusis (see Deubner, *Attische Feste*, 85 f.); he is son of Demeter (q.v.) and Iasion (Hesiod, *Theog.* 969 ff.). He is thus closely connected in idea with Pluton (*cf.* HADES), and presumably with the nymph Pluto, mother of Tantalus. Cf. Hesychius s.vv. εὔπλουτον, πλοῦτος. Demeter and Kore send him to those whom they favour (*Hymn. Hom. Cer.* 486 ff.). He appears mostly as a figure in popular, not merely literary, tradition, see especially the *Eiresione* (Ps.-Hdt. *Vit. Hom.* 465), in which he comes with Mirth and Peace to the house which the bearers of the *eiresione* visit. In art he is shown with Demeter in more than one connexion. In the higher literature he is mentioned as overthrowing the wealth which he once gave (Aesch. *Pers.* 163), wished in Tartarus because his blindness makes so much trouble (Timocreon, fr. 5 Diehl); and Aristophanes' *Plutus* takes up this theme, which may very well have been a popular proverb, and describes the curing of his blindness, after which, knowing where he goes, he visits honest men only. Here he is wealth in general, not only agricultural prosperity. *See* EIRENE.

H. J. R.

PNEUMA, *see* ANATOMY AND PHYSIOLOGY, paras. 2, 8, 13, 14.

PNIGOS, *see* METRE, GREEK, II. 5.

PNYX, the meeting-place of the Athenian Ecclesia, is a low hill west of the Acropolis. The earliest construction was probably due to Cleisthenes; the speaker faced the sea, the assembly sitting on a gently sloping hill. When it was rebuilt under the Thirty Tyrants, the speaker faced north (Plut. *Themist.* 19). The present massive retaining wall and rock-cut *bema* are a Hadrianic restoration.

K. Kourouniotes and H. A. Thompson, 'The Pnyx in Athens', *Hesperia* i. 90 ff.; H. A. Thompson, 'Pnyx and Thesmophorion', ibid. v. 151 ff. T. J. D.

PODALIRIUS, *see* MACHAON.

POETELIUS LIBO, GAIUS, with his fellow consul L. Papirius, is reputed to have carried a law during the troubled period of the Second Samnite War, as a measure of social appeasement (probably in 326 B.C., or else 313). It prohibited imprisonment for debt, and enacted that loans should henceforward be based on the security of the borrower's property, not on his personal liberty. If the right of personal execution was not abolished until much later in spite of the *Lex Poetelia de nexis*, at least it was mitigated and made dependent on judgement.

E. Pais, *Storia di Roma* iv. 233 ff. P. T.

POLA, at the southern end of the Istrian peninsula in the northern Adriatic, has always owed its importance to its fine land-locked harbour. This ancient town was probably founded by Illyrians, certainly not by Colchians in pursuit of Argonauts (reject Strabo 1. 46; 5. 215). Presumably it came under the Romans' control when they conquered the head of the Adriatic (178 B.C.: Livy 41. 13). Destroyed in the Civil Wars, Pola was rebuilt by Augustus as the colony *Pietas Iulia* and became a flourishing town whose magnificent Antonine amphitheatre still survives (Pliny *HN* 3. 129). E. T. S.

POLEMARCHUS (Πολέμαρχος), at Athens, one of the nine archons (*see* ARCHONTES). Originally he was, presumably, head of the military forces; but the only one whom we know to have commanded an army is Callimachus, at Marathon, and it is doubtful whether he was commander-in-chief. After the introduction of the lot in 487 the polemarch lost all his military duties. He conducted certain sacrifices and festivals of a military character (such as the yearly Epitaphia); but his main duties were judicial. He introduced private suits in which foreign residents (metics, q.v.) were involved, whether between themselves or with citizens (perhaps only when metics were defendants). A. W. G.

POLEMON (1) **I** of Pontus was the son of a wealthy rhetorician, Zeno of Laodicea. With his father he won Roman favour and probably Roman citizenship by defending his city against the Parthians in 40–39 B.C. Antony first made him ruler of Lycaonia and part of Cilicia Tracheia (38), then when he gave Tracheia to Cleopatra (36) compensated him with Pontus and later with Lesser Armenia. He accompanied Antony's Parthian expedition, was captured, and held to ransom. After Actium Augustus confirmed his title but withdrew Lesser Armenia from him. In 15 B.C. Agrippa awarded him the Bosporan kingdom and assisted him to occupy it. He was killed by Bosporan rebels in 8 B.C. T. R. S. B.

POLEMON (2) of Athens, head of the Academy from the death of Xenocrates (314–313 B.C.), who converted him from a dissolute life and whose zealous follower he was, to his own death in 270, when he was succeeded by his pupil Crates. He seems to have been impressive by his force of character, but nothing is known of any original contribution by him to philosophy, and Diogenes Laertius 4. 17 says he attached more importance to conduct than to dialectic.

See Zeller, *Phil. d. Griechen* ii. 1⁴. 993–4. W. D. R.

POLEMON (3), a Greek of Ilium (*fl. c.* 190 B.C.), Stoic geographer who collected geographical, epigraphic, and artistic material in Greece, published in Περὶ τῶν κατὰ πόλεις ἐπιγραμμάτων, including especially dedications and monuments at Delphi, Sparta, Athens. In another work P. attacked Eratosthenes (Ath. 6. 234 d; 10. 436 d; 442 e etc.). E. H. W.

POLEMON (4) of Laodicea (*c.* A.D. 88–145), a Sophist who won political influence at Smyrna by his eloquence. A historical work and certain speeches of his are lost; but two surviving Declamations give evidence of his impassioned Asianist style, which was, however, free from the worst excesses (Norden, *Ant. Kunstpr.* i. 389).

J. W. H. A.

POLEMONIACUS, *see* PONTUS.

POLICE, GREEK. Athens in the late fifth and early fourth centuries possessed a corps of Scythian archers, public slaves; but these were rather ushers in the assembly and law-courts than real policemen. Civic police first appear in the Roman period. Magistrates named νυκτοστράτηγοι are then found in some cities of Asia and (in the 3rd c. A.D.) in the *metropoleis* of Egypt; they commanded a corps of νυκτοφύλακες, who patrolled the town at night. Magistrates styled παραφύλακες occur throughout Asia Minor; they commanded mounted ὀροφύλακες and policed the city territory. More important than these were the εἰρηνάρχαι, who were instituted throughout the East (except in Egypt, where the corresponding εἰρηνάρχης νομοῦ does not appear till the 3rd c.) in the early second century A.D. They were appointed by the provincial governor from a list submitted by the city. Their principal duty was to catch brigands; they were assisted by mounted constables (διωγμῖται).

In Ptolemaic Egypt the police force was organized like the army. Its members were granted lots of land (κλῆροι), varying in size from the 30 arurae (*c.* 18 acres) of the mounted desert patrols (χερσέφιπποι) to the 10 of the ordinary constables (φυλακῖται). The police force of each village was commanded by the ἀρχιφυλακίτης τῆς κώμης, that of each nome by the ἐπιστάτης τῶν φυλακιτῶν. In the Roman period service in the police became a liturgy; the chief constable of each village was styled ἀρχέφοδος, his men φύλακες. More effective than these were the small detachments of the Roman army which were stationed all over the country.

Greek cities: O. Hirschfeld, *Kleine Schriften* (1891), 599–609; L. Robert, *Études anatoliennes* (1937), 98–110. Egypt: U. Wilcken, *Grundzüge und Chrestomathie der Papyruskunde* (1912), i. 411–16. A. H. M. J.

POLICE, ROMAN. Under the Republic little was done to preserve order in the streets of Rome, and men like Clodius found it easy to create serious disturbances. The magistrates were provided with lictors and *viatores* who would keep order in their immediate vicinity, but the only officials to whom the name police can be applied were the *triumviri capitales* or *nocturni*, whose duties included that of dealing with nocturnal disturbances. Augustus created three *cohortes urbanae*, whose number was later greatly increased. These were distinct from the *vigiles*, who were primarily concerned with fires, and may fairly be regarded as police. The function of their commander, the *praefectus urbi* (Tac. *Ann.* 6. 11) was to control the unruly element in the city. He differed from the Chief Constable of a modern city in possessing judicial power, which he evidently exercised in a summary way; his court was apt to compete with the *quaestiones perpetuae* (Tac. *Ann.* 14. 41). Urban cohorts were stationed at Lugdunum and Carthage, and in the provinces the preservation of order was a duty of the governor, who might make use of soldiers for the purpose even in senatorial provinces. G. H. S.

POLIS (πόλις), the Greek city-state. Its origin reaches back to the times of Homer and Hesiod, when the old monarchy was disappearing. The Polis arose as an anti-monarchic State, and it remained so, in spite of tyranny (q.v.). It was a State of small size, there being several reasons for political particularism in the Greek world—firstly, the natural division of the country into many separate districts, islands, peninsulas, etc.; further, the division of the Greek people into many larger or smaller tribes, and accordingly of the Greek religion into numerous local cults. Several hundreds of city-states existed, most of them extremely small. It seems almost impossible (and this not only for lack of information) to write a general history of all these States. We can only describe the most characteristic features of the type which was to become the Greek State *par excellence*.

2. The territory of a Polis (in contrast with the 'ethnos', or tribal State) included both town and country (hinterland). There always was only one town, mostly walled round, with the citadel, the original πόλις (later: 'acro-polis'), and the agora or market-place. The citizens resided alike in town and country, but the government of the State was entirely concentrated in the town. Membership of the citizen body would depend upon the constitution of each Polis, but in every case the Polis was identical with the totality of its citizens. Therefore the name of the State was taken from the citizens, not from the town or territory: οἱ Ἀθηναῖοι etc.; 'ἄνδρες γὰρ πόλις', says Thucydides (7. 77. 7). The citizens were a ruling class, not only in aristocracies and oligarchies (qq.v.), but even in democracies (q.v.); for besides the slaves there always was a population not belonging to the State, e.g. dependent lower classes, resident strangers (metics), inhabitants of surrounding districts (*perioeci*), etc. Even in citizenship (q.v.) there were different degrees, and for a long time the internal development of the Polis was a struggle for equality in citizenship and political rights, as well as in social and economic conditions.

3. The State consisted of its citizens, considered less as individuals than as forming smaller communities of kinship, of cult, of locality. Each individual was tied to the life of all these communities and of the State. Moreover, the State was not only a political community. To be a citizen meant adherence to the cults of the gods of the Polis, as well as military and economic service to the State, and obedience to its laws. The perfect Greek citizen was Aristotle's ζῷον πολιτικόν, at the same time attached to his Polis, and a free man.

4. Liberty, autonomy, autarky were the ideals of the Polis, and its chief claim was to be ruled by law (*nomos*).

In actual fact government remained a question of power, but the sacred 'nomos' always directed and regulated actual politics. Government was carried on mainly by three institutions: Assembly, Council, magistracies, all derived from earlier times. Each of these preponderated according to the various types of constitution. The Council held the chief political power in aristocracy and oligarchy, the Assembly in democracy. Jurisdiction was performed partly by the Council, partly by special officials, the final court being mostly the people, i.e. the Assembly. In democracies the dicasteries (q.v.) gathered almost all jurisdiction into their hands.

5. Remembering always that it is wrong to generalize from the institutions of any single Polis, all of which differed in many ways, we may consider the Athenian democracy as having reached (and gone beyond) the highest standard of a Polis, the organization of which strongly influenced other States. In Athens during the fifth and the fourth centuries the rule of the people was realized most completely. The Assembly, although in fact consisting of only part of the people, especially those living in town, was open to any citizen, and was the true sovereign (τὸ κύριον). All foreign policy, all military and naval questions, all legislation, and the control of all executive officials were treated and decided by the Assembly. Its functions and its power were really unlimited. But all matters presented to the Assembly were prepared by a *probouleuma* of the Council. Therefore the decrees (ψηφίσματα) were finally resolved by Council and people in common (ἔδοξε τῇ βουλῇ καὶ τῷ δήμῳ). But the Assembly could always reject, add, or amend. In addition to its main task of *probouleusis* the Council collaborated authoritatively with the magistracies and controlled public finance. The councillors were elected by lot and not allowed to be re-elected more than once. Thus the majority of those citizens who attended the Assembly were councillors once in their life. The Council formed a committee of the people, its membership changing yearly. It was not a restraining power, as the Areopagus formerly used to be. The magistracies had to execute the people's decrees, but some rights of initiative and command were given to the higher of them. There was no real political power connected with any magistracy, although some of them carried a certain measure of influence.

6. The Polis lost its power and its function of leadership in Greek politics partly through the corruption of democracy, but more so through the overwhelming power of Alexander's empire and the Hellenistic monarchies. However, it did not vanish, nor even cease to appear politically autonomous. There were still political and economical struggles between the parties of the Polis, and oligarchy was often renewed. Some of the city-states remained centres of cultural or economic life, and in the monarchies of Asia newly founded cities, many of them originally military colonies, became the agents of hellenization of the East. The Hellenistic age owed most of its intellectual life to the traditions of the Polis. Perhaps its greatest efficiency issued from its part in Greek philosophy. In the fourth century, when the Polis began to decline, Plato designed his immortal picture of the ideal State, and Aristotle created political science. For both of them political theory was theory of the Polis, and even the Stoics considered the world as the unity of 'cosmo-polis'.

G. Glotz, *The Greek City* (1929); F. E. Adcock, *CAH* iii, ch. 25; W. R. Halliday, *The Growth of the City-State* (1923); V. Ehrenberg, in Gercke-Norden, *Einleitung in die Altertumswissenschaft*[3] (1932), vol. iii, pt. 3; W. W. Tarn, *The Greeks in Bactria and India* (1938), ch. 1; A. H. M. Jones, *The Greek City from Alexander to Justinian* (1940). V. E.

POLITES, in mythology, son of Priam (q.v.) by Hecuba (q.v.), a swift runner and consequently employed as a scout (*Iliad* 2. 791 ff., cf. 24. 250). He takes a minor part in the fighting (13. 533; 15. 339). In Verg. *Aen.* 2. 526 ff. he is killed by Neoptolemus (q.v.); cf. Quint. Smyrn. 13. 214; source unknown. H. J. R.

POLLIO, GAIUS ASINIUS (76 B.C.–A.D. 5), fought on Caesar's side and later on Antony's in the Civil War. Consul in 40, he celebrated a triumph over the Parthini of Illyria in 39. After quarrelling with Antony he did not go over to Octavian but maintained a reserved attitude, consoling himself for political inactivity by devotion to literary pursuits.

In youth he had been an associate of Catullus and his circle, and later enjoyed the friendship of Horace (*Carm.* 2. 1. 1 ff.) and Virgil (*Ecl.* 4 is addressed to him). We hear that it was P. who suggested to Virgil that he should write a *carmen bucolicum*. P.'s own works included tragedies; *historiae*, an account of the Civil Wars (starting with the year 60 and ending possibly with Caesar's death) used by Plutarch and Appian; speeches, which, to judge from his criticism of Cicero, were Atticist in style (cf. Tac. *Dial.* 21. 13); poems (Verg. *Ecl.* 3. 86; Plin. *Ep.* 5. 3. 5); grammatical writings; and letters. As a literary critic P. was renowned for the severity of his judgements, among which is the celebrated sneer at Livy's *Patavinitas*. P. appears also as a patron of the arts. He founded the first public library in Italy (39) and organized the first *recitationes* of literary works. L. R. P.

POLLIO, see also POMPONIUS (6), VEDIUS.

POLLUX, see CASTOR.

POLLUX, JULIUS, of Naucratis (2nd c. A.D.), scholar and rhetorician. His *Onomasticon* was composed in the lifetime of Commodus, to whom are addressed epistles prefixed to each of its ten books: that introducing bk. 8 indicates that the author's appointment to a Chair at Athens (not before A.D. 178) preceded the completion of the work. In bks. 8–10 he replies to Phrynichus' criticism of points in 1–7. As an example of Atticism and other profitable vices of the age he comes under Lucian's lash in 'Ρητόρων Διδάσκαλος: cf. ch. 24—οὐκέτι Ποθεινὸς ὀνομάζομαι ἀλλ' ἤδη τοῖς Διὸς καὶ Λήδας παισὶν ὁμώνυμος γεγένημαι. Like his other works, the *Onomasticon* in its original form has perished: the extant manuscripts from which it is now known are derived from four incomplete, abridged, and interpolated copies from an early epitome possessed (and interpolated) by Arethas, Archbishop of Caesarea, *c.* A.D. 900. The arrangement is topical, not alphabetical. The work partly resembles a rhetorical handbook, e.g. in its collections of synonyms and of subject-vocabularies, in collections of compounds (ὁμο- and some others), in the fifty-two terms for use in praising a king, or the thirty-three terms of abuse to apply to a tax-collector. The story of Heracles' discovery of purple is added expressly as a light relief for the student. Wider philological and encyclopaedic interests appear in the citations from literature and in the treatment of music and the theatre. Besides these, his subjects include religion, private and public law, human anatomy and ethics, war, the sciences, arts, crafts, and trades, houses, ships, husbandry, cookery, children's games, and a host of other matters. But the work is predominantly a thesaurus of terms, not of information.

Editions: Hemsterhuys and others, 1706 (reprinted with additions, Dindorf, 1824); Bekker, 1846; Bethe, in Teubner's *Lexicog. Gr.* IX. i–iii, 1900–31. P. B. R. F.

POLUS of Agrigentum, Sophist, younger than Socrates (Pl. *Grg.* 463 e), pupil of Gorgias; like his teacher he confined himself in later years to teaching rhetoric. He wrote a rhetorical Τέχνη, the beginning of which may perhaps be seen in Pl. *Grg.* 448 c. He is mentioned often by Plato and once by Aristotle.

See Zeller, *Phil. d. Griechen* i³, 1323. W. D. R.

POLYAENUS (1) of Lampsacus, one of the chief direct disciples of Epicurus, who turned P.'s attention from mathematics to philosophy. He died before his master. Works: Περὶ φιλοσοφίας: Τὰ πρὸς τὸν Ἀρίστωνα: Περὶ ὅρων.

See Zeller, *Phil. d. Griechen*, iii. 1⁴. 379–80. W. D. R.

POLYAENUS (2), a Macedonian rhetorician, in his later years dedicated his collection of *Stratagems*, in eight books, to the Emperors Marcus and Verus, to aid them in Verus' Parthian War (A.D. 162). His examples, true or false, are taken from every people of the known world, gods included. Similar collections of extracts, called *hypomnemata*, on every subject and from all sorts of sources, had been common in Hellenistic literature, and Polyaenus, who produced his book very quickly, did not make his own extracts but utilized earlier compilations; theories about his sources are useless. Some items are historically valuable, others worthless; each one must be judged separately. W. W. T.

POLYBIUS (1) (*c.* 203?–*c.* 120 B.C.), the Greek historian of Rome, son of the Achaean statesman Lycortas, was born in Megalopolis probably towards 203 B.C. and, after a liberal education, entered politics early, following the Megalopolitan policy of Philopoemen and Lycortas. In 183 he carried Philopoemen's ashes, in 181–180 went on an embassy to Egypt, and in 169–168 was Hipparch of the Achaean League. After Pydna he was deported to Rome with the thousand Achaeans answering for their politics in the Third Macedonian War. Protected by Aemilius Paullus, he moved in Scipionic society, gaining the friendship of Scipio Aemilianus, and under their patronage began his great historical work. Free to travel in Italy, he also accompanied Scipio Aemilianus to Spain in 151, crossing to Numidia, and, perhaps on the return journey, saw south Gaul, the Alps, and Cisalpine Gaul. Returning to Achaea in 150, he again accompanied Scipio to Africa 147–146, exploring the coast of Mauretania. On the destruction of Corinth he helped in the settlement of Greece. He was probably at Numantia, and died, after a fall from a horse, towards 120.

2. Besides a panegyric on Philopoemen, a book on tactics, and a late work on the Numantine War, he wrote a *Universal History* in forty books on the period 220/219–145/144 B.C.; bks. 1–5 are fully preserved, bks. 6–40 in excerpts and in their use in Livy, Diodorus, Appian, and Plutarch. A προκατασκευή (bks. 1–2) gave a preliminary survey from the First Punic War, following on Timaeus. The main narrative first described the situation in Rome and Carthage (bk. 3) and the East (bks. 4–5) in 220–216 B.C., and then, after bk. 6, recorded by Olympiad years the course of events in the different theatres. Bks. 7–15 continued the Second Punic War, bks. 16–29 the Second Macedonian, Syrian, and Third Macedonian Wars, bks. 30–4 167/6–153/2 B.C., bks. 35–9 the final conquest of Spain, Africa, and Greece (to 145/4). At set points he balances his work, bk. 6 analysing the Roman constitution, bk. 12 discussing historiographical theory, bk. 34 Mediterranean geography, bk. 40 closing the work with a recapitulation and chronological survey.

3. Polybius' wide political and military experience, his access to official and historical records in Greece and Rome, and his intimate knowledge of personalities and events fitted him for his task. He followed the Roman Fabius Pictor and the pro-Carthaginian Philinus of Acragas for the First Punic War, Fabius Pictor for the Gallic Wars, the Roman senatorial tradition (e.g. perhaps Postumius Albinus) with (probably) Silenus from Hannibal's side for the Second Punic War, the senatorial tradition for events in the West in the second century B.C.; his use of Cato's *Origines* is doubtful. In Hellenistic affairs he had the Achaean tradition, including

Aratus' *Memoirs*, and histories such as those of the Rhodians Zeno and Antisthenes. He refers to archive records. Lycortas, Aemilius Paullus, and the Scipionic family gave eyewitness evidence for events before his own time.

4. Inspired by the rise of Rome, impressed with the strength and stability of her civic and confederate institutions, he saw in the protectorate of Rome over Greece by 168 B.C. an imperial fulfilment which admitted of political analysis. With this conception he began the writing of bks. 1–29, describing the Roman constitution in bk. 6 as an example of the ideal 'mixed' constitution of Peripatetic theory. Events after 168 then led him to treat the Roman domination, first to 153/2 (30–4) and later to the full conquest (35–40). His attitude to Rome became less favourable; senatorial degeneracy and Gracchan radicalism destroyed his faith in her constitutional stability. References in bk. 6 to 'cyclic' degeneration from the aristocracy of the Hannibalic War towards ochlocracy, which represent Stoic theory, accompanied by criticism of 'Flaminian' policy, indicate that in preparing the later books, which appeared after Scipio Aemilianus' death, probably posthumously, he was also engaged in revising the earlier books, especially bk 6.

5. An exponent of pragmatic historiography, in the tradition of Thucydides, like Hieronymus of Cardia, he brought to his historical analysis a mature appreciation of political causation, constitutional form, and character development. His conventional references to Fortune, in current Peripatetic phraseology, do not affect this historical position, which, together with the principle of full authenticity in narrative detail, he maintains against the rhetorical Isocratean elaboration of Timaeus and the dramatic Peripatetic technique of Phylarchus. His claims for himself cannot all be allowed. His pragmatism may work mechanically, for example, in combining Fabius Pictor and Philinus, or narrowly in estimating the mystical character of Scipio Africanus. His moralizing reflections, his characterization, of Philip V for example, even his historical criticism, of Phylarchus for example, may reflect political prejudice. And he conceals, or fails to realize, his own bias: Aetolian and Macedonian policy, pro-Roman politics in Achaea, the anti-Scipionic trends in Rome are vilified; Aratus, Philopoemen, Scipio Africanus, Aemilius Paullus, Scipio Aemilianus are glorified. Yet his theme was a great one, and he handled it with historical mastery, to illumine the imperial rise of Rome.

6. In composition he followed the Olympiad yearly division, modifying it for pragmatic or literary effect, e.g. at Cannae or after Zama. In narration he is circumstantial to the point of verbosity. His style is 'the style of the Chancellery', but with a lack of grace that is his own. Yet he may set details in vivid scenes and report speeches in a form betraying the influence of rhetorical and dramatic method. An historian to be used with care, a writer read with difficulty, he yet gives invaluable material to the historian and to the reader a narrative that repays effort. *See* HISTORIOGRAPHY, GREEK, para. 7.

TEXTS: J. Schweighäuser (1789–95); F. Hultsch (1867–71; 1888–92); Th. Büttner-Wobst (1882–1904); J. L. Strachan-Davidson, *Selections* (1888).

TRANSLATIONS: E. S. Shuckburgh (1889); W. R. Paton (1922–7, Loeb).

CRITICISM: O. Cuntz, *Polybius und sein Werk* (1902); J. B. Bury, *Ancient Greek Historians* (1909), 191; R. Laqueur, *Polybius* (1913); K. J. Beloch, *Hermes* 1915, 357; G. De Sanctis, *Stor. Rom.* iii, pt. 1 (1916), 200; F. Taeger, *Die Archäologie des Polybios* (1922); C. Wunderer, *Polybios* (1927); E. Norden, *Ant. Kunst.* i (1923; 4th impr.), 152; W. Siegfried, *Studien zur geschichtlichen Anschauung des Polybios* (1928); F. W. Walbank, *JHS* 1938, 55; *CQ* (1943), 73; (1945) 1; A. H. McDonald, *CHJ* 1939, p. 136.   A. H. McD.

POLYBIUS (2) was one of Claudius' freedmen and his secretary, especially for literary and perhaps for legal matters (*a studiis* and later *a libellis*). He translated

Homer into Latin and Virgil into Greek. Seneca addressed to him (probably in A.D. 43) a *Consolatio* (*Dial.* xi) for the death of one of his brothers, hoping that it might be construed as a petition for recall from exile. He was killed in 47 through the manœuvres of Messalina.

Consol. ad Polyb. in J. D. Duff's ed. of Seneca, *Dial. x, xi, xii* (1915). *PIR*, P 427; A. Momigliano, *Claudius* (1934), 103.   A. M.

POLYBOEA, (1) name of several mythological heroines; (2) a goddess, sister of Hyacinthus (q.v.), identified with Artemis and Kore (Paus. 3. 19. 4; Hesych. s.v.).

POLYBUS (1), in mythology, king of Corinth or Sicyon, a figure of some importance in the legends of Oedipus and Adrastus (qq.v.). Being childless, or at all events without sons, he and his wife adopt the infant Oedipus and rear him as their own (Soph. *OT* 1016 ff.). He is sonless again in the version preserved by schol. Pind. *Nem.* 9. 30, cf. Hdt. 5. 67. 4. In this tradition Adrastus is his daughter's son and inherits his kingdom. But he is either an extremely vague figure or a conflation of several persons, for we hear of him also as in Tenea (Strabo 8. 6. 22, p. 380), Boeotia (schol. Eur. *Phoen.* 28), and Argos (*Etym. Magn.* 207. 41 ff.).

See further Höfer in Roscher, s.v.   H. J. R.

POLYBUS (2), son-in-law of Hippocrates, *see* ANATOMY AND PHYSIOLOGY, para. 3.

POLYCLEITUS of Larisa, used by Eratosthenes as a geographical source. *See* ALEXANDER (3), Bibliography, Ancient Sources.

POLYCLETUS (Πολύκλειτος), Greek sculptor, a native of Argos, probably a younger contemporary of Phidias, and, like Phidias and Myron, a reputed pupil of Ageladas of Argos. He was the greatest exponent of the Peloponnesian tradition and school in the second half of the fifth century B.C., and he did not fall under the influence of Phidias and the Attic school. His earliest work is dated not before 452, his latest (the Spartan memorial for Aegospotami) at 405. Numerous Hellenistic and Roman copies of his work survive, and he had an immense popularity during his lifetime and after. By far the best copy is that of his famous 'Diadumenos', for which he was paid 100 talents, found at Delos, now in Athens. It is a late Hellenistic copy. He specialized in statues of Olympic victors, and three signed bases of such statues have been found at Olympia. His 'Spear-holder' is represented by a tolerably good Roman copy found at Pompeii, now in Naples Museum. The so-called 'Westmacott' athlete, a Roman copy in the British Museum, is thought to preserve the type of his statue of the Olympic victor Cyniscus. A copy of an Amazon, now at Berlin, is thought to reproduce the style of the sculptor. Polycletus worked mainly in bronze, but he also carved statues in marble and made the chryselephantine statue of Hera for the temple at Argos (after 423).   S. C.

POLYCRATES (1) seized Samos *c.* 540 B.C. with his brothers Pantagnotus and Syloson, but soon made himself sole tyrant. He made Samos a great naval power, annexed neighbouring islands (including Rheneia near Delos), and celebrated Delian Games. He formed alliances with Egypt and Cyrene, but later sent a force of disaffected Samians to help Cambyses against Egypt. These sailed back and attacked the tyrant unsuccessfully, though supported by a Spartan force, which Polycrates bought off with a bribe of specially struck false coins. *C.* 522 Polycrates was lured to the mainland by the satrap Oroetes, who pretended to be plotting against Darius, and there crucified. His piratical thalassocracy suggests a consistent effort, tempered by opportunism, to maintain an unconquered Samos as successor to Miletus (then under Persian rule). Polycrates built many public works (aqueduct, harbour, temple, bazaar), encouraged the woollen industry, and patronized artists and poets (Theodorus, Anacreon). Athenaeus associates him with Samian industries even before he became tyrant, a statement borne out by an inscription on the statue of his father Aeaces.

Herodotus, bk. 3; Thucydides 1. 13, 3. 104; Aristotle, *Politics* 1313 b; Athenaeus 540 d. E. Curtius, *Ath. Mitt.* 1906, 151 f.; P. N. Ure, *The Origin of Tyranny* (1922), ch. 3.   P. N. U.

POLYCRATES (2) (4th c. B.C.), Athenian rhetor censured by Isocrates on account of the trivial nature of his rhetorical exercises. His works included Βούσειρις, which drew from Isocrates a more effective panegyric on the same theme, the Κατηγορία Σωκράτους, to which Isocrates also replied (*Bus.* 5 ff.: cf. also Xen. *Mem.* 1. 2), the Ἑλένη, a παίγνιον written in emulation of a similar work by Isocrates, as well as Sophistic *encomia* on trifling themes (a pot, pebbles, etc.).   J. W. H. A.

POLYDAMAS (Πο(υ)λυδάμας), in mythology, son of Panthoos (Homer, loc. cit. infra). In the *Iliad* he takes some part in the fighting, but is chiefly noteworthy for his sage advice, which Hector rejects to his cost (18. 249 ff.). His death is nowhere recorded and he seems to be thought of as surviving the war.   H. J. R.

POLYDORUS (Πολύδωρος). There are some ten mythological persons bearing this name, the only ones of any importance being: (1) son of Cadmus (q.v.) and Harmonia, a purely genealogical figure, ignored by Euripides (*Bacch.* 43–4), but mentioned, e.g., by Herodotus (5. 59). (2) Youngest son of Priam and Hecuba (qq.v.). When the Trojan War was raging, Priam sent him with much gold to Polymestor, a Thracian king, who murdered him for the gold after the fall of Troy. His ghost speaks the prologue of Euripides, *Hecuba*, and an important part of the plot is Hecabe's discovery and avenging of the murder. Cf. Verg. *Aen.* 3. 22 ff.   H. J. R.

POLYEIDUS (1), a seer, one of the Melampodidae, a Corinthian. When Glaucus, son of Minos (q.v.) was drowned in a honey-jar, Polyeidus, after passing a test imposed by Minos, found the body and afterwards restored it to life by using a herb revealed by a snake.

See Hyginus, *Fab.* 136; Roscher's *Lexicon*, s.v.   H. J. R.

POLYEIDUS (2) 'the Sophist' is known only from Aristotle (*Poet.* 16, 17), who refers to the recognition scene in his *Iphigeneia* (if that was the title).

POLYGNOTUS (*fl. c.* 475–447 B.C.), painter, son and pupil of Aglaophon of Thasos; later an Athenian citizen. Friend of Cimon and probably of Sophocles. Pliny dates before 420 B.C. He painted the 'Iliupersis' in the Stoa Poikile soon after 460, the 'Iliupersis' and 'Nekyia' in the Cnidian Lesche at Delphi probably between 458 and 447; according to a very probable emendation he painted in the Theseum soon after 475. The 'Rape of the Leucippidae' in the Anakeion, the 'Suitor Slaying' in Plataea, the 'Achilles in Scyros' and the 'Nausicaa' (both later in the Pinakotheke) are undated. Contemporary and later vases, particularly the Niobid painter's Argonaut crater (Pfuhl, fig. 492), illustrate Polygnotan grouping and postures, as described by Pausanias, and the transparent drapery and freer treatment of the face, noted by Pliny. Many of the elements of his art had appeared sporadically before, but he combined them to represent men of high moral purpose (ἦθος) and 'better than ourselves', often either taking a decision or in the reaction after the event. For Theophrastus and others he was a primitive (he did not use shading), but still the first great painter.

Overbeck, 380, 614, 1042–79; Pfuhl, 688, 729; E. Löwy, *Polygnot* (1929); C. Dugas, *Rev. Ét. Gr.* 1938, 53.   T. B. L. W.

POLYMNESTUS, *see* MUSIC, § 10.

POLYNICES (Πολυνείκης), *see* ETEOCLES, ADRASTUS.

POLYPEMON, *see* PROCRUSTES.

POLYPERCHON (b. *c.* 380 B.C.), son of Simmias a Macedonian noble, first appears when promoted 'taxiarch' to command a brigade of Alexander's Macedonian infantry after Issus (333). Under Alexander he rose no higher, and his first independent command was in the Lamian War (321), when he showed some skill. This, with his seniority and want of personal ambition, inspired the regent Antipater to recommend the army to elect him his successor (319); but, lacking Antipater's prestige, he had no chance of controlling the 'separatist' generals. He failed even to hold Macedonia and retain possession ot the two kings, and degenerated into a mere general of mercenaries in Greece, employed alternately by Antigonus and Cassander against each other.

H. Berve, *Alexanderreich*, No. 654; W. W. Tarn, *CAH* vi, ch. 15.   G. T. G.

POLYPHEMUS, *see* CYCLOPES.

POLYPHRASMON (so spelt *IG* ii². 2325), son of the tragic poet Phrynichus, wrote a tetralogy on the subject of Lycurgus, presented in 467 B.C., but defeated by Aeschylus' Theban tetralogy and by Aristias (Arg. Aesch. *Sept.*).

POLYSTRATUS, perhaps a direct disciple of Epicurus, followed Hermarchus (successor of Epicurus) as head of the school. Works: Περὶ ἀλόγου καταφρονήσεως, frs. ed. C. Wilke, 1905: Περὶ φιλοσοφίας, frs. ed. Crönert, *Kolotes u. Menedemos*, 36.

See Zeller, *Phil. d. Griechen* iii. 1⁴. 381–2.

POLYXENA (Πολυξένη), in mythology, daughter of Priam (q.v.) and Hecuba (q.v.); not in Homer. In the *Cypria* she is mortally wounded at the fall of Troy and buried by Neoptolemus (fr. 26 Allen). In the *Iliu Persis* and later she is sacrificed to the ghost of Achilles (Proclus); cf., e.g., Eur. *Hec.* 220 ff.). Hence the story that Achilles in life was in love with her, e.g. Hyginus, *Fab.* 110.   H. J. R.

POLYZELUS, Athenian comic writer. Suidas mentions Νίπτρα, Ἀφροδίτης γοναί, Διονύσου γοναί, Μουσῶν γοναί, and Δημοτυνδάρεως. Titles containing the word γοναί suggest Middle Comedy, but Δημοτ. is clearly a fifth-century production, for it mentions (fr. 3) Theramenes, who died in 404 (Xen. *Hell.* 2. 3. 55) and Hyperbolus (fr. 5) who was killed in 411 (Thuc. 8. 73. 3).

FCG ii. 367 ff.; *CAF* i. 789 ff.; Demiańczuk, *Supp. Com.* 82 f.   M. P.

POMERIUM was the line demarcating an augurally constituted city, containing the *auspicia urbana*. The name was soon transferred to the strip between wall and urban property (Livy 1. 44; Plut. *Rom.* 11) and even to the *glacis* outside the wall (cf. *CIL* x. 1018, Pompeii). The original *pomerium* of Rome is the subject of conflicting statements: Tacitus (*Ann.* 12. 24) describes the Lupercal circuit, Varro (apud *Solin.* 1. 17) the augural *templum* of the Palatine. The earliest known boundary, containing (by inference) the Capitol, Quirinal, Viminal, Oppian, Caelian, and Palatine hills, is based upon Varro's description (*Ling.* 5. 46–54) of the lustration of the Four Regions. This remained unaltered until Sulla extended it 'auctis p. R. finibus' (Tac. *Ann.* 12. 23). On these grounds it was extended by Caesar (Dio Cass. 43. 50), Augustus (Tac. *Ann.* 12. 23; Dio Cass. 55. 6; a claim of thrice is made in *Bull. Com. Arch.* 1919, 24–32), Claudius (Tac. *Ann.* 12. 24; Aul. Gell. 13. 14. 7; *CIL* vi. 31537 *a–d*; *Not. Scav.* 1909, 44, 45; 1912. 197;

1913, 68), Vespasian (*CIL* vi. 930, 14–16; 31538 *a–c*), Hadrian (*CIL* vi. 31539 *a–c*), and Aurelian (S.H.A. *Aurelian* 21). The Imperial *pomerium*, thus loosely defined by *cippi*, is thought to have coincided on the east with the Republican wall, breaking away to include the Aventine and Emporium, the southern half of the Campus Martius, and all the Pincian hill, at the last point extending beyond Aurelian's Wall. *See also* AUSPICIUM.

M. Labrousse, *Mélanges d'arch.* 1937, 1 ff.   I. A. R.

POMONA, Roman goddess of *poma*, i.e. fruits, especially such as grow on trees, apples, etc. Her flamen (q.v.) was lowest in rank of all, corresponding apparently to the small importance of her province. She had a sacred place, *pomonal*, twelve miles out of Rome (Festus, p. 296, 15 ff. Lindsay), but no known festival. Ovid (*Met.* 14. 623 ff.) has a story (unconnected with facts of cult and clearly his own or another comparatively late author's invention) that Vertumnus (q.v.) loved her, pled his own cause in disguised shape, and finally won her.   H. J. R.

POMPAEDIUS (or, better, **POPPAEDIUS**) **SILO,** QUINTUS, a Marsian, was the chief Italian leader in the Social War. He ambushed and defeated Q. Caepio, but failed to force Marius to give battle. After most of the Italians had given up the struggle Pompaedius still remained in arms and retook Bovianum. He perished after being defeated by Metellus Pius in the last battle of the war (88 B.C.).   M. H.

POMPEIA, daughter of Q. Pompeius Rufus (*cos.* 88 B.C.) and of Mucia, Sulla's daughter, married Caesar in 67 and was divorced in 61, as Caesar's wife had to be above suspicion (*see* CLODIUS 1).

POMPEIANUS, TIBERIUS CLAUDIUS, *see* CLAUDIUS (15).

POMPEII, situated on a small volcanic hill, 5¼ miles south-east of Vesuvius, was not a small town according to ancient standards, having an area of *c.* 160 acres. Its sudden end in the eruption of Vesuvius in A.D. 79, which was described by the Younger Pliny (*Ep.* 16 and 20), struck the imagination of the ancient world as well as the modern. The site, forgotten in the Middle Ages, was rediscovered in 1748; since then intermittent excavation has proceeded. About two-fifths of it have now been uncovered.

2. Pompeii served in Strabo's time as a port of Nola, Nuceria, and Acerrae (5. 4. 8). Its commercial and strategic position at the mouth of the Sarnus, one of the gateways of Campania, explains its historical development. Strabo (ibid.) states that it was occupied successively by Oscans, Etruscans and Pelasgians, Samnites, and Romans,

3. The Oscans were the descendants of the neolithic inhabitants of Campania, as appears from their rough pottery. From the eighth century B.C. they came under the influence of the Greek colonies of the coast, and Greek pottery (geometric, proto-Corinthian, Corinthian) and bronzes appear in their graves. In the seventh century Etruscan influence becomes apparent, issuing doubtless from Capua and Nola, and from this time Greek and Etruscan features occur together. The Samnites invaded Campania in the fifth century, occupying Capua in 432 and Cumae in 420, and their penetration south of Vesuvius must have followed soon.

4. The town-plan of Pompeii seems to contain an older portion and a newer portion, of which the former may follow the plan of an early Oscan settlement. If so, the question arises: when was the town enlarged to its present size, and by whom? The fortifications of the enlarged town suggest a date in the fifth century B.C., but without further excavation it is impossible to decide whether the impulse came from the Greeks, Etruscans, or Samnites.

5. From the end of the fifth century B.C. till the age of

Sulla, Pompeii was a Samnite town. Its language was Oscan. Coinage suggests that it belonged to a league of which Nuceria was the head. Its chief magistrate was a *meddix tuticus*, and under him were quaestors and aediles. An assembly (*kombennion*) appears in inscriptions, though it is not known whether it was an assembly of all citizens or a town-council. The period was one of great prosperity, based on agriculture and commerce. Culturally the town passed through two phases, the line between them falling about the middle of the third century B.C. The first (in which limestone was the chief building material) may be called Italian in the sense that it is a reflection of a more or less homogeneous civilization which was spread over most of south Italy at the time (cf. the Oscan and Lucanian tomb-paintings in the Naples and Capua museums). The street-plan, temples, and houses show that it was strongly permeated with Etruscan influences. The second phase (so-called 'tufa' period) was Hellenistic and received a great impetus from the ever-widening trade connexions of Campania during the second century B.C. Increasing prosperity is reflected in the dignified monuments which date from the third and second centuries B.C. The main Forum, hitherto a rough and unsystematic market-place, was converted into a dignified civic centre. The region of the Foro Triangolare was rebuilt after the manner of a Greek gymnasium to be a centre of the town's cultural life. Objects like bronzes, marble tables, terra-cottas, and mosaics were imported in large quantities from Hellenistic factories or made by local workmen after Hellenistic designs. In houses wall-decoration became markedly Hellenistic, and the Greek peristyle was added to the Italian atrium.

6. In the Social War Pompeii joined the Italians (Appian, *BCiv.* 1. 39) and in 89 B.C. was attacked by L. Sulla. The outcome of the siege is unknown, but the war as a whole completely changed the position of Pompeii. With the rest of Italy it received Roman franchise and the citizens were enrolled in the *tribus Menenia*. As a punishment for resistance to Sulla's army a colony of Roman veterans was planted on the town under the leadership of P. Sulla, the Dictator's nephew (Cic. *Sull.* 60–2). At this time, except for the incipient use of Latin in place of Oscan as the language of official life, the romanization of Pompeii had not gone far, but hereafter it made rapid strides. The names and functions of the magistrates were brought into line with those of other Roman colonies. The Oscan language was replaced by Latin, and Oscan weights and measures by Roman standards. Houses, wall-painting, metal-work, and pavements all took on a Roman tinge. Romanization in architecture was indirectly assisted by an earthquake in A.D. 63. Seneca (*QNat.* 6. 1. 1–2) and Tacitus (*Ann.* 15. 22) say that it left much of the city in ruins, and this is confirmed by the remains. In the parts that were rebuilt before the eruption the influence of Rome was strong.

7. Local families and traditions were not, however, entirely swamped by the Roman colonists. Indeed, inscriptions suggest that after initial difficulties the two groups lived amicably side by side. Municipal elections continued to be contested with vigour, and except to deal with irregularities and disorder (e.g. the riot in the amphitheatre of A.D. 59; Tac. *Ann.* 14. 17) there was little interference from the central government. The remains of the last half-century before the eruption present the picture of a prosperous town—a market for the produce of a rich country-side, a port with wide connexions in the Mediterranean, and an industrial centre producing certain specialities (mill-stones, fish-sauce, perfumes, and cloth) for which the demand was more than local.

BIBLIOGRAPHY

ANCIENT SOURCES: (*a*) Inscriptions: *CIL* iv and x, 787–1079, 8143–57, 8348–61; *Eph. Epigr.* viii. 86–90, 202; *Not. Scav.* 1927, 89–116; 1929, 438–76; 1933, 277–331; 1936, 299–352. (*b*) Authors:

scattered references of which the most important are: Cic. *Pro Sulla*, 60–2; Strabo 5. 4. 3–8; Seneca, *QNat.* 6. 1. 1–2; Tac. *Annals*, 14. 17 and 15. 22; *Hist.* 1. 2; Pliny, *Ep.* 6. 16 and 20; Suetonius, *Titus* 8. 3 ff.; Dio Cassius, 66. 21–4.

MODERN WRITERS. For further bibliography, A. W. Van Buren, *A Companion to the Study of Pompeii and Herculaneum* (Rome, 1933). General works: A. Mau, *Pompeii, Its Life and Art* (tr. F. W. Kelsey, U.S.A. 1899); E. Pernice, *Pompeii* (1926); R. C. Carrington, *Pompeii* (1936); A. Sogliano, *Pompei nel suo sviluppo storico: Pompei preromana* (1937); M. Della Corte, *Case ed abitanti a Pompeii* (Pompei 1926); T. Frank, *Econ. History of Rome*² (1927), 245 ff.; H. H. Tanzer, *The Common People of Pompeii: a Study of the Graffiti* (U.S.A. 1939).   R. C. C.

POMPEIUS (1), QUINTUS, a *homo novus* and friend of Scipio Aemilianus, was consul in 141 B.C., when he succeeded his enemy Q. Metellus Macedonicus in Hispania Citerior. After failing to storm and blockade Numantia he accepted terms, receiving 30 talents. But on the arrival of his successor, M. Popillius Laenas, he disowned the treaty with senatorial connivance and escaped all punishment. Accused shortly afterwards of extortion, he was acquitted again. He returned to Spain as a legate of L. Furius Philus (136). He opposed Ti. Gracchus (133), and was censor with Metellus Macedonicus (131).

Drumann–Groebe, *Geschichte Roms*² iv. 313; A. Schulten, *Numantia* (1933), 69.   A. M.

POMPEIUS (2) **RUFUS**, QUINTUS (*cos.* 88 B.C.), was husband of Cornelia, daughter of Sulla; and father of Pompeia, Caesar's wife from 67 to 61. An active Optimate, Pompeius as tribune in 100 proposed the recall of Metellus (q.v. 6) Numidicus. He was praetor in 91, and consul with Sulla in 88. He was driven from Rome in the struggle against his former friend Sulpicius, besides losing a son in the riots; he fled to Sulla's army at Nola. After Sulla's march on Rome and departure for the East, Pompeius was to have superseded Pompeius Strabo in command of the force still in the field against the Marsi, but Strabo had him assassinated.

For coin-portrait see *B.M. Coins, Rom. Rep.* i. 484.   M. H.

POMPEIUS (3) **MAGNUS**, GNAEUS, see POMPEY.

POMPEIUS (4), GNAEUS, elder son of Pompey and Mucia, and son-in-law of Appius Claudius, in 49 secured an Egyptian fleet, with which before the battle of Dyrrhachium he destroyed Caesar's transports. Early in the African War he occupied the Balearics and crossed to Spain, where he was joined after Thapsus by his brother and Labienus, raised thirteen legions, and won most of the southern province. But after manœuvres which drove him south from Corduba he was defeated by Caesar in 45 in the hard-fought battle of Munda, and later captured and executed. He was both cruel and stupid (Cic. *Fam.* 15. 19, Plut. *Cic.* 39).   G. E. F. C.

POMPEIUS (5), SEXTUS, younger son of Pompey the Great, accompanied his father from Lesbos to Egypt after Pharsalus, proceeded to Africa after the murder of Pompey, and joined his brother in Spain after Thapsus. He commanded the garrison of Corduba during the campaign of Munda, subsequently contrived to raise an army (partly of Pompeian fugitives), and won appreciable successes against the governors of Further Spain, Carrinas and Pollio. In 44 B.C. a settlement was effected by Lepidus, and in 43 the Senate appointed Sextus commander of the fleet. Outlawed under the *Lex Pedia*, he employed his ships to rescue fugitives from the proscription and occupied Sicily, which he used as a base for raiding and blockading the Italian coast. He repelled an attack by Octavian's *legatus* Salvidienus in 42, supported Antony against Octavian in 40 (when his lieutenant Menodorus occupied Sardinia), and was given the governorship of Sicily, Sardinia, and Achaea by the treaty of Misenum. In 38 Octavian accused him of breaking the treaty and again attacked him, but was defeated in naval battles near Cumae and Messana.

In 36 the attack was renewed, and after Agrippa's victory off Mylae and Octavian's defeat off Tauromenium the war was decided by the battle of Naulochus. Sextus escaped with a few ships to Asia Minor, where he attempted to establish himself and was captured and executed by Antony's *legatus* M. Titius (35). His wife was Scribonia, daughter of L. Scribonius Libo.

ANCIENT SOURCES: *Bellum Hispaniense* 3 and 4; Cicero, *Letters and Philippics*; Velleius 2. 72–9; Appian, *BCiv.* 2–5; Dio Cassius 42–9. MODERN LITERATURE: J. Kromayer, *Philol.* lvi (1897); Drumann–Groebe, *Gesch. Roms* iv. 563–91; T. Rice Holmes, *Architect of the Roman Empire* i (1928); M. Hadas, *Sextus Pompey* (U.S.A. 1930).
                    G. W. R.

POMPEIUS (6) **SILO,** rhetor, some of whose arguments are cited by the elder Seneca.

POMPEIUS (7) **SATURNINUS,** orator, historian, poet whose verse, in the manner of Catullus and Calvus, Pliny greatly admired (*Ep.* 1. 8 and 16). Pliny sent him for criticism his speech at the opening of the Como library.

POMPEIUS (8) (5th c. A.D.), grammarian, author of a *Commentum artis Donati* (ed. Keil, *Gramm. Lat.* v. 95–312). Cf. Teuffel, § 472. 2; Schanz–Hosius, § 1102.

POMPEIUS LENAEUS, see LENAEUS.

POMPEIUS, *see also* FESTUS (2), STRABO (1), TROGUS.

POMPEY (GNAEUS POMPEIUS, called MAGNUS after 81) (106–48 B.C.) served with his father Strabo at Asculum, and throughout the Marian domination preserved an army in Picenum with which he won victories for Sulla in 83. Impressed by his forces and self-confidence Sulla sent him with *imperium* to Sicily, where he defeated and killed Carbo, and then to Africa, where he destroyed Cn. Domitius and King Iarbas. Pompey was still an *eques*, but a marked man, for Sulla grudgingly allowed him to triumph; and in 77, after assisting Catulus to overcome Lepidus, he obtained proconsular *imperium* to reinforce Metellus Pius against Sertorius (q.v.) in Spain. Thence he returned in 71 and co-operated with the reluctant Crassus in finishing off the Servile War. Again he triumphed, and extorted from the Senate the consulate, emphasizing the illegality by surrendering his horse with great ceremony to the censors, whose office he now restored; in this year, too, the tribunes recovered their rights, and L. Cotta reduced senatorial representation on the courts to one-third (70 B.C.). From both tribunes and *equites* Pompey reaped his reward: in 67 the *Lex Gabinia* created for him an *imperium* with unprecedented powers against the pirates, whom he destroyed in three months; and to this *imperium infinitum aequum* Manilius next year added Lucullus' Asiatic provinces and conduct of the Mithridatic War. His Eastern campaigns were his greatest achievement: Mithridates was defeated immediately, and though attempts to pursue him over the Caucasus failed, he committed suicide in the Crimea in 63. Further, Pompey founded colonies, annexed Syria, settled Judaea, and laid the foundation of all subsequent Roman organization of the East (though he reached no agreement with Parthia). In 62 he returned, disbanded his army, and triumphed, for the moment a *popularis* no longer (Cic. *Att.* 2. 1. 6). But he made two requests: settlement of his veterans and ratification of his Eastern *acta*. But the Senate, led on by the Metelli, whose kinswoman Mucia he had divorced, and by Lucullus and Cato, frustrated him, until he was driven into partnership with Crassus and Caesar; he married the latter's daughter Julia (q.v. 1) in 59. His demands were satisfied by Caesar as consul; but his popularity waned, and in 58–57 Clodius (q.v.) deliberately flouted him. In 57, after backing Cicero's recall, he received control of the corn-supply for five years; but no military power was attached, nor could he secure the commission to restore Ptolemy Auletes in Egypt next year. Again he wavered towards the *optimates*, but still preferred the 'Triumvirate', which was renewed at Luca in 56. Pompey became consul with Crassus for 55, and received Spain for five years; but he governed his province by proxy. The murder of Clodius in 52 caused his appointment as sole consul, with backing from extreme *optimates*. His immediate legislation, *de vi, de ambitu*, and *de iure magistratuum*, was designed only to end the corruption at elections; but the prolongation of his *imperium* for five years from this date destroyed the balance of power with Caesar; and he took as his colleague Metellus (q.v. 11) Scipio, whose daughter Cornelia he had married, Julia (q.v. 1) having died in 54. Gradually his new alliance led him to support demands that Caesar be recalled before he was sure of the consulate of 48; and in 50, when negotiations with Caesar were breaking down, he accepted from the consul C. Marcellus the command of the Republican forces in Italy. In 49 he transported his forces from Brundisium to Greece and spent the year mobilizing in Macedonia. He met Caesar on his arrival in 48 with a force powerful in every arm, and inflicted a serious reverse when Caesar attempted to blockade him at Dyrrhachium. But later (9 August), perhaps under pressure from his senatorial friends, he joined in a pitched battle at Pharsalus, and was irretrievably defeated. He fled to Egypt, but was stabbed to death as he landed (28 Sept. 48).

The violence and unconstitutional character of Pompey's early career invites comparison with Augustus, whom in his constitutional position he so often resembled: in 67 he had twenty-four *legati* with praetorian *imperium*; from 55 he governed Spain through *legati*, and while doing so was made consul in 52. But still more significant was his unofficial power: by 62 in Spain, Gaul, Africa, the East, and parts of Italy, there were colonists and *clientes* bound to him by the relationship of *fides* and surrounding him with a magnificence unsurpassed by a Roman senator hitherto; the climax was reached with the dedication of his theatre in the Campus Martius in 55. He owed all to his military genius, which must have been of the highest order even though other commanders, Metellus, Crassus, Lucullus, often paved the way to his successes. In politics, where his chief ambition lay, he was unimaginative and irresolute, but he genuinely tried to re-establish order and dignity in the government of the Roman Empire. His private life, too, was of a high standard for such an age, and two women, Julia and Cornelia, married to him for dynastic ends, fell deeply in love with him. Cicero's earlier eulogies may be discounted, and even in early years there were bitter criticisms (cf. *Att.* 1. 13. 4); but despite the disappointments and suspicions of the war years Pompey's death brought from him a heartfelt tribute: 'hominem enim integrum et castum et grauem cognoui' (*Att.* 11. 6. 5).

SOURCES: (a) Ancient: Plutarch, *Sertorius* and *Lucullus*, Appian, *BCiv.* 1. 80 f. and *Mithridatica* are evidence for P.'s early career, with Plutarch's *Pompey*, an excellent life based probably on Nepos; *see also under* CAESAR (1), GABINIUS (2), MANILIUS (2).
(b) To the general works mentioned s.v. CAESAR add C. Lanzani, 'Silla e Pompeio', *Historia* 1933; A. E. R. Boak, 'The extraordinary commands from 80 to 48 B.C.', *Amer. Hist. Rev.* 1918–19; P. Groebe, 'Zum Seeräuberkriege des Pompeius Magnus', *Klio* 1910, 374; F. Guse, 'Die Feldzüge des dritten Mithradatischen Krieges in Pontus und Armenien', *Klio* 1926, 332.   G. E. F. C.

POMPILIUS (*c.* 100 B.C.), epigrammatist quoted by Varro. Teuffel, § 146. 2; Baehr. *FPR* 274.

POMPONIUS (1) **BONONIENSIS** (*fl. c.* 100–85 B.C.), Latin poet, older contemporary of Novius (q.v.). These two made *fabulae Atellanae* literary and tended to fuse them with *palliatae*. Seventy known titles show the four stock Atellan characters (fool, boaster, old driveller, old sly-boots), various occupations, political satire,

religious and mythological themes; in popular language, with coarseness and farcical scenes. He perhaps wrote *satura* also.

Fragments: O. Ribbeck, *CRF*[2] 225 (3rd ed. Teubner, 1897).   E. H. W.

POMPONIUS (2) **RUFUS** wrote *Collecta* from which Valerius Maximus (4. 4 *ad init.*) quotes 'maxima ornamenta matronis liberos'.

POMPONIUS (3) **SECUNDUS**, PUBLIUS [?CALV]ISIUS SABINUS (Quint. *Inst.* 8. 3. 31; 10. 1. 98) (*cos. suff.* A.D. 44), friend of the elder Pliny who wrote his biography (Plin. *Ep.* 3. 5) and calls him 'consularem poetam' and 'uatem ciuemque clarissimum' (*HN* 7. 80; 13. 83). Endangered by prosecution under Tiberius, he survived (Tac. *Ann.* 5. 8). He wrote *Aeneas*, a praetexta. Under Claudius his verses on the stage drew insults from the mob (ibid. 11. 13). Legate of Upper Germany, he victoriously checked the Chatti in 50 (ibid. 12. 28). Pliny (*HN* 13. 83) mentions having seen the handwriting of the Gracchi, about two centuries old, in his possession. W. Otto (*Philol.* xc. 4 [N.F. xliv. 4]) argues that he died not in the late sixties A.D., as Cichorius holds, but between 51 and 57. He was perhaps step-brother of Caesonia, Gaius' wife. His brother Quintus (*cos. suff.* A.D. 41) favoured the restoration of the Republic after Gaius' death; as an accomplice of Camillus Scribonianus in 42, he committed suicide or was killed.

PIR, P 563; C. Cichorius, *Römische Studien* (1922), 423; Schanz-Hosius, *Röm. Literatur* ii⁴ (1935), 475; E. Ritterling, *Fasti des röm. Deutschlands* (1932), 15.   J. W. D. and A. M.

POMPONIUS (4) **MELA**, of Tingentera (near Gibraltar), wrote under Gaius (A.D. 37–41) or early in Claudius' reign, a geographical survey in Latin of the inhabited world (*De Chorographia*) in three books. He describes (bk. 1) the earth's division into north and south hemispheres, and five zones (two habitable, the southern being an island of *Antichthones*); then the relative positions and boundaries of the three continents, surrounded by Ocean which indented it by four seas, the Caspian (erroneously regarded as connected with the Northern Ocean), Persian Gulf, Red Sea, Mediterranean; then countries, Gibraltar Straits–Egypt, Palestine–Euxine; (bk. 2) Scythia, Thrace, Macedonia, Greece, Italy; south Gaul, Spain; then all the Mediterranean islands; then (bk. 3) the outer coasts of Spain, Gaul, Germany, unknown north Europe, and east Asia; British Isles, Thule, India, Persian Gulf, Red Sea; Ethiopians; west Africa. Inner Europe is neglected, so is inner though known Asia. Africa is all north of the equator. The work was a popular summary, with lists of names, but no mathematical details or distances, though there are some details of physical nature, climate, and customs of lands. Mela's idea of the known world is roughly that of Strabo.

Text: C. Frick (1880). Cf. E. Bunbury, *Hist. Anc. Geog.* (1879), ii. 352 ff.   E. H. W.

POMPONIUS (5) **BASSULUS**, MARCUS (? 1st c. A.D.) recorded in an inscription of Aeclanum (*CIL* 9. 1164) as a translator of Menander and writer of original comedies (probably not for performance).

POMPONIUS (6) **PROCULUS VITRASIUS POLLIO**, TITUS, entering upon a senatorial career under Hadrian, was consul between 138 and 140, being thereafter successively governor of Hispania Citerior (*c.* 146), of Lower Moesia (*c.* 147–9), and proconsul of Asia (*c.* 151–2). He served on the staff of Marcus Aurelius in the German War, down to 175, and held a second consulship in 176. He married Annia Fundania Faustina, granddaughter of that M. Annius Verus who was father of Faustina the Elder and grandfather of M. Aurelius.

PIR, P 558; P. Lambrechts, *La Composition du sénat romain . . . (117–192)* (1936), p. 88, no. 462.   C. H. V. S.

POMPONIUS (7), Sextus, a Roman jurist of the time of Hadrian and the Antonines. He held no official post nor (probably) had he the *ius respondendi*; thus he could devote his time to literary activity. He was one of the most productive legal writers (more than 300 *libri*). But though not without critical ability, he is rather a compiler. Roman legal literature owed to him its biggest work: his commentary on the Edict, composed at Hadrian's order, seems to have had over 150 books, as a passage of the 83rd book, preserved in the *Digest*, deals with a subject treated little more than half-way through the Edict. It is curious that the work was not excerpted directly for the *Digest* and is known only by quotations due to the later commentaries on the Edict (of Paulus and Ulpian). His other works are also extensive: two text-books of *ius civile*, *Ad Sabinum* (36 books) and *Ad Q. Mucium* (39 books); two (or one?) works of predominantly casuistic character, *Variae Lectiones* (41 books) and *Epistulae* (20 books). In addition, an epitome *Ex Plautio* and monographs on *Senatus consulta, Fideicommissa*, and *Stipulationes*. Especially notable is the booklet *Liber singularis enchiridii*, a short compendium of the history of Roman legal sources, magistrates, and legal science up to the time of Julian, Pomponius' contemporary (*Dig.* 1. 2. 2). This small compendium contains a good many mistakes, copied from older writings, and has been shortened and deformed by Justinian's compilers; it is, nevertheless, of value, since it gives some new details which are preserved nowhere else. There is no reason to deny the authorship of Pomponius, as has been tried in recent times. Pomponius had a perfect knowledge of the older legal literature, and he himself is often quoted by later writers, his reports of other jurists' opinions being careful and accurate. His works have been utilized for the *Digest* with particular predilection; his contribution to it is, after those of Paulus and Ulpian, one of the largest.

A comprehensive monograph is lacking. On the language of Pomponius: W. Kalb, *Roms Juristen nach ihrer Sprache dargestellt* (1890), 63 ff. On the chronological sequence of his works: H. Fitting, *Alter und Folge der Schriften röm. Juristen²* (1908), 33 ff. On the *Enchiridion*: F. Ebrard, *Sav. Zeitschr.* xlv (1925), 117 ff. (erroneous, cf. S. Riccobono, *Mélanges Cornil* ii (1926), 380). A. B.

POMPONIUS, *see also* ATTICUS, MARCELLUS, PORPHYRION.

POMPTINE MARSHES, a malaria-stricken region, formed by the stagnation of the Ufens and other streams, lying south-east of Rome between Volscian mountains and Tyrrhenian Sea. Pliny's statement that twenty-four cities once flourished here (*HN* 3. 59) is an exaggeration: Suessa Pometia, like the lands later assigned to citizens of the Pomptina and Oufentina tribes, lay outside the marshes proper (Livy 6. 21; 7. 15; 9. 20). The Via Appia crossed the marshes, but travellers apparently preferred to use the parallel, nineteen-mile-long ship-canal, since the marshes included highwaymen among other perils (Strabo 5. 233; Hor. *Sat.* 1. 5. 10 f.; Juv. 3. 307). From 160 B.C. or earlier numerous attempts were made by Cethegus, Trajan, and others to drain them—a task successfully accomplished only recently. E. T. S.

PONS MULVIUS carried the Via Flaminia across the Tiber north of Rome; it is first mentioned in 207 B.C. At the existing bridge of six arches, built by Aemilius Scaurus in 109 B.C., the Allobroges were trapped during the Catilinarian conspiracy in 63 B.C. and Maxentius was defeated by Constantine in A.D. 312. Of the four large 60-feet arches, only the southern pair remains. Above pointed cutwaters, both up- and downstream, are flood-arches. The road makes a sloping approach on each side.

R. Delbrück, *Hellenistische Bauten in Latium* i (1907); T. Frank, *Roman Buildings of the Republic* (1924), 141. I. A. R.

PONTICUS, an epic writer in Propertius' set, likened by him to Homer.

PONTIFEX, PONTIFICES. The word (cf. *artifex, aurifex*) means one skilled in the important magic of bridge-making (see Giuffrida–Ruggeri in *Journ. Roy. Anthropol. Inst.* 1918, 100; Birt in *Rh. Mus.* 1926, 115 ff.), and by extension a priest acquainted with the increasingly elaborate ceremonial of public cult (cf. Cicero, *Har.* 18). At Rome, and with local differences no doubt elsewhere, the *pontifices* were originally an advisory board (*collegium*) whose business it was to assist the chief magistrate in his sacral functions; this is strongly indicated by the fact that their normal meeting-place was the Regia (Pliny, *Ep.* 4. 11. 6). Their number seems to have been primitively three (this was the number at Colonia Genetiva Iulia, see *Lex Vrsonensis* [Bruns, *Fontes* 27], 67, and colonies were constituted on the model of Rome), but was successively increased to six, nine, fifteen, and finally (under Caesar) sixteen (Livy, *periocha* 89; Dio Cass. 42. 51. 4). In historical times the original meaning of their name was quite unheeded, and they presided over the State cult generally. Like all the State priesthood, the *pontifices* were originally patricians; but by the *Lex Ogulnia* of 300 B.C. (Livy 10. 6. 6; see Mommsen, *Staatsr.* ii³. 22) half the college was chosen from the plebeians. Their position as an advisory body remained unaltered, at least in theory, and their decisions were *decreta*, i.e. pronouncements on points submitted to them or coming within their competence; they were not laws and had in themselves no executive effect. In practice it does not seem that they were disregarded, but the magistracy, not the pontiffs themselves, must enforce them.

The head of the college was the *Pontifex Maximus*. The original manner of his appointment was presumably by choice either of the king or of the other pontiffs; in historical times (before 212 B.C., but the date is uncertain, see Mommsen, ibid. 27) he was elected by vote of seventeen of the thirty-five tribes, chosen by lot, and thus, by a curious compromise, never by a majority of the people, like secular magistrates. He was head of the whole State clergy, exercising disciplinary functions over some at least of them (Wissowa, *RK* 509 ff.).

The *collegium pontificum* included, besides the pontiffs themselves, the *flamines*, Vestals, and *rex sacrorum*, but not the augurs nor the minor colleges. In Imperial times the post of *pontifex maximus* was held by the reigning emperor, Gratian being the first to refuse it, about A.D. 375 (Zosimus 4. 36).

Literature: Mommsen and Wissowa, locc. citt. H. J. R.

PONTIUS (1), Gavius, Samnite general who trapped a Roman army in the Caudine Forks, 321 B.C., and imposed his own peace terms. Patriotic annalists invented the story that Rome immediately repudiated the peace and defeated Pontius (Livy 9. 2 f.; F. E. Adcock, *CAH* vii. 599). Pontius himself is probably no mere annalists' figment modelled on Pontius Telesinus, Sulla's Samnite opponent. But the story that in 292 he defeated Fabius Gurges, whose father Fabius Rullianus then proceeded to defeat, capture, and execute him, is fiction suggested by events of 213, when Fabius Cunctator was his own son's legate (Livy, *Epit.* 11; 24. 4). E. T. S.

PONTIUS (2) **TELESINUS,** a Samnite patriot, and leader of the last effort to break Rome's supremacy in Italy. After moving ostensibly to the relief of Praeneste in 82 B.C., he made a sudden night-march with 40,000 men upon the capital, then ungarrisoned. Sulla, arriving in the nick of time, defeated him at the Colline Gate after a terrible struggle. M. H.

PONTIUS (3) **AQUILA,** a wealthy man from Sutrium, was tribune of the plebs (45 B.C.). Because he did not stand up when Caesar passed in triumph after Munda, his properties were confiscated. He was among Caesar's murderers, was legate of D. Brutus in Cisalpine Gaul, and was killed at Mutina (43).

G. Niccolini, *I fasti dei tribuni della plebe* (1934), 343; E. Pais, *I fasti dei tribuni della plebe* (1918), 166, and *Dalle guerre puniche a Cesare Augusto* i (1918), 313.   A. M.

PONTIUS (4) **PILATUS,** procurator of Judaea (A.D. 26–36), under whom Jesus Christ died. Jewish opinion thought him 'inflexible, merciless, obstinate' (Philo, *Leg. ad Gaium*, 38). Summoned to Rome by Tiberius on a complaint of the Samaritans, he arrived shortly after the Emperor's death. Therewith he disappears from authentic history. Eusebius relates that he committed suicide. The Christian opinion was not always hostile. Tertullian estimated him 'pro sua conscientia christianus' (*Apol.* 21); he is canonized with his wife in the Coptic Church. Pilate's alleged report to Tiberius of the condemnation of Jesus is a forgery. The apocryphal literature on him is large.

G. A. Müller, *Pontius Pilatus der fünfte Procurator von Judäa* (1888); E. Schürer, *Gesch. d. jüd Volkes*[4] i. 488; H. Peter, *Neue Jahrb.* 1907, p. 1. For the legend A. Harnack, *Gesch. d. altchristl. Liter.* i, pp. 21, 865; ii. 1, p. 603.   A. M.

PONTUS (Πόντος), the sea mythologically personified; he is son of Earth (Hesiod, *Theog.* 131–2); father of Nereus, Ceto, and Eurybia (233 ff.); husband of Mare, i.e. Thalassa (Hyginus, *Fab.*, *praef.* 5).

PONTUS, a region of north Asia Minor including the south coast of the Euxine between the Halys and Colchis and extending southward to Cappadocia and Lesser Armenia. A series of mountain ranges with deep valleys runs parallel to the coast. Two small coastal plains are formed by the deltas of the Halys and the Iris, which break through the mountains and provide the main lines of drainage and communication. It has but one convenient cross-road from Amisus to Sebasteia. Pontus is well watered and fertile, with a mild climate at the coast and in the valleys. Olives and other fruits, nuts, timber, pasture, and grain abound near the coast, but the inland is comparatively bare. Iron was mined along the coast (*see* CHALYBES).

The social and political structure of Pontus resembled that of Cappadocia; the same village population organized in territorial units, the same large temple territories with numerous sacred slaves ruled by priests, and the same feudal iranized nobility. Some mountainous regions in eastern Pontus remained for long uncivilized tribal territories. The Greek colonies on the coast were simply trading stations with little or no territory.

The centre and strength of the Pontic kingdom was the Pontic territory proper, but the kings continually added to it until it reached its greatest extent under Mithridates VI (*see* MITHRIDATES I–VI, PHARNACES I). They apparently brought the priests and nobility under control, and established a regional administration, but they did little to develop cities. Pompey gave much of the kingdom to princes, Deiotarus of Galatia and the priest of Comana, and divided the rest among various centres, chosen with an excellent eye for natural advantages, which he raised to municipal status and included in the province of Bithynia and Pontus. Besides the coast cities these were Magnopolis, Amaseia, Cabeira-Diospolis, Zela, Megalopolis, Neapolis, and Pompeiopolis. Practically all of these reverted to native rulers under Antony, but in the early Empire they gradually resumed city form. The western part was known as Pontus Galaticus, with Amaseia as its metropolis. The eastern part remained under the rule of Polemon's dynasty, until it was annexed in A.D. 64, and retained

the name of Pontus Polemoniacus, with the former royal capital Neocaesarea (Cabeira-Diospolis) as metropolis. Thus Pontus became part of the Galatian-Cappadocian province, and it remained joined with Cappadocia from Trajan until Diocletian, who divided it between his two provinces of Diospontus and Polemoniacus. To the end Pontus kept much of its native character; the cities remained regional and artificial, the feudal aristocracy important, and in the eastern portion the native tribes were only slightly touched by Hellenic civilization.

Th. Reinach, *Mithridate Eupator* (1890); *Trois royaumes* (1888); *CAH* ix. 211 ff., 606 ff.; J. A. R. Munro, *JHS* xxi (1901), 52 ff.; J. G. C. Anderson, F. Cumont, H. Grégoire, *Studia Pontica* i–iii (1903–10); Jones, *Eastern Cities*, 148 ff.; J. G. C. Anderson in *Anatolian Studies presented to Sir William Ramsay* (1923), 1 ff.
                                    T. R. S. B.

PONTUS EUXINUS, *see* EUXINE SEA.

POPANA (πόπανα), a sort of cakes (q.v.).

POPILLIUS (1) **LAENAS,** GAIUS, consul in 172 B.C., when he defended M. Popillius, whose high-handed conduct in Liguria had incurred the Senate's disapproval, was envoy in Greece in 170, and in 168 led the embassy to Egypt which after Pydna forced Antiochus Epiphanes to withdraw his army immediately from Egypt: he demanded a decision before the king stepped outside a circle drawn by Popillius.

Livy 42. 10 and 21; 43. 17; 44. 19 and 29; 45. 10 ff.; Polyb. 28. 3–5; 29. 27.   A. H. McD.

POPILLIUS (2) **LAENAS,** PUBLIUS (*cos.* 132 B.C.), son of (1) above, was a vigorous opponent of Tiberius Gracchus; as consul he presided over the *Quaestio* for the trial of his supporters. He served in Sicily as praetor, and later built the Via Popillia from Capua to Rhegium (cf. Dessau, *ILS* 23). When C. Gracchus passed his declaratory law, 'ne quis de capite c. R. iniussu ciuium iudicaretur', Popillius left Rome, but was recalled after Gracchus' death by L. Bestia (tribune 121 or 120).
                                    M. H.

POPLICOLA, *see* VALERIUS (1).

POPPAEA SABINA, daughter of T. Ollius (d. A.D. 31), was married first to Rufrius Crispinus, then to Otho. She became Nero's mistress in 58. The murder of Agrippina and banishment of Octavia are attributed partly to her incitement. Nero married her in 62 and remained devoted to her till her death in 65. A daughter born in 63 died within four months.

Sources: *PIR*, P 630. For her interest in Judaism, Josephus, *AJ* 20. 8. 11, *Vit.* 3. Modern Literature: Ph. Fabia, *Rev. Phil.* N.S. xx–xxii (1896–8); B. W. Henderson, *Life and Principate of the Emperor Nero* (1903).   G. W. R.

POPULARES came into use as a political catchword towards the middle of the second century B.C. It has wrongly been rendered as if it meant 'democratic'. At that time there were no political parties, and the struggle was between the wealthy members of the senatorial oligarchy, who controlled public finance and administration, and the newly enriched class of middlemen, business men, etc. The latter sought the support of the poor with the pretext that they defended their rights and interests. They thus came to be called *populares*, which merely means that they relied upon the lower classes or that they belonged to the coterie of a *popularis vir*, such as Marius or Caesar.

H. M. Last, *CAH* ix. 137 ff.; W. Kroll, *Die Kultur d. ciceronischen Zeit* (1933), i. 70 ff.   P. T.

POPULATION (GREEK). Most Greek States, from at least the sixth century, had a census, of various degrees of accuracy and detail, of their citizen population. In Athens every boy at age 18 was registered in his deme, and the total of deme registers formed the list of those entitled to attend the Ecclesia. Every boy of 18 of zeugite census or over (*see* ZEUGITAI) was also entered in the hoplite-ranks of the army, and a list was kept of *thetes* (q.v.) liable for service in the fleet; boys and girls were entered as well into their phratries (q.v.). Metics (q.v.) were registered in their deme of residence; and there was perhaps a poll-tax on slaves. But, so far as we know, no ancient writer ever made use of such statistics, for Athens or any other State, to record the total population at any one time, still less the changes from one time to another. We have only (1) some approximate (and not always reliable) estimates by historians of total citizen populations, or of hoplite strengths in particular campaigns; (2) two or three Athenian lists (last third of the 4th c.), and a few more Boeotian lists (3rd c.), of men entered as hoplites at age 18. For the *thetes* we are even less well-informed: the light-armed troops were generally ill organized, and in the fleet foreigners (in various proportions) served as well as citizens. We have also figures, for one year, of the cereal production of Attica, and for another year those of cereal imports. These serve as a slight check on figures for total population.

2. A. *General*. There was undoubtedly a considerable natural increase of the Greek population during the great colonizing periods (10th to 6th cc. B.C.), for flourishing States were founded all over the Mediterranean, and the States of Greece proper were as populous as ever. In the fifth and fourth centuries over-population was still the Greek problem, and there was considerable emigration. After Alexander's conquests, particularly in the third century, very large numbers of Greeks settled in Asia. But Greece proper did not recover from this last drain on its numbers, and there the population declined in the third and second centuries. We do not know that the Roman peace produced any increase in numbers and prosperity.

3. B. *Separate States*. From the meagre evidence the following rough figures have been estimated for Attica (area, *c.* 2,500 sq. km.):

Date B.C.	Citizens: Men 18-59 Hoplites and cavalry	Thetes	Citizens: Total	Metics: Men 18-59	Total	Slaves: Total	Total population of Attica
480	15,000?	20,000?	140,000?	?	?	?	?
431	25,000	18,000	172,000	9,500	28,500	110,000	310,000
425	16,500	12,500	116,000	7,000	21,000	80,000	217,000
400	11,000?	11,000?	90,000	?	?	?	?
323	14,500	13,500	112,000	12,000?	42,000?	106,000?	260,000?
313	12,000	9,000	84,000	10,000	35,000	?	?

There must have been far fewer metics and slaves in 480, and again in 400 than in 431; but we have no figures even for a rough estimate. There was considerable emigration to colonies between 480 and 431, less between 400 and 323. Of the total population in 431 perhaps half lived in Athens, Piraeus, and environs (not entirely urban in character)—one-third of the citizens, nearly all the metics, and about two-thirds of the slaves; a hundred years later perhaps three-quarters of the total.

4. For other States we have only figures for the hoplite forces and their approximate areas. Argos (1,400 sq. km.) had in 400 a citizen population equal to that of Athens, but not as many metics and slaves; Corinth (880 sq. km.) in the fifth and fourth centuries less than half the hoplites of Athens in 400, so less than half the population—perhaps 80,000. Arcadia (4,700 sq. km.), a poor country from which men were always emigrating, had 6,000–7,000 hoplites in the fourth and third centuries; by comparison with Attica this would mean about 80,000–90,000 citizen population—two-thirds only of its population to-day—with but few slaves to add; there were probably far more men below the hoplite census. Elis, a much richer land, but rural in character, may have

had a population of 80,000. The population of Laconia (8,500 sq. km., of which Messenia had nearly 3,000) is much more difficult to estimate. It had much of the richest land in Greece, but it was thinly populated. The Spartiates of 21–50 years numbered some 3,000, so perhaps 4,000 in all (i.e. *c.* 12,000 total population); the *perioeci* in the army were also about 3,000, but in what proportion to the total of *perioeci* we do not know. Still less do we know the number of helots, except that they were more numerous relatively to the free population than in any other State.

5. Boeotia (2,600 sq. km.) was prosperous and agricultural, with few foreigners and slaves; it put 7,000 hoplites and 1,000 horse in the field in 424, and similar numbers in the fourth century; it had about 10,000 of hoplite rank in all the third century. In 424 there were 10,000 light-armed. This yields *c.* 25,000–30,000 adult males, 90,000–100,000 citizen population (rather larger than to-day). Of the islands Corcyra (720 sq. km.), parts of Euboea, Thasos (300), Lesbos (1,750), Chios (820), Samos (470), Naxos (450), Andros (400), Paros (200), and Rhodes (1460) were highly developed, and their density of population approached that of Athens in 323; Corcyra probably and Chios perhaps exceeded it, each with large numbers of slaves. Aegina (100 sq. km.) before its conquest by Athens, was exceptionally well populated (perhaps 25,000–30,000 persons, nearly half of them slaves). The cities of the Hellespont and Bosporus and those in the Euxine were very prosperous, but we have no figures. Ionia and especially Miletus, had declined since their conquest by Persia; Erythrae and Ephesus were the richest of the Ionian cities in the fifth century, but neither half so rich as Byzantium.

6. In the West Syracuse (4,700 sq. km.) rivalled Athens in population, and in the early fourth century easily out-distanced it. Acragas (4,300 sq. km.) was not far behind, and Selinus, Gela, Himera, Messene were all populous. In all the Greek cities of Sicily (25,500 sq. km.) there may have been 700,000–800,000 persons (including numerous slaves). In south and south-west Italy Tarentum became in the fourth century the most populous, not much behind contemporary Athens; Sybaris and Croton had surpassed it in the sixth and fifth centuries. The total Italiote population may have equalled that of the Greeks in Sicily.

K. J. Beloch, *Bevölkerung der griechisch-römischen Welt* (1886), and 'Griechische Aufgebote' (*Klio* 1905–6); A. W. Gomme, *Population of Athens* (1933).   A. W. G.

POPULATION (ROMAN WORLD). All estimates can, at best, be only approximate, for they depend largely not on direct statistics, but on indirect evidence, often capable of more than one interpretation. The considerations are mostly of a very general character—the area of cities and countries, the varying density of population, the proportion of civic to rustic districts, the proportion of males capable of bearing arms to the whole free population or of that population itself to the slaves. All that is possible here is a study of a very few of the more reliable data, and some not unreasonable estimates of the population of the Empire as a whole.

2. First in importance stand the figures of the Roman census, in theory held once every *lustrum* (four years), and extending from the reign of the king Servius Tullius to that of the Emperor Vespasian. If we neglect the figures before 443, when the office of censor was established, we can trust these statistics to give us a fairly reliable picture of the increase of the Roman civic body. The general upward movement of the figures answers to historical probability, and one or two occasional drops can be reasonably explained. The fact that some difficulties are left over is no serious objection: the very unexpectedness of some figures entitles them to serious consideration. To take a few examples only in round numbers, we have 262,000 (294–293 B.C.), 270,000 (234–233), 214,000 (204–203), 318,000 (131–130), 394,000 (125–124), 463,000 (86–85), 910,000 (70–69). Note the delay in increase due to the First Punic War, the severe fall in the Second, the sharp rises after the land legislation of Tiberius Gracchus and, again, after the Social War. The figures are usually and most reasonably taken to record the *libera capita*, all males above military age, about one-third of the total free population. The addition to be made for slaves will be small at first, increasingly large towards the close of the Republic. The Roman population of Italy will have amounted to about 1,000,000 in 294–293 B.C., to about 4,500,000 in 70–69. The figures under the Empire show much too large a rise to be explained simply by the extension of Roman citizenship. The 4,000,000 odd of 28 B.C., the 5,984,000 odd of A.D. 47, probably give the grand total of Romans, including women and children. It may be noted here that regular registration of births in Rome was only instituted by Marcus Aurelius.

3. Polybius has preserved an invaluable record of the total armed strength of Rome and her Italian allies, horse and foot, in 225 B.C.—nearly 800,000 in all. This fits in reasonably well with the figures of the Roman census, and leads to an estimate of about 3,500,000 Romans and allies.

4. For the city of Rome the numbers of recipients of free corn provide a useful control. The 320,000 of 53 B.C. were reduced by Caesar in 46 to 150,000, but raised by Augustus to 250,000 or more. From this it may be conjectured that Rome, at the beginning of the Empire, had not more than a million inhabitants.

5. Caesar's statements of the military strength of the Gallic tribes are perhaps somewhat exaggerated; they lead to an estimate of something like 5,000,000 inhabitants. Pliny gives a figure of nearly 700,000 for the three north-western districts of Tarraconensis, which might suggest about 6,000,000 inhabitants for the whole of Spain.

6. If the attempt must be made to estimate population for the Empire as a whole, the vast gaps in our exact knowledge can be filled in only from very rough-and-ready estimates of probability and arguments from analogy. Beloch's estimates, which may be regarded as a reasonable mean between the very high and the very low, give some 54,000,000 for the whole Empire—rather less than half in the West including Illyricum. Italy will have about 6,000,000, and Rome, the largest city of the Empire, something less than a sixth of these. The East, with its swarming cities, must have had many areas of relatively thick population. Seleuceia ad Tigrim, when taken by the Romans in 163, is said to have lost 300,000 or even 400,000 inhabitants: though outside the Empire, it may supply some measure for the great cities of the Roman East.

K. J. Beloch, *Die Bevölkerung der griechisch-römischen Welt* (1886); Frank, *Econ. Surv.*, see Index, s.v.; for Early Italy see A. Afzelius, *Die römische Eroberung Italiens* (1942).   H. M.

POPULUS meant the whole Roman community, independent of classes and social distinctions. Probably the original meaning was the citizens as a military body, as is shown by the title *magister populi* (*see* DICTATOR). During the struggle of the Orders *populus* indicated the community as distinguished from the plebs. Finally, at the time of the crisis of the nobility, *populus* designated the classes supporting the *populares* (q.v.) in their opposition to the Senate.

Mommsen, *Röm. Forsch.* i. 168 ff.; *Röm. Staatsr.* iii³. 3 ff. P. T.

PORCIA, a firm Republican, was daughter of Cato Uticensis and wife of Bibulus (*cos.* 59 B.C.) and afterwards of M. Brutus, Caesar's murderer. The best tradition (Plut. *Brutus* 53; Cic. *ad Brut.* 1. 9) proves that she died before Brutus in 43 B.C., despite the affirmation (Val. Max. 4. 6. 5) that she killed herself by swallowing live coals, after Brutus' death.   A. M.

PORCIUS (1) LĬCĬNUS (*fl.* 2nd half of the 2nd c. B.C.)—not the Licinius of Cic. *De Or.* 3. 225—wrote a literary-historical poem in trochaic septenarii, eleven of which are preserved in Suetonius' *vita Terentii*. They contain a virulent attack on Terence and his sycophantic relationship with the Scipionic circle. Gellius ascribes to P. an erotic epigram, an imitation of Callimachus, and the famous lines

> Poenico bello secundo Musa pinnato gradu
> intulit se bellicosam in Romuli gentem feram.

R. Büttner, *P. Licinus u. der litterarische Kreis des Q. Lutatius Catulus* (1893).   L. R. P.

PORCIUS (2) LATRO, MARCUS, Augustan rhetor; a Spaniard, contemporary and intimate friend of the elder Seneca. He was the most distinguished representative of the new rhetoric at Rome, more at home in the school than in the court but critical of its Asiatic excesses, and combined a vigorous and natural style with a vast capacity for work (Sen. *Controv.* 1 *pr.* 13–24); among his many admirers was Ovid, who borrowed ideas from him in his verse (*Controv.* 2. 2. 8). He died A.D. 4.   C. J. F.

PORCIUS, *see also* CATO, FESTUS.

PORFYRIUS, *see* OPTATIANUS.

PORPHYRION, POMPONIUS (early 3rd c. A.D.), scholar, whose commentary on Horace is still extant (ed. A. Holder, 1894), though not in its original form. Porphyrion's exposition, intended for school pupils, includes subject-matter, grammar, and style. He incorporated the work of earlier commentators, including Acron (q.v.).

Cf. Teuffel, § 379, 1; Schanz-Hosius, § 602.   J. F. M.

PORPHYRY (Πορφύριος) (A.D. 232/3–*c.* 305), scholar, philosopher, and student of religions. He was born at Tyre (or Batanea in Palestine); originally bore the Syrian name *Malchus*; studied under Longinus at Athens; became devoted personal disciple of Plotinus at Rome, 262–3; edited Plotinus' *Enneads*, after A.D. 300. His extremely numerous and varied writings (77 titles are listed by Bidez) fall into the following classes. (1) Early philosophico-religious works, written before his conversion to Plotinism: Περὶ τῆς ἐκ λογίων φιλοσοφίας (extensive fragments preserved, containing curious information about theurgic practices); Περὶ ἀγαλμάτων (fragments extant); perhaps Φιλόσοφος ἱστορία, a history of philosophy down to Plato, from which the extant Πυθαγόρου βίος is an excerpt. (2) Later works on philosophy and religion, written from the Plotinian standpoint. The following are completely or partially extant: Ἀφορμαὶ πρὸς τὰ νοητά, a disjointed collection of edifying thoughts, borrowed or adapted from Plotinus; Περὶ ἀποχῆς ἐμψύχων, a treatise on vegetarianism in four books, drawing on Theophrastus, etc.; Πρὸς Ἀνεβώ, a letter on theurgy, strikingly sceptical in tone; Πρὸς Μαρκέλλαν, an *epistola moralis* addressed to his wife. An essay *De regressu animae* is known from quotations in Augustine. The important treatise Κατὰ Χριστιανῶν, in fifteen books, was condemned to be burnt in 448, but interesting fragments survive, from which we learn that Porphyry used the modern weapon of historical criticism, e.g. to establish the lateness of the Book of Daniel. Elsewhere he similarly proved the 'Book of Zoroaster' to be a forgery. (3) Περὶ Πλωτίνου βίου καὶ τῆς τάξεως τῶν βιβλίων αὐτοῦ: this has the double character of a biography of Plotinus and a preface to P.'s edition of the *Enneads*. (4) Numerous philosophical commentaries on Plato, Aristotle, Theophrastus, Plotinus, of which only a school-commentary on Aristotle's *Categories* survives complete. Here belongs also the Εἰσαγωγὴ εἰς τὰς Ἀριστ. Κατηγορίας or Περὶ τῶν πέντε φωνῶν, which became a standard medieval textbook of logic.

(5) Philological works include Ὁμηρικὰ ζητήματα, a landmark in the history of Homeric scholarship which Schrader has reconstructed; and the extant Περὶ τοῦ ἐν Ὀδυσσείᾳ τῶν νυμφῶν ἄντρου, a specimen of allegorizing interpretation. Porphyry wrote also on grammar, rhetoric, and the history of scholarship. The Βίος Ὁμήρου falsely included in Plutarch's *Moralia* is sometimes attributed to Porphyry. (6) Extant works on technical subjects are a commentary (incomplete) on Ptolemy's *Harmonica*; an introduction to Ptolemy's *Tetrabiblos*; and a treatise on embryology, Πρὸς Γαῦρον περὶ τοῦ πῶς ἐμψυχοῦται τὰ ἔμβρυα (formerly attributed to Galen, but probably by Porphyry).

Though unoriginal and often uncritical, Porphyry is a remarkable polymath, and has the good habit of quoting his authorities by name; he has thus preserved many fragments of older learning. As a thinker he is unimportant: 'in the whole extant work of Porphyry there is not a thought or an image which one can confidently affirm to be his own' (Bidez).

Life and Works: J. Bidez, *Vie de Porphyre* (1913: includes collection of ancient sources and full bibliography). Texts: Π. τῆς ἐκ λογίων φιλοσοφίας, G. Wolff (1856); frs. of Π. ἀγαλμάτων and *De regressu animae* in Bidez, op. cit.; Πυθαγόρου βίος, Π. ἀποχῆς, Π. τοῦ ἐν Ὀδ. τῶν νυμφῶν ἄντρου, Πρὸς Μαρκ., and frs. of Φιλόσ. ἱστορία, Nauck, *Porphyrii opuscula*[2] (1886); Ἀφορμαί, B. Mommert (1907); Πρὸς Ἀνεβὼ in G. Parthey's ed. of Iamblichus, *Myst.* (1857); frs. of Κ. Χριστιανῶν, A. Harnack, *Abh. Berl. Ak.* 1916 and *Sitzb. Berl. Ak.* 1921; Π. Πλωτίνου βίου in editions of Plot.; works on Arist. in *Comm. in Arist. graeca* iv. 1; Ὁμηρικὰ ζητ., H. Schrader (1880–90); Εἰς τὰ Ἁρμονικὰ Πτολ., I. Düring (Göteborg, 1932); Εἰς τὴν ἀποτελεσματικὴν (Τετράβιβλον) Πτολ., H. Wolf (1559); Πρὸς Γαῦρον, K. Kalbfleisch, *Abh. Berl. Ak.* (1895, Anhang). An edition of the fragments, based on material assembled by the late Prof. Bidez, is in preparation.

E. R. D.

PORSEN(N)A, probably an Etruscan title interpreted by the Romans as the name of a chieftain. The story went that, summoned by the exiled Tarquinius Superbus, Porsenna of Clusium vainly laid siege to Rome. Another version, however, deriving from the Etruscan legend of Mastarna (q.v.), asserts that he ruled over Rome. Porsenna and Mastarna are therefore to be considered as the Roman and the Etruscan name of the same king who attained power at Rome towards the end of the sixth century. Later speculation fitted him into the list of the traditional kings of Rome only by equating Mastarna with Servius Tullius or by connecting the story of Porsenna with the fall of the Tarquins.

G. De Sanctis, *Klio* 1902; F. Schachermeyr, *PW*, s.v.; L. Pareti, *Studi etruschi* (1931), 154 ff.

P. T.

PORTICO. (1) In classical meaning (*porticus*: *stoa*), a colonnade, applied particularly to a roofed building in every Greek or Hellenistic town, consisting of a long rectangular unit with one row or two rows of columns in front, backed either by a wall or by a row of chambers used for shops or places of business. Good evidences of examples still existing are at Athens (Stoa of Attalus, etc.), Corinth, Delos, and other places. At Delos the 'Portico of Antigonus' (*c.* 254 B.C.) had a length of nearly 400 ft., including a projecting pavilion at each end; and the 'Portico of Philip' had two parallel porticoes divided by a wall. Often, as at Magnesia-on-Maeander, the Portico or Stoa formed one side of the large open space of the Market.

(2) As generally understood in modern times, a columned or pillared entrance feature—usually surmounted by a pediment—projecting from any important side or end of a classical building. In this sense the ends of Greek or Roman temples or the fronts of propylaea have porticoes, though the simplest form of temple entrance—'distyle-in-antis' (*see* TEMPLE)—is really a porch and can hardly be called a portico, as it forms an entrance enclosed between walls. In a different way, the projecting feature on the north side of the Erechtheum (q.v.) is appropriately termed a porch.

A. Marquand, *Greek Architecture* (1909), 320–3.

T. F.

A portico of Greek type was first erected in Rome in 193 B.C.; many more were constructed after that date, especially in the first century B.C. The most notable porticoes were (1) the porticus Minucia (110 B.C.), where public distributions of corn took place; (2) the porticus Pompeii (55 B.C.), adjacent to Pompey's theatre; (3) the porticus Octaviae (after 27 B.C.), which served as an art gallery.

M. C.

PORTORIA were duties on goods entering or leaving harbours, the upkeep of which was a charge on public funds. Such levies were made in Italian harbours under the Republic, though they were temporarily abolished between 60 B.C. and Caesar's dictatorship, and in provincial harbours such as Syracuse (Cic. *Verr.* 2. 185; cf. *ILS* 38. 1. 32 ff.). In the Principate a customs-duty was levied on goods crossing certain frontiers, and for this purpose several provinces might form a single unit, e.g. the Gallic and the Danubian provinces. The amount of this duty varied: it was 5 per cent. in Sicily, 2 per cent. in Spain, and 2½ per cent. in Gaul and elsewhere. There is some evidence that a higher charge was made at the frontiers of the Empire. The *portoria* were levied solely for revenue purposes and were not protective: the Empire was practically a free-trade unit. Their collection was let out to *publicani* (q.v.) during the Republic and the first two centuries of the Principate (Tac. *Ann.* 13. 50–1). The extent to which individual cities levied octroi dues is uncertain. Elaborate tariffs were imposed by Palmyra and the city of Zarai in Numidia.

G. H. S.

PORTRAITURE (GREEK). Commemorative statues were set up in Greece from early days, e.g. the statue of Pericles by Cresilas (q.v.); but until the fourth century they made no attempt to render a close likeness of their subject. Incipient realism in Greek portrait sculpture is discernible in the well-known statue of Demosthenes at Rome, which is probably a copy of a fourth-century original. But the aim of the Greek portraitists remained as before to bring out the distinctive *ethos* or personality of their subject, rather than to reproduce his features exactly. From the time of Lysippus (q.v.), who made a famous statue of Alexander the Great, portraiture attained a wide vogue. Hellenistic sculptors not only made authentic portraits of contemporary celebrities, but imaginary ones of earlier Greek worthies. Most of our surviving portraits are works by Hellenistic artists or copies of these.

Among Greek painters the only one to achieve a reputation as a portraitist was Apelles (q.v.), whose picture of Alexander ranked with Lysippus' statue. The only extant Greek portrait paintings are craftsmen's work from Greek cemeteries in Egypt.

J. J. Bernoulli, *Griechische Ikonographie* (2 vols., 1901); F. Poulsen, *Greek and Roman Portraits in English Country Houses* (1923).

M. C.

PORTRAITURE (ROMAN). The Roman ritual custom of preserving the features of departed ancestors by means of death-masks (*imagines*, q.v.) was a stimulus to the development of portrait art in Italy; but traces of death-masks are not common among existing portraits, and a Greek idealizing tradition, derived at first through Etruria and later by more direct contact, is generally present in some degree to modify Italic naturalism. The chronology of the earliest Italian portraits, which may go back to the early third century B.C., is still not entirely settled; they are of plastic materials, bronze, or clay. The use of marble began *c.* 100 B.C.; this was generally assisted by colour, of which traces occasionally remain. Late Republican portraits show a dry realistic style; historical identifications in this period are almost entirely fanciful.

In the case of Imperial portraits the coin-series provides a base for identification, while changes in the bust-form as well as in the sculptural style help to fix the date of private portraits. The bust, which in the late Republic included little more than head and neck, incorporated the shoulders by Flavian times, and in the early third century had grown into a half-length figure, after which it grew smaller again. Stylistically, the portraits of Augustus show a strongly idealizing and dignified character, which in the later Julio-Claudians becomes often frigid. Republican naturalism persisted in private portraits and became the official style under the Flavians, with greater technical resource and ability. Trajanic portraits continue this tradition with more dryness, but Hadrian went back to a Greek idealism, more academic than that of Augustus; with him begins the row of bearded emperors. The Antonine emperors show a distinctive pictorial style, the abundant hair and beard drilled, and the marble surfaces polished or left rough, to secure effects of light and shade. Under the military emperors of the third century this picturesque style gave way to simpler treatment; hair and beard close-cut and rendered by pitted surfaces; and this style, after a short-lived reversion under Gallienus to more florid portraiture, leads to the stiffer, frontal portraits of the fourth century.

A. Hekler, *Greek and Roman Portraits* (1912); R. Paribeni, *Il ritratto nell' arte antica* (1934); J. J. Bernoulli, *Römische Ikonographie* (1882–94); A. Zadoks-Jitta, *Ancestral Portraiture in Rome* (Amsterdam, 1934); R. Delbrück, *Spätantike Kaiserporträts* (1933). F. N. P.

PORTUS ITIUS, a harbour of the Morini, used by Caesar (*BGall.* 5. 2 and 5) in the second British expedition (54 B.C.). The words seem to mean 'Channel Harbour', so that Boulogne, the port normally used, is the obvious identification, though there are arguments for Wissant.

T. Rice Holmes, *Ancient Britain*, 552–95; *CR* xxiii. 77–81.
                                                              C. E. S.

PORUS, i.e. the Paurava king, ruled the country between the Jhelum and the Chenab when Alexander arrived. Defeated by Alexander in a desperate battle at the Jhelum crossing, he became his ally; and Alexander, when forced to turn back at the Beas, abandoned the hard-won eastern Punjab and handed it over to Porus, who again became independent. If Porus be Parvataka of the *Mudrārākshasa*, he subsequently aided Chandragupta to conquer north-west India from the Macedonians. He was killed (before 318) by the Macedonian Eudamus, who secured his elephants.

Berve, *Alexanderreich* ii. p. 340.   W. W. T.

POSEIDON (Ποσειδῶν, Doric Ποτειδάν), Greek god of earthquakes and of water, secondarily of the sea, since he appears to be native Greek, not pre-Hellenic, and it is fairly certain that their former habitat was inland, cf. the paucity of Greek names for fishes (examples of non-Greek fish-names in J. Huber, *De lingua antiquissimorum Graeciae incolarum* (1921), 8 ff.). The name is of doubtful etymology, but almost certainly Greek, and the first two syllables are usually supposed cognate with ποταμός, πόσις (drink), etc. His most significant titles are ἐνοσίχθων or ἐννοσίγαιος, 'earthshaker', and γαιήοχος, 'holder or possessor of earth', meaning probably husband of the earth-goddess. The latter is an appropriate name enough for a deity who, whatever his exact origins, certainly is closely connected with water, which fertilizes the earth; it need not be rain-water, though that is perhaps the most commonly spoken of in such a context (cf., e.g., Aesch. fr. 44 and Eurip. fr. 898, Nauck²). In general, the theory (Cook, *Zeus* ii. 582 ff.) that he is 'a specialized form of Zeus', or a sky-god of any kind, has the balance of evidence against it. Being a great god, he has functions not unlike those of his celestial brother, but the Greeks themselves consistently differentiate them. That he causes earthquakes is an idea which possibly reflects some early and crude attempt to explain

that phenomenon, cf. the later quasi-scientific theory (Seneca, *QNat.* 6. 6 ff.) that it was due to the action of water in some way.

2. Mythologically, Poseidon is one of the three sons of Kronos; in Homer he is younger than Zeus (*Iliad* 15. 204); in Hesiod and most later writers (*Theog.* 453 ff.), Zeus is the youngest son. He has but little mythology of his own; he was one of those swallowed by Kronos and afterwards spewed up (ibid. 459), although obscure legends say that Kronos was tricked into swallowing a foal instead (a young horse instead of the young Lord of Horses, see below; Paus. 8. 8. 2, from Arcadia), or that he threw Poseidon into the sea (Hyginus, *Fab.* 139. 1). When the three brothers, after the defeat of their father, drew lots for the universe the sea fell to his share (*Il.* loc. cit. 190). It is to be noticed that at least one probably more ancient god, Nereus (q.v.), is thus displaced from the position which it would seem that he once held. His consort is the unimportant Amphitrite, and some legends of little significance are told of his wooing (see Rose, *Handb. Gk. Myth.* 63 f.). Of his various amours, the most interesting is that with Medusa the Gorgon, who became by him mother of Pegasus (q.v.). With Apollo (q.v.) he built the walls of Troy for Laomedon, was cheated of his pay, and in revenge sent a sea-monster to ravage the land (*Il.* 21. 441 ff., where Poseidon alone builds the walls, Apollo herding Laomedon's cattle; cf. AEACUS, HERACLES). For his quarrel with Odysseus, *see* ODYSSEUS. He is commonly the father of strong but rough and brutal men, or monsters such as the giant Antaeus, his son by Earth (Apollod. 2. 115). There are also several tales of his begetting horses, besides Pegasus; for one *see* ARCADIAN CULTS, DEMETER.

3. In cult he is, of course, prominent as sea-god and worshipped on all occasions connected with the sea and navigation. In addition, as already suggested, he is worshipped as a god of fresh water (Krenouchos, Nymphagetes; see Farnell, p. 5), and sporadically as god of earthquakes (Strabo 1. 3. 16, 57, the Rhodians found a temple to him on the volcanic island of Thera with the title Asphalios, a by-form of which—Asphalion—is rightly interpreted by Macrobius, *Sat.* 1. 17. 22, as *terram stabiliens*). It is quite natural that a god of water should occasionally be a god of vegetation, Phytalmios, Plut. *Quaest. conv.* 675 f., which says the cult is practically universal in Greece. But it is less obvious why he should be Hippios, Lord of Horses. This cannot arise from a metaphor like Engl. 'white horses' for waves, since no such metaphor is known in Greek, and it is noteworthy that Cornutus (*Theolog. Graec.* 22, p. 44, 1 Lang) suggests only that it is because we use ships 'like horses', i.e. as means of transport. This is of course absurd, for cult-titles like this do not grow out of poetical figures. The real reason is, however, uncertain; possibly the title is due merely to the fact that the peoples worshipping him were themselves horse-breeders. That horses were bred and used in Thessaly is notorious, and the cult of Poseidon Hippios is especially Thessalian (Farnell, p. 23). In general, Poseidon is closely connected with the Minyans in mythical times, the Ionians in historical, though his cult spreads far wider than these parts of the Greek race.

4. Though popular and held in much reverence (partly because of his worship, as an ancestral god or otherwise, by many noble families; cf. the comparatively respectful handling of him by Aristophanes, whose conservatism is well known), he did not develop with the evolution of higher theological and ethical ideas, thus contrasting with Zeus and even with Hades. One reason for this may be the fact that these ideas were accompanied by a tendency towards monotheism, and hence Zeus hardly left room for another great god, even Hades being on occasion merely identified with him.

L. R. Farnell, *Cults of the Greek States* (1896–1909) iv. 1 ff., and the relevant arts. in the larger dictionaries.   H. J. R.

POSIDIPPUS (Ποσείδιππος) (1), New Comedy poet, born in Macedonia after 316 B.C.; he won four victories from 289/288 onwards. Fr. 12, a version of the famous story of Phryne's acquittal; fr. 28, a Thessalian maintains his right to speak his native dialect and not adopt Attic.

Posidippus' importance is clear: his Ἀποκλῃομένη was re-acted c. 180 B.C., his work was imitated on the Roman stage (Gell. 2. 23. 1), and his statue is extant.

FCG iv. 513 ff.; *CAF* iii. 335 ff.   W. G. W.

POSIDIPPUS (2)(*fl.* 270 B.C.), from Pella in Macedonia, was an epigrammatist, and a close friend of Hedylus and Asclepiades. He has about twenty fine poems in the Anthology, mostly about love and feasting: many of them can be paired with poems by Asclepiades (*Anth. Pal.* 7. 267, 284). Probably the works of the three friends were published together; still, Asclepiades was the leader, P. the follower.

R. Reitzenstein, *Epigramm und Skolion* (1893), 87; P. Schott, *Pos. epigrammata* (1905).   G. H.

POSIDONIUS (Ποσειδώνιος) (1) of Olbiopolis, Sophist and historian, author of a work on the Dniester region, Ἀττικαὶ ἱστορίαι and Λιβυκά, has been identified, though this is uncertain, with the Posidonius who, according to Plutarch (*Aem.* 19), was contemporary with Perseus of Macedon (179–168 B.C.) and described his reign, including the battle of Pydna.

FGrH ii. B, p. 893; BD, p. 596.   A. H. McD.

POSIDONIUS (2) (c. 135–c. 51–50 B.C.), born at Apamea on the Orontes, after studying philosophy at Athens under Panaetius devoted several years of his life to scientific research in the western Mediterranean provinces and in North Africa. He then settled down at Rhodes, which became his adoptive country. Towards the end of 87 Posidonius was sent to Rome on behalf of the Rhodians to appease Marius, and he conceived for him an intense dislike, to which he later gave vent in his historical works. In 78 Cicero attended the school of Posidonius, to whom he often pays tribute in his writings, although the philosopher declined to revise Cicero's account of the conspiracy of Catiline. Another famous visitor of Posidonius was Pompey, who met him twice, after defeating the pirates and on his return from the East. Posidonius was such an enthusiastic supporter of Pompey that he devoted a separate treatise to the narrative of Pompey's eastern campaigns; it was from this that Strabo drew his strongly rationalistic explanation of the work of Moses as a Jewish lawgiver. The wars of Pompey seem to have been dealt with by Posidonius as an appendix to his *Histories*, the fifty-two books of which started from the point where Polybius left off, and included the history of the Eastern and Western peoples with whom Rome had come into contact, from about 146 B.C. to the dictatorship of Sulla. The meagreness of the fragments, which we owe chiefly to the learned curiosity of Athenaeus, makes a reconstruction impossible. But the fact that his work exercised a widespread and lasting influence is sufficient to give us an idea of Posidonius' literary skill as well as of his accuracy and matter-of-factness. Sallust, Caesar, Tacitus, and Plutarch were respectively dependent on Posidonius for the conception of history, for the ethnology of the Gauls and of the Germans (whom Posidonius probably did not distinguish from the Celts), and for the history of Marius and Marcellus; while the so-called universal historians (e.g. Timagenes, Trogus, Diodorus) did not hesitate to borrow even his doctrine of the unity of history, symbolized by the 'cosmopolis', or city of God, in which, ruled ever as it is by His providence, all human beings have a share (*see* HISTORIOGRAPHY, GREEK, para. 7). In his *Histories*, which were biased in favour of the *nobilitas*, and consequently strongly opposed to the Gracchi and the equestrian party,

Posidonius aimed at showing that the Roman Empire, embracing as it did all the peoples of the known world, embodied the commonwealth of mankind and reflected the commonwealth of God, to which deserving statesmen and philosophers were to be admitted after the fulfilment of their earthly task. This theory Cicero expounds in his *Somnium Scipionis*, which is indisputably based upon the ideas of Posidonius or cognate thinkers. The *Histories* of Posidonius must therefore be considered as the complement and the practical application of his philosophical system. He thus vindicated Roman imperialism, which less civilized peoples were forced to accept, or rather to welcome, for the sake of their own improvement, while at the same time he gave a practical illustration of the doctrine of continual communion and mutual sympathy between the world of God and the world of man. According to Posidonius the end and destiny of the human race is exactly reflected in the vicissitudes of history. Political virtue, therefore, consists in turning humanity back to its state of prehistoric innocence, in which philosophers were the law-givers and instructors of their fellow-men and acted as intermediaries between the world of matter, in which men are compelled to live, and the world of God, from which alone law-abiding morality can spring. Thus politics and ethics are one, and any form of moral or political activity becomes a religious duty, by fulfilling which man frees himself and acquires knowledge of the gifts of the spirit, which enable him to enjoy a superior form of existence after death. Since the God of Posidonius is the creator neither of matter nor of soul, the latter cannot be considered immortal in itself. But since it is composed of the same substance as the heavenly bodies, it escapes from the human prison and returns to the sublime abode whence it originally came. Posidonius, moreover, introduced heroes and daemons as intermediary beings between man and God, in whose eternity they have a share. Their power and influence over earthly creatures is manifested in visions, divination, and oracles. The harmony which Posidonius observed in the world of man he discovered no less in nature. To prove that the same laws and processes were at work in both worlds, he devoted himself to scientific research. His study of primitive cultures led him to establish the principle that the present condition of semi-civilized peoples reflects the original stage of culture among those now civilized. His travels and observations enabled him to prove the connexion between tides and the phases of the moon, and to give an accurate description of the life and currents of the ocean. Nor was he merely a theorist; some important achievements witness his practical skill. For instance, he calculated the circumference of the earth, constructed a sphere, and drew a map. He showed also a lively interest in poetry, rhetoric, lexicography, geometry, etc. *See also* METEOROLOGY.

The contemporaries of Posidonius were more impressed by his personality and the width of his interests than by his system. His influence has often been over-emphasized, but it ought by no means to be under-estimated. Although it is uselessly dangerous to attempt to rebuild his system by a mere mechanical spoliation of Lucretius, Cicero, Manilius, Seneca, and Pliny the Elder, it cannot be seriously doubted that they as well as Virgil and the historians mentioned above were largely dependent upon Posidonius. In the history of ancient thought he can be compared to no one but Aristotle. As Aristotle forms the epilogue of the culture of classical Greece, so Posidonius collected the heritage of the Graeco-Roman civilization, or shaped it afresh, bequeathing to the Renaissance the legacy of the Hellenistic age.

TEXTS: Apart from I. Bake's antiquated edition, no collection of the fragments of Posidonius is available, except for the passages from his historical works, which have recently been edited, with an exhaustive commentary, by F. Jacoby, *FGrH* ii, no. 87. A new collection of 'the philosophical as well as the scientific material' is being prepared by L. Edelstein (cf. *AJPhil.* 1936, 322, n. 121).

MODERN LITERATURE: K. Reinhardt, *Poseidonios* (1921); *Kosmos u. Sympathie* (1926); *P. über Ursprung u. Entartung* (1928); L. Heinemann, *P. metaphysische Schriften* (2 vols., 1921, 1928); G. Rudberg, *Forsch. z. P.* (1918). A detailed bibliography is given in K. Praechter's appendix to Ueberweg's *Grundriss* i¹². 150 ff. **P. T.**

POSSESSIO. Roman terminology distinguished different kinds of *possessio*. *Possessio naturalis* signified physical control over the possessed object without regard to its rightfulness. *Possessio civilis* was such as was based on *iusta causa*, and was important in the province of the *ius civile*. *Possessio ad interdicta* was the true and proper *possessio*, protected by a remedy of praetorian law, *interdicta* (see LAW AND PROCEDURE, ROMAN, II. 11). This particular protection against disturbance by a third party represents one of the most characteristic marks of Roman *possessio*: it served exclusively to defend the existing condition of things, independently of ownership or other rights; but for the enjoyment of this kind of protection *possessio* must be *iusta*, i.e. not acquired violently or clandestinely or *precario* (if the holder was a tenant-at-will). In interdictal proceedings the possessor had only to prove a matter of fact, his possession, and no right. Acquisition of possession involved an objective element and a subjective one: effective control (*corpus*) and the consciousness and willingness to hold it (*animus possidendi*). For some methods of acquiring ownership possession was one of the principal elements, as in *traditio* (transfer of ownership of *res nec mancipi* by informal delivery of possession), *occupatio* (when possession was taken of an ownerless object), and *usucapio* (uninterrupted possession for a certain time, see DOMINIUM). An important distinction lay between *possessio bona fide* and *mala fide*, depending upon the circumstance whether the possessor believed or not that he did not violate another man's right by his possession. Only *possessio bona fide* might be the basis for *usucapio*, and only a *bona fide* possessor became entitled to the fruits of the object by *separatio*.

G. Cornil, *Traité de la possession* (1905); S. Riccobono, *Sav. Zeitschr.* 1910; *Bullettino dell' Istituto di Diritto Romano*, 1911; P. Bonfante, *Corso di Diritto romano* ii. 2 (1928), iii (1933). **A. B.**

POSSESSION. That a human being might become possessed by a supernatural power was a fairly common ancient belief. The effect might be a prophetic frenzy, as in the case of the Pythia (cf. APOLLO); such a person was ἔνθεος. It might also be some terrifying disease, as epilepsy (Hippoc. *De morbo sacro*, especially p. 592 f. Kühn). Or it might be insanity; the victim was then commonly said δαιμονᾶν, as Aesch. *Sept.* 1001, or κακοδαιμονᾶν, as Dinarchus, 1. 91. Latin called him *larvatus* or *cerritus*, possessed respectively by the Larvae or Ceres, e.g. Plautus, *Men.* 890. Later, under Oriental influence (cf., e.g., the numerous references to demoniacs in the N.T.), the belief grew stronger and commoner, and mentions of magical cures and the activity of exorcists, pagan and Christian, are extremely frequent.

Julius Tambornino, 'De antiquorum daemonismo' (1909; *RGVV* vii. 3). **H. J. R.**

POSTAL SERVICE (GREEK). In the Persian Empire couriers and horses were maintained at stations spaced at intervals of a day's journey (σταθμοί) along the royal roads, and government dispatches were carried by relays; the system was called ἀγγαρήιον. Antigonus I reorganized this service of couriers (βυβλιαφόροι) in 302 B.C., and the same system is found in Ptolemaic Egypt. We possess the day-book of a station, specifying the couriers who went out and came in and the documents that they carried. The post was probably a liturgy incumbent upon the mounted militiamen, and those who preferred not to serve personally paid the tax ἀνιππίας instead. Another papyrus records the wages of a postal staff; they comprise forty-four βιβλιοφόροι (here probably runners), one ὡρογράφος, one ἔφοδος, and one καμηλίτης. This station probably belonged to a local postal service, distinct from the mounted post.

F. Preisigke, *Klio* vii (1907), 241–77. **A. H. M. J.**

POSTAL SERVICE (ROMAN). Under the Republic no public post existed; both private individuals and government officials depended on hired *tabellarii* (q.v.). Augustus organized a regular *cursus publicus*, but this was employed simply for official dispatches, and only occasionally might individuals be granted a *diploma* entitling them to make use of it (Plin. *Ep.* 10. 120–1). At first (Suet. *Aug.* 49) relays of messengers were stationed along the roads, but later Augustus established posting-houses, where messengers travelling by carriage might change horses. The same messenger generally carried his dispatch to its destination (Tac. *Hist.* 2. 73). The cost of the post was usually borne by the local authorities, though several emperors temporarily transferred the burden to the fiscus (*ILS* 214). Even imperial letter-carriers often travelled on foot. The average speed attained by the Roman post has been estimated at fifty miles a day, though much higher speeds were possible if the news was urgent (A. M. Ramsay, in *JRS* xv. 60 ff.). The revolt of the Rhine army against Galba was known in Rome in about nine days, which implies a rate of about 160 miles a day. Dispatches were sent by sea if navigation was possible, but in winter normally travelled by land. The news of the accession of Pertinax, which occurred in the winter, took sixty-three days to reach Alexandria from Rome, a distance by road of rather over 3,000 miles. On the other hand, Galba's accession, which occurred in summer, was known in Alexandria within twenty-seven days, as it was possible to send the news by sea.

O. Hirschfeld, *Verwaltungsbeamten* (1905), 190 ff.; O. Seeck, *PW*, s.v. 'cursus publicus'. **G. H. S.**

POSTLIMINIUM. The legal position of a Roman citizen captured by the enemy was similar to that of a slave, but many of his rights remained in suspense until he returned to Roman territory. By virtue of the right of *postliminium*, which was said to be *moribus constitutum*, the captive after his return recovered with his freedom all his former rights just as if he had never been captured by the enemy. Such rights, however, depended on actual exercise and could not therefore be held in suspension indefinitely. According to Justinian's law the marriage continued in spite of the husband's captivity. If the *captivus* died in captivity, he died a slave; but a *Lex Cornelia* (of the dictator Sulla) enacted that his will, made before he was captured, remained valid, there being a fiction that he had died on Roman territory and as a free man and had never been captured. This so-called *fictio legis Corneliae* was applied to successions on intestacy and further extended by the jurists and Justinian.

The *ius postliminii* was applied also to things (slaves, ships, horses used in military service, and so on) and real estate which fell into the enemy's hand during war and were subsequently recovered by their owner.

L. Mitteis, *Röm. Privatrecht* (1908), 192 ff.; S. Solazzi, *Struttura del postliminio* (1918); W. W. Buckland, *A Text-book of Roman Law*² (1932), ch. 2; U. Ratti, 'Studi sulla captivitas', *Riv. ital. per le sc. giur.* 1926, 1927, *Bull. Ist. Dir. rom.* xxxv (1927), *Ann. Univ. Macerata* 1927 (1926); H. Krüger, 'Captivus redemptus', *Sav. Zeitschr.* li (1931), 203 ff.; E. Levy, 'Captivus redemptus', *CPhil.* xxxviii (1943), 159 ff. **A. B.**

POSTUMIUS (1) TUBERTUS, AULUS, appointed dictator in 431 B.C. by his son-in-law Cincinnatus, won a notable and undoubtedly historical victory over the Aequi on the Algidus (traditionally on 19 June), but details of the campaign, which closely resembles that of Cincinnatus in 458, must be rejected. O. Hirschfeld (*Kleine Schr.* 1913, 246 f.) has wrongly assumed that the legend of Cincinnatus grew out of the story of Postumius. **P. T.**

POSTUMIUS (2) **MEGELLUS**, LUCIUS (*cos.* I, 305 B.C.; II, 294; III, 291). The victories over the Samnites, which tradition assigns to his two first consulships, were probably reverses. His alleged triumph 'de Samnitibus Etrusceisque' in 294 is an anticipation of that of 291; he was not in Etruria. In 291 he helped to end the Third Samnite War by storming Venusia. He is said to have 'triumphed' and to have been fined for conducting the war against the wishes of the Senate. H. H. S.

POSTUMIUS (3) **ALBINUS**, AULUS, Roman senator and historian, praetor in 155 B.C., consul in 151, commissioner for the settlement of Achaea in 146, and an enthusiastic philhellene, wrote a history of Rome from its origins, in Greek. Pragmatic in treatment, it belongs to the Senatorial tradition. Cato mocked his apology for his Greek (Gellius, 11. 8. 2), but Polybius, if grudgingly, recognized his culture and influence (Polyb. 39. 1) and, though his excessive philhellenism and wordiness offended the older Romans, Cicero praises him as 'disertus' (*Brut.* 81). References to a poem and to his *de aduentu Aeneae* may point to one work; Macrobius' reference (3. 20. 5) may, but not necessarily, indicate a Latin version of his history.

H. Peter, *HRRel.* i, pp. cxxiv, 53; M. Gelzer, *Hermes* 1934, p. 48. A. H. McD.

POSTUMIUS (4) **ALBINUS**, AULUS, in the winter 110–109 B.C. was left by his brother Sp. Albinus, then consul, in charge of the Roman forces in Africa. He tried to finish the Jugurthine War at one stroke, by seizing Jugurtha in his treasure-city of Suthul, but was thwarted by Jugurtha's excellent intelligence service. Albinus was trapped with his army, and could only save it by 'passing under the yoke' and agreeing to leave Numidia in ten days. He is probably to be identified with the consul of 99, who was killed in a mutiny when serving as Sulla's legate at Pompeii in 89. He may be the adoptive father of Decimus Brutus, the tyrannicide. M. H.

POSTUMIUS (5) **ALBINUS**, SPURIUS, was sent as consul in 110 B.C. to renew the war with Jugurtha after Bestia's settlement of the Numidian question had been destroyed by Memmius' agitation. He made vigorous preparations, but no action was taken till his brother A. Albinus (while he himself was absent in Rome) attempted to entrap Jugurtha at Suthul. When this had failed (*see* POSTUMIUS 4) Sp. Albinus was condemned under the *Quaestio* of Mamilius. M. H.

POSTUMUS, MARCUS CASSIANIUS LATINIUS, left in military command on the Rhine by Gallienus, when he set out to crush Ingenuus in Moesia, quarrelled over the disposal of booty with Silvanus, Praetorian Prefect and guardian of the young prince, Saloninus, in Cologne (early A.D. 259). He took the city, put both guardian and prince to death, and established himself as independent emperor in Gaul. Attacked by Gallienus in 263, he was defeated, but allowed to escape by the half-hearted pursuit of Aureolus. Gallienus was wounded and withdrew, and Postumus was left to develop an Empire of the West, to which both Spain and Britain adhered. Postumus certainly abetted the revolt of Aureolus in 268, but had himself to meet the revolt of Laelianus in Moguntiacum (*Mainz*). He took the city, but was murdered by his own troops when he forbade the sack.

Postumus successfully defended the Rhine frontier against German invasion. He had his own senate and struck coins at several mints, among them Cologne. Cologne, Mainz, and Treves were his chief cities. Victorinus, who succeeded after Marius, was his general, but never his colleague. His usurpation weakened central authority, but saved the West.

CAH xii. 185 ff.; Parker, *Roman World*, 168, 175 ff., 188. H. M.

POTAMON of Alexandria, probably of the time of Augustus (31 B.C.–A.D. 14), founder of the Eclectic school. He attempted without much originality or consistency to combine Platonic and Peripatetic tenets with the Stoic creed (Diog. Laert. *prooem.* 21). The school had little influence.

See Zeller, *Phil. d. Griechen* iii. 1⁴. 639–41. W. D. R.

POTIDAEA, a Corinthian colony, founded *c.* 600 B.C. for trade with Macedonia and along the line of the later Via Egnatia. It struck coins from *c.* 550 B.C. A strongly fortified port, it withstood a siege by Artabazus (480–479). It joined the Delian Confederacy; but its connexion with Corinth, which supplied its annual chief magistrate, rendered it suspect to Athens. After an increase of its tribute to fifteen talents (434 B.C.) it revolted (432), but although it received help from Peloponnesus it was reduced in 430. Athenian cleruchs occupied the site until 404, when it passed to the Chalcidians. It was recovered by Athens in 363 and received another cleruchy in 361; but in 356 it fell into the hands of Philip II of Macedon. It was perhaps destroyed in the Olynthian War (348); but it was refounded by Cassander under the name of Cassandreia (*c.* 316). N. G. L. H.

POTĪTII and **PĪNARII**, *see* HERCULES.

POTITUS, *see* VALERIUS (2).

POTTERY. The earliest pottery of Greece, from neolithic deposits in Crete, is hand-made, of burnished dark clay, a ware characteristic of a wide Mediterranean area; the surface sometimes blacked, elsewhere reddened. In Asia Minor this ware persists through the Bronze Age and recurs later. Neolithic pottery from the Cyclades is so far unknown; on the mainland red polished and painted wares are followed by 'Dimini ware' with brown linear and spiral patterns on white, supposedly of Danubian origin. The recently discovered neolithic ware of Cyprus shows a similar sequence.

2. In the early Bronze Age the dark clay ware is followed by painted fabrics, dull dark on light ground. In Crete there is a change (*c.* 2300 B.C.) to light-on-dark painted ware, which continues throughout the Middle Minoan period. The slow potter's wheel is introduced, probably from Asia (*c.* 2100 B.C.), soon followed by the quick wheel. In the Late Minoan Age the dark-on-light technique returns, with a naturalistic style embracing floral and marine subjects. The Cyclades and Mainland favour the dark-on-light style throughout. On the Mainland an intrusive 'Minyan ware' appears *c.* 2000 B.C. of grey clay, wheel-made, the shapes recalling metal-work. After 1400 B.C. 'Mycenaean pottery' predominates, with lustrous brown ornament on buff, based mainly on Late Minoan; the pottery, found over a wide area, is remarkably uniform. Later the designs grow stylized, and in the sub-Mycenaean age are reduced to geometric elements.

3. Geometric pottery (1000–700 B.C.) develops from the earlier fabric with no change of technique, but with the addition of new patterns, such as the maeander, and an enrichment of the decoration, which now covers the whole vase in horizontal bands. In contrast to Mycenaean ware, Geometric falls into local schools, the most important being the Attic, where 'Dipylon' vases often have funeral scenes and chariot processions, conventionally rendered.

4. In the late eighth century the Geometric style passes into the Orientalizing, as the result of closer acquaintance with Eastern art. The decorative repertory is enriched by floral patterns, animals, winged monsters, etc., which replace the Geometric patterns in the horizontal bands. Experiments in technique—outline drawing, incised

lines, polychromy—are found, the human figure is drawn with increasing naturalism, and mythological representations begin. The local styles are again clearly distinguished; the seventh century sees the high-water mark of the Island and East Greek schools; the chief Mainland fabrics are the Athenian (proto-Attic), proto-Corinthian, and Laconian.

5. By 600 Athenian potters had substantially evolved the Attic black-figured style, and the sixth century sees the gradual assimilation of other local styles to this, and ultimately their disappearance as Athenian wares under the Pisistratids obtain a monopoly. In black-figure the design is laid in dark paint, improved to the brilliant black Attic glaze, on the reddish buff clay; inner markings are made by incised lines; white is used for the flesh of women, red for men's beards and hair, etc. The decorative patterns are reduced, and the field of the vase occupied by a mythological or other subject.

6. About 525 Athens introduces a new technique, the red-figured, in which the decoration is left in the ground-colour and the background filled with black; inner details are rendered in thin glazed lines; accessory colours are sparingly used in the fifth century. In this style greater freedom of drawing was possible, and the artists pass from archaic stiffness to the classic style of the mid-fifth and to the free style of the late fifth century. The vases of the fourth century are characterized technically by greater use of accessory colours and gilding. A subsidiary Attic fabric of the fifth century is the 'white-ground' ware, in which the background is white, with designs in black glaze at first, later in matt polychrome; these vases were mainly used for sepulchral purposes.

7. In the late fourth century Greek pottery undergoes a change. The large painted vases disappear with the red-figure style, and the potter's art is restricted to the production of cheap clay substitutes for the costly vessels of metal which Hellenistic taste preferred. Painted decoration is limited to floral scrolls and patterns: both light-on-dark and dark-on-light styles are found; but painted wares are secondary to the new metallic styles, in which relief ornament is predominant. Sometimes moulded reliefs are added to wheel-made vases; in other fabrics the vase is thrown in a mould, as in the hemispherical 'Megarian bowls', the most widespread Hellenistic fabric. In the third century the black ground-colour inherited from Athens is modified in East Greece into red or bronze, and from this develops the *terra sigillata* (q.v.), the standardized fine pottery of Roman times.

8. Italian pottery of the Neolithic and Bronze Ages is mainly of the dark-clay Mediterranean type; painted wares, dark on light, occur sporadically in the south and have been compared with the wares of the Balkan peninsula. In the early Iron Age the hand-made dark-clay ware ('impasto') continues in several local styles; among them the Latin, characterized by its funerary 'hut-urns', and the Villanovan of Tuscany and Bologna, with biconical urns and incised geometric decoration. The 'bucchero' of Etruria (700–500) is also dark-clay ware, but wheel made, with polished black surface; early decoration is incised, later decoration is in relief. Painted wares imitating the contemporary styles of Greece appear on the west coast about 700, and by 525 the native pottery is largely displaced by Greek (mainly Attic) imported vases and local copies. There are independent schools of pottery in Apulia which, while borrowing the painted technique from Greece, remain barbaric in style. The Italian red-figured style begins in south Italy about 440, perhaps introduced by immigrant Athenian potters. There are four main schools—the south Italian, the school of Paestum, the Campanian, and the Etruscan. A large production of vases, often of great size and elaborate decoration, continued into the early third century.

9. In the Hellenistic period Apulia and Campania are the chief areas of production. Light-on-dark painted ware and vases with applied reliefs are the main fabrics. Alexandria was the principal source of inspiration, and Italy long remained untouched by the East Greek experiments in red glazes and moulded wares; after 30 B.C., however, it took the lead in these with the appearance of Arretine ware (see TERRA SIGILLATA).

10. Apart from *terra sigillata*, the pottery of the Roman East is mainly plain earthenware, though moulded vases of the second to third century are not unknown. The pottery of the western provinces shows more character, and there are a number of local decorated fabrics, e.g. the Caistor ware of Britain, with elaborate relief ornament.

Prehellenic: E. J. Forsdyke, *Catalogue of Greek and Etruscan Vases in the British Museum* i, pt. 1, *Prehistoric Aegean Pottery* (1925). Hellenic painted wares: see VASE-PAINTING. Hellenic relief wares: F. Courby, *Les Vases grecs à reliefs* (1922). Early Italian pottery: T. E. Peet, *The Stone and Bronze Ages in Italy* (1909); D. Randall-MacIver, *Villanovans and Early Etruscans* (1924), and *The Iron Age in Italy* (1927); A. D. Trendall, *Frühitaliotische Vasen* (1938). Hellenistic pottery: H. A. Thompson, *Hesperia* iii (1934), 311–430; R. Pagenstecher, *Die Calenische Reliefkeramik* (1909). Roman Pottery: see TERRA SIGILLATA; also H. Sumner, *Excavations in New Forest Roman pottery sites* (1927). General: *Corpus Vasorum Antiquorum*, so far as published (examples of almost every fabric, with bibliographies); P. Jacobsthal and J. D. Beazley (edd.), *Bilder griechischer Vasen* (1930); G. M. A. Richter and M. J. Milne, *Shapes and Names of Athenian Vases* (U.S.A. 1935).   F. N. P.

PRAECONES, see APPARITORES.

PRAEFECTI CAPUAM CUMAS, see PRAEFECTURA, CAPUA, VIGINTISEXVIRI.

PRAEFECTURA means an assize-town in Roman territory. When Capua became a *municipium* (q.v.) prefects with authority delegated by the *praetor urbanus* were occasionally sent there to assist in judicial rearrangements consequent upon the grant of *civitas sine suffragio*. The practice spread later to all other *municipia* and also to *oppida* and *conciliabula* in the areas of full citizens (see CITIZENSHIP, OPPIDUM), and became annual. The *praefecti* did not replace but assisted the local authorities of *municipia*; in *oppida civium Romanorum* they were sometimes the only senior judicial authority. In Campania after the abolition of local autonomy following the revolt of 215–211 B.C. a new set of annual *praefecti*, minor magistrates elected at Rome, were instituted to take sole charge of local jurisdiction. Elsewhere the old system prevailed down to the Social War, but was not extended to the municipalities then incorporated. Between 89 and 44 B.C. the surviving *praefecti* were abolished and the *praefecturae* assimilated to *municipia*, though the title sometimes remained in use as a designation.

See the bibliography under MUNICIPIUM: Modern Views, Republic.   A. N. S.-W.

PRAEFECTUS. Before the Social War each *ala sociorum* had six *praefecti*, three of whom were Roman officers. In Caesar's armies *praefecti* were the commanders of cavalry contingents. Under the Principate *praefecti* were regular officers of equestrian rank. They commanded the Praetorians, *vigiles*, and imperial fleet; the urban cohorts were under the *praefectus urbi*.

The legions in Egypt were commanded by *praefecti* instead of the normal *legati*, and Septimius Severus followed this precedent when he raised Legiones Parthicae I–III. Gallienus substituted *praefecti* for senatorial *legati* in all the legions (see PRIMIPILUS). Each legionary camp had its commandant, called *praefectus castrorum* and later *praefectus (castrorum) legionis*, who was a promoted centurion.

In the *Auxilia* each *ala* and *cohors* was commanded by a *praefectus*, who was before Claudius a promoted centurion, and subsequently a young man starting his equestrian career.

Praefecti also held extraordinary appointments, e.g. *praef. levis armaturae*; *praef. orae maritimae*. See also ALIMENTA, ANNONA, FABRI, PRAEFECTUS PRAETORIO, PRAEFECTUS URBI, VIGILES.

A. von Domaszewski, *Die Rangordnung des römischen Heeres* (1908); C. W. Keyes, *The Rise of the Equites in the Third Century of the R. Empire* (U.S.A. 1915). H. M. D. P.

PRAEFECTUS PRAETORIO. The commanders of the Praetoriani (q.v.), chosen by the emperor usually from the equestrian order, were normally two in number (sometimes one or three). Though occasionally jurists (*see* PAPINIAN, ULPIAN, PAULUS), they were essentially soldiers, until under Constantine they became civil administrators, four in number. They served as general adjutants to the emperors, sometimes acquiring great influence over them and becoming their chief advisers on matters of high policy (*see* SEJANUS, BURRUS, TIGELLINUS, PLAUTIANUS). In cases of a disputed succession the prefects not infrequently played a decisive part in the choice of the next emperor. From the time of the Severi they perhaps became *ex officio* senators; they exercised a general jurisdiction in those civil and criminal cases which originated in Italy beyond the sphere of the Praefectus Urbi (i.e. 100 miles from Rome) and heard, *vice imperatoris*, appeals from the provinces. They overshadowed the Praefectus Annonae, were the most important members of the Consilium Principis, and gained increasing influence from the time of Diocletian in financial administration.

L. L. Howe, *The Praetorian Prefect from Commodus to Diocletian* (U.S.A. 1942); J.-R. Palanque, *Essai sur la préfecture du prétoire du Bas-Empire* (1933). H. H. S.

PRAEFECTUS URBI in early Rome was the deputy of the king, then of the consuls, in their absence from the city. With the institution of the praetorship such a deputy became unnecessary, although a *Praefectus Urbi Feriarum Latinarum* was needed. Following the precedent of Julius Caesar who had put prefects in charge of the city during his absence in Spain (late 46 B.C.), Augustus on occasion appointed a *Praefectus Urbi*. The office probably had become permanent before the end of his reign; it was held, for an indefinite tenure, by a senator of consular rank, who commanded the *cohortes urbanae* and was responsible for maintaining order in the city. The prefect's power of summary jurisdiction in criminal cases gradually increased; he encroached upon, and in the third century superseded, the *quaestiones*, when his criminal jurisdiction extended to 100 miles around Rome. H. H. S.

PRAEFICA, see DEAD, DISPOSAL OF, para. 7; NENIA.

PRAENESTE occupied a cool, lofty spur of the Apennines 23 miles east-south-east of Rome; nowadays *Palestrina*, with interesting polygonal walls. Traditionally founded in the mythical period (Verg. *Aen.* 7. 678), it enjoyed by 700 B.C. an advanced, etruscanized civilization. It is first mentioned in history in the fifth century B.C. as a powerful Latin city, its strategic site facing the Alban Hills being inevitably attacked by Aequi (q.v.). In the fourth century it frequently fought Rome and, after participating in the Latin War, was deprived of territory and became a *civitas foederata* which still possessed *ius exsilii* 200 years later (Polyb. 6. 14). Apparently Praeneste was a very privileged ally: Praenestines loyally resisted Pyrrhus (reject Florus 2. 18) and Hannibal, and actually preferred their own status to that of Roman citizens. After 90 B.C. Praeneste became a Roman *municipium* which Sulla's party sacked for its devotion to Marius' cause (82). Sulla transferred Praeneste to lower ground and settled veterans there. It remained a *colonia* in Imperial times, famed chiefly as a fashionable villa resort and seat of the ancient and

oracular *sortes Praenestinae* which Roman emperors, foreign potentates, and others consulted in the huge temple of Fortuna Primigenia, probably Italy's largest sanctuary (Polyb. 6. 11). Praeneste has yielded a spectacular marine mosaic, to which Pliny (*HN* 36. 25) possibly refers, the earliest specimen of Latin, whose peculiarities confirm Festus' statement (p. 157, 488 L.) that Praenestine Latin was abnormal, and Verrius Flaccus' calendar; Flaccus probably, and the Greek writer Aelian certainly, were natives of Praeneste. The Anicii were also prominent Praenestines.

Strabo 5. 238; Livy 2. 19; 3. 8; 6. 21, 26 f.; 8. 12 f.; 23. 19 f.; Diod. 16. 45; App. *BCiv.* 1. 65. 94; Cic. *Div.* 2. 41. R. S. Conway, *Italic Dialects* i (1897), 311; R. v. D. Magoffin, *Topographical and Municipal History of Praeneste* (U.S.A. 1908); H. C. Bradshaw, *BSR* ix (1920), 257; D. Randall-MacIver, *Iron Age in Italy* (1927). E. T. S.

PRAEROGATIVA was the *centuria* that had the right of voting first. Originally the right was granted to the eighteen *centuriae* of the knights; but not later than 215 B.C. it was conferred upon the one of the seventy *centuriae* of the first class which had been chosen by lot. The voting of the *centuria praerogativa* was considered to be binding on the course of the polling.

Mommsen, *Röm. Staatsr.* iii². 290 ff. P. T.

PRAETEXTA, see FABULA *and* DRAMA, para 2.

PRAETEXTATUS, see VETTIUS.

PRAETOR (etymologically connected with *prae-ire*, 'to lead', 'to precede') was originally the name borne by the highest Roman magistrate, later called consul (q.v.). His close connexion with military affairs is shown by the use of the adjective *praetorius* in such expressions as *praetorium, cohors praetoria*, and *porta praetoria*, and by the Greek translation of *praetor* as στρατηγός. According to tradition a praetor was first elected in 366 B.C. to supervise the administration of justice in Rome (*praetor urbanus*); the two earlier praetors would by that date have assumed their title of consuls. The view of De Sanctis (*Stor. d. Rom.* i. 404 ff.) that three original praetors divided their functions in 366, two (consuls) being responsible for military affairs, one (*praetor urbanus*) for legal, is discussed s.v. CONSUL. Plebeians were excluded from the praetorship until 337. Rome's closer relations with foreign Powers led to the creation (c. 242 B.C.) of a second praetor, called *praetor qui inter peregrinos ius dicit* (abbreviated to *praetor peregrinus*), who dealt with lawsuits in which either one or both parties were foreigners. The acquisition of overseas provinces greatly enlarged the sphere of the praetors' activities, so that in 227 B.C. their number was increased from two to four, to provide for the government of Sicily and Sardinia, and to six in 197 B.C., to administer Spain. By exercising the supreme provincial authority, the praetors became once again military magistrates, and in fact the difference of rank and power between them and the consuls decreased progressively, although the *praetor urbanus* was still subordinate to the consuls; he was preceded by six lictors only, and performed the consuls' functions of summoning the Senate and supervising the defence of Rome merely during their absence. In the second century the *praetor urbanus* and *peregrinus* dealt chiefly with the administration of justice. Sulla, who increased the praetors' number to eight, prescribed that all of them should remain in Rome as judges, or presidents of *quaestiones* (q.v.), and should proceed to the governorship of provinces in the following year by prorogation of their office. Sulla's reform, however, was abolished in the Augustan age. Although the beneficent influence of the praetorship in the domain of law continued to make itself felt under the emperors (thanks to the edicts in which it was customary for praetors to outline, on entering their office, the main principles of their jurisdiction), the praetorship nevertheless declined rapidly, and its functions were soon reduced to minor jurisdiction, e.g. in matters relating to guardianship, the status of liberty, etc., or financial duties, performed by the *praetores aerarii* from 23 B.C. to A.D. 44. It eventually became a merely honorary appointment, the main feature of which was that the *praetor urbanus* had to superintend the games provided by him on entering his office, to win the favour of the Roman populace.

Mommsen, *Röm. Staatsr.* ii². 1, 193 ff.; for the origins of praetor-ship cf. G. De Sanctis, *Riv. fil.* 1929, 1933.   P. T.

PRAETORIANS. During the last two centuries of the Republic generals normally had a bodyguard or *cohors praetoria*. After Philippi 8,000 veterans were organized in such cohorts and divided between Octavian and Antony. Out of these a permanent corps of nine cohorts was created by Augustus in 27 B.C. To avoid any suggestion of military despotism some were stationed outside Rome, others billeted about the city, and in 2 B.C. two prefects were appointed from the equestrian order.

In a sense Sejanus may be called the real founder of the Praetorians. Appointed sole prefect in A.D. 23, he concentrated the cohorts in a single camp just outside the Walls of Rome. From this event dates the political importance of the Guard and its commanders.

The number of cohorts was raised by Caligula to twelve. In 69 Vitellius cashiered the soldiers who had supported Otho, and constituted sixteen cohorts from the German legions. Vespasian, however, reverted to the Augustan figure; a tenth cohort was added, perhaps by Domitian, and this number, apart from a possible reduction by Diocletian, remained unchanged till the Praetorians were disbanded by Constantine in 312.

Each cohort was probably 500 strong, with some additional *equites* and *speculatores* (imperial bodyguard), till its numbers were doubled by Septimius Severus. Its commander was a tribune, who since Claudius was regularly a promoted *primipilus* centurion. Under him were centurions, the two senior of whom were the *trecenarius*, who commanded the *speculatores*, and the *princeps castrorum*.

During the first two centuries, apart from the Vitellian episode, the praetorians were recruited from Italy and the romanized provinces. A change was made by Septimius Severus, who substituted a new guard recruited mainly from the Illyrian legions.

The Praetorians attended the emperor and members of his family at home and abroad. They served for sixteen years, were paid three times as highly as the legionaries and received frequent and large donatives. On discharge they were granted *diplomata* (see DIPLOMA, DONATIVUM, SIGNA MILITARIA).

M. Durry, *Les Cohortes prétoriennes* (1938); A. Passerini, *Le coorti pretorie* (1939).   H. M. D. P.

PRAETORIUM denoted a general's tent (Livy 7. 12, 10. 32; Caes. *BCiv.* 1. 76) or his staff or council (Livy 26. 13. 6). Hence comes the *porta praetoria* of Roman castrametation (see CAMPS). By an extension of meaning *praetorium* signified the residence of a provincial governor (e.g. *ILS* 2298), a pleasure villa (e.g. Suet. *Tib.* 39), an official road-side rest-house (*CIL* iii. 6123), or an emperor's residence (*CIL* iii. 5050). It is also regularly used for the forces or services of the Praetorian Prefect (*CIL* v. 2837, viii. 9391, etc.). In permanent fortresses or forts it is distinguished from the *principia*, or headquarters building, and clearly refers to the commandant's house, a separate structural entity (Livy 28. 25; Tac. *Ann.* 1. 44; *CIL.* vii. 446, 703, 704; *JRS* xix. 215).

See Mommsen, *Hermes* xxxv, 437.   I. A. R.

PRATINAS of Phlius (see TRAGEDY) is stated by Suidas (s.v.) to have been the first to compose satyric plays; and of his fifty plays thirty-two were satyric. He competed

at Athens about the beginning of the fifth century B.C. A fragment of one of his satyric plays (Ath. 14, p. 617 b) attacks the growing predominance of the flute accompaniment over the words of the dithyramb. His Παλαισταί was brought out by his son Aristias in 467 B.C. (Arg. Aesch. *Persae*).

TGF 726. M. Pohlenz, *Das Satyrspiel und Pratinas von Phleius* (1926); A. W. Pickard-Cambridge, *Dithyramb, Tragedy, and Comedy* (1927), 28 ff., 92 ff.   A. W. P.-C.

PRATUM (or **PRATA**), meaning miscellany, title of a lost work by Suetonius. Cf. SILVA.

PRAXAGORAS of Cos (second half of 4th c. B.C.), the teacher of Herophilus, was numbered by Galen among the greatest physicians; the few data preserved do not give a clear picture of his achievements. Praxagoras' anatomy was a strange mixture of correct and false notions. He recognized the connexion of the brain with the spinal cord; on the other hand, he believed that the arteries, coming from the heart, taper away and finally turn into nerves. Respiration he called, though not the cause, yet the re-creating source of the soul, and considered the arteries as air-channels. The discovery of the arterial pulse was ascribed to him. Diseases he explained by the (eleven) humours, also emphasizing the importance of the pneuma; he was particularly interested in fevers. His therapy is almost unknown; his operation on the ileus is mentioned.

TEXT: Fragments, C. G. Kühn, *Opuscula Academica Medica et Philologica* ii (1828), 128 f.; cf. also *Anth. Plan.* 16. 273.
LITERATURE: Only survey, E. D. Baumann, *Janus* (1937). Surgery, K. Sudhoff, *Quellen u. Studien z. Gesch. d. Naturw. u. d. Med.* (1933). Date, about 300 B.C., W. Jaeger, *Diokles v. Karystos* (1938), following from later date of Diocles. An older and a younger P. (H. Schöne, *Rh. Mus.* 1903, p. 64), not yet clearly distinguished.   L. E.

PRAXIDIKAI, 'the exactors of justice'; goddesses worshipped at Haliartus (Paus. 9. 33. 3). Their temple was roofless (it is common for oaths to be taken in the open air) and they were sworn by, but not lightly. They were daughters of Ogygus, i.e. ancient Boeotian (Dionysius of Chalcis in Photius, s.v.). In sing. an epithet of Persephone (q.v.; *Hymn. Orph.* 29. 5).   H. J. R.

PRAXILLA (*fl.* 451 B.C. (Eusebius–Jerome)), poetess, of Sicyon, wrote dithyrambs (fr. 1), drinking-songs (Schol. Ar. *Vesp.* 1239), and hymns, including one to Adonis, in which a line was proverbial for its silliness (fr. 2, cf. Zenob. 4. 21).

Text: E. Diehl, *Anth. Lyr. Graec.* ii. 129–30.   C. M. B.

PRAXILLEION, see METRE, GREEK, III (15).

PRAXIPHANES of Mitylene, son of Dionysiphanes of Mitylene (*IG* 11. 4. 613; *Schol. Flor. Callim. PSI* 11. 1935, p. 146; Clem. *Strom.* 1. 309 a; *Vita Arati* Lat., p. 149 Maass), or Rhodes (Strabo 14. 655; Epiph. *Adv. Haeres.* 3. 2. 9, *Dox. Graec.* p. 592 Diels). Peripatetic writer. He was a pupil of Theophrastus (Procl. *in Tim.* 5 c, etc.) and is called the 'first grammarian' (Clem. l.c., etc.). As a literary critic he must have been well known; against him Callimachus wrote his book Πρὸς Πραξιφάνην (Callim. fr. 100 g Schn., cf. *Schol. Flor. Callim.* l.c.). He was honoured by the Delians (*IG* l.c.). He wrote a dialogue 'On poets' (Περὶ ποιητῶν) in which he introduced Isocrates talking to Plato on the latter's estate (Diog. Laert. 3. 8). Other writings are 'On poems' (Π. ποιημάτων, Phld. Π. ποιημ. col. 11) and 'On history' (Π. ἱστορίας, Marcellin. *Vita Thucyd.*, § 28 f.). He probably also composed an ethical dialogue (see Crönert).

L. Preller, *De P. Peripatetico*, etc. (1842, with the fragments); R. Hirzel, *Der Dialog* (1895) i. 310; F. Susemihl, *Gesch. griech. Litt. Alex.* i. 144; W. Crönert, *Kolotes u. Menedemos* (1906), 69 f.; K. O. Brink, *CQ* 1946 (with the fragments).   K. O. B.

PRAXITELES, sculptor, probably son of Cephisodotus (q.v. 1), Athenian. Pliny dates 364 B.C., probably by Aphrodite of Cnidos. Selected works, (i) *dated*: 1. Altar of Artemis at Ephesus, after 356. 2. Work on Mausoleum, after 351 (doubtful). 3. Artemis at Brauron, 346. According to Studniczka the bronze original of the Artemis of Gabii (Winter, *KB* 297. 6). 4. Signature from Leuctra, about 330. (ii) *Undated*: 5. Aphrodite of Cnidos. Marble; Lucian describes particularly the face and eyes and the setting which showed the front and back view (Pliny's 'undique conspici' is mistaken). Recognized from coins in many copies (ibid. 295. 3–5); fragment in the British Museum is contemporary. Other Aphrodites, including draped Aphrodite of Cos, are recorded. A draped Aphrodite in the Louvre is ascribed by the copyist to Praxiteles; the Aphrodite of Arles (ibid. 312. 2) is attributed on style. 6. Hermes with infant Dionysus in Heraeum at Olympia (ibid. 294. 1–2; 295. 1). Marble; original, not copy as recently suggested. Later than Cnidian Aphrodite, perhaps 343. 7. Apollo Sauroctonus (lizard-slayer). Bronze, known from several copies (ibid. 294. 3). Early, the head nearer Cephisodotus than no. 5. 8. Group of Apollo, Artemis, and Leto with Muses and Marsyas on the base, at Mantinea. Pausanias dates to third generation after Alcamenes. The base has been discovered (ibid. 296. 1–3); dated by parallels on vases not long after 350. 9. Dionysus, Inebriation, and 'the famous satyr'. Bronze, later in Rome. The Dresden satyr (ibid. 297. 7), stylistically near no. 7, may reproduce the satyr. The leaning satyr (ibid. 295. 2) reflects a later original, perhaps Praxiteles' satyr in the street of Tripods. 10. Eros of Thespiae, later in Rome. 11. Eros of Parium, Leto in Argos, Artemis in Anticyra are reproduced on coins. 12. Phryne, Praxiteles' mistress, at Delphi (and Thespiae), gilded or golden. 13. Soldier and horse, on grave at Athens. 14. Niobid group, see under Scopas. (iii) *Attributed*: 15. Head from Chios in Boston, original (ibid. 297. 3; attributed from likeness to no. 5 above). 16. Hermes Farnese, copy (ibid. 294. 4; attributed from likeness to no. 6 above). 17. Aberdeen head in British Museum, original; later and heavier than Hermes. 18. 'Eubuleus' head (ibid. 297. 2) from Eleusis, original (copies also survive). Perhaps Iacchus. 19. (Doubtful) Apollo Lyceius, described by Lucian (*Anach.* 7). 20. Women from Herculaneum, copies (Winter, *KB* 394. 1; probably Demeter and Persephone; attributed from likeness to no. 8 above). 21. Many copies, including ivory statuette from Athenian Agora.

Praxiteles was thought most successful in marble and to excel in representing emotion; he preferred those statues which Nicias (q.v.) painted. Intimate feeling can be appreciated in the surviving originals, nos. 6, 15, 17, 18. Nos. 5, 6, 7, 9, 16, 19 are skilfully composed for a single view (no. 5 also for back view). Contrast the tridimensionalism of Lysippus. The assumption of an earlier Praxiteles is uncertain; for Praxiteles' sons *see* CEPHISODOTUS (2).

Overbeck, 525, 1165, 1178, 1180–1, 1188–1300; G. E. Rizzo, *Prassitele* (1932); C. Blinkenburg, *Knidia* (1932); R. Carpenter, etc., *AJArch.* 1931, 249.   T. B. L. W.

PRAYER. Prayer was quite as prominent in ancient as in modern religions, and, then as now, could be formal or informal, accompanied by other acts of worship (in this case generally sacrifice) or used by itself. For the latter our earliest instance is *Iliad* 1. 37 ff., where Chryses prays to Apollo with no more ceremony than going away by himself to a retired place on the sea-shore, this probably for the practical reason that he did not want to be overheard by the men he was asking Apollo to injure. His prayer is formal and contains all the characteristic parts. First he addresses the god by complimentary phrases ('thou of the silver bow', 'thou who protectest Chryse and holy Cilla, mighty lord of Tenedos'), ending with his local title Smintheus. He then reminds Apollo of his own acts of piety and finally makes his petition, that the god shall avenge him on the Greeks. But informal prayers are common also in and after Homer; for instance, in *Iliad* 7. 179 f., all the Greeks pray to Zeus that the lot may fall on one of three leading champions to fight Hector; they say simply Ζεῦ πάτερ and then state their request, using the imperatival infinitive, common in prayers (cf., e.g., Aristophanes, *Ran.* 886 ff.; here the prayer is accompanied by an offering of incense). Even liturgies seem to have contained such informal petitions, for example the famous Eleusinian ὗε κύε (Hippolytus, *Haer.* 5. 7. 34, p. 87 Wendland), though this might be said to be artificial, even rhetorical brachylogy; cf. Schwenn, op. cit. infra, p. 7 f. Of elaborate formulae belonging to classical liturgies we have none left, the surviving specimens, when not literary or fragmentary, being late and magical; the most famous is that in the great Paris papyrus, *PGM* iv. 486 ff.; cf. A. Dieterich, *Mithrasliturgie* (ed. 3, with addenda by O. Weinreich, 1923); A. D. Nock in *JEg. Arch.* 15 (1929), 231.

For Italy we have a considerable amount of material; that concerning Rome is handily collected by Appel. Perhaps the most outstanding feature of the official prayers is the elaborate accuracy, like that of a legal document, with which they are phrased. Thus, the formula for the *consecratio* of a hostile city (Macrobius, *Sat.* 3. 9. 10–11; Appel, op. cit. infra, 14) not only invokes the appropriate gods but adds 'or by whatever other name it is lawful to name (you)', and is not content with mentioning the city which is to be destroyed by their help but goes on with 'which I feel that I am mentioning', lest there should be some other place with the same name. This savours on the one hand of the meticulosity of developed magical formulae, on the other of the exact and legalistic spirit of Roman public institutions generally; like precautions are taken in other prayers. The rest of Italy is represented, in this respect, by the famous *Tabulae Iguuinae* (q.v.; R. S. Conway, *Italic Dialects*, 356 ff.; C. D. Buck, *Oscan and Umbrian Grammar*, 260 ff.). They are hardly less exact and particular as to detail than the Roman formulae.

F. Schwenn, *Gebet und Opfer*, (1927); P. J. T. Beckmann, *Das Gebet bei Homer* (1932); G. Appel, *De Romanorum precationibus* (1909).   H. J. R.

PRECATIO TERRAE, PRECATIO OMNIUM HERBARUM, two short iambic litanies to Mother Earth and to All Herbs, probably post-Augustan.

Text w. transl., J. W. and A. M. Duff, *Minor Lat. Poets*, 1935.

PRIAM (Πρίαμος), in mythology, son of Laomedon, (q.v.) and king of Troy at the time of its destruction by Agamemnon. In Homer he is already an old man, father of fifty sons, some by Hecuba (q.v.), the rest by other wives or concubines (*Iliad* 24. 495–7). His non-Greek name (for the popular but absurd etymology *see* HESIONE) and his harem both suggest that some memory at least of a real Oriental prince survives into Epic. He is an amiable character, tender and considerate to Helen, although he disapproves of the war and its cause (*Il.* 3. 162 ff.), respected even by his enemies for his faith and wisdom (ibid. 105 ff., 20. 183), and esteemed by most of the gods, including Zeus (though Hera implacably hates him (4. 20 ff.) and Athena is hardly less hostile), because of his piety. He takes part in the treaty (3. 259 ff.) and has returned to the city before it is broken (305 ff.). He tries to induce Hector to come within the walls after the rout of the Trojans (22. 38 ff.) and after his death goes, encouraged by Iris, to ransom his body (24. 159 ff.), succeeding by help of Hermes (360 ff.) and by the impression which his appearance and words produce upon Achilles.

He did not survive the fall of Troy. The account in

the *Iliu Persis*, that he took refuge at the altar of Zeus Herkeios in his own palace and was there killed by Neoptolemus (q.v.), remained classical; its best-known telling in surviving literature is Virgil's (*Aen.* 2. 506 ff.). Apart from the above incidents he has no story of any account. His name became almost proverbial for a man who had known the extreme of contrasting fortunes (Arist. *Eth. Nic.* 1101ᵃ8, Juvenal, 10. 258 ff.).

He is a common figure in art; for examples see Höfer in Roscher's *Lexikon*, s.v. H. J. R.

PRIAPE(I)A, poems in honour of Priapus (q.v.). Among the Greeks poems had been addressed to him. The chief Latin collection contains eighty-five poems: two attributed to Tibullus, probably wrongly (Hiller, *Hermes* 18. 343); three from the *Catalepton*, possibly by Virgil (Teuffel, *Gesch. röm. Lit.* 230. 2); a series of eighty pieces (principally hendecasyllabic and elegiac) composed under Augustus and collected in the first century A.D. The two first of these eighty introduce the collection; the third is by Ovid (Sen. *Controv.* 1. 2. 22), the rest by unknown authors who show signs of Ovid's influence.

The subjects are mainly the shameful chastisements awaiting thieves, the phallus of the god, the offerings presented to him. Irreproachable in versification, lively and sometimes witty in style, they are, with rare exceptions, marked by extreme, even repulsive, obscenity.

Other *priapea*: Catullus, fr. 2; Horace, *Sat.* 1. 8; Tibullus 1. 4; Martial 6. 16, 49, 72, 73; Buecheler, *Carm. Epigr.* 193, 1504.

BIBLIOGRAPHY

Editions: E. Baehrens, *Poet. Lat. min.* i. 54 ff.; F. Buecheler, ed. minor of Petronius⁴, 1904 (86 poems, no. 80 being divided into two). See F. Buecheler, 'Vindiciae libri Priapeorum', *Rh. Mus.* xviii (1863); C. Cali, *Studi letterari* (1898); R. S. Radford, 'Priapea and Virgilian Appendix' (*Trans. Am. Phil. Ass.* 52 (1921); contentions questionable); R. F. Thomason, *The Priapea and Ovid* (U.S.A. 1931); M. Coulon, *La Poésie priapique dans l'antiquité et au moyen âge* (1932). C. F., transl. J. W. D.

PRIAPUS (Πρίαπος, Πρίηπος), a god of fertility, originally worshipped at Lampsacus on the Hellespont and in that neighbourhood. His symbol was the phallus, q.v., and indeed he himself may almost be said to have been a phallus provided with a grotesque body. It is clear that his original cult was important, and his local mythology connected him with great deities, for the Greek version of the story is that he was the son of Dionysus, his mother being either a local nymph or Aphrodite (i.e. the Oriental Great Mother) herself (Strabo 13. 1. 12; Paus. 9. 31. 2, who also testifies that he was the god most worshipped at Lampsacus). His local sacrifice was the ass; since this creature was thought of as the embodiment of lust quite as much as stupidity in antiquity, we may suppose that the purpose of the offering was to maintain the god's power of generation (aetiological account of the origin of the sacrifice, Ovid, *Fasti* 1. 391 ff.; an ass once brayed and woke a nymph, Lotis, who in *Met.* 9. 348-9, turns into a lotus-flower to escape him. It thus saved her from his attentions. He therefore hates asses). In any case, the victim is non-Greek, see Frazer on Ovid, *Fasti*, loc. cit.

His cult spread to Greece after Alexander, when interchange of ideas, religious and other, between East and West was common. It was popular also in the great Hellenistic cities, such as Alexandria, and made its way in due course to Italy. Greece had by that time outgrown most of the more crudely naturalistic worships, and Priapus seems to have been found broadly funny rather than impressive. He was adopted as a god of gardens, where his statue (a misshapen little man with enormous genitals) was a sort of combined scarecrow and guardian deity. For poems in his honour *see* PRIAPEA.

Hans Herter, *De Priapo* (1932) H. J. R.

PRIENE, an Ionian city on the south-east flank of Mt. Mycale, in the Maeander valley and opposite Miletus. It was one of the twelve Ionian cities and claimed a Boeotian origin. When Croesus fell to the Persians Priene, which had been under his control, was subdued. It remained an unimportant town until the fourth century B.C. when it was rebuilt as a whole. It was planned on a rectangular grid-plan, covering a series of terraces cut in the rocky hill-side, and held a population of some 4,000. The site was surrounded by a powerful city-wall with an acropolis on the mountain. The Agora is situated in the middle of the city, with a temple of Athena a little higher up, and higher still a theatre and an Ecclesiasterium. The two latter buildings are in an excellent state of preservation, the Ecclesiasterium being an unusual and remarkable building. The theatre has features not found elsewhere. At the lower levels are a gymnasium and a boys' school. The site as a whole is of great beauty and better preserved than any other of the period. The city-walls in some places are intact. Its remains give a good idea of a typical planned city.

M. Schede, *Priene* (1934); T. Fyfe, *Hellenistic Architecture* (1936). S. C.

PRIESTS (ἱερῆς, *sacerdotes*). In no ancient Greek or Italian State was there such a thing as a class or caste of priests, and none was under priestly dominance, as was often the case, for instance, in Egypt. This does not mean that priests had no influence or were not treated with great respect, nor that their office could not be hereditary; it results rather from the absence of any cleavage between the religious and secular life of the community, under normal circumstances at least. Whereas a priest, despite his office, was not generally interdicted from secular activities,* a magistrate was usually a priest as a part of his official functions, which is why, in Greek cities, they often wore wreaths, a very common mark of one engaged in religious duties, and in Rome all curule magistrates wore the *praetexta*. The gods were, during the classical epoch, a sort of superior class of citizens, and their servants were not normally cut off from the life of the State as a whole, any more than any other class of persons whose duties were chiefly directed towards some one part of the population, e.g. magistrates who, like Roman aediles and Greek *agoranomoi*, had to do mostly with traders.

2. Furthermore, the executive powers of a priest were as a rule narrowly defined. He was active chiefly as an expert adviser (cf. PONTIFEX), and was, for example, in sole charge of the conduct of a sacrifice or other piece of ritual which fell within his province. Thus, the priestess of Athena and no one else superintended the annual ritual of the Arrhephoroi (Paus. 1. 27. 3). But the clergy, in spite of responsibilities for sanctuaries, did not draw upon the public funds for the expenses of ritual; the revenues of a temple, usually not very large, were another matter. We have abundant records of the governing body of a State voting the money for sacral purposes, as it might for any other; for instance, in Athens, *IG*¹ i *supp.*, p. 66, no. 53 a (*SIG* 93) shows us the Council and People, not any sacral body, making the arrangements for some necessary work on a chapel sacred to Codrus and other worthies. *IG* i. 1 (*SIG* 42), though very fragmentary, is enough to show that innumerable details of the Eleusinian Mysteries, though of course not the secret ritual itself, were in the hands of the Athenian Government. At Rome Livy (22. 10. 1) gives the important evidence that according to the highest priestly authority of the day, the then pontifex maximus, a *ver sacrum* (q.v.) could not be vowed save by act of the popular Assembly ('iniussu populi uoueri non posse');

* In Rome, for example, the flamen Dialis very seldom held a magistracy, cf. Plutarch, *Quaest. Rom.* 113 and Rose ad loc., but there was no definite prohibition against his doing so; for the pontificate of the emperors *see* PONTIFEX.

accordingly, the vow was made in the form of a bill proposed to and passed by the Assembly. The chief pontiff did not even give his advice of his own motion, but after consulting his colleagues at the request of a secular magistrate. Even the possessions of a temple, though sacred, were not the absolute property of the deity, in fact at least, though in law they seem always to have been. Thucydides (2. 13. 3–4) represents Pericles as counting among the resources of the Athenian State the treasures of the various temples and even the golden ornaments of the cult-statue of Athena, and there is good inscriptional evidence (e.g. *IG* i. 32, *SIG* 91) that even in times of less stress than those of the Peloponnesian War the State felt at liberty to 'borrow' from the gods and, if able, to repay, thus re-establishing a reserve fund for emergencies. Since, then, the clergy of a State had neither executive nor economic independence, it is easy to see why they never were supreme.

3. In private life it seems to have been much the same. The average ancient did, indeed, commingle his religion with his daily occupations to a considerable extent, and hence must on occasion have needed priestly guidance in matters of ritual, for instance that of a professional diviner to tell him the best day for a marriage, or of a priest of some sort to perform the religious rites needed on that and sundry other occasions. But we have only to look at Theophrastus' sketch of the pietistic man (*Charact.* 16, especially §§ 7 and 12) to see that priestly interference in the normal household was slight. This man, whose foible is gross exaggeration of the religious practices in which his more sensible neighbours are moderate, consults the *exegetes* (q.v.) and goes monthly to the Orphic specialists to undergo their rites; we may conclude that the ordinary person did such things far less often.

4. As to the appointment of priests, in some cases the office was in the hands of a clan or family, as the Eumolpidae at Eleusis, or the Potitii and Pinarii in the cult of Hercules at the Ara Maxima. This presumably is the result of the rites having been originally domestic or clan-worships. Some priests served for life, while others were chosen to serve for a single year. Normally, a State priest was appointed in some way by the State, often by actual election; in Hellenistic times many priesthoods were publicly sold, e.g. *SIG* 1012 (Paton–Hicks, *Inscr. of Cos*, 27). Some were lucrative, but in later times priesthoods were often an expense. The tendency was towards abolishing rules which confined eligible candidates to any one class of citizens, although the restrictions remained in the case of some particularly venerable offices (*see* HIEROPHANTES); thus, the greater flamens at Rome remained patricians. Generally, no ethical tests were imposed, although some few positions were so hedged about with restrictions as to enforce at least an outward respectability of conduct.

5. Private religious organizations, permitted or tolerated by the State, and cults confined to a family, clan, or other group within the community, had their own rules, but these fall outside the scope of this article. H. J. R.

PRIMIPILUS was the senior centurion in a legion. Under the Principate each legion had in its complement of sixty centurions two officers bearing this title, the *primipilus* and the *primipilus iterum*. The *primipilus* commanded the leading century; on promotion he entered the equestrian order and after holding tribunates in the garrison troops at Rome might be appointed *primipilus bis*. As such he served on the staff of the *legatus*, retained his equestrian rank, and was qualified to receive command of the Egyptian legions or a senior procuratorship. *See* CENTURIO. H. M. D. P.

PRIMUS, MARCUS ANTONIUS, born at Tolosa in Gallia Narbonensis *c.* A.D. 20, was a turbulent and ambitious character—'strenuus manu, sermone promptus, serendae

in alios inuidiae artifex, discordiis et seditionibus potens, raptor, largitor, pace pessimus, bello non spernendus' (Tac. *Hist.* 2. 86). Exiled for his share in the forgery of a will (61), he was restored by Galba and put in charge of legio VII in Pannonia. In the summer of 69 he declared openly for Vespasian, won over the other Danubian armies and, spurning a cautious strategy, invaded Italy across the Julian Alps. His dash and vigour carried all before him to victory at the second battle of Bedriacum. He pressed on to Rome, but came too late to save Flavius Sabinus. For a short time he was in supreme control, but after the arrival of Mucianus he was gradually thrust aside. Lapsing into private life, he enjoyed a quiet and happy old age. R. S.

PRINCEPS. When Augustus selected 'Princeps' as the word which indicated most satisfactorily his own constitutional position, he chose, typically, a word which had good Republican associations.

2. It was not an abbreviation of 'Princeps Senatus', though that, also, was a Republican title and one which Augustus held. The 'Princeps Senatus', or First Senator, was, before the time of Sulla the man who had been placed by censors at the head of the list of members of the Senate, and ranked as the senior member of that body. Augustus in the census of 28 B.C. enrolled himself as 'Princeps Senatus' (Dio Cass. 53. 1; *Res Gest.*, c. 7), and succeeding emperors held the same position.

3. 'Principes' in the plural, meaning the 'chief men of the State', was a phrase commonly employed by late Republican writers, as Cicero, and it continued to be used in the Empire (Suet. *Aug.* 66; *Res Gest.*, c. 12).

4. It was the singular 'Princeps', however, applied to *one* prominent statesman, especially Pompey, in Republican times, which supplied Augustus with something of a precedent (e.g. Sallust, *Hist.* 3. 48. 23 M.; Cic. *Har. Resp.* 46, *Pis.* 25, *Domo* 66, *Sest.* 84, *Red. Sen.* 5 and 29, *Red. Pop.* 16). Early in 49 B.C. Cornelius Balbus wrote to Cicero (*Att.* 8. 9. 4): 'Nihil malle Caesarem quam principe Pompeio sine metu uiuere.' Cicero used this designation of other statesmen besides Pompey. In 46 B.C. he used it of Julius Caesar (*Fam.* 9. 17. 3). He used it also of himself in connexion with the renown that he won by his action against the Catilinarian conspirators (*Phil.* 14. 17) and by his rallying of the Senate against Antony at the end of 44 B.C. (*Fam.* 12. 24. 2). The phrase 'Princeps Ciuitatis' is also used of the 'Moderator Reipublicae' in Cicero's *De Republica* (5. 7. 9, where the reading is probably sound in spite of the doubts of Dessau, *Gesch. der röm. Kaiserzeit* i, 61, n. 2), though here, almost certainly, he was not thinking of Pompey. In this work Cicero foreshadows a Principate of the Augustan type, a revived Republic, with a statesman in the background strong enough to ensure that it should function properly. Augustus' choice of the word 'Princeps' to designate his position was typical of his 'ciuilis animus'; it contrasted strongly with the 'Dictatura' and the suspected monarchical intentions of Julius Caesar and, in indicating an unquestioned but not a narrowly defined or clearly determined primacy, the word suited perfectly Augustus' definition of his own authority in the *Res Gest.*, c. 34: 'Auctoritate omnibus praestiti, potestatis autem nihil amplius habui quam qui fuerunt mihi quoque in magistratu conlegae.' *Principatus* was in sharp opposition to *dominatio*, 'Princeps' to 'Dominus', and both Augustus and Tiberius took pains to suppress the use of the title 'Dominus', though it was a conventional form of polite address within the Roman family (Ovid, *Fasti* 2. 142; Suet. *Aug.* 53; Dio Cass. 57. 8). The importance of this choice of title was appreciated by Roman historians; cf. Tac. *Ann.* 1. 1: 'Cuncta discordiis ciuilibus fessa nomine principis sub imperium accepit'; 1. 9: 'Non regno tamen neque dictatura, sed principis nomine constitutam rem publicam' (cf. 3. 28).

5. 'Princeps' was not an *official* title (like, for example, *Pater Patriae*). It was assumed by Roman emperors at their accession and not conferred upon them by definite grant of the Senate; nor does it appear in the list of official titles in documents and inscriptions. On the other hand, by itself it might be used in inscriptions (e.g. on the funerary urn of Agrippina: 'Ossa Agrippinae . . . matris C. Caesaris Aug. Germanici principis', Dessau, *ILS* 180). Claudius, in his edict *de Anaunorum civitate*, wrote: 'Gai principatu' (Dessau, *ILS* 206). The Greek form of the word, ἡγεμών, appears in the fifth Cyrene Edict of Augustus (line 86, *JRS* 1927, 36): 'Αὐτοκράτωρ Καῖσαρ Σεβαστός, ἡγεμὼν ἡμέτερος.'

6. The nuance of the word, chosen by Augustus for its inoffensive character, was soon lost (though the use of the word itself persisted) as the government of the Roman emperors became more autocratic. It may be doubted whether the Greeks ever appreciated its subtlety; Dio Cassius, for instance, in recording Tiberius' very typical remark (57. 8. 2), 'I am *dominus* of my slaves, *imperator* of my troops, and *princeps* of the rest', loses the point by using, for 'Princeps', not ἡγεμών, but πρόκριτος, which means 'Princeps Senatus'. The title 'Princeps' in Latin survived the reorganization of Diocletian, though such phrases as 'Gloriosissimus Princeps' show that its original significance had been lost.

7. Further light is thrown on the significance of the word 'Princeps' by the title 'Princeps Iuventutis', meaning Leader of the Equestrian Order, or, more probably, of the 'Iuventus' of that Order (*see* PRINCEPS IUVENTUTIS), which was given in certain cases in the early Empire to princes of the Imperial house who might be considered as 'Heirs apparent', the relation of the 'Princeps Iuventutis' to the 'Princeps' being well illustrated by Ovid's words (*Ars Am.* 1. 194): 'Nunc iuuenum princeps, deinde future senum.'

M. Hammond, *The Augustan Principate* (U.S.A. 1933); Mommsen, *Röm. Staatsr.* ii. 2 (1887), p. 3. Further, see the bibliographies of M. Hammond, op. cit. and *CAH* x. 913 ff.   J. P. B.

PRINCEPS IUVENTUTIS or PRINCEPS IUVENUM.

The phrase occurs in the Roman Republic (Cicero, *Vatin.* 24, applies it to the younger Curio), but first appears with constitutional significance after the reorganization of the *Iuventus* by Augustus (*see* IUVENES). Probably in 5 and 2 B.C. respectively the *Ordo equester* gave silver shields and spears to Augustus' grandsons, Gaius and Lucius, and hailed them as *Principes Iuventutis*. The same honour was paid possibly to Germanicus and Drusus, son of Tiberius; certainly to Tiberius Gemellus, adopted son of Gaius, in A.D. 37; to Nero, after his adoption by Claudius and, much later, to Commodus. The title was retained by these princes when they were no longer *Iuvenes*, and had something of the significance of 'Crown Prince'. This was lost when, occasionally after Domitian, and regularly in the third century, reigning emperors used the title; its connexion with the *ordo equester* also disappeared in the third century.
                                J. P. B.

PRISCIANUS

(early 6th c. A.D.), grammarian, born at Caesarea in Mauretania, taught in Constantinople. His *Institutiones grammaticae* in eighteen books (ed. M. Hertz in Keil's *Gramm. Lat.*, vols. ii and iii) is the most voluminous work of any Latin grammarian. The first sixteen books deal with the parts of speech in great detail, the last two with points of syntax; but there are no sections devoted specifically to the *vitia et virtutes orationis* or to metre. Priscian made use of Greek grammars, and appears to have been well acquainted with all the more important of his Latin predecessors. His expositions are liberally illustrated by quotations from the standard school authors such as Cicero, Virgil, and Horace; he also drew, especially for bks. 5 to 10, on sources which afforded him many quotations from

Republican writers; and his Greek authorities provided him with Greek examples. During the Middle Ages this work was widely read and commentaries were written upon it. Besides the long treatise, we possess the following shorter works: (*a*) *De figuris numerorum*, (*b*) *De metris fabularum Terentii*, (*c*) *Praeexercitamina rhetorica*, (*d*) *Institutio de nomine et pronomine et verbo*, (*e*) *Partitiones XII versuum Aeneidos*, (*f*) *De accentibus* (of doubtful authenticity), (*g*) *De laude imperatoris Anastasii* (312 hexameters), (*h*) *Periegesis e Dionysio* (1087 hexameters). Of these, (*a*), (*b*), and (*c*) were dedicated to Symmachus (consul 485); (*a*)–(*f*) are in Keil, *Gramm. Lat.* iii. 406–528, (*g*) and (*h*) in Baehrens, *PLM* v. 264–312. *See also* SCHOLARSHIP, LATIN, and cf. Teuffel, § 481; Schanz–Hosius, §§ 1111–15.   J. F. M.

PRISCUS, *see* HELVIDIUS, NERATIUS.

PRISON. Roman criminal law did not recognize the imprisonment of free persons as a form of punishment. The public prison (*carcer*, *publica vincula*) served only for a short incarceration applied as a coercive measure (*coërcitio*) by magistrates for disobedience or recalcitrance against their orders. During inquiry in a criminal trial the accused person could be detained (*custodia reorum*) so as to be at the disposal of the authorities; condemned persons could be imprisoned so as to ensure the execution of the sentence, but as the rules were very lax and no term for such a detention was fixed, the magistrates postponed the arrest of the malefactors in order to give them the chance of going into voluntary exile (*see* EXSILIUM). Private, domestic prisons existed in larger households for the imprisonment of slaves. *See also* TULLIANUM.   A. B.

PRO CONSULE. This term was applied to a consul whose *imperium* had been extended by *prorogatio* (q.v.) after his year of office. In the later Republic it normally denoted the governor of a province, as this duty was rarely performed by a magistrate in office. The proconsulship came to be dissociated from the magistracy and was conferred, e.g., on Pompey in 77, 66, and 65 B.C., when he was a private citizen. In 52 a law of Pompey fixed an interval of five years between the magistracy and the promagistracy. In the Principate the term proconsul was applied to governors of senatorial provinces, whether *consulares* or *praetorii*. The power of the emperor himself was largely derived from his proconsular *imperium*.
                                G. H. S.

PROAGON, a kind of dress-parade in the Odeum of *choregi*, poets, actors, and choruses a few days before the Great Dionysia at Athens, and probably also before the Lenaea. Probably the names and subjects of the plays were announced. At the *proagon* next after the death of Euripides, Sophocles appeared in mourning and his actors and chorus did not wear the usual crowns (Aeschin. 3. 66–7 with schol.; Pl. *Symp.* 194 a; *Vit. Eurip.* and schol. on Ar. *Vesp.* 1104).   A. W. P.-C.

PROBA (4th c. A.D.), poetess, besides an epic on the civil war between Constantius and Magnentius, composed out of Virgilian scraps a cento (q.v.) on parts of the Old and New Testaments.

Text: K. Schenkl, *CSEL* 16 (1887); cf. Teuffel, § 422. 3.

PROBOULOI (πρόβουλοι). (1) A magistracy of eight members in Corinth, after the overthrow of the tyranny (early 6th c.); found also in Corcyra and a few other States.

(2) A body of ten men above age 40, appointed at Athens in 413 B.C. (after the Sicilian disaster), to act as a council to 'prepare business' (προβουλεύειν) more efficiently than the Boule of 500. It was the first break

with the democratic tradition. In 411 the oligarchs carried a proposal that they and twenty other elected citizens should form a commission of ξυγγραφεῖς to draw up proposals for constitutional change (*see* FOUR HUNDRED). A. W. G.

PRŎBUS (1), VALERIUS (late 1st c. A.D.), of Berytus, scholar. He interested himself in Republican authors and somewhat in the fashion of Aristarchus worked over the texts of Terence, Lucretius, Virgil, and Horace, indicating his views by critical signs. He himself published little (cf. Suet. *Gram.* 24), but communicated his learning in conversation with friends. It is improbable that he wrote full commentaries, but some information about his work on Terence and Virgil is found in scholia to those authors. He is not mentioned in the scholia to Horace. Aulus Gellius and later grammarians quote him with some frequency on points of grammar. The *Libri iuris notarum* (ed. Th. Mommsen in Keil's *Gramm. Lat.* iv. 271–6) attributed to him is not the original work. Other treatises: *Ars catholica, Instituta artium, Appendix Probi, De nomine,* and *De ultimis syllabis* (ed. Keil, *Gramm. Lat.* iv. 3–43, 47–192, 193–204, 207–16, 219–64) are neither genuine notes of Probus nor based on his writings; apocryphal also is the extant commentary on the *Eclogues* and *Georgics* of Virgil (ed. H. Hagen in Thilo's *Servius* iii. 2). As early as the fifteenth century a 'younger Probus' was conjured up to account for the false ascription of these works. *See* SCHOLARSHIP, LATIN, and cf. Teuffel, §§ 300–1; Schanz–Hosius, §§ 477–9.
J. F. M.

PROBUS (2), MARCUS AURELIUS, whose earlier career has become confused with that of Tenagino Probus and is little known, was in A.D. 276 in command of Syria and Egypt. Set up as rival to Florian after the death of Tacitus, he outmanœuvred Florian at Tarsus and succeeded him (summer of that year).

The main task of Probus was to restore peace and order to the reunited empire of Aurelian. Turning first to Gaul, which was overrun by Germans, he recovered the province in an arduous campaign and restored the Rhine frontier (277). Alamanni and Senones, Franks and Burgundians, all succumbed to his arms. Then, moving eastward, he defeated the Vandals on the Danube and put down the insurrection of Lydius (or Palfuerius?) at Cremna in Pisidia. In Egypt the Blemmyes captured Ptolemais and Coptos, but were defeated by Probus' generals. In 280 he settled the Bastarnae in Thrace. He celebrated a splendid triumph in Rome in 281. In 282 he was at Sirmium, preparing for a campaign against Persia, when the troops in Raetia proclaimed Carus, the Praetorian Prefect, emperor. A corps, sent by Probus, deserted to Carus, and Probus was killed by his own troops in the Iron Tower.

The rebellions of Saturninus in the East (277–8) and of Proculus and Bonosus in Gaul (280), and an attempt at revolt in Britain, though all successfully quelled, point to serious discontent in the army. The stern discipline of Probus and his employment of troops on the planting of vineyards were both unpopular. The danger of settling barbarians in the Empire was revealed by the exploit of a band of Franks, who made their way home after extensive ravages in the Mediterranean. Probus sought the co-operation of the Senate in government, but did not take the decisive step of putting senators back into military commands.

H. Mattingly, *CAH* xii, ch. 9, 313 ff.; Parker, *Roman World*, 215 ff. H. M.

PROCEDURE, CIVIL AND CRIMINAL, *see* LAW AND PROCEDURE.

PROCELEUSMATIC, *see* METRE, GREEK, III (4).

PROCESSION. Processions were very prominent features of Greek festivals. There are various kinds. Best known is that in which people who take part in a festival go in an orderly procession to the temple of the god; so, for instance, in the Panathenaic procession as represented on the Parthenon frieze (cf. PANATHENAEA). The gods are waiting for the procession; certain men look after its order; virgins carry sacred implements, elderly men green branches; youths conduct the sacrificial animals; chariots, which are to partake in the following contest, and the cavalry follow. Later the *peplos* brought to the goddess was hoisted on a ship set on wheels. Everyone's place in the procession was fixed and there was a special building, the Pompeion near the Dipylon gate, where the procession was arranged and from which it started. An inscription from Andania prescribes arrangements in detail (*SIG* 736). Sometimes a procession went to a mountain-top in order to perform a weather ceremony or fire-ritual, e.g. the Daidala to Mt. Cithaeron. Another kind of procession is due to a connexion between two cult-places. The outstanding example is the Iacchus procession, in which the people went to Eleusis in order to celebrate the mysteries. First the sacred things were brought to Athens, on the 14th Boedromion they were taken back to Eleusis together with the image of Iacchus, conducted by the priests, the magistrates, the ephebi, and the great mass of *mystae*. Sometimes a god was brought to visit another temple, e.g. Artemis from the suburb of Mesoa to Patrae; Dionysus was brought from his temple into the orchestra of the theatre in order to be present at the performances. Processions in which a god made his epiphany are peculiar to Dionysus. At the Anthesteria he was brought into the city on a ship set on wheels. Sometimes the image of a god was brought out to be cleansed; so that of Athena Polias in Athens was taken to the shore of Phaleron. The carrying of the image of a god in procession has always a special reason. In Greece, unlike many other countries, the god was not carried about in procession in order to give blessings and to be venerated. Blessings were distributed by carrying round sacred or rather magical things—the phallus, which was absent from hardly any Dionysiac procession, the 'may' (*eiresione*), the swallow, etc.; the last are rural processions, sometimes conducted by children collecting contributions.

E. Pfuhl, *De Atheniensium pompis sacris* (1900); M. P. Nilsson, *JDAI* xxxi (1916), 309 ff. M. P. N.

PROCLUS, *see* EPIC CYCLE.

PROCNE (*Πρόκνη*), *see* PHILOMELA.

PROCONSUL, *see* PRO CONSULE.

PROCŎPIUS, born at Caesarea in Palestine, was a notable personage of the Byzantine court during the reign of Justinian I. His career has two sides—the official and the literary. Beginning life as a professor of rhetoric at Constantinople he became secretary in A.D. 527 to the great general Belisarius, with whom he visited in turn Asia, Africa, and Italy, undertaking, apart from his secretarial duties, important charges in connexion with the commissariat and the navy. He returned with Belisarius to Constantinople in 542, was advanced to the rank of *illustris* and senator, and, in 562, became prefect of Constantinople. He died in 565.

He is best remembered for his literary activity. He had a quick mind, a lively interest in facts and events, and a good command of Greek style. His own experience of affairs and his long service under Belisarius gave him unique qualifications for writing the history of his own times. His general history of his age (in eight books) was devoted mainly to the Vandal War (two books), and the

Gothic Wars (four). A thorough acquaintance with good classical models enabled Procopius to shape his personal experience into a work of major historical importance. His knowledge of medical matters is considerable, but perhaps not enough to prove that he was himself a doctor. His religion seems to be a lukewarm and not very decided Christianity. Six books of Κτίσματα described buildings, and various orations are also preserved under his name.

The great historical puzzle connected with Procopius is the authorship of the 'Ἀνέκδοτα', 'Historia Arcana', a 'Chronique scandaleuse' of the age. This 'curious' book, with its malignant revelations about the great personages of the age—the early career of the Empress Theodora may be read as a choice sample—is a surprising and not very creditable production for a man of Procopius' rank and service. But Suidas directly assigns it to him, and the onus of proof seems to rest on those who deny his authorship.

J. B. Bury, *History of the later Roman Empire*[2] ii (1923). H. M.

PROCOPTAS, see PROCRUSTES.

PROCRIS (Πρόκρις), wife of the Attic hero Cephalus (q.v.). After sundry adventures, which have come down to us in late forms (Ovid, *Met.* 7. 794 ff.; Hyginus, *Fab.* 189), she was accidentally killed by him.

PROCRUSTES (Προκρούστης; also called **Damastes,** Δαμάστης, Apollod. *Epit.* 1. 4, Plut. *Thes.* 11, or **Poly-pemon,** Πολυπήμων, Paus. 1. 38. 5, or **Procoptas,** Προκόπτας, Bacchylides 17. 28). All these names refer to his activities. He lived in some part of Attica (see Jebb on Bacchyl. loc. cit.), and having 'overcome' (δαμάζειν) strangers would force them to lie down on one of his two beds. Here he caused them 'much woe' by hammering them out (προκρούειν) to a sufficient length to fit the longer bed (so Bacchyl. and Apollod.) or racking them out with weights (Hyginus, *Fab.* 38. 3). If they were longer than the shorter bed he lopped them (προκόπτειν). Theseus (q.v.) killed him in like manner. His father was Poseidon (Hyginus), or is called by one of the names elsewhere given to Procrustes himself (see, e.g., Bacchyl.).

See further Höfer in Roscher, *Lex.*, art. 'Polypemonides', and refs. there. H. J. R.

PROCULIANI, see SABINUS (2).

PROCULUS, a prominent Roman jurist of the first half of the first century A.D., was a teacher and had the *ius respondendi* (see JURISPRUDENCE). The School of Proculians took its name from him (see SABINUS 2). Author of *Epistulae* (11 bks.), a collection of opinions and discussions taken from his practice and of *Notae* to Labeo, the precursor of the School. He was frequently cited by later jurists. A. B.

PROCULUS, see also POMPONIUS (6).

PROCURATOR, an agent, especially a financial agent. Augustus, like any other Roman, employed such agents, and in his service they attained new rank and responsibilities.

Procurators of the emperor might be either knights or freedmen, but the knights always held the more important posts and, from Hadrian onwards, tended to displace freedmen. The title 'procurator Augusti' belonged strictly to the knight alone, who qualified for employment by serving in a number of officers' posts (usually three—'tres militiae'). Procurators came to be graded in salary-classes, *sexagenarii* and *centenarii* (60,000, 100,000 HS.: *vir egregius*) and *ducenarii* (200,000 HS.: *vir perfectissimus*).

The duties of procurators were essentially financial. (1) Procurators of provinces dealt with the imperial finances in their districts. Claudius gave them jurisdiction in cases affecting the *fiscus*. In the imperial provinces the procurator worked under the *legatus*, in the senatorial his position was more independent beside the governor and his quaestor. In both he could occasionally act as a check on the governor. In the third century the appointment of procurators to govern 'uice praesidis' was one of the main ways in which knights displaced senators in the provincial administration. The procurator had no troops under him, but could, at need, obtain small detachments from the governor.

(2) Procurators of a great variety of departments under the emperor's control—the mint, the gladiatorial schools, the mines, the *annona*, the *vicesima hereditatum* (see also ALIMENTA). The heads of departments, such as the *a rationibus* and *ab epistulis*, were regularly knights after Hadrian and stood high in the equestrian career.

(3) A third class of procurators governed minor provinces, such as Thrace and Judaea, which were assigned to the emperor, but had no important garrisons. These 'procuratores et praesides' were not restricted to finance and enjoyed the power of life and death (the *ius gladii*). In practice they might sometimes be placed in semi-dependence on the governors of larger provinces. The best known of such procurators is Pontius Pilate, who ordered the Crucifixion.

The knight who entered the imperial service, after serving as officer in the army or, from Hadrian, in such civil posts as those of the *advocati fisci*, spent most of his life passing, by advancement, from one procuratorship to another. Procurators first supervised the private collection of taxes and then undertook direct collection. The office continued into the fourth century, under the new name of *rationalis*.

O. Hirschfeld, *Die kaiserliche Verwaltungsbeamten*, etc. (1905); H. Mattingly, *The Imperial Civil Service of Rome* (1910); A. N. Sherwin-White, 'Procurator Augusti', *BSR* xv (1939), 11 ff. H. M.

PRODICUS of Ceos, a Sophist and a contemporary of Socrates. We have very little reliable information about his life. We learn from Plato that he was employed by his native city on diplomatic missions and that he took advantage of the opportunities these afforded to further his professional interests. He gained considerable repute in his profession and demanded high fees for his courses of instruction. These are described as being concerned with the right use of words and were marked by their subtle discriminations between the precise meanings of kindred terms. Plato represents Socrates as being on friendly terms with him and paying tribute to the value of his teaching, though always with a touch of irony. There are also references to discussions, or perhaps rather exhortations, on moral questions, and he was the author of the famous myth 'The Choice of Heracles'.

Testimonia and frs. in H. Diels, *Vorsokr.*[5] ii. 308–19. Zeller, i. 2[6]. 1311–15; T. Gomperz, *Griechische Denker* (Engl. Transl. i. 425–30). G. C. F.

PRODIGIA. A *prodigium* is an event contrary to the supposed or known workings of nature, taken as a sign that the *pax deorum* is broken or in danger of being broken; whereas an *omen* is commonly a natural and ordinary event, observed by a diviner under certain circumstances. Examples are frequent in Livy, and collected by Julius Obsequens, *Prodigiorum liber*, from him. For example, in 136 B.C. (Obs. 25) the town of Rhegium was mysteriously burned, many objects in various places struck by lightning, streams at Puteoli ran blood, and a slave-girl bore a monstrous child. To deal with such things (*procurare*), Etruscan experts were often summoned (cf. HARUSPICES), as in the above instance; by their advice the child was burned and his ashes thrown into the sea. Other examples are mysterious voices of warning (Obs. 24, in 137 B.C.); rains of milk, blood, etc. (ibid. 28, 30, 31, 35, 51, 54); meteors and other like phenomena; the *hastae Martis* or the *ancilia* moving of their own accord (ibid. 44 a, 47); earthquakes and eruptions; statues sweating or weeping (ibid. 6, 28, 52); phantoms of various kinds (ibid. 17, 18, 51). Sacrifices, lustrations, and a *nouendiale sacrum*, or ceremony lasting nine days, were among the commonest forms of *procuratio* (e.g., ibid. 4, 12, 23).

See bibliography to DIVINATION. H. J. R.

PROEDROI (πρόεδροι). (1) A general name for presidents. (2) At Athens, from early in the fourth century, the nine men who presided at the meetings of the Ecclesia and Boule (cf. PRYTANIS for the 5th c. practice). The *Epistates* of the *prytanis*, before each meeting of the Boule and of the Ecclesia, chose by lot one man from each of the *phylae* other than the *prytaneuousa*; these nine then chose their *epistates* from their own number, who was the actual chairman of the meeting. No one served as *proedros* more than once. A. W. G.

PROETUS (Προῖτος), a mythical king of the Argolid, who first appears in Homer, in the story of Bellerophon (q.v.). Later (Apollodorus 2. 24 ff.) he and Acrisius are sons of Abas son of Danaus (q.v.); for their quarrel *see* ACRISIUS. The only other legend of importance concerns his daughters. These insulted the statue of Hera, or would not receive the rites of Dionysus (the latter is the Hesiodic story, the former and more probably original from Acusilaus, Apollod. 26). They were driven mad by the offended deity and wandered about the country 'with all manner of unseemliness'. In particular, they fancied themselves cows (Verg. *Ecl.* 6. 48). Melampus (q.v.), being asked to heal them, demanded a third of the kingdom; this was refused, and they went madder still and killed their own children. Proetus now agreed to Melampus' terms, although they were raised to include another third for his brother Bias. The women were then caught at Sicyon and cured, except one, Iphinoe, who had died. H. J. R.

PROGYMNASMATA, or preliminary exercises, constituted the elementary stage of instruction in schools of rhetoric (1st c. B.C. or earlier), and were represented later in the Προγυμνάσματα of Aelius Theon, Hermogenes, and Aphthonius (Spengel, *Rhet.* ii. 59 ff., 3 ff., 21 ff.; see also Quint. 2. 4). Designed to introduce pupils to the art of speaking, these works expounded various devices which were held to contribute to that end, notably the use of μῦθος (fable), διήγημα (narrative), χρεία (moral essay), γνώμη (maxim), ἀνασκευή and κατασκευή (refutation and confirmation of a story), κοινὸς τόπος (amplification), ἐγκώμιον (panegyric), σύγκρισις (comparison), ἠθοποιία (character-drawing), ἔκφρασις (description), θέσις (abstract question). As manuals of composition in Sophistic school-practice such works were defective, but their later influence was considerable. Exercises in διήγημα prepared the way for Greek romances, while ἔκφρασις and ἠθοποιία were to persist as important elements in medieval Poetics (C. S. Baldwin, *Medieval Rhetoric and Poetic* (1928), 17, 35, etc.).

See also G. Saintsbury, *History of Criticism* (1900–4), i. 89 ff.; Kroll, *Rhetorik*, § 37. J. W. H. A.

PROLETARII were the citizens of the fifth class of the centuriate constitution (*see* CENTURIA), who were too poor to contribute to the State except by their children (*proles*). Originally they were exempted from military service, which depended on the financial resources of the citizens. But with increasing military, and especially naval, needs, the *proletarii*, whether identified with or distinguished from the *capite censi*, were called up and armed by the State. The reforms of Marius terminated the system of levying troops on the census.

G. W. Botsford, *The Roman Assemblies* (1909), 207 f. P. T.

PROLOGUE, see TRAGEDY, AESCHYLUS, SOPHOCLES, EURIPIDES.

PROMETHEUS (Προμηθεύς, 'the forethinker'; all other etymologies of his name are merely fantastic; the word is used as a common noun, Aesch. *PV* 86), an ancient and popular demi-god, one of the Titans (son of Iapetus, Hesiod, *Theog.* 510, where his mother is Clymene the Oceanid). Originally, his character is entirely non-moral; he is the supreme trickster (cf. the like figure, Coyote or another, in Amerindian mythologies, W. Schmidt, *Origin and Growth of Religion*, 189, citing Kroeber), and as such is on occasion opposed to Zeus, whom he outwits. It would appear that he developed in common belief into a supreme craftsman, and was worshipped as such by craftsmen, particularly in Attica (see L. Deubner, *Attische Feste* (1932), 211 f.). Probably it is in this connexion that he is associated with fire and with the creation of man.

Hesiod has two principal tales of him. The first is that when Zeus hid fire away from man, Prometheus stole it and brought it to earth again (*Theog.* 562 ff.). Zeus would not give fire to the ash-trees for man's use, i.e. prevented the hardwood fire-sticks from being effective when rubbed against the soft ones; Prometheus therefore stole from the gods enough fire to make the pith of a stalk of giant fennel smoulder, and from this men got fire once more. It is a tale of common enough type, see Stith Thompson, A 1415 and references. Hesiod gives it, what probably did not originally belong to it, a preface explaining why Zeus acted so. Prometheus had tricked him with regard to the respective share of gods and men in burnt offerings (*Theog.* 535 ff.); he wrapped all the poorest parts of the victim up in fat, the best parts in another bundle, and bade Zeus choose; the simple-minded god taking the fat, man has ever since kept all the best of the meat for himself. This is a manifest aetiological myth to explain sacrificial usage, and its hero may always have been Prometheus. The story is also given an epilogue. Zeus punished mankind in general by creating woman to their confusion; the first woman was called Pandora, because she had 'all gifts' from the gods (she probably is in reality an earth-goddess, the All-giver); Prometheus' simple brother Epimetheus ('After-thinker') married her despite his brother's warnings, and she let out all evils from the store-jar where they were kept (*Theog.* 570 ff., *Op.* 50 ff.). This tale, for which cf. the part played by Eve in the Hebrew myth, is a piece of satire against women with which Prometheus has no necessary connexion.

The other tale is the vengeance of Zeus on Prometheus. He chained him and sent an eagle to eat his liver, which was as immortal as the rest of him and grew at night as fast as the eagle could devour it by day. In this torment he remained until Heracles released him. In Hesiod the reason of the punishment is the deceit regarding the sacrifices (*Theog.* 534 ff.); in Aeschylus (*PV* 7 ff.) it is the theft of fire. But a further complication is introduced, by Aeschylus himself so far as we know. Prometheus knew the secret regarding Thetis (q.v.), and would not reveal it till, apparently, he at last gave it up as the price of his liberty. Aeschylus also gives Prometheus high moral dignity as the friend of man against the tyranny of Zeus.

Prometheus, as master-craftsman, makes man from clay (Paus. 10. 4. 4) or from clay plus bits of other animals (Horace, *Carm.* 1. 16. 13 ff.). H. J. R.

PRONUNCIATION, GREEK. The main features of ancient Greek pronunciation have been established by the skilful handling of very various types of evidence. For many details, naturally, only approximate accuracy can be claimed.

A. VOWELS AND DIPHTHONGS

(1) α, ι, υ. These symbols represented both short and long vowels. The exact quality of ᾰ and ῐ cannot be

certainly stated. It seems probable, however, that *a* sounded like *a* in Eng. *father*, that *ī* was a close vowel like *ee* in Eng. *meet*, and *ĭ* a short vowel of similar quality. *ŭ* and *ū* in Attic, Ionic, and some other dialects were modified approximately to the sound of French *u* or Germ. *ü*. (2) *ε*, *η*, *ει*. In the Ionic alphabet, which eventually came into universal use, *ε* is a close short vowel (*ĕ* as in Fr. *été*), *η* a long open vowel (*ę̄* as in Fr. *fête*). Consequently, in many dialects, including Attic and Ionic, the *ē̦* which resulted from contraction (*ε*+*ε*) or compensatory lengthening (e.g. *τιθενς* > *τιθε̄́ς*, later *τιθείς*) could not be expressed by *η*. It continued to be denoted by *ε* until at different periods in different places the original diphthong *ει* had changed in pronunciation from a true diphthong to a long *e* of close quality (*ē̦* like the *e* of Eng. *prey*). The symbol *ει* then became available to express *ē̦*, whether this sound had developed from an original diphthong or not. (3) *o*, *ω*, *ου*. Similarly *o* was a close short vowel (*ŏ* like the final syllable of Eng. *bellow*), *ω* a long open vowel (*ǭ* somewhat less open than *au* in Eng. *aught*). *ου* represented originally the diphthong, but when this became a simple *ǭ* the symbol was used to represent also the lengthened *o* (*ǭ*) which arose from contraction or compensatory lengthening. This *ǭ* (spelled *ου*) had developed by 350 B.C. into *ū*. (4) *αι*, *οι*, *υι* denote genuine diphthongs. Not until the second century A.D. did *αι* generally become an open long *e* (*ē̦*), although in Boeotian this change had already taken place by the fourth century B.C. Confusions between *οι* and *υ* in the third century A.D. show the development of *οι* to a monophthong, presumably *ü*, and again the change is evidenced for Boeotian many centuries before. In the diphthong *υι* (= *üi*) the *υ* seems to have shared the modification of *υ* mentioned above. (5) *ᾱι*, *ωι*, *ηι* were long diphthongs. Before the Christian era their second element (*ι*) was lost in pronunciation although retained in educated spelling. The use of *iota subscript* is a late Byzantine device. (6) *αυ* and *ευ* remained genuine diphthongs throughout the ancient period. Their *υ*-element did not share the development of simple *υ* into *ü*.

(7) *Later developments.* In Modern Greek distinctions of quantity have disappeared save that the stressed vowel is longer than the unstressed. *ι*, *η*, *ει*, *υ*, *οι*, and *υι* have all the sound of a close *i* (*i̭*); *αυ* and *ευ* have become *av* (*αβ*) and *ev* (*εβ*) before voiced sounds, *af* (*αφ*) and *ef* (*εφ*) before unvoiced.

B. Consonants

(1) Like the corresponding sounds in English, *π*, *τ*, *κ* were voiceless and *β*, *δ*, *γ* voiced stops. (By 'stop' one means a consonant involving a momentarily complete stoppage of the expiration, by 'voice' the vibration of the vocal chords, and 'voiceless' indicates the absence of such vibration.) *φ*, *θ*, *χ* were voiceless aspirates approximately like *ph*, *th*, and *kh* in Eng. *top-hat*, *pot-hook*, *ink-horn* respectively. (2) *μ* is the labial, *ν* the dental nasal. The guttural nasal (= *ng*) is usually expressed by *γ* (as in *ἄγγελος*), which in this use is called by the ancient grammarians *agma*. *ρ* was a trilled *r* pronounced with the tip of the tongue against the gums and voiced like the *r* in Scottish *hard*, except in the initial position (*ῥ-*) and in some other positions, where it was voiceless. (3) *σ* (*s*) was a voiceless dental spirant like *s* in Eng. *past*, except before voiced consonants in the combinations *σβ*, *σδ*, *σγ*, *σμ*, where it became the voiced spirant (= Fr. *z*). The *spiritus asper* was like Eng. *h*, a slight rustle of breath heard before the beginning of the vowel-sound; its absence was denoted by the *spiritus lenis*. (4) *ξ* and *ψ* represented *ks* and *ps* respectively. For *ζ* there is strong evidence of a pronunciation *zd* in the older period. Etymological considerations (e.g. *ἐλπιδιω* > *ἐλπίζω*) suggest also *dz*. Probably both pronunciations were current at different times or in different dialects. Already in the fourth century B.C. in Attic *ζ* had developed into

the voiced spirant *z*. (5) The Ionic *-σσ-* and the *-ττ-* which takes its place in Attic and some other dialects offer special difficulty. In the period of the *Koine* these represented *-ss-* and *-tt-* respectively, but in the older period the evidence points to a more complex sound. One suggestion is that *-σσ-* represented *š* (= Eng. *sh*) and that *-ττ-* denoted *t͡p* (= Eng. *tth* in *not thin*). There are other views, however, and no final decision has been reached. (6) Even after the introduction of the Ionic alphabet, *ϝ* (digamma) continued in some dialects to represent *u̯* (Eng. *w*). This was a voiced sound, but a voiceless form of it (*FH*, i.e. digamma + Eng. *H*, perhaps like Scottish *wh*, i.e. *hw*) is found in some dialects.

(7) *Later developments.* By the fourth century A.D. *β* and *δ* had become voiced spirants = Eng. *v* and *th* (as in *then*) respectively. In Modern Greek *γ* before *ε*, *ι*, *υ* is like our *y*: before *α* and *o* it has become a voiced guttural spirant (a sound which English does not possess, although the Scottish *ch* is its voiceless equivalent). *φ*, *θ*, *χ* became early in the Christian era voiceless spirants like Eng. *f*, *th* (as in *thin*), *ch* (as in Scottish *loch*) respectively.

C. Accent

(1) The Greek accent, up to at least the beginning of the Christian era, was an accent of pitch. The accented syllable of a word differed from the others mainly because it was pronounced on a higher musical note, and not (as in English and many other languages) with greater expiratory force or stress. No doubt the higher musical note involved also some degree of greater stress, but the preservation of the quality and quantity of vowels and the absence of syncope make it clear that for the ancient period any stress element was secondary. On the other hand, early in the Christian era the musical accent was yielding place to an ever-increasing stress accent. The beginning of the process can be detected as early as the third century B.C., and the change becomes really marked about the fourth century A.D., when we find the choliambics of Babrius so constructed that the penultimate syllable of the line always has an accent. Modern Greek has a stress accent, usually on the syllable which formerly carried the musical accent.

(2) The terminology employed in references to the accent (which begin with Plato, *Cra.* 399) is clearly musical in character. The signs were invented by Alexandrian grammarians (probably by Aristophanes). The Acute (*προσῳδία ὀξεῖα*), for which the sign was ´, indicated a note which we are told (Dion. Hal. *Comp.* 11) was a musical fifth higher than the Grave ` (*προσῳδία βαρεῖα*) of the other syllables. The circumflex, which could stand only on long vowels or diphthongs, denoted a combination of the other two accents whereby the voice first rose and then fell. The sign ῀ and the name *προσῳδία περισπωμένη* (where the participle means 'drawn round') indicate this peculiarity. The Grave meant the absence on any syllable of Acute and Circumflex and, eventually, was left undenoted except in the special case where an Acute on the last syllable of a word before another word in the same sentence underwent a lowering of tone (e.g. *ὁ ἀγαθὸς ἀνήρ*). Papyri, however, show older methods of accentuation which placed a Grave on several syllables of a word (e.g. *μὴσάμὲνοὶ*, *φὶλὴσὶστέφανον*), or on the syllable immediately before an Acute or Circumflex, which were then left unexpressed (e.g. *ἐλθὲ*, *κρατὲρωι*).

(3) In the Indo-European language from which Greek was derived the accent was free: in other words, it might rest on any syllable of a word. In Greek this freedom was so restricted that in a polysyllabic word only one of the last three syllables might bear the accent, and the third last (Antepenult) only if the last was short. For the conditions governing the accentuation of these syllables, as well as the complication introduced by the close attachment in pronunciation of some words

(Enclitics and Proclitics) to others, a Greek grammar should be consulted.

F. Blass, *Ueber d. Aussprache d. Griechischen* (1888; Engl. Transl. W. J. Purton, 1890); E. V. Arnold and R. S. Conway, *The Restored Pronunciation of Greek and Latin* (1907); E. H. Sturtevant, *The Pronunciation of Greek and Latin*[2] (U.S.A. 1940); E. Schwyzer, *Griech. Grammatik* i (1934), 174–232; J. P. Postgate, *Short Guide to the Accentuation of Ancient Greek* (1924); J. Vendryes, *Traité d'accentuation grecque* (1904).   J. W. P.

PRONUNCIATION, LATIN. For the pronunciation of Latin various types of evidence are available. Besides the tradition of the schools (inaccurate in several respects) we have numerous phonetic descriptions by Latin grammarians which, though sometimes lacking in clarity, yield valuable information when interpreted by experts. Important evidence is also derived from the forms which Latin loan-words assume in foreign languages, and again from changes in orthodox spelling or departures from that spelling made by people of inferior education who attempted to write as they pronounced. In addition, we have certain evidence furnished by phonetic change within the Latin period and by the development or preservation of Latin sounds in the various Romance languages. It must be remembered that for many of the conclusions thus reached about the pronunciation of a 'dead' language only approximate accuracy can be claimed.

A. Vowels and Diphthongs

The vowels *a, e, i, o, u* may be either long or short. It is probable that *a*, long and short, had approximately the same quality as the *a* of Eng. *father*. Between the long and the short forms of each of the other vowels there was a difference of quality. Thus while ĕ was open (ę̆) like *e* in Eng. *met*, ē was close (ę̄) like *é* in Fr. *été*. ĭ was open (ĭ) like *i* in Eng. *fit*, while ī was close (ī) like *ee* in Eng. *feed*. Similarly ŏ was open (ǫ) like *o* in Eng. *not*, and ō close (ǭ) like *au* in Fr. *faute*. ŭ was approximately like the *u* of Eng. *full* and ū like the *oo* of *fool*. There was also a modified *u* (*ü*) resembling Fr. *u* and Germ. *ü*, which, as in *maximus, maxumus*, was written sometimes as *u*, sometimes as *i*. In educated pronunciation of the classical period *ae* was a diphthong, approximately like *ai* in German *Kaiser*; in Imperial times it became an open long *e* (ę̄). *oe* was also a diphthong (like *oy* in Eng. *boy*) in classical times, becoming later close *e* (ę̄). *au* was normally a diphthong like *ow* in Eng. *how* throughout the Latin period. Sporadically, however, in vulgar usage *au* got the sound of ō and in some words (e.g. *coda* for *cauda*) this seems to have been a very general pronunciation. The rare *eu* must have sounded approximately like *ew* in Eng. *new*. *ui* in *cui* and *huic* seems to have contained the vowel *u* followed in the same syllable by the sound of *i*.

B. Consonants

(1) The voiceless stops *p, t, c* (*k*) and the voiced stops *b, d, g* must have been approximately like the corresponding sounds in English. *c*, even before *e* and *i*, remained a stop during the classical period (i.e. *Cicero* was pronounced *Kikero*) and for long afterwards. Romance developments show that in the late Imperial period it had in this position undergone some degree of assibilation, thereby starting the process of change which led to the pronunciation of *c* in Fr. *cent* and Ital. *cento*. Similarly *g* remained a stop in all positions until about A.D. 500, when before *e* and *i* it developed into a *y*-sound. *b* between vowels became the spirant (bilabial) *v* fairly generally by the third century A.D. (2) *f* was originally a bilabial but later a labio-dental spirant like Eng. *f*. *s* was a voiceless sibilant (like the voiceless *s* in Eng. *past*) in all positions. In contact with voiced stops it caused them to become voiceless, so that a word like *urbs* was pronounced *urps*. (3) *h* was weakly articulated from an early period. Uneducated pronunciation tended to drop it, and in the later Empire was lost altogether. The reaction against the tendency to omit it caused sometimes an intrusive 'h' in the affected pronunciation of some people (e.g.

hinsidiae for *insidiae*). This habit is satirized in Catullus, 84. (4) *n* before a guttural became the guttural nasal ŋ (*ng*); and *g* in *-gn-* probably had the same pronunciation. Thus *anguis* would be pronounced *aŋguis*, and *dignus* *diŋnus*. Final *m* before an initial vowel in the following word had a reduced pronunciation, of which the exact nature is disputed. Even before initial consonants final *m* eventually weakened and, except in monosyllables, leaves no trace in Romance. (5) *r* was trilled, with the point of the tongue probably against the gum. There were two varieties of *l*, one palatal approximately like Eng. *l*, the other velar or guttural like *ll* in Eng. *all*. Palatal *l* occurred before another *l* and before *i*; *l* final and before *a, o, u* or a consonant (except another *l*) was velar. (6) i̯ (written *i*) and u̯ (written *u*) were semi-vowels = Eng. *y* and *w* respectively. By the third century A.D. this u̯ had become a spirant, either bilabial or labio-dental *v*, except in the combinations *qu, gu*, which continued to be pronounced as in English *queen* and *anguish*.

C. Accent

(1) *Early accent.* Many scholars hold that at a period before the beginning of literature the first syllable of every word carried a stress accent or, in other words, was pronounced with greater expiratory force than the remainder. This theory explains most easily the syncope which many Latin words had undergone (e.g. *quindecim* for *quínquedecem*) and the changes which had affected vowels (e.g. in compounds: *caedo* but *incīdo, cado* but *incĭdo*). Authorities on Plautine prosody tell us that even in Plautus' period words consisting of four short syllables were still accentuated in the old way (e.g. fắcĭlĭŭs instead of the classical *facilius*).

(2) *Accent of the Classical and later periods. (a) Position.* If the above theory is correct, a change must have taken place in the accentuation of polysyllabic words in the period before Plautus. Thereafter the position of the accent is regulated by the Penultimate Law, whereby if the penult is long by nature or position, the accent rests on it, but goes back to the antepenult if the penult is short (*confringo* but *cóncĭdo*). Apart from some exceptions like *illĭc* (for *illĭce*), where a final syllable has been lost, disyllabic words were accented on the first syllable.

(b) *Nature.* Descriptions by Latin writers suggest that during the classical period, and for several centuries afterwards, the language had a pitch accent whereby the accented syllable was pronounced on a higher musical note than the others. The terms employed (*accentus acutus, gravis, circumflexus*) are all translations of the Greek musical terminology, and there is no hint in the Latin accounts that the Latin accent differed in character from that of Greek. Not until the fourth century A.D. do we find in the grammarians phraseology which clearly implies the presence of a stress accent. The form assumed by Latin words in the Romance languages points unmistakably to the existence of a stress accent in the Late Latin period.

Scholars differ about the interpretation of these facts. Some accept the grammarians' accounts at their face value and believe that the classical accent was musical but gave way to a stress accent in the late period. Others hold that the accent throughout was one of stress and that the evidence of Latin writers is vitiated by an unscientific dependence on Greek theory. Some, again, adopt an intermediate position and believe that, while evidence in the language itself points to a stress accent having always been predominant, especially in the pronunciation of the lower classes, the influence of Greek education on the higher classes in the classical period had brought about a considerable degree of musical accent.

E. Seelmann, *Die Aussprache des Lateins* (1885); W. M. Lindsay, *The Latin Language* (1894), 13–147; Stolz–Schmalz, *Lateinische Grammatik*[5] (1926–8 revised, M. Leumann and J. B. Hofmann), 50–4; E. H. Sturtevant, *The Pronunciation of Greek and Latin*[2] (U.S.A. 1940).   J. W. P.

PROOEMIUM. (1) *Verse.* See HOMERIC HYMNS *and* LYRIC POETRY, GREEK.

(2) *Prose.* With the development of Attic oratory in the last quarter of the fifth century B.C. the custom arose of compiling collections of stock openings to forensic and political speeches (also of perorations, ἐπίλογοι). The first collection was made by Cephalus (Suidas, s.v.), others by Antiphon, Critias, and Thrasymachus. The extant set attributed to Demosthenes numbers fifty-six, five of which are identical with the openings of Dem. 1, 4, 14, 15, 16. Blass argues cogently for the authenticity of the set, often impugned, pointing out that the historical background, in the few places where it is defined, is everywhere that of the *first* war against Philip, a restriction only explicable on the supposition that D. himself wrote the prooemia between 349 and 346, for his own use when required (cf. Cicero's practice, *Att.* 16. 6. 4), with the exception that some, including those to 14–16 (354–350), were specially composed for particular speeches. Ephorus wrote a prooemium to each book of his history, in which practice he was followed by Diodorus (Diod. Sic. 16. 76. 5). The theory of the prooemium is discussed by Aristotle (*Rh.* 3. 14), Hermogenes (*Inv.* 1. 1–5, and Apsines (*Rhet.* ad init.).

R. Swoboda, *De Dem. quae feruntur prooemiis* (1887); F. Blass, *Die attische Beredsamkeit* iii. 1² (1893), 322–8; E. Stemplinger, *Das Plagiat in d. griech. Lit.* (1912), 223–7.   J. D. D.

PROPEMPTIKON (προπεμπτικόν), a composition wishing a friend a prosperous voyage.

I. GREEK. The earliest extant example is Sappho's χαίροις ἔρχεο κ.τ.λ. (*Berl. Klassikertexte* 5. 2. 12 f.). Others are Erinna (?) fr. 2, Theoc. 7. 52–70, and Callim. fr. 114. Parthenius wrote one. The genre is discussed by Menander (q.v. 4) Rhetor (Spengel, *Rhet.* 3. 395–9).   J. D. D.

II. LATIN. The first propemptikon known in Latin literature is Helvius Cinna's poem written in Bithynia in 56 B.C. and addressed to Asinius Pollio when he was starting on a journey to Greece. This was an imitation of Parthenius and so obscure that Hyginus wrote a commentary on it. Other poems of this genre are Tibullus 1. 3, Propertius 1. 17 and 2. 26, and Ovid, *Am.* 2. 11. But the first complete specimen that faithfully adheres to the rules laid down by rhetoric is Statius, *Silvae* 3. 2. Horace, however, in *Carm.* 1. 3, a poem addressed to Virgil when on his way to Athens, departs from the usual schema in that instead of laying imprecations on the first inventor of ships he loses himself in wonder at the daring of the first mariner.

F. Jäger, *Das antike Propemptikon*, 1913.   L. R. P.

PROPERTIUS, SEXTUS (wrongly styled *Sextus Aurelius Nauta* in some MSS.), born between 54 and 48 B.C., probably at Assisi (4. 1. 121–6 *Asis*; Plin. *Ep.* 6. 15; 9. 22), though claims have been made by other Umbrian towns. His father was an *eques* and died while the poet was a boy; soon after his property was reduced by distribution of lands among veterans of Antony and Octavian (41–40); love and poetry claimed him early (4. 1. 127–34; 3. 15. 3–6). Beyond this little is known save the story of his love for Cynthia, a lady of easy virtue whose true name was Hostia (Apul. *Apol.* 10). The course of his love did not run smooth; he idealized her at first; but she was faithless and after five or six years (perhaps 29–24 B.C.) he broke with her (1. 1; 3. 24). Whether the breach was permanent is uncertain; later (4. 8) he describes a quarrel with her and again (4. 7) tells us of her death; both poems are probably retrospective. He may even have married; for Passennus Paulus, the poet-friend of Pliny, claimed to be descended from him (Plin. ll. cc.). Maecenas was his patron (2. 1 and 3. 9); if the poet who claims to be a second Callimachus (Hor. *Epist.* 2. 2. 100; cf. Prop. 4. 1. 64) was Propertius, he knew Horace and was disliked by him. Ovid was his

friend (*Tr.* 4. 10. 45); this reference (A.D. 2) to him shows that he was no longer alive; as the latest date assignable to any poem of Propertius is 16 B.C. (4. 11), his death must fall between those two dates.

2. WORKS. Four Books of Elegies survive (the division into five books found in some texts is without authority); they may be dated (precariously): bk. 1 (33–28 B.C.); bk. 2 (28–25); bk. 3 (24–22); bk. 4 (21–16). The first (known in antiquity as the *Cynthia Monobiblos* (Mart. 14. 189)) deals almost entirely with love, his own or others', and has a freshness and charm which is all its own. Books 2 and 3 are likewise mainly concerned with his love. But the first ecstasy is gone; neither he nor Cynthia is faithful; quarrels ensue to close in a brusque and violent renunciation (3. 24). But elements of another type begin to intrude; cf. the two elegies addressed to Maecenas (2. 1; 3. 9) and those in praise of Augustus (2. 10; 3. 4) together with poems on his own art (3. 1, 2, 3, 5, and esp. 2. 34 which closes with a fine panegyric of Virgil). To these must be added letters to friends (3. 12 and 22), general reflections on the wickedness of womankind, illustrated from myth and history, and two laments —for Paetus drowned and for the 'young Marcellus' (3. 7 and 18). In bk. 4 we find ourselves in a new world. Two poems only are directly concerned with Cynthia (7 and 8), the former tragic and deeply moving, the latter humorous. Of the remainder one (5) is a cynical *Ars Amoris*; one (3) is a letter from a wife to her husband at the wars, and another—his noblest work—an epitaph for the tomb of a noble Roman Lady (11). The remainder are, in the Alexandrian manner, poems on the origin of Roman cults (Vertumnus (2), Tarpeia (4), the anniversary of Actium (6), the Ara Maxima (9), and Jupiter Feretrius (10), all introduced by an obscure preface (1) in the form of a dialogue between the poet and an astrologer).

3. Propertius is not a flawless poet, and few of his poems are of sustained excellence. But they reveal a living, if not always an attractive, personality, and have many moments of real greatness. And this gift of exaltation is enhanced by his mastery of the metre, which in his hands has a weight, a force, and majesty which is unique in Latin. 'Sunt qui Propertium malint', said Quintilian (10. 1. 93) of Roman Elegists: and the same is true to-day. As his passion fades, his poetic ideals change, and he begins to claim Philetas and Callimachus as his masters— not in erotic verse, but in narrative coloured with mythological learning, finding their full expression in the legends of bk. 4, inspired by the *Aitia* of Callimachus. His later work has a harder and more mannered brilliance; but loss of freshness in feeling and colour is compensated by increased strength, incisiveness, and (cf. 3. 7; 4. 7 and 11) imagination as well. His metrical technique also changes; in bk. 1, three-, four-, or five-syllable endings to the pentameter are frequent (39 per cent.); in bk. 2 they drop to 14 per cent., in bk. 3 to 4 per cent., and in bk. 4 to 2 per cent. But there is no loss of beauty or of power. *See also* ELEGIAC POETRY, ALEXANDRIANISM.

4. The text of the poems presents a difficult problem— thought is often obscure and transitions violent. That lines have been lost or at times displaced is almost certain. But it is hard to justify wholesale transposition, and the attempts that have been made in this direction are not encouraging; nor has any satisfactory theory for such wholesale dislocation been forthcoming.

TEXTS: E. Baehrens (1880); A. Palmer (1880); J. P. Postgate, *Corp. Poet.* (1894); J. S. Phillimore (1901); C. Hosius, ed. 3 (1932); O. L. Richmond (1926).
COMMENTARIES: K. Lachmann (1816); P. J. Enk (1911); M. Rothstein, i² (1920), ii² (1924); H. E. Butler and E. A. Barber (1933). *Selections:* J. P. Postgate (1905).
TRANSLATIONS: J. S. Phillimore (1906); H. E. Butler (1912).
STUDIES: In addition to prefaces to editions (above): MSS., A. E. Housman, *Journ. Phil.* xxi (1893), 101–97; xxii (1894), 84– 128; O. L. Richmond, *Journ. Phil.* xxxi (1910), 162–96; B. L. Ullman, *CPhil.* (1911), 282–301.   H. E. B.

PROPHECIES (χρησμοί, *vaticinia*). Besides the oracles of the greater and lesser shrines, there were in circulation in antiquity a number of prophecies, sometimes nameless, often attached to the name of some inspired person. Of these, the most famous was the Sibyl, or the Sibyls (q.v.); but in addition, there were several men, some known to have lived during the historical period. Herodotus (1. 62. 4) mentions Amphilytus, a contemporary of Pisistratus, tyrant of Athens, and preserves the text of an oracle which he was suddenly inspired to give the latter. Such persons were known as χρησμῳδοί in Greek (e.g. [Plato], *Theages*, 124 d) or χρησμολόγοι; in Latin, *vates*; for a list of them, with some account of their lives or legends, see Bouché–Leclercq, *Histoire de la divination* ii, ch. 2. Naturally, their alleged utterances were particularly rife in times of stress; cf. Thucydides 2. 8. 2, who speaks both of oracular sayings (λόγια) quoted and χρησμολόγοι 'singing' their prophecies at the outbreak of the Peloponnesian War. In 2. 54. 2 he quotes the text of one nameless utterance, ἥξει Δωριακὸς πόλεμος καὶ λοιμὸς (or λιμὸς) ἅμ' αὐτῷ. This craze is a favourite subject for Aristophanes' mockery, particularly in the *Knights*; an especial butt is a certain Bacis (q.v.), whose oracles were extremely popular.

The most celebrated Italian *vates* was perhaps a certain Marcius, or a pair of brothers, the Marcii, for whom see Cicero, *Div.* 1. 115; 2. 113, with Pease's notes; Cicero also mentions one Publicius. Here again, such effusions were multiplied in times of crisis; Augustus collected and destroyed a number of unauthorized collections (Suetonius, *Aug.* 31), many of them in Latin, no doubt in large measure a legacy of the Civil Wars. H. J. R.

PROPHETES (προφήτης), the title of the mortal who speaks in the name of a god or interprets his will. It is properly used only of seers and functionaries attached to an established oracular shrine; the unattached seer is called *mantis*, etc. (*see* PROPHECIES). Moreover, it is more often used of the officials who interpreted signs at non-inspirational oracles or the cries of the god's medium at inspirational oracles than of the actual receivers of mantic inspiration. At Claros the prophet remained the direct mouthpiece of the god; but at Delphi and Didyma a woman who could be described as *prophetis* (προφῆτις) was directly inspired by Apollo. She was assisted by the male prophet, who interpreted her incoherent remarks and reduced them to an intelligible response. At Didyma the prophet was an annually elected magistrate. At Delphi the title was not used officially; the two magistrates, elected for life, who performed this office had the title of priest (ἱερεύς).

For further information and for bibliography *see* ORACLES; also E. Fascher, *ΠΡΟΦΗΤΗΣ* (1927). J. E. F.

PROPYLAEA, a monumental roofed gateway; but pre-eminently one of the most renowned buildings of antiquity, that on the west side of the Athenian Acropolis (q.v.) designed by Mnesicles (q.v.), built of Pentelic marble, with some steps of black Eleusis stone, *c.* 435 B.C. and still largely intact. The plan, with its deep 'hall', its Doric hexastyle porticoes fronting outwards and inwards, and with its single division-wall pierced by five doorways, is of early origin (cf. the 'South Propylaeum' at Cnossos); but Mnesicles provided wing-buildings of lesser height (the south one being curtailed) projecting from the front, forming loggias with Doric columns and rooms beyond. Larger wing-buildings to the east were intended. An inclined ramp continuing the slope of the natural rock formed the approach, and there were five steps at the doorways. The central avenue had a span of nearly 14 ft. and was flanked by Ionic colonnades; the ceilings were formed of marble beams

and of slabs with deeply hollowed square coffers, richly decorated in blue and gold. The room of the north wing was adorned with wall-paintings by Polygnotus.

Anderson, Spiers, and Dinsmoor, op. cit. under ARCHITECTURE, p. 133. T. F.

PROROGATIO. As early as the Samnite Wars (Livy 8. 23) the Romans realized the disadvantages inherent in their system of annual magistracies, and adopted the practice of retaining the services of magistrates after their period of office had expired. The activities of such men were confined to the *provincia* (q.v.) to which they had been appointed. At first a vote of the people was required for these extensions, but before long the Senate secured the power of prorogation (Polybius 6. 13). Flamininus (*cos.* 198 B.C.) retained his *imperium* till 194 and L. Lucullus (*cos.* 74) till 66. *Prorogatio* became the rule rather than the exception with the growth of the Empire. The practice of *prorogatio imperii* created the *proconsulare imperium* (*see* PRO CONSULE).

G. H. Stevenson, *Roman Provincial Administration* (1939), 55 ff. G. H. S.

PROSCRIPTIO. (*a*) A notice of sale of a debtor's property. (*b*) The publication of a list of persons who were declared outlaws and whose property was confiscated. This method was used by Sulla (82–81 B.C.) and by Antony, Lepidus, and Octavian (43–42) to rid themselves of their political and personal enemies. Rewards were offered for the execution of the proscribed, and in the former case their sons and grandsons were excluded from political office.

Ancient sources: Velleius 2. 28 and 66–7; Plutarch, *Sulla* 31 f., *Cicero* 46 f. and *Antony* 20; Appian, *BCiv.* 1. 95 and 4. 5 ff.; Dio Cassius, fr. 109 and 47. 3 ff. Modern Literature: H. Kloevekorn, *De proscriptionibus ann. 43 a. C.* (1891); Drumann–Groebe, *Gesch. Roms* i. 265 ff. and 470 ff., ii. 399 ff.; T. Rice Holmes, *Roman Republic* i (1923), 59–60; *Architect of the Roman Empire* i (1928), 72 ff. G. W. R.

PROSE-RHYTHM. By prose-rhythm we mean here the quantitative or accentual arrangement of syllables, articulating the sentence and defining its close. We exclude from discussion: rhythm in general (E. A. Sonnenschein, *What is Rhythm?* (1925); De Groot, *Der Rhythmus*); correspondence of sound and sense (Norden, *Die antike Kunstprosa*[2]); Gorgianic figures. For rhythm emphasized by rhyme *see* ASSONANCE. For *Hiatus in Greek Prose* see s.v.

2. *Ancient theory.* From Thrasymachus onwards, prose-rhythm (ῥυθμός, *numerus*) was a recognized branch of rhetoric. Our chief authorities are Aristotle, Demetrius, Dionysius, Cicero, Caesius Bassus, Quintilian. They are generally agreed that prose-rhythm should be distinct from verse-rhythm, varied, and not too obvious. Cicero adds that sentence-endings (*clausulae*) are rhythmically most important, though the rest of the sentence is not to be neglected. According to him, the last syllable of a clausula is *anceps*; Quintilian disagrees.

3. Extant Greek theory gives few precise details. Aristotle recommends $-\cup\cup\cup$ as an opening rhythm, $\cup\cup\cup-$ as a clausula (he perhaps has Plato in mind; in the *Ethics* $-\cup\cup\underline{\cup}$ is sought as a clausula and $\cup\cup\cup\cup$ somewhat avoided). Demetrius and Dionysius are vague, and neglect important contrasts of rhythm in the authors they quote.

4. Latin theorists confuse matters by borrowing from Greek theorists without regard to differences of language. Cicero (whose sources include Aristotle's *Rhetoric* and lost works of Ephorus, Theophrastus, Theodectes, Hieronymus of Rhodes) apparently recommends the clausulae $-\cup\cup-\underline{\cup}$, $-\cup\cup-\cup\underline{\cup}$, $\cup\cup\cup\underline{\cup}$, all of which he strongly avoids in practice. However, he also recommends certain of his favourite forms, e.g. $-\cup--\underline{\cup}$, $-\cup--\cup\underline{\cup}$, $-\cup-\underline{\cup}$, $-\cup\cup\cup-\underline{\cup}$. (See, further, Laurand,

Études; and *CQ* xxv. 18.) Bassus recommends several Ciceronian clausulae (e.g. – ∪ – ⏒ and its five 'resolutions') together with forms usually avoided. Quintilian prefers – ∪ – – to – ∪ – ∪. Diomedes (4th c. A.D.) is the first theorist to recommend expressly the quite common clausula – – – – ∪ ⏒.

5. *Modern research.* To establish the rhythms—clausulae especially—favoured by particular authors, modern scholars have used statistical methods. De Groot has shown that statistics must be *comparative*; since in the structure of any language some rhythms are commoner than others, preference for a clausula is shown, not by its absolute frequency, but by its frequency relative to 'unrhythmical' prose. Cicero's clausula – ∪ ∪ ∪ – ⏒ has a low absolute frequency (4·7 per cent.); but it has a high relative frequency, for it is about twice as common in Cicero as in unrhythmical prose (2·4 per cent.). A supplement to this external comparison is the internal comparison of sentence-rhythm and clausula-rhythm in the same author (De Groot, Skimina, Novotný, Broadhead; and Zielinski in his later work).

6. *Greek quantitative prose.* The rhythms of the Ionians—Heraclitus, Pherecydes, Herodotus—are reminiscent of epic. Hexameter openings and endings are common (ἁρμονίη ἀφανὴς φανερῆς κρείττων, Heraclit.; οὖτω μὲν Πέρσαι λέγουσι γενέσθαι, Hdt.). There is no distinct clausula.

7. Thrasymachus perhaps initiated a prose-rhythm differing from verse-rhythm; he was certainly regarded as an innovator (Cic. *Orat.* 39. 175), especially in his use of paeonic rhythm (Arist. *Rh.* 3. 1409ᵃ1). We are not told if he cultivated a distinct clausula, and his one short continuous fragment is inconclusive (twelve sentence-endings, of which five are – ∪ – ⏒ and one ∪ ∪ ∪ –). Gorgias resembles earlier writers in the verse-rhythms of the sentence, but he has a distinct clausula (– ∪ – – ⏒ in *Hel.*, – ∪ – ⏒ in *Pal.*).

8. Thucydides is proved by De Groot to be an almost 'unrhythmical' writer, i.e. to depart very little from the natural rhythms of the language. However, he shows some preference for the clausulae – ∪ ∪ – – ⏒ and ∪ ∪ ∪ ⏒.

9. The sentence-rhythm of Isocrates is too varied for analysis; he seeks as clausulae most forms with a long penultimate (– ∪ ∪ ∪ – ⏒, – ∪ ∪ – ⏒, – ∪ – ⏒, – ∪ – – ⏒; not – ∪ ∪ – – ⏒); is indifferent to – – – ⏒; favours final words of four syllables (as does Hyperides).

10. Demosthenes is concerned more with sentence-rhythm than with clausula-rhythm. His only well-defined clausula is – ∪ – ⏒. The rhythms – ∪ – – ∪ ⏒, – ∪ ∪ – ∪ ⏒, – ∪ ∪ – ⏒ occur often at the clausula, but oftener throughout the sentence. He avoids series of six or more long syllables. But his most characteristic practice is the avoidance everywhere of series of three or more short syllables ('Blass's Law'). Exceptions to this rule average 5 in 100 lines of D. (contrast Lysias, 23; Isocrates, 25; Aeschines, 21; Hyperides, 28). His technique here is of word-order rather than word-choice; his exceptions may perhaps be deliberate. Thus, though he continually uses πρότερον without breaking his rule, he has no scruples in 9. 60, 61. He once uses διαγίγνομαι with participle (23. 179, in a form which gives five shorts); but he does not substitute ἐπιβουλεύων διαγίγνεται for ἐπ. διατελεῖ (19. 326).

11. Plato's rhythmical preferences show considerable evolution. Throughout his work he favours the clausulae – ∪ – ∪ ⏒, – – – – ∪ ⏒, – ∪ ∪ – ∪ ⏒, and somewhat avoids – ∪ – – ⏒. In the earlier books of the *Republic* he seeks – ∪ – ⏒, – ∪ – ∪ ⏒, – ∪ – ∪ ∪ ⏒; is indifferent to – – – ⏒; avoids ∪ ∪ ∪ ⏒ and – ∪ ∪ ∪ – ⏒. In the *Laws* he seeks ∪ ∪ ∪ ⏒ and – ∪ ∪ ∪ – ⏒, avoiding – ∪ – ⏒ and increasing his avoidance of – ∪ ∪ – ⏒ (*Resp.* 7·0 per cent.; *Leg.* 1·3 per cent., probably the lowest figure in Greek). In the sentence his later work shows increasing

preference for series of short syllables, and he then writes κάθαπερ, μέχριπερ, τινα τρόπον for ὥσπερ, ἕωσπερ, τρόπον τινά. His average percentages of exceptions to 'Blass's Law' are: *Cri.*, 18; *Euthphr.* and *Chrm.*, 24; *Resp.* bks. 2–9, 25; *Resp.* bk. 1, 29; *Symp.*, 30; *Soph.*, 36; *Ti.*, 46; *Leg.* bk. 12, 56 (Vogel's statistics). His later preference for the clausula ∪ ∪ ∪ ⏒ is in accord with this; but he does not abandon – – – – ∪ ⏒, and his avoidance of – – – ⏒ is never very marked. The dactylo-trochaic rhythms of *Phdr.* are exceptional in his practice. Lucian's clausulae suggest imitation of Plato.

12. The rhythmical practice of other writers is summarized below. Clausulae alone are considered, and only well-marked preference or avoidance recorded.

∪ ∪ ∪ ⏒ Sought by Philo, Plutarch, Chariton, Xenophon Ephesius, Josephus; avoided by Lysias, Aeschines. – ∪ ∪ – ∪ ⏒ Sought by Lys., Alcidamas, Hyperides, Ph., Charit., Xen. Eph., Joseph. – ∪ – ⏒ Sought by Lys., Antisthenes (59·5 per cent.), Alcid., Isaeus, Xenophon, Hyp., Antiochus Rex, Ph., Plut., Charit. – ∪ – – ∪ ⏒ Sought by Lys., Alcid., Isae., Aeschin., Antioch. R., Ph., Charit., Xen. Eph. – ∪ – – ⏒ Sought by Alcid., Antioch. R., Ph., Charit., Joseph. – ∪ ∪ ∪ – ⏒ Sought by Alcid., Antioch. R., Ph., Plut.; avoided by Lys., Aeschin. – – – – ∪ ⏒ Sought by Lys., Aeschin., Isae., Antioch. R., Ph., Charit., Xen. Eph.; avoided by Alcid., Plut. – – – ⏒ Avoided by Antisth., Ph., Plut., Charit., Xen. Eph., Joseph. – ∪ ∪ – ⏒ Sought by Xen.; avoided by Lys., Antisth., Aeschin., Hyp., Ph., Plut., Charit., Xen. Eph., Joseph.

13. *Observations.* Antisth., Plato, Hyp., perhaps others, prefer a long final in certain clausulae. Though classical writers on the whole seek rhythms distinct from verse, a good deal of verse-rhythm remains in Isocrates and Demosthenes; few writers altogether escape iambic sequences (R. A. Pope counts fourteen perfect trimeters in Aeschines). King Antiochus, Philo, Plutarch, and the novelists belong to a Hellenistic school which replaced the variety of classical writers with a small canon of sought and avoided clausulae. Hegesias, an earlier representative of the same school, probably influenced Cicero and his followers. To this period belongs the preference for – ∪ – or – ∪ ∪ before – ∪ – ⏒, as also the general strong avoidance of – – – ⏒ and – ∪ ∪ – ⏒ as clausulae. (Among classical writers – – – ⏒ is little avoided; – ∪ ∪ – ⏒ is sought by Isocrates and Xenophon, and allowed by Demosthenes.)

14. *Greek accentual prose.* The origin of the Greek accentual clausula (*cursus*) is still uncertain. There are traces of it in the orator Menander (q.v. 4); it appears fully in Himerius, Procopius, S. Basil, and Byzantine writers generally. The forms most commonly sought have 2 or 4 unaccented syllables between the last two accents: ´~ ~ ´ ~, ´ ~ ~ ~ ´ ~, ´ ~ ~ ~ ~ ´ ~, ´ ~ ~ ~ ~ ´ ~ ~. Forms with no syllable between (χρηστὸς ἄνθρωπος) are sought by Procop.; those with 1, by Men. Rh., Him., Procop.; those with 3 or 5 are universally avoided. For details, see Skimina, De Groot.

15. *Latin quantitative prose.* Some fragments of C. Gracchus (cf. Cic. *De Or.* 3. 214, Gellius 11. 13) show the earliest traces of quantitative rhythms. Pre-Ciceronian orators (Metellus, Crassus, Titinius, Carbo) seek the clausulae – ∪ – – ⏒, – ∪ – ∪ ∪ ⏒, – ∪ – – ⏒, – ∪ – ⏒. *Auctor ad Herennium* seeks most Ciceronian forms except – ∪ ∪ ∪ – ⏒, – – – – ∪ ⏒.

16. *Cicero* throughout the sentence avoids series of choriambs and dactyls. He has a well-marked system of sought and avoided clausulae. The following are sought as sentence-endings: – ∪ – – ⏒ and its 'resolutions' ∪ ∪ ∪ – – ⏒, – ∪ ∪ ∪ – ⏒, – ∪ – ∪ ∪ ⏒, ∪ ∪ ∪ ∪ – ⏒, ∪ ∪ ∪ – – ⏒, – ∪ ∪ – ∪ ⏒, – ∪ – ∪ ∪ ⏒, – ∪ – ⏒, often preceded by – – –, – ∪ –, or – ∪ ∪. Commonly avoided, but used for special effects, is – – – ⏒; strongly avoided are – ∪ ∪ – ⏒, ∪ ∪ ∪ ⏒, – – ∪ ∪ ⏒,

−∪−∪−⌣, −∪∪−−⌣. The preferred clausulae reappear at the end of cola and commata, but with more
exceptions; −−−⌣ is commoner there, and −∪∪−⌣
less strictly avoided. The variations in C.'s practice
belong to subject-matter rather than chronology (see
Laurand); but there is a gradual diminution of the
'Asiatic' clausula −∪−⌣. C. shows in the clausula some
desire for coincidence of accent and ictus. For ⌐∪−⌐⌣
there is a coincidence of 60·5 per cent. in C. as against
54 in unrhythmical prose and 51 in Livy: for ⌐∪−⌐∪−,
63·5 as against 49·5 and 40; for ⌐−−⌐∪⌣, 35 as against
31·5 and 29. Broadhead and Zielinski exaggerate the
influence of accent.

17. We may here group together as a Ciceronian
school: Caesar, Nepos, Seneca, Suetonius, Quintilian,
the younger Pliny, Apuleius, Tertullian. Their clausulae
are in general Ciceronian, except that −−−−∪⌣ is
avoided by most of them, and that −−−⌣ is tolerated by
Caesar and Nepos. −∪∪∪−⌣ is avoided by Sen. and
Tert., and −∪−⌣ by Sen.

18. Opposed to Cicero's practice are Brutus ('Attic
school'), Sallust, Livy. They seek −∪−−∪⌣, but avoid
−∪−⌣, −∪−−⌣, −∪∪∪−⌣; and they tolerate or
seek −∪∪−⌣, −−∪∪⌣, −∪∪−⌣, and −−−⌣ (Livy
36·5 per cent.). Tacitus in his early work is fairly
Ciceronian, but always avoids −∪∪∪−⌣. In his mature
work he is indifferent to most clausulae, only favouring
somewhat −∪−−⌣ and −∪−−∪⌣.

19. The 'Greek' clausulae ∪∪∪⌣, −∪∪−∪⌣ have
little currency in Latin; but ∪∪∪⌣ seems to be sought
by Sallust (Cat.), Brutus, Pomponius Mela, Apuleius
(Met.), −∪∪−∪⌣ by Sallust (Jug.), Brutus, Mela,
Apuleius (Apol. Flor., Met.).

20. *Latin accentual prose.* There is a transitional
period when clausulae remain quantitative, but are
gradually restricted to forms where (a) accent and ictus
coincide, (b) there are 2 or 4 unaccented syllables between
the last two accents. Thus *ésse debétis, ésse confíteor*
are retained, but (núm)*quam relìquísset, dgere debétis* are
avoided. Alone among '3-forms', *ésse videátur* keeps a
certain prestige, but diminishes. The form *gladio pete-
batur* passes as a combination of quantitative −∪−−⌣
and accentual ∻ ~ ~ ~ ~ ∻ ~. These tendencies may be
observed in the choice of clausulae recommended by
Sacerdos (3rd c.; see Nicolau's commentary) and in the
detailed studies of Cyprian–Jerome, Arnobius, Faustus
by P. C. Knook, H. Hagendahl, A. G. Elg. For coincidence of ictus and accent compare these percentages
with Cicero's: ⌐∪−⌐−, Augustine 78, Arnobius 95,
Leo 93. ⌐∪−⌐∪⌣, Augustine 73·5, Arnobius 95·3,
Leo 99·5. Much material of this period has yet to be
investigated, and unless the works examined are of some
length the evidence is apt to be inconclusive; thus it is
perhaps impossible to decide whether the rhythms of
Niceta's *Te Deum* are purely quantitative or not.

21. In the Middle Ages quantity is neglected, and
favoured rhythms are practically reduced to the three
accentual cursus-forms: ∻ ~ ~ ∻ ~ (*planus*), ∻ ~ ~ ∻ ~ ~
(*tardus*), ∻ ~ ~ ~ ~ ∻ ~ (*velox*)—which are used, e.g.,
by Gregory of Tours, Bernard of Clairvaux, Héloïse,
Dante.

22. *Applications.* Study of prose-rhythm has been
useful in some questions of chronology (Plato) and
authenticity (for Plutarch's Συγκρίσεις, against *Consolatio ad Apollonium*). In textual criticism rhythmical
criteria may help to distinguish between manuscript
variants and to reject mistaken emendations. Original
emendation should be very cautious, taking into account
not only a writer's preferences but also his margin of
exceptions. In *Somnium Scipionis* 12, it is simple to
change 'ingeniique tui consiliique' to 'ingenique tui
consilique'; it would be rash to change πρὸς ἐμέ to πρός
με everywhere in Demosthenes, setting 'Blass's Law'
above normal usage.

BIBLIOGRAPHY

H. Bornecque, *Les Clausules métriques latines* (1907, fullest collec-
tion of Lat. theory). H. D. Broadhead, *Latin Prose Rhythm* (1922,
Cicero only). A. C. Clark, *Fontes prosae numerosae* (1909, select
theory and texts, Gk.-Lat.). A. W. de Groot, *Handbook of antique
Prose-Rhythm* (Groningen, 1919, chiefly Gk.); *Der antike Prosarhyth-
mus* (1921, Gk.-Lat.); *La Prose métrique des anciens* (1926, Gk.-Lat.).
L. Laurand, *Études sur le style des discours de Cicéron* ii⁴ (1938);
Pour mieux comprendre l'antiquité classique (1936, Lat. cursus).
M. G. Nicolau, *L'Origine du 'cursus' rythmique en latin* (1930, also
discusses methods). F. Novotný, *Eurhythmie* i (1918, fullest collection of Gk. theory; Czech commentary); *État actuel des études sur
le rythme de la prose latine* (1929). W. H. Shewring, *CQ* xxiv. 164,
xxv. 12 (Gk.-Lat.; criticized by Broadhead, *CQ* xxvi. 35, defended
by S. xxvii. 46). S. Skimina, *État actuel des études sur le rythme de la
prose grecque* i (1930, quantitative prose), ii (1930, accentual).
T. Zieliński, *Der constructive Rhythmus in Ciceros Reden* (1914).
Full bibliographies by Laurand: for Gk., *Musée Belge* xxv. 133–8
and *Études classiques* iv. 237–8; for Lat., *Rev. Ét. Lat.* vi. 73–90 and
xii. 419–23.
              W. H. S.

PROSERPINA, *see* PERSEPHONE.

PROSODIAC, *see* METRE GREEK, III (6).

PROSTITUTION, SACRED, existed in two main
forms. (1) The defloration of virgins before marriage
was originally a threshold rite, whereby the dangerous
task of having intercourse with a virgin was delegated
to a foreigner, since intercourse was in many, if not all,
cases limited to strangers. The custom was observed at
Babylon (Hdt. 1. 199) and at Heliopolis-Baalbek (Sozom.
Hist. Eccles. 5, 10; Socrates, *Hist. Eccles.* 1, 18, 48); in
Cyprus (Hdt. l.c.; Just. *Epit.* 18. 5), in Lydia (Hdt. 1. 93;
Ael. *VH* 4. 1), and at Sicca Veneria in Numidia (Val.
Max. 2. 6. 15) girls are said thus to have earned dowries.
In Acilisene well-born maidens were dedicated to Anaitis
as prostitutes for considerable periods (Strabo 532–3),
thus constituting a half-way step to (2) regular temple
prostitution, generally of slaves, such as existed in
Babylonia, in the cult of Ma at Comana Pontica (Strabo
559), of Aphrodite at Corinth (Strabo 378; Athen. 573),
and perhaps at Eryx (Strabo 272; Diod. 4. 83), and in
Egypt (*PTeb.* 6).

Nilsson would derive all sacred prostitution from the
first type, which, he further claims, was originally non-
religious, but readily became attached to fertility cults.
It might then develop into type 2, or as at Byblus in the
cult of Adonis (Lucian, *Syr. D.* 6), where, though the
original purpose had been lost, the 'market' was still
open only to strangers. The (unfulfilled) vow of the
citizens of Locri Epizephyrii to prostitute their virgins
(Just. *Epit.* 21. 3), unique in Greek annals, was a desperate
measure to secure divine aid in war. The hereditary
παλλακαί at Tralles were concubines, and perhaps
prophetesses, of the god, not temple prostitutes. The
evidence for Thebes in Egypt (Hdt. 1. 182; Str. 816) is
contradictory.

F. Cumont, *Rel. Or.*⁴ 258–9; L. R. Farnell, *Greece and Babylon*
(1911), 268–82; M. P. Nilsson, *Griechische Feste* (1906), 365–7.
Tralles: K. Latte, *Harv. Theol. Rev.* 1940; L. Robert, *Études
anatoliennes* (1937), 406–7. *See* ANAHITA, HIERODOULOI, MYLITTA.
              F. R. W.

PROTAGORAS of Abdera, one of the earliest and
most successful of the Sophists. His date is uncertain
but his birth cannot be placed much later than 485 B.C.,
and was probably earlier, while he was about seventy
years old at the time of his death. During forty of these
he practised the profession of Sophist with great success,
probably mainly at Athens. He claimed to teach 'virtue'
(ἀρετή), which can perhaps be better expressed as
efficiency in the conduct of life. He was evidently a man
of high character and generally respected. When
Thurii was founded by the Athenians in 444, he was
appointed to draw up a code of laws for the new colony.
The well-known story of his trial and condemnation at
Athens is inconsistent with the statements of Plato and
may probably be dismissed as an invention or error of
later writers.

His chief significance in the history of thought rests on the doctrine expressed in his well-known dictum 'Man is the measure of all things'. There can be little doubt that this was generally understood in antiquity as being a doctrine of the relativity of all knowledge or opinion to each particular person, and that it involved a complete scepticism about the claims of any science to universal validity. He also adopted an agnostic attitude towards belief in the gods. He does not, however, seem to have extended this scepticism to the claims of morality. Here he apparently adopted conventional moral ideas without much question, and advocated respect by each man for the moral code of his particular community.

Testimonia and Frs. in H. Diels, *Vorsokr.*[5] ii. 253–71. Histories of Ancient Philosophy, Zeller, i. 2[6]. 1296–1304; T. Gomperz, *Griechische Denker* (Engl. Transl. i. 438–75); L. Robin, *La Pensée grecque* (1923, Engl. Transl. 141–7); J. Burnet, *From Thales to Plato* (1914), ch. 7. G. C. F.

PROTESILAUS, in mythology, commander of the contingent before Troy from Phylace and other places in Thessaly. He was killed in landing by one of the defenders (*Iliad* 2. 695 ff.). Homer also states that 'his wife was left mourning and his house half-finished'. From this it is a natural conclusion that he was newly married, whence a touching legend developed, preserved almost solely in Latin authors (Catullus 68. 73 ff.; Ovid, *Her.* 13; Hyginus, *Fab.* 103 f.). Protesilaus had offended the gods by not sacrificing before he began his house (Catullus); or he knew that the first man ashore was fated to be killed and patriotically took it upon himself to fall (Hyginus). His wife Laodameia grieved so for his loss that the gods granted her prayer to see him again for three hours. At the end of that time she killed herself (Eustathius on the *Iliad*, p. 325, 23 ff., who makes Protesilaus the prime mover throughout, because owing to Aphrodite's anger he desired his wife even after his death); or she spent so much time with an image of him that her father Acastus burned it and she flung herself on the fire (Hyginus 114, cf. Ovid 151 ff.). The author and date of this legend are unknown.

For his cult see Farnell, *Hero-Cults*, p. 412, note 102. H. J. R.

PROTEUS (Πρωτεύς), a minor sea-god, herdsman of the flocks of the sea, seals, etc. In Homer (*Od.* 4. 385 ff.) he is an Egyptian daimon, servant of Poseidon, who has the power to take all manner of shapes, but if held till he resumes the true one, will answer questions. Virgil (*G.* 4. 387 ff.) imitates this. But in Euripides, *Helena* 4, Herodotus 2. 112 ff., he is a virtuous king of Egypt, who takes Helen (q.v.) and her wealth from Paris and keeps them safe till at length Menelaus arrives and claims them. The relation of this to Stesichorus' palinode is not clear. H. J. R.

PROTOGENES (late 4th c. B.C.), painter and sculptor, of Caunus; connected by anecdotes with Apelles, Aristotle, Demetrius Poliorcetes. His pictures included 'Ialysus', 'Resting Satyr', 'Alexander and Pan', 'Paralus and Hammonias' (allegories of the Athenian State galleys), portraits of Aristotle's mother, Antigonus, and Philiscus. He wrote two books on painting. His works showed excessive elaboration, but according to Apelles lacked charm (χάρις). T. B. L. W.

PROTREPTICUS, exhortation (to philosophy). The prose-form of the Greco-Roman *protrepticus* was based on the *protrepticus* to rhetorical and political education which the Sophists had first brought forward. The sophistic form again can be tracked back to the old poetical ὑποθῆκαι or παραινέσεις (exhortations) of Hesiod, Theognis, and others. The few Greek exhortations preserved (e.g. Galen's Π. ἐπ' ἰατρικήν) are only late examples of the genre. The most famous classical exhortation was Aristotle's *Protrepticus*, based partly on the sophistic *protrepticus* which Plato gives in the

Euthydemus (278e f.). Cicero wrote his *protrepticus Hortensius* after the model of Aristotle, but turned it into a dialogue. It was the reading of the *Hortensius* which led the young Augustine to philosophy.

P. Hartlich, *De exhortationum a Graecis Romanisque scriptarum historia* (Leipziger Studien 1889). *See also* ARISTOTLE, CICERO. P. Friedländer, *Hermes* 1913; P. Wendland, *Anaximenes von Lampsakos* 81 f.; W. Jaeger, *Paideia*, Engl. Transl., i. 30 f., passim (on the poetical and sophistic *protrepticus*). K. O. B.

PROVINCIA designated the sphere of action of a magistrate possessing *imperium*, and originally was applied to any district in Italy or overseas in which authority was exercised by a representative of Rome. Macedonia, for instance, and Spain were allotted to Roman generals as their 'provinces' long before their annexation. Italy itself might be the 'province' of one of the consuls whose colleague had a command elsewhere. The word was also applied to the duties of other magistrates: the *praetor urbanus* had the *provincia urbana*, and the *praetor peregrinus* the *provincia peregrina*. Later, however, the word was specially associated with the overseas possessions of Rome, which were sharply distinguished from Italy by the fact that their inhabitants paid tribute. The Roman confederacy in Italy was based on treaties involving military obligations but not taxation; but when extra-Italian districts were included in the Empire tribute was paid, except by individuals or communities who had been granted *immunitas* (q.v.).

2. When a province was annexed a *Lex Provinciae* was drawn up by a Roman general with the assistance of a commission of ten nominated by the Senate. In this document were laid down the general principles according to which the area was to be administered. It divided the province into administrative districts, and dealt with taxation, the administration of justice, and local government. Well-known examples are the *Lex Rupilia* of Sicily and the *Lex Pompeia* of Bithynia. Every governor on entering office supplemented the provisions of the *Lex Provinciae* by issuing an edict. This was mainly concerned with financial and judicial questions; but a governor had considerable freedom in making experiments which might or might not be taken over by his successor. Cicero conferred upon the cities of Cilicia a degree of autonomy to which they were not accustomed.

3. The earliest provinces were governed by magistrates specially elected for the purpose. Two additional praetors were elected from 227 B.C. to govern Sicily and Sardinia, and two more from 197 for the two Spanish provinces. No further addition, however, was made to the number of magistrates till the dictatorship of Sulla, though meantime several provinces had been acquired. Provinces were governed either by magistrates actually in office or by those whose imperium had been extended by *prorogatio* (q.v.), and fairly long commands became common. The Senate, which was normally responsible for the allocation of provinces, decided annually which were to be consular and which praetorian, after which the consuls and praetors settled the final distribution by lot. By a law of C. Gracchus the Senate was required to determine the consular provinces before the magistrates concerned were actually elected. In the last century of the Republic important commands were often conferred by plebiscitum, e.g. the appointment of Marius against Jugurtha, of Pompey against the pirates and Mithridates, and of Caesar in Gaul. Pompey in 52 fixed an interval of five years between the holding of a magistracy and of a provincial governorship. Under the Principate a distinction was made between 'senatorial' or 'public' and 'imperial' provinces. The former were governed by ex-consuls and ex-praetors with the title of proconsul, who normally held office for a year, while imperial provinces were entrusted to *legati Augusti propraetore* of senatorial rank, or to equestrian officials selected by the emperor, whose term of office was indefinite. Under

Augustus and Tiberius, Poppaeus Sabinus governed provinces for 24 years (Tac. *Ann.* 6. 39). Consular *legati* of imperial provinces had legions under their command. No legions were stationed permanently in senatorial provinces (except Africa), nor in imperial provinces of the second class. The equestrian *praefectus* of Egypt had a legionary force, but provinces governed by *procuratores* were garrisoned by *auxilia* only. The governor of a province under the Republic had supreme authority in both civil and military matters with the assistance of his quaestor (q.v.) and his *legati*, over whose appointment he had some control. In the Principate the financial administration of an imperial province was in the hands of an equestrian procurator, who was appointed independently of the *legatus* and was sometimes regarded as a rival. In senatorial provinces this duty belonged to the quaestor, but even in them procurators looked after the interests of the *fiscus* and *patrimonium*. Rome had so few official representatives in the provinces, even in the Principate, that government would have been impossible without the co-operation of local authorities. Accordingly, much was done to foster municipal life, which flourished greatly during the early centuries of the Principate, when the central government still allowed much local autonomy. With the growth of bureaucracy this autonomy was diminished by the encroachments of the central government, until the holding of municipal office came to be regarded as a burdensome duty.

4. The provinces of the Republic were acquired in a piecemeal fashion, and it is not till the Principate that a definite policy is apparent. As a result of the Punic Wars Rome acquired Sicily (241 B.C.), Sardinia and Corsica (231), and Hither and Farther Spain (197). Macedonia was annexed in 148 after an unsuccessful experiment in autonomy, and Achaea and Africa in 146, Asia in 133. Bithynia and Cyrene (74) were bequeathed to Rome by their kings. Southern Gaul became a province in 120, and Roman rule was extended over the whole of Gaul by Caesar. Pompey added Syria to the Empire, and by the first century B.C. Cilicia and Illyricum were regarded as provinces (their previous status is obscure). In the reign of Augustus the Danube was fixed as the northern frontier of the Empire, and the four Danubian provinces (Raetia, Noricum, Pannonia, and Moesia) were annexed. After the defeat of Varus in A.D. 9 no serious attempt was made to extend the Empire to the Elbe, though a considerable area in south-west Germany lay within the 'limes' connecting the Rhine with the Danube, the construction of which began in the Flavian period. Egypt became a province after the defeat of Antony and Cleopatra in 31 B.C. The most important provinces acquired after the reign of Augustus were Britain and Dacia, annexed by Claudius and Trajan, but certain regions previously ruled by 'client kings' were transformed into provinces, e.g. Cappadocia in A.D. 17, Mauretania in 40, and Thrace in 46. Most of the extensive conquests made by Trajan east of the Euphrates were abandoned, but the province of Arabia between Palestine and the Red Sea was retained and a province of Mesopotamia was organized under Marcus Aurelius. The process of subdividing the provinces, which began under Domitian and Trajan, was continued much farther in the period of Diocletian and Constantine.

ANCIENT SOURCES: Our chief sources of information for the provincial government of the later Republic are the speeches of Cicero (especially the *Verrines*) and his letters from Cilicia and to his brother Quintus. For the Principate we depend mainly on references in Tacitus, the Younger Pliny, etc. For details inscriptions are invaluable, and the *Natural History* of the Elder Pliny contains much statistical information. For the later period the *Digest* should be consulted.

MODERN BOOKS: F. F. Abbott and A. C. Johnson, *Municipal Administration in the Roman Empire* (1926); V. Chapot, *The Roman World* (1928); A. H. J. Greenidge, *Roman Public Life* (1901); J. Marquardt, *Röm. Staatsverw.* i and ii (1881); Mommsen, *The Provinces of the Roman Empire* (1909); G. H. Stevenson, *Roman Provincial Administration* (1939).   G. H. S.

PROVOCATIO in the regal period was the appeal to the royal grace, and in early Republican times it was a political weapon against arbitrary administration of justice. But it soon became a right which every male Roman enjoyed. Whatever the reasons for his condemnation to a capital punishment (or, at a later stage, to a fine), he was allowed to appeal (*provocare*) to the *Comitia Centuriata*, while the appeal against a fine was made to the *Comitia Tributa*. The magistrate who disregarded the appeal and executed the sentence was considered guilty of murder and punished, unless the right of appeal was suspended by proclaiming a state of siege (*see* SENATUS CONSULTUM ULTIMUM) or superseded by dictatorship. *Provocatio* was such a characteristic feature of the Republican conception of liberty and citizenship that the Romans thought of it as contemporary with the foundation of the Republic, and attributed a law *de provocatione* to Valerius Publicola (q.v.) which is a mere anticipation of the *Lex Valeria* (*c.* 300 B.C.). The right of appeal was introduced or reinforced by the decemvirs, and remained intact until superseded by *appellatio* (q.v.) in the imperial age.

Mommsen, *Röm. Strafr.* (1899), 167 f., 473 ff.; G. W. Botsford, *The Roman Assemblies* (1909), 239 ff.   P. T.

PROVOCATIO, in later classical jurisprudence, *see* APPELLATIO.

PROXENOS. Since Greek States did not send permanent diplomatic representatives abroad, local citizens served as *proxenoi* to look after the interests of other States in their community. By the beginning of the fifth century this system had developed from earlier practices of hospitality under which some relied on hereditary ties with foreign families and others on the more general respect for strangers and suppliants. Survivals from this were the continued existence of private friends in foreign States (ἰδιόξενοι) and the practice of a few States of appointing *proxenoi* to look after visitors. More commonly States selected their own *proxenoi* in other States and, in return for services already rendered and expected in the future, bestowed honours and privileges upon them. Such appointments were much coveted, and many voluntarily assumed the burdens in the hope of gaining the title. The position usually was hereditary. A *proxenos* must be a citizen of the State in which he served and not of the State he represented. Later, however, when honours were bestowed more freely and had little practical significance, *proxenia* and honorary citizenship frequently were combined in the same grant.

C. Phillipson, *The International Law and Custom of Ancient Greece and Rome* (1911), ch. 6; E. Szanto, *Das griechische Bürgerrecht* (1892), ch. 1.   J. A. O. L.

PRUDENTIUS AURELIUS CLEMENS (b. A.D. 348), the greatest of the Christian Latin poets, was a native of Spain (probably Tarraconensis). After a good education and a period devoted to vice he began a successful career as advocate and administrator and attained a position at court. He then broke with his past and dedicated himself to Christian poetry. After 405 traces of his life are lost. His works are remarkable for skill in various metres and for profound knowledge of pagan Latin poetry. The titles are *Cathemerinon*, 'The Diary'; a series of hymns, *Apotheosis*, in which he battles for the Catholic doctrine of the Trinity; *Hamartigenia* on the origin of sin; *Psychomachia*, 'The battle for the soul', an allegory; *Peristephanon*, 'On the (martyrs') crowns'; *Contra Symmachum*, where the events of 384 are vividly recalled after an interval of about twenty years (*see* SYMMACHUS 2); and the *Dittochaeon*, a collection of forty-nine hexameter tetrastichs on biblical topics.

Ed. W. Bergman (*CSEL* lxi, 1926); Concordance by Deferarri and Campbell (Medieval Academy of America, 1932).   A. S.

PRUSIAS, *see* BITHYNIA.

PRYTANIS (πρύτανις). (1) A general term for a presiding officer. (2) The chief magistrate of some States (e.g. Mytilene) in early times, or, as in Chios, the *eponymos*. Elsewhere (chiefly in Asia Minor), *prytaneis* were the magistrates who presided over the boule and the ecclesia. (3) In Athens, from the time of Cleisthenes, and elsewhere, the *prytaneis* were a section of the Boule, acting as a committee for the preparation of business. They consisted either of all the members of one *phyle* or of members chosen in equal numbers from each *phyle*. At Athens the fifty members from each of the ten *phylae* served as *prytaneis* for one-tenth part of the year in an order determined by lot (the φυλή πρυτανεύουσα). Their period of office was normally therefore 36 or 37 days, in intercalary years 38 or 39. When there were twelve *phylae* (after 307–306), their office lasted 30 or 31 days.

They met daily in the Tholos or Skias, a circular building near the Bouleuterion, and fed there. A third of their number must remain in the building night and day. They chose each day by lot one of their number as their *epistates* or chairman, who also presided over the Boule and Ecclesia, if they met on his day. (For later procedure *see* PROEDROI). The *prytaneis* summoned both Boule and Ecclesia and set out the agenda; they saw to it that only qualified persons attended the meetings. They received and introduced to the Boule all magistrates, private citizens, or foreign ambassadors who wished to meet it or were summoned to it. They had certain powers of arrest as a committee of the Boule (*see* BOULE). In Aristotle's time they were paid 6 obols a day. For the πρυτάνεις τῶν ναυκράρων *see* NAUKRARIAI. A. W. G.

PSAON OF PLATAEA, Hellenistic historian, continuing Diyllus from 297/6 B.C., covered partly the same period as Phylarchus and may have been contemporary with him; his work perhaps extended to Ol. 140 (220–217), where Polybius began, and was continued by Menodotus.

FGrH ii, A, p. 158; C, p. 131. A. H. McD.

PSELLUS, MICHAEL (earlier CONSTANTINE), probably of Nicomedia (A.D. 1018–78/9), after studying law at Constantinople held a judicial post at Philadelphia. Under Constantine IX (1042–55) he became professor of philosophy at the Academy in Constantinople. He was now one of the most influential figures in the Eastern Empire and was appointed State Secretary and Vestarch. Apart from a brief period of retirement in a monastery (1054–5), he was a member of all the governments at Constantinople until the reign of Michael VII (1071–8), under whom he became Prime Minister. The ingratitude of this emperor caused him to spend his last days in obscurity.

WORKS. (1) Scientific and philosophical treatises on mathematics, music, astronomy, physics, metaphysics, ethics, theology, alchemy, demonology, medicine, jurisprudence, topography, etc.; e.g. the miscellany *De Omnifaria Doctrina* (Διδασκαλία παντοδαπή), his literary masterpiece *De Operatione Daemonum* (Π. ἐνεργείας δαιμόνων), his discussion of Athenian judicial terminology, and his short account of the topography of Athens.

(2) Paraphrases of the *Iliad* and of Aristotle, *Categories*, an abridgement of Porphyry, *De Quinque Vocibus*, a commentary on Aristotle, *De Interpretatione*, a treatise on Plato, *Phaedrus*, and an allegorical study on Homer. Also works in letter-form on rhetoric, and poems on rhetoric, grammar, and Greek dialects.

(3) *Chronographia* (Χρονογραφία), a lively and colourful history of the century 976 to 1077, is valuable, though somewhat inadequate.

(4) Funeral orations, panegyrics, *apologiae* written in a style of persuasive dignity. His letters, of which about 500 survive, are interesting for their picture of Byzantine civilization and of their author himself.

(5) Rhetorical exercises and essays on set themes.

(6) Occasional verse, satirical and epigrammatic.

Psellus was a man of encyclopaedic learning and great literary gifts. At a time when scholarship was at a low ebb, he had a keen though rather self-conscious love of classical and patristic literature and was passionately devoted to Plato and the Neoplatonists. His own style owed much to Plato, Aelius Aristides, and Gregory Nazianzen.

In his public life he reflects the faults of the age. Amid the atmosphere of palace-intrigue and court-flattery, scruples and sincerity found no place, and his political career was disfigured by servility and unrestrained ambition.

J. P. Migne, *PG* cxii (1864); *De Operatione Daemonum*, F. Boissonade (1838); *Chronographia*, E. Rénauld (1926–8); *Scripta minora*, I *Orationes et dissertationes*, E. Kurtz – F. Drexl (1936); C. Sathas, *The History of Psellus* (1899). C. Zervos, *Un Philosophe néo-platonicien du XIe siècle* (1920); E. Rénauld, *Étude de la langue et du style de P.* (1920) and *Lexique choisi de P.* (1920); K. Svoboda, *La Démonologie de M. P.* (1927); J. Bidez, *Cat. des MS. alchim. grecs* vi (1928). J. F. L.

PSEUDEPIGRAPHIC LITERATURE. Antiquity has left us a number of writings which evidence, internal or external, proves not to be the work of the authors whose names are traditionally attached to them. The causes of this seem to be chiefly: (*a*) a tendency to ascribe anonymous pieces to a well-known author of like genre. Thus, the whole Epic Cycle and other hexameter poems were at one time or another ascribed to Homer; in Latin several compositions more or less epic in style, as the *Culex* and *Ciris*, have become attached to the name of Virgil, others, in elegiacs, to those of Tibullus and Ovid. (*b*) Works by the followers of a philosopher tended to be credited to their master; for instance, several short dialogues by members of the Academy bear the name of Plato, and, e.g., the *Problemata*, which are Peripatetic, are preserved as by Aristotle. (*c*) Rhetorical exercises in the form of speeches, letters, etc., supposed to be by well-known persons, now and then were taken for their real works. Thus, no. 11 of our collection of Demosthenes' speeches is a clever imitation of him, said by Didymus, *In Demosth.*, col. 11, 10, to come from the *Philippica* of Anaximenes of Lampsacus. The Epistles of Phalaris are the most notorious work of this kind, thanks to Bentley's exposure of them. (*d*) The existence of deliberate forgeries, made to sell (*see* FORGERIES, LITERARY), is vouched for by Galen (*In Hipp. de nat. hominis* 2, p. 57, 12 Mewaldt). (*e*) Various mechanical accidents of copying account for a few pseudepigraphies. (*f*) But the most frequent cases are of rather late date and connected with the craze for producing evidence of the doctrines one favoured being of great age. For instance, the numerous Neopythagorean treatises, whereof specimens are preserved chiefly in Stobaeus, are regularly attached to the names of prominent early Pythagoreans, including Pythagoras himself (q.v.), despite the fairly constant tradition that he wrote nothing. The Sibylline oracles (*see* SIBYLLA) are an outstanding instance of this; Phocylides (q.v.) is the alleged author of a long set of moralizing verses pretty certainly the work of an unknown Jew and of late date. Christian literature has some glaring examples of this practice, notably the Clementine Recognitions and Homilies, most certainly neither by Clement of Rome nor any contemporary, and the works attributed to Dionysius the Areopagite, really produced some three centuries or more after his death. Cf. also HERMES TRISMEGISTUS. H. J. R.

PSEUDO-ASCONIUS, *see* ASCONIUS.

PSEUDO-CALLISTHENES. The so-called *Alexander Romance* (Βίος Ἀλεξάνδρου τοῦ Μακεδόνος) is extant in three Greek versions. The oldest belongs to *c.* A.D. 300, but may contain elements derived from a romantic account of Alexander's life written soon after his death.

Text: W. Kroll, *Historia Alexandri Magni* (1926). A. Ausfeld, *Der griechische Alexanderroman* (1907). *See also* CALLISTHENES *and* NOVEL, GREEK. R. M. R.

PSEUDO-FRONTINUS, *see* FRONTINUS.

PSEUDO-OVIDIANA, *see* CONSOLATIO AD LIVIAM *and* ELEGIAE IN MAECENATEM; cf. *Nux* under OVID.

PSEUDO-QUINTILIAN, *see* DECLAMATIONES.

PSEUDO-VERGILIANA, *see* APPENDIX VERGILIANA.

PSYCHE, the soul or, in later usage, the soul as a butterfly, does not appear as a clearly individualized mythological being before the fourth or the fifth century B.C. The notion of the soul occupied the Greeks from very early times. It has been suggested that the soul was first conceived as a bird, on the strength of the passages in Homer where the soul of Patroclus utters a faint noise (*Il.* 23. 101) and the souls of wooers chirp like bats (*Od.* 24. 6). In art a bird is shown flying over the head of a dying hero and birds are often seated on funeral *stelae* (cf. *Sirenes*). But Homer explicitly depicts the soul as a kind of a double, resembling the dead in 'height, eyes, voice' and wearing the same garments (*Il.* 23. 66), and the archaeological evidence is ambiguous. The Homeric souls, often called *eidola*, disappear like smoke, in the manner of our ghosts, if somebody attempts to touch them (*Od.* 11. 206). They dwell in Hades on the barren asphodel meadow and lack the vitality and memory which they can regain only by drinking blood (*Od.* 11. 25, cf. 24. 1). The Homeric notion remained current down to Plato's times (*Phd.* 81 c, d). On vases we see the soul of Patroclus in full armour watching Achilles as he drags the corpse of Hector; the soul of Sarpedon leaving the body (E. Haspels, *Attic Black-Figure Lekythoi* (Paris 1936), 51); the souls of Achilles and Memnon weighed by Zeus; and the souls of commoners at a funeral, in the cemetery, and in Hades. On some vases they are shown with Charon, on others with Hermes Psychagogus.

Different notions of the soul were developed by Greek philosophers and poets. The most important change is the elevation of soul from a rather materialistically conceived double to a dematerialized divine being, of a nature totally different from the body. 'The body is the tomb of the soul', said the Orphics (*see* ORPHISM). The inscriptions honouring the warriors fallen at Potidaea claims that their souls were received by the aether, their bodies by earth (Kaibel, *Epigr. gr.* 21). The Homeric connexion with the individual had been severed so far that all *Psychai* could be conceived as female. The earliest representation of P. in that form, of the late fifth century, appears in south Italy, the home of Pythagoreans and Orphics. It would appear that the type which represents P. as a butterfly was evolved approximately at the same time. Plato's inspired vision of the chariots of souls in *Phaedrus* presupposes a connexion of Eros and P. Roughly contemporary with Plato are some beautiful bronze reliefs from Asia Minor (Devambez, *Les Grands Bronzes du Musée d'Istanbul*, 1935) on which Eros and P., a maiden, are shown in quiet harmony. They are united in the Hellenistic 'Invention of the Kiss', a marble group which was copied in Roman (E. Strong, *JRS* 1924, 71) and early Christian art, perhaps as symbol of heavenly happiness (F. Cumont, *Syria* 1929, 231). On the other hand, Eros (q.v.), who had before plagued individual victims of love, now turns also on P., since she, the soul, is recognized as the seat of passions. In Hellenistic poetry and art Eros is represented inflicting innumerable tortures upon P. (G. Hanfmann, *AJArch.*

1939, 240). In Apuleius (*Met.* 4. 28) the motif of the tormented Psyche is combined with a *märchen* of the Fairy Bridegroom type. The goddess P., who appears in some late writings, is according to Reitzenstein an Iranian goddess in Greek disguise.

E. Rohde, *Psyche* (1907); O. Waser in Roscher, *Lex.*, s.v. O. Weinreich in L. Friedländer, *Sittengeschichte* iv. 89; Apuleius, *The Story of Cupid and Psyche*, ed. L. C. Purser (1910); R. Reitzenstein, *Sitz. Heidelberg* 1914 and 1917. G. M. A. H.

PTAH, called *Φθά* or *Φθάs* and also Hephaestus by the Greeks, was an old deity of Memphis. Originally a god of artisans, a fashioner and maker of things, he acquired later a solar character and became one of the chief deities of Egypt. The temple of Ptah was one of the chief buildings in the complex of structures at Memphis which included the temple of Apis and others. T. A. B.

PTOLEMAEUS (1) of Ascalon, of uncertain date, is said by Steph. Byz. to have been a pupil of Aristarchus, and in Suidas to have been father (or teacher) of Archibius (a grammarian at Rome under Trajan). P. joined the Pergamenes and disputed the Aristarchan texts of Homer. He also wrote *Περὶ διαφορᾶς λέξεως*, *Περὶ ὀρθογραφίας*, and *Περὶ μέτρων*. P. B. R. F.

PTOLEMAEUS (2) **CHENNOS** ('quail') of Alexandria (*fl. c.* A.D. 100) wrote the *Sphinx*, a mythologico-grammatical work, perhaps in dramatic form (*ἱστορικὸν δρᾶμα*, Suid.), though this is disputed; *Ἀνθόμηρος*, in twenty-four rhapsodies, correcting Homer's errors; *Παράδοξος* (or *Καινὴ*) *ἱστορία*, of which Photius gives an extract.

A. Chatzis, *Der Philosoph und Grammatiker Ptolemaios Chennos* (1914). J. D. D.

PTOLEMAEUS (3) *ὁ ἐπιθέτης*, grammarian, pupil of Hellanicus the Chorizontist, and a pertinacious opponent of Aristarchus, wrote commentaries on Homer and Bacchylides and kindred monographs.

PTOLEMAEUS (4) of Mende, a priest, wrote on the *πράξεις* of the Egyptian kings in three books; he is scarcely the Ptolemaeus who published a life or history of Herod the Great, soon after 4 B.C.

FHG iv. 485: *FGrH* ii, BD, 625.

PTOLEMAEUS (5) of Naucratis (2nd c. A.D.), Egyptian rhetor, uninfluenced by the Second Sophistic, except in style, where he follows Polemon.

PTOLEMAEUS (6) **PINDARION** (i.e. commentator on Pindar) (2nd c. B.C.), a pupil of Aristarchus, wrote also on Homeric antiquities and on analogy. *See* CRATES (3) OF MALLOS.

PTOLEMAIA, *see* RULER-CULT.

PTOLEMAIS (1) (**ACE**). The Phoenician port of Ace was named Ptolemais *c.* 261 B.C. by Ptolemy II. From Antiochus IV's reign its people, renamed the 'Antiocheis in Ptolemais', issued municipal coins, sometimes inscribed 'Ace' in Phoenician. Claudius made Ptolemais a Roman colony, planting in it veterans from the four Syrian legions. A. H. M. J.

PTOLEMAIS (2) **HERMIOU,** a foundation of Ptolemy Soter, with a substantial Greek population and a Greek constitution, was the centre of Hellenism in Upper Egypt throughout the Graeco-Roman period; Strabo classed it with Memphis in importance, and later it ranked second to Alexandria. Hardly any remains of buildings are visible, but inscriptions have been found recording decrees of the Ptolemaic senate, and references in papyri from other districts show the continued influence of its citizens in Roman times.

G. Plaumann, *Ptolemais in Oberaegypten* (1910) J. G. M.

PTOLEMAIS (3) **THERON** ('of the Hunts'), on the west coast of the Red Sea, probably at Aquiq (Crowfoot, *Geog. Journ.* xxxvii. 523). Founded by Ptolemy II for elephant-hunts, it was used as a port for a trade-route to Meroe and the Nile.

Agatharchides (*GGM* i. 174); Strabo 17. 768–71. E. H. W.

PTOLEMY (1). The name of all the Macedonian kings of Egypt.

PTOLEMY I SOTER (*c.* 367/6–283 or 282 B.C.), son of the Macedonian Lagus and a certain Arsinoe, who was, perhaps, a mistress and not, as was later believed, a second cousin of Philip II. He was exiled as Alexander's friend, recalled after Philip's death, and appointed *hetairos*, *somatophylax*, and *edeatros* ('Companion', 'Life-guard', and 'Seneschal') to Alexander. He fought with distinction during Alexander's campaigns, which he subsequently described in an historical work. He married Artacama, Artabazus' daughter, in 324, divorced her after Alexander's death, and subsequently married Eurydice and (with or without divorce) Berenice I (q.v.). He became satrap of Egypt in late summer 323, executed Cleomenes (q.v. 3), and fought without much success against Antigonus Monophthalmus and Demetrius Poliorcetes (315–301). He declared himself king early in 304, finally conquered Palestine, Cyprus, and many possessions in the Aegean Sea and Asia Minor (*c.* 301–286), but took little active part in government after 285.

He was the originator of the cults of Sarapis and of Alexander in Egypt, and the founder of Ptolemais in Upper Egypt. The legal and military organization of his Empire—the army consisting of military settlers, mercenaries, and native levies—and the main outlines of Ptolemaic administration were due to him (cf. ALEXANDRIA, EGYPT UNDER THE GREEKS AND ROMANS, EPIMELETES, EPISTATES, NOMOS). Registers of land, houses, slaves, cattle, and tax-payers were compiled in the villages, and summaries of these were made for nome registers and the central register in Alexandria, which was used for preparing the State budget. The highest State office was that of the *dioecetes* (= manager) whose *oeconomi* administered the Empire like a royal estate. F. M. H.

Ptolemy I wrote, when king, the best of the histories of Alexander. He used Alexander's official *Journal* and other official material, but much was his own recollection; he was in a better position to know than almost anyone. So far as can be made out his book was a genuine history and not merely a military record; Alexander was a supreme figure, but yet a human man. Probably it was defective on the political side; when he wrote he had long lost sympathy with some of Alexander's ideas. He probably desired to correct current popular history and beliefs, and his silences were part of his criticism; but bad history ousted good, and, but for Arrian, practically all knowledge of his work would have perished. *See* ALEXANDER (3), Bibliography, Ancient Sources. W. W. T.

PTOLEMY II PHILADELPHUS (308–246 B.C.), son of Ptolemy I and Berenice I, was born at Cos, and married Arsinoë I *c.* 289–288. He was elected joint ruler with his father in 285, succeeded to the throne in 283–282 and married Arsinoë II *c.* 276–275, uniting her Aegean possessions with the Empire. He conquered important districts in Syria and Asia Minor during the First Syrian War (*c.* 276–271). In the Chremonidean War against Macedonia (266–261) he incurred slight losses; the Second Syrian War (*c.* 260–253) was indecisive, and was concluded by a marriage between Antiochus II and Berenice Syra (q.v.). East African and south Arabian coastal districts received garrisons as outposts for trade.

Ptolemy II and his advisers created most of the scientific system of Ptolemaic financial administration (cf. AGRICULTURE, BANKS, COMMERCE, FINANCE, INDUSTRY, MONOPOLIES, PASTURAGE, VITICULTURE), planted Greek settlements in Egypt, especially round L. Moeris (q.v.),

and instituted the Ptolemaic ruler-cult with its priests of Alexander and a growing number of deified members of the dynasty. He built the Pharus, the Museum, the Library, and other edifices and institutions of Alexandria as well as a canal from the Nile to the Red Sea.

PTOLEMY III EUERGETES, son of Ptolemy II and Arsinoë I, was born between 288 and 280 and died in 221 B.C. After his (presumable) adoption by Arsinoë II and his succession to the throne in 246 he married Berenice II (q.v.) and united Cyrene with Egypt. In the Third Syrian War (246–241) he acquired important towns in Syria and Asia Minor. Ptolemaic expansion ceased after this, perhaps owing to difficulties in Egypt.

PTOLEMY IV PHILOPATOR (*c.* 244–205 B.C.), son of Ptolemy III and Berenice II, married Arsinoë III (q.v.) in 217. The main events of his reign were: his succession to the throne (221); the poisoning of his consort Arsinoë III (q.v.); invasions of Palestine by Antiochus III (221 and 219–217). He gained a decisive victory over Antiochus (q.v. 3) at Raphia (217), but only with the help of the native Egyptians, who for decades revolted afterwards. Almost the whole Thebaid was ruled in consequence by the Nubian kings Harmachis and Anchmachis (208/7–187/6).

PTOLEMY V EPIPHANES (210–180 B.C.), son of Ptolemy IV and Arsinoë III. He was joint ruler with his father from 210; he succeeded to the throne in 205, the death of Ptolemy IV being kept a secret for a considerable time. The official succession (of uncertain date) was followed by revolts throughout two decades, and, from 203 onwards, by plans of the Seleucid and Macedonian kings to partition the outlying Egyptian territories, the consequence of which was the loss of most possessions in the Aegean, Asia Minor, and Palestine, where his troops suffered a final defeat at Panion in 200. The king was declared of full age in 197 and married the Seleucid princess Cleopatra I (q.v.) in 193. His *epistrategus* Hippalus reconquered the Thebaid in 187–186, and the last native revolt of this period in the Delta was quelled in 184/3.

PTOLEMY VI PHILOMETOR, son of Ptolemy V and Cleopatra I, was born in 186 or (perhaps) 184/3 and died in 145 B.C. He succeeded to the throne in 180 in joint rule with his mother, who died in 176; he formally married Cleopatra II in 175/4. In consequence of three invasions from Antiochus IV (170, 169, and 168), he established a joint rule with Ptolemy VIII and Cleopatra II from 170 to 164. He defeated native revolts, but fled from Ptolemy VIII, to return as sole ruler in 164/3. His struggle with this brother continued for a decade. After a successful campaign beginning in 150 he was elected Seleucid king in joint rule with Demetrius II, but was killed in a victorious battle against Alexander Balas.

PTOLEMY VII NEOS PHILOPATOR, son of Ptolemy VI and Cleopatra II, was born *c.* 162–161, became joint ruler with his father in 145, sole ruler from his father's death until Ptolemy VIII's return to Egypt, and was killed by his uncle's orders in August 144.

PTOLEMY VIII EUERGETES (*c.* 182/1–116 B.C.), brother of Ptolemy VI. He was joint ruler with Ptolemy VI and Cleopatra II in 170–164; sole ruler in 164–163; king of Cyrene in 163–145; returning to Egypt in 145. He married Cleopatra II in 144, and took Cleopatra III to wife in 142 without being able to divorce Cleopatra II, who led a successful revolt against him in 132. He reconquered Alexandria in 127, and an amnesty and a peaceful reign with the two queens followed from 124. The king's final testament gave all power to Cleopatra III. An earlier testament during his rule in Cyrene bequeathed his possessions to Rome.

PTOLEMY IX SOTER II (LATHYRUS) (*c.* 141–81 B.C.), eldest son of Ptolemy VIII and Cleopatra III. He was priest of Alexander from 135/4; subsequently became governor of Cyprus and married Cleopatra IV, his sister, during Ptolemy VIII's last years. Elected joint ruler with Cleopatra III against her wishes in 116, he divorced Cleopatra IV and married Cleopatra Selene, another sister. He had to accept his brother Ptolemy X as joint ruler in 110. He reconquered the kingdom, but another revolt of his brother compelled him to flee to Cyprus in 108/7, and from there to Seleucid Syria. Cleopatra Selene divorced him; but he reconquered Cyprus very soon, was victorious in Syria against the Jewish State allied with his mother, and reconquered Egypt in 89–88. Cleopatra Berenice, his daughter, returned from exile as joint ruler in 88, after Ptolemy X's death, and remained sole ruler from Ptolemy IX's death to 80. The Thebaid revolted against the new rule from 88 to 86.

PTOLEMY X ALEXANDER I (c. 140–88 B.C.), younger brother of Ptolemy IX, was governor of Cyprus from 116; was recalled to Egypt by his mother in 110, but resigned after a short joint rule with the title 'king' of Cyprus. Another joint rule in 108 prepared the way for his final third joint rule with Cleopatra III under pressure from the insurgent Alexandrians. After Cleopatra III's (possibly natural) death, the king married Cleopatra Berenice, daughter of Ptolemy IX, a few days later. Expelled from Egypt by a military revolt, he made successive attempts to recover his kingdom by land from Syria and by sea from Asia Minor, and died in a naval battle (89–88).

PTOLEMY XI ALEXANDER II (c. 100/99–80 B.C.), son of Ptolemy X and his unknown first wife. Sulla made him joint ruler with and husband of his step-mother Cleopatra Berenice. He murdered her nineteen days after the wedding, and was killed by the Alexandrians, in spite of his being the last legitimate male descendant of the dynasty. His (doubtfully genuine) testament gave Egypt to Rome.

PTOLEMY XII THEOS PHILOPATOR PHILADELPHUS NEOS DIONYSUS (AULETES), son of Ptolemy IX and a mistress, was born between 116 and 108 and died in 51 B.C. He succeeded to the throne in 80, and married Cleopatra V Tryphaena, his sister, in 80/79. He fled to Rome from the insurgent Alexandrians in 58, but was restored by Gabinius in 55.

PTOLEMY XIII, brother of Cleopatra VII (q.v.), was born in 63 and died in 47 B.C. In 51 he married his sister, who became joint ruler with him but was presently expelled by him. After the murder of Pompey by his ministers (48) he was forced by Caesar to share the throne again with Cleopatra. He subsequently made open war against Caesar, was defeated and drowned in the Nile.

PTOLEMY XIV (c. 59–44 B.C.), another brother of Cleopatra VII. Caesar made him king of Cyprus in 48, and joint ruler and husband of Cleopatra in 47. He was murdered by her orders.

PTOLEMY XV CAESARION, ostensible son of Caesar and Cleopatra VII, was born in 47 B.C., was made joint ruler with his mother in 43 or by Antonius in 34, and was killed by Octavian's orders in 30 B.C.

See APOLLONIUS 3, ARSINOË, BERENICE, CLEOMENES, CLEOPATRA.

Wilcken, PW, s.v. 'Arsinoe', 'Berenike'; Stähelin, ibid., s.v. 'Kleopatra'. E. Bevan, A History of Egypt under the Ptolemaic Dynasty (1927). A. Bouché-Leclercq, Histoire des Lagides i–iv (1903–7). CAH vii, chs. 3, 4, 22; viii, chs. 6, 9, 16; ix, chs. 8, 9, 16. G. Corradi, Studi Hellenistici (1929). W. Otto, Abhandlungen der bayrischen Akademie, Phil.-Hist. Klasse, 1928 no. 1, 1934 no. 11, 1938 no. 17, 1939 pt. 3; W. Peremans and J. Vergete, Papyrologisch Handboek (1942); Rostovtzeff, Hellenistic World. Numerous articles in JHS, JEg.Arch., Arch. Pap., and other periodicals. The administration of Ptolemaic Egypt is illustrated by inscriptions and numerous papyri (Greek and Demotic). A recent survey in Cl. Préaux, L'Économie royale des Lagides (1933), with complete bibliography and an index of important passages. F. M. H.

PTOLEMY (2) of Cyrene revived the sceptical school of philosophy about 100 B.C. (Diog. Laert. 9. 115).

See Zeller, Phil. d. Griechen iii. 2⁴. 2.

PTOLEMY (3) (CLAUDIUS PTOLEMAEUS) of Alexandria, born at Ptolemaïs ἡ Ἑρμείου, made observations between A.D. 121 and 151. His great work, originally called Μαθηματικὴ σύνταξις, became known as Μεγάλη σύνταξις, Great Collection, in contradistinction to the Μικρὸς ἀστρονομούμενος (τόπος), the 'Little Astronomy', comprising smaller introductory works; the Arabs turned μεγίστη into al-Majisti, whence Almagest. It is the definitive account of the Greek achievement in astronomy according to Hipparchus, with some additions of Ptolemy's own. Trigonometry is the method used; it is first applied in Book 1 to the calculation, by means of 'Menelaus' Theorem' and trigonometrical formulae based thereon, of a Table of Chords of arcs subtending angles from $\frac{1}{2}$° by steps of $\frac{1}{2}$° to 180°, equivalent to a Table of Sines of half the angles respectively. There follow formulae in the solution of spherical triangles for the purpose of relating arcs of the equator, ecliptic, horizon, and meridian, and so on. Book 3 is mainly on the length of the year and the motion of the sun on the eccentric and epicycle hypotheses; bks. 4, 5 on the lunar month, lunar theory, sizes and distances of sun, moon, and earth; bk. 6 on conjunctions and oppositions of sun and moon, solar and lunar eclipses; 7, 8 on the fixed stars and the precession of the equinoxes; 9–13 on the movements of the planets.

2. Other works extant in whole or in part are: (1) The Analemma, on orthogonal projection, in a Latin translation from the Arabic by William of Moerbeke, plus a few Greek fragments.

(2) The Planispherium, on stereographic projection, Latin translation from the Arabic.

(3) Φάσεις ἀπλανῶν ἀστέρων, on the fixed stars, Book 2 only.

(4) Ὑποθέσεις τῶν πλανωμένων, first book in Greek, second in Arabic.

(5) Inscription in Canobus.

(6) Προχείρων κανόνων διάτασις καὶ ψηφοφορία. (All these are included in Heiberg's edition, Teubner, 1898–1907.)

(7) Optics, five books (bk. 1 and end of 5 missing), translated from the Arabic by Admiral Eugenius Siculus in 12th c. (see Govi, L'Ottica di Claudio Tolomeo, 1884), remarkable as containing (bk. 5) the first attempt at a theory of refraction, details of experiments, etc.

(8) Geography (Γεωγραφικὴ ὑφήγησις), see below.

3. Other works attributed to Ptolemy are: Περὶ ῥοπῶν, on balancings or turnings of the scale; Περὶ διαστάσεως, on dimensions; three books of Mechanics. For Ptolemy's attempt to prove Euclid's Parallel Postulate, see Proclus on Eucl. I. T. H.

4. Ptolemy's Geography (Γεωγραφικὴ Ὑφήγησις) was a treatise in eight books, with an atlas of maps. Its object was 'to reform the map of the world' by bringing up to date the map of a previous geographer, Marinus of Tyre (c. A.D. 120?). Ptolemy's map extended from c. 20° S. to 65° N., and from a basic meridian through the Canary Islands to 180° E.; drawn from the standpoint of an astronomer, it was intersected by curved lines of latitude and longitude, to which all his data were (theoretically) referred.

5. Ptolemy's scientific ideal outstripped his practical application. Adopting Posidonius' estimate of 180,000 stades for the earth's circumference, in preference to Eratosthenes' more correct calculation of 250,000 stades, he systematically underrated the distance between any two positions of longitude, and the errors due to this false graduation accumulated in the outer or eastern portion of his map. Moreover, with rare exceptions, his positions were not really determined by astronomic

observation, but by dead reckoning from (often inexact) reports of travellers. Though Ptolemy recognized the danger of this method of computation, he tabulated all his data in exact terms of latitude and longitude, thus giving a delusive appearance of scientific certainty to his deductions. Furthermore, he rejected the theory of a circumfluent ocean round the three continents, and while he left blank the map of the unknown world to west, north, and east, he assumed the existence of a large sub-equatorial continent.

6. The most conspicuous errors in Ptolemy's map were the extension of the Eurasian land-mass over 180° of longitude (instead of 130°), and the invention of a Terra Australis connecting the east coast of Africa with China and converting the Indian Ocean into a huge lake. Of its innumerable errors and deficiencies of detail the following are most notable. (1) *Europe*. The Atlantic coast of the continent has an almost unbroken north-east trend. Scotland lies on its back in a west–east direction (probably the result of a wrong join of two sectional maps). Scandinavia is a small island. Germany, Poland, and Central and Northern Russia are largely left blank. The Sea of Azov is greatly magnified. (2) *Asia*. The Caspian Sea is correctly conceived as a lake, but is greatly elongated from west to east, and the Persian Gulf is similarly distorted. India is a rectangle with its main axis running from west to east, and Ceylon is magnified fourteen times. The Malay peninsula is determined with fair accuracy, but the Chinese coast curves away to east and south so as to meet Terra Australis. (3) *Africa*. The Mediterranean coast runs almost continuously from west to east. Two unidentifiable rivers, Gir and Nigir, cross north Africa in the same direction. The White Nile is correctly derived from two Central African lakes, but the mountains on either side are connected into a continuous west–east chain ('Mountains of the Moon').

7. But despite its faults, the treatise of Ptolemy was on the whole the most accurate of ancient geographical works, and it was the most comprehensive. It therefore remained standard until modern times.

Texts: C. Nobbe (1843); Ch. Müller and C. T. Fischer (bks. 1–3) (1883–1901). Commentary: E. H. Bunbury, *History of Ancient Geography* (1879), ii. 519 ff. Text, maps, and commentary: P. J. Fischer, *Cl. Ptolemaei Geographiae codex Urbinas Graecus* 82 (3 vols., 1932). E. H. W.

PUBLICANI were principally collectors of taxes, but this was only one of the functions performed by them for the Roman government. At least as early as the Second Punic War there existed a class of man (*ordo publicanorum*, Livy 25. 3) accustomed to undertake contracts for the State such as the erection of buildings, the provision of food for the armies, or the working of mines. In 167 B.C. the government decided to close the mines of Macedonia in order to avoid the necessity of employing *publicani* to exploit them (Livy 45. 18). The influence of the *publicani* was increased by the privileges conferred by C. Gracchus on the equestrian order, with which they were closely associated, and they acquired a great source of wealth in the collection of the *decumae* of the new province of Asia. In disputes with provincial governors the *publicani* could count on the support of the equestrian order in Rome. In the later Republic they were organized in *societates*, presided over by a *magister* with whom *socii* were associated. The *societates* were represented in the provinces by a *pro magistro* (Cic. *Verr.* 2. 169) with a staff of assistants. There is some evidence for the existence of a class of shareholders (*participes*) with a financial interest in the company: Polybius (6. 17) emphasizes that many people were affected by the terms on which contracts were let. The *publicani* were most prominent in the provinces which paid *decumae* (q.v.), but Cicero (*Verr.* 3. 27) enumerates a large number of provinces in which they were active, and it is probable

that their services were employed not only in the collection of indirect taxes but in connexion with the *stipendium* (q.v.). (For *pactiones* between the *publicani* and cities see Cic. *Att.* 5. 13. 1; *Prov. Cons.* 5. 10.)

In the early Principate *publicani* were still used for the collection of *vectigalia* (q.v.). In Nero's reign such complaints arose about their misbehaviour in the collection of *portoria* that measures were taken to control them (Tac. *Ann.* 13. 50–1). Their activities were from an early date supervised by imperial *procuratores*. The companies employed a large number of slaves and freedmen (*ILS* 1851–76). As late as the time of Trajan the word *publicanus* designated tax-collector (Tac. *Germ.* 29). In the course of the second century the *societates* disappear and are replaced by individual *conductores* (q.v.).

M. Rostovtzeff, 'Gesch. der Staatspacht' (*Philol.* Suppl. ix, p. 329 ff.); O. Hirschfeld, *Verwaltungsbeamten*[2] (1905), 81 ff.; G. H. Stevenson in *Comp. Lat. Stud.* 342 ff. G. H. S.

PUBLILIUS (1) **VOLERO**, tribune of the plebs in 471 B.C., is traditionally credited with a law that transferred the election of plebeian magistrates from the assembly of the *curiae* to the tribal assembly, i.e. officially recognized the tribunes. As such a concession by the patricians is unlikely at so early a date, the *rogatio Publilia* must be considered as an anticipation of the *Lex Publilia* (339 B.C.; *see* PUBLILIUS 2).

G. W. Botsford, *The Roman Assemblies* (1909), 270 ff., 300 f. P. T.

PUBLILIUS (2) **PHILO**, QUINTUS, the first plebeian dictator (339 B.C.), is credited with three laws which were a landmark in the struggle for social equality: (1) censorship should be opened to plebeians; (2) *plebiscita* should be binding on the whole community (an anticipation of the *Lex Hortensia*); (3) the *auctoritas patrum* should be reduced to the formal ratifying of proposals, before they went forward to the centuriate assembly. Publilius was the first plebeian praetor (337), and, as censor (332), helped towards creating the new tribes Maecia and Scaptia. As consul he besieged Naples (327) and was appointed pro-consul for 326 (the first known example of *prorogatio imperii*). The tradition which records his triumphs (over the Latins in 339, and over the Samnites and Palaeopolitae in 326) is not altogether trustworthy. He played a leading part in the recovery of Rome after the Caudine catastrophe, but details of his later career (e.g. his alleged implication in the rebellion of Capua in 314) are uncertain.

CAH vii. 482 f., 530 f., 595 ff.; G. W. Botsford, *The Roman Assemblies* (1909), 299 ff. P. T

PUBLILIUS (3) **SYRUS** (not Publius, Woelfflin, *Philol.* xxii (1865), 439) came to Rome as a slave in the first century B.C., presumably from Antioch (Plin. *HN* 35. 199). Intellectual ability, psychological discernment, and wit ensured him manumission. He devoted his gifts to the latinized form of the mime, where his one rival was the veteran knight Laberius (q.v.), whom he surpassed in the competition between them ordered by Julius Caesar. Only two of his titles, both doubtful, are recorded: *Putatores* (? *Potatores*) and *Murmidon* (Nonius, 2. 133; Priscian, *Inst.* K. 2. 532. 25). His clever improvisations suffered through being entrusted to the frail security of actors' copies, but some retained a scenic vogue at least until Nero's time. The elder Seneca commended his power of expressing some thoughts better than any other dramatist; Petronius seems to cite from him a passage of 16 lines; and Gellius quotes for their neatness 14 maxims (Sen. *Controv.* 7. 3. 8; Petron. 55; Gell. 17. 14).

In the first century A.D. it was realized that, whatever the harm wrought by the immorality of mimes, the apophthegms uttered by various dramatic personages might well be selected and alphabetically arranged to inculcate on schoolboys a proverbial wisdom founded on human experience. So it came about later that Jerome learned in class the line which he quotes twice, 'aegre reprehendas quod sinas consuescere' (Hieron. *Epist.* 107. 8; 128. 4). The great textual difficulty is to disengage truly Publilian *sententiae* from accretions due to paraphrases of genuine verses, or insertions of Senecan and pseudo-Senecan ideas, or such distortions of the original iambic senarii and trochaic septenarii as induced copyists to mistake them for prose.

There could be no unified ethical standard among maxims spoken by different characters in different scenes. Some are platitudes; some contradict others, as proverbs often do. Many advocate self-regarding behaviour; yet the prevailing terseness of expression is an undeniable attraction.

Text: J. K. Orelli, *Publii* [sic] *Syri Mimi et aliorum Sententiae* (1822; 791 iambics and 83 trochaics, with Scaliger's Greek verse translations. Editions: W. Meyer, *Publii* [sic] *Syri Sententiae* (1880; 733 lines). R. A. H. Bickford-Smith, *Pub. Syr. Sent.* (1895; 722 lines). Translation: J. Wight Duff and A. M. Duff in *Minor Latin Poets* (Loeb 1934, revised 1935; 734 lines). J. W. D.

PUDICITIA, personification of the chastity or modesty of women. According to Livy (10. 23), she was originally worshipped as Pudicitia Patricia in a small shrine in the Forum Boarium, but in 296 B.C. a rival cult of Pudicitia Plebeia was founded in the Vicus Longus. At first limited to women who had married but once, the cult degenerated and was forgotten.

For criticism see Wissowa, *Gesammelte Abhandlungen*, 254 ff.; Platner–Ashby, 433 ff., where more references are given; for other cults, see Wissowa, *RK* 334. H. J. R.

PUGILLARES, *see* BOOKS, II. 3.

PULCHER, *see* CLAUDIUS, CLODIUS.

PULVINAR, (1) a couch, such as was used for the images or symbols of gods at a *lectisternium* (q.v.; Horace, *Carm.* 1. 37. 3 and often). This seems to be a purely Greek rite, adopted in Rome. (2) A platform on which such objects were placed, either to be adored at a *supplicatio* (q.v.), or for other ritual purposes, see [Acro] on Horace, loc. cit. and literature under SUPPLICATIONES. H. J. R.

PUNIC WARS: three wars in which Rome gradually superseded Carthage as the dominant power in the western Mediterranean. The early relations of Rome and Carthage had been friendly. The interests of Rome, which were primarily agricultural and confined to Italy, did not clash with those of the Carthaginians, who gained a commercial monopoly in the Western Mediterranean. Treaties were negotiated (probably in 509 and 348 B.C.), confirming this Punic monopoly and guaranteeing Italian coast-towns against Carthaginian attack, while the hostility of Pyrrhus to both Rome and Carthage resulted in a supplementary agreement between the two powers (279). But in 264 when the Carthaginians occupied Messana in north-east Sicily a dangerous situation was created, since Rome was now the ally of the Greek cities in south Italy, who saw a threat to their trade or security if Carthage dominated Sicily and the Straits of Messana. When therefore the Mamertines (q.v.) in Messana appealed to Rome for help, the Senate hesitated, foreseeing the possibility of war with Carthage, but the People decided to accept the Mamertine alliance whatever the consequences. When Appius Claudius (q.v. 5) Caudex crossed to Sicily war was declared. In fact both Rome and Carthage had rushed in to secure a key position, but with different motives: defensive imperialism dominated Roman policy; an exploiting commercial imperialism actuated Carthage. Neither side used the Messana affair as an excuse for a predetermined war, but being different in race, culture, and religion, with divergent moral and material interests,

Rome and Carthage would gravitate more quickly towards conflict when the minor States between them had been eliminated or assimilated. In the Hellenistic East a common culture held the three great monarchies in a precarious balance of power, which Rome later tried to maintain when she had absorbed something of that culture. In the West dissimilarity made compromise more difficult.

2. THE FIRST PUNIC WAR (264–241) opened with a successful Roman offensive conducted by Appius Claudius Caudex and M. Valerius (q.v. 4) Messalla against the Carthaginians and Hieron in north-east Sicily; this resulted in Hieron entering into alliance with Rome (263). In 262 the Romans won Segesta and, after a siege, Agrigentum, but since Carthage continued fighting they realized that peace could be secured only by driving the Carthaginians completely out of Sicily: this involved challenging their naval supremacy. By a magnificent achievement the Romans built some 160 vessels equipped with grapnels (*corvi*) which helped to thwart their enemy's superior naval skill. The new fleet commanded by Duilius (q.v.) defeated the Carthaginians off Mylae (260). When no decisive result was reached in Sicily, the Romans sent an expeditionary force under Regulus (q.v. 1) to Africa; after the way had been opened by a great naval victory off Ecnomus, it landed in Africa (256), but was defeated in 255. A relieving fleet defeated the Punic navy off the Hermaean Promontory, evacuated the survivors of Regulus' army, but was wrecked by a storm off Pachynus on the way home. In Sicily the Romans captured Panormus (254), thus confining the Carthaginians to the western end of the island, but a newly raised fleet was wrecked off Cape Palinurus (253). Both sides were exhausted. After L. Metellus (q.v. 1) had repulsed a Punic attack on Panormus (250), the Romans blockaded Lilybaeum and Drepana. A naval attack by P. Claudius (q.v.) Pulcher on Drepana failed, while the rest of the fleet was wrecked off south Sicily (249); the Romans, however, seized Mt. Eryx (q.v.), thus cutting off the land-communications of Drepana. Despite the fresh efforts in Sicily of Hamilcar (q.v.) Barca, 247–241, the Romans at length raised a new fleet under C. Lutatius Catulus (q.v.), who defeated the Carthaginians off Aegates Insulae and negotiated peace-terms, which ultimately included the evacuation of Sicily and an indemnity of 3,200 talents to be paid in ten years.

3. Carthage immediately had to face a serious revolt of her mercenaries (the 'Truceless War'). Scarcely had she crushed this, when the Romans occupied Sardinia in answer to an appeal from some mercenaries there (238). To Carthaginian protests Rome replied by refusing arbitration and declaring war: Carthage had to submit, surrender Sardinia and Corsica, and pay an additional 1,200 talents. The desire to deprive Carthage of an island base against Italy may partly explain this wanton aggression, which embittered relations which were just becoming more friendly. Primarily as compensation for the loss of Sicily and Sardinia the imperialist party at Carthage turned to Spain, which would also furnish abundant natural wealth and man-power in the event of future hostilities with Rome. The conquest of Spain was achieved from 237 to 219 by Hamilcar, Hasdrubal, and Hannibal (qq.v.). By attacking Rome's ally, Saguntum, Hannibal deliberately precipitated the Second Punic War. The question of war-guilt is complicated. Possibly it was not a long-premeditated war of revenge championed by the family of Barca, but when the Romans interfered south of the Ebro (the Punic sphere of influence *de facto* and possibly *de jure*), Hannibal refused to contemplate a recurrence of bullying such as Carthage had suffered in 238: he struck before Rome was ready.

4. THE SECOND PUNIC WAR (218–201). The Romans prepared to send one army to Africa, a second to Spain, but were foiled by Hannibal's bold invasion of north

Italy (*see* HANNIBAL *and* SCIPIO 3). They wisely, however, sent an army to Spain where P. and Cn. Scipio (q.v. 4 and 3) prevented reinforcements reaching Hannibal, won a sea-battle which gave Rome naval supremacy, and took the offensive until their deaths (211); their successor Claudius Nero (q.v. 2) still held the line of the Ebro. Meantime Hannibal had defeated Roman armies at Trebia (218), Trasimene (217), and Cannae (216), but as Rome refused to admit defeat and retained the loyalty of central and northern Italy he attempted to encircle her with a ring of enemies. But this wider strategy ultimately failed: in the west his brother Hasdrubal's offensive in Spain was repulsed (215), while a Carthaginian landing in Sardinia proved abortive (215); in the north the hostile Gauls failed to take decisive action; in the east an alliance was made with Philip V of Macedon, who, however, un-aided by the Punic fleet, gradually lost interest in the First Macedonian War (214–205) and negotiated the Peace of Phoenice with Rome (*see* VALERIUS 5 *and* GALBA 2); in the south Greek cities were encouraged to revolt, but their leader Syracuse was reduced to submission by 211 by Marcellus (q.v. 1). Meantime in Italy Hannibal's strength was being worn down by Fabius, Sempronius Gracchus, Marcellus, and Fulvius (qq.v.) Flaccus, who avoided further pitched battles and recovered Capua (which had revolted after Cannae) in 211 and Tarentum in 209. Hasdrubal, who at length broke through to Italy from Spain, was defeated at the Metaurus by Claudius Nero and Livius Salinator (q.v.) in 207, and thereby Hannibal's last hope of receiving reinforcements died, despite the attempt of Mago (q.v.). Scipio (q.v.) Africanus victoriously drove the Carthaginians from Spain by his final victory at Ilipa (206) and led an expeditionary force to Africa where his successive victories forced the recall of Hannibal from Italy. Thanks to his tactical reforms and the help of Masinissa (q.v.), Scipio defeated Hannibal at the battle of Zama (q.v., 202). In 201 peace was signed: Carthage surrendered her navy and Spain, retained her autonomy and her territory within the Phoenician Trenches (i.e. roughly modern Tunisia), became a dependent ally of Rome, and paid an indemnity of 10,000 talents in fifty annual instalments. But the Romans evacuated Africa. Factors which gave Rome the victory included her superiority by sea and in man-power, the loyalty of the Italian allies, the wisdom of the Senate and the doggedness of the People, the blocking of reinforcements to Hannibal, the defensive strategy of Fabius in Italy combined with the offensive strategy of Scipio, who forged a weapon which drove the Carthaginians from Spain and vanquished Hannibal himself. Against such factors Hannibal's untiring gallantry and genius were unavailing. The war was a turning-point in ancient history; it had profound effects on the political, economic, social, and religious life of Italy, while thereafter for centuries no power could endanger Rome's existence.

5. THE THIRD PUNIC WAR (149–146). Carthage, no longer a great Mediterranean power, made a remarkably quick economic recovery, thanks partly to Hannibal's financial reforms, but she was continually provoked by Masinissa, whose aggression the Romans did little to check until they feared that his African kingdom might soon embrace Carthage itself. Cato (q.v. 1), from motives of revenge and fear, urged the destruction of Carthage; Nasica (*see* SCIPIO 10) advocated a more lenient policy. There is little evidence to suggest that Roman policy was dictated by commercial jealousy. Intervention was legally justified when Carthage was goaded into attacking Masinissa, Rome's ally (150). Rome declared war on Carthage (149), and a Roman army under Manilius (q.v. 1) landed in Africa. Carthage surrendered, handed over hostages and arms, and then heard the Roman terms that the city itself must be destroyed. Unexpectedly she refused to comply, and with desperate heroism withstood a Roman blockade until 146, when Scipio (q.v. 11) Aemili-anus stormed and sacked the city. Carthage having been destroyed, her territory was made into the Roman province of Africa.

BIBLIOGRAPHY

ANCIENT SOURCES: For the *First Punic War*, Polybius, bk. 1 based mainly upon the pro-Roman Fabius Pictor and the pro-Carthaginian Philinus (see F. W. Walbank, *CQ* 1945). For the *Second Punic War*, Polybius, bk. 3 and fragmentary notices in 7–15. He drew upon both Roman material (public archives, family records, oral tradition from survivors, and writers as Fabius) and Punic material (the Greek writers Sosylus and Silenus who lived with Hannibal). Livy, bks. 21–30, provides a detailed narrative, based partly upon Polybius, partly upon less trustworthy Roman annalists. For the *Third Punic War* Polybius' account is fragmentary (bks. 36–9). Appian's account (*Libyca*, 67–135) is based upon Polybius, though contaminated with inferior annalistic material. Subsidiary authorities add little.

MODERN LITERATURE: *General.* Tenney Frank and B. L. Hallward in *CAH* vii, ch. 21, and viii, chs. 2–5, 15; H. H. Scullard, *A History of the Roman World* (1935); S. Gsell, *Histoire ancienne de l'Afrique du Nord* i–iv (1913–20), esp. vol. iii; E. Pais, *Storia di Roma durante le guerre puniche* (1927); G. De Sanctis, *Stor. Rom.*, vol. iii, pts. 1, 2 (1916–17) which is of fundamental importance for the First and Second Wars; U. Kahrstedt, *Geschichte der Karthager von 218–146* (1913), containing detailed source criticism. For the separate battles J. Kromayer and G. Veith, *Antike Schlachtfelder* iii, iv (1912–31) and *Schlachten-Atlas zur antiken Kriegsgeschichte, röm. Abt.* i, ii (1922).

Special. W. W. Tarn, 'The Fleets of the First Punic War', *JHS* 1907; J. H. Thiel, *Studies on the History of Roman Sea-power* (Amsterdam, 1946), ch. ii. On the question of war-guilt, G. De Sanctis, *Problemi di storia antica* (1932) and E. Bickermann, *Revue de philologie*, 1936. H. H. Scullard, *Scipio Africanus in the Second Punic War* (1930); E. Groag, *Hannibal als Politiker* (1929); F. E. Adcock, 'Delenda est Carthago', *CHJ* 1946, 117 ff.

H. H. S.

PUPIENUS, *see* BALBINUS.

PUPIUS, PUBLIUS, contemporary with Horace, who calls his tragedies 'lacrimosa poemata' (*Epist.* 1. 1. 67).
Cf. Baehr. *FPR* 348; Morel *FPL* 112.

PUPIUS, *see* PISO (4).

PURPLE. The purple dye, which the Romans valued so highly that it became for them the symbol of power and luxury, was obtained from several species of shellfish —πορφύρα, κήρυξ, *purpura*, *murex*, *buccinum*. The fish had to be opened as soon as it was caught, for the dye was contained in a vein which dried up after death. When these veins had been extracted they were steeped in salt water for five days and the liquid was then boiled in vats. It was found that the dye from the purpura was very dark, while that from the murex was brighter, so that a mixture was often made, one part of purpura to two of murex. In this the wool was left for five hours, then taken out and dried, and finally given a second dipping until all the dye was absorbed. This was the famous twice-dyed Tyrian purple; a pound of wool so dyed cost 1,000 *denarii* (£40). Purple robes often formed part of the insignia of kings, magistrates, and commanders in the field. At Rome magistrates, senators, and *Equites* wore garments with a purple border. *See also* DYEING.
Pliny, *HN* 9. 36–65. D'A. W. Thompson, *A Catalogue of Greek Fishes* (1947), s.v. πορφύρα. F. A. W.

PUTEOLI, nowadays *Pozzuoli*, a town near Naples (*see* PAUSILYPUS MONS). Samian colonists from Cumae founded Dicaearchia here (*c.* 521 B.C.). When Dicaearchia became Puteoli is unknown (Strabo 5. 245 f.). Presumably Puteoli became a Roman dependency at the same time as Capua in 338 (cf. Festus p. 262 L.). In the Hannibalic War it was an important military and trading-port (Livy 24. 7; 26. 17), and in 194 became a citizen colony which was subsequently recolonized several times (Dessau, *ILS* 5317; Plut. *Sulla*, 37; Tac. *Ann.* 14. 27; Pliny, *HN* 3. 61). As the harbour of Rome, Puteoli became a great commercial entrepôt, by 125 B.C. second only to Delos (Festus p. 109 L.). All Rome's eastern imports and exports, including grain, passed through Puteoli (Strabo 3. 145; 17. 793; Pliny, *HN* 36. 70; Seneca, *Ep.* 77). Its trade guilds, fire-brigade, imperial post station, its special road (Via Domitiana) joining the Via Appia, its lighthouse, artificial harbour-works and surviving monuments (e.g. amphitheatre), attest a prosperity which survived the rivalry of Ostia. Devastations by Alaric (410), Genseric (455), and Totila (545) finally ruined Puteoli. In its heyday Puteoli was a fashionable villa resort, e.g. of Sulla, Cicero, Hadrian.

K. J. Beloch, *Campanien²* (1890); C. Dubois, *Pouzzuoles Antiques* (1907); K. Lehmann-Hartleben, *Antike Hafenanlagen des Mittelmeeres* (1923), 163; J. Bérard, *Bibliogr. topogr.* (1941), p. 83. E. T. S.

PYGMALION, (1) Legendary king of Tyre, brother of Elissa (Dido), whose husband, Acherbas or Sychaeus, he killed in the hope of obtaining his fortune. (See Verg. *Aen.* 1. 343–64, Justin. *Epit.* 18. 4, and DIDO.) (2) Legendary king of Cyprus, who having fashioned an ivory statue of a woman fell in love with it. Aphrodite gave it life, and the woman bore P. a daughter, Paphos, the mother of Cinyras (Ovid, *Met.* 10. 243–97), though according to Apollod. *Bibl.* 3. 14. 3 Cinyras was P.'s son-in-law. Philostephanus (*FHG* iii. 31, fr. 13) calls the statue a figure of Aphrodite. P. was perhaps, like Cinyras (q.v.), a priest-king, associated with the cult of Aphrodite-Astarte (cf. J. G. Frazer, *Adonis Attis Osiris* i, ch. 3). F. R. W.

PYGMIES, dwarfs of ridiculous appearance who live in Africa, or India, or Scythia. They are mentioned and discussed in Greek mythology in connexion with their fight against the cranes. Homer (*Il.* 3. 6) says that the cranes flee before the winter to the (Southern) stream of Oceanus and bring death to the Pygmies. Hecataeus of Miletus, who definitely located the P. in Southern Egypt, Ctesias, and the writers on India (e.g. Megasthenes) considerably elaborated the story. The P. disguise themselves as rams, or ride on rams and goats. They battle with the cranes to protect their fields, or even conduct operations to destroy the eggs of the cranes. Other mythographers invented explanations for the struggle, tracing the enmity back to a beautiful pygmy girl transformed into a crane (Boeus in Athen. 9. 393 e).

As Herodotus hinted (2. 32. 6) and Aristotle (*Hist. An.* 8. 12. 597 a) confirmed, the dwarfs of central Africa may have been the origin of the myth. Modern explorers report that the Akka dwarfs hunt cranes and that the birds vigorously resist. Around this core of fact, possibly conveyed to Greeks through Egyptian sources (R. Hennig, *Rh. Mus.* 1932), grew a solid shell of dwarf folklore (R. Dangel, *SMSR* 1931, 128) and novelistic invention. The geranomachy is often shown in Greek art, the François vase being the earliest instance. In Hellenistic art dwarfs or P. are often used for parodies of mythological and *genre* scenes, or shown in Nile landscapes (W. B. MacDaniel, *AJArch.* 1932, 260). G. M. A. H.

PYLAEMENES, in mythology, king of the Paphlagonian Eneti (*Iliad* 2. 851). He is distinguished chiefly for coming to life in *Il.* 13. 658, cf. 643, after being killed in 5. 576, a slip of Homer's from which most ridiculous consequences have been drawn by ancient and modern critics. H. J. R.

PYLOS was the name of three places in western Peloponnese (Strabo 8. 339; cf. Ar. *Eq.* 1059). *Messenian Pylos* lay at the north end of Navarino Bay, on a rocky peninsula joined by a sandspit to the mainland, and separated by a narrow channel from the island of Sphacteria. Uninhabited in 425 B.C., the Athenians fortified it and held it with a Messenian garrison until 409 (Diod. 13. 64). Its subsequent history is obscure. It is surprising that this fertile district, with one of the best harbours of Greece, was not more important; its only great period was the Mycenaean. A palace of the

thirteenth century has recently been discovered on a hill four miles to the north, with more than six hundred clay tablets inscribed in characters descended from the latest Minoan script. This may well be called the palace of Neleus and Nestor. There are also beehive-tombs near.

Thuc. bk. 4. R. M. Burrows, *JHS* 1896, 55 ff.; 1898, 147 ff. T. J. D.

PYLOS in Triphylia, a little south of Samikon, was taken by Strabo (followed by some moderns) for the Homeric town of that name. Rich beehive-tombs of the sixteenth century have been found in this district, near Kakovatos.

Strabo 8. 344 ff.; W. Dörpfeld and K. Müller, *Ath. Mitt.* 1908, 295 ff.; 1909, 269 ff. T. J. D.

PYRAMUS and **THISBE,** hero and heroine of a love-story almost unknown except from Ovid, *Met.* 4. 55 ff., who says, 53, that it is not a common tale. They were next-door neighbours in Babylon, and, as their parents would not let them marry, they talked with each other through the party-wall of the houses, which was cracked. Finally they arranged to meet at Ninus' tomb. There Thisbe was frightened by a lion coming from its kill; she dropped her cloak as she ran and the lion mouthed it. Pyramus, finding the bloodstained cloak and supposing her dead, killed himself; she returned, found his body, and followed his example. Their blood stained a mulberry-tree, whose fruit has ever since been black when ripe, in sign of mourning for them. H. J. R.

PYRENEES (Πυρήνη, τὰ Πυρηναῖα ὄρη; *Pyrenaeus mons*), the range of mountains between Gaul and Spain. The name was derived from a city, or port of call, frequented by traders from Massilia. Herodotus (2. 33) places near it the source of the Ister (*Danube*). Avienus (559) knew both the town and the mountains, the former near Portus Veneris (*Vendres*). Silius Italicus (3. 441) and Diodorus (5. 35) present other more imaginative derivations. The error of Polybius (34. 7. 4), ascribing a north–south direction for the range, was corrected by Pliny (4. 110), but all classical estimates as to length were excessive. The chief highway (Via Augusta) crossed the mountains near their eastern limit. It was supplemented by a road from Jaca to Pau (*Itin. Ant.* 452. 6), and another from Pamplona to Dax (ibid. 453. 4). Timber, hams, and bacon appear to have been the important contributions of the Pyrenees to the economic life of the peninsula.

Classical references in *PW*, s.v. 'Hispania'. Excellent modern description in M. Sorre, *Les Pyrénées* (1922). J. J. Van N.

PYRRHON (Πύρρων) of Elis (*c.* 360–*c.* 270 B.C.), son of Pleistarchus (Diocl. Magn. ap. Diog. Laert. 9. 61; Aristocl. ap. Euseb. 14. 18. 1; etc.), founder of Scepticism. The son of poor parents, he earned his livelihood by painting (Apollod. and Antig. Car. ap. D.L. 61 f.; etc.). He got his first philosophical lessons from the Megarian Bryson; later he joined the Democritean Anaxarchus, whom he accompanied on Alexander's expedition (Alex. Polyh. ap. D.L. 61; Suid. s.v. 'Pyrrhon' and 'Socrates'; etc.). In later years he lived a single and secluded life in modest circumstances at Elis, honoured and admired by his fellow citizens (Pausan. 6. 24. 5; D.L. 64). P. had several pupils, of whom Timon was the most important. He left no writings.

Pyrrhon aims at imperturbability of mind (Timon ap. Sext. Emp. *Math.* 5. 141, cf. *Pyr.* 1. 10). It is only possible to arrive at this end, he argues, if we understand the nature of things and our relation to them. Seeing that their nature makes it impossible for us to have any undeniable knowledge, P. drew the conclusion that we should not trouble about things we cannot really understand and refrain from idle talk and assertion (ἀφασία, Timon ap. Aristocl. ap. Euseb. 14. 18. 3 f.). Between 'yes' and 'no' there will be no difference. This equilibrium of judgement will immediately create the desired equilibrium in our soul and free us from passion and anxiety.

Pyrrhon's aim in putting forward his theory was ethical. It was not before its connexion with the logical theory of Arcesilaus that Pyrrhonism began to exercise any considerable influence upon philosophical thought. *See also* SCEPTICS.

For bibliography *see under* SCEPTICS.   K. O. B.

PYRRHUS (319–272 B.C.), the most famous of the Molossian kings of Epirus. After reigning as a minor from 307 to 303 he was driven out and followed the fortunes of Demetrius the Besieger. By the influence of Ptolemy II, whose step-daughter Antigone he married, and of Agathocles (q.v.), he became joint king with Neoptolemus (297). He removed Neoptolemus and attempted to set up a Hellenistic type of monarchy over Epirus and to emancipate Epirus from Macedonia. By intervening in a dynastic quarrel in Macedonia Pyrrhus obtained the frontier provinces of Parauaea and Tymphaea, together with Ambracia, Amphilochia, and Acarnania. On the death of Antigone he acquired Corcyra and Leucas as the dowry of his new wife, the daughter of Agathocles, and made an alliance with the Illyrian chief Bardylis, whose daughter he also married. Before he could consolidate his kingdom he went to war with Demetrius, now king of Macedon (291–286), obtaining half of Macedonia, Thessaly, and an alliance with Aetolia and Athens; but he was driven back by Lysimachus (283).

Pyrrhus next undertook to assist Tarentum against the Romans, and with a force of 25,000 men and twenty elephants he defeated the Romans at Heraclea (280). He marched close up to Rome, but failed to impose peace. In 279 he again defeated the Romans at Asculum, and then transferred his forces to Sicily, where he met the Carthaginians, at that time the allies of Rome. He almost expelled the Carthaginians from the island, but broke off the war and returned to Italy. After a drawn battle against the Romans at Beneventum (275), he retired to Epirus with one-third of his expeditionary force. In a new attempt to conquer Macedonia he penned up Antigonus Gonatas in Thessalonica but suddenly moved off to Peloponnesus, where he failed in a siege of Sparta and was killed in a street fight at Argos.

A brilliant tactician and adroit opportunist, Pyrrhus impressed his contemporaries but never won a lasting victory. His death left Epirus exhausted.

Plutarch, *Pyrrhus*; G. N. Cross, *Epirus* (1932).   N. G. L. H.

PYRRHUS, *see also* NEOPTOLEMUS.

PYTHAGORAS (1), son of Mnesarchus of Samos, emigrated c. 531 B.C., perhaps to escape the tyranny of Polycrates, to Croton. He was a devotee of Apollo, and the Crotoniates identified him with Apollo Hyperboreus. He wrote nothing (though works were later fathered on him) and already in Aristotle's day his life was obscured by legend; but a gibe of Xenophanes (fr. 7 Diels) establishes his belief in metempsychosis, and Heraclitus (frs. 40, 129), Empedocles (fr. 129), Ion of Chios (fr. 4), and Herodotus (4. 95) testify to his spiritual powers and learning. These and later statements indicate that he believed the soul to be a fallen divinity confined within the body as a tomb and condemned to a cycle of reincarnation as man, animal, or plant, from which, however, it may win release by cultivation of an Apolline purity. The spirit, he held, is purified by study; accordingly he taught a 'way of life' (Pl. *Resp.* 600 b), in which the investigation of nature (ἱστορίη) became a religion. He is reliably said to have discovered the numerical ratios determining the principal intervals of the musical scale,

whence he was led to interpret the world as a whole through numbers, the systematic study of which he thus originated (Aristox. fr. 23 Wehrli; Eudem. fr. 84 Spengel). He is possibly the discoverer (though not in its Euclidean form) of 'Pythagoras' Theorem' (Eucl. 1. 47).

In Croton P. founded a religious society, under the government of which this city rose to supremacy among the Achaean towns in Italy. A conspiracy under Cylon led, however, to P.'s retirement to Metapontum, where he died; and at some date between 460 and 400 the order was almost wholly destroyed. Survivors settled in Thebes (Lysis, Philolaus) and Phleius, some afterwards returning to Tarentum, which became the chief seat of the school till its extinction in the late fourth century B.C. Membership of the order, open to women equally with men, entailed a strict discipline of purity, elements in which were silence, self-examination (πῇ παρέβην, τί δ' ἔρεξα, τί μοι δέον οὐκ ἐτελέσθη; Diog. Laert. 8. 22), abstention from flesh, and the observation of precepts originally taboos but later interpreted symbolically (ἀκούσματα, σύμβολα). Fourth-century writers distinguish divergent religious and scientific groups, ἀκουσματικοί (Πυθαγορισταί) and μαθηματικοί (Πυθαγόρειοι).

Starting from P.'s discovery of the intervals, his followers devoted themselves to arithmetic, using a notation consisting probably of patterns of dots; the most important of these was the τετρακτύς, which represented the number ten as sum of the first four integers and was traditionally attributed to P. himself. They said the universe was produced by the First Unit (the Heaven) inhaling the Infinite (or Void), so as to form groups of units or numbers (Ar. *Metaph.* N 1091[a]15 f., *Phys.* 213[b]22 f.), and that all things (even, e.g., opinion, opportunity, injustice, Ar. *Metaph.* A 990[b]22) were numbers and had position. Their earlier geocentric astronomy was based on that of the early Ionians, but probably by about 500 B.C. they had reached the hypothesis that the earth is spherical. Aristotle attributes to them (*Cael.* 293[a]18 f.) an astronomical system presupposing a central fire, around which circle the celestial bodies, including sun, earth (which thus first becomes a planet), and counter-earth (ἀντίχθων, intended to account for lunar eclipses). This system, to which the older belief in a 'harmony of the spheres' was accommodated, appears to date at earliest from the late fifth century. *See also* ASTRONOMY, MATHEMATICS.

For Pythagorean writers of independent importance (Alcmaeon, Philolaus, Archytas, etc.) and for Neopythagoreanism see separate articles.

Diels, *Vorsokr.*[5] i. 96–113, 440–80; Mullach, *FPG* i. 485–509 (*Pythagoreorum Similitudines*); R. Hercher, *Epistolographi*, 601 (*Pythagoreorum Epistulae*); Burnet, *Early Greek Philosophy*[4], 80–112, 276–309; T. Heath, *History of Greek Mathematics* (1921) i. 65–117, 141–69; Zeller-Mondolfo, *La filosofia dei Greci* i[a] (1938), 288–685; E. Frank, *Plato und die sogenannten Pythagoreer* (1923).   A. H. C.

PYTHAGORAS (2), Greek sculptor of the first half of the fifth century B.C. A native of Samos and later resident at Rhegium in Italy, whither he probably emigrated on the fall of Samos in 494. He is reputed to have introduced greater realism into art and was the first to emphasize the importance of 'rhythm' and 'symmetry' in art. No work of his is known, and only one Roman copy is thought to reflect his style—the so-called 'Omphalos Apollo' at Athens.   S. C.

PYTHEAS (c. 310–306 B.C.), Greek navigator of Massalia. From Strabo, Diodorus, and Pliny mostly we learn (from evidence distrusted by the ancients) that, sailing from Gades (*Cadiz*) past Cape Ortegal, the Loire, north-west France, and Uxisame (*Ushant*), he visited Belerium (*Cornwall*) and the tin-depot at Ictis (*St. Michael's Mount*), circumnavigated Britain, described its inhabitants and climate, reported an island Thule (q.v.) (*Norway* or *Iceland*), sailed perhaps to the Vistula, and reported an estuary (*Frisian Bight?*) and an island (*Heligoland?*) abounding in amber. P. calculated closely the latitude of Massalia and laid bases for cartographic parallels through north France and Britain.

Cf. M. Cary and E. Warmington, *Ancient Explorers* (1929), 33 ff.; E. Warmington, *Greek Geog.* (1934), 169 ff.; G. E. Broche, *Pythéas le Massaliote* (1936). E. H. W.

PYTHERMUS (1), poet, of Teos, wrote drinking-songs, of which one line survives. He composed in the Ionian mode and was mentioned by Hipponax (Ath. 625 c).

E. Diehl, *Anth. Lyr. Graec.* ii. 60.

PYTHERMUS (2) of Ephesus, writing after Antiochus I or II and followed by Hegesandrus (*c.* 150 B.C.), published Ἱστορίαι in eight books, treating Hellenistic history.

FHG iv. 487.

PYTHIA, see APOLLO, para. 4.

PYTHIAN GAMES. From early times there had been a festival at Delphi in connexion with the oracle of Apollo, with a musical competition consisting of a hymn to the god—νόμος Πυθικός—sung to a cithara accompaniment. This took place every eighth year, but in 582 B.C. the festival was reorganized and placed under the management of the Amphictionic Council. Henceforth it was celebrated in the third year of each Olympiad. The musical competitions—in instrumental music,

singing, drama, and recitations in verse and prose—still took the first place, but to them now were added athletic and equestrian contests modelled on those at Olympia. The stadium for the foot-races lay close under Mount Parnassus, the chariot-races were held in the Crisaean plain, where a hippodrome was constructed. The prize was a crown of bay-leaves cut in the valley of Tempe. The Pythian Games ranked next in importance after the Olympic. F. A. W.

PYTHIUS of Priene (4th c. B.C.), architect. He designed the Mausoleum (q.v.) at Halicarnassus and the temple of Athena Polias at Priene, both in the Ionic Order. He held the opinion that architects should be well versed in the arts, and objected to the use of the Doric order in sacred buildings because of the complications arising from the spacing of the triglyphs. His books on the temple and the Mausoleum have not survived. (Vitruv. I. 1; 4. 3; 7, *praef.*) H. W. R.

PYTHON (mythological), see APOLLO, paras. 4 and 5.

PYTHON of Catana or Byzantium was said to be author of a satyric play called *Agen*, produced in 324 B.C. in the camp of Alexander the Great on the Hydaspes (in the Punjab); some attributed it to Alexander himself. It contained references to Harpalus and other contemporary persons in the style of the Old Comedy (Ath. 13. 95 f.).

TGF 810–11. A. W. P.-C.

Q

QUADI, a German tribe of the Suebic group, left the Main region (*c.* 8 B.C.) and went to Moravia; they were closely connected with the Marcomanni. Vannius established a kingdom between the March and the Waag, but was overthrown *c.* A.D. 50, his followers being settled by the Romans in Pannonia. After a war against Domitian the Quadi maintained peace till the great Marcomannic Wars. Though overwhelmed by Rome, they remained a permanent danger, and often with Marcomanni or Sarmatae-Jazyges plundered Roman land (e.g. under Valerian and Gallienus and in 282, 358, and 375). Later some of the Quadi joined the Vandals and Alani and went to Spain.

Franke, *PW*, s.v. 'Marcomanni'; C. Patsch, *Sitz. Wien*, 209 v (1929) and 217 i (1937); L. Schmidt, *Geschichte der deutschen Stämme. Die Westgermanen²* (1938); J. Klose, *Roms Klientel-Randstaaten am Rhein und an der Donau* (1934). F. A. W. S.

QUADRIGARIUS, see CLAUDIUS (11).

QUADRIGATUS, see COINAGE, ROMAN, para. 5.

QUADRIVIUM, see EDUCATION, I. 9.

QUAESTIO. The introduction of *quaestiones*, permanent criminal courts, composed of thirty or more jurymen under the presidency of a praetor, resulted in a thorough reform of criminal justice in Rome. First appointed as commissions for inquiry in exceptional cases, they became later a standing institution; the first *quaestio perpetua* was constituted by the *Lex Calpurnia* (149 B.C.) for the *crimen repetundarum* (see REPETUNDAE). This example was followed by several *leges*; under Sulla, Caesar, and Augustus the *quaestiones* were systematized and extended. They were never organized by a general statute, but Augustus' *Lex Iulia iudiciorum publicorum* brought some order into the variety of procedural rules produced by copious legislation. The

quaestiones were gradually extended to all the more serious crimes, superseding the jurisdiction of magistrates and *comitia*; for each category of such crimes new tribunals were created. Members of the jury were originally senators; subsequently, after long political struggles—for justice in criminal matters acquired a political character—*equites* (see EQUES) replaced them or shared the courts with them. (*See also* GRACCHUS (4), DRUSUS (2), COTTA (3).) *Tribuni aerarii* (q.v.), an intermediate class between *equites* and *plebs*, substantially independent, were admitted to the jury from 70 B.C. to the time of Augustus.

Criminal prosecutions in the *quaestiones* were not initiated by the magistrate, but by an accusation (*nominis delatio*), which could be made by any citizen who on request (*postulatio*) obtained an authorization from the chairman of the competent court. The accusation was presented in writing to the magistrate, who entered the charge in the official record (*nomen recipere*) and directed the trial. The court for judging each case was constituted with the co-operation of both the parties, accuser and accused. They had a limited right of challenging the jurors, who were chosen by lot from a panel of persons qualified for this function. The jurymen gave their verdict on the guilt of the accused by a majority of votes; the presiding magistrate had no right to vote, but he inflicted the statutory penalty. No appeal was admitted. The crimes for which particular *quaestiones* were instituted were *res repetundae* (q.v.); murder and poisoning (by the *Leges Sempronia* and *Cornelia de sicariis et veneficis*); murder of near relations (see PARRICIDIUM); *maiestas* (see PERDUELLIO); *peculatus* and *sacrilegium* (theft of *res publicae* and *sacrae*); bribery by candidates at elections (*ambitus*); falsification of coins, weights, documents, wills, etc. (*falsum*); grave cases of injury; violence (*vis*); traffic in free persons (*plagium*); adultery and contraventions against the provisioning of the people (annona). The *quaestiones* disappeared in the first half of the third century A.D., when criminal jurisdiction was conferred upon other organs of the State.

H. F. Hitzig, *Die Herkunft des Schwurgerichts im röm. Strafprozess* (1909); J. Lengle, 'Auswahl der Richter im röm. Quästionenprozess', *Sav. Zeitschr.* liii (1933); A. H. J. Greenidge, *The Legal Procedure of Cicero's Time* (1901), 415 ff. *See also* LAW AND PROCEDURE, ROMAN, III. A. B.

QUAESTOR. In spite of a definite statement of Tacitus (*Ann.* 11. 22), it is generally held that no quaestors existed under the monarchy, and that the office was created at the beginning of the Republic. At first they were nominated by the consuls, but from 449 B.C. were elected by the tribal assembly. Their number was originally two, but in 421, when the office was opened to plebeians, it was raised to four (Livy 4. 54). We do not hear of any increase till the time of Sulla, who fixed the number at twenty. Caesar appointed forty, but Augustus reverted to the number of twenty. In early times the quaestors exercised judicial powers (*quaestores parricidii* are mentioned in the XII Tables), but later they were concerned mainly with finance. Their connexion with the consuls was originally very close, and the relation between a quaestor and the higher official to whom he was attached was always considered to be that of a son to a father (Cic. *Planc.* 11. 28). The quaestorship, in spite of its antiquity, was the lowest office in the *cursus honorum* and was held by young men.

Among the quaestors the most important were the two *quaestores urbani*, who were responsible for the *aerarium* q.v.), in which were stored not only reserves of money but public documents such as decrees of the Senate and accounts. Quaestors conducted sales on behalf of the treasury, and sometimes made financial statements in the Senate, though they did not become regular members of that body till the time of Sulla. Under the Principate the *aerarium* was put in charge of more senior officials, but from A.D. 44 to 56 specially selected quaestors were chosen for this purpose and held office for three years (Tac. *Ann.* 13. 29; *ILS* 966). The remaining quaestors were attached to generals in the field and to provincial governors, and their duties, though primarily financial, were not exclusively so. As a provincial quaestor a young man gained experience which later would prove useful. He might command troops or administer justice, and might even be left in charge of a province as *quaestor pro praetore*. The *provinciae* of the quaestors were determined by the Senate and distributed among the various holders by lot, though a general might have a say in the choice of his quaestor. The practice of *prorogatio* (q.v.) must have been applied to the *provinciae* of quaestors if their number did not exceed four before Sulla's dictatorship. Each provincial governor had one and the governor of Sicily two. In addition to the *quaestores urbani* and the provincial quaestors there were *quaestores classici* and a *quaestor Ostiensis*, connected with the fleet and the corn-supply. In the Principate a quaestor was attached to the proconsuls of senatorial provinces (e.g. Tac. *Agr.* 6), while in the imperial provinces finance was in the charge of an equestrian procurator. The name quaestor was employed by municipal towns and by *collegia* to designate their financial officials.

A. H. J. Greenidge, *Roman Public Life* (1901), 212 ff., 369 ff. G. H. S.

QUEROLUS, the 'Grumbler', anonymous comedy, also called *Aulularia* because of a superficial resemblance to Plautus' *Aulularia*. It was written in Gaul, possibly *c.* A.D. 400. Rutilius, to whom it is dedicated, may thus be Rutilius Namatianus (q.v.); but this common view is not unchallengeable, and some evidence suggests a later date. The play is written in iambic and trochaic cadences, half-way between metre and prose.

Ed. L. Hermann (introd., app. crit., trans., 1937). O. S.

QUIETUS, *see* LUSIUS.

QUINCTILIUS, *see* MAXIMUS (2), VARUS.

QUINCTIUS CAPITOLINUS, TITUS, consul on six occasions between 471 and 439 B.C. His chief recorded achievement, dated 464, when (allegedly as proconsul appointed by a *senatus consultum ultimum*) he extricated the consul Furius from a trap set by the Aequi, bears so great a resemblance to the exploits of Cincinnatus (q.v.) as to suggest that it was an invention (cf. Valerius Antias; Livy 3. 4. 9 to 3. 5. 13). P. T.

QUINCTIUS, *see also* ATTA, CINCINNATUS, FLAMININUS.

QUINDECIMVIRI (originally **Duoviri**, then **Decemviri**, Livy 6. 37. 12, first mentioned as **Quindecimviri** in 51 B.C., Caelius in Cicero, *Fam.* 8. 4. 1) SACRIS FACIUNDIS, one of the *quattuor amplissima collegia* of the Roman clergy. They were originally custodians of the Sibylline books (Livy 5. 13. 5–6 and often), but their activities were probably widened to cover the supervision of all foreign cults recognized or tolerated in Rome (Wissowa, *RK* 543) on the authority of these books. They were of course originally patricians, but after 367 B.C., when their number was raised to ten, half of them were chosen from the plebs. The method was election, probably as for the *pontifices* (q.v.; Cicero above). Caesar increased them to sixteen (Dio Cassius 42. 51. 4), and supernumeraries were common under the Empire (cf. ibid. 51. 20. 3). H. J. R.

QUINQUATRUS, *see* MARS, MINERVA.

QUINQUIREME. The standard warship in the fleets of the Hellenistic States and of the Roman Republic was the quinquireme (πεντήρης), a galley accommodating more rowers than the smaller but similar trireme (q.v.) and gaining thus greater force. The crew on a Roman quinquireme numbered 300, in addition to the marines (Polyb. 1. 26. 7). The arrangement of rowers on a quinquireme is even more uncertain than that on a trireme; probably groups of five oarsmen pulled one large oar in the fashion of the medieval Venetian galleys *a scaloccio*. Since the quinquireme did not appear at Athens until 325 B.C., the report that Dionysius of Syracuse introduced the craft is doubtful; possibly it was Phoenician in origin. Expensive to maintain and difficult to man, this vessel lost its supremacy in the first century B.C. but it still found use in the Roman imperial navy. *See* TRIREME. C. G. S.

QUINTILIANUS, MARCUS FABIUS, born probably between A.D. 35 and 40 at Calagurris in Hispania Tarraconensis (Auson. *Prof. Burd.* 1. 7), the son perhaps (cf. *Inst.* 9. 3. 73) of a rhetorician, who may even have practised at Rome (Sen. *Controv.* 10. *pr.* 2). He was sent to Rome for his education and was, if we may believe the scholiast on Juv. 6. 451, a pupil of the *grammaticus* Remmius Palaemon; at a later date he attached himself to the famous orator Domitius Afer (*Inst.* 5. 7. 7; 10. 1. 86; Plin. *Ep.* 2. 14. 10), from whom he must have learned the practical side of rhetoric and the methods of the courts. Later (but not before A.D. 57 when he was present at the trial of Cossutianus Capito) he went back to Spain, but returned to Rome with Galba in 68 (Hieron. *Chron.*). There he became famous as a teacher and was appointed a salaried Professor of Rhetoric by Vespasian (Hieron. *Chron.* on A.D. 88; but his appointment must have been earlier). Pliny the Younger (l.c.) was one of his pupils. After teaching rhetoric and practising at the bar for twenty years (*Inst.* 1. *pr.* 1) he retired (perhaps in 88, more probably in 90, since he can hardly have settled down as a teacher during the civil wars of A.D. 69). He was well off (Juv. 7. 186–9), and devoted his retirement to writing (see below, WORKS i and ii). While thus engaged he was appointed by Domitian to instruct his two great-nephews (*Inst. 4. pr.* 2), and through the influence of their father Flavius Clemens received the *ornamenta consularia* (Auson. *Grat. Act.* 7. 31). Not long before his retirement he married a young wife who died at the age of 19, leaving him two sons, of whom the younger died when 5, the elder when 9 a few years later (*Inst. 6. pr.* 3 ff.). The date of his own death is uncertain; it is rashly assumed that he died before A.D. 100 on the strength of Pliny's words (l.c.) 'ita certe ex Quintiliano praeceptore meo audisse memini' (written 97–100).

WORKS

(i) *De causis corruptae eloquentiae*, of which nothing remains; our knowledge of its contents does not go beyond four brief references in the *Institutio*. It was begun at the time of the younger son's death (6. *pr.* 3); in view of the mother's youth, not more than three years or less than one can divide the two sons; the work was therefore begun from four to two years before the writing of *Inst.* 6. *pr.* 3.

(ii) *Institutio oratoria*, published c. A.D. 95; for it was composed in little more than two years (*Ep. ad Tryph.*) after long solicitation by his friends; Domitian was still alive when bk. 10 was written (10. 1. 91–2). The work opens with a letter to his publisher Trypho, followed by a dedication to Marcellus Vitorius. It covers the education of an orator—from his cradle almost to his grave. Bk. 1 discusses his education in boyhood, and is so sane, penetrating, and sympathetic in general outlook that it has real value even to-day, while its later chapters on grammar and language are of importance to every student of Latin. Bk. 2 deals with the Schools of Rhetoric and the declamations, which played such a large part in instruction, and with the nature and value of oratory. Bks. 3–9 are of a more technical character; in bk. 3 types of causes are analysed with excess of subtlety, bks. 4–6. 1 discuss the formal structure of a speech in great detail. The rest of bk. 6 provides an oasis on emotional appeal, which contains an illuminating and entertaining chapter (3) on wit and humour. Bk. 7 deals with arrangement, points of law, syllogistic argument, etc. Bk. 8 treats of style, propriety of words, ornament, general reflexions (*sententiae*), and metaphor; bk. 9 of figures of thought and speech, concluding with an interesting chapter (4) on artistic structure and rhythm. Quintilian apologizes for the dryness of his technical details; but through all these books there runs a vein of shrewd wisdom and a sense of reality; he denounces the fantastic absurdity which marked so many themes for declamation. Nevertheless, bk. 10 brings relief; in it he discusses the value of reading, merely as an aid to oratory, it is true; but his review of Greek and Latin authors is deservedly famous, and the exposition of the way in which a speech should be prepared forms a worthy close to an admirable book. Bk. 11 contains an interesting discussion of memory and mnemonics, while its chapter (3) on delivery, gesture, and dress is both instructive and amusing. Bk. 12 deals with higher themes. Accepting Cato's definition of an orator as 'a good man, skilled in speaking', he discourses on the importance of character, the educative value of philosophy, the ideals which should guide the orator, the appropriate use of different styles, and the age at which the orator should retire—a fine book written with grave and attractive dignity. The style is still under the influence of Ciceronianism, lucid, vigorous, and sound, yet marked by the compression and point learned in the schools of his age—a perfect vehicle for his purpose. And he leaves the impression of a man of high ideals, wise, kindly, and in the widest sense humane. *See also* LITERARY CRITICISM IN ANTIQUITY, II. 5; RHETORIC, LATIN, para. 4.

(iii) *Pro Naevio Arpiniano* (accused of throwing his wife out of a window), the sole speech published by himself (7. 2. 24). Two others in defence (1) of Queen Berenice (4. 1. 19), (2) of a woman accused of forgery (9. 2. 73), were published against his will from shorthand reports.

(iv) *Artes rhetoricae*. Two were published from lecture notes against his will (1. *pr.* 7).

(v) *Declamationes* (q.v.). Two collections, *Maiores* and *Minores*, survive under his name. The style and the fantastic nature of much of their contents prove them to be spurious. Their date is uncertain.

TEXTS: C. Halm (1868); F. Meister (1886–7); L. Radermacher (1907–35); with trans. H. Bornecque (1932).

COMMENTARIES: G. L. Spalding (1798–1816; suppl. vols. by C. T. Zumpt (1829) and E. Bonnell (1834)). Bk. 1, C. Fierville (1890); F. H. Colson (1924). Bk. 10, W. Peterson (1891). Bk. 12, A. Beltrami (1910).

TRANSLATIONS: J. S. Watson (1856); H. E. Butler (1921). *See* DECLAMATIONES PS.-Q., EDUCATION. H. E. B.

QUINTUS (1), anatomist and physician of the eclectic school in Rome, in the age of Hadrian (A.D. 117–38), and pupil of Marinus. He founded an important medical school, to which the teachers of Galen belonged. Later he was banished from Rome and died in Pergamum. He left no written works, but his anatomical teaching had great influence, e.g. on Galen. W. D. R.

QUINTUS (2) **SMYRNAEUS** (4th c. A.D.), epic poet, author of a Greek poem, the *Posthomerica*, found in Calabria, headed Ἡ ποίησις τοῦ Ὁμηρικοῦ Κοΐντου, on a manuscript containing also Colluthus, *Rape of Helen* (? 6th c. A.D.). Hence Quintus is sometimes called Calaber, but more often Smyrnaeus, from the single recorded fact about him, that in his youth he lived at Smyrna near the Hermus (Quint. Smyrn. 3. 306–13). The poem, continuing the story of the *Iliad* to the start of the Achaeans for home, shows thorough acquaintance with Homer, but some slight misunderstanding of Homeric Greek, and it may have been meant to form a substitute, in closer agreement with Homer, for the account of the events given in the Epic Cycle (q.v.). The sources are various, some Hellenistic, and one a poem of unknown identity much used by Virgil, possibly the poem indicated by Macrobius (*Sat.* 5. 2) under the name of Peisander. The poetry of Quintus is prolix, never exalted, and sometimes macabre; the parts are greater than the whole, which lacks structural unity; but it has some freedom, competence, eloquence in representing emotion, and pathos, and frequently the similes are attractive.

Texts: A. Zimmermann (1891); A. S. Way (Loeb, 1913); Criticism: F. A. Paley, *On Quintus Smyrnaeus and the 'Homer' of the Tragic Poets* (1876); C. A. Sainte-Beuve, *Étude sur Virgile* (1891); F. Kehmptzow, *De Quinti Smyrnaei fontibus ac mythopoeia* (1891); G. W. Paschal, *A Study of Quintus Smyrnaeus* (1904); W. F. J. Knight, *CQ* xxvi (1932), 178–89. W. F. J. K.

QUIRINAL, the northernmost hill of Rome, traditionally occupied by Sabines, and certainly the site of an early settlement (*Mon. Ant.* 15. 776 ff.) which became one of the Four Regions of Republican Rome. On it were many famous temples, including the age-old *Capitolium vetus* and those of Semo Sancus (466 B.C.), Salus Semonia (311 B.C.), Quirinus (293 B.C.), Honos (*CIL* vi. 30915), Fortuna Publica (204 B.C.), and Venus Erycina (181 B.C.). Later, the hill was the site of houses of famous associations or luxury, as of Atticus, Narcissus, and Martial. Domitian built the *templum gentis Flaviae* on the site of his ancestral home. Constantine erected large *thermae*. The north fringe of the hill was bordered by cemeteries and by Julius Caesar's gardens, which became the notorious *horti Sallustiani*. I. A. R.

QUIRINALIS, *see* CLODIUS (3).

QUIRINIUS, PUBLIUS SULPICIUS (*cos.* 12 B.C.), a *novus homo* from Lanuvium (on his career cf. Tacitus, *Ann.* 3. 48). Quirinius defeated the Marmaridae (Florus 2. 31), perhaps as proconsul of Crete and Cyrene (? *c.*

15 B.C.). Between 12 B.C. and A.D. 2 he subjugated the Homanadenses, 'Cilician' brigands on the southern borderland of the province of Galatia (Strabo 569). The precise date of this war and the command held by Quirinius are disputed. It has been argued that he must have been legate of Syria at the time; but the war could have been conducted only from the side of Galatia, which province, though normally governed by imperial legates of praetorian rank, might easily have been placed under a consular (cf. L. Calpurnius Piso, c. 13 B.C.). Quirinius prudently paid court to Tiberius at Rhodes, succeeded M. Lollius as guide and supervisor of C. Caesar in the East (A.D. 2), and shortly after married Aemilia Lepida, a descendant of Sulla and Pompey. Legate of Syria in A.D. 6, he superintended the assessment of Judaea when that territory was annexed after the death of Archelaus (Josephus, *AJ* 17. 1 ff., cf. *ILS* 2683; also Acts v. 37, which mentions the insurrection of Judas the Galilaean ἐν ταῖς ἡμέραις τῆς ἀπογραφῆς). In order to reconcile and explain St. Luke ii. 1 and establish a date for the Nativity before the death of Herod the Great (i.e. before 4 B.C.), various attempts have been made to discover an earlier governorship of Syria by Quirinius, and, by implication, an earlier census in Judaea. It is by no means certain that the acephalous elogium from Tibur (*ILS* 918) should be attributed to Quirinius, and, in any case, it cannot prove two governorships of Syria.

Quirinius lived to a wealthy and unpopular old age. In 21 he died and was granted a public funeral on the motion of Tiberius, who recounted his meritorious services (Tac. *Ann.* 3. 48).

E. Groag, *PW*, s.v. 'Sulpicius (90)'; L. R. Taylor, *AJPhil.* 1933, 120 ff.; R. Syme, *Klio* 1934, 122 ff., and *Roman Revolution* (1939), see Index. R. S.

QUIRINUS, a god of Sabine origin (Ovid, *Fasti* 2. 475 ff., whereon see Frazer), worshipped from very early times on the Quirinal. Except that his functions resembled those of Mars and that he had sacred arms (Festus, p. 238, 9 Lindsay), we know little of him; he regularly forms a third with Jupiter and Mars (qq.v.; e.g. Livy 8. 9. 6); his flamen (q.v.) is the lowest of the three *flamines maiores* and the third *spolia opima* belong to him (Servius on *Aen.* 6. 859). His flamen's activities are known only in the service of other deities (Gellius 7. 77. 7; Ovid, *Fasti* 4. 910; Tertullian, *De Spect.* 5). His festival is on 17 Feb.; his cult-partner is Hora (Gell. 13. 23. 2), of whom nothing is known. The name must mean 'he of *quirium*'; as this is not a possible word for the labializing Sabine speech, the most plausible etymology is that of Kretschmer (*Glotta* 10. 147 ff.), that it was originally *co-uiri-um*, 'assembly of the men', hence also *Quirites*. See further Wissowa, *RK* 153 ff.; cf. ROMULUS. H. J. R.

R

RABIRIUS (1), GAIUS, had, as a young man, been implicated in the death of Saturninus in 100 B.C. Early in 63 Caesar wished to stress the dangerous situations which might arise from the *senatus consultum ultimum.* At his instigation the tribune Labienus therefore charged Rabirius with murder, resuscitating for his purpose an obsolete method of impeachment. The Senate pronounced the sentence invalid; and when a more regular action was brought before the Comitia Centuriata Cicero himself defended Rabirius. The trial had served its purpose; and with Caesar's connivance the praetor Metellus Celer broke up the court by a convenient legal fiction.

See Cicero, *Pro Rabirio.* Cf. E. G. Hardy, *Journ. Phil.* xxxiv (1918). J. M. C.

RABIRIUS (2) **POSTUMUS,** GAIUS, known unofficially as *Postumus Curtius*, being posthumous son of C. Curtius, adopted under the will of his uncle C. Rabirius (q.v.). A banker like his father, he placed loans throughout the Empire, until to recover vast sums from Ptolemy Auletes he took up residence at Alexandria, called himself the king's minister, and requisitioned Egyptian supplies. After the condemnation of Gabinius (q.v. 2) in 54 Rabirius was prosecuted as receiver, but Cicero's extant speech secured his acquittal, mainly on technicalities; the defence of fact was merely that Rabirius was now poor. Caesar assisted him, and by 49 he was a senator, Caesar's ardent partisan, and was employed on commissariat work for the African War; by 45 he had designs on the consulate.

Cf. H. Dessau, *Hermes* 1911, 61 3ff. G. E. F. C.

RABIRIUS (3) GAIUS, epic poet mentioned alongside of Virgil by Velleius (2. 36. 3). Ovid alludes to his 'mighty utterance' (*Pont.* 4. 16. 5). He may have written the poem on Actium of which a fragment was recovered in papyrus 817 from Herculaneum. *See* BELLO AEGYPTIACO, CARMEN DE.

Teuffel, § 252. 9; Morel, *FPL.* J. W. D.

RACES, HORSE- AND CHARIOT-, *see* CIRCUS.

RAETIA, a Roman province in the Alps, including Tyrol and parts of Bavaria and Switzerland. The Raeti were partly Illyrian, partly Celtic, their language having been affected by Etruscan elements (cf. J. Whatmough, *Harv. Stud.* 1937, 181 ff.). After the Camunni and Vennones had been defeated by P. Silius Nerva (16 B.C.) Drusus and Tiberius in a combined operation from the south and from Gaul conquered the Raeti and the Celtic Vindelici, whose territory became a province together with the Vallis Poenina; the latter was disconnected from Raetia after Claudius and before M. Aurelius. At first under the command of the governor of Gaul (who appointed a *praefectus* in A.D. 16–17 after Germanicus had been recalled from the Rhine), Raetia got its own governor, who according to the *communis opinio* was an equestrian procurator with *ius gladii* (Ph. Horovitz, *Rev. Phil.* 1939, 61 ff., tries to prove that until Trajan the governors of Raetia were *praefecti*, and then were replaced by equestrian *procuratores*). The governor, who resided at Augusta Vindelicorum, commanded the troops: 4 *alae* and 11 *cohortes* in A.D. 107 (*CIL* xvi. 55), and 3 *alae* and 13 *cohortes* in 166 (op. cit. 121). During the Marcomannic Wars under M. Aurelius the newly raised Legio III Italica Concors was quartered in Raetia at Castra Regina, its commander becoming the provincial governor as a *legatus Aug. pro praetore.* At least since Gallienus Raetia was again placed under equestrian administration, and was divided under Diocletian for civil administration into Raetia I (capital probably Curia) and Raetia II (capital Augusta Vindelicorum), both provinces being under the military command of the *dux Raetiarum* who resided at Augusta Vindelicorum (on the frontier see R. Heuberger, *Klio* 1931, 348 ff.). Alamannic pressure increased and the Lake of Constance–Argen–Iller–Danube defence-line was given up soon after A.D. 389; the Alamanni occupied the relinquished territory, though temporarily forced back in 430. About

450 the Alamanni and other German tribes again mastered nearly the whole plain. Before 482 the last outposts on the Danube were evacuated and only the Alpine regions remained under control from Italy.

Haug, *PW*, s.v. 'Raeti' and 'Raetia'; F. Stähelin, *Die Schweiz in römischer Zeit*[2] (1931); R. Heuberger, *Raetien im Altertum und Frühmittelalter* i (1932); id., 'Das ostgothische Raetien', *Klio* 1937, 77 ff.; F. Hertlein–O. Paret–P. Goessler, *Die Römer in Württemberg* i–iii (1928–32). On the *limes Raeticus* see Fabricius, *PW* xiii. 605 ff. On roads see W. Cartellieri, *Philol.*, *Suppl.* xviii (1926); L. Castelpietra, *Raetia* (1935), 33 ff. (via Claudia Augusta); H. U. Instinsky, *Klio* 1938, 33 ff. (Septimius Severus).   F. A. W. S.

RAMNES, TITIES, LUCERES, *see* TRIBUS.

RAVENNA, an important port in Cispadane Gaul on the Adriatic. The name Ravenna is certainly Etruscan; the original population was probably Etruscan and Umbrian mixed. It is only legend that assigns its foundation to Thessalians. Pliny seems to be plainly in error when he calls it a city of the Sabines. Of its earlier history practically nothing is known. A *civitas foederata* in the later Republic, it received Roman citizenship in 89 B.C. or from Julius Caesar in 49 B.C. and ranked thenceforth as a *municipium*.

The course of the later history of Ravenna was determined by Augustus when he made it the station of his Italian fleet of the north, corresponding to Misenum in the south. The presence of the fleet ensured to Ravenna a certain permanent importance: occasionally, as in A.D. 69, it gave it a temporary historical significance. With the sea to the east and with marshes almost cutting off approach from the west, Ravenna was a natural residence of notable State prisoners: it was there that Maroboduus was interned by Tiberius. The life of Ravenna centred round the sea and the fleet. The *praefectus classis* was the most notable personage of the town, and the suburb by the harbour was itself called 'classis'. The local government presents unique features (cf. *CIL* xi, p. 6). There was a considerable export of wood, asparagus, and fish.

In A.D. 404 Ravenna became the main residence of the Emperor of the West, who was drawn thither by its uniquely protected position. Its mint came to dominate the Western coinage. After the fall of the Empire Odovacer and Theodoric still resided at Ravenna, and finally, when Justinian recovered Italy, Ravenna became the seat of the Imperial viceroy, the Exarch. The last phases of Ravenna's greatness are represented by mosaics of great interest and beauty.

Rosenberg, *PW*, s.v.   H. M.

REBILUS, CANINIUS, *see* CANINIUS REBILUS.

RECITATIO, the public reading of a literary work by the author himself. In Greece, Herodotus' reading of parts of his works may be taken as an anticipation of the Roman practice. At Rome Crates' lectures suggested the idea of a public reading of the verses of dead poets (Suet. *Gram.* 2). But the real creator of the *recitatio* was Asinius Pollio: he was the first Roman to read before an audience his own works (Sen. *Controv.* 4 *praef.* 2). Under the influence of the same causes which explain the expansion of Augustan literature the custom soon spread extraordinarily. It still flourished under Domitian. Afterwards we find fewer allusions to it, although it survives to the sixth century.

Before the construction of Hadrian's Athenaeum, no definite place set apart for *recitationes* existed. Very rarely they took place in a theatre, sometimes at a banquet, oftenest in some hall, hired by the author or lent by a patron; the reader had to supply the necessary furniture (Tac. *Dial.* 9), which cost him dear, as readings did not pay. So starving poets recited anywhere (forum, thermae, circus, etc.).

There were two kinds of *recitationes*: the one meant for

a restricted audience, the other for the public (Plin. *Ep.* 7. 17. 11–12). Invitations were given by the author himself, or by means of short notes (*codicilli*) and programmes (*libelli*). Women were not excluded. From a sort of platform the *recitator*, standing up, first delivered a preamble (*praefatio*), then read seated. Sometimes he preferred to get a freedman to read, supplying gestures himself (Plin. *Ep.* 9. 34. 2). Readings might extend over several days. They were chiefly of verse (epic, tragic, lyric), more rarely of prose (history, philosophy, discourses). The hearers expressed their approval—with occasional support from hired clappers—by applause and by cries ('effecte', 'euge', 'pulchre', 'sophos', etc.); they might even rise and kiss the reader.

The *recitatio* at first offered genuine advantages: by it an author made his works quickly known, realized whether they were worth publishing, and obtained the criticisms of competent judges. But very soon it degenerated, becoming an end in itself, encouraging the conceit of authors, and exercising on the literature of the Empire the same untoward influences as *declamatio* (q.v.)—love of the showy, of smart sayings, with defects in composition and neglect of depth in favour of form.

Th. Herwig, *De recitatione poetarum apud Romanos* (1864); L. Valmaggi, 'Le letture pubbliche a Roma nel primo secolo dell' era volgare' (*Riv. Fil.* xvi (1888)); J. E. B. Mayor, *Thirteen Satires of Juvenal* i (1893), 173–82; F. Orlando, *Le letture pubbliche in Roma imperiale* (1907); Funaioli in *PW* ii. A, s.v. 'Recitationes'; L. Friedlaender, *Sittengesch. Roms*[10], Bd. ii (1922), 225–30.
                                              C. F., transl. J. W. D.

RECUPERATORES were jurymen who acted in the second stage of Roman civil proceedings in place of *unus iudex*. They were first established by international treaties between Rome and other States, to act as exceptional courts for litigation between their citizens. The competence of *recuperatores* was extended to lawsuits between two *peregrini*, and by a later development to proceedings in which both parties were Roman citizens; for the procedure of this court enjoyed a great popularity by reason of its celerity (restricted number of witnesses, short limit of time for delivering of judgement), though the court was composed of three members. We find *recuperatores* in trials on different matters, so that a general rule for their competence cannot be laid down; probably they were competent above all for controversies which required an accelerated hearing. Presumably a petition of the litigants could induce the magistrate to allot the case to this court. In post-classical procedure there was no place for *recuperatores*. In Justinian's Digest the compilers deleted this term and replaced it by *iudices*.   A. B.

REDICULUS. When Hannibal, attempting to raise the siege of Capua in 211 B.C., made a demonstration against Rome, a shrine was erected to the unknown power which made him go back again, under the name of Rediculus (Festus, p. 354. 25; 355. 6 Lindsay). It stood outside the Porta Capena, and the deity may have been surnamed Tutanus (Varro, *Sat. Men.*, fr. 213 Buecheler).   H. J. R.

RED SEA (Ἐρυθρὰ or Ἐρυθραία Θάλασσα: *Rubrum Mare*. Derivation of name uncertain, perhaps from 'Red Men' = Phoenicians). This name was extended by the ancients to cover all eastern waters, including the Indian Ocean, but referred specifically, as it does now, to the Arabian Gulf. The Red Sea proper was navigated by the Egyptians, by Israelites and Phoenicians, and by the Persians, through whom it became known to the Greeks. It was mentioned by several of the Attic dramatists, and Herodotus (2. 11; 3. 107 ff.) was acquainted with its shape. In an attempt to circumnavigate Arabia, Alexander sent ships from Suez which sailed as far as Yemen (Theophrastus, *Hist. Pl.* 9. 4. 1). The Ptolemies opened up the Red Sea completely. Under Ptolemy I the west coast was explored; under Ptolemy II forts and stations for elephant-hunts were founded here (*see* BERENICE, MYOS HORMOS, PTOLEMAIS THERON) and the Arabian shore was made known as far as Hedjaz and Al 'Ula; under Ptolemy III piracy was suppressed, and in the first century B.C. a '*strategus* of the Red Sea' makes his appearance. Under the Caesars the Red Sea became an important channel for trade between the Roman Empire and the eastern seas.

Periplus Maris Rubri (translation and notes by W. H. Schoff, 1912); Cary–Warmington, *Explorers*, 67–8, 222.	E. H. W.

REGIA, the traditional home of King Numa, was the seat of authority under the Republic of the *pontifex maximus* and contained his archives. It was situated at the east end of the *forum Romanum*, between the Sacra Via and the precinct of Vesta. Its orientation by the cardinal points matched that of the pre-Sullan forum; foundations of the buildings of the early Republic, 390 B.C. and 148 B.C., still exist. The trapezoidal plan of the main existing structure, an elegant building in marble erected by Calvinus in 36 B.C., reconciles older and newer orientations. The view that the *fasti* (q.v.) *consulares* were affixed to its walls is now doubted (cf. A. Degrassi, *Rend. Pont.* xxi (1945–6) and *Inscr. Ital.* XIII. i (1947), who attributes them to the adjacent Arch of Augustus). The courtyard contained the *sacrarium Martis*, with *hastae* and *ancilla*, and the shrine of Ops Consiva. I. A. R.

REGIFUGIUM. 24 Feb. is marked on the calendars *Q(uando) R(ex) C(omitiauit) F(as)*. The even number indicates that it is not a lucky day; the only other even-numbered festival is the second Equirria (14 Mar.). 24 Mar. and 24 May have the same letters attached, for unknown reasons, but 24 Feb. was called the Regifugium, because the *rex sacrorum* (q.v.) concluded the ritual by running away from the Comitium (Plut. *Quaest. Rom.* 63, where see Rose for suggested interpretations). H. J. R.

REGILLUS, LUCIUS AEMILIUS, praetor in 190 B.C., defeated the fleet of Antiochus at Myonnesus, securing the Scipios' passage over to Asia Minor. He celebrated a naval triumph, vowing a temple to *Lares permarini*, which was dedicated in 179.

Livy, bk. 37 and 40. 52; Polyb. bk. 21; Appian, *Syr.* 27.

REGILLUS LACUS can probably be identified with the volcanic depression called *Pantano Secco* near Tusculum (T. Ashby, *Roman Campagna*, 148). Here Rome conquered the Latins *c.* 496 B.C. in a battle said to have been decided by the intervention of Castor and Pollux (Livy 2. 19; Dion. Hal. 6. 3 f.). E. T. S.

REGIO. (1) At Rome *regio* denoted particularly the city wards, four in number (Livy 1. 43; Varro, *Ling.* 5. 45) during the Republic, and assumed to represent a regal synoecism of the Palatine and Esquiline settlements. By 7 B.C. Augustus had reorganized the whole system, creating fourteen numbered *regiones* (*see* ROME, TOPO-GRAPHY) administered by *aediles, tribuni plebis*, and praetors chosen by lot (Dio Cass. 55. 8), and divided into *vici* (*see* VICOMAGISTRI). Under Hadrian the administration had passed to libertine *vicomagistri* and one, or two, *curatores* responsible to the *praefectus vigilum* (*CIL* vi. 975). Under Alexander Severus fourteen consular *curatores* were instituted (S.H.A. *Alex. Sev.* 33. 1) under the *praefectus urbi* (*CIL* x. 6507; xiv. 2078). Each ward possessed a sub-station (*excubitorium*) of the *vigiles*.

(2) *Regio* is also used of the eleven *regiones* of Italy, instituted by Augustus, probably as a basis for the census (*see* ITALY). I. A. R.

REGIUM, *see* RHEGIUM.

REGULUS (1), MARCUS ATILIUS, as consul reduced Brundisium (267 B.C.). As consul II in 256 with L. Manlius Vulso (q.v.) he won the naval battle of Ecnomus,

thus opening the way for the invasion of Africa. After Manlius' return Regulus was left in sole command in Africa. He defeated the Carthaginians but offered impossibly severe terms. In spring 255 he was defeated on ground chosen by Xanthippus (q.v.) and was captured; only 2,000 Romans escaped from this disaster, which ended the African expedition. Later (? 249) he was sent on parole to Rome to arrange an exchange of prisoners (or to negotiate peace-terms which he urged the Senate to decline) and returned to Carthage, where he died in captivity. The story of his death by torture on his voluntary return to Carthage became a national epic (Horace, *Carm.* 3. 5), but is probably untrue: the barbarity of the Carthaginians was perhaps invented to palliate the action of his widow in torturing some Punic prisoners in Rome. On the Regulus legend see E. Klebs, *PW*, s.v. 'Atilius (51)', and T. Frank, *CPhil.* 1926.
H. H. S.

REGULUS (2), MARCUS AQUILIUS, who had been a notorious informer in the Neronian period, was detested by the younger Pliny as 'the biggest scoundrel on two legs' ('omnium bipedum nequissimus', *Ep.* 1. 5. 14). His hysterical talent ('ingenium insanum', ibid. 4. 7. 4) and effrontery led many to take him for an orator; but for Herennius (q.v.) Senecio he was 'uir malus dicendi imperitus', exactly the opposite of Cato's famous definition. Defects notwithstanding, he secured many convictions in trials for *maiestas*. We know of two lost publications of his: (1) a pamphlet satirizing Arulenus (q.v.) Rusticus after his death; (2) a biography of his own dead son, of which he had 1,000 copies made for circulation. Martial mentions him several times in complimentary terms. J. W. D.

REHTIA, *see* RELIGION, ITALIC.

REIZIANUM, *see* METRE, GREEK, III (9).

RELEGATIO was at first the expulsion of a Roman citizen or a *peregrinus* decreed by a magistrate as a coercive measure. In this application it was a mere administrative act. As a penalty in criminal trials, introduced by several *leges, relegatio* was applied in different gradations; the mildest one was a simple temporary expulsion, without confinement or death penalty in case of return, and without loss of citizenship or property. The severest form was *deportatio* (introduced by Tiberius), a perpetual banishment to a certain place, combined with confiscation of property and loss of citizenship. *Relegatio* consisted either in the exclusion of the *relegatus* from residence in certain places or territories (Rome, Italy, or the provinces), or in his confinement to a particular place of abode. A very common form was *relegatio* (or *deportatio*) *in insulam* or *in Oasim* (near Egypt). Banishment in all its variations was especially a punishment for the higher classes (*see* HONESTIORES). The lower classes were punished for similar crimes with forced labour (*in opus publicum* or *in metalla*) or even with death.

Mommsen, *Röm. Strafr.* (1899); J. L. Strachan-Davidson, *Problems of Roman criminal law* i, ii (1912); E. Levy, *Röm. Kapitalstrafe* (1931); U. Brasiello, *La repressione penale in diritto romano* (1937); Z. Żmigryder-Konopka, *Rev. hist. de droit français* 1939, 307 ff. A. B.

RELICS. The cult of heroes (*see* HERO-CULT), at their real or supposed graves, had occasionally curious results. Naturally, many of these monuments were not real graves at all, as the Pelopion at Olympia; many places also claimed to possess the buried remains of heroes not native to them, and had legends explaining how they came there (Oedipus at Colonus in Attica, Soph. *OC.* 576 ff.; Eurystheus in the deme Pallene, Eur. *Heracl.* 1031; Hector at Thebes, see W. R. Halliday in *Liverpool Annals* xi. 3 ff.). Moreover, unburied remains were venerated here and there, as the 'honoured bones' mentioned by Pausanias at Asopus in Laconia (3. 22. 9), without even a name, and the bones of the Sibyl at Cumae (Paus. 10. 12. 8), in Apollo's temple. But this was not confined to the cult of heroes. The most remarkable instance of such a thing in the cult of a deity was the Hellotia in Crete, a festival of Athena (q.v., cf. Nilsson, *Griechische Feste*, 95 f.). Here a very large wreath, called a *hellotis*, was carried and said to contain the bones of Europa (q.v.; Seleucus in Athenaeus, 678 a–b). What the 'bones' really were is unknown. Furthermore, many relics were not bodies or parts of them. Aniconic cult-objects were occasionally explained as relics, as the stone at Delphi said to have been swallowed by Kronos (q.v.; Hesiod, *Theog.* 497 ff.), cf. the 'sceptre of Agamemnon' at Chaeronea (Paus. 9. 40. 11) and the 'shield of Diomedes' at Argos (I. R. Arnold in *AJArch.* xli. 436 ff.).

F. Pfister, *Der Reliquienkult im Altertum* (2 vols.; 1909–12).
H. J. R.

RELIGION, TERMS RELATING TO.

No word in either Greek or Latin corresponds exactly to English 'religion', 'religious'. In the former language perhaps ὅσιος and εὐσεβής, with their corresponding abstract nouns, come closest. ὁσία seems to mean primitively 'usage', 'custom', hence 'good, commendable, pious usage' or the feelings which naturally go with it. It tends to specialize into meaning that which is proper and lawful with regard to holy things, or to traditional morality; it is, for instance, ἀνόσιον to commit murder. To say that a man is εὐσεβής does not of itself mean that he is what we call pious, unless some such phrase as πρὸς τοὺς θεούς is added; the famous εὐσεβεῖς after whom the εὐσεβῶν χώρα in Sicily was named (see *Aetna*, 623 ff., and R. Ellis ad loc.) were loving and self-sacrificing sons, and so *pii* (see below). Cf. in general J. C. Bolkestein, Ὅσιος *en* Εὐσεβής: *Bijdrage tot de godsdienstige en zedelijke Terminologie van de Grieken* (1936). A word belonging essentially to the religious vocabulary in classical times is θέμις, since that which it is or is not θέμις to do is respectively allowed or disallowed by religious law or custom; but the Homeric θέμιστες are traditional laws, not purely religious. ἱερός means properly 'tabu', hence 'consecrated' to some deity, and a man careful in his religious duties may be called ἱερός, as Ar. *Ran.* 652; ἱερά are religious rites, or materials, especially victims, for them. δεισιδαίμων varies between 'pietistic' and 'pious', but is usually the former, see H. Bolkestein, 'Theophrastos' Charakter der Deisidaimonia' (*RGVV* xxi. 2; 1929). The word ἅγιος so distinctly indicates something belonging to the sacral sphere that it is tempting, despite the difference of breathing, to connect it etymologically with ἄγος, a tabu or the evil state resulting from the violation of one (see E. Williger, 'Hagios, Untersuchungen zur Terminologie des Heiligen', ibid. xix. 1; 1922). As regards outward observances, the simple word τιμή is common; a worshipper is often said to 'attend on' or 'serve' the gods, θεραπεύειν and synonyms (never δουλεύειν in a purely Greek context). To be a regular worshipper, e.g. of the gods of a State, is νομίζειν θεούς, which later comes to mean to believe in their existence (see J. Tate in *CR* l (1936), 3; li (1937), p. 3). Occasionally θρησκεύειν has the former sense (as Hdt. 2. 64. 3); θρησκεία is a common, though mostly late, word for 'worship'. A τελετή or τέλος is any rite, though in Hellenistic it tends to mean a mystical rite or even secret doctrine (see C. Zijderveld, Τελετή, diss. Purmerend, 1934; cf. H. Bolkestein, Τέλος ὁ γάμος, *Mededeelingen* lxxvi B, no. 2 (1933)).

In Latin *religio* seems to be properly a bond or restraint of a non-material kind, and so develops into 'sacral or religious observance or scruple'; *religiones*, a complex or system of such restraints, is perhaps the nearest Latin

for 'a religion'. Generally, *religio* has a good meaning, though to a materialist, as Lucretius, it is nearly 'superstition', and in Hor. *Sat.* 1. 9. 71 it is something to be slightly ashamed of. *Religiosus* usually means 'pietistic', but denotes a laudable quality in the mouth of an uneducated man (Petronius 44. 18). In its good sense *religio* approaches Hellenistic εὐλάβεια (K. Kerényi in *Byzantinisch-Neugriechische Jahrbücher* 1931, 306 ff.). *Sacer* is almost exactly 'tabu', opposed to *profanus*, that which is used in ordinary life, cf. CONSECRATION. It is thus ambivalent, meaning on occasion 'accursed'. That which is actually *sacer* might also be *profanus*, as a temple or a human being, whereas a god is *sanctus*, as is also a man of venerable life or conduct; the inviolable walls of a city are *sanctae res* (Gaius 2. 8, cf. Plut. *Quaest. Rom.* 27 and Rose, *Rom. Quest. of Plut.* (1924), 181), but a table, which may be used for domestic ritual, is *sacra* (Juv. 6. O 4). *Pius, pietas* correspond fairly closely to εὐσεβής and εὐσέβεια, see above; Virgil's Aeneas is *pius* because he observes right relations to all things human and divine. Outward observances are *ritus*, properly no more than 'customs', *honores*, again by no means a peculiarly religious term, *cura caerimoniaque* (Cicero, *Inv. Rhet.* 2. 161, cf. W. Warde Fowler, *Rel. Exper.* (1911), index s.v.), or simply *caerimoniae*. *Sacra* denotes the holy objects and the ritual (*sacra facere*, to perform a religious ceremony).
H. J. R.

RELIGION, CELTIC.

The subject of this article is the religion of the Celtic-speaking peoples, in so far as it was known to the Greeks and Romans. The term 'Celtic' will not be used in an anthropological sense, and no attempt will be made to distinguish among the component races of the Celtic population. They were scattered over a wide area, and their recorded history covers centuries. They must have had a great variety of beliefs and practices. But it is possible to recognize in the ancient accounts of the Celts certain common characteristics which justify us in speaking of Celtic religion, and the testimony of the classical writers finds some confirmation in the archaeological monuments and in Irish and Welsh literature. This evidence from neo-Celtic, however, is too late to be considered in the present discussion.

2. Notices of the Celts (Κελτοί; perhaps sometimes meant by Ὑπερβόρε(ι)οι—see HYPERBOREANS) are found in the classical writers from the time of Hecataeus, and there are occasional references to their worship in the historians who deal with the age of the migrations. But the most systematic ancient account of Celtic religion is that of Caesar in several familiar passages in the sixth book of the *De Bello Gallico* (chapters 13, 14, 17, 18). Caesar there deals with the three aspects of the subject which chiefly interested the Greeks and Romans: (1) the gods (17, 18); (2) the Druids (13); and (3) the ideas of a future life (14).

3. (1) With regard to the gods, Caesar declares that the Gauls worship Mercury above all others, and after him Apollo, Mars, Jupiter, and Minerva. They associate Mercury with the arts, with roads and travel, and with wealth and commerce; and of the remaining four divinities they entertain much the same opinion as other nations. In the next chapter (18) he adds Dispater to his list, saying that the Druids taught the people that Dispater was the father of their race, and that they consequently reckon time by nights and not by days.

4. Caesar's account is of course of very little use as a description of Celtic religion. In the terms in which it is given, with the identification of Gaulish and Roman divinities, it cannot possibly be true. And even if we accepted the existence of six greater divinities corresponding to those named, Caesar's conventional characterization would tell us very little of their nature and functions. It is comparable to Tacitus' description of the Germanic worship of Mercury, Hercules, and Mars;

but in the case of the Teutons a considerable body of later mythology has been preserved, whereas in Gaul we have little to build upon except the *interpretatio Romana*, q.v., which not only obscures Caesar's account, but also appears in the great majority of the inscriptions and monuments.

5. The archaeological evidence in part bears out Caesar's statements, in part corrects or qualifies them. Many monuments have been found which show the worship of the gods he names, or of divinities who were assimilated to them. But in the inscriptions the name of Mercury occurs much less frequently than that of Mars. This may mean that in the Gallo-Roman times, as apparently also in the earlier period of the invasions, the god of war was more worshipped than in Caesar's Gaul. It is possible also that the two names describe only different aspects of the same great Celtic god.

6. Caesar supplies us with no native names for his divinities, but Lucan (1. 444-6) mentions Teutates, Taranis, and Esus, and Lucian (*Heracles*, 1-3) gives an account of Ogmios. A few other Celtic names of gods are given by the authors, and the inscriptions supply many more, which usually occur as epithets accompanying the name of a Roman god.

7. Whether any of their names represent divinities with a widely diffused cult is a matter of dispute. Some authorities are disposed to deny the existence of any pantheon of greater gods among the Celts, and certainly most of the evidence points to a lower mythology with local cults. But the distribution of certain names in Celtic territory seems to indicate that there were a few greater gods. (*See also* DEAE MATRES, EPONA.)

8. (2) Of the Druidical priesthood Caesar speaks at some length. It is sometimes objected, to be sure, that the Druids were not properly a sacerdotal order, and they are doubtless to be distinguished from common priests, who are called by various other names (*sacerdotes, antistites,* and *gutuatri*). But Caesar clearly ascribes to them religious functions, as well as educational, judicial, and political. He describes them as a privileged class, exempt from taxes and military service. They practised divination and were present at sacrifices. They were organized and had a single chief, elected by the whole body, and there was a general assembly held every year among the Carnutes. They acted as judges in personal and inter-tribal disputes. One of their chief functions was the education of the young, whom they taught by oral tradition.

9. Caesar's statements are confirmed by many passages in other authors, who add various details. Pliny (*HN* 16. 249 ff.) describes one striking ceremony, the gathering of the mistletoe, in which the Druids took part. The authority for the subdivision of the order into δρυΐδαι, οὐάτεις, and βάρδοι comes not from Caesar but from Strabo (4. 197; cf. also Amm. Marc. 15. 9. 8 and Diod. Sic. 5. 31). Several writers speak of human sacrifice in Gaul (for example Lucan 1. 446 and Diod. Sic. 5. 31). But the accounts were probably exaggerated and there is no evidence that the Druids were responsible for the practice. We read (Pliny *HN* 30. 4. 13; Suetonius, *Claud.* 25) of a violent abolition of the Druids by Roman authority. But it is more likely that their influence declined when their rights and powers were withdrawn. The later history of the Druids, when they appear to have sunk to be a magic-mongering order, is reflected in Pliny (*HN* 29. 52-3) and Tacitus (*Hist.* 4. 54).

10. (3) The Druids were commonly described by the ancient writers as philosophers, and the teaching most often ascribed to them is that of immortality. In fact the Greeks and Romans were especially impressed by the vividness of the Celtic belief in a future life—witness the story told by Valerius Maximus (2. 6. 10) and Pomponius Mela (3. 2) of men who made loans against repayment in the next world. Some authors speak simply of their belief in a life beyond the grave (cf. Timagenes,

in Amm. Marc. 15. 29; Strabo 4. 197; Mela 3. 2; Lucan 1. 455 ff.). But others refer definitely to a doctrine of transmigration (q.v.), and associate the Druids with Pythagoras (cf. Val. Max. 2. 6. 10; Alex. Polyhistor, in Diod. Sic. 5. 28; Caesar, *BGall.* 6. 14). In the light of later Celtic tradition, Irish and Welsh, it seems not improbable that the ancient Celts held some sort of a doctrine of metempsychosis or rebirth. But there is no clear evidence that it carried with it any idea of moral retribution.

BIBLIOGRAPHY

General: J. A. MacCulloch, *The Religion of the Ancient Celts* (1911); G. Dottin, 'La Religion des Celtes' in his *Manuel pour servir à l'étude de l'antiquité celtique* (1913). For an account of Greek and Latin *testimonia* see H. d'Arbois de Jubainville, *Principaux auteurs de l'antiquité à consulter sur l'histoire des Celtes* (1902). Notices of Celts in Greek authors from Hecataeus to Posidonius are printed, with English translation, by W. Dinan, *Monumenta Historica Celtica,* vol. i (1911; no more published). Greek and Latin materials, from inscriptions as well as literature, are collected by A. Holder, *Altceltischer Sprachschatz* (1896-). On Gaulish religion in particular see A. Bertrand, *La Religion des Gaulois* (1897); C. Jullian, *Histoire de la Gaule* (1908); Charles Renel, *Les Religions de la Gaule,* etc. (1906); and J. Toutain, *Les Cultes païens dans l'empire romain.* On Druidism, in addition to the foregoing, H. d'Arbois de Jubainville, *Les Druides et les dieux celtiques à forme d'animaux* (1906); T. D. Kendrick, *The Druids* (1927). On the Celtic ideas of the future life there are valuable special studies by A. Nutt in Meyer and Nutt, *The Voyage of Bran* (1895). F. N. R.

RELIGION, ETRUSCAN. Our knowledge of Etruscan religion is limited by the imperfect nature of our sources. Archaeological material is abundant but ambiguous. Religious documents written in Etruscan are largely unintelligible. References to Etruscan religion in Greek and Roman sources are fragmentary and are derived from authors who may have contaminated Etruscan ideas with non-Etruscan notions (C. O. Thulin, *Die etruskische Disciplin* (1909), 1 ff.).

2. ETRUSCAN SOURCES. The Etruscan inscriptions are collected in the *Corpus Inscriptionum Etruscarum* (*CIE*). We have many shorter funeral inscriptions and dedications from archaic times on. Longer and more important inscriptions are: (1) the clay tablet from Capua assigned to the sixth or the fifth century B.C. on which names of several deities occur (*Studi Etruschi* 1934, 227); (2) lead tablets found at Magliano, Volterra, and Campiglia, perhaps, like their Greek and Roman parallels, curses (*CIE* 5237); (3) the Hellenistic bronze liver from Piacenza (discussed later); (4) a rectangular cippus found in Perugia, perhaps an agreement between two families about the division of a mausoleum (ibid. 4538); and (5) the comprehensive Etruscan text inscribed on the wrappings of an Egyptian mummy now in Zagreb (ibid., Suppl. Fasc. i, 1921, and M. Runes, *Der etruskische Text der Agrambinden* (1935)). The form of some passages suggests prayers, and names of gods and sacrificial implements have been recognized, but the significance of the whole is uncertain.

3. ROMAN SOURCES. Valuable information is found in Livy and in Cicero, *De Divinatione* (ed. A. S. Pease) and *De Haruspicum Responso.* Claudius Pulcher, Nigidius Figulus, Tarquitius Priscus, Aulus Caecina, Julius Aquila, Umbricius Melior, the Emperor Claudius, and many other Roman writers discussed various aspects of Etruscan religion, but we have only fragments of their work. Some of this writing was derived from Etruscan sources, but there was also a strong tendency to add assorted religious information or to interpret Etruscan material in the light of Hellenistic religion or Hellenistic philosophy. All these authors knew only the very latest phase of Etruscan religion. There is nothing in Greek classical writers that would elucidate the earlier phases; Plato's reference to 'Tyrrhenian' cults is thought to refer to the Samothracian Cabiri (P. Boyancé, *Le Culte des muses* (1937), p. 22, n. 1).

4. ETRUSCAN DISCIPLINE. Roman writers of Cicero's time seem to imply the existence of a code of Etruscan religious practices and beliefs. These books are variously referred to as Etruscan books, verses of Tages, books of Begoe; or, by their contents, as Books of Haruspices, Books on Lightning, Books on Ritual (Cic. *Div.* 1. 33. 72), Books on Fate (Livy 5. 15. 11), Books on Animal Gods (Serv. in *Aen.* 3. 168). It is not clear which of these were written in Etruscan and which in Latin; several names may refer to the same books. They must have contained genuine Etruscan beliefs with many later accretions. Many of these books had probably grown out of the records of answers given by Etruscan diviners and soothsayers to Romans; and all of them may, in some manner, have been fitted for Roman consumption, but we cannot doubt the antiquity of the Etruscan notion that thunderbolts are thrown by various gods and that these thunderbolts portend events in human life. Tinia, the chief god of the Etruscan pantheon (perhaps originally a great storm-god of the kind known in the religions of mountainous Asia Minor), threw three kinds of thunderbolts. Eight other gods threw one kind each, among them Juno and Minerva, the partners of Tinia in the great Etruscan triad of gods, and Vulcan (Sethlans?) the god of fire (Plin. *HN* 2. 138; Serv. in *Aen.* 1. 42). Spots which the thunderbolt had struck were sacred; the deity was propitiated with a sacrifice, the spot enclosed, and the thunderbolt regarded as buried (*fulmen conditum*). The wide porch in front of the Etruscan temples was probably used for observation of thunderbolts.

5. In an Etrusco-Latin bilingual from Pesaro (CIL xi. 6363) we see that the priest who interpreted thunderbolts (*fulguriator*) was also concerned with interpreting signs in the livers of victims (*haruspex*). This procedure was regarded as an Etruscan specialty: its antiquity is proved by the Etruscan mirror on which the Greek seer Calchas is shown so employed (E. Q. Giglioli, *L'arte etrusca* (1935), pl. 298. 1). On another mirror, of the third century B.C., a haruspex *Pavatarchies* foretells the future from the liver in the presence of the god Veltune (Vertumnus?) and the hero Tarchon (q.v.); some other representations of haruspices have been recognized from the peculiar costume (H. Dragendorff, *Studi Etruschi* 1928, p. 177). The Etruscan bronze liver from Piacenza (G. Körte, *Röm. Mitt.* 1905, 348) was divided into forty regions inscribed with the names of gods. The right half of the liver counted as lucky, the left as 'hostile' (Cic. *Div.* 2. 28), but the appearance and colour of the liver (Luc. 1. 618) were also taken into account in making predictions, of which we have some examples (Livy 5. 21. 8; Plin. *HN* 11. 90). Hepatoscopy was also known in the Near East, and in spite of differences in details a connexion with the Etruscan *haruspicia* appears possible.

6. The ritual appertaining to prophecy, greatly as it was valued by the Romans who called in Etruscan specialists, formed only a small part of the Etruscan discipline. Solemn foundation of cities, temples, and altars, and religious rites concerning distribution and division of land, are traced to Etruscan sources (Festus, p. 285 Müller; Blume–Lachmann–Rudorff, *Schriften d. röm. Feldmesser* i. 350). Processions, sacrifices, marriages, funerals, and funeral games are represented in Etruscan art. They, too, may have been codified in religious books. An interesting vase of the seventh century B.C. shows the 'Troy Game', apparently an ancestor of the Roman equestrian procession (E. Q. Giglioli, *Studi etruschi* 1929, 111), the *ludus Troiae*.

7. Much concern for the dead was shown by the Etruscans. The prevailing notion from the beginning to the end of Etruscan culture makes the dead continue their life in their house-like tombs. Other works of art show them on their journey to the lower world in the company of demons who are at times of ugly and terrifying character. Funeral games were held in honour of the deceased; gladiatorial games may have originated on these occasions (L. Malten, *Röm. Mitt.* 1923–4). The deification

of souls imputed to Etruscans by Arnobius (*Adv. Nat.* 2. 62) need imply no more than a belief in after-life. If phallic cippi really adorned male tombs, and house-urns female (R. Mengarelli, *Studi Etruschi* 1936, 90), it might be argued that the Etruscans regarded the sexual and procreative power as the lasting part of mankind. This would connect with the Roman belief in *genii* and *Junones* (see also L. Euing, *Die Sage von Tanaquil* (1933), 24). From the fourth century B.C. on credence was also given by some Etruscans to Greek ideas of an underworld presided over by Hades and Persephone to which Hermes Psychopompos brings the dead.

8. The Etruscans also had a peculiar system of world ages (*saecula*). They apparently believed that a certain number of *saecula* were allotted to each nation, this number being ten in the case of the Etruscans.

9. Etruscan mythology includes Etruscan, Greek, and Italic gods. Unquestionably Etruscan in name are *tinia, cilens, fufluns, sethlans, turms, culsu, acavisr, alpan, vecu* or Begoe, *mean, mlacuch, snenanth, thalna,* and some others. Early relations with Greece led to equation of *tinia* with Zeus, *fufluns* with Dionysus, *turms* with Hermes, *turan* with Aphrodite, *sethlans* with Hephaestus. As early as the sixth century B.C. the Etruscan cities of Caere and Spina (or their Greek inhabitants) had treasuries in the Delphic sanctuary; Greek dedications to Hera have been found in a temple precinct in Caere (R. Mengarelli, *Studi Etruschi* 1936, 67). Among the gods of their Italic subjects Juno and Minerva rose to a place in the highest Etruscan triad (F. Altheim in *PW*, s.v. 'Minerva'), and Mars, Neptune, Silvanus, and Janus were also among the Etruscan high gods. The Greek Heracles, Apollo, Artemis, Hades, Persephone, and Charon retained their Greek names, while many other gods, though Etruscan or Italic in name, retained their Greek functions and mythology. Native Etruscan gods such as *tinia* and *turan* probably had an original mythology of their own; *turan* carrying the child *tinia* (D. Levi, *Not. Scavi* 1931, 204) indicates a myth unknown in Greek tradition. Some traits of native mythology are perhaps reflected in the representations of Oriental deities in early Etruscan art and in the peculiar mythological variations which have been observed in the Etruscan representations of Heracles and Charon (J. Bayet, *Herclé* (1926); F. De Ruyt, *Charun* (1934)).

10. Many names of gods are related to names of cities or to family names. Nortia, Hostia, Soranus, Feronia, Angerona are often called family deities, i.e. deities which belonged first to one family and then became more popular. It is true that sometimes a deity is described as belonging to one particular family (*culsu leprenei* and *uni urmsnei*), but these formulae resemble the Latin *Fortuna Flavia* and should rather be taken as an indication that the family claimed a well-known deity as their special patron (H. J. Rose, *SMSR* 1928, 209). Possible theophoric names of cities are Populonia, connected with *fufluns,* and perhaps Vetulonia. In other instances the priority is not clear: Tarchon, Tarquinia, and the family of Tarquinii; the god *Vel, Veltune,* Voltumnus, the cities Volsinii, Veltur (Capua?), Volturnum, and numerous Etruscan names from the root *vel-* or *velz-* are good examples.

11. Apart from a few high gods such as *tinia, uni* (Juno), Minerva, Mars, Apollo, *turms, fufluns, sethlans,* and Heracles, we find that the Etruscan deities seem to belong to definite spheres. Some gods are known only from documents referring to the *disciplina.* Others such as Charun, Tuchulcha, Mantrns (Mantus), and Vanth are peculiar to the funerary sphere. On mirrors, which were primarily designed for women, *turan* as goddess of love and subsidiary deities such as *acavisr, thalna, snenanth* are prominent, and minor demons designated as *lasae* are frequent.

12. Etruscan religion is a complex phenomenon. Certain features, such as the combination of political and religious powers in the hands of the princely *lucumones*; the worship of Tinia on the mountains, and his importance as thunder-god; the ritualistic codification of beliefs; the prophecies from thunderbolts and from the liver; and the quality of fervid and strange mythological imagination are suggestive of pre-Greek, possibly Oriental religions. On the other hand, the significance attached to agriculture and to distribution of land and the peculiar designation of one god as belonging to another (*turms aitas* = Hermes of Hades) are reminiscent of Roman religion (Gellius 13. 23), and many scholars have recognized similarities between Etruscan rituals and the *Tabulae Iguuinae* (q.v., and K. Olzscha, *Klio*, Beiheft 1939). It would appear that the influence of primitive Italic religion extended not only to mythology but to belief as well. Greek influence produced genuine transformations of some Etruscan gods and added considerably to mythological variety. It failed to affect very deeply the ritual or the general tenor of Etruscan religion.

K. O. Müller and W. Deecke, *Die Etrusker* (1877); L. R. Taylor, 'Local Cults in Etruria', *Am. Ac. Rome* ii (1923); G. Herbig in Hastings, *ERE*, s.v. 'Etruscan Religion'; C. Clemen, *Die Religion der Etrusker* (1936); E. Fiesel, 'Die Namen des griech. Mythos im Etruskischen', *Zeitschr. f. vergleichende Sprachforschung, Ergänzungsheft*, vol. v (1928); F. Altheim, *A History of Roman Religion* (1938). *Studi Etruschi* i–xiii (1927–39) contain important articles, reports on new material, and bibliographies. Other articles in *Studi e materiali di storia delle religioni* iv–xii (1928–36), esp. vols. iv and v, and in Roscher, *Lex.*, and *PW* under the names of Etruscan deities. *See also* TAGES *and* TARCHON. G. M. A. H.

RELIGION, ITALIC. The history of a religion needs documents, and those written in the language of the people of whose religious beliefs and practices it is proposed to give an account. The documentary evidence from ancient Italy, other than Latin and Greek, is meagre or, in some cases, imperfectly understood. But it is enough to make certain two facts: (1) the development of religion among the Italic tribes was essentially parallel to what took place at Rome—the differences are differences of detail; (2) hence, as at Rome, so in Italy at large, religion during the period *c.* 400–90 B.C. (which is the only period in which its activity is attested and also remained comparatively independent) was a composite affair that had received contributions from a very old and persistent stratum of Mediterranean people, from the waves of trans-Alpine immigrants—starting in prehistoric times and including the Gauls—who brought several forms of Indo-European language into Italy, from Illyrian settlers on the east coast, from others on the west (the Etruscans—probably of Anatolian origin), from Greek colonists, and, through them, from the Near East. It was, therefore, especially by the end of that period, ripe for the identification of its deities with those of Rome, to whom many of them were sufficiently akin (e.g. Umbrian *cubrar matrer*, at Fulginia, gen. sing. 'Bonae matris', or Picene *dea Cupra*, cf. the Roman Bona dea), or even identical (e.g. Oscan *diúveí*, i.e. 'Ioui', *mamrt[ei]* 'Marti'), as well as for identification with Greek and other deities of the kind that went on in Roman religion. Greek cults are by no means missing from the dialect-records, e.g. Messapic *aprodita* and *damatar*, which interpret themselves; Oscan *apellun*—'Apollo' (Messana, Pompeii), *herekló*—'Hercules' (Lucania, Campania, Samnium, Vestini, Paeligni, and at Praeneste), *meelikiieís*—'Μειλιχίου' (Pompeii), *eukliíí*—'Εὐκόλῳ' (i.e. Hermes, in Samnium); and, in the fastness of Corfinium even, *perseponas* (i.e. Persephonae, gen. sing.), uranias 'Οὐρανίας'. If *líganakdíkeí* (Samnium) is a translation of Θεσμοφόρῳ rather than an independent compound (quasi *lignāco-dic-*, qualified by the epithet *entraí*, i.e. 'inmost-forest-revealing goddess'), then a Greek cult-title has been borrowed.

2. But there is much that is genuinely native, as the enumeration which follows shows (for the *Tabulae Iguuinae* see that article). The fundamental Italic conception of deity, like the Roman, was 'act rather than personality' (e.g. *herentas* 'desire' at Herculaneum and Corfinium, compare the Roman *Venus*, lit. 'charm'; *vezkeí*, perhaps 'Lucinae' [?], *patanaí* 'Pandae', *genetaí* 'Genitae', cf. the Roman Genita Mana Venus, Genetrix —these three all from the *Tabula Agnonensis*, Samnium). The greater part of the beliefs of Italic tribes were concerned with the innumerable aspects of natural order (*diumpaís* [cf. *Lumphieis, Νύμφαις CIL* i². 1624, Naples] and *anafríss* 'imbribus' both ibid.—and both with the epithet *kerríio*—'Cerealis', i.e. 'genialis', *cerfu semunu*, Corfinium, gen. pl., cf. Lat. *semunis* acc. pl., *Carm. Arv.*, *Semo Sancus*, and, for *cerfu*, Lat. *duonus cerus*, *Carm. Sal.*, ap. Varr.) or of human life (Venetic *re·i·tia*, called *sahnat·e·i* 'healer', Ven. *vrota* 'turner', cf. *Postuorta*, *Anteuorta*; or Ven. *lah·v·na*, cf. Messapic *logetibas* dat. pl., Sicel Λάγεσις, Messapic *lahona* dat. sign., perhaps all connected with Gr. Λοχία, and so maieutic; Osc. *ammaí*, *Tab. Agn.*, clearly nurturing in function, *maatuís* ibid., cf. 'Manibus' or possibly *Matutinus*, Mater Matuta [?]).

3. Then, too, just as in Roman religion, there are gentile cults, proper to certain families, e.g. Raetic *velχanu*, Ven. *Volkanus*; *Diua Plotina* (Ariminum), *Ancharia* (Asculum), *anagtiai diiviai* 'Angitiae Diae' (Samnium, also found among the Marsi and Vestini), and *Pelina* (Paeligni), the last named perhaps already tribal or local, like *Flanatica* (Histri), *Minerua Cabardiacensis* (Travi, Aemilia), *Matronae Vcellasiacae Concanaunae* or *Matronae Braecorium Gallianatium* (Transpadana). From Capua and Cumae comes a large group of inscriptions, which call themselves *iúvilas* (n. pl.), cf. *leima iuvila*, i.e. 'Lima Iouia' (Raetic). Each regularly bears a heraldic emblem and records or prescribes an annual sacrifice to certain tutelary deities, or in honour of the ancestors of the family, on a fixed date. Jupiter 'Flagius' (cf. *Ioui Flazzo*, *Flazo* at Pozzuoli) is expressly mentioned, and a goddess analogous to the Roman Lucina seems also to be concerned. The wording of these inscriptions is very similar to that of a number of early Theran inscriptions (e.g. *IG* 12. iii Suppl. 1324, cf. iii. 452), and this interpretation of them is thereby confirmed. During the Social War the confederate Italic tribes represented Italia on coins (*Vitelliú*), just as the Romans had *Roma* long before.

4. Last we have to note the recognition and worship of certain greater personalized powers, which, again as at Rome, were like enough to some of the Olympian deities to be identified with them, or had been borrowed from them—Jupiter himself, *regenaí peai cerie iovia* 'Reginae Piae Cereri Iouiae', Castor and Pollux (Paelignian *puclois iouiois* dat. pl.), and the 'first-born daughter of Jove' (*diouo filea primocenia*, Praeneste)—to name no others. Even Juno and Diana appear to have been Latin in the first place rather than Roman. To the most remote times goes back the worship of mother-goddesses, attested by non-epigraphic remains at opposite ends of the peninsula in Liguria and in Malta (compare the later Celtic *Matronae* in Cisalpina, also called *Iunones*), or of mother-earth (Sicel Ἄννα, Messapic *ana*, Osc. *Damia*, with a festival δάμεια at Tarentum, cf. Lat. *damium*, Osc. *damuse* . . . *'*Damosia'), whose cult was extremely ancient all through the Mediterranean basin, or of infernal deities (attested by several Oscan *defixiones*); and not much later is the worship of animals, often disguised subsequently as eponymous ancestors, Messapic *Daunus* (the wolf?), *Hirpus* (Sabini, Hirpini— also the wolf), Messapic *Menzana* (the horse), Sicel Ἰταλός (the bull), or of natural features such as the mountain-top (Celtic *Penninus* in the Alps, *ocres tarincris* gen. sg., Marrucini), hot springs (Ligurian *Bormo*), or rivers (*Padus pater*). Agricultural deities and festivals, like the Ligurian *Leucimalacus* ('apple-ripener') and *plostralia*, or the Oscan *fiuusasiais* (loc. pl., 'Floralibus'), are a commonplace. There is, in short, every reason to suppose that, together with the same elements (magic, taboo, animism) that are fundamental in early Roman religion, there went, among the Italic communities, the same kind of development of local and functional spirits as at Rome, worshipped in the same way by sacrifice, prayer, lustration, and vow.

BIBLIOGRAPHY

The primary sources are collected in R. S. Conway, *The Italic Dialects* (2 vols. 1897), and in R. S. Conway, J. Whatmough, and S. E. Johnson, *The Prae-Italic Dialects of Italy* (3 vols., 1933). J. Whatmough, *The Foundations of Roman Italy* (1937), includes brief surveys of the known facts from all the dialect-areas. A full discussion of the problems of Italic religion, with much theorizing and some questionable assertion, may be had in F. Altheim, *A History of Roman Religion* (1938; to be used with caution).   J. W.

RELIGION, MINOAN-MYCENAEAN. As very few finds of religious importance are reported from the Early and Middle Helladic (Bronze Age) periods of the mainland of Greece, our knowledge of the religion of the pre-Greek population of Greece is almost exclusively derived from Crete, where the Bronze Age is called the Minoan Age (q.v.). In the Late Helladic period the immigrant Greeks dominated the mainland, especially its eastern parts. (We revert later to this period, which is also called Mycenaean.) The cult-places in Minoan Crete were partly natural caves or rock-shelters. Some caves, e.g. at Psychro and Arkalochori, have yielded numerous votives, double axes, bronzes, rings, gems, etc. The rock-shelter at Petsofa is peculiar by reason of its terra-cottas representing limbs and parts of the body; they cannot, however, be votives to a healing god. There were no great temples, but rustic sanctuaries and small chapels in houses and palaces, e.g. at Cnossos, Gurnia, etc. Their type of façade is known from wall-paintings and pieces of gold foil; it has three compartments with columns and horns of consecration and is crowned by the same horns. At the back is a raised dais on which idols and vessels were placed, other vessels being placed on the floor. There were altars and several kinds of sacral vessels too. We very often see an object consisting of two hornlike projections united by a common base; it is called 'horns of consecration'. Sacred vessels or branches were put between the horns. 'Horns of consecration' were often used in a purely ornamental way on vase-pictures and buildings, etc. The symbol of Minoan religion is the double axe which is very often depicted on vases and found among votives; the blades are generally curved and so thin that they are useless for practical purposes. Paintings show it crowning a high pole beneath which a sacrifice is performed. Probably it is the sacrificial axe. In the opinion of Evans the cult of pillars was frequent, but most of the pillars have a structural purpose, and the columns surrounded by symmetrically grouped animals on gems, etc., seem to be an abbreviation of a temple. A few cases seem, however, to prove a cult of baetyls (sacred stones). Tree-cult is proved by many gems and especially by the paintings of the sarcophagus from H. Triada, showing a tree in a holy enclosure. Some representations show a dance of an ecstatic kind. The cult-idols are female, bell-shaped, and very primitive; they are often found in houses. A few of better workmanship carry snakes in their hands, e.g. the faience statuette from Cnossos and the chryselephantine statuette in Boston. Gems and seal-impressions show the epiphany of gods in bird-shape and also in human form, sometimes as small figures hovering down from the air, sometimes full-sized. There is further a great number of daemons, monsters, and fabulous animals.

2. Many scholars, headed by Evans, think that the Minoans believed in a Great Goddess who ruled this world and the Nether World and compare her with the Great Mother of Asia Minor. A famous seal-impression from Cnossos shows a goddess holding a spear, standing on a mountain between two lions; the similarity is undeniable, but does not prove identity. From this and other data a kind of monotheism is inferred, and when a boy god is joined with the Mother Goddess as her paramour, just as Attis with the Great Mother, it is even termed a 'dual monotheism'. This last suggestion is highly hypothetical. It is more likely that the Minoans, just as other peoples, had a polytheistic pantheon. On seals, rings, and gems we discern gods and goddesses of various functions, the goddesses being in a considerable majority: a master and a mistress of animals who also are gods of hunters, who worshipped the so-called Mother of Mountains mentioned above, a goddess of tree-cult whom the great gold ring from Mycenae shows seated under a tree and approached by votaries, a goddess seated on board a ship, and finally the snake-goddess. The snake is believed to characterize her as a goddess of the Underworld, but the snake is to this day, even in Greece, still more venerated in domestic cult than in the cult of the dead. Since the snake-idols are found in houses and house chapels, it is clear that the snake-goddess has her origin in the cult of the house-snake. She is a domestic goddess, not the Lady of the Underworld. Of the cult of the dead little is known except for the paintings of the sarcophagus from H. Triada which probably represent a deification of the dead man. The heavenly bodies are sometimes represented; it is uncertain whether worship was paid to them. The alleged bull-cult cannot be proved; the bull-ring which gave rise to the Minotaur myth was hardly anything other than a secular sport. Egyptian influence is apparent in details, Babylonian is less prominent; but, generally speaking, the Minoan religion has a native character of its own.

3. Since the beginning of the Mycenaean age the Greeks took over Minoan religion with Minoan culture. To judge from the monuments above, they seem to have been wholly minoized; very many rings, gems, etc., with quite Minoan representations, for a great part certainly made in Crete, have been found on the mainland. Differences are few. In a room at Asine there is a bench with idols and vessels just as in Crete; the difference is that the bench is located in a corner of a hall and that to the idols are added a stone axe and a large male head, perhaps Zeus. On a limestone tablet from Mycenae is painted a goddess covered with a great shield, probably a forerunner of Athena. In the shaft-graves at Mycenae were found gold leaves representing a nude woman with birds who is called Aphrodite; an Oriental origin is probable, for nudity (like the phallus) is not found in Minoan religion. But the Mycenaeans were Greeks and certainly had their own religion, though in art it was concealed by the Minoan exterior.

4. The Homeric epics, which go back into the Mycenaean age, set us on its track. The Greeks brought with them Zeus from their old home; their State of Gods is, just as always, modelled after the State of men; like the Mycenaean war-king Agamemnon, Zeus is surrounded by vassals, and there is even a popular assembly in which the small gods take part. The Greek State of the Gods corresponds precisely to the feudal organization of the Mycenaean age. There is in Homer a simple belief in Destiny which recurs among other warlike peoples and helps them to brave the risks of warfare; it probably developed during the warring Mycenaean age. Athena, the special protectress of certain heroes, is the Minoan palace-goddess—she, too, has the snake as her attribute—and the Mycenaeans transformed her into the warlike protectress of the king. Hera is perhaps another palace-goddess; her name signifies simply 'the Lady' (it is kindred with ἥρως, in Homer 'Lord', 'Sir'). Another discrepancy is that plenty of idols are found in Mycenaean

tombs and almost none in Minoan, except for the very end of the Minoan age when it was influenced by the Mycenaeans. The Mycenaeans built stately beehive tombs for their kings which have no parallel in Crete, and the dead were buried unburned. Homer, on the contrary, knows only cremation and speaks always of mounds. Cremation began at the end of the sub-Mycenaean age; the question is too difficult to be treated here; but offerings, though not the dead, were sometimes burned in Mycenaean tombs. The beehive tomb was covered by a mound, at least the top of which projected above the surface. A cult was of course given to the dead kings and princes, who when alive were heroes—to use the word as Homer does. The cult of ancestors ceases with the extinction of the family, but if the people also are devoted to it, it may survive the extinction of the family and even the forgetting of the name of the dead man. There is evidence that at one Mycenaean tomb the cult was continued down into the historical age—at Menidi (Acharnae), in fact, to the beginning of the Peloponnesian War.

5. The cult of heroes has its origin in the Mycenaean age. There is other evidence for cult continuity from Mycenaean to historical times; the temple of the city goddess was built on the ruins of the palace of the Mycenaean king at Athens, Mycenae, Tiryns. Thus Minoan religion was transformed by the Mycenaean Greeks and handed down to the historical age. Certain myths of an un-Greek appearance, especially the myth of the birth and death of Zeus, show that Minoan elements were taken over directly. Hyakinthos, whose Minoan origin his name proves, is another representative of the dying and revival of vegetation. The Divine Child abandoned by its mother and nourished by others represents another Minoan myth which is coupled with the former. Again, the concept of Elysium, or the Islands of the Blest, seems to be a Minoan heritage. The two great antitheses in Greek religion are not, as many say, the Olympian and the Chthonic religion, but the emotional Minoan and the sober Greek religion. Historical Greek religion is a fusion of the two, but the contrast lingered on in the archaic age and gave the mystic movements their force.

A. J. Evans, 'Mycenaean Tree and Pillar Cult' (*JHS* xxi (1901), 99 ff.); *The Palace of Minos*. M. P. Nilsson, *The Minoan-Mycenaean religion and its survival in Greek religion* (Lund, 1927); 'Homeric and Mycenaean religion' (*ARW* xxxiii (1936), 84 ff.; *Gesch. d. griech. Religion* i. 237 ff.).   M. P. N.

RELIGION, PERSIAN. The Greeks had, from about the fifth century B.C., a fairly good acquaintance with Persian religion, not always, however, with its native form, but with the mixed beliefs and practices brought about by the extension of Persian influence to Babylonia and elsewhere; hence, e.g., the frequent assertion that Zoroaster (q.v.) was an astrologer; cf. Bidez–Cumont, p. vj. Further colouring is due either to the general opinion that all barbarians are too stupid, or too sage, to worship any but the natural and visible gods, as heaven, earth, and sun (cf. Ap. Rhod. 3. 714 ff. [Colchians], Caesar, *BGall.* 6. 21. 2 [Germans]), or to the recurrent, but especially Hellenistic, craze for finding deep philosophical learning among Orientals. Hence the numerous statements about Persians worshipping the sun and earth should be read with caution, though some no doubt refer to real cults of Mithra (q.v.) and of a mother-goddess; and such passages as Dio Chrysostom, 36, 39 ff. von Arnim, which puts a quasi-Platonic myth into the mouths of the Magi, may be disregarded. Something was known of Persian gods from fairly early times, though the oldest surviving mentions of Mithra and Ahura-Mazda (ʼΩρομάσδης, ʽΩρομάζης, ʽΩρομάζης) respectively, Herodotus 1. 131. 3 and [Plato], *Alcib.* 1. 122 a, make the former a goddess, the latter Zoroaster's father. Of surviving authors, Plutarch, *Mor.* 369 d ff., 1026 b, gives a correct account of Ahura-Mazda and Añgra-Mainyu or Ahri-

man (Ἀρειμάνιος). Other statements substantially correct are, e.g., Herodotus 1. 132 and Phoenix of Colophon, f. 1 Powell, about the method of sacrifice; Strabo 15. 3. 15 on the holy fire; Cicero, *Leg.* 2. 26, on Persian objection to temples of Greek type, and numerous remarks about the Magi, although Hdt. 3. 61. 1 ff may be neglected in this context, because it rests on confusion between *magašu*, a palace official, and *magawan*, members of the priestly order (see F. W. König, *Der falsche Bardija* (1938), 93, 180). Some knowledge of their sacred writings may be presumed on the part of Hermippus (Pliny, *HN* 30. 4) and those who drew upon him; some were known by name and a certain amount of truth blended with the falsehoods told about them, see Bidez–Cumont, *passim*.

For bibliography *see* ZOROASTER, and add C. Clemen, *Fontes historiae religionis Persicae* (*Fontes historiae religionum*, fasc. 1, 1920); M. Haug, *Essays on the Religion of the Parsis*, ed. E. W. West, London, n.d., ch. 1.   H. J. R.

RELIGION, TEUTONIC. Information concerning Teutonic religious ideas and observances furnished by classical authors is a welcome supplement to the knowledge gained from the much more abundant Germanic sources, for two reasons particularly: the comparatively early date of the references, and their value as illustrating the religion of the south Germanic tribes, for which the vernacular materials are scanty. The inscriptions, extant in considerable number, transmit native divine names which are rarely found in the literary sources, the authors of which usually substitute the name of a Roman god who bears a real or fancied resemblance to the Teutonic deity (*see* INTERPRETATIO ROMANA).

2. Among ancient writers Tacitus has most to say concerning Germanic religion. His statements about Teutonic gods contradict directly the testimony of Caesar, *BGall.* 6. 21: 'Deorum numero eos solos ducunt, quos cernunt et quorum aperte opibus iuuantur, Solem et Vulcanum et Lunam, reliquos ne fama quidem acceperunt.' Tacitus says, *Germ.* 9: 'Deorum maxime Mercurium colunt, cui certis diebus humanis quoque hostiis litare fas habent. Herculem et Martem concessis animalibus placant.' *Mercurius* undoubtedly represents the Teutonic *Woðanaz (OE Wōden, ON Óðinn); dies Mercurii* is translated by *day of Wōðanaz* (OE *Wōdenes dæg*, Engl. *Wednesday*). Later references confirm this equation. Similarly, Mars = Teutonic *Tīwaz (etymologically related to Dyāus, Zeus, Jupiter), the Indo-European heaven-god who became among the Teutons a god of war. *Dies Martis* = OE *Tīwes dæg*, Engl. *Tuesday*. Hercules is usually (and probably rightly) equated with the Germanic thunder-god *Þunraz (ON. Þórr, Thor). But here the equation is not supported by *interpretatio Romana*, for OE *Þunres dæg*, Engl. *Thursday*, German *Donnerstag* = *dies Iouis*. The fourth chief deity of the Teutons, *Inguz or *Ingwaz, a god of fertility, appears *Germ.* 2 in the tribal name *Ingaevones*. Cf. Yngvi-Freyr in Scandinavia, whose statue 'cum ingenti priapo' in the temple at Uppsala is described by Adam of Bremen in the eleventh century. (*Ing-* related to Gr. ἔγχος 'lance', i.e. phallus, phallic image?). The names of the other two tribal groups, *Istaevones* and *Herminones*, may contain by-names of Wōðanaz and Tīwaz respectively.

3. We are better informed concerning the Teutonic names of female divinities, both from literary sources and from inscriptions. Tacitus describes (*Germ.* 40) the cult of the goddess Nerthus, *Terra mater*, whose name corresponds exactly to that of Njǫrðr, the Norse fertility-god. Nothing is known of two other goddesses mentioned by him, Tanfana (*Ann.* 1. 51) and Baduhenna (*Ann.* 4. 73), except that the latter name contains in its first element a Germanic word for 'battle'. The inscriptions show a large number of additional names: Nehalennia, Hludana, Haeva, Vagdavercustis, Sandraudiga,

Hariasa, Harimella, Garmangabis, Alateivia, Vihansa, and others. Many of these are recognizably Teutonic, but only partially capable of interpretation. A special group is constituted by the *Matres* and *Matronae*, who were also venerated in Celtic territory; *see* DEAE MATRES. In the case of male gods the names appear as by-names: *Mercurius Cimbrianus* or *Cimbrius*, *Mercurius Channinus* (*Channo?*), *Mercurius Leudisio*, and others; *Hercules Magusanus* (eight inscriptions); *Mars Halamarthus* (slayer of men?), *Mars Thingsus* (god of the thing or folk-moot; cf. German *Dienstag* vs. Engl. *Tuesday*). This last inscription, found at Housesteads near Hadrian's Wall, can be dated between A.D. 222 and 235, during the reign of Alexander Severus.

4. For an account of Teutonic ritual and sacrifice (in which fertility-cults played a prominent part from the early Bronze Age to the end of the pagan period), of priests and priestesses, and of oracles and prophecy, the reader is referred to Much's article cited below.

C. Clemen, *Fontes historiae religionis Germanicae*; *PW*, Suppl. 3. 579 ff. (R. Much); K. Helm, *Altgermanische Religionsgeschichte* i; J. de Vries, *Altgerm. Religionsgesch.* i (Pauls Grundriss³, 12/1).

F. S. C.

RELIGION, THRACIAN. This was crude and barbaric before Greek influences transformed it. There is evidence of primitive animal-worship, human sacrifice, magical ceremonies, orgiastic rites. The earliest evidence, however, shows a belief in a future life. They brought to their worship powerful religious emotions that were still evident in later times.

Their native gods were vaguely conceived until individualized in Greek forms. The chthonian powers were especially favoured by them. Dionysus (q.v.) was their greatest god and their chief contribution to Greek religion. He was a god of vegetation and fertility, worshipped in wild, ecstatic rites. He was closely related to Sabazius (q.v.), whose cult was widespread among Thracians and Phrygians. He was originally conceived in animal form, and the animals thought to embody the god were torn to pieces and devoured raw by his worshippers, who thereby filled themselves with the god's power.

Other important Thracian deities are Bendis (q.v.), goddess of the chase and fertility, identified with Artemis; the closely related Cotys (q.v.) or Cotyto; Bedy, a spring and river god; Heros, god of vegetation and the chase, guardian of houses and roads (*see* RIDER-GODS); the closely related Rhesus (q.v.), the mysterious Zalmoxis (q.v.), of whom we know little; water-spirits, identified with the Nymphs; a war-god, identified with Ares; the Cabiri (q.v.). Several Greek gods were widely worshipped: Apollo, Zeus, Hera, Hermes, Heracles, Helios, Hades, Persephone, Asclepius, Hygieia, Telesphorus. The Thracians had a well-developed cult of the dead, for whom they raised impressive mounds.

P. Perdrizet, *Cultes et mythes du Pangée* (1910); G. Kazarow, *CAH* viii. 547–53, and *PW* vi A. 472–551; H. J. Rose, in Hastings, *ERE* xii. 325–31.

J. E. F.

REMMIUS PALAEMON, QUINTUS, *see* PALAEMON.

REMUS, *see* ROMULUS.

REPETUNDAE (or more fully **Res repetundae**). Several Roman laws of the time of the Republic dealt with the repression of illicit enrichment of public officials at the cost of people subject to their power. Frequent cases of abuse committed by provincial governors and their subordinates led to the provision of a legal remedy. Wrongdoing of this character was called *crimen repetundarum*, since the original legal provisions conferred upon the person who suffered loss the right to demand return of *res* or *pecuniae* extorted. The first Republican law against these offences was the *Lex Calpurnia* (149 B.C.), which introduced a special criminal procedure (*quaestio*, q.v.), though the trial somewhat resembled a civil action,

being directed to the return of the *res repetundae*. Subsequent legislation extended farther the circle of persons responsible for such abuse, and enlarged considerably the sphere of illicit acts to be punished as *crimen repetundarum*. The last *lex* on the matter was the severe *Lex Iulia repetundarum* (59 B.C., by Caesar), the provisions of which were accepted in the *Digest*, together with extensions introduced by classical jurists. Finally, *pecuniae quas quis in magistratu, potestate, curatione, legatione uel quo alio officio, munere, ministerio publico cepit*, could be claimed back from all officials. Penalties varied in course of time and were not identical in all cases: fines, loss of political rights (removal from the Senate), *infamia* (q.v.), *deportatio*, in graver cases.

Besides the text-books on Roman Criminal Law (*see* LAW AND PROCEDURE, ROMAN, III), Kleinfeller, *PW* i A. 603 ff.; A. v. Premerstein, *Sav. Zeitschr.* xlviii (1928), 505 ff. On the *Leges Repetundarum*, A. Berger, *PW* xii, s.v. 'Leges Acilia, Calpurnia, Cornelia, Iulia, Iunia, Servilia'. Translation of *Lex Acilia* (123 B.C., very important for the procedure and in large part preserved) in E. G. Hardy, *Six Roman Laws* (1911). W. S. Ferguson, *JRS* 1921, 86; J. P. Balsdon, 'The History of the Extortion Court at Rome, 123–70 B.C.', *BSR* xiv (1938).

A. B.

REPOSIANUS (3rd c. A.D.), author of a poem in 182 hexameters on the intrigue between Mars and Venus, preserved in the codex Salmasianus.

Text with transl., J. W. and A. M. Duff, *Minor Lat. Poets* (Loeb, 1935).

REPUDIUM, *see* MARRIAGE, LAW OF, II. 6.

RES PRIVATA, a new department of imperial finance, distinct alike from *fiscus* and *patrimonium*, created by Septimius Severus to receive the enormous estates confiscated from his political enemies. Why Severus chose to apply this special treatment is not clear. He might well decline to merge them in the *fiscus*, but the *res privata* could no more remain private property than the *patrimonium*, and, actually, it passed from emperor to emperor. It was under a procurator of a special rank (*tricenarius*—300,000 HS per annum) and administered vast landed estates, especially in Asia Minor.

H. M.

RES REPETUNDAE, *see* REPETUNDAE.

RESCRIPTUM, *see* CONSTITUTIONES.

REX, the Roman word for 'King' (etymologically connected with *regere*, to lead), is in itself evidence for a period of monarchy, the existence of which is postulated by the general process of political development in the Greek and Roman world, and attested by literary tradition, by archaeology, and by juridical and religious survivals. The word *rex* occurs in the Lapis Niger inscription in the Roman Forum, but the doubtful date of this makes it a matter of dispute whether the *rex* referred to is actually a king or the *rex sacrorum* (q.v.). Moreover, the name *Regia*, meaning the palace of the supreme pontiff, and such compounds of *rex* as *rex sacrorum* (or *sacrificolus*) and *interrex* prove that these republican officials were preceded by kings, whose name and powers they inherited.

That the king had ritual duties is confirmed by the analogous obligations fulfilled by his counterpart in Athens, the (ἄρχων) βασιλεύς. But the question of the power actually held by the king, and the legal foundation of the Roman monarchy, cannot be answered satisfactorily, owing to the lack of contemporary evidence. The only documents mentioned by ancient authorities are an agreement between Tarquin the Elder and Gabii, and an alliance between Servius Tullius and the Latin League. Therefore, annalists and jurists, in setting forth their theory of kingship and in relating the history of the regal period, merely applied the political system of the Republic to the original constitution of the city, substituting for the consuls one magistrate called *rex*, who was supposed to have had the right of being preceded by twelve lictors, since he combined in his person the authority and power of the two consuls. Although Roman tradition wrongly connected the origins of several Republican functions and customs with the regal period, it seems certain that some of these rights were actually enjoyed, and some of these duties fulfilled, by the kings—e.g. the wearing of a purple robe, the triumphal procession after a victorious campaign, etc. The king administered justice sitting in an ivory chair on a chariot (hence the term *sella curulis*); he made war and peace; in time of war he assumed the chief command and exercised a supreme right of life and death over every soldier and citizen.

The Roman monarchy was supposed to be elective, and not hereditary, on the analogy of the procedure followed in consular elections. The traditional list of the seven kings provides no proof to the contrary, although it contains two Tarquins, since one Tarquin may be merely a duplication of the other. The traditional kings certainly represent neither gods nor the personification of the seven hills, but not all of them can be accepted as historical figures. If nearly all details referring to the history of the regal period must be rejected, yet tradition is indisputably right in dating the fall of monarchy at the end of the sixth century B.C. It is difficult to say whether this was due, as traditionally related, to a revolution, or to a gradual evolution, although the fact that legal measures were taken not later than the fourth century to prevent any attempt at the re-establishment of monarchy seems to favour the former alternative. The example and influence of the Hellenistic kingdoms caused at Rome a change of attitude towards both the conception of monarchy and its practice, thus paving the way for the monarchical restorations of Sulla, Caesar, and Augustus.

Mommsen, *Röm. Staatsr.* ii². 1. 4 ff.; A. Rosenberg, *PW* s.v.; K. J. Beloch, *Röm. Gesch.* (1926), 225 ff. On the idea of kingship in the age of Caesar see J. Carcopino, *Points de vue sur l'impérialisme romain* (1934), 102 ff. P. T.

REX NEMORENSIS, the 'king of the grove', i.e. Diana's grove near Aricia. This unique official was an escaped slave who acquired office by killing his predecessor, after a formal challenge in the shape of a violation of the grove by plucking a branch. See Strabo 5. 3. 12, p. 239; Suetonius, *Calig.* 35; Servius on *Aen.* 6. 136; more in Frazer, *GB* i, p. 11, note 1. The man was Diana's priest; for attempted explanations of his position see Frazer, op. cit. passim; A. Lang, *Magic and Religion*, 206 ff.; Rose, *Roman Questions of Plutarch*, 91. H. J. R.

REX SACRORUM. On the expulsion of the kings from Rome, their sacral functions were confided to a priest who bore the title of *rex sacrorum* officially, less formally *rex* simply; Livy (2. 2. 1), which see for the institution, calls him *rex sacrificolus* (not *sacrificulus*). He was subordinate to the Pontifex Maximus (ibid.), but superior to all the flamens, Festus, p. 198, 30 Lindsay. He was a patrician born of confarreate marriage (Gaius 1. 112), might hold no other post and was chosen for life (Dion. Hal. *Ant. Rom.* 4. 74. 4), and his wife, the *regina*, had certain sacral duties, Festus, p. 101. 6.

See Marquardt-Wissowa, *Staatsverw.* iii². 321 ff. H. J. R.

RHABDOMANCY, see DIVINATION, para. 6.

RHADAMANTHYS, in mythology, son of Zeus and Europa (q.v.); he did not die but went to Elysium (*Od.* 4. 564). There he is a ruler and judge (Pind. *Ol.* 2. 75 ff.). He is uniformly represented as just (id. *Pyth.* 2. 73 f., and often). He is one of the judges of the dead (Plato, *Apol.* 41 a), along with others renowned for their justice, and so often in later authors, e.g. Verg. *Aen.* 6. 566, where he presides over Tartarus. Apart from this he has not much legend; his genealogy varies, Cinaethon ap. Paus. 8. 53. 5 giving Cres–Talos–Hephaestus–Rhadamanthys.

See further Jessen in Roscher's *Lexikon*, s.v. H. J. R.

RHAETIA, see RAETIA.

RHAMPSINITUS, i.e. Ramses (III?), to whom a folk-tale (Stith Thompson, K 315. 1) is attached in Herodotus 2. 121. The builder of his treasury left a secret entrance and after his death his two sons stole therefrom. One being trapped, the other beheaded him, avoided capture himself, and at last was reconciled to the king. H. J. R.

RHAPSODES were reciters of epic poetry, ῥαπτῶν ἐπέων ἀοιδοί, as the Homeridae (q.v.) are called (Pind. *Nem.* 2. 1), including both poets themselves, even Homer (Pl. *Resp.* 600 d), and minstrels reciting the work of others. Minstrels mentioned by Homer partly extemporize and partly recite from memory. An important part of the duty of a minstrel was to select and join passages of existing poetry, adapting them with greater or less alteration, a method which is indicated by the frequent notices (especially Clem. Al. *Strom.* 6. 2. 25. 1–26. 3) of the appropriation or plagiarism by one poet of the work of another, and to which the name rhapsode is clearly suitable. Rhapsodes interpolated work of their own into Homer (schol. Pind. *Nem.* 2. 1); see CYNAETHUS. Later, rhapsodes came to be more distinct from poets, as a class making their living by recitation (Hdt. 5. 67); but they were expected to give their own interpretations of the poets (Pl. *Ion* 530 c), and always tended to expand the texts, the main source of the interpolations detected by the Alexandrians. At first they accompanied their own recitations on the lyre, but later they carried a staff, which suggested the ancient but improbable derivation of their name from ῥάβδος. Rhapsodes performed at an early date in Delos, where an unknown poet claims that he and Homer together sang hymns to Apollo, ῥάψαντες ἀοιδήν (Hes. fr. 34); the introduction of the custom of recitation at various places is recorded, as at Syracuse; see CYNAETHUS. At Athens Homer, and presumably recitations, had been introduced before the fighting for Sigeum (Hdt. 5. 94). The recitations at the Panathenaea were regulated by laws, sometimes attributed to Solon, Pisistratus, or Hipparchus (Lycurg. *Leoc.* 102; Diog. Laert. 1. 2. 9. 57; [Plato], *Hipparch.* 228 b, etc.). The facts are obscure; but apparently the requirements were that only the authentic poetry of Homer should be recited, and in correct sequence, not arbitrary extracts, and that more than one rhapsode should be available to recite in turn. Rhapsodes came to be unfavourably regarded; but their performances lasted at least till the time of Sulla.

T. W. Allen, *Homer, the Origins and Transmission* (1924), 42–50. W. F. J. K.

RHEA SILVIA, see ROMULUS.

RHEDA, see CARRIAGES.

RHEGIUM ('Ρήγιον: Regium is probably more correct, the name being pre-Greek), nowadays *Reggio*, a Greek colony in the 'toe' of Italy opposite Messana, was founded c. 720 B.C. by Chalcis (its inhabitants, however, included Messenians, after 600 at least). Originally an oligarchy using the legislation of Charondas of Catana (Arist. *Pol.* 2. 9; 5. 12), Rhegium later became subject to Anaxilas (q.v.), who extended its authority, e.g., over Messana (q.v.). But Syracuse, traditional enemy of Chalcidian cities, supported Rhegium's rival Locri and ultimately destroyed Rhegium (387: see DIONYSIUS 1). Soon rebuilt, Rhegium, although temporarily held by Campanian mercenaries (280–270), successfully resisted Bruttii, Pyrrhus, and Hannibal. Becoming a favoured and loyal Roman ally, it acquired municipal status after 90 B.C. (Cic. *Arch.* 3), and colonists but not colonial status under

Augustus. Despite frequent earthquakes it remained a populous, Greek-speaking city throughout Imperial times. The lyric poet Ibycus was born here.

Strabo 6. 257 f.; Hdt. 6. 23; 7. 165, 170; Thuc. bks. 4, 6, 7; Diod. bks. 11–16; Livy 23. 30; 36. 42. P. Larizza, *Rhegium Chalcidense* (1905); J. Bérard, *Bibliogr. topogr.* (1941), p. 85.　　　E. T. S.

RHENUS was the Celtic name for the Rhine. This river (850 miles long) became the Roman frontier in Caesar's time, and between the river Vinxt and Holland it always so remained, though from the Flavian period until *c.* A.D. 260 the frontier of Germania Superior lay farther east. In Classical times, as always, the river, with its important tributaries, was a great channel of commerce, and the Romans maintained a fleet on it from 12 B.C., the *classis Germanica*, with headquarters at Bonn and later at Cologne. The first extant description of the river is that of Caesar (*BGall.* 4. 10), who notes its rise in the St. Gotthard, enumerates the tribes along its banks, and mentions that it divides into several streams on nearing the sea. Ancient writers generally regarded the Rhine as having two or three mouths, probably the Waal (Vahalis), Old Rhine, and the Vecht (cf. Strabo 4. 193; Pliny, *HN* 4. 101; Ptolemy 2. 9. 1). Drusus canalized the Vecht outlet (*see* FLEVO L.), and he also raised a dike, near the delta, completed by Pompeius Paulinus in A.D. 55 (Tac. *Ann.* 13. 53), to regulate the flow of the Rhine. Civilis cut it in 70 to hinder the Roman pursuit (*Hist.* 5. 19). Corbulo dug a canal, the Vliet, between Rhine and Meuse (*Ann.* 11. 20). Roman bridges existed above Basle and at Mainz, Coblenz, and Cologne; Caesar's bridges were built near Andernach.

Haug, in *PW* i A. 733–56, s.v. 'Rhenus'.

Another Rhenus (*Reno*) flowed into the Po near Bononia, and on an island here the Second Triumvirate was formed in 43 B.C.　　　O. B.

RHESUS, in *Iliad* 10. 435 ff. a Thracian ally of Priam. On his first night before Troy Odysseus and Diomedes (qq.v.) stole upon his camp, killed him and twelve of his men, and carried off his magnificent horses. Homer makes him son of Eïoneus; [Euripides], *Rhesus*, 279, 393–4, of the river Strymon and a Muse (Euterpe, according to schol. *Il.* loc. cit.). The scholiast on *Iliad* loc. cit. says (cf. Verg. *Aen.* 1. 469 ff., with Servius auctus there) that if Rhesus' horses had tasted Trojan pasture and he and they drunk of the Scamander, Troy could not have fallen. As the *Rhesus* (962 ff.) says he shall not go to Hades but live on as a demi-god (ἀνθρωποδαίμων) in a cave, he is perhaps originally a Thracian deity.　　　H. J. R.

RHETOR, *see* EDUCATION, III. 3.

RHETORIC, GREEK. Rhetoric (τέχνη ῥητορική; the term ῥήτωρ appears first in Ar. *Ach.* (425 B.C.), ῥητορική first in Plato), or the art of oratory, was first taught at Athens by the Sicilians Corax and Tisias, followed by Gorgias and other Sophists. From the first the main object was held to be that of persuasion; and Corax and Tisias, concerned solely with oratory of the law-courts (forensic), prescribed as essentials plausible (εἰκός) arguments and their arrangement according to fixed rules. Ceremonial oratory (epideictic) was treated by Gorgias, who emphasized the value of an emotional appeal in winning persuasion. Aiming at prose expression which should rival poetry in its effects, he advocated the use of many devices, including symmetrical clauses, figures, and poetic diction; and thus laid the foundations of Sophistic rhetoric. Of Gorgias' contemporaries, Thrasymachus, moreover, indicated the value of the period and rhythmical effects in prose; Protagoras, Prodicus, and Hippias by their philological studies prepared the way for a more precise use of words; and further developments came from Polus with his tricks of expression, from Theodorus of Byzantium with his complicated rules, his divisions and subdivisions, while by Evenus the rules were presented in metrical form.

2. Criticism of this system came, however, from Plato, who condemned the spurious arguments based on probability (*Grg.* 453 ff.), the fixed divisions assigned to a forensic speech (*Phdr.* 266 e), as well as the mechanical use of stylistic ingenuities (*Grg.* 462 c). Such rhetoric he refused to recognize as an art, and described it as a mere knack (ibid. 463 b), empirically acquired and devoid of rational basis. On the other hand, he made some far-reaching suggestions when he insisted on the need for subject-matter based on truth (ibid. 453 ff.), or again, on the fact that organic unity (not arbitrary divisions) determined the form of a speech (*Phdr.* 264 c). He also pointed out that artificial devices were not enough, that native endowment (φύσις), a knowledge of art (ἐπιστήμη), and practice (μελέτη) were needed (ibid. 269 d), and that in all matters of expression psychological considerations were important (ibid. 270 ff.).

3. Meanwhile a new conception of rhetoric was being formulated by Isocrates, who regarded it as a cultural study in which fitting expression was sought for lofty themes. This study he described as a sort of practical philosophy, the best form of training for life and citizenship; and thus began the long conflict between philosophy and rhetoric in the educational sphere. In developing his theory Isocrates first decried the trivial subjects favoured by Polycrates and others, and then directed attention to those great political issues on which great utterance was possible. With interest thus centred on political oratory he elaborated what was largely a new technique, which gave to Attic prose fresh dignity and grace, and he established a tradition which, handed down by pupils and later writers, has persisted to the present day. He was, in short, one of the great formative influences in technical rhetoric.

4. Yet more significant was Aristotle's contribution when, in his *Rhetoric*, he defended the art against Plato's strictures and included it in his philosophical course, after modifying the prevailing conception of its nature. To him rhetoric was a genuine art, the counterpart of dialectic, both being branches of the art of reasoning; and its function he defined, not as persuasion, but as 'the observing of all the available means of persuasion' (*Rh.* 1. 1. 14). His approach is thus of a philosophical kind. He is primarily concerned with establishing sound sense as the main essential in oratory, in accordance with Plato's teaching. In bks. 1 and 2 he deals at length with processes of argument, with proofs sophistical and valid. He then proceeds to a consideration of style (bk. 3), based apparently on his earlier treatise, *Theodectia*; and his exposition of this branch is highly suggestive and illuminating. Here again, however, his philosophical bent affects his treatment. It is as if he distrusted stylistic effects in general, as appealing to the emotions instead of to the understanding; and two qualities alone he regards as essential, namely σαφήνεια and πρέπον, thus leaving to later writers a more complete analysis. Yet his achievement was of the first importance. With him originated the later threefold classification of rhetoric, as well as the systematic treatment of εὕρεσις, τάξις, and λέξις; and in general he may be said to have laid the foundations of philosophical rhetoric.

5. To the further advance of rhetorical study but little was contributed at this stage. The work of Theophrastus alone is of lasting importance, in that he developed the doctrines of Isocrates and Aristotle, and gave fresh impetus to the study of style. In his Περὶ λέξεως he described its main virtues (ἀρεταί) as four in number—Ἑλληνισμός, σαφήνεια, πρέπον, κατασκευή—and pointed out other effects, such as the value of ὑπόκρισις (action) in oratory, and of euphony and variety in all prose expression. His later influence was considerable, and is seen in the works of Cicero, Dionysius of Halicarnassus, and others.

6. A new phase began about the middle of the third century B.C., when great oratory ceased owing to political conditions, and rhetoric became merely a scholastic discipline in the spread of Greek culture. Of manuals dealing with this school rhetoric nothing survives. It seems to have been a continuation of Sophistic teaching, adapted for school purposes, and modified in the light of current literary tendencies. Those tendencies, already visible in the Attica of the fourth century B.C., developed later in Asiatic centres, and thus gave rise to florid and emotional styles subsequently known as 'Asianist', of which Hegesias of Magnesia was the chief representative. With the cultivation of these styles school rhetoric was largely concerned. It prescribed exercises of a declamatory kind, dealing often with fictitious and fantastic themes, besides panegyrics and memorial speeches, all written in accordance with fixed rules and methods. It provided instruction also in letter-writing; and characteristic of its methods were those *Progymnasmata* (q.v.) or preliminary exercises employed in the schools of the first century B.C.

7. In the meantime a renewed attack was being made on rhetoric by the philosophical schools, the main charges being that it possessed no clear subject-matter and no definite aims, and was thus of little use in education. The Peripatetics, it is true, were interested in matters of style. But for the rest, Epicurus had denied the value of rhetoric for either philosopher or statesman; while the Stoics, who treated of definitions, correct diction, and the like, also attached to it but little importance. This hostility was sustained in the second century B.C. by Carneades, Critolaus, and others. A reaction set in when Hermagoras (*c.* 150 B.C.) claimed for the subject-matter of rhetoric a more serious treatment. Maintaining that all non-technical problems (πολιτικὰ ζητήματα) fell within its scope, both particular (ὑπόθεσις) and general (θέσις) problems, he prescribed four questions (στάσεις) which he held to be adequate for the solution of all such problems, thus establishing a system which was to be discussed throughout later antiquity. With details of style he did not deal; and his contemporary, Athenaeus, did little to fill the gap, beyond perhaps inspiring the treatise on Figures by the first-century Gorgias. Meanwhile, fresh activities were developing at Rhodes under Apollonius and Molon; the philosophers Posidonius and Philon were adopting a less hostile attitude. And by the first century B.C. insistent demands for instruction came from Rome, to which Apollodorus and Theodorus (followers of Hermagoras) responded, thus carrying on the rhetorical tradition, with some differences, it is true (*see* ALEXANDER 12), into the Imperial period.

8. Of yet greater importance was the new direction given to rhetorical study by the Atticist movement, which assumed definite form *c.* 50 B.C. and stood, first, for a rejection of the prevailing Asianist styles (see Norden, *Ant. Kunstpr.* i. 131 ff.), and secondly, for a return to the standards of the great Attic writers. The reaction was due partly to Roman influence and good sense, still more to the tendency of Greek minds to revert under Roman domination to a glorious past. Earlier grammarians had preserved and explained something of the literary legacy of ancient Greece. And now the main object became that of imitation, and of modifying rhetorical principles in accordance with classical ideals. Among the main agents in effecting this change were Caecilius of Calacte, Dionysius of Halicarnassus, and later Demetrius and 'Longinus', all of whom, however, with their wider interests, subordinated technical instruction to criticism of an aesthetic kind (*see* LITERARY CRITICISM, GREEK). Nevertheless, the main developments at this stage are clear. Caecilius alone specifically condemned Asianism (*K. Φρυγῶν*); but all alike advocated the

doctrine of μίμησις, which, previously enunciated by Isocrates (*K. τῶν σοφιστῶν* 18), and intermittently practised by the Rhodians and others, was now restated and developed by Dion. Hal. (*De Imit.* A. III. 28) and 'Longinus' (*Π. ὕψους* 13. 2). The models commended were chiefly those comprised in the canon of the ten Attic orators (due to second-century grammarians, probably of Pergamum); and while Plato, Thucydides, Xenophon, and others were also included, Demosthenes was finally proclaimed as the greatest of them all. In the meantime efforts were devoted throughout the first century A.D. to the teaching of classical style. A systematized theory of Figures had been submitted by Caecilius; the three main types of style—grand, middle, and plain, as defined by earlier theorists—were expounded by Dion. Hal. and Demetrius; and new graces to be won by σύνθεσις (composition) were also pointed out by the same writers, notably the effects of an artistic word-order, euphony, rhythm, variety, and the like.

9. By the beginning of the second century A.D. ancient rhetoric was entering on its last phase (the so-called 'Second Sophistic'). Firmly entrenched by now in the educational system, and having received fresh impetus from a revival of the Greek spirit, it took on a new colouring from the Asiatic centres of that movement (Smyrna, Ephesus, Tarsus), and discarded for the most part first-century teaching. With the aim of reviving the glories of ancient Greece, epideictic oratory became now the main occupation (cf. Atticus Herodes and Aristides). Teachers of rhetoric sought to cultivate an ornate expression by adopting the methods of the earlier school rhetoric. And the characteristic contributions of the second and third centuries were thus Προγυμνάσματα (Theon, Minucianus, Hermogenes), τέχναι (Alexander, Aristides, Theon, Menander, Longinus, Apsines), μελέται (Adrianus, Polemon), and letters (Alciphron, Lesbonax). Of special interest historically was the work of Hermogenes, who, besides modifying the stasis-doctrine of Hermagoras, attempted to reduce the study of style to a fixed system. Taking over from others the conception of certain forms (ἰδέαι) of style (distinct from the ἀρεταί of Theophrastus and the three later types), he sought by analysis of his impressions of classical writers to arrive at definitive laws of style. The result was his Περὶ ἰδεῶν, a treatise notable for its obscure terminology, its endless classifications, distinctions, definitions, and rules, which added but little to the vital appreciation of style. Yet this work, together with his *Progymnasmata* and his stasis-teaching, represented the authoritative doctrine for later generations; and since poetry also entered into his treatment (under πανηγυρικός), his influence extended ultimately to medieval poetry as well as prose. Thus in the second and later centuries did Greek rhetoric revert to sterile scholastic standards and methods. It gave rise to a system which had disastrous effects on literature for centuries to come; and what was of value in the earlier teaching was left for later ages to rediscover.

BIBLIOGRAPHY

TEXTS, etc.: Walz, *Rhet. Graeci* (1832–6); L. Spengel, *Rhet. Graeci* (1853–6, vol. i², ed. C. Hammer 1894); Isocrates, *Works*, ed. G. Norlin (Loeb, 1928); Anaximenes, *Rhet. ad Alex.*, tr. E. S. Forster (works of Aristotle xi; 1924). Aristotle, *Rhetoric*, ed. Cope (with trs., 1878); tr. Welldon (1886); tr. Jebb-Sandys (1909); ed. J. H. Freese (Loeb, 1926); trs. (with comment.) Lane Cooper (1932). Theophrastus Περὶ λέξεως, ed. A. Mayer (1910); *Aristides*, ed. W. Schmid (Teubner, 1926); *Hermogenes*, ed. H. Rabe (Teubner, 1913). For Dion. Hal., Demetrius, and 'Longinus' *see* LITERARY CRITICISM, I. 5.

SPECIAL STUDIES: F. Blass, *Griech. Bereds. von Alex. bis Augustus* (1865); *Attische Bereds.*² (i–iii; 1887–98); E. Norden, *Ant. Kunstprosa* (1898); O. Navarre, *La Rhét. grec. avant Aristote* (1900); G. Saintsbury, *History of Criticism* (1900); R. Volkmann, *Rhet. der Gr. und Römer* (3rd ed. by C. Hammer, 1901); W. Süss, *Ethos* (1910); J. D. Denniston, *Greek Lit. Criticism* (1924); C. S. Baldwin, *Ancient Rhet. and Poetic* (1928); W. Rhys Roberts, *Greek Rhet. and Lit. Criticism* (1928); J. W. H. Atkins, *Lit. Criticism in Antiquity* (1934); W. Kroll, *Rhetorik* (1937).   J. W. H. A.

RHETORIC, LATIN. The study of rhetoric at Rome dates from the second century B.C. It formed part of those Greek traditions which were being assimilated by Romans; and although, then as later, its teaching rested mainly in Greek hands, Latin works (lost) came from Cato, and subsequently from M. Antonius and Hortensius, in which were expounded Hellenistic scholastic doctrines. During the first century B.C. efforts were made to adapt this instruction to Roman needs; and first came the attempt of L. Plotius Gallus (c. 95 B.C.) to drive out Greek teaching by founding a Roman school of rhetoric. More significant was the appearance of *Rhetorica ad Herennium* (q.v.: c. 86 B.C.), sometimes ascribed to Cornificius, which aimed at giving a Roman colouring by latinizing Greek terminology, omitting Greek subtleties, and supplying Latin illustrations, while submitting in schematic form Hellenistic doctrine, notably Hermagoras' stasis-teaching, figures, and the like. The treatise, moreover, is one of great historical interest. The first surviving work on rhetoric after a lapse of three centuries, and the first complete Latin manual, it throws valuable light on Hellenistic teaching; and, widely accepted later as Cicero's work, it exercised decisive influence on medieval poetic theory.

2. Yet more drastic were the modifications proposed by Cicero under Aristotelian and Rhodian influences; though his *De Inventione* (84 B.C.) and certain later writings provided merely conventional matter, and he wrote no complete manual. In his famous dialogues on oratory and orators (55–46 B.C.), however, he criticizes constructively the prevailing mechanical methods; and what he advocates is a more generous conception of rhetoric, an advance beyond the technical study of arguments and style, and in general the discarding of Hellenistic doctrine for the ideals and standards of classical Greece. He also applies his teaching to the solution of the contemporary Asianist-Atticist problem (*see* LITERARY CRITICISM IN ANTIQUITY, II. 2). Thus his contribution to rhetorical study was mainly critical in kind; it lay in suggesting the larger vision, and in pointing the way to more fruitful theories and methods.

3. Developments along these lines were, however, stayed by changed conditions in the Augustan era, when, owing to the decline of popular assemblies and alterations in legal procedure, oratory vanished from public life to be cultivated mainly in the schools. Some amount of theorizing still went on. Now began the controversy between Apollodorus (q.v. 5) and Theodorus (q.v. 3) in which the Apollodoreans M. Calidius and Clodius Turrinus, the Theodorean Vallius Syriacus, and others joined; the τέχνη of Apollodorus was translated by C. Valgius Rufus; while other contributions were Junius Otho's *Colores* and a dissertation on style by Domitius Marsus. But such activities were of academic interest only. In practice a new conception of rhetoric was forming in the schools, where study was limited to exercises in *controversiae* and *suasoriae* (q.v.), which aimed at inculcating a declamatory style suitable for scholastic show-pieces (*see* EDUCATION, III. 3). That this innovation was not without its effects is revealed by the elder Seneca. Moreover, from now on, rhetoric became the predominant factor in education, and a false idea of style invaded all branches of literature.

4. Nor, apart from Quintilian's *Institutio*, were substantial additions made to rhetorical theory during the first century A.D., despite Imperial patronage. Critical comments on the decline of style came from various quarters; and technical treatments of the subject from rhetors and others. Celsus (following Varro) had a section on rhetoric in his *Encyclopaedia*; manuals came from the elder Pliny, Verginius Flavus, Tutilius, and Visellius; and P. Rutilius Lupus translated the Περὶ σχημάτων of Gorgias (1st c. B.C.). From Quintilian alone came a contribution of value; and in his great treatise he does for school rhetoric what Cicero had tried to do for public oratory. Reviewing earlier teaching in the light of his own rich experience, and preserving both in form and substance what was valuable in that teaching, he propounds a new system, based on first principles and psychological grounds, and consisting mainly of a restatement of Cicero's classical ideals, yet with a full sense of the inevitability of development. Judicious in its outlook, illuminating and convincing in its methods, the *Institutio* is a lasting monument of the Latin genius, which, eminently practical, had little taste for abstract theorizing on a discipline originally Greek.

Special Studies: E. Norden, *Ant. Kunstprosa* (1898); G. Saintsbury, *History of Criticism* (1900); R. Volkmann, *Rhet. der Gr. und Römer* (3rd ed. by C. Hammer, 1901); J. Wight Duff, *Literary History of Rome* (2 vols., 1909 and 1927); J. W. H. Atkins, *Literary Criticism in Antiquity* (1934); W. Kroll, *Rhetorik* (1937). Cf. DECLAMATIO.
J. W. H. A.

RHETORICA AD HERENNIUM. The treatise on rhetoric addressed to C. Herennius (written c. 86–82 B.C.) is by an unknown author. Some, interpreting passages of Quintilian, assign it to 'Cornificius'. It is ascribed in the manuscripts to Cicero, and has often been printed with his works; but the Ciceronian authorship, first challenged in the fifteenth century, is no longer accepted. Its relationship to Cicero's *De Inventione* has not been satisfactorily determined. Rhetoric is treated in five divisions: Invention in judicial, deliberative, and demonstrative causes; Arrangement; Delivery; Memory (an important discussion); and, with abundant illustrations, Style (the oldest surviving treatment in Latin). The doctrine is a fusion of Greek systems; the illustrations, terminology, and spirit are Roman. The style is generally clear, and less archaic and 'plebeian' than scholars once maintained.

Best text: F. Marx, 1894 (with Proleg. and Index) and 1923 (Teubner).
H. C.

RHIANUS, of Bene, less probably of Ceraea, in Crete: a contemporary of Eratosthenes (born 276 B.C.), R. began life as a slave and custodian of a wrestling-school. After a belated education he attained fame as a poet and Homeric scholar, probably at Alexandria.

WORKS

Verse: R. wrote epic poems and epigrams, but was best known for the former (Ath. 11. 499 d), of which one was a *Heracleias*. Four others, *Thessalica*, *Achaeica*, *Eliaca*, *Messeniaca*, were tribal epics, rich in myth, history, and geography. The last was used by Pausanias (bk. 4, cf. especially 6. 1) as one source for the history of the Second Messenian War. Episodes in the poem seem to have been modelled on Homer or the rest of the cycle. More romantic scenes, e.g. the escape of Aristomenes from prison and the love-affair which betrayed the Messenians, show the influence of a later school of writing. The longest fragment (1) of R., possibly complete in itself, consists of twenty-one hexameters on the folly of mankind. Most of the epigrams (frs. 66–76) have a paederastic *motif*.

Prose: R. produced an edition of the *Iliad* and *Odyssey*. It was more conservative than that of Zenodotus, and the forty-five readings from it which have survived have led critics to judge it favourably.

To some extent R. falls into line with Apollonius Rhodius against Callimachus and his own contemporary Euphorion. Like Apollonius he preferred epic to epyllia, but his language seems to have been simpler than that of Apollonius. In the extant fragments he uses neologisms, but hardly any 'glosses'. His epics must have been agreeable reading, but it is possible, in view of the numerous citations by Stephanus of Byzantium, that they were too cumbered with geography.

Texts: J. U. Powell, *Collectanea Alexandrina* (1925), 9–21; E. Diehl, *Anth. Lyr. Graec.* vi (1924), 221–5 (epigrams only). General literature: W. Aly, 'Ριανός in *PW*, Zweite Reihe I, 781–90; A. Meineke, *Analecta Alexandrina* (1843), 171–212; C. Mayhoff, *De Rhiani studiis Homericis* (1870).
E. A. B.

RHINTHON, of Tarentum, a potter's son, writer of phlyax-plays (ἱλαροτραγῳδίαι, later known as *fabulae Rhintonicae*: see PHLYAKES); contemporary with Ptolemy I (early 3rd c. B.C.). He was honoured with an epitaph by the poetess Nossis of Locri in south Italy (*Anth. Pal.* 7. 414): she calls him Syracusan, and claims originality for his 'tragic *phlyakes*', i.e. for raising the crude phlyax-drama by comic treatment of tragic themes. Of thirty-eight pieces attributed to R. nine titles are known (almost all are burlesques of Euripides), but very meagre fragments survive. One (fr. 10) from Ὀρέστας (Doric form) mentions 'the metre of Hipponax', i.e. scazon: a character in the play (violating dramatic illusion) points out that a curse just uttered will not scan as a tragic iambic trimeter.

South Italian vases give scenes from the *phlyakes* of Rhinthon and others.

CGF 183 ff. W. G. W.

RHIPAEI MONTES (Ῥιπαῖα Ὄρη), the 'gusty' and ever snowy mountains, imagined from Homer onwards to exist north of the known parts of Europe. From them blew the North Wind; beyond, down to the Northern Ocean, dwelt Hyperboreans (q.v.). Herodotus ignored the Rhipaeans and Strabo denied their existence. Those who believed in them differed as to their location. Aeschylus and Pindar regarded them as the source of the Danube, and Posidonius thought originally that the Alps were meant. On the other hand, Aristotle placed them beyond Scythia, and Roman poets put them in the extreme north. In general, their latitude was moved northward as knowledge increased. Ptolemy, who considered that they were of moderate altitude, located them in Russia (lat. 57° 30'–63° 21'), between rivers flowing into Baltic and Euxine. They remained on maps until modern times.

Ptol. *Geog.* 3. 5, 15, 22; Kiessling, *PW*, s.v. Ῥιπαῖα Ὄρη. E. H. W.

RHODES, an island of about 420 square miles, close to the mainland of Caria, was settled by Dorian Greeks who formed three city-states, Ialysus, Lindus, and Camirus. Their development was normal for the time and place—colonization (including Gela, Rhegium, and Phaselis, all Lindian colonies), tyranny, Persian conquest. In the fifth century, till 412–411 B.C., they were members of the Athenian Confederacy, and their constitutions were presumably democratic.

The war with Athens (411–407) combined with internal stresses to produce the union ('Synoecism') of the three cities into one State with a new federal capital *Rhodos*, though the original cities kept the greatest possible local autonomy. The 'Rhodians' remained democrats, perhaps even extremists, till revolutionary disturbances (c. 397–388) resulted probably in a moderate democracy which was overthrown only for a period of Persian domination (355–333); its stability later depended on a compromise between the interests of the large citizen proletariat and of the wealthy citizens (see especially Strabo 14. 652).

The prosperity of Rhodes must always have come mainly from the carrying trade. It received a great impetus from the conquests of Alexander, giving unrestricted access to Egypt, Cyprus, and Phoenicia, and in the third century Rhodes became easily the richest of the Greek city-states. Politically, too, the partition of Alexander's empire after 323 enabled it to reassert its independence and steer its own course in foreign affairs. This independent policy provoked the famous siege by Demetrius (305–304); but its survival on this occasion increased its prestige and self-confidence, so that in the third century it successfully avoided subservience to any of the 'great powers'. Like Athens earlier, it stood as a centre of exchange and capital and the enemy of piracy

on the high seas. The Rhodian fleet was fairly large and always efficient: it was the 'senior service'—its officers were drawn from the best families, its crews (and the workers in the shipyards) from the poor citizens.

Rhodes (with Pergamum) was largely responsible for the first major intervention of Rome in eastern affairs (201). It co-operated with Rome (not previously an ally) in the wars against Philip V and Antiochus, and was rewarded with territory in Caria and Lycia. But Rome punished the equivocal attitude of Rhodes in the Third Macedonian War by proclaiming Delos a free port 167): this unfair competition, and perhaps an increase in piracy which Rhodes could no longer check, crippled it so severely that in three years its annual harbour revenues fell from a million to 150,000 drachmae. It became an ally of Rome on unfavourable terms, and ceased to be a power in the world. It successfully withstood a siege by Mithridates in 88, but was captured and pillaged by Cassius in 43. Nevertheless, under Roman rule Rhodes kept a modicum of prosperity and no small distinction as a beautiful city and a centre of higher education, with Panaetius and Posidonius its greatest savants.

Ancient sources: Inscriptions, especially *IG* xii, part 1 (1905), and A. Maiuri, *Nuova silloge epigrafica, Rodi e Cos* (1925). Literary sources are widely scattered: for the famous siege, Diodorus, book 20. 81–8 and 91–100. Modern literature: H. von Gelder, *Geschichte der alten Rhodier*; M. Rostovtzeff, *CAH* viii. 619 ff. (and Bibliography); *Hellenistic World* (1941). G. T. G.

RHODES, CULTS AND LEGENDS OF. The most noteworthy cult at Rhodes was that of Helios (q.v.); the festival was called Halieia, celebrated yearly with sacrifice of a four-horse team thrown into the sea (Festus, p. 190, 28 Lindsay) and quadrennially with more elaboration. An ancient cult at Lindos was directed to a goddess identified with Athena; she was, however, plainly chthonian, being worshipped with fireless offerings (Pind. *Ol.* 7. 48); for the remarkable chronicle-inscription of her temple see C. Blinkenberg, *La Chronique du temple lindien*, Acad. royale des sciences et des lettres, Copenhague, 1912, and *Die lindische Tempelchronik* (1915). There were also festivals to Kronos, Poseidon, Apollo (Sminthia), Dionysus, probably the Dioscuri, Heracles and his son Tlepolemus (the Tlapolemeia, an agonistic festival of some importance; cf., for such events in Rhodes, I. R. Arnold in *AJArch.* xl (1936), 432 ff.). For authorities, see M. P. Nilsson, *Griechische Feste* (1906), 478. Athenaeus, 360 c, records a custom of Lindos; children in the month Boedromion (presumably Badromios in the local dialect) went about singing a traditional song about the coming of the swallow and collecting contributions from the houses. This was called χελιδονίζειν.

A few legends are known. Helios himself chose the island, which had not then risen above the surface of the sea (Pind. *Ol.* 7. 54 ff.). His children by the nymph Rhodos, daughter of Aphrodite (ibid. 14), were instructed by him to offer sacrifice to Athena the day she was born. In their haste they forgot to bring fire (ibid. 39 ff.), hence the custom of fireless sacrifice (above). The sons of Helios were Lindus, Ialysus, and Camirus, eponyms of the three chief cities of the island (schol. rec. Pind. ibid. 34). H. J. R.

RHYME, see ASSONANCE.

RHYTHM, PROSE, see PROSE-RHYTHM.

RICINIATA sc. *fabula*: see FABULA.

RIDDLES. A riddle (γρῖφος) in its proper sense may be described as a species of αἴνιγμα or 'dark saying', which in turn belongs to the wider category of αἶνος ('story'). It is essentially designed to baffle or challenge the intelligence of the hearer; its subject-matter may be derived from a variety of sources, e.g. natural phenomena, social custom, or myth. The Oracle, for example, is typically expressed in enigmatic form. Early examples of riddles in Greek literature are Hesiod fr. 160 Rz. (contest of Calchas and Mopsus, perhaps rather to be described as a direct test of intelligence) and Theognis 1229 f.; the later *Certamen Hom. et Hes.* (ad fin.) preserves the traditional story of Homer and the Fishermen. By the fifth century B.C. the propounding of γρῖφοι had become a regular diversion of Greek society, especially at the symposium (Ar. *Vesp.* 20 f.); Aristotle (*Rh.* 3. 11. 6) mentions τὰ εὖ ᾐνιγμένα among the pleasurable seasonings of discourse. The authorship of early collections of riddles was ascribed to Cleobulus of Lindos and his daughter Cleobuline (Suidas; Wilamowitz, *Textgesch. d. gr. Lyr.* 40. 3; O. Crusius *Philol.* 55). The Peripatetic Clearchus of Soli (frs. 61–8 in *FHG*) composed a work Περὶ γρίφων, which was used by Athenaeus. Athenaeus himself (10. 448 b–459 b) gives a copious selection of riddles from comedy and other sources. A short collection of metrical examples is contained in *Anth. Pal.* 14. The general tendency to enigmatic expression, not unknown in earlier literature, becomes stronger with the Alexandrians, for example in the *Alexandra* of Lycophron.

Riddles occur sporadically in Latin literature. Aulus Gellius (12. 6) cites a metrical one from Varro; Petronius (58) provides examples of the popular type. The Greek term *aenigma* is habitually employed; Gell. (loc. cit.) gives *scirpus* as the native word. The metrical collection bearing the name of *Symphosius* (q.v.) (4th–5th century A.D.) is composed in imitation of the Greek convivial type.

As might be expected from the character of the two peoples, the Greeks liked a riddle—γρῖφος—and the Romans did not. 'The investigation of riddles', said the philosopher Clearchus, who divided them into seven classes, 'is not unconnected with philosophy: a riddle is a sportive problem, and to find the answer we have to use our intellect.' The most famous riddle was that proposed by the Sphinx and answered by Oedipus: 'What is that which walks on four legs, and two legs, and three legs?' Answer: 'Man.' Another was: 'A man and not a man, with a stone and not a stone, hit a bird and not a bird sitting on a tree and not a tree.' Answers: 'A eunuch, a pumice-stone, a bat, a fennel-stalk.' A third ran: 'What is the strongest of all things?' 'Love: iron is strong, but the blacksmith is stronger than iron, and love can subdue the blacksmith.'

W. Schultz, *PW* i A. 1 (1914), s.v. 'Rätsel'; *Rätsel aus d. hellen. Kulturkreise* (1909); K. Ohlert *R. u. Gesellschaftsspiele d. alt. Gr.²* (1912); E. Cougny ed. *Anth. Pal.* (1890), 3. 563 (metrical examples from various sources); Christ–Schmid–Stählin; Teuffel–Kroll⁶ 1 (1916), 3 (1913). W. M. E. and F. A. W.

RIDER-GODS AND HEROES. Theriomorphic gods were well-known to the Greeks in prehistoric times, witness Poseidon (Hades) and the Dioscuri and their association with the horse; we may add the wind-god Boreas. As the horse was unknown to the old Cretan civilization, the connexion of these gods with horses may be pure Greek. The god soon became a rider of a horse (as the dead man, originally represented as a horse, became a rider in the 6th c. B.C.). Epithets (Hippios, Hippia), sacrifices, priesthoods, myths, however, still remind us of the origin. Further evidence is afforded by works of art (cf. the horse's head on the so-called Totenmahl reliefs, on which the dead man is shown on a couch, banqueting). Very widespread is a type of relief on which a hero or god appears as a rider or hunter (the Dioscuri are shown mounted or standing beside their horses). We see them also on horseback in the air, approaching the festal table set ready for them (cf. their apparition to the Romans after the battle of Lake Regillus), see THEOXENIA. In Thrace and neighbouring countries the type was exceedingly popular during later periods and the Roman age. Copies of the 'Thracian rider' (hunter) were often found in shrines, dedicated 'to the Lord Hero' or to local deities, heroes or heroized dead.

L. Malten, 'Das Pferd im Totenglauben', *JDAI* xxix (1914), 181 ff.; Gawril I. Kazarow, *Die Denkmäler des thrakischen Reitergottes in Bulgarien* (Text und Tafelband, 1938). S. E.

RINGS (δακτύλιος, *anulus*) were used in Minoan and Mycenaean times both as signets and as ornaments. They are not mentioned in Homer and are rarely found in Early Iron Age deposits. Since the early sixth century they were in regular use as signets. The practice of wearing rings as ornaments is rare before the fourth century and reaches its height under the Roman Empire. Collections of rings are mentioned at this period. Rings also had special uses at Rome: the gold ring as a military decoration and as a mark of rank, originally limited to *nobiles* and *equites*, extended under the Empire to denote *ingenuitas*; and the betrothal ring, first of iron, later of gold (apparently unknown in Greece).

F. H. Marshall, *Catalogue of the Greek, Etruscan, and Roman Finger-rings in the British Museum* (1907); F. Henkel, *Die römischen Fingerringe der Rheinlande* (1913). F. N. P.

RIPARIENSES, *see* LIMITANEI.

RIVER-GODS. The cult of the river-gods was no doubt brought by the Greeks from their home in the north, but it was also a primitive inheritance surviving from the original population of the Greek peninsula. A number of rivers (and mountains) retained their names from this pre-Hellenic period (Ilissus, Pamisus, Peneius, Enipeus, etc.; in Asia, e.g., Scamandrus, Maeandrus). As for Italy we may suppose a parallel evolution.

All rivers, seas, etc., according to Homer (*Il.* 21. 196 f.), are ultimately derived from Oceanus (father of all rivers, Hesiod, *Theog.* 337 ff.), or they are 'fallen from heaven' (fed by rain; Xanthus in Homer is even 'son of Zeus'). The old superstition that river-gods had children by mortal women gave to the local rivers quite an exceptional position in Greek genealogies. The river Inachus is, e.g., the father of Io, and rivers are the ancestors of whole tribes and of the oldest heroes (for the offering of hair to rivers as κουροτρόφοι see Hom. *Il.* 23. 46, Aesch. *Cho.* 6, Paus. 8. 41. 3; cf. Agamemnon's oath, *Il.* 3. 276 ff.). A vision of rivers is a sign of offspring to the dreamer (Artem. 2. 38). Divine origin from local rivers is attested by many personal names, especially in Boeotia and Attica (Ismenodorus, Cephisodorus, etc.; cf. Bechtel, *Personennamen*, 145 ff. and 529). Yet the river belonged to a lower stratum of polytheism, 'the river power remained only half-personal, an animate nature-power, to whom altars might be erected, but rarely a temple' (Farnell, *Cults* v. 424). A reminiscence of religious primitivism is the ritual of casting victims such as horses and bulls into streams. The bovine nature of rivers is well attested, e.g., by coin-issues of Sicily (river-gods as man-headed bulls or horned youths), but full human shape became conventional, e.g. for Nile and Tiber. The widespread cult of Achelous, for which the Dodonaean oracle made an intense propaganda, is of special interest.

O. Waser, s.v. 'Flussgötter' in *PW* vi. 2774–815; L. R. Farnell, *Cults of the Greek States* v. 420–4 and in Hastings, *ERE* ix. 225–7. S. E.

ROADS. Paved roads were unusual in Greece except in the neighbourhood of important sanctuaries, such as Delphi; and there is no record of road-construction by Hellenistic kings. But from an early date in their history the Romans were aware of the importance of good communications, and their road-system was one of their outstanding achievements. The spread of Roman influence through Italy was marked by the construction of such roads as the Via Appia (312 B.C.) from Rome to Capua and later to Beneventum and Brundisium, and the Via Flaminia from Rome to Ariminum (268) which in 187 was extended to Bononia under the name of Via Aemilia. By the end of the Republic all parts of Italy were connected by good roads. In the Principate the main work of road-making was in the provinces, though the Republic had already constructed the Via Egnatia from Dyrrhachium to Thessalonica and the Via Domitia from the Rhône to the Pyrenees, and the Alps could be crossed easily by the pass of Mt. Genève. Augustus made roads across the Great and Little St. Bernard, and his stepson Drusus made one farther east 'from Altinum to the Danube' (*ILS* 208). Much information can be derived from milestones (q.v.) as to the part played by different emperors in road-building: we find, for instance, that Tiberius was specially interested in Dalmatia, Claudius in Gaul, and Hadrian in Africa and the Eastern Provinces. (For a useful summary of the development of the road-system, see H. S. Jones, *Companion to Roman History*, 40–5, and see in the present work the articles on the chief Roman roads, VIA AEMILIA, etc.)

Under the Republic the censors were responsible for the roads and let out the contracts for their construction and repair; but even before the Principate *curatores* of particular roads are found (*ILS* 5800, 5892). In 20 B.C. Augustus established a board of senatorial *curatores viarum*, and from the time of Claudius or Nero we find many *curatores* of particular Italian roads (*ILS* III. 1, pp. 359–60), usually of senatorial rank. No curatores of provincial roads are known: for them the governors were probably responsible.

The cost of the roads was probably divided between the public treasury (whether *aerarium* or *fiscus* is uncertain), the local authorities, and the owners of the land through which they passed, but the emperors often made large personal contributions. The arch of Ariminum (*ILS* 84) records that the Via Flaminia and the most important roads of Italy were repaired at the cost of Augustus. Hadrian added a sum to the amount contributed by the *possessores agrorum* to the cost of repairing part of the Via Appia, and paid for the bridges on a road in Africa (*ILS* 5872, 5875).

No general rule was followed in the construction of Roman roads. We generally find a foundation of flags covered by a layer of rubble and above it a bed of concrete. The metalling might consist of flagstones, of rammed gravel, or of concrete, according to the material available.

Roads were made by the Romans primarily for the rapid movement of troops to the frontier and from one part of the frontier to another. But their existence did much to foster trade and social intercourse, and so to create a homogeneous civilization within the Roman Empire.

L. Friedländer, i. 268–80; Sir W. Ramsay, 'Roads and Travel in the New Testament' (Hastings, *Dictionary of the Bible*); T. Codrington, *Roman Roads in Britain*³ (1918); G. H. Stevenson in *Legacy of Rome*, 141–72; O. Hirschfeld, *Verwaltungsbeamten* (1905), 205–11; H. F. Tozer, *Ancient Geography* (1935), 299 ff.   G. H. S.

ROBIGUS, the *numen* of rust in wheat. His festival (Robigalia) was on 25 Apr. (Ovid, *Fasti* 4. 905 ff., whereon see Frazer), at the fifth milestone of the Via Claudia (*Fasti Praenest.* on that date). The Flamen Quirinalis offered a dog and a sheep and prayed that rust might not attack the crops. Possibly the original intention was to destroy Robigus, Rose in *CR* xxxvi (1922), 17.

    H. J. R.

ROMANCE, see NOVEL.

ROMANUS, see AQUILA, JULIUS (10).

ROME (HISTORY)

   I. Early Italy and Regal Rome.
  II. Rome and Italy.
 III. Rome and the Mediterranean.
 IV. The Fall of the Republic.
  V. Augustus and the Julio-Claudian Emperors.
 VI. The Flavians and Antonines.
VII. Collapse and Recovery.
    Bibliography.

(*Note.* Separate articles will be found on nearly all the proper names and institutions mentioned in this brief summary. It has not been necessary, therefore, to insert constant cross-references.)

I. EARLY ITALY AND REGAL ROME

1. Long before the emergence of Rome as an influence in Italian affairs a variety of peoples, whose civilization outshone that of nascent Rome, had populated Italy (q.v.). After the early Terremaricoli and Villanovans the standard of civilized life was gradually raised by Etruscans, Oscans, and Greeks, and it is particularly against the background of the history of the Greeks in southern Italy and of the Etruscans in the centre and north that the development of early Rome must be set.

2. Of the Indo-European peoples who entered Italy from north of the Alps, the Umbrians and Sabellians formed one branch, the Latins another. The latter, who occupied the plain of Latium, soon developed a sense of common origin, from which in time there grew one or more Latin Leagues, and their early hill-top settlements gradually increased in size and influence. One of these shepherds' villages was Rome, perhaps founded as an offshoot from Alba Longa. It quickly surpassed many of its neighbours, thanks to its geographical position near the sea and the centre of Italy, its command of the Tiber-ford, and its control of a primitive salt-route from the Tiber mouth to the central hills. The Latin and Sabine settlements on the different hills gradually coalesced to form a city (see ROME, TOPOGRAPHY). Of primitive Rome we are ill-informed, since it was not until the end of the third century B.C. that the Romans began to write its history (see HISTORIOGRAPHY, ROMAN) and that at a time when national pride led them to connect their history with that of the Greek world and to forge links with Greek mythology. Hence were evolved the foundation-stories which attributed a Trojan origin to the Romans through Aeneas, and the founding of the city to his descendants Romulus and Remus (at varying dates: 814, 753, 751, 748, 729 B.C.). Tradition records six kings after Romulus: Numa Pompilius, Tullus Hostilius, Ancus Marcius, Tarquinius Priscus, Servius Tullius, and Tarquinius Superbus, some at least of whom were historical figures. There is no doubt that there were kings in early Rome and that some of them were Etruscan. The king (*rex*) was advised by the Senate, a council of elders, representatives of the noblest patrician clans (*gentes*), which enjoyed political and religious privileges. The People (*populus*), which included the less privileged classes (plebeians and clients), were divided into thirty *curiae*. To Servius Tullius are attributed administrative reforms, which in essence are probably his work. He created the *tribus*, which gradually increased to thirty-five, and divided the people into five *classes* and each class into *centuriae* on the basis of a registration of the citizens and their property (*census*). Gradually a new assembly (Comitia Centuriata) superseded in importance an older assembly of the *curiae* (Comitia Curiata).

3. Under the Etruscan kings Rome advanced in power and civilization. The process of urbanization was accelerated; commerce and industry increased; religious and political institutions underwent changes; the boundaries of the *ager Romanus* were extended to include some 350 square miles. But the debt to the Etruscans must not be exaggerated. Under the veneer of a dominating

Etruscan caste Rome remained essentially a Latin city, and agriculture remained her chief industry.

II. ROME AND ITALY (509–264 B.C.)

4. With the expulsion of Tarquinius Superbus (510) Rome threw off the Etruscan yoke, and despite the efforts at restoration by Lars Porsenna the monarchy was abolished. An aristocratic Republic was established, and two annually elected magistrates, later called consuls, were invested with *imperium*, though in times of national emergency they might temporarily be superseded by the appointment of a dictator. The history of the Republic during the next 250 years is marked by two struggles: an internal class-struggle, during which the Republican constitution was hammered out and which ended in a compromise, and an external struggle with surrounding peoples, which ended in the assertion of Rome's supremacy as the head of a confederacy which embraced all Italy.

5. The Roman citizens were divided into two classes, patricians and plebeians, perhaps as a result of economic development. The plebeians suffered grievances which they sought to redress by means of pressure brought by *secessiones* and by virtually creating a separate State within the State. The poorer plebeians sought more land, more liberal laws of debt and personal security against the oppression of patrician magistrates; the wealthier plebeians sought political and social equality with the patricians. During this struggle of the orders the plebeians (*see* PLEBS) established their own officers (tribunes and aediles) and assembly (*concilium plebis*) and gradually forced the patricians to recognize these. Landmarks in the struggle are the *Lex Publilia Voleronis* (471), the appointment of *Decemviri* and the codification and publication of the XII Tables, which formed the basis for the future development of Roman law (451–450), the Valerio-Horatian laws (449), the *Lex Canuleia* (445), the Licinian-Sextian rogations (367), the *Leges Publiliae* (339), the reforms of Cn. Flavius (304), the *Lex Ogulnia* (300), and finally the *Lex Hortensia* (287), which after earlier attempts (449, 339) gave *plebiscita* the force of laws binding on the whole community. Meantime, increase in public business, and, still more, patrician attempts to thwart the plebeian assaults on the patrician monopoly of office, led to the establishment of new magistracies. From 445 to 376 *tribuni militum consulari potestate*, an office open to plebeians, replaced the consuls, some of whose powers were transferred to newly established censors (443). The plebeians gradually gained admission to the quaestorship (421), the restored consulship (366), the dictatorship (356), the censorship (351), and in 337 to the praetorship, which had been established in 366 and led through the praetorian edict to the building up of Roman law.

6. Economic problems, such as shortage of food and land and harsh laws of debt, which tended to reduce freemen to serfdom, were attacked by legislators (e.g. Poetelius). Further, the conquest of Italy and the consequent distribution of land and establishment of colonies helped to alleviate economic distress. But while much hardship was lessened, only a small group of plebeian families became sufficiently rich and influential to enjoy the newly gained political privileges, and there grew up a new patricio-plebeian nobility which through the Senate and magistracies exercised a monopoly of government scarcely less exclusive than that enjoyed earlier by the patricians alone. But in theory the sovereignty of the People was at last established and the struggle of the orders was ended; by common sense and compromise the Romans, without bloodshed, had solved a problem which in many Greek States led to unending class-warfare.

7. Rome's external history was even more stormy. Following the collapse of Etruscan power in Latium the Romans, after a conflict with the Latins at Lake Regillus (496?), negotiated through Sp. Cassius a new alliance with the Latin League. Union in Latium was necessitated by external danger on all fronts: in the north were Etruscans, in the north-east Sabines, eastwards lay the Aequi, and south-east the Volsci. All these peoples were pressing on the plain of Latium. In the first half of the fifth century, in wars adorned by the exploits of Coriolanus and Cincinnatus, a Triple Alliance of Romans, Latins, and Hernici held their own against Aequi and Volsci; in the second half they moved to the offensive and victory. Then under Camillus' leadership Rome besieged and finally captured the Etruscan outpost, Veii (396), but thereafter a predatory horde of Celts led by Brennus swept down from the north, defeated the Roman army at Allia (387) and sacked the city, although Manlius held the Capitol. Thereafter the city was rebuilt and refortified, while Rome's shaken prestige and power in central Italy were slowly reestablished. In 358 the treaty between Rome and the Latin League was renewed on less favourable terms for the Latins, who later fought an unsuccessful war of independence (340–338), saw their League dissolved, and entered into fresh relations with Rome.

8. Roman interests were now spreading to Campania, where they became predominant after an alliance with Neapolis (326). This brought Rome into conflict with the Samnite hill-tribes, and bitter struggles ensued. After the perhaps apocryphal First Samnite War (343–341), the Second lasted intermittently from 326 till Roman victory in 304 and was marked by a major disaster at the Caudine Forks (321). Roman ascendancy in Etruria was extended, and alliances were made with Umbrian cities, the Picenes and Marsi, and with northern Apulia. Early in the third century the Samnites made a new bid for freedom; in alliance with fresh Gallic invaders, Etruscans, and Umbrians they were defeated at Sentinum (295) and finally subdued by 290. Further Celtic tribes and some Etruscan towns gave trouble until the Boii were defeated at Lake Vadimo (283) and again in 282. With the Samnites reduced, Rome was next drawn into southern Italy, where the Greek cities were being hard pressed by Lucanian tribes. When in 282 Rome sent a protective garrison to Thurii at that city's request, Tarentum resented Rome's interference in her sphere of influence, picked a quarrel with Rome, and summoned the help of Pyrrhus of Epirus, who landed in Italy (280). After two 'Pyrrhic' victories at Heraclea and Asculum he withdrew to Sicily (278); after his return (276) he was defeated by Rome (275) and retired to Greece, leaving Rome now undisputed mistress of Italy.

9. Rome's conquest of Italy had been achieved not merely by the sword; indeed, Rome was certainly no more aggressive than her neighbours, since the *ius fetiale* forbade wars of aggression. By founding Latin and Roman colonies at strategic points, and by the construction of roads, Rome had bound Italy together. But she had done more: she had created a political confederacy which embraced all Italy except Cisalpine Gaul. By the principle of incorporation Roman citizenship, in whole or part, had been extended to a large area of Italy, while the rest of the peninsula was bound to Rome by alliances of varying type, the most privileged being *ius Latii*. All citizens and allies alike, were subject to military service, but only the citizens paid direct taxes. Peace was thus at length substituted for war as the normal condition of life in Italy; very gradually, since Rome did not force her civilization on others, local languages, customs, and cults gave place to a common culture based on the Latin tongue and Roman law. Finally, by this political unification of Italy, Rome was no longer merely a Latin city but had become a world power, with whom Egypt entered into a treaty (273). The era to which later Romans looked back as the formative period of their national character, when life was simple and austere, was passing. Rome was now politically linked with the Greek South and in direct contact with Hellenic influences.

III. ROME AND THE MEDITERRANEAN (264–133 B.C.)

10. As a world power Rome came into contact with Carthaginian interests in the western Mediterranean and with the Hellenistic world in the East. Her conflicts with Carthage are described under PUNIC WARS; they resulted in the elimination of Carthage from the western Mediterranean and in the acquisition by Rome of overseas *provinciae*, Sicily (241), Sardinia (238), Spain (201), Africa (146). The Romans had to face another Gallic invasion of Italy, which was shattered at the battle of Telamon (225). Thereafter the northern frontier was secured by the defeat of the Boii and Insubres (224–220; 200–191), the pacification of Cisalpine Gaul, and the protection of its flanks by the reduction of the Ligurians (197–154), Istrians (178–177), and Dalmatian coast (156–155; 129). Thus Roman authority was extended from near Massilia (*Marseilles*) round the sweep of the Alps to Istria and thence down the west coast of the Balkan peninsula.

11. Meantime Rome had been drawn into Hellenistic affairs. As a police measure she had suppressed Illyrian piracy in the Adriatic and established a small protectorate in Illyricum (First Illyrian War, 229–228, Second 219; *see* TEUTA, DEMETRIUS 6). Then she had successfully faced Hannibal's ally, Philip V of Macedonia, in the First Macedonian War (214–205: *see* PUNIC WARS). Thereafter, when Philip launched a career of conquest in the eastern Mediterranean, Rhodes and Pergamum appealed for help to Rome. Actuated partly by a desire for future security against a possible threat from Philip's fleet or his ally Antiochus III of Syria, partly perhaps from philhellenic sentiments, the Romans somewhat reluctantly entered upon the Second Macedonian War (200–196), which terminated in the victory of Flamininus at Cynoscephalae. Macedonia was forced to surrender her conquests but survived as an independent State, while Rome proclaimed freedom for Greece; no territory was annexed, and by 194 all Roman troops had evacuated Greece. Rome was next involved with Antiochus, with whom Hannibal had sought refuge. When he invaded Greece he was defeated at Thermopylae by the Romans, who then for the first time crossed to Asia and again defeated him at Magnesia (189). By the treaty of Apamea Antiochus was forced back into Syria, while most of the Seleucid kingdom in Asia Minor was given to Pergamum and Rhodes; Rome annexed no territory. Macedonia remained quiet until the accession of Perseus, who challenged Rome, only to meet defeat at the hands of Aemilius Paullus at Pydna in 168 (Third Macedonian War, 172–167). Macedonia was divided into four republics, but after further disorders caused by Andriscus was at length annexed as a Roman province (147). The Achaean League was suppressed, and Corinth was destroyed by Mummius (146), not probably from motives of commercial jealousy but as an example to Greece that Roman patience was at an end. For half a century Rome had allowed Greece to enjoy or abuse her freedom: Rome's final intervention brought peace, if not prosperity. Meantime Rome had overawed the Hellenistic kingdoms of Bithynia, Galatia (*see* MANLIUS VULSO), Pergamum, and Rhodes, and had interfered in the politics of Egypt (*see* POPILLIUS 1) and Syria. In 133 Attalus of Pergamum bequeathed his kingdom to Rome, and it was formed into the province of Asia.

12. Meanwhile in the west Rome's attempt to administer and protect her provinces of Spain (acquired in 206 and organized in 197) led her into a long series of conflicts with the native tribes of the interior, especially Celtiberians and Lusitanians, which only ended with the destruction of Numantia by Scipio Aemilianus in 133 (*see* NUMANTIA, SPAIN, VIRIATHUS, etc.). Finally, after campaigns against Ligurians, Allobroges, and Arverni (125–121), southern Gaul was formed into the province of Gallia Transalpina or Narbonensis.

13. During this period of the establishing of an overseas empire, and more particularly in the latter part of it, economic and social life in Rome and Italy underwent profound changes. In many parts capitalist farming replaced peasant husbandry; with the acquisition of an empire there was a greater field for industry and commerce, which had little interest for the Roman nobility or influence on Roman policy, but enhanced the importance of the rich business men (*see* EQUES); slavery increased, both on the land and in the household; women gained greater freedom; life became more luxurious for the privileged classes, and public games increased; the city, adorned with new public buildings, assumed a fresh appearance. From the First Punic War, when Roman soldiers had fought in Grecian Sicily, the floodgates of Hellenism were open. Many nobles, as the Scipios and Flamininus, were ardent philhellenes, while the earliest Roman historians actually wrote in Greek; Cato's attempt to stem the tide was merely temporary. Fresh contacts were made with Greece in the Macedonian Wars, Greek philosophers lectured in Rome (155), while the group of intellectuals known as the Scipionic Circle attempted to reconcile the best aspects of Greek and Roman life. In all spheres, art and architecture, literature and religion, Greek influences prevailed. But despite these profound changes the governing class, drawn from a small number of families, retained many of its old virtues and its general control of public affairs.

IV. THE FALL OF THE REPUBLIC (133–31 B.C.)

14. Rome next had to grapple with many problems of which the solution became urgent. Of imperial problems that of safeguarding the frontiers was the least clamant. More pressing were the consequences of provincial administration, since the institutions of a city-state were ill-adapted to governing an empire, and the attempts made to modify them were not sufficiently fundamental. The standard of provincial administration fell. Some governors plundered their provinces for private gain, others were corrupted by desire for power. The army began to look rather to its commanders than to the State for the rewards of service, and when led by men of ambition formed a new and dangerous element in Roman life. Rome also faced grave domestic issues, and a struggle developed between *optimates* and *populares*. Difficulties which might have been settled by compromise were rendered more acute by the rise of ambitious personalities who sought to exploit political power for their own ends. Further, Rome's selfish policy towards her Italian allies, who had helped to win the empire but were deprived of many of its spoils, led to increasing discontent and ultimately to open war. Finally, there were urgent economic problems. The growth of *latifundia*, the promotion of pasturage at the expense of cereal production, and the system of land-tenure had all combined to drive the small farmer from the countryside to unemployment in the towns. There was pressing need to re-establish a small peasantry on the land and to rid the cities of idle hands.

15. Public attention was focused on many of these problems by the careers of Tiberius and Gaius Gracchus, who as tribunes representative of the sovereign authority of the Roman People challenged the senatorial monopoly of government. Their efforts, and the subsequent agrarian legislation, partially solved the economic problems, while Gaius championed the demands of the allies for Roman franchise and made the *Equites* a political force and a Third Estate. Their attempts at reform were followed by a conservative reaction and by the war with Jugurtha (112–106). This was conducted

by the Senate with such corruption and indolence that at length the People and *Equites* demanded energetic action, which was given by Marius in whom the People found a military leader.

16. Unrest in Sicily found expression in two Slave Wars (135–132, 103–101). German tribes were on the move, defeating Roman armies (114, 113), and finally wiped out two consular armies at Arausio (105). In this hour of national crisis Marius held repeated consulships (103–101), and thanks to his military reforms saved his country by defeating the Teutones near Aquae Sextiae (102) and the Cimbri near Vercellae (101). But a new danger was at hand: Marius at the head of a professional army, which had been raised partly from proletarians by voluntary enlistment and owed more to its leader than to the State, might threaten the Senate in the name of the People. But Marius was clumsy in politics: his temporary alliance with the leaders of the popular party, Saturninus and Glaucia (103–100), was followed by his own eclipse and a brief conservative reaction (99–91) which nearly proved fatal to Rome. The attempted reforms of Drusus (91) and his plan to enfranchise the Italians failed, while his assassination precipitated the revolt of the allies in the Social or Marsian War (91–87), the result of the Senate's selfish policy. Some of the allies fought to win Roman citizenship, others as the Samnites to destroy Roman predominance in Italy. By fighting and by political concessions (*see under* CAESAR (2), STRABO (1), PLAUTIUS (1)) the Romans gained victory by conceding the main issue at stake. Italy was now united, and all south of the Po received Roman citizenship.

17. A contention between Marius and Sulla for the command against Mithridates of Pontus led to Sulla's march on Rome at the head of Roman legions (88) and the inauguration of a period of civil war and bloodshed. Thereafter Sulla left for Greece, where he defeated the Pontic army at Chaeronea (86) and settled the East. He returned in 83 to overthrow in civil war the government which Cinna had established in his absence. By 82, after a proscription of his political opponents, he attained a quasi-monarchical position as dictator and attempted to re-establish the authority of the Senate over against the powers of the tribunate and the influence of army commanders by a series of measures which did not long survive his voluntary retirement in 79. Pompey, after defeating Sertorius, who had held Spain against the senatorial government from 80 to 72, enjoyed a joint-consulship in 70 with Crassus, who had suppressed a slave-revolt led by Spartacus in Italy. Backed by their armies these two ambitious leaders, both former lieutenants of Sulla, swept away much of Sulla's legislation. The tribunate once again became a dangerous weapon which might assert the wishes of the Roman People, now mainly the unruly populace of the capital and unrepresentative of Italy as a whole, and those of their unscrupulous and ambitious leaders. Through the tribunate Pompey was given in 67 an overriding command against the pirates, whom he swept out of the Mediterranean, and then against Mithridates, whose renewed aggression had been checked by Lucullus. Though Lucullus had invaded Pontus and defeated Tigranes of Armenia, he had been forced to retire, and thus it was reserved for Pompey to end the Mithridatic wars and to resettle the East (64–2), where he reorganized the client-kingdoms, established Syria as a Roman province (64), and promoted urbanization throughout Asia Minor. Other recent provincial changes affected Cisalpine Gaul, Bithynia, Cilicia, Crete, and Cyrene.

18. While Pompey was in the East, Crassus and Caesar intrigued in Rome against his return, using a tribune Rullus to further their ends. Catiline led a revolutionary scheme of broken men, which was unmasked by the consul Cicero (63), who began to hope for a *concordia ordinum*, a reconciliation of all moderate elements in the State. But the Senate foolishly withstood the demands of Pompey, who on his return from the East had loyally retired into private life, and also those of Caesar, who in 60 returned from a command in Spain. Pompey and Caesar together with Crassus were thus forced into an unofficial coalition, known as the First Triumvirate (60). In 59 Caesar as consul gained a prolonged command for himself in Gaul, which he added as a new province to the Empire, thus advancing the frontiers to the Rhine and the English Channel (58–50: *see* GALLIC WARS). Meantime, in a period of increasing electoral corruption and public disorder, fostered by gang-leaders as Clodius and Milo and resulting in the temporary exile of Cicero (58–7), the Triumvirate appeared to be breaking up, but was reaffirmed at a conference held at Luca (56). While Caesar made his name and won a devoted army in Gaul, Pompey controlled events in Rome and administered his Spanish province through *legati*. The death of Crassus at Carrhae (53) during a disastrous expedition against Parthia emphasized the rivalry of Pompey and Caesar, who gradually drifted into open conflict, with Pompey somewhat reluctantly supporting the senatorial cause. Caesar defeated the Pompeian army in Spain at Ilerda (49) and Pompey himself at Pharsalus (48); he won further victories in Asia at Zela (47), in Africa at Thapsus, where Cato's suicide exemplified the collapse of the Republican cause (46), and in Spain at Munda (45). Whether or not Caesar intended finally to end the Republic, as dictator he introduced the principle of personal autocracy into the constitution. His beneficial legislative reforms and his plans for safeguarding the Empire by military expeditions against Dacia and Parthia were cut short by his assassination by a group of short-sighted Republican conspirators, led by Cassius and Brutus (44).

19. Instead of a restoration of peace and the Republic another round of civil war followed. At first Octavian, Caesar's heir and avenger, supported by Cicero and the Republican party, struggled against Antony, who had been Caesar's helper. After the battle of Mutina (43) the three Caesarian leaders, Antony, Octavian, and Lepidus, formed an official coalition, the Second Triumvirate. The triumvirs defeated the forces of the Republicans led by Brutus and Cassius at Philippi (42). Gradually Octavian strengthened his hold on Italy and the western provinces, eliminating Sextus Pompeius and Lepidus. Meanwhile Antony had gone to the East, where he met Cleopatra, launched a disastrous expedition against Parthia, and finally became suspect of sacrificing Roman interests to Cleopatra. Thus the scene was set for a final clash between the Roman forces of the East and West which culminated in Antony's defeat by Octavian at Actium (31) and his death at Alexandria (30). The Roman world was reunited under the sole leadership of Octavian and peace was restored when he settled the East and annexed Egypt.

20. Despite civil wars, misgovernment, political corruption, the ambitions of the rival dynasts (*principes viri*), and the collapse of the Republican constitution, the Roman world still offered a foundation on which a new system could be constructed. Further, the political unification of Italy was reflected in the greater unity of Italian civilization. The whole of this period and especially the Ciceronian age witnessed a steady advance of oratory, art, and letters. If Cicero was the dominant literary figure, there were also Lucretius, Catullus, Varro, and Sallust. Political instability had not undermined all the productive activities of man.

V. AUGUSTUS AND THE JULIO-CLAUDIAN EMPERORS (31 B.C.–A.D. 68)

21. Within the framework of the Republic, which had collapsed through the attacks of military dictators and the lack of an adequate civil service, Augustus, as Octavian was then called, created a new system which endured. His own position as *princeps* (q.v.) made him in fact a disguised constitutional monarch—'auctoritate omnibus praestiti'—with control over legislation, criminal jurisdiction, the army, and to a large extent finance and provincial administration. He shared his functions with the Senate, but his power was undivided. The army was reformed and was made the protector instead of a potential destroyer of the State; the frontiers were secured; the provinces were administered with greater care. To secure an adequate supply of civil servants the senatorial and equestrian orders were reorganized; the new executive included boards of *curatores* and *praefecti*, especially the prefect of the newly formed Praetorian Guard, and a *consilium principis*. By new buildings (*see*, e.g., ARA PACIS, FORUM AUGUSTI), by care for the water- and food-supplies (*see* ANNONA), by creating cohorts of *vigiles* to prevent fire and urban cohorts as a police force, Augustus made Rome a worthy capital of the Empire. By renovating the State religion and by less successful legislation designed to encourage marriage and the restoration of morality Augustus hoped to create a new Roman People, the worthy exponents of that civilization which it was the great achievement of the Empire to spread to the provinces of the West. The Greco-Roman civilization of the Mediterranean now became one, but the centre of gravity of the Empire was fixed in Italy and the West. True, the pendulum was to swing gradually eastwards during the next 300 years, and the Augustan empire was radically modified in constitution and finally overrun by the barbarians, but not before it had done its great work of romanizing western Europe. Therein lies to a great measure the debt which the world owes to Augustus and his victory at Actium. Nor could Augustus have accomplished his task alone. He owed much to friends like Agrippa and Maecenas and not a little to writers such as Virgil, Horace, and Livy, who made this the Golden Age of Latin literature.

22. Though it was as peace-maker after the long series of civil wars that Augustus derived much of his popularity, he yet added much to the Empire, but for reasons of security rather than from desire for conquest. In the East ambitious plans were abandoned, an agreement was reached with Parthia, and Galatia was made a province (25 B.C.), as was Judaea in A.D. 6. Spain was finally pacified and, like Gaul, was reorganized. Local self-government was encouraged, the growth of towns fostered, and many colonies were founded. In the north Augustus advanced the frontier to the Danube and by the creation of a chain of provinces (Raetia, Noricum, Pannonia, and Moesia) protected the Balkans from invasion by the wild tribes of central Europe. His plan to advance beyond the Rhine to the Elbe was finally abandoned after the defeat of Varus, and the Rhine–Danube formed the frontier. The fostering of provincial *concilia* and the growth of the imperial cult increasingly gave a sense of unity to the Empire. With the frontiers thus secure and a stable central government the Mediterranean world enjoyed a new era of industrial advance and widespread commerce.

23. Not the least difficult problem which faced Augustus was the succession. His efforts to secure it in the direct line of the Julian house were thwarted by the deaths of Marcellus, Gaius Caesar, and Lucius Caesar. At length he made Tiberius co-regent and at his death the empire was handed on without a hitch. The prestige of his name and the methods which he had displayed determined to a large measure the decisions of his successors.

24. The reign of Tiberius (A.D. 14–37) saw the political advancement of the Senate at the expense of the People, but nevertheless the senatorial administration increasingly depended on the will of the *princeps*.

The career of Sejanus demonstrated the potential power of the Praetorian Prefect and Guard. Though the reign was marked by the growth of delation and ended in a Terror, the provincial administration was good. Tiberius followed the precept of Augustus not to extend the Empire beyond its existing boundaries, except that Cappadocia was made a province. The interlude of the extravagant reign of Gaius (37–41) emphasized the autocratic tendencies latent in the Principate. Claudius' reign (41–54) was notable for his development of the imperial civil service, in which freedmen were given greater influence, for a more liberal extension of Roman franchise, and for an energetic foreign policy which replaced client kingdoms by provinces, and added the two Mauretanias (42), Britain (43), Lycia (43), and Thrace (46) to the Empire. Nero's reign (54–68) might open well under the guidance of Seneca and Burrus, but his reconciliation with the Senate did not last and he gradually scandalized the aristocracy. Disorder followed in the provinces. In the East Nero adopted a more aggressive policy towards Armenia. This resulted in a clash with Parthia and the defeat of Paetus at Rhandeia (62), although the Armenian problem was settled thanks to Corbulo's display of Roman might. A revolt in Britain was led by Boudicca (61); rebellion spread through Judaea (66–70), while Vindex revolted in Gaul and Galba in Spain. Stoics, aristocrats, army chiefs, and private individuals opposed and hated Nero at home. Thus the Julio-Claudian dynasty collapsed amid rebellion and civil war, but the constructive work of Augustus and Claudius survived the disaster.

VI. THE FLAVIANS AND ANTONINES (A.D. 69–192)

25. The 'Year of the Four Emperors' (69) and the period of renewed civil war is important for its revelation that an emperor could be made elsewhere than at Rome, by the wishes of the armies in the provinces, who recognized, however, that their nominees were still pretenders until approved by the Senate. Galba from Spain was accepted by the Praetorian Guard and Senate, but in 69 the Praetorians acclaimed Otho and killed Galba. The Rhine armies, however, proclaimed Vitellius, on whose behalf Caecina and Valens defeated Otho's forces at Bedriacum. After Otho's suicide Vitellius was accepted as emperor, but meantime the eastern legions had declared for Vespasian, whose claim was soon accepted on the Danube. Vespasian's cause was led from Pannonia by Antonius Primus, who defeated the Vitellians and captured Rome. In 70 peace was re-established, Jerusalem was stormed, the rising of Civilis on the Rhine and the attempt of Classicus to create an Imperium Galliarum were thwarted. From the confusion there had emerged a second Augustus, a *restitutor orbis*, who restored peace, founded a new dynasty, and resumed the task of government.

26. It was the great achievement of Vespasian (69–79) to restore confidence and prosperity, to prevent the character of the Principate changing from civilian to military, and to minimize the risk of renewed civil war by founding the Flavian dynasty and securing the succession of his sons Titus (79–81) and Domitian (81–96). Under the Flavians there was a marked and increasing advance towards absolute monarchy, brought about by the example set by Vespasian of reviving the censorship and holding numerous consulates, and by Domitian's acceptance of semi-divine honours, even though such measures may have been taken primarily to enhance the prestige of the upstart dynasty. The Senate, which by the admission of more provincials became more representative of the Empire, was neglected by Vespasian and slighted by Domitian, who relied more on the *consilium principis*. Wise in the choice of their executive, the Flavians made increasing use of *Equites* in place of freedmen. By a prudent economy Vespasian restored

the State finances, which withstood Titus' prodigality and Domitian's heavy expenditure. In foreign policy the Flavians aimed at strengthening the existing frontiers, particularly by a valuable consolidation of the Rhine and Danube *limites*, although the rising power of Dacia was given only a taste of Roman might, and an advance was made into Scotland. In general the provinces enjoyed a period of uneventful prosperity, resting on the restored tranquillity of the central government. The Flavians had little to fear from Caecina and Antonius Saturninus, but the obstructive opposition of Stoic and Cynic philosophers (*see*, e.g., HELVIDIUS PRISCUS) was irritating, while after 88 discontented senatorial opposition led to the renewal of delation and charges of *maiestas* and to the Reign of Terror in which Domitian the tyrant perished.

27. The reigns of the 'Five Good Emperors', Nerva (96–8), Trajan (98–117), Hadrian (117–38), Antoninus Pius (138–61), M. Aurelius (161–80), culminated in the Indian Summer of the Antonines, that era which Gibbon regarded as the happiest known to man. During this period the Principate underwent considerable modification. Nerva was chosen as the 'best citizen' by the Senate, not by the legions, but he found the armies, especially the Praetorian Guard, difficult to control and compromised by adopting a soldier, Trajan, and making him co-regent. The next three rulers, none of whom had a son to succeed him, followed Nerva's example of adopting as son and successor a man of tried ability, thus averting further crises at their own deaths. Trajan by his tolerance won from a grateful Senate the title of Optimus Princeps. Hadrian, by his versatility, by his measures for the defence of the Empire and his care for its well-being, and above all by his personal activity in the provinces, won the respect of soldiers and civilians alike and peacefully handed over the reins of government to the senator Antoninus Pius, under whose beneficent influence the Empire entered upon one of the most secure periods of its history, although local self-government gradually weakened under the far-reaching paternalism of the central government. With the accession of M. Aurelius Stoicism was enthroned, and the philosopher manfully shouldered the responsibilities thrust upon him. But an era was passing. The joint rule of M. Aurelius and L. Verus (161–9) foreshadowed the division of imperial power. Further, through danger on the frontiers and a devastating plague the Empire was threatened with the loss of its margin of security and prosperity. When M. Aurelius, by promoting his son Commodus (180–93) to the throne, reverted to the dynastic principle of succession in place of the 'choice of the best', it was an ill day for the Empire. The moral basis of the Principate, emphasized by the recent emperors, was weakened by the misrule and corruption of Commodus. Gradually, with the swelling tide of Eastern religious ideas and with the victory of the military over the civilian conception of the Principate, the way was paved for the Dominate.

28. From Nerva to M. Aurelius the emperors maintained good relations with the Senate, which by the admission of more provincials became yet more representative of the Empire. But if it regained some of its former prestige, it recovered little of its power, although Tacitus might praise Nerva for reconciling *libertas* and *principatus*. From Hadrian's time the administrative civil service, now drawn nearly exclusively from the senatorial and equestrian orders, was organized on a larger and more rigid scale. Honorific titles marked grades of equestrian officials, whose military and civil careers were sharply distinguished. Under Hadrian also there were important changes in the Roman legal system, and here the *consilium principis* played a leading part. The Comitia had died a natural death and its legislative functions were superseded by imperial 'constitutions', which were marked by a spirit of humanity and equity. By careful economy and a modest court the emperors

were able to be liberal in public expenditure, establishing various *alimenta* and *congiaria*, endowing education and planning public works, although under M. Aurelius the *fiscus* began to feel the strain.

29. Throughout the provinces urbanization reached its widest extent. Under ruling aristocracies of public-spirited men, who often spent lavishly to endow and maintain their own cities, the municipalities flourished as never before, although occasionally the Roman government was forced to limit their liberties in order to maintain public order or to support their finances, which sometimes became inadequate under the strain of compulsory contributions imposed on the local magistrates and senators (*see* LITURGY, CURATOR). The care which the emperors exercised in the provinces is well illustrated by the correspondence between Trajan and Pliny or by Hadrian's thorough tours of inspection. Trajan and his three successors, who were all of Spanish or Gallic origin, were naturally liberal in granting Roman franchise.

30. There were few extensions of the Empire except under the warrior prince Trajan, who after two wars (101–2, 105–6) defeated Decebalus and annexed Dacia, which was quickly romanized. In the East Trajan annexed Nabataean Arabia in Transjordania and advanced over the Euphrates to wrest from Parthian control the new provinces of Armenia, Mesopotamia, and Assyria. By abandoning his predecessor's eastern conquests Hadrian reached a settlement with Parthia, which was temporarily upset under M. Aurelius. Thus in general Rome still held the line of the Euphrates, but the frontier was strengthened and straightened. Widespread Jewish revolts in 116 were quickly suppressed, while the establishment of a Roman colony in Jerusalem by Hadrian led to a second war in Palestine (131–4) and the ejection of all Jews from Jerusalem, although Hadrian's severe terms were modified by Antoninus. In Britain various attempts were made to secure the frontier: a Roman disaster led to the evacuation of Scotland and the construction of Hadrian's Wall (122–7); another extension of Roman influence into Scotland was followed by the establishment of the Antonine Wall (142–3). A greater crisis arose when Germanic tribes, the Marcomanni and Quadi, invaded the Danubian provinces and even raided north Italy. By resolute action M. Aurelius repelled the danger and planned to avert its repetition by advancing the frontier to the Carpathians and mountains of Bohemia, but after his death Commodus abandoned the plan. On the Rhine–Danube frontier precautions were taken, such as the rebuilding in stone of earth forts in Upper Germany and Raetia under Hadrian and the construction of an advance line under the Antonines. Administrative changes included the establishment of Upper and Lower Germany as separate provinces under Hadrian, the division of Pannonia into two provinces under Trajan and of Dacia under Hadrian.

31. Although the Roman army which secured the frontiers was as yet unconquerable, it was undergoing many changes. With Hadrian's system of local recruiting it became less mobile and predominantly provincial. Only the Praetorian Guard retained a Latin tradition; the provincial soldiers, although good fighters, had only a slight acquaintance with Roman political ideas or Graeco-Roman culture, while as a result of the gradual separation of military from civil careers the higher officers, who were still mainly of Italian stock, had little experience of civil government.

32. In the latter part of this period the Roman Empire attained its highest economic development with the peace that reigned throughout Mediterranean lands and the extension of the road-system. In agriculture and industry the provinces began to outrun Italy. Commerce extended beyond the bounds of Empire to Scandinavia, overland to China, and through the Indian Ocean to the

East. Industry and commerce promoted the growth of cities, while other new towns grew out of the military *canabae*. New buildings at Rome, as the Colosseum, Trajan's Forum, and the Pantheon, found their counterparts in the fora, theatres, amphitheatres, baths, aqueducts, and bridges which now adorned the chief provincial cities. Roman sculpture kept pace with architecture, and imperial ideals often conformed to the artistic traditions of the provinces. Schools and libraries exemplified State interest in education. Literature entered upon its Silver Age with the work of Martial and Juvenal, of Tacitus, Suetonius, and Quintilian, while there was a revival of Greek literature. Christian apologists developed a new branch of literature, and Roman jurisprudence reached its maturity. In every sphere, and especially in the religious, provincial influences spread, and the western stamp which Augustus had set upon the Empire gradually became less clear-cut. Christianity had taken root in Italy, Africa, and Gaul, and was developing that organization which was successfully to challenge the imperial régime. Rome had imposed no uniformity of culture, but had allowed the provincials to retain their varied customs and institutions. The predominantly Latin culture of the West was complementary to the Hellenism of the East. But despite diversity there was a real feeling of unity, and all looked to the emperor as to a universal Providence by whose unremitting care the *pax Romana* was preserved. True, some problems, such as the social evils of slavery and the pauperization of urban populations or the possibility of a wise policy of decentralization and provincial representation, were not taken in hand. True, the culture of the Empire meant less to the masses in the provinces than to the middle and upper classes for whose benefit the Empire chiefly existed, while there were many foreshadowings of unhealthy changes to come. Nevertheless, the barriers between Rome and the provinces had fallen, and in an age of general serenity and good will, when men had become more humane, the stability of the Empire may well have seemed assured and the 'Aeternitas Populi Romani' more than a pious hope or an empty dream.

VII. Collapse and Recovery (A.D. 193–330)

33. The death of Commodus ushered in a new period of civil war. The attempt of Pertinax to co-operate with the Senate failed through the renewed influence of the Praetorian Guard, which auctioned the Empire to Didius Julianus. Again, as in A.D. 69, provincial armies put forward their candidates for the throne, Clodius Albinus in Britain, Pescennius Niger in Syria, and Septimius Severus in Pannonia. Severus seized Rome, struck down his rivals, and established a new dynasty. His reign (193–211) was marked by the development of the power of the equestrian order, the reconstitution of the Praetorian Guard and the increased power of its prefect, and by the creation of the *res privata*, but above all by its military aspect: the civilian constitution of the Empire which Augustus had conceived was set aside. Abandoning all pretence of co-operation with the Senate, Severus openly showed that his authority rested on the support of the army. His restoration of order in northern Britain was followed by the evacuation of Scotland. In general the frontier fortifications were consolidated and the provinces were well administered, some being divided into two. His son Caracalla (M. Aurelius Antoninus, 211–17) developed the military tendencies of the father, and by his edict of 212 abolished all distinction between Italians and provincials, so that the Empire became a commonwealth of equal members. But Alamanni and Goths were ominously threatening the Danube frontier. After Macrinus' brief reign (217–18), Elagabalus (218–22) gave Rome an unwelcome insight into Eastern cult, Oriental pomp, and personal corruption. Alexander

Severus (221–35), guided by Julia Mamaea, attempted a *rapprochement* with the Senate and gave Rome a few years of comparative peace and tranquillity. But again the military element triumphed over the civil, and Alexander's murder was followed by half a century of military anarchy which nearly led to the final collapse of the Empire.

34. Emperors followed one another thick and fast: the Thracian peasant Maximinus (235–8), Gordian I, II, Pupienus, Balbinus (238), Gordian III (238–44), the Arabian Philip (244–9), the Illyrian Decius (249–51), Trebonianus Gallus (251–3), the Moor Aemilianus (253), and Valerian (253–60). While the armies played the game of emperor-making, the security and unity of the Empire were nearly destroyed. In the East the Parthian dynasty of the Arsacids was superseded by the aggressive Sassanidae who overran Syria (256), captured Valerian (259), and invaded Asia Minor. They were checked with the help of the caravan city of Palmyra, which under Zenobia now proceeded to challenge Roman supremacy in the East. In the West a pretender, Postumus, established an independent *imperium Galliarum*, which included Spain and Britain. Franks threatened the Lower Rhine, Saxon pirates ventured into the English Channel, Goths raided the Balkans and the Aegean, Alamanni crossed the Rhine and ravaged north Italy as far as Ravenna. With the Empire thus cracking and being rent asunder under his feet Valerian's son and successor Gallienus (253–68) had also to face a swarm of pretenders and rivals, the so-called Thirty Tyrants (q.v.). To his honour he brought the Empire through the crisis without complete disaster and laid the foundations of recovery. The tide was turned by his successors, the Illyrian emperors, Claudius Gothicus (268–70), who repelled the Gothic peril, and Aurelian (270–5), who, though evacuating Dacia, destroyed Palmyra (273), recovered Gaul, and justly earned the title of *Restitutor Orbis*. The great wall which he constructed around Rome was a bulwark of defence but also a symbol of the vanishing *pax Romana*. But still the army could not agree to a durable government and elevated a succession of emperors, many Illyrian, who had to fight rivals and barbarians alike: Tacitus (275–6), who defeated some Goths in Asia Minor, Florianus (276), Probus (276–82), who secured the Rhine and Danube frontiers and disposed of the rival Bonosus, Carus (282–3), who invaded Mesopotamia, Carinus (283–5), and Numerianus (283–4). Out of this welter of short-lived emperors emerged Diocletian, who held power for twenty years (284–305) and then voluntarily laid it aside.

35. In order to secure the protection of the Empire and an unchallenged succession Diocletian divided the Empire and imperial power. As joint Augustus with Maximian he established two junior Caesars, Galerius and Constantius, who should ultimately succeed. But when he insisted on retiring, fresh civil wars followed, in which Constantine by his defeat of Maxentius at the Milvian Bridge gained the Western Empire (312). In the East Licinius won supremacy by defeating Maximinus (313), but was defeated by Constantine in 314 and finally in 324, so that the Empire, West and East, was once more united under a resolute ruler. But the centre of gravity was shifting eastwards. The barbarian invasions had left emperors little time to spend in Rome, and Diocletian had set up his court at Nicomedia in Bithynia. Finally, by 330, Constantine had established at Byzantium a new capital, East Rome or Constantinople.

36. The Principate was dead; the military had triumphed over the civil aspect. Further, the basis of imperial authority had collapsed and a new sanction must be found. Eastern ideas of the king as the viceregent of heavenly authority were introduced. Thus Aurelian brought back to Rome the Persian worship of the Unconquered Sun, and Diocletian regarded himself as

Jovius the earthly representative of Jupiter. The climax came when Constantine took Christianity into partnership with the Empire. The long period of persecution (q.v.) was ended and the struggle, which had gradually assumed the form of State against Church rather than Christian against pagan, was resolved with Constantine reigning as the earthly representative of the Christians' God; thus the way was prepared for a reconciliation between the Christian Church and the culture of the ancient world. Further, the outward form of imperial authority changed no less than its basis, which was legally autocratic after 282, when Carus dispensed with the theory that his power derived from the Senate. In title *dominus* replaced *princeps*. Aurelian (*dominus et deus*) introduced the pomp of Oriental absolutism, while Diocletian and Constantine elaborated a court ceremonial in which the 'sacred' person of the emperor, arrayed in diadem, purple and gold, demanded prostration on the part of those admitted to audience. The *consilium principis* became a *sacrum consistorium*. The old Republican magistracies either died out or were divested of all executive authority. The Senate survived with undimmed prestige, but its authority was reduced to that of a local town council. Under Diocletian military were separated from civilian offices, and under Constantine the senatorial and equestrian orders united. Provincial administration was profoundly modified: the number of provinces rose to 70 and ultimately to 116, the Empire was grouped into prefectures and dioceses, and the officials (*praesides*, *vicarii*, *praefecti praetorio*, etc.) accordingly increased. Municipal patriotism and self-government declined, owing to impoverishment, financial pressure, and the growth of bureaucracy, so that under Constantine the *curiales* became a hereditary caste and the attempt to avoid office and its crushing responsibilities was checked by State action. Thanks to the military reforms of Diocletian and Constantine with frontier forces (*limitanei*) and mobile reserves (*comitatenses*), the Roman army, although profoundly changed, still guarded the frontiers and kept the barbarians at arm's length.

37. The mid-third century witnessed an economic as well as a political collapse. Rising costs of government led to depreciation of the coinage and the extension of a system of requisitions and compulsory labour. The monetary system was undermined and was partially replaced by payments in kind, although the improvement of the coinage under Diocletian and Constantine led to a slow revival of confidence and a gradual restoration of a money economy. A new taxation system (*annona*) was developed by Diocletian to remedy the injustices of the arbitrary requisitions which had become more common during the preceding upheavals, while he also extended the system of compulsory corporate responsibility for the collection of taxes and for the performance of other services. Gradually various industrial and commercial guilds were converted into hereditary castes in an attempt to maintain the economic life of the Empire, which had declined seriously in the third century as a result of civil wars and barbarian invasions, increasing difficulties of communication, and above all the general sense of insecurity and lack of confidence. Not all parts of the Empire declined as rapidly as did some, but industry, especially in the west, suffered severely and the total cultivated area and the size of the towns gradually diminished. Finally, through the growth of *latifundia*, some landed gentry in their fortified villas could live securely and at ease in a manner which foreshadowed medieval feudalism, but the tenants (*coloni*) on the large estates had gradually to surrender their liberty of movement and sank to a state of serfdom which received legal recognition under Constantine.

38. Social life declined in the towns and flourished rather among the country aristocracy. The State educational institutions were not neglected, and letters received some encouragement. After the third-century collapse both Latin and Greek literature enjoyed a mild revival, while Christian literature showed real vigour. Sculpture declined, but architecture maintained a technically high level, and the way was paved for the transition to 'late classical' art. Neoplatonism and Mithraism strove with Christianity for the allegiance of men, while in the country-side paganism still flourished. But the future lay with Christianity, and when Constantine, a Roman emperor, presided at the Council of Christian bishops at Nicaea in 325 an era in man's history was ended and the threshold of the Middle Ages was revealed.

39. Diocletian and Constantine had buttressed up the Empire, but the latter's unerring insight in founding a new Christian capital *in partibus Orientis* could not secure the unity of the whole. After his death and renewed civil war the Empire was temporarily reunited under Constantius and Julian, whose reign witnessed a reaction of paganism against Christianity, and again under Theodosius I (395), whose sons, theoretically joint rulers of a single empire, were in practice monarchs of East and West. In the East the Byzantine Empire survived until the Mohammedan capture of Constantinople in 1453. If its culture became predominantly Greek, it at any rate produced two of the greatest monuments of Roman law in the codes of Theodosius II and Justinian. East Rome was in fact the direct continuation of the Roman Empire, and to its resolute resistance to the storms of barbarism the modern world owes much of the preservation of the legacy of the ancient world. The West, separated from the East, could not long survive the storm of Germanic invasions. Picts, Scots, and Saxons overran Britain, which the Romans evacuated, Gaul was conquered by Franks and Burgundians, Spain by Suebi and Vandals, who, passing to north Africa (429), cut the Mediterranean in two. In 410 the Goth Alaric sacked Rome, and although the threat from Attila the Hun was averted (452) Rome was again raided and plundered by the Vandal Gaeseric in 455. When the German Odoacer deposed Romulus Augustulus in 476 the rule of Rome in the West was ended, but the survival of Roman law and the Latin tongue, the Roman Church, and the Holy Roman Empire continued to demonstrate the indestructibility of the Roman tradition.

BIBLIOGRAPHY

On the sources for Roman history *see* HISTORIOGRAPHY (ROMAN AND GREEK), ANNALS, FASTI, EPIGRAPHY, COINAGE (ROMAN), PAPYRI.

GENERAL HISTORIES. *The Cambridge Ancient History*, edited by S. A. Cook, F. E. Adcock, M. P. Charlesworth, and (vol. xii) N. H. Baynes: vii, *The Hellenistic Monarchies and the Rise of Rome* (1928); viii, *Rome and the Mediterranean, 218–133 B.C.* (1930); ix, *The Roman Republic, 133–44 B.C.* (1932); x, *The Augustan Empire, 44 B.C.–A.D. 70* (1934); xi, *The Imperial Peace, A.D. 70–192* (1936); xii, *The Imperial Crisis and Recovery, A.D. 193–324* (1939). Volumes of Plates, prepared by C. T. Seltman, iii (to vols. vii and viii), iv (to ix and x), v (to xi and xii).

Methuen's History of the Greek and Roman World, edited by M. Cary: vol. iv, *A History of the Roman World, 753–146 B.C.*, by H. H. Scullard (1935); v, *146–30 B.C.*, by F. B. Marsh (1934); vi, *30 B.C.–A.D. 138*, by E. T. Salmon (1944); vii, *A.D. 138–337*, by H. M. D. Parker (1935).

M. Rostovtzeff, *A History of the Ancient World*, vol. ii, *Rome* (1927). *European Civilization*, edited by E. Eyre, vol. ii, *Rome and Christendom*, by A. W. Gomme S. N. Miller, and W. E. Brown (1935).

M. Cary, *A History of Rome down to the Reign of Constantine* (1935). T. Frank, *A History of Rome* (1923). H. F. Pelham, *Outlines of Roman History*[5] (1926). A. E. R. Boak, *A History of Rome to A.D. 565*[3] (U.S.A. 1943).

Histoire ancienne, edited by G. Glotz. Part III: *Histoire romaine*: I, *Des origines à l'achèvement de la conquête*[2], by E. Pais and J. Bayet (1940); II, *La République romaine de 133 à 44 av. J.-C.*, by G. Bloch and J. Carcopino (1935–6); III, *Le Haut-Empire*, by L. Homo (1933); IV, *Le Bas-Empire jusqu'au 395*: i, *L'Empire romain de l'avènement des Sévères au concile de Nicée*, by M. Besnier (1937); ii, *L'Empire chrétien (325–395)*, by A. Piganiol (1947). A. Piganiol, *Histoire de Rome*[2] (1946).

J. Vogt and E. Kornemann, *Römische Geschichte* in Gercke-Norden, *Einleitung in die Altertumswissenschaft*[3] iii. 2 (1933). E. Kornemann, *Römische Geschichte* i (1939), ii (1940).

Storia d'Italia, i, *L'Italia Antica*, by P. Ducati (1936); ii, *L'Italia imperiale*, by R. Paribeni (1939). Of a projected *Storia di Roma* in 30 vols. the following have been published: vol. ii, *Roma nell' età delle guerre puniche* (1938), by G. Gianelli; iii, *Le grandi conquiste mediterranee* (1945), by G. Corradi; *Da Diocleziano alla caduta dell' Impero d'Occidente* (1941), by R. Paribeni; xviii, *La Religione di Roma antica*, by N. Turchi; xxiv, *La Letteratura di Roma repubblicana ed augustea*, by A. Rostagni; xxvi, *L'Arte in Roma dalle origini al secolo viii* by P. Ducati.

THE REPUBLIC. *General*: Mommsen, *History of Rome* (Engl. Transl.). W. E. Heitland, *The Roman Republic* (3 vols. 1909). T. Frank, *Roman Imperialism* (1914).

Early Italy: D. Randall-MacIver, *Italy before the Romans* (1928). J. Whatmough, *The Foundations of Roman Italy* (1937). L. Homo, *Primitive Italy* (Engl. Transl. 1927).

Later Republic: A. H. J. Greenidge, *A History of Rome, B.C. 133-104* (1904). A. H. J. Greenidge and A. M. Clay, *Sources for Roman History, 133-70 B.C.* (1903). T. Rice Holmes, *The Roman Republic* (3 vols. 1923), covering 70-44 B.C.

Transition to Empire: F. B. Marsh, *The Founding of the Roman Empire²* (1927). T. Rice Holmes, *The Architect of the Roman Empire* (2 vols. 1928, 1931). R. Syme, *The Roman Revolution* (1939).

A. Piganiol, *La Conquête romaine⁴* (1944). M. Holleaux, *Rome, la Grèce et les monarchies hellénistiques au iii⁰ siècle av. J.-C.* (reprint, 1936). G. Colin, *Rome et la Grèce de 200 à 146 av. J.-C.* (1904).

K. J. Beloch, *Römische Geschichte bis zum Beginn der punischen Kriege* (1926). F. Altheim, *Epochen der römischen Geschichte*, i (1934), ii (1936).

G. De Sanctis, *Storia dei Romani*, vols. i-iv, i (1907-23, down to 167 B.C.). E. Pais, *Storia di Roma dell' età regia sino alle vittorie su Taranto e Pirro* (1934); *Storia di Roma durante le guerre puniche* (2 vols. 1927); *Storia di Roma durante le grandi conquiste mediterranee* (1931); *Storia interna di Roma dalle guerre puniche alla rivoluzione graccana* (1931). E. Ciaceri, *Le origini di Roma* (1937).

ROMAN EMPIRE. *General*. J. B. Bury, *A History of the Roman Empire from its Foundation to the Death of Marcus Aurelius* (6th impression, 1913). M. P. Nilsson, *Imperial Rome* (1926). J. Wells and R. H. Barrow, *A Short History of the Roman Empire to the Death of Marcus Aurelius* (1931).

E. Albertini, *L'Empire romain³* (1939). L. Homo, *L'Empire romain* (1925).

H. Dessau, *Geschichte der römischen Kaiserzeit* (vols. I, II, i, ii, 1924-30). A. von Domaszewski, *Gesch. der röm. Kaiser³* (1922).

The Provinces. V. Chapot, *The Roman World* (Engl. Transl. 1928). A. H. M. Jones, *The Cities of the Eastern Roman Provinces* (1939). Mommsen, *The Provinces of the Roman Empire from Caesar to Diocletian* (Engl. Transl., reprinted 1909). G. H. Stevenson, *Roman Provincial Administration till the Age of the Antonines* (1939).

The Later Empire. F. Lot, *The End of the Ancient World* (Engl. Transl. 1931). E. Gibbon, *The Decline and Fall of the Roman Empire* (ed. by J. B. Bury, 7 vols. 1896-1900). O. Seeck, *Geschichte des Untergangs der antiken Welt* (6 vols. 1895-1921). E. Stein, *Geschichte des spätrömischen Reiches* (vol. i, 1928). A. Dopsch, *The Economic and Social Foundations of European Civilization* (Engl. Transl. 1938). J. B. Bury, *History of the later Roman Empire* (A.D. 395-A.D. 565) (1923); *The Invasion of Europe by the Barbarians* (1928). F. Lot, *Les Invasions germaniques* (1935). N. H. Baynes, *The Byzantine Empire* (1925). *Cambridge Medieval History*, vols. i, ii (1911-13). C. N. Cochrane, *Christianity and Classical Culture* (1940).

CONSTITUTIONAL, ETC. A. H. J. Greenidge, *Roman Public Life* (1901). L. Homo, *Roman Political Institutions* (Engl. Transl. 1929). Mommsen, *Römisches Staatsrecht* (3 vols. 1881-8); *Römisches Strafrecht* (1899). J. Marquardt, *Römische Staatsverwaltung* (3 vols. 1881-5). French translation of Mommsen and Marquardt, *Manuel des antiquités romaines* (19 vols. 1890-1907): i-vii, *Le Droit public romain*; viii, ix, *L'Organisation de l'empire romain*; x, *L'Organisation financière*; xi, *L'Organisation militaire*; xii, xiii, *Le Culte*; xiv, xv, *La Vie privée des Romains*; xvi, *Sources du droit romain*; xvii-xix, *Le Droit pénal romain*.

See also under SENATE, COMITIA, PRINCEPS, CONSUL, etc.

ECONOMIC AND SOCIAL. *An Economic Survey of Ancient Rome*, edited by T. Frank (5 vols. U.S.A.): i, *Rome and Italy of the Republic*, by T. Frank (1933); ii, *Roman Egypt*, by A. C. Johnson (1936); iii, *Roman Britain, Spain, Sicily and Gaul*, by R. G. Collingwood, J. J. van Nostrand, V. Scramuzza, and A. Grenier (1937); iv, *Roman Africa, Syria, Greece and Asia*, by R. M. Haywood, F. M. Heichelheim, J. A. O. Larsen, and T. R. S. Broughton (1938); v, *Rome and Italy of the Empire*, by T. Frank (1940); *General Index* (1940).

M. Rostovtzeff, *The Social and Economic History of the Roman Empire* (1926; revised German and Italian editions, 1931 and 1933; new English edition forthcoming). T. Frank, *An Economic History of Rome²* (U.S.A.) 1927). M. P. Charlesworth, *Trade Routes and Commerce of the Roman Empire²* (1926).

W. Warde Fowler, *Social Life at Rome in the Age of Cicero* (1909). *The British Museum Guide illustrating Greek and Roman Life*. L. Friedländer, *Roman Life and Manners under the Early Empire* (Engl. Transl. of 7th edition, 4 vols., 1908-13; new 11th German edition, 4 vols., 1921-3). S. Dill, *Roman Society from Nero to M. Aurelius²* (1905); *Roman Society in the last century of the Western Empire²* (1899). A. Grenier, *The Roman Spirit* (Engl. Transl. 1926). J. Carcopino, *Daily Life at the Zenith of the Empire* (1940).

Three small introductory books are M. Cary and T. J. Haarhoff,

Life and Thought in the Greek and Roman World (1940); R. W. Moore, *The Roman Commonwealth* (1942); and H. Grosse-Hodge, *Roman Panorama* (1944).

See also s.v. AGRICULTURE, COMMERCE, INDUSTRY, etc.

WORKS OF A GENERAL CHARACTER. *A Companion to Latin Studies*, edited by J. E. Sandys³ (1921). H. Stuart Jones, *Companion to Roman History* (1912).

BIBLIOGRAPHIES. Full bibliographies are contained in *CAH*. These may be supplemented by such annual works as *The Year's Work in Classical Studies*; *L'Année philologique* (edited by J. Marouzeau); and *Bibliotheca philologica classica* in Bursian's *Jahresbericht über die Fortschritte der klassischen Altertumswissenschaft*.   H. H. S.

ROME (TOPOGRAPHY). The Tiber valley at Rome is a deep trough, from ½ to 1½ miles wide, cut into the soft tufa floor of the river's lower basin. The edges of the trough are formed by steep weathered cliffs, seamed and even isolated by tributary streams. Thus were formed the famous hills of Rome, the Capitol, Palatine, and Aventine being cut off from the main hinterland, the Caelian, Oppian, Esquiline, Viminal, and Quirinal as flat-topped spurs. On the valley floor itself the river meanders in an S-shaped curve, the northern or upper twist containing the flat and mephitic Campus Martius and skirting the Vatican plain, the southern curve skirting the Capitol, *Forum Boarium*, and Aventine, and enclosing *Transtiberim*, a smaller plain at the foot of the Janiculan ridge. Just below the middle of the S-curve the river runs shallow and divides at Tiber island, traditionally erected by man upon a natural basis. The ford so made has no fellow between Rome and the sea, or for many miles upstream. Thus, while hills and spurs provided the natural strongholds beloved by primitive communities, traffic across the heavily populated Latian plain concentrated at the Tiber ford, the key to Rome's predominance.

2. Archaeology attests widespread primitive settlements on the Esquiline and Quirinal (qq.v.), associated with grave-goods going back to the ninth century B.C. Elsewhere space was more restricted: the Palatine or Capitoline cemeteries crowded the edges of the marshy valley of the *Forum Romanum* (q.v.), where burials cease by the sixth century B.C., attesting the synoecism brought about by the kings and coincident with the draining of the valley by the *cloaca maxima* (q.v.) and the creation of the *forum* market-place. The Wall of Servius (q.v.) on the Viminal, and cliffs elsewhere, made Rome a great promontory fortress comparable with Veii or Ardea, while the *pons sublicius* supplanted the ford. Regal ambition made a sacred acropolis of the Capitol, royal acres of the Campus Martius, a religious centre of the Aventine, with temple of Diana and *armilustrium*, and a *circus* (q.v.) of the Velabrum. The Republic kept the monuments, made of the Campus Martius a training-ground, and gradually concentrated civic activities in the Forum (q.v.). The Palatine became a residential centre. Markets lined the Tiber bank, near the bridge and in touch with river-traffic, or clustered behind the Forum, whence State buildings gradually ousted them. The city became crowded, especially in the valleys which formed the irregular arterial routes, and as early as the third century B.C. tenement houses, which were to become a feature of the capital, attest the overcrowding and squalor which beset the narrow thoroughfares, such as the *Vicus Tuscus*, *Vicus Iugarius*, or *Subura*. Civic pride and family ambition early endowed innumerable temples. The city wall was erected *c.* 378 B.C., enclosing the *Quattuor Regiones* (q.v.); aqueducts (q.v.) came later, in 312, 272, and 144 B.C.; quays, new Tiber bridges, *basilicae*, and porticoes later still, as in the great outburst of building activity in 184-176 B.C. Sulla was the first of the great dictators or *principes* to systematize large areas, linking the Forum and Capitol as an architectural unit by means of the *Tabularium* (q.v.). Pompey set a new fashion in theatres and porticoes, by the famous group of buildings centred upon his theatre and

Hecatostylon; while of Julius Caesar's grandiose schemes, including Tiber diversion (Cic. *Att.* 13. 33), only the *Forum Iulium* (q.v.) remains, though such buildings as the *basilica Iulia* and the *Saepta* (q.v.) were finished by Augustus.

3. Thus the monumental centres of the City had been determined by the Republic upon a basis inherited from the kings. Their surviving outward form, however, owes far more to the emperors, whose rebuildings or additions transformed or eclipsed the older monuments. Augustus built a new *Forum Augustum* (q.v.), novel in form and dedication, a modest palace on the Palatine, associated with the temple of Apollo, and three new aqueducts (q.v.), while many new monuments in the Campus (q.v.), including the *Mausoleum*, were erected by him or by his *viri triumphales*. It may be claimed that in the Campus he and Agrippa rivalled Pompey. Studied attention was paid to the archaic cult buildings of the Forum Romanum, in harmony with the religious revival, while the city was divided into fourteen new *regiones* (q.v.). The contributions of Tiberius, the *Castra Praetoria* on the outskirts of the Viminal and the enlarged *Domus Augustana* on the Palatine (q.v.), are curiously significant of his policy; while the freak building-schemes of Gaius reflect that disregard of public feeling which cost him his life. The only lasting building of Gaius, the *Circus* (q.v.) in *Transtiberim*, was to fix through the martyrs the centre of Christianity. The effect of all these building-schemes was to drive the residential quarters off the Palatine to the villas and parks of the Quirinal, Pincian, and Aventine. To supply these higher sites, Claudius built two sumptuous aqueducts. Nero's parkland palace (s.v. DOMUS AUREA) attests his Hellenistic tastes, as do his *Colossus* and monumental *Via Sacra* (q.v.), the sole street in Rome comparable with the great colonnaded streets of the Roman East or the newer Imperial cities of the West. His Baths and Gymnasium are more to Roman taste. The Flavians spent much energy in Romanizing the creations of the τύραννος, the *Colosseum* (q.v.), *Forum Vespasiani* (q.v.), and Baths of Titus taking their place. Nerva's *Forum Transitorium* is a curious essay in the monumental approach, linking *Forum Romanum* and *Subura*. Trajan's *Thermae* finally blotted out the *Domus Aurea*, while his monumental *Forum* (q.v.) and market represent the impact of the Syrian Apollodorus upon Roman taste—'in Tiberim defluxit Orontes!' The Aqua Traiana (s.v. AQUEDUCTS) was the first good water-supply in *Transtiberim*. Hadrian replaced the vestibule of the *Domus Aurea* by the temple of Venus and Rome, erected a new *Mausoleum* and the *pons Aelius*, and rebuilt the *Pantheon* and Baths of Agrippa in the Campus.

4. Then followed a pause in building activities: the Antonines could afford to live upon the prestige of their predecessors, adding only triumphal monuments and temples of the *Divi*. Later building-schemes, apart from repairs, take the form of isolated monumental buildings, chiefly of utility. Aurelian's *Templum Solis* is the one notable religious building. The typical erections are the great *Thermae*. But the policy of the Severi is illustrated by their vast extension of the Imperial palace on the Palatine (q.v.), with ornamental façade (*see* SEPTIZONIUM) on Via Appia, and the *Castra Equitum Singularium* on the Caelian. It is significant for the overcrowding in the City, as well as for the urgent need of cleanliness, that the sites for the great Baths had to be sought on the fringe, Caracalla picking the low ground outside Porta Capena, Diocletian selecting the Viminal, Constantine choosing the Quirinal. Great fires offered the only chance of rebuilding in the older regions: thus, the *Thermae Alexandrinae* were an enlargement of Nero's Baths in the Campus, while the fire of Carinus in 284 created space for the *basilica* of Maxentius, the noblest experiment in vaulting in the ancient world. The city

had now reached the climax of its development, and it is significant that Aurelian had again ringed it with a defensive wall (*see* WALL OF AURELIAN). Further changes belong to the medieval topography.

T. Ashby and S. Platner, *Topographical Dictionary of Ancient Rome* (1929); C. Hülsen and H. Jordan, *Topographie der Stadt Roms* (4 vols. 1871–1906); R. Lanciani, *Ruins and Excavations of Ancient Rome* (1897); *Forma Urbis Romae* (1893–1901); G. Lugli, *I monumenti antichi di Roma e del suburbio* (vols. i–iii, 1931–8; Engl. Transl., *The Classical Monuments of Rome*, vol. i; vol. i is now superseded by *Roma Antica, Il Centro Monumentale* (1946)); O. Gilbert, *Topographie der Stadt Rom* (1883–5); T. Ashby, *Aqueducts of Ancient Rome* (1935); I. A. Richmond, *City Wall of Imperial Rome* (1930); G. Saeflund, *Le Mura di Roma repubblicana* (1932).   I. A. R.

ROMULUS and **REMUS,** mythical founders of Rome. Their legend, though probably as old as the late fourth century B.C. in one form or another (the Ogulnii dedicated a statue of the she-wolf with the twins in 296 B.C., Livy 10, 23, 12; see further J. Carcopino, *La Louve du Capitole*), cannot be very old nor contain any popular element, unless it be the almost universal one of the exposed children who rise to a great position. The name of Romulus means simply 'Roman', cf. the two forms *Sicanus* and *Siculus*; Remus (who in the Latin tradition replaces the Rhomos of most Greek authors), if not a back-formation from local place-names such as Remurinus ager, Remona (Festus, pp. 344. 25 and 345. 10 Lindsay), is possibly formed from *Roma* by false analogy with such doublets as Κέρκυρα, Corcyra, where the *o* is short. The part played by a god in begetting children is against all provably native Italian tradition; the entire story moves on purely Greek lines, and the idea of having an eponym whose name explains that of a city is itself Greek. However, there is no doubt that the legend was shaped by someone well acquainted with Roman topography and having a not inconsiderable knowledge of Roman religion and custom; contrast the older stories preserved, e.g., in Festus, p. 326. 28 ff.

In its normal form (Livy 1. 3. 10 ff.; Dion. Hal. *Ant. Rom.* 1. 76. 1 ff.; Plutarch, *Romulus*, 3 ff.; more in Carter, Roscher's *Lexikon*, iv. 174. 14 ff., which article is an excellent summary of the whole matter, with relevant literature) the story runs thus. Numitor, king of Alba Longa, had a younger brother Amulius who deposed him. To prevent the rise of avengers he made Numitor's daughter, R(h)ea Silvia, a Vestal Virgin (q.v.). But she was violated by Mars himself, and bore twins. Amulius, who had imprisoned her, ordered the infants to be thrown into the Tiber. The river was in flood, and the receptacle in which they had been placed drifted ashore near the Ficus Ruminalis. There a she-wolf (Plutarch, *Rom.* 4, adds a woodpecker, both being sacred to Mars) tended and suckled them, until they were found by Faustulus, the royal herdsman (probably a by-form of Faunus, q.v.). He and his wife Acca Larentia (q.v.) brought them up as their own; they increased mightily in strength and boldness, and became leaders of the young men in daring exploits. In one of these Remus was captured and brought before Numitor; Romulus came to the rescue, the relationship was made known, they rose together against Amulius, killed him, and made Numitor king again. The twins then founded a city of their own on the site of Rome, beginning with a settlement on the Palatine; Romulus walled it, and he or his lieutenant Celer killed Remus for leaping over the walls. He opened an asylum on the Capitol for all fugitives, and got wives for them by stealing women from the Sabines, whom he invited to a festival. After a successful reign of some forty years he mysteriously vanished in a storm at Goat's Marsh and became the god Quirinus, q.v., one of the most obvious Greek touches in the whole story.

For literature see references in text.   H. J. R.

RORARII, *see* VELITES.

ROSALIA or **ROSARIA** (generally neut. plur., occasionally fem. sing., plur. **Rosaliae**). The Romans were extravagantly fond of roses and used them especially on all manner of festal occasions, at banquets both official (e.g. *Act. Arval.*, p. ccv, 13 Henzen) and private (e.g. Martial 9. 93. 5). It is therefore not remarkable that a feast of roses was a common event, although it never became a fixed public festival, except locally. The best-known occasions of this sort were commemorations of the dead, also called *dies rosationis*, when presumably the members of the family met at the grave and decked it with roses. Violets were also used, hence *uiolatio, dies uiolares* or *uiolae* (see A. de-Marchi, *Culto privato di Roma antica*, i (1896), 201). But quite apart from this, feasts of roses are recorded in a number of documents, none earlier than Domitian, at Capua on 5 May, at Rome on 23 May ('macellus rosa [*sic*] sumat', Philocalus) and 21 May, at Pergamum on 24–6 May, and at various places in northern Italy and central Europe on dates ranging from about 1 June to the middle of July; in other words, at the time of year when roses were to be had abundantly. There is no reason to suppose that all these developed out of the cult of the dead; rather is the reverse true, that the honours done in this manner to the dead were a particular case of inviting them to a feast or other entertainment at which the survivors were also present, or simply a development of the custom, common in antiquity as now, of decking graves with flowers, cf. Nilsson, *Rosenfest*, 136.

An interesting instance is the *Rosaliae signorum* in the calendar of Dura-Europos which has the entry *pridie kal. Iunias ob rosalias signorum supplicatio*. It seems probable that on that occasion the standards (q.v.) were garlanded with roses. See A. S. Hoey in *Harv. Theol. Rev.* xxx (1937), 15 ff.

M. P. Nilsson in *PW*, s.v. 'Rosalia' (full refs. to authorities); 'Das Rosenfest', in *Beiträge zur Religionswissenschaft* ii (1914–15: publ. 1915), 134 ff.   H. J. R.

ROSCIUS (1), Sextus, born in Ameria (Umbria), was accused of parricide in 80 B.C. by C. Erucius at the instigation of Chrysogonus, who had placed the father's name on the proscription list in order to confiscate the property. Defended by Cicero, he was acquitted. The political significance of the trial, possibly a protest against Sulla's tyranny, is doubtful.

Von der Mühll, *PW* i A. 1117; J. Carcopino, *Sylla* (1931), 147; E. Ciaceri, *Cicerone* i (1926), 22; J. Humbert, *Les Plaidoyers écrits de Cicéron* (1925), 100.   A. M.

ROSCIUS (2) **OTHO**, Lucius, a tribune in 67 B.C., opposed the *Lex Gabinia*. He carried a *Lex Roscia*, which restored to the men of equestrian rank and census a special place in the theatres. This unpopular law was defended by Cicero in 63.

ROSCIUS (3) **GALLUS**, Quintus, from Solonium by Lanuvium (Cic. *Nat. D.* 1. 79: *Div.* 1. 79), the famous actor, was of free birth, being brother-in-law to Quinctius (*Quinct.* 77). Sulla made him a knight. Handsome in person (*Arch.* 17), he had a squint (*Nat. D.* 1. 79) and wore a mask (*De Or.* 3. 221). Time moderated his natural vivacity (ibid. 1. 254; *Leg.* 1. 11); supreme in comedy, he also played tragic parts (*De Or.* 3. 102). His name became typical for a consummate artist (*Brut.* 290; *De Or.* 1. 130, 258), his popularity being prodigious (*Arch.* 17). His earnings were enormous (Plin. *HN* 7. 128; Cic. *QRosc.* 23). He was on intimate relations with Catulus (*Nat. D.* 1. 79), Sulla (Plut. *Sulla* 36), and Cicero, to whom he gave his first important brief (*Quinct.* 77), 81 B.C., and who later defended him in a private suit. Cicero mentions his death as recent in 62 B.C. (*Arch.* 17).   G. C. R.

ROSTRA. The earliest *rostra*, or speaker's platform, at Rome lay on the south side of the augurally constituted *comitium*; it existed in 338 B.C. when it was adorned with the prows (*rostra*) of ships captured from Antium, later with statues and a sundial. This platform is long, with a straight front, associated with the second level of the Comitium. When rebuilt, probably by Sulla (*JRS* xii (1922), 21–5), it had a curved front. On planning the *Curia Iulia* (q.v.) Caesar projected new *rostra* at the north end of the Forum, the core of these being contained within the curved steps built there by Augustus for his large rectangular platform of 42 B.C. The Augustan *rostra* were called the *rostra vetera* in contrast with the front of the *podium* of the Temple of Divus Julius (29 B.C.) also treated as *rostra* (Frontin. *Aq.* 129; Dio Cass. 56. 34) with ships' prows from Actium. A rough northward extension of the Augustan *rostra* of about A.D. 470 commemorates a naval victory over Vandals (*Röm. Mitt.* x. 59).   I. A. R.

ROXANE (the name may be connected with the hill-state of Roshan), daughter of the Bactrian baron Oxyartes, was married in 327 to Alexander, who hoped thus to reconcile the great barons of the north-eastern marches. Beyond the story that after Alexander's death she murdered his other wife Barsine (Stateira), little is heard of her; her son Alexander IV was born after Alexander's death, and she and the boy became pawns in the wars of the Successors till Cassander murdered them both. In Greek and Bactrian legend, however, she became a daughter of Darius III and ancestress, through her (supposed) daughter Apama, of the Seleucid and Euthydemid dynasties.

Berve, *Alexanderreich* ii. 346.   W. W. T.

RUBELLIUS, *see* BLANDUS.

RUBICO (commonly called **Rubicon**), a red-coloured but not certainly identified stream that flowed into the Adriatic, marking the boundary between Italy and Cisalpine Gaul. In 49 B.C. Julius Caesar, after some hesitation, precipitated Civil War by crossing it.

Plut. *Caes.* 32; Lucan 1. 213 f.; Suet. *Iul.* 31; Appian *BCiv.* 2. 35; H. Philipp in *PW*, s.v.   E. T. S.

RUBRENUS LAPPA, a tragedy-writer to whose *Atreus* Juvenal refers (7. 72–3).

RUFINUS (5th c. A.D.), grammarian (not identical with the translator of Eusebius). His *Commentarium in metra Terentiana* and his *De compositione et de metris oratorum* are extant (ed. Keil, *Gramm. Lat.* vi. 554–65; 565–78).

Cf. Teuffel, § 445. 5; Schanz–Hosius, § 1104.

RUFIUS FESTUS, *magister memoriae* under Valens, perhaps the Festus of Tridentum who was *magister memoriae* between A.D. 365 and 372 and proconsul of Asia, wrote a *Breviarium rerum gestarum populi Romani* from the origins to the accession of Valens. The first part described the conquest of the Roman provinces, the second the Eastern Wars from Sulla, especially the Parthian Wars. Dedicated to Valens, it appeared after the Gothic peace (A.D. 369), at the height of the Persian War. It represents ultimately the epitomized Livian tradition and a compendious Imperial history.

Ed. W. Förster (1874); C. Wagener (1886).   A. H. McD.

RUFUS (1), Publius Sulpicius, a great orator and statesman, *c.* 98 B.C. impeached the democrat Norbanus *de maiestate* for his action in 104; he remained an Optimate till his tribunate (88). He had been intimate with L. Crassus and the younger Drusus, whose reforms he supported. In 88, changing sides, he passed by force a series of laws, including the transference of Sulla's intended eastern command to Marius; the recall of those exiled by the Varian Commission of 91; and the distribution of the new citizens throughout the tribes. When Sulla marched on Rome Sulpicius Rufus was killed and his laws were declared to be invalid. Cinna later restored his distribution of the voters. His career marks the return, after Drusus' effort to associate the Senate with reform, to 'normal politics'. M. H.

RUFUS (2), SERVIUS SULPICIUS, prosecuted Murena (q.v.) when defeated by him in the consular elections for 62 B.C. He reappeared as a moderate, both as consul in 51, and in 49 when he attended Caesar's Senate; and though he retired to Samos after Pharsalus, he governed Achaea for Caesar in 46. He died on the embassy to Antony in January 43, and was honoured with a public funeral and a statue on the Rostra. The Ninth Philippic is Cicero's eulogy on him, a man of peace and great sanctity of character, chiefly famous as a jurisconsult. He wrote to Cicero two celebrated letters—a description of the murder of M. Marcellus (q.v.) and a consolation for Tullia's death (*Fam.* 4. 5. 12). G. E. F. C.

RUFUS (3), MARCUS EGNATIUS, won popularity as aedile (probably 21 B.C.) by organizing a private fire-brigade, was elected praetor for the following year, and presented himself (probably illegally) as a candidate for the consulship in 19 (one of the places having been left vacant for Augustus or declined by him). His candidature was rejected by the consul in office and rioting ensued. Rufus then plotted to assassinate Augustus on his return from the East, but was detected and executed.

Velleius 2. 91 and 92; Dio Cassius 53. 24. Stuart Jones, *CAH* x, p. 134, n. 4, and p. 145. G. W. R.

RUFUS (4), CURTIUS, of obscure origin and alleged by some to be the son of a gladiator, entered the Senate and won the praetorship, not without encouragement from Tiberius, who remarked 'Curtius Rufus uidetur mihi ex se natus'. The year of his consulate is unknown. Legate of Upper Germany in A.D. 47, he employed his troops with digging for silver in the territory of the Mattiaci and was rewarded with the *ornamenta triumphalia*. Later he was proconsul of Africa, thus fulfilling a prediction made to him in his humble beginnings. R. S.

RUFUS (5), QUINTUS CURTIUS, rhetorician and historian, writing under Claudius (10. 9. 4: *caliganti*, cf. Caligula; or under Vespasian: J. Stroux, *Philol.* 1929, 233), published a history of Alexander the Great in ten books. Our text begins at bk. 3 (333 B.C.) and has gaps between bks. 5 and 6 and in bk. 10. The tradition is partly panegyrical, from Clitarchus, but partly unfavourable and also 'contaminated' with the tradition of Ptolemy and Aristobulus. His aim was dramatic, in the Peripatetic fashion, and rhetorical; we find few technicalities, but emotional presentation, vivid detail, and the introduction of speeches. The style is classic, on the model of Livy, but with contemporary usage in sentence structure and vocabulary.

Editions: J. Mützell (1841), with commentary; E. Hedicke (1867; 2nd ed. 1908, ed. minor 1931); Th. Vogel (1881); P. H. Damsté (1897). S. Dosson, *Étude sur Q. Curce* (1887); E. Schwartz, *PW* iv. 1870; W. Kroll, *Studien zum Verständnis der röm. Lit.* (1924), 331; F. Helmreich, *Die Reden bei Curtius* (1927). Cf. on sources Schanz–Hosius, *Gesch. röm. Lit.* ii. 601. A. H. McD.

RUFUS (6), LUCIUS VERGINIUS, consul in A.D. 63, was afterwards legate of Upper Germany. In 68 he was prepared to make a deal with Vindex (q.v.), but, being compelled by his own soldiers to fight, he crushed the rebel. He refused to be hailed as emperor and recognized Galba, who, still suspicious, replaced him in Germany. Consul II under Otho, he again refused the sovereignty after Otho's death. He became an example of loyalty to the State, and Nerva chose him as his colleague in the consulate (97). He died that year or a

little later. His panegyric was pronounced by Tacitus, and his memory was celebrated by Pliny the Younger, whose *tutor* he had been (*Ep.* 2. 1). His epitaph is preserved (Pliny, *Ep.* 9. 9):

> Hic situs est Rufus, pulso qui Vindice quondam
> Imperium adseruit non sibi sed patriae.

PIR, V 284; E. Ritterling, *Fasti des römischen Deutschland unter dem Prinzipat* (1932), 18. A. M.

RUFUS (7), CLUVIUS, the Imperial historian, consul before A.D. 41. Nero's herald in the theatre, he became Galba's governor of Hispania Tarraconensis in 68. He first supported Otho, but later declared for Vitellius, defending Spain against Lucceius Albinus, and was witness, with Silius Italicus, at the truce between Vitellius and the Vespasians. His *historiae* may have begun with Gaius (Joseph. *AJ* 19. 1. 13 (91)) and ended with Otho (Plut. *Otho* 3); but in any event its main part covered the reign of Nero. Tacitus (*Ann.* 13. 20; 14. 2) may have followed him in the second part of the *Annals*.

H. Peter, *HRRel.* ii (1906), pp. clxv and 114; Ph. Fabia, *Les Sources de Tacite* (1893), 171, 376. A. H. McD.

RUFUS (8) of Ephesus, physician under Trajan (A.D. 98–117), probably studied in Alexandria; he knew Egypt well, visited Caria and Cos, and practised in Ephesus, at that time a famous medical centre.

Of numerous writings, mostly on dietetics and pathology, these are preserved: Π. ὀνομασίας τῶν κατ᾽ ἄνθρωπον μορίων. Ἰατρικὰ ἐρωτήματα. Π. τῶν ἐν νεφροῖς καὶ κύστει παθῶν. Π. σατυριασμοῦ καὶ γονορροίας. Π. τῶν κατ᾽ ἄρθρα νοσημάτων (Latin, *De podagra*).

Rufus was a dogmatist, though of no special creed, a man of great experience and independent mind; in commenting on Hippocrates he did not refrain from criticizing the master. Anatomy he held necessary for sound medical practice. Opposed to general theories, he mostly studied single diseases. He also renounced the usual prognosis and preferred to ask the patient about the history and symptoms of his case. His books, written in a lively and personal style, bear out the judgement of Galen that the objective critic finds nothing missing in Rufus' writings. His influence was greater in the Orient than in the Occident. *See* ANATOMY AND PHYSIOLOGY, para. 11.

TEXTS: Opera, Ch. Daremberg and E. Ruelle (1879); not genuine, Ὀνομασιῶν τῶν κατὰ ἄνθρωπον ἀ. Π. ἀνατομῆς τῶν τοῦ ἀνθρώπου μορίων. Π. ὀστῶν. Σύνοψις π. σφυγμῶν. De podagra, H. Mørland, *Symbolae Osloenses* (1933).
MODERN LITERATURE: J. Ilberg, *Abh. Sächs. Akad.* (1930), list of writings, also from Arabic, ibid., p. 47; cf. M. Wellmann, *Hermes* (1912); for Ephesus, J. Keil, *JÖAI* (1905; 1926). H. Gossen, *PW* i A. 1207. L. E.

RUFUS, *see also* POMPEIUS (2), POMPONIUS (2), RUTILIUS, SALVIDIENUS, SUILLIUS, VARIUS, VIBIUS (2).

RULER-CULT. I. GREEK. The essential characteristic of Greek ruler-worship is the rendering, as to a god or hero, of honour—τιμή—to individuals deemed superior to other men because of their achievements, position, or power. This tendency lies deeply rooted in the Greek mind and is not to be derived from similar practices in the ancient East.

In the aristocratic society of the Archaic Age, as in the classical *polis* of the fifth century, no man could reach a position of such generally acknowledged pre-eminence as to cause the granting of divine honours to be thought appropriate: the only approximation to deification is the posthumous heroization of oecists (*see* CITY-FOUNDERS). Only in the period of disintegration after Aegospotami and through the rise of individualism do we find divine honours given to living men, all persons of admitted superiority, usually due to their political or military achievements.

Ruler-cult in a developed form first appears during

the reign of Alexander the Great and is directly inspired by his conquests, personality, and, in particular, by his absolute and undisputed power. Alexander's attempt to force the Greeks and Macedonians in his entourage to adopt the Persian custom of prostration before the king—προσκύνησις (in itself not implying worship)—was an isolated and unsuccessful experiment without consequence. Much more important is his salutation as the son of Zeus by the priest of Zeus Ammon at Siwa in 331. Though the priest was merely employing the traditional salutation due to any Pharaoh, the prestige which the oracle of Ammon enjoyed throughout the Greek world had a decisive effect, not only on the Greeks, but also on the romantic imagination of the young king himself. It is probably the progressive development of these emotions which caused Alexander in 324, together with his order for the restoration of political exiles, to demand and receive formal recognition of his divinity from the Greek *poleis*. Alexander also secured heroic honours for his dead intimate Hephaestion, and it seems clear that his motives were primarily personal rather than political; that is, the desire that his career and personality should receive definite and official recognition from the Greeks.

Alexander demanded honours: they were *voluntarily* granted by the Greeks to his successors and their descendants, and thus the two generations after his death saw the rise of all the characteristic phenomena of Greek ruler-worship. These fall into five categories:

1. Dedications to rulers by individuals are necessarily difficult to interpret; the motives range from sincere devotion to the most interested flattery.

2. Like any oecist, a king was worshipped by cities which he had himself founded—but as a god, not a hero.

3. Rulers were sometimes honoured by having their statues placed in an already existing temple. The king was thought to share the temple with the god (as σύνναος θεός) and thus to partake in the honours rendered to the deity and, on occasion, in the deity's qualities.

4. The most characteristic method of deification was for a Greek *polis*, by legislative enactment, to enrol a king among its official divinities with his own cult and priest. This was a tactful way of honouring a suzerain and could also be an appropriate expression of thanks for the benefactions of a foreign ruler.

5. The Greek monarchies of the east in time created their own official cults. The dynastic cult of the Ptolemies at Alexandria (founded 285–284) in its developed form by the end of the third century consisted of a priest of Alexander, of each pair of deceased rulers, and of the reigning king and queen. In 280 Antiochus I deified his dead father Seleucus and dedicated to him a temple and precinct at Seleuceia in Pieria; it was probably also Antiochus I who established the imperial ruler-cult of the Seleucid Empire with high priests of the living king and his divine ancestors (πρόγονοι) in each province of the empire. In the later dynastic cult of the Attalids the kings were deified only after death.

Greek ruler-worship is essentially political and is free from any truly religious emotion (there is no known instance of any prayer addressed to a king). It reached full development only in an age when the effective political powers were supra-national imperial States. Its prevalence in the Hellenistic period is primarily caused by the fact that it was the only possible method for the expression of loyalty to such States.

E. Bickermann, *Institutions des Séleucides* (1938), ch. 7, 236 ff.; W. S. Ferguson, *American Historical Review* xviii (1912), 29 ff.; E. Meyer, *Kleine Schriften* (1924), ii. 265 ff.; A. D. Nock, *Harv. Stud.* xli (1930), 1 ff.; U. Wilcken, 'Zur Entstehung des hellenistischen Königskultes', *Sitz. Berlin* 1938, 298 ff.   C. F. E.

II. ROMAN. Hero-cult was not indigenous to Italy. The primitive Romans sacrificed to the ghosts of the dead (*Manes* q.v.) and conceived of a semi-independent spirit (*genius* q.v.) attached to living persons. But the myth of a deified founder, Romulus (q.v.), was only invented in or after the fourth century B.C. under Greek influence. From the time of Marcellus' conquest of Syracuse (212 B.C.), Roman officials received divine honours from Greek cities; notable instances are possibly Scipio Africanus (c. 200) and certainly the 'liberator' Flamininus (c. 191). At Rome such honours are met with only at the beginning of the first century B.C., and then exceptionally, as those offered privately to Marius (101) and popularly to the demagogue Gratidianus (86). Under Stoic influence the idea that worthy individuals might become divine after death appeared in Cicero's *Somnium Scipionis* (c. 51) and in the shrine which he planned for his daughter Tullia (d. 45). Caesar as dictator (45–44) received divine honours, probably by his own wish and perhaps with a reminiscence of Alexander. After his assassination the triumvirs, supported by popular agitation, secured from the Senate his deification (42).

Imperial emperor-worship falls into two aspects, the worship of the living ruler, including his identification with gods, and the apotheosis of the dead one, and into three types, provincial, municipal, and private. In Egypt Augustus succeeded to the religious position of the Ptolemies. Elsewhere the Greeks continued for him the Hellenistic concept of the divine ruler. And at Rome his titles included *Divi filius* and *Augustus*, which gave him a divine aura if not actual divinity. Officially, however, Augustus was usually joined with the goddess *Roma*. He particularly encouraged the cults maintained by the provincial assemblies (κοινά), e.g. for Asia at Pergamum (29 B.C.) and for Galatia at Ancyra. At Rome the poets constantly spoke of him as divine or divinely inspired. In c. 12–7 B.C. he joined his *genius* with the *Lares compitales* for the official cults of the 265 wards (*vici*) of the city. Throughout Italy, individuals, groups, and towns spontaneously offered worship to him or to his *genius*. In the western provinces Augustus established altars (not temples) to himself, probably in conjunction with *Roma*, and assemblies (*concilia*) for Gaul at Lyons (12–10 B.C.), for Germany at Cologne (c. 10 B.C.), and perhaps elsewhere. Municipal (e.g. at Narbo) and private worship seems, however, to have been less common in the West than in the East. After his death his cult as *divus Augustus* was formally instituted on the Palatine, and cities and provinces (e.g. Tarraco) throughout the Empire dedicated temples to him as *divus Augustus*.

Though his 'constitutional' successors, when consulted, deprecated worship of themselves, the Greeks continued to accord it. Of the 'absolutist' emperors, Gaius and Domitian required worship, but Nero and Commodus probably welcomed rather than demanded divine honours. The Senate rewarded deceased emperors who had pleased it with apotheosis. During the third century the spread of oriental cults was associated with the view that the emperor was especially under divine protection rather than himself a god, and when Constantine adopted Christianity (A.D. 311) this became the official doctrine. It was perpetuated in the theory of the divine right of kings (*rex Dei gratia*).

Emperor-worship was not merely a device to lend dignity and superhuman authority to the ruler or to secure the loyalty of subjects; it represented a spontaneous expression of gratitude to one who had saved and benefited his subjects by establishing peace and prosperity, an expression couched in terms of Hellenistic flattery and supported by the prevalent Stoicism. The practice was perhaps at first more widespread in the East than in the West, more sincere in private than in official (municipal or provincial) cult, and more spontaneous under Augustus than under his successors. In general, it probably contributed little or nothing to fill the religious needs of the population of the Empire. However, it acquired increasing political significance. In the towns of Italy the colleges of *seviri* or *Augustales* in charge of the imperial cult afforded an outlet for the ambition of freedmen, to whom public offices were closed. Augustus' hope that the provincial assemblies might become intermediaries between the cities and the emperor proved vain, but the provincial and municipal priesthoods and the presence of the provincial temple in a city were much sought-after honours. Emperor-worship enhanced the position of the ruler by contributing to court ceremonial and insignia. Either the ruler or his *genius* (in Greek, his 'Tyche') might be invoked with the gods to confirm oaths, a practice to be distinguished from oaths of loyalty to the emperor. Offenders against the emperor's divinity laid themselves open to the charge of treason (*crimen laesae maiestatis*). Though Pliny's detection of Christians by their refusal to sacrifice before the statues of the gods and Trajan (Bithynia *c.* A.D. 112) may not represent a general test, this test or that of refusal to confirm an oath by invoking the emperor had become regular in Tertullian's day (*c.* A.D. 200). Decius demanded sacrifice to the gods, together with offerings in honour of (not to) himself and an oath by his *genius* as evidence of loyalty from everyone, not merely Christians; cf. the Egyptian certificates (*libelli*) of A.D. 250. Finally, in the 4th century, emperor-worship, with its formality and its voluntary participation, yielded to the new, vital State church, the Christian, conformity to which became a compulsory political obligation.

For bibliography cf. *CAH* x. (1934), 951–2. General survey with bibliography, Herzog–Hauser, 'Kaiserkult' in *PW* suppl. iv (1924), 806 ff. Development through Augustan period, L. R. Taylor, *Divinity of the Roman Emperor* (1931). On special topics mentioned above, E. Kornemann, *Klio* i (1901); F. Blumenthal, *Arch. Pap.* v (1913); P. Riewald, *De imp. Rom. cum certis dis comparatione etc.* (1912); E. Bickermann, *ARW* xxvii (1929); M. Rostovtzeff, *Rev. Hist.* clxiii (1930); J. P. V. D. Balsdon, *The Emperor Gaius* (1934), 157 ff.; H. I. Bell, *Jews and Christians in Egypt*, 1 ff.; G. Schumann, *Hell. und griech. Elemente in der Regierung Neros* (1930), 21 ff.; K. Scott, *The Imp. Cult under the Flavians* (1936); Wittig, 'Messius (9)' (Decius) in *PW* xv (1932), 1279 ff.; L. Homo, *L'Emp. Aurélien* (1904), 184 ff.; N. H. Baynes, *Constantine the Great and the Christian Church* (1931); P. Guiraud, *Les Assemblées provinciales* (1887); J. Toutain, *Les Cultes païens etc.* i (1907), 17 ff.; A. Alföldi, *Röm. Mitt.* xlix (1934), l (1935); A. D. Nock, *Harv. Stud.* xli (1930) and chapters in *CAH* x, xii. M. Hammond.

RULLIANUS, see FABIUS (3).

RULLUS, PUBLIUS SERVILIUS, tribune in 63 B.C., introduced a comprehensive agrarian measure at the instigation of Caesar and Crassus. His ostensible aim was the redistribution of land in Italy and the provinces, and to this end a board of commissioners was to be established with far-reaching powers. In many respects he anticipated the later legislation of Caesar; but Cicero, divining that the real purpose of the bill was to strengthen the position of Caesar and Crassus at Pompey's expense, attacked the proposals so vigorously in the Senate and the assembly that they were withdrawn.

See Cicero, *Leg. Agr.* (of four speeches two survive in whole and one in part); E. G. Hardy, *Some Problems of Roman History* (1924). J. M. C.

RUMINA, an obscure goddess, who, if her name be not Etruscan (Schulze, *Latein. Eigennamen*, 580 f.), is to be connected with *ruma* (breast) and taken to be a *numen* of suckling. She had a shrine near the Lupercal, where milk, not wine, was offered, Varro, *Rust.* 2. 11. 5; Wissowa, *RK* 242. H. J. R.

RUPILIUS, PUBLIUS, a close friend of Scipio Aemilianus, brought the Slave War in Sicily to an end in 131 B.C.; with a senatorial commission he drew up a charter for the province (*Lex Rupilia*). As consul in 132, with his colleague Popillius, he vigorously prosecuted Tiberius Gracchus' adherents; and like him went into exile in 123. M. H.

RUTILIUS (1) RUFUS, PUBLIUS (*cos.* 105 B.C.), was a friend of Scipio Aemilianus, under whom he served at Numantia, and of the Mucii Scaevolae. A professed Stoic, and an Optimate in politics, he was responsible in some measure for the military reforms for which Marius is usually given the credit. He served with Metellus in Africa (109–107 B.C.) and was left in command when Metellus refused to meet his successor Marius. As consul in 105, after the defeat of his colleague Mallius in Gaul, Rutilius raised and trained the army which Marius later commanded against the Cimbri: he improved military swordsmanship by introducing the gladiators' methods. In 100 he took part in the resistance to Saturninus. His condemnation *de repetundis* (92) by the equestrian jury after his *legatio* under Q. Scaevola in Asia (94) led directly to the breach between *Optimates* and *Equites*, which the younger Drusus vainly tried to heal. He retired to the province he was alleged to have plundered; Cicero met him at Smyrna in 78. Later historians found his memoirs a valuable source. An eminent soldier, jurist, and orator, Rutilius combined Greek culture with the old Roman virtues. M. H.

RUTILIUS (2) LUPUS, PUBLIUS (early 1st c. A.D.), rhetorician, abridged in Latin a work on figures of speech by Gorgias, who taught at Athens in the first century B.C. (Quint. *Inst.* 9. 2. 102).

RUTILIUS (3) GALLICUS, GAIUS (*cos. suff. c.* A.D. 70, *cos.* II *c.* 90), from Augusta Taurinorum. Apart from the poem, with valuable details of his career, which Statius composed to celebrate Rutilius' recovery from an illness (*Silv.* 1. 4), the only evidence about this eminent senator comes from inscriptions. *ILS* 9499 contains his *cursus* down to the consulate (*inter alia* he had been legate of Galatia for nine years, partly under Cn. Domitius Corbulo). He was governor of Lower Germany in 78 (*ILS* 9052), when he defeated the Bructeri and captured the priestess Veleda (Statius, *Silv.* 1. 4. 89 f.; Tac. *Germ.* 8). By the year 89 he had been appointed *praefectus urbi*, in which post he may have died. R. S.

RUTILIUS, see also NAMATIANUS.

RUTUPIAE, modern *Richborough* (Kent), situated originally on an island of the now silted Thanet channel; a pair of ditches were very probably the defences of a Claudian landing-party (A.D. 43) and the site was used as a stores base for the conquest. *C.* 80–90 a deeply founded structure (trophy+sea-mark?) was built. Rutupiae was the principal landing-place from the Continent, so that in authors 'Rutupinus' = British. *C.* 250 the trophy, itself in ruins, but perhaps replaced by an equally strange cruciform structure, was surrounded by ditches, which were soon replaced by the stone Saxon shore-fort of *c.* 6 acres (Carausius? *c.* 290 or a little earlier). Quantities of late coins prove a long, perhaps post-Roman occupation.

J. P. Bushe-Fox, *First, Second, and Third Reports of Excavations*, 1926–32. Summaries of later results in *JRS*. General Summary, *Victoria County History, Kent* iii. 24–41. Coins: F. S. Salisbury, *Numismatic Chronicle*⁵ vii. 108–20; *Antiquaries Journal* vii. 268–81. C. E. S.

S

SAALBURG, a site on the Upper German *limes* which commanded a pass across the Taunus mountains. Under Domitian, who advanced the frontier to the outer slopes of the range, a small earth fort was constructed here. Shortly after 116 the *Cohors Raetorum Civium Romanorum* was brought from Wiesbaden and a fort built for it. The fort was rebuilt in 213 after a raid by the Alamanni, but was abandoned in 259–60. The successive forts and the adjoining civil settlement have been excavated, and the walls and main buildings of the cohort fort reconstructed.

Der obergermanisch-raetische Limes, B, Bd. ii. 1, no. 11, 1937. O. B.

SABAZIUS (Σαβάζιος, in Anatolia frequently Σαο(υ)ά-ζιος), a Thraco-Phrygian god, regarded by the Greeks now as purely foreign, again as identical with Dionysus. Wherever his place of origin, Phrygia and Lydia were the chief centres of his cult; the Attalid cult of S. at Pergamum (C. Michel, *Recueil d'Inscriptions grecques* (1897–1927), 46, 142–141 B.C.) was a foundation of the Cappadocian princess, Stratonice. Private associations worshipping S. existed at Athens from the late fifth century, and Demosthenes (xviii. 259–60) derides his purificatory rites, but evidence for the cult is scanty till Imperial times. S. was identified with the Κύριος Σαβαώθ of the Septuagint (cf. Val. Max. 1. 3. 2), and once called Theos Hypsistos (q.v.), and certain Jewish eschatological concepts are associated with him in the Vincentius frescoes at Rome (Dessau, *ILS* 3961). His chief attribute is the snake, important also in his mysteries. In art, S. appears either in Phrygian costume or, since he was frequently called Ζεὺς S., with the thunderbolt and eagle of Zeus. Noteworthy are the votive hands, making the 'benedictio Latina' and adorned with numerous cult symbols. *See also* ANATOLIAN DEITIES *and* MACEDONIAN CULTS.

See especially Eisele in Roscher, *Lex.* s.v., and F. Cumont, *CRAcad. Inscr.* 1906. F. R. W.

SABELLI, the name given collectively to those Italic peoples who spoke Oscan (q.v.). They expanded from their original habitat (reputedly Sabine Amiternum) by proclaiming Sacred Springs: all men born within a certain year were dedicated to a god; his sacred animal guided them, armed, to fresh lands, where they usually imposed their language and coalesced with the pre-Sabellian population. Thus originated Marrucini, Marsi, Paeligni, Vestini, Apuli, Samnites, Hirpini, Frentani, Campani, Lucani, Bruttii (Cato fr. 50 P.; Dion. Hal. 1. 16; Festus p. 93, 150, 235, 425, 519 L.; Livy 22. 10). These migrations were still continuing in the fifth century B.C. and later: Sabelli conquered Campania *c.* 450–420, Lucania *c.* 420–390; Bruttii appeared *c.* 356. But the Sabelli were more expansive than cohesive. The Samnites, whom ancient writers regard as Sabelli preeminently (see E. A. Sonnenschein, *CR* 1897, 339), had no feeling of political unity with their ancestors the Sabines, nor the Frentani with theirs, the Samnites.

Old Sabellic is the description inaccurately applied to some untranslated inscriptions from Picenum, including the oldest non-Etruscan inscriptions from Italy. The two dialects in question may be Illyrian (J. Whatmough, *Prae-Italic Dialects* ii (1933), 207). E. T. S.

SABINA, VIBIA, daughter of L. Vibius Sabinus and Matidia the Elder (child of Trajan's sister Marciana) and thus Trajan's grand-niece, married Hadrian (q.v.), A.D. 100, through Plotina's favour. Report described the marriage as unsuccessful, but, although Septicius Clarus

and Suetonius (q.v. 2) were dismissed, there is little evidence for this view. Sabina remained faithful; she received the honour of coinage with the title 'Augusta' in 128 (Hadrian now 'Pater Patriae'), accompanied Hadrian in Egypt (130), and was consecrated by him after her death (136 or 137), with a special coinage. Groundless scandal subsequently ascribed her death to Hadrian's poisoning, or to compulsory suicide.

S.H.A. *Had.*; *PIR*, V 414. B. W. Henderson, *Hadrian etc.* (1923), 22 ff.; H. Mattingly, *B.M. Coins, Rom. Emp.* iii (1936). C. H. V. S.

SABINI dwelt north-east of Rome principally in villages, politically disunited, often unwalled, and usually perched on Apennine hill-tops (Strabo 5. 228, 250). Their origin is unknown; ancient writers, observing their bravery and simple morality, thought them Lacedaemonians (Dion. Hal. 2. 49). They probably spoke Oscan (see SABELLI; cf. Varro, *Ling.* 7. 28), and were famous for their superstitious practices and strong religious feelings (Festus p. 434 L.; Cic. *Div.* 2. 80); many Roman religious institutions reputedly derived from them. Although the Rape of the Sabine Women is fiction, stories connecting Sabines with primitive Rome are not entirely untrustworthy. Peculiarities of the Latin language, duplicated usages in certain Roman religious practices, the double nature of the Roman burial customs, traditions concerning the Quirinal, Esquiline, and Numa Pompilius imply a Sabine element in the Roman population, the result not of Sabine conquest but of amalgamation or gradual infiltration (e.g. the Claudii: Livy 2. 16). Livy and Dionysius record numerous wars against Sabines from regal times until 449 B.C., embellishing them with accounts of the legendary Titus Tatius and victorious Valerii (figments doubtless of Valerius Antias' imagination); probably these were operations against sporadic Sabine bands. In 449 Rome won a resounding victory (Livy 3. 38 f.). Silence envelops the Sabines thereafter until 290, when M'. Curius Dentatus for some unrecorded reason suddenly conquered them (Livy, *Epit.* 11), confiscated some of their territory (T. Frank, *Klio* 1911, 367), and sold some Sabines into slavery, the remainder becoming *cives sine suffragio* (Vell. Pat. 1. 14). However, the fertile *Ager Sabinus* (nowadays *Sabina*; but its exact ancient limits are unknown) remained Sabine: personal names ending in *-edius* were common there (A. Schulten, *Klio* 1903, 235); *octoviri*, the annual magisterial board (prototype of the quattuorviral constitution of Roman *municipia?*), still administered Sabine towns. Becoming full citizens in 268 (Cic. *Balb.* 13), the Sabines were rapidly romanized and ceased to be a separate nation. Chief towns: Reate, Amiternum, Nursia, and, before 449, Cures, Nomentum, and Fidenae.

A. Schwegler, *Römische Geschichte* i (1853), 243 f.; A. Rosenberg, *Staat der alten Italiker* (1913), 40 f.; *CAH* iv, 455, 467 (Conway); vii. 368, 493 (Last); 615 (Adcock) (with bibliography); H. Rudolph, *Stadt und Staat im römischen Italien* (1935); J. Whatmough, *Foundations of Roman Italy* (1937), 285 f.; E. C. Evans, *Am. Ac. Rome* xi (1939). E. T. S.

SABINIAN SCHOOL, *see* SABINUS (2).

SABINUS (1), Ovid's friend, who composed imaginary replies to Ovid's letters from heroines (*Heroides*) and modelled a work on the *Fasti*.

SABINUS (2), MASURIUS, a Roman jurist of the first half of the first century A.D. Descended from a poor family, he lived on the contributions of his disciples; in his fiftieth year he obtained equestrian rank and was the first of this rank to receive the *ius respondendi*.

Sabinus was famous for a standard work, an exposition of the *ius civile* in three books, which served posterity as a model for systematic treatises on private law, entitled *Ex Sabino* or *Ad Sabinum* (as following the system and disposition of Sabinus' work). Other works: *Ad edictum praetoris urbani*; *De furtis*; *Responsa*, and some writings not of a juridical character.

Most of the jurists of the Imperial period up to the time of Salvius Julianus and Gaius were adherents of one or other of two jurists' schools (*scholae, sectae*). The one was called *Sabiniani* after Sabinus or *Cassiani* after his disciple Cassius, the other *Proculiani* after its leader Proculus. The antagonism of the two Schools was derived from the predecessors of these jurists, G. Ateius Capito (q.v.), teacher of Sabinus, and M. Antistius Labeo (q.v.). The individual contrast between these two jurists of the age of Augustus has nothing to do with the opposition of the Schools. Similarly, the contrast between the last great representatives of the Schools, Celsus (q.v. 3) and Julianus (q.v.), offers no clue to the real nature of this opposition. There is a long series of doctrines on which the opinions of the two Schools are divided, but the intrinsic bases of the antagonism cannot be ascertained. It was neither the contrast between *ius strictum* and *ius aequum*, nor that between the ancient national *ius civile* and the *ius gentium*, nor differences in philosophical doctrines or in the method of exposition, although the Sabinians had a predilection for systematic description and the Proculians rather for casuistic. The most considerable representatives of the Sabinians were, besides the founder, the jurists Cassius, Javolenus, Aburnius Valens, Julianus, and Gaius; chiefs of the other school were Proculus, the two Nervae (father and son), Pegasus, the two Celsus (father and son), and Neratius (qq.v.).

O. Lenel, *Sabinus-System* (1892); G. Baviera, *Le due scuole dei giur. rom.* (1898); B. Kübler, s.v. 'Rechtsschulen', in *PW* i A. 381 ff., an exhaustive exposition of the opposing school doctrines; S. Di Marzo, 'Cassiani e Sabiniani', *Riv. ital. per le scienze giurid*, 1910; V. Arangio-Ruiz, *Storia del dir. rom.* (1937), 265 ff.   A. B.

SABINUS (3), FLAVIUS (*cos. suff. anno incerto*), born *c.* A.D. 8, the elder brother of the Emperor Vespasian. He was legate of Moesia for seven years (*c.* 49–56) and *praefectus urbi* for twelve years (Tac. *Hist.* 3. 75, where some suspect the text) under Nero and Otho, though not continuously. When the Flavian forces approached Rome in Dec. 69, he all but completed negotiations for the abdication of Vitellius, when he was set upon by auxiliary troops of the German armies and killed with his friends after a siege on the Capitol, where he had taken refuge. 'Innocentiam iustitiamque eius non argueres; sermonis nimius erat' (Tac. *Hist.* 3. 75).   R. S.

SABINUS (4), TITUS FLAVIUS, son of (3) above, escaped from the burning of the Capitol in A.D. 69, was consul in 82 with Domitian, was married to Julia (Titus' daughter, then Domitian's mistress), and was killed by Domitian before the end of 84. His disgrace perhaps involved the banishment of Dio of Prusa.

Stein, *PW* vi. 2614.   A. M.

SABINUS, *see also* CALVISIUS, NYMPHIDIUS.

SACADAS, musician and poet, of Argos (Paus. 9. 30. 2), won three Pythian victories with the flute, composed tunes and elegiac poems set to tunes (Plut. *De mus.* 8), connected with the second establishment of music at Sparta in the first half of the seventh century B.C. Nothing of his work survives. See MUSIC, § 10. C. M. B.

SACAEA (Σάκαια, Strabo 11. 8. 4–5, p. 512; Σακέα, MSS. of Athenaeus, 639 c; τῶν Σακῶν ἑορτή, Dio Chrys. *Orat.* 4. 66), a Babylonian festival, perhaps of New Year (S. H. Hooke, *Orig. of Early Semitic Ritual* (1938), 59), kept up by the Persians. It was a time of general licence,

feasting, and disguising (Strabo), when slaves ruled their masters (Berosus in Athenaeus) and a criminal was given all royal rights for the five days the feast lasted and then put to death (Dio).

See Frazer, *GB*³, index s.v.   H. J. R.

SACERDOS, MARIUS PLOTIUS (3rd c. A.D.), grammarian and metrician. The first book of his *Artes grammaticae* (ed. Keil, *Gramm. Lat.* vi. 427–546) deals with the parts of speech and *vitia orationis* (but the introduction is lost); the second with nouns, verbs, and constructions; the third with metres. The three books seem not to have been published as a single work and the second is in essentials identical with the spurious *Ars catholica Probi* (cf. Keil, iv. 3–43). This work is the oldest Latin grammatical treatise extant in anything like its entirety.

Cf. Teuffel, § 394; Schanz–Hosius, §§ 604–5.   J. F. M.

SACRA VIA, *see* VIA SACRA.

SACRAMENTUM (LEGAL) signified in the oldest Roman civil proceedings the sum of money deposited *in iure* by both the litigants as a stake. The party whose claim was disproved in the hearing before the judge forfeited his deposit to the *aerarium*. The opposite assertions of the parties concerning the right claimed by the plaintiff formed a kind of wager, in accordance with which the judge had to settle in his sentence which party's *sacramentum* was *iustum*: thus the matter in dispute was indirectly decided. The amount of the *sacramentum*, 50 or 500 asses, depended on the value of the object under litigation: the larger sum was the money deposited as a stake in cases above 1,000 asses. *Sacramentum* was a sort of penalty for the loser of the process, but he forfeited it to the State, and not to his adversary. In its origins *sacramentum* was probably an oath (the soldiers' oath bore the same name), but as early as the times of the XII Tables it was merely a sum of money. Later *sacramentum* was not deposited but guaranteed by security (*praedes*). From the *sacramentum* the principal *legis actio* took its name: *legis actio sacramento* (*per sacramentum*). The proceedings are described by Gaius 4. 13 ff.

For bibliography *see* LAW AND PROCEDURE, ROMAN, II.   A. B.

SACRAMENTUM (MILITARY). In the pre-Marian period, when a new legion was levied, an oath of loyalty to the standards was administered by the tribunes to the soldiers. The formula was repeated by one soldier on behalf of his comrades, who repeated in unison 'idem in me'. This *sacramentum*, violation of which rendered the offender *sacer* (*see* RELIGION, TERMS RELATING TO), was binding for the duration of the campaign. After Marius it was extended to cover the whole period of service and thus became synonymous with *stipendium* (q.v.). In the Principate the army took an oath to the *princeps* as sole *imperator*. This was renewed on the anniversary of his accession and on 1 January annually.

H. M. D. Parker, *The Roman Legions* (1928).   H. M. D. P.

SACRED BAND (ἱερὸς λόχος), the picked corps of Thebans formed by Gorgidas (378 B.C.). It consisted of 300 men who were traditionally grouped as pairs of lovers. To Pelopidas was due the idea of keeping the band together and so fostering their *esprit de corps*. They fought under him at Tegyra (375) and on the attacking wing at Leuctra (371), and were said to have remained undefeated till their heroic annihilation at Chaeronea (338). Their exact equipment is not recorded, but evidently they were shock troops and were largely responsible for the military supremacy of Thebes. A similar corps was formed by the Carthaginians, perhaps in imitation of the Thebans.

Plutarch, *Pelopidas* 14 ff.; Ath. 13. 561 e; Polyaenus 2. 5. 1.   H. W. P.

SACRED SPRINGS, *see* SPRINGS, SACRED.

SACRED STONES, *see* STONES, SACRED.

SACRED WARS, the name of the wars declared by the Delphic Amphictiony against one or more of its members on the ground of sacrilege against Apollo.

The *First Sacred War* arose from a dispute between the Delphians and Cirrha about Cirrha's right to levy tolls on pilgrims. Solon is said to have urged Athens to join in the war, and Cirrha was annihilated *c.* 590 B.C. by the forces of Thessaly, Sicyon, and Athens. Delphi was declared independent, and Thessaly organized the Amphictiony to her interest.

The *Second Sacred War* was precipitated by a Phocian seizure of Delphi. The Spartans restored the Sanctuary to the Delphians. But soon afterwards the Athenians, led by Pericles, reinstated Phocis (448). We do not know when Delphi was again liberated; its independence was affirmed in the peace of Nicias (Thuc. 1. 112; 5. 18).

The *Third Sacred War* involved most of Greece and ended in the intervention of Philip II of Macedon. During the Theban Hegemony Thebes had controlled the Amphictiony, and in spring 356 B.C. passed through its council a threat of war, unless Phocian separatist leaders paid the fines imposed on them for cultivating the Crisaean plain (between Delphi and Cirrha), which was sacred to Apollo. The separatists, led by Philomelus, seized Delphi and repelled Boeotian and Locrian attacks. The Sacred War was finally begun in autumn 355, when the Thebans obtained an open declaration of hostilities from the Amphictiony. Philomelus, with passive allies in Sparta, Athens, Achaea, and others, raised mercenaries with Delphian funds to face the coalition of Thessaly, Locris, and Boeotia. Defeating the Thessalians, who withdrew from the war, Philomelus defended Phocis successfully but was killed at Neon (354). Onomarchus, his able successor, invaded Boeotia and subdued Doris, Locris, and part of Thessaly, where he twice defeated Philip of Macedon (353). In 352 Onomarchus, despite Athenian assistance, was defeated and killed by Philip in Thessaly; his successor, Phayllus, held Thermopylae with aid from Athens, Sparta, and Achaea, and prevented Philip from entering central Greece. He eventually fell ill and was succeeded by Phalaecus, who pillaged the shrine at Delphi. By 347 Phocis and Thebes were exhausted by guerrilla warfare; Thebes and Thessaly invited Philip to intervene, while a faction in Phocis invited Athens and Sparta; but Phalaecus, regaining power, rebuffed both. Athens then allied with Philip, and Phocis, isolated, surrendered to Philip, who reconvened the Amphictionic Council. The Phocians were disarmed and obliged to receive garrisons and to pay an indemnity. Their Amphictionic votes were transferred to Philip.

Diodorus, bk. 16. For the chronology see P. Cloché, *Étude chronologique sur la troisième guerre sacrée* (1915); N. G. L. Hammond, *JHS* 1937.
N. G. L. H.

SACRIFICE (from the Latin *sacrificium*, the performance of a sacred action).

I. A sacrifice, according to Plato (*Euthyphro* 14 c), is a gift to the gods, and this was the current view of antiquity (in which the subject was treated by various scholars, of whom Philochorus is especially noteworthy). Modern comparative method, however, combined with anthropological theory, has sufficiently shown the complexity of the problem. One ancient attempt to classify the confused mass of details is that of Theophrastus, who distinguished offerings of praise, of thanksgiving, and of supplication. We may also distinguish between gods, daemones (heroes), and the dead as recipients of the offerings, and between private and public sacrifices. Finally, we may lay stress on the material of the sacrifice, the difference between vegetable and animal offerings, and on the way in which the offerings were made over to the supernatural powers (communal-sacrificial feast, holocaust, burial, libation, etc.). In view of the prehistoric origin of most of the sacrificial ritual it is for the most part extremely difficult to detect the real source of the ritual in question, which is very often of a purely magical nature. Only insight into primitive mentality and evolutionary method can here give us a better understanding of the problems; and yet the religious and ethical notions of sacrifice in classical antiquity and in higher religions in general are quite different from those of primitive and savage worshippers.

II. *Bloodless offerings and blood offerings.* (1) Theophrastus and other ancient philosophers believed that man at first knew only vegetarian food and accordingly offered to the gods grass and roots, cereals, vegetables (even blades and leaves), fruits and non-intoxicating liquids (principally milk). Animal food is, however, probably of equal antiquity, but in many Greek cults, especially those of chthonian deities, vegetables were prescribed (all kinds of fruits in the procession for the Sun and the *Horai* at Athens, a dish of beans at the Pyanopsia for Apollo, etc.); in a number of cults cakes (q.v.) were customary (cf. Ar. *Plut.* 661 and schol.). We may add cheese, honey, and oil; and, no doubt, home-grown incense was from the remotest antiquity burnt for the gods (θύω originally means to 'fumigate', later commonly to 'sacrifice', as contrasted with ἐναγίζειν, which is used of offerings to the dead and the heroes).

(2) *Blood offerings* were the most popular form of ancient sacrifice, public and private. The deity was provided with the same food as the worshipper, meat from domesticated or wild animals and birds, and sometimes fish (q.v.). The meat, specially selected for the deity, was burnt on the altar, wine being simultaneously poured into the flames. Many details, known to us from Homer, may have had a magical character; the sacrificer washed his hands, sprinkled barley grains, threw some of the victim's hair into the fire, touched the altar (the centre of sanctity), and in a prayer praised the god, thanked him, or begged for his help. The entrails were separately cooked and tasted before the communal sacrificial feast started (on this point Greek and Roman usage agree remarkably). The deity was the honoured guest: this feature was still more prominent at the Theoxenia (q.v.; cf. the *lectisternia*, q.v., of the Romans). Epithets like 'goat-eater' (i.e. Hera), 'bull-eater' (Dionysus) bear witness to the original conception of the deity as really eating of the flesh of the victim. On many inscriptions the necessity of eating the flesh (being sanctified, *tabu*) within the holy precincts is enforced. We may infer that more indifferent worshippers often took it home; in other sacrifices this was quite correct. Concerning Roman ritual it is especially noteworthy that the sacrificer covered his head with his toga during the whole operation. Music (pipes, also lyre) was traditional in Greece as in Rome.

The choice of animals (which ought to be without blemish) was essential and intricate; the rules generally apply to the Greeks as well as the Romans. Male deities usually preferred male victims; bright (celestial) deities demanded light-haired victims, the nether world (and the dead) black victims. The virgins Athena and Artemis sometimes wanted unbroken cattle. A pregnant sow was offered to the earth-goddess in order to intensify her *mana* (her fertility), a cock to the war-god. To some deities animals unfit (or not used) for human food were sacrificed: dogs to Hecate, Eileithyia, Enyalios (Sparta); horses to Poseidon, the Sun (burnt-offering), the Winds (also the river Skamandros into which horses were thrown, according to the *Iliad*; cf. the *equus October* sacrificed to Mars at Rome); asses to Priapus and (at Tarentum) to the Winds. No doubt there existed a mysterious sympathy between these gods and their victims (cf. also the red dog sacrificed to the spirit of the mildew at the Roman Robigalia, *see* ROBIGUS); the gods were formerly believed to appear in the shape of these very animals, as legend and archaeological evidence still attest (so Poseidon as god of the earth and the underworld in the shape of a horse). So far we may here use the term communion-feast (see *infra*).

III. The offerings mentioned mostly belong to the regular gift type of sacrifice (honorific sacrifices). Some of them may originate in tithes (ἀπαρχαί, *primitiae*), the first-fruits of field and orchard, game and spoils. These were tabu and the due of the dead, heroes and gods alike. Other offerings, which are utterly destroyed, represent the *piacular* (propitiatory) or *purificatory* type. The buried corpses of the dead had to be fed (cf. the remains of Mycenaean tomb-cult); we know of a number of cases where the blood of the victims and other libations were led through a tube or hole into the mouth of the dead (cf. Paus. 10. 4. 10). The victim itself, being tabu, was burnt, and such burnt offerings (holocausts) were traditional in the cults of the heroes and chthonic deities; but we hear also of common meals of the family or of worshippers round the graves and the altars (as in the present-day grave-ritual of the East). The proper time was the evening, in contrast with the daytime which was prescribed for sacrifices to the Olympian gods.

The offering of a *human victim*, attested by Homer (*Il.* 23. 171 ff.) and Greek myth (Iphigenia; cf. the tradition of the Messenian Wars), is a relic of primitive propitiatory sacrifice, offered to the feared soul or enraged deity, mostly in times of emergency. The *ver sacrum*, q.v., and the *Argei*, q.v., cannot prove human sacrifice at Rome; but in the third century B.C. two pairs of Gaulish and Greek men and women were buried alive in the Forum Boarium in accordance with Sibylline oracles. In the cult of Dionysus a human victim was even rent to pieces, and in the ritual of Zeus Lykaios, on the remote Mt. Lykaion in Arcadia, there were practices reflecting real cannibalism (so King Tantalus feasted the gods on the flesh of his son). The Athenians, however, felt ashamed of the sacrifice of Persian prisoners before the battle at Salamis. The self-sacrifice of the Roman commander on the field of battle, combined with a prayer and curse, is a vicarious sacrifice, originating in magic (*see* DEVOTIO).

IV. Purely magic is the use of scapegoats, known from Athens (Hippon. fr. 6 ff. Diehl) and Massalia. This may have been a once widespread Mediterranean, later specifically Ionian practice, repeated at fixed intervals. In Athens it was attached to a festival of Apollo, the Thargelia (q.v.). A man, called a φαρμακός (or two men or a man and a woman), was treated according to a fixed ceremonial, and then, loaded with all the wickedness of the city, was driven out by the inhabitants. In Massalia a criminal was selected and finally killed.

Another type of magical practice is the *oath sacrifice*. The swearer touched a portion of the victim (or trod upon its genitals), and the contact filled him with its *mana*; thereupon the animal was buried or cast into the sea. As the oath involved a conditional curse, the danger from the communion established with the victim (and secondarily with the oath-gods) involved peril to the perjurer (cf., e.g., *Il.* 3. 103; 19. 267).

V. The ritual of the Athenian *Bouphonia* is peculiar. An ox 'of its own accord' approaches the altar, eats the corn upon it, and is thereupon slain by the priest, who flees into voluntary exile. The axe is adjudged guilty and cast into the sea. The flesh of the ox is eaten, its hide sewed together, and this sham ox is yoked to the plough. The family to which the priesthood of Zeus Polieus belonged was the Bouzygai (those who yoke oxen), who may have supervised the festival called Dipolieia, of which the Bouphonia was part, and the crime appears to be the 'murder' of the plough-ox (the totem theory is to be discarded).

VI. *Sacramental sacrifice.* The 'omophagies' of the Maenads, characteristic of the cult of the Thracian Dionysus—the rending of a bull or goat, the eating of its raw flesh and the drinking of its blood—are to be referred to the conception of the god incarnated in an animal (cf. DIONYSUS, ORPHISM). The citizens of Tenedos preserved reminiscences of a similar communion with the deity (personified as a calf, sacrificed to the god, Dionysus, himself, Ael. *NA* 12. 34). Different from this 'omophagy' is the sacrifice of a wolf to Apollo, a bear to Artemis (both being incarnated in the respective animals). *See* MAGIC, DIVINATION.

BIBLIOGRAPHY

L. R. Farnell, s.v. 'Sacrifice' (Greek) in Hastings, *ERE*; Ph.-E. Legrand and J. Toutain, s.v. 'Sacrificium' in Dar.-Sag.; L. Ziehen, s.v. 'Opfer' in *PW* xviii. 579 ff.; P. Stengel, *Die griech. Kultusalter-tümer*³; *Opferbräuche der Griechen* (1910); S. Eitrem, *Opferritus und Voropfer* (1915), and *Symb. Osl.* xviii (1938), 9 ff.   S. E.

SACROVIR, JULIUS, an Aeduan, whose family had received Roman citizenship, perhaps from Caesar. After having fought for the Romans, he rebelled in A.D. 21 with Julius Florus and collected a large army of his countrymen. He occupied Augustodunum, but was easily defeated by C. Silius and committed suicide. It is doubtful whether his name is inscribed on the arch of Orange.

A. Stein, *PW* x. 796; C. Jullian, *Histoire de la Gaule* iv (1913), 153. For the arch, literature in *CAH, Plates* iv. 192.   A. M.

SAEPTA IULIA was the voting-hall of the Roman people, in the Campus Martius, planned by Caesar and completed by Augustus and Agrippa in 26 B.C.; it replaced booths or pens known as *ovile*. It was over 400 m. long and 60 m. deep, in seven aisles formed by eight rows of columns. There were thus formed about eighty rooms, which Hülsen (Jordan, *Topographie d. Stadt Rom* iii. 561) relates to the double division of the thirty-five tribes. It is uncertain whether it had two stories, or whether the upper was the huge hall of the *Diribitorium* (Dio Cass. 55. 8. 3; 7 B.C.). As the building lost its political significance, it came to be used for public meetings and shows. After repairs following the fire of A.D. 80 it became a luxury bazaar (Mart. 9. 59) very like Nero's buildings on the Via Sacra (q.v.).   I. A. R.

S(A)EVIUS NICANOR (2nd–1st c. B.C.), grammarian, the first to gain fame by his teaching (Suet. *Gram.* 5), wrote *commentarii*, said to have been mainly borrowed, and a *satura*.

SAGITTARII, *see* ARMS AND ARMOUR, ROMAN.

SAGUNTUM, a city of the Edetani (or Arsetani; cf. *Arse* on coins) about 16 miles north of Valencia in Spain. It had close trade relations with Massilia. An alliance with Rome (contracted probably after 228 B.C.) did not save it from siege and capture by Hannibal in 219 B.C., an incident which precipitated the Second Punic War. In 217 the elder Scipios moved against it (traces of their camp at the neighbouring Almenara survive) and it fell by 212. The city and its walls were rebuilt by the Romans. Sertorius occupied it, but was driven out by Metellus and Pompey in 75. It became a *municipium civium Romanorum* under Augustus. It was noted for its cereals, a variety of fig, and a type of pottery. Some of the amphorae in Monte Testaccio at Rome came from Saguntum. There survive traces of the Iberian wall and Punic buildings on the citadel and a Roman theatre.

M. Gonzales Simancas, *Sagunto, sus monumentos y las excavaciones* (1929).   J. J. van N.

SALACIA, cult-partner of Neptunus (Gellius 13. 23. 2), probably the *numen* of springing water (root of *salire*; for the suffix cf. *salax*); Neptunus (q.v.) is a deity originally of fresh water.

SALAMIS (1), an island in the Saronic Gulf between the western coast of Attica and the eastern coast of the Megarid, closes the bay of Eleusis on the south. In the strait formed by the slopes of Mt. Aegaleus, the island of Psyttaleia, and the promontory of Cynosura southwards, and the small island of St. George northwards, the Persian fleet was crushingly defeated (Sept. 480 B.C.). Though probably colonized by, and originally belonging to, Aegina, and temporarily occupied by Megara (c. 600 B.C.), Salamis shared the fortunes of Athens from the age of Solon and Pisistratus. Declared a cleruchy soon after Cleisthenes' reforms, it was consequently exploited. In 318 it was conquered by Macedonia. Aratus restored it to Athens (c. 230).

C. N. Radas, *La Bataille de Salamine* (1915); L. Bürchner, *PW*, s.v.; D. Levi, G. De Sanctis, *Encicl. ital.*, xxx. 489 f. P. T.

SALAMIS (2), the principal Greek city of Cyprus, situated on the east coast within sight of Syria. It succeeded an inland settlement at Enkomi which has yielded very rich Mycenaean remains. It appears to have been the first Cypriot city to strike coins; from these a list of its kings can be recovered. *C.* 400 B.C. King Evagoras started a Hellenic revival against Phoenician encroachments in Cyprus and conquered most of the island. It was the scene of a notable naval victory by Demetrius the Besieger over Ptolemy I in 306. In the Roman period, from which most of its ruins date, it contained a large Jewish population. S. C.

SALARIUM ('salt-money') was a sum paid to officers and officials and to professional men (e.g. teachers and doctors), which was regarded not as a regular payment, but as a contribution to expenses incurred. If such honoraria were not paid the recipient could not enforce his claim to them, but could only appeal to a higher authority. Under the Republic all payments to public servants were of this character, but under the Principate fixed payments were made to provincial governors and to officers of the army. Details are lacking, but we know that a proconsul received HS 1,000,000 (Dio 78. 22). For the scale of payments to officers see A. von Domaszewski, 'Die Rangordnung des römischen Heeres', *Bonner Jahrb.* 1908, 140 ff. G. H. S.

SALEIUS BASSUS, *see* BASSUS.

SALII (from *salire* 'to dance'), an ancient ritual *sodalitas* (*see* SODALES) found in many towns of Italy, usually in association with the war-god. Outside Rome they are heard of at Lavinium, Tusculum, Aricia, Anagnia, and especially at Tibur, where they were attached to Hercules (Serv. ad *Aen.* 8. 285). At Rome they were connected with Mars, though it is possible that of their two companies, each twelve in number, the Palatini and the Collini (or Agonenses), the latter originally belonged to Quirinus; they were required to be of patrician birth and to have both father and mother living. They wore the old Italian war-dress, *tunica picta*, with breastplate covered by the short military cloak (*trabea*), and the conical felt hat known as the *apex* (Dion. Hal. 2. 70). A sword was girt by their side; on the left arm they carried the *ancilia*, 'figure of eight' shields, preserved in the *sacrarium Martis* in the Regia and said to be copies of the original *ancile*, which fell from heaven as a gift from Jupiter to Numa (Ov. *Fasti* 3. 365–92); in the right hand they carried a 'spear or staff' (Dion. Hal. l.c.). The Salii played a prominent part in the Quinquatrus of 19 Mar. and the Armilustrium of 19 Oct., which marked the opening and closing of the campaigning season. On certain days, too, during each of these two months, marked in the calendar by the note *arma ancilia mouent*, the Salii went in procession through the city. At certain spots they halted and performed elaborate ritual dances (*tripudium*, cf. Plut. *Num.* 13), beating their shields with their staves and singing the Carmen Saliare (q.v.) or *axamenta*, of which some fragments are preserved. In the evening they feasted and resumed their procession on the next appointed day. C. B.

SALINATOR, MARCUS LIVIUS, was born in 254 B.C.; Livius Andronicus (q.v.) was perhaps pedagogue in his father's house. As consul (219) he campaigned against the Illyrians. After his triumph he was accused of peculation and withdrew from Rome (218). His bitterness and the desertion of his father-in-law, Pacuvius of Capua, to the enemy explain his non-participation in the first part of the Hannibalic War. Recalled by the consuls in 210, he did not speak in the Senate till 208. As consul II (207) he was reconciled in national interests with his colleague C. Claudius Nero (q.v.), his former subordinate officer who had witnessed for the prosecution at the trial. Together they defeated Hasdrubal at Metaurus. Salinator was proconsul in Etruria (206–205) and censor (204), again with Nero for colleague, when he imposed a salt-tax. H. H. S.

SALLUST (GAIUS SALLUSTIUS CRISPUS) (86–c. 34 B.C.), was born at Amiternum of a plebeian family; at Rome Sallust entered the senatorial career and became quaestor. In 52, as tribune of the commons, he joined in opposing Cicero in the trial of Milo (Asc. *Mil.* 33). He was expelled from the Senate in 50 by the censors, Appius Claudius and L. Piso, for alleged immorality, but was reappointed quaestor by Caesar in 49. In 48–47 he commanded one of Caesar's legions, but was unsuccessful (Oros. 6. 15. 8; Dio 42. 52). As praetor in Africa he rendered Caesar important service (*BAfr.* 8 and 34) and was made proconsular governor of Numidia. On his return to Rome he was accused of plundering the province, but either was not brought to trial or was acquitted. He was wealthy enough to buy a fine estate in the Sixth Region, where he laid out beautiful gardens (the famous *Horti Sallustiani*) and spent the rest of his life in retirement.

WORKS

1. **Bellum Catilinae** (on titles see Ahlberg, *Proleg. in Sall.*, Göteborg, 1911, 115 ff.), apparently published in 43 B.C. After his usual philosophic introduction S. gives an account of the conspiracy. The chronology is distorted, the events of a few months being extended to over a year. Hence the work is valued, not for its historical importance, but for the vividness and artistry of the narrative and its fine character-sketches.

2. **Bellum Iugurthinum**, published about 41. An account of the war with the Numidian king (111–106), preceded by a philosophical introduction and the story of Jugurtha's previous life and his rise to power. S. had gathered personal information in Africa and had an abundance of good literary sources, including translations from the Punic (*Iug.* 17. 7): yet as history the *Iug.* is of slight value; chronology is indefinite or disregarded, and even the sequence of events is not strictly followed; but as a literary masterpiece of absorbing interest it ranks high.

3. **Historiae**, in five books, apparently composed after 39. It is preserved only in fragments, including, however, four speeches and two letters, published (in cod. V) for use in the schools; for although S. did not rank high as an orator (Quint. 4. 2. 45), the speeches in his works were generally admired.

4. *Disputed works.* In cod. V, in the same handwriting as the extracts from the *Historiae*, two anonymous *suasoriae* are preserved, entitled *Epistulae ad Caesarem senem de re publica*; also in some manuscripts of the *Bella* an *Invectiva in Ciceronem*, attributed to S., and an *Invectiva in Sallustium*, assigned to Cicero. The last-named is certainly spurious. Quintilian cites the *Inv. in Ciceronem* as if genuine, and Kurfess believes it to be

an early work of S. The second *suasoria* (dramatic date 50 or 49) is earlier than the first (dr. d. 46), which is often called an oration, but most editors retain the traditional names and order. The genuineness of the two *Epistulae* has been much discussed, exhaustively, with a full bibliography to date, by Last (*CQ* vii (1923) and viii), who admits that of the first, but denies that of the second. The authenticity of both has found many supporters (see Kurfess's ed.).

5. Sallust adopted a new branch of historiography, the monograph. By way of preparation he carefully studied Thucydides and Cato, and was supplied with an epitome of Roman history by Ateius Philologus (Suet. *Gram.* 10; p. 108 Reiff.). His devotion to the popular party was such that many suspect an ulterior purpose in his writings, but he professes impartiality, and shows it in depicting the character of Metellus in the *Iug.* and in not disguising the faults of his hero Marius. In style he followed Thucydides, and developed a terse and highly rhetorical manner characterized by asymmetry and antithesis. He used so many archaisms that he was accused of pilfering from Cato (Suet. *Gram.* 15; p. 112 Reiff.), but he used them with artistic effect (*see* ARCHAISM). In general, his effort was to avoid commonplace diction, and his style is effective and vivid; it found critics in his own day and later, but also admirers and imitators. As historian, Quintilian (10. 1. 101), Martial (14. 191), and Tacitus (*Ann.* 3. 30) give him high praise. In his personal character he presents an enigma; modern opinion is mostly unfavourable, but Kritz (*Proleg.* to commentary) ably defends him. On the whole, the charges against him are not supported by very good authority. Much weight is naturally given to Varro's accusation (Gell. 17. 18), but it is noteworthy that it finds no mention in connexion with Sallust's expulsion from the Senate, or even in the *Invective*.

BIBLIOGRAPHY

LIFE AND WORKS: Introd. to Commentaries and Translations.
TEXTS: Dietsch (1859), with word index; H. Jordan (Berlin, 1887). Cat. and Iug.: Teubner (Eussner, Ahlberg); Epistulae: Teubner (Kurfess, 1921); Invectivae: Teubner (Kurfess, 1914).
COMMENTARIES: Fr. Kritz (1856). Cat. and Iug.: R. Jacobs (ed. 11 by Wirz and Kurfess, 1922); W. W. Capes (1897); W. C. Summers (*Iug.*; 1902); A. M. Cook (*Cat.*; 1901 (reprinted))' E. Cesareo (*Iug.*; 1937). Hist.: B. Maurenbrecher (1891–3; text, word index); new fragments, *John Rylands papyrus*, 473 (ed. C. H. Roberts, 1938).
TRANSLATIONS: J. C. Rolfe (Loeb); Budé (Fr.).
STYLE AND DICTION: Introdd. to Commentaries and Translations.
SPECIAL STUDIES: A. Kurfess, 'De Invectivis', *Mnemos.* xl (1912); Bursian, *Jahresb.* Bd. clxxxiii (1920); L. Post, *Class. Weekly* 1928; W. Schur, *Sallust als Historiker* (1934).   J. C. R.

SALLUSTIUS (2) CRISPUS, GAIUS, great-nephew and adopted son of the historian, remained an *eques* and was adviser of Augustus and Tiberius. He was privy to the murder of Agrippa Postumus and arrested in A.D. 16 the false Agrippa. He owned copper-mines. To him is addressed Horace, *Carm.* 2. 2. He died in A.D. 20.

Stein, *PW* i A. 1955; E. Hohl, *Hermes* 1935, 350.   A. M.

SALMONEUS (Σαλμωνεύς), a son of Aeolus (q.v.). In post-Homeric tradition, e.g. Verg. *Aen.* 6. 585 ff., he was king of Elis, and pretended to be Zeus, flinging torches for lightnings and making a noise like thunder with his chariot; Zeus smote him with a real thunderbolt. It is very likely that this story originates in some rite of weather-magic, a mimic storm to make a real one; see Rose, *Handb. Gk. Myth.* 83, and references in notes 21, 22.   H. J. R.

SALONAE, a city of Dalmatia, near modern *Split* (*Spalato*). It served the Romans as a base of operations in the Dalmatian hinterland (L. Metellus, 119 B.C.; C. Cosconius, 78 B.C.; Octavian, 35–34 B.C.), and became the capital of the province Illyricum. In 27 B.C. it was constituted as a colony. It rose in prosperity under the Illyrian emperors of the later third century. Diocletian, who was a native of Salonae, retired there in A.D. 305 and built himself an immense palace on the pattern of a military camp. Considerable portions of this palace remain, as also of the town walls, basilica, thermae, theatre, and amphitheatre.   M. C.

SALTICA, sc. *fabula*: *see* FABULA.

SALUS, an old Roman goddess, later often identified with the Greek Hygieia (q.v.), the attendant of Asclepius.

The temple to *Salus publica* on the Quirinal is said to have been built in 302 B.C. by the dictator C. Junius Bubulcus. Under the Empire, *Salus publica* and *Salus Augusti* appear often side by side. Where the genitive 'Augusti' appears, Salus may be regarded as definitely a 'virtue' of this emperor, his saving power—not merely his health. An *augurium salutis*, which did not involve any personification of *salus*, was to be taken annually on a day free of all wars: this was an inquiry to ask whether it was permissible to pray for *salus* for the people. The constant wars of the last years of the Republic caused its frequent omission, but it was revived in 29 B.C. and performed on various occasions in the early Principate (Dessau, *ILS* 9337). Prayers 'pro salute Augusti' were commonly offered, as, for example, by the Arval Brethren.

Salus very frequently appears on coins, with the type of Hygieia, feeding out of her patera the sacred snake and holding the sceptre of divine majesty. A rarer attribute, ears of corn, may properly belong to the older Roman Salus.

G. Wissowa, *RK* 131 ff., 306 ff., and Index; A. S. Pease on Cic. *Div.* 1. 105.   H. M.

SALUTATIO. From six o'clock in the morning until eight most Romans under the Empire who had any social position, high or low, were occupied either in holding or attending a reception—*salutatio*. It was a tiresome business, but it had become recognized as part of the daily routine. The wealthy patron thought that his prestige was enhanced by a crowd of callers, the legacy hunter attended to ingratiate himself with the childless rich, and the needy client, though he might complain of long walks in the cold morning, received compensation in the form of a dole (*sportula*). *See also* CLIENS.

Juvenal 1. 95–102; 3. 127–30; 5. 19–23; Martial 4. 8. 1–6 and passim.   F. A. W.

SALVIANUS was born *c.* A.D. 400, probably at Trèves, where he witnessed the destruction wrought by the Franks, 418. He joined the holy community at Lérins (St. Honorat), and belonged to the intimate circle of St. Honoratus till the latter became bishop of Arles, 426. Later S. was a presbyter in Marseilles, and still alive there about 470. His most notable work is *De gubernatione Dei* (*De praesenti iudicio*), eight books (440) in which God's government of the world is set over against the moral obliquity of the times. Of Salvian's letters nine are preserved.

Ed. F. Pauly (*CSEL* 8).   A. S.

SALVIDIENUS RUFUS was one of Octavian's associates in 44 B.C. and later one of his chief *legati*. In 42 he was worsted by Sextus Pompeius in a naval battle near Messana. He played a prominent part in the Perusine War and was then sent to Gaul and designated consul. During the siege of Brundisium, however, he entered into treasonable communication with Antony, who subsequently informed Octavian. Denounced by the latter in the Senate, Salvidienus was declared a public enemy and either committed suicide or was executed (40).

Appian, *BCiv.* 4 and 5; Dio Cassius, bk. 48.   G. W. R.

SALVIUS JULIANUS (L. Octavius Cornelius P. Salvius Julianus Aemilianus) (*c.* A.D. 100–*c.* 169), a Roman jurist, born at the village of Pupput near Hadrumetum, disciple of Javolenus (q.v.), the last recorded leader of the Sabinian School. Even as a young man he enjoyed a high authority among his contemporaries, as is clearly proved by the fact that before he was thirty years old he was entrusted by Hadrian with the revision and rearrangement of the praetorian edict. This work procured him a wide reputation, and Justinian praised him for it in the highest terms (*Const.* 'Tanta' § 18, and still more in its Greek version, *Const.* Δέδωκεν § 18). His official career is given in an inscription (*ILS* 8973). He was: *decemuir stlitibus iudicandis, quaestor imp. Hadriani (cui diuos Hadrianus soli salarium quaesturae duplicauit propter insignem doctrinam), tribunus plebis, praetor, praefectus aerarii Saturni, item militaris, consul (ord.,* 148), *pontifex, curator aedium sacrarum, legatus Germaniae inferioris* (under Pius) and *Hispaniae Citerioris* (under Marcus Aurelius and Verus), *proconsul Africae*. Under Hadrian and Antoninus Pius he was a member of the imperial *consilium*. His principal works are *Digesta* (in 90 books), a systematic, richly casuistic treatise on civil and praetorian law, partly following the arrangement of the *edictum perpetuum*. A large number of passages have been inserted by the Compilers in the *Digest*, still more numerous (about 500) are the quotations of this work in later literature; Marcellus, Scaevola, and Paulus arranged new editions of it, supplemented by their own notes. Other works of Salvius are: Commentaries to less known jurists, Urseius Ferox and Minicius; a monograph *De ambiguitatibus*. Many of his *Responsa* were published by his pupil Caecilius (q.v. 6) Africanus.

Salvius is the most remarkable representative of Roman jurisprudence. He may justifiably be regarded as an epoch-making figure in Roman legal science, which reached with him the height of its development. His style is plain and lucid, the exposition precise and limpid, his explanation of legal conceptions and institutions is masterly and authoritative; his speciality was concise formulation. And finally, as a fine example of self-criticism, he says (*Dig.* 37. 5. 6) 'saepe animaduerti hanc partem edicti habere nonnullas reprehensiones'.

H. Buhl, *Salv. Julianus* (1888); L. Boulard, *Salv. Julianus* (1902); H. Fitting, *Alter und Folge der Schriften röm. Juristen*[2] (1908), 21 ff.; P. de Francisci *Rend. Ist. Lomb.* xli (1908), 442 ff., xlii (1909); O. Lenel, *Edictum perpetuum*[3] (1927), one of the standard works of the (Romanist) literature; A. Guarino, *Salvius Julianus* (1946).
A. B.

SALVIUS, see also OTHO.

SAMIAN WARE in the time of Plautus was a familiar pottery of an inexpensive kind. It is further mentioned by Martial, and by Pliny, who states that it was still in repute for dinner services. If this implies contemporary production, the ware was probably one of the East-Mediterranean fabrics of *terra sigillata* (q.v.); but the statement of Isidore (*Etym.* 20. 4. 3), that Samian vases were red in colour, would apply equally to *Sigillata* and to some Hellenistic wares, e.g. late Megarian bowls. Up to the present no kilns have been discovered on Samos which would make the identification certain. From Pliny old antiquarians mistakenly borrowed the phrase Samian ware as a label for the *sigillata* found on Roman sites in Britain.

Plautus, *Capt.* 291; Martial, 1. 53. 6, etc.; Pliny, *HN* 35. 160. For *terra sigillata* found in Samos see R. Eilmann, *Ath. Mitt.* lviii (1933), 50.
F. N. P.

SAMNIUM, a region in the southern Apennines whose inhabitants spoke Oscan (q.v.). The Samnite confederation comprised four cantons: Hirpini, Caudini, Caraceni, and the formidable Pentri (Frentani and other Sabelli (q.v.), although often called Samnites by ancient writers, were excluded). The Samnites, primitive but warlike, lived mostly in agricultural villages, frequently unwalled and unidentifiable, each administered by a *meddix* (q.v.; large Oscan cities sometimes had two *meddices*). In war-time these *meddices* elected a generalissimo to lead the confederation for one campaign; he was eligible for reelection. This confederation, however, was very loose; it lacked a federal assembly to direct policy, and ultimately Latin colonies at Saticula, Beneventum, and Aesernia enabled Rome to split it into its component cantons. In 354 B.C., owing to a Gallic scare, the Samnites signed a defensive alliance with Rome. But they soon recommenced expanding (Strabo 5. 249 f.), and their neighbours sought Roman protection. Samnite Wars inevitably resulted. The First (343–341), for control of Campania (q.v.), is generally but not quite convincingly reckoned apocryphal. The Second (328-[321, 315]–304), despite the Samnite success at the Caudine Forks (q.v.), prevented Samnite domination of Lucania and Apulia. The Third (298–290) involved, and decided the destiny of, all Central and Southern Italy. Samnium was depopulated by these wars but not completely subjugated; some cantons later supported Pyrrhus and Hannibal (Zonar. 8. 6; Livy 22. 61). Subsequently depopulation increased; pastoral pursuits gradually replaced agricultural and by 180 Samnium could accommodate transported Ligurians. The Samnites fought implacably in the Social War and against Sulla, who slaughtered all he could (Diod. 37. 2; Plut. *Sulla* 28 f.). The survivors were gradually romanized. Chief towns: Beneventum, Aeclanum, Abellinum (Hirpini), Caudium, Saticula (Caudini), Bovianum Vetus, Aufidena (Caraceni), Bovianum, Aesernia, Saepinum (Pentri). The Samnites taught the Romans to use maniple, *scutum,* and possibly *pilum.*

Ancient literature: Our principal source, Livy (bks. 8–10), depends on annalists more patriotic than trustworthy. The scanty information supplied by Diodorus (bks. 19, 20) and Polybius (2. 19 f.) is more reliable. Modern literature: F. E. Adcock, *CAH* vii. 581, with bibliography (for history); R. S. Conway, *Italic Dialects* i (1897), 180 (for language); A. Sambon, *Monnaies antiques de l'Italie* i (1903), 103 (for coins); F. Weege, *JDAI* (1909), 98, 141 (for material civilization); S. Weinstock, *Klio* xxiv (1931), 235 (for constitution).
E. T. S.

SAMOS, an island off western Asia Minor, colonized by Ionians *c.* 1100–1000 B.C. It long preserved a distinctive dialect. Samians settled in Amorgos *c.* 690 B.C., at Perinthos (601), Bisanthe, and Heraion Teichos in Thrace, at Naucratis, at Oasis in Libya, in Cilicia, and perhaps at Dicaearchia (Puteoli), and *c.* 490 at Zancle (Messana). Colaeus of Samos made a famous voyage to Tartessus *c.* 620; Ameinocles of Corinth had built warships for the Samians *c.* 704, Samian ships helped Sparta in the Second Messenian War. The rich landed class (γεωμόροι) continued influential till late in the fifth century (hence the oligarchic reactions in Samian history), but trade and industry flourished, especially in metal-work and woollen products. Sixth-century Samos was the home of notable architects, sculptors, and gem engravers (Rhoecus, Theodorus, Mnesicles), of moralists and poets (Aesop, Ibycus, Anacreon). A Samian engineer, Mandrocles, bridged the Bosporus for Darius. But the greatest of all Samians, Pythagoras, migrated to south Italy.

The consecutive history of Samos begins with the tyranny of Polycrates (q.v.), his steward Maeandrius, and his brother Syloson, the last a vassal of Darius. Samos joined the Ionian revolt, but her ships deserted at Lade (494). When the revolt was crushed the Persians allowed her a democratic government. She fought well for Xerxes at Salamis, but soon turned against the Persians and was an autonomous member of the Athenian Confederacy till her revolt in 441 which Pericles himself suppressed. During the oligarchic revolution of the 400 (411 B.C.) Samos was the stronghold of the democracy. For their loyal co-operation the Samians were made Athenian citizens after Aegospotami (405); but the city fell to Lysander in 404. About 394 she had a currency alliance with Ephesus, Cnidos, and Rhodes. In 365 Athens captured the island and planted Athenian cleruchs, who were expelled only after Alexander's death. She was eclipsed by Rhodes in the new Hellenistic world, in which her greatest achievement was to produce the astronomer Conon.

Herodotus; Thucydides; Xenophon, *Hellenica*; Polybius; Diodorus. E. Buschor, *Altsamische Standbilder* (1935); P. Gardner, *Samos and Samian Coins* (1882); *SIG* 10, 116, 117, 276, 312, 333.
P. N. U.

SAMOSATA (mod. *Samsât*), a fortified city on the right bank of the Euphrates; the residence of the kings of Commagene (q.v.). Like Zeugma, it guarded an important crossing of the river on one of the main caravan routes from East to West, and it was consequently of considerable strategic and commercial importance. Its formidable defences twice withstood a Roman siege, but in A.D. 72 it was forced to surrender, and it was garrisoned henceforth by a Roman legion. In 359 a Roman army was defeated here by the Persians; in 637 the city was finally captured by the Arabs. M. S. D.

SAMOTHRACE, an island of the north-east Aegean, consisting of a table-like mountain which rises to 5,250 ft., and containing but little cultivable land. Its Greek population was of Samian origin. It formed part of the two maritime confederacies of Athens; in the third century it frequently changed hands among the Hellenistic dynasts; under Roman rule it was a 'civitas libera'. Its chief importance lay in the mystery cult of its twin gods, the Cabiri (q.v.). This cult attained a wide vogue in the Hellenistic age, and its initiates included some Roman notables. The remains of the temple date back to the sixth century. M. C.

SANCHUNIATHON. Under this name Philon (q.v. 5) of Byblos appears to have published Φοινικικά, claiming pre-Trojan authority. In nine books the work, partly preserved in Eusebius, treated cosmogony, the rise of human society, theogony, and Phoenician cult-practice, in Euhemeristic and syncretistic fashion, using probably Hellenistic material based on Phoenician tradition.

O. Eissfeldt, *Ras Schamra und Sanchunjaton* (1939); *FHG* iii. 560 (*Philo Byblius*). A. H. McD.

SANDAS (Σάνδας, Σάνδης, Σάνδων), a god of Tarsus in Cilicia, perhaps of Luwian origin. At his festival a great pyre was erected and burned; the Greeks accordingly equated him with Heracles. Traces of his cult are found in Cappadocia, Lydia, and other nearby lands, but his real nature remains uncertain.

Philipp, *PW*, s.v. 'Sandon'; J. G. Frazer, *Adonis Attis Osiris*[1] (= *GB*[3] v), ch. 6. F. R. W.

SANDRACOTTUS (Chandragupta), the Maurya (perhaps a tribal name), founded the Mauryan empire. His origin is uncertain. After Alexander quitted India he overthrew the Nanda king of Magadha on the Ganges, the principal Indian kingdom (Greek Prasii), and took the crown; an Indian drama made Parvataka, supposed to be Porus, his helper. Subsequently he subdued all India north of the Nerbudda and the Vindhya mountains and east of the Indus; the two dates for his accession, 321 B.C. in Ceylonese and 313 (312) in Jain tradition, should refer respectively to the conquest of Magadha and the establishment of his empire. About 305 Seleucus attacked him. What happened is unknown, but a treaty was made by which Seleucus ceded to him Gandhāra and the Indian portions of Arachosia and Gedrosia, and gave him a daughter or niece, possibly for his son Bindusāra, receiving in return a large force of elephants and the lasting friendship of the dynasty. Chandragupta's empire, a complex of vassal kings and peoples, was described

for Greeks by Megasthenes (q.v.), Seleucus' ambassador at his court; he ruled it from Pātaliputra, with viceroys at Taxila and Ujjain. Traditionally he reigned twenty-four years; his personality is unknown.

F. W. Thomas, *Cambridge History of India* i, ch. 18. W. W. T.

SANNYRION, Athenian comic writer. Fragments of three mythological burlesques survive: Γέλως, Δανάη, and 'Ιώ. Δανάη may be dated after 408 B.C., as fr. 8 refers to the actor Hegelochus' famous mispronunciation γαλῆν ὁρῶ for γαλήν' ὁρῶ in Eur. *Or.* 279 (produced 408; cf. Ar. *Ran.* 304).

FCG ii. 873 ff.; *CAF* i. 793–5; Demiańczuk, *Suppl. Com.* 83. M. P.

SANTRA, a scholar of the Ciceronian age who wrote a *De antiquitate verborum* in at least three books (now lost). He also interested himself in questions of literary history.

Cf. Teuffel, § 211. 2; Schanz–Hosius, § 196. 1; G. Funaioli, *Gramm. Rom. Frag.* 384–9.

SAPPHO, poetess, daughter of Scamandronymus and Cleis, of Eresus and Mytilene in Lesbos, born *c.* 612 B.C. (Suidas s.v. Σαπφώ). As a child, no doubt owing to political troubles, she went into exile in Sicily (*Marm. Par.* 36), though apart from a passing reference to Panormus (fr. 7) no traces of this are left in her fragments. She returned to Mytilene, where she was the centre of some kind of θίασος which honoured Aphrodite and the Muses and had young girls for its members. With these she lived in great intimacy and affection, wrote poems about them, and celebrated their marriages with songs. She married Cercylas and had a child Cleis (Suidas l.c., cf. fr. 152 and *Philol.* 1939, 277–86). Her brother Charaxus angered her by his love for the courtesan Rhodopis or Doricha, whom Sappho is said to have rated (Hdt. 2. 135, Strab. 17. 808, cf. fr. 26). Little else is known of her life, and nothing of her death, since the old story that she threw herself over a cliff in love for Phaon (Ovid, *Ep. Sapph.*, passim) seems to be an invention of the New Comedy. Her work was collected in seven books. Book 1 contained poems in the Sapphic stanza and included an address to Aphrodite (fr. 1), which may have been written as a hymn for her companions, but seems to be strictly personal to herself, a poem to an unnamed girl, which was probably inspired by seeing her next to her bridegroom and shows the strength of Sappho's feelings for her (fr. 2), a poem wishing her brother a fair voyage home and offering forgiveness for his faults (fr. 25), lines on the beauty of Anactoria (fr. 27), and an invocation to Aphrodite to appear at a festival in the country (frs. 5–6). Book 2 contained poems in the Aeolic dactylic pentameter, such as lines of great feeling and intimacy to Cleis (frs. 40–1), and closed with a narrative poem on the wedding of Hector and Andromache, in which the presence of two Attic forms has raised grave doubts about its authenticity. Book 3 contained poems in the greater asclepiad, including lines of contempt to an uneducated woman (fr. 58) in which the theme that song confers immortality appears explicitly for the first time. Book 4 contained poems in ionic tetrameters mostly too fragmentary to be intelligible, though fr. 65 A seems to have told the story of Tithonus. Book 5 contained poems composed in stanzas of mixed character, especially fr. 98, on a girl who has gone to Lydia and is compared to the moon outshining the stars, and fr. 96, which gives a retrospect of happy days passed with another girl. Of bk. 6 nothing much survives except lines on a girl who is prevented by love from attending to her weaving (fr. 114)—a theme of folk-song. Book 7 probably contained wedding-songs of different character in different metres. In the hexameter fragments a bride is compared to an apple (fr. 116) and to a hyacinth (fr. 117). Fr. 131 gives a dialogue between the Bride and her Maidenhood, another traditional theme. In this book

Sappho was more colloquial than usual and showed an element of badinage (Demetr. *Eloc.* 167, cf. fr. 124). Something of her manner may perhaps be seen from Catullus' imitations of her in his poems 61 and 62. Sappho writes in the vernacular language of Lesbos, except in a small group of poems (frs. 55, 116-19) in which she admits some variations taken from the epic. Her subjects are usually personal; there are few traces of narrative, though some poems (frs. 114, 149) seem to be modelled on folk-songs. She wrote for herself and her friends, gave candid accounts of her and their feelings, had an excellent eye and ear for natural things, a command of verbal melody, and an unequalled directness and power.

TEXT: E. Diehl, *Anth. Lyr. Graec.* i. 4, pp. 3–85: E. Lobel, Σαπφοῦς μέλη (1925).

CRITICISM: U. von Wilamowitz-Moellendorff, *Sappho und Simonides* (1913), 17–101; G. Perrotta, *Saffo e Pindaro* (1936), 3–101; C. M. Bowra, *Greek Lyric Poetry* (1936), 186–247. C. M. B.

SARAPIS (usually in Latin **Serapis**), according to Tacitus (*Hist.* 4. 81) and Plutarch (*Mor.* 361 f–362 e), was brought to Egypt from Sinope by Ptolemy I. There is another tradition that places Sarapis in Babylon in the time of Alexander, and Tacitus reports that Sarapis was believed by some people to have come from Seleuceia in Syria, while others thought he came from Memphis. It now seems to have been established that the cult of Sarapis arose at Memphis in the temple above the underground chambers where the bodies of the deceased Apis bulls were entombed, and the projection of all these figures came to be addressed as Osorapis. The probability remains that the king established the worship in Alexandria and sought to make Sarapis an imperial deity. There is some evidence to show that the cult, along with that of Isis, was accepted and propagated by Greeks and Macedonians in the royal civil and military services. The cult of Sarapis did not grow rapidly at Alexandria, however. Although Isis and Sarapis were included in the royal oath by the end of the third century, they do not appear in the oath used in Alexandria. The creation of the cult was marked by the introduction of the worship into Alexandria and, according to tradition, was accomplished through the assistance of Demetrius of Phaleron, the Eumolpid Timotheus, and Manetho. In fact, Demetrius seems to have given the earliest testimony concerning the miraculous powers of Sarapis, since, in his *Paeans*, he is supposed to have shown his gratitude to the god for having restored his sight. The Sarapeum at Alexandria, accounted one of the wonders of the world, was said to have been designed by Parmeniscus, while the cult-statue, a great sitting figure adorned with precious metals, was attributed to Bryaxis. The tradition is consistently uniform that those who had a hand in shaping the external features of the cult were men of Greek speech and culture. Manetho, an Egyptian priest who assisted in the formation of the cult, had some familiarity with Hellenic culture, since he wrote in Greek. It is not surprising that this deity combined the attributes of many potent Hellenic gods with some of the characteristics of Osiris. He was represented with the benign and bearded countenance of Zeus, his head crowned with a modius (emblem of fertility). At the right knee of the seated god was the three-headed dog Cerberus, an attribute borrowed from Hades, while the upraised left hand grasped a staff or sceptre, reminiscent of Zeus and Asclepius. Sarapis was a healer of the sick, a worker of miracles, a deity who was superior to fate and who retained from Osiris the character of a god of the underworld. He spoke to his followers in dreams as Asclepius did, yet partook of their festive banquets as a jovial lord of Olympus might have done. He was identified at times not only with the gods already mentioned, but also with Dionysus, Helios, Jupiter, and others. He was associated with Dolichenus and other powerful deities. At Memphis, as well as at Abydos and elsewhere, we know of people called *katochoi* who seem to have considered themselves bound to the temple precincts until the god should set them free. Except when identified with another god, Sarapis seldom receives an epithet. Yet, in one inscription, a man with an Alexandrian deme name calls Sarapis the god of the city and addresses him as Sarapis Polieus. Sarapis was the chief god in the cult of the Egyptian deities. His cult usually went with that of Isis and Harpocrates, Anubis and others being included on occasion. In the Aegean area we find that most of the public cults of the Egyptian deities were called cults of Sarapis, even though other deities were included. In many Greek cities there were cult societies of *Sarapiastai* who held banquets on certain days, passed decrees, voted crowns to officials of the society and to distinguished strangers, and who set up *stelae* recording thereon their official acts. In the period of the Roman Empire, when the mysteries of Isis were quite widespread throughout the Mediterranean world, the worship of Isis tended to eclipse that of Sarapis. Since the worship of both these gods was spread by commercial contacts as well as by zealots, the cults were strong in those cities which had commercial connexions with the East. The acclamation 'There is one Zeus Sarapis', a cry of enthusiasm for the deity, has come down to us in numerous inscriptions.

BIBLIOGRAPHY

ANCIENT SOURCES. Th. Hopfner, *Fontes Historiae Religionis Aegyptiacae* (1922–5), contains the literary sources. The inscriptions are scattered through *IG, CIL, CIG,* and *Sammelbuch griechischer Urkunden aus Ägypten* (Preisigke). The Delian inscriptions are collected in P. Roussel, *Les Cultes égyptiens à Délos* (1916), and in *Inscriptions de Délos.* Papyri documents may be found in U. Wilcken, *Urkunden der Ptolemäerzeit* i (1922–7), and in *PCairo Zen., PTeb., POxy.,* and elsewhere. Other sources are collected in O. Weinreich, *Neue Urkunden zur Sarapis-Religion* (1919). Statuary: H. Haas, *Bilderatlas zur Religionsgeschichte,* 9–11 Lief. (1926).

MODERN LITERATURE. The classic discussion of the origin of Sarapis is found in part 1 of U. Wilcken, *Urkunden der Ptolemäerzeit* (1922–7). Other works are: F. Cumont, *Les Religions orientales dans le paganisme romain* (1929); G. Lafaye, *Histoire du culte des divinités d'Alexandrie* (1884); A. D. Nock, *Conversion* (1933); A. Rusch, *De Serapide et Iside in Graecia Cultis* (1906); J. Toutain, *Les Cultes païens dans l'empire romain* (1907–); O. Weinreich, *Neue Urkunden zur Sarapis-Religion* (1919). T. A. B.

SARCOPHAGI. While plain coffins of stone, clay, wood, or lead were usual in Classical Greece, more elaborate forms appear to have been mainly produced, under Oriental influence, for export. The sculptured tombs of south-west Asia Minor may have suggested the movable decorated sarcophagus. The usual Greek type had architectural decoration based on the Greek temple; other types in stone were: the Egyptianizing anthropoid coffin, limited to Cyprus and Phoenicia (5th–4th cc. B.C.); the chest with a recumbent figure on the lid, found in Carthage and Etruria; the banqueting-couch with reclining figures on the lid, favoured in Etruria; and the altar, the earliest to be used in Rome. These types were fully developed by early Hellenistic times; later, simpler forms are found, with decoration limited to garlands. With the increasing use of inhumation over the Roman Empire in the second century, there was a revival which lasted into Christian times; the earlier sculptured types reappeared and there was a new form, the basin (ληνός).

The most important sarcophagi in clay are the painted series from Asia Minor (6th–5th cc. B.C.), and the examples of the banquet class from Etruria. Wooden sarcophagi have only survived exceptionally (e.g. in the Crimea), while the most important specimens in lead come from Roman Syria.

W. Altmann, *Architectur und Ornamentik der antiken Sarkophage* (1902); C. Robert, *Die antiken Sarkophagreliefs* (1890–); C. R. Morey, *Sardis,* vol. v, pt. 1 (U.S.A. 1924). On painted sarcophagi see E. Pfuhl, *Malerei und Zeichnung der Griechen* (1923), i, § 101. F. N. P.

SARDES (Σάρδεις), the chief city of Lydia, lying under a fortified hill in the Hermus valley, near the junction of the roads from Ephesus, Smyrna, Pergamum, and inner Asia Minor. As the capital of the Lydian kingdom, especially under Croesus, and later as the headquarters of the principal Persian satrapy, it was the political centre of Asia Minor in the pre-Hellenistic period, and it also attained fame for its progress in the arts and crafts— it was the first city to mint gold and silver coins. It was captured and burnt by the Ionians in B.C. 499, and Xerxes mustered his troops at Sardes before he crossed the Hellespont. In the Macedonian period it belonged in succession to Antigonus, the Seleucids, and the Attalids, and in 133 B.C. it passed to the Romans, who made it the capital of a *conventus* in the province Asia. It was one of the 'Seven Churches' of the Apocalypse. Diocletian made it capital of the province Lydia. Its temple of Artemis has been excavated; among the most important finds were a number of inscriptions in the Lydian language.

H. C. Butler, *Sardis* (1922 ff.).   W. M. C.

SARDINIA (Σαρδώ), a large island off western Italy containing *nuraghi* and other megalithic monuments of its prehistoric inhabitants (traditionally a mixture of Libyans, Iberians, and Ligurians). It is more fertile, less mountainous, and much more unhealthy than Corsica. The Greeks apparently never colonized Sardinia. Carthage annexed it (*c.* 500 B.C.), but failed to pacify the rugged interior. Rome seized the island from Carthage in 238 B.C. (reject Diod. 15. 27) and organized it, with Corsica, as a province in 227 (Corsica became a separate province in Imperial times). The Romans despised the Sardinians ('Sardi uenales: alius alio nequior': Festus, p. 428 L.) and in Republican times allowed them not one free city; Sardinia was treated as conquered land that sent money and grain to Rome (it remained an important granary throughout antiquity). The frequent Sardinian revolts ceased in 114 B.C., but brigandage continued. This was gradually suppressed under the Empire (Tac. *Ann.* 2. 85) and Sardinia achieved a little prosperity: Carales obtained Roman civic rights; Turris Libisonis, Uselis, and Cornus became *coloniae*; and the silver- and iron-mines were worked. But the island never really flourished. Finally it fell successively to Vandals, Goths, Byzantine emperors, and Saracens.

Ancient writers mention Sardinia infrequently. The important references are: Strabo 5. 223 f.; Pliny, *HN* 3. 83 f.; Paus. 10. 17. 2 f.; Diod. 4. 29 f., 5. 15; Justin, bks. 18 and 19; Cic. *Pro Scauro*; Livy, bks. 21–30. Modern literature: E. S. Bouchier, *Sardinia in Ancient Times* (1917); E. Pais, *Storia della Sardegna e della Corsica* (1923); T. Ashby, *CAH* ii. 581; C. Bellieni, *La Sardegna e i Sardi* (1931); A. Taramelli, *Bibliografia romano-sarda* (1939).   E. T. S.

SARDUS, a prose writer whose style so charmed Pliny that he read and re-read him (*Ep.* 9. 31).

SARIS(S)A (σάρισα), see ARMS AND ARMOUR, GREEK.

SARMATAE (Σαρμάται, Σαυρομάται), a nomad tribe, closely related to the Scythians, and speaking a similar Indo-European language, but showing some points of difference in culture. Their women had a freer position, and, in the days of Herodotus at least, hunted and fought alongside the men (4. 116–17). Their troops were all mounted, but while the rank and file were archers, the chieftains and their retainers wore armour and used heavy lances. Until *c.* 250 B.C. the Sarmatae dwelt east of the river Tanais. During the next 300 years they moved slowly westwards, displacing the Scythians. Of their two main branches, the Roxolani advanced to the Danube estuary, the Iazyges crossed the Carpathians and occupied the plain between the middle Danube and the Theiss. The Roxolani, checked by the generals of Augustus and Nero, became clients of Rome; and the

Iazyges entered into similar relations, serving as a buffer between the Dacians and the province of Pannonia. In the second and third centuries the Sarmatae were again set moving by the pressure of German tribes. The Iazyges allied with the Marcomanni against M. Aurelius, and the Roxolani shared the Gothic raids into Moesia. Eventually large numbers of them were settled within Roman territory by Constantine; the rest were partly absorbed by their German neighbours, partly driven back into the Caucasus.

M. Rostovtzeff, *CAH* xi. 91–104.   M. C.

SARPEDON, in mythology, commander of the Lycian contingent of Priam's allies (*Iliad* 2. 876). He takes a prominent part in the fighting, leading an assaulting column of the allies on the Greek wall (12. 101), and making the first breach (290 ff.). He is finally killed by Patroclus (16. 426 ff.), mourned by his father Zeus (459 ff.), and carried off to Lycia for burial by Sleep and Death (666 ff.).

Post-Homeric accounts make him one of the sons of Zeus and Europa, the difference in mythological dating being got over by supposing that he lived for three generations (Apollod. 3. 6). Ancient critics had already noticed that his connexion with Crete was secondary, schol. *Il.* 6. 199, which makes the difference of time six generations. It is possible that some historical relationship between the two countries lies behind it. At all events, there was an historical cult of him in Lycia, with which the Homeric story of his burial is presumably to be connected; his hero-shrine is mentioned, for instance, by schol. *Il.* 16. 673. The rather wide distribution of place-names formed from his (see Immisch in Roscher's *Lexikon* iv. 393 ff.) suggests that his worship is old and famous, which may well have drawn Homer's attention to him.

H. J. R.

SASANIDS, *see* SASSANIDS.

SASERNA, a cognomen of the gens Hostilia. Two Sasernae, father and son, wrote on husbandry about the beginning of first century B.C. and were used by Varro, Pliny (*HN*), and Columella.

Teuffel, § 160; Schanz–Hosius i⁴ (1927), 242.

SASSANIDS, kings of the New Persian Empire A.D. 224–636. The dynasty derived its name from Sāsān, grandfather of Artaxerxes I (q.v.), who took over the inheritance of the Achaemenids and Arsacids. Their empire at its greatest extent stretched from Syria to India and from Iberia to the Persian Gulf. The Sassanids constantly sought to drive the Romans from Asia; and the forts of the Euphrates *limes* were fortified against attacks from them. Major campaigns were undertaken against them by various Roman emperors. Valerian was defeated and captured by Sapor I, Constantius defeated Sapor II in 345, Julian died on an invasion of Mesopotamia, Kavadh was defeated by Belisarius; Khosroes II conquered Asia Minor and even threatened Constantinople, but was driven back by Heraclius. On their north-east boundary the Sassanids were menaced by the Hephthalites ('White Huns') and Turks. They were driven from Mesopotamia by the Arabs (A.D. 636), but lingered on as a local dynasty in Iran.

The strongly centralized despotic government of the Sassanid Empire was upheld by the powerful priesthood of the Mazdaean State religion.

SOURCES: (1) Classical: Ammianus Marcellinus; Zosimus; Procopius, *Persica*; Agathias (based on the official records at Ctesiphon). (2) Oriental: various Pehlevi works and numerous traditions are partially preserved in the Avesta and in the works of Firdausi and many other Arab and Persian writers (T. Nöldeke, *Tabari*, 1879). (3) Numismatic: E. Herzfeld, *Kushano-Sasanian Coins*, Mem. Arch. Survey of India, no. 38 (1930); F. D. I. Paruck, *Sāsānian Coins* (Bombay, 1924).

MODERN WORKS: J. B. Bury, *History of the Later Roman Empire* ~ A. Christensen, *L'Empire des Sassanides* (1907), *L'Iran sous* ~(1936), *CAH* xii, ch. 4; K. Güterbock, *Byzanz und* Nöldeke, *Geschichte der Perser und Araber zur* ~ *Das national-iranische Epos* (1896-1904); ~ *Oriental Monarchy* (1876); *PW*, articles
M. S. D.

~trapavan), the title held by Persian ~ governors. The satrap was in effect a vassal ~, with wide powers within his own province (Xen. *Oec.* 4. 5), but owing allegiance to the Great King. Certain military and civil officials, responsible only to the latter, acted as checks on his autonomy. The political organization of the Persian Empire into satrapies, at first based on the boundaries of the conquered nations, was revised by Darius; his division into twenty satrapies (Hdt. 3. 89-94), though modified by subsequent territorial conquests and losses, remained the basis for later kings; Alexander preserved the satrapal system and it was continued by the Parthians. The Sassanids (q.v.) had local governors who partly corresponded in function to the old satraps.

H. Berve, *Das Alexanderreich* i (1926); A. Christensen, *Die Iranier* (1936); E. Meyer, *Geschichte des Altertums* iii. 3 (1937); *PW*, s.v. 'Satrap' (Lehmann–Haupt). M. S. D.

SATURA, satire, the only literary form created by Rome, was so free and personal that its character changed with each satirist. Still, it may be broadly defined as a piece of verse, or prose mingled with verse, intended to improve society by mocking its anomalies, and marked by spontaneity, topicality, ironic wit, indecent humour, colloquial language, frequent use of dialogue, constant intrusions of the author's personality, and incessant variety of tone and style.

2. NAME. *Satura*, from *satur*, 'full', means 'a medley' full of different things. A mixed stuffing was called *satura* too, and the legal formula *per saturam* meant 'en bloc' ('in a mixture'). Since variety was fundamental to satire, the Romans accepted this derivation: Livy alludes to it in his description of primitive satire. A plausible modern suggestion is the Etruscan *satir*, 'speech'; for satire had a distantly Etruscan origin, and was essentially speech.

3. ORIGINS. *Rome*. Livy (7. 2, probably quoting Varro) says that in 364 B.C. Etruscan dancers performed the first ballet ever seen in Rome. Hitherto the nearest approach to drama (q.v., para. 1) had been improvised dialogues in Fescennine verse; now amateurs, copying the dancers, added rhythmical miming to these improvisations. Finally, professional actors 'performed satires full of different rhythms', in which words, music, and miming all harmonized. So the original *satura* was a disjointed series of action-songs and musical sketches without a plot. Its variety, humour, spontaneity, love of dialogue, and mimic realism are traceable throughout later literary satire.

4. *Greece*. Quintilian (10. 1. 93), comparing Greek and Roman literature, remarks 'satura tota nostra est'. This is usually translated 'satire is a wholly Roman invention', but probably means 'we are supreme throughout satire' (Rennie, *CR*, 1922). Actually, many Greek influences, which Quintilian must have known, affected Roman satire.

5. First was the Hellenistic street-sermon, as delivered by travelling Cynic and Stoic preachers like Bion (fl. 250 B.C.). Upon ethical themes these men improvised amusing stump-speeches, full of philosophical propaganda made palatable by epigrams, fables, shocking colloquialisms, obscene jokes, vivid character-sketches, parodies of poetry, and dialogues with imaginary opponents. These informal talks were called διατριβαί, 'leisure hours'. Both Lucilius and Horace (cf. *Epist.* 2. 2. 60) similarly call their satires *sermones*. From the diatribe Roman satirists borrowed both the principle called σπουδογέλοιον, 'joking in earnest', and the devices

by which it held its audience; the same influence somewhat guided their choice of subjects.

6. Another powerful influence was Athenian Old Comedy, on which Horace (*Sat.* 1. 4. 6) says 'Lucilius entirely depends'. He means that Lucilius did for Roman satire what 'Eupolis atque Cratinus Aristophanesque poetae' did for Attic comedy, by making its bold imaginative humour carry serious criticism of contemporary society. Few close imitations of Aristophanes appear in Lucilius or his successors; but Lucilius' strong, harsh wit, his love for topical themes, his fearless persecution of prominent persons, and his passionate interest in social and political problems, while doubtless rooted in his character, gained conviction from the example of the great comedians.

7. A third, less potent influence was philosophical satire. From the Cynic Menippus (*fl. c.* 250) Varro borrowed the technique of interweaving prose with fragments of verse. The philosophical Dunciad called Σίλλοι, *Squints*, in mock-heroic verse, by the Sceptic Timon (*c.* 315-226), possibly guided Lucilius in preferring hexameters to invective iambics. But the Greek satirists were chiefly interested, not in improving society, but in scolding rival philosophers; this limited their influence on Roman satire.

8. DEVELOPMENT. *Ennius* (239-169 B.C.) was the first to write a poetic medley modelled on the stage *satura*. His satires are known to have contained (1) a debate between Life and Death, (2) Aesop's fable of the lark, (3) a parasite's monologue on his profession; and they were in varying metres. Thus, he emphasized (*a*) the variety of satire, (*b*) its moral intention, (*c*) its love of speech, (*d*) its use of devices borrowed from the diatribe —fable, character-sketch, personification. But his work was less directly critical than that of later satirists.

9. After him satire split into two branches: Lucilian, in hexameter verse; Varronian, in prose and verse intermingled. Horace (*Sat.* 1. 10. 66) called Ennius the *auctor* of satire, because he originated it; and *Lucilius* (180-102) its *inventor*, because he realized its true nature. Lucilius' great innovations were four. He made verse-satire a weapon of attack on the follies and vices of society, naming the fools and knaves he attacked. He fixed on the hexameter as its medium. He wrote chiefly on topical, personal subjects. And it was he who made the language of satire unliterary, colloquial, even coarse.

10. The Menippean satires of *Varro* (116-27) blended prose with all kinds of verse, and even Greek with Latin. Varro was chiefly interested in the application of philosophy to life. Realistic but whimsical, energetic but eccentric, his work lacked the bite of Lucilius' poems and had few imitators.

11. If Lucilius is the wasp and Varro the bee, *Horace* (65-8 B.C.) is the dragon-fly of satire, ornamental but stingless. Although a professed follower of Lucilius, he seldom 'broke his grinders on Lupus and Mucius' (Pers. 1. 115), but exposed mild folly (Hor. *Sat.* 2. 8) and oddities like social climbers (1. 9) and witches (1. 8). Never quite at home in satire, he eventually turned to the milder form of the poetic epistle. *The Pumpkinification of Claudius, Seneca*'s (4 B.C.-A.D. 65) gibe at the lately deified emperor, is in Varro's manner with a new infusion of venom.

12. *Persius* (A.D. 34-62) left six satires strongly tinged with Stoicism. They have the compression of Horace and the coarseness of Lucilius, but their contorted thought and allusive style prevent them from attaining the directness and energy of true satire.

13. *Petronius* (d. 66), the Brummell of Nero's court, produced a brilliant parody of Greek romance in a long Menippean satire describing the adventures of three rascally Greeklings. The largest fragment is the masterly *Banquet of Trimalchio*, where the dialogue-element of satire appears at its finest; the book also contains some remarkable folk-lore and many striking poems. The one element of satire which it lacks is moral intention—elegant, efficient, debauched, it reflects the character of its author.

14. Under the Principate it became dangerous to inveigh directly against the great. Therefore, although satire is essentially topical, satirists turned to attacking dead, symbolic, or insignificant people. Horace used many type-names from Lucilius; Persius, from Lucilius and Horace. *Juvenal* (c. 50–127) deliberately writes of the dead. When he mentions contemporaries, they are symbols or nonentities. Yet his fierce gloomy poems bear the imprint of life; he describes vice with the fascinated disgust of Swift. Despite his colloquial vocabulary, his tone is more rhetorical than conversational.

15. The powerful and dignified invectives of *Claudian* (c. 390) against court enemies are really panegyrics inverted, not true satires. Juvenal was the last genuine Roman satirist, and the Lucilian model, as strengthened and ennobled by him, inspired nearly all modern satirists.

BIBLIOGRAPHY

ANCIENT SOURCES: references collected in F. Marx's *Lucilii reliquiae* i (1904), pp. cxx–cxxv.
MODERN LITERATURE: (a) *General works*: A. Kiessling and R. Heinze, and P. Lejay, prefaces to their edns. of Hor. *Sermones*: W. Kroll, in *PW*, s.v. 'Satura'; J. Wight Duff, *Roman Satire* (1937).
(b) *Name*: A. Funck, *Arch. für latein. Lexikogr.* (1888), 33 ff.; F. Marx, op. cit. i, pp. ix–xvi; G. L. Hendrickson, *CPhil.* 1911; F. Muller, *Philol.* 1923; P. Meriggi, *Studi Etruschi* (1937).
(c) *Roman origins*: H. Nettleship, *Lect. and Essays*, 2nd ser. (1895); B. L. Ullman, *Stud. in Philol.* (U.S.A. 1920), reviewing the controversy; G. L. Hendrickson, *CPhil.* 1927; P. Boyancé, *Rev. Ét. Anc.* 1932.
(d) *Greek origins*: (i) *Diatribe*: O. Hense, *Teletis reliquiae* (1909), on Bion; A. Oltramare, *Origines de la diatribe rom.* (1926); N. Terzaghi, *Per la storia della sat.* (1932). (ii) *Greek satire*: C. Wachsmuth, *Corpusculum poesis epicae Gr. ludibundae* ii (1885); J. Geffcken, *Neue Jahrb.* 1911; G. C. Fiske, *Lucilius and Horace* (U.S.A. 1920); O. Immisch, *Neue Jahrb.* 1921.
(e) *Development*: T. Birt, *Zwei politische Satiren d. alt. Rom.* (1888); A. Kusch, *De saturae Rom. hexametro* (1915); A. H. Weston, *Latin satiric writing after Juvenal* (U.S.A. 1915).   G. H.

SATURNIAN METRE, a type of early Latin verse used, e.g., by Livius Andronicus (*Odyssia*; e.g. 'uirum mihi Camena / insece uersutum'), by Naevius (*Bellum Punicum*; e.g. 'nouem Iouis concordes / filiae sorores'), in inscriptions (e.g. Scipionic epitaphs), and presumably in the *versus Fescennini* (q.v.). About 160 indubitable examples are extant; few, if any, can be called primitive; the most frequently quoted is: 'dabunt malum Metelli / Naeuio poetae.' Ennius (*Ann.* 214 Vahl.) despised the metre; to Horace (*Epist.* 2. 1. 157) it was 'horridus', to Virgil (*G.* 2. 386) 'incomptus'. Roman grammarians (e.g. Caesius Bassus) in bewilderment tried to equate its many metamorphoses with various Greek metres; but Servius (ad Verg. *G.* 2. 385) speaks of it as composed 'ad rhythmum solum'. Modern scholars agree that each line falls into two parts; otherwise controversy reigns. Purely quantitative interpretations (e.g. L. Müller, F. Leo, C. Zander), despite the aid of elision, hiatus, synizesis, metrical lengthening, and emendation, are all unsatisfactory. The 'accentual' theory (e.g. O. Keller) which disregards quantity and imposes on Saturnians the rhythm of 'The queen was in her parlour / eating bread and honey' involves incredibly artificial accentuations (e.g. 'dédet Tempéstátébus'). W. M. Lindsay's view is that three ordinary word-accents in the first part of the line (normally of 7 syllables) and two in the second part (normally of 6 syllables) function as metrical stresses. Saturnians can, indeed, be so read; but most readers would unconsciously introduce a third (non-accentual) stress into the second part. W. J. W. Koster regards the metre as a double 'tripudium' (cf. 'enos Lases iuuate' in hymn of Fratres Arvales) which later came under the influence of Greek ideas of quantity. Mere syllable-counting, the structural use of word-accents at roughly

equal intervals, and quantitative schemes may all have played a part in the evolution of the Saturnian; but from our meagre remains we cannot confidently define its original nature or trace its history.

See Teuffel, § 62; Schanz–Hosius i, § 6; W. M. Lindsay in *AJPhil.* 1893, 139–70, 305–34; F. Leo, *Der saturnische Vers* (1905); C. Zander, *Versus Saturnii* (1918); W. J. W. Koster in *Mnemos.* 1929, 267–346; O. J. Todd, 'Servius on the Saturnian Metre', *CQ* 1940, 133–45.   J. F. M.

SATURNINUS (1), LUCIUS APPULEIUS, tribune in 103 and 100 B.C. and a revolutionary democrat. He was father of Appuleia, wife of Lepidus (q.v. 2, cos. 78). His career is known only from hostile sources, which represent him as a powerful but unprincipled demagogue, with no statesmanlike aims. As quaestor serving at Ostia he was embittered when the Senate transferred his duties to M. Scaurus, the Princeps Senatus. His laws in 103 included one giving land in Africa to Marius' veterans, a *lex de maiestate* establishing a new *quaestio perpetua*, and probably a *lex frumentaria*. In 102 Metellus Numidicus, as censor, tried to exclude Saturninus and Glaucia from the Senate, while in 101 Saturninus was arraigned for insulting an embassy from Mithridates. In 100 he proposed measures for founding colonies overseas in Sicily, Greece, and Macedonia and for settling veterans on allotments in Gaul (Cisalpine, or possibly Transalpine). When he attached a clause which imposed an oath of obedience Metellus went into exile rather than take the required oath. Saturninus pressed these laws in spite of tribunician vetoes and secured his own election to a third tribunate. There was also much violence at the consular elections for 99: Glaucia, though praetor in 100, was a candidate, and his rival Memmius was murdered. The *Equites*, whose alliance with the extreme democrats had been largely responsible for the earlier successes of Saturninus and Glaucia, took fright, and when the Senate's *ultimum decretum* was passed, Marius attacked his former ally Saturninus, who surrendered, on promise of trial, but was murdered by a body of *Equites*. His career marks the extreme application (following Gracchan ideas) of Greek principles and methods to Roman politics; some survived (e.g. Caesar used the *exsecratio* in 59). To Saturninus' years of power belong Rome's most serious effort (before the *Lex Gabinia*) to suppress piracy (q.v.).

E. Klebs, *PW* ii. 261; H. Last, *CAH* ix. 164–72.   M. H.

SATURNINUS (2), GAIUS SENTIUS (*cos.* 19 B.C.), of a Pompeian family, related to that Scribonia who married Octavian in 40 (*ILS* 8892). Consul in 19, without colleague for the greater part of the year, he dealt firmly with electoral disorders, refusing to admit the candidature of Egnatius Rufus (q.v.) and thwarting his alleged conspiracy. Proconsul of Africa (c. 14); legate of Syria (c. 9–6), Sentius next appears as legate under Tiberius in Germany (A.D. 4–5); in A.D. 6 he led the army of the Rhine eastwards to participate in the campaign against Maroboduus. Velleius praises warmly this useful public servant and friend of Tiberius—'uirum multiplicem in uirtutibus, nauum, agilem prouidum', etc. (2. 105. 1).   R. S.

SATURNINUS (3), LUCIUS ANTONIUS, governor of Upper Germany, proclaimed himself emperor at Moguntiacum (probably 1 Jan., A.D. 89). On receipt of the news Domitian left Rome and marched northwards. In the meantime, however, the governor of Lower Germany, Lappius Maximus, who remained loyal, defeated and killed Saturninus in a battle fought beside the Rhine (perhaps near Coblenz). It is stated that German allies of the usurper were unable to cross the Rhine to his assistance because of a sudden thaw (Suetonius, *Dom.* 6 f.; Dio 67. 11; Martial 4. 11; 9. 84; *CIL* vi. 2066 (*Acta fratrum arvalium*)).   R. S.

manner. The ancients themselves supposed that he was not a native god, but imported from Greece, a story which blends with the flight of Kronos from Zeus, as in Verg. *Aen.* 8. 319 ff. His name seems to find its nearest parallels in Etruria (F. Altheim, *Griechische Götter*, pp. 8, 178), both as to stem (if we reject the connexion with *satus*) and suffix. It is therefore by no means impossible that he is a very old importation from Etruria, and conceivable that the Romans were right in identifying him with Kronos (q.v.).

His temple, the ruins of which are still conspicuous, stands on the clivus Capitolinus, and served as a treasury (*aerarium Saturni*), see Platner–Ashby, 463 ff. His cult-partner is the obscure goddess Lua, whose name seems connected with *lues*, an odd colleague for a god of sowing, but more intelligible if he really had something of the grim character of Kronos. See Gellius 13. 23. 2.

Of the early history of his festival nothing is known; Livy (22. 1. 20) speaks as if it originated in 217 B.C., which is obviously not so, see above. At most, some modification of the ritual, in the direction of hellenization, took place then. In historical times it was the merriest festival of the year, 'optimus dierum', Catullus 14. 15. Slaves were allowed temporary liberty to do as they liked, presents were exchanged, particularly wax candles and little pottery images or dolls, *sigillaria* (q.v.); Macrob. *Sat.* 1. 7. 18 ff., see Wissowa op. cit. 206, note 2 ff., for more references. There was also a sort of mock king, or Lord of Misrule, *Saturnalicius princeps* (Seneca, *Apocol.* 8. 2). By about the fourth century A.D. much of this was transferred to New-year's Day, and so became one of the elements of the traditional celebrations of Christmas (Nilsson in *ARW* xix. 52 ff.). The resemblance to the Kronia was noticed by the ancients (Accius in Macrob. *Sat.* 1. 7. 36–7); it may be pointed out that there is also a resemblance to the Sacaea (q.v.), though the evidence for killing or pretended killing of the mock king is of the weakest (Frazer, *GB* ii. 310 ff.). The connexion between these various festivals is as yet very obscure.

H. J. R.

SATYRS and **SILENI** are 'spirits of wild life in woods and hills' (H. J. Rose, *Handbook of Greek Mythol.*, 156), bestial in their desires and behaviour, and having details of animal nature, either of a horse or of a goat. Classical authors constantly confused Satyrs and Sileni, but from the fourth century B.C. on Sileni are usually old and retain horse-ears, while Satyrs are usually young (Paus. 1. 23. 5) and have taken over from Pan the traits of a goat. It seems that Satyrs and Sileni had a different origin, but we are ill informed about the early history of the Satyrs. Hesiod (ap. Strabo 471) makes them brothers of the Nymphs (q.v.) and calls them 'good-for-nothing and mischievous'. Apollodorus refers to one Arcadian Satyr who stole cattle and was killed by Argus (2. 1. 2), but clearly identifiable Satyrs first appear in satyr-plays, such

them. There may have been many stories on this pattern. On the François vase Silenus is captured by two wild men named Oreios and Therytas. The story that became famous is that of King Midas who caught Silenus after having made him drunk (Theopomp. *FHG* i, frs. 74–7). Ovid links this story with the punishment of Midas for his avarice (*Met.* 11. 90). In Virgil (*Ecl.* 6) Silenus is caught by two young shepherds and sings them mythological stories. About the middle of the sixth century B.C. Silenus (or Sileni, the plural being a matter of small importance in this lower layer of folk mythology) is drawn into the circle of Dionysus. He accompanies Dionysus in the triumphant return of Hephaestus (F. Brommer, *JDAI* 1937, 198), goes along to fight the giants, frolics in the thiasus, rides in the *carrus navalis*, makes music, and helps to make and drink wine. The behaviour of the Sileni is not always the best, and they are apt to attack even Hera or Iris (E. Haspels, *Attic Black-Figured Lekythoi* (1936), p. 20). When Pratinas introduced the satyr-play, the Sileni provided the distinctive costume but suffered a transformation into comic drunkards and cowards. The Silenus *par excellence* in these plays is the old Papposilenus, who has many weaknesses but also has intellectual talents. He is entrusted with the education of Dionysus, and even voices a proverbial philosophy in Pindar (schol. Ar. *Nub.* 223) and in the story of Midas. The comparison of Socrates with Silenus is based not only on common ugliness but also on common irony and wisdom. Portraits of Socrates and idealized heads of Sileni show great similarity (C. Weickert, *Festschrift J. Loeb* (1930), 103). Silenus is often represented as a good father and the Satyrs as his children. Hellenistic art depicts Silenus either as dignified, inspired, and musical, as the painting of the Villa dei Misteri (P. B. Mudie Cook, *JRS* 1913, 157), or as an old drunkard, as in many sculptural and decorative groups.

Kuhnert in Roscher, *Lex.*, s.v. 'Satyros'; F. Brommer, *Satyroi* (1937).
G. M. A. H.

SATYRUS (1) (*fl.* 3rd c. B.C.), Peripatetic biographer from Callatis Pontica, wrote mainly at Oxyrhynchus and Alexandria. Works: (1) Βίοι of famous men of all types, including Philip II, Sophocles, Demosthenes, Pythagoras, etc. Frs. in Diog. Laert. and Ath.; also four pages of the Βίος Εὐριπίδου, found at Oxyrhynchus. (2) Περὶ χαρακτήρων (Ath. 4. 168 e). Περὶ δήμων Ἀλεξανδρέων is by another Satyrus.

Satyrus widened the scope of biography to include all celebrities; he takes an uncritical delight in anecdotes and personalities. The Oxyrh. fragment (in dialogue form) reveals a careful and attractive style.

FHG iii. 159–66; A. S. Hunt, *POxy.* ix (1912), no. 1176.
F. W. W.

SATYRUS (2) (2nd c. B.C.) nicknamed *Zeta*, pupil of Aristarchus, was perhaps the author of a collection of ancient myths (*FGrH* i. 20).

SATYRUS (3) (*fl. c.* 150 B.C.), physician, pupil of Quintus (q.v. 1) of Rome, and teacher of Galen at Pergamum. He was a faithful follower of Quintus in the exegesis of Hippocrates and in the teaching of anatomy and pharmacology.

PW ii A. 235.

SAXA, *see* DECIDIUS SAXA.

SAXON SHORE (*Litus Saxonicum*), name given to the coastline in Gaul and Britain exposed to Saxon raids (or possibly settled by Saxon *laeti*).

(1) *Not. Dign. occ.* (xxxvii, xxxviii) mentions two ports, Grannona and Marcae, under local military *duces*: their sites are uncertain (Grenier, *Manuel* i. 389, 392).

(2) In Britain the *Notitia* (*occ.* xxviii) lists nine forts under a *Comes litoris Saxonici*, who appears in Ammianus' narrative of A.D. 367 (27. 8. 1). They seem to be grouped in pairs (? for naval organization). Actually ten forts are known from Brancaster (Norfolk) to Porchester (Hants), nine of which are certainly those of the *Notitia* list. Outliers are found in Lincolnshire and Wales. All but two have external bastions and all but two others have roughly rectangular ground-plans. The areas are 6–10 acres. The original idea may be due to Carausius (not later), but one fort, Anderida (Pevensey, Sussex), is later (*c.* 330).

F. J. Haverfield in *PW* ii A. 327–34; G. Macdonald in *25 jahre R-G Kommission*, 107–13; *JRS* xxii. 60–72; R. G. Collingwood, *Archaeology of Roman Britain* (1930), 48–53; J. Mothersole, *Saxon Shore* (1924; popular but sound). C. E. S.

SAXONS, a German tribe first mentioned by Ptolemy (2. 11. 7) as settled in the Cimbric Chersonese (modern *Holstein*). By *c.* A.D. 200 they seem to have displaced and subdued the Chauci of the lower Elbe; their distinctive pottery is found in Frisia and towards the lower Rhine, where from the fourth century they engaged in warfare with the Franks, while eastward they reached Swabia and Thuringia, and even penetrated into Italy (568). At sea they attracted the attention of ancient authors by their ruthless piracy (cf. Sid. Apoll. 8. 6. 13–15). Their raids were succeeded by permanent settlement. In Gaul documents and place-names show them established around Bayeux, near Boulogne, and in south-west Flanders; while in conjunction with their neighbours the Angli and the mysterious Jutes, they began towards the middle of the fifth century to establish themselves permanently in Britain. Saxon settlements were mainly in the south (Wessex, Essex, Middlesex, Sussex), but their name was applied by themselves and others indiscriminately to all the Teutonic invaders.

Full bibliographies in Collingwood-Myres, *Roman Britain*; R. H. Hodgkin, *History of the Anglo-Saxons*[2] (1939); see also L. Schmidt, *Gesch. der deutschen Stämme*[2] (1937). C. E. S.

SCABILLARII, *see* PANTOMIMUS.

SCAEVA (? SCAEV(I)US) MEMOR, *see* MEMOR.

SCAEVOLA (1), GAIUS MUCIUS, according to some authors originally bore the *cognomen* Cordus, which he subsequently changed for Scaevola. This was an amulet worn by Roman children, but popular etymology wrongly connected it with *scaeva*, the left hand; thence arose the story of the brave Roman who, having failed to kill Porsenna, showed his indifference to physical pain by holding his right hand in fire. The surmise that the legend merely is a misinterpretation of a monument, which represented a young man stretching his right hand over an altar, is improbable.

G. De Sanctis, *Per la scienza dell' antichità* (1909), 321 ff. P. T.

SCAEVOLA (2), PUBLIUS MUCIUS (*cos.* 133 B.C.), was the first of his family to win distinction as a jurist: a master of the *ius Pontificium*. He advised Tiberius Gracchus on the provisions of his land-law. As consul he refused to countenance the use of force against the Gracchans, though he later approved the force used by Scipio Nasica. He succeeded his brother Crassus Mucianus as Pontifex Maximus. M. H.

SCAEVOLA (3), QUINTUS MUCIUS, 'AUGUR' (*cos.* 117 B.C.), was a great jurist and probably a moderate reformer in politics. His family connexions clearly suggest that he may have been influential in the democratic party, though perhaps not with the extremists. His granddaughter Licinia (daughter of L. Crassus) married the younger Marius; and it is not surprising that Scaevola refused to countenance Sulla when, in 88, he called upon the Senate to declare the elder Marius a public enemy. Scaevola educated his grandson, M'. Glabrio (*cos.* 67), before whom Verres was tried in 70; and Cicero as a youth attended his legal consultations.

F. Münzer, *Röm. Adelsparteien*, 275 ff. M. H.

SCAEVOLA (4), QUINTUS MUCIUS, 'PONTIFEX' (*cos.* 95 B.C.), was the son of (2) and cousin of (3) above. As consul with L. Crassus, he carried the *Lex Licinia Mucia*, expelling the Latins from Rome. As proconsul of Asia (94), he issued a provincial edict which served as a model to other governors, e.g. to Cicero in Cilicia. He lost his life in the Marian massacres of 82.

An excellent jurisprudent and teacher, Scaevola published the first systematic treatise on Civil Law. This was the basis of much subsequent work on the *ius civile*, books 'ad Quintum Mucium' being arranged according to his system. His *liber singularis ὅρων* (*Definitionum*) was the earliest work directly excerpted in Justinian's *Digest*. A. B.

SCAEVOLA (5), QUINTUS CERVIDIUS, legal adviser of Marcus Aurelius, teacher of Paulus, Tryphoninus, and (perhaps) Papinian, a famous figure among the Roman jurisprudents of the second century A.D. A sagacious casuist, he pronounced his decisions resolutely and tersely, in a language which is not free from vulgarisms and heaviness, a specialist in *responsa*. Some of his responses deal with cases presented by provincials and infiltrated with new ideas coming from the Hellenistic East. But Scaevola was not easily open to such innovations. His *responsa* fill a special collection (six books) and also a much larger publication, the *Digesta* (in 40 books), renowned as the most prominent work of casuistic literature, though this kind of juridical work did not normally include *responsa*. The relation between Scaevola's *Digesta* and *Responsa* is not quite clear; a new solution, which assumes both works to have been published long after the death of Scaevola has been proposed in recent times (F. Schulz, 'Überlieferungsgeschichte der Responsen Scaevolas', *Symbolae Friburgenses in honorem O. Lenel*, 1934). Other works of Scaevola: *Notae* to *Digesta* of Julian and Marcellus, *Regulae*, *Quaestiones*. A. B.

SCAMANDRIUS, *see* ASTYANAX.

SCANDINAVIA. The earliest information about Scandinavia is Pytheas' account (*c.* 325 B.C.) of Thule (q.v.), if its identification with Norway is correct. Mela (3. 3) mentions 'islands' in the Sinus Codanus 'north of the Elbe'; Pliny states (*HN* 4. 96) that the largest and most fertile of these is the island of Scatinavia and mentions Sevo Mons, which may be the mountains between south Sweden and Norway. Tacitus (*Germ.* 44, 45) knows of the Suiones (Svear, Swedes), a seafaring nation which evidently came within the ken of the amber traders at the mouth of the Vistula; Ptolemy mentions numerous tribes in Scandia. Jutland was better known to the Romans, a naval expedition having sailed as far as the Skaw in A.D. 5 (*Mon. Anc.* 26).

The Scandinavian Neolithic Age, fertilized by influences coming with the Megalithic culture from the south-west, was one of considerable achievement, and subsequent Bronze Age culture, in which the trade in Jutland amber (q.v.) with the south played an important part, was of a high order. There was a falling-off in the Early Iron Age, and by the end of the first century B.C. a number of peoples (Langobardi, Vandili, Burgundiones, Gutones) had migrated, in part at any rate, to the German mainland. The home-staying Scandinavians entered upon a new period of prosperity in the first century A.D. and enjoyed a lively intercourse with other peoples, as the great quantity of Roman goods in their graves show. In the third and fourth centuries they came under the influence of the culture stream from the Gothic settlements on the Black Sea and in the Danube lands.

H. Shetelig, H. Falk, and E. V. Gordon, *Scandinavian Archaeology* (1937); L. Schmidt, *Geschichte der deutschen Stämme*.   O. B.

SCAPULA, see OSTORIUS.

SCAPULOMANCY, see DIVINATION, para. 6.

SCAPUS, see BOOKS, I. 4.

SCARABS, see GEMS.

SCATO, see VETTIUS (2).

SCAURUS (1), MARCUS AEMILIUS (*cos.* 115 B.C.), was the husband of Caecilia Metella, afterwards Sulla's wife, and father of Aemilia, later wife of Pompey. Scaurus, though his family had no recent distinction, rose to be *Princeps Senatus*; to Cicero he stands out as the 'Grand Old Man' of the *Optimates*, but his early career is hard to understand. In 110 he presided over the *Quaestio Mamilia*, though he had himself served under Bestia in 111 and on the embassy to Jugurtha in 112: Sallust's attempt to portray him as a skilful villain is an unconvincing *tour de force*. It is not known that he was concerned in Opimius' persecution of Gracchans in 121; if he had had no share in Opimius' severities, he might be acceptable to the democrats in 110. With the fall of Opimius and his friends, Scaurus became one of the Optimate leaders; he was censor in 109, with the elder Drusus. His marriage with Caecilia Metella is best dated after 102 (see Münzer, *Adelsparteien*, p. 281). He played a prominent part, on the Optimate side, in the events of the years before and after 100, and as a strong supporter of Drusus' reforms was accused in 90 at Caepio's instigation under the Varian Commission. He died soon afterwards. He wrote *De vita sua* in three books.

G. Bloch, *Mélanges d'histoire ancienne* (1909); E. Pais, *Dalle guerre puniche a Cesare Augusto* i (1918), 91 ff.   M. H.

SCAURUS (2), MARCUS AEMILIUS, son of (1) above, was Pompey's quaestor in the Mithridatic War; he marched into Judaea and Nabataea. Aedile (58 B.C.), praetor (56), and propraetor in Sardinia, he was in 54 accused *de repetundis*, defended by Cicero and acquitted. Accused again *de ambitu*, he went into exile in 52. He married Mucia, previously Pompey's wife.

Klebs, *PW* i. 588.   A. M.

SCAURUS (3), MAMERCUS AEMILIUS, the last male member of the distinguished republican family of Aemilii Scauri, was a man of unsavoury character, but a distinguished orator and advocate (Sen. *Controv.* 10, praef. 2–3; Tac. *Ann.* 6. 29). Though disliked by Tiberius, he was suffect consul, probably in A.D. 21, but did not govern a province. Twice prosecuted for *maiestas*, in 32 and 34, on the second occasion he committed suicide.   J. P. B.

SCAURUS, see TERENTIUS.

SCAZON, see METRE, GREEK, II (2).

a theory of probability.

(3) Outside the Academy Pyrrhonism or scepticism was revived by Aenesidemus, if not earlier. The new Pyrrhonian school gives a systematic synthesis of Academic-Pyrrhonian teaching and the empiricism of the so-called empirical physicians. In the 'modes' (τρόποι) of Aenesidemus, Agrippa, and others we find criticism reduced to certain formulae. Sextus Empiricus gives in his preserved works an account of the whole system.

Bibliography (selection). E. Zeller, *Philos. d. Griechen* iii a⁴, 494 f.; iii b, 1 f.; V. Brochard, *Les Sceptiques grecs* (1887); R. Hirzel, *Unters. zu Cicero's philos. Schriften* iii; R. Richter, *Der Skeptiz. in Philos.* i (1904); A. Goedeckemeyer, *Die Geschichte d. griech. Skeptiz.* (1905); E. Bevan, *Stoics and Sceptics* (1913); Ueberweg–Praechter, *Grundriss*¹² §§ 63, 64, 75; M. M. Patrick, *The Greek S.* (1929); K. Deichgräber, *Die griechische Empirikerschule* (1930).   K. O. B.

SCHERIA (Σχερία, epic Σχερίη), the land of the Phaeacians, at which Odysseus (q.v.) arrives after his shipwreck (*Od.* 5. 451 ff., cf. 34). It is a fertile country, apparently an island (6. 204), having an excellent, almost land-locked harbour (263 ff.), by which its city stands, at least one river (5 loc. cit.), and a mild climate (cf. 7. 117 ff.; fruits grow all the year round). The population are enterprising and very skilful sea-farers, great gossips, boastful and rather impudent, not very warlike nor athletic, fond of pleasure, but kindly and willing to escort strangers in their wonderful ships. Various real places have been suggested as the original of Scheria, the most popular in ancient and modern times being Corfú; but as that is within some eighty miles of Ithaca, whereat Scheria is distant a night's voyage for one of the magical Phaeacian ships (*Od.* 13. 81 ff.), the identification is unlikely. See, however, A. Shewan, *Homeric Essays* (1935), 242 ff. That details of real places have been used for the picture is likely.   H. J. R.

SCHOLARSHIP IN MODERN TIMES: (a) RENAISSANCE TO 1800. A formal history of classical scholarship in modern times, i.e. from the Renaissance onwards, is too vast for the limits here possible. It must suffice to represent the subject by a general bibliography of works of reference and to indicate some of the features and of the greater names in the periods into which it may be divided. A supplementary selection of books largely biographical, and without claim to be exhaustive, will serve to illustrate features in these periods.

A. GENERAL WORKS OF REFERENCE
Bursian, C. *Geschichte der class. Philologie in Deutschland von den Anfängen bis zur Gegenwart.* 1883.
Gudeman, A. *Outlines of the Hist. of Class. Philology*³. U.S.A. 1902 [a compact summary].
—— *Grundriss der Geschichte der Klass. Philologie*². 1909.
Hallam, H. *Introd. to the Lit. of Europe in the Fifteenth, Sixteenth, and Seventeenth Centuries*⁶. 1860.

Kroll, W. *Geschichte der Klass. Philologie.* 1908, 1920 [a brief sketch].

Mayor, J. E. B. *Bibliographical Clue to Latin Literature.* 1875 [edited after E. Hübner with large additions].

Peck, H. T. *Hist. of Classical Philology.* 1911 [contains bibliographical index pp. 461–76].

Pökel, W. *Philologisches Schriftsteller-Lexikon.* 1882 [useful for dates and works of classical scholarship up to its time of publication: references under important names to biographical notices].

Sandys, J. E. *A History of Classical Scholarship,* vol. ii. 1908 [from Revival of Learning to end of 18th century in Italy, France, England, and the Netherlands].

—— do. vol. iii, *The Eighteenth Cent. in Germany and the Nineteenth in Europe and U.S.A.* 1908.

   [Both vols. have chronological tables, portraits, and bibliographies and furnish learned and well-written estimates of scholars.]

—— *Harvard Lectures on the Revival of Learning.* 1905.

Sathas, K.N. Νεοελληνικὴ φιλολογία· βιογραφίαι τῶν ἐν τοῖς γράμμασι διαλαμψάντων Ἑλλήνων (1453–1821). 1868.

B. PERIODS OF MODERN SCHOLARSHIP AND RELEVANT STUDIES

It will be convenient to follow, with some modification, Sandys's four periods, which he considered predominantly: I. Italian, II. French, III. English and Dutch, IV. German.

I. Of these the first is that of the Renaissance or Revival of Learning, especially in Italy from the death of Dante in 1321 for two centuries to the death of Leo X in 1521. It may be said to begin with Petrarch (1304–74) and to end with the contemporaries of Erasmus (1466–1536). It is the period of learned Greek immigrants in Italy, of the acceptance and promotion of the new learning by humanist scholars and educators, of an energetic quest for manuscripts, and of the extension of classical enthusiasm into many countries of Europe. Representative of a combined devotion to Greek and Latin study were Valla (1407–57), who was among the founders of historical criticism in his disproof of the authenticity of the *Donation of Constantine*; Politian (1454–94), professor of Greek and Latin at Florence, who stimulated a natural Italian interest in writers of the 'Silver Age'; and Ficino (1433–99), renowned as a commentator on and translator of Plato.

The new learning spread more slowly in the north. At Paris, Greek, though taught spasmodically from about 1458, scarcely established itself until after the arrival of Lascaris in 1495. Its introduction into Germany is associated with Rudolphus Agricola (1443–85) and Reuchlin (1455–1522), and in England with William of Selling in 1473 and with Linacre, Grocyn, Latimer, Colet, Sir John Cheke, and others. Typical fruit is seen in Roger Ascham's *Scholemaster*. Greek was taught at Louvain in 1517 and was fostered by Erasmus. More cosmopolitan than the Italian stylists and too sane to tolerate fastidious pedantry (see his *Ciceronianus*, 1528), Erasmus reached the high-water mark in the Renaissance appreciation of the purely literary attraction of the classics.

A limited number of works are here given as guide-posts.

Allen, P. S. *The Age of Erasmus.* 1914.
—— and H. M. Allen (with H. W. Garrod in later vols.). *Opus Epistolarum Desiderii Erasmi denuo recognitum et auctum* . . . 11 vols. 1906–47.
Baldelli, G. *Vita di Giovanni Boccaccio.* 1806.
Bandini, A. A. *Italorum et Germanorum Epistolae ad Petrum Victorium* (cum vita Victorii). 2 vols. 1758–60. [Important, as Pietro Vettori's many-sided learning advanced *inter alia* Aristotelian and Ciceronian scholarship.]
Boerner, C. F. *De doctis hominibus Graecis litterarum Graecarum in Italia instauratoribus.* Leipzig 1750. [On lives and writings of twelve Greek immigrants including Chrysoloras, Bessarion, Chalcondyles, etc.]

Boulting, W. *Aeneas Silvius* (Enea Silvio de' Piccolomini—Pius II) *Orator, Man of Letters, Statesman and Pope* (illust.). 1908.
Burckhart, J. *Die Cultur der Renaissance in Italien.* 1860 and many later edns. Engl. Transl. by S. G. C. Middlemore, 1878; subsequent issues include that of Phaidon Press, 1937. [Part iii is on humanism from 14th to 16th cent.]
Cambridge Bibliography of English Literature, 4 vols. (including index vol.). 1940. [Vol. i contains sections on scholars and translations; humanists, pp. 664 ff.; Latin and Greek learning, 1500–1660, pp. 859–63.]
Cambridge Modern History: The Renaissance, vol. i, 1907 [esp. ch. xvi by R. C. Jebb].
Christie, R. C. *Étienne Dolet, the Martyr of the Renaissance.* 1880 and 1899.
Comparetti, D. *Virgilio nel medio evo.* 2 vols. 1872 [ed. 2, 1896]. Engl. Transl. by E. F. M. Benecke. 1895.
Geiger, L. *Humanismus und Renaissance in Italien u. Deutschland von den Anfängen bis zur Gegenwart.* 1882.
—— *Johann Reuchlin.* 1871.
[The *Epistolae Obscurorum Virorum* in 1516–17 championed Reuchlin by parodying the barbarous Latin of his opponents. Latin text with Eng. rendering and historical introd., F. G. Stokes, 1925.]
Körting, G. *Petrarca: Leben und Werke.* 1878.
—— *Boccaccio: Leben und Werke.* 1880.
Lupton, J. H. *A Life of John Colet, D.D., Dean of St. Paul's.* 1887.
Maehly, J. A. *Angelus Politianus: ein Culturbild aus der Renaissance.* 1864.
Michelet, J. *Histoire de France,* vol. vii 'Renaissance'. 1855.
Nolhac, P. de. *Pétrarque et l'Humanisme.* 1892.
Pastor, L. *Geschichte der Päpste im Zeitalter der Renaissance bis zur Wahl Pius II.* 1886 ff. Engl. Transl. by F. I. Antrobus. 1891 ff.
Rashdall, H. *The Universities of Europe in the Middle Ages.* 3 vols. 1895; new ed. by F. M. Powicke and A. B. Emden, 1936.
Robinson, J. H., and Rolfe, H. W., *Petrarch the first Modern Scholar and Man of Letters* (with translations from his correspondence). U.S.A. 1898 and 1914.
Sabbadini, R. *Le scoperte dei codici latini e greci ne' secoli xiv e xv.* 1905. [Records Poggio's recovery of ancient MSS. on four expeditions.]
—— *Nuove ricerche.* 1914.
Saintsbury, G. *A History of Criticism and Literary Taste in Europe.* 3 vols.[2] 1905. [Vol. ii, bk. iv 'Renaissance Criticism' includes Erasmus and Italian editors of Aristotle's *Poetics*, e.g. Castelvetro.]
Seebohm, F. *The Oxford Reformers of 1498* (being a history of the fellow-work of Colet, Erasmus, and More). 1867.
Shepherd, W. *The Life of Poggio Bracciolini.* 1802.
Spingarn, J. E. *A History of Literary Criticism in the Renaissance* (with special reference to the influence of Italy in the formation and development of modern classicism). Columbia Univ., U.S.A. Ed. 1 1899; 5th impr. 1925. [Italian Transl. by Antonio Fusco, 1905, has additions by the author and preface by B. Croce.]
Strauss, D. F. *Ulrich von Hutten.* 2 vols. 1857–8; ed. 2, 1871. Engl. Transl. by Mrs. G. Sturge 1874.
Symonds, J. A. *Renaissance in Italy,* new ed. 7 vols. 1909–14. [Vol. ii is on 'The Revival of Learning'.]
Vahlen, J. *Lorenzo Valla.* Vienna 1864; Berlin 1870.
Voigt, G. *Die Wiederbelebung des class. Altertums oder das erste Jahrhundert des Humanismus.* 1859; ed. 3 by M. Lehnerdt, 2 vols. 1893.
Weiss, R. *Humanism in England during the 15th century.* 1941.
Woodward, W. H. *Vittorino da Feltre and other Humanist Educators.* 1897.

This was also the period of the earliest printing of classical authors. For a handy conspectus of *editiones principes*, Greek and Latin, with editor, printer, and place of printing, see Sandys, op. cit. ii. 102–5. Here France was considerably behind Italy. The elder Stephanus, Robert Estienne (1503–59), father of Henri (1528–98), links the first two of our periods, and his activities (including the *Thesaurus Linguae Latinae* and eight Greek *editiones principes* from 1544 onwards) take us far into the sixteenth century. The still greater performance of his son followed in the issue of 58 Latin authors and 74 Greek (18 of the latter being *editiones principes*) and of his *Thesaurus Graecae Linguae* and his Plato.

The following works may be consulted:

Botfield, B. *Prefaces to the first editions of the Greek and Roman Classics, etc.* 1861.
Dibdin, T. F. *Introd. to knowledge of rare and valuable editions of the Greek and Latin Classics*[4]. 1827.
Didot, A. Firmin. *Alde Manuce et l'hellénisme à Venise.* 1875.
Renouard, A. A. *Annales de l'imprimerie des Aldes*[3]. 3 vols. 1834.
—— *Annales de l'imprimerie des Estienne*[2]. 1843.

II. This period, opening approximately with the founding of the Corporation of Royal Readers (later, the Collège de France) by Francis I at the suggestion of the famous Greek scholar Budaeus (Budé) in 1530, and closing about the end of the seventeenth century, may with fairness be considered a French period. Its four outstanding names are those of (1) Julius Caesar Scaliger's still more eminent son Joseph Justus Scaliger (1540–1609), who, after editing several Latin poets and Festus, turned from textual criticism rather more to subject-matter (e.g. in his Manilius) and to the verification of ancient chronology; (2) a scholar who aimed at conveying to readers his own interest in ancient life, Isaac Casaubon (1559–1614), of Huguenot parentage, a famous editor of Persius and father of Méric Casaubon, whose education and scholarly activities are associated with England; (3) Justus Lipsius (Joest Lips, 1547–1606), who showed himself a great Latinist, not least in his editions of Tacitus and of Seneca; and (4) Salmasius (Claude de Saumaise, 1588–1653), who discovered the MS. of the Greek *Anthologia* of Cephalas and who as editor of several Latin historians earned his call to Leyden in 1631. In France there belong to this period also Ramus (Pierre de la Ramée); three Royal Readers in Greek, Turnebus, Dorat, and Lambinus (noted for his Horace); Muretus, Pithou, Petau, the Daciers, the distinguished palaeographer Mabillon, and others. France too holds the credit of Du Cange's glossary of medieval Latin, first published in 1678, and of Huet's series of Delphin classics (1670–80).

In the Netherlands Vivès, Spanish by birth, had left his mark on education at Louvain; Canter marked a new era by editing the Greek tragic poets; and Cruquius remains memorable for his edition of Horace, which gives our only information about the *codex antiquissimus Blandinius.* Among compatriots who handed on the tradition of scholarship in the seventeenth century were the elder Dousa and his two sons; Merula (*Ennii fragmenta,* 1595); Vossius the elder (an authority on rhetoric and grammar); Meursius; Daniel Heinsius, in whose Latin work Scaliger's influence appears, as it does in Grotius, whose *De Iure Belli et Pacis* is more widely known than his skilful Latin renderings from the Planudean Anthology. The next generation yielded distinguished names in Daniel Heinsius's son Niklaas, J. F. Gronovius (successor to D. Heinsius at Leyden in 1659), while Jacob Gronovius and Bentley's correspondent Graevius carried learning into the eighteenth century. The Dutch scholar Perizonius (Voorbroek) in his *Animadversiones Historicae,* 1685, first raised the question of the importance of primitive lays in the shaping of Roman legends.

Scholarship in England during the period is perhaps best remembered for the Tudor translators, among them Philemon Holland, and later for Dryden's *Virgil.* Ben Jonson's friend Farnaby edited among his Latin texts Seneca's tragedies and published a Latin grammar in 1641. Sir Henry Savile's *Chrysostom* was a triumph of erudition and printing; Gataker issued his *M. Aurelius* with a Latin translation; and to the learned jurist Selden we owe the rescue of the *Marmor Parium.* Scotland produced an eminent scholar in George Buchanan, translator of the Psalms, while Arthur Johnston also showed great skill in his Latin verse. This period, it may be noted, included the age of Milton and of the Cambridge Platonists. More than one scholar, Creech included, worked on the still misty text of Lucretius, and before the end of the century Potter wrote his *Antiquities of Greece.*

In Germany the generation succeeding Reuchlin witnessed the diligence of Melanchthon (Schwarzerd, 1497–1560), who merited the title of 'praeceptor Germaniae' by his editions of Greek and Latin classics and his grammars. His friend and biographer Camerarius (Kammermeister) is best known for a Plautus of 1552. Sturm (1507–89) was a staunch upholder of speaking and writing Latin. Greek texts were carefully edited by Xylander (= Holtzmann, 1532–76), whose *Pausanias* was completed by Sylburg. Janus Gruter (1560–1627),

who, though born at Antwerp and educated at Norwich, Cambridge, and Leyden, was long associated with Heidelberg, edited some seventeen Latin authors, and at Scaliger's instigation compiled a corpus of ancient inscriptions. The *Polyhistor* of Morhof (1639–91), professor at Rostock, should be mentioned as of interest to students of literary history.

In Italy Ciceronian study was furthered by the *Lexicon* of Nizolius (1498–1566): Sigonius worked on Livy and used his Ciceronian scholarship to forge a *Consolatio.* Robortelli edited the *Poetics* of Aristotle (1548) over twenty years before Castelvetro's edition. In both the sixteenth and the seventeenth centuries an increasing bent towards archaeology is discernible among Italian scholars.

A series of '*Delitiae*' showed the skill in Latin verse attained by the scholars of several different countries.

BIBLIOGRAPHY. For a fuller appraisal of scholarship in the sixteenth and seventeenth centuries see Sandys, op. cit., vol. ii.
The following is a selection of relevant works:

Bernays, J. *Joseph Justus Scaliger.* Berlin 1855.
Brown, P. Hume. *George Buchanan, Humanist and Reformer.* 1890; new ed. 1906.
Burigny, J. L. de. *La Vie de Grotius.* 2 vols. 1752. [Based on P. A. Lehmann's *Hugonis Grotii manes . . . vindicati,* 1727, which contains a full list of his writings with a biography.]
Butler, C. *Life of Hugo Grotius.* 1827.
Caumont, A. *Étude sur la vie et les travaux de Grotius.* 1862.
Desmaze, C. *Pierre de la Ramée, sa vie, ses écrits, sa mort.* 1864.
Legay. *Adrien Turnebus, lecteur royal.* 1878.
Meursius, J. (Jan de Meurs). *Athenae Batavae sive de urbe Leidensi et Academia.* 1625. [Contains an autobiography and an account of D. Heinsius, etc.]
Nazelle, J. J. *I. Casaubon, sa vie et son temps.* 1897.
Nisard, C. *Le Triumvirat littéraire au xvi siècle — Juste Lipse, Joseph Scaliger, et Isaac Casaubon.* 1852. [Bernays's biography gives a fairer estimate of Scaliger's character.]
Pattison, M. *Isaac Casaubon.* 1875; ed. H. Nettleship, 1892 (index added).
Rebitté, D. *Guillaume Budé, restaurateur des études grecques en France.* 1846.
Reiffenberg, A. de. *De Justi Lipsii vita et scriptis commentarius.* Brussels 1823.
Robinson, G. W. *Autobiography of Joseph Scaliger translated by G. W. R.* Harvard, U.S.A. 1927. [Includes the funeral orations by Daniel Heinsius and Dominicus Baudius.]
Russell, J. *Ephemerides Isaaci Casauboni cum praefat. et notis.* 2 vols. 1850. [The diary is a valuable testimony to Casaubon's character and learning.]

III. For scholarship in England, the eighteenth century may be described as the period from Bentley to Porson: the continuance of its influence into the next century is well marked by Cobet's acknowledgement of debt to his 'three Richards'—Bentley, Dawes, and Porson. Bentley's lead in insistence upon the fundamental necessity of sound texts, and his boldness in the purgation of what he judged to be corrupt, gave, in spite of some hostile critics, an enlivening impulse to textual criticism (q.v.) and chronology. Although Wood's *Essay on the Original Genius and Writings of Homer* (1769) influenced Wolf and Heyne abroad, Homeric scholarship did not equal that on the Greek drama; but the general vitality of works by English scholars is proved by translations into French and German and by notices in the Leyden *Bibliotheca Critica* founded by Wyttenbach with Ruhnken's approval. It is not surprising that in an age when classical quotation came readily to Chatham, Burke, Fox, and Pitt, the Public Schools should publish their verses, and several renderings be made of *Paradise Lost* and Gray's *Elegy.* Translation into English was carried on with equal vigour, and many examples might be specified besides the renderings of Homer by Pope and his associates. Studies of Aristotle's *Poetics,* of Horace's *Ars Poetica,* and of the treatise *On the Sublime* indicated growing attention to literary criticism, while other works were concerned with lexicography, ancient geography, topography, and the antiquities of Greece and Rome. Travel in Greece and Asia Minor fostered enthusiasm for archaeology, inscriptions, and ancient art; acquaintance with the East was responsible for Sir Wm. Jones's realization of the linguistic importance of Sanskrit (*see* COMPARATIVE PHILOLOGY); and Roman remains at home were the subject of Horsley's noteworthy *Britannia Romana*. Representative works of pure scholarship were Bentley's famous *Dissertation upon the Epistles of Phalaris* (1699, translated into Latin in 1777 and into German about 80 years later), his Horace (1711, containing over 700 textual changes), his Terence (frequently cited in the O.C.T. edition), and his Manilius; Wasse's Sallust (based on collation of 80 MSS.) and his manuscript commentary on Thucydides incorporated in Duker's Thucydides, Amsterdam, 1731; Markland's *Sylvae* of Statius; Taylor's Lysias; Dawes's *Miscellanea Critica*; Toup's *Emendationes in Suidam*; Tyrwhitt's *Poetics* of Aristotle; and, about the end of the century, Porson's editions of four plays of Euripides, marked by the wonderful memory and grasp of metre which made him the greatest Atticist of his day.

In Italy among the best-known names are those of the lexicographers Facciolati and Forcellini. Corsini's *Fasti Attici* signally advanced Greek chronology. France, like Italy, furthered archaeology, and included among its scholars possessing other interests Olivetus (Cicero), the three Capperoniers, and Montfaucon, who may be called the founder of Palaeography (q.v.). Of several Alsatian scholars, Brunck was eminent for his editions of Greek dramatists. Villoison's publication of the Venetian scholia to the *Iliad*, 1788, helped to fertilize Homeric studies anew. Germany's noteworthy names included J. A. Fabricius (*Bibliotheca Latina* and *Bibliotheca Graeca*), Gesner (*Scriptores Rei Rusticae, Thesaurus Linguae Latinae*, etc.), Scheller (*Lexicons*), Ernesti (Cicero), Reiske (*Oratores Graeci*, 12 vols., and edns. of many Greek classics), Heyne (Virgil, 4 vols. 1775; *Iliad*, 8 vols. 1802), and F. A. Wolf, author of the epoch-making *Prolegomena to Homer*, 1795, and editor of both Greek and Latin classics. The works of such pupils of Wolf as Boeckh, Bekker, Buttmann, and Bernhardy bear witness to his fertile and wide-reaching influence in the nineteenth century. Interest in ancient art was stimulated by Winckelmann and Lessing.

But no country of the time eclipsed the Netherlands. An imposing array consists of the two Burmans, uncle and nephew (both industrious editors of Latin authors and the younger widely known for his edition of the *Anthologia Latina*); Kuster (whose Suidas was published at Cambridge); Duker (whose Thucydides, we have seen, incorporated work by Wasse); Drakenborch (Livy, Silius); Hemsterhuys (whose mastery of Greek owed much to Bentley and who edited Pollux and the greater part of Lucian); Oudendorp (Lucan, Frontinus, Caesar, Apuleius); Valckenaer (Euripides' *Phoen.* and *Hipp.*, Theocritus, Callimachus); Ruhnken (edn. of Timaeus' *Lexicon vocum Platonicarum*, and *Historia Critica Oratorum Graecorum*); and Wyttenbach (biographer of Ruhnken and the indefatigable editor of Plutarch's *Moralia*, etc.).

BIBLIOGRAPHY. For the eighteenth century see Sandys, op. cit., vols. ii and iii, and his bibliographical notes. The following may be mentioned:

Chalmers, G. *Life of Thomas Ruddiman*. 1794.
Chasles, P. *Dissertation on Life and Works of Michael Maittaire*. 1839.
Ernesti, J. A. *Narratio de J. M. Gesnero*. 1796. ['An admirable biographical sketch', Sandys in *Companion to Latin Studies*.]
Heeren, A. H. L. *C. G. Heyne biographisch dargestellt*. 1813.
Hodgson, J. *An Account of Life and Writings of R. Dawes*. 1829.
Jebb, R. C. *Bentley* (Eng. Men of Letters series). 1882.
Johnstone, J. *The Works of Samuel Parr with Memoirs*. 1828. [Reviewed with other works on Parr in De Quincey's Essay 'Dr. Parr and his Contemporaries'.]
Körte, W. *Leben u. Studien F. A. Wolfs des Philologen*. 1833.
Mähly, J. A. *Richard Bentley: eine Biographie*. 1868.
Monk, J. H. *Life of Bentley*. 1830.
Müller, E. F. W. Lucian, *Gesch. der klass. Philologie in den Niederlanden*. 1868.
Nicoll, H. J. *Great Scholars*. 1880. [A popular account including Bentley, Porson, Parr, Ruddiman, Adam, and others.]

Ruhnken, D. *Elogium Hemsterhusii*. 1768, 1789; ed. Bergman 1824; ed. Frey 1875. [The *Elogium*, by a learned and devoted pupil, is 'one of the classics in the history of scholarship: it presents us with the living picture of the perfect critic' (Sandys).]
Watson, J. S. *Life of Richard Porson*. 1861.
Wolf, F. A. *Litterarische Analekten*. 1816 ff. [Not confined to German scholars.]
Wordsworth, Chr. *Bentley's Correspondence*. 2 vols. 1842.
—— *Scholae Academicae: some account of the studies at the English Universities in the xviiith cent.* 1877; reissue 1910. [Notably ch. ix 'Humanity', and Appendix ix 'A Chronological List of Eng. xviiith cent. edns. of ancient classics'.]
Wyttenbach, D. *Vita D. Ruhnkenii*. 1799; ed. Bergman 1824; ed. Frotscher 1846. [Besides its biographical interest, has value for its picture of contemporary scholarship.]   J. W. D.

SCHOLARSHIP IN MODERN TIMES: (b) 19TH AND 20TH CENTURIES. (Living scholars are not, as a rule, discussed in the articles on modern scholarship.)

I. INTRODUCTORY

1. The nineteenth century, based upon solid and indispensable foundations laid in the eighteenth, exhibited a deepening and widening of classical research productive of a fresh renaissance in which no single section of study seems self-sufficient. To this new humanism nothing which illumines the literature, languages, life, thought, or art of classical antiquity can be considered alien. Virtually it has realized the broad conception of the classics entertained by Wolf as a vast structure whose constituent parts should combine in a deep penetration into the infinite variety of Greek and Roman life. Brilliant services were rendered to textual criticism (q.v.), but establishment of a sound text, though fundamental, is only one of the functions of scholarship; for complete exegesis many other departments of learning have to be drawn upon. Verbal study may demand reinforcement from closer investigation of dialects Greek and Italic, or of archaic inscriptions or of Latin as late as the *Itinerarium Aetheriae*; much in Herodotus calls in anthropology; the dramatic value of some scenes of a Greek tragedy must be assessed in relation to conditions of theatrical representation or to half-forgotten elements of religious ritual. So ancient classics, to exert their full humanistic effect, need constant reinterpretation in the light of increasing knowledge in many different branches.

2. Some features of the period may be mentioned in illustration. It is marked by a stricter system of textual criticism (e.g. Lachmann), an intensified care in assessing the value of manuscripts and their interrelation, and the application of palaeographic knowledge (e.g. Traube). There has been a more scientific investigation of the grammar, syntax, and history of ancient languages in light of the steady development of comparative philology (q.v.). Lexicography has been advanced by the labours of scholars like Wölfflin in the *Archiv für latein. Lexikographie u. Grammatik* (1884–1909) and by the *Thesaurus Linguae Latinae*, still in progress. The *Greek–English Lexicon* of Liddell & Scott, as revised and augmented by Sir H. S. Jones and R. McKenzie, 1940, is deservedly hailed as one of the triumphs of recent scholarship.

3. Fresh interest in the earlier Latin authors is exemplified by works like Vahlen's *Ennius* (1854, 1903[2]), Marx's *Lucilius* (1904 f.), Bücheler's *Menippean Satires* of Varro (1922[6]), while the importance of those later writers who have rescued for us fragments of archaic literature is recognized in editions such as Hosius's *Gellius* (1903) and Lindsay's *Nonius Marcellus* (1903). The grammarians and rhetors of Greece and Rome have been carefully collected, and exact attention paid to the metres and prose-rhythms of Greek and Latin and to the principles of composition in prose and verse. The practice of composition in both languages has nowhere been more tastefully cultivated than in the universities and classical schools of Britain. Skill and felicity in serious translation of great modern poetry and even in renderings of light verse have been exhibited by some of the most distinguished British editors of the classics (e.g. Kennedy, Munro, Shilleto, Jebb, Headlam) and justify Wilamowitz's acknowledgement in his *Erinnerungen* that appreciation of his own verses was keener in England than in Germany.

4. The light thrown upon the life of ancient Greece and Rome by archaeology and epigraphy has served both literary and historical research, especially through the conduct of excavation on increasingly scientific lines. The late nineteenth century witnessed and welcomed the recovery in Egypt of papyri, some bearing on commercial and social life, and others containing literary works, e.g. several of Bacchylides' odes, the Ἀθηναίων πολιτεία, considerable portions of Menander's comedies and Herodas' mimes, all of which were at once a stimulus to interest and a challenge to skill in textual restoration. The comparatively new science of anthropology has illuminated much in ancient custom and religion (e.g. Frazer's edition of Ovid's *Fasti*).

5. The immeasurably extended range of subjects now embraced under classical learning may be gauged from the contents of the volumes of Müller's *Handbuch der Altertumswissenschaft*, Pauly's *Real-Encyclopädie* (1839–52) (of which a new edition, begun by Wissowa in 1893, is almost complete), or *A Companion to Greek Studies* and *A Companion to Latin Studies* (Camb. Univ. Press). The bibliographical sections in Nairn's *Classical Handlist* (1939²) provide further illustration.

6. A feature at once signalizing and aiding advance has been the collection of the results of past research which provide material for future work in the *Corpora* of inscriptions, of ecclesiastical writers and of writers on agriculture, astrology, geography, gromatics, medicine, metrology, music, etc. Add to these valuable collections of fragments such as those of the Greek and Roman dramatists, poets, and historians whose partial survival we owe largely to quotation by other ancient authors.

7. With this expansion of range the increase of Classical Societies or Academies has kept pace. Learned periodicals circulate in many languages to record and promote classical learning. The spread of Greek and Latin scholarship is significantly represented by the separate sections devoted in Sandys's *History of Classical Scholarship*, vol. iii, to the modern scholars of Scandinavia, Greece, Russia, and the United States of America. Of erudition so widely spread only a mere fraction can here come under notice.

II. GERMANY

8. In Germany scholarship during the nineteenth century was marked by a transmission of vital influence due to stimulating teachers. Much was achieved by suggestion of subjects for research to pupils destined sometimes to be collaborators with their professors. This transmission was so notable that a fair conception of modern German scholarship can be gained from observing the groups or 'schools' formed. Thus it has been usual to differentiate a grammatico-critical school continuing the Hermann tradition from the historico-antiquarian school continuing the Boeckh tradition—a convenient if not in every case a rigid division.

9. Gottfried Hermann (1772–1848), who had precursors among scholars of England and Holland and whose authority on metre is demonstrated in his editions of Greek poets, left a succession of students whose names represent, though they do not exhaust, the record of classical learning in the earlier part of the period. They include Näke (*Dirae, Lydia*); Reisig (especially devoted to Greek and Latin grammar); Thiersch (whose enthusiasm for Greek grammar, poetry, and epigraphy revived classics in Bavaria); Hercher (*Scriptores Erotici Graeci*; *Epistolographi Graeci*); Lobeck (the acknowledged learning of whose *Aglaophamus* contained good-humoured criticism of Creuzer's ultra-mysticism); Meineke (Aristophanes; Comic Fragments); K. F. Hermann (Greek Antiquities;

Juvenal); Trendelenburg (Aristotelian logic); Spengel (*Rhetores Graeci*); Classen (Thucydides); Ritschl (who opened a new era in the study of Plautus, his labour on nine of the plays being continued by his pupils Loewe, Goetz, and Schoell); Sauppe (co-editor with Baiter of *Oratores Attici*); Haupt (G. Hermann's son-in-law and editor of his posthumous Aeschylus, who convincingly separated the bucolics of Calpurnius and Nemesianus); Bergk (*Poetae Lyrici Graeci*); Koechly (editor of many Greek classics); Bonitz (Platonic and Aristotelian scholar); Passow (whose repeated re-editions of Schneider's lexicon formed a basis for Liddell and Scott); and Schaefer (specially interested in Demosthenes' times).

10. Dissen (1784–1837, a pupil of Heyne: *Greek Moods and Tenses*; editions of Pindar, Tibullus, and *De Cor.*), though representative of grammatical and critical study, disliked Hermann's method and was not of his school.

11. Wilhelm Dindorf (1802–83) edited most of the Greek poets, and his brother Ludwig (1805–71) most of the Greek historians. Together, they were the main editors of the *Thesaurus Linguae Graecae* (Paris, mid-19th c.).

12. The leader of the historico-antiquarian school was Boeckh (1785–1867; Pindar, 4 vols. 1811–22; *Corp. Inscript. Graec.* 1825–40, continued by Franz, E. Curtius, and Kirchhoff; *Public Economy of Athens*, 1st Germ. ed. 1817). Boeckh was himself a follower of Wolf, whose most distinguished pupils were Bekker (1786–1871; Demosthenes; *Oratores Attici*; Aristotle); Buttmann (*Lexilogus*, 1818–25); Heindorf (Plato; Theocritus) and Bernhardy (who wrote on both Greek and Roman literary history and issued a monumental Suidas, 1834–58).

13. Among Boeckh's own pupils the most prominent were K. O. Müller (1797–1840: *Die Dorier*; *Die Etrusker*; ed. of Varro, *De Ling. Latina*; *Lit. of Ancient Greece*); E. Curtius (1814–96; the historian whose influence largely contributed to the excavation of Olympia); Koehler (secretary of the German Archaeological Institute at Rome); and Kirchhoff (1826–1908; distinguished in the textual criticism of Euripides, Plotinus, and Aeschylus, as well as in epigraphy).

14. Here it is worth observing that the dissertations on the *Eumenides* (1833; Engl. transl. 1835) accompanying K. O. Müller's text are of a type which Boeckh, Dissen, and Welcker preferred to the exclusive method of verbal criticism followed by Hermann. Welcker's (1784–1868) *Die griechische Tragoedien*, 1841, still possesses value; for followers of the historical line of research were often drawn to the aesthetic side of the ancient world, and Welcker's aim was to view Greece under the threefold aspect of religion, poetry, and art, an aim colouring his editions of Hesiod's *Theogony*, etc., while his most extensive work dealt with Greek tragedies in relation to the epic cycle.

15. The influence bequeathed by teachers, whether purely Hermannic or Boeckhian, whether a blend of these or sometimes rather reminiscent of Heyne or Wolf, was a great and varied stimulus.

16. Lachmann (1793–1851), who was a junior colleague and collaborator at Göttingen of Dissen, Heyne's pupil, consistently upheld method in textual criticism when editing Latin and Greek authors, signally so in his masterpiece, Lucretius. It appeared exactly in the middle of the century with lasting effects. Similarly, Lobeck (1781–1860) at Königsberg passed on a portion of Hermann's influence to his pupil Lehrs (*De Aristarchi studiis Homericis*, 1833; 1882³); and Bernhardy—one of Wolf's pupils, as we have seen—taught Nauck (1822–92), who edited Homer, Sophocles, Porphyry; *Tragicorum Graecorum Fragmenta*, 1856, 1889², with *Index tragicae dictionis*. In his Euripides the influence of Porson and that of Elmsley are also evident.

17. Between the two rival schools there was a good deal

of interaction: e.g. K. O. Müller's student Schneidewin (1810–66), whose training was largely archaeological, is best known for his Sophocles; and Otto Jahn (1813–69), by some classed in the antiquarian school for numerous archaeological papers, was highly successful in editing many Greek and Latin authors, notably Persius. Ribbeck, whose life (1827–98) almost reached the close of the century, and who was pupil and biographer of G. Hermann's pupil Ritschl, may be selected as a further example of transmitted German influence—though he was a scholar of independence and ingenuity, as seen in his reconstruction of tragedies of the Roman Republic, in his theory of a double text for Juvenal (*Der echte u. d. unechte Iuvenal*), and in his text of Virgil.

18. As to influence, it is right to emphasize that of Bentley and Porson on German metrists and of Elmsley on specialists in Greek drama. G. Hermann had listened to Reiz in his lectures at Leipzig insisting on Bentley's example. Jahn in his courses at Bonn recommended Porson and Elmsley as masters to follow alongside of Hermann, Valckenaer, and Madvig; and Nettleship dates his appreciation of Bentley's greatness from attendance at Haupt's lectures on Horace.

19. Like Ribbeck, Lucian Müller (1836–98) selected for his domain the Latin poets (except Plautus and Terence). He dealt with their prosody and published the fragments of the chief early poets, besides editing Lucilius, Phaedrus, Horace, and Nonius Marcellus. A contemporary was Emil Baehrens (1848–88), to whom we owe the useful collections *Poetae Latini Minores* (not seldom too arbitrarily emended), *Fragmenta Poetarum Latinorum*, and Statius' *Silvae*.

20. Many names of the nineteenth century must be omitted, but mention should be made of the work done early in the century on the Greek Anthology by Jacobs and later on Greek dialects by Ahrens; Westphal on Greek rhythm and music; Rohde on the Greek novel and religion (*Der griechische Roman; Psyche*); Kock and Müller-Strübing on Aristophanes and Greek comic fragments; Halm on Cicero; Merkel on Ovid; Hiller on Tibullus; Urlichs and Detlefsen on the elder Pliny.

21. In the twentieth century among prominent German scholars who died in its first decade were Von Christ (1831–1906), whose *Griechische Literaturgeschichte* has been revised by Schmid and Stählin; Dittenberger (1840–1906), a Platonic and Aristotelian scholar and editor of Greek inscriptions; Blass (1848–1907), noted for *Die Attische Beredsamkeit*, and an authority on Greek pronunciation and prose-rhythm; Furtwängler (1853–1907), one of the most versatile of modern archaeologists, and successor to Brunn as professor in Munich; Zeller (1814–1908), the venerable historian of Greek philosophy. The Roman side lost within the same period by death Buecheler (1837–1908), an able textual critic, conversant with archaic Latin and Italic dialects, editor of Petronius and *Carmina Latina Epigraphica*; Wölfflin (1831–1908), the lexicographer already named who contributed much to the historical study of Latin syntax and edited some books of Livy; Schwabe (1835–1908), best known for work on Catullus and his revision of Teuffel's *Geschichte d. römischen Literatur*; Friedländer (1824–1909), whose works included a survey of Homeric criticism from Wolf to Grote, *Sittengeschichte Roms* (Engl. transl.), Petronius' *Cena Trimalchionis*, and Juvenal.

22. Of those who died within the next thirty years there should be mentioned, mainly on the Greek side, Wecklein (1843–1926), in particular a student of Attic drama; von Arnim (1859–1931), memorable for his labours on Stoic philosophy; Diels for his *Doxographi Graeci* (1879, rp. 1929), studies of commentaries on Aristotle, and editions of the pre-Socratics; Eduard Meyer (1855–1930), admirably represented by his elaborate *Geschichte des Altertums*, 5 vols.; and Birt (1852–1933), author of *Das antike Buchwesen*, etc. Wilamowitz-Moellendorff (1848–1931), one of the greatest Greek scholars of all time, produced a long series of works including important treatises on Homer, Pindar, Plato, Greek Tragedy, and the text of the lyric and bucolic poets, editions of Eur. *HF* and other plays, the epoch-making *Verskunst*, and the posthumous *Glaube der Hellenen*. His powerful genius embraced literature, art, archaeology, history, and other subjects as parts of a unified Hellenism.

23. On the Roman side there died in this period Leo, author of important studies of Plautus and Roman comedy, whose *The Archaic (Roman) Literature* (1913) was an instalment of his projected *Roman Literature*; Schanz(1842–1914), whose monumental *Römische Literaturgeschichte* has been revised by Hosius and others; Kroll (d. 1937), a student of Ciceronian society who shared in the reissue of Teuffel's *Röm. Lit.* and of Pauly–Wissowa, *Real-Encyclopädie*; Seeck (1850–1921), author of *Gesch. des Untergangs der antiken Welt*.

24. There also passed away Vollmer (1867–1923), a competent textual critic, editor of Horace and Statius and reviser of parts of Baehrens's *Poet. Lat. Minores*; Immisch (1862–1936), who added to many classical writings his *Horazens Epistel über die Dichtkunst*; Hosius (1866–1937), who edited A. Gellius (after Hertz) and Lucan, and also re-edited several volumes of Schanz; W. Heraeus (1862–1938), editor of Petronius and Martial; Dessau (1856–1931) is best known by his *Inscriptiones Latinae Selectae*, and Wissowa (1859–1931) is remembered equally for his *Religion u. Kultus der Römer* and for his editorship, after Pauly, of the *Realencyclopaedie*.

25. A few Austrian names may be added: Hartel (d. 1907) for Greek epigraphy; Swoboda (d. 1926) for competence in problems of Greek history; Kappelmacher (d. 1932) for work on Lucilius and other authors.

III. Great Britain

26. In Great Britain, for the early part of the nineteenth century a dominant feature was the survival of the Porsonian tradition of exact verbal scholarship. Its representatives were, at Oxford, Elmsley in separate plays of Euripides, Aristophanes, and Sophocles from 1806 to 1823, and the Cambridge scholars Dobree, who with his *Plutus* edited Porson's notes on Aristophanes, 1820; Blomfield, editor of five plays of Aeschylus, who had joined Monk in publishing Porson's *Adversaria . . . in poetas Graecos*, 1812; and Monk, author of *The Life of Bentley*, 1830, and editor of several plays of Euripides after 1840. They did not confine themselves to Greek drama: Elmsley published a Thucydides in six volumes; Dobree gave attention to the Attic orators, especially Demosthenes and Lysias. Badham (1813–84) united with his fidelity to Porson an enthusiasm for Cobet: he went in 1867 to Sydney, where, as Professor of Greek, he greatly furthered Australian education.

27. The tastes of Gaisford (1779–1855), Professor of Greek at Oxford, though he published Porson's notes on Pausanias, lay mainly elsewhere. He edited Cicero's *Tusculans* with Bentley's emendations and turned to Greek authors, *Poetae minores Graeci*, Herodotus, Suidas, Hephaestion, and Stobaeus.

28. Another factor operative at a time when in England a measure of lethargy weakened learning was direct touch with classical lands. Both before and after Greece won her independence, travel by scholarly observers was frequent. Their journals and drawings made Greece, Greek islands, Troy, and other parts of Asia Minor living attractions. There is permanent value in the works of Dodwell, Gell, Christopher Wordsworth, and Colonel Leake (an accomplished topographer and numismatist). Mure, whose five volumes on Greek literature were well received by the reading public in 1850, had issued his account of *A Tour in Greece and the Ionian Islands* in 1842; and Fellowes, the discoverer of the Xanthian marbles, published in various years after 1839 the journals he kept in Asia Minor. These heralded Newton's history of his discoveries at Halicarnassus, Cnidus, and elsewhere in the Levant, 1862–5. They paved the way for Bunbury and Tozer on ancient geography and for fresh explorations in Asia Minor from the eighties onwards by W. M. Ramsay and others.

29. But whatever the galvanizing effects of travel and the study of ancient art, the classics could not live a fully awakened life by these and the Porsonian tradition. There was justification for J. W. Donaldson's complaint in his *Varronianus*, 1844, that Latin scholarship was not flourishing in England, but lagged behind the standard reached by continental research.

30. Rectification was at hand. By the date of the third edition of *Varronianus*, 1860, Donaldson discerned proofs of a renewed devotion to the minutiae of Latin criticism. This was aided by recognition of the stimulating labours of continental scholars—Ritschl, Madvig, Lachmann. University Colleges in England were increasing in number, and the Scottish Universities developing fresh vigour. Glasgow provides an example. Lushington, senior classic at Cambridge in 1832, became Professor of Greek at Glasgow in 1838 and held the Chair for nearly forty years. An inspiring teacher, he possessed consummate skill in composition and breadth enough to combine admiration for both Hermann and Boeckh. Among his pupils were three distinguished scholars, all of whom went to Balliol: W. Y. Sellar, Professor of Humanity, Edinburgh, who began his literary works with *Roman Poets of the Republic*, 1863; Lewis Campbell, Professor of Greek, St. Andrews, editor of Sophocles 1871–81, and an accomplished writer of Greek verse; and D. B. Monro, Provost of Oriel, author of *A Grammar of the Homeric Dialect*, 1882 (2nd ed., 1891).

31. Henceforth the balance was more evenly held between Greek and Latin and there is steady achievement in the latter from the time of Conington, the first occupant of the Latin Chair at Oxford (1854–69) and H. A. J. Munro, first occupant of the Latin Chair at Cambridge (1869–72). Conington's early Aeschylean and Homeric works are not so memorable as his Virgil (1863), his verse translation of Horace, often extremely happy, and his Persius (Lat. and Engl.), edited after his death by his successor in the Latin Chair, Nettleship. Munro, who tempered his admiration for Ritschl and Lachmann with sturdy independence, had produced his *Aetna* and his famous Lucretius before he was Professor. His studies in Catullus appeared in 1878: the fragments of Lucilius and of Euripides occupied him, and his virile rendering of Gray's *Elegy* is a good specimen of his verse composition.

32. Other latinists in Britain during the later nineteenth century and in the twentieth should be mentioned. Several of the best scholars published grammars which have gone through many editions. *A Grammar of the Latin Language* by Roby first appeared in 1871: later he devoted attention to Roman private law. Lexicography was represented by Key in his unfinished dictionary published posthumously in 1888; and several of Nettleship's papers proved the increased interest in lexicography and ancient grammarians. John Wordsworth's *Fragments and Specimens of Early Latin* directed attention to the archaic documents and writers. W. Ramsay of Glasgow (d. 1865) had his unfinished *Mostellaria* of Plautus completed by his nephew G. G. Ramsay; and Plautine studies were later developed by Sonnenschein, Lindsay, and others. The elder Ramsay's *Roman Antiquities*, originally published 1851, was enhanced in usefulness by Lanciani's revision of 1901.

33. The achievement of the period in Latin can be appreciated from a selection of editions. Holden's Minucius Felix goes back to 1853, but by his Aristophanic and other work and his skill in composition he belongs to both languages. Sound scholarship was shown in Wickham's

Horace (1874–9), and in Palmer's *Satires* of Horace (1883): Palmer's ability in textual criticism was also exercised on Ovid's *Heroïdes*, Propertius, Plautus' *Amphitruo*, and Catullus, and among Greek authors on Bacchylides and Aristophanes. Another scholar who aided Horatian study was A. S. Wilkins in the *Epistles*: his *De Oratore* (3 vols., 1879–92) included a survey of ancient rhetoric. Authors of the Silver Age were represented in Furneaux's Tacitus (1884 ff.) and in Peterson's Quintilian X (1891) and Tacitus' *Dialogus* (1893). The Dublin physician, James Henry, gave years of close attention to the MSS. and interpretation of Virgil in his *Aeneidea* (1873–89). Over a long period, J. S. Reid, who became Professor of Ancient History in Cambridge, greatly advanced Ciceronian scholarship by editions of the *Academica*, *De Finibus*, and many of the speeches.

34. If one pursues the record for Latin into the twentieth century, other scholars emerge. Robinson Ellis (1834–1913), Professor of Latin at Oxford, an able textual critic, is especially associated with Catullus, Ovid's *Ibis*, Avianus, *Aetna*, and (1907) with the *Appendix Vergiliana*. Warde Fowler (1847–1921) had a wide range of interests— *Julius Caesar, The City State, Roman Festivals, Social Life in the Age of Cicero, Religious Experience in the Age of Cicero, The Messianic Eclogue* (with J. B. Mayor and R. S. Conway), and suggestive studies of some of the later books of the *Aeneid*. Postgate (d. 1926), Professor of Latin at Liverpool, an expert on grammar and style (*Sermo Latinus*), edited the *Corpus Poetarum Latinorum* (i, 1894, ii, 1905), to which he himself contributed Catullus, Propertius, Grattius, Columella, parts of Statius, Nemesianus, etc. Phillimore (1873–1926), tutor of Christ Church, Oxford, afterwards Professor of Greek and then of Humanity at Glasgow, edited Propertius, Statius' *Silvae*, etc. *Musa Clauda* shows his power of versification. Conway (1864–1933), Professor of Latin, Manchester, made his mark by his *Italic Dialects*; but, besides his eminence as a philologist and grammarian, he was a Virgilian enthusiast whether in lecturing or writing. His projected revision of Conington's *Aeneid* got no farther than Book I. With others he edited a great part of Livy (O.C.T.).

35. Housman (d. 1936), Professor of Latin, Cambridge, secured fame as an English poet, textual critic, and exact scholar. Perhaps nowhere are his qualities better seen than in his Manilius, the revised edition of which (5 vols.) was completed in 1937, the year after his death. To Postgate's *CPL* he contributed the *Ibis* and Juvenal, the latter being also separately edited 'editorum in usum' (1905, 2nd ed. 1931). A. C. Clark (1859–1937), Professor of Latin, Oxford, did work of great importance on Cicero (e.g. volumes of *Orationes*, O.C.T.) and on Latin prose-rhythm (*Fontes Prosae Numerosae*, etc.). Lindsay (1858–1937), Professor of Humanity, St. Andrews, produced his *Latin Language* in 1894, followed by *A Short Historical Latin Grammar* and *Early Latin Verse*. For O.C.T. he edited Plautus, Martial, Isidore, and in collaboration Terence, and for the Teubner series Nonius Marcellus and Festus. S. G. Owen (1858–1940), Reader in Latin, Oxford, devoted attention to Ovid, Persius, and Juvenal, and for a time edited *The Year's Work in Classical Studies*.

36. Some scholars serve as a bridge between Latinists and Hellenists, e.g. J. E. B. Mayor (1825–1910), whose many works include an edition of *Odyssey* ix–x, an elaborate Juvenal, Pliny, *Epistles III*, and *A Bibliographical Clue to Latin Literature* (based on Hübner); Shuckburgh (1843–1906), who divided his labours between history (*Augustus*), editions (Herodotus 5, 6, 8, 9), and a translation of Cicero's letters (4 vols., 1899–1900); and Tyrrell of Dublin (1844–1914), a tasteful translator into Greek and Latin verse, the editor of many classics in both languages (*Bacchae, Troades, Sophoclis, Tragoediae*, Plautus' *Mil. Glor.*) and, with Purser, of *The Correspondence of Cicero* (arranged chronologically with revision of text, commentary, and essays).

37. We go back to those who, after about the middle of the last century, were predominantly Hellenists. B. H. Kennedy (1804–89) after his Headmastership at Shrewsbury was for twenty-two years Professor of Greek at Cambridge. Though he produced a *Latin Primer* in 1866 (since revised for two generations) and a Virgil, he used both languages skilfully in *Sabrinae Corolla* and in *Between Whiles*. He translated the *Birds*, and edited (with transl.) *Agamemnon*, *Theaetetus*, and *Oedipus Tyrannus*. Shilleto (1809–76) was noted for his *De Falsa Legatione* (1844) and his Greek and Latin compositions. Blakesley (1808–85) brought geography and history to bear on his Herodotus (1852–3). Blaydes (1818–1908) concentrated on Aristophanes and Sophocles. Paley (1815–88), a fertile scholar, issued, after Propertius and the *Fasti*, his editions of Aeschylus (1855), Euripides (3 vols., 1856–60, 2nd ed. 1872–80), and the *Iliad* (1866).

38. The study of Roman history was materially helped at this period by the stimulating lectures and writings of Pelham (1846–1907), as well as those of Strachan-Davidson (1843–1916), Master of Balliol, an authority on Cicero, Republican politics, and the criminal law of Rome.

39. The study of Aristotle was continued by Cope's *Rhetoric* (1867) and by Sir A. Grant's *Ethics* (1857; 1884[4]), and Chandler's standard work on Greek accents (1862) should not obscure his deep knowledge of Aristotle; while the study of Plato was continued by Geddes's *Phaedo* (1863 and ed. 2 later), Riddell's *Apology* (1867), with a valuable digest of Platonic idioms, and by W. H. Thompson's *Phaedrus* (1868) and *Gorgias* (1871). In the same year Jowett, Professor of Greek in Oxford, made the *Dialogues* 'an English classic' and ten years later published his translation of Thucydides and the *Politics* in 1885. The year after his death (1894) his text of the *Republic* (with Campbell) came out. Archer-Hind (1849–1910), an excellent translator into Greek prose and verse, had issued a *Phaedo* (1883) and *Timaeus* (1888). James Adam (1860–1907), a profound student of Plato, edited various smaller dialogues and the *Republic* (1897). The substance of his Gifford lectures at Aberdeen appeared posthumously as *The Religious Teachers of Greece* (1908). The Platonic record was continued in the *Phaedo* (1911) of Burnet of St. Andrews, and his *Plato* (O.C.T.). He was extensively concerned with Early Greek philosophy. E. Abbott (1843–1901), editor of the *Hellenica* essays and joint translator of Duncker's *Greek History* (1896), issued Herodotus 5, 6 (1893), and later 9. Others who annotated books of Herodotus were Sayce, 1–3 (1883), and Macan, 4–5, 7–9 (1908).

40. Jebb (1841–1905) before exchanging the Greek Chair at Glasgow for that in Cambridge had produced his *Bentley*, his introduction to *Homer*, and his *Attic Orators*, and had begun his masterly edition of Sophocles (1887–96). *Bacchylides* came out in 1905 and his translation of Aristotle's *Rhetoric* was edited by Sandys in 1909. His volume of *Translations* with Jackson and Currey illustrated his felicity in versions from and into Greek and Latin prose and verse. Haigh (1855–1905), besides collaborating with Papillon on Virgil, gave attention to the stage of the Athenians in *The Attic Theatre* (1889; rev. 1898) and to the dramatists in *The Tragic Drama of the Greeks* (1896). W. G. Headlam (1866–1908) showed profound grasp of Greek lyric diction, particularly in Aeschylus: his *Agamemnon* (ed. A. C. Pearson) and his *Herodas* (with A. D. Knox) came out posthumously. Much of Headlam's work on Aeschylus first saw the light in George Thomson's edition of the *Oresteia*. Rutherford (1853–1907), an admirer of Cobet, produced a valuable work on Attic Greek in *The New Phrynichus* (1881), and edited Babrius' *Fables* (1883), Thucydides 4 (1889), and *Scholia Aristophanica* (1896). Butcher (1850–1910), Professor of Greek at Edinburgh,

is well remembered for his prose translation with Lang of the *Odyssey* (1879). His addresses at Harvard are naturally in lighter style than that in his Exposition of *Aristotle's Theory of Poetry and the Fine Arts* (with critical text of the *Poetics*). Verrall (1851–1912), ingenious, stimulating, often daring in hypothesis and exegesis, is well represented by *Studies in the Odes of Horace* (1884), *Euripides the Rationalist* (1895), and editions of *Agamemnon*, *Choephori*, *Eumenides*, and *Ion*. Bywater (1840–1914), Professor of Greek in Oxford, edited Heraclitus' fragments (1877), *Ethica Nicomachea* (1890), and the *Poetics* (1898). His contributions to *Journal of Philology* (1879–1914) were mainly on Aristotelian subjects. Beare (1857–1918), of Dublin, published his *Select Satires of Horace* (1882), *Greek Theories of Cognition* (1906), and his translation of the works (*Parva Naturalia*, etc.) contained in the Oxford *Works of Aristotle*, iii (1907). His colleague, Mahaffy (1839–1919), was a fertile writer on Greek literature and social life. His writings include *Prolegomena to Ancient History* (1871); *A History of Greek Classical Literature* (1880); *The Flinders-Petrie Papyri* with transcriptions, commentaries, index [with J. G. Smyly], 3 vols. 1891–1905. Merry (1835–1918) edited the *Odyssey* and, with congenial understanding, many plays of Aristophanes. His contemporary Rogers (1828–1919) published 1910–15 *The Comedies of Aristophanes*, edited, translated, and explained. Henry Jackson (1839–1921), Professor of Greek, Cambridge, contributed powerfully by his lectures to the study of Greek philosophy, especially of Plato and Aristotle. Valuable articles from his pen appeared in *Journal of Philology* (e.g. on Plato's later theory of Ideas), in *Transactions and Proceedings of the Cambridge Philological Society*, and in *Encycl. Brit.* R. A. Neil's (1852–1901) *Knights* is an outstanding edition. Sir Samuel Dill (1844–1924), Corpus Christi College, Oxford, Professor of Greek, Belfast, wrote two notable works, *Roman Society in the Last Century of the Western Empire* and *Roman Society from Nero to Marcus Aurelius*.

41. Bury (1861–1927) was an indefatigable worker. His bibliography includes the *Nemean* and *Isthmian Odes*, Greek and Latin verse, Valerius Flaccus (in Postgate's *CPL*), histories of Greece, of the Roman Empire, of the later Roman Empire, and many articles and reviews. On the Byzantine Empire he was an expert. He had been Professor of Greek in Dublin; there he had also been Professor of Modern History, and later in Cambridge held the corresponding chair.

42. Leaf (1852–1927) combined business activities with wide Homeric scholarship, linguistic and archaeological, especially in his *Iliad* (2 vols.).

43. Sir J. E. Sandys (1844–1922), Public Orator at Cambridge (1876–1914), edited various speeches of Demosthenes; *Bacchae* (1880; 1900[4]); Cicero, *Orator* (1885); *Aristotle's Constitution of Athens* (1893; 1912[2]). He was author of *A History of Classical Scholarship*, 3 vols.; *Latin Epigraphy* (1909); contributor to *Camb. Companion to Greek Studies*; editor of and contributor to *Companion to Latin Studies* 1910; 1921[3]; rp. 1935.

44. Sonnenschein (d. 1929) was a learned and productive grammarian: his Plautine works include editions of *Captivi* and *Rudens*. Farnell (1856–1934) proved his authority on Greek religion in *The Cults of the Greek States*, 5 vols., 1896–1909, in published series of lectures, and towards the end of his life in what was a long-cherished enthusiasm, an edition of Pindar, 1930–2.

IV. FRANCE

45. France in the nineteenth century made noteworthy contributions to scholarship. The study of the classics faced difficulties under the First Empire and Latin in schools met with set-backs from changes of government policy in education; but a renaissance can be traced to the foundation in 1866 of the *École pratique des Hautes-Études* by Duruy, himself an eminent historian, when Minister of Public Instruction. There were other factors. The wealth of MSS. in French libraries, the Roman remains in Provence and North Africa, the inspiration of the Louvre, the training of many classicists in the French Schools at Athens (from 1846) and at Rome (from 1873) all played a part as incentives. The attraction of archaeology and the establishment of two Schools abroad, with their varied influence, justify consideration of this subject in the first place.

ARCHAEOLOGY. **46.** Early in the century, among archaeologists A. L. Millin was the author of *Monuments antiques inédits* (1802–6) and produced full descriptions of Roman remains in southern France. Quatremère's *Le Jupiter Olympien* (1815), the Comte de Clarac's outline-engravings of sculptures in the Louvre (1826–30), Rochette's views on Pergamene art, all bequeathed material of value. The Lenormants, father and son, were active researchers in ancient art and numismatics. Mionnet on coins and Rayet on the Tanagra figurines merit attention. From the middle of the century the influence of the School at Athens was marked. A summary of its inspiration is given by Sandys (*Hist. Class. Scholarship* iii. 266–7) up to the directorate of Homolle at the beginning of the twentieth century. Radet published a history of the School, and the School itself published its results at first as *Archives*, then as a *Bulletin*, which in 1879 became the *Bulletin de Correspondance Hellénique*.

47. Archaeology was not the sole concern kept in view. The range into literature, grammar, history, and religion may be seen from a few names and titles by former members of the School who drew therefrom their stimulus towards researches for which afterwards they won fame. Beulé (*L'Acropole*, 1852–4: books on several Roman emperors); De Coulanges, in 1875 Professor of Ancient History at the Sorbonne; *La Cité Antique*, 1864, influential as a survey of political institutions; Decharme (*Euripide et l'esprit de son théâtre*, 1893); Collignon (*Sculpture grecque*, 2 vols.; completion of Rayet's *Céramique grecque*); Riemann 1853–91 (thesis on Livy's language and grammar 1879; collaborated with Goelzer in *Grammaire Comparée du Grec et du Latin*, 2 vols., 1897–1901; *Syntaxe Latine*, revised by Lejay and then by Ernout, reached its 8th ed. 1927); S. Reinach (*Cultes, mythes et religions*, 5 vols., 1902–23, and other works on religion and art; *Reliefs*, 1909–12); Hauvette (d. 1908; shared in exploration of Delos; wrote on Athenian *strategoi*, and on Herodotus, Simonides, Callimachus, his lectures in Paris being mainly on Greek literature); Monceaux (*Apulée*, 1889; *Les Africains*, 1894; *Hist. lit. de l'Afrique chrétienne*, 7 vols., 1902 ff.); and Homolle, as Director of the School responsible for the excavations at Delphi and Delos.

48. The School at Rome comes later (1873), and *La Bibliothèque des Écoles françaises d'Athènes et de Rome* includes valuable work on literature and history, e.g. *La Vie municipale dans l'Égypte* by Jouguet, the papyrologist, Albertini's *La Composition dans les ouvrages philosophiques de Sénèque*, and Carcopino's *Virgile et les origines d'Ostie*.

PALAEOGRAPHY and INSCRIPTIONS. **49.** B. E. C. Miller (1812–86) entered the MSS. department of the Paris Library in 1834 and became an expert palaeographer, examining MSS. in many countries, especially Medieval Greek. He joined with Beulé, de Presle, and d'Eichthal in founding the French Association for the Promotion of Greek Research. Egger (1813–85), editor of 'Longinus' and of Varro, *De Lingua Latina*, wrote on criticism among the Greeks, on papyri and inscriptions, and remains memorable for his work on Hellenism in France. A young scholar, Graux (1852–82), who lived less than thirty years, achieved notable proficiency in Greek

palaeography. He was a pupil of Tournier (1831–99), who edited Sophocles in 1867. Valckenaer (1771–1852), secretary of the Academy of Inscriptions in 1840, was a Horatian scholar and student of ancient geography. Desjardins also united keenness for geography and epigraphy. Renier (1809–85) edited the Roman inscriptions of Algeria. Cagnat, an epigraphic authority on North Africa, we shall mention again when we come to the twentieth century. L. Delisle, Director of the Bibliothèque Nationale (d. 1909) by his catalogues, palaeographical knowledge, and personal help rendered eminent services to classical scholars everywhere.

PURE CLASSICS. **50.** In Pure Classics, the record may begin with Boissonade, Larcher's successor as Professor of Greek in the University of Paris, 1813, and Gail's successor at the Collège de France, 1828. Boissonade's annotated Greek poets in 24 vols. saved some of them from oblivion; his editions of prose authors were mainly of the later Greek age. His services to the Greek *Thesaurus* should be recalled. J. L. Burnouf (1775–1844), famous for a Greek grammar, translated Tacitus; and Victor Cousin (1792–1867) the whole of Plato. Nearly contemporary with Cousin, Patin translated Horace and issued his studies, showing learning and judgement, of Greek tragic authors and of Latin poets.

51. T. H. Martin (1813–84) was led by his studies on Plato's *Timaeus*, 1841, to the domain of ancient science. A later generation saw Greek science treated by Tannery (1843–1904). Portions of Hippocrates and Galen, 1854–6, were translated by Daremberg, familiar as Saglio's coadjutor on the *Dictionnaire des Antiquités*. Another renowned lexicographer, Littré, also worked on Hippocrates, completing his edition and translation (10 vols., 1839–61). Alexandre (1797–1870), editor of the Sibylline oracles, deserves mention for his *Greek and French Dictionary*. Charles Thurot (1823–82), whose father and uncle were scholars, concerned himself in Greek with Aristotle and in Latin with the grammar of medieval schools. His international outlook is shown in his respect for Madvig's *Adversaria Critica*. An older scholar, Saint-Hilaire (1805–95), made Aristotle the concern of a long lifetime both as translator and expositor. Another authority on Aristotle and on aspects of ancient, medieval, and Renaissance philosophy was C. Waddington, of English descent. His cousin was W. H. Waddington, educated in Paris and Cambridge, who travelled in Greece and Asia Minor, served as ambassador of France to Great Britain 1883–93, and made his mark in epigraphy and numismatics.

52. Benoist (1831–87) worked chiefly on Latin. Those of his school included Waltz, Goelzer, Plessis, and Causeret. His larger edition of Virgil was published in 1876–80. He raised the standard of editing in France and with his pupil Riemann edited Livy 21–5.

53. In the history of literature and literary criticism there was a field where the genius of France shone and deserves a conspicuous place. The history of Greek literature can be studied in the five vols. of A. and M. Croiset (1888–99), a work of graceful lucidity. Couat's *Alexandrian Poetry under the First Three Ptolemies* is authoritative on a special period. Desiré Nisard (1806–88), Professor of Latin Eloquence at the Collège de France, produced attractive studies on the Latin poets of the decadence and the four great Latin historians: his brother Charles contributed French translations of several Latin authors edited by Desiré. Pichon's *Histoire de la littérature latine* has appeared in several editions well into the twentieth century, and has been followed in 1934 by Bayet's work on the same subject. Lamarre's account of the literature to the end of the Republic (4 vols., 1901) is over-elaborate in illustrative quotations. De la Ville de Mirmont published studies on the oldest Latin poetry in 1903, and Lejay, editor of Horace's *Satires* and Virgil, a history of Latin literature to Plautus, 1928. Labriolle records ably the *History of Latin Christian Literature*, 1924².

54. In studies of individual authors France has been prolific from Sainte-Beuve's *Étude sur Virgile* and Taine's *Essai sur Tite-Live* to such later works as Macé's *Suétone* (1900), Boissier's *Martial* in his *Tacite* (1904²), Villeneuve's *Perse* (1918), Bourgéry's *Sénèque le prosateur* (1922), Guillemin's *L'Originalité de Virgile* (1931), Bornecque's *Tite-Live* (1933).

55. France has always been strong in rhetoric. The Chair of Eloquence at the Sorbonne and the lectures of Villemain, brilliantly popular rather than deep, exemplified a national passion, although about the beginning of the twentieth century Navarre's *Essai sur la rhétorique grecque* expressed fears of a coming period of neglect. But books which kept the subject in view were Jullien's *Les Professeurs de littérature dans l'ancienne Rome*, 1886, Berger and Cucheval's *Hist. de l'éloquence romaine depuis la mort de Cicéron jusqu'à l'avènement de l'Empereur Hadrien*, 1892², and Cucheval's survey of *Roman Eloquence after Cicero*, 1893.

56. Bornecque too, besides editing and translating Seneca's *Controversiae et Suasoriae*, Cicero's *Orator*, 1921, and the *Rhet. ad Herennium*, 1932, had in 1902 published *Les Déclamations et les déclamateurs d'après Sénèque le père*. From Marouzeau's *Essai de stylistique latine* it is not a far step to the kindred subject of literary style in individual writers. Virtually all the main classical and patristic authors have been surveyed in French monographs.

57. To linguistics and grammar distinguished scholarship has been devoted. Riemann has been mentioned among ex-pupils of the School at Athens. Among Meillet's works may be cited *Les Dialectes indo-européens*, 1908, 1922; *Introd. à l'étude compar. des langues indo-européennes*, 1937⁸; *Aperçu d'une histoire de la langue grecque*, 1913, 1920²; *Esquisse d'une histoire de la langue latine*, 1933³. Meillet combined with Vendryes (author of *Le langage: introd. linguistique à l'histoire*, 1921) for a *Traité de grammaire comparée des langues classiques²*, 1927 and with Ernout, an authority on dialectic and archaic Latin, for a *Dict. étymologique de la langue latine*, 1931.

58. Among French scholars who lived into the twentieth century were Victor Henry (1850–1907) of the Sorbonne, well known for comparative grammars of Greek and Latin; the veteran Boissier (1823–1908), delightful for a winsome blend of literary brilliance and archaeological learning in *Cicéron et ses amis* (often republished since 1865; Engl. transl.), *La Religion romaine*, 1874, *L'Opposition sous les Césars*, 1875, *Promenades archéologiques*, 1880, *La Fin du paganisme*, 1891, *L'Afrique romaine*, 1895, etc.

59. Cagnat, epigraphist and historian, author of *Étude historique sur les impôts indirects chez les romains*, 1882, *Cours d'épigraphie latine*, 1885, 1914⁴, *Carthage Timgad Tebessa*, 1909, *L'Armée romaine d'Afrique*, 1912, *Inscriptiones graecae ad res romanas pertinentes*, 1901– ; Weil (1818–1909); *Euripides*, 7 plays, 1868; *Demosthenes*, chief speeches; *Aeschylus*, 1884, 1907²; *Études*, 1897–1900 (his pronounced Hellenism helped towards a fairer view of Euripides: obituaries by Bouché-Leclercq and others, Bursian's *Biog. Jahrb.* 1911); Havet (elected F.B.A. 1917, since deceased), *De Saturnio latinorum versu*, 1880; *Phaedri Fabulae*; *Manuel de critique verbale appliquée aux textes latins*, 1911.

60. Political history both of Greece and of Rome can be represented by Duruy (1811–94), already mentioned in another connexion. A new edition of his *Histoire des Romains* was issued 1917–20. More limited periods have been covered in books like that by De Presle (an expert in modern Greek) on the Greeks in Sicily and Greeks under Roman rule, or Mérimée's handling of Catiline and the Social War, and his collaboration in the *Histoire de César* by Napoleon III. In the twenties of this century an important series appeared under the broad title

of *L'Évolution de l'humanité*, to which competent scholars like Chapot, Glotz, Grenier, Homo, Jouguet, Lot, and Toutain contributed volumes on classical subjects covering a wide range from Aegean civilization to the Macedonian and from primitive Italy to the end of the ancient world.

61. There have been many special studies of individual historical figures and of emperors, of Roman towns in France and North Africa, and of economic and social problems (e.g. Wallon's learned account of ancient slavery, 1847, republished 1879). To Reinach's history of religions, already named, may be added Toutain's *Les Cultes païens dans l'empire romain*, 3 vols. 1908–20.

V. ITALY

62. In Italy the record of modern classical scholarship may open with Cardinal Mai (1782–1854), whose discoveries from palimpsests at the Ambrosian and Vatican Libraries led to his publication of the correspondence of M. Aurelius and Fronto (Milan, 1815; Rome, 1823). At Rome he edited large portions of Cicero *De Republica* from a Vatican palimpsest: later, his extensive collections from Vatican MSS. amounted to over thirty volumes. His publications from Greek included portions of Isaeus and Dionysius of Halicarnassus.

63. Peyron (1785–1870) edited fresh fragments from Cicero's speeches; but did not restrict himself to Latin, for he published fragments from Empedocles and Parmenides (1810), a commentary on Theodosius of Alexandria (1817), and accounts of Greek papyri at Vienna.

64. Vallauri (1805–97), the opponent of Ritschl's methods in critical study of Plautus, published editions of four plays 1853–9, followed by a critical text of the whole, 1873. Vallauri's history of Latin literature, 1849, was the predecessor of several works in the twentieth century.

65. De Vit (1810–92) was noted as a lexicographer: his enlarged Forcellini was completed (except for the unfinished *Onomasticon*) in 1879. Corradini (1820–88) laboured in the same field. His new edition of Forcellini was continued by Perin, 1864–90. Gandino (1827–1905) took special interest in ancient Latin (1878), was a valued contributor to the *Rivista di Filologia*, and author of a work on Latin style (1895).

66. It is intelligible that Greek in Italy should not have been studied in modern times with the fervour of the Renaissance. Mai and Peyron, it is true, had their Hellenic sides. So too had Bonghi (1828–95), who translated Plato, but also wrote a history of Rome and an account of Roman festivals.

67. In Comparative Philology the chief work of Pezzi (1844–1906) was *La lingua greca antica*, 1888, covering the phonology, morphology, and dialects of the Greek language. Ascoli, appointed to the Chair at Milan, attracted notice outside Italy and recognized the linguistic value of Celtic.

68. Archaeology throve in Italy. The Archaeological Institute had been founded in 1829, and Canina (1795–1856) published a second edition of his standard work *L'architettura antica*, 12 vols., 1844. E. A. Visconti (1751–1818) contributed much to the study of Greek and Roman art. Borghesi (1781–1860), an expert on coins and inscriptions, published fresh fragments of the *Fasti Consulares* (2 vols., 1818–20). The nine volumes of his *Collected Works* appeared from 1862 to 1884. The fame of Cavedoni (1795–1865) rested on his numismatic knowledge. Avellino (1788–1850), a professor of Greek, was founder of and frequent contributor to the *Bulletino Archeologico Napolitano*; Garrucci (1812–85) concerned himself with the *Graffiti di Pompei*, and in his later residence at Rome with collections of inscriptions of the Republic and coins of ancient Italy. Fabretti (1816–94) at Turin represented Etrurian antiquities, and Serradifalco with Cavallari handled those of Sicily (5 vols. fol. 1834–42). After the expulsion of the Bourbons Fiorelli (1824–96) became head of the museum at Naples, and director at Pompeii for fifteen years. In 1875 he took charge of museums and excavations in Rome. Bruzza (1812–83), notable for his collection of inscriptions from Vercelli, exercised a stimulus on the study of early Christian archaeology, and De Rossi (1822–94), an able epigraphist and topographer, was an expert not only on early inscriptions from Rome but also on the Christian inscriptions of the catacombs.

69. With monuments of classical antiquity available, with excavations scientifically conducted, and finds (as at Pompeii) skilfully restored, archaeology continued to flourish as in congenial soil. Lanciani, professor at Rome and Director of Excavations (1878), was the eminent author of *Forma Urbis Romae* and other works in Italian and English. He carried on his labours into this present century in *Storia degli scavi di Roma*, 1903, *Golden Days of the Renaissance* (Engl. transl. 1906), and *Wanderings in the Campagna*, 1909. Since his day exploration has been intensified, and its progress recorded in the *Notizie degli scavi* since 1877. Inside the capital itself and along its walls, investigations have been pursued (G. Boni 1859–1925): its more immediate surroundings have been closely examined (e.g. Tomasetti, *La campagna romana*, 3 vols., 1910–13). Pompeii has had many of its structures restored and much of its life re-created (e.g. Matteo della Corte, *Juventus*, 1924, etc.), and the Italian Government has faced the harder problem at Herculaneum (Maiuri, *Herculaneum*, illust. 1932). P. Orsi (1859–1935) rediscovered prehistoric Sicily; L. Pigorini (1842–1925) studied the *terra mare*. Overseas perhaps the most spectacular achievement has been in Crete, where an Italian Archaeological Mission headed by F. Halbherr discovered the great inscription of Gortyn (1884) and began its excavation in 1900 at Phaestos, second only to Cnossos as a Minoan palace: cf. Pernier, *Il palazzo Minoico di Festo*, 1935). Excavations in Cyrenaica have yielded among other objects important fragments of Augustan edicts (1927).

70. The *Rivista di filologia* was founded in 1873; the *Studi di filologia classica* in 1893. *Atene e Roma*, from 1898, has borne a share in quickening the interest in Greek (e.g. Bignone, its editor, has published studies in Theocritus, *Poeti Apollinei*, and *L'Aristotele Perduto e la formazione filosofica di Epicuro*, 2 vols., 1936). Perhaps it is symptomatic that two studies of Sophocles should be published in the same year, Perrotta's *Sofocle*, 1935, and Untersteiner's *Sofocle: studio critico*, 2 vols., 1935.

71. *Il Mondo Classico* also bears its share in reviewing books from different countries. For Latin authors the Paravia series was expressly designed under Pascal's editorship so that Italy should not be obliged to rely on foreign texts: another valuable collection of Latin and Greek writers is published by the Accademia dei Lincei.

72. Among Italian classical scholars of the twentieth century one of the greatest was G. Vitelli (1849–1935), a pioneer in papyrological research.

73. In literary history, Rostagni's *Storia della letteratura Greca*, 1937, made a worthy precursor to his *Letteratura di Roma repubblicana ed Augustea*, 1939. His bibliography records works written by Italian and foreign scholars on the primitive culture and languages of Italy, on archaic and classical authors, including texts. He had competent predecessors on the literary history of Rome in Giussani (1899), Amatucci (2 vols., 1912–16), Marchesi (2 vols., 1925–7; 1933³), and Ussani (1929). Cocchia in 1924–5 concentrated on Latin anterior to Hellenic influence. A history of the Latin language was written by G. Devoto (1940), who also published an edition of the *Tabulae Tigurinae* (2nd ed. 1940). E. Bignone started a new history of Latin literature in 1945. Distinguished research on Lucretius has been carried out by Bignone, on Varro by P. Fraccaro (1907), on the *Odes* of Horace by G. Pasquali (1920), on Horace *Ars Poetica* by A. Rostagni (1930) who wrote also a commentary on Aristotle's

Poetics (1927) and a much-discussed book on *Virgilis minore* (1933). G. Funaidi edited *Grammaticae Romanae fragmenta* I (1907) and studied the ancient commentators of Virgil (1930). Cicero was examined as a lawyer by E. Costa (2nd ed. 1927) and as a politician by E. Ciaceri (1926–30). C. Marchesi wrote on Seneca (3rd ed. 1944) and on Tacitus (1924). E. Malcovati edited the Fragments of the Roman Orators (1930).

74. Of editions, Giussani's Lucretius belongs to 1896–8, but has been re-edited by Stampini 1921 ff. Comparetti and Sabbadini were elected in 1916 and 1922 respectively as corresponding members of the British Academy. The former (b. 1835) was Professor of Greek at Pisa and Florence, published texts of Hyperides and Procopius, wrote on papyri from Herculaneum and the laws of Gortyn in Crete, though his fame chiefly rests on his *Virgilio nel medio evo* (Engl. transl. 1895). Sabbadini distinguished himself as an authority on texts of the Italian Renaissance in virtue of *Le scoperte dei codici latini e greci ne' secoli xiv e xv*, 1905, and *Nuove ricerche*, 1914. He edited Virgil, 2 vols., in 1930. Pasquali published *Storia della tradizione e critica del testi* in 1934.

75. In political history De Sanctis has written both on the Greeks (2 vols.) and on the Romans (4 vols., 1907–23). Pais followed his *Storia di Roma* (2 vols., 1898) and *Ancient Legends of Roman History* (1906) with a *Storia Critica di Roma* for the first five centuries (1913–20), and dealt also with the period of the Mediterranean conquests and the internal history from the Punic Wars to the Gracchan revolution (1931). The most noted of the works of Ferrero, who left Florence for Geneva (d. 1942), is *Grandezza e decadenza di Roma* (E.T. 1909).

76. The study of Roman law owes much to Italian scholars like I. Alibrandi (1823–84); P. Bonfante (1864–1932); V. Arangio-Ruiz; P. De Francisci; S. Riccobono. C. A. Nallino (1929) and E. Volterra (1937) discussed relations between Roman law and oriental laws. P. Fraccaro chiefly contributes to Roman Public Law.

VI. THE LOW COUNTRIES AND SCANDINAVIA

(a) HOLLAND. **77.** Dutch contact with British scholars, though often significant, was not so intimate as in the eighteenth century. We note first the influence of Wyttenbach, who held for forty-five years Chairs at Amsterdam, 1771–99, and at Leyden, 1799–1816. He died in 1820. Among his pupils were Mahne, his biographer; van Lennep, professor at Amsterdam for over half a century from 1799 (*Heroïdes*, Terentianus Maurus, Hesiod); van Heusde, keenly interested in Platonic philosophy; and Bake, notable for intercourse with English Porsonians and for works on Attic oratory and Ciceronian style.

78. Among Bake's pupils was Suringar (1805–95), author of *Ciceronis Commentarii de Vita sua* and *Annales Ciceroniani*, 1854. Geel (1789–1862) in his edition of *Phoenissae*, 1846, supported Valckenaer's views and showed Porson's influence. The group of Greek scholars round Bake and Geel at Leyden included the two brothers W. A. Hirschig (ed. *Scriptores Erotici Graeci*, 1856) and R. B. Hirschig (ed. *Gorgias*, 1873). Reuvens (1793–1835) became known abroad as an archaeologist (e.g. on orientation of the Parthenon and on adornments of Asinius Pollio's Library); his able work was continued (1806–69) by the epigraphist L. J. F. Janssen.

79. To S. Karsten of Utrecht we owe *Agamemnon* (1855), a study of Horace (1861), and works on Greek philosophy, and to his son H. T. Karsten a dissertation on Plato's *Letters*. His pupil C. M. Francken wrote his life and edited Lucan, 1896–7. *Varroniana* appeared in *Mnemosyne* when he was eighty. Peerlkamp (1786–1865), of French descent, was professor at Leyden 1822–48 and issued his much debated *Odes* of Horace 1834: the still less convincing *Ep. ad Pis.* followed 1845 and *Satirae* 1863. His *Aeneid* belongs to 1843.

80. His successor at Leyden was the great Greek scholar Cobet (1813–89). He spent years examining manuscripts in Italy, and the fruits are visible in *Commentationes Philologicae*, 1850–1; *Variae Lectiones*, 1854; *Novae Lectiones*, 1858; *Miscellanea Critica*, 1876; and texts of Greek classics. Exact experience of manuscripts and thorough knowledge of Greek, especially Attic, were essential elements in his methods for curing faulty texts. Concentrating mainly on Greek authors of the Golden Age, he inclined to over-regularize in accord with Attic usage, but he was a critic whose pronouncements could carry commanding authority without sacrificing geniality. Though German scholars like Reiske, the Dindorfs, Bergk, Meineke, Lehrs, and (in his best work) Nauck were valued highly by Cobet, he had by the time of his return from Italy admittedly freed himself from the German school, so that English methods increasingly won his admiration in his 'three Richards'—Bentley, Dawes, Porson—and the heirs of Porson's influence, Elmsley and Dobree. As a vigorous contributor to *Mnemosyne* (founded 1852) he gave fresh life to its second series from 1872.

81. Among Cobet's pupils were Naber (b. 1828; ed. of Josephus, Fronto, and Photius); Halbertsma (*Lectiones Lysiacae*, and posthumous *Adversaria Critica*, ed. Herwerden); and du Rieu (1829–96), proposer of a scheme for photographic reproduction of complete Greek and Latin manuscripts executed under his successor de Vries. These are comparable in utility with Chatelain's *Paléographie des classiques latins*, fol., Paris, 1884–1900, where, for example, the two Leyden manuscripts of Lucretius are finely done and the introduction is of value. Naber and Herwerden (b. 1831) are among Dutch scholars to whom Wilamowitz makes favourable reference in his *Erinnerungen*.

82. Cornelissen (1839–91), who succeeded Pluygers in the Latin Chair at Leyden, was an admirer of Cobet; and van der Vliet (1847–1902) studied Greek palaeography under Cobet and Latin under Pluygers, covering a wide range in his publications.

83. An example of other scholars who continued their labours into the twentieth century was van Leeuwen. After holding 1884–1914 the Chair vacated by Cobet he migrated to Switzerland. Besides papers in *Mnemos.*, he edited Menander (Lat. comm. 1919³), and *Iliad* and *Odyssey*, each in 2 vols. (Lat. comm.), 1912–17. He issued his Aristophanes (Lat. comm.; prolegg.) 1896 to 1909, commendably terse annotation replacing the Burman style of expansive comment. Long before, Boot's notes on *Epp. ad Atticum*, 1865–6 (2nd ed. 1886), had set a pattern of greater brevity.

84. J. J. Hartman of Leyden may be chosen to represent Latin—the indefatigable co-editor of and contributor to *Mnemos.* (e.g. *Propertiana*, 1922). He was the accomplished winner in 1899 of the Hoeufft medal for writing Latin verse (open to any nationality). The notice *in memoriam*, *Mnemos.* 1924, in a page of Latin prose deeply laments his loss.

85. The scholarly traditions of Holland have been worthily maintained in the best theses of its universities.

(*b*) BELGIUM. **86.** Louvain is the oldest university of Belgium—having been active, with some interruptions, from 1426. The other three, Liége, Ghent, Brussels belong to the nineteenth century. At first after 1830 they were staffed in part from abroad. In contrast to Dutch scholars, who on the whole specialized in textual criticism, the Belgian forte was archaeology and constitutional antiquity. De Witte (1808–89) illustrates this point. A traveller in the Near East, he was in touch with many French and Italian institutes, edited the *Gazette archéologique* and the *Revue numismatique*, and published collections illustrating ancient life. A constant correspondent of his was Roulez (1806–78), who became Professor of Greek at Ghent, lecturing on a wide range of subjects, archaeology, art, mythology, literature, and law.

87. Gantrelle (1809–93), Professor of Latin at Ghent, is associated mainly with Tacitus. He and his colleague Wagener (1829–96) were active in editing the *Revue de l'instruction publique*, the former with closer attention to grammar, the latter to archaeology and history. Educated in Germany and France, Wagener combined much that was best in the systems of both countries. Antiphon, Plutarch, Cicero, Tacitus engaged his special attention. A mission to Greece and Asia Minor deepened his knowledge, and after a considerable interval of politics and administrative experience he returned to Ghent to lecture on Greek epigraphy and constitutional history.

88. Roersch (1831–91) of Liége, an expert linguist, championed the study of the ancient world, and collated several manuscripts for his edition of Cornelius Nepos. His sketch of Belgian philology in the encyclopaedia *Patria Belgica* was an able performance. In 1885 with Professor Paul Thomas of Ghent he produced a good Greek grammar. Thomas had a distinguished Latin side commemorated in Brakman's well-deserved greeting on his seventieth birthday (*Mnemos.* 1922) honouring his services to the textual criticism of Terence, Manilius, Velleius, Seneca, Petronius, and other Latin authors.

89. Nève (1816–93) was an orientalist as well as a classic. In his memoir on the *Collegium Trilingue* (1856) he surveyed the study of the learned languages from the sixteenth to the eighteenth century, and much later he dealt with minor humanists of the southern Netherlands.

90. Thonissen (1816–91), for thirty-six years Professor of Criminal Law at Louvain, in a long series of historical and legal works ranged from law in primitive Greece to his study of modern socialism in comparison with the laws of Crete, Athens, Sparta, Rome, and Plato's ideal State.

91. Willems (1840–98), student at Louvain and foreign universities, Paris, Berlin, Leyden, found his life's work not directly in his earlier studies, whether oriental or literary, but mainly in the composition of standard books on the political institutions of Rome. He held a chair at Louvain 1865–98. In 1870 he published his treatise on Roman antiquities, entitled after its first edition *Le Droit public romain*, and 1878–85 his yet more renowned work *Le Sénat de la république romaine*. He founded the *Musée Belge* 1897.

92. To Belgian learning we are indebted in recent years for Cumont's studies of literature, philosophy, and religion (esp. Mithraism) in the Roman Empire.

(*c*) DENMARK. **93.** In the nineteenth century Denmark was distinguished for its contributions to linguistics and grammar. Rask (1787–1832), a student of Icelandic and of Eastern languages, first recognized the philological importance of Zend. To some extent he anticipated 'Grimm's Law'. Verner (1846–96) made his name later by elucidating the exceptions to that 'Law'. But the most famous Danish record was that of Madvig (1804–86), whose special field lay in grammar and verbal criticism. For over half a century he was professor at Copenhagen. By education a Danish product, versed early in legal documents, and later experienced in politics and administration, he brought to bear a judge-like discernment in weighing the truth of doubtful texts. Cicero, *de Finibus*, 1839, won him a European reputation and his Latin Grammar, 1841, was translated into almost every continental language. When he left the Ministry of Education, his interest in Roman constitutional history had as its outcome *Die Verfassung und Verwaltung des römischen Staates*, 1881–2, *Emendationes Livianae*, 1860, and, with Ussing, his pupil, Livy, 1861–6. *Adversaria Critica* on Greek and Latin writers came out 1871–3.

94. Ussing (1820–1905), though originally by bent and on Madvig's advice an archaeologist, published commentaries on Greek authors and a work on Greek and Roman education (translated from Danish into German, 1870), but was best known abroad for collaborating with Madvig on Livy and for his own annotated Plautus 1875–87.

95. In the 20th c. the leading scholars were J. L. Heiberg (d. 1928), A. B. Drachmann (d. 1935), C. Hude (d. 1936), and Ada Adler (d. 1946).

(*d*) NORWAY. **96.** For Norway a university was founded at Christiania (now Oslo), where Bugge (1833–1907), a well-equipped linguist, held for over forty years the Chair of Comparative Philology. Apart from his authority on Scandinavian literature and mythology, he proved a worthy pupil of Madvig by work on Italic dialects, emendations on Plautus, and an edition of *Mostellaria*.

(*e*) SWEDEN. **97.** The endeavour of Queen Christina of Sweden in the seventeenth century to create a Renaissance of the North inspired her invitations to foreign scholars, Grotius, Vossius, N. Heinsius and others, and her purchase of books and manuscripts from France and Italy.

98. Sandys gives a conspectus of professors at Upsala and Lund who contributed to classical learning. It is characteristic of Sweden that scarcity of manuscripts has meant more study in foreign universities, and travels in Italy and Greece have meant more attraction to archaeology. This comes out in typical names. Einar Löfstedt (1831–89), who studied in Germany, succeeded Spongberg in the Greek Chair at Upsala in 1874. He travelled in Italy and the Near East in 1876–7. Among his works was a Greek grammar, 1868; 1885³. A later Einar Löfstedt, of Lund, has earned acknowledged authority in Latin by his *Philologischer Kommentar zur Peregrinatio Aetheriae*, 1911, by *Vermischte Studien zur lateinischer Sprachkunde und Syntax*, 1936, and by *Syntactica*, 1928, 1933 (ed. 2, 1942).

99. Zander's *Versus Saturnii* reached a third edition at Lund, 1918. Lundström (d. 1940), of Göteborg, combined studies on Plautus, Columella, and other Latin authors with archaeology (*Undersökningar i Roms topographi*, 1929). Valmin's work on *The Swedish Messenia Expedition*, 1938, stands for a similar interest in archaeology. A pure scholar, Sjögren (1870–1934: obit. *Bursian*, 1940) was a pupil of Leo at Göttingen. He furthered Ciceronian scholarship by developing Lehmann's views on the text of the *Letters*: L. C. Purser and A. C. Clark thought highly of his work. His *Commentationes Tullianae* appeared 1910 and letters *Ad Familiares* (1925) and *Ad Atticum* (1916–32, not yet complete).

VII. SWITZERLAND

100. Switzerland holds an honourable record in devotion to the classics. In the forefront stands Iohann Caspar Orelli (1787–1849), of a scholarly family in Zürich and noted for editions of Plato, Cicero, Horace, and Tacitus. He is already mentioned in the German section. Baiter, also from Zürich, who studied at several German universities, joined Orelli and his colleague W. Winckelmann (b. Dresden) in editing Plato, 1839 ff. Baiter published Orelli's Horace³, 1850–2; and with Halm continued ed. 2 of Cicero's works, 1846–62, interrupted by Orelli's death. At Zürich, Baiter joined Sauppe (b. near Dresden) in the *Oratores Attici*.

101. Mähly (1828–1902), the author of biographies of Politian and of Bentley, made an important contribution to Latin scholarship in his *Varroniana*, but was interested in Greek as well as Latin lyrics.

102. Schweizer-Sidler (1815–94) edited Tacitus' *Germania* and in half a century at Zürich made his reputation in Latin and Sanskrit. Wirz (1842–1914) issued a critical edition of Sallust. Plüss (1845–1919) was the author of *Horazstudien*, 1882.

103. Among Hellenists may be noted: Hug (1833–95) for his *Anabasis, Cyropaedia*, Plato's *Symposium*, etc.; Hitzig (1843–1918) for his Pausanias in collaboration with Blümner, his German colleague at Zürich; Oeri (1844–1908) for works on Greek tragic writers; Kägi (1849–1923), for a Greek grammar prized in Switzerland; Finsler, for his Homeric learning; and Nicole for Greek papyrology.

104. In history, Billeter (1873–1929) wrote an inquiry on rates of interest in Greece and Rome and on the essence of the Greek character. Stähelin (b. 1873) chose a work of national significance in *Die Schweiz in römischer Zeit*.

105. Switzerland has nowhere proved her strength better than in linguistics, e.g. Wackernagel (1806–69); Thurneysen, whose specialities were Latin and Celtic; De Saussure, teacher of Meillet, the French scholar; Schwyzer (1874–1943), Hellenist and linguist who held professorial chairs in Zürich and in Germany. Wölfflin (1831–1908), already mentioned in the German section for services to the historical study of Latin syntax and to the *Thesaurus*, was born in Bâle, and his professional work in Zürich preceded that in Erlangen and Munich.

106. The classical periodical founded in 1943, *Museum Helveticum*, is intended to give fuller expression to Swiss scholarship.   J. W. D.

VIII. U.S.A.

107. The condition of classical learning in the United States of America at the start of European emigration to the west naturally depended on the qualifications of the particular teachers to be found among the emigrants. English influence was followed by Dutch, Irish (particularly of Ulster), and Scottish. The contributions made were not particularly striking before the nineteenth century, being cultural rather than erudite. With the advent of the nineteenth century, and more and more as the century proceeded, many of the best classical students of the American universities, both State and other, continued their education in the German universities, and that practice persisted into the twentieth century. Elegant compositions in Greek and Latin have never been a characteristic feature of American classical scholarship, but important contributions, as good as those from any European country, have been made in the fields of comparative philology, grammar in the widest sense, lexicography, epigraphy, palaeography, papyrology, history (especially economic and social), religion, and archaeology. Students in other countries will neglect at their peril such periodicals as the *American Journal of Archaeology* (1895–), *American Journal of Philology* (1880–), *Classical Philology* (1906–), *Classical Weekly* (long edited by Charles Knapp, 1907–), *Harvard Studies in Classical Philology* (1890–), and *Hesperia* (1932–).

108. Among notable editions of classical authors are Pind. *Ol.* and *Pyth.* by B. L. Gildersleeve (1885), Dem. *De Cor.* by W. Goodwin (1901), *Meid.* (1906), Amm. Marc., by C. U. Clark, etc. (1910–15), Cic. *Div.* by A. S. Pease (1920–3), Verg. *Aen. IV* by A. S. Pease (1935).

COMPARATIVE PHILOLOGY: C. D. Buck, *Compar. Gram. of Gk. and Lat.* (1937), *Introd. to Study of Gk. Dialects, Grammar of Oscan and Umbrian* (1928).

GREEK AND LATIN GRAMMAR: B. L. Gildersleeve and C. W. E. Miller, *Syntax of Classical Gk. from Hom. to Dem.* (1901–11), W. W. Goodwin, *Syntax of the Moods and Tenses of the Greek Verb*, new ed. (1889), H. W. Smyth, *Sounds and Inflexions of Gk. Dialects, Ionic* (1894), W. G. Hale, *The Cum Constructions* (1887–9), C. E. Bennett, *Syntax of Early Latin* (1910–14).

GREEK AND LATIN LEXICOGRAPHY: E. A. Sophocles, *Gk. Lexicon of the Rom. and Byz. Periods*, 3rd ed. (1914), G. Lodge, *Lexicon Plautinum* (1901–33), various contributors, in *Arch. latein. Lexikogr.* (1884–); W. A. Oldfather, *Concordance to Cic. epist.* (1938), to Sen. *Tragedies* (1918), and others.

PALAEOGRAPHY (especially by pupils of L. Traube (*ob.* 1907)): E. A. Lowe, *The Beneventan Script* (1914), *Scriptura Beneventana* (1929), *Codices Latini Antiquiores* (1934–), H. B. Van Hoesen, *Roman Cursive Writing* (1915), E. K. Rand, *The Script of Tours* (1929–), L. W. Jones, *The Script of Cologne* (1932), K. and S. Lake, dated Greek facsimiles (1934–).

PAPYROLOGY: especially *Michigan Papyri* (1931–47).

EPIGRAPHY: B. D. Meritt, *Greek Inscriptions* (1931), W. K. Prentice, *Greek and Latin Inscriptions* (1908), J. R. S. Sterrett, *Epigraphical Journey in Asia Minor, Wolfe Expedition to Asia Minor* (1888), A. B. West, 'Latin Inscriptions' (*Corinth Excavations* viii. 2 (1931)).

HISTORY: M. L. W. Laistner, *Survey of Ancient History to the Death of Constantine* (1929), etc., M. Rostovtzeff, numerous works by this Russian-born scholar, all of high importance, M. Hammond, *The Augustan Principate* (1933), T. Frank (editor and part author), *Economic Survey of Ancient Rome* (1933–40, 5 vols.).

RELIGION: A. D. Nock, *Conversion* (1933); C. H. Moore, *Religious Thought of the Greeks* (2nd ed. 1925).

ARCHAEOLOGY, Platner–Ashby, *Topographical Dictionary of Ancient Rome* (1929), E. B. van Deman, *Building of the Roman Aqueducts* (1934), G. M. A. Richter, *Sculpture and Sculptors of the Greeks* (2nd ed. 1930); parts of *Corpus Vasorum Antiquorum* by various authors, G. M. A. Richter, *Ancient Furniture* (1926).　　A. S.

BIBLIOGRAPHY

For obituary notices of many recent scholars, besides those in the list below, reference may be made to the *Class. Review, Brit. Acad. Proceedings, Necrologe* in *Biographisches Jahrbuch* in Bursian's *Jahresbericht*, and to other foreign classical periodicals like *Mnemosyne, American Journal of Philology* (Transactions and Proceedings), *Classical Philology*, etc.

Abbott, E., and Campbell, L. *The Life and Letters of Benjamin Jowett.* 2 vols., 1897.
Adcock, Heitland, Souter, *J. S. Reid.* Brit. Acad. Proc. 1927.
Bailey, C. *A. C. Clark.* Brit. Acad. Proc. 1937.
—— *R. S. Conway.* Brit. Acad. Proc. 1936.
Baynes, N. H. *A Bibliography of Works of J. B. Bury with Memoir.* 1929.
—— *J. B. Bury.* Brit. Acad. Proc. 1924.
Bell, H. I. *A. S. Hunt.* Brit. Acad. Proc. 1934.
Chapman, R. W. *The Portrait of a Scholar* [= Ingram Bywater] *and Other Essays.* 1920. [Title-page also printed in Memoir in W. W. Jackson, q.v.]
Clark, A. C. *L. C. Purser.* Brit. Acad. Proc. 1932.
Coon, R. H. *W. Warde Fowler: an Oxford Humanist.* 1934.
Evans, Joan. *Time and Chance: the Story of Arthur Evans and his Forbears.* 1943.
Evans, T. S. *Latin and Greek Verse with Memoir* by J. Waite. 1893.
Farnell, L. R. *An Oxonian Looks Back.* 1934.
Garrod, H. W. *Allen, P. S.* Brit. Acad. Proc. 1933.
Glover, T. R. *Cambridge Retrospect.* 1943.
Gow, A. S. F. *A. E. Housman: A Sketch together with list of his writings.* 1936.
Gudeman, A. *Imagines Philologorum* (160 Bildnisse—Renaissance bis zur Gegenwart). 1911.
Headlam, M. F. *Sir Thomas Heath.* Brit. Acad. Proc. 1940.
Hertz, M. *Karl Lachmann.* 1851.
Jackson, W. W. *Ingram Bywater: the Memoir of an Oxford Scholar.* Oxf. 1917.
Jebb, C. L. (Lady). *Life and Letters of Sir R. C. Jebb,* with chapter on Jebb as a scholar and critic by Dr. A. W. Verrall. 1907.
Kenyon, Sir F. G. *Sir E. Maunde Thompson.* Brit. Acad. Proc. 1929.
Klussmann, R. *Bibliotheca scriptorum classicorum et graec. et lat.* 2 vols., 1903–13. [Books published 1878–1896.]
Marett, R. R. *L. R. Farnell.* Brit. Acad. Proc. 1934.
—— *Sir J. G. Frazer.* Brit. Acad. Proc. 1941.
Marouzeau, J. *Dix années de bibliog. classique . . . pour 1914–24.* 2 vols., 1927–9.
—— *L'Année philologique bibliog. crit. et analytique de l'antiquité gréco-latine,* vols. i–xvi, 1924–44; published 1928–46.
Mayor, J. E. B. in the edition of his *Sermons* (1911) by H. F. Stewart.
Müller, Lucian. *Heinrich Ritschls Leben.* 1877.
Munro, H. A. J. *Translations into Latin and Greek Verse* with prefatory note by J. D. Duff. 1906.
Murray, G. *Margoliouth, D. S.* Brit. Acad. Proc. 1939.
Myres, Sir J. L. *Sir H. Stuart Jones.* Brit. Acad. Proc. 1940.
—— *Sir Arthur Evans.* Brit. Acad. Proc. 1941.
Nettleship, H. *Lectures and Essays: Moritz Haupt;* 1st ser. 1885. Ed. F. Haverfield, 2nd ser. 1895.
—— *Madvig:* also *Memoir* by M. Nettleship on H. N.
Owen, S. G. *J. P. Postgate.* Brit. Acad. Proc. 1927.
Parry, R. S. *Henry Jackson, O.M. A Memoir.* Camb. 1926.
Peck, H. T. *A Hist. of Class. Philol. . . .* (7th cent. B.C. to 20th cent. A.D.). New York, 1911.
Ranke, F. *August Meineke, Ein Lebensbild.* 1871.
Reinach, S. *Manuel de philologie classique.* 1883².
Ribbeck, E. *Otto Ribbeck, Ein Bild seines Lebens aus seinen Briefen 1846–1898.* 1901.
——, O. *F. W. Ritschl, Ein Beitrag z. Gesch. der Philologie.* 2 vols., 1881.
Rose, H. J. *W. M. Lindsay.* Brit. Acad. Proc. 1937.
Rutherford, W. G. Obituary on Cobet. *C.R.* 1889. [Bibliography by Cobet's pupil S. A. Naber in *Mnemos.* xxxiv and xxxv, 1906–7.]
Sandys, Sir J. E. *A Hist. of Class. Scholarship,* vol. iii, 46–523. Camb. 1908.
Smith, A. H. *Thomas Ashby.* Brit. Acad. Proc. 1931.
Symonds, J. A. *Miscellaneous Writings of John Conington,* with a Memoir by H. J. S. Smith, Savilian Professor of Geometry. 2 vols., 1872.
Verrall, A. W. 'Obituary on S. H. Butcher, with Greek Verses *In Memoriam',* *Class. Rev.* 1911.
Wilamowitz-Moellendorff, U. von. *Geschichte der Philologie (Einleitung in die Altertumswissenschaft* I Band I Heft, 1921; *Wilamowitz-Bibliographie 1868 bis 1929* (Berlin 1929).　　J. W. D.

SCHOLARSHIP, GREEK, IN ANTIQUITY.

Until the end of the sixth century B.C. Greek literature depended for its survival on oral tradition. Rhapsodes claimed to be exact about the actual words of Homer (Xen. *Mem.* 4. 2. 10). But textual corruption and variation were inevitable. Pisistratus is said to have had an official text of Homer compiled, but the method of recension is unknown, and interpolations were alleged in antiquity. From the sixth to the fourth century Homeric criticism was not so much philological as directed against the morality of his mythology, as in Plato's famous attack (*Resp.* 377 d). Texts were prepared by Antimachus and Aristotle; a treatise was written by Democritus, and a commentary by Ion of Ephesus, but their nature and value are uncertain.

2. Towards the end of the fifth century the popularity of the Athenian drama stimulated the development of the trade in books, and private collections became possible, though on a small scale (cf. the library of Euripides). But this development did not secure texts from corruption. The absence, in many cases, of an authoritative text, the difficulties presented to the copyist by the form of the fifth-century book, which lacked word-division and punctuation, careless or ignorant transcription, and, in the case of the drama, actors' tampering with the text, were continual sources of danger. Tragedy suffered so badly in the fourth century that in 330 B.C. Lycurgus ordered that a public copy of the text of the three great tragic poets should be deposited in the State archives. This was perhaps merely a copy of the best acting-version. That it was not regarded as presenting the original text of the poets seems clear from Alexandrian criticism. Autograph manuscripts of Plato and Aristotle may have been kept in the Academy and Lyceum. Aristotle made the first important contribution to literary history with his *Didascaliae*, and other Peripatetics devoted themselves to the history and criticism of literature and to grammatical and scientific scholarship, e.g. Theophrastus and Demetrius of Phalerum.

3. The last-named was credited with advising Ptolemy Soter (305–285 B.C.) to found a library at Alexandria. With the establishment of this library in the Brucheum, of the smaller library in the Serapeum, and of the collegiate body in the Museum, scholarship really began. The libraries contained a huge collection of papyrus rolls, which grew in number from 200,000 c. 285 B.C. to 700,000 in the first century B.C. The successive librarians were learned scholars (e.g. Zenodotus, Aristophanes). Research was facilitated by their careful classification of authors and texts (cf. Callimachus, *Pinakes*), by their determination of genuine and spurious works, and by their introduction of rolls of standard size, which made possible the division of large works, formerly inconvenient to handle, into groups of rolls. These Alexandrian scholars sought to reconstitute the original text of the classical writers, especially Homer. They adopted the sound practice of comparing manuscripts; but they also followed too subjective criteria. Caution grew with experience and knowledge, Aristophanes and Aristarchus modifying the arbitrary method of Zenodotus. Their work is best shown in the Venetian scholia to the *Iliad*. In their recensions (διορθώσεις) they used marginal signs, of which the most important were the *obelus* (ὄβελος —), used by Zenodotus and later scholars to mark a spurious line, the asterisk (ἀστερίσκος *), used by Aristophanes to mark incomplete sense and by Aristarchus to mark a verse wrongly repeated elsewhere, the κεραύνιον (T) marking a succession of spurious lines, the ἀντίσιγμα (ꓱ), used by Aristophanes to indicate erroneous repetition and by Aristarchus to mark disturbed word-order, the διπλῆ (>) marking anything noteworthy. The authors thus edited formed the basis of the Alexandrian canon of the best poets, later extended to include prose-writers. Besides such critical editions, the Alexandrians produced exegetical commentaries (ὑπομνήματα), filled with antiquarian and mythological lore, works of literary history and criticism, and lexicographical studies; they also pursued research in metric, grammar, and accentuation. Concurrently with the development of literary studies in Alexandria went the growth of Pergamum as a rival centre of learning with a large library, in which parchment was first used on a considerable scale for books. Here scholarship was exercised rather upon prose than upon poetry, and although editions and commentaries were produced (notably by Crates of Mallos), its best work was probably done in the fields of antiquarian and grammatical research.

4. From the second century B.C. the demand for popular editions and handbooks brought forth variorum commentaries, published separately from the text, but having lemmata (*see* SCHOLIA) and compilations (cf. especially the writings of Didymus), which preserved the best features of Alexandrian scholarship and from which much of the older scholia on classical authors is derived. These commentaries were of great importance in preventing a text's corruption, since the notes would fit only the particular text for which they had been written (cf. the excellent preservation of the nine annotated plays of Euripides, and the seven comedies of Aristophanes in the Venetian MS.).

5. From the time of Hadrian Greek scholarship declined. The systematic study of grammar (e.g. by Apollonius Dyscolus and Herodian), of metric (e.g. by Hephaestion), and the compilation of lexica (e.g. by Harpocration and Hesychius) continued the preservation of the results of Alexandrian research. But the steadily diminishing interest in Greek classical authors and the preference for select editions and anthologies (cf. the works of Proclus and Stobaeus) caused the disappearance of the writings of many earlier authors. The process of disappearance was further helped by the transfer of texts from the decaying papyrus rolls to durable vellum codices in the fourth and fifth centuries, when only such texts as were valued were copied. Marginal scholia, which had been rare in the papyrus rolls, now became common, and such annotated texts were more reliable than texts without scholia. Although the Roman and early Byzantine ages were a period of loss, texts were not seriously corrupted. The evidence of papyri shows that the quality of texts suffered little between the second and eleventh centuries. Poets were more fortunate than prose-writers in escaping corruption, thanks to the transmission of the Alexandrian commentaries, but some prose-authors, notably Herodotus, Isocrates, Plato, Demosthenes, have come down to us in a good state.

6. After the eighth century, which was the darkest age for Greek literature and scholarship, there came a revival in the ninth century, begun by Photius and Arethas, whose enthusiasm probably helped, along with the industry of lexicographers like 'Suidas', q.v. (10th c.), to save many texts, and many of our best manuscripts belong to this time. In the twelfth century Tzetzes annotated the *Iliad* and Eustathius produced his important Homeric commentary and struggled to secure the preservation of the monastic libraries. Under the Palaeologi, at Byzantium there was a renaissance of learning which produced editions of classical authors, commentaries, handbooks, and lexica. But scholars like Thomas Magister and Demetrius Triclinius (early 14th c.) were often wilful and drastic in textual criticism, and their unsatisfactory views of metre and language led them into frequent error. Their texts became current in Italy, and, but for the fall of Constantinople, their method would have left an indelible mark on Greek literature.

F. W. Hall, *A Companion to Classical Texts* (1913); J. W. White, *The Scholia on the 'Aves' of Aristophanes* (1914); A. C. Pearson, *The Fragments of Sophocles* i (1917); J. E. Sandys, *A History of Classical Scholarship* i³ (1921); U. v. Wilamowitz-Moellendorff, *Einleitung in die griechische Tragödie* (1921); Christ-Schmid-Stählin, *Geschichte der griechischen Literatur* ii⁶, *Die nachklassische Periode* (1920–4); C. Krumbacher, *Geschichte der byzantinischen Literatur²* (1897); D. L. Page, *Actors' Interpolations in Greek Tragedy* (1934).
J. F. L.

SCHOLARSHIP, LATIN, IN ANTIQUITY. Interest in systematic Latin scholarship began in Rome with the visit of Crates (q.v.) of Mallos *c.* 168 B.C. His influence may be seen in the orthographical and literary investigations of L. Accius (170–*c.* 85) and in the satires of Lucilius (180–102). But the first Roman 'scholar' was L. Aelius Stilo Praeconinus of Lanuvium (*c.* 154–*c.* 74), whose studies included, besides grammar and literary history (he made a list of the genuine plays of Plautus), etymological, antiquarian, and historical subjects. He inspired M. Terentius Varro (116–27) to his encyclopaedic studies: Varro's antiquarian researches (*Antiquitates rerum humanarum et divinarum*), his grammatical writings (*De lingua Latina*), his educational treatises (*Disciplinarum libri novem*) formed a storehouse and model for later critics and scholars. The interest aroused by Varro and his predecessors in grammar and the history of Roman literature is seen in Cicero, Horace, and Caesar amongst others. Varro's scholarship was rivalled by that of P. Nigidius Figulus (98–45), who wrote *Commentarii grammatici* and shares with Varro the credit of inventing the terminology of Latin grammar. Other professed scholars of the same period are L. Ateius Praetextatus and Valerius Cato. A great stimulus to scholarship was given by the founding of the Palatine Library with its collections of Greek and Latin literature in 28 B.C. and the appointment of C. Julius Hyginus (64 B.C.–A.D. 17) (who wrote a commentary on Virgil) as librarian. At the close of the Augustan period Fenestella's *Annales* continued the encyclopaedic scholarship of Varro; Verrius Flaccus wrote his *De orthographia* and in his *De verborum significatu* produced the first Latin lexicon, a storehouse of information later abridged by Pompeius Festus and drawn upon by all subsequent scholars. Later, in the first century A.D., Q. Remmius Palaemon, the teacher of Quintilian, wrote an *Ars Grammatica*, the first formal Latin grammar. The tradition of literary criticism was continued by L. Annaeus Seneca, Petronius, and Persius. Q. Asconius Pedianus (A.D. 3–88 or, according to others, 9 B.C.–A.D. 76) wrote a commentary on Cicero's orations and a defence of Virgil, and the elder Pliny (A.D. 23–79) wrote on *dubius sermo*. M. Valerius Probus (d. A.D. 88) of Berytus not merely studied the *sermo antiquus* (upon which he wrote a *Silva observationum*) but produced careful texts based upon a study of early manuscripts of a number of Latin authors. Fabius Quintilianus (d. 95?), in the *Institutio Oratoria*, summed up the current views upon grammar and literary criticism. In the next century C. Suetonius Tranquillus (d. *c.* 140) wrote, besides lives of orators, poets, and scholars (*De viris illustribus*), a treatise upon critical signs. His younger contemporary Aulus Gellius, in his *Noctes Atticae*, supplies valuable details on the earlier language and literature and on lexicography and grammar. At the end of the century Terentianus Maurus published a manual on prosody and metre; Acron commented on Terence and Horace; and Festus abridged Verrius Flaccus.

In the third century Porphyrion commented on Horace, C. Julius Romanus wrote on grammar, and Solinus wrote an epitome of Pliny, while the learned Censorinus compiled his *De die natali* (A.D. 238). Early in the next century Nonius Marcellus compiled his *De compendiosa doctrina* from the works of earlier scholars; C. Marius Victorinus wrote on metre and commented on Cicero; Aelius Donatus compiled his celebrated grammar, wrote a noted commentary on Terence and another on Virgil; Charisius and Diomedes compiled grammars. At the end of the century Maurus Servius Honoratus wrote his famous commentary on Virgil (extant in a longer and shorter form), omitting nothing but literary criticism. St. Jerome (c. 348–420) revised the Latin Bible, wrote *De viris illustribus* (after Suetonius), and translated the chronicle of Eusebius. At the end of the century Macrobius wrote a commentary on Cicero's *Somnium Scipionis*, and in his *Saturnalia* discussed Virgil and ancient Latin literature and language. Martianus Capella, early in the fifth century, summarized ancient learning in his *Nuptiae Philologiae et Mercurii*. The list of Latin scholars closes with the name of Priscian, early in the sixth century, who wrote a grammar in eighteen books, sixteen of which dealt with accidence, in which was summed up all the grammatical learning of previous centuries. *See also* LITERARY CRITICISM, II.

J. E. Sandys, *A History of Classical Scholarship* i (1903); J. W. H. Atkins, *Literary Criticism in Antiquity* ii (1934); W. Kroll, *Studien z. Verst. d. röm. Lit.* (1924), 87 ff., 308 ff.   R. M. H.

SCHOLIA. The word σχόλιον is first found in Cicero (*Att.* 16. 7. 3); its plural is now generally used to describe a body of notes (preserved in the margins of texts) which expound or criticize the language or subject-matter of an author. An individual scholium usually consists of a lemma (i.e. a word or phrase repeated from the text of the author) and an interpretation. In default of a lemma, a reference mark or the mere position of the item in the margin indicates the passage with which the note is concerned. Though the distinctions between scholia, glosses, and commentaries cannot be rigidly drawn, the term 'gloss' is usually applied to sporadic interpretations of the meanings of separate words and the term 'commentary' (*commentum, commentarius*) to an exposition which (except for interspersed lemmata) is continuous and is generally transmitted as a separate work (e.g. Porphyrius on Aristotle, Asconius on Cicero). Many items, however, in a body of scholia do not differ in length or substance from glosses, while others are clearly due to a learned pen. Most scholia, indeed, are the *disiecta membra* of lost commentaries; and it is often possible to trace them with some probability to their immediate or ultimate sources. The breaking up of a commentary into marginal scholia met the convenience of readers of a text, but inevitably caused the loss of much that we should have valued. Where space permitted, the successive owners of a manuscript would sometimes add notes of their own or excerpts from commentaries not previously incorporated; and this heterogeneous material was always at the mercy of copyists who sometimes curtailed or recast it. Yet despite many trivialities and much useless lumber, scholia often throw valuable light on points of fact or problems of exegesis (especially when based on the work of one of the great scholars of antiquity), and sometimes their interpretations contain evidence for the author's text. Their lemmata, however, which were frequently adjusted by copyists, need to be used with the utmost caution. Individual manuscripts or groups of manuscripts of a single author often present sets of scholia which bear little immediate relationship to each other; for example, the Homeric scholia in cod. Venetus A are quite distinct from those in cod. Venetus B, and both sets differ from the scholia in cod. Townleianus.

2. GREEK SCHOLIA. The notes found in the Venice codex (A) of Homer afford a good illustration of the origin of scholia. Though they cite the views of Zenodotus of Ephesus, Aristophanes of Byzantium, and Aristarchus, they are not based directly on the continuous commentaries (ὑπομνήματα) and special treatises (συγγράμματα) of the great Alexandrians. Nor are they directly derived from the work of the indefatigable Didymus Chalcenterus (1st c. B.C.), who summed up the countless Homeric προβλήματα, ζητήματα, and λύσεις of earlier scholars; for they contain references to Aristonicus (the younger contemporary of Didymus) and to Herodian and Nicanor (both of the 1st cent. A.D.) who wrote on Homer's prosody and on punctuation. Their chief immediate source is a lost commentary composed not earlier than the middle of the second century A.D.; and on the reliability of its author we depend for our knowledge of the work of his many predecessors. The extant scholia (or, rather, sets of scholia) on Hesiod, Pindar, Aeschylus, Sophocles, Euripides, and Aristophanes are all indebted ultimately to Didymus; but in every instance there are probably several intermediate stages between him and them. Behind the scholia on the Alexandrian poets Apollonius Rhodius, Theocritus, Lycophron, and Nicander lies the work of Theon, a scholar of the age of Tiberius. Scholia on prose authors, apart from Plato and Demosthenes, are comparatively scanty. Late manuscripts of the poets frequently contain scholia taken from Byzantine scholars such as Tzetzes (12th cent.), Eustathius (12th cent.), Demetrius Triclinius (early 14th cent.), and Thomas Magister (early 14th cent.).

3. LATIN SCHOLIA. None of the collections of scholia on Latin authors is earlier than the third century A.D. and many are as late as the sixth or seventh century. Despite attributions made in the Middle Ages, they are all several stages removed from the work of first- and second-century scholars (Cornutus, Probus, Velius Longus, Arruntius Celsus, Aemilius Asper, Terentius Scaurus). Of prose authors, only the speeches of Cicero have scholia. Terence is the only Republican poet whose text is thus annotated (the scholia in the cod. Bembinus being particularly important). The various but not extensive sets of scholia on Virgil are overshadowed by the great commentary of Servius, but the scholia Bernensia (closely related to Philargyrius) are valuable. For Horace there are collections attributed to Acron and Porphyrion (qq.v.) as well as the less important notes of the commentator Cruquianus. The *Ibis* of Ovid and the *Aratea* of Germanicus both have scholia; and of the poets of the first century A.D., Persius, Lucan, Statius, and Juvenal each has two or more sets of annotations.

A. Gudeman, art. 'Scholien' (Greek only) in *PW*; reports on scholia literature in Bursian, vols. clxxxviii (P. Wessner), ccxxxi, and cclii (Fr. Lammert); P. Faider, *Répertoire des éditions de scolies et commentaires d'auteurs latins* (1931); J. E. Sandys, *Hist. of Class. Scholarship* i² (1906); F. W. Hall, *Companion to Classical Texts* (1913). Ample information can be found in the sections devoted to individual authors in Christ–Schmid–Stählin, *Geschichte der Gr. Lit.*, and Schanz–Hosius, *Geschichte der Lat. Lit.*; to the editions there mentioned add: J. F. Mountford, *Scholia Bembina* (1934); H. J. Botschuyver, *Scholia in Horatium λφψ codicum Parisinorum* (1935); and P. Wessner, *Scholia in Iuvenalem vetustiora* (1931).   J. F. M.

SCHOOLS, *see* EDUCATION.

SCIPIO AFRICANUS, *see* SCIPIO (5) and (11) below.

SCIPIO (1) **BARBATUS,** LUCIUS CORNELIUS, consul 298 B.C.; his sarcophagus was the oldest discovered in the Scipios' tomb. The inscription subsequently carved on this sarcophagus records Scipio's exploits in Samnium and Lucania (Dessau, *ILS* 1), and is more trustworthy than Livy (10. 12 f.), who describes his Etruscan successes.   E. T. S.

SCIPIO (2), LUCIUS CORNELIUS, son of (1) above, was curule aedile, consul (259 B.C.), and censor (258). In 259 he attempted to use the new Roman fleet to deprive the Carthaginians of a naval base against Italy: he captured

Aleria and reduced Corsica, but failed to storm Olbia in Sardinia. Two inscriptions (Dessau, *ILS* 2, 3) record his career, but do not mention the triumph which the *Fasti Triumphales* assign to him. Near the Porta Capena he dedicated a temple to the Tempestates which had spared his fleet.   H. H. S.

SCIPIO (3) **CALVUS**, GNAEUS CORNELIUS, son of Lucius (2) above, brother of Publius (4), and uncle of Africanus Major (5). As consul in 222 B.C. he campaigned with his colleague Marcellus (q.v. 1) against the Insubres whom he routed at Mediolanum. In 218 he was sent to Spain to prevent reinforcements reaching Hannibal in Italy and to break the Carthaginian power in Spain. His strategy was to advance southwards along the coast, winning adequate bases and command of the sea. In 217 he won a decisive naval victory off the Ebro. His brother Publius arrived to take supreme command, and together they advanced to Saguntum (traces of their camp survive at Almenara, 5 miles north). In 215 they inflicted a crushing defeat near Ibera on Hasdrubal, who was attempting to break through to Italy. By 212 they had captured Saguntum, from which base they could advance farther south. In 211, while Publius was defeated on the upper Baetis, Gnaeus was destroyed with his army at Ilorci in the hinterland of Carthago Nova. (On the site see H. H. Scullard, *Scipio Africanus* (1930), 50 ff., 143.)
                                                              H. H. S.

SCIPIO (4), PUBLIUS CORNELIUS, was younger brother of Gnaeus (3) above, and father of Africanus Major (5). Consul in 218 B.C., Scipio had to divert his army, destined for Spain, to suppress a Gallic rising in north Italy. With fresh troops he reached the mouth of the Rhône, only to find that Hannibal had slipped past. Scipio hastened back to north Italy, where he hoped to fight delaying actions along the tributaries of the Po. Beaten back and wounded in a cavalry skirmish at Ticinus, he retired to Trebia where he was joined by Sempronius who insisted on engaging Hannibal. The Romans were defeated and lost two-thirds of their army (Dec. 218). In 217 Scipio was sent as proconsul to join his brother in Spain. For his campaign there and his death in 211 see Scipio (3).
                                                              H. H. S.

SCIPIO (5) **AFRICANUS MAJOR**, PUBLIUS CORNELIUS (236–184 B.C.), son of Publius (4) above, and husband of Aemilia, the sister of Paullus (q.v. 2); father of two sons (8 and 9 below) and two daughters, Cornelia, wife of Scipio (10) Nasica, and Cornelia (q.v.), mother of the Gracchi. Born in 236 B.C., Scipio is said to have saved his father's life at the battle of Ticinus (218) and as military tribune to have rallied the survivors of Cannae (216). After being curule aedile (213), he was appointed by the People to the command in Spain, being the first *privatus* to be invested with proconsular *imperium* (210). In Spain he followed his father's offensive strategy rather than the cautious policy of his own predecessor, Nero (q.v. 2). He seized the enemy's base, Carthago Nova (q.v.), by a brilliant *coup de main* (209). He drilled his army in new tactics, by which the three lines of the Roman army acted with greater mutual independence; he also adopted the Spanish sword and improved the *pilum*. In 208 he defeated Hasdrubal Barca at Baecula (*Bailen*) in Baetica: screened by his light troops, his main forces divided and fell on the enemy's flanks, a movement which was a complete break with traditional Roman tactics. He wisely avoided a wild-goose chase after the fleeing Hasdrubal (q.v.) and decided to fight on in Spain, where he finally defeated the two other Carthaginian armies at Ilipa (*Alcala del Rio*, near *Seville*): he held the enemy's main forces while the wings outflanked them (206). Thus Roman domination was established in Spain.

2. As consul for 205, Scipio carried through his determination to invade Africa, despite senatorial opposition

led by Fabius. With an army composed partly of volunteers he crossed to Sicily and succeeded in snatching Locri from Hannibal. In 204 he landed with perhaps 35,000 men in Africa, where he besieged Utica and wintered on a nearby headland (Castra Cornelia). Early in 203 he successfully attacked and burnt the camps of Syphax and Hasdrubal some six miles to the south. At Campi Magni (*Souk el Kremis*) on the upper Bagradas, Scipio defeated another enemy army by a double outflanking operation. When he captured Tunis, Carthage sought peace. During an armistice terms were referred to Rome, but after Hannibal's return to Africa the Carthaginians renewed the war in 202. After joining Masinissa, Scipio finally defeated Hannibal in the battle of Zama (q.v.), where neither side could outflank the other and the issue was decided by the Roman and Numidian cavalry, which broke off its pursuit of the Punic horsemen and fell on the rear of Hannibal's army. Scipio was named Africanus after the country he had conquered.

3. In 199 Scipio was elected censor and became *princeps senatus*. A keen supporter of a philhellenic policy, he prudently but vainly urged in his second consulship (194) that Greece should not be completely evacuated lest Antiochus of Syria should invade it. In 193 he was sent to Carthage to investigate a frontier dispute between Carthage and Masinissa. When his brother Lucius (7) was given the command against Antiochus (190), Africanus, who could not constitutionally yet be re-elected consul, was 'associated' with the command. After crossing to Asia, where he received back from Antiochus his captured son Lucius (9), Scipio fell ill and took no active part in his brother's victory at Magnesia (189). Meanwhile in Rome political attacks, led by Cato, were launched on the Scipios, culminating in the 'Trials of the Scipios', on which the ancient evidence is conflicting. Africanus intervened when Lucius was accused in 187; whether he himself was formally accused either in 187 or 184 is doubtful. But his influence was undermined and he withdrew embittered and ill to Liternum where he died soon afterwards (184).

4. An outstanding man of action, Scipio was nevertheless something of a mystic, in whom contemporary legend saw the spiritual descendant of Alexander the Great and the favourite of Jupiter Capitolinus. Profoundly convinced of his own powers, Scipio personified a new era in which Greek ideas swept over Roman life. By his tactical reforms and strategic ideals he forged a new weapon with which he asserted Rome's supremacy in Spain, Africa, and the Hellenistic East, championing Rome's imperial and protectorate mission in the world. He turned a city-militia into a semi-professional army. For ten years he commanded a devoted army, and his victory at Zama gave him the most powerful position yet held by a Roman general. But the time had not yet come when the individual challenged the power of the Senate. Scipio, who could make peace as well as war, sank back into the life of a private citizen, but he achieved less success as a statesman and was ultimately forced into virtual exile by personal rivalry and antagonism.

W. Schur, *Scipio Africanus und die Begründung der römischen Weltherrschaft* (1927); H. H. Scullard, *Scipio Africanus in the Second Punic War* (1930), to which add id., *JRS* 1936, 19 ff. on the site of the battle of Ilipa; R. M. Haywood, *Studies on Scipio Africanus* (U.S.A. 1933); A. H. McDonald, 'Scipio Africanus and Roman Politics in the Second Century B.C.', *JRS* 1938.
  On the ancient sources and Scipionic 'legend' see H. H. Scullard op. cit., ch. 1; Ed. Meyer, *Kleine Schriften* ii (1924), 331 ff. On the 'Trials' see Mommsen, *Römische Forsch.* ii; P. Fraccaro, *I processi degli Scipioni* (1911) and in *Athenaeum* 1939. For a possible coin portrait see *CAH Plates* iv, p. 57; but cf. *Num. Chron.* 1930 Proc., p. 4.   H. H. S.

SCIPIO (6) **NĀSĬCA**, PUBLIUS CORNELIUS (*cos.* 191 B.C.), son of Scipio (3), received the Magna Mater (204), was curule aedile (197), praetor in Further Spain (194), defeating the Lusitanians at Ilipa, and consul in 191, when he completed the subjugation of Boian territory (191–190). His failure in the censor elections of 189 and 184 marks the Scipionic decline, and apart from the founding of Aquileia (181) and his action as patron in the Spanish inquiry of 171, he played no further part in public life.

Livy 29. 11 and 14; 35. 1; 36.　　　　　　　A. H. McD.

SCIPIO (7) **ASIATICUS** (ASIAGENUS, ASIAGENES), LUCIUS CORNELIUS (*cos.* 190 B.C.), brother of Scipio Africanus, whose legate he was in Spain (207–206), Sicily (205), and Africa (204–202), was curule aedile (195) and praetor in Sicily (193). In 191 he was with M'. Acilius Glabrio at Thermopylae, and in 190 succeeded him as consul. This marked the Scipionic control of policy against Antiochus, and Scipio Africanus accompanied him to the East in effective command. Making a truce with the Aetolians, he crossed to Asia Minor to defeat Antiochus at Magnesia (probably Jan. 189). After preliminary peace negotiations he was succeeded by Manlius Vulso, returning to triumph in 188, with votive games in 186. The senatorial opposition to Africanus' dominance, however, brought on him a demand for accounts and for inquiry into monies received from Antiochus, and eventually a charge of peculation, on which he would have been imprisoned except for the intervention of Sempronius Gracchus (cf. s.v. PETILLIUS and MINUCIUS 3). Cato degraded him from equestrian status in 184. An undistinguished figure, his career follows that of his great brother.

Livy bks. 28–30; 36. 21; 37–8; Polyb. bks. 21, 23; Appian, *Syr.* 23 ff.; Diod. bk. 29; Gellius 4. 18. De Sanctis, *Stor. Rom.* iv. 1, pp. 180, 583; W. Schur, *Scipio Africanus* (1927); A. H. McDonald, *JRS* 1938, 158.　　　　　　　A. H. McD.

SCIPIO (8) PUBLIUS CORNELIUS, elder son of Africanus Major, adopted the later Africanus Minor before 160 B.C. Augur in 180, he was precluded from a public career by ill health; an outstanding orator, he also wrote an historical work in Greek. An inscription in Saturnian verse from the Tomb of the Scipios probably refers to him (Dessau, *ILS* 4).　　　　　　　H. H. S.

SCIPIO (9), LUCIUS CORNELIUS, son of Africanus Major, was captured in the war with Antiochus (192 B.C.), but was released unransomed before Magnesia in 190. He gained the praetorship (174) with the help of his father's secretary, but incurred the censors' displeasure. Details of his capture and personality are confused: see Münzer, *PW*, s.v. 'Cornelius (325)'.　　　　　　　H. H. S.

SCIPIO (10) **NASICA CORCULUM**, PUBLIUS CORNELIUS, curule aedile in 169 B.C., distinguished himself in the Pydna campaign (168); his account of it in an ἐπιστόλιον is preserved by Plutarch (*Aem.* 15–18). On account of irregular election, he resigned the consulship of 162. Censor in 159, he removed unauthorized statues from the Forum. Consul in 155, he ended the Dalmatian War. He checked the building of a theatre on grounds of public morality. Against Cato's policy of destroying Carthage, he urged the moral stimulus of Carthage to Rome, presumably representing the traditional liberal Scipionic policy in Africa. In 152 he forced Masinissa to withdraw from Carthaginian territory. He was envoy to Andriscus (150), Pontifex Maximus (150), and *princeps senatus* (147). Learned in pontifical and civil law, he upheld traditional standards of morality and politics, at home and abroad.

Livy, bks. 44–5; *Per.* 47–50. M. Gelzer, *Philol.* 1931, 261.　　　　　　　A. H. McD.

SCIPIO (11) **AEMILIANUS AFRICANUS NU-MANTINUS**, PUBLIUS CORNELIUS (185/4–129 B.C.), the second son of L. Aemilius Paullus (q.v. 2) Macedonicus,

was adopted by P. Scipio (8), the elder son of Scipio Africanus. He accompanied Paullus to Greece in 168, and fought at Pydna. His youthful development and family circumstances are described by Polybius (31. 23–9). In 151 he volunteered to serve as military tribune in Spain, distinguishing himself at Intercatia. On a mission to Masinissa (150), he shared in the negotiations between Numidia and Carthage after the outbreak of hostilities. In 149 he went as military tribune to Carthage where he dominated the fighting: οἶος πέπνυται, as Cato said (cf. *Od.* 10. 495). In 148 he settled the succession to Masinissa, dividing Numidia and undoing the king's work. He was elected consul for 147 by special dispensation on account of his youth, and received, also by special vote, the command against Carthage. Establishing efficiency in the army, he blockaded Carthage, and in 146 destroyed the city, enslaving its people and setting up the province of Africa. If he wept over the destruction (Appian, *Pun.* 132), it came from his own policy and strategy.

2. In 144 he gained control of policy in Spain by the commands of Q. Fabius and C. Laelius, and in 142 became censor, exercising his authority with traditional severity. His two years' embassy for settling relations with Egypt, Syria, Pergamum, and Greece is assigned either to 141–140 or to 136–135. Laelius' proposals for land-settlement, probably in 140, represent his policy of internal restoration. His prosecution of L. Aurelius Cotta in 138 shows his regard for good government. The *Lex Cassia* of 137, introducing the secret ballot in popular jurisdiction, reflects his aim of limiting the influence of clientship, abused by the senatorial houses. In Spain he opposed conciliation, rejecting Mancinus' agreement, and in 134 became consul for the second time, again by special dispensation, as re-election to the consulship had been prohibited in 151. Receiving the command in Spain, with a distinguished staff, he restored discipline in the army, and blockaded and destroyed Numantia in 133.

3. His hostility to the 'Flaminian' character of Tiberius Gracchus' agrarian programme and to his demagogy and constitutional irregularity was undisguised: ὡς ἀπόλοιτο καὶ ἄλλος ὅτις τοιαῦτά γε ῥέζοι (*Od.* i. 47). He publicly declared his opinion: 'si is occupandae rei publicae animum habuisset, iure caesum' (Vell. 2. 4. 4). He rejected Papirius Carbo's proposal to legalize the re-election of tribunes, and showed his contempt for the populace. He did not check the work of the Gracchan Land Commission, however, until it began to threaten the interests of the Italians: then he stepped in to hold the balance in State and Confederation with all his authority. His death after popular disorder at the Feriae Latinae of 129 raised the suspicion of assassination, although the official *laudatio* ignored this. He married Sempronia, sister of the Gracchi, but left no children.

4. Liberal in culture, Stoic in belief, literary in interests, the centre of the brilliant Scipionic Circle, he was yet traditional in his basis of thought. As a soldier he inherited the professional competence of Aemilius Paullus; as a statesman he practised the strict senatorial policy of civic and Confederate balance and provincial domination. Pre-eminent in authority, he appeared at the crisis of Roman constitutionalism, and his death removed the hope of stability; his life might well inspire Cicero's conception of a principate.

Livy, bk. 44; *Per.* 48–59; Polyb. bks. 32–9; Plutarch, *Aemilius Paullus, Ti. Gracchus*; Diod. bks. 30–4; Appian, *Pun.* 71, 98 ff.; *Hisp.* 49 ff.; *BCiv.* 1; Cicero, *De Republica, De Amicitia*; H. Malcovati, *Or. Rom. Frag.* i. 110, 233. E. Lincke, *P. Corn. Scipio Aemil.* (1898); A. Schulten, *Numantia* i. 273, 366; S. Gsell, *Histoire ancienne de l'Afrique du Nord* iii (1918), 336; F. Münzer, *Röm. Adelsparteien und Adelsfamilien* (1920), 225; J. Carcopino, *Autour des Gracques* (1928), 83; J. Kaerst, *Neue Jahrb.* 1929, 653; K. Bilz, *Die Politik des P. Corn. Scipio Aemil.* (1936); A. H. McDonald, *Cambr. Hist. Journ.* 1939, 144.　　　　　　　A. H. McD.

SCIPIO(12) NASICA SERAPIO, PUBLIUS CORNELIUS, consul in 138 B.C. and optimate leader against Tiberius Gracchus, was son of Scipio (10) and of Cornelia, a daughter of Scipio Africanus Major. He was a staunch upholder, like his father, of the old, simple manners. In 133, when disorder threatened on Ti. Gracchus' candidature for a second tribunate, Serapio called on the consuls to use force, and on their refusal, himself headed the majority of the senators in an attack, in which Tiberius lost his life. To avoid the consequent unpopularity, Serapio was sent on a mission to Asia, though he was Pontifex Maximus. He died soon after, at Pergamum.
M. H.

SCIPIONIC CIRCLE means the philosophic and literary coterie (mid-2nd cent. B.C.) headed by Publius Cornelius Scipio (q.v. 11) Aemilianus (Africanus Minor) and Gaius Laelius, both distinguished orators, whose friendship Cicero's *De Amicitia* commemorates. Admirers of Greek literature and learning, they cultivated a Hellenic purity of form and style in Latin literature, and attracted to themselves many educated Roman nobles similarly desirous of uniting the best of both civilizations. Scipio's own friendship with Polybius, the exiled Greek historian, did much to promote Greek studies, which were furthered by the transport to Rome (167 B.C.) of the library of Perseus of Macedon. Closely connected were C. Lucilius the satirist and the young African comic dramatist, Terence, who enjoyed such support that his plays were sneeringly attributed to his patrons. The dominating influence in philosophy and political thought was the Greek Stoic Panaetius. Other less prominent members appear as speakers in Cicero's *De Republica*.

R. M. Brown's *Study of the Scipionic Circle*, Iowa Studies, 1934, seeks to extend its personnel and date.
G. C. W.

SCIRAS, writer of phlyax-plays, like Rhinthon, also of Tarentum, probably in third century B.C. One title, Μελέαγρος, survives, with one fragment of 2 vv. (parody of Eur. *Hipp.* 75).

CGF 190.

SCIRON (Σκίρων), a brigand infesting the dangerous Scironian Way (Σκιρωνὶς ὁδός, Hdt. 8. 71. 2) over the Scironian Cliffs (Σκιρωνίδες πέτραι, Strabo 9. 1. 4) near Megara. He made passers-by wash his feet and, as they did so, kicked them over the cliff, where, according to some, they were devoured by a great tortoise (Apollod. *Epit.* 1. 2; Plut. *Thes.* 10; Hyginus, *Fab.* 38. 4; and other authors, see O. Waser in Roscher, art. 'Skiron'). Theseus (q.v.), on his way to Athens, threw him into the sea, where, according to Ovid, *Met.* 7. 444 ff., his bones turned into the cliffs bearing his name. The Megarian account made him no brigand but a most respectable and highly connected person (Plut. loc. cit.).
H. J. R.

SCIROPHORIA, an Athenian festival, also called *Scira*, celebrated the 12th Scirophorion (June/July), and, according to ancient texts, in honour of Demeter and Kore. (The attempt to claim it for Athena alone must be rejected.) The name indicates that something was carried, the σκίρα. The ancient interpretation that these were parasols is improbable, although it is said that the priestess of Athena Polias and the priest of Poseidon-Erechtheus went from the Acropolis to a place called Scira walking under a great white baldachino. The rites seem to have a connexion with those of the Thesmophoria.

E. Gjerstad, *ARW* xxvii (1929), 189 ff., justly criticized by L. Deubner, *Attische Feste*, 40 ff.
M. P. N.

SCOLIA, drinking-songs, especially Attic. Athenaeus (15. 693 f.) preserves a collection for the late sixth and early fifth centuries. They were sung in the Prytaneum;

a singer held a myrtle-branch and, when he had finished, passed the branch to another and called on him for a song. The process is illustrated in Ar. *Vesp.* 1216 ff., cf. schol. Pl. *Grg.* 451 e, Plut. *Quaest. conv.* 1. 1. 5. There were also choral σκόλια, possibly of a later date, like two pieces in a papyrus at Berlin (*Scol. Anon.* 30).

R. Reitzenstein, *Epigramm und Skolion* (1893), 3–44; C. M. Bowra, *Greek Lyric Poetry* (1936), 402–33.
C. M. B.

SCOLION METRE, see METRE, GREEK, IV (3).

SCOPAS (4th c. B.C.), sculptor, of Paros; possibly son of Aristander, who was working in 405 B.C., if the Parian sculptor, Aristander, son of Scopas, known from signatures of the first century B.C., is a descendant. Pliny dates him 420 B.C., perhaps by his birth. Selected works, (i) *dated*: 1. Temple of Athena Alea at Tegea; after 395 B.C. Scopas was ἀρχιτέκτων and made marble statues of Asclepius and Hygieia; he must have designed and supervised the pediments (A. Calydonian boar-hunt, B. Achilles and Telephus). The surviving fragments are the basis of all attributions (Winter, *KB* 300. 2–4). A copy of the Asclepius has been recognized. He also made a beardless Asclepius for Gortys (Arcadia). 2. One column in Artemis temple at Ephesus, after 356 B.C. Doubtful, since *una a Scopa* should perhaps read *imo scapo*. 3. East side of Mausoleum, after 351 B.C. Slab 1022 (Winter, *KB* 304. 3) recalls the Tegea sculptures in style.

(ii) *Undated*: 4. Heracles in Sicyon, marble. Copies have been recognized in the Lansdowne Heracles, etc. (Winter, *KB* 300. 8; 301. 1). 5. Bacchant, marble. Callistratus' description justifies recognition of Dresden Maenad (Winter, *KB* 306. 4) as copy. 6. Apollo from Rhamnus, later in Palatine temple. Marble, represented as Citharode. Reproduced on Sorrento base. 7. Poseidon, Thetis, Achilles, Nereids, Tritons, etc. In temple of Neptune at Rome (built by Cn. Domitius Ahenobarbus, 32 B.C.). The base has been recognized (Winter, *KB* 384. 5). The Tritoness of Ostia may derive from the group. 8. Seated Mars and Venus in temple of Mars at Rome (built by D. Junius Brutus Callaicus, 138 B.C.). 9. Apollo Smintheus at Chryse. Represented on coins. 10. Aphrodite Pandemus at Elis, bronze. Represented on coins. 11. Niobid group. Attributed to Scopas or Praxiteles. The style of surviving copies (Winter, *KB* 307) suggests neither.

(iii) *Attributed*: 12. Meleager (Winter, *KB* 300. 7, 301. 2). The Tegea sculptures are remarkable for the expression of violent emotion and movement. His influence is seen in many later works, e.g. the Pergamene gigantomachy (Winter, *KB* 352–5).

Overbeck, 755, 766, 1149–89, 1227; K. A. Neugebauer, *Studien über Skopas* (1913); C. Picard, *Rev. Ét. Gr.* 1934, 385; 1935, 475.
T. B. L. W.

SCOPELIANUS, famous Sophist in Smyrna, in the reigns of Domitian and Hadrian; author of an epic Γιγαντία.

Philostr. *VS* 1. 21.

SCORDISCI, a Celtic tribe, later intermingled with Illyrians and Thracians, dwelling south of the lower Savus as far as the upper Margus, first appeared in the third century B.C. The Romans, after occupying Macedonia, had frequently to repel raids of Scordisci against this province. Subdued by Tiberius in 15 B.C., the Scordisci remained loyal thereafter, and even supported Tiberius against the Pannonians in 12 B.C. Aelia Mursa was founded in their territory (A.D. 118).

Fluss, *PW*, s.v.; C. Patsch, *Sitz. Wien* 214 i (1932); R. Syme, *JRS* 1934, 117 ff.
F. A. W. S.

SCRIBAE meant originally all persons who practised writing. Subsequently, when copyists came to be called *librarii*, the term was restricted to secretaries of private individuals, who wanted assistance in correspondence and book-keeping, or of magistrates, especially those concerned with finance and municipal affairs. These public *scribae* were generally freeborn citizens, belonged to the class of the knights, and received a regular salary. They formed several corporations, e.g. the *scribae quaestorii*. Divided into three *decuriae*, they kept the archives of the Senate, transcribed documents, and acted as cashiers and accountants at the *aerarium*. With the growth of bureaucracy in the imperial age, *scribae* were generally appointed to assist any financial, military, or municipal magistracy.

Mommsen, *Röm. Staatsr.* i³ 346 ff.; C. Lécrivain, Dar.-Sag. iv. 2, 1123 f.; E. Kornemann, *PW*, s.v.　　　P. T.

SCRIBONIA, sister of L. Scribonius (q.v. 1) Libo, was married to Octavian (her third husband), for political reasons, in 40 B.C., and divorced in the following year. In 2 B.C. she accompanied her daughter Julia into exile.

Suetonius, *Aug.* 62; Appian, *BCiv.* 5. 53; Dio Cassius 48. 16 and 34; 55. 10.

SCRIBONIANUS (1), LUCIUS ARRUNTIUS CAMILLUS, was descended, probably, from Sex. Pompeius, and was consul in A.D. 32. He was legate of Dalmatia under Gaius and Claudius. In 42, at the instigation of Annius Vinicianus and many Roman senators and *equites*, he persuaded his two legions (VII and XI) to revolt against Claudius. After four days the legions abandoned the revolt, and he was murdered.　　　J. P. B.

SCRIBONIANUS (2), FURIUS (LUCIUS ARRUNTIUS SCRIBONIANUS), son of (1) above, was banished in A.D. 52 for consulting astrologers and died soon afterwards.

SCRIBONIUS (1) **LIBO**, LUCIUS (b. *c.* 90 B.C.?), brother of Scribonia (q.v.) and father-in-law of Sextus Pompeius, commanded a division of Pompey's fleet in the Adriatic in 49 and 48. He was proscribed in 43, and became one of the chief supporters of Sextus Pompeius, representing him in negotiations with Antony (40) and taking part in the conference near Misenum (39). After Naulochus Libo accompanied Sextus to Asia Minor, but abandoned him when he persisted in carrying on against hopeless odds (35). He was consul in 34.

Cicero, *Letters*; Caesar, *BCiv.* bks. 1 and 3; Appian, *BCiv.* bk. 5.　　　G. W. R.

SCRIBONIUS (2) **LIBO DRUSUS**, MARCUS. The trial of the highly born Libo Drusus before the Senate in A.D. 16 was the first of the important treason trials of Tiberius' principate. Tacitus (*Ann.* 2. 27 ff.) considered him an innocent, if half-witted, victim of conspiracy; possibly, however, he was a serious conspirator (cf. F. B. Marsh, *The Reign of Tiberius* (1931), 58 ff., 291 f.). He committed suicide during the trial.　　　J. P. B.

SCRIBONIUS (3) **LARGUS**, Roman physician *c.* A.D. 1-50, studied at Rome in the time of Tiberius. In 43 he accompanied Claudius on his British campaign, probably on the recommendation of his patron C. Julius Callistus, secretary to Claudius, who also procured the Emperor's patronage for Scribonius' writings. In gratitude Scribonius dedicated to Callistus his only work to come down to us, the *Compositiones* (prescriptions). The contents of this show him to be an empiricist in method, closely akin to Celsus. His work was largely used by (among other writers) Marcellus Empiricus.

Ed. G. Helmreich (1887); *PW* ii A. 876.　　　W. D. R.

SCRIBONIUS, *see also* APHRODISIUS, CURIO.

SCRINIUM, *see* BOOKS, II. 2.

SCRIPTORES HISTORIAE AUGUSTAE, *see* HISTORIA AUGUSTA.

SCRIPTURA MONUMENTALIS, *see* EPIGRAPHY, LATIN, para. 16.

SCROFA, GNAEUS TREMELLIUS, friendly with Cicero and Atticus, and chief interlocutor in the first two books of Varro's *De Re Rustica*. Importing elegance into his work on agriculture, he thought little of the matter-of-fact Sasernae (q.v.; Varro, *Rust.* 1. 2. 25). Varro, Pliny, Columella used him.　　　J. W. D.

SCULPTURE, GREEK. The origins of monumental sculpture in Greece are still uncertain, but some inheritance from Minoan and Mycenaean times must be taken for granted. Monumental sculptures of the Bronze Age are known, as, for instance, the Gate of the Lionesses at Mycenae, and cult statues at Mycenaean shrines must have survived the Dorian invasion and have been taken over by the invaders. Thus at Lindus in Rhodes there was a very ancient image, probably Mycenaean, that survived into Hellenic times. The Greeks therefore had instances of sculpture before their eyes to imitate. From the 'Geometric' period (*c.* 1000-700 B.C.) a stone base of a life-size statue found at Samos survives this time. On Geometric and Proto-Corinthian vases appear figures which can plausibly be identified as statues. The famous Apollo of Amyclae, described by Pausanias and represented on late coins of Laconia, appears to have been a statue of the eighth century.

2. But the earliest actual Greek statues which we possess cannot be dated before 650. These belong to a clearly defined style known as the Dorian, common in all Dorian lands, Crete, Sicily, Rhodes, Thera, and Peloponnesus. The marble statue dedicated by Nicandra and found at Delos is typical of this style, which as a whole is represented by a multitude of smaller works of art in bronze, terra-cotta, and ivory found throughout the Dorian world and dating from 690 to 600. A splendid version of the style is a small stone figure from Crete (the 'Auxerre lady', now in the Louvre); and a later group of architectural sculpture in the same style comes from Prinias in Crete. The Peloponnese and Crete may generally be taken as the centre from which this style emanated, and the priority in the making of statues therefore belongs to that part of Greece.

3. The origins of Attic sculpture are unknown, but by 600 statues larger than life-size were made in marble, with great technical efficiency. Examples are the *kouros* (young male figure) in New York, the *kouros* from Sunium, and the head of a *kouros* from the Dipylon cemetery. This vivid and vigorous style has nothing to do with the Dorian style, so that Attica can claim an independent school of sculpture at an early date.

4. Sculpture in eastern Greece began later. Two separate and distinct schools grew up there, one connected with Samos and Naxos, together with Miletus, the other with Siphnos, Paros, and Chios and perhaps other islands. Both styles were current in the mainland of Ionia, and semi-Hellenic communities like Lycia fell under the influence of the second style. The Heraeum at Samos and the Sacred Way at Branchidae near Miletus have produced most of the statues of the first style. Theodorus Rhoecus and Telecles were famous Samian sculptors. Micciades and Archermus of Chios are known to have worked there. The sculptures of the Siphnian Treasury at Delphi represent the work of that island. The school as a whole may be called 'Cycladic'. The period of the two schools is roughly the same, *c.* 560-500. Earlier work is known in Ionia itself, and some of the Samian sculpture may go back to 580. But no known Ionian work dates to the seventh century.

5. The Peloponnesian school developed in the sixth century, with the two sculptors Dipoenus and Scyllis as its most famous representatives. Sicyon became a famous artistic centre; its Treasury at Delphi and the statues of

Cleobis and Biton at the same shrine are typical of this school and period. *G.* 500 Canachus had a high repute at Argos.

6. The 'Cycladic' school achieved an immense popularity at the expense of the rival Samo-Milesian school. Its style deeply influenced Attic sculpture from 550 onwards, largely under the patronage of Pisistratus. Attic sculpture, of which the Acropolis *korai* (maidens) are typical for this age, closely but not slavishly follows 'Cycladic' conventions. The Peloponnese, on the other hand, retained its independence, and only one region, Laconia, showed influences from the east of Greece.

7. By 500 the gaiety and brilliance of the conventional 'Archaic' styles gave place to a powerful and general tendency towards experimentation, checked for a time by the disturbances of the Ionian revolt and the Persian wars. From 500 to 480 little work was done, though the island of Aegina showed great activity. The pediments of the temple of Aphaea are typical of these decades, and two sculptors, Callon and Onatas of Aegina, achieved great fame. But the controlling factor in the new experiments was the great popularity of the new processes of bronze-casting, which enabled sculptors to devise more free compositions than the limitations of stone-carving allow. From 480 to 450 some of the greatest masterpieces of Greek sculpture were produced. Pythagoras, Calamis, mere names to us, were influential experimentalists who advanced the art of sculpture. Myron, about whom we know more, also made important contributions. Many superb original masterpieces of this age survive, such as the Bronze god from Artemisium, the 'Ludovisi' Throne and the Charioteer of Delphi, all in excellent preservation. The influence of the Peloponnese now extended to Athenian sculpture. The Athenian artists Hegias, Critius, and Nesiotes were typical of the period immediately following the Persian wars. But the greatest surviving masterpiece of the age is the large group of sculpture (*c.* 75 per cent. of the whole) from the two pediments of the temple of Zeus at Olympia. Although the authorship of these works is entirely unknown, they are the work of a very great artist. These sculptures mark the climax of pure stone-carving in Greece. The figure of Apollo is unequalled in all art. The sculptures of the Parthenon on the other hand represent a totally different technique and outlook. (*See* PHIDIAS.)

8. *Circa* 450 Phidias led sculpture into a new direction and created the Classical style as such. He was a superlatively good artist who broke with the old traditions and invented new methods and compositions. But we know his work only at second-hand. His influence was now predominant in Greece, except in the Peloponnese, where Polycletus was only partly influenced by him, and sculpture became standardized in style and method. Almost every sculptor of 450–400 owed his inspiration to Phidias. Alcamenes, Agoracritus, Paeonius, and the sculptors of the Erechtheum and the Nike Temple Balustrade all derived from him. Elegance and refinement now took the place of the grandeur and solemnity of the work of the first half of the century. Just as the gaiety and exuberance of the sixth century gave place to the severe simplicity of the early fifth, so the sophisticated skill and brilliance of the later fifth century superseded the austerity of the preceding generation. The close of the Peloponnesian War marked a pause in artistic development, and artists like Cephisodotus at the beginning of the next century merely carried over the classical traditions of the past.

9. With Praxiteles sculpture in Greece took a new turn. Artists were now individuals and no longer members of regional schools. Sculpture now showed a tendency to become slightly self-conscious. Figures strike attitudes and demand an audience. But superlative technical skill and great charm mark works such as the Hermes holding the infant Dionysus, found at Olympia and now held by many to be a fine Roman copy

of an original by Praxiteles. Of Scopas we know almost nothing except that his style, as Pliny tells us, was indistinguishable from Praxiteles'.

10. With Lysippus the long and virile tradition of the Peloponnese took a new lease of life. Lysippus, whose style is best seen from the statue of Agias at Delphi, a contemporary copy of a bronze work from the sculptor's studio, foreshadowed new tendencies which heralded the Hellenistic styles of Greece. Lysippus was a carver of vigorous and active figures and a maker of portraits. True portraiture in Greece now begins and is represented by a large series of superb portraits of famous Hellenistic rulers, or of men like Demosthenes, known to all Greeks. Apart from portraiture Hellenistic sculpture was mainly an experiment in pastiches, with a permanent tendency to be synthetic rather than original. Few outstanding works are preserved, but the Victory of Samothrace and the sculptures in high relief from the Altar of the Gods at Pergamum show respectively a revival of fifth-century style and a new experiment in baroque, the first of its kind in Greece.

11. It would be difficult to say when Greek sculpture as such ceases. It merges into Roman and is the controlling element in all Roman work down to *c.* A.D. 350. Hellenistic styles and inventions, such as the Laocoon group or the Venus de Milo, led to fashions and imitations and deeply influenced Roman work.

G. M. Richter, *The Sculpture and Sculptors of the Greeks* (1930); J. D. Beazley and B. Ashmole, *Greek Sculpture and Painting* (1932); S. Casson, *The Technique of Early Greek Sculpture* (1933); J. Overbeck, *Die antiken Schriftquellen* (1868; ancient literary sources).
S. C.

SCULPTURE, ROMAN. Etruscan sculptors are recorded to have worked at Rome during the regal period, and some fragments in terracotta, of regal or early republican date, have recently been recovered. Etruscan sculpture is well known from the seventh to the first century B.C. The Etruscans produced votive sculpture in bronze and clay, and architectural sculpture in the latter material; stone they reserved for tomb sculpture and sarcophagi. Early sculptures of local style have also come to light in other regions of Italy. From the third century onward Greek artistic currents percolated into Rome through Etruria and Campania, and many Greek statues reached the city as war booty. But with the possible exception of portraiture (q.v.), sculpture does not seem to have been produced at Rome until the last century of the Republic, when marble (usually assisted by colour) came into use for statuary and architectural ornament.

The most important product of Roman sculpture is the great series of historical and commemorative reliefs on ornaments and buildings of the capital and other cities. The historical relief originated in Republican times, but came into prominence under the Empire. The Ara Pacis (q.v.) illustrates the idealizing Greek style introduced under Augustus, but in the next notable extant monument, the Arch of Titus, there was a return to Italian tradition with its greater feeling for atmosphere and pictorial effect. The columns of Trajan and Marcus Aurelius exemplify the 'continuous' style, in which the history of a campaign is unrolled around the shaft in separate episodes. There was a brief return to Greek classicism under Hadrian, but with the Antonines the pictorial style was resumed, with experiments in perspective, crowd-representation, and deep-cut contrasts of light and shade. The Arch of Septimius Severus closed this phase; little but portraits and sarcophagi was produced in the third century, and the contemporary reliefs on the Arch of Constantine marked the beginning of late antique art, with new and Oriental conceptions of relief-sculpture.

Other types of relief were: decorative, for interior walls (stucco and terracotta were here employed as well as marble); and sepulchral: from the second century until Christian times there was a large output of sarcophagi with mythological, battle, or genre scenes. Of Roman pedimental sculpture little remains, though some information is provided by coins and other representations. Sculpture in the round was largely confined to adaptations of Greek types; honorific portrait statues appear in toga, cuirass, or in heroic nudity. The sculpture of the provinces was largely, though not exclusively, sepulchral; the Eastern Provinces, possessing their own artistic traditions, in some respects led the capital; the Western Provinces followed Italy, though some stylistic phases of the metropolis were absent and there were local forms, e.g. the Jupiter-columns of Germany.

E. Strong, *Roman Sculpture* (1907) and *Scultura Romana* (1923–5); *CAH*, chs. on Republican and Early Imperial art by E. Strong in vols. ix, x, on the later Empire by G. Rodenwaldt in vols. xi, xii. *See also* ALTAR, PORTRAITURE, SARCOPHAGI, and individual monuments such as the ARA PACIS. For provincial sculpture see E. Espérandieu, *Recueil général des bas-reliefs de la Gaule romaine* (1907–28); S. Ferri, *Arte romana sul Reno* (1931), *sul Danubio* (1933).
F. N. P.

SCUTUM, see ARMS AND ARMOUR, ROMAN.

SCYLAX of Caryanda explored for Darius 'an Indian river' flowing eastward; from its mouth he returned by sea to the Isthmus (Hdt. 4. 44). Strabo quotes this 'ancient writer' on Troad geography; Aristotle, on India (*Pol.* 1332ᵇ23). Suidas mentions a life of Heracleides of Mylasa (Hdt. 5. 121). The extant *Periplus* is a fourth-century compilation in his name.
GGM 1. 565; *PW*, s.v.   J. L. M.

SCYLLA (Σκύλλη, -α), (1) a sea-monster, living in a cave opposite Charybdis (q.v.); she had six heads, each with a triple row of teeth, and twelve feet. She lived on fish of all sorts, but if a ship came near enough, she would seize six men at a time from it and devour them. The only way to restrain her was to implore the intervention of her mother Cratais. She was immortal and irresistible (see Homer, *Od.* 12. 85 ff., 245 ff.). Later authors (e.g. Verg. *Ecl.* 6. 75) say she had a girdle of dogs' heads about her loins. There were also stories, of uncertain date and origin, to the effect that she had once been of human shape but was turned by magic into a monster. E.g. Ovid (*Met.* 13. 730 ff., 14. 1 ff.) says she was loved by Glaucus (q.v. 2) the merman, and changed by Circe (q.v.), who was her rival. Tzetzes on Lycophron, 46 and 650, makes Poseidon the lover and Amphitrite the rival. Rationalizations of her into a rock (cf. Ovid, *Met.* 14. 73) or other natural danger of the sea are fairly common; her father is regularly Phorcys, q.v. She is often (as Verg. loc. cit.) confused with (2), daughter of Nisus (q.v.) king of Megara.   H. J. R.

SCYMNUS, a Greek of Chios, alleged author of a prose περιήγησις. He is not the author of the extant Π., an unpoetical geographical summary in iambics, written *c.* 90 B.C. or earlier: introduction, Europe, especially coasts of Spain, Italy, Sicily, Adriatic, Euxine; then Asia. The rest is lost. [S.], using various authors, is worth little, except on the Euxine, Ligurian, and Spanish coasts, and Greek colonies.
GGM 1, lxxiv ff., 196 ff.; *PW*, s.v.; E. H. Bunbury, *Hist. Anc. Geog.* (1879), ii. 69 ff.   E. H. W.

SCYTHIA was the name given by the Greeks to the country between the Carpathians and the river Don. Its eastern half (between the Don and the Dnieper) was mostly an arid steppe; but western Scythia, the 'land of the black earth', was one of the world's natural wheatfields. The valleys of the Dnieper and the Kuban (north of Mt. Caucasus) were seats of a prehistoric culture dating back to the third millennium; its inhabitants practised agriculture and metallurgy, and had a relatively high standard of art. But the whole country was exposed

to recurrent invasions by ruder nomadic peoples. In the seventh century it was occupied by the Scythians, a people of uncertain provenance, but of Indo-European speech. One section of the invaders also overran upper Mesopotamia and Syria (*c.* 650–620 B.C.), and another advanced across the Carpathians to the middle Danube; but the main body stayed on in South Russia.

The Scythian armies consisted of mounted archers who were well versed in elusive 'desert tactics'. The folk was divided into several tribes, each with its separate grazing area. Each tribe stood under kings and subordinate chiefs, who were buried in large mounds (*kurgans*) along with their horses and retainers. The Scythians remained true to their nomadic habits, exploiting the labour of the previous inhabitants, especially in the black-earth zone, whose surplus wheat they sold to the Greeks of the Black Sea coast. In return the Scythian chiefs avidly bought Greek pottery and metal-work. Their tombs have produced a profusion of ornaments in gold (probably from the Urals), showing animal *motifs* and hunting-scenes of the best Greek workmanship.

The Scythians beat off an invasion by the Persian king Darius (*c.* 512 B.C.), and *c.* 325 they destroyed an expedition under Alexander's general Zopyrion. But after 300 they were ousted from the Balkan lands and central Europe by the oncoming Celts, and in the last three centuries B.C. they were displaced in south Russia by the Sarmatae. Some remnants found refuge in the Crimea and the Dobrudja, but under the Roman Empire the Scythians pass out of history.

Herodotus 4. 1–144. E. H. Minns, *Scythians and Greeks* (1913); M. Rostovtzeff, *Iranians and Greeks in South Russia* (1922); *Skythien und der Bosporus* i (1931)—a survey of the literary and archaeological sources.   M. C.

SCYTHINUS of Teos, contemporary of Plato, wrote Ἴαμβοι which expressed Heraclitus' doctrine in verse, and also a prose work Περὶ φύσεως and a Ἱστορία which was a novelistic account of Heracles' deeds as benefactor of the human race.
Ed. Diels, *PPF* 169. *PW* iii A. 696.   W. D. R.

SEALS (σφραγίς, *signum, sigillum*) played an important part in ancient life, taking the place of the modern signature on documents and, to some extent, of locks and keys. The materials for sealings were lead and wax for documents; in commerce a lump of clay was commonly pressed down over the cordage. In Roman times small seal-cases were frequently employed to protect the impression from damage. The seal was usually a finger-ring with an intaglio cut on the bevel or on an inset stone. Some types of stones, set in swivels, were worn about the neck, but this custom was Oriental rather than Greek. Greek cities possessed civic seals, for public documents or public property; the Romans utilized a magistrate's personal seal. It was also customary to stamp with the maker's name a variety of products, from bread to bricks, as a trade-mark; for this purpose stamps of wood or metal, oblong, circular, or foot-shaped, were employed.
V. Chapot, Dar.-Sag., s.v. 'Signum'.   F. N. P.

SECESSIO means the 'withdrawal' of the plebs from the rest of the Roman community. Unlike a 'general strike', it implies detachment from public life and withdrawal from the town. The plebeians *en masse* retired outside the *pomerium*, often to the Aventine, which was turned over to them *c.* 450 B.C. We have no means of deciding how many secessions (five are recorded between 494 and 287 B.C.) actually occurred. It would be too radical to accept only the last, for the account of it differs widely from that of the earlier ones, so that a mere anticipation would be incomprehensible. The first secession (traditionally dated to 494), which was stopped by Menenius Agrippa (q.v.), and the second of 449, which is reputed to have caused the fall of the decemvirs, are perhaps fictitious. Nor is the third, with which Canuleius (q.v.) is credited, better supported, although the *Lex Canuleia* (445) may have been forced through by a secession. The fourth, which is not beyond suspicion, was merely a military rebellion (342). The fifth secession of 287 is indisputably historical. Social troubles, arising from the pressure of debts, led the plebs to withdraw to the Janiculum. A plebeian dictator, Q. Hortensius (q.v.), was appointed, and his law terminated the struggle of the Orders.

Ed. Meyer, *Kleine Schriften* i² (1924), 373 ff.; G. De Sanctis, *Stor. Rom.* ii. 4 ff.; M. Fluss, *PW*, s.v.   P. T.

SECTATORES, *see* CANDIDATUS.

SECULAR GAMES, scenic games (*ludi*) and sacrifices performed by the Roman State to commemorate the end of one *saeculum* and the beginning of a new one. The *saeculum*, defined as the longest span of human life, was fixed in the Republic as an era of a hundred years. The celebration was ordered by the Sibylline Books and was under the direction of the *duumviri* (later *decemviri* (q.v.) or *quindecimviri*) *sacris faciundis*. The ceremony took place in the Campus Martius, near the Tiber, at a spot which was known as Tarentum or Terentum. The gods honoured in the republican *ludi* are said to have been Dis and Proserpina, who had an altar near by. The games were associated in origin with the Valerian *gens*, and Valerius Corvus' first consulship, 348 B.C., may have been the date of the first celebration. The secular games of 249 B.C. are much better authenticated. Many scholars believe that the ceremony was actually introduced in that year from Tarentum, though the connexion of the site of the games with the south Italian city is by no means certain. The next celebration took place in 146 B.C. (a date attested by contemporary writers, and therefore more trustworthy than Livy's assignment of the games to 149. Like modern centennials, the *saeculum* was not always celebrated punctually.) No games were held a century later (although, if we may trust the indications of coins with symbols of the *saeculum* on them (Alföldi, *Hermes* lxv. 369 ff.), there were plans in 45–42 B.C. to celebrate the *ludi* in the near future. The Fourth Eclogue has been interpreted as a prediction—not fulfilled—of games to be held in 40 B.C.

Augustus' plans to celebrate the beginning of a new age were known to Virgil, who died two years before the games took place, and were referred to in the familiar words 'aurea condet saecula' (*Aen.* 6. 792–3). At Augustus' request the *quindecimviri* made calculations for the celebration and fixed the length of the *saeculum* at 110 years. Augustus' *ludi* in 17 B.C. are well known from Horace's *Carmen Saeculare* and from an inscription, found near the Tiber, which gives details of the complicated ritual. They consisted of three nights and three successive days of sacrifices and archaic scenic games, and of seven supplementary days of more modern entertainment in theatre and circus. Dis and Proserpina do not appear among the gods honoured. Each night Augustus and Agrippa made appropriate offerings and sacrifices beside the Tiber to the Moerae, to the Ilithyiae, and to Terra Mater. On the first two days they made sacrifices on the Capitol to Jupiter and Juno Regina; on the third day they made offerings to Apollo and Diana on the Palatine. The scenic games continued night and day, and 110 matrons held *sellisternia* for Juno and Diana. As we know from the inscription, it was after the offerings on the third day that twenty-seven boys and twenty-seven girls, whose fathers and mothers were living, sang Horace's hymn, first on the Palatine and then on the Capitol. In the hymn Horace brings into great prominence Augustus' patron god Apollo in his new Palatine temple.

The antiquarian emperor Claudius revived the *saeculum* of a hundred years and held games in A.D. 47 for the eight-hundredth birthday of Rome. Following his example, Philip in 248 celebrated the thousandth anniversary of the city. Domitian in 88 and Septimius Severus in 204 calculated their festivals by use of the Augustan *saeculum* of a hundred and ten years. From Septimius Severus' celebration extensive inscriptional records have been discovered, including a fragmentary secular hymn written in hexameters by an unknown poet.

Horace, *Carmen Saeculare* and the *scholia*; Censorinus, *D.N.* 17; Livy, *Per.* 49; Val. Max. 2. 4. 5; Zosimus 2. 1 ff.; *CIL* vi. 32323–36. For the recent discoveries of the inscription of Septimius Severus see *Not. Scav.* 1931, 313 ff.   L. R. T.

SECUNDUS, *see* JULIUS (11), POMPONIUS (3).

SECURITAS, commonly associated with the Emperor or the State as a 'virtue' or 'desirable state' (*res expetenda*). Securitas was commonly invoked when some imminent danger had been averted or on an occasion, like 10 Jan., A.D. 69, when the Arval Brethren sacrificed to her on the adoption of Piso. Her characteristic attribute is the column on which she leans.

G. Wissowa, *RK* 335.   H. M.

SECURITY in Roman law was given to the creditor in the form of rights over the property of the debtor. By the earliest real security, *fiducia*, the creditor acquired ownership of the pledged object, with the obligation to retransfer it to the debtor after payment of the debt. Restrictions of this fiduciary ownership, transferred to the creditor by *mancipatio* (q.v.) or *in iure cessio* (*see* DOMINIUM), could be laid down in a special agreement between creditor and debtor, concerning especially the creditor's obligation to reconvey the property. By the later form of pledge (*pignus*) the creditor acquired only possession of the object handed to him, with interdictal protection, but without right of *usucapio* (*see* POSSESSIO). From *pignus* arose later another form of security, practised particularly in relations between landlords and agricultural tenants, whereby the object pledged for the payment of rent (slaves, cattle, agricultural implements) was left in the hands of the tenant: the creditor acquired neither ownership nor possession. For this form of security the term *hypotheca* was later applied. The debtor could hypothecate the same object successively to several creditors, but the earlier mortgage had priority; later mortgagees might enforce their rights only if the preceding one was satisfied. Some mortgages, as for taxes due to the *fiscus* or for the dowry of a woman, were privileged (the latter by a reform of Justinian).   A. B.

SEDIGITUS, *see* VOLCACIUS (1).

SĒDŬLIUS (*fl. c.* A.D. 435), a Christian Latin poet, author of the *Paschale Carmen*, with a prose version *Paschale Opus*, in five books, a scriptural elegy, and a hymn to Christ.

Edition: Huemer, *CSEL* (1885).

SEGESTA (correct Greek form: Ἔγεστα. See Festus, p. 458 L.), a city of north-western Sicily. Segesta was thoroughly hellenized by the fifth century B.C., but actually was neither Greek, Phoenician, nor Sicanian (Strabo 6. 272, exceptionally, regards Ionian Phocaeans as founders of Doric-speaking Segesta). The Segestans reckoned themselves Trojans. Presumably they were Elymi (= Asiatics?). Against Selinus (q.v.), her traditional enemy, Segesta usually invoked outside aid, e.g. Cnidians and Rhodians in 580 B.C. The combatants in 454 are unknown, Diodorus' text (11. 86) erroneously mentioning Lilybaeum (q.v.). In 426 and 416 Athens supported Segesta, induced thereto by exaggerated notions of Segestan wealth (Thuc. 6. 6 f.; however, no poverty-stricken city built the magnificent surviving temple). The Athenian expedition, however, failed disastrously at Syracuse (413), whereupon Segesta sought Carthaginian help (410). Carthage responded, sacked Selinus, and obliterated Himera (409). Segesta thereby became a Carthaginian dependency which was temporarily seized by Agathocles (307), who treacherously razed it, and Pyrrhus (276). In the First Punic War Segesta immediately surrendered to, and was generously treated by, the Romans, who like the Segestans claimed Trojan descent. Segesta became a *civitas libera et immunis*, but declined rapidly after the Servile War (102). By Strabo's time its port, Emporium, had outstripped it. Subsequently Segesta disappeared.

Diod. 5. 9; 13. 43 f.; 14. 48, 53 f.; 20. 71; 36. 5; Cic. *Verr.* 3. 92; 4. 72; 5. 125.
E. T. S.

SEIA, an obscure Roman goddess, said to be the guardian of corn while underground (Augustine, *De civ. D.* 4. 8). Her statue, with that of Segesta and a third who must not be named indoors, stood in the Circus Maximus (Pliny, *HN* 18. 8; cf. Tert. *De Spect.* 8, Macrob. *Sat.* 1. 16. 8).
H. J. R.

SEJANUS (LUCIUS AELIUS SEIANUS; d. A.D. 31). The maternal ancestry of Sejanus was distinguished; his father was an *eques*, L. Seius Strabo. He was made his father's colleague as Prefect of the Praetorian Guard by Tiberius on his accession, and soon, on his father's appointment as Prefect of Egypt, he became sole commander of the Guard, whose strength he increased by quartering all the cohorts in a single barracks near the Porta Viminalis. Over Tiberius he exercised a steadily increasing influence. After the death of Tiberius' son Drusus in 23 (which Sejanus was suspected of compassing) his influence in the Senate was paramount, and in a succession of treason trials he attacked his enemies (chiefly friends and adherents of Agrippina). He failed to secure Tiberius' consent for a marriage with Livia, the widow of Tiberius' son Drusus, in 25, but his influence increased through Tiberius' retirement (which he encouraged) to Capreae in 27. In 29 he secured the arrest and deportation of Agrippina and her eldest son Nero; her second son Drusus was imprisoned in the Palace in 30. In 31 Sejanus appears to have planned to strike at the principate. He was consul, had perhaps been granted *imperium proconsulare*, and had hopes of *tribunicia potestas*. Tiberius, however, warned by Antonia, the widow of his brother Drusus, sent a letter to the Senate. Sejanus was arrested, brought before the Senate, and executed, the command of the Guard having been transferred to Macro (q.v.). The ease with which he was suppressed shows that his conspiracy was still in an early stage.
J. P. B.

SELENE, the moon-goddess of the Greeks. There was no cult of the Moon amongst the Greeks (that of the Sun may either be pre-Greek or, as e.g. in Rhodes, imported from the East). A real cult of the Moon in old Crete is very problematic and can hardly be proved from the rings and gems on which these heavenly bodies are represented (a cult of the Sun may be more acceptable). In Greek mythology, however, Sun and Moon had a significant place from olden times (but no doubt the Sun as the symbol of all physical life was the more important in the religious ideas of the Greeks). According to Hesiod they were both born of the Titan Theia, but Aeschylus made the Moon the daughter of the Sun, others again his wife. A number of goddesses and heroines have been equated with the Moon by mythologists—Hera, Io, Artemis, Hecate; 'whether Io (whose wanderings were compared with the course of the moon) or Hera had anything to do with the moon before the oriental influence (in the 7th c. B.C.), is a difficult question' (A. B. Cook, *Zeus* i. 456). But usually it is assumed that the Cretan Pasiphae, daughter

of Helios by Perseis, was a hypostasis of Selene (her oracular function at Thalamae may support this view). Much more important is the role which the Moon played in Greek poetry and folk-lore, especially sorcery, in which she was almost identified with Hecate (Artemis). The Greeks shared with most other peoples the superstition about the influence of the Moon on all organic and erotic life. The waxing Moon made everything prosper, the waning had the contrary effect (recommended for healing diseases, for malevolent magic); the full Moon was sometimes prescribed for love-charms (note the use of the stone selenites), the rising Moon for magical procedure in general. Eclipses of the Moon were due to sorceresses (Thessalian superstition). Selene was also thought to be the abode of the souls, at least in Hellenistic times.

F. Schwenn, art. 'Selene' in *PW*; Legrand, art. 'Luna' in Dar.–Sag.; W. H. Roscher, *Über Selene und Verwandtes* (1890).   S. E.

SELEUCEIA (1) **ON TIGRIS** was founded *c.* 312 B.C. by Seleucus I Nicator, as the capital of his empire. It became the great outpost of Greek civilization in the Orient, and replaced Babylon as the entrepôt of trade between east and west. Built beside the ancient Opis, on a natural lake where the Nahrmalka canal from the Euphrates joined the Tigris, Seleuceia was a port for maritime shipping (Strabo 16. 739). The city had a mixed Greek and Babylonian population and a large Jewish colony; Pliny estimated the total population as 600,000 in his day (*HN* 6. 122). Even after the centre of Seleucid power had shifted to Syria, Seleuceia maintained its essentially Greek character. When the Parthians conquered Babylonia, they preserved its free constitution, and kept their troops and administrative officials at Ctesiphon (q.v.) on the oppositive river bank. In the Parthian period Seleuceia was still a great commercial centre, in spite of the rivalry of Vologesocerta. But it became the seat of violent factions and dynastic quarrels; after a seven years' revolt (A.D. 35–42—Tac. *Ann.* 11. 9. 6) it was heavily punished. Excavations show that the city thenceforward gradually became orientalized; burnt down by Trajan, it was rebuilt in Parthian style. Its final destruction in A.D. 164 by Avidius Cassius marks the end of Hellenism in Babylonia.

M. Streck, 'Seleukeia und Ktesiphon', *Alte Orient* xvi. 3/4 (1917); O. Reuther, *Antiquity* 1929, 434 ff.; L. Waterman, *First and Second Prelim. Reports upon the Excavations at Tell Umar* (U.S.A. 1931–3); R. H. McDowell, 'Stamped Objects from Seleucia' and 'Coins from Seleucia' (*Univ. of Michigan Studies, Hum. Ser.* xxxvi and xxxvii, 1935).   M. S. D.

SELEUCEIA (2) **IN PIERIA** was founded *c.* 300 B.C. by Seleucus I as the seaport of Antioch. Captured by Ptolemy III *c.* 245, it was recovered in 219 by Antiochus III; its adult male citizens then numbered 6,000. It issued municipal coinage from Antiochus IV's reign, coined as one of the Brother Peoples (149–147), and in 108 received its freedom, which was confirmed by Pompey in reward for its resistance to Tigranes. It was the station of an imperial fleet; Vespasian improved the harbour.
A. H. M. J.

SELEUCUS (1) **I** (NICATOR) (*c.* 358–280 B.C.), son of Antiochus (presumably a Macedonian noble). He accompanied Alexander to Asia, but was never among his most prominent generals, though probably a close personal associate. After Alexander's death he obtained the satrapy of Babylonia (321), where he supported Antigonus against Eumenes, but nevertheless lost his satrapy and fled to Egypt (316). He regained Babylon by a spectacular exploit, and soon gained Media and Susiana also: from this year (312) the Seleucid Era begins.

Seleucus naturally joined the coalition of 'separatist' generals against Antigonus, and the victory of Ipsus (301) gave his kingdom access to the Mediterranean through

Syria and (296) Cilicia. Henceforth his policy had a predominantly western bias, as illustrated by the founding of Antioch (300) to balance Seleuceia (q.v. 1), by his marriage to Stratonice daughter of Demetrius (298), and by the avenues for expansion which he sought in Syria and Asia Minor. In the East he ceded the Indian provinces to Chandragupta early in his reign (304?). He finally won Asia Minor with the victory of Corupedium over Lysimachus (281), which also gave him hopes of seizing the vacant throne of Macedonia. He invaded Europe, but was murdered by Ptolemy Keraunos, who wanted Macedonia for himself.

The achievement of Seleucus was inferior only to that of Alexander, for he reassembled most of Alexander's empire in Asia. The dual character of his dominion, Mediterranean and continental, was implicit in his two capitals and his two wives (he never repudiated the Bactrian Apama, his wife since 324). But, unlike Alexander, he built his army, bureaucracy, and new cities primarily on Graeco-Macedonian immigrants as a foundation. In character he was the most humane, and one of the ablest, of the Successors.

ANCIENT SOURCES. For the Seleucids in general the sources are too scattered to be indicated briefly. See Bibliographies to *CAH* vi, ch. 15 (W. W. Tarn); vii, chs. 3 (Tarn), 5 (M. Rostovtzeff), and 22 (Tarn); viii, chs. 6 and 7 (M. Holleaux) and 16 (E. R. Bevan).
MODERN LITERATURE. *CAH* vi–viii; E. R. Bevan, *The House of Seleucus* (1902); E. Bikerman, *Institutions des Séleucides* (1938).
G. T. G.

SELEUCUS (2) **II** (CALLINICUS) (*c.* 265–226 B.C.) was the eldest son of Antiochus II and Laodice. In this reign (commencing in 247) the Seleucid Empire first suffered severely from the same centrifugal tendencies which had previously beset the Persian Empire. In the Far East, Bactria became definitely independent, and the native kingdom of Parthia also came into existence (248–247): in the West, Seleucid Asia Minor was lost temporarily. Seleucus was hampered throughout by dynastic troubles: first, the pretensions of his stepbrother which produced the invasion of Ptolemy III with its spectacular (though ephemeral) successes ('Third Syrian War', 246–1), and, later, the revolt of Antiochus Hierax in Asia Minor. Seleucus spent his life on campaign, but it remained for his son Antiochus ('the Great') to restore the kingdom.
G. T. G.

SELEUCUS (3) **III** (SOTER) (*c.* 245–223 B.C.), eldest son of Seleucus II, reigned three years only, being murdered (for reasons unknown) on a campaign against Attalus I of Pergamum.

SELEUCUS (4) **IV** (PHILOPATOR) (*c.* 218–175 B.C.), second son of Antiochus III, in whose lifetime he already held important commands. In his reign (which commenced in 187) he maintained correct relations with Rome and observed the terms of the peace of Apamea (188), which forbade political adventures in the West, and rendered them impossible by reason of the severe indemnity which it imposed upon him. But he also kept up friendly relations with Macedonia and Egypt, the two Powers of the Near East which remained independent of Rome.
G. T. G.

SELEUCUS (5) of Seleuceia on the Tigris (*c.* 150 B.C.), described by Strabo (16. 1. 6; 1. 1. 9) as a Chaldaean or Babylonian, stands alone as a thoroughgoing supporter of Aristarchus of Samos' heliocentric hypothesis, which he tried to demonstrate (Plut. *Quaest. Plat.* 8. 1, 1006 c; *Dox. Graec.* 383). He wrote on the tides in opposition to Crates of Mallos; he attributed the tides to the moon's resisting the rotation of the earth; Strabo (3. 5. 9) says that he discovered periodical inequalities in the flux and reflux of the Red Sea, which he attributed to the position of the moon in the zodiac.
T. H.

SELEUCUS (6) **HOMERICUS** of Alexandria was perhaps at the court of the Emperor Tiberius (Suet. *Tib.* 56). He is said to have written commentaries in Greek on practically every Greek poet. Besides works on Greek language and style and on Alexandrian proverbs, he wrote a criticism of the critical signs used by Aristarchus, a history of philosophy, a biographical work probably on literary figures, a theological treatise, a paradoxographical study, a miscellany, and a commentary on the *axones* of Solon.

FHG iii, 500; M. Müller, *de Seleuco Homerico* (1891); R. Reitzenstein, *Geschichte der griechischen Etymologiker* (1897). J. F. L.

SELIDES (σελίδες), *see* BOOKS, I. 5.

SELINUS (Σελινοῦς), a Greek city on the south-west coast of Sicily, founded from Megara Hyblaea (651 or 628 B.C.), quickly became prosperous, founding its own colony of Heraclea Minoa. Its earliest definite personalities are the tyrants Peithagoras and Euryleon the Spartan (510). Its isolated, westerly situation necessarily made Selinus opportunist; it even supported Carthage in the Himera campaign (480). In the fifth century B.C. Selinus flourished and built the temples whose impressive ruins survive at *Selinunte*. Ultimately, however, its traditional enmity with Segesta (q.v.) proved disastrous, provoking Athenian and Carthaginian intervention in Sicilian affairs; Carthage actually sacked Selinus (409). Selinus' refugees soon returned, but as Carthaginian tributaries. Such they remained, except occasionally, until Carthage evacuated and razed Selinus (250 B.C.), which thus disappeared from history (reject Pliny, *HN* 3. 91).

Strabo 6. 272; Thuc. 6. 4. 20; 7. 50, 58; Hdt. 5. 46; Diod. 5. 9; 11. 21 f.; 13. 54 f.; 114. J. Hulot–G. Fougères, *Sélinonte* (1910); J. Bérard, *Bibliogr. topogr.* (1941), 89. E. T. S.

SELLA CURULIS was an ivory folding seat, without back or arms, used by magistrates *cum imperio*. Its Etruscan origin is merely a conjecture of ancient authorities. The name was derived (Gell. 3. 18. 3 ff.) from the chariot (*currus*) in which the chief magistrate was conveyed to the place of judgement, and originally the *sella curulis* served as the seat of justice. Subsequently it became the attribute of all the higher ('curule') magistrates.

Mommsen, *Röm. Staatsr.* i³, 399 ff.; B. Kübler, *PW*, s.v. P. T.

SEMELE (Σεμέλη), otherwise called **Thyone** (Θυώνη), in mythology, a daughter of Cadmus and mother of Dionysus (qq.v.). Whether or not Semele is Zemelo and originally the name of a Thraco-Phrygian earth-goddess, it is certainly not Greek, whereas Thyone is. Such double namings are not uncommon, cf. Alexander-Paris. Her story consists almost wholly of her relations with Zeus and Dionysus. The former's association with her aroused Hera's jealousy, and the goddess, disguising herself (Ov. *Met.* 3. 259 ff.; Hyginus, *Fab.* 167, 179, from older sources, cf., e.g., Eur. *Bacch.* 6 ff.), advised her to test the divinity of her lover by bidding him come to her in his true shape. She persuaded him to give whatever she should ask, and he was thus tricked into granting a request which he knew would result in her death. The fire of his thunderbolts killed her, but made her son immortal (cf. Ov. *Fasti*, 3. 715 f.; Rose in *CR* 36 (1922), 116). Zeus put the unborn child in his thigh, whence he was born at full time, and, after coming to maturity, he descended into Hades and brought Semele up (Pind. *Ol.* 2. 25 ff.; Paus. 2. 37. 5—Argive legend of the place where he went down to fetch her; and elsewhere); she thus became an Olympian goddess. This, if she was originally a goddess, is evidently secondary. She had a cult in Thebes in historical times (Eur. loc. cit.; Paus. 9. 12. 3–4).

The statement of Hesychius, s.v. Ἐγχώ, that this was

another name for her, is pretty obviously due to a misunderstanding of a lost comedian's joke. Someone had said that Dionysus was son of 'Pour-out' or 'Fill-up' and his words had been taken seriously; see Rose in *CQ* xxvi (1932), 58. For Actaeon's love of her (in which case he can hardly have been her nephew) see Acusilaus in Apollod. 3. 30, and cf. ACTAEON. H. J. R.

SEMIRAMIS (Σεμίραμις), in Greek legend, the daughter of the Syrian goddess Derceto (*see* ATARGATIS). Exposed at birth, she was tended by doves till found by shepherds. Her first husband was Onnes, her second Ninus, king of Assyria, after whose death she ruled many years, renowned in war and as builder of Babylon (this point Berosus, *FHG* ii. 507, denies). At death she was changed into a dove, which was accordingly held sacred (Diod. Sic. 2. 4–20). The historical figure behind this legend is almost certainly Sammuramat, wife of the Assyrian king Shamshi-Adad V, and herself regent 810–805 B.C. in the minority of her son Adad-Nirari III. F. R. W.

SEMO SANCUS DIUS FIDIUS (for the full name see Dion. Hal. *Ant. Rom.* 4. 58. 4). A deity of puzzling origin and functions, said to be Sabine (e.g. Propert. 4. 9. 74; he is there identified with Hercules, q.v., apparently from the interpretation of Dius Fidius as *Iouis filius*, and Sancus is, as often, corrupted, whether by Prop. himself or a copyist, into Sanctus). Semo appears to be his name, and suggests the Semunes of the Arval hymn, usually taken to be deities of sowing; Sancus would seem to be an epithet, perhaps connected with *sancire*, cf. the adj. *sanqualis*, which also shows a *u*-stem. Fidius pretty certainly is to be explained as cognate with *fides*, and Dius is simply 'divine' or 'heavenly'. In historical times he is connected with oaths and treaties (Wissowa in Roscher's *Lexikon*, iv. 318 f., cf. *RK* 130 f.), hence the common oath *medius fidius*. Hence he has some connexion with thunder. His temple stood on the Quirinal (Platner–Ashby, 469 f.), and he had some sort of cult on Tiber island also (Wissowa, locc. cit.). Conceivably a deity of sowing had been absorbed by Jupiter (q.v.). H. J. R.

SEMONIDES, iambic and elegiac poet, originally of Samos, but connected especially with Amorgos (Suidas s.v. Σημωνίδης, Strabo, 487, Steph. Byz. s.v. Ἀμοργός). Suidas makes him a contemporary of Archilochus, Cyril places him in 664–661 (*Adv. Iul.* 1, p. 12), and modern critics have tended to place him later still because of an alleged dependence, not only on Archilochus (fr. 1 and Archil. fr. 84), but also on Phocylides (fr. 7 and Phoc. fr. 2). A piece of elegiac verse on the shortness of life which Stobaeus (4. 34) attributes to Simonides of Ceos has been ascribed with some reason to Semonides. He is also said to have written a history of Samos in two books of elegiacs (Suidas). Of his iambic fragments the longest, fr. 7, describes various types of women by comparing them to animals and shows the influence of popular fables; another, fr. 1, discourses on the illusions and uncertainties of life and prescribes a mean between desire and despair. Semonides has plenty of humour and some satirical gift; he writes easily. His language is Ionic. *See also* IAMBIC POETRY, GREEK.

Text: E. Diehl, *Anth. Lyr. Graec.* i. 3, pp. 50–64. C. M. B.

SEMOS of Delos (*c.* 200 B.C.) was a careful, scholarly compiler.

WORKS. (1) Geographical and antiquarian: *Delias* or *Deliaca*, on the geography, antiquities, institutions, products, etc., of Delos; *Nesias*, a work on islands; *On Paros, On Pergamum, Periodoi.*

(2) *On Paeans*, of which a valuable fragment survives describing the masks, dress, and performance of αὐτοκάβδαλοι, ἰθύφαλλοι, φαλλοφόροι (*FHG* iv. 492 ff.). J. F. L.

SEMPRONIUS, *see* ASELLIO, GRACCHUS, TUDITANUS.

SENATUS. I. REGAL AND REPUBLICAN ROME

(*a*) *Composition.* The Senate was the council of the kings and survived the monarchy. Tradition attributes to Romulus the institution of a Senate of 100 members, but the oldest certain number is 300, evidently connected with the 3 tribes and 30 curiae. Sulla increased the number to 600, Caesar to 900, and Augustus reverted to 600. The distinction between patrician and plebeian senators, whatever its origin, must have been already definite in the second half of the fifth century B.C. The patrician senators, called *patres*, continued to retain certain prerogatives (cf. below). Plebeian senators were called *adlecti* or *conscripti*. Patricians and plebeians together were called *qui patres qui conscripti* or *patres ⟨et⟩ conscripti*. *Senatores pedarii*, who voted but did not speak, were probably at first those who had not held magistracies, and later magistrates of low rank. The senators were chosen first by the kings, later by the consuls, and after the *plebiscitum* of Ovinius (q.v.) by the censors. Late in the third century it was the rule to choose first ex-curule magistrates, who could take part in the sessions before formal appointment. In the time of the Gracchi plebeian aediles and, by the *plebiscitum Atinium*, *tribuni plebis* secured the same privileges. Sulla made admission to the Senate depend mainly on the quaestorship. Thus the Senate was recruited indirectly by popular election. Censors could only remove qualified persons if guilty of misconduct; the exclusion could be revoked by their successors. Certain professions (e.g. petty industry) and certain civic punishments or moral transgressions disqualified from admission. Freedmen or sons of freedmen were not usually admitted. A property qualification (1,000,000 sesterces) was first imposed by Augustus, but the senators usually had at least equestrian census.

Senators wore the *clavus latus* (q.v.) and special shoes of red leather. They had reserved seats at religious ceremonies and public entertainments. They were not allowed to leave Italy without the Senate's permission. Being excluded from State contracts and the possession of large ships (*see* CLAUDIUS 7), they were predominantly a landlord class. They had at times an exclusive or privileged position as judges in criminal and civil courts (*see* QUAESTIO 8). As office depended mainly on wealth and birth, 'new men' were rare, and the Senate tended to become hereditary (*see* NOVUS HOMO, OPTIMATES). Membership being *de facto* permanent, senators exerted great influence on internal and foreign policy. The transformation of the Senate into a body of ex-magistrates avoided serious clashes between the *imperium* of the magistrates and the *auctoritas* of the Senate and made the Senate responsible in the last centuries B.C. for the direction of the Roman State. The Republic collapsed when military leaders destroyed the authority of the Senate.

(*b*) *Procedure.* The Senate was summoned by the presiding magistrates, either holders of *imperium* or, later, tribunes, according to an order of precedence. Sessions were held between dawn and sunset, but were forbidden by a *Lex Pupia* (2nd or 1st c. B.C.) during the Comitia. Only during the Empire were the times of meeting fixed—usually two each month. The meeting had to take place either in Rome (*see* CURIA 2), or within a mile of the city, in a place both public and consecrated. The first sitting of the year was in the temple of Jupiter Capitolinus.

Sittings were held in private, but with opened doors, the tribunes of the plebs sitting in the vestibule in the period before their admission to sessions. Each senator spoke from his seat. Freedom of speech was unlimited during the Republic. Augustus imposed a time-limit. First came the report (*relatio*) of the chairman or another magistrate, who submitted it in writing. Each senator was asked (*interrogatio*) his opinion (*sententia*), according to his rank (*censorii, consulares, praetorii, aedilicii,* etc.). Within each category the patricians took precedence, the senior patrician *censorius* of the *gentes maiores* (after 209 B.C. any patrician *censorius*) heading the list as *princeps senatus*. After Sulla the magistrate gave priority to the consuls designate or, in their absence, to any *consularis*; and *princeps senatus* became a merely social title open to plebeians. After the debate the different opinions were put to vote by a division (*discessio*). Sometimes *relatio* was followed by *discessio* without *interrogatio*. Certain resolutions required a quorum. Any resolution, called either *decretum* or, more commonly, *senatus consultum* (q.v.), could be vetoed by the tribunes. The urban quaestors kept the records in the *aerarium*. The publication of official reports in the *acta rerum urbanarum*, ordered by Caesar, was suppressed in part by Augustus. Improvements in short-hand made accurate reports possible.

(*c*) *Functions.* The Senate existed, formally, to advise the magistrates. The patrician senators retained two special functions. The first, which became a pure formality, was to ratify the deliberations of the People (and probably of the plebs) and was called *patrum auctoritas* (q.v.). The second was to elect an *interrex* (q.v.) for the arrangement of elections, if no magistrates were available.

The Senate advised the magistrates in matters of domestic and foreign policy, finance and religion, and on their legislative proposals. It could invalidate laws already voted by pointing out technical flaws in procedure. It suggested the nomination of a dictator, assigned the various duties to the magistrates, decided the *prorogatio imperii*, established the equipment (*ornatio*) for each magistrate and pro-magistrate, and marked out the two provinces destined for the consuls. In war-time it influenced the choice and the extension of commissions, fixed the number of the levies, and criticized the conduct of war. In finance it determined the rate of the tribute, supervised revenue and expenditure, and controlled the *aerarium*. It could order the censors to redraft contracts and regulated the coinage (at least of the mint of Rome). The practical decision of war, the conclusion of peace treaties, and the conduct of foreign policy were usually in the hands of the Senate, but the formal declaration of war and ratification of treaties belonged to the Comitia. It often received ambassadors and appointed senators to help the magistrates or pro-magistrates in concluding treaties and in settling the organization of conquered territory. The arbitration of the Senate was often asked by Italian communities, by provincials and client States. Religious life was controlled by the Senate, which contained the members of the principal priestly colleges and could order religious ceremonies and introduce new cults. In urgent cases the Senate could order dispensation from the observance of law, subject usually to ratification by the Comitia, and after the Gracchan period it could pass the *senatus consultum ultimum* (q.v.).

II. THE IMPERIAL AGE

(*a*) *The ordo.* In Augustus' view the preservation of the Senate's prestige was vital to his intended restoration of the Republic. The Senate was left to govern Italy and those provinces which required only small garrisons (*see* PROVINCIA). Consequently it retained the *aerarium*. But the emperor soon acquired control both of the *aerarium* and of the whole senatorial administration. The Senate retained only the supervision of copper coinage. Tiberius transferred to it the actual election of the magistrates, but the imperial *nominatio* and *commendatio* (q.v.) reduced the importance of elections to a minimum. Thus the self-recruitment of the Senate by the quaestorian elections was influenced by the will of the emperors, who could also, by *adlectio* (q.v.), directly introduce new members to any senatorial rank.

The Senate became a hereditary order, since, except for new men introduced by the emperor, only the sons of the senators could become senators. Most of the high offices in the State (governments of provinces, with few exceptions, commands of legions, *praefectus urbi, praefecti aerarii, legati iuridici, correctores,* etc.) were reserved for senators. The senators became a privileged class interested in preserving the Empire. Future senators served at first a year in the army as *tribuni laticlavii*, then held the vigintivirate and entered the Senate at twenty-five through the quaestorship. The senators were called *clarissimi*, a title extended during the second century to wife, sons, and daughters.

(*b*) *Functions and authority.* The Senate developed judicial functions from Republican precedents. A legislative power grew out of its advisory capacity. *Senatus consulta* had acquired full recognition as laws at least by A.D. 200. The emperor had the right of convening, presiding over and laying matters before the Senate, and had the titular position of *princeps senatus*. The *relatio* of the emperor took precedence. It was usually a written speech (*oratio*), which the later jurists quoted as authoritative rather than the subsequent *senatus consultum*. The number of senators attending meetings continually decreased. Mere *acclamationes* were often substituted for discussion. On the whole, the Senate lost its independence; its freedom was restricted to the choice of a new emperor when the throne was vacant, or during a revolution. The Senate, however, was always in formal connexion with the People, the true repository of the *imperium*: it conferred his powers on the *princeps*. The acknowledgement of the Senate, therefore, was the condition of the legitimacy of an emperor (*see* AUGUSTUS, PRINCEPS). Furthermore, the Senate preserved a tradition of discussion, of competence, of respect for the public interest and for Republican procedure, and represented a sort of public opinion—of the wealthy classes. Friendly relations between Senate and emperors were taken to distinguish 'good' emperors from tyrants. *Damnatio memoriae* (q.v.) depended on the Senate.

(*c*) *From the Principate to the Late Empire.* In the late Republic numbers of municipal Italians and even some provincials entered the Senate, especially under Julius Caesar. Under the Empire, the number of provincial senators increased almost continuously, but until the time of Septimius Severus the majority were Italian. In the first century the provincials came mostly from Spain and Gallia Narbonensis; afterwards Orientals and Africans prevailed. The Danubian provinces never supplied many members.

The distinction between senatorial and imperial provinces was gradually eliminated, and the *aerarium* became simply the city-treasury of Rome. Gallienus deprived senators of the command of legions and greatly reduced their share of provincial government. The increasing importance of the *Equites* resulted under Constantine in a virtual fusion of the two orders. This new senatorial order recovered much administrative authority. Consequently, the number of senators greatly increased (probably 2000, *c.* A.D. 350). Constantine matched the Senate of Rome with another in Constantinople, which in A.D. 359 was made completely equal to that of Rome. Entry to the Senate was now through the praetorship, and the usual imperial *adlectio* was *inter consulares*. Senators were divided into three groups: *clarissimi*; (*clarissimi et*) *spectabiles*; (*clarissimi et*) *illustres*. By 450 the two lower classes were excused from attendance in the capital. Under Justinian only the *illustres* were entitled to speak, *sententiam dicere*. The *praefectus urbi* usually presided. Senators were free from municipal burdens, but subject to special taxes. As a political body the Senate naturally declined still further; but it remained the representative of the Roman People and continued to legislate. As a body of great landlords, the Senate remained an essential element of the social structure of the Empire. In the fourth century senators led the defence of Paganism in Italy and in the fifth many assisted the barbarian generals to destroy imperial authority. The Roman Senate is last mentioned in A.D. 580.

BIBLIOGRAPHY

1. Mommsen, *Röm. Staatsr.* iii. 2 (1888) is fundamental, but does not entirely supersede earlier works (e.g. G. Bloch, *Les Origines du sénat romain* (1883); P. Willems, *Le Sénat de la république romaine*[2] (1885)). O'Brien Moore, *PW* Suppl. vi (1935), 660, is very good. A. H. J. Greenidge, *Roman Public Life* (1901), pp. 261, 377. For the origins see also G. Pacchioni, *Att. Acc. Scienze Torino* lx, 1925, 875.

2. *The Senate of the Principate*: Th. A. Abele, *Der Senat unter Augustus* (1907); M. Hammond, *The Augustan Principate* (1933); H. Volkmann, *Zur Rechtsprechung im Prinzipat des Augustus* (1935), 93; A. v. Premerstein, *Vom Werden und Wesen des Prinzipats* (1937), 218; O. T. Schulz, *Das Wesen des römischen Kaisertums der ersten zwei Jahrhunderte* (1916).

3. *The Transformation of the Senatorial Class*: P. Willems, op. cit.; F. Münzer, *Römische Adelsparteien und Adelsfamilien* (1920); H. Hill, 'Sulla's new senators in 81 B.C.', *CQ* 1932, 170; R. Syme, 'Caesar, the Senate and Italy', *BSR* 1938, p. 1; id., *The Roman Revolution* (1939); S. J. De Laet, *De Samenstelling van den Romeinschen Senaat gedurende de eerste eeuw van het Principaat* (1941); J. Willems, 'Le Sénat romain en l'an 65 a. J. Chr.', *Musée Belge* iv (1900), 236, v (1901), 82, and vi (1902), 100; B. Stech, 'Senatores Romani qui fuerint inde a Vespasiano usque ad Traiani exitum', *Klio, Beih.* x (1908); C. S. Walton, 'Oriental senators in the Service of Rome', *JRS* 1929, 38; P. Lambrechts, *La Composition du sénat romain de l'accession au trône d'Hadrien à la mort de Commode* (1936); id., *La Composition du sénat romain de Septime Sévère à Dioclétien* (1937).

4. *For the Late Empire*: Ch. Lécrivain, *Le Sénat romain depuis Dioclétien* (1888); J. B. Bury, *History of the Later Roman Empire* i[2] (1923); J. Sundwall, *Weströmische Studien* (1915); id., *Abhandlungen zur Geschichte des ausgehenden Römertums* (1919); E. Stein, *Bull. Acad. Belgique* 1939, 308.   A. M.

SENATUS CONSULTUM

SENATUS CONSULTUM was the advice of the Senate to the magistrates. In Republican times it had no legislative force, but *de facto* it was binding. If it was vetoed, it lost its binding force, but conserved the *senatus auctoritas*. During the Empire the *senatus consulta* were at first implemented by a clause in the praetor's edict; after Hadrian certain *senatus consulta* immediately had the force of law. The *senatus consultum* was drafted after the session of the Senate in the presence of the presiding magistrate and some witnesses, usually including the proposer. If necessary, it was translated into Greek. Many *senatus consulta* are preserved in their Greek translation.

A *senatus consultum* usually contained: (1) the name of the presiding magistrate, date, place of assembly, witnesses; (2) the magistrate's report; (3) the introductory formula: 'd(e) e(a) r(e) i(ta) c(ensuerunt)'; (4) the terms of the *consultum*, which often confirmed its own advisory nature in references to the magistrates such as s(i) e(is) u(idebitur); i(ta) u(tei) e(is) e r(e)p(ublica) f(ideue) s(ua) u(ideatur); (5) the letter *C* (= censuere), indicating senatorial approval. In the Imperial age was added the number of the senators present.

The texts of *senatus consulta* were deposited in the *aerarium*. Another copy was in ancient times given to the plebeian sanctuary of Ceres. The documents were classified, but not sufficiently to avoid losses and falsifications. The jurists often named them after one of the consuls of the year (*SC Orfitianum*) or more rarely after the emperor who proposed them (*SC Claudianum*) or after the occasion of the *SC* (*SC Macedonianum*).

Many *senatus consulta* are collected in Bruns, *Fontes*[7] (1909). For the Greek texts, P. Viereck, *Sermo graecus quo S P Q R magistratusque populi romani . . . usi sunt* (1888), is fundamental. P. Willems, *Le Sénat de la république romaine* i. 248; ii. 204; O'Brien Moore, *PW*, Suppl. vi, 800 (with a list of *SC*).   A. M.

SENATUS CONSULTUM ULTIMUM

SENATUS CONSULTUM ULTIMUM, a declaration of public emergency by the Senate, usually interpreted as authorizing the magistrates to employ every means of repression against public enemies (not necessarily specified *nominatim*), without being subjected to *provocatio* and *intercessio* (Sall. *Cat.* 29). The formula was: 'senatus decreuit darent operam consules ne quid respublica detrimenti caperet' (Sall. loc. cit., cf., e.g., Caes. *BCiv.* 1. 5). The proper name was *SC de republica defendenda*. The name *SC ultimum* is derived from Caesar, loc. cit.

Its first certain use concerned C. Gracchus. The other assured instances are: the 'tumultus' of Saturninus and Glaucia (100 B.C.), against Sulla (83), Lepidus (77), Catiline (63), in the disturbances of 62 (Metellus Nepos) and 52 (Clodius), against Caesar (49), M. Caelius Rufus (48), the disturbances of Dolabella (47), against M. Antonius and against Octavian (43). It was last employed against Salvidienus Rufus in 40.

The exercise of this power by the Senate was hotly contested, e.g. in connexion with C. Rabirius (q.v.). The law of Clodius *de capite civis Romani* in 58 was also a partial condemnation of the *senatus consultum ultimum*.

Mommsen, *Röm. Staatsr.* i. 687; ii. 1240; *Strafr.* 257; C. Barbagallo, *Una misura eccezionale dei Romani: il S.C.U.* (1900); J. L. Strachan-Davidson, *Problems of the Roman Criminal Law* i (1912), 225; E. G. Hardy, *Some Problems in Roman History* (1924), 27, 99; G. Plaumann, *Klio* xiii (1913), 321; H. Last, *CAH* ix. 84; id. *JRS* 1943, 94.   A. M.

SENECA

SENECA (1), LUCIUS (or perhaps MARCUS ANNAEUS), writer on rhetoric, was born of equestrian family at Corduba in Spain about 55 B.C. Of his life we know little; he was certainly in Rome both as a young man and after his marriage, and his knowledge of the contemporary schools of declamation implies that he spent much time there. He amassed a considerable fortune and may have held an official post in Spain or engaged in trade. By his marriage with Helvia, a fellow countrywoman, he had three sons—Annaeus Novatus, who after adoption by L. Junius Gallio became governor of Achaea, L. Annaeus Seneca (q.v. 2) the philosopher, and M. Annaeus Mela, the father of Lucan. He died between A.D. 37 and 41, after the death of Tiberius and before the exile of his son the philosopher.

His historical work, covering the period from the outbreak of the civil war to his death, is lost. The *Oratorum sententiae divisiones colores*, addressed to his sons, consists of extracts, supplied by his retentive memory, from the declaimers whom he had heard during his long life, interspersed with digressions and comments of his own. The work comprised ten books devoted to *controversiae*, each with a preface, and at least two devoted to *suasoriae*. In our manuscripts only five books (1, 2, 7, 9, and 10) of the *controversiae* and one of the *suasoriae* have survived and these have suffered some mutilation: an abridgement made for school use (probably 4th c.) gives us some knowledge of the contents of the missing books of *controversiae* and, what is more important, preserves, with some mutilation, seven of the prefaces.

Shrewd observation, a phenomenal memory, and an experience extending from Cicero's age into the reign of Gaius make Seneca's work a most valuable source for the literary history of the early Empire. The rhetorical schools were his lifelong interest, but he clearly recognized their excesses and dangers. While the new movement fascinated him, his own sympathies were with the oratorical tradition of Cicero. The specimens of the handling of some forty themes by more than a hundred *rhetores*, great and small, if they are not verbally exact quotations, show remarkable skill in reproducing the styles and mannerisms of others; they are relieved by pithy incidental criticisms and scraps of literary reminiscence which serve to maintain the atmosphere of informality. Seneca's own views, both on individual declaimers and on the general tendencies of his time, are developed at greater length in the prefaces, written in an easy but terse and incisive prose which represents the transition from the periodic to the pointed style. The work bears out the character ascribed to him by his son: he was 'maiorum consuetudini deditus', a man of old-fashioned Roman strictness, fair-minded but suspicious of novelty and of Greek culture, critical of the decadence of contemporary society but combining seriousness with a satiric humour. *See also* LITERARY CRITICISM, LATIN, para. 4.

Editions: A. Kiessling (Teubner, 1872), H. J. Müller (1887), H. Bornecque (1902, with Fr. tr. and notes); *Suas.*, W. A. Edward (1928, with tr. and comm.). General: H. Bornecque, *Les Déclamations et les déclamateurs d'après Sénèque le Père* (1902); W. Hoffa, *De Seneca patre quaestiones selectae* (1909).   C. J. F.

SENECA (2), LUCIUS ANNAEUS, born at Corduba, *c.* 5 or 4 B.C., was the second son of (1) above. The family was equestrian, wealthy, and distinguished. As a small child, Seneca was taken to Rome in charge of an aunt, his mother Helvia's sister, and by her care was pulled through an ailing childhood and early youth, while her influence helped him in early stages of his official life. At Rome he studied the rhetoric which was a natural prelude to a senatorial career, and (against his father's liking) the philosophy which, with money-making and the lesser hobby of viticulture, formed his lifelong unofficial pursuit. His first step in the *cursus*, the quaestorship, came perhaps shortly after A.D. 32. Details of his beginnings are lacking as definite dates, but we know that by Caligula's accession he ranked as an orator and writer of the first standing, and that this fact, as an affront to the Emperor's megalomania, nearly caused his death. Seneca was in his mid-forties when in Claudius' first year, 41, Messalina secured his banishment to Corsica for adultery with Julia Livilla, an improbable enough charge to suggest an ulterior but equally un-proven motive. In Corsica he remained, broken and unstoically despondent, till in 49 he was recalled by Agrippina's influence and, with Afranius Burrus, appointed tutor to Nero, a praetorship in 50 sealing his rehabilitation. With Nero's accession in 54, S., still asso-ciated with Burrus, passed from tutor to minister, obtain-ing in 55 or 56 a suffect consulate, which marks roughly the peak of his ministerial influence. He and Burrus were reluctant accessories to Agrippina's murder in 59, and it was Seneca who composed Nero's explanation to the Senate. On the death of Burrus, three years later, S., now nearing seventy, attempted to retire and relinquish his very great wealth to the Emperor, his relations with whom had become strained. Nero refused the gift, though in 64 he seems to have partially reconsidered the refusal in view of the need for restorations after the Great Fire; the retirement he permitted, at least tacitly, for Seneca henceforth spent little time in Rome and much in Campania, living in the leisure which the letters to Lucilius Junior incidentally reveal. When the Pisonian conspiracy foundered in 65, Seneca was named among those concerned by one of the conspirators; further evidence seems tenuous, but it sufficed. He faced the self-inflicted end he was permitted to choose with tran-quillity, and must be allowed a courage in his death which in his life had not been so evident. Seneca mar-ried twice: his infant son by his first wife died before the exile; his second, Pompeia Paulina, considerably younger than himself, would have died with him but for Nero's intervention.

2. Seneca's extant works do not comprise his whole literary performance. All his forensic oratory has vanished—a specially regrettable loss. There are scraps, titles, or mentions of some dozen other works not extant, and he himself speaks (*Dial.* 1 = *De Prov.* 1. 1, *Ep.* 106. 2) of a design for a comprehensive ethical survey; but the lateness of the references and perhaps his own temperament suggest that this was a design only. The survivals, containing few materials for dating them, leave the tracing of intellectual or stylistic development mainly conjectural.

3. We have first ten pieces passing under the mis-nomer of *Dialogi*. Of these, three are formal *consola-tiones—Ad Marciam*, *Ad Polybium*, and *Ad Helviam Matrem*, the first dateless but probably not late, the other two belonging to the early part of the exile. The remain-ing seven are philosophical or ethical treatises: *De Provi-dentia*, showing that the sufferings of the good under Providence are only apparent, dedicated to Lucilius and probably late; *De constantia sapientis*, on the impassibility of the Stoic adept, written after Caligula's death; *De ira*, a rather badly constructed discussion of the nature, futility, and cure of anger, addressed to his brother Novatus, and probably to be placed early in Claudius' reign; *De vita beata* (incomplete), an exposition of the Stoic theory of happiness, addressed to the same brother (but now as 'Gallio', hence later than *De ira*), containing an apologia for the philosophic millionaire which sounds personal, and hinting at a date not far before the sacrifice of 61; *De otio*, a fragment justifying retirement from public life for the Stoic, perhaps pointing to a slightly later phase of the same crisis; *De tranquillitate animi*, presenting Annaeus Serenus, who seeks advice on the occasional vacillations of the proficient, an imposing but irrelevant discourse on the disquiets of the idle and vicious, probably not early; *De brevitate vitae*, maintain-ing to Pompeius Paulinus that life is long enough if no time is wasted, written apparently in 49.

4. Three other prose treatises stand outside the *Dialogi*: *De clementia* (the autocrat should be merciful), seemingly addressed to Nero early in his reign, one book and a part out of an original three; *De beneficiis*, to one Aebutius Liberalis, on the nature of benefits, their proper recipients, and so forth, unsystematic and rather patchily readable, written intermittently after Claudius' death; *Naturales quaestiones*, dealing with curiosities of fire, air, and water, and the nature of winds, earthquakes, and comets, its recipient being Lucilius and its central date 63 (*see* METEOROLOGY). Of the *Epistulae morales*, to the same person and of the same period, we have 124, and know that others are lost; in these Seneca plays the part of philosophic and ethical director to a less advanced friend.

5. The *Apocolocyntosis*, in the medley of prose and verse proper to Menippean satire, is a venomous and moderately amusing skit on the deification of Claudius, written just after his death.

6. Seneca's prose is a highly rhetorical product, owing its stimulus to the practice of *recitatio* and the consequent need to sparkle, in an easily bored generation. His mastery is rather of epigrammatic point and the artifice appropriate to its presentment than of language as a sustained and flexible means of expression. So, too, his thought is rather spasmodic than consistent and his ethics ring truer in emotional appeal than in speculation. His letters are his most attractive work: their purpose makes no great demands on originality, and gives scope for an undoubted experience of men and an innocuous assump-tion of the superiority so necessary to his egoism, while the epistolary form allows the development of themes in isolation, without too much revealing a weakness in sustained and constructive thought, and admits relief in glimpses of personal circumstances and social conditions. His 'causidicalis argutia' and 'uernacula eruditio' (Gellius 12. 2) are there, but in this environment have a not unpleasant freshness.

7. His most important poetical works are nine tragedies: *Hercules* [*Furens*], based generally on the *Hercules Furens* of Euripides; *Troades*, with a dual source in Euripides' *Troades* and *Hecuba*; *Phoenissae*, so disjointed that it is doubted whether its episodes belong to one play; *Medea*, mainly empurpled Euripides, but other sources may here and there be latent; *Phaedra*, the myth debased to a not very subtle story of minx and misogynist; *Oedipus*, with a considerable Sophoclean basis; *Agamemnon*, in which a debt to Aeschylus is rather to be assumed than easily traced; *Thyestes*, a crassly horrific treatment of the gruesome myth, without extant source; *Hercules Oetaeus*, with but little in it, apart from subject, to suggest the *Trachiniae*—long, dull, and psychologically incredible.

8. A tenth tragedy, *Octavia* (q.v.), interesting as the sole surviving *praetexta*, and for its subject, but for little else, long and strangely ranked, against its own unequivocal evidence, as Seneca's; it is now recognized as Senecan pastiche.

9. That the tragedies were written for reader or listener rather than playgoer is shown by episodes unsuited for stage presentation. Their strength lies in passages of rhetorical and descriptive power; their weakness, glaringly emphasized beside Greek counterparts, in crude characterization and psychology. Conventional moralizing (mainly Stoic) companions the bloodily macabre, and peaks of emotional stress are seldom unpointed (or untravestied) by epigram. Their versification is polished but monotonous in texture, while the choruses, lacking the relief of strophic arrangement, frequently hammer at one short metrical phrase, without system-break or other diversion, *ad nauseam*.

10. The tragedies cannot be dated, but suggest the clever immaturity of a youngish man. Though false standards of taste and their peculiar survival-position gave them an undue influence on the early moulding of modern tragedy in England and elsewhere, it is now less by their own merits than as a clue to the author's character that they interest us.

11. Besides the tragedies we have seventy-seven epigrams, a few handed down under Seneca's name, and others attributed to him with more or less probability. A recent survey (Peyrani) allows more than forty of them, on linguistic and other grounds, a reasoned authenticity, but it is a fragile canon.

12. Seneca's character, with its lamentable rift between principle and practice in crises, is sometimes pronounced detestable. He preached detachment and was conspicuously a money-maker; defiance of circumstance, yet whined in Corsica and crawled before Polybius (q.v. 2); contempt for death and pain, yet, till finally trapped, evaded them by flagrant complaisance. He could vent spite, or curry favour, or both by clever sniggering at a dead and by no means contemptible emperor, yet five years later connives supinely at more than common murder by a vicious live one. With all this he affects the moral guide. Such is briefly the indictment. It may be observed, first, that most neurotics are superficially detestable either to a small or a large audience, but that the causes are preponderantly beyond their control, the problem more clinical than moral, and detestation irrelevant; second, that Seneca's life and works present a fairly clear-cut picture of neurosis. The early ill-health is significant: youthful designs of suicide (*Ep.* 78. 2) and a temporary leaning to occultism of the ascetic-ceremonial kind (*Ep.* 108. 17 ff.) point to neurotic maladjustment, despair over physical inferiority and, alternatively, flight from reality. The flight proceeds in his philosophy, which becomes a ready-made escape-system (analogous to but less obvious than the arbitrary system of complete paranoia) in which he moves a leader calm and unruffled, compensating and submerging his inferiorities, inadequacies, and dismal failures before the reality to which he can react only with discomfort or terror. Consistent with this are his thought and style, neither architectonic: the one capable of developing cleverly rather than profoundly a limited theme, but hardly of framing and supporting a consistent personal philosophy; the other aiming at point rather than period, and displaying at times a considerable eloquence of the propagandist type, with an appeal rather to emotion than intellect. In the tragedies, too, we meet no product or promise of a balanced artist-mind, but the primitive thought-forms, rough-hewn idola, and nightmares risen out of a tortured egoist's unconscious mind. Everywhere are traceable the erratic ability and the limitations which are common stigmata of paranoiac abnormality. Abnormal his character is; not devoid of a disfigured greatness in its mutilation, and one which it is more profitable to understand than to condemn unconditionally.

BIBLIOGRAPHY

TEXT: Dialogues, app. crit., Gertz (1886); edn. of x, xi, xii, comm. J. D. Duff (1915). De ben., De clem., Hosius (²1914). Nat. quaest., Gercke (1907). Epp. mor., Hense (1914); Beltrami (²1931); selections, Summers (1910). Apocolocyntosis, Bücheler–Heraeus (1922), Waltz (1932); Ball (with transl., 1902). Tragedies, Richter (1902). Poems, *Anth. Lat.* (1894–1926).

STUDIES: Chronological: A. Gercke, *Senecastudien* (1895), *PIR²*, A 617. Biographical: R. Waltz, *La Vie politique de Sénèque* (1909); C. Marchesi, *Seneca* (1920). Literary: E. Albertini, *La Composition dans les ouvrages philosophiques de S.* (1923). Dramatic influence: F. L. Lucas, *Seneca and Elizabethan Tragedy* (1922). Philosophical: C. Martha, *Les Moralistes sous l'empire romain* (1865); G. Boissier, *La Religion romaine d'Auguste aux Antonins* (1879).   E. P. B.

SENECIO, see HERENNIUS; SOSIUS.

SENONES, the last Gauls to settle in Italy, came from a parent stock which in Caesar's time inhabited the Seine basin (Caesar, *BGall.* 2. 2, etc.). In Italy, ousting the Umbrians, they established themselves on the Adriatic coast between Ariminum and Ancona, the Ager Gallicus of historical times. Diodorus and Livy, but not Polybius, say that Senones led the marauding Gallic band that captured Rome in 390 B.C. Thereafter Senones remained a constant menace for 100 years until Rome subjugated them in 283 (Polyb. 2. 17 f.; Diod. 14. 113 f.; Livy 5. 35). They then disappeared from Italy, being either expelled or massacred. Their territory was used partly for colonies (Sena, Ariminum), partly for the allotments which Flaminius assigned to individual Roman citizens in 232.

For bibliography *see* CISALPINE GAUL.   E. T. S.

SENTENTIA, in the language of Roman literary and rhetorical criticism, means the finished expression of a thought. In post-Augustan times the word is used especially to denote the terse, pointed, epigrammatic expression of a striking thought (cf. Quintilian 8. 5. 2), which often is of general application (in which case *sententia* is equivalent to 'aphorism', 'wise saw'), but is not necessarily so; any striking thought expressed in this terse, pointed manner can be denoted by the word *sententia*.

Such *sententiae* are found in early Latin literature, e.g. in the elder Cato (from whom Seneca (*Ep.* 94. 27) quotes 'emas non quod opus est, sed quod necesse est; quod non opus est, asse carum est', as an example of a thought 'packed into a *sententia*'). Quintilian (12. 10. 48) tells us that he finds such *sententiae* in Cicero; they are found also in the fragments of Varro's *Saturae Menippeae* and in the historian Sallust; and the mime of the late Republic afforded ample scope for their use (cf. the surviving *Sententiae* of Publilius Syrus (q.v.); e.g. 'tam dest auaro quod habet quam quod non habet'). It was in the Silver Age, however, when the influence of the rhetorical schools on literature became much more marked, that the employment of *sententiae* reached its full development. In prose, for instance, the moralizing essays of Seneca are full of them, and Tacitus uses them with masterly effect (e.g. *Agr.* 30. 7 'ubi solitudinem faciunt, pacem appellant'). So too in verse: e.g. the dramas of Seneca, the epic of Lucan (whom Quintilian, with references to this characteristic, calls 'sententiis clarissimus'; e.g. 1. 128 'uictrix causa deis placuit sed uicta Catoni'), the satires of Juvenal (e.g. 1. 74 'probitas laudatur et alget'), and, of course, the epigrams of Martial.

See W. C. Summers, *Select Letters of Seneca*, Introduction A ('The pointed style in Greek and Roman literature'); J. Wight Duff, *Lit. Hist. Rome* (*Silver Age*), Index and passim. *See also* GNOME (γνώμη).   W. S. W.

SENTIUS, *see* SATURNINUS (2).

SEPTIMIUS (1), PUBLIUS, a Republican writer on architecture mentioned by Vitruvius (7. *praef.* 14).

SEPTIMIUS (2) **SERENUS,** one of the 'neoteric' school in Hadrian's time, wrote rural poems.

Teuffel, § 353.

SEPTIMIUS, LUCIUS, *see* DICTYS.

SEPTIMIUS, *see also* GETA, ODAENATHUS, SEVERUS, VABALLATHUS.

SEPTIZONIUM, a famous ornamental façade, screening the south-east corner of the Palatine Hill at Rome, and dedicated by Severus in A.D. 203 (*CIL* vi. 31229). It closed the vista of the Via Appia like a stage-background, in which the elements were three large niches girt with three stories of colonnading. Earlier examples of *septizonia* occur in Rome (Suet. *Titus* 2, schol. cod. Berolin. fol. 337) and Lambaesis (*CIL* viii. 2657). The adjective ἑπτάζωνος is applied to the seven planets (Dio Cass. 37. 18), and although the word is not itself used metathetically of the days of the week which they govern (see Dombart, *PW*, s.v.), the representations of these gods upon calendars is a common-place. Perhaps, therefore, these great ornamental façades, filled with statuary, mosaics, and numbers, served as public calendars as well as embellishments.

Ch. Hülsen, *Das Septizonium des Septimius Severus*, Winckelmanns-program, n. 46 (1886); Th. Dombart, *Das Septizonium zu Rom* (1922). I. A. R.

SEPTUAGINT (in abbreviation, LXX), the collection of writings which became the Old Testament of the Greek-speaking Church. They are mainly translated from the Hebrew (or Aramaic), but include in the Apocrypha some pieces originally composed in Greek.

The name is derived from a story told in Greek by a Jewish writer in the Epistle of Aristeas to Philocrates to the effect that in response to a suggestion of his librarian, Demetrius of Phalerum, Ptolemy II Philadelphus asked for a copy of the Jewish law, and was sent from Jerusalem seventy-two learned Jews who at Alexandria made a translation of it for the royal library. The story which at first has some verisimilitude is embellished by later writers with legendary elements and extended to include beside the Law the other translated books.

The translation was evidently done by different hands at different times. Nearly all of it was finished before the Christian era. It was intended probably for use by those Jews whose first, or only, language was Greek, or possibly for use in attracting Gentiles to the synagogue. Apart from Jews or Christians, few writers show any knowledge of it. Greek and Roman references to things Jewish are not derived directly from the LXX. The single citation of Genesis in the anonymous treatise *On the Sublime* 9. 9 is an exception that proves the rule. The influence of the LXX is probably first manifest in less literary circles, as in the *Corpus Hermeticum* and in the magical papyri. The rendering varies in style and literalness; when not influenced by the underlying Semitic, the Greek as in the New Testament represents the vernacular Hellenistic (*Koine*).

Since the Hebrew from which the LXX was translated is older than the oldest Hebrew manuscripts extant, and even than the standardized (Massoretic) text, the LXX is invaluable in efforts at reconstructing the original text of the Old Testament. The LXX itself was corrupted in copying and was revised. Origen collated it in his famous *Hexapla* not only with the Hebrew, but with the Greek versions of Aquila, Symmachus, and Theodotion. It was (with some exceptions) the text used in scripture quotation by the New Testament and later Christian

writers, as well as by Philo and Josephus. It had some influence upon the Vulgate and other versions of the Old Testament.

Critical text: A. Rahlfs (1936), *Septuaginta* (ix. 1, x, xiii, xiv), Göttingen 1931– . Text with apparatus: A. E. Brooke and N. McLean (1906–), H. B. Swete 1907–12 (and later reprints). Textual criticism: F. G. Kenyon, *Text of the Greek Bible* (1937). Introduction: H. B. Swete (2 vols., ed. 1914). Handbook: R. R. Ottley (1920). Grammar: R. Helbing (1907), H. St. J. Thackeray (1909), Abel (Paris, 1927). Influence: A. Deissmann, 'Die Hellenisierung des semitischen Monotheismus' in *Neue Jahrb.* vi (1903); H. St. J. Thackeray, *The Septuagint and Jewish Worship* (2nd ed. 1923); C. H. Dodd, *The Bible and the Greeks* (1934); C. H. Roberts, *Two Biblical Papyri in the John Rylands Library* (Manchester, 1936); F. Wutz, 'Systematische Wege von der Septuaginta zum hebräischen Urtext', *JTS* xlv (1937), 158–61.
Aristeas. Text: Teubner (Wendland, 1900), Swete (see above). Translation: Thackeray (1917); H. G. Meecham, *The Oldest Version of the Bible* (1932); H. G. Meecham, *The Letter of Aristeas* (1935); W. W. Tarn, *The Greeks in Bactria and India* (1938, excursus). Concordance: Hatch and Redpath (1896–1906). H. J. C.

SERAPION (1) of Alexandria, founder of the empirical school of medicine (*c.* 200–150 B.C.), wrote (1) Πρὸς τὰς διαιρέσεις; (2) Θεραπευτικά. He placed individual observation and experiment first, the statements of recognized authorities second, and argument from analogy third—to be used when the other two are lacking. He is much praised by Galen.

PW ii A. 1667. W. D. R.

SERAPION (2) of Antiocheia, a mathematical geographer (2nd or 1st c. B.C.), held that the sun is eighteen times the size of the earth. He also wrote on astrology. He may probably be dated later than Hipparchus and Panaetius, and earlier than Ptolemy.

Ed. in *Catalogus Codicum Astrologorum*. *PW* ii A. 1666.
W. D. R.

SERAPIS, *see* SARAPIS.

SERENUS (1) **SAMMONICUS,** a voluminous writer of the time of Septimius Severus (A.D. 193–211), was murdered by Caracalla's orders in A.D. 212. His only known work is *Res reconditae*. He had a library of 62,000 books.

PW ii A. 1675.

SERENUS (2) (or **SERENIUS**), QUINTUS (or QUINCTIUS), author of a medical text-book in verse, *Liber medicinalis*, which may be dated between the end of the second and the fourth century. It depends in the main on the *Medicina Plinii* and on Pliny's Natural History. The author *may* have been the poet Serenus Sammonicus (son of the other Serenus Sammonicus, q.v.), who was a friend of Gordian I (b. *c.* A.D. 159) and the teacher of Gordian II (b. *c.* 192), and died before 235.

PW ii A. 1675. Ed. F. Vollmer, *CML* ii. 3 (1916).
W. D. R.

SERENUS (3), mathematician, from Antinoeia in Egypt (formerly thought to be of Antissa in Lesbos), may probably be dated between Pappus and Theon of Alexandria (i.e. *c.* A.D. 300–50). Two of his works are extant: Περὶ κυλίνδρου τομῆς and Περὶ κώνου τομῆς; both edited by J. L. Heiberg (1896). A commentary on the κωνικά of Apollonius of Perga has been lost. Serenus is not of first-rate importance, but preserves much that is of value from earlier writers, notably Apollonius.

PW ii A. 1677. W. D. R.

SERES, the Chinese and Tibetans, first known to Greeks left by Alexander in inner Asia. Aristotle knew vaguely of silk, but not of China. They became famous from Augustus' time as producers of silk sent by land to Asia Minor and by sea to Egypt. As trade developed, the name Seres was applied to Chinese and Tibetans as approached by land, 'Sinae' being their name as approached by sea from India. By Nero's reign further Chinese products were reaching the Roman Empire, the Seres were definitely placed above India, and some geographical details filtered through. In A.D. 97, after Chinese conquests in central Asia, Kan Ying visited Antioch, and c. 120 a 'Roman' Maes Titianus sent agents, probably to Kashgar and Daraut Kurghan (where 'Chinese' were met) and beyond. These learnt of cities— Daxata (*Singanfu*?, where Roman coins have been found) and Sera (*Loh Yang*?), seven months from Kashgar (or Daraut Kurghan), and gained rough ideas of Pamir, Tian Shan, and Altai Mountains, and of rivers (Hwang-ho and Yang tsze-Kiang?), but nothing of the sea east of China. They proved that silk was an animal product. Meanwhile one Alexander had explored from India to Cattigara (q.v.); others reached the Sinae in China itself, naming their capital 'Thinae' (*Nanking*?). Yet Ptolemy made the Chinese coast face west and join Africa. In 166 a mission reached China from Marcus Aurelius, another in 284. About 550, silk-moth eggs were smuggled to Constantinople.

Ptol. *Geog.* 6. 16. 1 ff. (Seres); 7. 3. 1 ff. (Sinae); Warmington, *Indian Commerce*, 36–7, 71–2, etc. F. Hirth, *China and the Roman Orient* (1885). Honigmann, *PW*, s.v. E. H. W.

SERFS. Various Greek States possessed unfree agricultural labourers that are best described as serfs. In opposition to slaves they consisted of groups of natives reduced to hereditary servitude. They normally had families and homes of their own on the estates of their masters; they turned over to the latter a part of the produce of the land and kept a part for themselves. Greek tradition attributed their status to conquest, and in the case of two groups (the *maryandynoi* of Heraclea Pontica and some of the *penestai* of Thessaly) reports a compact made between them and their masters. Serfdom has assumed so many forms that the name is not inappropriate, even if some of the features of Greek serfdom differ from those of the better-known examples. Thus the compacts mentioned forbid sale beyond the borders and so imply that sale within the borders was permitted, which, furthermore, is specifically attested for the *maryandynoi*. Best known of all are the helots (q.v.) of Sparta, the *penestai* of Thessaly, and the serfs of Crete, but serfdom is attested also for Argos, Sicyon, Byzantium, and Heraclea Pontica, and seems to have been common in Asia Minor, Magna Graecia, and Sicily. The distribution suggests that it was common particularly in Doric States. In Crete the great code of Gortyn does not seem to have differentiated between slaves and serfs, but later there were special names both for serfs on public (μνωῖται) and on private estates (ἀφαμιῶται and κλαρῶται). For the position of the *hektemoroi* of early Athens and the *coloni* of late Rome *see* HEKTEMOROI *and* COLONI.

ANCIENT SOURCES: Pollux 3. 83; Athen. 6. 263–71; other scattered references. Discussions of serfdom in individual States are common, but comprehensive accounts rare.
MODERN LITERATURE: *Encycl. Social Sciences*, s.v. 'Serfdom'; G. Busolt, *Griechische Staatskunde* (1920), 135–8, 283–8, and *passim*. J. A. O. L.

SERGIUS, author (date unknown) of *Explanationes in Donatum* (ed. Keil, *Gramm. Lat.* iv. 486–565; cf. also 475–85). In manuscripts his name is often confused with that of Servius.

SERGIUS, *see also* CATILINE.

SERMO bears a variety of meanings in Latin. Besides being used for conversation, verse in conversational manner and with satiric bent (as in Lucilius and Horace), for style, and for the language of a nation (*in Latino sermone*, Cic. *De Or.* 3. 42), *sermo* is in rhetoric especially applied to the sketch of effective lines of argument well illustrated in the set of shorter pseudo-Quintilianean *declamationes* (q.v.). J. W. D.

SERPENTS, SACRED. As the δεισιδαίμων in Theophrastus (*Char.* 16. 4) when he sees a snake in his house takes it for a warning to invoke a god or found a *heroon*, it may be assumed that less pietistic persons had similar feelings regarding some serpents. They are, indeed, the regular accompaniment of heroes and of some, especially chthonian, deities. Sabadius is mentioned in Theophrastus; the god whom Aeschines' mother is alleged to have served, apparently Attis (Demosth. 18. 260), had snakes in his ritual, which were handled by some of the officiants; Zeus Meilichius is represented by a huge snake (Harrison, *Prolegomena*, p. 18 and fig. 1). When, therefore, Alexander of Abonutichus produced his new god in serpent form (Lucian, *Alex.* 7 ff.) he was following time-honoured tradition. In Italy the serpent was connected with the genius (q.v.), cf. Cicero, *Div.* 2. 62, where Ti. Sempronius Gracchus, father of the tribunes, sees two snakes, a male and a female, in his bedroom and is told that according as he kills one or the other, he or Cornelia will die, which duly comes to pass. However, they are not found only in this context. Apart from foreign cults (as that of Aesculapius, see especially Ovid, *Met.* 15. 669 ff., where the god in serpent form follows the embassy sent to bring him to Rome) and stories of foreign colour (as Tacitus, *Ann.* 11. 11. 6), in the old Italian worship of Juno Sospita the serpent played a part (Prop. 4. 8. 3 ff.). *See also* ANIMALS, SACRED; ASCLEPIUS, para. 5; RELIGION, MINOAN–MYCENAEAN.
H. J. R.

SERRANUS, an epic poet who died prematurely, mentioned with Saleius Bassus (q.v.) by Quintilian (*Inst.* 10. 1. 89–90) and Juvenal (7. 80).

SERRANUS, *see* ATILIUS.

SERTORIUS, QUINTUS (*c.* 122–72 B.C.), was of Sabine extraction. He was *tribunus militum* in Spain (98) and legate in the Social War. Since Sulla barred his election to the tribunate, he declared for Marius, although he did not approve his Terror. Appointed governor of Hispania Citerior (83), he was proscribed by Sulla and escaped to Mauretania, where he defeated a Sullan army. He failed in an attempt to return to Spain and is said to have dreamed of fleeing to the Blessed Isles. Later, invited by the Lusitani, he successfully returned to Spain, where he gathered around him many Roman followers and gained the goodwill of the natives, who regarded his white fawn as a sign of divine protection. While his general Hirtuleius overran Hispania Citerior, Sertorius defeated Fufidius, legate of Ulterior (80) and, by guerrilla tactics, his successor Metellus Pius (79–78). Reinforcements under Perperna (q.v.) reached him in 77. Master of most of Spain, Sertorius created a rival Senate of 300 Romans and established a school for sons of native chiefs at Osca (*Huesca*), thereby incidentally gaining hostages.

Sertorius prevented Metellus joining Pompey, who arrived with reinforcements (77), and outmanœuvred Pompey near Lauro (76). But Metellus defeated Hirtuleius near Segovia (75), while control of Carthago Nova assured the communications of the senatorial commanders with Italy. After Sertorius had won a half-victory near the Sucro (Jucar), his enemies effected a junction (75). Sertorius negotiated an ineffective military alliance with Mithridates (75), but could not check the slow exhaustion of his movement. His popularity, and possibly his character, declined, until he was murdered by Perperna in 72.

Sertorius, like Caesar, was one of several Roman generals who tried to master Rome from the provinces. By necessity or inclination he dealt generously with his native supporters and linked himself with the enemies (Mithridates and pirates) of the senatorial government.

But despite military skill, chivalrous bravery, and personal integrity he failed to master and unify the movement.

Sources: Plutarch, *Sertorius*, from Sallust; fragments of Sallust's *Historiae*; Diodorus 37. 22; Appian, *BCiv.* 1. 108–15; Livy, *Per.* 90–6. See Schulten, *Fontes Hisp. Antiquae*, iv. Cf. *Rylands Papyri* iii, n. 473 (1938). Modern: A. Schulten, *Sertorius* (Leipzig, 1926); T. Rice-Holmes, *The Roman Republic* i (1923); V. Ehrenberg, *Ost und West* (1935), 177 (with bibliography).   A. M.

SERTORIUS, see also MACRO.

SERVASIUS, SULPICIUS LUPERCUS, JUNIOR ('Serbastus', cod. Leid. Voss. of Ausonius; 'Sebastus', Schryver, Baehrens; 'Servastus', Wernsdorf), a fourth-century A.D. schoolman of uncertain name, has left three Sapphic stanzas *De vetustate*, and forty-two elegiac lines *De cupiditate*.

Text w. tr.: J. W. and A. M. Duff, *Minor Latin Poets* (1935).
                                                          J. W. D.

SERVILIA (b. *c.* 100 B.C.) was daughter of Q. Servilius Caepio and Livia (the sister of M. Livius Drusus), step-sister of Cato Uticensis and mistress of Caesar. She married first M. Junius Brutus, to whom she bore Brutus, the murderer of Caesar, and next D. Junius Silanus (*cos.* 62). Her three daughters by Silanus became respectively wives of the triumvir Lepidus, P. Servilius (*cos.* 48), and C. Cassius, the murderer of Caesar. She was the real head of one of the most important aristocratic groups of Rome. After Caesar's death her influence on Brutus was considerable.

F. Münzer, *PW* ii A. 1817; R. Syme, *The Roman Revolution* (1939), see index.   A. M.

SERVILIUS (1) **AHALA,** GAIUS. The legend that Servilius saved his country in 439 B.C. by killing the usurper Sp. Maelius (q.v.) with a dagger concealed under his armpit was probably invented as an aetiological myth to explain the *cognomen* Ahala or Axilla (i.e. armpit) borne by the *gens Servilia*. When it was discovered that Servilii Ahalae occurred in the Fasti before 439, a different version was elaborated, according to which Servilius acted neither as a private citizen nor illegally, but as Master of Horse in Cincinnatus' second (fictitious) dictatorship. Later embellishments, due to political propaganda of Gracchan and Sullan times, include Servilius' exile from his ungrateful country. The legend of the tyrannicide and saviour of republican liberty decisively influenced a descendant of the *gens Servilia*, M. Brutus.

Mommsen, *Röm. Forsch.* ii. 199 ff.   P. T.

SERVILIUS (2) **VATIA ISAURICUS,** PUBLIUS (134–44 B.C.), assisted Sulla in his last campaigns against the Marians and was rewarded with a consulship in 79. As proconsul of Cilicia in 78–75 he made a systematic attempt to reduce the pirate haunts in south Asia Minor. In 77 he cleared east Lycia and Pamphylia by naval action and siege operations. Crossing Mt. Taurus into Isauria, he spent the campaigns in 76–75 in subduing its strongholds. These successes laid open the northward and more vulnerable side of Cilicia Trachea, the chief pirate base; but they were not followed up, because of the outbreak of the Mithridatic War. In 63 Servilius was defeated by Caesar in the competition for the office of Pontifex Maximus. In 57–56 he was active in the recall of Cicero and the repression of Clodius. As censor in 55–54 he repaired the Tiber embankment after a disastrous flood.

For his campaigns see H. A. Ormerod, *JRS* 1922, 35 ff.   M. C.

SERVILIUS (3) **VATIA ISAURICUS,** PUBLIUS, son of (2) above, in early life supported Cato, but became a Caesarian and Caesar's colleague as consul in 48 B.C. After suppressing the disturbances of Caelius he governed Asia, whence he corresponded with Cicero in 46. After Caesar's murder Cicero affected to regard him as an ally, but knew him for a man of straw or worse (cf. *ad Brut.* 2. 2. 3, if genuine), and in 43 Servilius betrothed his daughter to Octavian and became reconciled with Antony. Octavian jilted Servilia, but compensated her father with the consulate of 41, in which he showed his usual caution during the Perusine War.   G. E. F. C.

SERVILIUS (4) **NONIANUS,** MARCUS (*cos.* A.D. 35), famous for his *recitationes*, the applause on one occasion attracting Claudius Caesar to join his audience (Plin. *Ep.* 1. 13. 3). For his style in history see Quint. *Inst.* 10. 1. 102; Tac. *Dial.* 23; Peter, *HRRel.* ii, p. cxxviii. 98.

SERVILIUS, see also CAEPIO, CASCA, GLAUCIA, RULLUS.

SERVITUTES. Restrictions on ownership arising from the rights of other parties were already recognized in early Roman law. A particular group of these *iura in re aliena* formed *servitutes*: their essential mark was that the owner of a plot of land was entitled to exercise certain rights on a neighbouring estate (e.g. walking, using the roadway, driving or pasturing cattle, drawing water, etc.). Servitudes were a burden for the owner of the *praedium quod servit*, but they originated in the needs of agricultural economy, a dominant interest in ancient Rome. They ranked with *res mancipi* (see MANCIPATIO), and were considered as vested in the land itself (*iura praediorum*), so that they passed from one proprietor to another. A counterpart to these *servitutes praediorum rusticorum* were *servitutes praediorum urbanorum*, introduced later in the interest of buildings: a neighbour could be obliged not to build too high, or not to obstruct the access of light, etc. Whilst the rustic servitudes consisted in positive actions on the part of the owner of the dominant estate, the urban ones were mostly negative, and merely bound the owner of the servient tenement to abstain from certain actions.

Another category of rights over the property of other parties consisted in *servitutes personarum*. The qualification of these rights as 'servitudes' perhaps dates from Justinian or the post-classical period. To this class of rights belong: *usufructus* (a right to use and draw produce from another's property—land, or movables such as slaves and cattle); *usus* (a mere *ius utendi* without any right to profits); and rights analogous to *usus*, namely *habitatio*, relating to another person's house or lodging, and *operae servorum* or *animalium* (in which case *ius utendi* was restricted to the labour of slaves or animals). The category of personal servitudes was substantially reformed in post-classical times and by Justinian. The application of some general rules to all types of servitudes, and the equalization of the methods by which they were constituted and protected, made it possible to include all the personal servitudes in the same group as the predial servitudes.

P. Bonfante, *Corso di diritto romano* iii (1933); W. W. Buckland, *Law Quarterly Review* 1927, 1928, 1930; B. Biondi, *La categoria romana delle servitutes* (1938). See also the text-books of Roman Law under LAW AND PROCEDURE, ROMAN, I.   A. B.

SERVIUS (1) **TULLIUS,** the sixth king of Rome (traditionally 578–535 B.C.), is an indisputably historical figure, whose Roman or Latin origin (despite his later identification with the Etruscan *Mastarna*, q.v.) is attested by his having built the temple to the Latin goddess Diana on the Aventine. Here the text of a treaty between Rome and the Latin League, traditionally attributed to Servius and known to authors of the Augustan age, was preserved. There is no reason to doubt the authenticity of the treaty, the invention of which would have been wholly purposeless. The tradition that Servius was the son of a maidservant, and that he built the fortifications of Rome (*cf. under* WALL OF SERVIUS) must be rejected. The constitution attributed to him (as a reputedly liberal ruler) is probably a fictitious precedent for the laws passed in the fourth century on behalf of the plebs (see CENTURIA, CLASSIS).

H. Last, *CAH* vii. 391 ff. For papyrological evidence: *POxy.* 2088; M. A. Levi, *Riv. fil.* 1928; A. Piganiol, *Scritti in onore di B. Nogara* (1937), 373 ff. For a more conservative view of the Servian reforms see H. Last, *JRS* 1945, 30 ff.   P. T.

SERVIUS (2) (4th c. A.D.), grammarian and commentator (called *Marius* or *Maurus Servius Honoratus* in MSS. from the 9th c. onwards). His greatest work was a commentary on Virgil (in the order *Aen.*, *Ecl.*, *G.*), for which he directly or indirectly brought under contribution much of the earlier Virgilian criticism. He relied greatly on Aelius Donatus, though he names him only when he disagrees with him. Since his work was designed for school purposes, he stresses grammatical, rhetorical, and stylistic points, but he does not neglect subject-matter, on which some of his notes show considerable learning. By way of illustration he quotes freely not only from Virgil but also from Terence, Cicero, Sallust, Lucan, Statius, and Juvenal. Often he reports conflicting views, but he retains his own judgement and is always a keen defender of his author. The Servian commentary is found in a longer and a shorter version in manuscripts; but only the shorter was printed until Pierre Daniel in 1600 published the longer form, which he regarded as the original Servius. G. Thilo, however, in the nineteenth century showed that the so-called Servius Auctus or Servius Danielis consisted of (*a*) Servius and (*b*) the remains of a much more learned commentary (composed in the order *Ecl.*, *G.*, *Aen.*) which he attributed to some Irish monk of the seventh or eighth century (possibly Adamnan). In his edition he printed what he judged to belong to this hypothetical commentary in italics. The current opinion (cf., e.g., E. K. Rand in *CQ* 1916, 158–64) is that the 'additions' in Servius Danielis are virtually parts of the commentary of Aelius Donatus which S. himself had not incorporated. The standard edition is that of G. Thilo (vols. i, ii, iii. pt. 1, 1881–7; vol. iii. pt. 2 = *Appendix Serviana*, ed. H. Hagen, 1902); but a new edition (vol. ii, 1946) by a group of Harvard scholars is in course of publication. The other extant works of S. are: *Explanatio in artem Donati*, *De finalibus*, *De centum metris*, *De metris Horatii* (ed. Keil, *Gramm. Lat.* iv. 405–48, 449–55, 456–67, 468–72). The *Glossae Servii grammatici* (ed. G. Goetz, *Corp. Gloss. Lat.* ii. 507–33) are an apocryphal compilation. *See also* SCHOLARSHIP, LATIN, IN ANTIQUITY, and cf. Teuffel, § 431; Schanz–Hosius, § 248. 2 and § 835. J. F. M.

SERVIUS, *see also* SULPICIUS (2).

SESOSTRIS (Hdt. 2. 102–11) was a mythical Egyptian king to whom were ascribed great conquests in Africa and Asia. In Ptolemaic times he was regarded as a person who had once lived and been heroized. Little of historical value can be gained from the somewhat lengthy discussion of the story by Herodotus. The subject is discussed thoroughly by Wiedemann, *Herodots Zweites Buch.*   T. A. B.

SESTIUS, PUBLIUS, as quaestor (63 B.C.) helped Cicero against Catiline, and later actively promoted Cicero's recall from exile. As tribune (57) he struggled with an armed band against Clodius. In 56 he was accused *de vi* and *de ambitu*. In the accusation *de vi* he was defended by M. Crassus, Hortensius, Licinius Calvus, and Cicero (cf. *Pro Sestio*, and *In P. Vatinium testem interrogatio*; P. Vatinius was a witness against Sestius) and was acquitted. In 52 he was defended by Cicero on a charge of bribery and probably acquitted. Praetor (in 55?) and propraetor in Cilicia (49), he passed over to Caesar after Pharsalus and accompanied Domitius Calvinus against Pharnaces.

E. Ciaceri, *Cicerone* ii (1930), 76; cf. L. G. Pocock, *A Commentary on Cicero in Vatinium* (1926).   A. M.

SESTOS, a city of the Thracian Chersonese, possessing the best harbour in the Dardanelles, and commanding the chief crossing of the straits (to Abydos). Its original Greek population came from Lesbos. Darius returned by way of Sestos from his Scythian Expedition, and Xerxes here set foot on Europe, crossing the Dardanelles by a bridge of boats. Athenian interest in Sestos began with the occupation of the Chersonese by Miltiades; at this time perhaps it received an Athenian settlement. It was the first town to be freed from Persia by the Athenian fleet (479–478), and it was the chief Athenian station during the naval operations against Sparta in the Dardanelles (411–404). After a brief Spartan occupation (404 to 393 or 386) it reverted to Athens in 365. A rebellion against Athens in 357 led to its recapture by Chares, the enslavement of the population, and the establishment of an Athenian cleruchy (352). After a frequent change of overlords in the Hellenistic age it became a free city under Roman rule, but it lost its position as the principal crossing-point between Europe and Asia to Byzantium.

S. Casson, *Macedonia, Thrace and Illyria* (1926), 210–27.
M. C.

SET (called **Typhon** by the Greeks) was a god of Upper Egypt. He appears in the myth of Osiris as the wicked brother who murders the great god of the underworld and wounds his son Horus. The role of Set in this myth was well known to the Greeks, hence he is the wicked Typhon in Plutarch's essay concerning Isis and Osiris (13 ff.). The Greek Typhon (q.v.) was a wicked son of Gaea and Tartarus who was overcome by Zeus, just as Horus finally overcame Set.

A. Erman, *Die Religion der Ägypter* (1934); G. Roeder, art. 'Set' in Roscher's *Lexikon*.   T. A. B.

SEVERUS (1), LUCIUS SEPTIMIUS, Emperor A.D. 193–211. A native of Africa, after distinguished service under Marcus, he became consul in 190 and subsequently governor of Upper Pannonia. Saluted Emperor at Carnuntum (13 Apr. 193), he entered Rome on 9 June (see PERTINAX *and* DIDIUS JULIANUS). His first act was to dismiss the Praetorians and constitute a new guard for which all legionaries were eligible. The Senate he sought to conciliate by a promise to put no senator to death and the people by a *congiarium*. After the funeral and apotheosis of Pertinax he set out against his rival Pescennius Niger.

2. Victories by Septimius' guards at Perinthus, Cyzicus, and Nicaea were followed by a decisive battle at Issus (194; see PESCENNIUS NIGER), and after punitive expeditions against the Osroeni, Adiabeni, and Scaenite Arabs the war was ended. To prevent a recurrence of civil war Syria was divided into two provinces, Coele and Phoenice. The reason for the early termination of the war was fear of Albinus, who was alleged to be in treasonable correspondence with the Senate (see CLODIUS ALBINUS). Before leaving for Europe, Septimius raised his son Caracalla to the rank of Caesar and adopted himself into the family of the Antonines (196). After a brief visit to Rome he rejoined his army in Gaul, and the issue was settled at a battle near Lugdunum (Feb. 197). Britain, like Syria, was divided into two provinces, and a rigorous persecution of the adherents of Niger and Albinus initiated.

3. After a short stay in Rome Septimius was summoned East by news of a Parthian attack on Nisibis. A successful campaign culminated in the fall of Ctesiphon (198), in honour of which Caracalla was raised to the rank of Augustus and his brother Geta to that of Caesar. After two abortive attacks on the desert fortress of Hatra the war ended with the annexation of Mesopotamia (199). The next three years were spent in Palestine and Egypt, where Alexandria was given a municipal council. On 1 Jan. 202 Septimius and Caracalla became joint-consuls at Antioch, and then returned to Rome.

4. Septimius spent most of the next six years in Rome (*see* PLAUTIANUS). In 208 he set out with his wife and two sons for Britain. In the hope of intimidating the Caledonians Scotland was invaded, but the Roman losses were severe, and a temporary peace was patched up in the autumn of 210. Worn out by sickness and broken in spirit by Caracalla's unfilial conduct he died at York in 211.

5. *Administration.* Septimius' reign marks an important stage in the development of the powers of the equestrian order. Three new legions (I–III Parthicae) were commanded by equestrian *praefecti*, the new province of Mesopotamia was, like Egypt, governed by a knight, and *vicarii*, who were equestrian procurators, not infrequently replaced the regular senatorial governors in other provinces. Most significant are the additional powers given to the Praetorian Prefect, who became supreme criminal judge beyond the 100th milestone from Rome, and took over the control of the corn supply from the *praefectus annonae* (*see* PLAUTIANUS). By contrast the Senate was treated with disdain and became little more than a *claque* for applauding the emperor's proposals and messages. Yet there are, apart from political persecutions, few indications of misuse of power. Useful legislation based on equity and humanitarianism was passed, and the principle affirmed that the law is no respecter of persons.

6. In the sphere of finance the *fiscus* received the revenues of both imperial and senatorial provinces, together with the bulk of the emperor's *patrimonium*. The *aerarium* was reduced to a municipal treasury, and a new exchequer, *res privata principis*, was instituted to receive the profits of imperial confiscations. If Septimius' methods of raising money are open to criticism, his use of it was extravagant. In addition to *congiaria*, corn, oil, and medicine were distributed free to the populace of Rome, the alimentary system was revived, and the cost of the imperial post taken over by the *fiscus*. Rome was adorned with new buildings, an arch in the Forum, a palace on the Palatine, and the Septizonium or House of the Seven Planets, a monument to the emperor's faith in astrology, which had guided him to choose Julia Domna, a lady with a royal horoscope, for his second wife (*see* JULIA DOMNA).

7. The chief military reform was the constitution of the new Guard, which henceforth served as a seminary for officers. This change represents not a barbarization but a democratization of the army, just as the stationing of II Parthica at Albanum illustrates Septimius' policy of placing Italy on a level with the provinces. New concessions were made to the soldiers, who were allowed to marry during their service and on their discharge enjoyed special benefits.

8. In the provinces Hadrian's Wall was repaired and outposts south of the *Limes Tripolitanus* established. New colonies, which frequently received *ius Italicum*, were founded, notably in Africa and Syria. But Antioch, Byzantium, and Lugdunum, which had espoused the cause of Niger or Albinus, were harshly punished. Similarly conditions in the country-side varied; in the West there was probably less distress than in Lydia and Egypt, where the peasants were ground down by imperial agents or landlords. Severus was champion of neither town nor country. The army was the factor that determined his policy, and to maintain its cost the civil population was subjected to a variety of imperial requisitions. On his death-bed the Emperor is said to have exhorted his sons to live in peace, enrich the soldiers, and despise the rest of the world.

Herodian 2. 11–3. fin.; Dio Cassius, bks. 73–6; S.H.A. J. Hasebroek, *Untersuchungen zur Geschichte des Kaisers Septimius Severus* (1921); M. Platnauer, *The Life and Reign of the Emperor L. Septimius Severus* (1918); Parker, *Roman World*, 58–88, 115–38; S. N. Miller, *CAH* xii. 1–42.   H. M. D. P.

SEVERUS (2) ALEXANDER, MARCUS AURELIUS, Emperor A.D. 222–35. This was the title by which Alexianus son of Mamaea was known, when he was adopted by Elagabalus at the age of thirteen and became sole emperor (221–2). Of a friendly and amenable disposition, virtuous and honest, he was also vacillating and ineffective, and this weakness was accentuated by the possessive devotion of his mother, who had sought to shield him from the licentious influences of his cousin.

2. The first nine years of his reign, when first Maesa and then Mamaea controlled the government, were without incident, apart from the murder of the prefect Ulpian (q.v.) by the praetorians, who were restive under his strict command. The finances were rehabilitated without curtailing useful expenditure (e.g. on baths at Rome and road-making in the provinces). Alexander's reign is represented in the *Historia Augusta* (q.v.) as a resuscitation of senatorial power, but apparently the Senate recovered no more than the appearance of supremacy which Dio suggests in the speech of Maecenas to Augustus (52. 14 ff.). There were two important reforms in this direction. A new *consilium principis* (q.v.) was formed, comprising 20 jurisconsults from the equestrian order, and 70 senators. Although the senatorial members formed the majority, with men like Ulpian and Paulus (q.v.) taking part in the discussions, the real power lay with the bureaucrats. Secondly, the incompatibility between the status of a senator and a praetorian prefect was removed. But if this enhanced the Senate's prestige, it also extended the powers of the prefect, who could preside at senatorial trials. Further, there was no decline in the power of the soldiers in politics and it was, for instance, fear for his safety at their hands that led the Emperor to send the historian Dio (q.v.) to Bithynia during the year of his consulship. But because after his death the Senate declined as a political body, Alexander became the hero of those who regarded senatorial power as a panacea, and from such panegyrics grew up the historical novel which constitutes the Life of Severus Alexander in the *Historia Augusta*.

3. In 231 Alexander and his mother left Rome for Antioch, to repel an invasion of Mesopotamia by the Persian king Artaxerxes (q.v. 4). After quelling some mutinies he prepared for a campaign in the following spring, in which his army was divided into three divisions. The result was not an unqualified success, but Mesopotamia was recovered.

4. Alexander returned to a triumph in Rome (233), but his stay was short, as news of unrest in Germany necessitated his presence on the Rhine. The army, part of which was sent direct from Syria, was concentrated at Mainz, but Alexander made the fatal mistake of trying to buy peace. This pacifism was interpreted as cowardice by the European legions, which were further incensed at the favouritism shown by the Emperor and his mother to the Oriental troops. Looking for a leader of courage and energy, their choice fell on a Thracian peasant called Maximinus (235). Soon afterwards Alexander and his mother, deserted even by their Orientals, were murdered.

Herodian, bk. 6; Dio Cassius, bks. 79–80; S.H.A. A. Jardé, *Études critiques sur la vie et le règne de Sévère Alexandre* (1925); W. Thiele, *De Severo Alexandro Imperatore* (1909); Parker, *Roman World*, 102–14, 129–38; *CAH* xii, ch. 2, §§ 1, 2.   H. M. D. P.

SEVERUS (3), SEXTUS JULIUS, a Dalmatian by birth, rose to senatorial rank, pursuing under Hadrian (q.v.) a brilliant career. Preliminary and urban offices once discharged, he was successively commander of Legio XIV Gemina, governor of Dacia (*c.* 120–6?), consul (127), governor of Lower Moesia (128–30), of Britain (*c.* 130–3), of Judaea (*c.* 133–5), and then—the first to hold this office—of the newly formed Syria Palaestina.

PIR, I 374; P. Lambrechts, *La Composition du Sénat. romain . . . (117–92)* (1936), p. 41, no. 93.   C. H. V. S.

SEVERUS (4), FLAVIUS VALERIUS, a rough soldier and boon companion of Galerius, chosen at his wish to succeed as Caesar in the West in A.D. 305. On the death of Constantius Chlorus in 306 Severus succeeded him as Augustus, and Constantine, proclaimed in Britain, was fitted into the system as his Caesar. When Maxentius rose in Rome, Galerius ordered up Severus from Milan to suppress him. Baffled by the walls of Rome and deserted by his own men Severus retired to Ravenna and surrendered, on the promise of his life, to the old Maximian. When Galerius invaded Italy in 307, Severus was treacherously put to death by Maxentius at Tres Tabernae. H. M.

SEVERUS (5), SULPICIUS, a Christian writer of note, born soon after A.D. 350 in Aquitania. He was a successful advocate and married into a wealthy consular family, but he became a monk. His chief works include his *Chronica*, a chronicle reaching from Old Testament times to his own, and Dialogues that centre round Saint Martin of Tours.

Kappelmacher, *PW*, s.v. H. M.

SEVERUS, CASSIUS, *see* CASSIUS (9).

SEVIUS NICANOR, *see* SAEVIUS.

SEXTILIUS ENA, *see* ENA.

SEXTIUS (1), TITUS, was *legatus* to Caesar in Gaul and governor of Africa Nova (Numidia) from 44 B.C. After Mutina he was ordered by the Senate to transfer two of his legions to Italy and the third to Cornificius, governor of Africa Vetus. Later he attacked Cornificius, defeated him, and annexed his province (42 or 41). He handed over both provinces to Octavian's lieutenant Fango (on instructions from Lucius Antonius), recovered them during the Perusine War as Antony's representative, and surrendered them to Lepidus shortly afterwards.

Appian, *BCiv.* 3–5; Dio Cassius 48. 21–3. F. L. Ganter, *Provinzialverwaltung d. Triumvirn* (1892), and *Philol.* liii (1894), 144–6. G. W. R.

SEXTIUS (2), QUINTUS, philosopher of the time of Augustus, founded a philosophical school which met with great success at first but did not last long. He claimed to be the founder of a native school of philosophy, but was in fact an eclectic, borrowing from Stoicism his ethical views, from Plato the theory that the soul is an incorporeal entity, and from the Pythagoreans a belief in vegetarianism. *See* DIATRIBE. He is probably identical with the botanical and medical writer Sextius Niger, whose work Περὶ ὕλης ἰατρικῆς was used by Pliny and Dioscorides.

PW ii A. 2040. W. D. R.

SEXTIUS LATERANUS, *see under* STOLO.

SEXTIUS NIGER, *see* (2) above.

SEXTUS (1) of Chaeronea, nephew of Plutarch, Platonist, teacher of Marcus Aurelius and Varus.

PW ii A. 2057.

SEXTUS (2), called **Empiricus**, physician and sceptical philosopher, wrote in the last third of the second century A.D. His epithet Empiricus (so already Diog. Laert. 9. 116) shows that he belonged to the 'empirical' school of physicians (cf. [Galen], *Isagoge* 4). In one point, however, he disagrees with them (*Pyr.* 1. 236).

His medical writings are lost. As a philosopher S. lacks originality. He represents the new sceptical school founded by Aenesidemus, whose system he sets out with clarity though not wholly without errors and repetitions. Now and then he criticizes Aenesidemus from a more modern point of view. To us his writings are most valuable, being the only complete description of ancient scepticism.

His books are: *Outlines of Pyrrhonism* (Πυρρώνειοι ὑποτυπώσεις): bk. 1 gives a general account of the sceptical basic terms, and discusses the end and method of Pyrrhonism; bk. 2 refutes dogmatic logic and theory of knowledge, bk. 3 physics and ethics.

In detail we find this criticism in the five books of *Against the Dogmatists* (Πρὸς δογματικούς). A third work is *Against the Schoolmasters* (Πρὸς μαθηματικούς), in six books, criticizing the non-philosophical subjects of general teaching: grammar, rhetoric, mathematics, astronomy, music. The former work, which follows in the manuscripts after the latter, is also counted as Πρὸς μαθημ. 6–11.

Texts: I. Bekker (1842); H. Mutschmann (vols. i and ii, 1912–14; iii still lacking); Loeb (with Engl. Transl., without the last work). Studies: E. Pappenheim, *Lebensverhältnisse des S. E.* (1875); L. Haas, *Über d. Schriften des S. E.* (1882); A. Kochalsky, *De S. E. adv. logicos libr. quaestiones crit.* (Thesis, Marburg 1911); W. Heintz, *Studien zu S. E.* (1932); *P.W.* ii 2057 A. *See also* SCEPTICS. K. O. B.

SEXTUS (3), originator of a collection of gnomes, Σέξτου γνῶμαι, mentioned by Origen and translated into Latin by Rufinus, who gave it the name of *Anulus*. The Syriac translation bears the title *Dicta selecta sancti Xysti episcopi Romani*, but Jerome argues against the authorship of Xystus (A.D. 256–8) and calls the author Sextus Pythagoreus. The original collection was probably non-Christian and made in the second century A.D., but additions implying a Christian background were gradually made, though definite allusions to Christ or to Christian doctrine were avoided.

Ed. A. Elter (1891–2). *PW* ii A. 2061. W. D. R.

SHIPS. The shipping of the ancient Mediterranean consisted of two main types of vessels—the slim, light-draught war-galley (*see* TRIREME, QUINQUIREME) and the heavy, slow merchant ship. The distinction between these, which accompanied the separation of merchant and pirate in the archaic Greek period, reflects the wide difference in functions: the merchant ship kept the sea night and day with heavy cargoes, in all but the worst weather; for the war-ship, considerations of seaworthiness were subordinate to efficiency and handiness in battle. Fleets of war, in consequence, often found blockades and long cruises dangerous.

The proportion of length to breadth, in the galley about 7 : 1, approximated to 4 : 1 for the transport. Merchant and war-vessels alike were constructed from wood, chiefly larch, cypress, and fir (Theophrastus, *Hist. Pl.* 5. 7). As to-day, a keel was set upon ways in a dockyard; to this shipwrights attached ribs, upon which the planking of the hull was nailed. Strengthening cables seem to have taken the place of stringers parallel to the keel in some cases. The prow of the merchant vessel was simple, without ram or voluted prow-post; the stern-post, which curved back towards the prow, on cargo ships often resembled a goose's neck. While war-galleys were at most decked only on prow and stern, other craft were usually completely decked by 400 B.C. and had a cabin aft. In the stern was a ladder for use if the ship were beached, usually an anchor in addition to the prow-anchor, and the tutelary image of some god, from which the ship might take its name. This name, or some indicative symbol, was often placed on the prow. The steering-gear consisted of two large rudder-oars, one projecting on either side of the stern.

Merchant craft, having a permanent mast, relied chiefly on sail, though long sweeps could be used. At first they had one mast, which bore a square sail, made from linen or sometimes from hides; later a small forward mast was added, and in the Roman Empire two or three main masts are sometimes found, with triangular sails above the main yard. Such sailing-vessels apparently made three to four knots in normal conditions (*see* NAVIGATION).

With the spread of commerce merchant vessels increased in size. The unique *Alexandreia* of Hiero II rated at 3,310 tons, and the Alexandrian grain-ship *Isis*, of the second century A.D., measured roughly 140 by 36 feet, with a depth of 33 feet and a weight of 3,250 tons. These were exceptional; but by the Roman Empire the average *navis oneraria* rated perhaps at 50 tons.

Acts xxvii–xxviii; Lucian, *The Ship*. E. Assmann, 'Seewesen' in A. Baumeister's *Denkmäler des klassischen Altertums* (1888; numerous reproductions); F. Miltner, *PW*, s.v. 'Seewesen'; C. Torr, *Ancient Ships* (1894); A. B. Cook, *Comp. Gr. Stud.* ch. vi, § 11.
C. G. S.

SIBYLLA. This word, of uncertain etymology, appears first in Heraclitus (ap. Plut. *Pyth. Or.* 6; Clem. Al. *Strom.* 1. 70. 3), and was early used as a proper name (e.g. Ar. *Pax* 1095, 1116). As a single prophetic female the Sibyl was variously localized, and legends of her wanderings account for her presence at different spots, but as early as Heraclides Ponticus (Clem. *Strom.* 1. 108. 3) she became pluralized, and thereafter we find two, three, four, five, six, or ten Sibyls, in different places and some bearing individual names, since the term Sibyl had now become generic. Varro's *Res Divinae* (ap. Lact. *Inst.* 1. 6. 8–12) lists ten: 1. Persian; 2. Libyan; 3. Delphic; 4. Cimmerian (in Italy); 5. Erythraean; 6. Samian; 7. Cumaean (named Amalthea, Herophile, Demophile, or, in Verg. *Aen.* 6. 36, Deiphobe); 8. Hellespontic (at Marpessus near Troy); 9. Phrygian (at Ancyra); 10. Tiburtine (named Albunea). Sibyls at Delos, Clarus, Colophon, Sardis, Dodona, and elsewhere (A. Bouché-Leclercq, *Hist. de la divination*, ii (1880), 175, 183. Buchholz in Roscher, *Lexikon* iv. 796–803) are doubtful and perhaps to be identified with some of those in Varro's list. For a legend of the Cumaean Sibyl *see* APOLLO, para. 6.

The ecstatic character of Sibylline prophecy (cf. Heraclitus ap. Plut. loc. cit.) is described by Virgil, *Aen.* 6. 77–102. The content of such utterances was early reduced to written form, in Greek hexameter verses, the genuineness of which was often guaranteed by acrostics (Cic. *Div.* 2. 112; Dion. Hal. 4. 62. 6). They were originally, in the case of the Cumaean Sibyl (Varro ap. Serv. *Aen.* 3. 444), inscribed on palm-leaves. Collections of these verses were made for later consultation, and there is a famous story (Dion. Hal. 4. 62. 1–6; Plin. *HN* 13. 88; Lact. *Inst.* 1. 6. 10–11; Serv. *Aen.* 6. 72, etc.) of the sale to Tarquinius Priscus of one such collection which was put into the charge of a special priestly college (*see* QUINDECIMVIRI SACRIS FACIUNDIS), to be consulted only at the command of the Senate, in contrast to the unrestricted consultation of Sibyls elsewhere. After these Sibylline Books had been destroyed in the burning of the Capitol in 83 B.C. a new collection was made from various sources to replace them. To the Jewish-Hellenistic culture and later to Christian influence are due many blatant forgeries, and fourteen somewhat miscellaneous books of oracles are still extant (ed. by A. Rzach, 1891; J. Geffcken, 1902). The last known consultation of the books was in 363 (Amm. Marc. 23. 1. 7), and the official collection was burned in the time of Stilicho (Rut. Namat. 2. 52). The influence of Jewish and Christian interpolations, however, combined with the prophecy of the Cumaean Sibyl in Virgil's *Fourth Eclogue* to give to all the Sibyls a position in Christian literature and art somewhat similar to that accorded the Old Testament prophets.
A. S. P.

SICELIDAS, *see* ASCLEPIADES (2).

SICELS. The Sicels, or *Siculi*, were the native inhabitants of Sicily whom the Greeks found in possession of the island. They had unquestionably migrated long before from north Africa in consequence of the drying up of the Sahara. Some occupied the southern half of Italy, which explains the frequent classical references to *Siculi* even near Rome itself. They represent a pre-Aryan stratum (cf. under LIGURIANS) and their language may have been totally unrelated to Italic; possibly it was akin to the surviving Berber languages. The movement of *Siculi* from Italy to Sicily described by Thucydides, Philistus, and Hellanicus, who date by the Trojan war, refers to a far later period (middle or late Bronze Age).

Excavations, principally in eastern Sicily, give consecutive pictures of Siculan culture until it was killed out by the Greeks. The Neolithic period, arbitrarily termed 'Sicanian', is interesting chiefly for the incised pottery of Stentinello. The 'First Siculan' period is Chalcolithic and remarkable for unique painted wares with simple geometric patterns. The rock-hewn chamber-tombs are characteristic; wide commerce is already suggested. The 'Second Siculan' is full Bronze Age; it marks the zenith of the native culture. Mycenaean influence is then quite strong, marked especially by imports of the Late Minoan Third types. The 'Third Siculan' is Iron Age, beginning with the tenth century; it shows stagnation and decline. Intercourse with Greece of the Dipylon period, however, continued and resulted in some interesting native pottery.

T. E. Peet, *Stone and Bronze Age* (1908); 'Sicilien' in Ebert's *Real-Lexikon der Vorgeschichte* (bibliography and illustrations).
D. R.-MacI.

SICILY. PREHISTORY. Ancient writers know three native peoples: Sicani in western, Siculi in eastern (*see* SICELS), and Elymi in north-western Sicily. Thucydides (6. 2) attributes an Iberian origin to the Sicans, Italic to the Sicels, and Trojan to the Elymians. The Sicans are now often considered the Neolithic inhabitants. Despite the linguistic difficulty of separating Siculi from Sicani (Siculi : Sicani = Romuli : Romani), recent philological research tends to reinforce Thucydides' opinion and show that the Sicel language was Indo-European and more nearly connected with Latin than Osco-Umbrian, while some place-names in the Sican area may be connected with Iberia. The origin of the Elymians remains obscure, but toponymy renders a Ligurian connexion probable. It must also be noted that there is no distinction of culture between east and west corresponding to the distinction of Siculi and Sicani.

2. THE GREEK PERIOD. The extent of early Phoenician colonization in Sicily is unknown, but in historical times it was limited to Motya, Solus, and Panormus. The Elymians, whose principal towns were Segesta, Eryx, and Entella, became traditional allies of the Carthaginians. From c. 735 B.C. (the chief source, Thucydides 6. 3–5, is only approximately reliable) there followed a prolonged period of Greek colonization in the island (*see* COLONIZATION; also the several Greek cities). The natives were ejected from the best sites, when not reduced to serfdom, as at Syracuse. The penetration of Greek customs slowly transformed the Sicel peasant, but the assimilation was incomplete before Hellenistic times. The economic development was favourable. Wheat, wine, oil, cattle, and horses were exported. Abundant pottery imported from Corinth and Rhodes, later from Attica, proves a considerable trade with Greece. Carthaginian and south-Italian markets also were open, as was Rome from c. 500 B.C. (whither the Sicilian agrarian cult of Demeter passed). Many sixth-century temples attest the culture and wealth of this period, and the first Sicilian coinage belongs to the second half of the century. The Phoenicians, allied with the Etruscans, stood on the

defensive, but defeated the attempts of Pentathlus (c. 580) and Dorieus (c. 510) to colonize Lilybaeum.

3. Tyranny emerged, as in Greece, but the aristocracy was much stronger, Carthaginians and Sicels affected internal politics, and there was in general greater social instability. The early tyranny of Phalaris (q.v.) of Acragas led on to numerous revolutions after c. 550. Hippocrates (q.v.) of Gela founded the first great tyrannical State in Sicily, which his successor Gelon (q.v.) extended to Syracuse. A coalition of Anaxilaus (q.v.), the Carthaginians, Selinus, and Himera tried to check him and his ally Theron of Acragas, while the Greek homeland was involved in the Persian War. They were defeated at Himera (480). Under Gelon and Hieron, Sicilian culture reached its zenith. Greek culture penetrated deeply into the Phoenician colonies. The Elymian cities became half-Phoenician, half-Greek. After the deaths of Theron and Hieron (467–466) the tyrannies soon came to an end. The attempts of the Sicel chief Ducetius (q.v.) to organize a national movement proved abortive.

4. Leontini and Rhegium, the enemies of Syracuse, renewed a former alliance with Athens (433) which had ambitions towards the west. After a preliminary intervention on their behalf (427–424), Athens undertook the great expedition against Syracuse which ended in tragedy (413). Carthage now profited by the exhaustion of Syracuse to attempt the complete conquest of Sicily (409). Selinus and Himera fell in 409, Acragas and Gela in 406–405.

5. The Greeks could resist only by transforming their political structure. In Sicily democracy had been less productive than in Greece, but it had given rise to rhetoric. Under the tyranny of Dionysius I (q.v.) a Sicilian State was organized, which deprived the Greeks of their freedom and wealth, but repelled the Carthaginians to their former boundary. The price of power was internal dissolution. Chaos followed Dionysius' death, and petty tyrants established themselves in various cities. Timoleon (q.v.) beat off a fresh Carthaginian attack. After his death (c. 330) the restored free governments lost ground; many fell to adventurers like Agathocles (q.v.) who, on the basis of an anti-aristocratic and anti-Carthaginian policy, rebuilt a large but shortlived State in Sicily. New tyrants appeared, and many of the best men (e.g. Timaeus, Theocritus) abandoned Sicily in view of the patent dissolution of the Greek settlements. The Mamertines (q.v.) established themselves as landpirates in Messana (c. 288). To meet a fresh Carthaginian attack the Greeks sought the help of Pyrrhus (q.v.), who failed to expel the Carthaginians. Syracuse, under Hieron II (q.v.), made the final effort, checked the Mamertines, but allowed Carthage to occupy Messana. This precipitated Roman interference and the First Punic War (see PUNIC WARS), after which Sicily became a Roman province. Hieron's kingdom remained autonomous and prosperous till his death in 215, when Syracuse went over to Carthage. After Rome had reduced Syracuse (211) the State of Syracuse was incorporated in the Roman province.

6. THE ROMAN PROVINCE. The province was governed by a praetor with one quaestor in Syracuse and another in Lilybaeum. The provincial council of natives was merely an ornamental body; Messana and Tauromenium were theoretically considered as federated cities, because they had not fought against the Romans. A few communities became *liberae* and *immunes* (e.g. Segesta, Panormus). The remainder were either tithe-paying (*decumanae*) or tithe-and-rent paying (*censoriae*; the number of these is uncertain): in the *civitates censoriae* the land was considered *ager publicus*. All the cities enjoyed considerable independence in home affairs. The bronze coinage of the cities continued until after Augustus. The rules of the *decuma* (q.v.) were derived from a law of

Hieron II. During the Republic the Romans fostered wheat-growing. Many Romans bought estates in Sicily. Italian immigration was considerable. The development of *latifundia* favoured the rebellions of slaves (135–132; 104–100 B.C.). The governorship of C. Verres (73–71 B.C.) was only a small episode, but the fight between Sex. Pompeius and Octavian added a heavy burden. As Sicilian wheat lost importance, much ploughland was turned into pasture. *Latifundia* spread enormously. The emperors became the biggest landowners. Foreign trade, still flourishing in Republican times, declined.

7. The Sicilians apparently obtained the Latin rights by Caesar's gift. Antony published a scheme of Caesar to grant Roman citizenship to Sicily, but Octavian did not implement it. Under Augustus Messana and then a few other cities obtained Roman citizenship. Augustus founded colonies of veterans in Catana, Panormus, Syracuse, Tauromenium, Termae, and Tyndaris. The old system of administration was probably replaced with (a) tax-free Roman colonies and *municipia*; (b) tax-free Latin *municipia*; (c) tax-paying Latin *municipia*. A fixed levy replaced tithes. Latin and Greek culture long coexisted. In the fifth century the Vandals with their fleets partially held and totally controlled Sicily.

BIBLIOGRAPHY

GENERAL: J. Bérard, *Bibliographie topographique des principales cités grecques de l'Italie méridionale et de la Sicile* (1941).
PREHISTORY: P. Orsi, *A cura dell' archivo storico per la Calabria e la Lucania* (1935); *Reallexikon der Vorgeschichte* (esp. s.v. 'Sikuler', 'Sizilien', 'Stentinello-Kultur'); J. Whatmough, *The Foundations of Roman Italy* (1936) and *The Prae-Italic Dialects of Italy* (1933), ii 430; G. Patroni, *La preistoria*, i–ii (1937).
GREEK AND ROMAN PERIODS: General histories of Greece and Rome. E. A. Freeman, *History of Sicily*, 4 vols. (1890–4); E. Pais, *Storia della Sicilia e della Magna Grecia* i (1894); B. Pace, *Arte e civiltà della Sicilia antica* (1935–); L. Pareti, *Studi siciliani e italioti* (1914); E. Ciaceri, *Culti e miti nella storia dell' antica Sicilia* (1911); T. J. Dunbabin, *The Western Greeks* (1948). For the relations between Athens and the West see bibliography by A. E. Raubitschek, *TAPA* lxxv, 1944, 10.
O. Cuntz, 'Zur Geschichte Siziliens in der caesarisch-august. Epoche', *Klio* vi (1906), 466; V. Scramuzza, *Econ. Survey* iii; T. Frank, 'On the migration of Romans to Sicily', *AJPhil.* lvi (1935), 61.
INSCRIPTIONS: *IG* xiv (1890: G. Kaibel); *CIL* x. 2 (1883: Th. Mommsen).
COINS: G. F. Hill, *Coins of Ancient Sicily* (1903); W. Giesecke, *Sicilia numismatica* (1923); E. Gabrici, *La monetazione di bronzo della Sicilia antica* (1927). A. M.

SICINIUS, GNAEUS, tribune of the plebs (76 B.C.), attempted to repeal the law of Sulla about the tribunate, but was frustrated by the consuls and perhaps murdered.

SICINIUS, *see also* DENTATUS.

SICULUS FLACCUS, *gromaticus*, of unknown date; author of a treatise on categories of land-tenure in Italy.

SICYON, Corinth's western neighbour, stood in a rich plain two miles from the sea. The archaic town lay at the foot of a large triangular plateau which was the acropolis. Demetrius Poliorcetes transplanted it to the acropolis. The remains of this town include the theatre, stadium, agora with fountains and portico, and large Roman buildings.

Sicyon was founded from Argos, and owed Argos religious and originally also political duties. These were set aside by the tyranny which, begun by Orthagoras c. 660 B.C., and favouring the non-Dorian elements, lasted over 100 years. Its greatest power was attained under Cleisthenes, who led the forces which destroyed Crisa in the first Sacred War (c. 580), and also had relations farther west. He celebrated his daughter's wedding with fabulous magnificence (Hdt. 6. 127). Sparta put down the tyranny and Sicyon became her faithful ally. In the third century its chief citizen, Aratus, gave it an important position in the Achaean League. Sicyon was a famous centre of art. In the archaic period it was a home of painting and pottery (Plin. *HN* 35. 151–2), but the attribution of the proto-Corinthian vases to Sicyon is now discredited (H. Payne, *Necrocorinthia*, 1931, 35 ff.). In the fourth century it owned the leading school of painters and produced the sculptor Lysippus.

C. H. Skalet, *Ancient Sicyon* (U.S.A. 1928).   T. J. D.

SIDON, a city on the coast of Phoenicia, was ruled under Persia by a native dynasty which had close commercial relations with Athens and was already hellenized, as the sarcophagi of the kings show. The dynasty was confirmed by Alexander but suppressed in the early third century (the last known king was the Ptolemaic admiral Philocles), and Sidon became a republic, ruled by Suffetes. From Antiochus IV's reign it issued municipal coinage, still mostly inscribed in Phoenician. In 111 B.C. it gained its freedom, which was recognized by Pompey but taken away by Augustus in 20. It received, however, about this time a great accession of territory up to Mount Hermon (*see* ITURAEA), and was probably soon again freed. Under Elagabalus it became a Roman colony. Sidon was a great commercial city and also possessed two important industries, purple-dyeing and glass-blowing; the latter art was discovered in the first century B.C. at Sidon, and the names of many Sidonian glass-blowers of the early Principate are known, chiefly from signatures on extant pieces.

E. Honigmann, *PW* ii A (1923), 2216–29.   A. H. M. J.

SIDONIUS APOLLINARIS (GAIUS SOLLIUS MODE-STUS(?) APOLLINARIS SIDONIUS), a Gallo-Roman of noble family, was born at Lugdunum (*Lyons*) about A.D. 430. He married Papianilla, daughter of Avitus, and through her acquired the estate of Avitacum in Auvergne. Avitus was proclaimed emperor, July 455. Sidonius accompanied him to Rome, and there recited in his honour, 1 Jan. 456, a panegyric in verse (*Carm.* 7), which was rewarded with a statue in Trajan's Forum. Avitus was soon dethroned. S. then joined an insurrection with headquarters at Lyons, but was finally reconciled to Majorian, the new emperor, and delivered at Lyons (458) a panegyric on him (ibid. 5). In 459 or 460 he held some government post at Rome. After Majorian's fall (461) he spent some years in his native country. In 467 he led a Gallo-Roman deputation to the Emperor Anthemius at Rome. On 1 Jan. 468 he recited his third and last panegyric (ibid. 2), after which he became *praefectus urbi*. He returned to Gaul in 469 and accepted the bishopric of Auvergne with seat at Clermont-Ferrand. Although ill equipped for ecclesiastical office, he discharged his sacred duties with earnestness and success; above all, he upheld his people in resisting the Goths. In 475 Rome, to his dismay, ceded Auvergne to Euric. S. was subjected to a mild imprisonment in the fortress of Livia, near Carcassonne. Soon released, he was ultimately allowed to resume his bishopric. The usual date for his death, 479, is probably a little too early. He was canonized.

WORKS. (1) *Carmina*: (*a*) 1–8, the three long panegyrics (in reversed chronological order) together with prefaces and dedications; (*b*) 9–24, professedly youthful poems, ranging from 4 to 512 lines, practically all addressed to, or concerned with, friends. (2) *Epistulae*, nine books, addressed to many friends and relations. Bks. 1–2 belong to the period before his episcopate. Some letters were specially written for the collection, the others were carefully revised. Both poems and letters throw important light on the fifth century. They show S. as a genial and sympathetic man, a loyal friend and ardent patriot, but also as a rather narrow-minded aristocrat and literary pedant. His originality was limited, but he had a keen eye for external details. His language is absurdly stilted and obscure, with all manner of rhetorical tricks exaggerated *ad nauseam*.

Text: ed. Luetjohann (1887; life by Mommsen); Mohr (1895); with notes, Savaro (Paris, 1609); Sirmond (Paris, 1652); W. B. Anderson, with transl. and notes (bibliog.), vol. i (Poems and Letters, bks. 1–2, Loeb 1936); O. M. Dalton, free transl. of Letters (2 vols., 1915); C. E. Stevens, *Sidon. Apoll. and His Age* (bibliog.; 1933).
                                                         W. B. A.

SIEGECRAFT, GREEK. The limitations of Greek siegecraft before the fourth century B.C. were partly those of Greek engineering. They are best illustrated by the strategy of the Peloponnesian War, which was based on the fact that Athens was impregnable. Potidaea and Plataea (not great cities) had to be starved out; the famous siege of Syracuse was little more than an unsuccessful attempt at blockade. A beleaguered city, if well provisioned, had far more to fear from treachery within its walls than from the enemy without.

The problem for the besieger was the city-wall, how to go under it, over it, or through it. Undermining, scaling-ladders, or a movable tower, the ram—all these were tried in the fifth century or earlier, but the defence had effective if primitive replies (see, e.g., Thucydides 2. 71–8; 3. 20–4 and 52: Plataea). The invention of the catapult was important (*c.* 400, perhaps in Syracuse), because its missiles (stones or arrows) could clear a wall of its defenders while a ram breached it or a tower disgorged a boarding-party. Dionysius at Motya was the first to co-ordinate 'machines' and show that they could capture a strong island fortress (398: Diodorus 14. 47–53). Why the generals of Greece were so slow to imitate is uncertain: lack of money probably accounts for much, and also lack of stimulus among cities accustomed to wars of attrition rather than destruction. Philip of Macedon (359–336) had the first 'modern' siege-train in Greece, and he introduced a short era in which the attack was ahead of the defence, a development which probably had profound political effects, helping him to conquer Greece without a war *à outrance*.

The supreme success of Alexander in siege warfare was due less to a further technical advance than to the personal factor: by all reasonable standards Tyre was impregnable, but he took it (Arrian, *Anab.* 2. 16–24). Later, at natural strongholds like Aornos (q.v.) and 'the Sogdian rock', his machines might help him, but far more it was his obvious contempt for the natural obstacles that got him through. The siege of Rhodes by Demetrius (305: Diod. 20. 81–8 and 91–100) was, technically, the most elaborate in antiquity: Demetrius had an unprecedented siege-train, but the Rhodians, too, had artillery besides a good wall. Already, in fact, the balance had shifted back in favour of the defence. Catapults could serve both sides. A solid wall of dressed stone could withstand rams for a time, roofed battlements could protect its defenders, a ditch in front could hinder rams and towers from approaching. And all the old tricks remained: even the armoured 'Helepolis' of Demetrius was ultimately fired by the Rhodians. It was not so much degeneration in subsequent besiegers as the improved equipment of the besieged which fixed the acme of Greek siegecraft towards the end of the fourth century, and made the third century an age of few great sieges.

Aeneas Tacticus, *Poliorketika*; Athenaeus and Biton in K. Wescher, *Poliorcétique des Grecs* (1868). E. Schramm in J. Kromayer and G. Veith, *Heerwesen und Kriegführung der Griechen und Römer* (1928), ch. 5.   G. T. G.

SIEGECRAFT, ROMAN. Rome was slow in adopting Greek artillery and does not seem to have made any great contribution to its development.

Two types of heavy artillery were used, the *catapulta* and the *ballista*, the former for shooting arrows, the latter for stones. Their construction was based upon the elasticity of torsion produced by twisted strands of gut or horsehair made taut by a windlass, which when released forced the discharge of the projectile. Later we hear of the *onager*, so-called from its 'kicking' propensities, in which the strings were stretched horizontally and not vertically. For the *catapulta* see the tombstone of C. Vedennius Moderatus, a soldier of Legion XVI (*ILS* 2034).

These engines were used mainly for defensive purposes, as the projectiles, although effective in clearing the battlements of defenders, were not sufficiently heavy to breach solid walls. The principal attacking engine was the *aries*, a beam with an iron head, which is shown on Trajan's column. It was moved up to the walls in a *testudo* or frame which was protected against fire by a wooden roof covered with clay or hides. A variety of the *aries* was the *terebra* for boring into a wall, while the *falx muralis* loosened the stones on the top. Movable towers were employed by Caesar at Massilia, and in Titus' siege of Jerusalem.

Another method of assault was by driving an underground gallery into the town. The mining party was protected by a *musculus* or wooden shed, 60 feet long, 4 feet wide, and 5 feet high, with a sloping roof covered with fire-proof material. It was moved up to the wall on rollers. A variety of it was the *vinea* which had one of its sides left open; the *pluteus* was a screen capable of protecting a small squad.

H. S. Jones, *Companion to Roman History* (1912), 215–23; R. Schneider, *PW*, s.v. 'Geschütze'. H. M. D. P.

SIGILLARIA. The custom of making presents of little pottery figures at the Saturnalia (q.v.), was so firmly fixed at Rome that there was a regular market for them, where apparently other trifling wares were also sold (Ausonius, *Cent. nupt.*, p. 206, 7 Peiper). It was usual to give dependants money for this fair (e.g. Sueton. *Claud.* 5). The origin of the custom is not known; the date of the fair was, in Imperial times, the last of the seven days which the Saturnalia then lasted (Macrob. *Sat.* 1. 10. 24). H. J. R.

SIGNA MILITARIA. The earliest standard of the Roman Army was the *signum* of the maniple. Its primitive form was a hand on the top of a pole, which later was replaced by a spearhead decorated with *phalerae*, *coronae*, and zodiac emblems. It was used by the centurion commanding the maniple for giving orders or for rallying his troops. When the cohort superseded the maniple, the *signum* of the first maniple in each cohort was used as the standard of the cohort. The century had no separate *signum*.

In the pre-Marian army there were also five legionary standards, which were placed for safety in battle between the first two lines. In substitution for these Marius gave each legion an *aquila* of silver or gold with *coronae* as its sole decoration. The *aquila* was the *numen legionis*; its loss sometimes entailed the disbandment of the legion.

Under the Principate the legion retained its *aquila* and *signa*. The praetorians had only *signa* and *vexilla*. (For other uses of *vexilla*, see VEXILLUM.) The legions, urban cohorts, *vigiles*, and *auxilia* were also given *imagines*, which were medallions with the portrait of the reigning princeps.

A. von Domaszewski, *Die Fahnen im römischen Heere* (Abhandlungen des archäologisch-epigraphischen Seminars der Universität Wien, Heft 5, 1885). H. M. D. P.

SIGNATURES, *see* SUBSCRIPTIONES.

SIKINNIS, *see* DANCING.

SILANION (4th c. B.C.), sculptor, of Athens, dated by Pliny 328 B.C. Selected works: 1. Theseus, in Athens. 2. Dying Iocasta, bronze with admixture of silver in the face. 3. Sappho, in Syracuse, later in Rome. 4. Corinna.

5. Plato, erected in the Academy by Mithridates the Persian; after 387 (foundation of Academy). The original of surviving Plato busts (Winter, *KB* 317. 2), which differ too much to justify further attribution to Silanion. 6. The sculptor Apollodorus (noted mainly for his irritable temper). 'Nec hominem fecit sed iracundiam' (Plin. *HN* 34. 81). 7. The boxer Satyrus, at Olympia, after 327. 8. Signature from Miletus, about 328 B.C. Silanion wrote *Praecepta symmetriarum*. His pupil Zeuxiades made a statue of Hyperides, who died 322.

Overbeck, 1350–63; E. Schmidt, *JDAI* 1932, 239; 1934, 180; R. Boehringer, *Platon, Bildnisse und Nachweise* (1935). T. B. L. W.

SILANUS, DECIMUS JUNIUS, husband of Servilia (q.v.), when *consul designatus* in 63 B.C. proposed the 'extreme punishment' for the Catilinarian conspirators, but after Caesar's reply modified his opinion.

F. Münzer, *PW* x. 163.

SILENI, *see* SATYRS.

SILIUS (1), GAIUS, grandson of P. Silius Nerva (*cos.* 20 B.C.) and described as 'iuuentutis Romanae pulcherrimus', attracted the guilty passion of Messalina and was involved in a liaison, perhaps in a plot to displace Claudius. It is said that the lovers openly celebrated a marriage while the Emperor was absent at Ostia. The imperial freedmen, in alarm, took counsel together and compelled Claudius to act. Silius and his paramour were put to death (A.D. 48). R. S.

SILIUS (2) **ITALICUS** (a recent inscription (*CR* xlix. 216–17) mentions his full name, TIBERIUS CATIUS ASCONIUS SILIUS ITALICUS). His birthplace is uncertain, perhaps Padua (*CR* i. 56–8), but not Italica in Spain. He died *c.* A.D. 101 aged 75, from voluntary starvation to shorten an incurable ailment (Pliny, *Ep.* 3. 7): this fixes his birth in 26. As a pleader he won fame, and, after receiving a bad name as a Neronian informer, was consul in 68; he supported Vitellius for the succession (Tac. *Hist.* 3. 65), and later about 77 gained high praise for his administration of Asia. Thereafter, he enjoyed an elegant retirement amongst numerous friends in Rome and Campania; a connoisseur of books, pictures, and statuary, he owned many country-houses, including one of Cicero's, for whom he showed great reverence, as for Virgil, whose tomb in Naples he repaired. From Martial's flattering references to him after 88 it seems that his poetic interest began only late in life. His Stoic outlook and death are confirmed by his acquaintance with Epictetus (Arr. *Epict. diss.* 3. 8. 7).

WORKS. *Punica*, the longest Latin poem, an historical epic in 12,200 verses on the Second Punic War. The seventeen books begin with Hannibal's oath and, except for digressions on Regulus and Anna, proceed in regular order of events to Scipio's triumph after Zama. The poem was planned by 88, but probably only bks. 1–6 appeared under Domitian (E. Bickel, *Rh. Mus.* lxvi. 505); as 14. 686 dates from the close of Nerva's principate, hasty workmanship would explain the inferiority of the final books. Since he wrote 'maiore cura quam ingenio' (Plin. *Ep.* 3. 7. 5), sources should be traceable for his facts; though owing most to Livy's Third Decad, he is not a mere free versifier of Livy. His main additional historical authority was Valerius Antias. On geography Varro is his chief source, along with Hyginus; his ethnography rests ultimately on Posidonius. Of Ennius, who described the same war, there is little direct imitation. His poetry owes most to the *Aeneid*, but adaptations occur from Lucan's and the other epics.

The *Ilias Latina* (q.v.), sometimes ascribed to him as a youthful work, is perhaps by Baebius Italicus.

Despite his clinging to a mythological scheme and the outworn epic machinery, Silius is distinctive. His learning, displayed in endless epithets and catalogues, is tiresome; he has too many rhetorical speeches; his language is not really poetic, and accounts of battles are confused and gruesome; but the versification is not monotonous; similes, if excessive, are clear and lifelike; and short passages show good narrative skill or straightforward description. Scipio fails as hero, and Hannibal comes nearer the part. *See also* EPIC POETRY, LATIN, para. 3.

BIBLIOGRAPHY

LIFE AND WORKS: Pliny, *Ep.* 3. 7; Martial; A. Klotz, *PW*, s.v. 'Silius', 79 ff.
    TEXTS: A. Drakenborch (Utrecht, 1717); G. A. Ruperti (Göttingen, 1795–8); L. Bauer (Teubner, 1890–2); W. C. Summers, *CPL* (1905).
    TRANSLATION: With text, J. D. Duff (Loeb).
    SOURCES: A Klotz, *Rh. Mus.* lxxxii. 1–34; J. Nicol, *The Historical and Geographical Sources used by Sil. Ital.* (1936); B. Rehm, *Philol.* Suppl. xxiv. 2. 97 ff.
    RECENT LITERATURE. M. Schuster in Bursian, *Jahresb.* ccxii (1927), 125–30.   D. J. C.

SILK. In early times silk was exported from the Far East by overland routes to the countries of western Asia, and in the days of Herodotus the Persians regarded a silk robe as one of their choicest possessions. The pure silk robe—*vestis serica*—however, was not the same as the *vestis Coa* or the *vestis bombycina* with which it is sometimes confused. The Coan robe was made at Cos from the pierced cocoons of a worm—*bombyx*—which lived on oak and ash trees, the bombycine robe from the pierced cocoons of the true mulberry silkworm; and as in both cases it was impossible to unwind the cocoons, they were carded and then spun into a coarse silk. The Chinese alone knew the method of unwinding the entire cocoon, and the raw silk—μέταξα—was imported into Italy before the beginning of the Christian era. It was very expensive and at first a silk robe was only half silk—*subserica*—the warp of linen, the woof of silk; and even so was by law confined to women. In the late Empire the pure woven silk stuffs were imported, a pound of gold being paid for a pound of silk—*holoserica vestis*—and Elagabalus was the first to wear such a robe.   F. A. W.

SILLOI, *see* TIMON (2).

SILLYBOS (σίλλυβος), *see* BOOKS, I. 8.

SILO, *see* GAVIUS, POMPAEDIUS, POMPEIUS (6).

SILURES, a tribe in south-east Wales, an offshoot of the Iron Age B culture. Under the leadership of Caratacus, they gave trouble to the Roman armies, but were finally subdued by Frontinus (A.D. 74–8), who planted a legionary fortress at Isca (*Caerleon*). A Roman town in the plain (Venta Silurum, *Caerwent*) replaced their hill forts.

Collingwood–Myres, *Roman Britain*, 94–7, 110–12.   C. E. S.

SILVA, like ὕλη, could mean raw material, and, perhaps with a suggestion of its Ciceronian sense of a forest-like abundance, was extended as a literary title to work of varied content (cf. Suetonius' *Pratum*). Quintilian (*Inst.* 10. 3. 17) explains it as a rapid draft, and this applies to Statius' *Silvae*, which are occasional poems hastily composed. Ben Jonson's definition, 'the Ancients call'd that kind of body *Sylva*, or Ὕλη, in which there were workes of divers nature, and matter congested', indicates why it remained an appropriate title for miscellaneous verses into the Renaissance, e.g. Mantuanus' 'subitaria carmina' (Bologna, 1052) or Politian's 'Sylvae'.   J. W. D.

SILVANUS, the Roman god of uncultivated land beyond the boundaries of the tillage. He was thus uncanny and dangerous, *see* PILUMNUS. His personality also seems to have been very vague, for he has no name, *Siluanus* being merely an adjective, unless, with Wissowa, *RK* 213, we suppose that the substantive Faunus (q.v.), is to be supplied. Clearly it would be well to propitiate him when making inroads into his domain, so it is quite understandable that 'every estate has three Silvani' (Gromatici, p. 302, 14 Lachmann), one for the boundary, one *domesticus, possessioni consecratus* (watching over the farm-house itself?), and one for the herdsmen; of course a late and somewhat fossilized form of the worship, which itself dated from times when such land represented the felling of trees and other interferences with the wild country. Silvanus thus bears a kind of resemblance to Greek satyrs and Sileni, and is freely identified with them and with Pan (Wissowa, ibid. 215), also with foreign, especially barbarian, gods somehow connected with untilled land, or supposed to be, regardless of their relative importance. Silvanus also occurs as a title of Mars (q.v.; Cato, *Agr.* 83), unless *Marti Siluano* is archaic asyndeton for *Marti et Siluano*.

H. J. R.

SILVANUS, *see* PLAUTIUS (1), (3), and (5).

SILVER. Though known in remote antiquity, silver was for long a rarer and more valuable metal than gold, which could be easily obtained from alluvial deposits by simple washing, whereas silver had to be extracted by regular mining processes. The Phoenicians are said to have been the first to bring silver into general use; several of the silver objects mentioned in Homer have Sidonian associations. The main sources for classical Greece were Bactriana, Colchis, Lydia, Mt. Pangaeus in Thrace, and Laurium, which provided abundant supplies for Athens down to 413 B.C. In the western Mediterranean Spain was the most prolific source of supply, with Sardinia, Gaul, and Britain as minor sources. The conquests of Spain and Asia made silver plentiful at Rome, where it had previously been rare.

Silver was worked with a hammer into plates which were soldered or riveted together and then decorated with repoussé work (ἐμπαιστική), stamping, chasing, and engraving. Vases might be hammered or cast from a mould and were often adorned with reliefs (*emblemata*), let into the body of the vessel or *crustae* soldered upon the surface. To provide colour contrast silver objects were often gilded, a practice mentioned in the Acropolis inventories. Niello, a form of enamelling, does not appear until Roman Imperial times.

Less popular than gold for jewellery, silver was especially used for valuable and luxurious specimens of objects for which bronze was the common material. It was extensively used for statuettes, but rarely for larger sculpture; for the domestic furniture of wealthy Romans; and, above all, for services of dinner-plate. Many of these services (*ministeria*) have been preserved, examples being the Treasures of Hildesheim in Berlin, and of Boscoreale in Paris, both of the early Empire; and the Esquiline Treasure in London, of the late Empire. They include flat dishes for eating (*lances*), flat or hemispherical bowls for drinking (*calices, scyphi*), jugs (*urceoli*), saucepans (*trulli*), buckets for fruit (*situlae*), spoons (*cochlearia*), pepper-castors (*piperatoria*), etc. Cups were the special subjects of artists of whom Pliny gives a list dating from the fourth and third centuries B.C.; he remarks that while no names of goldsmiths have been preserved, the silversmiths (*argentarii*) are numerous.

Pliny, *HN* bk. 33; H. B. Walters, *Catalogue of Silver Plate in the British Museum* (1921).   F. N. P.

SILVIA, a name now generally discarded in the title of *Peregrinatio ad loca sancta* (q.v.).

SILVIUS, son of Aeneas (q.v.) and Lavinia, father of Silvius Aeneas and ancestor of the Alban royal house of Silvii (Verg. *Aen.* 6. 760–7; Liv. 1. 3). A legend due to the name, but unknown to Virgil, told that Lavinia, fearing the jealousy of Ascanius, fled to the woods and there gave birth to her son (Dion. Hal. 1. 70).   C. B.

SIMMIAS (1) (or **Simias**) of Thebes, a member of the inner circle of Socrates' friends, one of those who were prepared to put up money to secure his escape from prison, and who were with him on the day of his death. He had previously associated with the Pythagorean Philolaus, and in the *Phaedo* he ably defends Pythagorean theories. In the *Phaedrus* Plato praises highly his philosophical ability. Diogenes Laertius ascribes to him twenty-three dialogues (not extant), but it is doubtful whether this ascription is sound.

   PW iii A. 144.   W. D. R.

SIMMIAS (2) of Rhodes, poet and grammarian, lived in Rhodes (Strabo 364, 655) about 300 B.C., wrote three books of γλῶσσαι and four of ποιήματα (Suidas s.v. Σιμμίας). Of the first Athenaeus gives a few quotations (327 e, 472 e, 479 c, 677 c) about the meanings of words. The poems vary in character. Fragments survive of a hexametric epic on Apollo (fr. 1 Powell), and others called *Gorgo* and *Μῆνες* (frs. 6–8), and of lyrical poems (frs. 13–17). There are also three complete *Technopaegnia* called *Wings* (fr. 24), *Axe* (fr. 25) and *Egg* (fr. 26) and epigrams (frs. 18–22) which are in the epideictic manner of the time. His style shows affinities to the Coan circle of Theocritus, and though he calls himself Δωρία ἀηδών, he does not write in any single dialect.

   Text: E. Diehl, *Anth. Lyr. Graec.* ii. 257–75; J. U. Powell, *Coll. Alex.*, 109–20. Criticism: H. Fraenkel, *De Simia Rhodio* (1915).
                                                          C. M. B.

SIMON of Athens, a shoemaker, was according to a late tradition a friend of Socrates, who used to visit him in his workshop and discuss philosophical questions with him. He plays a considerable part in the (late) *Socraticae epistulae*, and Diogenes Laertius says he was the first to write reminiscences of Socrates in dialogue form. But he is never mentioned by Plato or Xenophon, and his very existence as a real personage is not quite certain.

   PW iii A. 163.   W. D. R.

SIMONIDES (c. 556–468 B.C.), lyric and elegiac poet, born at Iulis in Ceos c. 556 B.C. (fr. 147), the son of Leoprepes. In the last years of the sixth century he wrote Epinician Odes for Glaucus of Carystus (fr. 8, Paus. 6. 10. 1) and Eualcidas of Eretria (fr. 9, Hdt. 5. 102). He was the guest of Hipparchus at Athens ([Pl.] *Hipparch.* 228 c), and to this period may have belonged some of his fifty-six victories in dithyrambic competitions (fr. 79). A couplet honouring the murderers of Hipparchus, though attributed to him (fr. 76), is not necessarily by him, while his epitaph on Hippias' daughter, Archedice, shows his affection for the family (fr. 85). About 514 he went to Thessaly, where he was the guest of the Scopads, and celebrated their chariot victories (Theoc. 16. 42–7). He was miraculously preserved when their house fell and destroyed them (Callim. fr. 71, Cic. *De Or.* 2. 86). He lamented them in a Dirge (schol. Theoc. 16. 36). To the same period belong his dirge on Antiochus the son of Echecratidas (ibid. 44), but the only substantial fragment from this time is his lines to Scopas on the nature of virtue (fr. 4) in which he seeks to substitute a good conscience as the right test for a good man instead of all-round excellence. He was back in Athens in 490, when his epitaph on the fallen of Marathon was preferred to that of Aeschylus (*Vit. Aesch.*, p. 4). In the wars of 480–479 he rose to great prominence and wrote a commemorative hymn for the Spartans who fell at Thermopylae (fr. 5), a hymn of thanksgiving for the victory of

Artemisium (frs. 1–3), and epitaphs for the fallen, including his own friend Megistias (fr. 83) and the Spartans who died with Leonidas (fr. 92). At this time he was a friend of Themistocles (Plut. *Them.* 5, Cic. *Fin.* 2. 32. 104), in whose interest he carried on a verbal warfare with Timocreon (frs. 169–70, Diog. Laert. 2. 25, 40). About 476 B.C. he went to Syracuse as the guest of Hieron, with whom various stories connect him (Pl. *Ep.* 2, Ath. 656 d, Ael. *VH* 9. 1), and made peace between him and Theron (Timaeus ap. schol. Pind. *Ol.* 2. 29). He died in 468 (*Marm. Par.* 73) and was buried at Acragas (Callim. fr. 71). He was said to be ugly (Plut. *Them.* 5), fond of money (Ar. *Pax* 698, Callim. fr. 77), and the inventor of a technique for remembering (Cic. *De Or.* 2. 357). His work falls into the following classes: (1) Hymns, of which very little survives, except frs. 1–2, 5. (2) Scolia and Encomia, including his poem to Scopas (fr. 4) and his quatrain on the four best things (*Scol. Att.* 7). (3) Dirges, for which he was extremely renowned (Quint. *Inst.* 10. 1. 64), notably frs. 6–12. The famous lines on Danae (fr. 13) do not necessarily come from a Dirge. (4) Epinicians, written for many patrons, including Astylus of Croton (fr. 10), Crius of Aegina (fr. 13), Xenocrates of Acragas (fr. 6), Anaxilas of Rhegium (fr. 7). In these he seems to have been much more playful than Pindar. (5) Elegies, frs. 62–6, 84, 99, 128, 130, including both poems on public events such as the battle of Plataea and short, sympotic poems. (6) Inscriptional epigrams for dedications and epitaphs. The authenticity of these is very doubtful in many cases, as they were probably not collected till the fourth century and would not have the author's name on the stone. The most likely to be genuine are frs. 79, 83, 85, 91; *see* EPIGRAM, 1 (1). (7) Since many apophthegms are attributed to him, a collection of such may have existed. He was admired for his choice of words (Dion. Hal. ii, p. 205. 7, *De Imit.*), his sweetness (Cic. *Nat. D.* 1. 22), his harmonious style (Dion. Hal. *Comp.* 23).

   Text: E. Diehl, *Anth. Lyr. Graec.* ii. 61–118. Criticism: U. von Wilamowitz-Moellendorff, *Sappho und Simonides* (1913), 137–212; C. M. Bowra, *Greek Lyric Poetry* (1936), 317–401; A. Hauvette, *Les Épigrammes de Simonide*; M. Boas, *De Epigrammatis Simonideis* (1905).
                                                          C. M. B.

SIMYLUS, (1) Greek didactic iambographer, of whom a few fragments survive, of the third or second, or even of the first, century B.C. Probably not identical with a comic poet of the same name (*CAF* ii. 444). See LITERARY CRITICISM, GREEK, para. 4.

   (2) Greek author of an elegy or epigram on Tarpeia, perhaps slightly earlier than the Augustan age. *Anth. Lyr. Graec.* ii. 248.

   Meineke, *FCG*, praef. xiii ff.; J. E. Sandys, *History of Classical Scholarship* (1903), i. 56; J. W. H. Atkins, *Literary Criticism in Antiquity* (1924), i. 179; *PW* iii A. 1, 216–17.   J. D. D.

SIN. The various words which may be translated by 'sin' and the ideas which they represent fall into two classes, a lower and a higher. In the former the act is one which brings about undesirable relations between the agent and his supernatural environment; it may be the breach of a tabu, disobedience to the command of a supernatural being, departure from the recognized standard of conduct (ὁσία, *fas*) of his community. It need not be what we should regard as immoral; it does not necessarily connote any evil intention, or any intention at all, on the agent's part; it often is not individual in itself, very often not individual in its consequences. Indeed, the fact that its consequences are supposed to extend far beyond the sinner is the main reason for general objection to it. In the latter the act is itself considered wrong, offending a deity or deities because the god or gods are supposed to be righteous and interested in human morality. The history of Greek thought in this respect is a progress from the lower to the higher conception. Rome seems of herself to have made but small advance in this direction till enlightened by Greek theology.

2. Of the former stage, in Greece, Hesiod furnishes a good example (cf. SUPERSTITION). He forbids, with equal earnestness and apparently equal assuredness that divine vengeance will follow transgression, on the one hand a number of acts of which any moral code would disapprove, such as the ill-treatment of orphans and of one's own parents (*Op.* 330 ff.), and on the other purely ritual offences such as omitting to wash the hands before pouring libation (ibid. 724 ff.; full list in R. Pettazzoni, *La Confessione dei Peccati* iii (1936), 174 ff.). This is in a poem which repeatedly and emphatically insists on the justice of Zeus. In some archaic rites, such as that of the Samothracian gods, confession of offences was a preliminary to initiation; it does not appear that anything more was needed, the confession being simply a process of getting rid of the state of sinfulness and so leaving the candidate ritually pure; Pettazzoni, op. cit. 163 ff., cf. i. 60 ff.; *Harv. Theol. Rev.* xxx (1937), 1 ff., the last giving other examples of confession in ancient ritual, especially Oriental cults.

3. For Rome, a similar state of things can be detected for early times. It is significant that the word *scelus*, perhaps the nearest classical equivalent of 'sin', can also, in Plautus and other Republican authors, mean 'ill-luck', such as would naturally come mechanically from the violation of some tabu. A legend, the more significant because it is probably pure invention and therefore shows fairly early ideas of what is proper in such matters, represents grave consequences befalling as the result of a wholly accidental *vitium*, or shortcoming, in the celebration of games to Jupiter (Livy 2. 36). The XII Tables show at least the beginnings of a movement towards a more enlightened view, for they make provision for lenient treatment of a merely accidental homicide (Cicero, *Top.* 64).

4. Greece, as early as Homer and more articulately and detailedly in later authors down to about the end of the fifth century B.C., develops a theory which strongly stresses the moral aspect. Sin is the result of $\H{v}\beta\rho\iota\varsigma$ or overweening disregard of the rights of others; Theognis in a famous passage declares this due to $\kappa\acute{o}\rho o\varsigma$, satiety, in other words too much prosperity, but adds 'when wealth attends a base man' (Theog. 153, cf. Solon, fr. 3. 9 Diehl), while Aeschylus (*Ag.* 751 ff.) emphatically denies that prosperity of itself has any such result (contrast Hdt. 1. 32. 6–9). In any case, this $\H{v}\beta\rho\iota\varsigma$ results in $\check{a}\tau\eta$, a state of blindness to both moral and prudential considerations, in which 'the evil appears good' (Soph. *Ant.* 622, see Jebb ad loc.), and this brings about utter ruin. These sins appear in no case to be mere ritual offences, but serious wrongdoings. It was further held that punishment might not overtake the actual sinner, but either his descendants (as Solon, fr. 1. 29 ff. Diehl) or those somehow associated with him (Hesiod, op. cit. 240; cf., e.g., Horace, *Carm.* 3. 2. 29 f.), despite their innocence. This problem seems to have exercised Aeschylus greatly, for several of his plays deal with the problem of the hereditary curse, as the surviving trilogy and that of which the *Seven against Thebes* remains. His solution would appear to be that the children of the sinful inherit a certain tendency to sin, but are nevertheless free agents who may return to better ways.

5. Some of the more mystical religious systems, notably Orphism (q.v.), occupied themselves with the relations between sin and suffering, and seem to have found a solution in the theory that sins committed in one life may be atoned for in another, see especially Pind. *Ol.* 2. 56 ff. (probably Pythagorean). Orphism seems actually to have had a kind of dogma of original sin (Pind. fr. 127 Bowra, see Rose in *Greek Poetry and Life* (1936), 79 ff.).

6. Further examination of this and kindred problems

was mostly left to the philosophic schools (it is worth noting that the Christian word for sin, $\dot{a}\mu a\rho\tau\acute{\iota}a$, may derive from a Stoic technicality, see Wilamowitz-Moellendorff, *Glaube der Hellenen* ii (1932), 120). Many of the later, orientalizing cults elaborately developed the idea of punishment for sin after death, which in Homer hardly exists, save for the penalties inflicted on a few who had directly and personally offended the gods (*Od.* 11. 576 ff.), but expanded under philosophico-religious influences (Orphic-Pythagorean?) into such schemes of Hell, Purgatory, and Paradise as are found in Verg. *Aen.* 6 and became extremely minute and particular in later documents (see A. Dieterich, *Nekyia²*, 1913).

Literature: besides the works mentioned in the text, a good summary is A. W. Mair in Hastings, *ERE* xi. 545 ff., cf. J. S. Reid, ibid. 569 ff.　　　　　　　　　　　　　　　　　H. J. R.

SINIS, a brigand who lived on the Isthmus of Corinth. He made all comers contend with him at holding down a pine-tree, which, when they could no longer hold it, flung them into the air and so killed them (so Apollod. 3. 218 and others, see for details Wörner in Roscher, s.v.), or, more intelligibly, tied them to two such trees which were then let go and tore them asunder (so Diod. Sic. 4. 59. 3 and others). Hence he was surnamed Pityocamptes ($\Pi\iota\tau\nu o\kappa\acute{a}\mu\pi\tau\eta\varsigma$), i.e. pine-bender. Theseus (q.v.) on his way to Athens, killed him in the same manner, Plut. *Thes.* 8, who adds that Perigune ($\Pi\epsilon\rho\iota\gamma o\acute{\nu}\nu\eta$), Sinis' daughter, became the concubine first of Theseus and later of Deïoneus son of Eurytus of Oechalia.　　　　　H. J. R.

SINNIUS CAPITO, scholar of the Augustan age whose *Epistulae* (containing grammatical discussions), *Liber de syllabis*, and *Libri spectaculorum* are mentioned by later writers. Cf. Teuffel, § 260; Schanz–Hosius, § 353; G. Funaioli, *Gramm. Rom. Frag.* 458–66.

SINON, a pretended deserter from the Greek forces at Troy, who told the Trojans a long and false tale of the building of the Trojan Horse (Verg. *Aen.* 2. 57–194) and after it had been taken within the walls released the Greek soldiers inside it and joined in the sack of the city. The story is derived from the epic cycle and is treated by several extant writers.

O. Immisch in Roscher, *Lexikon* iv (1915), 935–46; A. C. Pearson, *Fragments of Sophocles* ii (1917), 181–3.　　　　　　A. S. P.

SINOPE, a town situated almost at the midpoint of the south shore of the Euxine on an easily defended peninsula with two good harbours about its base, and near the place where the crossing to the Crimea is shortest. The promontory is well watered and fertile (Strabo speaks of market gardens), the tunny catch was famous, and the mountains noted for their timber and cabinet woods. Founded by Miletus traditionally before 756 B.C., it was destroyed by the Cimmerians and refounded before 600. It early commanded the maritime trade of much of the Pontic region and established many colonies along the coast, some of which were tributary to it in Xenophon's time. In spite of mountain barriers it drew trade from the interior, notably in Sinopic earth (cinnabar). In 444 it was freed from a tyrant by Pericles. It was attacked and perhaps eventually captured by the Persian satrap Datames (c. 375). The town probably maintained its freedom under Alexander and his immediate successors, and with the assistance of Rhodes repelled Mithridates III of Pontus in 220, but was finally occupied by Pharnaces I in 183 and soon became the Pontic capital. In the Third Mithridatic War it was captured and constituted a free town by Lucullus. It was occupied and suffered severely at the hands of Pharnaces II (q.v.), but Caesar repaired its losses by settling a colony with the title of Colonia Iulia Felix Sinope. An abundant coinage attests its prosperity both in the early and the Imperial periods, and the appearance of men of Sinope all about the Euxine, the Aegean, at Athens, and at Rhodes attests the wide commercial connexions of the city. Its vigorous hellenism is shown by the names of Diogenes the Cynic, Diphilus the comic poet, and other men of letters. Strabo describes it as a city with fine buildings, market-place, porticoes, gymnasium, and fortifications.

Strabo 12. 545; D. M. Robinson, *Ancient Sinope* (1906); F. Miltner, *Anatolian Studies Presented to William Hepburn Buckler* (1939), 191 ff. T. R. S. B.

SIRENES, half women, half birds endowed with enchanting song. In the *Odyssey* (12. 39, 184) the S. live on an island near Scylla and Charybdis. Sailors charmed by their song land and perish; the meadow is full of decaying corpses. But Odysseus following the advice of Circe passes safely. Similarly Orpheus saves the Argonauts by competing with the S. (Ap. Rhod. 4. 893; Apollod. 1. 9. 25). In other stories the S. must die if a mortal can resist their song (Hyg. *Fab.* 141). The escape of Odysseus and of Orpheus and their defeat by the Muses (q.v.) lead to their death. The S. are omniscient and have the power to quiet the winds (with their song? Hes. fr. 69 Rzach). S. are sometimes called daughters of Earth; they sing the strains of Hades (Soph. fr. 861 Pearson), and they live in Hades (Pl. *Cra.* 403 d). S. accompany the dead on their voyage to the lower world and crown tombs, from very early times. This leads some authorities to assume that they were originally birds inhabited by souls of the dead. A poetical interpretation makes these funereal S. grieve for the dead with mournful songs just as they mourn for Persephone (Dositheus viii in Hyg. *Fab.* ed. Rose; Eur. *Hel.* 167 f.). When definite geographical locations began to be attached to Homeric geography, it was held that S. ranged along the coast of south Italy, where they were worshipped by the seafaring population (Strabo 1. 22) in Naples, Sorrentum, and Sicily. They probably figured in Timaeus (q.v.).

In art, S. begin as rapacious singing monsters, but like many other monsters they are ennobled in Classical art to mourning, beautiful beings; in Hellenistic art and literature they are representatives of music almost as much as Muses and are said to be daughters of a Muse (Ap. Rhod. 4. 896). Occasionally they are given an erotic character (Attic comedy).

Weicker in Roscher, *Lexikon*, s.v. 'Seirenen'; H. Payne, *Necrocorinthia* (1931), 139; E. Haspels, *Attic Black-Figured Lekythoi* (Paris, 1936), 150. G. M. A. H.

SIRMIUM, a town on the Savus in Pannonia (Inferior), founded by the Celtic Taurisci, was occupied by the Romans (perhaps by 35 B.C.) and became a colony under the Flavians. Important as a road-junction and as a base against Dacians and other Danube tribes, Sirmium had an arms factory (*Not. Dign. Occ.* 9. 18), a *statio classis primae Flaviae Aug.* (l.c. 32. 50), and an imperial mint which worked from A.D. 330 to 378. At Sirmium four Arian creeds were drafted (A.D. 347–59). Often in later times the residence of emperors and high officials, Sirmium, which was the most important town of Pannonia, was abandoned c. 400 by the Romans.

M. Fluss, *PW*, s.v.; C. Patsch, *Sitz. Wien*, 209 v (1929); *Strena Buliciana* (1924), 229–32. F. A. W. S.

SISCIA, a town in Pannonia (Superior) where the Colapis joins the Savus. Taken by Octavian (35 B.C.), Siscia developed quickly, and became a *colonia* (Flavia) under Vespasian; Septimius Severus apparently sent there fresh colonists (*colonia Septimia*). Its imperial mint worked from Gallienus till A.D. 387. Important through its natural strength, which was increased by a canal dug by Tiberius, and as a river-harbour, Siscia was a station of the *classis Aegentensium sive secundae Pannonicae* (*Not. Dign. Occ.* 32. 56), and also a customs-station.

M. Fluss, *PW*, s.v. On the coinage, A. Alföldi, *Siscia* (1931) and *Numizmatikai Közlöny* xxvi/xxvii (1927/8), 14–58. F. A. W. S.

SISENNA, LUCIUS CORNELIUS, the historian, praetor in 78 B.C., defended Verres (70), and was legate to Pompey in 67, dying in Crete. His *Historiae*, in at least twelve books (scarcely the twenty-three of fr. 132), after a reference to Roman origins treated the Social War and Sullan Civil War, certainly from 90 to 82, probably to Sulla's death; it may have continued the work of Sempronius Asellio (q.v.). The composition was literary, not chronological, the style vivid and striking, on the model of Cleitarchus (Cic. *Leg.* 1. 2. 7). This Hellenistic influence appears in his translation of Aristides' *Milesiaca*, associating him with Petronius and Apuleius. His historical authority, however, was recognized by Sallust and Varro. He is not the Plautine commentator of this name.

H. Peter, *HRRel.* i² (1914), pp. cccxxxiv, 276; A. Schneider, *De Sis. hist. reliquiis* (1882); C. Cali, 'La vita e le opere di L. Corn. Sisenna', *Studi letterari*, 1898, 93. A. H. McD.

SISPES, see JUNO.

SISYPHUS, in mythology, son of Aeolus (2), (q.v.). In *Od.* 11. 593 ff. he is one of those tormented in Hades, having eternally to roll a rock up a hill, from the top of which it always rolls down again. In *Il.* 6. 154–5 he lives in Ephyre in the Argolid and is grandfather of Bellerophon (q.v.), and 'most crafty of men'. The reason for his damnation is not stated in Homer; others, as Eustathius and the schol. on Homer, ll.cc. (cf. Rose, *Handbk. Gk. Myth.*, pp. 270, 294, and notes), connect it with his offence against Zeus in telling Aesopus where the god had taken his daughter Aegina. For the associated folk-tale of how Sisyphus befooled Death and Hades *see* THANATOS. Being clearly the familiar trickster of popular tales, he is naturally brought into association with Autolycus (q.v.); thus, Polyaenus (*Strat.* 6. 52, cf. Hyginus, *Fab.* 201) says Autolycus used to steal his cattle, but Sisyphus stopped him by attaching to their hooves lead tablets with the words 'stolen by Autolycus', whereby he tracked them. He is also father of Odysseus in post-Homeric accounts, cf. ANTICLEA. His name is a not infrequent nickname for cunning persons (see Wilisch in Roscher's *Lex.* iv, 964, 22 ff.). A more serious side of his character is reflected in his shrine, the Sisypheion, on the Acrocorinthus (Strabo 8. 6. 21) and his grave on the Isthmus (Paus. 2. 2. 2). H. J. R.

SITALCES, a Thracian king of the tribe of the Odrysae (in the Hebrus valley), who inherited from his father Teres a dominion over the entire eastern Balkan peninsula up to the Danube. He extended this empire to the middle Strymon. Common enmity against Macedonia brought him into alliance with Athens. In 431 B.C. he delivered to the Athenians some Corinthian and Spartan envoys on the way to Persia. In 429 he made a foray with massed forces into Macedonia, encountering no resistance. But failing to receive assistance as arranged from Athens, he could not capture any strongholds, and so fell back. He was killed in a campaign in the central Balkans (424); his empire broke up soon after.

Thucydides 2. 29. 67, 95–101. M. C.

SITOPHYLAKES, overseers of the cornmarket in Athens and a few other States. In Athens there were five for the city and five for the Piraeus (after 350 B.C. twenty and fifteen respectively). They supervised the sale of imported corn, wholesale and retail, not only looking after the quality, but controlling prices and the amount bought: no one merchant could purchase more than a certain quantity.

In other more self-supporting States the control was not so strict, and the duties of the *sitophylakes* were performed by the *agoranomoi* (q.v.).

Lysias, *Or.* 22. A. W. G.

SITTIUS, PUBLIUS, a Roman *eques* from Nuceria in Campania, went to Further Spain late in 64 B.C. as a free-lance speculator, thus severing his association with Catiline (so Cicero, *Sull*. 20. 56–9; contrast Sall. *Cat*. 21. 3). Later he established himself as a condottiere in Mauretania, and enjoyed great influence with Bocchus and Bogud. During the Civil War he gave valuable support to Caesar, joining with Bocchus in 46 to create a diversion in Numidia. He was rewarded with part of the territory of Masinissa and Juba, where he settled with his followers (Sittiani). Later he died through treachery.

J. M. C.

SKYTALE, a secret method of communication used by Spartan magistracies, especially between ephors and king or general, during war-time. Each of them had a stick of equal size, so that a message written on a strip of leather wound round the stick of the sender, and then detached, became illegible until the strip was rewound on the stick of the recipient. The skytale is described by Plut. *Lysander* 19, and Gell. 17. 9.

A. Martin, Dar.-Sag., s.v.   V. E.

SLAVERY, LAW OF. I. GREECE. Slaves could belong to the State (δοῦλοι δημόσιοι, being employed for public works or subordinate services in public offices), temples (ἱερόδουλοι), or private persons. Slaves had no legal personality, and generally their master could dispose of them as of the rest of the property. Their legal position was not uniform: slaves living in the master's household were in a worse condition than those who had economic independence with their own lodging and paid only a rent to their master. The former class (οἰκέται) could own no property or enter into transactions on behalf of their master. A slave of this class could be sued personally, if he did any damage, but his master would be liable under the judgement. Slaves of the second category (e.g. those who belonged to the State) had larger legal powers: as administrators of large estates or commercial undertakings they acted as their master's representatives, and their declarations were legally binding. It seems that they could be parties to a trial; their position may be characterized as half-free. There were also considerable differences in the laws of particular States; according to the law of Gortyn the distinction between free men and slaves was less sharp. Slaves were not debarred from public religious ceremonies nor from the army and navy; they were protected against cruelty on the part of their master, and they could take refuge in an asylum (*see* ASYLIA) and demand to be sold to another master. Penalties inflicted upon slaves were more severe: where a free man was punished with a pecuniary fine, slaves were flogged.

Slavery arose by birth, capture in war or kidnapping, sale of a free child by his father or of a debtor by the creditor (these two last measures were abolished at Athens by Solon). Release from slavery could be effected by will, by notification before witnesses, in public places or before altars, by consecration or sale to a divinity. By enfranchisement the slave acquired freedom, but not citizenship. His dependence on his master was not entirely abolished: he often remained for some years in the master's household and worked there as before for the master's profit, and he could not marry without his consent. He was obliged to pay him an annual fee, and when he died childless, his estate went to his master.

II. ROME. In ancient Rome slaves could not possess any rights, they were considered as objects in the ownership of their master and ranked with *res mancipi* (*see* MANCIPATIO). The development of Roman economic life, to which they contributed considerably, gradually enforced a recognition of their personality. As an instrument of the legal personality of his master the slave could acquire property and credits for him; by a later development (praetorian reforms) he could also oblige him if he was installed in the management of a commercial undertaking or ship by the master. The custom of entrusting slaves with money for their personal disposal (*peculium*) added to their liberty of trading, because this separate fund served to ensure the fulfilment of the obligations contracted by the slave. The *peculium* was subsequently considered as the slave's own property. This recognition of a restricted legal personality in slaves was accompanied by protective measures against bad treatment by their masters. Slaves who were the property of the State (*servi publici*) enjoyed a privileged condition at Rome too, as in Greece.

Children of a female slave were slaves, even if the father was free. Foreign prisoners of war became slaves of Rome; similarly Roman citizens captured by the enemy fell into slavery (*see* POSTLIMINIUM). According to an ancient rule a Roman could not become a slave on Roman soil, but he could be sold *trans Tiberim* by a magistrate for a penalty, or by a creditor for a default. New methods of enslavement were later recognized, even on Roman soil.

Slaves became free by manumission, which could be effected in various forms: by disposition of the master in his will (later by *fideicommissum*, q.v.); or *vindicta*, a solemn procedure before a magistrate (originally a fictitious claim of liberty); or by entry of the slave with the master's consent into the list of citizens (*census*) by the censors. Informal declarations (by letter of enfranchisement or before witnesses, *inter amicos*) were introduced later. The law of manumission, the effects of which were very various, underwent continual alteration; the Christian State added a new procedure of manumission *in ecclesia*.

BIBLIOGRAPHY

GREECE: L. Beauchet, *Histoire du droit privé de la République athénienne* ii (1897); A. Calderini, *Manomissione e condizioni dei liberti in Grecia* (1908); R. Taubenschlag, *Sav. Zeitschr.* (1930; papyri).
ROME: W. W. Buckland, *The Roman Law of Slavery* (1908), a standard work; A. M. Duff, *Freedmen in the Early Roman Empire* (1928); H. Lévy-Bruhl, *Quelques problèmes du très ancien droit romain* (1934); S. Brassloff, *Sozialpolitische Motive in der römischen Rechtsentwicklung* (1933); W. L. Westermann, art. 'Sklaverei' in *PW* Suppl. vi.   A. B.

SLAVES. In general the ancient world assumed slavery and seldom questioned its moral justification or economic utility. The State concerned itself little with slavery as such, though it defined specific rights; literature has little to say directly. In the study of slavery it is important (1) to observe the perpetual implicit conflict between the view that the slave is a chattel and that a slave is also a man, (2) to banish all associations clinging to the word slave from later history, (3) to note the steps in the development of slavery which prove that ultimately slavery paid only in so far as the condition of the slave approximated to that of the free man—which is the negation of slavery.

I. GREEK SLAVES

2. In the Homeric age slaves (δμῶες, δμωαί: δοῦλος only in *Il*. 3. 409, *Od*. 4. 12) were few, even in the richest families. They were acquired in war, though often the men were ransomed and the women and children spared, or by purchase (for prices, see *Il*. 23. 705, *Od*. 1. 430) or by piracy. Much household work was done by the family or free servants (ἀμφίπολοι, *Od*. 9. 206, though the word does not always imply freedom) and the hard work in the fields by hired labourers (θῆτες). Women were put to spin and weave; they often became the concubines of their masters, the child of master and slave being free (*Od*. 14. 200 f.). Though the slave was dependent on his master, his lot was not unhappy. There was no distinction between the work of slave and free; the lot of the free labourer, not the slave, is taken by Odysseus as the less enviable (*Od.* 11. 489).

3. The steps from Homeric to fifth-century slavery are obscure. After the self-sufficing patriarchal economy of the Homeric age, increasing wealth demanded more help in the household; the sale of the produce led to the development of industry and the investment of money in slaves. The cities of Asia Minor developed industry and with it slavery; Chios became a slave market. From such beginnings slavery spread, reaching some States early, others, e.g. Boeotia, Locris, Phocis, about the fourth century, as economic conditions demanded. Periander (c. 600 B.C.) regulated the extent of slavery, probably to prevent the growth of a leisured class. Solon's abolition of the right to sell self or children lasted into later times and was accepted widely outside Athens. The law of Gortyn has extensive legislation on the conditions of slavery.

4. After 500 B.C. the number of slaves greatly increased and their proportion to free men rose. The sources of slavery were (i) birth; (ii) exposure of a child and its rescue: probably few exposed children were saved, though later drama and papyri mention rescue; (iii) piracy; (iv) war and the selling of captives. Phrygia, Lydia, Caria, Paphlagonia, Thrace, Scythia were the chief markets. In a sale in 414 B.C. the prices range from about 70 to 300 *drachmae* (*IG²* i. 329). The usual word for a slave is δοῦλος: ἀνδράποδον is juristic; οἰκέτης, θεράπων, παῖς, are also loosely used. The number of slaves in Attica c. 430 B.C. has been estimated at 115,000 out of a total population of 315,000, and in Athens and Piraeus at 70,000 out of 155,000 (Gomme; see bibl.). Nicias is said to have had 1,000 slaves (Xen. *Vect.* 4. 14), but about 50 was perhaps the number employed by a rich man. Slaves were employed (i) by the State (δημόσιοι) in Athens and elsewhere, as servants of officials and the βουλή, and as police (Σκυθαί or τοξόται); they were paid a daily wage and could move about freely: after manumission they became full citizens; (ii) as ἱερόδουλοι: these were not common in Greece; (iii) as household slaves or as παιδαγωγοί, porters, etc.; (iv) in business or shops, or in professions (doctors, musicians, etc.). Often they were μισθοφοροῦντες or χωρὶς οἰκοῦντες, handing over their profits to their owners or working on a percentage basis; (v) on the land, but these were not as common as (vi) workers in the mines, e.g. at Laurium, where thousands of miners were employed. While healthy conditions were impossible in mines, the slaves were not treated as cruelly as those employed by the Ptolemies in Egypt or in the stone quarries at Syracuse. A miner cost about 180 *drachmae*.

5. After 400 B.C. industrial slaves increased, and their price rose. Employers often shared work with their slaves and factories were not large. Demosthenes' father employed twenty or thirty slaves in an arms factory and twenty in a bed factory.

6. Alexander's conquests did not increase slavery. In the Hellenistic age industry declined in Greece and free labour could perform most of the work, though slaves in industry were numerous in Asia. In Ptolemaic Egypt there was little agricultural slavery, and little domestic slavery except at Alexandria.

7. The Greek slave was not distinguished in dress from the free man (as vase-paintings show). Temples and religious rites were open to him, but not the palaestra or Ecclesia. Attic tragedy and comedy show human and friendly relations between slave and free man. From the third century Stoicism did something to improve the position of the slave through the doctrine of the brotherhood of man.

II. ROMAN SLAVES

8. Roman slavery was more extensive and elaborate than Greek. The chief sources of slaves were: (i) Capture in war. Prisoners were sold *sub hasta* or *sub corona*, e.g. after the siege of Veii, the northern campaigns of Marius, the Mithridatic wars, and Caesar's Gallic wars. Cicero treated the selling of slaves as a matter of course (*Att.* 5. 20), and in Imperial times enslavement on a large scale was known, as, e.g., of the Jews by Titus and Hadrian. Asiatic slaves probably reached Rome after the campaigns against Antiochus in 189 B.C. (ii) Piracy and brigandage, which became more profitable as wars became rarer and slaves more valuable. (iii) Exposure of children. This is a commonplace of Roman comedy. But the law-books and papyri show it existed; the law was in favour of liberty if free birth could be proved. (iv) Sale of children. Perhaps this was theoretically permitted (Cic. *Caecin.* 34) in the Republic, but the right is denied in Paul. 5. 1. 1. Sale of self was not valid, but might occur. (v) Enslavement for serious crime; *servi poenae* worked in mines and quarries. (vi) Birth. The child of a slave woman was usually a slave. The slave born in the household (*verna*) became increasingly common as the supply of prisoners diminished. But increase in *vernae* implied family life for the slave, and so conditions of slavery were much modified.

9. Slaves were drawn from all nationalities, but chiefly from the east Mediterranean. In the last two centuries of the Republic large slave-markets were established, e.g. at Delos, which distributed numbers of Asiatics, Syrians, Jews, Greeks, Egyptians. Many of the slaves were skilled and educated, often beyond their masters. Slaves captured in the north and west (e.g. Dacia, Moesia, Germany, Gaul) were rougher, and were generally employed in manual work.

10. The prices of slaves varied greatly with the qualifications of the slave and the state of the market. Prices given in Plautus are not easy to evaluate, and in the literature extravagant prices are generally quoted. Columella (3. 3. 8) gives 8,000 sesterces as a reasonable price for a skilled vine-dresser. Other prices include 8,000 sesterces for an accomplished young slave (Horace, *Ep.* 2. 2. 5) and 100,000 for *servi litterati* (Seneca, *Ep.* 27. 5; cf. Martial 1. 58. 1; 2. 63. 1); Horace also cites 500 *drachmae* (c. 2000 sesterces) for a slave. Papyri give various prices.

11. The main types of employment were: (i) In the household (*familia urbana*). In small households two or three performed all the work; in larger houses learned and professional slaves (doctors, etc.) were employed, specialists ministered to every luxury, and large numbers were maintained for display. (ii) In business and industry, sometimes as an extension of household service, sometimes independently. Slaves worked with their craftsman master or were put in charge of shops or workshops, often holding very responsible positions and being correspondingly well rewarded. (iii) On the land (*familia rustica*) as herdsmen, farm labourers, or bailiffs. In Republican Italy gangs of slave herdsmen worked under very primitive conditions: Cato said it was cheaper to work such slaves to death and to replace them than to treat them well. But in farming slavery was gradually found (see, e.g., Columella) to be expensive and inefficient, and it succeeded on the land only when conditions of life for a slave approached those of a free man. The *ergastula* (slave-barracks) therefore became rare and disappeared. (iv) In the public service of the State or township, particularly in the early Empire: such service gave superior social and legal status and carried a salary. The work was such as would now be carried out by some of the higher and all the lower branches of the Civil Service.

12. The number of slaves in Rome is difficult to assess. Modern estimates suggest 520,000 free to 280,000 slave (Beloch), 780,000 to 200,000 (Kahrstedt).

13. In the early days of slavery there was merciless exploitation, and in the early Empire cases of grossest cruelty occur, and the waste of life in the gladiatorial shows is notorious. But kindliness and affection are common. Though Cicero speaks kindly of slaves, there is clearly for him a gulf between slave and free. Pliny was a kindly master (see *Ep.* 1. 4; 2. 6; 2. 17; 8. 16; 8. 24). The literature of the Empire shows a growing humanity towards slaves, while hundreds of inscriptions testify to a very tolerable life for them. Family life for slaves was reckoned on (*see* CONTUBERNIUM) and protection of life and property was assured (*see* PECULIUM). A very extensive body of law testifies to the increasing care for the slave. Even though slavery might be compulsion, it was often an initiation into a higher culture. To this changed attitude Stoicism contributed much (cf. Seneca, *Ep.* 47).

14. Through intermarriage between slaves of different nationality and through marriage of slaves or freedmen with the free population, slavery contributed to the fusion of races, with its attendant mixture of culture and stock; in this some historians have seen a cause of the decay of the Empire.

See further s.v. FREEDMEN ; SERFS.

BIBLIOGRAPHY

GENERAL: H. Wallon, *Histoire de l'esclavage dans l'antiquité* (1879); E. Meyer, 'Die Sklaverei im Altertum' in *Kleine Schriften* (1910), 169 ff.; W. L. Westermann, s.v. 'Sklaverei' in *PW* Suppl. vi (1935), 894–1068.
GREEK: T. D. Seymour, *Life in the Homeric Age* (1907); A. Lang, *The World of Homer* (1910); R. J. G. Mayor in *Comp. Greek Stud.*; M. N. Tod in *CAH* v, pp. 7–11 and bibliography, pp. 493–4; A. E. Zimmern, *Greek Commonwealth*[5], (1931), part iii, chs. 7, 15, 16; A. E. Zimmern, *Solon and Croesus* (1928), 105–63; G. Glotz, *Ancient Greece at Work* (1926), esp. pp. 192–219; A. W. Gomme, *The Population of Athens* (1933); M. Cary, *A History of the Greek World from 323 to 146 B.C.* (1932); W. W. Tarn, *Hellenistic Civilization* (1929).
ROMAN: Becker and Göll, *Gallus* ii (1881), 115–86; J. Marquardt, *Das Privatleben der Römer*, ch. 4; G. Boissier, *La Religion romaine*[3] (1884) ii, ch. 4; W. Warde Fowler, *Social Life at Rome in the Age of Cicero* (1910), 204–36; R. H. Barrow, *Slavery in the Roman Empire* (1928; with bibliography which applies also to Republic). *See also* SLAVERY, LAW OF; FREEDMEN.   R. H. B.

SMYRNA (Σμύρνα or Ζμύρνα), a city on the west coast of Asia Minor at the head of the gulf into which flows the Hermus, the natural outlet of the trade of the Hermus valley and within easy reach of the Maeander valley, for whose trade it competed with Miletus and Ephesus. 'Old' (or 'Aeolian') Smyrna lay at the north-eastern corner of the gulf; it was conquered by Ephesus and Colophon and became a member of the Ionian Confederacy *c.* B.C. 688. After its capture by Alyattes of Lydia in 627 Smyrna ceased for 300 years to exist as a city; it was refounded on its present site around Mount Pagus by Antigonus and Lysimachus after Alexander's capture of Sardes, and at once became one of the chief cities of Asia. Throughout the Roman period it was famous for its wealth, its fine buildings, and its devotion to science and medicine. It sided with Rome against Mithridates, and in the Imperial period owed much to Roman favour. It was made a 'temple-warden' (νεωκόρος) in the imperial cult by Tiberius and was restored after its destruction by earthquakes in A.D. 178 and 180 by Marcus Aurelius. It was one of the 'Seven Churches' of the Apocalypse.

C. J. Cadoux, *Ancient Smyrna* (1938).   W. M. C.

SMYRNA (poem), *see* ZMYRNA.

SNAKES, SACRED, *see* SERPENTS.

SOCII. The Roman confederation consisted, apart from Latini (q.v.), of the *socii Italici* and allies from beyond Italy. The Italian peoples—Etruscan, Umbrian, Sabellian, and Greek—were allied to Rome by formal treaties, either *foedus aequum* or *foedus iniquum* (*see* FOEDUS). The frequent revolts of the allies led to the common substitution of the latter for the former type. Such allies provided Rome with troops *e formula togatorum*—the Greeks giving sailors for the fleet—both in defensive and offensive wars, and were bound in general to respect the dignity of Rome. Otherwise they were sovereign peoples, but tended in the second century B.C. to fall under the general supervision of Rome, until their autonomy became in practice limited. The allies sometimes imitated Roman institutions, notably at Bantia in Bruttium, which romanized its constitution (*see* MEDDIX), while Rome occasionally granted them certain privileges of the Latins, chiefly *commercium, conubium,* or *ius exsilii*. But generally the *socii Italici* differed from Rome and the Latins in language, custom, and laws, and being less privileged than the Latins felt more deeply the deterioration in the Roman attitude, which led to the Social War. This was fought in the defence of local liberty and personal equality over against the abuse of the unrestricted *imperium* by Roman magistrates, claims finally met by the grant of Roman citizenship under the Julian and Plautian laws of 90–89 B.C. (*see* CAESAR 2; PLAUTIUS 1).

From early times Rome had allies outside Italy, notably Carthage and Massilia. After 200 B.C. the number of these *civitates foederatae* rapidly increased. Greek city-states, confederations, and kings became allies, normally by *foedus aequum*. With Rome's rise to world power the position of these *foederati* deteriorated, till they became merely the most highly privileged class of provincial communities, though in theory their rights depended upon a bilateral agreement. They were never included in the *formula togatorum*, although they sometimes provided auxiliary troops, cavalry, or light-armed, nor did they normally receive the social *iura*, except occasionally *ius exsilii*. But they were immune from interference by provincial governors and in internal affairs were in practice freer than the Italian allies, notably in the right of coinage. *Foederati* did not commonly survive in the Western Provinces; for when they rebelled, Rome reduced them to the status either of ordinary provincial communities, *stipendiarii*, or of *civitates liberae*. The latter originally were the Greek States declared free by Flamininus in 196 B.C. Their freedom depended upon a revocable decision of Rome. This 'freedom' later became a substitute for or modification of direct provincialization, as in Macedon (167 B.C.), and Africa (145). Special conditions added to the declaration secured for Rome the substantial advantages—notably the payment of tribute—without the burden of provincial government. Such free States were also known as *socii*, or *socii et amici populi Romani*, terms also applied to the ordinary provincial subjects of Rome. In the Ciceronian age *socius* came to mean any community which had been received *in fidem populi Romani*.

ANCIENT SOURCES: Livy, Polybius, Cicero (esp. *pro Balbo*) *passim,* and many inscriptions in *CIL, SIG, OGI*.
MODERN LITERATURE: Inside Italy: R. L. Beaumont, *JRS* xxix (Carthaginian treaty); K. Beloch, *Der Italische Bund. Römische Geschichte*; P. Fraccaro in *Atti Congr. Int. Diritto. Rom.* 1934; A. Heuss, *Klio,* Beiheft xxxi (concerning *dediticii*); Mommsen-Marquardt, *Manuel* vi. 2 (*Röm. Staatsr.* iii. 1); A. Rosenberg, *Staat der alten Italiker* (1913). Outside Italy: above, and Abbott and Johnson, *Municipal Administration of the Roman Empire* (documents); E. W. Henze, *De Civitatibus Liberis* (1892); H. Horn, *Foederati* (Frankfurt-am-M., 1930); A. H. M. Jones, *Cities of the Eastern Provinces*; E. Taubler, *Imperium Romanum* (for the treaty forms, also Mommsen–Marquardt, i. 280–5 (*Röm. Staatsr.* i. 246); A. Heuss, *Klio* 1934); A. N. Sherwin-White, *The Roman Citizenship* (1939, esp. Part I).   A. N. S.-W.

SOCRATES (469–399 B.C.), son of Sophroniscus and Phaenarete, Athenian of the deme of Alopece. His father is said to have been a sculptor or stone-mason and was apparently reasonably well-to-do. At any rate Socrates served in the army as a hoplite, though he was reduced to poverty later. He married late in life Xanthippe, who became notorious in subsequent generations for the stories of her bad temper, though these are very likely to have been exaggerated. There is some indication that this may have been his second marriage.

2. In early life he was interested in the scientific philosophy of his time and was associated with Archelaus the physicist. It is quite likely that he attained considerable distinction in this line, though whether he was ever the head of a definite philosophical school, as has been conjectured, is extremely doubtful. But by the time at which we know most about him he had abandoned these interests and devoted himself to the work of inquiry into the right conduct of life, carried on by the familiar Socratic method of cross-questioning the people with whom he came in contact. This change of interest is probably to be dated some years before the Peloponnesian War and has been plausibly connected with the response made by the Delphic oracle to his friend Chaerephon, to the effect that no one was wiser than Socrates. Of the external events of his life we know comparatively little. He served in the army and we hear of him taking part in the fighting at Potidaea, Amphipolis, and Delium, where he gained a great reputation for courage. He found himself one of the Presidents of the Assembly at the time of the trial of the generals after Arginusae and courageously refused to put the illegal motion to the vote in spite of the fury of the multitude. After the fall of Athens we hear of him defying the orders of the Thirty Tyrants when they tried to implicate him in their misdeeds.

3. In 399 B.C. he was brought to trial before a popular jury on the charge of introducing strange gods and of corrupting the youth. There has been considerable dispute as to the precise significance of this charge. But the available evidence suggests that the accusation of introducing strange gods was never clearly formulated or pressed very hard. It may well have been put in just to create prejudice, while the real gravamen of the charge lay in the accusation of being a subversive influence on the minds of the young men. This was undoubtedly connected, whether avowedly or not, with his known friendship with some of the men who had been most prominent in attacks on democracy in Athens. After a not very conciliatory speech in his defence he was condemned to death. He refused to take advantage of a plan for his escape, made by some of his friends, and thirty days after the condemnation he drank the hemlock.

4. His general appearance and manner of life are probably more familiar to us than any figure in Greek history. He was a man of strong physique and great powers of endurance, and completely indifferent to comfort and luxury. He was remarkable for his unflinching courage, both moral and physical, and his strong sense of duty. Together with this went an extremely genial and kindly temperament and a keen sense of humour, while he was obviously a man of the greatest intellectual ability. It was the combination of these qualities which secured for him a devoted circle of friends of very varied types, from young men of good family looking forward to a public career to serious thinkers who seem to have come to him for light on the problems which interested them. His circle included both Athenians and men from other cities of Greece. Several of them became known later as founders of philosophical schools of their own representing very diverse views. Such were Plato and Antisthenes at Athens, Eucleides at Megara and, possibly, Phaedo at Elis.

5. Socrates' religious views have also been the subject of some debate. He was undoubtedly a man of strong religious sense and scrupulous in religious observances. But he is very likely to have applied the dissolvent influence of his critical method to some of the conventional religious beliefs of the time. On the other hand, there is no real evidence of definite membership of any unorthodox religious body or sect. One of the best-known things about him is the experience, which he had at intervals throughout his life, of a divine sign or warning which determined his action for him from time to time. The exact nature of this has been the subject of much discussion, but still remains a mystery.

6. The precise significance of Socrates' contribution to thought has been a matter of considerable debate in recent times. There are some who ascribe to him a great part of the positive philosophical doctrines usually associated with the name of Plato. But this does not commend itself to the majority of scholars, who accept as the literal truth the statement frequently ascribed to him by the earliest authorities that he had no set of positive doctrines to teach. None the less his influence on subsequent thought was undoubtedly very great. Later authors in ancient times represented him as being the first thinker to turn men's minds towards questions of morality and the conduct of life. This can hardly be literally true, as an interest in these matters seems to have been developing in Greece in the earliest years of his life. But he does seem to have been the first person to apply serious critical and philosophical thought to these questions, and to examine systematically the fundamental assumptions from which current discussions about conduct started. In the course of this he was the first to lay stress on the importance of systematic definition of the general terms used in discussion. In this way he may be regarded as the inspiration for the development, not only of moral philosophy, but also of logic. To understand his influence fully we have to remember both his own striking personality and the intellectual tendencies of the time. He worked in an age of widespread criticism and discussion which was beginning to produce a sceptical attitude about the foundations of morality and the possibility of knowledge alike. And the example of his strong moral sense and devotion to truth combined with his readiness or even eagerness to face squarely any criticism and discussion was what established his influence most firmly among the men of his age.

BIBLIOGRAPHY

ANCIENT SOURCES: Plato; Xenophon, *Mem., Ap., Symp.*; Aeschines Socraticus (fragments, Teubner text); Aristotle, *Metaph., Eth. Nic., Mag. Mor.* (for philosophical contribution).
MODERN AUTHORS: (a) *General*: Zeller, ii. 1⁴; Gomperz, Engl. Transl. ii; Robin; J. Burnet, *From Thales to Plato* (1914); H. Maier, *Sokrates* (1913); C. Ritter, *Sokrates* (1931); A. E. Taylor, *Socrates* (1932); A. K. Rogers, *The Socratic Problem* (1933); *PW* v A. 811.
(b) *On the Socratic controversy*, particularly relations of Socrates and Plato: A. E. Taylor, *Varia Socratica* (1911); W. D. Ross, *Aristotle's Metaphysics*, introd. ii (1924); A. Diès, *Autour de Platon* i (1927); G. C. Field, *Plato and his Contemporaries* (1930); R. Hackforth, *The Composition of Plato's Apology* (1933). G. C. F.

SODALES, 'companions' or 'associates', members of the minor priesthoods at Rome, which ranked below the *Collegia* (q.v.) and differed from them in that they acted only as a body and not as individuals. The chief of these were the Fetiales (q.v.), who had charge of the *ius fetiale* and made treaties (Liv. 1. 24) and declared war (Liv. 1. 32). Three other *sodalitates* were concerned with annual rites; the Salii (q.v.), priests of Mars, active in March and October, at the opening and closing of the campaigning season; the Luperci, executants of the ritual of the Lupercalia (q.v.) in February; and the Fratres Arvales (q.v.), celebrants of agricultural rites, associated later with the cult of the Imperial house. Besides these there were the Sodales Titii or Titienses, of whom nothing is known but their name; Roman tradition (Tac. *Ann.* 1. 54) connected them with the Sabine king Titus Tatius, some recent scholars look to the Etruscan deity Mutinus Titinius and suspect that their ritual was originally phallic. To these ancient *sodalitates* were added after the death of Augustus the Sodales Augustales, who were charged with the cult of the two Divi, Julius and Augustus; later Imperial families instituted Sodales Flaviales, Hadrianales, and Antoniniani. C. B.

SOL. The name of the Sun is given to two utterly different deities in Rome. The older is Sol Indiges, of whom we know that he had a sacrifice on 9 Aug. (Augustan calendars for that date: *Soli Indigiti in colle Quirinale*), while calendars for 11 Dec., especially the new Fasti Antiates, give AG(onium) IND(igetis). Nothing more is known with any certainty; the indication for 11 Dec. is supplemented by Lydus, *Mens.* 4. 155, p. 172. 22 Wuensch, who says that the festival was in honour of Helios. See Koch, *Gestirnverehrung im alten Italien* (1933), p. 63 ff., against Wissowa, *RK*, p. 317; but some of Koch's combinations are very hazardous, see Rose in *Harv. Theol. Rev.* xxx (1937), 165 ff. This cult was native, apparently.

Much later and certainly foreign (Syrian) was the worship of Sol Invictus, to give him his most characteristic title. Eastern sun-gods had been making their way in the west, helped no doubt by the current identification of Apollo with Helios (e.g. Horace, *Carm. Saec.* 9), for some time; but the first attempt to make the Sun's the chief worship was that of Elagabalus (218–22) (S.H.A. *Vit. Ant. Heliogab.* 6. 7 and 17. 8), who introduced the god of Emesa, whose priest and, apparently, incarnation he was, El Gabal. Elagabalus' excesses and consequent unpopularity and assassination checked the cult, but Aurelian (270–5) reintroduced a similar worship, also Oriental; he was himself the child of a priestess of the Sun (see S.H.A. *Vit. Aurel.* 5. 5 and 35. 3). This remained the chief imperial and official worship till Christianity displaced it, although the cult of the older gods, especially Jupiter, did not cease, but rather the new one was in some sort parallel to it, the Sun's clergy being called *pontifices Solis*, a significant name which was part of a policy of romanizing the Oriental god. Sol had a magnificent temple on the campus Agrippae, see Platner-Ashby, p. 491 ff. Its dedication day (*natalis*) was 25 Dec.

See Wissowa, op. cit. 365 ff.; Cumont, *Religions orientales*[4], 106 ff., and notes.   H. J. R.

SOLARIUM, *see* CLOCKS.

SOLINUS, GAIUS JULIUS, wrote (probably soon after A.D. 200) *Collectanea Rerum Memorabilium*, a geographical summary of parts of the known world, with remarks on origins, history, customs of nations, and products of countries. Almost the whole is taken from Pliny's *Natural History* and Mela without acknowledgement. There is a meagre addition about the British Isles which gives us Tanatus (*Thanet*); the stone jet, found abundantly in Britain; and the absence of snakes in Ireland. He introduced the name 'mare Mediterraneum'.

Best edition: Mommsen, 2nd ed. 1895. That of Saumaise, prefixed to his *Plinianae exercitationes* (1689), is still useful.
E. H. W.

SOLON (*c.* 640/635 to soon after 561/560 B.C.), Athenian statesman and poet, was of noble descent but of moderate means. He was prominent in the war with Megara for the possession of Salamis, urging his countrymen to renewed effort when they despaired of success (probably *c.* 600). In 594–593 (probably) he was appointed 'archon and reconciler' to terminate civil strife at Athens. At this time the nobles not only controlled the State (*see* EUPATRIDAE), but had got nearly all the land into their own hands; the poor were not only politically powerless and deprived of their lands, but many of them actually enslaved—for in hard times they were compelled to borrow from the rich, and soon the only security they could offer was that of their persons. Solon first cancelled all existing debts and mortgages, thereby freeing the peasants and their lands at a blow, and for the future forbade all borrowing on the security of the person. This reform was lasting and made an end of serfdom in Attica. Then by an alteration of the coinage and weights and measures to bring them into line with those of Euboea

and the western Greeks, and by offering citizenship to immigrant craftsmen, he greatly encouraged industry and commerce.

2. Finally he reformed the constitution. He reserved the chief offices (*see* ARCHONTES) and the Areopagus (q.v.) for the members of the highest of the four property-classes (*pentacosiomedimnoi, hippeis, zeugitai, thetes,* qq.v.), of which he was perhaps the author; but in so doing he threw them open to others than the old nobility of birth. He restricted the *thetes* to participation in the Ecclesia and the Heliaea (q.v.). But he defined the rights and duties of the Ecclesia for the first time, and, by the institution of a Boule (q.v.) of 400 to prepare business for the Ecclesia, he freed it from the control of the Areopagus. By the right of appeal to the Heliaea, he freed the individual from the unfettered power of the magistrates, and gave the people some control over them. He also issued a new and humane code of law, abolishing all Draco's laws except those of homicide, and defining the duties of the several magistrates.

3. Solon's constitutional reforms were not wholly successful: civil strife raged from 589 to 580, and internal peace was not secured till Pisistratus' final triumph. Yet his institutions remained as the basis of the State: the rights of all citizens to some share in the government had been made secure.

4. Solon travelled extensively, to Egypt, Cyprus, and probably Asia Minor, certainly after his archonship, perhaps before as well. His poems are the earliest Athenian literature, and as the work of a great public man they are unique. Though not great literature, they are fresh and direct, and reveal a transparent honesty which justifies his reputation for good faith and wisdom (see below).

Aristotle, *Ath. Pol.*, chs. 1–13; Plutarch, *Solon*. Later tradition about Solon became confused and anecdotic; but Aristotle and Plutarch preserve much good material, especially that derived from Solon's own poems. Chief modern works: F. E. Adcock, *CAH* iv, ch. 2 (with fuller bibliography); I. M. Linforth, *Solon the Athenian* (Univ. of California Publ., vol. vi (1919)); W. J. Woodhouse, *Solon the Liberator* (1938).   A. W. G.

5. SOLON'S POEMS. Solon expressed his opinions on personal and political matters in poems. He used elegiacs, in which he seems to have been influenced by Tyrtaeus, iambics, and trochaics, the traditional medium for gnomic verse. His fragments may be arranged approximately in chronological order. Frs. 12 and 13 are attributed to his early years and show the traditional aristocratic taste for pleasure. The elegy which summoned the Athenians to capture Salamis, of which eight lines survive, had originally one hundred and was admired by Plutarch (*Sol.* 8); Solon was said to have disguised himself as a herald and recited it in the agora at Athens. In it he certainly adopts a public role which recalls that of Tyrtaeus, and gives first a public warning, then a strong exhortation to the Athenians to fight. Fr. 3 is a long fragment, written before his archonship, in which he analyses the political situation and criticizes the careless presumption of the ruling class, transposes the traditional notion of ὕβρις into political life, and praises the virtues of εὐνομίη. Fr. 4, belonging to the same time, though probably not to the same poem, also attacks the arrogance and avarice of the nobles. Fr. 11, in which the political situation is compared to the sea, may belong to this period. Soon after his archonship he wrote fr. 5, in which he proclaims the impartiality of his actions and his fairness both to rich and to poor. In it he urges the populace to follow their leaders, and warns them against ὕβρις. The trochaic fr. 23 is an important defence of himself against critics who said that he should have made himself tyrant. He treats them with contempt and blames the corrupt ambitions of others. The iambics of fr. 24 belong to the same time. In them Solon answers critics who said that he did not go far enough, and claims that his work may be seen in his settlement of boundary-disputes and his liberation of the serfs. Fr. 7, to Philocyprus, is a poem of farewell to his host in Cyprus, the king of Soli, before going back to Athens (cf. Hdt. 5. 113). Fr. 9 belongs to the years after his return, before Pisistratus had made himself tyrant. Frs. 9 and 10 probably belong to the same poem. Solon foresees the coming of tyranny as a natural phenomenon whose signs are clear in the mad excitement of the people. Fr. 8 was written when this tyranny was a fact, and is addressed to those who after putting Pisistratus into power are now complaining; Solon points out that they have brought their suffering on their own heads because they have been deceived by specious words. Two important pieces are of uncertain date. Fr. 1, the longest extant fragment, is a meditative poem, addressed to the Muses, in which Solon seems to describe the different stages of ignorance in which man lives, from the criminal blindness of the wrongdoer to the deluded hopes of the trader and the partially enlightened state of the professional classes who work under the patronage of the gods. It may belong to his middle years. Fr. 19, on the stages in man's growth and decay, is a curious piece of proverbial wisdom which may belong to his old age. *See also* IAMBIC POETRY, GREEK.

TEXT: E. Diehl, *Anth. Lyr. Graec.* i. 1, 23–49.
COMMENTARY: I. M. Linforth, *Solon the Athenian* (U.S.A. 1919), 103–245.
CRITICISM: U. von Wilamowitz-Moellendorff, *Aristoteles und Athen* ii. 303–15; id., *Sappho und Simonides* (1913), 257–75; C. M. Bowra, *Early Greek Elegists* (1938), 73–104; W. Jaeger, *Solons Eunomie, Sitz. Preuss. Ak.* 1926; E. Römisch, *Studien zur älteren griechischen Elegie* (1933), 1–48, 60–81.   C. M. B.

SOPATER (Σώπατρος) of Paphos, Greek parodist and writer of *phlyakes*, *floruit* from the time of Alexander to that of Ptolemy II. Fr. 19 mentions Thibron, who put Harpalus to death in 324 B.C. S. lived in Alexandria (frs. 1, 13, 24). Fourteen titles of plays survive: three (Βακχίς, Βακχίδος μνηστῆρες, Βακχίδος γάμος) seem to form a triad, unless merely varied descriptions of the same piece; Ἱππόλυτος, Νεκυιά, Ὀρέστης are burlesques of mythology or tragedy (cf. MIDDLE COMEDY). From Γαλάται, *The Gauls*, fr. 6 (12 vv.)—the longest extant *phlyax*-fragment—contains raillery of the Stoics; this passage, far removed from the buffoonery of the original *phlyakes*, approaches the spirit and language of Attic Comedy.

CGF 192 ff.   W. G. W.

SOPHAENETUS of Stymphalus (*fl. c.* 400 B.C.), author of an *Anabasis* of Cyrus and one of the generals who led the Greek army back to the Black Sea. Where Diodorus' account of the expedition differs from Xenophon's, we may suppose that his source, Ephorus, drew his divergent information from S.

FGrH ii. 109; *FHG*. ii. 74.   G. L. B.

SŌPHILUS, Middle Comedy poet, from Sicyon or from Thebes (Suidas), towards the end of the period. Ἀνδροκλῆς is named after the usurer ridiculed by Menander (*Sam.* 261), and only one comedy has a mythological title (Τυνδάρεως ἢ Λήδα).

FCG iii. 581 ff.; *CAF* ii. 444 ff.   W. G. W.

SOPHISTIC, SECOND, see DECLAMATIO, para. 1.

SOPHISTS. The word σοφιστής does not appear to have been in use before the fifth century B.C. In its earliest use it simply means a wise man or a man skilled at any particular kind of activity. From the first there is, however, perhaps some suggestion of a man who made a special job of being wise, and it gradually came to be specially, though never exclusively, applied to members of a particular profession. This was the profession of itinerant teachers who went from city to city giving instruction for a fee. The subjects of instruction varied somewhat in content, but always had a

relation to the art of getting on, or of success in life. Some Sophists, such as Protagoras, claimed to teach 'virtue', which was almost equivalent to efficiency in the conduct of life. Others, like Gorgias and his successors, confined themselves to the teaching of oratory, which in democratic cities was one of the chief roads to success. Instruction in this was, indeed, included in the teaching even of those who made the wider claim. We hear of other aspects of their teaching, such as the system of memory-training ascribed to Hippias, but all have reference to this central practical aim. Their nearest modern parallel is to be found in the numerous institutions at the present day which advertise their ability to train people for success in business, or in life in general. Their activities met a very real demand for higher education, and the leading Sophists enjoyed great success and amassed large fortunes. *See also* EDUCATION, III. 2.

It is important to remember that the Sophists were a profession and not a school of thought, though some of them, such as Protagoras, taught definite philosophic views. But the very nature of the profession tended to produce a certain attitude of mind, which placed emphasis on material success and on the ability to argue for any point of view irrespective of its truth. The general influence of the Sophists was therefore necessarily in the direction of scepticism both about the claims of reasoning to arrive at the truth and about the claims of any moral code to determine one's conduct. At the best they taught no more than uncritical acceptance of the conventional moral code of one's particular society. At the worst, in the teaching, for instance, of men like Antiphon and Thrasymachus, they encouraged a cynical disbelief in all moral restraints on the pursuit of selfish, personal ambitions. Some of the early Sophists were men of high character and unblemished reputation. But others were not so, and there were apparently good grounds in their activities for the undesirable associations which the word came to have and which have passed over into its English derivative.

Under the Roman Empire, particularly from the second century A.D. onwards, the word acquired a more specialized meaning and became restricted to teachers and practitioners of rhetoric, which by this time was tending to become a purely literary exercise practised for its own sake. It was, however, a very popular pursuit, and successful practitioners in it enjoyed a high reputation. It became the most valued part of higher education, and teachers of rhetoric were endowed at many of the great centres of population. In later centuries the movement tended to become specially associated with paganism and died out after the final triumph of Christianity.

Fragments in Diels, *Vorsokr.*; Zeller, i. 2⁶; Gomperz (Engl. Transl. i); Robin; J. Burnet, *From Thales to Plato* (1914); W. Jaeger, *Paideia* (Engl. Transl. 1939).
Later Sophistic: Philostratus and Eunapius, for lives of the Sophists; E. Norden, *Die antike Kunstprosa* i (1909).   G. C. F.

SOPHOCLES (1). (*See also* TRAGEDY.)

I. LIFE (*c.* 496–406 B.C.)
Sophocles, son of Sophilus, a wealthy industrialist, was born in or about 496 B.C. at Colonus (*Marm. Par.* 56 and 64), to the praise of which one of his loveliest odes is dedicated (*OC* 668 ff.). His youthful beauty and his skill in dancing and music attracted attention, and he led the paean of victory after Salamis with his lyre. His master in music was Lamprus, one of the great teachers of the old school (*Life*: cf. Plut. *De mus.* 31). His first victory in tragedy was won in 468 B.C. (*Marm. Par.* 56: *IG²* ii. 2325), when he defeated Aeschylus; Plutarch (*Cim.* 8) says that it was his first appearance as a tragic poet—this has been doubted—and that owing to the excitement of popular feeling the archon entrusted the award of the prize to Cimon and his fellow-generals.

One of his plays on this occasion was probably the *Triptolemus*. In two other early plays he made his mark —as a ball-player in the character of Nausicaa (in the Πλύντριαι ἢ Ναυσικάα) and as a player on the lyre in that of Thamyras (in the play of that name); but the weakness of his voice caused him to give up acting in person (*Life*). His early life coincided with the expansion of the Athenian Empire, and he himself took an honourable share in the duties of citizenship. In 443/442 he was *Hellenotamias* or imperial treasurer (*IG*² i. 202); he was elected general twice at least—in 440, when he was a colleague of Pericles in the suppression of the Samian revolt (*Life*; Plut. *Per.* 8, etc.), and later with Nicias (Plut. *Nic.* 18); and after the Sicilian disaster he was one of the πρόβουλοι appointed to deal with the crisis (Arist. *Rh.* 3. 18, etc.). Whether he owed his appointment in 440 to the success of the *Antigone* may be doubted. There is a pleasant record of his conversations with Ion at Chios in the course of the Samian Expedition (Ath. 13, p. 603 ff.), and two other friends of Cimon are connected with him in different ways—Polygnotus, who depicted him in the *Stoa Poikile* holding the lyre, and Archelaus the philosopher, to whom he wrote an elegiac poem. He also wrote (about 441 B.C.) a poem to Herodotus, with whom there are a number of points of contact in his work (Plut. *An seni* 3). He was priest of the healing deity Amynos, Alcon, or Halon (the exact name is doubtful) and made his own house a place of worship for Asclepius until the temple built for him was ready (Plut. *Num.* 3, *Etym. Magn.* s.v. Δεξιών); in recognition of this he was honoured as a hero with the title Δεξιών after his death. He also composed a paean to Asclepius. These and other indications suggest that he accepted the religion of his day without misgivings, just as in other ways he showed himself a healthy minded and normal, as well as a distinguished, Athenian, and he is said to have refused all invitations to leave Athens for the courts of kings (*Life*, cf. fr. 789). His interest in the theory and criticism as well as in the writing of poetry was shown in the composition of a prose work *On the Chorus*, in the story of his discussion of poetical expressions with Ion (Ath. loc. cit.), and in his founding of a literary club (the θίασος of the Muses). He seems to have distinguished his own conscious technique from the inspiration which carried Aeschylus away (εἰ καὶ τὰ δέοντα ποιεῖς ἀλλ' οὐκ εἰδώς γε ποιεῖς). He died late in 406, and Aristophanes in the next year summed up his genial and kindly temperament in the line ὁ δ' εὔκολος μὲν ἐνθάδ', εὔκολος δ' ἐκεῖ (*Ran.* 82). It was characteristic that a few months before his death he appeared with his chorus and actors in mourning for Euripides at the *proagon* (q.v.) before the Great Dionysia. Phrynichus (the Comic poet) spoke of him as εὐδαίμων ἀνὴρ καὶ δεξιός, who died a good death and was taken from the evil to come.

He is said to have composed (probably) 123 plays, and with these he won 24 victories, which means that 96 of his plays were successful; in his other contests he was placed second, but never third.

II. Works

Sophocles, according to Plut. *De prof. virt.* 7, distinguished three periods in his own style: first the 'bombastic' style (ὄγκος) of Aeschylus; secondly, a harsh and artificial style (πικρὸν καὶ κατάτεχνον) of his own, and thirdly, the best type of style and most suited for the expression of character (ἠθικώτατον καὶ βέλτιστον). The extant plays, the earliest of which must fall about twenty-five years after his first appearance, seem all to belong to the third period, though the fragments of some lost early plays recall in matter and vocabulary some of the characteristics of Aeschylus, and some critics have professed to find traces of the second style (whatever Plutarch's words may mean) in the *Ajax* and *Antigone*.

The latter was probably produced in 441; the *Ajax* is probably rather earlier; for the *Oedipus Tyrannus* a year soon after 430 seems probable, and the *Trachiniae* may belong to the same period, though the indications are very uncertain. It is disputed whether the *Electra* preceded or followed Euripides' *Electra* (413), and it is variously placed by scholars between 418 and 410. The *Philoctetes* was produced in 409 (*Argum.*), and the *Oedipus Coloneus* posthumously in 401 (*Argum.*). The date of the satyric *Ichneutae* is uncertain (see Powell and Barber, *New Chapters* iii. 93 f.). Of the lost plays, the *Telepheia*, if it was in fact a Trilogy dealing with the story of Telephus (and consisting perhaps of the *Aleadae*, the *Mysi*, and the Ἀχαιῶν σύλλογος), is likely to have been an early group (see ibid. iii. 68 ff.). More than one-third of the known titles are those of plays taken from the Trojan cycle of legend (including that of the house of Atreus); the remainder cover a wide range; about twenty are those of satyric plays.

III. Character of his Work. (*See also* TRAGEDY.)

1. The chief changes made by Sophocles in the form of tragedy were the discontinuance of composition in trilogies, the increase of the number of the chorus from twelve to fifteen, and the introduction of the third actor and of scene-painting (Arist. *Poet.* 4). The abandonment of the trilogy-form involved a great reduction in the proportion of the play allotted to the chorus, the confinement of long descriptive passages mainly to the messengers' speeches (with which Greek tragedy seldom dispensed), and greater rapidity in the progress of the action.

2. The third actor is not used in the *Ajax* with the same freedom as in the later plays. His introduction went with the increasing concentration of interest upon the persons taking part in the action; the chorus, though intimately concerned and often closely attached to one of these persons, no longer had the same importance as in Aeschylus, and if still a religious, was no longer a dramatic, necessity. The poet's thought was mainly brought out by the course of events, though it might also be expressed in the reflections of the chorus. These are generally such as a normal spectator—religious, sympathetic, and right-minded—might make at each turn in the action—never lacking in dramatic appropriateness, but only exceptionally prophetic or philosophical. Sophocles employs a joyful song of the chorus with special skill at moments of relief or expectancy, or before the disaster which it darkens by contrast. The structure of many of the choral odes shows consummate art: that of the great Coloneus ode (*OC* 668 ff.)—to take the most striking instance—is a marvel of intricate symmetry. The language of the odes, where it is continuous and not broken up by dialogue, is always of surpassing beauty.

3. In the non-choral parts of the play Sophocles shows himself absolute master of all the possibilities of dialogue in every variety of tone, though the passages in which he uses the trochaic tetrameter in excited dialogue are very few and brief. In the setting out of the arguments in a dispute he had plainly taken advantage of the rhetorical teaching and practice of his day. Some of his characters such as Odysseus in the *Philoctetes* and Creon in the *Oedipus Coloneus*) recall the qualities of the typical 'sophist', as (e.g.) Plato saw him, and the scepticism expressed by others (for instance, Iocasta and Hyllus) in regard to gods and oracles and seers was probably fashionable in some intellectual circles, though in Sophocles it shows itself only to be confuted by the course of events. The use of moral and sententious maxims in the *Ajax* and *Antigone* is sometimes criticized as excessive, though it is, as a rule, thoroughly in character; in the later plays the use of such sentiments is as skilful and convincing as that of the other elements in

dialogue. Sophocles is reported to have had his moments of bathos (e.g. [Longinus], *Subl.* 33, etc.), but there is little trace of them in the extant plays.

4. The structure of the plays shows two principal types. The *Ajax, Antigone,* and *Trachiniae* fall each into two parts; the fate of the hero or heroine is accomplished in the first; in the second a consequential issue is brought to its conclusion—the honour to be paid to Ajax, the punishment of Creon, the death of Heracles. In the other plays the single plot covers the whole play, though the *Oedipus Coloneus* is perhaps not exactly in the shape in which Sophocles would have left it had he lived. But there is nothing in any play which is (in Aristotle's phrase) 'episodic' or irrelevant. Each stage in the action is linked with what has gone before by what Aristotle calls a necessary or probable connexion, even if the connexion is only revealed by a startling περιπέτεια or a recognition-scene, such as Sophocles employs to heighten the 'pity and fear' which his tragedies evoke in the highest degree. It is in keeping with the close relevance of every scene and word that Sophocles almost entirely avoids allusions to contemporary events, though the discussions of the rights of the individual against government and the assertion of a higher law than that of the State may have had a special meaning for his own day. The prologues (which are all in dialogue, with or without a longer opening speech) are all essential to the action, not (as sometimes in Euripides) almost outside it, and the arrangement of scenes and choral odes often shows a symmetry which, though not mathematically exact, is evidently deliberate. The regular alternation of *episodia* and *stasima* (see TRAGEDY) is often varied with good effect. The compression of events off the stage during a choral ode or a scene is never such as to rouse any sense of improbability. In a very few places— the opening speech of Deianeira in the *Trachiniae,* the monody of *Electra* at the beginning of the play, the appearance of Heracles *ex machina* in the *Philoctetes*— Sophocles may owe something to Euripides. The main interest of Sophocles is in the display of noble characters —not faultless, but nearer to the ideal than ordinary men and women, ὅμοιοι ἡμῖν ἀλλὰ καλλίους (Arist. *Poet.* 25)—confronted with some terrible crisis or subjected to some almost unendurable strain. They suffer out of proportion to any fault in themselves which may have contributed to the disaster, but without losing their nobility. There has generally been some fault—some hastiness or pride or excess of confidence, some breach of αἰδώς or σωφροσύνη, which makes the suffering, if not deserved, yet explicable and not wholly inappropriate. There may also have been some hereditary doom or some divine anger working itself out (cf. *Ant.* 582 f., 593 ff.), or some oracle which must be fulfilled, but Sophocles is never greatly concerned about the justification of such influences; he accepts them as part of the story or of the universal order, and throws his whole attention on to the characters affected by them, showing how they meet and surmount the suffering brought upon them. The tragedy of each character lies almost wholly within human life, and is not viewed, as by Aeschylus, against an ever-present background of divine and demoniacal influences; nor has he any doubt of human free-will. His view of life was that of the normal healthy-minded Athenian. He assumed the justice of the gods—the upholders of human piety and morality, and the veracity of the oracles (which could no more be questioned than are laws of nature to-day) and of the seers who revealed the divine will; but he also saw that life contained much unhappiness, falling often upon men and women relatively innocent, and this, too, he accepted as a fact. Sophocles expresses as few poets have done the sadness of the suffering incidental to the life of man; he even depicts men falling by an irony of fate into the very calamity which they are striving to avoid and bringing about the

exact reverse of their good intentions. Yet he is no pessimist. For either (1) the suffering, even if in excess of what is called guilt, may yet be the fulfilment of a law, whether it is brought about by some ὕβρις or excess, as with Ajax and Heracles (and even with Oedipus), or is the consequence of something in the past which cannot be undone; or (2) the man who suffers in this way is not a whit the worse man for it; Ajax is still worthy of honour; Oedipus in the *Coloneus* is righteous still; or (3) the suffering when accomplished is seen to have been worth while; Antigone vindicates the higher law for which she dies; the character of Oedipus has been subdued and purified; Philoctetes is made the means of a great deliverance. The agony has seldom been wasted, and when it is possible to see law, reason, and purpose, there is no pessimism.

5. The qualities inherent in each character are drawn out in a series of scenes in which they are confronted with characters of varying types, often contrasting sharply with their own and reacting quite differently to events. Their moods may change as the situation changes, but there is nowhere any real inconsistency. Not only the heroes, but all the persons of the drama, are drawn with the same perfect art; they are real persons, not mere types, but not more minutely analysed than the part they have to play demands. Perhaps the characters who come nearest to being merely typical are the Creons of the *Antigone* and the *Oedipus Coloneus*—the 'tyrant' as he was conventionally regarded—but even these are strongly individualized; both contrast strongly with the balanced reasonableness of Creon in the *Oedipus Tyrannus.*

6. In language Sophocles allows himself much freedom. He uses more words and forms taken from living literary Ionic than Aeschylus, and fewer Aeolic and merely archaic forms. It is said that 1,296 words appear first in his works, though it cannot be assumed that they were all coined by him. He employs a large number of slight variations of the ordinary forms of words and many unusual constructions, and he has a few mannerisms (e.g. certain kinds of redundant expression); his metaphors and other figures show perhaps less imagination, but also less obscurity, than are sometimes found in Aeschylus. It is seldom that his meaning is not perfectly clear or his expression anything but adequate and beautiful. He employs with almost terrifying effect what is called irony, whereby words used by a speaker in their ordinary and obvious meaning are charged with a more sinister meaning for those who know what the speaker cannot know.

7. It is a commonplace of both ancient and modern critics to liken Sophocles to Homer, on account not only of his choice of many subjects from the Trojan cycle, but also of his adherence to Homer in the character-drawing of his heroes and in some of their speeches, in his use of very many expressions and favourite idioms borrowed from or clearly modelled on the Homeric, and above all in the spirit of his work, in which the story is presented, as in Homer, for its own sake and for its human interest, not as the vehicle of a theory (see M. Lechner, *De Sophocle poeta* Ὁμηρικωτάτῳ, 1859).

BIBLIOGRAPHY

LIFE AND WORKS: A. E. Haigh, *Tragic Drama of the Greeks* (1896); M. Pohlenz, *Die griechische Tragödie* (1930); T. von Wilamowitz, *Die dramatische Technik des Sophokles* (1917); H. Weinstock, *Sophokles* (1931); T. B. L. Webster, *Introduction to Sophocles* (1936); A. von Blumenthal, *Sophokles* (1936); C. M. Bowra, *Sophoclean Tragedy* (1944).

TEXT: O.C.T. (A. C. Pearson, 1923).

COMMENTARIES: L. Campbell (1879–81); R. C. Jebb (each play separately with translation, 1883 onwards; *Ant., OT,* and *OC* in 3rd ed., *Phil.* in 2nd ed.); Fragments, ed. A. C. Pearson (1917); *Oedipus Tyrannus,* J. T. Sheppard (1920). See also C. Robert, *Oidipus* (1915). *Lexicon Sophocleum,* F. Ellendt (2nd ed. by H. Genthe (1867–72)).

TRANSLATIONS: Prose: R. C. Jebb. Verse: A. S. Way (1909), and G. Murray, *Oedipus Tyrannus* (1911). A. W. P.-C.

SOPHOCLES (2) the younger, son of Ariston and grandson of the great Sophocles, produced his grandfather's *Oedipus Coloneus* in 401 B.C., and plays of his own from 396 onwards. The numbers of his plays and victories are uncertain (Suidas s.v., Arg. Soph. *OC*).

SOPHONISBA (*Sophoniba* Livy; *Σοφωνίβα* Appian; the correct name is Saphanba'al), daughter of Hasdrubal (q.v. 3); she married Syphax, whom she thus won over to the Carthaginian cause. When Masinissa and Laelius overthrew Syphax (203 B.C.) Sophonisba took poison which according to the romantic story (Livy 30. 12–15) was sent to her by Masinissa, now enamoured of her and unable by any other means to save her from captivity at Rome. Details of her story (e.g. that before her marriage to Syphax she had been betrothed to Masinissa) may be false, but the outline need not be questioned.

H. H. S.

SOPHRON (*Σώφρων*) (c. 470–400 B.C.), Syracusan writer of mimes. His mimes were divided according to subject-matter into *ἀνδρεῖοι* and *γυναικεῖοι*. Some 170 short fragments remain, mostly cited by grammarians to illustrate the Doric dialect. Of the *ἀνδρεῖοι* may be mentioned *Θυννοθήρας* ('The Tunny-fisher') and *Ὡλιεύς* (i.e. ὁ ἁλιεύς) *τὸν ἀγρώταν* (possibly a dispute between a fisherman and a farmer); of the *γυναικεῖοι* —*Ἀκέστριαι* ('The Sempstresses'), *Συναριστῶσαι* ('Women at breakfast'), *Ταὶ γυναῖκες αἳ τὰν θεόν* (i.e. Hekate) *φαντι ἐξελᾶν* (i.e. 'The Sorceresses'). S.'s mimes were written in some kind of rhythmical prose (schol. Greg. Naz. (in Kaibel, *CGF* 153) *ῥυθμοῖς τισι καὶ κώλοις ἐχρήσατο*). Their subject-matter was the events of everyday life. S., who was probably the first writer to give literary form to the mime, was greatly admired by Plato (Ath. 11. 504 b; cf. Pl. *Resp.* 5. 451 c). Herodas possibly and Theocritus certainly owed much to him— a schol. on Theoc. 2 says that Theocritus adapted (*μεταφέρει*) one of S.'s mimes.

Kaibel, *CGF* 152 ff.; A. Olivieri, *Frammenti della Commedia Greca* (1930); P. Colombo, *Il Mimo di Sophrone e di Senarcho* (1934).

M. P.

SORANUS of Ephesus, physician under Trajan and Hadrian (98–138), studied in Alexandria and practised in Rome. He was one of the greatest physicians, a man of erudition, of objective judgement, full of love for his native Greece, critical towards the Romans of the world metropolis.

Of his books, almost twenty in number, dealing with history of medicine, terminological problems, and medicine proper, there are preserved in Greek: 1. *Γυναικεῖα* I–IV (I. Hygiene of midwife, conception, etc.; II. Childbed, care of the infant; III and IV. Pathology). 2. *Π. σημείων καταγμάτων* and *Π. ἐπιδέσμων*, fragments of a surgical treatise.

Soranus restored the Methodical school by moderating its exaggerations in the spirit of the new classical era and by harmonizing it with the tradition. Though believing in general symptoms, he did not neglect individual factors, distinguished the different forms of diseases, and observed accurately the course of an illness. A terse but excellent author, his books in Latin translations or adaptations were widely read in the Occident. *See* ANATOMY AND PHYSIOLOGY, para. 11.

TEXT: J. Ilberg, *CMG* iv (1927). The *βίος Ἱπποκράτους* spurious, L. Edelstein, *PW* Suppl. vi. 1293, s.v. 'Hippokrates'. Latin translations, Caelius Aurelianus, *De morbis acutis et chronicis* (cf. Ilberg, *Sitz. Leipz.* (1925)); Muscio, *Gynaeceia*. Ps.-Soran., see Rose, *Anecdota Graeca* ii.
LITERATURE: Survey, E. Kind, *PW* iii A. 1113. Text-history of *Gynaikeia*, Ilberg, *Abh. Sächs. Akad.* (1910). Doxography, H. Diels, *Dox. Graec.* 207, *Sitz. Berl.* (1893). Influence on Tertullian, H. Karpp, *Zeitschr. f. neutestamentl. Wiss.* (1934). Medicine, T. C. Allbutt, *Greek Medicine in Rome* (1921). L. E.

SORANUS, *see also* VALERIUS (11).

SORTES BIBLICAE, HOMERICAE, VERGILIANAE, *see* DIVINATION, para. 6.

SORTITION (*κλήρωσις*), election by lot, a method of appointing officials in Greek city-states, especially in democracies. It was based on the idea of equality. Little is known of its use except at Athens. It remains uncertain when sortition was introduced there, perhaps as early as Solon. From 487/6 B.C. the archons were appointed by lot out of nominated candidates (*πρόκριτοι*); later, this nonsensically became a double sortition. Since the archons were elected by lot, they lost political leadership. But all ordinary magistrates, a few excepted, were thus appointed; also the Council (a Prytany of fifty from each *phyle*) and the juries (by a very complicated procedure). Lot decided very many questions in political and social life. Politically, sortition entailed rotation in office, and electoral contests were avoided by it; moreover, the power of magistrates was reduced, and thus the sovereignty of the popular assembly was guaranteed. Sortition was practicable, as almost every citizen had a minimum of political experience, and nobody could be elected without having presented himself. Only oligarchs were opposed to sortition, but, except by a few critics like Socrates, it was never discussed on principle. It was, indeed, a necessary and fundamental element of the democratic Polis. But military officers and some technical (especially financial) magistracies were always appointed by voting. In later times sortition was gradually restricted.

Arist., *Ath. Pol.* T. W. Headlam, *Election by Lot at Athens* (1891, 2nd ed. 1933); V. Ehrenberg, *PW*, s.v. 'Losung'. V. E.

SOSIBIUS of Lacedaemon. In the reign of Ptolemy I (323–283 B.C.) he went to Egypt and became closely associated with the Alexandrian school. He is probably to be identified with the grammarian Sosibius *ὁ λυτικός*. Important for his studies in the history of Sparta (*Περὶ τῶν ἐν Λακεδαίμονι θυσιῶν* and *Χρόνων ἀναγραφή*).

FHG ii. 625. G. L. B.

SOSICRATES, Rhodian biographer, date uncertain. Works (*FHG* iv. 500–3): (1) *Φιλοσόφων διαδοχή*, a biographical study of various philosophers, following the teacher–pupil relation. S. used Hermippus and perhaps Satyrus. Whether he used Apollodorus is disputed: if a common source in Eratosthenes explains similarities, S. perhaps wrote the (2) *Κρητικά* (Ath. 6. 264 a; Diod. Sic. 5. 80. 4), which Apollodorus used. If S. is the Sosicrates mentioned in Timachidas (*Lind. Temp. Chron.* p. 317, Blinkenberg), he flourished 150–130 B.C.: but the identification is uncertain. F. W. W.

SOSIGENES, astronomer, earlier confused with a Stoic and a Peripatetic of the same name, was Caesar's astronomical expert in his introduction of the Julian calendar, in 47 B.C.

PW iii A. 1153.

SOSII. The Sosii are twice mentioned by Horace (*Epp.* 1. 20. 2; *A.P.* 345) as booksellers of his day; according to the scholiasts on these passages, they were two brothers.

Books (q.v.) were originally multiplied by individuals (or their slaves) making copies for private use, and this procedure remained common throughout antiquity (at no time was there any law of copyright). How far the professional production and sale of books bad developed in fifth-century Athens is uncertain: Plato (*Apol.* 26 d) makes Socrates say that a copy of Anaxagoras could sometimes be bought from the Orchestra (presumably that in the Agora) for a drachma at most, and Eupolis (Fr. 304, Kock) mentions a place 'where books are for sale'. In Hellenistic times the foundation of the great Library (*see* LIBRARIES) at Alexandria must have encouraged the development of the book-trade. At Rome professional booksellers (*librarii*, which also means 'copyists'; later *bibliopolae*), with staffs of copyists, are first mentioned in Cicero's day; many of Cicero's own works were published by Atticus, who kept a large number of slaves trained in all the operations of book-production. In Imperial times there are more frequent references in literature to professional booksellers (apparently often freedmen); e.g. Martial (1. 117. 11) describes the bookshop owned by one Atrectus in the Argiletum as having its *postes* covered with advertisements of books. There are few indications of the price of books: Book 13 of Martial was sold by the bookseller Tryphon for 4 sesterces (13. 3. 2); a handsome copy of another of his books was sold by Atrectus for 20 sesterces (1. 117. 17).

Th. Birt, *Das antike Buchwesen* (1882), Index, s.v. 'Buchhandel'; also *Kritik und Hermeneutik nebst Abriss des antiken Buchwesens* (1913), 307 ff.; Dziatzko in *PW* iii. 973 ff. (s.v. 'Buchhandel'); W. Schubart, *Das Buch bei den Griechen und Römern²* (1921), 146 ff.   W. S. W.

SOSIPATER (Σωσίπατρος), Greek comic poet: fr. 1, cookery—a sublime science. Apparently among the earlier writers of the New Comedy (v. 11 Chariades is named as living, whereas in Euphron fr. 1. 7 he appears to be dead).

FCG iv. 482 ff.; *CAF* iii. 314 ff.

SOSIPHANES of Syracuse, tragic poet, flourished about the last third of the fourth century B.C., though some date him later and there may have been two poets of the name. He is credited with seventy-three tragedies (Suidas, s.v.), and seven victories. He is included in some lists of the *Pleiad* (see TRAGEDY). A short but striking fragment on the transitoriness of human happiness survives.

TGF, 819–20.   A. W. P.-C.

SOSITHEUS, of Alexandria Troas, lived in Athens, Syracuse, and Alexandria, was a member of the *Pleiad* (see TRAGEDY), and wrote tragedies and satyric plays, including a *Daphnis or Lityerses*, in which a sarcastic reference to the Stoic Cleanthes occurred; 20 lines of this play survive, as well as a laudatory epigram on the poet by Dioscorides (*Anth. Pal.* 7. 707).

TGF, 821–4.   A. W. P.-C.

SOSIUS, GAIUS, quaestor to Antony c. 40 B.C., was appointed governor of Syria and Cilicia in 38 and captured Jerusalem in the interest of Herod in 37. Consul in 32, he joined Antony before the outbreak of war, was defeated by Agrippa in a naval engagement (31), and commanded the left wing of Antony's fleet at Actium. He was subsequently pardoned by Octavian. Sosius rebuilt the temple of Apollo near the theatre of Marcellus and took part as *quindecimvir sacris faciundis* in the Ludi Saeculares in 17 B.C.

Velleius 2. 85–6; Josephus, *AJ* 14. 15–16; Dio Cassius 49. 22—51. 2.
                                                                   G. W. R.

SOSIUS SENECIO, QUINTUS (*cos. ord.* A.D. 99, II *ord.* 107), is revealed by the convergence of casual evidence as one of the most important members of the governmental oligarchy under Trajan. Of his origin, family, and official career before the consulate nothing is recorded. The link with an influential consular (Sex. Julius Frontinus was his father-in-law) and the friendship of the new emperor explain his conspicuous advancement: Sosius and Cornelius Palma are the first pair of *consules ordinarii* appointed by Trajan. The date of his second consulate, held with the great Licinius Sura as colleague, and the honour of a public statue (Dio Cass. 68. 12. 2), support the conjecture that he held a high command in the Second Dacian War (A.D. 105–6). Sympathetic, like others of his class and rank (for example, C. Minicius Fundanus, *cos.*

suff. 107), to the pursuits of philosophy and letters, Sosius might be claimed for a representative figure in a 'proto-Antonine' period of imperial civilization—Plutarch of Chaeronea enjoyed his friendship and commemorated it by the dedication of several works.

Sosius did not leave a son to perpetuate the family, but his daughter married Q. Pompeius Falco (*cos. suff.* 108), and that line is prominent in the Antonine aristocracy, with manifold connexions and a much-advertised pedigree, as witness the polyonymous consul of A.D. 169 (Dessau, *ILS* 1104), who has thirty-four names, apart from *praenomina*.

PIR, S 560; E. Groag, *PW* iii A. 1180 ff.   R. S.

SOSPITA, see JUNO.

SOSTRATUS, surgeon and zoologist, probably practised in Alexandria after 30 B.C. His medical works dealt chiefly with gynaecology. In zoology he perhaps ranks next after Aristotle among the Greeks. Works: Περὶ ζῴων or Περὶ φύσεως ζῴων; Περὶ βλητῶν καὶ δακέτων. Aelian and the scholia to Nicander preserve much information about his zoological works.

PW iii A. 1203.   W. D. R.

SOSUS of Pergamum, an artist of the Hellenistic period, was memorable for two mosaic pavements: the *asarotos oikos*, which represented a floor strewn with the unswept débris of a banquet; and a panel (*emblema*) depicting birds drinking from a wine-cup. Roman copies of these two works have been recognized among mosaic pavements preserved in Italian museums.

Pliny, *HN* 36. 184; E. Pfuhl, *Malerei und Zeichnung der Griechen* (1923), §§ 862, 864.   F. N. P.

SOSYLUS of Lacedaemon, a freedman of Hannibal who wrote a methodical and impartial history of the latter (Περὶ Ἀννίβου πράξεων) towards the end of the third century B.C. One of the more important sources of Polybius, whose harsh verdict on him (Polyb. 3. 20. 1–5) must be toned down in the light of a recent papyrus fragment from his fourth book.

FGrH 176; *FHG* iii. 99.   G. L. B.

SOTADES (1), Middle Comedy poet, about the time of Demosthenes. In fr. 1 a cook magnifies his skill in preparing fish for table. Fr. 3 refers to the orator Hegesippus (under his nickname Crobylus). A new fragment (Demiańczuk, *Suppl. Com.*, p. 83) makes play upon παθεῖν, μαθεῖν (cf. Aesch. *Ag.* 177).

FCG iii. 585 ff.; *CAF* ii. 447 ff.   W. G. W.

SOTADES (2), Iambic poet, of Maronea, lived in the time of Ptolemy Philadelphus, of whose marriage with Arsinoë he disapproved strongly (Ath. 621 a, fr. 1 Powell). He invented the *versus sotadeus*, a minor ionic metre which allowed great variations. Some fragments of his work survive, notably from his transcription of the *Iliad* into sotadeans (frs. 4 a–c), and lines to the flute-player Theodorus (fr. 2). The sotadeans preserved by Stobaeus (frs. 6–14) are commonly thought not to be his, and may be moralizing verses composed for the education of Greek children in Egypt. *See* IAMBIC POETRY, GREEK.

Text: E. Diehl, *Anth. Lyr. Graec.* ii. 286–94; J. U. Powell, *Collectanea Alexandrina*, 238–45.   C. M. B.

SOTER (Σωτήρ), fem. **SOTEIRA** (Σώτειρα), a title of several deities, expressing their power to save their worshippers from dangers. It has no Latin equivalent (Cicero, *Verr.* 2. 2. 154), unless it be Juno's epithet Sispes or Sospita. It is used, for example, of Zeus (as Xenophon, *An.* 1. 8. 16, and often) and of Kore (Ar. *Ran.*, 379, cf. Farnell, *Cults* iii. 198). In Hellenistic times it comes to be used of men, especially kings, often implying some measure of deification; Antigonus Doson was called Euergetes in life, Soter after his death (Polybius 5. 9. 10). The most famous holder of the title was perhaps Ptolemy I. Like all such titles, it was later cheapened, being given, for instance, to the notorious Verres (Cicero, loc. cit.). Its transcendental use is Christian, cf. A. D. Nock in *Essays on the Trinity and the Incarnation* (ed. A. E. J. Rawlinson, 1928), 87 ff.   H. J. R.

SOTERIA. The term σωτήρια was appropriate for any sacrifice(s), with or without attendant *agones*, etc., performed either once or several times in commemoration, or in hope, of the deliverance of one man or a group from oppression, sickness, or danger. Commonly Σωτήρια designated certain more or less elaborate city or national festivals celebrated at regular intervals to commemorate major events. (Compare the (older) Ἐλευθέρια, at Plataea, Syracuse, Samos; a third usage consisted in naming festivals in honour of the deliverer himself, e.g. the Diogeneia at Athens after 230/29 B.C.). The known Soteria, some sixteen in all (*PW*, s.v.) are Hellenistic (or later), part of the efflorescence of festivals at that time. The Soteria at Delphi, to commemorate the defeat of Brennus and his Celts in winter 279/8 B.C., are best known: inscriptions furnish a considerable body of detail (as yet not synthesized) about the performances, and data important for third-century chronology. Soon after the departure of the Gauls, the Amphictiones founded annual Soteria. It was not until 243/2 that the Aetolians refounded the same festival: the positive dating in that year of the Athenian archon Polyeuctus has settled a controversy (*Hesperia* vii (1938), p. 121, no. 24; for the whole problem, R. Flacelière, *Les Aitoliens à Delphes*, 1937).

SOTERICHUS (c. A.D. 300), epic poet, author of Greek poems on Dionysus, Alexander, and other subjects (Suid.).

SOTION (1) of Alexandria, Peripatetic, wrote (? between 200 and 170 B.C.) (1) a Διαδοχὴ τῶν φιλοσόφων in thirteen books, in which each philosopher is treated as the definite successor of another; (2) a book on Timon's Σίλλοι. The former work is a main though not a direct source of Diogenes Laertius' information. Sotion seems to have introduced the ultra-simple division of the philosophical successions into Ionian and Italian.

PW iii A. 1235.   W. D. R.

SOTION (2), Peripatetic, not earlier than the reign of Tiberius (A.D. 14–37). Works: Κέρας Ἀμαλθείας; *Strange Stories* (ed. A. Westermann, in Παραδοξογράφοι, 1839, p. 183), about rivers, springs, and pools; Dioclean Disputations (against Epicurus); a commentary on the *Topics*.

PW iii A. 1237.   W. D. R.

SOUL. Apart from philosophic doctrines concerning the soul, there are traces in vocabulary and usage of comparatively primitive ideas surviving in both Greece and Italy. Savages not infrequently believe that a man has several souls (e.g. Frazer, *GB* iii. 27, 80); now in Greek, notably in Homer, there are several words which mean something like 'soul' and seem to refer to parts of a man having different functions. Ψυχή, to judge by its etymology, means the breath-soul, which corresponds to the unsubstantial nature of departed ψυχαὶ as phantoms, εἴδωλα (*Od.* 11. 51, cf. 83; *Il.* 23. 104). Such phantoms have no φρένες, midriff and the parts adjacent, vitals; to give them more than a faint semblance of life they need to drink blood. It seems not improbable that the θυμός, the 'hot' or 'reeking' part, is the blood-soul; to kill is to take away the θυμός, to save the θυμὸς is to save life (*Il.* 22. 68 and often; *Od.* 11. 105). In Latin the evidence is less strong, partly no doubt because early documents are lacking; *anima* and *animus* correspond rather to later, philosophical uses respectively of ψυχὴ and θυμὸς than

to the above meanings. But we may note the existence of *umbra* in the sense of ghost, suggesting belief in a shadow-soul; cf. Lucretius' insistence (4. 364 ff.), on the true nature of shadows. *See, further,* AFTER-LIFE, GENIUS, PSYCHE.

Rose in *Actes du congrès international d'histoire des religions tenu à Paris en octobre 1923* (1925), ii. 138 ff.   H. J. R.

SPAIN. 1. PREHISTORY. The story of prehistoric man in Spain is one of frequent intrusions from Africa and from continental Europe. Yet cultural development appears to have been gradual, without catastrophic change from palaeolithic times to the late Bronze Age. Noteworthy among prehistoric remains are the late palaeolithic cave-paintings (*Altamira*), megalithic structures (probably the first in Europe), and bronze utensils (Spain's gift to western Europe, possibly even to Italy). Writers of antiquity noted among the emerging culture-groups the Ligures, Iberi, and Celti. From them they named the peninsula Liguria, Iberia, or Celtica. The name Hispania, of unknown origin, prevailed.

2. PHOENICIANS AND GREEKS. Traders from Tyre discovered on the Atlantic coast the kingdom of Tartessus (q.v.), wealthy in silver and tin, and founded on its borders the colony of Gades (q.v.). Phocaeans also sought the rewards of trade through their colony Mainake (near modern *Malaga*) founded in the seventh century B.C. The subsequent rise of Carthage was followed by the absorption of Tartessus into her empire and the expulsion of the Phocaeans from Mainake and their ports of call, Dianium (*Denia*) and Ebusus (*Iviza*). Greek influence was thereby limited to the north-eastern corner of the peninsula, where Emporiae (*Ampurias*) and Rhodae (*Rosas*) had been established by Massilia c. 600 B.C. After the First Punic War Carthaginian influence was extended by arms and diplomacy to the east and north, with Carthago Nova (q.v.) as civil and military centre. A quarrel with Rome over Saguntum (q.v.) brought on the Second Punic War, which deprived Carthage of all her Spanish possessions and gave to Rome titular claim to the entire peninsula.

3. ROMAN SPAIN: REPUBLIC. For almost two centuries the Romans fought to impose their rule on the Spanish tribes. The most difficult to conquer were the Celtiberians, Astures, and Cantabri (qq.v.). Probably one half-million troops were used by the Romans before 133 B.C., when the fall of Numantia (q.v.) marked the end of organized resistance. Three serious wars were subsequently fought against Sertorius, leader of the Marian faction (78–72 B.C.), against the legions and the sons of Pompey (49–45 B.C.), and against the natives of Asturia and Cantabria (26–19 B.C.). Most famous among the generals sent out to aid in pacification were Scipio Africanus Major (210), Cato the Censor (196), Tiberius Sempronius Gracchus (179), Scipio Aemilianus (134), Pompey (77), Julius Caesar (61), and M. Agrippa (26). In 197 B.C. Spain was organized into two provinces whose boundaries remained for some time ill defined. Hispania Citerior centred in the hellenized district of the lower Ebro valley, with Tarraco (q.v.) as headquarters. Hispania Ulterior was based on the Baetis (*Guadalquivir*) valley, long pacified by the Carthaginians. Its chief cities were Corduba (q.v.) and Hispalis (*Seville*). A regulatory administrative act (*lex provinciae*) was drawn up for each province in 133 B.C. The tribute demanded was one-twentieth of the annual crops. The rich mines were confiscated, worked directly by the State up to 178, and then leased to *publicani*. The novelty of administering an unorganized area led to many experiments, as the account of Roman municipal settlements well illustrates. Graccuris in 179 was probably the first to be named after its founder. Carteia, about 170, settled by sons of mixed marriages, was granted the status of a Latin colony by senatorial decree. Valentia (q.v.) and Urso (q.v.) also had unusual features. Caesar's liberal extension of citizenship and his policy of extra-Italian colonization added thirty new towns to the sixteen established by his predecessors.

4. EARLY EMPIRE. The reorganization of Spain by Augustus was a recognition of past progress and an encouragement to further advance. The less urban portion of Hispania Ulterior was organized as the province Lusitania (q.v.). The wealthier and completely romanized remainder became a senatorial province, Baetica (q.v.). Hispania Citerior retained its unity; its multiple administrative problems were controlled by a governor and three *legati*. Three legions, stationed in the restless north-west, remained there until Vespasian's reign. Existing municipal foundations were doubled by Augustus; this brought the total to about one hundred. A comprehensive plan of road-building, an 'encircling system', bound the parts of the peninsula to one another and to Rome. The rapid growth of the imperial cult, in which the State, citizen, and subject were equally enthusiastic, proves the success of Augustus' reorganization. The fruits of Caesar's generous planting and Augustus' careful cultivation were reaped by Vespasian, who extended the Latin Right to all the municipalized units of Spain (*see* MALACA). He also reorganized the State-owned mines. Details of his measures have been preserved in two fragments of later date (*Lex Metalli Vipascensis*, see Bruns, *Fontes Iuris Romani*[7], 289–93). Trajan and Hadrian, although of Spanish origin, were not unduly generous to their native province. Under the latter the road system reached its peak and the mining regulations were revised. Spain as a whole, and especially Baetica, became 'more Roman than the Romans'. Many senators of Rome, including three emperors, Trajan, Hadrian, and Theodosius I, were from Spain. Among Spanish men of letters were M. Porcius Latro, Hyginus, the two Senecas, Lucan, Pomponius Mela, Columella, Quintilian, Martial, Prudentius, and Orosius. Exports included gold, silver, lead, iron, cinnabar, wheat, oil, wine, and many other items. Spain contributed numerous recruits to the Roman imperial forces; the Spanish sword was introduced into the Roman army by Scipio Africanus. The best-known extant monuments are the bridge at *Alcantara* and the aqueduct at Segovia.

5. LATER EMPIRE. The assimilation of Roman institutions is clearly proved by later Spanish history. It was Christian Spain that furnished the first extant record of a Church Council (Elvira). The greatest exponent of Latin culture in the sixth–seventh centuries was Isidore of Seville. Roman law and Roman orthodoxy were transmitted to the Visigothic conquerors. The language of Spain resembles most closely of all the derivatives the Latin mother tongue.

BIBLIOGRAPHY

CLASSICAL SOURCES: *Fontes Hispaniae Antiquae* i–v (1922–40), edited by A. Schulten, P. Bosch Gimpera, and L. Péricot, contain texts with commentary and Spanish translation of all literary references prior to Caesar (i, ii), and for the wars in Spain, 237–154 B.C. (iii), 154–72 B.C. (iv), 72 B.C.–A.D. 19 (v). Add Strabo (bk. 3); Pliny, *HN* (bk. 3 et passim); Ptolemy (bk. 2. 3–5). Inscriptions in *CIL* ii and supplementary lists. Coins in A. Vives y Escudero, *La Moneda Hispánica* (1928); G. F. Hill, *Ancient Coinage of Hispania Citerior* (Amer. Numism. Soc., Notes and Monogr. no. 50).

MODERN WORKS: (*a*) *General*: C. H. V. Sutherland, *The Romans in Spain 217 B.C.–A.D. 117* (1939); *CAH* viii, ch. 10 (A. Schulten), xi, ch. 12 (E. Albertini); A. Schulten in *PW*, s.v. 'Hispania'; M. Marchetti in Ruggiero's *Diz. Epig.*, s.v. 'Hispania'; A. Ballasteros y Beretta, *Historia de España* i (1919, largely bibliographical); *Historia de España*, tomo ii, *España Romana*, ed. R. Menéndez Pidal (1935); P. Paris, *Promenades archéologiques en Espagne* (1921); J. R. Mélida, *Arqueología española* (1929).

(*b*) *Early Spain*. P. Dixon, *The Iberians of Spain* (1940); P. Bosch Gimpera, *Etnología de la Península Ibérica* (1932); A. Schulten, *Tartessos* (1922); 'Die Etrusker in Spanien', in *Klio* 1930; R. Carpenter, *The Greeks in Spain* (1925).

(*c*) *Roman conquest*. See bibliographies s.v. SCIPIO AFRICANUS, VIRIATHUS, NUMANTIA, and SERTORIUS. R. Syme, 'The Spanish War of Augustus', *AJPhil.* 1934.

(*d*) *Administration, etc.* E. Albertini, *Les Divisions administratives de l'Espagne romaine* (1923); C. H. V. Sutherland, 'Aspects of Imperialism in Roman Spain', *JRS* 1934; R. K. McElderry, 'Vespasian's Reconstruction of Spain', *JRS* 1918; addenda in *JRS* 1919; M. I. Henderson, 'Julius Caesar and *Latium* in Spain', *JRS* 1942; E. S. Bouchier, *Spain under the Roman Empire* (1914).

(*e*) *Economic.* J. J. van Nostrand in T. Frank, *Econ. Surv.* ii (1937); L. C. West, *Imperial Roman Spain; the Objects of Trade* (1929).   J. J. Van N.

SPARTA. 1. NAME AND SITUATION. Σπάρτη is more probably derived from the prevalence of the plant σπάρτος ('Spanish broom' = *Spartium iunceum*) than from σπαρτή, meaning either 'the sown land' or 'the place of scattered settlements'. Whilst Σπάρτη and Λακεδαίμων are used indifferently in Homer for the dwelling-place of Menelaus, the latter is the official name in historic times, Σπάρτη having poetic or patriotic associations and never being used as an alternative to Λακεδαίμων to describe the territory as contrasted with the city. Sparta is situated on low hills and level ground *c.* 650–700 feet above sea-level on the west bank of the Eurotas, between two tributaries which flow from the slopes of Taÿgetus, and covered a roughly elliptical area measuring *c.* 2 miles (north to south) by 1¼, with the Acropolis slightly north of the centre. Though it received partial defences before the end of the fourth century, it was not surrounded with a continuous wall until the early second century B.C. The walls, described by Livy (34. 38) at the time of Flamininus' attack in 195 as defending the level places only, were destroyed in 188 but rebuilt, and the whole circuit (48 stades according to Polybius) completed in 184 (Livy 38. 34; Paus. 7. 8. 5). This figure agrees closely with the conclusions drawn from the surviving remains discovered in 1906. As a result of these and subsequent excavations several landmarks of Spartan topography have also been identified, including the sanctuary of Athena Chalkioikos on the Acropolis overlooking the vast theatre of early Imperial date which replaced a smaller Hellenistic structure; the sanctuary of Artemis Orthia, where the Spartan boys were flogged, in the 'Contest of the Whips', on the bank of the Eurotas, which fixes the position of the quarter 'Limnai'; the quarter of 'Pitane' to the north-west of the Acropolis; and, most probably, the Agora south-east of the theatre. The position of the other two quarters Kynosura and Mesoa remains uncertain, but with the data obtained, Pausanias' account of the topography of the city becomes much more intelligible.

2. HISTORY. No certain remains of pre-Dorian occupation have been found on the site of Sparta except a handful of Mycenaean potsherds from the Acropolis; but at Therapne (q.v.) across the Eurotas a modest Late-Helladic dwelling has been uncovered, and at Amyclae (q.v.) some four miles down-stream a prehistoric site of the same period, preceded by an earlier settlement dating back to 2000 B.C. at least, underlay the sanctuary of Apollo Amyclaeus; and a short distance farther south was the beehive tomb of Vaphio which yielded the famous gold cups and other valuable finds. Sparta was thus essentially a settlement of the Dorian invaders, and preserved throughout its history the appearance and the tradition of the villages of the earliest settlers (cf. Thuc. 1. 10). The synoecism of these villages, which is the most probable explanation of the dual kingship, made possible the conquest of the Eurotas valley and the subsequent expansion of Spartan rule over the rest of Laconia. The reduction of the conquered population, consisting of Achaean and other pre-Dorian stocks, to the status either of *Perioikoi* who retained partial independence subject to the obligation to serve in Sparta in war, or of helots who were serfs bound to the soil which they cultivated for their Spartan masters, belongs to this stage of her expansion. Whether the reforms of Lycurgus (q.v.), recognizing the existence of the two kings, the Gerousia, and the Apella, and the organization into Tribes and Obes should all be dated to the same period is much less certain.

3. The Messenian Wars, of which the dates are likewise much disputed (I. *c.* 725–705 (?); II. 685–668, or as late as *c.* 640–620?) and the details obscured by the more or less legendary exploits of Aristodemus and Aristomenes (qq.v.), furnished a valuable addition to the number of land-lots required to support the growing citizen-population. After the conquest of Messenia no fresh territory was annexed, and in the sixth century a new policy marks Sparta's foreign relations, Tegea (q.v.), which was finally overcome after a disastrous Spartan defeat, being allowed to retain her land and her independence. This policy, perhaps to be associated with the ephor Chilon (q.v.), culminated in the organization of the Peloponnesian Confederacy under Spartan hegemony, which attained its maximum of activity, if not success, in the reign of Cleomenes (q.v. 1).

4. Sparta's leadership in Greek affairs, which she maintained with increased credit in the invasion of Xerxes, began to decline soon after 479, partly as a result of the excesses of Pausanias (q.v. 1), the disgrace and exile of Leotychides (q.v.), the anti-Spartan activities of Themistocles, and, above all, the growth of the Delian Confederacy under Athens; and it was more seriously impaired by the loss of life in the earthquake of 464 B.C. and the strain of the Third Messenian War (*c.* 464–460). Owing, however, to the collapse of the Athenian land-empire and the defection of Megara, recognized by the Thirty Years' Peace, Sparta could face with revived confidence the prospects of the Peloponnesian War. The pre-eminence which she regained by the overthrow of Athens was nevertheless precariously based on a dwindling citizen-population, on the individualist ambitions of Lysander and Agesilaus (qq.v.), and on an increasing disregard for the traditional equality of posessions and for the prohibition of monied wealth and of the alienation of land-lots; and it is not surprising that she never recovered her strength after the disaster of Leuctra and the restoration of Messenian independence.

5. During the next hundred years or more the number of her citizens and her political importance were steadily declining. The deadening effects of her conservative régime were realized, far too late, in 242 B.C. by Agis III, whose proposals to revive the strictness of the Lycurgan training and to admit *Perioikoi* and foreigners to the citizen-body were obstructed by the ephors and the few remaining *Spartiatai*; and, after his violent death, by Cleomenes III, who by revolutionary methods abolished the ephorate and raised the number of citizens to 4,000, but, ruling as a tyrant, was opposed and overthrown by the Achaean League and Antigonus Doson at Sellasia (222 or 221). Of the various tyrants who followed him, Nabis, who styled himself king, was the most successful, but was defeated by Flamininus in 195, and Sparta was compelled to join the Achaean League and finally incorporated as a *civitas foederata* in the province of Achaea. A remarkable revival of prosperity under the Roman Empire, especially in the second century, is attested by inscriptions and architectural remains, and a revival of the Lycurgan régime is a picturesque, if unconvincing, feature of the age of Septimius Severus. Surviving the destructive raid of the Heruli in A.D. 267, Sparta finally succumbed in ruins at the hands of the Goths under Alaric in 395.

For the Spartan Constitution *see* EPHORS, HELOTS, LYCURGUS, PERIOIKOI; *see also* XENOPHON for his *Polity of the Lacedaemonians*. For the Spartan army *see* ARMIES, GREEK, para. 3.

BIBLIOGRAPHY

ANCIENT SOURCES: (*a*) *Documents*: *IG* v. 1 [1913]; *BSA* xxvi–xxx (1926–32). Public documents prior to Hellenistic times are extremely scarce, and the great majority of surviving inscriptions are statue-bases and lists of magistrates of the Imperial age.
(*b*) *Authors*. Poets: see Alcman and Tyrtaeus; Homer, esp. *Od.* iv. Prose: Hdt. 1. 65 ff.; bks. 5–6 passim (Cleomenes), bks. 7–9 (Persian Wars). Thuc. 1. 10, 18, 89 ff., 101–3, 128 ff. (Pausanias); bks. 2–8 passim (Peloponnesian War). Xenophon, *Hell.* (passim), *Lac.*; Aristotle, *Pol.* 2. 9; 5. 7 and passim. Plutarch, *Lycurgus, Lysander, Agesilaus, Agis* (III), *Cleomenes* (III), *Apophthegmata Laconica*. For topography, Strabo, 8. 4–6 (Laconia); Pausanias, 3. 11–20 (Sparta).
MODERN WORKS: K. O. Müller, *Dorians* (Engl. Transl. 1830) is still valuable and suggestive. On the Spartan Constitution, G. Gilbert, *Constitutional Antiquities* (E.T. 1895); A. H. J. Greenidge, *Handbook of Gk. Const. Hist.*; G. Busolt–H. Swoboda, *Gr. Staatskunde* (1926), 634 ff. (sound and cautious); U. Kahrstedt, *Gr. Staatsrecht* i (1922) (fully documented but often misleading); Ed. Meyer, *Forschungen* i. 269 ff. (Lycurgus). The article 'Sparta' in *PW* is a valuable summary, with exhaustive accounts of topography (E. Bölte), Constitution and History (V. Ehrenberg), Religion and Art (L. Ziehen).
EXCAVATIONS: *BSA* xii–xvi, xxvi–xxx; R. M. Dawkins and others, *The Sanctuary of Artemis Orthia at Sparta* (1929).
MAPS: *Graecia Antiqua* (Frazer and Van Buren, 1930), pl. xxxv.
A. M. W.

SPARTA, CULTS AND MYTHS. The former are well discussed in general by Ziehen in *PW*, 2° Reihe III, art. 'Sparta', 1453 ff. Prominent among them were those of Apollo at Amyclae (Hyacinthia, *see* HYACINTHUS; his throne and archaic statue there were famous, Paus. 3. 19. 1 ff.); of Artemis, who became identified with a Dorian goddess, Ortheia (the name has various forms, see 'Artemis Orthia', *JHS*, Supplement vol. v, 1929, especially pp. 399 ff.); Athena, whose principal temple was the Bronze House, hence her epithet Chalkioikos; Aphrodite, here worshipped as an armed goddess, Areia or ὡπλισμένη; Enyalios, apparently regarded as separate from Ares, with some interesting ritual, including sacrifice of puppies and a sham-fight; Zeus, who in Hellenistic times had (*inter alia*) the title of Agamemnon, a curious blend of the cults of a god and a hero, if the somewhat doubtful evidence is correct. Of heroes and heroines, the Dioscuri (q.v.), were prominent, often in connexion with Helen (q.v.); see F. Chapouthier, *Les Dioscures au service d'une déesse* (1935), especially pp. 143 ff. Helen herself was worshipped in a way indicating that she is more goddess than heroine. The Leucippides also (*see* DIOSCURI) had a cult. Of festivals, one of the most prominent was the Carneia (q.v.).

Really Spartan myths are quite uncommon, most of the fabulous history of the place representing attempts to attach pre-Dorian mythology to the Dorians. The Pelopidae, including Agamemnon, who is killed at Amyclae as early as Pindar, *Pyth.* 11. 31, the hint being taken from *Od.* 4. 514, are claimed as a kind of Spartans, and Heracles has a series of adventures there and is made out to be an ancestor, though he had little cult. H. J. R.

SPARTACUS, Thracian gladiator who led a revolt at Capua in 73 B.C. Numerous Thracian, Celtic, and German renegades quickly joined him. Spartacus defeated two Roman armies, then devastated southern Italy, continually attracting additional fugitives; ultimately his army numbered 90,000. In 72, after losing his Celtic associate Crixus, he defeated three Roman armies and reached Cisalpine Gaul whence, he hoped, his followers would disperse to their homes. They, however, preferred to plunder Italy. Spartacus accordingly marched south again, conquered two more Roman armies, desolated Lucania, and would have invaded Sicily, had not piratical transports failed him. In 71 Crassus, after unsuccessfully attempting to corner Spartacus in the 'toe' of Italy, finally caught and destroyed him in Lucania, subsequently crucifying any rebels he captured. Pompey, returning from Spain, annihilated the few who escaped. Spartacus quickly became a legend; he was competent, brave, physically powerful, and apparently humane.

Ancient Literature: the primary source was apparently Sallust's *Histories* (see extant fragments in Maurenbrecher's edition). Plutarch (*Crass.* 8 f.; *Pomp.* 21) and Appian (*BCiv.* 1. 116 f.) give continuous, but not wholly trustworthy, accounts, the writers who follow Livy (*Epit.* 95 f.; Florus 2. 8; Eutrop. 6. 7; Oros. 5. 24) sketchier versions. Modern literature: T. Rice Holmes, *Roman Republic* (1923), i. 156 f. (for topography); H. Last, *CAH* ix. 329 f. (with bibliography). E. T. S.

SPARTOCIDS, a dynasty which established itself at Panticapaeum in 438 B.C., and ruled most of the Crimea and the Taman peninsula until *c.* 110 B.C. It was called after its founder, Spartocus I, and two later kings of like name. The Spartocids were probably of Thracian origin, but soon became hellenized. The earlier members of the dynasty avoided regal style and were known simply as ἄρχοντες Βοσπόρου; but they kept a mercenary force and probably owned most of the Crimean land. From the time of Spartocus III (304–284) they bore the title of kings. They so developed the cultivation of wheat in their dominions as to become the greatest exporters of grain to Greece. In the fifth century they probably conceded a right of pre-emption to Athens; in the next two centuries they still cultivated the Athenian market, but dealt freely with other Aegean cities. Their wealth is attested by their magnificently furnished rock-tombs near Panticapaeum. In the second and first centuries the Spartocids suffered from Scythian and Sarmatian invasions of the Crimea, and *c.* 110 they were displaced by Mithridates VI of Pontus. A daughter of Mithridates' son Pharnaces, Queen Dynamis, founded a new dynasty, which survived under Roman protectorate until the fourth century A.D.

M. Rostovtzeff, *CAH* viii, ch. 18.   M. C.

SPARTOI, *see* CADMUS. Their descendants had a birthmark in the shape of a spear-head, Arist. *Poet.* 1454ᵇ22 (from Euripides' *Antigone?*), by which they could be known.

SPATHA, *see* ARMS AND ARMOUR, ROMAN.

SPES, a *res expetenda* rather than an actual 'virtue'. A temple was built to her by A. Atilius Calatinus in the First Punic War. Burnt down in 31 B.C., it was restored by Germanicus in A.D. 17. 'Spes P.R.' is the rising generation, the hope of the race, 'Spes Augusta' imperial promise centred in the princes (cf. *supplicatio Spei et Iuuentuti*, 18 Oct., for the *toga uirilis* of Augustus). She bears an opening flower and catches up her skirt as if in haste.

G. Wissowa, *RK*, 263, 329f.   H. M.

SPEUSIPPUS, son of Eurymedon and Potone, a sister of Plato. He was associated in the Academy with Plato, went with him to Syracuse on his last visit, and succeeded him as head of the Academy from 347 to 339 B.C. He appears to have been a man of considerably less austere character than Plato, though doubtless the stories in later writers of his bad temper and proneness to physical pleasures are exaggerated. We also hear of him as an agreeable companion in social intercourse.

He was a prolific author, but only a few stray fragments of his work survive. From these, and from references in later authors, we get the impression that his interests turned largely to the empirical side of knowledge. He seems to have emphasized the observable differences and resemblances of phenomena and deprecated attempts to reduce them to a common first principle. He was interested in biological investigation, and wrote a book, of which a few fragments survive, in which he attempted to classify the different species of animals and plants by their resemblances to each other. He also contributed to mathematical theory and to ethics. In the latter connexion he is mentioned by Aristotle as advocating the view that pleasure is in itself bad: he held, apparently, that the intermediate state between pleasure and pain was the sole good.

Frs. in Mullach, *FPG* iii. 62–99. Histories of ancient philosophy: Zeller, ii. 1⁴. 982–1010; Gomperz (Engl. Transl. iv. 2–5); Robin (Engl. Transl. 238o); P. Lang, *De Speusippi Academici Scriptis* (1911). *PW* iii A. 1636.   G. C. F.

SPHAERA BARBARICA, GRAECANICA, *see* CONSTELLATIONS, para. 10.

SPHAERUS of Borysthenes (b. *c.* 285 or 265, lived at least to 221 B.C.), a pupil first of Zeno, then of Cleanthes; friend and adviser of the Spartan reformer Cleomenes. His numerous writings dealt with all branches of philosophy (especially with morals and politics) and with certain of the older philosophers. His definitions were highly esteemed in the Stoic school.

Testimonia in von Arnim, *SVF* i. 139–42. *PW* iii A. 1683.   W. D. R.

SPHAIRAI (σφαῖραι), *see* BOXING.

SPHINX, a mythological monster, with human head and the body of a lion. Originating in Egypt, probably as a type of the king, the Sphinx became known early to Syrians, Phoenicians, and Mycenaean Greeks. Already in the Near East it was transformed into a female being and remained female in Greek literature, although in art bearded male Sphinxes are known in the archaic period (H. Payne, *Necrocorinthia*, 1931, p. 89). Sphinxes were at first adopted by the Greek artists as a type of ghost-like monsters who carry off boys or youths and are present at fatal combats. Like many other monsters, the Sphinx acquired an apotropaic significance and was placed on tombs (Diog. Laert. 1. 89) and depicted on shields (Aesch. *Sept.* 522). In Boeotia, the native land of Hesiod's great mythological system, the Sphinx became a central figure of the native cycle concerned with the mythical dynasty of the Labdacidae. In an early version the Sphinx, sent by Hera to Thebes, asked the Thebans the riddle about the three ages of men (Apollod. 3. 5. 7 f.; a piece of folk-lore). They failed to solve it, and after each effort the Sphinx carried away and devoured one of them, including Haemon, son of Creon (E. Haspels, *Attic Black-Fig. Lekythoi*, 1938, p. 131), until Oedipus (q.v.) solved the riddle. The Sphinx committed suicide, or was killed by Oedipus (Corinna in schol. Eur. *Phoen.* 26). Later accounts, attesting the growth of Delphic religion, make Apollo send the Sphinx. These versions were used by Sophocles (*OT*) and Euripides (*Phoen.*).

In art sphinxes appear in great abundance in the 'animal friezes' of the orientalizing period; marble statues of Sphinxes, such as the Sphinx of the Naxians in Delphi, are given as votives to Apollo (Ch. Picard, *Manuel d'archéol.* i, p. 570, fig. 197), or guard the tombs of Attica. In Classical art the Sphinx is humanized. The Sphinx from Aegina and those of later Attic vases have beautiful serious faces, sometimes female breasts. Instead of the Hesiodic monster, the child of Echidna and Orthros (*Theog.* 326), the Sphinx becomes the wise, enigmatic, and musical messenger of divine justice; the tragic poets call her 'the wise virgin' and say that she sang her riddle (Eur. *Phoen.* 48, 1507).

J. Ilberg in Roscher, *Lex.*, s.v.; H. J. Rose, *Handbook of Greek Mythol.*, pp. 188 and 297; P. Wolters, *Gnomon* 1925, 46.   G. M. A. H.

SPHONDULOMANCY, *see* DIVINATION, para. 6.

SPICULUM, *see* ARMS AND ARMOUR, ROMAN.

SPINA, a city of eastern Italy, near one of the southern estuaries of the river Po, and probably to be identified with an excavation-site near the Lago di Comacchio, where graves have been discovered with a rich furniture of Greek pottery and metal-ware, mostly of the sixth century. Ancient writers describe Spina as a Greek city, and mention that it had a treasure-house at Delphi. Its principal trade was probably with the Etruscans at Felsina (Bononia), but its Greek nationality need not be denied. With the decline of Etruscan power in the fourth century and the recession of the coastline Spina became derelict.

Strabo 5. 214. S. Aurigemma, *Il Regio Museo di Spina* (1936).   M. C.

SPINA, *see* CIRCUS.

SPINNING. In an ancient household a large amount of a woman's time was spent in wool-work; and on the tomb of a virtuous Roman matron the crowning words of praise were 'Lanam fecit'. The fleeces were brought into the house in their rough state and had first to be washed. The wool was then teased and pulled into fluff before being treated by an instrument called *epinetron* which separated the fibres and arranged them lengthways, making them ready for spinning. The spindle—κλωστήρ, *fusus*—was a straight piece of reed, wood, or metal about 12 inches long; the whorl was a disk of clay, wood, or ivory attached to the end of the spindle; and the operation of spinning was as follows. The wool was placed on the distaff (ἠλακάτη, *colus*), and from it a little was drawn, twisted, and fixed to a hook at the top of the spindle. With the help of the whorl the spindle was spun round, and as it spun more wool was paid out from the distaff and twisted into yarn.

H. Blümner, *Technologie der Griechen und Römer*[2] (1912) i. 120 ff.
F. A. W.

SPINTHER, *see* LENTULUS (5).

SPOLIA OPIMA were spoils offered by a Roman general who had slain an enemy leader in single combat. Three kinds are distinguished, *prima*, *secunda*, and *tertia* according to the rank of the winner. *Prima spolia* were dedicated in the temple of Jupiter Feretrius. These were traditionally won on three occasions. Romulus' victory, however, was obviously invented to credit him with the building of the temple of Jupiter Feretrius and the institution of the custom. But the historicity of the victories of A. Cornelius Cossus (q.v.) over Tolumnius (*c.* 428) and of M. Claudius Marcellus (q.v.) over Virdumarus (222 B.C.) is attested by epigraphical and literary evidence.

J. Marquardt, *Röm. Staatsverw.* ii. 560 f.; F. Lammert, in *PW*, s.v.
P. T.

SPONSALIA, *see* MARRIAGE, LAW OF, para. 6, *and* BETROTHAL.

SPONSIO, *see* STIPULATIO.

SPORTULA, *see* CLIENS.

SPRINGS, SACRED. The worship of springs (or wells), a phenomenon of the highest antiquity and widespread all over the world, is in essential points similar to that of rivers (*see* RIVER-GODS). Flowing water, especially when bubbling up from the interior of the earth, was to the primitive mind animate and divine, and the plastic creative imagination of the Greeks personified such spirits of fountains as nymphs (*see* NYMPHS). Fountains with extraordinary qualities gained special significance and acquired corresponding myths—warm healing fountains were attached to the cult of Hephaestus (and Heracles, sometimes Artemis). Mantic springs brought into existence the most famous oracles of antiquity, as those of Apollo at Branchidae near Miletus and at Delphi (Cassotis); cf. the spring at Claros, that of Daphne near Antioch, and that in the Troad near the grave of the Sibyl. Poseidon was said to have caused fountains to spring up (e.g. the salty fountain on the Athenian Acropolis, in the Erechtheum); so also Dionysus (thus a fountain near Haliartus reminded men of the wine-god and his nurses because of the ruddy colour of its waters: Plut. *Lys.* 28. 7). The fountain on the summit of the Boeotian Helicon, Hippocrene, was brought forth by a blow of the hoof of Pegasus, said to have been the horse of Poseidon. Fountains were also named after heroes, as Achilles and Agamemnon; those that disappear into the earth were considered as entrances to Hades (as Styx in Arcadia, Asterion in Argos, Cassotis near Delphi). A number of myths (cf. AMYMONE, SEMELE, DIRCE) and cults (cf. the nymphs of the spring) clearly show how

strong a fascination springs exercised on Greek minds. The Roman festival Fontinalia (13 Oct.), when flowers were thrown into the fountains, was important. The Romans also threw coins into the wells (Plin. *Ep.* 8. 8. 2). Horace sacrifices a kid to the Bandusian spring, *Carm.* 3. 13. 3.

O. Gruppe, *Gr. Mythologie und Rel. Gesch.* (1906), Index, s.v. 'Quelle' (p. 1913); E. Michon, J. A. Hild, 'Fons' in Dar.-Sag.
S. E.

SPURINNA, *see* VESTRICIUS.

STABERIUS EROS, a scholar, originally a slave, who taught the children of the Sullan *proscripti* free. Brutus and Cassius were his pupils (Plin. *HN* 35. 199; Suet. *Gram.* 13).

STADIUM. The Greek στάδιον, the running-track, was a long parallelogram, about 200 yards long and 30 yards wide. In the sprint race (also known as στάδιον) the competitors ran the length of the track; in the longer events they went up and down the straight, turning sharply round pillars at the end. When possible the stadium lay between two hills with an embankment at the two ends which were either left square or rounded in a half-circle, for the convenience of the spectators. The four best-known extant stadia are those at Delphi, Olympia, Epidaurus, and Athens. At Delphi the present structure, dating from the second century A.D., is largely due to Herodes Atticus, who also rebuilt the stadium at Athens with forty-six rows of marble seats holding some 50,000 people. In all four stadia the start and finish are marked with pillars and stone slabs divided into sections, one for each runner. At Epidaurus there are also small pillars every hundred feet on each side of the track, and a stone channel with basins at intervals to provide the spectators with water.

E. N. Gardiner, *Athletics of the Ancient World* (1930), 128 ff.
F. A. W.

STAGIRUS (later **Stagira**) (Στάγειρος, Στάγειρα), *see* ARISTOTLE.

STANDARDS, CULT OF. Every permanent station of a Roman military unit, especially a legion, and every camp regularly constructed contained a chapel, which, at least in Imperial times (Vegetius, *De re mil.* 2. 6), was under the charge of the first cohort, or headquarters company. In this were kept, besides the statues of gods worshipped by the troops and of the emperors, the standards of the unit and its component parts. These, from an unknown date (Pliny, *HN* 13. 23; our information does not go back to Republican times), received divine or quasi-divine honours. They were anointed and otherwise tended on feast-days (Pliny, ibid., cf. ROSALIA). A suppliant might take refuge at them (Tacitus, *Ann.* 1. 39. 7); an altar was on occasion dedicated at least partly to them, or at all events to the most important, the eagle of the legion (*CIL* iii. 7591; no. 14 v. Domaszewski); the *natalis* of the eagle, presumably the anniversary of the day when the unit was first commissioned, was celebrated (*CIL* ii. 6183; no. 3 v. Domaszewski); sacrifice was made to them particularly on the occasion of a victory (Josephus, *BJ* 6. 316, where the troops who took Jerusalem make offerings to their ensigns in the Temple, not in their camp). Tertullian even says with rhetorical exaggeration that the soldiers venerated them beyond all gods (*Apol.* 16). They are not precisely gods, but are associated with *genius* and *uirtus* (*CIL* iii. 7591, above), and are 'propria legionum numina' (Tac. *Ann.* 2. 17. 2). This perhaps goes to the heart of the matter; they are the embodiment of the luck or power of the unit to which they belong, and hence worthy of respect and to be kept sacredly.

A. von Domaszewski, *Die Religion des römischen Heeres* (*Westdeutsche Zeitschrift* xiv. 1895), pp. 9 ff.
H. J. R.

STAPHYLUS (1), personification of the grape-cluster, σταφυλή. He is vaguely attached to Dionysus, as his son by Ariadne (q.v.; Plutarch, *Thes.* 20); his favourite (schol. Ar. *Plut.* 1021); an Assyrian king who welcomes him during his Indian campaign (Nonnus, *Dionys.* 18. 5 ff.). Or he discovered the vine and informed Oeneus (q.v.; 'Probus' on Verg. *G.* 1. 9). H. J. R.

STAPHYLUS (2) of Naucratis, an Alexandrian to whom are assigned histories of Athens and Thessaly (Περὶ Ἀθηνῶν and Θεσσαλικά). Perhaps *c.* 300 B.C.

FHG. iv. 505.

STAR-MYTHS, see ANDROMEDA.

STASEAS of Naples, the first Peripatetic philosopher known to have settled in Rome. M. Calpurnius Piso became his pupil *c.* 92 B.C. He is frequently mentioned by Cicero. He seems to have occupied himself particularly with the problem of the normal length of human life.

PW iii A. 2153. W. D. R.

STASIMON, see TRAGEDY, para. 14.

STASINUS of Cyprus (? 8th c. B.C.), epic poet, possibly author of the *Cypria* (Ath. 15, p. 682 d). *See* EPIC CYCLE.

EGF 15–32.

STATARIA, sc. **fabula**: one of the three types of play according to Euanthius' division, *motoria* (lively), *stataria* (quiet), *mixta* (blended): see FABULA.

STATERA, see WEIGHING-INSTRUMENTS.

STATHMOS (σταθμός), see WEIGHING-INSTRUMENTS.

STATILIA, see MESSALINA.

STATILIUS TAURUS, TITUS (*cos. suff.* 37 B.C., *cos.* II 26 B.C.), the greatest Augustan marshal after Agrippa. Of uncertain origin (perhaps Lucanian), by military talent and steadfast loyalty he rose to wealth and honours; he was thrice acclaimed imperator by the legions and held several priesthoods (*ILS* 893; 893 a). His earliest recorded service for Octavian was as an admiral in the *Bellum Siculum* (36). After the conquest of Sicily he crossed to Africa and secured that province, holding a triumph in 34 (the amphitheatre erected in commemoration on the Campus Martius was completed in 30). He also fought in Illyricum (34–33), commanded the land army in the campaign of Actium (31), and conducted operations in Spain (29). After his second consulate (26) the only record of him is that he was put in charge of Rome as *praefectus urbi* in 16 when Augustus departed to the provinces of the West (Dio Cass. 54. 19. 6; Tac. *Ann.* 6. 11). He probably died not long after.

R. Syme, *Roman Revolution* (1939), see Index. R. S.

STATIUS, PUBLIUS PAPINIUS (*c.* A.D. 45–96), was born at Naples, where his father, himself a poet, was a schoolmaster. From his father, whom he eulogizes in *Silvae* 5. 3, he learned much of the poetic technique he was afterwards to develop. Settling in Rome, he established there his fame and popularity as a poet. From his *Silvae* we learn that he recited his works to fashionable audiences (cf. Juv. 7. 82–6), that he became intimately acquainted with several of the leading men of his day, and that he was admitted to the court of Domitian, to whose good graces he owed the running water in an estate he acquired at Alba (3. 1. 61 ff.), where his father was buried (5. 3. 35–40). He won the prize, probably in 89, at the annual festival instituted by Domitian at Alba, but was, much to his chagrin, unsuccessful at the quinquennial Capitoline contest, probably in 94. To his wife Claudia he pays graceful compliments (3. 5). They had no children, though Claudia had a daughter by a previous marriage

and Statius adopted a son who died young (5. 5). Statius' health was not robust, and we hear of one serious illness through which he was nursed by his wife. Towards the end of his life he retired to his native city, where he died, seemingly before the murder of Domitian (Sept. 96). He appears to have been of an amiable disposition, deeply attached to his relations and capable of warm friendship. Though not of great wealth, he was probably in easy circumstances, at any rate during his later years. Real hardship does not seem ever to have fallen to his lot and, generally speaking, it is only of the pleasant sides of life that we have glimpses in his poems. The least pleasing aspect of his nature is to be seen in the extravagant flattery lavished on Domitian (e.g. *Silv.* 4. 1–3), which may be partially extenuated by the conditions of the age.

2. WORKS. A poem on Domitian's German wars and the *Agave*, a libretto for a pantomimus mentioned by Juvenal 7. 87, have perished. The epic *Thebais*, published about 91, took twelve years to complete and tells in twelve books the story of the quarrel between Eteocles (q.v.) and Polynices. The *Achilleis*, brought to a conclusion in the second book by the poet's death, deals with the education of Achilles under the Centaur Chiron, his disguise as a girl during his sojourn at the court of Lycomedes in Scyros, his amour with Deidameia, his detection by Ulysses and Diomedes, and his departure for Troy. The *Silvae* in five books published at different times from 92 onwards, the fifth being posthumous, consist of thirty-two occasional poems addressed to the poet's friends celebrating their marriages, villas, baths, *objets d'art*, or public benefactions, offering congratulations on recovery from illness, the birth of an heir, or attainment of high office, or consolations on the loss of relatives, and sometimes dealing with lighter subjects. The most famous is the short address to Sleep (5. 4). These poems are mostly in hexameters, though four are in hendecasyllabics, one in sapphics, and one in alcaics. They were lost in medieval times till Poggio discovered a manuscript containing them at Constance in 1417.

3. Statius' verse is fluent and highly polished, even in the hastily composed *Silvae*. The *Thebais* requires episodic treatment and lacks a real hero. There are frequent imitations of Virgil in word and thought, and the gods take part in the action. Excessive use of hyperbole is perhaps the chief fault in taste. But the various episodes, highly coloured and rhetorical though they be, are generally successful regarded as separate wholes, the descriptive passages striking, and the narrative lively. The sentiment rarely reaches sublimity, but telling effects are achieved in 'pathetic' passages. The epics were much admired throughout medieval times, and Statius, regarded by Dante as a Christian, is an important character in the *Purgatorio*. He was a favourite also of Chaucer's. *See also* EPIC POETRY.

BIBLIOGRAPHY

LIFE: Vollmer's edition of *Silvae* (Teubner, 1898).
MSS. OF EPICS: Klotz in *Hermes* xl (1905). See, too, Garrod's edition of *Thebais* (1906), for theory (arising from nature of manuscript variants) of a second edition of *Thebais* by Statius himself. All manuscripts of *Silvae* derive from MS. Matritensis M31. For different views on problems connected with the tradition see Klotz's second Teubner edition (1911), and Phillimore's second edition (1917).
SOURCES AND MODELS: R. Helm, *De P. Papinii Statii Thebaide* (1892); Essenfeldt in *Philol.* 1904.
LITERARY APPRECIATION: L. Legras, *Étude sur la Thébaïde de Stace* (1905). E. J. W.

STELLA, ARRUNTIUS, see ARRUNTIUS.

STENOGRAPHY, see TACHYGRAPHY.

STENTOR, a man who could shout as loudly as fifty ordinary people (*Iliad* 5. 785–6). He is evidently known to Homer, but no later author has anything worth quoting to say of him.

STEPTERIA, see APOLLO, para. 4.

STEROPE or **ASTEROPE,** (1) one of the Pleiads, wife of Oenomaus (q.v.; Paus. 5. 10. 6). (2) daughter of Cepheus king of Tegea (Apollod. 2. 144). Heracles gave her (in Paus. 8. 47. 5, Athena gave Cepheus) some of the hair of Medusa, bidding her lift it thrice above the city wall, to put attackers to flight. H. J. R.

STERTINIUS, in the Augustan Age, turned Stoic tenets into Latin verse and, according to Acro (ad Hor. *Epist.* I. 12. 20), wrote 220 books.

STESICHORUS, lyric poet, said to have been born at Mataurus (Steph. Byz. s.v. Μάταυρος) and to have lived at Himera (Pl. *Phdr.* 244 a, Arist. *Rh.* 1393ᵇ). His real name was said to be Teisias (Suidas s.v. Στησίχορος), and it is quite possible that Στησίχορος was a title. His dates are confused by *Marm. Par.* 50, which places his arrival in Greece in 485 B.C. This seems a mistake, and there can be little doubt that he was alive in the first half of the sixth century, since he is connected with Phalaris (Arist. *Rh.* 1393ᵇ) and Suidas places his birth at 632–629 B.C. and his death 556–553 B.C. His works were collected in twenty-six books, and seem to have been lyrical poems composed on a big scale, in which the narrative element was strong. Titles of several poems survive and indicate that he told stories gathered from widely different epic sources. It is not known what type of poems he composed, though it is possible that some were Dithyrambs, since narrative predominated in this type, and Stesichorus may have been influenced by the voyage of Arion in the West. Though the fragments are scanty, something may be learned of his work. In his *Funeral-games of Pelias* he drew on the Argonautic saga and described the games in some detail (frs. 1–3). His *Geryoneis* told of Heracles' quest of the cattle of Geryon, and was remarkable for its knowledge of the silver-mines of Tartessus (fr. 4), its conception of Heracles as a great drinker (fr. 5), its account of the Sun's magic cup which Heracles borrowed for his voyage (fr. 6), and for the notion that Geryon was winged (schol. Hes. *Th.* 287), which was soon popularized by painters. His *Boar-hunters* (fr. 7) seems to have been about the Calydonian boar-hunt, and his *Eriphyle* (fr. 8) dealt with a famous Theban legend. His *Iliupersis* drew on the epic, and was interesting for its account of Epeus who made the Wooden Horse (fr. 9), though attempts to connect it with the legend of Aeneas remain unproved. In his *Helen* he seems to have told the conventional story in a first version, which contained an account of her marriage to Menelaus (fr. 10). But legend (Pl. *Phdr.* 243 a) told that he was blinded for this and did not recover until he recanted in a second poem, his famous *Palinode*, in which he denied that Helen ever went to Troy (fr. 11). Perhaps the truth behind this is that Stesichorus outraged opinion which regarded Helen as a goddess, as it did in Sparta. His *Oresteia* in two books seems also to have been sung at Sparta at a spring festival (frs. 13–14), and differed from Homer in placing the death of Agamemnon in Lacedaemon. It contained an account of Clytemnestra's dream (fr. 15), and gave some part to the nurse of Orestes (schol. Aesch. *Cho.* 733). The *Rhadine*, attributed to him, seems more likely to be a later, romantic work by another poet, perhaps of the same name (cf. *Marm. Par.* 73). The fragments show that he wrote in the traditional language of choral lyric, used a kind of 'dactylo-epitrite' metre, and was an ingenious inventor of episodes later very popular, such as the birth of Athene in full armour from the head of Zeus (*Etym. Magn.* 772. 49). He was admired for his dignity (Quint. *Inst.* 10. 1. 62) and grandeur in plot and character (Dion. Hal. *Vett. Cens.* 2. 27). *See also* PASTORAL POETRY, GREEK.

Text: E. Diehl, *Anth. Lyr. Graec.* ii. 39–48.
Criticism: J. Vürtheim, *Stesichoros' Fragmente und Biographie* (1919): C. M. Bowra, *Greek Lyric Poetry* (1936), 77–140. C. M. B.

STESIMBROTUS(*fl.* late 5th c. B.C.), biographer from Thasos, who taught at Athens. Works (*FGrH* ii B. 107): (1) Homeric studies; (2) Περὶ τελετῶν, on the Samothracian mysteries; (3) Περὶ Θεμιστοκλέους καὶ Θουκυδίδου καὶ Περικλέους (frs. in Plut.). While giving full biographical details, S. criticized Themistocles and Pericles and lauded Cimon; no preserved fragments concern Thucydides (son of Melesias). F. W. W.

STHENEBOEA, see BELLEROPHON.

STHENELUS, a tragic poet of the fifth century B.C., chosen by Aristotle (*Poet.* 22) as the example of a poet who avoided all use of poetic vocabulary and was in consequence commonplace in style. His insipidity is ridiculed by Aristophanes (*Vesp.* 1313), and Plato Com. (fr. 70) says that he appropriated other poets' verses. *TGF* 762. A. W. P.-C.

STHENNO, see GORGO.

STICHOMETRY. (1) GREEK. Στίχος means primarily a line of verse, and metrical texts were naturally measured by the number of their verses; but for bibliographical purposes the equivalent of a hexameter line was taken as a unit of measurement for prose works also. For this purpose the hexameter line was reckoned as approximately 16 syllables or 36 letters (Galen, *De placitis Hippocratis et Platonis* 8. 1, p. 655). This does not mean that prose works were habitually written in lines of this length. On the contrary, the evidence of papyri found in Egypt shows that the lines in prose manuscripts were usually not much more than half of this. The στίχος was simply a unit of measurement indicating the extent of the book, or of portions of a work, and serving to fix the remuneration of the copyist. Thus Josephus (*AJ* 20. 11. 3) states that his work consists of twenty books and 60,000 στίχοι, and according to Diogenes Laertius the works of Aristotle comprised 445,270 στίχοι; while the Edict of Diocletian fixes a scribe's wage at 25 or 20 *denarii* per 100 στίχοι. Callimachus, in his catalogue (πίνακες) of the Alexandrian Library, recorded the number of στίχοι in each work. Many extant manuscripts contain notes of the number of στίχοι (see Ritschl, op. cit. infra), e.g. several of the Herculaneum rolls, the Chester Beatty papyrus and the Codex Claromontanus of the Pauline Epistles, the Laurentian manuscripts of Herodotus and Sophocles, etc. A few manuscripts have a marginal numeration by στίχοι in hundreds.

(2) LATIN. In Latin manuscripts the same system was in force, the unit being the Virgilian line of 16 syllables. This is stated explicitly in Phillipps MS. 12266 at Cheltenham, where the writer, in order to check the dishonesty of copyists, states that he had calculated on this basis the number of lines in the books of the Bible and the writings of Cyprian. Stichometrical notes are, however, not common in Latin manuscripts.

Stichometry, a purely mechanical device, is distinct from colometry, the method of dividing texts according to sense-lines. This, according to Jerome (pref. to Isaiah) was common in manuscripts of Demosthenes and Cicero, and was adopted in his Vulgate version of the Prophets. There is no trace of it in extant Greek papyri, but it is found in bilingual manuscripts (where its utility is obvious), and in some later Vulgate manuscripts.

C. Graux, *Rev. Phil.* 1878, 97; F. Ritschl, *Opusc.* (1866), i. 74; V. Gardthausen, *Griechische Paläographie²* (1913), ii. 70–82; E. M. Thompson, *Introd. to Gr. and Lat. Palaeography* (1912), 67–71. F. G. K.

STICHOMYTHIA (στιχομυθία, Poll. 4. 113, τὸ παρ' ἓν ἰαμβεῖον ἀντιλέγειν) is a form of dramatic dialogue in which two characters speak a single line each for a considerable stretch (cf. *Henry VI*, III. iii. 2). Sometimes they speak two lines each with similar regularity (Eur.

Bacch. 935 ff.). As Gross shows, Aeschylus was less strict in his use of stichomythia in later plays than in earlier, whereas Euripides grew more strict. Sophocles, avoiding in this as in other respects stiffness in the structure of his iambic verse, is far freer than either; and in comedy, with its naturalistic technique of dialogue and ready tolerance of *antilabe* (breaking of a line between speakers), there is hardly a trace of stichomythia (Ar. *Ach.* 1097 ff., a special case; 305 ff., pairs; *Plut.* 163 ff.). Stichomythia can be highly effective, as in the tensely concentrated dialogue between Orestes and his mother (Aesch. *Cho.* 908 ff.), and that between Oedipus and the Herdsman (Soph. *OT* 1147 ff.); but it tends to involve the introduction of padding (e.g. Soph. *OT* 559, Eur. *Ion* 1002). Even in a long and otherwise regular series stichomythia is sometimes broken, particularly towards the end. Editors occasionally emend needlessly through a mistaken desire for symmetry.

A. Gross, *Die Stichomythie in d. griech. Trag. u. Kom.* (1905).
J. D. D.

STĬLO PRAECONINUS, Lucius Aelius (Suet. *Gram.* 3; Plin. *HN* 33. 29), the first great Roman scholar, born at Lanuvium about 150 B.C., of equestrian rank, and a Stoic by training. He interested himself in literary criticism, antiquities, grammar, and etymologies; though not an orator, he composed speeches for others. Amongst his pupils he numbered Varro and Cicero (*Brutus* 205–7), and his aims and methods profoundly influenced his own and succeeding generations. His work on literature included interpretations of the *carmina Saliorum*, comments on the language of the XII Tables, critical editions of Ennius and Lucilius, and the establishing of a canon of twenty-five plays of Plautus, whose language he rated highly (Quintil. 10. 1. 99). It is difficult to estimate his debt to Greek grammarians, but his treatise on sentences (*De proloquiis*; Gell. 16. 8. 1) was probably inspired by the Περὶ ἀξιωμάτων of Chrysippus.

Cf. G. Funaioli, *Gramm. Rom. Frag.*, pp. 57–76; Teuffel, § 148; Schanz–Hosius, § 76 a.
J. F. M.

STILPON (*c.* 380–300 B.C.), third head of the Megarian school, may have studied under Diogenes the Cynic, as well as under Eucleides the founder of the Megarian school. During his headship the school was the most popular in Greece; *inter alios* the originally Platonic school of Eretria came under its influence, and Zeno, the founder of Stoicism, acquired from Stilpon his skill in dialectic. Stilpon is said to have written at least twenty dialogues, and the names of some are preserved. In metaphysics he maintained the monism characteristic of the Megarian school, denied the Platonic distinction between universals and individuals, and asserted the wrongness of all assertion that was not tautologous; in ethics, under Cynic influence, he extolled the virtue of ἀπάθεια, but did not press the doctrine to such extremes as the Cynics. His influence, largely due to personality rather than to originality of view, soon passed away.

PW iii A. 2525.
W. D. R.

STIMULA, Roman goddess of unknown functions. She had a grove (Livy 39. 12. 4, cf. Ovid, *Fasti* 6. 503), where the Bacchanals met in 186 B.C.; hence identified with Semele (q.v.). Ovid (ibid.; August. *De civ. D.* 4. 11) derives her name 'de stimulis quibus . . . homo impellitur'.
H. J. R.

STIPENDIUM has two meanings: (*a*) years of military service and (*b*) pay.

(*a*) In the Republican period liability for military service was at first reckoned in terms of campaigns, and eligible citizens might be called upon to serve either 16 or 20. With the extension of Rome's military commitments the equivalent years of service came to be substituted for the number of campaigns. The following

regulations were made by Augustus in 13 B.C.: (1) legionary, 16 years+4 as a veteran; (2) praetorian, 12 years; (3) auxiliary, 25 years. In A.D. 5 legionary service was increased to 20 years+5 with the veterans, and praetorian to 16, although the former were often kept with the colours for 30 or 40 years. Under the Flavians legionaries served *sub aquila* for the same number of years as the auxiliary.

(*b*) M. Camillus (q.v.) is said to have introduced pay, but its origin may be earlier. It was probably a reimbursement of the soldier for his expenses upon equipment and commissariat. In the second century the legionaries received 120 *denarii* yearly, against which stoppages were made for food and clothing. After the Marian reforms, when soldiering became a profession, and higher wages were a necessity, Caesar doubled the pay, fixing it at 10 *asses* daily or 225 *denarii* yearly. This rate for the legions was maintained by Augustus, who fixed the praetorian scale at 750 *denarii* yearly, i.e. more than three times that of the legionary. The pay given to the auxiliaries is uncertain, but may have been 75 *denarii* yearly. The following table shows the rising scale under later emperors in *denarii*.

	Legionary	Legionary Centurion	Primi Ordines	Praetorian
Augustus . .	225	3,750	7,500	750
Domitian . .	300	5,000	10,000	1,000
Commodus . .	375 }			{ 625
Severus . .	500 }	6,250	12,500	{ 850
Caracalla . .	750	12,500	25,000	2,500

A. von Domaszewski, 'Der Truppensold der Kaiserzeit,' *Neue Heidelberger Jahrbücher*, vol. x (1900); H. M. D. Parker, *The Roman Legions* (1928).
H. M. D. P.

STIPULATIO, a formal contract concluded verbally in the form of question (made by the future creditor, *stipulator*: 'centum dare spondes?'), and answer (by the future debtor: 'spondeo'). From the use of the verb *spondeo* it derived the alternative name of *sponsio* (for this identification in the time of the XII Tables see the new fragment of Gaius, 4. 17 a). *Stipulatio* was one of the oldest institutions of Roman private law, and it gradually developed into a 'fulcrum' of the whole Roman system of obligations. Originally restricted to a fixed sum of money, it was subsequently extended to any specified article (*certa res*), and eventually to any legal transaction, and its use was thrown open to non-citizens. Thus it became a general and, indeed, the most usual mode of creating any kind of obligation. Other verbs (*promittere, dare, facere,* and Greek equivalents) were now permissible, but the classical law always required oral proceedings, the personal presence of the parties, and an immediate answer substantially appropriate to the question. Every obligation concluded in another form could be confirmed and transferred into stipulation. Its simple and elastic form admitted its use for accessory obligations (sureties) by which the creditor was guaranteed against insolvency or failure of the principal debtor. The surety (*sponsor*) obliged himself to the creditor by a new *stipulatio*, called *sponsio* (in a narrower sense), to undertake the same obligation as the promissor of the first *stipulatio*. Since *sponsio* was open only to *cives* another form of *stipulatio*, *fidepromissio*, was created for non-citizens, whereby the verb *fidepromitto* obliged the surety. If the principal debt did not arise from a *stipulatio*, the stipulation for suretyship had to be in the form of *fideiussio*.

Stipulatio was largely applied in civil proceedings, e.g. to oblige a defendant or his representative to fulfil a judgement (*judicatum solvi*); representatives of the plaintiff assured the ratification of their action by a *cautio de rato*. In many cases a *stipulatio* could be ordered by a magistrate, especially by the praetor (*stipulationes praetoriae*), both in order to make more stringent an already existing obligation, and to create a new obligation for the protection of an interest otherwise not protected, for lack of *ius civile* (e.g. in case of usufruct, legacy, guardianship, or damage threatened to a neighbour's property by the dangerous condition of a building, etc.).

Since *stipulatio* took place without witnesses, it soon became usual to draw up a written note (*instrumentum, cautio*) to provide evidence of its conclusion. By a post-classical development the document was deemed sufficient, *stipulatio* being taken for granted. The requirement of oral form was thus considerably relaxed, if not abandoned, and a later imperial rescript abolished the necessity of solemn words. Under Justinian the simultaneous presence of the parties was the only surviving requirement, and this was assumed if the parties had been in the same place on the day mentioned in the document.

E. Levy, *Sponsio fidepromissio* (1906); S. Riccobono, *Sav. Zeitschr.* xxxv, xlii, and *Corso di diritto Romano: Stipulationes, Contractus, Pacta* (1935). See also bibliography s.v. LAW AND PROCEDURE, ROMAN, I.
A. B.

STIPULATIO AQUILIANA, see AQUILIUS (4).

STOA, see PORTICO.

STOA, philosophical school or sect, founded by Zeno of Citium in about 300 B.C., named after the Stoa Poikile, a public hall in Athens, in which Zeno and his successors used to teach. Though the school was probably less strictly organized than the Academy and the Peripatos, it had a continuous succession of official heads (προστάται) from Zeno to at least A.D. 260 (the latest date known) and probably some time later. But it had faded out long before Justinian closed the last philosophical schools at Athens in A.D. 529.

The history of the school is usually divided into three periods: (I) The Early Stoa (from Zeno to the first half of the second century B.C.); (II) the Middle Stoa (second and first centuries B.C.); (III) The Late Stoa (time of the Roman Empire).

I. The *Early Stoa* is represented by: (1) Zeno (until 263); (2) disciples of Zeno: Cleanthes (προστάτης from 263 to 232), Ariston of Chios, Herillus of Carthage, Dionysius 'ὁ Μεταθέμενος', Persaeus, Aratus of Soli; (3) disciples of Cleanthes: Chrysippus (προστάτης from 232 to 207) and Sphaerus; (4) disciples of Chrysippus: Zeno of Tarsus and Diogenes the Babylonian, who followed Zeno of Tarsus as προστάτης (exact date unknown); (5) disciples of Diogenes: Antipater of Tarsus (προστάτης from *c.* 150 to 129 B.C.), Archedemus of Tarsus, and Boethus of Sidon.

Zeno was the author of all the fundamental doctrines of the Early Stoa. His system was taken over in its entirety by Cleanthes—while Ariston and Herillus developed doctrines of their own and were later considered heretics—and it was elaborated and corrected by Chrysippus. The philosophy of Chrysippus became later so much identified with Stoic orthodoxy that it superseded the Zenonian system in the mind of posterity. This makes it difficult to determine exactly in what respects Chrysippus differed from his predecessors, since neither his nor their works have survived.

The system of the Early Stoics was divided into three parts: (*a*) τὸ λογικόν (comprising theory of knowledge, logic, rhetoric); (*b*) τὸ φυσικόν (ontology, physics, theology); (*c*) τὸ ἠθικόν (ethics). Their main doctrines were the following:

(1) Virtue is based on knowledge. Only the wise man who not only knows the truth but also knows with certainty that he knows it can be really virtuous. Since knowledge is the agreement of one's mental conceptions with reality, the wisdom of the wise man consists in his having such mental conceptions as are caused by real things, correspond exactly to (or are accurate images of) these things, and could not have been produced by other causes. Conceptions of this kind are called καταληπτικαὶ

φαντασίαι. In the first part of their system (τὸ λογικόν) the Stoics tried to prove that such conceptions are possible and discussed how they are acquired, how they differ from other conceptions, and how they can be expressed in language.

(2) It is the aim of the philosopher to live in harmony (Zeno), or, as Chrysippus added, in harmony with nature (ὁμολογουμένως φύσει ζῆν). The formative and guiding principle in nature is the λόγος (reason), which is identified with God and manifests itself as εἱμαρμένη (fate, necessity) and πρόνοια (divine providence). In a special way it manifests itself in human reason. Among the elements fire is most closely related to the λόγος. The universe is periodically consumed by fire, from which in due course a new world arises.

(3) To be virtuous, that is to live in harmony with reason, is the only good, not to be virtuous the only evil. Everything else is indifferent (ἀδιάφορον). But the orthodox Stoics—in contrast to heretics like Ariston—admitted that there were also προηγμένα (for instance: self-preservation, health) which the wise man chooses and ἀποπροηγμένα (death, illness, pain, etc.) which he avoids if he can do so without acting unvirtuously. Yet their presence or absence does not affect his happiness. For since he always acts in harmony with reason he is always possessed of the only real good and therefore completely independent of the vicissitudes of fortune. He is also absolutely brave, since he knows that pain and death are no evils; absolutely continent, since he knows that pleasure is not a good; and absolutely just, since he is not influenced by prejudice or favour.

II. The *Middle Stoa* is chiefly represented by Panaetius, Diogenes the Babylonian's successor as προστάτης, and by his disciples Posidonius and Hecaton.

Zeno of Tarsus and his disciples had begun to doubt some special doctrines of their predecessors, for instance the doctrine of a periodical world conflagration (ἐκπύρωσις). Panaetius was the first to reject this doctrine altogether and to undertake a thorough revision of the whole Stoic system of philosophy, partly under the influence of Platonic and Aristotelian ideas. In ethics he rejected the belief that only the absolutely wise man can be virtuous. He considered it the duty of the philosopher to help those who without aspiring to absolute wisdom are making progress in wisdom and virtue (προκόπτοντες). He tried to adapt Stoic ethics to the needs of active statesmen and soldiers. It was through him that Stoicism became so important an element in the life of the best representatives of Roman nobility. His ethical views had great influence on P. Scipio Aemilianus, in whose company he spent some years of his life, and on Scipio's friends P. Rutilius Rufus, C. Laelius, Q. Aelius Tubero, Q. Mucius Scaevola the augur, Q. Mucius Scaevola the pontifex and famous jurist, etc. Through his writings he influenced the younger Cato, Brutus, and Cicero, though the latter professed himself an Academic. His disciple Hecaton created a system of moral casuistry, discussing in detail how the virtuous man would act under certain circumstances, especially when there is a seeming conflict of duties. Posidonius subjected the system of the Early Stoics to an even more thorough revision than Panaetius. He was the author of a new natural philosophy comprising all sciences. Mainly through him Stoicism influenced many scientists, like the astronomers Geminus and Cleomedes, the geographer Strabo, and many others.

III. During the latest period in the history of the Stoa purely theoretical questions, though still discussed (cf. Seneca's *Quaestiones Naturales*, and, in the second century, the dispute between Academics, Peripatetics, and Stoics over the categories), receded into the background, giving way to a philosophy which was almost exclusively concerned with ethical questions.

Most important among the Stoic philosophers of the

first century after Christ were L. Annaeus Seneca, L. Annaeus Cornutus, C. Musonius Rufus, and, towards the end of the century, Epictetus. At the same time Stoicism gave a philosophical foundation for the aristocratic opposition to those of the emperors who tried to rule without or against the Senate. Helvidius Priscus, Paetus Thrasea, Rubellius Plautus, the famous opponents of Nero, and Junius Rusticus, who was condemned to death under Domitian, professed Stoicism.

The most important representative of Stoicism in the second century was the Emperor M. Aurelius. The names of a great many Stoic philosophers of minor importance who lived at that time have come down to us. None of the important representatives of the school taught in Athens during that period.

From the third century onward the school gradually faded out. But Stoic doctrine had an important influence on later Neoplatonism and on the philosophy of some of the Fathers of the Christian Church. While the Stoic school ceased to exist, Stoicism spread far beyond the ranks of professional philosophers, and continued to exercise an important influence on the life and thought of many.

See also ALLEGORY, GREEK, para. 3; ASTROLOGY; ARCESILAUS (1) (for the sceptical criticism of the Stoic doctrine of knowledge).

Stoicorum veterum fragmenta, coll. von Arnim, 4 vols. (1921-4); A. Schmekel, *Die Philosophie der mittleren Stoa* (1892); W. L. Davidson, *The Stoic Creed* (1907); E. Bevan, *Stoics and Sceptics* (1913); O. Rieth, *Grundbegriffe der stoischen Ethik* (1933).
K. von F.

STOA OF EUMENES, *see* ACROPOLIS.

STOBAEUS ('Ιωάννης Στοβεύς), author of an anthology of excerpts from poets and prose-writers, intended in the first instance for the instruction of his son Septimius. The work was probably composed in the fifth century A.D.; it consisted originally of four books, which came to be grouped later under the titles 'Εκλογαί and 'Ανθολόγιον, though subject-matter and treatment are essentially homogeneous. It deals with a variety of topics, from metaphysics to household economy; from bk. 2 onwards it is concerned chiefly with ethical questions. The illustrative extracts, which S. probably owed in large measure to earlier collectors, are arranged under successive headings, being grouped generally in the same order, beginning with the poets. Photius (9th c.) commends the work for its usefulness, especially to writers and speakers. Its value for us consists in the large number of citations from earlier literature, which not only supplement our knowledge of classical authors, but often throw light upon difficulties in the regular manuscript tradition.

Suidas (s.v. 'Ιωάννης); Photius, *Bibl.*, cod. 167. Editions: T. Gaisford (1822, 1850); C. Wachsmuth and O. Hense (1884-1912). Criticism: A. Elter, *De Ioh. St. cod. Phot.* (1880); id., *De gnom. graec. hist. et orig.* (1893).
W. M. E.

STOLA, *see* DRESS, para. 3.

STOLO, GAIUS LICINIUS, and L. Sextius Lateranus, traditionally tribunes of the plebs from 376 to 367 B.C., were celebrated as the authors of the law that opened the consulship to the plebs, by enacting that one consul might be a plebeian. L. Sextius was in all likelihood the first plebeian consul and he may have been appointed in 366: but the details of the long struggle, which preceded the passing of the Licinian-Sextian laws, and most of the laws themselves, must be rejected either as anticipating events of the Gracchan Age, or as inventions of Licinius Macer designed to glorify his family. By the enactment which increased from two to ten the number of the officials who superintended various religious ceremonies, the plebeians secured an equal representation. The existence of a law on debts and usury, providing that

interest should be deducted from the principal and the balance paid in three equal annual instalments, is sometimes denied. By far the most disputed measure is that which limited tenancies of public land; even if Stolo took some such step to meet the economic crisis of his time, the details are obviously borrowed from the agrarian policy of the Gracchan Age, especially from the law carried by the tribune of 145, with which Licinius Macer is likely to have credited his ancestor.

B. Niese, *Hermes* 1888; F. Münzer, *PW* xiii. 464 ff.; H. Stuart Jones and H. Last, *CAH* vii. 524 ff., 538 ff.; J. Carcopino, *République romaine* i (1935), 153 f., 167 f.; G. Niccolini, *Fasti d. tribuni d. plebe* (1934), 56 ff.; H. H. Scullard, *Hist. Roman World* (1935), 99 ff.
P. T.

STONES, SACRED. The Greeks (and Romans) preserved many survivals of religious primitivism, some of which may be due to the pre-Greek (and the pre-Roman) culture (especially where there was no clear explanation or legend). Good specimens are the many stones (and rocks) that because of their remarkable appearance or mysterious efficacy were regarded as holy, possessing unusual power (or *mana*), in fact fetishes (cf. the Greek *baitylos*). Unhewn stones were the Eros of Thespiai, the Charites of Orchomenus, the healing 'Heracles' at Hyettus (characteristically all Boeotian cults), the 'Zeus Descender' (Καππῶτας) at Gythium (probably a meteorite); at Delphi was shown the very stone which Kronos swallowed in place of the new-born Zeus, and oil was daily poured on it. Here they also possessed the much revered Omphalos, q.v. (presumably a relic from the previous Gaea-cult at Delphi). Thirty squared stones were reverenced at Pharae and had individual divine names; an obelisk at Megara was named Apollon Karinos, and the small stone columns which commonly stood before the doors of Athenian houses were called by the name of Apollo Agyieus. At Pheneus in Arcadia solemn oaths were taken by the *petroma* of Demeter, which was 'two great stones joined to one another' (Paus. 8. 15. 1). We know of representations of Zeus as a pillar (Tarentum) (pillar-cult was well known to the Cretans of pre-Greek times), as a pyramid (Sicyon), and as an omphalos (on Mount Casius). Herms were extremely popular—square columns with human heads and a *membrum virile*. From the Near East we may adduce the black stone (a meteorite) belonging to the Mother of the Gods at Pessinus, the white conical stone of Aphrodite at Paphos, and the cones and pyramids which often occur on coins from Asia Minor.

At Rome an ancient boundary-stone on the Capitol passed as the Jupiter Terminus, who here followed on the old god Terminus. The Romans also swore on 'Jupiter the stone', cf. E. Harrison, *Essays Ridgeway*, 92 ff.; and the *lapis manalis*, which was carried from the Porta Capena by the pontifices and over which water was probably poured, was important as a rain charm.

M. W. de Visser, *Die nicht menschengestaltigen Götter der Griechen* (1903).
S. E.

STRABO (1), GNAEUS POMPEIUS (*cos.* 89 B.C.), a vigorous commander with a reputation for cruelty, avarice, and perfidy. In the Social War, as legate of P. Rutilius Lupus, he was defeated by Afranius (Lafrenius) in 90 B.C.; was besieged at Firmum in Picenum where he had estates; and, after its relief, himself besieged Asculum. In 89, as consul, he introduced a law admitting the Transpadanes to the Latin Right; he defeated the Italians on the Adriatic coast, and then in the regions north of Samnium, which he thus isolated; finally, he took Asculum. In 88 the Senate relieved him of his command; he handed over his army, but was believed to have instigated the murder of his successor, Q. Pompeius Rufus (*cos.* 88). In 87, when the Marians attacked Rome, he moved so slowly that he was held to have betrayed the cause of the Optimates when it could have been saved. After an indecisive battle with Cinna and Sertorius outside the Colline Gate, he was saved from assassination by his son's prudence and vigour; but he was killed by lightning or died of disease soon afterwards.

On his grant of franchise to some Spanish horsemen, see Dessau, *ILS* 8888 and cf. G. H. Stevenson, *JRS* 1919, 95 ff.   M. H.

STRABO (2) (64/63 B.C.–A.D. 21 at least), historian and geographer, a Greek (partly Asiatic in descent) of Amaseia, Pontus. He studied grammar under Aristodemus, and, later, geography under Tyrannion, philosophy under Xenarchus, and knew Posidonius. He was in Rome in 44–35, c. 31, and 7 B.C.; in Egypt 25–c. 19 B.C. (collecting geographical material); and in Amaseia c. 7 B.C. to his death. A Peripatetic, S. became a Stoic, with some contempt for religion, and admired the Romans and their empire; independent but no great traveller, he knew various parts of Asia Minor and Egypt, but little of Greece or Italy, and probably wrote for persons in political positions (he emphasizes the use of geography in public affairs—1. 1. 16–18), but whether at Rome for Romans or at Amaseia or Alexandria for Greeks is disputed. Apparent ignorance and omissions do point to some special purpose.

His *Historical Sketches* (Ἱστορικὰ ὑπομνήματα), forty-seven books excluding the era covered by Polybius, are lost; his *Geography* (Γεωγραφία), seventeen books, has survived. Books 1–2: introductory. 1. Homer; Eratosthenes criticized. 2. Mathematical geography; criticism of Eratosthenes and Polybius, examination of Posidonius (especially zones); Eudoxus' voyages. S.'s opinions on the earth; cartography on sphere and plane. 3. Spain, Scillies. 4. Gaul, Britain, etc. 5–6. Italy, Sicily; the Roman Empire. 7. North and east Europe, north Balkans (some is lost). 8–10. Greece (very antiquarian and mythological). 11. Euxine-Caspian, etc., Taurus, Armenia. 12–14. Asia Minor (some mythology and history). 15. India, Persia. 16. Mesopotamia, Palestine, Ethiopian coasts, Arabia. 17. Egypt, Ethiopia, north Africa.

Strabo brings Eratosthenes more up to date. On a geocentric sphere, the one land-mass is ocean-girt. S. knows Mediterranean lands, Egypt, Asia Minor; little of British Isles; nothing of northernmost Europe and Asia; Caspian by Alexander's writers and Megasthenes; Africa is a triangle north of the equator. S. gives geographical and historical information readably, without details except where interesting or important. Having moderate (and not up-to-date) mathematical and astronomical knowledge, S. underestimates both; latitudes, longitudes, and 'climata' he treats lightly, and is inadequate in physical geography and phenomena, being predisposed towards his own ideas of what is important. He reveres Homer, undervalues Herodotus, scorns Pytheas. He adds Roman to Greek authorities, despising (rightly?) Roman geographers. But his work is a storehouse of information, an historical geography, and a philosophy of geography.

Text, translation, and full bibliographies in H. L. Jones, *The Geog. of S.* (Loeb).   E. H. W.

STRABO, GAIUS JULIUS 'VOPISCUS' CAESAR, *see* CAESAR (8) STRABO.

STRATEGI (στρατηγοί), a general term for commanders of armies or fleets, but also for magistrates with mainly military duties; *strategi* are found in most Greek States, varying in number according to the size and organization of the State. In Athens they formed a college of ten, first instituted (probably) in 501–500, one from each *phyle*, each to command the hoplite regiment of his *phyle*, and together to form a council of war to the polemarch (q.v.). Like all officials of whom technical skill was required, they were elected by vote by the Assembly, for one year, and could be re-elected any number of times.

In 487, when the polemarch ceased to command the army, the *strategi* became the highest military officers, their regimental commands devolving upon a new body, the ten *taxiarchoi*. Like all other Athenian officials, they were subject to *euthyna* (q.v.), and might be suspended by the Ecclesia to stand immediate trial for misconduct. When they were re-elected their *euthyna* was postponed.

2. Since 487 the *strategi* were the most important magistrates at Athens. They were responsible for the garrison of Attica, the fleet, the protection of commerce against piracy. In war they were appointed to take single or joint command in particular campaigns; if several were appointed, one *strategus* might be given supreme command. They sometimes received power to conclude treaties or terms of surrender or to decide the size of an expeditionary force (στρατηγοὶ αὐτοκράτορες), subject only to the usual *euthyna* when they left office. In the field *strategi* had special disciplinary powers; and like other magistrates they had judicial duties within their own sphere—i.e. they introduced to the dicastery and presided over the trial of military offences (desertion, cowardice, etc.). At home, they alone of magistrates had the right of sitting with the Boule, and could ask it to summon a special meeting of the Ecclesia; but they had no special powers in the Ecclesia.

3. In the fifth century most of the leading politicians were elected *strategi* and led armies and navies (though some *strategi* were not politicians). In the fourth, when specialization of military functions went farther, *strategi* and politicians were seldom the same men; only Phocion tried (unsuccessfully) to combine the two duties. *Circa* 350 B.C. the functions of individual *strategi* began to be specialized: one *strategus* was elected to command at home, two in the Piraeus (these three as well to have control of the *Ephebi*, q.v.), one for service abroad, and one for administrative services in connexion with the trierarchy (*see* TRIERARCHY *and* SYMMORIAI). Later, one was appointed for the navy and one for foreign troops.

4. Some outstanding *strategi* obtained frequent re-election (as Cimon, Pericles—often between 460 and 445, and every year from 443 to 429,—Phocion, 40 times). This led to the relaxation and (c. 330) to the abolition of the rule requiring all the *phylae* to be represented on the board of the *strategi*.

5. In most other States the position of the *strategi* was, as far as we know, similar to that in Athens. An exception was the single *strategus*, the highest magistrate with both military and political powers, in the Achaean and Aetolian Leagues (qq.v.).

6. In the territorial monarchies of the Hellenistic age the *strategi* were district governors. They maintained order within their province and exercised administrative jurisdiction.

Aristotle, *Ath. Pol.* ch. 61.   A. W. G.

STRATOCLES (c. 350–292 B.C.) was one of Demosthenes' accusers in the Harpalus trial (324–323). He became the agent of Demetrius Poliorcetes in Athens from 307 and directed the immoderate adulation shown to him. In 303 his authority was upheld by Demetrius against an attempted revolt by the party of Cassander, but was shattered after Demetrius' defeat at Ipsus (301). In 294 he was reinstated by Demetrius, but had to share his power with more moderate politicians. His main characteristic was unscrupulous demagogy.

W. B. Dinsmoor, *Archons of Athens* (1931).   F. W. W.

STRATON (1) (Στράτων) of Lampsacus (d. 270–268 B.C.; Apollod. ap. Diog. Laert. 5. 58), son of Arcesilaus, Peripatetic philosopher. He was a pupil of Theophrastus. For some time he acted as teacher to Ptolemy Philadelphus in Alexandria (l.c., cf. 37). After Theophrastus' death in 288–286 he became president of the school, which he governed for eighteen years up to his death (l.c.).

In spite of the logical, ethical, and historical treatises he wrote (D.L. 58 f.), S. was a specialized physicist. He transformed the Aristotelian philosophy into a materialistic science. Of the greatest influence on ancient mechanics and medicine was his theory of space. S. showed that the Democritean 'empty space' does not exist as a 'continuum' under natural conditions, but only as intermittent discontinuous reality within bodies. Whenever by artificial conditions a continuous empty space is created, the molecular parts of the bodies try to close it at once (Diels, *Dox. Graec.* Index, s.v.; Simpl. in Arist. *Phys.*, Index, s.v.; Heron, *Spiritalia*, Introd.).

E. Zeller, *Aristotle*, etc., Engl. Transl., 2. 450 f.; M. Siebeck, *Gesch. der Psychologie* i. 2; T. Gomperz, *Greek Thinkers*, Engl. Transl., 4. 499; H. Diels, *Zum phys. System des S.* (Berlin Akad. 1893; important work); W. Jaeger, *Hermes* 1913; *PW* iv. 278.
K. O. B.

STRATON (2), New Comedy poet. The only extant fragment (for which see Guéraud and Jouguet, *Livre d'écolier*, 1938, 35 ff.) is a skit upon the glossomania of the time, in which a bombastic cook describes common things in obsolete poetical words and phrases, and causes his patron to call him 'ex-slave of some kind of rhapsode' (ῥαψῳδοτοιούτου τινὸς | δοῦλος γεγονώς), and therefore filled with Homeric vocables. The play *Phoenicides* (*Phoenix*, according to Suidas) is dated *c.* 300 B.C. by the reference (v. 43) to the work of Philetas of Cos.

FCG iv. 545 f.: *CAF* iii. 361 f. W. G. W.

STRATON (3) of Sardis (*fl.* A.D. 125) is the author of about 100 epigrams in the *Greek Anthology*, the core of bk. 12. Almost all deal with homosexual love, using the erotic conventions elaborated by Alexandrian poets; but they are usually either coarse or mawkish, and are neither sociologically nor aesthetically interesting.

J. Geffcken in *PW*, s.v. G. H.

STRATONICUS (*fl. c.* 410–360 B.C.), of Athens, musician and wit, contemporary of Timotheus and Polyeidus (Ath. 8. 352 a–b) and of the actor Simycas (ibid. 348 a). His witticisms, Εὐτράπελοι λόγοι, were well known soon after his death and excerpts made of them (Ath. 350 d). Characteristic examples are: 'Who is more barbarous—the Boeotians or the Thessalians? The Eleans' (ibid. 350 b); and on a small city: αὕτη οὐ πόλις ἐστίν, ἀλλὰ μόλις (ibid. 352 a). C. M. B.

STRATTIS, writer of Athenian comedy; dramatic activity *c.* 409–375 B.C. Suidas lists seventeen comedies, mainly mythological burlesques (e.g. Ἀταλάντη; Ἀνθρωπορέστης), parodies (e.g. Μήδεια; Φιλοκτήτης; Μυρμιδόνες), and personal attacks (e.g. Κινησίας; Μακεδόνες ἢ Παυσανίας).

FCG ii. 763 ff.; *CAF* i. 711 ff.; Demiańczuk, *Suppl. Com.* 84 ff. M. P.

STRENAE. This name was given by the Romans to the luck-bringing twigs which at the New Year were brought from the grove of the goddess Strenia and were exchanged by way of gift as bearers of luck and blessing. This oldest form of *strenae* was preserved in cult, since on the old New Year's Day (1 March) the old laurel branches before the doors of the *rex sacrorum*, the great *flamines*, the *Curiae*, and the temple of Vesta were replaced by new branches. The *strena* is a Spring ceremony and is related to the German May tree. Later it came to be a gift, usually money, but twigs retained an aspect of luck in popular usage. The fact that the use involved an omen led to the word *strena* receiving the meaning 'omen' as early as Plautus.

L. Deubner, *Glotta* iii (1912), 34 ff.; M. P. Nilsson, *PW* iv A. 351 ff.; U. Wilcken, *Arch. Pap.* xi. 297. L. D.

STROPHIC RESPONSION, *see* METRE, GREEK, V.

STYX, a river of Arcadia, which plunges from a snow-fed spring on the north-east side of Mt. Chelmos, down a black rock to a depth of 600 feet, and flows through a wild gorge to join the Crathis. Its water was thought poisonous. It was one of the nine rivers of the underworld; the gods in Homer, and the Arcadians in fact, took oath by it (Hdt. 6. 74).

Hesiod, *Theog.* 775 ff.; Paus. 8. 17–18, and Frazer ad loc.
T. J. D.

SUASORIA, one of the two main exercises in *declamatio* (q.v.), was the rhetorical speech of advice imagined as applicable to a crisis in the career of some eminent figure in history, e.g. Juvenal's school exercise (1. 16) supposed to urge abdication on the dictator Sulla. Though a less advanced exercise than the *controversia* (q.v.), it involved for success historical knowledge, psychological penetration, and dramatic ability. In the elder Seneca's collection, now imperfect, seven examples remain, argued in detail; e.g. 'Alexander deliberates whether he should sail the Ocean', 'Cicero deliberates whether he should beg Antony to spare his life'. As in the *controversiae*, and with similar rhetorical devices, Seneca's method is to recall briefly but dexterously the mode of treatment of such themes followed by prominent rhetors of the time of Augustus and Tiberius. In this he displays a marvellous memory for the general line taken, and a Boswellian gift for reproducing the style of different speakers on the same problem. The *suasoria* was the exercise in which Ovid as a student excelled: the *controversia* did not appeal to his genius ('molesta illi erat omnis argumentatio', Sen. *Controv.* 2. 2. 12). *See also* EDUCATION, III. 3.

Texts: H. J. Müller, *L. Annaei Senecae Oratorum et Rhetorum Sententiae Divisiones Colores* (1887); H. Bornecque (with Fr. Transl., 1902); W. A. Edward, *The Suasoriae of Seneca the Elder* (introd., text, Engl. Transl., notes; 1928). For fuller bibliogr., Wight Duff's *Lit. Hist. of Rome in Silver Age*, p. 42. *See also* DECLAMATIO, RHETORIC, SENECA THE ELDER. J. W. D.

SUBSCRIPTIONES. (1) GREEK. In rolls of the classical period (so far as extant evidence goes) information as to the contents of a manuscript is appended at the end (like the colophons in early printed books), not prefixed. This information was principally the name of the author and title of the work. This seems to suggest that when a roll had been read, it was put back on the shelf with the end of the roll outside, leaving to the next person who wished to read it the task of rolling it backwards to the beginning (*JTS* xl. 56). In extant papyri the subscriptions are of this simplest type. In one of the earliest Biblical papyrus codices (Chester Beatty Pap. II, of the Pauline Epistles), the number of στίχοι in each epistle has been added, but in a different hand.

Medieval codices often add more information, such as the name of the scribe, the fact that the text has been corrected, or the date of writing. Thus the *Codex Sinaiticus* has notes at the end of Esdras and Esther recording the correction of the text from a manuscript by Pamphilus. In later times prayers for faithfulness in transcription, or curses against inaccuracy or theft, are sometimes added.

(2) LATIN. Early Latin classical manuscripts not infrequently have subscriptions recording the name of a corrector, often a man of considerable standing; e.g. the Medicean codex of Virgil, 'Turcius Rufius Apronianus Asterius . . . legi et distinxi codicem fratris Macharii'. Asterius, who was consul in 494, also revised Sedulius. Other subscriptions are: (Martial) 'Ego Torquatus Gennadius emendaui feliciter'; (Apuleius) 'Ego Crispus Sallustius emendaui Romae felix' (with dates = 395 and 397); (Persius) 'Flauius Julius temptaui emendare sine antigrapho' (A.D. 402). These belong to the time when educated Romans, finding no outlet in public life, retired to their country houses and literature.

In some cases these revisions affected the textual tradition; e.g. nearly all the manuscripts of Terence contain the text as revised by Calliopius, and all manuscripts but one of the first decade of Livy bear the subscriptions of Nicomachus Flavianus, his son Nicomachus Dexter, and of Victorianus, all men of senatorial rank about A.D. 400.

V. Gardthausen, *Gr. Palaeographie* ii (1913), 425; Jahn, 'Die Subscriptionen in den Handschriften römischer Klassiker', in *Sitz. Sächs. Gesellsch. d. Wissenschaften* 1851, 327.   F. G. K.

SUBURA, the valley between the Viminal and Esquiline Hills of Rome, opening out of the Argiletum and Forum Transitorium. The district was notorious for its bustle, noise, dirt, and shady morality. Its reputable traders sold provisions and delicacies, and manufacturing trades are also known (*CIL* vi. 1953, 9284, 9399, 9491, 33862). Here lay a Jewish synagogue (*CIG* 6447). Distinguished residents included Julius Caesar.

See Juv. 11. 51. 141; Martial 2. 17; 5. 22. 5–9; 7. 31; 10. 94. 56; 12. 18. 2; Pers. 5. 32.   I. A. R.

SUEBI, an important Germanic people (including the Semnones, Hermunduri, Marcomanni, Quadi, Naristi, Vangiones, Nemetes, Triboci) which began to expand south-westwards from its home in the Mark of Brandenburg and Mecklenburg-Strelitz during the second century B.C., the various tribal divisions becoming differentiated during the process. The Semnones remained in Brandenburg; they were regarded as the parent stem and controlled a sanctuary venerated by all Suebic tribes. Soon after 100 B.C. the Suebi reached the Rhine; after the campaigns of Ariovistus (q.v.) the Vangiones, Nemetes, and Triboci were left where they had settled in the Palatinate and Alsace. The Suebi who occasioned Caesar's passage of the Rhine were probably the Quadi. Drusus marched against the Transrhenane Suebi in 9 B.C., and this led to their migration, the Quadi going to Moravia, the Marcomanni to Bohemia. A few remained behind (e.g. the Suebi Nicretes around Ladenburg). The Marcomannic kingdom of Maroboduus (q.v.) encouraged Roman traders and had a wide influence on German culture. The advance of the Goths upset the Suebi, and the Marcomannic War (168–79) resulted. About the same time the Semnones began to migrate south-westwards, and later, as the Alamanni (q.v.), became dangerous foes of the Empire.

L. Schmidt, *Geschichte der deutschen Stämme, Die Westgermanen²* (1938), 128 ff. Tacitus, *Germania*, ed. Anderson (1938), 178 ff.
                                                        O. B.

SUEIUS, a pedantic writer of rural idylls. Ribbeck identifies him with Seius, a friend of Cicero and of Varro.

Baehr. *FPR* 285; Morel, *FPL* 53.

SUETONIUS (1) PAULINUS, GAIUS, as ex-praetor in A.D. 41, commanded against the Mauretanians and was the first Roman to cross the Atlas mountains, of which he wrote a description (Pliny, *HN* 5. 14). He was probably *consul suffectus c.* 42. In 59 he was appointed governor of Britain and at once began a forward movement reaching the Irish Sea and subduing Mona (Anglesey), a stronghold of Druidism. During the campaign he learnt of Boudicca's revolt (61) and swiftly returned with his advance-guard, but unable to concentrate an adequate force was compelled to abandon Londinium and Verulamium to sack. Retreating (along Watling Street) to his main force, he routed Boudicca's attack. His severity towards the rebels led to discords with the *procurator* Classicianus and his own recall (61). In 69 he supported Otho, and took a leading part in the campaign of Bedriacum, after which he came to terms with Vitellius.

*PIR*¹, S 278; *PW* iv A. 591–3; Collingwood-Myres, *Roman Britain*, 98–104.   C. E. S.

SUETONIUS (2) TRANQUILLUS, GAIUS (*c.* A.D. 69–*c.* 140), born probably in Rome (Macé, *Essai sur Suét.* 33), of equestrian rank, son of Suet. Laetus, tribune in a legion at Bedriacum (*Otho* 10). He practised law for a time; took no part in political life; and, when made a military tribune through Pliny's influence, had the post transferred to a relative (Plin. *Epist.* 3. 8). That he was a teacher lacks evidence. He received from Trajan the *ius trium liberorum*, but without fulfilling its conditions (Plin. *Ep.* 10. 94 and 95). He was secretary (*ab epistulis*) to Hadrian, probably while Septicius Clarus was Praetorian Prefect (119–21 or 122). Both were dismissed by the Emperor, apparently for some breach of court etiquette (S.H.A. *Hadr.* 11). After that we hear no more of S.; he seems to have passed his remaining life in retirement and literary work.

WORKS

1. *De viris illustribus*, composed 106–13, biographies of literary men, of which we have *De grammaticis et rhetoribus* (p. 98 f. Reiff.) and a few Lives of Roman writers, differing in the extent of their abridgement and interpolation. Jerome lists thirty-three from *De poetis*, of which *Terence, Horace,* and *Lucan* are generally regarded as Suetonian; *Virgil, Tibullus* (greatly abridged), and *Persius* are accepted by many, although the last-named is directly attributed to Valerius Probus (q.v.) of Berytus (*fl. c.* A.D. 56–80), who edited the earlier writers with biographies of the Alexandrian type as introductions (Suet. *Gram.* 24; p. 118 Reiff.). Of Jerome's list of fifteen from *De oratoribus* (p. 80 Re) we have a brief abstract of the *Life of Passienus Crispus* (p. 88 Re) and of his list of six from *De historicis* (p. 91 Re) the *Life of Pliny the Elder*.

2. *De vita Caesarum* (published *c.* 121), biographies of Julius to Domitian, complete except for the first few chapters of *Julius*, apparently lost between the sixth and eighth centuries.

3. *Lost Works* in Greek and Latin, catalogued by Suidas, s.v. Τράγκυλλος, preserved only in fragments, differently arranged by various scholars: *On Famous Courtesans* (Joh. Lydus 3. 64, Suet. *Rel.* Reiff., p. 349); *On the Kings* (Auson. *Epist.* 23, p. 267 Peiper; *Epist.* 19, Suet. *Rel.* Reiff., p. 315); *On Public Offices* (Macé, op. cit., pp. 300 ff.; Suet. *Rel.* Reiff., p. 346); *Roma* (pp. 147 ff. Re); *The Games of the Greeks* (part of *Ludicra Historia*, Gell. 9. 7. 3; p. 322 Re); *On Cicero, De Re Publica* (p. 352 Re); *Pratum* or *Prata* (Prisc. *Gramm. Lat.* 2. 387. 24 Keil; Suet. *Rel.* Reiff., pp. 147 ff.); *On Terms of Abuse in Greek* (p. 273 Re); *De rebus variis* (Charisius, *Gramm.* 2. 236. 17 Keil; p. 353 Re); *On Critical Marks in Books* (pp. 137 ff. Re); *Historia*, title uncertain (Gell. 15. 4. 4; p. 354 Reiff.). How many of these were separate books is doubtful; of his miscellany, *Pratum*, ten books are cited, of which eight may be on various topics antiquarian and scientific.

The importance of Suetonius is due to his surviving works, because of their intrinsic interest, their place in the history of biography, and their influence on historiography, which took a biographic turn from Tacitus to Ammianus. His influence extended to the Christian writers, and through Einhard's *Life of Charles the Great* to Petrarch and the Renaissance. His place in the history of biography is important. Although he credited Varro with introducing Roman biography after Greek models, he was not dependent on these, since, clearly, long before the days of book biography the Romans had moulded for themselves a prose form devoted to the history and appreciation of a person (Stuart, p. 219: see bibliog. infra). Furthermore, the Lives are in accord with his mental and literary processes. A grammarian, he collected and classified his data about his human subjects as he would have done in a work on grammar (Macé, op. cit., p. 54). S. had successors in Marius Maximus and

Aelius Junius Cordus, whose works exist only in fragments; after his time Roman biography rapidly degenerated, reaching its lowest ebb in the *Scriptores Historiae Augustae*. Suetonius' style has generally been underestimated; Mackail's too severe verdict (*Lat. Lit.* p. 231) was directly contradicted (in advance) by Nettleship (*Anc. Lives of Virgil*, p. 29); see also J. D. Duff, *Journ. Phil.* xxxiii. 165. He is often charged with scandalmongery and prurience, but he conscientiously collected material of every kind and presented it with the same judicial coldness. (See Peck's edn. of *Jul.* and *Aug.*, Pref.) He does not give a fair estimate of the emperors, since he drew indiscriminately on their friends and their enemies; but the lives are of absorbing interest, with a wealth of varied information (see Mackail, op. cit., p. 230).

BIBLIOGRAPHY

LIFE AND WORKS: Mommsen, *Hermes* iii. 43 ff.; A. Macé, *Essai sur Suétone* (1900; Introd. to Texts, Commentaries, and Translations). Leo, *Griech. röm. Biographie* (1901); D. R. Stuart, *Epochs of Gk. and Rom. Biography* (U.S.A. 1928); Funaioli, *PW* iv A. 593.
TEXTS: *Caesars*: M. Ihm (1907); Teubner (Roth, Ihm). *Other Works*: Suet. *Praeter Caesarum Libros Reliquiae*, A. Reifferscheid (1860); R. P. Robinson, *Gram. et Rhet.* (Paris, 1925).
COMMENTARIES: Baumgarten-Crusius (1816–18) (with *Clavis Suetoniana*; cf. *Index to Suet.*, A. A. Howard and C. N. Jackson, U.S.A. 1931), issued with additions by C. B. Hase (Paris, 1928). *On separate Lives*: Julius, H. E. Butler and M. Cary (Oxford, 1927); Jul.-Aug., H. T. Peck (2nd ed. 1893), Westcott and Rankin (U.S.A. 1918); Aug., Shuckburgh (1896), M. Adams (1939); Tib.-Nero, J. B. Pike (U.S.A. 1903); Claud., H. Smilda (1896); Galba-Vit., C. Hofstee (1898); Titus, H. Price, Univ. Penn. diss. 1919; Vespasian, A. W. Braithwaite (1927); Domitian, J. Janssen (Groningen, 1919); De poetis, A. Rostagni (1944); *see also* Translations.
TRANSLATIONS: Philemon Holland (1606); J. C. Rolfe (with text; Loeb, 1914); Budé Series (Fr.); *Galba-Domitian*, with text and commentary, G. W. Mooney (Dublin, 1930).
STYLE AND DICTION: L. Damasso, *La Gramm. di C. S. T.* (1906); Introdd. to Commentaries and Translations.
SPECIAL STUDIES: W. Dennison, 'Epigraphic Sources of Suet.', *AJArch.* Ser. 2, vol. ii; R. J. Rietra, *Tib.* 24–40 (1927). J. C. R.

SUFFECTIO was the procedure by which a substitute (*suffectus*) was appointed, whenever a magistrate resigned or died during his term of office. It was employed to fill vacancies even of very short duration: there are examples of *suffecti* who exercised their power only for a few hours. Under the Empire, when the consulship ceased to be a yearly magistracy, the consuls appointed after the original pair were also called *suffecti*. No *suffectus* ever gave his name to the year, although he kept the rank and title of an ex-magistrate (e.g. *vir consularis, praetorius, quaestorius*, etc.).

Mommsen, *Röm. Staatsr.* i³. 592; B. Kübler, *PW*, s.v. P. T.

SUFFETES, see CARTHAGE, SYRIA.

SUIDAS (correctly, ἡ Σοῦδα) is the name of a lexicon, not an author: the word is borrowed from Latin and means *Fortress* or *Stronghold*: see F. Dölger, *Der Titel d. S.* (reviewed, *Gnomon* xiii (1937), 575), who instances other fanciful names of such collections, e.g. Pamphilus' Λειμών. The lexicon was compiled about the end of the tenth century A.D. Texts (with scholia) of Homer, Sophocles, Aristophanes, and the *Anth. Pal.* were directly consulted; otherwise, the work is mainly based not on copies of the writings of authors or commentators but on abridgements and selections from these made by late hands, e.g. the Συναγωγή (*see* LEXICA SEGUERIANA), Harpocration, and Diogenianus (qq.v.). The historians are quoted from the *Excerpts* of Constantine Porphyrogenitus; biography comes mainly from Hesychius of Miletus; Babrius and Athenaeus are among the other authors consulted. The work is marred by contradictions and other ineptitudes. Many of its sources were already corrupt, and like most works of its kind it has suffered from interpolation. Nevertheless, it is of the highest importance, since it preserves (however imperfectly)

much that is ultimately derived from the earliest or best authorities in ancient scholarship, and includes topics from many departments of Greek learning and civilization.

Editions: Küster, 1705; Gaisford, 1834; Bekker, 1854; Bernhardy, 1853; Adler (Teubner's *Lexicog. Gr.* I, i–v), 1929–38. P. B. R. F.

SUILLIUS RUFUS, PUBLIUS, was half-brother to Corbulo and to Caesonia, wife of the Emperor Gaius. Banished by Tiberius, he was allowed to return to Rome by Gaius. He became consul and, under Claudius, won a sinister series of successes as prosecutor. He returned to banishment during the reign of Nero. J. P. B.

SULLA (1), LUCIUS CORNELIUS (138–78 B.C.), born of an obscure patrician family, followed a tardy senatorial career undistinguished save for the part which he played in the arrest of Jugurtha when quaestor in 107, until he won a considerable military reputation in the Social War. This gained him, late in life, the consulship of 88 and the command of the impending war against Mithridates. He now married his fourth wife, Caecilia Metella, widow of Aemilius Scaurus (q.v.)—an important political alliance. The legislative activity of the tribune Sulpicius drew him for the first time into party politics as an opponent of the *populares*, to prevent the proposed transfer of his military command to Marius. When the proposal was passed, Sulla, with a disregard for the constitution which shocked *optimates* as well as *populares*, inaugurated the period of military dictatorships by marching on Rome with his legions. He reversed the legislation of Sulpicius, who perished while his supporters fled, and left for the East without taking any serious steps to muzzle the *populares*. There he was later joined by the opponents of the Cinnan régime, and so formed a closer connexion with the *optimates*. After the sack of Athens and the victories of Chaeronea and Orchomenus, Sulla, eager to return to Italy, granted Mithridates fairly favourable terms. By the Peace of Dardanus, August 85, Mithridates surrendered his fleet, paid an indemnity, and regained his former kingdom. The client kings were restored, the supporters of Mithridates punished, and the province of Asia reorganized. Having secured the loyalty of his troops by generous rewards and a relaxation of older standards of discipline, Sulla and his optimate friends returned to Italy (83) to settle with the Cinnan government, which had declared him a public enemy. Civil war ensued, the strength of the *populares* coming from the irreconcilable Samnites and the newly enfranchised *populi Italici*, who for a time believed that Sulla proposed to upset their privileges. The victory of the Colline Gate (82) left Sulla master of Rome and Italy. By a special law (81) he secured himself a special dictatorship with extraordinary powers, assumed the cognomen Felix, and, after persecuting the remnants of the popular leaders with proscriptions whose object was largely financial, set about reconstructing the Roman Constitution. The Senate was to be the seat of supreme authority. The censorship fell into abeyance and with it censorial control of the personnel of the Senate. By closing the senatorial career to future tribunes the political importance of the tribunate was annihilated. In addition, the tribunes' powers of legislation and veto were limited, and their judicial powers were transferred to the senatorial *quaestiones*. Thus the divided sovereignty which had rent Rome since the Gracchi was suppressed. Closer control over magistrates and pro-magistrates was secured by legislation that defined and limited their powers and duties, and prescribed penalties for provincial governors guilty of treasonable conduct. Office was confined to older men by amendments of the *Lex Villia annalis*: men were prevented from commencing a senatorial career before the age of thirty, while the ten years' interval between iteration of office was re-enforced. The Senate was to be regularly recruited from the quaestors, whose numbers were raised to twenty, and its sources enlarged. The development of the pro-magistracy as the normal method of provincial government was encouraged, especially by an increase in the number of praetors, designed to provide, with the two proconsuls, a yearly supply of new pro-magistrates for the regular provinces. Sulla thus constructed a self-sufficient governmental machine which, while it would enable the Senate to control the Roman State, was far from favourable to the ambitions of individual *optimates*. He also supplemented the administration of criminal law, where the judicial machinery was inadequate, by the creation of new *quaestiones*, making seven in all: this was the most enduring feature of Sulla's reforms. Membership of the juries was transferred back to the senatorial order. In Italy, by the harsh treatment of those municipalities which had opposed him, notably in Etruria, and by the settlement of his veterans in colonies amid the vanquished, Sulla prepared future discontents, and even in his own time was unable to establish perfect discipline (cf. OFELLA). The quasi-regal character of Sulla's dictatorship, unlimited in power and duration, set the model for the undisguised monarchies of Caesar and the second Triumvirate, while the memory of the Sullan régime, especially of its cruelty, clouded the atmosphere of the next generation.

Sulla probably derived his political ideas from the group of moderate *optimates* earlier headed by Aemilius Scaurus and including the Caecilii Metelli and the Lutatii Catuli, with which he was doubly allied by marriage. But he was not the servant of this or any clique, and as dictator held an independent, autocratic position, often criticized by his closest allies. The deposition of the dictatorship (79) was not the end of his authority, and may have been due either to knowledge that his serious work was done, combined with a dislike of routine administration and a hankering for the leisured life (both of which traits are evident in his early career), or possibly to consciousness of the disease of which he died suddenly in Campania the year following (78 B.C.). He was buried with spectacular public ceremonies in the Campus Martius.

ANCIENT SOURCES: Appian, *BCiv.* bk. 1; Plutarch, *Sulla*; Sallust, *Histories* (fragments) and *Jug.* (early career); Cicero, *Pro Roscio Amerino* (contemporary, 80 B.C., partly satirical). Scattered references in Greenidge and Clay, *Sources for Roman History*, 133–70 B.C.

MODERN: J. Carcopino, *Sylla* (1931, an incomplete monarchy); H. M. Last, *CAH* ix, ch. 6 (the constitution); M. A. Levi, *Silla* (Milan, 1924); Mommsen, *History of Rome* (hammer of the optimates). Also H. Hill (on recruitment of senators), *CQ* 1932.
                                                                        A. N. S.-W.

SULLA (2) PUBLIUS CORNELIUS, a wealthy nephew of the dictator, was elected consul for 65 B.C. with P. Autronius Paetus; but both were found guilty of bribery and were deprived of office. Sulla was almost certainly implicated in the abortive conspiracy to murder the new consuls which Catiline and Autronius set on foot, but he took no active part in it. In 62 he was accused of complicity in Catiline's second conspiracy. Cicero himself undertook his defence and he was acquitted. He acted as a lieutenant of Caesar in the Civil War (Caesar, *BCiv.* 3. 51. 89). He died in 45 B.C.

See Cicero, *Pro Sulla* (ed. J. S. Reid, 1882).   J. M. C.

SULLA (3), FAUSTUS CORNELIUS, son of the dictator by Caecilia Metella, and husband of Pompeia, Pompey's daughter, was Pompey's follower. In 63 B.C. he was the first to mount the walls of the temple of Jerusalem. In 52 he received the charge to rebuild the Curia Hostilia, henceforward Curia Cornelia. After Thapsus (46) he was captured and killed.

F. Münzer, *PW* iv. 1515.   A. M.

SULPICIA (1), daughter of Servius Sulpicius Rufus, and ward of Valerius (q.v. 15) Messalla Corvinus, is not to be confused with her namesake celebrated by Martial (10. 35 and 38). She composed six short elegies incorporated in the Tibullus collection (4. 7–12), in which with unique frankness and rare warmth she passionately avows her love for Cerinthus, a young gentleman of her own sphere, not a freedman or the Cornutus mentioned by Tibullus (2. 2 and 3). Though Sulpicia's literary remains amount to only forty lines and show traces of amateurishness, they nevertheless completely lack conventionality and affectation and constitute a splendid human document. Here is the first poetry we have written by a *docta puella*, and it throws light on certain social tendencies of the Augustan Age. *See also* ELEGIAC POETRY.

Text in editions of Tibullus; commentaries in editions of K. F. Smith and Postgate (*see* TIBULLUS). In chronological order, G. Némethy, *Tibulli Carmina, Acc. Sulpiciae Elegidia* (1905). Cf. 'Sulpicia (114)' in *PW*; Schanz-Hosius, *Gesch. röm. Lit.* ii (1935).
                                                                        J. H.

SULPICIA (2), wife of Calenus, in Martial's time, and by him praised as authoress of poetry of honourable love (10. 35 and 38). A 'satira' of 70 lines is questionably ascribed to her.

Text in O. Jahn's ed. of Persius and Juvenal. See J. W. Duff, *Roman Satire*, 1937.

SULPICIUS (1) **BLITHO** (1st c. B.C.), one of Nepos' sources (*Hannibal* 13. 1). For confusion with Sulpicius Galba, grandfather of the Emperor Galba, see Schanz–Hosius i, § 112. 6; Peter, *HRRel.*, p. ccclxxix.

SULPICIUS (2), SERVIUS, author of love-poems, mentioned by Horace (*Sat.* 1. 10. 86) and Ovid (*Tr.* 2. 441).

SULPICIUS (3) **CAMERINUS**, QUINTUS, epic poet (Ovid, *Pont.* 4. 16. 19) and possibly same as consul of A.D. 9.

SULPICIUS (4) **APOLLINARIS** (2nd c. A.D.), scholar, the teacher of Aulus Gellius and the Emperor Pertinax. He wrote learned letters (*epistolicae quaestiones*, now lost), verse summaries of the *Aeneid* (6 hexameters for each book; see Baehrens, *Poet. Lat. Min.* iv. 169), and metrical summaries of the plays of Terence (cf. e.g. W. M. Lindsay's ed. of Ter.).

Cf. Teuffel, § 357; Schanz-Hosius, § 597.   J. F. M.

SULPICIUS, *see* GALBA, GALLUS, QUIRINIUS, RUFUS, SEVERUS.

SUMMANUS, perhaps originally an epithet of Jupiter (q.v.), as 'dweller in the most high places'; but distinguished from him (Festus, p. 254. 3) as the god who sends nocturnal thunderbolts. He had a temple founded during the war with Pyrrhus (Platner–Ashby, p. 502), and wheel-shaped cakes called *summanalia* were offered to him (Festus, p. 474. 17). His identification with Pluto (Martianus Capella, 2. 161) is fanciful.

See Wissowa, *RK* 135.   H. J. R.

SUNIUM, a bold promontory at the south apex of Attica. It was crowned by a marble temple of Poseidon, built in the late fifth century on the foundations of a temple destroyed by the Persians before completion. There was also an Ionic temple of Athena. A mass of Egyptian objects found here testifies to Athens' early overseas trade (Pendlebury, *Aegyptiaca*, 82 ff.). Sunium was fortified in 413 for the security of the Athenian corn-ships; the circuit of the walls and the boat-houses are well preserved.

B. Στάης, τὸ Σούνιον (1920); Ἀρχ. Ἐφ. 1900, 133 ff.; 1917, 168 ff. W. Wrede, *Attische Mauern* (1933), p. 43 ff.   T. J. D.

SUPERSTITION. The word 'superstition' is relative, for it may be taken to mean indulgence in beliefs or practices which have been abandoned by general, or at least by educated opinion of the time. For instance, the Emperor Tiberius cannot be called superstitious for believing in astrology, but a modern could be, since its falsity is now well known. It is doubtful whether a Greek or Latin word exists for superstition, since δεισιδαιμονία (cf. RELIGION), when derogatory, as it most often is, means rather excessive pietism or religiosity, whereas *superstitio* itself is implied by Virgil to be unenlightened and meaningless worship ('uana superstitio ueterumque ignara deorum', *Aen.* 8. 187, see W. Warde Fowler, *Aeneas at the Site of Rome*, 1918, p. 57), perhaps with reference especially to Oriental cults of the poet's day. It is hardly possible here to do more than give examples of the existence of magico-religious rites or beliefs known to have been condemned by the more enlightened people of the time.

Whereas Homer evidently writes for a remarkably free-thinking public, he has traces of a state nearer the primitive. For example, although his Achaean characters regard fish merely as very poor food, he speaks of one as ἱερός, holy or tabu (*Il.* 16. 407). This plainly refers to some belief like that of the Syrians with regard to the holy fish of their goddess (Hyg. *Fab.* 197). Hesiod, writing some time later but from a peasant environment, is full of scruples which a Homeric hero would laugh at, e.g. *Op.* 750, against a boy of twelve years or twelve months sitting on a tomb; 753, against a man using a woman's bath, besides the elaborate observation of certain days of the month, 765 ff., if that is really Hesiodic.

The prevalent use of amulets (q.v.) was evidently regarded as superstition by the more enlightened minds of the fifth and fourth centuries B.C.; hence the point of the story in Theophrastus, ap. Plut. *Pericles* 38, that that statesman during his last illness apologized to a friend for having one about his neck, put there by the women of his household, saying that he must be very low to submit to such folly. A similar contempt is expressed by Plato, *Resp.* 2. 364 b ff., for practitioners of magic (q.v.), and some of the lower forms of purificatory rites which clung to the fringes of Orphism (q.v.). The former of these gained ground with the degeneracy of natural science, as may be seen by comparing the earlier works on medicine, e.g. the Hippocratic corpus, above all *De morbo sacro*, which protests against the unscientific ascription of diseases to supernatural agencies, with some of the later productions, especially the extraordinary mixture of traditional remedies and conjuring which has come down to us from Marcellus of Bordeaux.

In Rome one of the most frequently denounced forms of superstition is the adoption of fragments of foreign ritual, especially the more spectacular kinds. Thus Juvenal's women consult all manner of foreign diviners, indulge in extraordinary orgiastic rites, and perform more or less Egyptian penances (*Sat.* 6. 314 ff., 511 ff.). A fairly common form of this seems to have been the observance of some Jewish rites, especially the Sabbath, by those who were neither Jews nor proselytes (Juv. 14. 96, cf. Hor. *Sat.* 1. 9. 69).

With the coming of Christianity, many who were superstitiously inclined developed two new forms of their aberration. One was the retention, despite all the Doctors of the Church could say, of purely pagan beliefs; e.g. St. Augustine complains, *Expos. epist. ad Galat.* 35, of Christians who tell him 'to his face' that they will not start on a journey the day after the Kalends, which in pagan Roman belief was *religiosus* (cf. Plut. *Quaest. Rom.* 25). The other was the employment of Christian names, holy books, etc., for magic, as the Christian charms, Preisendanz ii. 189 ff., and cf. the strictures of St. Augustine (in *Iohan. evang. tract.* vii. 12) against those who use a Gospel as a remedy for headache. Similar uses had long been made of Jewish formulae, etc., see, e.g., M. Rist in *Journ. Bib. Lit.* lvii (1938), 289 ff.

There is no comprehensive and authoritative work, but material will be found in all large treatises on ancient religion, especially those dealing with the earliest and latest periods. H. J. R.

SUPPLICATIONES. On the occasion of a great national calamity (as after the battle of Lake Trasumene, Livy 22. 10. 8) or success (as after the crushing of Vercingetorix' revolt, Caesar, *BGall.* 7. 90. 8) it was the custom at Rome and elsewhere, cf. *ILS* 108 (Cumae), to give opportunity for general adoration of the gods, or certain of them, by providing access to their statues or other emblems, often at least placed on *puluinaria* (q.v.). This was known as a *supplicatio*, from the kneeling or prostrations of the worshippers (commoner in Italy than Greece, C. Sittl, *Gebärden*, 177–8, but cf. H. Bolkestein, *Theophrastos' Charakter der Deisidaimonia*, 23 ff.). It was at least on occasion associated with a *lectisternium* (q.v.), as in Livy, loc. cit., but is to be distinguished from it, as Livy there does. It is apparently a genuinely Roman procedure, older than the foreign use of statues to represent the gods. That it is often said to have taken place *ad (circa) omnia puluinaria* is held by Wissowa, *RK* 424, to indicate, along with the fact that it generally followed a consultation of the Sibylline Books, that in the form familiar from our authorities it was fully hellenized; but see A. K. Lake in *Quantulacumque* (1937), 243 ff.
H. J. R.

SURA, LUCIUS LICINIUS, born in Hispania Tarraconensis, after pursuing a senatorial career, commanded Legio I Minervia at Bonn (*c.* A.D. 93–7), became governor of Gallia Belgica (97), and consul. A fellow countryman of Trajan and, like him, versed in frontier-defence, he became his intimate, and possibly influenced Nerva in the adoption of Trajan. Governor of Lower Germany, and *cos.* II (*ordinarius*) in 102, he served with distinction on Trajan's staff in both Dacian Wars, became *cos.* III (*ordinarius*) in 107—a rare honour—and died soon after 110. Rich and cultured, he wielded immense influence. Pliny in one letter submits a physical problem to him (*Ep.* 4. 30), and in another a psychic one (ibid. 7. 27). He was a patron of Martial (6. 64. 12–13), who admired the old-fashioned ring of his oratory (7. 47. 1–2). It is recorded that he composed speeches for Trajan (S.H.A. *Hadr.* 3. 11).

E. Groag, *PW*, s.v. 'Licinius (167)'; *PIR*, L 174.
C. H. V. S. and J. W. D.

SURA, see LENTULUS (4), PALFURIUS.

SURENAS, i.e. the Suren. The Surens, one of the seven great Parthian families, ruled Seistan as vassals of the Arsacids, with their capital at Alexandria-Prophthasia. Surenas, whose personal name is unknown, was a tall foppish young man with ideas; he thought that the long-range weapon, the bow, would be irresistible if sufficiently munitioned and mobile, and therefore formed a highly trained professional army of 10,000 horse-archers, with 1,000 swift Arabian camels carrying a huge reserve of arrows. With this force he overthrew Mithridates III and restored Orodes II to his throne, and then defeated Crassus' invasion (*see* CARRHAE). For a moment his genius had made the horse-archer, the common man who had won Carrhae, potential master of the world; but the Parthian nobles were jealous, and Orodes put to death his too brilliant vassal.

W. W. Tarn, *CAH* ix. 606 ff.; E. Herzfeld, *Sakastan* (1932), 70 ff.
W. W. T.

SURGERY. I. BEFORE 300 B.C.

1. In the Homeric poems references to surgery are mainly in the *Iliad* and concerned with the 147 wounds there recorded. The wound is cleaned; blood squeezed or sucked out; edges united by bandaging; and an analgesic of dried herbs rubbed in and applied as an

air-tight pad. The only wound-spell is in the *Odyssey* (19. 457-8 ἐπαοιδή, cf. Pindar, *Pyth.* 3. 45 ff.). Homeric treatment resembles the best Egyptian practice. Moreover, instruments early in Greek use, notably the trephine, closely resemble Mesopotamian finds. Thus there is presumption that Greek surgery drew on the traditions of both these civilizations. The first historic Greek practitioner after Asclepius and his sons (*Il.* 2. 731-2; 4. 194; 11. 518 and 614, etc., and Hesiod, *Epic Cycle, Sack of Ilium*, 5) was Democedes of Croton. He treated King Darius surgically and had certainly Persian contacts (Hdt. 3. 125, 129, 137).

2. The surgical part of the Hippocratic Collection is in confusion. *Fractures, Dislocations* (i.e. ἀρθρῶν, *of joints*), and *Wounds of the head* are of about 400 B.C., the two former being parts of a larger work. *The nature of bones* is of about 350 B.C. *On surgery* and *Mochlicon* (= *Instruments of reduction*) are later abbreviations of earlier works, but the introductory chapter of *Mochlicon* is the displaced first part of *The nature of bones*. Treatises covering the whole medical field were, Galen indicates, commonly called 'Concerning the things of surgery'. Some idea of such a work is gained by reading the above works in the following order: *On Surgery*, being a greatly abbreviated introduction to the whole; introductory chapter of *Mochlicon*, being descriptions of the bones; *The nature of bones*, a sketch of theoretical anatomy for the surgeon, omitting bones (despite title); *Fractures*; *Dislocations*; remaining chapters of *Mochlicon*; *Wounds of the head*. It must be remembered that the parts differ greatly in age and state and that there is repetition and overlapping.

3. Startlingly modern are the minute directions for preparation of the operating room, and such points as the management of light—both artificial and natural—scrupulous cleanliness of hands, care and use of instruments with special precautions for those of iron, decencies of the operating chamber, modes of dressing wounds, use of splints, and need for tidiness, cleanliness, aftercare, and nursing. The directions for bandaging and for diagnosis and treatment of dislocations and fractures, especially of depressed fractures of the skull, are very impressive. In *Fractures* and *Dislocations* certain procedures for reduction are identical with those now in use, but other passages are incompatible with the facts of anatomy. *Wounds of the head* has a special place in the history of surgery. It is a practical work by a highly skilled craftsman, and every sentence suggests experience. Although its treatment of depressed fractures has been criticized from an early date, the book was in current use until the middle of the eighteenth century. It introduces technical terms, two of which, *bregma* and *diploe*, survive in modern usage.

4. Among instruments described is the 'bench of Hippocrates', a bed for reducing dislocations, especially of the hip. The form is so ancient as to antecede the screw as a mechanical power. Lever, crank, windlass, and pulley are employed. With minor changes it was in continuous use for at least 2,000 years. There is no reason to associate it with Hippocrates; it may well be more ancient than he, but the name is late.

II. ALEXANDRIA AND THE EMPIRE

5. After 300 B.C. anatomical knowledge enters surgery from the Alexandrian school. Thus *Dislocations* has an obvious interpolation (on the anatomy of the shoulder-joint) of at least a century later than the main text. Similarly the surgeon Hegetor can be approximately dated from a fragment of his work (preserved by Apollonius of Citium) describing the anatomy of the hip joint in a way only discoverable by dissection. We have no complete surgical work of Alexandrian origin.

6. Passing by the stories of Pliny, the first professed surgeon at Rome of whom we have news is Meges of Sidon early in the first century A.D. Heliodorus soon after gave the first account of ligation and torsion of blood-vessels, treated stricture by internal section, performed radical cures for hernias, and was especially skilled in skull operations. Amputations were fully described by Archigenes of Apamea. Antyllus treated cataracts surgically and removed aneurysms by applying two ligatures and cutting down between them—an operation still known by his name alternatively with that of John Hunter (1728-93). These Roman operators of the first and second centuries A.D. acted with resource and confidence. The fragments of their works have the authentic tang of experience.

7. The standard account of Roman surgery of the first century A.D. is the seventh book of *De medicina* of Aulus Cornelius Celsus. The professional standing of Celsus—whether lay or professional, bond or free—and the character of his book—whether translated from a Greek text, or product of personal experience, or a compilation—are disputed, but it is certain from the articulation of the book that its author or compiler had practical surgical experience. He gives details of the very dangerous operations for extirpating a goitre and for cutting for stone, and describes well what might be thought to be the modern operation for removing tonsils and for other procedures on the face and mouth and for the removal of polypus from the nose. He gives the first account of dental practice, which includes wiring of loose teeth and use of a dental mirror. His attitude and line of treatment are sensible and humane.

8. Galen was no surgeon but his works include accounts of his surgical predecessors. Useful details are also preserved in the works of later Greek writers, notably Oribasius and Paul of Aegina. (For organization of the surgical service in the Imperial army *see* MEDICINE.)

9. Graphic representations have a place in the history of surgery. The most important are: (*a*) A kylix of about 490 B.C., painted by Sosias, of Achilles bandaging Patroclus. The drawing is excellent, but the bandaging execrable. (*b*) A vase-painting of about 400 B.C. of a surgeon treating patients in his surgery. (*c*) A few votives, murals, memorial slabs, etc., showing instruments for operations. The best is a tablet of instruments from the Asclepieum at Athens. (Details of (*a*), (*b*), and (*c*) are discussed by Charles Singer, *Greek Medicine and Greek Biology*, 1922.) (*d*) Surgical instruments. The best collection is from Pompeii, where over 200 have been found. (*e*) Trajan's column shows an advanced dressing-station of a legion. (*f*) A Laurentian manuscript of about 900, copied from one of the first century B.C., contains illustrations of Soranus of Ephesus *On bandaging* and *On the uterus* and of Apollonius of Citium *On reduction of dislocations*. (For references to (*d*), (*e*), and (*f*) see bibliography of MEDICINE.)

10. There was interest in veterinary surgery, especially under the Empire. The army had hospitals for animals (Hyginus, *Liber de munitionibus castrorum* 21. 22). Much can be gleaned from agricultural writings, but there was also a considerable veterinary literature. The *Mulomedicina Chironis* of about A.D. 100 survives in a philologically curious Latin version of about A.D. 300. It formed the basis for the larger *Digesta artis mulomedicinae* of Publius Vegetius Renatus (383-450), unexpectedly scientific and well arranged, which long remained in use. Abstracts of a collection of ancient works called *Hippiatrica*, said to have been made for Constantine Porphyrogenitus (905-59), have been in use ever since his time.

BIBLIOGRAPHY

The surgical works of 'Hippocrates' are mostly in vol. iii of the Loeb *Hippocrates* by E. T. Withington (1927). Two older works of permanent importance are: J. E. Petrequin, *Chirurgie d'Hippocrate* (2 vols., 1877-8), product of 30 years' study by an accomplished surgeon, and Francis Adams, *The Genuine Works of Hippocrates* (2 vols., 1849), by the last great Greek scholar who practised under almost the circumstances of an ancient surgeon. For Celsus the

Loeb edition of W. G. Spencer (3 vols., 1936–8) covers most needs. M. Wellmann, *Celsus, eine Quellenuntersuchung* (1913), is important. For texts, H. Kühlewein, *Hippocratis Opera Omnia* (2 vols., 1894–1902); F. Marx, *Celsi opera quae supersunt* (1915); U. C. Bussemaker and C. Daremberg, *Œuvres d'Oribase* (6 vols., 1851–76). The notes and comments of Francis Adams, *The Seven Books of Paulus Aegineta* (3 vols., 1844–7), are without rival. Werner R. Lewek, 'Die Bank des Hippokrates', *Janus* xl (1936) is exhaustive.

Veterinary Surgery: Sir Frederic Smith, *Early History of Veterinary Literature* (1919); E. Lommatzsch, *P. Vegeti Renati Mulomedicina* (1903); H. Ahlquist, *Studien zur Mulomedicina Chironis* (1909). C. S.

SURVIVAL after death, *see* AFTER-LIFE.

SUSA, the 'city of lilies', was the capital of Elam, and afterwards of the Achaemenids, where Darius I built his palace (Apadāna). Under Seleucids and Parthians its name was Seleuceia-on-the-Eulaeus; the excavations have furnished numerous Greek inscriptions. In A.D. 1 there were still Greek cleruchs in charge of the citadel, i.e. some early Seleucid had planted a military colony there; probably it became a *polis* under Antiochus III. In A.D. 21 it was still a full Greek city, with a Council, Assembly, and elected magistrates whose qualifications were scrutinized; it could send embassies, and was therefore a State; though subject to Parthia, it had more than local autonomy. Beside Greeks, other peoples can be traced—Persians, Syrians, Jews, Anatolians, Babylonians, Elymaeans; its city-goddess was the Elamite Nanaia, renamed Artemis, in whose temple Greeks manumitted their slaves. Four Greek poems are known, one a lyric ode (1st c. B.C.) addressed to Apollo by a Syrian title, Mara (Lord); it belongs to a known class of acrostic poems, and that and the forms of decrees and manumissions show that Susa was well within the Greek culture-sphere.

SEG vii. 1–33; Fr. Cumont in *CRAcad. Inscr.* 1930–3; W. W. Tarn, *The Greeks in Bactria and India* (1938), pp. 27, 39, 68. W. W. T.

SUSARION, inventor (? mythical) of Comedy, first mentioned in the Parian Marble (*c.* 260 B.C.) under some year between 581 and 560 as an Athenian. But the name is doubtfully Attic and another tradition says he was a Megarian. The one recorded fragment, however, is written in Attic and contains the definitely Attic word δημόται. If he existed, we may regard Susarion as one of those who wrote the words for the primitive Attic κῶμος-comedy (*see* COMEDY, OLD). It is possible, however, that no such man existed and that the non-Attic name was invented to square with the tradition of the Megarian origin of comedy.

FCG ii. 3 f.; *CGF* 77 f.; A. W. Pickard-Cambridge, *Dithyramb, Tragedy, and Comedy*, 280 ff. M. P.

SYBARIS (Σύβαρις), an Achaean-Troezenian foundation (*c.* 720 B.C.) near a similarly named river on the Gulf of Tarentum, near the modern *Sibari*, an area formerly fertile, now derelict. By expanding its territory, dispatching colonies (Laus, Scidrus, Posidonia-Paestum), and monopolizing Etruscan trade Sybaris became powerful; her wealthy luxuriousness was proverbial. But in 510 internal dissensions enabled Croton to obliterate Sybaris. Sybarite exiles, after twice unsuccessfully attempting to refound Sybaris, joined the Athenian foundation at Thurii (q.v.) (443). Thurii quickly expelled them, whereupon they established a new Sybaris on the river Traeis, never an important place.

Strabo 6. 263; Hdt. 5. 44 f.; Diod. 12. 9 f.; Ath. 12. 518 f. P. N. Ure, *CAH* iv. 113; D. Randall-MacIver, *Greek Cities of Italy and Sicily* (1931); J. Bérard, *Bibliogr. topogr.* (1941), p. 94. See, too, bibliography s.v. MAGNA GRAECIA. E. T. S.

SYCOPHANTS (συκόφανται). Athens had no public prosecutors in the modern sense. Solon permitted citizens to prosecute any wrongdoers. Inducements were offered to volunteers in certain cases (γραφὴ ξενίας, φάσις, ἀπογραφή) by granting them a liberal share of fines and moneys recovered for the treasury. The system

worked: there was no lack of prosecutors. But *c.* 450 B.C. abuses appeared. Men began to make a profession of prosecutions for personal, political, and financial reasons. These were called sycophants.

In spite of constant references by Aristophanes and the orators, there survives no legal definition of a sycophant. Among the direct measures taken against sycophancy were γραφὴ συκοφαντίας, εἰσαγγελία, and προβολή. The only known law under which sycophants could be prosecuted was the law against those who deceived a court by promises. The procedure in this case was εἰσαγγελία. Provision was also made by law for the annual presentation (προβολή) of not more than six alleged sycophants—three citizens and three metics. A προβολή was not a formal indictment but a general charge of sycophancy. The vote was not a verdict. If it was hostile, the Ecclesia could try the case itself or turn it over to a dicastery.

The most dangerous type of sycophant was the blackmailer who extorted money, so that the guilty escaped punishment and the innocent paid blackmail. An indirect check on blackmail was a law providing a penalty of 1,000 drachmas for dropping a suit once it was started. But often money was extorted by the mere threat of litigation. The means of relief from this form of extortion were ineffectual, for blackmail was not in itself a crime. A different way of checking sycophants was the law providing that a prosecutor who failed to obtain one fifth of the votes should be fined 1,000 drachmas and deprived of the right to bring a similar type of suit in the future.

Freedom of prosecution was one of the corner-stones of democracy. There was always the danger that honest volunteers might be discouraged. This explains why no ancient writer ever suggested the repeal or modification of Solon's law.

R. J. Bonner and G. Smith, *The Administration of Justice from Homer to Aristotle* ii (U.S.A. 1938), ch. 3. R. J. B.

SYENE (*Assuan*), on the southern frontier of ancient Egypt, on the right bank of the Nile, just below the First Cataract. It was a trading town, and from its quarries came the valuable 'syenite' stone. Under the Ptolemies it replaced Elephantine as the frontier outpost; in 25 B.C. it was freed from Ethiopian invaders by the Romans, who established a garrison there. The fact that the sun's rays fell vertically at Syene in midsummer was utilized by Eratosthenes (q.v.) to make a remarkable calculation of the earth's circumference. E. H. W.

SYLE (ἡ σύλη, τὸ σῦλον) was (1) robbery, cattle-reiving in general; (2) an act of reprisal by an injured person or his kinsmen for a deed of violence or a default on a debt. In early Greece this was often the only means of obtaining satisfaction from members of another tribe or city, and was therefore sanctioned by custom. In time of war *syle* was permitted against all enemy traders. From the sixth century it was gradually circumscribed by commercial treaties and by grants of *asylia* (q.v.) to certain individuals, cities, or sanctuaries. But even in Hellenistic times belligerent States still licensed privateering, and *syle* did not disappear until the Roman era.

H. A. Ormerod, *Piracy in the Ancient World* (1924), ch. 2. M. C.

SYMBOLON. With the growth of commerce in Greece, it became increasingly important that there should be some guarantee of security for the person and property of a merchant in foreign ports. This was accomplished by judicial treaties known as σύμβολα. Over half a dozen treaties negotiated between cities on the coast and islands of the Aegean are extant.

In the earlier treaties only immunity from forcible seizure of goods and restriction upon reprisals were secured. Out of these simple treaties grew the more elaborate σύμβολα of the period of the Confederacy of

Delos. Suits tried under the provisions of these treaties were called δίκαι ἀπὸ συμβόλων. It was the common practice to avoid using the commercial codes of the contracting cities, either by providing for the use of the code of a third city, or by including in the treaty a commercial code and procedure involving, no doubt, all the elements common to the codes of the contracting parties. Where Athens was concerned, naturally her commercial code would be dominant. The place of trial was the home of the defendant.

In Athens these treaties were ratified by a Heliastic court. After the formation of the Confederacy of Delos the judicial treaties concluded between Athens and her allies continued in force even when the allies had been reduced to subjection.

J. H. Lipsius, *Das Attische Recht* (1915), pp. 965 ff.; H. Grant Robertson, 'The Administration of Justice in the Athenian Empire', *University of Toronto Studies, History and Economics* iv. 2, 1924.
R. J. B.

SYMMACHIA (συμμαχία, 'fellowship in fighting') was used with several meanings: informal co-operation in war, a treaty of alliance, and a confederacy of allies. Treaties of alliance, of which the earliest Greek example preserved dates from the sixth century, could be of two kinds: defensive (*epimachia*) or offensive and defensive. The latter generally included a clause pledging the signatories to have the same friends and enemies. In such treaties the contracting States frequently had equal rights, but the clause could be so expanded as to subordinate one partner to the other. Thus in 404 B.C. Athens promised to have the same friends and enemies as the Lacedaemonians and follow their leadership. *Symmachia* has been used in a special sense as the name for a confederacy of allies under the *hegemonia* (leadership) of one State. The *hegemonia* included command in war and generally also the presidency of the assembly of the allies. Such leagues were not federal States but recognized the freedom of their members and could continue to exist even under the King's Peace. The Peloponnesian and Delian Leagues are described in separate articles. More advanced was the Second Athenian League organized *c.* 378 B.C., when a congress or constitutional convention of allies of Athens met and adopted by decrees (δόγματα) the principles or constitution of the League, which was ratified by treaties between Athens and the members. Athens next in the spring of 377 issued a decree inviting States to join on the terms of freedom, self-government, and exemption from garrisons and the payment of tribute. Other documents show that the entire war-policy of members was controlled by the League. Athens held the *hegemonia*, and the members of the assembly (*synedrion*) of the allies, in which each State cast one vote, remained permanently in Athens so that meetings could be called on short notice. The policy of 'the Athenians and their Allies' was determined by agreement between the *synedrion* and the Athenian Ecclesia. The *synedrion* also exercised some judicial authority. The guarantee against tribute (φόρος) did not prevent the collection of contributions (συντάξεις) from members. The League finally was dissolved in 338 B.C. A special variety of *symmachia* is constituted by the Hellenic Leagues of Philip II, Antigonus Monophthalmus, and Antigonus Doson, in which the *hegemonia* was held by kings, while a committee selected from its members presided over the assembly.

ANCIENT SOURCES: collected by R. von Scala, *Die Staatsverträge des Altertums* (1898).
MODERN LITERATURE. *General*: A. Martin, Dar.-Sag., and W. Schwahn, *PW*, s.v. 'Symmachia'; W. S. Ferguson, *Greek Imperialism* (U.S.A. 1913), chs. 1–3 and 7; G. Busolt, *Griechische Staatskunde* ii (1926), 1250 ff. and 1320 ff.; V. Martin, *La Vie internationale dans la Grèce des cités* (1940), 121–281.
Special: F. H. Marshall, *The Second Athenian Confederacy* (1905); F. Hampl, *Die griechischen Staatsverträge des 4. Jahrhunderts* (1938). The latter work (reviewed by Larsen in *CPhil.* 1939) contains references to many recent studies.
J. A. O. L.

SYMMACHUS (1) (*fl. c.* A.D. 100) wrote a commentary with ὑποθέσεις on Aristophanes which owed much to Didymus and was one of the main sources of the oldest scholia to Aristophanes. He probably produced the first edition of the latter's select plays.

SYMMACHUS (2), QUINTUS AURELIUS (*c.* A.D. 340–*c.* 402), belonged to a distinguished family. Trained by a Gallic *rhetor*, he became the greatest orator of his day, and thus attained the highest positions in the State. In 369 he was sent on deputation to Gaul and there won the close friendship of Ausonius (q.v.). In 373 he was appointed proconsul of Africa. Holding fast to the pagan religion, he proved the most prominent opponent of Christianity in his time. The influence of Julian had in part re-established paganism, and a storm arose over an altar of Victory in the senate-house at Rome, when Gratian in 382 forbade pagan worship. The pagan party struggled for supremacy, especially when Symmachus was *praefectus urbi* (384, 385), but was defeated especially through the efforts of Ambrose (q.v.). Symmachus nevertheless attained the consulship in 391 and lived till about 402.

During this last period he wrote the greater part of the numerous letters that have come down to us. Fragments of his carefully composed speeches are also preserved. The letters, in ten books, are addressed to leading persons of the day; their arrangement imitates that of the younger Pliny, nine books private, one official correspondence.

Ed. O. Seeck (1883).
A. S.

SYMMORIA. An official group of taxpayers in Athens in the fourth century B.C., which performed certain public services as a corporate body. The law of Periander (357–356 B.C.) introduced a reform of the *trierarchy*, which was later improved by Demosthenes. It divided the twelve hundred wealthiest citizens into twenty equal *symmoriai*. The upkeep of a number of ships was allotted to them on a proportional basis. Their *epimeletai*, who were, perhaps, identical with the *symmoriarchai*, the wealthiest members of a *symmoria*, divided the *symmoria* into *synteleiai* of members according to their wealth, so that each *synteleia* found one ship.

Earlier in date than Periander's law were the *symmoriai* created in 378–377 in connexion with the reform of the *eisphora* (q.v.). These included practically all Athenian taxpayers and special *symmoriai* of *metoikoi*. They seem to have been organized in the same way as the trierarchic *symmoriai*. Outside Athens, in Teos and possibly Nysa, the term meant bodies analogous to the Attic γένη, and in later antiquity private clubs. *See* EISPHORA; LITURGY; TRIERARCHY.

A. M. Andreades, *A History of Greek Public Finance* (U.S.A. 1933), Index, s.v.; G. Busolt–H. Swoboda, *Griechische Staatskunde* i, ii (1920–6), Index, s.v.; F. Poland, in *PW*, s.v. 'Symmoria', 'Symmoriarches'.
F. M. H.

SYMPHOSIUS (or **SYMPOSIUS**), CAELIUS FIRMIANUS (4th–5th c. A.D.), the reputed author of a series of a hundred riddles, each consisting of three hexameter lines, which according to the prologue to the work were composed for use at the Saturnalia. Two other short poems are erroneously attributed to him, *De fortuna*, in fifteen choriambic tetrameters, and *De livore*, in twenty-five hendecasyllabics.

See Baehrens, *PLM* iv. 364 ff.
A. L. P.

SYMPLEGADES (Συμπληγάδες, sc. πέτραι), the Clashing Rocks through which the Argonauts (q.v.) had to pass into the Hellespont. The story is essentially the same as that of the Planctae (Πλαγκταί, *Odyssey* 12. 59 ff.), i.e. the Wandering Rocks, which not even the doves which carry ambrosia to Zeus can get through without losing one of their number; these, however, are not definitely located. The Argo is said there to have passed them, whence it seems that Planctae is the older name, though later authors (as Apoll. Rhod. 4. 860 ff.) suppose two sets of clashing or moving rocks, one to the east and the other to the west of the Mediterranean. There is no need to seek a rationalizing explanation of either, see J. Bacon, *Voyage of the Argonauts*, p. 79.

H. J. R.

SYMPOLITEIA (the sharing of citizenship or political life) is employed—as it was by Polybius—as a descriptive name for a federal State, while the word used in documents as a part of the name was *koinon* (commonwealth). In English these federal States are called leagues but must be distinguished from *symmachiai* (q.v.), for which the same word is used. Characteristic is a division of power between the central and local governments and a double citizenship and allegiance, local and federal, symbolized at times by such identifications as 'an Aetolian from Naupactus'. To the federal government belonged foreign affairs, the army, and jurisdiction in cases of treason; in local government and institutions there was a tendency to uniformity. While a citizen normally could exercise political rights only in one community, he apparently possessed civil rights, including the right to acquire real property (*enctesis*), in all communities within the league. Exceptions were the Thessalian League organized by Flamininus and other leagues founded under Roman influence. (For accounts of the chief *sympoliteiai*, see ACHAEAN LEAGUE, AETOLIAN LEAGUE, *and* FEDERAL STATES.) *Sympoliteia* is applicable also to any merging of citizenship, and the related verb is used in a Phocian inscription of the second century B.C. referring to the absorption of the city of Medeon by Stiris. Similar expressions are common in connexion with the union of cities in Asia Minor.

ANCIENT SOURCES: *Koinon* in League names: *SIG* 653. 'Aetolian from Naupactus': ibid. 380 and 500; Stiris–Medeon: ibid. 647 (cf. 546 B).

MODERN LITERATURE: E. Szanto, *Das griechische Bürgerrecht* (1892), ch. 3; G. Busolt, *Griechische Staatskunde* (1920), i. 156 ff.; W. Schwahn, *PW*, s.v. The nature of federal citizenship is discussed by W. Kolbe in *Sav. Zeitschr.* 1929; Anatolian *sympoliteiai*, by L. Robert, *Villes d'Asie Mineure* (1935), 54–65.   J. A. O. L.

SYMPOSIUM (συμπόσιον). Nominally a symposium was a drinking-party, but actually at Athens drinking was the least important part of the entertainment. The Romans and the Macedonians were fond of an occasional drinking-bout, but at Athens moderation both in drinking and eating was the rule. Wine was seldom drunk neat, and the proportions of wine and water in the mixing-bowl—*crater*—were often one to three. Music by flute-girls, performances by hired entertainers, songs by the guests, impromptu verse and riddles—these were the ordinary diversions; but above all there was conversation and discussion of every sort of subject.

Plato, *Symposium*; Xenophon, *Symposium*; Aristophanes, *Wasps*, 1174–1325.   F. A. W.

SYMPOSIUM LITERATURE. Banquets bulked large in Greek life and hence also in literature from Homer (*Il.* 2. 402, *Od.* 9. 1, etc.) onwards. After the meal the company would turn to drinking and general conversation, sometimes on set themes. Such discussions gave rise to a minor literary *genre*. They suggested to Plato the setting for his *Symposium* (drinking-party), which with Xenophon's *Symp.* (probably later than Plato's) supplied later writers with stock methods, characters (e.g. the unbidden guest), and incidents, serving as a framework for dialogues on literary, philosophical, and many other topics. The dialogue-form, the mixture of grave and gay, characterization, historical interest—these were the marks of the 'Socratic' symposium, a type which includes Plutarch's *Symp.* and *Quaest. conv.* and the *Deipnosophists* of Athenaeus, though here the artistry is lacking, and the post-classical tendency to substitute miscellaneous learning for philosophic thought is much in evidence. Lost works of this

type include Aristotle's *Symp.* (Ath. 674 f.), perhaps concerned with Homeric questions and resembling the later 'grammatical' symposia, such as Herodian's, rather than Xenophon; Epicurus also wrote a symposium (criticized by Ath. 186 e).

A different but related type is the satirical, initiated by Menippus and exemplified for us by Lucian (and in Latin by Horace, *Sat.* 2. 8, and Petronius). Unlike the 'Socratic' symposia, Lucian's contains nothing serious (save the moral drawn by the narrator); and the dialogue is secondary to the description of the farcical incidents.

The *Saturnalia* of Macrobius (q.v.) furnishes a Latin example of the serious literary symposium influenced by Gellius; it is supposed to be held among learned guests at the house of Vettius Praetextatus.

Descriptive works with little or no dialogue were strictly Δεῖπνα rather than συμπόσια. To this class belong the δειπνητικαὶ ἐπιστολαί of Hippolochus and Lynceus (Ath. 128 a), concerned with the food and displays of magnificence; and the *Symp.* of Heraclides of Tarentum (Ath. 120 b). (Philosophy is not necessarily excluded by such works any more than gastronomy by Athenaeus.) There were also verse-symposia in this group; some were descriptive or didactic (on diet and cookery), others were parodies, like the mock-epic of Matron (quoted by Ath. 134 d).

J. Martin, *Symposion*, 1931 (useful but often fantastic), and literature there cited.   J. T.

SYMPOSIUS, *see* SYMPHOSIUS.

SYNCOPATION, *see* METRE, GREEK, III (1).

SYNCRETISM, a word with a curious history, for which see J. Moffatt in Hastings, *ERE*, s.v. It is now used to denote a phenomenon very common in the later stages of ancient religion. While in the earlier periods the theory of the identity of the gods of different nations (cf. INTERPRETATIO ROMANA) was prevalent, in practice each community normally continued to worship its own deities, or if it imported those of another, regarded them as foreign and often gave them a more or less foreign cult. But from about the generation after Alexander it became more and more usual to identify gods of various nations in practice, thus producing cults of a mixed nature, and also to blend together deities of the same racial or national origin but different functions. Perhaps the earliest example of the former process is the Alexandrian cult of Sarapis (q.v.). Here we have an Egyptian god, Usar-Api, i.e. Osiris-Apis, himself no doubt the result of a certain amount of blending of native worships. But his cult-legend represents him as coming from the Black Sea, the foundation of his Alexandrian ritual was partly due to the Eumolpid Timotheus, the initiative in the matter was taken by Ptolemy I, the god was variously identified with Asclepius, Zeus, and Pluto (Tac. *Hist.* 4. 83 f.), and the statue was a Greek work, a Hades with some attributes foreign to him on Greek soil. All this was a State cult, intended perhaps to reconcile Greek and Egyptian elements in the mixed Ptolemaic kingdom. It does not appear to have excited any opposition or nationalistic feeling, at all events among Greeks, if only because earlier movements had tended somewhat in the same direction (see O. Kern, *Relig. d. Griech.* iii. 145 ff.). Certainly the spread of similar mixed cults was rapid, and current theological speculation at least kept pace with the facts of actual worship. At once an example of these movements and an instance of syncretism involving comparatively little but the blending of native elements is the very common Hellenistic identification of Apollo (q.v.) with Helios, and hence with various non-Greek sun-gods.

Naturally, syncretism is most conspicuous in those worships which never had been national within the classical area, for instance that of Isis. The *locus classicus* for this is Apuleius, *Met.* 11. 5, where a long speech put into the goddess's mouth identifies her with ten different figures of Mediterranean or Anatolian cult. Mithraism (q.v.) manifestly had syncretistic elements; indeed, solar religions seem to have lent themselves especially to it, see, e.g., the long and fantastic list of identifications of the 'Heracles' of Tyre, Nonnus, *Dion.* 40. 369 ff., while theoretically the tendency in late times to identify all gods with the sun (Macrob. *Sat.* 1. 17. 2) worked in the same direction. Two incidental results were the occasional formation of compound names for deities, as Κουραφροδίτη (Proclus, *Hymn* 5. 1), and the not uncommon occurrence of late statues showing one god with the attributes of one or several others. Syncretism is perhaps especially characteristic of magic (q.v.): see S. Eitrem in *Symb. Oslo.* 19 (1939), 57 ff.

Literature. No one important work is devoted to the subject, but all treatises on Hellenistic and Imperial cults have chapters or sections dealing with it. H. J. R.

SYNOECISMUS (συνοικισμός), the joining of several communities into one city-state (*see* POLIS). According to the common Greek opinion it was a single act, performed by a single person, as in the case of the most famous synoecismus, that of Athens by Theseus. In fact, the unification of Attica into one State was produced by a long-continued development, and so it may have been in many other instances. There were different kinds of synoecismus. (1) Several towns of a district effected a political union, the government being centred in one of them, or in a newly founded city. (2) In districts containing only one town the rural population was gathered into this as the only fortified place. (3) Two cities were amalgamated into one, perhaps by the will of some superior authority, e.g. a Hellenistic king. (4) In a tribal State a city was founded as a political centre for the districts occupied by villages and farms. In the second and third type of synoecismus the population was actually transplanted; in most cases the synoecismus was a merely political act (cf. Thuc. 2. 15).

U. Kahrstedt, *PW*, s.v. 'Synoikismos'. V. E.

SYNTHESIS (garment), *see* DRESS, para. 3.

SYPHAX (Σόφαξ), chief of a Numidian tribe, the Masaesyles, in north Africa, with capitals at Siga and Cirta. He wore a diadem like a Hellenistic monarch, while Phoenician, not Berber, was his official court language. In a war against Carthage (ending in 212 B.C.), he received some support from the Scipios in Spain. He overran part of the territory of his neighbour Masinissa (q.v.) and tried to retain the friendship of both Rome and Carthage, but was won over to the latter by Sophonisba (q.v.). He fought against the Roman expeditionary force under Scipio, who burnt his camp. Defeated at Campi Magni, he fled to his kingdom where he was beaten in battle and captured by Laelius and Masinissa (203). He died in imprisonment in Italy.

For coinage see L. Charrier, *Description des Monnaies de la Numidie* (1912). H. H. S.

SYRACUSE, a Corinthian colony founded *c.* 734 B.C. (Thuc. 6. 3). The colony was soon prosperous in trade and agriculture; *c.* 598 it founded Camarina. Its first known government was an aristocracy of landlords (γαμόροι), who had reduced the natives to serfdom (κυλλύριοι). A constitution was attributed to the hero Diocles (q.v.). The Demos and serfs expelled the landlords (*c.* 485); the latter received the help of Gelon (q.v.) who became tyrant and forcibly transported the population of neighbouring Greek cities to Syracuse. The old double city on the isle (Ortygia) and on the mainland (Achradina) became insufficient: new quarters were built, Tyche and Temenites (later called Neapolis). Gelon defeated the Carthaginians at Himera (480) and made Syra-

cuse the most important city of the Western World after Carthage. His successor Hieron I (q.v.) extended its influence to south Italy, and gave it a cultural splendour second only to that of Athens. After his death (467) Syracuse lost her empire. The moderate democracy worked through an Assembly and Senate (βουλή): two other councils, the σύγκλητος, perhaps an extraordinary assembly, and the ἔσκλητος are not clearly known. The yearly *strategi* (in variable number) were heads of the State. The People had a προστάτης τοῦ δήμου, probably an unofficial spokesman. The first years of the new Government were difficult. The new citizens of Gelon were expelled. A procedure of ostracism (πεταλισμός) was temporarily introduced. But Syracuse won the wars against Ducetius (q.v.) and Acragas. Two Athenian attempts to intervene in Sicily (427–424; 415–413) were repulsed by Syracuse, and Hermocrates' (q.v.) policy of intervention in the affairs of Greece led to his banishment and constitutional changes: the presidency of the popular assembly was probably transferred from the *strategi* to archons chosen by lot.

2. In face of another Carthaginian attack and subsequent complications Syracuse submitted to the tyranny of Dionysius I (q.v.). The troubled period of Dionysius II (367–344) was interrupted by a long exile (357–347), in which the two Academics Dion and Callippus and two other sons of Dionysius I treacherously replaced one another. Timoleon (q.v.), to save the supremacy of Syracuse in Sicily, introduced new colonists, and a new democratic constitution. The senate of 600 members gradually developed into an oligarchy of which the leaders were later banished. But the democratic leader Agathocles (q.v.) carried out a revolution by which he became στρατηγὸς αὐτοκράτωρ (317) and king (304). With his death (289) the last great period of Greek expansion in Italy passed away.

3. A new tyrant, Hicetas (288–278 B.C.) was beaten by the Carthaginians. The Carthaginians besieged Syracuse, but Pyrrhus (q.v.), who drove them back, was not able to renew the State of Dionysius and Agathocles. Hieron II (q.v.) defeated the Mamertines, but indirectly provoked the intervention of the Romans whose honoured vassal he became. His nephew Hieronymus (215–214 B.C.) did not follow his policy. After his murder, the struggle between a pro-Roman aristocratic party and a pro-Carthaginian party led to the Roman siege. Despite a heroic defence, in which Archimedes played his part, Marcellus mastered Ortygia by treachery and Achradina by surrender (211). In the Roman province, Syracuse was a *civitas decumana*, but remained a beautiful city, the residence of the governor. Settlers were sent by Augustus in 21 B.C.: Syracuse became a colony. In A.D. 280 it was plundered by the Franks. Famous catacombs show the development of Christianity.

For bibliography cf. SICILY. J. Bérard, *Bibliogr. topogr.* (1941), 96; L. Wickert, *PW* iv A. 1478; L. Giuliano, *Storia di Siracusa antica*[3] (1936); W. Hüttl, *Verfassungsgeschichte von Syrakus* (1929). For the topography: K. Fabricius, 'Das antike Syrakus', *Klio*, Beih. xxviii (1932). Coins: E. Boehringer, *Die Münzen von Syrakus* (1929). A. M.

SYRIA. This country (often called by the Greeks Coele Syria, to distinguish it from 'Syria between the rivers' or Mesopotamia) was a satrapy ('Beyond the River') of the Persian Empire till in 332 B.C. it was conquered by Alexander. On his death (323) it was assigned to Laomedon, who was in 319–318 ejected by Ptolemy I. Thereafter it was disputed between Ptolemy and Antigonus, till on the latter's death in 301 it was partitioned between Seleucus I, who occupied the north (Syria Seleucis), and Ptolemy I, who retained the south, to which the name Coele Syria was now restricted; the boundary was the river Eleutherus. Despite the three Syrian wars this arrangement remained substantially unchanged till in 201 Antiochus III conquered Coele Syria. During this period the four Phoenician dynasties which had ruled most of the coast were suppressed, and the maritime towns became republics, governed by *suffetes*. The Seleucids, especially Seleucus I, colonized their area intensively, founding at least eight cities and six military colonies of Macedonians. The Ptolemies seem to have founded no colonies and governed the interior on a bureaucratic system like the Egyptian. Antiochus IV (175–163) encouraged the hellenization of the upper classes, which had already made some progress, and its corollary, civic autonomy. He allowed both the principal Greek colonies and the chief Phoenician towns to issue their own coins, and granted civic charters to many native towns in the interior.

2. After Antiochus IV's death the Seleucid power gradually declined owing to constant wars between rival claimants to the throne, complicated by Ptolemaic interventions. Taking advantage of the weakness of the central Government, many of the cities asserted their freedom, and scores of local chiefs carved out principalities for themselves, while four native dynasties, those of Commagene, the Ituraeans, the Jews, and the Nabataeans (q.v.), built up considerable kingdoms. The two branches of the Seleucid house were gradually pushed back to Antioch and to Damascus and its neighbourhood, to which the term Coele Syria was now restricted. Finally, in 83, Tigranes of Armenia occupied the country, and on his defeat Pompey made Syria a Roman province (64–63). Pompey re-established a number of cities which had been subdued or destroyed by dynasts, notably those subject to the Jewish kingdom, but in general confirmed the existing situation. The province of Syria thus comprised besides the cities, a few of which were free, the client kingdoms of Commagene and Arabia, the ethnarchy of the Jews, the tetrarchy of the Ituraeans, and many minor tetrarchies in the north. The Parthians invaded Syria in 40 and were ejected by Ventidius in 39. Antony gave to Cleopatra the Ituraean tetrarchy, the coast up to the Eleutherus (except Tyre and Sidon), Damascus and Coele Syria, and parts of the Jewish and Nabataean kingdoms.

3. Syria (which probably included Cilicia Pedias from *c.* 44 B.C. to A.D. 72) was under the Principate an important military command; its legate, a consular, had down to A.D. 70 normally four legions at his disposal. The client kingdoms were gradually annexed. Commagene (q.v.) was finally incorporated in the province in A.D. 72, Ituraea partly in 24 B.C., partly (Agrippa II's kingdom) *c.* A.D. 93. Judaea, at first governed by procurators, became in A.D. 70 a regular province ruled by a praetorian legate, who commanded a legion withdrawn from Syria; under Hadrian the province, henceforth usually known as Syria Palaestina, became consular, a second legion being added. The Nabataean kingdom became in A.D. 105 the province of Arabia, ruled by a praetorian legate with one legion. Septimius Severus divided Syria into a northern province with two legions (Syria Coele) and a southern with one legion (Syria Phoenice). Urbanization made little progress under the Empire. Commagene and Arabia were on annexation partitioned into cities, but much of Ituraea was added to the territories of Berytus, Sidon, and Damascus, and in the rest the villages became the units of government. In Judaea the centralized bureaucracy established by the Ptolemies and maintained by the Seleucids, Maccabees, and Herodians survived in some areas throughout the Principate; in others cities were founded by Vespasian, Hadrian, and the Severan emperors. Of the minor

principalities some, such as Chalcis ad Belum, Emisa, and Arca, became cities, but most seem to have been incorporated in the territories of existing towns. Cities being so scarce, Syria remained a predominantly rural country—hence its importance as a recruiting-ground both for the local legions and for many auxiliary units—and only superficially hellenized: not only the peasants of the wide city territories but even the proletariat of the towns always continued to speak Aramaic.

4. Wine was grown for export in many parts, chiefly along the coast. Other agricultural products of commercial importance were nuts, various fruits, such as the plums of Damascus or the dates of Jericho, and vegetables, e.g. Ascalonite onions. The principal industries were linen-weaving (at Laodicea and in several Phoenician and north Palestinian towns), wool-weaving (at Damascus), purple-dyeing (on the Phoenician and Palestinian coast), and glass-blowing (at Sidon). The country was also enriched by the transit trade from Babylonia, Arabia Felix, and the Far East, much of which passed by caravan over the Arabian desert to such emporia as Palmyra, Damascus, Bostra, and Petra, and thence to the coastal ports.

Mommsen, *The Provinces of the Roman Empire* ii (1886), 1–231; G. A. Harrer, *Studies in the History of the Roman Province of Syria* (1915); E. S. Bouchier, *Syria as a Roman Province* (1916); U. Kahrstedt, 'Syrische Territorien in hellenistischer Zeit', *Abh. Ges. Gött., phil.-hist. Kl.,* N.F. xix (1926); R. Dussaud, *Topographie historique de la Syrie antique et médiévale* (1927); E. Honigmann, *PW* iv A (1932), 1549–1727; F. Cumont, *CAH* xi, ch. 15; Jones, *Eastern Cities,* 227–95; F. M. Heichelheim, *An Economic Survey of Ancient Rome* iv (1938), 120–257.   A. H. M. J.

SYRINX (Σύριγξ), a nymph loved by Pan (q.v.). She ran away from him and begged the earth, or the river-nymphs, to help her; she became a reed-bed, from which Pan made his pipe (σύριγξ).

Ovid, *Met.* 1. 689 ff.; Servius on Verg. *Ecl.* 2. 31.

SYRINX, see MUSIC, § 9 (ii).

SYRTES, the shallow waters lying between Tunisia, Tripolitania, and Cyrenaica. The Greater Syrtis (*Gulf of Sidra*) formed the south-east corner of this ill-reputed Mediterranean bay, the Lesser Syrtis (*Gulf of Gabès*) the south-west. Legends, possibly propagated to protect Phoenician trade-monopoly, exaggerated the dangers of the Syrtic Sea, which failed to hamper the commerce of the Phoenician Tripolis to the south or the Greek Pentapolis to the west; to the west Meninx (*Djerba*), the mythical island of the Lotus-eaters, did a prosperous trade in purple dye, and Tacape (*Gabès*) and Taparura (*Sfax*) were flourishing ports.   W. N. W.

SYRUS, see PUBLILIUS (3).

SYSSITIA (συσσίτια; also known as ἀνδρεῖα or φιδίτια) were mess-companies, among which the citizen body was apportioned at Sparta and in the cities of Crete. At Sparta each mess was about fifteen strong. Membership (which was obtained by co-optation) was a necessary qualification for full citizenship, and each mess-mate was bound to provide from his estate a fixed minimum ration of food on pain of disfranchisement. The Cretan *syssitia* were formed by voluntary grouping round a leader of good family; their upkeep was at State cost.

According to Aristotle (*Pol.* 1272ᵇ33) *syssitia* also existed at Carthage. These probably were confined to the aristocracy.

Plutarch, *Lycurgus* 12; Strabo 10. 480, 483.   M. C.

T

TABELLAE, *see* BOOKS, II. 3.

TABELLARII were freedmen or slaves employed as couriers, and formed part of the *familia* of every individual or company with correspondents in the provinces. Their services were shared by groups of friends. During Caesar's Gallic campaigns Oppius arranged for the sending of letters to him and his officers (Cic. *QFr.* 3. 1. 8). In the Civil Wars *tabellarii* were often stopped and their letters read (Cic. *Fam.* 12. 12. 1). In the Principate private *tabellarii* were still required, as the Public Post carried no private correspondence (*see* POSTAL SERVICE). The imperial *tabellarii* (*ILS* 1701-11) were organized in groups under *praepositi* and *optiones*. *Tabellarii* had to travel on foot unless provided with a *diploma* entitling them to the use of the *cursus publicus* (Plin. *Ep.* 10. 64).
G. H. S.

TABERNARIA, sc. **fabula,** *see* FABULA.

TABULA BANTINA, a bronze tablet, found at Bantia in 1793, and now at Naples. On it is inscribed in the Latin alphabet an Oscan inscription containing a series of municipal regulations for the town of Bantia. A Latin inscription (*CIL* i². 582) on the other side dates it *c.* 125 B.C. It is of vital importance for the study of Oscan.

C. D. Buck, *A Grammar of Oscan and Umbrian²* (texts, glossary, bibliography; 1928). P. S. N.

TABULA PONTIFICUM, a whitened board set up yearly by the Pontifex Maximus in the Regia, with the magistrates' names, recorded by the day events in which the pontifical college took ceremonial action, e.g. dedications, festivals, triumphs, eclipses, famines, prodigies; political events entered solely in their sacral connexion. From the first full registration of prodigies in Livy (296–295 B.C.), the first recorded eclipse (if this is dated 13 June 288, reading 'quadringentesimo' in Cicero, *Rep.* 1. 16. 25), and the first regular accuracy of the *fasti* (q.v.), it appears to have begun about 300 B.C., presumably on the Ogulnian reform of the pontifical college. It formed the basis for the composition of the *annales maximi* (*c.* 123 B.C.), with the incorporation of fuller political records.

Cicero, *De Or.* 2. 12. 52; Servius ad Verg. *Aen.* 1. 373; Cato *Origines*, bk. 4, fr. 77 (Peter). O. Seeck, *Die Kalendartafel der Pontifices* (1885); L. Cantarelli, *Riv. fil.* 1898, 209; De Sanctis, *Stor. Rom.* i. 16; K. J. Beloch, *Röm. Geschichte*, 86; J. E. A. Crake, *CPhil.* 1940. A. H. McD.

TABULAE IGUVINAE. At Gubbio, the ancient Iguvium (Umbria), there were discovered in 1444 nine bronze tablets of varying sizes (the largest now surviving measures 33 by 22 in., the smallest 16 by 12), engraved on one or both sides partly in the native, partly in the Latin alphabet. Two of them were taken to Venice in 1540 and lost; the remaining seven are still at Gubbio. These are the famous Iguvine Tables. The oldest was written *c.* 400 B.C., and the latest not later than 90 B.C. The text contains the proceedings and liturgy of a brotherhood of priests, the *frater atiieřiur* ('Fratres Atiedii', apparently in origin a *nomen gentilicium*), not unlike the Roman Arval brethren, viz.: regulations for the lustration of Iguvium, for an assembly of the *populus* (Umb. *puplum* acc. sing.) of Iguvium (presumably in connexion with the *lustrum*), concluding sacrifice of the lustrum on behalf of the Brotherhood, an optional sacrifice of a dog to the infernal deity *Hontus*, assembly and sacrifices at the 'decurial' festivals of federated clans (ten in number), directions for sacrifice to Jupiter, Pomonus (called *pupřike* dat. sing., quasi *Pubi-dicus and connected with initiation-rites?), Vesuna, and other deities on stated occasions, and various administrative resolutions of the Brotherhood. Among the other deities worshipped were *Trebus, Tefer* (connected with burnt offerings?), *Torra* (all three designated *Iouius* or *Iouia*), *Praestita* (called *Cerria*), *Cerrus Martius, Mars Hodius, Hule* (an infernal deity), *Mars Grabovius* ('the oak-tree', an epithet of Illyrian associations or origin), *Fisus* and *Fisouius, Picu(u)ius Martius, Coredius, Vofio* ('hearer of vows'?), *Tursa* (a goddess of dread), *Purtupite* (the recipient of offerings). In scope, content, and antiquity the Iguvine Tables surpass all other documents for the study of Italic religion. *See* LUSTRATION. They are also the main source of our knowledge of Umbrian.

F. Buecheler, *Umbrica* (1883), is still important. C. D. Buck, *A Grammar of Oscan and Umbrian²* (1928; texts and glossary); A. von Blumenthal, *Die iguvinischen Tafeln* (1931), discusses numerous details, but is prone to dubious conjecture; G. Devoto, *Tabulae Iguvinae* (1937), gives much attention to matters of religion; I. Rosenzweig, *Ritual and Cults of Pre-Roman Iguvium* (1937), is a usable compilation. See also the bibliography to the article RELIGION, ITALIC. J. W.

TABULARIUM. (1) The record-office at Rome, probably serving chiefly the adjacent *aerarium Saturni*, built by Q. Lutatius Catulus in 78 B.C. Its rear façade, standing upon a huge substructure, masked the ridge between the two summits of the Capitol and closed the west end of Sulla's forum, overshadowing the temples of Concord and Saturn. A stairway from the Forum climbed through the ground-floor of the substructure to the front hall of the building. The first floor contained a service corridor, leading from the top of the *Porticus Deorum Consentium* to two floors of eastern strong-rooms. The façade is formed by an arcade with shops or offices, and masks two inaccessible vaulted undercrofts suggestive of two large asymmetrical halls, now vanished, at the level of the upper Corinthian façade, a Flavian restoration.

See Delbrueck, *Hellenistische Bauten in Latium* i (1907), 23–46.

(2) Other *tabularia* in Rome were the Aventine *Templum Cereris*, for plebiscites and *senatus consulta*; *Atrium Libertatis*, the censors' registry of punishments and citizen-rolls; *Aedes Nympharum*, the censors' tax-registry; *Tabularium Caesaris*, for cadastral records; *Tabularium castrense*, for the Imperial household.

(3) Taxation sub-offices (*CIL* vi. 8431).

(4) *Tabularium Caesaris* in provinces for Imperial rescripts, etc. (*CIL* x. 7852).

(5) *Tabularium Caesaris* in provincial capitals for tax-returns, census, imperial domain-land, birth-registration (S.H.A. *Vit. Marc.* 6).

(6) Military *tabularia* in legionary fortresses and frontier forts (*CIL* viii. 2852; vi. 3196).

(7) *Tabularia civitatum* for municipal or cantonal records and local taxation.

See for (2)–(7) O. Hirschfeld, *Die kaiserlichen Verwaltungsbeamten²* (1905), 59 ff., 325; J. Marquardt, *Römische Staatsverw.²* i, ii (1881–4); Mommsen, *Gesamm. Schrift.* v. 329. I. A. R.

TACFARINAS, a Numidian, formerly an auxiliary trooper, took to brigandage and stirred up a serious insurrection in Africa (A.D. 17). Despite victories won by three proconsuls in succession, Furius Camillus, L. Apronius, and Q. Junius Blaesus (the last of whom was acclaimed *imperator* by the troops), the elusive enemy prosecuted his depredations until trapped and killed at Auzia by P. Cornelius Dolabella (24). R. S.

TACHYGRAPHY. (1) GREEK. Diogenes Laertius (*Vit. Xen.* 2. 48) says that Xenophon was the first to use signs to represent spoken words (πρῶτος ὑποσημειωσάμενος τὰ λεγόμενα); but whether this represents anything like systematic tachygraphy is quite uncertain. The same may be said of the word ὀξυγράφος in the LXX version of Ps. xlv. 2. Nothing is really known of Greek shorthand except from papyri and wax-tablets found in Egypt, which give specimens of tachygraphy from the second century A.D. onwards, and portions of manuals from the end of the third century. These show a fully organized system, composed of a syllabary and a (so-called) Commentary, consisting of groups of words, arranged in fours or occasionally eights, with a sign attached to each, which had to be memorized. The tetrads include some element of association (e.g. one sign represents Γανυμήδης, οἰνοχοεῖ, νέκταρ, μιξοβάρβαρος), but oftener it is not discernible. Such a system is referred to in Basil. *De Virg.* 31 (Migne, *PG* xxx. 733). The British Museum has a portion of two manuals (Papp. 2561, 2562), and a wax-tablet book with exercises; and this material is supplemented by papyri from Antinoë and elsewhere.

(2) LATIN. According to Plutarch (*Cato Mi.* 23), Cicero introduced shorthand at Rome, and as he refers to it by a Greek name (διὰ σημείων, *Att.* 13. 32) he probably derived it from Greece. The Latin system, which shows affinity with the Greek, is associated with the name of Cicero's freedman, Tiro, and the lists of symbols which have come down to us are known as *notae Tironianae*, but the medieval representations of them have been elaborated to an extent that would make them useless for actual reporting. They are sometimes used for scholia.

In the ancient systems of shorthand, as in the modern, one sign may have several interpretations, and in order to interpret shorthand records it is necessary to have a clue to the subject, and (often) to remember something of what was said. Thus stock phrases such as ὦ ἄνδρες Ἀθηναῖοι or τί δεῖ μακρολογεῖν were represented by single signs.

The recently discovered material is in H. J. M. Milne, *Greek Shorthand Manuals* (1934); the earlier literature in C. Wessely, *Ein System altgriechischer Tachygraphie* (1895); A. Mentz in *Arch. Pap.* viii. 34; F. W. G. Foat in *JHS.* xxi. 238; V. Gardthausen, *Griechische Palaeographie*² (1913), ii. 270–84; E. M. Thompson, *Introd. to Gr. and Lat. Palaeography* (1912), 71–4. F. G. K.

TACITUS (1), CORNELIUS. We do not know exactly the parentage, year of birth and death, or even *praenomen*, of Tacitus. He was born *c.* A.D. 55, possibly of North Italian stock, and began his official career under Vespasian. He married Agricola's daughter in 77, and became *praetor* and *XVvir sacris faciundis* in 88 (*Agr.* 9; *Hist.* I. 1; *Ann.* II. 11). Away from Rome when Agricola died in 93, he returned to witness three deadening years of Domitian's savagery (*Agr.* 2 and 44). *Consul suffectus* in 97, he pronounced the funeral oration over Verginius Rufus (q.v.), and in 100 led Pliny in prosecuting Marius Priscus for extortion; famous by now for eloquence, he attracted students 'ex admiratione ingenii' (Pliny, *Ep.* 4. 13). He was proconsul of Asia, probably in 112–13 (*AJArch.* xl (1936), 71); a passage in *Ann.* 2. 61 must have been written after 115. That is all.

2. The *Dialogus*, now after much controversy regarded as Tacitean by most scholars, takes rank as his earliest work, composed *c.* A.D. 80. Purporting to be a discussion on reasons for the decline of oratory, it is written with great charm, skill in characterization, and with some foretaste of T.'s later style. Then came silence till Domitian's death. The *De vita Iulii Agricolae*, published in 98, describes the life of his father-in-law, the larger part being devoted to the scene of Agricola's greatest achievements, Britain. It belongs to a well-known *genre*, and is frankly laudatory towards its subject and critical of his jealous master, Domitian. Military and topographical details are subordinated to the depicting of Agricola's character; 'bonum uirum facile crederes, magnum libenter'.

3. To 98, too, belongs the *De origine et situ Germanorum*, a description of the various tribes inhabiting the regions north of Rhine and Danube. Again Tacitus employs a familiar *genre*, though probably more than one motive impelled him to write. Considering its sources, the account appears careful and reliable. Throughout there is a contrast, sometimes open, sometimes implied, between the robust simplicity of a vast and virile nation and the immorality and corruption of the over-civilized empire threatened by it; 'tam diu Germania uincitur'.

4. These are short monographs. Two longer works narrate imperial history from A.D. 14–96. The first has no manuscript title, but is usually called the *Histories*: beginning in 69, it presumably ended with Domitian's assassination. Four books and twenty-six chapters of the fifth alone survive, but they give a comprehensive picture of Civil War, containing an extraordinary gallery of ambitious intriguers and incompetent rulers, with one emperor who 'changed for the better', Vespasian. What Tacitus related of Domitian may be gauged from the *Agricola*, and from the portrait of him in 70—'nondum ad curas intentus, sed stupris et adulteriis filium principis agebat' (*Hist.* 4. 2).

5. The second is the *Annals*, a conventional title (cf. *Ann.* 4. 32), for in the First Medicean manuscript the heading is 'ab excessu diui Augusti'. We know of sixteen books, though 7–10 are completely missing, and book 16 breaks off in A.D. 66, before Nero's death. Indeed, the exact number of books in *Histories* and *Annals* is uncertain: St. Jerome writes as though there were thirty (*Comment. in Zachariam,* 3. 14), but scholars cannot decide whether the *Annals* contained eighteen books and the *Histories* twelve, or sixteen and fourteen. For each year Tacitus makes a division into affairs concerning the Princeps and his provinces, and affairs concerning the Senate and its provinces. Occasionally, for artistic or historical clarity, he oversteps the year's limit, but the reason alleged is characteristic,—'quo requiesceret animus a domesticis malis' (*Ann.* 6. 38). Attempts, by Ross in 1878 and Hochart in 1890, to prove the *Annals* a Renaissance forgery, are easily refuted; we possess in them the genuine Tacitus at the height of his powers.

6. What of the man himself? In composing these works Tacitus could draw partly on previous authors, now non-existent (Aufidius Bassus, Cluvius Rufus, Fabius Rusticus, or Vipstanus Messalla), partly on his own experience. He quotes and chooses between conflicting accounts (*Hist.* 3. 28; *Ann.* 13. 20; 14. 2), and we need not doubt his thoroughness and care (Pliny, *Ep.* 7. 33). Fabia's thesis, that Tacitus always slavishly copied one source, is both unlikely and unacceptable.

7. But his view is also coloured by his own experience. Reacting against the Principate, Tacitus looks back longingly on the 'free' institutions of the Republic ('libertatem et consulatum', *Ann.* 1. 1; cf. 4. 63); the Principate may have benefited the provinces and secured peace (*Ann.* 1. 2; *Hist.* 1. 1), but the overwhelming power thus centred in one man blunted the moral sense of even experienced rulers (*Ann.* 6. 48), and rapidly reduced the ruled to servility and flattery. Thus the Principate tended towards *regnum*, where T. found 'fugas ciuium, urbium euersiones, fratrum coniugum parentum neces aliaque solita regibus' (*Hist.* 5. 8; cf. *Ann.* 6. 1, and 12. 66) and even Augustus is damned with faint praise, or belauded only for contrast with his worse successors (e.g. *Ann.* 1. 46; 3. 5; 13. 3). Roman *virtus* had stagnated into an inactive and inglorious temper; Augustus had lured citizens into the Principate 'dulcedine otii'; *pax* merely cloaked *ignavia*. The emperors had neglected military glory: Tiberius preferred diplomacy to arms

(*Ann.* 2. 64 and 4. 32); Caligula's campaigns were a farce (*Germ.* 37 and *Hist.* 4. 15); Claudius had merely reconquered Britain (*Agr.* 13); and Nero's crimes had alienated the soldiery (*Ann.* 15. 67). Domitian had been warlike, but in the wrong way, and Tacitus shrinks from enumerating the Roman lives he lost (Orosius 7. 10. 4).

8. Nor was the vaunted *pax Augusta* fruitful or prosperous, at least in Rome (*Hist.* 1. 1; *Ann.* 1. 10); what galls Tacitus is the lack of independence and courage among those who should most have shown it. While lower ranks provided shining examples of loyalty and heroism (*Ann.* 13. 44 and 15. 57), most nobles and senators could only cringe to a despot, 'homines ad seruitutem paratos' (*Ann.* 3. 65; cf. 14. 13), and though L. Silanus *did* put up a fight (*Ann.* 16. 9), the 'patientia seruilis' of Nero's victims rouses Tacitus' scornful pity (*Ann.* 16. 16). Yet he disapproves the Stoic-minded and their theatrical gestures: his ideal was the prudence of Agricola (*Agr.* 42) or of L. Piso (*Ann.* 6. 10).

9. Throughout those eighty odd years, T. discerns the wrath of the gods working, gods more eager to punish than to save (*Hist.* 1. 3; *Ann.* 4. 1; 16. 16). His task is gloomy, to record the suspicions of Tiberius, played upon by informers; Claudius the helpless tool of freedmen or wives; the vanity and vice of Nero—all resulting in baseless accusations and judicial murders. 'Primum facinus noui principatus' (*Ann.* 1. 6) is echoed by 'prima nouo principatu mors' (*Ann.* 13. 1) for the reign of Nero. Given the opportunity of recounting victories won by Germanicus or Corbulo, Tacitus can expand indeed (*Ann.* 2. 18; 13. 39); otherwise he feels a painful contrast with Republican historians—'nobis in arto et inglorius labor' (*Ann.* 4. 32). Better times undeniably had come with Nerva (*Agr.* 3; *Hist.* 1. 1), but he fears that the past century, in his account, will seem a sombre period (*Ann.* 4. 33).

10. To dissipate this feeling of monotony and rivet the reader's attention T. marshals all his resources, forming a style unique and perfectly adapted to purpose. He keeps us continually on the alert. His vocabulary is large and varied: note the different phrases for dying or committing suicide or for 'evening was approaching'. To the classical word Tacitus prefers an older, a simple verb to the usual compound, new forms to hackneyed. Echoes of poetry, subtle reminiscences of Virgil, Graecisms, all make their appeal. Words are left uncoupled, grouped in strange and striking order ('tamen' pushed to the end; *Ann.* 2. 57), or thrust into violent prominence.

11. Though Tacitus can elaborate sentences of length and complexity, he prefers (like Sallust) rapidity and shortness; periodic structure is deliberately abandoned. Gone are the temporal clauses of Livy, gone the superlatives of Cicero. Instead we have intensity and brevity, gained by skilful use of Historic Infinitives, or adjectives that become practically Active Past Participles ('gnarus', 'certus', 'dubius'), by omission of verbs, by compression. Doublings or treblings are rare: every noun, every adjective holds its last drop of meaning. So intensely personal is his style that he rarely quotes, save for damning effect—a phrase revealing Tiberius' tortured soul, a brutal joke of Nero, a tribune's bluntness (*Ann.* 6. 6; 14. 59; 15. 67; 16. 4).

12. Throughout shines the quality Pliny noted in Tacitus' speeches, elevation. Tacitus believes in the dignity and moral effect of history (*Ann.* 3. 65). He will not chronicle petty events (*Ann.* 13. 31): his unwillingness to mention spades and shovels (*Ann.* 1. 65), or a garden-cart (*Ann.* 11. 32) leads to circumlocutions recalling French tragedy, but he never drops into mere pomposity; he knows history is a great theme, to be adorned by *fides* and *eloquentia* worthy of it (*Ann.* 4. 34). This consciousness informs his whole manner, whether in comment on nobles who competed at Nero's bidding, 'quos fato perfunctos ne nominatim tradam, maioribus

eorum tribuendum puto' (*Ann.* 14. 14), or sad reflection on the 'ludibria rerum mortalium cunctis in negotiis' (*Ann.* 3. 18).

13. The style, indeed, is inescapable, making its effect sometimes by long passages, sometimes by sentences, sometimes by one phrase of psychological insight. We may instance Agrippina's murder by her son (*Ann.* 14. 1–9), or the rise and collapse of the Pisonian conspiracy (*Ann.* 15. 48–71); Vitellians and Vespasianists fighting ferociously in the heart of Rome, while onlookers applaud (*Hist.* 3. 82–3), or Germanicus' visit to the Varian camp (*Ann.* 1. 61–2), or the terrible picture of Tiberius' end (*Ann.* 6. 50–1). Great and fatal characters stalk across the stage—Tiberius, Sejanus, the younger Agrippina, Nero—and these are drawn at length, but Tacitus can in a phrase sum up person or situation: Galba, 'capax imperii nisi imperasset' (*Hist.* 1. 49); Vitellius, 'principatum ei detulere qui ipsum non nouerant' (*Hist.* 3. 86); Claudius Sanctus, pusillanimous leader of disgraced troops, 'effosso oculo dirus ore, ingenio debilior' (*Hist.* 4. 62).

14. Always the irony remains keen—'proprium humani ingenii est odisse quem laeseris' (*Agr.* 42), 'acerrima proximorum odia' (*Hist.* 4. 70), 'obliuione magis quam clementia' (*Ann.* 6. 14)—or we have Nero's admiral advising him to destroy Agrippina; and after?— 'additurum principem defunctae templum et aras et cetera ostentandae pietati' (*Ann.* 14. 3).

15. His bias against the dynastic system is plain; yet his accuracy, though severely probed by modern criticism, can rarely be impugned. Though sometimes an unfavourable interpreter of his facts, he will not blacken even Tiberius or Nero by crediting stupid rumours about them (*Ann.* 4. 11; 16. 6). His picture of capital and court is terrible, but its general truth is incontestable. His gaze is focused upon Rome; when he looks farther he approves the sturdy simplicity of North Italy and the provinces (*Ann.* 16. 5), and can pen a moving appeal for the preservation of the Empire (*Hist.* 4. 74). Though mistrustful of 'civilization' and of its debilitating effects, he never despairs of human nature: even the Civil War produced examples of heroism, loyalty, and friendship (*Hist.* 1. 3), and virtue is not confined to past ages (*Ann.* 3. 55). Napoleon called Tacitus a 'traducer of humanity': from one who spent his powers in annihilating humanity this verdict is interesting, but simply untrue. In independent research and judgement, in essential truth, in the dramatic power and nobility of an enthralling style, Tacitus claims his place among the greatest historians.

16. Yet his survival hangs upon a slender thread. He was little read in succeeding centuries; later, Orosius (q.v.) and Sidonius (q.v.) appear to know him, and Iordanes paraphrases a passage from the *Agricola*. Then darkness falls, though in the ninth century monks at Fulda apparently possessed the early *Annals*, and the *Germania*. Even now we are dependent upon one manuscript (discovered about 1510) for *Annals* 1–6, and upon one manuscript (the Second Medicean, discovered about 1430) for *Annals* 11–16 and *Histories* 1–5. So near came Tacitus to mortality. *See also* LITERARY CRITICISM, LATIN, para. 5.

BIBLIOGRAPHY

LIFE AND WORKS: G. Boissier, *Tacite*[4] (1923); C. Marchesi, *Tacito* (1924); L. Schwabe in *PW* iv. 1566; E. E. Sikes in *CAH* xi. 737; W. C. Summers in *Silver Age of Latin Lit.*; J. Wight Duff in *Lit. Hist. of Rome* (Silver Age), 559–98 (with full bibliography).

TEXTS: O.C.T. (C. D. Fisher; Furneaux); Teubner (Halm-Andresen–Köstermann).

COMMENTARIES: Annals 1–6 (Furneaux, ed. 2, 1896); 11–16 (Furneaux–Pelham-Fisher, 1907); (E. Köstermann, 1932–4). Agr., J. H. Sleeman (1914, repr. 1923); H. Furneaux and J. G. C. Anderson (1922). Dial., W. Peterson (1893); A. Gudeman (ed. 2, 1914). Germ., J. H. Sleeman (with Agr.); W. Reeb (1930); J. G. C. Anderson (1938). Hist., W. A. Spooner (1891); C. Halm and G. Andresen (ed. 5, 1916).

TRANSLATIONS: Agr. (with Dial. and Germ.), M. Hutton (Loeb,

1914). *Hist.*, W. H. Fyfe (1912); G. G. Ramsay (1915); C. H. Moore (Loeb, 1925–31). *Ann.*, G. G. Ramsay (1904); J. Jackson, (Loeb, 1931).

STYLE, DICTION, AND THOUGHT. Besides studies under 'Life and Works' see: E. Courbaud, *Les Procédés d'art de T. dans les 'Histoires'* (1918); N. Eriksson, *Studien zu den Annalen des T.* (1934); A. Draeger, *Über Syntax und Stil des T.³* (1882); Ph. Fabia, *Les Sources de T.* (1893); Ed. Fraenkel, 'Tacitus', *Neue Jahrb.* viii (1932), 218; G. A. Harrer, 'Tacitus and Tiberius', *AJPhil.* xli (1920), 57; J. S. Reid, 'T. as a Historian', *JRS* xi (1921), 191; R. Reitzenstein, *T. und sein Werk* (Neue Wege . . . IV) 1926.

LEXICON: A. Gerber and A. Greef, *Lexicon Taciteum* (1903).
M. P. C.

TACITUS (2), MARCUS CLAUDIUS, was chosen by the Senate to succeed Aurelian in September A.D. 275, being then an elderly senator, already twice consul. Consul for the third time in 276, he marched East, against Persia (?), gained a victory, through Florian, over the Goths in Pontus, but succumbed to murder, or the threat of it, from his own troops at Tyana (*c.* March). The misgovernment of his kinsman, Maximinus, as governor of Syria, had brought discredit on his rule.

A senator himself of high character and reputation, Tacitus certainly favoured the Senate, but he did not effectively restore its authority or give back to it the commands in the army. After Tacitus and his halfbrother, Florian (q.v.), the 'militaris potentia conualuit' under Probus. Tacitus was probably responsible for some salutary reforms, such as forbidding the debasement of metals at the mint, but it was only the hopeful fancy of later historians that painted his reign as a late summer of constitutional government under the Senate.

CAH xii. 311 ff.; Parker, *Roman World*, 212 ff.   H. M.

TAENARUM (*Ταίναρον*, more rarely *Ταίναρος*). (1) The central peninsula of south Peloponnesus and its terminal cape, near which stood a Temple of Poseidon. Near the temple, of which scanty traces remain, is a cave, through which Heracles traditionally dragged up Cerberus from Hades. The sanctuary enjoyed a right of asylum (cf. the adventure of Pausanias, Thuc. 1. 133), and private slaves were manumitted there, before an ephor (*IG* v. 1, 1228 ff.). In the later fourth century the Taenarum district was an important headquarters for mercenaries.

(2) A city on the west coast of the above peninsula, probably founded by Augustus, and a member of the Eleutherolaconian League.   A. M. W.

TAGES, an important figure of Etruscan mythology, child-like in appearance but of divine wisdom. T. was unearthed by a peasant in the fields near Tarquinia and revealed the Etruscan discipline (*libri Tagetici*) to the twelve *lucumones* of Etruria.

Cf. A. S. Pease on Cic. *Div.* 2. 50.   G. M. A. H.

TAGUS (*ταγός*), the title of the Thessalian headmagistrates, who were elected intermittently to deal with an emergency involving the whole country. In practice, *tagi* usually retained their office till their death, thus securing an advantage over the leaders of rival baronial families. The term *tagus* is avoided by historians apart from Xenophon, but the principal leaders, such as Thorax the Aleuad who negotiated the submission to Xerxes, certainly held the *tageia*. Jason (q.v. 2) revived the office in 374 B.C. to legalize his control of Thessaly, but Alexander (5), who claimed the *tageia*, cannot have been legitimately elected. When a new Thessalian League was formed under Theban influence (*c.* 369), the federal *tageia* ceased to exist, and the principal magistrate was an *ἄρχων*. A municipal *tageia*, as is attested by inscriptions, survived until Roman times.

E. Meyer, *Theopomps Hellenika* (1909), 218–49; A. Momigliano, *Athenaeum* 1932, 51–3.   H. D. W.

TALOS (*Τάλως, Τάλος*), perhaps originally a god (*ταλῶς* is the Sun and Talaios a Cretan title of Zeus, Hesych. s.vv.), but in mythology the guardian of Crete (originally

of Europa, Ap. Rhod., infra). He is generally said to have been made of bronze by Hephaestus, but animated; for other accounts see Roscher's *Lex.*, s.v. He kept strangers off by throwing stones (Ap. Rhod.), or burned them (Simonides in schol. Plat. *Resp.* 337 a), or heated himself red-hot and then clasped them in his arms (Eustathius on Homer, p. 1893. 6). His vital fluid was kept in by a membrane in his foot; Medea (q.v.) cast him into a magic sleep and cut the membrane, thus killing him.

See Ap. Rhod. *Argon.* 4. 1638 ff., the most circumstantial account, and A. B. Cook, *Zeus* i. 719 ff.   H. J. R.

TALTHYBIUS, Agamemnon's herald (*Iliad* 1. 320). For some reason his name remains familiar in later writings, while his comrade Eurybates (ibid.) is forgotten. He was the eponym of a herald-clan at Sparta, the Talthybiadae (see Hdt. 7. 134. 1).

TANAGRA, the chief town of east Boeotia, with a territory extending to the sea, was more closely bound with Attica, with which it had easy connexions, than was the rest of Boeotia (cf. Hdt. 5. 57). It was an early rival to Thebes; after the Persian Wars it probably stood at the head of the Boeotian League (Head, *Historia Numorum²*, p. 348). In 457 the Athenians were defeated here by the Spartans and their allies, and the battles of Oenophyta and Delium were also fought in this district. In the fourth century Tanagra declined in importance, contributing only one boeotarch to the League, but it flourished in Hellenistic and Roman times (Strabo, p. 403). It is now best known for the lively little Hellenistic terracotta figures, women and groups from daily life, found in its graves. It was the birthplace of the poetess Corinna. The walls are preserved, but little else. *See also* FEDERAL STATES, para. 3.

Paus. 9. 20, and Frazer, ad loc.   T. J. D.

TANAÏS, the river Don, and a city at its estuary. The river was usually regarded as the boundary between Europe and Asia. A trade route to Central Asia, by which Ural gold came to the Black Sea, and Greek textiles were carried as far as Mongolia, probably followed the Tanaïs valley. But the Greeks knew little of the river: Aristotle and Alexander mistook it for a branch of the Jaxartes (q.v.).

The city of Tanaïs was probably founded by Panticapaeum *c.* 500 B.C. (to judge by the fairly rich finds beginning at that date). In the first century A.D. it was rebuilt higher up the river, near modern Rostov, but it lost its former prosperity.

E. H. Minns, *Scythians and Greeks* (1913), 566–9.   M. C.

TANTALUS (*Τάνταλος*), in mythology, king of Sipylos and the neighbourhood in Lydia, son of Zeus and Plutô (*Πλουτώ*), Hyginus, *Fab.* 82. 1; the name is variously corrupted in sundry authors, see Scheuer in Roscher's *Lexikon* v. 75. 26 ff. Plutô being a minor being of the same kind as Plutus (q.v.), this would seem one of the numerous variants of a union of the sky-father with the earth-mother. It is natural, therefore, that their child should be proverbially wealthy (*Ταντάλου τάλαντα*, Anacreon in Photius, s.v., is an older equivalent of 'the riches of Croesus') and king of a fertile district. He is the ancestor of the Pelopidae (*see* PELOPS), the line being

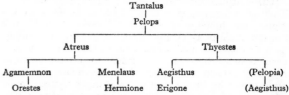

and also father of Niobe (q.v.). His chief legends deal with his crime and its punishment. For one form of the former *see* PELOPS; there are various others, one of the best known being that he stole the food of the gods, to whose society he had been admitted, and gave it to mortals (Pindar, *Ol.* 1. 60 ff.). All agree that in some way he abused the privileges which he had been granted. But he was immortal (Pindar, ibid.), having eaten divine food, and so his penalty must be everlasting, for he could not be killed. In Homer (*Od.* 11. 582 ff.) and in most authors (it became almost proverbial for 'tantalizing' in our sense, see Plato, *Prt.* 315 c) he is hungry and thirsty; he stands in water up to his chin, with fruit-laden trees over his head, but when he tries to drink, the water disappears, and if he reaches for the fruit, the wind blows it away. Pindar (ibid. 57 ff.) says a great stone is hung over his head, always threatening to fall, so that the penalty is everlasting fear. Euripides (*Or.* 4 ff.) follows this version, putting Tantalus in the air, not, as usual, in Tartarus.   H. J. R.

TANUSIUS GEMINUS, historian mentioned in Suet. *Iul.* 9, and for his 'ponderosi' *Annales* in Sen. *Ep.* 93. 11, where 'scis . . . quid uocentur' supports the identification of T. with Catullus' 'Volusius' from Padua (36. 1 and 18–20; 95. 7). He may have written *Annales* in verse before his *historia*.

Peter, *HRRel.* 49 ff.   J. W. D.

TAPROBANE (also **Palaesimundu;** later **Salice** and **Sielediba**), Ceylon. First described by Onesicritus and Megasthenes (*c.* 325–300 B.C.) as an island south of India, it was believed by many to be a large land-mass projecting towards Africa (Strabo 15. 690–1; *Peripl. M. Rubr.* 61). It was rediscovered by accident *c.* A.D. 50 (Plin. *HN* 6. 84 ff.); Ceylonese envoys visited Rome, and Greek traders henceforth frequented the island. Yet Ptolemy (*Geog.* 7. 4. 1 ff.), while giving considerable detail and the correct shape, made it fourteen times too large. Many Roman coins, dating from the third century, have been found in Ceylon, though western trade was now conducted intermediately through the Axumites.

Warmington, *Indian Commerce*, esp. 117 ff.; H. Codrington, *Ceylon Coins* (1924); Still, *Journ. R. Asiatic Soc.*, Ceylon Branch xix.
                                                       E. H. W.

TARAXIPPOS, *see* GLAUCUS (3).

TARCHON, founder of Tarquinia and, according to some authorities, of the Etruscan dodecapolis. T. is the son of Tyrrhenus, the legendary leader of the Etruscans on their migration from Lydia (Strabo 5, p. 219), and an ally of Evander (Verg. *Aen.* 8. 506). He is shown on an Etruscan mirror in Florence, watching the examination of a liver for omens (E. Q. Giglioli, *Arte etrusca*, 1934, pl. 299).   G. M. A. H.

TARENTINI LUDI, *see* SECULAR GAMES.

TARENTUM (*Τάρας*), a leading city of south Italy. Situated on an isthmus between a sheltered bay and a tidal lagoon, it was the first port of call for westward-bound ships from Greece, and it derived wealth from the fisheries and the purple-mussels of the lagoon. Its coast was good orchard country, and its hinterland provided the best sheep-downs in Italy.

Mycenaean and geometric pottery on the site prove unbroken intercourse with Greece from *c.* 1200 B.C. The first permanent Greek settlement was made *c.* 700, when refugees from Sparta, the Partheniae, founded a colony. Although of Spartan origin, Tarentum had a normal constitutional development. Its early aristocracy gave way (*c.* 475) to a long-lived democracy, in which the fishermen played a predominant part. The territorial expansion of Tarentum was long delayed by the resistance of the Messapian tribes; *c.* 475 a Tarentine army suffered a resounding defeat at their hands. But the decline of Croton after 450 gave Tarentum ascendancy among the Greeks of south Italy; in

433–432 it founded a colony at Heraclea (q.v. 1), which became the seat of a league of Italiote Greeks. Under the administration of the philosopher Archytas (q.v.) Tarentum reached the height of its prosperity in the fourth century. Its textile industry was now supplemented by ceramic manufactures of Attic style, and finds of Tarentine coins in the Po valley prove the growth of its trade in the Adriatic. Its wealth was reflected in a magnificent series of gold coins. But after Archytas' death the democracy became engrossed in its festivities, and it relied increasingly on mercenary captains who served it indifferently. King Archidamus II of Sparta was defeated by the Lucanians (338); Alexander I of Epirus overcame the Lucanians, but quarrelled with his employers (334); Cleonymus of Sparta sustained defeat and quarrelled into the bargain (303); finally, Pyrrhus of Epirus abandoned Tarentum to the Romans.

The Tarentines, concerned at the advance of the Romans into south Italy and towards the Adriatic, had pledged them by treaty (334 B.C.?) not to send warships into the Gulf of Otranto. In 282, when Rome assumed protectorate over the city of Thurii and sent a fleet into Tarentine waters, they forced on a war, relying upon assistance from Pyrrhus. The latter, after some early victories over Rome, retired from Italy in 275 and withdrew his garrison in 272. Tarentum obtained a lenient treaty from Rome, and one of its war captives, Livius Andronicus (q.v.), became the founder of Latin literature. In 213 the city fell to Hannibal by treachery; recaptured by Rome in 209, it was thoroughly plundered. This disaster, and the foundation of a Latin colony at the rival port of Brundisium, led to its decay. Attempts by Gaius Gracchus and by Nero to revive it with Italian settlers merely led to its transformation into an Italian town. In 37 B.C. Antony and Octavian renewed the Second Triumvirate at Tarentum. Little is heard of the city thereafter.

Strabo 6. 279–82. E. Ciccotti, *Storia della Magna Grecia* (1927–8), i, ch. 4, ii, ch. 8; A. J. Evans, *The Horsemen of Tarentum* (1889; coinage); P. Wuilleumier, *Tarente, Des Origines à la conquête romaine* (1939).   M. C.

TARPEIAN ROCK. The site of this famous cliff (*rupes*), whence murderers and traitors were thrown, is located by Dionysius (7. 35. 4; 8. 78. 5) as overhanging the Roman forum, while Varro (*Ling.* 5. 41) and others, equating *saxum Tarpeium* with *rupes*, place it close to the temple of Jupiter Capitolinus. Lucan (3. 154) connects it with the temple of Saturn. This leads to the conclusion that the cliff was at the south-west corner of the Capitol.

See H. Jordan, *Topographie der Stadt Rom*, i. 2 (1871), 127–31.
                                                       I. A. R.

TARQUINII was the oldest of Etruscan cities and head of the Confederation of Twelve. Its name is derived from the family of Tarchon (q.v.) which gave two kings to Rome. Situated in the Tuscan Maremma about sixty miles from Rome, the city stood on a high plateau, five miles from its port, Graviscae. The extensive cemeteries, though looted for generations, have yet furnished a valuable local museum. But the glory of Tarquinii is its series of painted tombs, illustrating Etruscan life and religion. Often at war with Rome (e.g. 359–351 and 310–308), Tarquinii lost its independence in the third century B.C.

M. Pallottino, *Tarquinii* (1937).   D. R.-MacI.

TARQUINIUS (1) **PRISCUS** according to tradition was the fifth king of Rome (616–579 B.C.) and the son of Demaratus of Corinth, who is said to have settled at Tarquinii in Etruria. Tarquinius was probably an historical figure, though the stories of his relations with his wife Tanaquil and with Graia Caecilia, of his Greek descent, and of his coming to Rome from Tarquinii are probably late inventions. His Etruscan origins, however, are indirectly proved by the story of Mastarna (q.v.), and confirmed by the Roman belief that Tarquin brought to Rome Etruscan customs, cults, and craftsmen. The foundation of the temple of the Capitoline Triad and other public works are attributed to Tarquin, and undoubtedly this building activity belongs to the period when he is said to have been king. His wars against neighbouring States also are probably historical, but they betray so much similarity with those fought by Tarquinius Superbus as to suggest that Priscus and Superbus are merely duplicate names for the same king.

H. Last, *CAH* vii. 387 ff.; F. Schachermeyr, *PW*, s.v.; A. Blakeway, 'Demaratus', *JRS* 1935, 129 ff.   P. T.

TARQUINIUS (2) SUPERBUS. The historicity of the last king of Rome (traditionally 534–510 B.C.) is probably proved by the treaty between Rome and Gabii ascribed to him, which survived in the temple of Semo Sancus till the time of Augustus—(the forgery of such a document would be unintelligible). But, as the name 'Superbus' would not appear in its text, the treaty proves only that *a* King Tarquinius existed, thereby confirming the suggestion that the two Tarquins are merely a duplication of the same king. The records of the Tarquinian sovereignty were later embellished by tradition in order to justify the surname of *Superbus* and to explain the fall of monarchy, popular legends (e.g. of Lucretia, q.v.) being combined with tales of probable or indisputable Greek origin, such as Tarquinius' conspiracy against Servius Tullius and the decapitation of the tallest poppies at Gabii. For the story of his fall *see* LUCRETIA, BRUTUS (1).

H. Last, *CAH* vii. 393 ff.; F. Schachermeyr, *PW*, s.v.   P. T.

TARQUINIUS (3) COLLATINUS, LUCIUS, was traditionally the husband of Lucretia (q.v.). When her story was connected with the fall of the monarchy, Collatinus was regarded as a founder of the Republic, and one of the first consuls (509 B.C.). The legend of his consulship also served to harmonize the double tradition about the dedication of the temple of the Capitoline Triad, which was associated both with a Tarquin and with the beginning of the Republic: a consul Tarquinius replaced his royal namesake.   P. T.

TARQUITIUS PRISCUS is known to us only from a few scattered references. He is mentioned by Pliny, together with Caecina, as one of his sources for 'Etruscan lore', though it is not certain that Pliny had direct access to his writings. Macrobius (e.g. *Sat.* 3. 7. 3) quotes from a book of his, *Ostentarium*, a translation of an Etruscan work on prognostication, and from his *Prognostication from Trees*. The evidence seems to indicate that he was an important intermediary for the transmission of Etruscan learning to the Romans.   A. L. P.

TARRACO (nowadays *Tarragona*) was an Iberian settlement, perhaps the port of, or settled by, the neighbouring Cissa (cf. Cesse on coins). It was used as headquarters by the Scipios in 218 B.C. The phrase 'opus Scipionum' (Pliny, *HN* 3. 21) applies to the second layer of the town walls, but this may be Iberian. Overshadowed at first by Carthago Nova, Tarraco later became the first city of Roman Spain. Caesar or Augustus, following his wishes, gave it colonial rank (Colonia Victrix Triumphalis Iulia) and it became the capital of Hispania Tarraconensis. An altar to Augustus and a temple to *divus* Augustus indicate its support of the provincial imperial cult. After its sack by the Franks in A.D. 264 Tarraco was refortified, and survived into the Visigothic period. Coins, objects of art, numerous inscriptions, some 200 yards of aqueduct, and the so-called 'Tomb of the Scipios' remain, but only traces of villas, temples, and buildings. Tarraco, situated at the junction of the military highway (Via Augusta) from north to south and the road to Ilerda, was primarily a military and administrative centre, with no extensive economic interests, though its wine was famed for its quality.

S. M. de Navascués, *Tarragona* (1929); A. Fick, in *Arch. Anz.* 1933, on the walls; G. S. Vilaro, *Rivista di Archeologia Cristiana*, 1937, on extensive necropolis.   J. J. van N.

TARSUS. Though Tarsus later claimed Triptolemus, Perseus, or Heracles as its founder, it was probably a native Cilician town. It was the capital of the Cilician kings and of the Persian satraps, but the Greek coins which it issued during the fifth and fourth centuries B.C. show that it was early hellenized and autonomous. It was renamed 'Antioch on the Cydnus' by Seleucus I or Antiochus I and issued municipal coins under this name from Antiochus IV's reign; on its later autonomous coins it used its old name. Annexed by Pompey in 66 it was granted freedom and immunity by Antony; it was the capital of the province of Cilicia from c. A.D. 72. Its constitution was timocratic, a fee of 500 drachmas being charged for admission to citizen rights. This disfranchised the mass of the population, the workers in the linen industry, on which the city's prosperity was based. During the first century B.C. Tarsus was the seat of a celebrated philosophical school.

W. Ruge, *PW* iv A (1932), 2413–39.   A. H. M. J.

TARTESSUS, a region of south Spain, round the middle and lower Baetis (*Guadalquivir*). The name was also given to the river and to a town at its mouth. Probably visited by the Minoans, it was temporarily occupied by the Phoenicians. *C.* 650 B.C. the Samian Colaeus was driven there; c. 600 Phocaeans came, making friends with the Tartessian ruler. The trade of Tartessus with Phoenicians and Carthaginians and (in tin) with Brittany and south-west Britain made it proverbially wealthy. *C.* 500 the town was probably destroyed by the Carthaginians. Geographic writers confused it with Gades. Later poets used Tartessus of all Spain or all west Europe. Tartessus was probably the Biblical Tarshish.

Hdt. 1. 163, 4. 152, 196; Strabo 3. 148–51; Mela 1. 2. 6; Avienus, *Ora Maritima* 224 ff. A. Schulten, *Tartessos* (1922), and in *PW*, s.v.   E. H. W.

TATIUS, TITUS, a Sabine king, who after the Romans had carried off the Sabine women is said to have captured the Capitol; after the women had effected a reconciliation, Tatius and Romulus ruled jointly over the two peoples. Tatius probably was a king of Rome, as there is evidence that he enlarged the city and established several cults. The suggestions that he was the eponymus of the Roman tribe Titienses, or that his connexion with Romulus was invented as a precedent for collegiate magistracy are equally uncertain.   P. T.

TAURISCUS (1), an anomalist grammarian, pupil of Crates (q.v. 3) of Mallos, first used τρόπος (trope) as contrasted with κυριολεξία: cf. Sext. Emp. *Math.* 1. 248 f.

TAURISCUS (2) (1st c. B.C.), sculptor, son of Artemidorus, of Tralles. Works (owned by Asinius Pollio): 1. Hermerotes, probably a pair of herms with bodies and heads of Erotes. 2 (with his brother, Apollonius). Marble group from Rhodes of Zethus, Amphion, Dirce, and the bull, inspired by a painting and by earlier sculpture. The Farnese bull from the baths of Caracalla (Winter, *KB* 357. 1) is a copy with the added figure of Antiope, etc.   T. B. L. W.

TAUROBOLIUM, *see* CYBELE.

TAUROMENIUM (Ταυρομένιον: nowadays *Taormina* with beautiful ancient theatre), was founded in eastern Sicily c. 403 B.C., allegedly by Siculi, on a hill overlooking Naxos (q.v.), which Dionysius had destroyed. Dionysius' mercenaries soon expelled the Siculi; also Naxian refugees settled here (358) (reputedly led by Andromachus, whose role his historian son Timaeus has doubtless exaggerated). Becoming thus a Greek city, Tauromenium quickly prospered. Its successive masters were Timoleon, Agathocles (who exiled Timaeus), Tyndarion, and Hieron of Syracuse. When Hieron died during the Second Punic War, Tauromenium submitted to Rome and became a favoured *civitas foederata*. The Servile War (*c.* 133) and Sextus Pompeius' operations (36) damaged it severely; but becoming an Augustan *colonia* it flourished under the Empire.

Diod. bks. 14–16; Strabo p. 268 (confused); Cic. *Verr.* 2. 160; 3. 13; 5. 49; App. *Sic.* 5; *BCiv.* 5. 103, 105, 109, 116. J. Bérard, *Bibliogr. topogr.* (1941), 111. E. T. S.

TAURUS MONS, properly the mostly well-wooded heights (average 7,000 feet) beginning in south-west Asia Minor, and continuing along the Lycian coast and through Pisidia and Isauria to the borders of Cilicia and Lycaonia. It then divides into: (i) Antitaurus, apparently the heights going north-east through Cappadocia (Mons Argaeus) and Armenia (Mons Capotes) towards the Caucasus; (ii) Abus or Macis (Massis), through Armenia towards the Caspian, keeping the name Taurus and sending southwards Mons Amanus (q.v.) and (beyond the Euphrates) Mons Masius. There were subsidiary ranges south of the Euphrates, and Mt. Zagrus separating Media from Assyria and Babylonia. The name Taurus was extended to include not only the heights of north Iran, but also the Paropamisus (*Hindu Kush*) and Emodus or Imaus (*Himalayas*); and was continued by hearsay to the Eastern Ocean at 'Tamus Headland'. The whole range was regarded as the backbone of Asia, and along it Dicaearchus (*c.* 300 B.C.) fixed for geographers a parallel or median in cartography, dividing the land mass into the cool and warm regions. E. H. W.

TAXES, see FINANCE, GREEK, *and* FINANCE, ROMAN.

TAXILES, i.e. 'king Taxila', his personal name being Omphis (Āmbhi), king of the country between the Indus and the Jhelum with his capital at Taxila. From fear of his neighbour Porus he welcomed Alexander; Taxila became Alexander's advanced base, and Taxiles fought for him against Porus. At first Taxiles was subjected to the Macedonian satrap Philippus; after Philippus' murder he ruled nominally as Alexander's governor but soon in complete independence. By 312 B.C. at latest the Taxila kingdom had become part of Chandragupta's empire. W. W. T.

TE DEUM LAUDAMUS, see NICETA OF REMESIANA.

TECHNOPAIGNIA, poems intended to show the author's skill, especially by the shape which they make on the page. This art was popular at the beginning of the third century B.C., which produced Simmias' *Axe*, *Wings*, and *Egg*, Theocritus' *Pipe*, and Dosiadas' *Altar*. C. M. B.

TEGEA lay in the south-east Arcadian plain, across the roads from Sparta to the Argolid and the Isthmus. In this exposed position it developed politically before the other Arcadian towns. *C.* 550 B.C. Sparta came to terms with Tegea after a long war; and for two centuries it followed the Spartan lead, though at times unwillingly, for the Tegeans were tough fighters (cf. Hdt. 9. 26). It was a favourite place of residence for Spartan and other exiles (Leotychidas; Micythus of Rhegium; King Pausanias). *C.* 471 Tegea revolted and joined Argos, but submitted after a defeat (*Anth. Pal.* 7. 512; Hdt. 9. 35). Later, out of hostility to Mantinea (q.v.), Tegea was pro-Spartan. She looked unfavourably on the foundation of Megalopolis.

The temple of Athena Alea, burnt down in 395, was rebuilt with great magnificence, with Scopas as architect and sculptor (Paus. 8. 45. 5).

Ancient authorities: *IG* v. 2, 1 ff. V. Bérard, 'Tegée et la Tegéatide', *BCH* 1892, 529 ff.; 1893, 1 ff.; Hiller von Gaertringen, *PW*, s.v. 'Tegea'; C. Dugas and others, *Sanctuaire d'Aléa Athéna à Tegée* (1924); *BCH* 1921, 335 ff. (older temple). T. J. D.

TEIRESIAS, see TIRESIAS.

TELAMON, in mythology, brother of Peleus (q.v.). On his banishment he settled in Salamis, and as a reward for helping Heracles against Troy received Hesione (q.v.) as his slave-concubine. He was a stern father to her son Teucer (q.v.), and on the latter returning from Troy without Aias (q.v.), Telamon banished him (Eur. *Helena*, 91 ff.). For his hero-cult see, e.g., Herodotus 8. 64. 2. H. J. R.

TELCHINES (Τελχῖνες), semi-divine beings living in Rhodes and skilled in all manner of metal-work, therefore also in magic and consequently dangerous, mischievous, and having the Evil Eye. Our accounts of them are late and contradictory, but agree more or less in the above points, and also that they were finally destroyed by one of the greater gods, Zeus, Poseidon, or Apollo, or at least driven from Rhodes. They have a certain resemblance to the dwarfs or gnomes of northern European mythology.

See especially Strabo 14. 2. 7, pp. 653–4; Eustathius ad *Iliad*. p. 771. 55 ff. (from Strabo and Suetonius); Suidas, s.v.; more in Friedländer in Roscher, s.v., with literature; Herter in *PW*, s.v. See also MAGIC, 4. H. J. R.

TELECLIDES (*fl. c.* 450–420 B.C.), writer of Athenian comedy, won eight victories. His Ἀμφικτύονες depicts the Golden Age, the Πρυτάνεις the peace and luxury of the period succeeding the Persian Wars. He attacked Pericles (frs. 42–4).

FCG ii. 361 ff.; *CAF* i. 209 ff.; Demiańczuk, *Suppl. Com.* 86. M. P.

TELEGONIA, see EPIC CYCLE.

TELEMACHUS (Τηλέμαχος), son of Odysseus and Penelope (qq.v.). He is prominent in the *Odyssey*, where his character develops throughout those parts of the poem in which he appears. At first he is an untried youth, a good and dutiful son but timid and unenterprising. At the behest of Athena he bids his mother's suitors depart, and when they will not, still with her help he takes ship, goes to the mainland, and then inquires after his father, first from Nestor and then from Menelaus (*Od.* 1–4). Athena warns him to return home and sail by a different route, since the one by which he came is beset by the suitors, who plan to kill him. He does so, and on the way takes the fugitive prophet Theoclymenus aboard. He shows from now on more energy and resource, even before meeting his father (*Od.* 15–16. 153); and, having met him, acts as an intelligent and even enterprising helper, astonishing his mother by taking command of the house (21. 343 ff.) and fighting valiantly against the suitors (22. 91 ff.).

Outside Homer he appears in a few episodes. Palamedes, to detect Odysseus' feigned madness, put Telemachus, then a baby, in the road of his father's plough (Hyginus, *Fab.* 95. 2). After his father's death he married Circe (q.v.), *Telegonia* (in Proclus). H. J. R.

TELEMUS (Τήλεμος), in mythology, a prophet who foretold to Polyphemus the Cyclops that Odysseus (q.v.) should one day blind him; *Od.* 9. 507 ff.

TELEPHUS (1) (Τήλεφος), in mythology, son of Heracles (q.v.) and Auge, daughter of King Aleos, the eponym of Alea in Arcadia. She bore him in a shrine of Athena; a pestilence ensued, and Aleos when he discovered the matter had the child exposed and gave Auge to be sold overseas. She came into the possession of Teuthras, king and eponym of Teuthrania in Mysia, who married her; the child was suckled by a hind and picked up by shepherds, who called him Telephus (as if from θηλᾶν, to suckle, and ἔλαφος, a deer or hind; Apollod. 2. 146). In the version preserved by Hyginus (*Fab.* 99. 3) Auge was adopted by Teuthras, who was childless. For some reason (accounts vary in different authors) Telephus when he grew up went to Mysia; here, according to Hyginus' story (very doubtfully traced to Sophocles), Auge was given him in marriage, and they discovered their relationship at the last moment. At all events he became king of Mysia, and here joins with the Epic tradition (post-Homeric), the first part of his story being apparently Tragic. In the *Cypria* the Greeks on their way to Troy mistook Teuthrania for it; Telephus resisted them and was wounded by Achilles. The wound would not heal, and he (at least according to Euripides, *Telephus*) made his way to the Greek camp at Aulis and in accordance with an oracle asked Achilles to cure him; this was done by applying the rust of the spear, for the oracle had said that the wounder should be the healer. He then guided the Greeks to Troy. See further Schmidt in Roscher, s.v.   H. J. R.

TELEPHUS (2) of Pergamum (2nd c. A.D.), a Stoic grammarian, teacher of Verus, wrote on Homer, on the history of literature and of scholarship, on bibliography and antiquities, and on *Attic Syntax* (5 books); he compiled an alphabetical lexicon of things in common use, and an Ὠκυτόκιον (in 10 books) of adjectives for the aid of writers and orators. His works are lost.   P. B. R. F.

TELES (*Τέλης*) (*fl. c.* 235 B.C.), Cynic philosopher, probably of Megara, is the oldest of the many authors of Cynic or Stoic διατριβαί (short ethical discussions), frs. of whose works have been preserved (in his case, in the pages of Stobaeus). His διατριβαί have no claim to philosophical distinction; they simply commend the Cynic way of life in popular language; but he is interesting because of his references to earlier writers like Bion of Borysthenes, Stilpon, and Crates the Cynic.

Ed. O. Hense² (1909). *PW* v A. 375.   W. D. R.

TELESILLA (*Τελέσιλλα*), Argive poetess of the fifth century B.C., famous for arming the women of Argos after its defeat by Cleomenes (Hdt. 6. 76 ff., Polyaen. 8. 33). Nine fragments of her work survive, and seem to come from Hymns, especially to Apollo and Artemis, with whom six are concerned. The Telesilleion (see METRE, GREEK, III (9)) or acephalous glyconic is called after her. She seems to have written mainly for women (Paus. 2. 20. 8). An Epidaurian Hymn to the Mother of the Gods ascribed to her seems to be a later imitation.

FRAGMENTS: E. Diehl, *Anth. Lyr. Graec.* ii. 61; J. M. Edmonds, *Lyra Graeca* ii. 236–45.
CRITICISM: U. von Wilamowitz-Moellendorff, *Textg. d. gr. Lyr.* (1900), 76; P. Maas, *Epidaurische Hymnen* (1933), 134–41.
                                                     C. M. B.

TELESILLEION, see METRE, GREEK, III (9).

TELESINUS, see PONTIUS.

TELESPHORUS (*Τελεσφόρος*), a child-god associated with Asclepius (q.v.). He is commonly shown in art, but seldom mentioned in literature; his name occurs on several inscriptions in his honour, however.

See Schmidt in Roscher, s.v.; Schwen in *PW*, s.v.   H. J. R.

TELESTES, dithyrambic poet of Selinus (Ath. 616 f, Diod. Sic. 46. 6), won victory at Athens 402/1 B.C. (*Marm. Par.* 79). Titles of his Dithyrambs are *Argo*, *Asclepius*, and *Hymenaeus*, of which in all four fragments survive. The comedian Theopompus referred to him (Ath. 501 f).

In style and music he resembled Timotheus and Philoxenus (Dion. Hal. *Comp.* 132). Alexander read him (Plut. *Alex.* 8), and the tyrant Aristratus of Sicyon put up a statue to him (Plin. *HN* 35. 109).

E. Diehl. *Anth. Lyr. Graec.* ii. 153.   C. M. B.

TELETE (*τελετή*). Being related to τελεῖν as, for instance, ταφή to θάπτειν, this word properly means no more than 'accomplishment', 'performance', which suits its very rare non-sacral use (perhaps only *Batrachom.* 303, where it is equivalent to the usual Epic τέλος). But from a comparatively early date it was specialized (it does not occur in any sense earlier than Pindar) to mean the accomplishment of a religious or quasi-religious ceremony. So Pindar, *Ol.* 10. 52, uses it of the first celebration of the Olympic Games by Heracles; *Pyth.* 9. 97 and *Nem.* 10. 34, of Athenian festivals including athletic contests; *Ol.* 3. 40, of the celebration of *theoxenia* (q.v.). Only in the last case is the rite purely religious. In Euripides (Aeschylus and Sophocles use only τέλος) it repeatedly means a rite, and perhaps especially one somewhat out of the ordinary, as those of Dionysus, *Bacch.* 22, or any orgiastic ceremonies, ibid. 73. Aristophanes uses it for rites of any kind, as *Pax* 418–20. But there seems to have been a growing tendency about this time to use it especially of mystic ceremonials; thus, Herodotus employs it in speaking of those of Demeter and Dionysus, Andocides (1. 111) of the Eleusinian Mysteries, while it is a favourite word of Plato to signify an initiation. After Alexander this tendency is accentuated, the word very frequently meaning a rite supposed to contain some hidden philosophic or gnostic meaning. It also can signify a magical or supernatural action or even force. This finally develops, especially in Philon of Alexandria, into the sense of 'inner meaning', even 'allegorical interpretation'.

C. Zijderveld, *Τελετή; Bijdragen tot de kennis der religieuse terminologie in het Grieksch* (1934).   H. J. R.

TELLUS, the Roman earth-goddess, probably very old, though her temple dates only from 268 B.C. (Platner-Ashby, p. 511). For the question of Greek influence on her ritual see F. Altheim, *Terra Mater* (1931); St. Weinstock in *PW*, s.v. 'Terra Mater'. She is associated in cult with Tellumo (Varro in August. *De civ. D.* 7. 23); with Altor ('Feeder') and Rusor ('Ploughman'?), ibid.; perhaps with the doubtful Tellurus (Mart. Capella i. 49). No festival is named after her and she has no flameu; but she is the deity concerned in the *feriae sementivae* (Ovid, *Fasti* 1. 657 ff., whereon see Frazer); the Fordicidia of 15 April (ibid. 4. 629 ff., whereon see Frazer; the offering, a cow in calf, is typical for powers of fertility); and the sacrifice of the *porca praecidanea* (Varro in Nonius, p. 163 M., Gellius 4. 6. 8, who adds Ceres), a sin-offering for neglect of rites, especially those of the dead.

See further Weinstock, loc. cit.   H. J. R.

TEMENOS (*τέμενος*), in Homeric usage, signifies either a king's or a god's domain, an area marked off and assigned to his use. In later times it is nearly always used of a god's domain.

In the narrower sense it is the sanctuary (ἱερόν) or precinct (περίβολος), the consecrated and enclosed area surrounding the god's altar, which was the centre of worship and the only indispensable cult structure. It usually included a temple also, whose primary purpose was to house the image and votive offerings. Larger precincts, like Apollo's at Delphi, or the Altis at Olympia, also enclosed the treasuries built to house the offerings of a single city, sacred groves, statues, theatres, and the temples of associated deities. The rules governing the sanctity of precincts varied from cult to cult; entrance was sometimes forbidden except to certain persons at certain times. In most cults whoever entered the precinct had to be purified first. The Roman *fanum* or *templum* (in the original sense) corresponds to *temenos* in this narrower meaning.

In the broader sense the *temenos* is all the land that belongs to a god's cult. Some cults owned large areas of forest, pasture, cultivable land, and even factories and fisheries, from which they received revenues. Though sometimes cultivation of the god's domain was forbidden, it was usually worked either by the god's slaves or by contractors.

Ancient Sources: see *SIG* 977–94, and many of the inscriptions in Prott-Ziehen, *Leges Graecorum sacrae e titulis collectae* (1896–1906) for cult-laws relating to this subject. Modern Literature: P. Stengel, *Griechische Kultusaltertümer* (1920), 17–21; A. Fairbanks, *Handbook of Greek religion* (1910), 65–74. For Roman religion see G. Wissowa, *RK* 467–79.　　　　　　　　　　　　　J. E. F.

TEMENUS (*Τήμενος*), (1) king of Stymphalus, founder of the cult of Hera as Maid, Wife, and Widow, *see* HERA, ARCADIA; Paus. 8. 22. 2. (2) Son of Phegeus king of Psophis; he and his brother Axion murdered Alcmaeon (q.v.), Paus. 8. 24. 10. (3) One of the Heraclidae (q.v.; exact genealogy uncertain). After taking a prominent part in the Return of the Heraclidae, he got Argos for his portion of the conquered land. He had a daughter Hyrnetho, and favoured her husband Deïphontes (q.v.) above his own sons, who therefore murdered their father. The people then decided that Deïphontes and Hyrnetho should be king and queen (see Apollod. 2. 172 ff.). One of Temenus' sons (Perdiccas, according to Hdt. 8. 137; Archelaus, Hyginus, *Fab.* 219; the latter account is somehow connected with Euripides, *Archelaus*) founded the royal house of Macedonia.

See further O. Waser in Roscher's *Lex.*, art. 'Temenos'. H. J. R.

TEMPE, a narrow valley, nearly five miles in length, in northern Thessaly, through which the Peneus flows between the massifs of Olympus and Ossa. The gorge, which was caused by erosion and not, as Greek tradition maintained, by an earthquake, was strategically important, since the principal route to Macedonia could here be closed by a very small force. In 480 B.C. the Greeks sent troops to hold Tempe against Xerxes, but they evacuated it owing to distrust of the Thessalians. Tempe was the scene of operations in 336, when Alexander overcame Thessalian opposition, and in the Third Macedonian War.　　　　　　　　　　　　　H. D. W.

TEMPLE. Greek temples, except circular ones (usually dedicated to Asclepius), were primarily of uniform type, a rectangular chamber (*naos*, cella) containing the image of the deity, with doorway at east end and porch (*pronaos*) produced by thrusting forward the side walls of the cella; there was sometimes a rear porch (*opisthodomos*, *posticum*) in addition. This type of building, considerably elongated, and having a surrounding verandah of columns (*peripteros*, *pteron*, peristyle) has been traced back to *c.* the tenth century B.C. By second quarter of sixth century (Heraeum at Olympia even earlier) it became established, and in that century one Doric and two Ionic temples attained an area of over 60,000 sq. ft. Most small temples were non-peripteral, the cella being exposed, with a porch at one end or both. Usual varieties of porch arrangement are (*a*) 'Distyle-in-antis' (2 columns between ends—*antae*—of side walls); (*b*) 'Prostyle-tetrastyle' (4 columns standing clear of *antae*); (*c*) 'Prostyle-hexastyle' (6 columns do. do.). The great majority of peripteral temples were hexastyle, with 6 columns at each end and 12 to 14 on flanks.

As roof support was the chief structural problem, the larger temples had a single or (usually) double row of columns in the cella, but some of the largest temples may have been 'hypaethral', i.e. with an unroofed (or partially unroofed) cella. The larger Ionic temples of Asia Minor were usually 'dipteral', with a double row

of columns in the peristyle; 'pseudo-dipteral' temples (e.g. Artemis, Magnesia) having a similar position for the outer row of columns and the inner row omitted. At Ephesus, Samos, Sardes, and Didyma the entrance end was further emphasized by increasing the depth of the porch and providing an avenue of columns. The peripteral plan greatly increased the size of the form common to all temples and unified the noble simplicity of the main idea—an unbroken rectangle having a simple low-pitched roof and a gable (pediment) at each end, the whole governed by the strong horizontal lines of stylobate and entablature (*see* ARCHITECTURE). No original example of a normal Greek Ionic temple exists; there are several fairly complete Doric ones, but the marble roof slabs, the decorations (*acroteria*) above the pediments, the doors or grilles which closed the entrance, and the colouring of the entire structure—chiefly concentrated on the frieze, the cresting (*sima*) of the cornice, and the ceilings—must be imagined. The Temple of Poseidon, Paestum, and the Theseum, Athens, give the best complete impression. Buildings which contained such masterpieces as the Athena Parthenos and the Zeus at Olympia must have been magnificent inside: the flat ceilings of marble or wood panels probably admitted light, borrowed from special roof slabs in prepared positions.

Roman temples closely resembled Greek ones in external form and treatment, but the Corinthian Order, with steeper pediments and richly carved friezes, was generally used. The temple floor was on a raised platform enclosed by a wall-base (plinth) and this was thrust forward beyond the porch—which was given great importance—to enclose the entrance stepway; ideas probably borrowed from non-peripteral Etruscan temples in Italy, and Roman temples were often non-peripteral, or pseudo-peripteral (i.e. with engaged columns on the flanks). Internally, the architectural treatment sometimes given to the west end of the cella (e.g. in the Temple of Bacchus, Baalbek) is significant in its resemblance to the sanctuary element of the Christian church.

See also ARCHITECTURE.

D. S. Robertson, op. cit. under ARCHITECTURE; A Marquand, *Greek Architecture* (1909); L. V. Solon, *Polychromy* (U.S.A. 1924). T. F.

TEMPLE OFFICIALS. A priest (q.v.) presided over every temple and sanctuary in the Greek and Italian States. No other official was needed in the numerous small cults. But at the larger shrines the priest received the assistance of minor officials.

In the administration of the cult and the performance of ritual he was assisted by *hieropoioi* (ἱεροποιοί), who likewise received, as their due, portions of the sacrifices and other honours and perquisites. In Athens two boards of *hieropoioi* of ten each were chosen by lot: one (οἱ ἐπί τὰ ἐκθύματα) to perform all sacrifices appointed by oracle, the other (οἱ κατ' ἐνιαυτόν) to administer the four-yearly festivals except the Panathenaea (Arist. *Ath. Pol.* 54). Directly charged with the offering of sacrifices were θύται, among whom a higher rank was sometimes distinguished, the ἱεροθύται or ἀρχιεροθύται. The larger and more important the cult, the more attendants were necessary at the sacrifices. We find mention of sacred heralds (ἱεροκήρυκες), libation-pourers (οἰνοχόοι), overseers (ἐπιμεληταί).

In the care and management of the temple and precinct the priest was assisted by ναοφύλακες, νεωποιοί, or νεωκόροι. They guarded the sanctuary, kept it clean, and purified entrants.

In the administration of cult-finances, sacred treasures, votive offerings, and the revenue-producing parts of the god's domain, the priest was assisted by treasurers or stewards (ἱεροταμίαι). In some cities, as Miletus, a board of ἱεροταμίαι was appointed that looked after the properties of all State-cults.

Since there was no fixed hierarchy in Greek religion, and each State, even each cult, was a law to itself, the evidence shows great variety of practice and much overlapping of the functions of the three principal types of subordinate cult-official. There were also such minor functionaries as cantors (ἀοιδοί), musicians, and agonothetai, who supervised the sacred games. *See also* AEDITUUS.

ANCIENT SOURCES: for inscriptions concerning Greek temple officials see *SIG*³ 1002-54; C. Michel, *Recueil d'Inscriptions grecques* (1897-1927), 669-735, 810-39, 857-78; many inscriptions in von Prott-Ziehen, *Leges Graecorum sacrae e titulis collectae* (1896-1906).

MODERN LITERATURE: A. Fairbanks, *Handbook of Greek religion* (1910), 76-83; P. Stengel, *Griechische Kultusaltertümer*³ (1920), 31-54. J. E. F.

TEMPLUM, see AUGURES, DIVINATION, TEMENOS.

TENES (*Τένης*), the eponym of Tenedos, for whose story, probably not very early, see Plutarch, *Quaest. Graec.* 28 (*Mor.* 350 d-f), with Halliday there and in *CQ* 21 (1927), 37 ff. He was son of Apollo, but nominally of Cycnus king of Coloni; his step-mother accused him as Potiphar's wife did Joseph, and Cycnus set him and his sister Hemithea adrift in a chest which landed at Tenedos. Later, Cycnus discovered the truth and tried to be reconciled, but Tenes with an axe cut the moorings of his boat when Cycnus visited Tenedos, hence the proverb 'Tenedian axe' for a rash deed. Tenes was finally killed by Achilles in defending Hemithea; hence at his heroshrine Achilles may not be named nor a flute-player enter, because a flute-player bore false witness against him to Cycnus. H. J. R.

TEPIDARIUM, see BATHS.

TEREBRA, see SIEGECRAFT, ROMAN.

TERENCE (PUBLIUS TERENTIUS AFER, ? 195-159 B.C.), is said by Suetonius to have been born in Carthage of Libyan stock, and to have come to Rome as a slave in the household of the senator Terentius Lucanus, who gave the handsome, gifted boy a good education, and set him free; his talents obtained for him entry into a circle of noble Romans interested in literature. Encouraged by them, he entered, somewhat as an outsider, on his dramatic career, which we may perhaps reconstruct as follows. In 166 he produced his first play, the *Andria* (which, according to one story, he had previously read to Caecilius). This play was based on the *Andria* of Menander, but differed from it in certain respects (see below); the elderly dramatist Luscius Lanuvinus and his friends seized on these differences as a means of discrediting a possible rival; Terence consequently found himself compelled, contrary to his intention, to write a prologue, not to explain the plot (a procedure which he detested) but to reply to the charge of 'contamination' and ask for a fair hearing. Apparently he tried to produce the *Hecyra* in 165 without a prologue, but failed because of a rumour of more interesting sideshows such as rope-dancing. In 163 came the *Heautontimorumenos*, the prologue to which was spoken (contrary to custom) by the chief actor, Ambivius Turpio, who managed by his prestige to secure a hearing for the play. In 161, at the Ludi Megalenses, came the *Eunuchus*, the success of which probably led to the production of the *Phormio* at the Ludi Romani of the same year. In 160, at the funeral games of Aemilius Paulus, Terence produced the *Adelphi*, but again failed with the *Hecyra*; this play was finally produced at the Ludi Romani of the same year, the prologue being delivered by Ambivius. In 159 Terence is said to have visited Greece, a journey from which he never returned. He left some property as a dowry to his daughter, who married a senator: such biographical

details, however, were a subject of controversy even in ancient times.

2. The *didascaliae* inform us that all Terence's plays were produced by Ambivius Turpio, and that the music was composed by Flaccus, slave of Claudius. Our other information is mainly derived from the commentary of Donatus.

3. In his prologues Terence replies to the charges that he 'contaminated' or 'spoilt' his originals, stole characters and scenes from plays already translated, derived help from his noble friends, and lacked ability; he asserts that earlier dramatists also took liberties with their originals—the liberty to which he himself confesses being his practice of combining parts of different plays—and that he is innocent of intentional plagiarism from *Latin* dramatists. Politeness forbade him to do more than evade the charge of receiving help from his friends; for the rest, he taunts Lanuvinus with being 'a good translator but a bad writer'. Donatus' commentary leads us to suspect that many of the alterations introduced by Terence were due to his own invention, his motives being to introduce effective dialogues and interesting contrasts in character.

4. A brief summary of two of the plays will serve to illustrate some of Terence's departures from his Greek originals.

(1) *Andria* ('The Girl from Andros'). Simo has forced his son Pamphilus to become engaged to the daughter of Chremes; Chremes, learning that Pamphilus is in love with the supposed orphan Glycerium, wishes to break off the engagement; Simo pretends to Pamphilus that it still holds; Pamphilus, on the advice of his slave Davus, tries to out-manœuvre Simo by feigning submission, but finds himself cornered when Simo persuades Chremes to withdraw his refusal. Glycerium bears a child; Davus lets Chremes see it; Chremes definitely refuses to let his daughter marry Pamphilus. Finally it transpires that Glycerium is also the child of Chremes; she can now marry Pamphilus, while Chremes' other daughter is given to her faithful lover Charinus.

Sources (according to the prologue): Menander's Ἀνδρία and Περινθία. Terence, according to Donatus, changed the opening monologue of the Ἀνδρία into a dialogue by introducing the slave Sosia, who appears only in this scene (πρόσωπον προτατικόν); he also added the second lover, Charinus, with his slave—apparently out of free invention ('non sunt apud Menandrum')—in order, we may presume, to provide foils to Pamphilus and Davus. Donatus fails to indicate convincingly Terence's debt to the Περινθία.

(2) *Adelphi* ('The Brothers'). Demea has two sons; the younger, Ctesipho, he brings up strictly; the elder, Aeschinus, he entrusts to his easy-going brother Micio. Both boys go astray; Aeschinus, reckless if generous, seduces Pamphila and, on his timid brother's behalf, kidnaps a music-girl, to Pamphila's alarm. After a tardy confession to Micio he is allowed to marry Pamphila; meanwhile Demea, disappointed with the results of his own methods, decides to court popularity by a show of affability, and thus turns the tables on Micio. Original by Menander; the kidnapping scene borrowed from Diphilus' Συναποθνήσκοντες. Most modern and perhaps finest of Terence's plays.

5. Apart from the *Adelphi*, the only clear example of borrowing from a second original is the addition to the Menandrian framework of the *Eunuchus* (his liveliest and most popular play) of two characters, Thraso and the parasite, from Menander's Κόλαξ. On the other hand, Donatus points out several instances of alteration made by Terence which owed nothing to any Greek original. It seems possible that this was the real charge against Terence, and that he tried to evade it by concentrating on the minor point of his occasional borrowings from secondary Greek originals.

6. Of his other plays it is useful to indicate the primary Greek original. *Hecyra* ('The Mother-in-law') had for its source Apollodorus' *Ἑκυρά*, and is an excellent example of the *comédie larmoyante*, with no unlikeable characters. *Heautontimorumenos* ('The Self-tormentor') was derived from Menander: its opening scene is famous and its intrigue complicated. *Phormio* was based on Apollodorus' *Ἐπιδικαζόμενος*, and its lively intrigue was imitated by Molière in *Les Fourberies de Scapin*.

7. Julius Caesar praised Terence as a polished dramatist, who lacked only *vis comica*. His polish is apparent not only in his unequalled style but also in the urbane and humanitarian tone of his plays. He gives us kindly masters, faithful slaves, affectionate parents and children, even generous courtesans; behaviour may be lax, but is seldom brutal. Lacking Plautus' metrical gift and power to excite laughter, he was nevertheless an original dramatic artist, deeply interested in the complexities of life and the contrasts of character.

Text: R. Kauer and W. M. Lindsay (O.C.T. 1926). Text and commentary: S. G. Ashmore (1908). See also Ph. Fabia, *Les Prologues de Térence* (1888); G. Norwood, *The Art of T.* (1923). Dziatzko's commentaries on Phormio⁴ and Adelphi² are standard.
W. B.

TERENTIA was Cicero's wife. Her family was wealthy. Since her half-sister, Fabia, a Vestal, was suspected of intercourse with Catiline, the encouragement Cicero had from Terentia in acting against him might have family motives. She was often, especially in the trial of Clodius, suspected of influencing her husband. Firm and careful, she sustained him in exile and always helped him in his financial difficulties. After his return a growing coldness between them resulted in divorce (46 B.C.). Cicero immediately married Publilia, and it is uncertain whether Terentia ever got back her property. It is related that she afterwards married Sallust the historian, and then Messalla Corvinus, and that she died aged 103. Cicero had by her a daughter, Tullia, and a son, Marcus.

L. Neubauer, *Wiener Studien* 1910, p. 271; St. Weinstock, *PW* v A. 710.
A. M.

TERENTIANUS MAURUS (late 2nd c. A.D.), grammarian and metrist. His *De litteris syllabis et metris Horatii* (ed. Keil, *Gramm. Lat.* vi. 325–413) is written entirely in verse (2,981 lines).

See also SCHOLARSHIP, LATIN, and cf. Teuffel, § 373 a; Schanz–Hosius, § 514.
J. F. M.

TERENTIUS (1) **AFER**, PUBLIUS, *see* TERENCE.

TERENTIUS (2) **SCAURUS**, QUINTUS (early 2nd c. A.D.), grammarian. His *Ars grammatica* and his commentary (in at least ten books) on Horace are lost. The *Liber de orthographia* (ed. Keil, *Gramm. Lat.* vii. 11–33) attributed to him is probably genuine.

Cf. Teuffel, § 352. 2; Schanz–Hosius, §§ 594–5.
J. F. M.

TERENTIUS, *see also* CULLEO, VARRO.

TERMINUS, a boundary-mark; in Roman religion, especially the *numen* of such marks, which were set up with ceremony, sacrifice being made and blood and other offerings, with the ashes of the fire, put into the hole which was to contain the *terminus* (Siculus Flaccus in *Gromat. Lat.* 141. 4 ff. Lachmann). This filling of the mark with power was reinforced by a yearly sacrifice and feast (Ovid, *Fasti* 2. 638 ff.) by the neighbours, on 23 Feb. (Terminalia). It is therefore not remarkable that there was a god Terminus, a kind of concentration of the *numen* of all the boundary-marks. Traditionally, the Terminus on the Capitol had been there before the temple of Jupiter Optimus Maximus was built, and refused to move; he therefore was left inside the temple, with an opening in the roof above, as he must be under the open sky (Ovid, ibid. 669 ff.).

See Wissowa, *RK* 136 ff.; Frazer on Ovid, loc. cit. H. J. R.

TERPANDER (*Τέρπανδρος*) (*fl.* 647 B.C. Hieron.–Eus., 645 B.C. *Marm. Par.* 34), musician and poet, of Antissa in Lesbos (Timoth. *Pers.* 240), but worked in Sparta (Ath. 635 d) in the middle of the seventh century. He is said to have written: (1) Nomes, in which he set his own or Homer's lines to lyre-music (Plut. *De mus.* 3); (2) *Προοίμια* or Preludes, which may have been of the same *genre* as the Homeric Hymns (ibid.); (3) scolia (ibid. 28). It is doubtful whether any of the fragments ascribed to him are genuine. Fr. 1 is a libation-song, but indicates a later date in its use of pure spondees, its theology, and its play on the word *ἀρχά*. Fr. 4 seems to be an adaptation of Pind. *Ol.* 13. 22–3. Fr. 2 and fr. 3 have been less disputed. But it may be doubted whether his works were known at Alexandria. *See also* MUSIC, § 10.

Diehl, *Anth. Lyr. Graec.* ii. 3–5; Wilamowitz, *Timotheos* (1903), 92–3.
C. M. B.

TERRACOTTAS. Sculpture on a large scale in terracotta was rare in Greece, except in primitive times. In Etruria terracotta long remained the favourite material for temple sculpture, often on a colossal scale. Cyprus has also yielded many large votive terracotta statues.

2. Clay figurines (*κοραί*, *sigillaria*) are found from the earliest periods; Minoan examples of the second millennium B.C. already show elaborate detail of costume. In Greece they become common from the seventh century. They served as votive offerings, as funeral furniture, as toys, and, later, as house-ornaments. Figurines of the archaic period are hieratic in character, types of seated or standing goddesses being most popular. From the fourth century the art is secular in feeling, as exemplified in the figurines of women in everyday garb from Tanagra, Myrina in Aeolis, etc. Production fell off after A.D. 100.

3. Relief work other than architectural is rare and mainly confined to votive tablets. The series of 'Melian reliefs' with mythological scenes belongs to the early fifth century.

4. For sepulchral purposes chests (*λάρνακες*) and jars (*πίθοι*) were used in Bronze-Age Crete. Large painted sarcophagi are found in Clazomenae and Rhodes at the end of the sixth century. Sarcophagi with reclining figures modelled on the lids were used in Etruria during late archaic and Hellenistic times, and small reproductions of these were used for urns in cremations.

5. In architecture sun-dried bricks (*πλίνθοι ὠμαί*, *lateres crudi*), the universal primitive building-material, were largely replaced in the Hellenistic period by baked bricks (*πλίνθοι ὀπταί κέραμοι*, *lateres cocti*, *testae*). As a result of the abundance of stone, brick construction was rarer in Greece than in Rome, where it remained the principal material of Republican and Imperial buildings. The gable-roofs of early Greek temples were generally composed of flat terracotta tiles (*στεγαστῆρες*, *σωλῆνες*, *tegulae*), rounded covering-tiles (*καλυπτῆρες*, *imbrices*), finial ornaments (*ἀκρωτήρια*, *antefixae*), and gutters with lion-head spouts (*κεραμίδες λεοντοκέφαλοι*, *leontochasmata*); and wooden framing was frequently covered with terracotta slabs, painted or moulded. In Greece, after the archaic period, these features were usually translated into stone, but in Italy the use of terracotta long persisted. Moulded terracotta slabs were employed in Imperial times to decorate Roman house interiors.

R. Kekulé, *Die Antiken Terrakotten* (4 vols., 1880–93); G. M. A. Richter, *Etruscan Terracotta Warriors in the Metropolitan Museum of Art* (U.S.A. 1937); D. Burr, *Terracottas from Myrina in Boston* (Vienna, 1934); P. Jacobsthal, *Die Melischen Reliefs* (1931); D. S. Robertson, *Handbook of Greek and Roman Architecture* (1929), 349.
F. N. P.

TERRA SIGILLATA, pottery made in moulds; by modern archaeologists the term is restricted to the fine red-glazed table-ware in general use over the Roman Empire, and formerly known as Samian Ware (q.v.). In this sense it includes not only the decorated vases produced from moulds, but also the plain wheel-made varieties. *Terra sigillata* imitates metal-ware in its embossed decoration and in its forms, which are standardized, some shapes being regularly decorated, others invariably plain; they are of moderate size, mainly handleless drinking-bowls and plates. The origin of the ware is to be sought in the Eastern Mediterranean, where moulded relief-ware was popular from the late fourth century (*see* POTTERY), and experiments in red glaze began in the third century. Precise information, such as has been obtained in the West from study of the actual pottery sites, is not yet available for the East, and the place and date of the appearance of the bright sigillata glaze are still unknown; some excavators' reports set the date as high as 150 B.C. In any case the Eastern *sigillata* never equalled the Western in artistic and technical quality, being limited to plain forms; and the bulk of it is subsequent to, and influenced by, the spread of Arretine ware.

2. The western fabrics are better known. That of Arretium in Etruria began shortly after 30 B.C.; some of the early potters bear Oriental names. Here was developed the decorated *sigillata*, bowls surrounded with designs taken from the repertory of Neo-Attic art. Arretine ware, plain and decorated, was widely exported, and about the beginning of the Christian era, to lessen cost of transport, branch potteries for the production of plain ware were established round the Mediterranean. Those in South Gaul commenced about A.D. 20 to produce independently decorated ware, and before their competition the Arretine potteries lost ground, though production did not cease until Flavian times. In their turn the South Gaulish potteries (of which La Graufesenque was the largest centre) were replaced after the first century by others nearer the frontiers (Lezoux in the Auvergne; Rheinzabern, Trier, etc., in Germany). In the second century manufacture extended to Aquincum in Pannonia and Colchester in Britain. The wars of the mid-third century proved disastrous to the industry, and production ceased for a time.

3. In the Roman East several fabrics, all of plain ware, have been distinguished. One pottery-site has been located, near Pergamum, of Tiberio-Claudian times; and it is surmised from Pliny (*HN* 35. 60) that Samos was a centre of production. The period of greatest activity was the early first century, after which the pottery falls off in quantity and quality. On present evidence it would appear that the East used little decorated ware, and what has been found is Western import.

4. The fourth century witnessed a revival, both in the East (where Egypt may have led the way) and in the West (potteries in the district of the Marne). This late ware is characterized by the use of stamped decoration, a technique which survived into Coptic and Frankish times.

Eastern fabrics: J. H. Iliffe, 'Sigillata Wares in the Near East' (*Quarterly of the Department of Antiquities in Palestine* vi (1938), 4–53). Western fabrics. General: F. Oswald and T. D. Pryce, *Terra Sigillata* (1920). Arretine: A. Oxé, *Arretinische Reliefgefässe vom Rhein* (1933). Gaulish: A. Oxé, *Frühgallische Reliefgefässe vom Rhein* (1934); J. Déchelette, *Les Vases céramiques ornés de la Gaule romaine* (1904); F. Hermet, *La Graufesenque* (1934). Spain: M. Cazurro, *Inst. d'Estudis Catalans*, Anuari 1909–10, p. 296. Fourth-century fabrics: (West) W. Unverzagt, *Terra Sigillata mit Rädchenverzierung* (1919); (East) K. Kubler, 'Spätantike Stempelkeramik' (*Ath. Mitt.* lvi (1931), 75).   F. N. P.

TERREMARE.

A Terramara has been aptly described as 'a Lake-dwelling on land'. But it is a 'lake-dwelling' of unique shape and kind, trapezoidal in outline, enclosed by a rampart of earth and surrounded by a moat fed from a stream. Such constructions are known only in the eastern half of the Po valley, particularly around Parma and Modena. The word is derived from Italian country-speech and its plural is Terremare. Chronologically the Terremare belong to the Bronze Age and begin at the earliest stages of that period. Discoveries in the Po valley began in 1862. In 1900 Pigorini launched his theory, which has found its way into every text-book but has lately been subjected to criticism long overdue. The theory maintains that (1) at the end of the Neolithic Age a new race appeared in Italy; which, unlike the Neolithics, cremated its dead. These newcomers came from the Danube valley. They were the direct ancestors of all the Italic tribes. At the end of the Bronze Age they left the Po valley and occupied the whole of Italy. (2) This people introduced the use of bronze and should be regarded as leading the whole civilization of Italy in its day.

2. In the first controversies which arose it was undoubtedly established (*a*), as against Brizio, that the Terramaricoli were not indigenous but immigrants, and (*b*), as against Sergi, that their structures were not Roman camps misunderstood by the excavators. But what was never proved was the postulated archaeological connexion between Bronze-Age Terramaricoli and Iron-Age Villanovans (q.v.).

3. The few cemeteries which are intermediate in date are not demonstrably intermediate in quality. The supposed pedigree, therefore, passing from Terramaricoli through Villanovans to Romans is weak at its most crucial point. That the Terramaricoli were the ancestors of the Italici becomes merely a pious opinion. Much of Pigorini's theory appears now as a somewhat rash prophecy which it was assumed that the future would confirm with more material. Only a more recent and complete regional survey could disprove Colini's over-statement that the whole Iron Age in Italy was uniform and its several phases the 'dialects of a common language'. It has required the experience of nearly thirty years since then to show that Villanovan culture was definitely restricted in its area and could never be made to cover more than a fraction of the Italici, though perhaps the most interesting fraction. If the supposed march of the Terramaricoli from the Po to the heel of Italy is not wholly a myth, as some critics maintain, there are at any rate no clear traces of it. Probably few still believe in the outlying Terramara at Taranto.

4. Yet though the first part of Pigorini's theory can no longer be held to be convincing there is no sufficient reason for the present to consider the second part of it unsound. The importance of the Terramaricoli will still be considerable if they can safely be regarded as the pioneers and introducers of the Bronze Age. This claim has recently been attacked because there is an important Bronze-Age culture on many sites unrelated to Terremare—a fact suddenly emphasized by recent discoveries. The '*extra*-terramaricoli', as Rellini terms them, are certainly more important than the world supposed. But the orthodox opinion still holds good that the Italian Bronze Age is the legitimate child of Central Europe. If, therefore, the Terramaricoli lived originally somewhere near Bohemia and Hungary, they may well have brought in the knowledge of bronze-working from those regions.

The best account is still T. E. Peet, *The Stone and Bronze Ages in Italy* (1909). For the 'Extra-terramaricoli' see *Mon. Ant.* 34 (1932). The whole Terramara culture is pictorially illustrated by O. Montelius, *La Civilisation primitive en Italie* (plates 12, 26). G. Säflund, *Le Terremare* (Lund, 1939), is an important statement of recent research.   D. R.-MacI.

TERTULLIAN

(QUINTUS SEPTIMIUS FLORENS TERTULLIANUS) (*c.* A.D. 160–*c.* 225), a native of the Roman province Africa of pagan parentage, received a thorough training as a lawyer. Most of his life was spent at Carthage. His ardent yet sarcastic temperament persisted after his conversion, when, though apparently remaining a layman, he devoted his pen to the furtherance of the Christian religion, as he understood it. His later writings are more markedly ascetic, due to his devotion to the Montanistic sect. He wrote both in Latin and in

Greek, but none of his Greek works has survived. There can be no doubt that he had read the leading Greek and Latin pagan authors, of whom Herodotus and Varro may be named. He is the earliest writer known to us to formulate the doctrine of the Trinity, and, as a creator of Latin Christian terminology his importance is capital. Of all Latin prose writers he is perhaps the most difficult to master.

Of his surviving works, over thirty in number, the following may be considered the most important: *Ad nationes* (A.D. 197), *Apologeticus* (Ἀπολογητικός [*sc. λόγος*], 197), *De testimonio animae* (197–200), *De spectaculis* (200), *De praescriptione haereticorum* (200), *De oratione*, *De baptismo*, *Adversus Iudaeos* (these between 200 and 206), *Adversus Marcionem* (207–11), *De pallio* (209), *De anima*, *De carnis resurrectione* (208–11), *De corona* (211), and *Adversus Praxean* (after 213).

The *Apology* has been styled 'the noblest oration among all which antiquity has left us'. It was addressed to Roman governors and naturally avoids Christian technicalities. But the author knows the history and character of persecution as well as he knows Roman law. He successfully rebuts all the charges made against Christians and also shows clearly what Christianity is within the Roman Empire.

Ed. F. Oehler (Lipsiae, 1853); *Apology*, ed. J. E. B. Mayor (tr. A. Souter) (1917), T. R. Glover (Loeb, 1931), H. Hoppe (1939).
A. S.

TESSERA, a ticket or token, used in Rome, as in all ages, for a great variety of purposes, and represented by small pieces, often circular, of lead, bronze, terracotta, bone, etc.

The *tesserae nummulariae*, formerly known erroneously as *tesserae gladiatoriae*, were tabs attached to bags of silver denarii, to show that they had been tested for genuineness (*specto*). The surviving examples belong to the last century of the Republic.

Under the Empire there were *tesserae frumentariae*, for the recipients of free corn, *tesserae* for games and public shows, and *tesserae* given in largesse by the Emperor and exchangeable for various presents. Many of these *tesserae* bear types, similar to those of coins, but less often legends, and are often of lead. One series of bronze *tesserae* shows imperial heads on the obverse and numbers on the reverse. The attribution of *tesserae* to their particular uses is largely conjectural, but the principles of classification have been determined by Rostovtzeff.

Tesserae were, of course, used in private, as well as in public life. Among private *tesserae* may be mentioned the *tesserae hospitales*, which established the claim of the bearer to hospitality on his travels abroad, and *tesserae lusoriae*, used for games.

K. Regling, *PW*, s.v.; M. Rostovtzeff, 'Römische Bleitesserae', *Klio*, Beiheft 3, 1905.
H. M.

TESTA, see TREBATIUS.

TESTAMENTUM, see INHERITANCE.

TESTAMENTUM PORCELLI, a satiric parody (3rd or 4th c. A.D.) of a will imagined to be by a pig, Grunnius Corocotta, just before being killed. It is mentioned by Jerome (praef. *Comment. in Isaiam*) as causing amusement in boys' schools.

Text at end of Bücheler's ed. of Petronius.
J. W. D.

TESTIMONIUM signifies in its widest sense all types of evidence (Gai. 3. 131; Cic. *Top*. 19. 73); the term *instrumentum* was later used in the same sense (Dig. 22. 4. 1). In a narrower sense the term signifies the testimony of a witness (*testis*), which was in ancient times the only evidence in legal proceedings. It maintained its importance also in the classical period, though documentary proof gained more and more ground. In the oldest law we already find another activity of witnesses: some solemn legal transactions and acts required for their validity the presence of witnesses, e.g. *mancipatio* and other transactions *per aes et libram* (five witnesses), *confarreatio* (ten), also some important acts in civil procedure (as *in ius vocatio, litis contestatio*) and such legal acts as the opening of a will. When a crime (e.g. of *furtum*) was being investigated, some processes open to the parties to the case required the participation of witnesses. But the widest field of their activity was in testamentary law, because in all forms of will their presence was necessary for the validity of the act. The two functions were closely connected, for presence at a legal transaction entailed an obligation on the witness to give evidence if there was litigation. Refusal of testimony made a man *intestabilis*, i.e. incapable of being a witness or calling a witness, and hence also of making a will.

2. In course of time various forms of written evidence (*instrumenta, documenta*) were developed. On the one hand, a transaction may itself be made in writing and attested by witnesses; on the other, some event or act may be recorded in writing and the truth of the record attested by persons who have been present at the occurrence; or again, a person may make some statement and other persons simply attest the identity of the deponent and the fact that he made the statement. The object of this last process is to make the evidence available in subsequent court proceedings, when it can be read aloud in the absence of the witness himself.

3. Some persons were generally excluded from testimony: slaves, *impuberes*, women (only from transactions), *intestabiles*, persons convicted of crimes, and those who followed an infamous profession. In particular cases all persons connected by a bond of kinship or moral obligation with a party interested in the lawsuit or in the transaction (*testimonium domesticum*) were excluded. Capacity to witness a will was regulated by special rules.

4. The deposition of a witness was made personally and usually under oath. Recitation of a written *testatio*, which became the later practice, carried less conviction. Apart from witnesses to legal transactions, persons could not be forced to give evidence except in criminal proceedings. Citation of a witness was called *denuntiatio*. In post-classical law, under the influence of the Hellenistic East, documents acquired greater evidentiary value than the evidence of witnesses, which became more and more distrusted. The testimony of one witness had no value at all.

5. False witness was severely punished (*Lex Cornelia testamentoria*); according to some laws even with death (XII Tables: 'deicere e saxo Tarpeio'; *Lex Cornelia de sicariis*).

Modern literature: S. Riccobono, *Sav. Zeitschr.* xxxiv (1913), 231 ff.; L. Wenger, art. 'Signum', in *PW* ii A; M. Kaser, s.v. 'Testimonium', ibid. v A; W. Hellebrand, *Das Prozesszeugnis im Rechte der Papyri* (1934).
A. B.

TESTUDO, see SIEGECRAFT, ROMAN.

TETHYS (Τηθύς), in mythology, daughter of Earth and Heaven, sister of Ocean (Hesiod, *Theog.* 136); becomes the consort of Ocean and bears the Rivers, also the three thousand Oceanids, whose work it is to aid the rivers and Apollo to bring young men to their prime, and Styx, chief of them all (ibid. 337 ff.).
H. J. R.

TETRALOGY, see TRAGEDY, para. 12.

TETRARCHY (τετραρχία, i.e. the fourth part of an ἀρχή) was first used to denote one of the four political divisions of Thessaly ('tetrad' being a purely geographical term). The tetrarchies—Thessaliotis, Hestiaeotis, Pelasgiotis, and Phthiotis—may have formed separate tribal States before Thessaly became a single κοινόν. After this union they continued to exist for purposes of local government, but the rapid development of cities towards the end of the fifth century, together with the decay of the κοινόν, caused them to lose much of their importance. In 342 B.C. Philip of Macedon, now Archon of Thessaly, revived the tetrarchies in order to overcome the resistance of the cities through tetrarchs who were his partisans. How long this system lasted is unknown.

The term found its way to the Hellenistic East and was applied to the four divisions into which each of the three tribes of the Galatians was subdivided. In Roman times many hellenized princes in Syria and Palestine were styled 'tetrarch', but the number of tetrarchies in any political organization ceased to be necessarily four, the term denoting merely the realm of a subordinate dynast.

A. Momigliano, *Athenaeum* 1932, 47–51; W. Schwahn, *PW*, s.v. 'Tetrarch'.　　　　　　　　　　　　　　　　　H. D. W.

TETRICUS, GAIUS PIUS ESUVIUS, governor of Aquitania, was made Emperor on the death of Victorinus by Victorinus' mother, Victoria. Ruling from A.D. 270 to 274 he suffered much from his disorderly troops and an insubordinate governor, Faustinus. Despairing of his Empire, he made no move against Rome and, finally, appealed to Aurelian, 'eripe me his, inuicte, malis', and, when Aurelian invaded Gaul, deserted his army at the battle of Châlons. Led in triumph, he was afterwards appointed 'corrector Lucaniae'. His son, Tetricus II, shared his fortunes as Caesar, then for a short time as Augustus, and again as a senator of Rome.　　　H. M.

TEUCER (1) (*Τεῦκρος*), (1) ancestor of the Trojan kings, the genealogy being

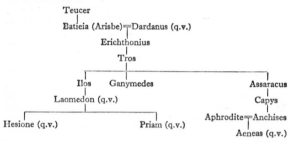

Teucer
|
Bateia (Arisbe)═Dardanus (q.v.)
|
Erichthonius
|
Tros
|
Ilos　　Ganymedes　　　　　　　Assaracus
|　　　　　　　　　　　　　　　　|
Laomedon (q.v.)　　　　　　　　Capys
|　　　　　　　　　　　　　　　|
Hesione (q.v.)　　Priam (q.v.)　Aphrodite═Anchises
　　　　　　　　　　　　　　　　　|
　　　　　　　　　　　　　　　Aeneas (q.v.)

For authorities, see Schmidt in Roscher, v. 406. Ramsay, *Asianic Elements*, 225, identifies him with the Hittite god Tarku. (2) Son of Telamon (q.v.) by Hesione. Throughout the *Iliad* he is a valiant archer, and faithful comrade of his half-brother, the greater Aias. This character is maintained in later works, e.g. the *Ajax* of Sophocles. He was absent at the time of Aias' suicide (*Ajax*, 342–3), but returned (974) in time to take a leading part in the struggle to secure him honourable burial. After his banishment (*see* TELAMON) he founded Salamis in Cyprus (Horace, *Carm.* 1. 7. 27 ff., and often). There is no consistent tradition of the manner or place of his death.　　　　　　　　　　　　　　　　　　H. J. R.

TEUCER (3) of Cyzicus (1st c. B.C.) wrote on the Mithridatic Wars, Tyre, the Arabs, Jewish history, Byzantium, and Cyzicus, his work covering Pompey's settlement of the East, and reflecting the part played by Cyzicus at this time. His *Περὶ χρυσοφόρου γῆς* does not necessarily identify him with Teucer of Babylon (q.v.).

FHG iv. 508.　　　　　　　　　　　　　　A. H. McD.

TEUCER (4) of Babylon (probably the Babylon in Egypt), astrologer, is conjectured to belong to the first century A.D. He expounded the traditional astrology of Egypt and united with it Oriental and Greek elements. He had a great influence on Arabian and medieval astrology, through his description of the constellations. Frs. of his works have been preserved.

Ed. F. Boll, *Sphaera* (1903), pp. 16, 31; *PW* v A. 1132.　　　　　　　　　　　　　　　　　　　　　W. D. R.

TEUTA, Illyrian queen and regent after Agron's death in 231 B.C., followed up his victory over the Aetolians at Medeon by aggression against Epirus, and directed Illyrian piracy against Italian commerce with Greece. She refused Rome satisfaction for the murder of Italian merchants in 230 and even for an attack on the Roman envoys. In 229 she took Corcyra, defeating the Achaeans, and was besieging Issa and Dyrrhachium when Rome intervened, in the First Illyrian War, and forced her to withdraw and submit.

Polyb. 2. 2–12. M. Holleaux, *CAH* vii. 827.　　A. H. McD.

TEUTHRAS, *see* TELEPHUS.

TEUTOBURGIENSIS, SALTUS, the district where, in A.D. 9, the army of P. Quinctilius Varus (q.v.) was destroyed on the march from summer to winter quarters, by the Cheruscan prince Arminius (q.v.). Despite much discussion, the *Saltus Teutoburgiensis* has not been located, neither is it certain whether *saltus* here means a forest or a mountain pass. The Teutoburger Wald of modern maps is an archaizing name given in the seventeenth century. The site of the disaster must lie somewhere between the middle Weser and the upper Ems, between the Lippe and the Dümmer See.

A. Franke, s.v. 'Teut. Saltus' in *PW* v A. 1166–71.　　O. B.

TEUTONES, a German tribe, first encountered by Pytheas (*c.* 325 B.C.) on the Holstein coast; Thy, in north Jutland (NW. of Limfjorden), preserves their name. They wandered forth with the Cimbri (q.v.) and after many vicissitudes were annihilated by Marius at Aquae Sextiae (*Aix-en-Provence*) in 102 B.C. With them were the Ambrones, who are thought to have come from the Frisian islands. The name Teuton became a synonym for German, and poets of the Empire still wrote of the 'furor teutonicus' long after the disappearance of the tribe, but for a small group near Miltenberg (if this is a correct deduction from *ILS* 9377) and elements among the Aduatuci of Gaul (Caes. *B Gall.* 2. 29).　　O. B.

TEXTUAL CRITICISM. 'Textual criticism, a general term given to the skilled and methodical application of human judgement to the settlement of texts. . . . The aim of the "textual critic" may then be defined as the restoration of the text, as far as possible, to its original form if by "original form" we understand the form intended by its author' (J. P. Postgate in *Enc. Brit.*[14]). More briefly: it is the branch of knowledge concerned with the genuineness of texts.

Textual criticism may be divided into (A) statement showing what is the 'transmitted text' (*recensio*); (B) examination of this text concerning its genuineness (*examinatio*); (C) conjectural restoration, as far as possible, of the original text, where the transmitted text is insufficient.

A. *Recensio* may be divided into: (i) collection of witnesses (including extracts, translations, quotations, imitations, etc.); and (ii) statement of the interrelationship between these witnesses ('stemmatics').

B. *Examinatio* may be divided into: (i) choice (*selectio*) between variants, i.e. between two or more readings which have been proved by the recension to be transmitted ('substantive', 'authoritative'); and (ii) localization of corruptions.

C. Conjectural restoration may be divided into (i) emendation of corrupt passages; and (ii) supplementing of passages that have suffered physical damage.

Some important particular methods and notions may now be explained.

(1) There are several methods of stemmatics (A. ii). The most commonly used is that of 'significant errors' (*errores significativi*), which are either *separative* (i.e. showing that one witness is independent of another),

or *conjunctive* (showing that two witnesses are more closely connected each with the other than with any third witness).

The different types of interrelationship which can be ascertained by 'significant errors' are 3 if 2 witnesses are extant; 22 if 3; 250 if 4; about 4,000 if 5; and so on!

If of two witnesses (*A* and *B*), *A* contains no separative error when compared with *B*, while *B* contains one or more separative errors when compared with *A*, then *B* can, and in longer texts must, be regarded as derived from *A*, and in consequence must be eliminated from the substantive witnesses.

(2) Where one witness depends on two or more other witnesses, i.e. where the transmission is 'contaminated' and the stemma 'convergent', it is seldom possible to ascertain the type of interrelationship by stemmatics.

(3) In a split transmission the lost witness with which the splitting of the transmission begins is called the *archetype*. Lost derivatives of the archetype which are represented by two or more extant witnesses are conveniently called *hyparchetypes*. An extant witness which proves to be the source of all the others is called *testis unicus*.

(4) *Selectio* (B i) depends (*a*) on the intrinsic value of the variants; (*b*) on the degree of probability that one of them has originated from the other. The same principles apply *mutatis mutandis* to the choice between conjectural emendations (C i).

(5) The period during which the corruption must be shown to have been possible is, in the case of variants, that between the archetype and the witness for the rejected variant; in the case of conjectures, that between the original text and the archetype or the *testis unicus*. For this reason it is important to know as much as can be known about the history of the transmission.

(6) Modern critical editions represent the results of textual criticism by varying systems of terms, signs, and arrangements, which are often confusing. There is a tendency towards uniformity in this technique which should be encouraged by all editors.

Typical stemma of a split transmission

With such a stemmatic type, neither the age of the witnesses *A*, *B*, and *C*, nor their quality (in so far as it depends on the number and gravity of the corruptions in each of them) is of decisive importance for the *selectio*.

BIBLIOGRAPHY

The most comprehensive recent books are: L. Havet, *Manuel de critique verbale appliquée aux textes latins*, 1911: F. W. Hall, *Companion to Classical Texts*, 1913: G. Pasquali, *Storia della tradizione e critica del testo*, 1934.

Havet hides his valuable theoretical remarks among too many examples of doubtful aptness. Hall gives much useful technical help and well-chosen examples. Pasquali treats predominantly the problems of abnormal transmission.

There are, besides, three modern condensed accounts by writers who think independently: J. P. Postgate, in *Enc. Brit.*[14] (1929), s.v. 'Textual Criticism'; P. Maas, *Textkritik*, in Gercke–Norden, *Einleitung in die Altertumswissenschaft*, i[3], Heft 2 (1927); G. Pasquali, in *Enciclopedia Italiana* (1932), s.v. 'Edizione critica'.

The textual criticism of Shakespeare offers many similar problems relating to choice between variants, conjectures, history of trans-

mission, etc.: see especially the relevant work of A. W. Pollard and W. W. Greg.

The following is a selection of studies and examples in the different branches of the subject:

A i. (Collection of witnesses.) For the infinite variety of problems, see the prefaces of modern critical editions. Among catalogues of MSS. outstanding examples are: *Codices Vaticani graeci rec.*, I. Mercati et P. Franchi de Cavalieri I (1923); and (for technical authors) *Catalogus codicum astrologorum graecorum*, ed. W. Kroll and others (1898–). Among collections of fragments, especially valuable are those for *Greek Comedy*, by A. Meineke (1839–57); *Greek Tragedy*, by A. Nauck[2] (1891); the *Presocratics*, by H. Diels and W. Kranz[5] (1934–8); *Greek Historians*, by F. Jacoby (1923–).

A ii. (Stemmatics): P. Maas, 'Leitfehler und stemmatische Typen', *Byz. Zeitschrift* 1937, 289.

B i. (Principles of choice between variants): A. E. Housman, ed. of Manilius I (1903), praef. ch. iv.

C ii. (Texts which are physically damaged): E. Lobel, editions of papyri of Sappho (1925), Alcaeus (1927), Callimachus (*Hermes* 1934, 1935), *POxy.* col. 18 (1941).

HISTORY OF TRANSMISSION: U. von Wilamowitz-Moellendorff, *Herakles*[1] (1889), reprinted as *Einleitung in die Griechische Tragoedie*. Classics in medieval times, *Greek*: P. Maas in Gercke–Norden, op. cit. i[3], *Anhang* (1927), cf. *Byz. Zeitschr.* 1938, 409; *Latin*: E. Norden in Gercke–Norden, op. cit. i[3], Heft 4 (1927), 93.

CORRUPTION: (*a*) *Interpolations*: G. Jachmann, 'Binneninterpolation', in *Nachrichten Gött. Ges. Wiss. Fachgruppe i*, Bd. i (1936), 123, 185. On the additional verses in Juvenal, *Sat.* 6, see U. Knoche, *Philologus* xciii (1938), 196. (*b*) *Omission of lines in prose*: A. C. Clark, *Descent of MSS.* (1918). (*c*) *Medieval conjectures*: P. Maas, 'Eustathios als Konjekturalkritiker', *Byz. Zeitschr.* 1935, 1936.

CONTAMINATED TRANSMISSION: Examples of this desperate case are Homer, *Iliad* (most complete ed. T. W. Allen (1931)); and the Greek New Testament (most complete ed. H. von Soden (1913); *Ev. Marc.* and *Ev. Matt.*, ed. S. C. E. Legg (1935 and 1940): for an important new reading of *Ev. Matt.* 6. 28, see T. C. Skeat in *Zeitschr. für Neutest. Wiss.* 1938, 211).

TECHNIQUE OF CRITICAL EDITIONS: O. Stählin, *Editionstechnik*[2] (1914); Union Académique Internationale, J. Bidez et A. B. Drachmann, *Emploi des signes critiques*[2] (1938). Edition of a text with complicated transmission: *Codex Theodosianus*, ed. Th. Mommsen (1906); of fragments with compendious apparatus: *Anthologia lyrica graeca*, ed. E. Diehl, i[2] (1933–7), ii[2] (1942).

HISTORY OF TEXTUAL CRITICISM: see SCHOLARSHIP IN ANTIQUITY and SCHOLARSHIP IN MODERN TIMES under Aristarchus, Eustathius of Thessalonika, Bentley, Porson, G. Hermann, Lachmann, Wilamowitz-Moellendorff, A. E. Housman. P. M.

THALES of Miletus was universally accounted one of the Seven Sages and author of numerous aphorisms. As statesman he advised the Ionians to resist Persian aggression by establishing a federal council at Teos. As scientist he predicted to within a year, probably from knowledge of Babylonian calendars, the solar eclipse which occurred during the Battle of the Halys on 28 May 585 B.C. He is further reliably said (though he wrote nothing) to have introduced into Greece and generalized Egyptian methods of mensuration (thus founding 'geometry') and to have connected the Nile-floods with the Etesian winds. His view that the world not only originates from but consists of and returns to water, on which the earth floats, marks the beginning of physical science. *See also* ASTRONOMY.

Diels, *Vorsokr.*[5] i. 67–81; Burnet, *Early Greek Philosophy*, 40–50; *PW* v A. 1210; Zeller-Mondolfo, *La filosofia dei Greci* i. 2 (1938), 100–34. A. H. C.

THALETAS, of Gortyn in Crete (Paus. 1. 14. 4), worked at Sparta in the seventh century B.C. (Plut. *De mus.* 9). He wrote songs which exhorted to law-abidingness (Plut. *Lyc.* 4) and paeans (Plut. *De mus.* 10, but cf. 42). Nothing of his work survives. He used paeonic and cretic rhythms (Plut. *De mus.* 10). C. M. B.

THALLUS published a chronological work in three books, from the Trojan War to Ol. 167 (112–109 B.C.) according to Eusebius; but on the evidence of the fragments, from Belus to at least the death of Christ. If Eusebius is right, Thallus' work must have been later extended. Euhemeristic in character, it was used by the Christian apologists. He may, perhaps, be the Samaritan Thallus, Augustus' secretary or Tiberius' freedman.

FGrH ii, B. 1156; BD. 835. A. H. McD.

THALYSIA (θαλύσια), *see* FIRST FRUITS.

THAMUGADI (modern *Timgad*), an agricultural settlement in Numidia twenty miles east of Lambaesis (q.v.). Founded in A.D. 100 by Trajan as a colony (*ILS* 6841), the original town was designed on camp lines; *cardo* and *decumanus* intersected at right angles, *curia*, basilica, and forum were placed at this intersection, and smaller streets ran parallel to the two main roads. Thamugadi had many public baths and a theatre, and public-spirited citizens gave it a library and a market-place. When it outgrew its original rectangle, an enormous Capitoline temple was built outside the walls.

The fertile country-side brought great prosperity under the Septimian dynasty; but later its fortunes declined owing to blood-stained religious quarrels. Saharan raiders sacked and burnt it; the Byzantines built a protecting fortress, but it fell to the first Arab invasion.

Excepting Leptis, Timgad has the most complete Roman remains in Africa. Its forum commemorates the African sportsman's ideal: 'uenari, lauari, ludere, ridere, occ est uiuere' (*CIL* viii, *Suppl.* 17938).

A. Ballu, *Les Ruines de Timgad*[2] (1904); R. Cagnat, *Carthage, Timgad, etc.*[2] (1909). W. N. W.

THAMYRIS (Θάμυρις) or **THAMYRAS** (Θαμύρας), a bard, who boasted that he would win a contest even if the Muses opposed him, whereat they blinded him and made him forget his skill (*Iliad* 2. 594 ff.). Later authors attribute a multitude of musical inventions to him and add some unimportant tales; see Höfer in Roscher, s.v. H. J. R.

THANATOS. Death, as a person, hardly rises to the level of a mythological figure, belonging rather to folklore or poetical fancy. Thus he is a healer (Eur. *Hipp.* 1373, i.e. only death will ease Hippolytus' pain); he keeps Polybus in the grave (Soph. *O.T.* 942); he begat the poison which kills Heracles (Soph. *Trach.* 833); he is the only god who loves not gifts (Aesch. in Ar. *Ran.* 1392, i.e. death is inexorable, and, incidentally, is not worshipped as a god). In Epic he is a little more concrete; he is the brother of Sleep, and the two carry away the body of Sarpedon (*Iliad* 14. 231; 16. 671 ff.). Cf. Hesiod, *Theog.* 212 (Death, son of Night), 764 (he is iron-hearted, hated even by gods).

In Eur. *Alcestis* he is a clearly defined figure, the 'dark-robed lord of the dead' (843), armed with a sword (76), and Euripides borrows him from Phrynichus (Serv. Dan. on *Aen.* 4. 694), who very likely had him from popular belief. Heracles rescues Alcestis (q.v.) by literal physical wrestling with Thanatos. Except for its successful issue, this is not unlike the modern Greek stories of a hero contending with Charos.

A merry tale of Sisyphus (q.v.) is preserved from Phrynichus (fr. 119 Jacoby) by schol. *Iliad* 6. 153. Sisyphus told Asopus what had become of Aegina (q.v.), and Zeus therefore sent Thanatos against him; but Sisyphus bound Thanatos, so no one died until Ares rescued him and gave Sisyphus to him. Before dying, Sisyphus bade his wife Merope give him no funeral dues; she obeyed, and he got permission from Hades to re-ascend to earth and remonstrate. He neglected to return till he died of old age, and Hades set him to roll the rock to keep him from running away again.

For Thanatos in art see O. Waser in Roscher s *Lex.*, s.v. H. J. R.

THARGELIA, an Ionian festival attributed to Apollo and celebrated the 7th Thargelion (May–June), also known from Asia Minor (Hipponax), Abdera, Massilia. The most discussed rite took place the day before. A man (the φαρμακός) was fed, led around in the town, flogged with green plants, driven out, and sometimes stoned or killed. He is certainly a scapegoat, absorbing all evil and then removed. On the other hand, certain rites point to the conception of a spirit of vegetation whose power is to be reinforced. The festival is named after the θάργηλα which were brought on the chief day, first fruits of the still-unripe crops cooked in a pot; the word signifies also the first bread baked of the new crop. The mixing of the two mentioned motifs is explained by the fact that the Thargelia were celebrated a little before the harvest, partly to protect and partly to promote the crops. The θάργηλα rite has been interpreted as the breaking of the tabu on the unripe crops.

L. Deubner, *Attische Feste*, 179 ff.; M. P. Nilsson, *Griech. Feste*, 105 ff.; J. E. Harrison, *Proleg. to the Study of Greek Religion*, 77 ff.; the *pharmakos* is much discussed, e.g. Frazer, *GB*[3] ix; Nilsson, *Gesch. d. griech. Religion* i. 97 ff. M. P. N.

THASOS, an island of the north Aegean, colonized from Paros, probably *c.* 680 B.C. From the gold-mines in its soil (the first exploitation of which Herodotus ascribed, probably without good reason, to the Phoenicians), and from others on the mainland under Mt. Pangaeus, it derived a revenue rising to 2–300 talents. A dispute with Athens about the mainland mines led to its secession from the Delian League (465), followed by its reduction (463). If we may judge by the fluctuations in the tribute of Thasos (3 talents in 454, and 30 in 446), it was deprived of the mainland mines in 463, but recovered them soon after. Despite a massacre of its Athenian partisans by Lysander (404), it again allied with Athens in 389 and was a permanent member of Athens' Second Confederacy. In 340 it was subdued by Philip, and it remained a Macedonian dependency until freed by the Romans in 196. After 300 its waning revenues from the mines were supplemented by the profits of a carefully regulated export of wine. The volume of this trade is attested by widely distributed finds of wine-jars (identified by an official stamp) in the Balkan lands, where Thasian coinage also circulated freely.

Thasos had a flourishing school of sculpture from the seventh to the sixth century, and it was the home of the painter Polygnotus. It preserves impressive remains of its fifth-century walls.

S. Casson, *Macedonia, Thrace and Illyria* (1926), passim; F. v. Hiller in *PW*, s.v. M. C.

THEAETETUS (*c.* 414–369 B.C.) of Athens, mathematician, friend and pupil of Plato in philosophy and of Theodorus of Cyrene in mathematics, contributed much to the foundations (*a*) of Euc. bk. 10, by investigating the various species of irrationals (cf. Pl. *Tht.* 147 d–148 b), and (*b*) of Euc. bk. 13, by constructing theoretically the five regular solids and discovering the methods of inscribing them in spheres.

PW v A. 1351. W. D. R.

THEAGENES (1) of Megara slaughtered the flocks and herds of the wealthy, secured a bodyguard, and made himself tyrant; constructed a tunnelled conduit and pillared fountain; married his daughter to Cylon of Athens, and supported Cylon's unsuccessful attempt to make himself tyrant. He was himself subsequently banished from Megara. The date of Theagenes' tyranny depends on that of Cylon (victor Olymp. XXXV, coup before Draco), and in spite of recent questionings is probably to be put between 640 and 620 B.C.

Aristotle, *Politics* 1305 a, *Rhetoric* 1. 2; Pausanias 1. 28, 40, 41; Thucydides 1. 126; Plutarch, *Quaest. Graec.* 18. B. Dunkley, *BSA* xxxvi. 145 f. P. N. U.

THEAGENES (2) of Rhegium (*fl. c.* 525 B.C.), contemporary of Cambyses, was the first scholar to attempt an allegorical interpretation of Homer by suggesting that the names of the gods represented either human faculties or natural elements (*see* ALLEGORY).

Diels, *Vorsokr.*[5] i. 51 f.; F. Wehrli, *Zur Geschichte der allegorischen Deutung Homers im Altertum* (1928). J. F. L.

THEAGES, pupil of Socrates. Plato refers in the *Republic* (496 b) to 'the bridle of Theages', the bad health which kept him out of politics and saved him for philosophy. On the basis of this reference an imitator of Plato wrote a *Theages* dealing with the relation between philosophy and politics, and this is included in the corpus of Plato's works.

PW v A. 1350. W. D. R.

THEANO is said to have been the wife of Pythagoras, but another tradition describes her as being among his pupils, and the wife of his disciple Brotinus or Brontinus. Several apocryphal books were ascribed to her in antiquity. Seven apocryphal letters are to be seen in R. Hercher, *Epistolographi*, 603–7.

PW v A. 1379. W. D. R.

THEATRES, STRUCTURE OF. Greek and Hellenistic theatres were unroofed and placed where natural ground-slope assisted seating, thus reducing substructures to a minimum. The auditorium or *cavea* was rather more than a semicircle on plan, and seating was of stone or marble slabs, unless natural rock was cut to shape and wooden seats were added. Narrow stepways were arranged radially. The lowest seat tier was sometimes a special one with continuous backs, or even separate armchairs, finely shaped and finished in marble (Dionysus Theatre, Athens, and Priene, Asia Minor), and separated by a gangway from the seats above; in larger theatres there was a similar concentric gangway half-way up. In the centre of the *cavea* was the orchestra or chorus space, usually a complete circle. Stepped raking and balustraded walls closed each end of the *cavea* and formed one side of wing-passages (*parodoi*), the front of the stage being set back the width of the passage at least. The stage (*skene*) was probably of wood in earlier examples. Theatres of late fourth century had built loggias (*proskenia*) in front, and it is therefore assumed that their stages were raised considerably. The theatre at Epidaurus (*c.* 330 B.C.) is over 360 ft. across the *cavea* and must have seated well over 7,000; owing to the favourable conformation of the ground its natural acoustic properties are unsurpassed; that at Syracuse (*c.* 400 B.C.), in excellent preservation, has fine evidences of balustraded backs to its upper concentric gangway.

Roman theatres conformed to a type which made a complete building, though, in larger examples, the auditorium—a semicircle—was probably only partly roofed. The stage, certainly roofed and close to the semicircular 'orchestra', was a wide and fairly deep raised platform, backed by a wall (*scenae frons*) as high as the top of the *cavea*, treated as an elaborate front towards the stage, with columns, niches, etc. Substructures of *cavea* and stage consisted of vaulted passages, etc., with staircases, and the outer walls enclosing the back of the *cavea*, sometimes squared, were of arched construction in tiers, with order treatments. Good examples are at Pompeii (small theatre, early, partly Greek, *c.* 80 B.C.), Orange, Aspendus, Athens (Odeon), Miletus, Taormina, and Dougga (N. Africa).

D. S. Robertson, op. cit. under ARCHITECTURE, pp. 164 and 271. T. F.

THEATRICAL PRODUCTION (1) GREEK, see TRAGEDY, COMEDY; (2) ROMAN, see DRAMA, para. 7.

THEBAIS, see EPIC CYCLE.

THEBES (1), on the south edge of the east plain of Boeotia, was the chief Mycenaean city in Central Greece (the Phoenician origin of Cadmus, the founder of its dynasty, is no longer credited). The gruesome fates of its princes were, next to the tale of Troy, the favoured material of Greek epic and tragedy. It was destroyed by the Argives, and lay waste (the Catalogue of Ships names only Ὑποθῆβαι; *Il.* 2. 505). After the Boeotian invasion Thebes outstripped the other Boeotian towns, but was never strong enough to combine them into a unitary State. It was friendly with the Pisistratids (Hipparchus made a dedication to Apollo Ptoos, *BCH* 1920, 237 ff.); its hostility to Athens dates from the Athenian reception of the Plataeans (q.v.) in 509 B.C. As a punishment for the support which it gave to the Persians in 480–479, Thebes lost its predominant position in the Boeotian League, and recovered it only in 446. During the Peloponnesian War it grew at the expense of its small neighbours. Its territory, with subject towns, was nearly half Boeotia, and it elected four of eleven boeotarchs (*Hell. Oxy.* xii. 3). Dissatisfied with the Spartan peace in 404, Thebes joined Athens and Argos in the Corinthian War. The peace of 387 enabled the Spartans to detach the other Boeotian towns from Thebes, and in 382 they garrisoned the citadel. The Thebans retook it in 378, and at Leuctra in 371 drove the Spartans out of Central Greece. For a brief period Thebes, led by Epaminondas (q.v.) was the chief power of Greece; but its hegemony did not survive him. Thebes joined Athens in resisting Philip; it was punished by destruction for a revolt against Alexander, and though refounded was never again a great city. Thebes was a pleasant place, with trees and fresh water ([Dicaearchus] 1. 12 ff. in *FHG* ii. 258). The temple of Ismenian Apollo and the prehistoric city and palace have been excavated. *See also* FEDERAL STATES (third paragraph).

L. Ziehen, *PW*, s.v. 'Thebai'; A. W. Gomme, *BSA* 17. 29 ff. (topography). T. J. D.

THEBES (2), formerly capital of Egypt, was still an important city at the Greek conquest, but suffered considerably during revolts in 206 and 88 B.C. of which it was the centre. It was sacked by Cornelius Gallus in 30 or 29 B.C.; Strabo found it a group of villages. The temples prospered under the Ptolemies: building was done on the east bank, and the temple of Deir-el-Medineh on the west was begun under Philopator. Occasional records of works occur till *c.* A.D. 150. Thebes had then become a tourist centre, the great attractions, as shown by graffiti, being the statue of 'Memnon' and the Pharaonic tombs. Papyri and numerous ostraca have been found there, almost all dealing with finance or taxation.

The fullest account of the buildings is in Baedeker's *Egypt* (1929). J. G. M.

THEIAS, see CINYRAS.

THEMIS, a goddess originally akin to or even identical with Gaea (Aesch. *Eum.* 2; *PV* 209–10). In the former passage the oracle at Delphi was once hers; in the latter, she is still a prophetess, and warns her son Prometheus of the future. The same powers are shown in Pindar, *Isthm.* 8. 34 ff., cf. THETIS. In all probability, her name means 'steadfast' (root θε). In Hesiod, *Theog.* 135 she is a daughter of Earth; ibid. 901 ff. she is Zeus' second consort, mother of the Horae and Moerae. But, as her name is used also to mean 'firmly established custom or law, justice', she tends to become an abstraction, Justice or Righteousness. For example, Medea, when betrayed, invokes her as guardian of oaths (Eur. *Med.* 160 ff.); Plato, *Laws*, 936 e, suggests an oath by Zeus, Apollo, and Themis. Her several cults may be supposed to have originated with her earlier nature for the most part; see further, Weniger in Roscher, s.v. H. J. R.

THEMISON of Laodicea, pupil of Asclepiades and precursor of Thessalus of Tralles, lived in Rome under Augustus (31 B.C.–A.D. 14). His views being most inconsistent, his system is no unity. He agreed with Asclepiades in the theory of corpuscles. On the other hand, he introduced into medicine the conception of the *communia* ('status strictus, fluens, et mixtus'), referring to excretion which is either too much or too little, or too much from one part, too little from another. This defect, which he probably thought to hinder the free movement of the atoms, he tried to remedy by an alteration of the state of the body as the physician finds it. Moreover, he was the first to study methodically the problem of chronic diseases and to encourage their treatment by physicians.

TEXT. Fragments, not collected. Π. τῶν ὀξέων καὶ χρονίων νοσημάτων (R. Fuchs, *Rh. Mus.* 1903) not Themison but Herodotus, M. Wellman, *Hermes* 1905, 1913.
LITERATURE. General survey, K. Deichgräber, *PW* v A. 1632. Th. Meyer-Steineg, 'Das medizinische System d. Methodiker', *Jenaer med.-hist. Beiträge* 1916. Themison not the founder of the Methodical school, L. Edelstein, *PW*, Suppl. vi, 358, s.v. 'Methodiker'.
L. E.

THEMISTO, name of several heroines, the only one of importance being the daughter of Hypseus (Nonnus, *Dionys.* 9. 305 f.), wife of Athamas (q.v.). Herodorus, in schol. Ap. Rhod. 2. 1144, makes her his first wife and mother of several children, including Phrixus and Helle.

See Höfer in Roscher, s.v. H. J. R.

THEMISTOCLES (*c.* 528–*c.* 462 B.C.), Athenian statesman, of the poor but noble family of the Lycomids. He held a wardenship of aqueducts, and in 493–492, when he was eponymous archon, he secured the transformation of the Piraeus into a fortified port, and advocated an increase in the Athenian navy against the menace from Aegina and from Persia. At the time of Marathon he was eclipsed by Miltiades (q.v.), who checked Themistocles' policy of naval expansion. After Miltiades' death (489) Themistocles obtained supremacy in Athens by having his rivals ostracized. In 483, when the necessity for a powerful fleet had been brought home to the Athenians in an unsuccessful war against Aegina, Themistocles persuaded the Athenians to build at least 100 new warships with the proceeds of some new silver-mines at Laurium (q.v.), thus breaking with the custom of distributing surpluses of revenue. Henceforth the future of Athens lay on the sea, and the poorer classes, from whom the seafaring population was drawn, came to play a decisive part in Athenian politics. As a champion of national unity in 480 he had the Athenian exiles recalled, and took joint direction of the Persian war with his former antagonist Aristides (q.v.). He held the Persians at Artemisium; after the disaster at Thermopylae he secured the evacuation of Athens, and he persuaded the Spartan admiral-in-chief Eurybiades (q.v.) to fight a decisive battle at Salamis. The stories that he enticed Xerxes to fight by a confidential message, and that he suggested the cutting of the Hellespont bridges, are of doubtful value.

No sooner had the Persians withdrawn from Greece than Themistocles effected the reconstruction of the walls of Athens in the face of Spartan opposition, and to check possible retaliation by Sparta he sponsored democratic movements in Peloponnesus. He probably sounded Pausanias (q.v.) for a revolution at Sparta, and through him he perhaps established contact with Xerxes. At Athens he lost ground to the party of Cimon (q.v.), which stood for friendship with Sparta and vigorous prosecution of the Persian War, and *c.* 470 he was ostracized and retired to Argos. After an abortive attempt to foment revolts against Sparta in Peloponnesus he was denounced by Sparta as an accomplice of Pausanias in medism and was condemned to death by the Athenians in default (*c.* 468). He escaped to Asia after an adventurous flight by way of Corcyra, Epirus, and Macedonia, and was appointed by the Persian king Artaxerxes I as overlord of Magnesia-ad-Maeandrum, Lampsacus, and Myus (since Lampsacus and Myus were in the Delian League, his lordship over these towns was purely nominal). He died at Magnesia *c.* 462. The fable of his suicide, known to Aristophanes (*Eq.* 83), was disproved by Thucydides. The story that he played a part in the overthrow of the Areopagus (Aristotle, *Ath. Pol.* 25) is now generally discredited.

Themistocles had a bad reputation for vanity and acquisitiveness, but his strategic genius was widely recognized. He was the chief architect of the Greek victory over Persia, and though he cannot be connected with any democratic reforms at Athens, his naval policy was rightly regarded by ancient writers as the foundation of the radical Athenian democracy. *See also* PERSIAN WARS.

Hdt. bks. 7–8; Thuc. 1. 93, 135–8; Plutarch, *Themistocles*. A. Bauer, *Themistokles* (1881; good survey of sources); U. Kahrstedt, *PW*, s.v. 'Themistokles'; K. J. Beloch, *Gr. Gesch.* ii². 2. 134 ff.; G. De Sanctis, *Atthis²* (1912), 364 ff.; id. in *Riv. Fil.* 1924, 1930, 1937; L. I. Highby, *The Erythrae Decree* (1936), 45 ff., 81 ff.; H. T. Wade-Gery, *BSA* xxxvii. 263. P. T.

THEMISTOGENES of Syracuse, quoted by Xenophon (*Hell.* 3. 1. 2) as the author of an *Anabasis* of Cyrus. Suidas' vague notice accepts this statement, but it is unlikely that there was a third account of the expedition in addition to those of Xenophon and Sophaenetus. Themistogenes was probably the pseudonym under which Xenophon published his *Anabasis*.

FGrH ii. 108; *FHG* ii. 74. G. L. B.

THEOCRITUS, of Syracuse, son of Praxagoras and Philina. The alternative tradition that T. was a Coan is to be rejected. Arg. c, *Id.* IV puts T.'s *floruit* at 284–280 B.C., but the evidence of the poems suggests this is at least ten years too early. XVI is dated *c.* 276–275 by its references to Hieron and was written in Sicily. It is probably the earliest extant poem. Soon after 276–275 T. went to Cos (Arg. b, *Id.* VII) and joined Philetas' circle. But his stay there cannot have been long, since XV and XVII (both composed in Egypt) were written before June 270 (death of Arsinoë), cf. 15. 24, 109 ff.; 17. 128 ff., where reference is made to the queen as still alive. Later T. seems to have left Alexandria and returned to Cos or at any rate the Eastern Aegean. His life may have covered *c.* 310–250. The dating of the poems, apart from those mentioned above, is very controversial.

2. XI and XIII are addressed to Nicias, a doctor (Arg. c, *Id.* XI makes him a schoolfellow of the famous Erasistratus), who also wrote verse. T. apparently made his acquaintance on his first visit to Cos, and XI at any rate was probably composed then. Later Nicias married Theugenis and practised at Miletus. T. visited his friends there (XXVIII; *Ep.* 8), but this was after his stay in Egypt, since XXVIII goes naturally with the other Aeolica, XXIX, XXX, XXXI (*PAntin.* p. 59) and in XXIX T. describes himself as growing old. XVIII, which has echoes of Sappho, may belong to the same period, as also may XII. In Egypt T. composed XV, XVII, probably the lost *Berenice* (Ath. 7. 284 a), and possibly the Hymns XXII and XXIV (cf. now *PAntin.* p. 55), as also the epyllion XIII, despite the dedication to Nicias. XIV seems post-Egyptian, as does II. The scene of both is perhaps Rhodes. Of the remaining pieces VIII is possibly and IX certainly not by T. IV and V, if not composed while T. was still in the West, belong to the first stay in Cos. VII must have been written in Cos, but probably after the Egyptian visit, cf. 45–8 (T. sides with Callimachus in the literary controversy), 93 (? an allusion to Philadelphus' patronage). I, III, VI, and X were probably written in Cos, VI and X perhaps before, I and III after, the stay in Alexandria. The dating of the Epigrams is uncertain. *Ep.* 18, apparently intended for a statue of Epicharmus in Syracuse, may have been written there: others (17, 19, 21–2) were probably composed in the East.

3. So far as any conclusions are possible, T.'s poetic development seems as follows. His first poem (XVI)

adapts to hexameters themes made familiar by the classical Lyric Poets. One of these, Stesichorus, may have introduced him to Daphnis, the hero of Greek Bucolic. But it is in Cos that T. becomes a pastoralist, influenced by Philetas and his associates, but also reacting against them. In Egypt XVII shows him as a formal panegyrist, but in XV he adapts a Mime of Sophron to compliment the Court and continues this experiment in XIV and II, the latter poem, which has no ulterior purpose, marking his highest achievement in pure art. XIII, XXII, and XXIV are tributes to the Alexandrian fashion, but the Bucolic interest survives and I and VII show it enriched by the new contacts. Finally, as he grows older, T. takes up the Lesbian poets and produces the Aeolica and kindred pieces.

4. Of the other poems included in the Bucolic Corpus only XXI, XXV, and XXVI have any claim to be by T., and the claim can scarcely be admitted even in the case of XXV, a poem of considerable merit. Various other works ascribed to T. by Suidas, e.g. *Proetides*, *Elpides*, *Epikedeia*, *Elegies*, *Iambi*, are now lost.

5. Theocritus was an accomplished craftsman who succeeded in nearly every *genre* that he chose to handle. Modern scholarship has emphasized the element of parody, *pastiche*, and topical allusion in nearly all the Bucolics. The criticism is just, though disguised references to individuals are unproved except for VII, but, while T. was led to Pastoral by literary influences and remained subject to those influences all his life, his combination of realism and romanticism in this sphere is what gives his verse its unique charm. In his manipulation of the hexameter T. eschews the refinements of Callimachus, but varies the metrical form according to the subject, sometimes even in the same poem—compare XV, 1–99 with 100–44. The literary Doric which he uses for most of his pieces probably came naturally to him, but the employment in other poems of the Epic, Ionic, and Aeolic dialects, if not equally successful, at least shows an adaptability only surpassed by Callimachus. *See also* PASTORAL POETRY, GREEK, *and* EPYLLION.

TEXTS: U. von Wilamowitz-Moellendorff, *Bucolici Graeci²* (1910); Ph. Legrand, *Bucoliques grecs* (1925–7); J. M. Edmonds, *The Greek Bucolic Poets* (Loeb, 1912); R. J. Cholmeley, *The Idylls of Theocritus²* (1919); A. S. Hunt and J. Johnson, *Two Theocritus Papyri* (1930); C. Wendel, *Scholia in Theocritum Vetera* (1914).

GENERAL LITERATURE: von Blumenthal, 'Theokritos (1)', in *PW*, Zweite Reihe X, 2001–25; Ph. Legrand, *Étude sur Théocrite* (1898); U. von Wilamowitz-Moellendorff, *Die Textgeschichte der Griechischen Bukoliker* (1906).   E. A. B.

THEODAISIA, see THEOXENIA.

THEODECTES (c. 375–334 B.C.), born at Phaselis (in Lycia), probably lived mainly at Athens, where he studied under Plato, Isocrates, and Aristotle and won fame as an orator (Cicero, *Orat.* 5. 1, praises his polished style), a writer on rhetorical subjects, and a composer of popular riddles in verse. As a tragic poet he composed 50 plays and in 13 competitions won 8 victories (Suidas, s.v.), of which 7 were at the Great Dionysia (*IG²* ii. 2325). He died at the age of 41 and was buried on the way to Eleusis([Plut.] *X Orat.* 837 d, Steph. Byz. s.v. Φασηλίς); his monument at Phaselis was honoured by Alexander the Great, his fellow student under Aristotle (Plut. *Alex.* 17). His plays included a *Lynceus* (the crisis of which is praised by Aristotle, *Poet.* 11), a *Mausolus* (in honour of the late king of Caria, but the treatment is unknown), and a *Philoctetes* (Aristotle, *Eth. Nic.* 7. 8, refers to the hero's brave resistance to pain; his hand, not, as in Sophocles, his foot, had been bitten by the serpent). The fragments consist mainly of rather commonplace but well-expressed reflections, and suggest that the poet was in the Euripidean tradition (*TGF* 801–7).   A. W. P.-C.

THEODOREANS (*Theodorei*), followers of Theodorus (q.v.) from Gadara, who taught Tiberius rhetoric ('Tiberius ipse Theodoreus', Sen. *Suas.* 3. 7; Suet. *Tib.* 57; Quint. *Inst.* 2. 11. 2; 3. 1. 17–18; 3. 11. 26; 4. 2. 32). Their τέχνη represented a broader Attic school than that of the Apollodoreans (q.v.).

Piderit, *De Apoll. Pergameno et Theod. Gadarensi rhetoribus*, diss. Marb., 1842; *PIR¹*, T 119.   J. W. D.

THEODORIDAS (second half of 3rd c. B.C.), Syracusan poet, wrote poems against his contemporaries in the form of sepulchral epigrams, against Mnasalces (*Anth. Pal.* 13. 21), and Euphorion (ibid. 7. 406). Also genuine epitaphs (ibid. 7. 282, 439, 527, 528) and dedications (ibid. 6. 155, 156). Also Poem to Eros (Ath. 475 f), dithyramb *The Centaur* (id. 699 e), iambic and hexameter poems (id. 229 b, 302 c), cinaedic songs (Suid., s.v. 'Sotades').

Cf. F. Susemihl, *Gesch. gr. Litt. Alex.* (1891), i. 246. 24, ii. 541 ff.   C. M. B.

THEODORUS (1), of Samos, a Greek artist of c. 550 B.C. He made a silver bowl for Croesus, and an emerald seal for Polycrates. He was said to have invented the line, rule, lathe, and lever, and to have been associated with Rhoecus in inventing, or introducing into Samos, the arts of modelling in clay and of casting images in bronze and iron. Pliny describes a bronze self-portrait by him, and includes him in his list of notable painters. Athenagoras (*Legatio*, ch. 17) says that he and Telecles made the Pythian Apollo at Samos; and Diodorus (1. 98) that they brought back the canon of proportion for the human figure from Egypt. Pausanias mentions a building called 'Scias' at Sparta, apparently an assembly hall, which was attributed to him; and Vitruvius cites a book by him on the Heraeum at Samos which (according to Herodotus) was built for Croesus by Rhoecus, and which is probably identical with the 'Labyrinth' which Pliny attributes to Theodorus himself. Diogenes Laertius (2. 103) says that he advised the inclusion of a layer of charcoal in the foundations of the Artemisium at Ephesus.

Herodotus 1. 51, 3. 41, 60; Plato, *Ion* 533 b; Vitruvius 7, *praef.*; Pliny *HN* 7. 198; 34. 83; 35. 146, 152; 36. 95; Pausanias 3. 12. 10; 9. 41. 1.   H. W. R.

THEODORUS (2) of Cyrene (b. c. 460 B.C.), mathematician, teacher of Plato and Theaetetus (Pl. *Tht.* 147 d–148 b), was originally a pupil of Protagoras but turned early to mathematics. Plato represents him as proving separately that √3, √5, and the roots of the other non-square numbers up to 17 are irrational (the irrationality of √2 being known already).

PW v A. 1811.   W. D. R.

THEODORUS (3) of Gadara (*fl.* 33 B.C.), rhetor and younger rival of Apollodorus (q.v.). He taught Tiberius at Rhodes, and his writings (lost) included works on grammar and rhetoric (Π. θέσεως, Π. ῥήτορος δυνάμεως), besides Π. ἱστορίας and Π. πολιτείας. His importance lies in the school he founded, and among his followers were the author of Π. ὕψους and Alexander, son of Numenius. The different principles upheld by the Apollodoreans and Theodoreans (Schanz, *Hermes* xxv (1890)) may be gathered from Anon. Seguerianus (Spengel, *Rhet.* i. 427 ff.), Seneca (*Controv.* 2. 1. 36), Quintilian, and Augustine. *See* RHETORIC, LATIN, para. 3; THEODOREANS.   J. W. H. A.

THEODOSIUS I and II.

(1) THEODOSIUS I, surnamed 'the Great', son of Theodosius, the general who, after recovering Britain for Valentinian I, died in unmerited disgrace, was called in by Gratian to help him repair the disaster of Adrianople (A.D. 379). Appointed Augustus of the East, Theodosius succeeded in a few years in overcoming the Gothic peril, partly by victories, partly by wise conciliation and by enlisting Goths as allies in the imperial service. The

price was a heavy one, the barbarization of the Eastern army. When Maximus in 383 rose in Britain and Gratian died near Lugdunum, Theodosius recognized the new emperor in the West. But Valentinian II still held Italy and Africa, and, when Maximus in 387–8 forced a quarrel on him and invaded Italy, Theodosius was driven to take sides, to receive the young emperor, and declare war on Maximus. Victorious at Siscia, Theodosius pursued and captured Maximus near Aquileia, and allowed rather than ordered his execution. Theodosius had two sons, Arcadius, already made Augustus in 383, and the younger Honorius, also destined to Empire. Valentinian, nominally restored to power, was actually under the tutelage of Theodosius; he resided in Gaul until his murder in 392, when the patrician, Eugenius, was set up by the Franks as puppet-emperor in his place. Again Theodosius was forced to interfere. Invading Italy in 393, he won the decisive battle of the Frigidus. Honorius was created Augustus in Rome, and the general Stilicho was prepared for the post of guardian to the two young princes. Soon afterwards, in 395, Theodosius died.

Theodosius won the title of the 'Great' by his settlement of the Gothic problem and by an able administration, which maintained peace with little interruption in the East and restored imperial unity, after two civil wars, in the West. A strict Athanasian, he was the first emperor to impose orthodoxy throughout his dominion and to break down the lingering resistance of paganism, especially in its stronghold of Rome. His submission to the penance demanded by St. Ambrose of Milan in 390 for the massacre of Thessalonica is famous.

(2) THEODOSIUS II, son of Arcadius, was created Augustus in 402, while still a child, and succeeded his father in 408. For long years he was under tutelage, first of the prefect Anthemius, 408–14, then of his own sister, Pulcheria, who was made Augusta in 414. Eudoxia, whom he married in 421, also played a leading part in politics. Peace in the East was interrupted only by two short Persian wars, but the Balkans were threatened by Ostro-Goths, and soon after 440, by Attila and his Huns, and a policy of diplomacy and subsidies was used to compensate for military weakness. In the West, on the death of Honorius Valentinian III and his mother, Galla Placidia, were restored in 423, after the brief usurpation of Johannes. Valentinian married Eudoxia, daughter of Theodosius, and remained under Eastern influence. An expedition against the Vandals in Africa in 431 was unsuccessful. The publication of the Codex Theodosianus in 438 was the one great achievement of a long reign (408–50), lacking in immediate distinction, but important in the orderly development of the great Byzantine Empire.

Camb. Med. Hist. i; J. B. Bury, *Hist. of later Roman Emp.*[2] (1923).
H. M.

THEODOSIUS (3) of Bithynia (probably between 150 and 70 B.C.), mathematician and astronomer, mentioned by Strabo, is probably to be identified with Theodosius the inventor of a sun-dial for use in any locality, mentioned by Vitruvius, and with an author Theodosius mentioned by Suidas. Works: extant (1) Σφαιρικά, the oldest extant Greek work on sections of the sphere, a compilation of earlier discoveries, (2) Περὶ οἰκήσεων (astronomical tables for different parts of the earth), (3) Περὶ ἡμερῶν καὶ νυκτῶν; lost (1) Ὑπόμνημα εἰς τὸ Ἀρχιμήδους ἐφόδιον; (2) Ἀστρολογικά; (3) Διαγραφαὶ οἰκιῶν.

PW v A. 1930. *Sphaerica*, ed. J. L. Heiberg, 1927.　W. D. R.

THEODOTUS, *see* JEWISH GREEK LITERATURE.

THEOGNETUS, one of the later poets of the New Comedy. Fr. 1 ridicules excessive preoccupation with philosophy, fr. 2 mentions Pantaleon, whom Chrysippus describes as ὁ πλάνος.

FCG iv. 549 f.; *CAF* iii. 364 f.

THEOGNIS (1) (*fl.* 544–541 B.C.; Suidas, s.v. Θέογνις), elegiac poet, of Megara. Some 1389 lines survive in good manuscripts under his name, and there is much dispute about their authenticity. The chief difficulties are: (1) among these lines are passages written by other poets, or only slightly altered from them, notably Mimnermus (795–6, 1020–2), Tyrtaeus (935–8, 1003–6), Solon (227–32, 315–18, 585–90, 1253–4), Euenus (465–96 and possibly 667–82, 1345–50). These are not cases of the practice of 'paradiorthosis', by which a line was taken and slightly altered in a different sense, as in most cases they are either unaltered or altered in some quite trivial way. (2) In the text of Theognis there are repetitions, which look like variations of the same theme, and it is hard to believe that both sets were written by the same man. (3) There are chronological difficulties. 894 refers to the Cypselids, who disappear from history c. 580 B.C., while 773–82 is a prayer to Apollo to keep the Medes away from Megara and cannot be earlier than 490 B.C. (4) the existing text does not agree with either of the two books mentioned by Suidas, the *Maxims* in 2,800 verses and the *Gnomology to Cyrnus*. It seems therefore probable that the original work of Theognis has been supplemented, especially as we find many variations on a given theme, which suggest that the book is a collection of σκόλια intended for the use of singers who had to cap one song with another on a similar subject. A clue for detecting the authentic Theognis ought to lie in 19–23, where the poet speaks of a 'seal' on his work which cannot be stolen or replaced by a substitute, but there is no agreement on what this seal is. It has been thought to be the excellence of the work, the name 'Theognis' in 22, the name Cyrnus, which appears in many poems. If the last is right we may perhaps have a means for restoring at least the *Gnomology to Cyrnus* which Suidas mentions. Otherwise the problem seems insoluble. The poems to Cyrnus show marked individuality. Their poet has a strong aristocratic bias, is very frank about his emotions, uses bold and vivid metaphors, went into exile (1197–2000), believed in traditional tenets of Greek morality, and was not without some worldly wisdom. The whole collection agrees with this section in its political temper, and we may conjecture that it was popular, if not composed, in aristocratic circles in Athens in the fifth century. The separate poems are sympotic elegies, and the book may have been a song-book used by those who did not wish to improvise when called on for a song over the wine. Book II, which consists of love-poems, seems to be Athenian, and the whole collection begins with four introductory pieces whose themes recall those of Attic σκόλια. But otherwise it is hard to mark breaks in the collection, though some regard the promise of immortality to Cyrnus, 237–54, as the end of one section and 753–6 as the end of another. The section 1–254 is much more quoted by fourth-century writers than the rest of the book, and may perhaps have had a separate circulation. The whole collection is interesting as being the poetry of a small class with clear ideas about morals and politics and a strong interest in personal relations. Reference in it to Simonides (469, 667, 1349) and to Onomacritus (503) may be to the familiar bearers of these names.

BIBLIOGRAPHY

Text: E. Diehl, *Anth. Lyr. Graec.* i. 2, pp. 1–87. Commentary: T. Hudson-Williams, *The Elegies of Theognis* (1910). Criticism: E. Harrison, *Studies in Theognis* (1902); T. W. Allen, *Theognis* (1934); F. Jacoby, *Theognis* (Sitz. d. Preussischen Akademie d. Wissenschaften 1931); J. Kroll, *Theognis-interpretationen* (1936); C. M. Bowra, *Early Greek Elegists* (1938), cap. 5.　C. M. B.

THEOGNIS (2), a tragic poet spoken of contemptuously by Aristophanes (*Ach.* 11, 140; *Thesm.* 170) as one who ψυχρὸς ὢν ψυχρῶς ποιεῖ. He is identified by some with the Theognis who was one of the Thirty Tyrants. If so, he resembled Critias in combining 'tyranny' with poetry.
A. W. P.-C.

THEOGONIA, (1) *see* EPIC CYCLE, (2) *see* HESIOD.

THEOI PATROOI, PATRIOI: DI PATRII (θεοὶ πατρῷοι, πάτριοι).

Of the two adjectives, the former means *connected with a father*, or *fathers*, as οὐσία πατρῴα, an estate inherited from one's father; the latter, in dialects (such as Attic) which use both, is vaguer, meaning *ancestral, time-honoured, traditional*. Applied to gods, the former has therefore the more intimate meaning; a θεὸς πατρῷος is at least the god whom the speaker's father, or his ancestors generally, worshipped, while a πάτριος θεός may be merely one whom it is customary to worship in his community, or in the Greek world generally.

The narrowest and most exact meaning of πατρῷος θεός is a god from whom descent is claimed. Aesch. fr. 162 Nauck may serve as an example:

οἱ θεῶν ἀγχίσποροι
οἱ Ζηνὸς ἐγγύς, ὧν κατ' Ἰδαῖον πάγον
Διὸς πατρῴου βωμός ἐστ' ἐν αἰθέρι,
κοὔπω σφιν ἐξίτηλον αἷμα δαιμόνων.

'Those near akin to the gods, close to Zeus, whose altar of Zeus Patroos lies on Ida's heaven-kissing slope, in whose veins the blood of the deities is yet fresh.' The exact context is unknown, but clearly the poet is speaking of heroes who are but a generation or two from their ancestor Zeus. It is in this sense that Athenians worshipped Apollo Patroos. Every candidate for the archonship was tested, and one of the questions put was whether he had a cult of Zeus Herkeios and Apollo Patroos. The former question was meant to ensure that he belonged to a respectable family, having its own proper domestic cult; the latter, to make it clear that he was, what all Athenians claimed to be, a good Ionian, since Ion (q.v.) is son of Apollo and ancestor of the Ionian stock. See Arist. *Ath. Pol.* 55. 3. Another not uncommon use of πατρῷος is in such a context as Ar. *Nub.* 1468 (paratragic), καταιδέσθητι π. Δία. Here Zeus is named by a father appealing to his son's sense of duty. He is evidently the god who cares for fathers and their rights. When Orestes (Eur. *El.* 671) says ὦ Ζεῦ πατρῷε καὶ τρόπαι' ἐχθρῶν ἐμῶν, he may very well be combining the two senses, for Zeus is his ancestor (*see* TANTALUS) and he wants his help to revenge the murder of Agamemnon.

But that πατρῷος cannot always have this sense is clear from the fact that it is used as a title of Artemis at Sicyon (Paus. 2. 9. 6), where her rude and archaic image testified the antiquity of her cult, but clearly, being virgin, she was not an ancestress. Again, the epithet is applied to Hestia, *IG* xiv. 980 (from Rome), and certainly Hestia is uniformly virgin; the dedicator perhaps meant to differentiate her from the Roman Vesta (q.v.). In much the same manner, other inscriptions in the same collection (nos. 971, 962, 972) apply the title to the Palmyrene gods and the (Thracian?) Ares. This is in contrast, on the one hand with πατρῷος applied to the obscure Eumelos as ancestor-god of the Eumelidae (ibid. 715), on the other hand with the use, not of πατρῷος but of πάτριος of Aeneas in an inscription from Ilium, *CIG* 3606, where the dedicators might certainly claim him as an ancestor. A long list of examples will be found in Roscher's *Lexikon* iii. 1688–9, of gods of all sorts, from (probably) actual ancestors thought of as deified to ordinary gods traditionally worshipped by the persons in question, who seem to be called quite indifferently πατρῷοι or πάτριοι, with one or two instances of θεοὶ μητρῷοι, whether deified maternal ancestors or gods worshipped in the household of the dedicator's mother.

In Rome, *di patrii* manifestly cannot have the narrower sense of θεοὶ πατρῷοι, at least in official cult, since no Roman god was officially an ancestor; the theories, e.g., about the identity of Romulus and Quirinus (qq.v.) had no effect on the State cult of the latter. A good example of its use is in Verg. *G.* 1. 498, 'di patrii Indigetes et Romule Vestaque mater'. The expression is ambiguous, but either he calls the Indigetes, Quirinus and Vesta, all *patrii*, or he uses that epithet of the first of these only; the former is the more likely. Since no one, even mythologically, seems to have claimed the Indigetes (q.v.) for ancestors, and certainly no one laid such a claim to Vesta, the sense 'worshipped by our fathers, ancestral' is perfectly clear. Nor does it mean only those gods to whom the epithet *pater* (or *mater*) is applied, for while such titles are known for Quirinus and Vesta, no such collocation as *Indigetes patres* is to be found. There is, however, a somewhat specialized sense in which the word is used; it applies above all to the Penates. In this sense *paternus* is once or twice employed; the evicted tenant in Horace, *Carm.* 2. 18. 26 goes his way 'paternos (πατρῷους) in sinu ferens deos'. These would be his *di penates*, represented by images or other symbols, which he piously takes away as Anchises did his in leaving Troy (Verg. *Aen.* 2. 717), though here they are called *patrii*, appropriately, for they are not merely the gods of the individual house but the future objects of national Roman worship, the *Penates publici*, which are not venerated because they formed part of anyone's *sacra domestica*, but because they had been adored by Rome and the States supposedly her ancestors from time immemorial, cf. PENATES. Examples of this use are: Cicero, *Har.* 37, 'patrii penatesque di'; *Dom.* 144; cf. Dion. Hal. *Antiquit.* 1. 67. 3, some say *di penates* means Πατρῷοι (θεοί).

Roscher's *Lexikon*, arts. 'Patrii di' (J. Ilberg), 'Patrioi theoi', 'Patroa' (Höfer), 'Patrooi theoi' (Ilberg). H. J. R.

THEOLOGUMENA ARITHMETICAE. This work has been thought to be by Iamblichus, because Iamblichus apparently wrote about the properties of the Monad. But it does not bear the name of Iamblichus in the manuscripts, and is merely a compilation from Anatolius and Nicomachus.

Ed. V. de Falco (1922). W. D. R.

THEON (1) of Alexandria (1st c. A.D.), son of Artemidorus of Tarsus, and successor of Apion (q.v.) at Alexandria. He wrote, *inter alia*, alphabetical lexica of Tragedy and Comedy, probably based (mainly) on the unalphabetical collections of Didymus; commentaries on the chief Alexandrian poets (completing his father's unfinished work on Callimachus); and one of the first treatises on Greek syntax.

C. Giese, *De Theone eiusque reliquiis* (1867). P. B. R. F.

THEON (2) of Smyrna (*fl. c.* A.D. 115–40), Platonist, author of an extant work Τὰ κατὰ τὸ μαθηματικὸν χρήσιμα εἰς τὴν Πλάτωνος ἀνάγνωσιν, and of a lost commentary on the *Republic* and a lost work on the order of Plato's writings. The extant book is an elementary work on arithmetic (especially on the types of numbers), the theory of musical harmony, and astronomy.

Ed. E. Hiller (1878). *PW* v A. 2067. W. D. R.

THEON (3), AELIUS, of Alexandria (2nd c. A.D.), rhetor, wrote commentaries on Xenophon, Isocrates, and Demosthenes, also a Τέχνη and Ζητήματα περὶ συντάξεως λόγου (lost). His Προγυμνάσματα (Spengel, *Rhet.* ii. 59) is a manual of some merit, which rivalled in popularity the work of Hermogenes. J. W. H. A.

THEOPHANES of Mytilene, the historian of Pompey, after a pro-Roman part in home politics, accompanied P. in the Third Mithridatic War, and, receiving Roman citizenship, fought in the Civil War. His work appears to have treated only P.'s campaigns, which he compared to those of Alexander, and was written probably in 63/2 B.C. to further P.'s cause in Rome.

FGrH ii, B, p. 919; BD, p. 614: R. Laqueur, *PW* v. 2090.
A. H. McD.

THEOPHILUS, Middle Comedy poet, late in the period: he won a victory in 330/329 B.C. Eight or nine titles survive (two of them mythological burlesques, the rest from daily life). Fr. 1, the mutual devotion of master and slave.

FCG iii. 626 ff.; *CAF* ii. 473 ff.   W. G. W.

THEOPHORIC NAMES, *see* NAMES, THEOPHORIC.

THEOPHRASTUS (372/369–288/285 B.C.; Apollod. ap. Diog. Laert. 5. 36; 40; 58), Peripatetic philosopher. He was born at Eresus in Lesbos, his father being the wealthy fuller Melantas (Athenod. ap. D.L. 5. 36). When he came to Athens he is said to have attended Plato's lectures (D.L. l.c.). Probably during Aristotle's stay in Assos and Mitylene T. joined him (see Jaeger, *Aristotle*, Engl. transl., 115. 1), and became his most faithful pupil. When Aristotle left Athens in 323/322 T. took over the presidentship of the school (Apollod. l.c.). The Peripatos had the greatest external development under this famous scholar and writer. Important and productive pupils worked under him. Up to 2,000 students are said to have attended his lectures (D.L. 37). He had connexions with such powerful princes as Cassander and Ptolemy (l.c.). As a pupil of Aristotle he was subject to political attacks in Athens (l.c.). His pupil Demetrius of Phalerum enabled him to purchase an estate for the school, which aliens actually were not entitled to do (D.L. 39; 52). His testament proves him a wealthy and careful man (D.L. 51 f.).

WORKS

Preserved: *Enquiry into plants* (Περὶ φυτῶν ἱστορίας) in nine books and *Aetiology of plants* (Περὶ φυτῶν αἰτιῶν) in six books, the first a classification and description, the latter a physiology, of plants. In these great works T. used the biological principles of Aristotle to build up for the first time a system of botany.

The *Characters* (Χαρακτῆρες), a collection of thirty short pictures of typical characters, such as the loquacious, the mean, etc. His descriptions are rich in delightful features. The idea of the work can be traced back to the typology of human characters Aristotle gives in the *Ethics*.

'From the Metaphysics' (Θεοφράστου τῶν μετὰ τὰ φυσικά), a short collection of problems in which difficulties are discussed arising out of the Aristotelian metaphysics.

There are several little scientific treatises dealing with mineralogical, meteorological, and physiological subjects: *On stones, On fire, On winds, On weather signs, On odours, On weariness, On swooning, On sweat, On paralysis.*

The treatise *On sense-perception* (Περὶ αἰσθήσεως καὶ αἰσθητῶν) is part of the great work on the history of Physics (Φυσικῶν δόξαι, including Metaphysics; see PHILOSOPHY, HISTORY OF). Another historical work was his big collection of laws in 24 books which is almost entirely lost.

Other examples of the lost part of T.'s enormous work may be gathered from the bibliography. Lists of his writings are to be found in Diogenes Laertius (5. 42 f., cf. Usener, *Analecta Theophrastea*, 1858). T. as an original philosopher cannot be compared with Aristotle or even with Zeno or Epicurus. His critical but at the same time susceptible and refined mind was captured by Aristotle at a time when the new basis the master had laid required application, development, enlargement, and criticism. This task T., more a scholar than a philosopher, fulfilled with productive and masterly skill. His power of work was fabulous. He wrote standard works in Botany and History of Philosophy. He carried on Aristotelian ideas in Logic, Rhetoric, Poetics, Ethics, Politics, and Science, so that his works together with the

Aristotelian dialogues represented the Peripatetic school throughout the Hellenistic age.

BIBLIOGRAPHY

LIFE AND WORKS: Diogenes Laertius 5; C. A. Brandis, *Handbuch der Geschichte der . . . Philos.* iii. 1. 250 f.; E. Zeller, *Aristotle*, etc., Engl. transl., 2. 348 f.; T. Gomperz, *Greek Thinkers*, Engl. transl., 4. 461 f.; Ueberweg–Praechter, *Grundriss*[12], 401 f.; O. Regenbogen in *PW*, Suppl. vol. vii, s.v. 'Theophrastos'.
TEXTS (selection): Schneider (5 vols., 1818 f.); F. Wimmer in Teubner series (3 vols., 1854–62, or (with Lat. transl.) Paris, 1866 (insufficient)). *Char.*: H. Diels (Oxford, 1909); *De igne*: A. Gercke (1896); *Metaph.*: H. Usener (1890).
WITH COMMENTARY OR TRANSLATION: *Hist. pl.*: Loeb (together with *On odours*; *On weather signs*). *Caus. pl.*: R. E. Dengler, book 1, Thesis Philadelphia, 1927. *Char.*: R. C. Jebb and J. E. Sandys (1909); J. M. Edmonds and G. E. V. Austen (1904); Budé; Loeb. *Metaph.*: W. D. Ross and F. H. Fobes (1929). Περὶ αἰσθ.: G. M. Stratton (U.S.A. 1917).
STUDIES ON PRESERVED AND LOST WORKS (SELECTION): O. Regenbogen, art. 'Theophrastos', *PW*, Suppl. vol. vii. *Botany*: H. Bretzl, *Botanische Forschungen des Alexanderzuges* (1903); L. Hindenlang, *Sprachliche Unters. zu T. bot. Schriften* (Diss. philol. Argentor. vol. 14); G. Senn, *Die Entwick. d. biolog. Forschungsmethode in der Antike*, etc. (1933); O. Regenbogen, *Hermes* (1934); R. Strömberg, *Theophrastea*, Thesis Göteborg 1937. *Psychology*: L. Philippson, Ὕλη ἀνθρωπίνη ii (1831). Φυσικῶν δόξαι: H. Diels, *Dox. Graec.* (1879); G. Bergsträsser, *Sitz. Akad. Heidelberg* 1918; E. Reitzenstein, 'T. und Epikur' (*Orient und Antike* 1924). *Laws*: H. Usener, *Kleine Schriften* i. 114 f. *Ethics*: F. Dirlmeier, *Die Oikeiosis-Lehre T.'* (1937). Περὶ γάμου: E. Bickel, *Diatribe in Senecae philosophi fragm.* i(1915). Π. εὐσεβείας: J. Bernays, *T.' Schrift üb. Frömmigkeit* (1866). Π. φιλίας: G. Heylbut, *De T. libris π. φιλ.*, Thesis Bonn, 1876. *Rhetoric*: J. Stroux, *De T. virtutibus dicendi* (1912). *Logic*: K. Prantl, *Gesch. der Logik* i. *Literary criticism*: A. Rostagni, *Stud. Ital.* 1922. T., Stoa, and Epicurus: see Φυσικῶν δόξαι, and E. Bignone, *L'Aristotele perduto*, etc. (1936), Index, s.v., and Dirlmeier (see above).   K. O. B.

THEOPOMPUS (1), a king of Sparta and leader in the First Messenian War (Tyrtaeus fr. 3; *see* MESSENIA). He was credited by fourth-century writers with two constitutional reforms—the subjection of resolutions by the Apella to a veto by the kings and Gerousia, and the institution of the ephorate. It is probable that the ephorate was of earlier origin (*see* EPHORS), but that it obtained its wide executive powers under Theopompus.   M. C.

THEOPOMPUS (2), Athenian writer of comedy; dramatic activity c. 410–370 B.C. Suidas lists 24 plays, including mythological burlesques (e.g. Ἄδμητος; Πηνελόπη), 'political' plays (e.g. Εἰρήνη; Μῆδος), and comedies of manners (e.g. Βατύλη ('The Dwarf'); Καπηλίδες).

FCG ii. 792 ff.; *CAF* i. 733 ff.; Demiańczuk, *Suppl. Com.* 86 f.   M. P.

THEOPOMPUS (3) of Chios (b. c. 378 B.C.), historian, banished with his father Damasistratus c. 334 for Spartan sympathies and restored by Alexander as a supporter against the pro-Persian oligarchy. On the latter's death he fled to Egypt.

Theopompus, a contemporary of Ephorus, was a pupil of Isocrates and adopted his view of history as the handmaid of politics. Little remains of numerous writings except fragments from the two works on which his fame rests, the *Hellenica* (Ἑλληνικαὶ ἱστορίαι) and *Philippica* (Φιλιππικά). The former, a continuation of Thucydides from 411, reached the battle of Cnidos, 394, in 12 books, and took the supremacy of Sparta as its main theme. Our knowledge of the *Hellenica* is meagre unless we accept R. Laqueur's recent arguments (*PW*, s.v. 'Theopompus') for the identification of the author of the Oxyrhynchus *Hellenica* (see OXYRHYNCHUS, THE HISTORIAN FROM) with Theopompus. These arguments rest on style, methods, and the evidence of personal views and research embodied in the papyrus agreeing with characteristics of T.

Theopompus was able to view events in Greece from a detached standpoint, as is shown by his choice of Philip of Macedon as the connecting theme of the 58 books of *Philippica*. Beginning with Philip's accession, this prolific work was a world history depicted in a series of extensive digressions. Certain of these acquired separate titles (*Τὰ θαυμασία, Περὶ δημαγωγῶν*, etc.). T. was remarkable for wide and critical research and for the harshness of his verdicts. *See also* HISTORIOGRAPHY, GREEK, para. 4.

FHG i. 278; iv. 643; FGrH. ii. 115; E. Meyer, *Theopomps Hellenika* (1909); *Hellenica Oxyrhynchia* (O.C.T.).   G. L. B.

THEORIKA, State allowances made to the poorer citizens of Athens to enable them to visit the theatres, introduced, it is said, by Pericles. Two obols were paid per head at each performance to all persons registered for the purpose on the roll of citizens. Later, allowances were paid on other occasions also. In the fourth century B.C. a regulation was made that all surpluses of the State should be used for *theorika* (except during war-time, as an enactment of Demosthenes provided). Another law of the same period punished with death anyone suggesting the use of these funds for army purposes during times of peace. The administrators of the *theorika*, οἱ ἐπὶ τὸ θεωρικόν, were elective magistrates who had considerable, and during the time of Eubulus (q.v.) even a controlling, power over financial administration.

The term occurs in Roman Egypt, too, where it seems to mean funds for religious local festivals, which had to be supplied by taxation.

A. M. Andreades, *A History of Greek Public Finance* (U.S.A. 1933), Index, s.v. 'Theorikon'; G. Busolt-H. Swoboda, *Griechische Staatskunde* i, ii (1920–6), Index, s.v.; W. Schwahn, in *PW*, s.v. 'Theorikon'.   F. M. H.

THEOROI (θεωροί), 'observers', a word originally applied to sight-seeing travellers and to the attendants at festivals of distant cities. It became an official title given to a city's representatives at another city's festival. The great panhellenic festivals were attended by theoric delegations (θεωρίαι) from every Greek State. Cities to which *theoroi* regularly came assigned the duty of receiving them to official *theorodokoi* (θεωροδόκοι). At the festivals the *theoroi* offered sacrifices in the name of their cities, and so the title was likewise given to the envoys that a city sent to a distant shrine to offer sacrifice in its name and to the envoys that it sent to consult a distant oracle. The envoys that were sent round to announce the coming celebration of a festival and, after the creation of new panhellenic agonistic festivals in the third century B.C. and later, to announce the new games to all the Greek States were also called *theoroi*. It thus became the accepted title of all sacred envoys. The religious functions of *theoroi* eventually obscured the original purpose of their office, and as early as Thucydides several cities gave the title to annually elected religious magistrates. At Thasos the *theoroi* were eponymous magistrates.

F. Poland, *De legationibus Graecorum publicis* (Leipzig, 1885); C. P. Bill, *TAPA* xxxii (1901), 196–204; P. Boesch, *Θεωρός* (1908); A. Boethius, *Die Pythais* (Uppsala, 1918).   J. E. F.

THEOS (θεός) denotes a god, especially one of the great gods, from his anthropomorphic aspect; from the aspect of power he is also called δαίμων (*see* DAIMON). When there is no room for doubt, θεός often takes the place of the proper noun: thus ἡ θεός is at Athens Athena. There is no reason for assuming anonymous gods. At Eleusis τὼ θεώ are Demeter and Kore, ὁ θεός and ἡ θεά Pluto and Persephone. The indefinite expressions θεός τις, θεοί alternate in Homer with δαίμων to denote some unknown divine power; in later authors τὸ θεῖον is an equivalent. This abstraction becomes finally an expression for the irrational in human life, that which cannot be explained by natural causes. No plausible etymology exists. Plato's derivation from θεῖν 'to run' (*Cratylus* 397 d), depends on his opinion that the innate power of motion of the celestial bodies is a sign of their divinity.   M. P. N.

THEOXENIA (Θεοξένια), or **THEODAISIA** (Θεοδαίσια), a Greek rite 'held on certain fixed days on the supposition that the gods in person were visiting the cities' (schol. Pind. *Ol.* 3, p. 105, 14 ff. Drachmann). The statement of Hesych., s.v., that it was 'a festival in common for all the gods', may go back to a gloss relating to a particular (unknown) example. The characteristic feature was that a god or gods were considered to be present as guests at a banquet given by their worshippers. This might apparently be a public or private ceremony; if the former, it was often an important one, hence the fairly common occurrence of a month called Theoxenios or Theodaisios. The best-known was at Delphi, in Theoxenios (March–April); for this the sixth Paean of Pindar (q.v.) was written. Here presumably Apollo (q.v.) was the chief guest of honour, but not the only one: θεῶν ξενίᾳ (Pind. op. cit. 60); for an indication that Leto was present cf. Ath. 372 a. The meal was shared by human beings, witness the setting aside, as late as Plutarch's time (*De sera* 557 f), of a portion for Pindar's descendants. Another was that in honour of the Dioscuri and Helen (qq.v.) at Acragas, Pind. *Ol.* 3; this seems to have been rather a domestic feast of the Eumenidae on a magnificent scale than a public festival proper. Several other instances are recorded; see F. Pfister in *PW*, s.v. 'Theodaisia', 'Theoxenia'.   H. J. R.

THERA, one of the Sporades, a treeless semi-circular island, forming part of the cone of an ancient volcano, and famous for its wine. According to tradition it was originally settled by Phoenicians. Later came colonists from Laconia, who built the temple to the Carnean Apollo. Owing to dissensions the older population migrated to Cyrene. The islanders took no part in the Persian wars, but, though Dorians, appear as allies of Athens in the Peloponnesian war. The island was a Ptolemaic naval base during the third and part of the second century B.C.

German archaeological excavations (1895–1902) have revealed a fine capital city, with a theatre, of Hellenistic and Roman times.

Hdt. 4. 147 ff. Cf. Bursian ii. 520 ff.; *Thera*, ed. H. von Gaertringen (1899–1902). Pfuhl, *Ath. Mitt.* xxviii. 1–288 (tombs, etc.). Dörpfeld, *Ath. Mitt.* xxix. 57–72 (theatre).   W. A. L.

THERAMENES (b. c. 455 B.C.), Athenian statesman. He was one of the principals in establishing the Four Hundred (q.v.). Four months later he was active in overthrowing them and establishing the Five Thousand; he is said to have prosecuted the oligarchic leaders himself. He acquiesced in the subsequent restoration of the full democracy, and assisted Alcibiades in restoring Athens' naval supremacy (*see* PELOPONNESIAN WAR). At Arginusae (406) he was ordered to help the ships wrecked after the battle; he laid the blame for the failure to rescue the crews on the *strategi*, and escaped prosecution. In 404 he was sent to negotiate peace with Sparta, and is said deliberately to have wasted three months in discussion while Athens was closely besieged. But he was sent again and brought back the final terms of peace. He was elected one of the 'Thirty Tyrants' (q.v.), but soon quarrelled with the extremists, especially Critias (q.v.), who had him condemned and executed.

His character was violently censured in antiquity, for his frequent change of sides and attacks on former friends, by some of the democrats (as Lysias) and the extreme oligarchs; some (as Aristotle) warmly defended him, as one who would serve Athens under any constitutional government. Aristophanes makes fun of his cleverness, but genially. We have now no means of judging his sincerity.   A. W. G.

THERAPNE, the site of an early sanctuary on a steep cliff on the left bank of the Eurotas, to the south-east of Sparta. On an adjacent hill-top remains of a modest Late

Helladic settlement were excavated in 1910. The massive remains of a fifth-century building (excavated by the British School at Athens in 1909) represent the altar (and temple?) of Helen, who was worshipped here, together with the Dioscuri and Menelaus. The cult of the Twins was later transferred to Sparta itself. Polybius calls the sanctuary Menelaion, Pausanias the temple of Menelaus. Votive offerings attest a cult from the early Geometric period to the fourth century B.C. A. M. W.

THERMAE, see BATHS.

THERMOPYLAE (i.e. 'Hot Gates'), so-called from its hot sulphur springs, formed an important defence line of Greece, separating Phocis from Thessaly; it followed Mt. Oeta and the Spercheius valley. There were three passes, one westward and another eastward of Anthela, where the central pass (Thermopylae proper) lay, and where the Phocians had built a wall against Thessalian attacks. Notwithstanding their narrowness, the passes could be turned, outflanking the defenders. Thus Xerxes (August 480 B.C.), Brennus (279), and M' Acilius Glabrio (191) forced Thermopylae against the resistance of, respectively, the Spartans, the Aetolians, and Antiochus III.

F. Stählin, *PW*, s.v. 'Thermopylen'; Y. Béquignon, *La Vallée du Sperchéios* (1937), 43 ff., 235 ff. P. T.

THERMUM, religious centre of Aetolia. Situated north-east of L. Trichonis on a natural rock-castle, it commanded the central plains of Aetolia and formed the meeting-place for the Aetolian League. Extensive excavation has revealed its occupation from the Bronze Age and its importance as a cult centre for the worship of Apollo Thermios, Apollo Lyseios, and Artemis; oval houses, early type of *megaron*, three temples of c. 600 B.C., and terra-cotta metopes and antefix heads revealing Corinthian influence are the most important discoveries. Its historical importance coincides with the Aetolian League, until its sack in 218 B.C. by Philip V of Macedon.

Ἀρχ. Ἐφ. 1900, 167 f.; Ἀρχ. Δελτ. 1915 and 1916; W. J. Woodhouse, *Aetolia* (1897), 252 f. N. G. L. H.

THERON, tyrant of Acragas (488–472 B.C.), father-in-law of Gelon, with whom he defeated the Carthaginians at Himera (480). His reign was distinguished by love of peace and culture. He was closely attached to Pindar and Simonides, and he made Acragas into one of the most beautiful Greek cities. In the quarrel between Gelon's brothers Hieron and Polyzelus (c. 476) he took the latter's side. But actual war between Theron and Syracuse was avoided, and Hieron betrayed to Theron the plot of the Himeraeans against his son.

Hdt. 7. 165 f. Pindar, *Ol.* 2, 3, fr. 118 f., and scholia. Diod. bk. 11. Schachermeyr, *PW*, s.v. 'Theron'. V. E.

THERSANDER (Θέρσανδρος), name of five mythological persons, for whom see Höfer in Roscher, s.v.; the one of most genealogical importance is son of Polynices and Argeia (*see* ADRASTUS), from whom Theron of Acragas claimed descent (Pindar, *Ol.* 2. 43 ff.); he was one of the Epigoni (q.v.). H. J. R.

THERSITES, in mythology, an ugly, foul-tongued fellow, who rails at Agamemnon (*Iliad* 2. 212 ff.), until beaten into silence by Odysseus. Evidently, from his description, he is of low (non-Achaean) birth; but in post-Homeric tradition (schol. *Il.* ibid.) he is of good family, son of Agrios brother of Oeneus (q.v.), therefore akin to Diomedes (q.v.). Hence, when Achilles slays him for railing at him when he mourns for Penthesilea (*Aethiopis*), a quarrel arises and Achilles goes to Lesbos to be purified. H. J. R.

THESAUROI, see TREASURIES.

THESEUS (Θησεύς), son of Aegeus (q.v.) or Poseidon, i.e., of a sea-god, and national hero of Athens. This explains his prominence in ancient, especially Attic, literature; the chief surviving continuous accounts of him, however, are Plutarch, *Theseus*, and Apollod. 3. 216 ff., continued by *Epit.* 1. His legend had manifestly been influenced by that of Heracles (q.v.; encounters with brigands and monsters; campaign against the Amazons), and it is not surprising that he is made Heracles' friend and contemporary. There is no proof that any real person lies behind the legend, but that is not impossible.

2. *Childhood and youth.* When Aegeus departed from Troezen, he left instructions with Aethra that when her son was able, he should lift a certain rock, under which Aegeus had hidden a sword and sandals. Meanwhile, the boy was educated by Pittheus, his tutor being a certain Connidas, a hero honoured in Attica the day before the Theseia (Plut. op. cit. 4). On reaching young manhood (sixteen years old, Paus. 1. 27. 8) he lifted the rock easily (Plut. 6) and determined not to sail to Athens to find his father but go the more dangerous way by land. He thus encountered Periphetes, or Corynetes, Sinis, Sciron, Procrustes, Phaea the sow of Crommyon (qq.v.), and other dangerous men and beasts; the exact numbers and names vary in different accounts. Plutarch (9) says that Theseus was eager to emulate Heracles, and in fact this is one of the most obvious places in which the latter's legend has influenced his.

3. *Attic and Cretan adventures.* Arrived in Attica, he was in danger from Medea (q.v.), who persuaded Aegeus to send him against the Marathonian bull, which in some accounts was Pasiphae's bull brought from Crete by Heracles (q.v.). On the way there, an old woman named Hecale hospitably entertained him; having killed the bull, he found her dead on his return, and ordered that her memory should be honoured (Callim., frs. of *Hecale*, p. 240 ff. Mair; Plut. 14). Coming back to Athens, he narrowly escaped an attempt of Medea to poison him (Apollod. *Epit.* 1, 5), thanks to Aegeus recognizing him in time. He now heard of the tribute yearly sent to the Minotaur (q.v.), and volunteered, or was specially chosen by Minos, to be one of the youths included in it (Plut. 17). On the voyage to Crete he proved his divine ancestry by leaping overboard and coming back safely from the palace of Amphitrite with a gold ornament which Minos had thrown in (Bacchyl. 16). In Crete he killed the Minotaur by the help of Ariadne (q.v.), who gave him a clue of thread to find his way out of the Labyrinth and afterwards fled with him. He left her at Dia (Naxos); in the original story this was probably due to some magical forgetfulness (cf. Theocr. 2. 45–6), but this detail having fallen out, various reasons were given for his ingratitude (Plut. 20). Thence he sailed to Delos, where he and his comrades danced a complicated figure, in commemoration of the Labyrinth, said to be preserved in the traditional Delian dance known as the 'crane' (Plut. 21). This may serve as an example of the numerous ceremonies, Attic and other, said in later times to commemorate some part of his adventures. For his return cf. AEGEUS.

4. *Kingship.* Theseus succeeded his father and is supposed to have brought about the συνοικισμός, or union of the various communities of Attica into one State with Athens for the capital (Plut. 24). The event is itself historical, but its age and author unknown. He took part with Heracles in the expedition against the Amazons, or went against them on his own account, and won Antiope, or Hippolyte (cf. HIPPOLYTUS) for himself; the Amazons in their turn invaded Attica, held the Areopagus against Theseus, and were finally defeated in a desperate battle. Pirithous the Lapith raided Marathon, was met by Theseus, and became his friend and ally; Theseus came to his wedding-feast and took part in the

resultant fight with the Centaurs (q.v.), and later helped Pirithous to invade the lower world in an attempt to carry off Persephone (q.v.). According to the most familiar of the many versions of this story, Theseus was ultimately rescued by Heracles from imprisonment, but Pirithous remained below. Theseus also carried off Helen (q.v.) while she was very young, and consequently Attica was invaded by the Dioscuri (q.v.).

5. *Death and posthumous honours.* Apart from the variant of his permanent detention by Hades (Verg. *Aen.* 6. 617–18, perhaps already in *Od.* 11. 631) his reign is generally said to have been ended by a rebellion (headed by Menestheus, a descendant of Erechtheus, q.v., Plut. 32), which led to his banishment; he went to Scyros and was there murdered by king Lycomedes (Plut. 35). Long after, some bones alleged to be his were brought from Scyros by Cimon (Plut. 36), and a hero-shrine built for them (not the temple now popularly called the Theseum).

6. *Contact with other legends.* Besides Heracles, Theseus is said to have been one of the helpers of Meleager (q.v.) in the boar-hunt (Plut. 29), and an Argonaut (q.v., ibid.); he brought about the burial of the bodies of the Seven against Thebes (Eur. *Suppl.*), and kindly received Oedipus (q.v., Soph. *OC*).

Steuding in Roscher's *Lexikon*, s.v. (abundant references to ancient literature and art); H. Herter in *Rh. Mus.* 85 and 88. H. J. R.

THESIS in metre, *see* METRE, GREEK, I.

THESMOPHORIA, a women's festival common to all Greeks, regularly celebrated in the autumn. In Athens it took place on the 11th–13th Pyanopsion (Oct./Nov.). The women erected bowers with couches of plants and sat on the ground. The second day was a fast. The name of the third day, Καλλιγένεια, hints at the fecundity of mankind also, but the chief purpose of the festival was to promote the fertility of the corn which just was to be sown. Pigs had been thrown down into subterranean caves (μέγαρα), probably at the Scirophoria; the putrefied remains were brought up, laid on an altar, and mixed with the seed-corn. The myth of Eubuleus, the swineherd swallowed up by the earth when Pluto carried off Kore, is an *aition* to account for this custom. *See* DEMETER.

M. P. Nilsson, *Griech. Feste*, pp. 313 ff.; J. E. Harrison, *Proleg. to the Study of Greek Religion*, 120 ff.; L. Deubner, *Attische Feste*, 50 ff. The interpretation of Demeter θεσμοφόρος as *legifera* is to be rejected. M. P. N.

THESMOTHETAI, the six junior archons at Athens (*see* ARCHONTES), sitting as a college. They were first instituted presumably (before the publication of law codes) to keep record of judicial decisions as well as to act as judges. Later their functions were purely judicial. They had charge in principle of cases in which the interests of the community as a whole were immediately concerned, and in practice of all cases not specifically within the province of other magistrates. They conducted the *dokimasia* (q.v.) of all magistrates and elections by lot; and they allotted the days for trials and the courts to the presiding magistrates. A. W. G.

THESPIAE, near the east foot of Mt. Helicon, was the chief town of south Boeotia. The Thespians, alone of Boeotians, fought in full strength at Thermopylae and Plataea. They took a prominent part in the restored Boeotian League after 446 B.C., providing two boeotarchs. The Spartans used Thespiae as a base for their anti-Theban policy after 382, and it remained important after their expulsion. It was in Roman times still one of the chief Boeotian cities (Strabo, pp. 403, 410). Visitors came to see the Eros of Praxiteles (Cic. *Verr.* 2. 4. 135), and the sanctuary and games of the Muses (*see* HELICON).

Fiehn in *PW*, s.v. 'Thespeia'. T. J. D.

THESPIS won a prize for tragedy at Athens about 534 B.C. (*Marm. Par.*). Some authorities (e.g. Suidas, s.v.) say that he came from Icaria (in Attica). He was the first to appear as an actor separate from the chorus, and speaking a prologue and set speeches (Aristotle ap. Themistium *Orat.* 26, p. 316; Diog. Laert. 3. 56), his face disguised in various ways and ultimately in a linen mask—the disguise which would most easily allow an actor to change from one character to another (Suidas, s.v.). Suidas states that he wrote plays called *The Contests of Pelias* or *Phorbas*, *The Priest*, *The Young Man*, and *Pentheus* (*TGF* 832–3), but the plays passing under his name in the fourth century B.C. were known to be forgeries (Diog. Laert. 5. 92). Horace's description of him (*Ars P.* 275 ff.) as taking his plays about on waggons, with a chorus, whose faces were stained with wine-lees, probably rests on a confusion of early tragedy with early comedy. *See also* TRAGEDY. A. W. P.-C.

THESPROTI, *see* EPIRUS.

THESSALONICA, a city of Macedonia, founded by Cassander, who synoecized the small towns at the head of the Thermaic Gulf; perhaps on the site of Therme (Strabo, fr. 24). It was named after Cassander's wife. It stood at the junction of the Morava–Vardar route from Europe with the route from the Adriatic to Byzantium (the later Via Egnatia). An open roadstead sheltered by Chalcidice, Thessalonica became the chief Macedonian port, displacing Pella when its harbour was silted up. Strongly fortified, it withstood the Roman siege, surrendered after the battle of Pydna, and became the capital of the Roman province (146 B.C.); in the Civil War it served as Pompey's base. A free State and the main station on the Via Egnatia, it enjoyed great prosperity, shown by its prolific coinage, and was made a Roman colony by Decius *c.* A.D. 250. The population included a large Roman element and a Jewish colony, visited by St. Paul, one of whose disciples, Aristarchus, became the first Bishop of Thessalonica. Second city to Constantinople in the Byzantine Empire, Thessalonica reached a height of prosperity to which the extant walls and early Byzantine churches bear witness, until it was sacked by Saracens in 904.

E. Oberhummer, *PW*, s.v. 'Thessalonika'. N. G. L. H.

THESSALUS (1) of Cos (*fl. c.* 421–411 B.C.), the more famous of Hippocrates' two sons. Galen considered him to be the author of bks. 5 and 7, and the part-author of bks. 2 and 6, of the Hippocratic work on epidemics, and thinks he may have been the author of the Κατ' ἰητρεῖον.

PW vi A. 165. W. D. R.

THESSALUS (2) of Tralles, the *Iatronikes* as he styled himself, lived in Rome and died before A.D. 79. Pliny the Elder quotes his epitaph. The new medical school to which he laid claim in a letter to Nero was that of the Methodists.

Thessalus accepted Themison's doctrine of the *communia* but did not understand them as a dogmatic conception. He rather took them to mean the morbid change visible in the patient which indicates with necessity what the physician should do: change the existing state into its opposite. In short, he interpreted the *communia* as a true sceptic would (Sext. Emp. *Pyr.* 1. 236). The degree of the necessary change he determined by considering the size of the *communia*, the locality affected, and the seasons, so that his treatment did not much differ from the usual one. Medical theory, however, was greatly simplified in this way. Thessalus' school was the only new sect seriously to compete with the older Hellenistic schools. Galen's attacks are such as one would expect from a reactionary archaist without understanding of the modernist attitude of Nero's time.

TEXT. Fragments not collected. The treatise on remedies (F. Cumont, *Rev. Phil.* 1918), probably not by Thessalus.
LITERATURE. H. Diller, *PW* vi A. 168; cf. L. Edelstein, *PW*, Suppl. vi. 358, s.v. 'Methodiker'. Medical doctrine, Th. Meyer-Steineg, *Das medizinische System d. Methodiker*, Jenaer med.-hist. Beiträge (1916); T. C. Allbutt, *Greek Medicine in Rome* (1921).
L. E.

THESSALY, a district of northern Greece. Thessaly proper, comprising the four tetrads, Thessaliotis, Hestiaeotis, Pelasgiotis, and Phthiotis (q.v. for the distinction between Thessaly and its Perioecis), consists of two large and level plains separated by hilly country. Mountain barriers impede communication by land with neighbouring areas, and the only outlet to good harbours is a low pass leading to the Gulf of Pagasae. Owing to the extent of its plains Thessaly was richer in grain, horses, and cattle than other parts of Greece, but extremes of temperature discouraged the growth of olives and vines.

After producing an important prehistoric culture Thessaly was overrun by waves of northern invaders. Most of these pressed on southwards, but the Thessali, who migrated from Thesprotia, remained and dominated the plains, reducing the conquered to serfdom or driving them into the mountains. A few baronial families gradually became supreme, and their enterprise in organizing a loosely-knit national State headed by a *tagus* (q.v.) made Thessaly a formidable power in the sixth century. The rivalries of aristocratic houses and the medism of the Aleuadae (q.v.) soon caused a decline, which was intensified during the fifth century by social unrest, as the urbanization of this backward district gradually broke down baronial domination. In the wars between Athens and Sparta the Thessalians favoured the former but rendered little assistance, and the foundation of a Spartan colony at Heraclea (q.v. 4) Trachinia illustrates their impotence.

Late in the fifth century Lycophron (q.v.) established a tyranny at Pherae, and a protracted struggle began between the Pheraean tyrants and the bulk of the Thessalians led by Larissa, where the Aleuadae had become a city aristocracy. This conflict was disastrous, since both sides enlisted external support from powers who aimed at selfish domination of a valuable district. It was only during the tyranny of Jason (q.v. 2), who revived the national State and had himself elected *tagus*, that Thessaly was united and formidable to the rest of Greece. Anarchy returned under Alexander (q.v. 5) of Pherae and his successors, and Thessaly fell an easy prey to Philip of Macedon, who adroitly turned local quarrels to his own advantage. In theory the Thessalians retained their independence, but the kings of Macedon held the archonship of the Thessalian League for life, and Thessaly remained virtually a Macedonian province. Its contingent of cavalry was invaluable to Alexander in Asia. An unsuccessful attempt was made in the Lamian War to throw off Macedonian suzerainty, and in the Hellenistic period Thessaly was often overrun by rival powers, some parts falling under Aetolian control.

In 196 Rome liberated Thessaly from Macedonian rule and established a new Thessalian League, which was maintained even after 148, when Thessaly was absorbed in the Roman province of Macedonia.

Geography and Topography: F. Stählin, *Das hellenische Thessalien* (1924). History: H. D. Westlake, *Thessaly in the Fourth Century B.C.* (1935); F. Hiller von Gaertringen, *PW*, s.v. 'Thessalia (Geschichte)'. Political and Social Development: U. Kahrstedt, *Gött. Nachr.* 1924, pp. 128–55; G. Busolt, *Griechische Staatskunde* ii (1926), 1478–1501.
H. D. W.

THESTIUS, in mythology, king of Pleuron, father of Lynceus and Idas (Argonauts and hunters of the Calydonian boar) and of Althaea, wife of Oeneus (q.v.; Ovid, *Met.* 8. 304, 446 and elsewhere).

THESTOR (Θέστωρ). Of the five persons so called (Höfer in Roscher, s.v.), the least obscure is the father of Calchas (q.v.; *Iliad* 1. 69). He has no legend, the tale in Hyginus, *Fab.* 190, being manifestly late romance.

THETES (θῆτες), in general, wage-labourers. At Athens they constituted the lowest of the four census-classes, men with property producing less than 200 *medimnoi* of corn or the equivalent in other produce or money. By the constitution of Solon (q.v.) they were made members of the Ecclesia and Heliaea; but could not hold magistracies. This limitation was never formally abrogated; but from c. 450 B.C. they were in practice admitted to all offices. Because they could not afford a suit of armour they did not serve in the hoplite ranks; but when Athens became mainly a naval power, they had the even more important duty of serving as rowers, marines, and navigation officers, for which the State provided the equipment. On land some of them served as 'light-armed' men, i.e. as a transport and labour corps. *See* PENTACOSIOMEDIMNOI, HIPPEIS, ZEUGITAI.
A. W. G.

THETIS (Θέτις), a Nereid, who was fated to bear a son mightier than his father. This being revealed by Themis to the gods, Pindar, *Isthm.* 8. 34 ff. (in Aesch. *Prom. Bound* and *Prom. Unbound* she reveals it to her son Prometheus, who discloses it as the price of his liberation; cf. PROMETHEUS), Zeus and Poseidon gave up all thoughts of possessing her, and instead gave her to Peleus (q.v.), as the most deserving of mankind. Their wedding was attended by all the gods, who brought various gifts (Pind. *Pyth.* 3. 92 ff.; Catullus 64. 31 ff., etc.). She bore one child, Achilles (q.v., *Iliad* 18. 55 ff.; Pindar, ibid. 100); Lycophron, 178, says there were seven, of whom the rest perished in the fire when she tried to make them immortal, cf. PELEUS. See further Roscher's *Lexikon*, arts. 'Peleus', 'Thetis'.
H. J. R.

THEVESTE (modern *Tebessa*), an old Berber town, at the east end of the High Plateaux, commanding the upper Ampsaga. Hanno conquered it for Carthage in the third century B.C. It became an important road-centre, linking up with Carthage, Cirta, Tacapae, and Lambaesis. The Flavians moved the legion from Ammaedara (*Haidra*) and made Theveste its permanent camp. When the legion occupied Lambaesis (probably near the beginning of Trajan's reign), Theveste became a colony.

Its strategical importance led to its refortification by the Byzantines in a manner which laid down the pattern of medieval fortifications.

R. Cagnat, *Carthage, Timgad, Tebesse²* (1909). W. N. W.

THIRTY TYRANTS (1). At the end of the Peloponnesian War (April 404 B.C.) the oligarchs at Athens already had the upper hand, Critias leading the extremists, Theramenes the moderates. Both sections joined in asking Lysander for help against the democrats; under pressure from him the Ecclesia was compelled to appoint thirty ξυγγραφεῖς to draw up a new constitution κατὰ τὰ πάτρια. The Thirty at once seized full power, constituted a new Boule under their control, and a board of Ten to rule Piraeus, abolished the dicasteries, and began the removal of obnoxious democrats and *sykophantai* (June). This developed into a reign of terror, many respectable citizens and metics being executed and their property confiscated; a Spartan garrison was stationed on the Acropolis; no new constitution was promulgated. To meet the protests of Theramenes, Critias agreed to draw up a list of 3,000 to constitute the citizen body, but he never published it, and he stifled further opposition from Theramenes by executing him. 1,500 men in all are said to have been executed; many were exiled or fled. But the Thirty failed to prevent the capture of Piraeus by a band of exiles under Thrasybulus (q.v.), and Critias was killed in a battle (Dec.–Jan. 404/3). They were now deposed by the moderate oligarchs, who constituted themselves as the 3,000, and were replaced by a board of Ten who eventually became reconciled with Thrasybulus' party, by the good offices of the Spartan king Pausanias (q.v.). The full democracy was now restored (June 403), and the remnant of the Thirty, who had retired to Eleusis, were exterminated there two or three years later.

Xenophon, *Hell.* 2. 3. 4; Aristotle, *Ath. Pol.* 34. 3–41. 1 (less trustworthy than Xenophon, especially in chronology); Diodorus 14. 3–6 (from Ephorus). Details in Lysias (esp. *Or.* 12 and 13), Andocides, and Isocrates. A. W. G.

THIRTY TYRANTS (2), the name given in the *Historia Augusta* to the swarm of pretenders that arose in the provinces about the middle of the third century A.D., mainly under Gallienus. Name and number are derived from the notorious tyrants of Athens after the Peloponnesian War. As the *Historia* (Pollio) on more than one occasion gives the number as 'twenty' instead of 'thirty', one might conjecture behind the longer list a shorter one of twenty. The order of arrangement seems to be haphazard.

In Gaul we have *Postumus*, Postumus Junior, *Lollianus* (*Laelianus*), *Marius*, *Victorinus*, Victorinus Junior, *Tetricus, Tetricus Junior*: in Illyricum, *Regilianus* (*Regalianus*), Ingenuus, Valens Superior and Aureolus: in Greece, Piso and Valens: in Isauria, Trebellianus: in Syria, Cyriades, Macrianus Senior, *Macrianus Junior*, Ballista, and *Quietus*: in Palmyra, Odaenathus, Herodes, Herennianus, Maeonius, and Timolaus: in Egypt, Aemilianus: in Africa, Celsus: uncertain place, Saturninus. Two 'female tyrants', Victoria (Gaul) and *Zenobia* (Palmyra), complete the thirty; but, to dispense with women, Titus (under Maximin I) and Censorinus (under Claudius II) are appended. The names italicized above are known from coins; of the others some, like the younger Postumus and Victorinus, are mere shadows: others, like Piso and Valens, though known to history, are very doubtfully classed as pretenders.

CAH xii. 169 ff.; Parker, *Roman World*, 167 ff. H. M.

THISBE, see PYRAMUS.

THOAS (Θόας), in mythology, (1) the father, (2) the son by Jason of Hypsipyle (q.v.).

THOMAS MAGISTER (*Theodulos*) of Thessalonica was the Secretary of Andronicus II (A.D. 1282–1328), but withdrew to a monastery, where he devoted himself to scholarship.

WORKS. (1) *Ecloga Vocum Atticarum* (Ἐκλογὴ ὀνομάτων καὶ ῥημάτων Ἀττικῶν), based especially on Phrynichus, Ammonius, Herodian, and Moeris, but with much added material that is less valuable, drawn from his own reading, e.g. in Herodotus, Thucydides, Aelius Aristides, and Synesius.

(2) Scholia, which are almost valueless, to Aeschylus, Sophocles *Aj.*, *El.*, *OT*, Euripides *Hec.*, *Or.*, *Phoen.*, Aristophanes *Plut.*, *Nub.*, *Ran.*; the Pindar scholia ascribed to him are probably the work of Triclinius. Lives of these poets appear under his name in some manuscripts.

(3) Declamations on set themes in the manner of the ancient orators, e.g. *De Regis Officiis* (Π. βασιλείας); panegyrics on famous personalities of earlier date, e.g. Gregory Naz.; eulogistic addresses to contemporaries; deliberative discourses on questions of the moment.

(4) Letters.

Ecloga, F. Ritschl (1832); J. P. Migne, *PG* cxlv (1865); T. Hopfner, *Sitz. Wien. Akad.* 1912. J. F. L.

THRACE was in historic times the eastern half of the Balkan peninsula. Originally extending to the Adriatic, the Thracians were driven back to the river Axius by Illyrian invaders c. 1300 B.C.; after 480 they lost the land west of the Strymon to the Macedonians, who also took from them the Pangaeus district c. 350. Thrace, even in the restricted sense, was not a uniform country: it included the grain and orchard lands of the Hebrus valley, the wooded massif of Mt. Haemus, and the steppe of the Dobrudja. The Thracian people spoke the same (Indo-European) tongue, but fell into some twenty independent and mutually discordant tribes, chief among them the Getae by the Danube, the Bessi on Mt. Haemus, and the Odrysae in the Hebrus valley. Each tribe was a loosely compacted monarchy, with a fighting and hunting aristocracy, and a folk engaged in tillage, lumbering, or (as among the Getae) stock-raising. The Thracians were not without a native culture. Their bronze age resembled that of Mycenaean Greece; they cultivated poetry and music; their nature deities, Dionysus (the vegetation-spirit) and Zalmoxis, were also powers of the underworld who gave men life after death. But their savage methods of fighting, their human sacrifices, their habits of tattooing and of eating butter, made them appear barbarous to the Greeks, and unlike their Macedonian neighbours they took on no more than a veneer of Greek civilization.

Greek colonists settled on the south and east coasts of Thrace after 700. In exchange for pottery, metal-ware, and wine, they obtained timber and slaves. Greek concessionaires worked the gold and silver mines of Mt. Pangaeus (which also supplied some Thracian dynasts with silver for coinage), and Greek recruiting officers (especially in the fourth century) enlisted Thracian 'peltasts' or light-armed fighters. After a period of vassalage to Persia (c. 512–479), the Thracians united under the Odrysian chiefs Teres and Sitalces (q.v.), but by 400 they had again fallen apart. In 342 the southern tribes were subdued by Philip of Macedon; these furnished Alexander with a valuable corps of light troops. From 323 to 281 most of Thrace came under Lysimachus, and henceforth the country stood open to Greek traders; but after Lysimachus' death it reverted to independence and dissension.

In the first century B.C. the Roman governors of Macedonia made occasional retaliatory raids upon marauding Thracian tribes; in 29–28 M. Crassus and c. 12 B.C. L. Piso subdued the country systematically. In A.D. 46 the Emperor Claudius, to end recurrent unrest, made southern and central Thrace into a province, and annexed the north to Moesia. Later emperors developed the road-system (centring on Byzantium), and from the time of Trajan constituted cities of Greek type. But the continuous barbarian invasions of the third and following centuries condemned Thrace to remain essentially a military province.

S. Casson, *Macedonia Thrace and Illyria* (1926), pt. 1; G. Kazarow, *CAH* viii, ch. 17; G. A. Short, *Annals of Archaeology and Anthropology* 1937, 141–55 (Greek colonies on the Black Sea); Jones, *Eastern Cities*, ch. 1; B. Lenk and A. Betz, *PW*, s.v. 'Thrake'. M. C.

THRACIAN SEA, see AEGEAN SEA.

THRASEA PAETUS, PUBLIUS CLODIUS (*cos. suff.* A.D. 56), Stoic, renowned for his uprightness and republican sympathies. He modelled himself on Cato Uticensis, of whom, utilizing Munatius Rufus, he composed a *Life* which Plutarch consulted (*Cato Min.* 25, 37). Condemned under Nero (A.D. 66), he ended his life in noble fashion (Tac. *Ann.* 14. 12, 48–9; 15. 20–22; 16. 21–35). *See also* ARRIA MINOR. G. C. W.

THRASYBULUS (d. 388 B.C.), son of Lycus, Athenian general and statesman. In 411 he was a leader of the democratic State formed by the navy at Samos in opposition to the Four Hundred. He was responsible for the recall of Alcibiades and contributed largely to the naval success of the following years.

He was banished by the Thirty and fled to Thebes where he organized a band of seventy exiles and occupied Phyle (late autumn, 404). When his followers had increased to a thousand, he seized the Piraeus and defeated the troops of the Thirty. Thanks to an amnesty proclaimed at the instance of Sparta, he led his men to Athens, and the democracy was restored. In the Corinthian War he played a prominent part, and in 389/8 he commanded a fleet which gained many allies but suffered from lack of financial support. At Aspendus his troops plundered the natives, who murdered him in his tent.

Thrasybulus clung obstinately to an imperialistic policy when Periclean ambitions were far beyond the resources of Athens. But he was long remembered as a staunch champion of democracy who nevertheless avoided the excesses of contemporary party-struggles.

Thucydides, bk. 8; Xenophon, *Hell.* bks. 1–4; Diodorus, bks. 13–14; Nepos, *Thrasybulus.* H. D. W.

THRASYLLUS of Alexandria (d. A.D. 36), astrologer. Tiberius made his acquaintance during his stay in Rhodes (6 B.C.–A.D. 2) and came to believe in him implicitly; Thrasyllus remained till his death in close contact with the Emperor. He was a man of good education and a serious student of astrology. Works: (1) a work or works on astrology, epitomized later in a Συγκεφαλαίωσις τοῦ Ἱεροκλέα Θρασύλλου πίνακος; (2) Περὶ τῶν ἔπτα τόνων. In addition he was, with Dercyllides, responsible for the division of Plato's works into tetralogies.

PW vi A. 581. W. D. R.

THRASYMACHUS of Chalcedon (*fl. c.* 430–400 B.C.), sophist and rhetorician, is best known from his defence, in the *Republic*, of the thesis that justice is the interest of the stronger. He played an important part in the development of Greek oratory, by his elaboration of the appeal to the emotions by means of elocution and 'action', and in the development of prose style by his attention to rhythm and to the building up of periods.

Testimonia and frs. in Diels, *Vorsokr.*⁵ 2. 319–26; *PW* vi A. 584. W. D. R.

THRASYMEDES (Θρασυμήδης), a son of Nestor who takes a minor part in the *Iliad* 10. 255; 16. 321 ff., and elsewhere. In the Wooden Horse, Quint. Smyrn. 12. 319.

THRENOS, *see* DIRGE.

THUBURSICU(M) NUMIDARUM (modern *Khamissa*), a market-town on the road from Hippo Regius (q.v.) to Theveste. Lying in the richly phosphated Bagradas valley, it became a prosperous centre of the agricultural life which Masinissa introduced into his territory. Its traditional loyalty to the Numidian royal house survived in Roman times in the worship of Gauda and Hiempsal. Attacked in A.D. 23 by Tacfarinas and his Garamantian allies, it was relieved by the proconsul, Dolabella. After being administered jointly by native chieftains and military prefects, it was made a municipium by Trajan, and became a colony in A.D. 270. Its extensive ruins have yielded many excellent specimens of Greek and Roman art.

S. Gsell and C. A. Joly, *Khamissa, Mdaourouch, Announa* (Paris 1922). W. N. W.

THUCYDIDES (1), Athenian statesman, son of Melesias; related by marriage to Cimon (q.v.), whom he succeeded as 'leader of the rich' in 449 B.C. He must then have been elderly, if his son was contemporary with Aristides' son (Plato, *Laches,* init.). Plato speaks of his

military activities, but he is known only as a politician. He was a bitter opponent of Pericles till his ostracism in 443 or 442. According to Plutarch he organized an oligarchic and anti-imperialist party. If so, the party disappeared after his ostracism. He later returned to Athens in his old age, and appears to have been prosecuted on some charge (Ar. *Ach.* 705 ff.). Aristotle and Plutarch vouch for his respectability and his statesmanship, as recognized by all; for the latter there is no evidence. A. W. G.

THUCYDIDES (2), author of the (incomplete) History of the War between Athens and Sparta, 431–404 B.C., in 8 books.

1. LIFE. He was born probably between 460 and 455 B.C.: he was general in 424 (4. 104) and must then have been at least 30 years old; while his claim in 5. 26. 5 that he was of years of discretion from beginning to end of the war perhaps suggests that he was not much more than grown up in 431. He probably died about 400. He shows no knowledge of fourth-century events. The revival of Athenian sea power under Conon and Thrasybulus, from 394 on, made the decision of Aegospotami less decisive than it seemed to T. (compare e.g. 5. 26. 1 with Xen. *Hell.* 5. 1. 35). Of the three writers who undertook to complete his History, only Xenophon took his view that the story ended in 404 (or 401). Theopompus took it down to 394, and so probably did Cratippus (Plut. *Mor.* 345 d). If, as seems most likely, the very respectable author of the *Hellenica Oxyrhynchia* is Cratippus, then both his work and Theopompus' are on a very much larger scale than Xenophon's, a scale like Thucydides' own. This fact, as well as considerations of language and outlook, makes it likely that Xenophon's continuation (*Hell.* bks. 1–2) was written earlier than the others, and indeed, before the battle of Coronea in 394. But if this be so, then T. cannot have lived more than a year or so into the fourth century. Marcellinus, in his *Life,* c. 34, says that T. was 'over 50' when he died. If he was born about 455 and died about 400, this will be true. The figure may be from Cratippus, who evidently gave some biographical data: Marcellinus quotes him just before (33) for the view that T. died in Thrace.

Thucydides, then, was part of that ardent youth whose abundance on both sides seemed to him to distinguish the war he wrote of. Something of his ardour may be felt in 2. 31: his pride in the soldier's profession and his devotion to the great commander, Pericles.

He caught the Plague, some time between 430 and 427, but recovered, and in 424 failed in the task of saving Amphipolis from Brasidas. Not to have been a match for Brasidas does not prove him a bad soldier: from his history one receives the impression of a first-rate regimental officer, ashore or afloat, who saw war as a matter of style; perhaps his defence of the generals before Megara in 4. 73. 4 (cf. 108. 5) says worse of his judgement of problems of high command than his failure against Brasidas. He was exiled for this (424 winter) and returned 20 years later, after the war was over, and died within a few years.

He had property and influence in the mining district of Thrace (4. 105. 1). His father's name was Olorus (4. 104. 4), the name of Cimon's Thracian grandfather; his tomb was in Cimon's family vault. It is almost certain he was related by blood to Cimon, and probably to Thucydides the statesman (*JHS* 52. 210); born in the anti-Pericles opposition, he followed Pericles with a convert's zeal.

2. PARTS OF THE HISTORY. The incomplete history falls into five parts: A, an introduction (bk. 1). B, the 10 years war (2. 1–5. 24). C, the precarious peace (5. 25–end). D, The Sicilian war (6 and 7). E, fragment of the Decelean war (8). It is convenient to take first B and D, the two complete wars.

B is enclosed between two statements that 'the continuous war has herein been described'. It was therefore provisionally finished (if these are T.'s words). It contains one allusion to the fall of Athens (2. 65. 12) and several allusions to events late in the 27 years: these are no doubt additions made to an already existing narrative, since one passage certainly (2. 23. 3) was not written as late as the last decade of the century. The narrative gets rather more summary after T.'s exile (424): e.g. after the futile embassy to Artaxerxes I (4. 50) nothing is said of the important negotiations with Darius II.

D is the most finished portion. As it stands it is adapted to a history of the whole war (6. 7. 4, 6. 93. 4, 7. 18. 4, cf. 7. 9 etc., also 7. 44. 1, 7. 87. 5), and twice at least refers to events of 404 or later (7. 57. 2, 6. 15. 3-4). But these may be revisions and it has been suggested that T. published it separately; and this opinion, though little held now, is not disproved. B and D are connected by C, sequel to B and introduction to D, and provided accordingly with a second preface. For symptoms of incompleteness, see below. It covers $5\frac{1}{2}$ years, very unequally. Its two outstanding features are the description of the Mantinea campaign, and the Melian Dialogue. The former should perhaps be regarded, with B and D, as a third completed episode. The latter foreshadows the dramatic style of D; but if we read 5. 111 with 8. 27 we shall draw no facile moral (see 8. 27. 5).

E has the same symptoms of incompleteness as C and, moreover, stops abruptly in the middle of a narrative. It is very full, covering barely two years in its 109 chapters.

A consists of (i) 1. 1-23, a long preface, illustrating the importance of T.'s subject by comparison with earlier history (the so-called 'archaeology') and stating his historical principles: (ii) the causes of the war—that is, for the most part, an account of the political manœuvres of 433-2; he adds important digressions, especially 1. 89-117, a history of the years 479/8-440/39, partly to illustrate his view that the war was an inevitable result of Athens' power, partly to make his history follow without interval on that of Herodotus (1. 97. 2). The second motive perhaps explains the length of another digression (1. 128-38) on the fate of Pausanias and Themistocles.

3. INCOMPLETENESS. E stops in mid narrative, in winter 411: T. intended to go down to 404 (5. 26. 1). It shares with (roughly) C two peculiarities, absence of speeches and absence of documents, which are thought to show incompleteness; for these see below. The plan to make of BCDE a continuous history of the 27 years is only superficially achieved, even to 411: e.g. there is nothing of Atheno-Persian relations between 424 and 412, vital though these were (2. 65. 12). We shall see below that T. kept his work by him and revised continually; so he left double treatments of the same theme, one of which he meant no doubt to suppress. E.g. the tyrannicides (1. 20, 6. 54-9); possibly 1. 23. 1-3 is a short early variant of 1. 1-19; 3. 84 of part of 82-3 (Schwartz 286 f.). It may be even suspected that 8. 82. 2 is a less accurately informed version of 86. 4-5 and the two have been merely harmonized by 85. 4. If this last suspicion were just, it would be good evidence that T.'s remains were put into shape by an editor, whose hand may be further suspected in the misplacement of 3. 17, in 1. 56-7 (whose author —as it stands—surely misconceived the course of events), perhaps even in 1. 118. 2 (where the last sentence seems to leap from the 'fifties to 432); an editorial hand has, indeed, been suspected wholesale. Though no single case is quite decisive, it is unlikely T. left his unfinished work in need of no editing. If we look for an editor, one thinks naturally of Xenophon, who wrote the continuation (it seems) immediately after T.'s death; the suggestion was made in antiquity (Diog. Laert. 2. 57). His soldierly (if not his intellectual) qualities might commend him to T., but if it was indeed he, he worked with

extreme piety, and his hand is very little apparent. Xenophon's limits and virtues alike disqualify him for the authorship of 1. 56-7.

4. SPEECHES AND DOCUMENTS. Ancient craftsmen, and T. notably, aimed at exactness; but in his speeches, T. admits (1. 22. 1) that exactness was beyond his powers of memory. Here, then, as in reconstructing the far past (1. 20-1), he had to trust to his historical imagination, whose use generally he planned to avoid (ὡς ἂν ἐδόκουν ἐμοὶ εἰπεῖν: this meant applying to the speeches the sort of rationalizing schematism that, e.g., Hecataeus applied to geography); and even here, he promises he will control its use as rigorously as he can by the tenor of the actual words. It is much debated whether he made this profession early or late; and it has been much explained away. But it is unreasonable to doubt that from the start T. took notes himself, or sought for hearers' notes, of the speeches he considered important. But since he used speeches dramatically, to reveal the workings of men's minds and the impact of circumstance, it is clear that verbatim reports would not have served even if he could have managed to get them, and he was bound to compromise (unconsciously) between dramatic and literal truth. It is likely that, as his technique developed, dramatic truth would tend to prevail; it is tempting to put his profession of method early, a young man's intention. Even so, while we cannot suppose that, at a moment when morale was vital, Pericles used the words in 2. 64. 3; while it is unlikely that the Athenian debater at Melos developed exactly the same vein of thought as Phrynichus before Miletus (5. 111.-8. 27); while Pericles' first speech (1. 140 ff.) is perhaps composite, and hard to assign to a single occasion; it is yet dangerous to treat the speeches as free fiction: their dramatic truth was combined with the greatest degree of literal truth of which T. was capable. He tried to recreate real occasions.

There are no speeches in E, and (except the Melian Dialogue) none in C: Cratippus (a younger contemporary) says T. had decided to drop their use. Modern critics treat their absence as a symptom of incompleteness; they would have been added had he lived. But it is possible that these parts without speeches are experiments in new techniques. T. may have felt, as many readers do, that the narrative of the 10 years is a compromise between the methods of tragedy and of a laboratory notebook, so that between the profoundest issues and the particular detail the middle ranges (e.g. an intelligible account of strategy) are neglected. In the later narrative the methods are more separated. The Sicilian war was capable of almost purely dramatic treatment; C and E evidently not. And in consequence in E at least a new technique is developed, less like either drama or chronicle, more of an organized narrative, with more of the writer's own judgements of values and interpretations of events. It is questionable if E would be improved by speeches, that is, could be profitably (or at all?) transformed into the style of B or D: was Cratippus perhaps right about T.'s intention?

This would not prevent some of the speeches in bks. 1-4 being composed (or revised) very late. The new experiment would not entail eliminating the dramatic from those books; T. experimented to the end and never solved his problem. It is commonly thought that the Funeral Speech was written or rewritten after Athens' fall; and 2. 64. 3 surely was. The Corcyra debate (1. 31-44), on the contrary, has good chances of being an actual report, written up soon after delivery. Though some speeches aim at dramatic characterization (Gorgiastic, 4. 61. 7: Laconic, 1. 86), all are in Thucydides' idiom. But the personalness of this idiom is often overestimated (Finley, op. cit. infra).

It is noteworthy that those portions which lack speeches have (instead?) transcriptions of documents: that is,

E and (roughly speaking) C.* If, then, we take C and E as experiments in a new method, the experiment begins in the latter part of B. These documents are usually thought (like the absence of speeches) a sign of incompleteness, since they offend against a 'law of style' which forbids the verbatim use of foreign matter in serious prose. We need not debate the general validity of this law: with so inventive a writer as T., his laws of style are to be deduced from his practice, and 5. 24. 2 (cf. 2. 1) suggests that the end of B is provisionally finished. Are they part of the experiment? One may be surprised (though grateful) that T. thought the full text of the Armistice (4. 118–19) worth its room. One of the documents (5. 47) is extant in fragments (IG. i² 86) and confirms the substantial accuracy of the copies. One conflicts gravely with the narrative (5. 23, 5. 39. 3): it would seem the narrative was written in ignorance of the exact terms, and has not been revised.

5. 'EARLY' AND 'LATE'. T. says (1. 1. 1) he began to write his history as soon as war started; and it is at least arguable that much of the existing narrative, in all five parts of the work, was written, substantially as we have it, very soon after the events. But he worked slowly, and, as he says at 1. 22. 3, laboriously; correcting in the light of better information (we only detect this process where it is incomplete; e.g. 5. 39. 3 was due for correction in the light of 5. 23) or of later events (1. 97. 2; 4. 48. 5, where the qualification ὅσα γε may have been put merely *ex abundanti cautela*, but more likely when the troubles started again in 410). If his point of view, or his method, changed materially during this process, it becomes of importance to know from which point of view this or that portion is written. Almost a century ago, Ullrich called attention to this, believing that an important change of approach came with his discovery (announced in the second preface, 5. 26) that the war had not ended in 421.

Two criteria have been used to determine earliness or lateness: (a) reference to, or ignorance of, datable events or conditions; (b) the stage in T.'s own development which a passage reveals.

(a) References to late events cannot be written early, but they may be inserted in early contexts: e.g. those who think D early regard 6. 15. 3–4 and 7. 57. 2 as additions. Ignorance of late events is very much harder to establish: those same who think D early may suspect in 6. 41. 3 ignorance of Dionysius' tyranny, or even (a very slippery question) in 6. 54. 1 ignorance of Herodotus' history—but cannot prove their suspicions; yet where such ignorance is certain (see below), we may be sure that the narrative (or line of thought) which warrants them was conceived early. The results of this method are modest: e.g. (i) 1. 10. 2 was not written after the catastrophe of 404: therefore the war against which earlier wars are being measured is not the completed 27 years, and the 'end of war' mentioned in 1. 13. 3–4, 1. 18. 1, is presumably 421; (ii) 2. 23. 3 was not written after the loss of Oropus in 411: therefore some of the narrative of B was written much as we have it before 411; (iii) 2. 65. 12 refers to the fall of Athens: therefore B received additions down to 404 at least.

(b) More has been hoped from the second method. T. worked from his twenties to his fifties, his material growing under his eyes: there must surely be some intellectual or spiritual growth, some change of outlook. The best exponent of this method is Schwartz, who gives (op. cit. infra 217–42) an eloquent account of T.'s growth. The danger of this method is evident: in the ablest hands it yields quite different results (Meyer, Schwartz), and its first postulate may be doubted, namely, that T.'s opinion on the 'true cause' of the war (1. 23. 6) was not

* Not exactly C: C ends with the Melian Dialogue (which in colour belongs to D ?) and B has documents instead of speeches in its latter part, i.e. after the occasion of T.'s exile.

formed till after the fall of Athens. No doubt that was his view after 404; no doubt 1. 23. 6 and 1. 88 were written (inserted?) pretty late. But much the same view is expressed by the Corcyran envoy in 1. 33. 3 (cf. 42. 2); and whether the envoy said it or not it was surely Pericles' view. Pericles believed that if Athens used her opportunity in 433 she was bound to provoke in Sparta an enmity that must be faced; all his career, against Cimon and his successors, he had fought for his conviction that Athens and Sparta were natural enemies and Greece not large enough for both. His admirers held that this clear principle (1. 140. 1) was obscured in debate by the irrelevant particulars (1. 140. 4–141. 1). We have not to consider whether Pericles was right: rather, the effect on T. The devout disciple saw the story unfold in the terms his master had foreseen (2. 65). How far such a 'Pericles-fixation' may have warped T.'s judgement, see below.

If this first postulate go, the second will follow it, viz. that only after 404 was Pericles given the importance he now has in bks. 1–2, since after 404 T. started to rewrite his history as a 'defence of Pericles' (Schwartz 239). It hardly needs to be said that many hold to these postulates and the present writer's disbelief is as subjective as their belief. If these are untrue, truer postulates may be found: the attempt to recreate T.'s experience should (and will) never be dropped.

6. TRUTHFULNESS. Perhaps no good historian is impartial; T. certainly not, though singularly candid. His tastes are clear: he liked Pericles and disliked Cleon. He had for Pericles a regard comparable to Plato's for Socrates, and an equal regard for Pericles' Athens. These things were personal: but in principle, concentrations of energy (like Athens or Alcibiades) were to his taste. Their impact on a less dynamic world was likely to be disastrous—but whose fault was that? The world's, he says, consistently (1. 99; 1. 23. 6 etc.; 6. 15; 6. 28; cf. 2. 64. 3–5): and though this consistency may surprise us, we need not quarrel with it. Such judgements are rare, since T. conceives his task as like medical research (see below, and cf. 3. 82. 2) where blame is irrelevant; the disconcerting simplicity of 2. 64. 3 (power and energy are absolute goods) is the more striking.

We need not here investigate T.'s possible mistakes. The present writer believes that Pericles (having planned an offensive war) lost his striking power, first because Potidaea revolted, next because of the Plague. Forced to the defensive, he left that as his testament. T. was reluctant to face the fact of this failure, and accepted the testament, siding with the defeatist officer class against the revived offensive of Cleon (4. 27. 5, 28. 5, 65. 4, 73. 4: cf. 5. 7. 2). This is why Pericles' huge effort against Epidaurus (6. 31. 2; motive, cf. 5. 53) is recorded as a minor futility (2. 56. 4); why Phormion's first campaign in Acarnania (2. 68. 7–9; of 432?) is left timeless; why we hear nothing of the purpose of the Megara decree; why, when that nearly bore fruit at last, T. suggests that the capture of Megara was of no great moment (4. 73. 4; but cf. 72. 1).

Such criticisms hardly detract much from his singular truthfulness. Readers of all opinions will probably agree that he saw more truly, inquired more responsibly, and reported more faithfully than any other ancient historian. That is a symptom of his greatness, but not its core. Another symptom is his style: it is innocent of those clichés of which Isocrates hoped to make the norm of Attic style; in its 'old-fashioned wilful beauty' (Dionysius) every word tells. Like English prose before Dryden and Addison, it uses a language largely moulded by poets: its precision is a poet's precision, a union of passion and candour. After T. history mostly practised the corrupting art of persuasion (cf. Isocr. 4. 8): his scientific tradition survived in the antiquarians, of whom he is the pioneer (1. 8. 1, 2. 15. 2, 3. 104. 4–6, 6. 55. 1), but the instinctive exactness of early Greek observation was lost. To combine his predecessors' candour of vision with his successors' apparatus of scholarship was a necessity laid on him by his sense of the greatness of his subject: he could no more distort or compromise with what he wished to convey than Shakespeare or Michelangelo could.

Thucydides would no doubt prefer to substitute, for these great names, the practice of any honest doctor. He was not modest, but in his statement of his principles he is singularly unaware of his unique equipment, and claims rather that he has spared no pains. The proper context for this statement (1. 20–2) is, first, his very similar statement about his own account of the Plague (2. 48. 3), and then the physician Hippocrates' maxim, 'ars longa vita brevis'. The 'art' which outlasts individual lives is the scientific study of man: the physician studied his clinical, T. his political, behaviour. To know either so well that you can control it (and civilization is largely made up of such controls) is a task for many generations: a piece of that task well done is something gained for ever (1. 22. 4). H. T. W.-G.

7. STYLE. In a famous sentence (*Thuc.* 24) Dionysius gives as the four 'tools' in Thucydides' work-shop τὸ ποιητικὸν τῶν ὀνομάτων, τὸ πολυειδὲς τῶν σχημάτων, τὸ τραχὺ τῆς ἁρμονίας, τὸ τάχος τῶν σημασιῶν. The first, third, and fourth of these criticisms are undoubtedly true. T.'s style has a poetical and archaistic flavour (it is often difficult to distinguish clearly between the two), as a reader sees at once when he turns from T. to Andocides and Lysias. His consistent use of αἰεί for ἀεί, ξύν for σύν, and σσ for ττ is one of the signs of this tendency. 'Roughness' is to be seen in his bold changes of construction and his violent hyperbata, in which he wrests an emphatic word from its natural place in the sentence to give it more prominence (1. 19 κατ' ὀλιγαρχίαν, 1. 93. 4 τῆς θαλάσσης). 'Speed' is perhaps the most striking of all his characteristics. He achieves an extreme concision, hardly to be paralleled in Greek prose except in the gnomic utterances of Democritus. A sentence like δοκεῖ ... καταστροφή (2. 42. 2) is gone in a flash, and no orator, composing for the ear, could have risked such brevity. At 2. 37. 1 μέτεστι ... προτιμᾶται two antitheses are telescoped into one. τὸ πολυειδὲς τῶν σχημάτων is much more open to question, especially as Dionysius has just before credited T. with the use of the θεατρικὰ σχήματα (parisosis, paronomasia, and antithesis) affected by Gorgias and other writers of the sophistic school. T.'s thought is, it is true, markedly antithetical in cast (e.g. 1. 70. 6), and antithesis is sometimes strained (e.g. 2. 43. 3). But, unlike the Gorgianists, he has no affection for merely external antithesis, and he often deliberately avoids formal balance (e.g. 4. 59. 2). He eschews almost entirely certain other common adornments of style. He is too austere to use metaphor at all freely, or asyndeton (more suited to the spoken word). He does employ certain devices of assonance, neither, like Gorgias, as ἡδύσματα, nor, like Demosthenes, for emphasis pure and simple, but for the emphasizing of a contrast (3. 82. 8 εὐσεβείᾳ ... εὐπρεπείᾳ, 6. 76. 2 κατοικίσαι ... ἐξοικίσαι, 76. 4 ἀξυνετωτέρου ... κακοξυνετωτέρου). He has a strong leaning, as Dionysius observed (*Amm.* 2. 5), towards abstract expression (e.g. 3. 82–3), sometimes carried to the length of personification (πόλεμος 1. 122. 1, ἐλπίς 5. 103. 1). He probably coined abstracts (especially in -σις) freely, as Euripides did, according to the fashion of the late fifth century, and sometimes used them out of season (7. 70. 6, ἀποστέρησιν, and the odd-looking negatived abstracts, 1. 137. 4 οὐ διάλυσιν, etc.). Like Antiphon, he experimented freely with the use of neuter adjective, or even participle (1. 142. 8 ἐν τῷ μὴ μελετῶντι), to convey an abstract idea. His periods are usually loosely constructed (e.g. 3. 38. 4–7), of clauses longer in actual

words, and far richer in content, than those of other Greek prose-writers (e.g. 2. 43. 2–6). J. D. D.

BIBLIOGRAPHY

TEXTS: H. Stuart-Jones (O.C.T. 1898–1902, reprinted 1942, with *apparatus criticus* revised by J. E. Powell); C. Hude (Teubner, Ed. maior 1913–25, ed. minor 1920–8, with scholia).
TRANSLATIONS: Thomas Hobbes 1629 (= vol. viii–ix in Hobbes's English works, 1843); R. Crawley (*Everyman* 1910).
COMMENTARIES: E. C. Marchant (bks. 1–3, 6, and 7, 1891–1905); in German, J. Classen (bks. 1–2 ed. 5, bks. 3–8 ed. 3, revised by J. Steup, 1892–1922); in Latin, E. F. Poppo (ed. 3, revised by J. M. Stahl, 1886); a commentary is in preparation by A. W. Gomme (Bk. 1 published 1945).
CRITICISM. Ancient: Cratippus, *FGrH* 64: Dion. Hal. *Thuc.* [cf. *ad Amm. de T. idiom., ad Pomp.*] (= *opuscula*, ed. Usener-Radermacher, i. 325 ff. [421 ff., ii. 221 ff.]); Marcellinus, *Life of T.*, prefixed to most texts of T. Modern: C. N. Cochrane, *T. and the Science of History* (1929; relation to Hippocratics); J. H. Finley, *Thucydides* (U.S.A. 1942); A. W. Gomme, *Essays in Gk. Hist. and Lit.* (1937, nos. vi–ix); G. B. Grundy, *T. and the History of his Age*[2] (1948); W. Jaeger, *Paideia* (1936), Eng. tr. by G. G. A. Highet 1938, pp. 379 ff.); W. R. M. Lamb, *Clio Enthroned* (1914); E. Meyer, *Forschungen* ii (1899, no. v); H. Patzer, *Das Problem der Geschichtsschreibung des T.* (1937; 'nothing much written before 404'); G. De Sanctis, *Rendiconti Acc. Lincei* vi (1930), 229 ff.; id., *Postille Tucididee* (Melian dialogue, bk. 8); W. Schadewaldt, *Die Geschichtsschreibung des T.* (1929; esp. bks. 6–7); E. Schwartz, *Das Geschichtswerk des T.* (1919; *Stilgesetz*, pp. 28 ff.); F. W. Ullrich, *Beiträge zur Erklärung des T.* (1846–52); and esp. on the speeches: A. W. Gomme, op. cit. no. ix, *The Speeches*; M. Pohlenz, *Gött. Nachr.* 1919, 95 ff.; 1920, 56 ff.; *T.-studien, Gött. Anz.* 1936, 281 ff., 'Die T.-frage'; R. Zahn, *Die erste Periklesrede*, Diss. 1934 (notes by Jacoby; accepts 'true cause' as criterion of lateness).
INDEX: M. H. N. von Essen, *Index Thucydideus*, 1887.
H. T. W.-G.

THUGGA (modern *Dougga*), a hill-town west of the military road from Carthage to Theveste. The site was occupied in neolithic times. The Berbers built the market-town of Thukka on the hill slopes, for the sale of wheat, barley, oil, beans, and grapes from the fertile Oued Kaled valley. Phoenicians from the coast cities joined them, improved their agricultural methods, established government by shophets (*see* CARTHAGE), and built temples to Baal and Taanit. Marius settled some veterans at Thugga, and Roman *pagus* and native *civitas* existed side by side. By A.D. 100 the shophets had become *duumviri*; in the second century there was great building activity by generous citizens, and in the third the town became Colonia Licinia Septimia Aurelia Alexandriana Thugga. Its best-known ruins are the beautiful Capitoline temple, the theatre and the Berber mausoleum with its bilingual inscription.

L. Carton, *Dougga* (Tunis, 1929). W. N. W.

THULE (Θούλη), a northern land first heard of and described by Pytheas (q.v.). It lay six days' sail to north of Britain. At midsummer the sun's and the Bear's paths, as seen at Thule, coincided, and neither set. The inhabitants ate berries, 'millet' (oats?) threshed in barns because of the dampness and lack of sun, herbs, fruits, roots, and honey. Round Thule everything was held in an impalpable mass 'like a jelly-fish' (thick fog?) which Pytheas himself saw. It is uncertain whether Thule was Iceland or Norway. Nothing further was discovered about it, but it was henceforth regarded as the northernmost part of the inhabited world. Eratosthenes drew a parallel through Thule at 66° (Arctic circle), which remained for long on maps. Ptolemy gave Thule a N.–S. extension of 55 miles and located it at Mainland (Shetland), though he retained the belief in its midsummer midnight sun. The land of Thule which Agricola's fleet claimed to have seen (Tac. *Agr.* 10) was no doubt a Shetland island.

Strabo 63–4, etc.; Plin. *HN* 2. 187, 4. 104; Geminus, *Elem. Astron.* 6; Ptol. *Geog.* 2. 3, 14, 2. 6. 22, 8. 3. 3. Cary-Warmington, *Explorers*, 36 ff.; G. E. Broche, *Pythéas le Massaliote* (1936), 145 ff.
E. H. W.

THURII (Θούριοι), Pericles' panhellenic foundation (443 B.C.), which Herodotus and Lysias reputedly joined. Its site, near to, possibly identical with, that of Sybaris (q.v.), is certain (H. Philipp in *PW* vi A. 646 f.). It was originally inhabited by Messapii (J. Whatmough, *Foundations of Roman Italy* (1937), 336). Despite *stasis*, quarrels with other Greeks, and Lucanian wars, Thurii flourished for a time, but finally became voluntarily a Roman dependency, and as such opposed Pyrrhus. To revive Thurii after its spoliation by Hannibal Rome founded the Latin colony of Copia here, 193 B.C. (App. *Hann.* 57; Livy 35. 9). But, although remaining strategically important, Thurii gradually declined and ultimately was abandoned (App. *BCiv.* 1. 117; 5. 56. 58; Diod. 12. 9 f.; Strabo 6. 263).

J. Bérard, *Bibliogr. topogr.* (1941), 94; K. Freeman, *Greece and Rome*, 1941, 49 ff.; V. Ehrenberg, *AJPhil.* 1948, 149 ff.   E. T. S.

THYESTES, see AEGISTHUS, ATREUS.

THYIA (Θυία), apparently the same word as θυιάς, a Bacchante. There being a spot so named at Delphi (Hdt. 7. 178. 2), she is occasionally heard of (as ibid.) as the nymph of the place.

THYIADES, see MAENADS.

THYMOETES (Θυμοίτης) (1), a brother of Priam, Hom. *Il.* 3. 146; Verg. *Aen.* 2. 32, whereon see Servius for his quarrel with Priam; Diod. Sic. 3. 67. 5. (2) Son of the above, Diod. Sic. ibid.

THYONE, see SEMELE.

THYSDRUS (modern *El Djem*), a Tunisian market-town, lying inland south of Hadrumetum. It was captured by Caesar in 46 B.C., and fined for supporting the Pompeians. Subsequently it became the centre of a prosperous agricultural district; its amphitheatre, of which striking ruins survive, was built for 60,000 spectators. The elder Gordian (q.v.) was proclaimed emperor at Thysdrus.   W. N. W.

TIBER rises as a creek in the Apennines near Arretium, develops into Central Italy's greatest river, meanders south to Narnia (confluence with the Nar), then SW. past Rome (where it divides about the *Insula Tiberina*), and enters the Tyrrhenian Sea at Ostia. The silt it carries down with it on its 250-mile journey accounts for its tawny colour ('flauus Tiberis'); it accumulates at its mouth to choke the harbour works (*portus*) built by Trajan and others (Claudius even excavated a separate, artificial mouth), and constantly advances the coastline at Ostia. Tributaries: Tinia-Clitumnus, Clanis, Nar, Anio, Allia and numerous brooks (Pliny's 42 is actually an underestimate). Navigation, although possible as far as Narnia, was hazardous owing to the swift current. Inundations are first recorded in 241 B.C. (Oros. 4. 11), but were frequent in all periods, even after Augustus instituted *curatores riparum et alvei Tiberis* (Suet. *Aug.* 37). The salt deposits at its mouth were worked in very early times, although the settlement at Ostia which traditionally dates from Ancus Marcius' period is not demonstrably older than the fourth century B.C. The Tiber formed the eastern border of Etruria (and hence is frequently called *Tyrrhenus* or *Lydius*) and the northern boundary of Latium. In Imperial times opulent villas studded the banks of its lower course.

Strabo 5. 218; 232 f.; Pliny, *HN* 3. 53 f.; Dion. Hal. 3. 44. S. A. Smith, *Tiber and its tributaries* (1877); G. Calza in *Capitolium* 1937.   E. T. S.

TIBERIANUS, in Gaul as *praefectus praetorio*, A.D. 335 (Hieron. Chron. ad ann. 2352), was a poet whose best-known piece is the *Amnis ibat*, 20 trochaic tetrameters. Its feeling for nature prompted Baehrens' suggestion that Tiberianus also composed the *Pervigilium Veneris* (q.v.). For his other brief poems and fragments (text and tr.) see J. W. and A. M. Duff, *Minor Lat. Poets*, 1935.   J. W. D.

TIBERIAS, on L. Galilee, was founded by Herod Antipas (q.v.). Despite its Greek constitution, it was a completely Jewish city. It was the capital of a toparchy, and also of Galilee, till Nero gave Galilee to Agrippa II. In the Jewish war the proletariat was anti-Roman, but the aristocracy on the whole loyal to the king and to Rome; it surrendered to Vespasian and was spared. After the Second Jewish War Tiberias was paganized by Hadrian, but it later became once more a thoroughly Jewish city, the seat of a rabbinical school.   A. H. M. J.

TIBERIUS (1), the Emperor (TIBERIUS JULIUS CAESAR AUGUSTUS), was the son of Ti. Claudius Nero and Livia, born in 42 B.C. His mother was divorced, in order to marry Octavian, early in 38 shortly before the birth of her second son Drusus. From 20 B.C., when, accompanying Augustus to the East, he received back the standards lost to the Parthians at Carrhae, until A.D. 12, when he returned to Rome after retrieving the situation on the Rhine after the disaster of Varus, Tiberius had a brilliant military career (interrupted only from 6 B.C. to A.D. 4). Between 12 and 9 B.C. he reduced Pannonia. From 9 B.C. (after the death of his brother) to 7 B.C. and again from A.D. 4 to 6 he campaigned in Germany. From A.D. 6 to 9 he was engaged in suppressing the great revolts of Pannonia and Illyricum. (See, for details of these campaigns, R. Syme, *CAH* x, ch. 12.)

2. After Agrippa's death Tiberius was forced in 12 B.C. to divorce Vipsania Agrippina, mother of his son Drusus, in order to marry Augustus' daughter, Agrippa's widow, Julia. A son born of this—most unhappy—marriage died in infancy. In 6 B.C. Tiberius was granted *tribunicia potestas* for five years and invited to carry out a diplomatic mission in the East. Augustus hoped, however, to be succeeded by one of his young grandsons, Gaius or Lucius, and, perhaps through pique on that account, Tiberius retired to Rhodes in 6 B.C. He returned to Rome, though not to Augustus' favour, in A.D. 2. In A.D. 4, both his grandsons having died, Augustus was forced to recognize Tiberius as his likely successor. He adopted him, together with Agrippa Postumus, forcing Tiberius to adopt his nephew Germanicus. Tiberius was given *tribunicia potestas* for ten years, and this was renewed in A.D. 13 for a further ten years. He was also, at the time of his adoption and again in A.D. 13, given *imperium proconsulare*, like that held by Augustus.

3. Augustus died on 19 August A.D. 14 and Tiberius, in virtue of the *imperium* which he already possessed, was able to discharge urgent administrative duties in the interval before September 17, when (*Fast. Amitern.*, *CIL* I, i², p. 244), after an embarrassing and unprecedented debate (Tac. *Ann.* 1, 10–13) he was, on the proposal of the consuls, proclaimed Emperor. He reigned until his death on 16 March A.D. 37.

4. Loyalty to Augustus was the keystone of Tiberius' policy. While Augustus was consecrated and a *templum divi Augusti* was built at Rome, Tiberius refused to accept any extravagant honours for himself (Tac. *Ann.* 4. 37 f.; cf. the inscriptions from Gythium, Ἑλληνικά i (1928), 7 ff., 152 ff.). In foreign policy he followed the 'consilium coercendi intra terminos imperii' bequeathed to him by Augustus (Tac. *Ann.* 1. 11) and, when Germanicus was recalled from the Rhine at the end of 16, the project of conquering Germany was at last abandoned. Cappadocia was made a province on the death of its king Archelaus in 17. The revolt of Florus and Sacrovir in Gallia Lugdunensis in 21 was suppressed with little difficulty by the Upper German army. Trouble with Parthia threatened on two occasions, but was settled by diplomatic negotiation, by Germanicus in 18 and by L. Vitellius at the very end of Tiberius' principate. Tiberius' only innovation in provincial administration lay in lengthening the tenure of office of imperial *legati* in the

provinces, whether from slackness or of set purpose (see Marsh, op. cit. infra, 157 ff.). In finance Tiberius exercised rigid economy, built little, gave donations sparingly and games hardly at all; he therefore bequeathed great wealth (more than 2,000 millions of sesterces; Suet. *Calig.* 37, Dio. Cass. 59. 2).

5. Tiberius' difficulties in administration were many. His accession coincided with legionary revolts in Pannonia and in Lower Germany, the German legions being ready to proclaim their commander, Germanicus, Emperor. In the Senate he was persistently irritated and insulted by such men as L. Arruntius and Asinius Gallus (q.v.). Within his own family there was jealousy concerning the selection of his prospective successor. After the death of Germanicus in 19 and of Tiberius' son Drusus in 23, the way lay open to the sons of Agrippina and Germanicus: Nero, Drusus, and Gaius. Nero and Drusus fell through the schemes of Sejanus, and Gaius, while his life was saved, received little preparation for government from Tiberius.

6. The reign of Tiberius was disfigured (cf. Tac. *Ann.* 1. 72 f.; 4. 6, 'legesque, si maiestatis quaestio eximeretur, bono in usu') by the heavy incidence, especially after 23, of trials, chiefly before the Senate, for *maiestas* and *perduellio* (on the distinction, not explicit in Tacitus, and on the figures and details of the law and its administration, see Rogers, op. cit. infra). There is record of more than 100 such prosecutions, of which those of M. Scribonius (q.v. 2), Libo Drusus in 16 and of Cn. Calpurnius Piso (q.v. 7) in 20 were outstanding. Tiberius' own responsibility is hard to assess. Though he showed no vindictiveness or cruelty (cf. Tac. *Ann.* 3. 51), a stronger man might have checked the abuse. There is no evidence that he was ever in serious danger of assassination; yet he had a morbid fear of it, and was encouraged in this fear by L. Aelius Sejanus (q.v.), prefect of the Praetorian Guard and, after 23, Tiberius' chief adviser. Tiberius was encouraged by him to leave Rome for Capreae in 26; he did not return to Rome again, but corresponded by letter with the Senate. Agrippina and Nero were arrested in 26, Drusus in 30, and were all subsequently put to death or committed suicide. Sejanus himself was arrested and executed in Rome on the charge of conspiracy, in 31. His death was followed by that of many of his supporters.

7. While stories of Tiberius' vice on Capreae may be discounted, his mind was almost unhinged in the last six years of his life (cf. Tac. *Ann.* 6. 6). Lacking the affability ('ciuile ingenium') of his brother Drusus and nephew Germanicus, apt to speak in language of obscure and, it was thought, sinister ambiguity (cf. especially Dio Cass. 57. 1), austere, not even possessing, like his son Drusus, the pardonable and popular weakness of fondness for games, he neither sought popularity nor won it; in Rome itself the news of his death was welcomed.

BIBLIOGRAPHY

ANCIENT SOURCES: We have a contemporary account of Tiberius' campaigns under Augustus and of the first sixteen years of his reign in Velleius Paterculus 2. 94-131. This account (published in A.D. 30) is favourable to Tiberius (and also to Sejanus). It is in sharp contrast to the other Roman accounts of the reign, viz. Tacitus, *Annals* 1-6 (most of book 5, with its account of the arrest and trial of Sejanus, is lost), Suetonius, *Tiberius*, and Dio Cassius, bks. 57 f. Tacitus' bias against Tiberius, displayed often in strikingly inept comment and innuendo, has been variously explained. Possibly he saw in Tiberius the prototype of Domitian; though, for a different explanation, see T. S. Jerome, *Aspects of the Study of Roman History* (U.S.A. 1923), chs. 15-17. Without doubt Tacitus' chief sources, the historians who wrote at the end of the Julio-Claudian period, whose works have perished (e.g. Servilius Nonianus, Aufidius Bassus and, in her memoirs, to which Tacitus once refers, *Ann.* 4. 53, the younger Agrippina), gave an extremely unfavourable account of Tiberius. See, on Tacitus' sources, P. Fabia, *Les Sources de Tacite* (1893), and F. B. Marsh, *The Reign of Tiberius* (1931), appendix 1. The Jewish writers, Philo–a contemporary–and Josephus, are friendly to Tiberius and unfriendly to Sejanus.

MODERN LITERATURE: F. B. Marsh, *The Reign of Tiberius* (1931), and M. P. Charlesworth, *CAH* x, chapter 19, both with complete bibliographies; R. S. Rogers, *Criminal Trials and Criminal Legislation under Tiberius* (U.S.A. 1935); *Studies in the Reign of Tiberius* (1943); E. Ciaceri, *Tiberio²* (1944); D. M. Pipidi, *Autour de Tibère* (1944). See, on the Gythium inscriptions, E. Kornemann, *Neue Dokumente zum lakonischen Kaiserkult* (1929) and M. Rostovtzeff, *Rev. Hist.* clxiii (1930). J. P. B.

TIBERIUS (2) **JULIUS CAESAR GEMELLUS**, one of twin sons born in A.D. 19 to Drusus, son of Tiberius, and Livia. Tiberius made him joint heir with Gaius to his personal property. Though the Senate annulled the will, Gaius adopted Tiberius Gemellus and allowed him to be hailed as *Princeps Iuventutis*. He was put to death, however, during the first year of Gaius' principate.

J. P. B.

TIBERIUS (3) **JULIUS ALEXANDER**, of an opulent Jewish family of Alexandria, nephew of Philon (q.v. 4), but a renegade from the ancestral faith, rose high in the service of Rome. He was procurator governing Judaea (*c.* A.D. 46–8), when he executed the sons of Judas the Galilean; general staff officer under Corbulo in Armenia (63) and soon after Prefect of Egypt. His long edict, published soon after Galba's accession, has been preserved (*OGI* 669). Tiberius Alexander made his troops take the oath in the name of Vespasian on 1st July 69, which date was adopted as the 'dies imperii'. Enjoying high favour with the new dynasty, he was present with Titus at the siege of Jerusalem in the same function as he had held under Corbulo. He vainly tried to have the Temple preserved.

O. W. Reinmuth, *Trans. Am. Phil. Ass.* 1934. R. S.

TIBIAE, *see* MUSIC, § 9 (ii).

TIBULLUS, ALBIUS (48?–19 B.C.), Roman elegiac poet, pre-eminently 'tersus atque elegans' (Quintilian, 10. 1. 93). Little is known of him except what can be gathered from his poetry and references and poems by Horace and Ovid. There is also an anonymous and corrupt *Vita*, going back perhaps to Suetonius, containing, however, little not found in his poetry. It is preceded by an epigram of Domitius Marsus (recently argued to be the author of the *Vita*), which fixes the date of his death.

2. An arresting personality, well educated, of equestrian rank, he, like other Augustan poets, lost a considerable portion of his patrimony during the civil wars. Notwithstanding his complaints of 'paupertas', not to be taken seriously, he had enough left to lead a comfortable existence in Rome or on his estate between Praeneste and Tibur. He became the poet laureate of the republican literary circle, headed by Messalla Corvinus (q.v.), whom, according to some, he accompanied to Gaul—a view inacceptable to the present writer. He accompanied Messalla to the East, but, falling ill at Corcyra, returned to Italy.

3. The collection under T.'s name (*Corpus Tibullianum*) contained originally three books, which Italian scholars of the fifteenth century divided into four. Only the first two definitely belong to him. The first was published about 26 B.C. Elegies 1, 2, 3, 5, 6, were inspired by Delia, a woman of plebeian extraction, whose real name, according to Apuleius, was Plania. She is somewhat of a mystery, described now as single, now as having a 'coniunx', probably in the euphemistic sense. Her faithlessness put an end to the poet's idyllic dream of a happy life with her in the country. Elegies 4, 8, 9 deal with Marathus, a 'puer delicatus', whom T. admired, perhaps in order to forget Delia's fickleness. Elegy 7 is a birthday poem in honour of Messalla, mentioned also in other elegies; elegy 10 contrasts the blessings of peace with the savagery of war.

4. Book II consists of six elegies; its lacunae are due to the ravages of time, not to posthumous publication. The heroine of 3, 4, 6 is Nemesis, a greedy, unscrupulous

courtesan, who almost became the Nemesis of the poet's life. Elegy 1 gives a charming description of the Ambarvalia festival; the occasion for 2 is the birthday of his friend Cornutus. Elegy 5 celebrates the installation of Messalla's son, Messalinus, as one of the xv-viri. This elegy is important because in it alone T. touches upon national topics; yet even here the erotic element intrudes, namely his love for Nemesis (111–20).

5. Book III is the literary property of Lygdamus (q.v.). Book IV opens with the Panegyricus (q.v.) Messallae. Elegies 2–6, however, known as the Garland of Sulpicia, treat incidents of Sulpicia's love for Cerinthus. They are artistic counterparts to elegies 7–12, written by Sulpicia herself (q.v.). The author of 2–6, likewise of 13–14, is undoubtedly Tibullus. The two latter probably refer to his love affair with Glycera mentioned by Horace (Carm. 1. 33).

6. One thing is certain—the entire collection emanated from Messalla's circle; later, perhaps during Claudius' reign, an editor (some think Lygdamus) published the entire poetry of the circle in the form transmitted.

7. Tibullus' poetry was limited to two main topics: love and longing for idyllic country life. These themes he handles in masterly fashion, through a series of small pictures skilfully woven into a harmonious and artistic whole. By his art that hid art, by his exquisite Latin and melodious verse freed from the burdensome pedantry of Alexandrian learning, he became the poet who contributed most to the perfection of Roman elegy. Respected by his contemporaries, he enjoyed a solid reputation throughout the ages and notwithstanding some adverse criticism in recent years he has stood the test of time. See also ELEGIAC POETRY, LATIN.

BIBLIOGRAPHY

Exhaustive list, Schanz–Hosius, Gesch. röm. Lit. 2 Teil (1935); F. Marx, s.v. 'Albius', PW i (1894); cf. under LYGDAMUS, PANEGYRICUS MESSALLAE, SULPICIA, ELEGIAC POETRY (LATIN).
EDITIONS: J. P. Postgate (1915); M. Ponchont (1924); F. Calonghi (1927); F. W. Lenz (1937); with commentary: K. F. Smith (U.S.A. 1913); E. Cesareo (1938). Selections: Postgate (1928); K. Harrington (U.S.A. 1914). Translations (verse): T. C. Williams (U.S.A. 1905); A. S. Way (1936). Translation (prose): J. P. Postgate (Loeb, 1912).
STUDIES: A. Cartault, A propos du Corpus Tibullianum (1906); Le Distique élégiaque chez Tib. Sulp. Lygd. (1911); M. Ponchont, Étude sur le texte de T. (1923); K. Witte, Die Geschichte der röm. Elegie, I: Tibullus (1924); J. Hammer, Prolegomena (see 'Messalla'); M. Schuster, Tibull-Studien (1930); N. Salanitro, Tibullo (1938). J. H.

TIBUR, nowadays Tivoli with numerous monuments. Famed for fruits, building-stone (travertine), and cults (e.g. Hercules, Vesta, Albunea), it lies 18 miles ENE. of Rome, where the Anio (q.v.) leaves the Sabine mountains (Strabo 5. 238). Founded before Rome, possibly by Siculi, Tibur was a powerful member of the Latin League with several dependent towns (Pliny, HN 16. 237; Dion. Hal. 1. 16; Cato fr. 58 P.). In the fourth century B.C., aided occasionally by Gauls or Praenestines, it frequently fought Rome until deprived of territory in 338 (Livy 7–8. 14). Tibur, however, remained independent and could harbour Roman exiles (Dessau, ILS 19; Livy 9. 30). Acquiring Roman citizenship c. 90 B.C. (App. BCiv. 1. 65), it became a fashionable resort: Catullus, Horace (possibly), Augustus, and Hadrian had Tiburtine villas. Propertius' Cynthia and captive potentates like Syphax (201 B.C.) and Zenobia (A.D. 273) also sojourned here.

Catullus 44; Prop. 3. 16; Livy 30. 45; S. H. A. Tyr. Trig. 30. 27; E. Bourne, A Study of Tibur (U.S.A. 1916); G. Cascioli, Bibliografia di Tivoli (1923); R. Paribeni, Hadrian's Villa at Tibur (Rome, n.d. 1932?); C. Carducci, Tibur (Rome, 1940); J. Mancini, Inscriptiones Italiae (1936), i 1. E. T. S.

TICIDAS, one of the neoterici (q.v.), wrote erotic poems to 'Perilla', i.e. Metella (Ovid, Tr. 2. 433; Apul. Apol. 10). See Baehr. FPR 325; Morel, FPL 90.

TIGELLINUS, GAIUS (?) OFONIUS, a man of low birth and morals, was exiled by Gaius in 39 for adultery with Agrippina. Under Claudius he lived in obscurity, but found favour with Nero, upon whom he had the worst influence. Promoted first to the post of praefectus vigilum, he was in 62 made praefectus praetorio. In 65 he received the triumphalia ornamenta and other distinctions for his loyalty in the Pisonian conspiracy. In 68 he swore allegiance to Galba, though he was compelled to resign from his position of praefectus praetorio. Under Otho Tigellinus was forced to commit suicide. His memory was universally execrated.

Stein, PW, s.v. 'Ofonius Tigellinus'. R. L. J.

TIGRANES (1) I 'the Great', son (?) of Artavasdes; king of Armenia. He was set on the Armenian throne c. 94 B.C. by Parthian troops, in return for 'seventy valleys' in Armenia (Strabo 11. 532). He rapidly consolidated his power, and his alliance with Mithridates of Pontus led to an interference in Asia Minor which Rome would not tolerate. In 92 B.C. Sulla was sent; an agreement between Rome and Parthia failed to curb Tigranes, who embarked on remarkable conquests in the north of the Parthian Empire. At the height of his career he ruled Gordyene, Adiabene, and Media Atropatene, and even part of the Seleucid possessions in Cilicia and Phoenicia, and he assumed the imperial title 'King of kings' (Joseph. AJ 13. 419–21; Plut. Luc. 21). This empire, of which Tigranocerta (q.v.) was founded as the capital, was short-lived. In 69 war was resumed by Rome, Lucullus captured Tigranocerta, but the issue remained undecided until Pompey succeeded in separating the Armenian and Pontic kings. Tigranes' son rebelled and fled to Pompey; together they marched on Artaxata and Tigranes finally surrendered. He lost all his possessions except Armenia proper. Henceforward, though engaging in frontier disputes with Parthia, he kept peace with Rome.

F. Tournebize, Histoire politique et religieuse de l'Arménie (1911); PW, s.v. 'Tigranes' (F. Geyer); see also ARMENIA, LUCULLUS, POMPEY. M. S. D.

TIGRANES (2) II (20 B.C.–c. 6 B.C.) son of King Artavasdes of Armenia. Captured and sent to Egypt by Antony, he lived for many years in Rome. After the murder of his brother Artaxes, the Armenians sent a request to Augustus that he be sent to reign instead (Tac. Ann. 2. 3). Tiberius accompanied him with an army, and Tigranes was crowned without opposition. Armenia was thus restored to the ostensible control of Rome. M. S. D.

TIGRANES (3) III (c. 2 B.C.), son of Tigranes II. On his father's death he was crowned by the pro-Parthian party in Armenia, to reign jointly with his sister-consort Erato. He was expelled by the Romans, but returned after the murder of the Roman nominee a few years later. Attacked by Augustus' adoptive son C. Caesar, he made overtures for peace, but died fighting on his eastern frontier. M. S. D.

TIGRANES (4) V, great-grandson of Archelaus of Cappadocia (Tac. Ann. 14. 26). In A.D. 60 he was sent from Rome to replace Tiridates (q.v. 3) on the throne of Armenia. When he proceeded to lay Adiabene waste, Vologeses of Parthia sent his general Monaeses to invade Armenia, and Tigranes was shut up in Tigranocerta; but the siege was raised after negotiations. He was withdrawn by the Romans in 62 and disappeared from history. M. S. D.

TIGRANOCERTA, city in Armenia, in Arzanene; later rechristened Martyropolis. Founded by Tigranes I (Appian, Mithr. 67), it replaced Artaxata (q.v.) as the capital of Armenia; it was colonized by Armenians and Cappadocian Greeks (Strabo 12. 2. 7; Plut. Luc. 25. 29) and strongly fortified. In 69 B.C. the battle of Tigranocerta marked the culmination of the Mithridatic wars and the victory of Lucullus (q.v. 2); it was the centre of the struggle between Tiridates and Corbulo (q.v.), and in the wars of Sapor II against Rome and Armenia in the fourth century A.D. it was destroyed by the Sassanians.

The site of Tigranocerta is disputed; see C. F. Lehmann-Haupt, *Armenien einst und jetzt* (1910–31); *PW*, s.v. 'Tigranocerta'; T. Rice Holmes, *Roman Republic* (1923) i. 409 ff. M. S. D.

TIGRIS, the more easterly of the Two Rivers of Mesopotamia. Rising in Armenia, it flows south-east through Assyria and Babylonia to the Persian Gulf. On its left bank it receives three main tributaries, the Greater and Lesser Zâb and the Diyâla. The great Nahrwân canal ran parallel to the east of it. At Seleuceia it is only *c*. 18 miles from the Euphrates (q.v.) and the rivers were joined in antiquity by a network of canals. At the double mouth of the Tigris were the kingdoms of Mesene and Characene. Both rivers frequently change their course. The Tigris is the faster; the journey downstream could be made on rafts, Seleuceia being the limit for shipping. M. S. D.

TIMACHIDAS of Lindus in Rhodes (*c*. 100 B.C.), wrote commentaries on several Greek authors, a δεῖπνον (in eleven books or more—Ath. 1. 5 a) and a miscellaneous glossary.

TIMAEUS (1) of Locri in Italy, Pythagorean, the chief speaker in Plato's *Timaeus*. We have no knowledge of him independent of this, and he may have been a fictitious character. The work in ps.-Doric dialect Περὶ ψυχᾶς κόσμω καὶ φύσιος, which passes under the name of Timaeus Locrus, is a late (probably 1st century A.D.) and unintelligent paraphrase of the *Timaeus*: ed. (with Plato's *Timaeus*) C. F. Herman (Leipzig 1852).

Testimonia in Diels, *Vorsokr.*[5] i. 441. *PW* vi A. 1203. W. D. R.

TIMAEUS (2) of Tauromenium (*c*. 356–260 B.C.). His father Andromachus became tyrant of Tauromenium when he settled there with the Naxians expelled by Dionysius II (358), and by his moderate rule succeeded in retaining his position after the liberation of Sicily by Timoleon (343). However, T. fled to Athens, either in 317, when Agathocles drove his enemies from Syracuse to Acragas, or when he seized Tauromenium (312). There he remained for fifty years, studied rhetoric under Philiscus, pupil of Isocrates, came into contact with the Peripatetic School, and probably returned to Sicily under Hieron II.

The *History* ('Ιστορίαι) in 38 books was primarily concerned with Sicily, and its importance was great in standardizing previous accounts of Sicilian history and origins. It included events in Italy and Carthage, frequently mentioned affairs in Greece, and reached its conclusion with Pyrrhus' death (272). The books on Agathocles and Pyrrhus (34–8) seem to have been added to the original plan, perhaps after T.'s return.

Timaeus' faults largely resulted from his rhetorical training and were common to most of his contemporaries. He showed little critical ability, and his rationalizing of myths is clumsy. But charges of wilful ignorance or falsification (Diod. Sic. 13. 90; Polyb. 12. 25) cannot be substantiated; and we must recognize in him the cultivation of wide interests characteristic of the Peripatetics, diligence in collecting information, and a reasonable impartiality, except in the case of Agathocles.

FHG i. 193. G. L. B.

TIMAEUS (3) (probably 4th c. A.D.), under the influence of Neoplatonism, compiled an extant lexicon of Plato.

Editions: Ruhnken (1789); Koch (1833); Dübner (in Baiter's *Plato*, 1839).

TIMAGENES of Alexandria, captured and brought to Rome in 55 B.C., where he taught rhetoric and knew Augustus, but subsequently fell out of favour with him. He was a friend of Asinius Pollio, at whose villas he lived. The reference to him in Hor. *Epist.* 1. 19. 15 is obscure. He wrote a *History of Kings* (Βασιλεῖς), which was used by Pompeius Trogus.

FHG iii. 317–23; *FGrH* ii. 88; *PW* vi A. 1. 1063–71. J. D. D.

TIMANTHES (late 5th c. B.C.), painter, of Cythnus, later of Sicyon, contemporary of Zeuxis; famed for his *ingenium*. In his 'sacrifice of Iphigenia' he showed degrees of grief culminating in the veiled Agamemnon (reflections on late reliefs, Pfuhl, figs. 638–9). He also painted an ideal Hero, and a sleeping Cyclops with a tiny Satyr beside him. T. B. L. W.

TIME-RECKONING. The ancients, like all civilized peoples, were faced with a grave difficulty in the reckoning of time, apart from the incidental ones which must have confronted their earliest attempts to observe its passage accurately. For reasons of 'ancestral custom', quite as much religious as scientific or practical, they tried 'to conduct their years in accordance with the sun, their days and months in accordance with the moon' (Geminus of Rhodes, 8. 7). Now the three natural divisions of time, day, lunar month, and solar year, are incommensurables. Taking the day as 1, the lengths of the other two are approximately $29\frac{1}{2}$ and $365\frac{1}{4}$ respectively, but these last two figures are far from accurate, and the inaccuracy is bound to show itself in any calendar, however carefully reckoned, which tries to combine them.

2. THE DAY (ἧμαρ, ἡμέρα, *dies*). Although the Babylonians, with whose astronomy the Greeks early became to some extent acquainted, divided day and night (24 hours, νυχθήμερον in Greek) into twelve periods (double hours, cf. Hdt. 2. 109. 3, but see J. E. Powell in *CR* 54, 69 f.), the Greeks made little use of this measurement for any but purely scientific calculations till Hellenistic times (*cf.* CLOCKS). Ordinarily, in classical times, they did not speak of hours but of 'cock-crow', 'time of full market' (i.e. mid-morning), 'noon', 'lamp-lighting', 'time of first sleep', and the like. When hours were used, they were not of fixed length, but each 1/12 of the day (or night), consequently varying with the season. Our hour is the ὥρα ἰσημερινή, *hora aequinoctialis*, 1/12 of the day or night at the equinox. Besides the natural reckoning of the day from dawn, it was common in Greece to reckon it officially, for calendar purposes, from sunset to sunset; the Romans reckoned from midnight.

3. THE WEEK was little used, save, in Hellenistic times, by believers in astrology (see ASTROLOGY). It is a grouping of days in accordance with the supposed governing of the first hour of each by the planet whose name it bears; for details see F. H. Colson, *The Week*, (1926; not always quite accurate, but the fullest and best account in English). Strictly speaking, neither Jews nor Christians observe a week, since both officially reject astrology, but a festival (Sabbath and Sunday respectively) which occurs at intervals of seven days. The planetary week becomes important about the third century A.D., and is called ἑβδομάς, *septimana*. In Italy it was customary to have market-days (*nundinae*) at intervals of eight days (a *nundinum*). This might loosely be called a week, but was of very small importance for reckoning time. On calendars it was marked by a continuous series of letters, A–H, the first being the day of the *nundinae*.

4. MONTHS (*see further* CALENDARS) were (except as noted below) lunar, more or less accurately reckoned. They always consisted of an integral number of days, which varied slightly so that the average length approximated to 29½ days in any given calendar. It was early noticed that while 12 of these months were about equal to a (solar) year (354 or 355 days as against 365¼) the difference was great enough for such a calendar to be about three months too short in eight years. Hence the practice (date and author unknown) of arranging the years in groups of eight (called *oktaeteris*) and inserting in them three extra months (μῆνες ἐμβόλιμοι). The total number of days would thus be about right (2,922, if the intercalation was accurately made). Astronomers, beginning with Meton and Eudoxus (qq.v.), constructed more elaborate and accurate cycles (see, e.g., Geminus 8. 50), but the influence of these on the civic calendars was apparently slow and slight.

5. THE YEAR (ἔτος, ἐνιαυτός, *annus*) consequently was unsatisfactory, since it never exactly coincided with the solar year. As the chief industry of antiquity was agriculture, a demand existed, and was met by the above-named astronomers and others after them, for a perpetual calendar which should show the astronomical facts* and the supposed meteorological events (prevailing winds, etc.) connected with them. Examples of these are the calendar at the end of Geminus (see bibliography, infra), the fragments of a calendar found at Miletus in 1899 (Kubitschek, op. cit. infra, p. 173), and the so-called Italian rustic calendars (ibid., p. 120). They are founded upon the signs of the zodiac, not on civic months. Since a movable pin often enabled the owner to note the day of the local calendar alongside the day given on the perpetual one, the name παράπηγμα was commonly given to such a device. But in Egypt, from very early times, there had been in use a calendar beginning with the rising of Sirius (considered as the sign of the coming rise of the Nile) which consisted of 365 days divided into 12 months having nothing to do with the moon but consisting of 30 days each, with 5 extra days (ἐπαγόμεναι in Greek) at the end of the year. This, of course, meant that in four years the calendar was a day wrong, and in 1,460 years (a Sothis-period, so called from the Egyptian name of Sirius) it righted itself. This difference was well known and its reform proposed (Decree of Canopus, 238 B.C.; see Kubitschek, p. 89) by the insertion of a day every fourth year. On this basis Caesar's reform was founded (*see* CALENDARS), and adopted by Romans and to some extent by others.

6. ERAS. Ancient years, however calculated, were not numbered on any generally understood system, as with us, but merely named ('in the archonship of so-and-so', 'in the consulate of X and Y', 'in the tenth year of the reign of A', etc.), which was next to useless for chronology. This defect was felt, especially by historians, and several eras were proposed. The most familiar were the Olympiads (first celebration of Olympic games, traditionally 776 B.C., thereafter every four years), used quite commonly by chronologists from the fourth century B.C. on; the years from the foundation of Rome, A(nno) V(rbis) C(onditae) or A(b) V(rbe) C(ondita), an event reckoned by Varro (q.v. 2) at 753 B.C. in our dating; and some important local eras, as that of the Seleucidae (kings of Pergamon), from 312 B.C.; several Roman provinces had eras of their own, see Kubitschek, pp. 76 ff. Chronographers from Eratosthenes (q.v.) to the great Christian historian Eusebius of Caesarea and his Latin adapter St. Jerome (see Rose, *Handbook of Lat. Lit.*, 492) also used, for earlier dates, such events as the fall of Troy (1183 B.C., Eratosthenes) or the birth of Abraham (2016 B.C., Eusebius). Our era was introduced by the abbot Dionysius Exiguus (d. *c.* A.D. 540); the practice of reckoning early dates backwards from it is quite recent and a little complicated by the fact that astronomers do

* The Greek peasant was a tolerable practical astronomer from the days of Hesiod and earlier, see, e.g., *Op.* 383; so must the Italian farmers have been.

and historians generally do not insert a year 0 between 1 B.C. and A.D. 1.

Literature: mostly cited in text. The most convenient summary of relevant facts, with good account of earlier works, is W. Kubitschek, *Grundriss der antiken Zeitrechnung* (1928). The most important ancient author, Geminus of Rhodes, is best edited by Manitius (1898; critical text and German version). *See also* CALENDARS.

H. J. R.

TIMESITHEUS, GAIUS FURIUS SABINUS AQUILA, like most of the bureaucrats of the third century A.D., rose from the ranks and entered the equestrian service by way of the centurionate. His career is remarkable for its accumulation of vicarial procuratorships held under Severus Alexander, Maximinus, and Gordian III. In 241 he was appointed Praetorian Prefect and till his death at Nisibis in the winter of 243–4 exercised over his young master a domination that made him virtually emperor. His unscrupulousness is perhaps reflected in the Latin writers' version of his name, Misitheus.

ILS 1330, and see under GORDIAN III. H. M. D. P.

TIMGAD, *see* THAMUGADI.

TIMOCLES, Middle Comedy poet, late in the period, but he practised with wit and originality the ἰαμβικὴ ἰδέα of the Old Comedy, attacking, among many others, Demosthenes and Hyperides. Almost one-half of the fragments touch upon personal ridicule. Of 27 known titles four denote mythological burlesques (Ἥρωες, Κένταυρος), two refer to characters (Ἐπιχαιρέκακος, Πολυπράγμων). An original formation is Ὀρεσταυτοκλείδης, i.e. Autocleides suffering the fate of Orestes—obsessed, however, not by Furies, but by beldames of this world. The latest date to be found in T. is the reference to the γυναικονόμοι of Demetrius of Phalerum, fr. 32. 3—after 317 B.C. Fr. 1, the strange gods of Egypt; fr. 6, consolation from Tragedy, which outdoes human woes; fr. 8, defence of the parasite's life; fr. 12, Demosthenes 'never uttered an antithesis'.

FCG iii. 590 ff.: *CAF* ii. 451 ff.: Demiańczuk, *Suppl. Com.* 88 ff. W. G. W.

TIMOCREON (first half of 5th c. B.C.), lyric and elegiac poet of Ialysus in Rhodes (fr. 1. 3, Plut. *Them.* 21). He probably took the Persian side when they occupied Rhodes, went to Susa as the guest of the Great King (Ath. 10. 415 f), engaged in controversy with Themistocles after 479 for failing to take him home, and mocked him for his failure to win favour at the Isthmus, and, apparently, for not being made general *c.* 477 B.C. He also had interchanges with Simonides, who criticized his style (fr. 162) and character (fr. 99). He was a pentathlic victor and a great glutton (Ath. l.c.). He wrote σκόλια (fr. 5, with a possible reference to his taking money from the Persians) and epigrams (fr. 6; with a possible reference to Themistocles) in a mixture of colloquial and literary language.

Text: E. Diehl, *Anth. Lyr. Graec.* ii, pp. 120–3.
Criticism: C. M. Bowra, *Greek Lyric Poetry* (1936), 369–73. C. M. B.

TIMOLEON, Corinthian general who fought for Syracuse against Dionysius II (q.v.), Hicetas, tyrant of Leontini, and the Carthaginians (345 B.C. ff.). At Corinth he had proved himself an anti-tyrannic and unselfish citizen. Arriving in Sicily at the invitation of the Syracusan patriots, he fought successfully with a small mercenary force against overwhelming odds. He drove Dionysius from the citadel of Syracuse, and recaptured the rest of the city from Hicetas, who was left in the lurch by his Carthaginian allies. With the assistance of other Greek cities which now joined him he invaded the Carthaginian province, and decisively defeated on the banks of the Crimisus a large and newly levied army from Carthage (341). After some further hard and partly unsuccessful campaigns he made peace with Carthage. He next removed the remaining tyrants in Sicily, resettled some important cities, and restored their autonomy. Growing blind, he withdrew from politics (about 337). The date of his death is unknown. Sicily, enjoying a short time of peace and wealth, honoured him highly after death. But his work was soon undone by Agathocles (q.v.): the soldier overcame the idealist.

Main sources, all depending on his panegyrist Timaeus: Plutarch, *Timoleon*; Nepos, *Timoleon*; Diodorus, bk. 16. Literature: Hackforth, *CAH* vi. 285 ff.; Stier, *PW*, s.v.   V. E.

TIMON (*Τίμων*) (1) of Athens, the famous misanthrope, a semi-legendary character. He seems to have lived in the time of Pericles. Aristophanes is the first to allude to him. He became known to Shakespeare through Plutarch (*Ant.* 70) and Lucian's dialogue.

Prosop. Att. 13845.   V. E.

TIMON (2), son of Timarchus from Phlius, sceptic philosopher, *c.* 320–*c.* 230 B.C. (Apollon. Nicaensis ap. Diog. Laert. 9. 109). Like his master Pyrrhon he came from a poor family; he earned his living as a dancer. After attending the lectures of the Megarian philosopher Stilpon he met Pyrrhon in Elis, and became his pupil and prophet. After a life of wandering as a sophist he had saved enough money to live independently in Athens. There he died at 90 years of age (Antig. Car. ap. Diog. Laert. 9. 112).

Timon was the literary exponent of the old sceptic school, a versatile and witty writer. His prose writings are lost except for a few fragments. Of his poetry (tragedies, comedies, etc.) only fragments of philosophic caricatures are preserved. The 'Silloi' (i.e. mock-poetry) in three books ridicule in parodic pseudo-homeric hexameters all dogmatic philosophers. In the *Indalmoi* (i.e. ideas, opinions) he proclaimed the theory of scepticism and refuted dogmatic errors.

Fragments: K. Wachsmuth, *Sillographi Graeci*[2] (1885); H. Diels, *PPF* (1901); Studies: *PW* vi A. 1301; *see also* SCEPTICS.   K. O. B.

TIMOSTRATUS (early 2nd c. B.C.), one of the latest comic poets of Athens whose fragments survive. A man of good Athenian family, T. obtained in 188 B.C. fifth place with *Λυτ[ρούμενος*, in 183 third place with *Φιλοίκειος* (*IG* ii². 2322, lines 141, 155).

FCG iv. 595 f.; *CAF* iii. 355 ff.   W. G. W.

TIMOTHEUS (1) (*c.* 450–*c.* 360 B.C.; *Marm. Par.* 76), dithyrambic poet, of Miletus. After failures in Athens he succeeded with the *Persae*, a lyric nome, for which Euripides wrote the prologue (Satyr. *Vit. Eur.* fr. 39, col. 22) *c.* 419–416 B.C. Large portions of this are preserved in a papyrus of the fourth century B.C. It is an account of Salamis, in which a crude realism is combined with a grotesque imitation of the high style. It closes with the poet's claim to have revolutionized music. Though written out as prose, the *Persians* is constructed on easily distinguishable metrical principles. It is astrophic and composed of various *metra*. His works were collected in eighteen books, but few other fragments are of interest except fr. 7, in which he proclaims the newness of his art. He is said to have influenced Euripides, and parallels have been noted between the speech of the Phrygian in *Persians* 152 with that of the Phrygian in Eur. *Or.* 1365 ff. *See* MUSIC, § 10.

Text: E. Diehl, *Anth. Lyr. Graec.* ii, pp. 134–52.
Commentary: U. von Wilamowitz-Moellendorff, *Timotheos: Die Perser* (1903).   C. M. B.

TIMOTHEUS (2), son of Conon and pupil of Isocrates. Elected *strategus* in 378 B.C., when the Second Athenian Confederacy was founded, he won many members for the Confederacy by his tour of NW. Greece in 375. Recalled in 374, he broke the peace just concluded with Sparta by restoring democratic exiles in Zacynthus, and was

given the command against Sparta in 373. Paralysed by lack of funds, he was impeached but acquitted; to restore his fortunes he served for Persia against Egypt. Upon the fall of Callistratus in 366 he returned to power with an imperialist policy, which alienated Persia and the Confederacy; in spite of Epaminondas' naval campaign he achieved considerable success, but failed repeatedly to capture Amphipolis. Discontent among the Confederates, which his policy evoked, resulted in the Social War; in 356 Timotheus, Iphicrates, and Chares, sharing the command at Embata, failed to co-operate, and impeached by Chares, he was sentenced to a fine of 100 talents, left Athens, and died in 354. A wealthy aristocrat with little sympathy for the demos, he pursued an individualist and short-sighted policy with outstanding ability.

P. Cloché, *La Politique étrangère d'Athènes 404–338 B.C.* (1934).
                    N. G. L. H.

TIMOTHEUS (3), Greek sculptor of the fourth century B.C., who worked on the sculptures of the sanctuary of Asclepius at Epidaurus and later on the Mausoleum of Halicarnassus, in company with other artists. An inscription at Epidaurus records payments made to him for making reliefs (or models) and acroterial figures for the temple. The surviving sculptures from Epidaurus give us some indication of his style, which appears to have been in the Attic manner.   S. C.

TIN, as a component of bronze, occurs very early in Mesopotamia, apparently derived from a distant source, probably Drangiana. Bronze is found sporadically in the later Early Minoan period, and regularly from Middle Minoan times; it probably reached the rest of Europe at a rather later date. The principal sources available to the classical world were the Erzgebirge (cf. Scymnus 493) and western Europe. Small quantities were mined in Etruria in pre-Roman times, and tin was worked near Delphi. The Phoenicians tried at times to monopolize the western sources, but by the third century Massilia established an overland route. The main Punic source was probably Galicia. Breton tin was worked at an early date, but not much in Roman times; the mines of central Gaul closed soon after the Roman conquest. Cornish tin was hardly known before the Late Bronze Age; it was worked all through the Roman period under native supervision. In Cornwall must be located the Cassiterides. They were known to Massiliots from the fifth century, but the sea-route thither from Spain was discovered by P. Crassus (q.v. 2) probably about 95 B.C. *See also* CASSITERIDES.

Metallic tin must have been known to alloy in exact proportions with copper; little has survived, mainly owing to oxidization, but also because it was not of great use unalloyed. Classical writers confuse tin and lead, because they had no clear idea of the atomic difference of metals. Mining was largely in placers; in Cornwall vein-mining was not started before late medieval times.

See especially Strabo 3. 175–6, Polybius 34. 10. H. Hencken, *Archaeology of Cornwall and Scilly* (1932); W. C. Borlase, *Tin-mining in Spain Past and Present* (1897); O. Davies, *Roman Mines in Europe* (1935); *Proc. Belfast Natural History Society* 1931/2, 41.
                    O. D.

TINGI(S) (modern *Tangier*), a seaport nearly facing Gibraltar across the Straits. Phoenician sailors established a trading-station there and fitted it with an elaborate water-supply, for use on their voyages to Tartessus and the Canaries. After Bocchus' death it passed to Juba II. Tingi received municipal rights and became the capital of the procurator of Mauretania Tingitana under Claudius. It was cut off from Rusaddir (*Melilla*) by the Riff mountains, but was connected with Volubilis (q.v.) and Sala by military roads. Among the auxiliaries which protected Tingi was a detachment of British cavalry.   W. N. W.

TIQUADRA, *see* BALEARES INSULAE.

TIRESIAS (*Τειρεσίας*), a legendary blind Theban seer, so wise that even his ghost still has its wits (*φρένες*, cf. SOUL) and is not a mere phantom (*Odyssey* 10. 493–5). Later legends account for his wisdom and blindness chiefly thus: (*a*) He saw Athena bathing; since his mother was her friend, she did not cause his death, but blinded him and gave him the power of prophecy by way of compensation (Callimachus, *Lav. Pall.* 57 ff.). (*b*) He one day saw snakes coupling and struck them with his stick, whereat he became a woman; later the same thing happened again and he turned into a man. Being asked by Zeus and Hera to settle a dispute as to which sex had more pleasure of love, he decided for the female; Hera was angry and blinded him, but Zeus recompensed him by giving him long life and power of prophecy. So Hyginus, *Fab.* 75, see Rose, ad loc. His advice was sought throughout the times of the Labdacidae, and he finally died after the evacuation of Thebes when besieged by the Epigoni, from drinking of the spring Tilphussa (Apollod. 3. 84, cf. Athenaeus, 41 e).   H. J. R.

TIRIDATES (1) **II** was the throne-name of some Parthian, not an Arsacid, who was probably Monaeses, the general who had defeated Antony's invasion. He revolted against Phraates IV, apparently in 32 B.C., and expelled him; but in 30 Phraates was restored by the Suren from Seistan. Tiridates escaped to Syria, and in 27 invaded Mesopotamia; as he had learnt that only an Arsacid could hold the throne successfully, he set up as joint-king with himself Phraates' young son Phraates, but by 25 Phraates IV had recovered Parthia, and the boy-king had fled to Augustus. Tiridates' end is unknown.

W. W. Tarn, *Mélanges Glotz* ii. 831.   W. W. T.

TIRIDATES (2) **III,** grandson of Phraates IV, was sent by Tiberius to contest the Parthian throne, with the military support of L. Vitellius, governor of Syria (Tac. *Ann.* 4. 32). Expelling Artabanus II, he was welcomed by the pro-Roman faction in the cities of Mesopotamia, and was crowned at Ctesiphon (A.D. 35); he was subsequently again driven out by Artabanus.   M. S. D.

TIRIDATES (3), brother of Vologeses I (q.v.) of Parthia, who set him on the throne of Armenia (A.D. 54). He fled before the Romans and was temporarily displaced by Tigranes V (q.v.), but was reinstated by Vologeses. By a compromise with Corbulo (q.v.) T. agreed to journey to Rome and receive the crown of Armenia ceremonially from Nero (A.D. 66).   M. S. D.

TIRO, MARCUS TULLIUS, freedman, secretary, and friend of Cicero, wrote a biography of him and perhaps collected his notable sayings. He also published original works (*De usu atque ratione linguae Latinae*, a miscellany [*Πανδέκται*], *Epistulae*) and perhaps prepared a tragedy. He edited some parts of Cicero's works and assisted in the collection of the letters. He invented a system of shorthand (*notae Tironianae* is a modern name), which is preserved with modifications (*see* TACHYGRAPHY).

W. Drumann, *Geschichte Roms* vi² (1929), 356; H. Peter, *HRRel.* ii, p. xvii; Schanz–Hosius, *Röm. Literatur*⁴ i (1927), 590.   A. M.

TIRO, *see also* JULIUS (12).

TIROCINIUM, *see* IUVENES.

TIRONIANAE NOTAE, *see* TACHYGRAPHY.

TIRYNS occupies a rocky hill in the Argive plain, 2½ miles north of Nauplia and 1 mile from the sea. A few neolithic fragments show that the site was early inhabited,

and with the Early Bronze Age (*c.* 2800–2100 B.C.) it became important. A round house, perhaps that of the chief, stood on the summit with huts clustered round, and the main settlement spread in the plain below. In the Middle Bronze Age a settlement on the hill with the pottery, houses, and tombs characteristic of the age seems to have been fortified. Its inhabitants belonged to what was probably the first wave of Greek-speaking people in Greece. To this succeeded (1600–1400) in the Late Bronze Age a prince's house of which only a few fresco fragments remain. About 1400 Tiryns began to assume its present form. In the first stage a great wall was built round the south of the hill with a gate on the east. In the second stage the fortress was enlarged at a higher level created by terracing. The wall was extended to the north to include the middle part of the hill, and on the east a great gate, like the Lion Gate at Mycenae, was built. In the third stage the vaulted galleries with store chambers on the south and east were added. A bastion with a side gate was thrown out on the west and a massive wall was built round the north of the hill to protect flocks and herds and refugees. Within the south citadel arose a complex of buildings comprising an earlier and a later royal residence. The earlier palace on the east is well built though small, and is approached through a court. The west or great megaron was a noble hall entered through two courts with propylons, and the inner court contained an altar and a colonnade. It was richly decorated with frescoes, like its predecessors, and by the hearth was a place for a throne. At the side were a bathroom and chambers with upper stories. The lower town on the plain developed similarly, and Tiryns at this time was a rich and powerful State. Attempts to reconcile the plans of the palace and the two megara with the Homeric house divided into men's and women's apartments are based on the false assumption that the two megara were contemporaneous and parts of one homogeneous structure. The palace perished by fire at the end of the Late Bronze Age, but Tiryns continued to be inhabited through the geometric and archaic periods, and a temple seems to have arisen on the ruins of the palace. Tiryns survived into the classical period as an independent town and sent a contingent to Plataea, but was destroyed by Argos *c.* 470 B.C.

H. Schliemann, *Tiryns* (1886); A. Frickenhaus, G. Rodenwaldt, K. Müller, *Tiryns* i–iv (1912–39); G. Karo, *Führer durch Tiryns*² (1934).   A. J. B. W.

TISIAS of Syracuse (5th c. B.C.), pupil of Corax and teacher of Gorgias, Isocrates, and Lysias, wrote a *τέχνη* based on that of Corax. To him have been attributed the Doric fragments on rhetoric in *POxy.* iii, pp. 27 ff. (see W. R. Roberts, *CR* xviii (1904), 18 ff.).

T. W. H. A.

TISSAPHERNES, satrap of the Anatolian coastal provinces from 413 B.C., after he had suppressed the revolt by Pissuthnes of Lydia. In 412, prompted by Alcibiades, he began the policy of intervention in the Peloponnesian War, though his support for Sparta was intermittent and half-hearted, his real objective being the exhaustion of both sides. The conspiracy of his brother Terituchmes against Darius II may have been a contributory factor in Tissaphernes' relegation to Caria in 408, when Cyrus initiated a vigorous pro-Spartan policy. In 401, when Cyrus began to mobilize his army, Tissaphernes, who had previously denounced him on Artaxerxes' accession, rode post-haste to warn the Great King. At Cunaxa his cavalry charge decided the day. He was restored to his command of the coastal provinces, and had to bear the brunt of the Spartan offensive which followed. Though he diplomatically diverted most of the attacks against Pharnabazus, he was crushingly defeated by Agesilaus near Sardis in 395. The hatred of Parysatis (Artaxerxes' daughter) had long made his position insecure, and after his disaster Artaxerxes decided to remove him. He was lured by Tithraustes to Colossae and assassinated.

W. Judeich, *Kleinasiatische Studien* (1892), ch. 2. D. E. W. W.

TITAN (Τιτάν,-ῆν), one of the older gods who were before the Olympians, children of Heaven and Earth. Hesiod (*Theog.* 132 ff.), lists Oceanus, Coeus, Crius, Hyperion, Iapetos, Theia, Rhea, Themis, Mnemosyne, Phoebe, Tethys, and Kronos. These names are an odd mixture of Greek and non-Greek, personal names and abstractions. For the battle between them and Zeus *see* KRONOS. The etymology of Τιτῆνες is highly uncertain; Hesiod (ibid. 209) fancifully derives it from τιταίνειν, to strain, and τίσις, vengeance, in allusion to their relations with their father. Later poetry often uses Titan and Titanis for Hyperion and Phoebe, Sun and Moon. *See also* ORPHISM. H. J. R.

TITANOMACHIA, *see* EPIC CYCLE.

TITHE, δεκάτη, the tenth part of a revenue offered as thankoffering to a god; the sense is often the same as that of votive offering, ἀπαρχή (q.v.). E.g. a certain Aeschines offered a statue to Athena as δεκάτη (*IG* i². 543). Best known are the tithes which the Athenians brought to the Eleusinian goddesses and in a decree exhorted all Greeks to bring (*IG* i². 76; 2; *SIG* 83). M. P. N.

TITIANUS, JULIUS (2nd c. A.D.), epistolographer (Ciceronian in style), miscellanist, and grammarian. His studies of Virgil are mentioned by Servius ad *Aen.* 10. 18. His son wrote prose fables. The elder Titianus was nicknamed 'ape' (*simia*, Sid. Apoll. *Ep.* 1. 1. 2) by his fellow *Frontoniani* (q.v.) in disapproval of his copying Cicero's epistolary style.

Teuffel, § 364. J. W. D.

TITIES, RAMNES, LUCERES, *see* TRIBUS.

TITINIUS (1), Latin poet; earliest known composer of *fabulae togatae* of the type called *tabernariae*, in lively popular Plautine style. He survived Terence, with whom he was classed in character-drawing, especially feminine. *See* DRAMA, ROMAN, para. 5.

Fragments: O. Ribbeck, *CRF*² 133 (3rd ed. Teubner, 1897). E. H. W.

TITINIUS (2) **CAPITO,** GNAEUS OCTAVIUS, belonged to the younger Pliny's circle and is praised by him as an upholder of high literary standards (*Ep.* 8. 12). His *recitationes* included obituaries of prominent citizens. Pliny addresses to him a very interesting comparison between history and oratory (*Ep.* 5. 8). For the inscription recording his career see *ILS* 1448. J. W. D.

TITIUS (1), GAIUS (2nd c. B.C.), orator and tragic writer. The abundance of *argutiae* in his speeches is mentioned by Cicero, *Brut.* 167.

See Teuffel, § 141.

TITIUS (2) MARCUS, served as Antony's quaestor in the Parthian expedition (36 B.C.), and hunted down Sextus Pompeius in the following year. He went over to Octavian in 32, was *consul suffectus* in 31, and fought in the campaign of Actium. He was later governor of Syria.

Plutarch, *Antony*; Appian, *BCiv.* bk. 5; Dio Cassius, bks. 48–50. G. W. R.

TITIUS (3) **PROBUS,** GAIUS, an epitomator whose relation to Julius Paris, abbreviator of Valerius Maximus, is obscure. The difficulty was felt by Vossius, *De Historicis Latinis*, prefixed to Leyden edn. of Val. Max. 1655.

Teuffel, § 279. 11.

TITUS (TITUS FLAVIUS VESPASIANUS, A.D. 39–81), the son of the future emperor Vespasian, was educated with Claudius' son Britannicus. He served in Germany and Britain as *tribunus militum*, and accompanied his father, eventually serving as *legatus legionis*, to Palestine. When Vespasian departed to assume the principate, Titus was left to carry on the Jewish war, which he completed in 70 with the capture of Jerusalem. On his return to Rome he triumphed with Vespasian and was promoted to virtual partnership in the government. He was given the *proconsulare imperium* and the *tribunicia potestas*, held the censorship (73) and seven consulships with his father, and was made *praefectus praetorio* without colleague. He was thus marked out for the succession, and on Vespasian's death was declared princeps automatically (A.D. 79).

Under his father Titus had conducted a most unpopular liaison with Berenice, sister of Herod Agrippa, and as *praefectus praetorio* he had shown himself cruel. Only the soldiers adored him. But as princeps Titus rapidly won universal affection. Possessed of good looks, intelligence, and charm, he introduced an era of fabulous generosity. His father's carefully garnered wealth enabled him to indulge his love of giving, and nobody was turned away from his door. His own house was set in order, Berenice finally dismissed, and Vespasian's modest way of living retained.

There were no executions or trials for *maiestas*, and informers were publicly scourged and expelled. By these and other means the Senate was mollified and its opposition practically ceased. Titus showed the utmost leniency to conspirators, even promoting participants. With his brother Domitian his relations were unhappy; feeling that he could not trust him, he did not promote Domitian from his post of *princeps iuventutis*.

Two disasters befell Italy during the reign, the eruption of Vesuvius (24 August 79), which destroyed Pompeii and Herculaneum, and the plague and great fire in Rome (A.D. 80). Titus generously helped the sufferers, and took in hand an extensive building programme to replace the damage of the fire. He completed the Colosseum and built the Thermae that carry his name.

Titus died in 81. His death caused universal sorrow, and this 'darling of the human race' (Suetonius) was at once enrolled among the gods. Probably his lavish expenditure would soon have caused a crisis; but men remembered his short reign as a period of ideal happiness.

Suet. *Titus*; Dio Cass. bk. 66; PIR, F 264; Weynand, *PW*, s.v. 'Flavius (207)'; *PIR²*, F 399. *See also* VESPASIAN. R. L. J.

TITYUS, a son of Earth, whom Odysseus saw in Hades, covering nine acres of ground, while two vultures tore at his liver, as a punishment for assaulting Leto (*Od.* 11. 576–81). The seat of desire is appropriately punished. He was killed by Zeus (Hyginus, *Fab.* 55), Apollo (Apoll. Rhod. 1. 759 ff.), Artemis (Pindar, *Pyth.* 4. 90; in Euphorion, fr. 105 Powell, she was defending herself, not her mother), or Apollo and Artemis (Apollod. 1. 23). For variants in his story, which are numerous, see Waser in Roscher, s.v. H. J. R.

TLEPOLEMUS, *see* LICYMNIUS.

TMOLUS (Τμῶλος), the deity of the Lydian mountain so named. He appears, with Midas, as judge of the contest between Apollo and Pan (Ovid, *Met.* 11. 156 ff.), and as a coin-figure.

TOGA. The toga was the conventional town dress of the respectable Roman citizen, corresponding to our black morning-coat. It was uncomfortable and expensive; but to wear it on public occasions in Rome was an ancestral custom which had to be observed. The material was fine white wool, with the distinguishing mark of a purple border for curule magistrates and for youths till they reached manhood, *toga praetexta*. In shape it was like two large segments of a circle equal in size placed with the straight edges together. In length it was nearly three times, in width about twice, the height of the wearer; and it required very careful adjustment. Before putting on it was folded lengthwise, bunched into thick folds, and thrown over the left shoulder with a third of its total length hanging in front. The rest of the cloth was passed across the back, brought forward under the right arm, and again thrown back over the left shoulder, covering nearly all the left arm. Then the back portion was spread out to cover the right shoulder, and the front was drawn up at the breast so as to make a mass of folds, *sinus*, which served as a pocket.

Quintilian, 11. 3. 137; Tertullian, *De Pallio* 5. L. Wilson, *The Roman Toga* (1924).   F. A. W.

TOGATA sc. **fabula**, *see* FABULA.

TOILET. Most of the aids to beauty known to-day were to be found in ancient times on a lady's toilet table; and both in Greece and Rome men gave much more attention to their bodies than is usual with us. The Greeks were constantly rubbing themselves with olive-oil, and the Romans under the Empire devoted much time to massage and bathing: dandies went further and would remove the hair from every part of their body with tweezers, pitch-plaster, and depilatories.

Many specimens have been found of ancient toilet implements, such as mirrors, combs, razors, scissors, curling-tongs, hair-pins, safety-pins, nail-files, and ear-picks. Mirrors were usually made of burnished metal, for though glass was known it was seldom used. Combs were of the tooth-comb pattern, with one coarse and one fine row of teeth. Razors, made of bronze, were of various shapes, the handle often beautifully engraved. Safety-pins (*fibulae*) and brooches had many forms elaborately inlaid with enamel and metal. Ear-picks—*auriscalpia*—were in general use at Rome.

Cosmetics and perfumes were freely used. Athenian wives attached importance to white cheeks, as distinguishing them from sunburned working women; they applied white lead, and also used a rouge made from orchid. Roman ladies also had a great variety of salves, unguents, and hair-dyes, kept in a toilet box with separate compartments for powders, paints, and tooth-pastes. Several recipes for these commodities are given by Ovid in his mock-didactic poem *De medicamine faciei*, the strangest being one for a lotion 'halcyon cream', made apparently from birds' nests and guaranteed to cure spots on the face.

Greek women usually wore their hair arranged simply in braids, with a parting in the middle, drawn into a knot behind; and the same style was frequently adopted in Rome. But under the Empire a fashion arose of raising a structure of hair on the top of the head, painfully arranged by a lady's maid. Blondes were fashionable in Rome, and brunettes could either dye their hair or use the false hair which was freely imported from Germany.

Men in early Greece and Rome wore beards and allowed the hair of the skull to grow long. From the fifth century the Greeks cut the hair of their skulls short, and from the time of Alexander they shaved their chins. The Romans followed suit in the third century B.C., but from the time of Hadrian they again wore beards.

Ovid, *De medicamine faciei*.   F. A. W.

TOLOSA, town in Gallia Narbonensis, modern *Toulouse*, a typical river-plain site (of pre-Roman origin), which under Augustus completely superseded the important Halstatt-La Tène *oppidum* of Vieille-Toulouse. In 106 B.C. Tolosa was wantonly sacked by the consul Cn. Servilius Caepio, who carried off a huge spoil. Under the Empire Tolosa possessed *ius Latii* and perhaps the title of colony (Ptolemy 2. 10. 6). Famous for literary culture, its most famous son was, however, the warrior Antonius Primus. Since 418 it was the capital of the Visigothic kingdom (*regnum Tolosanum*). Its ancient remains are scanty.

C. E. Stevens, *PW* vi A. 1685–93.   C. E. S.

TOMIS (Τόμις, Τόμαι; Tomi; mod. *Costanza*) was a Milesian colony of the seventh century. It had a trade route to the Danube across the Dobrudja, but until the third century it played a subordinate part to its neighbour Istria (q.v.). It was brought under Roman rule by M. Lucullus (72 B.C.), but continued to suffer from raids by the hinterland peoples until it was incorporated in the province of Moesia. Under Roman rule, if not before, it was the head of a league of neighbouring Greek cities. The poet Ovid, who was relegated to Tomis by Augustus, held rank there as ἀγωνοθέτης.   M. C.

TORCH-RACE, a relay race in which sacred fire was carried by competing teams from one altar to another. At Athens it formed part of the Prometheia, Hephaesteia, and Panathenaea, and was extended to other cults, as that of Pan (Hdt. 6. 105). In the festival of Bendis at Piraeus it was a horse-race (Pl. *Resp.* 328 a). The contest probably originated in the belief that fire through use loses its purity, and that fresh fire must be periodically fetched from the altar of a fire-god. The ritual was common to many cults in all Greece and maintained its sacral character throughout antiquity.

See articles 'Lampadedromia' in *PW* and Dar.-Sag. F. R. W.

TORQUATUS, *see* MANLIUS (4).

TORTURE was applied in the Roman criminal procedure at an early time, but only to slaves to make them confess when accused or to force the truth out of them as witnesses. The procedure was called *quaestio*; a slave's evidence was never *testimonium*. In Republican times the use of torture was fairly common, but the emperors of the first two centuries A.D. tried to restrict it by admitting it only in cases of grave crime and when the delinquent was so near conviction, 'ut sola confessio seruorum deesse . . . uideatur'. (See the discussion in *Dig.* 48. 18.) From the time of Tiberius the application of torture extended to free persons (to witnesses in the second century), except the *honestiores* (q.v.). Stricter provisions were introduced with regard to some special crimes such as adultery and *crimen maiestatis*, where slaves could be examined under torture against their *domini*, though normally they were not allowed to give evidence against them. In post-classical times torture was extended to civil proceedings (*Cod. Theod.* 2. 27. 1. 2 a), and even Justinian with his distrust of witnesses maintained it, though with restriction to low-born and suspected individuals.   A. B.

TOWNS. I. GREEK AND HELLENISTIC. Very little was known about the residential planning of Greek towns of the fifth century B.C. before the recent excavations at Olynthus in Macedonia. These have disclosed a regular formation of domestic buildings opening to long straight streets, as in the much earlier towns of Egypt; an arrangement obviously suitable for a flat site. The only other evidences of this period or earlier are those from some fortified hill-towns, where remains within the walls are too scanty to enable any substantial conclusions to be drawn. Hippodamus of Miletus (q.v.) is credited with the adoption of the 'Gridiron' system of planning in squares, with all streets at right angles to one another, and it is evident that Priene (fourth, third, and second centuries) which is on a hill slope, wonderfully preserved, shows no attempt to depart from parallel rectangular formations; these suited the plan types of the larger units formed by Greek temples and civic buildings, the particularly large one of the agora or market—an open court with colonnades all round—being conspicuous. The Stoa or Portico (q.v.) and (particularly) the Stadium were also units of considerable size, but the latter was usually on the outskirts of the town proper. The Temple (q.v.) was given a position of importance, and the Theatre (q.v.) utilized the rising ground which governed the selection of a site.

On the more monumental side, Selinus in Sicily shows the most complete early evidences, though, as at Paestum and Hipponium in Magna Graecia, there is little left except some fine walls and the temples or their foundations. Hellenistic sites with substantial evidences are Pergamum, Miletus, and Corinth. At Pergamum, which is a fortified town of the third and second centuries, placed on a hill, the evidences of gymnasia, temples and their precincts, a library, a great altar, upper and lower palaces, and a theatre overlooking a long terrace, are remarkably complete and show skilful planning with wise abandonment of Hippodamian principles. Unfortunately very little is left of Hellenistic Antioch so far as can be known, and of Hellenistic Alexandria still less. Dura-Europus (Seleucid, third century) was also mostly of parallel formation; but it is clear from Miletus that large Hellenistic towns on flat sites had groups of civic buildings which were arranged round open courts, though there is little attention to symmetry or axial formality.

II. GRAECO-ROMAN AND ROMAN. Graeco-Roman and Roman towns show adhesion in essentials to Greek and Hellenistic principles of domestic planning—Timgad, N. Africa (second century A.D.), of 'Gridiron' formation, with closely packed units, might be six centuries earlier —but, in general, the Roman town, whatever its geographical position, conformed to the usages of a military camp in its surrounding wall (*vallum*), its main street (*cardo*), cross streets (*decumani*) and groups of buildings in *insulae*. The important Roman towns in the Near East—Palmyra, Gerasa (Jerash) and, in N. Africa, Leptis Magna—had monumental buildings (Baths, Basilicas, Theatres (qq.v.), Nymphaea, etc.) sometimes planned on axial lines—one of the most remarkable being those associated with the Temple of Artemis at Gerasa—and additional monumental quality in their colonnaded streets, providing shelter for the footways, with 'tetrapylons' at the main intersections and arched gateways at their ends. The temples occupied the same commanding positions as in the cities of Greece. This involved, on flat sites (e.g. Aezani, Palmyra) raised platforms on made ground of great extent, with surrounding walls and covered ways.

Ostia, Pompeii, and Herculaneum—three provincial centres or seaside resorts quite near Rome—have afforded the most vivid evidences of town life. At Ostia there were streets with continuous blocks of houses of three stories. At Pompeii there are two distinct elements— the forum and temple one, which has monumental quality, and the residential one, in which the wealthy type of house predominates. Herculaneum was a seaside resort laid out with remarkable orderliness, fronted towards the sea by a wide terrace protected by a moat. It is clear from the two latter sites that the principles of house planning and disposition, though certain local features were introduced, did not differ materially from those at the close of the Hellenistic period which can be seen at Delos. In Rome the Forum had important buildings in it and around it, the adjacent Palatine Hill containing the palaces of the Caesars; the extent of the residential element must be imagined, but without difficulty, as so many larger evidences still remain.

A. von Gerkan, *Griechische Städteanlagen* (1924). D. S. Robertson, op. cit. under ARCHITECTURE, ch. 12. T. Fyfe, *Hellenistic Architecture* (1936), ch. 8. T. F.

TOXARIS, a Scythian visitor to Athens, given heroic honours there after his death in gratitude for good medical advice sent by him in a dream in time of plague, Lucian, *Scythes* 1.

TOYS (παίγνια, *ioculi*). Specimens from children's tombs, and representations on Greek painted vases (in particular on small Attic red-figure jugs, which are surmised to have been presents to children on the feast of Choes) provide our knowledge of ancient toys, which did not differ essentially from modern ones. For the infant there were clappers and rattles (πλαταγή, *crepitaculum*), hinged surfaces of wood or revolving circles with bells or rings of metal, or in animal form with loose pebbles inside. *Crepundia* (γνωρίσματα) were miniature objects and charms hung around the infant's neck; in literature these often served to identify abandoned or kidnapped children. Bells (κώδων, *tintinnabulum*) served the double purpose of amusement and of averting the evil eye. For a more advanced age the doll of rag, bone, wood, or clay was the customary plaything; the limbs were often movable (νευρόσπαστα). Doll's house furniture, chairs, couches, toilet and kitchen utensils, were used as toys as well as for votive offerings; it was customary for girls on marriage and for boys on arrival at puberty to dedicate their playthings to deities. Animals, chariots and horses in wood or clay, go-carts, and whip-tops are represented in museums, while the use of the ball (σφαῖρα, *pila*) and hoop (τροχός, *trochus*) is illustrated on vase-paintings, as are the swing and see-saw. Regular games were played with knucklebones (ἀστράγαλος, *talus*), dice (κύβος, *tessara*), and other pieces.

Anita E. Klein, *Child Life in Greek Art* (U.S.A. 1932); *British Museum Guide to the Exhibition illustrating Greek and Roman Life*, s.v. 'Toys'; L. Becq de Fouquières, *Les Jeux des anciens* (1873). F. N. P.

TRABEA, QUINTUS, Latin writer of *comoediae palliatae*, contemporary with Caecilius; could stir the emotions, says Varro. Two fragments in O. Ribbeck, *CRF*[2] 31 (3rd ed. Teubner, 1897).

TRABEATA sc. fabula: *see* FABULA.

TRACHALUS, *see* GALERIUS (2).

TRAGEDY, GREEK (Introductory). At the beginning of the fifth century B.C. Tragedy at Athens formed part of the Great Dionysia, the spring festival of Dionysus Eleuthereus, probably organized some decades earlier by Pisistratus and reorganized towards the turn of the century by Cleisthenes. Three poets competed, each presenting three tragedies and one satyric play. In the former, the actors—originally one only, but Aeschylus introduced a second very early in the century—and the chorus all presented human beings or divine beings in human form; in the latter the chorus were disguised as satyrs, mainly human in form but with the ears and tails of horses and indecently costumed, and the play presented parts of ancient legend which were grotesque in themselves or could easily be made so. Contests of dithyrambs, danced by 50 singers in circular formation (whereas the tragic chorus was arranged in a rectangle), were performed at the festival before the end of the century; the addition of the satyric plays to the tragedies probably took place about 500 B.C.

2. The scenes of a tragedy consisted of set speeches or dialogue as might be required; in the earliest play of Aeschylus (the *Supplices*) dialogue is mostly between an actor and the chorus leader and there is little conversation between two actors. The scenes are separated by choral odes of considerable length and of high excellence as lyric poetry. This suggests that tragedy sprang from a performance which was entirely lyric, and in fact the introduction of a single actor, delivering a prologue and set speeches, is attributed, on what seems to be good authority, to Thespis (q.v.), who gave a performance at Athens about 534 B.C. and probably began the use of the iambic trimeter metre for such speeches, though the trochaic tetrameter was never entirely abandoned for dialogue. The actors and chorus in tragedy wore masks (the actor's mask having been introduced by Thespis, after other experiments in disguise), and must have had some kind of σκηνή or tent to change in. The number of the chorus employed by Thespis and by Aeschylus in his early days is disputed; some scholars think that it was fifty, as in the dithyramb, and argue that as in Aeschylus' earliest extant play the chorus represented the fifty daughters of Danaus, it must have contained fifty singers; others, who doubt the derivation of tragedy from dithyramb, point to the fact that the chorus in other plays of Aeschylus consisted of twelve or, later, fifteen singers.

3. The attempt to trace back the development of tragedy before the fifth century is beset with uncertainties at every point. Phrynichus, indeed, a slightly senior contemporary of Aeschylus, seems to have written plays predominantly lyric and not unlike the early plays of Aeschylus himself. But of Thespis nothing more is certainly known than what has been stated above, though one account brings him to Athens from Icaria (in Attica), where his performances may have been connected with the autumn festival of the vintage, and some scholars, relying upon late and doubtful notices, think that these or some similar performances may have been a grotesque affair, which, developing in different directions, gave rise to both tragedy and comedy. No ancient authority attributes satyric plays or satyr-choruses to Thespis. We hear (Pollux 4. 123) of a time 'before Thespis' when 'someone' got up on a table and answered the chorus, and Thespis may have turned this 'someone' into a regular actor impersonating a character. A late notice (Suidas, s.v. Ἀρίων) ascribes to Arion of Corinth (about 600 B.C.) the invention of the τραγικὸς τρόπος, i.e. probably the style or mode in music which afterwards belonged to tragedy, and a statement (Joannes Diaconus in Hermogenem) attributed to Solon says that Arion composed the first δρᾶμα τῆς τραγῳδίας. Further, Herodotus (5. 67) records that at Sicyon the τραγικοὶ χοροί commemorating the sufferings of the hero Adrastus were transferred by the tyrant Cleisthenes to the worship of Dionysus, and very late sources (Suidas, s.v. Ἀριών and οὐδὲν πρὸς τὸν Διόνυσον) mention a 'tragic poet' Epigenes of Sicyon, who was upbraided for introducing into the worship of Dionysus themes which had nothing to do with the god. Possibly inventions or innovations of Epigenes may have had some influence later on the embryo tragedy of Athens, and it may have been some such originally Dorian performance into which Thespis imported an actor. Some scholars believe that the story of Thespis' performances in Icaria was a late invention, intended to deprive the Dorians of the credit for an Athenian institution. The connexion of early tragic lyrics with Dorian peoples is supported by language. The language of tragedy is, in its main substance, Attic, but not only is there a considerable infusion of Epic and Ionic forms (due to a tradition from days when 'Homer' in a broad sense was the only literature), but in the lyric portions the use of ᾱ for η is probably Doric in origin. A considerable number of Doric words and forms is also to be found in the iambic, as well as in the lyric, portions of tragedy. The explanations which treat these forms as old Attic are less probable (see Pickard-Cambridge, *Dithyramb, Tragedy, and Comedy*, pp. 146 ff., 417 f., and refs. there given). Such forms (as well as the Ionic) doubtless came naturally to a poet who was moved to express himself in language possessing greater distinction than ordinary speech. The theory of the origin of tragedy which is probably still most popular is based mainly on the literal acceptance of statements made by Aristotle (*Poet.* 3–5). According to this theory, the original lyric performance was identical with dithyramb, and its chorus was composed of satyrs, exhibiting some of the physical characteristics of goats (τράγοι). The actor was developed out of the leader (ἐξάρχων) of the dithyramb; the abandonment of the grotesque language and dancing of the satyrs coincided with the introduction of the iambic trimeter, a more serious metre than the trochaic tetrameter, and the plots, originally short, became longer. Suidas' statement that Pratinas of Phlius (about 500 B.C.) was the first to compose satyric plays is explained away by supposing that the original satyr-plays or tragedies (there being at first *ex hypothesi* no difference) had been drifting too far from Dionysus and subjects connected with him, and that what Pratinas really did was to re-introduce from Phlius the old type of satyric play, which now or shortly afterwards became a pendant to three non-satyric tragedies. (The date at which tragedy on this view discarded the satyric dress for its chorus is not specified.)

4. In support of this theory are usually adduced the names τραγῳδία and τραγῳδοί (goat-singers), explained as referring to the goat-like satyrs, and transferred, it is supposed, to the horse-tailed satyrs of Attica; and the fact that Suidas ascribes to Arion the composition of literary dithyrambs and the production of satyrs speaking verse, as well as the invention of the τραγικὸς τρόπος, it being assumed that in all three points one and the same type of composition is referred to—an assumption for which there seems to be no ground. It is also the fact that in the fifth century satyric plays were always the work of the same composers as tragedies, and were generally like tragedies in structure.

5. But this theory presents great difficulties. There is no evidence that a dithyramb was ever danced in satyr-costume, nor is there any trace of dramatic elements in dithyramb before Bacchylides (well on into the fifth century); the dithyrambic chorus was circular, the tragic rectangular. Suidas' notice about Pratinas is more naturally interpreted to mean that he introduced satyric plays for the first time into a festival of non-satyric tragedies; the names 'dithyramb' and 'tragedy' or 'tragic chorus' are never interchangeable in the Classical period, and Arion's 'tragic' song and the tragic choruses of Sicyon were probably quite distinct from dithyramb; the word τραγῳδοί, 'goat singers', may mean, not singers in goat-costume (a meaning inappropriate to the equine satyrs of Attic drama), but singers competing for the goat as a prize (such as Thespis received), or at the sacrifice of a goat (as perhaps at Icaria, though the evidence is not very satisfactory). Possibly, therefore, Aristotle was theorizing, inferring that the more crude and primitive satyr-drama must have preceded the finer tragedy, and that both might have sprung from the dithyramb, which had come by his own day to include dramatic elements, and which was also known once to have had more riotous forms than later, so that it would not be absurd to connect it with satyr-play. It is difficult to imagine that the noble seriousness of tragedy can have grown so quickly, if at all, out of the ribald play of satyrs.

6. It seems more probable that early in the sixth century experiments in lyrics of a serious or 'tragic' kind, dealing with heroic legend (and with no special preference for stories connected with Dionysus) were made in the northern towns of the Peloponnese, especially Corinth and Sicyon, and in the latter place at least came to be associated with the worship of Dionysus; that later in the century Thespis made his experiment at Athens, combining his choruses with an actor delivering set speeches, and probably imparting a higher tone to what may have been a rough kind of performance; that these Athenian plays came under the influence of the Peloponnesian and Dorian lyric 'tragedy'; and that the

two strains came to be blended, and so arose the tragedy of Phrynichus and Aeschylus, associated with the Great Dionysia and, in that festival, with dithyramb and with the Satyric drama brought by Pratinas from Phlius. (For a full presentation and discussion of the evidence see Pickard-Cambridge, *Dithyramb, Tragedy, and Comedy*, chs. 1 and 2, and Ziegler, art. 'Tragoedia' in *PW*. The former also discusses the theories of Sir William Ridgeway and Dr. Gilbert Murray, of whom the one derives tragedy from rites said to have been enacted at the tombs of heroes, the other from a supposed ritual-sequence representing the death and resurrection of the Year, in the form of a δαίμων or hero. These theories do not appear to have won any very wide acceptance.)

7. The history of tragedy in the fifth century will mainly be found in the articles on Aeschylus, Sophocles, and Euripides (*see also* AGATHON, ION, IOPHON). The present article deals mainly with some general aspects of tragedy, its subjects, form, production, etc.

8. Tragedy in Greece was a religious ceremony in the sense that it formed part of the festivals of Dionysus, and that it dealt with grave religious problems; but it was not an act of worship in the same way as was dithyramb, in which the chorus represented the Athenian people itself paying honour to the god, and its members remained in their own persons. The tragic chorus was always dramatic and 'in character', and from the first the action and the lyrics had most commonly no reference to Dionysus, but presented in dramatic form themes chosen freely from the whole range of epic story and floating legend, gradually settling down, as Aristotle says (*Poet.* 14) to a narrower range (largely non-Dionysiac) as it was found that the legends of certain houses furnished better material than others for dramatic treatment. If the chorus sings an ode to Dionysus, it is because the dramatic situation suggests it (as in Sophocles, *Ant.* 1115), not as an Athenian act of worship. But the tragedy of the three great poets and their contemporaries was always religious in the sense that the interest was not simply in the action as an exciting series of events, nor simply in the study of striking characters (though both these interests were strong), but in the meaning of the action as exemplifying the relation of man to the powers controlling the universe, and the relation of these powers to his destiny. In the choral odes, and implicitly in the action, the character of these ultimate powers is set forth, and even if (as often with Euripides) the conclusion drawn or to be inferred is a sceptical one, the spectator or reader is always in contact with the ultimate problems of human life and world-order. (The articles on the three great tragedians will illustrate this.) At the same time, tragedy shows a growing interest in the character of human beings as such. The personages of Aeschylus, though they include some very striking individuals, tend to be types or embodiments of a principle; Sophocles devotes himself mostly to displaying the effect upon certain noble and well-marked, but not abnormal, characters, of some terrible crisis or strain; the characters of Euripides are less raised above ordinary human life; his plays are often studies in distracted or abnormal mentality; he specializes and analyses with a minuteness entirely foreign to Aeschylus and almost absent from the plays of Sophocles.

9. With the growing interest in individual character went an increasing attention to art. Aeschylus is never entirely free from the crudities of primitive drama; in Sophocles we find the perfectly balanced and controlled use of all the resources of tragedy; in Euripides an indulgence, highly skilful, but in the judgement of many critics excessive, in more sensational effects both in action and in language. The importance of the actor's art grew correspondingly, until in the fourth century Aristotle (*Rhet.* 3. 1) could say that the actors now counted for more than the poets. Where attention is

concentrated on the performer there is less attention to the message; and whereas Aeschylus was a teacher and a prophet, and Sophocles always maintained the highest religious and moral earnestness, and Euripides was taken so seriously as to provoke strong antagonism, there is no reason to suppose that tragedy was so taken in the fourth century. It was simply a form of art, and perhaps not a particularly successful one; and the chorus, which had embodied the essence of the poet's teaching a century before, came to be, very often, only a singer of interludes. Aristotle does not allude to the religious interest of tragedy at all.

10. The poets were free to vary the legends which they found current, for the sake either of their moral or of dramatic art. Aeschylus made some modifications for the sake of religious truth; Euripides, for whom the legends had little religious value and were merely human inventions, himself invents freely; but it was Agathon who first composed a tragedy in which both characters and plot were entirely invented (Arist. *Poet.* 9). Very rarely a subject might be taken from contemporary or recent history; Phrynichus' *Phoenissae* and *Taking of Miletus*, Aeschylus' *Persae*, Theodectes' *Mausolus*, and Moschion's *Men of Pherae* are instances.

11. The poets might also be teachers in politics, though only to a subordinate extent. In Sophocles, indeed, there is little discernible allusion to contemporary issues, and he keeps wholly within the limits of his heroic plot. But in Aeschylus the contemporary reference and the moral are often unmistakable, while Euripides sometimes offers political discourses out of all proportion to their dramatic appropriateness, and alludes frequently to events and questions of his own day. Indeed, hatred of Sparta sometimes leads him to insert passages suggested as much by the contemporary as by the dramatic situation. That in all three poets there should be passages in praise of Athens is natural enough, and both Aeschylus and Euripides like to trace back to a legendary source the beginnings of some honoured institution, religious or political. The poets tend also to modify in the direction of constitutional monarchy or democracy the legendary traditions of absolute power.

12. The presentation of tragedies at the Great Dionysia in groups of three, followed by a satyric play, was regular throughout the fifth century, though the satyric play might be replaced by a fourth tragedy or by a play which, if not a tragedy, was at least of a serious kind, like the *Alcestis* of Euripides, who wrote very few satyric plays. From about the middle of the fourth century the satyric play dropped out, except for the performance of a single one at the beginning of each festival. (This is first recorded for 341 B.C. (*IG* ii². 2320).) Aeschylus often presented groups of plays, trilogies or tetralogies, connected in subject; the practice was probably his invention and was little followed by other poets, but Polyphradmon composed a Λυκούργεια, dramatizing the story of Lycurgus, Sophocles (possibly, but not certainly) a Τηλέφεια, Philocles a Πανδιονίς, and Meletus an Οἰδιπόδεια; and now and then there seems to have been a looser connexion of subject between a group of plays exhibited by Euripides, as, for instance, between the *Alexander, Palamedes*, and *Troades* in 415, and between the *Chrysippus, Oenomaus*, and *Phoenissae* about 409. It was only occasionally that the satyric play presented a lighter version of part of the same story as the preceding trilogy, as did the *Sphinx* and *Lycurgus* and probably the *Amymone* of Aeschylus.

13. The addition of an actor to the original chorus was attributed to Thespis (see above), and Aristotle in his brief summary (*Poet.* 4) says that Aeschylus increased the number of actors to two, diminished the part taken by the chorus, and made the dialogue predominant; Sophocles introduced a third actor and scene-painting. (Both these innovations were adopted by Aeschylus in

his latest plays.) In the *Oedipus Coloneus*, written in his last years, Sophocles probably required four actors. As the importance of the actor's part increased, tragedy passed from oratorio into drama; but not completely, for the lyric element long remained an essential part, and there was never a complete presentation of the action. The critical or fatal act took place, with the rarest exceptions, off the scene or even outside the play; the dialogue and the speeches of the actors lead up to it or develop its consequences, but on the scene itself there is very little action. Exceptions will be found at the end of Aesch. *Agam.*, and in the *Supplices* and *Eumenides*; in Soph. *OC*, and Eur. *Andr.* and *Heraclidae*. Obviously the interplay of characters and motives was impossible until there were more actors than one, and on this side of dramatic art Aeschylus himself only gradually acquired the consummate skill which he shows in the *Agamemnon*. The single actor could do little more than narrate or ask and answer questions. (The name ὑποκρίτης by which he was called probably means 'answerer', though other interpretations have been offered.)

14. In the first play of Aeschylus it is the fortunes of the Chorus which are the subject of the play; and in his work the Chorus never loses its importance as the vehicle of his most profound reflection and the lessons which he draws from the action; when not itself the leading personage (as in the *Supplices* and *Eumenides*) it is always closely connected with the hero and his fortunes, and may take a not unimportant share in the development of the action. In Sophocles, though it takes no part in the action, it is intimately interested in it and usually attached closely to one of the leading personages, though the choral odes may lack some of the religious intensity of those of Aeschylus, and their reflections may be rather those of a wise and right-minded spectator, not deficient in relevance or appropriateness. In some plays of Euripides, on the other hand, the chorus seem to be on the spot accidentally and may even be in the way; they may be detached from the hero and the action, and their chants may at times seem to be almost callously irrelevant, though there is usually some good reason for this. Neither in Sophocles nor in Euripides have the choral odes the magnitude which they regularly display (except in the *Prometheus*) in Aeschylus. With Agathon (according to Arist. *Poet.* 18) the chorus is said to have been reduced to the singing of interludes unconnected with the play, and this may often have happened in the fourth century. The entry of the chorus is very commonly made to the accompaniment of marching anapaests, and these with the lyric ode which follows when the chorus is in position for dancing (or the lyric or semi-lyric passage substituted for it) form the *parodos* or entrance-song. The succeeding choral odes are termed *stasima*; but there is a form of lyric dialogue between the chorus and a principal actor, the κομμός, which often takes the place of a *stasimon* and probably reproduces a traditional form of lamentation such as is recorded in Homer (e.g. *Il.* 18. 49 ff., 24. 720 ff.), though it is not, in tragedy, confined to lamentations. The parodos is regularly preceded (after the two earliest plays of Aeschylus) by a speech or a scene forming a prologue, and after the parodos the normal structure may be said to be a regular alternation of *epeisodia* or Acts (in which the actors take the main part, though the chorus may join in dialogue or make brief comments on the speeches) and *stasima*. The number of *epeisodia* and *stasima* may be as small as three of each or as many as five or six, according to the view taken of the composition of the particular play. But the limits of variation in this typical structure are very wide. In Aeschylus in particular there are frequently scenes which are mainly lyric, with brief speeches by an actor or snatches of dialogue between the lyrics, the whole sometimes forming a more or less (though not completely) symmetrical structure of the type known as

epirrhematic (lyrics and *epirrhemata* of speech or dialogue), and in most plays of Sophocles and several of Euripides there are similar reminiscences of what may have been an original epirrhematic form. This form is also not rare in the κομμός. Again, an *epeisodion* (particularly if long) may be broken up by the insertion of lyrics or anapaests, or (more rarely) the strophe and antistrophe of a choral ode may be separated and interlaced with the parts of an *epeisodion*. The structure of some plays of Euripides (e.g. the *Hippolytus*, *Hercules Furens*, and *Troades*) is in parts very free, though the normal alternation of *epeisodia* and *stasima* is always observed in considerable parts of the play. Rarely in Aeschylus or Sophocles, much more commonly in Euripides, an anapaestic or lyric monody by one of the actors may be introduced, and in such monodies (and more rarely in choral lyrics), the regular antistrophic form of composition (in strophe and antistrophe, with or without epode) may be abandoned for free lyrics (μέλος ἀπολελυμένον) in which the music as well as the words was highly emotional (*see* EURIPIDES). Scholars differ as to the extent to which the choral lyrics printed continuously in our manuscripts were divided up, particularly at moments of excitement or uncertainty, between several members of the chorus; but there was certainly the possibility of expressing conflicting views through the two halves of the chorus. In some plays there was a secondary chorus (for instance in the *Supplices* and *Eumenides* of Aeschylus, the *Hippolytus* of Euripides and some lost plays), which might play a not unimportant part (see Lammers, *Die Doppel- und Halb-Chöre in der antiken Tragödie*, 1931). The beginning and end of an *epeisodion*, or the entrance of a character, were often marked, particularly in Aeschylus, by a passage in anapaestic dimeters. The play concluded with a final scene (*exodos*) very variable in structure; but there was never a great choral finale, like that of a modern oratorio; the chorus at most speak a few quiet words.

15. It is certain that the several metres used by the poets possessed different emotional values, though they can no longer be fully appreciated. In dialogue the trochaic tetrameter usually implies greater excitement than the iambic trimeter in which dialogue and set speeches are mainly composed. The anapaestic dimeter is used either in marching (and in similar movements at the beginning and end of a scene), or, with less strict metrical rules, in lamentation; in the latter case, and possibly in the former, the words were sung. Hexameter passages are very rare; there is a remarkable lament in elegiacs in Euripides' *Andromache*. Of purely lyric metres, the dochmiac expresses the greatest emotional excitement or distress.

16. The plot of an ancient tragedy displays far less variety than a play of Shakespeare, and Aristotle regards as the ideal plot one in which each step arises out of what precedes it as its necessary or probable consequence, and everything irrelevant to the main causal sequence is excluded, though the poet's skill is shown in so arranging the sequence that pity, fear, and surprise are aroused in the highest degree. (On the value of surprise he lays great stress, and it should be noted that he states that even the best-known plots were known only to few.) So he prefers plots in which the crisis is a περιπέτεια, in which the action brings about just the reverse of what the agent intends or the spectator is led to expect, or an ἀναγνωρισμός, the revelation at the critical moment of a close relationship, unsuspected until some dreadful deed was done or about to be done, or events had reached an *impasse*. (Many forms of recognition are classified in *Poetics* 16.) Best of all is a plot in which περιπέτεια and ἀναγνωρισμός are combined. It is noteworthy that Aeschylus, whom Aristotle almost leaves out of account, seems to have made little use of either.

17. The fact that the Chorus was normally present

throughout the action imposed certain conditions upon tragedy from which the modern dramatist is free. The action must take place out of doors, and change of place is very rare, though it occurs, e.g., in Aeschylus' *Eumenides* and Sophocles' *Ajax*, the chorus having been sent away for sufficient reasons; interiors of houses, otherwise invisible, may be displayed by means of the ἐκκύκλημα or the throwing open of doors. It might be expected that the constant presence of the Chorus would also require that the action should be continuous in time; but in fact this so-called 'Unity of Time' was not strictly observed. Aristotle (*Poet.* 5) notes that it was the usual practice to represent (in a play lasting up to 3 hours) events which could fall within about 24 hours, so that considerable intervals of time might be supposed to elapse during a choral ode, and if usually the intervals were not long enough to cause any trouble with audiences accustomed to the convention, they might if required be much longer, as in Aeschylus' *Agamemnon* and *Eumenides*; there is great compression of the events happening off the stage in Sophocles' *Trachiniae*, Euripides' *Andromache* and *Supplices*, and some other plays; the choral ode separated the scenes as effectively and unobjectionably as a modern curtain. In a number of plays, all, of course, acted in broad daylight, the action is supposed to take place at early dawn or even at night. There is no reason to suppose that a Greek audience was more troubled by this than an Elizabethan.

18. Tragedy in Athens was probably performed at first in a circular orchestra in the precinct of Dionysus with no fixed background, except possibly the tent or shelter in which the actors dressed. In the earliest plays of Aeschylus all the scenery that is needed is a raised structure on the far side of the orchestra from the audience, to serve in the *Supplices* as a stepped altar, with the statues of a number of gods grouped round behind it; in the *Persae* as the Tomb of Darius; in the *Septem* again as an altar, with statues of gods, and in all three plays the plain background (probably the side of the actors' σκήνη) could represent whatever the play required —the wall of Artemis' sacred precinct (*Supp.* 144–6), the Persian council chamber (*Pers.* 140–1), possibly the palace of Eteocles (or any building on the Theban acropolis) in the *Septem*. There can have been no raised stage, as is shown by the movements of the chorus, and the orchestra must have been large enough to accommodate considerable crowds. It is probable, but not certain, that a few stones still remain to mark the position of this early orchestra. The *Prometheus Vinctus* raises complicated scenic problems which cannot be discussed here; the edition of G. Thomson offers a solution more probable than any so far suggested. By the date of the *Oresteia* Aeschylus had evidently adopted the painted background, introduced first by Sophocles and representing a palace or temple-front, and this remained the normal setting of tragedy to the end of the classical period. The façade was probably not raised above the orchestra on a stage, though there may very likely have been a broad step (with images of gods, if required), and often an altar, in front of the central door; few scholars can now be found to defend the existence of a raised stage in the fifth century, and it seems clear that chorus and actors had complete freedom of access to one another, though the actors probably performed for the most part against the background. In the *Ajax* of Sophocles the background represents the tent of Ajax, though there are difficult scenic problems connected with the play; special scenery must have been arranged for the *Philoctetes* and *Oedipus Coloneus*, Sophocles' two last plays, and stagecraft had doubtless developed considerably by the end of the century. In the satyric *Ichneutae* a very simply decorated background may have represented the χλωρὸς ὑλώδης πάγος, with the entrance to Cyllene's Cave, and the *Cyclops* of Euripides, with the cave of

Polyphemus, may have been somewhat similarly staged. The normal façade suffices for most plays of Euripides, with additions or modifications when required, e.g. in the *Electra*, in which the front is that of a workman's cottage, and in the *Andromache*, in which the shrine of Thetis as well as the palace of Neoptolemus was required. In four plays the scene was laid before a temple (*Heraclidae*, *Supplices*, *Ion*, *Iphigenia in Tauris*), in front of which in the *Heraclidae* must have been a large stepped altar, while the *Iphigenia* and probably the *Ion* need a portico. In other plays the background consists of one or more tents. The indications in the plays of Euripides (as in those of Sophocles) are against a raised stage, and the *Rhesus*, which many scholars suppose to be a fourth-century play, still requires that chorus and actors shall be on the same level (see line 684). The raised stage is thought by some scholars to have been introduced when the theatre was remodelled in the latter part of the fourth century—the chorus having ceased to be an integral part of the play, but the more probable date of the change is early in the second century. The extant remains of the theatre at Athens afford no certainty on this point, and it must not be assumed that the change was made everywhere in the Greek world at the same time. Some of the new theatres springing up in many parts of Greece and Asia Minor may have been the first to introduce the stage.

19. The Athenian poets made use of various somewhat crude mechanical devices, the γέρανος, the μηχανή and θεολογεῖον to display actors (usually gods) in the air, the ἐκκύκλημα to reveal the interior of a house or temple, and others; the precise use of these in particular plays is keenly debated. Probably Aeschylus experimented freely; Sophocles used such devices little if at all; Euripides certainly used the μηχανή and θεολογεῖον in many plays, though perhaps he employed the ἐκκύκλημα less often than is sometimes supposed.

20. *Tragedy at the Lenaea and Rural Dionysia.* Of Tragedy at the Lenaea in the fifth century all that is known is that in 419 and 418 two poets competed, each with three tragedies (no satyric play) (*IG* ii². 2319), and that Agathon won a victory in 416 (Ath. 5. 217 a). There are many records of Lenaean tragedy for the fourth century (*IG* ii². 2325; Diod. Sic. 15. 74; Plut. *X Orat.* 839 d) and among the victors named are Dionysius of Syracuse, Aphareus, Theodectes, and Astydamas. At the Rural Dionysia there were frequent performances of tragedy, which may have helped to familiarize the inhabitants of Attica with the great masterpieces. The festival at the Piraeus seems to have been of special importance, and here and at Salamis new plays were sometimes produced. We hear also of festivals at Collytus, Eleusis, and Icaria, and an inscription from Aixone records the exhibition of tragedies (including Sophocles' Τηλέφεια) and comedies there (see A. E. Haigh, *Attic Theatre*, pp. 29, 30, and A. W. Pickard-Cambridge in Powell and Barber, *New Chapters* iii. 69 ff.).

21. *Later Tragedy.* In the century after his death the influence of Euripides on the drama was probably stronger than it was in his life-time, and a certain inferiority of contemporary writers to the great three of the fifth century seems to have been acknowledged: old plays were sometimes performed (*IG* ii². 2318, Wilhelm p. 23), and from about 341 B.C. one such play was regularly exhibited at the beginning of the festival after the single satyric play (*IG* ii². 2320). Dramatic festivals now came to be held all over the Greek world and theatres sprang up everywhere, though we have little evidence as to the plays presented. Aeschines acted in the *Oenomaus* and *Antigone* of Sophocles, which Demosthenes (18. 180, 19. 246) speaks of as often exhibited. The extant *Rhesus*, ascribed to Euripides, is probably a fourth-century play. in which some of the characteristic idioms of all three of the great tragedians are imitated; but if not strong in character-drawing, it is a good acting play with an impressive final scene. The century was more famous for great actors than great poets (see above); but the reputation of Theodectes, Astydamas, and others must have had some foundation. Apart from the historical plays mentioned above, mythological subjects unknown to the fifth century were sometimes chosen, such as the stories of Adonis and of Leda. There may have been experiments in form, such as the *Centaur* of Chaeremon (q.v.), and Chaeremon and others either wrote to be read, not acted, or at least are regarded by Aristotle as better fitted for reading (ἀναγνωστικοί), being characterized by a vivid descriptive style (γραφικὴ λέξις, as opposed to ἀγωνιστική) (Arist. *Rh.* 3. 12). The fact that several of the poets of the century were rhetoricians as well as (or more than) poets may be connected with this. In the third century, when Alexandria was the chief literary centre of the world, we hear of the *Pleiad* of seven tragic poets at the court of Ptolemy Philadelphus (285–247 B.C.); five of these were Homerus, Lycophron, Philicus, Sositheus, and Alexander Aetolus (qq.v.); for the remaining two places various names are given. Over 60 names of tragic poets of the Hellenistic period are preserved; the titles of their plays suggest that they often took subjects seldom, if at all, treated in the classical period.

22. In the fourth and third centuries satyric plays were sometimes composed which were more like comedies in their topical and personal allusions. (*See* PYTHON, LYCOPHRON, SOSITHEUS.) There seems to have been some revival of this form of composition under the influence of Sositheus, and it did not die out entirely, at least outside Athens, before the Christian era.

23. It appears that new tragedies were occasionally composed down to the second century A.D., but not later (see Haigh, *Tragic Drama*, p. 444).

BIBLIOGRAPHY

GENERAL: A. E. Haigh, *Tragic Drama of the Greeks* (1896); G. Norwood, *Greek Tragedy* (1920); M. Pohlenz, *Die griechische Tragödie* (1930); A. Lesky, *Die griechische Tragödie* (1938); U. von Wilamowitz-Moellendorff, *Einleitung in die griechische Tragödie* (1907); A. W. Pickard-Cambridge, *Dithyramb, Tragedy, and Comedy* (1927); H. D. F. Kitto, *Greek Tragedy* (1939).

ESSAYS, SPECIAL ASPECTS, ETC.: H. Weil, *Études sur le drame antique* (1897); L. Campbell, *Tragic Drama in Aeschylus, Sophocles, and Shakespeare* (1904); E. Petersen, *Die attische Tragödie als Bild- und Bühnen-Kunst* (1915); L. E. Matthaei, *Studies in Greek Tragedy* (1918); W. Schadewaldt, *Monolog und Selbstgespräch* (1926); W. Kranz, *Stasimon* (1933).

GREEK TRAGEDY AND GREEK ART: J. H. Huddilston, *Greek Tragedy in the Light of Vase-paintings* (1898) and *The Attitude of the Greek Tragedians towards Art* (1898); L. Séchan, *Études sur la Tragédie Grecque* (1926); T. B. L. Webster, *Greek Art and Literature* (1939).

THEATRE, PERFORMANCE, ETC.: A. E. Haigh, *Attic Theatre*[3] (1907) (out of date as to Theatre of Dionysus); R. C. Flickinger, *The Greek Theater and its Drama*[3] (U.S.A. 1936); M. Bieber, *Die Denkmäler zum Theaterwesen im Altertum* (1920) and *The History of the Greek and Roman Theater* (1939); H. Bulle, *Untersuchungen an griechischen Theatern* (1928); E. R. Fiechter, *Das Dionysos-Theater in Athen* (1935–6); A. W. Pickard-Cambridge, *The Theatre of Dionysus in Athens* (1946). A. W. P.-C.

TRAGEDY, LATIN, see DRAMA, ROMAN.

TRAGICOCOMOEDIA (τραγικοκωμῳδία), a play blending tragic and comic elements (Plaut. *Amph.* 50–63).

TRAGULA, see ARMS AND ARMOUR, ROMAN.

TRAJAN (MARCUS ULPIUS TRAIANUS), Roman Emperor A.D. 98–117, son of M. Ulpius (q.v. 1) and a Spanish mother, born at Italica in Baetica on 18 Sept. A.D. 53 (less probably 56), served his vigintivirate (*c.* 70), and spent the next ten years as military tribune, accompanying his father to Syria (*c.* 75); he was subsequently quaestor and (before 86) praetor. During a legionary command in Spain, he was called to counter the revolt of Saturninus (q.v. 3) in Upper Germany (*c.* 88); he was consul (*ordinarius*) in 91. Governor of Upper Germany in 97, he there learned of his adoption by Nerva (q.v.). The choice was interesting. Trajan was Spanish-born, his family

was 'new'; he had seen little of Rome; and Nerva had collateral kinsmen. But Trajan was an experienced soldier, respected but popular as a general, and probably possessing influence at Rome (*see* SURA).

2. After Nerva's death Trajan (now *cos.* II), unwilling to hasten to Rome or to stress his Nervan connexion (honoured but never emphasized), preferred to inspect and organize the Rhine and Danube frontiers: this, with his execution of the mutinous Praetorians (*see* NERVA), and his halving of the normal donative, showed his strength. Senatorial privileges were at once confirmed. Early in 99 he returned to Rome, amid general welcome, and in 100 held his third consulship (refused in 99; others in 101, 103, 112). Pliny's *Panegyric*, delivered that year, elaborated his character. Popular with the army, affable to senators, protector of the people, he was *princeps*, not *dominus*; a natural leader, he did not abuse his powers. Personally modest and simple like his wife, Plotina (q.v.), he insisted on traditional forms.

3. His social and financial policy, however, was the reverse of reactionary. *Congiaria* (presumably of 75 *denarii* a head) were given in 99 and 102. Free distributions of corn continued, with more recipients, and the corn-supply received special attention. The system of *alimenta* (q.v.) was extended; accession-gifts were remitted; the scope of the Inheritance Tax was narrowed; provincial burdens were lightened. There was an ever-increasing programme of public works, at first mainly repairs, supervision, and sundry road-building, but after 107 building increased; this (with the vast *congiarium* paid in 107: 500 *denarii* a head) was doubtless the result of the treasure won in the Second Dacian War (5 million lb. weight of gold and double of silver; the figures are not easily disproved). New baths, the Aqua Traiana, the Naumachia, the magnificent Forum Traiani (q.v.), and new roads and bridges, at home and abroad, were constructed after 107, when there were also sumptuous games celebrating the Dacian conquest.

4. For Trajan's Dacian and Parthian wars there was justification. Domitian's arrangement with Decebalus (q.v.) left the Danube (and Moesia) unsafe. Trajan left Rome in 101, crossed the Danube at Lederata and marched by way of Bersovia and Aizis (Priscian, *Inst. Gramm.* 6. 13) to Tibiscum, to be joined perhaps by a parallel column proceeding *via* Tsierna (cf. *ILS* 5863) and the Teregova Keys pass. At Tapae he fought an apparently indecisive battle, and retired to winter on the Danube. In 102 he advanced up the Aluta valley to the Red Tower pass, and, helped by Lusius (q.v.) Quietus, finally forced the surrender of Decebalus and his capital Sarmizegethusa. Trajan returned to Rome to claim his triumph and title 'Dacicus'. The peace was short; by 105 Decebalus had attacked the Iazyges and besieged the Roman garrisons left in Dacia. Trajan, proceeding through Illyricum to Drobetae, relieved the garrisons. In 106 he crossed Apollodorus' great new bridge at Drobetae, recaptured Sarmizegethusa, and drove Decebalus to suicide. Dacia was annexed as a province, with its capital at Sarmizegethusa, now a colony. The gold- and salt-mines were quickly operated; one legion, XIII Gemina, soon sufficed as a garrison, with *auxilia*. Dacia thus became at last a bastion protecting the lower Danube. The Tropaeum Traiani at Adam-klissi (q.v.), commemorated Trajan's triumph.

5. In Numidia Roman occupation was quietly strengthened by the founding of Thamugadi and Lambaesis (qq.v.). In the east, too, Trajan began modestly in 105–6 with the annexation of Arabia Petraea or Nabataea (q.v.) by A. Cornelius Palma (q.v.); thus the Flavian eastern frontier was rounded off. But Parthia was still a menace, and when, after 110, its king Osroes dethroned Axidares (Rome's Parthian vassal) in Armenia, Trajan set out (Oct. 113), probably intending to annex Armenia. He advanced to Elegeia; Armenia, falling easily into his hands, was incorporated with Cappadocia and Lesser Armenia (114). Trajan (now officially 'Optimus'), perhaps elated by effortless conquest, moved south into Upper Mesopotamia, taking Nisibis and (through Lusius Quietus) Singara: coins proclaimed *Armenia et Mesopotamia in potestatem p. R. redactae*. In 115 he crossed and descended the Tigris, and captured Ctesiphon, the Parthian capital, while a parallel force descended the Euphrates: winter found him (now 'Parthicus') at the Tigris mouth. With Mesopotamia and its valuable trade-routes captured, consolidation and organization were now essential. But in 116 southern Mesopotamia revolted, while Parthian forces successfully attacked Trajan's base-lines—Armenia, Adiabene, and north Mesopotamia. Trajan suppressed the revolt, making Parthamaspates client-king at Ctesiphon (cf. coins, *Rex Parthis datus*); Lusius Quietus repelled attacks in the north. But the Empire was restless: Jews were in savage revolt in Cyrene, Egypt, Cyprus, and the Levant; Trajan himself was infirm. Leaving his new and precarious conquests, he turned homeward in 117, dying in Cilicia *c.* August 8th (*see* HADRIAN). While the Dacian wars had brought solid gain, the expense of the Parthian campaigns was out of all proportion to their material advantages.

6. General administration was economical and strict, but humane and progressive. Provincial governors, lax under Nerva, were well chosen; provincial and local finances, often unsound, were entrusted to special administrators (like Pliny in Bithynia and Maximus in Achaea) and to local *curatores* (q.v.). *Equites* continued to replace freedmen in the Civil Service; more provincials —eastern as well as western—were made senators. But, as Pliny's correspondence shows, the burden of administration lay with Trajan; and provincial initiative received no encouragement. Trajan himself was fully conscious of his imperial mission, to secure Felicitas, Securitas, Aequitas, Iustitia—Salus Generis Humani; and his ruling on the Christians (Plin. *Ep.* 10. 97) illustrates his combined firmness and humanity in general legislation. The principate was a burden laid by heaven upon an earthly vice-gerent (cf. Plin. *Pan.* 80. 3), the servant of mankind, a public exemplar. The title 'Optimus', used unofficially as early as 100, emphasized by the great *Optimo Principi* coin-series of 103 onwards, and official from 114, rehabilitated the principate in the mystical glory (second only to that of Jupiter Optimus Maximus) enjoyed by Augustus but since dissipated. Trajan's consecration was no mere compliment; and his tradition (cf. Eutropius 8. 5) remained alive.

BIBLIOGRAPHY

A. ANCIENT SOURCES. *Literary*: Dio Cassius, bk. 68; Pliny, *Pan.* and *Ep.* (esp. bk. 10, *ad Traianum*), etc. (see *CAH.* xi, p. 886 f.). One sentence of Trajan's Dacian Commentaries is preserved (Priscian, *Inst. Gramm.* 6. 13).
Inscriptions are numerous. On the wars see *CAH* xi, p. 889; also *PIR*, V 575.
Coins: H. Mattingly, *B.M. Coins, Rom. Emp.* iii (1936); H. Mattingly and E. A. Sydenham, *The Roman Imperial Coinage*, ii (1930); P. L. Strack, *Untersuchungen zur römischen Reichsprägung des zweiten Jahrhunderts* ii (1933); M. Durry, *Rev. Hist.* lvii (1932), 316 ff.; H. Mattingly, *Num. Chron.*[5] vi (1926), 232 ff.
B. MODERN LITERATURE. *General*: R. Paribeni, *Optimus Princeps* (2 vols., 1926–7); C. de la Berge, *Essai sur le règne de Trajan* (1877); R. P. Longden, *CAH* xi, chs. 5 and 6; B. W. Henderson, *Five Roman Emperors* (1927), chs. 8–12.
Special: (a) *Finance, and the Dacian treasure*: J. Carcopino in *Dacia* i (1924), 28 ff.; F. Heichelheim, *Klio* 1932, 124 ff.; R. Syme, *JRS* 1930, 55 ff.; C. H. V. Sutherland, *JRS* 1935, 150 ff. (b) *Public works*: R. Paribeni, op. cit. ii, chs. 14–16. (c) *Wars.* (i) *Dacia, and Trajan's column*: C. Cichorius, *Die Reliefs der Traianssäule* (2 vols., 1896–1900); G. A. T. Davies, *JRS* 1917, 74 ff.; 1920, 1 ff.; K. Lehmann-Hartleben, *Die Traianssäule* (1926); E. Petersen, *Trajans dakische Kriege* (2 vols., 1899–1903); I. A. Richmond, *BSR* xiii (1935), 1 ff.; H. Stuart Jones, ibid. v (1910), 435 ff.; E. T. Salmon, *Trans. Am. Phil. Ass.* 1936; C. Patsch, *Der Kampf um den Donauraum unter Domitian und Trajan* (1937). (ii) *Parthia, etc.*: R. P. Longden, *JRS* (1931), 1 ff.; J. Guey, *Essai sur la guerre parthique de Trajan* (1937). *See also under* ALIMENTA, EQUES, SENATUS.
                                                                        C. H. V. S.

TRAJAN'S COLUMN, *see* FORUM TRAIANI.

TRALLES (Τράλλεις, also Τράλλις), a city sometimes attributed to Lydia, sometimes to Caria, on a strong position on the north side of the richest section of the Maeander valley; its wealth and commercial advantages are inherited by the modern Aidin. First mentioned by Xenophon, it was an important city in the Hellenistic (for part of which it was called Seleuceia) and Republican periods; under the early Empire it received a large body of Italian inhabitants and the epithet Caesarea. Its organization and cult are relatively well known from numerous coins and inscriptions. Its Church received a Letter from Ignatius.   W. M. C.

TRANSMIGRATION. Although the belief that the soul after the death of the body passes into some other corporeal substance is widespread, cogent evidence is lacking that it existed in Greece otherwise than as a philosophical tenet or theological doctrine of non-popular origin. There is even less trace of it in Italy. It was certainly taught by the Pythagoreans and regarded as one of their most characteristic dogmas, e.g., Horace, *Carm.* 1. 28. 10, where see commentators; cf. Empedocles, 375, Pindar, *Ol.* 2. 56 ff. It is also Orphic, as Pindar, fr. 127 Bowra. Hence opinions as to its ultimate origin must vary with the theories held as to the sources of these systems. From one or both of them it passes into Platonism (e.g., Plato, *Resp.* 10. 614 D ff.), and so, e.g., to the mixed eschatology of Verg. *Aen.* 6. 713 ff. Its existence outside the then civilized world was remarked, e.g., among the Druids (Caesar, *BGall.* 6. 14. 5; Lucan 1. 454 ff.).   H. J. R.

TRANSVECTIO EQUITUM, *see* CASTOR AND POLLUX; EQUES.

TRAPEZA (table), *see* FURNITURE.

TRAPEZUS, a colony of Sinope, traditionally founded in 756 B.C. as a trading-post on the south-east coast of the Euxine. Its mediocre harbour and inhospitable neighbours retarded its development, so that in 399 it was still a small town tributary to Sinope. It formed part of the kingdoms of Mithridates VI, Deiotarus, and the line of Polemon, and grew steadily in importance in the early Empire, since it was the nearest port to the Armenian frontier. It became a free city in A.D. 64 and received harbour works from Hadrian, but its prosperity was destroyed when it was sacked by the Goths in 259.

F. Cumont, *Studia Pontica* ii (1906), 362 ff.; Jones, *Eastern Cities*.
                                                                        T. R. S. B.

TRAVEL. Among the Greeks there was much travel, not only by soldiers and merchants, but by visitors to the great religious centres (pilgrims, athletes, actors), and by sightseers (e.g. to Athens); but the organization of travel was as yet little developed. The establishment of the Pax Romana, the union of the civilized world under one government, and the construction of good roads throughout the Empire provided facilities for communication which cannot be paralleled till modern times. The Roman government imposed no restrictions on travel, and as a result there was constant movement between Italy and the provinces, and between the several provinces. Under the Republic many Italians lived permanently or temporarily in the provinces (*see* CONVENTUS). There was a large Italian settlement in Delos. Southern Gaul was full of Roman citizens (Cic. *Font.* 11), and when Mithridates invaded the province of Asia the number of Romans and Italians massacred by him was estimated at 80,000. Many of these were *publicani* or *negotiatores*, but it is probable that some settled on the land, especially in Africa (*JRS* viii. 34 ff.). Conversely many provincials moved to Italy. Settlements of Syrians are found in ports like Puteoli, and Juvenal complains that the Orontes had poured into the Tiber.

Members of the Roman 'governing class' had occasion to travel widely in the performance of their duties. A speaker in Tacitus (*Ann.* 3. 33), who declares that he had spent forty years in service abroad but had always left his wife in Italy, must have visited her sometimes. All active members of the senatorial class held appointments in several provinces in the course of their career. Many Roman soldiers were stationed in parts of the Empire far from their homes, in which they often settled when their period of service had expired (Tac. *Ann.* 14. 27). Artists and philosophers and religious teachers like St. Paul moved freely from province to province. The satirists are full of references to the risks which merchants would incur for the sake of gain: one merchant boasts in an inscription that he had made 72 voyages from the Peloponnese to Italy. Roman traders ventured far outside the limits of the Empire, and were fairly familiar with India. Ptolemy's Geography shows that some knowledge of Indo-China existed in the Roman Empire in the second century, and finds of Roman coins in the countries of northern Europe show that traders went far beyond the Rhine and the Danube. Wealthy Romans travelled freely for pleasure, and often made long stays in the more attractive cities of Greece and Asia Minor.

By modern standards travelling was not comfortable in the Roman Empire. Aelius Aristides emphasized the discomforts of his journey from Asia Minor to Rome in A.D. 155, and the conditions under which Horace travelled to Brundisium (*Sat.* 1. 5) were not luxurious. Travelling was not free from danger even in Italy: travellers were liable to be attacked by highwaymen even on the Via Appia and Flaminia. On the whole, however, travel was safer than it has been at most periods of history. Bodies of troops were stationed at intervals on the main roads of Italy, and in the provinces it was the duty of governors to secure safety of communications.

On the accommodation of travellers *see* INNS. *See also* NAVIGATION, ROADS.

L. Friedländer, *Roman Life and Manners* i, chs. 6–7; H. S. Jones, *Companion to Roman History* (1912), 40–51, 316–37; G. H. Stevenson in *Legacy of Rome*, 141–72; Cary–Warmington, *Explorers* (1929); E. H. Warmington, *Commerce between the Roman Empire and India* (1928); O. Brogan, 'Trade between the Roman Empire and the free Germans' (*JRS* xxvi. 195 ff.); M. P. Charlesworth, *Trade Routes and Commerce of the Roman Empire* (1926). G. H. S.

TREASURIES (θησαυροί). This term is usually applied by ancient authors, and consistently employed by Pausanias, to a type of small building erected at the major Greek sanctuaries for the purposes of housing the archives and treasures of a particular Greek city-state or community. These buildings were invariably small in size and built like miniature Greek temples *in antis*, with two main supporting columns. Sites of at least twenty such treasuries have been identified at Delphi and twelve at Olympia. The treasuries were mostly built of the material most characteristic of the city or area which they represented. The Treasury of Sicyon at Delphi was made of Sicyonian limestone, that of Siphnos of island marble, while the Treasury of Megara was adorned with terra-cottas in Megarian clay. The Treasury of Cyrene at Olympia contained sculptures of African limestone. Each contained some of the principal portable or precious minor objects belonging to the State it represented. There were also treasuries at the sanctuary of Apollo at Delos. The official name for a treasury was οἶκος, the 'communal house' in which were kept the *sacra*. The treasury served especially for official *theoroi* who came as delegates to festivals. Records were kept in them also, and inscriptions concerning nationals were cut on the walls of each treasury. Two treasuries at Delphi survive to us more or less intact, or capable of complete restoration,

that of the island of Siphnos and that of Athens. The former in the Ionian style was the richest and most highly adorned at Delphi. It was built *c.* 540 B.C. The latter is a severe Doric building and was built *c.* 510. The earliest treasury known is of the late seventh century and the latest of the fourth century. S. C.

TREBATIUS TESTA, GAIUS, a Roman jurist, contemporary of Augustus, and a friend of Cicero, who dedicated to him his *Topica*, and Horace. Recommended by Cicero to Caesar as legal adviser, he enjoyed his favour. As a legal writer Trebatius is known as the author of an extensive treatise on sacred and pontifical law (*De religionibus*) and of a work *De iure civili*. He was highly esteemed as a jurist who could take an independent attitude; the fact that Labeo was his disciple procured him the reputation of a good teacher. A. B.

TREBIUS NIGER (? 2nd c. B.C., Teuffel, 132; but placed under Empire by Cichorius, *Röm. Studien*, 1922) is several times quoted on points in natural history by Pliny (e.g. 9. 80; 89; 93; 10. 40; 32. 15).

TREBONIANUS GALLUS, GAIUS VIBIUS (emperor A.D. 251–3), was proclaimed emperor by his army after the battle of Abrittus and subsequently raised his son Volusianus to the rank of Augustus (*see* DECIUS 4). His reign was disastrous. The Persians overran Mesopotamia, the Goths, temporarily bought off, re-entered Moesia, and plague was rampant. The situation on the Danube was, however, restored by Aemilianus (q.v.) in 252; but next year Aemilianus marched into Italy and advanced to Interamna, anticipating the reinforcements that Trebonianus had ordered Valerian to bring from Raetia (*see* VALERIANUS). In the ensuing battle Trebonianus and his son were murdered by their troops. H. M. D. P.

TREBONIUS, GAIUS, quaestor *c.* 60 B.C., *tribunus plebis* in 55, when he carried the *Lex Trebonia* conferring five-year commands on Pompey and Crassus. As *legatus* he did good service in Gaul (55–0) and in 49 conducted the siege of Massilia. Praetor in 48, he was sent next year to Spain, but failed against the Pompeians. Though appointed *consul suffectus* by Caesar in 45, he is said to have plotted against him in that year, and he took part in the actual assassination in 44, detaining Antony outside. Proconsul of Asia in 43, he was treacherously murdered by Dolabella at Smyrna. He published a collection of Cicero's witticisms.

F. Münzer, *PW* vi A. 2274–82. C. E. S.

TREES, SACRED. Tree worship, characteristic of primitive religion, took a prominent place in old Cretan religion. Not only growing trees, often seen inside the doors of shrines or behind walls, but also boughs were the objects of adoration and sacrifice (orgiastic dancing apparently belonged to the ritual). Prehistoric Crete knew trees as deities (epiphanies of goddesses are recognizable in some tree-cults); to the Greeks, however, trees (and groves) were only holy. The tree, 'having its own soul' (Sil. Ital., cf. δρυάς and art. NYMPHS), was only the abode or the property of a deity (just as springs, mountains, etc. were): so in the story of the Thessalian king, Erysichthon (q.v.), who cut down the holy oak (or attacked the holy grove of poplars) and was correspondingly punished by Demeter. In general it seems to have been a common custom, when clearing a virgin forest, to leave a tree or a clump of trees unhewn, as 'holy' (often dedicated to Artemis). The oak (cf. the mantic oak of Dodona) was mostly associated with Zeus (an inheritance from Indo-European times), the olive-tree with Athena, the laurel with Apollo (cf. the metamorphosis of Daphne), the plane sometimes with Dionysus (cf. his epithet δενδρίτης), the myrtle with

Aphrodite, the agnus castus (important for medicine) with Asclepius. But trees and plants were often sacred to a deity simply because they grew near to his or her temple or altar (cf. the wild olive used for crowns at Olympia). Cypress, elms, white poplar may have adorned burial places and were accordingly characteristic of the infernal regions. Sacrifices and all sorts of gifts to sacred trees are known from Homeric times. Greek mythology knows the Tree of Life (the Gardens of the Hesperides), but not the originally Oriental World-tree (cf. the Scandinavian Yggdrasil).

In the Forum of Rome the sacred *ficus Ruminalis* or fig-tree of Romulus was one of the most holy emblems of the Eternal City (cf. the cornel-tree on the Palatine, Plut. *Rom.* 20).

C. Boetticher, *Der Baumkultus der Hellenen* (1856); W. Mannhardt, *Wald- und Feldkulte*[2] (1904); J. G. Frazer, *GB* ii. 9 ff.; O. Gruppe, *Gr. Mythologie* ii. 779–92, 'Pflanzenfetische'. S. E.

TREMELLIUS SCROFA, see SCROFA.

TRESVIRI, *see* TRIUMVIRI.

TRES (TRIUM) VIRI CAPITALES, *see* VIGINTI-SEXVIRI.

TREVERI, a Gallic tribe in the Moselle basin. Strong Germanic admixture is attested by ancient authors, who are supported by archaeological evidence of German penetration *c.* 200 B.C. They furnished cavalry to Caesar, but gave him much trouble to subdue; and were active in rebellion under the early Empire (29 B.C., A.D. 21, A.D. 70), so that they lost their privilege of 'libertas'. Nevertheless, the presence of the Rhine army as a market tempted them to loyalty; and the second century shows an era of great prosperity based on large-scale agricultural organization (cf. the Igel-Saüle of the Secundinii). The invasions of the third century destroyed this culture, but the land recovered somewhat with the establishment of the emperor's and prefect's court at Trier (Augusta Treverorum, q.v.). Trier fell finally to the barbarians *c.* 430.

J. Steinhausen, *Siedelungskunde des Triererlandes* (1936); Rau, *PW* vi A. 2301–2353. C. E. S.

TRIBONIANUS (d. A.D. 543–5), a confidant and the most intimate collaborator of the Emperor Justinian in the composition and publication of his legislative works. His birth-place was (probably) Side in Pamphylia. He began as an advocate, but soon he rose to the high offices of the *magister officiorum* and *quaestor sacri palatii* which he occupied several times. As a lawyer of great learning, especially in the legal literature of the past centuries (Justinian says it in particular praise of him) he was invited by the Emperor to assist in the work of codification, first in the composition of the first Codex as an ordinary member of the Commission and subsequently, when he had given proof of his quality in this task, as the director (*gubernator*) of the work on the compilation of the Digest. He chose his collaborators for this mighty undertaking by commission from the Emperor himself. It may be that the idea of making and the plan for constructing the great collection originated in his mind. In the same manner the direction of the work on the *Institutiones* was entrusted to him. He took an equally prominent part in the edition of the second Codex, for which he was especially qualified, having been the intellectual author of the collection of *Quinquaginta Decisiones* published in the time between the two Codes (*Inst. Iust.* 1. 5. 3).

Tribonian is considered the responsible editor of Justinian's Codification, and so all alterations and insertions executed by the Compilers have been put to his account, and are sometimes called 'emblemata Triboniani'. The expression is hardly correct, for he, though the soul and creator of the whole Codification, cannot be considered the author of all interpolations, a good share of which may well have been the work of his collaborators. However, having regard to the high praise which the Emperor gave him, we must admit that Tribonian's part in the imperial legislative work was decisive.

There are notices of Tribonian in Procopius (*Pers.* 1. 24–5), Hesychius, and Suidas. The last named has articles on two distinct Tribonians. If the identity of these two persons is assumed (as B. Kübler tried to demonstrate), Tribonianus might be the author of some philosophical writings and of dissertations about planets, prosody, and various other topics.

B. Kübler, s.v. 'Tribonianus' in *PW* vi A; 'Die Gehilfen Justinians bei der Kodifikation', *Acta Congr. iurid. internaz.* Rome 1934, i. 22 ff. A. B.

TRIBUNI AERARII were the magistrates or officials who collected the war-tax and distributed pay to the soldiers of the several tribes (although they were soon superseded in this office by the *quaestores*). Whether they originally were the heads of the tribes is doubtful, as these officials later were named *curatores*. In the first century B.C. the tribunes appear as a class somewhat similar to, but less wealthy than, the knights, and from them the third *decuria* of judges was taken (70 B.C.). A *Lex Iulia* (46) exempted them from this task.

Mommsen, *Staatsr.* iii[3]. 189 ff., 532 f.; J. Lengle, *PW*, s.v. P. T.

TRIBUNI MILITUM in the Republican Army were the senior officers of the legions. Elected by the people, they ranked as magistrates, and six were assigned to each legion. They were employed in administrative duties and only rarely held a tactical command. When the number of legions was increased, only the tribunes of the four *legiones urbanae* were elected by the people; the remainder were nominated by the consuls.

In the Caesarian period the tribunes were knights and their importance declined with the rise of *legati*. Under the Principate the tribunate in the legions was reserved for young men starting a senatorial (*laticlavii*) or an equestrian career (*angusticlavii*), the latter outnumbering the former.

Tribuni also commanded cohorts in the Household Troops and *cohortes milliariae* in the *Auxilia*. In the Constantinian army the title is borne by officers in command of units (e.g. *legio*, *vexillatio*, etc.) in the field army. H. M. D. P.

TRIBUNI PLEBIS (or PLEBI, δήμαρχοι) were officers of the plebs first created in 500–450 B.C. The name is evidently connected with *tribus*, but it is uncertain whether the tribunes were at first chiefs of the tribes, who later became officers of the plebs, or whether the name simply imitated that of the *tribuni militum* already existing. The original number of the tribunes is variously given as two, four, or five; but the only certain fact is that before 449 B.C. it had risen to ten. The tribunes were charged with the defence of the lives and property of the plebeians. Their power was not derived from any statute, but from an oath of the plebeians to uphold their *sacrosanctitas* or inviolability—an oath which the patricians never effectually challenged. The tribunes asserted a right of veto (*intercessio*) against any act performed by the magistrates, against elections, laws, *senatus consulta*. The only magistrates exempted were (until *c.* 300 B.C.) the dictator, and perhaps the *interrex*. The tribunes further summoned the plebs to assemblies (*concilia plebis*, more usually called *comitia plebis tributa*), elicited resolutions (*plebiscita*), and asserted a right of enforcing the decrees of the plebs and their own rights (*coercitio*). *Coercitio* probably could go as far as the infliction of death. Connected with the *coercitio* was a certain amount of jurisdiction. Tribunes were elected by the *comitia plebis*. Each tribune could stop the action of his colleagues by veto. Thus the office was better equipped for obstruction than for getting things done.

This revolutionary power was gradually recognized by the State. The tribunes became indistinguishable from magistrates of the State, although without *imperium* and insignia. The full acknowledgement of their power coincided with the recognition of *plebiscita* as laws with binding force (*c*. 287 B.C.). The tribunes were first admitted to listen to the debates of the Senate; at least from the third century B.C. they obtained the right of convening the Senate; in the second century the tribunate became a sufficient qualification for entry to the Senate. From the fourth and third centuries B.C. the tribunate became partially an instrument by which the Senate could control the magistrates through the veto. But the tribunate never forgot its revolutionary traditions. In this period a custom sprang up which rendered reelection to the tribunate unconstitutional; but this custom was broken by C. Gracchus. From the time of Gracchus the tribunician veto was curtailed by special clauses of laws and *senatus consulta*. Sulla excluded the tribunes from the magistracies of the Roman People and abolished or curtailed their power of moving legislation and their judicial powers. In 75 B.C. they were readmitted to the magistracies, and in 70 the tribunician power was restored to its full extent. The builders of the Principate appreciated the value of the tribunician power in the construction of their personal power. Caesar assumed at least the tribunician *sacrosanctitas*. Augustus, probably in three steps (36, 30, 23 B.C.), obtained a permanent *tribunicia potestas*. The Republican tribunate remained, but lost all its independence and nearly every practical function. Until the third century A.D. the tribunate remained a step in the senatorial career for plebeians alternatively with the aedileship. There is still evidence for the tribunate in the fifth century A.D.

BIBLIOGRAPHY

Mommsen, *Staatsr.* ii. 1 (1887), 272; A. H. J. Greenidge, *Roman Public Life* (1901), 93; E. Meyer, *Kleine Schriften* i² (1924), 333; G. De Sanctis, *Stor. Rom.* ii. 26, iv. 1. 534; K. J. Beloch, *Röm. Gesch.*, 264; G. Niccolini, *Il tribunato della plebe* (1932); id., *I fasti dei tribuni della plebe* (1934); J. L. Myres, *Essays presented to C. G. Seligman* (1934), 227; Lengle, *PW* vi A. 2454; H. Siber, *Die plebejischen Magistraturen bis zur Lex Hortensia* (1936); C. H. Brecht, 'Zum römischen Komitialverfahren', *Sav. Zeitschr. Röm. Abt.* lix (1939), 261; F. Altheim, *Lex Sacrata. Die Anfänge der plebeischen Organisation* (1940). Cf. PLEBS.   A. M.

TRIBUS. In Rome the tribe was a division of the State. An analogous division existed in Etruscan Mantua (Serv. ad *Aen.* 10. 202). The *trifu* of the *Tabulae Iguvinae* is on the contrary the whole community. The connexion of *tribus* with *tres* is uncertain. The three original Roman tribes were Titienses (Tities), Ramnenses (Ramnes), and Luceres. It is nearly certain that these tribes were originally ethnic and not local; they probably included the plebs from the first.

The ethnic tribes were virtually eliminated by the creation of new local tribes, which consisted of four urban tribes and an increasing number of 'rustic' tribes. The urban tribes were traditionally ascribed to Servius Tullius; but this tradition is not universally accepted by modern scholars. The sixteen oldest rustic tribes bore the names of patrician families, who evidently owned a large part of their territory. The newer tribes included territories in which settlements of Roman citizens were founded, or citizenship was conferred on the native inhabitants. The number of thirty-five, which was attained in 241 B.C. by the progressive addition of rustic tribes, was never exceeded. Later enrolments of citizens into tribes were made without reference to geographic contiguity.

All citizens were probably registered at all times in the local tribes, but at least for some part of the third century B.C. the lower social orders were usually confined to the urban tribes. The punishment of 'expulsion from

a tribe' (*tribu movere*), which the censors possessed, had by the second century come to mean relegation to an urban tribe.

The extension of the Roman franchise to a great part of Italy after the Social War introduced the question of the balance between new and old citizens. The attempt to confine new citizens to a few tribes in order to check their importance in the *comitia* ultimately failed. But in general freedmen were admitted only to the urban tribes. From the Ciceronian age the name of the tribe in abbreviated form had a regular place in the citizen's full name (the first instance of a regulation of the matter in *CIL* i². 583). Provincials, both individuals and *civitates*, who in Imperial times received the Roman citizenship, had to be enrolled in some specified tribe. No absolute rule was followed, but for instance people or *civitates* of Gallia Narbonensis were enrolled by preference in tribus Voltinia, the Orientals in the Collina and Quirina.

The territorial tribes were the units for census, taxation, and the military levy. Officials called *tribuni aerarii* (q.v.) long had charge of the financial obligations of the tribe. The relation between the *tribuni aerarii* and other officers called *curatores tribuum* is uncertain. The assemblies of the plebs and special less important assemblies of the whole people were arranged by territorial tribes (*see* COMITIA).

There is evidence also for the tribes as a voting section of the citizens in some *municipia* (Lilybaeum) and *coloniae* (Genetiva Urso, Iconium).

Mommsen, *Röm. Staatsr.* iii (1887), 161; A. H. J. Greenidge, *Roman Public Life* (1901); W. Kubitschek, *De Romanorum tribuum origine ac propagatione* (1882); id., *Imperium Romanum tributim descriptum* (1889); E. Meyer, *Kleine Schriften* i². 333; A. Rosenberg, *Der Staat der alten Italiker* (1913), 118; G. De Sanctis, *Stor. Rom.* i. 247; ii, pp. 16, 230; K. J. Beloch, *Röm. Geschichte*, 264; G. Niccolini, 'Le tribu locali romane', *Studi in onore Bonfante* ii (1930), 235; E. Täubler, 'Die umbrisch-sabellischen und die römischen Tribus', *Sitz. Heidelb. Akad.* 1929–30; P. Fraccaro, 'Tribules ed aerarii', *Athenaeum*, 1933, 142; H. Last, *AJPhil.* 1937, 467; id. *JRS* 1945, 30.
                                      A. M.

TRIBUTUM was a direct tax, as distinguished from a *vectigal* (q.v.). Under the Republic the term *stipendium* was more commonly employed (e.g. Cic. *Verr.* 3. 12), but in the Principate *tributum* was in general use, especially in imperial provinces (Gaius 2. 21). Between 404 and 167 B.C. a *tributum* was intermittently imposed on Roman citizens to meet the cost of wars. This was regarded rather as a compulsory loan than as a tax, and might be repaid out of the spoils of war. After 167 the word was applied only to provincial taxation. Provinces which paid a fixed *tributum* or *stipendium* were distinguished from those subject to variable *decumae* (q.v.). In the Principate a distinction was made between the *tributum soli*, which was imposed on all provincial land except that on which the *ius Italicum* had been conferred, and the *tributum capitis*, which was charged on other forms of property. Until the reign of Diocletian Italy was exempt from *tributum*, but all provincials, whether in possession of Roman citizenship or not, paid *tributum*. The assessment to *tributum* was based on the *census* (q.v.), but nothing is known as to the rate at which it was levied. Exemptions were given by grants of *immunitas* (q.v.) to communities or individuals. *See* FINANCE, ROMAN, para. 3.   G. H. S.

TRICLINIUM, the dining-room in a Roman house, or more commonly the arrangement of the three couches about the dining-table on three of its four sides. These couches each held three guests, who reclined upon their left elbow, and were known as *Lectus summus, medius, imus*. The first, on the right hand of the service, was reserved for the chief guests, but the place of honour was the third cushion on the middle couch—*locus consularis*—the host generally sitting next on the first cushion of the lowest couch.   F. A. W.

TRICLINIUS, Demetrius (early 14th c.), the outstanding critic of his day, lived probably at Constantinople. He was a scholar of considerable learning, with a particular interest in metric, but the quality of his scholarship was affected by the unfavourable conditions of the time, and his emendations are of unequal merit.

His transcript of Hesiod, with scholia in his own handwriting, survives in *Cod. Marcianus gr.* 464 (dated 1316). His annotated text of Pindar, now represented in a family of twenty-eight manuscripts, is of little value. His text of Aeschylus is preserved in *Cod. Farnesianus* I.E. 5; his extant notes, largely metrical, to five plays, occasionally present successful corrections. To his annotated edition of Sophocles, now represented by the *libri Tricliniani*, we owe some good readings. His scholia to Euripides are practically useless. Of his work on Aristophanes and Theocritus little is known.

T. Hopfner, *Sitz. Wien. Akad.* 1912. J. F. L.

TRIERARCHY. A liturgy (q.v.), for naval purposes, the trierarchy was of special importance at Athens, from which a few other States copied the institution. From the early fifth century the Athenian *strategi* chose for one year from the wealthy adult citizens a number of trierarchs corresponding to the number of triremes to be manned. Furnished with the hull and tackling of a trireme, along with the pay and food of the crew, the trierarch, who acted also as captain, bore all expense of maintenance and repair, totalling some forty to sixty *minae* (Lysias 21. 2, 32. 26–7). After 411 B.C. two citizens usually shared each trierarchy; revisions in 357 and again, at the urging of Demosthenes (*De Corona* 102 ff.), in 340 spread the burden more equitably. Demetrius of Phalerum abolished the liturgy in 317–307 B.C. Elsewhere in Greece the term 'trierarch' denoted merely captain of a trireme; in the Hellenistic and Roman periods, a trierarch might command any warship.

Orations of Demosthenes, especially 14 (*On the Symmories*) and 51 (*On the Crown of the Trierarchy*). M. Brillant, Dar.-Sag., s.v. 'Trierarchia' (1918). C. G. S.

TRILOGY, see TRAGEDY, para. 12.

TRINUNDINUM was the interval between three *nundinae*, i.e. the space of 24 days (by inclusive reckoning), required between moving and voting a resolution, or between the nomination of candidates and the polling, or between the promulgation and execution of a sentence, etc. The legal force of this measure of publicity, which also guaranteed the legislative power against any abuse on the part of the executive, was confirmed by the *Lex Caecilia Didia* (98 B.C.).

Mommsen, *Röm. Staatsr.* iii³. 1229 ff. P. T.

TRIOPAS (Τριόπας), in mythology, father (Callimachus, *Cer.* 79) of Erysichthon (q.v.); the latter's sin and punishment are sometimes ascribed to him, as Hyginus, *Poet. Astr.* 2. 14. Triopas (occasionally called Triops, Τρίοψ) is usually Thessalian, but appears in bewildering and mutually contradictory genealogies (see Mayer in Roscher's *Lexikon*, s.v.). There seems to be no doubt that he is somehow connected with the place Triopion in Caria (Steph. Byzant. s.v.). It is also possible that his name ('Three-eye') covers an old sky-god, cf. the three-eyed Zeus in Paus. 2. 24. 3. H. J. R.

TRIPOLIS (in Phoenicia) was a joint colony of Tyre, Sidon, and Aradus. From Antiochus IV's reign it issued municipal coinage. In 111 B.C. it gained its freedom, but it later fell under a tyrant, who was executed by Pompey; its liberty was not restored. Its territory produced a noted wine. A. H. M. J.

TRIPTOLEMUS, see DEMETER, MYSTERIES.

TRIREME. The earliest type of Greek warship, the simple *pentekontor* with twenty-five oarsmen on a side, was supplanted in the sixth century B.C. by the more complex trireme, which remained the standard war-galley throughout the ancient period, except in Hellenistic times (see QUINQUIREME). Light in structure, undecked, and slim in comparison with merchant craft, the Athenian trireme of the fourth century B.C., probably standard, measured about 120 ft. by 20 ft. The prow of the galley, rising into a lofty prow-post which was given a hooked shape by the Greeks and was voluted by the Romans, bore a ram of wood and bronze. On each side of this was painted a large apotropaic eye. A cross-beam, introduced in the Peloponnesian War, strengthened the prow and projected from the sides sufficiently to protect the 'oar-box', an outrigger construction which compensated for the curving sides of the galley.

The trireme in part sacrificed seaworthiness for efficiency in battle. During storms and at night it was often beached, for its crew (about 200 men) had but cramped quarters. It made an average speed of some four to five knots, aided by a square sail. In battle the mast was lowered or put on shore, and the trireme, formidable chiefly for its ram (see DIEKPLUS), was propelled by the easily-directed force of oarsmen.

The arrangement of these rowers, which marks the great advance of the trireme over the *pentekontor*, has been much debated, for the ancient evidence is obscure. The long-accepted view that the rowers sat in three superimposed banks is now generally rejected; it seems probable that, the rowing-benches being slanted forward, the rowers sat three on a bench, each rower pulling an individual oar.

E. Assmann, *Seewesen* in A. Baumeister's *Denkmäler des Klassischen Altertums* (1888; full reproduction of ancient representations); W. W. Tarn, 'The Greek Warship', *JHS* 25 (1905) and *Hellenistic Military and Naval Developments* (1930); F. Brewster, 'The Arrangement of Oars in the Trireme', *Harv. Stud.* 44 (1933). C. G. S.

TRITOGENEIA, see ATHENA, para 2.

TRITON (Τρίτων), the merman of Greek, or rather pre-Greek mythology. The meaning of the name is unknown, but since the syllable *trit-* recurs in the name of the sea-goddess Amphitrite, also non-Greek, it is permissible to suppose that it is a pre-Hellenic vocable meaning something like 'water'. The Tritons remain quite vague figures, mostly appearing as a decoration of sea-pieces and other works of art, but they sometimes play a subordinate part in a legend. For example, a Triton in human form appears to the Argonauts (q.v), at Lake Tritonis and gives them the clod of earth which was the pledge of future possession of Cyrene; Virgil (*Aen.* 6. 171 ff.) has a story of a Triton who, furious at the presumption of the human trumpeter Misenus in daring to challenge him to a contest (Tritons are commonly represented as playing on conches), drowns him. Pausanias (9. 20. 4; 21. 1) had seen what were represented as bodies of Tritons, possibly sea-beasts of some kind. H. J. R.

TRITOPATORES(Τριτοπάτορες), **TRITOPATREIS** (Τριτοπάτρεις), obscure figures of Attic cult, worshipped at Marathon on the eve of the Skira (Deubner, *Att. Feste*, p. 44). Their name seems to mean 'great-grandfathers', and they are said to be wind-gods, also the first ancestors of mankind, and to be prayed to for children before a marriage (Photius, s.v.). H. J. R.

TRITTYES (τριττύες, 'thirds'), divisions of *phylae* (q.v.) at Athens; territorial in character (both in the old and new *phylae*), but for State, not local administration. The old *trittyes* each formed a group of four *naukrariai* (q.v.); the new ones were simply local divisions of the *phylae*, used for the mustering of crews for triremes.

Plato speaks of *trittyarchoi* as officers of minor rank (in the army or the navy?), but nothing else is known of them. The *trittyes* did not form separate corporative units, like the *phylae* and the *demoi*.   A. W. G.

TRIUMPHAL ARCHES

TRIUMPHAL ARCHES were erected by the Romans to commemorate victories, and in honour of individual emperors. Though resembling other arches erected to mark the pomerium (q.v.) or to lend dignity to approaches of towns, bridges, and fora, they seldom had any practical function, and were frequently entirely detached from any walls. Pliny refers to arches designed to carry statuary as 'recently introduced'. The façades were usually of marble and ornamented with applied Orders (Corinthian or Composite), free-standing columns being usual in the later examples, engaged columns or pilasters in the earlier. A heavy attic story with a large inscribed tablet was usually superimposed above the cornice; and the whole structure generally served as a pedestal for a group of statuary. The earlier examples are mostly of the single-arch type, but this was later superseded by a large central arch flanked by two smaller ones. The most notable examples in Rome itself are those of Constantine (A.D. 312: commemorating his victory over Maxentius); of Titus (82: taking of Jerusalem); and of Septimius Severus (203: the Parthian Victories). Outside Rome those of Trajan at Ancona (112), built on a bridge-head, and at Beneventum (114) deserve notice. The example at Orange may perhaps date from the reign of Augustus. It is an early specimen of the triple-arched type, and unusual in having pediments and a double attic story. Most of the earlier arches are in Italy or Gaul: many of the later in North Africa.   H. W. R.

TRIUMPHUS (cf. θρίαμβος) was the processional return of a victorious Roman general, when he went to offer sacrifice to Jupiter on the Capitol. The Senate granted triumphs in accordance with certain rules. They were reserved for magistrates with *imperium*, who had been in command on the day of the victory. In the late Republic, triumphs were regularly celebrated by proconsuls and propraetors. Generals remained outside Rome until granted permission to retain their *imperium* within the city on the day of the triumph. *Legati* of a general could not triumph, but the rule was broken by Caesar and afterwards by the triumvirs. The victory had to be won against foreigners, not in civil wars.

The procession comprised the magistrates and Senate, trumpeters, the spoils of the enemy (including pictorial descriptions and allegorical figures), the white oxen destined for sacrifice, the principal captives in chains, the lictors, the *triumphator* in a chariot with four horses, while the army followed behind. The *triumphator* wore the dress of a king or of Jupiter (this important question is doubtful); he had laurel, sceptre, and crown and his face was painted red. His children rode with him. To avoid the evil eye an amulet was worn, and a slave whispered: 'Hominem te memento.' The army followed shouting 'Io triumphe', praises of the general, and coarse expressions or verses. The procession entered Rome by the Porta Triumphalis, passed through the Circus Flaminius and reached the Via Sacra and the Forum. At the Clivus Capitolinus the principal captives were generally taken away and put to death. At the Capitol the laurel was deposited on the lap of the god. Triumphs might last longer than one day. The *triumphator* preserved the privilege of appearing at public spectacles in special dress; his name was inscribed in the *Fasti Triumphales*.

The triumph on the Alban Mount was a procession to the Temple of Jupiter Latiaris there. It probably derived from the times of the Latin League, and it was used by generals when the Senate refused a regular triumph. It was recorded in the Fasti. A *triumphus navalis* was equally possible, but no details are known.

During the Empire the triumph became an imperial prerogative. The *ornamenta triumphalia* (the right to appear at festivals in triumphal dress) were bestowed on other generals. From the time of the Antonines, triumphal dress was worn by every consul on entry into office and other special occasions. The emperors used triumphal costume freely.

Mommsen, *Röm. Staatsr.* i³. 412; E. Pais, *Fasti triumphales populi romani* (1920); R. Laqueur, 'Über das Wesen des römischen Triumphs', *Hermes* 1909, 214; A. Bruhl, 'Les Influences hellénistiques dans le triomphe romain', *Mélanges d'arch.* 1929, 77; L. Deubner, 'Die Tracht des römischen Triumphators', *Hermes* 1934, 316; A. Alföldi, 'Insignien und Tracht der römischen Kaiser', *Röm. Mitt.* 1935, 25; W. W. Fowler, *CR* 1916, 153.   A. M.

TRIUMVIRI (*tresviri*), any board or commission of three, e.g. *tresviri capitales* (police magistrates), *tresviri monetales* (masters of the mint), *triumviri agris dandis assignandis* (commissioners appointed under an agrarian law). The term is specially applied, (a) in modern usage to Pompey, Caesar, and Crassus after their political alliance in 60 B.C.; (b) (officially) to Antony, Lepidus, and Octavian, after the *Lex Titia* of 27 Nov. 43 B.C., which appointed them *triumviri rei publicae constituendae* with practically absolute powers, for five years. They retained the office after its legal termination, and it was renewed for a second quinquennium after the Treaty of Tarentum. Lepidus was deposed in 36. Antony contrived to use the title after 33, though Octavian appears to have dropped it.

First Triumvirate: Cicero, *Letters*; Velleius 2. 44; Plutarch, *Crassus* 14, *Pompey* 47, *Caesar* 13–14; Appian, *BCiv.* 2. 9; Dio Cassius 37. 54 ff. Second Triumvirate: Augustus, *Mon. Anc.* 7; Plutarch, *Antony* 19 ff.; Suetonius, *Aug.* 27; Appian, *BCiv.* 4. 2 ff. and 5. 95; *Illyrica* 28; Dio Cassius 46. 54 ff. and 47. 2. Modern Literature: T. Rice Holmes, *Roman Republic* (1923) i and ii, *Architect of the Roman Empire* i; M. Cary and F. E. Adcock, *CAH* ix, chs. 12 and 15; M. P. Charlesworth and W. W. Tarn, *CAH* x, chs. 1–3.   G. W. R.

TRIVIA, Latin translation of Τριοδῖτις, title of Hecate (q.v.) as goddess of cross-roads. Since the identification of Hecate with Artemis and Selene was popular in Hellenistic times and Diana (q.v.) was identified with Artemis, the epithet is often used of Diana, as Lucretius 1. 84; Catullus 34. 15; cf. Verg. *Aen.* 6. 35 (Hecate and Diana).   H. J. R.

TRIVIUM, see EDUCATION, I. 9.

TROAS, the mountainous north-west corner of Asia Minor forming a geographical unit dominated by the Ida massif and washed on three sides by the sea. Its name derives from the belief that all this area was once under Trojan rule. The interior is inaccessible, and the more important cities were situated on the coast. The historical significance of the Troad derives from its strategic position flanking the Hellespont (a factor which may already have weighed with the Achaeans in their attack on Troy). From the sixth century Athens became increasingly interested in holding the straits, but after Aegospotami Persia nominally controlled the Troad. It became the battlefield in the struggle between east and west when Alexander routed the Persian first line of resistance at the Granicus. Later the Troad was ruled by Antigonus, who founded Antigoneia—afterwards Alexandria Troas—and from him the country passed successively under the power of Lysimachus, the Seleucids, and Attalus I of Pergamum. The Attalids bequeathed it to Rome, and the Troad suffered severely in the wars of the Republic; but under the Empire it enjoyed a long period of tranquillity until the Arab incursions of the eighth century.

W. Leaf, *Strabo on the Troad* (1923).   D. E. W. W.

TROGLODYTAE (Τρωγλοδύται, 'Cave-dwellers') were a primitive people who dwelt in natural or artificial caves, mostly on the Red Sea coast south of Egypt, but also on the Arabian and Iranian coasts, in north-west Africa, and on the north side of the Caucasus. Their lands on the Red Sea coast were explored by agents of Ptolemy II and III. They mostly went naked, ate the bones and hides as well as the flesh of their cattle, and drank a mixture of milk and blood. They squeaked like bats, talked gibberish, and buried their dead by pelting them with stones. They kept women in common, but were governed by 'tyrants'.

Hdt. 4. 183; Diod. 3. 32–3 (from Agatharchides); Strabo 16. 775–6.
E. H. W.

TROGUS, POMPEIUS, the Augustan historian, a Vocontian from Gallia Narbonensis, whose grandfather was enfranchised by Pompey and whose father served under Caesar, wrote zoological, and perhaps botanical, works, used by the Elder Pliny, and a Universal History in forty-four books, entitled *Historiae Philippicae*. Beginning with the Ancient Orient and Greece (bks. 1–6), he treated Macedon (bks. 7–12) and the Hellenistic kingdoms to their fall before Rome (bks. 13–40). Bks. 41–2 contained Parthian history to 20 B.C., bks. 43–4 the kingly period of Rome, and Gallic and Spanish history to Augustus' Spanish victory. His source, which is independent of the patriotic Roman tradition, may possibly be Timagenes of Alexandria. The narrative was elaborate, in the Hellenistic, especially the Peripatetic, fashion, with dramatic presentation and a moralizing tendency; speeches were as a rule reported indirectly (Justin. 38. 3. 11; but note Mithridates' speech, 38. 4). This character is reflected in the epitome of Justinus (q.v.) by which, in addition to the *prologi* (tables of contents), the work is preserved.

L. E. Hallberg, *De Trogo Pompeio* (1869); F. Seck, *De Pomp. Trog. sermone* (1881); E. Schneider, *De Pomp. Trog. hist. Philipp. consilio et arte* (1913); A. Momigliano, *Athenaeum* 1934, 56; on sources, see Schanz–Hosius, *Gesch. der röm. Lit.* ii (1935), 323.
A. H. McD.

TROIAE HALOSIS, poem on the taking of Troy in the *Satyricon* of Petronius (q.v. 2).

TROILUS (Τρωΐλος), son of Priam (q.v.), mentioned *Iliad* 24. 257 as dead. Later accounts, as the *Cypria* (Proclus), specify that he was slain by Achilles (q.v.; cf. Verg. *Aen.* 1. 474 and Servius thereon; more in Mayer in Roscher, s.v.). 'Troilus and Cressida' (i.e. Chryseis) is a purely medieval fiction, having no connexion with antiquity.
H. J. R.

TROPHONIUS (Τροφώνιος), apparently 'the Feeder', a Boeotian oracular god (description of his shrine at Lebadea, P. Philippson, *Symb. Osl. fasc. suppl.* ix, pp. 11 ff.). Of him and his brother Agamedes practically the same story is told as that of the architect of Rhampsinitus (q.v.; Paus. 9. 37. 4 ff.). His oracle was held in great reverence, and visited with elaborate and obviously archaic ritual, after which the inquirer was supposed to be snatched away underground and given direct revelations (ibid. 39. 5 ff.); for its legend see ibid. 40. 1 f.
H. J. R.

TROPHIES (τρόπαια, trophaea, from τροπή). An ancient victory was marked and consecrated by the erection of a mound, a heap of stones, or more often a trophy of captured arms. There were two kinds of trophies, the *tumulus* or mingled heap of arms, and the single panoply set on a stake, corresponding to the mêlée and the duel; the second form eventually became more popular. The trophy was erected generally on the battlefield, sometimes in the sanctuary of the deity to whom the victory was ascribed. Naval trophies stood on the coast near the battle-site or in the home port of the victorious fleet, and were composed of captured prows or sterns, or the fore-part of a ship on which a statue of a deity or the commanding admiral might be erected.

Regularly observed in the fifth century, the practice later grew rarer, and the Macedonians did not originally erect trophies, though there are occasional Hellenistic examples. At Rome naval trophies were frequently exhibited in the Forum. Under the Empire the trophy often became the crowning ornament of a permanent stone memorial; examples are the Trophies of Augustus at La Turbie and of Trajan at Adamklissi.

A. Reinach, Dar.–Sag., s.v. 'trophaeum'.
F. N. P.

TROS (Τρώς), an early Trojan prince, for whose genealogical position *see* TEUCER.

TROY (mod. *Hissarlik*) stood 4 miles from the east side of the Aegean entrance to the Dardanelles, and in the north-east corner of the triangular plateau between the rivers identified as the Scamander and Simoïs. Excavation has revealed nine well-defined strata. The earliest town, Troy I, began early in the Bronze Age; it had a crude brick wall on a battered stone base with projecting gate towers. The second stratum was larger; it was defended by a similar wall with projecting towers and pierced by gates approached by ramps. Near its centre, within a court entered by a propylon, was a large megaron-like building flanked by others, presumably the residence of the ruler. To this settlement belonged the great treasure found by Schliemann. It was followed by two more settlements of the Early Bronze Age, slightly larger but apparently unfortified. The fifth settlement marked the transition from the Early to the Middle Bronze Age. The sixth stratum covered the Middle and most of the Late Bronze Age. It was much larger and was protected by a high well-built wall of limestone. It was entered by a great gate at the south, and there were two smaller gates. Within a series of terraces stood large houses with interior columns. Outside was a cremation cemetery. This rich and well-populated town passed through three stages: (*a*) and (*b*) before and after the construction of the wall; (*c*) after the addition of its towers. The last two stages were of the Late Bronze Age. Troy VI was wrecked by an earthquake, and its reconstruction (known as Troy VII A) may be identified with the Troy of Priam, for its destruction by fire befell about the traditional date for the Trojan War. Troy VII B shows Danubian and Thracian contacts and covers the Early Iron Age. Troy VIII was the town of the Greek colonial and archaic period. Troy IX was the Hellenistic and Graeco-Roman Ilium, which flourished till after the days of Constantine. The earlier 'cities' were, like Mycenae and Tiryns, the fortified residences of kings, but the Graeco-Roman Ilium had its citadel on the hill of Hissarlik (then devoted to the temple of Athena), and spread over the plateau to the south-east. Of all the prehistoric sites in the Troad Hissarlik is the largest and most important and corresponds best with the Homeric accounts of Troy. Of the other excavated sites suggested for Troy some have not revealed any prehistoric remains at all and others have proved insignificant. The site on Bally Dagh by the Bunarbashi springs, which before Schliemann's day was held to be Troy, has little or no correspondence with Homeric descriptions. Excavation has shown that its walls were not older than the classical period, and that the earliest remains were contemporary with Troy VIII (c. 800 B.C.). The lately revived theory that Hissarlik was not an inhabited site, but a polyandrion or incineration necropolis, needs no refutation.

H. Schliemann, *Troy and its Remains* (1875), *Ilios* (1880), *Troja* (1884); W. Dörpfeld, *Troja und Ilion* Athens, 1902); W. Leaf, *Troy* (1912); C. W. Blegen, *Excavations at Troy* (*AJArch.* 1932–9).
A. J. B. W.

TRYPHIODORUS (5th c. A.D.), epic poet, believed to have lived in Egypt; he was influenced by Nonnus and influenced Colluthus. His poems include an *Iliu Halosis*, still extant, which is partly dependent on Quintus Smyrnaeus (q.v.), and partly, besides others, on a lost poetic source unknown to Quintus but used by Virgil. The poem lacks brilliance, but has some rhythm, music, and vitality.

Text: W. Weinberger, 1896. Criticism: W. Weinberger, *Wien. Stud.* xviii (1896), 116–59; L. Castiglioni, *Riv. fil.* liv, N.S. iv (1926), 501–17; E. Cesareo, *Studi ital. di filol. class.*, N.S. vi (1928), 231–50, vii. (1929), 251–300; W. F. J. Knight, *CQ*, xxvi (1932), 178–89. W. F. J. K.

TRYPHON, son of Ammonius, an important Greek grammarian at Rome under Augustus. His works, which were used by his contemporary Didymus, by Apollonius Dyscolus, and very freely by Herodian, included musical, botanical, zoological, and important dialect glossaries; as Atticist and analogist (*see* GLOSSA (Greek) *and* CRATES (3) of Mallos) he wrote Περὶ Ἑλληνισμοῦ, Περὶ ὀρθογραφίας, on disputed breathings, and on etymological pathology, which 'science' (including, for him, dialectal variation) he founded. His works are lost. Our T. Περὶ παθῶν is a late abridgement.

J. Wackernagel, *De pathologiae veterum initiis* (1896). P. B. R. F.

TUBILUSTRIUM, *see* MARS.

TUCCA, *see* PLOTIUS.

TUDITANUS (1), PUBLIUS SEMPRONIUS (*cos.* 204 B.C.), military tribune at Cannae (216), curule aedile in 214, praetor in 213, commanding at Ariminum until 211, became censor in 209. A leading diplomat, he closed the First Macedonian War by the Peace of Phoenice (205). Consul in 204, he won a success over Hannibal near Croton, dedicating a temple to *Fortuna Primigenia* (194). His Greek experience placed him on the embassy to Greece, Syria, and Egypt in 200, which opened the new Roman policy in the East, with the Second Macedonian War.

Livy 24. 43 ff.; 29. 12–13 and 36; 31. 2. G. De Sanctis, *Stor. Rom.* iii. 2. 432; M. Holleaux, *Rome, la Grèce et les monarchies hellénistiques* (1921), 255. Cf. A. H. McDonald and F. W. Walbank, *JRS* 1937, 180. A. H. McD.

TUDITANUS (2), GAIUS SEMPRONIUS, consul in 129 B.C. when he triumphed over the Iapydes, wrote *Libri magistratuum* in at least thirteen books, treating intercalation, the *maius* and *minus imperium*, the origin of the tribunate, and the *nundinae*. Fragments about the Aborigines, the books of Numa, the death of Regulus, and (probably) Flamininus' triumph, indicate an historical work.

H. Peter, *HRRel.* i² (1914), pp. cci; 143. Cf. C. Cichorius, *Wiener Stud.* 1902, 588. A. H. McD.

TULLIA (1), the younger daughter of Servius Tullius, was said to have impelled her brother-in-law, the future Tarquinius Superbus, to murder her husband, Aruns Tarquinius, and her father, in order that she might marry him and become his queen. Tullia then drove her chariot over her dead father's body, in a street thereafter named Vicus Sceleratus. The story, for which a Greek origin has wrongly been claimed, is probably an aetiological myth invented to explain the street name and the gesture of a statue, which was popularly believed to represent Servius Tullius. P. T.

TULLIA (2), Cicero's beloved daughter (Tulliola), born *c.* 78 B.C., married in 63 C. Calpurnius Piso Frugi, who died in 57, then in 56 Furius Crassipes, and finally in 50 P. Cornelius Dolabella. Separated from her third husband in 46, she died in 45. Cicero considered building a temple to her. Her death was a turning-point in his mental life. A. M.

TULLIANUM, the underground execution-cell of the prison at Rome, flanking the *comitium*, and connected with Servius Tullius (Varro, *Ling.* 5. 151; Festus 356). The derivation from **tullus*, a spring, is more attractive, for the existing work is a well-chamber, once circular, built in coursed peperino (Tenney Frank, *Buildings of the Roman Republic*, 39–47) of the third century B.C. The room above it has a travertine front repaired in A.D. 22 or 45 (*CIL* vi. 31674; cf. *ILS* iii, p. 342). The frontal orientation, as of the *comitium*, is by the cardinal points. A spring still rises in the present floor, higher than the original. Here were executed most State prisoners, including Jugurtha, the Catilinarian conspirators, and Vercingetorix. I. A. R.

TULLIUS ('Tully' esp. in 18th-cent. English), *see* CICERO. *See also* TIRO.

TULLIUS LAUREA, MARCUS, *see* LAUREA.

TULLUS HOSTILIUS, traditionally the third king of Rome (673–642 B.C.), is probably an historical figure, and the suggestion that he is a duplication of Romulus need not be discussed. His capture of Alba Longa, which ceased to be an independent commonwealth during the regal period, and his founding of the *Curia Hostilia*, may be accepted as facts. The Curia was indisputably built by an eponymous king, because no consul Hostilius is mentioned in the early Fasti, nor did the gens Hostilia come to power till the end of the second century B.C. The laws and reform, however, attributed to Tullus are, like his public works, pure inventions.

H. Last, *CAH* vii. 377, 401 f. P. T.

TUMULTUS was the state of fear (*timor*) and confusion resulting from a war fought on the frontiers of Italy (or, originally, near the walls of Rome). Cicero (*Phil.* 8. 1. 3) attests that there were only two examples of *tumultus*, namely *tumultus Italicus* (i.e. war in Italy and, later, civil war) 'quod erat domesticus' and *tumultus Gallicus* (as Gaul was the only province that had a common frontier with Italy), 'quod erat Italiae finitimus'. The term probably came into use after the Gallic capture of Rome (387 B.C.). When the *tumultus* was announced, business and the administration of justice stopped (*justitium*), army leave was cancelled, and all the citizens, wearing the military dress called *sagum*, were levied, even if previously exempted from service, to form a supplementary corps named *tumultuarii milites*.

E. Pottier, Dar.-Sag., s.v.; Kromayer-Veith, *Heerwesen u. Kriegführung* (1928), 285, 305. P. T.

TUNICA, *see* DRESS, para. 3.

TURBASIA, *see* DANCING.

TURBO (QUINTUS MARCIUS TURBO FRONTO PUBLICIUS SEVERUS), of equestrian rank, was sent in A.D. 117 by Trajan to quell Jewish trouble in Egypt. Dispatched by Hadrian (immediately after accession) to subdue revolt in Mauretania, as imperial procurator, he thus displaced Lusius (q.v.) Quietus. Early in 118 Hadrian appointed him to the special and temporary command of Pannonia with Dacia, with distinguishing rank equivalent to that of *praefectus Aegypti*, though hardly with this title (see S.H.A. *Had.* 7. 3). In 119 he replaced Attianus (q.v.) as *praefectus praetorio*: his prefecture, loyal and unselfishly industrious, probably continued until 135, if not longer. He himself may have survived into Antoninus' reign.

S.H.A. *Had.*; Dio Cassius, bk. 69; *PIR*, M 179; R. H. Lacey, *The Equestrian Officials of Trajan and Hadrian*, etc. (Diss. Princeton, 1917), p. 17, no. 39. C. H. V. S.

TURIA, wife of Q. Lucretius Vespillo (*cos.* 19 B.C.), concealed her husband during the proscriptions of 43–42 until his pardon was obtained. She is usually identified with the subject of the so-called 'Laudatio Turiae' (*ILS* 8393).

Appian, *BCiv.* 4. 44; Val. Max. 6. 7. 2. Modern Literature on the Laudatio: Mommsen, *Ges. Schr.* i (1905), 395 ff.; W. Warde Fowler, *CR* xix (1905), 261 ff. The identification with Turia is disputed by D. Vaglieri, *Not. Scavi* (1898), 412 ff., and Hirschfeld, *Wien. Stud.* xxiv (1902), 233 ff. G. W. R.

TURNUS (1), Italian hero, son of Daunus and the nymph Venilia, and brother of the nymph Juturna; king of the Rutulians, whose capital was Ardea. He was the accepted suitor of Lavinia, daughter of Latinus (q.v.), but Latinus subsequently betrothed her to Aeneas against the will of his wife Amata. The Latins, roused by Juno, join with the Rutulians to make war on the Trojans. Turnus fights bravely, leads the attack on the Trojan camp and defends Lavinium. He slays Pallas, son of Evander, and is twice saved by Juno from Aeneas, who finally pursues and kills him (*Aen.* 7–12). C. B.

TURNUS (2), satirist under Domitian, brother of the tragic poet Scaeva Memor (q.v.), and credited with 'ingentia pectora' by Martial (7. 97. 7; 11. 10; Probus (Vallae) *ad Iuven.* 1. 20; Rut. Namat. 1. 603–4; Lydus, *Mag.* 1. 41).

TURPILIUS, SEXTUS (died old, 103 B.C.), Latin composer of *comoediae palliatae*, livelier and more popular than Terence's. Of thirteen surviving titles six come from Menander. *See* DRAMA, ROMAN, para 4. Fragments: O. Ribbeck, *CRF²* 85 (3rd ed. Teubner 1897). E. H. W.

TURPIO, AMBIVIUS, *see* AMBIVIUS.

TURRANIUS GRACILIS (of uncertain date), an authority on Spain, used by the elder Pliny (*HN*, bks. 3, 9, and 18, *index auctorum*).

TURRINUS, CLODIUS, name of two rhetoricians, father and son, discussed by the elder Seneca (*Controv.* 10, *pr.* 14–16). The senior lost force in speaking by too strict adherence to Apollodorean rules: he held an important appointment in Spain. The son, in whom Seneca saw high promise, was treated as one of his own sons. J. W. D.

TUSCULUM, a city near *Frascati* 15 miles south-east of Rome. Its extensive remains occupy a strong, bracing site 2,198 feet above sea-level. Myths shroud its origin, but Tusculum was certainly powerful in early Latium. Its dictator Octavius Mamilius allegedly supported his son-in-law Tarquinius Superbus (508 B.C.); but traditions associating Tusculum with Etruscans may be mere aetiological fictions to explain its name. More credibly, Tusculum reputedly led the Latins at Lake Regillus (q.v.) *c.* 496, when Mamilius himself fell. Thereafter, however, being exposed to Aequian attacks via Algidus, it became Rome's ally and staunchly resisted Aequi, Volsci, and Gauls. Tusculum, the first Latin city to obtain Roman citizenship (381), supplied Rome with several illustrious families (Mamilii, Fulvii, Fonteii, Juventii, Porcii). Some Tusculans joined the Latin revolt in 340 B.C. but usually Tusculum remained loyal (e.g. against Hannibal). A *municipium* under late Republic and early Empire, Tusculum was a fashionable resort where wealthy Romans sojourned: Lucullus, Maecenas, and especially Cicero, who composed several philosophical treatises in his Tusculan villa (at Poggio Tulliano?). Subsequently Tusculum is seldom mentioned, but was still an important stronghold when destroyed in medieval times. Cato the Censor was born here.

Strabo 5. 239; Livy 1. 49; 2. 15 f.; 3. 7 f.; 4. 33 f.; 6. 21; 8. 7 f.; 26. 9; Dion. Hal. bk. 10 passim. G. McCracken, *A Short History of Ancient Tusculum* (U.S.A. 1939). E. T. S.

TUTANUS, *see* REDICULUS.

TUTELAGE, *see* GUARDIANSHIP.

TŪTĬCĀNŬS, friend of Ovid from youth, whose name could not appear in elegiac verse without the playful scansions of *Pont.* 4. 12. 10–11: cf. 4. 14. He retold Homeric themes in Latin.

TWELVE TABLES, the earliest Roman code of laws, and the starting-point in the development of Roman law. The circumstances under which it was drawn up are not clear, and the authenticity of the Twelve Tables has therefore been called into doubt by some scholars. But it may be regarded as certain that the Twelve Tables were actually drawn up by a special commission of *decemviri legibus scribundis* in 451–450 B.C. (*see* DECEMVIRI). Enacted by the *Comitia Centuriata* as a statute (*lex duodecim tabularum* appears often in the sources), the Twelve Tables were published in the Forum on tablets of bronze (or wood). The original Tables perished when Rome was burnt by the Gauls. The object of the code was to collect the most important rules of the existing customary law, the knowledge of which had been till then confined to the *pontifices*, and the levelling of existing legal customs by the abolition of patrician privilege. Thus they had both a codificatory and a legislative character. How far the *decemviri* fulfilled these tasks is very difficult to estimate, in default of authentic sources about the law in pre-decemviral times, and for lack of a complete text of the Code, which is known only through fragments surviving in legal and lay literature (altogether about 128, probably a third of the whole). The surviving text is mostly in a later and modernized Latin, but it contains a few passages in archaic language, whose meaning is not always clear. But it is beyond doubt that its legislative innovations may have been important, since the high constitutional position of the *decemviri* must have authorized them to make reforms. Some few reminiscences of Greek institutions in the Code may be brought into connexion with an embassy to Athens, which preceded the decemviral work. The Twelve Tables contained rules from all spheres of law: private and criminal law and procedure, sacral and public law. But the statement of Livy (3. 34. 6) that they were 'fons omnis publici priuatique iuris' is an exaggeration, for they were only a selection. The principal rules are mentioned in the separate articles on institutes of Roman law; for the important part which they played in the evolution of Roman Law, *see* LAW AND PROCEDURE, ROMAN, I. The Twelve Tables were never abolished (even in Cicero's youth schoolboys learnt them by heart); but it is clear that the later development of Roman law must have made them obsolete. Some fundamental rules nevertheless remained operative until Justinian.

Reconstructions of the decemviral code have been attempted since the 16th century; the best one is that of R. Schoell, *Legis duodecim tabularum reliquiae* (1866). Modern editions are to be found in the collections of *Fontes iuris Romani* by Bruns–Mommsen–Gradenwitz, Girard, and Riccobono (second edition i, 1941)—*see* LAW AND PROCEDURE, ROMAN, I.

G. Baviera, *Studi Perozzi* (1925, printed 1914); E. Täubler, *Untersuchungen zur Geschichte des Dezemvirats und der XII Tafeln* (1921); H. F. Jolowicz, *Historical Introduction to the Study of Roman Law* (1932); A. Berger, *Studi Riccobono* i (1933); *Atti del Congresso Internazionale di diritto romano*, Roma 1933, i (1934); A. Berger, *PW* iv A, s.v. 'Tabulae Duodecim'. See also the various text-books of Roman law. A. B.

TYCHE. Since τύχη, 'fortune', contains the stem of τυγχάνειν, 'to hit the mark', the notion of *good* fortune must have been prominent, though the word may, like *moira*, refer simply to one's 'lot', whether good or bad. It is not found in Homer (cf. Macrob. *Sat.* 5. 16. 8), but

Hesiod (*Theog.* 360) includes Tyche among the Oceanids, and in the Homeric *Hymn to Demeter* (420) she appears as a companion of Persephone. When Alcman (fr. 62 Bergk, 44 Diehl) gives her a moral pedigree as daughter of Forethought and sister of Loyalty and Persuasion, she is more an abstraction than a deity. Archilochus (fr. 16 Bergk, 8 Diehl) aids the process of personification when he says that 'fortune and fate (*moira*) give all things to man'. Pindar hailed Tyche as patroness of Himera (*Ol.* 12), and numbered her among the Moirai (Paus. 7. 26. 8), probably in the place of Lachesis. We find the word first used as a common noun in the Homeric *Hymn to Athena* (11. 5), in the sense of 'good fortune'. In Tragedy it is of frequent occurrence, but there are comparatively few cases in which Tyche is clearly personified (e.g., Soph. *O.T.* 977, 1080; Eur. *Hec.* 786, *Ion* 1514), and even here her influence on the course of events is negligible as compared with that of Fate. As a goddess, Tyche came to greatest prominence in Hellenistic and Roman times, being identified with the Latin Fortuna (q.v.). Yet she found no place in myth, and had little importance in cult except as Agathe Tyche and as patroness of various cities, e.g. Caesarea (Sozomen. *Hist. eccl.* 5. 4. 2), Antioch (Julian, *Apophth.* 176, p. 223 Bidez–Cumont), and even Constantinople (*Chron. pasc.*, a. 328 = Migne, *PG* 92. 709). Tyche was portrayed in sculpture as early as the sixth century B.C. by Bupalus of Chios (Paus. 4. 30. 6); more celebrated, however, in later times was the Tyche of Antioch by Eutychides of Sicyon.

For Thucydides *tyche* was no divine power, but merely a term denoting those phases of a situation which men often prove powerless to anticipate or control, however intelligently they may have striven. 'Therefore', as he makes Pericles say (1. 140. 1), 'we are accustomed to blame chance for everything that happens unexpectedly.' In the same spirit Nicias, on the eve of the Sicilian expedition, argues for laying one's plans with all possible care, leaving as little as may be to chance (6. 23. 3; cf. 5. 16. 1). When the Melians express their trust in some *divine* fortune that will help them resist Athenian agression (5. 104. 1; cf. 5. 112. 2), we perceive that the historian is only dramatizing their piety. Thucydides seems, therefore, to anticipate the philosophical conception of *tyche* as chance, the unforeseen element in human affairs which men use as an 'excuse for their own ill counsel' (Democritus ap. Stob. *Ecl.* 2. 8, p. 156 W.; cf. Anaximenes and Epicurus, ibid., pp. 156, 159). Plato develops in the tenth book of his *Laws* the principle that all things are due to three causes, nature, Chance, and art, while for Aristotle chance is the incalculable in the human sphere, corresponding to 'spontaneity' among the lower animals.

In the Greek romances Tyche is often one of the operative forces, usually malicious (cf. Chariton 1. 14. 7; 2. 8. 6; 4. 1. 12 and passim, cf. p. 133 ed. Blake; Achilles Tatius 4. 9; 5. 7 and passim), rarely benevolent (e.g. Chariton 1. 10. 2), and sometimes as a symbol of the unpredictable (cf. Chariton 2. 8. 3). Not unlike a romance in some respects is an autobiography of the sophist Libanius (*Or.* 1), who reviews the influence which Tyche has exerted upon his life.

BIBLIOGRAPHY
Detailed discussion of the numerous contexts of *tyche*: L. Ruhl, in Roscher, *Lex.* v. 1310–57; Waser, ibid. 1357–80; S. G. Stock, 'Fortune (Greek)', in Hastings's *ERE* vi. 93 ff.; G. Busch, *Untersuchungen zum Wesen der τύχη in den Tragödien des Euripides* (Diss., Heidelberg, 1937); F. Allègre, *Étude sur la déesse grecque Tyche* (1889); A. Bouché-Leclercq in *Rev. del'hist. des religions* xxiii (1891), 273–307; A. D. Nock, *Sallustius* (1926), lxxiv–lxxv; S. Eitrem in *Symb. Osl.* xiii (1934), 47–51. R. A. P.

TYDEUS (Τυδεύς), in mythology, father, by Deipyle daughter of Adrastus (q.v.), of Diomedes (q.v. 2), and son of Oeneus (q.v.) (Apollod. 1. 75). He was a small but powerful and valiant man (*Iliad* 5. 801). Being sent on an embassy to Thebes by the Seven, he took part in sports there and defeated all the rest; the Thebans laid an ambush for him, but he killed all but one of the fifty who composed it (4. 384 ff.). Later poems, drawing more or less on the Cyclic Thebaid, and still later ones which use the *Thebais* of Antimachus, tell of his part in the attack on Thebes, his furious battle-rage (as Aesch. *Sept.* 377 ff.), and the manner of his death (*see* MELANIPPUS). H. J. R.

TYNDAREOS (Τυνδάρεως or -ος), in mythology, husband of Leda and father, real or putative, of Helen, Clytemnestra, and the Dioscuri (qq.v.). He was king of Lacedaemon (Apollod. 2. 145, and often), brother of Leucippus (q.v. 1), and of Aphareus and Icarius (Apollod. 1. 87); for his varying genealogy, see Roscher's *Lexikon* v. 1406 f. He has not much legend of his own; Hesiod (fr. 93 Rzach) says that when sacrificing to the gods he forgot Aphrodite, who therefore made his daughters light and unfaithful. He is also associated with Heracles (q.v.); the hero had a serious quarrel with Hippocoon and his sons, wherefore he invaded Lacedaemon, their kingdom, overcame and killed them in a desperate battle in which he lost his brother Iphicles (q.v.), and gave Lacedaemon to Tyndareos (Alcman, fr. 1. 5 Diehl; Apollod. 2. 143 ff.). H. J. R.

TYNNICHUS, poet of unknown place and date, whose reputation rested on a single poem, a paean to Apollo, of which nothing survives, but which was admired by Aeschylus (Porph. *Abst.* 2. 18) and mentioned with high praise by Plato.

J. M. Edmonds, *Lyra Graeca* (Loeb), ii. 234–5.

TYPHON, TYPHOEUS (Τυφών, Τυφωεύς), a monster, often confused with the Giants (q.v.), as Horace, *Carm.* 3. 4. 53, but originally and properly distinct from them. He was born by Earth to Tartarus after the defeat of the Titans (Hesiod, *Theog.* 820 ff.). He had a hundred heads of dragon-shape, which uttered the sounds of all manner of beasts, also mighty hands and feet (presumably a hundred, or a hundred pairs, of each, though Hesiod does not say so) and would have done enormous harm if Zeus had not at once attacked him with his thunderbolts, overthrown him, and cast him into Tartarus, setting Aetna on fire by the way (in Homer, *Il.* 2. 783, he lies in the land of the Arimi; cf. Verg. *Aen.* 9. 715–16, and commentators on both passages). His shape suggests Oriental rather than Greek myth, and this is confirmed by his regular connexion with Cilicia. The story, therefore, in Apollod. 1. 41–4, Nonnus, *Dion.* 1. 154 ff., may be Eastern and ancient. Typhon strove with Zeus, stole his thunderbolts, and cut out his sinews with his own sword; but Hermes and Aegipan stole all back (or Cadmus, q.v., disguised as a shepherd, beguiled Typhon with his music), so Zeus was finally victorious, and buried Typhon under Aetna. H. J. R.

TYRANNIO (1) the Elder (early 1st c. B.C.). Theophrastus, son of Epicratides, of Amisus (where his teacher nicknamed him Tyrannio), afterwards a pupil of Dionysius Thrax, was brought by Lucullus as prisoner to Rome, where he was freed and enjoyed the patronage of Pompey, being the first Aristarchan to teach in the city. He was among those who examined the manuscripts brought by Sulla from Athens, 86 B.C. His works, on metre (a comparatively rare topic), on Homeric and other criticism and exegesis, and on grammar (which, under Atticist influence, he defined as θεωρία μιμήσεως) have perished. P. B. R. F.

TYRANNIO (2) the Younger, son of Artemidorus, a Phoenician, was brought as a prisoner to Rome and freed by Terentia. He was a pupil of T. the Elder, and became an eminent grammarian at Rome, Strabo being among his pupils. He wrote on accents and other grammatical topics, but his works have been confused with those of the elder T., the fate of which they have shared.   P. B. R. F.

TYRANNY (τυραννίς, perhaps a Lydian word) was the illegal monarchy which was usurped by individuals in many oligarchic city-states of the seventh and the sixth centuries B.C., the 'age of tyrants'. It was not a special form of constitution or a reign of terror; that bad sense was attached to it later, especially by the democratic *polis* of the fifth century which glorified the tyrannicide, and by the political philosophers, e.g. Plato, to whom tyranny meant the worst constitution possible. Tyranny hardly ever lasted more than two generations. The best known of the tyrants were Pheidon, Polycrates, Periander, Cleisthenes of Sicyon, Pisistratus (qq.v.). The last representatives of the early period of tyranny were the Syracusan tyrants Gelon and Hieron. A second epoch of tyranny was introduced by Dionysius I (q.v.). Tyranny of the older type mostly arose from political and economic leadership of the lower classes, and often prepared the rise of democracy. The outlines of the constitution did not change, but the tyrants used laws and institutions as the instrument of their own policy. In general they contributed greatly to the enrichment and civilization of their States, and without being 'business men' they participated in the great economic changes of their time. Later tyrants were mostly military adventurers.

H. Swoboda, *Griechische Staatsaltertümer* (1913); P. N. Ure, *The Origin of Tyranny* (1922).   V. E.

TYRE (Τύρος, *Tyrus*), HELLENISTIC AND ROMAN, an important city on the Phoenician coast, some twenty miles south of Sidon. In 332 B.C. it offered an obstinate resistance to Alexander and was only captured after a famous siege. Though destroyed, it made a rapid recovery and remained under a native dynasty till 274, when it became a republic, ruled by *Suffetes*. From the reign of Antiochus IV it issued a municipal coinage, mostly inscribed in Phoenician, and in 125 it became free. It early struck a *foedus* with Rome, and its freedom was respected till 20, when Augustus withdrew it, probably for a time only. It was colonized with veterans by Septimius Severus, who granted it the *ius Italicum*, and also made it the capital of Syria Phoenice. It was a great commercial city, maintaining a *statio* at Puteoli and at Rome during the Principate, and was the seat of a famous purple-dyeing industry. It ruled a large territory, stretching to the upper waters of the Jordan.
                                                A. H. M. J.

TYRO, see NELEUS.

TYRRHENUS (Τυρρηνός), eponym of the Tyrrhenians (Etruscans, q.v. para. 3), Dion. Hal. *Ant. Rom.* 1. 27. 1, where he is son of King Atys and comes from Maeonia; in schol. Plat. *Tim.* 25 b, he is Atys' grandson; son of Heracles, Dion. Hal. 1. 28. 1, or of Telephus (q.v.) ibid.; apparently god of the Tyrrhenian Sea (Valerius Flaccus 4. 715). He invented trumpets (Hyginus, *Fab.* 274. 20).
                                                H. J. R.

TYRSENI, see ETRUSCANS, para. 3.

TYRTAEUS, elegiac poet of the seventh century B.C., said by some to be an Athenian schoolmaster, who was sent to Sparta as the result of an oracle (Pl. *Leg.* 629 a, Paus. 4. 15. 6). It seems more likely that he was really a Spartan, since he was a general (Ath. 14. 630 f, Diod. Sic. 8. 36), and his fragments show him giving orders (frs. 1 and 8), which would hardly be tolerated by Spartans in a foreigner. He led the Spartans in the second Messenian

War and helped to take Messene (Suidas s.v. Τυρταῖος). His poems were collected at Alexandria in five books and contained: (1) war-songs, of which two specimens have been recognized in pieces of undoubted Spartan origin but not necessarily his (frs. 15–16 Bergk = *Carm. Pop.* 18–19); (2) exhortations in elegiac verse; and (3) a poem called Πολιτεία for the Lacedaemonians. Most of the existing fragments seem to belong to the second class. Fr. 1 seems to be concerned with some definite occasion in war, since it gives orders for tactical arrangements and is concerned with a siege. Fr. 6–7 is a single poem which begins by praising the virtue of dying for one's country and ends by urging the young men to valour. Fr. 8 begins with a general praise of courage at a time that seems to be after a defeat and ends with specific advice on conduct in battle. Fr. 9 is more elaborate; it is concerned with the nature of ἀρετή and of the ἀνὴρ ἀγαθός, whom Tyrtaeus finds in the brave fighter. There is no good reason to suspect the authenticity of these pieces, since the type of warfare which they describe belongs to the seventh century, and all show a similar use of language, even of repeated phrases. Other fragments may belong to the third class, notably fr. 2 on the origin of the Spartans, fr. 3 on the alleged Delphian origin of their constitution, frs. 4 and 5 on the First Messenian War. T. was certainly connected with the political reforms of his time, though he was not necessarily a prophet of the so-called Lycurgan constitution. He writes in an epic language, with many echoes of Homer, and at times he is unskilful in his adaptation of a Homeric motive to new uses (fr. 6–7. 21–6 and *Il.* 22. 71–6, fr. 8. 29–34 and *Il.* 16. 215–17). His importance is more political than literary, though he seems to have influenced Solon. The Spartans are said to have sung his songs on the march (Ath. 630 e).

Text: E. Diehl, *Anth. Lyr. Graec.* i. 1. 6–22. Commentary: T. Hudson-Williams, *Early Greek Elegy* (1926), 106–15. Criticism: U. von Wilamowitz-Moellendorff, *Textgeschichte der gr. Lyriker* (1900), 97–118; W. Jaeger, 'Tyrtaios über die wahre ἀρετή', *Sitz. Preuss. Ak.* 1932; C. M. Bowra, *Early Greek Elegists* (1938), 39–70.
                                                C. M. B.

TZETZES, JOHANNES (12th c. A.D.), a copious, careless, quarrelsome, Byzantine polymath. In his youth he wrote (A.D. 1143) a commentary on the *Iliad*, followed by *Allegories* on *Iliad* and *Odyssey* (in 10,000 verses), and other verse works on *Antehomerica, Homerica*, and *Posthomerica*. His other writings included scholia on Hesiod, Aristophanes, Lycophron, and others, and a poem on prosody. His chief work, Βίβλος Ἱστορική, by its first editor named Χιλιάδες, is a review (in 12,674 verses) of Greek literature and learning, with quotations from over 400 authors. In regard to his poverty and slighted merits Tzetzes displays an engaging lack of reticence. He was not always without taste or discretion; e.g., once, when reduced to selling the rest of his library he retained his Plutarch; nor is felicity of expression lacking in (for example) his objurgation of Thucydides' cross-word style (λοξοσυστρόφοις λόγοις). Generally, however, his manner is dull, and he is extremely inaccurate (perhaps owing to his frequent separation from his books). His uncorroborated evidence is accordingly viewed with much suspicion. Nevertheless, he preserves much valuable information from ancient scholarship.

Editions: *Letters*, Pressel, 1851; *Chiliades*: Kiessling, 1826; (scholia) Cramer, *Anecd. Ox.* 3 (1836); *Allegories* (*Il.* and *Od.*): Matranga, *Anecd. Gr.* 1 (1850); (*Iliad*): Boissonade, 1851; (scholia) Cramer, *Anecd. Ox.* 3. On *Iliad*: Hermann, 1812–14; Bachmann (in schol. *Iliad*) 1835–8; *Homerica, AnteH., PostH.*: Jacobs, 1793; Bekker, 1816; (reprinted, Lehrs, 1868); On *Theogony*: Matranga, *Anecd. Gr.* (2), 1850; *Schol. on W.D. and Shield*: Gaisford, *Poet. Gr. Min.* 3. *Schol. on Aristophanes*: Studemund, *Anecd. Gr. varia*, 1886; *Schol. on Lycophron*: Müller, 1811. *Allegories ἐκ τῆς χρονικῆς* etc.: Morellus, 1616; Studemund, *Anecd. Gr. varia*, 1886; *Schol. on Oppian*: Bussemaker (Didot), 1849; Περὶ διαφορᾶς ποιητῶν, etc.: Cramer, *Anecd. Ox.* 3 (1836). *On Death of Emperor Manuel* (1180): Matranga, *Anecd. Gr.* 2 (1850).   P. B. R. F.

U

UBII, a German tribe on the east of the Rhine, between the Main and the Westerwald, which besought Caesar's help against the Suebi (q.v.) in 55 B.C. Under renewed Suebic pressure in 38 B.C. Agrippa brought them across the river at their own request, and settled them on land formerly belonging to the Eburones, in which Cologne was later to rise (*see* COLONIA AGRIPPINENSIS). The Ubii furnished recruits to the Roman army; they only joined Civilis in A.D. 70 under duress and returned to their allegiance to Rome at the earliest possible moment.

O. B.

ULPIAN (1) (DOMITIUS ULPIANUS, d. A.D. 228), born at Tyre, one of the last Roman jurists of the classical period; his teacher is unknown. Banished by Elagabalus, he was recalled by Alexander Severus and appointed *magister libellorum.* He held several official posts, and finally (from 222) he was *praefectus praetorio.* He was killed (228) by the mutinous Praetorians, ostensibly for his severity and some plans of reform unfavourable to this privileged corps. He was a contemporary of Paulus and his colleague in some official posts, but in the sphere of scientific activity they were rivals (they do not cite one another). Ulpian was as voluminous a writer as Paulus, superior to him in clarity and ease of exposition, but not in originality and acuteness of judgement. He was mostly a compiler, but not a slavish copyist. He was a man of great learning, profoundly versed in the earlier literature, which he sifted with the critical acumen of a practitioner. His reports are exact and trustworthy, and though his contributions to the works of his predecessors were not very considerable, his merits cannot be denied. His works—nearly 280 books—published mostly in 211–17, were the chief source from which Justinian's compilers drew material for the *Digest*: one-third of the whole compilation comes from Ulpian's pen. His principal works are: *Ad edictum libri* 81, a long commentary on the Praetor's Edict, following the text of the Edict word by word, with an annex in two books on the Edict of the *aediles curules*; a comprehensive work *Ad Sabinum* in 51 books (probably two editions) with several supplementary monographs on various *Leges* or on special branches of the private law (*sponsalia, fideicommissa*); general works for practitioners (*Disputationes, Responsa, Opiniones,* the last probably a post-classical compilation); short text-books: *Institutiones Regulae* (7 books), and a *Liber singularis Regularum.* (The text of this last work preserved in the manuscript Cod. Vat. Reg. 1128 is rather a fragment of an epitome or compilation, composed between 320 and 342, by an unknown writer with many post-classical transformations of classical texts taken from Gaius, Ulpian, and other jurists.) Some of Ulpian's monographs describe the functions of magistracies such as those of Proconsul, Consul, Quaestor, Praefectus urbi, Praetor tutelaris, etc.

O. Karlowa, *Röm. Rechtsgeschichte* i (1885), 739 ff.; P. Jörs, *PW,* s.v. 'Domitius Ulpianus'; H. Fitting, *Alter und Folge der Schriften röm. Juristen*[2] (1908), 99 ff.; F. Schulz, *Sabinus-Fragmente in Ulp. Sabinus-Kommentar* (1906); B. Kübler, *Gesch. des röm. Rechts* (1925), 279 ff.
   On the *Liber singularis Regularum*: V. Arangio-Ruiz, *Bull. dell' Ist.* xxx (1921), 178 ff., xxxv (1927), 191 ff. Editions: B. Kübler and E. Seckel in Huschke, *Jurispr. anteiust.*[6] i (1908); G. Baviera in the Italian edition of *Fontes iuris rom. anteiust.* (1909, 2nd ed., 1940); F. Schulz, *Die Epitome Ulpiani* (1926); W. W. Buckland, *Law Quarterly Review* xl (1912), 185–201; liii (1937), 508–18.
A. B.

ULPIAN (2) of Emesa taught rhetoric at Antioch in the reign of Constantine (A.D. 324–37) and wrote a number of declamations and rhetorical works. He is the reputed author of scholia to eighteen speeches of Demosthenes; they are of little independent value.

ULPIUS TRAIANUS, MARCUS, father of the Emperor Trajan (q.v.), was a native of Italica in Baetica, of which province he later became governor. He commanded Legio X Fretensis in the Jewish War (c. A.D. 67–8), becoming consul (the first of his family to reach this rank) soon afterwards. In 73–4 he was created a patrician. Governor of Syria c. 75–6 (cf. *Ann. épigr.* 1933, no. 205), he won *ornamenta triumphalia* (*ILS* 8970), doubtless due to his wise handling of Parthian threats, and became proconsul of Asia c. 79–80. He died before 100 (cf. Plin. *Pan.* 89); consecrated (c. 112), he was honoured on his son's coinage as *Divus Pater Traianus.*

PIR, V 574; B. Stech, *Klio,* Beiheft x (1912) s.v.; R. Paribeni, *Optimus Princeps* i (1926), 45 ff.; H. Mattingly, *B.M. Coins, Rom. Emp.* iii (1936).
C. H. V. S.

ULPIUS, *see also* MARCELLUS (10); TRAJAN.

UMBILICI, *see* BOOKS, II. 2.

UMBRIAN, *see* DIALECTS (ITALIC).

UMBRIANS. The Umbrians, Sabellians, and Oscans form the P-speaking branch of the Italici, as contrasted with the Q-speaking Latins. These two Italic branches differ in (a) dialect (e.g. Latin Q is replaced in Umbrian by P thus: 'Quis' = 'Pis', cf. the 'Iguvian tablets' of Gubbio); and (b) burial practice: the Latins cremate, the Umbrians bury. It is impossible to say which arrived first in Italy; perhaps the geographical distribution rather suggests that the Umbrians were the earliest. There may have been several waves of Italici beginning c. 2,000 B.C. (or possibly earlier) and ending before 1,000 B.C. Evidently at one time the Umbrians occupied Etruria, for Herodotus (1. 94) says that the Etruscans landed among the 'Ομβρικοί. Since Herodotus lived at Thurii, a Greek colony, which must have known a great deal about the Etruscans, his phrase is probably correct. A few place-names also support this view. The Umbrians, therefore, being driven from Etruria and hemmed in on all sides by aggressive neighbours, were eventually confined to their historic province in central Italy. If Patroni's attractive suggestion that 'Umbri' is really the ethnical name of the people whom archaeologists nickname 'Villanovans' could be accepted, they would then cease to be shadowy and acquire a very vivid personality. Patroni supposes that the name Umbria did not originally belong to the central province but was given to it by the Villanovans, who at some time conquered it. He compares the naming in historic days of Lombardy from the Lombards. His view is unfortunately difficult to prove.
D. R.-MacI.

UNIVERSITIES, *see* EDUCATION, III.

URBANUS, a Virgilian scholar repeatedly cited by Servius in his commentary on Virgil. He is certainly later than Cornutus (q.v.) whom he criticizes; and Thilo, *Serv. praef.* 16, puts him as late as the fourth century (Teuffel–Kroll 379. 9).

URBICUS, *see* LOLLIUS.

URICONIUM, *see* VIROCONIUM.

URSO (nowadays *Osuna*), a native settlement in Spain about sixty miles east of Seville. A centre of Pompeian resistance in 45 B.C., it was stormed by Caesar, who later replaced the inhabitants with colonists. Bronze tablets containing part of the charter giving it colonial status (*Lex Coloniae Genetivae Iuliae*) survive. The charter is an administrative regulation (*lex data*) based on a legislative act (*lex rogata*) issued by M. Antonius on behalf of Julius Caesar. The colonists came apparently from Rome and included freedmen who were granted the exceptional right of holding colonial magistracies. Noteworthy are the decorated cave-tombs for pagan burials. A translation, with commentary, of the *Lex Ursonensis* is given in E. G. Hardy, *Roman Laws and Charters* (1913).

J. J. Van N.

USUCAPIO, see DOMINIUM, POSSESSIO.

USURAE MARITIMAE, see BOTTOMRY LOANS.

USURY. Loans at interest were not customary in Greece and Italy during the early Iron Age, except perhaps for cattle and seed. Our earliest records come from Megara, and from Athens, where Solon removed all restrictions of interest, and made provisions for all types of loans. Usury with or without security became a profitable business during the classical period, both for private individuals and for temples and State institutions. Athens, from Solon's time, most Hellenic States, and Rome forbade lending on the security of the debtor's person, a practice prevalent in the East until the Hellenistic age, which was a period of large borrowing transactions throughout the civilized world. Usury was absolutely forbidden at Rome in 357 B.C., but the law became inoperative from the second century. The pitiless treatment of debtors by the upper classes at Rome during the later Republic is only too well known. Since 51 B.C. interest might not exceed 12 per cent., except for seed

loans; but usury by legal subterfuge is attested by authors and papyri. These evasions were gradually made more difficult, until in the Late Roman period a limit was fixed (50 per cent.!), extending to seed loans. Unlimited usury was henceforth illegal.

See BOTTOMRY LOANS; INTEREST, RATE OF. M. Schnebel, *Aegyptus* xiii (1933), 35 f. F. M. H.

USUS, see MANUS.

UTICA, traditionally the oldest Phoenician settlement on the north African coast, some thirty miles north-west of Carthage; its ruins now lie five miles inland. Founded *c.* 1100 B.C., Utica became a flourishing port for the produce of the Bagradas valley. She remained jealously independent of the growing power of Carthage, joining the rebel African mercenaries in 238. Utica was besieged by Scipio (204) and supported Masinissa (q.v.) against Carthage in 149. Rome rewarded Utica with lands of the fallen city and made her the capital of the Roman province of Africa; Italian financiers and merchants settled in the Free City. Pompey made the port his base for the swift campaign which won Africa from the Marians (81). Later Utica remained loyal to the Pompeian cause against the forces of Curio and Caesar, and was the scene of Cato's suicide. Heavily fined for its senatorial sympathies, Utica lost ground as Roman Carthage became important, but received municipal rights under Augustus and colonial under Hadrian.

W. N. W.

V

VABALLATHUS, SEPTIMIUS, or in Greek ATHENODORUS, the son of Odaenathus (q.v.) by his second wife Zenobia (q.v.), was an infant when his father was killed but was his titular successor, under the guardianship of his mother. He at first assumed the title of king of kings and *corrector totius orientis*. In A.D. 270 Aurelian recognized him as *vir consularis, rex, imperator, dux Romanorum*. In 271 he was proclaimed *Imperator Caesar Vaballathus Athenodorus Augustus*. In 274 he was carried in Aurelian's triumph, but was spared and granted a pension. A. H. M. J.

VACUNA, a Sabine goddess, Horace, *Epist.* 1. 10. 49. He probably puns on her name, as if she were 'uacationis dea' (so Cruquius' commentator ad loc.), but her real functions were already forgotten. Varro identified her with Victoria (q.v.; 'Acron' ad loc.), others with Bellona, Diana, Minerva, and Venus (qq.v.; ibid. and Porphyrio ad loc.). She had groves at Reate and by the Lacus Velinus (Pliny, *HN* 3. 109).

See E. C. Evans, *Cults of the Sabine Territory* (1939), index s.v. H. J. R.

VAGELLIUS (name doubtful), Neronian poet and friend of Seneca (*QNat.* 6. 2. 8). Morel *FPL* 124. The same name is accepted by Ribbeck and others, but queried by Schanz, for the doubtful 'Vallegius' mentioned by Donatus (auctarium, Suet. *Vit. Ter.*) as a witness to the younger Scipio's share in Terence's plays. J. W. D.

VALENS, FABIUS (*cos. suff.* A.D. 69), born at Anagnia of equestrian family, 'procax moribus neque absurdus ingenio' (Tac. *Hist.* 1. 62). Commander of Legio I in Germania Inferior, he supported Galba, suppressed the governor Fonteius Capito, and incited Vitellius to proclaim himself emperor. An army-commander in the

invasion of Italy and at Bedriacum, and honoured by Vitellius, he was impeded by ill health from reaching northern Italy in time to oppose the troops of Antonius Primus. Learning of the fall of Cremona, he made his way to Gallia Narbonensis, but was captured there and subsequently put to death. R. S.

VALENS, see also VETTIUS (5).

VALENTIA (nowadays *Valencia*), a foundation of the Edetani in Hispania Citerior. Decimus Brutus settled the veterans of Viriathus (138 B.C.) either here or at another Valentia (? *Valença do Minho* in Portugal). Its inhabitants supported Sertorius' cause even after his death. The expression 'uterque ordo' (*CIL* ii. 3475) suggests a second veteran settlement, possibly by Pompey at the close of the Sertorian war. The prosperity of the city is proved by Iberian ceramics, Ibero-Roman coins, numerous inscriptions, and the fact of Byzantine occupation. J. J. Van N.

VALERIANUS, PUBLIUS LICINIUS (emperor A.D. 253–60), Gallus' emissary in Raetia, was during Aemilianus' reign saluted emperor by his troops and after the latter's assassination accepted by the Senate (*see* TREBONIANUS GALLUS *and* AEMILIANUS). He reached Rome in 253 and appointed his son, Gallienus (q.v.), Augustus and joint ruler of the Empire. In 256–7 Valerian left Rome for the East and repelled a Persian invasion. Meanwhile the Goths entered Asia Minor. Valerian attempted to relieve Bithynia, but was recalled by a new Persian attack. Owing to plague in his army he attempted negotiations, but by a perfidious ruse was arrested by King Sapor and carried off to die in captivity (260).

During his reign there was a further persecution of the Christians, and two edicts were issued imposing penalties for recalcitrance upon clergy and laity. Yet Valerian was neither a fool nor a knave, and in a more peaceful age might have governed with unoffending moderation.

Zosimus 1. 29–36; Zonaras 12. 23; Victor, *De Caesaribus* 32. Parker, *Roman World*, 163–71; *CAH* xii, ch. 6, § 5.
H. M. D. P.

VALĔRIUS (1) **POPLICOLA**, PUBLIUS, traditionally one of the first consuls in 509 B.C., is a figure of doubtful historicity. His story rests mainly on the account of Valerius Antias, who claimed descent from him, and was the main source of Plutarch's biography. His alleged victories over Rome's neighbours, his work as a popular lawgiver (e.g. a *Lex Valeria*, establishing the right of *provocatio*), his consequent *cognomen* Poplicola (*populum colere*), his raising the number of senators, and his institution of the quaestorship are all suspect.   P. T.

VALERIUS (2) **POTITUS**, LUCIUS, and M. Horatius Barbatus, the consuls who are said in 449 B.C. to have replaced the Decemvirs, were traditionally patrician benefactors of the plebs who reconciled the Orders. In all likelihood they acted as peacemakers, although their programme of appeasement probably consisted (apart from the restoration of the consulship) in the *de facto* recognition of the measures taken by the plebeians for their government (tribal assemblies) and their defence (the appointment of plebeian magistrates). The laws ascribed to Valerius and Horatius (Livy 3. 55) were: (1) the recognition that *plebiscita* bound the whole community; (2) the restoration of the right of appeal; (3) the sacrosanctity of plebeian magistrates. They must be rejected because *plebiscita* were given force of law only by the *Lex Hortensia* (c. 287 B.C.); the right of appeal had already been secured by the XII Tables; and the recognized sacrosanctity of plebeian magistrates, however welcome, juridically meant nothing except that they were now magistrates of the Roman community. They were attributed to the consuls of 449 because the fall of the Decemvirs seemed a landmark in the plebeian advance, or rather because the annalists liked to connect the basic elements of the Roman constitution with either the beginnings of the Republic (laws attributed to Valerius Poplicola) or the restoration of the consulship.

F. Münzer, *PW* viii. 2328 ff.; G. De Sanctis, *Stor. Rom.* ii. 51 ff.; G. W. Botsford, *The Roman Assemblies* (1909), 274 ff.; H. Stuart Jones, *CAH* vii. 480 ff.; H. H. Scullard, *Hist. Roman World* (1935), 454 f.   P. T.

VALERIUS (3) **CORVUS**, MARCUS. Roman hero of the fourth century B.C., traditionally a simple farmer who lived to be a hundred. He was consul in 348 (when only 22 years old), 346, 343, 335, 300, 299 (*suffectus*), dictator in 342, 301; altogether he occupied the curule chair twenty-one times. When military tribune (349) he engaged a giant Gaul in single combat: a raven (*corvus*), by flapping in the Gaul's eyes, presented Valerius with victory and a cognomen. Valerius is also said to have defeated Volsci (346), Samnites (343), the inhabitants of Cales (335), Aequi (300), Etrusci (299), and to have quelled a mutiny (342) and promulgated a law of appeal (300). Even Livy (cf. 7. 42; 10. 3) hesitated to ascribe all these exploits to him. Some of the exaggerations in surviving accounts probably derive from Valerius Antias. Modern writers are more critical.

Livy, bks. 7–10; Val. Max. 8. 13. 1; 8. 15. 5; App. *Gall.* 10; *BCiv.* 3. 88; Aul. Gell. 9. 11; Zonar. 7. 25; [Aur. Vict.] *De vir. ill.* 29. F. Münzer, *De gente Valeria*, Diss. Berlin 1891.   E. T. S.

VALERIUS (4) **MESSALLA**, MARCUS, as consul in 263 B.C., reduced the district around Aetna and drove back Hieron (q.v. 2), who then deserted the Carthaginian for the Roman cause. For this diplomatic success and for having freed Messana, Valerius received the cognomen Messalla, which his predecessor Claudius (q.v. 5) may rather have deserved. He decorated a wall of the Senate-house with a painting of his success. He was censor in 252.   H. H. S.

VALERIUS (5) **LAEVINUS**, MARCUS, praetor in 227 B.C. and again in 215, commanded a fleet on the Illyrian coast against Philip V in 214, and in 212–211 entered into alliance with the Aetolians and Attalus of Pergamum in the First Macedonian War. Consul in 210, he captured Agrigentum, completing Marcellus' work in Sicily, which he governed for three years; in 208 he defeated a Punic fleet. In 205 he brought the Magna Mater from Pessinus to Rome. He died in 200. The records of a consulship in 220 (*CIL* i². 140) and a command in Greece in 201 (Livy 31. 3) are false.

Livy 23. 30 ff.; 26. 24 ff.; 27. 29; 29. 11. G. De Sanctis, *Stor. Rom.* iii. 2, pp. 309, 411.   A. H. McD.

VALERIUS (6) **FLACCUS**, LUCIUS, the friend and colleague of Cato, curule aedile (201 B.C.), praetor in Sicily (199), was consul with Cato in 195, defeating the Boians and Insubrians (195–194). Military tribune at Thermopylae (191), he was triumvir in 190–189, reinforcing Placentia and Cremona and founding Bononia. Censor with Cato (184), he became *princeps senatus* on the death of Scipio Africanus; he died in 180. Capable but not outstanding, he maintained a conservative traditionalism against Hellenism in Rome.

Livy 33. 42–3; 34. 22, 42, and 46; 36. 17 ff.; 39. 40 ff.; Polyb. 20. 9 ff.; Plutarch, *Cato maior*. G. De Sanctis, *Stor. Rom.* iv. 1, p. 580.
A. H. McD.

VALERIUS (7) **FLACCUS**, LUCIUS, consul (100 B.C.) with Marius whom he helped to repress Saturninus and Glaucia, was censor (97), and *princeps senatus*. As *interrex* (82) he carried the law investing Sulla with the dictatorship and became his *magister equitum*.

VALERIUS (8) **FLACCUS**, LUCIUS, curule aedile in 98 B.C., praetor (between 96 and 89), was elected *consul suffectus* to replace Marius in 86 to hold office with Cinna. He carried a *Lex de aere alieno* which remitted three-quarters of all outstanding loans. Sent by the democrats to supersede Sulla in his Eastern command against Mithridates, Flaccus crossed to Greece; his troops began to desert to Sulla; he quarrelled with his legate Fimbria, by whom he was ultimately murdered while marching through Bithynia (85).   M. H.

VALERIUS (9) **AEDITUUS** (*fl. c.* 100 B.C.), like Lutatius Catulus and Porcius Licinus, wrote epigrams, often erotic, after Greek models. Gellius (19. 9. 10) praises the verses of all three as unequalled for neatness and charm.

See J. Wight Duff, *Lit. Hist. Rome to Golden Age*, 246–7; Morel, *FPL*.   J. W. D.

VALERIUS (10) **ANTIAS**, the Sullan annalist, wrote a history of Rome in at least seventy-five books, from the origins to his own times. Bk. 2 included Numa, bk. 22 Mancinus at Numantia, bk. 45 (probably) the year 110 B.C.; the latest date preserved is 91 B.C., the latest book 75. This shows an increase in scale for contemporary events, but even for early times he wrote more fully than the records justified (Livy 3. 5. 12). He represents the Hellenistic, particularly the Isocratean, fashion in historiography, elaborating battle-scenes, inventing casualty figures, and rhetorically composing reports of debates and speeches. To information often false he added confusion and misrepresentation, under the political and family influences of his time, e.g. on early Valerian tradition. Livy criticizes his numbers (26. 49. 3; 33. 10. 8; 36. 38. 6), but followed him throughout his work. His style was vigorous and rhetorical, if without grace, bringing annalistic history to its highest literary point before Livy.

H. Peter, *HRRel.* i² (1914), pp. ccv; 238; K. W. Nitzsch, *Die röm. Annalistik* (1873), 349; F. Münzer, *De gente Valeria* (1891); W. Soltau, *Livius' Geschichtswerk* (1897); M. Gelzer, *Hermes* 1935, 269.   A. H. McD.

VALERIUS (11) **SORANUS** (i.e. of Sora), QUINTUS, *trib. pleb.* 82 B.C., was a linguistic and antiquarian scholar often quoted by Varro, *Ling.*: cf. Gell. 2. 10. 3.; Cic. *De Or.* 3. 43; *Brut.* 169. Two hexameters of his on the fatherhood of Jupiter are quoted from Varro by St. Augustine, *De civ. D.* 7. 9.

See Morel, *FPL.* Schmekel (*Die Philosophie der mittleren Stoa* (1892), 446), placed him in the Scipionic Circle, and Büttner (*Porcius Licinus u. der litter. Kreis des Lutatius Catulus*, 123) sought to identify him with Valerius (q.v. 9) Aedituus.   J. W. D.

VALERIUS (12) **CATO**, PUBLIUS (b. *c.* 100 B.C.), poet, teacher, and critic, born in Cisalpine Gaul, became head of the neoteric school of poets to which Catullus belonged. He wrote an *Indignatio*, protesting his free birth and lamenting early privations, when as an orphan he lost his heritage in Sullan times. An inspiring teacher, he was called the Latin Siren (Suet. *Gram.* 11). Besides editing Lucilius, he wrote grammatical works. Two poems attributed to him were especially praised by Suetonius (loc. cit.). The *Lydia*, celebrating a mistress, was learnedly erotic in the Alexandrian manner. The *Diana* (or *Dictynna*), now lost, followed Callimachus in treating the story of the Cretan nymph Britomartis, who, pursued by Minos, flung herself into the sea but was caught in a fisherman's net. Some scholars believe the *Diana* to form the second half of the *Dirae*, preserved in the *Appendix Vergiliana* (q.v.).   L. R. P.

VALERIUS (13) **FLACCUS**, LUCIUS, son of (8) above, as praetor (63 B.C.) helped Cicero against Catiline. He was governor of Asia (62/1). Accused of extortion, he was defended in 59 by Cicero (cf. the extant oration *Pro Flacco*) and acquitted. He was a legate of the proconsul L. Calpurnius Piso Caesoninus in Macedonia in 57.

P. Willems, *Le Sénat de la république romaine* (1885), i. 464; J. Humbert, *Les Plaidoyers écrits de Cicéron* (1925).   A. M.

VALERIUS (14) **MESSALLA NIGER**, MARCUS, a 'conservative' for whom Cicero avowed great respect (*Att.* 1. 14. 6), was praetor in 65 B.C., consul for 61, and censor in 55. As consul he favoured strong measures against Clodius (q.v.), who was accused of sacrilege, and a special court of inquiry was established; but his colleague M. Pupius Piso, a friend of Clodius, secured that the jury be chosen in the usual way, and Clodius was able to buy his acquittal (Cic. *Att.* 1. 13, 14, 16).   J. M. C.

VALERIUS (15) **MESSALLA CORVINUS**, MARCUS (64 B.C.–A.D. 8), soldier, orator, statesman, and patron of letters, first distinguished himself at Philippi (42 B.C.) as supporter of Brutus and Cassius. Declining command of the Republican army after that disaster, he transferred his allegiance to Antony; but, disgusted with Antony's conduct, he joined Octavian (how soon, however, is not clear). He fought for Octavian against Sextus Pompeius (36) and in the Illyro-Pannonian War (35–34), subdued the Alpine Salassi (34–33), and as consul with Octavian (31) took part in the battle of Actium. After service in the East, as proconsul in Gaul he conquered the Aquitani, celebrating a triumph in 27. Already member of the College of Augurs, he became the first permanent *curator aquarum* in 11, and it was he who proposed the title of *Pater Patriae* for Augustus (2 B.C.). He reconstructed part of the Via Latina and several public buildings, gained fame as orator and historian, dabbled

in poetry and philosophy, and was the patron of a literary circle—Tibullus, Lygdamus, Sulpicia, and the author of the *Panegyricus Messallae* (q.v., and see PASTORAL POETRY, LATIN, para. 2). Titles of several of his grammatical and stylistic treatises have survived.

Though he served under Octavian, Messalla was, as shown by his resignation of the *praefectura urbis* (26) after only a few days in office, one of that small group of republican gentlemen who had the courage during most perilous times to assert their principles.

Historical fragments, H. Peter, *HRRel.* ii, pp. lxxviii ff. and 65 ff.; grammatical, H. Funaioli, *Gramm. Rom. Frag.* i. 503 ff.; rhetorical, H. Malcovati, *ORF* iii. 188 ff. See also J. Hammer, *Prolegomena to an Edition of the Panegyricus Messallae* (U.S.A. 1925); R. Kuthan, *De duabus Messalae expeditionibus* (1923); R. Syme, *The Roman Revolution* (1939), see Index; J. Carcopino, *Rev. Phil.* 1946, 96–117.   J. H.

VALERIUS (16) **MESSALLA MESSALLINUS**, MARCUS (*cos.* 3 B.C.), son of (15) above, and a person of some distinction and oratorical talent but not to be compared with his parent. Legate of Illyricum in A.D. 6 and present with Tiberius on the campaign against Maroboduus, he was sent back to deal with the rebellious Pannonians and Dalmatians and reached Siscia after fighting a battle; he received *ornamenta triumphalia.* Later Messallinus spoke in the Senate on several occasions during the principate of Tiberius. His election as one of the *quindecimviri* in charge of the Sibylline books is celebrated in the longest poem (2. 5) of Tibullus, who enjoyed the patronage of Messallinus' father.   R. S.

VALERIUS (17) **MAXIMUS**, a Roman historian in Tiberius' reign with strong rhetorical and philosophical bias. A poor man, he was befriended by Sextus Pompeius (*cos.* A.D. 14), and accompanied him to his governorship in Asia about A.D. 27. After his return Valerius composed a handbook of illustrative examples for rhetoricians, *Factorum ac dictorum memorabilium libri IX*. This is dedicated to Tiberius, to whom constant flattery is addressed; and the violent denunciation of Sejanus (9. 11 Ext. 4) suggests that it was published soon after his downfall in 31. The subject-matter of the nine books has no clearly defined plan, but is divided under headings mostly moral or philosophical in character (e.g. Omens, Moderation, Gratitude, Chastity, Cruelty), which are usually illustrated by Roman (*domestica*) and foreign (*externa*) examples. The latter, chiefly Greek, are admittedly less important, and in keeping with the strongly national spirit of the compilation are outnumbered by the *domestica* by two to one. The work is shallow, sententious, and bombastic, full of the boldest metaphor and rhetorical artifices of the Silver Age, especially forced antitheses and far-fetched epigrams, only occasionally relieved by touches of poetic fancy or neat passages of narrative or dialogue. His chief sources seem to have been Livy and Cicero, but there are indications of many others, such as Varro, Coelius Antipater, Pompeius Trogus, and several Greek writers. His use of this material is almost entirely non-critical, and varies greatly in extent and accuracy. Yet the variety and convenience of the compilation ensured some measure of success in antiquity, and considerably more in the Middle Ages. It is referred to by Pliny the Elder, Plutarch, and others. Most significant, however, is the existence of two later epitomes. The first is by Julius Paris (fourth cent.?) and has attached to it a summary on Roman names, *De praenominibus*, ascribed to a certain C. Titius Probus and elsewhere erroneously included in manuscripts as bk. 10 of Valerius' own work. The second, by Januarius Nepotianus (5th c.?), breaks off early in bk. 3.

Editions: A. Torrenius (1726; notes and index); C. Kempf (1854; good *Prolegomena*); Teubner (1888). Translation: W. Speed (1678).   G. C. W.

VALERIUS (18) **ASIATICUS**, a wealthy Roman, born at Vienna (Narbonensis), was consul in A.D. 46. Involved in Gaius' death, he later fell a victim to Messallina for alleged aspiration to the Empire (47). Claudius attacked his memory in a famous speech (Dessau, *ILS* 212).

PIR, V 25; Ph. Fabia, *La Table claudienne de Lyon* (1929), 104.
A. M.

VALERIUS (19) **FLACCUS** (two subscriptions in the Vatican manuscript of his *Argonautica* give his name fully as C. Valerius Flaccus Balbus Setinus (bk. 2), or as C. V. F. Setinus Balbus (bk. 5), but the last two names are uncertain). Nothing is known of his life save that he was a *quindecimvir sacris faciundis* (1. 5, 8. 239–41), that he probably began his poem in A.D. 80 (see references to Titus and his *Templum Divi Vespasiani*, 1. 13–16, and to the eruption of Vesuvius, 3. 208–9, 4. 507–9), and that premature death overtook him before he completed his eighth book in 92 or 93; for the only certain reference to him in Roman literature is Quintilian's brief expression of regret at his demise (*Inst.* 10. 1. 90).

His only known work is the *Argonautica*, which is indebted to but not a close imitation of the similar work of Apollonius Rhodius (q.v.), in so far as Valerius is less concerned with deliberate displays of learning and with passages which tend to lower the heroic standard of the epic. He is more pathetic than Apollonius and invests his characters and theme with a Roman dignity. The poem takes the reader in the company of the Argonauts from Iolcos to Colchis, where Jason secures the Golden Fleece and escapes with Medea, but it breaks off abruptly with the pursuit of the Argo by her brother Absyrtus. Had Valerius lived to complete his poem, he would probably have brought his heroes back via the Danube and either the Adriatic as did Apollonius, or the North Sea in order to pay a compliment to the memory of Vespasian, who had once served in Britain (cf. 1. 7–9).

Valerius is strongly influenced by both Virgil and Ovid, like the other epic writers of the early Empire, but is probably a truer poet than they, in so far as he is less obviously rhetorical than Lucan and a more original genius than Statius. Unlike them, however, he was unknown in the Middle Ages until the Florentine humanist Poggio Bracciolini discovered at St. Gall in 1416 a manuscript (now lost) of the first three books and part of the fourth. Vat. Lat. 3277 (*saec.* ix *in.*), possibly from Fulda, is the principal surviving authority for the text. See also EPIC POETRY, LATIN, para 3.

BIBLIOGRAPHY

LIFE AND WORK: G. Thilo, *Proleg.* i; J. Peters, *De C. Valerii Flacci Vita et Carmine* (1890); Giarratano, *Proleg.* ii; R. Syme, *CQ* 1929, 129; K. Scott, *Riv. Fil.* 1934, 474; R. J. Getty, *CPhil.* 1936, 53.

TEXTS: G. Thilo (1863; best critical apparatus); J. B. Bury, Postgate's *Corp. Poet. Lat.* (1905); C. Giarratano (1904; highly conservative); O. Kramer (Teubner, 1913).

COMMENTARIES: P. Burman (1724; useful variorum edition); P. Langen (1897). Index, W. H. Schulte (U.S.A. 1935).

TRANSLATION: J. H. Mozley (Loeb, 1934).

STUDIES. (a) General: K. Schenkl, *Stud. z. d. Argonautica* (1871); W. C. Summers, *A Study of the Argonautica* (1894); F. Mehmel, *Valerius Flaccus* (1934). (b) Textual: A. C. Clark, *CR* 1899, 119; P. Krenkel, *De Codicis Valeriani Carrionis Auctoritate* (1909); B. L. Ullman, *CPhil.* 1931, 21; R. J. Getty, *The Lost St. Gall MS. of Valerius Flaccus* (1934). R. J. G.

VALERIUS (20) **LICINIANUS**, LUCIUS, from Bilbilis (Mart. 1. 61. 11; 4. 55. 1), an advocate whom Martial considered a Spanish Cicero, was exiled by Domitian, but permitted by Nerva to settle in Sicily, where he professed oratory (Plin. *Ep.* 4. 11).

VALERIUS, see also BABRIUS, DIOCLETIAN, HARPOCRATION, JULIUS, LICINIUS, MAXIMIAN, MAXIMINUS (2), MAXIMUS, PROBUS, SEVERUS (4).

VALETUDINARIUM, see MEDICINE, § III.

VALGIUS RUFUS (*cos. suff.* 12 B.C.), one of the poetic circle patronized by Maecenas (Hor. *Sat.* 1. 10. 82), was consoled by Horace (*Carm.* 2. 9) on the death of a favourite slave, Mystes, whom he had himself commemorated in elegiac laments. He composed epigrams, translated Apollodorus' rhetorical precepts (Quint. *Inst.* 3. 1. 18), wrote on grammatical questions and on herbs.

See *PIR*; Teuffel; Schanz; Baehrens, *FPR*. J. W. D.

VALLIUS SYRIACUS, a distinguished rhetorician in the elder Seneca's *Controversiae* (1. 1. 11 and 21; 2. 1. 34 ff.; 7. 6. 11; 9. 4. 18). He proclaimed himself a pupil of Theodorus (q.v. 3), and therefore not a slavish employer of *narratio* (q.v.) in his speeches.

VANDALS, a Germanic race, who moved from their original home on the Baltic to the Hungarian plain about A.D. 170. There they developed mailed cavalry, armed with lance and bow, and raided Raetia and Italy. In A.D. 406 they crossed the Rhine at Moguntiacum (*Mainz*) in conjunction with the Germanic Suebi and the non-Germanic Alans, and three years later invaded Spain. They were acknowledged as *foederati*, and the Asding Vandals shared Galicia with the Suebi, while the Siling Vandals received Baetica and the Alans Lusitania. Visigoth attacks annihilated the Silings and cut up the Alans. Remnants of the latter joined the Asdings, and Gunderic became king of the Vandals and Alans.

Alone among the Germanic invaders the Vandals built a fleet, with which they overran the Balearic Islands. In A.D. 429 Gaiseric led his mixed nation into Mauretania (q.v.) Tingitana. The Vandals, who had become Arians, received the support of rebellious Moors, and Donatist and Circumcellion victims of Catholic repression. After some opposition Gaiseric seized Carthage (439), where he ruled as a practically independent king, controlling Italy's corn-supply. Making Carthage once more a great naval power, he attacked Sicily, Sardinia, and Corsica, and in 455 sent his fleet to the Tiber. The Vandal sack of Rome, though comparatively mild, avenged the fate of their Phoenician predecessors six centuries earlier. Gaiseric was the most dreaded power in the Mediterranean till his death (477).

The Vandals remained a tyrannical and persecuting minority of Arian landowners among their Catholic subjects. The Romano-Berber population served their illiterate masters with menial and manual labour. The Vandal leaders paid no taxes on their large estates; the old financial system disappeared; and, though corn, marbles, and minerals were still exported, African commerce dwindled. Justinian found an excuse to intervene, and Belisarius' expeditionary force crushed the Vandal armies (533). Subsequent revolts ended in the transportation of the fighting-men to different parts of the Empire, and the extirpation of the Vandal race from Africa.

Letters of St. Augustine; Procopius, *De Bello Vandalico*. E. Gautier, *Genséric, roi des Vandales* (1932); L. Schmidt, *Geschichte der Vandalen* (1901). W. N. W.

VARGUNTEIUS, QUINTUS (2nd c. B.C.), junior to Lampadio (q.v.) among early lecturers on old Latin poets, expounded Ennius in public lectures, attracting large audiences (Suet. *Gram.* 2).

VARIUS RUFUS, a distinguished elegiac, epic, and tragic Augustan poet, friend of Virgil (*Catal.* 7; *Ecl.* 9. 35), Maecenas, and Horace (*Sat.* 1. 5. 40; 6. 55), who praises his epic highly (*Carm.* 1. 6; *Sat.* 1. 10. 43). His recorded epics are the *De morte* (based perhaps on Epicurean principles with special reference to Julius Caesar's death) and a *Panegyric* on Augustus. His tragedy *Thyestes*, performed at the games after Actium (29 B.C.), won deep admiration and comparison with the Greek masterpieces (Quint. 3. 8. 45, 10. 1. 98; Tac. *Dial.* 12). Assisted by Plotius Tucca (q.v.), he edited the *Aeneid* by Augustus' orders after Virgil's death.

Morel, *FPL*.　　　　　　　　　　　　　　　　G. C. W.

VARRO (1), GAIUS TERENTIUS (*cos.* 216 B.C.), was represented in the hostile aristocratic tradition as of humble origin (a butcher's son) and as a radical demagogue opposed to the Senate (cf. C. Flaminius), whereas his career shows that he enjoyed the Senate's confidence, while his father may have been a rich merchant. He was praetor in 218 B.C. As consul he commanded at Cannae (q.v.); he was probably no more responsible than his colleague, L. Aemilius Paullus, for the subsequent disaster, after which he was thanked by the Senate for not despairing of the State. He served as proconsul in Picenum (215–213), held Etruria against Hannibal's advance (208–207), and went as an ambassador to Africa in 200.　　　　　　　　　　　　　　　　　　H. H. S.

VARRO (2), MARCUS TERENTIUS (116–27 B.C.), was probably born at Reate in the country of the Sabines (Symmachus, *Ep.* 1. 2. 21; according to Augustine, *De civ. D.* 4. 1, 'Romae natus et educatus'). He was a pupil of the first Roman philologist L. Aelius Stilo, who made himself known by his researches into the genuineness of the comedies bearing Plautus' name. At Athens his teacher of philosophy was the Academic Antiochus of Ascalon. In public life Varro rose to be a praetor. He fought as a partisan of Pompey in Spain in 49, but without success. Caesar restored him to favour and appointed him keeper of the future public library in 47. After Caesar's death he was outlawed by Antony in 43, but escaped death. His libraries, however, were plundered. When the Civil War was over he was allowed to devote himself entirely to peaceful study. According to Gellius (3. 10. 17) he had already edited 490 books at the beginning of his 78th year. We know the titles of fifty-five works, a catalogue of Varro's writings (but not of all) having been preserved in a fragment of Hieronymus (Ritschl, *Opusc.* iii. 522 ff.). We possess only two of his works substantially: *De lingua Latina* (in part) and *Rerum rusticarum libri iii.*

WORKS

1. *De lingua Latina libri XXV*, of which bks. 5–10 are partly extant (only 5 and 6 entirely). Book 1 contained an introduction, probably a general view of the subject, books 2–7 explained how words had originated and were applied to things and ideas, 8–13 treated declension and conjugation, 14–25 dealt with syntax. Books 2–4 were dedicated by Varro to his quaestor Septumius, but starting from bk. 5 the remaining books are dedicated to Cicero. The work was published before Cicero's death, probably in 43 B.C. The derivations are often fanciful, but the work has preserved many quotations, especially from the old Latin poets.

2. *Rerum rusticarum libri III* (37 B.C.); bk. 1 treats of agriculture in general; 2 of cattle- and sheep-breeding; 3 of the smaller live stock kept on a farm, such as birds, bees, fishes, etc. Varro's aim was to rouse the diminished interest in country-life. The author has a tiresome tendency to group subject-matter under various headings and divide these again into subdivisions, but his prefaces are enjoyable and his book is not without wit.

Of Varro's lost works we may mention:

1. *Saturarum Menippearum libri CL*, probably between 81 and 67 B.C., humorous essays seasoned with verses, in which Varro followed, but in his own original way, the dialogues of the Cynic philosopher Menippus of Gadara (first half of 3rd c. B.C.). Varro proves himself here an enemy to the luxury and other foibles of his

time. Ninety titles and 600 fragments have come down to us.

2. *Antiquitatum rerum humanarum et divinarum libri XLI* (47 B.C.). The first twenty-five books dealt with res humanae, and the last sixteen books with res divinae (Augustine, *De civ. D.* 6. 3). To arrange his subject-matter he put the questions: Who? Where? When? What? After an introductory book, 2–25 were divided into four parts: 2–7 treated of persons (e.g. inhabitants of Italy), 8–13 of places (e.g. Rome, Italy), 14–19 of the times, 20–25 of the actions of men.

The sixteen books that contained the res divinae began with an introductory book; the rest were divided into five parts: 27–9, priests; 30–2, temples, etc.; 33–5, festal days, games, etc.; 36–8, *sacra*; 39–41 the gods.

3. *Logistoricon libri LXXVI* (44 B.C.–?), a collection of dialogues on various subjects—education of children, madness, chastity, etc. Every book took its name from a celebrated character, e.g. *Marius de fortuna*, *Tubero de origine humana*.

4. *Hebdomades vel de imaginibus* (libri xv; 39 B.C.). This work treated of famous Romans and Greeks, and contained 700 portraits illustrating the text (Plin. *HN* 35. 11). It was called *Hebdomades* (Gellius, 3. 10. 1), because the number 7 played an important part throughout.

5. *Disciplinarum libri IX*, an encyclopaedia of the *artes liberales*, i.e. of the branches of learning essential for a free-born man (cf. ENCYCLOPAEDIC LEARNING).

Varro's writings cover nearly every domain of science—history (*De vita populi Romani*, 'a social history of the Roman people'), geography, rhetoric, jurisprudence (*De iure civili lib. XV*), philosophy, music, medicine, architecture, literary history (*De scaenicis originibus lib. III*; *De comoediis Plautinis*). He was the greatest scholar among the Romans; as to his method, he was a pupil of the Greeks, but he collected his matter largely himself. His works were a mine of information for pagan and Christian authors, and even for medieval compilers. *See also* GRAMMAR; SCHOLARSHIP, LATIN.

BIBLIOGRAPHY

LIFE AND WORKS. G. Boissier, *La Vie et les ouvrages de M. T. Varron* (1861); H. Dahlmann, *PW*, Suppl. vi (1935), 1172.

TEXTS: Ling. Lat.: Weidmann (Spengel), Teubner (Schoell and Goetz); Rer. rust.: Teubner (Goetz); Fragm. Gramm. and Lit.: G. Funaioli, *Gramm. Rom. fragm.* i. 183 (Teubner); Sat. Men.: Weidmann (Bücheler-Heraeus, Petron. *Sat.* 1922, 181); Antiq.: R. Merkel, *Ovidi Fasti* (1841), p. cvi; P. Mirsch, *Leipz. Stud.* v. 1 (1882); Logist., Imag.: Ch. Chappuis, *Fragm. des ouvr. de Varron* (1868); Disc.: F. Ritschl, *Opusc.* iii. 372; Hist. fr.: H. Peter, *HRRel.* ii (1906), p. 9.

COMMENTARIES: Rer. Rust.: J. G. Schneider, *Script. rei rust.* i (1794); H. Keil, *Comment. in Varronis rer. rust. libros tres* (critical, 1891).

TRANSLATIONS: Ling. Lat.: R. G. Kent (with text, Loeb); Rer Rust. 1: L. Storr-Best (1912); W. D. Hooper and H. B. Ash (w. text, Loeb).

STYLE AND DICTION: G. Heidrich, *Der Stil des Varro* (1892); R. Krumbiegel, *De Varroniano scribendi genere quaestiones* (1892); E. Norden, *Kunstprosa* i (1909), 194.

SPECIAL STUDIES: Ling. Lat.: H. Dahlmann, *V. und die hellenistische Sprachtheorie* (1932); Sat. Men.: L. Riccomagno, *Studio sulle Sat. Men. di Varrone* (1931); J. W. Duff, *Roman Satire* (U.S.A. 1936); F. della Corte, *La Poesia di V. ricostituita* (1938); Antiq.: R. Agahd, *Fleck. J. Suppl.* 1898; Logist.: R. Müller, *Klass. Phil. Stud.* xii (1938); De gente Pop. Rom.: P. Fraccaro, *Studi Varroniani* (1907); De vita Pop. Rom.: B. Riposati (1939).

P. J. E.

VARRO (3) ATACINUS, PUBLIUS TERENTIUS, was born at Atax in Narbonese Gaul in 82 B.C. and died shortly before 35 B.C. Of his life nothing is known but his attachment to a pseudonymous Leucadia, to whom he addressed elegies. Besides these, which Propertius and Ovid seem to respect, he wrote *Argonautica*, imitating or translating Apollonius Rhodius, a geographical poem named *Chorographia*, a poetical calendar entitled *Epimenis* (but both word and authorship are disputed), apparently based on Aratus' *Phaenomena*, a *Bellum*

Sequanicum on Caesar's campaign of 58, and, Horace testifies, some ineffective satire. The ancients thought well of his versions from the Greek, and fragments tend to corroborate them: the *Bellum Sequanicum*, which might interest us most, seems not to have attracted them. *See* DIDACTIC POETRY, LATIN.

Morel, *FPL* 93. E. P. B.

VARRO (4) MURENA, AULUS TERENTIUS, in 25 B.C. ruthlessly subdued the Salassi of the Val d'Aosta. His camp became later Augusta Praetoria (q.v.). While consul with Augustus (23), he was involved in a conspiracy with Fannius Caepio and was executed. His sister married Maecenas. To him is addressed Hor. *Carm.* 3. 19.

M. Fluss, *PW* v A. 706; H. Stuart Jones, *CAH* x. 136; R. Syme, *Roman Revolution* (1939), see Index. A. M.

VARUS (1), PUBLIUS ATTIUS, praetor, then propraetor in Africa, in 49 B.C. after having opposed Caesar in Picenum, crossed to Africa. As the effective leader of the Pompeians he defeated Curio. After Pharsalus he had to resign to Scipio the supreme command. He fell at Munda. A. M.

VARUS (2), PUBLIUS QUINCTILIUS (*cos.* 13 B.C.), of a patrician family that had been of no importance for centuries. He owed his career to the favour of Augustus, being the husband of Claudia Pulchra, the grand-niece of the Princeps, and was able to acquire some political influence (his two sisters made good marriages, cf. the table in *PW* xvii. 870). Varus became proconsul of Africa (? 7–6 B.C.), and then legate of Syria. When Judaea revolted after the death of Herod the Great he marched rapidly southwards and dealt firmly with the insurgents (Josephus, *BJ* 2. 39 ff., etc.). Varus is next heard of as legate of the Rhine army in A.D. 9. When marching back with three legions from the summer-camp near the Weser, he was treacherously attacked in difficult country by Arminius (q.v.) whose professions he had trusted. The Roman army was destroyed in the Saltus Teutoburgiensis and Varus took his own life (Dio 56. 18–22; Velleius 2. 117–20; Florus 2. 30). Varus was made the scapegoat for the signal failure of Augustus' whole German policy. He is alleged to have been grossly extortionate in Syria, torpid and incompetent in his German command—'ut corpore ita animo immobilior, otio magis castrorum quam bellicae adsuetus militiae' (Velleius 2. 117. 2). On the site of his defeat see bibliography, *CAH* x. 943. R. S.

VARUS (3), QUINCTILIUS, son of the general defeated by the Germans in A.D. 9, was as a speaker trained under the pre-Tiberian rhetor Cestius Pius from Smyrna.

VARUS (4), ARRIUS, a Roman knight, served with distinction as *praefectus cohortis* under Corbulo, but later defamed his old commander to Nero. In A.D. 69, when a *primus pilus* in one of the Danubian legions, he lent vigorous help to Antonius Primus on the Flavian side in the invasion of Italy, being rewarded after the final victory with the office of *praefectus praetorio*. Mucianus, however, soon arrived at Rome, put a check upon his ambitions (cf. the treatment of Antonius Primus), and reduced him to the post of *praefectus annonae*. He is not heard of afterwards. R. S.

VARUS (5), P. ALFENUS, *see* ALFENUS.

VASE-PAINTING. NINTH TO EIGHTH CENTURY B.C. *Geometric.* Athenian 'Dipylon' vases have rhythmical bands (often divided into metopes) of complicated pattern and figure-scenes, battles, dances, funerals, etc., in silhouette. Local variants, mostly with fewer figure-scenes, occur elsewhere.

2. SEVENTH CENTURY. *Orientalizing.* From *c.* 725 B.C. patterns become more naturalistic and the decoration less orderly, with larger figures in partial outline; later the black-figure style (silhouette with incised inner markings) comes in. Athenian vases are divided into Early Proto-Attic (reminiscent of geometric), 'black and white', Late Proto-Attic (predominantly black-figure). In Corinth Middle and Late Proto-Corinthian, 700–625 (neat and orderly; some small polychrome vases of superlative merit), is followed by Early Corinthian, 625–600 (black-figure; animal friezes and heroic scenes). Melian vases have large, untidy, heroic scenes. East Greek vases have processions of animals on white ground; figure-scenes are rare.

3. SIXTH CENTURY. *Black-figure.* In Athens two lines can be traced: 1. *Vigorous style.* Massive figures and often violent scenes. Originates in seventh century with Nessus painter. Continued by Sophilus, *c.* 570, the painter of Siana cups, 575–550, Saconides ('the Lydian'), 560–530, Execias (q.v.), Andocides (q.v.) painter, and Leagrus group, *c.* 515. 2. *Delicate style.* Drawing neat and fine, sometimes formal. Begins with Clitias, 560, and painters of Little Master cups, *c.* 550, then Amasis (q.v.) painter and the Affecter; and after 525 Antimenes painter and Menon painter (*see* ANDOCIDES).

4. Corinthian vase-painting continues till about 550, with some excellent pictures, e.g. 'Departure of Amphiaraus'. Chalcis carries on the best Corinthian tradition until 520, but the later Phineus group shows Ionian influence. The finest Laconian vases, e.g. Arcesilas cup, are produced 590–550. The chief East Greek styles are Fikellura, 570–500 (derives from Rhodian; drawing often witty), Clazomenian, 560–530, including Northampton group (formal and decorative), Caeretan, 540–525 (lively scenes of 'Heracles and Busiris', etc.; perhaps made in Italy, but, unlike Pontic and allied groups, shows no Etruscan influence).

5. 530–400. *Red-figure.* Figures reserved against black background, inner markings in black or brown. In Athens starts with Andocides (q.v.) painter and Menon painter. The vigorous style is continued by Euphronius (q.v.), Euthymides (q.v.), Cleophrades painter (*see* EPICTETUS 1), Panaetius painter (*see* EUPHRONIUS), Brygus (q.v.) painter; and the delicate style by Epictetus (q.v. 1), Phintias (formal and elaborate), Berlin painter (rhythmical line and quiet beauty), Pan painter (mannerist), Duris (q.v.). After 480 Niobid painter and Penthesilea painter (*see* EUPHRONIUS) reflect composition of Micon and Polygnotus (q.v.); Chicago painter and painter of Boston phiale are quieter. White-ground vases, particularly *lecythi*, are now common; Achilles painter, 460–440, develops tradition of Berlin painter; Reed painter (430–410) is more passionate. In red-figure Eretria painter (440–420) begins a rich style which Meidias painter elaborates (*see* MEIDIAS); Berlin Dinus painter is realistic and vigorous. Red-figure painting starts in south Italy about 440 and at first is strongly influenced by Athens.

6. FOURTH CENTURY. In Athens the rich style continues in the work of Meidias painter's successors. The vigorous style can be traced through successive groups of Kertch vases. In south Italy local groups, Lucanian, Tarentine (including Gnathia), Apulian, Paestan, etc., develop on their own lines; their subjects are sometimes interesting, the drawing usually unpleasing, and the decorative value marred by excessive use of white and yellow paint. Gnathia ware has interesting echoes of Sicyonian painting. Vase-painting ends in the third century.

Recent works: General: *Corpus Vasorum antiquorum*; *Classification des céramiques antiques*; E. Pfuhl, *Malerei und Zeichnung der Griechen* (1923); *Masterpieces of Greek Drawing and Painting* (1926); E. Buschor, *Greek Vase-painting* (1921); P. Jacobsthal, *Ornamente griechischer Vasen* (1927). Special. Geometric: J. L. Myres, *Who were the Greeks?* (1930), 473. Seventh century, Proto-Attic: J. M. Cook, *BSA* xxxv. 165. Corinthian: H. G. G. Payne, *Necrocorinthia*

(1931); *Protokorinthische Vasenmalerei* (1933). Island: H. G. G. Payne, *JHS* 1926, 203. East Greek: A. Rumpf, *Jahrb.* 1933, 55. Sixth century. Black-figure: J. D. Beazley, *Attic Black-figure* (1930); *BSA* xxxii. 1; *JHS* 1932, 167 (Little Master cups); New York Metrop. Museum v. 93; M. Robertson, *JHS* 1935, 224 (Siana cups); C. E. Haspels, *Attic Black-figured Lekythoi* (1936); S. Papaspiridi-Karusu, *Ath. Mitt.* lxii. 111 (Sophilus); A. Rumpf, *Sakonides* (1937). Chalcidian: Rumpf, *Chalkidische Vasen* (1927); H. R. W. Smith, *Origin of Chalcidian Ware* (1932). Laconian: E. A. Lane, *BSA* xxxiv. 99. Fikellura: R. M. Cook, *BSA* xxxiv. 1. Clazomenian: J. D. Beazley, *BSR* xi. 1. Caeretan: E. Pottier, *Mon. Piot* (1933), 1. Pontic, etc.: T. Dohrn, *Die schwarzfigurigen etruskischen Vasen* (1937). Red-figure: J. D. Beazley, *Attic Red-figured Vases in American Museums* (1918); *Attische Vasenmaler* (1925); *Greek Vases in Poland* (1928); *Der Berlinermaler* (1930); *Der Panmaler* (1931); T. B. L. Webster, *Der Niobidenmaler* (1935); K. Schefold, *Untersuchungen zu den Kertscher Vasen* (1934). White ground: J. D. Beazley, *Attic White Lekythoi* (1938). Italian: A. D. Trendall, *Frühitaliotische Vasen* (1938); *Paestan Pottery* (1936); C. W. L. Scheurleer, *Arch. Anz.* 1936, 285 (Gnathia). T. B. L. W.

VATES, *see* PROPHECIES.

VATIA, *see* SERVILIUS (2) and (3).

VATICAN, originally the district on the west bank of the Tiber extending from the territory of Veii to the reaches below Rome, but in the chorography of Rome restricted to the ridge (*mons* or *montes*) confining the river from Pons Milvius to the Janiculum (Cic. *Att.* 13. 33. 4). A still more restricted topographical use is represented by *Vaticana vallis* (Tac. *Ann.* 14. 14) and *Vaticanum* (Plin. *HN* 8. 37; 16. 237; 18. 20), the unhealthy plain which the valley drained. Here lay the *Naumachia* and the *Circus Gai et Neronis*, the latter the scene of early Christian martyrdoms and close to the site of St. Peter's *basilica*. *Vaticanus* was also attached to a shrine of the Magna Mater, whose altars (*CIL* vi. 497–504) have been found on the site of St. Peter's façade and which seems to have been an important cult-centre, with branches in Gaul and Germany (*CIL* xiii. 1751, 7281).
I. A. R.

VATICINATIO, *see* DIVINATION, para 4.

VATINIUS, PUBLIUS, tribune 59 B.C., sponsored the bills granting Caesar (q.v.) Cisalpine Gaul and Illyricum, and confirming Pompey's Eastern settlement, and figured prominently in the attacks on Bibulus and in the Vettius affair. In 56 Cicero, defending Sestius (q.v.), delivered the invective *In P. Vatinium testem interrogatio*, but in 54, obedient to the triumvirs, successfully defended Vatinius on a bribery charge. After serving with Caesar in Gaul, Vatinius won a victory in the Adriatic in 47, and in December received the consulate, an office he always boasted he would hold. His proconsulate, in Illyricum, was recognized by a *supplicatio* in 45; and despite his surrender to Brutus in 43 he triumphed in 42. The best-hated man of his time, he was made an easy butt by his personal disabilities, weak legs, and scrofulous swellings; but he took raillery well, and in later life was genuinely reconciled with Cicero, to whom in 45 he wrote *Fam.* 5. 10. (Cf. Catullus, 14. 3 and 52–3.)

L. G. Pocock, *A Commentary on Cicero In Vatinium* (1926).
G. E. F. C.

VECTIGAL meant an indirect tax, though it is sometimes loosely used as equivalent to *tributum*. It was applied to revenue derived from public land, mines, salt-works, etc., and in general to rents derived from State property. Apart from such charges the only *vectigalia* of the Republican period were the *portoria* (q.v.) and the *vicesima libertatis*, a tax of 5 per cent. on the value of manumitted slaves. In the Principate the number of the *vectigalia* was increased, and they provided a considerable part of the State revenue. Only *vectigalia* were paid by the inhabitants of Italy, who were exempt from tributum. The most important of the *vectigalia* were the *portoria*. In order to raise revenue for the provision of pensions to old soldiers Augustus founded the *aerarium militare*,

into which was paid the yield of two new taxes, the *centesima rerum venalium*, a tax of 1 per cent. on sales by auction, and the *vicesima hereditatum*. The latter was a charge of 5 per cent. on all sums above 100,000 sesterces bequeathed to persons other than near relatives. The death-duties were paid by citizens only, and their introduction was resented by Italians, who objected to any form of taxation. The extension of the citizenship had the effect of increasing their yield. Another *vectigal* was the *quinta et vicesima venalium mancipiorum*, a 4 per cent. tax on sales of slaves. The collection of *vectigalia* was even in the Principate let out to companies of *publicani* (q.v.). In the second century single *conductores* (q.v.) took their place, and subsequently *vectigalia* were collected by State officials. *See also* EMPHYTEUSIS.
G. H. S.

VEDIOVIS, VEIOVIS, VEDIVS, an ancient deity, worshipped at Rome between the Arx and Capitol and on Tiber island (Platner–Ashby, p. 548 f.) and at Bovillae. His offering was a she-goat, sacrificed *ritu humano* (Gell. 5. 12. 12), whether that means on behalf of the dead (cf. Festus, p. 91. 24 Lindsay) or as a surrogate for a human victim (Preller–Jordan, *Rom. Mythol.*[3] i. 265). This suggests a chthonian god, but his name is puzzling. The ancients, deriving *Iuppiter* from *iuuare*, took Vediouis as 'the non-helper' (Gell. ibid. 8), i.e. harmful, or as 'little Iuppiter', on the analogy of *uegrandis* (Ovid, *Fasti* 3. 445–8, cf. Festus, p. 519. 22 Lindsay, both from Verrius Flaccus); Wissowa, *RK*, p. 237, as a sort of anti-Iuppiter, a god of the dead; C. Koch, *Der römische Juppiter*, p. 68, as meaning an abnormal form of Iuppiter. His festival was on 21 May (calendars) and his statue of Apolline type (Gell. ibid. 11 f.).
H. J. R.

VEDIUS POLLIO, PUBLIUS, a freedman's son, was friend of Augustus, who made him a knight; rich and cruel, he used to feed his lampreys with human flesh. He was active in the civil service in Asia after Actium, and was widely honoured. He died in 15 B.C. bequeathing to Augustus the villa of Pausilypon (q.v.).

PIR, V 213; K. Scott, *AJPhil.* 1939, 459; R. Syme, *Roman Revolution* (1939), 410.
A. M.

VEIENTO, FABRICIUS, impeached A.D. 62 for his satiric 'Codicilli' against senators and priests, was banished by Nero and had his publications burned (therefore much in demand, 'conquisitos lectitatosque', says Tacitus); but under Domitian became active in Rome as a delator and one of Juvenal's satiric council on the Emperor's turbot (Tac. *Ann.* 14. 50; Juv. 3. 185; 4. 113 and 123; 6. 113).
J. W. D.

VEII, the most southern of Etruscan cities, only nine miles north of Rome, was a perpetual menace to it in early times ('assidui et anniuersarii hostes', Florus 1. 12). Dennis aptly calls it the 'Troy of Italy', recalling the legends of the siege which ended Veii's wars with Rome in 396 B.C. Till then the Romans had not mastered the west bank of the Tiber. The captured land was soon formed into four new rustic tribes. Veii was about seven miles in circumference. Livy (1. 15; 5. 2) testifies to its early strength, Florus and Plutarch (*Camillus*) to its wealth, but it had become desolate by the time of Augustus (Propertius 10. 27), when it was made a *municipium Augustum*. Probably the materials were used in building Rome. Veii was especially famous for its statuary. Pliny (*HN* 35. 157) has preserved the name of Vulca, commissioned to furnish statues for Jupiter's temple on the Roman Capitol. From Vulca's school came the terracotta statue of Apollo found in 1916, now in the Museo di Villa Giulia at Rome.
D. R.-MacI.

VEIOVIS, *see* VEDIOVIS.

VEIOVIS AEDES, *see* CAPITOL.

VELABRUM was the low ground between the Capitol and Palatine in Rome, originally a swamp open to Tiber floods. The Cloaca Maxima (q.v.) passed riverwards through it, and by draining made of it one of the busiest centres in the city (Macrob. 1. 10. 15), contained between the Vicus Tuscus and Vicus Iugarius and carrying all traffic between the Forum and the river. Here lay Acca Larentia's shrine.   I. A. R.

VELIA, now a narrow ridge or spur connecting the Palatine and Oppian hills of Rome at the head of the Via Sacra (q.v.). The summit was probably modified by levelling for the vestibule of Nero's *Domus Aurea* in A.D. 64, where later stood the temple of Venus and Rome, dedicated in A.D. 135. The saddle was crowned by the Arch of Titus (*CIL* vi. 945).   I. A. R.

VELITES. In the early Republican army the light-armed troops were recruited from citizens unable to provide themselves with hoplite armour and were called *rorarii*. By the Second Punic War their title had been changed to *velites*. The number in each legion was the same as that of *hastati* or *principes*. In battle they were employed probably as *iaculatores* (γροσφομάχοι) in conjunction with the cavalry to open the attack and were regularly stationed on the flanks. They were abolished by Marius and their place was taken by foreign contingents (e.g. Balearic slingers). *See also* ARMS, ROMAN.

Kromayer-Veith, *Heerwesen und Kriegführung der Griechen und Römer* (1928).   H. M. D. P.

VELIUS LONGUS (early 2nd c. A.D.), scholar, who interested himself in the language of Republican authors and wrote a commentary on the *Aeneid*. Only his *De orthographia* (ed. Keil, *Gramm. Lat.* vii. 46–81) is extant.

Cf. Teuffel, § 352. 3 a; Schanz-Hosius, § 596.

VELLEIUS PATERCULUS, GAIUS (*c.* 19 B.C.–after A.D. 31), was of Campanian descent. We owe our knowledge of his origin and personal history to the naïve family pride with which he refers to the exploits of his forefathers and his own career. His maternal ancestors included Decius Magius, who remained faithful to Rome when Capua joined Hannibal, and Minatius Magius, who received Roman citizenship for raising a legion which fought for Rome in the Social War. V.'s paternal grandfather was *praefectus fabrum* under Pompeius, and his father served in the cavalry in Germany. He himself served as a tribune in Thrace and Macedonia and accompanied Gaius Caesar to the East in 1 B.C. He served for eight years under Tiberius as prefect of horse and *legatus* in Germany and Pannonia, and, on Tiberius' recommendation was elected quaestor in A.D. 6 and praetor in 15. There is no evidence that he held further office.

The *Historiae Romanae* is a compendium of Roman history addressed to V.'s friend M. Vinicius (who married Julia, daughter of Germanicus) on attaining the consulship, A.D. 30. Bk. 1, of which the opening and the part dealing with the period from Romulus to the battle of Pydna are missing, begins with the history of the Orient and Greece and ends with the fall of Carthage and Corinth (146 B.C.); bk. 2, covering the period 146 B.C. to A.D. 30, becomes more detailed as it approaches the author's own day, doubtless because, as he tells us, he projected a fuller history from the Civil War onwards. He inserted two historical excursuses, on Roman colonization (1. 14–15) and on the Roman provinces (2. 38–9), and three on literary topics, one on early Latin literature (2. 9), and another on the Ciceronian and Augustan period (2. 36), in which he couples Virgil with the minor poet Rabirius, while a third (1. 16–17) points out that the flourishing periods in Greek and Latin literature were confined within very brief limits. He shows some knowledge of Greek literature, mentioning Homer, Hesiod, tragic and comic writers, Isocrates, Plato, Aristotle. He cites Cato, Hortensius, and the *Memoirs* of Augustus among his sources (1. 7. 3; 2. 16. 3 and 124. 3). A considerable controversial literature discusses authors possibly used by him (see Schanz).

Velleius is the typical retired officer who has turned amateur historian. He is enthusiastic rather than critical and has all the pretentiousness of the novice who has fallen under the spell of contemporary rhetoric. Though his work is the earliest extant specimen of post-Augustan prose, his style has all the characteristics of the Silver Age. His attempts at pointed phraseology, though occasionally effective, are often puerile. He indulges in lengthy sentences which are not periods but mere strings of clauses interspersed with parentheses, and he has an irritating fondness for exclamations and interrogations. He admits that he wrote hurriedly, and the stream of his narrative, if it sometimes carries the reader along with it, certainly lacks profundity. His interest is chiefly biographical, and he portrays, often with some skill, the lesser lights as well as the protagonists of history. His admiration for his old chief Tiberius and for the whole imperial house is unbounded; even Tiberius' ministers, such as Sejanus, can do no wrong. His work is a valuable source for the reigns of Augustus and Tiberius and a useful corrective for the diatribes against Tiberius of Tacitus and Suetonius.

BIBLIOGRAPHY
LIFE AND WORKS: Schanz-Hosius, § 422; Teuffel, § 278; J. Wight Duff, *Lit. Hist. Rome, Silver Age*, 83 ff.; W. C. Summers, *Silver Age of Lat. Lit.* 139 ff.; H. Sauppe, *Schweiz. Museum* (1837) i. 133; A. Pernice, *De Vell. fide historica* (1862); J. Stanger, *De Vell. fide* (1863); W. Goeke, *De Vell. Tiberii imagine* (1876); F. A. Schöb, *Vell. und s. literar.-histor. Abschnitte* (1908); F. Münzer, *Zur Komposition des Vell. in Festschrift zur 49. Versammlung deutscher Philologen u. Schulmänner in Basel im Jahre* 1907, 247 ff.; W. Schaefer, *Tiberius und s. Zeit im Lichte der Tradition des Vell.* (1912).
TEXTS: O.C.T. (R. Ellis); Teubner (Haase, Halm).
COMMENTARIES: Gruter (1607); N. Heinsius (1678); Burman (1719); Krause (1800); Ruhnken-Frotscher (1830–9); Lemaire (1822); Orelli (1835); Kritz (1840); Rockwood (Civil War and reigns of Augustus and Tiberius) (1900).
TRANSLATIONS: Newcome (1721); Baker (1814); Watson (Bohn); F. W. Shipley, with text (Loeb, 1924).
STYLE AND DICTION: N. Oestling, *De elocutione Vell.* (1874); C. de Oppen, *De Vell.* (1875); H. Georges, *De elocutione Vell.* (1877); O. Lange, *Zum Sprachgebr. des Vell.* (1878); F. Milkau, *De Vell. genere dicendi* (1888); C. von Morawski, *Philol.* xxxv. 715; E. Norden, *Kunstpr.* 302.   E. S. F.

VELLUM, *see* BOOKS, I. 12, 13.

VENANTIUS HONORIUS CLEMENTIANUS FORTUNATUS was born, probably after A.D. 530, near Treviso in northern Italy, and was educated at Ravenna. He left Italy for Gaul in 565. There he visited the grave of St. Martin at Tours, and there he continued to live till his death about 600. With him the Latin poetry of Gaul ends. The most notable of his many poems is the *De virtutibus S. Martini* in four books, of 2243 hastily composed hexameters.

Best ed. of his verse and prose, F. Leo and B. Krusch in *MGH* (1881–5).   A. S.

VENATIONES. Fights of man against beast or beast against beast were introduced into Rome in the second century B.C. They grew more elaborate, until under the Empire the whole world was ransacked for animals, which were brought by sea to Ostia and kept in cages under the arena. Lions, panthers, bears, bulls, hippopotami, crocodiles were either matched against each other or against human *bestiarii*. Five thousand wild and four thousand tame animals were slaughtered, some of them by women, when the Flavian amphitheatre was opened; eleven thousand when Trajan celebrated his triumph over the Dacians.

Friedländer ii. 62–74.   F. A. W.

VENETI (1), Gallic tribe occupying modern *Morbihan*. Their strongly 'Atlantic' culture was but slightly touched by Celticism in the La Tène period, but they themselves strongly influenced south-west British cultures by their trade, which stimulated their resistance to Caesar. They were defeated by D. Brutus in a naval battle (57 B.C.). Under the Empire their commerce declined, but a prosperous agricultural life is indicated by villa-finds. The region was occupied by emigrant Britons in the fifth century.

Caes. *BGall*. 3. 8–16. C. Jullian, *Hist. de la Gaule* ii. 486–94; vi. 437–49. C. E. S.

VENETI (2) inhabited the fertile areas about the head of the Adriatic. Chief cities: Ateste in prehistoric times, Patavium in historic (*see* ANTENOR). Inscriptions, dating from the fifth to the first century B.C., show that the Veneti spoke an Illyrian language (cf. Hdt. 1. 196). Archaeological evidence reveals that they immigrated into north Italy *c*. 950; here they preceded and later successfully resisted Etruscans and Gauls. They were highly civilized, preferred horse-breeding and commerce to war, and early organized the Baltic amber (q.v.) trade. They particularly worshipped a goddess of healing, Rehtia. Always friendly to Rome, the Veneti aided her against Gauls (390 B.C.) and Hannibal. Later from allies they became subjects, though retaining local autonomy. Presumably they obtained Latin rights in 89, full citizenship in 49 B.C. Their romanization ensued.

Strabo 5. 212; Polyb. 2. 17 f.; Livy 1. 1; 5. 33; 10. 2. R. S. Conway, *CAH* iv. 441; *Prae-Italic Dialects* i (1933), 230; J. Whatmough, *Foundations of Roman Italy* (1937), 171 (with bibliography). For their alleged Paphlagonian origin see Serv. ad *Aen*. 1. 242; Hom. *Il*. 2. 852; Strabo 12. 543. E. T. S.

VENILIA, a goddess of forgotten nature and functions. It is implied by Varro (*Ling*. 5. 72) that she is associated with Neptunus (q.v., cf. August. *De civ. D*. 7. 22). Some insignificant stories, patently late inventions, are told of her by poets.

VENNONIUS, an early Roman author, now lost, whose history Cicero greatly regrets not to have at hand (*Att*. 12. 3. 1; cf. *Leg*. 1. 6). He is cited by Dionysius of Halicarnassus, 4. 15.

Peter, *HRRel*. i. 142.

VENTIDIUS, PUBLIUS (*cos. suff*. 43 B.C.), the proverbial upstart of the Roman revolutionary wars; probably of quite reputable municipal origin. Captured in infancy at Asculum and led in the triumph of Pompeius Strabo (89 B.C.), he made his livelihood with difficulty. Abusively designated as a *mulio*, he was probably an army-contractor (cf. Gellius 15. 4, the best account of his early life). Like other representatives of the defeated and impoverished Italians, he became an adherent of Caesar, through whose patronage he entered the Senate. Praetor in 43, Ventidius, who had been raising three legions in his native Picenum, reinforced Antony, after his defeat at Mutina. As a reward, he became consul later in the year. In 41–40 B.C. he intervened indecisively in the *Bellum Perusinum*. After the Pact of Brundisium he was sent to drive the Parthians out of Asia and Syria, in which task he won brilliant victories at the Cilician Gates and at Mt. Amanus (39), and at Gindarus (38). Superseded by Antony (there were allegations of taking bribes from the king of Commagene), he returned to Rome to celebrate his Parthian triumph (38), and died soon after, being honoured with a public funeral. His Parthian triumph was long remembered (cf. Tac. *Germ*. 37. 4: 'infra Ventidium deiectus Oriens'). No official or contemporary evidence gives P. Ventidius the *cognomen* 'Bassus'; nor can he quite be proved identical with Sabinus, the *mulio* of Virgil, *Catal*. 10.

R. Syme, *Roman Revolution* (1939), see Index. R. S.

VENUS, an Italian goddess, not originally Roman (Varro, *Ling*. 6. 33: 'cuius nomen ego antiquis litteris . . . nusquam inueni'). She is so obscure that the only clues to her functions are her name, a few passing remarks of antiquaries, and her identification. The name should by all analogies be neuter and apparently is feminine merely because it denotes a female; as a common noun it means 'charm, beauty', and so may be compared to Charis (q.v.). Varro (op. cit. 6. 20) says that on the Vinalia Rustica (a day mistakenly supposed to be her festival) gardeners keep holiday. Cf. *Rust*. 1. 1. 6, Venus has *procuratio hortorum*; Festus, pp. 322. 19; 366. 35, Lindsay; Pliny, *HN* 19. 50. Add Naevius, *fr. com*. 122 Ribbeck, who speaks of eating 'Venus that has felt Vulcan's power', i.e. boiled vegetables. We may therefore suppose that she was the *numen* whose power made herb-gardens look 'charmingly' prosperous and fertile. There is not the smallest evidence that she had anything to do with animal fertility, including that of mankind. However, perhaps through the association of Aphrodite (q.v.) with Charis, or the Charites, she somehow became identified with her at an unknown date. It would seem that the cult of Aphrodite of Eryx (Venus Erucina) was the first point of contact (temple in 217 B.C., see Platner–Ashby, p. 551). To classical Rome Venus was Aphrodite; so much so that the Greek metonymies (Aphrodite = love-making, highest throw at dice, luck, etc.) were taken over by her. As Venus Genetrix (= mother of the *gens Iulia*) she was prominent in Imperial cult.

Wissowa, *RK* 288 ff.; Keune in Roscher's *Lexikon*, s.v. H. J. R.

VENUSIA, a town, probably of Peucetian origin, in Apulia near the Lucanian border, famed as Horace's birthplace (*Sat*. 2. 1. 34); nowadays *Venosa*. When Rome took Venusia it was a populous Oscan-speaking city, 292 B.C.; it received a Latin colony one year later (Dion. Hal. 17–18. 5 incredibly numbers the colonists at 20,000). Venusia immediately became a military stronghold and important station on the Via Appia (Strabo 5. 250). Resisting Hannibal, it harboured the fugitives from Cannae, thereby repeating the rôle it had probably played in 280 after Heraclea (Polyb. 3. 116 f.; Zonar. 8. 3). In 200 Rome reinforced Venusia (Livy 31. 49). Roman arrogance presumably provoked its defection in the Social War (Malcovati, *Fragm. Orat. Rom*. ii. 140; App. *BCiv*. 1. 39). In 43 the Triumvirs settled veterans here and Venusia remained a *colonia* in Imperial times (App. *BCiv*. 4. 3).

N. Jacobone, *Venusia* (1909). E. T. S.

VER SACRUM, literally, consecrated (produce of the) spring. In times of distress, or merely when the population was superabundant, Italian communities and others, including Greek, also (Dionysius, Strabo) used to consecrate to a god, often Jupiter, all that should be born in the spring. The beasts were apparently sacrificed; but the human beings (*sacrani*), when twenty years old (Festus, p. 150. 21), were veiled and sent out of the country. They might go where they would and found a new settlement.

Festus, pp. 150, 424, 519 Lindsay; Dion. Hal. *Antiquit*. 1. 16; Strabo 5. 4. 12, p. 250. Cf. Livy 22. 10. H. J. R.

VERBENA, VERBENARIUS, *see* FETIALES.

VERBORUM A GRAECIS TRACTORUM LIBRI, *see* CLOATIUS.

VERCINGETORIX, son of Celtillus, formerly king of the Arverni, raised the revolt against Caesar in 52 B.C., and was acclaimed king of the tribe and general of the confederates. Defeated by Caesar's cavalry at Noviodunum Biturigum, he adopted 'Fabian' tactics, hampering Caesar's supply by systematic destruction. With this was combined the strategy of tempting Caesar to attack or ingloriously decline the attack on impregnable ground. The policy succeeded admirably near Avaricum, where Caesar did not attack, and at Gergovia, where he did. Vercingetorix was led to risk another attack on Caesar in the field, which was badly defeated, so that he retreated to another prepared fortress, Alesia (q.v.). Caesar had an unexpected weapon, the circumvallation, with which he beat off not only Vercingetorix but the Gallic army summoned from outside to break it. Vercingetorix surrendered and was put to death after Caesar's triumph (46).

Caes. *BGall.* bk. 7. C. Jullian, *Vercingetorix* (1921). C. E. S.

VERGILIOMASTIX, 'the scourge of Virgil', is a bombastic name given perhaps to any of the rampant critics of Virgil. See Servius ad *Ecl.* 2. 23; *Aen.* 5. 521; Ribbeck, *Proleg. ad Verg.*, ch. 8 (1866); Donatus, 16. 61–2 (E. Diehl, *Die Vitae Vergilianae u. ihre antike Quellen*, 1911). R. M.

VERGINIA was traditionally slain by her own father to save her from the cupidity of the decemvir Appius Claudius. This murder is said to have precipitated a revolution leading to the overthrow of the decemvirs (449 B.C.). The poetical details of this legend show that the story, although probably based on that of Lucretia, was not invented by jurists as a precedent for the protection of individual liberty, or by annalists desirous of explaining the fall of the decemvirs. The late connexion of the legend with the story of Appius Claudius' lust and tyranny is proved by the fact that the so-called plebeian heroes Verginius and Verginia in fact belonged to a family that was indisputably patrician.

C. Appleton, *Rev. hist. droit franç.* (1924). P. T.

VERGINIUS FLAVUS, a famous Neronian teacher who had Persius for a pupil. His renown brought exile on him (Tac. *Ann.* 15. 71). Quintilian held his authority in great respect, mentioning him in several passages.

Teuffel, § 297. 9.

VERGINIUS, *see also* RUFUS (6).

VERNA, *see* SLAVES, para 8.

VERONA, a town on the river Athesis in Cisalpine Gaul, astride the routes to the Brenner Pass in fertile wine-producing country (Verg. *G.* 2. 94). Although probably founded by Raeti, it is first mentioned in history as a town of the Cenomani (Pliny, *HN* 3. 130; Livy 5. 35). Prior to Imperial times little is known of Verona except that it was Catullus' birthplace. A large, flourishing city, Verona had the title of *colonia* in A.D. 69 (Strabo 5. 212; Tac. *Hist.* 3. 8). Numerous Roman remains (including magnificent first-century amphitheatre, third-century walls, etc.) and the fact that Constantine (312), Theodoric (499), and the Lombards (568) thought it worth while to occupy it, demonstrate its importance.

A. M. Allen, *History of Verona* (1910); P. Marconi, *Verona Romana* (1938). For its Raetic origin see J. Whatmough, *Harv. Stud.* xlviii (1937), 181. E. T. S.

VERRES, GAIUS, was a notorious governor of Sicily, chiefly known through the speeches of Cicero. His public career began in 84 B.C., when he was quaestor to the Marian consul Cn. Papirius Carbo. He deserted Carbo in order to attach himself to Sulla, who gave him some land at Beneventum. In 80 he went to the East as *legatus* and later *legatus pro quaestore* of Dolabella, the governor of Cilicia. Verres and his chief co-operated in plundering the provincials, but when Dolabella was prosecuted on his return in 78 Verres secured his own safety by giving evidence against him. In 74 he obtained the praetorship by bribery, and made use of his office to enrich himself. In his governorship of Sicily (73–70) he

showed, according to Cicero, a complete disregard of the rights both of the provincials and of Roman citizens. On his return he was prosecuted for *res repetundae* before a court consisting of senators. Though Verres secured the support of Q. Hortensius, Cicero produced such strong evidence that he abandoned his defence and went into exile at Massilia. Cicero's 'Actio Secunda' was therefore never delivered. Verres seems to have spent the rest of his life at Massilia. In 43 he was proscribed by Antony, who is said to have coveted the works of art which he had stolen from the provincials. G. H. S.

VERRIUS FLACCUS, *see* FLACCUS.

VERTUMNUS, an Etruscan god (Varro, *Ling.* 5. 46; Prop. 4. 2. 4, who says he came from Volsinii). A statue of him stood in the Vicus Tuscus, and Propertius (ibid. 13 ff.) indicates that the tradespeople there made frequent offerings to him. Nothing is known of his functions; his name may be connected with the Etruscan family *ultimni*, latinized Veldumnius. The Romans etymologized it from *uertere*, e.g. Prop. ibid. 21 ff.

See Wissowa in Roscher, s.v. H. J. R.

VERULAMIUM, town in Britain, near modern St. Albans (Herts.). According to Tacitus (*Ann.* 14. 33), it was sacked by Boudicca in A.D. 61. He speaks of 'municipium V.' which has been almost universally, though rashly, interpreted as a technical term of status; Verulamium was, however, certainly a cantonal capital (Catuvellauni). A shrine of the martyr St. Alban (date uncertain), close by, was visited by St. Germanus in 429 (*Script. rer. Meroving.* vii. 262).

Excavations carried out since 1930 have added much knowledge. It appears that a Belgic city, defended by forest and on its open side by slight earthworks, was built *c.* 15 B.C. by Tasciovanus on a plateau above the valley of the Ver (not therefore Cassivellaunus' *oppidum*). After the Roman conquest the site was moved to the river valley, and after Boudicca's sack (61) an area of *c.* 150 acres was enclosed by an earth-bank. This was succeeded *c.* 130 by a new walled town *c.* 200 acres in area, on a slightly different site. Portions of the Forum, two triumphal arches, a theatre, a gymnasium (?), temples, houses, and shops have been uncovered, all built *c.* 130–70. In the third century the town decayed (possibly London diverted its trade) and by 300 'bore some resemblance to a bombarded city' (*Verulamium*, 28). A thorough reconstruction *c.* 300 restored prosperity for a time, but the population declined in numbers and in standard of life, until after the English conquest the site was waste.

R. E. M. and T. V. Wheeler, *Verulamium* (1936); summary of earlier data, *Victoria County History, Herts.* i. 125–39. See also M. Kenyon, *Archaeologia* lxxxiv. 213–61 f. (theatre); *Antiquaries Journal* xvii. 28–55; *Transactions of the St. Alban's and Hertfordshire Architect. and Archaeological Society* iv. 243–75; v. 25–30, 152, 214–21. C. E. S.

VERUS, LUCIUS (L. Ceionius Commodus) (A.D. 130–169), son of L. Aelius (q.v. 4), was born at Rome, and on Aelius' death passed to the Aurelian family, being adopted by Antoninus Pius (q.v.) in 138, and brought up with M. Aurelius (q.v.), who directed his studies. He assumed the *toga virilis* in 145, became quaestor in 153 and consul in 154, with a second consulship in 161. Thus, on Pius' death he lacked all the special standing of his adoptive 'twin' Marcus Aurelius, ten years his senior; but Marcus at once created him (as 'L. Aurelius Verus') Augustus and colleague with tribunician power, and married him to Lucilla (q.v.) in 164. He was weak and indulgent—defects which made his administration (*see* AURELIUS) an embarrassment to his partner, and his death perhaps a relief to the Empire.

S.H.A. *Verus*; Dio Cassius, bks. 71–2; *PIR²*, C 606; *see also under* AURELIUS. P. Lambrechts, *Ant. class.* iii (1934), 173; C. H. Dodd, *Num. Chron.* 1911, 209. C. H. V. S.

VESPAE IUDICIUM COCI ET PISTORIS IUDICE VULCANO, contest between baker and cook in ninety-nine hexameters by a travelling rhetorician Vespa. The poem shows no trace of Christianity and is familiar with mythology and Roman folk-lore, but cannot be older than the third century A.D. because of its prosody (*in caccabŏ, quāsi, Meleāger*). Metre is pleasing, although final syllable is admitted in the fifth rise (e.g. 'potest superorum').

Baehrens, *PLM* iv. 326. O. S.

VESPASIAN (TITUS FLAVIUS VESPASIANUS), emperor A.D. 69–79. Born A.D. 9, at Sabine Reate, the son of a tax-gatherer, Flavius Sabinus, he was *tribunus militum* in Thrace, *quaestor Cretae et Cyrenarum*, aedile in 38, praetor in 40. As *legatus* of Legio II Augusta, he received the *triumphalia ornamenta* for his services in Britain (44). In 51 he was *consul suffectus*, and subsequently (? *c.* 63) proconsul of Africa. In 66 he accompanied Nero to Greece, but fell into disfavour because he went to sleep at one of the Emperor's recitals. Nero, however, suddenly appointed him to quell the Jewish rebellion (late 66). On 1 July 69 the legions at Alexandria hailed Vespasian as Imperator, and their example was followed on the 3rd by those in Judaea. On 22 December, with the death of Vitellius, the Senate formally appointed Vespasian emperor.

2. The new emperor was well fitted to carry out the heavy task of reconstruction which lay before him. The keynote of his character was a sturdy common-sense which despised all ostentation. A typical countryman, he was blunt, straight-forward, and honest, with a strong and somewhat coarse sense of humour. His immediate task was to restore public confidence and to repair the damage of the civil wars. Titus, the Emperor's eldest son, was left to carry on the war in Palestine, and two competent generals, Annius Gallus and Petilius Cerialis, were appointed to suppress the revolt of Civilis (q.v.). By the end of 70 Vespasian could boast that there was peace on all frontiers, and in 71 the temple of Janus was ceremonially closed. In the same year Vespasian and Titus celebrated a magnificent triumph for the capture of Jerusalem.

3. The new era of peace and reconstruction was ushered in by the rebuilding of the Capitoline Temple, which was started in 70. Next, Vespasian turned to the pressing problem of imperial finance. He stated himself that forty thousand million sesterces (*c.* £400,000,000) were needed to make the State solvent. Retrenchment alone was not sufficient. The tributes of the provinces generally were raised and strictly exacted, public land unlawfully occupied was resumed for the State, and various new taxes were devised. Vespasian incurred a reputation for parsimony as a result of these measures, but the whole Empire benefited. In Rome itself magnificent buildings, such as the Temple of Peace and the Colosseum, were erected, while money in the provinces was freely spent on building, road-making, and the encouragement of art and education.

4. It was largely for financial reasons that Vespasian assumed the censorship with Titus in 73, but he also honoured the most distinguished of the Italians and provincials by means of *adlectio* (q.v.), and so filled up the numbers of the Senate, depleted by civil war and persecution. He thus obtained valuable recruits for the administration, and from this time dates the gradual substitution of *equites* for freedmen in the imperial government. In keeping with this liberal outlook was his edict conferring Latin rights on all the towns of Spain. The founding of numerous colonies in backward provinces furthered romanization, and Vespasian's general policy was to encourage municipal life. He also exerted the strictest control over governors and officials, and severely punished maladministration.

5. In foreign policy Vespasian aimed at consolidation and strengthening of existing frontiers. The number of legions was maintained at twenty-eight. In the East Vespasian substituted three armies with a total of six legions in Syria, Cappadocia, and Judaea, for the old four-legion army in Syria. In 72 the kingdoms of Commagene and Armenia Minor were annexed. In Britain the subjugation of Wales was completed, and the Roman frontier was advanced into Scotland (*see* CERIALIS, FRONTINUS, AGRICOLA). In Germany the frontier was pushed forward by means of roads and forts, to strengthen the angle between the Upper Rhine and the sources of the Danube (73–4).

6. Vespasian made little direct change in the constitution. The position assigned to Titus of virtual partnership in the administration was of especial importance. Titus commanded the praetorians and performed many of the tasks of government. Vespasian thus assured the succession, and he made it plain that Titus was to be succeeded by Domitian. Together with Titus Vespasian held the ordinary consulship in every year except 73 and 78; this was probably due to a desire to enhance the dignity of the new imperial house. The Senate was formally consulted on all occasions, but the tendency was towards autocracy. This was resented by certain of the Stoic aristocracy, who, in alliance with the Cynics, attacked in particular the arrangements for the succession. The tolerant Vespasian was forced eventually to execute their leader, Helvidius Priscus (q.v.), and to exile, and in one or two cases kill, Cynic philosophers. The only direct plot was that of A. Caecina and Eprius Marcellus in 79, which Titus summarily suppressed.

7. Vespasian died in 79, and was deified by the Senate. His reign had restored the prosperity of the Roman world and brought back sanity into the Empire.

PRINCIPAL ANCIENT SOURCES: Tac. *Hist.* bks. 2–4; Suet. *Vesp.*; Dio Cass. bks. 65–6. H. C. Newton, 'The Epigraphical Evidence for the Reigns of Vespasian and Titus' (*Cornell Stud. in Class. Philol.* 1901); H. Mattingly and E. Sydenham, *The Roman Imperial Coinage* ii. 1–213.

MODERN LITERATURE: *PIR*[1], F 263; *PIR*[2], F 398; Weynand, *PW*, s.v. 'Flavius (206)'; M. P. Charlesworth, *CAH* xi, ch. 1; M. Rostovtzeff, *Social and Economic History of the Roman Empire* (1926), chs. 5–8. R. L. J.

VESTA, VESTALS. Vesta is the Roman hearth-goddess, the etymological equivalent of Hestia (q.v.), as she is in cult. She was prominent in family worship (*see* WORSHIP, HOUSEHOLD; PENATES), and is sometimes depicted in *lararia* (as Boyce, *Am. Ac. Rome* xiv, plate 24) with her favourite beast, the ass ([Verg.] *Copa*, 26). Not much is known of her domestic ritual, but see Cato, *Agr.* 143. 2.

For her as for Hestia it is evident that the royal hearth-cult must have been supremely important in early times. Hence it is very natural that her State worship (*Vesta publica populi Romani Quiritium*) should not be in a temple but in a round building near the Regia, doubtless an imitation in stone of the ancient round hut (the modern *capanna*). This contained no image (Ovid, *Fasti* 6. 295–6), but a fire which never was let out ('ignis inextinctus', ibid. 297; 'ignem illum sempiternum', Cicero, *Dom.* 144). Curtained off from the rest of the building was the *penus* (Festus, p. 296. 12 Lindsay), which was opened for some days at the Vestalia, 9 June, a time of ill-omen, for the building was cleaned then and the days were *religiosi* and *nefasti* till the dirt had been disposed of on 15 June, Q(*uando*) ST(*ercus*) D(*elatum*) F(*as*). The *penus* contained various sacred objects, but as none but the Vestals might enter it, their nature was never known but widely guessed at (e.g. Livy 26. 27. 14; cf. Dion. Hal. *Ant. Rom.* 2. 66. 3). This cult, though old (founded by Numa, Dion. Hal. ibid. 1 and other authors), was not primitive, for the Forum is not part of the oldest Rome. Preceding it was the cult of

Caca, on the Palatine (Servius on *Aen.* 8. 190), of like character.

Vesta was served by the Vestal Virgins, representing the daughters of the royal house (see Rose in *Mnemos.* liv (1926), 2 ff.). They are said to have been originally two, then four, but in historical times normally six (Plut. *Numa* 10). They served originally for five years (Dion. Hal. 1. 76. 3), in historical times for thirty, during which time they must remain virgin, but after which they might marry, though few did, as it was supposedly unlucky (Plut. ibid.). Candidates must be between the ages of six and ten, and were chosen by the *Pontifex Maximus*, with the formula *te, Amata, capio*, from a total of twenty (if so many offered). They were not necessarily patricians. They received numerous honours, including emancipation from their fathers' tutelage, but were under the control of the Pontifex, who could scourge any who let the sacred fire out or committed other offences short of unchastity; for that the culprit was entombed alive (an obvious ordeal; Vesta might set her free if she was innocent). See Plut. loc. cit.; Gellius 1. 12.

Not much is known of the ritual, save that it was old-fashioned, not using water from mains and relighting the fire, if ever it went out, by friction of wood (Wissowa, 254). The Vestals wore the old sacral dress otherwise used by brides only. *See* MIRACLES, ATRIUM VESTAE.

Wissowa in Roscher's *Lexikon*, s.v. H. J. R.

VESTRICIUS SPURINNA, a distinguished military commander, praised by Pliny for lyrics in Greek and Latin (*Ep.* 2. 7; 3. 1): see Schanz–Hosius, § 416.

VESUVIUS, a famous volcano in central Italy, long dormant (Diod. Sic. 4. 21. 5), whose crater, where wild vines grew, served as a fortress refuge for Spartacus (q.v.). Strabo (5. 8) describes the slopes as well cultivated, the summit as flat and barren. After a preliminary earthquake on 5 Feb. A.D. 63 (Seneca, *QNat.* 6. 1; cf. Tac. *Ann.* 15. 22), which severely damaged Pompeii and Herculaneum, with slighter effects at Naples and Nuceria, a very violent eruption took place, after warning rumblings, on 24–5 Aug. 79, in which Pliny the Elder perished, as his nephew describes (Plin. *Ep.* 6. 16. 20). This buried Pompeii in sand, stones, and mud, Herculaneum in liquid tufa, Stabiae in ashes. Further eruptions are recorded in 202 (Dio Cass. 77. 2), 472 (*Chron. Marcell.* A.D. 472), and 512 (Procop. *Goth.* 4. 35). The existing mountain is a huge crater, of which one side and part of the floor alone remain, and are dwarfed by a large central cone (Vesuvio, 1,303 m.).

P. Preusse, *Klio* 1934, 295; M. Baratta, *Athenaeum* 1935, 205; C. F. C. Letts, *The Eruption of Vesuvius* (U.S.A. 1937); E. de Martonne, *Traité de géographie physique*[6] (1935), ii. 725; F. A. Perret, *The Vesuvius Eruption of 1906* (U.S.A. 1924). I. A. R.

VETERA, near Xanten, on the Rhine opposite the Lippe, was one of the chief bases in the Augustan invasions of Germany, and *c.* 16–14 B.C. became the permanent headquarters of two legions. Their fortress was rebuilt in A.D. 43, and a magnificent headquarters building or praetorium and legate's palace belonging to it have been excavated. Around it a large civil settlement grew up. All was destroyed by Civilis in 70, and a new fortress for a single legion was erected on a fresh site. In 100 Trajan built a fortified military colony nearby, but the legion was maintained here until the end of the Roman Empire. O. B.

VETERINARY SCIENCE, see HIPPIATRICI, MULO-MEDICINA, SURGERY, para. 10.

VETTIUS (1) PHILOCOMUS, a friend of Lucilius, on whose satires, like Laelius Archelaus, he lectured and commented (Suet. *Gram.* 2).

VETTIUS (2) SCATO, PUBLIUS, an Italian general in the Social War, who had the distinction, in 90 B.C., of defeating both the Roman consuls (L. Caesar and P. Rutilius Lupus) in the same year.

VETTIUS (3), LUCIUS, a professional informer, gained notoriety in 62 B.C. by charging Caesar with complicity in the Catilinarian Conspiracy (Suet. *Iul.* 16). In 59 he professed to have knowledge of a conspiracy to assassinate Pompey. The plot was revealed through the younger Curio, in whom Vettius confided. On cross-examination before the Senate, and before Caesar in the forum, Vettius implicated several well-known members of the senatorial party; shortly afterwards he died in prison in suspicious circumstances. It remains unknown whether the plot was genuine, and, if so, who was behind it. It may merely have been fabricated by Vettius for his own ends.

Cic. *Att.* 2. 24, *Vatin.* 24–6, *Sest.* 132; Suet. *Iul.* 20; Dio 37. 41, 38. 9; Appian, *BCiv.* 2. 12; Plutarch, *Lucullus*, 42. J. M. C.

VETTIUS (4) BOLANUS commanded a legion under Corbulo in Armenia (A.D. 62), and was sent by Vitellius as legate of Britain (69–71), where he failed to keep firm control of the Brigantes. He was proconsul of Asia, and raised to the patriciate perhaps by Vespasian.

Statius, *Silv.* 5. 2. R. G. Collingwood, *Roman Britain*[2] (1937), 107. A. M.

VETTIUS (5) VALENS, astrological writer of the second century A.D.

Ed. W. Kroll, 1908.

VETTIUS (6) AGORIUS PRAETEXTATUS (d. A.D. 384) was a resolute opponent of Christianity, who held many high offices in the State, both priestly and administrative. We have from him a notable epitaph, with a long poem in iambic *senarii*, showing how a synthesis of pagan cults was attempted in face of the common enemy, Christianity. He prepared a Latin translation of Themistius' adaptation of Aristotle's *Categories*. He also did something for the purification of the texts of various Latin authors. His career was in many ways parallel to that of his contemporary Symmachus (q.v. 2).

CIL vi. 1779 (= Dessau, *ILS* 1259); *Carm. Epigr.* no. 111. A. S.

VETTIUS, *see also* JUVENCUS.

VETUS, *see* ANTISTIUS.

VEXILLUM, in the Republican army, was the standard of the legionary cavalry. Under the Principate it was sometimes the standard of the auxiliary *alae*, but more commonly was used as the standard of a detachment or of a corps of veterans after their period of service under the *aquila* had been completed. Hence it came to mean a detachment (*vexillatio*) of infantry, and in the Constantinian army of cavalry, or a body of veterans (*sub vexillo tendentes*).

H. M. D. Parker, *The Roman Legions* (1928); A. von Domaszewski, 'Die Fahnen im römischen Heere', *Abhandlungen des archäologisch-epigraphischen Seminars der Universität Wien*, 1885, 1–80; M. Rostovtzeff, 'Vexillum and Victory', *JRS* 1942. H. M. D. P.

VIA AEMILIA, named after its builder M. Aemilius Lepidus, *cos.* 187 B.C. (Livy 39. 2), and subsequently repaired by Augustus and Trajan, ran from Ariminum 176 miles north-west to Placentia (with later extensions to Augusta Praetoria, to Segusio, to Aquileia, all somewhat inaccurately called Via Aemilia). The Aemilia helped to romanize Cisalpine Gaul rapidly. It touched every important city of the district (still called Emilia) except Ravenna.

M. Aemilius Scaurus, censor 109 B.C., built another Via Aemilia prolonging the Via Aurelia (q.v.) to Dertona and Vada Sabatia.

Strabo 5. 217. N. Lamboglia, *Athenaeum* 1937 E. T. S.

VIA APPIA, the Romans' principal route to south Italy and beyond (Strabo 6. 283). Appius Claudius Caecus, censor 312 B.C., built and named the 132-mile section from Rome to Capua (Livy 9. 29). It had probably been extended by 244 through Beneventum, Venusia, and Tarentum to Brundisium (234 miles). Paving of the Appia commenced in 295 and apparently was complete by Gracchan times (Livy 10. 23; Plut. *C. Gracch.* 7; reject Diod. 20. 36). In Imperial times a praetorian *curator* kept the road in order. Its exact line can be traced most of the way to Beneventum, but not beyond, since the shorter route to Brundisium via Canusium and Barium, which Horace (*Sat.* 1. 5. 77 f.) and later the Via Traiana used, led to neglect of the Appia. Between Rome and Beneventum, however, one can still see roadside tombs (e.g. the Scipios', Caecilia Metella's), the ancient pavement (*c.* 20 ft. wide at *Itri*), a rock-cutting (at Tarracina), embankments (e.g. at Aricia and *Itri*), bridges (three between Caudium and Beneventum), and milestones. One of these proves that, even though travellers preferred the 19-mile-long ship-canal, the Appia from its earliest days crossed the Pomptine marshes (q.v.) (C. Hülsen, *Röm. Mitt.* 1889, 83 f.). Various branches, e.g. the Via Popillia to Rhegium, were also somewhat inaccurately called Via Appia.

T. Ashby, *Roman Campagna* (1927), 174 f.   E. T. S.

VIA AURELIA, important highway (Cic. *Phil.* 12. 9) of unknown date, but presumably built before its extension, the Via Aemilia Scauri of 109 B.C. It was 175 miles long, running from Rome north-west to Alsium, thence along the Etruscan coast to Vada Volaterrana. Later prolongations to Dertona and to Arelate are also called Via Aurelia in the Itineraries.

D. Anziani, *Mélanges d'arch.* 1913.   E. T. S.

VIA DOMITIA, a very ancient route from the Rhône to Spain, improved by the Romans apparently before the death of Polybius (124 B.C.; cf. 3. 39. 8), but owing its name to the conqueror of Narbonensis, M. Domitius Ahenobarbus (121). It was repaired by M. Fonteius (*c.* 75), and under the Empire by Tiberius (A.D. 31–2— earliest inscribed milestones), Claudius (41), Antoninus Pius (145), Maximinus (235–8), and Diocletian (284–305).

Grenier, *Manuel* ii. 26–9.   C. E. S.

VIA EGNATIA, Roman road built *c.* 130 B.C. from the Adriatic coast to Byzantium; named after Egnatia on the Apulian coast, where the corresponding road from Rome to Brindisi touched the sea, the Via Egnatia was the main route from Rome to the East. Two branches of the road, starting respectively from Dyrrhachium and Apollonia, united in the Skumbi valley, crossed the Balkan range by Lake Lychnidus (*Ochrida*), and descended to Thessalonica via Heraclea, Eordaea, Aegae, and Pella, whence it followed the Thracian coast to Byzantium. It followed the line of a trade-route through the Balkan range which Corinth had exploited.   N. G. L. H.

VIA FLAMINIA, the great northern highway of Italy, built 220 B.C. by C. Flaminius, when censor (Livy *Epit.* 20; reject Strabo 5. 217). It was 209 miles long from Rome via Narnia, Mevania, Nuceria, and Helvillum to Fanum Fortunae, where it turned north-west and followed the Adriatic coastline via Pisaurum to Ariminum. After A.D. 69 the section between Narnia and Nuceria was provided with an alternative, six-mile longer route via Interamna, Spoletium, and Fulginium. From its earliest days the Flaminia was much frequented; its importance was, if anything, enhanced in late Imperial times when the imperial court was at Milan or Ravenna. Large towns grew up along its tomb-lined course (Livy 22. 11; Cic. *Phil.* 12. 9; Tac. *Hist.* 1. 86; 2. 64; Juv. 1.

61. 171). The road was often repaired: by C. Gracchus, Augustus (parts of whose bridge at Narnia, and an honorific arch at Ariminum survive), Vespasian (whose tunnel through Intercisa Pass still exists near Calles), Trajan, Hadrian. Various branches, e.g. from Nuceria to Ancona, were also inaccurately called Via Flaminia.

T. Ashby–R. A. L. Fell, *JRS* 1921.   E. T. S.

VIA LATINA, perhaps the earliest of the highways radiating from Rome, is not named after its builder—a fact suggesting high antiquity. It ran south-east and by 334 B.C. probably already reached Cales (q.v.). Pyrrhus and Hannibal both used it, presumably because it followed an easier line than the Appia. After surmounting the outer rim of the Alban Hills at Algidus, the Latina followed the Trerus valley through the Hernici country where the Via Labicana joined it near Anagnia. It crossed the Liris at Fregellae, then proceeded via Aquinum, Casinum, Venafrum, Teanum, and Cales across the Volturnus to Casilinum where it merged with the Appia. (A later short cut via Rufrae avoided Venafrum.) The 135-mile Latina was much frequented (Strabo 5. 237); important branches ran from it into Samnium. Its exact line can still be traced without much difficulty.

T. Ashby, *Roman Campagna* (1927), 153 f.   E. T. S.

VIA POSTUMIA, north Italian highway centring on Cremona, whence it ran in one direction through Dertona to Genua and in the other through Mantua to Aquileia. (There was also a branch from Bedriacum through Verona to the Brenner Pass.) This road, built by Sp. Postumius Albinus, *cos.* 148 B.C., consolidated the conquest of Liguria. The Itineraries regard it as part of the Via Aurelia, and ancient authors virtually ignore it.

Dessau, *ILS* 5806, 5946; Tac. *Hist.* 3. 21.   E. T. S.

VIA SACRA (or **SACRA VIA**), the street connecting the *Forum Romanum* with the Velia, affording access to the Palatine. The name probably comes from the hallowed buildings which the street passed, connected with the shrines of Vesta and the Regia. The earliest known monument at its end is the *fornix Fabianus* (*JRS* 1922, 27–8) of 121 B.C., whence the road straggled towards the Velia, passing many private houses and shops, its pavement being still visible. In A.D. 64 Nero planned the street anew as a noble colonnaded avenue flanked by large bazaars for jewellers, florists, and luxury-traders. The northern bazaar was smaller and was obliterated by the basilica of Maxentius; the southern, though curtailed by Hadrian's extensions of the Atrium Vestae (q.v.), occupied the considerable space between that house and the Arch of Titus.   I. A. R.

VIA VALERIA, important highway running north-east from Rome to Aternum on the Adriatic. Its first 18 miles comprised the very ancient Via Tiburtina. This was prolonged, possibly *c.* 300 B.C., to Carsioli, Alba Fucens, and apparently Cerfennia (Livy 10. 1. 3; Diod. 20. 90, emending Σερεννία. Livy 9. 43 records a road-building Valerius, censor 306 B.C.). This extension later became a paved highway, perhaps in the censorship of M. Valerius Messalla (154 B.C.), and was the Via Valeria proper (cf. Strabo 5. 238). Finally the Emperor Claudius continued the road as the Via Claudia Valeria from Cerfennia to the Adriatic (R. Gardner, *BSR* ix. 1920). Pliny's estimate of 136 miles as the breadth of Italy is based on the Valeria (*HN* 3. 44).   E. T. S.

VIATORES were public bailiffs, mostly freedmen or of low birth, whose chief business was to run errands for the magistrates and summon senators to meetings. They also seized confiscated goods, made arrests, and executed the commands and sentences issued by their respective magistrates. They formed a corporation divided into several *decuriae* according to the rank of the magistracies (the first was therefore the *decuria consularis*). Municipal magistrates also employed *viatores* chiefly to collect taxes.

Mommsen, *Röm. Staatsr.* i³. 360 ff.   P. T.

VĪBIUS (1) **MARSUS**, GAIUS (*cos. suff.* A.D. 17), legate of Germanicus in the East, proconsul in Africa (27–30); accused of *maiestas*, he narrowly escaped death (37). Legate of Syria (42–5), he was hostile to King Agrippa.

PIR, V 388; R. S. Rogers, *Criminal Trials under Tiberius* (1935), 162.   A. M.

VIBIUS (2) **RUFUS**, GAIUS (*cos. suff.* A.D. 16), a declaimer of Tiberius' reign, married Cicero's widow. His arguments are often cited in the elder Seneca's *Controversiae* (e.g. 2. 1. 2 and 28; 2. 3. 8; 2. 6. 10; 7. 3. 4; 9. 2. 2).

VIBIUS (3) **CRISPUS**, QUINTUS, a dangerously persuasive *delator* with a pleasant style of oratory (Quint. *Inst.* 10. 1. 119; 12. 10. 11; Tac. *Ann.* 14. 28; *Hist.* 2. 10; 4. 41 and 43; *Dial.* 8 and 13.)

VIBIUS (4) **MAXIMUS**, GAIUS, *praefectus coh. III Alpinorum* in Dalmatia A.D. 93 (*CIL* iii. 859), prefect of Egypt in 104, was a friend of both Martial (11. 106) and Statius, whose *Silv.* 4. 7 was written in his honour. Its close suggests that V. rivalled the terseness of Sallust and Livy in a Universal History.

Peter, *HRRel.* ii, p. clxxi.   J. W. D.

VIBIUS, *see also* PANSA, SABINA, TREBONIANUS.

VICA POTA, a goddess, whose shrine lay on the Velia (Livy 2. 7. 12). Though it existed in his time, her functions were unknown, some explaining her as Victory (q.v.; *uincere, potiri*; Cicero, *Leg.* 2. 28), some as goddess of food and drink (*uictus, potus*; Arnobius, *Adv. Nat.* 3. 25).   H. J. R.

VICARIUS. During the first two centuries A.D. *vicarius* meant a substitute for an absent or deceased provincial governor. In the third century *vicarii* were equestrian procurators who were specially appointed by the emperor to administer provinces in place of the regular senatorial governors. When Diocletian divided the Empire into dioceses, each was entrusted to a *vicarius* with the exception of Italy, which had two *vicarii*. (*See* DIOECESIS.)   H. M. D. P.

VICESIMA HEREDITATUM, *see* FINANCE, ROMAN, para 4.

VICOMAGISTRI were presidents of sub-districts (*vici*) in town or city wards (*regiones*), known to have existed in Rome and her colonies under the Republic (*CIL* vi. 2221), and charged with the upkeep of local cults and the presidency of religious festivals. Examples also occur in Italian communities at Delos (*BCH* xxxvi. 154 ff.). These men were free-born, but of low social standing, and their organization could be used politically. It was in fact misused and quashed in 64 B.C. (Cic. *Pis.* 4. 9), revived in 58, to Cicero's disgust (*Red. Sen.* 13. 33; *Sest.* 15. 34; 25. 55), and perhaps again abolished by Caesar (Suet. *Iul.* 42. 3). As revived by Augustus in 7 B.C. (Dio Cass. 54. 2: *CIL* vi. 343, 2222) and earlier (op. cit. 449, 452), the *vicomagistri* furnish an example of his subtle transformation of Republican institutions. They were connected with his creation of Fourteen Regions (*see* REGIO) and each *vicus* elected four. Their cult of the *lares compitales* now included the *lares Augusti* and *genius* of the emperor (*ILS* 3612–21, Rome; *ILS* 3611, Naples; *ILS* 3622, Verona). Municipal duties included assistance with the *census* (Suet. *Aug.* 40) and fire-fighting until A.D. 6. Under Hadrian two *curatores*, a *denuntiator*, and four *magistri* went to each *vicus*, all

now freedmen and acting under the *praefectus vigilum* (*CIL* vi. 975). In Pliny's day (*HN* 3. 9. 13) there were 1060 for the 265 *vici* of Rome, while in the fourth century there were 48 to each *regio*, excepting one of 49, making 673 in all.   I. A. R.

VICTIMARIUS. At a Roman sacrifice, the officiant did not, at least normally and in the classical epoch, kill the victim himself; this was done by a *victimarius* or sacred slaughterman. These formed a *collegium* in Imperial times, attendant (*CIL* vi. 971) on the emperor, priests, and magistrates.   H. J. R.

VICTORIA, the Roman equivalent of Nike (q.v.). There is no evidence that she is anything more, mentions of an early cult of Victory being referable to Vacuna or Vica Pota (qq.v.; Dion. Hal. *Ant. Rom.* 1. 15. 1; Asconius, *Pis.*, p. 13. 15 Clark). She is associated in cult with Jupiter (Victor), as in the *acta Arualium*, p. cxcviii Henzen, oftener with Mars, as ibid., p. clxv, also with other deities. She was worshipped by the army, as was natural (Domaszewski, *Rel. des röm. Heeres* (*Westd. Zeit.* 1895), pp. 4 ff.), and hence is given surnames associating her with particular legions and more commonly still with emperors (list in Roscher, vi. 299; cf. J. Gagé, *Rev. Arch.*, 5th Ser., xxxii (1930), 1 ff., *Rev. Hist.* clxxi (1933), 1 ff.). Her temple on the Palatine dates from 294 B.C., see Platner–Ashby, p. 570. Her most famous monument was perhaps her altar in the senate-house, put there at the beginning of the Empire, removed under Constantius, replaced by the pagan party in Rome, removed again by Gratian in 382, replaced for a short time by Eugenius and perhaps once more by Stilicho, and finally vanishing with the other vestiges of pagan cult (Ambrosius, *Epp.* 17; 18; 57. 6, cf. Paulinus, *Vit. Ambros.* 26; Symmachus, *Relat.* 3; Claudian, 28. 597).

See Latte in Roscher, s.v.   H. J. R.

VICTORIATUS, *see* COINAGE, ROMAN, paras. 5 and 7.

VICTORINUS (1), GAIUS MARIUS (4th c. A.D.), was the author of philosophical (Neoplatonic), rhetorical, and grammatical works. His reputation was such that a statue in his honour was set up in the forum Traianum. After becoming a Christian, he wrote theological treatises. Most of his *Ars grammatica* (ed. Keil, *Gramm. Lat.* vi. 3–184) has been ousted in our manuscripts by the *De metris* of Aphthonius (q.v.). His translations of Plato, Aristotle, and Porphyrius are lost, as is his commentary on Cicero's *Topica*; but his *explanationes* of the *De inventione* of Cicero are preserved (ed. Halm, *Rhet. Lat. Min.* 155–304). His Christian writings (in Migne *PL* viii) included commentaries on some Pauline epistles, *De trinitate contra Arium*, *De ὁμοουσίῳ recipiendo*, and possibly a work against the Manichaeans.

Cf. Teuffel, § 408; Schanz–Hosius, §§ 828–31 a.   J. F. M.

VICTORINUS (2), MAXIMUS, grammarian of unknown date, author of a *De ratione metrorum* (ed. Keil, *Gramm. Lat.* vi. 216–28). Certain other treatises: *Ars Victorini*, *De metris*, *De finalibus metrorum* (ed. Keil, *Gramm. Lat.* 6. 187–205; 206–215; 229–224) are attributed in manuscripts to an unspecified 'Victorinus'.

Cf. Teuffel, § 408. 4–5; Schanz–Hosius, § 829.   J. F. M.

VI(C)TORIUS MARCELLUS, orator, to whom Quintilian dedicated his *Institutes* as a manual for Marcellus' son and for his own boy, of whom, however, he was bereaved before his work was half completed (*Inst.* 1, prooem. 6; 6, prooem. 1–16). Statius addresses *Silvae*, bk. 4, to him (prooem. 1).   J. W. D.

VICUS was the smallest agglomeration of buildings forming a recognized unit, either a country village or a ward of a town. The former were subordinate to the *pagus* in which they were situated, the latter directly to the municipal authority. *Vici* could also exist on private or imperial estates withdrawn from the municipal system, where they depended upon the local landlord or imperial procurator. They were administered by *magistri* or *aediles* elected by the villagers. Priestly officials, *dicatores*, are also known. *Vici* in towns, too, had their *vicomagistri* (q.v.). Those of Rome, revived by Augustus, had charge of the street shrines, and for a while of the fire-brigade. A *vicus* could be a *praefectura* (q.v.) but was normally subordinate to an intermediate authority.

For bibliography *see under* MUNICIPIUM (REPUBLIC).

A. N. S.-W.

VIENNA, town in Gallia Narbonensis, modern *Vienne*; capital of the Allobroges. Perhaps created *colonia Latina* by M. Antonius (43 B.C.); given probably by Gaius the title of *colonia civium Romanorum*. In the third century A.D. it possessed *ius Italicum*. In 69 it narrowly escaped destruction from Vitellius' army, encouraged by its jealous neighbour Lugdunum. A large straggling town with Augustan *enceinte* is partially preserved. Its most notable surviving building is the temple of Rome and Augustus, enlarged and rededicated by Tiberius. Like Lugdunum, it was an important seat of early Christianity.

CIL xii, p. 217; Grenier, *Manuel* i. 323-8.

C. E. S.

VIGILES (νυκτοφύλακες). Except for the existence of *triumviri nocturni*, about whose function little is known, the city of Rome under the late Republic possessed neither fire brigade nor police force. After the fire of 23 B.C. Augustus established a fire brigade of 600 slaves commanded at first by the aediles but after 7 B.C. (when Rome was divided into 14 *regiones* and 265 *vici*, each with four *vicomagistri*) by the *vicomagistri*. After another serious fire (A.D. 6) Augustus effected a lasting reorganization. He created a corps of 7,000 *Vigiles*, all freedmen, who were organized in seven cohorts, each consisting of seven centuries, and each commanded by a tribune. Over the whole body was set a *Praefectus Vigilum*, who was appointed directly by the emperor; he was an *eques* and ranked below the *Praefectus Annonae* and *Praefectus Praetorio* (Dio Cass. 55. 26; Suet. *Aug.* 30). From Trajan's time he was assisted by a Sub-Prefect. To his original duties were added later those of a judge, and he presided over trials for incendiarism and petty larceny (*Digest* 1. 15. 3); in the third century A.D. the office, like that of *Praefectus Praetorio*, was held by eminent jurists.

Each cohort of *Vigiles* was responsible for two *regiones* of the city. The troops were quartered at first in private houses (Dio Cass. 57. 19. 6; cf. Suet. *Tib.* 37), but later had sub-stations, *excubitoria*, one in each *regio*. They were occasionally called on in emergencies to perform military duties, e.g. in A.D. 31, at the time of the arrest of Sejanus, when the loyalty of the praetorians was uncertain (Dio Cass. 58. 9-13), and in A.D. 69. In such emergencies they normally came, with their prefect, under the command of the *Praefectus Urbi*.

P. K. Baillie Reynolds, *The Vigiles of Imperial Rome* (1926).

J. P. B.

VIGINTISEXVIRI. This collective denomination—the reason of which is not quite clear—embraces twenty-six Roman civil *magistratus minores* who had no special official titles, being indicated only by their functions and number (*duoviri, tresviri, quattuorviri*). Some of them were endowed with particular juridical competence. Thus the *decemviri stlitibus iudicandis* were a special tribunal for lawsuits on freedom; from the time of Augustus they presided over the several sections of the centumviral College (*see* CENTUMVIRI). Another group were the four *praefecti* (*iure dicundo*) *Capuam Cumas*, exercising jurisdiction as delegates of the *praetor urbanus* in ten Campanian towns. The remainder had administrative functions:

the *tresviri* (*triumviri*) *monetales* (more precise title: *tresviri aere argento auro flando feriundo*), the masters of the mint; the *quattuorviri viis in urbe purgandis*, and the *duoviri viis extra urbem purgandis*, who provided for the maintenance of the streets in Rome and in the environs respectively; and finally the *tresviri capitales* responsible for prisons (*carceris custodia*) and executions. In their capacity as guardians of nocturnal peace they were also called *tresviri nocturni*. Under Augustus the number of these magistrates was reduced to twenty, six of them (four *praefecti Capuam Cumas* and *duoviri viis extra urbem purgandis*) having been abolished. Hence their new collective name: *vigintiviri*. One of these magistracies was, as it seems, a necessary preliminary to the quaestorship.

A. B.

VIGINTIVIRI, *see* VIGINTISEXVIRI.

VILICUS, *see* COLONUS.

VILLA was the Latin name for a rural dwelling associated with agriculture. The traditional Italian farm of this kind is described in detail by Varro (*Rust.* 1. 11-13) and Vitruvius (6. 6. 1) as a courtyard edifice comprising house, stables, and workshops, run by slave labour for the benefit of an urban proprietor. Such farms, however, were always matched by those of smallholders and yeomanry, and Campanian examples of both kinds have been studied (R. Carrington, *JRS* xxi. 110 f.) and may be compared with Istrian farms of the same type (Gnirs, *JÖAI* xviii (1915) Beiblatt 101). *See* AGRICULTURE. The residential villa, or country seat of the well-to-do, is a later development of the second century B.C., wherein are seen the first relations of architectural design to landscape or vistas and the development of large courtyard houses or seaside palaces.

In the provinces the development of country houses is primarily of the Imperial age, our knowledge of Republican examples being negligible. Local types of house undoubtedly existed, though understanding of their development is very uneven as between provinces. In Syria the age-old eastern type of courtyard house (*liwan*) existed side by side with smaller flat-roofed dwellings, while in Africa mosaics attest a two-story house based upon a corridor, with larger tower-like rooms at either end. This type of house occurs very widely throughout the north-west provinces on estates of medium size, while larger houses there follow the more Roman courtyard type or the open-fronted style associated with landscape architecture. In Britain and Belgica there were hybrids between large courtyard houses and the open-fronted corridor-house, while native tradition also survived in the so-called basilican house, a barn-like building of nave and aisles. Socially, most of the provincial villas known to us are the dwellings of large landowners or small-holders, and there is little trace of the Italian *latifundia*. In the north-west provinces economic life tended to concentrate in these, to the exclusion of the towns, wherein is to be sought one reason for the rapid disappearance of Roman tradition under the impact of barbarian invasions.

C. Swoboda, *Römische und romanische Paläste* (1919); A. Gnirs, *JÖAI* x (1907) Beiblatt; ibid. xviii (1915); P. Gauckler, *Mon. Piot* iii (1897), 185 ff.; id., *Inventaire des mosaïques* ii. 1 (Tunisie), no. 940; E. Littman, *Ruinenstätten und Schriftdenkmäler Syriens* (1917) 31; H. C. Butler, *Publ. of an Amer. Arch. Exped. to Syria, 1899-1900,* i-iv (1904-5), *Publ. of Princeton Univ. Exp. to Syria, 1904-5,* i-iii, (1907-16); F. Cumont, *Comment la Belgique fut romanisée²* (1918); A. Grenier, *Habitations gauloises et villas latines dans la cité des Mediomatrices* (1906); P. Steiner, *Römische Landhäuser im Trierer Bezirk* (1923); F. Oelmann, *Bonner Jahrb.* cxxxiii. 51-152; R. G. Collingwood, *Archaeology of Roman Britain* (1930), 113-36; I. A. Richmond, *JRS* xxii. 96-106.

I. A. R.

VILLANOVANS. 'Villanovan' is not an ancient word, and it is only by a convention that it is applied to a particular period and people. It is derived from the modern name of a small town near Bologna. Here in 1853 was found an early Iron-Age cemetery of cremation. Subsequent excavation has shown Villanova to be only one of many similar cemeteries in the provinces of Bologna, Faenza, Forli, and Ravenna. The dates are of all stages between 1000 and 500 B.C. Three periods, termed First Benacci, Second Benacci, Arnoaldi, have been defined. The Benacci sites (roughly 1,000 to 700 B.C.) have their equivalent in the contemporary culture of Etruria and Latium. It is therefore inferred that all three regions were occupied by kindred peoples, so that the name of *Northern Villanovans* is given to the Bolognese, while the occupants of Latium and Etruria are called *Southern Villanovans*. Into Etruria, however, had come by the eighth century a new people, the Etruscans (q.v.), and to disentangle their work and products from those of the native Italians has always been a task of great complexity. Bologna has furnished a valuable key, for archaeology has proved conclusively that the Etruscans did not come to Bologna before *c.* 500 B.C. Consequently everything Bolognese before 500 is likely to be definitely Villanovan and not Etruscan. Similarly, everything in Latium and Etruria which resembles the Bolognese must be Villanovan. Presumably the Villanovans represent the Q-branch of the Italic peoples; they can be distinguished from their neolithic predecessors as well as from the P-branches of the Italics by their custom of cremation of the dead (cf. s.v. UMBRIANS). Like the people of the Terremare (q.v.) they came in as invaders from north of the Alps, and they are regarded by Pigorini's school as direct descendants of the Terramaricoli. This theory is unprovable. Most recent writers prefer to regard the Villanovans as newcomers, representing an invasion of about the eleventh century. A large body of the immigrants settled permanently round Bologna, the rest crossed the Apennines. In Etruria they formed the core of a State presently to be ruled by Etruscans; in Latium they were the forefathers of the Latins. They appear as a vigorous, inventive, hard-working people. Their earliest settlements, in the Etrurian district of Tolfa and Allumiere and in the Alban hills, only slightly antedate the first graves in the prehistoric cemetery of the Forum at Rome. It must be noted, however, that mingled with the cremation-graves in the Forum are inhumation-graves of equal antiquity, which may reasonably be attributed to the Sabines (cf. the literary tradition of the founding of Rome). Models of the dwelling-houses of these first Romans occur in some graves. They were round huts, built of wattle and daub, and roofed with carved beams. The Rome not only of Romulus and Numa but of several centuries later must have consisted mainly of such huts. Traces of similar buildings have been found also at Bologna. But the dwellers in these huts were already finished craftsmen. Their workmanship can best be studied at Bologna, because that region was wholly free from any Mediterranean influences. The First Benacci period there is remarkable for its fine bronzework (weapons, armlets, fibulae, horse-gear, and decorated belts); the second for its masterpieces in hammered vessels. Similar work is found in Etruria, which raises the question of priority. At Bologna there is no trace of oriental commerce, but the frequent amber and certain foreign swords indicate the use of transalpine traderoutes. In the Arnoaldi period (700–500 B.C.) there are some indications of trade with the Etruscans, but even the Etruscan foundation of the neighbouring Felsina (500 B.C.) had little effect on the native Villanovan culture, which was only destroyed in the fourth century by the Gauls.

D. Randall-MacIver, *Villanovans and Early Etruscans* (1924), *Italy before the Romans* (1928); J. Sundwall, *Villanovastudien* (1928); F. von Duhn, *Italische Gräberkunde* (1924); F. Messerschmidt, *Bronzezeit und frühe Eisenzeit in Italien* (1935). D. R.-MacI.

VILLIUS, LUCIUS, as tribune of the plebs, in 180 B.C. carried a law (*Lex Villia annalis*) determining the interval which must elapse between tenure of one office and candidature for a higher one, thereby establishing a *certus ordo magistratuum*, the terms of which (with slight modifications by Sulla) remained in force until the early Imperial age.

Mommsen, *Röm. Staatsr.* i³. 529 ff., 537 ff.; F. Münzer, *Röm. Adelsparteien* (1920), 151 f., 197 f. P. T.

VINDEX, GAIUS JULIUS, of regal Aquitanian family, son of a Roman senator (who had presumably been adlected by Claudius), rebelled against Nero (early spring, A.D. 68) when legate of Gallia Lugdunensis, for unknown reasons. He sought to inveigle other provincial governors, vainly, except Sulpicius Galba (q.v. 1), whose claims to the throne he promised to support. Masses of native Gauls, the notables, and their clients joined Vindex. The city of Vienna in Narbonensis declared for him, but the Roman veteran colony of Lugdunum refused to admit him. In the meantime, Verginius Rufus (q.v. 6) mustered the army of Germania Superior and marched to crush the rising. Vindex was defeated and killed in a great battle at Vesontio.

Fluss, *PW*, s.v. 'Julius (534)'. R. S.

VINDICATIO was the action by which a quiritary owner (see DOMINIUM), if deprived of the possession of an object, demanded its restitution from the actual possessor. The term signified in the early Roman process the formal assertions of the right of ownership made by both the parties. The plaintiff in *rei vindicatio* had to prove that he had acquired ownership according to the principles of *ius civile*, and if he had acquired it from another person, that the latter's title was equally valid, which might be difficult to prove. These difficulties could be avoided by proving that he possessed the object at issue in conditions which sufficed for *usucapio* (see DOMINIUM, POSSESSIO). In this case he could make use of another action, called *Publiciana*. The defendant, when condemned, had to restore the object together with its increments; the possessor *mala fide* was more severely treated (see POSSESSIO). In the formulary process, however, the winning plaintiff was compelled to content himself with the value of the vindicated object, if the defendant refused to return it; the value was fixed according to the estimate made by the plaintiff under oath.

A. B.

VINDOBONA, now *Vienna* on the Danube, was originally inhabited by a Celtic population. It was the camp, first of *ala I Flavia Domitiana Britannica c(ivium) R(omanorum)*, later of Legio XIII Gemina, which began building a stone fortress completed by Legio XIV Gemina. (The chronology of the building activities and troop movements remains disputed: according to Polaschek, op. cit. infra, 6 ff., Legio XIII Gemina came to Vindobona after A.D. 96, and started converting the cavalry camp into a legionary fortress between 98 and 107; it was relieved by Legio XIV Gemina, which continued building till 114 or earlier when transferred to Carnuntum, its place being taken by Legio X Gemina P.F.), Vindobona, which became a *municipium* under Caracalla, was also a *statio* of the *classis Histrica* (*Not. Dign. Occ* xxxiv. 28). Though not the equal of Carnuntum, Vindobona was an important fortress, especially in the Marcomannic Wars, during which it was apparently destroyed, though it was rebuilt again. M. Aurelius died there. In 395 part of the camp was burnt down, and later (perhaps *c.* 406) Vindobona was abandoned by the Romans.

A. v. Domaszewski in *Geschichte der Stadt Wien* i (1897), 37 ff.; F. Kenner, ibid. 42–159; E. Nowotny, *Mitteilungen des Vereines für Geschichte der Stadt Wien* iv (1923), 5–22; E. Polaschek, ibid. xv (1935), 1–14. A guide to Vindobona by Polaschek is said to be in preparation. F. A. W. S.

VINDONISSA, modern *Windisch*, Switzerland, a prehistoric site on the lower Aar, occupied *c.* A.D. 12 by Legio XIII, which was replaced in 45–6 by Legio XXI Rapax, whose violent behaviour to the Helvetii in 69 induced Vespasian to send it elsewhere. Its place was taken by Legio XI Claudia Pia Fidelis, until *c.* 100 when it was realized that Vindonissa was too far from any theatre of war. A considerable civil population remained for whom the military fortress was reconstructed *c.* 260 under pressure of Alamannic attacks. The fortress and the *forum* of the *canabae* have been partially excavated. It was an important centre of lamp manufacture.

R. Laur-Belart, *Vindonissa, Lager and Vicus* (1935). C. E. S.

VINEA, *see* SIEGECRAFT, ROMAN.

VINICIANUS, ANNIUS, son of Vinicianus who conspired in A.D. 42, and son-in-law of Corbulo, was legate of Legio V Macedonica in 63 when he was not yet quaestor. In 65 he escorted Tiridates to Rome. He gave his name to a plot against Nero at Beneventum (66).

Stein, *PW*, Suppl. iii. 407; *PIR*[2], A 700. A. M.

VINICIUS (1), MARCUS (*cos. suff.* 19 B.C.), a *novus homo* from Cales in Campania, is first mentioned as legate of Augustus in Gaul (25 B.C.). In Illyricum (13, perhaps as proconsul) he and Agrippa began the *Bellum Pannonicum* terminated by Tiberius (12–9). Vinicius is next (and last) heard of in A.D. 1 or 2 as commander of the Rhine army. The acephalous elogium from Tusculum, recording operations against Transdanubian peoples (*ILS* 8965) is now generally attributed to Vinicius, but the details and dating of that campaign are uncertain (14–13, 10, and *c.* 1 B.C. have been suggested). The historian Velleius Paterculus enjoyed the patronage of the Vinicii, dedicating his work to the grandson, M. Vinicius.

R. Syme, *CQ* 1933, 142 ff.; A. v. Premerstein, *JÖAI* 1934, 60 ff. R. S.

VINICIUS (2), PUBLIUS (*cos.* A.D. 2), Augustan orator and declaimer; an admirer of Ovid who combined originality with good taste (Sen. *Controv.* 7. 5. 11, 10. 4. 25).

VINICIUS (3), LUCIUS (*cos. suff.* 5 B.C.), Augustan orator and declaimer; famous for his quick wit (Sen. *Controv.* 2. 5. 20).

VIPSANIUS, *see* AGRIPPA (3).

VIRGA, *see* APEX.

VIRGIL (PUBLIUS VERGILIUS MĀRO; 70–19 B.C.), poet. Several versions of the 'Life' of Virgil have come down to us, attributed to Donatus and others, and based on a Life by Suetonius; they contain many legendary details, but the following facts appear to be well established. Virgil (the spelling with *i* is traditional in English, though inscriptions prove *Vergilius* as the Latin form) was born on the Ides (15th) of October, 70 B.C., at Andes, a *pagus* in the neighbourhood of Mantua. The locality of Andes has been much disputed, but it is traditionally identified with the modern Pietole. His *nomen* and *cognomen* have been thought to imply Celtic or Etruscan origin, but the evidence is slight. His father was a man of humble birth, a potter according to some, or a courier in the employment of one Magius, whose daughter Magia he married. He seems to have acquired land and to have made money by bee-keeping.

2. Virgil's education began at Cremona, and there on his fifteenth birthday, 15 Oct. 55, he assumed the *toga virilis*; tradition said that Lucretius (q.v.) died on the same day. From Cremona he went to Milan for a short time and then to Rome, where he learned rhetoric under prominent teachers and also medicine and astronomy,

but ultimately abandoned these pursuits and the writing of verses for the sake of studying philosophy in the school of Siro, the Epicurean (*Catal.* 5). Virgil's youthful poems must be assigned to this Roman period, when he was under the influence of the Alexandrian school, and had probably formed friendships with Cornelius Gallus, Asinius Pollio, and Alfenus Varus. It is possible, too, that at this time he conceived the idea of writing an epic.

3. In 42 the lands round Cremona and Mantua were distributed to the veterans of the Civil Wars, and *Ecl.* ix, in which Menalcas is clearly Virgil, shows that he lost his estate. If Tityrus in *Ecl.* i is also Virgil, it may be that he recovered it by an appeal to Octavian through his powerful friends, but the identification is uncertain. In Virgil's first published work, the *Eclogues* or *Bucolics*, poems are dedicated to each of his three friends. Asconius states that these poems were begun when Virgil was 28 (42 B.C.) and finished in three years. This tallies well with the date of the quarrel over his lands, and also with the certain date of *Ecl.* iv, which is dedicated to Pollio in his consulship (40 B.C.). The tenth *Eclogue*, dedicated to Gallus, must, however, be placed as late as 37 B.C.

4. By this time Virgil was fully established in the friendship of Maecenas and had become intimate with Horace, who in *Sat.* 1. 5. tells how Virgil with Varius and Tucca, afterwards his literary executors, joined Maecenas and himself on a journey which they were making in order to negotiate the 'treaty of Tarentum' with Antony in 37. The next seven years of Virgil's life were occupied in the writing of the *Georgics*. The mention of the Portus Iulius (2. 161–4), which was completed in 37 B.C., gives the earliest date and the reference to Octavian's campaign in the East (4. 560–2) after Actium, 31–29 B.C., the latest. The poem was written largely in honour of Maecenas, who may have suggested it as a support to the policy of an agricultural revival in Italy, but contains many passages of direct eulogy of Octavian, to whom Virgil recited the poem at Atella after his return from the East in 29. During the latter part of this period Virgil was living at Naples (4. 563–4), and the opening of *Georg.* 3 suggests that he may have paid a visit to Greece (cf. Hor. *Carm.* 1. 3).

5. During the last ten years of his life Virgil was engaged on the composition of the *Aeneid*, living at or near Naples and occasionally in Sicily. Augustus was deeply interested in the work and when absent in Spain in 26 and 25 wrote urging him to send the draft or sections of the poem. Virgil refused, but subsequently recited Books ii, iv, and vi to Augustus and Octavia; this must have been after the death of Marcellus in 23 (see *Aen.* 6. 860–86). In 19 Virgil started with the intention of travelling in Greece and Asia for three years and completing the *Aeneid*, after which he meant to devote himself to philosophy. At Athens, however, he met Augustus and was persuaded to return with him. He fell ill at Megara, and was brought back to Brundisium, where he died on 20 Sept.; his remains were taken to Naples and buried on the road to Puteoli in a tomb with the inscription, attributed to Virgil himself:

> Mantua me genuit, Calabri rapuere, tenet nunc
> Parthenope; cecini pascua, rura, duces.

Before he left Italy Virgil had caused Varius, to whom with Tucca he left his writings, to promise to burn the *Aeneid*, if anything should happen to him. Augustus ordered the executors to disregard this wish, and the poem was published in its unfinished state.

6. According to tradition Virgil was tall and firm-set, dark and of a rustic appearance, and suffered from ill-health. His personal modesty won him the nickname of 'Parthenias' at Naples, and, when in Rome, he is said to have avoided all appearances in public. Through the generosity of his benefactors he amassed a considerable fortune.

7. WORKS

(1) *Early Poems.* Fourteen short poems (**Catalepton**) and five longer works, **Culex, Ciris, Copa, Moretum,** and **Aetna,** were traditionally attributed to Virgil in his youth, but in modern times the attribution has in regard to many of them been disputed. These poems and their authorship are discussed separately under the head *Appendix Vergiliana* (q.v.).

(2) *Eclogues* ('Εκλογαί, 'Select Poems') or **Bucolics** (Βουκολικά, 'Pastorals', a title taken from Theocritus), composed between 42 and 37 B.C. With the exception of iv and vi the *Eclogues* are modelled on the *Idylls* of Theocritus. In general the 'plot' is derived from one or more of the *Idylls*, e.g. iii from *Id.* iv and v, viii from *Id.* i and ii, ix from *Id.* vii. The phraseology is based on that of the *Idylls* imitated, but with frequent additions from other *Idylls*. Sometimes the translation is close (in 8. 58 perhaps a mistranslation), sometimes there is a free paraphrase, sometimes an idea is adopted and worked out independently. The 'amoebean' dialogue is frequently employed and the setting and scenery are for the most part Sicilian. The general influence of the Alexandrian school is seen in the use of 'literary' epithets, and metrically in the frequency of the 'bucolic diaeresis' and the employment of Greek forms of hiatus and line-terminations.

But with this close adherence to Theocritus Virgil has combined an Italian realistic element. Mantua, Cremona, and the river Mincius appear amid Sicilian scenery, and contemporary personages are either disguised as shepherds (e.g. Tityrus in i and Menalcas in ix are probably Virgil himself and Daphnis in v Julius Caesar), or appear in person, Pollio in iii and viii, Gallus in vi and x, Varus in vi and ix (the Varus of vi may be Quintilius and not Alfenus), while the rival poets Bavius and Mevius are mentioned in iii. Moreover, contemporary events are introduced; i and ix are concerned with the evictions round Mantua and with Virgil's appeal to Octavian, v is probably a reference to the deification of Julius Caesar, whose 'star' is referred to again in ix. 47, and iv prophesies the birth of a boy, under whose rule the world will be at peace. (The child has usually been taken to be the expected offspring of Octavian and Scribonia, who proved in fact to be a daughter, but there is much to be said for the recent suggestion (W. W. Tarn, *JRS* 1932, 154) that it was the expected child of Antony and Octavia.) Further, not only is Theocritus imitated, but also Latin writers, and in particular Lucretius in the cosmological passage of vi, which nevertheless is not necessarily to be regarded as Epicurean. In vi, too, there are allusions to the *Ciris*, which some recent critics believe to have been the work of Gallus.

But with all this confusion of Greek and Italian elements, of ideal pastoral with present-day history, the *Eclogues* show much of Virgil's art and charm, and in spite of an occasional jarring note they have a characteristic tone and unity.

(3) *Georgics* (Γεωργικά, 'husbandry'), a poem in four books, dealing with the farmer's life and occupations, written from 36 to 29 B.C. The first book deals with the cultivation of crops, the second with that of fruit-trees, especially of the vine, the third with the farm animals, including horses, and the fourth with bee-keeping.

The *Georgics* are often said to be based on the *Works and Days* of Hesiod, and Virgil himself claims (2. 176) that he is 'singing the song of Ascra through the towns of Rome', but the relation is much less close than that of the *Eclogues* to the *Idylls* of Theocritus. Two passages in bk. i, the description of the plough (169–75) and the account of the days of the month favourable or unfavourable for work (276–86), are directly imitated from Hesiod, and here and there a phrase or a precept is due to him.

But if Virgil truly owes a debt to Hesiod, it is rather for the main idea of a didactic poem on agriculture, and for the generally pervasive spirit of hard work. In direct imitation Virgil owed almost more to three Alexandrian poets. From Aratus' *Diosemeia* ('Signs of the Sky') he took much of the matter for the discussion of prognostics of the weather (1. 204 ff.), in a section of which (375–87) he closely followed a Latin translation by Varro Atacinus; from the *Phaenomena* come some lines in the description of the *mundus* (1. 244–6). From Eratosthenes comes the description of the zones of the sky (1. 233–51). To Nicander's *Georgica* Virgil may have owed something, and in bk. iv to his *Melissurgica*. In the *Georgics*, too, Virgil begins his imitation of Homer, especially in similes and in the narration of the story of Aristaeus (4. 315–558), which according to Servius was substituted for a eulogy of Gallus, after he had fallen into disgrace.

Much of the subject-matter of the *Georgics* is due to the Latin prose-writers on agriculture, Cato and Varro, though it is not easy to point to obvious imitation. Of other Latin authors Virgil now draws upon Ennius, and all the four books are full of reminiscences of Lucretius, to whom he addresses a famous eulogy in 2. 490–2.

Notwithstanding this debt to other writers, the *Georgics* are Virgil's own and many critics have regarded them as his greatest work. There has been much discussion whether they form a practical guide to husbandry, but at least Virgil must have drawn on his own experience on his father's farm. Metre and expression are freer and more mature than in the *Eclogues*, the books are full of observation of animals and of nature, and in many passages there is the characteristic Virgilian pathos and sympathy. The grandeur of the whole conception and many sustained portions of the writing can bear comparison with the *Aeneid*.

(4) **Aeneid,** 'The story of Aeneas', the title, *Aenēis*, being modelled on 'Ιλιάς and 'Οδύσσεια. The connexion of the Trojans and Aeneas with Rome first appears in Latin literature in Naevius. As soon as Rome came into contact with Greece, there was a desire to associate the history of Rome with the Greek world, but politically a connexion with the Trojans, the enemies of the Greeks, was more natural than with the Greeks themselves. Aeneas, the son of Anchises and Aphrodite, is the one Trojan hero in the *Iliad* with a future, and a kingdom is prophesied for his descendants (*Il.* 20. 307). The story of his wanderings may have been based on the dissemination at different spots in Greece of the cult of Aphrodite Aeneas (*see* AENEAS 1); this would bring him to Sicily, from whence it was no long step to Cumae and to Rome.

Virgil adopted this story as the most comprehensive legend of the origins of Rome—that of Romulus was too local and too narrow—but he intended his poem to be much more than the mere narration of an ancient legend. The *Aeneid* is in fact an epic of Rome, the embodiment of its history and greatness in the past (see especially the parade of the Roman heroes in 6. 756 ff. and the scenes on the shield of Aeneas, 8. 626 ff.), and of the prevailing sense of a new era inaugurated by Augustus. It is a mistake to regard the *Aeneid* as an allegory—Aeneas is not a mere puppet-reproduction of Augustus—but the new hope is never absent.

The *Aeneid* may be said to be based on Homer. The first six books, which relate Aeneas' wanderings, are modelled on the first half of the *Odyssey*, culminating in a similar way in a visit to the lower world, and adopting in ii and iii the device of a personal narrative by the hero, whereas the last six, which tell the story of the war with the Rutulians, are modelled on the *Iliad*. In detail, too, there are many echoes of Homer in the phraseology and particularly in the similes. Other Greek writers are also laid under contribution, Apollonius Rhodius' description of the love of Jason and Medea assisting in the composition of iv. In the *Aeneid*, too, Virgil embodies far more frequently than in the earlier poems the phrases and thoughts of his Latin predecessors. Lucretius is still imitated, and now the older writers find their place, expecially Ennius, and occasionally Naevius, Pacuvius, and Lucilius. This embodiment of the work of his predecessors is not to be regarded as 'plagiarism', but rather as a compliment to those whose words are enshrined. The *Aeneid* commemorates the literature as well as the history of Rome.

The books of the *Aeneid* were not written by Virgil in the order in which they now stand, and it is not difficult to discover inconsistencies of narrative between them. The general plan of the structure of the poem seems to be that the even-numbered books are more thrilling and dramatic, the odd quieter and lower in tone. On the whole, the poem fails as a story, partly perhaps through its length and the magnitude of the conception, partly because of the inevitable artificiality of the 'learned' epic as opposed to the straightforward simplicity of Homer. But it rises from time to time to magnificent heights, and bks. ii, iv, vi, and xii will always stand out as unsurpassed.

The character of Aeneas and his insistent 'piety' have always proved a stumbling-block to modern readers, who feel an instinctive sympathy with his opponent Turnus (as with Hector in the *Iliad*), and with the deserted Dido. But to a Roman reader Aeneas' duty to the gods and to the destiny of Rome would rightly override his personal inclinations, and a closer study of the poem shows a continual development in his character, as his destiny is revealed to him. Book vi, in which he first comes to realize the future greatness of Rome, is the pivot of the poem; from that time he has a new confidence and decision, which raise him to the rank of a hero. Many of the minor characters are finely drawn—Turnus and Dido, Pallas, Mezentius, Nisus, and Euryalus.

In the *Aeneid* Virgil reaches the full command of Latin poetic diction and of the hexameter as its vehicle. The *ars* of the Alexandrians and the genuine Latin *ingenium* are welded into a whole, which alike in its uniformity and its variety stands out as essentially Latin. If the poem as a whole lacks the unity of the *Georgics*, yet in the grandeur of its theme and the perfection of its execution it must be looked on as Virgil's greatest work.

8. Virgil's merits were fully acknowledged by his contemporaries (see, e.g., Hor. *Sat.* 1. 10. 44, Prop. 2. 34. 65), and he became the inevitable model for all subsequent Latin writers of epic and even influenced the style of prose-writers like Livy. Posterity has acknowledged him as the greatest of Roman poets. His style is that of the 'learned' poet; his mind was stocked with ancient legends and associations and he makes full use of them, often applying the 'local epithet' where it has no immediate significance; his syntax and his phraseology are deeply influenced by his predecessors both Greek and Latin. But his learning never degenerates, as it did with some of his contemporaries, into pedantry or frigidity; he is master of his tools and shapes his work to that delicacy and subtlety of expression which has always been recognized as 'Virgilian'. He attained the full perfection of technique in the writing of hexameters and gave them a smoothness which is never monotonous. His themes in *Georgics* and *Aeneid* were lofty, and he treated them with majesty and dignity and at the same time with a sympathetic insight and feeling which were all his own. It was this quality of tenderness, humanity, and deep religious sentiment, together with the supposed Messianic prophecy of *Eclogue* iv, which caused him to be regarded in the Middle Ages as the herald of Christianity, and led Dante to choose him as his guide in the *Divina Commedia*. A debased form of this reverence looked upon him as a magician, and legends gathered round his tomb at Naples. He soon became a school text-book and was selected by later writers as the standard of Latin grammar. Modern criticism has revealed difficulties and weaknesses in his work, but has done nothing to dislodge him from his position in the small company of the greatest poets of the world.

See also ALEXANDRIANISM; DIDACTIC POETRY, LATIN; EPIC POETRY; EPYLLION; PASTORAL POETRY, LATIN.

BIBLIOGRAPHY

TEXTS: O. Ribbeck (1894–5), A. Hirtzel (1900), G. Janell (1920), R. Sabbadini (1930).
COMMENTARIES: Servius, ed. G. Thilo and H. Hagen (1881–7), J. Conington, revised by H. Nettleship and F. Haverfield (latest editions 1883–98). *Aeneid*: J. Henry *Aeneidea* (1873–89), J. W. Mackail (1930). Separate books: *Aen.* i, R. S. Conway (1935); iv, A. S. Pease (U.S.A. 1935); vi, E. Norden (3rd ed. 1926), H. E. Butler (1920); vii, viii, xii, W. Warde Fowler (1916, 1917, 1919).
TRANSLATIONS. *Verse*: J. Dryden, J. Rhoades (1893). *Prose*: J. W. Mackail (1889, 1905), J. Jackson (1908).
LEXICONS: H. Merguet (1912), M. N. Wetmore (U.S.A. 2nd ed. 1930).
ANCIENT LIVES: ed. H. Nettleship (1879), E. Diehl (1911), J. Brummer (1912).
CRITICAL ESSAYS: W. Y. Sellar (3rd ed. 1897), T. R. Glover (5th ed. 1923), Tenney Frank (1927).
SPECIAL STUDIES: F. Skutsch, *Aus Vergils Frühzeit* (1901); B. Nardi, *The Youth of Virgil* (tr. B. P. Rand, U.S.A. 1930); R. Heinze, *Virgils epische Technik*[2] (1928); T. F. Royds, *Beasts, Birds and Bees of Virgil*[2] (1914); J. Sargeaunt, *Trees, Shrubs and Plants of Virgil* (1920); C. Bailey, *Religion in Virgil* (1935); J. B. Mayor, R. S. Conway, and W. Warde Fowler, *Virgil's Messianic Eclogue* (1907); J. Sparrow, *Half-lines and Repetitions in Virgil* (1931); D. Comparetti, *Virgil in the Middle Ages* (tr. E. F. M. Benecke, 1895); H. J. Rose, *The Eclogues of Virgil* (1942). C. B.

VIRIATHUS, a shepherd, led the Lusitanian rebellion against the Romans which Ser. Sulpicius Galba's butcheries had provoked in 150 B.C. The first to utilize guerrilla tactics in the mountains, a form of warfare for which Romans were not prepared, Viriathus also profited by the wars in which Rome was entangled in Africa and in Greece. He beat a series of Roman governors in Spain and mastered nearly all Hispania Ulterior and part of Citerior. In 145 Rome sent out a consul, Q. Fabius Maximus Aemilianus, and two legions. Viriathus lost liberty of movement (144), but the extension of the rebellion to the Celtiberians gave his effort new life, although the two peoples never co-operated effectively. In 143–142 a general, Quinctius (probably the consul Q. Caecilius Metellus Macedonicus), and the consul L. Caecilius Metellus Calvus were defeated. In 141 Viriathus forced the proconsul, Q. Fabius Maximus Servilianus to surrender. A treaty was concluded in which full possession of their territory was recognized to the Lusitanians, and Viriathus was styled an ally and friend of the Roman People. But in 140 the consul Cn. Servilius Caepio induced the Senate to break the pact and renewed the war. Viriathus' army was now exhausted. Viriathus, whose political ability was inferior to his military skill, hoped for a new peace. He sent three friends to Caepio, but they were bribed to murder him. He was killed sleeping and his unorganized State collapsed (139).

The principal source is Appian, *Hisp.* 60 ff. (from Polybius: the beginning of § 66 is hopelessly corrupt). Cf. *Fontes Hispaniae Antiquae* iv (Barcelona 1937); A. Schulten, *Neue Jahrb.* 1917, 209 (fundamental); id. *CAH* ix. 314; Kromayer, *Schlachten Atlas*, col. 56. For the chronology, E. Kornemann, *Klio*, Beiheft ii (1904), 96; F. Münzer, *PW* vi. 1811. A. M.

VIROCONIUM (*Uriconium*), town in Roman Britain, modern *Wroxeter* (Shropshire). The site was occupied c. 48–9 (cf. *Antiquaries Journal* xviii. 34) by a fortress of the fourteenth and twentieth legions which has not been located. It was succeeded by a town, itself the successor perhaps of a neighbouring hill-fort, the Wrekin, which became the cantonal capital of the Cornovii. This town, built c. 80, had an earth-bank and timber houses, but very ambitious public buildings were intended. They were not completed, and by 130 a less ambitious forum and basilica was built (cf. *JRS* xiv. 244). Houses were now rebuilt in stone, and a stone town-wall was added enclosing *c.* 107 acres. The new basilica was burnt and rebuilt *c.* 160 and burnt finally *c.* 300. The town itself seems to have decayed to annihilation. Coins of Carausius with mint-mark BRI have been claimed for Viroconium (= Briconium) (*Num. Chron.*⁵ v. 336).

Summary of old excavations, *Victoria County History, Shropshire*, i. 220–52, later Bushe-Fox, *1st, 2nd, and 3rd Reports*; K. M. Kenyon, *Excavations at Wroxeter*, 1936 and 1937. D. Atkinson, *Report on Excavations at Wroxeter (Viroconium), 1923–7* (1942). No full report of forum excavations (Atkinson), summary in Macdonald, *Roman Britain* (1914–28), 89–97. C. E. S.

VIRTUS and HONOS, *see* HONOS.

VITELLIUS (1), AULUS (A.D. 15–69), emperor in A.D. 69, was a friend of Gaius and Claudius. He was consul in 48, proconsul in Africa and legate there under his brother. In 68 he was sent by Galba to command the legions of Lower Germany. On 2 Jan. 69 he was hailed as emperor by his troops, at the instigation of his legates Caecina Alienus and Fabius Valens, and was immediately recognized by Upper Germany. He obtained the adherence of Gaul, Raetia, and Spain. His expeditionary force to Italy had started before news arrived of Galba's death. Caecina and Valens converged on north Italy and easily overcame Otho (q.v.). Vitellius was still in Germany when he heard of the victory. His march to Rome (May–June) was like that of a conqueror. He posed as the successor of Nero and later adopted the title of *consul perpetuus*. He humiliated the defeated soldiers, and doubled his mistake by not dismissing them. He disbanded only the Praetorians and *cohortes urbanae*. He was incompetent and became notorious for his gluttony. The Eastern legions swore allegiance to him, yet immediately afterwards they hailed Vespasian (q.v.) as their emperor. The Danubian troops, many of whom had fought for Otho, went over to Vespasian and invaded Italy under Antonius Primus. Valens was ill, and Vitellius had to rely on Caecina, who was plotting with the commander of the fleet at Ravenna. Vitellius, with four legions, decided to hold the line of the Po at Cremona and Hostilia. The troops at Hostilia refused to support the treacherous course which Caecina proposed, and retired to Cremona after having arrested their commander. A battle before Cremona, with a demoralized army, was a defeat for the absent Vitellius (Oct. 69). Valens, who had recovered, failed to organize a second army in Gaul. In Germany Civilis (q.v.) rose in arms. The fleet at Misenum abandoned Vitellius. In Rome, Vespasian's brother, Flavius Sabinus (q.v.), had nearly persuaded Vitellius to abdicate, but the mob compelled him to remain. Vitellius had to attack Sabinus in the Capitol, where the temple of Jupiter was burned. Primus arrived and defeated the Vitellians after a desperate resistance. Vitellius was discovered hiding, led through the Forum and cruelly killed (20 Dec. 69).

Sources: Suetonius, *Vitellius*, etc. *See further under* GALBA. A. M.

VITELLIUS (2), LUCIUS (*cos.* A.D. 34, *cos.* II 43, *cos.* III 47), son of P. Vitellius (a Roman knight from Nuceria, procurator of Augustus), was an intimate friend of the Emperor Claudius and the most successful politician of the age: when he died he was honoured with a public funeral and a statue in the Forum bearing the inscription 'pietatis immobilis erga principem' (Suetonius, *Vitellius* 3). Legate of Syria from A.D. 35 to 37, he displayed great vigour, dealing firmly with Parthian affairs, inducing Artabanus to pay homage to Rome and conciliating the Jews: 'regendis prouinciis prisca uirtute egit' (Tac. *Ann.* 6. 32). At Rome, however, he earned a different reputation—'exemplar apud posteros adulatorii dedecoris habetur' (ibid.). Claudius chose him for colleague in the censorship (47). Vitellius had a large share in

devising the ruin of Valerius Asiaticus; and, cleverly adopting the cause of Agrippina, he acted as the mouthpiece of a loyal Senate in advocating her marriage to Claudius. He probably died soon after. R. S.

VITICULTURE. The vine and its cultivation were known in Eastern Mediterranean countries as far back as the neolithic period. Minoan Crete had vines in plenty, as had the larger landowners of the periods of Homer and Hesiod. In many parts of Greece, and in Italy after 150 B.C. grapes were a more important crop than corn. Famous wines came from Cos, Cnidos, Thasos, Chios, Lesbos, Rhodes, Ephesus, and Aminea, Berytus and Laodicea, Tarraco in Spain, several districts of Sicily, the *Falernus mons* in Campania, etc. Plantations in which vines grew side by side with fruit-trees and vegetables were often preferred to those confined to the vine alone, though these became more usual after the Hellenistic age. The plantations were enclosed by walls or fences. The methods of Greco-Roman culture are familiar to us from the recorded practice of Hellenistic Egypt and Roman Italy, which later spread to the Roman provinces.

Many species of vines were known, some being imported. In laying out a vineyard the land was first ploughed and dug over, and provision was made for irrigation. Then the vines were planted into long trenches and bound with bast to reeds or stakes or (as often in Greece and Italy) to trees, and subsequently pruned. The whole vineyard was next dug over and manured, and the soil was loosened (*ablaqueatio*) so as to lead more water to the roots. There followed a second digging, a picking off of young sterile shoots. a third digging, a second picking of shoots. The vines were tied up and a thorough irrigation undertaken before the crop was harvested. The vineyards had to be well guarded against thieves, a precaution as necessary then as it is to-day. In course of time new vines had to be planted to replace those that had died. An Italian model vineyard of *c.* 66 acres described by Cato needed 2 oxen, 3 asses, and many implements, with a slave overseer, his wife, and 16 slaves to work it.

States took a great interest in viticulture. A law of Thasos dating from the fourth century B.C. protected native growers by forbidding the import of foreign, and regulating dealings in home-produced wines. Rome seems to have put restrictions on viticulture in certain areas outside Italy with a similar view. Ptolemaic Egypt introduced heavy duties on wine imports, together with State control of the culture of vines in the Nile country by imposing a special tax, the *apomoira*.

See AGRICULTURE. For the Thasian wine-law see *BCH* xlv (1921), 46. S. Loeschke, *Denkmäler vom Weinbau aus der Zeit der Römerherrschaft an Mosel, Saar und Ruwer* (1934); P. Remark, 'Der Weinbau im Römerreich' (*Tusculum Schriften* 13–15; 1927). F. M. H.

VITIUM, in augury, *see* AUSPICIUM.

VITRASIUS, *see* POMPONIUS (6).

VITRUVIUS POLLIO, a Roman architect and military engineer under Augustus. He built a basilica at Fanum; but his fame rests chiefly on a treatise, *De architectura*, on architecture and engineering, compiled partly from his own experience, and partly from similar works by Hermogenes (q.v.) and other noted architects, mostly Greeks. His outlook is essentially Hellenistic, and there is a marked absence of reference to important buildings of Augustus' reign. *De architectura*, the only work of its kind which has survived, is divided into ten books. Book i treats of town-planning, architecture in general, and of the qualifications proper in an architect; ii of building-materials; iii and iv of temples and of the 'Orders'; v of other civic buildings; vi of domestic buildings; vii of pavements and decorative plaster-work;

viii of water-supplies; ix of geometry, mensuration, astronomy, etc.; x of machines, civil and military. The information on materials and methods of construction in ii and vii, and on rules of proportion in iii and iv is of great value. Many editions of Vitruvius have been published since 1486. There is a good translation by J. H. Morgan (U.S.A. 1914).   H. W. R.

VOCONIUS ROMANUS, an able orator in Pliny's circle who wrote letters which read as if the Muses were speaking in Latin (*Ep.* 2. 13. 7)—a hint at the propriety of a poetic ingredient in letter-writing.

VOLATERRAE (Etruscan *Velathri*) was the most northern Etruscan lordship. From its formidable position, 1,800 feet above the sea, it commanded a huge area including the sea-port Luna and perhaps Populonia. Important in the eighth century, it is seldom mentioned before Cicero (*Dom.* 30). It was the native town of the Caecina family, and birthplace of Persius. Surviving tracts of ancient wall and remarkable gateways may be assigned very conjecturally to 300 B.C. In the Florence Museum are contents of several important graves of 900–800 B.C. But hundreds of alabaster sarcophagi of 300 and 200 B.C. in the local museum are aesthetically degenerate.   D. R.-MacI.

VOLCACIUS (1) **SEDIGITUS** (*fl. c.* 100 B.C.) is the author of thirteen senarii, in which ten writers of the *comoedia palliata* are enumerated and characterized by him with great self-confidence. Gellius (15. 24) quotes the verses from V.'s lost work *De poetis.* In his list Caecilius Statius is first, Plautus second, Naevius third, Licinius fourth, Atilius fifth, Terence sixth, Turpilius seventh, Trabea eighth, Luscius ninth, and Ennius tenth 'causa antiquitatis' (cf. Suet. *Vit. Ter.* 7). These lines are almost all that we have of this eccentric critic of early Roman poetry.

See Baehrens, *FPR* (Teubner, 1886); W. Morel, *FPL* (Teubner, 1927).   A. S.

VOLCACIUS (2) **MOSCHUS,** rhetor, a Greek from Pergamum (Porphyr. ad. Hor. *Epist.* 1. 5. 9) who owed Roman citizenship perhaps to Volcacius Tullus the consul of 33 B.C. (Kiessling, *Hermes* xxvi, 634–5). Exiled after a trial for poisoning, he opened a school at Marseilles, where he died about A.D. 25. A speaker of some distinction but too much concerned with tricks of style (Sen. *Controv.* 10 pr. 10, 2. 5. 13; Tac. *Ann.* 4. 43).
                                                  C. J. F.

VOLCANUS (VOLKANUS, VULCANUS), an ancient Italian fire-god, apparently of volcanic fire (this would explain why he is worshipped at Puteoli, near the *zolfatare,* Strabo 5. 246; perhaps also his association with Maia, Gellius 13. 23. 2, 'Maiam Volcani', if her name is to be derived from rt. *MAG* and explained as the power which makes something, perhaps crops, increase; cf. also Pliny, *HN* 2. 240, fire comes out of the ground near Mutina 'statis Volcano diebus'), certainly of destructive fire, which explains why his temple should always stand outside a city (Vitruvius 1. 7. 1), on the authority of the Etruscan haruspices. He was worshipped at Rome from the earliest known times, having a flamen (q.v.) and a festival, the Volcanalia, on 23 Aug. (calendars). His shrine, the Volcanal, stood in the Comitium, i.e. outside the Servian walls; a newer one was in the Campus Martius (see for both Platner–Ashby, p. 583 f.). His name is certainly not Latin, the nearest to it in sound being the Cretan ϝελχανός (for whom see A. B. Cook, *Zeus* ii. 946 ff.), who, however, seems to have no resemblance to him in functions. For Etruscan names suggesting Volcanus see Altheim, *Griechische Götter,* p. 172. It is thus possible, but unproved, that he came in from the eastern Mediterranean, through Etruria. He seems to have been worshipped principally to avert fires, hence his by-name Mulciber ('qui ignem mulcet'), his title Quietus, and his association with Stata Mater (Dessau, *ILS* 3295, 3306), apparently the goddess who makes fires stand still. On the Volcanalia, when sacrifice was also made to Juturna, the Nymphs, Ops Opifera, and Quirinus, he was given a curious and (at least for Rome), unexampled sacrifice, live fish from the Tiber being flung into a fire (see calendars and Varro, *Ling.* 6. 20, Festus, p. 274, 35 ff. Lindsay). This also can be readily explained as an offering of creatures usually safe from him to induce him to spare those things which at so hot a time of year are particularly liable to be burned. He had a considerable cult at Ostia, where he seems to have been the chief god (J. Carcopino, *Virgile et les origines d'Ostie,* 42 ff.). In classical times he is fully identified with Hephaestus, q.v.

Wissowa in Roscher's *Lexikon,* s.v.; Rose in *JRS* 1933, 46 ff.
                                                  H. J. R.

VOLERO, see PUBLILIUS (1).

VOLOGESES I, King of Parthia, A.D. 52—*c.* 80. Much of his reign was spent in wars with Rome and on his eastern frontier. In 54 Vologeses set his brother Tiridates (q.v. 3) on the throne of Armenia (Tac. *Ann.* 13. 6). Cn. Corbulo (q.v.), sent to re-establish Roman influence, was at first successful, Vologeses being occupied on his eastern frontier with a rebellion. Tiridates fled, and a Roman nominee Tigranes (q.v. 4) was crowned. But Vologeses returned to continue the war, and at one time gained an advantageous treaty from Corbulo's colleague Paetus. Finally peace was made and Tiridates did homage to Nero for his throne. Vologeses' later relations with Rome were friendlier; he sought Vespasian's help against the invading Alani (Suet. *Domitian* 2. 2). In his reign Zoroastrianism made great advances, and the books of the Avesta were collected. He founded Vologesocerta near Babylon, as a commercial rival to Seleuceia.

On the wars with Corbulo see M. Hammond, *Harv. Stud.* xlv (1934); A. Momigliano, *Atti del II° congresso naz. di studi romani* i (1931), 368–75; W. Schur, *Klio* xix (1925), 75–96, and xx (1926), 215–22.   M. S. D.

VOLSCI descended from central Italy in the sixth century B.C. and by 500 had established themselves in the middle Liris valley and regions south-east of the Alban Hills. Chief towns: Sora, Arpinum, Atina, Privernum, Ecetra, Antium, Circeii, Anxur (= Tarracina), Velitrae, and possibly Suessa Pometia. Casual mention of Volsci in regal times is untrustworthy, but thereafter they became, and for 200 years remained, a threat which Rome met by signing an alliance with Latins and Hernici c. 493 (see CASSIUS 1). The Aequi (q.v.) aided the Volsci. Fifth-century Volscian operations are known only from garbled Roman accounts; but Coriolanus' exploits and defensive Latin colonies at Signia (495), Norba (492), and Ardea (442) imply Volscian successes. In 431, however, the Latin allies defeated the Aequi, then repulsed the Volsci; Latin colonies at Circeii (393), Satricum (385), Setia (382) mark their advance. Volsci opposed Rome in the Latin War, but were defeated by C. Maenius (q.v.). By 304 all Volsci were subject to Rome and so rapid and complete was their romanization that their original civilization can scarcely be discovered. The surviving specimen of their language displays affinities with Umbrian (cf. Festus, p. 204 L.). Their degree of political unity is uncertain. Usually they are represented as a united nation; yet apparently some Volscian cities were left to face Rome unaided, e.g. Pometia and Ecetra in the fifth century, Antium and Privernum in the fourth.

Diodors Römische Annalen, ed. Drachmann xi. 37—xiv. 102; Livy, bks. 2–8; Dion. Hal., bks. 6–11, 14. *CAH* vii, passim (H. Last); R. S. Conway, *Italic Dialects* i (1897), 267. For their alleged Illyrian origin see Serv. ad *Aen.* 12. 842; J. Whatmough, *Foundations of Roman Italy* (1937), 300.   E. T. S.

VOLSINII, an Etruscan city; the original site was probably Orvieto. Only after the conquest of this strong fortress and rebellious people in 280 B.C. was the community transported to the Lago di Bolsena (cf. the Roman treatment of the Faliscans). The Romans are said to have looted 2,000 statues from Volsinii, but only one head is now in the museum of Florence. Somewhere near Bolsena, perhaps at Montefiascone, was the Fanum Voltumnae, the shrine of an Etruscan god at which the heads of the Confederation held their meetings.

D. R.-MacI.

VOLTACILIUS PITHOLAUS (? *Plotus*, Reifferscheid), Lucius, according to Nepos the first freedman to write history, opened a school of rhetoric, 81 B.C. He had as a pupil Pompeius Magnus, whose biography, as well as his father's, he wrote (Suet. *Rhet.* 3).

VOLTUMNA, an Etruscan goddess, at whose shrine the Etruscan federal council met (Livy 4. 23. 5; 25. 7; 61. 2; 5. 17. 6; 6. 2. 2). Nothing more is known of her and the site of the shrine is uncertain (*see* VOLSINII).

See L. R. Taylor, *Local Cults of Etruria* (1923), 230 ff.

VOLUBILIS (Modern *Oubili*), a Moorish agricultural town in the Djebel Zerhoun plain. Phoenician colonists joined with the natives to make it a centre of the oil-trade. Greek bronzes excavated at Volubilis point to its inclusion in the dominions of Juba II. Governed successively by shophets (*suffetes*), shophet-duumvirs, and duumvirs, it was rewarded by Claudius with the rank of *municipium* for its loyalty during Aedemon's rebellion. The beautiful arch of Caracallus and Julia Domna testifies to its prosperity under the Severi.

A. Momigliano, *Claudius* (1934), 66, 114; L. Chatelain, *Le Maroc des romains* (1944), 139–250. W. N. W.

VOLUMNIUS, Publius, a philosopher who accompanied M. Brutus in his campaign against the triumvirs. He recorded, perhaps in a biography, prodigies which preceded Brutus' last battle (Plut. *Brut.* 48).

VOLUSIUS, *see* MAECIANUS.

VOTIENUS MONTANUS, orator, from Narbo; prosecuted for treason under Tiberius; died in exile, A.D. 27. He condemned the showiness of declamations (Sen. *Controv.* 9. *praef.* 1). His passion for repetitions which did not leave well alone led to his being called 'the Ovid of speakers'.

See *PIR*, V 674. J. W. D.

VOTING. (1) *In Greek city-states* most resolutions of the Assembly, as well as elections of magistracies, were decided by show of hands (χειροτονία), in some rare cases by acclamation, e.g. in the case of the Spartan ephors. For questions concerning individuals (ἐπ' ἀνδρί), voting was accomplished by secret ballot (ψήφισμα from ψῆφος = voting-stone); but already in early times *all* decrees of people were so called. The same method was used for passing sentences by juries, and voting by sherds was similar (*see* OSTRACISM). V. E.

(2) *At Rome* voting took place in the assemblies of the *curiae*, centuries, and tribes. The procedure was roughly the same, especially after the introduction of the ballot in the latter half of the second century B.C. It was generally preceded by a *contio* (q.v.). When the presiding magistrate dissolved this and ordered the voting to begin (*discedere*), non-citizens were summoned to withdraw (*populus summouetur*), and ropes were stretched across the Assembly to divide it into as many enclosures as there were centuries or tribes. According to the formalities of the polling, voters then entered the enclosures, called at first *licium*, then *ovile*, and finally *saepta* (q.v.). Under Augustus a *diribitorium* was constructed on the Campus Martius for the tellers (*diribitores*). The enclosures were connected with the platform of the magistrate by galleries (*pontes*). In each compartment the votes were taken singly and orally, and officials called *rogatores* marked off the names of the candidates on special tablets (*ferre punctum*). From 139 to 107 B.C. several *leges tabellariae* were enacted to secure secrecy of vote, which had to be written on official tablets (*tabellae*). The formulas, however, did not change: in legislation, *Uti rogas* (V.) and *antiquo* (A.), this negative answer properly meaning: 'I confirm the old state of things'; in jurisdiction *libero* (L.) and *damno* or *condemno* (hence the abbreviated form C.); in elections, *dico* or *facio*. A century named *praerogativa* (q.v.) voted first. The tablets were then thrown into an urn (*cista*) at the exit of each *pons* under the control of guardians (*custodes*), who forwarded it to the *diribitores*. They counted the votes until a relative majority was obtained. A system of group-voting was characteristic: a majority of votes in a century determined the vote of that century, and a majority of the centuries determined the will of the whole Assembly. Voting was allowed only between sunrise and sunset, on days especially appointed in the Calendar.

Mommsen, *Röm. Staatsr.* iii². 397 ff.; G. W. Botsford, *The Roman Assemblies* (1909), 466 ff. P. T.

VOTIVE OFFERINGS are gifts of a permanent character to supernatural beings (ἀναθήματα, later ἀναθέματα, as distinct from δῶρα, gifts to human beings), thus differing from sacrifices and taxes (tithes and first-fruits are here not included). They have their source in religious feeling and in the worship of divine powers affecting man as benefactors and protectors or the opposite. This dedication is a voluntary act, but it may have been recommended by religious tradition or sometimes ordered by an oracle (e.g. for unbelief, breach of religious custom, blood-guilt; cf. the two statues of the Spartan regent Pausanias dedicated in the Brazen House of Athena). For the gods they may mean an increase of their authority: the gift and its publicity 'magnify' the gods, at the same time intensifying the feeling of connexion and sympathy on both sides. The social and merely economical aspect must also be taken into account, and again the often contagious pride and joy of giving and delight in embellishing sanctuaries, especially national centres.

2. The motives generally are: thanksgiving (e.g. for deliverance from sickness, perils on the sea, and all sorts of calamity), intercession (sometimes accompanied by sacrifice, or taking its place, or reminding the deity of it), or propitiation (each Athenian archon swore to dedicate a golden statue, probably not a portrait of himself, if he broke his oath; cf. corresponding sacrifices from similar motives). The occasions are manifold. States (or monarchs) returned thanks for victory in war and thus commemorated other forms of divine aid (so tripods of gold were sent to Delphi after the battles of Plataeae, Himera, Cumae, Diod. 11. 21). Statues of Victory were common as war-dedications (cf. the Athenian temple inventories, the most famous examples being the Nike of Paeonius at Olympia, and the Nike of Samothrace now in the Louvre). The statue of Nemesis at Rhamnus was a memorial of the Persian War, the temple of Athena at Pergamum of the defeat of the Gauls. A crown of honour was dedicated to the Athenian people by 'the Euboeans saved and set free', as Demosthenes informs us (xxiv. 180). The people (alone, or with the Boule) dedicated statues of officials in sacred precincts; later such compliments to the Roman emperors became quite commonplace (at their accession to the throne, on their birthdays, on their visits to the provinces, etc.).

3. We must not forget the many feasts and ceremonials, often annually repeated, which served the State or

private individuals as occasions to show their loyalty or gratitude to the State divinities or national heroes. Many finds of innumerable standardized figures in the earliest strata of ancient shrines may have their origin in such festivals, e.g. miniature reproductions of the cult-image of the temple or other forms of the deity in question (as the votive offerings, to (Artemis) Orthia at Sparta), objects of use, robes (cf. Hecuba's gift to Athena in the *Iliad*), mirrors, weapons, etc., finally the ἀνδριάντες and κόραι of all sizes and different materials (falling into disuse in the 5th c. B.C.). We may especially mention the *peplos* offered at the Panathenaea at Athens. Sacred missions (θεωρίαι, *see* THEOROI) regularly brought with them offerings for dedication, thus supplementing their sacrifices.

4. Private people dedicated on similar principles, for help in disease (cf. the sanctuaries of Asclepius), in danger and every sort of calamity, for good luck and further aid, often accompanying the offering with a prayer and sacrifice for further success. Victories in games and contests of other kinds (cf. the legendary competition between Homer and Hesiod) were eagerly glorified, the offering of the prize becoming traditional and often compulsory (cf. the many statues of athletes, and the Charioteer at Delphi). We may add as appropriate occasions of offering: every great moment or crisis of human life, birth, puberty (e.g. the offering of one's hair), marriage, election to an office, acquittal in court, etc. We only need to look through the well-turned dedicatory poems of bk. vi of the *Anthology* or the treasure-lists of Athens (the treasures of Athena, Artemis Brauronia, or Asclepius), Delos, Delphi to have an impression of the endless varieties of motive; dedication of slaves, chiefly as a form of emancipation, is also to be noted. The holy precincts thus in course of time were filled with gifts; they became real museums. Treasure-houses were built, and in the inner chambers of the temples (the *opisthodomoi*) their always increasing treasures were kept, but still these overflowed. The clearing-up did not mean destroying, since the ex-votos were commonly tabu and accordingly much can still be found by archaeologists within the sacred enclosures.

5. As for the meaning of these ex-votos, and the objects dedicated, they might be of direct use to the god. In myth or history many temples are recorded as being due to the gratitude of heroes, monarchs, cities (Danaus, Heracles, Theseus; the temple of Apollo at Bassae commemorates deliverance from pestilence). We may add altars (often with inscriptions), colonnades, idols, garments for the idols, etc. The throne of Xerxes, the manger of Mardonius, and other trophies were offered to the gods; cf. also the many statues of the Apollo or Kouros type. But pious people dedicated also what had been useful to themselves, thanks to the benevolence of a god or the gods; artisans their tools, etc. (also specimens of their skill and their gains), a shipowner an image of his ship (cf. Catullus 4; Agamemnon dedicated his rudder to Hera at Samos), a courtesan her mirror—in general things well used or now useless, or but once used (so a cauldron used for the bride's bath before marriage) and for ever to be remembered. Acts, blessed by the gods (birth, victory, etc.) were also thus immortalized, and a representation of a sacrifice offered to the god was as good as the sacrifice itself. We easily imagine how important an impulse was in this way given to art (e.g. sculpture) and even to poetry. The historians drew facts from the inscriptions employed, and the makers of legend a fresh start for their imagination (cf. the Lindian

temple-chronicle). The homage thus paid to the gods is also a reliable barometer as to the curve of religious feeling in antiquity (as to-day in the Catholic Church). The parallelism with the offerings to the dead is noteworthy.

E. Reisch, *Griechische Weihgeschenke* (1890). The chief work is W. H. D. Rouse, *Greek Votive Offerings* (1902). S. E.

VOTUM. Greeks and Romans alike made promises to gods that, if this or that favour was granted, they would do this or that act in return, and felt under an obligation to do as they had promised. Nevertheless, the practical and juridical character of Roman religion, as distinct from Greek, is seen in the Roman public use of vows, *uota*, public or private, which oblige either of the two parties engaged in the act to keep the bargain if the god (or gods) is willing, and even in the formulae of many private vows: *u(otum) s(oluit) l(ibens) m(erito)* and in the phrases *uoti reus, uoti damnatus*. The reciprocity involves the State (or the private individual) taking the initiative. In the name of the State the magistrate undertakes to offer to the god or the gods sacrifices, games, the building of a temple, the dedication of an altar, a share of the booty, or some other thing if the god on his side will give his assistance in winning the war, averting the famine or pestilence, achieving some success, etc. The publicity of such vows was compulsory. The vows made by the State were in most cases extraordinary, but vows were also made regularly for a definite period, e.g. the annually renewed *uota* of the higher magistrates for the welfare of the State (on 1 January, before the first regular sitting of the Senate) and the *uota* at the termination of the *lustrum*. The periodicity of public *uota* may originate in the terms defined for the magistrates. Such vows found their direct continuation under the Empire in the *uota pro salute imperatoris* (for the emperor and his family, since 30 B.C., the periodicity becoming regular *uota quinquennalia, decennalia*, etc.). Vows for the safe return of the emperor (from expeditions or war), for his health, his reign, for the delivery of the empress, etc. were customary. The text of the *uotum* was regularly fixed in the presence of the pontifices, and the document went into the archives. As modalities of the *uotum* we have to consider the devotion of the enemy's army (*see* DEVOTIO) and the evocation of the gods of a besieged city (*see* EVOCATIO). Good examples of private vows are Verg. *Aen.* 5. 235 (Cloanthus vows a bull if he wins the boat-race) and Hor. *Carm.* 1. 5.

G. Wissowa, *RK* 380 ff. J. Toutain, art. 'Votum' in Dar.-Sag. W. Warde Fowler, *The Religious Experience of the Roman People*, 200 ff. S. E.

VULCA, *see* VEII.

VULCI, unknown in classical literature, was one of the wealthiest Etruscan cities, situated on the Fiora, half-way between Monte Argentario and Tarquinii. The immense cemeteries were ruthlessly sacked by avaricious owners in the mid-nineteenth century, and no records published. Most of what was saved from 20,000 graves found its way eventually to the Louvre and British Museum. This miscellaneous loot consists principally of Greek painted vases and gold ornaments. Unique, except for similar finds from Caere, are the enormous red jars of the seventh century in the Louvre (Campana collection).

G. Dennis, *Cities and Cemeteries of Etruria*; S. Gsell, *Fouilles de Vulci* (1891). D. R.-MacI.

VULSO, *see* MANLIUS (5).

WALL OF ANTONINUS, a Roman frontier-wall, 37 miles long, running from Bridgeness on the Forth to Old Kilpatrick on the Clyde, built for Antoninus Pius (S.H.A. *Pius*, 5. 4) in A.D. 142 by Q. Lollius (q.v. 4) Urbicus. The wall was of turf, standing upon a cobbled foundation 14 feet wide and systematically built (*JRS* xi. 1 f.) in long sectors by Legions II, VI, and XX, who marked their work by inscribed slabs (*CIL* vii. 1088, 1121, 1122, 1126, 1130–3 a, 1135–8, 1140–2). Twenty feet or more in front of the wall lay a ditch, approaching 40 feet wide and not less than 12 feet deep. Forts occur at Carriden, Kinneil, Inveravon, Mumrills (6½ acres), Falkirk, Rough Castle (1 acre), Seabegs, *Castlecary* (3½ acres), Westerwood (2 acres), Croy Hill (1½ acres), Bar Hill (3 acres), Auchendavy (3 acres), Kirkintilloch, Cadder (2 acres), *Balmuildy* (4 acres), New Kilpatrick (3½ acres), Castlehill (1½ acres), Duntocher, Old Kilpatrick (4 acres), those italicized having stone walls. Minor structures are signalling-platforms, occurring in pairs at high points, and a guard-post for the passage of the northward road at Watling Lodge, near Falkirk. Thus, the Antonine Wall is structurally an advance upon Hadrian's Turf Wall (see WALL OF HADRIAN) in its economy of material and rubble foundation, allowing better drainage, while its garrison was distributed in small close-spaced forts instead of large forts and mile-castles. Beyond the wall outpost-forts of the north road were held as far as Strathearn on the east, while on the west a road led towards Dumbarton, to a fortified port as yet unknown. Posts on the flanks are also still undiscovered.

History. Excavation of the forts reveals three periods of occupation, between A.D. 142 and the close of the century. Epigraphy discloses campaigning in the north under Julius Verus in 155–8 (*Eph. Epigr.* ix. 1163, 1230, and 1108, Brough), and this is taken to be the opening of the second period of occupation, though literature also records disturbances in Britain in 162 (S.H.A. *Marcus*, 8. 7), which were suppressed by Calpurnius Agricola (q.v.), not to mention those before the campaigning of 184, when the overthrow of a frontier-wall is mentioned (Dio Cass. 71. 16) and not reflected in the archaeology of Hadrian's Wall. The final abandonment of the wall is represented by an orderly evacuation, in complete contrast with the violent attack upon Hadrian's Wall in 197. This is shown to have followed upon a short occupation.

Sir G. Macdonald, *The Roman Wall in Scotland*[2] (1934).
I. A. R.

WALL OF AURELIAN, the City Wall of Rome, constructed by Aurelian in A.D. 271–5 in anticipation of a sudden barbarian inroad (S.H.A. *Aurel.* 21. 9; 39. 2; Aurel. Vict. *Caes.* 35; Ioh. Malalas, *Chron.* xii, p. 299), was completed by Probus (Zosim. 1. 49). The original wall was some 20 feet high excluding the wide-set battlements. It extended for 12 miles, with 381 rectangular towers, at an interval of *c.* 100 feet, except on the long river-walls. The wall was usually solid but occasionally galleried and sometimes treated as a revetment-wall. It frequently embodied earlier structures, such as the retaining-wall of the Horti Aciliani (*muro torto*), the *castra praetoria*, private houses and tenements, the so-called *amphitheatrum castrense*, the *domus Lateranorum*, and the pyramid-tomb of Cestius. It surrounded the Fourteen Regions, enclosing, however, a relatively small part of *Transtiberim*. The gates, mostly named from the principal roads, were Portae *Flaminia*, Pinciana, Salaria, Nomentana, 'Chiusa', Tiburtina, Praenestina-Labicana, Asinaria, Metrobia, Latina, *Appia*, *Ostiensis*,

Portuensis, Aurelia-Pancraziana, Septimiana, Aurelia-Sancti Petri. All were flanked by simple semicircular towers, those italicized having twin portals originally. There were also at least six postern-gates. The wall was thus designed to repel a raid rather than stand siege. The wall was doubled in height by adding a gallery, while gates were remodelled and fitted with vantage-courts, by Maxentius (A.D. 306–12), who also began a ditch. Wall, and especially gates, were repaired by Stilicho in 401–3 (*CIL* vi. 1188–90; Claud. *VI Cons. Hon.* 529). Later repairs occurred under Valentinian III, probably after the earthquake of 442, and under Theodoric in 507–11. Belisarius, in preparation for the siege of 536, refurbished the wall and dug a large ditch in front of it.

I. A. Richmond, *The City Wall of Imperial Rome* (1930).
I. A. R.

WALL OF HADRIAN, a frontier-wall of Roman Britain, running for 80 Roman miles from Wallsend-on-Tyne to Bowness-on-Solway. Erected in A.D. 122–8, it was first designed to start at *Pons Aelius*, Newcastle-upon-Tyne, the eastern 45 miles being in stone (10 feet thick and some 15 feet high, excluding battlements), and the western 31 miles in turf (20 feet thick at the base and some 12 feet high). Twenty feet in front of the wall ran a V-shaped ditch (27 feet wide and 15 feet deep). Patrols lay in attached fortlets or mile-castles, with towered gates to north, at every 1620 yards, and in intermediate turrets (20 feet square) at every 540 yards. As work progressed, changes came. The Stone Wall was changed to 7½ feet in width, and extended 4 miles eastwards, to Wallsend, and 4 miles westward (replacing the Turf Wall) to Banks. Garrison forts were also built, at Wallsend, Newcastle, *Benwell*, *Rudchester*, *Halton*, *Chesters*, *Housesteads*, Carvoran, *Birdoswald*, Castlesteads, Stanwix, *Burgh-by-Sands*, and *Bowness* (those italicized being of standard pattern for a *cohors milliaria* or an *ala quingenaria*). The rest probably held *cohortes quingenariae* and were soon augmented by Carrawburgh and Greatchesters. Forts and turrets continued down the Cumberland coast to Moresby; outpost-forts existed at Birrens, Netherby, and Bewcastle.

Behind the wall, enclosing all forts but Carvoran on the Stanegate (see below), ran a boundary-ditch (20 feet wide, 10 feet deep, and 8 feet across the flat bottom) with upcast disposed in two equidistant turf-kerbed mounds, 100 feet apart from crest to crest. A patrol-track ran along the south side of the ditch, reached by causeways at the mile-castles. Public passages pierced both mounds at the forts and crossed the ditch on a causeway faced in stone and barred by a non-defensive gate. Lateral communication was first supplied by branches from the Stanegate, the pre-Hadrianic road from Corbridge to Carlisle. Later, the Military Way, between the boundary-ditch and wall, connected forts and mile-castles.

History. The Turf Wall was entirely replaced in stone during the second century, and the boundary-ditch was slighted. But relations between the Wall of Antoninus (q.v.) and Hadrian's Wall are obscure. The garrison was depleted by Albinus in A.D. 196–7, and on his defeat the wall was savagely overthrown, to be restored by Severus in 200–5. In place of the Antonine Wall, a forward zone was now held by outpost-forts at Risingham, High Rochester, Bewcastle, and Netherby, a system which kept peace until the defeat of Allectus in 297 invited another inroad, followed by the restoration of Constantius I. Under Constans in 343 and Julian in

360 the forward zone suffered, and was abandoned after attacks by Picts, Scots, and Saxons in 367-9, which again overwhelmed the wall. Finally, the wall was evacuated by Magnus Maximus (383-8), who left the frontier in the care of Lowland *foederati*.

J. C. Bruce, *The Handbook to the Roman Wall*[10] (edited by I. A. Richmond, 1947); R. G. Collingwood, *JRS* 1921, 37-66, 1931, 36-64; F. G. Simpson and I. A. Richmond, *JRS* 1935, 1 ff.; I. A. Richmond, *Northumberland County History* xv for outpost-forts.

I. A. R.

WALL OF SERVIUS, the city-wall of Republican Rome, traditionally assigned to King Servius Tullius, actually belongs to 378 B.C. It is of Grotta Oscura tufa, built in headers and stretchers, 4·50 m. thick and at least 8·50 m. high, retaining an earth bank or terrace, and is comparable with the contemporary wall of Pompeii II (*see* FORTIFICATIONS). The masons' marks, with Hellenistic affinities, suggest Greek contractors. The wall enclosed an irregular area dictated by contours, embracing the Quirinal, Viminal, Oppian, Caelian, Aventine, and fortified Capitoline hills. There is, however, room for difference of opinion (cf. von Gerkan, *Röm. Mitt.* xlvi, 1931, 153-88) as to the course between the last two points, while the time-space relation of the Palatine fortification to the wall is another crux. Gates are well-known by name, hardly by structure. In the second century B.C. the wall was heightened to some 50 feet (cf. Pompeii III), and was also supplied with casemates for *ballistae*, covering approaches to the gates. During the first century B.C. neglect and encroachment made the course hard to find by the time of Augustus.

The original work of Servius is represented by the *agger*, which, revetted by the Republican Wall just described, crosses the neck of land between Quirinal and Oppian. It is a typical promontory defence, as at Ardea, and covered tombs of the sixth century B.C. in Villa Spithoever. It is later than such works as the *murus terreus Carinarum*, which, if defensive, would mark an independent Oppian circuit. The rest of the fortification, as at Ardea, would depend upon scarped cliffs, 'ex omni parte arduis praeruptisque montibus', as Cicero observed (*Rep.* 2. 6. 11).

G. Saeflund, *Le mura di Roma repubblicana* (1932). I. A. R.

WAR, ART OF (GREEK). Homer was commonly credited by ancient readers with having intended to provide instruction in the art of war. But the attempt to deduce some kind of theory from military practice does not seem properly to have begun till the latter half of the fifth century, when the Sophists applied their abstract methods to this subject among others. Of the text-books derived from this movement there are only preserved the small treatise of Xenophon on the duties of a cavalry officer and an extract dealing with siege-warfare from a comprehensive text-book by Aeneas Tacticus. The other technical writers on the subject date from the Roman period. Of contemporary historians Thucydides, Xenophon, and Polybius in their different ways show appreciation of the art of war as a factor in history.

2. The Homeric battles cannot be reduced to technical terms. Sometimes they consist of duels between chieftains, taking place in front of masses of imperfectly armed retainers; at others the Greeks and Trojans meet in ranks of infantry, called phalanxes, and ranged closely shoulder to shoulder. Chariots are normally used to convey chieftains into or out of the fighting-line.

3. In Tyrtaeus the references to warfare are too full of Homeric echoes to give independent evidence on archaic warfare. The chief source of information before the Peloponnesian War is Herodotus. From him it appears that Greek warfare till his day was based on the hoplite (q.v.). Campaigning was mostly confined to the period of the year from March to October, the only season when (in the absence of military roads) it was easy to move bodies of heavy troops. Wars were usually limited to the border struggles of neighbouring States; the invader's objective was to destroy the corn and fruit-trees of the enemy and so compel them to offer battle or capitulate. There was no science of manœuvring before or during action, the only tactical device being the ambush. When hoplites met on level ground the deciding factor was usually weight of numbers. The troops were massed in ranks reckoned as the depth of so many shields. The side which first broke under pressure was defeated. The victors set up a trophy: the vanquished asked for a truce to bury their dead. Light-armed troops were quite unorganized; cavalry also were few, and were not used with any special effect.

4. The Peloponnesian War revealed the absurdity of annual raids on the enemy's corn-lands. The Athenians by retiring into their fortified area and importing their food-supplies were able to ignore the Spartan invasions. Hence the Spartans were forced at last to adopt the method of creating a permanent fortified base at Decelea. Also the constant fighting in various kinds of terrain showed up the lack of adaptability of the hoplites and the advantages of the occasional use of light-armed troops. The development of the peltast (q.v.) in the early fourth century provided a more mobile unit, which did not cost so much to maintain all the year round.

5. The hoplite battle was first revolutionized by Epaminondas (q.v.). It had been a convention to put the best troops on the right of the line, but Epaminondas placed a massed body on the left to crush the enemy's right in a slanting advance, and by this element of surprise he broke the Spartan front at Leuctra. This manœuvre was only a more intelligent use of an old Boeotian device, but out of it Philip and Alexander, by means of the Macedonian phalanx (q.v.), developed the method of attacking with part of their front, while the rest held back. For the purpose of delivering the main thrust Alexander used the excellent cavalry which Thessaly and Macedon provided, and exploited the charge from the flank. The further step of holding part of one's forces in reserve to use at a later point in the action is not found before the battle of Arbela. The other special innovation in Alexander's warfare is the pressing of pursuit, by which the enemy was prevented from re-forming.

6. After Alexander there were no drastic changes. The main evolution consists in the further modification of the phalanx. Also a few special varieties of warfare added to the complexity of fighting: heavy-armed cavalry and elephants (q.v.) were first known from oriental sources, but were soon used throughout the Hellenistic world. Generally war became more and more an activity for professionals and was too complex for the ordinary citizen; but as it became more specialized, it also became more stereotyped. Alexander's attack in its fresh vigour was never twice the same, but the Hellenistic generals' methods were quite fixed when the Romans met them on Greek soil.

Ancient text-books: Xenophon, *Hipparchicus*; Aeneas Tacticus. Later technical writers are not of great value. Modern discussions: J. Kromayer and G. Veith, *Heerwesen und Kriegführung der Griechen und Römer* (1928). Hoplite war: G. B. Grundy, *Thucydides and His Age* (1911). Hellenistic warfare: W. W. Tarn, *Hellenistic Military and Naval Developments* (1930). H. W. P.

WAR, ART OF (ROMAN). The earliest Roman battle order was probably the phalanx (*see* preceding article.) In the fourth century (after the Gallic invasions or during the Samnite Wars) this was replaced by the manipular system, a type of warfare of which an essential feature was open-order fighting. This innovation was accompanied by the adoption of *pilum* and *gladius* as the national weapons, the effective use of which required space for free movement. In this system the legion was drawn up in three lines of maniples with intervals equal to the frontage of each unit between the maniples, and with a distance of varying depth between each line, the units in the rear lines covering off the intervals in the line in front of them. The plan of battle was at first schematic. After preliminary skirmishing by light-armed troops and cavalry stationed on the flanks of the legions, the front line (*hastati*) on coming into range hurled their *pila* and, if successful, advanced and decided the issue by hand-to-hand fighting with the *gladius*; if unsuccessful, they retired through the gaps in the second line, and their place was taken by the *principes*. Finally a stand might be made with closed ranks at the third line (*triarii*), which at first retained the *hasta*.

2. During the Punic Wars much practical experience was acquired. Each line of maniples became more independent of the others, and experiments were made with a larger unit, the cohort, which after Marius permanently superseded the maniple. The fullest development was reached under Caesar. The *triplex acies* was no longer rigidly adhered to (e.g. *BGall.* 3. 24. 1), but dispositions varied with topographical conditions. The possibilities of flank attacks or of holding troops in reserve for the decisive onslaught were frequently exploited, while archers and slingers were increasingly employed in country unsuited to heavy infantry. Roman warfare was thus emancipated from stereotyped theories. Its success depended partly on the general's ability but mainly on the discipline of the soldiers.

3. During the first two centuries A.D. tactics for the most part followed the Caesarian model. But with the increasing efficiency of the auxiliary cavalry and light infantry a greater variety of manœuvres resulted. The legions still normally sustained the brunt of attack and defence, but the auxiliaries not infrequently played a decisive part (e.g. Tac. *Hist.* 2. 25; 2. 41; 5. 18; *Agr.* 35). Later the Roman army gradually lost its national character and its ability to give effect to the Roman art of war.

4. Another feature of Roman warfare was camp construction. Even on short campaigns a camp with ditch and rampart was laid out as a base for attack and a safe retreat in the event of defeat (*see* CAMPS). During the Republic these camps were usually temporary, but in the scheme of frontier defence gradually perfected in the Principate permanent garrisons for legions and *auxilia* were established (*see* LIMES).

5. Two methods of advance were commonly adopted. If attack was not expected, the army moved in one long column with a vanguard of scouts and cavalry, which also protected the flanks and rear (Josephus *BJ.* 3. 6. 2). If danger was anticipated, a formation easily convertible into an *acies* was adopted (*agmen quadratum*, Tac. *Ann.* 1. 51).

6. Despite the lack of maps, converging movements involving long marches and careful synchronization were increasingly attempted and sometimes succeeded. On the whole Roman strategy aimed at the destruction of the enemy in pitched battle rather than at a war of attrition.

J. Kromayer and G. Veith, *Heerwesen und Kriegführung der Griechen und Römer* (1928); H. Delbrück, *Geschichte der Kriegskunst*[3] (1920); T. Rice Holmes, *Caesar's Conquest of Gaul*[2] (1911); F. E. Adcock, *The Roman Art of War under the Republic* (U.S.A. 1940). H. M. D. P.

WAR, RULES OF. These, like other international law, depended on custom and showed a constant conflict between the higher standard of the best public opinion and harsher measures permitted by usage, while passion and expediency frequently caused the most fundamental rules to be violated. Thus, the temptation to profit from a surprise at times led to the opening of hostilities without a declaration of war. Probably the law most generally

observed was that of the sanctity of heralds, for heralds were essential to communications between belligerents. Nor did Greeks frequently refuse a defeated army a truce for burying its dead, for the request of such a truce meant an admission of defeat and usually was followed by retreat. Beyond this there were few restraints except humanitarian considerations and the universal condemnation of excessive harshness. Plundering and the destruction of crops and property were legitimate, and were carried on both by regular armies and fleets, and by informal raiding-parties and privateers, and even the sanctity of temples was not always respected. Prisoners, if not protected by special terms of surrender, were at the mercy of their captors, who could execute them or sell them into slavery. The warfare of the Hellenistic Age was somewhat more humane, though with the wars of Rome and Philip V deterioration began once more. Roman warfare at its worst was extremely cruel and sometimes went to the length of killing all living things, even animals, in cities taken by storm, but it was often tempered by mercy. Though surrender (*deditio*) gave full power to the captors, it was unusual to use extreme measures against a city that surrendered and appealed to the *fides* of Rome. The protection of the rules of war was not extended to pirates and not always to barbarians.

C. Phillipson, *The International Law and Custom of Ancient Greece and Rome* (1911), chs. xxii–xxviii; M. Rostovtzeff, *The Social and Economic History of the Hellenistic World* (1941), 140–3, 192–204, 603–10, 1258–9. J. A. O. L.

WARS, SACRED, *see* SACRED WARS.

WATER, according to the Ionian philosopher, Thales, was the primal element, the origin of all things; Hesiod thought likewise, speaking not of water but of the mythical Oceanus; similarly the Orphic theogony of Hellanicus placed water at the beginning of the world. In all purificatory rites water (as well as fire) is exceedingly important. The new-born child, the bride and bridegroom, also the mourner and the combatant (i.e. those who have come into contact with death or the dead), have to be washed or bathed; likewise the *mystai* (cf. MYSTERIES). Water washed away all uncleanness and (according to Euripides) all sins; running water or water from a spring is particularly pure, likewise sea-water. It was fertilizing to nature and even gave new life to man. To the dead it was a usual gift (together with milk, wine, honey, and oil, cf. the vases on the graves with pierced bottoms, the *lutrophoroi*). Water (and fire) are traditional in all sorts of magic. The Orphics knew the water of Memory as well as of Forgetfulness in the other world, and we hear also of mantic water (cf. SPRINGS).

S. Eitrem, *Opferritus und Voropfer der Griechen und Römer* (1915), ch. 2; M. Ninck, 'Die Bedeutung des Wassers im Kult und Leben der Alten' (*Philol. Supp.* XIV. ii, 1921). S. E.

WEAVING. The weaving of cloth for ordinary household use in Greece and Rome was usually done at home. The more elaborate forms of weaving were left to professional craftsmen, and the best specimens of their work, often imported from Persia, Egypt, and Phoenicia, seem by the descriptions in literature to have been equal to the finest modern tapestry. These were all made by hand on an upright loom (ἱστός, *tela*) differing very little in principle from that used by Penelope in the *Odyssey*. Its operation was as follows.

The framework was simple: two upright posts joined at the top by a transverse beam (ζυγόν, *jugum*). To this beam were fastened the threads of the warp (πηνίον, *stamina*) with weights attached at the bottom to make them hang straight. These threads were then divided into two groups by means of two horizontal rods (κανόνες, *arundines*) so that the shuttle (κερκίς, *radius*) might pass alternately over and under them. The warp was much stouter than the weft thread, which was placed on a bobbin (πήνη, *panus*) revolving on a cane and delivering the thread through a hole in the front of the shuttle. After the shuttle had passed to and fro several times the weft was driven upwards by a comb (κτείς, *pecten*) the teeth of which were inserted between the warp threads. For weaving in its simplest form this was all that was necessary; when a pattern was required a system of leashes and heddles, such as we have now, was used and worked by hand. In early times the web began at the top and the weaver worked standing; but some time in the last century B.C. the Egyptian fashion of sitting and starting at the bottom was introduced in Rome.

H. Blümner, *Technologie der Griechen und Römer*² (1912) i. 135 ff.
F. A. W.

WEIGHING-INSTRUMENTS. The balance (σταθμός, *libra*, *bilanx*) of two pans at equal distances from the point of suspension is an invention of primitive times; it is a frequent symbol in Minoan tablets, and Homer is familiar with its use, which persisted through antiquity. The steelyard, in which the rod is unequally divided, the object to be weighed being suspended from the short arm against a sliding weight on the longer, does not appear before Roman times (*statera*: originally *statera campana*, from an alleged Campanian origin); but from its greater convenience it became the most popular form of balance. Examples in museums show great variety; several scales and as many suspension-points may be combined; the pans may be replaced by hooks or by receptacles for liquids. *Trutina* is a pan-balance for large masses; *momentana* and *moneta* are for small objects, or coins.

E. Michon, Dar.-Sag., s.v. 'Libra'; M. della Corte, *Mon. Ant.* xxi (1912), 1–42.
F. N. P.

WEIGHTS. Weights of the Greek Bronze Age are usually flattened cylinders of stone or metal, incised circles on the upper surface indicating the denomination. Other forms are the duck and bull's head, the slingstone of haematite, and from Cnossos comes a flattened stone pyramid, the weight of a light talent (29,000 gm.) or of a standard copper ingot. Several standards appear to have been current, extant Minoan weights having been related to the Egyptian, Babylonian, and Phoenician systems.

The typical weight of historic Greece is a square plaque of lead with a badge, and sometimes the denomination and the name of the issuing city, on the top in relief. The principal types on Attic weights, which are widespread outside Attica, are the tortoise, amphora, and dolphin. There were many other forms, as caprice or local custom dictated. Roman weights show less variety, the common form being a spheroid of stone or metal, with flattened top and bottom; the denomination is generally expressed in punctured characters on the top.

Several weight standards were used in Greece; the principal were the Aeginetic, traditionally associated with Pheidon of Argos, and the Euboic, introduced by Solon into Attica. The Attic-Euboic in later times tended to oust the Aeginetic. The historical origin of these standards is disputed; the Greeks held that they were based on natural units, e.g. in the Attic–Euboic system on the barley-corn, of which twelve went to the obol. Extant weights often show considerable variations from the norm. The theoretical Greek table is:

	Attic-Euboic standard	Aeginetic standard
The *obol*, or metal spit	0·72 gm.	1·05 gm.
The *drachma*, bundle of six spits	4·31 ,,	6·30 ,,
The *mina*, 100 *drachmae*	431·00 ,,	630·00 ,,
The *talent*, 60 *minae*	36·86 kg.	37·80 kg.

The talent represented a man's load. The Attic-Euboic mina weighed almost a pound avoirdupois.

The Roman system was based upon the pound, *libra*, of 327·45 grammes = 0·721 of the pound avoirdupois, which was divided into 12 ounces, *unciae*. The names and symbols of the subdivisions are:

libra or *as*	1 pound	I
deunx	11 oz.	S ⚌ ⚌ —
dextans	10 ,,	S ⚌ ⚌
dodrans	9 ,,	S ⚌ —
bes	8 ,,	S ⚌
septunx	7 ,,	S—
semis	6 ,,	S
quincunx	5 ,,	⚌ ⚌ —
triens	4 ,,	⚌ ⚌
quadrans	3 ,,	⚌
sextans	2 ,,	⚌
sescuncia	1½ ,,	≷—
uncia	1 ,,	—
semuncia	½ ,,	Ƨ
sicilicus	¼ ,,	Ɔ
sextula	⅙ ,,	Ƨ
semisextula	¹⁄₁₂ ,,	ƨ
scripulum	¹⁄₂₄ ,,	Ͽ

A. J. Evans, 'Minoan Weights', in *Corolla Numismatica* (1906), 336 ff.; *British Museum Guide to the Exhibition illustrating Greek and Roman Life* (1929), s.v. 'Weights'; E. Michon, Dar.-Sag., s.v. 'Libra', 'Pondus'; O. Viedebandt, *Antike Gewichtsnormen* (1923); W. Ridgeway, *Origin of Metallic Currency and Weight Standards* (1892).
F. N. P.

WIND-GODS were worshipped both by the Greeks and the Romans. Their ruler, Aeolus, might shut them up in a sack (Homer), but they were also regarded as well-defined personalities (so especially Boreas and Zephyrus). Originally they were represented as horses (the swift-footed horses of Achilles are the offspring of Zephyrus and one of the Harpies), later as anthropomorphic, often winged (under Oriental influence). The earth-born (volcanic) Oriental Typhon retained his serpent's feet. Homer speaks of four winds (later also the traditional number), Hesiod names three as children of Astraeus (the Starry Man) and Eos (the Dawn). The winds were regarded as fertilizing or impregnating, and astrologers assigned them to the planet Jupiter; they were also regarded as destructive, and their cult had a corresponding character (a black lamb is sacrificed to the 'typhos' according to Aristophanes, *Ran.* 847–8). The Athenians were especially interested in Boreas, for whom they organized a state-cult because he destroyed the Persian fleet. (Dedication to the winds at Pergamum, *Ath. Mitt.* xxxv. 547.) Even magic practices were employed in order to conciliate the winds (cf. the 'wind-lullers' at Corinth, Hesych., s.v.).

In Italy the name of the north wind (*aquilo*) still reminds us of the idea of the wind as a mighty bird. Here the west wind, Favonius (Zephyrus), was the favourite. The Romans had a temple of the *Tempestates* (near to the Porta Capena) from the third century B.C. In Imperial times the winds were often represented on sarcophagi.

Steuding, art. 'Windgötter', in Roscher; F. Cumont, *Rev. Arch.* VI Sér. xiii (1939), 26 ff.
S. E.

WINE. Both in Greece and in Italy wine was very cheap, and formed part of a slave's daily ration. At Athens the average price for the common sort was twopence a gallon, at Rome sixpence. The process of wine-making in both countries was as follows. The grapes were gathered, trodden, and then pressed. Some of the juice (γλεῦκος, *mustum*), was used at once and drunk unfermented; some was boiled down into jelly (*defrutum*) and used later for enriching poor wine. The rest of the must was poured into jars, *dolia*, and left to ferment for nine days. The jars were then closed and once a month opened for examination and treatment until the wine was fit for use. The common wines were drunk from the jar; the choicer kinds were drawn off and put into bottles (*amphorae*) which were then sealed, labelled, and stored in *apothecae*, usually at the top of the house to catch the heat from the bath-furnace.

The simplest classification of wines is by colour, of which the Greeks recognized three sorts, the Romans four. There was white wine (λευκός, *albus*); brown wine (κιρρός, *fulvus*); and red wine (ἐρυθρός, μέλας) subdivided by the Romans into light red—*sanguineus*, and dark red (*niger*). As for locality we need only consider here the wines of Greece and Italy. Of the Greek wines the best were those made at Chios, the Thasian, Lemnian, and Coan coming next. Of the Italian the Setine, grown on the hills near the Pomptine marshes, came first; then in order the Caecuban, Falernian, and Alban. The best of the Greek wines were light and dry (λεπτός, αὐστηρός); the Italian had more body and were sweeter, especially the *vinum dulce* and the raisin wine (*passum*). The Greek vintages reached maturity in seven years; many Italian wines required twenty.

Athenaeus, bks. 1–10; Columella, *De Re Rustica*, bk. 12; Pliny, *HN.* bk. 14.

F. A. W.

WOMEN, POSITION OF.

In the course of ancient history the social and economic position of women passed through many phases, and it is necessary to distinguish six periods: Early Greece, the fifth century at Athens, Hellenistic Greece, Republican Rome, Imperial Rome, Christian Rome. The changes were sometimes due to the difference between European and Asiatic ideas of women, sometimes to the effect on family life of long-continued foreign wars, sometimes to the influence of an ascetic religion. Only a brief summary can be given here, and it must be understood that in every period there were many exceptions to the general rule.

2. In the society pictured in the Homeric poems, and especially in the *Odyssey*, women held an honoured place. In the households of Odysseus, Menelaus, and Alcinous the wives, Penelope, Helen, and Arete. take their full share in the governing of the home and are treated with all due respect. This comparative equality of the sexes was in later ages always retained at Sparta, but in Ionia during the seventh century B.C. an idea became prevalent, perhaps due to Asiatic influence, that women were inferior beings. The early satirists, Simonides and Hipponax, vented their spleen on the female sex, and to them 'Women are the greatest evil that God ever created'.

3. After 500 B.C. the Athenians adopted Ionian ideas of womanhood, and the whole structure of Athenian social life was arranged for men's sole benefit. No education was thought necessary for girls, a marriage was arranged for them as soon as possible, and after that the less that was heard or seen of them the better. The Athenian house was small, dark, and uncomfortable; but women spent most of their time indoors, for nearly all forms of outdoor recreation were closed against them.

4. The conquests of Alexander swept away many Greek prejudices and enlarged the social as well as the political horizon. The ideas that all men but Greeks were barbarians and that all females were inferior to males were both seen to be false. Macedonian women had always been more independent than their Athenian sisters, and in the dynasties established by Alexander's successors there were a number of women as energetic, as ambitious, and as unscrupulous as any man. Their influence spread downwards, and in Alexandria and Antioch, the two great cities of the Hellenistic world, women had their full share of the pleasures of life. The Alexandrian poets always had a female audience in mind, and the fifteenth idyll of Theocritus will show how different an Alexandrian household was from an Athenian.

5. The Roman matron from the first enjoyed a higher status than was customary at Athens, but it was as a wife and a mother that she was held in esteem. As a woman she passed by law at marriage from her father's control into that of her husband and remained *in manu* until his death. The Roman family was governed by the will of the *paterfamilias* by right of *patria potestas*, and the only restrictions were those imposed by custom and religion. During the long series of foreign wars in which Rome was engaged during the third and second centuries B.C. women in their husband's absence controlled the home, and finally the form of marriage by *usus* gave them independence (*see* MARRIAGE, LAW OF). Under the later Republic women received at least an elementary education; they met their husband's guests at dinner, and they were free to attend most outdoor entertainments.

6. In the last century B.C. and under the early emperors many Roman women of high position abused their freedom. Ladies like Sempronia, Clodia, and the two Julias rivalled men in looseness of life, and although Augustus tried to mend matters by his social legislation he met with no great success, as may be seen from Juvenal's Sixth Satire. But in Italy as a whole the old Roman traditions generally remained in honour.

7. With the rise of Christianity in Rome women were put back into a position of relative subservience. A century after Juvenal, Tertullian writes to his 'beloved sisters': 'You are the gateway of the devil, you are the unsealer of the forbidden tree, you are the first rebel against the divine law.' The finances of the early Christian Church owed much to the liberality of wealthy women converts, but both St. Augustine and St. Jerome were convinced that woman was the weaker vessel; and the Church followed their lead.

Companion Gr. Stud., 610 ff.; *Comp. Lat. Stud.*, 185 ff.; A. W. Gomme, *Essays in Greek History and Literature*, ch. 5; Friedländer, i, ch. 5.

F. A. W.

WORSHIP, HOUSEHOLD.

A Greek householder might have a particularly close association with some god or hero (as Ariston king of Sparta with Astrabacus, Hdt. 6. 69. 3; Pindar with Alcmeon, *Pyth.* 8. 56 ff., and with the Mother of the Gods, *Pyth.* 3. 77 ff.: for private *sacra* cf. Theopomp. ap. Porph. *Abst.* 2. 16), but this was exceptional, and no part of domestic cult proper. The centre of the latter seems to have been the hearth, respectful treatment of which is recommended as early as Hesiod, *Op.* 733–4. At the ordinary family meals it was customary to begin by offering a little of the food, probably to Hestia (q.v.; Theophrastus in Porph. *Abst.* 2. 20). Before drinking wine, which formed a regular part of the meal, a little was poured on the floor to the Good Daimon, i.e. the luck of the house, and a little drunk neat, thus establishing a communion with him (cf. W. W. Tarn, *JHS* xlviii (1928), 210 ff.; Athenaeus, 692 ff.; Ar. *Eq.* 85 (with schol.), 106). After a more formal dinner, when the tables were cleared and the drinking-bout (*symposium*) began, it was customary, at all events in Athens, to offer three libations, to Zeus, the heroes, and Zeus Soter (Aeschylus, fr. 55 Nauck; see further Cook, *Zeus* ii. 1123, note 7). Of these, Zeus Soter is not the great Zeus, but rather a domestic deity, see H. Sjövall, *Zeus im altgr. Hauskult* (Diss. Lund, 1931), 85 ff.; see the whole dissertation for various domestic deities called Zeus, including Zeus Ktesios (pp. 53 ff.), who is hardly more than a deified store-jar in origin; cf. Cook, p. 1092 ff. A householder also made private celebrations of recognized public festivals (Nock, *Harv. Theol. Rev.* xxix (1936), 85, n. 105; cf. *SIG* 695, 86 ff.).

For Rome cf. CHILDREN, LARES, PENATES, VESTA. The cult was essentially the same as the Greek, though there were marked differences in detail; the objects of worship were the hearth (Vesta), the *numina* of the store-cupboard (Penates), and the Lar Familiaris; but there might be added to the *lararium*, or domestic chapel, at all events in classical times, almost any deity the householder fancied, as is shown by the figures represented in the Pompeian *lararia* (see Boyce in *Am. Ac. Rome* xiv, and add S.H.A. *Alex. Sev.* 29. 2). Cf. Hor. *Sat.* 2. 2. 123 ff. for a domestic cult of Ceres. *See also* MEALS, SACRED; VESTA.

There is no treatise on the subject as a whole. The handbooks of private antiquities are inadequate here. Some useful works are cited above; add M. P. Nilsson in *Symb. Philol. Danielsson* (Uppsala, 1932), 218 ff. H. J. R.

WRESTLING. To the Greeks wrestling was both a science and an art. Victory alone was not sufficient; the winner must win gracefully and according to the precepts of the schools. Wrestling was one of the sports in which women were allowed by some States to take part, competing even against men. There were separate rules for men and boys, and the different movements, grips, and throws were taught on a progressive system; textbooks were used, and fragments of one such manual have recently been found on an Egyptian papyrus. The two principal styles were upright wrestling, in which the object was to throw one's opponent to the ground, three falls being necessary for victory; and ground wrestling, in which the struggle was continued until one of the combatants yielded. F. A. W.

X

XANTHIPPE, *see* SOCRATES.

XANTHIPPUS (1), husband of Cleisthenes' niece Agariste and father of Pericles. As a political ally of the Alcmaeonids (q.v.), he probably brought Miltiades (q.v.) to trial in 493 B.C., and he secured his condemnation in 490–489. He was ostracized in 484, but was recalled in the general amnesty before Xerxes' invasion. Elected general for 479 he commanded the Athenian contingent at Mycale and had a large share in this victory. In 478, after a winter siege, he captured Sestos and had the Persian governor and his children massacred.

J. Kirchner, *Prosopographia Attica* ii. 152 f., no. 11169; J. Carcopino, *L'Ostracisme athénien* (1935), 148 f., and passim; H. Willrich, *Perikles* (1936), 62 ff. P. T.

XANTHIPPUS (2), a Spartan mercenary captain, helped Carthage against Regulus (q.v.). He reorganized the Carthaginian army and annihilated the Roman expeditionary force, making brilliant use of the Carthaginian elephants and cavalry to outflank and mow down the Romans (255 B.C.). After this victory he left Carthage. The story that he was treacherously killed on his homeward journey may be rejected. Perhaps he is the same Xanthippus who later served Ptolemy Euergetes. H. H. S.

XANTHUS (1), poet of Magna Graecia or Sicily in seventh century B.C., mentioned by Stesichorus (Ath. 12. 513 a), who is said to have drawn on his *Oresteia* for his own (ibid.). He said that Electra was originally called Laodice, but had her name changed by the Argives because she remained unmarried (Ael. *VH* 4. 26).

J. M. Edmonds, *Lyra Graeca* (Loeb), ii. 12–13. C. M. B.

XANTHUS (2), son of Candaules, a Lydian, born 'about the capture of Sardis' (Suidas), described a drought in Artaxerxes' reign (464–424 B.C.) and is coupled with Hellanicus and Damastes as 'coming down to Thucydides' time' (Dion. Hal. *Thuc.* 5). But Ephorus thought he 'gave a starting-point' to Herodotus (Ath. 12. 515 d). The authenticity of his Λυδιακά (4 books) was disputed by Artemon, but there was a summary by Menippus (Diog. Laert. 6. 101). Eratosthenes and Dion. Hal. used him and Nicolas of Damascus copiously. He wrote also Μαγικά and a *Life of Empedocles*. In Ionic dialect and simple graphic style he recorded romances, folk-tales, and popular customs; quoted a Lydian king-list, and discussed geological and botanical questions.

FHG i. 36–44; iv. 628–9; *FGrH* ii. 90 (Nic. Dam.); L. Pearson, *Early Ionian Historians* (1939), ch. iii. J. L. M.

XENAGORAS (*fl. c.* 90 B.C.), a Greek, wrote Χρόνοι (Chronologies) of Greek (and Italian?) towns, and Περὶ νήσων.

XENARCHUS (1), Sicilian mime-writer (*see* MIMUS) of the late fifth century B.C., son of Sophron (q.v.).

Arist. *Poet.* 1447ᵇ3; Kaibel, *CGF*, p. 182.

XENARCHUS (2), Middle Comedy poet, of considerable frankness and liveliness; 8 titles survive, mainly from daily life. Fr. 1, parody of tragic style: fr. 7, illegal watering of fish; fr. 14, happy cicalas, their wives have no voice.

FCG iii. 614 ff.; *CAF* ii. 467 ff.

XENOCLES (1), son of the elder Carcinus (q.v. 1), is said (Aelian *VH* 2. 8) to have defeated Euripides in 415 B.C. with a group of plays consisting of *Oedipus*, *Lycaon*, *Bacchae*, and *Athamas* (satyric). His *Licymnius* was parodied by Aristophanes (*Nub.* 1264–5), and there are contemptuous references to him in Ar. *Thesm.* 169, *Ran.* 86. Epithets applied to him (μηχανοδίφης, δωδεκαμήχανος) may refer to a fondness for strange mechanical devices (*TGF*, p. 770).

(2) Son of the younger Carcinus (q.v. 2), wrote tragedies in the fourth century B.C. (schol. Ar. *Ran.* 86).

A. W. P.-C.

XENOCRATES (1) of Chalcedon, son of Agathenor, disciple of Plato and head of the Academy from 339 to 314 B.C. He is presented to us as a man of impressive personality, with a combination of austere dignity and kindliness which exercised a great influence on all who came in contact with him. He was generally respected in Athens and was employed by the citizens as ambassador to Antipater in 322 B.C.

His philosophical contributions, so far as we can reconstruct them from the scanty evidence, were less impressive. He seems, in general, to have attempted to reproduce Plato's thought in a stereotyped and formalized system, though on one or two points he probably preserved the correct tradition of interpretation as against Aristotle. He also interested himself in giving a systematic account of the nature of the gods and daemons and their relations to the heavenly bodies, in a way which foreshadowed the fantasies of later Neoplatonism. From the titles of his works we may conjecture that his chief interest lay in moral questions, but rather in the direction of teaching a practical morality than of ethical analysis, a line which his immediate successors in the Academy appear to have followed.

Histories of Ancient Philosophy: Zeller, 2. 1⁴. 1010–32; Gomperz (Engl. Transl. 4. 5–11); R. Heinze, *Xenocrates* (1892). G. C. F.

XENOCRATES (2) of Aphrodisias, physician of the time of Nero and the Flavians (54–96). Works: Περὶ τῆς ἀπὸ τοῦ ἀνθρώπου καὶ τῶν ζῴων ὠφελείας, full of superstitious means of treatment, borrowed largely from previous works such as Ps.-Democritus' Λιθογνώμων, a lexicon of gems (frs. ed. M. Wellmann in *Quellen u. Studien zur Geschichte der Naturwissenschaften u. der Medizin*, 1935); Περὶ τῆς τῶν ἐνύδρων τροφῆς; *On the healing properties of plants*; *On the names of plants*; *On the meaning of the flight of birds*.

Frs. ed. J. L. Ideler in *Physici et Medici Graeci Minores* (1841), i. 121.   W. D. R.

XENON, a friend often mentioned in Cicero's *Letters*: not to be identified with Zeno of Sidon, also mentioned by Cicero.

See Zeller, *Phil. d. Griechen* iii. 1⁴. 385.

XENOPHANES of Colophon left Ionia at the age of twenty-five, probably on the Persian conquest in 545 B.C., and lived an exile's life for at least sixty-seven years, at some time in Zancle and Catana, and latterly perhaps at the court of Hieron of Syracuse. He is said to have written epic verses on the Foundation of Colophon and the Colonization of Elea, but extant fragments are either from his *Satires* (Σίλλοι) in hexameters (including those traditionally attributed to a philosophic poem) or from elegiac occasional pieces.

An accomplished and original writer in the tradition of Tyrtaeus and Solon, X. became the poet in Magna Graecia of the Ionian intellectual enlightenment. In ruthless criticism of Homer and Hesiod he denies that the gods act dishonourably or have human shape or understanding; there is a single supreme Deity who, without stirring, sways the universe through thought. His physical theories, based on keen, though perhaps not independent, observation, show the same rejection of traditional myth. In his elegies he turns his criticism to society, denouncing the accepted canons of ἀρετή (athletic and military prowess) as of less social value than intellectual achievement. Throughout he claims for his views not truth but probability and propriety. Neither sceptic nor mystic, he is more a searching and constructive critic of convention than a systematic thinker, and he is falsely claimed as the founder of the Eleatic school. But as the first philosophic theologian he exercised a lasting influence on religious thought.

Diels, *Vorsokr.*⁵ i. 113–39; Diehl, *Anthologia Lyrica Graeca*² i. 1. 64–76; Burnet, *Early Greek Philosophy*⁴, 112–29; C. M. Bowra, *Early Greek Elegists* (1938), 106–35; W. Jaeger, *The Theology of the Early Greek Philosophers* (1947), ch. iii.   A. H. C.

XENOPHON (1), *c.* 430 (not 440 or earlier, as supposed prior to W. Mitford, *History of Greece*² iv. 292 f.) to *c.* 354 B.C. (not 360, as Stesiclides ap. Diog. Laert. 2. 56), son of Gryllus of the Athenian deme Erchia, a man of means. He became a disciple of Socrates, but does not claim to have known him intimately. Probably he served in the Athenian cavalry. In 401, on the invitation of the Theban Proxenus, and despite the warning of Socrates (*Anab.* 3. 1. 5), he joined the expedition of Cyrus against Artaxerxes, unaware of its true objective. After the murder of the generals he was chosen to succeed Proxenus as general, and, according to his own account, gradually won paramount influence with the army. With Chirisophus the Spartan he led the army to Trapezus, which was reached early in 400. Subsequently he took service under the Thracian prince Seuthes. Early in 399 he handed over the Cyrean troops to Thibron the Spartan general. When he married Philesia is unknown, but in 394 his sons, Gryllus and Diodorus, were old enough to be educated at Sparta (Plut. *Ages.* 20, Dinarchus ap. D.L. 2. 54). He was apparently still in Asia when he heard that he was banished (*An.* 7. 8. 57; cf. D.L. 2. 51, a confused statement). The specific charge is unknown, but doubtless *laconism* and friendship with Cyrus were alleged against him. He probably served under Thibron's successor Dercylidas (from 399 autumn; cf. *Hell.* 3. 2. 7), certainly under Agesilaus (from 396), of whom he became a close friend and admirer. In 394 he accompanied the king to Greece and saw, possibly fought in, the battle of Coronea,

though not as commander of the Cyreians. He then went to Sparta, where he was joined by his wife and sons. He was presented by the Spartan government with an estate at Scillus, near Olympia, and lived there as a country gentleman. When the Eleans recovered Scillus from Sparta (probably 371) he lost the estate and migrated to Corinth. The decree of exile was rescinded, probably in 369, when Athens concluded an alliance with Sparta (*Hell.* 6. 5. 49; 7. 1). X. sent his sons to Athens to serve in the cavalry and was probably there himself occasionally. He died at Corinth (Demetrius Magnes ap. D.L. 56).

2. WORKS

(1) **Anabasis** (Κύρου ἀνάβασις), an account of the expedition under Cyrus the Younger of the Greek mercenaries and of their subsequent adventures (401–399), now, but not originally, in seven books. X. first published his *Anabasis* under the pseudonym Themistogenes of Syracuse (*Hell.* 3. 1. 2; Plut. *De glor. Ath.* 345), but whether that work included all seven books or only i–iv is uncertain. In v–vii Xenophon represents his conduct and judgement as almost invariably correct, and may be answering detractors. Though finished long after the events narrated (5. 3. 7), the *Anabasis* shows remarkable freshness.

(2) **Hellenica** (Ἑλληνικά), a history from the close of Thucydides (411) to the battle of Mantinea (362), in seven books. It consists of two separate works, (*a*) to the close of the Peloponnesian War (2. 3. 9 or 10), in imitation of Thuc., with an appendix on the Thirty (to ii end); (*b*) the rest in a different manner, still unfinished in 358 (6. 5. 37). The theory that there is another break at 3. 5. 1 is discredited. In (*b*) there are serious omissions, and X. shows bias in favour of Sparta and against Thebes, and there is cheap moralizing; but it contains some notable speeches (6. 5. 38; 7. 1. 2). The *Hellenica* was overrated by the Atticists.

(3) **Cyropaedia** (Κύρου παιδεία), an idealized biography of Cyrus the Elder, in eight books, the most highly finished of X.'s works, but too long, monotonous, and repetitive. The education of Cyrus, which accounts for his subsequent success, is based on principles that X. ascribes elsewhere to Socrates. X. makes Cyrus the embodiment of his own notions of the good ruler (cf. Cicero, *QFr.* 1. 1. 23). The descriptions of battles are vivid, and there is much instruction for military commanders in the form of concrete examples. There are many romantic touches, especially 6. 5; 7. 3, which influenced later Greek romance writers. Bk. 8. 8 is a palinode, showing how all went to pieces after Cyrus' death; it is inconsistent in details with the main work and its genuineness is disputed, but the language suggests X.

(4) **Polity of the Lacedaemonians** (Λακεδαιμονίων πολιτεία), a laudatory account, cursory and unequal, of Spartan institutions. They are due to Lycurgus, to whom X. attributes ideas of his own. Ch. 14 is a palinode prompted by disgust at the conduct of Spartan harmosts, probably added in 378.

(5) **Agesilaus** (Ἀγησίλαος), an encomium of King Agesilaus, written apparently just after his death (360). Despite free use of rhetorical embellishments in the manner of Gorgias, it betrays signs of haste. Substantial parts are repeated with stylistic changes from *Hell.* 3. 4. 2 f.; 4. 2 f. It is now generally thought genuine, but some question Ch. 11, a summary.

(6) **Memorabilia** (Ἀπομνημονεύματα), memoirs of Socrates in four books. They consist of (1) a defence of Socrates (1. 1–2), shown by Cobet to be a reply to the Sophist Polycrates; (2) anecdotes illustrating the defence point by point (to end of bk. 1); (3) a miscellany originally written at different times, of which some parts form a series of conversations connected in subject. At the opening of seventeen of these X. states, or at least implies,

that he had heard them; but this is of no historical value. X. draws on Plato and other Socratics, and attributes to Socrates many of his own ideas. His credibility as a witness to the historical Socrates is much debated. The belief that large portions are interpolations is discarded.

(7) **Apology** (Ἀπολογία Σωκράτους), designed to show why Socrates did not defend himself better. The writer professes to record what he heard from Hermogenes. Some parts occur in the *Memorabilia* with little difference; 18 is in *Symp.* 4. 41; 14 may owe something to Plato, *Ap.* 21 a; 23 to *Crito* 44 b; 27 = Gorgias, *Palamedes* 1. It is an inferior production, but the language favours the view that it is by X.

(8) **Oeconomicus** (Οἰκονομικός), a discussion on estate management between Socrates and Critobulus. The first third is a preamble to an account by Socrates of a conversation between himself and Ischomachus, a landowner. The sentiments are entirely X.'s, reflecting his life at Scillus. Though disfigured by platitudes, the work has charm.

(9) **Symposium** (Συμπόσιον), a pleasant record of an imaginary drinking-party in the house of Callias, celebrating the success of Autolycus at the Panathenaic festival in 422 (Athenaeus 5. 216; 11. 504), with Socrates among the guests. There are notable anachronisms, and X., then aged about 8, states that he was present. There is much light banter, but the address of Socrates to Callias (8. 6 f.) is serious.

(10) **Hieron** (Ἱέρων), a conversation between the elder H. of Syracuse and Simonides of Ceos, who visited Syracuse in 476. The theme is double: (a) is the private citizen or the despot the happier? (b) how must a despot rule to win the affection of his people? There is little attempt at characterization; from ch. 8 Simonides is the mouthpiece of X. It is generally thought that X. was prompted by some event, probably the accession of Dionysius II (367), and by a political, or even personal, motive; more likely he is merely discussing problems that interested the Socratics.

(11) **Hipparchicus** (Ἱππαρχικός), on the duties of a cavalry commander, addressed to one about to hold the position, with suggestions for improvement of the cavalry. It falls into two parts: (a) Memoranda (1–3. 1); (b) proposals for putting these into practice. (a) resembles *Mem.* 3. 3.

(12) **On Horsemanship.** (Περὶ ἱππικῆς), an authoritative and well-constructed manual, supplementary to 11 (12. 14). It is the oldest complete treatise existing on the subject.

(13) **Ways and Means** (Περὶ πόρων), suggestions for improving Athenian finances. It supports a peace, such as was advocated by Eubulus, and is to be dated 355–354. Style, language, and matter prove it to be genuine.

(14) **Cynegeticus** (Κυνηγετικός), a hortatory treatise on hunting, especially of the hare. To the technical part (2–11) is prefixed a rhetorical proem, enumerating the disciples of Chiron. After 11 comes an epilogue in praise of hunting, and then a bewildering attack on the sophists, who 'do no good to anyone'. The genuineness of this medley, in whole or in part, especially that of the proem, is much debated. Nothing in 2–11 is inconsistent with X.: 12 contains passages similar to his acknowledged writings, and opinions expressed in 13 resemble his. Of those who accept the work most think that it was written before X. left Athens in 401.

The Polity of the Athenians (Ἀθηναίων Πολιτεία) is proved by language and contents not to be by X.; it was written by an Athenian oligarch, probably when X. was a child.

3. Xenophon is not a great, but a meritorious and versatile, author. He can write in a style suitable to every prose form, can depict a scene and draw a character. He is an amateur philosopher, historian, and economist, but a master of military, especially of cavalry, tactics. His works show a persistent moral and pedagogic tendency: he has at hand a cheap remedy for moral, social, and economic evils. His thoughts, repeated again and again, are commonplace, and he is often tedious. He is a great borrower from other writers: had we more of the Socratic works, especially those of Antisthenes, his borrowings would be even more apparent. His style is habitually simple, but sometimes he uses the devices of rhetoric. The vocabulary is multifarious, containing colloquial, dialectic, and poetic elements.

4. As a man, despite his sententiousness and self-satisfaction, he deserves respect, even admiration, for his wide sympathies and interests, for his courage and comradeship, and for his simple piety. *See also* HISTORIO-GRAPHY, GREEK, para. 4.

BIBLIOGRAPHY

LIFE AND WORKS: Diogenes Laertius ii. 48–59; G. Grote, *H.G.* viii, *Plato* iii; W. Mure, *Lang. and Lit. of Greece* v (1857) (severe); A. Roquette, *de X. vita* (1884); H. G. Dakyns, *Works of X.* (laudatory and discursive); J. Pantazides, *Anab.* (1900); K. Münscher, *Philol. Supp.* xiii (1920, influence of X. on subsequent writers).

TEXTS: O.C.T. (Marchant); Teubner (Gemoll, Hude, Thalheim, Ruhl). *Opuscula*, G. Pierleoni² (1937).

COMMENTARIES: *An.*, A. von W. Vollbrecht (1907–12); **Hell.,** G. E. Underhill (1906); B. Büchsenschütz (1860–76); **Cyr.,** L. Breitenbach (1875); **Cyr., Oec.,** Hieron, H. A. Holden (1883–90); **Lac. Pol.,** F. Ollier (1934); **Ages.,** H. Hailstone (1879); **Mem.,** J. R. Smith (U.S.A. 1903); R. Kühner (1858); Hipparch., Hipp., P. L. Courier (1807); **Hipp.,** E. Pollack (1889–90); **Vect.,** J. H. Thiel (1922); [Ath. Pol.], E. Kalinka (1913).

TRANSLATIONS: H. G. Dakyns (*Everyman*, 1890); M. H. Morgan, *Art of Horsemanship* (U.S.A. 1894). With text, Loeb Series; *Budé Series* (French).

STYLE AND DICTION: G. Sauppe, *X. opera I* (1845); W. G. Rutherford, *New Phrynichus*; H. Richards, *X. and others* (1907); A. Schacht, *de X. studiis rhetoricis* (1890); W. Horn, *Quaestiones ad X. elocutionem pertinentes* (1926); L. Gautier, *La Langue de X.* (1911); A. W. Persson, *Zur Textgeschichte X.* (1915).

STUDIES OF PARTICULAR WORKS: *An.*, J. Mesk, *Wien. Stud.* 1922–3; **Hell.,** M. MacLaren, *Am. J. Phil.* 1934; **Cyr.,** L. Castiglioni, *Studi Senofontei V*, 1922; **Ages.,** W. Seyffert, *Jb. cl. Phil.* 1909; **Mem.,** E. Richter, *Jahrb. f. cl. Phil. Supp.* xix, 1892; A. Delatte, *Le 3ᵐᵉ livre des Souvenirs*, 1933; **Ap.,** H. Gomperz, *Neue Jahrb.* 1924; **Oec.,** N. Festa, *Riv. indo-greco-italica di filol.* 1920; Symp., G. F. Rettig, *Philol.* 1879; Hieron, C. Watermann, *de X. Hier.* 1914; Hipparch., E. Ekman, *Zu X.'s H.*, 1933; **Cyn.,** O. Manns, *Ueber die Jagd bei den Griechen* (1889–90); L. Radermacher, *Rh. Mus.* 1896–7 (*Cyn.* spurious); W. A. Baehrens, *Mnem.* 1926 (*Cyn.* genuine); **Vect.,** K. von der Lieck (1933). E. C. M.

XENOPHON (2), author of a Greek novel called the *Ephesiaca* or *Anthia and Habrocomes* (Τὰ κατὰ Ἀνθίαν καὶ Ἀβροκόμην Ἐφεσιακά), is known, on the authority of Suidas, as Xenophon of Ephesus; but he may have been associated with Ephesus only because of the title of his book and to distinguish him from Xenophon of Cyprus, author of the *Cypriaca* or *Cinyra, Myrrha, and Adonis*, and Xenophon of Antioch, author of the *Babyloniaca*, neither extant. X.'s topographical description of Ephesus, which is untrue of his own period, is largely derived from literary sources. His precise date is uncertain, but it was after Trajan's reign and probably before A.D. 263, when the temple of Artemis at Ephesus was destroyed by the Goths. Suidas, who mentions other works now lost, says that the *Ephesiaca* comprised ten books; since only five are extant, modern critics often assume that they represent an abridgement, thereby excusing the disjointedness of the narrative. Whether full or abridged, it is the weakest of the extant novels. The usual themes are exploited, but the presentation is uninspired and unskilful and suggests that the author, or his abridger, was almost illiterate. The simplicity of thought and expression lacks the charm that may be felt in Chariton (q.v.) and serves only to expose the poverty of the material.

Text and Translation: Budé (Dalmeyda). Commentary: A. Locella (1796). Life and Work: G. Dalmeyda in the Introduction to the Budé edition (1926); O. Schissel von Fleschenberg, *Die Rahmenerzählung in den Ephesischen Geschichten des X.* (1909); K. Bürger, *Hermes*, 1892; B. Lavagnini, *Annali delle Università Toscane*, 44 (1926); Ch. Picard, *Ephèse et Claros* (1922). See also on the NOVEL, GREEK. R. M. R.

XERXES I (*Khshaiarsha*), son of Darius and Atossa, king of Persia 485–465 B.C. He inherited from his father the task of punishing the Greeks for their participation in the Ionian revolt. Securing the co-operation of Carthage, and promises of support from several Greek States, he prepared a great fleet and army, bridged the Hellespont, and dug a canal through the Athos peninsula. In the spring of 480 his forces set out. At first they met with success; the fleet was victorious at Artemisium, the army forced Thermopylae, Attica was laid waste, and the Greeks forced back to their last line of defence, the Isthmus of Corinth. But at Salamis Themistocles with the Greek fleet won a victory which decided the future of Greece. His supplies from Asia cut off, Xerxes was forced to retreat; Mardonius, whom he left in command, was defeated at Plataea, and a final Persian failure at Mycale encouraged the defection of the Greeks of Asia Minor.

Of Xerxes' subsequent career little is known. In his reign the circumnavigation of Africa was attempted. A violent and intolerant ruler, he attempted to instal the sole cult of Ahura Mazda. He built extensively at Persepolis, Ecbatana, etc. But the Empire, though still vast in extent and resources, was weakened by court intrigues, in one of which he was murdered.

K. J. Beloch, *Griechische Geschichte* ii (1916); G. B. Grundy, *The Great Persian War* (1901); E. Obst, 'Der Feldzug des Xerxes', *Klio*, Beiheft vii (1913); *CAH* iv, ch. 9, 10; *see also* PERSIA, PERSIAN WARS.   M. S. D.

XUTHUS (*Ξοῦθος*), *see* CREUSA (1), ION.

Z

ZAGREUS, *see* DIONYSUS, ORPHISM, PERSEPHONE.

ZALEUCUS, the lawgiver of Italian Locri. As his laws are said to have been the first Greek codification, he probably lived c. 650 B.C. His legislation was notorious for its severity. The older tradition (4th c.) seems to have preserved some good material, e.g. his use of the *lex talionis* ('eye for eye') and prescription of exact penalties for each crime. Like other Greek lawgivers, he also issued sumptuary laws. Zaleucus was famous, too, as a conciliator of social factions; the constitution of Locri, however, remained extremely aristocratic. His laws were accepted by many cities of Italy and Sicily. The later tradition about him (especially in Diodorus) is mostly legendary.

F. E. Adcock, *Cambr. Hist. Journ.* ii (1927); M. Mühl, *Klio*, Beiheft xxii (1929).   V. E.

ZALMOXIS (Salmoxis) (*Ζάλμοξις, Σάλμοξις*), the deity of the Getae (Hdt. 4. 94–6). He seems to have been a god of the dead, for the Getae are said to 'make immortal' a man every four years, by throwing him upon spear-points, after charging him with messages for the other world. Plato (*Chrm.* 156 d) speaks of certain 'physicians of Zalmoxis' and their doctrines; this seems his own invention. Other authors (see commentators *ad locc.*) add nothing but a conjecture of Mnaseas (in Photius, s.v. *Ζάμολξις* [*sic*]) that he was the same as Kronos (q.v.).

Cf. A. D. Nock, *CR* xl (1926), 184 ff.   H. J. R.

ZAMA was the name of more than one town in North Africa. One (*colonia Zamensis*) was at Sidi Abd el Djedidi, 31 miles north-west of Kairouan. Farther west lay Zama Maior (perhaps modern Jama) and Zama Regia (now fixed through two inscriptions at Ksar Toual Zouameul, rather than 4½ miles farther west at Seba Biar: see *Rev. Arch.* xx (1942–3), 178–9); some scholars believe that these two Zamas should be identified with each other. Zama Regia in the Numidian kingdom was besieged unsuccessfully by Metellus during the Jugurthine War (109 B.C.); later it was Juba's capital, and after capture by T. Sextius (41 B.C.) it was temporarily destroyed. It became a *municipium* c. 29 B.C. and a colony under Hadrian. Zama is best known as the traditional site of Hannibal's defeat by Scipio Africanus in 202, an identification which rests on no better authority than Nepos. The battle was almost certainly not fought there, although Hannibal camped at western Zama before advancing still farther west to the actual battlefield which Polybius calls Margaron (otherwise unknown) and Livy Naraggara (Sidi Youssef); it probably lay between Naraggara and western Zama in a plain Draa-el-Metnan, south-west of Sicca Veneria (El Kef).

See T. Rice Holmes, *The Roman Republic* iii (1923), 536; H. H. Scullard, *Scipio Africanus in the Second Punic War* (1930), 310. For the *municipium*, M. Grant, *From Imperium to Auctoritas* (1946), 182.   H. H. S.

ZANCLE = MESSANA (q.v.)

ZELA, an ancient town of Pontus, with a considerable and fertile territory, and a large slave population attached to a Persian temple. Here Mithridates VI defeated Triarius in 67, and Caesar Pharnaces II (q.v.) in 47. Originally under the rule of priests, it received municipal status from Pompey. It became a temple State again under Antony, but at some later date (probably A.D. 64) became a city again. Under the Roman Empire it lay off the main-road system and fell into insignificance.

F. Cumont, *Studia Pontica* ii (1906), 188–94; iii (1910), 233–56; J. A. R. Munro, *JHS* xxi (1901), 52 ff.; Jones, *Eastern Cities*.
T. R. S. B.

ZENO (*Ζήνων*) (1) of Elea, pupil and friend of Parmenides, was born, according to Plato, c. 490 B.C. (*Prm.* 127 b). He wrote probably a single book in Attic prose, supporting Parmenides' monism by drawing contradictory conclusions from the premisses of its opponents; whence Aristotle calls him the inventor of dialectic. Some of his arguments survive; those concerning motion are (in summary):

(*a*) Before a moving body can reach the end of a line, it must reach the mid-point, before this the mid-point again, and so on. Therefore it can never start at all.

(*b*) Achilles can never overtake the tortoise since, when he reaches its starting-point, the tortoise is a little farther on, and so *ad infinitum*.

(*c*) The flying arrow is always opposite a length of ground equal to itself, and is therefore at every given moment at rest.

(*d*) Suppose two groups of equal units moving in a race-course with equal speed in opposite directions alongside a stationary group of similar units; then a unit of one moving group will in a given time pass twice as many units of the other as a unit of this will pass of the stationary group. Since the speeds and distances traversed are equal, the given time is therefore equal to half itself.

Of these arguments the first pair apparently presupposes (and thus refutes) the hypothesis that being is infinitely divisible, the second pair the hypothesis that it is composed of indivisible magnitudes. Zeno's other important surviving arguments show that, if being is many, it must be both infinitely small and infinitely great, and both limited and unlimited in number. *See also* MATHEMATICS.

Diels, *Vorsokr.*⁵ i. 247–58; Burnet, *Early Greek Philosophy*⁴, 310–20; W. D. Ross, *Aristotle's Physics* (1936), xi–xii, 71–85, 479–80, 655–6; H. D. P. Lee, *Zeno of Elea* (1936).   A. H. C.

ZENO (2) (335–263 B.C.), son of Mnaseas of Citium (Cyprus), probably of Phoenician race, founder of the Stoic school. He came to Athens in 313 and attended the lectures of Polemon, head of the Academy, and of the Megaric philosopher Diodorus ὁ Κρόνος, but was converted to Cynicism by Crates of Thebes. His earlier writings, especially his πολιτεία, are said to have been entirely Cynic in outlook. Later he turned to Socratic philosophy through study of the works of Antisthenes, and finally developed his own system. He taught in the Stoa Poikile, a public hall in Athens, from which the name of his school is derived, and soon acquired a large audience, though he tried to keep out the general public and wanted to teach real philosophers only. He became a friend of King Antigonus Gonatas and was invited to stay with him at his court at Pella, but declined and sent his disciple Persaeus instead.

Unlike most of the Socratics he created a complete philosophical system, consisting of logic and theory of knowledge (λογικόν), physics (φυσικόν and θεολογικόν), and ethics (ἠθικόν). In physics he admittedly followed Heraclitus, but was also strongly influenced by Aristotelian philosophy. In logic and theory of knowledge he was influenced by Antisthenes and Diodorus, the Megaric. His ethical doctrine gave great comfort to many during the troubled times of the successors of Alexander. According to this doctrine the only real good is virtue, the only real evil moral weakness. Everything else, including poverty, death, pain, is indifferent. Since nobody can deprive the wise man of his virtue he is always in possession of the only real good and therefore happy.

H. von Arnim, *SVF* i (1921), 3–72; Diogenes Laertius 7. 1–160; M. Pohlenz, 'Zenon und Chrysipp', *Nachricht. Götting. Gesellsch.*, Fachgruppe i, N.F. ii, no. 9.   K. von F.

ZENO (3) of Tarsus, Stoic, successor of Chrysippus as head of the school in 204 B.C. He left behind him few books but many disciples.

Testimonia in von Arnim, *SVF* iii. 209. See Zeller, *Phil. d. Griechen* iii. 1⁴. 45–6.

ZENO (4) of Rhodes (early 2nd c. B.C.), wrote a history of Rhodes from the beginnings to his own times, which Polybius used (with Antisthenes), although he criticized his patriotic exaggeration (Polyb. 16. 14); his tradition may also appear in Diodorus.

FHG iii. 174.

ZENO (5) of Sidon (b. *c.* 150 B.C.), Epicurean, pupil of Apollodorus and probably head of the school between him and Phaedrus. Cicero heard him lecture in Athens in 79–78. Philodemus' Περὶ παρρησίας was a selection from Z., and his Περὶ σημείων borrows lectures by Z. He is probably the source of part of Cic. *Nat. D.* i.

See Zeller, *Phil. d. Griechen* iii. 1⁴. 384–6.   W. D. R.

ZENO (6) of Sidon, Stoic, pupil of Diodorus Cronus (Diog. Laert. 38. 16).

See Zeller, *Phil. d. Griechen* iii. 1⁴. 40.

ZENO, *see also under* APOLLONIUS (3).

ZENOBIA (Septimia), or in Aramaic *Bat Zabbai*, the second wife of Odaenathus (q.v.). She was probably responsible for the murder of her husband and his son by a previous marriage; at any rate she thereupon

secured the power for herself in the name of her infant son Vaballathus (q.v.). Gallienus sent Heraclianus against her, but he was defeated, and Zenobia, having secured Syria, in A.D. 269 conquered Egypt, and next year overran Asia Minor except Bithynia. Aurelian at first acquiesced, granting to Vaballathus the same position as his father, but when in 271 Zenobia, not content with this partial recognition, proclaimed her son Augustus, he marched against her. His general Probus conquered Egypt; he himself reoccupied Asia Minor with little resistance, defeated Zabdas, Zenobia's general, at Antioch and again at Emesa, and finally captured Palmyra and the queen herself and her son. Having been exhibited at Aurelian's triumph she was granted a pension and a villa at Tibur. Zenobia is highly praised for her beauty, intelligence, and virtue, but was evidently a ruthless and unscrupulous woman. She sacrificed to her personal ambition the fortune of her native city, which Odaenathus had by his loyalty to the empire preserved. *See also* AURELIANUS.

J. G. Février, *Histoire de Palmyre* (1931), 103–41.   A. H. M. J.

ZENODORUS, author, between 200 B.C. and A.D. 90, of a treatise Περὶ ἰσομέτρων σχημάτων. Several propositions from it are preserved in the commentary of Theon of Alexandria on Bk. 1 of Ptolemy's *Syntaxis*. He was followed closely in his treatment of the subject by Pappus, whose treatment is, however, more complete. His style is not unlike that of Euclid and Archimedes.   W. D. R.

ZENODOTUS of Ephesus (b. *c.* 325 B.C.), pupil of Philetas, became the first head of the Library at Alexandria (*c.* 284) and undertook the classification of the Greek epic and lyric poets, some of whom he edited.

WORKS

(1) Lexicography: *Homeric Glossary* (Γλῶσσαι), which often relied on guesswork to give the meaning of difficult words, but opened the way for the scholarly study of language; Λέξεις ἐθνικαί, a compilation of foreign expressions. (2) Editions (διορθώσεις). His recension of the *Iliad* and *Odyssey*, in which for the first time the poems were divided into twenty-four books, represented the first scientific attempt to get back to the original Homeric text by the collation of several manuscripts. He marked lines of the genuineness of which he felt doubt with an *obelus* (see SCHOLARSHIP, GREEK, para. 3), and altered the text by the transposition or telescoping of verses, by the introduction of new readings, and sometimes even by the insertion of new lines. But the extremely subjective nature of his criteria made him sometimes rash in emendation. He produced also recensions of Hesiod, *Theog.*, Anacreon, Pindar (*P.Oxy.* v. 841).

H. Düntzer, *De Zenodoti studiis Homericis* (1843); K. Lehrs, *De Aristarchi studiis Homericis*³ (1882); A. Römer, *Über die Homerrezension des Zenodot* (1886); D. B. Monro, *Homer's Odyssey*, Appendix (1901); G. M. Bolling, *External Evidence for Interpolation in Homer* (1925).   J. F. L.

ZENON, *see* ZENO, *and also* APOLLONIUS (3).

ZEPHYRUS, god of the West Wind, sometimes said to be husband of Iris (rainy wind and rainbow), as Alcaeus, fr. 8 Diehl; a subordinate figure in a few legends, as that of Hyacinthus (q.v.). His parents are Eos and Astraeus (Hesiod, *Theog.* 379). *Cf.* WIND-GODS.

ZETES, *see* CALAÏS.

ZETHUS, *see* AMPHION.

ZEUGITAI in the original sense were owners of a ζεῦγος or pair of oxen. At Athens they constituted the third census-class, with an estimated revenue of 200–300 *medimnoi* of corn, or the equivalent in other produce or money. By the constitution of Solon (q.v.) they were full citizens, except that they were eligible only to the minor magistracies. From the time of Cleisthenes (q.v.), they could be elected *strategoi*, and in 457 they became eligible for the archonship. The majority of farmers and craftsmen of Athens belonged to this class; and these formed the bulk of the infantry in war-time, each man providing his own arms (*see* HOPLITES). A. W. G.

ZEUGMA (mod. *Bâlkîs*), on the right bank of the Euphrates at its chief crossing, between Europus and Samosata. Twin colonies Seleuceia and Apamea were founded by Seleucus I at this point, which came to be known by the generic name Zeugma ('junction'); it superseded an earlier Zeugma near Thapsacus. Originally in Commagene, Zeugma was added to the province of Syria in A.D. 58. As a frontier post and a meeting-place of trade-routes from East and West across the Parthian Empire, it became extremely prosperous. Justinian fortified it against the Sassanids, but in 639 it fell to the Arabs. M. S. D.

ZEUS is the only Greek god whose Indo-European origin can be proved with certainty. He is found as 'Father', which attribute is very common in Greek too, among the Romans, Indians, and Illyrians (Jupiter, Dyaus pita, Deipatyros); the name of the German god Ziu (cf. Tuesday) is akin. The word signifies 'sky', and according to a general opinion the bright sky; yet this is of no importance to primitive man, and the cults prove that Zeus is the weather-god, i.e. the sky as the sphere of atmospheric phenomena, thunder, rain, etc. Mountain peaks give weather signs, and Zeus is enthroned on them; Olympus is a pre-Greek word signifying 'mountain'; and among other peoples also the thunder-god became the supreme god. The epithet 'Father' is generally understood according to the Homeric phrase 'Father of gods and men'. But Zeus created neither gods nor men and it is unbelievable that in Indo-European times a nobility traced its descent from Zeus—this is probably due to the heroic Mycenaean age; again, the divine children of Zeus, Athena, Artemis, Apollo, Ares, Dionysus, include pre-Greek and immigrant gods. Consequently 'Father' is to be taken in the sense of *pater familias*, protector and ruler of the family. This implies a moral notion, the maintenance of customary laws; and these, e.g. the respect for suppliants and guest-friends (Zeus Hikesios, Xenios), were always bound up with Zeus. This explains why Zeus was the god of the courtyard and the household (Zeus Herkeios, Ktesios). The Greek State being founded on the family, Zeus was, as Homer shows, the protector of the king and his rights. The Mycenaean age formed the supreme god and the State of the gods after the model of its mighty kings and knights. Zeus is surrounded by recalcitrant vassals who sometimes show him respect, sometimes mock him. He rules according to power rather than according to righteousness, and has innumerable loves and children.

Homer impressed this Zeus upon the Greek mind. In the historical age, although kingship was abolished, Zeus was not dethroned. Zeus became the highest civic god, often with the epithet Polieus and together with Athena Polias, the old Mycenaean palace goddess and protectress of the king. As protector of political freedom he was called Soter, Eleutherios, and festivals were instituted in his honour. He had little to do with other concerns of the people—agriculture, war, crafts, etc. It was never forgotten that Zeus was the protector of law and morals. Hesiod invokes him as such in his cry for justice and places Dike at his side. The loftiest conception of Zeus is found in Aeschylus, who enhances his righteousness and overwhelming power. In the classical age Zeus was very prominent in art and literature, but among the people he receded into the background, being either the

weather-god of the rustics or the high civic god who received more respect than attention. In the Hellenistic age his name was very freely given to the chief deity of any non-Greek tribe or region. Cosmological ideas were not in any large measure attached to Zeus; Stoic philosophy, however, identified him with its highest principle, fire, which at the same time is the reason which pervades and animates the universe. This idea is expressed very beautifully in the hymn by Cleanthes (q.v.).

Certain myths are important, among them the most peculiar Cretan myth of the birth of Zeus, according to which the child was hidden in a cave in order that Kronos might not swallow it up, and nourished by animals, and the Curetes danced around it. The Cretans told also that Zeus was dead and buried. This is certainly a Minoan conception, the spirit of vegetation, as born and dying annually. Zeus dethroned Kronos and together with the Olympian gods fought against the Titans and imprisoned them. The Titans are believed to be pre-Greek gods but the evidence is slight. The myth is perhaps modelled on the cosmological myth according to which Kronos dethroned his father Uranus. These myths are mixed up with the folk-tale motives.

A. B. Cook, *Zeus* (1914–40); M. P. Nilsson in *ARW* xxxv (1938), 156 ff.; *Gesch. d. griech. Rel.* i. 364 and 483 (the Titans). M. P. N.

ZEUXIADES, *see under* SILANION.

ZEUXIS, painter, of Heraclea in Lucania, pupil of Neseus of Thasos or Damophilus of Himera. Pliny dates him 397 B.C., and rejects 424. Quintilian dates both him and Parrhasius in the time of the Peloponnesian War. In Plato's *Protagoras* (dramatic date about 430) he is young and a new-comer in Athens. His rose-wreathed Eros is mentioned in Ar. *Ach.* 991–2 (425). He painted Alcmena for Acragas before 406, and Archelaus' palace between 413 and 399. He 'entered the door opened by Apollodorus and stole his art'; he added the use of highlights to shading, and Lucian praises in the Centaur family (an instance of the unusual subjects which Zeuxis preferred) the subtle gradation of colour from the human to the animal body of the female Centaur; his grapes were said to have deceived the birds. His figures lacked the ἦθος of Polygnotus, although his Penelope was morality itself, and his Helen, for Croton, an ideal picture compiled from several models; πάθος rather than ἦθος distinguished the Autoboreas with Titan look and wild hair, and the Menelaus drenched in tears. He also painted monochromes on white, and *figlina opera* (clay plaques).

Overbeck, 1077, 1121, 1647–91; Pfuhl, 739; O. Brendel, *JDAI* 1932, 191. T. B. L. W.

ZMYRNA or **Smyrna** (= Myrrha), a lost poem by Helvius Cinna (q.v. 4), dealt in Alexandrian fashion and under the influence of Parthenios, with the unnatural passion of Myrrha for her father Cinyras. It was elaborated through nine years (Catull. 95; Quint. *Inst.* 10. 4. 4; Serv. ad Verg. *Ecl.* 9. 35). Martial (10. 21. 3–4) banters a literary contemporary for preferring to Virgil this recondite and obscure work. J. W. D.

ZOÏLUS (Ζωΐλος) of Amphipolis (4th c. B.C.), the cynic philosopher, pupil of Polycrates and teacher of Anaximenes, is described by Suidas as ῥήτωρ καὶ φιλόσοφος, by Aelian, *VH* 11. 10, as κύων ῥητορικός and ψογερός. He was notorious for the bitterness of his attacks on Isocrates, Plato, and especially Homer.

WORKS.

(1) *Against Isocrates*. (2) *Against Plato*, favourably mentioned by Dion. Hal. *Pomp.* 1. (3) *Against Homer* (Καθ' Ὁμήρου or Κατὰ τῆς Ὁμήρου ποιήσεως or perhaps Ὁμηρομάστιξ, which became the author's nickname).

This work was chiefly devoted to severe, though often captious, criticism of the poet's invention, of the credibility of incidents (e.g. *Il.* 23. 100), and of the characters (e.g. *Il.* 1. 50). (4) *Censure of Homer* (Ψόγος Ὁμήρου), probably a declamation. (5) *Panegyric on the People of Tenedos.* (6) *On Figures,* a technical rhetorical treatise; his definition σχῆμά ἐστιν ἕτερον μὲν προσποιεῖσθαι ἕτερον δὲ λέγειν is criticized by Quintilian (9. 1. 14). He was the first to use σχῆμα in this technical sense. (7) *On Amphipolis.* (8) A history of Greece from the Theogony to the death of Philip of Macedon.

FGrH ii. A. 71; U. Friedländer, *De Zoilo aliisque Homeri obtrectatoribus* (1895).   J. F. L.

ZONAS of Sardis (*fl.* 90 B.C.) was a distinguished orator, and the author of some excellent epigrams in the *Greek Anthology*; the finest is a lovely epitaph asking Charon to help the little dead boy who cannot walk very well in his first sandals (*Anth. Pal.* 7. 365). He also bore the name Diodorus, and some epigrams attributed to the other Diodorus may be his.   G. H.

ZOOLOGY. Excellent early vase-paintings of animals are scattered over the Greek world with special schools in Cyprus, Boeotia, Chalcis, etc. Marine creatures are particularly well rendered. The name for a painter, *zōgraphos*, suggests attention to animal forms. Much accurate observation is displayed on coins and mosaics, both Greek and Imperial, and on some of them the actual species of small marine invertebrates can be easily recognized.

2. With some effort a classificatory system may be read into the arrangements of animals by habit in *On diet* of the Hippocratic Collection. More scientific are various fragments of the Sicilian school on the structure of animals (*see* ANATOMY AND PHYSIOLOGY, para. 2). In the true scientific tradition is a work of the Hippocratic Collection (artificially divided under titles *On Generation, On the Nature of the Embryo,* and *On Diseases,* Book iv) of about 380 B.C. It sets forth in some detail a doctrine of pangenesis astonishingly like that of Darwin (*Animals and Plants under Domestication,* 1868). To explain heredity it supposes that vessels reach the seed carrying samples from all parts of the body. It contains the first account of a controlled biological experiment. 'Take 20 eggs and let them be incubated by hens. Each day, from the second to that of hatching, remove an egg, break it, and examine it. You will find that the nature of the bird can be likened to that of man. The membranes proceed from the umbilical cord, and all that I have said on the subject of the infant you will find in the bird's egg, in which you will be surprised to find an umbilical cord.'

3. With almost the sole exception of this able work, ancient zoology begins and ends with Aristotle. Among his positive contributions are:

(*a*) Records of the life, breeding, habits, and structure of about 540 species of animals.

(*b*) Investigations of the developing chick, which has ever since been the classical embryological subject.

(*c*) Accounts of the habits and development of octopuses and squids, in some cases surpassed only in quite modern times.

(*d*) Anatomical accounts of the four-chambered stomach of ruminants, of the complex relations of the ducts, vessels, and organs in the mammalian generative system, and of the mammalian character of porpoises, dolphins, and whales, all unsurpassed until the seventeenth century.

(*e*) Accounts of exceptional modes of development of fish, among them of a dog-fish the young of which is linked to the womb by a navel cord and placenta much as in a mammal. Nothing has contributed

more to Aristotle's modern scientific reputation than the rediscovery of this phenomenon a century ago.

(*f*) Observations on paternal care in fish, verified only in the last century.

(*g*) Stress on the heart and vascular system on embryological grounds. He is often quoted as calling the heart 'the first to live and last to die'. The idea is in his works but the phrase is not.

(*h*) A permanent addition to the technique of scientific instruction was his introduction of diagrams to explain anatomical relations. Some of his diagrams can be restored from his descriptions.

4. There is no system of classification of animals in Aristotle's works, but from them can fairly be extracted an intelligible scheme which was hardly improved until the time of Cuvier in the early nineteenth century. Aristotle also emphasizes that living things can be arranged in a sort of ladder, the *scala naturae* discussed by naturalists until the mid-nineteenth century. 'Nature proceeds little by little from things lifeless to animal life in such a way that it is impossible to determine the exact line of demarcation, nor on which side thereof an intermediate form should lie. Thus, next after lifeless things in the upward scale comes the plant, and of plants one will differ from another as to its amount of apparent vitality; and, in a word, the whole of plant-kind, while devoid of life compared with an animal, is endowed with life as compared with other corporeal entities. Indeed, there is observed in plants a continuous scale of ascent towards the animal.' (*Hist. An.* 588 b 4 ff.)

5. Aristotle's view on generation is that the material substance is contributed by the female, the male giving the principle of life. The male he compares to the sculptor, the female to the marble. It is, therefore, theoretically unnecessary for conception that anything material should pass from male to female. This view is linked with controversies involving the ideas of 'spontaneous generation' and of 'parthenogenesis' which have lasted ever since and constantly present new facets with advancing knowledge.

6. Aristotle's theory of the actual mechanism of generation is of great historic importance. He specifically rejects pangenesis. He considers that the nutritive material distributed by the blood contains a number of fractions each of which accords to a particular organ and is elaborated for that organ by the vital principle. Before distribution each fraction yields up a minute part to the semen. Because the semen thus contains representatives of every organ—and therefore of every feature—the offspring resembles its father. It resembles its mother because she also contributes to the offspring parts separated off from her blood before distribution, as does the father. In her case, however, these parts are contained in the catamenia (or their equivalents), which, suppressed during pregnancy, provide the material of the body of the offspring. (*Gen. An.* 1. 18–22.)

7. It calls for remark that Aristotle, having thought deeply on heredity, considered only the relation of parent to offspring and not the general principle as extended to descent. This is one of the several points at which he approaches, without crossing, the frontier of evolutionary doctrine. His theory turns up in Lucretius (4. 1229–31) and also in the *Wisdom of Solomon* (7. 2), an Alexandrian Jewish work with Stoic influence approximately contemporary with the beginning of the Christian era. Galen comments on Aristotle's theory (*De sanitate tuenda* 1. 2 and *Nat. Fac.* 1. 6–7). After Aristotle there is no scientific observation of a zoological character. (However, *see* ANATOMY AND PHYSIOLOGY, paras. 12, 18.)

8. The largest collections of animal stories are those of Pliny and Aelian. Much accurate nature-knowledge can be gleaned from general literature, especially Latin.

Roman country gentlemen had their game preserves and aviaries, of which Varro gives details (*Rust.* 3. 49. 13). A mural in the Villa Livia shows a bird-sanctuary. Under the Empire many strange beasts were brought to Rome for the circus. Lions, tigers, elephants both African and Indian, rhinoceroses, bears, bisons, boars, leopards, panthers, hyenas, and crocodiles were in the imperial menageries. These sometimes contained prodigious numbers; Trajan owned 11,000 beasts, Augustus 420 tigers, Nero 400 bears, and Gordian I 300 ostriches. Curiosity accounted for the presence of serpents, camels, hippopotamuses, antelopes, zebras, and giraffes. The first giraffe came to Europe for Commodus about 190, and Gordian I (237) is said to have had 100 of them.

BIBLIOGRAPHY

The Hippocratic work *On Generation* is given in the edition of E. Littré, vol. iii (1851). Practically all the zoological work of Aristotle is in his three works *Historia animalium, De partibus animalium, De generatione animalium* (see ARISTOTLE). Discussion with bibliography in Charles Singer, *Studies in the History and Method of Science* ii (1921), and *Greek Biology and Greek Medicine* (1922). Representation of animals in ancient art: Imhof-Blumer and O. Keller, *Tier- und Pflanzenbilder auf Münzen und Gemmen des klassischen Altertums* (1889); J. Morin, *Dessins des animaux en Grèce* (1911). Menageries in great detail by G. Loisel, *Histoire des ménageries* (3 vols., 1912). C. S.

ZOPYRUS, writer on physiognomy, known from his judgement on Socrates' appearance.

See Förster, *Scriptores Physiognomonici* i, prol. vii ff.

ZOROASTER (Ζωροάστρης), the best-known form of the name of Zarathuštra; for others see Bidez–Cumont, i. 36 ff. The Greeks had heard of him as early as the fifth century B.C. (Xanthus of Lydia in Diog. Laert. proem, 2), and mentions of him are common in the Hellenistic period. Apart from an aberrant tradition,

due perhaps to Ctesias (q.v.), which made him a king of Bactria conquered by Ninus and Semiramis (Bidez–Cumont, ii. 41 ff.), a fairly correct idea of his teachings was current in philosophic circles from about the time of Plato, the intermediary being probably Eudoxus of Cnidos. Legendary details of all sorts accumulated about him, some doubtless of Oriental origin, and he was credited with the authorship of an immense number of works (2,000,000 lines or some 10,000,000 words, Hermippus in Pliny, *HN* 30. 4, were ascribed to him), dealing with theology, natural science, astrology, magic, etc., much of their contents being not only spurious but also quite foreign to his real interests and teachings.

J. Bidez and F. Cumont, *Les Mages hellénisés* (1938). H. J. R.

ZOSIMUS (1), a Greek historian, an *advocatus fisci* and a *comes*, under Theodosius II, who wrote six books on 'The decline of Rome', from Augustus to A.D. 410. There is a gap from Probus to the year 303. The work was not finished until after 425. Zosimus used excellent authorities—notably Dexippus and Eunapius—and is not without historical judgement and a sense of style. He is well informed on Eastern affairs—his account of the wars of Aurelian against Palmyra is easily the best that survives—not so well on the West. He is not strong on exact dating and handles many topics too cursorily. One serious defect of Zosimus as a pure historian has its special interest for us. An avowed enemy of the triumphant Christian Church, he never tires of recounting the services rendered to the Empire by the old gods and the disasters that followed their neglect.

Ed. L. Mendelssohn (1887). H. M.

ZOSIMUS (2), writer on alchemy (q.v.) of the third or fourth century A.D.

APPENDIX I

GENERAL BIBLIOGRAPHY

(*Note.* This list contains the main bibliographic and encyclopaedic publications used in 1948. For earlier works of similar character see the article SCHOLARSHIP, MODERN. For special bibliographies see the article concerned.)

A. Complete bibliographies, issued shortly after publication of the works (books, articles, reviews) which they register.

1. *Bibliotheca philologica classica* (in progress?), 65 vols., 1873–1941 (for 1938).
   This is part of or an appendix to *Bursians Jahresbericht* (see B. 1), and gives titles of works only.
2. *Revue des revues*, appearing as an appendix at the end of each volume of *Revue de Philologie*, nouvelle [2nd] série, 49 vols., 1877–1925.
   Gives mainly abstracts of articles.
3. J. Marouzeau, *Dix années de bibliographie classique* [1914–24], 2 vols., published 1927 and 1928 by 'Les Belles Lettres', Paris.
   Gives titles of books (including reviews) and abstracts of articles.
4. J. Marouzeau, *L'Année philologique* (in progress), 17 vols. [for 1924–46], published 1928–48 by 'Les Belles Lettres', Paris.
   Gives titles of books (including reviews) and abstracts of articles.
On the relationship of 2–4 with 1 see *Bulletin de l'Association G. Budé*, Suppl. critique x (1939, for 1938), pp. 7–9.

B. Collections of critical reports on main subjects (e.g. grammar, literature, history, archaeology) in systematic order.

1. Complete collection: *Bursians Jahresbericht* (in progress?), 284 vols., 1873–1943.
   Full title: *Jahresbericht über die Fortschritte der klassischen Altertumswissenschaft.*
   Publisher: (since 1898) O. R. Reisland, Leipzig; (before 1898) Calvary, Berlin.
   Main successive editors: Bursian, Iwan Müller, Kroll, Münscher, Thierfelder.
   'Generalregister' for volumes i–lxxxvii appeared 1897 (without volume number).
   Indexes to reports: vol. cxxxviii (1908), p. 143; vol. clxvi (1914), p. 119; vol. cci (1925), p. 205.
      Since 1938 there has been one such index yearly, the last on pp. 3 ff. of the preliminary to vols. cclxxxi–cclxxxiv (1943).
   Appendices: (*a*) *Bibliotheca philologica classica* (above A. 1).
               (*b*) *Biographisches Jahrbuch* (obituaries of classical scholars) at the end of each 'Jahrgang'. Last part vol. cclxxxiv (1943); last survey vol. ccii B (1925).
2. Selective collections:
   a. *Year's Work in Classical Studies* (in progress), 34 vols., 1906–39.
      First editor: W. H. D. Rouse for the Council of the Classical Association.
      Last editor before the war of 1939–45: S. G. Owen for the Classical Journals Board.
      Present editor: Prof. G. B. A. Fletcher.
   b. *Bulletin de l'Association Guillaume Budé*, nouvelle série (in progress), 4 numbers, 1946–7. Publishers and editors of the *Bulletin* not named. Contains useful surveys on classical studies in different countries during the 1939–45 war.

C. Collections of comprehensive presentations of main subjects in systematic order.

1. Iwan von Müllers *Handbuch* (in progress), 9 parts with many extensive subdivisions, 1885–1946.
   Full title: (1885–1920) *Handbuch der klassischen Altertumswissenschaft.*
              (since 1920) *Handbuch der Altertumswissenschaft.*
   Publisher: O. Beck, later C. H. Beck, at Nördlingen (Bavaria), later Munich.
              (since 1945) Biederstein, Munich.
   Successive editors: Iwan von Müller (d. 1917), R. Pöhlmann (d. 1914), Walter Otto (d. 1941).
   The first edition, 1885–91 (9 vols.), has now been almost completely superseded by new editions, the latest of which are enormously enlarged. Since 1920 many new subjects concerning especially prehistory and the Ancient East have been added.
2. Gercke–Norden, *Einleitung*, 3rd (partly 4th) ed., 3 vols., 1921–35.
   Full title: *Einleitung in die Altertumswissenschaft.*
   Publisher: Teubner.
   Editors: A. Gercke (d. 1922) and E. Norden (d. 1941).
      Vol. i, 3rd ed. (10 subsections), 1921–7, with index.
      Vol. ii, 4th ed. (6 subsections), 2 half-vols. with separate indexes, 1932, 1933.
      Vol. iii, 3rd ed. (4 subsections), 1932–5 (no index).
   The subsections have separate pagination and were on sale separately.
   On the scheme of the first edition (3 vols., 1910, 1912) see *Bursians Jahresbericht* ccii B (1925), pp. 188 ff.

D. Collection of articles in alphabetical order.

  1. Pauly–Wissowa, *Real-Encyclopädie* (in progress), 33 vols., 1893–1943.
       Full title: *Paulys Real-Encyclopädie der classischen Altertumswissenschaft. Neue Bearbeitung.*
       Publisher: J. B. Metzler, Stuttgart.
       Successive editors: Wissowa, W. Kroll, Mittelhaus. [A. Pauly (d. 1845) began the edition of a similar encyclopaedia at Stuttgart in 1839.]
       The work is complete for the words from A to Tyrrhener, except for two-thirds of the letter P.
       There are 7 vols. of supplements. There is an index to Suppl. vols. i–v after the article *molaris lapis* (1932).
       The published volumes contain more than 50,000 columns of 68 lines each.
       On the scheme for the work see *Bursians Jahresbericht* ccxlv (1934), pp. 126–8.
  2. *Lübker's Reallexicon*, 8th ed., 1914.
       Full title: *Friedrich Lübkers Reallexikon des klassischen Altertums.*
       Publisher: Teubner.
       Editors: Geffcken and Ziebarth.
       The work is very similar to the present dictionary.
       The first edition was made by F. Lübker (d. 1867) in 1855, 'für Gymnasien' (secondary schools).

E. General encyclopaedias in alphabetical order with numerous articles on classical subjects.

  1. *Enciclopedia italiana*, 37 vols., 1929–39.
  2. *Der grosse Brockhaus*, 21 vols., 1928–35.

F. General catalogues of printed books.

  1. British Museum, *Catalogue of Printed Books*, 89 vols., 1881–1900; *Supplement*, 6 vols., 1900–7.
  2. British Museum, *General Catalogue of Printed Books* (in progress), 41 vols., 1931–47 (A–CONR).

G. Various items.

  1. Nairn's *Classical Hand-list*, 2nd ed., 1939, published by B. H. Blackwell, Oxford (excellent selection of important works, with book-prices).
  2. *Byzantinische Zeitschrift*, 'Generalregister' for vols. i–xii (1892–1903), 1909 (by P. Marc).
  3. *Revue des études grecques*, 'Tables générales' for vols. xxxi–l (1918–37), 1937.
  4. *Journal of Hellenic Studies*, Index to vols. xliii–lx (1923–40), 1941.
  5. Two modern surveys on results and tasks:
       (a) *Mémorial des études latines, offert à J. Marouzeau* = *Revue des études latines*, vol. xxi (1943).
       (b) H. Fuchs, 'Rückschau und Ausblick im Arbeitsgebiet der lateinischen Philologie', *Museum Helveticum* iv (1947), pp. 147–98.
  6. *Wilamowitz-Bibliographie* (for 1868 to 1929), 1929.

APPENDIX II
BIBLIOGRAPHY OF THE HISTORY OF GREEK AND LATIN LITERATURE

A. GREEK

  1. Period from Homer till about the end of the 5th century B.C. (Thucydides, Democritus, and Hippocrates not yet treated).

       Iwan von Müllers *Handbuch*, Abteilung VII: *Geschichte der griechischen Literatur*, 4 vols., by W. Schmid (b. 1859), 1929–46. A volume on the literature of the 4th century B.C., by H. Herter, is in preparation. Meanwhile, for this period see Geffcken, *Griechische Literaturgeschichte*, vol. ii, 1934 (not included in the *Handbuch*).

  2. Period from Alexander the Great to Justinian.

       Iwan von Müllers *Handbuch*, Abteilung VII: 'Schmid–Stählin', *Geschichte der griechischen Literatur*, 2 vols., by W. Schmid and O. Stählin, 1920, 1924.
       For the literature of *c.* 320–*c.* 1 B.C. the following work (not included in the *Handbuch*) is still indispensable: Susemihl (1826–1901), *Geschichte der griechischen Literatur in der Alexandrinerzeit*, 2 vols. (*c.* 1680 pp.), 1891, 1892.

  3. Period from Justinian till A.D. 1453.

       Iwan von Müllers *Handbuch*, Abteilung IX, 1: Krumbacher (1856–1909), *Geschichte der Byzantinischen Literatur*, 2nd ed. 1897.

B. LATIN

       Iwan von Müllers *Handbuch*, Abteilung VIII and IX, 2.

  1. Period from the beginning to Hadrian.

       'Schanz–Hosius', 2 vols., 1927, 1935 (Martin von Schanz, 1842–1914; obituary in *Bursians Jahresbericht* ccxlix (1935), pp. 50–87).

2. Period from Hadrian to Constantine.
   'Schanz'[3], vol. iii, edited by Hosius and G. Krüger, 1922.

3. Period from Constantine to Justinian.
   'Schanz', vol. iv, in two parts (the second finished by Hosius and G. Krüger), 1914, 1920.

4. Period from Justinian till the end of the 12th century.
   'Manitius', 3 vols., 1911–31 (Max Manitius, born 1858).

APPENDIX III
BIBLIOGRAPHY OF GREEK GRAMMAR

1. 'Kühner–Blass' and 'Kühner–Gerth'.
   R. Kühner (1802–78), *Ausführliche Grammatik der griechischen Sprache*, appeared first in 1834–5, with second edition in 1869–71 (the first edition contained also in the title the following words, afterwards omitted: *wissenschaftlich und mit Rücksicht auf den Schulbetrieb ausgearbeitet*). The third edition consists of two parts, each of two volumes: Part I, containing phonology and morphology, by F. Blass (1843–1907: obituary by W. Crönert, *Bursians Jahresb.* cxlv (1910), 1–32), 1890–2; Part II, containing syntax, by B. Gerth, 1898–1904.

2. Schwyzer, *Griechische Grammatik* (in Iwan von Müllers *Handbuch* ii. i) (E. Schwyzer, 1874–1943; obituary by A. Debrunner, *Museum Helveticum* i (1944), 1–12).
   Vol. i (1939), containing general part, phonology, morphology, word-formation, 842 pp.
   Vol. ii, containing syntax and indexes, is being made ready for publication by Professor A. Debrunner (Berne), and is expected to appear in 1949.

   Both works are equally indispensable. If we accept J. B. Hofmann's distinction of the 'diachronical' and the '(idio)synchronical' types of grammar (*Lat. Grammar*, 5th ed., 1928, pp. 11 ff.), then Kühner–Blass belongs to the synchronical, Schwyzer to the diachronical. In other words, Kühner–Blass gives grammar as a tool for interpretation of the texts, and especially of the Greek classical texts; Schwyzer uses all sorts of texts from the beginning of Indo-European speech to modern living Greek as sources for the history of innumerable phenomena of Greek language.

3. C. D. Buck, *Introduction to the Study of the Greek Dialects*, 1928.

4. J. D. Denniston, *The Greek Particles*, 1934.

5. 'Buck–Petersen': *A Reverse Index of Greek Nouns and Adjectives*, by C. D. Buck and W. Petersen (d. 1939), 1944. Next to Liddell and Scott, the most important modern contribution to the study of Greek lexicography.

PRINTED IN GREAT BRITAIN
AT THE UNIVERSITY PRESS, OXFORD
BY VIVIAN RIDLER
PRINTER TO THE UNIVERSITY